Standard Catalog of®

WORLD COINS

1601-1700

5th Edition

George S. Cuhaj
Editor

Thomas Michael
Market Analyst

Harry Miller
U.S. Market Analyst

Deborah McCue
Database Specialist

Kay Sanders
Database & Editorial Assistant

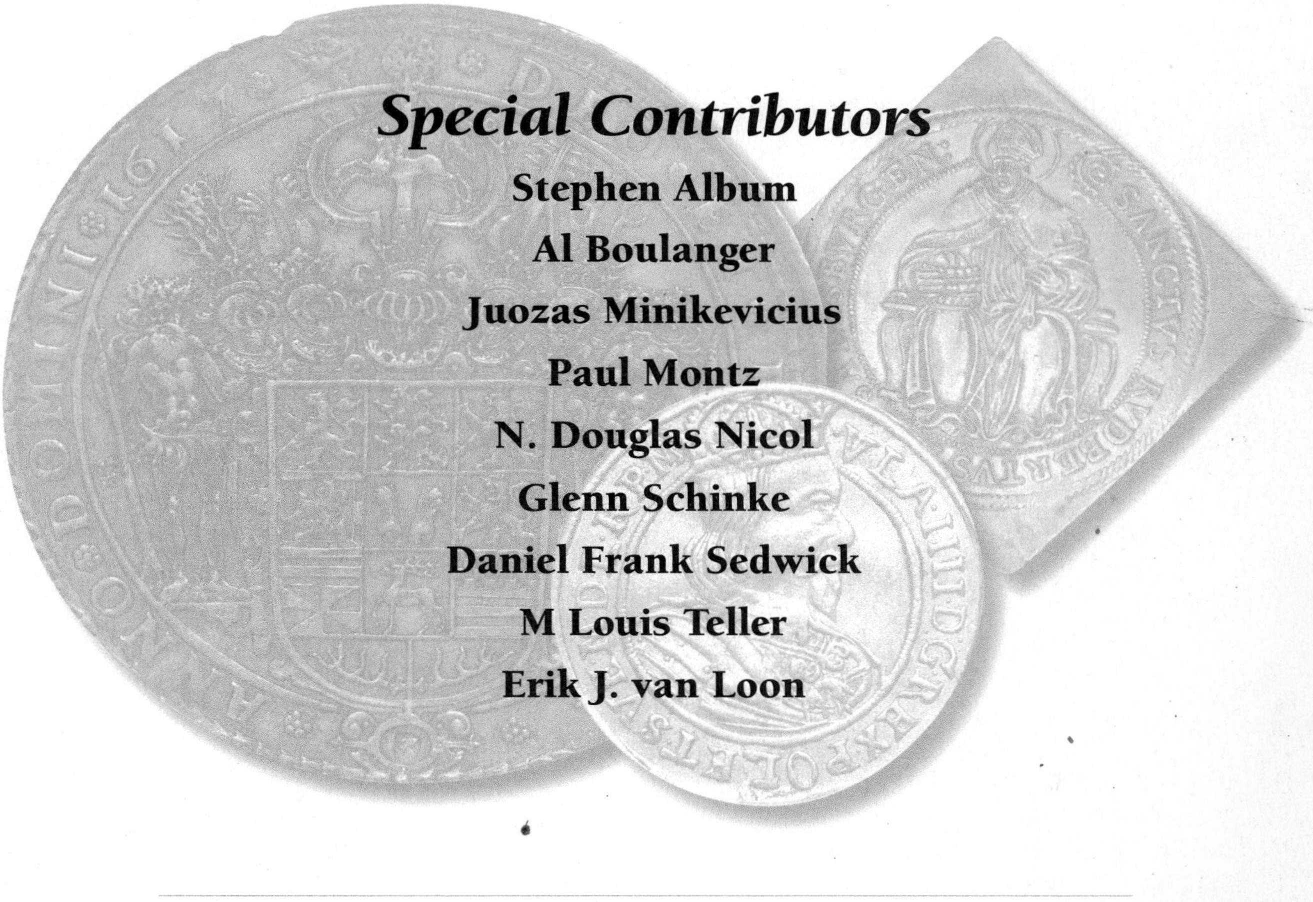

Special Contributors

Stephen Album
Al Boulanger
Juozas Minikevicius
Paul Montz
N. Douglas Nicol
Glenn Schinke
Daniel Frank Sedwick
M Louis Teller
Erik J. van Loon

Bullion Value (BV) Market Valuations

Valuations for all platinum, gold, palladium and silver coins of the more common, basically bullion types, or those possessing only modest numismatic premiums are presented in this edition based on the market levels of:

$1,550 per ounce for **platinum** • **$1,750** per ounce for **gold**
$600 per ounce for **palladium** • **$35** per ounce for **silver**

Published by

Krause Publications, a division of F+W Media, Inc.
700 East State Street • Iola, WI 54990-0001
715-445-2214 • 888-457-2873
www.krausebooks.com

To order books or other products call toll-free 1-800-258-0929
or visit us online at www.shopnumismaster.com

ISBN-13: 978-1-4402-1704-3
ISBN-10: 1-4402-1704-1

Cover Design by Jana Tappa
Designed by Sandi Carpenter
Edited by George Cuhaj

Cover images courtesy of Heritage Auctions.

Printed in the United States of America

INTRODUCTION

Welcome to our new 5th edition of the 17th Century Standard Catalog of World Coins. This most recent version of our ever changing and evolving series of comprehensive reference catalogs is designed to meet the needs of those with serious interest in the coins of our numismatic heritage. More than half of the pages within this reference are devoted to early European coinage, with a significant portion of this book displaying the vast array of Germanic coins stuck during this time period.

Still, the Standard Catalog of World Coins 1601-1700 provides an abundance of coin listings for nations around the globe. You will find coins from worldwide territories of the European powers, including issues meant for circulation in Portuguese India, Danish Tranquebar, Spanish Netherlands and Colonial North America, countermarked coins from Brazil and cob coins from Colombia and Bolivia. Listings for the remnants of the Hapsburg Empire can be found throughout this volume with coins struck for use in Austria, Bohemia, Hungary and Salzburg. Coins of Spain, France and the French States are here as well, alongside crowns from Transylvania, plus coins from the Middle Eastern areas of Turkey and Syria.

But some of the greatest areas of interest probably reside with this catalogs listings for pre-unified territories. The massive section for German States coinage has experienced a comprehensive revision for all values on minor coins, crowns and thalers, and gold ducats and their multiples. The same is true of the Swiss Cantonal issues, Independent Kingdoms of India, coinage of the Provinces of the Netherlands and those coins struck for use in the various Italian States and cities. All of these collecting areas have witnessed a great rebirth of activity and very significant boosts to individual coin values.

It just goes to show that the classics never go out of style. There will always be a healthy market for coins of this era, hammered or milled, specialists will always be interested in 17th Century types.

So this easy to use catalog, arranged in a basic alphabetic fashion by country, with groupings for political structure, coinage type and denomination to help better organize the data, will always be an important volume in any numismatic library. You will find photographs of many 17th Century coins, information on metal content, obverse and reverse descriptions, legends, types and variety details, date listings and of course values presented in multiple grades of preservation. In short, just about all the information you could want on the classic coins of the old world and its early extensions into the East and West of the globe.

All this data has not come easily into the book you hold before you. A generation of numismatists has worked diligently to lay the foundations on which current experts can build and to them we own a debt of gratitude.

Continuing this work are some seventy contributing coin dealers, collectors and researchers who have lent their knowledge to the compiling of this new edition, providing our staff with updated values, new images, newly discovered dates and expanded listings. The accuracy of the data offered in this volume is assured through their kind assistance. To them we offer a heartfelt "Thank you!" for their generosity and dedication to the advancement of our shared field of coin collecting.

Finally to you, the reader, we extend our wishes that you may enjoy using this catalog as much as we enjoyed it's production. Look it over, put it to good use and please let us know if you have any comments or questions.

Best Wishes,
The Editorial Staff of the
Standard Catalog of World Coins

CONTRIBUTING TO THE CATALOG

SENDING SCANNED IMAGES

- Scan images with a resolution of 300 dpi
- Set size at 100%
- Scan in true 4-color
- Save images as 'jpeg'
- Specify the state, denomination and diameter of coin
- Send images to the editor at **George.Cuhaj@fwmedia.com**

OFFERING DATA CORRECTIONS

- Refer to coins by state and catalog number
- Be as clear and specific as possible
- Send your comments to the editor at **George.Cuhaj@fwmedia.com**

SUGGESTING VALUE CHANGES

- Reference the coin's state and catalog number
- Specify date and grade
- Explain your sources
- Send your suggestions to the market analyst at **Tom.Michael@fwmedia.com**

ACKNOWLEDGMENTS

Many numismatists have contributed countless changes, which have been incorporated in this edition. While all cannot be acknowledged here, special appreciation is extended to the following individuals and organizations who have exhibited a special dedication - revising and verifying historical and technical data and coin listings, reviewing market valuations and sharing digital images - for this edition.

Dr. Lawrence A. Adams
Stephen Album
Scott Annechino
Dr. Luis Alberto Asbun-Karmy
Mitchell A. Battino
Gonzalo Barinaga
Dr. Bernd Becker
Jan Bendix
Allen G. Berman
Joseph Boling
Al Boulanger
Klaus Bronny
Adolfo Cayón
Clemente Cayón
Fred L. Colombo
Scott E. Cordry
Jean-Paul Divo
Wilhelm R. Eglseer
Thomas F. Fitzgerald
Arthur Friedberg
Tom Galway
Ron Guth
Marcel Häberling
Don Hanlon
Flemming Lyngbeck Hansen
Emmanuel Henry
Wade Hinderling
Serge Huard
Ton Jacobs
Héctor Carlos Janson
Craig Keplinger
John M. Kleeberg
Lawrence C. Korchnak
Peter Kraneveld
Ronachai Krisadaolarn
Samson Kin Chiu Lai
Joseph E. Lang
Dirk Löbbers
Jürgen Mikeska
Juozas Minikevicius
Robert Mish
Paul Montz
Horst-Dieter Müller
N. Douglas Nicol
Alberto Paashaus
Frank Passic
Tom Passon
Marc Pelletier
William Rosenblum
Remy Said
Jacco Scheper
Glenn Schinke
Dr. Wolfgang Schuster
Daniel Frank Sedwick
Olav Sejerøe
Alexander I. Shapiro
Clark Smith
Jørgen Sømod
Dr. Sebastian Steinbach
Vladimir Suchy
Alim A. Sumana
M. Louis Teller
Archie Tonkin
Anthony Tumonis
Erik J. van Loon
Justin C. Wang
Paul Welz
Stewart Westdal
John Wilkison
Ertekin Yenisey

Auction Houses

Aureo & Calicó
Baldwin's Auctions Ltd.
Classical Numismatic Group
Daniel Frank Sedwick, LLC
Dix, Noonan, Webb, Ltd.
Dmitry Markov Coins & Medals
Jean Elsen S.A.
Frankfurter Münzhandlung
Ira & Larry Goldberg Coins & Collectibles, Inc.
Hauck & Aufhäuser
Heidelberg Münzhandlung Herbert Grün
Gorny & Mosch – Giessener Münzhandlung
Auktion Heidrun Höhn
Helios Numismatik
Heritage World Coin Auctions
Hess-Divo Ltd.
Gerhard D. Hirsch Nachfolger
Thomas Høiland Møntauktion
Fritz Rudolf Künker Münzhandlung
Leipziger Münzhandlung
LHS Numismatik AG
Maison Palombo
Auktionshaus Meister & Sonntag
Münzenhandlung Harald Möller, GmbH
Münzen & Medaillen Deutschland, GmbH
Moneti i Medali
MPO
Münz Zentrum Köln
Noble Numismatics, Pty. Ltd.
Numismatica Ars Classica
Numismatik Lanz München
Dr. Busso Peus Nachfolger
Ponterio & Associates
Bruun Rasmussen
Auktionshaus H.D. Rauch GmbH
Riibe Mynthandel AS
Schulman BV
Sotheby's
Spink - Smythe
St. James Auction Ltd.
Stack's - Coin Galleries
UBS, AG, Gold & Numismatics
Jean Vinchon Numismatique
Westfälische Auktionsgesellschaft
World Wide Coins of California

COUNTRY INDEX

HOW TO USE THIS CATALOG

This catalog series is designed to serve the needs of both the novice and advanced collectors. It provides a comprehensive guide to over 400 years of world coinage. It is generally arranged so that persons with no more than a basic knowledge of world history and a casual acquaintance with coin collecting can consult it with confidence and ease. The following explanations summarize the general practices used in preparing this catalog's listings. However, because of specialized requirements, which may vary by country and era, these must not be considered ironclad. Where these standards have been set aside, appropriate notations of the variations are incorporated in that particular listing.

ARRANGEMENT

Countries are arranged alphabetically. Political changes within a country are arranged chronologically. In countries where Rulers are the single most significant political entity a chronological arrangement by Ruler has been employed. Distinctive sub-geographic regions are listed alphabetically following the countries main listings. A few exceptions to these rules may exist. Refer to the Country Index.

Diverse coinage types relating to fabrication methods, revaluations, denomination systems, non-circulating categories and such have been identified, separated and arranged in logical fashion. Chronological arrangement is employed for most circulating coinage, i.e., Hammered coinage will normally precede Milled coinage, monetary reforms will flow in order of their institution. Non-circulating types such as Essais, Piefort, Patterns, Trial Strikes, Mint and Proof sets will follow the main listings, as will Medallic coinage and Token coinage.

Within a coinage type coins will be listed by denomination, from smallest to largest. Numbered types within a denomination will be ordered by their first date of issue.

IDENTIFICATION

The most important step in the identification of a coin is the determination of the nation of origin. This is generally easily accomplished where English-speaking lands are concerned, however, use of the country index is sometimes required. The coins of Great Britain provide an interesting challenge. For hundreds of years the only indication of the country of origin was in the abbreviated Latin legends. In recent times there have been occasions when there has been no indication of origin. Only through the familiarity of the monarchical portraits, symbols and legends or indication of currency system are they identifiable.

The coins of many countries beyond the English-language realm, such as those of French, Italian or Spanish heritage, are also quite easy to identify through reference to their legends, which appear in the national languages based on Western alphabets. In many instances the name is spelled exactly the same in English as in the national language, such as France; while in other cases it varies only slightly, like Italia for Italy, Belgique or Belgie for Belgium, Brasil for Brazil and Danmark for Denmark.

This is not always the case, however, as in Norge for Norway, Espana for Spain, Sverige for Sweden and Helvetia for Switzerland. Some other examples include:

DEUTSCHES REICH - Germany 1873-1945
BUNDESREPUBLIC DEUTSCHLAND -
Federal Republic of Germany.
DEUTSCHE DEMOKRATISCHE REPUBLIK -
German Democratic Republic.
EMPIRE CHERIFIEN MAROC - Morocco.
ESTADOS UNIDOS MEXICANOS -
United Mexican States (Mexico).
ETAT DU GRAND LIBAN -
State of Great Lebanon (Lebanon).

Thus it can be seen there are instances in which a little schooling in the rudiments of foreign languages can be most helpful. In general, colonial possessions of countries using the Western alphabet are similarly identifiable as they often carry portraits of their current rulers, the familiar lettering, sometimes in combination with a companion designation in the local language.

Collectors have the greatest difficulty with coins that do not bear legends or dates in the Western systems. These include coins bearing Cyrillic lettering, attributable to Bulgaria, Russia, the Slavic states and Mongolia, the Greek script peculiar to Greece, Crete and the Ionian Islands; The Amharic characters of Ethiopia, or Hebrew in the case of Israel. Dragons and sunbursts along with the distinctive word characters attribute a coin to the Oriental countries of China, Japan, Korea, Tibet, Viet Nam and their component parts.

The most difficult coins to identify are those bearing only Persian or Arabic script and its derivatives, found on the issues of nations stretching in a wide swath across North Africa and East Asia, from Morocco to Indonesia, and the Indian subcontinent coinages which surely are more confusing in their vast array of Nagari, Sanskrit, Ahom, Assamese and other local dialects found on the local issues of the Indian Princely States. Although the task of identification on the more modern issues of these lands is often eased by the added presence of Western alphabet legends, a feature sometimes adopted as early as the late 19th Century, for the earlier pieces it is often necessary for the uninitiated to laboriously seek and find.

Except for the cruder issues, however, it will be found that certain characteristics and symbols featured in addition to the predominant legends are typical on coins from a given country or group of countries. The toughra monogram, for instance, occurs on some of the coins of Afghanistan, Egypt, the Sudan, Pakistan, Turkey and other areas of the late Ottoman Empire. A predominant design feature on the coins of Nepal is the trident; while neighboring Tibet features a lotus blossom or lion on many of their issues.

To assist in identification of the more difficult coins, we have assembled the Instant Identifier section presented on the following pages designed to provide a point of beginning for collectors by allowing them to compare unidentified coins with photographic details from typical issues.

We also suggest reference to the comprehensive Country Index.

DATING

Coin dating is the final basic attribution consideration. Here, the problem can be more difficult because the reading of a coin date is subject not only to the vagaries of numeric styling, but to calendar variations caused by the observance of various religious eras or regal periods from country to country, or even within a country. Here again with the exception of the sphere from North Africa through the Orient, it will be found that most countries rely on Western date numerals and Christian (AD) era reckoning, although in a few instances, coin dating has been tied to the year of a reign or government. The Vatican, for example dates its coinage according to the year of reign of the current pope, in addition to the Christian-era date.

Countries in the Arabic sphere generally date their coins to the Muslim era (AH), which commenced on July 16, 622 AD (Julian calendar), when the prophet Mohammed fled from Mecca to Medina. As their calendar is reckoned by the lunar year of 354 days, which is about three percent (precisely 2.98%) shorter than the Christian year, a formula is required to convert AH dating to its Western equivalent. To convert an AH date to the approximate AD date, subtract three percent of the AH date (round to the closest whole number) from the AH date and add 622. A chart converting all AH years from 1010 (July 2, 1601) to 1421 (May 25, 2028) is presented as the Heijra Chart elsewhere in this volume.

The Muslim calendar is not always based on the lunar year (AH), however, causing some confusion, particularly in Afghanistan and Iran, where a calendar based on the solar year (SH) was introduced around 1920. These dates can be converted to AD by simply adding 621. In 1976 the government of Iran implemented a new solar calendar based on the foundation of the Iranian monarchy in 559 BC. The first year observed on the new calendar was 2535 (MS), which commenced March 20, 1976. A reversion to the traditional SH dating standard occurred a few years later.

Several different eras of reckoning, including Christian and Muslim (AH), have been used to date coins of the Indian subcontinent. The two basic systems are the Vikrama Samvat (VS), which dates from Oct. 18, 58 BC, and the Saka era, the origin of which is reckoned from March 3, 78 AD. Dating according to both eras appears on various coins of the area.

Coins of Thailand (Siam) are found dated by three different eras. The most predominant is the Buddhist era (BE), which originated in 543 BC. Next is the Bangkok or Ratanakosindsok (RS) era, dating from 1781 AD; followed by the Chula- Sakarat (CS) era, dating from 638 AD. The latter era originated in Burma and is used on that country's coins.

Other calendars include that of the Ethiopian era (EE), which commenced seven years, eight months after AD dating; and that of the Jewish people, which commenced on Oct. 7, 3761 BC. Korea claims a legendary dating from 2333 BC, which is acknowledged in some of its coin dating. Some coin issues of the Indonesian area carry dates determined by the Javanese Aji Saka era (AS), a calendar of 354 days (100 Javanese years equal 97 Christian or Gregorian calendar years), which can be matched to AD dating by comparing it to AH dating.

The following table indicates the year dating for the various eras, which correspond to 2011 in Christian calendar reckoning, but it must be remembered that there are overlaps between the eras in some instances.

Christian era (AD)	2011
Muslim era (AH)	AH1432
Solar year (SH)	SH1389
Monarchic Solar era (MS)	MS2570
Vikrama Samvat (VS)	VS2068
Saka era (SE)	SE1933
Buddhist era (BE)	BE2554
Bangkok era (RS)	RS230
Chula-Sakarat era (CS)	CS1373
Ethiopian era (EE)	EE2004
Korean era	4344
Javanese Aji Saka era (AS)	AS1944
Fasli era (FE)	FE1421
Jewish era (JE)	JE5771
Roman	MMXI

Coins of Asian origin - principally Japan, Kor
Turkestan and Tibet and some modern gold issue
key - are generally dated to the year of the gove
dynasty, reign or cyclic eras, with the dates indica
Asian characters which usually read from right to le
recent years, however, some dating has been accor
to the Christian calendar and in Western numerals.
Japan, Asian character dating was reversed to read fro
left to right in Showa year 23 (1948 AD).

More detailed guides to less prevalent coin dating systems, which are strictly local in nature, are presented with the appropriate listings.

Some coins carry dates according to both locally observed and Christian eras. This is particularly true in the Arabic world, where the Hejira date may be indicated in Arabic numerals and the Christian date in Western numerals, or both dates in either form.

The date actually carried on a given coin is generally cataloged here in the first column (Date). Dates listed alone in the date column which do not actually appear on a given coin, or dates which are known, but do not appear on the coin, are generally enclosed by parentheses with 'ND' at the left, for example ND(1926).

Timing differentials between some era of reckoning, particularly the 354-day Mohammedan and 365-day Christian years, cause situations whereby coins which carry dates for both eras exist bearing two year dates from one calendar combined with a single date from another.

Countermarked Coinage is presented with both 'Countermark Date' and 'Host Coin' date for each type. Actual date representation follows the rules outlined above.

NUMBERING SYSTEM

Some catalog numbers assigned in this volume are based on established references. This practice has been observed for two reasons: First, when world coins are listed chronologically they are basically self-cataloging; second, there was no need to confuse collectors with totally new numeric designations where appropriate systems already existed. As time progressed we found many of these established systems incomplete and inadequate and have now replaced many with new KM numbers. When numbers change appropriate cross-referencing has been provided.

Some of the coins listed in this catalog are identified or cross-referenced by numbers assigned by R.S. Yeoman (Y#), or slight adaptations thereof, in his Modern World Coins, and Current Coins of the World. For the pre-Yeoman dated issues, the numbers assigned by William D. Craig (C#) in his Coins of the World (1750-1850 period), 3rd edition, have generally been applied.

In some countries, listings are cross-referenced to Robert Friedberg's (FR#) Gold Coins of the World or Coins of the British World. Major Fred Pridmore's (P#) studies of British colonial coinage are also referenced, as are W.H. Valentine's (V#) references on the Modern Copper Coins of the Muhammadan States. Coins issued under the Chinese sphere of influence are assigned numbers from E. Kann's (K#) Illustrated Catalog of Chinese Coins and T.K. Hsu's (Su) work of similar title. In most cases, these cross-reference numbers are presented in the descriptive text for each type.

DENOMINATIONS

The second basic consideration to be met in the attrition of a coin is the determination of denomination. Since denominations are usually expressed in numeric, rather than word form on a coin, this is usually quite easily accomplished on coins from nations, which use Western numerals, except in those instances where issues are devoid of any mention of face value, and denomination must be attributed by size, metallic composition or weight. Coins listed in this volume are generally illustrated in actual size. Where size is critical to proper attribution, the coin's millimeter size is indicated.

The sphere of countries stretching from North Africa through the Orient, on which numeric symbols generally unfamiliar to Westerners are employed, often provide the collector with a much greater challenge. This is particularly true on nearly all pre-20th Century issues. On some of the more modern issues and increasingly so as the years progress, Western-style numerals usually presented in combination with the local numeric system are becoming more commonplace on these coins.

Determination of a coin's currency system can also be valuable in attributing the issue to its country of origin.

The included table of Standard International Numeral Systems presents charts of the basic numeric designations found on coins of non-Western origin. Although denomination numerals are generally prominently displayed on coins, it must be remembered that these are general representations of characters, which individual coin engravers may have rendered in widely varying styles. Where numeric or script denominations designation forms peculiar to a given coin or country apply, such as the script used on some Persian (Iranian) issues. They are so indicated or illustrated in conjunction with the appropriate listings.

MINTAGES

Quantities minted of each date are indicated where that information is available, generally stated in millions, and usually rounded off to the nearest 10,000 pieces. On quantities of a few thousand or less, actual mintages are generally indicated. For combined mintage figures the abbreviation "Inc. Above" means Included Above, while "Inc. Below" means Included Below. "Est." beside a mintage figure indicates the number given is an estimate or mintage limit.

MINT AND PRIVY MARKS

The presence of distinctive, but frequently inconspicuously placed, mintmarks indicates the mint of issue for many of the coins listed in this catalog. An appropriate designation in the date listings notes the presence, if any, of a mint mark on a particular coin type by incorporating the letter or letters of the mint mark adjoining the date, i.e., 1883CC or 1890H.

The presence of mint and/or mintmaster's privy marks on a coin in non-letter form is indicated by incorporating the mint letter in lower case within parentheses adjoining the date; i.e. 1827(a). The corresponding mark is illustrated or identified in the introduction of the country.

In countries such as France and Mexico, where many mints may be producing like coinage in the same denomination during the same time period, divisions by mint have been employed. In these cases the mint mark may appear next to the individual date listings and/or the mint name or mint mark may be listed in the Note field of the type description.

Where listings incorporate mintmaster initials, they are always presented in capital letters separated from the date by one character space; i.e., 1850 MF. The different mintmark and mintmaster letters found on the coins of any country, state or city of issue are always shown at the beginning of listings.

METALS

Each numbered type listing will contain a description of the coins metallic content. The traditional coinage metals and their symbolic chemical abbreviations sometimes used in this catalog are:

Platinum - (PT)	Copper - (Cu)
Gold - (Au)	Brass -
Silver - (Ag)	Copper-nickel- (CN)
Billion -	Lead - (Pb)
Nickel - (Ni)	Steel -
Zinc - (Zn)	Tin - (Sn)
Bronze - (Ae)	Aluminum - (Al)

During the 18th and 19th centuries, most of the world's coins were struck of copper or bronze, silver and gold. Commencing in the early years of the 20th century, however, numerous new coinage metals, primarily non-precious metal alloys, were introduced. Gold has not been widely used for circulation coinages since World War I, although silver remained a popular coinage metal in most parts of the world until after World War II. With the disappearance of silver for circulation coinage, numerous additional compositions were introduced to coinage applications.

OFF-METAL STRIKES

Off-metal strikes previously designated by "(OMS)" which also included the wide range of error coinage struck in other than their officially authorized compositions have been incorporated into Pattern listings along with special issues, which were struck for presentation or other reasons.

Collectors of Germanic coinage may be familiar with the term "Abschlag" which quickly identifies similar types of coinage.

PRECIOUS METAL WEIGHTS

Listings of weight, fineness and actual silver (ASW), gold (AGW), platinum or palladium (APW) content of most machine-struck silver, gold, platinum and palladium coins are provided in this edition. This information will be found incorporated in each separate type listing, along with other data related to the coin.

The ASW, AGW and APW figures were determined by multiplying the gross weight of a given coin by its known or tested fineness and converting the resulting gram or grain weight to troy ounces, rounded to the nearest ten-thousandth of an ounce. A silver coin with a 24.25-gram weight and .875 fineness for example, would have a fine weight of approximately 21.2188 grams, or a .6822 ASW, a factor that can be used to accurately determine the intrinsic value for multiple examples.

The ASW, AGW or APW figure can be multiplied by the spot price of each precious metal to determine the current intrinsic value of any coin accompanied by these designations.

Coin weights are indicated in grams (abbreviated "g") along with fineness where the information is of value in differentiating between types. These weights are based on 31.103 grams per troy (scientific) ounce, as opposed to the avoirdupois (commercial) standard of 28.35 grams. Actual coin weights are generally shown in hundredths or thousands of a gram; i.e., 2.9200 g., SILVER, 0.500 oz.

WEIGHTS AND FINENESSES

As the silver and gold bullion markets have advanced and declined sharply in recent years, the fineness and total precious metal content of coins has become especially significant where bullion coins - issues which trade on the basis of their intrinsic metallic content rather than numismatic value - are concerned. In many instances, such issues have become worth more in bullion form than their nominal collector values or denominations indicate.

Establishing the weight of a coin can also be valuable for determining its denomination. Actual weight is also necessary to ascertain the specific gravity of the coin's metallic content, an important factor in determining authenticity.

TROY WEIGHT STANDARDS

24 Grains = 1 Pennyweight
480 Grains = 1 Ounce
31.103 Grams = 1 Ounce

UNIFORM WEIGHTS

15.432 Grains = 1 Gram
0.0648 Gram = 1 Grain

AVOIRDUPOIS STANDARDS

27-11/32 Grains = 11 Dram
437-1/2 Grains = 1 Ounce
28.350 Grams = 1 Ounce

HOMELAND TYPES

Homeland types are coins which colonial powers used in a colony, but do not bear that location's name. In some cases they were legal tender in the homeland, in others not. They are listed under the homeland and cross-referenced at the colony listing.

COUNTERMARKS/COUNTERSTAMPS

There is some confusion among collectors over the terms "countermark" and "counterstamp" when applied to a coin bearing an additional mark or change of design and/or denomination.

To clarify, a countermark might be considered similar to the "hall mark" applied to a piece of silverware, by which a silversmith assured the quality of the piece. In the same way, a countermark assures the quality of the coin on which it is placed, as, for example, when the royal crown of England was countermarked (punched into) on segmented Spanish reales, allowing them to circulate in commerce in the British West Indies. An additional countermark indicating the new denomination may also be encountered on these coins.

Countermarks are generally applied singularly and in most cases indiscriminately on either side of the "host" coin.

Counterstamped coins are more extensively altered. The counterstamping is done with a set of dies, rather than a hand punch. The coin being counterstamped is placed between the new dies and struck as if it were a blank planchet as found with the Manila 8 reales issue of the Philippines.

PHOTOGRAPHS

To assist the reader in coin identification, every effort has been made to present actual size photographs of every coinage type listed. Obverse and reverse are illustrated, except when a change in design is restricted to one side, and the coin has a diameter of 39mm or larger, in which case only the side required for identification of the type is generally illustrated. All coins up to 60mm are illustrated actual size, to the nearest 1/2mm up to 25mm, and to the nearest 1mm thereafter. Coins larger than 60mm diameter are illustrated in reduced size, with the actual size noted in the descriptive text block. Where slight change in size is important to coin type identification, actual millimeter measurements are stated.

TRADE COINS

From approximately 1750-1940, a number of nations, particularly European colonial powers and commercial traders, minted trade coins to facilitate commerce with the local populace of Africa, the Arab countries, the Indian subcontinental, Southeast Asia and the Far East. Such coins generally circulated at a value based on the weight and fineness of their silver or gold content, rather than their stated denomination. Examples include the sovereigns of Great Britain and the gold ducat issues of Austria, Hungary and the Netherlands. Trade coinage will sometimes be found listed at the end of the domestic issues.

VALUATIONS

Values quoted in this catalog represent the current market and are compiled from recommendations provided and verified through various source documents and specialized consultants. It should be stressed, however, that this book is intended to serve only as an aid for evaluating coins, actual market conditions are constantly changing and additional influences, such as particularly strong local demand for certain coin series, fluctuation of international exchange rates and worldwide collection patterns must also be considered. Publication of this catalog is not intended as a solicitation by the publisher, editors or contributors to buy or sell the coins listed at the prices indicated.

All valuations are stated in U.S. dollars, based on careful assessment of the varied international collector market. Valuations for coins priced below $100.00 are generally stated in full amounts - i.e. 37.50 or 95.00 - while valuations at or above that figure are rounded off in even dollars - i.e. $125.00 is expressed 125. A comma is added to indicate thousands of dollars in value.

It should be noted that when particularly select uncirculated or proof-like examples of uncirculated coins become available they can be expected to command proportionately high premiums. Such examples in reference to choice Germanic Thalers are referred to as "erst schlage" or first strikes.

TOKEN COINAGE

At times local economic conditions have forced regular coinage from circulation or found mints unable to cope with the demand for coinage, giving rise to privately issued token coinage substitutes. British tokens of the late 1700s and early 1880s, and the German and French and French Colonial emergency emissions of the World War I era are examples of such tokens being freely accepted in monetary transactions over wide areas. Tokens were likewise introduced to satisfy specific restricted needs, such as the leper colony issues of Brazil, Colombia and the Philippines.

This catalog includes introductory or detailed listings with "Tn" prefixes of many token coinage issues, particularly those which enjoyed wide circulation and where the series was limited in diversity. More complex series, and those more restricted in scope of circulation are generally not listed, although a representative sample may be illustrated and a specialty reference provided.

MEDALLIC ISSUES

All medallic issues can be found in the current edition of Unusual World Coins.

RESTRIKES, COUNTERFEITS

Deceptive restrike and counterfeit (both contemporary and modern) examples exist of some coin issues. Where possible, the existence of restrikes is noted. Warnings are also incorporated in instances where particularly deceptive counterfeits are known to exist. Collectors who are uncertain about the authenticity of a coin held in their collection, or being offered for sale, should take the precaution of having it authenticated by the American Numismatic Association Authentication Bureau, 818 N. Cascade, Colorado Springs, CO 80903. Their reasonably priced certification tests are widely accepted by collectors and dealers alike.

EDGE VARIETIES

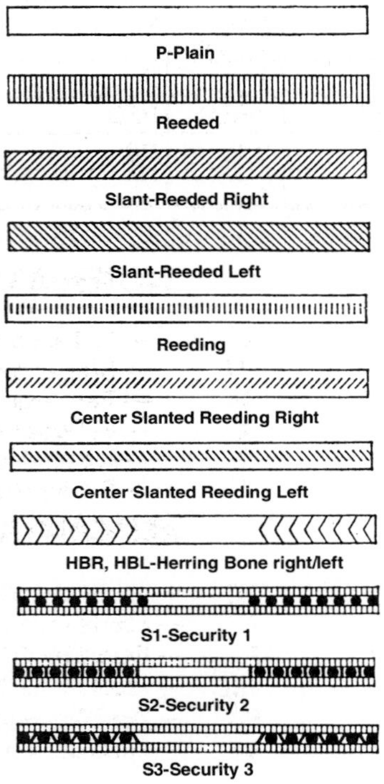

CONDITIONS/GRADING

Wherever possible, coin valuations are given in four or five grades of preservation. For modern commemoratives, which do not circulate, only uncirculated values are usually sufficient. Proof issues are indicated by the word "Proof" next to the date, with valuation proceeded by the word "value" following the mintage. For very recent circulating coins and coins of limited value, one, two or three grade values are presented.

There are almost no grading guides for world coins. What follows is an attempt to help bridge that gap until a detailed, illustrated guide becomes available.

In grading world coins, there are two elements to look for: 1) Overall wear, and 2) loss of design details, such as strands of hair, feathers on eagles, designs on coats of arms, etc.

The age, rarity or type of a coin should not be a consideration in grading.

Grade each coin by the weaker of the two sides. This method appears to give results most nearly consistent with conservative American Numismatic Association standards for U.S. coins. Split grades, i.e., F/VF for obverse and reverse, respectively, are normally no more than one grade apart. If the two sides are more than one grade apart, the series of coins probably wears differently on each side and should then be graded by the weaker side alone.

Grade by the amount of overall wear and loss of design detail evident on each side of the coin. On coins with a moderately small design element, which is prone to early wear, grade by that design alone. For example, the 5-ore (KM#554) of Sweden has a crown above the monogram on which the beads on the arches show wear most clearly. So, grade by the crown alone.

For Brilliant Uncirculated (BU) grades there will be no visible signs of wear or handling, even under a 30-power microscope. Full mint luster will be present. Ideally no bags marks will be evident.

For Uncirculated (Unc.) grades there will be no visible signs of wear or handling, even under a 30-power microscope. Bag marks may be present.

For Almost Uncirculated (AU), all detail will be visible. There will be wear only on the highest point of the coin. There will often be half or more of the original mint luster present.

On the Extremely Fine (XF or EF) coin, there will be about 95% of the original detail visible. Or, on a coin with a design with no inner detail to wear down, there will be a light wear over nearly all the coin. If a small design is used as the grading area, about 90% of the original detail will be visible. This latter rule stems from the logic that a smaller amount of detail needs to be present because a small area is being used to grade the whole coin.

The Very Fine (VF) coin will have about 75% of the original detail visible. Or, on a coin with no inner detail, there will be moderate wear over the entire coin. Corners of letters and numbers may be weak. A small grading area will have about 66% of the original detail.

For Fine (F), there will be about 50% of the original detail visible. Or, on a coin with no inner detail, there will be fairly heavy wear over all of the coin. Sides of letters will be weak. A typically uncleaned coin will often appear as dirty or dull. A small grading area will have just under 50% of the original detail.

On the Very Good (VG) coin, there will be about 25% of the original detail visible. There will be heavy wear on all of the coin.

The Good (G) coin's design will be clearly outlined but with substantial wear. Some of the larger detail may be visible. The rim may have a few weak spots of wear.

On the About Good (AG) coin, there will typically be only a silhouette of a large design. The rim will be worn down into the letters if any.

Strong or weak strikes, partially weak strikes, damage, corrosion, attractive or unattractive toning, dipping or cleaning should be described along with the above grades. These factors affect the quality of the coin just as do wear and loss of detail, but are easier to describe.

In the case of countermarked/counterstamped coins, the condition of the host coin will have a bearing on the end valuation. The important factor in determining the grade is the condition, clarity and completeness of the countermark itself. This is in reference to countermarks/counterstamps having raised design while being struck in a depression.

Incuse countermarks cannot be graded for wear. They are graded by the clarity and completeness including the condition of the host coin which will also have more bearing on the final grade/valuation determined.

STANDARD INTERNATIONAL GRADING TERMINOLOGY AND ABBREVIATIONS

	PROOF	UNCIRCULATED	EXTREMELY FINE	VERY FINE	FINE	VERY GOOD	GOOD	POOR
U.S. and ENGLISH SPEAKING LANDS	PRF	UNC	EF or XF	VF	F	VG	G	PR
BRAZIL	—	(1)FDC or FC	(3) S	(5) MBC	(7) BC	(8) BC/R	(9) R	UT GeG
DENMARK	M	0	01	1+	1	1÷	2	3
FINLAND	00	0	01	1+	1	1?	2	3
FRANCE	FB Flan Bruni	FDC Fleur de Coin	SUP Superbe	TTB Très très beau	TB Très beau	B Beau	TBC Très Bien Conservée	BC Bien Conservée
GERMANY	PP Polierte Platte	STG Stempelglanz	VZ Vorzüglich	SS Sehr schön	S Schön	S.G.E. Sehr gut erhalten	G.E. Gut erhalten	Gering erhalten
ITALY	FS Fondo Specchio	FDC Fior di Conio	SPL Splendido	BB Bellissimo	MB Molto Bello	B Bello	M	—
JAPAN	—	未使用	極美品	美品	並品	—	—	—
NETHERLANDS	— Proef	FDC Fleur de Coin	Pr. Prachtig	Z.f. Zeer fraai	Fr. Fraai	Z.g. Zeer goed	G	—
NORWAY	M	0	01	1+	1	1÷	2	3
PORTUGAL	—	Soberba	Bela	MBC	BC	MREG	REG	MC
SPAIN	Prueba	SC	EBC	MBC	BC+	BC	RC	MC
SWEDEN	Polerad	0	01	1+	1	1?	2	—

BRAZIL

FE — Flor de Estampa
S — Soberba
MBC — Muito Bem Conservada
BC — Bem Conservada
R — Regular
UTGeG — Um Tanto Gasto e Gasto

DENMARK

O — Uncirkuleret
01 — Meget Paent Eksemplar
1+ — Paent Eksemplar
1 — Acceptabelt Eksemplar
1 —Noget Slidt Eksemplar
2 — Darlight Eksemplar
3 — Meget Darlight Eskemplar

FINLAND

00 — Kiitolyonti
0 — Lyontiveres
01 — Erittain Hyva
1+ — Hyva
1? — Keikko
3 — Huono

FRANCE

NEUF — New
SUP — Superbe
TTB — Tres Tres Beau
TB — Tres Beau
B — Beau
TBC — Tres Bien Conserve
BC — Bien Conserve

GERMANY

VZGL — Vorzüglich
SS — Sehr schön
S — Schön
S.g.E. — Sehr gut erhalten
G.e. — Gut erhalten
G.e.S. — Gering erhalten Schlecht

ITALY

Fds — Fior di Stampa
SPL — Splendid
BB — Bellissimo
MB — Molto Bello
B — Bello
M — Mediocre

JAPAN

未使用 — Mishiyo
極美品 — Goku Bihin
美品 — Bihin
並品 — Futuhin

NETHERLANDS

Pr. — Prachtig
Z.F. — Zeer Fraai
Fr. — Fraai
Z.g. — Zeer Goed
G — Goed

NORWAY

0 — Usirkuleret eks
01 — Meget pent eks
1+ — Pent eks
1 — Fullgodt eks
1- — Ikke Fullgodt eks
2 — Darlig eks

ROMANIA

NC — Necirculata (UNC)
FF — Foarte Frumoasa (VF)
F — Frumoasa (F)
FBC — Foarte Bine Conservata (VG)
BC — Bine Conservata (G)
M — Mediocru Conservata (POOR)

SPAIN

EBC — Extraordinariamente Bien Conservada
SC — Sin Circular
IC — Incirculante
MBC — Muy Bien Conservada
BC — Bien Conservada
RC — Regular Conservada
MC — Mala Conservada

SWEDEN

0 — Ocirkulerat
01 — Mycket Vackert
1+ — Vackert
1 — Fullgott
1? — Ej Fullgott
2 — Dalight

STANDARD INTERNATIONAL NUMERAL SYSTEMS

Prepared especially for the *Standard Catalog of World Coins*© 2010 by Krause Publications

Western	0	½	1	2	3	4	5	6	7	8	9	10	50	100	500	1000
Roman			I	II	III	IV	V	VI	VII	VIII	IX	X	L	C	D	M
Arabic-Turkish	٠	١/٢	١	٢	٣	٤	٥	٦	٧	٨	٩	١٠	٥٠	١٠٠	٥٠٠	١٠٠٠
Malay-Persian	٠	١/٢	١	٢	٣	۴	۵	٦ or ۶	٧	٨	٩	١٠	۵٠	١٠٠	۵٠٠	١٠٠٠
Eastern Arabic	۰	۱/۲	۱	۲	۳	۴	۵	۶	۷	۸	۹	۱۰	۵۰	۱۰۰	۵۰۰	۱۰۰۰
Hyderabad Arabic	٠	١/٢	١	٢	٣	۴	۵	۶	٧	٨	٩	١٠	۵٠	١٠٠	۵٠٠	١٠٠٠
Indian (Sanskrit)	०	१/२	१	२	३	४	५	६	७	८	९	१०	५०	१००	५००	१०००
Assamese	০	১/২	১	২	৩	৪	৫	৬	৭	৮	৯	১০	৫০	১০০	৫০০	১০০০
Bengali	০	১/২	১	২	৩	৪	৫	৬	৭	৮	৯	১০	৫০	১০০	৫০০	১০০০
Gujarati	૦	૧/૨	૧	૨	૩	૪	૫	૬	૭	૮	૯	૧૦	૫૦	૧૦૦	૫૦૦	૧૦૦૦
Kutch	०	१/२	१	२	३	४	५	६	७	८	९	१०	५०	१००	५००	१०००
Devavnagri	०	१/२	१	२	३	४	५	६ or ६	७	८	९ or ९	१०	५०	१००	५००	१०००
Nepalese	०	१/२	१	२	३	४	५	६	७	८	९	१०	५०	१००	५००	१०००
Tibetan	༠	༡/༢	༡	༢	༣	༤	༥	༦	༧	༨	༩	༡༠	༥༠	༡༠༠	༥༠༠	༡༠༠༠
Mongolian	᠐	᠑/᠒	᠑	᠒	᠓	᠔	᠕	᠖	᠗	᠘	᠙	᠑᠐	᠕᠐	᠑᠐᠐	᠕᠐᠐	᠑᠐᠐᠐
Burmese	၀	၁/၂	၁	၂	၃	၄	၅	၆	၇	၈	၉	၁၀	၅၀	၁၀၀	၅၀၀	၁၀၀၀
Thai-Lao	๐	๑/๒	๑	๒	๓	๔	๕	๖	๗	๘	๙	๑๐	๕๐	๑๐๐	๕๐๐	๑๐๐๐
Lao-Laotian	໐		໑	໒	໓	໔	໕	໖	໗	໘	໙	໑໐				
Javanese	꧐		꧑	꧒	꧓	꧔	꧕	꧖	꧗	꧘	꧙	꧑꧐	꧕꧐	꧑꧐꧐	꧕꧐꧐	꧑꧐꧐꧐
Ordinary Chinese Japanese-Korean	零	半	一	二	三	四	五	六	七	八	九	十	十五	百	百五	千
Official Chinese			壹	貳	叁	肆	伍	陸	柒	捌	玖	拾	拾伍	佰	佰伍	仟
Commercial Chinese			〡	〢	〣	〤	〥	〦	〧	〨	〩	十	〥十	〡百	〥百	〡千
Korean		반	일	이	삼	사	오	육	칠	팔	구	십	오십	백	오백	천
Georgian			ა	ბ	გ	დ	ე	ვ	ზ	ჱ	თ	ი	ნ	რ	უ	ჩ
			11 ია	20 კ	30 ლ	40 მ	60 ჲ	70 ო	80 პ	90 ჟ	200 ს	300 ტ	400 ჳ	600 ფ	700 ქ	800 ღ
Ethiopian	◆		፩	፪	፫	፬	፭	፮	፯	፰	፱	፲	፶	፻	፭፻	፲፻
				20 ፳	30 ፴	40 ፵	60 ፷	70 ፸	80 ፹	90 ፺						
Hebrew			א	ב	ג	ד	ה	ו	ז	ח	ט	י	נ	ק	תק	
				20 כ	30 ל	40 מ	60 ס	70 ע	80 פ	90 צ	200 ר	300 ש	400 ת	600 תר	700 תש	800 תת
Greek			Α	Β	Γ	Δ	Ε	Τ	Ζ	Η	Θ	Ι	Ν	Ρ	Φ	Α
				20 Κ	30 Λ	40 Μ	60 Ξ	70 Ο	80 Π		200 Σ	300 Τ	400 Υ	600 Χ	700 Ψ	800 Ω

ILLUSTRATED GUIDE TO EASTERN MINT NAMES

Compiled by Dr. N. Douglas Nicol, 2006

Abarquh (Iran) ابرقوه

'Abdullahnagar (Pihani) عبدالله نگر

Abivard ابي ورد ابيورد باورد

Abu Arish (the Yemen) ابو عريش

Abushahr (Bushire - Iran) ابو سهر

'Adan (Aden-the Yemen) عدن

Adoni (Imtiyazgarh-Mughal) ادوني

Adrana (see Edirne)

Advani (Adoni - Mughal) ادواني

Afghanistan افغانستان

Agra (Mughal) اگره

Ahmadabad (Gujarat Sultanate, Mughal, Maratha, Bombay Presidency, Baroda) احمداباد

Ahmadnagar (Ahmadnagar Sultanate, احمدنگر

Ahmadnagar Farrukhabad (state, Afghanistan) احمدنگر فرخ اباد

Ahmadpur (Bahawalpur, Afghanistan) احمدپور

Ahmadshahi (Qandahar - Afghanistan) احمدشاهي

Ahsanabad (Kulbarga - Mughal) احسن اباد

Ajman (United Arab Emirates) عجمان

Ajmer (Salimabad - Mughal, Maratha, Gwalior, Jodhpur) اجمير

Ajmer Salimabad (Mughal) اجمير سليم اباد

Akalpurakh (Kashmir, Sikh) اكال پورخ

Akbarabad (Agra - Mughal, Maratha, Bharatpur) اكبراباد

Akbarnagar (Rajmahal - Mughal) اكبرنگر

Akbarpur (Tanda - Mughal) اكبرپور

Akbarpur Tanda (Mughal) اكبرپور تانده

Akhshi, Akhshikath (Central Asia) اخشي اخشيكاث

Akhtarnagar (Awadh - Mughal) اخترنگر

'Akka (Ottoman Turkey) عكّا عكّة

Aksu (China - Sinkiang) اقسو اقصو

al-Aliya العالية

'Alamgirnagar (Mughal, Koch Bihar) عالمگيرنگر

'Alamgirpur (Bhilsa, Vidisha-Mughal, Gwalior) عالم گيرپور

Amul (Iran) آمل

al-'Arabiya as-Sa'udiya (Saudi Arabia) العربية السعودية

al-'Ara'ish (Larache - Morocco) العرائش

Algeria (al-Jaza'ir) الجزائر

'Alinagar (Calcutta - Mughal) علي نگر

'Alinagar Kalkatah (Calcutta - Bengal Pres.) علي نگر كلكته

Allahabad (Mughal, Awadh) الله اباد

Almora (Gurkha)

Alwar (Mughal) الوار

Amaravati (Hyderabad) امراوتي

Amasya (Amasia - Turkey) اماسية

Amid (Turkey) آمد

Amritsar (Ambratsar - Sikh) امبرت سر امرت سر

Amirkot (Umarkot - Mughal) اميركوت

Anandghar (Anandpur - Mughal) انندگهره

Andijan (Andigan - Central Asia) اندجان اندگان

Anhirwala Pattan (Mughal) انحيروالا پتن

Ankaland (Bi-Ankaland - in England, Birmingham and London mints for Morocco) انكلند بانكلند

Ankara (Anguriya, Engüriye - Turkey) انگورية انقرية انقرة

Anupnagar Shahabad (Mughal) انوپنگر شاه باد

Anwala (Anola - Mughal, Rohilkhand, Afghanistan) انوله

Aqsara (Aqsaray, Aksara - the Yemen) اقصرا اقصراي اكصرا

Ardabil (Iran) اردبيل

Ardanuç (Turkey) اردنوج اردانيج

Ardanush (Iran) اردنوش

Arjish (Iran) ارجيش

Arkat (Arcot - Mughal, French India, Madras Presidency) اركات

Asafabad (Bareli - Mughal, Awadh) اصف اباد

Asafabad Bareli (Mughal, Awadh) اصفاباد

Asafnagar (Aklooj - Mughal, Rohilkhand, Awadh) اصف نگر اصفنگر

Asfarayin (Central Asia, Iran) اسفراين

Asfi (Safi - Morocco) اسفي

Asir (Asirgarh - Mughal) اسير

Astarabad (Central Asia, Iran) استراباد

Atak (Attock - Mughal, Afghanistan) اتك

Atak Banaras (Mughal) اتك بنارس

Atcheh (Sultanate, Netherlands East Indies) اچه

Athani (Maratha) اثاني

Aurangabad (Khujista Bunyad - Mughal, Hyderabad) اورنگ اباد

Aurangnagar (Mughal, Maratha) اورنگ نگر

Ausa (Mughal) اوسا

Awadh (Oudh, Khitta - Awadh state) اوده

Awbah (Central Asia) اوبه

Ayasluk (Ayasoluq, Ephesus - Turkey) اياسلق اياثلق

Aydaj (Iran) ايدج

Azak (Azow - Turkey) آزاق آزق

A'zamnagar (Gokak - Mughal) اعظم نگر

A'zamnagar Bankapur (Mughal) اعظم نگر بنكاپور

A'zamnagar Gokak (Belgaum - Mughal, اعظم نگر گوكاك

'Azimabad (Patna - Mughal, Bengal Presidency) عظيم اباد

Badakhshan (Mughal, Central Asia, Afghanistan) بدخشان

Bagalkot (Maratha) بگلكوت

Bagchih Serai (Krim) باغچه سراي

Baghdad (Bagdad - Iraq) بغداد

Bahadurgarh (Mughal) — بهادرگره

Bahawalpur (Bahawalpur state, Afghanistan) — بهاولپور

Bahraich (Mughal) — بهرايچ بهريچ

Bahrain (al-Bahrayn) — البحرين

Bairata (Mughal) — بيراتة

Bakhar (Bakkar, Bakhar, Bhakhar, Bhakkar - Mughal, Sind, Afghanistan) — بهكّر بهكهر

Baku (Bakuya - Iran) — باكو باكويه

Balanagor Gadha (Mandla - Maratha) — بالانگر گدها

Balapur (two places - one in Kandesh, one in Sira - Mughal) — بالاپور

Balhari (Bellary - Mysore) — بلهاري

Balikesir (Turkey) — بالكسير

Balkh (Mughal, Central Asia, Afghanistan) — بلخ

Balwantnagar (Jhansi - Mughal, Maratha, Gwalior) — بلونت نگر

Banaras (Benares, Varanasi - Mughal, Bengal Presidency, Awadh) — بنارس

Banda Malwari (Maratha) — بنده ملواري

Bandar (Iran) — بندر

Bandar Abbas (Iran) — بندر عباس

Bandar Abu Shahr (Iran) — بندر ابو شهر

Bandar Shahi (Mughal) — بندرشاهي

Bandhu (Qila - Mughal) — بندهو

Bangala (Mughal) — بنگالة

Banjarmasin (Netherlands East Indies) — بنجرمسن

Bankapur (Mughal) — بنكپ بنكاپور

Baramati (Sultanate, Mughal) — بنده ملواري

Bareli (Bareilly - Mughal, Rohilkhand, Awadh, Afghanistan) — بريلي

Bariz (Paris, in Paris - Morocco) — باريز بباريز

Baroda (Vadodara - Baroda state) — بروده

Basoda (Gwalior) — بسوده

al-Basra (Basra - Iraq) — البصرة

Batan (Baltistan? - Ladakh) — بتان

Bela (Las Bela state) — بيله

Belgrad (Turkey) — بنگالور

Bengalur (Bangalor - Mysore) — بنگالور

Berar (Mughal) — برار

Berlin (for Morocco) — برلين

Bhakkar, Bhakhar (See Bakkar)

Bharatpur (Braj Indrapur) — بهرت پور

Bhaunagar (Mughal) — بهاونگر

Bhelah (See Bela) — بهله

Bhilsa (Alamgirpur - Mughal) — بهيلسة

Bhilwara (Mewar) — بهيلوارا

Bhopal (Bhopal state) — بهوپال

Bhuj (Kutch) — بهوج

Bhujnagar (Bhuj - Kutch) — بهوج نگر

Bidlis (Bitlis - Turkey) — بدليس بتليس

Bidrur (Mughal) — بدرور

Bihbihan (Behbehan - Iran) — بهبهان

Bijapur (Bijapur Sultanate, Mughal) — بيجاپور

Bikanir (Mughal, Bikanir state) — بيكانير

Bindraban (Vrindavan - Mughal, Bindraban state) — بندربن

Bisauli (Rohilkhand) — بسولے بسولي

Bistam (Central Asia) — بسطام

Biyar (Iran) — بيار

Borujerd (Iran) — بروجرد

Bosna (Sarajevo - Turkey) — بوسنه

Bosna Saray (Sarajevo - Turkey) — بوسنة سراي

Braj Indrapur (Bharatpur) — برج اندرپور

Broach (Baroch, Bharoch - Mughal, Broach state, Gwalior) — بروني

Brunei (Malaya) — بروني

Bukhara (Central Asia) — بخارا

Bukhara-yi Sharif (Central Asia) — بخاراي شريف

Bundi (Bundi state) — بوندي

Burhanabad (Mughal) — برهان اباد

Burhanpur (Mughal, Maratha, Gwalior) — برهانپور

Bursa (Brusa - Turkey) — برسه بروسه

Bushanj (Iran) — بوشنج

Bushire (see Abushahr)

Çaniçe (Chanicha - Turkey) — چانيچه چاينيچه

Chakan (Maratha) — چاكن

Champanir (Gujarat Sultanate) — چانپانير

Chanda (Maratha) — چانده

Chanderi (Gwalior) — چنديري

Chandor (Maratha, Indore) — چاندور

Chhachrauli (Kalsia) — چهچرولي

Chhatarpur (Chhatarpur state) — چترپور

Chikodi (Maratha) — چكودي

Chinapattan (Madras - Mughal) — چيناپتن

Chinchwar (Maratha) — چنچور

Chitor (Akbarpur - Mughal) — چيتور

Chunar (Mughal) — چنار

Cuttack (see Katak)

Dadiyan (Iran) — داديان

Dalipnagar (Datia) — دليپ نگر

Damarvar (Mysore) — دماروار

Damghan (Central Asia) — دامغان

al-Damigh (the Yemen) — الدامغ

Damla (Mughal) — داملا

Darband (Derbent - Azerbaijan, Iran) — دربند

Darfur (see al-Fashir)

Darur (Mughal) — درور دارر

Daulatabad (Deogir - Mughal, Hyderabad) — دولت اباد دولتاباد

Daulat Anjazanchiya (see Comoros) — دولة انجزنچية

Daulatgarh (Rahatgarh - Bharatpur, Gwalior) — دولت گره

Daulat Qatar (State of Qatar - Qatar) دولة قطر

Dawar (Iran) داور

al-Dawla al-Mughribiya (Empire of Morocco) الدولة المغربية

Dawlatabad (Iran) دولتاباد

Dawraq (Iran) دورق

Dehdasht (Iran) دهدشت

Dehli (Shahjahanabad - Mughal, Afghanistan) دهلي

Deli (Netherlands East Indies) دلي

Deogarh (Partabgarh) ديوگره

Deogir (Daulatabad - Mughal) ديوگير

Dera (Derah - Mughal, Sikh, Afghanistan) ديره

Derajat (Mughal, Sikh, Afghanistan) ديره جات

Dewal Bandar (Mughal) ديول بندر

Dezful (Iran) دزفول

Dhamar (the Yemen) ذمار ذمر

Dharwar (Mysore) دهاروار

Dholapur (Dholapur state) دهولپور دہولپور

Dicholi (Mughal, Maratha) ديچولي

Dilshadabad (Mughal, Narayanpett) دلشاداباد

Dimashq (Damascus - Syria) دمشق

Diyar Bakr (Turkey) ديار بكر

Djibouti (Jaibuti - French Somaliland) جيبوتي

Dogam (Dogaon - Mughal) دوگام

Dogaon (Mughal) دوگاون

Edirne (Adrianople - Turkey) ادرنه

Elichpur (Mughal, Hyderabad) ايلچپور

Erzurum (Theodosiopolis - Turkey) ارزروم

Faiz Hisar (Gooty - Mysore) فعز حصار

Farahabad (Iran) فرح اباد

Farkhanda Bunyad (Hyderabad - Mughal) فرخنده بنياد

Farrukhabad (Ahmadnagar - Mughal, Bengal Presidency) فرخ اباد

Farrukhi (Feroke - Mysore) فرخي

Farrukhnagar (Mughal) فرخ نگر

Farrukhyab Hisar (Chitradurga - Mysore) فرخياب حصار

Fas (Fez - Morocco) فاس

Fas al-Jadid (see al-Madina al-Bayda' - Morocco) فاش الجديد

al-Fashir (Darfur, Sudan) الفشير

Fathabad Dharur (Mughal) فتح اباد دهرور

Fathnagar (Aurangabad - فتحنگر

Fathpur (Nusratabad, Sikri - Mughal) فتحپور

Fedala (Fadalat al-Muhammadiya - Morocco) فضالة

Fergana (Central Asia) فرغانة

Filastin (Palestine) فلسطين

Filibe (Philipopolis, Plovdiv - Turkey) فيليپ فلبه

Firozgarh (Yadgir - Mughal) فيروزگره

Firoznagar (Mughal, Hyderabad) فيروزنگر

al-Fujaira (United Arab الفجيرة

Fuman (Iran) فومان

Gadraula (Mughal) گدرولة

Gadwal (Hyderabad) گدوال

Gajjikota (Mughal) گجيكوتا

Ganja (Ganjah, Genje - Elizabethpol, Kirovabad in Azerbaijan, Iran, Turkey) گنجه

Ganjikot (Genjikot - Mughal) گنجيكوت

Gargaon (Assam) گرگاو

Garha (Mughal) گارحة

Gelibolu (Gallipoli - Turkey) گليبولي

Ghazni (Afghanistan) غزني

al-Ghurfa (Hadhramaut) الغرفة

Gilan (Iran) گنلان

Gobindpur (Mughal) گوبندپور

Gohad (Mughal, Dholapur) گوهد

Gokak (Belgaum, 'Azamnagar - Mughal) گوكاك

Gokul (Bindraban) گوكل

Gokulgarh (Mughal) گوكل گره

Gorakpur (Muazzamabad - Mughal) گوركپور

Gözlü (see Shahr-Gözlü - Krim) گوزلو

Gulbarga (Kulbarga, Ahsanabad - Mughal) گلبرگة

Gulkanda (Golkona - Sultanate, Mughal) گلكندة

Gulshanabad (Nasik - Mughal, Maratha) گلشن اباد

Gümüsh-hane (Turkey) گمشخانه

Guti (Gooty - Mughal, Mysore) گوتي

Guzelhisar (Turkey) گوزلحصر

Gwaliar (Mughal, Gwalior state, گواليار

Hafizabad (Mughal) هافظاباد

Haidarabad (Hyderabad, Haidrabad, Farkhanda Bunyad - Golkanda Sultanate, Mughal, Hyderabad state, Sind, Afghanistan) حيدراباد

Haidarnagar (Bednur, Nagar - Mysore) حيدرنگر

Hajipur (Mughal) حجيپور

Halab (Aleppo - Syria) حلب

Hamadan (Iran) همدان

Hansi (Qanauj - Mughal, Awadh) هانسي

al-Haramayn ash-Sharifayn (Mecca and Medina in Arabia - Ottoman Turkey) الحرمين الشريفين

al-Harar (Ethiopia) الهرر

Hardwar (Haridwar, Tirath - Mughal, Saharanpur) هاردوار

Harput, Harburt (see Khartapirt)

Harran (Turkey) حران

Hasanabad (Mughal) حسن اباد

Hathras (Mughal, Awadh) هاتهرس

Hathrasa (Hathras) هاتهرسا

Hawran (Horan - Syria) حوران

Hawta (the Yemen) حوطة

Hawz (Morocco) حوز

al-Hejaz (Saudi Arabia) الحجاز

Herat (Afghanistan, Central Asia, Iran) هراة هرات

al-Hilla (Hille - Iraq) الحلة

Hinganhat (Maratha) حنگنهات

Hisar (Central Asia) حصر حصار

Hisar Firoza (Mughal) حصار فيروزة

al-Hisn (el-Hisin - Turkey) الحصن

Hizan (Khizan - Turkey) هزان خيزان

Hukeri (Mughal, Maratha) هوكري

Husaingarh (Mughal) حسين گره

Huwayza (Iran) حويزة

Ibb (the Yemen) ايب

Ilahabad (Allahabad) اله اباد

Ilahabas (Mughal) اله اباس

Ili (China - Sinkiang) الي

al-Imarat al-'Arabiya al-Muttahida (United Arab Emirates) امتيازگره

Imtiyazgarh (Adoni - Mughal) امتيازگره

Indore (Indore state) اندور

Inebolu (Turkey) اينه بولى

Inegöl (Turkey) اينه كول

Iran ايران

al-Iraq

Iravan (Eravan, Erewan, Revan – Iran, Yeravan – Armenia) ايروان

'Isagarh (Gwalior) عيسى گره

Isfahan (Iran) اصفهان

Islamabad (Mathura – Mughal, Bindraban) اسلام اباد

Islam Bandar (Rajapur – Mughal) اسلام بندر

Islambul (Istanbul – Turkey) اسلامبول

Islamnagar (Navanagar – Mughal) اسلام نگر

Ismailgarh (Mughal) اسمعيل گره

Italian Somaliland (Somalia) الصومال الايطاليانية

Itawa (Mughal, Maratha, Rohilkhand, Awadh) اتاوه اتاوا

Izmir (Turkey) ازمير ازمر

Jabbalpur (Mughal) جَبالپور

Ja'farabad urf Chandor (Indore) جعفراباد عرف چاندور

Jahangirnagar (Dacca - Mughal, Bengal Presidency) جهانگيرنگر

Jaipur (Sawai - Mughal) جي پور

Jaisalmir (Jaisalmir state) جيسلمير

Jalalnagar (Mughal) جلال نگر

Jalalpur (Mughal) جلالپور

Jalaun (Jalon - Maratha) جلون

Jalesar (Mughal) جليسار

Jallandar (Jullundur - Mughal) جالندر جلّندر

Jalnapur (Jalna - Mughal) جالنة پور

Jambusar (Baroda) جمبوسر

Jammu (Jamun - Kashmir) جمون

Jaora (Jaora state) جاوره

Jaunpur (Mughal) جونپور

Java (Netherlands East Indies) جاو جاوا

Jaytapur (Jaiyatpur - Mughal) جيت پور

Jaza'ir (Algiers) جزائر

Jaza'ir Gharb (Algiers) جزائر غرب

al-Jaza'ir-i Gharb (Algiers) الجزائر غرب

Jelu (Jelou - Iran) جلو

Jerba (Cerbe, Gabes - جربة

Jering (Jaring, Jerin - جريج جرين

Jhalawar (Jhalawar state) جهالاوار

Jinji (Nusratgarh - جنجي

Jind (Jind state) جيند

Jodhpur (Mughal, Jodhpur state) جودهپور

Jordan (al-Urdunn) الاردن

al-Jumhuriya al-'Arabiya al-Muttahida (The United Arab Republic - Egypt, Syria and the Yemen) الجمهورية العربية المتحدة

al-Jumhuriya al-'Arabiya al-Suriya (The Arab Republic of Syria) الجمهورية العربية السورية

al-Jumhuriya al-'Arabiya al-Yamaniya (The Arab Republic of the Yemen) الجمهورية العربية اليمنية

al-Jumhuriya al-'Iraqiya (The Republic of Iraq) الجمهورية العراقية

al-Jumhuriya al-Libiya (The Republic of Libya) الجمهورية الليبية

al-Jumhuriya al-Lubnaniya (The Republic of Lebanon) الجمهورية اللبنانية

al-Jumhuriya as-Somal (The Republic of Somalia) الجمهورية الصومال

al-Jumhuriya as-Sudan (The Republic of the Sudan) الجمهورية السودان

al-Jumhuriya as-Sudan al-Dimuqratiya (The Democratic Republic of the Sudan) الجمهورية السودان الديمقراطية

al-Jumhuriya as-Suriiya (The Republic of Syria) الجمهورية السورية

al-Jumhuriya at-Tunisiya (The Republic of Tunisia) الجمهورية العراقية

al-Jumhuriya al-Yaman al-Dimuqratia al-Shu'ubiya (The Peoples' Democratic Republic of the Yemen) الجمهورية اليمن الديمقراطية الشعبية

Jumhuriyeti Turkiye (The Republic of Turkey) جمهوريتى توركيه

Junagarh (Junagadh - Mughal) جونة گره

al-Junub al-Arabi (South Arabia) الجنوب العربي

Kabul (Mughal, Afghanistan) كابل

Kaffa (Krim) كفّة

Kalanur (Mughal) كالانور

Kalat (Kalat state) قلات كلات

Kalian (Kalayani - Hyderabad) كليان

Kalikut (Calicut, Kozhikode - Mysore) كليكوت

Kalkatah (Calcutta, Alinagar - Mughal, Bengal Presidency) كلكته

Kalpi (Mughal, Maratha) كلپي

Kanauj (Qanauj - Mughal, Awadh) قنوج

Kanauj urf Shahgarh (Qanauj - Mughal, Awadh) قنوج عرف شاه گره

Kanbayat (Kambayat, Kanbat, Khambayat - Mughal, Cambay state) كمبايت كهنبايت كنبات كنبايت

Kandahar (see Qandahar)

Kangun (Hosakote - Mughal) كنگون

Kanji (Conjeeveram - Mughal) كنجي

Kankurti (Mughal, Maratha) كانكرتي

Kara Amid (Turkey) قره آمد

Karahisar (Qara-Hisar - Turkey) قراحصار قره حسار

Kararabad (Karad - Mughal) كراراباد

Karatova (Kratova - Turkey) قراطوه قراطوه

Karauli (Karauli state) كرولي

Karimabad (Mughal) — كريم اباد

Karmin (Central Asia) — كرمين

Karnatak (Carnatic - Mughal) — كرناتك

Karpa (Kurpa - Mughal) — كرپا

Kars (Qars - Turkey) — قارص قارس

Kashan (Iran) — كاشان

Kashgar (China - Sinkiang) — كاشغر كشقر

Kashmir (Srinagar - Kashmir Sultanate, Mughal, Sikh, Afghanistan) — كشمير

Kastamonu (Turkey) — قسطمونى

Katak (Cuttack - Mughal, Maratha) — كتك

Katak Banaras (Mughal) — كتك بنارس

Kawkaban (the Yemen) — كوكبان

Kayseri (Turkey) — قيصري قيسري

Kedah (Straits Settlements, Malaya) — كداه

Kelantan (Straits Settlements, Malaya) — كلنتن

Kemasin (Straits Settlements, Malaya) — كماسن

Khairabad (Mughal) — خيراباد

Khairnagar (Mughal) — خيرنگر

Khairpur (Mughal, Sind) — خيرپور

Khaliqabad (Dindigal - Mysore) — خالق اباد

Khambayat (Kanbayat - Mughal) — كمنبايت

Khanabad (Afghanistan) — خان اباد

Khanja (Canca, Hanca - Turkey) — خانجة خانجا

Khanpur (Bahawalpur) — خانپور

Khartapirt (Harput, Harburt - Turkey) — خرتبرت
خربت خربرت

Khizan (Turkey) — خيزان

Khoqand (Central Asia) — خوقند

Khotan (Khutan, China - Sinkiang) — خوتن ختن

Khoy (Khoi, Khui - Iran) — خوي

Khujista Bunyad (Aurangabad - Mughal, Hyderabad) — خجسته بنياد

al-Khurfa (the Yemen) — الخرفاة

Khurshid Sawad (Mysore) — خورشيد سواد

Khwarizm (Central Asia) — خوارزم

Kighi (Turkey) — كيغي

Kirman (Kerman - Iran) — كرمان

Kirmanshahan (Kermanshah - Iran) — كرمانساهان

Kish (Central Asia) — كش

Kishangar (Kishangar state) — كشنگره

Kishtwar (Mughal) — كشتوار

Koçaniye (Kochana - Turkey) — قوچانية

Koilkunda (Mughal) — كويلكونده

Kolapur (Mughal, Kolhapur) — كولاپور كلاپور

Konya (Turkey) — قونية

Kora (Mughal, Maratha, Awadh) — كورا

Kosantina (see Qusantinia)

Kosova (Kosovo - Turkey) — قوصوه قوسوه

Kostantaniye (see Qustantaniya)

Kotah (Kotah state) — كوته

Kotah urf Nandgaon — كوته عرف نندگانو

Kubrus (Cyprus - Turkey) — قبرص

Kuch Hijri (Kunch) — كوچ حجري

Kuchaman (Mughal) — كچامن

Kuche (China - Sinkiang) — كوچا

Kufan (Kufin - Central Asia) — كوفن كوفين

Kulbarga (see Gulbarga)

Kumber (Kumbar - see Maha Indrapur)

Kunar (Maratha) — كنار

Kunch (Maratha) — كونچ

Kurdasht (Azerbaijan) — كرداشت كردشت

Kuwait (al-Kuwayt) — الكويت

Ladakh (Ladakah - Kashmir, Afghanistan) — لداكه لداخ

Lahej (the Yemen) — لحج

Lahijan (Iran) — لاهيجان

Lahore (Lahur - Mughal, Sikh, Afghanistan) — لاهور

Lahri Bandar (Mughal) — لهري بندر

Langar (Central Asia) — لنگر

Lar (Iran) — لار

Larenda (Turkey) — لارندة

Lashkar (Gwalior) — لاشكار

Lebanon (Lubnan) — لبنان

Legeh (Thailand) — لغكه

Libya — ليبيا

Lucknow (Lakhnau - Mughal, Awadh) — لكهنو

Machhli Bandar (Masulipatam) — مچهلي بندر

Machhlipatan (Masulipatam - Mughal, French India, Madras Pres.) — مچهلي پتن

Madankot (Mughal) — مدنكوت

al-Madina al-Bayda' (see Fas al-Jadid - Morocco) — المدينة البيضاء

Madrid (for Morocco) — مدريد

al-Maghrib (Morocco) — المغرب

Maha Indrapur (Dig, Kumbar - Mughal, Bharatpur) — مهه اندرپور

Mahle (Male - Maldive Islands) — محلي

Mahmud Bandar (Porto Novo - Mughal) — محمودبندر

Mahoba (Maratha) — مهوبة

Mailapur (Madras - Mughal) — ميلاپور

Makhsusabad (Murshidabad - Mughal) — مخصوص اباد

Malharnagar (Indore, also for Maheshwar) — ملهارنگر

Malher (Malhar, Mulher - Mughal) — ملهر

Maliknagar (Mughal) — ملك نگر

Malnapur (Mughal) — مالناپور

Malpur (Mughal) — مالپور

Maluka (Netherlands East Indies) — ملوكة

al-Mamlaka al-'Arabiya as-Sa'udiya (The Kingdom of Saudi Arabia) — المملكة
العربية السعودية

al-Mamlaka al-Libiya (The Kingdom of Libya) — المملكة الليبية

al-Mamlaka al-Maghribiya (The Kingdom of Morocco) — المملكة المغربية

al-Mamlaka al-Misriya (The Kingdom of Egypt) — المملكة المصرية

al-Mamlaka al-Mutawakkiliya al-Yamaniya (The Mutawakkilite Kingdom of the Yemen) — المملكة
المتوكلية اليمنية

al-Mamlaka al-Tunisiya (The Kingdom of Tunisia) — المملكة التونسية

al-Mamlaka al-Urdunniya al-Hashimiya (The Hashimite Kingdom of Jordan) — الاردنية الهاسمية

Manastir (Turkey) — مناستر

Mandasor (Gwalior) — منديسور

Mandla (Maratha) — مندلا

Mandu (Mughal) — مندو

Mangarh (Mughal) — مانگره

Manghir (Monghyr - Bihar) — مانگهير

Manikpur (Mughal) — مانكپور

Maragha (Azerbaijan, Iran) — مراغة

Marakesh (Marrakech - Morocco) — مراكش

Mar'ash (Turkey) — مرعش

Mardin (Turkey) — ماردين

Marv (Central Asia, Iran) — ماروار

Marwar (Jodhpur, Nagor, Pali, Sojat) — ماروار

al-Mu'askar (Mascara - Algeria) — المعسكر

Mashhad (Iran) — مشهد

Mashhad Imam Rida (Iran) — مشهد امام رضى

Mathura (Islamabad - Mughal, Bindraban) — متهره

Mazandaran (Iran) — مازندران

Mecca (Makkah - al-Hejaz) — مكّة

Medea (Algeria) — مدية

Meknes (Miknas - Morocco) — مكناس

Menangkabau (Netherlands East Indies) — منڨكابو

Merta (Mirath - Mughal, Jodhpur) — ميرتة ميرتا

Misr (Egypt, Turkey) — مصر

Modava (Moldava - Turkey) — مداوه موداوه

Mombasa (Kenya) — ممباسة

Mosul (al-Mawsil - Iraq) — الموصل موصل

Muazzamabad (Gorakpur - Mughal, Awadh) — معظم اباد

Muhammadabad (Udaipur - Mughal) — محمداباد

Muhammadabad Banaras (Mughal, Awadh, Bengal Presidency, fictitious for Lucknow) — محمداباد بنارس

Muhammadabad urf Kalpi (Kalpi) — محمداباد عرف كلپي

al-Muhammadiya (al-Masila - Morocco) — المحمدية

al-Muhammadiya ash-Sharifa (Morocco) — المحمدية الشريفة

Muhammadnagar Tandah (Awadh) — محمدنگر تانده

Muhiabad Poona (Maratha) — محيى اباد پونه

Mujahidabad (Mughal) — مجاحداباد

Mujibalanagar (Rohilkhand) — مجى بالانگر

al-Mukala (the Yemen) — المكلا

Mukha (Mocca - the Yemen) — مخا

Mukhtara (the Yemen) — مختارة

Müküs (Turkey) — مكس

Multan (Mughal, Sikh, — ملتان

Muminabad (Bindraban) — مؤمن اباد

Munbai (Mumbai, Bombay - Mughal, Bombay Presidency) — منبي

Mungir (Mughal) — مهنگير

Muradabad (Mughal, Rohilkhand, Awadh, Afghanistan) — مراداباد

Murshidabad (Makhsusabad - Mughal, French India, Bengal Pres.) — مرشداباد

Murtazabad (Mughal) — مرتضاباد

Muscat (Oman) — مسقط

Mustafabad (Rampur - Rohilkhand) — مصطفاباد

Muzaffargarh (Jhajjar - Mughal) — مظفرگره

Mysore (Mahisur - Mysore state) — مهي سور مهيسور

Nabha (Sirkar - Nabha state) — سركار نابهه

Nagar (Ahmadnagar, Bednur - Maratha, Mysore) — نگر

Nagar Ijri (Srinagar in Bundelkand) — نگر يجري

Nagor (Mughal, Jodhpur) — ناگور

Nagpur (Maratha) — ناگپور

Nahan (Sirmur) — ناهن

Nahtarnagar (Trichinopoly - Arcot) — نهتر نگر

Najafgarh (Mughal, Rohilkhand) — نجف گره

Najibabad (Mughal, Sikh, Rohilkhand, Awadh, Afghanistan) — نجيبباباد نجيب اباد

Nakhjuvan (Iran, Azerbaijan) — نخجوان

Nandgaon (Nandgano - Kotah) — نندگانو

Nandgaon urf Kotah — نندگانو عرف كوته

Narnol (Mughal) — نارنول

Narwar (Sipri - Mughal, Gwalior, Narwar state) — نرور

Nasaf (Central Asia) — نسف

Nasirabad (Sagar, Wanparti - Hyderabad) — نصر اباد

Nasirabad (Dharwar - Mughal) — نصيراباد

Nasiri (Iran) — ناصري

Nasrullahnagar (Rohilkhand) — نصرالله نگر

Nazarbar (Mysore) — نظربار

Nejd (Saudi Arabia) — نجد

Nigbolu (Turkey) — نگبولو

Nihavand (Iran) — نهاوند

Nimak (Sikh) — نمك

Nimruz (Central Asia, Iran) — نيمروز نمرز

Nipani (Maratha) — نپني

Nisa (Iran) — نسا

Nishapur (Naysabur - Iran) — نيشاپور

Novabirda (Novoberda - Turkey) — نوابرده

Novar (Turkey) — نوار

Nukhwi (Iran, Azerbaijan) — نخوي

Nusratabad (Dharwar, Nasratabad, Fathpur - Mughal) — نصرت اباد

Nusratgarh (Jinji - Mughal) — نصرت گره

Ohri (Okhri, Ochrida - Turkey) — اوخرى

Oman ('Uman) — عمان

Omdurman (Umm Durman - the Sudan) — ام درمان

Orchha (Orchha state) — اورچحه

Ordu-Bagh (Iran) — اوردوباغ

Ordu-yi Humayun (Turkey) — اردو همايون

Orissa (Mughal) — اوريسة

Pahang (Straits Settlements) — فاحغ

Pakistan — پاكستان

Palembang	(Netherlands East Indies)	فلمبغ
Palestine	(see Filastin)	
Pali	(Jodhpur)	پالي
Panahabad	(Iran, Karabagh)	پناه اباد
Panipat	(Mughal)	پاني پت
Parenda	(Purenda - Mughal)	پرنده پرينده
Parnala (Qila)	(Mughal)	پرنالا (قلع)
Patan	(Seringapatan - Mysore)	پتن
al-Patani	(Patani - Thailand)	الفطاني
Pathankot		پثنكوت
Patna	(Azimabad - Mughal, Bengal Presidency)	پتنة
Pattan	(Anhirwala - Mughal)	پتن
Pattan Deo	(Somnath – Mughal)	پتن ديو
Perak	(Straits Settlements, Malaya)	فيرق
Peshawar	(Mughal, Sikh, Afghanistan, Iran)	پشاور
Petlad	(Baroda)	پتلاد
Phonda	(Mughal)	پهونده
Pondichery	(Pholcheri - French India)	پهلچري
Pondichery	(Porcheri - French India)	پرچري
Poona	(Punah, Pune, Muhiabad - Mughal, Maratha)	پونه
Pulu Malayu	(Island of the Malays - Sumatra, Netherlands East Indies)	فولو ملايو
Pulu Penang	(Penang, Prince of Wales Island - Straits Settlements, Malaya)	فولو فنيغ
Pulu Percha	(Island of Sumatra - Netherlands East Indies)	فولو فرج
Punamali	(Mughal)	پونامالي
Punch	(Mughal)	پونچ
Purbandar	(Porbandar - Mughal)	پوربندر
Qafsa	(Capsa - Tunis, Tunisia)	قفصة
al-Qahira	(Cairo - Egypt)	القاهرة
Qaiti	(the Yemen)	القعياطي
Qamarnagar	(Karnul - Mughal)	قمرنگر
Qanauj	(see Kanauj)	
Qandahar	(Ahmadshahi - Mughal, Afghanistan, Iran)	قندهار
Qarshi	(Central Asia)	قرشي
Qasbah Panipat	(Rohilkhand)	قصبة پاني پت
Qatar wa Dubai	(Qatar and Dubai - Qatar)	قطر و دبي
Qayin	(Central Asia)	قاين
Qazvin	(Iran)	قزوين
Qubba	(Azerbaijan)	قبة
Qumm	(Qomm - Iran)	قم
Qunduz	(Central Asia)	قندوز
Qusantinia	(Qustantina, Qusantina - Constantine, Algiers)	قسنطينية قسنطينة قسطنطينة
Qustantaniya	(Constantinople - Turkey)	قسطنطنية
Rabat	(Morocco)	رباط
Rabat al-Fath	(Rabat - Morocco)	رباط الفتح
Rada'	(the Yemen)	راداء
Radhanpur	(Radhanpur state)	رادهنپور
Rajapur	(Islam Bandar - Mughal)	راجاپور
Rajgarh	(Alwar)	راج گره
Ramhurmuz	(Iran)	رامهرمز
Ra'nash	(Ramhurmuz - Iran)	رعنش
Rangpur	(Assam)	رنگپور
Ranthor	(Ranthambhor - Mughal)	رنتهور
Ras al-Khaima	(United Arab Emirates)	رأس الخيمة
Rasht	(Resht - Iran)	رشت
Ratlam	(Ratlam state)	رتلام
Ravishnagar Sagar	(Garhakota - Maratha - Gwalior)	روش نگر ساگر
Rehman	(Reman - Thailand)	رحمن
Revan	(Iravan - Armenia)	روان
Rewan	(Rewa)	ريوان
Reza'iyeh	(Urumi - Iran)	رضائية
Rikab	(Rekab - Afghanistan, Iran)	ركاب
Rohtas	(Rohtak - Mughal)	رهتاس رحتاس
Rudana	(Taroudant - Morocco)	ردانة
Ruha	(al-Ruha - Turkey)	رهى رها الرها
Sa'adnagar	(Aklaj - Mughal)	سعدنگر
Sabzavar	(Iran)	سبزوار
Sa'da	(the Yemen)	صعدة
Sagar	(Maratha, Bengal Pres.)	ساگر
Saharanpur	(Mughal)	سهارنپور
Sahibabad Hansi	(Hansi state)	صاحب اباد هنسي
Sahrind	(Sarhind - Mughal, Cis-Sutlej Patiala, Afghanistan)	سرهند سهرند
Sailana	(Sailana state)	سيلانه
Saimur	(Mughal)	سيمور
al-Saiwi	(Sai, Saiburi, Teluban - Thailand)	السيوي
Sakiz	(Saqyz, Scio - Turkey)	ساقز سكيز
Sakkhar	(Mughal)	سكهر
Sala	(Sale - Morocco)	سلا
Salamabad	(Satyamangalam - Mysore)	سلام اباد
Salimabad	(Ajmer - Mughal)	سليم اباد
Samandra	(Turkey)	سمندره
Samarqand	(Central Asia)	سمرقند
San'a	(the Yemen)	صنعاء
Sanbal	(Sambhal - Mughal)	سنبل
Sanbhar	(Sambhar - Mughal)	سانبهر
Sangamner	(Mughal)	سنگمنر
Sangli	(Maratha)	سنگلي
al-Saniya	(Turkey)	السنية
Sarakhs	(Iran)	سرخس
Sarangpur	(Mughal)	سارنگپور
Saray	(Turkey)	سراي
Sari	(Iran)	ساري
Sari Pol	(Afghanistan)	سر پل
Sarhind	(see Sahrind)	
Sashti	(in Devanagari) (Maratha)	
Satara	(Mughal)	ستارا

- **Saudi Arabia** (see al-Hejaz, Nejd) — العربية السعودية
- **Sawai Jaipur** (Jaipur, fictitious for Karauli) — سواي جيپور
- **Sawai Madhopur** (Jaipur, fictitious for Sikar) — سواي مادهوپور
- **Sawuj Balaq** (Iran) — ساوج بلاق
- **Selam** (Selam state) — سيلم
- **Selanghur** (Selangor - Straits Settlements, Malaya) — سلاغور
- **Selanik** (Salonika - Turkey) — سلانيك
- **Selefke** (Turkey) — سلفكه
- **Semnan** (Simnan - Iran) — سمنان
- **Serbernik** (Turkey) — سربرنيك
- **Serez** (see Siroz - Turkey) — سرز سريز
- **Seringapatan** (Mysore)
- **Shadiabad Urf Mandu** (Mughal) — شادياباد ارف مندو
- **Shadman** (Central Asia) — شادمان
- **Shadora** (Gwalior) — شادهوره
- **Shahabad** (Awadh) — شاه اباد قنوج شاهاباد
- **Shahabad Qanauj** (Mughal, Rohilkhand, Awadh) — شاه اباد قنوج
- **Shahgarh Qanauj** (Mughal) — شاه گره قنوج
- **Shahjahanabad** (Dehli - Mughal, Bhilwara, Bindraban, Chitor, Mathura, Shapura, Udaipur, also fictitious for Bagalkot, Jaisalmir, Satara-EIC) — شاه جهان اباد
- **Shahr-Gözlü** (see Gözlü - Krim) — شهرگوزلو
- **Shakola** (Mughal) — شكولا
- **Shamakhi** (Shamakha, Shemakhi - Iran, Azerbaijan) — شماخي شماخه
- **Sharakat Almaniya** (German East Africa Co.) — شراكة المانيا
- **ash-Sharja** (Sharja - United Arab Emirates) — الشارجة
- **Shekki** (Iran) — شكّى
- **Sheopur** (Gwalior) — شيوپور
- **Shergarh** (Shirgarh - Mughal) — شيرگره
- **Sherkot** (Mughal) — شيركوت
- **Sherpur** (Shirpur - Mughal) — شيرپور
- **Shikarpur** (Sind) — شكارپور
- **Shiraz** (Iran) — شيراز
- **Shirvan** (Azerbaijan, Iran, Turkey) — شيروان شروان
- **Sholapur** (Mughal) — شولاپور
- **Shustar** (Iran) — شوستر
- **Siak** (Netherlands East Indies) — سيك
- **Sidrekipsi** (Turkey) — بسدره قپسى
- **Siirt** (Sa'irt - Turkey) — سعرت
- **Sijilmasa** (Sizilmassa - Morocco) — سجلماسة
- **Sikakul** (Chicacole - Mughal) — سيكاكل
- **Sikandarah** (Sikandra – Mughal) — سكندره
- **Sind** (Mughal, Sind state, Afghanistan, Iran) — سند
- **Singgora** (Thailand) — سڠگورا
- **Sira** (Mughal) — سيرة
- **Sironj** (Mughal, Indore, Tonk) — سرونج
- **Siroz** (see Serez - Turkey) — سيروز
- **Sistan** (Iran) — سيستان
- **Sitamau** (Sitamo) — سيتامو
- **Sitapur** (Mughal) — سيتاپور
- **Sitpur** (Sidhpur in Gujarat? - Mughal) — سيتپور
- **Sivas** (Siwas - Turkey) — سيواس
- **Sofia** (Turkey) — صوفية
- **Sojat** (Jodhpur) — سوجت
- **al-Somal al-Italyaniya** (Italian Somaliland, Somalia) — الصومال الايطاليانية
- **Srebernice** (Serbernichna - Turkey) — سربرنيچه
- **Sri** (Amritsar) — سري
- **Sri Akalpur** (Malkarian) — سري اكلپور
- **Srinagar** (Mughal, Garhwal, Kashmir) — سرينگر
- **Srinagar** (in Bundelkhand - Maratha) — سرينگر
- **Sultanabad** (Iran) — سلطاناباد
- **Sultanpur** (Mughal) — سلطانپور
- **Sumenep** (Netherlands East Indies) — سمنف
- **Surat** (Mughal, French India, Bombay Presidency, fictitious for Chand) — سورت
- **Suriya** (Syria) — سورية
- **al-Suwair/al-Suwaira** (Essaouir, Essaouira - Mogador, Morocco) — السوير الصويرة
- **Tabaristan** (Iran) — طبرستان
- **Tabriz** (Iran, Turkey) — تبريز
- **Tadpatri** (Mughal) — تدپتري
- **Ta'izz** (the Yemen) — تعز
- **Tanah Malayu** (Land of the Malays - Sumatra, Malacca, Straits Settlements) — تانة ملايو
- **Tana Ugi** (Land of the Bugis - Netherlands East Indies) — تانة اغيسى
- **Tanda** (Akbarpur - Bengal Sultanate, Mughal, Awadh) — تانده
- **Tanja** (Tangier - Morocco) — طنجة
- **Tappal** (Mughal) — ابرقوه
- **Taqidemt** (Algiers) — تاقدمت
- **Tarablus** (Tripoli in Lebanon) — طرابلس
- **Tarablus Gharb** (Tripoli West - in Libya) — طرابلس غرب
- **Tarapatri** (Mughal) — تراپتري
- **Tarim** (the Yemen) — تريم
- **Tashkand** (Tashkent - Central Asia) — تشكند
- **Tashqurghan** (Afghanistan) — تاشقورغان
- **Tatta** (Tattah - Mughal, Sind, Afghanistan) — تته
- **Tehran** (Iran) — طهران
- **Tellicherry** (French India, Bombay Presidency) — تلجري تالچري
- **Termez** (Central Asia) — ترمذ
- **Tetuan** (Tetouan, Titwan - Morocco) — تطوان
- **Tibet** (Mughal, Ladakh) — تبت
- **Tiflis** (Georgia, Iran) — تفليس
- **Tilimsan** (Tlemcen, Aghadir - Algiers) — تلمسان
- **Tirat Hardwar** (Hardwar) — تيرتهردوار
- **Tire** (Turkey) — تيره
- **Tokat** (Tuqat - Turkey) — توقاط توقات دوقات طوقات
- **Tonk** (Tonk state) — تونك
- **Toragal** (Mughal, Maratha) — تورگل توراگال
- **Trabzon** (Trebizond - Turkey) — طرابزون طرابزن
- **Trengganu** (Straits Settlements, Malaya) — ترغگانو

Tun (Central Asia) — تون

Tunis (Tunisia) — تونس

Turbat (Central Asia) — تربت

Tuyserkan (Iran) — توي سركان

Udaipur (Muhammadabad - Mughal) — اوديپور اديپور

Udgir (Mughal) — اجين

Ujjain (Mughal, Gwalior) — اجين

Ujjain Dar al-Fath (Gwalior) — اجين دارالفتح

Ujjainpur (Mughal) — اجين پور

Umarkot (Mughal) — امركوت

Umm al-Qaiwain (United Arab Emirates) — ام القيوين

United Arab Emirates (see al-Imarat al-'Arabiya al-Muttahida)

Urdu (Camp mint - Mughal, Central Asia, Iran) — اردو

Urdu Dar Rahi-i-Dakkin (Mughal) — اردو دار راه دكين

Urdu Zafar Qirin (Mughal) — اردو ظفر قرين

al-Urdunn (Jordan) — الاردن

Urumchi (China - Sinkiang) — ارومچي

Urumi (Urumia, Urmia, Reza'iya - Iran) — ارومي ارومية ارمية

Ushi (China - Sinkiang) — اوش

Usküp (Uskub, Skopje, Kosovo - Turkey) — اسكوپ

Van (Wan - Turkey, Armenia) — وان

Varne (Turkey) — ورنه

al-Yaman (the Yemen) — اليمن

Yarkand (China - Sinkiang) — يارقند

Yarkhissarmaran (China - Sinkiang) — ياركسارمرن

Yazd (Iran) — يزد

Yazur (Cemtral Asia) — يازر

Yenishehr (Larissa - Turkey) — ينكى شهر

Za (Taorirt - Morocco) — صا

Zabid (the Yemen) — زبيد

Zafarabad (Bidar - Mughal, Gurramkonda - Mysore) — ظفراباد

Zafarnagar (Fathabad - Mughal) — ظفرنگر

Zafarpur (Mughal) — ظفرپور

Zain-ul-Bilad (Ahmadabad - — زين البلاد

Zanjibar (Zanjibara - Zanzibar) — زنجبار زنجبارا

Zebabad (Mughal, Sardhanah) — زيب اباد

Zegam (Zigam - Iran) — زگام

Zinjan (Zanjan - Iran) — زنجان

al-Zuhra (the Yemen) — الزهرة

MINT EPITHETS

Geographical Terms:

Baldat (City - Agra, Allahabad, Burhanpur, Bikanir, Patna, Sarhind, Ujjain) — بلدات

Bandar (Port - Dewal, Hari, Surat, Machhlipatan) — بندر

Dakhil (Breach, Entrance - Chitor) — داخل

Dawla/Daula (State, State of) — دولة

Hazrat (Royal Residence - Fas, Marakesh, Dehli) — حضرة

Khitta (District - Awadh, Kalpi, Kashmir, Lakhnau) — خطة

Negri (State of - Straits Settlements, Malaya, Netherlands East Indies, Thailand) — نكري

Qasba (Town - Panipat, Sherkot) — قصبة

Qila (Fort - Agra, Alwar, Bandhu, Gwalior, Punch) — قلعة قلع

Qila Muqam (Fort Residence - Gwalior) — قلعة مقام

Qita (District - Bareli) — قطة

Sarkar (County - Lakhnau, Torgal) — سركار

Shahr (City - Anhirwala Pattan) — شهر

Suba (Province - Awadh) — سوبة

Tirtha (Shrine - Hardwar) — ترتة

Poetic Allusion:

Ashraf al-Bilad (Most Noble of Cities - Qandahar/Ahmadshahi) — اشراف البلاد

Baldat-i-Fakhira (Splendid City - Burhanpur) — بلدات فخيرة

Bandar-i-Mubarak (Blessed Port - Surat) — بندر مبارك

Dar-ul-Aman (Abode of Security - Agra, Jammu, Multan, Sarhind) — دار الامان

Dar-ul-Barakat (Abode of Blessings - Jodhpur, Nagor) — دار البركات

Dar-ul-Fath (Seat of Conquest - Ujjain) — دار الفتح

Dar-ul-Islam (Abode of Islam - Bahawalpur, Dogaon, Mandisor) — دار الاسلام

Dar-ul-Jihad (Seat of Holy War - Hyderabad) — دار الجهاد

Dar-ul-Khair (Abode of Beneficence - Ajmer) — دار الخير

Dar-ul-Khilafa (Abode of the Caliphate - Agra, Ahmadabad, Akbarabad, Akbarpur Tanda, Awadh, Bahraich, Daulatabad, Dogaon, Gorakpur, Gwalior, Jaunpur, Kanauj, Lahore, Lakhnau, Malpur, Shahgarh, Shahjahanabad, Tehran, the Yemen) — دار الخلافة

Dar-ul-Mansur (Abode of the Victorious - Ajmer, Jodhpur) — دار المنصور

Dar-ul-Mulk (Seat of Kingship - Dehli, Fathpur, Kabul) — دار الملك

Dar an-Nusrat (Abode of Succor - Herat) — دار النصرات

Dar-ur-Riyasa (Seat of the Chief of State - Jaisalmir) — دار الرياسة

Dar-us-Salam (Abode of Peace - Dogaon, Mandisor, Legeh) — دار السلام

Dar-us-Saltana (Seat of the Sultanate - Ahmadabad, Burhanpur, Fathpur, Herat, Kabul, Kora, Lahore) — دار السلطنة

Dar-ul-Surur (Abode of Happiness - Bahawalpur, Burhanpur, Saharanpur) — دار السرور

Dar-uz-Zafar (Seat of Victory - Advani, Bijapur) — دار الظفر

Dar-uz-Zarb (Seat of the Mint - Jaunpur, Kalpi, Patna) — دار الضرب

Farkhanda Bunyad (Of Auspicious Foundation - Hyderabad) — فرخنده بنياد

Hazrat (Venerable - Dehli) — حضرت

Khujista Bunyad (Of Fortunate Foundation - Aurangabad) — خجستة بنياد

Mustaqarr-ul-Khilafa (Residence of the Caliphate - Akbarabad, Ajmer) — مستقر الخلافة

Mustaqarr-ul-Mulk (Abode of Kingship - Akbarabad, Azimabad) — مستقر الملك

Sawai (One-fourth, i.e. "a notch better" - Jaipur) — سواي

Umm al-Bilad (Mother of Cities - Balkh) — ام البلاد

Zain-ul-Bilad (The Most-Beautiful of Cities – Ahmadabad) — زين البلاد

FOREIGN EXCHANGE TABLE

The latest foreign exchange rates below apply to trade with banks in the country of origin. The left column shows the number of units per U.S. dollar at the official rate. The right column shows the number of units per dollar at the free market rate.

COUNTRY	Official #/$	Market #/$
Afghanistan (New Afghani)	45	–
Albania (Lek)	100	–
Algeria (Dinar)	72	–
Andorra uses Euro	.715	–
Angola (Readjust Kwanza)	93	–
Anguilla uses E.C. Dollar	2.7	–
Antigua uses E.C. Dollar	2.7	–
Argentina (Peso)	4.0	–
Armenia (Dram)	368	–
Aruba (Florin)	1.79	–
Australia (Dollar)	.986	–
Austria (Euro)	.715	–
Azerbaijan (New Manat)	.795	–
Bahamas (Dollar)	1.0	–
Bahrain Is. (Dinar)	.377	–
Bangladesh (Taka)	71	–
Barbados (Dollar)	2.0	–
Belarus (Ruble)	3,016	–
Belgium (Euro)	.715	–
Belize (Dollar)	1.95	–
Benin uses CFA Franc West	471	–
Bermuda (Dollar)	1.0	–
Bhutan (Ngultrum)	45	–
Bolivia (Boliviano)	7.0	–
Bosnia-Herzegovina (Conv. marka)	1.40	–
Botswana (Pula)	6.59	–
British Virgin Islands uses U.S. Dollar	1.0	–
Brazil (Real)	1.65	–
Brunei (Dollar)	1.27	–
Bulgaria (Lev)	1.40	–
Burkina Faso uses CFA Franc West	471	–
Burma (Kyat)	6.42	1,250
Burundi (Franc)	1,236	–
Cambodia (Riel)	4,039	–
Cameroon uses CFA Franc Central	470	–
Canada (Dollar)	.973	–
Cape Verde (Escudo)	79	–
Cayman Islands (Dollar)	0.82	–
Central African Rep.	471	–
CFA Franc Central	471	–
CFA Franc West	471	–
CFP Franc	85	–
Chad uses CFA Franc Central	470	–
Chile (Peso)	474	–
China, P.R. (Renminbi Yuan)	6.6	–
Colombia (Peso)	1,894	–
Comoros (Franc)	352	–
Congo uses CFA Franc Central	470	–
Congo-Dem.Rep. (Congolese Franc)	923	–
Cook Islands (Dollar)	1.36	–
Costa Rica (Colon)	502	–
Croatia (Kuna)	5.29	–
Cuba (Peso)	1.00	27.00
Cyprus (Euro)	.403	–
Czech Republic (Koruna)	17.4	–
Denmark (Danish Krone)	5.3	–
Djibouti (Franc)	178	–
Dominica uses E.C. Dollar	2.7	–
Dominican Republic (Peso)	38	–
East Caribbean (Dollar)	2.7	–
Ecuador (U.S. Dollar)	1.00	–
Egypt (Pound)	5.9	–
El Salvador (U.S. Dollar)	1.00	–
Equatorial Guinea uses CFA Franc Central	470	–
Eritrea (Nafka)	15.0	–
Estonia (Kroon)	11.2	–
Ethiopia (Birr)	16.7	–
Euro	.715	–
Falkland Is. (Pound)	.615	–
Faroe Islands (Krona)	5.3	–
Fiji Islands (Dollar)	1.83	–
Finland (Euro)	.715	–
France (Euro)	.715	–
French Polynesia uses CFP Franc	85	–
Gabon (CFA Franc)	470	–
Gambia (Dalasi)	29	–
Georgia (Lari)	1.72	–
Germany (Euro)	.715	–
Ghana (New Cedi)	1.52	–
Gibraltar (Pound)	.615	–
Greece (Euro)	.715	–
Greenland uses Danish Krone	5.33	–
Grenada uses E.C. Dollar	2.7	–
Guatemala (Quetzal)	7.76	–
Guernsey uses Sterling Pound	.615	–
Guinea Bissau (CFA Franc)	471	–
Guinea Conakry (Franc)	7,650	–
Guyana (Dollar)	205	–
Haiti (Gourde)	40	–
Honduras (Lempira)	19	–
Hong Kong (Dollar)	7.79	–
Hungary (Forint)	194	–
Iceland (Krona)	115	–
India (Rupee)	45	–
Indonesia (Rupiah)	8,792	–
Iran (Rial)	10,325	–
Iraq (Dinar)	1,169	–
Ireland (Euro)	.715	–
Isle of Man uses Sterling Pound	.615	–
Israel (New Sheqalim)	3.62	–
Italy (Euro)	.715	–
Ivory Coast uses CFA Franc West	471	–
Jamaica (Dollar)	86	–
Japan (Yen)	82	–
Jersey uses Sterling Pound	.615	–
Jordan (Dinar)	.707	–
Kazakhstan (Tenge)	146	–
Kenya (Shilling)	83	–
Kiribati uses Australian Dollar	.986	–
Korea-PDR (Won)	135	–
Korea-Rep. (Won)	1,115	–
Kuwait (Dinar)	.278	–
Kyrgyzstan (Som)	47	–
Laos (Kip)	8,050	–
Latvia (Lats)	.505	–
Lebanon (Pound)	1,502	–
Lesotho (Maloti)	6.88	–
Liberia (Dollar)	73	–
Libya (Dinar)	1.22	–
Liechtenstein uses Swiss Franc	.925	–
Lithuania (Litas)	2.47	–
Luxembourg (Euro)	.715	–
Macao (Pataca)	8.0	–
Macedonia (New Denar)	44	–
Madagascar (Franc)	1,998	–
Malawi (Kwacha)	152	–
Malaysia (Ringgit)	3.03	–
Maldives (Rufiya)	12.8	–
Mali uses CFA Franc West	471	–
Malta (Euro)	.715	–
Marshall Islands uses U.S.Dollar	1.00	–
Mauritania (Ouguiya)	283	–
Mauritius (Rupee)	29	–
Mexico (Peso)	12.0	–
Moldova (Leu)	12.0	–
Monaco uses Euro	.715	–
Mongolia (Tugrik)	1,248	–
Montenegro uses Euro	.715	–
Montserrat uses E.C. Dollar	2.7	–
Morocco (Dirham)	8.0	–
Mozambique (New Metical)	31	–
Namibia (Rand)	6.88	–
Nauru uses Australian Dollar	.986	–
Nepal (Rupee)	72	–
Netherlands (Euro)	.715	–
Netherlands Antilles (Gulden)	1.79	–
New Caledonia uses CFP Franc	85	–
New Zealand (Dollar)	1.35	–
Nicaragua (Cordoba Oro)	22	–
Niger uses CFA Franc West	471	–
Nigeria (Naira)	154	–
Northern Ireland uses Sterling Pound	.615	–
Norway (Krone)	5.6	–
Oman (Rial)	.385	–
Pakistan (Rupee)	85	–
Palau uses U.S.Dollar	1.00	–
Panama (Balboa) uses U.S.Dollar	1.00	–
Papua New Guinea (Kina)	2.57	–
Paraguay (Guarani)	4,465	–
Peru (Nuevo Sol)	2.77	–
Philippines (Peso)	43	–
Poland (Zloty)	2.84	–
Portugal (Euro)	.715	–
Qatar (Riyal)	3.64	–
Romania (New Leu)	3.01	–
Russia (Ruble)	28	–
Rwanda (Franc)	600	–
St. Helena (Pound)	.615	–
St. Kitts uses E.C. Dollar	2.7	–
St. Lucia uses E.C. Dollar	2.7	–
St. Vincent uses E.C. Dollar	2.7	–
San Marino uses Euro	.715	–
Sao Tome e Principe (Dobra)	17,907	–
Saudi Arabia (Riyal)	3.75	–
Scotland uses Sterling Pound	.615	–
Senegal uses CFA Franc West	471	–
Serbia (Dinar)	74	–
Seychelles (Rupee)	12.2	–
Sierra Leone (Leone)	4,292	–
Singapore (Dollar)	1.27	–
Slovakia (Sk. Koruna)	22	–
Slovenia (Euro)	.715	–
Solomon Islands (Dollar)	7.79	–
Somalia (Shilling)	1,600	–
Somaliland (Somali Shilling)	1,600	4,000
South Africa (Rand)	6.88	–
Spain (Euro)	.715	–
Sri Lanka (Rupee)	110	–
Sudan (Pound)	2.55	–
Surinam (Dollar)	3.3	–
Swaziland (Lilangeni)	6.88	–
Sweden (Krona)	6.35	–
Switzerland (Franc)	.925	–
Syria (Pound)	47	–
Taiwan (NT Dollar)	29	–
Tajikistan (Somoni)	4.43	–
Tanzania (Shilling)	1,519	–
Thailand (Baht)	30	–
Togo uses CFA Franc West	471	–
Tonga (Pa'anga)	1.81	–
Transdniestra (Ruble)	12.0	–
Trinidad & Tobago (Dollar)	6.35	–
Tunisia (Dinar)	1.40	–
Turkey (New Lira)	1.60	–
Turkmenistan (Manat)	14,250	–
Turks & Caicos uses U.S. Dollar	1.00	–
Tuvalu uses Australian Dollar	.986	–
Uganda (Shilling)	2,384	–
Ukraine (Hryvnia)	7.94	–
United Arab Emirates (Dirham)	3.67	–
United Kingdom (Sterling Pound)	.615	–
Uruguay (Peso Uruguayo)	19	–
Uzbekistan (Sum)	1,667	–
Vanuatu (Vatu)	95	–
Vatican City uses Euro	.715	–
Venezuela (New Bolivar)	4.29	8.1
Vietnam (Dong)	20,835	–
Western Samoa (Tala)	2.38	–
Yemen (Rial)	214	–
Zambia (Kwacha)	4,730	–
Zimbabwe (Dollar)	–	–

HEJIRA DATE CONVERSION CHART

HEJIRA (Hijira, Hegira), the name of the Muslim era (A.H. = Anno Hegirae) dates back to the Christian year 622 when Mohammed "fled" from Mecca, escaping to Medina to avoid persecution from the Koreish tribemen. Based on a lunar year the Muslim year is 11 days shorter.

*=Leap Year (Christian Calendar)

AH Hejira	AD Christian Date
1010	1601, July 2
1011	1602, June 21
1012	1603, June 11
1013	1604, May 30
1014	1605, May 19
1015	1606, May 9
1016	1607, April 28
1017	1608, April 17
1018	1609, April 6
1017	1608, April 28
1018	1609, April 6
1019	1610, March 26
1020	1611, March 16
1021	1612, March 4
1022	1613, February 21
1023	1614, February 11
1024	1615, January 31
1025	1616, January 20
1026	1617, January 9
1027	1617, December 29
1028	1618, December 19
1029	1619, December 8
1030	1620, November 26
1031	1621, November 16
1032	1622, November 5
1033	1623, October 25
1034	1624, October 14
1035	1625, October 3
1036	1626, September 22
1037	1627, September 12
1038	1628, August 31
1039	1629, August 21
1040	1630, August 10
1041	1631, July 30
1042	1632, July 19
1043	1633, July 8
1044	1634, June 27
1045	1635, June 17
1046	1636, June 5
1047	1637, May 26
1048	1638, May 15
1049	1639, May 4
1050	1640, April 23
1051	1641, April 12
1052	1642, April 1
1053	1643, March 22
1054	1644, March 10
1055	1645, February 27
1056	1646, February 17
1057	1647, February 6
1058	1648, January 27
1059	1649, January 15
1060	1650, January 4
1061	1650, December 25
1062	1651, December 14
1063	1652, December 2
1064	1653, November 22
1065	1654, November 11
1066	1655, October 31
1067	1656, October 20
1068	1657, October 9
1069	1658, September 29
1070	1659, September 18
1071	1660, September 6
1072	1661, August 27
1073	1662, August 16
1074	1663, August 5
1075	1664, July 25
1076	1665, July 14
1077	1666, July 4
1078	1667, June 23
1079	1668, June 11
1080	1669, June 1
1081	1670, May 21
1082	1671, May 10
1083	1672, April 29
1084	1673, April 18
1085	1674, April 7

AH Hejira	AD Christian Date
1086	1675, March 28
1087	1676, March 16*
1088	1677, March 6
1089	1678, February 23
1090	1679, February 12
1091	1680, February 2*
1092	1681, January 21
1093	1682, January 10
1094	1682, December 31
1095	1683, December 20
1096	1684, December 8*
1097	1685, November 28
1098	1686, November 17
1099	1687, November 7
1100	1688, October 26*
1101	1689, October 15
1102	1690, October 5
1103	1691, September 24
1104	1692, September 12*
1105	1693, September 2
1106	1694, August 22
1107	1695, August 12
1108	1696, July 31*
1109	1697, July 20
1110	1698, July 10
1111	1699, June 29
1112	1700, June 18
1113	1701, June 8
1114	1702, May 28
1115	1703, May 17
1116	1704, May 6*
1117	1705, April 25
1118	1706, April 15
1119	1707, April 4
1120	1708, March 23*
1121	1709, March 13
1122	1710, March 2
1123	1711, February 19
1124	1712, February 9*
1125	1713, January 28
1126	1714, January 17
1127	1715, January 7
1128	1715, December 27
1129	1716, December 16*
1130	1717, December 5
1131	1718, November 24
1132	1719, November 14
1133	1720, November 2*
1134	1721, October 22
1135	1722, October 12
1136	1723, October 1
1137	1724, September 19
1138	1725, September 9
1139	1726, August 29
1140	1727, August 19
1141	1728, August 7*
1142	1729, July 27
1143	1730, July 17
1144	1731, July 6
1145	1732, June 24*
1146	1733, June 14
1147	1734, June 3
1148	1735, May 24
1149	1736, May 12*
1150	1737, May 1
1151	1738, April 21
1152	1739, April 10
1153	1740, March 29*
1154	1741, March 19
1155	1742, March 8
1156	1743, February 25
1157	1744, February 15*
1158	1745, February 3
1159	1746, January 24
1160	1747, January 13
1161	1748, January 2
1162	1748, December 22*
1163	1749, December 11
1164	1750, November 30
1165	1751, November 20
1166	1752, November 8*
1167	1753, October 29
1168	1754, October 18
1169	1755, October 7
1170	1756, September 26*
1171	1757, September 15
1172	1758, September 4
1173	1759, August 25
1174	1760, August 13*
1175	1761, August 2
1176	1762, July 23

AH Hejira	AD Christian Date
1177	1763, July 12
1178	1764, July 1*
1179	1765, June 20
1180	1766, June 9
1181	1767, May 30
1182	1768, May 18*
1183	1769, May 7
1184	1770, April 27
1185	1771, April 16
1186	1772, April 4*
1187	1773, March 25
1188	1774, March 14
1189	1775, March 4
1190	1776, February 21*
1191	1777, February 1
1192	1778, January 30
1193	1779, January 19
1194	1780, January 8*
1195	1780, December 28*
1196	1781, December 17
1197	1782, December 7
1198	1783, November 26
1199	1784, November 14*
1200	1785, November 4
1201	1786, October 24
1202	1787, October 13
1203	1788, October 2*
1204	1789, September 21
1205	1790, September 10
1206	1791, August 31
1207	1792, August 19*
1208	1793, August 9
1209	1794, July 29
1210	1795, July 18
1211	1796, July 7*
1212	1797, June 26
1213	1798, June 15
1214	1799, June 5
1215	1800, May 25
1216	1801, May 14
1217	1802, May 4
1218	1803, April 23
1219	1804, April 12*
1220	1805, April 1
1221	1806, March 21
1222	1807, March 11
1223	1808, February 28*
1224	1809, February 16
1225	1810, February 6
1226	1811, January 26
1227	1812, January 16*
1228	1813, January 6
1229	1813, December 24
1230	1814, December 14
1231	1815, December 3
1232	1816, November 21*
1233	1817, November 11
1234	1818, October 31
1235	1819, October 20
1236	1820, October 9*
1237	1821, September 28
1238	1822, September 18
1239	1823, September 8
1240	1824, August 26*
1241	1825, August 16
1242	1826, August 5
1243	1827, July 25
1244	1828, July 14*
1245	1829, July 3
1246	1830, June 22
1247	1831, June 12
1248	1832, May 31*
1249	1833, May 21
1250	1834, May 10
1251	1835, April 29
1252	1836, April 18*
1253	1837, April 7
1254	1838, March 27
1255	1839, March 17
1256	1840, March 5*
1257	1841, February 23
1258	1842, February 12
1259	1843, February 1
1260	1844, January 22*
1261	1845, January 10
1262	1845, December 30
1263	1846, December 20
1264	1847, December 9
1265	1848, November 27*
1266	1849, November 17
1267	1850, November 6

AH Hejira	AD Christian Date
1268	1851, October 27
1269	1852, October 15*
1270	1853, October 4
1271	1854, September 24
1272	1855, September 13
1273	1856, September 1*
1274	1857, August 22
1275	1858, August 11
1276	1859, July 31
1277	1860, July 20*
1278	1861, July 9
1279	1862, June 29
1280	1863, June 18
1281	1864, June 6*
1282	1865, May 27
1283	1866, May 16
1284	1867, May 5
1285	1868, April 24*
1286	1869, April 13
1287	1870, April 3
1288	1871, March 23
1289	1872, March 11*
1290	1873, March 1
1291	1874, February 18
1292	1875, February 7
1293	1876, January 28*
1294	1877, January 16
1295	1878, January 5
1296	1878, December 26
1297	1879, December 15
1298	1880, December 4*
1299	1881, November 23
1300	1882, November 12
1301	1883, November 2
1302	1884, October 21*
1303	1885, October 10
1304	1886, September 30
1305	1887, September 19
1306	1888, September 7*
1307	1889, August 28
1308	1890, August 17
1309	1891, August 7
1310	1892, July 26*
1311	1893, July 15
1312	1894, July 5
1313	1895, June 24
1314	1896, June 12*
1315	1897, June 2
1316	1898, May 22
1317	1899, May 12
1318	1900, May 1
1319	1901, April 20
1320	1902, April 10
1321	1903, March 30
1322	1904, March 18*
1323	1905, March 8
1324	1906, February 25
1325	1907, February 14
1326	1908, February 4*
1327	1909, January 23
1328	1910, January 13
1329	1911, January 2
1330	1911, December 22
1332	1913, November 30
1333	1914, November 19
1334	1915, November 9
1335	1916, October 28*
1336	1917, October 17
1337	1918, October 7
1338	1919, September 26
1339	1920, September 15*
1340	1921, September 4
1341	1922, August 24
1342	1923, August 14
1343	1924, August 2*
1344	1925, July 22
1345	1926, July 12
1346	1927, July 1
1347	1928, June 20*
1348	1929, June 9
1349	1930, May 29
1350	1931, May 19
1351	1932, May 7*
1352	1933, April 26
1353	1934, April 16
1354	1935, April 5
1355	1936, March 24*
1356	1937, March 14
1357	1938, March 3
1358	1939, February 21
1359	1940, February 10*

AH Hejira	AD Christian Date
1360	1941, January 29
1361	1942, January 19
1362	1943, January 8
1363	1943, December 28
1364	1944, December 17*
1365	1945, December 6
1366	1946, November 25
1367	1947, November 15
1368	1948, November 3*
1369	1949, October 24
1370	1950, October 13
1371	1951, October 2
1372	1952, September 21*
1373	1953, September 10
1374	1954, August 30
1375	1955, August 20
1376	1956, August 8*
1377	1957, July 29
1378	1958, July 18
1379	1959, July 7
1380	1960, June 25*
1381	1961, June 14
1382	1962, June 4
1383	1963, May 25
1384	1964, May 13*
1385	1965, May 2
1386	1966, April 22
1387	1967, April 11
1388	1968, March 31*
1389	1969, March 20
1390	1970, March 9
1391	1971, February 27
1392	1972, February 16*
1393	1973, February 4
1394	1974, January 25
1395	1975, January 14
1396	1976, January 3*
1397	1976, December 23*
1398	1977, December 12
1399	1978, December 2
1400	1979, November 21
1401	1980, November 9*
1402	1981, October 30
1403	1982, October 19
1404	1984, October 8
1405	1984, September 27*
1406	1985, September 16
1407	1986, September 6
1409	1987, August 26
1409	1988, August 14*
1410	1989, August 3
1411	1990, July 24
1412	1991, July 13
1413	1992, July 2*
1414	1993, June 21
1415	1994, June 10
1416	1995, May 31
1417	1996, May 19*
1418	1997, May 9
1419	1998, April 28
1420	1999, April 17
1421	2000, April 6*
1422	2001, March 26
1423	2002, March 15
1424	2003, March 5
1425	2004, February 22*
1426	2005, February 10
1427	2006, January 31
1428	2007, January 20
1429	2008, January 10*
1430	2008, December 29
1431	2009, December 18
1432	2010, December 8
1433	2011, November 27*
1434	2012, November 15
1435	2013, November 5
1436	2014, October 25
1437	2015, October 15*
1438	2016, October 3
1439	2017, September 22
1440	2018, September 12
1441	2019, September 1*
1442	2020, August 20
1443	2021, August 10
1444	2022, July 30
1445	2023, July 19*
1446	2024, July 8
1447	2025, June 27
1448	2026, June 17
1449	2027, June 6*
1450	2028, May25

ALGERIA

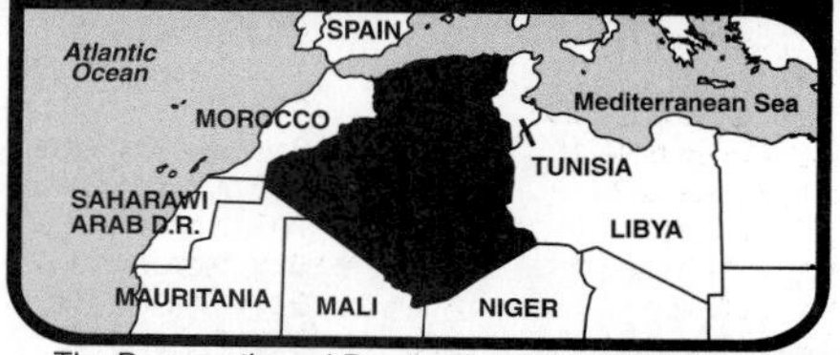

The Democratic and Popular Republic of Algeria, a North African country fronting on the Mediterranean Sea between Tunisia and Morocco. Capital: Algiers (Alger).

Algiers, the capital and chief seaport of Algeria, was the site of Phoenician and Roman settlements before the present Moslem city was founded about 950. Nominally part of the sultanate of Tilimsan, Algiers had a large measure of independence under the amirs of its own. In 1492 the Jews and Moors who had been expelled from Spain settled in Algiers and enjoyed an increasing influence until the imposition of Turkish control in 1518. For the following three centuries, Algiers was the headquarters of the notorious Barbary pirates as Turkish control became more and more nominal.

RULER

Ottoman, until 1830

ALGIERS

MINT NAMES

جزائر

Jaza'ir

جزائر غرب

Jaza'Ir Gharb
AH1012-1115/1603-1703AD

تلمسان

Tilimsan
AH964-1026/1556-1617AD

NOTE: The dots above and below the letters are integral parts of the letters, but for stylistic reasons, are occasionally omitted.

MONETARY SYSTEM

(Until 1847)

14-1/2 Asper (Akche, Dirham Saghir) = 1 Kharub
2 Kharuba = 1 Muzuna
24 Muzuna = 3 Batlaka (Pataka) = 1 Budju

NOTE: Coin denominations are not expressed on the coins, and are best determined by size and weight. The silver Budju weighed about 13.5 g until AH1236/1821AD, when it was reduced to about 10.0 g. The fractional pieces varied in proportion to the Budju. They had secondary names, which are given in the text. In 1829 three new silver coins were introduced and Budju became Tugrali-rial, Tugrali-batlaka = 1/3 Rial = 8 Muzuna and Tugrali-nessflik = 1/2 Batlaka = 4 Muzuna. The gold Sultani was officially valued at 108 Muzuna, but varied in accordance with the market price of gold expressed in silver. It weighed 3.20-3.40 g. The Zer-i Mahbub was valued at 80 Muzuna & weighed 2.38-3.10 g.

OTTOMAN

Mehmed III

AH1003-1012/1595-1603AD

HAMMERED COINAGE

KM# A1 MANGIR

Copper

Date	Mintage	VG	F	VF	XF	Unc
ND	—	100	—	—	—	—

KM# 1 SULTANI

3.4500 g., Gold **Note:** Two reverse varieties are known.

Date	Mintage	VG	F	VF	XF	Unc
AH1003	—	500	700	900	1,000	—

KM# 2 DEBASED DINAR

4.2050 g., Gold

Date	Mintage	VG	F	VF	XF	Unc
AH1003	—	500	600	850	1,000	—

Ahmed I

AH1012-1026/1603-1617AD

HAMMERED COINAGE

KM# A3 MANGIR

2.5200 g., Copper

Date	Mintage	Good	VG	F	VF	XF
AH1012 Rare	—	—	—	—	—	—

KM# B3 SULTANI

3.4000 g., Gold

Date	Mintage	VG	F	VF	XF	Unc
ND Rare	—	—	—	—	—	—

KM# 3 SULTANI

Gold **Note:** Weight varies: 3.08-3.45 grams. Varieties exist.

Date	Mintage	VG	F	VF	XF	Unc
AH1011 (Error)	—	300	400	650	1,100	—
AH1012	—	225	375	600	1,000	—
AH1102 (Error); Rare	—	—	—	—	—	—
AH1015	—	225	375	600	1,000	—
AH1017	—	225	375	600	1,000	—
AH1018	—	225	375	600	1,000	—

KM# 4 DEBASED DINAR

2.0680 g., Gold

Date	Mintage	VG	F	VF	XF	Unc
AH1012	—	—	—	600	850	—

Mustafa I

AH1031-1032/1622-1623AD - Second reign

HAMMERED COINAGE

KM# 5 SULTANI

3.4500 g., Gold

Date	Mintage	VG	F	VF	XF	Unc
AH1031	—	—	—	—	—	—

Murad IV

AH1032-1049/1623-1640AD

HAMMERED COINAGE

KM# 7 SULTANI

3.4500 g., Gold **Note:** Varieties exist.

Date	Mintage	VG	F	VF	XF	Unc
AH1028 (Error for 1038)	—	250	400	600	1,000	—
AH1033	—	250	400	600	1,000	—
AH1032	—	250	400	600	1,000	—
AH1038 Rare	—	—	—	—	—	—
AH1040	—	250	400	600	1,000	—
AH1041	—	250	400	600	1,000	—
AH1042	—	250	400	600	1,000	—
AH1043	—	250	400	600	1,000	—
AH1045	—	250	400	600	1,000	—
AH1046	—	250	400	600	1,000	—

Ibrahim

AH1049-1058/1640-1648AD

HAMMERED COINAGE

KM# 9 SULTANI

Gold, 21-22 mm. **Note:** Weight varies: 3.00-3.46 grams. Size varies.

Date	Mintage	VG	F	VF	XF	Unc
AH1049	—	250	400	600	1,000	—
AH1050//1049	—	250	400	600	1,000	—
Note: 1050 on obverse, 1049 on reverse						
AH10xx	—	250	400	600	1,000	—
AH1051	—	250	400	600	1,000	—
AH1052	—	250	400	600	1,000	—

Mehmed IV

AH1058-1099/1648-1687AD

HAMMERED COINAGE

KM# 11.2 SULTANI

Gold **Note:** Varieties exist.

Date	Mintage	VG	F	VF	XF	Unc
AH1058	—	—	—	—	—	—
AH1061	—	250	400	600	1,000	—
AH1076	—	250	400	600	1,000	—
AH1078	—	250	400	600	1,000	—
AH1086	—	250	400	600	1,000	—
AH1090	—	250	400	600	1,000	—
AH1092	—	250	400	600	1,000	—

KM# 11.1 SULTANI

Gold, 22-24 mm. **Note:** Weight varies: 3.30-3.45 grams. Size varies.

Date	Mintage	VG	F	VF	XF	Unc
ND	—	600	850	1,150	1,600	—

Mustafa II

AH1106-1115/1695-1703AD

HAMMERED COINAGE

KM# 13 SULTANI

3.4500 g., Gold, 21 mm.

Date	Mintage	VG	F	VF	XF	Unc
AH1110	—	—	—	—	—	—

ORAN

Coins were struck in Spain at the Madrid and Toledo Mint to use while the Spanish were occupying the area. In 1708 the city fortress fell to the Ottomans.

SPANISH OCCUPATION

Carlos II

LOCAL COINAGE

(Hammered)

KM# L4 4 MARAVEDIS

Copper **Obv:** Crowned arms of Castile and Leon **Rev:** Crowned 'IHS' below 'ORAN' **Mint:** Madrid

Date	Mintage	Good	VG	F	VF	XF
1691	—	—	—	—	350	—

KM# L5 8 MARAVEDIS

Copper **Obv:** Crowned arms of Castile and Leon **Rev:** Crowned 'IHS' above 'ORAN'. **Mint:** Madrid

Date	Mintage	Good	VG	F	VF	XF
1691	—	50.00	100	200	350	—

Philip III

LOCAL COINAGE

(Hammered)

KM# L1 2 MARAVEDIS

Copper **Obv:** Crowned arms of Castile and Leon **Rev:** ORAN in center

Date	Mintage	Good	VG	F	VF	XF
1618T	—	125	225	375	485	—

KM# L2 4 MARAVEDIS

Copper **Obv:** Crowned arms of Castile and Leon **Rev:** ORAN

Date	Mintage	Good	VG	F	VF	XF
1618	—	175	250	400	525	775

KM# L3 8 MARAVEDIS
Copper **Obv:** Crowned arms of Castile and Leon **Rev:** ORAN in center of legend

Date	Mintage	Good	VG	F	VF	XF
1618T	—	200	325	400	525	775

ANGOLA

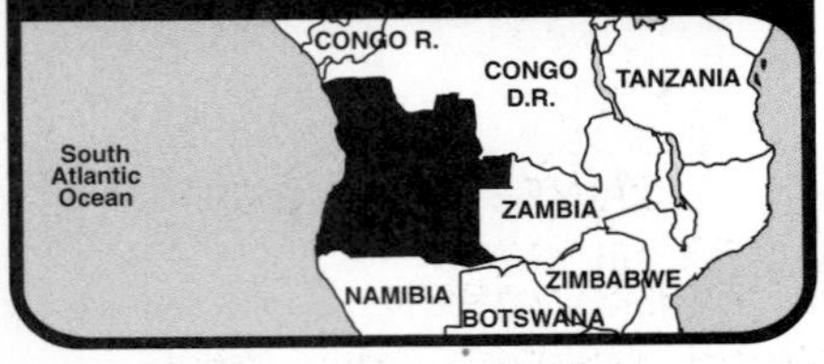

Angola is a country on the west coast of southern Africa. The population is predominantly Bantu in origin.

Angola was discovered by Portuguese navigator Diogo Cao in 1482. Portuguese settlers arrived in 1491, and established Angola as a major slaving center which sent about 3 million slaves to the New World.

RULER
Portuguese until 1975

MONETARY SYSTEM
(Until 1860)
50 Reis = 1 Macuta

PORTUGUESE COLONY

COLONIAL COINAGE

KM# 3 5 REIS (V)
Copper **Note:** The 1749 V Reis formerly listed here as KM#6 can be found under Brazil KM#159. This coin was struck for Brazil but also circulated in Angola.

Date	Mintage	VG	F	VF	XF	Unc
1695	—	300	525	875	1,950	—
1696	—	275	500	850	1,950	—

KM# 2 10 REIS (X)
Copper **Note:** The 1715-1749 X Reis formerly listed here as KM#4 can be found under Brazil KM#108 and KM#142. These coins were struck for Brazil but also circulated in Angola.

Date	Mintage	VG	F	VF	XF	Unc
1693 Unique	—	—	—	—	—	—
1694	—	100	200	350	750	—
1696	—	70.00	145	250	450	—
1697	—	25.00	48.00	95.00	210	—
1699	—	25.00	48.00	95.00	210	—

KM# 1 20 REIS (XX)
Copper **Note:** Similar to 5 Reis, KM#3. The 1715-1749 XX Reis formerly listed here as KM#5 can be found under Brazil KM#109 and KM#143. These coins were struck for Brazil but also circulated in Angola.

Date	Mintage	VG	F	VF	XF	Unc
1693	—	100	250	475	750	—
1694	—	60.00	110	225	400	—
1695	—	85.00	175	400	675	—
1697	—	8.00	16.00	35.00	75.00	—
1698	—	8.00	16.00	35.00	75.00	—
1699	—	7.50	14.00	28.00	65.00	—

ARMENIA

Presently the Republic of Armenia (formerly Armenian S.S.R.) is bounded in the north by Georgia, to the east by Azerbaijan and to the south and west by Turkey and Iran (Persia). It has an area of 11,506 sq. mi. (29,800 sq. km).

The earliest history of Armenia records continuous struggles with expanding Babylonia and later Assyria. In the sixth century B.C. it was called Armina. Later under the Persian empire it enjoyed the position of a vassal state. Conquered by Macedonia, it later defeated the Seleucids and Greater Armenia was founded under the Artaxis dynasty. Christianity was established in 303 A.D. which led to religious wars with the Persians and Romans who divided it into two zones of influence. The Arabs succeeded the Persian Empire of the Sassanids which later allowed the Armenian princes to conclude a treaty in 653 A.D. In 862 A.D. Ashot V was recognized as the "prince of princes" and established a throne recognized by Baghdad and Constantinople in 886 A.D. The Seljuks overran the whole country and united with Kurdistan which eventually ran the new government. In 1240 A.D. onward the Mongols occupied almost all of western Asia until their downfall in 1375 A.D. when various Kurdish, Armenian and Turkoman independent principalities arose. After the defeat of the Persians in 1516 A.D. the Ottoman Turks gradually took control over a period of some 40 years, with Kurdish tribes settling within Armenian lands. In 1605 A.D. the Persians moved thousands of Armenians as far as India developing prosperous colonies. Persia and the Ottoman Turks were again at war, with the Ottomans once again prevailing. The Ottomans later gave absolute civil authority to a Christian bishop allowing them free enjoyment of their religion and traditions.

RULER
Persian, until 1724

MINT NAMES

روان

Revan, (Erevan, now Yerevan)

OTTOMAN EMPIRE

STANDARD COINAGE

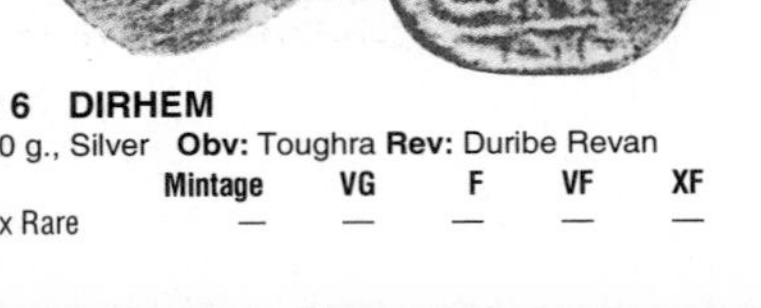

KM# 6 DIRHEM
1.9000 g., Silver **Obv:** Toughra **Rev:** Duribe Revan

Date	Mintage	VG	F	VF	XF	Unc
AHxxxx Rare	—	—	—	—	—	—

Mustafa I

STANDARD COINAGE

KM# 10 DIRHEM
1.8400 g., Silver **Obv:** Toughra with 4 lines **Rev:** Ruler and mint name

Date	Mintage	VG	F	VF	XF	Unc
AH1031 Rare	—	—	—	—	—	—

AUSTRIA

Presently the Republic of Austria, a parliamentary democracy located in mountainous central Europe, has an area of 32,374 sq. mi. (83,850 sq. km.) and a population of 8.08 million. Capital: Wien (Vienna). Austria is primarily an industrial country. Machinery, iron, steel, textiles, yarns and timber are exported.

The territories later to be known as Austria were overrun in pre-Roman times by various tribes, including the Celts. Upon the fall of the Roman Empire, the country became a margravate of Charlemagne's Empire. Premysl II of Otaker, King of Bohemia, gained possession in 1252, only to lose the territory to Rudolf of Habsburg in 1276. Thereafter, until World War I, the story of Austria was conducted by the ruling Habsburgs.

During the 17th century, Austrian coinage reflected the geopolitical strife of three wars. From 1618-1648, the Thirty Years' War between northern Protestants and southern Catholics produced low quality, "kipperwhipper" strikes of 12, 24, 30, 60, 75 and 150 Kreuzer. Later, during the Austrian-Turkish War, 1660-1664, coinages used to maintain soldier's salaries also reported the steady division of Hungarian territories. Finally, between 1683 and 1699, during the second Austrian-Turkish conflict, new issues of 3, 6 and 15 Kreuzers were struck, being necessary to help defray mounting expenses of the war effort.

RULERS
Rudolf II, 1576-1612
Matthias II, 1612-1619
Ferdinand II, 1619-1637
Ferdinand III, 1637-1657
Leopold I, 1657-1705

MINT MARKS
A, W, WI - Vienna (Wien)
(a) - Vienna (Wien)
AI,AL-IV,C-A,E,GA - Karlsburg (Alba Iulia, Transylvania)
B,K,KB - Kremnica (Kremnitz, Hungary)
BE,BE/V,BEZ,B.T. - Bistrice (Romania)
CB,CI,CI-BI(NI),CW,H,HS - Hermannstadt (Sibiu) (Transylvania)
CV (1693-94),FT,KV (1694-1700) - Klausenburg (Cluy, Transylvania)
D - Salzburg
D,G,GR - Graz (Styria)
F, HA - Hall
G,H,P-R - Gunzburg
GM - Mantua (Mantova)
(h) Shield - Vienna (Wien)
M - Milan (Milano, Lombardy)
MB 1693-1697, 1702 - Breh (Brzeg)
NB - Nagybanya (Baia Mare, Hungary)
O - Olmutz (Olomouc)
O - Oravicza (Oravita, Hungary)
S - Schmollnitz (Smolnik, Hungary)
V - Venice (Venice, Venetia)
(v) Eagle - Hall
W - Breslau (Wroclaw, Vratislav, Poland)

MINT IDENTIFICATION

To aid in determining an Austrian (Habsburg) coin's mint it is necessary to first check the coat of arms. In some cases the coat of arms will dominate the reverse. The Hungarian Madonna and child is a prime example. On more traditional Austrian design types the provincial coat of arms will be the only one on the imperial eagle's breast. When a more complicated coat of arms is used the provincial arms will usually be found in the center or at the top center usually overlapping neighboring arms.

Legend endings frequently reflect the various provincial coats of arms. Sometimes mint marks appear on coins such as the letter W for Breslau. Mintmaster's and mint officials' initials or symbols also appear and can be used to confirm the mint identity.

The following pages will present the mint name, illustrate or describe the provincial coats of arms, legend endings, mint marks, and mint officials' initials or symbols with which the mint identity can be determined.

AUGSBURG MINT

BRUNN MINT

(Brno)
(in Moravia)

MINT MARKS

Privy Mark	Description	Date	Names
(B)	Circled B	1624, 1625, 1627	

MINT OFFICIALS' INITIALS

Initials	Dates	Names
GR	1621-23	Georg Ritter
HG	1624	Hans Gebhart
BZ	1624	B. Zwirner

MINT OFFICIALS' PRIVY MARKS

Privy Mark	Description	Date	Names
CW(c) - CW	CW monogram	1623-27	Christoph Wonsiedler
(cs) -	Crenalated square	1621-23	Cons. De Witte
(ct) -	Circle in triangle or triangle in circle	1646-48	Johann Jan Conrad Richthausen
(d)	Dot in center of diamond		
(h) - HP HP	Conjoined HP, metal hook	1619-20	Peter Hema
		1619-22	Hans Peca
(o)	Dot in triangle		
(s)	Snowflake		

FÜRTH MINT

(in Bavaria)

Coat of arms, like Vienna, fills the lower left quarter of the shield on the imperial eagle's breast.

MINT OFFICIALS' INITIALS

Initials	Date	Name
CS	1630	Conrad Stutz, in Nurnberg

GRAZ MINT

(in Province of Styria)

Coat of arms, rampant panther similar to Bohemian lion, usually found on imperial eagle's breast. Legend usually ends: STY, STYR or STYRIAE.

MINT MARKS

D, G, GR - Graz (Styria)

MINT OFFICIALS' INITIALS

Initials	Dates	Names
CH, SH	1665-66	Sebastian Haydt
HCK	1657-65	Hans Caspar Khendimayer
IA	1694-1705	Johann Jacob Aigmann
IAN	1670-1694	Johann Anton Nowak
IGH	1671-73	-
IGW, IW	1671	Johann Georg Weiss
L	1660-82	-
MAX K		Maximillian Konig, engraver
M-IS	1649	Hans Ulrich Mark
MM	1690	Michael Miller, engraver

MINT OFFICIALS' PRIVY MARKS

Privy Mark	Description	Dates	Names
(m) - M	Stylized M	1648-49	Hans Ulrich Mark

HALL MINT

(in Tyrol)

Coat of arms are on eagle's breast. Legends usually end: TYR or TYROL.

MINT OFFICIALS' INITIALS

Initials	Dates	Names
CO, co	1613-18	Christoph Orber
IAK	1693-1701, 1704, 1706	Johann anton Konig, die-cutter

KLAGENFURT MINT

(in Province of Carinthia)

Coat of arms usually found in legend or as the middle arms on the imperial eagle's breast. Legend usually ends CAR or CARINTHIAE. This mint closed in 1622 and moved to Saint Veit.

MINT OFFICIALS' INITIALS

PS - P. Sigharter

KRAIN MINT

MAINZ MINT

(Germany)

MINT OFFICIALS' PRIVY MARK

Privy Mark	Description	Dates	Names
(s) -		1685	Ulrich Burkhart Wildering

NEUBURG am INN MINT

(in upper Austria)

Coat of arms, like Vienna, or quartered arms on imperial eagle's breast.

MINT OFFICIALS' PRIVY MARK

Privy mark	Description	Date	Name
(t) -	Triangle	1664-65	Bartholomaus Triangel

NIKOLSBURG MINT

(Mikulov)
(in Moravia)

For coat of arms, see Vienna. This mint opened in 1627 and closed in 1628.

MINT OFFICIALS' PRIVY MARKS

Privy marks	Description	Dates	Names
CW	C above W	1625	Christoph Wansidler

OLMÜTZ MINT

(Olomouc)
(in Moravia)

Coat of arms, see Vienna. This mint was captured and occupied by Sweden from June, 1642 until July, 1650 when it moved to Brunn. In 1664 it was closed.

MINT MARKS

(O) 1620, 1624, 1628

MINT OFFICIALS' INITIALS

Initials	Dates	Names
BZ	1620-24	Balthasar Zwirner, mintmaster
CC	1619-20	Cristoph Cantor
GR	1621-23	Georg Ritter, die cutter
HH	1636	Jan Krystof Huber, warden

MINT OFFICIALS' PRIVY MARKS

Privy Mark	Description	Dates	Names
ICH	C above IH	1635-36	Tobias Sonnenschein, mintmaster
		1636-38	Mrs. Dorota Sonnenschein
MF	Ligate MF, MF and anchor between crescents	1625-27, 29-35	Martin Fritsch
(a) -	Anchor	1628-40	-
(d) -	Crenalated diamond	1622-23	-
(h) - HP	HP & hook	1621	Peter Hema
(i)	Lamb in oval	1638-42	Adam Schafer, mintmaster
(l)	Leaf		
(o)	O in circle		

SAINT POLTEN MINT

Coat of arms, see Vienna.

MINT OFFICIALS' PRIVY MARKS

Privy mark	Description	Dates	Names
(c) -	Inverted chevron in circle	1624-25	Matthias Fellner v. Feldegg
(d)	Double trefoil in circle	1624-25	Johann Joachim Edling
			Donat Starkh, die-cutter
(f) - II E	Fleur de lis in circle between II & E	1625	Johann Joachim Edling
(r) -	Rosette	1625-26	Martin Turba

SAINT VEIT MINT

(in Carinthia)

Coat of arms, see Klagenfurt, are usually found on top center of the massive coat of arms on the imperial eagle's breast. Legend usually ends CAR or CARINTHIAE. This mint moved from Klagenfurt and opened in October, 1622. It closed in 1720.

MINT OFFICIALS' INITIALS

Initials	Dates	Names
CCS	1696	Carl Georg Christoph Strauss v. Straussenegg
CS	1690, 1692-1700	
DS	1622	Donat Stockh, die-cutter
GCVS	1689, 1693	Carl Georg Christoph
GSVS	1689, 91, 94	Strauss V. Straussenegg
G, GS, GCS	1668-72	Georg Christoph Strauss v. Straussenegg
HGP	1630, 38, 42	Hans Georg Perro
HL, LS	1693	-
IGR, IR	1679-89	John Georg Rabensteiner
IIP, IP	1699-1705	Johann Josef Preiss
IW	1700	-
P	1627	H. G. Perro
p-HS	1649	H. J. Stadler

MINT OFFICIALS' MONOGRAMS

Monogram	Description	Dates	Names
(g) - HG	HG monogram	1627-28	Hans Georg, die-cutter
(h) - M	HM monogram	1623-25	Hans Matz
(is) - IS	IS monogram	1645, 50, 54, 57	H. J. Stadler
(m) - MH	MH monogram		
(p) -	PS monogram	1624-28	Paul Sigharter

VIENNA MINT

(Wien)

Coat of arms, usually found in the legend or as the middle arms on a multiple arms shield or alone on the imperial eagle's breast. Legend usually ends TY, TYR or TYROL.

MINT OFFICIALS' INITIALS

Initials	Dates	Names
AP	1628, 30	Andreas Peter, die-cutter
BZ	1624	Balthasar Zwirner
CH	1610-11	Caspar Haidler, die-cutter
CM	1609-12	Christian Maler, die-cutter
DS	1624-37	Donat Starkh, die-cutter
HH	1659	?
HS	1655, 57-58	Hans Stadler
IMH, MH	1680-1736	Johann Michael Hofmann

MINT OFFICIALS' PRIVY MARKS

Privy mark	Description	Dates	Names
(b)	Bird		
(bs) -	Bird standing in circle	1637-48	Hans Jacob Stadler
(bw) -	Rooster walking right	1605-12, 22	Andreas Handl
(c) -	Chevrons within circles	1648-59	Johann Conrad Richthausen
(ca) -	CA monogram	1660-65	Andrea Cetto
(cv) -	Crowned CV monogram in circle	1636-37	Virgilius Constanz v. Vestenburg
(lf) -	Floweret	1659-60	Franz Faber
(ic)	Inverted chevron & inverted Y	1612-17, 19-36	Matthias Feliner v.Feldegg
(if)	Large flower	1622-23	Martin Turba, warden
(mm) -	MM monogram	1679-95, 1703-05, 07-08	Matthias Mittermayer
(r) -	Rosette	1659-60, 66-79	Franz Faber v. Rosenstock
(ri) -	Ring	1588-1604	Lorenz Huebmer
(t) -	Tree on shield	1617-19	Isaias Jessensky
(v)	VC monogram in circle		

WÜRZBURG MINT

(in Germany)

Coat of arms, like Vienna.

MINT OFFICIALS' PRIVY MARKS

Privy mark	Description	Date	Name
(t) -	Stylized A	1685	

HOLY ROMAN EMPIRE

STANDARD COINAGE

KM# 10 4 HELLER (Vierer)

Silver **Ruler:** Rudolf II **Obv:** Coat of arms within legend **Rev:** Eagle in inner circle **Mint:** Hall **Note:** Prev. KM#580.

Date	Mintage	VG	F	VF	XF	Unc
1601	—	60.00	95.00	175	280	—
1603	—	60.00	95.00	175	280	—
1604	—	60.00	95.00	175	280	—
1605	—	60.00	95.00	175	280	—
1606	—	60.00	95.00	175	280	—

KM# 12 PFENNIG

Silver **Ruler:** Ferdinand II **Obv:** Divided arms with date above in diamond **Mint:** Klagenfurt **Note:** Uniface. Varieties exist. Local issue for Archduke Ferdinand. Prev. KM#985.

Date	Mintage	VG	F	VF	XF	Unc
1601	—	12.00	25.00	40.00	60.00	—
1602	—	12.00	25.00	40.00	60.00	—
1603	—	12.00	25.00	40.00	60.00	—
1604	—	12.00	25.00	40.00	60.00	—
1605	—	12.00	25.00	40.00	60.00	—
1606	—	12.00	25.00	40.00	60.00	—
1607	—	12.00	25.00	40.00	60.00	—
1608	—	12.00	25.00	40.00	60.00	—
1609	—	12.00	25.00	40.00	60.00	—
1610	—	12.00	25.00	40.00	60.00	—
1612	—	12.00	25.00	40.00	60.00	—
1613	—	12.00	25.00	40.00	60.00	—
1614	—	12.00	25.00	40.00	60.00	—
1616	—	12.00	25.00	40.00	60.00	—
1617	—	12.00	25.00	40.00	60.00	—
1618	—	12.00	25.00	40.00	60.00	—

KM# 11 PFENNIG

Silver **Ruler:** Ferdinand II **Obv:** Griffin in shield with date above in diamond **Mint:** Graz **Note:** Uniface. Varieties exist. Prev. KM#555.

Date	Mintage	VG	F	VF	XF	Unc
1601	—	5.00	15.00	25.00	40.00	—
1602	—	5.00	15.00	25.00	40.00	—
1603	—	5.00	15.00	25.00	40.00	—
1604	—	5.00	15.00	25.00	40.00	—
1605	—	5.00	15.00	25.00	40.00	—
1608	—	5.00	15.00	25.00	40.00	—
(1)609	—	5.00	15.00	25.00	40.00	—
1610	—	5.00	15.00	25.00	40.00	—
1611	—	5.00	15.00	25.00	40.00	—
1612	—	5.00	15.00	25.00	40.00	—
1613	—	—	—	—	—	—
Note: Reported, not confirmed						
1614	—	5.00	15.00	25.00	40.00	—
1615	—	5.00	15.00	25.00	40.00	—
1616	—	5.00	15.00	25.00	40.00	—
1617	—	5.00	15.00	25.00	40.00	—

KM# 133 PFENNIG

Billon **Ruler:** Matthias II **Obv:** Shield of arms divides date in diamond **Mint:** Vienna **Note:** Uniface. Prev. KM#1725.

Date	Mintage	VG	F	VF	XF	Unc
1612	—	—	—	—	—	—

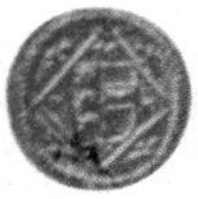

KM# 467 PFENNIG

Billon **Ruler:** Ferdinand II **Obv:** Carinthian arms in diamond, one digit of date on each side **Mint:** Saint Veit **Note:** Uniface. Prev. KM#1585.

Date	Mintage	VG	F	VF	XF	Unc
1624 (g)	—	30.00	50.00	90.00	150	—
1625 (h)	—	30.00	50.00	90.00	150	—
1627 (g)	—	30.00	50.00	90.00	150	—
1629 (g)	—	30.00	50.00	90.00	150	—

KM# 466 PFENNIG

Billon **Ruler:** Ferdinand II **Obv:** Shield of arms at center of diamond, date at sides and top **Mint:** Graz **Note:** Uniface. Varieties exist. Prev. KM#335.

Date	Mintage	VG	F	VF	XF	Unc
1624	—	9.00	22.00	45.00	75.00	—
1625	—	9.00	22.00	45.00	75.00	—
1626	—	9.00	22.00	45.00	75.00	—
1627	—	9.00	22.00	45.00	75.00	—
1628	—	9.00	22.00	45.00	75.00	—
1629	—	9.00	22.00	45.00	75.00	—
1630	—	9.00	22.00	45.00	75.00	—
1631	—	9.00	22.00	45.00	75.00	—
1632	—	9.00	22.00	45.00	75.00	—
1633	—	9.00	22.00	45.00	75.00	—
1634	—	9.00	22.00	45.00	75.00	—
1635	—	9.00	22.00	45.00	75.00	—
1636	—	9.00	22.00	45.00	75.00	—
1637	—	9.00	22.00	45.00	75.00	—

KM# 765 PFENNIG

Billon **Ruler:** Ferdinand III **Obv:** Date numerals left and right **Mint:** Saint Veit **Note:** Varieties exist. Uniface. Prev. KM#1620.

Date	Mintage	VG	F	VF	XF	Unc
1631	—	5.00	12.00	25.00	40.00	—
1636	—	5.00	12.00	25.00	40.00	—
1637	—	5.00	12.00	25.00	40.00	—
1639	—	5.00	12.00	25.00	40.00	—
1652	—	5.00	12.00	25.00	40.00	—
1653	—	5.00	12.00	25.00	40.00	—
1654	—	5.00	12.00	25.00	40.00	—

KM# 826 PFENNIG

Billon **Ruler:** Ferdinand III **Obv:** Oval shield of arms **Mint:** Graz **Note:** Uniface. Prev. KM#415.

Date	Mintage	VG	F	VF	XF	Unc
1637	—	4.00	9.00	18.00	30.00	—
1638	—	4.00	9.00	18.00	30.00	—
1639	—	4.00	9.00	18.00	30.00	—
1640	—	4.00	9.00	18.00	30.00	—

KM# 848 PFENNIG

Billon **Ruler:** Ferdinand III **Obv:** Flat-topped shield of arms **Mint:** Graz **Note:** Prev. KM#416.

Date	Mintage	VG	F	VF	XF	Unc
1638	—	4.00	9.00	18.00	30.00	—

KM# 905 PFENNIG

Billon **Ruler:** Ferdinand III **Obv:** Arms in cartouche at center of diamond, date at sides and bottom **Mint:** Graz **Note:** Prev. KM#417.

Date	Mintage	VG	F	VF	XF	Unc
1642	—	4.00	9.00	18.00	30.00	—
1643	—	4.00	9.00	18.00	30.00	—
1645	—	4.00	9.00	18.00	30.00	—
1647	—	4.00	9.00	18.00	30.00	—

KM# 906 PFENNIG

Billon **Ruler:** Ferdinand III **Obv:** Oval arms **Mint:** Saint Veit **Note:** Prev. KM#1621.

Date	Mintage	VG	F	VF	XF	Unc
1642	—	5.00	12.00	22.00	50.00	—
1645	—	5.00	12.00	22.00	50.00	—
1649	—	5.00	12.00	22.00	50.00	—

KM# 923 PFENNIG

Billon **Ruler:** Ferdinand III **Obv:** Date at sides and top **Mint:** Graz **Note:** Varieties exist. Prev. KM#418.

Date	Mintage	VG	F	VF	XF	Unc
1645	—	4.00	9.00	18.00	30.00	—
1648	—	4.00	9.00	18.00	30.00	—
1649	—	4.00	9.00	18.00	30.00	—
1650	—	4.00	9.00	18.00	30.00	—
1653	—	4.00	9.00	18.00	30.00	—

KM# 945 PFENNIG

Billon **Ruler:** Ferdinand III **Obv:** Small shield of arms divides date in diamond, F above shield, W below **Mint:** Vienna **Note:** Uniface. Prev. KM#1815.

Date	Mintage	VG	F	VF	XF	Unc
1647	—	10.00	20.00	35.00	65.00	—
1648	—	10.00	20.00	35.00	65.00	—

KM# 994 PFENNIG

Billon **Ruler:** Ferdinand III **Obv:** Flat-topped shield of arms at center of quatrefoil, date at sides and bottom **Mint:** Graz **Note:** Prev. KM#419.

Date	Mintage	VG	F	VF	XF	Unc
1656	—	4.00	9.00	18.00	30.00	—
1657	—	4.00	9.00	18.00	30.00	—

KM# 1111 PFENNIG

Billon **Ruler:** Leopold I **Obv:** Carinthian arms in diamond, one digit of date on each side **Mint:** Saint Veit **Note:** Uniface. Prev. KM#1635.

Date	Mintage	VG	F	VF	XF	Unc
1658	—	5.00	10.00	25.00	70.00	—
1659	—	5.00	10.00	25.00	70.00	—
1660	—	5.00	10.00	25.00	70.00	—
1664	—	5.00	10.00	25.00	70.00	—
1669	—	5.00	10.00	25.00	70.00	—
1681	—	5.00	10.00	25.00	70.00	—
1682	—	5.00	10.00	25.00	70.00	—
1684	—	5.00	10.00	25.00	70.00	—
1690	—	5.00	10.00	25.00	70.00	—
1693	—	5.00	10.00	25.00	70.00	—
1695	—	5.00	10.00	25.00	70.00	—
1696	—	5.00	10.00	25.00	70.00	—

KM# 1168 PFENNIG

Billon **Ruler:** Leopold I **Obv:** Oval arms divide date **Mint:** Graz **Note:** Uniface. Prev. KM#445.

Date	Mintage	VG	F	VF	XF	Unc
1660	—	5.00	10.00	20.00	40.00	—
1661	—	5.00	10.00	20.00	40.00	—
1662	—	5.00	10.00	20.00	40.00	—
1666	—	5.00	10.00	20.00	40.00	—
1671	—	5.00	10.00	20.00	40.00	—
1673	—	5.00	10.00	20.00	40.00	—
1674	—	5.00	10.00	20.00	40.00	—
1675	—	5.00	10.00	20.00	40.00	—

KM# 1286 PFENNIG

Billon **Ruler:** Leopold I **Obv:** Oval arms in diamond **Mint:** Graz **Note:** Varieties exist. Prev. KM#446.

Date	Mintage	VG	F	VF	XF	Unc
1676	—	5.00	10.00	20.00	40.00	—
1677	—	5.00	10.00	20.00	40.00	—
1678	—	5.00	10.00	20.00	40.00	—
1679	—	5.00	10.00	20.00	40.00	—
1680	—	5.00	10.00	20.00	40.00	—
1682	—	5.00	10.00	20.00	40.00	—
1684	—	5.00	10.00	20.00	40.00	—
1685	—	5.00	10.00	20.00	40.00	—
1686	—	5.00	10.00	20.00	40.00	—
1687	—	5.00	10.00	20.00	40.00	—
1688	—	5.00	10.00	20.00	40.00	—
1689	—	5.00	10.00	20.00	40.00	—
1691	—	5.00	10.00	20.00	40.00	—
1692	—	5.00	10.00	20.00	40.00	—
1693	—	5.00	10.00	20.00	40.00	—

KM# 14 2 PFENNIG

Silver **Ruler:** Ferdinand II **Obv:** Two crowned shields with date below, in trilobe **Mint:** Graz **Note:** Uniface. Varieties exist. Prev. KM#556.

Date	Mintage	VG	F	VF	XF	Unc
(1)601	—	8.00	17.00	30.00	50.00	—
(1)602	—	8.00	17.00	30.00	50.00	—
(1)603	—	8.00	17.00	30.00	50.00	—
(1)604	—	8.00	17.00	30.00	50.00	—
(1)605	—	8.00	17.00	30.00	50.00	—
1606	—	8.00	17.00	30.00	50.00	—
(1)608	—	8.00	17.00	30.00	50.00	—
(1)610	—	8.00	17.00	30.00	50.00	—
(1)611	—	8.00	17.00	30.00	50.00	—
(1)612	—	8.00	17.00	30.00	50.00	—
(1)613	—	8.00	17.00	30.00	50.00	—
(1)614	—	8.00	17.00	30.00	50.00	—
(1)615	—	8.00	17.00	30.00	50.00	—
(1)616	—	8.00	17.00	30.00	50.00	—
(1)617	—	8.00	17.00	30.00	50.00	—

KM# 13 2 PFENNIG

5.5000 g., Silver, 23.6 mm. **Ruler:** Ferdinand II **Obv:** Two crowned shields with date below in trilobe **Mint:** Klagenfurt **Note:** Uniface. Varieties exist. Local issue for Archduke Ferdinand. Prev. KM#986.

Date	Mintage	VG	F	VF	XF	Unc
1601	—	10.00	20.00	35.00	65.00	—
1602	—	10.00	20.00	35.00	65.00	—
1603	—	10.00	20.00	35.00	65.00	—
1604	—	10.00	20.00	35.00	65.00	—
1605	—	10.00	20.00	35.00	65.00	—
1606	—	10.00	20.00	35.00	65.00	—
1607	—	10.00	20.00	35.00	65.00	—
1608	—	10.00	20.00	35.00	65.00	—
1609	—	10.00	20.00	35.00	65.00	—
1610	—	10.00	20.00	35.00	65.00	—
1611	—	10.00	20.00	35.00	65.00	—
1612	—	10.00	20.00	35.00	65.00	—
1613	—	10.00	20.00	35.00	65.00	—
1614	—	10.00	20.00	35.00	65.00	—
1615	—	10.00	20.00	35.00	65.00	—
1616	—	10.00	20.00	35.00	65.00	—
1617	—	10.00	20.00	35.00	65.00	—
1618	—	10.00	20.00	35.00	65.00	—

KM# 252 2 PFENNIG

Billon **Ruler:** Ferdinand II **Obv:** Three shields of arms, top shiled divides date **Mint:** Saint Veit **Note:** Varieties exist. Uniface. Prev. KM#1586.

Date	Mintage	VG	F	VF	XF	Unc
ND	—	20.00	40.00	70.00	125	—
1620	—	20.00	40.00	70.00	125	—
1623	—	20.00	40.00	70.00	125	—
1623 (m)	—	20.00	40.00	70.00	125	—
1624	—	20.00	40.00	70.00	125	—
1624 (m)	—	15.00	25.00	50.00	100	—
1625 (m)	—	15.00	25.00	50.00	100	—
1625 (h)	—	15.00	25.00	50.00	100	—
1625 (p)	—	18.00	35.00	50.00	100	—
1626 (p)	—	18.00	35.00	50.00	100	—
1627 (p)	—	18.00	35.00	50.00	100	—

KM# 251 2 PFENNIG

Billon **Ruler:** Ferdinand II **Obv:** Three shields of arms, one above two **Mint:** Klagenfurt **Note:** Uniface. Prev. KM#950.

Date	Mintage	VG	F	VF	XF	Unc
ND	—	20.00	40.00	70.00	120	—

KM# 377 2 PFENNIG

Billon **Ruler:** Ferdinand II **Obv:** Three shields of arms, one above two, date divided by top shield **Mint:** Graz **Note:** Uniface. Varieties exist. Prev. KM#336.

Date	Mintage	VG	F	VF	XF	Unc
1622	—	9.00	22.00	40.00	60.00	—
1623	—	9.00	22.00	40.00	60.00	—
1624	—	9.00	22.00	40.00	60.00	—
1625	—	9.00	22.00	40.00	60.00	—
1626	—	9.00	22.00	40.00	60.00	—
1627	—	9.00	22.00	40.00	60.00	—
1628	—	9.00	22.00	40.00	60.00	—
1629	—	9.00	22.00	40.00	60.00	—
1630	—	9.00	22.00	40.00	60.00	—
1631	—	9.00	22.00	40.00	60.00	—
1632	—	9.00	22.00	40.00	60.00	—

KM# 435 2 PFENNIG

Silver **Ruler:** Ferdinand II **Obv:** Three coat of arms **Mint:** Krain **Note:** Uniface. Prev. KM#1010.

Date	Mintage	VG	F	VF	XF	Unc
1623 K Rare	—	—	—	—	—	—

KM# 566 2 PFENNIG

Silver **Ruler:** Ferdinand II **Obv:** Shields reversed, crown divides arched date **Mint:** Vienna **Note:** Prev. KM#1766.

Date	Mintage	VG	F	VF	XF	Unc
1625	—	10.00	30.00	60.00	110	—
1626	—	10.00	30.00	60.00	110	—
1627	—	10.00	30.00	60.00	110	—
1628	—	10.00	30.00	60.00	110	—
1629	—	10.00	30.00	60.00	110	—
1630	—	10.00	30.00	60.00	110	—
1631	—	10.00	30.00	60.00	110	—
1632	—	10.00	30.00	60.00	110	—
1633	—	10.00	30.00	60.00	110	—
1634	—	10.00	30.00	60.00	110	—
1635	—	10.00	30.00	60.00	110	—
1636	—	10.00	30.00	60.00	110	—

KM# 564 2 PFENNIG

Billon **Ruler:** Ferdinand II **Obv:** Large shields **Mint:** Saint Veit **Note:** Varieties exist. Uniface. Prev. KM#1587.

Date	Mintage	VG	F	VF	XF	Unc
1625	—	18.00	35.00	60.00	120	—
1626	—	18.00	35.00	60.00	120	—
1627	—	18.00	35.00	60.00	120	—

KM# 565 2 PFENNIG

Silver **Ruler:** Ferdinand II **Obv:** Crown above two shields of arms divides flat date **Mint:** Vienna **Note:** Uniface. Prev. KM#1765.

Date	Mintage	VG	F	VF	XF	Unc
1625	—	—	—	—	—	—

KM# 688 2 PFENNIG

Billon **Ruler:** Ferdinand II **Obv:** Two-digit date between bottom two shields **Mint:** Saint Veit **Note:** Prev. KM#1588.

Date	Mintage	VG	F	VF	XF	Unc
(16)28	—	20.00	40.00	90.00	150	—
(16)29	—	20.00	40.00	90.00	150	—
(16)30	—	20.00	40.00	90.00	150	—

KM# 801 2 PFENNIG

Billon **Ruler:** Ferdinand II **Obv:** Heart-shaped shields **Mint:** Graz **Note:** Prev. KM#337.

Date	Mintage	VG	F	VF	XF	Unc
1633	—	9.00	22.00	45.00	75.00	—
1634	—	9.00	22.00	45.00	75.00	—
1635	—	9.00	22.00	45.00	75.00	—
1637	—	9.00	22.00	45.00	75.00	—

KM# 804 2 PFENNIG

Billon **Ruler:** Ferdinand III **Obv:** Oval arms **Mint:** Saint Veit **Note:** Varieties exist. Uniface. Prev. KM#1622.

Date	Mintage	VG	F	VF	XF	Unc
1634	—	6.00	13.00	25.00	60.00	—
1637	—	6.00	13.00	25.00	60.00	—
1638	—	6.00	13.00	25.00	60.00	—
1640	—	6.00	13.00	25.00	60.00	—
1641	—	6.00	13.00	25.00	60.00	—
1642	—	6.00	13.00	25.00	60.00	—
1645	—	6.00	13.00	25.00	60.00	—
1646	—	6.00	13.00	25.00	60.00	—
1648	—	6.00	13.00	25.00	60.00	—
1649	—	6.00	13.00	25.00	60.00	—
1651	—	6.00	13.00	25.00	60.00	—
1653	—	6.00	13.00	25.00	60.00	—
1655	—	6.00	13.00	25.00	60.00	—

KM# 827 2 PFENNIG

Billon **Ruler:** Ferdinand III **Obv:** Larger, longer shields, arched date above crown **Mint:** Vienna **Note:** Prev. KM#1816.

Date	Mintage	VG	F	VF	XF	Unc
1637	—	8.00	16.00	30.00	50.00	—
1638	—	8.00	16.00	30.00	50.00	—
1639	—	8.00	16.00	30.00	50.00	—
1640	—	8.00	16.00	30.00	50.00	—
1641	—	8.00	16.00	30.00	50.00	—
1642	—	8.00	16.00	30.00	50.00	—
1643	—	8.00	16.00	30.00	50.00	—
1647	—	8.00	16.00	30.00	50.00	—
1653	—	8.00	16.00	30.00	50.00	—

KM# 849 2 PFENNIG

Billon **Ruler:** Ferdinand III **Obv:** Three shields of arms **Mint:** Graz **Note:** Varieties exist. Uniface. Prev. KM#420.

Date	Mintage	VG	F	VF	XF	Unc
1638	—	4.00	9.00	18.00	33.00	—
1639	—	4.00	9.00	18.00	33.00	—
1640	—	4.00	9.00	18.00	33.00	—
1641	—	4.00	9.00	18.00	33.00	—
1642	—	4.00	9.00	18.00	33.00	—
1643	—	4.00	9.00	18.00	33.00	—
1644	—	4.00	9.00	18.00	33.00	—
1645	—	4.00	9.00	18.00	33.00	—
1646	—	4.00	9.00	18.00	33.00	—
1647	—	4.00	9.00	18.00	33.00	—
1648	—	4.00	9.00	18.00	33.00	—
1651	—	4.00	9.00	18.00	33.00	—
1653	—	4.00	9.00	18.00	33.00	—
1655	—	4.00	9.00	18.00	33.00	—
1656	—	4.00	9.00	18.00	33.00	—
1657	—	4.00	9.00	18.00	33.00	—

KM# 872 2 PFENNIG

Billon **Ruler:** Ferdinand III **Obv:** Flat-topped shields **Mint:** Graz **Note:** Prev. KM#872.

Date	Mintage	VG	F	VF	XF	Unc
1639	—	5.00	10.00	25.00	55.00	—

KM# 1112 2 PFENNIG

Silver **Ruler:** Leopold I **Obv:** Bottom shields flat at center **Mint:** Saint Veit **Note:** Uniface. Prev. KM#1636.

Date	Mintage	VG	F	VF	XF	Unc
1658	—	8.00	16.00	35.00	65.00	—
1664	—	8.00	16.00	35.00	65.00	—

KM# 1131 2 PFENNIG

Billon **Ruler:** Leopold I **Obv:** Three shields of arms **Mint:** Graz **Note:** Varieties exist. Uniface. Prev. KM#447.

Date	Mintage	VG	F	VF	XF	Unc
1659	—	4.00	8.00	16.00	35.00	—
1660 L	—	4.00	8.00	16.00	35.00	—
1661 L	—	4.00	8.00	16.00	35.00	—
1662 L	—	4.00	8.00	16.00	35.00	—
1666 L	—	4.00	8.00	16.00	35.00	—
1669 L	—	4.00	8.00	16.00	35.00	—
1671 L	—	4.00	8.00	16.00	35.00	—
1672 L	—	4.00	8.00	16.00	35.00	—
1673 L	—	4.00	8.00	16.00	35.00	—
1674 L	—	4.00	8.00	16.00	35.00	—
1675 L	—	4.00	8.00	16.00	35.00	—
1676 L	—	4.00	8.00	16.00	35.00	—
1677 L	—	4.00	8.00	16.00	35.00	—
1678 L	—	4.00	8.00	16.00	35.00	—
1679 L	—	4.00	8.00	16.00	35.00	—
1680 L	—	4.00	8.00	16.00	35.00	—
1682 L	—	4.00	8.00	16.00	35.00	—
1682	—	4.00	8.00	16.00	35.00	—
1685	—	4.00	8.00	16.00	35.00	—
1686	—	4.00	8.00	16.00	35.00	—
1688	—	4.00	8.00	16.00	35.00	—
1692	—	4.00	8.00	16.00	35.00	—
1698	—	4.00	8.00	16.00	35.00	—
1700	—	4.00	8.00	16.00	35.00	—

KM# 1195 2 PFENNIG

Silver **Ruler:** Leopold I **Obv:** Three shields of arms - one above two, top shield divides date in straight line **Mint:** Vienna **Note:** Varieties exist. Uniface. Prev. KM#1850.

Date	Mintage	VG	F	VF	XF	Unc
1662	—	6.00	12.00	25.00	48.00	—
1664	—	6.00	12.00	25.00	48.00	—
1665	—	6.00	12.00	25.00	48.00	—
1667	—	6.00	12.00	25.00	48.00	—
1668	—	6.00	12.00	25.00	48.00	—
1669	—	6.00	12.00	25.00	48.00	—
1670	—	6.00	12.00	25.00	48.00	—
1671	—	6.00	12.00	25.00	48.00	—
1672	—	6.00	12.00	25.00	48.00	—
1675	—	6.00	12.00	25.00	48.00	—
1676	—	6.00	12.00	25.00	48.00	—
1680	—	6.00	12.00	25.00	48.00	—
1681	—	6.00	12.00	25.00	48.00	—
1683	—	6.00	12.00	25.00	48.00	—
1684	—	6.00	12.00	25.00	48.00	—
1685	—	6.00	12.00	25.00	48.00	—

KM# 1228 2 PFENNIG

Silver **Ruler:** Leopold I **Obv:** Bottom shields round **Mint:** Saint Veit **Note:** Uniface. Prev. KM#1637.

Date	Mintage	VG	F	VF	XF	Unc
1665	—	7.00	13.00	27.50	60.00	—
1668	—	7.00	13.00	27.50	60.00	—
1679	—	7.00	13.00	27.50	60.00	—
1683	—	7.00	13.00	27.50	60.00	—
1691	—	7.00	13.00	27.50	60.00	—
1693	—	7.00	13.00	27.50	60.00	—
1695	—	7.00	13.00	27.50	60.00	—

KM# 1337 2 PFENNIG

Silver **Ruler:** Leopold I **Obv:** Three shields of arms - one above two, divided date in arc **Mint:** Vienna **Note:** Varieties exist. Uniface. Prev. KM#1851.

Date	Mintage	VG	F	VF	XF	Unc
1686	—	6.00	12.00	25.00	48.00	—
1687	—	6.00	12.00	25.00	48.00	—
1688	—	6.00	12.00	25.00	48.00	—
1689	—	7.00	14.00	27.50	55.00	—
1690	—	6.00	12.00	25.00	48.00	—
1691	—	6.00	12.00	25.00	48.00	—
1692	—	6.00	12.00	25.00	48.00	—
1693	—	6.00	12.00	25.00	48.00	—
1694	—	6.00	12.00	25.00	48.00	—
1698	—	6.00	12.00	25.00	48.00	—
1699	—	6.00	12.00	25.00	48.00	—
1700	—	6.00	12.00	25.00	48.00	—

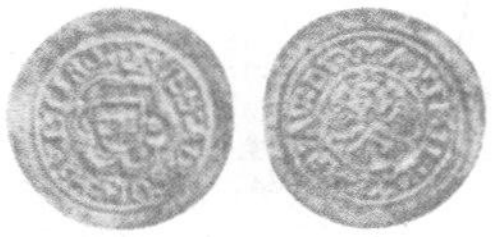

KM# 132 VIERER (4 Heller)

Silver **Ruler:** Maximilian **Mint:** Hall **Note:** Prev. KM#760.

Date	Mintage	VG	F	VF	XF	Unc
ND(1612-19)	2,311,000	100	225	300	525	—

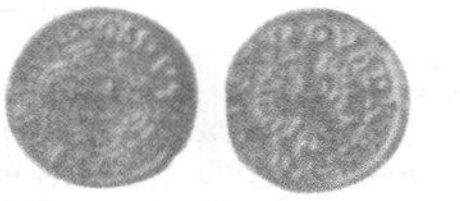

KM# 235 VIERER (4 Heller)

Silver **Ruler:** Leopold **Mint:** Hall **Note:** Prev. KM#785.

Date	Mintage	VG	F	VF	XF	Unc
ND(1619)	—	12.50	25.00	37.50	70.00	—

KM# 956 VIERER (4 Heller)

Silver **Ruler:** Ferdinand Charles **Rev:** Eagle with wreath **Mint:** Hall **Note:** Prev. KM#826.

Date	Mintage	VG	F	VF	XF	Unc
ND(1648-62)	2,483,000	10.00	20.00	35.00	60.00	—

KM# 955 VIERER (4 Heller)

Silver **Ruler:** Ferdinand Charles **Obv:** Austrian shield **Rev:** Eagle **Mint:** Hall **Note:** Prev. KM#825.

Date	Mintage	VG	F	VF	XF	Unc
ND(1648-62)	289,000	10.00	20.00	35.00	60.00	—

KM# 31 KREUZER

Silver **Ruler:** Rudolf II **Obv:** Bust, date below **Rev:** Two crosses at 45 degree angle with shield in circle at center **Mint:** Hall **Note:** Prev. KM#581.

Date	Mintage	VG	F	VF	XF	Unc
1602	—	25.00	50.00	100	185	—
1603	—	25.00	50.00	100	185	—

KM# 51 KREUZER

Silver **Ruler:** Rudolf II **Obv:** Inner circle and two-digit date **Mint:** Hall **Note:** Prev. KM#582.

Date	Mintage	VG	F	VF	XF	Unc
(16)04	—	25.00	42.00	100	210	—

KM# 52 KREUZER

Silver **Ruler:** Rudolf II **Obv:** Inner circle **Rev:** Inner circle **Mint:** Hall **Note:** Prev. KM#583.1.

Date	Mintage	VG	F	VF	XF	Unc
1604	—	20.00	40.00	80.00	130	—
1605	—	20.00	40.00	80.00	130	—
1606	—	20.00	40.00	80.00	130	—
1607	—	20.00	40.00	80.00	130	—
1608	—	20.00	40.00	80.00	130	—
1609	—	20.00	40.00	80.00	130	—
1610	—	20.00	40.00	80.00	130	—
1611	—	20.00	40.00	80.00	130	—

KM# 61 KREUZER

Silver **Ruler:** Rudolf II **Obv:** Two-digit date **Mint:** Hall **Note:** Prev. KM#584.

Date	Mintage	VG	F	VF	XF	Unc
(16)05	—	25.00	50.00	100	185	—
(16)08	—	25.00	50.00	100	185	—
(16)09	—	25.00	50.00	100	185	—

KM# 62 KREUZER

Silver **Ruler:** Rudolf II **Obv:** 1605 **Rev:** 1602 **Mint:** Hall **Note:** Mule. Prev. KM#585.

Date	Mintage	VG	F	VF	XF	Unc
1605-02	—	150	300	500	800	—

KM# 116 KREUZER

Silver **Ruler:** Rudolf II **Mint:** Vienna **Note:** Prev. KM#1710.

Date	Mintage	VG	F	VF	XF	Unc
1610	—	—	—	—	—	—

KM# 53.1 KREUZER

Silver **Ruler:** Rudolf II **Mint:** Hall **Note:** Thick planchet. Prev. KM#583.2.

Date	Mintage	VG	F	VF	XF	Unc
1610	—	22.00	45.00	90.00	175	—

KM# 134 KREUZER

Silver **Ruler:** Maximilian **Mint:** Hall **Note:** Prev. KM#761.

Date	Mintage	VG	F	VF	XF	Unc
ND(1612) CO	58,000	200	375	700	1,150	—
1613	142,000	200	375	700	1,150	—
1615	62,000	200	375	700	1,150	—
1616 CO	78,000	200	375	700	1,150	—
1617	62,000	200	375	700	1,150	—
1618 CO	214,000	200	375	700	1,150	—

KM# 185 KREUZER

Silver **Ruler:** Ferdinand II **Obv:** Bust right in inner circle **Rev:** Crowned arms in inner circle, date in legend **Mint:** Klagenfurt **Note:** Local issue for Archduke Ferdinand. Prev. KM#987.

Date	Mintage	VG	F	VF	XF	Unc
1614	—	100	175	300	500	—

KM# 236 KREUZER

Silver **Ruler:** Leopold **Obv:** Austrian arms **Rev:** Eagle arms on double cross **Mint:** Hall **Note:** Prev. KM#786.

Date	Mintage	VG	F	VF	XF	Unc
ND(1619-22)	—	7.00	15.00	30.00	55.00	—

KM# 253 KREUZER

Silver **Ruler:** Leopold **Obv:** Robed bust **Rev:** Eagle shield on double cross **Mint:** Hall **Note:** Prev. KM#787.

Date	Mintage	VG	F	VF	XF	Unc
ND	—	7.00	15.00	30.00	55.00	—

KM# 254 KREUZER

Silver **Ruler:** Ferdinand II **Obv:** Laureate bust right in inner circle, value at bottom **Rev:** Long cross with arms at center in inner circle **Mint:** Klagenfurt **Note:** Varieties exist. Prev. KM#951.

Date	Mintage	VG	F	VF	XF	Unc
ND	—	20.00	40.00	70.00	100	—

KM# 255 KREUZER

Silver **Ruler:** Ferdinand II **Obv:** Bust right **Rev:** Arms in double cross **Mint:** Klagenfurt **Note:** Prev. KM#952.

Date	Mintage	VG	F	VF	XF	Unc
ND	—	20.00	40.00	70.00	100	—

KM# 285 KREUZER

Silver **Ruler:** Ferdinand II **Obv:** Bust right **Rev:** Panther shield on double eagle **Mint:** Graz **Note:** Prev. KM#338.

Date	Mintage	VG	F	VF	XF	Unc
ND	—	10.00	20.00	35.00	60.00	—
1621	—	10.00	20.00	35.00	60.00	—

KM# 286 KREUZER

Silver **Ruler:** Ferdinand II **Obv:** Laureate bust right in inner circle **Rev:** Crowned imperial eagle with value on breast in inner circle **Mint:** Vienna **Note:** Prev. KM#1767.

Date	Mintage	VG	F	VF	XF	Unc
1621	—	12.50	25.00	45.00	70.00	—
1622 (c)	—	12.50	25.00	45.00	70.00	—
1624 (c)	—	12.50	25.00	45.00	70.00	—
1630	—	12.50	25.00	45.00	70.00	—

KM# 378 KREUZER

Silver **Ruler:** Ferdinand II **Obv:** Bust with plain collar **Mint:** Graz **Note:** Prev. KM#339.

Date	Mintage	VG	F	VF	XF	Unc
1622	—	10.00	20.00	35.00	60.00	—

KM# 379 KREUZER

Silver **Ruler:** Ferdinand II **Obv:** Bust with ruffled collar **Mint:** Graz **Note:** Prev. KM#340.

Date	Mintage	VG	F	VF	XF	Unc
1622	—	10.00	20.00	35.00	60.00	—
1623	—	10.00	20.00	35.00	60.00	—

KM# 380 KREUZER

Silver **Ruler:** Ferdinand II **Obv:** Bust with ruffled collar **Mint:** Graz **Note:** Kipper Kreuzer. Prev. KM#341.

Date	Mintage	VG	F	VF	XF	Unc
1622	—	10.00	20.00	35.00	60.00	—

KM# 381 KREUZER

Silver **Ruler:** Ferdinand II **Mint:** Vienna **Note:** Kipper Kreuzer. Prev. KM#1769.

Date	Mintage	VG	F	VF	XF	Unc
1622 (c)	—	—	—	—	—	—

KM# 437 KREUZER

Silver **Ruler:** Ferdinand II **Obv:** Laureate bust right in inner circle, value below, date below bust **Rev:** Long cross with arms at center in inner circle **Mint:** Saint Veit **Note:** Varieties exist. Prev. KM#1589.

Date	Mintage	VG	F	VF	XF	Unc
1623	—	18.00	30.00	50.00	100	—
1624	—	18.00	30.00	50.00	100	—
1624 (h)	—	15.00	25.00	45.00	90.00	—
1625 (p)	—	15.00	25.00	45.00	90.00	—
1626 (p)	—	15.00	25.00	45.00	90.00	—
1627 (p)	—	15.00	25.00	45.00	90.00	—
1627 (p)	—	16.00	28.00	50.00	100	—
1627 (p)	—	16.00	28.00	50.00	100	—
1628 (g)	—	16.00	28.00	50.00	100	—

KM# 487 KREUZER

Silver **Ruler:** Ferdinand II **Obv:** Laureate bust right in inner circle **Rev:** Crowned imperial eagle with shield on breast in inner circle, date in legend **Mint:** Saint Polten **Note:** Varieties exist. Prev. KM#1571.

Date	Mintage	VG	F	VF	XF	Unc
1624 (c)-IIE	—	25.00	45.00	90.00	160	—
1624 (c)-(d)	—	25.00	45.00	90.00	160	—
1624 (d)	—	25.00	45.00	90.00	160	—
1625 (c)-IIE	—	25.00	45.00	90.00	160	—

KM# 484 KREUZER

Silver **Ruler:** Ferdinand II **Obv:** Bust right with ruffled collar **Rev:** Value on double eagle **Mint:** Nikolsburg **Note:** Prev. KM#1220.

Date	Mintage	VG	F	VF	XF	Unc
1624 N-CW	—	40.00	70.00	120	200	—
1624 N	—	40.00	70.00	120	200	—
1627 N	—	40.00	70.00	120	200	—
1628 N	—	40.00	70.00	120	200	—

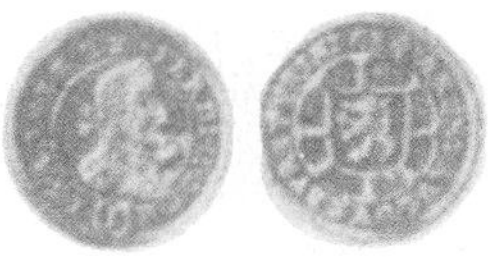

KM# 481 KREUZER

Silver **Ruler:** Ferdinand II **Obv:** Panther shield on double cross **Mint:** Graz **Note:** Prev. KM#342.

Date	Mintage	VG	F	VF	XF	Unc
1624	—	10.00	20.00	35.00	60.00	—
1626	—	10.00	20.00	35.00	60.00	—
1630	—	10.00	20.00	35.00	60.00	—
1631	—	10.00	20.00	35.00	60.00	—

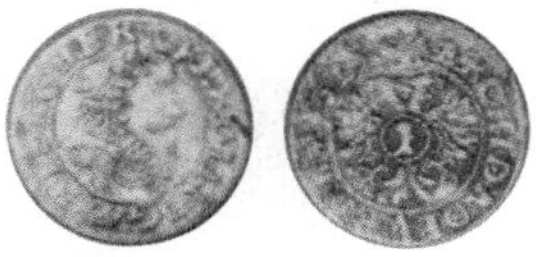

KM# 480 KREUZER

Silver **Ruler:** Ferdinand II **Rev:** Without shield below eagle **Mint:** Brunn **Note:** Prev. KM#201.

Date	Mintage	VG	F	VF	XF	Unc
1624 B-CW	—	8.00	17.00	33.00	60.00	—
1624 CW	—	8.00	17.00	33.00	60.00	—
1624 B	—	8.00	17.00	33.00	60.00	—
1625 B-CW	—	8.00	17.00	33.00	60.00	—
1625 CW	—	8.00	17.00	33.00	60.00	—
1626 CW	—	8.00	17.00	33.00	60.00	—

KM# 486 KREUZER

Silver **Ruler:** Ferdinand II **Obv:** Laureate bust right, date below **Rev:** Long cross with shield of arms at center **Mint:** Saint Polten **Note:** Prev. KM#1570.

Date	Mintage	VG	F	VF	XF	Unc
1624	—	30.00	50.00	80.00	150	—

KM# 479 KREUZER

Silver **Ruler:** Ferdinand II **Obv:** Bust right **Rev:** Small shield between eagle, value on eagle **Mint:** Brunn **Note:** Prev. KM#200.

Date	Mintage	VG	F	VF	XF	Unc
1624 B-CW	—	—	—	—	—	—

KM# 575 KREUZER

Silver **Ruler:** Leopold **Obv:** Crowned bust **Rev:** Eagle shield on double cross **Mint:** Hall **Note:** Prev. KM#788.

Date	Mintage	VG	F	VF	XF	Unc
ND(1625-32)	—	7.00	15.00	30.00	55.00	—

KM# 577 KREUZER

Silver **Ruler:** Ferdinand II **Obv:** Bust right **Rev:** Value on double eagle **Mint:** Olmutz **Note:** Varieties exist. Prev. KM#1230.

Date	Mintage	VG	F	VF	XF	Unc
1625 MF	—	8.00	17.00	33.00	60.00	—
1626 MF	—	8.00	17.00	33.00	60.00	—
1627 MF	—	8.00	17.00	33.00	60.00	—
1628 O	—	8.00	17.00	33.00	60.00	—
1629 O	—	8.00	17.00	33.00	60.00	—
1630 O	—	8.00	17.00	33.00	60.00	—
1630 MF-O	—	8.00	17.00	33.00	60.00	—
1631 MF-O	—	8.00	17.00	33.00	60.00	—
1632 MF	—	8.00	17.00	33.00	60.00	—
1632	—	8.00	17.00	33.00	60.00	—
1633 MF	—	8.00	17.00	33.00	60.00	—
1633	—	8.00	17.00	33.00	60.00	—
1634	—	8.00	17.00	33.00	60.00	—
1634 MF	—	8.00	17.00	33.00	60.00	—
1635 O-ICH	—	8.00	17.00	33.00	60.00	—
1635 ICH	—	8.00	17.00	33.00	60.00	—
1636 O-ICH	—	8.00	17.00	33.00	60.00	—
1636 O-HH	—	8.00	17.00	33.00	60.00	—

KM# 625 KREUZER

Silver **Ruler:** Ferdinand II **Rev:** Date divided below arms **Mint:** Saint Veit **Note:** Varieties exist. Prev. KM#1590.

Date	Mintage	VG	F	VF	XF	Unc
1626 (p)	—	16.00	28.00	60.00	100	—
1627 (g)	—	16.00	28.00	60.00	100	—
1628 (g)	—	16.00	28.00	60.00	100	—
1629	—	16.00	28.00	60.00	100	—
1630	—	16.00	28.00	60.00	100	—
1631	—	16.00	28.00	60.00	100	—
1636	—	16.00	28.00	60.00	100	—
1637	—	16.00	28.00	60.00	100	—

KM# 668 KREUZER

Silver **Ruler:** Ferdinand II **Obv:** Bust right with plain collar **Mint:** Nikolsburg **Note:** Prev. KM#1221.

Date	Mintage	VG	F	VF	XF	Unc
1627 N	—	40.00	70.00	120	200	—
1628 N	—	40.00	70.00	120	200	—

KM# 766 KREUZER

Silver **Ruler:** Ferdinand II **Obv:** Bust with plain collar **Mint:** Vienna **Note:** Varieties exist. Prev. KM#1768.

Date	Mintage	VG	F	VF	XF	Unc
1631 (c)	—	12.50	25.00	45.00	70.00	—
1631 (v)	—	12.50	25.00	45.00	70.00	—
1633	—	12.50	25.00	45.00	70.00	—
1634	—	12.50	25.00	45.00	70.00	—
1635	—	12.50	25.00	45.00	70.00	—
1636 (v)	—	12.50	25.00	45.00	70.00	—

KM# 779 KREUZER

Silver **Ruler:** Ferdinand II **Obv:** Flat-topped shield **Mint:** Graz **Note:** Prev. KM#344.

Date	Mintage	VG	F	VF	XF	Unc
1632	—	10.00	20.00	35.00	60.00	—
1633	—	10.00	20.00	35.00	60.00	—

KM# 778 KREUZER

Silver **Ruler:** Ferdinand II **Obv:** Heart-shaped shield **Mint:** Graz **Note:** Prev. KM#343.

Date	Mintage	VG	F	VF	XF	Unc
1632	—	10.00	20.00	35.00	60.00	—

KM# 802 KREUZER

Silver **Ruler:** Ferdinand II **Obv:** Without denomination below bust **Mint:** Graz **Note:** Prev. KM#345.

Date	Mintage	VG	F	VF	XF	Unc
1633	—	10.00	20.00	35.00	60.00	—

KM# 805 KREUZER

Silver **Ruler:** Ferdinand II **Obv:** Denomination below bust **Mint:** Graz **Note:** Prev. KM#346.

Date	Mintage	VG	F	VF	XF	Unc
1634	—	10.00	20.00	35.00	60.00	—
1635	—	10.00	20.00	35.00	60.00	—
1636	—	10.00	20.00	35.00	60.00	—

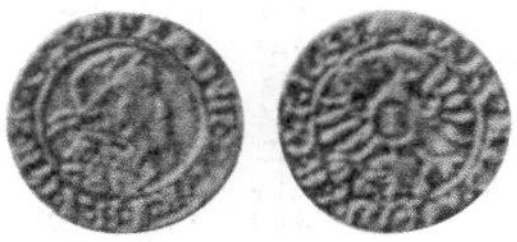

KM# 829 KREUZER

Silver **Ruler:** Ferdinand III **Obv:** Bust right **Rev:** Value on imperial eagle **Mint:** Olmutz **Note:** Prev. KM#1252.

Date	Mintage	VG	F	VF	XF	Unc
1637 O	—	8.00	18.00	35.00	65.00	—
1638 O	—	8.00	18.00	35.00	65.00	—
1639 O	—	8.00	18.00	35.00	65.00	—
1640 O	—	8.00	18.00	35.00	65.00	—
1641 O	—	8.00	18.00	35.00	65.00	—

KM# 830 KREUZER

Silver **Ruler:** Ferdinand III **Obv:** Laureate bust right in inner circle **Rev:** Crowned imperial eagle with value on breast in inner circle **Mint:** Vienna **Note:** Varieties exist. Prev. KM#1817.

Date	Mintage	VG	F	VF	XF	Unc
1637	—	10.00	20.00	35.00	65.00	—
1639	—	10.00	20.00	35.00	65.00	—
1641	—	10.00	20.00	35.00	65.00	—
1643	—	10.00	20.00	35.00	65.00	—
1644	—	10.00	20.00	35.00	65.00	—
1647	—	10.00	20.00	35.00	65.00	—

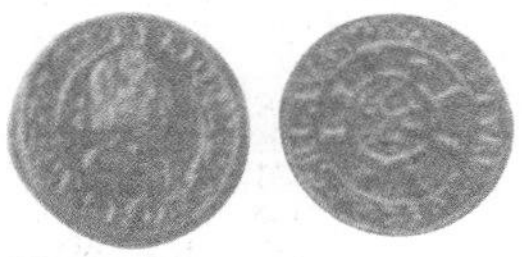

KM# 850 KREUZER

Silver **Ruler:** Ferdinand III **Obv:** Portrait and titles of Ferdinand III **Mint:** Graz **Note:** Varieties exist. Prev. KM#850.

Date	Mintage	VG	F	VF	XF	Unc
1638	—	10.00	20.00	35.00	65.00	—
1639	—	10.00	20.00	35.00	65.00	—
1640	—	10.00	20.00	35.00	65.00	—

Date	Mintage	VG	F	VF	XF	Unc
1641	—	10.00	20.00	35.00	65.00	—
1644	—	10.00	20.00	35.00	65.00	—
1645	—	10.00	20.00	35.00	65.00	—
1646	—	10.00	20.00	35.00	65.00	—
1648	—	10.00	20.00	35.00	65.00	—
1650	—	10.00	20.00	35.00	65.00	—
1652	—	10.00	20.00	35.00	65.00	—
1654	—	10.00	20.00	35.00	65.00	—

KM# 873 KREUZER

Silver **Ruler:** Ferdinand III **Mint:** Saint Veit **Note:** Prev. KM#1623.

Date	Mintage	VG	F	VF	XF	Unc
1639	—	12.00	25.00	40.00	70.00	—
1640	—	12.00	25.00	40.00	70.00	—
1641	—	12.00	25.00	40.00	70.00	—
1642	—	12.00	25.00	40.00	70.00	—
1645	—	12.00	25.00	40.00	70.00	—
1647	—	12.00	25.00	40.00	70.00	—
1649	—	12.00	25.00	40.00	70.00	—
1650	—	12.00	25.00	40.00	70.00	—
1651	—	12.00	25.00	40.00	70.00	—
1652	—	12.00	25.00	40.00	70.00	—
1655	—	12.00	25.00	40.00	70.00	—
1657	—	12.00	25.00	40.00	70.00	—

KM# 892 KREUZER

Silver **Ruler:** Ferdinand III **Mint:** Graz **Note:** Klippe. Prev. KM#423.

Date	Mintage	VG	F	VF	XF	Unc
1641	—	—	—	—	—	—

KM# 946 KREUZER

Silver **Ruler:** Ferdinand Charles **Obv:** Crowned bust **Rev:** Arms **Mint:** Hall **Note:** Prev. KM#827.

Date	Mintage	VG	F	VF	XF	Unc
ND(1647-62)	2,344,000	10.00	20.00	35.00	60.00	—

KM# 1135 KREUZER

Silver **Ruler:** Leopold I **Obv:** Laureate bust right in laurel inner circle **Rev:** Arms on St. George and St. Andrew crosses in laurel inner circle **Mint:** Hall **Note:** Prev. KM#620.

Date	Mintage	VG	F	VF	XF	Unc
ND	—	12.00	25.00	40.00	65.00	—

KM# 1136 KREUZER

Silver **Ruler:** Leopold I **Obv:** Solid inner circle **Rev:** Solid inner circle **Mint:** Hall **Note:** Prev. KM#621.

Date	Mintage	VG	F	VF	XF	Unc
ND	—	12.00	25.00	40.00	65.00	—

KM# 1134 KREUZER

Silver **Ruler:** Leopold I **Obv:** Portrait and titles of Leopold I **Mint:** Graz **Note:** Varieties exist. Prev. KM#448.

Date	Mintage	VG	F	VF	XF	Unc
1659	—	8.00	17.00	33.00	65.00	—
1660	—	8.00	17.00	33.00	65.00	—
1662	—	8.00	17.00	33.00	65.00	—
1664	—	8.00	17.00	33.00	65.00	—
1665	—	8.00	17.00	33.00	65.00	—

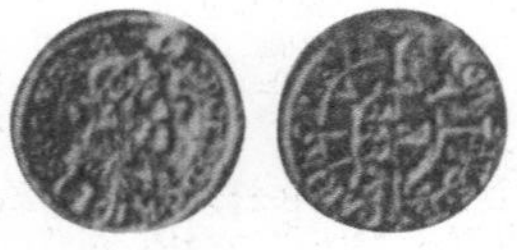

KM# 1137 KREUZER

Silver **Ruler:** Leopold I **Mint:** Saint Veit **Note:** Varieties exist. Prev. KM#1638.

Date	Mintage	VG	F	VF	XF	Unc
1659	—	14.00	30.00	60.00	100	—
1662	—	14.00	30.00	60.00	100	—
1665	—	14.00	30.00	60.00	100	—
1668	—	14.00	30.00	60.00	100	—
1679 IR	—	14.00	30.00	60.00	100	—
1681 IR	—	14.00	30.00	60.00	100	—
1682 IR	—	14.00	30.00	60.00	100	—
1683 IR	—	14.00	30.00	60.00	100	—
1685 IR	—	14.00	30.00	60.00	100	—
1689 IR	—	14.00	30.00	60.00	100	—
1693 GCS	—	14.00	30.00	60.00	100	—
1695 CS	—	14.00	30.00	60.00	100	—
1696 CCS	—	14.00	30.00	60.00	100	—
1700 IP	—	14.00	30.00	60.00	100	—

KM# 1208 KREUZER

Silver **Ruler:** Sigismund Franz **Mint:** Hall **Note:** Prev. KM#850.

Date	Mintage	VG	F	VF	XF	Unc
ND(1663-65)	1,052,000	10.00	20.00	35.00	60.00	—

KM# 1229 KREUZER

Silver **Ruler:** Leopold I **Mint:** Vienna **Note:** Varieties exist. Prev. KM#1852.

Date	Mintage	VG	F	VF	XF	Unc
1665	—	8.00	17.00	33.00	60.00	—
1666	—	8.00	17.00	33.00	60.00	—
1667	—	8.00	17.00	33.00	60.00	—
1668	—	8.00	17.00	35.25	65.00	—
1669	—	8.00	17.00	33.00	60.00	—
1670	—	8.00	17.00	33.00	60.00	—
1672	—	8.00	17.00	33.00	60.00	—
1673	—	8.00	17.00	33.00	60.00	—
1674	—	8.00	17.00	35.25	65.00	—
1675	—	8.00	17.00	33.00	60.00	—
1676	—	8.00	17.00	33.00	60.00	—
1677	—	8.00	17.00	33.00	60.00	—
1681	—	8.00	17.00	33.00	60.00	—
1695	—	8.00	17.00	33.00	60.00	—
1696	—	8.00	17.00	33.00	60.00	—
1697	—	8.00	17.00	33.00	60.00	—
1698	—	8.00	17.00	33.00	60.00	—
1699	—	8.00	17.00	33.00	60.00	—
1700	—	8.00	17.00	33.00	60.00	—

KM# 1240 KREUZER

Silver **Ruler:** Leopold I **Obv:** Portrait and titles of Leopold I **Rev:** Date divided below arms **Mint:** Graz **Note:** Varieties exist. Prev. KM#449.

Date	Mintage	VG	F	VF	XF	Unc
1666	—	8.00	17.00	33.00	60.00	—
1667	—	8.00	17.00	33.00	60.00	—
1669	—	8.00	17.00	33.00	60.00	—
1670	—	8.00	17.00	33.00	60.00	—
1672	—	8.00	17.00	33.00	60.00	—
1673	—	8.00	17.00	33.00	60.00	—
1674	—	8.00	17.00	33.00	60.00	—
1675	—	8.00	17.00	33.00	60.00	—
1676	—	8.00	17.00	33.00	60.00	—
1677	—	8.00	17.00	33.00	60.00	—
1678	—	8.00	17.00	33.00	60.00	—
1679	—	8.00	17.00	33.00	60.00	—
1680	—	8.00	17.00	33.00	60.00	—
1682	—	8.00	17.00	33.00	60.00	—
1684	—	8.00	17.00	33.00	60.00	—
1685	—	8.00	17.00	33.00	60.00	—
1686	—	8.00	17.00	33.00	60.00	—
1688	—	8.00	17.00	33.00	60.00	—
1690	—	8.00	17.00	33.00	60.00	—
1691	—	8.00	17.00	33.00	60.00	—
1692	—	8.00	17.00	33.00	60.00	—
1693	—	8.00	17.00	33.00	60.00	—
1694	—	8.00	17.00	33.00	60.00	—
1695	—	8.00	17.00	33.00	60.00	—
1696	—	8.00	17.00	33.00	60.00	—
1697	—	8.00	17.00	33.00	60.00	—
1698	—	8.00	17.00	33.00	60.00	—
1699	—	8.00	17.00	33.00	60.00	—
1700	—	8.00	17.00	33.00	60.00	—

KM# 1355 KREUZER

Silver **Ruler:** Leopold I **Mint:** Hall **Note:** Prev. KM#622.

Date	Mintage	VG	F	VF	XF	Unc
1691	—	15.00	30.00	45.00	70.00	—
1692	—	15.00	30.00	45.00	70.00	—
1693	—	15.00	30.00	45.00	70.00	—
1694	—	15.00	30.00	45.00	70.00	—
1695	—	15.00	30.00	45.00	70.00	—

KM# 1381 KREUZER

Silver **Ruler:** Leopold I **Obv:** Laureate bust of Leopold I right in inner circle **Rev:** Crowned double-headed eagle with value on breast in inner circle, crown divides date **Mint:** Augsburg **Note:** Prev. KM#5.

Date	Mintage	VG	F	VF	XF	Unc
1695A	2,892,000	—	—	—	—	—

KM# 1383 KREUZER

Silver **Ruler:** Leopold I **Rev:** Value on breast of eagle **Mint:** Vienna **Note:** Prev. KM#1853.

Date	Mintage	VG	F	VF	XF	Unc
1695	—	12.00	25.00	40.00	70.00	—

KM# 1397 KREUZER

Silver **Ruler:** Leopold I **Mint:** Hall **Note:** Varieties exist. Prev. KM#623.

Date	Mintage	VG	F	VF	XF	Unc
1699	1,339,000	15.00	30.00	45.00	70.00	—

KM# 124 2 KREUZER

Silver **Ruler:** Ferdinand II **Obv:** Half-figure right in inner circle **Rev:** Crowned arms in inner circle, date in legend **Mint:** Klagenfurt **Note:** Varieties exist. Local issue for Archduke Ferdinand. Prev. KM#988.

Date	Mintage	VG	F	VF	XF	Unc
1611	—	55.00	100	180	300	—
1614	—	55.00	100	180	300	—
1616	—	55.00	100	180	300	—
1617	—	55.00	100	180	300	—

KM# 383 2 KREUZER

Silver **Ruler:** Ferdinand II **Obv:** Double eagle **Rev:** Crowned oval arms **Mint:** Saint Veit **Note:** Prev. KM#1000.

Date	Mintage	VG	F	VF	XF	Unc
1622	—	—	—	—	—	—

KM# 384 2 KREUZER

Silver **Ruler:** Ferdinand II **Obv:** Crowned bust right **Rev:** Heraldic imperial eagle **Mint:** Saint Veit **Note:** Prev. KM#1001.

Date	Mintage	VG	F	VF	XF	Unc
1622	—	—	—	—	—	—

KM# 382 2 KREUZER

Silver **Ruler:** Leopold **Obv:** Tyrolean eagle **Rev:** Four-line inscription, value below in Roman numerals **Mint:** Hall **Note:** Prev. KM#789.

Date	Mintage	VG	F	VF	XF	Unc
1622	—	12.00	25.00	48.00	80.00	—
1623	—	12.00	25.00	48.00	80.00	—

KM# 490 2 KREUZER

Silver **Ruler:** Ferdinand II **Obv:** Laureate bust right **Rev:**

Crowned arms in inner circle **Mint:** Saint Veit **Note:** Varieties exist. Prev. KM#1591.

Date	Mintage	VG	F	VF	XF	Unc
1624 (m)	—	30.00	50.00	90.00	150	—
1625 (m)	—	30.00	50.00	90.00	150	—

KM# 488 2 KREUZER

Silver **Ruler:** Ferdinand II **Obv:** Laureate bust right **Rev:** Crowned shield with lion **Mint:** Graz **Note:** Varieties exist. Prev. KM#347.

Date	Mintage	VG	F	VF	XF	Unc
1624	—	15.00	30.00	65.00	100	—
1625	—	15.00	30.00	65.00	100	—
1626	—	15.00	30.00	65.00	100	—
1627	—	15.00	30.00	65.00	100	—

KM# 489 2 KREUZER

Silver **Ruler:** Ferdinand II **Obv:** Laureate bust right **Rev:** Denomination below shield **Mint:** Graz **Note:** Prev. KM#348.

Date	Mintage	VG	F	VF	XF	Unc
1624	—	15.00	30.00	65.00	100	—

KM# 17 3 KREUZER

Silver **Ruler:** Rudolf II **Obv:** Portrait right **Rev:** Heraldic imperial eagle **Mint:** Vienna **Note:** Prev. KM#1711.

Date	Mintage	VG	F	VF	XF	Unc
1601	—	35.00	75.00	145	225	—
1603	—	35.00	75.00	145	225	—
1604	—	35.00	75.00	145	225	—
1610	—	35.00	75.00	145	225	—

KM# 15 3 KREUZER

Silver **Ruler:** Ferdinand II **Obv:** Crowned bust right, value below **Rev:** Three shields, points together, date in legend **Mint:** Graz **Note:** Prev. KM#557.

Date	Mintage	VG	F	VF	XF	Unc
1601	—	—	—	—	—	—
(1)601	—	—	—	—	—	—

KM# 16 3 KREUZER

Silver **Ruler:** Ferdinand II **Obv:** Crowned half-figure right in inner circle **Rev:** Crowned arms in inner circle, date in legend **Mint:** Klagenfurt **Note:** Varieties exist. Local issue for Archduke Ferdinand. Prev. KM#989.

Date	Mintage	VG	F	VF	XF	Unc
1601	—	40.00	100	175	300	—
1602	—	40.00	100	175	300	—
1603	—	40.00	100	175	300	—
1604	—	40.00	100	175	300	—
1605	—	40.00	100	175	300	—
1606	—	40.00	100	175	300	—
1607	—	40.00	100	175	300	—
1608	—	40.00	100	175	300	—
1609	—	40.00	100	175	300	—
1610	—	40.00	100	175	300	—
1611	—	40.00	100	175	300	—
1612	—	40.00	100	175	300	—
1613	—	40.00	100	175	300	—
1614	—	40.00	100	175	300	—
1617	—	40.00	100	175	300	—
1618	—	40.00	100	175	300	—
1619	—	40.00	100	175	300	—

KM# 32 3 KREUZER

Silver **Ruler:** Ferdinand II **Obv:** Inner circles added **Rev:** Inner circles added **Mint:** Graz **Note:** Varieties exist. Prev. KM#558.

Date	Mintage	VG	F	VF	XF	Unc
1602	—	30.00	65.00	140	225	—
1603	—	30.00	65.00	140	225	—
1605	—	30.00	65.00	140	225	—
1606	—	30.00	65.00	140	225	—
1607	—	30.00	65.00	140	225	—
1608	—	30.00	65.00	140	225	—
1609	—	30.00	65.00	140	225	—
1613	—	30.00	65.00	140	225	—
1617	—	30.00	65.00	140	225	—

KM# 41 3 KREUZER

Silver **Ruler:** Rudolf II **Obv:** Armored bust in ruffled collar right in inner circle, date below bust **Rev:** Three shields with value below in inner circle **Mint:** Hall **Note:** Prev. KM#586.

Date	Mintage	VG	F	VF	XF	Unc
1603	—	75.00	150	285	475	—

KM# 42 3 KREUZER

Silver **Ruler:** Rudolf II **Obv:** Laureate armored bust right within inner circle **Rev:** Value above three shields within inner circle **Mint:** Hall **Note:** Prev. KM#587.

Date	Mintage	VG	F	VF	XF	Unc
1603	—	45.00	90.00	160	310	—
1604	—	45.00	90.00	160	310	—

KM# 43.1 3 KREUZER

Silver **Ruler:** Rudolf II **Obv:** Bust right, high ruffled collar **Rev:** Value encircled above three shields without inner circle **Mint:** Hall **Note:** Prev. KM#588.1.

Date	Mintage	VG	F	VF	XF	Unc
1603	—	45.00	90.00	180	350	—
1605	—	45.00	90.00	180	350	—

KM# 43.2 3 KREUZER

Silver **Ruler:** Rudolf II **Mint:** Hall **Note:** Thick planchet. Prev. KM#588.2.

Date	Mintage	VG	F	VF	XF	Unc
1605	—	45.00	90.00	180	350	—

KM# 91 3 KREUZER

Silver **Ruler:** Matthias II **Mint:** Vienna **Note:** Coronation commemorative. Prev. KM#1727.

Date	Mintage	VG	F	VF	XF	Unc
1608 CH	—	15.00	30.00	55.00	85.00	—

KM# 117 3 KREUZER

Silver **Ruler:** Rudolf II **Obv:** Laureate bust right with ruffled collar divides date **Rev:** Value above three shields within inner circle **Mint:** Hall **Note:** Prev. KM#589.

Date	Mintage	VG	F	VF	XF	Unc
1610	—	35.00	75.00	150	300	—
1611	—	35.00	75.00	150	300	—

KM# 125 3 KREUZER

Silver **Ruler:** Rudolf II **Obv:** Laureate bust right, ruffled collar **Rev:** Value below three shields without inner circle **Mint:** Hall **Note:** Prev. KM#590.

Date	Mintage	VG	F	VF	XF	Unc
1611	—	35.00	75.00	150	300	—

KM# 135 3 KREUZER

Silver **Ruler:** Maximilian **Obv:** Armored bust right, ruffled collar **Rev:** Three shields with date encircled above within inner circle **Mint:** Hall **Note:** Prev. KM#762.

Date	Mintage	VG	F	VF	XF	Unc
ND(1612) CO	40,000	350	600	1,000	1,500	—
1613	56,000	350	600	1,000	1,500	—
1616	16,000	350	600	1,000	1,500	—
1617 CO	7,999	350	600	1,000	1,500	—
1618	18,000	350	600	1,000	1,500	—

KM# 161 3 KREUZER

Silver **Ruler:** Matthias II **Obv:** Armored bust in ruffled collar right in inner circle **Rev:** Crowned imperial eagle with sword and scepter in inner circle, date in legend **Mint:** Vienna **Note:** Prev. KM#1728.

Date	Mintage	VG	F	VF	XF	Unc
1613 (c)	—	12.00	25.00	50.00	80.00	—
1616	—	12.00	25.00	50.00	80.00	—

KM# 186 3 KREUZER

Silver **Ruler:** Matthias II **Obv:** Head in ruffled collar right in inner circle **Rev:** Crowned imperial eagle in inner circle, value below, date in legend **Mint:** Vienna **Note:** Prev. KM#1726.

Date	Mintage	VG	F	VF	XF	Unc
1614 (c)	—	10.00	20.00	35.00	60.00	—
1615	—	10.00	20.00	35.00	60.00	—
1617 (t)	—	10.00	20.00	35.00	60.00	—
1618	—	10.00	20.00	35.00	60.00	—
1619	—	10.00	20.00	35.00	60.00	—

KM# 215 3 KREUZER

Silver **Ruler:** Ferdinand II **Obv:** Bust divides date **Mint:** Graz **Note:** Varieties exist. Prev. KM#559.

Date	Mintage	VG	F	VF	XF	Unc
1617	—	40.00	80.00	175	275	—

KM# 226 3 KREUZER

Silver **Ruler:** Matthias II **Mint:** Vienna **Note:** Klippe. Prev. KM#1730.

Date	Mintage	VG	F	VF	XF	Unc
1618	—	—	—	—	—	—
1619	—	—	—	—	—	—

KM# 225 3 KREUZER

Silver **Ruler:** Matthias II **Obv:** Bust right **Rev:** Heraldic imperial eagle **Mint:** Vienna **Note:** Prev. KM#1729.

Date	Mintage	VG	F	VF	XF	Unc
1618 (t)	—	12.00	25.00	50.00	80.00	—
1619	—	12.00	25.00	50.00	80.00	—

KM# 238 3 KREUZER

Silver **Ruler:** Leopold **Obv:** Robed bust **Rev:** Three shields within circle **Mint:** Hall **Note:** Prev. KM#790.

Date	Mintage	VG	F	VF	XF	Unc
ND(1619-25)	—	10.00	20.00	35.00	65.00	—

KM# 256 3 KREUZER

Silver **Ruler:** Ferdinand II **Mint:** Vienna **Note:** Varieties exist. Prev. KM#1770.

Date	Mintage	VG	F	VF	XF	Unc
1620 (c)	—	12.00	22.00	40.00	65.00	—
1621 (c)	—	12.00	22.00	40.00	65.00	—
1622 (c)	—	12.00	22.00	40.00	65.00	—
1622 (c)	—	12.00	22.00	40.00	65.00	—
1622 (r)	—	12.00	22.00	40.00	65.00	—
1623 (c)	—	12.00	22.00	40.00	65.00	—
1624 (c)	—	12.00	22.00	40.00	65.00	—
1624 (c)-BZ	—	12.00	22.00	40.00	65.00	—
1625 (c)	—	12.00	22.00	40.00	65.00	—
1626 (c)	—	12.00	22.00	40.00	65.00	—
1627 (c)	—	12.00	22.00	40.00	65.00	—
1628 (c)	—	12.00	22.00	40.00	65.00	—
1629 (c)	—	12.00	22.00	40.00	65.00	—
1630 (c)	—	12.00	22.00	40.00	65.00	—
1631 (c)	—	12.00	22.00	40.00	65.00	—
1632 (c)	—	12.00	22.00	40.00	65.00	—
1633 (c)	—	12.00	22.00	40.00	65.00	—
1634 (c)	—	12.00	22.00	40.00	65.00	—
1635 (c)	—	12.00	22.00	40.00	65.00	—
1636 (c)	—	12.00	22.00	40.00	65.00	—
1636 (v)	—	12.00	22.00	40.00	65.00	—
1637 (v)	—	12.00	22.00	40.00	65.00	—

KM# 290 3 KREUZER

Silver **Ruler:** Ferdinand II **Obv:** Large crowned bust right in inner circle **Rev:** Crowned imperial eagle with arms on breast, date in legend, value below **Mint:** Klagenfurt **Note:** Varieties exist. Prev. KM#954.

Date	Mintage	VG	F	VF	XF	Unc
1621	—	35.00	65.00	125	200	—

KM# 288 3 KREUZER

Silver **Ruler:** Ferdinand II **Obv:** Crowned imperial eagle with value on breast in inner circle **Rev:** Crowned arms in Order collar and inner circle, crown divides date **Mint:** Graz **Note:** Prev. KM#353.

Date	Mintage	VG	F	VF	XF	Unc
1621	—	20.00	40.00	75.00	125	—
1622	—	20.00	40.00	75.00	125	—

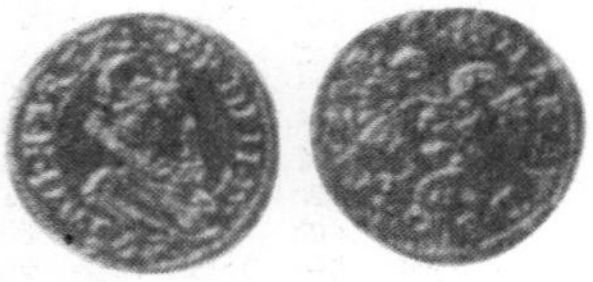

KM# 287 3 KREUZER

Silver **Ruler:** Ferdinand II **Obv:** Crowned bust right in inner circle **Rev:** Crowned imperial eagle with shield on breast, crown divides date **Mint:** Graz **Note:** Kipper 3 Kreuzer. Varieties exist. Prev. KM#349.

Date	Mintage	VG	F	VF	XF	Unc
1621	—	15.00	25.00	45.00	75.00	—
1622	—	15.00	25.00	45.00	75.00	—
1623	—	15.00	25.00	45.00	75.00	—

KM# 289 3 KREUZER

Silver **Ruler:** Ferdinand II **Obv:** Crowned imperial eagle in inner circle, value below **Mint:** Klagenfurt **Note:** Kipper 3 Kreuzer. Prev. KM#953.

Date	Mintage	VG	F	VF	XF	Unc
1621	—	35.00	65.00	125	200	—

KM# 393 3 KREUZER

Silver **Ruler:** Ferdinand II **Obv:** Crowned bust right in inner circle **Rev:** Crowned imperial eagle in inner circle, value below, date in legend **Mint:** Saint Veit **Note:** Prev. KM#1592.

Date	Mintage	VG	F	VF	XF	Unc
1622	—	12.00	25.00	45.00	85.00	—
1623	—	12.00	25.00	45.00	85.00	—

KM# 388 3 KREUZER

Silver **Ruler:** Ferdinand II **Obv:** Crowned bust right in ornamented inner circle, date below bust **Rev:** Crowned imperial eagle in inner circle, value below **Mint:** Graz **Note:** Prev. KM#354.

Date	Mintage	VG	F	VF	XF	Unc
1622	—	20.00	40.00	75.00	125	—
1623	—	20.00	40.00	75.00	125	—

KM# 387 3 KREUZER

Silver **Ruler:** Ferdinand II **Obv:** Bust right **Rev:** Heraldic double eagle **Mint:** Brunn **Note:** Prev. KM#202.

Date	Mintage	VG	F	VF	XF	Unc
1622 (h)	—	9.00	18.00	35.00	65.00	—
1624 B-BZ	—	9.00	18.00	35.00	65.00	—
1624 B-CW	—	9.00	18.00	35.00	65.00	—
1624 CW	—	9.00	18.00	35.00	65.00	—
1625 CW	—	9.00	18.00	35.00	65.00	—
1626 CW	—	9.00	18.00	35.00	65.00	—
1627 CW	—	9.00	18.00	35.00	65.00	—

KM# 389 3 KREUZER

Silver **Ruler:** Ferdinand II **Obv:** Bust in plain circle **Mint:** Graz **Note:** Prev. KM#355.

Date	Mintage	VG	F	VF	XF	Unc
1622	—	20.00	40.00	75.00	125	—

KM# 390 3 KREUZER

Silver **Ruler:** Ferdinand II **Obv:** Small crowned bust **Mint:** Klagenfurt **Note:** Prev. KM#955.

Date	Mintage	VG	F	VF	XF	Unc
1622	—	35.00	65.00	155	240	—

KM# 391 3 KREUZER

Silver **Ruler:** Ferdinand II **Obv:** Crowned imperial eagle in inner circle, value below **Rev:** Arms in cartouche, date in legend **Mint:** Klagenfurt **Note:** Varieties exist. Prev. KM#956.

Date	Mintage	VG	F	VF	XF	Unc
1622	—	35.00	65.00	155	240	—

KM# 493 3 KREUZER

Silver **Ruler:** Ferdinand II **Obv:** Laureate bust right in inner circle, value below **Rev:** Three shields of arms, points together, in inner circle, date at top **Mint:** Graz **Note:** Varieties exist. Prev. KM#350.

Date	Mintage	VG	F	VF	XF	Unc
1624	—	15.00	25.00	45.00	75.00	—
1625	—	15.00	25.00	45.00	75.00	—
1626	—	15.00	25.00	45.00	75.00	—

KM# 498 3 KREUZER

Silver **Ruler:** Ferdinand II **Obv:** Bust right with ruffled collar **Mint:** Saint Polten **Note:** Varieties exist. Prev. KM#1572.

Date	Mintage	VG	F	VF	XF	Unc
1624 (c)	—	18.00	35.00	65.00	125	—
1624 (d)	—	18.00	35.00	65.00	125	—
1625 (c)	—	—	—	—	—	—
1625 (d)	—	18.00	35.00	65.00	125	—
1625 (r)	—	18.00	35.00	65.00	125	—
1626 (r)	—	18.00	35.00	65.00	125	—

KM# 499 3 KREUZER

Silver **Ruler:** Ferdinand II **Mint:** Saint Veit **Note:** Varieties exist. Prev. KM#1593.

Date	Mintage	VG	F	VF	XF	Unc
1624 (h)	—	10.00	20.00	40.00	75.00	—
1624 (h)	—	10.00	20.00	40.00	75.00	—
1625 (h)	—	10.00	20.00	40.00	75.00	—
1625 (h)	—	10.00	20.00	40.00	75.00	—
1625 (p)	—	10.00	20.00	40.00	75.00	—
1626 (p)	—	10.00	20.00	40.00	75.00	—
1627 (g)	—	10.00	20.00	40.00	75.00	—
1627 (p)	—	10.00	20.00	40.00	75.00	—
1628 (g)	—	10.00	20.00	40.00	75.00	—
1628 (p)	—	10.00	20.00	40.00	75.00	—
1628	—	10.00	20.00	40.00	75.00	—
1629	—	10.00	20.00	40.00	75.00	—
1630 (g)	—	10.00	20.00	40.00	75.00	—
1630	—	10.00	20.00	40.00	75.00	—
1631	—	10.00	20.00	40.00	75.00	—
1632	—	10.00	20.00	40.00	75.00	—
1633	—	10.00	20.00	40.00	75.00	—
1634	—	12.00	25.00	50.00	90.00	—
1635	—	10.00	20.00	40.00	75.00	—
1636	—	10.00	20.00	40.00	75.00	—
1637	—	10.00	20.00	40.00	75.00	—

KM# 501 3 KREUZER

Silver **Ruler:** Ferdinand II **Obv:** Date below bust **Mint:** Saint Veit **Note:** Varieties exist. Prev. KM#1595.

Date	Mintage	VG	F	VF	XF	Unc
1624	—	12.00	25.00	50.00	90.00	—
1628	—	12.00	25.00	50.00	90.00	—
1629	—	12.00	25.00	50.00	90.00	—

KM# 496 3 KREUZER

Silver **Ruler:** Ferdinand II **Obv:** Bust right with ruffled collar **Rev:** Heraldic double eagle **Mint:** Nikolsburg **Note:** Prev. KM#1222.

Date	Mintage	VG	F	VF	XF	Unc
1624 Z	—	35.00	65.00	120	200	—
1627 N	—	35.00	65.00	120	200	—

KM# 497 3 KREUZER

Silver **Ruler:** Ferdinand II **Obv:** Bust right with ruffled collar **Rev:** Heraldic imperial eagle **Mint:** Olmutz **Note:** Prev. KM#1231.

Date	Mintage	VG	F	VF	XF	Unc
1624 BZ/(l)	—	8.00	17.00	33.00	60.00	—
1626 MF	—	8.00	17.00	33.00	60.00	—
1627 MF	—	8.00	17.00	33.00	60.00	—
1627 O	—	8.00	17.00	33.00	60.00	—
1628 O	—	8.00	17.00	33.00	60.00	—
1628 OL	—	8.00	17.00	33.00	60.00	—
1637 O	—	8.00	17.00	33.00	60.00	—

KM# 494 3 KREUZER

Silver **Ruler:** Ferdinand II **Obv:** Bust right **Rev:** Value above three coat of arms and ornamentation **Mint:** Krain **Note:** Prev. KM#1011.

Date	Mintage	VG	F	VF	XF	Unc
1624 Rare	—	—	—	—	—	—

KM# 500 3 KREUZER

Silver **Ruler:** Ferdinand II **Mint:** Saint Veit **Note:** Prev. KM#1594.

Date	Mintage	VG	F	VF	XF	Unc
1624	—	12.00	25.00	50.00	90.00	—

KM# 584 3 KREUZER

Silver **Ruler:** Ferdinand II **Obv:** Bust right with plain collar **Mint:** Nikolsburg **Note:** Prev. KM#1233.

Date	Mintage	VG	F	VF	XF	Unc
1625 N-(c)	—	35.00	65.00	120	200	—
1627 N	—	35.00	65.00	120	200	—
1627 N-(c)	—	35.00	65.00	120	200	—
1628 N	—	35.00	65.00	120	200	—

KM# 582 3 KREUZER

Silver **Ruler:** Ferdinand II **Mint:** Brunn **Note:** Klippe. Prev. KM#203.

Date	Mintage	VG	F	VF	XF	Unc
1625 CW	—	—	—	—	—	—

KM# 583 3 KREUZER

Silver **Ruler:** Leopold **Obv:** Crowned bust **Mint:** Hall **Note:** Prev. KM#791.

Date	Mintage	VG	F	VF	XF	Unc
ND(1625-32)	—	10.00	20.00	40.00	70.00	—

KM# 626 3 KREUZER

Silver **Ruler:** Ferdinand II **Mint:** Graz **Note:** Varieties exist. Prev. KM#351.

Date	Mintage	VG	F	VF	XF	Unc
1626	—	15.00	25.00	45.00	75.00	—
1627	—	15.00	25.00	45.00	75.00	—
1628	—	15.00	25.00	45.00	75.00	—

KM# 693 3 KREUZER

Silver **Ruler:** Ferdinand II **Obv:** Bust right with plain collar **Mint:** Olmutz **Note:** Varieties exist. Prev. KM#1232.

Date	Mintage	VG	F	VF	XF	Unc
1628 O	—	8.00	17.00	33.00	60.00	—
1629 O	—	8.00	17.00	33.00	60.00	—
1630 O	—	8.00	17.00	33.00	60.00	—
1630 (a)	—	8.00	17.00	33.00	60.00	—
1631 O	—	8.00	17.00	33.00	60.00	—
1632 (a)	—	8.00	17.00	33.00	60.00	—
1632 O	—	8.00	17.00	33.00	60.00	—
1633 (a)	—	8.00	17.00	33.00	60.00	—
1634 (a)	—	8.00	17.00	33.00	60.00	—
1635 MF	—	8.00	17.00	33.00	60.00	—

KM# 694 3 KREUZER

Silver **Ruler:** Ferdinand II **Obv:** Date **Rev:** Date **Mint:** Saint Veit **Note:** Prev. KM#1596.

Date	Mintage	VG	F	VF	XF	Unc
1628	—	12.00	25.00	50.00	90.00	—

KM# 709 3 KREUZER

Silver **Ruler:** Ferdinand II **Mint:** Graz **Note:** Varieties exist. Prev. KM#352.

Date	Mintage	VG	F	VF	XF	Unc
1629	—	15.00	25.00	55.00	90.00	—
1630	—	15.00	25.00	55.00	90.00	—
1631	—	15.00	25.00	55.00	90.00	—
1632	—	15.00	25.00	55.00	90.00	—
1633	—	15.00	25.00	55.00	90.00	—
1634	—	15.00	25.00	55.00	90.00	—
1635	—	15.00	25.00	55.00	90.00	—
1636	—	15.00	25.00	55.00	90.00	—
1637	—	15.00	25.00	55.00	90.00	—

KM# 743 3 KREUZER

Silver **Ruler:** Ferdinand II **Mint:** Fürth **Note:** Similar to 1 Thaler, KM#746. Prev. KM#285.

Date	Mintage	VG	F	VF	XF	Unc
1630 F Rare	—	—	—	—	—	—

KM# 833 3 KREUZER

Silver **Ruler:** Ferdinand III **Obv:** Portrait and titles of Ferdinand III **Mint:** Graz **Note:** Prev. KM#424.

Date	Mintage	VG	F	VF	XF	Unc
1637	—	15.00	25.00	45.00	80.00	—
1673	—	15.00	25.00	45.00	80.00	—
1638	—	15.00	25.00	45.00	80.00	—
1639	—	15.00	25.00	45.00	80.00	—
1640	—	15.00	25.00	45.00	80.00	—
1641	—	15.00	25.00	45.00	80.00	—
1642	—	15.00	25.00	45.00	80.00	—
1643	—	15.00	25.00	45.00	80.00	—
1644	—	15.00	25.00	45.00	80.00	—
1645	—	15.00	25.00	45.00	80.00	—
1646	—	15.00	25.00	45.00	80.00	—
1647	—	15.00	25.00	45.00	80.00	—
1648	—	15.00	25.00	45.00	80.00	—
1649	—	15.00	25.00	45.00	80.00	—
1650	—	15.00	25.00	45.00	80.00	—
1651	—	15.00	25.00	45.00	80.00	—
1652	—	15.00	25.00	45.00	80.00	—
1653	—	15.00	25.00	45.00	80.00	—
1654	—	15.00	25.00	45.00	80.00	—
1655	—	15.00	25.00	45.00	80.00	—
1656	—	15.00	25.00	45.00	80.00	—
1657	—	15.00	25.00	45.00	80.00	—

KM# 834 3 KREUZER

Silver **Ruler:** Ferdinand III **Obv:** Bust right **Rev:** Heraldic double eagle **Mint:** Olmutz **Note:** Prev. KM#1253.

Date	Mintage	VG	F	VF	XF	Unc
1637 O	—	10.00	20.00	35.00	65.00	—
1638 O	—	10.00	20.00	35.00	65.00	—
1639 O	—	10.00	20.00	35.00	65.00	—
1640 O	—	10.00	20.00	35.00	65.00	—
1640 (s)	—	10.00	20.00	35.00	65.00	—
1641 O	—	10.00	20.00	35.00	65.00	—
1641 (s)	—	10.00	20.00	35.00	65.00	—

KM# 836 3 KREUZER

Silver **Ruler:** Ferdinand III **Mint:** Saint Veit **Note:** Klippe. Prev. KM#1625.

Date	Mintage	VG	F	VF	XF	Unc
1637	—	—	—	—	—	—

KM# 837 3 KREUZER

Silver **Ruler:** Ferdinand III **Mint:** Vienna **Note:** Varieties exist. Prev. KM#1818.

Date	Mintage	VG	F	VF	XF	Unc
1637 (b)	—	12.00	25.00	45.00	75.00	—
1638 (b)	—	12.00	25.00	45.00	75.00	—
1639 (b)	—	12.00	25.00	45.00	75.00	—
1640 (b)	—	12.00	25.00	45.00	75.00	—
1641 (b)	—	12.00	25.00	45.00	75.00	—
1642 (b)	—	12.00	25.00	45.00	75.00	—
1643 (b)	—	12.00	25.00	45.00	75.00	—
1644 (b)	—	12.00	25.00	45.00	75.00	—
1645 (b)	—	12.00	25.00	45.00	75.00	—
1646 (b)	—	12.00	25.00	45.00	75.00	—
1647 (b)	—	12.00	25.00	45.00	75.00	—
1651 (b)	—	12.00	25.00	45.00	75.00	—
1657 (c)	—	12.00	25.00	45.00	75.00	—

KM# 835 3 KREUZER

Silver **Ruler:** Ferdinand III **Mint:** Saint Veit **Note:** Varieties exist. Prev. KM#1624.

Date	Mintage	VG	F	VF	XF	Unc
1637	—	12.00	25.00	50.00	85.00	—
1638	—	12.00	25.00	50.00	85.00	—
1639	—	12.00	25.00	50.00	85.00	—
1640	—	12.00	25.00	50.00	85.00	—
1641	—	12.00	25.00	50.00	85.00	—
1642	—	12.00	25.00	50.00	85.00	—
1643	—	12.00	25.00	50.00	85.00	—
1644	—	12.00	25.00	50.00	85.00	—
1645	—	12.00	25.00	50.00	85.00	—
1646	—	12.00	25.00	50.00	85.00	—
1647	—	12.00	25.00	50.00	85.00	—
1648	—	12.00	25.00	50.00	85.00	—
1649	—	12.00	25.00	50.00	85.00	—
1650	—	12.00	25.00	50.00	85.00	—
1652	—	12.00	25.00	50.00	85.00	—
1653	—	12.00	25.00	50.00	85.00	—
1655	—	12.00	25.00	50.00	85.00	—
1657	—	12.00	25.00	50.00	85.00	—

KM# 851 3 KREUZER

Silver **Ruler:** Ferdinand Charles **Rev:** Three shields **Mint:** Hall **Note:** Prev. KM#828.

Date	Mintage	VG	F	VF	XF	Unc
1638	688,000	8.00	17.00	35.00	65.00	—

KM# 852 3 KREUZER

Silver **Ruler:** Ferdinand Charles **Obv:** Crowned bust right divides date **Rev:** Two shields, value below **Mint:** Hall **Note:** Prev. KM#829.

Date	Mintage	VG	F	VF	XF	Unc
1638	1,100,000	8.00	17.00	33.00	60.00	—
1639	2,133,000	8.00	17.00	33.00	60.00	—
1640	1,308,000	8.00	17.00	33.00	60.00	—
1641	1,563,000	8.00	17.00	33.00	60.00	—
1642	2,353,000	8.00	17.00	33.00	60.00	—
1643	1,877,000	8.00	17.00	33.00	60.00	—
1644	1,907,000	8.00	17.00	33.00	60.00	—
1645	1,927,000	8.00	17.00	33.00	60.00	—
1646	2,344,000	8.00	17.00	33.00	60.00	—
1647	898,000	8.00	17.00	33.00	60.00	—
1648	1,727,000	8.00	17.00	33.00	60.00	—
1649	—	8.00	17.00	33.00	60.00	—
1650	1,787,000	8.00	17.00	33.00	60.00	—
1651	1,494,000	8.00	17.00	33.00	60.00	—
1652	1,594,000	8.00	17.00	33.00	60.00	—
1653	—	8.00	17.00	33.00	60.00	—
1654	1,910,000	8.00	17.00	33.00	60.00	—
1655	1,891,000	8.00	17.00	33.00	60.00	—
1656	1,971,000	8.00	17.00	33.00	60.00	—
1657	2,185,000	8.00	17.00	33.00	60.00	—
1658	3,377,000	8.00	17.00	33.00	60.00	—
1659	—	8.00	17.00	33.00	60.00	—
1660	3,909,000	8.00	17.00	33.00	60.00	—
1661	6,431,000	8.00	17.00	33.00	60.00	—
1662	5,113,000	8.00	17.00	33.00	60.00	—

KM# 947 3 KREUZER

Silver **Ruler:** Ferdinand III **Mint:** Graz **Note:** Klippe. Prev. KM#425.

Date	Mintage	VG	F	VF	XF	Unc
1647	—	—	—	—	—	—

KM# 1117 3 KREUZER

Silver **Ruler:** Ferdinand III **Mint:** Vienna **Note:** Posthumous issue. Prev. KM#1819.

Date	Mintage	VG	F	VF	XF	Unc
1658 (c)	—	—	—	—	—	—

KM# 1116 3 KREUZER

Silver **Ruler:** Leopold I **Obv:** Bust right in inner circle **Obv. Legend:** LEOPOLDVS • D • G • R • I • .... **Rev:** Three shields in inner circle **Mint:** Saint Veit **Note:** Varieties exist. Prev. KM#1639.

Date	Mintage	VG	F	VF	XF	Unc
1658	—	10.00	22.50	45.00	90.00	—
1659	—	10.00	22.50	45.00	90.00	—
1661	—	10.00	22.50	45.00	90.00	—
1662	—	10.00	22.50	45.00	90.00	—
1663	—	10.00	22.50	45.00	90.00	—
1664	—	10.00	22.50	45.00	90.00	—
1665	—	10.00	22.50	45.00	90.00	—
1666	—	10.00	22.50	45.00	90.00	—
1667	—	10.00	22.50	45.00	90.00	—
1668 GCS	—	10.00	22.50	45.00	90.00	—
1668 GS	—	10.00	22.50	45.00	90.00	—
1669	—	10.00	22.50	45.00	90.00	—
1669 GCS	—	10.00	22.50	45.00	90.00	—
1680 IR	—	10.00	22.50	45.00	90.00	—
1681 IR	—	10.00	22.50	45.00	90.00	—
1682 IR	—	10.00	22.50	45.00	90.00	—
1683 IR	—	10.00	22.50	45.00	90.00	—
1686 IR	—	10.00	22.50	45.00	90.00	—
1692 CS	—	10.00	22.50	45.00	90.00	—
1693 C-S	—	10.00	22.50	45.00	90.00	—
1695 CS	—	10.00	22.50	45.00	90.00	—
1695 I-R	—	10.00	22.50	45.00	90.00	—
1695 IA	—	10.00	22.50	45.00	90.00	—
1695	—	10.00	22.50	45.00	90.00	—
1696 CS	—	10.00	22.50	45.00	90.00	—
1696 C-S	—	10.00	22.50	45.00	90.00	—
1696	—	10.00	22.50	45.00	90.00	—
1697 CS	—	10.00	22.50	45.00	90.00	—
1697	—	10.00	22.50	45.00	90.00	—
1698 CS	—	10.00	22.50	45.00	90.00	—
1699 CS	—	10.00	22.50	45.00	90.00	—
1699 IP	—	10.00	22.50	45.00	90.00	—
1700 IP	—	10.00	22.50	45.00	90.00	—
1700 CS	—	10.00	22.50	45.00	90.00	—
1700 IW	—	10.00	22.50	45.00	90.00	—

KM# 1115 3 KREUZER

Silver **Ruler:** Leopold I **Obv:** Portrait right and titles of Leopold I **Rev:** Three shields in inner circle, date at top **Mint:** Graz **Note:** Varieties exist. Prev. KM#450.

Date	Mintage	VG	F	VF	XF	Unc
1658 HCK	—	8.00	17.00	33.00	60.00	—
1659 HCK	—	8.00	17.00	33.00	60.00	—
1659 L	—	8.00	17.00	33.00	60.00	—
1660 HCK	—	8.00	17.00	33.00	60.00	—
1660 L	—	8.00	17.00	33.00	60.00	—
1661 L	—	8.00	17.00	33.00	60.00	—
1662 L	—	8.00	17.00	33.00	60.00	—
1662	—	8.00	17.00	33.00	60.00	—
1663 L	—	8.00	17.00	33.00	60.00	—
1664 L	—	8.00	17.00	33.00	60.00	—
1665 SH	—	8.00	17.00	33.00	60.00	—
1666 SH	—	8.00	17.00	33.00	60.00	—
1666	—	8.00	17.00	33.00	60.00	—
1667	—	8.00	17.00	33.00	60.00	—
1668	—	8.00	17.00	33.00	60.00	—
1669 IGN	—	8.00	17.00	33.00	60.00	—
1669 IAN	—	8.00	17.00	33.00	60.00	—
1670 IGW	—	8.00	17.00	33.00	60.00	—
1671 IAN	—	8.00	17.00	33.00	60.00	—
1673 IAN	—	8.00	17.00	33.00	60.00	—
1674 IAN	—	8.00	17.00	33.00	60.00	—
1675 IAN	—	8.00	17.00	33.00	60.00	—
1676 IAN	—	8.00	17.00	33.00	60.00	—
1677 IAN	—	8.00	17.00	33.00	60.00	—
1678 IAN	—	8.00	17.00	33.00	60.00	—
1679 IAN	—	8.00	17.00	33.00	60.00	—
1681 IAN	—	8.00	17.00	33.00	60.00	—
1682 IAN	—	8.00	17.00	33.00	60.00	—
1684 IAN	—	8.00	17.00	33.00	60.00	—
1686 IAN	—	8.00	17.00	33.00	60.00	—
1688 IAN	—	8.00	17.00	33.00	60.00	—
1693	—	8.00	17.00	33.00	60.00	—
1694	—	8.00	17.00	33.00	60.00	—
1695 IA	—	8.00	17.00	33.00	60.00	—
1696 IA	—	8.00	17.00	33.00	60.00	—
1697 IA	—	8.00	17.00	33.00	60.00	—
1698 IA	—	8.00	17.00	33.00	60.00	—
1699 IA	—	8.00	17.00	33.00	60.00	—
1700 IA	—	8.00	17.00	33.00	60.00	—

KM# 1141 3 KREUZER

Silver **Ruler:** Leopold I **Rev:** Vienna arms below eagle **Mint:** Vienna **Note:** Varieties exist. Prev. KM#1854.

Date	Mintage	VG	F	VF	XF	Unc
1659	—	8.00	17.00	35.00	65.00	—
1659 HH	—	8.00	17.00	35.00	65.00	—
1660	—	8.00	17.00	35.00	65.00	—

KM# 1169 3 KREUZER

Silver **Ruler:** Leopold I **Rev:** Vienna arms on breast of eagle **Mint:** Vienna **Note:** Varieties exist. Prev. KM#1855.

Date	Mintage	VG	F	VF	XF	Unc
1660 (ca)	—	8.00	17.00	33.00	60.00	—
1661 (ca)	—	8.00	17.00	33.00	60.00	—
1662 (ca)	—	8.00	17.00	33.00	60.00	—
1663 (ca)	—	8.00	17.00	33.00	60.00	—
1664 (ca)	—	8.00	17.00	33.00	60.00	—
1665 (ca)	—	8.00	17.00	33.00	60.00	—
1666 (r)	—	8.00	17.00	33.00	60.00	—
1667 (r)	—	8.00	17.00	33.00	60.00	—
1668 (r)	—	8.00	17.00	33.00	60.00	—
1669 (r)	—	8.00	17.00	33.00	60.00	—
1670 (r)	—	8.00	17.00	33.00	60.00	—
1672 (r)	—	8.00	17.00	33.00	60.00	—
1673 (r)	—	8.00	17.00	33.00	60.00	—
1674 (r)	—	8.00	17.00	33.00	60.00	—
1693	—	—	—	—	—	—
1694	—	—	—	—	—	—
1695	—	—	—	—	—	—

KM# 1209 3 KREUZER

Silver **Ruler:** Sigismund Franz **Mint:** Hall **Note:** Prev. KM#851.

Date	Mintage	VG	F	VF	XF	Unc
1663	9,705,000	8.00	17.00	33.00	60.00	—
1664	5,624,000	8.00	17.00	33.00	60.00	—
1665	2,728,000	8.00	17.00	33.00	60.00	—

KM# 1231 3 KREUZER

Silver **Ruler:** Leopold I **Obv:** Value below bust right **Rev:** Shield on double eagle's breast, crown above **Mint:** Neuburg am Inn **Note:** Varieties exist. Prev. KM#1215.

Date	Mintage	VG	F	VF	XF	Unc
1665	—	5.00	8.00	15.00	30.00	—

KM# 1245 3 KREUZER

Silver **Ruler:** Leopold I **Mint:** Hall **Note:** Varieties exist. Prev. KM#624.

Date	Mintage	VG	F	VF	XF	Unc
1667	—	8.00	17.00	33.00	60.00	—
1668	—	8.00	17.00	33.00	60.00	—
1669	—	8.00	17.00	33.00	60.00	—
1670	—	8.00	17.00	33.00	60.00	—
1671	—	8.00	17.00	33.00	60.00	—
1672	—	8.00	17.00	33.00	60.00	—
1673	—	8.00	17.00	33.00	60.00	—
1674	—	8.00	17.00	33.00	60.00	—
1675	—	8.00	17.00	33.00	60.00	—
1676	—	8.00	17.00	33.00	60.00	—
1677	—	8.00	17.00	33.00	60.00	—
1678	—	8.00	17.00	33.00	60.00	—
1679	—	8.00	17.00	33.00	60.00	—
1680	—	8.00	17.00	33.00	60.00	—
1681	—	8.00	17.00	33.00	60.00	—
1682	—	8.00	17.00	33.00	60.00	—
1683	—	8.00	17.00	33.00	60.00	—
1684	—	8.00	17.00	33.00	60.00	—
1685	—	8.00	17.00	33.00	60.00	—
1686	—	8.00	17.00	33.00	60.00	—
1687	—	8.00	17.00	33.00	60.00	—
1688	—	8.00	17.00	33.00	60.00	—
1689	—	8.00	17.00	33.00	60.00	—
1690	—	8.00	17.00	33.00	60.00	—

KM# 1346 3 KREUZER

Silver **Ruler:** Leopold I **Rev:** Ornamental shields, value below **Mint:** Hall **Note:** Prev. KM#625.

Date	Mintage	VG	F	VF	XF	Unc
1690	—	8.00	17.00	33.00	60.00	—
1691	—	8.00	17.00	33.00	60.00	—

KM# 1356 3 KREUZER

Silver **Ruler:** Leopold I **Obv:** Value below bust **Mint:** Hall **Note:** Varieties exist. Prev. KM#626.

Date	Mintage	VG	F	VF	XF	Unc
1692	—	8.00	17.00	33.00	60.00	—
1693	—	8.00	17.00	33.00	60.00	—
1694	—	8.00	17.00	33.00	60.00	—

KM# 291 4 KREUZER

Silver **Ruler:** Leopold **Obv:** Tirolean eagle **Rev:** Five-line inscription **Mint:** Hall **Note:** Prev. KM#792.

Date	Mintage	VG	F	VF	XF	Unc
1621	—	20.00	35.00	80.00	140	—

KM# 33.1 6 KREUZER

Silver **Ruler:** Rudolf II **Obv:** Armed bust in ruffled collar right in inner circle **Rev:** Four shields in angles of cross in inner circle, date in legend **Mint:** Hall **Note:** Prev. KM#591.1.

Date	Mintage	VG	F	VF	XF	Unc
1602	—	35.00	75.00	145	300	—
ND(1603)	—	—	—	—	—	—

KM# 33.2 6 KREUZER

Silver **Ruler:** Rudolf II **Mint:** Hall **Note:** Thick planchet. Prev. KM#591.2.

Date	Mintage	VG	F	VF	XF	Unc
1602	—	35.00	75.00	145	300	—

KM# 53 6 KREUZER

Silver **Ruler:** Rudolf II **Obv:** Date below bust **Mint:** Hall **Note:** Prev. KM#592.

Date	Mintage	VG	F	VF	XF	Unc
1604	—	35.00	75.00	145	300	—

KM# 75 6 KREUZER

Silver **Ruler:** Rudolf II **Rev:** Oval shields in angles of cross **Mint:** Hall **Note:** Prev. KM#593.

Date	Mintage	VG	F	VF	XF	Unc
1606	—	35.00	75.00	145	300	—

KM# 76 6 KREUZER

Silver **Ruler:** Rudolf II **Obv:** Bust left, date below **Rev:** Four oval shields in angles of cross **Mint:** Hall **Note:** Prev. KM#594.

Date	Mintage	VG	F	VF	XF	Unc
1606	—	35.00	75.00	145	300	—

KM# 136 6 KREUZER

Silver **Ruler:** Maximilian **Obv:** Bust right within inner circle **Rev:** Plain Austrian shield on bottom **Mint:** Hall **Note:** Prev. KM#763.

Date	Mintage	VG	F	VF	XF	Unc
ND(1612)	—	350	650	1,100	1,650	—

KM# 137 6 KREUZER

Silver **Ruler:** Maximilian **Obv:** Bust right with high ruffled collar **Rev:** Ornamented shields **Mint:** Hall **Note:** Prev. KM#764.

Date	Mintage	VG	F	VF	XF	Unc
ND(612)	—	350	650	1,100	1,650	—

KM# 138 6 KREUZER

Silver **Ruler:** Maximilian **Rev:** Round shields **Mint:** Hall **Note:** Prev. KM#765.

Date	Mintage	VG	F	VF	XF	Unc
ND(1612) CO	—	350	650	1,100	1,650	—

KM# 139 6 KREUZER

Silver **Ruler:** Maximilian **Obv:** Bust right, high ruffled collar **Rev:** Plain Hapsburg shield at bottom **Mint:** Hall **Note:** Prev. KM#766.

Date	Mintage	VG	F	VF	XF	Unc
ND(1612)	—	350	650	1,200	1,750	—

KM# 292 6 KREUZER

Silver **Ruler:** Leopold **Obv:** Tirolean eagle **Rev:** Four-line inscription, value below in Roman numerals **Mint:** Hall **Note:** Prev. KM#793.

Date	Mintage	VG	F	VF	XF	Unc
1621	—	18.00	35.00	75.00	150	—
1622	—	18.00	35.00	75.00	150	—
1623	—	18.00	35.00	75.00	150	—

KM# 744 6 KREUZER

Silver **Ruler:** Ferdinand II **Mint:** Fürth **Note:** Similar to 1 Thaler, KM#746. Prev. KM#286.

Date	Mintage	VG	F	VF	XF	Unc
1630 Rare	—	—	—	—	—	—

KM# 1185 6 KREUZER

Silver **Ruler:** Leopold I **Mint:** Vienna **Note:** Varieties exist. Prev. KM#1856.

Date	Mintage	VG	F	VF	XF	Unc
1661	—	8.00	20.00	40.00	70.00	—
1662	—	8.00	20.00	40.00	70.00	—
1664	—	8.00	20.00	40.00	70.00	—
1665	—	8.00	20.00	40.00	70.00	—
1674	—	8.00	20.00	40.00	70.00	—
1676	—	8.00	20.00	40.00	70.00	—
1677	—	8.00	20.00	40.00	70.00	—
1678	—	8.00	20.00	40.00	70.00	—
1679	—	8.00	20.00	40.00	70.00	—
1680	—	8.00	20.00	40.00	70.00	—
1681	—	8.00	20.00	40.00	70.00	—
1682	—	8.00	20.00	40.00	70.00	—
1683	—	8.00	20.00	40.00	70.00	—
1684	—	8.00	20.00	40.00	70.00	—
1685	—	8.00	20.00	40.00	70.00	—
1686	—	8.00	20.00	40.00	70.00	—
1687	—	8.00	20.00	40.00	70.00	—
1688	—	8.00	20.00	40.00	70.00	—
1689	—	8.00	20.00	40.00	70.00	—
1690	—	8.00	20.00	40.00	70.00	—
1691	—	8.00	20.00	40.00	70.00	—
1692	—	8.00	20.00	40.00	70.00	—

KM# 1196 6 KREUZER

Silver **Ruler:** Leopold I **Rev:** Date in legend **Mint:** Vienna **Note:** Prev. KM#1857.

Date	Mintage	VG	F	VF	XF	Unc
1662	—	—	—	—	—	—

KM# 1234.1 6 KREUZER

Silver **Ruler:** Leopold I **Obv:** Hair style in curls **Mint:** Neuburg am Inn **Note:** Prev. KM#1216.1.

Date	Mintage	VG	F	VF	XF	Unc
1665	—	5.00	15.00	25.00	45.00	—

KM# 1234.2 6 KREUZER

Silver **Ruler:** Leopold I **Obv:** Hair style wavy **Mint:** Neuburg am Inn **Note:** Prev. KM#1216.2.

Date	Mintage	VG	F	VF	XF	Unc
1665	—	5.00	15.00	25.00	45.00	—

KM# 1233 6 KREUZER

Silver **Ruler:** Leopold I **Obv:** Leopold I **Mint:** Graz **Note:** Varieties exist. Prev. KM#452.

Date	Mintage	VG	F	VF	XF	Unc
1665 SH	—	10.00	20.00	45.00	75.00	—
1669 IGW	—	10.00	20.00	45.00	75.00	—
1670 IGW	—	10.00	20.00	45.00	75.00	—
1670 IAN	—	10.00	20.00	45.00	75.00	—
1671 IGW	—	10.00	20.00	45.00	75.00	—
1672 IAN	—	10.00	20.00	45.00	75.00	—
1673 IAN	—	10.00	20.00	45.00	75.00	—
1674 IAN	—	10.00	20.00	45.00	75.00	—
1675 IAN	—	10.00	20.00	45.00	75.00	—

KM# 1257 6 KREUZER

Silver **Ruler:** Leopold I **Obv:** Laureate bust right, value below **Mint:** Saint Veit **Note:** Varieties exist. Prev. KM#1640.

Date	Mintage	VG	F	VF	XF	Unc
1669 G-S	—	25.00	60.00	150	250	—
1670 G-S	—	25.00	60.00	150	250	—
1671 G-S	—	25.00	60.00	150	250	—
1671	—	25.00	60.00	150	250	—
1672 G	—	25.00	60.00	150	250	—
1672	—	25.00	60.00	150	250	—
1673	—	25.00	60.00	150	250	—
1674	—	25.00	60.00	150	250	—
1675	—	25.00	60.00	150	250	—

KM# 1288 6 KREUZER

Silver **Ruler:** Leopold I **Obv:** Crowned arms in Order collar and inner circle, crown divides date **Mint:** Graz **Note:** Varieties exist. Prev. KM#453.

Date	Mintage	VG	F	VF	XF	Unc
1676 IAN	—	10.00	20.00	45.00	75.00	—
1679 IAN	—	10.00	20.00	45.00	75.00	—
1680 IAN	—	10.00	20.00	45.00	75.00	—
1681 IAN	—	10.00	20.00	45.00	75.00	—
1682 IAN	—	10.00	20.00	45.00	75.00	—
1683 IAN	—	10.00	20.00	45.00	75.00	—
1684 IAN	—	10.00	20.00	45.00	75.00	—
1685 IAN	—	10.00	20.00	45.00	75.00	—
1686 IAN	—	10.00	20.00	45.00	75.00	—
1687 IAN	—	10.00	20.00	45.00	75.00	—
1688 IAN	—	10.00	20.00	45.00	75.00	—
1689 IAN	—	10.00	20.00	45.00	75.00	—
1690 IAN	—	10.00	20.00	45.00	75.00	—
1691 IAN	—	10.00	20.00	45.00	75.00	—
1692 IAN	—	10.00	20.00	45.00	75.00	—

KM# 1307 6 KREUZER

Silver **Ruler:** Leopold I **Obv:** Value in Roman numerals, without inner circle **Rev:** Without inner circle, arms in oval shield **Mint:** Saint Veit **Note:** Prev. KM#1641.

Date	Mintage	VG	F	VF	XF	Unc
1680	—	40.00	80.00	160	295	—
1680 IR	—	40.00	80.00	160	295	—
1681 IR	—	40.00	80.00	160	295	—
1682 IR	—	40.00	80.00	160	295	—

KM# 1317 6 KREUZER

Silver **Ruler:** Leopold I **Obv:** Without inner circle **Rev:** Without inner circle **Mint:** Graz **Note:** Prev. KM#454.

Date	Mintage	VG	F	VF	XF	Unc
1682	—	12.00	25.00	45.00	80.00	—

KM# 1322 6 KREUZER
Silver **Ruler:** Leopold I **Obv:** Inner circle added **Mint:** Saint Veit **Note:** Prev. KM#1642.

Date	Mintage	VG	F	VF	XF	Unc
1683 IR	—	40.00	80.00	160	295	—
1684 IR	—	40.00	80.00	160	295	—
1686 H-L	—	40.00	80.00	160	295	—
1690 CS	—	40.00	80.00	160	295	—

KM# 1334 6 KREUZER
Silver **Ruler:** Leopold I **Obv:** With inner circle **Rev:** With inner circle **Mint:** Saint Veit **Note:** Prev. KM#1643.

Date	Mintage	VG	F	VF	XF	Unc
1685	—	40.00	80.00	160	295	—
1686	—	40.00	80.00	160	295	—

KM# 1340 6 KREUZER
Silver **Ruler:** Leopold I **Obv:** Laureate bust right in inner circle **Rev:** Crown above two ornamental shields, value below, crown divides date **Mint:** Hall **Note:** Prev. KM#628.

Date	Mintage	VG	F	VF	XF	Unc
1687	—	8.00	18.00	45.00	90.00	—

KM# 1366 6 KREUZER
Silver **Ruler:** Leopold I **Obv:** Value in Arabic numeral below bust **Mint:** Hall **Note:** Prev. KM#1366.

Date	Mintage	VG	F	VF	XF	Unc
1693	—	8.00	18.00	45.00	90.00	—
1694	123,000	8.00	18.00	45.00	90.00	—

KM# 1644x 6 KREUZER
Silver **Ruler:** Leopold I **Obv:** Without inner circle **Rev:** Flat-topped shield, without inner circle **Mint:** Saint Veit

Date	Mintage	VG	F	VF	XF	Unc
1693 C-S	—	30.00	60.00	135	250	—

KM# 1374 6 KREUZER
Silver **Ruler:** Leopold I **Obv:** Value in Roman numeral below bust **Mint:** Hall **Note:** Prev. KM#630.

Date	Mintage	VG	F	VF	XF	Unc
1694	Inc. above	8.00	18.00	45.00	90.00	—

KM# 438.1 10 KREUZER
Silver **Ruler:** Leopold **Obv:** Rounded features on small bust **Mint:** Hall **Note:** Prev. KM#794.1.

Date	Mintage	VG	F	VF	XF	Unc
1623	—	30.00	60.00	120	200	—
1624	—	30.00	60.00	120	200	—

KM# 438.2 10 KREUZER
Silver **Ruler:** Leopold **Obv:** Angular features on large bust **Rev:** Rosettes flank arms **Mint:** Hall **Note:** Prev. KM#794.2.

Date	Mintage	VG	F	VF	XF	Unc
1625	—	30.00	60.00	120	200	—

KM# 589.1 10 KREUZER
Silver **Ruler:** Leopold **Mint:** Hall **Note:** Prev. KM#795.1.

Date	Mintage	VG	F	VF	XF	Unc
1625	—	20.00	40.00	75.00	135	—
1626	—	20.00	40.00	75.00	135	—
1627	—	20.00	40.00	75.00	135	—
1628	—	20.00	40.00	80.00	145	—
1629	—	20.00	40.00	80.00	145	—
1630	—	15.00	35.00	65.00	125	—

KM# 695 10 KREUZER
Silver **Ruler:** Ferdinand II **Mint:** Saint Veit **Note:** Prev. KM#1597.

Date	Mintage	VG	F	VF	XF	Unc
1628	—	20.00	40.00	85.00	150	—
1637	—	20.00	40.00	85.00	150	—

KM# 696 10 KREUZER
Silver **Ruler:** Ferdinand II **Obv:** Value divides date below bust **Mint:** Saint Veit **Note:** Prev. KM#1598.

Date	Mintage	VG	F	VF	XF	Unc
1628	—	25.00	50.00	90.00	150	—

KM# 589.2 10 KREUZER
Silver **Ruler:** Leopold **Obv:** Bust with striped sash **Mint:** Hall **Note:** Prev. KM#795.2.

Date	Mintage	VG	F	VF	XF	Unc
1632	—	15.00	35.00	65.00	125	—

KM# 1142 10 KREUZER
Silver **Ruler:** Leopold I **Rev:** Value in Arabic numerals **Mint:** Vienna **Note:** Prev. KM#1858.

Date	Mintage	VG	F	VF	XF	Unc
1659	—	—	—	—	—	—

KM# 1210 10 KREUZER
Silver **Ruler:** Sigismund Franz **Obv:** Armored bust right **Rev:** Crown above arms divides date **Mint:** Hall **Note:** Prev. KM#852.

Date	Mintage	VG	F	VF	XF	Unc
1663	252,000	15.00	25.00	45.00	80.00	—

KM# 1318 10 KREUZER
Silver **Ruler:** Leopold I **Obv:** Leopold I right, value below shoulder **Rev:** Three oval shields below date **Mint:** Graz **Note:** Varieties exist. Prev. KM#455.

Date	Mintage	VG	F	VF	XF	Unc
1682	—	25.00	50.00	115	210	—

KM# 1320 10 KREUZER
Silver **Ruler:** Leopold I **Obv:** Older bust right, value in Roman numerals **Rev:** Vienna arms on breast of eagle **Mint:** Vienna **Note:** Prev. KM#1859.

Date	Mintage	VG	F	VF	XF	Unc
1682	—	25.00	50.00	90.00	150	—

KM# 1319 10 KREUZER
Silver **Ruler:** Leopold I **Mint:** Saint Veit **Note:** Prev. KM#1645.

Date	Mintage	VG	F	VF	XF	Unc
1682 IR	—	30.00	60.00	150	295	—

KM# 295 12 KREUZER
Billon **Ruler:** Ferdinand II **Obv:** Bust with ruffled collar right in inner circle **Rev:** Crowned double-headed eagle in inner circle, value below, date in legend **Mint:** Vienna **Note:** 12 Kipper Kreuzer. Varieties exist. Prev. KM#1771.

Date	Mintage	VG	F	VF	XF	Unc
1621	—	15.00	25.00	45.00	75.00	—

KM# 195 15 KREUZER

Silver **Ruler:** Ferdinand II **Obv:** Crowned bust right in inner circle, value below **Rev:** Crowned cruciform arms in inner circle, crown divides date **Mint:** Graz **Note:** Prev. KM#560.

Date	Mintage	VG	F	VF	XF	Unc
1615	—	—	—	—	—	—

KM# 395 15 KREUZER

Silver **Ruler:** Ferdinand II **Mint:** Brunn **Note:** Klippe. Prev. KM#205.

Date	Mintage	VG	F	VF	XF	Unc
1622	—	—	—	—	—	—
1623	—	—	—	—	—	—

KM# 394 15 KREUZER

Silver **Ruler:** Ferdinand II **Obv:** Bust right **Rev:** Heraldic imperial eagle **Mint:** Brunn **Note:** Prev. KM#204.

Date	Mintage	VG	F	VF	XF	Unc
1622	—	—	—	—	—	—
1623	—	—	—	—	—	—

KM# 1144 15 KREUZER

Silver **Ruler:** Leopold I **Mint:** Vienna **Note:** Varieties exist. Prev. KM#1860.

Date	Mintage	VG	F	VF	XF	Unc
1659	—	15.00	28.00	60.00	125	—

KM# 1145 15 KREUZER

Silver **Ruler:** Leopold I **Obv:** Inner circles added **Rev:** Inner circles added **Mint:** Vienna **Note:** Varieties exist. Prev. KM#1861.

Date	Mintage	VG	F	VF	XF	Unc
1659	—	10.00	22.00	40.00	85.00	—
1660	—	10.00	22.00	40.00	85.00	—
1661	—	10.00	22.00	40.00	85.00	—
1662	—	10.00	22.00	40.00	85.00	—

KM# 1170 15 KREUZER

Silver **Ruler:** Leopold I **Rev:** Crown divides date **Mint:** Vienna **Note:** Varieties exist. Prev. KM#1862.

Date	Mintage	VG	F	VF	XF	Unc
1660	—	10.00	20.00	40.00	80.00	—
1663	—	10.00	20.00	40.00	80.00	—
1664	—	10.00	20.00	40.00	80.00	—
1674	—	10.00	20.00	40.00	80.00	—
1675	—	10.00	20.00	40.00	80.00	—
1676	—	10.00	20.00	40.00	80.00	—
1683	—	10.00	20.00	40.00	80.00	—
1684	—	10.00	20.00	40.00	80.00	—
1685	—	10.00	20.00	40.00	80.00	—
1693	—	10.00	20.00	40.00	80.00	—
1694	—	10.00	20.00	40.00	80.00	—
1695	—	10.00	20.00	40.00	80.00	—
1696	—	10.00	20.00	40.00	80.00	—

KM# 1186 15 KREUZER

Silver **Ruler:** Leopold I **Obv:** Value in Roman numeral below **Mint:** Graz **Note:** Varieties exist. Prev. KM#456.

Date	Mintage	VG	F	VF	XF	Unc
1661/0	—	10.00	20.00	45.00	90.00	—
1663	—	10.00	20.00	45.00	90.00	—
1664 L	—	10.00	20.00	45.00	90.00	—
1664 SH	—	10.00	20.00	45.00	90.00	—
1664	—	10.00	20.00	45.00	90.00	—
1665 SH	—	10.00	20.00	45.00	90.00	—

KM# 1187 15 KREUZER

Silver **Ruler:** Leopold I **Obv:** Ornamented inner circle **Mint:** Graz **Note:** Prev. KM#457.

Date	Mintage	VG	F	VF	XF	Unc
1661	—	10.00	20.00	45.00	90.00	—

KM# 1197 15 KREUZER

Silver **Ruler:** Leopold I **Obv:** Tall, awkward laureate bust to top of coin **Mint:** Vienna **Note:** Prev. KM#1863.

Date	Mintage	VG	F	VF	XF	Unc
1662	—	12.00	25.00	45.00	90.00	—

KM# 1198 15 KREUZER

Silver **Ruler:** Leopold I **Obv:** Ornamented inner circle **Mint:** Vienna **Note:** Varieties of ornamentation exist. Prev. KM#1864.

Date	Mintage	VG	F	VF	XF	Unc
1662	—	12.00	25.00	45.00	90.00	—
1663	—	12.00	25.00	45.00	90.00	—

KM# 1211 15 KREUZER

Silver **Ruler:** Leopold I **Obv:** Laureate bust right, value below **Rev:** Round shield within Order chain on eagle's breast **Mint:** Saint Veit **Note:** Prev. KM#1646.

Date	Mintage	VG	F	VF	XF	Unc
1663	—	20.00	40.00	95.00	195	—
1663 H-S	—	20.00	40.00	95.00	195	—
1664	—	20.00	40.00	95.00	195	—
1675	—	20.00	40.00	95.00	195	—

KM# 1219 15 KREUZER

Silver **Ruler:** Sigismund Franz **Obv:** Armored bust right, value below **Rev:** Crown above two shields **Mint:** Hall **Note:** Prev. KM#853.

Date	Mintage	VG	F	VF	XF	Unc
1664	2,249,000	10.00	20.00	50.00	95.00	—

KM# 1220.1 15 KREUZER

Silver **Ruler:** Leopold I **Obv:** Legend breaks between R and I **Obv. Legend:** DG • R • • - I • S • **Mint:** Neuburg am Inn **Note:** Prev. KM#1217.1.

Date	Mintage	VG	F	VF	XF	Unc
1664	—	12.00	25.00	60.00	110	—

KM# 1220.2 15 KREUZER

Silver **Ruler:** Leopold I **Obv:** Legend breaks between G and R **Obv. Legend:** DG • - R • I • S • **Mint:** Neuburg am Inn **Note:** Prev. KM#1217.2.

Date	Mintage	VG	F	VF	XF	Unc
1664	—	12.00	25.00	60.00	110	—

KM# 1235 15 KREUZER

Silver **Ruler:** Leopold I **Obv:** Value in Arabic numerals, plain inner circle **Mint:** Graz **Note:** Prev. KM#458.

Date	Mintage	VG	F	VF	XF	Unc
1665 SH	—	10.00	20.00	45.00	90.00	—

KM# 1280 15 KREUZER

Silver **Ruler:** Leopold I **Mint:** Saint Veit **Note:** Prev. KM#1647.

Date	Mintage	VG	F	VF	XF	Unc
1675 G-S	—	20.00	40.00	85.00	175	—
1675 GC-S	—	20.00	40.00	85.00	175	—

KM# 1281 15 KREUZER

Silver **Ruler:** Leopold I **Obv:** Plain inner circle **Rev:** Plain inner circle **Mint:** Saint Veit **Note:** Prev. KM#1648.

Date	Mintage	VG	F	VF	XF	Unc
1675 GC-SS	—	20.00	40.00	85.00	175	—
1689 GC-VS	—	20.00	40.00	85.00	175	—
1693	—	20.00	40.00	85.00	175	—
1693 GC-VS	—	20.00	40.00	85.00	175	—

KM# 1279 15 KREUZER

Silver **Ruler:** Leopold I **Mint:** Graz **Note:** Varieties exist. Prev. KM#459.

Date	Mintage	VG	F	VF	XF	Unc
1675 IAN	—	10.00	20.00	45.00	95.00	—
1676 IAN	—	10.00	20.00	45.00	95.00	—
1677 IAN	—	10.00	20.00	45.00	95.00	—
1678 IAN	—	10.00	20.00	45.00	95.00	—
1679 IAN	—	10.00	20.00	45.00	95.00	—
1680 IAN	—	10.00	20.00	45.00	95.00	—
1682 IAN	—	10.00	20.00	45.00	95.00	—
1689 IAN	—	10.00	20.00	45.00	95.00	—
1694 IAN	—	10.00	20.00	45.00	95.00	—

KM# 1289 15 KREUZER

Silver **Ruler:** Leopold I **Mint:** Hall **Note:** Varieties exist. Prev. KM#631.

Date	Mintage	VG	F	VF	XF	Unc
1676	—	10.00	20.00	45.00	90.00	—
1687	—	10.00	20.00	45.00	90.00	—
1691	—	10.00	20.00	45.00	90.00	—
1694	—	10.00	20.00	45.00	90.00	—
1697	—	10.00	20.00	45.00	90.00	—

KM# 1302 15 KREUZER

Silver **Ruler:** Leopold I **Obv:** Bust right, value in Roman numerals **Rev:** Crowned imperial eagle **Mint:** Saint Veit **Note:** Varieties exist. Prev. KM#1649.

Date	Mintage	VG	F	VF	XF	Unc
1679 I-G-R	—	16.50	35.00	75.00	140	—
1680 I-R	—	16.50	35.00	75.00	140	—
1681 I-R	—	16.50	35.00	75.00	140	—
1689 GS-VS	—	16.50	35.00	75.00	140	—
1690 CS	—	16.50	35.00	75.00	140	—
1693	—	16.50	35.00	75.00	140	—
1693 C-S	—	16.50	35.00	75.00	140	—
1693 L-S	—	16.50	35.00	75.00	140	—
1693 GCS	—	16.50	35.00	75.00	140	—
1693 GC-VS	—	16.50	35.00	75.00	140	—
1694	—	16.50	35.00	75.00	140	—
1694 C-S	—	16.50	35.00	75.00	140	—
1694 G-S	—	16.50	35.00	75.00	140	—
1694 GS-VS	—	16.50	35.00	75.00	140	—
1695	—	16.50	35.00	75.00	140	—
1696	—	16.50	35.00	75.00	140	—
1697 C-S	—	16.50	35.00	75.00	140	—
1697	—	16.50	35.00	75.00	140	—
1700	—	16.50	35.00	75.00	140	—

KM# 1335 15 KREUZER

Silver **Ruler:** Leopold I **Mint:** Mainz **Note:** The House of Hohenlohe. Varieties exist. Prev. KM#1175.

Date	Mintage	VG	F	VF	XF	Unc
1685 (s)	—	15.00	30.00	70.00	130	—
1685 B-W	—	15.00	30.00	70.00	130	—
1685 VB Monogram /W-(S)	—	15.00	30.00	70.00	130	—

KM# 1336 15 KREUZER

Silver **Ruler:** Leopold I **Mint:** Würzburg **Note:** Struck by the House of Hohenlohe. Prev. KM#1989.

Date	Mintage	VG	F	VF	XF	Unc
1685 (a)	—	—	—	—	—	—

KM# 1341 15 KREUZER

Silver **Ruler:** Leopold I **Rev:** Value below shields **Mint:** Hall **Note:** Prev. KM#632.

Date	Mintage	VG	F	VF	XF	Unc
1687	—	10.00	20.00	40.00	80.00	—

KM# 1344 15 KREUZER

Silver **Ruler:** Leopold I **Obv:** Laurreate armored bust right, wavy hair **Rev:** Crown above two shields, value below **Mint:** Hall **Note:** Prev. KM#633.

Date	Mintage	VG	F	VF	XF	Unc
1688	—	10.00	20.00	40.00	80.00	—
1690	—	10.00	20.00	40.00	80.00	—

KM# 1375 15 KREUZER

Silver **Ruler:** Leopold I **Obv:** Laureate bust right, roman numeral value below shoulder **Rev:** Crown divides date above complex arms within order chain **Mint:** Graz **Note:** Prev. KM#460.

Date	Mintage	VG	F	VF	XF	Unc
1694	—	10.00	20.00	45.00	90.00	—
1694 IA	—	10.00	20.00	45.00	90.00	—
1695 IA	—	10.00	20.00	45.00	90.00	—
1696 IA	—	10.00	20.00	45.00	90.00	—

KM# 303 24 KREUZER

Silver **Ruler:** Ferdinand II **Obv:** Laureate bust right in inner circle **Rev:** Crowned imperial eagle in inner circle, value below **Mint:** Graz **Note:** 24 Kipper Kreuzer. Prev. KM#356.

Date	Mintage	VG	F	VF	XF	Unc
1621	—	25.00	50.00	110	175	—
1622	—	25.00	50.00	110	175	—

KM# 305 24 KREUZER

Billon **Ruler:** Ferdinand II **Obv:** Laureate bust right in inner circle **Rev:** Crowned imperial eagle in inner circle, value below, date in legend **Mint:** Vienna **Note:** 24 Kipper Kreuzer. Varieties exist. Prev. KM#1772.

Date	Mintage	VG	F	VF	XF	Unc
1621	—	12.00	22.00	45.00	85.00	—
1622	—	12.00	22.00	45.00	85.00	—
1623	—	12.00	22.00	45.00	85.00	—

KM# 302 24 KREUZER

Silver **Ruler:** Ferdinand II **Mint:** Brunn **Note:** Klippe. Prev. KM#207.

Date	Mintage	VG	F	VF	XF	Unc
1621	—	—	—	—	—	—
1622	—	—	—	—	—	—
162x	—	—	—	—	—	—

KM# 301 24 KREUZER

Silver **Ruler:** Ferdinand II **Obv:** Bust right **Rev:** Heraldic imperial eagle **Mint:** Brunn **Note:** Prev. KM#206.

Date	Mintage	VG	F	VF	XF	Unc
1621 (h)	—	13.00	32.50	65.00	125	—
1622	—	13.00	32.50	65.00	125	—
1623	—	13.00	32.50	65.00	125	—

KM# 399 24 KREUZER

Silver **Ruler:** Ferdinand II **Obv:** Crowned bust right in ornamented inner circle **Rev:** Crowned imperial eagle in inner circle, value below, crown divides date **Mint:** Saint Veit **Note:** Varieties exist. Prev. KM#1599.

Date	Mintage	VG	F	VF	XF	Unc
1622	—	—	—	—	—	—
1623	—	—	—	—	—	—

KM# 397 24 KREUZER

Silver **Ruler:** Ferdinand II **Obv:** Crowned bust right **Rev:** Crowned imperial eagle with arms on breast, value below, crown divides date **Mint:** Saint Veit **Note:** 24 kipper Kreuzer. KM#384 is a product of either the Saint Veit or Klagenfurt Mints. Prev. KM#1002.

Date	Mintage	VG	F	VF	XF	Unc
1622	—	—	—	—	—	—

KM# 442 24 KREUZER

Silver **Ruler:** Ferdinand II **Obv:** Plain inner circle **Mint:** Saint Veit **Note:** Varieties exist. Prev. KM#1600.

Date	Mintage	VG	F	VF	XF	Unc
1623	—	—	—	—	—	—

KM# 309 30 KREUZER

Silver **Ruler:** Ferdinand II **Obv:** Bust right **Rev:** Heraldic imperial eagle **Mint:** Brunn **Note:** Prev. KM#208.

Date	Mintage	VG	F	VF	XF	Unc
1621 (h)	—	—	—	—	—	—

KM# 310 30 KREUZER

Silver **Ruler:** Leopold **Mint:** Hall **Note:** Prev. KM#796.

Date	Mintage	VG	F	VF	XF	Unc
1621	—	250	450	750	1,200	—
1623	—	250	450	750	1,200	—

KM# 317 48 KREUZER

Billon **Ruler:** Ferdinand II **Mint:** Vienna **Note:** 48 Kipper Kreuzer. Varieties exist. Prev. KM#1773.

Date	Mintage	VG	F	VF	XF	Unc
1621 (c)	—	10.00	20.00	50.00	85.00	—
1622 (c)	—	10.00	20.00	50.00	85.00	—
1623 (b)	—	10.00	20.00	50.00	85.00	—
1623 (c)	—	10.00	20.00	50.00	85.00	—

KM# 316 48 KREUZER

Silver **Ruler:** Ferdinand II **Obv:** Bust right **Rev:** Heraldic imperial eagle **Mint:** Olmutz **Note:** Prev. KM#1233.

Date	Mintage	VG	F	VF	XF	Unc
1621 BZ	—	—	—	—	—	—
1622 BZ	—	—	—	—	—	—

KM# 311 48 KREUZER

Silver **Ruler:** Ferdinand II **Obv:** Bust right **Rev:** Heraldic imperial eagle **Mint:** Brunn **Note:** Prev. KM#209.

Date	Mintage	VG	F	VF	XF	Unc
1621 (h)	—	14.00	30.00	65.00	120	—
1622 (h)	—	14.00	30.00	65.00	120	—

KM# 314 48 KREUZER

Silver **Ruler:** Ferdinand II **Obv:** Crowned imperial eagle with value on breast in inner circle **Rev:** Crowned oval arms in order collar and inner circle, date in legend **Mint:** Klagenfurt **Note:** Varieties exist. Prev. KM#957.

Date	Mintage	VG	F	VF	XF	Unc
1621	—	40.00	80.00	175	270	—
1622	—	40.00	80.00	175	270	—

KM# 312 48 KREUZER

Silver **Ruler:** Ferdinand II **Mint:** Brunn **Note:** Klippe. Prev. KM#210.

Date	Mintage	VG	F	VF	XF	Unc
1621 (h)	—	—	—	—	—	—

KM# 313 48 KREUZER

Silver **Ruler:** Ferdinand II **Obv:** Crowned imperial eagle with value on breast in inner circle **Rev:** Crowned arms in Order collar and inner circle, crown divides date **Mint:** Graz **Note:** 48 Kipper Kreuzer. Prev. KM#357.

Date	Mintage	VG	F	VF	XF	Unc
1621	—	15.00	30.00	65.00	120	—

KM# 405 48 KREUZER

Silver **Ruler:** Ferdinand II **Obv:** Crowned bust right in inner circle **Rev:** Crowned imperial eagle with panther shield on breast in inner circle, crown divides date **Mint:** Graz **Note:** Prev. KM#358.

Date	Mintage	VG	F	VF	XF	Unc
1622	—	15.00	30.00	65.00	120	—

KM# 409 48 KREUZER

Silver **Ruler:** Ferdinand II **Obv:** Crowned bust right in inner circle **Rev:** Crowned imperial eagle in inner circle, value at bottom, crown divides date **Mint:** Klagenfurt **Note:** Varieties exist. KM#409 is a product of either the Klagenfurt or Saint Veit mints. Prev. KM#958.

Date	Mintage	VG	F	VF	XF	Unc
1622	—	40.00	90.00	175	275	—
1623	—	40.00	90.00	175	275	—

KM# 407 48 KREUZER

Silver **Ruler:** Ferdinand II **Obv:** Date below bust **Mint:** Graz **Note:** Prev. KM#360.

Date	Mintage	VG	F	VF	XF	Unc
1622	—	15.00	30.00	65.00	125	—
1623	—	15.00	30.00	65.00	125	—

KM# 408 48 KREUZER

Silver **Ruler:** Ferdinand II **Obv:** Plain inner circle **Mint:** Graz **Note:** Prev. KM#361.

Date	Mintage	VG	F	VF	XF	Unc
1622	—	15.00	30.00	65.00	125	—
1623	—	15.00	30.00	65.00	125	—

KM# 406 48 KREUZER

Silver **Ruler:** Ferdinand II **Obv:** Ornamented inner circle **Mint:** Graz **Note:** Prev. KM#359.

Date	Mintage	VG	F	VF	XF	Unc
1622	—	15.00	30.00	65.00	125	—

KM# 410 48 KREUZER

Silver **Ruler:** Ferdinand II **Mint:** Saint Veit **Note:** 48 Kipper Kreuzer. Prev. KM#A1601.

Date	Mintage	VG	F	VF	XF	Unc
1622	—	—	—	—	—	—

KM# 443 48 KREUZER

Silver **Ruler:** Ferdinand II **Obv:** Date **Mint:** Klagenfurt **Note:** Prev. KM#959.

Date	Mintage	VG	F	VF	XF	Unc
1623	—	40.00	90.00	175	275	—

KM# 243 60 KREUZER

Silver **Ruler:** Leopold **Obv:** Bust right divides date **Rev:** Crowned arms **Mint:** Hall **Note:** Similar to 1 Thaler, KM#264.1. Prev. KM#798.

Date	Mintage	VG	F	VF	XF	Unc
ND(1619)	—	60.00	120	225	375	—
1623	—	60.00	120	225	375	—
16Z4	—	60.00	120	225	375	—

KM# 321 60 KREUZER

Silver **Ruler:** Ferdinand II **Obv:** Bust right **Rev:** Heraldic imperial eagle **Mint:** Brunn **Note:** Prev. KM#211.

Date	Mintage	VG	F	VF	XF	Unc
1621 (d)	—	16.50	40.00	75.00	150	—
1621 (d)-(h)	—	16.50	40.00	75.00	150	—
1621 (h)	—	16.50	40.00	75.00	150	—

KM# 322 60 KREUZER

Silver **Ruler:** Leopold **Obv:** Crown above two shields **Rev:** Legend **Mint:** Hall **Note:** Prev. KM#797.

Date	Mintage	VG	F	VF	XF	Unc
1621	—	300	550	950	1,600	—
1622	—	300	550	950	1,600	—
1623	—	300	550	950	1,600	—

KM# 323 60 KREUZER

Silver **Ruler:** Ferdinand II **Obv:** Bust right **Rev:** Heraldic imperial eagle **Mint:** Olmutz **Note:** Prev. KM#1234.

Date	Mintage	VG	F	VF	XF	Unc
1621 BZ/(I)	—	25.00	45.00	90.00	140	—
1621 BZ	—	25.00	45.00	90.00	140	—

KM# 411 75 KREUZER

Silver **Ruler:** Ferdinand II **Obv:** Bust right **Rev:** Heraldic imperial eagle **Mint:** Brunn **Note:** Prev. KM#212.

Date	Mintage	VG	F	VF	XF	Unc
1622	—	16.50	35.00	90.00	140	—
1622 (d)	—	16.50	35.00	90.00	140	—

KM# 412 75 KREUZER

Silver **Ruler:** Ferdinand II **Mint:** Brunn **Note:** Klippe. Prev. KM#213.

Date	Mintage	VG	F	VF	XF	Unc
1622	—	—	—	—	—	—

KM# 413 75 KREUZER

Silver **Ruler:** Ferdinand II **Obv:** Crowned bust right in inner circle **Rev:** Crowned imperial eagle with panther shield on breast in inner circle, crown divides date **Mint:** Graz **Note:** 75 Kipper Kreuzer. Prev. KM#362.

Date	Mintage	VG	F	VF	XF	Unc
1622	—	30.00	60.00	110	195	—

KM# 415 75 KREUZER

Silver **Ruler:** Ferdinand II **Obv:** Crowned bust right in inner circle, value at bottom **Rev:** Crowned imperial eagle in inner circle, crown divides date **Note:** 75 Kipper Kreuzer. Varieties exist. This coin is a product of either the Saint Veit or Klagenfurt Mints. Prev. KM#1003.

Date	Mintage	VG	F	VF	XF	Unc
1622	—	100	200	375	650	—

KM# 416 75 KREUZER

Silver **Ruler:** Ferdinand II **Obv:** Oval arms on eagle **Note:** This coin is a product of either the Saint Veit or Klagenfurt Mints. Prev. KM#1004.

Date	Mintage	VG	F	VF	XF	Unc
1622	—	—	—	—	—	—

KM# 417 75 KREUZER

Billon **Ruler:** Ferdinand II **Obv:** Laureate bust right in inner circle **Rev:** Crowned imperial eagle in inner circle, date in legend **Mint:** Vienna **Note:** 75 Kipper Kreuzer. Varieties exist. Prev. KM#1774.

Date	Mintage	VG	F	VF	XF	Unc
1622 (b)	—	15.00	25.00	50.00	90.00	—

KM# 414 150 KREUZER

Silver **Ruler:** Ferdinand II **Obv:** Ornamented inner circle **Rev:** Panther shield on breast in inner circle **Mint:** Graz **Note:** 150 Kipper Kreuzer. Varieties exist. Prev. KM#363.

Date	Mintage	VG	F	VF	XF	Unc
1622	—	50.00	100	195	250	—

KM# 423 150 KREUZER

Billon **Ruler:** Ferdinand II **Obv:** Bust right with high ruffled collar, value below **Rev:** Crowned double imperial eagle, shield on breast **Mint:** Vienna **Note:** 150 Kipper Thaler Kreuzer. Varieties exist. Prev. KM#1775.

Date	Mintage	VG	F	VF	XF	Unc
1622 (b)	—	14.00	30.00	60.00	110	—
1622 (c)	—	14.00	30.00	60.00	110	—
1622 (r)	—	14.00	30.00	60.00	110	—
1623 BZ	—	14.00	30.00	60.00	110	—

KM# 422 150 KREUZER

Silver **Ruler:** Ferdinand II **Obv:** Bust right **Rev:** Heraldic imperial eagle **Mint:** Graz **Note:** Prev. KM#1235.

Date	Mintage	VG	F	VF	XF	Unc
1622 (I) Rare	—	—	—	—	—	—
1623 (I) Rare	—	—	—	—	—	—

KM# 418 150 KREUZER

Silver **Ruler:** Ferdinand II **Obv:** Bust right **Rev:** Heraldic imperial eagle **Mint:** Brunn **Note:** Prev. KM#214.

Date	Mintage	VG	F	VF	XF	Unc
1622 (s)	—	20.00	50.00	100	200	—
1622	—	20.00	50.00	100	200	—
1623	—	20.00	50.00	100	200	—

KM# 419 150 KREUZER

Silver **Ruler:** Ferdinand II **Obv:** Plain inner circle **Mint:** Graz **Note:** Varieties exist. Prev. KM#364.

Date	Mintage	VG	F	VF	XF	Unc
1622	—	50.00	100	200	350	—

KM# 420 150 KREUZER

Silver **Ruler:** Ferdinand II **Note:** 150 Kipper Kreuzer. Varieties exist. This coin is a product of either the Saint Veit or Klagenfurt Mints. Prev. KM#1005.

Date	Mintage	VG	F	VF	XF	Unc
1622	—	125	250	450	725	—

KM# 424 150 KREUZER

Billon **Ruler:** Ferdinand II **Mint:** Vienna **Note:** Klippe. Prev. KM#1776.

Date	Mintage	VG	F	VF	XF	Unc
1622 (b)	—	14.00	27.50	48.00	80.00	—
1622 (r)	—	14.00	27.50	48.00	80.00	—

KM# 444 150 KREUZER

Silver **Ruler:** Ferdinand II **Mint:** Olmutz **Note:** Klippe. Prev. KM#1236.

Date	Mintage	VG	F	VF	XF	Unc
1623 (l) Rare	—	—	—	—	—	—

KM# 1246 1/10 THALER

Silver **Ruler:** Leopold I **Obv:** Crowned half-figure right with sword and scepter, value below **Rev:** Crowned eagle in Order collar and inner circle **Mint:** Hall **Note:** Prev. KM#634.

Date	Mintage	VG	F	VF	XF	Unc
ND	—	80.00	175	350	600	—

KM# 1247 1/10 THALER

Silver **Ruler:** Leopold I **Mint:** Hall **Note:** Prev. KM#635.

Date	Mintage	VG	F	VF	XF	Unc
1667	—	100	200	400	650	—

KM# 1248 1/10 THALER

Silver **Ruler:** Leopold I **Obv:** Date in front of figure **Mint:** Hall **Note:** Prev. KM#636.

Date	Mintage	VG	F	VF	XF	Unc
1667	—	100	200	400	650	—

KM# 20 1/4 THALER

Silver **Ruler:** Rudolf II **Obv:** Armored bust in ruffled collar right in inner circle **Rev:** Crowned imperial eagle with sword and scepter in inner circle, date in legend **Mint:** Vienna **Note:** Prev. KM#1712.

Date	Mintage	VG	F	VF	XF	Unc
1601	—	—	—	—	—	—

KM# 44 1/4 THALER

Silver **Ruler:** Rudolf II **Obv:** Armored bust in ruffled collar right in inner circle, date below bust **Rev:** Crowned flat-topped shield in Order collar in inner circle **Mint:** Hall **Note:** Prev. KM#595.

Date	Mintage	VG	F	VF	XF	Unc
1603	—	50.00	100	175	300	—
1604	—	50.00	100	175	300	—

KM# 54 1/4 THALER

Silver **Ruler:** Rudolf II **Obv:** Laureate bust right, high ruffled collar **Rev:** Crowned oval arms in garlands in inner circle **Mint:** Hall **Note:** Prev. KM#596.

Date	Mintage	VG	F	VF	XF	Unc
1604	—	50.00	100	175	300	—
1605	—	50.00	100	175	300	—

KM# 55 1/4 THALER

Silver **Ruler:** Rudolf II **Obv:** Laureate armored bust left, date below **Rev:** Crowned complex arms **Mint:** Hall **Note:** Prev. KM#597.

Date	Mintage	VG	F	VF	XF	Unc
1604	—	60.00	120	200	350	—

KM# 140 1/4 THALER

Silver **Ruler:** Rudolf II **Obv:** Bust left in laurel inner circle **Mint:** Hall **Note:** Prev. KM#598.

Date	Mintage	VG	F	VF	XF	Unc
1612	—	60.00	120	200	350	—

KM# 141 1/4 THALER

Silver **Ruler:** Maximilian **Mint:** Hall **Note:** Similar to 1 Thaler, KM#205.1. Prev. KM#755.

Date	Mintage	VG	F	VF	XF	Unc
1612	—	400	750	1,300	2,100	—
ND	—	400	750	1,300	2,100	—

KM# 162 1/4 THALER

Silver **Ruler:** Maximilian **Obv:** Bust right **Rev:** Crowned arms with Teutonic Order cross **Mint:** Hall **Note:** Prev. KM#756.

Date	Mintage	VG	F	VF	XF	Unc
1613	—	400	750	1,300	2,100	—

KM# 163 1/4 THALER

Silver **Ruler:** Maximilian **Mint:** Hall **Note:** Klippe. Prev. KM#757.

Date	Mintage	VG	F	VF	XF	Unc
1613	—	—	—	—	—	—

KM# 324 1/4 THALER

Silver **Ruler:** Ferdinand II **Obv:** Half figure right, holding scepter, in inner circle **Rev:** Three shields, points together **Mint:** Graz **Note:** Struck with dies of 3 Kreuzer, weight of 1/4 Thaler. Klippe. Prev. KM#561.

Date	Mintage	VG	F	VF	XF	Unc
ND Rare	—	—	—	—	—	—

KM# 325 1/4 THALER

Silver **Ruler:** Ferdinand II **Obv:** Crowned bust right in inner circle **Rev:** Crowned imperial eagle with oval arms on breast in inner circle **Mint:** Klagenfurt **Note:** Varieties exist. Prev. KM#960.

Date	Mintage	VG	F	VF	XF	Unc
ND	—	200	400	700	1,350	—

KM# 329 1/4 THALER

Silver **Ruler:** Ferdinand II **Obv:** Laureate bust right in inner circle **Rev:** Crowned imperial eagle in inner circle, date in legend **Mint:** Vienna **Note:** Prev. KM#1777.

Date	Mintage	VG	F	VF	XF	Unc
1621	—	50.00	100	200	350	—
1623	—	50.00	100	200	350	—

KM# 326 1/4 THALER

Silver **Ruler:** Ferdinand II **Obv:** Date below bust **Mint:** Klagenfurt **Note:** Prev. KM#961.

Date	Mintage	VG	F	VF	XF	Unc
1621	—	200	400	700	1,300	—

KM# 327 1/4 THALER

Silver **Ruler:** Ferdinand II **Obv:** Crown divides date **Mint:** Klagenfurt **Note:** Prev. KM#962.

Date	Mintage	VG	F	VF	XF	Unc
1621	—	200	400	700	1,300	—

KM# 328 1/4 THALER

Silver **Ruler:** Ferdinand II **Rev:** Crown divides date **Mint:** Klagenfurt **Note:** Prev. KM#963.

Date	Mintage	VG	F	VF	XF	Unc
1621	—	200	400	700	1,300	—

KM# 445 1/4 THALER

Silver **Ruler:** Ferdinand II **Obv:** Laureate bust, date below bust **Rev:** Crowned arms in Order collar and inner circle **Mint:** Graz **Note:** Prev. KM#365.

Date	Mintage	VG	F	VF	XF	Unc
1623	—	30.00	60.00	150	250	—
1630	—	30.00	60.00	150	250	—
1634	—	30.00	60.00	150	250	—
1638/4	—	30.00	60.00	150	250	—

KM# 590 1/4 THALER

Silver **Ruler:** Leopold **Mint:** Hall **Note:** Prev. KM#799.

Date	Mintage	VG	F	VF	XF	Unc
ND(1625)	—	60.00	120	225	375	—
1626	—	60.00	120	225	375	—
1629	—	60.00	120	225	375	—
1632	—	50.00	100	200	350	—

KM# 506 1/4 THALER

Silver **Ruler:** Ferdinand II **Obv:** Small bust right in inner circle **Mint:** Vienna **Note:** Prev. KM#1778.

Date	Mintage	VG	F	VF	XF	Unc
1625	—	50.00	100	200	350	—

KM# 591 1/4 THALER

13.5700 g., Silver **Ruler:** Ferdinand II **Mint:** Graz **Note:** Klippe. Weight of 1/2 Thaler. Prev. KM#367.

Date	Mintage	VG	F	VF	XF	Unc
1625	—	—	—	—	—	—

KM# 672 1/4 THALER

Silver **Ruler:** Ferdinand II **Obv:** Laureate bust right in inner circle **Mint:** Vienna **Note:** Prev. KM#1779.

Date	Mintage	VG	F	VF	XF	Unc
1627 (c)	—	40.00	90.00	180	300	—
1628 (c)	—	40.00	90.00	180	300	—
1629 (c)	—	40.00	90.00	180	300	—
1630 (c)	—	40.00	90.00	180	300	—
1631 (c)	—	40.00	90.00	180	300	—
1632 (c)	—	40.00	90.00	180	300	—
1633 (c)	—	40.00	90.00	180	300	—
1634 (c)	—	40.00	90.00	180	300	—
1635 (c)	—	40.00	90.00	180	300	—
1636 (v)	—	40.00	90.00	180	300	—

KM# 670 1/4 THALER

Silver **Ruler:** Ferdinand II **Mint:** Graz **Note:** Klippe. Prev. KM#366.

Date	Mintage	VG	F	VF	XF	Unc
1627	—	—	—	—	—	—

KM# 671 1/4 THALER

14.0000 g., Silver **Ruler:** Ferdinand II **Mint:** Graz **Note:** Prev. KM#368.

Date	Mintage	VG	F	VF	XF	Unc
1627	—	—	—	—	—	—

KM# 815 1/4 THALER

Silver **Ruler:** Ferdinand II **Mint:** Vienna **Note:** Klippe. Prev. KM#1780.

Date	Mintage	VG	F	VF	XF	Unc
1636 Rare	—	—	—	—	—	—

KM# 838 1/4 THALER

Silver **Ruler:** Ferdinand III **Obv:** Laureate bust right in inner circle **Mint:** Vienna **Note:** Varieties exist. Prev. KM#1820.

Date	Mintage	VG	F	VF	XF	Unc
1637	—	150	250	400	650	—
1639	—	150	250	400	650	—
1640	—	150	250	400	650	—
1641	—	150	250	400	650	—
1642	—	150	250	400	650	—
1643	—	150	250	400	650	—
1644	—	150	250	400	650	—
1645	—	150	250	400	650	—
1646	—	150	250	400	650	—
1647	—	150	250	400	650	—
1648	—	150	250	400	650	—

KM# 874 1/4 THALER

Silver **Ruler:** Ferdinand III **Mint:** Vienna **Note:** Klippe. Prev. KM#1821.

Date	Mintage	VG	F	VF	XF	Unc
1639	—	—	—	—	—	—

KM# 927 1/4 THALER

Silver **Ruler:** Ferdinand Charles **Mint:** Hall **Note:** Similar to 5 Ducat, KM#793. Prev. KM#831.

Date	Mintage	VG	F	VF	XF	Unc
ND(1646)	—	80.00	160	275	450	—

KM# 982 1/4 THALER

Silver **Ruler:** Ferdinand Charles **Obv:** Armored bust right, value below **Rev:** Crowned arms within Order chain **Mint:** Hall **Note:** Prev. KM#830.

Date	Mintage	VG	F	VF	XF	Unc
1654	—	75.00	150	250	400	—

KM# 1173.1 1/4 THALER

Silver **Ruler:** Leopold I **Obv:** Laureate bust right, value below, lion face on shoulder **Rev:** Crowned arms within Order chain **Mint:** Hall **Note:** Prev. KM#637.1.

Date	Mintage	VG	F	VF	XF	Unc
ND	—	90.00	185	350	600	—

KM# 1173.2 1/4 THALER

Silver **Ruler:** Leopold I **Obv:** Denomination below lion's head on shoulder **Rev:** Crowned complex arms within Order chain **Mint:** Hall **Note:** Prev. KM#637.2.

Date	Mintage	VG	F	VF	XF	Unc
ND	—	90.00	185	350	600	—

KM# 1271 1/4 THALER

Silver **Ruler:** Leopold I **Mint:** Vienna **Note:** Prev. KM#1865.

Date	Mintage	VG	F	VF	XF	Unc
1671 Rare	—	—	—	—	—	—

KM# 1376 1/4 THALER

Silver **Ruler:** Leopold I **Mint:** Graz **Note:** Prev. KM#461.

Date	Mintage	VG	F	VF	XF	Unc
1694 IA	—	50.00	100	210	350	—

KM# 22 1/2 THALER

Silver **Ruler:** Rudolf II **Mint:** Vienna **Note:** Prev. KM#1713.

Date	Mintage	VG	F	VF	XF	Unc
1601	—	100	200	350	600	—
1602	—	100	200	350	600	—
1605	—	100	200	350	600	—
1606	—	100	200	350	600	—
1607	—	100	200	350	600	—
1608	—	100	200	350	600	—
1609	—	100	200	350	600	—

KM# 21 1/2 THALER

Silver **Ruler:** Ferdinand II **Obv:** Crowned half figure right, holding scepter, in inner circle **Rev:** Crowned arms in Order collar, date in legend **Mint:** Klagenfurt **Note:** Varieties exist. Local issue for Archduke Ferdinand. Prev. KM#990.

Date	Mintage	VG	F	VF	XF	Unc
1601	—	65.00	125	225	400	—
1602	—	65.00	125	225	400	—
1610	—	65.00	125	225	400	—
1611	—	65.00	125	225	400	—

KM# 35 1/2 THALER

Silver **Ruler:** Ferdinand II **Obv:** Crowned half figure right holding scepter, in inner circle **Rev:** Crowned arms in Order collar, date in legend **Mint:** Graz **Note:** Prev. KM#562.

Date	Mintage	VG	F	VF	XF	Unc
1602 Rare	—	—	—	—	—	—

KM# 45 1/2 THALER

Silver **Ruler:** Rudolf II **Mint:** Hall **Note:** Prev. KM#599.

Date	Mintage	VG	F	VF	XF	Unc
1603	—	125	250	400	700	—

KM# 64 1/2 THALER

Silver **Ruler:** Rudolf II **Mint:** Vienna **Note:** Klippe. Prev. KM#1714.

Date	Mintage	VG	F	VF	XF	Unc
1605	—	—	—	—	—	—

KM# 92 1/2 THALER

Silver **Ruler:** Matthias II **Mint:** Vienna **Note:** Coronation commemorative. Prev. KM#1731.

Date	Mintage	VG	F	VF	XF	Unc
1608 CH	—	200	350	675	1,150	—

KM# 93 1/2 THALER

Silver **Ruler:** Matthias II **Mint:** Vienna **Note:** Klippe. Prev. KM#1732.

Date	Mintage	VG	F	VF	XF	Unc
1608 CH	—	—	—	—	—	—

KM# 101 1/2 THALER

Silver **Ruler:** Matthias II **Obv:** Portrait right **Rev:** Heraldic imperial eagle **Mint:** Vienna **Note:** Prev. KM#1733.

Date	Mintage	VG	F	VF	XF	Unc
1609	—	—	—	—	—	—

KM# 142 1/2 THALER

Silver **Ruler:** Rudolf II **Obv:** Bust right in rope inner circle, date in front of bust **Mint:** Hall **Note:** Prev. KM#600.

Date	Mintage	VG	F	VF	XF	Unc
1612	—	120	225	375	650	—

KM# 164 1/2 THALER

Silver **Ruler:** Matthias II **Obv:** Armored bust in ruffled collar right **Mint:** Vienna **Note:** Prev. KM#1734.

Date	Mintage	VG	F	VF	XF	Unc
1613 (c)	—	125	250	425	750	—
1615	—	125	250	425	750	—
1616	—	125	250	425	750	—
1617	—	125	250	425	750	—
1617 (t)	—	125	250	425	750	—
1618	—	125	250	425	750	—
1619	—	125	250	425	750	—

KM# 260 1/2 THALER

Silver **Ruler:** Ferdinand II **Mint:** Klagenfurt **Note:** Varieties exist. Prev. KM#964.

Date	Mintage	VG	F	VF	XF	Unc
ND	—	65.00	125	250	450	—

KM# 261 1/2 THALER

Silver **Ruler:** Ferdinand II **Mint:** Vienna **Note:** Prev. KM#1781.

Date	Mintage	VG	F	VF	XF	Unc
1620 (c)	—	35.00	75.00	135	225	—
1621 (c)	—	35.00	75.00	135	225	—
1622 (c)	—	35.00	75.00	135	225	—
1623 (c)	—	35.00	75.00	135	225	—
1624 (c)	—	35.00	75.00	135	225	—

KM# 330 1/2 THALER

Silver **Ruler:** Ferdinand II **Obv:** Date below bust **Mint:** Klagenfurt **Note:** Varieties exist. Prev. KM#965.

Date	Mintage	VG	F	VF	XF	Unc
1621	—	65.00	125	250	450	—

KM# 331 1/2 THALER

Silver **Ruler:** Ferdinand II **Rev:** Crown divides date **Mint:** Klagenfurt **Note:** Prev. KM#966.

Date	Mintage	VG	F	VF	XF	Unc
1621	—	65.00	125	250	450	—

KM# 446 1/2 THALER

Silver **Ruler:** Ferdinand II **Mint:** Graz **Note:** Prev. KM#369.

Date	Mintage	VG	F	VF	XF	Unc
1623	—	35.00	75.00	175	275	—
1624	—	35.00	75.00	175	275	—
1625	—	35.00	75.00	175	275	—
1627	—	35.00	75.00	175	275	—

KM# 447 1/2 THALER

Silver **Ruler:** Leopold **Mint:** Hall **Note:** Prev. KM#800.

Date	Mintage	VG	F	VF	XF	Unc
1623	—	60.00	120	225	375	—
1624	—	60.00	120	225	375	—

KM# 514 1/2 THALER

Silver **Ruler:** Ferdinand II **Obv:** Plain collar **Mint:** Vienna **Note:** Varieties exist. Prev. KM#1782.

Date	Mintage	VG	F	VF	XF	Unc
1624 (c)	—	35.00	75.00	135	225	—
1625 (c)	—	35.00	75.00	135	225	—
1626 (c)	—	35.00	75.00	135	225	—
1627 (c)	—	35.00	75.00	135	225	—
1628 (c)	—	35.00	75.00	135	225	—
1629 (c)	—	35.00	75.00	135	225	—
1630 (c)	—	35.00	75.00	135	225	—
1631 (c)	—	35.00	75.00	135	225	—
1632 (c)	—	35.00	75.00	135	225	—
1633 (c)	—	35.00	75.00	135	225	—
1634 (c)	—	35.00	75.00	135	225	—
1635 (c)	—	35.00	75.00	135	225	—
1636 (c)	—	35.00	75.00	135	225	—
1636 (v)	—	35.00	75.00	135	225	—

KM# 513 1/2 THALER

Silver **Ruler:** Ferdinand II **Obv:** Laureate bust right in inner circle **Rev:** Crowned arms in Order collar in inner circle, date in legend **Mint:** Saint Polten **Note:** Prev. KM#1573.

Date	Mintage	VG	F	VF	XF	Unc
1624 IIE Rare	—	—	—	—	—	—
1625 IIE Rare	—	—	—	—	—	—

KM# 511 1/2 THALER

Silver **Ruler:** Ferdinand II **Obv:** Bust right **Rev:** Heraldic imperial eagle **Mint:** Brunn **Note:** Prev. KM#215.

Date	Mintage	VG	F	VF	XF	Unc
1624 B-CW	—	—	—	—	—	—

KM# 515 1/2 THALER

Silver **Ruler:** Ferdinand II **Mint:** Vienna **Note:** Prev. KM#1784.

Date	Mintage	VG	F	VF	XF	Unc
1624 (c)	—	40.00	80.00	145	250	—

KM# 592.1 1/2 THALER

Silver **Ruler:** Leopold **Obv:** Horizontal stripes below breast plate **Rev:** Crown above arms **Mint:** Hall **Note:** Prev. KM#801.1.

Date	Mintage	VG	F	VF	XF	Unc
1625	—	60.00	120	225	375	—
1626	—	60.00	120	225	375	—
1629	—	60.00	120	225	375	—
1632	—	40.00	90.00	175	300	—

KM# 673 1/2 THALER

Silver **Ruler:** Ferdinand II **Mint:** Graz **Note:** Klippe. Prev. KM#370.

Date	Mintage	VG	F	VF	XF	Unc
1627	—	—	—	—	—	—
1629	—	—	—	—	—	—

KM# 698 1/2 THALER

Silver **Ruler:** Ferdinand II **Mint:** Graz **Note:** Klippe. Weight of 1 Thaler. Prev. KM#371.

Date	Mintage	VG	F	VF	XF	Unc
1627	—	—	—	—	—	—

KM# 592.2 1/2 THALER

Silver **Ruler:** Leopold **Obv:** Dot in square pattern below breast plate **Mint:** Hall **Note:** Prev. KM#801.2.

Date	Mintage	VG	F	VF	XF	Unc
1629	—	60.00	120	225	375	—

KM# 710 1/2 THALER

Tin **Ruler:** Ferdinand II **Mint:** Graz **Note:** Prev. KM#370a.

Date	Mintage	VG	F	VF	XF	Unc
1629/7	—	—	—	—	—	—

KM# 807 1/2 THALER

Silver **Ruler:** Ferdinand II **Mint:** Vienna **Note:** Klippe. Prev. KM#1783.

Date	Mintage	VG	F	VF	XF	Unc
1635 (c) Rare	—	—	—	—	—	—

KM# 839 1/2 THALER

Silver **Ruler:** Ferdinand III **Mint:** Vienna **Note:** Prev. KM#1822.

Date	Mintage	VG	F	VF	XF	Unc
1637 (b)	—	75.00	150	275	450	—
1638 (b)	—	75.00	150	275	450	—
1639 (b)	—	75.00	150	275	450	—
1640 (b)	—	75.00	150	275	450	—
1641 (b)	—	75.00	150	275	450	—
1642 (b)	—	75.00	150	275	450	—
1643 (b)	—	75.00	150	275	450	—
1644 (b)	—	75.00	150	275	450	—
1645 (b)	—	75.00	150	275	450	—
1646 (b)	—	75.00	150	275	450	—
1647 (b)	—	75.00	150	275	450	—
1648 (b)	—	75.00	150	275	450	—
1649 (c)	—	75.00	150	275	450	—

KM# 854 1/2 THALER

Silver **Ruler:** Ferdinand III **Obv:** Portrait and titles of Ferdinand III **Rev:** Crowned arms in Order collar and inner circle **Mint:** Graz **Note:** Prev. KM#426.

Date	Mintage	VG	F	VF	XF	Unc
1638	—	30.00	65.00	150	275	—

KM# 855 1/2 THALER

Silver **Ruler:** Ferdinand III **Mint:** Graz **Note:** Klippe. Prev. KM#427.

Date	Mintage	VG	F	VF	XF	Unc
1638	—	100	175	400	650	—

KM# 856 1/2 THALER

Silver **Ruler:** Ferdinand III **Mint:** Vienna **Note:** Klippe. Prev. KM#1823.

Date	Mintage	VG	F	VF	XF	Unc
1638	—	—	—	—	—	—

KM# 974 1/2 THALER

0.8330 Silver **Ruler:** Ferdinand III **Mint:** Vienna **Note:** Prev. KM#1824.

Date	Mintage	VG	F	VF	XF	Unc
1651 (c)	—	90.00	175	300	525	—
1652 (c)	—	90.00	175	300	525	—
1653 (c)	—	90.00	175	300	525	—
1655 (c)	—	90.00	175	300	525	—
1656 (c)	—	90.00	175	300	525	—

KM# 983 1/2 THALER

Silver **Ruler:** Ferdinand Charles **Mint:** Hall **Note:** Prev. KM#832.

Date	Mintage	VG	F	VF	XF	Unc
1654	—	90.00	175	300	500	—

KM# 1002 1/2 THALER

0.8330 Silver **Ruler:** Ferdinand III **Obv:** Large head reaches top of coin, date below bust **Mint:** Vienna **Note:** Prev. KM#1825.

Date	Mintage	VG	F	VF	XF	Unc
1657	—	90.00	175	300	525	—

KM# 1147 1/2 THALER

Silver **Ruler:** Leopold I **Obv:** Young laureate bust right in inner circle **Mint:** Hall **Note:** Prev. KM#638.

Date	Mintage	VG	F	VF	XF	Unc
ND	—	70.00	150	325	600	—

KM# 1148 1/2 THALER

Silver **Ruler:** Leopold I **Obv:** KM#638 **Rev:** Archduke Ferdinand Karl **Mint:** Hall **Note:** Mule. Prev. KM#639.

Date	Mintage	VG	F	VF	XF	Unc
ND	—	70.00	150	325	600	—

KM# 1149 1/2 THALER

Silver **Ruler:** Leopold I **Mint:** Hall **Note:** Prev. KM#640.

Date	Mintage	VG	F	VF	XF	Unc
ND	—	70.00	150	325	600	—

KM# 1150 1/2 THALER

Silver **Ruler:** Leopold I **Obv:** Similar to KM#640 with value below bust **Mint:** Hall **Note:** Prev. KM#641.

Date	Mintage	VG	F	VF	XF	Unc
ND	—	70.00	150	325	600	—

KM# 1151 1/2 THALER

0.8330 Silver **Ruler:** Leopold I **Obv:** Laureate bust right in inner circle **Rev:** Crowned imperial eagle in inner circle, crown divides date **Mint:** Vienna **Note:** Varieties exist. Prev. KM#1866.

Date	Mintage	VG	F	VF	XF	Unc
1659 Rare	—	—	—	—	—	—
1664	—	—	—	—	—	—
1671	—	100	165	275	450	—

KM# 1258 1/2 THALER

Silver **Ruler:** Leopold I **Mint:** Graz **Note:** Varieties exist. Prev. KM#462.

Date	Mintage	VG	F	VF	XF	Unc
1669 IGW	—	40.00	80.00	175	275	—
1674 IAN	—	40.00	80.00	175	275	—
1676 IAN	—	40.00	80.00	175	275	—
1678 IAN	—	40.00	80.00	175	275	—
1684 IAN	—	40.00	80.00	175	275	—
1694	—	40.00	80.00	175	275	—
1696	—	40.00	80.00	175	275	—

KM# 1368 1/2 THALER

0.8330 Silver **Ruler:** Leopold I **Obv:** Thin bust right in inner circle **Rev:** Crowned imperial eagle in inner circle, crown divides date **Mint:** Vienna **Note:** Varieties exist. Prev. KM#1867.

Date	Mintage	VG	F	VF	XF	Unc
1693	—	40.00	100	175	300	—

KM# 25 THALER

Silver **Ruler:** Rudolf II **Obv:** Armored bust in ruffled collar right **Mint:** Vienna **Note:** Dav. #3002. Prev. KM#1715.

Date	Mintage	VG	F	VF	XF	Unc
1601	—	65.00	125	200	350	—
1602	—	65.00	125	200	350	—
1603	—	65.00	125	200	350	—
1604	—	65.00	125	200	350	—
1605	—	65.00	125	200	350	—
1606	—	65.00	125	200	350	—
1607	—	65.00	125	200	350	—
1608	—	65.00	125	200	350	—
1609	—	65.00	125	200	350	—

KM# 23 THALER

Silver **Ruler:** Ferdinand II **Obv:** Crowned and armored half figure with scepter on shoulder right in inner circle **Rev:** Crowned flat-topped arms in Order collar of The Golden Fleece, date in legend at upper left **Mint:** Graz **Note:** Dav. #3307. Prev. KM#563.

Date	Mintage	VG	F	VF	XF	Unc
1601	—	125	225	450	800	—
1602	—	125	225	450	800	—

KM# 24 THALER

Silver **Ruler:** Ferdinand II **Mint:** Klagenfurt **Note:** Dav. #3314. Local issue for Archduke Ferdinand. Prev. KM#991.

Date	Mintage	VG	F	VF	XF	Unc
1601/0	—	100	200	400	750	—
1601	—	100	200	400	750	—
1602	—	100	200	400	750	—
1609	—	100	200	400	750	—
1610	—	100	200	400	750	—
1611	—	100	200	400	750	—
1612	—	100	200	400	750	—
1613	—	100	200	400	750	—
1614	—	100	200	400	750	—
1615	—	100	200	400	750	—
1616	—	100	200	400	750	—
1617	—	100	200	400	750	—
1618	—	100	200	400	750	—
1619	—	100	200	400	750	—
1620	—	100	200	400	750	—

KM# 36 THALER

Silver **Ruler:** Ferdinand II **Obv:** KM#566 **Rev:** KM#563 **Mint:** Graz **Note:** Dav. #3310A. Mule. Klippe. Prev. KM#567.

Date	Mintage	VG	F	VF	XF	Unc
1602 Rare	—	—	—	—	—	—

KM# 37.1 THALER

28.2800 g., Silver **Ruler:** Rudolf II **Obv:** Date below draped armored bust, clasp on shoulder **Mint:** Hall **Note:** Dav. #3005. Prev. KM#601.1.

Date	Mintage	VG	F	VF	XF	Unc
1602	—	50.00	100	210	375	—
1603	—	50.00	100	210	375	—
1605	—	50.00	100	210	375	—

KM# 56.1 THALER

Silver **Ruler:** Rudolf II **Obv:** Legend broken at lower right between R-OM: **Mint:** Hall **Note:** Dav. #3005A. Prev. KM#602.1.

Date	Mintage	VG	F	VF	XF	Unc
1604	—	50.00	100	210	275	—

KM# 37.2 THALER

Silver **Ruler:** Rudolf II **Obv:** Bust with tassel behind neck, without drapery or clasp **Mint:** Hall **Note:** Dav. #3005B. Varieties exist. Prev. KM#601.2.

Date	Mintage	VG	F	VF	XF	Unc
1605	—	50.00	100	210	375	—
1606	—	50.00	100	210	375	—
1607	—	50.00	100	210	375	—
1612	—	50.00	100	210	375	—

KM# 37.3 THALER

Silver **Ruler:** Rudolf II **Obv:** Longer ribbon tails, without tassel **Mint:** Hall **Note:** Dav. #3005C. Prev. KM#601.3.

Date	Mintage	VG	F	VF	XF	Unc
1605	—	50.00	100	210	375	—

KM# 65 THALER

Silver **Ruler:** Ferdinand II **Rev:** Inner circle added **Rev. Legend:** DVX • BVRGVND... **Mint:** Graz **Note:** Dav. #3307A. Prev. KM#564.

Date	Mintage	VG	F	VF	XF	Unc
(1)605	—	100	200	450	750	—

KM# 56.2 THALER

Silver **Ruler:** Rudolf II **Obv:** Legend broken at lower right between RO-M: **Mint:** Hall **Note:** Varieties exist. Prev. KM#602.2.

Date	Mintage	VG	F	VF	XF	Unc
1605	—	50.00	100	200	375	—

KM# 81 THALER

Silver **Ruler:** Rudolf II **Obv:** Front of armored bust through inner circle, date in legend above **Mint:** Hall **Note:** Dav. #3006. Prev. KM#603.

Date	Mintage	VG	F	VF	XF	Unc
1607	—	50.00	100	210	375	—
1609	—	50.00	100	210	375	—
1610	—	50.00	100	210	375	—

KM# 82 THALER

Silver **Ruler:** Rudolf II **Obv:** Bust with Alchemistry symbols on shoulder **Rev:** Cronwed complex arms within Order chain **Mint:** Hall **Note:** Dav. #3006A. Prev. KM#604.

Date	Mintage	VG	F	VF	XF	Unc
1607	—	50.00	100	200	375	—

KM# 94 THALER

Silver **Ruler:** Ferdinand II **Rev:** Round Order collar without inner circle **Mint:** Graz **Note:** Dav. #3308. Prev. KM#565.

Date	Mintage	VG	F	VF	XF	Unc
1608	—	100	200	450	800	—

KM# 95 THALER

Silver **Ruler:** Rudolf II **Obv:** Different armored bust right in inner circle **Mint:** Hall **Note:** Dav. #3006B. Prev. KM#605.

Date	Mintage	VG	F	VF	XF	Unc
1608	—	50.00	100	210	375	—

KM# 96 THALER

Silver **Ruler:** Matthias II **Mint:** Vienna **Note:** Coronation commemorative. Prev. KM#1735.

Date	Mintage	VG	F	VF	XF	Unc
1608 CH Rare	—	—	—	—	—	—

KM# 102 THALER

Silver **Ruler:** Ferdinand II **Rev:** Inner circle within Order collar **Mint:** Graz **Note:** Dav. #3310. Prev. KM#566.

Date	Mintage	VG	F	VF	XF	Unc
1609	—	75.00	150	350	700	—
1610	—	75.00	150	350	700	—

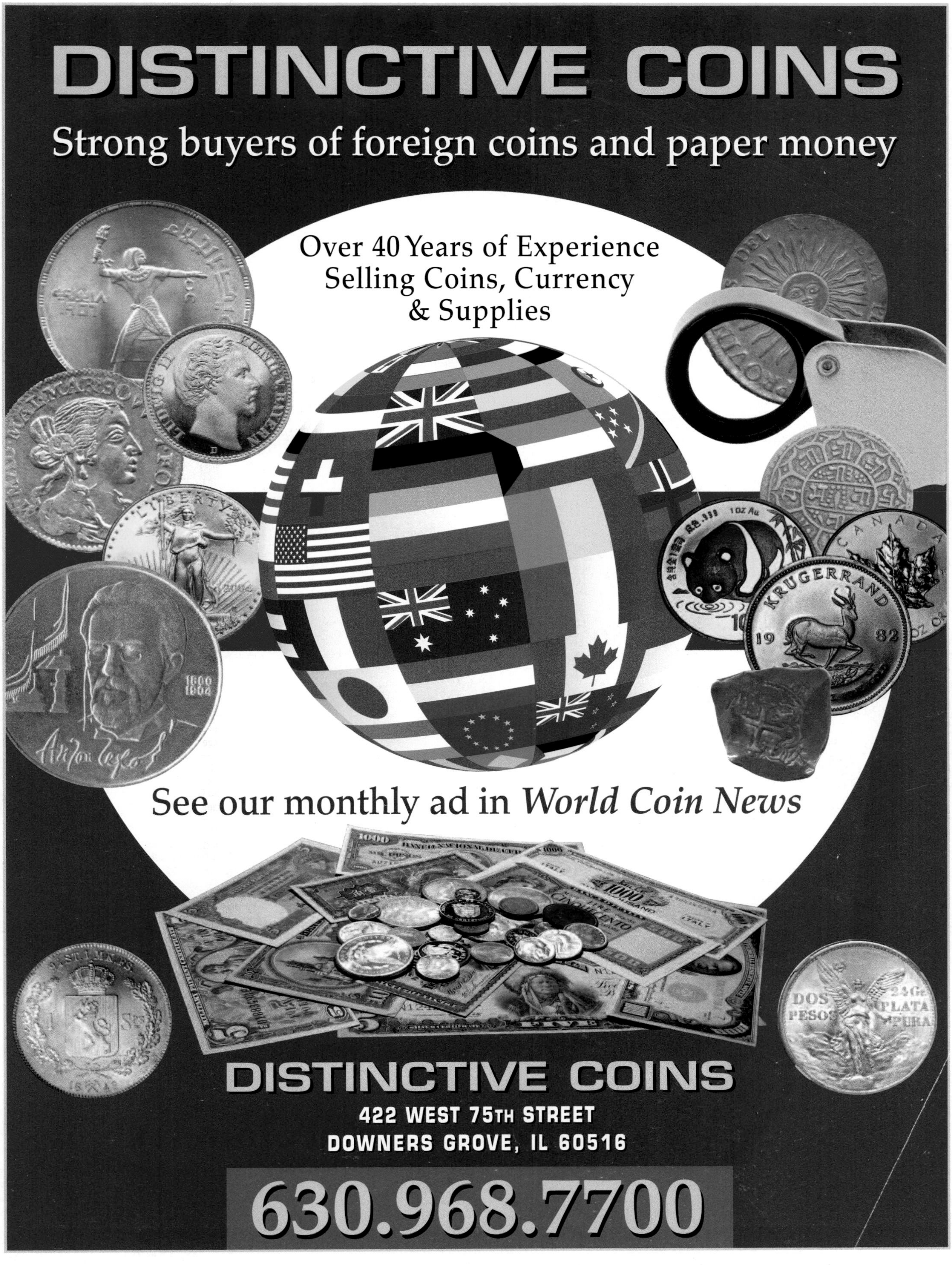
DISTINCTIVE COINS
Strong buyers of foreign coins and paper money
Over 40 Years of Experience
Selling Coins, Currency
& Supplies
See our monthly ad in World Coin News
DISTINCTIVE COINS
422 WEST 75TH STREET
DOWNERS GROVE, IL 60516
630.968.7700

Subscribe Today and Save 56%

Get all the coin information you need in one place! Order *World Coin News* now and you'll get 12 issues packed with international coin news, emerging market trends and tips on how you can cash in on them, recaps of coin shows, auctions, events and more!

SUBSCRIBE ONLINE TODAY

12 ISSUES

GET A FULL YEAR OF

World Coin News

FROM THE PUBLISHERS OF THE STANDARD CATALOG OF WORLD COINS®

FOR JUST

$25.99

TO ORDER, VISIT

subscribe.worldcoinnews.net

In Canada, add $15 (includes GST/HST). Outside the U.S. and Canada, add $30. Outside the U.S., remit payment in U.S. funds with order. Please allow 4-6 weeks for first-issue delivery. Annual newsstand rate $59.88. *World Coin News* is published 12 times per year which may include an occasional special, combined or expanded issue that may count as two issues.

Or call 386-246-3434. Or mail orders to Subscription Processing, P.O. Box 420235, Palm Coast FL 32142-0235. Mention offer code J1CHAD.

KM# 103 THALER

Silver **Ruler:** Matthias II **Obv:** Crowned bust in ruffled collar right in inner circle **Rev:** Crowned arms in Order collar in inner circle, date in legend **Mint:** Vienna **Note:** Titles as King of Bohemia. Dav. #3037. Prev. KM#1736.

Date	Mintage	VG	F	VF	XF	Unc
1609	—	125	250	425	750	—
1610	—	125	250	425	750	—

KM# 104 THALER

Silver **Ruler:** Matthias II **Obv:** Larger crowned bust with crown touching inner circle **Mint:** Vienna **Note:** Titles as King of Bohemia. Dav. #3038. Prev. KM#1737.

Date	Mintage	VG	F	VF	XF	Unc
1609	—	300	550	1,000	1,700	—

KM# 122 THALER

Silver **Ruler:** Matthias II **Obv:** Smaller bust in inner circle **Mint:** Vienna **Note:** Titles as King of Bohemia. Dav. #3039. Prev. KM#1738.

Date	Mintage	VG	F	VF	XF	Unc
1610	—	125	250	425	750	—
1611	—	125	250	425	750	—

KM# 118.1 THALER

Silver **Ruler:** Rudolf II **Obv:** Date in front of bust with additional shoulder ornamentation, legend divided **Obv. Legend:** RO-IM: **Rev:** Crowned complex arms within Order chain **Mint:** Hall **Note:** Dav. #3007. Prev. KM#606.1.

Date	Mintage	VG	F	VF	XF	Unc
1610	—	50.00	100	200	375	—

KM# 118.2 THALER

Silver **Ruler:** Rudolf II **Obv:** Laureate armored bust right, ornaments on armor, date at right **Rev:** Crowned complex arms within Order chain **Rev. Legend:** ...TIROL **Mint:** Hall **Note:** Dav. #3007C. Prev. KM#606.2.

Date	Mintage	VG	F	VF	XF	Unc
1610	—	50.00	100	210	375	—

KM# 118.3 THALER

Silver **Ruler:** Rudolf II **Obv:** Laureate armored bust right, date at right **Rev:** Crowned complex arms **Rev. Legend:** ...TIRO **Mint:** Hall **Note:** Dav. #3007D. Prev. KM#606.3.

Date	Mintage	VG	F	VF	XF	Unc
1610	—	50.00	100	210	375	—

KM# 118.4 THALER

Silver **Ruler:** Rudolf II **Obv:** Armored bust right, legend divided. **Obv. Legend:** DG: - RO. **Rev:** Crowned complex arms within Order chain **Rev. Legend:** ...TIRO **Mint:** Hall **Note:** Dav. #3007A. Prev. KM#606.4.

Date	Mintage	VG	F	VF	XF	Unc
1610	—	50.00	100	200	375	—

KM# 120 THALER

Silver **Ruler:** Rudolf II **Obv:** Laureate armored bust right, legend divided **Obv. Legend:** ROM-: IM: **Rev:** Crowned complex arms **Mint:** Hall **Note:** Dav. #3007B. Prev. KM#607.

Date	Mintage	VG	F	VF	XF	Unc
1610	—	50.00	100	200	375	—

KM# 121 THALER

Silver **Ruler:** Rudolf II **Obv:** Cloaked bust without horn on shoulder **Rev:** Ornamented shield **Mint:** Hall **Note:** Dav. #3008. Prev. KM#608.

Date	Mintage	VG	F	VF	XF	Unc
1610	—	50.00	100	200	375	—

KM# 126.2 THALER

Silver **Ruler:** Rudolf II **Obv:** Legend broken at lower right **Mint:** Hall **Note:** Dav. #3009. Prev. KM#609.2.

Date	Mintage	VG	F	VF	XF	Unc
1611	—	55.00	110	200	400	—
161Z	—	55.00	110	200	400	—

KM# 126.1 THALER

Silver **Ruler:** Rudolf II **Obv:** Draped bust with lion's head on shoulder in laurel wreath, unbroken legend **Mint:** Hall **Note:** Dav. #3009A. Prev. KM#609.1

Date	Mintage	VG	F	VF	XF	Unc
1611	—	55.00	110	200	400	—

KM# 143 THALER

Silver **Ruler:** Rudolf II **Obv:** Bust divides date **Mint:** Hall **Note:** Dav. #3010. Prev. KM#610.

Date	Mintage	VG	F	VF	XF	Unc
161Z	—	55.00	110	200	400	—

KM# 169 THALER

Silver **Ruler:** Matthias II **Obv:** Laureate, armored bust right in inner circle **Rev:** Crowned imperial eagle with shield on breast with sword and scepter in inner circle, date in legend **Mint:** Vienna **Note:** Titles as Emperor. Dav. #3043. Prev. KM#1741.

Date	Mintage	VG	F	VF	XF	Unc
1613	—	125	250	425	750	—
1614	—	125	250	425	750	—

KM# 130 THALER

Silver **Ruler:** Matthias II **Obv:** Crowned bust in ruffled collar right in inner circle **Rev:** Crowned arms in Order collar in inner circle, date in legend **Mint:** Vienna **Note:** Titles as King of Bohemia. Dav. #3040. Prev. KM#1739.

Date	Mintage	VG	F	VF	XF	Unc
1611	—	350	650	1,150	1,850	—
1612	—	350	650	1,150	1,850	—

KM# 165 THALER

Silver **Ruler:** Maximilian **Obv:** Bust right in decorated inner circle **Mint:** Hall **Note:** Dav. #3315. Prev. KM#767.

Date	Mintage	VG	F	VF	XF	Unc
ND	—	250	450	775	1,600	—

KM# 37.4 THALER

28.1800 g., Silver **Ruler:** Rudolf II **Obv:** Laureate bust right, longer ribbon tails, without tassel **Obv. Legend:** RUDOLPHVS II • DG • RO.IM • SEM • AV • GE • HVNG • BOH • REX **Rev:** Crowned arms in Order chain **Rev. Legend:** NEC NON ARCHIDVCES AV:DVC:BVR:COM:TIRO **Mint:** Hall **Note:** Dav.#3005C.

Date	Mintage	VG	F	VF	XF	Unc
1612	—	50.00	100	210	375	—

KM# 167 THALER

Silver **Ruler:** Maximilian **Obv:** Larger bust dividing legend at lower right with date **Mint:** Hall **Note:** Dav. #3317. Prev. KM#769.1.

Date	Mintage	VG	F	VF	XF	Unc
1613	—	75.00	150	265	525	—

KM# 144 THALER

Silver **Ruler:** Matthias II **Obv:** Smaller bust and crown **Mint:** Vienna **Note:** Titles as King of Bohemia. Dav. #3041. Prev. KM#1740.

Date	Mintage	VG	F	VF	XF	Unc
1612	—	350	650	1,150	1,850	—
1613	—	350	650	1,150	1,850	—

KM# 166 THALER

Silver **Ruler:** Maximilian **Obv:** Laurels form inner circle **Rev:** Laurels form inner circle; continuous legend with date below bust **Mint:** Hall **Note:** Dav. #3316. Prev. KM#768.

Date	Mintage	VG	F	VF	XF	Unc
1613	—	75.00	150	265	525	—

KM# 168 THALER

Silver **Ruler:** Maximilian **Obv:** Bust divides date **Mint:** Hall **Note:** Dav. #3318. Prev. KM#769.2.

Date	Mintage	VG	F	VF	XF	Unc
1613	—	75.00	150	265	525	—

KM# 187 THALER

Silver **Ruler:** Ferdinand II **Rev:** Crowned arms in Order collar in inner circle, crown divides date **Mint:** Graz **Note:** Dav. #3311. Prev. KM#568.

Date	Mintage	VG	F	VF	XF	Unc
1614	—	65.00	145	350	900	—
1617	—	65.00	145	350	900	—
1618	—	65.00	145	350	900	—

KM# 188.1 THALER

Silver **Ruler:** Maximilian **Obv:** Date in front of bust with Co below **Mint:** Hall **Note:** Dav. #3319. Prev. KM#770.1.

Date	Mintage	VG	F	VF	XF	Unc
1614 CO	—	200	350	575	1,150	—

KM# 188.2 THALER

Silver **Ruler:** Maximilian **Obv:** Bust divides date with Co below **Mint:** Hall **Note:** Dav. #3320. Prev. KM#770.2.

Date	Mintage	VG	F	VF	XF	Unc
1614 Co	—	200	350	575	1,150	—

KM# 188.3 THALER

Silver **Ruler:** Maximilian **Obv:** Bust divides punctuated date with large CO below **Mint:** Hall **Note:** Dav. #3321. Prev. KM#770.3.

Date	Mintage	VG	F	VF	XF	Unc
1615 CO	—	50.00	100	200	400	—

KM# 196 THALER

Silver **Ruler:** Matthias II **Rev:** Larger crown above eagle **Mint:** Vienna **Note:** Titles as Emperor. Dav. #3044. Prev. KM#1742.

Date	Mintage	VG	F	VF	XF	Unc
1615	—	125	250	425	750	—
1616	—	125	250	425	750	—

KM# 188.4 THALER

Silver **Ruler:** Maximilian **Obv:** Bust divides date with small co below **Mint:** Hall **Note:** Dav. #3321A. Prev. KM#770.4.

Date	Mintage	VG	F	VF	XF	Unc
1615 co	—	50.00	100	200	400	—

KM# 188.5 THALER

Silver **Ruler:** Maximilian **Obv:** Smaller bust divides date with small co below **Mint:** Hall **Note:** Dav. #3321B. Prev. KM#770.5.

Date	Mintage	VG	F	VF	XF	Unc
1615 co	—	50.00	100	200	400	—

KM# 205.1 THALER

Silver **Ruler:** Maximilian **Obv:** Bust with large drapery divides date with small co below **Mint:** Hall **Note:** Dav. #3322. Prev. KM#771.1.

Date	Mintage	VG	F	VF	XF	Unc
1616 co	—	50.00	100	200	400	—

KM# 206 THALER

Silver **Ruler:** Matthias II **Rev:** Smaller crown above eagle **Mint:** Vienna **Note:** Titles as Emperor. Dav. #3046. Prev. KM#1743.

Date	Mintage	VG	F	VF	XF	Unc
1616	—	125	250	425	750	—
1617	—	125	250	425	750	—

KM# 205.2 THALER

Silver **Ruler:** Maximilian **Obv:** With CO in legend below bust **Mint:** Hall **Note:** Dav. #3322A. Prev. KM#771.2.

Date	Mintage	VG	F	VF	XF	Unc
1616 CO	—	50.00	100	200	400	—

KM# 217 THALER

Silver **Ruler:** Ferdinand II **Obv:** Crowned bust without scepter **Rev:** Crown divides date **Mint:** Graz **Note:** Dav. #A3312. Prev. KM#570.

Date	Mintage	VG	F	VF	XF	Unc
1617	—	50.00	100	220	575	—
1618	—	50.00	100	220	575	—

KM# 221 THALER

Silver **Ruler:** Matthias II **Obv:** Laureate bust with wide ruffle **Mint:** Vienna **Note:** Titles as Emperor. Dav. #3048. Varieties exist. Prev. KM#1744.

Date	Mintage	VG	F	VF	XF	Unc
1617	—	125	250	425	750	—
1618	—	125	250	425	750	—
1619	—	125	250	425	750	—

KM# 216 THALER

Silver **Ruler:** Ferdinand II **Rev:** Date in legend **Mint:** Graz **Note:** Dav. #3312. Prev. KM#569.

Date	Mintage	VG	F	VF	XF	Unc
1617	—	50.00	100	220	575	—

KM# 218.1 THALER

Silver **Ruler:** Maximilian **Obv:** Small bust divides date with small outlined CO below **Mint:** Hall **Note:** Dav. #3323. Prev. KM#772.1.

Date	Mintage	VG	F	VF	XF	Unc
1617 co	—	40.00	90.00	210	375	—

KM# 218.2 THALER

Silver **Ruler:** Maximilian **Obv:** Bust barely dividing legend, with CARENTA **Mint:** Hall **Note:** Dav. #3323A. Prev. KM#772.2.

Date	Mintage	VG	F	VF	XF	Unc
1617	—	40.00	90.00	200	375	—

KM# 218.3 THALER

Silver **Ruler:** Maximilian **Obv:** Bust with lance rest on chest **Obv. Legend:** ... CAREN **Mint:** Hall **Note:** Dav. #3323B. Prev. KM#772.3.

Date	Mintage	VG	F	VF	XF	Unc
1617	—	40.00	90.00	210	375	—

KM# 218.4 THALER

Silver **Ruler:** Maximilian **Obv:** With CO in legend below bust **Obv. Legend:** MAXIMIL: DG: ARG: - :co: AV: DVX: BVR: STIR: **Mint:** Hall **Note:** Dav. #3323C. Prev. KM#772.4.

Date	Mintage	VG	F	VF	XF	Unc
1617	—	35.00	80.00	210	350	—

KM# 218.5 THALER

Silver **Ruler:** Maximilian **Obv. Legend:** MAXIMIL: DG: AR-C: co: AV: DVX: BVR: STIR: **Mint:** Hall **Note:** Dav. #3323D. Prev. KM#772.5.

Date	Mintage	VG	F	VF	XF	Unc
1617	—	35.00	80.00	210	325	—

KM# 218.6 THALER

28.4700 g., Silver **Ruler:** Maximilian **Obv:** Bust right divides date **Obv. Legend:** * MAXIMIL: DG: ARC: - :OO: AV: DVX: BUR: STIR **Rev:** Crowned arms **Rev. Legend:** ET: CARN: MAG: PRVSS: AD: COM: H: ET: TIROL **Mint:** Hall **Note:** Dav.#3323V.

Date	Mintage	VG	F	VF	XF	Unc
1617	—	50.00	100	175	350	—

KM# 219 THALER

Silver **Ruler:** Maximilian **Obv:** Bust with lance rest on shoulder **Mint:** Hall **Note:** Dav. #A3324. Prev. KM#773.

Date	Mintage	VG	F	VF	XF	Unc
1617	—	30.00	70.00	210	350	—

KM# 220 THALER

Silver **Ruler:** Maximilian **Obv:** Bust with shoulder ornamentation **Mint:** Hall **Note:** Dav. #A3324. Prev. KM#782.

Date	Mintage	VG	F	VF	XF	Unc
1617	—	30.00	70.00	210	350	—

KM# 227.2 THALER

Silver **Ruler:** Maximilian **Obv:** Ruffled collar bust right divides date **Obv. Legend:** MAXIMILI: D G ... CARN: **Rev:** Crowned arms **Mint:** Hall **Note:** Dav. #3324A. Prev. KM#774.2.

Date	Mintage	VG	F	VF	XF	Unc
1618	—	35.00	80.00	210	350	—

KM# 227.1 THALER

Silver **Ruler:** Maximilian **Obv:** Bust right divides date, high ruffled collar, cross on chain around neck **Obv. Legend:** MAXIMIL: D G ... CARN **Rev:** Crowned complex arms **Mint:** Hall **Note:** Dav. #3324. Prev. KM#774.1.

Date	Mintage	VG	F	VF	XF	Unc
1618	—	40.00	80.00	210	350	—

KM# 228 THALER

Silver **Ruler:** Matthias II **Mint:** Vienna **Note:** Titles as Emperor. Dav. #3048A. Klippe. Prev. KM#1745.

Date	Mintage	VG	F	VF	XF	Unc
1618 Rare	—	—	—	—	—	—

KM# 244 THALER

Silver **Ruler:** Ferdinand II **Obv:** Crowned bust right in inner circle **Rev:** Crowned imperial eagle with oval arms on breast in inner circle **Mint:** Klagenfurt **Note:** Varieties exist. Prev. KM#967.

Date	Mintage	VG	F	VF	XF	Unc
ND Rare	—	—	—	—	—	—

KM# 245 THALER

Silver **Ruler:** Matthias II **Rev:** Ornament after TYR ... **Mint:** Vienna **Note:** Titles as Emperor. Dav. #3049. Prev. KM#1746.

Date	Mintage	VG	F	VF	XF	Unc
1619	—	125	250	425	750	—

KM# 262.1 THALER

Silver **Ruler:** Ferdinand II **Obv:** Date below bust, legend **Obv. Legend:** FERDINANDVS • II • DG • RO • IM • S • A • GER • H • B • REX • **Rev:** Crowned imperial eagle with round arms, legend **Rev. Legend:** ARCHI • AVSTRIA • DVX • BVRGVN • STYRIAE • ETC • **Mint:** Graz **Note:** Prev. KM#372.1.

Date	Mintage	VG	F	VF	XF	Unc
1620	—	65.00	125	250	400	—

KM# 266 THALER

Silver **Ruler:** Ferdinand II **Rev:** Flat-topped shield of arms **Mint:** Klagenfurt **Note:** Dav. #3114. Prev. KM#969.

Date	Mintage	VG	F	VF	XF	Unc
1620	—	125	275	450	800	—

KM# 264.1 THALER

28.3800 g., Silver **Ruler:** Leopold **Obv. Legend:** LEOPOLDVS: NECNON: CAETERI: D: G: ARCHID: AUSTRI **Rev. Legend:** DVC: BVRG: STYR: CAR: ET: CARN: COM: TYROL: **Mint:** Hall **Note:** Dav. #3328. Prev. KM#802.1.

Date	Mintage	VG	F	VF	XF	Unc
1620	—	60.00	125	300	500	—
1621	—	60.00	125	300	500	—

KM# 268.1 THALER

Silver **Ruler:** Ferdinand II **Mint:** Vienna **Note:** Dav. #3074. Prev. KM#1785.1.

Date	Mintage	VG	F	VF	XF	Unc
16Z0	—	65.00	125	200	350	—

KM# 268.2 THALER

Silver **Ruler:** Ferdinand II **Obv:** Laureate wreath without bow **Rev:** Crowned double eagle, shield on breast surrounded by Order chain **Mint:** Vienna **Note:** Dav. #3076. Prev. KM#1785.2.

Date	Mintage	VG	F	VF	XF	Unc
16Z0 (c)	—	50.00	100	210	350	—
16Z1 (c)	—	50.00	100	210	350	—

KM# 263 THALER

Silver **Ruler:** Ferdinand II **Obv. Legend:** ...ROM. IMP. S. A. GER... **Rev:** Arms in flat-topped shield, date divided at top **Mint:** Graz **Note:** Dav. #3099. Prev. KM#374.

Date	Mintage	VG	F	VF	XF	Unc
1620	—	65.00	125	250	400	—

KM# 262.2 THALER

Silver **Ruler:** Ferdinand II **Obv. Legend:** ...D • G • - RO • IMP • S • A • G • HVN • ET • BO • REX • **Rev. Legend:** ...B-VRGVNDIAE... **Mint:** Graz **Note:** Varieties exist. Dav. #3098. Prev. KM#372.2.

Date	Mintage	VG	F	VF	XF	Unc
1620	—	65.00	125	250	400	—

KM# 264.2 THALER

Silver **Ruler:** Leopold **Obv:** Bust right divides date **Obv. Legend:** *LEOPOLDVS: D: G: A: ANEC: NON CAETERI: ARCH: AUST **Rev:** Crowned arms with furls at upper left and right **Rev. Legend:** DVX BVRG: STIR: CAR-ET: CARN: COM: TIRO **Mint:** Hall **Note:** Dav.#3329.

Date	Mintage	VG	F	VF	XF	Unc
16Z0	—	60.00	125	300	500	—

KM# 264.3 THALER

Silver **Ruler:** Leopold **Obv:** Bust right divides date **Obv. Legend:** * LEOPOLDVS: D: G: A: NEC: NON CAETERI: ARCH: AUST **Rev:** Crowned plain arms **Rev. Legend:** DVX BVRG: STIR: CAR-ET: CARN: COM: TIRO **Mint:** Hall **Note:** Dav. #3329V.

Date	Mintage	VG	F	VF	XF	Unc
16Z0	—	60.00	125	300	500	—

KM# 264.4 THALER

Silver **Ruler:** Leopold **Obv:** Bust right divides date **Obv. Legend:** * LEOPOLDVS: D: G: A: NEC: NON CAETERI: ARCH: AUST **Rev:** Crowned slightly ornate arms **Rev. Legend:** DVX BVRG: STIR: CA-RET: CARN: COM: TI • **Mint:** Hall **Note:** Dav. #3329.

Date	Mintage	VG	F	VF	XF	Unc
16Z0	—	60.00	125	300	500	—

KM# 265 THALER

Silver **Ruler:** Ferdinand II **Rev:** Crown divides date **Mint:** Klagenfurt **Note:** Varieties exist. Dav. #3112. Prev. KM#968.

Date	Mintage	VG	F	VF	XF	Unc
1620	—	125	250	400	650	—

KM# 264.5 THALER

28.7900 g., Silver **Ruler:** Leopold **Obv. Legend:** LEOPOLDVS D G ARCHID AUSTRIAE DVX BVRG S CAES M...ET RELIQ **Rev. Legend:** ARCHIDVC GVBERNATOR PLENARIVS COM TIROL **Mint:** Hall **Note:** Portrait varieties exist. Prev. KM#802.2.

Date	Mintage	VG	F	VF	XF	Unc
16Z1	—	60.00	125	300	500	—
16ZZ	—	60.00	125	300	500	—
16Z3	—	60.00	125	300	500	—
16Z4	—	60.00	125	300	500	—
16Z5	—	60.00	125	300	500	—

KM# 335 THALER

Silver **Ruler:** Ferdinand II **Obv:** Standing figure right between two shields **Rev:** Heraldic imperial eagle **Mint:** Brunn **Note:** Prev. KM#216.

Date	Mintage	VG	F	VF	XF	Unc
1621 GR-(h) Rare	—	—	—	—	—	—
1621 GR Rare	—	—	—	—	—	—
1622 GR Rare	—	—	—	—	—	—

KM# 338 THALER

Silver **Ruler:** Ferdinand II **Obv:** Laureate bust with ruffled collar right divides date **Rev:** Crowned complex arms within Order chain **Mint:** Hall **Note:** Dav. #A3125. Prev. KM#615.

Date	Mintage	VG	F	VF	XF	Unc
1621	—	125	250	450	1,100	—
1622	—	125	250	450	1,100	—
1623	—	125	250	450	1,100	—

KM# 347 THALER

Silver **Ruler:** Ferdinand II **Obv:** Standing Kaiser holding scepter and orb **Rev:** Crowned imperial eagle, arms on breast, date in legend left of crown **Mint:** Olmutz **Note:** Klippe. Dav. A3147. Prev. KM#A1237.

Date	Mintage	VG	F	VF	XF	Unc
1621 BZ	—	750	1,250	2,000	3,000	—
1622	—	750	1,250	2,000	3,000	—

KM# 336 THALER

Silver **Ruler:** Ferdinand II **Obv:** Date below bust **Obv. Legend:** ...D-G. RO. IM...HV. BO. REX **Rev:** Round arms on eagle's breast **Rev. Legend:** DVX-BVRGVN. STYRIAE. ETC. **Mint:** Graz **Note:** Varieties exist. Dav. #3100. Prev. KM#373.

Date	Mintage	VG	F	VF	XF	Unc
1621	—	65.00	125	250	400	—

KM# 337 THALER

Silver **Ruler:** Ferdinand II **Obv. Legend:** ...HV. B. REX. **Rev:** Date divided above by crown **Rev. Legend:** ...ET. **Mint:** Graz **Note:** Dav. #3102. Prev. KM#375.

Date	Mintage	VG	F	VF	XF	Unc
1621	—	65.00	125	250	400	—

KM# 339 THALER

Silver **Ruler:** Ferdinand II **Obv:** Tall, thin crowned bust **Rev:** Crown divides date **Mint:** Klagenfurt **Note:** Dav. #3118. Prev. KM#970.

Date	Mintage	VG	F	VF	XF	Unc
1621	—	650	1,200	2,000	3,500	—

KM# 340 THALER

Silver **Ruler:** Ferdinand II **Obv:** Crowned bust with high ruffled collar right, date below **Rev:** Crowned double eagle with shield on breast **Mint:** Klagenfurt **Note:** Varieties exist. Dav. #3115. Prev. KM#971.

Date	Mintage	VG	F	VF	XF	Unc
1621	—	85.00	175	350	550	—

KM# 341 THALER

Silver **Ruler:** Ferdinand II **Obv:** Crown divides date **Rev:** Order chain surrounds shield on crowned double eagle's breast **Mint:** Klagenfurt **Note:** Varieties exist. Dav. #3116. Prev. KM#972.

Date	Mintage	VG	F	VF	XF	Unc
1621	—	85.00	175	350	550	—

KM# 342 THALER

Silver **Ruler:** Ferdinand II **Rev:** Oval arms **Mint:** Klagenfurt **Note:** Dav. #3116. Prev. KM#A973.

Date	Mintage	VG	F	VF	XF	Unc
1621 Rare	—	—	—	—	—	—

KM# 343 THALER

Silver **Ruler:** Ferdinand II **Obv:** Date below bust **Obv. Legend:** S. A. G. HV. BO. REX **Mint:** Klagenfurt **Note:** Dav. #3120. Prev. KM#B973.

Date	Mintage	VG	F	VF	XF	Unc
1621	—	85.00	175	350	550	—

KM# 344 THALER

Silver **Ruler:** Ferdinand II **Obv:** Crowned bust divides date at collar height **Mint:** Klagenfurt **Note:** Dav. #3121. Varieties exist. Prev. KM#973.

Date	Mintage	VG	F	VF	XF	Unc
1621	—	85.00	175	350	550	—

KM# 345 THALER

Silver **Ruler:** Ferdinand II **Obv:** Bust divides date at shoulder height **Mint:** Klagenfurt **Note:** Dav. #3121A. Prev. KM#A974.

Date	Mintage	VG	F	VF	XF	Unc
1621	—	85.00	175	350	550	—

KM# 348 THALER

Silver **Ruler:** Ferdinand II **Mint:** Vienna **Note:** Klippe. Dav. #3076A. Prev. KM#1786.

Date	Mintage	VG	F	VF	XF	Unc
16Z1 (c) Rare	—	—	—	—	—	—

KM# 264.6 THALER

28.6600 g., Silver **Ruler:** Leopold **Obv:** Bust right divides date **Obv. Legend:** *LEOPOLDVS: D: G: ARCHID: AVSTRIAE DVX BVRG S CAES: M ET R LI **Rev:** Crowned arms with small ornaments left and right **Mint:** Hall **Note:** Dav. #3330V.

Date	Mintage	VG	F	VF	XF	Unc
16ZZ	—	30.00	125	300	500	—
16Z4	—	60.00	125	300	500	—

KM# 346 THALER

Silver **Ruler:** Ferdinand II **Obv:** Ornamented inner circle **Rev:** Round arms **Mint:** Klagenfurt **Note:** Dav. #3121A. Varieties exist. Prev. KM#974.

Date	Mintage	VG	F	VF	XF	Unc
1622	—	85.00	175	350	550	—

KM# 453 THALER

Silver **Ruler:** Ferdinand II **Obv:** Plain collar on Ferdinand **Mint:** Graz **Note:** Dav. #3104. Prev. KM#377.

Date	Mintage	VG	F	VF	XF	Unc
16Z3	—	35.00	100	210	300	—
16Z4/3	—	35.00	100	210	300	—
16Z4	—	35.00	100	210	300	—

KM# 456 THALER

Silver **Ruler:** Ferdinand II **Obv:** Older bust **Mint:** Vienna **Note:** Dav. #3078. Prev. KM#A1787.

Date	Mintage	VG	F	VF	XF	Unc
1623 (c)	—	50.00	100	200	350	—
1624 (c)	—	50.00	100	200	350	—

KM# 451 THALER

19.8700 g., Silver **Ruler:** Ferdinand II **Mint:** Brunn **Note:** Klippe. Prev. KM#216a.

Date	Mintage	VG	F	VF	XF	Unc
1623 GR Rare	—	—	—	—	—	—

KM# 452 THALER

Silver **Ruler:** Ferdinand II **Obv:** Laureate bust with high ruffled collar right, date below **Obv. Legend:** ...I: S: A: G: H: B: REX. **Rev:** Crowned arms in Order chain **Rev. Legend:** ...AVST: DVX:-BVR: STYRIAE: ETC. **Mint:** Graz **Note:** Dav. #3103. Prev. KM#376.

Date	Mintage	VG	F	VF	XF	Unc
1623	—	40.00	110	200	300	—

KM# 454 THALER

Silver **Ruler:** Ferdinand II **Obv:** Shield added on each side of Kaiser **Mint:** Olmutz **Note:** Klippe. Dav. #3147. Prev. KM#B1237.

Date	Mintage	VG	F	VF	XF	Unc
1623	—	750	1,250	2,000	3,000	—

KM# 455 THALER

Silver **Ruler:** Ferdinand II **Obv:** Bust right in inner circle, date below bust **Rev:** Crowned arms in Order collar and inner circle **Mint:** Saint Veit **Note:** Dav. #A3123. Prev. KM#1601.

Date	Mintage	VG	F	VF	XF	Unc
1623	—	125	250	400	800	—

KM# 521 THALER

Silver **Ruler:** Ferdinand II **Obv:** Laureate bust right in laurel wreath border **Rev:** Crowned complex arms within Order chain **Mint:** Graz **Note:** Dav. #3106. Prev. KM#379.

Date	Mintage	VG	F	VF	XF	Unc
1624	—	35.00	100	200	300	—
1625	—	35.00	100	200	300	—
1626	—	35.00	100	200	300	—

KM# 531 THALER

Silver **Ruler:** Ferdinand II **Mint:** Vienna **Note:** Dav. #3087. Varieties exist. Prev. KM#1790.

Date	Mintage	VG	F	VF	XF	Unc
1624 (c)	—	100	175	300	500	—
1625 (c)	—	100	175	300	500	—

KM# 526 THALER

Silver **Ruler:** Ferdinand II **Obv:** Laureate armored bust right, date below **Rev:** Crowned complex arms within Order chain **Mint:** Saint Veit **Note:** Dav. #3123. Varieties exist. Prev. KM#1602.

Date	Mintage	VG	F	VF	XF	Unc
1624 (m)	—	75.00	150	300	650	—
1625 (m)	—	75.00	150	300	650	—
1625 (p)	—	75.00	150	300	650	—

KM# 517.1 THALER

19.8700 g., Silver **Ruler:** Ferdinand II **Obv:** Laureate bust with high ruffled collar right **Rev:** Order chain surrounds shield on double eagle breast **Mint:** Brunn **Note:** Dav. #3144. Prev. KM#217.1.

Date	Mintage	VG	F	VF	XF	Unc
1624 B/HG-(c)	—	200	400	650	1,000	—
1624 B-(c)	—	200	400	650	1,000	—

KM# 518 THALER

19.8700 g., Silver **Ruler:** Ferdinand II **Mint:** Brunn **Note:** Klippe. Dav. #3146A. Prev. KM#218.

Date	Mintage	VG	F	VF	XF	Unc
1624 (c) Rare	—	—	—	—	—	—

KM# 517.2 THALER

19.8700 g., Silver **Ruler:** Ferdinand II **Obv:** Legend in circle followed by D. G... **Obv. Legend:** FERDINANDVS. II. B **Mint:** Brunn **Note:** Dav. #3146. Prev. KM#217.2.

Date	Mintage	VG	F	VF	XF	Unc
1624 B/HG	—	200	400	650	1,000	—
1624 B-(c)	—	200	400	650	1,000	—
1624 (c)	—	200	400	650	1,000	—

KM# 519 THALER

16.5500 g., Silver **Ruler:** Ferdinand II **Mint:** Brunn **Note:** Klippe. Prev. KM#218a.

Date	Mintage	VG	F	VF	XF	Unc
1624 B-(c) Rare	—	—	—	—	—	—

KM# 520 THALER

Silver **Ruler:** Ferdinand II **Obv:** Without Roman numeral II in legend **Mint:** Graz **Note:** Dav. #3104A. Prev. KM#378.

Date	Mintage	VG	F	VF	XF	Unc
1624	—	35.00	100	175	250	—

KM# 522 THALER

Silver **Ruler:** Ferdinand II **Mint:** Hall **Note:** Dav. #3330A. Klippe. Prev. KM#803.

Date	Mintage	VG	F	VF	XF	Unc
1624	—	—	—	—	—	—

KM# 525.1 THALER

Silver **Ruler:** Ferdinand II **Obv:** Laureate bust right **Obv. Legend:** FERDINANDVS. II. D., mint mark, G. R. I. S. A. G. HV. BO. REX **Rev:** Crowned arms in Order chain, date **Rev. Legend:** ARCHID. AVS. DVX. -BVR. CO. TYR **Mint:** Saint Polten **Note:** Dav. #3092. Prev. KM#1574.1.

Date	Mintage	VG	F	VF	XF	Unc
1624 (c)-IIE	—	350	600	1,000	1,750	—
1624 (d)	—	350	600	1,000	1,750	—

KM# 527 THALER

Silver **Ruler:** Ferdinand II **Obv:** Half-length figure right **Rev:** Five shields below crown **Mint:** Vienna **Note:** Dav. #3080. Prev. KM#B1787.

Date	Mintage	VG	F	VF	XF	Unc
1624 (c)	—	150	300	500	800	—

KM# 528 THALER

Silver **Ruler:** Ferdinand II **Obv:** Bust with ruffled collar right, legend without II **Mint:** Vienna **Note:** Dav. #3081. Prev. KM#C1787.

Date	Mintage	VG	F	VF	XF	Unc
1624 (c)	—	100	175	300	500	—

KM# 529 THALER

Silver **Ruler:** Ferdinand II **Obv:** Laureate armored bust right **Rev:** Crown above five shields **Mint:** Vienna **Note:** Dav. #3085. Prev. KM#1789.

Date	Mintage	VG	F	VF	XF	Unc
1624 (c)	—	100	175	300	500	—

KM# 530 THALER

Silver **Ruler:** Ferdinand II **Obv:** Larger head and different drapery **Rev:** Different crown, differently shaped shields **Mint:** Vienna **Note:** Dav. #3086. Prev. KM#A1789.

Date	Mintage	VG	F	VF	XF	Unc
1624 (c)	—	150	300	500	800	—

KM# 532 THALER

Silver **Ruler:** Ferdinand II **Obv:** Bust with thick striated collar right **Rev:** Crown above five shields with decorations between **Mint:** Vienna **Note:** Dav. #3083. Prev. KM#A1790.

Date	Mintage	VG	F	VF	XF	Unc
1624 (c)	—	100	175	300	500	—

KM# 533 THALER

Silver **Ruler:** Ferdinand II **Obv:** Bust with thin striated collar right **Rev:** Rearranged shields **Mint:** Vienna **Note:** Dav. #3084. Prev. KM#B1790.

Date	Mintage	VG	F	VF	XF	Unc
1624 (c)	—	100	175	300	500	—

KM# 534 THALER

Silver **Ruler:** Ferdinand II **Mint:** Vienna **Note:** Dav. #3087A. Klippe. Prev. KM#1791.

Date	Mintage	VG	F	VF	XF	Unc
1624 (c) Rare	—	—	—	—	—	—

KM# 599 THALER

Silver **Ruler:** Ferdinand II **Mint:** Vienna **Note:** Dav. #3091. Varieties exist. Prev. KM#1787.

Date	Mintage	VG	F	VF	XF	Unc
1625 (c)	—	35.00	100	200	350	—
1626/5 (c)	—	35.00	100	200	350	—
1626 (c)	—	35.00	100	200	350	—
1627 (c)	—	35.00	100	200	350	—
1628 (c)	—	35.00	100	200	350	—
1629 (c)	—	35.00	100	200	350	—
1630 (c)	—	35.00	100	200	350	—
1631 (c)	—	35.00	100	200	350	—
1632 (c)	—	35.00	100	200	350	—
1633 (c)	—	35.00	100	200	350	—
1634 (c)	—	35.00	100	200	350	—
1635 (c)	—	35.00	100	200	350	—
1636 (c)	—	35.00	100	200	350	—
1636 (v)	—	35.00	100	200	350	—
1637 (v)	—	35.00	100	200	350	—
1638 (v)	—	35.00	100	200	350	—

KM# 600 THALER

Silver **Ruler:** Ferdinand II **Mint:** Vienna **Note:** Klippe. Dav. #3091A. Varieties exist. Prev. KM#1788.

Date	Mintage	VG	F	VF	XF	Unc
1625 (c) Rare	—	—	—	—	—	—
1628 (c) Rare	—	—	—	—	—	—
1630 (c) Rare	—	—	—	—	—	—
1633 (c) Rare	—	—	—	—	—	—
1634 (c) Rare	—	—	—	—	—	—
1635 (c) Rare	—	—	—	—	—	—
1637 (v) Rare	—	—	—	—	—	—

KM# 525.2 THALER

Silver **Ruler:** Ferdinand II **Obv:** Bust in laurel wreath **Obv. Legend:** FERDINANDVS: II: D:, mint mark, : G. R: I: S: A: G: HV: BO: REX: **Mint:** Saint Polten **Note:** Dav. #3093. Prev. KM#1574.2.

Date	Mintage	VG	F	VF	XF	Unc
1625 (d)	—	350	600	1,100	1,900	—

KM# 525.3 THALER

Silver **Ruler:** Ferdinand II **Obv:** Bust in laurel wreath within circle **Mint:** Saint Polten **Note:** Dav. #3094. Prev. KM#1574.3.

Date	Mintage	VG	F	VF	XF	Unc
1625 (c)	—	350	600	1,100	1,900	—

KM# 525.4 THALER

Silver **Ruler:** Ferdinand II **Obv:** Bust in inner circle, mint mark divides IL-E below **Obv. Legend:** ...G. H. B. REX. **Rev:** Smaller Order chain **Mint:** Saint Polten **Note:** Dav. #3095. Prev. KM#1574.4.

Date	Mintage	VG	F	VF	XF	Unc
1625 (d)-IIE	—	350	600	1,100	1,900	—

KM# 525.5 THALER

Silver **Ruler:** Ferdinand II **Obv:** Bust in three circles **Obv. Legend:** ...G. R. IM. S. A. G. H. B. REX. **Mint:** Saint Polten **Note:** Dav. #3096. Prev. KM#1574.5.

Date	Mintage	VG	F	VF	XF	Unc
1625 (r)	—	350	600	1,100	1,900	—

KM# 598 THALER

Silver **Ruler:** Ferdinand II **Obv:** Armored laureate bust right **Obv. Legend:** ... COM. TYR. **Mint:** Vienna **Note:** Similar to KM#599. Dav. #3088. Prev. KM#D1787.

Date	Mintage	VG	F	VF	XF	Unc
1625 (c)	—	50.00	100	210	350	—

KM# 628 THALER

Silver **Ruler:** Ferdinand II **Rev:** Ornamented shield of arms, different crown **Mint:** Graz **Note:** Dav. #3108. Varieties exist. Prev. KM#380.

Date	Mintage	VG	F	VF	XF	Unc
1626	—	35.00	100	210	300	—
1627	—	35.00	100	210	300	—
1628	—	35.00	100	210	300	—
1629	—	35.00	100	210	300	—
1630	—	35.00	100	210	300	—
1631/0	—	35.00	100	210	300	—
1631	—	35.00	100	210	300	—

KM# 629.1 THALER

Silver **Ruler:** Leopold **Obv:** Crossed half figure in armor with sword and scepter, date in front **Rev:** Crowned arms with decorations on sides **Mint:** Hall **Note:** Dav. #3337. Prev. KM#804.1.

Date	Mintage	VG	F	VF	XF	Unc
1626	—	45.00	100	210	300	—
1627	—	45.00	100	210	300	—

KM# 630 THALER

Silver **Ruler:** Leopold **Mint:** Hall **Note:** Dav. #3337A. Klippe. Prev. KM#A805.

Date	Mintage	VG	F	VF	XF	Unc
16Z6	—	500	900	1,950	3,950	—

KM# 631 THALER

Silver **Ruler:** Ferdinand II **Obv:** Bust in laurel wreath **Rev:** Fuller Order chain **Mint:** Saint Polten **Note:** Dav. #3097. Varieties exist. Prev. KM#1574.6.

Date	Mintage	VG	F	VF	XF	Unc
1626 (r)	—	350	600	1,100	1,950	—

KM# 677 THALER

28.4000 g., Silver **Ruler:** Leopold **Subject:** Wedding of Leopold and Claudia **Obv:** Crowned busts of royal couple right within inner circle **Rev:** Imperial eagle within inner circle **Mint:** Hall **Note:** Mule. Struck on 1/2 Thaler dies. Dav. #3334. Prev. KM#806.

Date	Mintage	VG	F	VF	XF	Unc
ND Rare	—	—	—	—	—	—

KM# 678 THALER

Silver **Ruler:** Ferdinand II **Mint:** Saint Veit **Note:** Dav. #3124. Varieties exist. Prev. KM#1603.

Date	Mintage	VG	F	VF	XF	Unc
1627 (g)	—	75.00	150	300	650	—
1628 (g)	—	75.00	150	300	650	—
1632	—	75.00	150	300	650	—

KM# 676 THALER

Silver **Ruler:** Ferdinand II **Obv:** Date below bust **Rev:** Crowned ornamented shield of arms **Mint:** Graz **Note:** Klippe. Prev. KM#382.

Date	Mintage	VG	F	VF	XF	Unc
1627 Rare	—	—	—	—	—	—

KM# 629.2 THALER

Silver **Ruler:** Leopold **Obv:** Different armor **Rev:** Order chain around arms **Rev. Legend:** ... TIROLIS **Mint:** Hall **Note:** Dav. #3338. Prev. KM#804.2.

Date	Mintage	VG	F	VF	XF	Unc
1628	—	45.00	100	200	300	—
1630	—	45.00	100	200	300	—
1632	—	45.00	100	200	300	—

KM# 700 THALER

Silver **Ruler:** Ferdinand II **Obv:** Laureate bust right with ruffled collar **Mint:** Olmutz **Note:** Dav. #3148. Prev. KM#1237.

Date	Mintage	VG	F	VF	XF	Unc
1628 H-N(I) Rare	—	—	—	—	—	—
1630 (o)/M-F Rare	—	—	—	—	—	—

KM# 714 THALER

Silver **Ruler:** Ferdinand III **Rev:** Radiant Madonna and child with HP monogram below **Rev. Legend:** FECIT MAGNA POTENS **Mint:** Glatz **Note:** Dav. #3359A. Prev. KM#A304.

Date	Mintage	VG	F	VF	XF	Unc
1629 (h)//(h)	—	350	600	1,100	1,950	—

KM# 746 THALER

Silver **Ruler:** Ferdinand II **Mint:** Fürth **Note:** Dav. #3167. Prev. KM#287.

Date	Mintage	VG	F	VF	XF	Unc
1630 CS Rare	—	—	—	—	—	—

KM# 749.1 THALER

Silver **Ruler:** Ferdinand II **Obv. Legend:** ...D. G. ROM. IMP. S. A. G. H. BO. REX. **Rev:** Large crown and arms **Rev. Legend:** ...BVRG... **Mint:** Graz **Note:** Dav. #3110. Prev. KM#384.

Date	Mintage	VG	F	VF	XF	Unc
1630	—	35.00	100	210	300	—
1631	—	35.00	100	210	300	—
1632	—	35.00	100	210	300	—
1632/1	—	35.00	100	210	300	—
1633	—	35.00	100	210	300	—
1633/2	—	35.00	100	210	300	—
1636	—	35.00	100	210	300	—

KM# 748 THALER

Silver **Ruler:** Ferdinand II **Obv:** Ornamented inner circle **Mint:** Graz **Note:** Dav. #3110A. Prev. KM#383.

Date	Mintage	VG	F	VF	XF	Unc
1630 Rare	—	—	—	—	—	—

KM# 749.3 THALER

Silver **Ruler:** Ferdinand II **Rev:** Crowned plain shield without ornamentation **Mint:** Graz **Note:** Dav. #3110B. Prev. KM#384.3.

Date	Mintage	VG	F	VF	XF	Unc
1631	—	35.00	100	210	300	—
1632	—	35.00	100	210	300	—

KM# 750 THALER

Silver **Ruler:** Ferdinand II **Mint:** Graz **Note:** Dav. #3110C. Klippe. Prev. KM#385.

Date	Mintage	VG	F	VF	XF	Unc
1632 Rare	—	—	—	—	—	—
1633/2 Rare	—	—	—	—	—	—
1636 Rare	—	—	—	—	—	—

KM# 629.3 THALER

Silver **Ruler:** Leopold **Rev. Legend:** ... AVSTIÆ (error) **Mint:** Hall **Note:** Dav. #3338A. Prev. KM#804.3.

Date	Mintage	VG	F	VF	XF	Unc
1632	—	35.00	85.00	200	300	—

KM# 629.4 THALER

Silver **Ruler:** Leopold **Obv:** Crowned 1/2-length figure right with scepter and sword **Obv. Legend:** LEOPOLDVS • D: G: ARCHIDVX • AVSTRIÆ **Rev:** Crowned arms within Order chain **Rev. Legend:** DVX • BVRGVND: — COMES • TIROLIS **Mint:** Hall **Note:** Dav. #3338B. Prev. KM#804.4.

Date	Mintage	VG	F	VF	XF	Unc
1632	—	35.00	85.00	200	300	—

KM# 783 THALER

Silver **Ruler:** Leopold **Rev. Legend:** ... TIROLI • **Mint:** Hall **Note:** Prev. KM#A804.3.

Date	Mintage	VG	F	VF	XF	Unc
1632	—	22.50	45.00	150	250	—

KM# 784 THALER

Silver **Ruler:** Leopold **Obv:** Fancier embroidery on jacket **Mint:** Hall **Note:** Prev. KM#A804.4.

Date	Mintage	VG	F	VF	XF	Unc
1632	—	22.50	45.00	150	250	—

KM# 785 THALER

Silver **Ruler:** Leopold **Mint:** Hall **Note:** Dav. #3338C. Klippe. Prev. KM#805.

Date	Mintage	VG	F	VF	XF	Unc
1632	—	450	750	1,950	3,500	—

KM# 817 THALER

Silver **Ruler:** Ferdinand II **Obv. Legend:** FERDINAN: II: D • - G • **Mint:** Graz **Note:** Dav. #3111. Prev. KM#381.

Date	Mintage	VG	F	VF	XF	Unc
1636	—	35.00	100	210	300	—

KM# 840 THALER

0.8330 Silver **Ruler:** Ferdinand III **Obv:** Laureate bust with lace collar right **Rev:** With flat-topped shield on breast **Mint:** Vienna **Note:** Dav. #3174. Varieties exist. Prev. KM#1826.

Date	Mintage	VG	F	VF	XF	Unc
1637 (b)	—	65.00	125	200	350	—
1638 (b)	—	65.00	125	200	350	—
1639 (b)	—	65.00	125	200	350	—
1640 (b)	—	65.00	125	200	350	—
1641 (b)	—	65.00	125	200	350	—
1642 (b)	—	65.00	125	200	350	—
1643 (b)	—	65.00	125	200	350	—
1644 (b)	—	65.00	125	200	350	—
1645 (b)	—	65.00	125	200	350	—
1646 (b)	—	65.00	125	200	350	—
1647 (b)	—	65.00	125	200	350	—
1648 (b)	—	65.00	125	200	350	—
1648 (c)	—	65.00	125	200	350	—
1649 (c)	—	65.00	125	200	350	—

KM# 841 THALER

0.8330 Silver **Ruler:** Ferdinand III **Mint:** Vienna **Note:** Klippe. Dav. #3174A. Prev. KM#1827.

Date	Mintage	VG	F	VF	XF	Unc
1637 Rare	—	—	—	—	—	—

KM# 857 THALER

Silver **Ruler:** Ferdinand III **Obv:** Laureate bust, date below **Rev:** Crowned ornamental arms with flat-topped shield **Mint:** Graz **Note:** Dav. #3185. Prev. KM#428.

Date	Mintage	VG	F	VF	XF	Unc
1638	—	45.00	100	250	500	—

KM# 858 THALER

Silver **Ruler:** Ferdinand III **Mint:** Saint Veit **Note:** Dav. #3192. Prev. KM#1626.

Date	Mintage	VG	F	VF	XF	Unc
1638	—	75.00	150	300	650	—
1642	—	75.00	150	300	650	—

KM# 881 THALER

Silver **Ruler:** Ferdinand III **Obv:** Punctuated date below bust - 1.6.4.0. **Mint:** Graz **Note:** Dav. #3186. Prev. KM#429.

Date	Mintage	VG	F	VF	XF	Unc
1640	—	45.00	100	250	500	—

KM# 882 THALER

0.8330 Silver **Ruler:** Ferdinand III **Obv:** Oval shield on eagle **Mint:** Vienna **Note:** Dav. #3175. Varieties exist. Prev. KM#1828.

Date	Mintage	VG	F	VF	XF	Unc
1640 (b)	—	75.00	150	250	400	—
1641 (b)	—	75.00	150	250	400	—
1643 (b)	—	75.00	150	250	400	—
1645 (b)	—	75.00	150	250	400	—

KM# 883 THALER

0.8330 Silver **Ruler:** Ferdinand III **Mint:** Vienna **Note:** Dav. #3175A. Prev. KM#1829.

Date	Mintage	VG	F	VF	XF	Unc
1640 Rare	—	—	—	—	—	—
1641 Rare	—	—	—	—	—	—

KM# 895 THALER

Silver **Ruler:** Ferdinand III **Obv:** Ornamental inner circle **Rev:** Date divided above crown **Mint:** Graz **Note:** Dav. #3187. Prev. KM#430.

Date	Mintage	VG	F	VF	XF	Unc
1641	—	45.00	100	250	500	—

KM# 896 THALER

Silver **Ruler:** Ferdinand III **Mint:** Graz **Note:** Dav. #3187A. Klippe. Prev. KM#431.

Date	Mintage	VG	F	VF	XF	Unc
1641	—	300	600	1,350	2,250	—

KM# 920 THALER

Silver **Ruler:** Ferdinand III **Obv:** Plain inner circles **Rev:** Date above crown **Mint:** Graz **Note:** Dav. #3189. Prev. KM#432.

Date	Mintage	VG	F	VF	XF	Unc
1644	—	35.00	100	200	450	—
1646	—	35.00	100	200	450	—
1650	—	35.00	100	200	450	—

KM# 924 THALER

Silver **Ruler:** Ferdinand III **Mint:** Saint Veit **Note:** Dav. #3194. Varieties exist. Prev. KM#1627.

Date	Mintage	VG	F	VF	XF	Unc
1645	—	75.00	150	300	650	—
1649	—	75.00	150	300	650	—
1650	—	75.00	150	300	650	—
1654	—	75.00	150	300	650	—
1657	—	75.00	150	300	650	—

KM# 929.1 THALER

Silver **Ruler:** Ferdinand III **Obv. Legend:** FERDINANDVS • III • D: G: MM. R: I: S: A: G: HVN: BO: REX. **Rev. Legend:** ARCHID: AVS: D: VX:, arms, BVR: C: TYR: C:, date **Mint:** Brunn **Note:** Dav. #3216. Prev. KM#223.1.

Date	Mintage	VG	F	VF	XF	Unc
1646 (o)	—	550	1,000	1,850	2,850	—
1648 (o)	—	550	1,000	1,850	2,850	—

KM# 932.1 THALER

Silver **Ruler:** Ferdinand Charles **Obv:** Bust right with date in front **Rev:** Crowned arms in Order chain **Mint:** Hall **Note:** Dav. #3365. Prev. KM#833.1.

Date	Mintage	VG	F	VF	XF	Unc
1646	—	75.00	150	275	550	—

KM# 930 THALER

Silver **Ruler:** Ferdinand III **Obv:** Date below bust **Rev:** Date divided by crown **Mint:** Graz **Note:** Dav. #3189A. Prev. KM#433.

Date	Mintage	VG	F	VF	XF	Unc
1646//1646	—	35.00	100	200	450	—

KM# 931 THALER

Silver **Ruler:** Ferdinand III **Mint:** Graz **Note:** Dav. #3189B. Klippe. Prev. KM#434.

Date	Mintage	VG	F	VF	XF	Unc
1646//1646	—	225	400	600	1,000	—

KM# 929.2 THALER

Silver **Ruler:** Ferdinand III **Obv. Legend:** ... ROM: IM: SE: AV: GE: HV: BO: REX • **Rev:** Eagle arms below eagle **Mint:** Brunn **Note:** Dav. #3217. Prev. KM#223.2.

Date	Mintage	VG	F	VF	XF	Unc
1647 (t)	—	550	1,000	1,650	2,500	—

KM# 957 THALER

Silver **Ruler:** Ferdinand III **Obv:** Larger laureate bust **Obv. Legend:** FERDINAND • III • D • G • ROM • IMP • S • A • G • H • B • REX • **Mint:** Graz **Note:** Dav. #3190. Prev. KM#435.

Date	Mintage	VG	F	VF	XF	Unc
1648	—	35.00	100	250	500	—
1649	—	35.00	100	250	500	—
1650	—	35.00	100	250	500	—
1651	—	35.00	100	250	500	—
1653	—	35.00	100	250	500	—
1654	—	35.00	100	250	500	—

KM# 958 THALER

0.8330 Silver **Ruler:** Ferdinand III **Obv:** Bust with plain collar **Rev:** Flat-topped shield of arms **Mint:** Vienna **Note:** Dav. #3177. Prev. KM#1830.1.

Date	Mintage	VG	F	VF	XF	Unc
1648	—	85.00	165	300	550	—
1649	—	85.00	165	300	550	—

KM# 959 THALER

0.8330 Silver **Ruler:** Ferdinand III **Obv:** Bust with plain collar and lapels **Mint:** Vienna **Note:** Dav. #3179. Prev. KM#1830.2.

Date	Mintage	VG	F	VF	XF	Unc
1648	—	85.00	165	300	550	—
1649	—	85.00	165	300	550	—

KM# 972 THALER

0.8330 Silver **Ruler:** Ferdinand III **Mint:** Vienna **Note:** Dav. #3180. Prev. KM#1831.

Date	Mintage	VG	F	VF	XF	Unc
1650 (c)	—	85.00	165	300	550	—

KM# 975 THALER

0.8330 Silver **Ruler:** Ferdinand III **Obv:** Bust with heavy drapery **Mint:** Vienna **Note:** Dav. #3181. Prev. KM#1832.

Date	Mintage	VG	F	VF	XF	Unc
1651 (c)	—	85.00	165	300	550	—

KM# 977 THALER

0.8330 Silver **Ruler:** Ferdinand III **Obv:** Bust with light drapery **Mint:** Vienna **Note:** Dav. #3183. Varieties exist. Prev. KM#1833.

Date	Mintage	VG	F	VF	XF	Unc
1652 (c)	—	100	200	375	750	—
1653 (c)	—	100	200	375	750	—
1654 (c)	—	100	200	375	750	—
1655 (c)	—	100	200	375	750	—

KM# 932.2 THALER

Silver **Ruler:** Ferdinand Charles **Obv:** Older, larger bust **Rev:** Smaller arms **Mint:** Hall **Note:** Dav. #3366. Prev. KM#833.2.

Date	Mintage	VG	F	VF	XF	Unc
1652	—	75.00	150	275	550	—

KM# 933.3 THALER

Silver **Ruler:** Ferdinand Charles **Obv:** Older, thinner bust **Mint:** Hall **Note:** Dav. #3367. Prev. KM#833.3.

Date	Mintage	VG	F	VF	XF	Unc
1654	—	50.00	120	250	500	—

KM# 1003 THALER

Silver **Ruler:** Ferdinand III **Obv:** Older laureate bust with short beard, date above **Mint:** Graz **Note:** Dav. #3191. Prev. KM#436.

Date	Mintage	VG	F	VF	XF	Unc
1657 HCK	—	200	350	600	1,150	—

KM# 1004 THALER

0.8330 Silver **Ruler:** Ferdinand III **Obv:** Large bust **Rev:** Crowned oval arms **Mint:** Vienna **Note:** Dav. #A3184. Prev. KM#1834.

Date	Mintage	VG	F	VF	XF	Unc
1657 (c)	—	100	200	350	750	—

KM# 1005 THALER

0.8330 Silver **Ruler:** Ferdinand III **Obv:** Small laureate bust right in plain inner circle, punctuated date below bust **Rev:** Crowned arms in flat-topped shield in Order collar and inner circle **Mint:** Vienna **Note:** Dav. #3184. Prev. KM#1835.

Date	Mintage	VG	F	VF	XF	Unc
1657	—	100	200	350	750	—

KM# 1118 THALER

1.7000 g., Silver **Ruler:** Leopold I **Mint:** Vienna **Note:** Dav. #3223. Prev. KM#1868.

Date	Mintage	VG	F	VF	XF	Unc
1658 (c)	—	350	700	1,250	2,500	—

KM# 1156 THALER

Silver **Ruler:** Leopold I **Obv:** Laureate bust right, wavy hair **Rev:** Hapsburg arms on breast of eagle **Mint:** Vienna **Note:** Dav. #3224. Prev. KM#1869.

Date	Mintage	VG	F	VF	XF	Unc
1659 (c)	—	300	550	1,100	2,000	—

KM# 1175 THALER

Silver **Ruler:** Leopold I **Obv:** Laureate bust right, date above **Obv. Legend:** LEOPOLDVS. -D. G. R.I. S. A. G. H. ET. B. REX. **Rev. Legend:** ... BVR. STYRIAE. ET. C. **Mint:** Graz **Note:** Dav. #3231. Prev. KM#463.

Date	Mintage	VG	F	VF	XF	Unc
1660	—	250	400	650	1,000	—
1662	—	250	400	650	1,000	—
1669 IGW	—	250	400	650	1,000	—

KM# 1176 THALER

Silver **Ruler:** Leopold I **Mint:** Saint Veit **Note:** Varieties exist. Dav. #3236. Prev. KM#1652.

Date	Mintage	VG	F	VF	XF	Unc
1660	—	400	750	1,500	2,500	—
1670	—	400	750	1,500	2,500	—

KM# 932.4 THALER
Silver **Ruler:** Ferdinand Charles **Obv:** Larger bust dividing legend at top **Rev:** Date above crown **Mint:** Hall **Note:** Dav. #3368. Prev. KM#833.4.

Date	Mintage	VG	F	VF	XF	Unc
1662	—	175	350	550	900	—

KM# 1200 THALER
Silver **Ruler:** Sigismund Franz **Rev:** Date above crown **Mint:** Hall **Note:** Dav. #3369. Prev. KM#854.

Date	Mintage	VG	F	VF	XF	Unc
1662 Rare	5,415	—	—	—	—	—

KM# 1237 THALER
Silver **Ruler:** Leopold I **Obv:** KM#643 **Rev. Legend:** DVV. BVRGVNDI: -COM: TYROLIS. **Mint:** Hall **Note:** Dav. #3239. Mule. Prev. KM#1237.

Date	Mintage	VG	F	VF	XF	Unc
1665	—	40.00	100	200	375	—

KM# 1238 THALER
Silver **Ruler:** Leopold I **Obv:** With lion's head in shoulder drapery **Rev. Legend:** ARCHID: AVST: -DVX. BV: CO: TYR **Mint:** Hall **Note:** Dav. #3240. Prev. KM#643.

Date	Mintage	VG	F	VF	XF	Unc
1665	—	40.00	100	200	400	—
1668	—	40.00	100	200	400	—

KM# 1239.1 THALER
Silver **Ruler:** Sigismund Franz **Obv. Legend:** ...AVS: **Rev:** Crown divides dates **Mint:** Hall **Note:** Dav. #3370. Prev. KM#855.1.

Date	Mintage	VG	F	VF	XF	Unc
1665	39,000	125	250	400	750	—

KM# 1239.2 THALER
Silver **Ruler:** Sigismund Franz **Obv. Legend:** ...AVST: **Rev:** Crown divides dates **Mint:** Hall **Note:** Dav. #3370A. Prev. KM#855.2.

Date	Mintage	VG	F	VF	XF	Unc
1665	Inc. above	125	250	400	750	—

KM# 1268.1 THALER
Silver **Ruler:** Leopold I **Rev:** Vienna arms on breast of eagle **Mint:** Vienna **Note:** Dav. #3225. Prev. KM#1870.1.

Date	Mintage	VG	F	VF	XF	Unc
1670 (r)	—	75.00	135	275	475	—

KM# 1268.2 THALER
Silver **Ruler:** Leopold I **Obv:** Large bust divides legend at bottom **Rev:** Larger Vienna arms **Mint:** Vienna **Note:** Dav. #3226. Prev. KM#1870.2.

Date	Mintage	VG	F	VF	XF	Unc
1671 (r)	—	65.00	125	250	450	—

KM# 1272 THALER
Silver **Ruler:** Leopold I **Obv. Legend:** ROM: IM: SE: AV: GE: HVN: BOH: **Rev:** Date divided by crown above arms **Mint:** Graz **Note:** Dav. #3232. Prev. KM#464.

Date	Mintage	VG	F	VF	XF	Unc
1671 IGW	—	60.00	125	250	400	—
1672 IAN	—	60.00	125	250	400	—
1674 IAN	—	60.00	125	250	400	—
1676 IAN	—	60.00	125	250	400	—
1678 IAN	—	60.00	125	250	400	—
1682 IAN	—	60.00	125	250	400	—
1684 IAN	—	60.00	125	250	400	—
1687 IAN	—	60.00	125	250	400	—
1688 IAN	—	60.00	125	250	400	—

KM# 1275.1 THALER
Silver **Ruler:** Leopold I **Obv:** Older bust **Rev:** Complex heart-shaped arms on eagle's breast **Mint:** Vienna **Note:** Dav. #3227. Prev. KM#1871.1.

Date	Mintage	VG	F	VF	XF	Unc
1672 Rare	—	—	—	—	—	—

KM# 1303.1 THALER

Silver **Ruler:** Leopold I **Obv:** Armored bust without lion's head in shoulder drapery **Rev:** Crowned arms within Order chain **Mint:** Hall **Note:** Dav. #3241. Prev. KM#644.1.

Date	Mintage	VG	F	VF	XF	Unc
1679	—	30.00	90.00	210	350	—
1680	—	30.00	90.00	210	350	—
1682	—	30.00	90.00	210	350	—
1683	—	30.00	90.00	210	350	—
1686	—	30.00	90.00	210	350	—

KM# 1308 THALER

Silver **Ruler:** Leopold I **Mint:** Hall **Note:** Dav. #3241A. Klippe. Prev. KM#645.

Date	Mintage	VG	F	VF	XF	Unc
1680 Rare	—	—	—	—	—	—

KM# 1275.2 THALER

Silver **Ruler:** Leopold I **Obv. Legend:** ...G. H. ET. B. REX. **Rev. Legend:** ARCHID. AVST. (mint mark)DVX. B. COM. TYR. **Mint:** Vienna **Note:** Dav. #3228. Prev. KM#1871.2.

Date	Mintage	VG	F	VF	XF	Unc
1681 Rare	—	—	—	—	—	—
1683 With mint mark	—	—	—	—	—	—
1683	—	—	—	—	—	—

KM# 1321 THALER

Silver **Ruler:** Leopold I **Obv:** Older laureate bust right **Rev:** Crowned arms in Order collar, crown divides date **Mint:** Saint Veit **Note:** Varieties exist. Dav. #3237. Prev. KM#1653.

Date	Mintage	VG	F	VF	XF	Unc
1682 I-R Rare	—	—	—	—	—	—
1693 H-L	—	700	1,150	1,850	3,200	—

KM# 1348.1 THALER

Silver **Ruler:** Leopold I **Obv. Legend:** ...D. G. (decoration) ROM: IMP: SE: AV: G: H: B: REX: **Mint:** Graz **Note:** Dav. #3233. Prev. KM#465.1.

Date	Mintage	VG	F	VF	XF	Unc
1690	—	40.00	100	210	350	—

KM# 1349 THALER

Silver **Ruler:** Leopold I **Obv:** Laureate bust within inner circle, lion face on shoulder **Rev:** Crowned arms in Order chain, crown divides date **Mint:** Hall **Note:** Dav. #3242. Prev. KM#646.

Date	Mintage	VG	F	VF	XF	Unc
1690	—	30.00	90.00	210	350	—
1691	—	30.00	90.00	210	350	—
1694	—	30.00	90.00	210	350	—

KM# 1303.2 THALER

Silver **Ruler:** Leopold I **Obv:** Bust with lion's head in ornate shoulder drapery **Rev:** Crowned arms within Order chain **Mint:** Hall **Note:** Dav. #3243. Prev. KM#644.2.

Date	Mintage	VG	F	VF	XF	Unc
1691	—	30.00	90.00	200	350	—
1693	—	30.00	90.00	200	350	—
1694	—	30.00	90.00	200	350	—

KM# 1275.3 THALER

Silver **Ruler:** Leopold I **Obv:** Older portrait **Rev. Legend:** ...TYRO: 16 (crown) **Mint:** Vienna **Note:** Dav. #3229. Prev. KM#1871.3.

Date	Mintage	VG	F	VF	XF	Unc
1692	—	35.00	100	210	350	—
1693	—	35.00	100	210	350	—
1695	—	35.00	100	210	350	—

KM# 1348.2 THALER

Silver **Ruler:** Leopold I **Obv. Legend:** ...D. G. -R. I. S. A... **Mint:** Graz **Note:** Dav. #3234. Prev. KM#465.2.

Date	Mintage	VG	F	VF	XF	Unc
1693	—	40.00	100	210	350	—

KM# 1303.3 THALER

Silver **Ruler:** Leopold I **Obv:** Legend continuous below bust **Rev:** Crowned arms within Order chain **Mint:** Hall **Note:** Dav. #3244. Prev. KM#644.3.

Date	Mintage	VG	F	VF	XF	Unc
1694	—	30.00	90.00	210	350	—

KM# 1303.4 THALER

Silver **Ruler:** Leopold I **Obv:** Old laureate bust right in inner circle **Obv. Legend:** LEOPOLDVS • D: G: ROM: IMP: SE: A: G: H: B: REX • **Rev:** Crowned arms within Order chain **Rev. Legend:** ARCHID: AVST: DVX: BV: COM: TYR: **Mint:** Hall **Note:** Dav. #3245. Varieties exist. Prev. KM#644.4.

Date	Mintage	VG	F	VF	XF	Unc
1694 IAK	—	30.00	90.00	210	350	—
1695	—	30.00	90.00	210	350	—
1695 IAK	—	30.00	90.00	210	350	—
1696 IAK	—	30.00	90.00	210	350	—
1698	—	30.00	90.00	210	350	—
1700	—	30.00	90.00	210	350	—

KM# 1275.4 THALER

Silver **Ruler:** Leopold I **Obv:** Older portrait **Rev. Legend:** ...TYRO: 16: (crown) **Mint:** Vienna **Note:** Dav. #3229A. Prev. KM#1871.4.

Date	Mintage	VG	F	VF	XF	Unc
1695	—	35.00	100	200	350	—

KM# 1275.5 THALER

Silver **Ruler:** Leopold I **Obv:** Fatter bust **Rev. Legend:** ...TYRO **Mint:** Vienna **Note:** Dav. #3230. Prev. KM#1871.5.

Date	Mintage	VG	F	VF	XF	Unc
1696	—	35.00	100	200	350	—
1698	—	35.00	100	200	350	—
1699	—	35.00	100	200	350	—
1700	—	35.00	100	200	350	—

KM# 1303.5 THALER

Silver **Ruler:** Leopold I **Obv:** Narrow bust **Rev:** Crowned arms within Order chain **Mint:** Hall **Note:** Dav. #3245A. Prev. KM#644.5.

Date	Mintage	VG	F	VF	XF	Unc
1696	—	30.00	90.00	210	350	—
1699	—	30.00	90.00	210	350	—

KM# 1348.3 THALER

Silver **Ruler:** Leopold I **Obv. Legend:** ...D. G. spray ROM: OIMP:... **Mint:** Graz **Note:** Varieties exist. Dav. #3235. Prev. KM#465.3.

Date	Mintage	VG	F	VF	XF	Unc
1698	—	40.00	100	200	350	—

KM# 1408 THALER

Silver **Ruler:** Leopold I **Mint:** Vienna **Note:** Dav. #3230A. Klippe. Prev. KM#1873.

Date	Mintage	VG	F	VF	XF	Unc
1700 Rare	—	—	—	—	—	—

KM# 786 1-1/4 THALER

Silver **Ruler:** Ferdinand II **Obv:** Laureate bust right in inner circle, date below bust **Rev:** Crowned arms in Order collar and inner circle **Mint:** Graz **Note:** Klippe. Prev. KM#386.

Date	Mintage	VG	F	VF	XF	Unc
1632 Rare	—	—	—	—	—	—

KM# 537 1-1/2 THALER

Silver **Ruler:** Ferdinand II **Obv:** Laureate bust right in inner circle **Rev:** Crown above five shields of arms in inner circle, date in legend **Mint:** Vienna **Note:** Klippe. Dav. #A3083. Prev. KM#1792.

Date	Mintage	VG	F	VF	XF	Unc
1624 (c) Rare	—	—	—	—	—	—

KM# 26 2 THALER

Silver **Ruler:** Ferdinand II **Obv:** Crowned and armored half figure with scepter on shoulder in inner circle **Rev:** Crowned flat-topped arms in Order collar of The Golden Fleece in inner circle, date in legend at upper left **Mint:** Graz **Note:** Dav. #3306. Prev. KM#571.

Date	Mintage	VG	F	VF	XF	Unc
1601 Rare	—	—	—	—	—	—
1602 Rare	—	—	—	—	—	—

KM# 27 2 THALER

Silver **Ruler:** Ferdinand II **Mint:** Graz **Note:** Dav. #3306A. Klippe. Prev. KM#572. Illustration reduced.

Date	Mintage	VG	F	VF	XF	Unc
1601	—	2,210	3,800	7,000	12,500	—

KM# 57.2 2 THALER

Silver **Ruler:** Rudolf II **Obv:** Bust of Rudolph II right in inner circle **Obv. Legend:** RVDOLPHVS II: DG: ROM: IM: SEM: AV: GER: HV: BO: REX • **Mint:** Hall **Note:** Dav. #3004. Legend error. Prev. KM#611.2.

Date	Mintage	VG	F	VF	XF	Unc
1604	—	325	600	1,200	2,000	—

KM# 57.1 2 THALER

57.1900 g., Silver **Ruler:** Rudolf II **Obv. Legend:** RVDOLPHVS II: D G ... **Mint:** Hall **Note:** Dav. #3004. Prev. KM#611.1.

Date	Mintage	VG	F	VF	XF	Unc
1604	—	220	425	825	1,500	—

KM# 69 2 THALER

Silver **Ruler:** Ferdinand II **Rev. Legend:** DVX • BVRGUNDI... **Mint:** Graz **Note:** Dav. #A3307. Prev. KM#575.

Date	Mintage	VG	F	VF	XF	Unc
1605 Rare	—	—	—	—	—	—

KM# 70 2 THALER

Silver **Ruler:** Ferdinand II **Mint:** Graz **Note:** Dav. #A3307A. Klippe. Prev. KM#576.

Date	Mintage	VG	F	VF	XF	Unc
1605 Rare	—	—	—	—	—	—

KM# 83 2 THALER

Silver **Ruler:** Rudolf II **Obv:** Armored bust in ruffled collar right **Mint:** Vienna **Note:** Dav. #3001. Prev. KM#1716.

Date	Mintage	VG	F	VF	XF	Unc
1607	—	450	750	1,250	2,000	—

KM# 105 2 THALER

Silver **Ruler:** Ferdinand II **Rev. Legend:** DVX • BVRGUNDI... **Mint:** Graz **Note:** Dav. #3309. Prev. KM#577.

Date	Mintage	VG	F	VF	XF	Unc
1609 Rare	—	—	—	—	—	—

KM# 106 2 THALER

Silver **Ruler:** Ferdinand II **Mint:** Graz **Note:** Dav. #A3309. Klippe. Prev. KM#578.

Date	Mintage	VG	F	VF	XF	Unc
1609 Rare	—	—	—	—	—	—

KM# 107 2 THALER

Silver **Ruler:** Matthias II **Obv:** Crowned bust in ruffled collar right in inner circle **Rev:** Crowned arms in Order collar in inner circle, date in legend **Mint:** Vienna **Note:** Titles as designated King of Bohemia. Dav. #A3037. Prev. KM#1747.

Date	Mintage	VG	F	VF	XF	Unc
1609 Rare	—	—	—	—	—	—

KM# 123 2 THALER

Silver **Ruler:** Ferdinand II **Mint:** Klagenfurt **Note:** Dav. #3313. Similar to 1 Thaler, KM#24. Local issue for Archduke Ferdinand. Prev. KM#992.

Date	Mintage	VG	F	VF	XF	Unc
1610 Rare	—	—	—	—	—	—
1611 Rare	—	—	—	—	—	—
1613 Rare	—	—	—	—	—	—
1620 Rare	—	—	—	—	—	—

KM# 131 2 THALER

Silver **Ruler:** Matthias II **Mint:** Vienna **Note:** Titles as King of Bohemia. Dav. #A3040. Prev. KM#1748.

Date	Mintage	VG	F	VF	XF	Unc
1611 Rare	—	—	—	—	—	—

KM# 145 2 THALER

Silver **Ruler:** Matthias II **Obv:** Smaller bust and crown **Mint:** Vienna **Note:** Titles as King of Bohemia. Dav. #A3041. Prev. KM#1749.

Date	Mintage	VG	F	VF	XF	Unc
1612	—	2,000	4,000	6,000	9,500	—

KM# 170 2 THALER

Silver **Ruler:** Maximilian **Mint:** Hall **Note:** Dav. #A3316. Similar to 1 Thaler, KM#166. Prev. KM#775.

Date	Mintage	VG	F	VF	XF	Unc
1613 Rare	—	—	—	—	—	—

KM# 189 2 THALER

Silver **Ruler:** Matthias II **Obv:** Laureate, armored bust right in inner circle **Rev:** Crowned imperial eagle with shield on breast with sword and scepter in inner circle, date in legend **Mint:** Vienna **Note:** Titles as Emperor. Dav. #A3042. Prev. KM#1750.

Date	Mintage	VG	F	VF	XF	Unc
1614	—	1,000	1,850	3,500	7,000	—

KM# 197 2 THALER

Silver **Ruler:** Matthias II **Rev:** Larger crown above eagle **Mint:** Vienna **Note:** Titles as Emperor. Dav. #A3044. Prev. KM#1751.

Date	Mintage	VG	F	VF	XF	Unc
1615	—	950	1,750	3,500	5,500	—

KM# 207 2 THALER

Silver **Ruler:** Matthias II **Rev:** Smaller crown above eagle **Mint:** Vienna **Note:** Titles as Emperor. Dav. #3045. Prev. KM#1752.

Date	Mintage	VG	F	VF	XF	Unc
1616	—	1,000	1,850	3,500	6,000	—
1617	—	1,000	1,850	3,500	6,000	—

KM# 229.1 2 THALER

Silver **Ruler:** Matthias II **Obv:** Laureate bust with wide ruffle **Mint:** Vienna **Note:** Titles as Emperor. Dav. #A3047. Thick planchet. Prev. KM#1753.1.

Date	Mintage	VG	F	VF	XF	Unc
1618	—	1,000	1,850	3,500	6,000	—

KM# 229.2 2 THALER

Silver **Ruler:** Matthias II **Mint:** Vienna **Note:** Titles as Emperor. Thin planchet. Prev. KM#1753.2.

Date	Mintage	VG	F	VF	XF	Unc
1619	—	1,000	1,850	3,500	6,000	—

KM# 271 2 THALER

Silver **Ruler:** Ferdinand II **Obv:** Crowned half-length figure right **Rev:** Crowned arms **Mint:** Klagenfurt **Note:** Prev. KM#975.

Date	Mintage	VG	F	VF	XF	Unc
1620 Rare	—	—	—	—	—	—

KM# 273.1 2 THALER

Silver **Ruler:** Ferdinand II **Mint:** Vienna **Note:** Dav. #A3074. Similar to 1 Thaler, KM#268.1. Prev. KM#1793.1.

Date	Mintage	VG	F	VF	XF	Unc
16Z0	—	325	550	1,100	1,850	—

KM# 272 2 THALER

Silver **Ruler:** Ferdinand II **Obv:** Crowned bust right in inner circle **Rev:** Crowned imperial eagle with flat-topped shield of arms on breast in inner circle, crown divides date **Mint:** Klagenfurt **Note:** Dav. #3113. Varieties exist. Prev. KM#976.

Date	Mintage	VG	F	VF	XF	Unc
1620	—	550	1,050	1,950	3,100	—

KM# 356 2 THALER

Silver **Ruler:** Ferdinand II **Obv:** Tall, thin crowned bust **Mint:** Klagenfurt **Note:** Dav. #3117. Prev. KM#977.

Date	Mintage	VG	F	VF	XF	Unc
1621 Rare	—	—	—	—	—	—

KM# 273.2 2 THALER

Silver **Ruler:** Ferdinand II **Obv:** Without bow knot on laureate wreath **Mint:** Vienna **Note:** Dav. #3075. Similar to 1 Thaler, KM#268.1. Prev. KM#1793.2.

Date	Mintage	VG	F	VF	XF	Unc
16Z1	—	325	550	1,100	1,850	—
16Z2	—	325	550	1,100	1,850	—

KM# 357 2 THALER

Silver **Ruler:** Ferdinand II **Obv:** Crowned bust right **Rev:** Heraldic imperial eagle **Mint:** Klagenfurt **Note:** Prev. KM#978.

Date	Mintage	VG	F	VF	XF	Unc
1621 Rare	—	—	—	—	—	—

KM# 355 2 THALER

Silver **Ruler:** Ferdinand II **Obv:** Crowned bust with high ruffled collar right, lion's face on shoulder **Obv. Legend:** FERDINANDVS • II • D • G • ROM • IMP • S • A • GER • HVNG • ET • BO • REX • **Rev:** Crowned imperial eagle, complex arms within Order chain on breast **Rev. Legend:** ARCHI • AVSTRIAE • DVX •. B - VRGVNDIAE • STYRIAE • ETC • **Mint:** Graz **Note:** Dav. #3301A. Varieties exist. Prev. KM#387.

Date	Mintage	VG	F	VF	XF	Unc
1621	—	275	550	1,100	1,850	—

KM# 457 2 THALER

Silver **Ruler:** Ferdinand II **Obv:** Standing figure right **Rev:** Heraldic imperial eagle **Mint:** Brunn **Note:** Klippe. Prev. KM#219.

Date	Mintage	VG	F	VF	XF	Unc
1623 GR Rare	—	—	—	—	—	—

KM# 273.3 2 THALER

Silver **Ruler:** Ferdinand II **Obv:** Older bust **Mint:** Vienna **Note:** Dav. #3077. Varieties exist. Prev. KM#1793.3.

Date	Mintage	VG	F	VF	XF	Unc
1623	—	325	550	1,100	1,850	—
1624	—	325	550	1,100	1,850	—

KM# 545 2 THALER

Silver **Ruler:** Ferdinand II **Obv:** Laureate bust with plain collar right in inner circle **Rev:** Crown above five shields of arms in inner circle, date in legend **Mint:** Vienna **Note:** Dav. #3082. Prev. KM#1795.

Date	Mintage	VG	F	VF	XF	Unc
1624	—	325	550	1,000	1,650	—
1625	—	325	550	1,000	1,650	—

KM# 546 2 THALER

Silver **Ruler:** Ferdinand II **Mint:** Vienna **Note:** Dav. #3082A. Klippe. Prev. KM#1796.

Date	Mintage	VG	F	VF	XF	Unc
1624 Rare	—	—	—	—	—	—

KM# 541 2 THALER

Silver **Ruler:** Ferdinand II **Obv:** Bust right **Rev:** Heraldic imperial eagle **Mint:** Brunn **Note:** Dav. #3145. Prev. KM#220.

Date	Mintage	VG	F	VF	XF	Unc
1624 B-(c) Rare	—	—	—	—	—	—

KM# 544 2 THALER

Silver **Ruler:** Ferdinand II **Obv:** Laureate half-figure right in inner circle **Mint:** Vienna **Note:** Dav. #A3080. Prev. KM#1794.

Date	Mintage	VG	F	VF	XF	Unc
1624	—	3,250	5,000	7,500	12,500	—

KM# 273.4 2 THALER

Silver **Ruler:** Ferdinand II **Obv:** Older ruffld collar laureate bust right **Obv. Legend:** + FERDINANDVS • II • D: G • RISAVG • G • HVN • BOH • REX **Rev:** Jeweled crown above imperial eagle **Rev. Legend:** ARCHID • AVS • DVX • (shield) BUR • GO • TYR • **Mint:** Vienna **Note:** Dav.#3079.

Date	Mintage	VG	F	VF	XF	Unc
1624	—	325	550	1,100	1,850	—

KM# 542 2 THALER

Silver **Ruler:** Ferdinand II **Mint:** Brunn **Note:** Hexagonal klippe. Dav. #3145A. Prev. KM#221.

Date	Mintage	VG	F	VF	XF	Unc
1624 B-(c) Rare	—	—	—	—	—	—

KM# 610 2 THALER

Silver **Ruler:** Ferdinand II **Rev:** Different decorations between shields **Mint:** Vienna **Note:** Dav. #A3087. Prev. KM#A1795.

Date	Mintage	VG	F	VF	XF	Unc
1625 (c) Rare	—	—	—	—	—	—

KM# 609.1 2 THALER

Silver **Ruler:** Leopold **Obv:** Crowned half-length armored figure with sword and scepter **Rev:** Wreath above crowned eagle **Mint:** Hall **Note:** Dav. #3335. Prev. KM#807.1.

Date	Mintage	VG	F	VF	XF	Unc
ND(1625)	—	195	350	950	1,500	—

KM# 611 2 THALER

Silver **Ruler:** Ferdinand II **Rev:** Crowned imperial eagle in inner circle, date in legend **Mint:** Vienna **Note:** Dav. #3090. Varieties exist. Prev. KM#1797.

Date	Mintage	VG	F	VF	XF	Unc
1625 (c)	—	325	550	1,000	1,650	—
1626 (c)	—	325	550	1,000	1,650	—
1629 (c)	—	325	550	1,000	1,650	—
1631 (c)	—	325	550	1,000	1,650	—
1633 (c)	—	325	550	1,000	1,650	—
1634 (c)	—	325	550	1,000	1,650	—
1636 (v)	—	325	550	1,000	1,650	—

KM# 605 2 THALER

Silver **Ruler:** Ferdinand II **Obv:** Laureate bust right in inner circle of laurel, date below bust **Rev:** Crowned flat-topped arms in Order collar and inner circle **Mint:** Graz **Note:** Dav. #3105. Prev. KM#388.

Date	Mintage	VG	F	VF	XF	Unc
1625	—	275	550	1,000	1,650	—

KM# 606 2 THALER

Silver **Ruler:** Ferdinand II **Mint:** Graz **Note:** Dav. #3105A. Klippe. Prev. KM#389.

Date	Mintage	VG	F	VF	XF	Unc
1625 Rare	—	—	—	—	—	—

KM# 607 2 THALER

Silver **Ruler:** Ferdinand II **Obv:** Date above bust **Rev:** Crowned oval arms **Mint:** Graz **Note:** Dav. #3107. Prev. KM#390.

Date	Mintage	VG	F	VF	XF	Unc
1625	—	275	550	1,100	1,900	—
16Z6/5	—	275	550	1,100	1,900	—
1632/30/26	—	275	550	1,100	1,900	—

KM# 608 2 THALER

Silver **Ruler:** Ferdinand II **Mint:** Graz **Note:** Dav. #3107A. Klippe. Prev. KM#391.

Date	Mintage	VG	F	VF	XF	Unc
1625	—	550	1,050	2,000	3,500	—
1626	—	550	1,050	2,000	3,500	—

KM# 639 2 THALER

Silver **Ruler:** Leopold **Subject:** Wedding of Leopold and Claudia **Obv:** Conjoined busts of Leopold and Claudia right **Rev:** Crowned eagle within inner circle, legend around **Mint:** Hall **Note:** Dav. #3331. Prev. KM#808.

Date	Mintage	VG	F	VF	XF	Unc
ND(1626)	—	120	250	700	1,000	—

KM# 640 2 THALER

Silver **Ruler:** Leopold **Mint:** Hall **Note:** Dav. #3331A. Klippe. Prev. KM#809.

Date	Mintage	VG	F	VF	XF	Unc
ND(1626) Rare	—	—	—	—	—	—

KM# 641 2 THALER

Silver **Ruler:** Leopold **Obv:** More ornate crowns and robes **Rev:**

Larger wreath above eagle **Mint:** Hall **Note:** Dav. #3332. Prev. KM#810.

Date	Mintage	VG	F	VF	XF	Unc
ND(1626)	—	140	275	950	1,500	—

KM# 643 2 THALER

Silver **Ruler:** Leopold **Obv:** Similar to KM#808. **Rev:** Wreath surrounds crowned eagle's head, without inner circle **Mint:** Hall **Note:** Dav. #3333. Prev. KM#822.

Date	Mintage	VG	F	VF	XF	Unc
ND(1626)	—	—	—	—	—	—

KM# A644 2 THALER

Silver **Ruler:** Leopold **Obv:** Jugate busts right **Obv. Legend:** LEOPOLDVS • ARCHID • AVS • ET • CLAVDIA • ARCHIDVCISA • AVS • MEDIC **Rev:** Wreath around crowned head of eagle with wings outspread **Rev. Legend:** ARCHIDVX: AVST: DVX: BVR: COM: TYROLIS **Shape:** Klippe **Mint:** Hall

Date	Mintage	VG	F	VF	XF	Unc
ND(1626)	—	—	—	—	—	—

KM# 609.2 2 THALER

Silver **Ruler:** Leopold **Obv:** Date in front of figure **Rev:** Large wreath above eagle **Mint:** Hall **Note:** Dav. #3336. Prev. KM#807.2.

Date	Mintage	VG	F	VF	XF	Unc
ND(1625)	—	195	325	950	1,500	—

KM# 642 2 THALER

Silver **Ruler:** Leopold **Obv:** Similar to KM#808 **Rev:** Similar to KM#810 **Mint:** Hall **Note:** Dav. #A3334. Mule. Prev. KM#821.

Date	Mintage	VG	F	VF	XF	Unc
ND(1626)	—	—	—	—	—	—

KM# 644 2 THALER

Silver **Ruler:** Leopold **Obv:** KM#808 **Rev:** Obverse KM#810 **Mint:** Hall **Note:** Dav. #A3334. Mule. Prev. KM#823.

Date	Mintage	VG	F	VF	XF	Unc
ND(1626)	—	—	—	—	—	—

KM# 609.3 2 THALER

Silver **Ruler:** Leopold **Mint:** Hall **Note:** Dav. #A3338. Similar to 1 Thaler, KM#629.3. Prev. KM#807.3.

Date	Mintage	VG	F	VF	XF	Unc
1628	—	195	325	950	1,560	—

KM# 718 2 THALER

Silver **Ruler:** Ferdinand II **Rev:** Similar to 1 Thaler, KM#1237 **Mint:** Olmutz **Note:** Dav. #3149. Prev. KM#1238.

Date	Mintage	VG	F	VF	XF	Unc
1629 (o) Rare	—	—	—	—	—	—

KM# 768 2 THALER

56.8300 g., Silver **Ruler:** Ferdinand II **Obv:** Plain inner circle, date below bust **Rev:** Ornamental shield of arms **Mint:** Graz **Note:** Dav. #A3109. Prev. KM#392.

Date	Mintage	VG	F	VF	XF	Unc
1631	—	275	550	1,100	2,000	—

KM# 769 2 THALER

Silver **Ruler:** Ferdinand II **Mint:** Graz **Note:** Klippe. Dav. #3109B. Prev. KM#394.

Date	Mintage	VG	F	VF	XF	Unc
1631 Rare	—	—	—	—	—	—

KM# 876.1 2 THALER

Silver **Ruler:** Ferdinand III **Obv:** Laureate bust right, date below **Rev:** Crowned oval arms **Mint:** Graz **Note:** Dav. #A3186. Broad planchet. Prev. KM#437.1.

Date	Mintage	VG	F	VF	XF	Unc
1639	—	275	500	1,100	2,500	—
1641/39	—	275	500	1,100	2,500	—

KM# 897 2 THALER

Silver **Ruler:** Ferdinand II **Mint:** Graz **Note:** Dav. #A3109A. Posthumous date. Prev. KM#393.

Date	Mintage	VG	F	VF	XF	Unc
1640/31	—	275	550	1,100	1,700	—

KM# 876.2 2 THALER

Silver **Ruler:** Ferdinand III **Rev:** Crowned flat-topped arms **Mint:** Graz **Note:** Dav. #B3186. Thick planchet. Prev. KM#437.2.

Date	Mintage	VG	F	VF	XF	Unc
1640	—	275	500	1,100	2,200	—
1641/0	—	275	500	1,100	2,200	—

KM# 884 2 THALER
Silver **Ruler:** Ferdinand III **Obv:** Laureate bust right in inner circle **Rev:** Crowned imperial eagle with flat-topped shield on breast in inner circle, date in legend **Mint:** Vienna **Note:** Dav. #3173. Varieties exist. Prev. KM#1836.

Date	Mintage	VG	F	VF	XF	Unc
1640 Rare	—	—	—	—	—	—
1641 Rare	—	—	—	—	—	—

KM# 925 2 THALER
Silver **Ruler:** Ferdinand III **Rev:** Oval arms **Mint:** Vienna **Note:** Dav. #3176. Prev. KM#1837.

Date	Mintage	VG	F	VF	XF	Unc
1645 Rare	—	—	—	—	—	—

KM# 933 2 THALER
Silver **Ruler:** Ferdinand III **Obv:** Without scalloped inner circle **Rev:** Crowned oval arms, date divided above **Mint:** Graz **Note:** Dav. #3188. Prev. KM#438.

Date	Mintage	VG	F	VF	XF	Unc
1646	—	275	500	950	1,500	—

KM# 934 2 THALER
Silver **Ruler:** Ferdinand Charles **Obv:** Uncrowned bust with lion face on shoulder **Mint:** Hall **Note:** Dav. #3363. Prev. KM#834.

Date	Mintage	VG	F	VF	XF	Unc
ND(1646)	—	165	325	950	1,500	—

KM# 937 2 THALER
Silver **Ruler:** Ferdinand Charles **Mint:** Hall **Note:** Klippe. Prev. KM#835.

Date	Mintage	VG	F	VF	XF	Unc
ND(1646) Rare	—	—	—	—	—	—

KM# 960 2 THALER
Silver **Ruler:** Ferdinand III **Mint:** Brunn **Note:** Dav. #3215. Similar to 1 Thaler, KM#929.1. Prev. KM#224.

Date	Mintage	VG	F	VF	XF	Unc
1648 (o) Rare	—	—	—	—	—	—

KM# 967 2 THALER
Silver **Ruler:** Ferdinand III **Mint:** Saint Veit **Note:** Dav. #3193. Varieties exist. Prev. KM#1628.

Date	Mintage	VG	F	VF	XF	Unc
1649	—	275	550	1,100	2,050	—
1650	—	275	550	1,100	2,050	—
1654	—	275	550	1,100	2,050	—
1657	—	275	550	1,100	2,050	—

KM# 968 2 THALER
Silver **Ruler:** Ferdinand III **Obv:** Armored bust right **Rev:** Flat-topped shield on eagle's breast **Mint:** Vienna **Note:** Dav. #3178. Prev. KM#A1838.

Date	Mintage	VG	F	VF	XF	Unc
1649 Rare	—	—	—	—	—	—

KM# 976 2 THALER
Silver **Ruler:** Ferdinand III **Mint:** Graz **Note:** Dav. #A3190. Similar to 3 Thaler, KM#877. Prev. KM#442.

Date	Mintage	VG	F	VF	XF	Unc
1651	—	275	500	950	1,500	—

KM# 984 2 THALER
56.5100 g., Silver **Ruler:** Ferdinand Charles **Obv:** Uncrowned bust with armored shoulder **Mint:** Hall **Note:** Dav. #3363A. Prev. KM#836.

Date	Mintage	VG	F	VF	XF	Unc
ND(1654)	—	140	300	950	1,500	—

KM# 985 2 THALER
57.2600 g., Silver **Ruler:** Ferdinand Charles **Obv:** Crowned bust with armored shoulder **Mint:** Hall **Note:** Dav. #3364. Prev. KM#837.

Date	Mintage	VG	F	VF	XF	Unc
ND(1654)	—	275	550	1,100	2,400	—

KM# 986 2 THALER
Silver **Ruler:** Ferdinand Charles **Obv:** Crowned bust with lion face on shoulder **Mint:** Hall **Note:** Dav. #3364A. Prev. KM#845.

Date	Mintage	VG	F	VF	XF	Unc
ND(1654)	—	375	725	1,400	2,750	—

KM# 992 2 THALER
Silver **Ruler:** Ferdinand III **Obv:** Laureate bust right with light drapery, date below bust in inner circle **Rev:** Crowned arms in flat-topped shield in Order collar and inner circle **Mint:** Vienna **Note:** Dav. #3182. Prev. KM#1838.

Date	Mintage	VG	F	VF	XF	Unc
1655 Rare	—	—	—	—	—	—

KM# 1269x 2 THALER
Silver, 65 mm. **Ruler:** Leopold I **Mint:** Graz **Note:** Varieties exist. Dav. #A3232. Prev. KM#466. Illustration reduced.

Date	Mintage	VG	F	VF	XF	Unc
1670 IAN	—	275	600	1,300	2,200	3,250
1670 IGW	—	275	600	1,300	2,200	3,500
1675 IAN	—	275	600	1,300	2,200	3,250
1678 IAN	—	275	600	1,300	2,200	3,250
1682 IAN	—	275	600	1,300	2,200	3,250
1684 IAN	—	275	600	1,300	2,200	3,250

KM# 1119.1 2 THALER
56.5300 g., Silver **Ruler:** Leopold I **Obv:** Lion's head in shoulder drapery **Mint:** Hall **Note:** Dav. #3247. Prev. KM#648.1.

Date	Mintage	VG	F	VF	XF	Unc
ND(1670)	—	165	325	900	1,550	—

KM# 1119.2 2 THALER
Silver **Ruler:** Leopold I **Obv:** Lion's head in ornate shoulder drapery **Mint:** Hall **Note:** Dav. #3249. Prev. KM#648.2.

Date	Mintage	VG	F	VF	XF	Unc
ND	—	165	325	900	1,550	—

KM# 1121 2 THALER
Silver **Ruler:** Leopold I **Obv:** Similar to 2 Thaler, KM#648 **Rev. Legend:** DVX • BVRGVNDIAE • COMES • TYROLIS **Mint:** Hall **Note:** Dav. #3253. Prev. KM#658.

Date	Mintage	VG	F	VF	XF	Unc
ND	—	110	220	750	1,500	—

KM# 1323 2 THALER
Silver **Ruler:** Leopold I **Obv:** Bust right in inner circle **Rev:** Crowned arms in Order collar, crown divides date **Mint:** Saint Veit **Note:** Dav. #3238. Prev. KM#1654.

Date	Mintage	VG	F	VF	XF	Unc
1683/2	—	1,250	2,200	3,500	5,000	—

KM# 1120.1 2 THALER
Silver **Ruler:** Leopold I **Obv:** Armored bust without lion's head **Mint:** Hall **Note:** Dav. #3250. Prev. KM#656.1.

Date	Mintage	VG	F	VF	XF	Unc
ND	—	120	275	850	1,500	—

KM# 1120.2 2 THALER
Silver **Ruler:** Leopold I **Obv:** Lion's head in ornate shoulder drapery **Mint:** Hall **Note:** Dav. #3251. Prev. KM#656.2.

Date	Mintage	VG	F	VF	XF	Unc
ND	—	12.00	275	850	1,500	—

KM# 1338 2 THALER
Silver **Ruler:** Leopold I **Obv:** Finer style armored bust, hair curls in rows **Mint:** Hall **Note:** Dav. #3252. Prev. KM#657.

Date	Mintage	VG	F	VF	XF	Unc
ND1686-96	—	110	250	800	1,500	—

KM# 645 2-1/2 THALER
Silver **Ruler:** Ferdinand II **Obv:** Laureate bust right in inner circle of laurel, date at top **Rev:** Crowned oval arms in Order collar and inner circle **Mint:** Graz **Note:** Klippe. Prev. KM#395.

Date	Mintage	VG	F	VF	XF	Unc
1626/5 Rare	—	—	—	—	—	—

KM# 59 3 THALER
Silver **Ruler:** Rudolf II **Mint:** Hall **Note:** Dav. #3003. Prev. KM#612.

Date	Mintage	VG	F	VF	XF	Unc
1604	—	825	1,400	2,400	4,500	—

KM# 190 3 THALER
Silver **Ruler:** Matthias II **Obv:** Laureate, armored bust right in inner circle **Rev:** Crowned imperial eagle with shield on breast with sword and scepter in inner circle, date in legend **Mint:** Vienna **Note:** Titles as Emperor. Dav. #B3042. Prev. KM#1754.

Date	Mintage	VG	F	VF	XF	Unc
1614 Rare	—	—	—	—	—	—

KM# 208 3 THALER
Silver **Ruler:** Matthias II **Obv:** Smaller crown above eagle **Mint:** Vienna **Note:** Titles as Emperor. Dav. #A3045. Prev. KM#1755.

Date	Mintage	VG	F	VF	XF	Unc
1616 Rare	—	—	—	—	—	—
1617 Rare	—	—	—	—	—	—

KM# 230 3 THALER
Silver **Ruler:** Matthias II **Obv:** Laureate bust with wide ruffle **Mint:** Vienna **Note:** Titles as Emperor. Dav. #3047. Thick planchet. Prev. KM#1756.

Date	Mintage	VG	F	VF	XF	Unc
1618 Rare	—	—	—	—	—	—

KM# 359 3 THALER
Silver **Ruler:** Ferdinand II **Obv:** Crowned bust right in inner circle **Rev:** Crowned imperial eagle in inner circle, arms in flat-topped circle, crown divides date **Mint:** Graz **Note:** Dav.#3101. Prev.#KM396.

Date	Mintage	VG	F	VF	XF	Unc
1621 Rare	—	—	—	—	—	—

KM# 547 3 THALER
Silver **Ruler:** Ferdinand II **Obv:** Laureate bust right **Obv. Legend:** FERDINANDVS. II. B in circle; D. G. R. I. S. A. G. H. B. REX. **Rev:** Crowned imperial eagle **Rev. Legend:** ARCHID. AVS. DVX, arms, BVR. MA. MO., date, CW **Mint:** Brunn **Note:** Dav. #A3145. Prev. KM#222.

Date	Mintage	VG	F	VF	XF	Unc
1624 B-(c) Rare	—	—	—	—	—	—

KM# 615 3 THALER
Silver **Ruler:** Ferdinand II **Mint:** Graz **Note:** Dav. #A3107. Prev. KM#397.

Date	Mintage	VG	F	VF	XF	Unc
1625	—	850	1,500	2,500	4,650	—

KM# 616 3 THALER
Silver **Ruler:** Ferdinand II **Obv:** Laureate bust right with lion face on shoulder, laureate chain surrounds **Rev:** Crowned round complex arms within Order chain **Mint:** Graz **Note:** Dav. #A3107A. Klippe. Prev. KM#399.

Date	Mintage	VG	F	VF	XF	Unc
1625	—	—	—	7,500	10,000	—
16Z6/5	—	—	—	7,500	10,000	—

KM# 617.1 3 THALER
Silver **Ruler:** Leopold **Mint:** Hall **Note:** Dav. #A3335. Similar to 2 Thaler, KM#609.1 Prev. KM#811.1.

Date	Mintage	VG	F	VF	XF	Unc
ND(1625)	—	1,400	2,500	4,000	6,000	—

KM# 617.2 3 THALER
Silver **Ruler:** Leopold **Mint:** Hall **Note:** Dav. #A3336. Similar to 2 Thaler, KM#807.2. Prev. KM#811.2.

Date	Mintage	VG	F	VF	XF	Unc
1626	—	1,400	2,500	3,850	5,500	—

KM# 647 3 THALER
Silver **Ruler:** Ferdinand II **Obv:** Undivided date at top **Rev:** Oval arms **Mint:** Graz **Note:** Dav. #B3107. Prev. KM#398.

Date	Mintage	VG	F	VF	XF	Unc
1626/5	—	825	1,500	2,850	5,000	—
1632/30/26	—	825	1,500	2,850	5,000	—

KM# 648 3 THALER
Silver **Ruler:** Leopold **Subject:** Wedding of Leopold and Claudia **Mint:** Hall **Note:** Dav. #A3331. Prev. KM#812.

Date	Mintage	VG	F	VF	XF	Unc
ND(1626)	—	—	—	—	—	—
ND(1626) Rare	—	—	—	—	—	—

KM# 649 3 THALER
Silver **Ruler:** Leopold **Mint:** Hall **Note:** Dav. #A3331A. Klippe. Prev. KM#813.

Date	Mintage	VG	F	VF	XF	Unc
ND(1626) Rare	—	—	—	—	—	—

KM# 770 3 THALER
Silver **Ruler:** Ferdinand II **Obv:** Plain inner circle, date below bust **Rev:** Ornamental shield of arms **Mint:** Graz **Note:** Dav. #3109. Prev. KM#400.

Date	Mintage	VG	F	VF	XF	Unc
1631	—	950	1,650	3,250	5,500	—

KM# 787 3 THALER
Silver **Ruler:** Ferdinand II **Obv:** Laureate bust right in inner circle **Rev:** Crowned imperial eagle in inner circle, date in legend **Mint:** Vienna **Note:** Varieties exist. Prev. KM#1798.

Date	Mintage	VG	F	VF	XF	Unc
1632 Rare	—	—	—	—	—	—
1636 Rare	—	—	—	—	—	—

KM# 877 3 THALER
Silver **Ruler:** Ferdinand III **Obv:** Laureate bust, date below **Rev:** Crowned arms **Mint:** Graz **Note:** Dav. #LS290. Broad planchet. Prev. KM#439. Illustration reduced.

Date	Mintage	VG	F	VF	XF	Unc
1639 Rare	—	—	—	—	—	—
1641 Rare	—	—	—	—	—	—

KM# 885 3 THALER

Silver **Ruler:** Ferdinand III **Obv:** Laureate bust right in inner circle **Rev:** Crowned imperial eagle with flat-topped shield on breast in inner circle, date in legend **Mint:** Vienna **Note:** Dav. #A3173. Prev. KM#1839.

Date	Mintage	VG	F	VF	XF	Unc
1640 Rare	—	—	—	—	—	—

KM# 886 3 THALER

Silver **Ruler:** Ferdinand III **Rev:** Oval arms **Mint:** Vienna **Note:** Dav. #A3175. Prev. KM#1840.

Date	Mintage	VG	F	VF	XF	Unc
1640 Rare	—	—	—	—	—	—

KM# 961 3 THALER

Silver **Ruler:** Ferdinand III **Mint:** Brunn **Note:** Dav. #3214. Similar to 1 Thaler, KM#929.1. Prev. KM#225.

Date	Mintage	VG	F	VF	XF	Unc
1648 (o) Rare	—	—	—	—	—	—

KM# 1122.1 3 THALER

Silver **Ruler:** Leopold I **Mint:** Hall **Note:** Similar to 2 Thaler, KM#1119.1. Dav. #3246. Prev. KM#655.1.

Date	Mintage	VG	F	VF	XF	Unc
ND Rare	—	—	—	—	—	—

KM# 1122.2 3 THALER

Silver **Ruler:** Leopold I **Mint:** Hall **Note:** Similar to 2 Thaler, KM#1119.2. Dav. #3248. Prev. KM#655.2.

Date	Mintage	VG	F	VF	XF	Unc
ND Rare	—	—	—	—	—	—

KM# 1388 3 THALER

Silver **Ruler:** Leopold I **Mint:** Vienna **Note:** Dav. #A3229. Similar to 1 Thaler, KM#1275.3. Prev. KM#1910.

Date	Mintage	VG	F	VF	XF	Unc
1695 Rare	—	—	—	—	—	—

KM# 650 3-1/4 THALER

94.0000 g., Silver **Ruler:** Ferdinand II **Obv:** Laureate bust right in inner circle of laurel, date in legend above head **Rev:** Crowned oval arms in Order collar and inner circle **Mint:** Graz **Note:** Prev. KM#401.

Date	Mintage	VG	F	VF	XF	Unc
1626 Rare	—	—	—	—	—	—

MB# 727 4 THALER

Silver **Ruler:** Ferdinand II **Obv:** Crowned busts of 3 emperors to left, date at end of legend **Obv. Legend:** ✠ MAXI. CARO. ET. FERD. D.G. RO. CÆS. REG. HISP. **Rev:** Imperial eagle, 2-fold arms of Castile and Austria on breast **Rev. Legend:** HVNG. BO. DAL. CRO. & ARCHID. AVST. D. BVR. **Mint:** Hall **Note:** Dav.#A8104.

Date	Mintage	VG	F	VF	XF	Unc
(15)90	—	—	—	—	—	—

KM# 191 4 THALER

Silver **Ruler:** Matthias II **Obv:** Laureate, armored bust right in inner circle **Rev:** Crowned imperial eagle with shield on breast with sword and scepter in inner circle, date in legend **Mint:** Vienna **Note:** Titles as Emperor. Dav. #3042. Prev. KM#1757.

Date	Mintage	VG	F	VF	XF	Unc
1614 Rare	—	—	—	—	—	—

KM# 618 4 THALER

Silver **Ruler:** Ferdinand II **Obv:** Laureate bust right in inner circle **Rev:** Crown above five shields of arms in inner circle, date in legend **Mint:** Vienna **Note:** Dav. #A3087A. Prev. KM#1799.

Date	Mintage	VG	F	VF	XF	Unc
1625 Rare	—	—	—	—	—	—

KM# 788 4 THALER

Silver **Ruler:** Ferdinand II **Rev:** Crowned imperial eagle in inner circle, date in legend **Mint:** Vienna **Note:** Dav. #3089. Varieties exist. Struck with Thaler and double thaler dies. Prev. KM#1800.

Date	Mintage	VG	F	VF	XF	Unc
1632 Rare	—	—	—	—	—	—

KM# 908 4 THALER

Silver **Ruler:** Ferdinand III **Obv:** Laureate bust right in inner circle **Rev:** Crowned imperial eagle in inner circle, date in legend **Mint:** Vienna **Note:** Dav. #A3173. Prev. KM#1841.

Date	Mintage	VG	F	VF	XF	Unc
1642 Rare	—	—	—	—	—	—

KM# 962 4 THALER

113.7500 g., Silver **Ruler:** Ferdinand III **Mint:** Brunn **Note:** Dav. #A3214. Similar to 1 Thaler, KM#929.1. Prev. KM#226.

Date	Mintage	VG	F	VF	XF	Unc
1648 (o) Rare	—	—	—	—	—	—

KM# 551 5 THALER

Silver **Ruler:** Ferdinand II **Obv:** Old ruffled bust right **Rev:** Crowned imperial eagle, shield on breast **Mint:** Vienna **Note:** Dav. #A3077. Prev. KM#A1801.

Date	Mintage	VG	F	VF	XF	Unc
1624 (c) Rare	—	—	—	—	—	—

KM# 550 5 THALER

Silver **Ruler:** Ferdinand II **Obv:** Laureate bust right with ruffled collar **Rev:** Crown above five shields of arms, crowned imperial eagle **Mint:** Vienna **Note:** Prev. KM#1801.

Date	Mintage	VG	F	VF	XF	Unc
1624 Rare	—	—	—	—	—	—

KM# 552 5 THALER

Silver **Ruler:** Ferdinand II **Obv:** Bust with plain collar **Mint:** Vienna **Note:** Prev. KM#1802.

Date	Mintage	VG	F	VF	XF	Unc
1624 Rare	—	—	—	—	—	—

KM# 619 5 THALER

Silver **Ruler:** Ferdinand II **Obv:** Laureate bust right in inner circle of laurel, date below bust **Rev:** Crowned arms in flat-topped shield in Order collar and inner circle **Mint:** Graz **Note:** Dav. #3105. Prev. KM#402.

Date	Mintage	VG	F	VF	XF	Unc
1625 Rare	—	—	—	—	—	—

KM# 361 12-1/2 THALER

Silver **Ruler:** Ferdinand II **Obv:** Silesian eagle within legend; M and HR in corners **Mint:** Glogau **Note:** Uniface. Klippe. Prev. KM#332. Illustration reduced.

Date	Mintage	VG	F	VF	XF	Unc
1621 Rare	—	—	—	—	—	—

REVOLUTIONARY COINAGE

1620-1621

KM# 239 3 KREUZER

Silver **Ruler:** Ferdinand II **Obv:** Eagle **Rev:** Monument **Mint:** Olmutz **Note:** Prev. KM#1255.

Date	Mintage	VG	F	VF	XF	Unc
1619 CC	—	10.00	18.00	40.00	70.00	—
16Z0 CC	—	10.00	18.00	40.00	70.00	—

KM# 237 3 KREUZER

Silver **Ruler:** Ferdinand II **Obv:** Checkered eagle **Rev:** Monument **Mint:** Brunn **Note:** Prev. KM#230.

Date	Mintage	VG	F	VF	XF	Unc
1619	—	25.00	36.00	70.00	120	—
1619 (h)	—	25.00	36.00	70.00	120	—
1620 (h)	—	25.00	36.00	70.00	120	—

KM# 241 12 KREUZER

Silver **Ruler:** Ferdinand II **Obv:** Eagle **Rev:** Monument **Mint:** Olmutz **Note:** Prev. KM#1256.

Date	Mintage	VG	F	VF	XF	Unc
1619 CC	—	12.00	27.50	48.00	70.00	—
1620 CC	—	12.00	27.50	48.00	70.00	—
16Z0 BZ	—	12.00	27.50	48.00	70.00	—

KM# 240 12 KREUZER

Silver **Ruler:** Ferdinand II **Obv:** Checkered eagle **Rev:** Monument **Mint:** Brunn **Note:** Prev. KM#231.

Date	Mintage	VG	F	VF	XF	Unc
1619 HP	—	35.00	60.00	140	275	—
1620 (h)	—	35.00	60.00	140	275	—

KM# 257 12 KREUZER

Silver **Ruler:** Ferdinand II **Mint:** Brunn **Note:** Klippe. Prev. KM#232.

Date	Mintage	VG	F	VF	XF	Unc
1620 (h)	—	—	—	—	—	—

KM# 242 24 KREUZER

Silver **Ruler:** Ferdinand II **Mint:** Olmutz **Note:** Similar to 48 Kreuzer, KM#259. Prev. KM#1257.

Date	Mintage	VG	F	VF	XF	Unc
1619 CC	—	12.00	27.50	60.00	100	—
1619	—	12.00	27.50	60.00	100	—
1620 CC	—	12.00	27.50	60.00	100	—

KM# 259 48 KREUZER

Silver **Ruler:** Ferdinand II **Mint:** Olmutz **Note:** Prev. KM#1258.

Date	Mintage	VG	F	VF	XF	Unc
1620 BZ	—	15.00	37.50	95.00	160	—
1621 BZ	—	15.00	37.50	95.00	160	—

KM# 267 THALER

Silver **Ruler:** Ferdinand II **Mint:** Olmutz **Note:** Prev. KM#1259.

Date	Mintage	VG	F	VF	XF	Unc
1620 CC Rare	—	—	—	—	—	—
1620 BZ Rare	—	—	—	—	—	—

KM# 276 5 DUCAT

17.5000 g., 0.9860 Gold 0.5547 oz. AGW **Ruler:** Ferdinand II **Mint:** Olmutz **Note:** Struck with 1 Thaler dies, KM#267. Prev. KM#1262.

Date	Mintage	VG	F	VF	XF	Unc
1620 BZ Rare	—	—	—	—	—	—

KM# 278 10 DUCAT

35.0000 g., 0.9860 Gold 1.1095 oz. AGW **Ruler:** Ferdinand II **Mint:** Olmutz **Note:** Struck with 1 Thaler dies, KM#267. Prev. KM#1263.

Date	Mintage	VG	F	VF	XF	Unc
1620 BZ Rare	—	—	—	—	—	—

KM# 279 25 DUCAT

87.5000 g., 0.9860 Gold 2.7737 oz. AGW **Ruler:** Ferdinand II **Mint:** Olmutz **Note:** Struck with 1 Thaler dies, KM#267. Prev. KM#1264.

Date	Mintage	VG	F	VF	XF	Unc
1620 BZ Rare	—	—	—	—	—	—

TRADE COINAGE

KM# 1282 1/12 DUCAT

0.2917 g., 0.9860 Gold 0.0092 oz. AGW **Ruler:** Leopold I **Obv:** Laureate bust right in inner circle, value at shoulder **Rev:** Crowned imperial eagle **Mint:** Vienna **Note:** Prev. KM#1874.

Date	Mintage	VG	F	VF	XF	Unc
1675	—	100	165	325	725	—

KM# 1283 1/6 DUCAT

0.5834 g., 0.9860 Gold 0.0185 oz. AGW **Ruler:** Leopold I **Obv:** Laureate bust right, value at shoulder **Rev:** Crowned imperial eagle in inner circle **Mint:** Vienna **Note:** Prev. KM#1875.

Date	Mintage	VG	F	VF	XF	Unc
1675	—	165	275	425	825	—

KM# 1261 1/4 DUCAT

0.8750 g., 0.9860 Gold 0.0277 oz. AGW **Ruler:** Leopold I **Obv:** Laureate bust right in inner circle, value at shoulder **Rev:** Crowned imperial eagle **Mint:** Graz **Note:** Prev. KM#467.

Date	Mintage	VG	F	VF	XF	Unc
ND	—	100	220	350	775	—
1669	—	100	220	350	775	—

KM# 1377 1/4 DUCAT

0.8750 g., 0.9860 Gold 0.0277 oz. AGW **Ruler:** Leopold I **Obv:** Laureate bust right in inner circle, value at shoulder **Rev:** Crowned imperial eagle **Mint:** Vienna **Note:** Prev. KM#1876.

Date	Mintage	VG	F	VF	XF	Unc
1694	—	140	220	425	825	—

KM# 1284 1/3 DUCAT

1.1667 g., 0.9860 Gold 0.0370 oz. AGW **Ruler:** Leopold I **Obv:** Laureate bust right in inner circle, value at shoulder **Rev:** Crowned imperial eagle in inner circle **Mint:** Vienna **Note:** Prev. KM#1877.

Date	Mintage	VG	F	VF	XF	Unc
1675	—	140	250	450	875	—

KM# 969 1/2 DUCAT

1.7500 g., 0.9860 Gold 0.0555 oz. AGW **Ruler:** Ferdinand Charles **Obv:** Armored bust right **Rev:** Tyrolean eagle with shield of arms on breast **Mint:** Hall **Note:** Prev. KM#838.

Date	Mintage	VG	F	VF	XF	Unc
ND(1649)	—	185	375	1,100	1,950	—

KM# 1389 1/2 DUCAT

1.7500 g., 0.9860 Gold 0.0555 oz. AGW **Ruler:** Leopold I **Obv:** Laureate bust right in inner circle **Rev:** Crowned imperial eagle in inner circle **Mint:** Vienna **Note:** Prev. KM#1878.

Date	Mintage	VG	F	VF	XF	Unc
1695	—	165	275	525	1,000	—

KM# 6 DUCAT

3.5000 g., 0.9860 Gold 0.1109 oz. AGW **Ruler:** Ferdinand II **Obv:** Ferdinand standing facing divides date in inner circle **Rev:** Crowned arms in Order collar **Mint:** Klagenfurt **Note:** Prev. KM#993.

Date	Mintage	VG	F	VF	XF	Unc
ND	—	220	500	1,350	2,450	—
1598	—	220	500	1,350	2,450	—
1599	—	220	500	1,350	2,450	—
1601	—	220	500	1,350	2,450	—
160Z	—	220	500	1,350	2,450	—
1602	—	220	500	1,350	2,450	—
1604	—	220	500	1,350	2,450	—
1606	—	220	500	1,350	2,450	—
1607	—	220	500	1,350	2,450	—

KM# 28 DUCAT

3.5000 g., 0.9860 Gold 0.1109 oz. AGW **Ruler:** Rudolf II **Mint:** Vienna **Note:** Prev. KM#1717.

Date	Mintage	VG	F	VF	XF	Unc
1601	—	220	450	1,250	2,500	—
1602	—	220	450	1,250	2,500	—
1603	—	220	450	1,250	2,500	—
1604	—	220	450	1,250	2,500	—
1605	—	220	450	1,250	2,500	—
1606	—	220	450	1,250	2,500	—
1607	—	220	450	1,250	2,500	—
1608	—	220	450	1,250	2,500	—

KM# 97 DUCAT

3.5000 g., 0.9860 Gold 0.1109 oz. AGW **Ruler:** Ferdinand II **Obv:** Standing figure right divides date in inner circle **Mint:** Klagenfurt **Note:** Prev. KM#994.

Date	Mintage	VG	F	VF	XF	Unc
1608	—	220	500	1,350	2,450	—
1609	—	220	500	1,350	2,450	—
1610	—	220	500	1,350	2,450	—
1611	—	220	500	1,350	2,450	—
1612	—	220	500	1,350	2,450	—
1613	—	220	500	1,350	2,450	—
1614	—	220	500	1,350	2,450	—
1615	—	220	500	1,350	2,450	—
1616	—	220	500	1,350	2,450	—
1617	—	220	500	1,350	2,450	—
1618	—	220	500	1,350	2,450	—
1619	—	—	—	—	—	—
1620	—	—	—	—	—	—

KM# 5.1 DUCAT

3.5000 g., 0.9860 Gold 0.1109 oz. AGW **Ruler:** Ferdinand II **Obv:** Crowned and armored standing figure of Ferdinand facing holding scepter over right shoulder, date between feet **Obv. Legend:** FERDINANDVS - D • G • ARCHIDVX • **Rev:** Crowned 12-fold arms with central shield of Styria in Spanish shield, Order of Golden Fleece around, date divided at left under crown and at right **Rev. Legend:** AVSTRIÆ • DVX • - BVRGVNDI • STYRI • **Mint:** Graz **Note:** Prev. KM#573. Fr.#(119).

Date	Mintage	VG	F	VF	XF	Unc
(1)608//(1)608	—	275	550	1,300	2,500	—

KM# 109 DUCAT

3.5000 g., 0.9860 Gold 0.1109 oz. AGW **Ruler:** Matthias II **Obv:** Bust right **Rev:** Crowned arms **Mint:** Vienna **Note:** Prev. KM#1758.

Date	Mintage	VG	F	VF	XF	Unc
1609	—	180	375	1,100	2,000	—
1610	—	180	375	1,100	2,000	—
1611 (b)	—	180	375	1,100	2,000	—
1612 (c)	—	180	375	1,100	2,000	—

KM# 5.2 DUCAT

3.5000 g., 0.9860 Gold 0.1109 oz. AGW **Ruler:** Ferdinand II **Obv:** Crowned and armored standing Ferdinand facing with hands on hips **Obv. Legend:** FERDINANDV - S - D • G • ARCHIDVX • **Rev:** Crowned 12-fold arms with central shield of Styria in Spanish shield divide date, Order of Golden Fleece around **Rev. Legend:** AVSTRIÆ • DVX • - BVRGVNDI • STYRI • **Mint:** Graz **Note:** Fr.#119.

Date	Mintage	VG	F	VF	XF	Unc
1609	—	300	600	1,250	2,200	—

KM# 108 DUCAT

3.5000 g., 0.9860 Gold 0.1109 oz. AGW **Ruler:** Maximilian **Mint:** Hall **Note:** Prev. KM#777.

Date	Mintage	VG	F	VF	XF	Unc
ND(1609-12)	5,539	425	1,250	3,500	6,000	—

KM# 5.3 DUCAT

3.5000 g., 0.9860 Gold 0.1109 oz. AGW **Ruler:** Ferdinand II **Obv:** Crowned and armored Ferdinand facing holding sceptre over right shoulder, date between feet **Obv. Legend:** FERDINANDV - S - D • G • ARCHIDVX **Rev:** Crowned 12-fold arms with central shield of Syria in Spanish shield, Order of Golden Fleece around, date divided by crown at top **Rev. Legend:** AVSTRIÆ • DVX • - BVRG • STYRIÆ • **Mint:** Graz **Note:** Fr.#119.

Date	Mintage	VG	F	VF	XF	Unc
1610	—	300	600	1,200	2,000	—

KM# 147 DUCAT

3.5000 g., 0.9860 Gold 0.1109 oz. AGW **Ruler:** Matthias II **Obv:** Matthias standing right with scepter and orb **Rev:** Crowned imperial eagle with large shield **Mint:** Vienna **Note:** Prev. KM#1759.

Date	Mintage	VG	F	VF	XF	Unc
1612	—	220	450	1,400	2,200	—
1613	—	220	450	1,400	2,200	—
1614	—	220	450	1,400	2,200	—
1617 (c)	—	220	450	1,400	2,200	—
1617 (t)	—	220	450	1,400	2,200	—
1618	—	220	450	1,400	2,200	—

KM# 146 DUCAT

3.5000 g., 0.9860 Gold 0.1109 oz. AGW **Ruler:** Maximilian **Obv:** Armored figure standing 3/4 right **Rev:** Crowned arms **Mint:** Hall **Note:** Prev. KM#778.

Date	Mintage	VG	F	VF	XF	Unc
ND(1612)	—	425	1,250	3,500	6,000	—

KM# 171 DUCAT

3.5000 g., 0.9860 Gold 0.1109 oz. AGW **Ruler:** Ferdinand II **Rev:** Crowned ornamented oval arms **Mint:** Graz **Note:** Prev. KM#574.

Date	Mintage	VG	F	VF	XF	Unc
1613	—	375	850	2,200	5,500	—
1616	—	375	850	2,200	5,500	—
1617	—	375	850	2,200	5,500	—

KM# 5.4 DUCAT

3.5000 g., 0.9860 Gold 0.1109 oz. AGW **Ruler:** Ferdinand II **Obv:** Standing crowned and armored Ferdinand holding scepter over right shoulder, date between feet **Obv. Legend:** FERDINANDV - D • - G • ARCHIDVX • **Rev:** Crowned oval 8-fold arms in baroque frame, Order of Golden Fleece around, date divided by crown at top **Rev. Legend:** AVSTRIÆ • DVX • - BVRG • STYRIÆ • **Mint:** Graz **Note:** Fr.#119.

Date	Mintage	VG	F	VF	XF	Unc
1613	—	300	600	1,200	2,000	—

KM# 231 DUCAT

3.5000 g., 0.9860 Gold 0.1109 oz. AGW **Ruler:** Maximilian **Obv:** Arms of Tyrol in inner circle **Rev:** Crowned arms of Austria in inner circle **Mint:** Hall **Note:** Interregnum in Tyrol. Prev. KM#781.

Date	Mintage	VG	F	VF	XF	Unc
1618	1,971	550	1,650	3,650	6,500	—
1619	—	550	1,650	3,650	6,500	—

KM# 247 DUCAT

3.5000 g., 0.9860 Gold 0.1109 oz. AGW **Ruler:** Friedrich **Obv:** Ferdinand II standing facing in inner circle **Rev:** Crowned arms in inner circle, crown divides date **Mint:** Klagenfurt **Note:** Prev. KM#979.

Date	Mintage	VG	F	VF	XF	Unc
ND	—	220	450	1,100	1,950	—
1619	—	220	450	1,100	1,950	—
1620	—	220	450	1,100	1,950	—
1621	—	220	450	1,100	1,950	—
1622	—	220	450	1,100	1,950	—

KM# 246 DUCAT

3.5000 g., 0.9860 Gold 0.1109 oz. AGW **Ruler:** Leopold **Mint:** Hall **Note:** Prev. KM#814.

Date	Mintage	VG	F	VF	XF	Unc
ND(1619) Rare; CO monogram	—	—	—	—	—	—

KM# 248 DUCAT

3.5000 g., 0.9860 Gold 0.1109 oz. AGW **Ruler:** Matthias II **Obv:** Matthias standing facing **Mint:** Vienna **Note:** Prev. KM#1760.

Date	Mintage	VG	F	VF	XF	Unc
1619	—	220	450	1,400	2,200	—

KM# 274 DUCAT
3.5000 g., 0.9860 Gold 0.1109 oz. AGW **Ruler:** Ferdinand II **Mint:** Vienna **Note:** Prev. KM#1803.

Date	Mintage	VG	F	VF	XF	Unc
1620 (c)	—	180	260	600	1,900	—
1622 (c)	—	180	260	600	1,900	—
1628 (c)	—	180	260	600	1,900	—
1629 (c)	—	180	260	600	1,900	—
1630 (c)	—	180	260	600	1,900	—
1631 (c)	—	180	260	600	1,900	—
1632 (c)	—	180	260	600	1,900	—
1633 (c)	—	180	260	600	1,900	—
1634 (c)	—	180	260	600	1,900	—

KM# 363 DUCAT
3.5000 g., 0.9860 Gold 0.1109 oz. AGW **Ruler:** Ferdinand II **Obv:** Seated figure **Rev:** Heraldic imperial eagle **Mint:** Klagenfurt **Note:** Prev. KM#980.

Date	Mintage	VG	F	VF	XF	Unc
1621	—	750	1,650	3,850	6,750	—

KM# 364 DUCAT
3.5000 g., 0.9860 Gold 0.1109 oz. AGW **Ruler:** Ferdinand II **Obv:** Seated figure **Rev:** Heraldic imperial eagle **Mint:** Klagenfurt **Note:** Prev. KM#995.

Date	Mintage	VG	F	VF	XF	Unc
1621	—	750	1,650	3,850	6,750	—

KM# 425 DUCAT
3.5000 g., 0.9860 Gold 0.1109 oz. AGW **Ruler:** Ferdinand II **Obv:** Facing ruler seated on throne in inner circle **Rev:** Crowned imperial eagle in inner circle, crown divides date **Mint:** Graz **Note:** Prev. KM#403.

Date	Mintage	VG	F	VF	XF	Unc
1622	—	275	550	1,150	2,200	—
1623	—	275	550	1,150	2,200	—
1625	—	275	550	1,150	2,200	—
1627	—	275	550	1,150	2,200	—

KM# 426 DUCAT
3.5000 g., 0.9860 Gold 0.1109 oz. AGW **Ruler:** Ferdinand II **Obv:** Seated figure **Rev:** Heraldic imperial eagle **Mint:** Saint Veit **Note:** Prev. KM#1604.

Date	Mintage	VG	F	VF	XF	Unc
1622	—	220	450	1,100	2,000	—
1625	—	220	450	1,100	2,000	—

KM# 460 DUCAT
3.5000 g., 0.9860 Gold 0.1109 oz. AGW **Ruler:** Ferdinand II **Mint:** Graz **Note:** Prev. KM#404.

Date	Mintage	VG	F	VF	XF	Unc
1623	—	180	300	625	1,800	—
1625	—	180	300	625	1,800	—
1627	—	180	300	625	1,800	—
1629	—	180	300	625	1,800	—
1631	—	180	300	625	1,800	—
1633	—	180	300	625	1,800	—

KM# 620 DUCAT
3.5000 g., 0.9860 Gold 0.1109 oz. AGW **Ruler:** Leopold **Obv:** Crowned bust **Mint:** Hall **Note:** Prev. KM#817.

Date	Mintage	VG	F	VF	XF	Unc
ND(1625-30)	—	—	—	—	—	—
1631	—	—	—	—	—	—

KM# 657 DUCAT
3.5000 g., 0.9860 Gold 0.1109 oz. AGW **Ruler:** Ferdinand II **Mint:** Hall **Note:** Prev. KM#616.

Date	Mintage	VG	F	VF	XF	Unc
ND(ca.1626)	—	325	650	1,400	3,250	—

KM# 681 DUCAT
3.5000 g., 0.9860 Gold 0.1109 oz. AGW **Ruler:** Ferdinand II **Obv:** Standing figure right **Rev:** Heraldic imperial eagle **Mint:** Saint Veit **Note:** Prev. KM#1605.

Date	Mintage	VG	F	VF	XF	Unc
1627	—	220	450	1,100	2,000	—

KM# 723 DUCAT
3.5000 g., 0.9860 Gold 0.1109 oz. AGW **Ruler:** Ferdinand II **Obv:** Ferdinand II standing right **Rev:** Heraldic imperial eagle **Mint:** Olmutz **Note:** Prev. KM#1239.

Date	Mintage	VG	F	VF	XF	Unc
1629 (o)	—	220	450	1,100	2,000	—

KM# 757 DUCAT
3.5000 g., 0.9860 Gold 0.1109 oz. AGW **Ruler:** Leopold **Obv:** Standing figure with scepter facing front **Rev:** Standing saint **Mint:** Hall **Note:** Prev. KM#816.

Date	Mintage	VG	F	VF	XF	Unc
ND(1630-32)	—	350	1,000	2,750	4,250	—

KM# 758 DUCAT
3.5000 g., 0.9860 Gold 0.1109 oz. AGW **Ruler:** Ferdinand II **Obv:** Bust right **Mint:** Olmutz **Note:** Prev. KM#1240.

Date	Mintage	VG	F	VF	XF	Unc
1630 MF	—	275	550	1,400	2,750	—

KM# 771 DUCAT
3.5000 g., 0.9860 Gold 0.1109 oz. AGW **Ruler:** Leopold **Obv:** Arms in Order chain, legend **Obv. Legend:** LEOPOLDVS • D - G:... **Rev:** St. Leopold standing facing with banner, holding church model in left hand **Note:** Posthumous issue. Fr.#119a. Prev. KM#283.

Date	Mintage	VG	F	VF	XF	Unc
ND(1631-34)	—	1,150	2,300	4,600	7,800	—

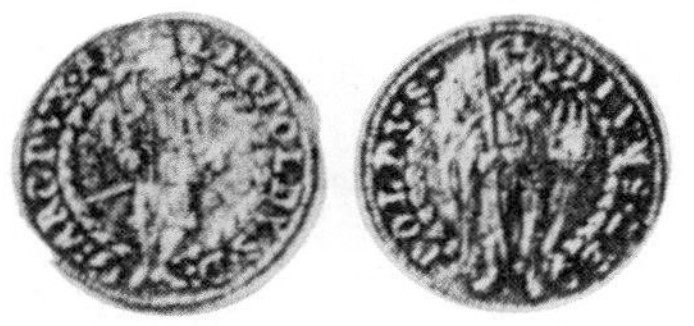

KM# 772 DUCAT
3.5000 g., 0.9860 Gold 0.1109 oz. AGW **Ruler:** Leopold **Obv:** Standing figure of Leopold right in inner circle **Rev:** Standing figure of St. Leopold right with banner in inner circle **Mint:** Hall **Note:** Prev. KM#815.

Date	Mintage	VG	F	VF	XF	Unc
ND	—	300	1,000	2,750	3,850	—
1631	—	300	1,000	2,750	3,850	—

KM# 808 DUCAT
3.5000 g., 0.9860 Gold 0.1109 oz. AGW **Ruler:** Ferdinand Charles **Obv:** Armored bust right **Rev:** Crowned oval arms in Order collar **Mint:** Hall **Note:** Prev. KM#839.

Date	Mintage	VG	F	VF	XF	Unc
ND Rare	—	—	—	—	—	—

KM# 809 DUCAT
3.5000 g., 0.9860 Gold 0.1109 oz. AGW **Ruler:** Ferdinand Charles **Obv:** Standing figure of Ferdinand Karl right in laurel circle **Rev:** Standing figure of St. Leopold facing with banner in laurel circle **Mint:** Hall **Note:** Prev. KM#840.

Date	Mintage	VG	F	VF	XF	Unc
ND	—	220	450	1,400	2,000	—

KM# 860 DUCAT
3.5000 g., 0.9860 Gold 0.1109 oz. AGW **Ruler:** Ferdinand III **Obv:** Ferdinand III standing facing in inner circle **Rev:** Crowned imperial eagle, crown divides date **Mint:** Graz **Note:** Prev. KM#440.

Date	Mintage	VG	F	VF	XF	Unc
1638	—	180	450	850	2,000	—
1640	—	180	450	850	2,000	—
1643	—	180	450	850	2,000	—
1644	—	180	450	850	2,000	—
1645	—	180	450	850	2,000	—
1647	—	180	450	850	2,000	—
1648	—	180	450	850	2,000	—
1652	—	180	450	850	2,000	—
1657	—	180	450	850	2,000	—

KM# 861 DUCAT
3.5000 g., 0.9860 Gold 0.1109 oz. AGW **Ruler:** Ferdinand III **Mint:** Saint Veit **Note:** Klippe. Prev. KM#1630.

Date	Mintage	VG	F	VF	XF	Unc
1638	—	325	550	1,250	2,750	—

KM# 878 DUCAT
3.5000 g., 0.9860 Gold 0.1109 oz. AGW **Ruler:** Ferdinand III **Obv:** Ferdinand III standing right in inner circle **Rev:** Crowned imperial eagle in inner circle **Mint:** Vienna **Note:** Prev. KM#1842.

Date	Mintage	VG	F	VF	XF	Unc
1639	—	180	325	575	1,650	—
1641	—	180	325	575	1,650	—
1642	—	180	325	575	1,650	—
1645	—	180	325	575	1,650	—
1646	—	180	325	575	1,650	—
1647	—	180	325	575	1,650	—

KM# 950 DUCAT
3.5000 g., 0.9860 Gold 0.1109 oz. AGW **Ruler:** Ferdinand III **Obv:** Crowned shield of arms added at each side of standing figure **Mint:** Vienna **Note:** Prev. KM#1843.

Date	Mintage	VG	F	VF	XF	Unc
1647	—	180	325	575	1,650	—
1648	—	180	325	575	1,650	—
1651	—	180	325	575	1,650	—
1652	—	180	325	575	1,650	—
1653	—	180	325	575	1,650	—
1654	—	180	325	575	1,650	—
1655	—	180	325	575	1,650	—
1656	—	180	325	575	1,650	—
1657	—	180	325	575	1,650	—

KM# 948 DUCAT
3.5000 g., 0.9860 Gold 0.1109 oz. AGW **Ruler:** Ferdinand III **Obv:** Laureate bust right **Rev:** Crowned imperial eagle, crown divides date **Mint:** Brunn **Note:** Prev. KM#227.

Date	Mintage	VG	F	VF	XF	Unc
1647	—	300	550	1,100	2,000	—

KM# 949 DUCAT
3.5000 g., 0.9860 Gold 0.1109 oz. AGW **Ruler:** Ferdinand III **Obv:** Ferdinand III standing right in inner circle **Rev:** Crowned imperial eagle, date in legend **Mint:** Saint Veit **Note:** Prev. KM#1629.

Date	Mintage	VG	F	VF	XF	Unc
1647	—	275	500	1,000	1,800	—

KM# 1158 DUCAT
3.5000 g., 0.9860 Gold 0.1109 oz. AGW **Ruler:** Leopold I **Obv:** Laureate head right in inner circle **Rev:** Crowned imperial eagle in inner circle, crown divides date **Mint:** Graz **Note:** Prev. KM#468.

Date	Mintage	VG	F	VF	XF	Unc
1659	—	200	425	825	1,750	—
1661	—	200	425	825	1,750	—
1667	—	200	425	825	1,750	—

KM# 1159 DUCAT
3.5000 g., 0.9860 Gold 0.1109 oz. AGW **Ruler:** Leopold I **Obv:** Leopold I on horseback right **Mint:** Graz **Note:** Prev. KM#469.

Date	Mintage	VG	F	VF	XF	Unc
1659	—	875	2,500	4,750	7,900	—
1660	—	875	2,500	4,750	7,900	—
1661	—	875	2,500	4,750	7,900	—

KM# 1181 DUCAT
3.5000 g., 0.9860 Gold 0.1109 oz. AGW **Ruler:** Leopold I **Mint:** Graz **Note:** Prev. KM#471.

Date	Mintage	VG	F	VF	XF	Unc
1660	—	180	375	750	1,650	—
1661	—	180	375	750	1,650	—
1667	—	180	375	750	1,650	—
1676 IAN	—	180	375	750	1,650	—
1679 IAN	—	180	375	750	1,650	—
1680 IAN	—	180	375	750	1,650	—
1682 IAN	—	180	375	750	1,650	—

KM# 1182 DUCAT

3.5000 g., 0.9860 Gold 0.1109 oz. AGW **Ruler:** Leopold I **Obv:** Leopold standing right flanked by crowned shields in inner circle **Rev:** Crowned imperial eagle in inner circle, date in legend **Mint:** Vienna **Note:** Prev. KM#1879.

Date	Mintage	VG	F	VF	XF	Unc
1660	—	275	550	1,100	2,200	—

KM# 1212 DUCAT

3.5000 g., 0.9860 Gold 0.1109 oz. AGW **Ruler:** Sigismund Franz **Obv:** Bust right **Rev:** Crowned arms in Order collar **Mint:** Hall **Note:** Prev. KM#856.

Date	Mintage	F	VF	XF	Unc	BU
ND(1663-65) Rare	4,233	—	—	—	—	—

KM# 1251 DUCAT

3.5000 g., 0.9860 Gold 0.1109 oz. AGW **Ruler:** Leopold I **Obv:** Laureate bust right in inner circle **Rev:** Crowned imperial eagle in inner circle, crown divides date **Mint:** Vienna **Note:** Prev. KM#1880.

Date	Mintage	VG	F	VF	XF	Unc
1667	—	180	350	725	1,250	—
1668	—	180	350	725	1,250	—
1671	—	180	350	725	1,250	—
1673	—	180	350	725	1,250	—
1676	—	180	350	725	1,250	—
1680	—	180	350	725	1,250	—

KM# 1250 DUCAT

3.5000 g., 0.9860 Gold 0.1109 oz. AGW **Ruler:** Leopold I **Obv:** Laureate bust right **Rev:** Crowned arms in Order collar **Mint:** Hall **Note:** Prev. KM#649.

Date	Mintage	VG	F	VF	XF	Unc
ND(1667)	—	550	1,250	2,650	5,300	—

KM# 1255 DUCAT

3.5000 g., 0.9860 Gold 0.1109 oz. AGW **Ruler:** Leopold I **Obv:** Laureate bust right in inner circle **Rev:** Crowned imperial eagle, date at upper left **Mint:** Saint Veit **Note:** Prev. KM#1655.

Date	Mintage	VG	F	VF	XF	Unc
1668 GS	—	220	450	875	1,950	—
1670	—	220	450	875	1,950	—

KM# 1290 DUCAT

3.5000 g., 0.9860 Gold 0.1109 oz. AGW **Ruler:** Leopold I **Obv:** Leopold standing facing in ornamental inner circle **Rev:** Crowned arms in Order collar, crown divides date **Mint:** Graz **Note:** Prev. KM#470.

Date	Mintage	VG	F	VF	XF	Unc
1676 IAN	—	275	550	1,100	2,200	—

KM# 1309 DUCAT

3.5000 g., 0.9860 Gold 0.1109 oz. AGW **Ruler:** Leopold I **Obv:** Laureate bust right in inner circle **Rev:** Crowned imperial eagle, crown divides date **Mint:** Saint Veit **Note:** Prev. KM#1656.

Date	Mintage	VG	F	VF	XF	Unc
1680 IR	—	180	475	850	1,850	—
1682 IR	—	180	475	850	1,850	—
1687	—	180	475	850	1,850	—
1690 CS	—	180	475	850	1,850	—

KM# 1123 DUCAT

3.5000 g., 0.9860 Gold 0.1109 oz. AGW **Ruler:** Leopold I **Rev:** Crowned round arms in Order collar **Mint:** Hall **Note:** Prev. KM#650.

Date	Mintage	VG	F	VF	XF	Unc
ND	—	550	1,250	2,650	5,300	—

KM# 1124 DUCAT

3.5000 g., 0.9860 Gold 0.1109 oz. AGW **Ruler:** Leopold I **Obv:** Laureate bust right in inner circle **Rev:** Crowned arms with concave sides in Order collar **Mint:** Hall **Note:** Prev. KM#651.

Date	Mintage	VG	F	VF	XF	Unc
ND1680	—	550	1,250	2,650	5,300	—

KM# 1125 DUCAT

3.5000 g., 0.9860 Gold 0.1109 oz. AGW **Ruler:** Leopold I **Obv:** Laureate armored bust right in inner circle **Rev:** Crowned arms in Order collar in inner circle **Mint:** Hall **Note:** Prev. KM#652.

Date	Mintage	VG	F	VF	XF	Unc
ND1680	—	550	1,250	2,650	5,300	—

KM# 1324 DUCAT

3.5000 g., 0.9860 Gold 0.1109 oz. AGW **Ruler:** Leopold I **Obv:** Older portrait **Rev:** Crowned oval arms **Mint:** Graz **Note:** Prev. KM#472.

Date	Mintage	VG	F	VF	XF	Unc
1683 IAN	—	180	375	800	1,675	—
1684 IAN	—	180	375	800	1,675	—
1686 IAN	—	180	375	800	1,675	—
1687 IAN	—	180	375	800	1,675	—
1689 IAN	—	180	375	800	1,675	—

KM# 1325 DUCAT

3.5000 g., 0.9860 Gold 0.1109 oz. AGW **Ruler:** Leopold I **Obv:** Large laureate bust right divides legend **Rev:** Crowned imperial eagle, crown divides date **Mint:** Vienna **Note:** Prev. KM#1890.

Date	Mintage	VG	F	VF	XF	Unc
1683	—	180	350	725	1,250	—
1684	—	180	350	725	1,250	—
1685	—	180	350	725	1,250	—
1686	—	180	350	725	1,250	—
1687	—	180	350	725	1,250	—
1689	—	180	350	725	1,250	—
1693	—	180	350	725	1,250	—
1694	—	180	350	725	1,250	—
1695	—	180	350	725	1,250	—
1697	—	180	350	725	1,250	—
1700	—	180	350	725	1,250	—

KM# 1372 DUCAT

3.5000 g., 0.9860 Gold 0.1109 oz. AGW **Ruler:** Leopold I **Obv:** Large laureate bust right to edge of coin **Rev:** Crowned arms in Order collar, crown divides date **Mint:** Graz **Note:** Prev. KM#473.

Date	Mintage	VG	F	VF	XF	Unc
1693	—	450	875	1,750	3,250	—

KM# 1410 DUCAT

3.5000 g., 0.9860 Gold 0.1109 oz. AGW **Ruler:** Leopold I **Obv:** Laureate bust right **Rev:** Crowned imperial eagle, crown divides date **Mint:** Saint Veit **Note:** Prev. KM#1657.

Date	Mintage	VG	F	VF	XF	Unc
1700	—	220	450	875	1,950	—

KM# 110 2 DUCAT

7.0000 g., 0.9860 Gold 0.2219 oz. AGW **Ruler:** Maximilian **Mint:** Hall **Note:** Similar to 1 Ducat, KM#146. Prev. KM#779.

Date	Mintage	VG	F	VF	XF	Unc
ND(1609)	—	725	1,500	4,250	7,500	—

KM# 172 2 DUCAT

7.0000 g., 0.9860 Gold 0.2219 oz. AGW **Ruler:** Matthias II **Mint:** Vienna **Note:** Varieties exist. Prev. KM#1761.

Date	Mintage	VG	F	VF	XF	Unc
1613	—	380	925	2,750	6,350	—
1615	—	380	925	2,750	6,350	—
1616	—	380	925	2,750	6,350	—
1619	—	380	925	2,750	6,350	—

KM# 275 2 DUCAT

7.0000 g., 0.9860 Gold 0.2219 oz. AGW **Ruler:** Ferdinand II **Obv:** Ferdinand II standing right **Mint:** Vienna **Note:** Prev. KM#1804.

Date	Mintage	VG	F	VF	XF	Unc
1620 (c)	—	380	800	2,000	5,200	—
1621 (c)	—	380	800	2,000	5,200	—
1622 (c)	—	380	800	2,000	5,200	—
1623 (c)	—	380	800	2,000	5,200	—
1624 (c)	—	380	800	2,000	5,200	—
1626 (c)	—	380	800	2,000	5,200	—
1627 (c)	—	380	800	2,000	5,200	—
1628 (c)	—	380	800	2,000	5,200	—
1629 (c)	—	380	800	2,000	5,200	—
1630 (c)	—	380	800	2,000	5,200	—
1631 (c)	—	380	800	2,000	5,200	—
1632 (c)	—	380	800	2,000	5,200	—
1633 (c)	—	380	800	2,000	5,200	—
1634 (c)	—	380	800	2,000	5,200	—
1635 (c)	—	380	800	2,000	5,200	—

KM# 365 2 DUCAT

7.0000 g., 0.9860 Gold 0.2219 oz. AGW **Ruler:** Ferdinand II **Obv:** Ruler seated facing throne in inner circle **Rev:** Crowned imperial eagle in inner circle, crown divides date **Mint:** Graz **Note:** Prev. KM#405.

Date	Mintage	VG	F	VF	XF	Unc
1621	—	450	925	2,200	5,300	—
1627	—	450	925	2,200	5,300	—

KM# 682 2 DUCAT

7.0000 g., 0.9860 Gold 0.2219 oz. AGW **Ruler:** Ferdinand II **Obv:** Standing figure right **Rev:** Heraldic imperial eagle with oval arms **Mint:** Saint Veit **Note:** Struck with 1 Ducat dies. Prev. KM#1606.

Date	Mintage	VG	F	VF	XF	Unc
1627 (g)	—	800	1,650	3,400	6,500	—

KM# 725 2 DUCAT

7.0000 g., 0.9860 Gold 0.2219 oz. AGW **Ruler:** Ferdinand II **Obv:** Uncrowned figure standing right **Rev:** Heraldic imperial eagle **Mint:** Olmutz **Note:** Prev. KM#1241.

Date	Mintage	VG	F	VF	XF	Unc
1629 (o) MF	—	380	775	1,500	4,950	—

KM# 760 2 DUCAT

7.0000 g., 0.9860 Gold 0.2219 oz. AGW **Ruler:** Ferdinand II **Obv:** Crowned figure **Mint:** Olmutz **Note:** Prev. KM#1242.

Date	Mintage	VG	F	VF	XF	Unc
1630	—	450	875	2,200	5,300	—

KM# 789 2 DUCAT

7.0000 g., 0.9860 Gold 0.2219 oz. AGW **Ruler:** Ferdinand Charles **Obv:** Armored bust right **Rev:** Tyrolean eagle with shield of arms on breast **Mint:** Hall **Note:** Prev. KM#841.

Date	Mintage	VG	F	VF	XF	Unc
ND(1632-62)	—	950	2,150	4,650	8,500	—

KM# 790 2 DUCAT

7.0000 g., 0.9860 Gold 0.2219 oz. AGW **Ruler:** Ferdinand II **Mint:** Klagenfurt **Note:** Prev. KM#981.

Date	Mintage	VG	F	VF	XF	Unc
1632	—	475	925	2,500	6,000	—

KM# 791 2 DUCAT

7.0000 g., 0.9860 Gold 0.2219 oz. AGW **Ruler:** Ferdinand II **Obv:** Standing figure **Rev:** Shield-shaped arms **Mint:** Saint Veit **Note:** Prev. KM#1607.

Date	Mintage	VG	F	VF	XF	Unc
1632	—	800	1,600	3,300	6,200	—

KM# 899 2 DUCAT

7.0000 g., 0.9860 Gold 0.2219 oz. AGW **Ruler:** Ferdinand III **Obv:** Ferdinand III standing right in inner circle **Rev:** Crowned imperial eagle in inner circle **Mint:** Vienna **Note:** Prev. KM#1844.

Date	Mintage	VG	F	VF	XF	Unc
1641	—	380	800	2,200	5,000	—
1642	—	380	800	2,200	5,000	—
1643	—	380	800	2,200	5,000	—
1644	—	380	800	2,200	5,000	—
1645	—	380	800	2,200	5,000	—
1646	—	380	800	2,200	5,000	—
1647	—	380	800	2,200	5,000	—
1648	—	380	800	2,200	5,000	—
1649	—	380	800	2,200	5,000	—
1650	—	380	800	2,200	5,000	—
1652	—	380	800	2,200	5,000	—
1653	—	380	800	2,200	5,000	—
1654	—	380	800	2,200	5,000	—
1656	—	380	800	2,200	5,000	—
1657	—	380	800	2,200	5,000	—

KM# 909 2 DUCAT

7.0000 g., 0.9860 Gold 0.2219 oz. AGW **Ruler:** Ferdinand Charles **Obv:** Emperor on horseback right above city view **Mint:** Hall **Note:** Prev. KM#842.

Date	Mintage	VG	F	VF	XF	Unc
1642	—	700	1,500	3,500	6,000	—

KM# 936 2 DUCAT

7.0000 g., 0.9860 Gold 0.2219 oz. AGW **Ruler:** Ferdinand III **Mint:** Saint Veit **Note:** Prev. KM#1631.

Date	Mintage	VG	F	VF	XF	Unc
1646	—	380	850	2,250	5,200	—
1648	—	380	850	2,250	5,200	—
1652	—	380	850	2,250	5,200	—
1653	—	380	850	2,250	5,200	—
1655	—	380	850	2,250	5,200	—

KM# 973 2 DUCAT

7.0000 g., 0.9860 Gold 0.2219 oz. AGW **Ruler:** Ferdinand III **Obv:** Ferdinand III standing facing in inner circle **Rev:** Crowned arms in inner circle, crown divides date **Mint:** Graz **Note:** Prev. KM#441.

Date	Mintage	VG	F	VF	XF	Unc
1650	—	380	950	2,350	5,300	—

KM# 1161 2 DUCAT

7.0000 g., 0.9860 Gold 0.2219 oz. AGW **Ruler:** Leopold I **Obv:** Leopold standing left flanked by shields of arms **Rev:** Crowned imperial eagle, date in legend **Mint:** Vienna **Note:** Prev. KM#1891.

Date	Mintage	VG	F	VF	XF	Unc
1659	—	475	1,000	2,750	7,700	—

KM# 1160 2 DUCAT

7.0000 g., 0.9860 Gold 0.2219 oz. AGW **Ruler:** Leopold I **Mint:** Saint Veit **Note:** Prev. KM#1659.

Date	Mintage	VG	F	VF	XF	Unc
1659	—	850	1,650	3,750	8,000	—

KM# 1183 2 DUCAT

7.0000 g., 0.9860 Gold 0.2219 oz. AGW **Ruler:** Leopold I **Obv:** Laureate bust right **Rev:** Crowned imperial eagle in inner circle, date in legend **Mint:** Vienna **Note:** Prev. KM#1892.

Date	Mintage	VG	F	VF	XF	Unc
1660	—	525	1,100	3,150	9,000	—
1661	—	525	1,100	3,150	9,000	—
1662	—	525	1,100	3,150	9,000	—

KM# 1223 2 DUCAT

7.0000 g., 0.9860 Gold 0.2219 oz. AGW **Ruler:** Leopold I **Obv:** Older laureate bust right in inner circle **Rev:** Crowned imperial eagle in inner circle, crown divides date **Mint:** Vienna **Note:** Prev. KM#1893.

Date	Mintage	VG	F	VF	XF	Unc
1664	—	525	1,100	3,150	9,000	—
1669	—	525	1,100	3,150	9,000	—
1682	—	525	1,100	3,150	9,000	—

KM# 1276 2 DUCAT

7.0000 g., 0.9860 Gold 0.2219 oz. AGW **Ruler:** Leopold I **Obv:** Older laureate bust right in inner circle **Rev:** Crowned arms in Order collar, crown divides date **Mint:** Graz **Note:** Prev. KM#474.

Date	Mintage	VG	F	VF	XF	Unc
1672 IAN	—	475	1,000	2,750	7,700	—
1674 IAN	—	475	1,000	2,750	7,700	—
1676 IAN	—	475	1,000	2,750	7,700	—
1678 IAN	—	475	1,000	2,750	7,700	—
1680 IAN	—	475	1,000	2,750	7,700	—
1682 IAN	—	475	1,000	2,750	7,700	—
1684 IAN	—	475	1,000	2,750	7,700	—
1685 IAN	—	475	1,000	2,750	7,700	—
1687/6 IAN	—	475	1,000	2,750	7,700	—

KM# 1126 2 DUCAT

7.0000 g., 0.9860 Gold 0.2219 oz. AGW **Ruler:** Leopold I **Obv:** Laureate bust right in inner circle **Rev:** Crowned eagle with wreath around head in inner circle **Mint:** Hall **Note:** Prev. KM#653.

Date	Mintage	VG	F	VF	XF	Unc
ND(1680)F	—	550	1,150	3,250	9,250	—

KM# 1312 2 DUCAT

7.0000 g., 0.9860 Gold 0.2219 oz. AGW **Ruler:** Leopold I **Obv:** Laureate bust right **Rev:** Crowned imperial eagle, crown divides date **Mint:** Saint Veit **Note:** Prev. KM#1660.

Date	Mintage	VG	F	VF	XF	Unc
1681 IR	—	825	1,650	3,850	8,750	—
1685 IR	—	825	1,650	3,850	8,750	—
1686 HL/VP	—	825	1,650	3,850	8,750	—

KM# 77 3 DUCAT

10.5000 g., 0.9860 Gold 0.3328 oz. AGW **Ruler:** Rudolf II **Mint:** Vienna **Note:** Prev. KM#1718.

Date	Mintage	VG	F	VF	XF	Unc
1606	—	2,750	4,700	7,250	12,500	—

KM# 806 3 DUCAT

10.5000 g., 0.9860 Gold 0.3328 oz. AGW **Ruler:** Ferdinand II **Mint:** Graz **Note:** Klippe. Prev. KM#411.

Date	Mintage	VG	F	VF	XF	Unc
1634 Rare	—	—	—	—	—	—

KM# 910 3 DUCAT

10.5000 g., 0.9860 Gold 0.3328 oz. AGW **Ruler:** Ferdinand Charles **Obv:** Emperor on horseback right in circle of arms **Mint:** Hall **Note:** Prev. KM#843.

Date	Mintage	VG	F	VF	XF	Unc
1642	—	1,150	3,150	7,250	10,500	—

KM# 995 3 DUCAT

10.5000 g., 0.9860 Gold 0.3328 oz. AGW **Ruler:** Ferdinand III **Obv:** Laureate bust right in inner circle **Rev:** Crowned imperial eagle in inner circle **Mint:** Vienna **Note:** Struck with 1 Ducat dies, KM#950. Prev. KM#1845.

Date	Mintage	VG	F	VF	XF	Unc
1656	—	825	1,550	4,400	8,000	—

KM# 1127 3 DUCAT

10.5000 g., 0.9860 Gold 0.3328 oz. AGW **Ruler:** Leopold I **Obv:** Laureate bust right in inner circle **Rev:** Crowned imperial eagle in inner circle **Mint:** Hall **Note:** Prev. KM#654.

Date	Mintage	VG	F	VF	XF	Unc
ND	—	750	1,700	4,500	9,250	—

KM# 148 4 DUCAT

14.0000 g., 0.9860 Gold 0.4438 oz. AGW **Ruler:** Matthias II **Mint:** Joachimstal **Note:** Prev. KM#A890.

Date	Mintage	VG	F	VF	XF	Unc
1612 Rare	—	—	—	—	—	—

KM# 366 4 DUCAT

14.0000 g., 0.9860 Gold 0.4438 oz. AGW **Ruler:** Ferdinand II **Obv:** Laureate bust right in inner circle **Rev:** Crowned imperial eagle in inner circle **Mint:** Vienna **Note:** Prev. KM#1805.

Date	Mintage	VG	F	VF	XF	Unc
1621 (c)	—	—	—	—	—	—
1622 (c)	—	1,100	2,750	6,500	10,000	—
1628 (c)	—	1,100	2,750	6,500	10,000	—
1634 (c)	—	1,100	2,750	6,500	10,000	—

KM# 683 4 DUCAT

14.0000 g., 0.9860 Gold 0.4438 oz. AGW **Ruler:** Ferdinand II **Obv:** Standing figure right **Rev:** Heraldic imperial eagle **Mint:** Saint Veit **Note:** Klippe. Struck with 1 Ducat dies. Prev. KM#1608.

Date	Mintage	VG	F	VF	XF	Unc
1627	—	2,750	4,700	8,750	12,500	—

KM# 1128 4 DUCAT

14.0000 g., 0.9860 Gold 0.4438 oz. AGW **Ruler:** Leopold I **Obv:** Young laureate bust right in inner circle **Rev:** Crowned imperial eagle in inner circle **Mint:** Saint Veit **Note:** Prev. KM#1661.

Date	Mintage	VG	F	VF	XF	Unc
1658	—	1,300	2,750	6,500	10,500	—

KM# 1162 4 DUCAT

14.0000 g., 0.9860 Gold 0.4438 oz. AGW **Ruler:** Leopold I **Mint:** Vienna **Note:** Prev. KM#1894.

Date	Mintage	VG	F	VF	XF	Unc
1659	—	1,300	2,750	6,500	10,500	—

KM# 1203 4 DUCAT

14.0000 g., 0.9860 Gold 0.4438 oz. AGW **Ruler:** Leopold I **Mint:** Vienna **Note:** Prev. KM#1896.

Date	Mintage	VG	F	VF	XF	Unc
1662	—	1,300	2,750	6,500	10,500	—

KM# 84 5 DUCAT

17.5000 g., 0.9860 Gold 0.5547 oz. AGW **Ruler:** Rudolf II **Mint:** Vienna **Note:** Prev. KM#1719.

Date	Mintage	VG	F	VF	XF	Unc
1607	—	4,600	7,200	10,500	17,000	—

KM# 179 5 DUCAT
17.5000 g., 0.9860 Gold 0.5547 oz. AGW **Ruler:** Matthias II **Mint:** Vienna **Note:** Thick planchet. Struck with 1/2 Thaler dies, KM#164. Prev. KM#1762.

Date	Mintage	VG	F	VF	XF	Unc
1613	—	1,200	2,400	4,950	9,900	—
1617	—	1,200	2,400	4,950	9,900	—
1618	—	1,200	2,400	4,950	9,900	—

KM# 277 5 DUCAT
17.5000 g., 0.9860 Gold 0.5547 oz. AGW **Ruler:** Ferdinand II **Mint:** Vienna **Note:** Prev. KM#1806.

Date	Mintage	VG	F	VF	XF	Unc
1620 (c)	—	1,000	1,700	3,500	7,000	—
1621 (c)	—	1,000	1,700	3,500	7,000	—
1622 (c)	—	1,000	1,700	3,500	7,000	—
1623 (c)	—	1,000	1,700	3,500	7,000	—

KM# 367 5 DUCAT
17.5000 g., 0.9860 Gold 0.5547 oz. AGW **Ruler:** Ferdinand II **Obv:** Crowned bust right **Rev:** Heraldic imperial eagle **Mint:** Saint Veit **Note:** Prev. KM#1609.

Date	Mintage	VG	F	VF	XF	Unc
1621 Rare	—	—	—	—	—	—

KM# 553 5 DUCAT
17.5000 g., 0.9860 Gold 0.5547 oz. AGW **Ruler:** Ferdinand II **Obv:** Bust with plain collar **Rev:** Five coats of arms **Mint:** Vienna **Note:** Prev. KM#1807.

Date	Mintage	VG	F	VF	XF	Unc
1624 (c)	—	1,000	1,700	3,500	7,000	—

KM# 660 5 DUCAT
17.5000 g., 0.9860 Gold 0.5547 oz. AGW **Ruler:** Ferdinand II **Rev:** Crowned imperial eagle in inner circle **Mint:** Vienna **Note:** Prev. KM#1808.

Date	Mintage	VG	F	VF	XF	Unc
1626 (c)	—	725	1,600	3,450	6,900	—
1627 (c)	—	725	1,600	3,450	6,900	—
1628 (c)	—	725	1,600	3,450	6,900	—
1632 (c)	—	725	1,600	3,450	6,900	—
1634 (c)	—	725	1,600	3,450	6,900	—
1636 (c)	—	725	1,600	3,450	6,900	—
1637 (v)	—	725	1,600	3,450	6,900	—
1637 (v)	—	725	1,600	3,450	6,900	—

KM# 659 5 DUCAT
17.5000 g., 0.9860 Gold 0.5547 oz. AGW **Ruler:** Leopold **Subject:** Wedding of Leopold and Claudia **Mint:** Hall **Note:** Prev. KM#818.

Date	Mintage	VG	F	VF	XF	Unc
ND(1626) Rare	—	—	—	—	—	—

KM# 684 5 DUCAT
17.5000 g., 0.9860 Gold 0.5547 oz. AGW **Ruler:** Ferdinand II **Obv:** Uncrowned bust right **Rev:** Crowned arms **Mint:** Saint Veit **Note:** Prev. KM#1610.

Date	Mintage	VG	F	VF	XF	Unc
1627 (g) Rare	—	—	—	—	—	—

KM# 726 5 DUCAT
17.5000 g., 0.9860 Gold 0.5547 oz. AGW **Ruler:** Ferdinand II **Obv:** Bust right **Rev:** Heraldic imperial eagle **Mint:** Olmutz **Note:** Struck wtih 1 Thaler dies, KM#718. Prev. KM#1243.

Date	Mintage	VG	F	VF	XF	Unc
1629 (o)	—	900	1,700	3,600	7,500	—

KM# 761 5 DUCAT
17.5000 g., 0.9860 Gold 0.5547 oz. AGW **Ruler:** Ferdinand II **Mint:** Olmutz **Note:** Struck wtih 1 Thaler dies, KM#700. Prev. KM#A1244.

Date	Mintage	VG	F	VF	XF	Unc
1630 (o) MF	—	950	1,750	3,850	7,700	—

KM# 792 5 DUCAT
17.5000 g., 0.9860 Gold 0.5547 oz. AGW **Ruler:** Ferdinand II **Obv:** Bust right **Rev:** Crowned arms **Mint:** Graz **Note:** Prev. KM#406.

Date	Mintage	VG	F	VF	XF	Unc
1632	—	950	1,750	4,600	8,000	—
1633	—	950	1,750	4,600	8,000	—

KM# 793 5 DUCAT
17.5000 g., 0.9860 Gold 0.5547 oz. AGW **Ruler:** Ferdinand Charles **Mint:** Hall **Note:** Prev. KM#844.

Date	Mintage	VG	F	VF	XF	Unc
ND(1632-46) Rare	—	—	—	—	—	—

KM# 863 5 DUCAT
17.5000 g., 0.9860 Gold 0.5547 oz. AGW **Ruler:** Ferdinand III **Mint:** Saint Veit **Note:** Struck wtih 1 Thaler dies, KM#858. Prev. KM#1632.

Date	Mintage	VG	F	VF	XF	Unc
1638 Rare	—	—	—	—	—	—

KM# 912 5 DUCAT
17.5000 g., 0.9860 Gold 0.5547 oz. AGW **Ruler:** Ferdinand III **Obv:** Laureate bust right **Rev:** Crowned imperial eagle, arms on breast, holding upright sword and scepter **Mint:** Vienna **Note:** Struck with 1/2 Thaler dies, KM#839. Prev. KM#1846.

Date	Mintage	VG	F	VF	XF	Unc
1642	—	950	1,300	2,910	6,500	—
1643	—	950	1,300	2,910	6,500	—
1644	—	950	1,300	2,910	6,500	—
1646	—	950	1,300	2,910	6,500	—
1655	—	950	1,300	2,910	6,500	—

KM# 1163 5 DUCAT
17.5000 g., 0.9860 Gold 0.5547 oz. AGW **Ruler:** Leopold I **Obv:** Leopold laureate bust right **Rev:** Crowned imperial eagle **Mint:** Vienna **Note:** Prev. KM#1895.

Date	Mintage	VG	F	VF	XF	Unc
1659	—	—	—	6,500	9,500	—

KM# A1203 5 DUCAT
17.5000 g., 0.9860 Gold 0.5547 oz. AGW **Ruler:** Leopold I **Obv:** Laureate bust right **Obv. Legend:** LEOPOLDVS DG R.... **Rev:** Crowned imperial eagle **Rev. Legend:** ARCHD • AVS • D • BVR • COM • TIRO **Mint:** Vienna **Note:** Prev. KM#PnC22, PnD22, PnF22. Fr#262.

Date	Mintage	VG	F	VF	XF	Unc
1661 ca	—	—	—	12,500	20,000	—
1662 ca	—	—	—	12,500	20,000	—
1663 ca	—	—	—	12,500	20,000	—

KM# 1263 5 DUCAT
17.5000 g., 0.9860 Gold 0.5547 oz. AGW **Ruler:** Leopold I **Obv:** Leopold bust right **Rev:** Crowned imperial eagle **Mint:** Vienna **Note:** Prev. KM#1897.

Date	Mintage	VG	F	VF	XF	Unc
1669 Rare	—	—	—	—	—	—

KM# 1270 5 DUCAT
17.5000 g., 0.9860 Gold 0.5547 oz. AGW **Ruler:** Leopold I **Obv:** Laureate bust right in inner circle **Rev:** Crowned imperial eagle in inner circle **Mint:** Graz **Note:** Prev. KM#475.

Date	Mintage	VG	F	VF	XF	Unc
1670 IGW	—	950	1,850	4,500	9,600	—
1671 IW	—	950	1,850	4,500	9,600	—
1672	—	950	1,850	4,500	9,600	—
1690 IAN	—	950	1,850	4,500	9,600	—

KM# 98 6 DUCAT
21.0000 g., 0.9860 Gold 0.6657 oz. AGW **Ruler:** Rudolf II **Mint:** Vienna **Note:** Struck with 1 Thaler dies, KM#25. Prev. KM#1722.

Date	Mintage	VG	F	VF	XF	Unc
1608 Rare	—	—	—	—	—	—

KM# 111 6 DUCAT
21.0000 g., 0.9860 Gold 0.6657 oz. AGW **Ruler:** Rudolf II **Mint:** Vienna **Note:** Struck with 1/2 Thaler dies, KM#22. Prev. KM#1723.

Date	Mintage	VG	F	VF	XF	Unc
1609 Rare	—	—	—	—	—	—

KM# 661 6 DUCAT
21.0000 g., 0.9860 Gold 0.6657 oz. AGW **Ruler:** Leopold **Subject:** Wedding of Leopold and Claudia **Mint:** Hall **Note:** Similar to 5 Ducat, KM#818 but klippe. Prev. KM#819.

Date	Mintage	VG	F	VF	XF	Unc
ND(1626) Rare	—	—	—	—	—	—

KM# 701 6 DUCAT
21.0000 g., 0.9860 Gold 0.6657 oz. AGW **Ruler:** Ferdinand II **Obv:** Bust right **Rev:** Crowned arms **Mint:** Saint Veit **Note:** Struck with 1 Thaler dies, KM#678. Prev. KM#1611.

Date	Mintage	VG	F	VF	XF	Unc
1628 (g) Rare	—	—	—	—	—	—

KM# 702 6 DUCAT
21.0000 g., 0.9860 Gold 0.6657 oz. AGW **Ruler:** Ferdinand II **Obv:** Bust right **Rev:** Crowned imperial eagle **Mint:** Vienna **Note:** Struck with 1/2 Thaler dies, KM#514. Prev. KM#1809.

Date	Mintage	VG	F	VF	XF	Unc
1628 Rare	—	—	—	—	—	—

KM# 794 6 DUCAT
20.9000 g., 0.9860 Gold 0.6625 oz. AGW **Ruler:** Ferdinand II **Obv:** Bust right **Rev:** Crowned arms **Mint:** Graz **Note:** Prev. KM#407.

Date	Mintage	VG	F	VF	XF	Unc
1632	—	1,450	3,000	7,200	11,000	—

KM# 864 6 DUCAT
21.0000 g., 0.9860 Gold 0.6657 oz. AGW **Ruler:** Ferdinand III **Mint:** Saint Veit **Note:** Struck wtih 1 Thaler dies, KM#858. Prev. KM#A1633.

Date	Mintage	VG	F	VF	XF	Unc
1638 Rare	—	—	—	—	—	—

KM# 938 6 DUCAT
21.0000 g., 0.9860 Gold 0.6657 oz. AGW **Ruler:** Ferdinand III **Mint:** Brunn **Note:** Similar to 10 Ducats, KM#939.1. Prev. KM#228.

Date	Mintage	VG	F	VF	XF	Unc
1646 (o)	—	1,450	3,000	6,600	10,500	—

KM# 150 6-1/2 DUCAT
22.7500 g., 0.9860 Gold 0.7212 oz. AGW **Ruler:** Rudolf II **Obv:** Laureate bust of Rudolph II right **Rev:** Crowned arms **Mint:** Ensisheim **Note:** Prev. KM#A276.

Date	Mintage	VG	F	VF	XF	Unc
1611 Rare	—	—	—	—	—	—

KM# 773 7 DUCAT
24.5000 g., 0.9860 Gold 0.7766 oz. AGW **Ruler:** Ferdinand II **Obv:** Bust right **Rev:** Crowned arms **Mint:** Graz **Note:** Prev. KM#408.

Date	Mintage	VG	F	VF	XF	Unc
1631 Rare	—	—	—	—	—	—

KM# 865 7 DUCAT
24.5000 g., 0.9860 Gold 0.7766 oz. AGW **Ruler:** Ferdinand III **Mint:** Saint Veit **Note:** Struck wtih 1 Thaler dies, KM#858. Prev. KM#1633.

Date	Mintage	VG	F	VF	XF	Unc
1638 Rare	—	—	—	—	—	—

KM# 151 8 DUCAT
28.0000 g., 0.9860 Gold 0.8876 oz. AGW **Ruler:** Matthias II **Mint:** Vienna **Note:** Struck with 1 Thaler dies, KM#130. Prev. KM#A1763.

Date	Mintage	VG	F	VF	XF	Unc
1612 Rare	—	—	—	—	—	—

KM# 232 8 DUCAT
28.0000 g., 0.9860 Gold 0.8876 oz. AGW **Ruler:** Ferdinand II **Mint:** Klagenfurt **Note:** Struck with 1 Thaler dies, KM#24. Prev. KM#999.

Date	Mintage	VG	F	VF	XF	Unc
1618 Rare	—	—	—	—	—	—

KM# 662 8 DUCAT
28.0000 g., 0.9860 Gold 0.8876 oz. AGW **Ruler:** Leopold **Subject:** Wedding of Leopold **Obv:** Crowned busts of the royal couple right **Rev:** Crowned imperial eagle right **Mint:** Hall **Note:** Prev. KM#820.

Date	Mintage	VG	F	VF	XF	Unc
ND(1626) Rare	—	—	—	—	—	—

KM# 795 8 DUCAT
28.0000 g., 0.9860 Gold 0.8876 oz. AGW **Ruler:** Ferdinand II **Obv:** Bust right **Rev:** Crowned arms **Mint:** Saint Veit **Note:** Struck with 1 Thaler dies, KM#678. Prev. KM#1612.

Date	Mintage	VG	F	VF	XF	Unc
1632	—	—	—	14,000	21,500	—

KM# 866 8 DUCAT
28.0000 g., 0.9860 Gold 0.8876 oz. AGW **Ruler:** Ferdinand III **Mint:** Saint Veit **Note:** Struck wtih 1 Thaler dies, KM#858. Prev. KM#A1634.

Date	Mintage	VG	F	VF	XF	Unc
1638 Rare	—	—	—	—	—	—

KM# 796 9 DUCAT
31.5000 g., 0.9860 Gold 0.9985 oz. AGW **Ruler:** Ferdinand II **Obv:** Bust right **Rev:** Crowned arms **Mint:** Saint Veit **Note:** Struck with 1 Thaler dies, KM#678. Prev. KM#1613.

Date	Mintage	VG	F	VF	XF	Unc
1632 Rare	—	—	—	—	—	—

KM# 1256 9 DUCAT
31.5000 g., 0.9860 Gold 0.9985 oz. AGW **Ruler:** Leopold I **Mint:** Hall **Note:** Struck with 1 Thaler dies, KM#1238. Prev. KM#647.

Date	Mintage	VG	F	VF	XF	Unc
1668 Rare	—	—	—	—	—	—

KM# 85 10 DUCAT
35.0000 g., 0.9860 Gold 1.1095 oz. AGW **Ruler:** Rudolf II **Mint:** Vienna **Note:** Struck with 1 Thaler dies, KM#25. Prev. KM#1721.

Date	Mintage	VG	F	VF	XF	Unc
1607 Rare	—	—	—	—	—	—

KM# 155 10 DUCAT
35.0000 g., 0.9860 Gold 1.1095 oz. AGW **Ruler:** Matthias II **Mint:** Vienna **Note:** Struck with 1 Thaler dies, KM#144. Prev. KM#B1763.

Date	Mintage	VG	F	VF	XF	Unc
1612	—	1,900	2,500	5,000	9,200	—

KM# 181 10 DUCAT
35.0000 g., 0.9860 Gold 1.1095 oz. AGW **Ruler:** Matthias II **Mint:** Vienna **Note:** Struck with 1/2 Thaler dies, KM#164. Prev. KM#1763.

Date	Mintage	VG	F	VF	XF	Unc
1613 (c) Rare	—	—	—	—	—	—

KM# 192 10 DUCAT
35.0000 g., 0.9860 Gold 1.1095 oz. AGW **Ruler:** Matthias II **Mint:** Vienna **Note:** Struck with 1 Thaler dies, KM#169. Prev. KM#A1764.

Date	Mintage	VG	F	VF	XF	Unc
1614 Rare	—	—	—	—	—	—

KM# 198 10 DUCAT
35.0000 g., 0.9860 Gold 1.1095 oz. AGW **Ruler:** Matthias II **Mint:** Vienna **Note:** Struck with 1 Thaler dies, KM#196. Prev. KM#B1764.

Date	Mintage	VG	F	VF	XF	Unc
1615 Rare	—	—	—	—	—	—

KM# 211 10 DUCAT
35.0000 g., 0.9860 Gold 1.1095 oz. AGW **Ruler:** Matthias II **Mint:** Vienna **Note:** Struck with 1 Thaler dies, KM#206. Prev. KM#1764.

Date	Mintage	VG	F	VF	XF	Unc
1616 Rare	—	—	—	—	—	—

KM# 371 10 DUCAT
35.0000 g., 0.9860 Gold 1.1095 oz. AGW **Ruler:** Ferdinand II **Obv:** Bust right **Rev:** Crowned imperial eagle **Mint:** Vienna **Note:** Struck with 1 Thaler dies, KM#268.2. Prev. KM#1810.

Date	Mintage	VG	F	VF	XF	Unc
16Z1 (c)	—	2,500	4,250	7,700	12,500	—
16ZZ/1 (c)	—	2,500	4,250	7,700	12,500	—

KM# 370 10 DUCAT
35.0000 g., 0.9860 Gold 1.1095 oz. AGW **Ruler:** Ferdinand II **Obv:** Ruffled collar **Mint:** Olmutz **Note:** Prev. KM#1244.

Date	Mintage	VG	F	VF	XF	Unc
1621 BZ Rare	—	—	—	—	—	—
1628 (o) Rare	—	—	—	—	—	—

KM# 368 10 DUCAT
3.5000 g., 0.9860 Gold 0.1109 oz. AGW **Ruler:** Ferdinand II **Obv:** Bust right **Rev:** Crowned arms **Mint:** Hall **Note:** Prev. KM#617.

Date	Mintage	VG	F	VF	XF	Unc
1621 Rare	—	—	—	—	—	—

KM# 369 10 DUCAT
35.0000 g., 0.9860 Gold 1.1095 oz. AGW **Ruler:** Ferdinand II **Obv:** Crowned bust right **Rev:** Heraldic imperial eagle **Mint:** Klagenfurt **Note:** Prev. KM#982.

Date	Mintage	VG	F	VF	XF	Unc
1621 Rare	—	—	—	—	—	—

KM# 622 10 DUCAT
35.0000 g., 0.9860 Gold 1.1095 oz. AGW **Ruler:** Ferdinand II **Mint:** Vienna **Note:** Struck with 1 Thaler dies, KM#599. Prev. KM#1811.

Date	Mintage	VG	F	VF	XF	Unc
1625 (c)	—	2,500	4,250	7,700	12,500	—
1626 (c)	—	2,500	4,250	7,700	12,500	—
1628 (c)	—	2,500	4,250	7,700	12,500	—
1630 (c)	—	2,500	4,250	7,700	12,500	—
1631 (c)	—	2,500	4,250	7,700	12,500	—
1636 (v)	—	2,500	4,250	7,700	12,500	—
1637 (v)	—	2,500	4,250	7,700	12,500	—

KM# 730 10 DUCAT
35.0000 g., 0.9860 Gold 1.1095 oz. AGW **Ruler:** Ferdinand II **Obv:** Plain collar **Mint:** Olmutz **Note:** Prev. KM#1245.

Date	Mintage	VG	F	VF	XF	Unc
1629 (o) Rare	—	—	—	—	—	—
1630 (o) MF Rare	—	—	—	—	—	—
1633 (o) Rare	—	—	—	—	—	—
1636/3 (o) Rare	—	—	—	—	—	—

KM# 803 10 DUCAT
35.0000 g., 0.9860 Gold 1.1095 oz. AGW **Ruler:** Ferdinand II **Obv:** Bust right **Rev:** Crowned arms **Mint:** Graz **Note:** Prev. KM#409.

Date	Mintage	VG	F	VF	XF	Unc
1633 Rare	—	—	—	—	—	—

KM# 867 10 DUCAT
35.0000 g., 0.9860 Gold 1.1095 oz. AGW **Ruler:** Ferdinand III **Mint:** Saint Veit **Note:** Struck wtih 1 Thaler dies, KM#858. Prev. KM#1634.

Date	Mintage	VG	F	VF	XF	Unc
1638 Rare	—	—	—	—	—	—

KM# 900 10 DUCAT
35.0000 g., 0.9860 Gold 1.1095 oz. AGW **Ruler:** Ferdinand III **Mint:** Vienna **Note:** Struck with 1 Thaler dies, KM#840. Prev. KM#A1848.

Date	Mintage	VG	F	VF	XF	Unc
1641 (b) Rare	—	—	—	—	—	—
1642 (b) Rare	—	—	—	—	—	—

KM# 913 10 DUCAT
35.0000 g., 0.9860 Gold 1.1095 oz. AGW **Ruler:** Ferdinand III **Obv:** Large laureate bust right **Rev:** Crowned imperial eagle, arms on breast, holding upright sword and scepter **Mint:** Vienna **Note:** Struck with 1 Thaler dies, KM#839. Prev. KM#1847.

Date	Mintage	VG	F	VF	XF	Unc
1642 (b)	—	2,750	4,400	8,500	12,500	—
1643 (b)	—	2,750	4,400	8,500	12,500	—

KM# 926 10 DUCAT
35.0000 g., 0.9860 Gold 1.1095 oz. AGW **Ruler:** Ferdinand III **Mint:** Vienna **Note:** Struck with 1 Thaler dies, KM#882. Prev. KM#B1848.

Date	Mintage	VG	F	VF	XF	Unc
1645 (b) Rare	—	—	—	—	—	—

KM# 939.2 10 DUCAT
35.0000 g., 0.9860 Gold 1.1095 oz. AGW **Ruler:** Ferdinand III **Obv:** Without inner beaded circle **Rev:** Without inner beaded circle **Mint:** Brunn **Note:** Struck with 1 Thaler dies, KM#929.1. Prev. KM#229.1.

Date	Mintage	VG	F	VF	XF	Unc
1646 (o) Rare	—	—	—	—	—	—

KM# 939.1 10 DUCAT
35.0000 g., 0.9860 Gold 1.1095 oz. AGW **Ruler:** Ferdinand III **Obv:** With inner beaded circle **Rev:** With inner beaded circle **Mint:** Brunn **Note:** Prev. KM#229.2.

Date	Mintage	VG	F	VF	XF	Unc
1648 (o) Rare	—	—	—	—	—	—

KM# 993 10 DUCAT
35.0000 g., 0.9860 Gold 1.1095 oz. AGW **Ruler:** Ferdinand III **Obv:** Large, more ornate laureate bust right **Mint:** Vienna **Note:** Prev. KM#1848.

Date	Mintage	VG	F	VF	XF	Unc
1655	—	3,000	5,000	9,000	14,500	—

KM# 996 10 DUCAT
35.0000 g., 0.9860 Gold 1.1095 oz. AGW **Ruler:** Ferdinand III **Obv:** Small laureate bust right **Mint:** Vienna **Note:** Prev. KM#1849.

Date	Mintage	VG	F	VF	XF	Unc
1656	—	2,750	4,500	8,500	12,500	—
1657	—	2,750	4,500	8,500	12,500	—

KM# 1326 10 DUCAT
35.0000 g., 0.9860 Gold 1.1095 oz. AGW **Ruler:** Leopold I **Mint:** Hall **Note:** Struck with 1 Thaler dies, KM#1303.1. Prev. KM#A659.

Date	Mintage	VG	F	VF	XF	Unc
1683 Rare	—	—	—	—	—	—

KM# 1327 10 DUCAT
Gold **Ruler:** Leopold I **Obv:** Leopold I laureate bust right in inner circle **Rev:** Crowned arms in Order chain, crown divides date **Mint:** Saint Veit **Note:** Struck with 2 Thaler dies, KM#1323. Prev. KM#1662.

Date	Mintage	VG	F	VF	XF	Unc
1683/2	—	—	—	14,000	21,500	—

KM# 1350 10 DUCAT
35.0000 g., 0.9860 Gold 1.1095 oz. AGW **Ruler:** Leopold I **Obv:** Armored laureate bust right **Obv. Legend:** LEOPOLDVS: D: ROM: IMP: S: A: G: H: B: REX: **Rev:** Crowned arms within Order chain **Rev. Legend:** ARCHID: AVST: DVX: BV: CO: TYR • 16 **Mint:** Hall **Note:** Struck with 1 Thaler dies, KM#1349. Prev. KM#659.

Date	Mintage	VG	F	VF	XF	Unc
1690 Rare	—	—	—	—	—	—

KM# 797 12 DUCAT
42.0000 g., 0.9860 Gold 1.3314 oz. AGW **Ruler:** Ferdinand II **Obv:** Bust right **Rev:** Crowned arms **Mint:** Saint Veit **Note:** Struck with 1 Thaler dies, KM#678. Prev. KM#1614.

Date	Mintage	VG	F	VF	XF	Unc
1632 Rare	—	—	—	—	—	—

KM# 820 12 DUCAT
42.0000 g., 0.9860 Gold 1.3314 oz. AGW **Ruler:** Ferdinand II **Obv:** Bust right **Rev:** Heraldic imperial eagle **Mint:** Olmutz **Note:** Prev. KM#1246.

Date	Mintage	VG	F	VF	XF	Unc
1636/3 (o) Rare	—	—	—	—	—	—

KM# 1264 12 DUCAT
42.0000 g., 0.9860 Gold 1.3314 oz. AGW **Ruler:** Leopold I **Obv:** Laureate bust right **Rev:** Crowned imperial eagle **Mint:** Vienna **Note:** Prev. KM#A1899.

Date	Mintage	VG	F	VF	XF	Unc
1669 Rare	—	—	—	—	—	—

KM# 1313 12 DUCAT
42.0000 g., 0.9860 Gold 1.3314 oz. AGW **Ruler:** Leopold I **Mint:** Vienna **Note:** Struck with 1 Thaler dies, KM#1275.2. Prev. KM#1899.

Date	Mintage	VG	F	VF	XF	Unc
1681 Rare	—	—	—	—	—	—

KM# 821 15 DUCAT
52.5000 g., 0.9860 Gold 1.6642 oz. AGW **Ruler:** Ferdinand II **Obv:** Bust right **Rev:** Heraldic imperial eagle **Mint:** Olmutz **Note:** Prev. KM#1247.

Date	Mintage	VG	F	VF	XF	Unc
1636/3 (o) Rare	—	—	—	—	—	—

KM# 372 20 DUCAT
70.0000 g., 0.9860 Gold 2.2190 oz. AGW **Ruler:** Ferdinand II **Obv:** Crowned bust right **Rev:** Heraldic imperial eagle **Mint:** Olmutz **Note:** Prev. KM#1248.

Date	Mintage	VG	F	VF	XF	Unc
1621 BZ Rare	—	—	—	—	—	—

KM# 427 20 DUCAT
70.0000 g., 0.9860 Gold 2.2190 oz. AGW **Ruler:** Ferdinand II **Obv:** Crowned bust right **Rev:** Heraldic imperial eagle **Mint:** Klagenfurt **Note:** Prev. KM#983.

Date	Mintage	VG	F	VF	XF	Unc
1622 Rare	—	—	—	—	—	—

KM# 664 20 DUCAT
70.0000 g., 0.9860 Gold 2.2190 oz. AGW **Ruler:** Leopold **Subject:** Wedding of Leopold and Claudia **Mint:** Hall **Note:** Struck with 3 Thaler dies, KM#648. Prev. KM#824.

Date	Mintage	VG	F	VF	XF	Unc
ND(1626) Rare	—	—	—	—	—	—

KM# 822 20 DUCAT
70.0000 g., 0.9860 Gold 2.2190 oz. AGW **Ruler:** Ferdinand II **Obv:** Bust right with value XX stamped in field **Rev:** Crowned arms **Mint:** Graz **Note:** Prev. KM#410.

Date	Mintage	VG	F	VF	XF	Unc
1636 Rare	—	—	—	—	—	—

KM# 823 20 DUCAT
70.0000 g., 0.9860 Gold 2.2190 oz. AGW **Ruler:** Ferdinand II **Obv:** Bust right **Mint:** Olmutz **Note:** Prev. KM#1249.

Date	Mintage	VG	F	VF	XF	Unc
1636/3 (o) Rare	—	—	—	—	—	—

KM# 940 20 DUCAT
70.0000 g., 0.9860 Gold 2.2190 oz. AGW **Ruler:** Ferdinand Charles **Mint:** Hall **Note:** Struck with 2 Thaler dies, KM#934. Prev. KM#849.

Date	Mintage	VG	F	VF	XF	Unc
ND(1646) Rare	—	—	—	—	—	—

PATTERNS

Including off metal strikes

KM#	Date	Mintage	Identification	Mkt Val
PnPR1	1602	—	Ducat. Silver. Klippe.	—
PnKN2	1604	—	Klein Pfennig. Gold. KM#1015	—
PnPR2	1604	—	Maley Groschen. Gold. KM#1295.	—
PnPR3	1604	—	3 Kreuzer. Gold. KM#1297. Weight of 1 Ducat.	—
PnJO1	1607	—	1/4 Thaler. Gold. KM#867, weight of 3 Ducat.	—
PnHA1	1612	—	Kreuzer. Gold. KM#583	—
PnHA2	ND(1612-19)	—	Vierer. Gold. Weight of 1/4 Ducat, KM#760.	—
PnVI6	1613	—	3 Kreuzer. Gold. KM#1728, weight of 3 Ducat.	—
PnVI9	1616	—	3 Kreuzer. Gold. KM#1728, weight of 5 Ducat.	—
PnSV1	ND	—	Kreuzer. Gold. Weight of 1/2 Ducat.	—
PnSV2	1621	—	48 Kreuzer. Gold. Weight of 4 Ducat.	—
PnKL1	ND	—	Kreuzer. Gold. KM#951, weight of 1/2 Ducat.	—
PnKL2	ND	—	Kreuzer. Gold. KM#952, weight of 1/2 Ducat.	—
PnKL3	1621	—	48 Kreuzer. Gold. KM#957, weight of 4 Ducat.	—
PnKL4	1622	—	48 Kreuzer. Gold. KM#958, weight of 4 Ducat.	—
PnSV3	1622	—	48 Kreuzer. Gold. Weight of 4 Ducat.	—
PnPR24	1623 (e)	—	10 Ducat. Silver. KM#1400. Weight of 1 Thaler.	—
PnPR25	1623 (e)	—	10 Ducat. Silver. KM#1400. Weight of 2 Thaler.	—
PnPR26	1623 (e)	—	10 Ducat. Silver. KM#1400. Weight of 3 Thaler.	—
PnPR28	1624 (c)	—	10 Ducat. Silver. KM#1400. Weight of 1 Thaler.	—
PnHA3	ND(1625-32)	—	Kreuzer. Gold. Weight of 1/2 Ducat, KM#788.	—
PnHA4	1626	—	10 Kreuzer. Bronze. KM#795.	—
PnSV4	1627	—	Thaler. Gold. Weight of 5 Ducat; KM#1603.	—
PnKL5	1628	—	10 Kreuzer. Gold. Weight of 3 Ducat.	—
PnSV5	1628	—	10 Kreuzer. Gold. Weight of 2 Ducat; KM#1597.	—
PnSV6	1628	—	10 Kreuzer. Gold. Weight of 3 Ducat; KM#1597.	—
PnSV7	1628	—	10 Kreuzer. Gold. Weight of 3 Ducat; KM#1598.	—
PnKL6	1628	—	10 Kreuzer. Gold. Weight of 2 Ducat.	—
PnHA8	ND(1632)	—	2 Thaler. Pewter. KM#807.	—
PnSV11	1637	—	3 Kreuzer. Gold. Weight of 1 Ducat; KM#1624.	—
PnSV12	1637	—	3 Kreuzer. Gold. Weight of 1 Ducat; KM#1625. Klippe.	—
PnGR9	1638/4	—	2 Ducat. Gold.	—
PnSV13	1638	—	2 Pfennig. Gold. KM#1622.	—
PnSV14	1638	—	3 Kreuzer. Gold. Weight of 1 Ducat. KM#1622.	—
PnSV15	1638	—	3 Kreuzer. Gold. Weight of 1 Ducat. KM#1625. Klippe.	—
PnPR29	1639	—	Ducat. Silver. KM#1417. Klippe.	—
PnSV21	1639	—	Pfennig. Gold. KM#1620.	—
PnSV22	1639	—	Kreuzer. Gold. KM#1623; weight of 1/2 Ducat.	—
PnSV23	1640	—	Kreuzer. Gold. KM#1623; weight of 1/2 Ducat.	—
PnSV24	1641	—	2 Pfennig. Gold. KM#1622.	—
PnHA9	1642	—	2 Ducat. Silver. KM#842.	—
PnSV25	1642	—	2 Pfennig. Gold. KM#1622.	—
PnVI18	1642	—	2 Pfennig. Gold. KM#1816.	—
PnGR10	1644	—	2 Pfennig. Gold. KM#420	—
PnVI19	1644	—	2 Pfennig. Gold. KM#1850.	—
PnGR11	1645	—	Pfennig. Gold. KM#418	—
PnGR12	1645	—	Kreuzer. Gold. KM#422; weight of 1/2 Ducat.	—
PnGR13	1646	—	Kreuzer. Gold. KM#422	—
PnVI20	1647	—	2 Pfennig. Gold. KM#1816.	—
PnHA11	ND(1647-62)	—	Kreuzer. Gold. KM#827.	—
PnGR14	1648	—	2 Pfennig. Gold. KM#420	—
PnVI21	1648	—	Kreuzer. Gold. KM#91; weight of 1/2 Ducat	—
PnSV26	1653	—	Pfennig. Gold. KM#1620.	—
PnSV27	1653	—	2 Pfennig. Gold. KM#1622; weight of 1/4 Ducat.	—
PnKN4	1654	—	Pfennig. Lead. KM#1100	—
PnJO3	1659	—	Thaler. Lead. KM#935	—
PnJO5	1663	—	15 Kreuzer. Gold. KM#932	—
PnJO6	1663	—	1/4 Thaler. Lead. KM#933	—
PnJO7	1663	—	1/2 Thaler. Lead. KM#934	—
PnJO4	1664	—	15 Kreuzer. Lead. KM#932	—
PnVI22	1696	—	15 Kreuzer. Brass.	—

TRIAL STRIKES

KM#	Date	Mintage	Identification	Mkt Val
TSHA1	ND(1626)	—	2 Thaler. Lead. KM#822.	—

AUSTRIAN STATES

AUERSPERG

Auersberg

The Auersperg princes were princes of estates in Austrian Carniola, a former duchy with estates in Laibach and Silesia, a former province in southwestern Poland and Swabia, one of the stem-duchies of medieval Germany. They were elevated to princely rank in 1653, and the following year were made dukes of Muensterberg, which they ultimately sold to Prussia.

RULER
Johann Weikard, 1615-1677

MONETARY SYSTEM
120 Kreuzer = 1 Convention Thaler

PRINCIPALITY

STANDARD COINAGE

KM# 3 THALER
Silver **Ruler:** Johann Weikard **Obv:** Facing bust with date below **Rev:** Crowned arms in Order chain **Note:** Dav. #3371.

Date	Mintage	VG	F	VF	XF	Unc
1654	—	1,350	2,100	3,400	5,300	—

TRADE COINAGE

KM# 10 DUCAT
3.5000 g., 0.9860 Gold 0.1109 oz. AGW **Ruler:** Johann Weikard **Obv:** Bust of Johann Weikard in inner circle **Rev:** Shield of arms in inner circle

Date	Mintage	VG	F	VF	XF	Unc
ND Rare	—	—	—	—	—	—

BRIXEN

A city near the Brenner Pass that was the seat of a bishopric from 992. The bishops were given the coinage right in 1179. Brixen was given to Austria in 1802.

RULER
Karl of Austria, 1613-1624

NOTE: Ruler listing includes only coin issuers and not all bishops.

BISHOPRIC

STANDARD COINAGE

KM# 5 3 KREUZER
Silver **Ruler:** Karl

Date	Mintage	VG	F	VF	XF	Unc
1614	—	22.50	45.00	80.00	175	—
1620	—	22.50	45.00	80.00	175	—

KM# 6 THALER
Silver **Ruler:** Karl **Obv:** Bust right **Rev:** Several coast of arms **Note:** Dav. #3457.

Date	Mintage	VG	F	VF	XF	Unc
1614	—	750	1,250	2,500	4,050	—

KM# 7 THALER
Silver **Ruler:** Karl **Note:** Dav. #3459.

Date	Mintage	VG	F	VF	XF	Unc
1615	—	725	1,200	2,400	3,900	—
1618	—	725	1,200	2,400	3,900	—

KM# 8 2 THALER
Silver **Ruler:** Karl **Obv:** Bust right **Rev:** Several coat of arms **Note:** Dav. #3456.

Date	Mintage	VG	F	VF	XF	Unc
1614 Rare	—	—	—	—	—	—

KM# 17 2 THALER
Silver **Ruler:** Karl **Note:** Similar to 1 Thaler, KM#7. Dav. #3458.

Date	Mintage	VG	F	VF	XF	Unc
1618	—	3,400	5,300	—	—	—

KM# 10 3 THALER
Silver **Ruler:** Karl **Obv:** Bust right **Rev:** Several coat of arms **Note:** Dav. #3456A.

Date	Mintage	VG	F	VF	XF	Unc
1614 Rare	—	—	—	—	—	—

KM# 11 4 THALER
Silver **Ruler:** Karl **Obv:** Bust right **Rev:** Several coat of arms **Note:** Dav. #3456B.

Date	Mintage	VG	F	VF	XF	Unc
1614 Rare	—	—	—	—	—	—

TRADE COINAGE

KM# 18 1/2 DUCAT
1.7500 g., 0.9860 Gold 0.0555 oz. AGW **Ruler:** Karl **Obv:** Bust of Karl right **Rev:** Crowned arms flanked by mitred arms

Date	Mintage	VG	F	VF	XF	Unc
1618	—	700	1,450	3,300	4,800	—

KM# 12 DUCAT
3.5000 g., 0.9860 Gold 0.1109 oz. AGW **Ruler:** Karl **Obv:** Bust of Karl right **Rev:** Crowned arms flanked by mitred arms

Date	Mintage	VG	F	VF	XF	Unc
1614	—	950	2,050	4,000	7,200	—
1618	—	950	2,050	4,000	7,200	—

KM# 13 3 DUCAT
10.5000 g., 0.9860 Gold 0.3328 oz. AGW **Ruler:** Karl **Obv:** Bust of Karl right in inner circle **Rev:** Crowned arms in inner circle

Date	Mintage	VG	F	VF	XF	Unc
1614 Rare	—	—	—	—	—	—

KM# 15 5 DUCAT
17.5000 g., 0.9860 Gold 0.5547 oz. AGW **Ruler:** Karl **Obv:** Bust of Karl right in inner circle **Rev:** Crowned arms in inner circle

Date	Mintage	VG	F	VF	XF	Unc
1614 Rare	—	—	—	—	—	—

KM# 16 7 DUCAT
24.5000 g., 0.9860 Gold 0.7766 oz. AGW **Ruler:** Karl **Note:** Struck with 1 Thaler dies, KM#6.

Date	Mintage	VG	F	VF	XF	Unc
1614 Rare	—	—	—	—	—	—

KM# 20 10 DUCAT
35.0000 g., 0.9860 Gold 1.1095 oz. AGW **Ruler:** Karl **Note:** Struck with 1 Thaler dies, KM#7.

Date	Mintage	VG	F	VF	XF	Unc
1618 Rare	—	—	—	—	—	—

Note: UBS Auction 50, 1-01, nearly XF realized approximately $12,150.

DIETRICHSTEIN

A noble Carinthian family traceable from 1000, it was not until after 1500 that the first coins were made. The coinage was sporadic and Karl Ludwig was the last to issue coins in 1726.

RULERS
Pulsgau Line
Sigismund Ludwig, 1631-1664
Sigismund Helfried, 1664-1698
Karl Ludwig, 1698-1732
Nicolsburg Line
Ferdinand Josef, 1655-1698

NOTE: Ruler listing includes only coin issuers and not all rulers of the various line of this family.

COUNTY

STANDARD COINAGE

KM# 5 1/2 KREUZER (2 Pfennig)
Billon **Ruler:** Sigismund Ludwig **Obv:** Crowned arms **Note:** Uniface.

Date	Mintage	VG	F	VF	XF	Unc
1650	—	45.00	85.00	170	300	—

KM# 1 THALER
Silver **Ruler:** Sigismund Ludwig **Rev:** Double eagle above large crowned arms **Note:** Dav. #3372. Varieties exist.

Date	Mintage	VG	F	VF	XF	Unc
1638	—	250	500	825	1,300	—
1644	—	250	500	825	1,300	—
1647	—	250	500	825	1,300	—

KM# 7 THALER
Silver **Ruler:** Sigismund Ludwig **Rev:** Large double eagle above small crowned arms **Note:** Dav. #3373.

Date	Mintage	VG	F	VF	XF	Unc
1640	—	265	525	875	1,400	—
1641	—	265	525	875	1,400	—

KM# 9 THALER
Silver **Ruler:** Sigismund Ludwig **Rev:** Larger arms with Order chain around **Note:** Dav. #3374. Varieties exist.

Date	Mintage	VG	F	VF	XF	Unc
1646	—	250	500	825	1,300	—
1651	—	250	500	825	1,300	—
1653	—	250	500	825	1,300	—

KM# 12 THALER
Silver **Ruler:** Sigismund Helfried **Obv:** Bust right **Rev:** Crowned arms **Note:** Dav. #3375.

Date	Mintage	VG	F	VF	XF	Unc
1664	—	575	975	1,750	3,000	—

KM# 10 2 THALER
Silver **Ruler:** Sigismund Ludwig **Note:** Similar to 1 Thaler, KM#7. Dav. A3373.

Date	Mintage	VG	F	VF	XF	Unc
1641	—	1,800	3,000	5,300	9,000	—

TRADE COINAGE

KM# 8 DUCAT
3.5000 g., 0.9860 Gold 0.1109 oz. AGW **Ruler:** Sigismund Ludwig **Obv:** Bust right in inner circle **Rev:** Crowned imperial eagle with F III on breast over small arms in inner circle

Date	Mintage	VG	F	VF	XF	Unc
1640	—	875	1,700	3,950	6,600	—
1651	—	875	1,700	3,950	6,600	—

KM# 2 5 DUCAT
17.5000 g., 0.9860 Gold 0.5547 oz. AGW **Ruler:** Sigismund Ludwig **Note:** Struck with 1 Thaler dies, KM#6.

Date	Mintage	VG	F	VF	XF	Unc
1638 Rare	—	—	—	—	—	—

KM# 3 6 DUCAT
21.0000 g., 0.9860 Gold 0.6657 oz. AGW **Ruler:** Sigismund Ludwig **Note:** Struck with 1 Thaler dies, KM#9.

Date	Mintage	VG	F	VF	XF	Unc
1638 Rare	—	—	—	—	—	—

KM# A12 6 DUCAT
21.0000 g., 0.9860 Gold 0.6657 oz. AGW **Ruler:** Sigismund Ludwig **Note:** Struck with 1 Thaler dies, KM#9.

Date	Mintage	VG	F	VF	XF	Unc
1653 Rare	—	—	—	—	—	—

KM# 11 10 DUCAT
35.0000 g., 0.9870 Gold 1.1106 oz. AGW **Ruler:** Sigismund Ludwig **Note:** Struck with 1 Thaler dies, KM#7.

Date	Mintage	VG	F	VF	XF	Unc
1641 Rare	—	—	—	—	—	—

KM# B12 10 DUCAT
35.0000 g., 0.9870 Gold 1.1106 oz. AGW **Ruler:** Sigismund Ludwig **Note:** Struck with 1 Thaler dies, KM#9.

Date	Mintage	VG	F	VF	XF	Unc
1653 Rare	—	—	—	—	—	—

COUNTY

Nikolsburg Line

STANDARD COINAGE

KM# 20 THALER
Silver **Ruler:** Ferdinand Josef **Obv:** Bust right **Rev:** Crowned arms **Note:** Dav. #3376.

Date	Mintage	VG	F	VF	XF	Unc
1695	—	265	525	900	1,450	—

TRADE COINAGE

KM# 21 DUCAT
3.5000 g., 0.9860 Gold 0.1109 oz. AGW **Ruler:** Ferdinand Josef **Obv:** Bust of Ferdinand Josef right **Rev:** Crowned arms in order collar; date divided at top

Date	Mintage	VG	F	VF	XF	Unc
1695	—	1,000	1,800	4,600	7,500	—
1696	—	1,000	1,800	4,600	7,500	—

EGGENBERG

An old Styrian family first mentioned in 1448. Two members made free barons in 1598 after service in the Dutch wars. Made a prince in 1623. Bought Italian properties of Aquileia and Gradiska in 1641. Passed to Herberstein in 1774 after death of the line.

RULERS
Johann Ulrich, 1623-1634
Johann Anton, 1634-1649
Johann Christoph, 1649-1710
Johann Seyfried, 1649-1713

PRINCIPALITY

STANDARD COINAGE

KM# 19 3 KREUZER
Silver **Ruler:** Johann Anton

Date	Mintage	VG	F	VF	XF	Unc
1647	—	70.00	135	265	450	—
1649	—	70.00	135	265	450	—

KM# 52 3 KREUZER
Silver **Ruler:** Johann Christoph

Date	Mintage	VG	F	VF	XF	Unc
1677	—	48.00	100	200	400	—

KM# 39 1/4 THALER
Silver **Ruler:** Johann Christoph

Date	Mintage	VG	F	VF	XF	Unc
1655	—	265	525	950	1,500	—
1658	—	265	525	950	1,500	—

KM# 40 1/2 THALER
Silver **Ruler:** Johann Christoph

Date	Mintage	VG	F	VF	XF	Unc
1654	—	425	825	1,500	2,500	—
1658	—	425	825	1,500	2,500	—

KM# 5 THALER
Silver **Ruler:** Johann Ulrich **Obv:** Crowned arms **Rev:** Heraldic double eagle **Note:** Dav. #3377.

Date	Mintage	VG	F	VF	XF	Unc
1625	—	1,200	2,000	3,300	5,500	—

KM# 6 THALER
Silver **Ruler:** Johann Ulrich **Note:** Similar to 2 Thaler, KM#7. Dav. #3379.

Date	Mintage	VG	F	VF	XF	Unc
1625	—	1,200	2,000	3,300	5,500	—

KM# 8 THALER
Silver **Ruler:** Johann Ulrich **Obv:** Crowned arms in order chain, 1-6-2-5 **Note:** Dav. #3380. Varieties exist.

Date	Mintage	VG	F	VF	XF	Unc
1629 Rare	—	—	—	—	—	—

KM# 9 THALER
Silver **Ruler:** Johann Ulrich **Obv:** EG and scroll below ruffled bust **Rev:** Crowned oval arms in order chain, date in legend **Note:** Dav. #3382.

Date	Mintage	VG	F	VF	XF	Unc
1629	—	575	1,050	1,750	2,900	—

KM# 15 THALER
Silver **Ruler:** Johann Ulrich **Rev:** Crowned shield shaped arms **Note:** Dav. #3383.

Date	Mintage	VG	F	VF	XF	Unc
1630	—	425	750	1,500	2,500	—
1631	—	425	750	1,500	2,500	—
1633	—	425	750	1,500	2,500	—

KM# 16 THALER
Silver **Ruler:** Johann Ulrich **Obv:** Date below ruffled bust **Note:** Dav. #3384. Varieties exist.

Date	Mintage	VG	F	VF	XF	Unc
1633 Rare	—	—	—	—	—	—

KM# 20 THALER
Silver **Ruler:** Johann Anton **Obv:** Bust right **Rev:** Crowned arms, date divided **Note:** Dav. #3385.

Date	Mintage	VG	F	VF	XF	Unc
1638	—	650	1,100	1,750	3,000	—

KM# 25 THALER
Silver **Ruler:** Johann Anton **Rev:** Date left of crown **Note:** Dav. #3387.

Date	Mintage	VG	F	VF	XF	Unc
1642	—	175	350	625	1,400	—
1643	—	175	350	625	1,400	—
1644	—	175	350	625	1,400	—

KM# 27 THALER
Silver **Ruler:** Johann Anton **Obv:** Older bust, different drapery **Rev:** Ornate arms in order chain **Note:** Dav. #3389.

Date	Mintage	VG	F	VF	XF	Unc
1644	—	325	575	975	1,950	—
1649	—	325	575	975	1,950	—

KM# 28 THALER

Silver **Ruler:** Johann Anton **Note:** Klippe. Dav. #3389A. Illustration reduced.

Date	Mintage	VG	F	VF	XF	Unc
1644 Rare	—	—	—	—	—	—

KM# 32 THALER

Silver **Ruler:** Johann Anton **Obv:** Bust divides legend at top **Rev:** Crowned ornate, oval arms **Note:** Dav. #3390.

Date	Mintage	VG	F	VF	XF	Unc
1645	—	450	825	1,650	2,700	—

KM# 33 THALER

Silver **Ruler:** Johann Christoph **Obv:** 2 facing busts above date **Rev:** Crowned oval with 6 smaller arms **Note:** Klippe. Dav. #3391.

Date	Mintage	VG	F	VF	XF	Unc
1652 Rare	—	—	—	—	—	—

KM# 37 THALER

Silver **Ruler:** Johann Christoph **Obv:** 2 facing busts below date **Rev:** Crowned oval arms **Note:** Dav. #3392. Previous KM#36.

Date	Mintage	VG	F	VF	XF	Unc
1653	—	325	575	900	1,500	—

KM# 41 THALER

Silver **Ruler:** Johann Christoph **Obv:** 2 facing busts above date, scroll border in inner circle **Note:** Dav. #3393. Previously KM#38.

Date	Mintage	VG	F	VF	XF	Unc
1654	—	210	325	575	975	—

KM# 45 THALER

Silver **Ruler:** Johann Christoph **Obv:** Longer busts **Rev:** Different frame around arms **Note:** Dav. #3395.

Date	Mintage	VG	F	VF	XF	Unc
1658	—	210	325	575	975	—

KM# 46 1-1/4 THALER

Silver **Ruler:** Johann Christoph **Note:** Similar to 1 Thaler, KM#39. Dav. #A3395.

Date	Mintage	VG	F	VF	XF	Unc
1658 Rare	—	—	—	—	—	—

KM# 7 2 THALER

Silver **Ruler:** Johann Ulrich **Obv:** Crowned arms **Rev:** Heraldic double eagle **Note:** Dav. #3378.

Date	Mintage	VG	F	VF	XF	Unc
1625	—	4,000	7,000	12,000	19,000	—

KM# 10 2 THALER

Silver **Ruler:** Johann Ulrich **Note:** Similar to 1 Thaler, KM#9. Dav. #3381.

Date	Mintage	VG	F	VF	XF	Unc
1629	—	2,800	4,600	8,000	14,000	—

KM# 26 2 THALER

Silver **Ruler:** Johann Anton **Note:** Similar to 1 Thaler, KM#25. Dav. #3386.

Date	Mintage	VG	F	VF	XF	Unc
1642	—	3,300	5,600	8,800	15,500	—
1643	—	3,300	5,600	8,800	15,500	—
1644	—	3,300	5,600	8,800	15,500	—

KM# 29 2 THALER

Silver **Ruler:** Johann Anton **Obv:** Bust extends to edge of coin on bottom **Rev:** Crowned arms **Note:** Dav. #3388.

Date	Mintage	VG	F	VF	XF	Unc
1644	—	3,300	5,600	8,800	15,500	—
1649	—	3,300	5,600	8,800	15,500	—

KM# 38 2 THALER

Silver **Ruler:** Johann Christoph **Note:** Similar to 1 Thaler, KM#36. Dav. #A3392. Previously KM#37.

Date	Mintage	VG	F	VF	XF	Unc
1653	—	3,300	5,600	8,800	15,500	—

KM# 47 2 THALER

Silver **Ruler:** Johann Christoph **Note:** Similar to 1 Thaler, KM#39. Dav. #3394. Previously KM#41.

Date	Mintage	VG	F	VF	XF	Unc
1658	—	3,300	5,600	8,800	15,500	—

KM# 30 3 THALER

Silver **Ruler:** Johann Anton **Note:** Similar to 2Thaler, KM#29. Dav. A3388.

Date	Mintage	VG	F	VF	XF	Unc
1644 Rare	—	—	—	—	—	—

Note: Kinker Auction #163, 1-10, VF-XF realized approx. $45,000

KM# 31 4 THALER

Silver **Ruler:** Johann Anton **Note:** Similar to 1 Thaler, KM#25. Dav. #A3386.

Date	Mintage	VG	F	VF	XF	Unc
1644 Rare	—	—	—	—	—	—

TRADE COINAGE

KM# 22 DUCAT

3.5000 g., 0.9860 Gold 0.1109 oz. AGW **Ruler:** Johann Anton **Obv:** Bust of Johann Anton right **Rev:** Crowned arms

Date	Mintage	VG	F	VF	XF	Unc
1638	—	5,300	8,300	12,000	20,500	—

KM# 43 DUCAT

3.5000 g., 0.9860 Gold 0.1109 oz. AGW **Ruler:** Johann Christoph **Obv:** Busts of Johann Christoph and Johann Seyfried facing in inner circle **Rev:** Crowned arms in inner circle

Date	Mintage	VG	F	VF	XF	Unc
1654	—	5,800	9,000	13,000	22,500	—

KM# 34 5 DUCAT

17.5000 g., 0.9860 Gold 0.5547 oz. AGW **Ruler:** Johann Christoph **Note:** Struck with 1 Thaler dies, KM#35.

Date	Mintage	VG	F	VF	XF	Unc
1652 Rare	—	—	—	—	—	—

KM# 49 5 DUCAT

17.5000 g., 0.9860 Gold 0.5547 oz. AGW **Ruler:** Johann Christoph **Note:** Struck with 1 Thaler dies, KM#39.

Date	Mintage	VG	F	VF	XF	Unc
1658 Rare	—	—	—	—	—	—

KM# 18 8 DUCAT

28.0000 g., 0.9860 Gold 0.8876 oz. AGW **Ruler:** Johann Ulrich **Note:** Struck with 1 Thaler dies, KM#9.

Date	Mintage	VG	F	VF	XF	Unc
1629	—	—	—	20,500	28,000	—

KM# 35 10 DUCAT

35.0000 g., 0.9860 Gold 1.1095 oz. AGW **Ruler:** Johann Christoph **Note:** Struck with 1 Thaler dies, KM#35.

Date	Mintage	VG	F	VF	XF	Unc
1652 Rare	—	—	—	—	—	—

KM# A36 10 DUCAT

35.0000 g., 0.9860 Gold 1.1095 oz. AGW **Ruler:** Johann Christoph **Note:** Struck with 1 Thaler dies, KM#38.

Date	Mintage	VG	F	VF	XF	Unc
1654 Rare	—	—	—	—	—	—

KM# 36 15 DUCAT

52.5000 g., 0.9860 Gold 1.6642 oz. AGW **Ruler:** Johann Christoph **Note:** Struck with 1 Thaler dies, KM#35.

Date	Mintage	VG	F	VF	XF	Unc
1652 Rare	—	—	—	—	—	—

GARSTEN

A Benedictine Abbey located in Upper Austria endowed by the Margrave Ottokar in the Steiermark. The Abbot issued a thaler for the official jubilee of the city of Steyer and the Ironmakers Guild in 1679.

ABBEY

STANDARD COINAGE

KM# 5 THALER

Silver **Ruler:** Roman Rauscher von Steyr **Obv:** 11-line inscription within sprays **Rev:** 3 shields in frame, bishop miter above **Note:** Dav. #3460.

Date	Mintage	VG	F	VF	XF	Unc
1679	—	575	1,150	2,000	3,000	—

OLMUTZ

In Moravia

Olmutz (Olomouc), a town in the eastern part of the Czech Republic which was, until 1640, the recognized capital of Moravia, obtained the right to mint coinage in 1144, but exercised it sparingly until the 17th century, when it became an archbishopric.

RULERS

Franz von Dietrichstein
Prince-Bishop, 1599-1636
Johann XIX Ernst von Plattenstein, 1636-1637
Leopold Wilhelm of Austria, 1637-1662
Karl Josef of Austria, 1663-1664
Karl II von Liechtenstein-Castelcorn, 1664-1695
Karl III Josef Herzog von Lothringen, 1695-1711

BISHOPRIC

STANDARD COINAGE

KM# 60.1 HELLER

Silver **Ruler:** Franz **Obv:** 3 shields on trilobe below hat, bottom of shields point towards center of coin **Note:** Uniface. Prev. KM#5.1.

Date	Mintage	Good	VG	F	VF	XF
(1)614	—	18.00	30.00	42.00	90.00	125

KM# 60.2 HELLER

Silver **Ruler:** Franz **Obv:** 3 baroque style shields on trilobe below hat, bottom of shields pont towards bottom of coin **Note:** Uniface. Prev. part of #60.2

Date	Mintage	Good	VG	F	VF	XF
ND	—	18.00	30.00	42.00	70.00	110

KM# 60.3 HELLER

Silver **Ruler:** Franz **Obv:** 3 square-topped shields on trilobe below hat, bottom of shields pont towards bottom of coin **Note:** Uniface. Prev. KM#60.2 and 5.2.

Date	Mintage	Good	VG	F	VF	XF
(1)615	—	10.00	14.00	30.00	55.00	100
(1)616	—	10.00	14.00	30.00	55.00	100
(1)617	—	10.00	14.00	30.00	55.00	100

KM# 316 1/2 KREUZER

Silver **Ruler:** Leopold Wilhelm **Obv:** 3 shields on trilobe **Note:** Prev. KM#A50.

Date	Mintage	Good	VG	F	VF	XF
ND	—	18.00	30.00	42.00	90.00	125

KM# 318 1/2 KREUZER

Silver **Ruler:** Karl II **Obv:** 3 shields, 1/2 in parenthesis **Note:** Uniface. Varieties exist. Prev. KM#86.

Date	Mintage	VG	F	VF	XF	Unc
1681	—	25.00	42.00	85.00	140	—
1682	—	18.00	36.00	70.00	110	—
1683	—	12.00	25.00	49.00	85.00	—
1684	—	18.00	36.00	70.00	110	—

KM# 325 1/2 KREUZER

Silver **Ruler:** Karl II **Obv:** 3 shields, denomination - S 1/2 S **Note:** Uniface. Prev. KM#95.

Date	Mintage	VG	F	VF	XF	Unc
1694	—	18.00	36.00	70.00	110	—
1695	—	18.00	36.00	70.00	110	—

KM# 15 KREUZER

Silver **Ruler:** Franz **Obv:** Arms on cross **Rev:** Mitre with sword and staff **Note:** Varieties exist. Prev. KM#6.

Date	Mintage	VG	F	VF	XF	Unc
ND	—	22.50	36.00	70.00	125	—

KM# 185 KREUZER

Silver **Ruler:** Leopold Wilhelm **Obv:** Bust right **Rev:** 3 shields in trilobe **Rev. Legend:** ...PRO., PRIN. or PRINC **Note:** Varieties exist. Prev. KM#50.

Date	Mintage	VG	F	VF	XF	Unc
1650	—	8.00	18.00	42.00	85.00	—
1651	—	7.00	14.00	35.00	75.00	—
(16)52	—	8.00	18.00	42.00	85.00	—
1652	—	8.00	18.00	42.00	85.00	—
(16)53	—	8.00	18.00	42.00	85.00	—
1653	—	8.00	18.00	42.00	85.00	—
(16)54	—	—	—	—	—	—
1654	—	6.00	12.00	27.50	70.00	—
1655	—	7.00	14.00	35.00	75.00	—

KM# 190.1 KREUZER

Silver **Ruler:** Leopold Wilhelm **Rev. Legend:** C. or COMES **Note:** Prev. KM#52.1.

Date	Mintage	VG	F	VF	XF	Unc
1656	—	10.00	19.00	55.00	100	—
1658	—	10.00	19.00	55.00	100	—

KM# 190.2 KREUZER

Silver **Ruler:** Leopold Wilhelm **Obv:** Bust right **Rev:** 2 shields in circle **Note:** Prev. KM#52.2.

Date	Mintage	VG	F	VF	XF	Unc
1658	—	8.00	18.00	42.00	85.00	—
1659	—	10.00	19.00	44.75	90.00	—

KM# 62 2 KREUZER

Silver **Ruler:** Franz **Obv:** Arms below hat **Rev:** 2 shields with staff and sword **Note:** Prev. KM#7.

Date	Mintage	VG	F	VF	XF	Unc
ND	—	30.00	48.00	105	170	—

KM# 63 3 KREUZER

Silver **Ruler:** Franz **Obv:** Bust 3/4 profile **Rev:** 3 shields in trilobe **Note:** Prev. KM#11.

Date	Mintage	VG	F	VF	XF	Unc
(1)614	—	12.00	25.00	49.00	90.00	—
(1)616	—	12.00	25.00	49.00	90.00	—
(1)617	—	12.00	25.00	49.00	90.00	—

KM# 50 3 KREUZER

Silver **Ruler:** Franz **Obv:** Arms below hat **Rev:** Madonna and child **Note:** Prev. KM#8.

Date	Mintage	VG	F	VF	XF	Unc
ND	—	—	—	—	—	—

KM# 51 3 KREUZER

Silver **Ruler:** Franz **Obv:** Bust right **Rev:** 3 shields in trilobe **Note:** Prev. KM#9.

Date	Mintage	VG	F	VF	XF	Unc
ND	—	12.00	25.00	49.00	90.00	—

KM# 52 3 KREUZER

Silver **Ruler:** Franz **Obv:** Bust right **Rev:** Ornamentation between shields **Note:** Varieties exist. Prev. KM#10.

Date	Mintage	VG	F	VF	XF	Unc
ND	—	12.00	25.00	49.00	90.00	—

KM# 90 3 KREUZER

Silver **Ruler:** Franz **Obv:** Bust right **Rev:** 3 shields in circle **Note:** Varieties exist. Prev. KM#12.

Date	Mintage	VG	F	VF	XF	Unc
(1)618	—	12.00	25.00	49.00	90.00	—
(1)619	—	12.00	25.00	49.00	90.00	—
(16)19	—	25.00	36.00	65.00	105	—

KM# 186 3 KREUZER
Silver **Ruler:** Leopold Wilhelm **Obv:** Bust right **Rev:** 3 shields with ornamentation, date **Rev. Legend:** ...PRIN **Note:** Varieties exist. Prev. KM#51.

Date	Mintage	VG	F	VF	XF	Unc
1650	—	12.00	25.00	49.00	100	—
1651	—	12.00	25.00	49.00	100	—
1652	—	25.00	30.00	55.00	110	—
1654	—	8.00	18.00	42.00	85.00	—
1655	—	8.00	18.00	42.00	85.00	—

KM# 192.1 3 KREUZER
Silver **Ruler:** Leopold Wilhelm **Obv:** Bust right **Rev:** 3 shields with ornamentation, date **Rev. Legend:** ...CO. or COM **Note:** Prev. KM#53.1.

Date	Mintage	VG	F	VF	XF	Unc
1656	—	8.00	18.00	42.00	85.00	—
1657	—	8.00	18.00	42.00	85.00	—
(16)5.7.	—	8.00	18.00	42.00	85.00	—

KM# 192.2 3 KREUZER
Silver **Ruler:** Leopold Wilhelm **Rev:** 2 shields in circle **Note:** Prev. KM#53.2.

Date	Mintage	VG	F	VF	XF	Unc
1658	—	8.00	18.00	42.00	85.00	—
1659	—	8.00	18.00	42.00	85.00	—

KM# 192.3 3 KREUZER
Silver **Ruler:** Leopold Wilhelm **Rev:** Arms below mitre and crown **Note:** Prev. KM#53.3.

Date	Mintage	VG	F	VF	XF	Unc
1660	—	10.00	19.00	55.00	100	—
1662	—	14.00	36.00	70.00	120	—

KM# 227.1 3 KREUZER
Silver **Ruler:** Karl II **Obv:** Small bust right within inner circle **Rev:** Arms **Note:** Many varieties exist. Prev. KM#65.1.

Date	Mintage	VG	F	VF	XF	Unc
1664	—	7.00	18.00	42.00	70.00	—
1667	—	7.00	18.00	42.00	70.00	—
1668	—	6.00	14.00	35.00	55.00	—
1669	—	5.00	12.00	31.50	55.00	—

KM# 227.2 3 KREUZER
Silver **Ruler:** Karl II **Obv:** Large bust right breaks inner circle **Note:** Many varieties exist. Prev. KM#65.2.

Date	Mintage	VG	F	VF	XF	Unc
1665	—	6.00	14.00	35.00	55.00	—
1666	—	6.00	14.00	35.00	55.00	—
1667	—	6.00	14.00	35.00	55.00	—
1668	—	2.50	12.00	35.00	55.00	—
1669	—	2.50	12.00	31.50	55.00	—
1670	—	2.50	12.00	31.50	55.00	—
Note: More than 150 varieties exist for this date.						
1673	—	7.00	18.00	42.00	70.00	—

KM# 227.3 3 KREUZER
Silver **Ruler:** Karl II **Rev:** Arms, SAS below, date at top **Note:** Prev. KM#65.3.

Date	Mintage	VG	F	VF	XF	Unc
1676	—	—	—	—	—	—

Note: Existance is questionable. SAS is an abbreviation for die cutter Simon Andreas Sinopi, who worked at the mint from 1677 to 1684 and 1689 to 1699.

KM# 227.4 3 KREUZER
Silver **Ruler:** Karl II **Rev:** Round or oval arms, without SAS **Note:** Prev. KM#65.4.

Date	Mintage	VG	F	VF	XF	Unc
1693	—	6.00	14.00	35.00	55.00	—

KM# 227.5 3 KREUZER
Silver **Ruler:** Karl II **Rev:** Round or oval arms, SAS below, date at top **Note:** Varieties exist. Prev. KM#65.5

Date	Mintage	VG	F	VF	XF	Unc
1695	—	6.00	14.00	35.00	55.00	—

KM# 335 3 KREUZER
Silver **Ruler:** Karl III Josef **Obv:** Bust right **Rev:** Crowned arms on cross **Note:** KM#335 has more than 5 minor varieties. Prev. KM#102.

Date	Mintage	VG	F	VF	XF	Unc
1699	—	18.00	50.00	105	140	—

KM# 236.1 6 KREUZER
Silver **Ruler:** Karl II **Obv:** Small bust right **Rev:** Arms, legends ends with date **Note:** Prev. KM#71.1.

Date	Mintage	VG	F	VF	XF	Unc
1665	—	14.00	30.00	85.00	165	—
1669	—	14.00	30.00	85.00	165	—

KM# 236.2 6 KREUZER
Silver **Ruler:** Karl II **Obv:** Large bust right **Rev:** Round arms, date divided by mitre and crown **Note:** Prev. KM#71.2.

Date	Mintage	VG	F	VF	XF	Unc
1673	—	12.00	25.00	55.00	110	—
1674	—	11.00	22.50	55.00	105	—
1675	—	11.00	22.50	55.00	105	—
1676	—	12.00	25.00	55.00	110	—
1677	—	14.00	27.50	65.00	120	—
1678	—	12.00	25.00	55.00	110	—
1679	—	14.00	27.50	65.00	120	—
1685	—	14.00	27.50	65.00	120	—
1693	—	11.00	22.50	55.00	105	—

KM# 236.3 6 KREUZER
Silver **Ruler:** Karl II **Rev:** SAS below arms **Note:** Prev. KM#71.3

Date	Mintage	VG	F	VF	XF	Unc
1678	—	14.00	27.50	65.00	120	—
1680	—	11.00	22.50	55.00	105	—
1681	—	14.00	27.50	65.00	120	—
1682	—	11.00	22.50	55.00	105	—
1683	—	12.00	25.00	55.00	110	—
1684	—	12.00	25.00	55.00	110	—

KM# 210 15 KREUZER
Silver **Ruler:** Leopold Wilhelm **Obv:** Bust right **Rev:** Arms below mitre and crown **Note:** Varieties exist. Prev. KM#58.

Date	Mintage	VG	F	VF	XF	Unc
1659	—	25.00	55.00	100	170	—
1661	—	25.00	55.00	100	170	—
1662	—	30.00	60.00	125	210	—

KM# 225 15 KREUZER
Silver **Ruler:** Karl Josef **Obv:** Bust facing **Rev:** Arms topped by mitre and crown **Note:** Prev. KM#60.

Date	Mintage	VG	F	VF	XF	Unc
1663	—	55.00	105	300	500	—
1664	—	49.00	105	300	500	—

KM# 230 15 KREUZER
Silver **Ruler:** Karl II **Obv:** Bust facing **Rev:** Arms **Note:** Prev. KM#66.

Date	Mintage	VG	F	VF	XF	Unc
1664	—	49.00	100	240	400	—

KM# 231.1 15 KREUZER
Silver **Ruler:** Karl II **Obv:** Bust right **Rev:** Arms, legend ends with date **Note:** Prev. KM#80.1.

Date	Mintage	VG	F	VF	XF	Unc
1664	—	25.00	42.00	90.00	150	—

KM# 231.2 15 KREUZER
Silver **Ruler:** Karl II **Rev:** Round arms, date at top between mitre and crown **Note:** Prev. KM#80.2.

Date	Mintage	VG	F	VF	XF	Unc
1675	—	25.00	42.00	90.00	150	—
1676	—	18.00	30.00	70.00	105	—
1677	—	42.00	60.00	150	270	—

KM# 231.3 15 KREUZER
Silver **Ruler:** Karl II **Rev:** Oval arms, SAS below **Note:** Prev. KM#80.3.

Date	Mintage	VG	F	VF	XF	Unc
1679	—	27.50	55.00	105	195	—

KM# 231.4 15 KREUZER
Silver **Ruler:** Karl II **Rev:** Heart-shaped arms **Note:** Prev. KM#80.4.

Date	Mintage	VG	F	VF	XF	Unc
1686	—	27.50	55.00	105	195	—

KM# 231.5 15 KREUZER
Silver **Ruler:** Karl II **Rev:** Arms straight on top, round on the bottom **Note:** Prev. KM#80.5.

Date	Mintage	VG	F	VF	XF	Unc
1687	—	25.00	42.00	90.00	180	—
1688	—	30.00	55.00	115	205	—
1689	—	30.00	55.00	115	205	—
1690	—	30.00	55.00	115	205	—
1691	—	30.00	55.00	115	205	—
1693	—	25.00	42.00	90.00	180	—
1694	—	25.00	42.00	90.00	180	—

KM# 231.6 15 KREUZER
Silver **Ruler:** Karl II **Rev:** Arms with two-tablet bottom **Note:** Prev. KM#80.7.

Date	Mintage	VG	F	VF	XF	Unc
1692	—	25.00	45.00	70.00	125	—
1693	—	20.00	35.00	60.00	100	—
1694	—	12.00	20.00	40.00	90.00	—

KM# 231.7 15 KREUZER

Silver **Ruler:** Karl II **Rev:** SAS below arms **Note:** Prev. KM#80.6

Date	Mintage	VG	F	VF	XF	Unc
1694	—	14.00	25.00	55.00	125	—

KM# 65 GULDEN (1/2 Thaler)

Silver **Ruler:** Franz **Obv:** Bust right **Rev:** Madonna and child, 2 shields **Note:** Prev. KM#13.

Date	Mintage	VG	F	VF	XF	Unc
ND Rare	—	—	—	—	—	—

KM# 75 GULDEN (1/2 Thaler)

Silver **Ruler:** Franz **Obv:** Bust 3/4 profile **Rev:** Madonna and child, 2 shields **Note:** Prev. KM#14.

Date	Mintage	VG	F	VF	XF	Unc
ND Rare	—	—	—	—	—	—

KM# 195 GULDEN (1/2 Thaler)

Silver **Ruler:** Leopold Wilhelm **Obv:** Bust right **Rev:** Arms with crown and miter **Note:** Prev. KM#A52.

Date	Mintage	VG	F	VF	XF	Unc
1656 Rare	—	—	—	—	—	—

KM# 196 1/2 THALER

Silver **Ruler:** Leopold Wilhelm **Obv:** Bust right **Rev:** Arms below mitre and crown **Note:** Prev. KM#A56.

Date	Mintage	VG	F	VF	XF	Unc
1656 Rare	—	—	—	—	—	—

KM# 20 THALER

Silver **Ruler:** Franz **Obv:** 3 shields in cloverleaf, 8 in center **Rev:** Saint Wenceslaus standing with arms at right, holding flag **Note:** Dav. #3461. Prev. KM#16.

Date	Mintage	VG	F	VF	XF	Unc
ND(1608-14) Rare	—	—	—	—	—	—

KM# 21 THALER

Silver **Ruler:** Franz **Obv:** Bust 3/4 profile **Rev:** Madonna and child behind 2 shields **Rev. Legend:** A-LA-RVM... **Note:** Dav. #3465. Varieties exist. Prev. KM#17.

Date	Mintage	VG	F	VF	XF	Unc
ND	—	1,600	3,000	5,000	8,000	—

KM# 22 THALER

Silver **Ruler:** Franz **Obv:** Bust right **Obv. Legend:** FRAN • CARD • A... **Rev:** Madonna and child **Note:** Dav. #3463. Varieties exist. Prev. KM#18.

Date	Mintage	VG	F	VF	XF	Unc
ND	—	2,000	4,000	7,000	11,000	—

KM# 35 THALER

Silver **Ruler:** Franz **Note:** Klippe. Dav. #3468A. Prev. KM#22.

Date	Mintage	VG	F	VF	XF	Unc
ND Rare	—	—	—	—	—	—

KM# 36 THALER

Silver Gilt **Ruler:** Franz **Note:** Klippe. Prev. KM#22a.

Date	Mintage	VG	F	VF	XF	Unc
ND Rare	—	—	—	—	—	—

KM# 45 THALER

Silver **Ruler:** Franz **Obv:** Narrower bust **Rev. Legend:** AL-A-RVM **Note:** Dav. #3466. Prev. KM#19.

Date	Mintage	VG	F	VF	XF	Unc
ND	—	1,600	3,000	5,000	8,000	—

KM# 55 THALER

Silver **Ruler:** Franz **Rev. Legend:** AL-LA-RVM **Note:** Dav. #3467. Prev. KM#20.

Date	Mintage	VG	F	VF	XF	Unc
ND	—	1,600	3,000	5,000	8,000	—

KM# 67 THALER

Silver **Ruler:** Franz **Rev. Legend:** A-LA-RVM **Note:** Dav. #3468. Prev. KM#21.

Date	Mintage	VG	F	VF	XF	Unc
ND Rare	—	—	—	—	—	—

KM# 76 THALER

Silver Gilt **Ruler:** Franz **Rev:** Madonna and child, 2 shields **Note:** Dav. #3469. Prev. KM#23.

Date	Mintage	VG	F	VF	XF	Unc
ND Rare	—	—	—	—	—	—

KM# 100 THALER

Silver **Ruler:** Franz **Obv:** Capped bust right **Rev:** Madonna and child behind 2 shields **Note:** Dav. #3470. Prev. KM#35.

Date	Mintage	VG	F	VF	XF	Unc
1624	—	3,600	7,200	12,000	20,000	—

KM# 101 THALER

Silver **Ruler:** Franz **Obv:** Bare bust right **Rev:** Madonna and child divide date above 2 shields **Note:** Dav. #3471. Prev. KM#36.

Date	Mintage	VG	F	VF	XF	Unc
1624	—	1,200	2,400	4,000	7,000	—

KM# 102 THALER

Silver **Ruler:** Franz **Note:** Klippe. Dav. #3471A. Prev. KM#37.

Date	Mintage	VG	F	VF	XF	Unc
1624 Rare	—	—	—	—	—	—

KM# 110 THALER

Silver **Ruler:** Franz **Obv:** Hatted arms **Rev:** Madonna and child on a half moon, date in legend **Note:** Dav. #3473. Prev. KM#38.

Date	Mintage	VG	F	VF	XF	Unc
1626 Rare	—	—	—	—	—	—

KM# 130 THALER

Silver **Ruler:** Franz **Obv:** Bust right **Rev:** Larger Madonna and child behind smaller shields, P-A and 1-6-2-8 below **Note:** Dav. #3474. Prev. KM#41.

Date	Mintage	VG	F	VF	XF	Unc
1628 P-A	—	1,200	2,400	4,000	7,000	—

KM# 131 THALER

Silver **Ruler:** Franz **Rev:** Oval shields, 16-28 below **Rev. Legend:** A-LL-ARVM... **Note:** Dav. #3475. Prev. KM#42.

Date	Mintage	VG	F	VF	XF	Unc
1628 Rare	—	—	—	—	—	—

KM# 140 THALER

Silver **Ruler:** Franz **Obv:** Date below bust **Rev:** Madonna and child above 2 small oval shields **Note:** Dav. #3477. Prev. KM#43.

Date	Mintage	VG	F	VF	XF	Unc
1629 Rare	—	—	—	—	—	—
1630 Rare	—	—	—	—	—	—

KM# 165 THALER

Silver **Ruler:** Franz **Obv:** Scroll work within inner circle **Rev:** Madonna and child above 2 shields, divided date below, scroll work in inner circle **Note:** Dav. #3478. Prev. KM#46.

Date	Mintage	VG	F	VF	XF	Unc
1634 Rare	—	—	—	—	—	—
1636 Rare	—	—	—	—	—	—

KM# 205 THALER

Silver **Ruler:** Leopold Wilhelm **Obv:** Armored bust right **Rev:** Arms topped by mitre and crown with mitre dividing date **Note:** Dav. #3479. Prev. KM#56.

Date	Mintage	VG	F	VF	XF	Unc
1658 Rare	—	—	—	—	—	—

KM# 245 THALER

Silver **Ruler:** Karl II **Obv:** Bust right **Obv. Legend:** CAROLVS • EX • COMM **Rev:** Capped arms divide date **Rev. Legend:** REGIAE - CAPELLAE • BOHEMAE **Note:** Dav. #3480. Prev. KM#72.

Date	Mintage	VG	F	VF	XF	Unc
1666 Rare	—	—	—	—	—	—

KM# 260 THALER

Silver **Ruler:** Karl II **Obv. Legend:** CAROL' D: G' EPVS... **Rev. Legend:** REG: - CAP: BOHE: ... **Note:** Dav. #3481. Prev. KM#76.

Date	Mintage	VG	F	VF	XF	Unc
1671	—	550	1,100	1,800	3,000	—

KM# 278 THALER

Silver **Ruler:** Karl II **Obv. Legend:** DVX • S • R • I • PCEPS **Note:** Dav. #3482. Prev. KM#81.

Date	Mintage	VG	F	VF	XF	Unc
1676	—	550	1,100	1,800	3,000	—

KM# 294 THALER

Silver **Ruler:** Karl II **Obv:** Larger bust breaks legend at top **Rev:** Arms with crown and mitre above, date in ornamentation at sides **Note:** Dav. #3484. Prev. KM#82.

Date	Mintage	VG	F	VF	XF	Unc
1678	—	550	1,100	1,800	3,000	—

KM# 320 THALER

Silver **Ruler:** Karl II **Obv:** Smaller bust in inner circle **Rev:** Date between crown and mitre above arms **Note:** Dav. #3485. Prev. KM#87.

Date	Mintage	VG	F	VF	XF	Unc
1683	—	600	1,200	2,000	3,500	—

KM# 327 THALER

Silver **Ruler:** Karl II **Obv:** Large bust breaks legend at top **Rev:** Mitre, date above crown divide legend at top **Note:** Dav. #3486. Prev. KM#96.

Date	Mintage	VG	F	VF	XF	Unc
1695	—	400	800	1,500	2,500	—

KM# 25 1-1/2 THALER

Silver **Ruler:** Franz **Obv:** Bust 3/4 profile **Rev:** Madonna and child, 2 shields **Note:** Dav. #3462. Prev. KM#24.

Date	Mintage	VG	F	VF	XF	Unc
ND Rare	—	—	—	—	—	—

KM# 37 2 THALER

Silver **Ruler:** Franz **Obv:** Bust right **Rev:** Madonna and child, 2 shields **Note:** Dav. #3464. Prev. KM#25.

Date	Mintage	VG	F	VF	XF	Unc
ND Rare	—	—	—	—	—	—

KM# 111 2 THALER

Silver **Ruler:** Franz **Obv:** Arms below crown, mitre and staff **Rev:** Madonna and child on a half moon **Note:** Dav. #3472. Prev. KM#39.

Date	Mintage	VG	F	VF	XF	Unc
1626 Rare	—	—	—	—	—	—

KM# 150 2 THALER
Silver **Ruler:** Franz **Obv:** Bust right, date below **Rev:** Madonna and child above 2 shields **Note:** Dav. #3476. Prev. KM#45.

Date	Mintage	VG	F	VF	XF	Unc
1630 Rare	—	—	—	—	—	—

KM# 296 2 THALER
Silver **Ruler:** Karl II **Note:** Similar to 1 Thaler, KM#82. Dav. #3483. Prev. KM#83.

Date	Mintage	VG	F	VF	XF	Unc
1678 Rare	—	—	—	—	—	—

KM# 26 3 THALER
Silver **Ruler:** Franz **Obv:** Bust right **Rev:** Madonna and child, 2 shields **Note:** Dav. #A3464.

Date	Mintage	VG	F	VF	XF	Unc
ND Rare	—	—	—	—	—	—

TRADE COINAGE

KM# 240 1/12 DUCAT
0.2917 g., 0.9860 Gold 0.0092 oz. AGW **Ruler:** Karl II **Obv:** Bust right **Rev:** Eagle **Note:** Prev. KM#A67.

Date	Mintage	VG	F	VF	XF	Unc
ND Rare	—	—	—	—	—	—

KM# 256 1/6 DUCAT
0.5833 g., 0.9860 Gold 0.0185 oz. AGW **Ruler:** Karl II **Obv:** Bust right **Rev:** Crowned and mitred arms **Note:** Prev. KM#68.

Date	Mintage	VG	F	VF	XF	Unc
ND	—	90.00	180	450	900	1,500

KM# 262 1/6 DUCAT
0.5833 g., 0.9860 Gold 0.0185 oz. AGW **Ruler:** Karl II **Obv:** Bust right **Rev:** Eagle with star on breast **Note:** Prev. KM#77.

Date	Mintage	VG	F	VF	XF	Unc
1671	—	120	240	550	1,400	—

KM# 80 1/4 DUCAT
0.8750 g., 0.9860 Gold 0.0277 oz. AGW **Ruler:** Franz **Obv:** Crowned F **Rev:** Cardinal's hat above arms **Note:** Prev. KM#27.

Date	Mintage	VG	F	VF	XF	Unc
ND	—	80.00	150	325	575	—
1616	—	80.00	150	325	575	—

KM# 252 1/4 DUCAT
0.8750 g., 0.9860 Gold 0.0277 oz. AGW **Ruler:** Karl II **Obv:** Bust right **Rev:** Arms **Note:** Prev. KM#69.

Date	Mintage	VG	F	VF	XF	Unc
ND	—	—	—	—	—	—

Note: Reported, not confirmed

KM# 170 1/2 DUCAT
1.7500 g., 0.9860 Gold 0.0555 oz. AGW **Ruler:** Franz **Obv:** Arms of Dietrichstein **Rev:** Arms of Olmutz **Note:** Prev. KM#47.

Date	Mintage	VG	F	VF	XF	Unc
1636	—	240	425	950	2,000	—

KM# 175 1/2 DUCAT
1.6600 g., 0.9860 Gold 0.0526 oz. AGW **Ruler:** Karl II **Obv:** Bust right **Rev:** Coat of arms **Note:** Prev. KM#67.

Date	Mintage	VG	F	VF	XF	Unc
ND	—	240	425	925	1,900	—

KM# 263 1/2 DUCAT
1.6600 g., 0.9860 Gold 0.0526 oz. AGW **Ruler:** Karl II **Obv:** Bust right **Rev:** Arms **Note:** Prev. KM#A70.

Date	Mintage	VG	F	VF	XF	Unc
ND Rare	—	—	—	—	—	—

KM# 115 DUCAT
3.5000 g., 0.9860 Gold 0.1109 oz. AGW **Ruler:** Franz **Obv:** Arms below hat **Rev:** Madonna and child facing seated in inner circle **Note:** Varieties exist. Prev. KM#40.

Date	Mintage	VG	F	VF	XF	Unc
1626	—	550	1,100	3,000	7,200	—
1628	—	550	1,100	3,000	7,200	—
1629	—	550	1,100	3,000	7,200	—
ND	—	550	1,100	3,000	7,200	—

KM# 207 DUCAT
3.5000 g., 0.9860 Gold 0.1109 oz. AGW **Ruler:** Leopold Wilhelm **Obv:** Bust right **Rev:** 2 shields of arms topped by mitre and crown **Note:** Prev. KM#57.

Date	Mintage	VG	F	VF	XF	Unc
1658	—	1,200	2,400	4,800	8,400	—

KM# 280 DUCAT
3.5000 g., 0.9860 Gold 0.1109 oz. AGW **Ruler:** Karl II **Obv:** Bust right **Rev:** Crowned and mitred arms **Note:** Prev. KM#89.

Date	Mintage	VG	F	VF	XF	Unc
1676	—	850	1,800	3,600	7,200	—
1684	—	725	1,450	3,000	6,000	—
ND	—	350	725	1,450	3,000	—

KM# 267 2 DUCAT
7.0000 g., 0.9860 Gold 0.2219 oz. AGW **Ruler:** Karl II **Obv:** Bust right in inner circle **Rev:** Crowned and mitred arms **Note:** Prev. KM#85.

Date	Mintage	VG	F	VF	XF	Unc
1672	—	725	1,800	3,900	6,700	—
1678	—	725	1,800	3,900	6,700	—
1680	—	725	1,800	3,900	6,700	—
1684	—	725	1,800	3,900	6,700	—
1691	—	725	1,800	3,900	6,700	—
1693	—	725	1,800	3,900	6,700	—
ND	—	725	1,800	3,900	6,700	—

KM# 220 3 DUCAT
10.5000 g., 0.9860 Gold 0.3328 oz. AGW **Ruler:** Leopold Wilhelm **Obv:** Bust right **Rev:** Crowned and mitred arms

Date	Mintage	VG	F	VF	XF	Unc
1660	—	1,150	2,400	5,100	9,000	—

KM# 298 3 DUCAT
10.5000 g., 0.9860 Gold 0.3328 oz. AGW **Ruler:** Karl II **Obv:** Bust right **Rev:** Crowned and mitred arms **Note:** Prev. KM#88.

Date	Mintage	VG	F	VF	XF	Unc
1678	—	1,150	2,400	5,100	9,000	—

KM# 30 4 DUCAT
13.6600 g., 0.9860 Gold 0.4330 oz. AGW **Ruler:** Franz **Obv:** Bust right **Rev:** Madonna with child behind small CoA **Note:** Struck with 1/2 Thaler dies of KM#15.

Date	Mintage	VG	F	VF	XF	Unc
ND Rare	—	—	—	—	—	—

KM# 197 4 DUCAT
14.0000 g., 0.9860 Gold 0.4438 oz. AGW **Ruler:** Leopold Wilhelm **Obv:** Bust right in inner circle **Rev:** Arms topped by mitre and crown in inner circle **Note:** Prev. KM#54.

Date	Mintage	VG	F	VF	XF	Unc
1656	—	—	—	—	—	—

Note: Reported, not confirmed

KM# 250 4 DUCAT
13.6600 g., 0.9860 Gold 0.4330 oz. AGW, 36 mm. **Ruler:** Karl II **Obv:** Bust of Karl II, right, in circle **Rev:** CoA with straight vertical lines

Date	Mintage	VG	F	VF	XF	Unc
1666 Rare	—	—	—	—	—	—

KM# 300 4 DUCAT
12.7200 g., 0.9860 Gold 0.4032 oz. AGW, 45 mm. **Ruler:** Karl II **Obv:** Bust of Karl II right, breaks inner circle at top **Rev:** CoA nearly round **Note:** Struck with Thaler dies of KM#294.

Date	Mintage	VG	F	VF	XF	Unc
1678 Rare	—	—	—	—	—	—

KM# 301 4 DUCAT
12.7200 g., 0.9860 Gold 0.4032 oz. AGW **Ruler:** Karl II **Obv:** Bust right **Rev:** Arms, topped by mitre and crown **Note:** Prev. KM#A78.

Date	Mintage	VG	F	VF	XF	Unc
1678	—	—	—	9,000	15,000	—

KM# 160 5 DUCAT
17.5000 g., 0.9860 Gold 0.5547 oz. AGW **Ruler:** Franz **Obv:** Bust right, within circle **Rev:** Madonna with child **Note:** Struck with 1/2 Thaler dies of KM#65.

Date	Mintage	VG	F	VF	XF	Unc
ND Rare	—	—	—	—	—	—

KM# 161 5 DUCAT
17.5000 g., 0.9860 Gold 0.5547 oz. AGW **Ruler:** Franz **Obv:** Bust 3/4 profile **Rev:** Madonna with child **Note:** Struck with 1/2 Thaler dies of KM#75.

Date	Mintage	VG	F	VF	XF	Unc
ND Rare	—	—	—	—	—	—

KM# 167 5 DUCAT
17.5000 g., 0.9860 Gold 0.5547 oz. AGW, 38.5 mm. **Ruler:** Franz **Obv:** Bust right, cuts inner circle at top **Obv. Legend:** FRAN • CARD • A • DIETRICHSTAIN • EPS • OLOMVC • 8 **Rev:** Madonna wearing 4 point crown; child above 2 straight shield; Dietrichstein on left and Olmutz on right **Rev. Legend:** SVB VMBRAA LA RVM TVARVM **Edge:** Plain **Note:** Struck with Thaler dies, KM#140. Prev. KM#15.

Date	Mintage	F	VF	XF	Unc	BU
1634 Rare	—	—	—	—	—	—

KM# 269 5 DUCAT
17.5000 g., 0.9860 Gold 0.5547 oz. AGW, 37.5 mm. **Ruler:** Karl II **Obv:** Bust of Karl II right **Rev:** CoA **Note:** Struck with 1/2 Thaler dies of an unknown type. Prev. KM#78.

Date	Mintage	VG	F	VF	XF	Unc
1672	—	—	—	8,300	13,000	22,000
1672 PRNICEPS error	—	—	—	9,900	15,000	25,000
1676	—	—	—	8,300	13,000	22,000
1678	—	—	—	8,300	13,000	22,000
ND	—	—	—	8,300	13,000	22,000

KM# 303 5 DUCAT
17.5000 g., 0.9860 Gold 0.5547 oz. AGW, 44 mm. **Ruler:** Karl II **Obv:** Bust of Karl II right **Rev:** CoA **Note:** Struck with Thaler dies of KM#294.

Date	Mintage	VG	F	VF	XF	Unc
1678	—	—	—	8,300	13,000	—

KM# 330 5 DUCAT
17.5000 g., 0.9860 Gold 0.5547 oz. AGW, 44 mm. **Ruler:** Karl II **Obv:** Bust of Karl II right **Rev:** CoA **Note:** Struck with Thaler dies of KM#327.

Date	Mintage	VG	F	VF	XF	Unc
1695	—	—	—	8,300	13,000	—

KM# 168 6 DUCAT
20.2000 g., 0.9860 Gold 0.6403 oz. AGW **Ruler:** Franz **Obv:** Bust right **Rev:** Madonna with child and shield **Note:** Struck with Thaler dies of KM#165.

Date	Mintage	VG	F	VF	XF	Unc
1634 Rare	—	—	—	—	—	—

KM# 305 6 DUCAT
20.6200 g., 0.9860 Gold 0.6536 oz. AGW, 36 mm. **Ruler:** Karl II **Obv:** Bust right in inner circle **Rev:** Arms topped by mitre and crown in inner circle **Note:** Struck with 1/2 Thaler dies of an unknown type. Prev. KM#70.

Date	Mintage	VG	F	VF	XF	Unc
1678	—	—	—	9,900	16,500	—

KM# 306 6 DUCAT
20.6200 g., 0.9860 Gold 0.6536 oz. AGW, 45 mm. **Ruler:** Karl II **Obv:** Bust right, touches top **Rev:** Arms below mitre and crown which touch outer boarder **Note:** Struck with Thaler dies of KM#294.

Date	Mintage	VG	F	VF	XF	Unc
1678	—	—	—	9,900	16,500	—

KM# 155 8 DUCAT
26.2500 g., 0.9860 Gold 0.8321 oz. AGW, 45 mm. **Ruler:** Franz **Obv:** Bust right in inner circle **Rev:** Madonna with child in Gloriole **Note:** Struck with Thaler dies of KM#140.

Date	Mintage	VG	F	VF	XF	Unc
1630	—	—	—	9,900	16,500	—

KM# 308 8 DUCAT
28.0000 g., 0.9860 Gold 0.8876 oz. AGW **Ruler:** Karl II **Note:** Struck with 1 Thaler dies, KM#294. Prev. KM#92.

Date	Mintage	VG	F	VF	XF	Unc
1678 Rare	—	—	—	—	—	—

KM# 332 9 DUCAT
30.9800 g., 0.9860 Gold 0.9820 oz. AGW, 44.5 mm. **Ruler:** Karl II **Obv:** Bust right **Rev:** Arms topped by mitre and crown in inner circle **Note:** Struck with Thaler dies of an unknown type.

Date	Mintage	VG	F	VF	XF	Unc
1695	—	—	—	—	—	—

Note: Reported, not confirmed

KM# 135 10 DUCAT

35.0000 g., 0.9860 Gold 1.1095 oz. AGW **Ruler:** Franz **Rev:** Madonna **Note:** Struck with 1 Thaler dies, KM#130. Prev. KM#49.

Date	Mintage	VG	F	VF	XF	Unc
1628 P-A Rare	—	—	—	—	—	—

KM# 172 10 DUCAT

35.0000 g., 0.9860 Gold 1.1095 oz. AGW **Ruler:** Franz **Note:** Struck with Thaler dies of KM#165.

Date	Mintage	VG	F	VF	XF	Unc
1636 Rare	—	—	—	—	—	—

Note: H.D. Rauch Auction 84, 5-09, nearly XF realized approximately $10,200.

KM# 120 10 DUCAT

35.0000 g., 0.9860 Gold 1.1095 oz. AGW **Ruler:** Franz **Note:** Struck with Thaler dies of KM#20.

Date	Mintage	VG	F	VF	XF	Unc
ND Rare	—	—	—	—	—	—

KM# 121 10 DUCAT

35.0000 g., 0.9860 Gold 1.1095 oz. AGW **Ruler:** Franz **Obv:** Three shields in cloverleaf **Rev:** Saint Wenzeslaus standing **Note:** Struck with Thaler dies of KM#20.

Date	Mintage	VG	F	VF	XF	Unc
ND Rare	—	—	—	—	—	—

KM# 198 10 DUCAT

35.0000 g., 0.9860 Gold 1.1095 oz. AGW **Ruler:** Leopold Wilhelm **Obv:** Bust right in inner circle **Rev:** Arms topped by mitre and crown in inner circle **Note:** Prev. KM#55.

Date	Mintage	VG	F	VF	XF	Unc
1656 Rare	—	—	—	—	—	—
1658 Rare	—	—	—	—	—	—

Note: UBS Auction 66, 9-06, VF realized approximately $48,600.

KM# 265 10 DUCAT

35.0000 g., 0.9860 Gold 1.1095 oz. AGW **Ruler:** Karl II **Obv:** Bust right, within inner circle **Note:** Struck with 1 Thaler dies, KM#260. Prev. KM#93.

Date	Mintage	VG	F	VF	XF	Unc
1671 Rare	—	—	—	—	—	—

KM# 282 10 DUCAT

35.0000 g., 0.9860 Gold 1.1095 oz. AGW **Ruler:** Karl II **Obv:** Bust right, within inner circle **Note:** Struck with Thaler dies of KM#278.

Date	Mintage	VG	F	VF	XF	Unc
1676 Rare	—	—	—	—	—	—

KM# 310 10 DUCAT

35.0000 g., 0.9860 Gold 1.1095 oz. AGW **Ruler:** Karl II **Obv:** Bust right, dividing legend at top **Note:** Struck with Thaler dies of KM#294.

Date	Mintage	VG	F	VF	XF	Unc
1678 Rare	—	—	—	—	—	—

Note: H.D. Rauch Auction 81, 11-07, XF+ realized approximately $47,450.

KM# 312 11 DUCAT

38.0300 g., 0.9860 Gold 1.2055 oz. AGW, 47.5 mm. **Ruler:** Karl II **Obv:** Bust right **Rev:** Coat of arms **Note:** Struck with Thaler dies of KM#294.

Date	Mintage	VG	F	VF	XF	Unc
1678 Rare	—	—	—	—	—	—

KM# 284 20 DUCAT

69.2000 g., 0.9860 Gold 2.1936 oz. AGW, 48.5 mm. **Ruler:** Karl II **Obv:** Bust right **Rev:** Coat of arms **Note:** Struck with Thaler dies of KM#278.

Date	Mintage	VG	F	VF	XF	Unc
1676 Rare	—	—	—	—	—	—

KM# 286 30 DUCAT

104.0000 g., 0.9860 Gold 3.2967 oz. AGW, 48 mm. **Ruler:** Karl II **Obv:** Bust right **Rev:** Coat of arms **Note:** Struck with Thaler dies of KM#278.

Date	Mintage	VG	F	VF	XF	Unc
1676 Rare	—	—	—	—	—	—

PATTERNS

Including off metal strikes

KM#	Date	Mintage	Identification	Mkt Val
Pn1	ND	—	Thaler. Pewter.	—
Pn2	1624	—	Thaler. Pewter.	—

ORTENBURG

A district of Carinthia with its own counts from c.1100 to 1421. Eventually it became property of the emperor who assigned it to a Spanish noble in 1524. This line died out in 1640. The Widmanns, an Italian family, ruled from 1640 to 1662 and produced the only coins. In 1662 Ortenburg passed to Porcia and was finally mediatized to Austria in 1805.

RULER

Christopher Widmann, 1640-1660

COUNTY

STANDARD COINAGE

KM# A3 1/2 THALER (Show - Schau)

Silver **Ruler:** Christopher Widmann **Obv:** Bust of Hans Widman right **Obv. Legend:** HANS WIDMAN AIGENTVMBSHERR DER (1631) **Rev:** Helmeted shield **Rev. Legend:** HER SCHAFTEN SOMMERÖGG VND PATERNIAN

Date	Mintage	VG	F	VF	XF	Unc
1631	—	1,000	2,000	3,500	—	—

KM# 3 THALER

Silver **Ruler:** Christopher Widmann **Note:** Dav. #3397.

Date	Mintage	VG	F	VF	XF	Unc
1656	—	275	550	1,000	1,750	2,750

TRADE COINAGE

KM# 6 DUCAT

3.5000 g., 0.9860 Gold 0.1109 oz. AGW **Ruler:** Christopher Widmann **Obv:** Bust in cardinal's garb **Rev:** Circular arms below cardinal's hat, date in legend

Date	Mintage	VG	F	VF	XF	Unc
1658	—	1,800	3,950	6,500	9,400	—

KM# 7 2 DUCAT

7.0000 g., 0.9860 Gold 0.2219 oz. AGW **Ruler:** Christopher Widmann **Note:** Similar to 1 Ducat, KM#6.

Date	Mintage	VG	F	VF	XF	Unc
1657 Rare	—	—	—	—	—	—

KM# 4 5 DUCAT

17.5000 g., 0.9860 Gold 0.5547 oz. AGW **Ruler:** Christopher Widmann **Note:** Struck with 1 Thaler dies, KM#3.

Date	Mintage	VG	F	VF	XF	Unc
1656	—	2,900	5,000	8,600	14,000	—

KM# 5 10 DUCAT

35.0000 g., 0.9860 Gold 1.1095 oz. AGW **Ruler:** Christopher Widmann **Note:** Struck with 1 Thaler dies, KM#3.

Date	Mintage	VG	F	VF	XF	Unc
1656 Rare	—	—	—	—	—	—

SALZBURG

A town on the Austro-Bavarian frontier which grew up around a monastery and bishopric that was founded circa 700. It was raised to the rank of archbishopric in 798. In 1803 Salzburg was secularized and given to an archduke of Austria. In 1803 it was annexed to Austria but years later passed to Bavaria, returning to Austria in 1813. It became a crownland in 1849, remaining so until becoming part of the Austrian Republic in 1918.

RULERS

Wolf Dietrich, 1587-1612
Marcus Sitticus, 1612-1619
Paris von Lodron, 1619-1653
Guidobald, 1654-1668
Max Gandolph, 1668-1687
Johann Ernst, 1687-1709

MONETARY SYSTEM

4 Pfenning = 1 Kreutzer
120 Kreutzer = 1 Convention Thaler

ARCHBISHOPRIC

STANDARD COINAGE

KM# 6 HELLER

Silver **Ruler:** Wolfgang Dietrich **Obv:** Shield of arms with date above in diamond **Rev:** Shield of arms in diamond

Date	Mintage	VG	F	VF	XF	Unc
1607	—	10.00	20.00	40.00	70.00	—
1608	—	10.00	20.00	40.00	70.00	—

KM# 33 HELLER

Silver **Ruler:** Markus Sittich **Obv:** Shield of arms with date above and/or at sides in diamond **Rev:** Shield of arms in diamond with annulets in corners

Date	Mintage	VG	F	VF	XF	Unc
1614	—	5.50	12.00	20.00	45.00	—
1615	—	5.50	12.00	20.00	45.00	—
1616	—	5.50	12.00	20.00	45.00	—
1618	—	5.50	12.00	20.00	45.00	—

KM# 72 HELLER

Silver **Ruler:** Paris **Obv:** Shield of arms divides date, "P" above **Note:** Kipper Heller. Uniface.

Date	Mintage	VG	F	VF	XF	Unc
1621	—	6.00	12.00	20.00	45.00	—
1622	—	6.00	12.00	20.00	45.00	—

KM# 10 PFENNING

Silver **Ruler:** Wolfgang Dietrich **Obv:** Shield of arms divides W-T, date below in diamond **Note:** Uniface.

Date	Mintage	VG	F	VF	XF	Unc
1610	—	5.50	12.00	20.00	45.00	—
1611	—	5.50	12.00	20.00	45.00	—

KM# 11 PFENNING
Silver **Ruler:** Markus Sittich **Obv:** Shield of arms, date above in diamond **Note:** Uniface.

Date	Mintage	VG	F	VF	XF	Unc
(1)612	—	5.50	12.00	20.00	45.00	—
1612	—	5.50	12.00	20.00	45.00	—
(1)613	—	5.50	12.00	20.00	45.00	—
(1)614	—	5.50	12.00	20.00	45.00	—
(1)615	—	5.50	12.00	20.00	45.00	—
(1)616	—	5.50	12.00	20.00	45.00	—
(1)617	—	5.50	12.00	20.00	45.00	—
(1)618	—	5.50	12.00	20.00	45.00	—
(1)619	—	5.50	12.00	20.00	45.00	—

KM# 55 PFENNING
Silver **Ruler:** Paris **Obv:** Cap above two shields of arms in trilobe, date below **Note:** Uniface.

Date	Mintage	VG	F	VF	XF	Unc
(1)620	—	6.00	12.00	25.00	50.00	—

KM# 73 PFENNING
Silver **Ruler:** Paris **Obv:** Cap above two shields of arms in trilobe, date below **Note:** Kipper Pfenning.

Date	Mintage	VG	F	VF	XF	Unc
(1)621	—	6.00	12.00	25.00	50.00	—
(1)622	—	6.00	12.00	25.00	50.00	—

KM# 82 PFENNING
Silver **Ruler:** Paris **Obv:** Shield of arms, "P" above **Rev:** Shield of arms, with date above

Date	Mintage	VG	F	VF	XF	Unc
1623	—	5.00	10.00	20.00	45.00	—
1624	—	5.00	10.00	20.00	45.00	—
1625	—	5.00	10.00	20.00	45.00	—
1626	—	5.00	10.00	20.00	45.00	—
1627	—	5.00	10.00	20.00	45.00	—
1628	—	5.00	10.00	20.00	45.00	—
1629	—	5.00	10.00	20.00	45.00	—
1630	—	5.00	10.00	20.00	45.00	—
1631	—	5.00	10.00	20.00	45.00	—
1632	—	5.00	10.00	20.00	45.00	—
1633	—	5.00	10.00	20.00	45.00	—
1634	—	5.00	10.00	20.00	45.00	—
1635	—	5.00	10.00	20.00	45.00	—
1636	—	5.00	10.00	20.00	45.00	—
1638	—	5.00	10.00	20.00	45.00	—
1639	—	5.00	10.00	20.00	45.00	—
1640	—	5.00	10.00	20.00	45.00	—
1641	—	5.00	10.00	20.00	45.00	—
1642	—	5.00	10.00	20.00	45.00	—
1643	—	5.00	10.00	20.00	45.00	—
1644	—	5.00	10.00	20.00	45.00	—
1645	—	5.00	10.00	20.00	45.00	—
1646	—	5.00	10.00	20.00	45.00	—
1647	—	5.00	10.00	20.00	45.00	—
1648	—	5.00	10.00	20.00	45.00	—
1649	—	5.00	10.00	20.00	45.00	—
1650	—	5.00	10.00	20.00	45.00	—
1652	—	5.00	10.00	20.00	45.00	—
1653	—	5.00	10.00	20.00	45.00	—

KM# 157 PFENNING
Silver **Ruler:** Guidobald **Obv:** Date above two shields of arms, G below **Note:** Uniface.

Date	Mintage	VG	F	VF	XF	Unc
1654	—	—	—	—	—	—

KM# 174 PFENNING
Silver **Ruler:** Guidobald **Obv:** Date above two shields, different right shield, G below

Date	Mintage	VG	F	VF	XF	Unc
1655	—	4.00	8.00	18.00	35.00	—
1656	—	4.00	8.00	18.00	35.00	—
1657	—	4.00	8.00	18.00	35.00	—
1658	—	4.00	8.00	18.00	35.00	—
1659	—	4.00	8.00	18.00	35.00	—
1660	—	4.00	8.00	18.00	35.00	—
1661	—	4.00	8.00	18.00	35.00	—
1662	—	4.00	8.00	18.00	35.00	—
1663	—	4.00	8.00	18.00	35.00	—
1664	—	4.00	8.00	18.00	35.00	—
1665	—	4.00	8.00	18.00	35.00	—
1666	—	4.00	8.00	18.00	35.00	—
1667	—	4.00	8.00	18.00	35.00	—
1668	—	4.00	8.00	18.00	35.00	—

KM# 186 PFENNING
Silver **Ruler:** Maximilian Gandolph **Obv:** Date above two shields, different right shield, MG below **Note:** Uniface.

Date	Mintage	VG	F	VF	XF	Unc
1668	—	4.00	8.00	18.00	35.00	—
1669	—	4.00	8.00	18.00	35.00	—
1670	—	4.00	8.00	18.00	35.00	—
1671	—	4.00	8.00	18.00	35.00	—

Date	Mintage	VG	F	VF	XF	Unc
1672	—	4.00	8.00	18.00	35.00	—
1673	—	4.00	8.00	18.00	35.00	—
1674	—	4.00	8.00	18.00	35.00	—
1675	—	4.00	8.00	18.00	35.00	—
1676	—	4.00	8.00	18.00	35.00	—
1677	—	4.00	8.00	18.00	35.00	—
1678	—	4.00	8.00	18.00	35.00	—
1679	—	4.00	8.00	18.00	35.00	—
1680	—	4.00	8.00	18.00	35.00	—
1681	—	4.00	8.00	18.00	35.00	—
1682	—	4.00	8.00	18.00	35.00	—
1683	—	4.00	8.00	18.00	35.00	—
1684	—	4.00	8.00	18.00	35.00	—
1685	—	4.00	8.00	18.00	35.00	—
1686	—	4.00	8.00	18.00	35.00	—
1687	—	4.00	8.00	18.00	35.00	—

KM# 5 2 PFENNING
Silver **Ruler:** Wolfgang Dietrich **Obv:** Three shields in trilobe, date below **Note:** Uniface.

Date	Mintage	VG	F	VF	XF	Unc
1601	—	5.50	12.00	20.00	45.00	—
(1)601	—	5.50	12.00	20.00	45.00	—
1603	—	5.50	12.00	20.00	45.00	—
(1)603	—	5.50	12.00	20.00	45.00	—
1604	—	5.50	12.00	20.00	45.00	—
1605	—	5.50	12.00	20.00	45.00	—
(1)606	—	5.50	12.00	20.00	45.00	—
(1)607	—	5.50	12.00	20.00	45.00	—
(1)608	—	5.50	12.00	20.00	45.00	—
(1)610	—	5.50	12.00	20.00	45.00	—
(1)611	—	5.50	12.00	20.00	45.00	—

KM# 12 2 PFENNING
Silver **Ruler:** Markus Sittich **Obv:** Shield of arms, hat above in trilobe, date below **Note:** Uniface.

Date	Mintage	VG	F	VF	XF	Unc
(1)612	—	5.50	12.00	20.00	45.00	—
1612	—	5.50	12.00	20.00	45.00	—
(1)613	—	5.50	12.00	20.00	45.00	—
1614	—	5.50	12.00	20.00	45.00	—
1615	—	5.50	12.00	20.00	45.00	—
1616	—	5.50	12.00	20.00	45.00	—
1617	—	5.50	12.00	20.00	45.00	—
1618	—	5.50	12.00	20.00	45.00	—
1619	—	5.50	12.00	20.00	45.00	—
1661 Error date	—	5.50	12.00	20.00	45.00	—

KM# 268 2 PFENNING
Silver **Ruler:** Johann Ernst **Obv:** Date above 2 shields, "IE" below **Note:** Uniface.

Date	Mintage	VG	F	VF	XF	Unc
1688	—	4.00	8.00	16.00	30.00	—
1689	—	4.00	8.00	16.00	30.00	—
1690	—	4.00	8.00	16.00	30.00	—
1691	—	4.00	8.00	16.00	30.00	—
1692	—	4.00	8.00	16.00	30.00	—
1693	—	4.00	8.00	16.00	30.00	—
1694	—	4.00	8.00	16.00	30.00	—
1695	—	4.00	8.00	16.00	30.00	—
1696	—	4.00	8.00	16.00	30.00	—
1697	—	4.00	8.00	16.00	30.00	—
1698	—	4.00	8.00	16.00	30.00	—
1699	—	4.00	8.00	16.00	30.00	—
1700	—	4.00	8.00	16.00	30.00	—

KM# 83 1/2 KREUZER
Silver **Ruler:** Paris **Obv:** Hat above shield of arms **Rev:** Shield of arms, value divides date at top

Date	Mintage	VG	F	VF	XF	Unc
1623	—	4.00	8.00	16.00	30.00	—
1624	—	4.00	8.00	16.00	30.00	—
1625	—	4.00	8.00	16.00	30.00	—
1627	—	4.00	8.00	16.00	30.00	—
1629	—	4.00	8.00	16.00	30.00	—
1630	—	4.00	8.00	16.00	30.00	—
1631	—	4.00	8.00	16.00	30.00	—
1633	—	4.00	8.00	16.00	30.00	—
1635	—	4.00	8.00	16.00	30.00	—
1636	—	4.00	8.00	16.00	30.00	—
1637	—	4.00	8.00	16.00	30.00	—
1638	—	4.00	8.00	16.00	30.00	—
1640	—	4.00	8.00	16.00	30.00	—
1642	—	4.00	8.00	16.00	30.00	—
1643	—	4.00	8.00	16.00	30.00	—
1645	—	4.00	8.00	16.00	30.00	—
1646	—	4.00	8.00	16.00	30.00	—
1647	—	4.00	8.00	16.00	30.00	—
1648	—	4.00	8.00	16.00	30.00	—
1649	—	4.00	8.00	16.00	30.00	—
1651	—	4.00	8.00	16.00	30.00	—
1652	—	4.00	8.00	16.00	30.00	—
1653	—	4.00	8.00	16.00	30.00	—

KM# 158 1/2 KREUZER
Silver **Ruler:** Guidobald **Obv:** Value divides date above two shields of arms, G above

Date	Mintage	VG	F	VF	XF	Unc
1654	—	3.50	7.00	16.00	30.00	—

Date	Mintage	VG	F	VF	XF	Unc
1655	—	3.50	7.00	16.00	30.00	—
1656	—	3.50	7.00	16.00	30.00	—
1657	—	3.50	7.00	16.00	30.00	—
1658	—	3.50	7.00	16.00	30.00	—
1659	—	3.50	7.00	16.00	30.00	—
1660	—	3.50	7.00	16.00	30.00	—
1661	—	3.50	7.00	16.00	30.00	—
1662	—	3.50	7.00	16.00	30.00	—
1663	—	3.50	7.00	16.00	30.00	—
1665	—	3.50	7.00	16.00	30.00	—
1667	—	3.50	7.00	16.00	30.00	—

KM# 221 1/2 KREUZER
Silver **Ruler:** Maximilian Gandolph **Obv:** Value divides date above two shields of arms, different right shield, MG below **Note:** Uniface.

Date	Mintage	VG	F	VF	XF	Unc
1671	—	4.00	8.00	16.00	30.00	—
1677	—	4.00	8.00	16.00	30.00	—
1680	—	4.00	8.00	16.00	30.00	—
1681	—	4.00	8.00	16.00	30.00	—
1682	—	4.00	8.00	16.00	30.00	—
1683	—	4.00	8.00	16.00	30.00	—
1684	—	4.00	8.00	16.00	30.00	—
1685	—	4.00	8.00	16.00	30.00	—
1686	—	4.00	8.00	16.00	30.00	—
1687	—	4.00	8.00	16.00	30.00	—

KM# 247 1/2 KREUZER
Silver **Ruler:** Johann Ernst **Obv:** Value divides date above 2 shields , "IE" below **Note:** Uniface.

Date	Mintage	VG	F	VF	XF	Unc
1687	—	4.00	8.00	16.00	30.00	—
1688	—	4.00	8.00	16.00	30.00	—
1689	—	4.00	8.00	16.00	30.00	—
1690	—	4.00	8.00	16.00	30.00	—
1691	—	4.00	8.00	16.00	30.00	—
1693	—	4.00	8.00	16.00	30.00	—
1694	—	4.00	8.00	16.00	30.00	—
1695	—	4.00	8.00	16.00	30.00	—
1696	—	4.00	8.00	16.00	30.00	—
1697	—	4.00	8.00	16.00	30.00	—
1698	—	4.00	8.00	16.00	30.00	—
1699	—	4.00	8.00	16.00	30.00	—
1700	—	4.00	8.00	16.00	30.00	—

KM# 84 KREUZER
Silver **Ruler:** Paris **Obv:** Hat above shield of arms **Obv. Legend:** PARIS D G ARCHIEPS **Rev:** Round arms in eight-armed cross, date in legend

Date	Mintage	VG	F	VF	XF	Unc
1623	—	4.00	8.00	18.00	35.00	—
1624	—	4.00	8.00	18.00	35.00	—
1627	—	4.00	8.00	18.00	35.00	—
1628	—	4.00	8.00	18.00	35.00	—
1629	—	4.00	8.00	18.00	35.00	—
1630	—	4.00	8.00	18.00	35.00	—
1631	—	4.00	8.00	18.00	35.00	—
1632	—	4.00	8.00	18.00	35.00	—
1633	—	4.00	8.00	18.00	35.00	—
1634	—	4.00	8.00	18.00	35.00	—
1636	—	4.00	8.00	18.00	35.00	—
1637	—	4.00	8.00	18.00	35.00	—
1638	—	4.00	8.00	18.00	35.00	—
1639	—	4.00	8.00	18.00	35.00	—
1640	—	4.00	8.00	18.00	35.00	—
1641	—	4.00	8.00	18.00	35.00	—
1642	—	4.00	8.00	18.00	35.00	—
1643	—	4.00	8.00	18.00	35.00	—
1644	—	4.00	8.00	18.00	35.00	—
1645	—	4.00	8.00	18.00	35.00	—
1646	—	4.00	8.00	18.00	35.00	—
1647	—	4.00	8.00	18.00	35.00	—
1648	—	4.00	8.00	18.00	35.00	—
1649	—	4.00	8.00	18.00	35.00	—
1650	—	4.00	8.00	18.00	35.00	—
1651	—	4.00	8.00	18.00	35.00	—
1652	—	4.00	8.00	18.00	35.00	—
1653	—	4.00	8.00	18.00	35.00	—

KM# 159 KREUZER
Silver **Ruler:** Guidobald **Obv. Legend:** GVIDOBALD D G AR EPS **Rev:** Round arms in eight-armed cross in inner circle, date in legend

Date	Mintage	VG	F	VF	XF	Unc
1654	—	4.00	8.00	18.00	35.00	—
1655	—	4.00	8.00	18.00	35.00	—
1656	—	4.00	8.00	18.00	35.00	—
1657	—	4.00	8.00	18.00	35.00	—

Date	Mintage	VG	F	VF	XF	Unc
1658	—	4.00	8.00	18.00	35.00	—
1659	—	4.00	8.00	18.00	35.00	—
1660	—	4.00	8.00	18.00	35.00	—
1661	—	4.00	8.00	18.00	35.00	—
1662	—	4.00	8.00	18.00	35.00	—
1663	—	4.00	8.00	18.00	35.00	—
1664	—	4.00	8.00	18.00	35.00	—
1665	—	4.00	8.00	18.00	35.00	—
1666	—	4.00	8.00	18.00	35.00	—
1667	—	4.00	8.00	18.00	35.00	—
1668/7	—	4.00	8.00	18.00	35.00	—
1668	—	4.00	8.00	18.00	35.00	—

KM# 185 KREUZER

Silver **Ruler:** Guidobald **Obv. Legend:** GVIDOBALD D G ARCHI EPS **Rev:** Date divided at top

Date	Mintage	VG	F	VF	XF	Unc
1660	—	6.00	12.00	25.00	40.00	—
1661	—	6.00	12.00	25.00	40.00	—
1662	—	6.00	12.00	25.00	40.00	—
1663	—	6.00	12.00	25.00	40.00	—

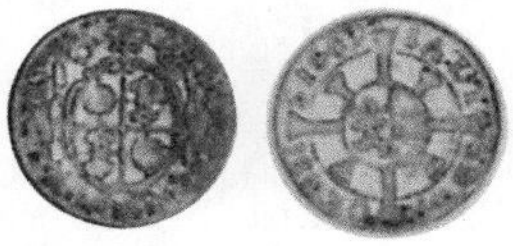

KM# 187 KREUZER

Silver **Ruler:** Maximilian Gandolph **Obv. Legend:** MAX GAND DG AR EPS **Rev:** Round arms in eight-armed cross, date in legend

Date	Mintage	VG	F	VF	XF	Unc
1668	—	4.00	8.00	18.00	35.00	—
1669	—	4.00	8.00	18.00	35.00	—
1670	—	4.00	8.00	18.00	35.00	—
1671	—	4.00	8.00	18.00	35.00	—
1672	—	4.00	8.00	18.00	35.00	—
1673	—	4.00	8.00	18.00	35.00	—
1674	—	4.00	8.00	18.00	35.00	—
1675	—	4.00	8.00	18.00	35.00	—
1676	—	4.00	8.00	18.00	35.00	—
1677	—	4.00	8.00	18.00	35.00	—
1678	—	4.00	8.00	18.00	35.00	—
1679	—	4.00	8.00	18.00	35.00	—
1680	—	4.00	8.00	18.00	35.00	—
1681	—	4.00	8.00	18.00	35.00	—
1682	—	4.00	8.00	18.00	35.00	—
1683	—	4.00	8.00	18.00	35.00	—
1684	—	4.00	8.00	18.00	35.00	—
1685	—	4.00	8.00	18.00	35.00	—
1686	—	4.00	8.00	18.00	35.00	—

KM# 226 KREUZER

Silver **Ruler:** Maximilian Gandolph **Obv. Legend:** MAX GAND DG ARCHIEPS **Rev:** Date at top in legend

Date	Mintage	VG	F	VF	XF	Unc
1674	—	6.00	12.00	25.00	40.00	—
1675	—	6.00	12.00	25.00	40.00	—
1676	—	6.00	12.00	25.00	40.00	—

KM# 248 KREUZER

Silver **Ruler:** Johann Ernst **Obv:** Oval arms with cardinals' hat above **Obv. Legend:** IO : ERNEST : D : G : ARCHIEP **Rev:** Round shield within double cross and circle

Date	Mintage	VG	F	VF	XF	Unc
1687	—	4.00	8.00	16.00	30.00	—
1688	—	4.00	8.00	16.00	30.00	—
1689	—	4.00	8.00	16.00	30.00	—
1690	—	4.00	8.00	16.00	30.00	—
1691	—	4.00	8.00	16.00	30.00	—
1692	—	4.00	8.00	16.00	30.00	—
1693	—	4.00	8.00	16.00	30.00	—
1694	—	4.00	8.00	16.00	30.00	—
1695	—	4.00	8.00	16.00	30.00	—
1696	—	4.00	8.00	16.00	30.00	—
1697	—	4.00	8.00	16.00	30.00	—
1698	—	4.00	8.00	16.00	30.00	—
1699	—	4.00	8.00	16.00	30.00	—
1700	—	4.00	8.00	16.00	30.00	—

KM# 276 2 KREUZER

Silver **Ruler:** Johann Ernst **Obv:** Hat above two shields of arms, value below **Rev. Legend:** SALZB/LAND/MINZ/1692

Date	Mintage	VG	F	VF	XF	Unc
1692	—	5.00	10.00	15.00	35.00	—

KM# 85 2 KREUZER (1/2 Landbatzen)

Silver **Ruler:** Paris **Obv:** Hat above two shields of arms in inner circle **Obv. Legend:** PARIS D G ARCHIEPS SALIS **Rev:** St. Rupert in inner circle, value below, date in legend

Date	Mintage	VG	F	VF	XF	Unc
1623	—	7.00	18.00	36.00	60.00	—

KM# 86 2 KREUZER (1/2 Landbatzen)

Silver **Ruler:** Paris **Obv. Legend:** PARIS D G ARCHIEPS **Rev:** Shield of arms in inner circle, value below, date above shield

Date	Mintage	VG	F	VF	XF	Unc
1623	—	6.00	12.00	25.00	40.00	—
1624	—	6.00	12.00	25.00	40.00	—
1625	—	6.00	12.00	25.00	40.00	—
1626	—	6.00	12.00	25.00	40.00	—
1629	—	6.00	12.00	25.00	40.00	—
1630	—	6.00	12.00	25.00	40.00	—
1631	—	6.00	12.00	25.00	40.00	—
1632	—	6.00	12.00	25.00	40.00	—
1633	—	6.00	12.00	25.00	40.00	—
1635	—	6.00	12.00	25.00	40.00	—
1636	—	6.00	12.00	25.00	40.00	—
1637	—	6.00	12.00	25.00	40.00	—

KM# 280 2 KREUZER (1/2 Reichsbatzen)

Silver **Ruler:** Johann Ernst **Obv:** Cardinals' hat above oval shield **Rev:** Oval shield within frame and circle with divided date above, value below

Date	Mintage	VG	F	VF	XF	Unc
1694	—	6.00	12.00	25.00	40.00	—
1695	—	6.00	12.00	25.00	40.00	—
1696	—	6.00	12.00	25.00	40.00	—
1697	—	6.00	12.00	25.00	40.00	—
1698	—	6.00	12.00	25.00	40.00	—
1699	—	6.00	12.00	25.00	40.00	—
1700	—	6.00	12.00	25.00	40.00	—

KM# 74 3 KREUZER

Silver **Ruler:** Paris **Obv:** Hat above two shields of arms in inner circle **Rev:** St. Rupert in inner circle, value below, date in legend

Date	Mintage	VG	F	VF	XF	Unc
1621	—	40.00	80.00	175	300	—
1622	—	40.00	80.00	175	300	—

KM# 156 3 KREUZER

Silver **Ruler:** Paris **Obv:** Hat above shield of arms, value below **Obv. Legend:** PARIS D G ARCHIEPS **Rev:** Shield of arms, date in legend **Note:** Kipper 3 Kreuzer.

Date	Mintage	VG	F	VF	XF	Unc
1653	—	25.00	48.00	95.00	210	—

KM# 228 3 KREUZER

Silver **Ruler:** Maximilian Gandolph **Obv:** Two shields of arms, date above, value below in inner circle **Obv. Legend:** MAX GAND... **Rev:** St. Rupert with salt box and crozier in inner circle

Date	Mintage	VG	F	VF	XF	Unc
1678	—	6.00	15.00	35.00	50.00	—
1679	—	6.00	15.00	35.00	50.00	—
1680	—	6.00	15.00	35.00	50.00	—
1681	—	6.00	15.00	35.00	50.00	—
1682	—	6.00	15.00	35.00	50.00	—
1683	—	6.00	15.00	35.00	50.00	—
1684	—	6.00	15.00	35.00	50.00	—
1685	—	6.00	15.00	35.00	50.00	—

KM# 249 3 KREUZER

Silver **Ruler:** Johann Ernst **Obv. Legend:** IO ERNEST...

Date	Mintage	VG	F	VF	XF	Unc
1687	—	6.00	15.00	35.00	50.00	—
1688	—	6.00	15.00	35.00	50.00	—
1689	—	6.00	15.00	35.00	50.00	—
1690	—	6.00	15.00	35.00	50.00	—
1691	—	6.00	15.00	35.00	50.00	—
1692	—	6.00	15.00	35.00	50.00	—

KM# 277 4 KREUZER (Batzen)

Silver **Ruler:** Johann Ernst **Obv:** Hat above two shields of arms, value below **Rev. Legend:** SALZB / LAND / MINZ / 1692

Date	Mintage	VG	F	VF	XF	Unc
1692	—	6.00	15.00	30.00	45.00	—

KM# 77 6 KREUZER

Silver **Ruler:** Paris **Obv:** Hat above shield of arms in inner circle **Rev:** St. Rupert in inner circle, value below, date in legend **Note:** Kipper 6 Kreuzer.

Date	Mintage	VG	F	VF	XF	Unc
(i)622	—	60.00	120	240	425	—
1622	—	60.00	120	240	425	—

KM# 78 12 KREUZER

Silver **Ruler:** Paris **Obv:** Hat above shield of arms in inner circle **Rev:** St. Rupert in inner circle, value below, date in legend **Note:** Kipper 12 Kreuzer.

Date	Mintage	VG	F	VF	XF	Unc
1622	—	90.00	180	300	475	—

KM# 230 15 KREUZER

Silver **Ruler:** Maximilian Gandolph **Obv:** Hat above shield of arms **Obv. Legend:** MAX GAND... **Rev:** St. Rupert in inner circle, value below, date in legend

Date	Mintage	VG	F	VF	XF	Unc
1681	—	12.50	25.00	45.00	90.00	—
1683	—	12.50	25.00	45.00	90.00	—
1684	—	12.50	25.00	45.00	90.00	—
1685	—	12.50	25.00	45.00	90.00	—
1686	—	12.50	25.00	45.00	90.00	—

KM# 250 15 KREUZER
Silver **Ruler:** Johann Ernst **Obv. Legend:** IO ERNEST...

Date	Mintage	VG	F	VF	XF	Unc
1687	—	12.50	25.00	45.00	90.00	—
1688	—	12.50	25.00	45.00	90.00	—
1689	—	12.50	25.00	45.00	90.00	—
1690	—	12.50	25.00	45.00	90.00	—
1692	—	12.50	25.00	45.00	90.00	—

KM# 278 15 KREUZER
Silver **Ruler:** Johann Ernst **Rev:** Saints Rupert and Virgil in diamond with value below in Arabic numerals

Date	Mintage	VG	F	VF	XF	Unc
1694	—	22.50	42.00	95.00	145	—

KM# 279 15 KREUZER
Silver **Ruler:** Johann Ernst **Rev:** Value in Roman numerals

Date	Mintage	VG	F	VF	XF	Unc
1694	—	22.50	42.00	95.00	145	—

KM# 56 24 KREUZER
Silver **Ruler:** Paris **Obv:** Hat above shield of arms in inner circle **Rev:** St. Rupert in inner circle, value below, date in legend **Note:** Kipper 24 Kreuzer.

Date	Mintage	VG	F	VF	XF	Unc
1620	—	120	210	350	600	—
1621	—	120	210	350	600	—

KM# 75 48 KREUZER
Silver **Ruler:** Paris **Obv:** Hat above value and two shields of arms in inner circle **Rev:** St. Rupert in inner circle, date in legend **Note:** Kipper 48 Kreuzer.

Date	Mintage	VG	F	VF	XF	Unc
1621	—	70.00	150	270	475	—

KM# 60 120 KREUZER
Silver **Ruler:** Paris **Obv:** Hat above value above two shields of arms within inner circle **Note:** Kipper 120 Kreuzer.

Date	Mintage	VG	F	VF	XF	Unc
1620 Rare	—	—	—	—	—	—
1621 Rare	—	—	—	—	—	—
1622 Rare	—	—	—	—	—	—

KM# 79 1/9 THALER
Silver **Ruler:** Paris **Obv:** Hat above shield of arms **Obv. Legend:** PARIS D G... **Rev:** St. Rupert in inner circle, value below, date in legend

Date	Mintage	VG	F	VF	XF	Unc
1622	—	40.00	80.00	150	250	—
1624	—	40.00	80.00	150	250	—
1626	—	40.00	80.00	150	250	—
1627	—	40.00	80.00	150	250	—
1628	—	40.00	80.00	150	250	—
1630	—	40.00	80.00	150	250	—
1633	—	40.00	80.00	150	250	—
1634	—	40.00	80.00	150	250	—
1635	—	40.00	80.00	150	250	—
1636	—	40.00	80.00	150	250	—
1638	—	40.00	80.00	150	250	—
1640	—	40.00	80.00	150	250	—
1642	—	40.00	80.00	150	250	—
1643	—	40.00	80.00	150	250	—
1644	—	40.00	80.00	150	250	—

KM# 150 1/9 THALER
Silver **Ruler:** Paris **Note:** Klippe.

Date	Mintage	VG	F	VF	XF	Unc
1643	—	55.00	110	205	325	—
1644	—	55.00	110	205	325	—

KM# 180 1/9 THALER
Silver **Ruler:** Guidobald

Date	Mintage	VG	F	VF	XF	Unc
1656	—	45.00	90.00	150	250	—
1660	—	45.00	90.00	150	250	—
1666	—	45.00	90.00	150	250	—

KM# 179 1/9 THALER
Silver **Ruler:** Guidobald **Note:** Similar in design to KM#180.

Date	Mintage	VG	F	VF	XF	Unc
1656	—	70.00	145	240	350	—

KM# 214 1/9 THALER
Silver **Ruler:** Maximilian Gandolph **Note:** Klippe.

Date	Mintage	VG	F	VF	XF	Unc
1669	—	45.00	90.00	170	280	—
1672	—	45.00	90.00	170	280	—
1673	—	45.00	90.00	170	280	—

KM# 222 1/9 THALER
Silver **Ruler:** Maximilian Gandolph **Obv. Legend:** MAX GAND D G... **Note:** Similar in design to KM#180.

Date	Mintage	VG	F	VF	XF	Unc
1673	—	45.00	90.00	175	285	—

KM# 269 1/9 THALER
Silver **Ruler:** Johann Ernst **Obv. Legend:** IO ERNEST D G... **Note:** Similar in design to KM#180.

Date	Mintage	VG	F	VF	XF	Unc
1688	—	45.00	90.00	150	250	—

KM# 270 1/9 THALER
Silver **Ruler:** Johann Ernst

Date	Mintage	VG	F	VF	XF	Unc
1688	—	45.00	90.00	150	250	—

KM# 7.1 1/8 THALER
Silver **Ruler:** Wolfgang Dietrich **Obv:** Oval arms with value above in inner circle **Obv. Legend:** WOLF TEO D G... **Rev:** St. Rupert in inner circle, date in legend

Date	Mintage	VG	F	VF	XF	Unc
ND	—	250	500	900	1,500	—

KM# 7.2 1/8 THALER
Silver **Ruler:** Wolfgang Dietrich

Date	Mintage	VG	F	VF	XF	Unc
1607	—	165	300	550	900	—
1609	—	165	300	550	900	—
1610	—	165	300	550	900	—
1612	—	165	300	550	900	—

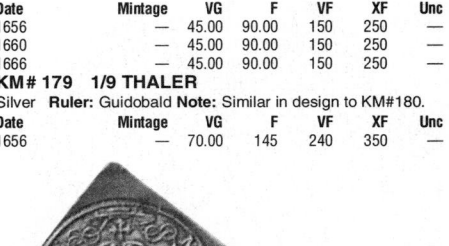

KM# 8 1/8 THALER

Silver **Ruler:** Wolfgang Dietrich **Note:** Klippe.

Date	Mintage	VG	F	VF	XF	Unc
1609	—	165	300	550	925	—
1610	—	165	300	550	925	—
1612	—	165	300	550	925	—

KM# 14 1/8 THALER

Silver **Ruler:** Markus Sittich **Note:** Klippe.

Date	Mintage	VG	F	VF	XF	Unc
1612	—	275	500	825	1,300	—
1613	—	275	500	825	1,300	—
1615	—	275	500	825	1,300	—
1616	—	275	500	825	1,300	—

KM# 13 1/8 THALER

Silver **Ruler:** Markus Sittich **Obv. Legend:** MARCVS SITTICVS D G…

Date	Mintage	VG	F	VF	XF	Unc
1612	—	200	400	650	1,000	—
1613	—	200	400	650	1,000	—
1614	—	200	400	650	1,000	—
1615	—	200	400	650	1,000	—
1616	—	200	400	650	1,000	—

KM# 57 1/8 THALER

Silver **Ruler:** Paris **Obv:** Shield of arms with value above, in inner circle **Obv. Legend:** PARIS D G…

Date	Mintage	VG	F	VF	XF	Unc
1620	—	45.00	90.00	165	275	—
1622	—	45.00	90.00	165	275	—
1623	—	45.00	90.00	165	275	—
1624	—	45.00	90.00	165	275	—

KM# 106 1/8 THALER

Silver **Ruler:** Paris **Note:** Klippe.

Date	Mintage	VG	F	VF	XF	Unc
1627	—	60.00	120	200	350	—

KM# 107.1 1/6 THALER

Silver **Ruler:** Paris **Obv:** Madonna and child above shield of arms in inner circle **Obv. Legend:** PARIS D G… **Rev:** St. Rupert with value above arms in inner circle, date in legend

Date	Mintage	VG	F	VF	XF	Unc
1627	—	50.00	100	185	300	—
1628	—	50.00	100	185	300	—
1630	—	50.00	100	185	300	—
1634	—	50.00	100	185	300	—

KM# 108 1/6 THALER

Silver **Ruler:** Paris **Note:** Klippe.

Date	Mintage	VG	F	VF	XF	Unc
1627	—	70.00	130	250	425	—
1642	—	70.00	130	250	425	—
1646	—	70.00	130	250	425	—
1647	—	70.00	130	250	425	—
1648	—	70.00	130	250	425	—
1651	—	70.00	130	250	425	—
1652	—	70.00	130	250	425	—

KM# 107.2 1/6 THALER

Silver **Ruler:** Paris **Rev:** Round shield below St. Rupert

Date	Mintage	VG	F	VF	XF	Unc
1638	—	75.00	135	250	400	—
1642	—	75.00	135	250	400	—
1645	—	75.00	135	250	400	—
1646	—	75.00	135	250	400	—
1648	—	75.00	135	250	400	—

KM# 160 1/6 THALER

Silver **Ruler:** Guidobald **Note:** Klippe.

Date	Mintage	VG	F	VF	XF	Unc
1654	—	38.50	75.00	150	250	—
1656	—	38.50	75.00	150	250	—
1658	—	38.50	75.00	150	250	—
1661	—	38.50	75.00	150	250	—
1663	—	38.50	75.00	150	250	—
1666	—	38.50	75.00	150	250	—

KM# 181 1/6 THALER

Silver **Ruler:** Guidobald **Obv:** Hat above shield of arms **Obv. Legend:** GUIDOBALD D G… **Rev:** St. Rupert in inner circle, value below, date in legend

Date	Mintage	VG	F	VF	XF	Unc
1656	—	44.00	90.00	160	265	—
1658	—	44.00	90.00	160	265	—
1661	—	44.00	90.00	160	265	—
1666	—	44.00	90.00	160	265	—

KM# 215 1/6 THALER

Silver **Ruler:** Maximilian Gandolph **Note:** Klippe.

Date	Mintage	VG	F	VF	XF	Unc
1669	—	65.00	110	195	325	—
1674	—	65.00	110	195	325	—
1677	—	65.00	110	195	325	—
1679	—	65.00	110	195	325	—

KM# 227 1/6 THALER

Silver **Ruler:** Maximilian Gandolph **Obv. Legend:** MAX GAND D G…

Date	Mintage	VG	F	VF	XF	Unc
1677	—	100	175	275	450	—

KM# 251 1/6 THALER

Silver **Ruler:** Johann Ernst **Obv. Legend:** IO ERNEST D G… **Note:** Klippe.

Date	Mintage	VG	F	VF	XF	Unc
1687	—	—	—	—	—	—
1688	—	110	220	325	550	—

KM# 15 1/4 THALER

Silver **Ruler:** Markus Sittich **Obv:** Hat above shield of arms dividing date **Obv. Legend:** MARCVS SITTICVS D. G. **Rev:** St. Rupert in inner circle, value below

Date	Mintage	VG	F	VF	XF	Unc
1612	—	240	425	725	1,200	—
1613	—	240	425	725	1,200	—

KM# 16 1/4 THALER

Silver **Ruler:** Markus Sittich **Note:** Klippe.

Date	Mintage	VG	F	VF	XF	Unc
1612	—	195	325	550	925	—
1613	—	195	325	550	925	—

KM# 35 1/4 THALER

Silver **Ruler:** Markus Sittich **Note:** Klippe.

Date	Mintage	VG	F	VF	XF	Unc
1614	—	110	220	375	650	—
1615	—	110	220	375	650	—
1616	—	110	220	375	650	—

KM# 34 1/4 THALER

Silver **Ruler:** Markus Sittich **Rev:** Date at end of outer legend

Date	Mintage	VG	F	VF	XF	Unc
1614	—	165	275	500	775	—
1615	—	165	275	500	775	—
1616	—	165	275	500	775	—

KM# 58 1/4 THALER

Silver **Ruler:** Paris **Note:** Klippe.

Date	Mintage	VG	F	VF	XF	Unc
1620	—	110	220	325	600	—
1622	—	110	220	325	600	—

KM# 80 1/4 THALER

Silver **Ruler:** Paris **Obv:** Hat above shield of arms **Obv. Legend:** PARIS D G… **Rev:** St. Rupert in inner circle, date in legend

Date	Mintage	VG	F	VF	XF	Unc
1622	—	130	240	450	725	—

KM# 88 1/4 THALER

Silver **Ruler:** Paris **Note:** Klippe.

Date	Mintage	VG	F	VF	XF	Unc
1624	—	90.00	165	275	500	—
1625	—	90.00	165	275	500	—
1626	—	90.00	165	275	500	—
1631	—	90.00	165	275	500	—
1638	—	90.00	165	275	500	—
1639	—	90.00	165	275	500	—
1651	—	90.00	165	275	500	—
1652	—	90.00	165	275	500	—

KM# 97 1/4 THALER

Silver **Ruler:** Paris **Rev:** St. Rupert in inner circle, value below, date in legend

Date	Mintage	VG	F	VF	XF	Unc
1625	—	110	220	375	650	—
1626	—	110	220	375	650	—
1639	—	110	220	375	650	—
1652	—	110	220	375	650	—

KM# 98 1/4 THALER

Silver **Ruler:** Paris **Obv:** Madonna and child above shield of arms **Obv. Legend:** PARIS D G... **Rev:** St. Rupert above value and arms in inner circle, date in legend

Date	Mintage	VG	F	VF	XF	Unc
ND	—	110	220	375	650	—
1626	—	110	220	375	650	—
1633	—	110	220	375	650	—
1634	—	110	220	375	650	—
1636	—	110	220	375	650	—
1637	—	110	220	375	650	—
1640	—	110	220	375	650	—
1642	—	110	220	375	650	—

KM# 103 1/4 THALER

Silver **Ruler:** Paris **Note:** Klippe.

Date	Mintage	VG	F	VF	XF	Unc
1626	—	75.00	150	270	500	—
1633	—	75.00	150	270	500	—
1636	—	75.00	150	270	500	—
1640	—	75.00	150	270	500	—
1642	—	75.00	150	270	500	—

KM# 140 1/4 THALER

Silver **Ruler:** Paris **Subject:** Cathedral Dedication **Note:** Similar to 1/2 Thaler, KM#141.

Date	Mintage	VG	F	VF	XF	Unc
1628	—	—	—	—	—	—

KM# 161 1/4 THALER

Silver **Ruler:** Guidobald **Note:** Klippe.

Date	Mintage	VG	F	VF	XF	Unc
1654	—	55.00	110	195	425	—
1658	—	55.00	110	195	425	—
1668	—	55.00	110	195	425	—

KM# 182 1/4 THALER

Silver **Ruler:** Guidobald **Obv:** Hat above shield of arms **Obv. Legend:** GVIDOBALDVS D G... **Rev:** St. Rupert in inner circle, value below, date in legend

Date	Mintage	VG	F	VF	XF	Unc
1656	—	70.00	140	220	450	—
1658	—	70.00	140	220	450	—
1660	—	70.00	140	220	450	—
1661	—	70.00	140	220	450	—
1663	—	70.00	140	220	450	—

KM# 216 1/4 THALER

Silver **Ruler:** Maximilian Gandolph **Obv:** Hat above shield of arms **Obv. Legend:** MAXIM GANDOL D G...

Date	Mintage	VG	F	VF	XF	Unc
1669	—	55.00	110	220	350	—
1672	—	55.00	110	220	350	—
1675	—	55.00	110	220	350	—

KM# 231 1/4 THALER

Silver **Ruler:** Maximilian Gandolph **Obv:** Inscription **Obv. Inscription:** MAX / GAND EX CO / MIT DE KOEN / BURG ARCHIEP ET / PR SALISBS SED / AP LEG SAZCVLO / VNDECIMO FVN / DATI ARCHI / EPTVS **Rev:** Hat above shield of arms divides date, triangle above

Date	Mintage	VG	F	VF	XF	Unc
1682	—	65.00	130	255	450	—

KM# 245 1/4 THALER

Silver **Ruler:** Maximilian Gandolph **Obv:** Hat above two shields of arms **Obv. Legend:** MAXIM GANDOL D G... **Rev:** St. Rupert in inner circle, value below, date in legend

Date	Mintage	VG	F	VF	XF	Unc
1684	—	130	265	375	650	—

KM# 246 1/4 THALER

Silver **Ruler:** Maximilian Gandolph **Note:** Klippe.

Date	Mintage	VG	F	VF	XF	Unc
1684	—	70.00	140	250	425	—

KM# 252 1/4 THALER

Silver **Ruler:** Johann Ernst **Obv:** Hat above two shields of arms in inner circle **Obv. Legend:** IO ERNEST D G... **Note:** Klippe.

Date	Mintage	VG	F	VF	XF	Unc
1687	—	49.50	100	180	300	—

KM# 281 1/4 THALER

Silver **Ruler:** Johann Ernst **Obv:** Hat above shield of arms

Date	Mintage	VG	F	VF	XF	Unc
1694	—	70.00	130	220	375	—

KM# 282 1/4 THALER

Silver **Ruler:** Johann Ernst **Obv:** Madonna and Child above shield of arms in inner circle **Rev:** St. Rupert above value and arms in inner circle, date in legend

Date	Mintage	VG	F	VF	XF	Unc
1694	—	33.00	65.00	140	275	—
1695	—	33.00	65.00	140	275	—
1696	—	33.00	65.00	140	275	—
1699	—	33.00	65.00	140	275	—
1700	—	33.00	65.00	140	275	—

KM# 294 1/4 THALER

Silver, 30 mm. **Ruler:** Johann Ernst **Subject:** Enthronement of the archbishop **Obv:** Bust right, star below **Rev:** Legend, date below **Rev. Legend:** IN MANV DOMINI SORTS MEA

Date	Mintage	VG	F	VF	XF	Unc
1699	—	105	215	350	600	—

KM# 17 1/2 THALER

Silver **Ruler:** Markus Sittich **Obv:** Hat above shield of arms, hat divides date **Obv. Legend:** MARCVS SITTICVS D G... **Rev:** St. Rupert in inner circle

Date	Mintage	VG	F	VF	XF	Unc
1612	—	350	650	1,100	1,800	—

KM# 18 1/2 THALER

Silver **Ruler:** Markus Sittich **Note:** Klippe.

Date	Mintage	VG	F	VF	XF	Unc
1612	—	325	600	1,000	1,700	—

KM# 37 1/2 THALER
Silver **Ruler:** Markus Sittich **Note:** Klippe.

Date	Mintage	VG	F	VF	XF	Unc
1614	—	165	325	600	1,000	—
1615	—	165	325	600	1,000	—
1617	—	165	325	600	1,000	—
1619	—	165	325	600	1,000	—

KM# 36 1/2 THALER
Silver **Ruler:** Markus Sittich **Rev:** Date at end of legend

Date	Mintage	VG	F	VF	XF	Unc
1614	—	250	450	775	1,250	—
1615	—	250	450	775	1,250	—
1617	—	250	450	775	1,250	—

KM# 59 1/2 THALER
Silver **Ruler:** Paris **Obv:** Hat above shield of arms in inner circle **Obv. Legend:** PARIS D G… **Rev:** St. Rupert in inner circle, date in legend **Note:** Klippe.

Date	Mintage	VG	F	VF	XF	Unc
1620	—	375	650	1,100	1,800	—
1622	—	375	650	1,100	1,800	—

KM# 76 1/2 THALER
Silver **Ruler:** Paris **Obv:** Hat above shield of arms in inner circle **Rev:** St. Rupert in inner circle, value below, date in legend **Note:** Kipper 1/2 Thaler.

Date	Mintage	VG	F	VF	XF	Unc
1621	—	85.00	175	300	500	—
1622	—	100	200	350	600	—

KM# 90 1/2 THALER
Silver **Ruler:** Paris **Note:** Klippe. Varieties exist.

Date	Mintage	VG	F	VF	XF	Unc
1624	—	275	450	825	1,500	—
1625	—	275	450	825	1,500	—
1626	—	275	450	825	1,500	—
1627	—	275	450	825	1,500	—
1629	—	275	450	825	1,500	—
1631	—	275	450	825	1,500	—
1636	—	275	450	825	1,500	—
1638	—	275	450	825	1,500	—
1639	—	275	450	825	1,500	—

KM# 89 1/2 THALER
Silver **Ruler:** Paris **Obv:** Madonna and child above shield of arms in inner circle **Rev:** St. Rupert above arms in inner circle

Date	Mintage	VG	F	VF	XF	Unc
1624	—	375	650	1,100	1,800	—
1625	—	375	650	1,100	1,800	—
1626	—	375	650	1,100	1,800	—
1627	—	375	650	1,100	1,800	—

KM# 141 1/2 THALER
14.5500 g., Silver **Ruler:** Paris **Subject:** Cathedral Dedication

Date	Mintage	VG	F	VF	XF	Unc
1628	—	65.00	125	250	425	—

KM# 188 1/2 THALER
Silver **Ruler:** Maximilian Gandolph **Obv:** Hat above shield of arms, date divided below in inner circle **Obv. Legend:** MAXIMM. GANDOLPH… **Rev:** St. Rupert in inner circle

Date	Mintage	VG	F	VF	XF	Unc
1668	—	210	350	600	1,000	—

KM# 189 1/2 THALER
Silver **Ruler:** Maximilian Gandolph

Date	Mintage	VG	F	VF	XF	Unc
1668	—	70.00	150	275	500	—

KM# 232 1/2 THALER
Silver **Ruler:** Maximilian Gandolph **Subject:** 1100th Year of the Bishopric

Date	Mintage	VG	F	VF	XF	Unc
1682	—	65.00	125	250	475	—

KM# 253 1/2 THALER
Silver **Ruler:** Johann Ernst **Obv:** Hat above shield of arms, date divided near bottom in inner circle **Rev:** SS. Rupert and Virgil

Date	Mintage	VG	F	VF	XF	Unc
1687	—	49.50	95.00	180	325	—
1694	—	49.50	95.00	180	325	—
1695	—	49.50	95.00	180	325	—
1698	—	49.50	95.00	180	325	—
1699	—	49.50	95.00	180	325	—
1700	—	49.50	95.00	180	325	—

KM# 19 THALER
Silver **Ruler:** Markus Sittich **Obv:** Similar to KM#38 but date divided near bottom of arms **Note:** Dav. #3488.

Date	Mintage	VG	F	VF	XF	Unc
1612	—	130	325	525	850	—
1613	—	130	325	525	850	—

KM# 20 THALER
Silver **Ruler:** Markus Sittich **Note:** Dav. #A3488. Klippe.

Date	Mintage	VG	F	VF	XF	Unc
1612	—	290	725	1,200	2,000	—
1613	—	290	725	1,200	2,000	—

KM# 39 THALER
Silver **Ruler:** Markus Sittich **Note:** Klippe. Dav. #A3492.

Date	Mintage	VG	F	VF	XF	Unc
1614	—	290	725	1,200	2,000	—
1615	—	290	725	1,200	2,000	—
1616	—	290	725	1,200	2,000	—
1617	—	290	725	1,200	2,000	—
1618	—	290	725	1,200	2,000	—
1619	—	290	725	1,200	2,000	—

KM# 38 THALER

Silver **Ruler:** Markus Sittich **Rev:** Date in legend **Note:** Dav. #3492.

Date	Mintage	VG	F	VF	XF	Unc
1614	—	130	325	525	850	—
1615	—	130	325	525	850	—
1616	—	130	325	525	850	—
1617	—	130	325	525	850	—
1618	—	130	325	525	850	—
1619	—	130	325	525	850	—

KM# 28 THALER

Silver **Ruler:** Markus Sittich **Obv:** Tower **Rev:** Saint on throne **Note:** Klippe. Mule. Dav. #3493.

Date	Mintage	VG	F	VF	XF	Unc
ND/1615 Rare	—	—	—	—	—	—
1593/1615 Rare	—	—	—	—	—	—
1593/1617 Rare	—	—	—	—	—	—

KM# 61 THALER

Silver **Ruler:** Paris **Obv. Legend:** PARIS D G... **Note:** Dav. #3497.

Date	Mintage	VG	F	VF	XF	Unc
1620	—	55.00	125	210	350	—
1621	—	55.00	125	210	350	—
1622	—	55.00	125	210	350	—
1623	—	55.00	125	210	350	—
1624	—	55.00	125	210	350	—

KM# 62 THALER

Silver **Ruler:** Paris **Note:** Dav. #3497A. Klippe.

Date	Mintage	VG	F	VF	XF	Unc
1620	—	205	500	875	1,300	—
1622	—	205	500	875	1,300	—

KM# 87 THALER

Silver **Ruler:** Paris **Obv:** Madonna above shield of arms **Rev:** St. Rupert standing facing **Note:** Dav. #3504. Varieties exist.

Date	Mintage	VG	F	VF	XF	Unc
1623	—	39.50	100	175	350	—
1624	—	39.50	100	175	350	—
1625	—	39.50	100	175	350	—
1626	—	39.50	100	175	350	—
1627	—	39.50	100	175	350	—
1628	—	39.50	100	175	350	—
1629	—	39.50	100	175	350	—
1630	—	39.50	100	175	350	—
1631	—	39.50	100	175	350	—
1632	—	39.50	100	175	350	—
1633	—	39.50	100	175	350	—
1634	—	39.50	100	175	350	—
1635	—	39.50	100	175	350	—
1636	—	39.50	100	175	350	—
1637	—	39.50	100	175	350	—
1638	—	39.50	100	175	350	—
1639	—	39.50	100	175	350	—
1640	—	39.50	100	175	350	—
1641	—	39.50	100	175	350	—
1642	—	39.50	100	175	350	—
1643/2	—	39.50	100	175	350	—
1644	—	39.50	100	175	350	—
1645	—	39.50	100	175	350	—
1646	—	39.50	100	175	350	—
1647	—	39.50	100	175	350	—
1648	—	39.50	100	175	350	—
1649	—	39.50	100	175	350	—
1650	—	39.50	100	175	350	—
1651	—	39.50	100	175	350	—
1652	—	39.50	100	175	350	—
1653	—	39.50	100	175	350	—

KM# 91 THALER

Silver **Ruler:** Paris **Note:** Dav. #3504A. Klippe.

Date	Mintage	VG	F	VF	XF	Unc
1624	—	205	500	875	1,300	—
1625	—	205	500	875	1,300	—
1628	—	205	500	875	1,300	—
1629	—	205	500	875	1,300	—
1631	—	205	500	875	1,300	—
1632	—	205	500	875	1,300	—
1636	—	205	500	875	1,300	—
1638	—	205	500	875	1,300	—

KM# 110 THALER

Silver **Ruler:** Paris **Subject:** Consecration of the Cathedral **Note:** Dav. #3499.

Date	Mintage	VG	F	VF	XF	Unc
1628	—	90.00	230	400	550	—

KM# 162 THALER

Silver **Ruler:** Guidobald **Obv. Legend:** GVIDOBALD D G... **Note:** Dav. #3505.

Date	Mintage	VG	F	VF	XF	Unc
1654	—	39.50	100	175	350	—
1655	—	39.50	100	175	350	—
1656	—	39.50	100	175	350	—
1657	—	39.50	100	175	350	—
1658	—	39.50	100	175	350	—
1659	—	39.50	100	175	350	—
1660	—	39.50	100	175	350	—
1661	—	39.50	100	175	350	—
1662	—	39.50	100	175	350	—
1663	—	39.50	100	175	350	—
1664	—	39.50	100	175	350	—
1665	—	39.50	100	175	350	—
1666	—	39.50	100	175	350	—
1667	—	39.50	100	175	350	—
1668	—	39.50	100	175	350	—

KM# 190 THALER

Silver **Ruler:** Maximilian Gandolph **Obv. Legend:** MAX: GAND: D: G:... **Note:** Dav. #3508. Illustration reduced.

Date	Mintage	VG	F	VF	XF	Unc
1668	—	39.50	100	175	350	—
1669	—	39.50	100	175	350	—
1670	—	39.50	100	175	350	—
1671	—	39.50	100	175	350	—
1672	—	39.50	100	175	350	—
1673	—	39.50	100	175	350	—
1674	—	39.50	100	175	350	—
1675	—	39.50	100	175	350	—
1677	—	39.50	100	175	350	—
1680	—	39.50	100	175	350	—
1685	—	39.50	100	175	350	—
1686	—	39.50	100	175	350	—

KM# 233 THALER

Silver **Ruler:** Maximilian Gandolph **Subject:** 1100th Year of the Bishopric **Note:** Dav. #3509.

Date	Mintage	VG	F	VF	XF	Unc
MDCLXXXII (1682)	—	90.00	230	400	700	—
1682 PS	—	—	—	—	—	—

KM# 254 THALER

Silver **Ruler:** Johann Ernst **Obv:** Madonna and child above Cardinals' hat and shield **Obv. Legend:** IO: ERNEST: D:G: ... **Rev:** St. Rupert above shield in frame, date in legend **Rev. Legend:** S: RUDBERTUS: EPS .... **Note:** Dav.#1234.

Date	Mintage	F	VF	XF	Unc	BU
1687	—	100	175	350	650	—
1688	—	100	175	350	650	—
1690	—	100	175	350	650	—
1691	—	100	175	350	650	—
1692	—	100	175	350	650	—
1693	—	100	175	350	650	—
1694	—	100	175	350	650	—
1695	—	100	175	350	650	—
1696	—	100	175	350	650	—
1697	—	100	175	350	650	—
1698	—	100	175	350	650	—
1699	—	100	175	350	650	—
1700	—	100	175	350	650	—

KM# 43 1-1/2 THALER

Silver **Ruler:** Markus Sittich **Obv:** Hat above oval shield of arms in inner circle **Obv. Legend:** MARCVS. SITTICVS. D. G... **Rev:** St. Rupert in inner circle, date in legend **Note:** Klippe. Dav. #3491.

Date	Mintage	VG	F	VF	XF	Unc
1617 Rare	—	—	—	—	—	—

KM# 21 2 THALER

Silver **Ruler:** Markus Sittich **Obv:** Hat above oval shield of arms in inner circle, date divided near bottom of arms **Obv. Legend:** MARCVS. SITTICVS. D. G... **Rev:** St. Rupert in inner circle **Note:** Klippe. Dav. #3487.

Date	Mintage	VG	F	VF	XF	Unc
1612 Rare	—	—	—	—	—	—
1613 Rare	—	—	—	—	—	—

KM# 40 2 THALER

Silver **Ruler:** Markus Sittich **Note:** Dav. #3490. Similar to 1 Thaler, KM#39.

Date	Mintage	VG	F	VF	XF	Unc
1614	—	1,050	1,600	2,500	3,850	—
1615	—	1,050	1,600	2,500	3,850	—
1616	—	1,050	1,600	2,500	3,850	—
1617	—	1,050	1,600	2,500	3,850	—
1618	—	1,050	1,600	2,500	3,850	—
1619	—	1,050	1,600	2,500	3,850	—

KM# 44 2 THALER

Silver **Ruler:** Markus Sittich **Note:** Dav. #3490A. Similar to 1 Thaler, KM#38.

Date	Mintage	VG	F	VF	XF	Unc
1617 Rare	—	—	—	—	—	—

KM# 63 2 THALER

Silver **Ruler:** Paris **Obv. Legend:** PARIS D G... **Note:** Dav. #3496. Similar to 1 Thaler, KM#62. Klippe.

Date	Mintage	VG	F	VF	XF	Unc
1620	—	900	1,500	2,400	3,600	—

KM# 92 2 THALER

Silver **Ruler:** Paris **Note:** Dav. #3503. Similar to 1 Thaler, KM#87. Klippe.

Date	Mintage	VG	F	VF	XF	Unc
1624	—	500	825	1,400	2,200	—
1625	—	500	825	1,400	2,200	—
1629	—	500	825	1,400	2,200	—
1631	—	500	825	1,400	2,200	—
1632	—	500	825	1,400	2,200	—
1636	—	500	825	1,400	2,200	—

KM# A111 2 THALER

Silver **Ruler:** Paris **Subject:** Consecration of the Cathedral **Note:** Dav. #3498.

Date	Mintage	VG	F	VF	XF	Unc
1628	—	1,000	1,650	2,750	3,850	—

KM# 111 2 THALER

Silver **Ruler:** Paris **Note:** Dav. #3498A. Klippe.

Date	Mintage	VG	F	VF	XF	Unc
1628	—	1,750	2,700	4,200	6,000	—

KM# 138 2 THALER

Silver **Ruler:** Paris **Note:** Dav. #3503A. Similar to 1 Thaler, KM#87.

Date	Mintage	VG	F	VF	XF	Unc
1629	—	550	1,000	1,650	2,750	—

KM# 113 2 THALER

Silver **Ruler:** Maximilian Gandolph **Obv:** City view of Salzburg **Obv. Legend:** MAX: GAND: D: G... **Note:** Dav. #3507. Illustration reduced.

Date	Mintage	VG	F	VF	XF	Unc
ND Rare	—	—	—	—	—	—

KM# 48 3 THALER

Silver **Ruler:** Markus Sittich **Obv:** Hat above oval shield of arms in inner circle **Obv. Legend:** MARCVS. SITTICVS. D. G... **Rev:** St. Rupert in inner circle, date in legend **Note:** Dav. #3489. Klippe.

Date	Mintage	VG	F	VF	XF	Unc
1618 Rare	—	—	—	—	—	—

KM# 81 3 THALER

Silver **Ruler:** Paris **Obv. Legend:** PARIS D G... **Note:** Dav. #3495. Klippe. Similar to 1 Thaler, KM#62.

Date	Mintage	VG	F	VF	XF	Unc
1622 Rare	—	—	—	—	—	—

KM# 99 3 THALER

Silver **Ruler:** Paris **Obv:** Madonna and child above shield of arms in inner circle **Rev:** St. Rupert above shield of arms in inner circle, date in legend **Note:** Dav. #3502. Klippe.

Date	Mintage	VG	F	VF	XF	Unc
1625	—	1,500	2,400	3,600	5,400	—
1629	—	1,500	2,400	3,600	5,400	—
1631	—	1,500	2,400	3,600	5,400	—

KM# 114 3 THALER

Silver **Ruler:** Paris **Subject:** Consecration of the Cathedral **Note:** Dav. #3498B. Similar to 1 Thaler, KM#110.

Date	Mintage	VG	F	VF	XF	Unc
1628 Rare	—	—	—	—	—	—

KM# 115 3 THALER

Silver **Ruler:** Paris **Note:** Dav. #3498C. Klippe.

Date	Mintage	VG	F	VF	XF	Unc
1628 Rare	—	—	—	—	—	—

KM# 64 4 THALER

Silver **Ruler:** Paris **Obv:** Hat above shield of arms in inner circle **Obv. Legend:** PARIS. D. G... **Rev:** St. Rupert in inner circle, date in legend **Note:** Dav. #3494. Klippe.

Date	Mintage	VG	F	VF	XF	Unc
1620 Rare	—	—	—	—	—	—

KM# 100 4 THALER

Silver **Ruler:** Paris **Note:** Dav. #3501. Klippe. Illustration reduced.

Date	Mintage	VG	F	VF	XF	Unc
1625 Rare	—	—	—	—	—	—
1629 Rare	—	—	—	—	—	—
1632 Rare	—	—	—	—	—	—

KM# 101 4 THALER

Silver **Ruler:** Paris **Note:** Dav. #3501A. Design similar to KM#100.

Date	Mintage	VG	F	VF	XF	Unc
1625 Rare	—	—	—	—	—	—

KM# 116 4 THALER

Silver **Ruler:** Paris **Subject:** Consecration of the Cathedral **Note:** Dav. #3498D.

Date	Mintage	VG	F	VF	XF	Unc
1628 Rare	—	—	—	—	—	—

KM# 117.1 4 THALER

Silver **Ruler:** Paris **Note:** Dav. #3498E. Klippe. Illustration reduced.

Date	Mintage	VG	F	VF	XF	Unc
1628 Rare	—	—	—	—	—	—

KM# 117.2 4 THALER

Silver **Ruler:** Paris **Note:** Three-sided klippe.

Date	Mintage	VG	F	VF	XF	Unc
1628 Rare	—	—	—	—	—	—

KM# 118 4 THALER

Silver **Ruler:** Maximilian Gandolph **Obv:** City view of Salzburg in inner circle **Obv. Legend:** MAX: GAND: D: G:... **Rev:** Hat above oval arms, a saint seated at each side in inner circle **Note:** Dav. #3506.

Date	Mintage	VG	F	VF	XF	Unc
ND Rare	—	—	—	—	—	—

KM# 119 5 THALER

Silver **Ruler:** Paris **Subject:** Consecration of the Cathedral **Note:** Dav. #3498F. Klippe. Similar to 4 Thaler, KM#117.1.

Date	Mintage	VG	F	VF	XF	Unc
1628 Rare	—	—	—	—	—	—

KM# 120 6 THALER

Silver **Ruler:** Paris **Subject:** Consecration of the Cathedral **Note:** Dav. #3498G. Klippe.

Date	Mintage	VG	F	VF	XF	Unc
1628 Rare	—	—	—	—	—	—

KM# 139 6 THALER

Silver **Ruler:** Paris **Note:** Dav. #3500. Similar to KM#145.

Date	Mintage	VG	F	VF	XF	Unc
1629 Rare	—	—	—	—	—	—

KM# 145 6 THALER

Silver **Ruler:** Paris **Note:** Dav. #3500A.

Date	Mintage	VG	F	VF	XF	Unc
1631 Rare	—	—	—	—	—	—

COUNTERMARKED COINAGE

1681

Prior to 1681 the confusion of the various types of Germanic coinage continued, particularly in regards to the many debased coins in circulation. In order to save his country from greater difficulties, Max Gandolph Kuenburg in 1681, ordered that all thalers and half thalers in circulation be countermarked with the Arms of the See including the date 1681. As the charge for this was one kreuzer for each thaler and two pfennige for each half thaler, the desired result was not attained. Partly through fear of innovation, partly through meanness, very few coins were handed in and all these countermarked pieces are comparitively rare.

KM# 217 GROSCHEN

Silver **Ruler:** Maximilian Gandolph **Countermark:** Arms of the See, date **Note:** Countermark on Bohemia-Prague Mint 1 Groschen of Wenceslaus III.

CM Date	Host Date	Good	VG	F	VF	XF
ND(1681)	1601-19 Rare	—	—	—	—	—

KM# 218 1/2 GULDEN

Silver **Ruler:** Maximilian Gandolph **Countermark:** Arms of the See, date **Note:** Countermark on Germany-Brandenburg 1/2 Gulden.

CM Date	Host Date	Good	VG	F	VF	XF
ND1681	1671 Rare	—	—	—	—	—
ND(1681)	1671 Rare	—	—	—	—	—

KM# 219 GULDEN

Silver **Ruler:** Maximilian Gandolph **Countermark:** Arms of the See, date **Note:** Countermark on Germany-Reuss-Schleiz Gulden.

CM Date	Host Date	Good	VG	F	VF	XF
1681	1678 Rare	—	—	—	—	—
ND(1681)	1678 Rare	—	—	—	—	—

KM# A229 2/3 THALER

Silver **Ruler:** Maximilian Gandolph **Countermark:** Arms of the See **Note:** Countermark on Goslar 24 Mariengroschen, KM#69.

CM Date	Host Date	Good	VG	F	VF	XF
ND(1681)	1674 CH	—	325	550	775	—

KM# 229.9 THALER

Silver, 40 mm. **Ruler:** Maximilian Gandolph **Countermark:** Arms of the See, date **Note:** Countermarked on Austria, Hall mint 1 Thaler, Dav.#3005.

CM Date	Host Date	Good	VG	F	VF	XF
ND(1681)	1607	—	—	—	—	—

KM# 229.2 THALER

Silver **Ruler:** Maximilian Gandolph **Countermark:** Arms of the See, date **Note:** Countermark on Austria - Hall Mint 1 Thaler, Dav. #3125.

CM Date	Host Date	Good	VG	F	VF	XF
ND(1681)	1622	—	550	900	1,500	2,150

KM# 229.3 THALER

Silver **Ruler:** Maximilian Gandolph **Countermark:** Arms of the See, date **Note:** Countermark on Austria - Hall Mint 1 Thaler, Dav. #3330.

CM Date	Host Date	Good	VG	F	VF	XF
ND(1681)	1632	—	550	900	1,500	2,150

KM# 229.4 THALER

Silver **Ruler:** Maximilian Gandolph **Countermark:** Arms of the See, date **Note:** Countermark on Austria - Hall Mint 1 Thaler, Dav. #3370.

CM Date	Host Date	Good	VG	F	VF	XF
ND(1681)	1665	—	550	900	1,500	2,150

KM# 229.6 THALER

Silver **Ruler:** Maximilian Gandolph **Countermark:** Arms of the See, date **Note:** Countermark on Austria - Salzburg 1 Thaler of Maximiliam Gandolf von Kuenberg.

CM Date	Host Date	Good	VG	F	VF	XF
ND(1681)	1624	—	600	1,100	1,800	2,400

KM# 229.5 THALER

Silver **Ruler:** Maximilian Gandolph **Countermark:** Arms of the See, date **Note:** Countermark on Austria - Salzburg 1 Thaler of Wolf Dietrich von Raitenau.

CM Date	Host Date	Good	VG	F	VF	XF
ND(1681)	ND(1612)	—	600	1,100	1,800	2,400

KM# 229.1 THALER

Silver **Ruler:** Maximilian Gandolph **Countermark:** Arms of the See, date **Note:** Countermark on Austria 1 Thaler of Leopold I.

CM Date	Host Date	Good	VG	F	VF	XF
ND(1681)	1621	—	550	900	1,500	2,150

KM# 229.8 THALER

Silver **Ruler:** Maximilian Gandolph **Countermark:** Arms of the See, date **Note:** Countermark on Germany - Teutonic Order 1 Thaler, Dav. #5848.

CM Date	Host Date	Good	VG	F	VF	XF
ND(1681)	1603	—	475	850	1,450	2,100

KM# 229.7 THALER

Silver **Ruler:** Maximilian Gandolph **Countermark:** Arms of the See, date **Note:** Countermark on Austria - Salzburg 1 Thaler, Dav. #3505.

CM Date	Host Date	Good	VG	F	VF	XF
ND(1681)	1654	—	475	850	1,450	2,100
ND(1681)	1665	—	475	850	1,450	2,100

TRADE COINAGE

MB# 400 GOLDGULDEN

3.5000 g., 0.9860 Gold 0.1109 oz. AGW **Ruler:** Georg **Obv:** 3 small shields of arms, one above two, in trilobe, upper lobe divides 1 - 5, rest of date below **Obv. Legend:** ★ GEORGIVS • D • G • ARCHIEPS • SALZ • APO • SE • L • **Rev:** Saint seated on throne, holding salt celler and crozier **Rev. Legend:** SANCTVS • RVDBERTVS • EPVS **Note:** Fr.#646.

Date	Mintage	VG	F	VF	XF	Unc
1586	—	850	1,650	3,000	5,000	—

KM# 51 GOLDGULDEN

0.6850 g., 0.9040 Gold 0.0199 oz. AGW **Ruler:** Markus Sittich **Obv:** Two shields below hat in inner circle **Rev:** St. Rupert standing divides date in inner circle

Date	Mintage	VG	F	VF	XF	Unc
1619	—	900	1,750	3,750	6,000	—

KM# 155 1/4 DUCAT

0.8750 g., 0.9860 Gold 0.0277 oz. AGW **Ruler:** Paris **Obv:** Arms below hat, value below **Obv. Legend:** PARIS… **Rev:** St. Rupert seated facing half right

Date	Mintage	VG	F	VF	XF	Unc
1652	—	100	200	400	750	—

KM# 163 1/4 DUCAT

0.8750 g., 0.9860 Gold 0.0277 oz. AGW **Ruler:** Guidobald **Obv. Legend:** GVIDOB…

Date	Mintage	VG	F	VF	XF	Unc
1654	—	60.00	100	185	275	550
1655	—	60.00	100	185	275	550
1658	—	60.00	100	185	275	550
1659	—	60.00	100	185	275	550
1660	—	60.00	100	185	275	550
1662	—	60.00	100	185	275	550
1668	—	100	175	400	550	750

KM# 191 1/4 DUCAT

0.8750 g., 0.9860 Gold 0.0277 oz. AGW **Ruler:** Maximilian Gandolph **Obv. Legend:** MAX GAND…

Date	Mintage	VG	F	VF	XF	Unc
1668	—	60.00	100	185	275	350
1669	—	60.00	100	185	275	350
1670	—	60.00	100	185	275	350
1671	—	60.00	100	185	275	350
1672	—	60.00	100	185	275	350
1675	—	60.00	100	185	275	350
1676	—	60.00	100	185	275	350
1678	—	60.00	100	185	275	350
1682	—	60.00	100	185	275	350
1686	—	60.00	100	185	275	350

KM# 255 1/4 DUCAT

0.8750 g., 0.9860 Gold 0.0277 oz. AGW **Ruler:** Johann Ernst **Obv:** Cardinals' hat above oval shield **Obv. Legend:** IO ERNEST… **Rev:** St. Rupert, value within oval circle below

Date	Mintage	VG	F	VF	XF	Unc
1687	—	50.00	90.00	165	225	300
1688	—	50.00	90.00	165	225	300
1699	—	50.00	90.00	165	225	300
1700	—	50.00	90.00	165	225	300

KM# 151 1/2 DUCAT

1.7500 g., 0.9860 Gold 0.0555 oz. AGW **Ruler:** Paris **Obv:** Arms below hat **Obv. Legend:** PARIS… **Rev:** St. Rupert seated facing

Date	Mintage	VG	F	VF	XF	Unc
1643	—	85.00	150	350	600	—
1644	—	85.00	150	350	600	—
1648	—	85.00	150	350	600	—
1649	—	85.00	150	350	600	—
1650	—	85.00	150	350	600	—
1651	—	85.00	150	350	600	—
1652	—	85.00	150	350	600	—

KM# 152 1/2 DUCAT

1.7500 g., 0.9860 Gold 0.0555 oz. AGW **Ruler:** Paris **Note:** Klippe.

Date	Mintage	VG	F	VF	XF	Unc
1643	—	250	400	1,000	1,600	—
1644	—	250	400	1,000	1,600	—
1649	—	250	400	1,000	1,600	—
1650	—	250	400	1,000	1,600	—

KM# 164 1/2 DUCAT

1.7500 g., 0.9860 Gold 0.0555 oz. AGW **Ruler:** Guidobald **Obv. Legend:** GVIDO…

Date	Mintage	VG	F	VF	XF	Unc
1654	—	75.00	125	225	350	—
1658	—	75.00	125	225	350	—
1659	—	75.00	125	225	350	—
1662	—	75.00	125	225	350	—
1663	—	75.00	125	225	350	—
1664	—	75.00	125	225	350	—
1665	—	75.00	125	225	350	—
1666	—	75.00	125	225	350	—

KM# 192 1/2 DUCAT

1.7500 g., 0.9860 Gold 0.0555 oz. AGW **Ruler:** Maximilian Gandolph **Obv. Legend:** MAX GAND…

Date	Mintage	VG	F	VF	XF	Unc
1668	—	65.00	110	250	400	—
1669	—	65.00	110	250	400	—
1670	—	65.00	110	250	400	—
1684	—	65.00	110	250	400	—
1686	—	65.00	110	250	400	—

KM# 193 1/2 DUCAT

1.7500 g., 0.9860 Gold 0.0555 oz. AGW **Ruler:** Maximilian Gandolph **Note:** Klippe.

Date	Mintage	VG	F	VF	XF	Unc
1668	—	110	165	350	600	—

KM# 256 1/2 DUCAT

1.7500 g., 0.9860 Gold 0.0555 oz. AGW **Ruler:** Johann Ernst **Obv:** Cardinals' hat above oval shield **Obv. Legend:** IO : ERNEST : D : G : ... **Rev:** St. Rupert **Rev. Legend:** SALISBVRG • 1705 • S: RVD....

Date	Mintage	VG	F	VF	XF	Unc
1687	—	75.00	125	275	450	—
1690	—	75.00	125	275	450	—
1699	—	75.00	125	275	450	—
1700	—	75.00	125	275	450	—

KM# 2 DUCAT

3.5000 g., 0.9860 Gold 0.1109 oz. AGW **Ruler:** Wolfgang Dietrich **Obv:** Oval 6-fold arms with central shield of Raitenau, legate's hat above **Obv. Legend:** WOLF • TEOD • D • G • AREPS • SAL • A • S • L • **Rev:** St. Rupert seated on throne holding salt cellar and crozier, date at end of legend **Rev. Legend:** SANCTVS • RVDBERTVS • EPS • SALZ • **Note:** Fr.#662.

Date	Mintage	VG	F	VF	XF	Unc
160Z	—	300	700	1,500	2,000	—

KM# 3 DUCAT

3.5000 g., 0.9860 Gold 0.1109 oz. AGW **Ruler:** Wolfgang Dietrich **Obv:** Oval 6-fold arms with central shield of Raitenau, legate's hat above **Obv. Legend:** WOLF • TEOD • D • G • AREPS • SAL • A • S • L • **Rev:** Saint seated on throne holding salt cellar and crozier, date at end of legend **Rev. Legend:** SANCTVS • RVDBERTVS • EPS • SALZ • **Shape:** Klippe **Note:** Fr.#663.

Date	Mintage	VG	F	VF	XF	Unc
160Z	—	600	1,200	2,400	3,600	—

KM# 22 DUCAT

3.5000 g., 0.9860 Gold 0.1109 oz. AGW **Ruler:** Markus Sittich **Obv:** Arms below hat **Obv. Legend:** MARC SIT... **Rev:** St. Rupert seated facing

Date	Mintage	VG	F	VF	XF	Unc
161Z	—	250	500	1,000	1,850	—
1613	—	250	500	1,000	1,850	—
1614	—	250	500	1,000	1,850	—
1615	—	250	500	1,000	1,850	—
1616	—	250	500	1,000	1,850	—
1617	—	250	500	1,000	1,850	—
1618	—	250	500	1,000	1,850	—

KM# 29 DUCAT

3.5000 g., 0.9860 Gold 0.1109 oz. AGW **Ruler:** Markus Sittich **Note:** Klippe.

Date	Mintage	VG	F	VF	XF	Unc
1613	—	350	800	1,600	2,200	—
1614	—	350	800	1,600	2,200	—

KM# 65 DUCAT

3.5000 g., 0.9860 Gold 0.1109 oz. AGW **Ruler:** Paris **Obv. Legend:** PARIS...

Date	Mintage	VG	F	VF	XF	Unc
1620	—	145	285	575	975	—
1622	—	145	285	575	975	—
1623	—	145	285	575	975	—
1625	—	145	285	575	975	—
1627	—	145	285	575	975	—
1629	—	145	285	575	975	—
1630	—	145	285	575	975	—
1631	—	145	285	575	975	—
1632	—	145	285	575	975	—
1633	—	145	285	575	975	—
1634	—	145	285	575	975	—
1635	—	145	285	575	975	—
1636	—	145	285	575	975	—
1637	—	145	285	575	975	—
1638	—	145	285	575	975	—
1639	—	145	285	575	975	—
1640	—	145	285	575	975	—
1641	—	145	285	575	975	—
1642	—	145	285	575	975	—
1643	—	145	285	575	975	—
1644	—	145	285	575	975	—
1645	—	145	285	575	975	—
1646	—	145	285	575	975	—
1647	—	145	285	575	975	—
1648	—	145	285	575	975	—
1649	—	145	285	575	975	—
1650	—	145	285	575	975	—
1652	—	145	285	575	975	—
1653	—	145	285	575	975	—

KM# 109 DUCAT

3.5000 g., 0.9860 Gold 0.1109 oz. AGW **Ruler:** Paris

Date	Mintage	VG	F	VF	XF	Unc
1627	—	300	750	1,500	2,250	—
1628	—	300	750	1,500	2,250	—
1631	—	300	750	1,500	2,250	—
1632	—	300	750	1,500	2,250	—
1634	—	300	750	1,500	2,250	—
1636	—	300	750	1,500	2,250	—
1637	—	300	750	1,500	2,250	—
1638	—	300	750	1,500	2,250	—
1640	—	300	750	1,500	2,250	—
1641	—	300	750	1,500	2,250	—
1642	—	300	750	1,500	2,250	—
1644	—	300	750	1,500	2,250	—
1645	—	300	750	1,500	2,250	—
1646	—	300	750	1,500	2,250	—
1647	—	300	750	1,500	2,250	—
1648	—	300	750	1,500	2,250	—
1649	—	300	750	1,500	2,250	—
1650	—	300	750	1,500	2,250	—
1651	—	300	750	1,500	2,250	—

KM# A165 DUCAT

3.5000 g., 0.9860 Gold 0.1109 oz. AGW **Ruler:** Paris **Note:** Klippe

Date	Mintage	VG	F	VF	XF	Unc
1640	—	350	900	1,800	2,700	—

KM# 165 DUCAT

3.5000 g., 0.9860 Gold 0.1109 oz. AGW **Ruler:** Guidobald **Obv. Legend:** GVIDOBALD...

Date	Mintage	VG	F	VF	XF	Unc
1654	—	120	225	475	750	1,250
1655	—	120	225	475	750	1,250
1656	—	120	225	475	750	1,250
1657	—	120	225	475	750	1,250
1658	—	120	225	475	750	1,250
1659	—	120	225	475	750	1,250
1660	—	120	225	475	750	1,250
1661	—	120	225	475	750	1,250
1662	—	120	225	475	750	1,250
1663	—	120	225	475	750	1,250
1664	—	120	225	475	750	1,250
1665	—	120	225	475	750	1,250
1666	—	120	225	475	750	1,250
1667	—	120	225	475	750	1,250
1668	—	120	225	475	750	1,250

KM# 175 DUCAT

3.5000 g., 0.9860 Gold 0.1109 oz. AGW **Ruler:** Guidobald **Note:** Klippe.

Date	Mintage	VG	F	VF	XF	Unc
1655	—	140	275	650	1,200	—
1657	—	140	275	650	1,200	—
1666	—	140	275	650	1,200	—

KM# 195 DUCAT

3.5000 g., 0.9860 Gold 0.1109 oz. AGW **Ruler:** Maximilian Gandolph **Note:** Klippe.

Date	Mintage	VG	F	VF	XF	Unc
1668	—	300	650	1,400	2,700	—
1669	—	300	650	1,400	2,700	—
1672	—	170	325	775	1,500	—
1674	—	170	325	775	1,500	—

KM# 194 DUCAT

3.5000 g., 0.9860 Gold 0.1109 oz. AGW **Ruler:** Maximilian Gandolph **Obv. Legend:** MAX GAND...

Date	Mintage	VG	F	VF	XF	Unc
1668	—	200	450	950	1,850	—
1669	—	200	450	950	1,850	—
1670	—	120	220	475	750	1,250
1671	—	120	220	475	750	1,250
1672	—	120	220	475	750	1,250
1673	—	120	220	475	750	1,250
1674	—	120	220	475	750	1,250
1675	—	120	220	475	750	1,250
1676	—	120	220	475	750	1,250
1677	—	120	220	475	750	1,250
1678	—	120	220	475	750	1,250
1679	—	120	220	475	750	1,250
1680	—	120	220	475	750	1,250
1681	—	120	220	475	750	1,250
1682	—	120	220	475	750	1,250
1683	—	120	220	475	750	1,250
1684	—	120	220	475	750	1,250
1685	—	120	220	475	750	1,250
1686	—	120	220	475	750	1,250
1687	—	120	220	475	750	1,250

KM# 257 DUCAT

3.5000 g., 0.9860 Gold 0.1109 oz. AGW **Ruler:** Johann Ernst **Obv:** Cardinals' hat above oval shield **Obv. Legend:** IO : ERNEST : .... **Rev:** St. Rupert **Rev. Legend:** S: RVDBERTVS • EPS • SALISBVRG •

Date	Mintage	VG	F	VF	XF	Unc
1687	—	130	275	550	950	1,500
1688	—	130	275	550	950	1,500
1689	—	130	275	550	950	1,500
1690	—	130	275	550	950	1,500
1691	—	130	275	550	950	1,500
1692	—	130	275	550	950	1,500
1693	—	130	275	550	950	1,500
1694	—	130	275	550	950	1,500
1695	—	130	275	550	950	1,500
1696	—	130	275	550	950	1,500
1697	—	130	275	550	950	1,500
1698	—	130	275	550	950	1,500
1699	—	130	275	550	950	1,500
1700	—	130	275	550	950	1,500

MB# 460 2 DUCAT

7.0000 g., 0.9860 Gold 0.2219 oz. AGW **Ruler:** Wolfgang Dietrich **Obv:** Oval 6-fold arms with central shield of Raitenau, legate's hat above **Obv. Legend:** WOLF • TEOD • D • G • - AREPS • SAL • A • S • L • **Rev:** 2 saints seated facing each other **Rev. Legend:** + S • RVDBERTVS • ET • S • VIRGILIVS • EPI • SALZ • **Note:** Fr.#659.

Date	Mintage	VG	F	VF	XF	Unc
ND(1587-1612)	—	275	500	900	1,500	—

MB# 461 2 DUCAT

7.0000 g., 0.9860 Gold 0.2219 oz. AGW, 28 mm. **Ruler:** Wolfgang Dietrich **Obv:** Oval 6-fold arms with central shield of Raitenau, legate's hat above **Obv. Legend:** WOLF • TEOD • D • G • - AREPS • SAL • A • S • L • **Rev:** 2 saints seated facing each other **Rev. Legend:** + S • RVDBERTVS • ET • S • VIRGILIVS • EPI • SALZ • **Note:** Fr.#658. Klippe.

Date	Mintage	VG	F	VF	XF	Unc
ND(1587-1612)	—	325	600	1,100	1,800	—

MB# 462 2 DUCAT

7.0000 g., 0.9860 Gold 0.2219 oz. AGW **Ruler:** Wolfgang Dietrich **Note:** Fr.#659. Klippe.

Date	Mintage	VG	F	VF	XF	Unc
ND(1587-1612)	—	1,200	2,150	3,950	6,600	—

KM# 4.1 2 DUCAT

7.0000 g., 0.9860 Gold 0.2219 oz. AGW **Ruler:** Wolfgang Dietrich **Obv:** Oval 6-fold arms with central shield of Raitenau, legate's hat above **Obv. Legend:** WOLF • TEOD • D.G • AREPS • SAL • A:S •L: **Rev:** St. Rupert seated on throne holding salt cellar and crozier, date at end of legend **Rev. Legend:** SANCTVS • RVDBERTVS • EPS • SALZ • **Note:** Fr.#660.

Date	Mintage	VG	F	VF	XF	Unc
1601	—	275	525	1,000	2,000	—
1602	—	275	525	1,000	2,000	—
160Z	—	275	525	1,000	2,000	—
1603	—	275	525	1,000	2,000	—
1604	—	275	525	1,000	2,000	—
1605	—	275	525	1,000	2,000	—
1606	—	275	525	1,000	2,000	—
1607	—	275	525	1,000	2,000	—
1608	—	275	525	1,000	2,000	—
1609	—	275	525	1,000	2,000	—
1610	—	275	525	1,000	2,000	—
1611	—	275	525	1,000	2,000	—

KM# 23 2 DUCAT

7.0000 g., 0.9860 Gold 0.2219 oz. AGW **Ruler:** Markus Sittich **Obv. Legend:** MARCVS SITTICVS

Date	Mintage	VG	F	VF	XF	Unc
1612	—	400	950	1,850	3,000	—
1613	—	400	950	1,850	3,000	—
1614	—	400	950	1,850	3,000	—
1616	—	400	950	1,850	3,000	—

KM# 9 2 DUCAT

7.0000 g., 0.9860 Gold 0.2219 oz. AGW **Ruler:** Wolfgang Dietrich **Rev:** St. Rupert and St. Virgil **Note:** Klippe.

Date	Mintage	VG	F	VF	XF	Unc
ND	—	650	1,450	4,300	7,300	—

KM# 30 2 DUCAT

7.0000 g., 0.9860 Gold 0.2219 oz. AGW **Ruler:** Markus Sittich **Note:** Klippe.

Date	Mintage	VG	F	VF	XF	Unc
1613	—	500	1,100	2,250	4,500	—
1615	—	500	1,100	2,250	4,500	—

KM# 93 2 DUCAT

7.0000 g., 0.9860 Gold 0.2219 oz. AGW **Ruler:** Paris **Note:** Klippe.

Date	Mintage	VG	F	VF	XF	Unc
1624	—	500	1,100	3,500	5,500	—
1634	—	500	1,100	3,500	5,500	—
1638	—	500	1,100	3,500	5,500	—
1639	—	500	1,100	3,500	5,500	—
1640	—	500	1,100	3,500	5,500	—
1641	—	500	1,100	3,500	5,500	—
1642	—	500	1,100	3,500	5,500	—
1643	—	500	1,100	3,500	5,500	—
1644	—	500	1,100	3,500	5,500	—
1645	—	500	1,100	3,500	5,500	—
1646	—	500	1,100	3,500	5,500	—
1648	—	500	1,100	3,500	5,500	—
1651	—	500	1,100	3,500	5,500	—

KM# 104 2 DUCAT

7.0000 g., 0.9860 Gold 0.2219 oz. AGW **Ruler:** Paris **Obv:** Madonna above arms in inner circle **Obv. Legend:** PARIS... **Rev:** St. Rupert standing with arms below in ornate inner circle

Date	Mintage	VG	F	VF	XF	Unc
1626	—	400	1,000	3,000	5,250	—

KM# 105 2 DUCAT

7.0000 g., 0.9860 Gold 0.2219 oz. AGW **Ruler:** Paris **Note:** Klippe.

Date	Mintage	VG	F	VF	XF	Unc
1626	—	650	1,450	4,600	7,600	—

KM# 121 2 DUCAT

7.0000 g., 0.9860 Gold 0.2219 oz. AGW **Ruler:** Paris **Obv:** Cathedral divides date with saints at sides in inner circle, arms below **Rev:** Reliquary carried by eight bishops, two angels below religuary in inner circle

Date	Mintage	VG	F	VF	XF	Unc
1628	—	—	—	—	—	—

KM# 122 2 DUCAT

7.0000 g., 0.9860 Gold 0.2219 oz. AGW **Ruler:** Paris **Obv:** Arms below hat **Obv. Legend:** PARIS... **Rev:** St. Rupert seated facing half right

Date	Mintage	VG	F	VF	XF	Unc
1628	—	450	1,000	3,150	5,500	—
1629	—	450	1,000	3,150	5,500	—
1631	—	450	1,000	3,150	5,500	—
1633	—	450	1,000	3,150	5,500	—
1634	—	450	1,000	3,150	5,500	—
1647	—	450	1,000	3,150	5,500	—
1648	—	450	1,000	3,150	5,500	—

KM# 166 2 DUCAT

7.0000 g., 0.9860 Gold 0.2219 oz. AGW **Ruler:** Guidobald **Obv. Legend:** GVIDOBALDVS... **Rev:** St. Rupert seated facing

Date	Mintage	VG	F	VF	XF	Unc
1654	—	325	775	2,150	3,750	—
1659	—	325	775	2,150	3,750	—
1662	—	325	775	2,150	3,750	—

KM# 196 2 DUCAT

7.0000 g., 0.9860 Gold 0.2219 oz. AGW **Ruler:** Maximilian Gandolph **Obv:** Cardinal's hat above shield **Obv. Legend:** MAX GAND... **Rev:** Figure seated 1/4 left

Date	Mintage	VG	F	VF	XF	Unc
1668	—	250	500	1,000	2,000	—
1673	—	250	500	1,000	2,000	—

KM# 223 2 DUCAT

7.0000 g., 0.9860 Gold 0.2219 oz. AGW **Ruler:** Maximilian Gandolph **Note:** Klippe.

Date	Mintage	VG	F	VF	XF	Unc
1673	—	500	1,150	3,000	5,000	—

KM# 234 2 DUCAT

7.0000 g., 0.9860 Gold 0.2219 oz. AGW **Ruler:** Maximilian Gandolph **Subject:** 1100th Anniversary of Salzburg **Obv:** Radiant symbol above Cardinal's hat over shield **Rev:** Inscription

Date	Mintage	VG	F	VF	XF	Unc
1682	—	375	750	1,950	3,500	—

KM# 272 2 DUCAT

7.0000 g., 0.9860 Gold 0.2219 oz. AGW **Ruler:** Johann Ernst **Note:** Klippe.

Date	Mintage	VG	F	VF	XF	Unc
1688	—	425	850	2,200	3,900	—

KM# 271 2 DUCAT

7.0000 g., 0.9860 Gold 0.2219 oz. AGW **Ruler:** Johann Ernst **Obv:** Arms **Obv. Legend:** IO ERNEST... **Rev:** Saint Rupert on throne

Date	Mintage	VG	F	VF	XF	Unc
1688	—	275	550	1,350	2,500	—

MB# 467 3 DUCAT

10.5000 g., 0.9860 Gold 0.3328 oz. AGW **Ruler:** Wolfgang Dietrich **Obv:** Oval 6-fold arms with central shield of Raitenau, legate's hat above **Obv. Legend:** WOLF • TEOD • D • G • AREPS • SAL • A • S • L • **Rev:** 2 saints seated facing each other **Rev. Legend:** S • RVDBERTVS • ET • S • VIRGILIVS • EP • **Note:** Fr.#656.

Date	Mintage	VG	F	VF	XF	Unc
ND(1587-1612)	—	—	2,750	4,950	8,300	—

MB# 471 3 DUCAT

10.5000 g., 0.9860 Gold 0.3328 oz. AGW **Ruler:** Wolfgang Dietrich **Obv:** Oval 6-fold arms with central shield of Raitenau, legate's hat above **Obv. Legend:** WOLF • TEOD • D • G • AREPS • SAL • A • S • L • **Rev:** 2 saints seated facing each other **Rev. Legend:** S • RVDBERTVS • ET • S • VIRGILIVS • EP • **Note:** Fr.#656.

Date	Mintage	VG	F	VF	XF	Unc
ND(1587-1612)	—	—	2,750	4,950	8,300	—

MB# 465 3 DUCAT

10.5000 g., 0.9860 Gold 0.3328 oz. AGW, 35.5 mm. **Ruler:** Wolfgang Dietrich **Obv:** Saint seated on throne holding salt cellar and crozier, oval 6-fold arms with central shield of Raitenau below **Obv. Legend:** SANCTVS • RVDBE - RTVS • EPS • SALISBV • **Rev:** Tower in storm-tossed sea, winds from clouds to either side blowing on it, date at end of legend **Rev. Legend:** + IN • DOMINO • SPERANS • NON • INFIRMABOR • **Note:** FR.#687/695.

Date	Mintage	VG	F	VF	XF	Unc
ND(1587-1612)	—	—	2,500	4,700	7,700	—

MB# 466 3 DUCAT

10.5000 g., 0.9860 Gold 0.3328 oz. AGW **Ruler:** Wolfgang Dietrich **Obv:** Saint seated on throne holding salt cellar and crozier, oval 6-fold arms with central shield of Raitenau below **Obv. Legend:** SANCTVS • RVDBE - RTVS • EPS • SALISBV • **Rev:** Tower in storm-tossed sea, winds from clouds to either side blowing on it, date at end of legend **Rev. Legend:** + IN • DOMINO • SPERANS • NON • INFIRMABOR • **Note:** Fr.#688. Klippe.

Date	Mintage	VG	F	VF	XF	Unc
ND(1587-1612)	—	—	3,000	5,400	9,600	—

MB# 468 3 DUCAT

10.5000 g., 0.9860 Gold 0.3328 oz. AGW **Ruler:** Wolfgang Dietrich **Obv:** Oval 6-fold arms with central shield of Raitenau, legate's hat above **Obv. Legend:** WOLF • TEOD • D • G • AREPS • SAL • A • S • L • **Rev:** 2 saints seated facing each other **Rev. Legend:** S • RVDBERTVS • ET • S • VIRGILIVS • EP • **Note:** Fr.#657. Klippe.

Date	Mintage	VG	F	VF	XF	Unc
ND(1587-1612)	—	—	3,200	5,700	9,300	—

MB# 469 3 DUCAT

10.5000 g., 0.9860 Gold 0.3328 oz. AGW **Ruler:** Wolfgang Dietrich **Obv:** Oval 6-fold arms with central shield of Raitenau, legate's hat above **Obv. Legend:** WOLF • TEOD • D • G • - AREPS • SAL • A • S • L • **Rev:** 2 saints seated facing each other **Rev. Legend:** + S • RVDBERTVS • ET • S • VIRGILIVS • EPI • SALZ • **Note:** Fr.#(657). Klippe.

Date	Mintage	VG	F	VF	XF	Unc
ND(1587-1612)	—	—	3,800	6,000	10,000	—

MB# 470 3 DUCAT
10.5000 g., 0.9860 Gold 0.3328 oz. AGW **Ruler:** Wolfgang Dietrich **Obv:** Oval 6-fold arms with central shield of Raitenau, legate's hat above **Obv. Legend:** WOLF • TEOD • D • G • - AREPS • SAL • AP • SE • L • **Rev:** Saint seated on throne holding salt cellar and crozier **Rev. Legend:** SANCTVS • RVDBERTVS • EPS • SALZBV • **Note:** Fr#657. Klippe.

Date	Mintage	VG	F	VF	XF	Unc
ND(1587-1612)	—	—	3,600	6,000	10,000	—

MB# 472 3 DUCAT
10.5000 g., 0.9860 Gold 0.3328 oz. AGW **Ruler:** Wolfgang Dietrich **Obv:** 2 adjacent shields of Salzburg and Keutschach joined by hanger loop above, date below **Rev:** 2 saints seated facing each other **Rev. Legend:** + S • RVDBERTVS • ET • S • VIRGILIVS • EPI • SALZ • **Note:** Klippe.

Date	Mintage	VG	F	VF	XF	Unc
ND(1513)//(1587-1612)	—	—	—	—	—	—

Note: Mule. Obverse die of MB#48 used with reverse die of MB#469.

KM# 24 3 DUCAT
10.5000 g., 0.9860 Gold 0.3328 oz. AGW **Ruler:** Markus Sittich **Note:** Klippe.

Date	Mintage	VG	F	VF	XF	Unc
1612	—	—	1,750	4,200	7,200	—

KM# 45 3 DUCAT
10.5000 g., 0.9860 Gold 0.3328 oz. AGW **Ruler:** Markus Sittich **Obv:** Arms below hat **Obv. Legend:** MARCVS SITTICVS... **Rev:** St. Rupert seated facing

Date	Mintage	VG	F	VF	XF	Unc
1617	—	—	1,450	3,300	6,100	—

KM# A46 3 DUCAT
10.5000 g., 0.9860 Gold 0.3328 oz. AGW **Ruler:** Markus Sittich **Note:** Klippe.

Date	Mintage	VG	F	VF	XF	Unc
1617	—	—	2,050	4,800	8,400	—

KM# 66 3 DUCAT
10.5000 g., 0.9860 Gold 0.3328 oz. AGW **Ruler:** Paris **Obv. Legend:** PARIS...

Date	Mintage	VG	F	VF	XF	Unc
1620	—	—	1,650	4,250	7,200	—

KM# 94 3 DUCAT
10.5000 g., 0.9860 Gold 0.3328 oz. AGW **Ruler:** Paris **Note:** Klippe.

Date	Mintage	VG	F	VF	XF	Unc
1624	—	—	1,700	4,400	7,200	—
1629	—	—	1,700	4,400	7,200	—
1638	—	—	1,700	4,400	7,200	—
1642	—	—	1,700	4,400	7,200	—

KM# 123 3 DUCAT
10.5000 g., 0.9860 Gold 0.3328 oz. AGW **Ruler:** Paris **Obv:** Cathedral divides date with saints at sides in inner circle, arms below **Rev:** Reliquary carried by eight bishops, two angels below reliquary in inner circle

Date	Mintage	VG	F	VF	XF	Unc
1628	—	—	1,250	3,050	5,200	—

KM# 146 3 DUCAT
10.5000 g., 0.9860 Gold 0.3328 oz. AGW **Ruler:** Paris **Obv:** Madonna above arms in inner circle **Obv. Legend:** PARIS... **Rev:** St. Rupert standing with arms below in ornate inner circle

Date	Mintage	VG	F	VF	XF	Unc
1631	—	—	1,650	4,250	7,200	—
1638	—	—	1,650	4,250	7,200	—
1642	—	—	1,650	4,250	7,200	—

KM# 183 3 DUCAT
10.5000 g., 0.9860 Gold 0.3328 oz. AGW **Ruler:** Guidobald **Obv:** Arms below hat in inner circle **Obv. Legend:** GVIDOBALDVS... **Rev:** Cathedral with saints at sides in inner circle

Date	Mintage	VG	F	VF	XF	Unc
1656	—	—	2,000	4,400	7,200	—

KM# 220 3 DUCAT
10.5000 g., 0.9860 Gold 0.3328 oz. AGW **Ruler:** Maximilian Gandolph **Obv:** Arms below hat **Obv. Legend:** MAXIM GANDOL... **Rev:** St. Rupert seated facing

Date	Mintage	VG	F	VF	XF	Unc
1670	—	—	2,000	4,400	7,400	—
1673	—	—	2,000	4,400	7,400	—

KM# 224 3 DUCAT
10.5000 g., 0.9860 Gold 0.3328 oz. AGW **Ruler:** Maximilian Gandolph **Note:** Klippe.

Date	Mintage	VG	F	VF	XF	Unc
1673	—	—	2,600	5,700	9,000	—

KM# 235 3 DUCAT
10.5000 g., 0.9860 Gold 0.3328 oz. AGW **Ruler:** Maximilian Gandolph **Subject:** 1100th Anniversary of Salzburg **Obv:** Arms below radiant triangle in inner circle **Obv. Legend:** A. MAX GAND. **Rev:** Five standing saints; five-line inscription in exergue

Date	Mintage	VG	F	VF	XF	Unc
1682	—	—	1,450	3,300	5,500	—

KM# 236 3 DUCAT
10.5000 g., 0.9860 Gold 0.3328 oz. AGW **Ruler:** Maximilian Gandolph **Subject:** 1100th Anniversary of Salzburg **Obv:** Nine-line inscription **Rev:** Arms below radiant triangle

Date	Mintage	VG	F	VF	XF	Unc
1682	—	—	1,600	4,150	6,600	—

KM# 275 3 DUCAT
10.5000 g., 0.9860 Gold 0.3328 oz. AGW **Ruler:** Johann Ernst **Obv. Legend:** IOAN ERNEST...

Date	Mintage	VG	F	VF	XF	Unc
1690	—	—	1,400	3,300	5,500	—

MB# 474 4 DUCAT
14.0000 g., 0.9860 Gold 0.4438 oz. AGW **Ruler:** Wolfgang Dietrich **Obv:** Saint seated on throne holding salt cellar and crozier, oval 6-fold arms with central shield of Raitenau below **Obv. Legend:** SANCTVS • RVDBE - RTVS • EPS • SALISBV • **Rev:** Tower in storm-tossed sea, winds from clouds to either side blowing on it, date at end of legend **Rev. Legend:** + IN • DOMINO • SPERANS • NON • IMFIRMABOR • **Note:** Fr.#693.

Date	Mintage	VG	F	VF	XF	Unc
ND(1587-1612)	—	—	—	9,400	15,000	—

MB# 475 4 DUCAT
14.0000 g., 0.9860 Gold 0.4438 oz. AGW **Ruler:** Wolfgang Dietrich **Obv:** Saint seated on throne holding salt cellar and crozier, oval 6-fold arms with central shield of Raitenau below **Obv. Legend:** SANCTVS • RVDBE - RTVS • EPS • SALISBV • **Rev:** Tower in storm-tossed sea, winds from clouds to either side blowing on it, date at end of legend **Rev. Legend:** + IN • DOMINO • SPERANS • NON • INFIRMABOR • **Note:** Fr.#694. Klippe.

Date	Mintage	VG	F	VF	XF	Unc
ND(1587-1612)	—	—	—	12,500	19,500	—

MB# 476 4 DUCAT
14.0000 g., 0.9860 Gold 0.4438 oz. AGW **Ruler:** Wolfgang Dietrich **Obv:** Oval 6-fold arms with central shield of Raitenau, legate's hat above **Obv. Legend:** WOLF • TEOD • D • G • AREPS • SAL • A • S • L • **Rev:** 2 saints seated facing each other **Rev. Legend:** S • RVDBERTVS • ET • S • VIRGILIVS • EP • **Note:** Fr.#655. Klippe, 36.5 x 36.5 mm.

Date	Mintage	VG	F	VF	XF	Unc
ND(1587-1612) Rare	—	—	—	—	—	—

MB# 477 4 DUCAT
14.0000 g., 0.9860 Gold 0.4438 oz. AGW, 33.5 mm. **Ruler:** Wolfgang Dietrich **Obv:** 4-fold arms of Salzburg and Raitenau (globe), legate's hat above **Obv. Legend:** WOLF • TEOD • D • G • ARE - PS • SALZ • AP • SE • LEG • **Rev:** 2 saints seated facing eaach other **Rev. Legend:** S • RVDBERTVS • ET S • VIRGILIVS • EP • **Note:** Fr.#654.

Date	Mintage	VG	F	VF	XF	Unc
ND(1587-1612)	—	—	—	12,500	19,500	—

MB# 478 4 DUCAT
14.0000 g., 0.9860 Gold 0.4438 oz. AGW, 34 mm. **Ruler:** Wolfgang Dietrich **Obv:** Oval 6-fold arms with central shield of Raitenau, legate's hat above **Obv. Legend:** WOLF • TEOD • D • G • AREPS • SAL • A • S • L • **Rev:** 2 saints seated facing each other **Rev. Legend:** S • RVDBERTVS • ET • S • VIRGILIVS • EP • **Note:** Fr.#654.

Date	Mintage	VG	F	VF	XF	Unc
ND(1587-1612)	—	—	—	12,500	19,500	—

MB# 543 4 DUCAT
14.0000 g., 0.9860 Gold 0.4438 oz. AGW, 40 mm. **Ruler:** Wolfgang Dietrich **Obv:** Saint seated on throne holding salt cellar and crozier, oval 4-fold arms of Salzburg and Raitenau below **Obv. Legend:** SANCTVS • RVDBERTVS • EPS • EPS • SALZBVRG • **Rev:** Tower in storm-tossed sea, winds from clouds to either side blowing on it, R.N. date in legend **Rev. Legend:** RESISTIT + MDXCIII + IMMOTA • **Note:** Fr.#685.

Date	Mintage	VG	F	VF	XF	Unc
MDXCIII (1593)	—	—	—	6,100	9,900	—

KM# 25 4 DUCAT
14.0000 g., 0.9860 Gold 0.4438 oz. AGW **Ruler:** Markus Sittich

Obv: Arms below hat **Obv. Legend:** MARCVS SITTICVS... **Rev:** St. Rupert seated facing

Date	Mintage	VG	F	VF	XF	Unc
161Z	—	—	—	6,100	9,900	—
1614	—	—	—	6,100	9,900	—
1615	—	—	—	6,100	9,900	—
1617	—	—	—	6,100	9,900	—

KM# 41 4 DUCAT
14.0000 g., 0.9860 Gold 0.4438 oz. AGW **Ruler:** Markus Sittich

Date	Mintage	VG	F	VF	XF	Unc
1615	—	—	—	6,100	9,900	—
1616	—	—	—	6,100	9,900	—
1618	—	—	—	6,100	9,900	—

KM# 67 4 DUCAT
14.0000 g., 0.9860 Gold 0.4438 oz. AGW **Ruler:** Paris **Obv:** Arms below hat **Obv. Legend:** PARIS... **Rev:** St. Rupert seated facing

Date	Mintage	VG	F	VF	XF	Unc
1620	—	—	—	4,400	7,200	—

KM# 68 4 DUCAT
14.0000 g., 0.9860 Gold 0.4438 oz. AGW **Ruler:** Paris **Note:** Klippe.

Date	Mintage	VG	F	VF	XF	Unc
1620	—	—	—	5,500	8,300	—

KM# 95 4 DUCAT
14.0000 g., 0.9860 Gold 0.4438 oz. AGW **Ruler:** Paris

Date	Mintage	VG	F	VF	XF	Unc
1624	—	—	—	5,800	8,800	—
1625	—	—	—	5,800	8,800	—
1629	—	—	—	5,800	8,800	—
1638	—	—	—	5,800	8,800	—

KM# 96 4 DUCAT
14.0000 g., 0.9860 Gold 0.4438 oz. AGW **Ruler:** Paris **Note:** Klippe.

Date	Mintage	VG	F	VF	XF	Unc
1624	—	—	—	8,800	13,000	—

KM# 124 4 DUCAT
14.0000 g., 0.9860 Gold 0.4438 oz. AGW **Ruler:** Paris

Date	Mintage	VG	F	VF	XF	Unc
1628	—	—	1,300	2,750	4,400	—

KM# 125 4 DUCAT
14.0000 g., 0.9860 Gold 0.4438 oz. AGW **Ruler:** Paris **Note:** Klippe.

Date	Mintage	VG	F	VF	XF	Unc
1628	—	—	1,750	4,150	6,600	—

KM# 176 4 DUCAT
14.0000 g., 0.9860 Gold 0.4438 oz. AGW **Ruler:** Guidobald **Obv. Legend:** GVIDOBALDVS...

Date	Mintage	VG	F	VF	XF	Unc
1655	—	—	1,750	4,150	6,600	—

KM# 197 4 DUCAT
14.0000 g., 0.9860 Gold 0.4438 oz. AGW **Ruler:** Maximilian Gandolph **Obv. Legend:** MAXIMIL GANDOLPH...

Date	Mintage	VG	F	VF	XF	Unc
1668	—	—	4,000	9,000	14,000	—

KM# 225 4 DUCAT
14.0000 g., 0.9860 Gold 0.4438 oz. AGW **Ruler:** Maximilian Gandolph **Obv:** Arms below hat **Obv. Legend:** MAXIM GANDOL... **Rev:** St. Rupert seated facing

Date	Mintage	VG	F	VF	XF	Unc
1673	—	—	—	6,100	9,900	—

KM# 237 4 DUCAT
14.0000 g., 0.9860 Gold 0.4438 oz. AGW **Ruler:** Maximilian Gandolph **Subject:** 1100th Anniversary of Salzburg **Obv:** Arms below radiant triangle in inner circle **Obv. Legend:** A MAX GAND... **Rev:** Five standing saints; five-line inscription in exergue

Date	Mintage	VG	F	VF	XF	Unc
1682	—	—	1,300	3,050	4,950	—

KM# 258 4 DUCAT
14.0000 g., 0.9860 Gold 0.4438 oz. AGW **Ruler:** Johann Ernst **Obv. Legend:** IOAN ERNESTUS...

Date	Mintage	VG	F	VF	XF	Unc
1687	—	—	1,300	3,050	5,200	—

MB# 413 5 DUCAT
17.5000 g., 0.9860 Gold 0.5547 oz. AGW **Ruler:** Georg **Obv:** 4-fold arms of Salzburg and Küenburg divide date, legate's hat above **Obv. Legend:** ★ GEORGIVS • D • G • AR • EPS • SALZ • A • S • L • **Rev:** 2 saints seated facing each other **Rev. Legend:** S • RVDBERTVS • ET S • VIRGILIVS • EP • **Note:** Fr.#639.

Date	Mintage	VG	F	VF	XF	Unc
(15)86 Rare	—	—	—	—	—	—

MB# 480 5 DUCAT
17.5000 g., 0.9860 Gold 0.5547 oz. AGW **Ruler:** Wolfgang Dietrich **Obv:** Saint seated on throne holding salt cellar and crozier, oval 6-fold arms with central shield of Raitenau below **Obv. Legend:** SANCTVS • RVDBE - RTVS • EPS • SALISBV • **Rev:** Tower in storm-tossed sea, winds from clouds to either side blowing on it, date at end of legend **Rev. Legend:** + IN • DOMINO • SPERANS • NON • INFIRMABOR • **Note:** Fr.#692.

Date	Mintage	VG	F	VF	XF	Unc
ND(1587-1612)	—	—	—	10,000	16,000	—

MB# 481 5 DUCAT
17.5000 g., 0.9860 Gold 0.5547 oz. AGW **Ruler:** Wolfgang Dietrich **Obv:** Saint seated on throne holding salt cellar and crozier, oal 6-fold arms with central shield of Raitenau below **Obv. Legend:** SANCTVS • RVDBE - RTVS • EPS • SALISBV **Rev:** Tower in storm-tossed sea, winds from clouds to either side blowing on it, date at end of legend **Rev. Legend:** + IN • DOMINO • SPERANS • NON • INFIRMABOR • **Note:** Fr.#684. Klippe.

Date	Mintage	VG	F	VF	XF	Unc
ND(1587-1612)	—	—	—	12,000	20,500	—

MB# 482 5 DUCAT
17.5000 g., 0.9860 Gold 0.5547 oz. AGW **Ruler:** Wolfgang Dietrich **Obv:** 4-fold arms of Salzburg and Raitenau (globe), legate's hat above **Obv. Legend:** WOLF • TEOD • D • G • ARE - PS • SALZ • AP • SE • LEG • **Rev:** 2 saints seated facing each other **Rev. Legend:** S • RVDBERTVS • ET S • VIRGILIVS • ET S • VIRGILIVS • EP • **Note:** Fr.#653.

Date	Mintage	VG	F	VF	XF	Unc
ND(1587-1612)	—	—	—	12,000	20,500	—

MB# 545 5 DUCAT
17.5000 g., 0.9860 Gold 0.5547 oz. AGW **Ruler:** Wolfgang Dietrich **Obv:** Saint seated on throne holding salt cellar and crozier, oval 6-fold arms with central shield of Raitenau below **Obv. Legend:** SANCTVS • RVDBE - RTVS • EPS • SALISBV • **Rev:** Tower in storm-tossed sea, winds from clouds to either side blowing on it, R.N. date in legend **Rev. Legend:** RESISTIT + MDXCIII + IMMOTA • **Note:** Fr.#683.

Date	Mintage	VG	F	VF	XF	Unc
MDXCIII (1593)	—	—	—	7,800	12,000	—

KM# 27 5 DUCAT
17.5000 g., 0.9860 Gold 0.5547 oz. AGW **Ruler:** Markus Sittich **Note:** Klippe.

Date	Mintage	VG	F	VF	XF	Unc
1612	—	—	—	8,400	14,500	—
1617	—	—	—	8,400	14,500	—

KM# 26 5 DUCAT
17.5000 g., 0.9860 Gold 0.5547 oz. AGW **Ruler:** Markus Sittich **Obv:** Arms below hat **Obv. Legend:** MARCVS SITTICVS... **Rev:** Tower in stormy sea

Date	Mintage	VG	F	VF	XF	Unc
1612	—	—	—	6,600	11,000	—

KM# 69 5 DUCAT
17.5000 g., 0.9860 Gold 0.5547 oz. AGW **Ruler:** Paris **Obv. Legend:** PARIS... **Rev:** St. Rupert seated facing

Date	Mintage	VG	F	VF	XF	Unc
1620	—	—	—	7,800	12,000	—

KM# 126 5 DUCAT
17.5000 g., 0.9860 Gold 0.5547 oz. AGW **Ruler:** Paris **Obv:** Cathedral divides date with saints at sides in inner circle, arms below **Rev:** Reliquary carried by eight bishops, two angels below reliquary, in inner circle

Date	Mintage	VG	F	VF	XF	Unc
1628	—	—	—	4,800	8,400	—

KM# 127 5 DUCAT
17.5000 g., 0.9860 Gold 0.5547 oz. AGW **Ruler:** Paris **Note:** Klippe.

Date	Mintage	VG	F	VF	XF	Unc
1628	—	—	—	7,800	12,000	—

KM# 177 5 DUCAT
17.5000 g., 0.9860 Gold 0.5547 oz. AGW **Ruler:** Guidobald **Obv. Legend:** GVIDOBALDVS...

Date	Mintage	VG	F	VF	XF	Unc
1655	—	—	—	5,800	9,400	—

KM# 198 5 DUCAT
17.5000 g., 0.9860 Gold 0.5547 oz. AGW **Ruler:** Maximilian Gandolph **Obv. Legend:** MAXIMIL GANDOLPH...

Date	Mintage	VG	F	VF	XF	Unc
1668	—	—	—	6,000	9,000	—

KM# 199 5 DUCAT
17.5000 g., 0.9860 Gold 0.5547 oz. AGW **Ruler:** Maximilian Gandolph **Obv:** Arms below hat **Obv. Legend:** MAXIMIL GANDOLPH... **Rev:** St. Rupert seated facing

Date	Mintage	VG	F	VF	XF	Unc
1668	—	—	—	6,600	11,000	—

KM# 238 5 DUCAT
17.5000 g., 0.9860 Gold 0.5547 oz. AGW **Ruler:** Maximilian Gandolph **Subject:** 1100th Anniversary of Salzburg **Obv:** Arms below radiant triangle in inner circle **Obv. Legend:** A MAX GAND... **Rev:** Five standing saints; five-line inscription in exergue

Date	Mintage	VG	F	VF	XF	Unc
1682	—	—	—	6,000	9,600	—

KM# 259 5 DUCAT
17.5000 g., 0.9860 Gold 0.5547 oz. AGW **Ruler:** Johann Ernst **Obv:** Arms below hat in inner circle **Obv. Legend:** IOAN ERNESTUS... **Rev:** Two saints seated, facing each other with croziers, church in foreground

Date	Mintage	VG	F	VF	XF	Unc
1687	—	—	—	3,900	6,000	—

MB# 485 6 DUCAT
21.0000 g., 0.9860 Gold 0.6657 oz. AGW **Ruler:** Wolfgang Dietrich **Obv:** 2 adjacent shields of arms, Salzburg on left, Raitenau (globe) on right, legate's hat above **Obv. Legend:** WOLF • TEOD • D • G • AREPS • SAL • AP • SE • LE • **Rev:** 2 saints seated facing each other **Rev. Legend:** + S • RVDBERTVS • ET S • VIRGILIVS • EPI • SALZBVRGN • **Note:** Fr.#652.

Date	Mintage	VG	F	VF	XF	Unc
ND(1587-1612) Rare	—	—	—	—	—	—

KM# 42 6 DUCAT
21.0000 g., 0.9860 Gold 0.6657 oz. AGW **Ruler:** Markus Sittich **Obv. Legend:** SANCTVS RUDBERTVS... **Note:** Klippe.

Date	Mintage	VG	F	VF	XF	Unc
1616	—	—	—	9,600	14,500	—
1617	—	—	—	9,600	14,500	—

KM# 46 6 DUCAT
21.0000 g., 0.9860 Gold 0.6657 oz. AGW **Ruler:** Markus Sittich

Date	Mintage	VG	F	VF	XF	Unc
1617	—	—	—	8,400	12,000	—

KM# 49 6 DUCAT
21.0000 g., 0.9860 Gold 0.6657 oz. AGW **Ruler:** Markus Sittich **Obv. Legend:** MARCVS SITTICVS...

Date	Mintage	VG	F	VF	XF	Unc
1618	—	—	—	8,400	12,000	—

KM# 128 6 DUCAT
21.0000 g., 0.9860 Gold 0.6657 oz. AGW **Ruler:** Paris **Obv:** Madonna above arms in inner circle **Obv. Legend:** PARIS • D: G: ARCHI EPS • SALIS • 1625 **Rev:** St. Rupert standing with arms below in ornate inner circle

Date	Mintage	VG	F	VF	XF	Unc
1625	—	—	—	9,600	14,500	—
1628	—	—	—	9,600	14,500	—

KM# 129 6 DUCAT
21.0000 g., 0.9860 Gold 0.6657 oz. AGW **Ruler:** Paris **Obv:** Cathedral divides date with saints at sides in inner circle, arms below **Rev:** Reliquary carried by eight bishops, two angels below reliquary, in inner circle

Date	Mintage	VG	F	VF	XF	Unc
1628	—	—	—	5,100	9,000	—

KM# 178 6 DUCAT
21.0000 g., 0.9860 Gold 0.6657 oz. AGW **Ruler:** Guidobald **Obv:** Arms below hat in inner circle **Obv. Legend:** GVIDOBALDVS... **Rev:** Cathedral with saints at sides in inner circle

Date	Mintage	VG	F	VF	XF	Unc
1655	—	—	—	6,000	9,300	—

KM# 200 6 DUCAT
21.0000 g., 0.9860 Gold 0.6657 oz. AGW **Ruler:** Maximilian Gandolph **Obv:** Arms below hat **Obv. Legend:** MAXIMIL GANDOLPH... **Rev:** St. Rupert seated facing

Date	Mintage	VG	F	VF	XF	Unc
1668	—	—	—	8,400	12,000	—

KM# 201 6 DUCAT
21.0000 g., 0.9860 Gold 0.6657 oz. AGW **Ruler:** Maximilian Gandolph **Obv:** Arms below hat in inner circle **Obv. Legend:** MAXIMIL GANDOLPH... **Rev:** Two saints seated, facing each other with croziers, church in foreground

Date	Mintage	VG	F	VF	XF	Unc
1668	—	—	—	6,000	8,400	—

KM# 239 6 DUCAT
21.0000 g., 0.9860 Gold 0.6657 oz. AGW **Ruler:** Maximilian Gandolph **Obv:** Arms below radiant triangle in inner circle **Obv. Legend:** A MAX GAND... **Rev:** Five standing saints; five-line inscription in exergue

Date	Mintage	VG	F	VF	XF	Unc
1682	—	—	—	8,400	12,000	—

KM# 260 6 DUCAT
21.0000 g., 0.9860 Gold 0.6657 oz. AGW **Ruler:** Johann Ernst **Obv. Legend:** IOAN ERNESTUS...

Date	Mintage	VG	F	VF	XF	Unc
1687	—	—	—	6,000	9,600	—

MB# 487 7 DUCAT
24.5000 g., 0.9860 Gold 0.7766 oz. AGW **Ruler:** Wolfgang Dietrich **Obv:** 2 adjacent shields of arms, Salzburg on left, Raitenau (globe) on right, legate's hat above **Obv. Legend:** WOLF • TEOD • D • G • AREPS • SAL • AP • SE • LE • **Rev:** 2 saints seated facing each other **Rev. Legend:** + S • RVDBERTVS • ET S • VIRGILIVS • EPI • SALZBVRGN • **Note:** Fr.#651.

Date	Mintage	VG	F	VF	XF	Unc
ND(1587-1612) Rare	—	—	—	—	—	—

KM# 50 7 DUCAT
24.5000 g., 0.9860 Gold 0.7766 oz. AGW **Ruler:** Markus Sittich **Obv:** Arms below hat **Obv. Legend:** MARCVS SITTICVS... **Rev:** Tower in stormy sea **Note:** Klippe.

Date	Mintage	VG	F	VF	XF	Unc
1618	—	—	—	12,000	17,000	—

KM# 240 7 DUCAT
24.5000 g., 0.9860 Gold 0.7766 oz. AGW **Ruler:** Maximilian Gandolph **Subject:** 1100th Anniversary of Salzburg **Obv. Legend:** A MAX GAND...

Date	Mintage	VG	F	VF	XF	Unc
1682 Rare	—	—	—	—	—	—

KM# 261 7 DUCAT
24.5000 g., 0.9860 Gold 0.7766 oz. AGW **Ruler:** Johann Ernst **Obv:** Arms below hat in inner circle **Obv. Legend:** IOAN ERNESTUS ... **Rev:** Two saints seated, facing each other with croziers, church in foreground

Date	Mintage	VG	F	VF	XF	Unc
1687	—	—	—	9,000	14,000	—

MB# 490 8 DUCAT
28.0000 g., 0.9860 Gold 0.8876 oz. AGW **Ruler:** Wolfgang Dietrich **Obv:** Saint seated on throne holding salt cellar and crozier, oval 6-fold arms with central shield of Raitenau below **Obv. Legend:** SANCTVS • RVDBE — RTVS • EPS • SALISBV • **Rev:** Tower in storm-tossed sea, winds from clouds to either side blowing on it, date at end of legend **Rev. Legend:** IN • DOMINO • SPERANS • NON • INFIRMABOR • **Note:** Fr.#691.

Date	Mintage	VG	F	VF	XF	Unc
ND(1587-1612)	—	—	—	12,000	21,000	—

MB# 491 8 DUCAT
28.0000 g., 0.9860 Gold 0.8876 oz. AGW **Ruler:** Wolfgang Dietrich **Obv:** 2 adjacent shields of arms, Salzburg on left, Raitenau (globe) on right, legate's hat above **Obv. Legend:** WOLF • TEOD • D • G • AREPS • SAL • AP • SE • LE • **Rev:** 2 saints seated facing each other **Rev. Legend:** + S • RVDBERTVS • ET S • VIRGILIVS • EPI • SALZBVRGN • **Note:** Fr.#650.

Date	Mintage	VG	F	VF	XF	Unc
ND(1587-1612) Rare	—	—	—	—	—	—

KM# 31 8 DUCAT
28.0000 g., 0.9860 Gold 0.8876 oz. AGW **Ruler:** Markus Sittich **Obv:** Arms below hat **Obv. Legend:** MARCVS SITTICVS... **Rev:** Tower in stormy sea

Date	Mintage	VG	F	VF	XF	Unc
1613	—	—	—	12,000	17,000	—

KM# 70 8 DUCAT
28.0000 g., 0.9860 Gold 0.8876 oz. AGW **Ruler:** Paris **Obv. Legend:** PARIS... **Rev:** St. Rupert seated facing

Date	Mintage	VG	F	VF	XF	Unc
1620	—	—	—	10,000	15,000	—

KM# 71 8 DUCAT

28.0000 g., 0.9860 Gold 0.8876 oz. AGW **Ruler:** Paris **Note:** Klippe.

Date	Mintage	VG	F	VF	XF	Unc
1620	—	—	—	12,000	20,000	—

KM# 102 8 DUCAT

28.0000 g., 0.9860 Gold 0.8876 oz. AGW **Ruler:** Paris **Obv:** Maddona above arms in inner circle **Obv. Legend:** PARIS... **Rev:** St. Rupert standing with arms below in ornate inner circle

Date	Mintage	VG	F	VF	XF	Unc
1625	—	—	—	14,500	21,000	—
1628	—	—	—	14,500	21,000	—

KM# 130 8 DUCAT

28.0000 g., 0.9860 Gold 0.8876 oz. AGW **Ruler:** Paris **Obv:** Cathedral divides date with saints at sides in inner circle, arms below **Rev:** Reliquary carried by eight bishops, two angels below reliquary in inner circle

Date	Mintage	VG	F	VF	XF	Unc
1628	—	—	—	10,000	14,500	—

KM# 131 8 DUCAT

28.0000 g., 0.9860 Gold 0.8876 oz. AGW **Ruler:** Paris **Note:** Klippe.

Date	Mintage	VG	F	VF	XF	Unc
1628 Rare	—	—	—	—	—	—

KM# 167 8 DUCAT

28.0000 g., 0.9860 Gold 0.8876 oz. AGW **Ruler:** Guidobald **Obv:** Arms below hat **Obv. Legend:** GVIDOBALDVS... **Rev:** Cathedral with saints at sides in inner circle

Date	Mintage	VG	F	VF	XF	Unc
1654	—	—	—	10,000	14,500	—

KM# 202 8 DUCAT

28.0000 g., 0.9860 Gold 0.8876 oz. AGW **Ruler:** Maximilian Gandolph **Obv:** Arms below hat in inner circle **Obv. Legend:** MAXIMIL GANDOLPH... **Rev:** Two saints seated facing each other with croziers, church in foreground

Date	Mintage	VG	F	VF	XF	Unc
1668	—	—	—	10,000	14,500	—

KM# 241 8 DUCAT

28.0000 g., 0.9860 Gold 0.8876 oz. AGW **Ruler:** Maximilian Gandolph **Subject:** 1100th Anniversary of Salzburg **Obv:** Arms below radiant triangle in inner circle **Obv. Legend:** A MAX GAND... **Rev:** Five standing saints; five-line inscription in exergue

Date	Mintage	VG	F	VF	XF	Unc
1682	—	—	—	12,000	17,000	—

KM# 262 8 DUCAT

28.0000 g., 0.9860 Gold 0.8876 oz. AGW **Ruler:** Johann Ernst **Obv. Legend:** IOAN ERNESTUS...

Date	Mintage	VG	F	VF	XF	Unc
1687	—	—	—	10,000	14,500	—

KM# 203 9 DUCAT

31.5000 g., 0.9860 Gold 0.9985 oz. AGW **Ruler:** Maximilian Gandolph **Obv:** Arms below hat in inner circle **Obv. Legend:** MAXIMIL GANDOLPH... **Rev:** Two saints seated facing each other with croziers, church in foreground

Date	Mintage	VG	F	VF	XF	Unc
1668	—	—	—	10,000	15,000	—

KM# 32 10 DUCAT

35.0000 g., 0.9860 Gold 1.1095 oz. AGW **Ruler:** Markus Sittich **Note:** Klippe.

Date	Mintage	VG	F	VF	XF	Unc
1613 Rare	—	—	—	—	—	—

KM# 47 10 DUCAT

35.0000 g., 0.9860 Gold 1.1095 oz. AGW **Ruler:** Markus Sittich **Obv:** Arms below hat **Obv. Legend:** MARCVS SITTICVS... **Rev:** Tower in stormy sea

Date	Mintage	VG	F	VF	XF	Unc
1617	—	—	—	14,500	21,500	—

KM# 132 10 DUCAT

35.0000 g., 0.9860 Gold 1.1095 oz. AGW **Ruler:** Paris

Date	Mintage	VG	F	VF	XF	Unc
1628	—	—	—	8,100	11,500	—

KM# 134 10 DUCAT

35.0000 g., 0.9860 Gold 1.1095 oz. AGW **Ruler:** Paris **Obv:** Madonna above arms in inner circle **Obv. Legend:** PARIS... **Rev:** St. Rupert standing, arms below

Date	Mintage	VG	F	VF	XF	Unc
1628	—	—	—	15,000	22,000	—
1631	—	—	—	15,000	22,000	—

KM# 133 10 DUCAT
35.0000 g., 0.9860 Gold 1.1095 oz. AGW **Ruler:** Paris **Note:** Klippe. Illustration reduced.

Date	Mintage	VG	F	VF	XF	Unc
1628	—	—	—	14,500	17,500	—

KM# 168 10 DUCAT
35.0000 g., 0.9860 Gold 1.1095 oz. AGW **Ruler:** Guidobald **Obv:** Arms below hat **Obv. Legend:** GVIDOBALDVS... **Rev:** Cathedral with saints at sides in inner circle

Date	Mintage	VG	F	VF	XF	Unc
1654	—	—	—	14,500	17,500	—

KM# 204 10 DUCAT
35.0000 g., 0.9860 Gold 1.1095 oz. AGW **Ruler:** Maximilian Gandolph **Obv:** Arms below hat in inner circle **Obv. Legend:** MAX GAND... **Rev:** Two saints seated facing each other with croziers, church in foreground

Date	Mintage	VG	F	VF	XF	Unc
1668	—	—	—	14,000	21,000	—

KM# 205 10 DUCAT
35.0000 g., 0.9860 Gold 1.1095 oz. AGW **Ruler:** Maximilian Gandolph **Note:** Klippe.

Date	Mintage	VG	F	VF	XF	Unc
1668 Rare	—	—	—	—	—	—

KM# 242 10 DUCAT
35.0000 g., 0.9860 Gold 1.1095 oz. AGW **Ruler:** Maximilian Gandolph **Subject:** 1100th Anniversary of Salzburg

Date	Mintage	VG	F	VF	XF	Unc
1682	—	—	—	10,000	14,500	—

KM# 243 10 DUCAT
35.0000 g., 0.9860 Gold 1.1095 oz. AGW **Ruler:** Maximilian Gandolph **Note:** Klippe.

Date	Mintage	VG	F	VF	XF	Unc
1682	—	—	—	12,000	17,000	—

KM# 263 10 DUCAT
35.0000 g., 0.9860 Gold 1.1095 oz. AGW **Ruler:** Johann Ernst **Obv. Legend:** IOAN ERNESTUS... **Rev:** Two saints seated facing

Date	Mintage	VG	F	VF	XF	Unc
1687	—	—	—	8,100	11,500	—

MB# 495 12 DUCAT
42.0000 g., 0.9860 Gold 1.3314 oz. AGW **Ruler:** Wolfgang Dietrich **Obv:** 2 adjacent shields of arms, Salzburg on left, Raitenau (globe) on right, legate's hat above **Obv. Legend:** WOLF • TEOD • D • G • AREPS • SAL • AP • SE • LE • **Rev:** 2 saints seated facing each other **Rev. Legend:** + S • RVDBERTVS • ET S • VIRGILIVS • EPI • SALZBVRGN • **Note:** Fr.#648.

Date	Mintage	VG	F	VF	XF	Unc
ND(1587-1612) Rare	—	—	—	—	—	—

KM# 53 12 DUCAT
42.0000 g., 0.9860 Gold 1.3314 oz. AGW **Ruler:** Markus Sittich **Note:** Struck with 1 Thaler dies, KM#19.

Date	Mintage	VG	F	VF	XF	Unc
1612 Rare	—	—	—	—	—	—

KM# 135 12 DUCAT
42.0000 g., 0.9860 Gold 1.3314 oz. AGW **Ruler:** Paris **Obv:** Cathedral divides date with saints at sides in inner circle, arms below **Rev:** Reliquary carried by eight bishops, two angels below reliquary in inner circle

Date	Mintage	VG	F	VF	XF	Unc
1628 Rare	—	—	—	—	—	—

KM# 169 12 DUCAT
42.0000 g., 0.9860 Gold 1.3314 oz. AGW **Ruler:** Guidobald **Obv. Legend:** GVIDOBALDVS...

Date	Mintage	VG	F	VF	XF	Unc
1654	—	—	—	16,000	22,000	—

KM# A207 12 DUCAT
42.0000 g., 0.9860 Gold 1.3314 oz. AGW **Ruler:** Maximilian Gandolph **Obv:** Arms below hat in inner circle **Obv. Legend:** MAXIMIL GRANDOLPH... **Rev:** Two saints seated facing each other with croziers, church in foreground

Date	Mintage	VG	F	VF	XF	Unc
1668	—	—	—	14,500	19,000	—

KM# A208 12 DUCAT
42.0000 g., 0.9860 Gold 1.3314 oz. AGW **Ruler:** Maximilian Gandolph **Obv. Legend:** MAXIMIL GANDOLPH... **Note:** Prev. KM#206.

Date	Mintage	VG	F	VF	XF	Unc
1668 Rare	—	—	—	—	—	—

KM# 207 12 DUCAT
42.0000 g., 0.9860 Gold 1.3314 oz. AGW **Ruler:** Maximilian Gandolph **Note:** Klippe.

Date	Mintage	VG	F	VF	XF	Unc
1668 Rare	—	—	—	—	—	—

KM# 244 12 DUCAT
42.0000 g., 0.9860 Gold 1.3314 oz. AGW **Ruler:** Maximilian Gandolph **Subject:** 1100th Anniversary of Salzburg **Obv:** Arms below radiant triangle in inner circle **Obv. Legend:** A MAX GAND... **Rev:** Five standing saints; five-line inscription in exergue **Note:** Klippe.

Date	Mintage	VG	F	VF	XF	Unc
1682 Rare	—	—	—	—	—	—

KM# 264 12 DUCAT
42.0000 g., 0.9860 Gold 1.3314 oz. AGW **Ruler:** Johann Ernst **Obv:** Arms below hat in inner circle **Obv. Legend:** IOAN ERNESTUS... **Rev:** Two saints seated facing each other with croziers, church in foreground

Date	Mintage	VG	F	VF	XF	Unc
1687 Rare	—	—	—	—	—	—

KM# 54 14 DUCAT
49.0000 g., 0.9860 Gold 1.5533 oz. AGW **Ruler:** Markus Sittich **Note:** Struck with 1 Thaler dies, KM#19.

Date	Mintage	VG	F	VF	XF	Unc
1612 Rare	—	—	—	—	—	—

KM# 208 15 DUCAT
52.5000 g., 0.9860 Gold 1.6642 oz. AGW **Ruler:** Maximilian Gandolph **Obv:** Arms below hat in inner circle **Obv. Legend:** MAXIMIL GRANDOLPH... **Rev:** Two saints seated facing each other with croziers, church in foreground

Date	Mintage	VG	F	VF	XF	Unc
1668 Rare	—	—	—	—	—	—

KM# 265 15 DUCAT
52.5000 g., 0.9860 Gold 1.6642 oz. AGW **Ruler:** Johann Ernst **Obv. Legend:** IOAN ERNESTUS...

Date	Mintage	VG	F	VF	XF	Unc
1687 Rare	—	—	—	—	—	—

KM# 136 16 DUCAT
56.0000 g., 0.9860 Gold 1.7752 oz. AGW **Ruler:** Paris **Obv:** Cathedral divides date with saints at sides in inner circle, arms below **Rev:** Reliquary carried by eight bishops, two angels below reliquary in inner circle

Date	Mintage	VG	F	VF	XF	Unc
1628 Rare	—	—	—	—	—	—

KM# 170 16 DUCAT
56.0000 g., 0.9860 Gold 1.7752 oz. AGW **Ruler:** Guidobald **Obv. Legend:** GVIDOBALDVS...

Date	Mintage	VG	F	VF	XF	Unc
1654 Rare	—	—	—	—	—	—

MB# 497 20 DUCAT
70.0000 g., 0.9860 Gold 2.2190 oz. AGW, 40 mm. **Ruler:** Wolfgang Dietrich **Obv:** 2 adjacent shields of arms, Salzburg on left, Raitenau (globe) on right, legate's hat above **Obv. Legend:** WOLF • TEOD • D • G • AREPS • SAL • AP • SE • LE • **Rev:** 2 saints seated facing each other **Rev. Legend:** + S • RVDBERTVS • ET S • VIRGILIVS • EPI • SALZBVRGN • **Note:** Fr.#647.

Date	Mintage	VG	F	VF	XF	Unc
ND(1587-1612) Rare	—	—	—	—	—	—

KM# 137 20 DUCAT
70.0000 g., 0.9860 Gold 2.2190 oz. AGW **Ruler:** Paris **Obv:** Cathedral divides date with saints at sides in inner circle, arms below **Obv. Legend:** ECCLES: METROP: SALISB: DEDICATVR 25 SEPT: APARIDE... **Rev:** Reliquary carried by eight bishops, two angels below reliquary in inner circle

Date	Mintage	VG	F	VF	XF	Unc
1628	—	—	—	22,000	33,000	—

KM# 171 20 DUCAT
70.0000 g., 0.9860 Gold 2.2190 oz. AGW **Ruler:** Guidobald **Obv:** Arms below hat **Obv. Legend:** GVIDOBALDVS... **Rev:** Cathedral with saints at sides in inner circle

Date	Mintage	VG	F	VF	XF	Unc
1654	—	—	—	15,000	22,000	—

KM# 209 20 DUCAT
70.0000 g., 0.9860 Gold 2.2190 oz. AGW **Ruler:** Maximilian Gandolph **Obv. Legend:** MAXIMIL GANDOLPH...

Date	Mintage	VG	F	VF	XF	Unc
1668 Rare	—	—	—	—	—	—

KM# 210 20 DUCAT
70.0000 g., 0.9860 Gold 2.2190 oz. AGW **Ruler:** Maximilian Gandolph **Note:** Klippe. Illustration reduced.

Date	Mintage	VG	F	VF	XF	Unc
1668 Rare	—	—	—	—	—	—

KM# 266 20 DUCAT
70.0000 g., 0.9860 Gold 2.2190 oz. AGW **Ruler:** Johann Ernst **Obv. Legend:** IOAN ERNESTUS...

Date	Mintage	VG	F	VF	XF	Unc
1687	—	—	—	21,000	30,000	—

KM# 172 24 DUCAT

84.0000 g., 0.9860 Gold 2.6627 oz. AGW **Ruler:** Guidobald **Obv:** Arms below Bishops hat **Obv. Legend:** GVIDOBALDVS • D:G: ARCHI: EPS: SALISBVRG: SED: AP: LEG: **Rev:** Bishops holding up Cathedral within inner circle **Rev. Legend:** SS: RVDBERTVS • ET • VIRGILIVS • PATRONI • SALISBVRGENSES •

Date	Mintage	VG	F	VF	XF	Unc
1654 Rare	—	—	—	—	—	—

KM# 211 25 DUCAT

87.5000 g., 0.9860 Gold 2.7737 oz. AGW **Ruler:** Maximilian Gandolph **Obv:** Arms below hat in inner circle **Obv. Legend:** MAXIMIL GANDOLPH... **Rev:** Two saints seated facing each other with croziers, church in foreground

Date	Mintage	VG	F	VF	XF	Unc
1668 Rare	—	—	—	—	—	—

KM# 212 25 DUCAT

87.5000 g., 0.9860 Gold 2.7737 oz. AGW **Ruler:** Maximilian Gandolph **Note:** Klippe.

Date	Mintage	VG	F	VF	XF	Unc
1668 Rare	—	—	—	—	—	—

KM# 213 44 DUCAT

140.0000 g., 0.9860 Gold 4.4379 oz. AGW **Ruler:** Maximilian Gandolph **Obv:** Arms below hat in inner circle **Obv. Legend:** MAXIMIL GANDOLPH... **Rev:** Two saints seated facing each other with croziers, church in foreground

Date	Mintage	VG	F	VF	XF	Unc
1668 Rare	—	—	—	—	—	—

KM# 173 50 DUCAT

175.0000 g., 0.9860 Gold 5.5474 oz. AGW **Ruler:** Guidobald **Obv:** Arms below hat **Obv. Legend:** GVIDOBALDVS... **Rev:** Cathedral with saints at sides in inner circle **Note:** Klippe.

Date	Mintage	VG	F	VF	XF	Unc
1654 Rare	—	—	—	—	—	—

KM# 267 50 DUCAT

175.0000 g., 0.9860 Gold 5.5474 oz. AGW **Ruler:** Johann Ernst **Obv:** Arms below hat in inner circle **Obv. Legend:** IOAN ERNESTUS... **Rev:** Two saints seated facing each other with croziers, church in foreground

Date	Mintage	VG	F	VF	XF	Unc
1687 Rare	—	—	—	—	—	—

PATTERNS

Including off metal strikes

KM#	Date	Mintage	Identification	Mkt Val
Pn1	(1)610	—	2 Pfenning. Gold. KM#5.	—
Pn2	(1)613	—	2 Pfenning. Gold. KM#12.	—
Pn3	1615	—	2 Pfenning. Gold. KM#12.	—
Pn4	(1)617	—	Pfenning. Gold. KM#11.	—
Pn5	(1)618	—	Pfenning. Gold. KM#11.	—
Pn6	1628	—	4 Ducat. Silver. KM#124.	—
Pn7	1628	—	10 Ducat. Lead. KM#132.	—
Pn8	1636	—	Kreuzer. Gold. KM#84.	—
Pn9	1638	—	1/4 Thaler. Gold. KM#88.	—

SINZENDORF

An old Austrian house which was divided into two branches. The elder line was advanced to the rank of count in 1613. His successors seemingly acquired the mint right a few years later. They became extinct in 1766.

Members of the younger line, who became counts in 1653 and princes in 1803, struck no coins.

RULERS

Pilgrim III, 1579-1620
Georg Ludwig, 1616-1680
Christian Ludwig, 1681-1687
Philipp Ludwig, 1687-1742

COUNTY

STANDARD COINAGE

KM# 4 1/2 THALER

Silver **Ruler:** Georg Ludwig **Obv:** Capped bust of Georg Ludwig right **Rev:** Crowned arms in order collar

Date	Mintage	VG	F	VF	XF	Unc
1676	—	600	1,000	2,000	3,500	—

KM# 5 THALER

Silver **Ruler:** Georg Ludwig **Obv:** Capped bust of Georg Ludwig right **Rev:** Crowned arms in order collar **Note:** Dav. #3414.

Date	Mintage	VG	F	VF	XF	Unc
1676	—	500	900	1,750	3,000	—

TRADE COINAGE

KM# 6 DUCAT

3.5000 g., 0.9860 Gold 0.1109 oz. AGW **Ruler:** Georg Ludwig **Obv:** Bust of Georg Ludwig right **Rev:** Crowned arms in Order collar **Note:** Fr. #3289.

Date	Mintage	VG	F	VF	XF	Unc
1676	—	1,250	2,750	5,000	8,500	—

TRAUTSON

An old Tyrolean family that traced its lineage back to 1134. During the reign of Paul Sixtus I (1589-1621), who was Imperial Governor of the Tyrol, the mint right was given to this house. Members of this house held high imperial offices until 1775 when the house passed to Auersperg.

RULERS

Paul Sixtus I, 1589-1621
Johann Franz, 1621-1663
Franz Eusebius, 1663-1728
Johann Leopold, 1663-1724

PRINCIPALITY

STANDARD COINAGE

KM# 5 3 KREUZER

Silver **Ruler:** Paul Sixtus I **Obv:** Bust right **Rev:** Coat of arms

Date	Mintage	VG	F	VF	XF	Unc
ND	—	15.00	25.00	45.00	80.00	—
1617	—	15.00	25.00	45.00	80.00	—
1618	—	15.00	25.00	45.00	80.00	—
1619	—	15.00	25.00	45.00	80.00	—

KM# 21 3 KREUZER

Silver **Ruler:** Paul Sixtus I **Obv:** Eagle **Rev:** Arms

Date	Mintage	VG	F	VF	XF	Unc
1621	—	12.00	20.00	40.00	75.00	—

KM# 25 1/4 THALER

Silver **Ruler:** Johann Franz

Date	Mintage	VG	F	VF	XF	Unc
1634	—	180	325	550	1,000	—

KM# 26 1/4 THALER

Silver **Ruler:** Johann Franz **Rev:** Crowned oval arms

Date	Mintage	VG	F	VF	XF	Unc
1634	—	250	425	650	1,200	—

KM# 27 1/4 THALER

Silver **Ruler:** Johann Franz **Rev:** Crowned shield-shaped arms

Date	Mintage	VG	F	VF	XF	Unc
1639	—	285	475	775	1,400	—

KM# A7 1/2 THALER

Silver **Ruler:** Paul Sixtus I **Note:** Similar to 1 Thaler, KM#20.

Date	Mintage	VG	F	VF	XF	Unc
ND(1615-21)	—	750	1,450	2,750	5,000	—

KM# 6 1/2 THALER

Silver **Ruler:** Paul Sixtus I **Obv:** Eagle **Rev:** Arms **Note:** Varieties exist.

Date	Mintage	VG	F	VF	XF	Unc
1620	—	245	475	850	1,550	—

KM# 8.1 THALER

Silver **Ruler:** Paul Sixtus I **Obv:** Bust right, bare headed, cape with order collar **Note:** Dav. #3418.

Date	Mintage	VG	F	VF	XF	Unc
1617	—	220	375	650	1,250	—

KM# 7 THALER

Silver **Ruler:** Paul Sixtus I **Obv:** Bust right with hat **Note:** Dav. 3416

Date	Mintage	VG	F	VF	XF	Unc
1617	—	500	850	1,500	2,250	—

KM# 8.2 THALER

Silver **Ruler:** Paul Sixtus I **Obv:** Larger bust **Note:** Similar to KM#8.3. Dav. #3422.

Date	Mintage	VG	F	VF	XF	Unc
1618	—	125	200	350	650	—

KM# 8.3 THALER

Silver **Ruler:** Paul Sixtus I **Note:** Dav. #3423.

Date	Mintage	VG	F	VF	XF	Unc
1619	—	125	200	350	650	—
16Z0	—	125	200	350	650	—

KM# 9 THALER

Silver **Ruler:** Paul Sixtus I **Obv:** Bow knot on shoulder **Note:** Dav. #3425.

Date	Mintage	VG	F	VF	XF	Unc
16Z0	—	125	200	350	650	—

KM# 20 THALER

Silver **Ruler:** Paul Sixtus I **Obv:** Arms in order chain **Rev:** Crowned double headed eagle above crown **Note:** Dav. #3426.

Date	Mintage	VG	F	VF	XF	Unc
ND	—	375	725	1,250	2,400	—

KM# 28.1 THALER

Silver **Ruler:** Johann Franz **Rev:** Double eagle above helmeted arms **Note:** Dav. #3427.

Date	Mintage	VG	F	VF	XF	Unc
1634	—	220	375	650	1,200	—
1635	—	220	375	650	1,200	—

KM# 28.2 THALER

Silver **Ruler:** Johann Franz **Obv:** Large bust **Rev:** Similar to KM#28.3 **Note:** Dav. #3428.

Date	Mintage	VG	F	VF	XF	Unc
1634	—	220	375	650	1,200	—

KM# 28.3 THALER

Silver **Ruler:** Johann Franz **Note:** Dav. #3429.

Date	Mintage	VG	F	VF	XF	Unc
1636	—	200	350	600	1,100	—
1637	—	200	350	600	1,100	—
1638	—	200	350	600	1,100	—
1639	—	200	350	600	1,100	—

KM# 10 2 THALER

Silver **Ruler:** Paul Sixtus I **Note:** Similar to 1 Thaler, KM#7. Dav. #3415.

Date	Mintage	VG	F	VF	XF	Unc
1617 Rare	—	—	—	—	—	—

KM# 11.1 2 THALER

Silver **Ruler:** Paul Sixtus I **Note:** Similar to 1 Thaler, KM#8.1. Dav. #3417.

Date	Mintage	VG	F	VF	XF	Unc
1617	—	900	1,500	2,500	4,750	—

KM# 11.2 2 THALER

Silver **Ruler:** Paul Sixtus I **Obv:** Bare head right, cape with chain hung all across **Note:** Dav. #3421.

Date	Mintage	VG	F	VF	XF	Unc
1618	—	900	1,500	2,500	4,750	—

KM# 11.3 2 THALER

Silver **Ruler:** Paul Sixtus I **Obv:** Larger bust with bow knot on shoulder **Note:** Dav. #3424.

Date	Mintage	VG	F	VF	XF	Unc
1620	—	900	1,500	2,500	4,750	—

KM# 12 2 THALER

Silver **Ruler:** Paul Sixtus I **Note:** Klippe. Dav. #3424A.

Date	Mintage	VG	F	VF	XF	Unc
16Z0 Rare	—	—	—	—	—	—

KM# 13.1 3 THALER

Silver **Ruler:** Paul Sixtus I **Note:** Similar to 1 thaler, KM#8.1. Dav. #3424A.

Date	Mintage	VG	F	VF	XF	Unc
1617 Rare	—	—	—	—	—	—

KM# 13.2 3 THALER

Silver **Ruler:** Paul Sixtus I **Note:** Dav. #3420.

Date	Mintage	VG	F	VF	XF	Unc
1618	—	2,000	3,500	5,000	9,000	—

KM# 14 4 THALER

Silver **Ruler:** Paul Sixtus I **Note:** Similar to 1 Thaler, KM#7. Dav. #A3415.

Date	Mintage	VG	F	VF	XF	Unc
1617 Rare	—	—	—	—	—	—

KM# 15 4 THALER

Silver **Ruler:** Paul Sixtus I **Note:** Similar to 1 Thaler, KM#11.2. Dav. #3419.

Date	Mintage	VG	F	VF	XF	Unc
1618 Rare	—	—	—	—	—	—

KM# 16 6 THALER

Silver **Ruler:** Paul Sixtus I **Note:** Similar to 2 Thaler, KM#11.2. Dav. #A3419.

Date	Mintage	VG	F	VF	XF	Unc
1618 Rare	—	—	—	—	—	—

TRADE COINAGE

KM# 29 1/4 DUCAT

0.8750 g., 0.9860 Gold 0.0277 oz. AGW **Ruler:** Johann Franz **Obv:** Bust right

Date	Mintage	VG	F	VF	XF	Unc
1635	—	250	500	1,000	2,000	—

KM# A30 1/2 DUCAT

1.7200 g., 0.9860 Gold 0.0545 oz. AGW **Ruler:** Johann Franz

Date	Mintage	VG	F	VF	XF	Unc
1635	—	700	1,400	2,500	4,000	—

KM# 17 DUCAT

3.5000 g., 0.9860 Gold 0.1109 oz. AGW **Ruler:** Paul Sixtus I

Date	Mintage	VG	F	VF	XF	Unc
ND	—	1,200	2,250	4,500	7,500	—

KM# 30 DUCAT

3.5000 g., 0.9860 Gold 0.1109 oz. AGW **Ruler:** Johann Franz **Obv:** Bust right **Rev:** Crowned imperial eagle above crowned arms

Date	Mintage	VG	F	VF	XF	Unc
1634	—	600	1,000	2,250	3,750	—
1636	—	1,000	2,000	4,000	6,500	—
1638	—	600	1,000	2,250	3,750	—

KM# 18 4 DUCAT

14.0000 g., 0.9860 Gold 0.4438 oz. AGW **Ruler:** Paul Sixtus I

Date	Mintage	VG	F	VF	XF	Unc
1618	—	1,800	3,600	7,000	12,500	—

KM# A22 5 DUCAT

17.0900 g., 0.9860 Gold 0.5417 oz. AGW **Ruler:** Paul Sixtus I

Date	Mintage	VG	F	VF	XF	Unc
1620 Rare	—	—	—	—	—	—

Note: Künker Auction 160, 9-09,VF realized approx. $17,500

KM# 22 10 DUCAT

35.0000 g., 0.9860 Gold 1.1095 oz. AGW **Ruler:** Paul Sixtus I **Note:** Struck with 1 Thaler dies.

Date	Mintage	VG	F	VF	XF	Unc
1617 Rare	—	—	—	—	—	—

KM# 23 10 DUCAT

35.0000 g., 0.9860 Gold 1.1095 oz. AGW **Ruler:** Paul Sixtus I **Note:** Struck with 1 Thaler dies, KM#8.2.

Date	Mintage	VG	F	VF	XF	Unc
1618 Rare	—	—	—	—	—	—

KM# A31 10 DUCAT

35.0000 g., 0.9860 Gold 1.1095 oz. AGW **Ruler:** Johann Franz **Note:** Struck with 1 Thaler dies, KM#28.3.

Date	Mintage	VG	F	VF	XF	Unc
1638 Rare	—	—	—	—	—	—

TROPPAU-JAEGENDORF

Troppau was an old upper Silesian duchy with its capital in the town of the same name located 90 miles southeast of Breslau. The capital of an Upper Silesian duchy Troppau fell to Austria 1528-1614 except for a short period in the 1550's. In 1614 Count Carl of Liechtenstein was created duke of Troppau for his military services. This coinage was intended for circulation in Troppau and in Jaegendorf.

RULERS

Carl, 1614-1627
Karl Eusebius, 1627-1684

MINT OFFICIALS' INITIALS & MONOGRAMS

Initials	Description	Dates	Names
BH	Ligate H	1614-16	Burghard Haase
CC	Crossed flags divide CC	1617-29	Krystof Cantor
	M above W		Michal Wilke
(j)	JZ monogram	1616-17	Jan Ziesler
(t)	TS monogram	1629-30	Tobias Sommerschein

DUCHY

JOINT COINAGE

KM# 1 3 KRAJCAR

Silver **Ruler:** Carl **Obv:** Bust of Carl right **Rev:** Capped ornate shield

Date	Mintage	VG	F	VF	XF	Unc
1614 BH	—	35.00	65.00	120	200	—

KM# 2 3 KRAJCAR

Silver **Ruler:** Carl **Rev:** Capped eagle

Date	Mintage	VG	F	VF	XF	Unc
1614 BH	—	40.00	70.00	135	225	—

KM# 3 3 KRAJCAR

Silver **Ruler:** Carl **Rev:** 2 ornate shields capped

Date	Mintage	VG	F	VF	XF	Unc
1614 BH	—	40.00	70.00	135	225	—

KM# 13 3 KRAJCAR

Silver **Ruler:** Carl **Rev:** 2 plain shields capped

Date	Mintage	VG	F	VF	XF	Unc
1615 BH	—	25.00	50.00	100	200	—
1615 (t)	—	25.00	50.00	100	200	—
1616 BH	—	25.00	50.00	100	200	—
1616 (t)	—	25.00	50.00	100	200	—
1617 (t)	—	25.00	50.00	100	200	—
1618 (f) c	—	25.00	50.00	100	200	—
1619 (f) c	—	25.00	50.00	100	200	—

KM# 32 KREUZER

Silver **Ruler:** Karl Eusebius **Obv:** Bust of Karl right **Rev:** Capped shield of arms

Date	Mintage	VG	F	VF	XF	Unc
1629 MW	—	35.00	60.00	120	225	—

KM# 33 3 KREUZER

Silver **Ruler:** Karl Eusebius **Obv:** Bust of Karl right **Rev:** Capped shield of arms

Date	Mintage	VG	F	VF	XF	Unc
1629 (t)	—	30.00	50.00	100	185	—

KM# 5 THALER

Silver **Ruler:** Carl **Obv:** Bust right **Rev:** Capped and helmeted arms **Note:** Dav. #3430.

Date	Mintage	VG	F	VF	XF	Unc
(1)614 BH	—	1,600	2,700	4,200	6,500	—

KM# 6 THALER

Silver **Ruler:** Carl **Rev:** Capped and helmeted arms divide B-H at lower edge **Note:** Dav. #3431.

Date	Mintage	VG	F	VF	XF	Unc
1614 BH	—	1,600	2,700	4,200	6,500	—

KM# 7 THALER

Silver **Ruler:** Carl **Rev:** Plain field arms divide B-H **Note:** Dav. #3432.

Date	Mintage	VG	F	VF	XF	Unc
1614 BH	—	1,600	2,700	4,200	6,500	—

KM# 14 THALER

Silver **Ruler:** Carl **Obv:** Different portrait **Rev:** 2 shields capped and helmeted **Note:** Dav. #3434.

Date	Mintage	VG	F	VF	XF	Unc
1615 BH	—	725	1,300	2,250	4,000	—
1616 BH	—	725	1,300	2,250	4,000	—

KM# 28 THALER

Silver **Ruler:** Carl **Obv:** Smaller bust **Rev:** Troppau arms at right **Note:** Dav. #3435.

Date	Mintage	VG	F	VF	XF	Unc
1619 CC	—	750	1,400	2,350	4,200	—

KM# 29 THALER

Silver **Ruler:** Carl **Rev:** Troppau arms at left **Note:** Klippe. Dav. #3435A. Illustration reduced.

Date	Mintage	VG	F	VF	XF	Unc
1619 CC Rare	—	—	—	—	—	—

KM# 30 THALER

Silver **Ruler:** Carl **Rev:** Troppau arms at right **Note:** Klippe. Dav. #3435B.

Date	Mintage	VG	F	VF	XF	Unc
1619 CC Rare	—	—	—	—	—	—

KM# 35 THALER

Silver **Ruler:** Karl Eusebius **Obv:** Bust right **Rev:** Crowned arms, date in legend **Note:** Dav. #3437.

Date	Mintage	VG	F	VF	XF	Unc
1629 MW	—	1,600	2,700	4,200	6,500	—

KM# 15 2 THALER

Silver **Ruler:** Carl **Obv:** Bust right **Rev:** Capped shield of arms **Note:** Dav. #A3432.

Date	Mintage	VG	F	VF	XF	Unc
1615 BH	—	4,200	6,500	9,000	14,000	—

KM# 17 2 THALER

Silver **Ruler:** Carl **Note:** Similar to 1 Thaler, KM#14. Dav. #3433.

Date	Mintage	VG	F	VF	XF	Unc
1616 BH	—	2,750	4,500	6,500	11,500	—

KM# 19 2 THALER

Silver **Ruler:** Carl **Obv:** Bust right in sprays **Rev:** Capped shield of arms in sprays **Note:** Dav. #3436.

Date	Mintage	VG	F	VF	XF	Unc
ND Rare	—	—	—	—	—	—

KM# 20 3 THALER

Silver **Ruler:** Carl **Note:** Similar to 2 Thaler, KM#19. Dav. #3436A.

Date	Mintage	VG	F	VF	XF	Unc
ND Rare	—	—	—	—	—	—

KM# 21 4 THALER

Silver **Ruler:** Carl **Note:** Similar to 2 Thaler, KM#19. Dav. #3436B.

Date	Mintage	VG	F	VF	XF	Unc
ND Rare	—	—	—	—	—	—

KM# 22 5 THALER

Silver **Ruler:** Carl **Obv:** Bust right **Obv. Legend:** CAROLVS D • G • PRINCEPS DE LICHTENSTEIN **Rev:** Crowned arms **Rev. Legend:** DVX OPPAVIÆ - ET CARNOVIA ... **Note:** Dav. #3436C.

Date	Mintage	VG	F	VF	XF	Unc
ND Rare	—	—	—	—	—	—

JOINT TRADE COINAGE

KM# 8 DUCAT

3.4900 g., 0.9860 Gold 0.1106 oz. AGW **Ruler:** Carl **Obv:** Bust of Carl right in inner circle **Rev:** Capped shield of arms in inner circle **Note:** Restrikes exist.

Date	Mintage	VG	F	VF	XF	Unc
1614 BH	—	1,000	2,000	4,000	8,000	—
1617	—	1,000	2,000	4,000	8,000	—
1618	—	1,000	2,000	4,000	8,000	—

KM# 9 2 DUCAT

7.0000 g., 0.9860 Gold 0.2219 oz. AGW **Ruler:** Carl **Obv:** Bust of Carl right in inner circle **Rev:** Capped ornate shield of arms in inner circle

Date	Mintage	VG	F	VF	XF	Unc
1614 BH	—	3,750	7,500	11,500	18,000	—
1616	—	3,750	7,500	11,500	18,000	—

KM# 10 3 DUCAT

10.5000 g., 0.9860 Gold 0.3328 oz. AGW **Ruler:** Carl **Obv:** Bust of Carl right in inner circle **Rev:** Crowned shield of arms in inner circle, date in legend

Date	Mintage	VG	F	VF	XF	Unc
1614 Unique	—	—	—	—	—	—

KM# 16 3 DUCAT

10.5000 g., 0.9860 Gold 0.3328 oz. AGW **Ruler:** Carl **Rev:** 2 shields capped in inner circle

Date	Mintage	VG	F	VF	XF	Unc
(1)618 CC	—	—	—	—	11,500	—

KM# 27 3 DUCAT

10.5000 g., 0.9860 Gold 0.3328 oz. AGW **Ruler:** Carl **Note:** Klippe.

Date	Mintage	VG	F	VF	XF	Unc
1619 Restrike	—	—	—	—	750	—

KM# 25 4 DUCAT

14.0000 g., 0.9860 Gold 0.4438 oz. AGW **Ruler:** Carl **Obv:** Bust of Carl right in inner circle

Date	Mintage	VG	F	VF	XF	Unc
1618	—	—	—	19,000	27,000	—

KM# A16 5 DUCAT

17.5000 g., 0.9860 Gold 0.5547 oz. AGW **Ruler:** Carl **Obv:** Bust of Carl right in inner circle **Rev:** Capped shield of arms in inner circle

Date	Mintage	VG	F	VF	XF	Unc
1615 BH	—	—	—	19,000	27,000	—

KM# 24 6 DUCAT

21.0000 g., 0.9860 Gold 0.6657 oz. AGW **Ruler:** Carl **Obv:** Bust of Carl right in inner circle

Date	Mintage	VG	F	VF	XF	Unc
1617	—	—	—	—	30,000	—

KM# 23 10 DUCAT

35.0000 g., 0.9860 Gold 1.1095 oz. AGW **Ruler:** Carl **Note:** Struck with 1 Thaler dies, KM#14.

Date	Mintage	VG	F	VF	XF	Unc
1616	—	—	—	—	37,500	—

AUSTRIAN NETHERLANDS

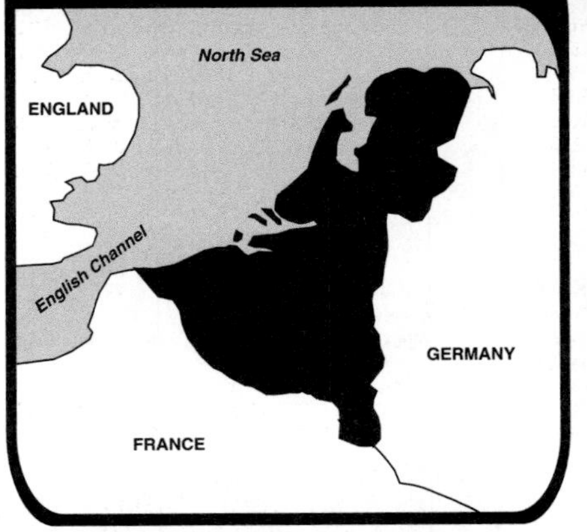

The Austrian Netherlands, which corresponds roughly to present-day Belgium, came into being on April 11, 1713, when the Treaty of Utrecht awarded the lands to Austria as part settlement following the war with Spain. It passed to France in 1795, was part of the Kingdom of Netherlands from 1815 to 1830, and became the present Belgium as the result of the revolution of 1830 against William I, Prince of Orange and King of the Netherlands.

RECKHEIM

A barony in Limburg which was raised to a county in 1624. Was in the hands of the van Lynden family and mediatized in 1803.

RULERS

Herman of Aspremont- Lynden, 1590-1603
Ernst, 1603-1636
Ferdinand, 1636-1665
Francois-Gobert and Ferdinand-Gobert of Aspremont-Lynden, 1665-1703

COUNTY

STANDARD COINAGE

KM# 21 DUIT

Copper **Ruler:** Ernst **Obv:** Shield of arms in inner circle **Rev:** TRA/REC/HEM in inner circle, date in legend at top

Date	Mintage	Good	VG	F	VF	XF
1616	—	12.00	25.00	50.00	80.00	150

KM# 22 DUIT

Copper **Ruler:** Ernst **Obv:** Crowned arms **Rev:** FRI / CIR / date in wreath of leaves **Note:** Varieties exist.

Date	Mintage	Good	VG	F	VF	XF
1617	—	7.00	15.00	30.00	55.00	110
1619	—	7.00	15.00	30.00	55.00	110
1620	—	7.00	15.00	30.00	55.00	110
1621	—	7.00	15.00	30.00	55.00	110
1631	—	7.00	15.00	30.00	55.00	110
1632	—	7.00	15.00	30.00	55.00	110
1633	—	7.00	15.00	30.00	55.00	110
1634	—	7.00	15.00	30.00	55.00	110

KM# 23 DUIT

Copper **Ruler:** Ernst **Obv:** Crowned arms **Obv. Legend:** NISI. DEVS-NOBISCVM **Rev:** FRI / DER / 1619 in laurel wreath

Date	Mintage	Good	VG	F	VF	XF
1619	—	10.00	20.00	40.00	70.00	140

KM# 30 DUIT

Copper **Ruler:** Ernst **Obv:** Crowned arms **Rev:** FRI / DER / date in laurel wreath

Date	Mintage	Good	VG	F	VF	XF
1620	—	10.00	20.00	40.00	70.00	140
1621	—	10.00	20.00	40.00	70.00	140

KM# 45 DUIT

Copper **Ruler:** Ernst **Rev:** FRI/SA/1633 in wreath and leaves

Date	Mintage	Good	VG	F	VF	XF
1633	—	10.00	20.00	40.00	70.00	140

KM# 47 DUIT

Copper **Ruler:** Ernst **Obv:** Shield of arms in laurel branches **Rev:** IMP / R with eagle above

Date	Mintage	Good	VG	F	VF	XF
ND	—	10.00	20.00	40.00	70.00	140

KM# 48 DUIT

Copper **Ruler:** Ernst **Obv:** Crowned arms in laurel branches **Rev:** BVL / LONEN / SIS in wreath, shield at bottom

Date	Mintage	Good	VG	F	VF	XF
ND	—	10.00	20.00	40.00	70.00	140

KM# 49 DUIT

Copper **Ruler:** Ernst **Rev:** FRI/CUA

Date	Mintage	Good	VG	F	VF	XF
ND	—	10.00	20.00	40.00	70.00	155

KM# 51 DUIT

Copper **Ruler:** Ferdinand **Obv:** Crowned arms **Rev:** FRI/CIR/ date

Date	Mintage	Good	VG	F	VF	XF
ND	—	6.00	12.00	20.00	35.00	70.00
1638	—	6.00	12.00	20.00	35.00	70.00
1639	—	6.00	12.00	20.00	35.00	70.00
1641	—	6.00	12.00	20.00	35.00	70.00
1642	—	6.00	12.00	20.00	35.00	70.00
1643	—	6.00	12.00	20.00	35.00	70.00
1644	—	6.00	12.00	20.00	35.00	70.00
1646	—	6.00	12.00	20.00	35.00	70.00
1651	—	6.00	12.00	20.00	35.00	70.00
1653	—	6.00	12.00	20.00	35.00	70.00
1655	—	6.00	12.00	20.00	35.00	70.00
1661	—	6.00	12.00	20.00	35.00	70.00

KM# 52 DUIT

Copper **Ruler:** Ferdinand **Obv:** Crowned arms **Rev:** FER / DIN / 1640 in wreath

Date	Mintage	Good	VG	F	VF	XF
ND	—	10.00	20.00	40.00	70.00	140
1640	—	10.00	20.00	40.00	70.00	140

KM# 87 DUIT

Copper **Ruler:** Francois and Ferdinand Gobert **Obv:** Crowned arms in palm branches

Date	Mintage	Good	VG	F	VF	XF
ND	—	10.00	20.00	40.00	70.00	140

KM# 88 DUIT

Copper **Ruler:** Francois and Ferdinand Gobert **Obv:** Shield of arms in garland

Date	Mintage	Good	VG	F	VF	XF
ND	—	10.00	20.00	40.00	70.00	140

KM# 89 DUIT

Copper **Ruler:** Francois and Ferdinand Gobert **Rev:** TRA / REC in quatrelobe

Date	Mintage	Good	VG	F	VF	XF
ND	—	10.00	20.00	40.00	70.00	140

KM# 90 DUIT

Copper **Ruler:** Francois and Ferdinand Gobert **Rev:** TRA / REC / HEM in wreath

Date	Mintage	Good	VG	F	VF	XF
ND	—	10.00	20.00	40.00	70.00	140

KM# 92 DUIT

Copper **Ruler:** Francois and Ferdinand Gobert **Obv:** Crowned eagle shield in palm branches **Rev:** TRA / REC / HEM in wreath

Date	Mintage	Good	VG	F	VF	XF
ND	—	10.00	20.00	40.00	70.00	140

KM# 96 DUIT

Copper **Ruler:** Francois and Ferdinand Gobert **Obv:** Bend sinister in shield

Date	Mintage	Good	VG	F	VF	XF
ND	—	10.00	20.00	40.00	70.00	140

KM# 97 DUIT

Copper **Ruler:** Francois and Ferdinand Gobert **Obv:** Crowned arms with lion supporters **Rev:** TRA/REC/NEM in wreath

Date	Mintage	Good	VG	F	VF	XF
ND	—	12.00	25.00	50.00	80.00	150

KM# 93 DUIT

Copper **Ruler:** Francois and Ferdinand Gobert **Rev:** DA/E TR/TRIA in inner circle and wreath **Note:** Legend: D(ENARIUS) AE (REUS) T(ERRITORII) R(ECKHEIMANSIS) I(MPERIALIS) A(SPREMONTIS), other legend varieties exist.

Date	Mintage	Good	VG	F	VF	XF
ND	—	10.00	20.00	40.00	70.00	140

KM# 46 DUIT

Copper **Ruler:** Ernst **Obv:** Crowned arms in wreath **Rev:** TRAN / MOESA / A.R. in wreath **Note:** Varieties exist.

Date	Mintage	Good	VG	F	VF	XF
ND	—	10.00	20.00	40.00	70.00	140

KM# 91 DUIT

Copper **Ruler:** Francois and Ferdinand Gobert **Obv:** Crowned oval arms **Rev:** O: D / FER / DIN in wreath **Note:** Varieties exist.

Date	Mintage	Good	VG	F	VF	XF
ND	—	10.00	20.00	40.00	70.00	140

KM# 94 DUIT

Copper **Ruler:** Francois and Ferdinand Gobert **Obv:** Ornamental shield of arms with cross of Lynden at bottom **Rev:** IN / REC / KVM in wreath **Note:** Varieties exist.

Date	Mintage	Good	VG	F	VF	XF
ND	—	10.00	20.00	40.00	70.00	155

KM# 95 DUIT

Copper **Ruler:** Francois and Ferdinand Gobert **Obv:** Ornamentation in bottom of shield of arms **Rev:** TRA / REC / KUM **Note:** Varieties exist.

Date	Mintage	Good	VG	F	VF	XF
ND	—	10.00	20.00	40.00	70.00	125

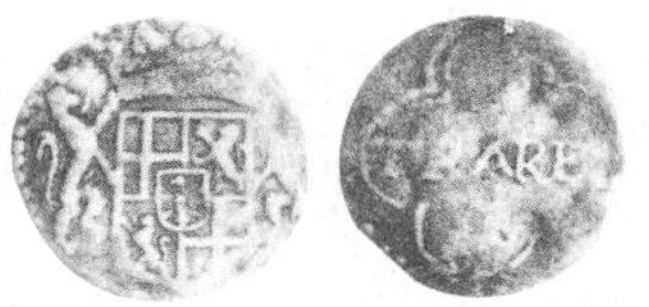

KM# 98 DUIT

Copper **Ruler:** Francois and Ferdinand Gobert **Rev:** TRAREC in quatrelobe **Note:** Varieties exist.

Date	Mintage	Good	VG	F	VF	XF
ND	—	12.00	25.00	50.00	80.00	150

KM# 85 DUIT

Copper **Ruler:** Ferdinand **Obv:** Small shield of arms, 2 digit date at top right **Rev:** FRI / CIA / R in wreath

Date	Mintage	Good	VG	F	VF	XF
(16)64	—	10.00	20.00	40.00	70.00	155

KM# 86 DUIT

Copper **Ruler:** Ferdinand **Obv:** Laurel branches around arms

Date	Mintage	Good	VG	F	VF	XF
(16)64	—	10.00	20.00	40.00	70.00	125

KM# 99 DUIT

Copper **Ruler:** Francois and Ferdinand Gobert **Obv:** Ornamental shield with ornamentation below bend **Rev:** FRAN / EG. LV / R.M in wreath **Note:** Varieties exist.

Date	Mintage	Good	VG	F	VF	XF
ND	—	12.00	25.00	50.00	80.00	150

KM# 100 DUIT

Copper **Ruler:** Francois and Ferdinand Gobert **Obv:** Crowned arms with lion supporters, VVTREH below **Rev:** / TRAREC / 1681 in quatrelobe **Note:** Varieties exist.

Date	Mintage	Good	VG	F	VF	XF
1681	—	12.00	25.00	50.00	80.00	150

KM# 68 1/2 LIARD (Gigot)

Copper **Ruler:** Ferdinand **Obv:** Crowned arms in inner circle **Obv. Legend:** FER...DE. REC **Rev:** Crowned arms on cross fleury, R-M at sides

Date	Mintage	Good	VG	F	VF	XF
ND	—	30.00	50.00	90.00	175	—

KM# 69 1/2 LIARD (Gigot)

Copper **Ruler:** Ferdinand **Obv:** Crowned arms **Rev:** Crowned double cross between 3 shields of arms, 2 above

Date	Mintage	Good	VG	F	VF	XF
ND	—	25.00	40.00	75.00	150	—

KM# 70 1/2 LIARD (Gigot)

Copper **Ruler:** Ferdinand **Rev:** Value divided at bottom

Date	Mintage	Good	VG	F	VF	XF
ND	—	25.00	40.00	75.00	150	—

KM# 71 1/2 LIARD (Gigot)

Copper **Ruler:** Ferdinand **Obv:** Crowned different arms in inner circle **Obv. Legend:** COM. REC

Date	Mintage	Good	VG	F	VF	XF
ND	—	25.00	40.00	75.00	150	—

KM# 72 1/2 LIARD (Gigot)

Copper **Ruler:** Ferdinand **Obv:** Crowned different arms (bend sinister) in inner circle **Obv. Legend:** MON. NO. DE. REC

Date	Mintage	Good	VG	F	VF	XF
ND	—	25.00	40.00	75.00	150	—

KM# 73 1/2 LIARD (Gigot)

Copper **Ruler:** Ferdinand **Rev:** Value divided at bottom

Date	Mintage	Good	VG	F	VF	XF
ND	—	25.00	40.00	75.00	150	—

KM# 74 1/2 LIARD (Gigot)

Copper **Ruler:** Ferdinand **Obv:** Crowned arms with bend **Obv. Legend:** FERDI. C. D. LIN. REC

Date	Mintage	Good	VG	F	VF	XF
ND	—	25.00	40.00	75.00	150	—

KM# 67 1/2 LIARD (Gigot)

Copper **Ruler:** Ferdinand **Obv:** Crowned arms **Obv. Legend:** REC. BAR. IN. BORS **Rev:** Crown above cross fleury **Rev. Legend:** FER-COM-LIN

Date	Mintage	Good	VG	F	VF	XF
1646	—	25.00	50.00	90.00	175	—

KM# 18 LIARD

Copper **Ruler:** Ernst **Obv:** Crown above 3 shields of arms, 2 above 1 **Obv. Legend:** ERNESTVS. DE. LYNDEN. LIBER **Rev:** Crowned arms **Rev. Legend:** BARO. IMPER. IN. RECHEM

Date	Mintage	Good	VG	F	VF	XF
ND	—	15.00	30.00	60.00	90.00	195

KM# 19 LIARD

Copper **Ruler:** Ernst **Obv:** Crowned arms divide A-I in inner circle **Rev:** Crowned arms divide P-P in inner circle

Date	Mintage	Good	VG	F	VF	XF
ND	—	15.00	30.00	60.00	90.00	195

KM# 15 LIARD

Copper **Ruler:** Ernst **Obv:** Bust of Ernest left **Obv. Legend:** ERNESTVS. DE. LYNDEN. LIBER **Rev:** Crowned arms **Rev. Legend:** BARD. IMPERIALIS. IN. RECHEIM **Note:** Varieties exist.

Date	Mintage	Good	VG	F	VF	XF
ND	—	18.00	35.00	65.00	100	205
1614	—	18.00	35.00	65.00	100	205

KM# 16 LIARD

Copper **Ruler:** Ernst **Obv:** Crown above 3 shields of arms, 2 above 1 **Obv. Legend:** ERNESTVS. DE. LYNDEN. LIBER **Rev:** Crowned arms **Rev. Legend:** BARO. IMPERI. RECHEIM **Note:** Varieties exist.

Date	Mintage	Good	VG	F	VF	XF
ND	—	15.00	30.00	60.00	90.00	195

KM# 17 LIARD

Copper **Ruler:** Ernst **Obv:** Crowned arms **Obv. Legend:** ERNESTVS. DE. LYNDEN. LIBER **Rev:** Crown above 3 shields of arms, 2 above 1 **Rev. Legend:** BARO. IMPERIALIS. IN. REKEIM **Note:** Varieties exist.

Date	Mintage	Good	VG	F	VF	XF
ND	—	15.00	30.00	60.00	90.00	195

KM# 20 LIARD

Copper **Ruler:** Ferdinand **Obv:** Crown above 3 shields of arms, 2 above 1 **Obv. Legend:** FERD. COM. DE. LIN. RECHEM **Rev:** Crowned arms divide date in inner circle **Rev. Legend:** FERDIN. ET. ELISABETH **Note:** Varieties exist.

Date	Mintage	Good	VG	F	VF	XF
1611(sic) Error	—	10.00	20.00	40.00	70.00	165
1640	—	10.00	20.00	40.00	70.00	165
1641	—	10.00	20.00	40.00	70.00	165
1645	—	10.00	20.00	40.00	70.00	165
1646	—	10.00	20.00	40.00	70.00	165

KM# 61 LIARD

Copper **Ruler:** Ferdinand **Obv:** Soldier with sword above shoulder divides R-O in inner circle **Obv. Legend:** DOMINVS. MIHI. ADIVTOR **Rev:** Crowned arms on cross in inner circle **Rev. Legend:** MON. NOVA. COM. D. REC

Date	Mintage	Good	VG	F	VF	XF
ND	—	15.00	30.00	60.00	90.00	180

KM# 62 LIARD

Copper **Ruler:** Ferdinand **Obv:** Soldier with sword above shoulder divides F-R in inner circle

Date	Mintage	Good	VG	F	VF	XF
ND	—	15.00	30.00	60.00	90.00	180

KM# 64 LIARD

Copper **Ruler:** Ferdinand **Obv:** Soldier with sword above shoulder divides F-O in inner circle **Obv. Legend:** COM. DE. LIND. REC **Rev. Legend:** FERD. II. DG. ROM. IMP

Date	Mintage	Good	VG	F	VF	XF
ND	—	15.00	30.00	60.00	90.00	180

KM# 58 LIARD

Copper **Ruler:** Ferdinand **Rev:** Crowned differnet arms in inner circle

Date	Mintage	Good	VG	F	VF	XF
ND	—	18.00	35.00	65.00	100	205

KM# 56 LIARD

Copper **Ruler:** Ferdinand **Obv:** Bust of Ferdinand left **Obv. Legend:** FERDINAN. COME **Rev:** Crowned arms **Rev. Legend:** DOMINVS. CO. BORS

Date	Mintage	Good	VG	F	VF	XF
ND	—	18.00	35.00	65.00	100	205

KM# 59 LIARD

Copper **Ruler:** Ferdinand **Obv:** Crowned arms in inner circle **Obv. Legend:** FERDINANDVS...REC **Rev:** Crown above F-R and double cross in inner circle **Rev. Legend:** FERDINANDVS. III. D. G. RO. IM **Note:** Varieties exist.

Date	Mintage	Good	VG	F	VF	XF
ND	—	15.00	30.00	60.00	90.00	180

KM# 60 LIARD

Copper **Ruler:** Ferdinand **Obv:** Crowned different arms in inner circle **Note:** Varieties exist.

Date	Mintage	Good	VG	F	VF	XF
ND	—	15.00	30.00	60.00	90.00	180

KM# 57 LIARD

Copper **Ruler:** Ferdinand **Obv:** Crowned bust of Emperor Ferdinand III left **Obv. Legend:** FERDINANDUS. DG. RO. IMP **Rev:** Crowned arms divide date in inner circle **Rev. Legend:** BARO. BORS. THIEN

Date	Mintage	Good	VG	F	VF	XF
1640	—	18.00	35.00	65.00	100	205
1641	—	18.00	35.00	65.00	100	205

KM# 55 LIARD

Copper **Ruler:** Ferdinand **Obv:** Crown above 3 shields of arms, 2 above 1 **Obv. Legend:** FERD. COM. DE. LIN. RECHEM **Rev:** Crowned arms divide date **Rev. Legend:** BARO. DE. BORS. THIEN

Date	Mintage	Good	VG	F	VF	XF
1640	—	15.00	30.00	60.00	90.00	180

KM# 63 LIARD

Copper **Ruler:** Ferdinand **Rev:** Date above crown

Date	Mintage	Good	VG	F	VF	XF
1640	—	15.00	30.00	60.00	90.00	180

KM# 66 LIARD

Copper **Ruler:** Ferdinand **Obv:** Crowned different arms divide date in inner circle **Obv. Legend:** F. C. ASPREM. ET. REC. Z **Rev. Legend:** DEVS. PROTECTOR. NOSTER **Note:** Varieties exist.

Date	Mintage	Good	VG	F	VF	XF
1644	—	15.00	30.00	60.00	90.00	180

KM# 80 LIARD
Copper **Ruler:** Ferdinand **Obv:** Bust of Ferdinand right **Obv. Legend:** MONETANOVA. COMITIS. AS. Z **Rev:** Crowned arms of Zeeland, date in legend at upper left **Rev. Legend:** DEVS. PROTECTOR. NOR 1657 **Note:** Varieties exist.

Date	Mintage	Good	VG	F	VF	XF
1657	—	12.00	25.00	50.00	85.00	175

KM# 81 LIARD
Copper **Ruler:** Ferdinand **Rev:** Crown divides date **Note:** Varieties exist.

Date	Mintage	Good	VG	F	VF	XF
1657	—	12.00	25.00	50.00	85.00	175

KM# 105 3 KREUZER
Billon **Ruler:** Ernst **Obv:** Crowned arms **Obv. Legend:** MONETA. NO. ARG. R. 3. D **Rev:** Crowned imperial eagle with value on breast **Rev. Legend:** FER. II. D. G. RO. IMP. S. AV

Date	Mintage	Good	VG	F	VF	XF
ND	—	90.00	175	325	600	—

KM# 4 SOL (1/2 Gros Stuiver)
Billon **Ruler:** Ernst **Obv:** St. Peter kneeling between 2 shields of arms in inner circle **Obv. Legend:** SS - PETRV-PATR **Rev:** Long cross with stars in angles in inner circle **Rev. Legend:** SIT NOMEN DOMINI BENEDICTVM E. C. D. R...SSI. S. W

Date	Mintage	Good	VG	F	VF	XF
ND	—	125	250	400	775	—

KM# 5 SOL (1/2 Gros Stuiver)
Billon **Ruler:** Ernst **Obv:** Crowned arms divide value (1-S) in inner circle **Obv. Legend:** E. C. ASPREMONT. REP **Rev:** Ornamental cross with rosette at center **Rev. Legend:** DEVS. PROT. ECTO. NOST **Note:** Varieties exist.

Date	Mintage	Good	VG	F	VF	XF
ND	—	65.00	125	200	425	—

KM# 6 SOL (1/2 Gros Stuiver)
Billon **Ruler:** Ferdinand **Obv:** Crowned arms **Obv. Legend:** F. C. ASPREMON...OS **Rev:** Ornate cross **Rev. Legend:** DEVS PROT-ECTO NOST

Date	Mintage	Good	VG	F	VF	XF
ND	—	65.00	125	200	425	—

KM# 7 SOL (1/2 Gros Stuiver)
Silver **Ruler:** Ferdinand **Obv:** Different arms

Date	Mintage	Good	VG	F	VF	XF
ND	—	65.00	125	200	425	—

KM# 8 2 SOLS (2 Stuiver Gros)
Billon **Ruler:** Ernst **Obv:** St. Peter kneeling between 2 shields of arms in inner circle **Obv. Legend:** S. S. PETRV-M PATRO **Rev:** Long cross with stars in angles in inner circle **Rev. Legend:** SIT. NOMEN. DNI. BENEDICTVM/ E. C. D. R. 1 ST. S. W **Note:** Varieties exist.

Date	Mintage	Good	VG	F	VF	XF
ND	—	150	300	500	925	—

KM# 9 3 SOLS (3 Stuiver)
Silver **Ruler:** Ernst **Obv:** Crowned arms in sprays **Obv. Legend:** ERNESTVS. COMES. IMP. RO...RE **Rev:** Floriated cross with lion at center in inner circle **Rev. Legend:** SIDERVS. PRONOBIS. QVIS. COR...

Date	Mintage	Good	VG	F	VF	XF
ND	—	60.00	120	200	425	—

KM# 10 4 SOLS (4 Stuivers)
Silver **Ruler:** Ernst **Obv:** Crowned arms in inner circle **Obv. Legend:** ERNESTVS. DE. LVNDEN. LI **Rev:** Crowned double-headed eagle in inner circle **Rev. Legend:** BARON. IMPEV. IN. RECH. IIII-ST **Note:** Varieties exist.

Date	Mintage	Good	VG	F	VF	XF
ND	—	75.00	150	300	550	950

KM# 12 4 SOLS (4 Stuivers)
Silver **Ruler:** Ernst **Rev:** Different arms **Note:** Varieties exist.

Date	Mintage	Good	VG	F	VF	XF
ND	—	50.00	100	200	350	700

KM# 11 4 SOLS (4 Stuivers)
Silver **Ruler:** Ernst **Obv:** Crowned double-headed eagle in inner circle **Obv. Legend:** MATH. II. D. G. ROM. IMP. SEMP. AVGV **Rev:** Different crowned arms in inner circle **Rev. Legend:** MO: NO: ARG. RECHEIM. IIII. ST

Date	Mintage	Good	VG	F	VF	XF
ND	—	40.00	85.00	165	285	550

KM# 33 4 SOLS (4 Stuivers)
Silver **Ruler:** Ernst **Obv:** Crowned double-headed eagle in inner circle **Obv. Legend:** FERDINAN. II. D. E. ROM. IMP. SE. AUG **Rev:** Crowned different arms divide date in inner circle **Rev. Legend:** ERNESTVS. COMES. DE. RECHEIM **Note:** Varieties exist.

Date	Mintage	Good	VG	F	VF	XF
1626	—	60.00	120	250	400	750

KM# 35 1/3 ESCALIN (Peerdeken)
Billon **Ruler:** Ernst **Obv:** RECM in exergue **Rev:** Different arms on cross

Date	Mintage	Good	VG	F	VF	XF
ND	—	50.00	100	165	325	—

KM# 34 1/3 ESCALIN (Peerdeken)
Billon **Ruler:** Ernst **Obv:** Knight on horseback brandishing sword to right in inner circle, REHM in exergue **Rev:** Arms on cross in inner circle **Rev. Legend:** MONET. A. NOVA-RECH-MENSIS **Note:** Varieties exist.

Date	Mintage	Good	VG	F	VF	XF
ND	—	50.00	100	165	325	—

KM# 36 ESCALIN
Silver **Ruler:** Ernst **Obv:** Rampant lion to left holding sword and shield in inner circle **Obv. Legend:** ERNESTVS. DE. IS. ER. COMES **Rev:** Crowned arms divide date in inner circle **Rev. Legend:** IMPERI-ALIS. IN. RECHEM

Date	Mintage	Good	VG	F	VF	XF
1626	—	90.00	180	300	575	—

KM# 43 ESCALIN
Silver **Ruler:** Ernst **Obv:** Crowned arms in branchs in inner circle, date above crown **Rev:** Floreated cross in inner circle **Rev. Legend:** DEVS. FORTI. ET. SPES-NOSTR

Date	Mintage	Good	VG	F	VF	XF
1629	—	60.00	120	200	425	—

KM# 50 ESCALIN
Silver **Ruler:** Ernst **Obv:** Rampant lion left holding sword and shield in inner circle **Obv. Legend:** MONETA. NOVA. COM. R. DEVS. MEVS. ADIVTOR **Rev:** Crowned different arms divide date in inner circle **Rev. Legend:** ER-NESTVS-COM-ES. IM. DR-C **Note:** Varieites exist.

Date	Mintage	Good	VG	F	VF	XF
1636	—	75.00	150	250	475	—

KM# 65 ESCALIN
Silver **Ruler:** Ferdinand **Obv. Legend:** FERDINANDVS. ET. ELISABETH. CO **Rev:** Arms similar to those of Spain divides date **Rev. Legend:** VISA. IN. NIMOD

Date	Mintage	Good	VG	F	VF	XF
1640	—	60.00	120	200	425	—

KM# 38 PATARD
Silver **Ruler:** Ferdinand **Obv:** Crowned arms without inner circle **Rev:** Ornate cross **Rev. Legend:** MONE NOVA ARGE RECH

Date	Mintage	Good	VG	F	VF	XF
ND	—	50.00	100	185	350	—

KM# 37 PATARD
Silver **Ruler:** Ferdinand **Obv:** Crowned arms in inner circle **Obv. Legend:** FERDINANDVS. CO. IN. RE(C)HEI **Rev:** Ornate cruciform **Rev. Legend:** DEVS. PROT. ECTO. NOST **Note:** Varieties exist.

Date	Mintage	Good	VG	F	VF	XF
ND	—	50.00	100	185	350	—

KM# 39 FLORIN (Gulden - 24 Mariengroschen)
Silver **Ruler:** Ferdinand **Obv:** Shield of arms with 3 helmets above **Obv. Legend:** FRANC. ET. FERD. FRAT. COM. IN. ASPERM. ET. RECKE **Rev:** XXIII / MARIEN / GROSCHEN at center **Rev. Legend:** GRAFL. RECKHEIM. MVNT

Date	Mintage	Good	VG	F	VF	XF
ND	—	—	—	—	—	—

KM# 40 1/16 THALER (1/16 Daalder-Peerdeken)
Billon **Ruler:** Ernst **Obv:** Crowned arms divide date in inner circle **Obv. Legend:** ERNESTVS. COMES. DE. RECHE M **Rev:** Crowned imperial eagle with value on breast in inner circle **Rev. Legend:** FERDINAN. II. DG. RO. IM. SEM. AV

Date	Mintage	Good	VG	F	VF	XF
16Z6	—	85.00	165	275	525	—

KM# 24 1/4 THALER (1/4 Daalder)
Silver **Ruler:** Ernst **Obv:** Crowned arms divide in inner circle **Obv. Legend:** ERNESTVS. DE. LYNDEN. LI. BA. IN. IM. R **Rev:** Crowned imperial eagle **Rev. Legend:** FERDINAND. II. D. G. RO. IM. S. AU

Date	Mintage	Good	VG	F	VF	XF
1619	—	120	225	345	550	950

KM# A13 1/4 THALER (1/4 Daalder)
Silver **Ruler:** Ernst **Obv:** Helmeted arms **Obv. Legend:** (Heart) ERNESTVS. DE LYNDEN. LI. BA. IN. R. **Rev:** Crowned imperial eagle **Rev. Legend:** FERDINAND. II. DG. RO. IM. S. AV.

Date	Mintage	Good	VG	F	VF	XF
ND(1619-36)	—	—	—	—	—	—

KM# 101 2/3 THALER (2/3 Daalder)
Silver **Ruler:** Francois and Ferdinand Gobert **Obv:** Bust of Francois-Gobert to right **Obv. Legend:** OMNIA. FORTITVDINE: ST. PRVDSENTIA **Rev:** Crowned arms in palm branches, date above crown **Rev. Legend:** FR. G. ET. FERG. COM. DE. A. ET. R. FR

Date	Mintage	Good	VG	F	VF	XF
1687 Rare	—	—	—	—	—	—

KM# 31 THALER (Daalder)
Silver **Ruler:** Ernst **Obv:** Helmeted arms **Obv. Legend:** ERNESTVS. DE. LYNDEN. LI: BA: IMP. IN. REC **Rev:** Crowned double-headed eagle in inner circle **Rev. Legend:** MATHIAS. D. G. ELEC. ROM. IMP. SEMP-AVE **Note:** Dav. #4505.

Date	Mintage	Good	VG	F	VF	XF
ND Rare	—	—	—	—	—	—

KM# 32 THALER (Daalder)
Silver **Ruler:** Ernst **Obv:** Helmeted arms **Obv. Legend:** ERNESTVS. DE. LYNDEN. L. B. A. IMP. RECHEM **Rev:** Crowned imperial eagle, crown divides date **Rev. Legend:** FERDINANDVS. II. D. G. ROM. IM. SEM. AV **Note:** Dav. #4507.

Date	Mintage	Good	VG	F	VF	XF
16Z0 Rare	—	—	—	—	—	—

KM# 28 2 THALER (2 Daalder)
Silver **Ruler:** Ernst **Obv:** Helmeted arms **Obv. Legend:** ERNESTVS. DE. LYNDEN. LI: BA: IMP. IN. REC **Rev:** Crowned imperial eagle **Rev. Legend:** MATHIAS. D. G. ELEC. ROM. IMP. SEMP-AVE **Note:** Dav. #4504.

Date	Mintage	Good	VG	F	VF	XF
ND Rare	—	—	—	—	—	—

KM# 29 2 THALER (2 Daalder)
Silver **Ruler:** Ernst **Obv:** Helmeted arms **Obv. Legend:** ERNESTVS. DE. LYNDEN. L. B. A. IMP. RECHEM **Rev:** Crowned imperial eagle, crown divides date **Rev. Legend:** FERDINANDVS. II. D. G. ROM. IM. SEM. AV **Note:** Klippe. Dav. #4506.

Date	Mintage	Good	VG	F	VF	XF
16Z0 Rare	—	—	—	—	—	—

TRADE COINAGE

KM# 42 GOLDGULDEN (Florin D'or)
3.5000 g., 0.9860 Gold 0.1109 oz. AGW **Ruler:** Ferdinand **Obv:** Soldier standing left with banner **Obv. Legend:** FERD: ASPREMON: LIND: RECHEIM. COM. **Rev:** Helmeted arms **Rev. Legend:** BEAT. GOB. COM.-ASPEREMON **Note:** Fr.#232b.

Date	Mintage	Good	VG	F	VF	XF
ND	—	350	650	1,250	2,500	4,500

Ancient home of Scythian tribes and known under the Romans as Albania and to the Arabs as Arran, the country of Azerbaijan was formed at the time of its invasion by Seliuk Turks and grew into a prosperous state under Persian suzerainty. From the 16th century the country was a theatre of fighting and political rivalry between Turkey, Persia and later Russia. Baku was first annexed to Russia by Czar Peter I in 1723 and remained under Russian rule for 12 years. After the Russian retreat the whole of Azerbaijan north of the Aras River became a khanate under Persian control. Czar Alexander I, after an eight-year war with Persia, annexed it in 1813 to the Russian empire.

RULERS

Mehmed III, AH1003-1012/1595-1603AD
Ahmed I, AH1012-1026/1603-1617AD

MINT NAMES

گنجه

Ganja (Elisabethpol, Kirovabad)

نخجوان

Nakhjavan

شماخي شماخه

Shemakhi

شيروان شروان

Shirvan

OTTOMAN

Mehmed III

HAMMERED COINAGE

MB# 26 BESLIK
2.0500 g., Silver **Obv:** Toughra **Rev:** Perso-Turkish-*duribe-Nackhchawan* **Mint:** Nakhjavan

Date	Mintage	Good	VG	F	VF	XF
AHxxxx	—	65.00	120	200	225	—

MB# 35 BESLIK
1.8200 g., Silver **Mint:** Shemakhi

Date	Mintage	Good	VG	F	VF	XF
AH1003	—	125	225	400	—	—
AHxxxx	—	125	225	400	—	—

MB# 36 BESLIK
1.8000 g., Silver **Obv:** Toughra **Rev:** Stylized fish, Perso-Turkish-*duribe Shamakhi* **Mint:** Shemakhi

Date	Mintage	Good	VG	F	VF	XF
AHxxxx	—	125	225	400	—	—

MB# 45 BESLIK
1.8000 g., Silver **Obv:** Toughra **Rev:** Perso-Turkish-*duribe Shirvan* **Mint:** Ganja

Date	Mintage	Good	VG	F	VF	XF
AHxxxx Rare	—	—	—	—	—	—

MB# 25 BESLIK
Silver **Obv:** Toughra **Rev:** Perso-Turkish-*duribe-Nackhchawan* **Mint:** Nakhjavan **Note:** Weight varies 1.92-1.97 grams.

Date	Mintage	Good	VG	F	VF	XF
AHxxxx	—	65.00	120	200	225	—

Ahmed I

HAMMERED COINAGE

MB# 56 BESLIK
1.8000 g., Silver **Obv:** Toughra **Rev:** Perso-Turkish-*duribe Shirvan* **Mint:** Shirvan **Note:** Varieties exist.

Date	Mintage	Good	VG	F	VF	XF
AHxxx	—	80.00	150	400	—	—

MB# 22 BESLIK
Silver **Obv:** Toughra **Rev:** Perso-Turkish-*duriba Shirvan* **Mint:** Shirvan **Note:** Weight varies 1.40-1.80 grams. Size varies 24-25 millimeters. Varieties of obverse exist.

Date	Mintage	Good	VG	F	VF	XF
AH1012	—	80.00	150	400	—	—
AHxxxx	—	80.00	150	400	—	—
AH1013	—	80.00	150	400	—	—
AH1014	—	80.00	150	400	—	—

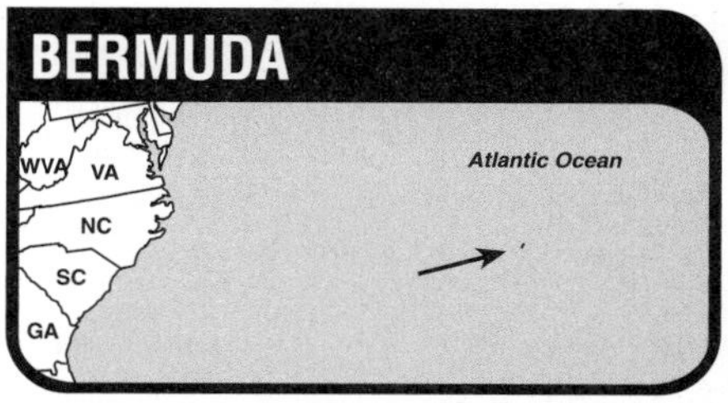

Situated in the western Atlantic Ocean 660 miles (1,062 km.) east of North Carolina, has an area of 20.6 sq. mi. (53 sq. km).

Bermuda was discovered by Juan de Bermudez, a Spanish navigator, in about 1503. British influence dates from 1609 when a group of Virginia-bound British colonists under the command of Sir George Somers was shipwrecked on the islands for 10 months. The islands were settled in 1612 by 60 British colonists from the Virginia Colony and became a crown colony in 1684. The earliest coins issued for the island were the "Hogge Money" series of 2, 3, 6 and 12 pence, the name derived from the pig in the obverse design, a recognition of the quantity of such animals then found there. The next issue for Bermuda was the Birmingham coppers of 1793; all locally circulating coinage was demonetized in 1842, when the currency of the United Kingdom became standard. Internal autonomy was obtained by the constitution of June 8, 1968.

BRITISH COLONY

HOGGE MONEY COINAGE

Coins of great rarity, sometimes known as "Hogge" money. Undated and struck in brass (or a brass alloy), originally silver washed, the Bermuda atmospheric conditions soon removed any trace of silver. Coins with a silver trace are of very great rarity. It has been alleged that denominations of one penny and four pence exist, but these are unknown.

KM# 1 2 PENCE (II Pence)
1.7000 g., Brass **Issuer:** Sommer Islands Company **Obv:** Hog standing facing left, II above **Rev:** Two-masted sailing ship between S and I

Date	Mintage	Good	VG	F	VF	XF
ND(c.1616) *16-18 known	—	—	—	—	—	—

Note: Stack's John J. Ford, Jr. Part XVIII, 5-07, VF-25 realized $86,250

KM# 2 3 PENCE (III Pence)
1.9600 g., Brass **Issuer:** Sommer Islands Company **Obv:** Hog standing facing left, III above **Rev:** Two-masted sailing ship between S and I

Date	Mintage	Good	VG	F	VF	XF
ND(c.1616) Rare	—	—	—	—	—	—

KM# 3 6 PENCE (VI Pence)
3.8000 g., Brass **Issuer:** Sommer Islands Company **Obv:** Hog facing left, VI above within circle **Obv. Legend:** SOMMER * ILANDS * **Rev:** Three-masted sailing ship, large portholes

Date	Mintage	Good	VG	F	VF	XF
ND(c.1616) *37 known	—	—	—	—	—	—

Note: Heritage Long Beach sale, 5-08, AU-50 realized $43,125; Spink sale 5010, 6-05, VF-XF realized $15,235

KM# 4 6 PENCE (VI Pence)
3.8000 g., Brass **Issuer:** Sommer Islands Company **Rev:** Small portholes

Date	Mintage	Good	VG	F	VF	XF
ND(c.1616)	—	—	—	—	—	—

Note: A combined total of *37 examples of all VI Pence are known

KM# A5 12 PENCE (XII Pence)
5.8600 g., Brass **Issuer:** Sommer Islands Company **Obv:** Hog facing left, XII above within circle **Obv. Legend:** SOMMER * ILANDS * **Rev:** Three-masted sailing ship with three small sails

Date	Mintage	Good	VG	F	VF	XF
ND(c.1616) *18 Known	—	—	—	—	—	—

KM# A6 12 PENCE (XII Pence)
5.8600 g., Brass **Issuer:** Sommer Islands Company **Rev:** Large sails

Date	Mintage	Good	VG	F	VF	XF
ND(c.1616) *6 known	—	—	—	—	—	—

Note: Stack's John J. Ford, Jr. Part XVIII, 5-07, EF-40 realized $109,250

Böhmen

The large and important Kingdom of Bohemia is located in Central Europe between Bavaria and Austria on the south, Saxony and Silesia on the north, Franconia and the Upper Palatinate to the west, and the Margraviate of Moravia to the east. The region was early settled by the Celtic Boii and controlled by the Czechs, a Slavic people, from the fifth century. Bohemia was at first a duchy and produced a series of rulers dating from the late 9th century. The first hereditary king was Wladislaw II, who ruled 1140-1173. During the later Middle Ages, the kingdom was acquired through marriage to various dynasties of the region, notably the Margraves of Moravia, the Electors of Brandenburg and emperors as well. By the late 15th century, the ruler was another Wladislaw II, a son of the King of Poland, and he was also the King of Hungary. His son, Ludwig, was killed in 1526 at the Battle of Mohacz, fighting against the Turks. His sister was the wife of Emperor Ferdinand I and thus, Bohemia passed to the Hapsburgs.

Bohemia, however, was an electoral monarchy and the king was chosen by the leading nobles at the capital, Prague. In most instances, the succession of one emperor to the next made electing the new emperor as king of Bohemia a mere formality. Very often, the heir apparent to the emperor was elected King of Bohemia prior to his father's passing. By the early 17th century, Protestantism had made great inroads among the Czech nobility and anti-Catholic/anti-Hapsburg sentiments were at a peak. Before Emperor Matthias died in 1619, the nobles had been forced to elect Archduke Ferdinand (II) in 1617. When two governors, appointed by Matthias, were thrown from a window of the palace in Prague in May 1618, in what became known as the Defenestration of Prague, the event precipitated a revolt by the Bohemian Estates (Die böhmischen Stände). The Estates were constituted of the noble lords, the knights and the cities, who deposed Emperor Ferdinand II as king and elected the Protestant Friedrich V, Count Palatine and Elector of the Rhine, in his place. Hostilities had already begun between some of the Protestant German princes and the Emperor, but the elevation of Friedrich to the Bohemian throne galvanized imperial resolve and made the new king's reign very short. Coinage was struck under the authority of firstly, the Estates, and then King Friedrich. The Hapsburgs regained Bohemia in 1620 and except for the later short reign of Karl Albrecht of Bavaria in 1741-42, continued until 1918, although it ceased to be viewed as a separate entity after the dissolution of the Holy Roman Empire by Napoleon in 1806.

RULERS

Ludwig, 1516-1626
Rudolf II, 1572-1612
Matthias, 1612-19
Friedrich von der Pfalz, 1619-20
Ferdinand II, 1620-37
Ferdinand III, 1637-57
Leopold I, 1657-1705

MINT MARKS

A – Vienna Mint
(c) – crossed hammers, 1695, 1711-12
S – Schmöllnitz Mint

BUDWEIS MINT

MINT OFFICIALS' INITIALS & PRIVY MARKS

Letters or Initials	Privy mark	Date	Name
(bf)=	Dog's head left in shield	1584-1611	Christoph Mattighofer, mintmaster
(bg)=	Dog's head left, but not in shield	1584-1611	Christoph Mattifghofer, mintmaster

ARMS

Crowned lion rampant, usually to left.

GLATZ MINT

(in Bohemia)

Coat of arms, like Vienna, on imperial eagle's breast, legends end like Breslau. This mint closed in 1660.

MINT MARKS

G, g, Glatz, 1628

MINT OFFICIALS' INITIALS and PRIVY MARKS

Initials	Dates	Names
AP	1627-28	Andreas Peter, die-cutter
G	1637-38	-
GW	1658-60	Georg Werner
HG	1629	Huser Glacensis, die-cutter
IR	1632	-
O	1636	Vacant

Privy Mark	Description	Dates	Names
(b)=	Circles in circle with wavy line	1627-28	Johann Jacob Huser
(r)=	Ligate HR	1631-36	Hans Rossner
(h)=	HP monogram	1628-31	Peter Hema

JOACHIMSTHAL MINT

Letters or Initials	Privy marks	Date	Name
(ah)=	Double fleur de lis in circle	1600-04	Christoph Taubenreutter, mintmaster
(ai)=		1604-06	Hans Gipfel, mintmaster
(aj)=	Lion's head left	1606-20	Centurio Lengefelder, mintmaster
(ak)=	Bird's wing	1621-37	Gregor Steinmüller, mintmaster
(al)=		1637-49	David Knobloch, mintmaster
(am)=	Bird flying left	1649-50	Johann Freistein, mintmaster
(an)=	Crown	1650-68	Johann Jakob Kittner, mintmaster
(ao)=		1668-70	Paul Wenzel Seling, mintmaster

KUTTENBERG MINT

Letters or Initials	Privy mark	Date	Name
(y)=	Goat's head left	1599-1603	Hans Spiess, mintmaster
(z)=	Eagle's head left in circle or shield	1603-1608	David Enderle, mintmaster
(aa)=		1608-12	Paul Skréta Sotnovsky von Závorice, mintmaster
(bb)=		1612-13	Johann Sultys, mintmaster
(cc)=	Bird left holding pole over wing	1614-15	August Schmilauer, mintmaster
(dd)=		1616-17, 1632-33	Vacant mintmaster's position
(ee)=		1617-32	Sebastian Hölzl, mintmaster
(ff)=		1633-35	Hans Prunz, mintmaster
(gg)=		1635	Lorenz Neumann, mint contractor
(hh)=	Arm left holding 3 arrows	1636-43	Daniel Kavka, mintmaster
(ii)=	Arm left holding hammer	1651-77	Gregor Hackl, mintmaster
(jj)=	CK or CK	1677-1702	Christoph Kroh, mintmaster

PRAGUE MINT

(Praha)
(in Bohemia)

Coat of arms on imperial eagle's breast. Legend usually ends BO, BOH, BOHEMIAE REX

Letters or Initials	Privy marks	Date	Name
(j)=		1600-09	Hans Lasanz, mintmaster
(k)=	Bird's wing	1609-10	Samuel Salvart, mintmaster
(l)=		1610-30	Benedikt Huebiner, mintmaster
(m)=		1619-20	Skréta Sotnovsky, mintmaster
(n)=	Upper half of griffin left	1623-25	Hans Suttner, mintmaster
(o)=	Boar's head right, I behind	1630-31	Eliseus du Bois, mintmaster
(p)=		1631-37	Tobias Schuster, mintmaster
(q)=		1637-66	Jakob W. Wolker, mintmaster
(qx)=		Used in 1651 only	Jakob W. Wolker
(r)=		1655-62	Christoph Margolik, mintmaster
(s)=		1668-88	Anton von Janinalli, mintmaster
(t)=	Crown and/or MV	1688-94	Matthias Vaist, mintmaster
PM		1694, 1710-11	Prague mint, during vacancies
GE		1694-1710	Gregor Egerer, mintmaster

KINGDOM

STANDARD COINAGE

MB# 238 HELLER

Silver **Ruler:** Rudolf II **Mint:** Kuttenberg **Note:** Uniface. Crowned R divides date. Varieties exist.

Date	Mintage	VG	F	VF	XF	Unc
1606	—	35.00	70.00	145	250	—

MB# 280 HELLER

Silver **Ruler:** Rudolf II **Mint:** Prague **Note:** Uniface. Crowned R divides date.

Date	Mintage	VG	F	VF	XF	Unc
1583 (i)	—	—	—	—	—	—

MB# 331 HELLER

Silver **Ruler:** Rudolf II **Obv:** Crowned R divides R - B, date below **Mint:** Kuttenberg **Note:** Uniface.

Date	Mintage	VG	F	VF	XF	Unc
1601	—	30.00	60.00	125	200	—
160Z	—	30.00	60.00	125	200	—
1603	—	30.00	60.00	125	200	—
1604	—	30.00	60.00	125	200	—
1605	—	30.00	60.00	125	200	—
1606	—	30.00	60.00	125	200	—
1607	—	30.00	60.00	125	200	—
1608	—	30.00	60.00	125	200	—
1609	—	30.00	60.00	125	200	—
1610	—	30.00	60.00	125	200	—
1611	—	30.00	60.00	125	200	—
161Z	—	30.00	60.00	125	200	—

KM# 150 HELLER

Silver **Ruler:** Matthias II **Obv:** Crowned M divides R - B, date below **Mint:** Kuttenberg **Note:** Uniface. Prev. KM#1045.

Date	Mintage	VG	F	VF	XF	Unc
1613	—	30.00	60.00	125	200	—
1614	—	30.00	60.00	125	200	—
1615	—	30.00	60.00	125	200	—
1616	—	30.00	60.00	125	200	—
1617	—	30.00	60.00	125	200	—
1618	—	30.00	60.00	125	200	—
1619	—	30.00	60.00	125	200	—

MB# 246 PFENNIG

Silver **Ruler:** Rudolf II **Obv:** Crowned Bohemian lion left in circle, date **Obv. Legend:** RVDOL. SECVN **Mint:** Kuttenberg **Note:** Uniface. Prev. KM#1016.

Date	Mintage	VG	F	VF	XF	Unc
1601	—	10.00	20.00	35.00	65.00	—
1602	—	10.00	20.00	35.00	65.00	—
1603	—	10.00	20.00	35.00	65.00	—
1604	—	10.00	20.00	35.00	65.00	—
1607	—	10.00	20.00	35.00	65.00	—
1608	—	10.00	20.00	35.00	65.00	—
1609	—	10.00	20.00	35.00	65.00	—
1610	—	10.00	20.00	35.00	65.00	—
1611	—	10.00	20.00	35.00	65.00	—

KM# 12 PFENNIG

Silver **Ruler:** Rudolf II **Obv:** Crowned Bohemian lion left in inner circle **Rev:** Date in center of empty field **Mint:** Joachimstal **Note:** Prev. KM#860.

Date	Mintage	VG	F	VF	XF	Unc
1602 (ah)	—	12.00	25.00	45.00	75.00	—

KM# 13 PFENNIG

Silver **Ruler:** Rudolf II **Obv:** Crowned Bohemian lion left in inner circle, date **Obv. Legend:** RVDOL. II. D.G... **Mint:** Kuttenberg **Note:** Klippe. Prev. KM#1017.

Date	Mintage	VG	F	VF	XF	Unc
1601	—	—	—	—	—	—

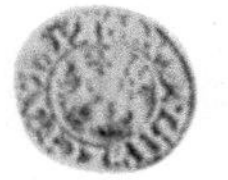

KM# 108 PFENNIG

Silver **Ruler:** Matthias II **Obv:** Crowned Bohemian lion left in circle, date **Obv. Legend:** MATHI. SECVN. **Mint:** Kuttenberg **Note:** Uniface. Prev. KM#1046.

Date	Mintage	VG	F	VF	XF	Unc
1612	—	25.00	45.00	100	180	—

KM# 175 PFENNIG

Silver **Ruler:** Matthias II **Obv:** Lion right, date **Obv. Legend:** MATTHIAS. R.B. **Mint:** Kuttenberg **Note:** Prev. KM#1047.

Date	Mintage	VG	F	VF	XF	Unc
1615	—	25.00	45.00	100	180	—
1616	—	25.00	45.00	100	180	—

KM# 202 PFENNIG

Silver **Ruler:** Matthias II **Obv:** Lion left **Mint:** Kuttenberg **Note:** Prev. KM#1048.

Date	Mintage	VG	F	VF	XF	Unc
1617	—	25.00	45.00	100	180	—
1618	—	25.00	45.00	100	180	—
1619	—	25.00	45.00	100	180	—

KM# 207 PFENNIG

Silver **Ruler:** Matthias II **Obv:** Legend, date **Obv. Legend:** MATTHIAS. R.H.B. **Mint:** Kuttenberg **Note:** Prev. KM#1049.

Date	Mintage	VG	F	VF	XF	Unc
1618	—	25.00	45.00	100	180	—

MB# 233 GROSCHEN

Silver **Ruler:** Rudolf II **Obv:** Bohemian lion left, titles of Rudolf II **Rev:** Crowned imperial eagle **Mint:** Kuttenberg **Note:** Varieties exist. Prev. KM#1020.

Date	Mintage	VG	F	VF	XF	Unc
1601 (y)	—	16.00	32.00	60.00	100	—
1602 (y)	—	16.00	32.00	60.00	100	—
1603 (z)	—	16.00	32.00	60.00	100	—
1604 (z)	—	16.00	32.00	60.00	100	—
1605 (z)	—	16.00	32.00	60.00	100	—
1608 (z)	—	16.00	32.00	60.00	100	—
1609 (z)	—	16.00	32.00	60.00	100	—
1609 (aa)	—	16.00	32.00	60.00	100	—
1610 (aa)	—	16.00	32.00	60.00	100	—

MB# 251 GROSCHEN

Silver **Ruler:** Rudolf II **Obv:** Bohemian lion left, titles of Rudolf II **Rev:** Crowned imperial eagle **Mint:** Prague **Note:** Varieties exist. Prev. KM#1296.

Date	Mintage	VG	F	VF	XF	Unc
1601 (j)	—	20.00	35.00	55.00	90.00	—
1604 (j)	—	20.00	35.00	55.00	90.00	—
1605 (j)	—	20.00	35.00	55.00	90.00	—

MB# 260 GROSCHEN

Silver **Ruler:** Rudolf II **Obv:** Bohemian lion left **Obv. Legend:** * RVDOL • II • D G - R • I • S • A • G • H • B O • R **Rev:** Crowned imperial eagle **Rev. Legend:** ARCHID • AVST • DVX • B • M • M • **Shape:** Square **Mint:** Kuttenberg **Note:** Klippe. Prev. KM#1021.

Date	Mintage	VG	F	VF	XF	Unc
1604 (z)	—	—	—	—	—	—

KM# 155 GROSCHEN

Silver **Ruler:** Matthias II **Obv:** Crowned Bohemian lion left in circle, titles of Matthias **Rev:** Crowned imperial eagle, Austria-Burgundy arms on breast, date in legend **Mint:** Prague **Note:** Prev. KM#1383.

Date	Mintage	VG	F	VF	XF	Unc
1613 (l)	—	12.00	25.00	40.00	75.00	—
1615 (l)	—	12.00	25.00	40.00	75.00	—
1616 (l)	—	12.00	25.00	40.00	75.00	—
1617 (l)	—	12.00	25.00	40.00	75.00	—
1618 (l)	—	12.00	25.00	40.00	75.00	—
1619 (l)	—	12.00	25.00	40.00	75.00	—
ND (l)	—	12.00	25.00	40.00	75.00	—

KM# 178 GROSCHEN

Silver **Ruler:** Matthias II **Obv:** Crowned Bohemian lion left **Rev:** Crowned imperial eagle **Mint:** Joachimstal **Note:** Prev. KM#880.

Date	Mintage	VG	F	VF	XF	Unc
1615 (aj)	—	35.00	75.00	145	275	—
1617 (aj)	—	35.00	75.00	145	275	—
1618 (aj)	—	35.00	75.00	145	275	—

KM# 192 GROSCHEN

Silver **Ruler:** Matthias II **Obv:** Crowned Bohemian lion left **Rev:** Crowned imperial eagle **Mint:** Kuttenberg **Note:** Prev. KM#1052.

Date	Mintage	VG	F	VF	XF	Unc
1616 (dd)	—	12.00	25.00	40.00	75.00	—
1617 (ee)	—	12.00	25.00	40.00	75.00	—
1618 (ee)	—	12.00	25.00	40.00	75.00	—
1619 (ee)	—	12.00	25.00	40.00	75.00	—

MB# 240 MALEY GROSCHEN

Silver **Ruler:** Rudolf II **Obv:** Crowned Bohemian lion left in circle, titles of Rudolf II **Rev:** Crowned R, value, and date **Mint:** Prague **Note:** Prev. KM#1295.

Date	Mintage	VG	F	VF	XF	Unc
1601 (j)	—	14.00	22.50	42.00	85.00	—
160Z (j)	—	14.00	22.50	42.00	85.00	—
1604 (j)	—	14.00	22.50	42.00	85.00	—
1605 (j)	—	14.00	22.50	42.00	85.00	—
1606 (j)	—	14.00	22.50	42.00	85.00	—
1609 (j)	—	14.00	22.50	42.00	85.00	—
1609 (k)	—	14.00	22.50	42.00	85.00	—

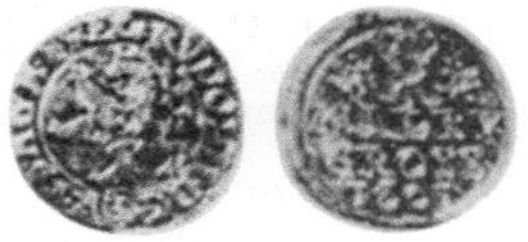

MB# 241 MALEY GROSCHEN

Silver **Ruler:** Rudolf II **Obv:** Crowned Bohemian lion left in circle, titles of Rudolf II **Rev:** Crowned R, value, and date **Mint:** Joachimstal **Note:** Prev. KM#861.

Date	Mintage	VG	F	VF	XF	Unc
1601 (ag)	—	5.00	10.00	22.00	45.00	—
1601 (ah)	—	5.00	10.00	22.00	45.00	—
ND (ag)	—	5.00	10.00	22.00	45.00	—
1602 (ah)	—	5.00	10.00	22.00	45.00	—
1603 (ah)	—	5.00	10.00	22.00	45.00	—
1604 (ah)	—	5.00	10.00	22.00	45.00	—
1606 (aj)	—	10.00	20.00	35.00	65.00	—
1607 (aj)	—	10.00	20.00	35.00	65.00	—
1608 (aj)	—	10.00	20.00	35.00	65.00	—
1609 (aj)	—	10.00	20.00	35.00	65.00	—
1610 (aj)	—	10.00	20.00	35.00	65.00	—
1611 (aj)	—	10.00	20.00	35.00	65.00	—
161Z (aj)	—	10.00	20.00	35.00	65.00	—

MB# 250 MALEY GROSCHEN

Silver **Ruler:** Rudolf II **Obv:** Crowned Bohemian lion left in circle, titles of Rudolf II **Rev:** Crowned R, value, and date **Mint:** Kuttenberg **Note:** Varieties exist. Prev. KM#1018.

Date	Mintage	VG	F	VF	XF	Unc
1601 (y)	—	5.00	12.00	30.00	55.00	—
160Z (y)	—	5.00	12.00	30.00	55.00	—
1603 (y)	—	5.00	12.00	30.00	55.00	—
1603 (z)	—	4.00	8.00	20.00	38.00	—
1604 (z)	—	4.00	8.00	20.00	38.00	—
1605 (z)	—	4.00	8.00	20.00	38.00	—
1606 (z)	—	4.00	8.00	20.00	38.00	—
1607 (z)	—	4.00	8.00	20.00	38.00	—
1608 (aa)	—	4.00	8.00	20.00	38.00	—
1608 (z)	—	4.00	8.00	20.00	38.00	—
1609 (aa)	—	4.00	8.00	20.00	38.00	—
1610 (aa)	—	4.00	8.00	20.00	38.00	—
1611 (aa)	—	4.00	8.00	20.00	38.00	—
161Z	—	4.00	8.00	20.00	38.00	—

MB# 269 MALEY GROSCHEN

Silver **Ruler:** Rudolf II **Obv:** Bohemian lion rampant left in circle **Obv. Legend:** RVDOL.II.D.G.-R.I.S.A.G.H.B.R. **Rev:** Crowned 'R' between two floral ornaments, three-line inscription with date below. **Rev. Inscription:** MALEY/GROSS/(date) **Mint:** Kuttenberg **Note:** Klippe. Prev. KM#1019.

Date	Mintage	VG	F	VF	XF	Unc
1606 (z)	—	—	—	—	—	—
1607 (z)	—	—	—	—	—	—

MB# 298 MALEY GROSCHEN

Silver **Ruler:** Rudolf II **Mint:** Joachimstal **Note:** Klippe. Prev. KM#864.

Date	Mintage	VG	F	VF	XF	Unc
1607 (aj)	—	—	—	—	—	—
1609 (aj)	—	—	—	—	—	—
1611 (aj)	—	—	—	—	—	—

KM# 47 MALEY GROSCHEN

Silver **Ruler:** Rudolf II **Rev:** Crowned R divides date, value below **Mint:** Joachimstal **Note:** Prev. KM#862.

Date	Mintage	VG	F	VF	XF	Unc
1604 (ai)	—	16.00	32.00	55.00	100	—
1605 (ai)	—	16.00	32.00	55.00	100	—
1606 (ai)	—	16.00	32.00	55.00	100	—

KM# 48 MALEY GROSCHEN

Silver **Ruler:** Rudolf II **Mint:** Joachimstal **Note:** Klippe. Prev. KM#863.

Date	Mintage	VG	F	VF	XF	Unc
1604 (ai)	—	—	—	—	—	—

KM# 76 MALEY GROSCHEN

Silver **Ruler:** Rudolf II **Mint:** Kuttenberg **Note:** Klippe. Prev. KM#1019.

Date	Mintage	VG	F	VF	XF	Unc
1606	—	—	—	—	—	—
1607	—	—	—	—	—	—

KM# 75 MALEY GROSCHEN

Silver **Ruler:** Rudolf II **Obv:** Crowned Bohemian lion left in circle, titles of Rudolf II **Rev. Legend:** ZVM / NEVEN / IAHR / date **Mint:** Prague **Note:** New Year Commemorative

Date	Mintage	VG	F	VF	XF	Unc
1606 (j)	—	—	—	—	—	—

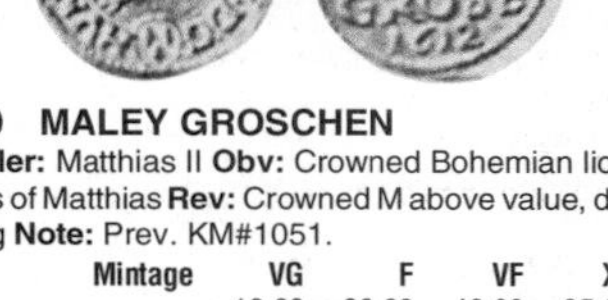

KM# 110 MALEY GROSCHEN

Silver **Ruler:** Matthias II **Obv:** Crowned Bohemian lion left in circle, titles of Matthias **Rev:** Crowned M above value, date **Mint:** Kuttenberg **Note:** Prev. KM#1051.

Date	Mintage	VG	F	VF	XF	Unc
1612 (bb)	—	12.00	22.00	40.00	85.00	—
1613 (bb)	—	12.00	22.00	40.00	85.00	—
1614 (bb)	—	12.00	22.00	40.00	85.00	—

KM# 111 MALEY GROSCHEN

Silver **Ruler:** Matthias II **Obv:** Crowned M divides date, value below **Mint:** Joachimstal **Note:** Prev. KM#879.

Date	Mintage	VG	F	VF	XF	Unc
1612 (aj)	—	30.00	60.00	125	245	—

KM# 153 MALEY GROSCHEN

Silver **Ruler:** Matthias II **Obv:** Crowned Bohemian lion left **Rev:** Crowned M divides date above value **Mint:** Kuttenberg **Note:** Prev. KM#1051.

Date	Mintage	VG	F	VF	XF	Unc
1613 (ee)	—	10.00	20.00	35.00	65.00	—
1615 (ee)	—	10.00	20.00	35.00	65.00	—
1617 (ee)	—	10.00	20.00	35.00	65.00	—
1618 (ee)	—	10.00	20.00	35.00	65.00	—
1619 (ee)	—	10.00	20.00	35.00	65.00	—

KM# 177 MALEY GROSCHEN

Silver **Ruler:** Matthias II **Obv:** Crowned Bohemian lion left **Rev:** Crowned M **Mint:** Prague **Note:** Prev. KM#1325.

Date	Mintage	VG	F	VF	XF	Unc
1615 (l)	—	38.00	75.00	150	250	—
1616 (l)	—	38.00	75.00	150	250	—
1617 (l)	—	38.00	75.00	150	250	—

KM# 191 MALEY GROSCHEN

Silver **Ruler:** Matthias II **Obv:** Crowned Bohemian lion left **Rev:** Crowned M divides date above value **Mint:** Prague **Note:** Prev. KM#1326.

Date	Mintage	VG	F	VF	XF	Unc
1616	—	35.00	60.00	120	200	—
1617	—	35.00	60.00	120	200	—
1617 (l)	—	35.00	60.00	120	200	—
1618 (l)	—	35.00	60.00	120	200	—
1619	—	35.00	60.00	120	200	—

KM# 203 MALEY GROSCHEN

Silver **Ruler:** Matthias II **Obv:** Crowned Bohemian lion left **Rev:** Crowned M divides date above value **Mint:** Joachimstal **Note:** Prev. KM#879.

Date	Mintage	VG	F	VF	XF	Unc
1617 (aj)	—	30.00	60.00	125	245	—
1618 (aj)	—	30.00	60.00	125	245	—
1619 (aj)	—	30.00	60.00	125	245	—

KM# 233 1/4 KREUZER

Silver **Ruler:** Ferdinand II **Obv:** Bohemian lion arms divide date in rhombus **Mint:** Kuttenberg **Note:** Uniface. Prev. KM#1066.

Date	Mintage	VG	F	VF	XF	Unc
1620	—	30.00	40.00	75.00	135	—
1623	—	30.00	40.00	75.00	135	—
1624	—	30.00	40.00	75.00	135	—
1625	—	30.00	40.00	75.00	135	—
1626	—	30.00	40.00	75.00	135	—
1628	—	30.00	40.00	75.00	135	—
1629	—	30.00	40.00	75.00	135	—
1630	—	30.00	40.00	75.00	135	—
1633	—	30.00	40.00	75.00	135	—

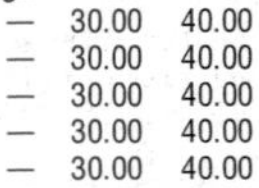

KM# 280 1/4 KREUZER

Silver **Ruler:** Matthias II **Obv:** Crowned Bohemian lion left, 4 below, all in circle **Rev. Legend:** FER. II. D.G. R.B., date **Mint:** Kuttenberg **Note:** Uniface. Prev. KM#1065.

Date	Mintage	VG	F	VF	XF	Unc
16Z1	—	35.00	80.00	150	225	—
16Z1 (ee)	—	35.00	80.00	150	225	—
16ZZ	—	35.00	80.00	150	225	—

KM# 442 1/4 KREUZER

Silver **Ruler:** Ferdinand III **Obv:** Bohemian lion arms divide date in rhombus **Mint:** Kuttenberg **Note:** Prev. KM#1100.

Date	Mintage	VG	F	VF	XF	Unc
1640	—	25.00	50.00	90.00	150	—
1654	—	25.00	50.00	90.00	150	—

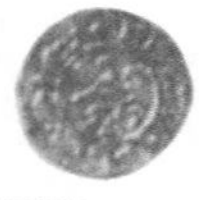

KM# 281 1/2 KREUZER

Silver **Ruler:** Ferdinand II **Obv:** Rampant lion left **Mint:** Kuttenberg **Note:** Prev. KM#1067.

Date	Mintage	VG	F	VF	XF	Unc
1621	—	25.00	50.00	90.00	150	—

KM# 321 1/2 KREUZER

Silver **Ruler:** Ferdinand II **Obv:** Crowned Bohemian lion left in trelobe divides F-II, date below **Mint:** Kuttenberg **Note:** Uniface. Prev. KM#1068.

Date	Mintage	VG	F	VF	XF	Unc
1622	—	25.00	50.00	90.00	150	—
1623	—	25.00	50.00	90.00	150	—

KM# 340 1/2 KREUZER

Silver **Ruler:** Ferdinand II **Obv:** Date above crown over two adjacent arms of imperial eagle and Bohemian lion **Mint:** Kuttenberg **Note:** Prev. KM#1069.

Date	Mintage	VG	F	VF	XF	Unc
1623	—	20.00	50.00	90.00	135	—
1624	—	20.00	50.00	90.00	135	—
1626	—	20.00	50.00	90.00	135	—
1627	—	20.00	50.00	90.00	135	—
1628	—	20.00	50.00	90.00	135	—
1629	—	20.00	50.00	90.00	135	—
1630	—	20.00	50.00	90.00	135	—
1631	—	20.00	50.00	90.00	135	—
1632	—	20.00	50.00	90.00	135	—
1633	—	20.00	50.00	90.00	135	—
1634	—	20.00	50.00	90.00	135	—

KM# 385 1/2 KREUZER

Silver **Ruler:** Ferdinand II **Obv:** Date above crown over two adjacent arms of imperial eagle and Bohemian lion, all in trefoil **Mint:** Prague **Note:** Uniface. Prev. KM#1365.

Date	Mintage	VG	F	VF	XF	Unc
1626 (l)	—	10.00	20.00	40.00	70.00	—

KM# 387 1/2 KREUZER

Silver **Ruler:** Ferdinand II **Obv:** Date above crown over two adjacent arms of imperial eagle and Bohemian lion **Mint:** Joachimstal **Note:** Uniface. Prev. KM#890.

Date	Mintage	VG	F	VF	XF	Unc
1626 (ak)	—	65.00	120	185	300	—
1629 (ak)	—	65.00	120	185	300	—

KM# 388 1/2 KREUZER

Silver **Ruler:** Ferdinand I **Obv:** Crown above two shields of arms, date above crown **Mint:** Prague **Note:** Uniface.

Date	Mintage	VG	F	VF	XF	Unc
1626 (e)	—	65.00	120	185	300	—
1629 (e)	—	65.00	120	185	300	—

KM# 386 1/2 KREUZER

Silver **Ruler:** Ferdinand II **Obv:** Three-digit date at bottom **Mint:** Prague **Note:** Prev. KM#1366.

Date	Mintage	VG	F	VF	XF	Unc
1628	—	5.00	10.00	22.00	45.00	—

KM# 443 1/2 KREUZER

Silver **Ruler:** Ferdinand III **Obv:** Date above crown over two adjacent arms of imperial eagle and Bohemian lion **Mint:** Joachimstal **Note:** Prev. KM#910.

Date	Mintage	VG	F	VF	XF	Unc
1640 (al)	—	—	—	—	—	—

KM# 477 1/2 KREUZER

Silver **Ruler:** Ferdinand III **Obv:** Crowned Bohemian lion left, F-III divided above, date to right **Mint:** Joachimstal **Note:** Prev. KM#911.

Date	Mintage	VG	F	VF	XF	Unc
1651	—	100	175	275	—	—
1652 (an)	—	100	175	275	—	—

KM# 479 1/2 KREUZER

Silver **Ruler:** Ferdinand III **Obv:** Crowned Bohemian lion left, F-III divided above, date to right **Mint:** Kuttenberg **Note:** Prev. KM#1101.

Date	Mintage	VG	F	VF	XF	Unc
1654 (ii)	—	20.00	40.00	70.00	180	—
1656 (ii)	—	20.00	40.00	70.00	180	—

KM# 483 1/2 KREUZER

Silver **Ruler:** Ferdinand III **Obv:** Crowned Bohemian lion left, F-III divided above, date to right **Mint:** Prague **Note:** Prev. KM#1405.

Date	Mintage	VG	F	VF	XF	Unc
1655 (r)	—	20.00	40.00	70.00	180	—

KM# 484 1/2 KREUZER

Silver **Ruler:** Leopold I **Obv:** Crowned L divides date, mintmaster's symbol and "1/2" all in laurel wreath **Mint:** Prague **Note:** Prev. KM#1425.

Date	Mintage	VG	F	VF	XF	Unc
1658 (r)	—	5.00	10.00	20.00	40.00	—
1661 (r)	—	5.00	10.00	20.00	40.00	—
1662 (r)	—	5.00	10.00	20.00	40.00	—
1663 (r)	—	5.00	10.00	20.00	40.00	—

KM# 490 1/2 KREUZER

Silver **Ruler:** Leopold I **Obv:** Crowned Bohemian lion left **Mint:** Kuttenberg **Note:** Uniface. Varieties exist. Prev. KM#1115.

Date	Mintage	VG	F	VF	XF	Unc
1661 (ii)	—	4.00	9.00	18.00	30.00	—
1663 (ii)	—	4.00	9.00	18.00	30.00	—
1667 (ii)	—	4.00	9.00	18.00	30.00	—
1668 (ii)	—	4.00	9.00	18.00	30.00	—
1669 (ii)	—	4.00	9.00	18.00	30.00	—
1670 (ii)	—	4.00	9.00	18.00	30.00	—
1674 (ii)	—	4.00	9.00	18.00	30.00	—
1675 (ii)	—	4.00	9.00	18.00	30.00	—
1678 (jj)	—	4.00	9.00	18.00	30.00	—
1680 (jj)	—	4.00	9.00	18.00	30.00	—
1681 (jj)	—	4.00	9.00	18.00	30.00	—
1683 (jj)	—	4.00	9.00	18.00	30.00	—
1686 (jj)	—	4.00	9.00	18.00	30.00	—
1688 (jj)	—	4.00	9.00	18.00	30.00	—
1689 (jj)	—	4.00	9.00	18.00	30.00	—
1690 (jj)	—	4.00	9.00	18.00	30.00	—
1691 (jj)	—	4.00	9.00	18.00	30.00	—
1692 (jj)	—	4.00	9.00	18.00	30.00	—
1693 (jj)	—	4.00	9.00	18.00	30.00	—
1694 (jj)	—	4.00	9.00	18.00	30.00	—
1696 (jj)	—	4.00	9.00	18.00	30.00	—
1697 (jj)	—	4.00	9.00	18.00	30.00	—
1698 (jj)	—	4.00	9.00	18.00	30.00	—
1699 (jj)	—	4.00	9.00	18.00	30.00	—
1700 (jj)	—	4.00	9.00	18.00	30.00	—

KM# 560 1/2 KREUZER

Silver **Ruler:** Leopold I **Obv:** Two adjacent shields, L and first half of date in left, Bohemian lion and last half of date in right, crown above, "1/2" in center, mintmaster's symbol below **Mint:** Prague **Note:** Prev. KM#1425.

Date	Mintage	VG	F	VF	XF	Unc
1665 (r)	—	6.00	12.00	25.00	50.00	—

KM# 602 1/2 KREUZER

Silver **Ruler:** Leopold I **Obv:** Crowned rampant lion left, "L-I" divided by lion's head, date down right side **Mint:** Prague **Note:** Uniface. Varieties exist. Prev. KM#1425.

Date	Mintage	VG	F	VF	XF	Unc
1695 GE	—	5.00	10.00	20.00	40.00	—
1698 GE	—	5.00	10.00	20.00	40.00	—
1699 GE	—	5.00	10.00	20.00	40.00	—
1700 GE	—	5.00	10.00	20.00	40.00	—

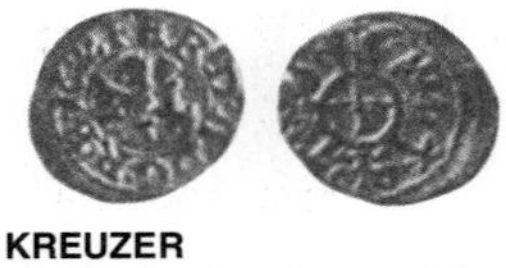

KM# 322 KREUZER

Silver **Ruler:** Ferdinand II **Obv:** Crowned Bohemian lion left in circle, titles of Ferdinand II and date **Rev:** Imperial eagle in circle, orb on breast with "1" **Mint:** Kuttenberg **Note:** Known struck on thick flan. Prev. KM#1070.

Date	Mintage	VG	F	VF	XF	Unc
1622	—	25.00	45.00	80.00	150	—

KM# 367 KREUZER

Silver **Ruler:** Ferdinand II **Obv:** Crowned imperial eagle, "I" in shield on breast, titles of Ferdinand II **Rev:** Crowned Bohemian lion left in circle, date in legend **Mint:** Kuttenberg **Note:** Prev. KM#1071.

Date	Mintage	VG	F	VF	XF	Unc
1624 (ee)	—	10.00	20.00	35.00	65.00	—
1625 (ee)	—	10.00	20.00	35.00	65.00	—
1627 (ee)	—	10.00	20.00	35.00	65.00	—

KM# 392 KREUZER

Silver **Ruler:** Ferdinand II **Obv:** Laureate bust right, titles of Ferdinand II **Rev:** Crowned imperial eagle, "I" in shield on breast, date in legend **Mint:** Prague **Note:** Prev. KM#1367.

Date	Mintage	VG	F	VF	XF	Unc
1624 (e)	—	10.00	20.00	35.00	65.00	—
1627 (l)	—	10.00	20.00	35.00	65.00	—
1637 (q)	—	10.00	20.00	35.00	65.00	—

KM# 368 KREUZER

Silver **Ruler:** Ferdinand II **Obv:** Crowned imperial eagle, value on breast in inner circle **Rev:** Rampant lion left in inner circle, date in legend **Mint:** Joachimstal **Note:** Prev. KM#891.

Date	Mintage	VG	F	VF	XF	Unc
1624 (ak)	—	10.00	20.00	35.00	65.00	—
1627 (ak)	—	10.00	20.00	35.00	65.00	—
1634 (ak)	—	10.00	20.00	35.00	65.00	—

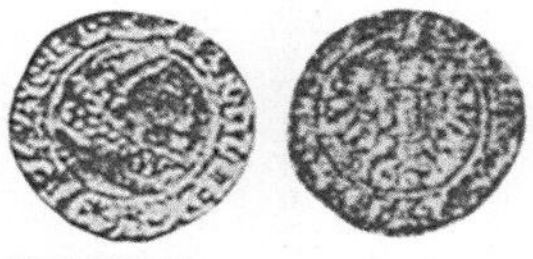

KM# 393 KREUZER

Silver **Ruler:** Ferdinand II **Obv:** Laureate bust right, titles of Ferdinand II **Rev:** Crowned imperial eagle, "I" in shield on breast, date in legend **Mint:** Kuttenberg **Note:** Prev. KM#1072.

Date	Mintage	VG	F	VF	XF	Unc
1627 (ee)	—	35.00	60.00	125	250	—

KM# 411 KREUZER

Silver **Ruler:** Ferdinand III **Obv:** Bust right, value (I) below, titles of Ferdinand III **Rev:** Crowned imperial eagle, Bohemian arms on breast, date in legend **Mint:** Prague **Note:** Prev. KM#1406.

Date	Mintage	VG	F	VF	XF	Unc
1637	—	25.00	45.00	75.00	135	—
1638 (q)	—	25.00	45.00	75.00	135	—
1639 (q)	—	25.00	45.00	75.00	135	—
1640 (q)	—	25.00	45.00	75.00	135	—
1642 (q)	—	25.00	45.00	75.00	135	—

KM# 408 KREUZER

Silver **Ruler:** Ferdinand III **Obv:** KM#411 **Rev:** KM#392 **Mint:** Prague **Note:** Mule.

Date	Mintage	VG	F	VF	XF	Unc
1637	—	—	—	—	—	—

KM# 445 KREUZER

Silver **Ruler:** Ferdinand III **Obv:** Laureate bust of Ferdinand III **Rev:** Crowned imperial eagle **Mint:** Prague **Note:** Prev. KM#1407.

Date	Mintage	VG	F	VF	XF	Unc
1639 (q)	—	15.00	30.00	60.00	100	—
1641 (q)	—	15.00	30.00	60.00	100	—
1642 (q)	—	15.00	30.00	60.00	100	—
1645 (q)	—	15.00	30.00	60.00	100	—
1646 (q)	—	15.00	30.00	60.00	100	—
1653 (q)	—	15.00	30.00	60.00	100	—

KM# 444 KREUZER

Silver **Ruler:** Ferdinand III **Obv:** Head of Ferdinand III right in inner circle **Rev:** Crowned imperial eagle in inner circle, date in legend **Mint:** Joachimstal **Note:** Prev. KM#912.

Date	Mintage	VG	F	VF	XF	Unc
1640 (al)	—	35.00	65.00	125	200	—
1641 (al)	—	35.00	65.00	125	200	—
1643 (al)	—	35.00	65.00	125	200	—
1646	—	35.00	65.00	125	200	—

KM# 446 KREUZER

Silver **Ruler:** Ferdinand III **Obv:** Laureate bust of Ferdinand III **Rev:** Crowned imperial eagle **Mint:** Joachimstal **Note:** Prev. KM#913.

Date	Mintage	VG	F	VF	XF	Unc
1640 (al)	—	40.00	75.00	145	225	—
1651 (an)	—	40.00	75.00	145	225	—
1652 (an)	—	40.00	75.00	145	225	—
1653 (an)	—	40.00	75.00	145	225	—

KM# 480 KREUZER

Silver **Ruler:** Ferdinand III **Obv:** Laureate bust of Ferdinand III **Rev:** Crowned imperial eagle **Mint:** Kuttenberg **Note:** Prev. KM#1102.

Date	Mintage	VG	F	VF	XF	Unc
1654 (ii)	—	50.00	90.00	175	250	—

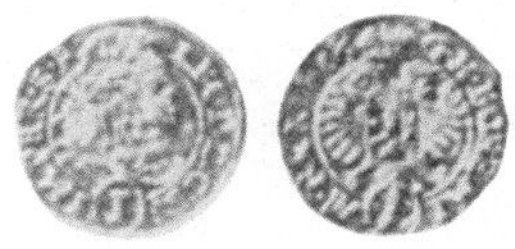

KM# 485 KREUZER

Silver **Ruler:** Leopold I **Obv:** Young laureate bust right, "1" below **Rev:** Crowned imperial eagle **Mint:** Kuttenberg **Note:** Prev. KM#1116.

Date	Mintage	VG	F	VF	XF	Unc
1659 (ii)	—	7.00	15.00	30.00	65.00	—
1660 (ii)	—	7.00	15.00	30.00	65.00	—
1661 (ii)	—	7.00	15.00	30.00	65.00	—
1663 (ii)	—	7.00	15.00	30.00	65.00	—
1664 (ii)	—	7.00	15.00	30.00	65.00	—
1665 (ii)	—	7.00	15.00	30.00	65.00	—
1666 (ii)	—	7.00	15.00	30.00	65.00	—
1667 (ii)	—	7.00	15.00	30.00	65.00	—
1668 (ii)	—	7.00	15.00	30.00	65.00	—
1671 (ii)	—	7.00	15.00	30.00	65.00	—
1672 (ii)	—	7.00	15.00	30.00	65.00	—
1675	—	7.00	15.00	30.00	65.00	—

KM# 491 KREUZER

Silver **Ruler:** Leopold I **Obv:** Young laureate bust right, value "1" in oval below, titles of Leopold I **Rev:** Crowned imperial eagle, oval Bohemian arms on breast, date in legend **Mint:** Prague **Note:** Prev. KM#1427.

Date	Mintage	VG	F	VF	XF	Unc
1659 (r)	—	7.00	15.00	30.00	65.00	—
1660 (r)	—	7.00	15.00	30.00	65.00	—
1663 (r)	—	7.00	15.00	30.00	65.00	—
1670 (s)	—	7.00	15.00	30.00	65.00	—
1673 (s)	—	7.00	15.00	30.00	65.00	—

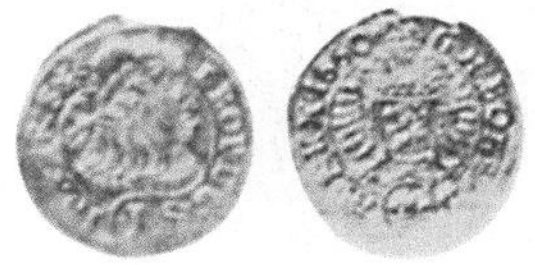

KM# 550 KREUZER

Silver **Ruler:** Leopold I **Obv:** Laureate bust of Leopold I, value below **Rev:** Crowned imperial eagle **Mint:** Joachimstal **Note:** Prev. KM#930.

Date	Mintage	VG	F	VF	XF	Unc
1660 (an)	—	75.00	135	225	—	—

KM# 582 KREUZER

Silver **Ruler:** Leopold I **Obv:** Older laureate bust right, "1" below **Rev:** Crowned imperial eagle, crown divides date **Mint:** Kuttenberg **Note:** Varieties exist. Prev. KM#1117.

Date	Mintage	VG	F	VF	XF	Unc
1680 (jj)	—	7.00	15.00	30.00	65.00	—
1681 (jj)	—	7.00	15.00	30.00	65.00	—
1683 (jj)	—	7.00	15.00	30.00	65.00	—
1684 (jj)	—	7.00	15.00	30.00	65.00	—
1686 (jj)	—	7.00	15.00	30.00	65.00	—
1687 (jj)	—	7.00	15.00	30.00	65.00	—
1688 (jj)	—	7.00	15.00	30.00	65.00	—

Date	Mintage	VG	F	VF	XF	Unc
1689 (jj)	—	7.00	15.00	30.00	65.00	—
1690 (jj)	—	7.00	15.00	30.00	65.00	—
1691 (jj)	—	7.00	15.00	30.00	65.00	—
1692 (jj)	—	7.00	15.00	30.00	65.00	—
1693 (jj)	—	7.00	15.00	30.00	65.00	—
1694 (jj)	—	7.00	15.00	30.00	65.00	—
1696 (jj)	—	7.00	15.00	30.00	65.00	—
1697 (jj)	—	7.00	15.00	30.00	65.00	—
1698 (jj)	—	7.00	15.00	30.00	65.00	—
1699 (jj)	—	7.00	15.00	30.00	65.00	—
1700 (jj)	—	7.00	15.00	30.00	65.00	—

KM# 603 KREUZER

Silver **Ruler:** Leopold I **Obv:** Young laureate bust right with long wig, value in oval below, titles of Leopold I **Rev:** Crowned imperial eagle holding sword and scepter in talons, oval Bohemian arms on breast, date divided by crown **Mint:** Prague **Note:** Varieties exist. Prev. KM#1427.

Date	Mintage	VG	F	VF	XF	Unc
1695 GE	—	6.00	12.00	25.00	50.00	—
1696 GE	—	6.00	12.00	25.00	50.00	—
1697 GE	—	6.00	12.00	25.00	50.00	—
1698 GE	—	6.00	12.00	25.00	50.00	—
1699 GE	—	6.00	12.00	25.00	50.00	—
1700 GE	—	6.00	12.00	25.00	50.00	—

KM# 604 KREUZER

Silver **Ruler:** Leopold I **Rev:** Date divided by crown and legend **Rev. Legend:** BOEMISCHE - LAND. MVN(T)Z **Mint:** Kuttenberg

Date	Mintage	VG	F	VF	XF	Unc
1695 (ll)	—	—	—	—	—	—

KM# 605 KREUZER

Silver **Ruler:** Leopold I **Rev. Legend:** BOEMISCHE - LANDMVNTZ **Mint:** Prague

Date	Mintage	VG	F	VF	XF	Unc
1695 GE	—	—	—	—	—	—

KM# 193 3 KREUZER

Silver **Ruler:** Matthias II **Obv:** Crowned rampant lion **Rev:** Crowned imperial eagle **Mint:** Kuttenberg **Note:** Varieties exist. Prev. KM#1050.

Date	Mintage	VG	F	VF	XF	Unc
1616	—	20.00	35.00	65.00	110	—
1617	—	20.00	35.00	65.00	110	—
1618	—	20.00	35.00	65.00	110	—
1619	—	20.00	35.00	65.00	110	—

KM# 204 3 KREUZER

Silver **Ruler:** Matthias II **Mint:** Joachimstal **Note:** Titles of Matthias. Prev. KM#881.

Date	Mintage	VG	F	VF	XF	Unc
1617	—	30.00	65.00	135	265	—
1618	—	30.00	65.00	135	265	—

KM# 283 3 KREUZER

Silver **Ruler:** Ferdinand II **Obv:** Imperial eagle **Rev:** Rampant lion left **Mint:** Joachimstal **Note:** Prev. KM#892.

Date	Mintage	VG	F	VF	XF	Unc
1621	—	12.00	25.00	50.00	90.00	—

KM# 327 3 KREUZER

Silver **Ruler:** Ferdinand II **Obv:** Laureate bust in inner circle, value below **Rev:** Crowned imperial eagle in inner circle, date in legend **Mint:** Joachimstal **Note:** Prev. KM#893.

Date	Mintage	VG	F	VF	XF	Unc
1622 (e)	—	10.00	20.00	40.00	75.00	—
1623 (E)	—	10.00	20.00	40.00	75.00	—

KM# 394 3 KREUZER

Silver **Ruler:** Ferdinand II **Mint:** Kuttenberg **Note:** Klippe. Prev. KM#1077.

Date	Mintage	VG	F	VF	XF	Unc
1637	—	—	—	—	—	—

KM# 415 3 KREUZER

Silver **Ruler:** Ferdinand II **Obv:** Bare head **Mint:** Kuttenberg **Note:** Prev. KM#1103.

Date	Mintage	VG	F	VF	XF	Unc
1638	—	15.00	27.00	45.00	85.00	—
1639	—	15.00	27.00	45.00	85.00	—
1640	—	15.00	27.00	45.00	85.00	—
1641	—	15.00	27.00	45.00	85.00	—

KM# 590 3 KREUZER (Groschen)
Silver **Ruler:** Leopold I **Obv:** Bust left in long wig **Rev:** Crowned imperial arms with sword and scepter **Mint:** Prague **Note:** Varieties exist. Prev. KM#1430.

Date	Mintage	VG	F	VF	XF	Unc
1688 MV	—	10.00	22.00	40.00	75.00	—
1691 MV	—	10.00	22.00	40.00	75.00	—
1693 MV	—	10.00	22.00	40.00	75.00	—
1694 MV	—	10.00	22.00	40.00	75.00	—
1694 PM	—	10.00	22.00	40.00	75.00	—
1694 GE	—	7.00	15.00	30.00	60.00	—
1695 GE	—	7.00	15.00	30.00	60.00	—
1696 GE	—	7.00	15.00	30.00	60.00	—
1697 GE	—	7.00	15.00	30.00	60.00	—
1698 GE	—	7.00	15.00	30.00	60.00	—
1699 GE	—	7.00	15.00	30.00	60.00	—
1700 GE	—	7.00	15.00	30.00	60.00	—

KM# 606 3 KREUZER (Groschen)
Silver **Ruler:** Leopold I **Obv:** Laureate bust right in inner circle **Mint:** Kuttenberg **Note:** Varieties exist. Prev. KM#1120.

Date	Mintage	VG	F	VF	XF	Unc
1695 (jj)	—	7.00	12.00	25.00	55.00	—
1696 (jj)	—	7.00	12.00	25.00	55.00	—
1697 (jj)	—	7.00	12.00	25.00	55.00	—
1698 (jj)	—	7.00	12.00	25.00	55.00	—
1699 (jj)	—	7.00	12.00	25.00	55.00	—
1700 (jj)	—	7.00	12.00	25.00	55.00	—

KM# 234 3 KREUZER (Groschen)
Silver **Ruler:** Ferdinand II **Obv:** Crowned imperial eagle, value (3) below, Austria-Burgundy arms on breast, titles of Ferdinand II **Rev:** Crowned Bohemian lion left in circle, date in legend **Mint:** Kuttenberg **Note:** Prev. KM#1073.

Date	Mintage	VG	F	VF	XF	Unc
1620 (ee)	—	15.00	30.00	50.00	90.00	—
1621 (ee)	—	15.00	30.00	50.00	90.00	—

KM# 282 3 KREUZER (Groschen)
Silver **Ruler:** Ferdinand II **Obv:** Crowned imperial eagle, value (3) below, Austria-Burgundy arms on breast, titles of Ferdinand II **Rev:** Crowned Bohemian lion left in circle, date in legend **Mint:** Prague **Note:** Prev. KM#1368.

Date	Mintage	VG	F	VF	XF	Unc
16Z1 (l)	—	8.00	16.00	32.00	65.00	—

KM# 324 3 KREUZER (Groschen)
Silver **Ruler:** Ferdinand II **Obv:** Laureate bust right, value (3) below, titles of Ferdinand II **Rev:** Crowned imperial eagle, Austria-Burgundy arms on breast, date in legend **Mint:** Prague **Note:** Prev. KM#1369.

Date	Mintage	VG	F	VF	XF	Unc
1622 (l)	—	12.00	25.00	45.00	85.00	—
1623 (l)	—	10.00	22.00	40.00	75.00	—

KM# 326 3 KREUZER (Groschen)
Silver **Ruler:** Ferdinand II **Obv:** Laureate bust in inner circle, value below **Rev:** Crowned imperial eagle in inner circle, date in legend **Mint:** Joachimstal **Note:** Prev. KM#893.

Date	Mintage	VG	F	VF	XF	Unc
1622 (ak)	—	12.00	30.00	65.00	115	—
1623 (ak)	—	12.00	30.00	65.00	115	—

KM# 325 3 KREUZER (Groschen)
Silver **Ruler:** Ferdinand II **Obv:** Laureate bust right, value (3) below, titles of Ferdinand II **Rev:** Crowned imperial eagle, Austria-Burgundy arms on breast, date in legend **Mint:** Kuttenberg **Note:** Prev. KM#1074.

Date	Mintage	VG	F	VF	XF	Unc
1622	—	15.00	30.00	50.00	90.00	—
1622 (ee)	—	15.00	30.00	50.00	90.00	—

KM# 370 3 KREUZER (Groschen)
Silver **Ruler:** Ferdinand II **Obv:** Bust right in ruffled collar **Rev:** Crowned imperial eagle **Mint:** Kuttenberg **Note:** Prev. KM#1075.

Date	Mintage	VG	F	VF	XF	Unc
1624 (ee)	—	7.00	12.00	25.00	55.00	—
1625 (ee)	—	7.00	12.00	25.00	55.00	—
1626 (ee)	—	7.00	12.00	25.00	55.00	—
1627 (ee)	—	7.00	12.00	25.00	55.00	—
1628 (ee)	—	7.00	12.00	25.00	55.00	—
1629 (ee)	—	7.00	12.00	25.00	55.00	—
1630 (ee)	—	7.00	12.00	25.00	55.00	—
1631 (ee)	—	7.00	12.00	25.00	55.00	—
1631	—	7.00	12.00	25.00	55.00	—
1632 (ee)	—	7.00	12.00	25.00	55.00	—
1633	—	7.00	12.00	25.00	55.00	—
1633 (dd)	—	7.00	12.00	25.00	55.00	—
1633 (ee)	—	7.00	12.00	25.00	55.00	—
1633 (ff)	—	7.00	12.00	25.00	55.00	—
1634 (dd)	—	7.00	12.00	25.00	55.00	—
1634 (ff)	—	7.00	12.00	25.00	55.00	—

KM# 369 3 KREUZER (Groschen)
Silver **Ruler:** Ferdinand II **Obv:** Bust right in ruffled collar **Rev:** Crowned imperial eagle **Mint:** Prague **Note:** Prev. KM#1370. Varieties exist.

Date	Mintage	VG	F	VF	XF	Unc
1624 (n)	—	8.00	15.00	30.00	60.00	—
1625 (l)	—	8.00	15.00	30.00	60.00	—
1625 (n)	—	8.00	15.00	30.00	60.00	—
1626 (l)	—	8.00	15.00	30.00	60.00	—
1626 (n)	—	8.00	15.00	30.00	60.00	—
1627 (l)	—	8.00	15.00	30.00	60.00	—
1628 (l)	—	8.00	15.00	30.00	60.00	—
1629 (l)	—	8.00	15.00	30.00	60.00	—
1630 (l)	—	8.00	15.00	30.00	60.00	—
1630 (o)	—	8.00	15.00	30.00	60.00	—
1631 (o)	—	8.00	15.00	30.00	60.00	—
1631 (p)	—	8.00	15.00	30.00	60.00	—
1632 (p)	—	8.00	15.00	30.00	60.00	—
1633 (p)	—	8.00	15.00	30.00	60.00	—
1634 (p)	—	8.00	15.00	30.00	60.00	—
1635 (p)	—	8.00	15.00	30.00	60.00	—
1636 (p)	—	8.00	15.00	30.00	60.00	—
1637 (p)	—	8.00	15.00	30.00	60.00	—
1637 (q)	—	8.00	15.00	30.00	60.00	—
1638 (q)	—	8.00	15.00	30.00	60.00	—

KM# 371 3 KREUZER (Groschen)
Silver **Ruler:** Ferdinand II **Rev:** Crowned imperial eagle, value below **Mint:** Joachimstal **Note:** Prev. KM#894. Varieties exist.

Date	Mintage	VG	F	VF	XF	Unc
1624 (ak)	—	7.00	15.00	28.00	55.00	—
1625 (ak)	—	7.00	15.00	28.00	55.00	—
1626 (ak)	—	7.00	15.00	28.00	55.00	—
1627 (ak)	—	7.00	15.00	28.00	55.00	—
1628 (ak)	—	7.00	15.00	28.00	55.00	—
1629 (ak)	—	7.00	15.00	28.00	55.00	—
1630 (ak)	—	7.00	15.00	28.00	55.00	—
1631 (ak)	—	7.00	15.00	28.00	55.00	—
1632 (ak)	—	7.00	15.00	28.00	55.00	—
1633 (ak)	—	7.00	15.00	28.00	55.00	—
1634 (ak)	—	7.00	15.00	28.00	55.00	—
1635 (ak)	—	7.00	15.00	28.00	55.00	—
1636 (ak)	—	7.00	15.00	28.00	55.00	—
1637 (ak)	—	7.00	15.00	28.00	55.00	—

KM# 405 3 KREUZER (Groschen)
Silver **Ruler:** Ferdinand II **Mint:** Kuttenberg **Note:** Prev. KM#1076. Varieties exist.

Date	Mintage	VG	F	VF	XF	Unc
1635 (dd)	—	7.00	12.00	25.00	55.00	—
1636 (hh)	—	7.00	12.00	25.00	55.00	—
1637 (hh)	—	7.00	12.00	25.00	55.00	—

KM# 409 3 KREUZER (Groschen)
Silver **Ruler:** Ferdinand II **Mint:** Prague **Note:** Prev. KM#1371. Klippe.

Date	Mintage	VG	F	VF	XF	Unc
1637 (q) Rare	—	—	—	—	—	—

KM# 412 3 KREUZER (Groschen)
Silver **Ruler:** Ferdinand III **Obv:** Bare-headed bust right, value below **Rev:** Crowned imperial eagle **Mint:** Prague **Note:** Prev. KM#1408.

Date	Mintage	VG	F	VF	XF	Unc
1638 (q)	—	10.00	20.00	38.00	75.00	—
1639 (q)	—	10.00	20.00	38.00	75.00	—
1640 (q)	—	10.00	20.00	38.00	75.00	—
1641 (q)	—	10.00	20.00	38.00	75.00	—

KM# 413 3 KREUZER (Groschen)
Silver **Ruler:** Ferdinand III **Obv:** Bust of Ferdinand III right **Rev:** Crowned imperial eagle **Mint:** Kuttenberg **Note:** Prev. KM#1076.

Date	Mintage	VG	F	VF	XF	Unc
1638 (hh)	—	7.00	12.00	25.00	55.00	—
1639 (hh)	—	7.00	12.00	25.00	55.00	—
1640 (hh)	—	7.00	12.00	25.00	55.00	—
1641 (hh)	—	7.00	12.00	25.00	55.00	—

KM# 414 3 KREUZER (Groschen)
Silver **Ruler:** Ferdinand III **Obv:** Head right in inner circle, value (3) below **Rev:** Crowned imperial eagle, date in legend **Mint:** Joachimstal **Note:** Prev. KM#914.

Date	Mintage	VG	F	VF	XF	Unc
1638 (al)	—	35.00	70.00	125	225	—
1639 (al)	—	35.00	70.00	125	225	—
1640 (al)	—	35.00	70.00	125	225	—
1641 (al)	—	35.00	70.00	125	225	—
1642 (al)	—	35.00	70.00	125	225	—
1643 (al)	—	35.00	70.00	125	225	—

KM# 448 3 KREUZER (Groschen)
Silver **Ruler:** Ferdinand III **Obv:** Laureate bust right **Rev:** Crowned imperial eagle **Mint:** Prague **Note:** Prev. KM#1409.

Date	Mintage	VG	F	VF	XF	Unc
1640 (q)	—	9.00	18.00	36.00	70.00	—
1641 (q)	—	9.00	18.00	36.00	70.00	—
1642 (q)	—	9.00	18.00	36.00	70.00	—
1643 (q)	—	9.00	18.00	36.00	70.00	—
1644 (q)	—	9.00	18.00	36.00	70.00	—
1645 (q)	—	9.00	18.00	36.00	70.00	—
1646 (q)	—	9.00	18.00	36.00	70.00	—
1647 (q)	—	9.00	18.00	36.00	70.00	—
1648 (q)	—	9.00	18.00	36.00	70.00	—
1649 (q)	—	9.00	18.00	36.00	70.00	—
1650 (q)	—	9.00	18.00	36.00	70.00	—
1651 (q)	—	9.00	18.00	36.00	70.00	—
1652 (q)	—	9.00	18.00	36.00	70.00	—
1653 (q)	—	9.00	18.00	36.00	70.00	—
1654 (q)	—	9.00	18.00	36.00	70.00	—
1655 (q)	—	9.00	18.00	36.00	70.00	—
1655 (r)	—	9.00	18.00	36.00	70.00	—
1656 (r)	—	9.00	18.00	36.00	70.00	—
1657 (r)	—	9.00	18.00	36.00	70.00	—

KM# 449 3 KREUZER (Groschen)
Silver **Ruler:** Ferdinand III **Obv:** Laureate bust of Ferdinand III right **Rev:** Crowned imperial eagle **Mint:** Kuttenberg **Note:** Prev. KM#1104 and #1105. Varieties exist.

Date	Mintage	VG	F	VF	XF	Unc
1641 (hh)	—	12.00	22.00	40.00	65.00	—
1642 (hh)	—	12.00	22.00	40.00	65.00	—
1654 (ii)	—	12.00	22.00	40.00	65.00	—
1655 (ii)	—	12.00	22.00	40.00	65.00	—
1656 (ii)	—	12.00	22.00	40.00	65.00	—
1657 (ii)	—	12.00	22.00	40.00	65.00	—

KM# 464 3 KREUZER (Groschen)
Silver **Ruler:** Ferdinand III **Obv:** Laureate head right in inner circle, value below **Rev:** Crowned imperial eagle, date in legend **Mint:** Joachimstal **Note:** Prev. KM#915. Varieties exist.

Date	Mintage	VG	F	VF	XF	Unc
1643 (al)	—	30.00	55.00	110	200	—
1644 (al)	—	30.00	55.00	110	200	—
1645 (al)	—	30.00	55.00	110	200	—
1646 (al)	—	30.00	55.00	110	200	—
1647 (al)	—	30.00	55.00	110	200	—
1648 (al)	—	30.00	55.00	110	200	—
1649 (am)	—	30.00	55.00	110	200	—
1650 (am)	—	30.00	55.00	110	200	—
1651 (an)	—	30.00	55.00	110	200	—
1654 (an)	—	30.00	55.00	110	200	—
1657 (an)	—	30.00	55.00	110	200	—

KM# 487 3 KREUZER (Groschen)

Silver **Ruler:** Leopold I **Obv:** Laureate bust right **Rev:** Crowned imperial eagle **Mint:** Kuttenberg **Note:** Prev. KM#1118.

Date	Mintage	VG	F	VF	XF	Unc
1658 (ii)	—	8.00	16.00	32.00	60.00	—
1659 (ii)	—	8.00	16.00	32.00	60.00	—
1660 (ii)	—	8.00	16.00	32.00	60.00	—
1661 (ii)	—	8.00	16.00	32.00	60.00	—
1662 (ii)	—	8.00	16.00	32.00	60.00	—
1663 (ii)	—	8.00	16.00	32.00	60.00	—
1664 (ii)	—	8.00	16.00	32.00	60.00	—
1665 (ii)	—	8.00	16.00	32.00	60.00	—
1666 (ii)	—	8.00	16.00	32.00	60.00	—
1667 (ii)	—	8.00	16.00	32.00	60.00	—
1668 (ii)	—	8.00	16.00	32.00	60.00	—
1669 (ii)	—	8.00	16.00	32.00	60.00	—

KM# 486 3 KREUZER (Groschen)

Silver **Ruler:** Leopold I **Obv:** Young bust right **Rev:** Crowned imperial arms **Mint:** Prague **Note:** Prev. KM#1428. Varieties exist.

Date	Mintage	VG	F	VF	XF	Unc
1658 (r)	—	15.00	30.00	55.00	90.00	—
1659 (r)	—	15.00	30.00	55.00	90.00	—
1660 (r)	—	15.00	30.00	55.00	90.00	—
1661 (r)	—	15.00	30.00	55.00	90.00	—
1662 (r)	—	15.00	30.00	55.00	90.00	—
1663 (r)	—	15.00	30.00	55.00	90.00	—

KM# 492 3 KREUZER (Groschen)

Silver **Ruler:** Leopold I **Obv:** Laureate bust of Leopold I right, value below **Rev:** Crowned imperial eagle **Mint:** Joachimstal **Note:** Prev. KM#931.

Date	Mintage	VG	F	VF	XF	Unc
1659 (an)	—	35.00	65.00	115	185	—
1660 (an)	—	35.00	65.00	115	185	—
1663 (an)	—	35.00	65.00	115	185	—

KM# 554 3 KREUZER (Groschen)

Silver **Ruler:** Leopold I **Obv:** Older laureate bust right **Rev:** Crowned imperial arms **Mint:** Prague **Note:** Prev. KM#1429.

Date	Mintage	VG	F	VF	XF	Unc
1664 (r)	—	10.00	22.00	40.00	70.00	—
1668 (r)	—	10.00	22.00	40.00	70.00	—
1670 (s)	—	10.00	22.00	40.00	70.00	—
1675 (s)	—	10.00	22.00	40.00	70.00	—
1676 (s)	—	10.00	22.00	40.00	70.00	—
1677 (s)	—	10.00	22.00	40.00	70.00	—
1678 (s)	—	10.00	22.00	40.00	70.00	—
1679	—	10.00	22.00	40.00	70.00	—

KM# 568 3 KREUZER (Groschen)

Silver **Ruler:** Leopold I **Obv:** Large laureate bust right **Mint:** Kuttenberg **Note:** Prev. KM#1119.

Date	Mintage	VG	F	VF	XF	Unc
1670 (ii)	—	8.00	16.00	32.00	60.00	—
1671 (ii)	—	8.00	16.00	32.00	60.00	—
1673 (ii)	—	8.00	16.00	32.00	60.00	—

Date	Mintage	VG	F	VF	XF	Unc
1675 (ii)	—	8.00	16.00	32.00	60.00	—
1676 (ii)	—	8.00	16.00	32.00	60.00	—
1677 (ii)	—	8.00	16.00	32.00	60.00	—
1678 (jj)	—	8.00	16.00	32.00	60.00	—
1679 (jj)	—	8.00	16.00	32.00	60.00	—

KM# 580 3 KREUZER (Groschen)

Silver **Ruler:** Leopold I **Obv:** Large laureate bust right **Rev:** Crowned imperial arms **Mint:** Kuttenberg **Note:** Prev. KM#1120.

Date	Mintage	VG	F	VF	XF	Unc
1679 (jj)	—	10.00	22.00	40.00	70.00	—
1680 (jj)	—	10.00	22.00	40.00	70.00	—
1681 (jj)	—	10.00	22.00	40.00	70.00	—
1682 (jj)	—	10.00	22.00	40.00	70.00	—
1683 (jj)	—	10.00	22.00	40.00	70.00	—
1684 (jj)	—	10.00	22.00	40.00	70.00	—
1685 (jj)	—	10.00	22.00	40.00	70.00	—
1686 (jj)	—	10.00	22.00	40.00	70.00	—
1687 (jj)	—	10.00	22.00	40.00	70.00	—
1688 (jj)	—	10.00	22.00	40.00	70.00	—
1689 (jj)	—	10.00	22.00	40.00	70.00	—
1690 (jj)	—	10.00	22.00	40.00	70.00	—
1691 (jj)	—	10.00	22.00	40.00	70.00	—
1692 (jj)	—	10.00	22.00	40.00	70.00	—
1693 (jj)	—	10.00	22.00	40.00	70.00	—
1694 (jj)	—	10.00	22.00	40.00	70.00	—

KM# 555 6 KREUZER

Silver **Ruler:** Leopold I **Obv:** Laureate bust right **Rev:** Crowned imperial eagle with sword and scepter **Mint:** Prague **Note:** Prev. #1431.

Date	Mintage	VG	F	VF	XF	Unc
1664 (r)	—	12.00	25.00	45.00	85.00	—
1665 (r)	—	12.00	25.00	45.00	85.00	—
1674 (s)	—	12.00	25.00	45.00	85.00	—
1678 (s)	—	12.00	25.00	45.00	85.00	—
1681 (s)	—	12.00	25.00	45.00	85.00	—
1682 (s)	—	12.00	25.00	45.00	85.00	—
1683 (s)	—	12.00	25.00	45.00	85.00	—

KM# 573 6 KREUZER

Silver **Ruler:** Leopold I **Obv:** Laureate bust right, value "VI" in oval below, titles of Leopold I **Rev:** Crowned imperial eagle, Bohemian arms on breast, holding sword and scepter in talons, date in legend **Mint:** Prague

Date	Mintage	VG	F	VF	XF	Unc
1674 (s)	—	—	—	—	—	—

KM# 584 6 KREUZER

Silver **Ruler:** Leopold I **Obv:** Laureate bust right **Mint:** Prague **Note:** Varieties exist. Prev. #1431 and #1432.

Date	Mintage	VG	F	VF	XF	Unc
1684 (s)	—	12.00	25.00	45.00	85.00	—
1685 (s)	—	12.00	25.00	45.00	85.00	—
1686 (s)	—	12.00	25.00	45.00	85.00	—
1687 (s)	—	12.00	25.00	45.00	85.00	—
1688 MV	—	20.00	40.00	75.00	120	—
1689 MV	—	20.00	40.00	75.00	120	—
1691 MV	—	20.00	40.00	75.00	120	—

KM# 591 6 KREUZER

Silver **Ruler:** Leopold I **Rev:** Date divided by crown at top **Mint:** Prague **Note:** Prev. KM#1430.

Date	Mintage	VG	F	VF	XF	Unc
1688 MV	—	6.00	12.00	25.00	65.00	—
1691 MV	—	6.00	12.00	25.00	65.00	—
1692	—	6.00	12.00	25.00	65.00	—
1693	—	6.00	12.00	25.00	65.00	—

KM# 286 12 KREUZER

Silver **Ruler:** Ferdinand II **Obv:** Laureate bust right **Rev:** Crowned imperial eagle **Mint:** Kuttenberg **Note:** Prev. KM#1078.

Date	Mintage	VG	F	VF	XF	Unc
1621 (ee)	—	—	—	—	—	—

KM# 285 12 KREUZER

Silver **Ruler:** Ferdinand II **Obv:** Bust right in ruffled collar **Rev:** Crowned imperial eagle **Mint:** Prague **Note:** Prev. KM#1372.

Date	Mintage	VG	F	VF	XF	Unc
1621 (l)	—	15.00	30.00	50.00	90.00	—

KM# 287 15 KREUZER

Silver **Ruler:** Ferdinand II **Obv:** Laureate bust right **Rev:** Crowned imperial eagle **Mint:** Kuttenberg **Note:** Prev. KM#1079.

Date	Mintage	VG	F	VF	XF	Unc
1621 (ee)	—	65.00	120	200	325	—
1622 (ee)	—	65.00	120	200	325	—

KM# 328 15 KREUZER

Silver **Ruler:** Ferdinand II **Obv:** Bust right in ruffled collar **Rev:** Crowned imperial eagle **Mint:** Prague **Note:** Prev. KM#1373.

Date	Mintage	VG	F	VF	XF	Unc
1622 (l)	—	15.00	25.00	40.00	75.00	—
1623 (l)	—	15.00	25.00	40.00	75.00	—

KM# 329 15 KREUZER

Silver **Ruler:** Ferdinand II **Obv:** Laureate bust in ruffled collar right in inner circle, value below **Rev:** Crowned imperial eagle **Mint:** Joachimstal **Note:** Prev. KM#895.

Date	Mintage	VG	F	VF	XF	Unc
1622 (ak)	—	65.00	120	200	325	—
1623 (ak)	—	65.00	120	200	325	—

KM# 494 15 KREUZER

Silver **Ruler:** Leopold I **Obv:** Laureate bust right **Rev:** Crowned imperial eagle **Mint:** Prague **Note:** Prev. KM#1433.

Date	Mintage	VG	F	VF	XF	Unc
1659 (r)	—	15.00	25.00	45.00	85.00	—
1663 (r)	—	15.00	25.00	45.00	85.00	—
1664 (r)	—	15.00	25.00	45.00	85.00	—

KM# 552 15 KREUZER

Silver **Ruler:** Leopold I **Obv:** Laureate bust of Leopold I right, value below **Rev:** Crowned imperial eagle **Mint:** Joachimstal **Note:** Prev. KM#932.

Date	Mintage	VG	F	VF	XF	Unc
1663 (an) Rare	—	—	—	—	—	—

KM# 574 15 KREUZER

Silver **Ruler:** Leopold I **Obv:** Laureate bust with long wig right **Rev:** Crowned imperial eagle **Mint:** Prague **Note:** Varieties exist. Prev. KM#1433.

Date	Mintage	VG	F	VF	XF	Unc
1674 (s)	—	15.00	25.00	45.00	90.00	—
1693 MV	—	15.00	25.00	45.00	90.00	—
1693 (t) MV	—	15.00	25.00	45.00	90.00	—
1694 MV	—	17.50	30.00	65.00	125	—
1694 PM	—	22.00	50.00	95.00	160	—
1694 GE	—	22.00	50.00	95.00	160	—
1695 GE	—	22.00	50.00	95.00	160	—
1696 GE	—	22.00	50.00	95.00	160	—

KM# 596 15 KREUZER

Silver **Ruler:** Leopold I **Obv:** Laureate bust right **Rev:** Crowned imperial eagle **Mint:** Kuttenberg **Note:** Prev. KM#1121.

Date	Mintage	VG	F	VF	XF	Unc
1694 CK	—	15.00	25.00	45.00	90.00	—
1695 CK	—	15.00	25.00	45.00	90.00	—
1696 CK	—	15.00	25.00	45.00	90.00	—

KM# 330 24 KREUZER

Silver **Ruler:** Ferdinand II **Obv:** Laureate bust right, value below **Rev:** Crowned imperial eagle **Mint:** Kuttenberg **Note:** Prev. KM#1080.

Date	Mintage	VG	F	VF	XF	Unc
1622 (ee)	—	—	—	—	—	—

KM# 342 24 KREUZER

Silver **Ruler:** Ferdinand II **Obv:** Bust right in ruffled collar **Rev:** Crowned imperial eagle **Mint:** Prague **Note:** Prev. KM#1374.

Date	Mintage	VG	F	VF	XF	Unc
1623 (l)	—	15.00	25.00	45.00	85.00	—

KM# 245 30 KREUZER

Silver **Ruler:** Ferdinand II **Obv:** Laureate bust right in ruffled collar **Rev:** Crowned imperial eagle **Mint:** Prague **Note:** Prev. KM#1375.

Date	Mintage	VG	F	VF	XF	Unc
1620 (m)	—	45.00	90.00	165	275	—
1621 (l)	—	45.00	90.00	165	275	—
1621 (m)	—	45.00	90.00	165	275	—
1622	—	45.00	90.00	165	275	—

KM# 288 30 KREUZER

Silver **Ruler:** Ferdinand II **Obv:** Laureate bust right **Rev:** Crowned imperial eagle **Mint:** Kuttenberg **Note:** Prev. KM#1081.

Date	Mintage	VG	F	VF	XF	Unc
1621 (ee)	—	—	—	—	—	—

KM# 289 37 KREUZER

Silver **Ruler:** Ferdinand II **Obv:** Laureate bust right **Rev:** Crowned imperial eagle **Mint:** Kuttenberg **Note:** Prev. KM#1082.

Date	Mintage	VG	F	VF	XF	Unc
1621 (ee)	—	125	325	575	1,000	—
1622 (ee)	—	125	325	575	1,000	—

KM# 290 37-1/2 KREUZER

Silver **Ruler:** Ferdinand II **Obv:** Laureate bust right **Rev:** Crowned imperial eagle **Mint:** Kuttenberg **Note:** Prev. KM#1083.

Date	Mintage	VG	F	VF	XF	Unc
1621 (ee)	—	—	—	—	—	—

KM# 294 48 KREUZER

Silver **Ruler:** Ferdinand II **Obv:** Laureate bust right **Rev:** Crowned imperial eagle **Mint:** Kuttenberg **Note:** Prev. KM#1084.

Date	Mintage	VG	F	VF	XF	Unc
1621 (ee)	—	115	250	500	850	—

KM# 293 48 KREUZER

Silver **Ruler:** Ferdinand II **Obv:** Laureate bust right in ruffled collar **Rev:** Crowned imperial eagle **Mint:** Prague **Note:** Prev. KM#1376.

Date	Mintage	VG	F	VF	XF	Unc
1621 (l)	—	115	250	500	850	—
1622 (l)	—	115	250	500	850	—

KM# 295 48 KREUZER

Silver **Ruler:** Ferdinand II **Obv:** Laureate bust right in inner circle **Mint:** Joachimstal **Note:** Prev. KM#896.

Date	Mintage	VG	F	VF	XF	Unc
1621 (ak)	—	—	—	—	—	—

KM# 260 60 KREUZER

Silver **Ruler:** Ferdinand II **Obv:** Laureate bust right **Rev:** Crowned imperial eagle **Mint:** Kuttenberg **Note:** Prev. KM#1085.

Date	Mintage	VG	F	VF	XF	Unc
1620 (ee)	—	30.00	60.00	120	225	—
1621 (ee)	—	30.00	60.00	120	225	—

KM# 259 60 KREUZER

Silver **Ruler:** Ferdinand II **Obv:** Laureate bust right in ruffled collar **Rev:** Crowned imperial eagle **Mint:** Prague **Note:** Prev. KM#1377.

Date	Mintage	VG	F	VF	XF	Unc
1620 (m)	—	120	275	525	900	—
1620 (n)	—	120	275	525	900	—
1621 (l)	—	120	275	525	900	—

KM# 297 60 KREUZER

Silver **Ruler:** Ferdinand II **Obv:** Laureate bust right in ruffled collar, value below **Rev:** Crowned imperial eagle **Mint:** Joachimstal **Note:** Prev. KM#897.

Date	Mintage	VG	F	VF	XF	Unc
1621 (aj)	—	115	250	500	850	—
1621 (ak)	—	115	250	500	850	—

KM# 262 70 KREUZER

Silver **Ruler:** Friedrich von der Pfalz **Obv:** Value below bust **Mint:** Prague **Note:** Prev. KM#1331.

Date	Mintage	VG	F	VF	XF	Unc
1620 (m)	—	—	—	—	—	—

KM# 264 70 KREUZER (1/2 Taler)

Silver **Ruler:** Ferdinand II **Obv:** Laureate bust right **Rev:** Crowned imperial eagle **Mint:** Kuttenberg **Note:** Prev. KM#1086.

Date	Mintage	VG	F	VF	XF	Unc
1620 (ee)	—	110	240	450	750	—
1621 (ee)	—	110	240	450	750	—

KM# 299 75 KREUZER (1/2 Taler)

Silver **Ruler:** Ferdinand II **Obv:** Laureate bust right **Rev:** Crowned imperial eagle **Mint:** Kuttenberg **Note:** Prev. KM#1087.

Date	Mintage	VG	F	VF	XF	Unc
1621 (ee)	—	85.00	160	275	600	—
1622 (ee)	—	85.00	160	275	600	—

KM# 298 75 KREUZER (1/2 Taler)

Silver **Ruler:** Ferdinand II **Obv:** Laureate bust right in ruffled collar **Rev:** Crowned imperial eagle in inner circle, date in legend **Mint:** Kuttenberg **Note:** Prev. KM#1378.

Date	Mintage	VG	F	VF	XF	Unc
1621 (l)	—	75.00	140	270	700	—
1622 (l)	—	75.00	140	270	700	—
1623 (l)	—	75.00	140	270	700	—
1623 (n)	—	75.00	140	270	700	—

KM# 331 75 KREUZER (1/2 Taler)

Silver **Ruler:** Ferdinand II **Obv:** Laureate bust right in ruffled collar **Rev:** Crowned imperial eagle in inner circle, date in legend **Mint:** Joachimstal

Date	Mintage	VG	F	VF	XF	Unc
1622 (ak)	—	110	240	550	900	—
1623 (ak)	—	110	240	550	900	—

KM# 266 120 KREUZER (Taler)

Silver **Ruler:** Ferdinand II **Obv:** Laureate bust right in ruffled collar **Rev:** Crowned imperial eagle **Mint:** Prague **Note:** Prev. KM#1379.

Date	Mintage	VG	F	VF	XF	Unc
1620 (m)	—	45.00	90.00	200	325	—
1621 (l)	—	45.00	90.00	200	325	—

KM# 307 120 KREUZER (Taler)

Silver **Ruler:** Ferdinand II **Obv:** Laureate bust right in ruffled collar **Rev:** Crowned imperial eagle **Mint:** Joachimstal **Note:** Prev. KM#899.

Date	Mintage	VG	F	VF	XF	Unc
1621 (ak)	—	50.00	100	220	350	—
1622 (ak)	—	50.00	100	220	350	—

KM# 304 120 KREUZER (Taler)

Silver **Ruler:** Ferdinand II **Mint:** Prague **Note:** Klippe. Prev. KM#1380.

Date	Mintage	VG	F	VF	XF	Unc
1621 (l) Rare	—	—	—	—	—	—

KM# 305.1 120 KREUZER (Taler)

Silver **Ruler:** Ferdinand II **Obv:** Laureate bust right in ruffled collar **Rev:** Crowned imperial eagle **Mint:** Kuttenberg **Note:** Prev. KM#1088.

Date	Mintage	VG	F	VF	XF	Unc
1621 (ee)	—	65.00	130	290	450	—
1622 (ee)	—	65.00	130	290	450	—

KM# 305.2 120 KREUZER (Taler)

Silver **Ruler:** Ferdinand II **Obv:** Value as (1110) **Mint:** Kuttenberg **Note:** Prev. KM#1089.

Date	Mintage	VG	F	VF	XF	Unc
1621 (ee) Error	—	75.00	150	325	425	—

KM# 268 140 KREUZER (Taler)

Silver **Ruler:** Ferdinand II **Obv:** Laureate bust right in ruffled collar **Rev:** Crowned imperial eagle **Mint:** Kuttenberg **Note:** Prev. KM#1090.

Date	Mintage	VG	F	VF	XF	Unc
1620 (ee)	—	85.00	160	350	600	—
1621 (ee)	—	85.00	160	350	600	—

KM# 267 140 KREUZER (Taler)

Silver **Ruler:** Ferdinand II **Obv:** Laureate bust right in ruffled collar **Rev:** Crowned imperial eagle **Mint:** Prague **Note:** Prev. KM#1381.

Date	Mintage	VG	F	VF	XF	Unc
1620 (m)	—	50.00	100	220	350	—
1621 (l)	—	50.00	100	220	350	—

KM# 309 150 KREUZER (Taler)

Silver **Ruler:** Ferdinand II **Obv:** Laureate bust right in ruffled collar **Rev:** Crowned imperial eagle **Mint:** Kuttenberg **Note:** Prev. KM#1091.

Date	Mintage	VG	F	VF	XF	Unc
1621 (ee)	—	45.00	90.00	180	300	—
1622 (ee)	—	45.00	90.00	180	300	—
1623 (ee)	—	45.00	90.00	180	300	—

KM# 308 150 KREUZER (Taler)

Silver **Ruler:** Ferdinand II **Obv:** Value below bust **Mint:** Prague **Note:** Prev. KM#1382.

Date	Mintage	VG	F	VF	XF	Unc
1621 (l)	—	35.00	65.00	130	240	—
1622 (l)	—	35.00	65.00	130	240	—
1623 (n)	—	35.00	65.00	130	240	—

KM# 310 150 KREUZER (Taler)

Silver **Ruler:** Ferdinand II **Obv:** Laureate bust right in ruffled collar **Rev:** Crowned imperial eagle **Mint:** Joachimstal **Note:** Prev. KM#900.

Date	Mintage	VG	F	VF	XF	Unc
1621 (ak)	—	40.00	90.00	200	300	—
1622 (ak)	—	40.00	90.00	200	300	—
1623 (ak)	—	40.00	90.00	200	300	—

KM# 333 300 KREUZER (2 Taler)

Silver **Ruler:** Ferdinand II **Obv:** Laureate bust right in ruffled collar, value below bust **Rev:** Crowned imperial eagle **Mint:** Kuttenberg **Note:** Prev. KM#1092.

Date	Mintage	VG	F	VF	XF	Unc
1622 (ee)	—	70.00	145	325	550	—

KM# 432 1/8 THALER (1/2 Reichsort)

Silver **Ruler:** Ferdinand III **Obv:** Bust right in circle, titles of Ferdinand III **Rev:** EIN / HALB / REICHS / ORTH / date in oval baroque frame, titles continuous **Mint:** Prague **Note:** Prev. KM#1410.

Date	Mintage	VG	F	VF	XF	Unc
1639 (q)	—	800	1,400	2,250	3,500	—
1648 (q)	—	—	—	—	—	—

Note: Reported, not confirmed

MB# 252 1/4 THALER

Silver **Ruler:** Rudolf II **Obv:** Young armored bust of Rudolf II right **Rev:** Crowned imperial eagle **Mint:** Prague **Note:** Varieties exist.

Date	Mintage	VG	F	VF	XF	Unc
1601 (y)	—	85.00	175	300	525	—
160Z (y)	—	85.00	175	300	525	—

MB# 277 1/4 THALER

Silver **Ruler:** Rudolf II **Obv:** Young armored bust in ruffed collar right in inner circle **Rev:** Crowned double-headed eagle with sword and scepter in inner circle, date in legend **Mint:** Joachimstal **Note:** Varieties exist. Prev. KM#865.

Date	Mintage	VG	F	VF	XF	Unc
160Z (ah)	—	65.00	135	250	450	—
1604 (ai)	—	65.00	135	250	450	—

KM# 15 1/4 THALER

Silver **Ruler:** Rudolf II **Obv:** Full-length crowned and armored figure, turned slightly right, holding scepter and orb, small crowned shields of Bohemia left and Hungary right, titles of Rudolf II **Rev:** Crowned imperial eagle, arms of Austria-Burgundy on breast, date in legend **Mint:** Prague **Note:** Prev. KM#1298.

Date	Mintage	VG	F	VF	XF	Unc
1601 (j)	—	300	550	900	1,500	—
1602 (j)	—	300	550	900	1,500	—

KM# 21 1/4 THALER

Silver **Ruler:** Rudolf II **Mint:** Prague **Note:** Klippe. Prev. KM#1299.

Date	Mintage	VG	F	VF	XF	Unc
1602 (j)	—	—	—	—	—	—

KM# 20 1/4 THALER

Silver **Ruler:** Rudolf II **Mint:** Joachimstal **Note:** Klippe. Prev. KM#866.

Date	Mintage	VG	F	VF	XF	Unc
1602 (ah) Rare	—	—	—	—	—	—

KM# 33 1/4 THALER

Silver **Ruler:** Rudolf II **Mint:** Prague **Note:** Klippe. Prev. KM#1301.

Date	Mintage	VG	F	VF	XF	Unc
1603 (j)	—	—	—	—	—	—
1605 (j)	—	—	—	—	—	—
1605	—	—	—	—	—	—

KM# 34 1/4 THALER

Silver **Ruler:** Rudolf II **Obv:** Armored bust right, titles of Rudolf II **Rev:** Crowned imperial eagle **Mint:** Kuttenberg **Note:** Prev. KM#1025.

Date	Mintage	VG	F	VF	XF	Unc
1603 (z)	—	45.00	75.00	145	250	—
1604 (z)	—	45.00	75.00	145	250	—
1605 (z)	—	45.00	75.00	145	250	—
1606	—	45.00	75.00	145	250	—
1609 (aa)	—	45.00	75.00	145	250	—
1610 (aa)	—	45.00	75.00	145	250	—
1611 (aa)	—	45.00	75.00	145	250	—

KM# 49 1/4 THALER

Silver **Ruler:** Rudolf II **Obv:** Armored bust right, titles of Rudolf II **Rev:** Crowned imperial eagle **Mint:** Prague **Note:** Prev. KM#1300.

Date	Mintage	VG	F	VF	XF	Unc
1604 (j)	—	300	550	950	1,600	—
1605	—	300	550	950	1,600	—
1607 (j)	—	300	550	950	1,600	—
1608 (j)	—	300	550	950	1,600	—
1609	—	300	550	950	1,600	—
1610 (k)	—	300	550	950	1,600	—
1611 (l)	—	300	550	950	1,600	—

KM# 62 1/4 THALER

Silver **Ruler:** Rudolf II **Mint:** Joachimstal **Note:** Klippe. Prev. KM#868.

Date	Mintage	VG	F	VF	XF	Unc
1605 Rare	—	—	—	—	—	—

KM# 60 1/4 THALER

Silver **Ruler:** Rudolf II **Mint:** Kuttenberg **Note:** Klippe. Prev. KM#1026.

Date	Mintage	VG	F	VF	XF	Unc
1605 (z)	—	—	—	—	—	—
1607 (z)	—	—	—	—	—	—

KM# 61 1/4 THALER

Silver **Ruler:** Rudolf II **Obv:** Older bust **Rev:** Crowned imperial eagle with square-topped shield n breast, without sword and scepter **Mint:** Joachimstal **Note:** Prev. KM#867.

Date	Mintage	VG	F	VF	XF	Unc
1605 (aj)	—	65.00	135	250	450	—
1607 (aj)	—	65.00	135	250	450	—
1610 (aj)	—	65.00	135	250	450	—

KM# 116 1/4 THALER

Silver **Ruler:** Matthias II **Obv:** Crowned bust right in inner circle **Rev:** Crowned arms divide date in order collar **Mint:** Joachimstal **Note:** Prev. KM#882.

Date	Mintage	VG	F	VF	XF	Unc
1612 (aj)	—	50.00	90.00	185	350	—

KM# 115 1/4 THALER

Silver **Ruler:** Matthias II **Obv:** Crowned bust right, titles of Matthias **Rev:** Crowned four-fold arms with central shield of Austria-Burgundy divide date, surrounded by Order of the Golden Fleece, date in legend **Mint:** Prague **Note:** Prev. KM#1328.

Date	Mintage	VG	F	VF	XF	Unc
1612 (l)	—	—	—	—	—	—

KM# 157 1/4 THALER

Silver **Ruler:** Matthias II **Obv:** Bust right, titles of Matthias **Rev:** Crowned imperial eagle, arms of Austria-Burgundy on breast with chain of order around, date in legend **Mint:** Prague **Note:** Prev. KM#1329.1.

Date	Mintage	VG	F	VF	XF	Unc
1613 (l)	—	200	400	700	1,500	—
1614 (l)	—	200	400	700	1,500	—

Date	Mintage	VG	F	VF	XF	Unc
1616 (l)	—	200	400	700	1,500	—
1617 (l)	—	200	400	700	1,500	—
1618 (l)	—	200	400	700	1,500	—

KM# 158 1/4 THALER

Silver **Ruler:** Matthias II **Obv:** Bust in ruffled collar right **Rev:** Crowned imperial eagle **Mint:** Kuttenberg **Note:** Varieties exist. Prev. KM#1053.

Date	Mintage	VG	F	VF	XF	Unc
1613 (bb)	—	185	350	700	1,200	—
1614 (cc)	—	185	350	700	1,200	—
1615 (cc)	—	185	350	700	1,200	—
1616 (dd)	—	185	350	700	1,200	—
1617 (ee)	—	185	350	700	1,200	—
1618 (ee)	—	185	350	700	1,200	—
1619 (ee)	—	185	350	700	1,200	—

KM# 179 1/4 THALER

Silver **Ruler:** Matthias II **Mint:** Prague **Note:** Thick planchet. Prev. KM#1329.2.

Date	Mintage	VG	F	VF	XF	Unc
1615	—	—	—	—	—	—

KM# 194 1/4 THALER

Silver **Ruler:** Matthias II **Obv:** Bust in ruffled collar right in inner circle **Rev:** Crowned imperial eagle in inner circle, date in legend **Mint:** Joachimstal **Note:** Prev. KM#883.

Date	Mintage	VG	F	VF	XF	Unc
1616 (aj)	—	40.00	80.00	160	275	—
1617 (aj)	—	40.00	80.00	160	275	—
1618 (aj)	—	40.00	80.00	160	275	—

KM# 209 1/4 THALER

Silver **Ruler:** Ferdinand II **Obv:** Crowned full-length armored figure turned slightly to right holding scepter and orb, titles of Ferdinand II **Rev:** Crowned imperial eagle in inner circle, date in legend **Mint:** Joachimstal **Note:** Mule. Prev. KM#884.

Date	Mintage	VG	F	VF	XF	Unc
1618 (aj) Rare	—	—	—	—	—	—

KM# 312 1/4 THALER

Silver **Ruler:** Ferdinand II **Obv:** Laureate bust right, titles of Ferdinand II **Rev:** Crowned imperial eagle, Austria-Burgundy arms on breast, date in legend **Mint:** Joachimstal

Date	Mintage	VG	F	VF	XF	Unc
1621 (ak)	—	—	—	—	—	—

KM# 372 1/4 THALER

Silver **Ruler:** Ferdinand II **Mint:** Prague **Note:** Klippe. Prev. KM#1385.

Date	Mintage	VG	F	VF	XF	Unc
1623 (n) Rare	—	—	—	—	—	—
1624 (n) Rare	—	—	—	—	—	—

KM# 345 1/4 THALER

Silver **Ruler:** Ferdinand II **Obv:** Standing figure holding orb and scepter in inner circle **Rev:** Crowned imperial eagle in inner circle **Mint:** Joachimstal **Note:** Prev. KM#901.

Date	Mintage	VG	F	VF	XF	Unc
1623 (ak)	—	125	275	550	950	—
1624 (ak)	—	125	275	550	950	—
1625 (ak)	—	125	275	550	950	—
1627 (ak)	—	125	275	550	950	—
1628 (ak)	—	125	275	550	950	—

KM# 344 1/4 THALER

Silver **Ruler:** Ferdinand II **Obv:** Laureate bust right in ruffled collar **Rev:** Crowned imperial eagle **Mint:** Kuttenberg **Note:** Varieties exist. Prev. KM#1093.

Date	Mintage	VG	F	VF	XF	Unc
1623 (ee)	—	110	240	450	750	—
1624 (ee)	—	110	240	450	750	—
1625 (ee)	—	110	240	450	750	—
1626 (ee)	—	110	240	450	750	—
1627 (ee)	—	110	240	450	750	—
1628 (ee)	—	110	240	450	750	—
1629 (ee)	—	110	240	450	750	—
1630 (ee)	—	110	240	450	750	—
1631 (ee)	—	110	240	450	750	—
163Z (ee)	—	110	240	450	750	—
1633 (dd)	—	110	240	450	750	—
1633 (ff)	—	120	275	550	925	—
1634 (ff)	—	120	275	550	925	—
1637 (hh)	—	120	275	550	925	—
1638 (hh)	—	120	275	550	925	—

KM# 343 1/4 THALER

Silver **Ruler:** Ferdinand II **Obv:** Standing figure of Ferdinand II **Rev:** Crowned imperial eagle, crowned Bohemian arms surrounded by Order of the Golden Fleece on breast, date in legend **Mint:** Prague **Note:** Varieties exist. Prev. KM#1384.

Date	Mintage	VG	F	VF	XF	Unc
1623 (n)	—	75.00	140	250	575	—
1624 (n)	—	75.00	140	250	575	—
1625 (n)	—	75.00	140	250	575	—
1625 (l)	—	75.00	140	250	575	—
1630 (l)	—	75.00	140	250	575	—
1630 (o)	—	75.00	140	250	575	—
1631 (p)	—	75.00	140	250	575	—
1632 (p)	—	75.00	140	250	575	—
1633 (p)	—	75.00	140	250	575	—
1635 (p)	—	75.00	140	250	575	—
1637 (q)	—	75.00	140	250	575	—

KM# 346 1/4 THALER

Silver **Ruler:** Ferdinand II **Mint:** Prague **Note:** Weight of 1/2 Thaler. Prev. KM#1386.

Date	Mintage	VG	F	VF	XF	Unc
1623 Rare	—	—	—	—	—	—

KM# 416 1/4 THALER

Silver **Ruler:** Ferdinand III **Obv:** Bust of Ferdinand III right **Rev:** Crowned imperial eagle **Mint:** Kuttenberg **Note:** Prev. KM#1106.

Date	Mintage	VG	F	VF	XF	Unc
1638 (hh)	—	150	300	550	950	—
1641 (hh)	—	150	300	550	950	—

KM# 434 1/4 THALER

Silver **Ruler:** Ferdinand III **Obv:** Bare bust of Ferdinand III right in inner circle **Rev:** Crowned imperial eagle in inner circle, date in legend **Mint:** Joachimstal **Note:** Prev. KM#916.

Date	Mintage	VG	F	VF	XF	Unc
1639 (al)	—	125	275	550	950	—
1643 (al)	—	125	275	550	950	—
1656 (al)	—	125	275	550	950	—

KM# 433 1/4 THALER

Silver **Ruler:** Ferdinand III **Obv:** Bare-headed bust right **Rev:** Crowned imperial eagle **Mint:** Prague **Note:** Prev. KM#1411.

Date	Mintage	VG	F	VF	XF	Unc
1639 (q)	—	100	200	350	550	—
1640 (q)	—	100	200	350	550	—
1641 (q	—	100	200	350	550	—

KM# 462 1/4 THALER

Silver **Ruler:** Ferdinand III **Obv:** Laureate bust right **Rev:** Crowned imperial eagle **Mint:** Prague **Note:** Varieties exist. Prev. KM#1412.

Date	Mintage	VG	F	VF	XF	Unc
1642 (q)	—	100	200	350	550	—
1646 (q)	—	100	200	350	550	—
1647 (q)	—	100	200	350	550	—
1648 (q)	—	100	200	350	550	—
1653 (q)	—	100	200	350	550	—
1655 (q)	—	100	200	350	550	—
1656 (q)	—	100	200	350	550	—
1656 (r)	—	100	200	350	550	—
1657 (r)	—	100	200	350	550	—

KM# 495 1/4 THALER

Silver **Ruler:** Leopold I **Obv:** Laureate bust of Leopold I right **Rev:** Crowned imperial eagle **Mint:** Joachimstal **Note:** Prev. KM#933.

Date	Mintage	VG	F	VF	XF	Unc
1659 (an) Rare	—	—	—	—	—	—
1663 (an) Rare	—	—	—	—	—	—

KM# 592 1/4 THALER

Silver **Ruler:** Leopold I **Obv:** Laureate bust right **Rev:** Crowned imperial eagle with sword and scepter **Mint:** Prague **Note:** Varieties exist. Prev. KM#1435.

Date	Mintage	VG	F	VF	XF	Unc
1693 (t) MV	—	125	275	550	950	—
1693 (t)	—	125	275	550	950	—
1695 GE	—	125	275	550	950	—

KM# 593 1/4 THALER

Silver **Ruler:** Leopold I **Obv:** Bust right in inner circle **Rev:** Crowned imperial eagle in inner circle, value below, crown divides dates **Mint:** Prague **Note:** Prev. KM#1434.

Date	Mintage	VG	F	VF	XF	Unc
1693 MV	—	375	650	1,150	—	—

Note: Value on reverse is 1/2-an error coin

MB# 253 1/2 THALER

Silver **Ruler:** Rudolf II **Obv:** Armored bust of Rudolf II right **Rev:** Crowned imperial eagle **Mint:** Kuttenberg **Note:** Varieties exist. Prev. KM#1027.

Date	Mintage	VG	F	VF	XF	Unc
1601 (y)	—	115	250	500	900	—
160Z (y)	—	115	250	500	900	—

MB# 262 1/2 THALER

Silver **Ruler:** Rudolf II **Obv:** Young armored bust in ruffled collar right in inner circle **Rev:** Crowned imperial eagle with sword and scepter in inner circle, date in legend **Mint:** Joachimstal **Note:** Prev. KM#869.

Date	Mintage	VG	F	VF	XF	Unc
1601 (ah)	—	115	250	500	900	—

MB# 293 1/2 THALER

Silver **Ruler:** Rudolf II **Mint:** Prague

Date	Mintage	VG	F	VF	XF	Unc
1585 (i)	—	—	—	—	—	—

MB# 323 1/2 THALER

Silver **Ruler:** Rudolf II **Obv:** Standing figure **Rev:** Crowned imperial eagle **Mint:** Prague **Note:** Varieties exist. Prev. KM#1302.

Date	Mintage	VG	F	VF	XF	Unc
1601 (j)	—	200	450	750	1,350	—
160Z (j)	—	200	450	750	1,350	—
1603 (j)	—	200	450	750	1,350	—
1604 (j)	—	200	450	750	1,350	—
1606 (J)	—	200	450	750	1,350	—

KM# 16 1/2 THALER

Silver **Ruler:** Rudolf II **Obv:** Standing figure, half right, holding scepter and orb, shield of arms on each side **Mint:** Prague **Note:** Prev. KM#1302.

Date	Mintage	VG	F	VF	XF	Unc
1601	—	200	400	750	1,350	—
1602	—	200	400	750	1,350	—
1603	—	200	400	750	1,350	—

Date	Mintage	VG	F	VF	XF	Unc
1606	—	200	400	750	1,350	—
1608	—	200	400	750	1,350	—
1609 (b)	—	200	400	750	1,350	—
1610 (b)	—	200	400	750	1,350	—
1610 (c)	—	200	400	750	1,350	—
1611	—	200	400	750	1,350	—

KM# 22 1/2 THALER

Silver **Ruler:** Rudolf II **Mint:** Kuttenberg **Note:** Klippe.

Date	Mintage	VG	F	VF	XF	Unc
1602 Rare	—	—	—	—	—	—

KM# 24 1/2 THALER

Silver **Ruler:** Rudolf II **Mint:** Prague **Note:** Klippe. Prev. KM#1032.

Date	Mintage	VG	F	VF	XF	Unc
160Z (j) Rare	—	—	—	—	—	—
1604 (j) Rare	—	—	—	—	—	—

KM# 23 1/2 THALER

Silver **Ruler:** Rudolf II **Obv:** Young armored bust in ruffled collar in inner circle **Mint:** Joachimstal **Note:** Klippe. Prev. KM#875.

Date	Mintage	VG	F	VF	XF	Unc
1602 (ah) Rare	—	—	—	—	—	—
1603 (ah) Rare	—	—	—	—	—	—

KM# 35 1/2 THALER

Silver **Ruler:** Rudolf II **Obv:** Bust right of Rudolf II **Rev:** Crowned imperial eagle **Mint:** Kuttenberg **Note:** Prev. KM#1029.

Date	Mintage	VG	F	VF	XF	Unc
1603 (z)	—	85.00	165	325	600	—
1604 (z)	—	85.00	165	325	600	—
1605 (z)	—	85.00	165	325	600	—
1606 (z)	—	85.00	165	325	600	—
1608 (z)	—	85.00	165	325	600	—
1610 (aa)	—	85.00	165	325	600	—
1611 (aa)	—	85.00	165	325	600	—

KM# 51 1/2 THALER

Silver **Ruler:** Rudolf II **Obv:** Older bust **Rev:** Crowned imperial eagle with square-topped shield on breast, without sword and scepter **Mint:** Joachimstal **Note:** Prev. KM#872.

Date	Mintage	VG	F	VF	XF	Unc
1604 (ai)	—	100	200	350	650	—
1606 (ai)	—	100	200	350	650	—
1606 (aj)	—	100	200	350	650	—
1607 (aj)	—	100	200	350	650	—
1609 (aj)	—	100	200	350	650	—
1610 (aj)	—	100	200	350	650	—

KM# 52 1/2 THALER

Silver **Ruler:** Rudolf II **Mint:** Joachimstal **Note:** Klippe. Prev. KM#873.1.

Date	Mintage	VG	F	VF	XF	Unc
1604 (ai) Rare	—	—	—	—	—	—
1608 Rare	—	—	—	—	—	—

KM# 50 1/2 THALER

Silver **Ruler:** Rudolf II **Mint:** Joachimstal **Note:** Struck from dies of 1/4 Taler, MB#277. Prev. KM#871.

Date	Mintage	VG	F	VF	XF	Unc
1604 (ai) Rare	—	—	—	—	—	—

KM# 67 1/2 THALER

Silver **Ruler:** Rudolf II **Obv:** Armored bust right in inner circle **Rev:** Crowned imperial eagle in inner circle, date in legend **Mint:** Budweis **Note:** Prev. KM#235.

Date	Mintage	VG	F	VF	XF	Unc
1605 (bf)	—	35.00	70.00	160	275	—
1606 (bf)	—	35.00	70.00	160	275	—
1608 (bf)	—	35.00	70.00	160	275	—
1609 (bf)	—	35.00	70.00	160	275	—
1610 (bf)	—	35.00	70.00	160	275	—

KM# 65 1/2 THALER

Silver **Ruler:** Rudolf II **Mint:** Kuttenberg **Note:** Klippe. Struck from 1/4 Taler dies, KM#34. Prev. KM#1030.

Date	Mintage	VG	F	VF	XF	Unc
1605 (z) Rare	—	—	—	—	—	—

Note: Stack's International sale 3-88 VF realized $15,400. Leu Numismatik Auction 75, 10-99, XF realized $38,665.

KM# 66 1/2 THALER

Silver **Ruler:** Rudolf II **Mint:** Joachimstal **Note:** Prev. KM#873.2. Struck from 1/4 Taler dies, KM#867.

Date	Mintage	VG	F	VF	XF	Unc
1605 (aj) Rare	—	—	—	—	—	—
1608 (aj) Rare	—	—	—	—	—	—

KM# 77 1/2 THALER

Silver **Ruler:** Rudolf II **Obv:** Armored bust right in ruffled collar **Rev:** Crowned imperial eagle **Mint:** Prague **Note:** Prev. KM#1304.

Date	Mintage	VG	F	VF	XF	Unc
1606 (j)	—	250	450	800	1,500	—
1608 (j)	—	250	450	800	1,500	—
1609 (k)	—	250	450	800	1,500	—
1610 (k)	—	250	450	800	1,500	—
1610 (l)	—	250	450	800	1,500	—
1611 (l)	—	250	450	800	1,500	—

KM# 97 1/2 THALER

Silver **Ruler:** Matthias II **Rev:** 15-fold arms **Mint:** Prague **Note:** Prev. KM#1330.

Date	Mintage	VG	F	VF	XF	Unc
1611 (l) Rare	—	—	—	—	—	—

KM# 98 1/2 THALER

Silver **Ruler:** Matthias II **Obv:** Crowned and ruffled bust right in inner circle **Mint:** Prague **Note:** Prev. KM#1331.

Date	Mintage	VG	F	VF	XF	Unc
1611 (l) Rare	—	—	—	—	—	—
1612 (l) Rare	—	—	—	—	—	—

KM# 119 1/2 THALER

Silver **Ruler:** Matthias II **Obv:** Three crowned busts to right, names and titles of Masimilian I, Karl V, and Ferdinand I **Rev:** Imperial eagle, Castile-Austria arms on breast, titles continuous **Mint:** Prague **Note:** Prev. KM#1333.

Date	Mintage	VG	F	VF	XF	Unc
ND(1612-19) Rare	—	—	—	—	—	—

KM# 118 1/2 THALER

Silver **Ruler:** Rudolf II **Obv:** Crowned and ruffled bust right in inner circle **Rev:** Crowned arms divide date in order collar **Mint:** Joachimstal **Note:** Prev. KM#885.

Date	Mintage	VG	F	VF	XF	Unc
1612 (aj) Rare	—	—	—	—	—	—

KM# 159 1/2 THALER

Silver **Ruler:** Rudolf II **Obv:** Bust right **Rev:** Crowned imperial eagle **Mint:** Prague **Note:** Prev. KM#1332.

Date	Mintage	VG	F	VF	XF	Unc
1613 (l)	—	200	475	825	1,600	—
1614 (l)	—	200	475	825	1,600	—
1615 (l)	—	200	475	825	1,600	—
1616 (l)	—	200	475	825	1,600	—
1617 (l)	—	200	475	825	1,600	—
1618 (l)	—	200	475	825	1,600	—
1619 (l)	—	200	475	825	1,600	—

KM# 160 1/2 THALER

Silver **Ruler:** Matthias II **Obv:** Bust in ruffled collar right **Rev:** Crowned imperial eagle **Mint:** Kuttenberg **Note:** Prev. KM#1054.

Date	Mintage	VG	F	VF	XF	Unc
1613 (bb)	—	350	725	1,125	1,900	—
1614 (cc)	—	350	725	1,125	1,900	—
1615 (cc)	—	350	725	1,125	1,900	—
1616 (ee)	—	350	725	1,125	1,900	—
1617 (ee)	—	350	725	1,125	1,900	—
1618 (ee)	—	350	725	1,125	1,900	—
1619 (ee)	—	350	725	1,125	1,900	—

KM# 195 1/2 THALER

Silver **Ruler:** Matthias II **Obv:** Bust right in inner circle **Rev:** Crowned imperial eagle in inner circle, date in legend **Mint:** Joachimstal **Note:** Prev. KM#886.

Date	Mintage	VG	F	VF	XF	Unc
1616 (aj)	—	—	—	—	—	—

KM# 230 1/2 THALER

Silver **Ruler:** Matthias II **Mint:** Kuttenberg **Note:** Prev. KM#1055. Struck on thick flan from dies of 1/4 Taler, KM#158.

Date	Mintage	VG	F	VF	XF	Unc
1619 (ee) Rare	—	—	—	—	—	—

KM# 335 1/2 THALER

Silver **Ruler:** Ferdinand II **Mint:** Prague **Note:** Klippe. Prev. KM#1389.

Date	Mintage	VG	F	VF	XF	Unc
1622 (n)	—	200	300	500	950	—
1625 (l)	—	250	350	650	1,150	—

KM# 348 1/2 THALER

Silver **Ruler:** Ferdinand II **Mint:** Prague **Note:** Klippe. Prev. KM#1389. Struck from 1/4 Taler dies, KM#343 on square flan.

Date	Mintage	VG	F	VF	XF	Unc
16Z3 (n) Rare	—	—	—	—	—	—

KM# 349 1/2 THALER

Silver **Ruler:** Ferdinand II **Obv:** Standing figure of Ferdinand **Rev:** Crowned imperial eagle **Mint:** Kuttenberg **Note:** Prev. KM#1094. Varieties exist.

Date	Mintage	VG	F	VF	XF	Unc
1623 (ee)	—	35.00	75.00	160	325	—
1624 (ee)	—	35.00	75.00	160	325	—
1625 (ee)	—	35.00	75.00	160	325	—
1626 (ee)	—	35.00	75.00	160	325	—
1627 (ee)	—	35.00	75.00	160	325	—
1628 (ee)	—	35.00	75.00	160	325	—
1629 (ee)	—	35.00	75.00	160	325	—
1630 (ee)	—	35.00	75.00	160	325	—
1631 (ee)	—	35.00	75.00	160	325	—
163Z (ee)	—	35.00	75.00	160	325	—
1633 (dd)	—	35.00	75.00	160	325	—
1633 (ff)	—	35.00	75.00	160	325	—
1634 (ff)	—	35.00	75.00	160	325	—

KM# 350 1/2 THALER

Silver **Ruler:** Ferdinand II **Obv:** Standing figure **Rev:** Crowned imperial eagle **Mint:** Joachimstal **Note:** Prev. KM#902.

Date	Mintage	VG	F	VF	XF	Unc
1623 (ak)	—	85.00	160	300	650	—
1624 (ak)	—	85.00	160	300	650	—
1625 (ak)	—	85.00	160	300	650	—
1626 (ak)	—	85.00	160	300	650	—
1627 (ak)	—	85.00	160	300	650	—
1628 (ak)	—	85.00	160	300	650	—

KM# 347 1/2 THALER

Silver **Ruler:** Ferdinand II **Obv:** Standing figure of Ferdinand II **Rev:** Crowned imperial eagle **Mint:** Prague **Note:** Varieties exist. Prev. KM#1387.

Date	Mintage	VG	F	VF	XF	Unc
1623 (n)	—	100	220	475	875	—
1624 (n)	—	100	220	475	875	—
1625 (n)	—	100	220	475	875	—
1625 (l)	—	100	220	475	875	—
1626 (l)	—	100	220	475	875	—
1630 (l)	—	100	220	475	875	—
1630 (o)	—	100	220	475	875	—
1631 (p)	—	100	220	475	875	—
1632 (p)	—	100	220	475	875	—
1633 (p)	—	100	220	475	875	—
1635 (p)	—	100	220	475	875	—
1637 (q)	—	100	220	475	875	—

KM# 397 1/2 THALER

Silver **Ruler:** Ferdinand II **Mint:** Prague **Note:** Muled with 1/4 Thaler die. Prev. KM#1388.

Date	Mintage	VG	F	VF	XF	Unc
1631 (g) Rare	—	—	—	—	—	—

KM# 417 1/2 THALER

Silver **Ruler:** Ferdinand III **Obv:** Bare-headed bust right in lace collar **Rev:** Crowned imperial eagle **Mint:** Prague **Note:** Prev. KM#1413.

Date	Mintage	VG	F	VF	XF	Unc
1638 (q)	—	65.00	125	220	375	—
1639 (q)	—	65.00	125	220	375	—
1640 (q)	—	65.00	125	220	375	—
1641 (q)	—	65.00	125	220	375	—

KM# 418 1/2 THALER

Silver **Ruler:** Ferdinand III **Obv:** Bare-headed bust right **Rev:** Crowned imperial eagle **Mint:** Kuttenberg **Note:** Prev. KM#1107.

Date	Mintage	VG	F	VF	XF	Unc
1638 (hh)	—	120	250	500	825	—
1641 (hh)	—	120	250	500	825	—

KM# 436 1/2 THALER

Silver **Ruler:** Ferdinand III **Obv:** Bare-headed bust of Ferdinand III right **Rev:** Crowned imperial eagle **Mint:** Joachimstal **Note:** Prev. KM#917.

Date	Mintage	VG	F	VF	XF	Unc
1639 (al) Rare	—	—	—	—	—	—

KM# 437 1/2 THALER

Silver **Ruler:** Ferdinand III **Obv:** Laureate bust right **Rev:** Crowned imperial eagle **Mint:** Joachimstal **Note:** Prev. KM#918.

Date	Mintage	VG	F	VF	XF	Unc
1639 (al) Rare	—	—	—	—	—	—
1643 (al) Rare	—	—	—	—	—	—
1656 Rare	—	—	—	—	—	—

KM# 452 1/2 THALER

Silver **Ruler:** Ferdinand III **Obv:** Laureate bust right in lace collar **Rev:** Crowned imperial eagle **Mint:** Prague **Note:** Prev. KM#1414.

Date	Mintage	VG	F	VF	XF	Unc
1641 (q)	—	65.00	125	220	375	—
1644 (q)	—	65.00	125	220	375	—
1646 (q)	—	65.00	125	220	375	—
1647 (q)	—	65.00	125	220	375	—
1648 (q)	—	65.00	125	220	375	—
1649 (q)	—	65.00	125	220	375	—
1653 (q)	—	65.00	125	220	375	—
1655 (rr)	—	65.00	125	220	375	—
1656 (rr)	—	65.00	125	220	375	—

KM# 466 1/2 THALER

Silver **Ruler:** Ferdinand III **Obv:** Laureate bust of Ferdinand III **Rev:** Crowned imperial eagle **Mint:** Kuttenberg **Note:** Prev. KM#1111.

Date	Mintage	VG	F	VF	XF	Unc
1643 (hh) Rare	—	—	—	—	—	—

KM# 496 1/2 THALER

Silver **Ruler:** Leopold I **Obv:** Laureate bust of Leopold I right **Rev:** Crowned imperial eagle **Mint:** Joachimstal **Note:** Prev. KM#934.

Date	Mintage	VG	F	VF	XF	Unc
1659 (an) Rare	—	—	—	—	—	—

Note: Restrike reported

KM# 570 1/2 THALER

Silver **Ruler:** Leopold I **Obv:** Laureate bust right **Rev:** Crowned imperial eagle **Mint:** Kuttenberg **Note:** Prev. KM#1122.

Date	Mintage	VG	F	VF	XF	Unc
1671 (ii) Rare	—	—	—	—	—	—

KM# 577 1/2 THALER

Silver **Ruler:** Leopold I **Obv:** Small laureate bust right **Rev:** Crowned imperial eagle **Mint:** Prague **Note:** Prev. KM#1436.

Date	Mintage	VG	F	VF	XF	Unc
1676 (s)	—	100	200	375	650	—

KM# 594 1/2 THALER

Silver **Ruler:** Leopold I **Obv:** Large laureate bust right **Rev:** Crowned imperial eagle holding sword and scepter **Mint:** Prague **Note:** Prev. KM#1438.1.

Date	Mintage	VG	F	VF	XF	Unc
1693 MV	—	110	240	500	825	—
1693 (t)	—	110	240	500	825	—

KM# 609 1/2 THALER

Silver **Ruler:** Leopold I **Mint:** Prague **Note:** Prev. KM#1438.2.

Date	Mintage	VG	F	VF	XF	Unc
1695 GE	—	80.00	150	300	500	—

KM# 610 1/2 THALER

Silver **Ruler:** Leopold I **Obv:** Older bust right **Rev:** Crowned imperial eagle **Mint:** Kuttenberg **Note:** Prev. KM#1123.

Date	Mintage	VG	F	VF	XF	Unc
1695 (jj) Rare	—	—	—	—	—	—

MB# 257 THALER

Silver **Ruler:** Rudolf II **Obv:** Bust right **Rev:** Stylized crowned imperial eagle **Mint:** Budweis **Note:** Varieties exist. Dav. #3029. Prev. KM#236.

Date	Mintage	VG	F	VF	XF	Unc
1601 (bg)	—	375	550	1,100	1,750	—
160Z (bg)	—	375	550	1,100	1,750	—
1603 (bg) Rare	—	—	—	—	—	—

MB# 255 THALER

Silver **Ruler:** Maximilian II **Obv:** Young armored bust in ruffled collar right, lion and three dots below **Rev:** Crowned imperial eagle **Mint:** Kuttenberg **Note:** Dav. #8079. Varieties exist. Prev. KM#1031.

Date	Mintage	VG	F	VF	XF	Unc
1601 (y)	—	100	170	265	500	—
160Z (y)	—	100	170	265	500	—

MB# 256 THALER

Silver **Ruler:** Rudolf II **Obv:** Young armored bust in ruffled collar right **Rev:** Crowned imperial eagle with sword and scepter **Mint:** Joachimstal **Note:** Dav. #3020. Varieties exist.

Date	Mintage	VG	F	VF	XF	Unc
1601 (ah)	—	70.00	130	235	450	—
160Z (ah)	—	70.00	130	235	450	—
1603 (ah)	—	70.00	130	235	450	—
1604 (ah)	—	70.00	130	235	450	—

MB# 300 THALER

Silver **Ruler:** Rudolf II **Obv:** Standing figure **Mint:** Prague **Note:** Dav. #8075. Prev. KM#1305. Varieties exist.

Date	Mintage	VG	F	VF	XF	Unc
1601 (j)	—	200	400	650	1,050	—
1602 (j)	—	200	400	650	1,050	—
1602	—	200	400	650	1,050	—

MB# 305 THALER

Silver **Ruler:** Rudolf II **Mint:** Prague **Note:** Klippe. Prev. KM#1306.

Date	Mintage	VG	F	VF	XF	Unc
1602 Rare	—	—	—	—	—	—

KM# 17 THALER

Silver **Ruler:** Rudolf II **Obv:** Standing figure, half right, holding scepter and orb, shield of arms on each side **Rev:** Crowned imperial eagle with shield on breast in inner circle, date in legend **Mint:** Prague **Note:** Prev. KM#1305.

Date	Mintage	VG	F	VF	XF	Unc
1601	—	200	400	650	1,050	—
1602	—	200	400	650	1,050	—

KM# 29 THALER

Silver **Ruler:** Rudolf II **Obv:** Armored bust in ruffled collar right in inner circle, ornamentatin in lower border **Mint:** Prague **Note:** Prev. KM#1306.

Date	Mintage	VG	F	VF	XF	Unc
1602 Rare	—	—	—	—	—	—

KM# 27 THALER

Silver **Ruler:** Rudolf II **Obv:** Wide bust right **Rev:** Eagle with square-topped shield on breast without sword and scepter **Mint:** Joachimstal **Note:** Varieties exist. Dav. #3021. Prev. KM#875.

Date	Mintage	VG	F	VF	XF	Unc
1602 (ah) Rare	—	—	—	—	—	—
1604 (ah) Rare	—	—	—	—	—	—
1604 (ai) Rare	—	—	—	—	—	—
1605 (ai) Rare	—	—	—	—	—	—
1606 (ai) Rare	—	—	—	—	—	—
1606 (aj) Rare	—	—	—	—	—	—
1607 (aj) Rare	—	—	—	—	—	—
1608 (aj) Rare	—	—	—	—	—	—
1609 (aj) Rare	—	—	—	—	—	—

KM# 26 THALER

Silver **Ruler:** Rudolf II **Obv:** Older, wider bust in ruffled collar **Mint:** Kuttenberg **Note:** Varieties exist. Dav. #3028. Prev. KM#1034.

Date	Mintage	VG	F	VF	XF	Unc
1602 (y)	—	85.00	170	265	450	—
1603 (y)	—	85.00	170	265	450	—
1603 (z)	—	85.00	170	265	450	—
1604 (z)	—	85.00	170	265	450	—
1605 (z)	—	85.00	170	265	450	—
1606 (z)	—	85.00	170	265	450	—
1607 (z)	—	85.00	170	265	450	—
1608 (z)	—	85.00	170	265	450	—
1608 (aa)	—	85.00	170	265	450	—
1609 (z)	—	85.00	170	265	450	—
1609 (aa)	—	85.00	170	265	450	—
1610 (aa)	—	85.00	170	265	450	—
1611 (aa)	—	85.00	170	265	450	—
1612 (aa)	—	85.00	170	265	450	—

KM# 28 THALER

Silver **Ruler:** Rudolf II **Obv:** Lion below older bust, without dots **Mint:** Kuttenberg **Note:** Prev. KM#1032.

Date	Mintage	VG	F	VF	XF	Unc
1602	—	85.00	170	265	450	—

KM# 37 THALER

Silver **Ruler:** Rudolf II **Obv:** Older, larger bust, lion and arabesques below **Mint:** Kuttenberg **Note:** Prev. KM#1033.

Date	Mintage	VG	F	VF	XF	Unc
1603 (c)	—	85.00	170	265	450	—

KM# 36 THALER

Silver **Ruler:** Rudolf II **Obv:** Bust right, lion below **Rev:** Crowned imperial eagle **Mint:** Budweis **Note:** Dav. #3030. Prev. KM#237.

Date	Mintage	VG	F	VF	XF	Unc
1603 (bf)	—	85.00	170	265	450	—
1604 (bf)	—	85.00	170	265	450	—
1605 (bf)	—	85.00	170	265	450	—
1606 (bf)	—	85.00	170	265	450	—
1607 (bf)	—	85.00	170	265	450	—
1608 (bf)	—	85.00	170	265	450	—
1609 (bf)	—	85.00	170	265	450	—
1610 (bf)	—	85.00	170	265	450	—
1611 (bf)	—	85.00	170	265	450	—

KM# 25 THALER

Silver **Ruler:** Rudolf II **Obv:** Armored bust in ruffled collar **Rev:** Crowned imperial eagle **Mint:** Prague **Note:** Varieties exist. Dav. #3019. Prev. KM#1307.

Date	Mintage	VG	F	VF	XF	Unc
1603 (j)	—	200	400	650	1,150	—
1604 (j)	—	200	400	650	1,150	—
1605 (j)	—	200	400	650	1,150	—
1606 (j)	—	200	400	650	1,150	—
1607 (j)	—	200	400	650	1,150	—
1608 (j)	—	200	400	650	1,150	—
1609 (k)	—	200	400	650	1,150	—
1610 (k)	—	200	400	650	1,150	—
1610 (l)	—	200	400	650	1,150	—
1611 (l)	—	200	400	650	1,150	—

KM# 53 THALER

Silver **Ruler:** Rudolf II **Mint:** Prague **Note:** Klippe. Dav. #3019A. Prev. KM#1308.

Date	Mintage	VG	F	VF	XF	Unc
1604 (j) Rare	—	—	—	—	—	—
1606 (j) Rare	—	—	—	—	—	—
1607 (j) Rare	—	—	—	—	—	—

KM# 93 THALER

Silver **Ruler:** Rudolf II **Obv:** Crowned bust right in ruffled collar **Rev:** Crowned shield in collar of the Golden Fleece **Mint:** Joachimstal **Note:** Dav. #3022. Prev. KM#876.

Date	Mintage	VG	F	VF	XF	Unc
1610 aj Rare	—	—	—	—	—	—
1611 aj Rare	—	—	—	—	—	—
1612 aj Rare	—	—	—	—	—	—

KM# 122 THALER

Silver **Ruler:** Rudolf II **Obv:** Crowned bust right in inner circle **Rev:** Crowned arms divide date in order collar **Mint:** Joachimstal **Note:** Prev. KM#876.

Date	Mintage	VG	F	VF	XF	Unc
1610 Rare	—	—	—	—	—	—
1611 Rare	—	—	—	—	—	—
1612 (aj) Rare	—	—	—	—	—	—

KM# 94 THALER

Silver **Ruler:** Rudolf II **Obv:** Older bust **Mint:** Joachimstal **Note:** Prev. KM#876.

Date	Mintage	VG	F	VF	XF	Unc
1610 (c) Rare	—	—	—	—	—	—
1611 (c) Rare	—	—	—	—	—	—
1612 (c) Rare	—	—	—	—	—	—

KM# 100 THALER

Silver **Ruler:** Rudolf II **Obv:** Crowned bust right **Rev:** Crowned shield in collar of the Golden Fleece **Mint:** Prague **Note:** Dav. #3057. Prev. KM#1334.

Date	Mintage	VG	F	VF	XF	Unc
1611 (l)	—	325	625	1,200	1,900	—
ND	—	325	600	1,100	1,800	—

KM# 101 THALER

Silver **Ruler:** Rudolf II **Obv:** Crowned bust right in ruffled collar **Rev:** Crowned shield in collar of the Golden Fleece **Mint:** Prague **Note:** Dav. #3058. Prev. KM#1335.

Date	Mintage	VG	F	VF	XF	Unc
1611 (l)	—	200	400	650	1,050	—
1612 (l)	—	200	400	650	1,050	—

KM# 124 THALER

Silver **Ruler:** Matthias II **Obv:** Bust right in ruffled collar **Rev:** Maximilian I, Charles V and Ferdinand I **Mint:** Prague **Note:** Dav. #3064.

Date	Mintage	VG	F	VF	XF	Unc
ND (l)	—	875	1,600	3,300	6,000	—

KM# 123 THALER

Silver **Ruler:** Matthias II **Obv:** Crowned conjoined busts of Maximilian I, Charles V and Ferdinand I **Rev:** Crowned imperial eagle **Mint:** Prague **Note:** Dav. #3066. Prev. KM#1339.

Date	Mintage	VG	F	VF	XF	Unc
ND(1612-19)	—	875	1,600	3,300	6,000	—

KM# 121.1 THALER

Silver **Ruler:** Rudolf II **Obv:** Crowned and armored bust **Mint:** Joachimstal **Note:** Dav. #3067. Prev. KM#887.1. Thick planchet variety exists.

Date	Mintage	VG	F	VF	XF	Unc
1612 (aj)	—	200	400	725	1,200	—

KM# 120 THALER

Silver **Ruler:** Rudolf II **Obv:** Crowned and armored bust right **Mint:** Kuttenberg **Note:** Dav. #3069. Prev. KM#1056.

Date	Mintage	VG	F	VF	XF	Unc
1612 (aa)	—	200	325	550	875	—
1612 (bb)	—	200	325	550	875	—
1613 (aa)	—	200	325	550	875	—
1613 (bb)	—	200	325	550	875	—

KM# 126 THALER

Silver **Ruler:** Matthias II **Obv:** Bust of Matthias right in inner circle **Rev:** Crowned busts of Maximilian I, Charles V, and Ferdinand I right in inner circle **Mint:** Prague **Note:** Prev. KM#1338.

Date	Mintage	VG	F	VF	XF	Unc
ND	—	775	1,400	2,400	4,200	—

KM# 121.2 THALER

Silver **Ruler:** Rudolf II **Mint:** Joachimstal **Note:** Thick planchet.

Date	Mintage	VG	F	VF	XF	Unc
1612 aj	—	240	450	875	1,400	—

KM# 125 THALER

Silver **Ruler:** Matthias II **Mint:** Joachimstal **Note:** Thick planchet. Prev. KM#887.2.

Date	Mintage	VG	F	VF	XF	Unc
1612	—	200	400	650	1,050	—

KM# 161 THALER

Silver **Ruler:** Matthias II **Obv:** Bust right in ruffled collar **Rev:** Crowned imperial eagle **Mint:** Prague **Note:** Prev. KM#1336. Dav. #3061.

Date	Mintage	VG	F	VF	XF	Unc
1613 (l)	—	100	210	425	700	—
1614 (l)	—	100	210	425	700	—
1615 (l)	—	100	210	425	700	—
1616 (l)	—	100	210	425	700	—
1617 (l)	—	100	210	425	700	—
1618 (l)	—	100	210	425	700	—
1619 (l)	—	100	210	425	700	—

KM# 163 THALER

Silver **Ruler:** Matthias II **Obv:** Bust in ruffled collar right in inner circle **Rev:** Crowned imperial eagle in inner circle, date in legend **Mint:** Joachimstal **Note:** Prev. KM#888. Dav. #3068. Varieties exist.

Date	Mintage	VG	F	VF	XF	Unc
1613 (aj)	—	200	400	725	1,200	—
1614 (aj)	—	200	400	725	1,200	—
1615 (aj)	—	200	400	725	1,200	—
1616 (aj)	—	200	400	725	1,200	—
1617 (aj)	—	200	400	725	1,200	—
1618 (aj)	—	200	400	725	1,200	—
1619 (aj)	—	200	400	725	1,200	—

KM# 162 THALER

Silver **Ruler:** Matthias II **Obv:** Bust in ruffled collar **Rev:** Crowned imperial eagle **Mint:** Kuttenberg **Note:** Prev. KM#1057. Dav. #3071. Varieties exist.

Date	Mintage	VG	F	VF	XF	Unc
1613 (bb)	—	140	240	425	700	—
1614 (bb)	—	140	240	425	700	—
1614 (cc)	—	140	240	425	700	—
1615 (cc)	—	140	240	425	700	—
1615 (dd)	—	140	240	425	700	—
1616 (aa)	—	140	240	425	700	—
1616 (cc)	—	140	240	425	700	—
1616 (dd)	—	140	240	425	700	—
1616 (ee)	—	140	240	425	700	—
1617 (ee)	—	140	240	425	700	—
1618 (ee)	—	140	240	425	700	—
1619 (ee)	—	140	240	425	700	—

KM# 180 THALER

Silver **Ruler:** Matthias II **Obv:** Bust right in ruffled collar **Rev:** Crowned imperial eagle in inner circle, date in legend **Mint:** Prague **Note:** Klippe. Dav. #3061A. Prev. KM#1337.

Date	Mintage	VG	F	VF	XF	Unc
1615 (l) Rare	—	—	—	—	—	—

KM# 210 THALER

Silver **Ruler:** Matthias II **Obv:** Smaller bust right in inner circle **Mint:** Kuttenberg **Note:** Prev. KM#1058.

Date	Mintage	VG	F	VF	XF	Unc
1618	—	170	265	450	725	—
1619	—	170	265	450	725	—

KM# 270 THALER

Silver **Ruler:** Ferdinand II **Obv:** Crowned full-length armored figure holding scepter and orb, turned slightly right, crowned arms of Bohemia and Electoral Pfalz to left and right, titles of Friedrich **Rev:** Round five-fold arms, date in legend **Mint:** Prague **Note:** Prev. KM#99(1558).

Date	Mintage	VG	F	VF	XF	Unc
1620 (m)	—	—	—	—	—	—

KM# 313 THALER

Silver **Ruler:** Ferdinand II **Obv:** Laureate bust right in inner circle **Rev:** Crowned imperial eagle, date in legend **Mint:** Joachimstal **Note:** Prev. KM#314. Dav. #3140.

Date	Mintage	VG	F	VF	XF	Unc
1621 (ak)	—	400	725	1,200	2,000	—
1622 (ak)	—	400	725	1,200	2,000	—

KM# 314 THALER

Silver **Ruler:** Ferdinand II **Obv:** Laureate bust right in inner circle **Mint:** Joachimstal **Note:** Prev. KM#903.

Date	Mintage	VG	F	VF	XF	Unc
1621 (e)	—	400	725	1,200	2,000	—
1622 (e)	—	400	725	1,200	2,000	—

KM# 354 THALER

28.8500 g., Silver **Ruler:** Ferdinand II **Rev:** Arms of Bohemia on eagle's breast **Mint:** Prague **Note:** Prev. KM#1390.1. Dav. #3136.

Date	Mintage	VG	F	VF	XF	Unc
1623 (n)	—	50.00	130	220	425	—
1624 (n)	—	50.00	130	220	425	—
1625 (n)	—	50.00	130	220	425	—
1625 (l)	—	50.00	130	220	425	—
1626 (l)	—	50.00	130	220	425	—
1627 (l)	—	50.00	130	220	425	—
1628 (l)	—	50.00	130	220	425	—
1629 (l)	—	50.00	130	220	425	—
1630 (l)	—	50.00	130	220	425	—
1630 (o)	—	50.00	130	220	425	—
1631 (o)	—	50.00	130	220	425	—
1631 (p)	—	50.00	130	220	425	—
1632 (p)	—	50.00	130	220	425	—
1633 (p)	—	50.00	130	220	425	—
1634 (p)	—	50.00	130	220	425	—
1635 (p)	—	50.00	130	220	425	—
1637 (p)	—	50.00	130	220	425	—
1637 (q)	—	50.00	130	220	425	—
1638 (q)	—	50.00	130	220	425	—

Note: 1638 coins are posthumous

KM# 353 THALER

Silver **Ruler:** Ferdinand II **Obv:** Full-length crowned and armored figure slightly right, with scepter and orb, crowned arms of Bohemia and Hungary to left and right, titles of Ferdinand II **Rev:** Crowned imperial eagle, Austria-Burgundy arms on breast, date in legend **Mint:** Prague

Date	Mintage	VG	F	VF	XF	Unc
1623 (n)	—	—	—	—	—	—

KM# 356 THALER

Silver **Ruler:** Ferdinand II **Mint:** Joachimstal **Note:** Dav. #3141. Prev. KM#904. Varieties exist.

Date	Mintage	VG	F	VF	XF	Unc
1623 (ak)	—	45.00	120	210	325	—
1624 (ak)	—	45.00	120	210	325	—
1625 (ak)	—	45.00	120	210	325	—
1626 (ak)	—	45.00	120	210	325	—
1627 (ak)	—	45.00	120	210	325	—
1630 (ak)	—	45.00	120	210	325	—
1631 (ak)	—	45.00	120	210	325	—
1632 (ak)	—	45.00	120	210	325	—

KM# 355 THALER

Silver **Ruler:** Ferdinand II **Obv:** Standing figure of Ferdinand **Rev:** Crowned imperial eagle **Mint:** Kuttenberg **Note:** Dav. #3143. Prev. KM#1095. Varieties exist.

Date	Mintage	VG	F	VF	XF	Unc
1623 (ee)	—	55.00	140	240	475	—
1624 (ee)	—	55.00	140	240	475	—
1625 (ee)	—	55.00	140	240	475	—
1626 (ee)	—	55.00	140	240	475	—
1627 (ee)	—	55.00	140	240	475	—
1628 (ee)	—	55.00	140	240	475	—
1629 (ee)	—	55.00	140	240	475	—
1630 (ee)	—	55.00	140	240	475	—
1631 (ee)	—	55.00	140	240	475	—
163Z (ee)	—	55.00	140	240	475	—
1633 (ee)	—	55.00	140	240	475	—
1633 (dd)	—	55.00	140	240	475	—
1633 (ff)	—	55.00	140	240	475	—
1634 (ff)	—	55.00	140	240	475	—
1636 (ff)	—	55.00	140	240	475	—
1636 (hh)	—	55.00	140	240	475	—
1637 (hh)	—	55.00	140	240	475	—

KM# 376 THALER

Silver **Ruler:** Ferdinand II **Obv:** No arms to left or right of figure **Mint:** Prague

Date	Mintage	VG	F	VF	XF	Unc
1624 (n)	—	—	—	—	—	—

KM# 377 THALER

Silver **Ruler:** Ferdinand II **Mint:** Prague **Note:** Klippe. Dav. #3136A. Prev. KM#1391.1.

Date	Mintage	VG	F	VF	XF	Unc
1624 (n) Rare	—	—	—	—	—	—

KM# 389 THALER

Silver **Ruler:** Ferdinand II **Obv:** Standing figure, "g" between feet **Mint:** Prague **Note:** Dav. #3136C. Prev. KM#1403. Varieties exist.

Date	Mintage	VG	F	VF	XF	Unc
1626 (l)	—	50.00	130	220	425	—

KM# 395 THALER

Silver **Ruler:** Ferdinand II **Obv:** Standing figure, slightly right, holding orb and scepter, titles of Ferdinand II **Rev:** Crowned imperial eagle **Mint:** Prague **Note:** Dav. #3137. Prev. KM#1392.

Date	Mintage	VG	F	VF	XF	Unc
1629 (l)	—	55.00	145	240	450	—
1630 (l)	—	55.00	145	240	450	—
1631 (p)	—	55.00	145	240	450	—

KM# 420 THALER

Silver **Ruler:** Ferdinand III **Obv:** Bare-headed bust right in lace collar **Rev:** Crowned imperial eagle **Mint:** Prague **Note:** Dav. #3204. Prev. KM#1415.

Date	Mintage	VG	F	VF	XF	Unc
1638 (q)	—	100	200	325	575	—
1639 (q)	—	100	200	325	575	—
1640 (q)	—	100	200	325	575	—
1641 (q)	—	100	200	325	575	—

KM# 421 THALER

Silver **Ruler:** Ferdinand III **Obv:** Bare-headed bust right **Rev:** Crowned imperial eagle **Mint:** Kuttenberg **Note:** Dav. #3212. Prev. KM#1108.

Date	Mintage	VG	F	VF	XF	Unc
1638 (hh)	—	130	235	400	650	—
1639 (hh)	—	130	235	400	650	—
1641 (hh)	—	130	235	400	650	—

KM# 440 THALER

Silver **Ruler:** Ferdinand III **Obv:** Laureate bust right **Rev:** Crowned imperial eagle **Mint:** Kuttenberg **Note:** Dav. #3213. Prev. KM#1109.

Date	Mintage	VG	F	VF	XF	Unc
1639 (hh)	—	130	235	400	650	—

Date	Mintage	VG	F	VF	XF	Unc
1641 (hh)	—	130	235	400	650	—
1643 (hh)	—	130	235	400	650	—

KM# 439 THALER

Silver **Ruler:** Ferdinand III **Obv:** Bust right in inner circle **Rev:** Crowned imperial eagle in inner circle, date in legend **Mint:** Joachimstal **Note:** Dav. #3208. Prev. KM#919.

Date	Mintage	VG	F	VF	XF	Unc
1639 (al)	—	130	235	400	650	—
1641 (al)	—	130	235	400	650	—
1642 (al)	—	130	235	400	650	—
1643 (al)	—	130	235	400	650	—

KM# 453 THALER

Silver **Ruler:** Ferdinand III **Obv:** Laureate bust right **Rev:** Crowned imperial eagle **Mint:** Prague **Note:** Dav. #3205. Prev. KM#1416.

Date	Mintage	VG	F	VF	XF	Unc
1641 (q)	—	100	200	325	575	—
1642 (q)	—	100	200	325	575	—
1643 (q)	—	100	200	325	575	—
1644 (q)	—	100	200	325	575	—
1645 (q)	—	100	200	325	575	—
1646 (q)	—	100	200	325	575	—
1647 (q)	—	100	200	325	575	—
1648 (q)	—	100	200	325	575	—
1649 (q)	—	100	200	325	575	—
1653 (q)	—	100	200	325	575	—
1656 (r)	—	100	200	325	575	—

KM# 467 THALER

Silver **Ruler:** Ferdinand III **Obv:** Laureate bust right in inner circle **Rev:** Crowned imperial eagle in inner circle, date in legend **Mint:** Joachimstal **Note:** Dav. #3210. Prev. KM#920.

Date	Mintage	VG	F	VF	XF	Unc
1643 (al)	—	130	235	400	650	—
1644 (al)	—	130	235	400	650	—
1656 (an)	—	130	235	400	650	—

KM# 497 THALER

Silver **Ruler:** Ferdinand III **Obv:** Large laureate bust right **Rev:** Crowned imperial eagle **Mint:** Kuttenberg **Note:** Dav. #3282. Prev. KM#1124.

Date	Mintage	VG	F	VF	XF	Unc
1659 (ii) Rare	—	—	—	—	—	—
1666 (ii)	—	550	925	1,550	2,350	—
1669 (ii)	—	550	925	1,550	2,350	—
1671 (ii)	—	550	925	1,550	2,350	—

KM# 498 THALER

Silver **Ruler:** Leopold I **Obv:** Laureate bust of Leopold I right **Rev:** Crowned imperial eagle **Mint:** Joachimstal **Note:** Prev. KM#935. Dav. #3281. Restrikes reported.

Date	Mintage	VG	F	VF	XF	Unc
1659 (an) Rare	—	—	—	—	—	—

KM# 575 THALER

Silver **Ruler:** Leopold I **Obv:** Laureate bust right **Rev:** Crowned imperial eagle holding sword and scepter **Mint:** Prague **Note:** Prev. KM#1439. Dav. #3278.

Date	Mintage	VG	F	VF	XF	Unc
1674 (s) Rare	—	—	—	—	—	—

KM# 611 THALER

Silver **Ruler:** Leopold I **Obv:** Large laureate bust right in long wig, lion's head at shoulder **Rev:** Crowned imperial eagle holding sword and scepter **Mint:** Prague **Note:** Prev. KM#1440.1. Dav. #3279.

Date	Mintage	VG	F	VF	XF	Unc
1695 GE	—	155	300	550	1,100	—

KM# 612 THALER

Silver **Ruler:** Leopold I **Obv:** Older large laureate bust right **Rev:** Crowned imperial eagle **Mint:** Kuttenberg **Note:** Prev. KM#1126. Dav. #3284.

Date	Mintage	VG	F	VF	XF	Unc
1695 (jj)	—	400	725	1,200	2,000	—

KM# 616 THALER

Silver **Ruler:** Leopold I **Obv:** Large laureate bust right in long wig, without lion head at shoulder **Mint:** Prague **Note:** Prev. KM#1440.2. Dav. #1006.

Date	Mintage	VG	F	VF	XF	Unc
1696 GE	—	145	240	425	1,000	—

KM# 128 1-1/2 THALER

Silver **Ruler:** Matthias II **Obv:** Bust right in ruffled collar **Rev:** Crowned busts of Maximilian, Charles V, and Ferdinand I **Mint:** Prague **Note:** Prev. KM#1340. Dav. #A3063.

Date	Mintage	VG	F	VF	XF	Unc
ND (l) Rare	—	—	—	—	—	—

KM# 127 1-1/2 THALER

Silver **Ruler:** Matthias II **Obv:** Crowned busts of Maximilian, Charles V, and Ferdinand I **Rev:** Crowned imperial eagle **Mint:** Prague **Note:** Prev. KM#1341.

Date	Mintage	VG	F	VF	XF	Unc
ND(1612-19) Rare	—	—	—	—	—	—

MB# 312 2 THALER

Silver **Ruler:** Rudolf II **Obv:** Young armored bust in ruffled collar right in inner circle **Rev:** Crowned imperial eagle with sword and secpter in inner circle, date in legend **Mint:** Joachimstal **Note:** Dav. #8077, A3020. Prev. KM#877.

Date	Mintage	VG	F	VF	XF	Unc
1602 (ah)	—	—	—	—	—	—
1603 (ah)	—	—	—	—	—	—

MB# 320 2 THALER

Silver **Ruler:** Matthias II **Obv:** Armored bust in ruffled collar right **Rev:** Crowned imperial eagle **Mint:** Prague **Note:** Dav. #3018. Prev. KM#1309.

Date	Mintage	VG	F	VF	XF	Unc
1602 (j)	—	725	1,200	2,400	4,200	—
1603 (j)	—	725	1,200	2,400	4,200	—
1604 (j)	—	725	1,200	2,400	4,200	—
1605 (j)	—	725	1,200	2,400	4,200	—
1606 (j)	—	725	1,200	2,400	4,200	—
1608 (j)	—	725	1,200	2,400	4,200	—
1609 (j)	—	725	1,200	2,400	4,200	—
1609 (k)	—	725	1,200	2,400	4,200	—
1610 (k)	—	725	1,200	2,400	4,200	—
1610 (l)	—	725	1,200	2,400	4,200	—
1611 (l)	—	725	1,200	2,400	4,200	—

KM# 38 2 THALER

Silver **Ruler:** Rudolf II **Rev:** Oval four-fold arms of Bohemia and Hungary with central shield of Austria-Burgundy on eagle's breast **Mint:** Kuttenberg **Note:** Dav. #3027. Prev. KM#1035.

Date	Mintage	VG	F	VF	XF	Unc
1603 (Y)	—	—	—	—	—	—

KM# 39 2 THALER

Silver **Ruler:** Rudolf II **Obv:** Bust right, lion below **Rev:** Crowned imperial eagle **Mint:** Kuttenberg **Note:** Dav. #3027A. Prev. KM#1036.

Date	Mintage	VG	F	VF	XF	Unc
1603 (z)	—	95.00	180	290	500	—
1604 (z)	—	95.00	180	290	500	—
1605 (z)	—	95.00	180	290	500	—
1606 (z)	—	95.00	180	290	500	—
1607 (z)	—	95.00	180	290	500	—
1608 (z)	—	95.00	180	290	500	—
1608 (aa)	—	95.00	180	290	500	—
1609 (aa)	—	95.00	180	290	500	—
1610 (aa)	—	95.00	180	290	500	—
1611 (aa)	—	95.00	180	290	500	—

KM# 54 2 THALER

Silver **Ruler:** Rudolf II **Mint:** Prague **Note:** Klippe. Dav. #3018A.

Date	Mintage	VG	F	VF	XF	Unc
1604 (j) Rare	—	—	—	—	—	—
1606 (j) Rare	—	—	—	—	—	—

KM# 70 2 THALER

Silver **Ruler:** Rudolf II **Mint:** Kuttenberg **Note:** Klippe. Dav. #3027B. Prev. KM#1037.

Date	Mintage	VG	F	VF	XF	Unc
1605 (z) Rare	—	—	—	—	—	—

KM# 71 2 THALER

Silver **Ruler:** Rudolf II **Obv:** Older armored bust right, lion and two arabesques below **Mint:** Joachimstal **Note:** Dav. #A3021. Prev. KM#878.1.

Date	Mintage	VG	F	VF	XF	Unc
1605 (ai) Rare	—	—	—	—	—	—
1606 (ai) Rare	—	—	—	—	—	—

KM# 91 2 THALER

Silver **Ruler:** Rudolf II **Mint:** Budweis

Date	Mintage	VG	F	VF	XF	Unc
1609 (bf) Rare	—	—	—	—	—	—

KM# 90 2 THALER

Silver **Ruler:** Rudolf II **Obv:** Without arabesques below bust **Mint:** Joachimstal **Note:** Prev. KM#878.2.

Date	Mintage	VG	F	VF	XF	Unc
1609 (aj) Rare	—	—	—	—	—	—

KM# 103 2 THALER

Silver **Ruler:** Rudolf II **Obv:** Crowned bust right **Rev:** Crowned shield in collar of the Order of the Golden Fleece **Mint:** Prague **Note:** Prev. KM#1342. Dav. #A3057.

Date	Mintage	VG	F	VF	XF	Unc
1611 (l) Rare	—	—	—	—	—	—

KM# 104 2 THALER

Silver **Ruler:** Rudolf II **Obv:** Crowned bust right in ruffled collar **Rev:** Crowned shield in collar of the Order of the Golden Fleece **Mint:** Prague

Date	Mintage	VG	F	VF	XF	Unc
1611 (l)	—	1,200	2,000	3,300	5,400	—
1612 (l)	—	1,200	2,000	3,300	5,400	—

KM# 131 2 THALER

Silver **Ruler:** Matthias II **Obv:** Crowned conjoined busts of Maximilian I, Charles V and Ferdinand I **Rev:** Crowned imperial eagle **Mint:** Prague **Note:** Dav. #3065. Prev. KM#1349.

Date	Mintage	VG	F	VF	XF	Unc
ND(1612-19) (l) Rare	—	—	—	—	—	—

KM# 130 2 THALER

Silver **Ruler:** Matthias II **Obv:** Large crowned bust right **Rev:** Crowned shield divides date in order collar **Mint:** Kuttenberg **Note:** Dav. #A3069. Prev. KM#1059.

Date	Mintage	VG	F	VF	XF	Unc
1612 (aa) Rare	—	—	—	—	—	—
1612 (bb) Rare	—	—	—	—	—	—

KM# 132 2 THALER

Silver **Ruler:** Matthias II **Obv:** Bust of Matthias right **Rev:** Crowned bust of Maximilian I, Charles V and Ferdinand I **Mint:** Prague **Note:** Dav. #B3063. Prev. KM#1348.

Date	Mintage	VG	F	VF	XF	Unc
ND(1612-19) Rare	—	—	—	—	—	—

KM# 166 2 THALER

Silver **Ruler:** Matthias II **Obv:** Large bust right **Rev:** Crowned imperial eagle **Mint:** Kuttenberg **Note:** Dav. #3070. Prev. KM#1060 and #1061. Varieties exist.

Date	Mintage	VG	F	VF	XF	Unc
1613 (bb)	—	875	1,450	2,400	3,950	—
1614 (bb)	—	875	1,450	2,400	3,950	—
1615 (cc)	—	875	1,450	2,400	3,950	—
1616 (aa)	—	875	1,450	2,400	3,950	—
1616 (dd)	—	875	1,450	2,400	3,950	—
1617 (ee)	—	875	1,450	2,400	3,950	—
1618 (ee)	—	875	1,450	2,400	3,950	—
1619 (ee)	—	875	1,450	2,400	3,950	—

KM# 165 2 THALER

Silver **Ruler:** Matthias II **Obv:** Bust right in ruffled collar **Rev:** Crowned imperial eagle **Mint:** Prague **Note:** Dav. #3060. Prev. KM#1344.

Date	Mintage	VG	F	VF	XF	Unc
1613 (l)	—	325	725	1,700	3,300	—
1614 (l)	—	325	725	1,700	3,300	—
1615 (l)	—	325	725	1,700	3,300	—
1616 (l)	—	325	725	1,700	3,300	—
1618 (l)	—	325	725	1,700	3,300	—
1619 (l)	—	325	725	1,700	3,300	—

KM# 184 2 THALER

Silver **Ruler:** Matthias II **Obv:** Matthias standing flanked by shield **Rev:** Crowned imperial eagle **Mint:** Prague **Note:** Dav. #3062. Prev. KM#1346.1.

Date	Mintage	VG	F	VF	XF	Unc
1615 (l)	—	875	1,550	2,650	4,600	—
1616 (l)	—	875	1,550	2,650	4,600	—
1617 (l)	—	875	1,550	2,650	4,600	—
1619 (l)	—	875	1,550	2,650	4,600	—

KM# 183 2 THALER

Silver **Ruler:** Matthias II **Obv:** Bust right in ruffled collar **Rev:** Crowned imperial eagle **Mint:** Prague **Note:** Klippe. Dav. #3060A. Prev. KM#1345.

Date	Mintage	VG	F	VF	XF	Unc
1615 (l) Rare	—	—	—	—	—	—

KM# 181 2 THALER

Silver **Ruler:** Matthias II **Obv:** Full-length figure of emperor turned slightly to right, holding orb and scepter, small crowned shield of Bohemian arms at left, Hungarian to right, titles of Matthias **Rev:** Crowned imperial eagle, arms of Austria-Burgundy on breast, chain of order around, date in legend **Mint:** Prague **Note:** Thick planchet. Dav. #3062A. Prev. KM#1347.

Date	Mintage	VG	F	VF	XF	Unc
1615 (l)	—	875	1,450	2,500	4,300	—
1618	—	875	1,450	2,500	4,300	—

KM# 211 2 THALER

Silver **Ruler:** Matthias II **Obv:** Bust in ruffled collar right in inner circle **Rev:** Crowned imperial eagle, date in legend **Mint:** Joachimstal **Note:** Dav. #A3068. Prev. KM#889.

Date	Mintage	VG	F	VF	XF	Unc
1618 (aj) Rare	—	—	—	—	—	—

KM# 315 2 THALER

Silver **Ruler:** Ferdinand II **Obv:** Laureate bust right in inner circle **Rev:** Crowned imperial eagle in inner circle, date in legend **Mint:** Joachimstal **Note:** Prev. KM#905.

Date	Mintage	VG	F	VF	XF	Unc
1621 (ak) Rare	—	—	—	—	—	—

KM# 362 2 THALER

Silver **Ruler:** Ferdinand II **Obv:** Ferdinand II standing holding orb and scepter in inner circle **Mint:** Joachimstal **Note:** Prev. KM#906. Dav. #A3141.

Date	Mintage	VG	F	VF	XF	Unc
1623 (ak)	—	725	1,300	2,150	3,250	—
1624 (ak)	—	725	1,300	2,150	3,250	—
1625 (ak)	—	725	1,300	2,150	3,250	—
1626 (ak)	—	725	1,300	2,150	3,250	—
1627 (ak)	—	725	1,300	2,150	3,250	—
1630 (ak)	—	725	1,300	2,150	3,250	—
1631 (ak)	—	725	1,300	2,150	3,250	—
1632 (ak)	—	725	1,300	2,150	3,250	—

KM# 361 2 THALER

Silver **Ruler:** Ferdinand II **Obv:** Standing figure of Ferdinand II holding orb and scepter **Rev:** Crowned imperial eagle **Mint:** Kuttenberg **Note:** Prev. KM#1096. Dav. #3142. Varieties exist.

Date	Mintage	VG	F	VF	XF	Unc
1623 (ee)	—	725	1,300	2,150	3,600	—
1624 (ee)	—	725	1,300	2,150	3,600	—
1625 (ee)	—	725	1,300	2,150	3,600	—
1626 (ee)	—	725	1,300	2,150	3,600	—
1627 (ee)	—	725	1,300	2,150	3,600	—
1628 (ee)	—	725	1,300	2,150	3,600	—
1630 (ee)	—	725	1,300	2,150	3,600	—
1631 (ee)	—	725	1,300	2,150	3,600	—
1632 (ee)	—	725	1,300	2,150	3,600	—
1634 (ff)	—	725	1,300	2,150	3,600	—

KM# 359 2 THALER

Silver **Ruler:** Ferdinand II **Obv:** Laureate bust right **Rev:** Crowned imperial eagle **Mint:** Prague **Note:** Prev. KM#1393.

Date	Mintage	VG	F	VF	XF	Unc
1623 (n) Rare	—	—	—	—	—	—

KM# 360 2 THALER

Silver **Ruler:** Ferdinand II **Obv:** Standing figure of Ferdinand II **Rev:** Crowned imperial eagle **Mint:** Prague **Note:** Prev. KM#1394. Dav. #3135. Varieties exist.

Date	Mintage	VG	F	VF	XF	Unc
1623 (n) Rare	—	—	—	—	—	—
1629 (l) Rare	—	—	—	—	—	—
1630 (l) Rare	—	—	—	—	—	—
1632 (p) Rare	—	—	—	—	—	—

KM# 358 2 THALER

Silver **Ruler:** Ferdinand II **Mint:** Prague **Note:** Dav. #3134.

Date	Mintage	VG	F	VF	XF	Unc
1623 (n) Rare	—	—	—	—	—	—

KM# 396 2 THALER

Silver **Ruler:** Ferdinand II **Obv:** Laureate bust facing in ruffled collar **Rev:** Crowned imperial eagle **Mint:** Prague **Note:** Prev. KM#1395. Dav. #3138.

Date	Mintage	VG	F	VF	XF	Unc
1630 (l) Rare	—	—	—	—	—	—

KM# 422 2 THALER

Silver **Ruler:** Ferdinand III **Obv:** Bare-headed bust right **Rev:** Crowned imperial eagle **Mint:** Kuttenberg **Note:** Prev. KM#1110. Dav. #3211.

Date	Mintage	VG	F	VF	XF	Unc
1638 (hh) Rare	—	—	—	—	—	—

KM# 454 2 THALER

Silver **Ruler:** Ferdinand III **Obv:** Bare head of Ferdinand III right in inner circle **Rev:** Crowned imperial eagle in inner circle, date in legend **Mint:** Joachimstal **Note:** Prev. KM#921. Dav. #3207.

Date	Mintage	VG	F	VF	XF	Unc
1641 (al) Rare	—	—	—	—	—	—
1643 (al) Rare	—	—	—	—	—	—

KM# 564 2 THALER

Silver **Ruler:** Leopold I **Obv:** Bust right **Rev:** Crowned imperial eagle **Mint:** Kuttenberg

Date	Mintage	VG	F	VF	XF	Unc
1666 Rare	—	—	—	—	—	—

KM# 198 2-1/2 THALER

Silver **Ruler:** Matthias II **Obv:** Matthias standing holding scepter and orb in inner circle **Rev:** Crowned imperial eagle in inner circle; date in legend **Mint:** Prague **Note:** Klippe.

Date	Mintage	VG	F	VF	XF	Unc
1616 (c) Rare	—	—	—	—	—	—

KM# 40 3 THALER

Silver **Ruler:** Rudolf II **Obv:** Armored bust in ruffled collar right **Rev:** Crowned imperial eagle, oval shield on breast **Mint:** Kuttenberg **Note:** Dav. #3026. Prev. KM#1038.

Date	Mintage	VG	F	VF	XF	Unc
1603 Rare	—	—	—	—	—	—

KM# 41 3 THALER

Silver **Ruler:** Rudolf II **Obv:** Bust right in ruffled collar **Rev:** Crowned imperial eagle, flat-topped shield on breast **Mint:** Kuttenberg **Note:** Dav. #3026A. Prev. KM#1039.

Date	Mintage	VG	F	VF	XF	Unc
1603 (z) Rare	—	—	—	—	—	—
1607 (z) Rare	—	—	—	—	—	—
1608 (z) Rare	—	—	—	—	—	—

MB# 324 3 THALER

Silver **Ruler:** Rudolf II **Mint:** Prague **Note:** Dav. #A8074.

Date	Mintage	VG	F	VF	XF	Unc
1603 (y) Rare	—	—	—	—	—	—

KM# 135 3 THALER

Silver **Ruler:** Matthias II **Obv:** Bust of Matthias right in ruffled collar **Rev:** Crowned conjoined busts of Maximilian I, Charles V, and Ferdinand I **Mint:** Prague **Note:** Prev. KM#1352. Dav. #C3063.

Date	Mintage	VG	F	VF	XF	Unc
ND (l) Rare	—	—	—	—	—	—

KM# 134 3 THALER

Silver **Ruler:** Matthias II **Obv:** Crowned bust of Maximilian I, Charles V, and Ferdinand I **Rev:** Crowned imperial eagle **Mint:** Prague **Note:** Prev. KM#1353.

Date	Mintage	VG	F	VF	XF	Unc
ND(612-19) Rare	—	—	—	—	—	—

KM# 199 3 THALER

Silver **Ruler:** Matthias II **Obv:** Matthias standing holding scepter and orb **Rev:** Crowned imperial eagle **Mint:** Prague **Note:** Dav. #B3059. Prev. KM#1351.

Date	Mintage	VG	F	VF	XF	Unc
1616 (l) Rare	—	—	—	—	—	—

KM# 364 3 THALER

Silver **Ruler:** Matthias II **Mint:** Prague **Note:** Prev. KM#365.

Date	Mintage	VG	F	VF	XF	Unc
1623 (n) Rare	—	—	—	—	—	—

KM# 455 3 THALER

Silver **Ruler:** Ferdinand III **Obv:** Bare head of Ferdinand III **Mint:** Joachimstal **Note:** Prev. KM#923. Dav. #3206.

Date	Mintage	VG	F	VF	XF	Unc
1641 (al) Rare	—	—	—	—	—	—

KM# 472 3 THALER

Silver **Ruler:** Ferdinand III **Obv:** Laureate head of Ferdinand III **Mint:** Joachimstal **Note:** Prev. KM#924. Dav. #B3209.

Date	Mintage	VG	F	VF	XF	Unc
1644 (al) Rare	—	—	—	—	—	—

KM# 42 4 THALER

Silver **Ruler:** Rudolf II **Obv:** Armored bust in ruffled collar right **Rev:** Crowned imperial eagle **Mint:** Kuttenberg **Note:** Prev. KM#35. Dav. #A3026.

Date	Mintage	VG	F	VF	XF	Unc
1603 (z) Rare	—	—	—	—	—	—
1604 (z) Rare	—	—	—	—	—	—

KM# 137 4 THALER

Silver **Ruler:** Matthias II **Obv:** Bust of Matthias right **Rev:** Crowned busts of Maximilian I, Charles V, and Ferdinand I **Mint:** Prague **Note:** Prev. KM#1354. Dav. #3063.

Date	Mintage	VG	F	VF	XF	Unc
ND (l) Rare	—	—	—	—	—	—

KM# 473 4 THALER

Silver **Ruler:** Matthias II **Obv:** Laureate bust right in inner circle **Rev:** Crowned imperial eagle in inner circle, date in legend **Mint:** Joachimstal **Note:** Prev. KM#925. Dav. #3209.

Date	Mintage	VG	F	VF	XF	Unc
1644 (al) Rare	—	—	—	—	—	—

KM# 187 5 THALER

Silver **Ruler:** Matthias II **Obv:** Matthias standing holding scepter and orb **Rev:** Crowned imperial eagle **Mint:** Prague **Note:** Prev. KM#1355. Dav. #3059.

Date	Mintage	VG	F	VF	XF	Unc
1615 (l) Rare	—	—	—	—	—	—
1619 (l) Rare	—	—	—	—	—	—

KM# 400 6 THALER

Silver **Ruler:** Ferdinand II **Obv:** Standing figure of Ferdinand holding orb and scepter **Rev:** Crowned imperial eagle **Mint:** Kuttenberg **Note:** Prev. KM#1097. Dav. #A3142.

Date	Mintage	VG	F	VF	XF	Unc
1631 (ee) Rare	—	—	—	—	—	—

TRADE COINAGE

KM# 587 1/4 DUCAT

0.8750 g., 0.9860 Gold 0.0277 oz. AGW **Ruler:** Leopold I **Obv:** Laureate bust right, titles of Leopold I **Rev:** Crowned imperial eagle holding sword and scepter in talons, Bohemian arms on breast, date divided by crown at top, titles continuous **Mint:** Kuttenberg **Note:** Prev. KM#1128.

Date	Mintage	VG	F	VF	XF	Unc
1690 (jj) Rare	—	—	—	—	—	—

KM# 598 1/4 DUCAT

0.8750 g., 0.9860 Gold 0.0277 oz. AGW **Ruler:** Leopold I **Obv:** Older laureate bust right in long wig **Rev:** Crowned imperial eagle with sword and scepter **Mint:** Prague **Note:** Prev. KM#1441.

Date	Mintage	VG	F	VF	XF	Unc
1694 PM	—	195	350	600	1,100	—
1694 GE	—	195	350	600	1,100	—
1695 GE	—	195	350	600	1,100	—

KM# 79 1/2 DUCAT

1.7500 g., 0.9860 Gold 0.0555 oz. AGW **Ruler:** Rudolf II **Subject:** New Years **Mint:** Prague **Note:** Prev. KM#1311.

Date	Mintage	VG	F	VF	XF	Unc
1606	—	—	—	—	—	—

KM# 562 1/2 DUCAT

1.7500 g., 0.9860 Gold 0.0555 oz. AGW **Ruler:** Rudolf II **Obv:** Laureate bust right **Rev:** Crowned imperial eagle **Mint:** Prague **Note:** Prev. KM#1442.

Date	Mintage	VG	F	VF	XF	Unc
1665 (r)	—	215	400	650	1,150	—

KM# 588 1/2 DUCAT

1.7500 g., 0.9860 Gold 0.0555 oz. AGW **Ruler:** Rudolf II **Mint:** Kuttenberg **Note:** Prev. KM#1129.

Date	Mintage	VG	F	VF	XF	Unc
1690 (jj) Rare	—	—	—	—	—	—

KM# 614 1/2 DUCAT

1.7500 g., 0.9860 Gold 0.0555 oz. AGW **Ruler:** Rudolf II **Obv:** Laureate bust right **Rev:** Crowned imperial eagle with sword and scepter **Mint:** Prague **Note:** Prev. KM#1442.

Date	Mintage	VG	F	VF	XF	Unc
1695 GE	—	215	400	650	1,150	—

MB# 316 DUCAT

Silver **Ruler:** Rudolf II **Rev:** Arms of Austria-Burgundy on breast of eagle with Order of the Golden Fleece **Mint:** Prague **Note:** Varieties exist. Prev. KM#1312.

Date	Mintage	VG	F	VF	XF	Unc
1601 (j)	—	155	265	650	1,100	—
1602 (j)	—	155	265	650	1,100	—
1603 (j)	—	155	265	650	1,100	—
1604 (j)	—	155	265	650	1,100	—
1605 (j)	—	155	265	650	1,100	—

KM# 81 DUCAT

Silver **Ruler:** Rudolf II **Rev:** Crowned imperial eagle **Mint:** Prague **Note:** Varieties exist. Prev. KM#1313.

Date	Mintage	VG	F	VF	XF	Unc
1606 (j)	—	155	265	650	1,100	—
1608 (j)	—	155	265	650	1,100	—
1609 (k)	—	155	265	650	1,100	—
1610 (k)	—	155	265	650	1,100	—
1610 (l)	—	155	265	650	1,100	—
1611 (l)	—	155	265	650	1,100	—

KM# 106 DUCAT

Silver **Ruler:** Matthias II **Obv:** Matthias standing dividing date **Rev:** St. Wenceslas **Mint:** Prague **Note:** Prev. KM#1356.

Date	Mintage	VG	F	VF	XF	Unc
1611 (l)	—	260	425	900	1,800	—
1612 (l)	—	260	425	900	1,800	—
ND (l)	—	260	425	900	1,800	—

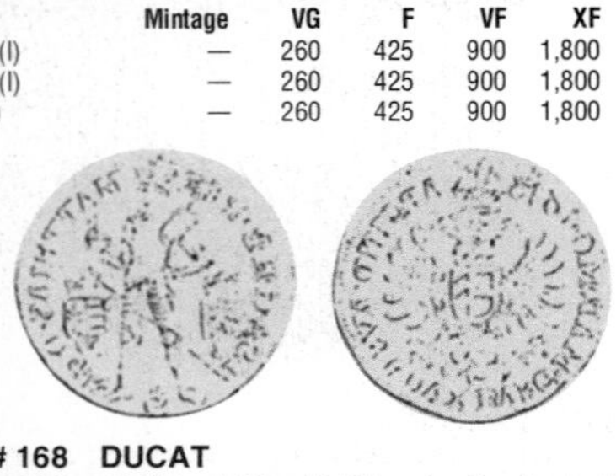

KM# 168 DUCAT

Silver **Ruler:** Matthias II **Obv:** Matthias standing flanked by two shields **Rev:** Crowned imperial eagle **Mint:** Prague **Note:** Prev. KM#1357.

Date	Mintage	VG	F	VF	XF	Unc
1613 (l)	—	215	400	725	1,200	—
1614 (l)	—	215	400	725	1,200	—
1615 (l)	—	215	400	725	1,200	—
1616 (l)	—	215	400	725	1,200	—
1617 (l)	—	215	400	725	1,200	—
1618 (l)	—	215	400	725	1,200	—
1619 (l)	—	215	400	725	1,200	—

KM# 275 DUCAT

Silver **Ruler:** Ferdinand II **Obv:** Standing figure of Ferdinand II between two shield, with Golden Fleece **Rev:** Crowned imperial eagle **Mint:** Prague **Note:** Varieties exist. Prev. KM#1396.

Date	Mintage	VG	F	VF	XF	Unc
1620 (m)	—	195	300	725	1,200	—
1623 (n)	—	195	300	725	1,200	—
1626 (l)	—	195	300	725	1,200	—
1627 (l)	—	195	300	725	1,200	—
1628 (l)	—	195	300	725	1,200	—
1629 (l)	—	195	300	725	1,200	—
1630 (l)	—	195	300	725	1,200	—
1630 (o)	—	195	300	725	1,200	—
1631 (o)	—	195	300	725	1,200	—
1632 (p)	—	195	300	725	1,200	—
1633 (p)	—	195	300	725	1,200	—
1634 (p)	—	195	300	725	1,200	—
1635 (p)	—	195	300	725	1,200	—
1636 (p)	—	195	300	725	1,200	—
1637 (p)	—	195	300	725	1,200	—
1637 (q)	—	260	350	900	1,500	—

KM# 390 DUCAT

Silver **Ruler:** Ferdinand II **Obv:** Shield without Golden Fleece **Mint:** Prague **Note:** Prev. KM#1397.

Date	Mintage	VG	F	VF	XF	Unc
1626 (l)	—	195	300	725	1,200	—
1627 (l)	—	195	300	725	1,200	—
1628 (l)	—	195	300	725	1,200	—

KM# 424 DUCAT

Silver **Ruler:** Ferdinand III **Obv:** Bare head right in lace collar **Rev:** Crowned imperial eagle **Mint:** Prague **Note:** Prev. KM#1417.

Date	Mintage	VG	F	VF	XF	Unc
1638 (q)	—	215	325	775	1,300	—
1639 (q)	—	215	325	775	1,300	—
1640 (q)	—	215	325	775	1,300	—

KM# 457 DUCAT

Silver **Ruler:** Ferdinand III **Obv:** Laureate bust right in lace collar **Rev:** Crowned imperial eagle **Mint:** Prague **Note:** Prev. KM#1418.

Date	Mintage	VG	F	VF	XF	Unc
1641 (q)	—	195	300	725	1,200	—
1645 (q)	—	195	300	725	1,200	—
1646 (q)	—	195	300	725	1,200	—
1648 (q)	—	195	300	725	1,200	—
1649 (q)	—	195	300	725	1,200	—
1651 (q)	—	195	300	725	1,200	—
1652 (q)	—	195	300	725	1,200	—
1655 (r)	—	195	300	725	1,200	—
1656 (r)	—	230	325	850	1,450	—

KM# 500 DUCAT

Silver **Ruler:** Ferdinand III **Obv:** Youthful bust right **Rev:** Crowned imperial eagle **Mint:** Prague **Note:** Prev. KM#1443.

Date	Mintage	VG	F	VF	XF	Unc
1659 (r) Rare	—	—	—	—	—	—

KM# 578 DUCAT

Silver **Ruler:** Ferdinand III **Obv:** Older laureate bust right in inner circle **Rev:** Crowned imperial eagle with sword and scepter in inner circle **Mint:** Prague **Note:** Varieties exist. Prev. KM#1444.

Date	Mintage	VG	F	VF	XF	Unc
1676 (s)	—	195	300	725	1,200	—
1680 (s)	—	195	300	725	1,200	—
1684 (s)	—	195	300	725	1,200	—
1685 (s)	—	195	300	725	1,200	—
1692 MV	—	195	300	725	1,200	—
1693 (t) MV	—	195	300	725	1,200	—
1693 MV	—	195	300	725	1,200	—
1694 MV	—	195	300	725	1,200	—

KM# 599 DUCAT

3.5000 g., 0.9860 Gold 0.1109 oz. AGW **Ruler:** Leopold I **Obv:** Older laureate bust right without inner circle **Rev:** Crowned imperial eagle with sword and scepter without inner circle **Mint:** Prague **Note:** Prev. KM#1445. Varieties exist.

Date	Mintage	VG	F	VF	XF	Unc
1694 PM	—	215	325	775	1,400	—
1694 GE	—	215	325	775	1,400	—
1695 GE	—	215	325	775	1,400	—
1696 GE	—	215	325	775	1,400	—
1698 GE	—	215	325	775	1,400	—
1699 GE	—	215	325	775	1,400	—
1700 GE	—	215	325	775	1,400	—

MB# 329 2 DUCAT

7.5000 g., 0.9860 Gold 0.2377 oz. AGW **Ruler:** Rudolf II **Mint:** Prague **Note:** Similar to KM#15, probably struck from dies intended for that denomination.

Date	Mintage	VG	F	VF	XF	Unc
1598 (i)	—	425	925	2,000	3,300	—

KM# 55 2 DUCAT

7.5000 g., 0.9860 Gold 0.2377 oz. AGW **Ruler:** Rudolf II **Obv:** Armored bust right, titles of Rudolf II **Rev:** Crowned imperial eagle, arms of Austria-Burgundy on breast, titles continuous, date **Mint:** Prague **Note:** Struck from 1/4 Thaler dies, KM#45.

Date	Mintage	VG	F	VF	XF	Unc
1604 (j)	—	450	1,000	2,150	3,650	—
1609 (k)	—	450	1,000	2,150	3,650	—
1610 (l)	—	450	1,000	2,150	3,650	—
1611 (l)	—	450	1,000	2,150	3,650	—

KM# 82 2 DUCAT

7.5000 g., 0.9860 Gold 0.2377 oz. AGW **Ruler:** Rudolf II **Obv:** Armored bust right, titles of Rudolf II **Rev:** Crowned imperial eagle, arms of Austria-Burgundy on breast, titles continuous, date **Mint:** Prague **Note:** Prev. KM#1314.

Date	Mintage	VG	F	VF	XF	Unc
1606	—	450	1,000	2,150	3,650	—
1610	—	450	1,000	2,150	3,650	—

KM# 138 2 DUCAT

7.5000 g., 0.9860 Gold 0.2377 oz. AGW **Ruler:** Rudolf II **Mint:** Joachimstal

Date	Mintage	VG	F	VF	XF	Unc
1612 (aj) Rare	—	—	—	—	—	—

KM# 173 2 DUCAT

7.5000 g., 0.9860 Gold 0.2377 oz. AGW **Ruler:** Matthias II **Obv:** Bust right in wreath and feather cap **Rev:** Crowned inscription in laureate wreath **Mint:** Prague **Note:** Fr.#13. Prev. KM#1358.

Date	Mintage	VG	F	VF	XF	Unc
1614 (l)	—	400	650	1,200	2,400	—
1618 (l)	—	400	650	1,200	2,400	—

KM# 365 2 DUCAT

7.5000 g., 0.9860 Gold 0.2377 oz. AGW **Ruler:** Ferdinand II **Obv:** Standing figure of Ferdinand II, two shields flanking **Rev:** Crowned imperial eagle **Mint:** Prague **Note:** Fr. #40. Varieties exist. Prev. KM#1398.

Date	Mintage	VG	F	VF	XF	Unc
1623 (l)	—	325	575	1,150	2,200	—
1623 (p)	—	325	575	1,150	2,200	—
1624 (l)	—	325	575	1,150	2,200	—
1624 (n)	—	325	575	1,150	2,200	—
1627 (l)	—	325	575	1,150	2,200	—
1628 (l)	—	325	575	1,150	2,200	—
1629 (l)	—	325	575	1,150	2,200	—
1630 (o)	—	325	575	1,150	2,200	—
1631 (p)	—	325	575	1,150	2,200	—
1632 (p)	—	325	575	1,150	2,200	—
1633 (p)	—	325	575	1,150	2,200	—
1634 (p)	—	325	575	1,150	2,200	—
1635 (p)	—	325	575	1,150	2,200	—
1636 (p)	—	325	575	1,150	2,200	—
1637 (p)	—	325	575	1,150	2,200	—
1637 (q)	—	325	575	1,150	2,200	—

KM# 366 2 DUCAT

7.0000 g., 0.9860 Gold 0.2219 oz. AGW **Ruler:** Ferdinand II **Obv:** Ferdinand II standing facing half right flanked by two shields **Rev:** Crowned imperial eagle in inner circle, date in legend **Mint:** Prague **Note:** Prev. KM#1398.1.

Date	Mintage	VG	F	VF	XF	Unc
1623 (c)	—	300	575	1,150	2,200	—

KM# 382 2 DUCAT

7.0000 g., 0.9860 Gold 0.2219 oz. AGW **Ruler:** Ferdinand II **Obv:** Ferdinand II standing right between two shields **Rev:** Crowned imperial eagle **Mint:** Joachimstal **Note:** Prev. KM#907.

Date	Mintage	VG	F	VF	XF	Unc
1625 (ak)	—	450	1,300	2,600	4,300	—

KM# 425 2 DUCAT

7.0000 g., 0.9860 Gold 0.2219 oz. AGW **Ruler:** Ferdinand II **Obv:** Bare-headed bust right in lace collar **Rev:** Crowned imperial eagle **Mint:** Prague **Note:** Prev. KM#1419.

Date	Mintage	VG	F	VF	XF	Unc
1638 (q)	—	375	725	1,450	2,650	—
1639 (q)	—	375	725	1,450	2,650	—
1640 (q)	—	375	725	1,450	2,650	—

KM# 458 2 DUCAT

7.0000 g., 0.9860 Gold 0.2219 oz. AGW **Ruler:** Ferdinand III **Obv:** Laureate bust right **Rev:** Crowned imperial eagle **Mint:** Prague **Note:** Varieties exist. Prev. KM#1420.

Date	Mintage	VG	F	VF	XF	Unc
1641 (q)	—	300	575	1,150	2,200	—
1642 (q)	—	300	575	1,150	2,200	—
1643 (q)	—	300	575	1,150	2,200	—
1644 (q)	—	300	575	1,150	2,200	—
1645 (q)	—	300	575	1,150	2,200	—
1646 (q)	—	300	575	1,150	2,200	—
1647 (q)	—	300	575	1,150	2,200	—
1648 (q)	—	300	575	1,150	2,200	—
1650 (q)	—	300	575	1,150	2,200	—
1651 (q)	—	300	575	1,150	2,200	—
1651 (qx)	—	300	575	1,150	2,200	—
1652 (q)	—	300	575	1,150	2,200	—
1653 (q)	—	300	575	1,150	2,200	—
1654 (q)	—	300	575	1,150	2,200	—
1655 (q)	—	300	575	1,150	2,200	—
1655 (r)	—	300	575	1,150	2,200	—
1656 (r)	—	300	575	1,150	2,200	—
1657 (r)	—	300	575	1,150	2,200	—

KM# 501 2 DUCAT

7.0000 g., 0.9860 Gold 0.2219 oz. AGW **Ruler:** Leopold I **Obv:** Young laureate bust right **Rev:** Crowned imperial eagle **Mint:** Prague **Note:** Prev. KM#1446.

Date	Mintage	VG	F	VF	XF	Unc
1659 (r)	—	550	1,000	2,150	3,650	—
1660 (r)	—	550	1,000	2,150	3,650	—
1662 (r)	—	550	1,000	2,150	3,650	—

KM# 569 2 DUCAT

7.0000 g., 0.9860 Gold 0.2219 oz. AGW **Ruler:** Ferdinand II **Obv:** Laureate bust right **Rev:** Crowned imperial eagle **Mint:** Kuttenberg **Note:** Prev. KM#1130.

Date	Mintage	VG	F	VF	XF	Unc
1670 (ii) Rare	—	—	—	—	—	—

KM# 585 2 DUCAT

7.0000 g., 0.9860 Gold 0.2219 oz. AGW **Ruler:** Leopold I **Obv:** Older laureate bust right **Rev:** Crowned imperial eagle with sword and scepter **Mint:** Prague **Note:** Prev. KM#1447.

Date	Mintage	VG	F	VF	XF	Unc
1684 (s)	—	500	1,000	2,100	3,600	—

KM# 43 3 DUCAT

10.5000 g., 0.9860 Gold 0.3328 oz. AGW **Ruler:** Rudolf II **Rev:** Crowned shield **Mint:** Prague **Note:** Prev. KM#1315.

Date	Mintage	VG	F	VF	XF	Unc
1603 (j)	—	1,450	2,350	4,600	8,600	—
1604 (j)	—	1,450	2,350	4,600	8,600	—
1605 (j)	—	1,450	2,350	4,600	8,600	—

KM# 56 3 DUCAT

10.5000 g., 0.9860 Gold 0.3328 oz. AGW **Ruler:** Rudolf II **Mint:** Prague **Note:** Struck with 1/4 Thaler dies, KM#228.

Date	Mintage	VG	F	VF	XF	Unc
1604 (j)	—	1,450	2,350	4,600	8,600	—

KM# 83 3 DUCAT

10.5000 g., 0.9860 Gold 0.3328 oz. AGW **Ruler:** Rudolf II **Mint:** Prague **Note:** Prev. KM#1316.

Date	Mintage	VG	F	VF	XF	Unc
1606	—	1,450	2,350	4,600	8,600	—

KM# 80 3 DUCAT

10.5000 g., 0.9860 Gold 0.3328 oz. AGW **Ruler:** Matthias II **Rev:** Crowned imperial eagle **Mint:** Prague **Note:** Prev. KM#1359.

Date	Mintage	VG	F	VF	XF	Unc
1606 (j)	—	2,150	3,300	5,300	10,500	—

KM# 85 3 DUCAT

10.5000 g., 0.9860 Gold 0.3328 oz. AGW **Ruler:** Rudolf II **Mint:** Joachimstal **Note:** Struck from 1/4 Thaler dies, KM#232.

Date	Mintage	VG	F	VF	XF	Unc
1607 (aj) Rare	—	—	—	—	—	—

KM# 139 3 DUCAT

10.5000 g., 0.9860 Gold 0.3328 oz. AGW **Ruler:** Rudolf II **Mint:** Prague **Note:** Similar to 1/2 Thaler, KM#265.

Date	Mintage	VG	F	VF	XF	Unc
1612 (l) Rare	—	—	—	—	—	—

KM# 205 3 DUCAT

10.5000 g., 0.9860 Gold 0.3328 oz. AGW **Ruler:** Rudolf II **Mint:** Prague **Note:** Prev. KM#1359.

Date	Mintage	VG	F	VF	XF	Unc
1617 (l)	—	2,150	3,300	5,300	10,500	—

KM# 57 4 DUCAT

14.0000 g., 0.9860 Gold 0.4438 oz. AGW **Ruler:** Rudolf II **Rev:** Crowned imperial eagle **Mint:** Prague **Note:** Prev. KM#1317. Struck with 1/2 Thaler dies, MB#323.

Date	Mintage	VG	F	VF	XF	Unc
1604 (j)	—	2,150	3,300	6,200	11,500	—

KM# 140 4 DUCAT

14.0000 g., 0.9860 Gold 0.4438 oz. AGW **Ruler:** Matthias II **Mint:** Joachimstal

Date	Mintage	VG	F	VF	XF	Unc
1612 (aj) Rare	—	—	—	—	—	—

KM# 426 4 DUCAT

14.0000 g., 0.9860 Gold 0.4438 oz. AGW **Ruler:** Ferdinand III **Mint:** Prague **Note:** Struck with 1/2 Thaler dies, KM#417.

Date	Mintage	VG	F	VF	XF	Unc
1638 (q) Rare	—	—	—	—	—	—

KM# 475 4 DUCAT

14.0000 g., 0.9860 Gold 0.4438 oz. AGW **Ruler:** Ferdinand III **Mint:** Prague **Note:** Struck with 1/2 Thaler dies, KM#452.

Date	Mintage	VG	F	VF	XF	Unc
1644 (q) Rare	—	—	—	—	—	—

MB# 327 5 DUCAT

17.5000 g., 0.9860 Gold 0.5547 oz. AGW **Ruler:** Rudolf II **Obv:** Rudolf II standing **Mint:** Prague **Note:** Prev. KM#1318. Struck from dies or intended dies for 1/2 Thaler, MB#323.

Date	Mintage	VG	F	VF	XF	Unc
1603 (j)	—	—	—	7,800	12,000	—
1604 (j)	—	—	—	7,800	12,000	—
1605 (j)	—	—	—	7,800	12,000	—
1606 (j)	—	—	—	7,800	12,000	—
1610 (k)	—	—	—	7,800	12,000	—
1610 (l)	—	—	—	7,800	12,000	—
1611 (l)	—	—	—	7,800	12,000	—

KM# 73 5 DUCAT

17.5000 g., 0.9860 Gold 0.5547 oz. AGW **Ruler:** Rudolf II **Obv:** Rudolf II standing **Mint:** Prague **Note:** Struck from 1/2 Thaler dies, KM#77.

Date	Mintage	VG	F	VF	XF	Unc
1605 (j) Rare	—	—	—	—	—	—

KM# 141 5 DUCAT

17.5000 g., 0.9860 Gold 0.5547 oz. AGW **Ruler:** Matthias II **Obv:** Rudolf II standing **Mint:** Prague **Note:** Struck from Thaler dies, KM#123.

Date	Mintage	VG	F	VF	XF	Unc
ND(1612-19) Rare	—	—	—	—	—	—

KM# 170 5 DUCAT

17.5000 g., 0.9860 Gold 0.5547 oz. AGW **Ruler:** Matthias II **Obv:** Matthias standing **Mint:** Prague **Note:** Prev. KM#1360.

Date	Mintage	VG	F	VF	XF	Unc
1612 (l) Rare	—	—	—	—	—	—
1613 (l) Rare	—	—	—	—	—	—
1615 (l) Rare	—	—	—	—	—	—
1616 (l) Rare	—	—	—	—	—	—
1618 (l) Rare	—	—	—	—	—	—
1619 (l) Rare	—	—	—	—	—	—

KM# 142 5 DUCAT

17.5000 g., 0.9860 Gold 0.5547 oz. AGW **Ruler:** Matthias II **Obv:** Bust right in ruffled collar **Rev:** Crowned imperial eagle **Mint:** Prague

Date	Mintage	VG	F	VF	XF	Unc
1612 (l) Rare	—	—	—	—	—	—

KM# 277 5 DUCAT

17.5000 g., 0.9860 Gold 0.5547 oz. AGW **Ruler:** Ferdinand II **Mint:** Prague **Note:** Struck from Thaler dies, KM#270.

Date	Mintage	VG	F	VF	XF	Unc
1620 (m) Rare	—	—	—	—	—	—

KM# 317 5 DUCAT

17.5000 g., 0.9860 Gold 0.5547 oz. AGW **Ruler:** Ferdinand II **Obv:** Standing figure of Ferdinand II between two shields **Rev:** Crowned imperial eagle **Mint:** Prague **Note:** Varieties exist. Prev. KM#1399.

Date	Mintage	VG	F	VF	XF	Unc
1621 (l)	—	1,600	2,400	4,200	6,600	—
1622 (l)	—	1,600	2,400	4,200	6,600	—
1623 (n)	—	1,600	2,400	4,200	6,600	—
1624 (n)	—	1,600	2,400	4,200	6,600	—
1628 (l)	—	1,600	2,400	4,200	6,600	—
1629 (l)	—	1,600	2,400	4,200	6,600	—
1631 (p)	—	1,600	2,400	4,200	6,600	—
1633 (p)	—	1,600	2,400	4,200	6,600	—
1634 (p)	—	1,600	2,400	4,200	6,600	—

Date	Mintage	VG	F	VF	XF	Unc
1635 (p)	—	1,600	2,400	4,200	6,600	—
1636 (p)	—	1,600	2,400	4,200	6,600	—
1637 (p)	—	1,600	2,400	4,200	6,600	—
1637 (q)	—	1,600	2,400	4,200	6,600	—

KM# 428 5 DUCAT

17.5000 g., 0.9860 Gold 0.5547 oz. AGW **Ruler:** Ferdinand III **Obv:** Bare-headed bust right in lace collar **Rev:** Crowned imperial eagle **Mint:** Prague **Note:** Prev. KM#1421. Struck with 1/2 Thaler dies, KM#417.

Date	Mintage	VG	F	VF	XF	Unc
1638 (q)	—	1,300	2,150	3,900	6,600	—
1640 (q)	—	1,300	2,150	3,900	6,600	—

KM# 459 5 DUCAT

17.5000 g., 0.9860 Gold 0.5547 oz. AGW **Ruler:** Ferdinand III **Obv:** Laureate bust right **Rev:** Crowned imperial eagle **Mint:** Prague **Note:** Prev. KM#1421. Struck with 1/2 Thaler dies, KM#452.

Date	Mintage	VG	F	VF	XF	Unc
1641 (q)	—	1,600	2,400	4,200	6,600	—
1642 (q)	—	1,600	2,400	4,200	6,600	—
1643 (q)	—	1,600	2,400	4,200	6,600	—
1644 (q)	—	1,600	2,400	4,200	6,600	—
1645 (q)	—	1,600	2,400	4,200	6,600	—
1647 (q)	—	1,600	2,400	4,200	6,600	—
1648 (q)	—	1,600	2,400	4,200	6,600	—
1654 (q)	—	1,600	2,400	4,200	6,600	—
1655 (r)	—	1,600	2,400	4,200	6,600	—

KM# 470 5 DUCAT

17.5000 g., 0.9860 Gold 0.5547 oz. AGW **Ruler:** Ferdinand III **Mint:** Joachimstal **Note:** Struck with 1/2 Thaler dies, KM#437.

Date	Mintage	VG	F	VF	XF	Unc
1643 (al)	—	2,000	3,500	6,500	10,000	—
1644 (al)	—	2,000	3,500	6,500	10,000	—

KM# 502 5 DUCAT

17.5000 g., 0.9860 Gold 0.5547 oz. AGW **Ruler:** Leopold I **Obv:** Young laureate bust right **Rev:** Crowned imperial eagle **Mint:** Prague **Note:** Prev. KM#1448.

Date	Mintage	VG	F	VF	XF	Unc
1659 (r) Rare	—	—	—	—	—	—
1661 (r) Rare	—	—	—	—	—	—

Note: H.D. Rauch, 1-09, XF realized approximately $35,000.

KM# 557 5 DUCAT

17.5000 g., 0.9860 Gold 0.5547 oz. AGW **Ruler:** Leopold I **Obv:** Older laureate bust right **Rev:** Crowned imperial eagle **Mint:** Prague **Note:** Prev. KM#1449.

Date	Mintage	VG	F	VF	XF	Unc
1664 (r)	—	1,200	2,050	2,900	6,300	—
1675 (s)	—	1,200	2,050	2,900	6,300	—
1676 (s)	—	1,200	2,050	2,900	6,300	—
1689 MV	—	1,200	2,050	2,900	6,300	—
1691 MV	—	1,200	2,050	2,900	6,300	—

KM# 565 5 DUCAT

17.5000 g., 0.9860 Gold 0.5547 oz. AGW **Ruler:** Leopold I **Obv:** Laureate bust right **Rev:** Crowned imperial eagle **Mint:** Kuttenberg **Note:** Prev. KM#1131.

Date	Mintage	VG	F	VF	XF	Unc
1669 (ii) Rare	—	—	—	—	—	—

KM# 95 6 DUCAT

0.9860 Gold **Ruler:** Leopold I **Mint:** Prague

Date	Mintage	VG	F	VF	XF	Unc
1610 (l) Rare	—	—	—	—	—	—

KM# 143 6 DUCAT

0.9860 Gold **Ruler:** Leopold I **Mint:** Prague **Note:** Struck with Thaler dies, KM#124.

Date	Mintage	VG	F	VF	XF	Unc
ND(1612-19) (l) Rare	—	—	—	—	—	—

MB# 235 10 DUCAT

35.0000 g., 0.9860 Gold 1.1095 oz. AGW **Ruler:** Rudolf II **Obv:** Armored bust right, titles of Rudolf II **Rev:** Crowned imperial eagle, arms of Austria-Burgundy on breast, no legend **Mint:** Prague

Date	Mintage	VG	F	VF	XF	Unc
ND Rare	—	—	—	—	—	—

MB# 308 10 DUCAT

35.0000 g., 0.9860 Gold 1.1095 oz. AGW **Ruler:** Rudolf II **Obv:** Rudolf II standing **Rev:** Crowned imperial eagle **Mint:** Prague **Note:** Prev. KM#1319. Varieties exist.

Date	Mintage	VG	F	VF	XF	Unc
1601 (j)	—	—	—	13,000	20,500	—
1603 (j)	—	—	—	13,000	20,500	—
1604 (j)	—	—	—	13,000	20,500	—
1605 (j)	—	—	—	13,000	20,500	—
1606 (j)	—	—	—	13,000	20,500	—
1608 (j)	—	—	—	13,000	20,500	—
1610 (k)	—	—	—	13,000	20,500	—
1610 (l)	—	—	—	13,000	20,500	—
1611 (l)	—	—	—	13,000	20,500	—

KM# 30 10 DUCAT

35.0000 g., 0.9860 Gold 1.1095 oz. AGW **Ruler:** Rudolf II **Obv:** Armored bust in ruffled collar **Rev:** Crowned imperial eagle **Mint:** Prague

Date	Mintage	VG	F	VF	XF	Unc
1602 Rare	—	—	—	—	—	—
1602 (j) Rare	—	—	—	—	—	—
1604 (j) Rare	—	—	—	—	—	—

KM# 44 10 DUCAT

35.0000 g., 0.9860 Gold 1.1095 oz. AGW **Ruler:** Rudolf II **Mint:** Kuttenberg **Note:** Prev. KM#1041.

Date	Mintage	VG	F	VF	XF	Unc
1603 (y) Rare	—	—	—	—	—	—

KM# 146 10 DUCAT

35.0000 g., 0.9860 Gold 1.1095 oz. AGW **Ruler:** Matthias II **Mint:** Prague **Note:** Struck with Thaler dies, KM#101.

Date	Mintage	VG	F	VF	XF	Unc
1612 (l) Rare	—	—	—	—	—	—

KM# 144 10 DUCAT

35.0000 g., 0.9860 Gold 1.1095 oz. AGW **Ruler:** Matthias II **Mint:** Prague **Note:** Struck with Thaler dies, KM#123.

Date	Mintage	VG	F	VF	XF	Unc
ND(1612-19) Rare	—	—	—	—	—	—

KM# 145 10 DUCAT

35.0000 g., 0.9860 Gold 1.1095 oz. AGW **Ruler:** Matthias II **Mint:** Prague **Note:** Struck with Thaler dies, KM#124.

Date	Mintage	VG	F	VF	XF	Unc
ND(1612-19) (l) Rare	—	—	—	—	—	—

KM# 171 10 DUCAT

35.0000 g., 0.9860 Gold 1.1095 oz. AGW **Ruler:** Matthias II **Obv:** Matthias standing right, holding sceptre and orb withing inner circle **Rev:** Crowned imperial eagle, shield on breast **Mint:** Prague **Note:** Prev. KM#1361, 1362, 1364.

Date	Mintage	VG	F	VF	XF	Unc
1613 (l) Rare	—	—	—	—	—	—
1616 (l) Rare	—	—	—	—	—	—
1617 (l) Rare	—	—	—	—	—	—
1618 (l) Rare	—	—	—	—	—	—
1619 (l) Rare	—	—	—	—	—	—

KM# 278 10 DUCAT

35.0000 g., 0.9860 Gold 1.1095 oz. AGW **Ruler:** Ferdinand II **Mint:** Prague **Note:** Struck with Thaler dies, KM#270. Prev. KM#1400.

Date	Mintage	VG	F	VF	XF	Unc
1620 (m)	—	—	—	14,000	22,000	—

KM# 318 10 DUCAT

35.0000 g., 0.9860 Gold 1.1095 oz. AGW **Ruler:** Ferdinand II **Obv:** Bust right **Rev:** Crowned imperial eagle **Mint:** Joachimstal **Note:** Struck with Thaler dies, KM#314. Prev. KM#908.

Date	Mintage	VG	F	VF	XF	Unc
1621 (ak) Rare	—	—	—	—	—	—

KM# 319 10 DUCAT

35.0000 g., 0.9860 Gold 1.1095 oz. AGW **Ruler:** Ferdinand II

Obv: Standing figure of Ferdinand II between two shields **Rev:** Crowned imperial eagle **Mint:** Prague **Note:** Prev. KM#1400. Varieties exist.

Date	Mintage	VG	F	VF	XF	Unc
1621 (l)	—	—	—	14,000	22,000	—
1622 (l)	—	—	—	14,000	22,000	—
1623 (n)	—	—	—	14,000	22,000	—
1624 (n)	—	—	—	14,000	22,000	—
1625 (l)	—	—	—	14,000	22,000	—
1627 (l)	—	—	—	14,000	22,000	—
1628 (l)	—	—	—	14,000	22,000	—
1629 (l)	—	—	—	14,000	22,000	—
1630 (o)	—	—	—	14,000	22,000	—
1631 (p)	—	—	—	14,000	22,000	—
1633 (p)	—	—	—	14,000	22,000	—
1634 (p)	—	—	—	14,000	22,000	—
1635 (p)	—	—	—	14,000	22,000	—
1636 (p)	—	—	—	14,000	22,000	—
1637 (p)	—	—	—	14,000	22,000	—
1637 (q)	—	—	—	14,000	22,000	—

KM# 380 10 DUCAT

35.0000 g., 0.9860 Gold 1.1095 oz. AGW **Ruler:** Ferdinand II **Obv:** Standing figure of Ferdinand II without shields **Rev:** Crowned imperial eagle **Mint:** Prague **Note:** Prev. KM#1401.

Date	Mintage	VG	F	VF	XF	Unc
1624 (n)	—	—	—	14,000	22,000	—

KM# 401 10 DUCAT

35.0000 g., 0.9860 Gold 1.1095 oz. AGW **Ruler:** Ferdinand II **Obv:** Facing bust in ruffled collar **Rev:** Crowned imperial eagle **Mint:** Prague **Note:** Prev. KM#1402. Struck with Thaler dies, KM#395.

Date	Mintage	VG	F	VF	XF	Unc
1631 (p) Rare	—	—	—	—	—	—

KM# 402 10 DUCAT

35.0000 g., 0.9860 Gold 1.1095 oz. AGW **Ruler:** Ferdinand II **Obv:** Standing figure of Ferdinand II holding globe and scepter **Rev:** Crowned imperial eagle **Mint:** Kuttenberg **Note:** Prev. KM#1098.

Date	Mintage	VG	F	VF	XF	Unc
1633 (dd) Rare	—	—	—	—	—	—

KM# 429 10 DUCAT

35.0000 g., 0.9860 Gold 1.1095 oz. AGW **Ruler:** Ferdinand III **Obv:** Bare-headed bust right in lace collar **Rev:** Crowned imperial eagle **Mint:** Prague **Note:** Prev. KM#1422. Struck with Thaler dies, KM#420.

Date	Mintage	VG	F	VF	XF	Unc
1638 (q)	—	—	—	10,000	19,000	—
1639 (q)	—	—	—	10,000	19,000	—
1640 (q)	—	—	—	10,000	19,000	—

KM# 460 10 DUCAT

35.0000 g., 0.9860 Gold 1.1095 oz. AGW **Ruler:** Ferdinand III **Obv:** Laureate bust right in lace collar **Rev:** Crowned imperial eagle **Mint:** Prague **Note:** Prev. KM#1423. Struck with Thaler dies, KM#453.

Date	Mintage	VG	F	VF	XF	Unc
1641 (q)	—	—	—	11,500	20,000	—
1642 (q)	—	—	—	11,500	20,000	—
1643 (q)	—	—	—	11,500	20,000	—
1644 (q)	—	—	—	11,500	20,000	—
1645 (q)	—	—	—	11,500	20,000	—
1646 (q)	—	—	—	11,500	20,000	—
1647 (q)	—	—	—	11,500	20,000	—
1648 (q)	—	—	—	11,500	20,000	—
1651 (q)	—	—	—	11,500	20,000	—
1652 (q)	—	—	—	11,500	20,000	—
1654 (q)	—	—	—	11,500	20,000	—
1655 (r)	—	—	—	11,500	20,000	—

KM# 503 10 DUCAT

35.0000 g., 0.9860 Gold 1.1095 oz. AGW **Ruler:** Leopold I **Obv:** Laureate bust right **Rev:** Crowned imperial eagle **Mint:** Prague **Note:** Prev. KM#1450.

Date	Mintage	VG	F	VF	XF	Unc
1659 (r)	—	2,750	4,500	14,000	22,000	—
1661 (r)	—	2,750	4,500	14,000	22,000	—
1663 (r)	—	2,750	4,500	14,000	22,000	—

KM# 558 10 DUCAT

35.0000 g., 0.9860 Gold 1.1095 oz. AGW **Ruler:** Leopold I **Obv:** Laureate bust right **Rev:** Crowned imperial eagle with sword and scepter **Mint:** Prague **Note:** Prev. KM#1451.

Date	Mintage	VG	F	VF	XF	Unc
1664 (r)	—	—	—	14,000	22,000	—
1675 (s)	—	—	—	14,000	22,000	—

KM# 566 10 DUCAT

35.0000 g., 0.9860 Gold 1.1095 oz. AGW **Ruler:** Leopold I **Obv:** Laureate bust right **Rev:** Crowned imperial eagle **Mint:** Kuttenberg **Note:** Prev. KM#1132.

Date	Mintage	VG	F	VF	XF	Unc
1669 (ii) Rare	—	—	—	—	—	—

KM# 147 15 DUCAT

Gold **Ruler:** Matthias II **Mint:** Prague **Note:** Struck with Thaler dies, KM#123.

Date	Mintage	VG	F	VF	XF	Unc
ND(1612-19) Rare	—	—	—	—	—	—

KM# 148 20 DUCAT

Gold **Ruler:** Matthias II **Mint:** Prague **Note:** Struck with Thaler dies, KM#101.

Date	Mintage	VG	F	VF	XF	Unc
1612 (l) Rare	—	—	—	—	—	—

KM# 189 25 DUCAT

Gold **Ruler:** Matthias II **Mint:** Prague **Note:** Klippe. Struck with Thaler dies, KM#181.

Date	Mintage	VG	F	VF	XF	Unc
1615 (l) Rare	—	—	—	—	—	—

BOHEMIAN ESTATES

STANDARD COINAGE

KM# 214 HELLER

Silver **Ruler:** Friedrich von der Pfalz **Obv:** Crowned F divides R - B, date below **Mint:** Kuttenberg **Note:** Uniface. Prev. KM#1064.

Date	Mintage	VG	F	VF	XF	Unc
1619	—	—	—	—	—	—
Note: Reported, not confirmed						
1620	—	80.00	160	250	450	—

KM# 213 HELLER

Silver **Ruler:** Friedrich von der Pfalz **Obv:** Crowned FRI divides R - B, date below **Mint:** Kuttenberg **Note:** Uniface. Prev. KM#1160.

Date	Mintage	VG	F	VF	XF	Unc
1619	—	100	180	275	500	—

KM# 215 HELLER

Silver **Ruler:** Friedrich von der Pfalz **Obv:** Crowned FII divides R - B, date below **Mint:** Kuttenberg **Note:** Uniface. Prev. KM#1160.

Date	Mintage	VG	F	VF	XF	Unc
1619	—	120	200	300	550	—
1620	—	120	200	300	550	—

KM# 216 PFENNIG

Silver **Ruler:** Friedrich von der Pfalz **Obv:** Crowned Bohemian lion left in circle, legend, date **Obv. Legend:** IN. DEO. F.(OR)T.(I)T.(U)D.O. **Mint:** Kuttenberg **Note:** Uniface. Prev. KM#1155.

Date	Mintage	VG	F	VF	XF	Unc
1619	—	125	225	350	600	—

KM# 217 PFENNIG

Silver **Ruler:** Friedrich von der Pfalz **Obv:** Crowned Bohemian lion right in circle, legend, date **Obv. Legend:** FRIDER. REX. BO **Mint:** Kuttenberg **Note:** Uniface. Prev. KM#1161.

Date	Mintage	VG	F	VF	XF	Unc
1619	—	85.00	165	275	500	—
1620	—	85.00	165	275	500	—

KM# 232 PFENNIG

Silver **Ruler:** Friedrich von der Pfalz **Obv:** Crowned Bohemian lion left, date **Obv. Legend:** FRIDER. REX. B. **Mint:** Kuttenberg **Note:** Uniface. Prev. KM#1162.

Date	Mintage	VG	F	VF	XF	Unc
1620	—	85.00	165	275	500	—

KM# 218 KREUZER

Silver **Ruler:** Friedrich von der Pfalz **Obv:** Large crown over date in circle **Obv. Legend:** MONE. REG. BOHEMI. **Rev:** Crowned Bohemian lion to right in circle, value "I" at bottom **Rev. Legend:** IN. DEO. FOR - TITVDO. **Mint:** Kuttenberg **Note:** Prev. KM#1156.

Date	Mintage	VG	F	VF	XF	Unc
1619 (ee)	—	90.00	175	275	500	—

KM# 219 3 KREUZER (Groschen)

Silver **Ruler:** Friedrich von der Pfalz **Obv:** Large crown over date, MONET REGNI BOHEMIAE **Rev:** Crowned Bohemian lion left in circle, value (3) at bottom, IN DEO FOR - TITVDO **Mint:** Kuttenberg **Note:** Kipper 3 Kreuzer. Prev. KM#1157.

Date	Mintage	VG	F	VF	XF	Unc
1619 (ee)	—	60.00	100	180	325	—

KM# 220 3 KREUZER (Groschen)

Silver **Ruler:** Friedrich von der Pfalz **Obv:** Large crown after date **Rev:** Crowned Bohemian lion left, value below **Mint:** Joachimstal **Note:** Prev. KM#940.

Date	Mintage	VG	F	VF	XF	Unc
1619 (aj)	—	40.00	80.00	150	325	—

KM# 222 12 KREUZER

Silver **Ruler:** Friedrich von der Pfalz **Obv:** Crown above date **Rev:** Bohemian lion, value at bottom **Mint:** Prague **Note:** Kipper. Prev. KM#91 (1550).

Date	Mintage	VG	F	VF	XF	Unc
1619 (l)	—	25.00	50.00	100	205	—

KM# 223 12 KREUZER

Silver **Ruler:** Friedrich von der Pfalz **Obv:** Crown above date **Rev:** Bohemian lion, value at bottom **Mint:** Kuttenberg **Note:** Prev. KM#1158.

Date	Mintage	VG	F	VF	XF	Unc
1619 (ee)	—	50.00	100	200	500	—

KM# 224 12 KREUZER

Silver **Ruler:** Friedrich von der Pfalz **Obv:** Crown over date **Rev:** Crowned Bohemian lion left **Mint:** Joachimstal **Note:** Prev. KM#941.

Date	Mintage	VG	F	VF	XF	Unc
1619 (aj)	—	40.00	80.00	150	325	—
1620 (aj)	—	40.00	80.00	150	325	—

KM# 236 12 KREUZER

Silver **Ruler:** Friedrich von der Pfalz **Obv:** Crowned bust right **Rev:** Crossed arms **Mint:** Kuttenberg **Note:** Prev. KM#1163.

Date	Mintage	VG	F	VF	XF	Unc
1620 (ee)	—	70.00	120	200	350	—

KM# 235 12 KREUZER

Silver **Ruler:** Friedrich von der Pfalz **Obv:** Crowned bust right, value (12) below, titles of Friedrich **Rev:** Crowned two-fold arms of Bohemia and Electoral Pfalz, date in legend **Mint:** Prague **Note:** Kipper. Prev. KM#92 (1551).

Date	Mintage	VG	F	VF	XF	Unc
1620 (m)	—	25.00	50.00	100	205	—

KM# 227 24 KREUZER

Silver **Ruler:** Friedrich von der Pfalz **Obv:** Crown over date **Rev:** Bohemian lion left **Mint:** Kuttenberg **Note:** Prev. KM#1159.

Date	Mintage	VG	F	VF	XF	Unc
1619 (ee)	—	25.00	50.00	90.00	195	—
1620 (ee)	—	25.00	50.00	90.00	195	—

KM# 226 24 KREUZER

Silver **Ruler:** Friedrich von der Pfalz **Obv:** Crown over date **Rev:** Bohemian lion left **Mint:** Prague **Note:** Kipper. Prev. KM#93 (1552)

Date	Mintage	VG	F	VF	XF	Unc
1619 (l)	—	30.00	75.00	145	275	—
1620 (m)	—	30.00	75.00	145	275	—

KM# 228 24 KREUZER

Silver **Ruler:** Friedrich von der Pfalz **Obv:** Crown over date **Rev:** Crowned Bohemian lion left **Mint:** Joachimstal **Note:** Prev. KM#942.

Date	Mintage	VG	F	VF	XF	Unc
1619 (aj)	—	35.00	85.00	160	300	—
1620 (aj)	—	35.00	85.00	160	300	—

KM# 239 24 KREUZER

Silver **Ruler:** Friedrich von der Pfalz **Obv:** Crowned bust right, value (24) below, titles of Friedrich **Rev:** Ornate squarish two-fold arms of Bohemia and Electoral Pfalz divide date, titles continuous **Mint:** Joachimstal **Note:** Prev. KM#945.

Date	Mintage	VG	F	VF	XF	Unc
(16)20 (aj)	—	85.00	160	265	475	—

KM# 242 24 KREUZER

Silver **Ruler:** Friedrich von der Pfalz **Rev:** Round arms **Mint:** Joachimstal **Note:** Prev. KM#946.

Date	Mintage	VG	F	VF	XF	Unc
1620 (aj)	—	40.00	90.00	175	300	—

KM# 237 24 KREUZER

Silver **Ruler:** Friedrich von der Pfalz **Obv:** Crowned bust right, value (24) below, titles of Friedrich **Rev:** Ornate squarish two-fold arms of Bohemia and Electoral Pfalz divide date, titles continuous **Mint:** Prague **Note:** Kipper. Prev. KM#94

Date	Mintage	VG	F	VF	XF	Unc
(16)20 (m)	—	80.00	150	250	450	—

KM# 240 24 KREUZER

Silver **Ruler:** Friedrich von der Pfalz **Obv:** Crowned bust right, value (24) below, titles of Friedrich **Rev:** Round six-fold arms with central shield of Electoral Pfalz, date in legend **Mint:** Prague **Note:** Known struck on thick flan of unlisted weight. Prev. KM#95.1 (1554)

Date	Mintage	VG	F	VF	XF	Unc
1620 (m)	—	45.00	100	200	375	—

KM# 238 24 KREUZER

Silver **Ruler:** Friedrich von der Pfalz **Obv:** Crowned bust right, value (24) below, titles of Friedrich **Rev:** Ornate squarish two-fold arms of Bohemia and Electoral Pfalz divide date, titles continuous **Mint:** Kuttenberg **Note:** Prev. KM#1164. Known struck on thick flan of unknown weight.

Date	Mintage	VG	F	VF	XF	Unc
(16)20 (ee)	—	80.00	150	250	450	—

KM# 241 24 KREUZER

Silver **Ruler:** Friedrich von der Pfalz **Obv:** Crowned bust right, value (24) below, titles of Friedrich **Rev:** Round six-fold arms **Mint:** Kuttenberg **Note:** Prev. KM#1165.

Date	Mintage	VG	F	VF	XF	Unc
1620 (ee)	—	40.00	90.00	175	300	—

KM# 243 24 KREUZER

Silver **Ruler:** Friedrich von der Pfalz **Obv:** Smaller bust **Rev:** Round six-fold arms **Mint:** Kuttenberg **Note:** Prev. KM#1166.

Date	Mintage	VG	F	VF	XF	Unc
1620 (ee)	—	45.00	95.00	185	325	—

KM# 250 48 KREUZER

Silver **Ruler:** Friedrich von der Pfalz **Obv:** Value below bust **Mint:** Joachimstal

Date	Mintage	VG	F	VF	XF	Unc
1620 (aj)	—	125	245	475	1,000	—

KM# 255 48 KREUZER

Silver **Ruler:** Friedrich von der Pfalz **Mint:** Prague **Note:** Klippe.

Date	Mintage	VG	F	VF	XF	Unc
1620 (m)	—	—	—	—	—	—

KM# 248 48 KREUZER

Silver **Ruler:** Friedrich von der Pfalz **Obv:** Value at bottom **Rev:** Date in margin **Mint:** Kuttenberg **Note:** Prev. KM#1167.

Date	Mintage	VG	F	VF	XF	Unc
1620 (ee)	—	100	200	350	—	—

KM# 252 48 KREUZER

Silver **Ruler:** Friedrich von der Pfalz **Obv:** Large bust **Rev:** Crown above large arms **Mint:** Kuttenberg **Note:** Prev. KM#1168.

Date	Mintage	VG	F	VF	XF	Unc
1620 (ee)	—	85.00	175	300	—	—

KM# 256 48 KREUZER

Silver **Ruler:** Friedrich von der Pfalz **Obv:** Ruffled collar bust right **Rev:** Crowned round seven-fold arms **Mint:** Kuttenberg **Note:** Prev. KM#1169.

Date	Mintage	VG	F	VF	XF	Unc
1620 (ee)	—	75.00	145	250	625	—

KM# 249 48 KREUZER

Silver **Ruler:** Friedrich von der Pfalz **Obv:** Crowned bust right **Rev:** Shield-shaped arms **Mint:** Joachimstal **Note:** Prev. KM#947.

Date	Mintage	VG	F	VF	XF	Unc
1620 (aj)	—	125	245	475	1,000	—

KM# 253 48 KREUZER

Silver **Ruler:** Friedrich von der Pfalz **Obv:** Large bust **Rev:** Crown above large arms **Mint:** Joachimstal **Note:** Prev. KM#948.

Date	Mintage	VG	F	VF	XF	Unc
1620 (aj)	—	120	225	450	925	—

KM# 254.1 48 KREUZER
Silver **Ruler:** Friedrich von der Pfalz **Obv:** Large bust **Rev:** Crowned round seven-fold arms **Mint:** Prague **Note:** Prev. KM#96.1 (1555).

Date	Mintage	VG	F	VF	XF	Unc
1620 (m)	—	110	220	450	875	—

KM# 254.2 48 KREUZER
Silver **Ruler:** Friedrich von der Pfalz **Obv:** Crowned small bust right **Rev:** Crowned round seven-fold arms **Mint:** Prague **Note:** Prev. KM#96.2 (1705).

Date	Mintage	VG	F	VF	XF	Unc
1620 (m)	—	110	220	450	875	—
1621 (m)	—	110	220	450	875	—

KM# 251 48 KREUZER
Silver **Ruler:** Friedrich von der Pfalz **Obv:** Large bust **Rev:** Crown above large arms **Mint:** Prague **Note:** Prev. KM#97(1556).

Date	Mintage	VG	F	VF	XF	Unc
1620 (m)	—	175	350	675	1,250	—

KM# 258 60 KREUZER
Silver **Ruler:** Ferdinand II **Obv:** Laureate bust right, value below **Rev:** Round coat of arms **Mint:** Kuttenberg **Note:** Prev. KM#1170.

Date	Mintage	VG	F	VF	XF	Unc
1620 (ee)	—	40.00	75.00	150	300	—

KM# 263 70 KREUZER
Silver **Ruler:** Ferdinand II **Obv:** Value below bust **Mint:** Kuttenberg **Note:** Prev. KM#1171.

Date	Mintage	VG	F	VF	XF	Unc
1620 (ee)	—	—	—	—	—	—

TRADE COINAGE

KM# 274 DUCAT
Silver **Ruler:** Friedrich von der Pfalz **Obv:** Crowned bust right, titles of Friedrich **Rev:** Arms of Electoral Pfalz superimposed on crowned Bohemian lion to left, date below, titles continuous **Mint:** Prague

Date	Mintage	VG	F	VF	XF	Unc
1620	—	1,800	2,400	3,850	5,500	—
1620 (m)	—	1,800	2,400	3,850	5,500	—

KM# 272 DUCAT
Silver **Ruler:** Friedrich von der Pfalz **Obv:** Crowned full-length armored figure right, holding scepter, titles of Friedrich **Rev:** Crowned four-fold arms in circle, titles continuous **Mint:** Prague **Note:** Prev. KM#100(1559).

Date	Mintage	VG	F	VF	XF	Unc
ND(1620) Rare	—	—	—	—	—	—

KM# 273 DUCAT
Silver **Ruler:** Friedrich von der Pfalz **Obv:** Crowned full-length armored figure right, holding orb and scepter **Rev:** Ornately-shaped arms, date in legend **Mint:** Prague **Note:** Prev. KM#101(1560).

Date	Mintage	VG	F	VF	XF	Unc
1620 (m) Rare	—	—	—	—	—	—

EGER

FREE CITY

STANDARD COINAGE

KM# 1 PFENNIG (Weisspfennig)
Copper **Obv:** Oval city arms, date at end of legend **Obv. Legend:** VIER HERRN ... **Note:** Ref. Sn(AE)#1. Uniface.

Date	Mintage	VG	F	VF	XF	Unc
1616	—	12.00	30.00	55.00	95.00	—

KM# 2 PFENNIG (Weisspfennig)
Copper **Obv:** Oval city arms, date at end of legend, final 'N' reversed **Obv. Legend:** VIER HERRN ... **Note:** Ref. Sn(AE)#2. Uniface.

Date	Mintage	VG	F	VF	XF	Unc
1618	—	12.00	30.00	55.00	95.00	—

KM# 3 PFENNIG (Weisspfennig)
Copper **Obv:** Round city arms, date at end of legend, final 'N' reversed **Obv. Legend:** VIER HERRN ... **Note:** Ref. Sn(AE)#3. Uniface.

Date	Mintage	VG	F	VF	XF	Unc
1622	—	12.00	30.00	55.00	95.00	—

KM# 4 PFENNIG (Weisspfennig)
Copper **Obv:** Oval city arms, date at end of legend **Obv. Legend:** ★ HERRN. O E V N G V R **Note:** Ref. Sn(AE)#4. Uniface.

Date	Mintage	VG	F	VF	XF	Unc
1628	—	10.00	25.00	45.00	85.00	—

FRIEDLAND

Albrecht Wenzel Eusebius von Wallenstein, prominent leader of the empire until his assassination in 1634, was made count of the empire in 1622, duke of Friedland in 1623, duke of Sagan in 1627 and was duke of Mecklenburg from 1628 to 1632. During this time Wallenstein became powerful and had additional ambitions even to the reorganization of the empire. This was seen as a threat by higher powers in the empire and Wallenstein was assassinated February 25, 1634.

RULER
Albrecht von Wallenstein, 1583-1634

COUNTY

STANDARD COINAGE

KM# 66 1/2 KREUZER
Billon **Ruler:** Albrecht **Obv:** 3 shields 1 above 2, top shield divides date **Note:** Uniface.

Date	Mintage	VG	F	VF	XF	Unc
1632	—	18.00	33.00	55.00	100	—

KM# 5 3 KREUZER
Silver **Ruler:** Albrecht **Obv:** Bust of Albrecht 1/2 right in inner circle **Rev:** Crowned eagle shield in inner circle, date divide by crown **Rev. Legend:** SAO. ROM. IMPERI. PRINCES **Note:** Varieties exist.

Date	Mintage	VG	F	VF	XF	Unc
1626	—	17.00	27.50	49.50	100	—

KM# 11 3 KREUZER
Silver **Ruler:** Albrecht **Obv:** Bust of Albrecht right in inner circle **Note:** Varieites exist.

Date	Mintage	VG	F	VF	XF	Unc
1627	—	17.00	27.50	44.00	85.00	—
1697 Error	—	17.00	27.50	44.00	85.00	—

KM# 12 3 KREUZER
Silver **Ruler:** Albrecht **Rev:** Date in legend at upper left **Note:** Varieites exist.

Date	Mintage	VG	F	VF	XF	Unc
1627	—	20.00	33.00	55.00	100	—
1628	—	20.00	33.00	55.00	100	—

KM# 24 3 KREUZER
Silver **Ruler:** Albrecht **Note:** Varieties exist.

Date	Mintage	VG	F	VF	XF	Unc
1628	—	17.00	27.50	44.00	85.00	—
1629	—	17.00	27.50	44.00	85.00	—
1630	—	17.00	27.50	44.00	85.00	—

KM# 32 3 KREUZER
Silver **Ruler:** Albrecht **Obv:** Bust of Albrecht 1/2 right in inner circle **Note:** Varieties exist.

Date	Mintage	VG	F	VF	XF	Unc
1629	—	19.00	30.25	48.50	95.00	—
1630	—	19.00	30.25	48.50	95.00	—

KM# 51 3 KREUZER
Silver **Ruler:** Albrecht **Obv:** Bust of Albrecht right in inner circle **Note:** Varieties exist.

Date	Mintage	VG	F	VF	XF	Unc
1630	—	17.00	33.00	55.00	100	—
1631	—	17.00	33.00	55.00	100	—
1632	—	17.00	33.00	55.00	100	—
1633	—	17.00	33.00	55.00	100	—
1634	—	17.00	33.00	55.00	100	—

KM# 50 3 KREUZER
Silver **Ruler:** Albrecht **Rev:** 3 shields with points together in inner circle **Note:** Titles of Duke of Friedland, Sagan and Mecklenburg. Varieties exist.

Date	Mintage	VG	F	VF	XF	Unc
1630	—	17.00	33.00	55.00	100	—
1631	—	17.00	33.00	55.00	100	—

KM# 6 1/2 GULDEN
Silver **Ruler:** Albrecht **Obv:** Bust of Albrecht 1/2 right in inner circle **Rev:** Crowned eagle shield with rosettes at sides, date divided by crown **Note:** Titles of Duke of Friedland. Varieties exist.

Date	Mintage	VG	F	VF	XF	Unc
1626	—	825	1,650	3,300	—	—
1627	—	825	1,650	3,300	—	—

KM# 25 1/2 GULDEN
Silver **Ruler:** Albrecht **Obv:** Bust of Albrecht right in inner circle **Rev:** Date left of crown in legend, plain field at sides of shield **Note:** Titles of Duke of Friedland and Sagan.

Date	Mintage	VG	F	VF	XF	Unc
1628	—	1,250	2,750	6,100	—	—

KM# 58 1/2 GULDEN
Silver **Ruler:** Albrecht **Obv:** Bust of Albrecht 1/2 right in inner circle **Rev:** Crowned arms in order collar in inner circle, date in legend **Note:** Titles of Duke of Friedland, Sagan and Mecklenburg.

Date	Mintage	VG	F	VF	XF	Unc
1631	—	725	1,400	3,050	5,200	—

Date	Mintage	VG	F	VF	XF	Unc
1632	—	725	1,400	3,050	5,200	—
1633	—	725	1,400	3,050	5,200	—

KM# 68 1/2 GULDEN

Silver **Ruler:** Albrecht **Note:** Klippe.

Date	Mintage	VG	F	VF	XF	Unc
1633	—	1,150	2,150	4,300	7,200	—

KM# 7 GULDEN

Silver **Ruler:** Albrecht **Obv:** Bust of Albrecht 1/2 right in inner circle **Rev:** Crowned eagle shield in inner circle, date divided by crown **Rev. Legend:** DOMINUS. PROTECTOR. MEVS **Note:** Titles of Duke of Friedland.

Date	Mintage	VG	F	VF	XF	Unc
1626	—	1,450	3,000	6,600	—	—

KM# 8 GULDEN

Silver **Ruler:** Albrecht **Rev. Legend:** SAC. ROM. IMPERI. PRINCEPS **Note:** Varieties exist.

Date	Mintage	VG	F	VF	XF	Unc
1626	—	1,200	2,400	5,000	9,600	—

KM# 26 GULDEN

Silver **Ruler:** Albrecht **Obv:** Bust of Albrecht right in inner circle **Note:** Titles of Duke of Friedland and Sagan. Varieties exist.

Date	Mintage	VG	F	VF	XF	Unc
1628	—	1,500	3,300	7,200	—	—

KM# 33 GULDEN

14.3600 g., Silver **Ruler:** Albrecht **Obv:** Large bust of Albrecht 1/2 right in inner circle

Date	Mintage	VG	F	VF	XF	Unc
1629	—	1,800	3,600	7,800	—	—

KM# 38 GULDEN

Silver **Ruler:** Albrecht **Rev:** Crown breaks outer legend, date in legend at upper left **Note:** Dav. #3448.

Date	Mintage	VG	F	VF	XF	Unc
1629	—	1,150	2,000	3,300	6,000	—

KM# 40 GULDEN

Silver **Ruler:** Albrecht **Obv. Legend:** ALBERTVS D: G: DVX MEGAP:.. **Rev:** Crowned arms divides "G-E" in order collar, date in legend **Note:** Dav. #3450.

Date	Mintage	VG	F	VF	XF	Unc
1629 GE	—	1,200	2,100	3,550	6,600	—

KM# 52 GULDEN

Silver **Ruler:** Albrecht **Note:** Klippe. Titles of Duke of Friedland, Sagan and Mecklenburg.

Date	Mintage	VG	F	VF	XF	Unc
1630	—	2,100	4,200	7,200	11,000	—

KM# 59 GULDEN

Silver **Ruler:** Albrecht **Rev:** Crowned arms in order collar in inner circle, date in legend **Note:** Varieties exist.

Date	Mintage	VG	F	VF	XF	Unc
1631	—	1,150	2,100	3,900	7,200	—
1632	—	1,200	2,650	4,800	7,800	—
1633	—	1,200	2,650	4,800	7,800	—

KM# A9 1/4 THALER

Silver **Ruler:** Albrecht **Obv:** Bust of Albrecht **Rev:** Crowned arms **Rev. Legend:** DEVS PROTECTOR MEVS **Note:** Klippe.

Date	Mintage	VG	F	VF	XF	Unc
1626	—	400	775	1,300	2,350	—

KM# 9 THALER

Silver **Ruler:** Albrecht **Rev:** Small crown **Rev. Legend:** DOMINUS. PROTECTOR. MEVS **Note:** Dav. #3438. Varieties exist.

Date	Mintage	VG	F	VF	XF	Unc
1626	—	925	2,000	3,950	6,600	—

KM# 10 THALER

Silver **Ruler:** Albrecht **Rev:** Large crown **Rev. Legend:** SAC. ROM. IMPERIL. PRINCEPS **Note:** Dav. #3439. Varieties exist.

Date	Mintage	VG	F	VF	XF	Unc
1626	—	875	1,700	3,300	6,000	—
1627	—	900	1,750	3,400	6,200	—

KM# 13 THALER

Silver **Ruler:** Albrecht **Rev:** Plain field at sides of arms, date in legend **Note:** Dav. #3440. Varieties exist.

Date	Mintage	VG	F	VF	XF	Unc
1627	—	875	1,700	3,300	5,900	—
1628	—	875	1,700	3,300	5,900	—

KM# 14 THALER

Silver **Ruler:** Albrecht **Rev:** Scrolls at sides of shield **Note:** Dav. #3441. Varieties exist.

Date	Mintage	VG	F	VF	XF	Unc
1627	—	875	1,700	3,400	6,100	—
1628	—	875	1,700	3,400	6,100	—

KM# 27 THALER

Silver **Ruler:** Albrecht **Note:** Dav. #3442. Varieties exist.

Date	Mintage	VG	F	VF	XF	Unc
1628	—	1,000	1,800	3,000	5,600	—

KM# 28 THALER

Silver **Ruler:** Albrecht **Note:** Dav. #3443. Varieties exist.

Date	Mintage	VG	F	VF	XF	Unc
1628	—	1,000	1,800	3,000	5,600	—

KM# 34 THALER

Silver **Ruler:** Albrecht **Obv:** Similar to KM#35 **Rev:** Crowned arms with decorations at sides in inner circle, date in legend **Note:** Dav. #3444. Varieties exist.

Date	Mintage	VG	F	VF	XF	Unc
1629	—	1,100	2,000	3,300	5,900	—

KM# 35 THALER

Silver **Ruler:** Albrecht **Obv. Legend:** ...DUX. FRIDLA. ET. SAGANAE **Mint:** Wismar **Note:** Dav. #3445. Struck at Wismar Mint.

Date	Mintage	VG	F	VF	XF	Unc
1629 Rare	—	—	—	—	—	—

Note: Leu Numismatik Auction 75, 10-99, VF realized $12,000

KM# 36 THALER

Silver **Ruler:** Albrecht **Rev:** Mint mark at bottom in outer legend **Mint:** Sagan **Note:** Dav. #3446. Struck at Sagan Mint.

Date	Mintage	VG	F	VF	XF	Unc
1629 S-HZ Rare	—	—	—	—	—	—

KM# 37 THALER

Silver **Ruler:** Albrecht **Obv:** Date below bust **Rev:** Crowned arms in order collar **Note:** Dav. #3447.

Date	Mintage	VG	F	VF	XF	Unc
1629	—	1,150	2,100	3,600	6,200	—

KM# 39 THALER

Silver **Ruler:** Albrecht **Obv. Legend:** ALBERTVS. D. G. DVX. ME-GA. FRI. ET. SA. P. VA **Note:** Dav. #3449.

Date	Mintage	VG	F	VF	XF	Unc
1629	—	1,150	2,100	3,600	6,200	—

KM# 53 THALER

Silver **Ruler:** Albrecht **Obv. Legend:** ALBERT. D. G. DVX. ME-GA. FRID. ET. SA. PR. VA **Note:** Dav. #3451.

Date	Mintage	VG	F	VF	XF	Unc
1630	—	1,150	2,100	3,600	6,200	—

KM# 54 THALER

Silver **Ruler:** Albrecht **Obv. Legend:** ALBERT. D.G. DVS. MEGA.. **Rev:** Crowned arms in order collar in inner circle, date in legend, ornamentation above crown **Note:** Dav. #3452.

Date	Mintage	VG	F	VF	XF	Unc
1630	—	1,200	2,200	3,850	7,000	—

KM# 60 THALER

Silver **Ruler:** Albrecht **Obv. Legend:** ALBERT. D. G. DVX. MEGA. FRID. ET. SAG. PR. VAN **Note:** Dav. #3455. Varieties exist.

Date	Mintage	VG	F	VF	XF	Unc
1631	—	1,150	2,150	3,850	6,600	—
1632	—	1,150	2,100	3,600	6,200	—
1633	—	1,400	2,400	4,200	7,500	—

KM# A68 1-1/2 THALER

Silver **Ruler:** Albrecht **Note:** Klippe. Similar to 1 Thaler, KM#60. Dav. #3454.

Date	Mintage	VG	F	VF	XF	Unc
1633 Rare	—	—	—	—	—	—

KM# 15 2 THALER

Silver **Ruler:** Albrecht **Rev. Legend:** SACRi. ROMANI. IMPE. PRINCEPS **Note:** Dav. #A3439.

Date	Mintage	VG	F	VF	XF	Unc
1627 Rare	—	—	—	—	—	—

KM# 16 2 THALER

Silver **Ruler:** Albrecht **Rev:** Plain field at sides of arms, date in legend **Note:** Dav. #A3440.

Date	Mintage	VG	F	VF	XF	Unc
1627 Rare	—	—	—	—	—	—

Note: Leu Numismatik Auction 75, 10-99 VF realized $19,665

KM# 17 2 THALER

Silver **Ruler:** Albrecht **Rev:** Scrolls at sides of shield **Note:** Dav. #A3441.

Date	Mintage	VG	F	VF	XF	Unc
1627 Rare	—	—	—	—	—	—

KM# 67 2 THALER

Silver **Ruler:** Albrecht **Note:** Similar to 1 Thaler, KM#60.

Date	Mintage	VG	F	VF	XF	Unc
1632 Rare	—	—	—	—	—	—

TRADE COINAGE

KM# 18 DUCAT

3.4800 g., 0.9860 Gold 0.1103 oz. AGW **Ruler:** Albrecht **Obv:** Bust of Albrecht 1/2 right in inner circle **Rev:** Crowned arms in cartouche in inner circle, date in legend **Mint:** Gitschin

Date	Mintage	VG	F	VF	XF	Unc
1627	—	2,200	4,400	9,400	18,000	—

KM# 19 DUCAT

3.4500 g., 0.9860 Gold 0.1094 oz. AGW **Ruler:** Albrecht **Rev:** Crowned oval arms in inner circle, date in legend

Date	Mintage	VG	F	VF	XF	Unc
1627	—	2,200	4,400	9,400	18,000	—

KM# 20 DUCAT

3.2000 g., 0.9860 Gold 0.1014 oz. AGW **Ruler:** Albrecht **Rev:** Crowned straight sided shield in inner circle; date in legend

Date	Mintage	VG	F	VF	XF	Unc
1627	—	1,650	4,150	8,300	15,000	—
1628	—	1,650	4,150	8,300	15,000	—

KM# 29 DUCAT

3.4000 g., 0.9860 Gold 0.1078 oz. AGW **Ruler:** Albrecht **Obv:** Bust of Albrecht right in inner circle **Rev:** Crowned round arms in cartouche in inner circle, date in legend **Note:** Varieties exist.

Date	Mintage	VG	F	VF	XF	Unc
1628	—	1,650	4,150	8,300	15,000	—
1629	—	1,650	4,150	8,300	15,000	—

KM# 41 DUCAT

3.4000 g., 0.9860 Gold 0.1078 oz. AGW **Ruler:** Albrecht **Obv:** Bust of Albrecht with broad face **Rev:** Crowned arms in order chain, date in legend

Date	Mintage	VG	F	VF	XF	Unc
1629	—	1,650	4,150	8,300	15,000	—

KM# 55 DUCAT

3.4000 g., 0.9860 Gold 0.1078 oz. AGW **Ruler:** Albrecht **Obv:** Bust of Albrecht with pointed face

Date	Mintage	VG	F	VF	XF	Unc
1630	—	3,050	5,800	10,500	18,000	—

KM# 61 DUCAT

3.4900 g., 0.9860 Gold 0.1106 oz. AGW **Ruler:** Albrecht **Obv:** Bust of Albrecht with large head **Rev:** Crowned arms in order collar, date in legend

Date	Mintage	VG	F	VF	XF	Unc
1631 Rare	—	—	—	—	—	—

Note: Kunker Auction 141, 6-08, VF+ realized approximately $14,715.

KM# 62 DUCAT

3.4200 g., 0.9860 Gold 0.1084 oz. AGW **Ruler:** Albrecht **Obv:** Small head **Note:** Varieties exist.

Date	Mintage	VG	F	VF	XF	Unc
1631 Rare	—	—	—	—	—	—

Note: Kunker Auction 141, 6-08, nearly XF realized approximately $21,685.

Date	Mintage	VG	F	VF	XF	Unc
1633	—	2,400	4,600	9,400	14,500	—
1634	—	2,400	4,600	9,400	14,500	—

KM# 21 2 DUCAT

6.9000 g., 0.9860 Gold 0.2187 oz. AGW **Ruler:** Albrecht **Obv:** Bust of Albrecht 1/2 right in inner circle **Rev:** Crowned arms in inner inner circle, date in legend **Mint:** Gitschin

Date	Mintage	VG	F	VF	XF	Unc
1627 Rare	—	—	—	—	—	—

Note: Kunker Auction 141, 6-08, VF realized approximately $23,235.

KM# 63 2 DUCAT

6.8000 g., 0.9860 Gold 0.2156 oz. AGW **Ruler:** Albrecht **Rev:** Crowned arms in order collar, date in legend **Note:** Varieties exist.

Date	Mintage	VG	F	VF	XF	Unc
1631	—	—	—	—	—	—

Note: Leu Numismatik Auction 75, 10-99, XF realized $16,665

Date	Mintage	VG	F	VF	XF	Unc
1633	—	4,950	8,300	14,000	—	—
1634	—	4,400	7,700	12,500	—	—

KM# 22 5 DUCAT

17.1300 g., 0.9860 Gold 0.5430 oz. AGW **Ruler:** Albrecht **Obv:** Bust of Albrecht 1/2 right in inner circle **Rev:** Crowned arms in inner circle, date in legend **Mint:** Gitschin

Date	Mintage	VG	F	VF	XF	Unc
1627 Rare	—	—	—	—	—	—

Note: Leu Numismatik Auction 75, 10-99, VF realized $32,000

KM# 30 5 DUCAT

17.4000 g., 0.9860 Gold 0.5516 oz. AGW **Ruler:** Albrecht **Obv:** Bust of Albrecht right in inner circle

Date	Mintage	VG	F	VF	XF	Unc
1628 Rare	—	—	—	—	—	—

KM# 42 5 DUCAT

17.2000 g., 0.9860 Gold 0.5452 oz. AGW **Ruler:** Albrecht **Obv:** Bust of Albrecht 1/2 right in inner circle **Rev:** Crowned arms in order collar, date in legend

Date	Mintage	VG	F	VF	XF	Unc
1629 Rare	—	—	—	—	—	—

KM# 56 5 DUCAT

17.2000 g., 0.9860 Gold 0.5452 oz. AGW **Ruler:** Albrecht **Obv:** Head of Albrecht completely within inner circle **Mint:** Sagan

Date	Mintage	VG	F	VF	XF	Unc
1630	—	—	—	—	—	—

Note: Leu Numismatik Auction 75, 10-99, better than VF realized, $11,335

KM# 64 5 DUCAT
17.3500 g., 0.9860 Gold 0.5500 oz. AGW **Ruler:** Albrecht **Obv:** Bust of Albrecht with pointed face 1/2 right in inner circle **Mint:** Sagan

Date	Mintage	VG	F	VF	XF	Unc
1631 Rare	—	—	—	—	—	—
1633 Rare	—	—	—	—	—	—
1634 Rare	—	—	—	—	—	—

KM# 23 10 DUCAT
34.5000 g., 0.9860 Gold 1.0936 oz. AGW **Ruler:** Albrecht **Obv:** Bust of Albrecht 1/2 right in inner circle **Rev:** Crowned oval arms in cartouche in inner circle **Mint:** Gitschin

Date	Mintage	VG	F	VF	XF	Unc
1627 Rare	—	—	—	—	—	—

KM# 31 10 DUCAT
34.6000 g., 0.9860 Gold 1.0968 oz. AGW **Ruler:** Albrecht **Obv:** Bust of Albrecht right in inner circle

Date	Mintage	VG	F	VF	XF	Unc
1628 Rare	—	—	—	—	—	—

KM# 43 10 DUCAT
34.9000 g., 0.9860 Gold 1.1063 oz. AGW **Ruler:** Albrecht **Obv:** Bust of Albrecht 1/2 right in inner circle

Date	Mintage	VG	F	VF	XF	Unc
1629 Rare	—	—	—	—	—	—

KM# 44 10 DUCAT
34.6000 g., 0.9860 Gold 1.0968 oz. AGW **Ruler:** Albrecht

Date	Mintage	VG	F	VF	XF	Unc
1629 Rare	—	—	—	—	—	—
1630 Rare	—	—	—	—	—	—

KM# 57 10 DUCAT
34.6000 g., 0.9860 Gold 1.0968 oz. AGW **Ruler:** Albrecht **Mint:** Sagan

Date	Mintage	VG	F	VF	XF	Unc
1630 GE Rare	—	—	—	—	—	—

KM# 65 10 DUCAT
34.6000 g., 0.9860 Gold 1.0968 oz. AGW **Ruler:** Albrecht **Obv:** Bust of Albrecht with pointed face 1/2 right in inner circle **Rev:** Crowned arms in order collar in inner circle, date in legend **Mint:** Gitschin

Date	Mintage	VG	F	VF	XF	Unc
1631 Rare	—	—	—	—	—	—

Note: Kunker Auction 141, 6-08, VF realized approximately $74,350. Leu Numismatik Auction 75, 10-99, XF realized, $38,665. Stack's International sale 3-88 VF realized $15,400.

GLATZ

The origins of the lordship of Glatz, which was centered on the town of the same name, present-day Klodzko in southern Poland, 48 miles (80 kilometers) south of Wroclaw (Breslau), follow the fortunes of the early dukes of Lower Silesia (Niederschlesien). Boleslaw I of Schweidnitz inherited Glatz in 1290, but his son Boleslaw II of Münsterberg sold the lordship to Bohemia in 1322. Georg Podiebrad von Kunstadt, King of Bohemia 1458-1471, divided various territories among his sons and Heinrich I (1492-1498) received Glatz as part of his inheritance. In the first year of Heinrich's rule, Emperor Friedrich III (1440-93) raised Glatz to a countship. Heinrich's son, Karl I (1498-1536) sold Glatz to Ulrich, Count of Hardeck. From that point onwards, Glatz passed from one family to another, eventually becoming part of the Habsburg possessions in Silesia. It was taken, along with much of Silesia, by Friedrich II the Great in 1740 and the following years of war between Austria and Prussia.

RULERS
Albrecht, Herzog von Bayern,
To Austria 1567-1623
Georg Friedrich, Graf von Hardeck, ca. 1613
Karl, Erzherzog von Österreich, 1623-1628
To Austria 1628-1740

MINT OFFICIALS' INITIALS

Initials	Date	Name
	1624	Hans Beghart, mintmaster
(a)=	1627-28	Johann Jakob Huser, mintmaster
(b)=	1627-28	Johann Jakob Huser, mintmaster
	1627	Daniel von Breen, warden
AP	1627	Andreas Peter, die-cutter
(c)=	1628-31	Peter Hema, mintmaster
	1629	Melchior Schirmer, warden
HG/F or (gothic g)	1629	Huserus Glatzensis, die-cutter
HR (ligature)	1631-34; 1634-37	Hans Rossner, warden; mintmaster
	1634-?	Georg Andrae Huebmer, warden
GW	1640; 1641-60	Georg Werner, die-cutter; mintmaster and contractor
	1649-?	Melchior Wilhelm Baumgart, warden

ARMS

Lower case Gothic g (gothic g), later crowned and double-tailed Bohemian lion combined with 2 curved bars from upper left to lower right, as well as other devices.

REFERENCE

F/S = Ferdinand Friedensburg and Hans Seger, ***Schlesiens Münzen und Medaillen der neueren Zeit***, Breslau, 1901 (reprint Frankfurt/Main, 1976).

S/Schl = Hugo Frhr. Von ***Saurma-Jeltsch, Schlesische Münzen und Medaillen,*** Breslau, 1883.

J/M = Norbert Jaschke and Fritz P. Maercker, ***Schlesische Münzen und Medaillen,*** Ihringen, 1985.

S = Hugo Frhr. Von Saurma-Jeltsch, ***Die Saurmasche Münzsammlung deutscher, schweizerischer und polnischer Gepräge von etwa dem Beginn der Groschenzeit bis zur Kipperperiode,*** Berlin, 1892

Sch = Wolfgang Schulten, ***Deutsche Münzen aus der Zeit Karls V.*** Frankfurt am Main, 1974.

COUNTSHIP

STANDARD COINAGE

KM# 52 PFENNIG
Silver **Ruler:** To Austria **Obv:** Shield with imperial eagle divides date, crown above, F.III below, all in quatrefoil **Note:** Prev. Austria KM#847. Uniface.

Date	Mintage	VG	F	VF	XF	Unc
1638	—	25.00	45.00	85.00	175	—

KM# 40 1/2 KREUZER (2 Pfennig)
Silver **Ruler:** To Austria **Obv:** 2 adjacent shields of arms, bottoms tilted outward, large crown above divides date, F.III under crown, mintmaster's symbol or initials at bottom **Note:** Ref. F/S#2861, 2865, 2880. Prev. Austria KM#741. Uniface.

Date	Mintage	VG	F	VF	XF	Unc
1630 (c)	—	15.00	30.00	60.00	120	—
1631 (c)	—	15.00	30.00	60.00	120	—
1637 HR	—	15.00	30.00	60.00	120	—
1638 HR	—	15.00	30.00	60.00	120	—

KM# 58 1/2 KREUZER (2 Pfennig)
Silver **Ruler:** To Austria **Obv:** 3 small shields of arms, 1 above divides date over 2 below, mintmasters initials at bottom **Note:** Ref. F/S#2893. Prev. Austria KM#891. Uniface.

Date	Mintage	VG	F	VF	XF	Unc
1641 GW	—	18.00	35.00	70.00	150	—
1644 GW	—	18.00	35.00	70.00	150	—

KM# 9 KREUZER
Silver **Ruler:** To Austria **Obv:** Ruff-collared bust right, titles of Ferdinand III as King of Bohemia, value I in oval below **Rev:** Shield of 2-fold arms (Austria and Glatz, 2 curved bars) superimposed on cross in circle, titles ocntinued and date **Note:** Ref. F/S#2833, 2835, 2842, 2857, 2860, 2864, 2870, 2872, 2875. Prev. Austria KM#690.

Date	Mintage	VG	F	VF	XF	Unc
16Z8 (a)	—	12.00	25.00	50.00	85.00	—
16Z8 (b)	—	12.00	25.00	50.00	85.00	—
16Z8 (c)	—	12.00	25.00	50.00	85.00	—
16Z9 (c)	—	12.00	25.00	50.00	85.00	—
1630 (c)	—	12.00	25.00	50.00	85.00	—
1631 (c)	—	12.00	25.00	50.00	85.00	—
163Z HR	—	12.00	25.00	50.00	85.00	—
1633 HR	—	12.00	25.00	50.00	85.00	—
1635 HR	—	12.00	25.00	50.00	85.00	—
1636 HR	—	12.00	25.00	50.00	85.00	—

KM# 8 KREUZER
Silver **Ruler:** To Austria **Obv:** Ruff-collared bust right, titles of Ferdinand III as King of Bohemia, value I in oval below **Rev:** Bohemian lion left in circle, titles continued and date **Note:** Ref. F/S#2834. Prev. Austria KM#689.

Date	Mintage	VG	F	VF	XF	Unc
16Z8 (a)	—	35.00	75.00	150	350	—

KM# 62 KREUZER
Silver **Ruler:** To Austria **Obv:** Laureate bust right, value I in cartouche below, titles of Leopold I **Rev:** Crowned imperial eagle, small oval shield of arms on breast, mintmaster's initials in oval at bottom, titles continued and date **Note:** Ref. F/S#2904. Prev. Austria KM#1133.

Date	Mintage	VG	F	VF	XF	Unc
1659 GW	—	40.00	80.00	160	375	—

KM# 4 3 KREUZER (Groschen)
Silver **Ruler:** To Austria **Obv:** Ruff-collared bust right in circle, value (3) below, titles of Ferdinand III as King of Bohemia **Rev:** 3 small shields of arms arranged wtih bottoms toward center in trefoil design, titles continued and date **Note:** Ref. F/S#2829-32, 2839-40. Prev. Austria KM#669. Varieties exist.

Date	Mintage	VG	F	VF	XF	Unc
1627	—	20.00	40.00	80.00	175	—
1627 (a)	—	20.00	40.00	80.00	175	—
1628 (a)	—	20.00	40.00	80.00	175	—
1628 (b)	—	20.00	40.00	80.00	175	—
1628 (c)-g	—	20.00	40.00	80.00	175	—
16Z8 (c)-G	—	20.00	40.00	80.00	175	—

KM# 12 3 KREUZER (Groschen)
Silver **Ruler:** To Austria **Obv:** Ruff-collared bust right in circle, value (3) below, titles of Ferdinand III as King of Bohemia **Rev:** Crowned 4-fold arms with central shield, titles continued and date **Note:** Ref. F/S#2841, 2856, 2859, 2863, 2868-69, 2871, 2873-74, 2878-79. Prev. Austria KM#692. Varieties exist.

Date	Mintage	VG	F	VF	XF	Unc
1628 (c)	—	12.00	25.00	45.00	75.00	—
1629 (c)	—	12.00	25.00	45.00	75.00	—
1630 (c)	—	12.00	25.00	45.00	75.00	—
1631 (c)	—	12.00	25.00	45.00	75.00	—
1631 HR	—	12.00	25.00	45.00	75.00	—
163Z HR	—	12.00	25.00	45.00	75.00	—
1633 HR	—	12.00	25.00	45.00	75.00	—
1634 HR	—	12.00	25.00	45.00	75.00	—
1635 HR	—	12.00	25.00	45.00	75.00	—
1636 HR	—	12.00	25.00	45.00	75.00	—
1637 HR	—	12.00	25.00	45.00	75.00	—

KM# 50 3 KREUZER (Groschen)

Silver **Ruler:** To Austria **Obv:** Ruff-collard bust right in circle, value (3) below, titles of Ferdinand III as emperor **Rev:** Crowned imperial eagle, 2-fold arms on breast, titles continued and date **Note:** Ref. F/S#2881-82, 2884-86. Prev. Austria KM#832. Varieties exist.

Date	Mintage	VG	F	VF	XF	Unc
1637 G	—	12.00	25.00	45.00	75.00	—
1637 HR	—	12.00	25.00	45.00	75.00	—
1638 G	—	12.00	25.00	45.00	75.00	—
1639 G	—	12.00	25.00	45.00	75.00	—
1640 G	—	12.00	25.00	45.00	75.00	—

KM# 56 3 KREUZER (Groschen)

Silver **Ruler:** To Austria **Obv:** Laureate bust right, not in circle, 3 in oval below, titles of Ferdinand III **Rev:** Crowned imperial eagle not in circle, 2 fold arms on breast, titles continued and date **Note:** Ref. F/S#2887, 2889-92, 2894-2902. Prev. Austria KM#893. Varieties exist.

Date	Mintage	VG	F	VF	XF	Unc
1640 GW	—	12.00	25.00	45.00	75.00	—
1641 GW	—	12.00	25.00	45.00	75.00	—
164Z GW	—	12.00	25.00	45.00	75.00	—
1643 GW	—	12.00	25.00	45.00	75.00	—
1644 GW	—	12.00	25.00	45.00	75.00	—
1645 GW	—	12.00	25.00	45.00	75.00	—
1646 GW	—	12.00	25.00	45.00	75.00	—
1647 GW	—	12.00	25.00	45.00	75.00	—
1648 GW	—	12.00	25.00	45.00	75.00	—
1649 GW	—	12.00	25.00	45.00	75.00	—
1650 GW	—	12.00	25.00	45.00	75.00	—
1651 GW	—	12.00	25.00	45.00	75.00	—
1653 GW	—	12.00	25.00	45.00	75.00	—
1654 GW	—	12.00	25.00	45.00	75.00	—

KM# 64 3 KREUZER (Groschen)

Silver **Ruler:** To Austria **Obv:** Laureate bust right, not in circle, 3 in oval below, titles of Leopold I **Rev:** Crowned imperial eagle not in circle, 2 fold arms on breast, titles continued and date **Note:** Ref. F/S#2903, 2905. Prev. Austria KM#1140.

Date	Mintage	VG	F	VF	XF	Unc
1659 GW	—	30.00	60.00	120	225	—
1660 GW	—	30.00	60.00	120	225	—

KM# 2 THALER

Silver **Ruler:** Georg Friedrich **Obv:** Arms of Hardeck, 3 helmets above, titles of Georg Friedrich **Rev:** Standing figure of St. George slaying dragon which divides date **Rev. Legend:** MONETA. ARG. A VETERI. RECVSA. COMITVM. IN. HARDECC.Zc. **Note:** Dav#3396. Prev. Austrian States - Glatz KM#5.

Date	Mintage	VG	F	VF	XF	Unc
1613 Rare	—	—	—	—	—	—

KM# 5 THALER

Silver **Ruler:** Karl **Obv:** Armored bust of Ferdinand III wearing ruffled collar right **Rev:** Crowned ornate oval arms in Order chain **Mint:** Glatz **Note:** Dav#3356. Prev. Austria KM#675.

Date	Mintage	VG	F	VF	XF	Unc
1627 (a)	—	650	1,250	2,000	3,500	—

KM# 14.1 THALER

Silver **Ruler:** To Austria **Obv:** Armored bust of Ferdinand III wearing wide ruffled collar right **Rev:** Crowned ornate flat-topped arms in Order chain **Mint:** Glatz **Note:** Dav#3357. Varieties exist. Prev. Austria KM#699.1.

Date	Mintage	VG	F	VF	XF	Unc
1628 (c)	—	300	700	1,350	2,750	—
1629 (c)	—	300	700	1,350	2,750	—

KM# 14.2 THALER

Silver **Ruler:** To Austria **Obv:** Armored bust of Ferdinand III wearing wide ruffled collar right, without HP Monogram **Rev:** Crowned ornate flat-topped arms in Order chain **Mint:** Glatz **Note:** Dav#3357A. Prev. Austria KM#699.2.

Date	Mintage	VG	F	VF	XF	Unc
1629	—	300	700	1,350	2,750	—

KM# 19 THALER

Silver **Ruler:** To Austria **Rev:** Radiant Madonna and child with HP monogram below **Rev. Legend:** FECIT MAGNA POTENS **Mint:** Glatz **Note:** Dav#3358. Prev. Austria KM#712. Varieties exist.

Date	Mintage	VG	F	VF	XF	Unc
1629 (c) Rare	—	—	—	—	—	—

Note: Künker auction 184, 3-11, VF realized approximately $16,770.

KM# 20 THALER

Silver **Ruler:** To Austria **Obv:** Armored bust of Ferdinand III wearing wide ruffled collar right, HP monogram below **Rev:** Hungarian shield at left, and Bohemian shields at right, Vienna shield at bottom in legend **Mint:** Glatz **Note:** Dav#3359. Prev. Austria KM#713.

Date	Mintage	VG	F	VF	XF	Unc
1629 (c)	—	700	1,300	3,000	5,000	—
1630 (c)	—	700	1,300	3,000	5,000	—

KM# 18 THALER

Silver **Ruler:** To Austria **Rev:** Crowned plain arms in Order chain **Mint:** Glatz **Note:** Dav#3360. Prev. Austria KM#711.

Date	Mintage	VG	F	VF	XF	Unc
1629 (c)	—	500	1,000	1,800	3,000	—
1630	—	500	1,000	1,800	3,000	—
1630 (c)	—	500	1,000	1,800	3,000	—
1631 HR	—	500	1,000	1,800	3,000	—

KM# 14.3 THALER

Silver **Ruler:** To Austria **Obv:** Armored bust of Ferdinand III wearing narrow ruffled collar right **Rev:** Crowned ornate flat-topped arms in Order chain **Mint:** Glatz **Note:** Dav#3361. Prev. Austria KM#699.3.

Date	Mintage	VG	F	VF	XF	Unc
1629 HG	—	500	1,000	1,800	3,000	—

KM# 42 THALER
Silver **Ruler:** To Austria **Obv:** Armored bust of Ferdinand III wearing wide ruffled collar 3/4 right **Rev:** Crowned ornate arms in Order chain **Mint:** Glatz **Note:** Dav#3362. Prev. Austria KM#747.

Date	Mintage	VG	F	VF	XF	Unc
1630 (c) Rare	—	—	—	—	—	—

KM# 46 THALER
Silver **Ruler:** To Austria **Obv:** Robed bust of Ferdinand III right **Rev:** Crowned ornate arms in Order chain **Mint:** Glatz **Note:** Dav#A3363. Prev. Austria KM#816.

Date	Mintage	VG	F	VF	XF	Unc
1636 Rare	—	—	—	—	—	—

KM# 6 2 THALER
Silver **Ruler:** Karl **Obv:** Armored bust of Ferdinand III wearing ruffled collar right **Rev:** Crowned ornate oval arms in Order chain **Mint:** Glatz **Note:** Dav#A3356. Prev. Austria KM#680.

Date	Mintage	VG	F	VF	XF	Unc
1627 (a) Rare	—	—	—	—	—	—

KM# 24 2 THALER
Silver **Ruler:** To Austria **Rev:** Radiant Madonna and child with HP monogram below **Rev. Legend:** FECIT MAGNA POTENS **Mint:** Glatz **Note:** Dav#A3358. Prev. Austria KM#717.

Date	Mintage	VG	F	VF	XF	Unc
1629 (c) Rare	—	—	—	—	—	—

KM# 23 2 THALER
Silver **Ruler:** To Austria **Rev:** Crowned ornate arms **Mint:** Glatz **Note:** Dav#A3361. Prev. Austria KM#715.

Date	Mintage	VG	F	VF	XF	Unc
1629 HG Rare	—	—	—	—	—	—

KM# 44 2 THALER
Silver **Ruler:** To Austria **Obv:** Armored bust of Ferdinand III wearing wide ruffled collar 3/4 right **Rev:** Crowned ornate arms in Order chain **Mint:** Glatz **Note:** Dav#A3362. Prev. Austria KM#751.

Date	Mintage	VG	F	VF	XF	Unc
1630 (c) Rare	—	—	—	—	—	—

KM# 25 3 THALER
Silver **Ruler:** To Austria **Obv:** Armored bust of Ferdinand III wearing wide ruffled collar right **Rev:** Crowned ornate flat-topped arms in Order chain **Mint:** Glatz **Note:** Dav#A3361. Prev. Austria KM#721.

Date	Mintage	VG	F	VF	XF	Unc
1629 (c) Rare	—	—	—	—	—	—

TRADE COINAGE

KM# 28 DUCAT
3.5000 g., 0.9860 Gold 0.1109 oz. AGW **Ruler:** To Austria **Obv:** Ferdinand III standing facing 3/4 right **Rev:** Crowned arms in Order chain, crown divides date **Mint:** Glatz **Note:** Prev. Austria KM#722.

Date	Mintage	VG	F	VF	XF	Unc
1629 (c)	—	600	1,250	3,000	7,000	—
1631 (c)	—	600	1,250	3,000	7,000	—
1631 HR	—	600	1,250	3,000	7,000	—
1636 HR	—	600	1,250	3,000	7,000	—

KM# 54 DUCAT
3.5000 g., 0.9860 Gold 0.1109 oz. AGW **Ruler:** To Austria **Rev:** Crowned imperial eagle in Order chain **Mint:** Glatz **Note:** Prev. Austria KM#859.

Date	Mintage	VG	F	VF	XF	Unc
1638	—	600	1,250	3,000	7,000	—
1640	—	600	1,250	3,000	7,000	—
1641	—	600	1,250	3,000	7,000	—
1645	—	600	1,250	3,000	7,000	—
1647	—	600	1,250	3,000	7,000	—

KM# 30 2 DUCAT
7.0000 g., 0.9860 Gold 0.2219 oz. AGW **Ruler:** To Austria **Obv:** Ferdinand III standing right **Rev:** Madonna and child **Mint:** Glatz **Note:** Prev. Austria KM#724.

Date	Mintage	VG	F	VF	XF	Unc
1629 (c)	—	1,250	2,750	5,500	11,500	—
1630 (c)	—	1,250	2,750	5,500	11,500	—
1631 (c)	—	1,250	2,750	5,500	11,500	—
1631 HR	—	1,250	2,750	5,500	11,500	—

KM# 48 5 DUCAT
17.5000 g., 0.9860 Gold 0.5547 oz. AGW **Ruler:** To Austria **Mint:** Glatz **Note:** Fr#192. Prev. Austria KM#819.

Date	Mintage	VG	F	VF	XF	Unc
1636 HR Rare	—	—	—	—	—	—

KM# 33 8 DUCAT
28.0000 g., 0.9860 Gold 0.8876 oz. AGW **Ruler:** To Austria **Obv:** Armored bust of Ferdinand III wearing narrow ruffled collar right **Rev:** Crowned ornate flat-topped arms in Order chain **Mint:** Glatz **Note:** Fr#191. Prev. Austria KM#727.

Date	Mintage	VG	F	VF	XF	Unc
1629 (c) Rare	—	—	—	—	—	—

KM# 35 9 DUCAT
31.5000 g., 0.9860 Gold 0.9985 oz. AGW **Ruler:** To Austria **Obv:** Armored bust of Ferdinand III wearing narrow ruffled collar right **Rev:** Crowned ornate flat-topped arms in Order chain **Mint:** Glatz **Note:** Fr#190. Prev. Austria KM#728.

Date	Mintage	VG	F	VF	XF	Unc
1629 HG Rare	—	—	—	—	—	—

KM# 16 10 DUCAT
35.0000 g., 0.9860 Gold 1.1095 oz. AGW **Ruler:** To Austria **Obv:** Armored bust of Ferdinand III wearing wide ruffled collar right **Rev:** Crowned ornate flat-topped arms in Order chain **Mint:** Glatz **Note:** Fr#189. Prev. Austria KM#703.

Date	Mintage	VG	F	VF	XF	Unc
1628 (c) Rare	—	—	—	—	—	—

KM# 17 10 DUCAT
35.0000 g., 0.9860 Gold 1.1095 oz. AGW **Ruler:** To Austria **Obv:** Armored bust of Ferdinand III wearing narrow ruffled collar right **Rev:** Crowned ornate flat-topped arms in Order chain **Mint:** Glatz **Note:** Fr#189. Prev. Austria KM#729.

Date	Mintage	VG	F	VF	XF	Unc
1629 HG Rare	—	—	—	—	—	—

KM# 38 12 DUCAT
42.0000 g., 0.9860 Gold 1.3314 oz. AGW **Ruler:** To Austria **Obv:** Armored bust of Ferdinand III wearing narrow ruffled collar right **Rev:** Crowned ornate flat-topped arms in Order chain **Mint:** Glatz **Note:** Fr#188. Prev. Austria KM#731.

Date	Mintage	VG	F	VF	XF	Unc
1629 HG Rare	—	—	—	—	—	—

PATTERNS

Including off metal strikes

KM#	Date	Mintage	Identification	Mkt Val
Pn1	1627 (a)	—	Thaler. Gold. KM#5, weight of 10 Ducat	—
Pn2	1629 HG	—	Thaler. Gold. KM#14.2, weight of 10 Ducat.	—
Pn3	1629 HG	—	Thaler. Gold. KM#14.3, weight of 12 Ducat.	—

LOBKOWITZ-STERNSTEIN

The Bohemian lords of Lobkowitz had long distinguished themselves in the service of the Holy Roman Empire. For his role on the side of the emperor in the opening phase of the Thirty Years' War, Dzenko Adalbert was given the countship of Sternstein in Upper Bavaria in 1623 and raised to the rank of Prince of the Empire. The lands in Bavaria were mediatized in 1805.

RULERS
Zdenko Adalbert, 1623-1628
Wenseslaus Franz Eusebius, 1628-1677
Ferdinand August Leopold, 1677-1715

MINT MARKS
VI = Vienna Mint

PRINCIPALITY

STANDARD COINAGE

KM# 7 1/2 THALER
Silver **Ruler:** Franz Joseph Maximilian **Obv:** Bust of Franz Joseph Maximillan right **Rev:** Crowned and mantled arms

Date	Mintage	VG	F	VF	XF	Unc
1615	—	—	—	—	—	—

Note: Reported, not confirmed

KM# 5 THALER
Silver **Ruler:** Zdenko Adalbert **Obv:** Bust of Zdenko Adalbert right **Rev:** Crowned 4-fold arms of Lobkowitz and Zerotin, surrounded by chain of the Order of the Golden Fleece **Note:** Show Thaler.

Date	Mintage	VG	F	VF	XF	Unc
ND	—	—	—	—	—	—

TRADE COINAGE

KM# 6 DUCAT
3.5000 g., 0.9860 Gold 0.1109 oz. AGW **Ruler:** Ferdinand August Leopold **Obv:** Armored bust right **Rev:** Crowned arms

Date	Mintage	VG	F	VF	XF	U
ND	—	2,600	4,300	7,800	12,000	

ROSENBERG

The counts of Rosenberg in Bohemia trace their origins back to the lords of Krumlau in the second half of the 12th century. Two lines were established early, but only the elder branch in Krumlau issued coins. In 1592, Count Wilhelm was raised to the rank of prince and awarded the right to strike coins. The line came to an end in 1611 and title passed to the Habsburgs until 1622, then to Eggenberg until 1719 and finally to Schwarzenberg from that year. The younger branch was raised to

Count of the Empire in 1648 and then prince in 1790. The various territories of Rosenberg were mediatized during the Napoleonic Empire. All coinage of Rosenberg was produced at the Reichenstein mint in Silesia.

RULERS

Elder Line
Jobst III, 1505-1539
Peter V, 1505-1545
Wilhelm, 1539-1592
Peter Wok von Ursini, 1592-1611

MINT OFFICIALS' INITIALS

Initials	Date	Name
MA	1584-86	Markus Ambrosius von Brosenthat

ARMS

Upper and lower fields divided by horizontal bar in which an eel, upper field a 5-petaled rose, lower field 5 alternately shaded bars diagonally from upper left to lower right.

REFERENCES

F/S = Ferdinand Friedensburg and Hans Seger, ***Schlesiens Münzen und Medaillen der neueren Zeit***, Breslau, 1901 (reprint Frankfurt/Main, 1976).

J/M = Norbert Jaschke and Fritz P. Maercker, ***Schlesische Münzen und Medaillen,*** Ihringen, 1985.

S = Hugo Frhr. Von Saurma-Jeltsch, ***Die Saurmasche Münzsammlung deutscher, schweizerischer und polnischer Gepräge von etwa dem Beginn der Groschenzeit bis zur Kipperperiode***, Berlin, 1892.

S/Sch = Hugo Frhr. Von Saurma-Jeltsch***, Schlesische Münzen und Medaillen***, Breslau, 1883.

Sch = Wolfgang Schulten, ***Deutsche Münzen aus der Zeit Karls V.*** Frankfurt am Main, 1974.

COUNTSHIP

STANDARD COINAGE

MB# 37 PFENNIG

Silver **Ruler:** Peter Wok von Ursini **Obv:** Rosenberg arms, 'W' above **Note:** Uniface.

Date	Mintage	VG	F	VF	XF	Unc
ND(1592-1611)	—	7.00	14.00	30.00	60.00	—

SCHLICK

Heinrich Schlick was the Bürgermeister (mayor) of Lazan in western Bohemia, but owned land in Passaun (Bassano in Italy, north of Vicenza and Padua) and Weisskirchen (at that time, Ujvár in Hungary, now in Romania) 45 miles (75 kilometers) east of Belgrade. Heinrich was given a patent for bearing a coat of arms by Emperor Sigismund (1410-37) in 1416. His son, Caspar (1436-49), was given the title of Count of Bassano in 1437. Therefore, Schlick was always included as the family name, but the title was Count of Passaun and Weisskirchen. The count obtained the mint right in 1489 and began coining silver from the mines of Joachimsthal and Michaelsburg about 1517. The large Guldengroschen struck from the mined silver came to be called a Joachimsthaler, later shorted to "Thaler", the origin of the "dollar" in English. The mint right was confiscated by the Bohemian crown in 1528 and Joachimsthal was also made a royal mint in 1545. The mint right was restored to the family in 1626. The last coins of Schlick were struck in the 1760's and by the dissolution of the Holy Roman Empire by Napoleon in 1806 the mint right was forfeited. The line of counts continued well into the 19th century, however.

RULERS
Georg Ernst, 1547-1612
Heinrich IV, 1612-1650
Franz Ernst, 1650-1675
Franz Josef, 1675-1740
Leopold Josef, 1675-1723

ARMS:

Schlick – 3 annulets divided by inverted 'V', 2 annulets to left and right of point, third lower inside the inverted figure.

Passaun (Bassano) – 2 rampant panthers facing each other and holding crenelated tower between them. This is usually the central shield of the family's manifold arms.

Weisskirchen – lion rampant left holding church model in left front paw.

REFERENCE:

S = Hugo Frhr. Von Saurma-Jeltsch, ***Die Saurmasche Münzsammlung deutscher, schweizerischer und polnischer Gepräge von etwa dem Beginn der Groschenzeit bis zur Kipperperiode,*** Berlin, 1892

Sch = Wolfgang Schulten, ***Deutsche Münzen aus der Zeit Karls V.*** Frankfurt am Main, 1974.

COUNTY

STANDARD COINAGE

KM# 5 KREUZER

Silver **Ruler:** Heinrich IV **Obv:** Arms **Rev:** Crowned imperial eagle with value on breast

Date	Mintage	VG	F	VF	XF	Unc
1630	—	20.00	30.75	55.00	100	—

KM# 6 3 KREUZER

Silver **Ruler:** Heinrich IV **Obv:** Arms **Rev:** Heraldic imperial eagle

Date	Mintage	VG	F	VF	XF	Unc
1628	—	13.00	25.00	46.25	85.00	—
1631	—	13.00	25.00	46.25	85.00	—
1632	—	13.00	25.00	46.25	85.00	—
1635	—	13.00	25.00	46.25	85.00	—
1637	—	13.00	25.00	46.25	85.00	—
1638	—	13.00	25.00	46.25	85.00	—

KM# 7 1/2 THALER

Silver **Ruler:** Heinrich IV

Date	Mintage	VG	F	VF	XF	Unc
1627	—	145	240	425	725	—

KM# 20.1 1/2 THALER

Silver **Ruler:** Franz Ernst **Obv:** Madonna with child and St. Anne, above crowned arms **Rev:** Double-headed imperial eagle with large heads

Date	Mintage	VG	F	VF	XF	Unc
1661	—	100	200	350	600	—

KM# 20.2 1/2 THALER

Silver **Ruler:** Franz Ernst **Obv:** Madonna with child and St. Anne, above crowned arms **Rev:** Double-headed imperial eagle with small heads **Rev. Legend:** LEOPOLD: ROM: IMP: - SEMPER • AVGVSTVS

Date	Mintage	VG	F	VF	XF	Unc
1661	—	350	625	1,050	1,750	—

KM# 25 1/2 THALER

Silver **Ruler:** Franz Josef **Obv:** Madonna with child with St. Anne separating S-A behind arms, small shield in legend separating I-G **Rev:** Crowned double-headed imperial eagle with arms on breast

Date	Mintage	VG	F	VF	XF	Unc
1677	—	290	500	925	1,450	—

KM# 8.1 THALER

Silver **Ruler:** Heinrich IV **Obv:** Crowned imperial eagle with arms on breast **Rev:** Madonna and child with St. Anne separating S-A behind arms, small shield in legend separating I-G **Note:** Dav. #3398.

Date	Mintage	VG	F	VF	XF	Unc
1627	—	175	290	500	875	—

KM# 8.2 THALER

Silver **Ruler:** Heinrich IV **Obv:** Madonna and child with St. Anne closer together behind oval arms separating date **Rev. Legend:** FERDINANDVS • I • ROM • IMP • SEMPER • AVGVSTVS **Note:** Dav. #3399.

Date	Mintage	VG	F	VF	XF	Unc
1629	—	700	1,250	3,500	6,500	—
1630	—	700	1,250	3,500	6,500	—

KM# 8.3 THALER

Silver **Ruler:** Heinrich IV **Obv:** Madonna and child with St. Anne dividing SAN-NA **Note:** Dav. #3400.

Date	Mintage	VG	F	VF	XF	Unc
1630	—	290	475	850	1,800	—

KM# 8.4 THALER

Silver **Ruler:** Heinrich IV **Obv:** Madonna and child with St. Anne dividing S. A-NNA **Note:** Dav. #3401.

Date	Mintage	VG	F	VF	XF	Unc
1632	—	290	475	850	1,800	—

KM# 8.5 THALER

Silver **Ruler:** Heinrich IV **Obv:** Shield dividing S. AN-NA **Note:** Dav. #3402.

Date	Mintage	VG	F	VF	XF	Unc
1634	—	290	475	850	1,800	—

KM# 8.6 THALER

Silver **Ruler:** Heinrich IV **Note:** Klippe. Dav. #3402A.

Date	Mintage	VG	F	VF	XF	Unc
1634 Rare	—	—	—	—	—	—

KM# 8.7 THALER

Silver **Ruler:** Heinrich IV **Rev. Legend:** FERDINAND: III • ROM - IMP • SEMPER • AVGVST **Note:** Klippe. Dav. #3404. Varieties exist.

Date	Mintage	VG	F	VF	XF	Unc
1641	—	290	475	850	1,450	—
1642	—	290	475	850	1,450	—

KM# 8.8 THALER

Silver **Ruler:** Heinrich IV **Note:** Klippe. Dav. #3404A.

Date	Mintage	VG	F	VF	XF	Unc
1641 Rare	—	—	—	—	—	—
1642 Rare	—	—	—	—	—	—

KM# 8.9 THALER

Silver **Ruler:** Heinrich IV **Obv:** Order chain around arms **Note:** Dav. #3406.

Date	Mintage	VG	F	VF	XF	Unc
1644	—	300	500	900	1,500	—

KM# 9 THALER

Silver **Ruler:** Heinrich IV **Obv:** Larger figures above shield **Note:** Almost every date is a different variety. Dav. #3408.

Date	Mintage	VG	F	VF	XF	Unc
1645	—	375	600	1,050	2,200	—
1646	—	375	600	1,050	2,200	—
1647	—	375	600	1,050	2,200	—
1648	—	375	600	1,050	2,200	—
1649	—	375	600	1,050	2,200	—

KM# 21.1 THALER

Silver **Ruler:** Franz Ernst **Obv:** Madonna and child with St. Anna above shield divides SAN NA **Rev:** Crowned double-headed imperial eagle with shield on breast **Rev. Legend:** FERDINAND: III... **Note:** Dav. #3409.

Date	Mintage	VG	F	VF	XF	Unc
1651	—	375	600	1,050	2,200	—
1652	—	375	600	1,050	2,200	—
1654	—	375	600	1,050	2,200	—

KM# 21.2 THALER

Silver **Ruler:** Franz Ernst **Obv:** Madonna and child with St. Anna above shield divides SAN NA **Rev:** Crowned double-headed imperial eagle with shield on breast **Rev. Legend:** LEOPOLDVS. I. ROM... **Note:** Dav. #3410.

Date	Mintage	VG	F	VF	XF	Unc
1658	—	375	625	1,150	2,250	—

KM# 21.3 THALER

Silver **Ruler:** Franz Ernst **Obv:** Madonna and child with St. Anne in cloud above crowned arms **Rev:** Crowned double-headed imperial eagle with shield on breast **Note:** Every date is a different variety. Dav. #3412.

Date	Mintage	VG	F	VF	XF	Unc
1660	—	375	600	1,050	2,200	—
1661	—	375	600	1,050	2,200	—
1663	—	375	600	1,050	2,200	—

KM# 26 THALER

Silver **Ruler:** Franz Josef **Obv:** Madonna and child with St. Anne in cloud above crowned arms dividing date and breaking legend at top and bottom **Obv. Legend:** Titles of Franz Josef **Rev:** Crowned double-headed imperial eagle with shield on breast, within circle of beads **Rev. Legend:** Titles of Leopold **Note:** Dav. #3413.

Date	Mintage	VG	F	VF	XF	Unc
1677	—	625	1,150	1,900	3,750	—

KM# 10 1-1/2 THALER

Silver **Ruler:** Heinrich IV **Note:** Klippe. Similar to 1 Thaler, KM#8.7. Dav. #A3404.

Date	Mintage	VG	F	VF	XF	Unc
1642 Rare	—	—	—	—	—	—

KM# 11.1 2 THALER

Silver **Ruler:** Heinrich IV **Note:** Similar to 1 Thaler, KM#8.4. Dav. #A3401.

Date	Mintage	VG	F	VF	XF	Unc
1632	—	2,200	3,650	5,600	10,500	—

KM# 11.2 2 THALER

Silver **Ruler:** Heinrich IV **Note:** Similar to 1 Thaler, KM#8.5. Dav. #A3402.

Date	Mintage	VG	F	VF	XF	Unc
1634	—	2,200	3,650	5,600	10,500	—

KM# 11.3 2 THALER

Silver **Ruler:** Heinrich IV **Note:** Klippe. Similar to 1 Thaler, KM#8.5. Dav. #A3402A.

Date	Mintage	VG	F	VF	XF	Unc
1634 Rare	—	—	—	—	—	—

KM# 12 2 THALER

Silver **Ruler:** Heinrich IV **Note:** Klippe. Dav. #3403.

Date	Mintage	VG	F	VF	XF	Unc
1641	—	2,250	3,750	7,500	18,000	—
1642	—	2,250	3,750	7,500	18,000	—

KM# 11.4 2 THALER

Silver **Ruler:** Heinrich IV **Note:** Similar to 1 Thaler, KM#8.7. Dav. #A3403.

Date	Mintage	VG	F	VF	XF	Unc
1642 Rare	—	—	—	—	—	—

KM# 11.5 2 THALER

Silver **Ruler:** Heinrich IV **Note:** Similar to 1 Thaler, KM#8.9. Dav. #3405.

Date	Mintage	VG	F	VF	XF	Unc
1644	—	2,200	3,650	5,600	10,500	—

KM# 16 2 THALER

Silver **Ruler:** Heinrich IV **Note:** Similar to 1 Thaler, KM#9. Dav. #3407.

Date	Mintage	VG	F	VF	XF	Unc
1645	—	2,200	3,650	5,600	10,500	—

KM# 22.1 2 THALER

Silver **Ruler:** Franz Ernst **Note:** Similar to 1 Thaler, KM#21.1. Dav. #A3409.

Date	Mintage	VG	F	VF	XF	Unc
1651 Rare	—	—	—	—	—	—

KM# 22.2 2 THALER

Silver **Ruler:** Franz Ernst **Note:** Similar to 1 Thaler, KM#21.3. Dav. #3411.

Date	Mintage	VG	F	VF	XF	Unc
1660 Rare	—	—	—	—	—	—

KM# 13 3 THALER

Silver **Ruler:** Heinrich IV **Note:** Similar to 1 Thaler, KM#8.9. Dav. #A3405.

Date	Mintage	VG	F	VF	XF	Unc
1644 Rare	—	—	—	—	—	—

TRADE COINAGE

KM# 14 DUCAT

3.5000 g., 0.9860 Gold 0.1109 oz. AGW **Ruler:** Heinrich IV **Obv:** Madonna and child with St. Anne above arms in inner circle **Rev:** Crowned imperial eagle in inner circle **Rev. Legend:** FERDINAND:II • DG: ROM: IMP: SEMP: AV:

Date	Mintage	VG	F	VF	XF	Unc
1628	—	900	1,550	3,600	8,400	—
1629	—	900	1,550	3,600	8,400	—
1630	—	2,100	4,200	7,200	—	—
1631	—	900	1,550	3,600	8,400	—
1634	—	900	1,550	3,600	8,400	—
1636	—	900	1,550	3,600	8,400	—
1637	—	900	1,550	3,600	8,400	—
1638	—	900	1,550	3,600	8,400	—

KM# A19 5 DUCAT

17.5000 g., 0.9860 Gold 0.5547 oz. AGW **Ruler:** Heinrich IV **Obv:** Madonna and child with St. Anne above arms in inner circle **Rev:** Crowned imperial eagle in inner circle **Note:** Struck with 1 Thaler dies, KM#9.

Date	Mintage	VG	F	VF	XF	Unc
1634	—	—	—	10,000	15,500	—
1646	—	—	—	10,000	15,500	—
1649	—	—	—	10,000	15,500	—

KM# B19 5 DUCAT

17.5000 g., 0.9860 Gold 0.5547 oz. AGW **Ruler:** Franz Ernst **Note:** Struck with 1 Thaler dies, KM#21.1. Previous KM#19.

Date	Mintage	VG	F	VF	XF	Unc
1652 Rare	—	—	—	—	—	—

KM# 23 5 DUCAT

17.5000 g., 0.9860 Gold 0.5547 oz. AGW **Ruler:** Franz Ernst **Obv:** Crowned imperial eagle **Rev:** Madonna, child and St. Anne

Date	Mintage	VG	F	VF	XF	Unc
1661 Rare	—	—	—	—	—	—

Note: USB Auction 66, 9-06, nearly XF realized approximately $26,725.

Date	Mintage	VG	F	VF	XF	Unc
1662 Rare	—	—	—	—	—	—

KM# 17 10 DUCAT

35.0000 g., 0.9860 Gold 1.1095 oz. AGW **Ruler:** Heinrich IV **Note:** Struck with 1 Thaler dies, KM#8.1.

Date	Mintage	VG	F	VF	XF	Unc
1627 Rare	—	—	—	—	—	—

Note: USB Auction 66, 9-06, VF realized approximately $25,900.

KM# 18 10 DUCAT

35.0000 g., 0.9860 Gold 1.1095 oz. AGW **Ruler:** Heinrich IV **Note:** Struck with 1 Thaler dies, KM#8.

Date	Mintage	VG	F	VF	XF	Unc
1634 Rare	—	—	—	—	—	—

Note: USB Auction 66, 9-06, XF realized approximately $68,000.

KM# 19 10 DUCAT

35.0000 g., 0.9860 Gold 1.1095 oz. AGW **Ruler:** Heinrich IV **Note:** Struck with 1 Thaler dies, KM#9.

Date	Mintage	VG	F	VF	XF	Unc
1646 Rare	—	—	—	—	—	—

Note: USB Auction 66, 9-06, good VF realized approximately $20,245.

BOLIVIA

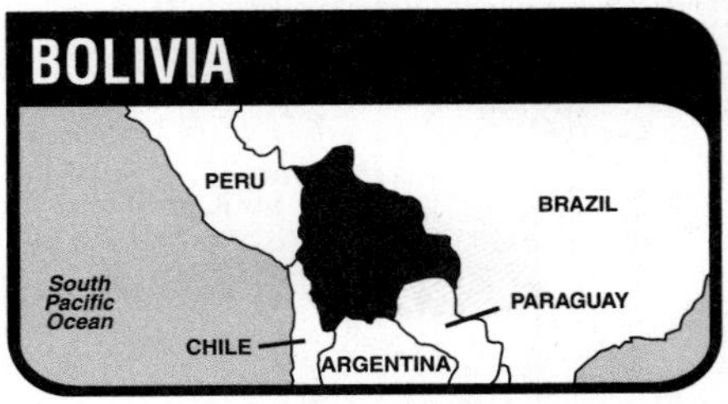

Bolivia, a landlocked country in west central South America, has an area of 424,165 sq. mi. (1,098,580 sq. km.).

Much of present day Bolivia was first dominated by the Tiahuanaco Culture ca.400 BC. It had in turn been incorporated into the Inca Empire by 1440AD prior to the arrival of the Spanish, in 1535, who reduced the Indian population to virtual slavery. When Joseph Napoleon was placed upon the throne of occupied Spain in 1809, a fervor of revolutionary activity quickened throughout Alto Peru - culminating in the 1809 Proclamation of Liberty. Sixteen bloody years of struggle ensued before the republic, named for the famed liberator Simon Bolivar, was established on August 6, 1825. Since then Bolivia has survived more than 16 constitutions, 78 Presidents, 3 military juntas and over 160 revolutions.

The Imperial City of Potosi, founded by Villarroel in 1546, was established in the midst of what is estimated to have been the world's richest silver mines (having produced in excess of 2 billion dollars worth of silver).

The first mint, early in 1574, used equipment brought over from Lima. Before that it had been used at La Plata where the operation failed. The oldest type was a cob with the Hapsburg arms on the obverse and cross with quartered castles and lions on the reverse. To the heraldic right of the shield (at the left as one faces it) is a "p" and, under it, the assayer's initial, although in some early examples the "P" and assayer can appear to the right of the shield. While production at the "Casa de Moneda" was enormous, the quality of the coinage was at times so poor that some 50 were condemned to death by their superiors.

Therefore, by royal decree of February 17, 1651, the design was changed to the quartered castles and lions for the obverse and two crowned pillars of Hercules floating above the waves of the sea for the reverse. A new transitional series was introduced in 1651-1652 followed by a new standard design in 1652 and as the last cob type continued on for several years along with the milled pillars and bust pieces from 1767 through 1773. In the final years under Charles III the planchet is compact and dumpy, very irregular and of poor style, contrasting sharply with their counterpart denominations of the pillar and bust types.

Rarely, and at very high prices, we may be offered almost perfectly round cobs, with the dies well-centered, showing the legend and date completely. These have gained importance in the last decades and are known as "royal" or "presentation" pieces. Every year a few of these specimens were coined, using dies in excellent condition and a specially prepared round planchet, to prove the quality of the minting to the Viceroy or even to the King.

Most pre-decimal coinage of independent Bolivia carries the assayers' initials on the reverse near the rim to the left of the date, in 4 to 5 o'clock position. The mint mark or name appears in the 7 to 8 o'clock area.

RULER

Spanish until 1825

MINT MARKS

PTA monogram - La Plata (Sucre)
P or PTS monogram - Potosi

ASSAYERS' INITIALS

There is little information available to establish the chronology of the assayers during the reign of Phillip II, 1555-1598, so the assayers initials are listed in alphabetical order. Calbeto in *Compendio de las Piezas de Ocho Reales* describes a piece with A overstruck over B, indicating A was later.

Initial	Date	Name
B	1596-1605	Hernando Ballesteros
C	1613	Augustin de la Quadra (Cuadra)
C	1678-79	Manuel de Cejas
E	1651-78	Antonio de Ergueta
F	1697-1701	?
M	1616-17	Juan Munoz
O	1649-51	Juan Rodriguez de Rodas
P	1620-31	Pedro Perez de Carrion
P	1622-26, 28-29, 46-47	Luis de Peralta
P, PO	1624-26	Pedro Martin de Palencia
Q	1613-17	Augustin de la Quadra
R	191-1618	Gaspar Ruiz
R	1605-13	?
R	1645-48	Felipe Ramirez Arellano
R, RL	1591-98, 1610-13, 18-23, 27-36, 44-48	Balthasar Ramos Leceta
T	1618-23, 27-36, 44-48	Juan Ximenez de Tapia
TR	1636-48	Pedro Trevino
V	1646	Geronimo Velasquez
V, VR	1679-84	Pedro de Villar
Z	1647-49	Pedro Zambrano

SYMBOLS

Letter and Symbol		Dates	Name
(c)=		1697	Sebastian de Chavarria
(o)=		1649-51	Juan Rodrigues de Roas
(t)R=		1636-40	Pedro Trevino
(tr)R=		1640-43	Pedro trevino
(tre)R=		1643-97	?

NOTE: These names are based on data put forth by Dr. E.A. Sellschopp in Las *Acunaciones de las Cecas de Lima, La Plata Y Potosi*, J. Pelliceri Bru in *Glosario de Maestros de Ceca y Ensayadores* and archival research in the *Casa Moneda Nacional de Bolivia*.

MONETARY SYSTEM
16 Reales = 1 Escudo

COLONIAL

COLONIAL COB COINAGE

MB# A1 1/4 REAL

0.8458 g., 0.9310 Silver 0.0253 oz. ASW **Ruler:** Philip II **Obv:** Castle **Rev:** Rampant lion **Note:** Prev. KM#A0001.

Date	Mintage	Good	VG	F	VF	XF
ND(1574-86)P R at right	—	125	200	350	550	—
ND(1574-86)P R at left	—	125	200	350	550	—
ND(1574-86)P M Rare	—	—	—	—	—	—

MB# B1 1/4 REAL

0.8458 g., 0.9310 Silver 0.0253 oz. ASW **Ruler:** Philip II **Obv:** Castle with assayer's initials and mint mark flanking **Rev:** Rampant lion **Note:** Prev. KM#B0001.

Date	Mintage	Good	VG	F	VF	XF
ND(1575-86)P B-P	—	100	175	300	500	—

KM# A6 1/4 REAL

Silver **Ruler:** Philip III

Date	Mintage	Good	VG	F	VF	XF
ND(1598-1605) P B Rare	—	—	—	—	—	—

MB# 1.1 1/2 REAL

1.6917 g., 0.9310 Silver 0.0506 oz. ASW **Ruler:** Philip II **Obv:** PHILIPPVS monogram **Obv. Legend:** DEI GRATIA HISPANIARVM **Rev:** Cross of Jerusalem, lions and castles in quarters **Rev. Legend:** ET INDIARVM REX **Note:** Prev. KM#0001.1.

Date	Mintage	Good	VG	F	VF	XF
ND(1574-86) P R at right	—	100	200	300	400	—
ND(1574-86) P R at left	—	100	200	300	400	—

MB# 1.2 1/2 REAL

1.6917 g., 0.9310 Silver 0.0506 oz. ASW **Ruler:** Philip II **Obv:** Mint mark at left, assayer's initial below monogram **Note:** Prev. KM#0001.2.

Date	Mintage	Good	VG	F	VF	XF
ND(1574-79) P M Rare	—	—	—	—	—	—
ND(1574-79) P L Rare	—	—	—	—	—	—
ND(1574-79)P S 1 known, Rare	—	—	—	—	—	—
ND(1574-79) P C Rare	—	—	—	—	—	—
ND(1574-79)P B with retrograde B at right Rare	—	—	—	—	—	—
ND(1574-79)P B at right Rare	—	—	—	—	—	—

MB# 1.3 1/2 REAL

1.6921 g., 0.9310 Silver 0.0506 oz. ASW **Ruler:** Philip II **Obv:** Assayer's initial below PHILIPPVS monogram **Note:** Prev. KM#0001.3.

Date	Mintage	Good	VG	F	VF	XF
ND(1574-86)P B	—	50.00	85.00	125	175	—
ND(1574-86)P small R Rare	—	—	—	—	—	—
ND(1586-89) P A Rare	—	—	—	—	—	—

MB# 1.4 1/2 REAL

1.6917 g., 0.9310 Silver 0.0506 oz. ASW **Ruler:** Philip II **Obv:** Border of X's **Rev:** Border of X's **Note:** Prev. KM#0001.4.

Date	Mintage	Good	VG	F	VF	XF
ND(1574-86)P B	—	50.00	100	175	250	—

MB# 1.5 1/2 REAL

1.6917 g., 0.9310 Silver 0.0506 oz. ASW **Ruler:** Philip II **Obv:** Border of squares **Rev:** Border of squares **Note:** Prev. KM#0001.5.

Date	Mintage	Good	VG	F	VF	XF
ND(1574-86)P B	—	50.00	100	175	250	—

KM# 6.1 1/2 REAL

1.6921 g., 0.9310 Silver 0.0506 oz. ASW **Ruler:** Philip III **Obv:** Mint mark and assayer's initials flanking PHILIPPVS monogram **Obv. Legend:** PHILIPPVS III D G

Date	Mintage	Good	VG	F	VF	XF
ND(1598-1605) P B-P Rare	—	—	—	—	—	—
ND(1605-13) P P-R	—	50.00	75.00	110	150	—
ND(1605-13) P R-P	—	50.00	75.00	110	150	—
ND(1613-17) P P-Q	—	50.00	75.00	110	150	—
ND(1613-17)P Q-P	—	50.00	75.00	110	150	—
1617P M Rare	—	—	—	—	—	—
1618P PAL Rare	—	—	—	—	—	—
1618P T/PAL Rare	—	—	—	—	—	—
1618P T Rare	—	—	—	—	—	—

KM# 6.3 1/2 REAL

1.6921 g., 0.9310 Silver 0.0506 oz. ASW **Ruler:** Philip III **Obv:** Assayer's initials and mint mark to left of monogram **Obv. Legend:** PHILIPPVS III DG

Date	Mintage	Good	VG	F	VF	XF
ND(1605-13)P R	—	50.00	75.00	110	150	—
ND(1618-21)P T	—	50.00	75.00	110	150	—

KM# 6.2 1/2 REAL

1.6921 g., 0.9310 Silver 0.0506 oz. ASW **Ruler:** Philip III **Obv:** Without mint mark

Date	Mintage	Good	VG	F	VF	XF
ND(1613-17)P Q	—	50.00	75.00	110	150	—
ND(1616-17)P M	—	50.00	75.00	110	150	—

KM# 11.1 1/2 REAL

1.6921 g., 0.9310 Silver 0.0506 oz. ASW **Ruler:** Philip III **Obv:** Monogram without assayer's initial or mint mark

Date	Mintage	Good	VG	F	VF	XF
ND	—	50.00	75.00	110	175	150

KM# A12.2 1/2 REAL

1.6921 g., 0.9310 Silver 0.0506 oz. ASW **Ruler:** Philip III **Rev. Legend:** POTOSI ANO 1652 EL PERU **Rev. Inscription:** ...PL-V-SV above L-T-RA

Date	Mintage	Good	VG	F	VF	XF
1652P	—	75.00	125	175	275	—

KM# A12.3 1/2 REAL

1.6921 g., 0.9310 Silver 0.0506 oz. ASW **Ruler:** Philip III **Rev. Inscription:** ...P-LV-SV above LT-R-A

Date	Mintage	Good	VG	F	VF	XF
1652P	—	75.00	125	175	275	—

KM# A12.4 1/2 REAL

1.6921 g., 0.9310 Silver 0.0506 oz. ASW **Ruler:** Philip III **Rev. Inscription:** ...PL-VS-VL above T-R-A

Date	Mintage	Good	VG	F	VF	XF
1652P	—	75.00	125	175	275	—

KM# A12.5 1/2 REAL

1.6921 g., 0.9310 Silver 0.0506 oz. ASW **Ruler:** Philip III **Rev. Inscription:** ...P-LV-SV above L-TR-A

Date	Mintage	Good	VG	F	VF	XF
1652P	—	75.00	125	175	275	—

KM# A12.6 1/2 REAL

1.6921 g., 0.9310 Silver 0.0506 oz. ASW **Ruler:** Philip III **Rev. Inscription:** ...P-LV-SV above L-T-RA

Date	Mintage	Good	VG	F	VF	XF
ND(1652)P	—	75.00	125	175	275	—

KM# 12.7 1/2 REAL

1.6921 g., 0.9310 Silver 0.0506 oz. ASW **Ruler:** Philip III **Rev. Inscription:** ...PL-V-SV above LT-R-A

Date	Mintage	Good	VG	F	VF	XF
1652P	—	75.00	125	175	275	—

KM# A12.1 1/2 REAL

1.6917 g., 0.9310 Silver 0.0506 oz. ASW **Ruler:** Philip IV **Rev:** Pillars and waves **Rev. Legend:** POTOSI ANO 1652 EL PERU **Rev. Inscription:** ...PL-V-SV above L-T-RA

Date	Mintage	Good	VG	F	VF	XF
1652P	—	75.00	125	175	275	—

KM# C12 1/2 REAL

1.6917 g., 0.9310 Silver 0.0506 oz. ASW **Ruler:** Philip IV **Obv:** Cross of Jerusalem with lions and castles in quarters **Obv. Legend:** PHILIPPVS IIII DG **Rev:** PHILIPPVS monogram superimposed on Cross of Jerusalem with P-H-5-2 in quadrants

Date	Mintage	Good	VG	F	VF	XF
1652P Rare	—	—	—	—	—	—

KM# B12 1/2 REAL

1.6921 g., 0.9310 Silver 0.0506 oz. ASW **Ruler:** Philip IV **Obv:** Monogram of PHILIPVS IIII superimposed on Cross of Jerusalem **Rev:** Crowned arms **Note:** Prev. KM#A12.1.

Date	Mintage	Good	VG	F	VF	XF
ND(1653-66)P Date off flan	—	20.00	30.00	45.00	50.00	—
1654/3P PE Rare	—	—	—	—	—	—
1654P PER Rare	—	—	—	—	—	—
1654P E PE	—	35.00	75.00	125	175	—
1654P E	—	35.00	50.00	75.00	100	—
1655P	—	35.00	50.00	75.00	100	—
1655P PH	—	35.00	50.00	75.00	100	—
1657P	—	35.00	50.00	75.00	100	—
1658P E	—	35.00	50.00	75.00	100	—
1659P E	—	35.00	50.00	75.00	100	—
1660P E	—	35.00	50.00	75.00	100	—
1661P E	—	35.00	50.00	75.00	100	—
1662P E	—	35.00	50.00	75.00	100	—
1663P E	—	35.00	50.00	75.00	100	—
1664P E	—	35.00	50.00	75.00	100	—
1665P E	—	35.00	50.00	75.00	100	—
1666P E	—	35.00	50.00	75.00	100	—

KM# A12.7 1/2 REAL

1.6921 g., 0.9310 Silver 0.0506 oz. ASW **Ruler:** Philip IV **Obv:** PHILIPPVS monogram superimposed on Cross of Jerusalem

Date	Mintage	Good	VG	F	VF	XF
1656P	—	50.00	75.00	150	225	—

KM# 22 1/2 REAL

1.6921 g., 0.9310 Silver 0.0506 oz. ASW **Ruler:** Philip IV **Obv:** Cross of Jerusalem, lions and castles in quarters, partial date below **Rev:** CAROLVS monogram, date below

Date	Mintage	Good	VG	F	VF	XF
ND(1667-1700) P Date off flan	—	20.00	30.00	40.00	50.00	—
1667P	—	30.00	40.00	60.00	100	—
1668P	—	30.00	40.00	60.00	100	—
1669P	—	30.00	40.00	60.00	100	—
1670P	—	30.00	40.00	60.00	100	—
1671P	—	30.00	40.00	60.00	100	—
1672P	—	30.00	40.00	60.00	100	—
1673P	—	30.00	40.00	60.00	100	—
1674P	—	30.00	40.00	60.00	100	—
1675P	—	30.00	40.00	60.00	100	—
1676P	—	30.00	40.00	60.00	100	—
1677P	—	30.00	40.00	60.00	100	—
1678P	—	30.00	40.00	60.00	100	—
1679/8P	—	—	—	—	—	—
1679P	—	30.00	40.00	60.00	100	—
1680P	—	30.00	40.00	60.00	100	—
1681P	—	30.00	40.00	60.00	100	—
1682P	—	30.00	40.00	60.00	100	—
1683/82P	—	—	—	—	—	—
1683P	—	30.00	40.00	60.00	100	—
1684P	—	30.00	40.00	60.00	100	—
1685P	—	30.00	40.00	60.00	100	—
1686P	—	30.00	40.00	60.00	100	—
1687P	—	30.00	40.00	60.00	100	—

Date	Mintage	Good	VG	F	VF	XF
1688P	—	30.00	40.00	60.00	100	—
1689P	—	30.00	40.00	60.00	100	—
1690P	—	30.00	40.00	60.00	100	—
1691P	—	30.00	40.00	60.00	100	—
1692P	—	30.00	40.00	60.00	100	—
1693P	—	30.00	40.00	60.00	100	—
1694P	—	30.00	40.00	60.00	100	—
1695P	—	30.00	40.00	60.00	100	—
1696P	—	30.00	40.00	60.00	100	—
1697P	—	30.00	40.00	60.00	100	—
1698P	—	30.00	40.00	60.00	100	—
1699P	—	30.00	40.00	60.00	100	—
1700P	—	30.00	40.00	60.00	100	—

MB# 2.1 REAL

3.3834 g., 0.9310 Silver 0.1013 oz. ASW **Ruler:** Philip II **Obv:** Crowned arms with mint mark above assayer's initials to right, denomination to left **Obv. Legend:** PHILIPPVS D.G. HISPANIARVM **Rev:** Cross of Jerusalem in quatrefoil, lions and castles in quarters **Rev. Legend:** ET INDIARVM **Note:** Prev. KM#0002.1.

Date	Mintage	Good	VG	F	VF	XF
ND(1574-86)P R	—	75.00	125	185	300	—

MB# 2.2 REAL

3.3834 g., 0.9310 Silver 0.1013 oz. ASW **Ruler:** Philip II **Obv:** Crowned arms with mint mark above assayer's initials to left, denomination to right **Note:** Prev. KM#0002.2.

Date	Mintage	Good	VG	F	VF	XF
ND(1574-79)P M	—	75.00	125	185	300	—
ND(1574-86)P R	—	75.00	125	185	300	—
ND(1574-86)P L	—	75.00	125	185	300	—
ND(1574-86)P B	—	40.00	65.00	100	150	—
ND(1574-86)P C Rare	—	—	—	—	—	—
ND(1574-86) P small R	—	50.00	75.00	110	175	—
ND(1586-89)P A	—	50.00	75.00	110	175	—

MB# 2.3 REAL

3.3841 g., 0.9310 Silver 0.1013 oz. ASW **Ruler:** Philip II **Obv:** Border of X's **Rev:** Border of X's **Note:** Prev. KM#0002.3.

Date	Mintage	Good	VG	F	VF	XF
ND(1574-86)P B	—	40.00	65.00	100	150	—

MB# 2.4 REAL

3.3841 g., 0.9310 Silver 0.1013 oz. ASW **Ruler:** Philip II **Obv:** Border of squares **Rev:** Border of squares **Note:** Prev. KM#0002.4.

Date	Mintage	Good	VG	F	VF	XF
ND(1574-86)P B	—	40.00	65.00	100	150	—

KM# 7 REAL

3.3834 g., 0.9310 Silver 0.1013 oz. ASW **Ruler:** Philip III **Obv. Legend:** PHILIPPVS III D G HISPANIARVM **Note:** Prev. KM#7.1.

Date	Mintage	Good	VG	F	VF	XF
ND(1596-1605)P B Rare	—	—	—	—	—	—
ND(1598-1621)P Date off flan	—	30.00	50.00	75.00	100	—
ND(1605-13)P small R	—	40.00	65.00	100	150	—
ND(1613-17)P Q	—	35.00	60.00	90.00	135	—
ND(1616-17)P M	—	35.00	60.00	90.00	135	—
1617P M Rare	—	—	—	—	—	—
1618P PAL/M Rare	—	—	—	—	—	—
1618P T Rare	—	—	—	—	—	—
1620P T Rare	—	—	—	—	—	—

KM# 12 REAL

3.3834 g., 0.9310 Silver 0.1013 oz. ASW **Ruler:** Philip IV **Obv. Legend:** PHILIPPVS IIII D G HISPANIARVM **Note:** Previous KM#12.4.

Date	Mintage	Good	VG	F	VF	XF
ND(1622)P Date off flan	—	30.00	50.00	75.00	100	—
1622P P/T	—	50.00	100	150	225	—

KM# 12a REAL

Silver **Ruler:** Philip IV **Obv. Legend:** PHILIPPVS IIII D G HISPANIARVM **Note:** .700-.931 fineness.

Date	Mintage	Good	VG	F	VF	XF
ND(1626-1648)P Date off flan	—	30.00	50.00	75.00	100	—
1626P P Rare	—	—	—	—	—	—
1628P P Rare	—	—	—	—	—	—
1628P P/T Rare	—	—	—	—	—	—
1628P T Rare	—	—	—	—	—	—

Date	Mintage	Good	VG	F	VF	XF
1629P T Rare	—	—	—	—	—	—
1630P T Rare	—	—	—	—	—	—
1631P T Rare	—	—	—	—	—	—
1632P T Rare	—	—	—	—	—	—
1633P T Rare	—	—	—	—	—	—
1634P T Rare	—	—	—	—	—	—
1636P T Rare	—	—	—	—	—	—
1636P TR Rare	—	—	—	—	—	—
1637P TR Rare	—	—	—	—	—	—
1638P TR Rare	—	—	—	—	—	—
1639P TR Rare	—	—	—	—	—	—
1640P FR Rare	—	—	—	—	—	—
1641P FR Rare	—	—	—	—	—	—
1642P FR Rare	—	—	—	—	—	—
1643P FR Rare	—	—	—	—	—	—
1644P FR Reported, not confirmed	—	—	—	—	—	—
1644P T Reported, not confirmed	—	—	—	—	—	—
1644P TR Rare	—	—	—	—	—	—
1645P T Rare	—	—	—	—	—	—
1646P V Rare	—	—	—	—	—	—
1647P Z Rare	—	—	—	—	—	—
1648P Z Rare	—	—	—	—	—	—
1648P Z/(tr) Reported, not confirmed	—	—	—	—	—	—

KM# 12b REAL

3.3834 g., 0.8960 Silver 0.0975 oz. ASW **Ruler:** Philip III **Obv. Legend:** PHILIPPVS IIII D G HISPANIARVM

Date	Mintage	Good	VG	F	VF	XF
ND(1649-51)P Date off flan	—	30.00	50.00	75.00	100	—
1649P (o)/Z Rare	—	—	—	—	—	—
1649P (o) Rare	—	—	—	—	—	—
1650P (o) Rare	—	—	—	—	—	—
1651P E Rare	—	—	—	—	—	—
1651P (o) Rare	—	—	—	—	—	—

KM# 13 REAL

3.3841 g., 0.9310 Silver 0.1013 oz. ASW **Ruler:** Philip IV **Obv:** Cross of Jerusalem, castles and lions in quarters **Obv. Legend:** PHILIPVS IV, D. G. HISPANIARUM REX **Rev:** Pillars and waves with 3-line inscription: Mint mark I, assayer's initial/ PLV-SVL-TRA/ date, mint mark

Date	Mintage	Good	VG	F	VF	XF
ND(1652-66)P Date off flan	—	30.00	40.00	60.00	90.00	—
1652P E I. PH. 6	—	40.00	90.00	150	275	—
1653P E PH	—	40.00	60.00	100	175	—
1654P E-PH	—	35.00	50.00	75.00	135	—
1655P E PH	—	35.00	50.00	75.00	135	—
1656P E	—	35.00	50.00	75.00	135	—
1657P E	—	35.00	50.00	75.00	135	—
1658P E	—	35.00	50.00	75.00	135	—
1659P E	—	35.00	50.00	75.00	135	—
1660P E	—	35.00	50.00	75.00	135	—
1661P E	—	35.00	50.00	75.00	135	—
1662P E	—	35.00	50.00	75.00	135	—
1663P E	—	35.00	50.00	75.00	135	—
1664P E	—	35.00	50.00	75.00	135	—
1665P E	—	35.00	50.00	75.00	135	—
1666P E	—	35.00	50.00	75.00	135	—

	Type I	Type II
Obverse	I I • • P E • •	I I A O P E 5 2
Reverse	F I IIII PLV SVL TRA E I E	A I O PLV SVL TRA E I E

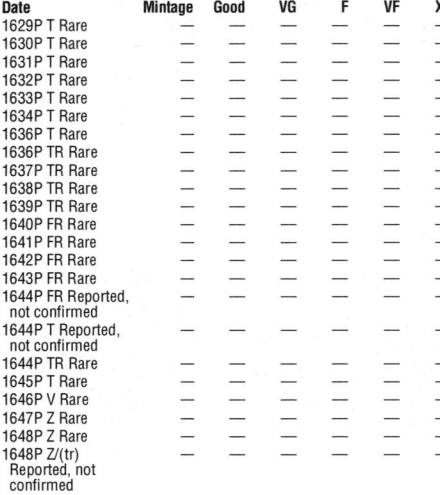

P I IIII
PLV SVL TRA
E • E
Type III

KM# A13.1 REAL

3.3834 g., 0.9310 Silver 0.1013 oz. ASW **Ruler:** Philip IV **Obv:** Castles and lions in shield **Obv. Legend:** PHILIPPVS IIII D G HISPANIARVM **Rev:** Pillars and waves **Rev. Legend:** POTOSI ANO 1652 EL PERU **Note:** Type I inscription.

Date	Mintage	Good	VG	F	VF	XF
1652P E Rare	—	—	—	—	—	—

KM# A13.2 REAL

3.3841 g., 0.9310 Silver 0.1013 oz. ASW **Ruler:** Philip IV **Obv:** Castles and lions in shield **Obv. Legend:** PHILIPPVS IIII D G HISPANIARVM **Rev:** Pillars and waves **Rev. Legend:** POTOSI ANO 1652 EL PERU **Note:** Type II inscription.

Date	Mintage	Good	VG	F	VF	XF
1652P E	—	75.00	125	175	250	—

KM# A13.3 REAL

3.3841 g., 0.9310 Silver 0.1013 oz. ASW **Ruler:** Philip IV **Obv:** Castles and lions in shield **Obv. Legend:** PHILIPPVS IIII D G HISPANIARVM **Rev:** Pillars and waves **Rev. Legend:** POTOSI ANO 1652 EL PERU **Note:** Type II inscription.

Date	Mintage	Good	VG	F	VF	XF
1652P E Rare	—	—	—	—	—	—

KM# A13.4 REAL

3.3841 g., 0.9310 Silver 0.1013 oz. ASW **Ruler:** Philip IV **Obv:** Castles and lions in shield **Obv. Legend:** PHILIPPVS IIII D G HISPANIARVM **Rev:** Pillars and waves **Rev. Legend:** POTOSI ANO 1652 EL PERU **Note:** Type II obverse inscription. Type IIII reverse inscription.

Date	Mintage	Good	VG	F	VF	XF
1652P E	—	75.00	125	175	250	—

KM# B13.1 REAL

3.3834 g., 0.9310 Silver 0.1013 oz. ASW **Ruler:** Philip IV **Obv:** Cross of Jerusalem with castles and lions in quarters, mint mark to left, assayer's initial to right, date below **Note:** Type III reverse inscription

Date	Mintage	Good	VG	F	VF	XF
1652P E	—	75.00	125	175	250	—

KM# B13.2 REAL

3.3834 g., 0.9310 Silver 0.1013 oz. ASW **Ruler:** Philip IV **Obv:** Cross of Jerusalem with castles and lions in quarters, mint mark to left, assayer's initial to right, date below **Note:** Type I reverse inscription

Date	Mintage	Good	VG	F	VF	XF
1652P E	—	75.00	125	175	250	—

KM# 23 REAL

3.3841 g., 0.9310 Silver 0.1013 oz. ASW **Ruler:** Charles II **Obv:** Cross of Jerusalem **Obv. Legend:** CAROLVS II

Date	Mintage	Good	VG	F	VF	XF
ND(1667-1701)P Date off flan	—	30.00	40.00	60.00	90.00	—
1667P E	—	35.00	50.00	75.00	135	—
1668P E	—	35.00	50.00	75.00	135	—
1669P E	—	35.00	50.00	75.00	135	—
1670P E	—	35.00	50.00	75.00	135	—
1671P E	—	35.00	50.00	75.00	135	—
1672/1P E Rare	—	—	—	—	—	—
1672P E	—	35.00	50.00	75.00	135	—
1672P E Dot between 7 and 2; Rare	—	—	—	—	—	—
1673/2P E Rare	—	—	—	—	—	—
1673P E	—	35.00	50.00	75.00	135	—
1674P E	—	35.00	50.00	75.00	135	—
1675//(17)65P E Rare	—	—	—	—	—	—
1675P E	—	35.00	50.00	75.00	135	—
1676P E	—	35.00	50.00	75.00	135	—
1677/6P E Rare	—	—	—	—	—	—
1677P E	—	35.00	50.00	75.00	135	—
1678P E	—	35.00	50.00	75.00	135	—
1678P C, E Rare	—	—	—	—	—	—
1678P C/E Rare	—	—	—	—	—	—
1678P C	—	35.00	50.00	75.00	135	—
1679P C	—	35.00	50.00	75.00	135	—
1679P C/E Reported, not confirmed	—	—	—	—	—	—
1679P V	—	35.00	50.00	75.00	135	—
1680P V	—	35.00	50.00	75.00	135	—
1680P V Rare	—	—	—	—	—	—
Note: Mint mark at upper right						
1681P V	—	40.00	50.00	75.00	135	—
1681/0P V Repoted, not confirmed	—	—	—	—	—	—
1682P V	—	40.00	50.00	75.00	135	—
1683P V	—	40.00	50.00	75.00	135	—
1684P V	—	40.00	50.00	85.00	150	—
1684P VR	—	40.00	50.00	85.00	150	—
1685P VR	—	40.00	50.00	80.00	150	—
1686P VR	—	40.00	50.00	80.00	150	—
1687P VR	—	40.00	50.00	80.00	150	—

Date	Mintage	Good	VG	F	VF	XF
1688P VR	—	40.00	50.00	80.00	125	—
1689P VR	—	40.00	50.00	80.00	150	—
1690P VR	—	40.00	50.00	80.00	150	—
1691P VR	—	40.00	50.00	80.00	150	—
1692P VR	—	40.00	50.00	80.00	150	—
1693P VR	—	40.00	50.00	80.00	150	—
1693P VR	—	40.00	50.00	80.00	150	—
1693P VR 1 and 3 inverted; Reported, not confirmed	—	—	—	—	—	—
1694P VR	—	40.00	50.00	80.00	150	—
1695P VR	—	40.00	50.00	80.00	150	—
1696P VR	—	40.00	50.00	80.00	150	—
1697P VR	—	40.00	65.00	80.00	150	—
1697P CH	—	70.00	90.00	150	275	—
1697P F	—	40.00	60.00	80.00	150	—
1697P F/CH Rare	—	—	—	—	—	—
1698P F	—	35.00	50.00	75.00	135	—
1699P F	—	35.00	50.00	75.00	135	—
1700P F	—	35.00	50.00	75.00	135	—

MB# 3.1 2 REALES

6.7668 g., 0.9310 Silver 0.2025 oz. ASW **Ruler:** Philip II **Obv:** Arms, mint mark above assayer's initial to right, denomination to left **Obv. Legend:** PHILIPVS II D. G. HISPANIARVM **Rev:** Cross of Jerusalem in quatrefoil, lions and castles in quarters **Rev. Legend:** ET INDIARVM REX **Note:** Prev. KM#0003.1.

Date	Mintage	Good	VG	F	VF	XF
ND(1574-79)P M	—	100	150	250	375	—

MB# 3.2 2 REALES

6.7668 g., 0.9310 Silver 0.2025 oz. ASW **Ruler:** Philip II **Obv:** Mint mark above assayer's initial to left, denomination to right **Note:** Prev. KM#0003.2.

Date	Mintage	Good	VG	F	VF	XF
ND(1574-86)P R	—	100	150	250	375	—
ND(1574-79)P M	—	—	—	—	—	—
ND(1574-86)P L/M Rare	—	—	—	—	—	—
ND(1574-86)P L	—	—	—	—	—	—
(1574-86)P B/S Rare	—	—	—	—	—	—
ND(1574-86)P B	—	—	—	—	—	—
ND(1574-86)P C Rare	—	—	—	—	—	—
ND(1574-86)P small R	—	—	—	—	—	—
ND(1586-89)P A	—	—	—	—	—	—

MB# 3.3 2 REALES

6.7668 g., 0.9310 Silver 0.2025 oz. ASW **Ruler:** Philip II **Obv:** "ii" over P-M to right **Note:** Prev. KM#0003.3.

Date	Mintage	Good	VG	F	VF	XF
ND(1574-86)P L Rare	—	—	—	—	—	—
ND(1574-86)P B/L Rare	—	—	—	—	—	—

MB# 3.4 2 REALES

6.7668 g., 0.9310 Silver 0.2025 oz. ASW **Ruler:** Philip II **Obv:** Border of X's **Rev:** Border of X's **Note:** Prev. KM#0003.4.

Date	Mintage	Good	VG	F	VF	XF
ND(1574-86)P B	—	75.00	100	150	225	—

MB# 3.5 2 REALES

6.7668 g., 0.9310 Silver 0.2025 oz. ASW **Ruler:** Philip II **Obv:** Border of squares **Rev:** Border of squares **Note:** Prev. KM#0003.5.

Date	Mintage	Good	VG	F	VF	XF
ND(1574-86)P B	—	75.00	100	150	225	—

KM# 8 2 REALES

6.7682 g., 0.9310 Silver 0.2026 oz. ASW **Ruler:** Philip III **Obv. Legend:** PHILIPPVS III D. G:HISPANIARVM

Date	Mintage	Good	VG	F	VF	XF
ND(1596-1605)PB Rare	—	—	—	—	—	—
ND(1605-13)P R Note: Curved leg R	—	50.00	75.00	125	175	—
ND(1605-13)P RL	—	50.00	75.00	125	175	—
ND(1613-17)P Q	—	50.00	75.00	125	175	—
ND(1616-17)P M	—	50.00	75.00	125	175	—
ND(1617-21)P Date off flan	—	45.00	70.00	90.00	125	—
1617P M	—	125	180	250	375	—
1617P M/C Rare	—	—	—	—	—	—
1618P RL	—	125	200	300	400	—
1618P T	—	125	180	250	375	—
1618P T/RL Rare	—	—	—	—	—	—
1618P T/RL and T to right Rare	—	—	—	—	—	—
1619P T	—	125	180	250	375	—
1620P T	—	125	180	250	375	—
1621P T	—	125	180	250	375	—

KM# 14 2 REALES

6.7668 g., 0.9310 Silver 0.2025 oz. ASW **Ruler:** Philip IV **Obv. Legend:** PHILIPPVS IV D.G. HISPANIARVM REX **Note:** Prev. KM#14.1.

Date	Mintage	Good	VG	F	VF	XF
ND(1622-23)P Date off flan	—	45.00	70.00	90.00	125	—
1622P P Rare	—	—	—	—	—	—
16ZIIIP P Rare	—	—	—	—	—	—

KM# 14a 2 REALES

Silver .700-.931 **Ruler:** Philip IV **Obv. Legend:** PHILIPPVS IV D. G. HISPANIARVM REX **Note:** .700-.931 fineness

Date	Mintage	Good	VG	F	VF	XF
ND(1626-48)P Date off flan	—	45.00	70.00	90.00	125	—
1626P P Rare	—	—	—	—	—	—
1626P T/P Rare	—	—	—	—	—	—
1626P T Rare	—	—	—	—	—	—
1627P T Rare	—	—	—	—	—	—
1628P P Rare	—	—	—	—	—	—
1628P T Rare	—	—	—	—	—	—
1629P T Rare	—	—	—	—	—	—
1630P T Rare	—	—	—	—	—	—
1631/0P T Rare	—	—	—	—	—	—
1631P T Rare	—	—	—	—	—	—
1632P T Rare	—	—	—	—	—	—
1633P T Rare	—	—	—	—	—	—
1634P T Rare	—	—	—	—	—	—
1635P T Rare	—	—	—	—	—	—
1637P T or TR Rare	—	—	—	—	—	—
1638P TR Rare	—	—	—	—	—	—
1639P TR Rare	—	—	—	—	—	—
1640P FR Reported, not confirmed	—	—	—	—	—	—
1641P FR Rare	—	—	—	—	—	—
1642P FR Rare	—	—	—	—	—	—
1643P FR Reported, not confirmed	—	—	—	—	—	—
1644P TR Rare	—	—	—	—	—	—
1645P T/R Reported, not confirmed	—	—	—	—	—	—
1645P TR Rare	—	—	—	—	—	—
1646P P Rare	—	—	—	—	—	—
1646P V/TR Rare	—	—	—	—	—	—
1648P TR Rare	—	—	—	—	—	—
1648P Z/T Rare	—	—	—	—	—	—

KM# 14b 2 REALES

6.7668 g., 0.8590 Silver 0.1869 oz. ASW **Ruler:** Philip IV **Obv. Legend:** PHILIPPVS IV D. G. HISPANIARVM REX **Note:** Early examples exist with castles and lions transposed.

Date	Mintage	Good	VG	F	VF	XF
ND(1649-52)P Date off flan	—	45.00	70.00	90.00	125	—
1649P (o) Rare	—	—	—	—	—	—
1649P Z Rare	—	—	—	—	—	—
1650P (o) Rare	—	—	—	—	—	—
1651P E Rare	—	—	—	—	—	—
1652P E Rare	—	—	—	—	—	—

KM# A16.2 2 REALES

6.7682 g., 0.9310 Silver 0.2026 oz. ASW **Ruler:** Philip IV **Obv:** Cross of Jerusalem with castles and lions in quarters, mint mark to left, assayer's initial to right **Rev:** Type I

Date	Mintage	Good	VG	F	VF	XF
1652P E	—	200	300	450	700	—

KM# 15.1 2 REALES

6.7682 g., 0.9310 Silver 0.2026 oz. ASW **Ruler:** Philip IV **Obv:** Type I, crowned shield with castles and lions **Obv. Legend:** PHILIPPVS IIII D. G. HISPANIARVM **Rev:** Type I, pillars and waves, inscription **Rev. Legend:** POTOSI ANO 1652 EL PERV

Date	Mintage	Good	VG	F	VF	XF
1652P E	—	200	300	450	700	—

Obverse	Type I	Type II	Type III
	A O	A O	A O
	P E	P E	P E
	2 52	2 5/2	5 2

Reverse	Type I	Type II
	F 2 IIII	P H E
	PLV SVL TRA	PLV SVL TRA
	E 2 E	E 2 P

KM# 15.2 2 REALES

6.7682 g., 0.9310 Silver 0.2026 oz. ASW **Ruler:** Philip IV **Obv:** Type II **Rev:** Type II

Date	Mintage	Good	VG	F	VF	XF
1652	—	200	300	450	700	—

KM# 15.3 2 REALES

6.7682 g., 0.9310 Silver 0.2026 oz. ASW **Ruler:** Philip IV **Obv:** Type III **Rev:** Type II

Date	Mintage	Good	VG	F	VF	XF
1652P E	—	200	300	450	700	—

KM# A16.1 2 REALES

6.7682 g., 0.9310 Silver 0.2026 oz. ASW **Ruler:** Philip IV **Obv:** Cross of Jerusalem with castles and lions in quarters, mint mark to left, assayer's initial to right **Rev:** Type II **Note:** Prev. KM#16.1.

Date	Mintage	Good	VG	F	VF	XF
1652P E	—	200	300	450	700	—

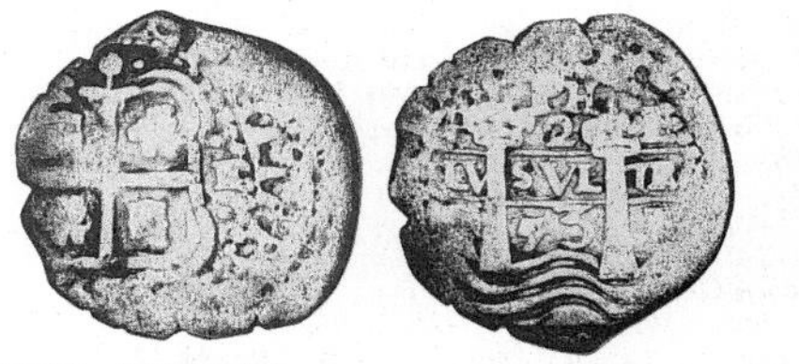

KM# 16 2 REALES

6.7682 g., 0.9310 Silver 0.2026 oz. ASW **Ruler:** Philip III **Obv:** Cross of Jerusalem **Rev:** P. O. E **Note:** Prev. KM#16.2.

Date	Mintage	Good	VG	F	VF	XF
ND(1652-67)P Date off flan	—	45.00	70.00	90.00	125	—
1652P I-PH-6	—	65.00	110	185	275	—
1653P E-PH	—	60.00	100	175	275	—
1654P E-PH	—	60.00	100	175	275	—
1655/4P E-PH Rare	—	—	—	—	—	—
1655P E-PH	—	60.00	100	175	275	—
1656P E-PH	—	60.00	100	175	275	—
1657P E	—	60.00	80.00	125	200	—
1658P E	—	50.00	75.00	100	150	—
1659P E	—	50.00	75.00	100	150	—
1660P E	—	50.00	75.00	100	150	—
1661P E	—	50.00	75.00	100	150	—
1662P E	—	50.00	75.00	100	150	—
1663P E	—	50.00	75.00	100	150	—
1664P E	—	50.00	75.00	100	150	—
1665P E	—	50.00	75.00	100	150	—
1666P E	—	50.00	75.00	100	150	—
1667P E	—	50.00	75.00	100	150	—

KM# 24 2 REALES

6.7682 g., 0.9310 Silver 0.2026 oz. ASW **Ruler:** Charles II **Obv:** Cross of Jerusalem, castles and lions in quarters **Obv. Legend:** CAROLVS II **Rev:** Crowned pillars of Hercules and waves, value at top center

Date	Mintage	Good	VG	F	VF	XF
ND(1667-1701)P Date off flan	—	45.00	70.00	90.00	125	—
1667P E	—	50.00	75.00	100	150	—
1668/7P E Rare	—	—	—	—	—	—
1668P E	—	50.00	75.00	100	150	—
1669P E	—	50.00	75.00	100	150	—
1670/69P E Rare	—	—	—	—	—	—
1670P E	—	50.00	75.00	100	150	—
1671/0P E Rare	—	—	—	—	—	—
1671P E	—	50.00	75.00	100	150	—
1672P E	—	50.00	75.00	100	150	—
1673P E	—	50.00	75.00	100	150	—
1674P E	—	50.00	75.00	100	150	—

Date	Mintage	Good	VG	F	VF	XF
1675P E	—	50.00	75.00	100	150	—
1676P E	—	50.00	75.00	100	150	—
1677P E	—	50.00	75.00	100	150	—
1678P E	—	50.00	75.00	100	150	—
1679P C	—	50.00	75.00	100	150	—
1679P V	—	50.00	75.00	100	150	—
1680P V	—	50.00	75.00	100	150	—
1681/0P V Reported, not confirmed	—	—	—	—	—	—
1681P V	—	50.00	75.00	100	150	—
1682P V	—	50.00	75.00	100	150	—
1683P V	—	60.00	90.00	125	175	—
1684P V	—	60.00	90.00	125	175	—
1684P V, VR Rare	—	—	—	—	—	—
1684P VR	—	60.00	90.00	125	175	—
1685P VR	—	60.00	90.00	125	175	—
1686P VR	—	60.00	90.00	125	175	—
1687P VR	—	60.00	90.00	125	175	—
1688P VR	—	60.00	90.00	125	175	—
1689P VR	—	60.00	90.00	125	175	—
1690P VR	—	60.00	90.00	125	175	—
1691P VR	—	60.00	90.00	125	175	—
1692/1P VR Reported, not confirmed	—	—	—	—	—	—
1692P VR	—	60.00	90.00	125	175	—
1693P VR	—	600	90.00	125	175	—
1694P VR	—	60.00	90.00	125	175	—
1695P VR	—	60.00	90.00	125	175	—
1696P VR	—	60.00	90.00	125	175	—
1697P (c)	—	60.00	100	200	300	—
1697P F	—	60.00	90.00	125	175	—
1697P F/(c) Rare	—	—	—	—	—	—
1697P VR	—	60.00	90.00	125	175	—
1698P F	—	60.00	90.00	125	175	—
1699P F	—	60.00	90.00	125	175	—
1700P F	—	60.00	90.00	125	175	—

MB# 4.1 4 REALES

13.5337 g., 0.9310 Silver 0.4051 oz. ASW **Ruler:** Philip II **Obv:** Crowned arms, mint mark above assayer's initial to right, denomination to left **Obv. Legend:** PHILIPPVS D.G. HISPANIARVM **Rev:** Cross in quatrefoil, lions and castles in quarters **Rev. Legend:** ET INDIARVM REX **Note:** Prev. KM#0004.1.

Date	Mintage	Good	VG	F	VF	XF
ND(1574-86)P R	—	250	375	500	750	—
ND(1574-79)P M	—	200	300	475	750	—
ND(1574-86)P L	—	200	275	475	750	—

MB# 4.2 4 REALES

13.5337 g., 0.9310 Silver 0.4051 oz. ASW **Ruler:** Philip II **Obv:** Mint mark above assayer's initial to left, denomination to right **Note:** Prev. KM#0004.2.

Date	Mintage	Good	VG	F	VF	XF
ND(1574-86)P R	—	100	150	225	350	—
ND(1574-86)P M	—	70.00	100	175	225	—
ND(1574-86)P L	—	100	150	225	350	—
ND(1574-86)P B	—	90.00	125	160	300	—
ND(1574-86)P C	—	100	150	225	350	—
ND(1586-89)P A	—	80.00	110	150	275	—
ND(1590-95)P small R, RL	—	80.00	110	150	275	—

MB# 4.3 4 REALES

13.5337 g., 0.9310 Silver 0.4051 oz. ASW **Ruler:** Philip II **Obv:** Border of X's **Rev:** Border of X's **Note:** Prev. KM#0004.3.

Date	Mintage	Good	VG	F	VF	XF
ND(1574-86)P B	—	60.00	90.00	150	210	—

MB# 4.4 4 REALES

13.5337 g., 0.9310 Silver 0.4051 oz. ASW **Ruler:** Philip II **Obv:** Border of squares **Rev:** Border of squares **Note:** Prev. KM#0004.4.

Date	Mintage	Good	VG	F	VF	XF
ND(1574-86)P B	—	60.00	90.00	150	225	—

KM# 9 4 REALES

13.5365 g., 0.9310 Silver 0.4052 oz. ASW **Ruler:** Philip III **Obv. Legend:** PHILIPPVS III D.G. HISPANIARVM **Note:** Previous KM#9.1.

Date	Mintage	Good	VG	F	VF	XF
ND(1596-1605)P B Rare	—	—	—	—	—	—
ND(1605-13)P R	—	60.00	90.00	150	225	—

Note: Curved leg R

Date	Mintage	Good	VG	F	VF	XF
ND(1613-17)P Q	—	60.00	90.00	150	225	—
ND(1616-17)P M	—	60.00	90.00	150	225	—
ND(1617-21)P Date off flan	—	60.00	90.00	140	200	—
1617P M Rare	—	—	—	—	—	—
1618P PAL Rare	—	—	—	—	—	—
1618P T Rare	—	—	—	—	—	—
1620P T Rare	—	—	—	—	—	—
1621P T Rare	—	—	—	—	—	—

Note: Early examples exist with castles and lions transposed

KM# 17 4 REALES

13.5365 g., 0.9310 Silver 0.4052 oz. ASW **Ruler:** Philip IV **Obv:** Crowned arms **Obv. Legend:** PHILIPPVS IIII **Rev:** Cross of Jerusalem, lions and castles in quarters

Date	Mintage	Good	VG	F	VF	XF
ND(1622)P Date off flan	—	60.00	90.00	140	200	—
1622P P Rare	—	—	—	—	—	—

KM# 17a 4 REALES

0.7000 Silver .700-.931 fineness **Ruler:** Philip IV **Obv:** Crowned arms **Obv. Legend:** PHILIPPVS IIII **Rev:** Cross of Jerusalem, lions and castles in quarters

Date	Mintage	Good	VG	F	VF	XF
ND(1624-47)P Date off flan	—	60.00	90.00	140	200	—
1624P P or T Rare	—	—	—	—	—	—
1627P T Rare	—	—	—	—	—	—
1628P T Rare	—	—	—	—	—	—
1629P P Rare	—	—	—	—	—	—
1629P T Rare	—	—	—	—	—	—
1630P T Rare	—	—	—	—	—	—
1631P T Rare	—	—	—	—	—	—
1632P T Rare	—	—	—	—	—	—
1633P T Rare	—	—	—	—	—	—
1635P T Reported, not confirmed	—	—	—	—	—	—
1639P TR Rare	—	—	—	—	—	—
1640P FR Rare	—	—	—	—	—	—
1643P TR or FR Rare	—	—	—	—	—	—
1644P T, TR or FR Rare	—	—	—	—	—	—
1646P V/T Rare	—	—	—	—	—	—
1647P P Reported, not confirmed	—	—	—	—	—	—

KM# 17b 4 REALES

13.5339 g., 0.8590 Silver 0.3738 oz. ASW **Ruler:** Philip IV **Obv:** Crowned arms **Obv. Legend:** PHILIPPVS IIII **Rev:** Cross of Jerusalem, lions and castles in quarters

Date	Mintage	Good	VG	F	VF	XF
ND(1649-51)P Date off flan	—	60.00	90.00	140	200	—
1649P (o)	—	135	190	275	400	—
1649P (o)/Z Rare	—	—	—	—	—	—
1649P Z Rare	—	—	—	—	—	—
1650P (o)	—	135	190	275	400	—
1651P E	—	135	190	275	400	—
1651P (o)	—	135	190	275	400	—

KM# 18 4 REALES

13.5365 g., 0.9310 Silver 0.4052 oz. ASW **Ruler:** Philip IV **Obv:** Crowned cross of Jerusalem, lions and castles in quarters **Rev:** Crowned pillars and waves, inscription includes mint mark, denomination, assayer's initial/PLV-SVL-TRA/assayer's initial; date-mint mark **Note:** Prev. KM#18.1.

Date	Mintage	Good	VG	F	VF	XF
ND(1652-66)P Date off flan	—	90.00	85.00	140	200	—
1652P E 1-PH-6 Reported, not confirmed	—	—	—	—	—	—
1653/2P E Rare	—	—	—	—	—	—
1653P E-PH	—	125	190	250	375	—
1654P E-PH	—	125	190	250	375	—
1655P E-PH	—	125	190	250	375	—
1656P E-PH	—	150	225	325	450	—
1657P E	—	125	190	250	375	—
1658P E	—	125	190	250	375	—
1659//(16)58P E Rare	—	—	—	—	—	—
1659P E	—	125	190	250	375	—
1660P E	—	125	190	250	375	—
1661P E	—	125	190	250	375	—
1662P E	—	150	225	325	450	—
1664P E	—	125	190	250	375	—
1665P E	—	125	190	250	375	—
1666P E	—	125	190	250	375	500

KM# A18 4 REALES

13.5337 g., 0.9310 Silver 0.4051 oz. ASW **Ruler:** Philip IV **Obv:** Crowned arms, lions and castles in quarters, A/P/4 at left, O/E/52 at right **Obv. Legend:** PHILIPPVS IIII D.G. HISPANIARVM **Rev:** Pillars and waves **Rev. Legend:** POTOSI ANO 1652 EL PERU **Rev. Inscription:** ... PLV - SVL - TRA/ E-4-E

Date	Mintage	Good	VG	F	VF	XF
1652P E Rare	—	—	—	—	—	—

KM# B18 4 REALES

13.5337 g., 0.9310 Silver 0.4051 oz. ASW **Ruler:** Philip IV **Obv:** Crowned cross of Jerusalem, castles and lions in quarters, mint mark to left, assayer's initial to right, date below

Date	Mintage	Good	VG	F	VF	XF
1652P E Rare	—	—	—	—	—	—

KM# 25 4 REALES

13.5365 g., 0.9310 Silver 0.4052 oz. ASW **Ruler:** Charles II **Obv:** Cross of Jerusalem, castles and lions at quarters **Rev:** Crowned pillars of Hercules and waves, value at top center

Date	Mintage	Good	VG	F	VF	XF
ND(1667-1701)P Date off flan	—	60.00	90.00	140	200	—
1667P E	—	150	225	325	375	—
1668P E	—	125	190	250	375	—
1669P E	—	125	190	250	375	—
1670P E	—	125	190	250	375	—
1671/0P E Rare	—	—	—	—	—	—
1671P E	—	125	190	250	375	—
1672P E	—	125	190	250	375	—
1673P E	—	125	190	250	375	—
1674P E	—	125	190	250	375	—
1675P E	—	125	190	250	375	—
1676P E	—	125	190	250	375	—
1677P E	—	125	190	250	375	—
1678P E	—	125	190	250	375	—
1679P C	—	125	190	250	375	—
1679P C/E Rare	—	—	—	—	—	—
1679P V	—	125	190	250	375	—
1680P V	—	125	190	250	375	—
1681P V	—	125	190	250	375	—
1682P V	—	125	190	250	375	—
1683P V	—	150	225	325	450	—
1684P V	—	150	225	325	450	—
1684P VR	—	150	225	325	450	—
1685P VR	—	150	225	325	450	—
1686P VR	—	150	225	325	450	—
1687P VR	—	150	225	325	450	—
1688P VR	—	150	225	325	450	—
1689P VR	—	150	225	325	450	—
1690P VR	—	150	225	325	450	—
1691P VR	—	150	225	325	450	—
1692P VR	—	150	225	325	450	—

Date	Mintage	Good	VG	F	VF	XF
1693P VR	—	150	225	325	450	—
1694P VR	—	150	225	325	450	—
1695P VR	—	150	225	325	450	—
1696P VR	—	150	225	325	450	—
1697P CH	—	200	300	400	575	—
1697P F/CH Rare	—	—	—	—	—	—
1697P F Rare	—	—	—	—	—	—
1697P VR	—	150	225	325	450	—
1698P F	—	150	225	325	450	—
1699P F	—	150	225	325	450	—
1700P F Rare	—	—	—	—	—	—

MB# 5.1 8 REALES

27.0674 g., 0.9310 Silver 0.8102 oz. ASW **Ruler:** Philip II **Obv:** Crowned arms, mint mark and assayer's initial to left, denomination to right **Obv. Legend:** PHILIPPUS D(EI).G. HISPANIARVM **Rev:** Cross of Jerusalem in tressure, castles and lions in quarters **Rev. Legend:** ET INDIARVM REX **Note:** Prev. KM#0005.1.

Date	Mintage	Good	VG	F	VF	XF
ND(1574-86)P R ISPANIARVM Rare	—	—	—	—	—	—
Note: Swiss Bank auction #20, 8-88, almost XF realized $22,780						
ND(1574-79)P M ISPANIARVM	—	1,000	2,000	3,500	5,000	—
ND(1574-86)P L ISPANIARVM	—	750	1,500	2,000	2,500	—
ND(1574-86)P B	—	150	200	350	500	—
ND(1574-86)P S/X Rare	—	—	—	—	—	—
ND(1574-86)P B/S/X	—	200	275	375	575	—
ND(1574-86)P C (under erasure of B/S/X)	—	750	1,750	2,500	3,500	—
ND(1574-86)P B/C (under erasure of B/S/X)	—	750	1,000	1,500	2,000	—
ND(ca.1580)P RL	—	150	225	375	575	—
ND(1586-89)P A	—	150	225	375	575	—

MB# 5.5 8 REALES

27.0703 g., 0.9310 Silver 0.8102 oz. ASW **Ruler:** Philip II **Obv:** Border of X's **Rev:** Border of X's **Note:** Prev. KM#0005.5.

Date	Mintage	Good	VG	F	VF	XF
ND(1574-86)P B	—	150	200	300	450	—

MB# 5.6 8 REALES

27.0674 g., 0.9310 Silver 0.8102 oz. ASW **Ruler:** Philip II **Obv:** Border of rectangles **Rev:** Border of rectangles **Note:** Prev. KM#0005.6.

Date	Mintage	Good	VG	F	VF	XF
ND(1574-86)P B	—	150	200	300	450	—

KM# 10 8 REALES

27.0674 g., 0.9310 Silver 0.8102 oz. ASW **Ruler:** Philip III **Obv. Legend:** PHILIPPVS (PHILIPVS or PHYLYPVS) III D.G. HISPANIARVM **Note:** Some examples exist with castles and lions, elements of the arms transposed.

Date	Mintage	Good	VG	F	VF	XF
ND(1596-1605)P B Rare	—	—	—	—	—	—
ND(1605-13)P R/B Curved leg R, Rare	—	—	—	—	—	—
ND(1605-13)P R Curved leg R	—	75.00	150	225	300	—
ND(1613-17)P Q/R Curved leg R, Rare	—	—	—	—	—	—
ND(1613-1617)P Q	—	75.00	150	225	300	—
ND(1613)P C/Q Rare	—	—	—	—	—	—
ND(1613)P C Rare	—	—	—	—	—	—
ND(1613-17)P Q/c Rare	—	—	—	—	—	—
ND(1616-17)P M/Q Rare	—	—	—	—	—	—
ND(1616-17)P M	—	75.00	150	225	300	—
ND(1617-21)P Date off flan	—	75.00	100	150	220	—
1617P M	—	250	500	750	1,000	—
1617P PAL Unique mule	—	—	—	—	—	—
1618P PAL	—	500	750	1,000	1,750	—
1618P T/PAL Rare	—	—	—	—	—	—
1618P T/PAL Rare	—	—	—	—	—	—
Note: Additional T to right						
1619P T	—	150	200	300	400	—
1620P T	—	150	200	300	400	—
1612P T (error for 1621); Rare	—	—	—	—	—	—
1621P T	—	150	200	300	400	—

KM# 19 8 REALES

27.0703 g., 0.9310 Silver 0.8102 oz. ASW **Ruler:** Philip IV **Note:** Prev. KM#19.1.

Date	Mintage	Good	VG	F	VF	XF
ND(1622-24)P Date off flan	—	75.00	125	175	275	—
1622P T	—	150	200	300	400	—
1622P P/T Rare	—	—	—	—	—	—
1622P P	—	150	200	300	400	—
1623 (16ZIII)P T	—	200	350	500	750	—
1623(16ZIII)P P Rare	—	—	—	—	—	—
1624P T Rare	—	—	—	—	—	—
1624P P Rare	—	—	—	—	—	—

KM# 19a 8 REALES

Silver **Ruler:** Philip IV **Note:** .700-.931 fineness.

Date	Mintage	Good	VG	F	VF	XF
ND(1625-48)P Date off flan	—	75.00	125	175	275	—
1625P P Rare	—	—	—	—	—	—
1626P T Reported, not confirmed	—	—	—	—	—	—
1626P P Rare	—	—	—	—	—	—
1627P T	—	200	300	400	500	—
1628P T	—	150	200	350	475	—
1628P P/T Rare	—	—	—	—	—	—
1628P P	—	150	200	350	475	—
1629P T	—	150	200	300	400	—
1629P P Rare	—	—	—	—	—	—
1630P T	—	150	200	300	400	—
1631P T	—	150	200	325	450	—
1632P T	—	150	200	350	475	—
1633P T	—	150	200	350	475	—
1634P T	—	150	200	350	475	—
1635P T	—	150	200	350	475	—
1636P T Rare	—	—	—	—	—	—
1636P TR Rare	—	—	—	—	—	—
1637P TR Rare	—	—	—	—	—	—
1638P TR Rare	—	—	—	—	—	—
1639P TR Rare	—	—	—	—	—	—
1640P FR Rare	—	—	—	—	—	—
1640P TR Rare	—	—	—	—	—	—
1641P FR Rare	—	—	—	—	—	—
1642P FR Rare	—	—	—	—	—	—
1643P FR Rare	—	—	—	—	—	—
1643P T Rare	—	—	—	—	—	—
1643P TR Rare	—	—	—	—	—	—
1644P T Rare	—	—	—	—	—	—
1644P FR Rare	—	—	—	—	—	—
1644P TR Rare	—	—	—	—	—	—
1645/4P R Rare	—	—	—	—	—	—
1645P TR Rare	—	—	—	—	—	—
1645P T (16455); Rare	—	—	—	—	—	—
1645P T	—	150	200	350	475	—
1646P R Reported, not confirmed	—	—	—	—	—	—
1646P T Rare	—	—	—	—	—	—
1646P V/T Rare	—	—	—	—	—	—
1646P V Rare	—	—	—	—	—	—
1646P P Reported, not confirmed	—	—	—	—	—	—
1647P TR Rare	—	—	—	—	—	—
1647P P Unique	—	—	—	—	—	—
1647P T Rare	—	—	—	—	—	—
1647P Z Rare	—	—	—	—	—	—
1648P Z/R Rare	—	—	—	—	—	—
1648P Z	—	150	200	350	475	—
1648P T Rare	—	—	—	—	—	—

KM# 19b 8 REALES

27.0674 g., 0.8590 Silver 0.7475 oz. ASW **Ruler:** Philip IV **Note:** Scarce examples of coins dated 1650 and 1651 with different "5's" and some with single dot or five dot ornaments between and flanking the digits of the date exist.

Date	Mintage	Good	VG	F	VF	XF
ND(1649-52)P Date off flan	—	75.00	125	175	275	—
1649P Z	—	150	200	300	425	—
1649P (o)/Z Rare	—	—	—	—	—	—
1649P (o)	—	100	175	275	400	—
1650/49P (o) Rare	—	—	—	—	—	—
1650P (o)	—	100	175	275	400	—
1651P (o)	—	100	175	275	400	—
1651P E/(o)	—	150	200	300	450	—
1651P E	—	100	175	275	400	—
1652P E Rare	—	—	—	—	—	—

KM# 21 8 REALES

27.0703 g., 0.9310 Silver 0.8102 oz. ASW **Ruler:** Philip IV **Obv:** Crowned cross of Jerusalem, castles and lions in quarters **Obv. Legend:** PHILIPVS IIII **Rev:** Crowned pillars and waves **Rev. Legend:** POTOSI ANO....

Date	Mintage	Good	VG	F	VF	XF
1652P 1-PH-6	—	175	325	500	750	—
ND(1652-67)P Date off flan	—	75.00	125	175	225	—
1653P E-PH	—	125	175	275	400	—
1654P E-PH	—	125	175	275	400	—
1655P E-PH	—	125	175	275	400	—
1656P E-PH	—	125	175	275	400	—
1657P E-PH	—	125	175	275	400	—
1657P E	—	125	175	275	400	—
1657P E Rare	—	—	—	—	—	—
Note: (E to left of cross)						
1658P E	—	125	175	275	400	—
1659P E	—	125	175	275	400	—
1660P E	—	125	175	275	400	—
1661/0P E Rare	—	—	—	—	—	—
1661P E	—	125	175	275	400	—

Date	Mintage	Good	VG	F	VF	XF
1662P E	—	125	175	275	400	—
1663P E	—	125	175	275	400	—
1664P E	—	125	175	275	400	—
1665P E	—	125	175	275	400	—
1666P E	—	125	240	325	500	—
1666P E Rare	—	—	—	—	—	—
Note: With 666 below pillars						
1667P E Rare	—	—	—	—	—	—

Obverse

A O
P E
8 52

Reverse F 8 IIII PL VSVL TRA Type I	F 8 IIII PLV SVL TRA E E Type II
F 8 IIII PLV SVL TRA E • E Type III	F 8 IIII PLV SVL TRA E 8 E Type IV
F 8 IIII PLV SVL TRA E 52 E Type V	HP P 8 E PLV SVL TRA E 52 E Type VI
HP P 8 E PLV SVL TRA E 52 P Type VII	I • PH • 6 P 8 E PLV SVL TRA E 52 P Type VIII

KM# A20.1 8 REALES

27.0674 g., 0.9310 Silver 0.8102 oz. ASW **Ruler:** Philip IV **Obv:** Crowned arms, castles and lions **Obv. Legend:** PHILIPPUS IIII D.G. HISPANIARUM **Rev:** Type I. Crowned pillars and waves **Rev. Legend:** POTOSI ANO 1652 EL PERV **Note:** Prev. KM#19.3.

Date	Mintage	Good	VG	F	VF	XF
1652P E Rare	—	—	—	—	—	—

KM# A20.2 8 REALES

27.0674 g., 0.9310 Silver 0.8102 oz. ASW **Ruler:** Philip IV **Obv:** Arms **Rev:** Type II

Date	Mintage	Good	VG	F	VF	XF
1652P E Rare	—	—	—	—	—	—

KM# A20.3 8 REALES

27.0674 g., 0.9310 Silver 0.8102 oz. ASW **Ruler:** Philip IV **Obv:** Arms **Rev:** Type III **Note:** Prev. KM#19.5.

Date	Mintage	Good	VG	F	VF	XF
1652P E	—	200	500	750	1,250	—

KM# A20.4 8 REALES

27.0674 g., 0.9310 Silver 0.8102 oz. ASW **Ruler:** Philip IV **Obv:** Arms **Rev:** Type IV **Note:** Prev. KM#19.4.

Date	Mintage	Good	VG	F	VF	XF
1652P E	—	200	500	750	1,250	—

KM# A20.5 8 REALES

27.0674 g., 0.9310 Silver 0.8102 oz. ASW **Ruler:** Philip IV **Obv:** Arms **Rev:** Type V **Note:** Prev. KM#19.6.

Date	Mintage	Good	VG	F	VF	XF
1652P E	—	200	500	750	1,250	—

KM# A20.6 8 REALES

27.0674 g., 0.9310 Silver 0.8102 oz. ASW **Ruler:** Philip IV **Obv:** Crowned Spanish shield with arms of Castile **Rev:** Type VI

Date	Mintage	Good	VG	F	VF	XF
1652P E Rare	—	—	—	—	—	—

KM# A20.7 8 REALES

27.0674 g., 0.9310 Silver 0.8102 oz. ASW **Ruler:** Philip IV **Obv:** Arms **Rev:** Type VII

Date	Mintage	Good	VG	F	VF	XF
1652P E Rare	—	—	—	—	—	—

KM# A20.8 8 REALES

27.0674 g., 0.9310 Silver 0.8102 oz. ASW **Ruler:** Philip IV **Obv:** Arms **Rev:** Type VIII **Note:** Prev. KM#20.1.

Date	Mintage	Good	VG	F	VF	XF
1652P E Rare	—	—	—	—	—	—

KM# 20.1 8 REALES

27.0703 g., 0.9310 Silver 0.8102 oz. ASW **Ruler:** Philip IV **Obv:** Cross of Jerusalem, castles and lions in quarters, mint mark to left, assayer's initial to right **Rev:** Type V, crowned pillars and waves **Rev. Legend:** POTOSI ANO 1652 EL PERV **Note:** Prev. KM#20.2.

Date	Mintage	Good	VG	F	VF	XF
1652P E	—	275	450	750	1,250	—

KM# 20.2 8 REALES

27.0674 g., 0.9310 Silver 0.8102 oz. ASW **Ruler:** Philip IV **Obv:** Cross of Jerusalem, castles and lions in quarters, mint mark to left, assayer's initial to right **Rev:** Type VII

Date	Mintage	Good	VG	F	VF	XF
1652P E Rare	—	—	—	—	—	—

KM# 26 8 REALES

27.0703 g., 0.9310 Silver 0.8102 oz. ASW **Ruler:** Charles II **Obv:** Cross of Jerusalem, castles and lions in quarters **Obv. Legend:** CAROLVS II D.G. HISPANIA **Rev:** Crowned pillars of Hercules and waves, value at top center

Date	Mintage	Good	VG	F	VF	XF
ND(1667-1701)P Date off flan	—	100	125	175	225	—
1667P E	—	125	175	275	400	—
1667P E Rare	—	—	—	—	—	—
Note: King's name as CARDLVS						
1668P E	—	125	175	275	400	—
1668P E Rare	—	—	—	—	—	—
Note: Mint mark to left and right						
1669/8P E	—	—	—	—	—	—
Note: Reported, not confirmed						
1669P E	—	125	175	275	400	—
1669P E Small date, Rare	—	—	—	—	—	—
1670/69P E Rare	—	—	—	—	—	—
1670P E	—	125	175	275	400	—
1671/0P E Rare	—	—	—	—	—	—
1671P E	—	125	175	275	400	—
1672P E	—	125	175	275	400	—
1673P E	—	125	175	275	400	—
1674/2P E Rare	—	—	—	—	—	—
1674P E	—	125	175	275	400	—
1675P E	—	125	175	275	400	—
1676P E	—	125	175	275	400	—
1677P E	—	125	175	275	400	—
1678/7P E Rare	—	—	—	—	—	—
1678P E	—	125	175	275	400	—
1679P C/E Rare	—	—	—	—	—	—
1679P C	—	125	175	275	400	—
1679P V/C	—	150	200	325	450	—
1679P V	—	125	175	275	400	—
1680P V	—	125	175	275	400	—
1681P V	—	125	175	275	400	—
1682P V	—	150	200	325	450	—
1683P V	—	150	200	325	450	—
1684P V	—	150	200	325	450	—
1684P V, VR Rare	—	—	—	—	—	—
1684P VR	—	150	200	325	450	—
1685P VR	—	150	200	325	450	—
1686//(16)85P VR Rare	—	—	—	—	—	—
1686P VR	—	150	200	325	450	—
1687P VR	—	150	200	325	450	—
1688P VR	—	150	200	325	450	—
1689P VR	—	150	200	325	450	—
1690P VR	—	150	200	325	450	—
1691P VR	—	150	200	325	450	—
1692P VR	—	150	200	325	450	—
1693P VR	—	150	200	325	450	—
1694//(16)93P VR	—	—	—	—	—	—
Note: Reported, not confirmed						
1694P VR	—	150	200	325	450	—
1695P VR	—	150	200	325	450	—
1696P VR	—	150	200	325	450	—
1697P VR	—	150	200	325	450	—
1697P F/CH Rare	—	—	—	—	—	—
1697P CH	—	150	300	550	900	—
1697P F	—	150	200	325	450	—
1698/7P F	—	—	—	—	—	—
Note: Reported, not confirmed						
1698P F	—	150	200	325	450	—
1699P F	—	150	200	325	450	—
1700P F	—	150	200	325	450	—

ROYAL COINAGE

Struck on specially prepared round planchets using well centered dies in excellent condition to prove the quality of the minting to the Viceroy or even to the King

KM# R-B12 1/2 REAL

1.6917 g., 0.9310 Silver 0.0506 oz. ASW **Ruler:** Philip IV **Obv:** Monogram of PHILIPVS IIII superimposed on Cross of Jerusalem **Rev:** Crowned arms

Date	Mintage	Good	VG	F	VF	XF
1655P E Rare	—	—	—	—	—	—
1662P E Rare	—	—	—	—	—	—

KM# R13 REAL

3.3834 g., 0.9310 Silver 0.1013 oz. ASW **Ruler:** Philip IV **Obv:** Cross of Jerusalem, castles and lions in quarters **Obv. Legend:** PHILIPVS IV **Rev:** Pillars and waves with 3-line inscription consisting of mint mark, I-assayer's initial, PLV-SVL-TRA, assayer's initial, date, mint mark

Date	Mintage	Good	VG	F	VF	XF
1654P E PH Rare	—	—	—	—	—	—

KM# R23 REAL

3.3834 g., 0.9310 Silver 0.1013 oz. ASW **Ruler:** Charles II **Obv:** Cross of Jerusalem **Obv. Legend:** CAROLVS II

Date	Mintage	Good	VG	F	VF	XF
1677P E Rare	—	—	—	—	—	—
1679P C Reported, not confirmed	—	—	—	—	—	—

KM# R15.3 2 REALES

6.7668 g., 0.9310 Silver 0.2025 oz. ASW **Ruler:** Philip IV **Obv:** Arms **Rev:** Type II

Date	Mintage	Good	VG	F	VF	XF
1652P E Rare	—	—	—	—	—	—

KM# R-A16.1 2 REALES

6.7668 g., 0.9310 Silver 0.2025 oz. ASW **Ruler:** Philip IV **Obv:** Cross of Jerusalem with castles and lions in quarters, mint mark to left, assayers initial to right **Rev:** Pillars and waves

Date	Mintage	Good	VG	F	VF	XF
1652P E Rare	—	—	—	—	—	—

KM# R-A16.2 2 REALES

6.7668 g., 9.3100 Silver 2.0254 oz. ASW **Ruler:** Philip IV **Rev:** Type I

Date	Mintage	Good	VG	F	VF	XF
1654P E Rare	—	—	—	—	—	—
1656P E Rare	—	—	—	—	—	—
1659P E Rare	—	—	—	—	—	—
1660P E Rare	—	—	—	—	—	—

KM# R24 2 REALES

6.7668 g., 0.9310 Silver 0.2025 oz. ASW **Ruler:** Charles II **Obv. Legend:** CAROLVS II

Date	Mintage	Good	VG	F	VF	XF
1671P E Rare	—	—	—	—	—	—
1683P V Rare	—	—	—	—	—	—
1685P VR Rare	—	—	—	—	—	—
1686P VR Rare	—	—	—	—	—	—
1687P VR Rare	—	—	—	—	—	—
1691P VR Rare	—	—	—	—	—	—
1692P VR Rare	—	—	—	—	—	—
1696P VR Rare	—	—	—	—	—	—
1697P VR Rare	—	—	—	—	—	—

KM# R18 4 REALES

13.5337 g., 0.9310 Silver 0.4051 oz. ASW **Ruler:** Philip IV **Obv:** Crowned cross of Jerusalem, lions and castles in quarters **Rev:** Crowned pillars and waves, inscription: mint mark, denomination, assayer's initial, PVS-SVL-TRA, assayer's initial, date, mint mark

Date	Mintage	Good	VG	F	VF	XF
1656P E Rare	—	—	—	—	—	—
1659P E Rare	—	—	—	—	—	—

KM# R25 4 REALES

13.5337 g., 0.9310 Silver 0.4051 oz. ASW **Ruler:** Charles II

Date	Mintage	Good	VG	F	VF	XF
1675P E Reported, not confirmed	—	—	—	—	—	—
1677P E Rare	—	—	—	—	—	—
1678P E Rare	—	—	—	—	—	—
1679P C Rare	—	—	—	—	—	—
1697P VR Rare	—	—	—	—	—	—

KM# R19.a 8 REALES

27.0674 g., 0.9310 Silver 0.8102 oz. ASW **Ruler:** Philip IV

Date	Mintage	Good	VG	F	VF	XF
1630P T Rare	—	—	—	—	—	—
1631P T Rare	—	—	—	—	—	—
1637P TR Rare	—	—	—	—	—	—
1638P TR Rare	—	—	—	—	—	—
1639P T Rare	—	—	—	—	—	—
1639P TR Rare	—	—	—	—	—	—
1640P FR Rare	—	—	—	—	—	—
1640P TR Rare	—	—	—	—	—	—
1641P FR Rare	—	—	—	—	—	—
1643P TR Rare	—	—	—	—	—	—
1644P FR Rare	—	—	—	—	—	—
1644P TR Rare	—	—	—	—	—	—
1646P T Rare	—	—	—	—	—	—
1647P T Rare	—	—	—	—	—	—
1648P T Rare	—	—	—	—	—	—

KM# R19.b 8 REALES

27.0674 g., 0.9310 Silver 0.8102 oz. ASW **Ruler:** Philip IV

Date	Mintage	Good	VG	F	VF	XF
1649P (o) Rare	—	—	—	—	—	—
1649P Z Rare	—	—	—	—	—	—
1650P (o) Rare	—	—	—	—	—	—
1651P (o) Rare	—	—	—	—	—	—
1651P E Rare	—	—	—	—	—	—

KM# R-A20.1 8 REALES

27.0674 g., 0.9310 Silver 0.8102 oz. ASW **Ruler:** Philip IV **Obv:** Crowned arms, castles and lions **Obv. Legend:** PHILIPPUS IIII D.G. HISPANIARUM **Rev:** Type I, crowned pillars and waves **Rev. Legend:** POTOSI ANO...

Date	Mintage	Good	VG	F	VF	XF
1652P E Transitional Type I, Rare	—	—	—	—	—	—

KM# R-A20.2 8 REALES

27.0674 g., 0.9310 Silver 0.8102 oz. ASW **Ruler:** Philip IV **Obv:** Arms **Rev:** Type II

Date	Mintage	Good	VG	F	VF	XF
1652P E Transitional Type II, Rare	—	—	—	—	—	—

KM# R-A20.3 8 REALES

27.0674 g., 0.9310 Silver 0.8102 oz. ASW **Ruler:** Philip IV **Obv:** Arms **Rev:** Type III

Date	Mintage	Good	VG	F	VF	XF
1652P E Transitional Type III, Rare	—	—	—	—	—	—

KM# R-A20.4 8 REALES

27.0674 g., 0.9310 Silver 0.8102 oz. ASW **Ruler:** Philip IV **Obv:** Arms **Rev:** Type IV

Date	Mintage	Good	VG	F	VF	XF
1652P E Rare	—	—	—	—	—	—

KM# R-A20.5 8 REALES

27.0674 g., 0.9310 Silver 0.8102 oz. ASW **Ruler:** Philip IV **Obv:** Arms **Rev:** Type V

Date	Mintage	Good	VG	F	VF	XF
1652P E Rare	—	—	—	—	—	—

KM# R-A20.6 8 REALES

27.0674 g., 0.9310 Silver 0.8102 oz. ASW **Ruler:** Philip IV **Obv:** Arms **Rev:** Type VI

Date	Mintage	Good	VG	F	VF	XF
1652P E Rare	—	—	—	—	—	—

KM# R21 8 REALES

27.0674 g., 0.9310 Silver 0.8102 oz. ASW **Ruler:** Philip IV **Obv:** Crowned cross of Jerusalem, castles and lions in quarters **Obv. Legend:** PHILIPVS IIII **Rev:** Crowned pillars and waves **Rev. Legend:** POTOSI ANO...

Date	Mintage	Good	VG	F	VF	XF
1652P E Rare	—	—	—	—	—	—
1653P E Rare	—	—	—	—	—	—
1654P E Rare	—	—	—	—	—	—
1655P E Rare	—	—	—	—	—	—
1656P E Rare	—	—	—	—	—	—
1657P E Rare	—	—	—	—	—	—

Date	Mintage	Good	VG	F	VF	XF
1658P E/P Reported, not confirmed	—	—	—	—	—	—
1658P E Rare	—	—	—	—	—	—
1659P E Rare	—	—	—	—	—	—
1660P E Rare	—	—	—	—	—	—
1661P E Rare	—	—	—	—	—	—
1662/1P E Rare	—	—	—	—	—	—
1662P E Rare	—	—	—	—	—	—
1663P E Rare	—	—	—	—	—	—
1664P E Rare	—	—	—	—	—	—
1665P E Rare	—	—	—	—	—	—
1666P E 666 between pillars, Rare	—	—	—	—	—	—
1666P E 66 between pillars, Rare	—	—	—	—	—	—

KM# R26 8 REALES

27.0674 g., 0.9310 Silver 0.8102 oz. ASW **Ruler:** Charles II **Obv:** Cross of Jerusalem, lions and castles in quarters **Obv. Legend:** CAROLVS II D.G. HISPANIA **Rev:** Pillars of Hercules and waves, value at top center

Date	Mintage	Good	VG	F	VF	XF
1667P E Rare	—	—	—	—	—	—
1668P E Rare	—	—	—	—	—	—
1669/8P E Rare	—	—	—	—	—	—
1669P E Rare	—	—	—	—	—	—
1670P E Rare	—	—	—	—	—	—
1671P E Rare	—	—	—	—	—	—
1672P E Rare	—	—	—	—	—	—
1673P E Rare	—	—	—	—	—	—
1674P E Rare	—	—	—	—	—	—
1675P E Rare	—	—	—	—	—	—
1676P E Rare	—	—	—	—	—	—
1677P E Rare	—	—	—	—	—	—
1678P E Rare	—	—	—	—	—	—
1679P C Rare	—	—	—	—	—	—
1680P V Rare	—	—	—	—	—	—
1681P V Rare	—	—	—	—	—	—
1682P V Rare	—	—	—	—	—	—
1683P V Rare	—	—	—	—	—	—
1684P VR Rare	—	—	—	—	—	—
1685P VR Rare	—	—	—	—	—	—
1686P VR Rare	—	—	—	—	—	—
1687P VR Rare	—	—	—	—	—	—
1688P VR Rare	—	—	—	—	—	—
1689P VR Rare	—	—	—	—	—	—
1690P VR Rare	—	—	—	—	—	—
1691P VR Rare	—	—	—	—	—	—
1692P VR Rare	—	—	—	—	—	—
1693P VR Rare	—	—	—	—	—	—
1694P VR Rare	—	—	—	—	—	—
1695P VR Rare	—	—	—	—	—	—
1696P VR Rare	—	—	—	—	—	—
1697P VR Rare	—	—	—	—	—	—
1698P F Rare	—	—	—	—	—	—
1700P F Rare	—	—	—	—	—	—

COUNTERMARKED COINAGE

1651-1652

Problems with debasement of the coinage struck at Potosi in the 1620s-1640s prompted a visit by the Royal Inspector Don Francisco de Nestares Marin, under orders by King Philip IV of Spain, at the end of 1648. Upon completion of the investigation, the order was given in October of 1650 to recall all coinage minted at Potosi since 1625 and prior to the accession of Juan Rodriguez de Rodas (assayer O with dot in middle) to the post of assayer in 1649. All half, 1, and 2 Reales , as well as any 4 and 8 Reales that were found to be heavily debased, were ordered to be melted, with all 4 Reales devalued to 3 Reales and 8 Reales devalued to 6 Reales. To differentiate the good new coinage from 1649 until a completely new design could be implemented in 1652, various countermarks were applied on the 4 and 8 Reales to reflect their higher net values of 3-3/4 Reales and 7-1/2 Reales respectively. Most of these countermarks bear a crown at the top, with either an initial or monogram or symbol below, all contained within a beaded circle (most common) or simple circle (single line, no beads) or beaded pentagon (rare) or no border (rarest). It is believed that each different countermark was applied in a different location within the Spanish colonies, but it is not known which countermark corresponds to which locale

KM# C17.2 3-3/4 REALES

13.5337 g., 0.8590 Silver 0.3738 oz. ASW **Ruler:** Philip IV **Countermark:** Crowned •F• in beaded circle **Note:** Countermark on 4 Reales, KM#17b.

CM Date	Host Date	Good	VG	F	VF	XF
ND(1651-52)	1650P o	175	275	400	500	—
ND(1651-52)	1651P E	200	300	400	525	—

KM# C17.3 3-3/4 REALES

13.5337 g., 0.8590 Silver 0.3738 oz. ASW **Ruler:** Philip IV **Countermark:** Crowned L in beaded circle **Note:** Countermark on 4 Reales, KM#17b.

CM Date	Host Date	Good	VG	F	VF	XF
ND(1651-52)	1649P o	175	275	400	500	—
ND(1651-52)	1650P o	175	275	400	500	—
ND(1651-52)	1651P	175	275	400	500	—

KM# C17.4 3-3/4 REALES

13.5337 g., 0.8590 Silver 0.3738 oz. ASW **Ruler:** Philip IV **Countermark:** Crowned A in beaded circle **Note:** Countermark on 4 Reales, KM#17b.

CM Date	Host Date	Good	VG	F	VF	XF
ND(1651-52)	ND(1649-51)P Rare	—	—	—	—	—

KM# C17.5 3-3/4 REALES

13.5337 g., 0.8590 Silver 0.3738 oz. ASW **Ruler:** Philip IV **Countermark:** Crowned C in beaded circle **Note:** Countermark on 4 Reales, KM#17b.

CM Date	Host Date	Good	VG	F	VF	XF
ND(1651-52)	1650P o Rare	—	—	—	—	—

KM# C17.6 3-3/4 REALES

Silver **Ruler:** Philip IV **Countermark:** Crowned P in beaded circle **Note:** Countermark on 4 Reales, KM#17b.

CM Date	Host Date	Good	VG	F	VF	XF
ND(1651-52)	ND(1649-51)P Rare	—	—	—	—	—

KM# C17.7 3-3/4 REALES

13.5337 g., 0.8590 Silver 0.3738 oz. ASW **Ruler:** Philip IV **Countermark:** Crowned Philip IV monogram in circle **Note:** Countermark on 4 Reales, KM#17b.

CM Date	Host Date	Good	VG	F	VF	XF
ND(1651-52)	1650P o	225	375	500	600	—

KM# C17.8 3-3/4 REALES

13.5337 g., 0.8590 Silver 0.3738 oz. ASW **Ruler:** Philip IV **Countermark:** Crowned retrograde L in circle

Note: Countermark on 4 Reales, KM#17b.

CM Date	Host Date	Good	VG	F	VF	XF
ND(1651-52)	1649-51P Rare	—	—	—	—	—

KM# C17.9 3-3/4 REALES

13.5337 g., 0.8590 Silver 0.3738 oz. ASW **Ruler:** Philip IV **Countermark:** Crowned O in beaded circle **Note:** Countermark on 4 Reales, KM#17b.

CM Date	Host Date	Good	VG	F	VF	XF
ND(1651-52)	1649-51P Rare	—	—	—	—	—

KM# C17.10 3-3/4 REALES

13.5337 g., 0.8590 Silver 0.3738 oz. ASW **Ruler:** Philip IV **Countermark:** Crowned arms, pomegranate below in beaded circle **Note:** Countermark on 4 Reales, KM#17b.

CM Date	Host Date	Good	VG	F	VF	XF
ND(1651-52)	1651P Rare	—	—	—	—	—

KM# C17.1 3-3/4 REALES

13.5337 g., 0.8590 Silver 0.3738 oz. ASW **Ruler:** Philip IV **Countermark:** Crown in beaded circle **Note:** Countermark on shield side of 4 Reales, KM#17b.

CM Date	Host Date	Good	VG	F	VF	XF
ND(1651-52)	1649P o/Z	200	300	400	525	—
ND(1651-52)	1649P o	175	275	400	525	—
ND(1651-52)	1649P Z	200	375	500	675	—
ND(1651-52)	1651P E	100	175	275	375	—

KM# C19.14 7-1/2 REALES

27.0674 g., 0.8590 Silver 0.7475 oz. ASW **Ruler:** Philip IV **Countermark:** Crown (varieties) in beaded circle **Note:** Countermark on 8 Reales, KM# 19.b.

CM Date	Host Date	Good	VG	F	VF	XF
ND(1651-52)	1649P Rare	—	—	—	—	—
ND(1651-52)	1650P o Rare	—	—	—	—	—
ND(1651-52)	1651P E/o Rare	—	—	—	—	—
ND(1651-52)	1651P o Rare	—	—	—	—	—

KM# C19.10 7-1/2 REALES

27.0674 g., 0.8590 Silver 0.7475 oz. ASW **Ruler:** Philip IV
Countermark: Crowned Philip IV monogram in circle **Note:** Countermark on 8 Reales, KM#19b.

CM Date	Host Date	Good	VG	F	VF	XF
ND(1651-52)	1649P o	125	250	400	575	—
ND(1651-52)	1650P o	125	250	400	575	—
ND(1651-52)	1651P E	125	250	400	575	—
ND(1651-52)	1651P o	125	250	400	575	—

KM# C19.2 7-1/2 REALES

27.0674 g., 0.8590 Silver 0.7475 oz. ASW **Ruler:** Philip IV
Countermark: Crowned L in beaded circle **Note:** Countermark on 8 Reales, KM#19b.

CM Date	Host Date	Good	VG	F	VF	XF
ND(1651-52)	1649P o/Z	100	175	300	475	—
ND(1651-52)	1649P o	90.00	150	285	435	—
ND(1651-52)	1649P Z	100	175	300	475	—
ND(1651-52)	1650P o	90.00	150	285	435	—
ND(1651-52)	1651P o	90.00	150	285	435	—
ND(1651-52)	1651P E	90.00	150	285	435	—

KM# C19.3 7-1/2 REALES

27.0674 g., 0.8590 Silver 0.7475 oz. ASW **Ruler:** Philip IV
Countermark: Crowned •F• in beaded circle **Note:** Countermark on 8 Reales, KM#19b.

CM Date	Host Date	Good	VG	F	VF	XF
ND(1651-52)	1649P o/Z	100	175	300	435	—
ND(1651-52)	1649P o	90.00	150	285	435	—

Note: Host coin dated 1649Z exists with c/m on obverse (crowned arms) and is considered rare

CM Date	Host Date	Good	VG	F	VF	XF
ND(1651-52)	1650P o	90.00	150	285	435	—
ND(1651-52)	1651P o	90.00	150	285	435	—
ND(1651-52)	1651P E	90.00	150	285	435	—
ND(1651-52)	1652P E	300	750	1,250	2,500	—

KM# C19.4 7-1/2 REALES

27.0674 g., 0.8590 Silver 0.7475 oz. ASW **Ruler:** Philip IV
Countermark: Crowned large O in beaded circle **Note:** Countermark on 8 Reales, KM#19b.

CM Date	Host Date	Good	VG	F	VF	XF
ND(1651-52)	1649P o	125	225	375	550	—
ND(1651-52)	1649P Z	150	240	400	575	—
ND(1651-52)	1650P o	125	225	375	550	—
ND(1651-52)	1651P E/o	200	300	400	600	—
ND(1651-52)	1651P E	125	225	375	550	—
ND(1651-52)	1651P o	125	225	375	550	—

KM# C19.5 7-1/2 REALES

27.0674 g., 0.8590 Silver 0.7475 oz. ASW **Ruler:** Philip IV
Countermark: Crowned S in beaded circle **Note:** Countermark on 8 Reales, KM#19b.

CM Date	Host Date	Good	VG	F	VF	XF
ND(1651-52)	1649P o	125	250	400	575	—
ND(1651-52)	1650P o	125	250	400	575	—
ND(1651-52)	1651P o	125	250	400	575	—

KM# C19.7 7-1/2 REALES

27.0674 g., 0.8590 Silver 0.7475 oz. ASW **Ruler:** Philip IV
Countermark: Crowned C in beaded circle **Note:** Countermark on 8 Reales, KM#19b.

CM Date	Host Date	Good	VG	F	VF	XF
ND(1651-52)	1649P o Rare	—	—	—	—	—
ND(1651-52)	1650P o Rare	—	—	—	—	—
ND(1651-52)	1651P E Rare	—	—	—	—	—
ND(1651-52)	1651P o Rare	—	—	—	—	—

KM# C19.8 7-1/2 REALES

27.0674 g., 0.8590 Silver 0.7475 oz. ASW **Ruler:** Philip IV
Countermark: Crowned G in beaded circle **Note:** Countermark on 8 Reales, KM#19b.

CM Date	Host Date	Good	VG	F	VF	XF
ND(1651-52)	1650P o	150	240	400	575	—
ND(1651-52)	1651P o Rare	150	240	400	575	—

KM# C19.12 7-1/2 REALES

27.0674 g., 0.8590 Silver 0.7475 oz. ASW **Ruler:** Philip IV
Countermark: Crowned Z in beaded circle **Note:** Countermark on 8 Reales, KM#19b.

CM Date	Host Date	Good	VG	F	VF	XF
ND(1651-52)	ND(1649-51)P Rare	—	—	—	—	—

KM# C19.13 7-1/2 REALES

27.0674 g., 0.8590 Silver 0.7475 oz. ASW **Ruler:** Philip IV
Countermark: Crowned 1652 in beaded pentagon **Note:** Countermark on 8 Reales, KM#19b.

CM Date	Host Date	Good	VG	F	VF	XF
ND(1651-52)	1650P o	200	300	450	675	—
ND(1651-52)	1651P E/o	125	200	285	375	—

KM# C19.15 7-1/2 REALES

27.0674 g., 0.8590 Silver 0.7475 oz. ASW **Ruler:** Philip IV
Countermark: Crown in circle **Note:** Countermark on 8 Reales, KM#19b.

CM Date	Host Date	Good	VG	F	VF	XF
ND(1651-52)	1649P o Rare	—	—	—	—	—
ND(1651-52)	1649P Z Rare	—	—	—	—	—
ND(1651-52)	1650P o Rare	—	—	—	—	—
ND(1651-52)	1651P E Rare	—	—	—	—	—

KM# C19.16 7-1/2 REALES

27.0674 g., 0.8590 Silver 0.7475 oz. ASW **Ruler:** Philip IV
Countermark: Crowned "a" in beaded circle **Note:** Countermark on 8 Reales, KM#19b.

CM Date	Host Date	Good	VG	F	VF	XF
ND(1651-52)	1649P o Rare	—	—	—	—	—
ND(1651-52)	1650P o Rare	—	—	—	—	—

KM# C19.17 7-1/2 REALES

27.0674 g., 0.8590 Silver 0.7475 oz. ASW **Ruler:** Philip IV
Countermark: Crowned •F• with two dots above crown **Note:** Countermark on 8 Reales, KM#19b.

CM Date	Host Date	Good	VG	F	VF	XF
ND(1651-52)	1651P E/o Rare	—	—	—	—	—

KM# C19.18 7-1/2 REALES

27.0674 g., 0.8590 Silver 0.7475 oz. ASW **Ruler:** Philip IV
Countermark: Crowned •G• in beaded circle **Note:** Countermark on 8 Reales, KM#19b.

CM Date	Host Date	Good	VG	F	VF	XF
ND(1651-52)	1650P o Rare	—	—	—	—	—

KM# C19.19 7-1/2 REALES

27.0674 g., 0.8590 Silver 0.7475 oz. ASW **Ruler:** Philip IV
Countermark: Crowned retrograde L in beaded circle **Note:** Countermark on 8 Reales, KM#19b.

CM Date	Host Date	Good	VG	F	VF	XF
ND(1651-52)	ND(1649-51)P Rare	—	—	—	—	—

KM# C19.20 7-1/2 REALES

27.0674 g., 0.8590 Silver 0.7475 oz. ASW **Ruler:** Philip IV
Countermark: Crowned o in beaded circle **Note:** Countermark on 8 Reales, KM#19b.

CM Date	Host Date	Good	VG	F	VF	XF
ND(1651-52)	1649P o Rare	—	—	—	—	—
ND(1651-52)	1650P o Rare	—	—	—	—	—
ND(1651-52)	1651P E Rare	—	—	—	—	—

KM# C19.21 7-1/2 REALES

27.0674 g., 0.8590 Silver 0.7475 oz. ASW **Ruler:** Philip IV
Countermark: Crowned •T• in circle **Note:** Countermark on 8 Reales, KM#19b.

CM Date	Host Date	Good	VG	F	VF	XF
ND(1651-52)	1651P E	—	—	—	—	—

KM# C19.22 7-1/2 REALES

27.0674 g., 0.8590 Silver 0.7475 oz. ASW **Ruler:** Philip IV
Countermark: Crowned arms, pomegranate below in circle **Note:** Countermark on 8 Reales, KM#19b.

CM Date	Host Date	Good	VG	F	VF	XF
ND(1651-52)	1649P Z	—	—	—	—	—
ND(1651-52)	1650P o	—	—	—	—	—
ND(1651-52)	1651P E/o	—	—	—	—	—
ND(1651-52)	1651P	—	—	—	—	—

KM# C19.23 7-1/2 REALES

27.0674 g., 0.8590 Silver 0.7475 oz. ASW **Ruler:** Philip IV
Countermark: Crowned 1605 in beaded pentagon **Note:** Countermark on 8 Reales, KM#19b.

CM Date	Host Date	Good	VG	F	VF	XF
ND(1651-52)	1650P o Rare	—	—	—	—	—

KM# C19.24 7-1/2 REALES

27.0674 g., 0.8590 Silver 0.7475 oz. ASW **Ruler:** Philip IV
Countermark: Crowned castle, BAIRES below **Note:** Countermark on 8 Reales, KM#19b. BAIRES = Buenos Aires.

CM Date	Host Date	Good	VG	F	VF	XF
ND(1651-52)	1649-51P o Rare	—	—	—	—	—

KM# C19.11 7-1/2 REALES

27.0674 g., 0.8590 Silver 0.7475 oz. ASW **Ruler:** Philip IV
Countermark: Crowned T in beaded circle **Note:** Countermark on 8 Reales, KM#19b. Three varieties of this countermark exist.

CM Date	Host Date	Good	VG	F	VF	XF
ND(1651-52)	1650P o Rare	—	—	—	—	—
ND(1651-52)	1651P E Rare	—	—	—	—	—

KM# C19.9 7-1/2 REALES

27.0674 g., 0.8590 Silver 0.7475 oz. ASW **Ruler:** Philip IV
Countermark: Crowned P in beaded circle **Note:** Countermark on 8 Reales, KM#19b. Two varieties of this countermark exist.

CM Date	Host Date	Good	VG	F	VF	XF
ND(1651-52)	1649P o Rare	—	—	—	—	—
ND(1651-52)	1650P o Rare	—	—	—	—	—

KM# C19.1 7-1/2 REALES

27.0674 g., 0.8590 Silver 0.7475 oz. ASW **Ruler:** Philip IV
Countermark: Plain crown in beaded circle **Note:** Countermark on 8 Reales, KM#19b.

CM Date	Host Date	Good	VG	F	VF	XF
ND(1651-52)	1649P o	90.00	150	285	435	—
ND(1651-52)	1649P Z	100	175	300	475	—
ND(1651-52)	1650P o	90.00	150	285	435	—
ND(1651-52)	1651P E	90.00	150	285	435	—
ND(1651-52)	1651P o	90.00	150	285	435	—

KM# C19.6 7-1/2 REALES

27.0674 g., 0.8590 Silver 0.7475 oz. ASW **Ruler:** Philip IV
Countermark: Crowned A in beaded circle **Note:** Countermark on 8 Reales, KM#19b.

CM Date	Host Date	Good	VG	F	VF	XF
ND(1651-52)	1649-51P Rare	—	—	—	—	—

Brazil, which comprises half the continent of South America and is the only Latin American country deriving its culture and language from Portugal, has an area of 3,286,488 sq. mi. (8,511,965 sq. km.

Brazil was discovered and claimed for Portugal by Admiral Pedro Alvares Cabral in 1500. Portugal established a settlement in 1532 and proclaimed the area a royal colony in 1549. During the Napoleonic Wars, Dom Joao VI established the seat of Portuguese government in Rio de Janeiro. When he returned to Portugal, his son Dom Pedro I declared Brazil's independence on Sept. 7, 1822, and became emperor of Brazil. The Empire of Brazil was maintained until 1889 when the federal republic was established. The Federative Republic was established in 1946 by terms of a constitution drawn up by a constituent assembly. Following a coup in 1964 the armed forces retained overall control under a dictatorship until civilian government was restored on March 15, 1985. The current constitution was adopted in 1988.

RULERS

Dutch Occupation, 1624-1661
Portuguese
Alfonso VI, 1656-1667
Pedro,
As Prince Regent, 1667-1683
As Pedro II, 1683-1706

MINT MARKS

B - Bahia
P - Pernambuco
R - Rio de Janeiro

MONETARY SYSTEM

(Until 1833)
120 Reis = 1 Real
6400 Reis 1 Peca (Dobra = Johannes (Joe) = 4 Escudos

PORTUGUESE COLONY

OCCUPATION COINAGE

Geotroyerde Westindishe Compangnie

The Dutch issuer was established in Brazil in 1624 remaining there until 1661.

KM# 8 10 STUIVERS
Silver **Obv:** Monogram of company with value above, date below **Note:** Uniface.

Date	Mintage	VG	F	VF	XF	Unc
1654 Rare	—	—	—	—	—	—

KM# 9 10 STUIVERS
Silver **Obv:** Monogram of company with value above, date below **Note:** Uniface.

Date	Mintage	VG	F	VF	XF	Unc
1654 Rare	—	—	—	—	—	—

KM# 10 20 STUIVERS
Silver **Obv:** Monogram of company with value above, date below **Note:** Uniface.

Date	Mintage	VG	F	VF	XF	Unc
1654 Rare	—	—	—	—	—	—

KM# 12 40 STUIVERS
Silver **Obv:** Monogram of company with value above, date below **Note:** Uniface.

Date	Mintage	VG	F	VF	XF	Unc
1654 Rare	—	—	—	—	—	—

Note: Silver emergency issues of 1654 are of questionable origin

KM# 5.1 3 FLORIN
1.8000 g., Gold **Rev:** Diamond after Brasil **Note:** Klippe.

Date	Mintage	VG	F	VF	XF	Unc
1645 Rare	—	—	—	—	—	—

KM# 5.2 3 FLORIN
1.8000 g., Gold **Obv:** Without periods **Rev:** Without periods **Note:** Klippe.

Date	Mintage	VG	F	VF	XF	Unc
1646 Rare	—	—	—	—	—	—

KM# 5.3 3 FLORIN
1.8000 g., Gold **Obv:** Period after III **Rev:** Period after Brasil **Note:** Klippe.

Date	Mintage	VG	F	VF	XF	Unc
1646 Rare	—	—	—	—	—	—

KM# 6.1 6 FLORIN
3.7000 g., Gold **Rev:** Diamond after Brasil **Note:** Klippe.

Date	Mintage	VG	F	VF	XF	Unc
1645 Rare	—	—	—	—	—	—

KM# 6.2 6 FLORIN
3.7000 g., Gold **Obv:** Without periods **Rev:** Without periods **Note:** Klippe.

Date	Mintage	VG	F	VF	XF	Unc
1646 Rare	—	—	—	—	—	—

KM# 6.3 6 FLORIN
3.7000 g., Gold **Obv:** Period after VI **Rev:** Period after Brasil **Note:** Klippe.

Date	Mintage	VG	F	VF	XF	Unc
1646 Rare	—	—	—	—	—	—

KM# 7.1 12 FLORIN
7.6000 g., Gold **Rev:** Diamond after Brasil **Note:** Klippe.

Date	Mintage	VG	F	VF	XF	Unc
1645 Rare	—	—	—	—	—	—
1646 Rare	—	—	—	—	—	—

KM# 7.2 12 FLORIN
7.6000 g., Gold **Obv:** Period after XII **Rev:** Period after Brasil **Note:** Klippe.

Date	Mintage	VG	F	VF	XF	Unc
1646 Rare	—	—	—	—	—	—

COUNTERMARKED COINAGE

Type I

c/m: Crowned 60, 120, 240, or 480 in countoured frame. Authorized by decree of February 26, 1643 on spanish Colonial 1, 2, 4, and 8 Reales "cob" coins. Value was raised 50%

KM# 1 60 REIS
3.3800 g., Silver **Countermark:** Type I **Note:** Countermark on Spanish Colonial 1 Real.

CM Date	Host Date	Good	VG	F	VF	XF
ND(1643)	ND	33.00	60.00	85.00	215	—

KM# 2 120 REIS
6.7700 g., Silver **Countermark:** Type I **Note:** Countermark on Spanish Colonial 2 Reales.

CM Date	Host Date	Good	VG	F	VF	XF
ND(1643)	ND	36.00	70.00	110	240	—

KM# 3 240 REIS
13.5400 g., Silver **Countermark:** Type I **Note:** Countermark on Spanish Colonial 4 Reales.

CM Date	Host Date	Good	VG	F	VF	XF
ND(1643)	ND	43.25	85.00	145	325	—

KM# 4 480 REIS
27.0700 g., Silver **Countermark:** Type I **Note:** Countermark on Spanish Colonial 8 Reales.

CM Date	Host Date	Good	VG	F	VF	XF
ND(1643)	ND	70.00	145	250	500	—

COUNTERMARKED COINAGE

Type III

c/m: Crowned 75, 150, 300, or 600 in contoured frame. Authorized by Decree of March 22, 1663 on Spanish Colonial 1, 2, 4, and 8 Reales cob coins. Value was raised 25%.

KM# 16 75 REIS
3.3800 g., Silver **Countermark:** Type III **Note:** Countermark on Spanish Colonial 1 Real.

CM Date	Host Date	Good	VG	F	VF	XF
ND(1663)	ND	33.00	55.00	90.00	150	—

KM# 17 150 REIS
6.7700 g., Silver **Countermark:** Type III **Note:** Countermark on Spanish Colonial 2 Reales.

CM Date	Host Date	Good	VG	F	VF	XF
ND(1663)	ND	38.50	60.00	95.00	175	—

KM# 18.2 300 REIS
Silver **Countermark:** Type III **Note:** Countermark on Bolivia 4 Reales, KM#18.

CM Date	Host Date	Good	VG	F	VF	XF
ND(1663)	ND	175	290	500	775	—

KM# 18.3 300 REIS
Silver **Countermark:** Type III **Note:** Countermark on Peru Star of Lima 4 Reales, KM#17.

CM Date	Host Date	Good	VG	F	VF	XF
ND(1663)	1659 Rare	—	—	—	—	—

KM# 18.1 300 REIS
Silver **Countermark:** Type III **Note:** Countermark on Spanish Colonial 4 Reales.

CM Date	Host Date	Good	VG	F	VF	XF
ND(1663)	ND	60.00	95.00	175	290	—

KM# 19.1 600 REIS
Silver **Countermark:** Type III **Note:** Countermarked on Spanish Colonial 8 Reales.

CM Date	Host Date	Good	VG	F	VF	XF
ND(1658)	ND	70.00	145	265	500	—

KM# 19.2 600 REIS
Silver **Countermark:** Type III **Note:** Countermarked on Bolivia 8 Reales, KM#21.

CM Date	Host Date	Good	VG	F	VF	XF
ND(1663)	1658	240	400	650	1,000	—

KM# 19.3 600 REIS
Silver **Countermark:** Type III **Note:** Countermarked on Peru Star of Lima 8 Reales, KM#18.

CM Date	Host Date	Good	VG	F	VF	XF
ND(1663)	1659	1,900	3,250	5,000	7,200	—

COUNTERMARKED COINAGE

Type IV

c/m: Crowned 50, 60, 100, 120, 125, 200, 250, or 500 in contoured frame. Authorized by amendment on July 7, 1663 to Decree of March 22, 1663 on Portuguese coins of John IV and Alfonso VI.

KM# 21 50 REIS
Silver **Countermark:** Type IV **Note:** Countermarked on Portugal 1/2 Tostao (value 5 as S).

CM Date	Host Date	Good	VG	F	VF	XF
ND(1663)	ND	36.00	60.00	110	205	—

KM# 23 50 REIS
Silver **Countermark:** Type IV **Note:** Countermarked on Portugal 1/2 Tostao.

CM Date	Host Date	Good	VG	F	VF	XF
ND(1663)	ND	36.00	60.00	110	205	—

KM# 20 50 REIS
Silver **Countermark:** Type IV **Note:** Countermarked on Portugal 40 Reis (5 in value as S).

CM Date	Host Date	Good	VG	F	VF	XF
ND(1663)	ND	36.00	60.00	110	205	—

KM# 22 50 REIS
Silver **Countermark:** Type IV **Note:** Countermarked on Portugal 40 Reis, KM#34.

CM Date	Host Date	Good	VG	F	VF	XF
ND(1663)	ND	36.00	60.00	110	205	—

KM# 25 60 REIS
Silver **Countermark:** Type IV **Note:** Countermarked on Portugal 1/2 Tostao.

CM Date	Host Date	Good	VG	F	VF	XF
ND(1663)	ND	43.25	70.00	120	215	—

KM# 24 60 REIS
Silver **Countermark:** Type IV **Note:** Countermarked on Portugal 40 Reis.

CM Date	Host Date	Good	VG	F	VF	XF
ND(1663)	ND	43.25	70.00	120	215	—

KM# 26 75 REIS
Silver **Countermark:** Type IV **Note:** Countermarked on Portugal 1/2 Tostao.

CM Date	Host Date	Good	VG	F	VF	XF
ND(1663)	ND	42.00	65.00	115	210	—

KM# 28 100 REIS
Silver **Countermark:** Type IV **Note:** Countermarked on Portugal 1/2 Tostao.

CM Date	Host Date	Good	VG	F	VF	XF
ND(1663)	ND	42.00	65.00	115	210	—

KM# 27 100 REIS
Silver **Countermark:** Type IV **Note:** Countermarked on Portugal 80 Reis.

CM Date	Host Date	Good	VG	F	VF	XF
ND(1663)	ND	42.00	65.00	115	210	—

KM# 29 120 REIS
Silver **Countermark:** Type IV **Note:** Countermarked on Portugal 80 Reis.

CM Date	Host Date	Good	VG	F	VF	XF
ND(1663)	ND	50.00	80.00	140	270	—

KM# 30 125 REIS
Silver **Countermark:** Type IV **Note:** Countermarked on Portugal 1 Tostao.

CM Date	Host Date	Good	VG	F	VF	XF
ND(1663)	ND	70.00	115	175	350	—

KM# 31 150 REIS
Silver **Countermark:** Type IV **Note:** Countermarked on Portugal 1 Tostao.

CM Date	Host Date	Good	VG	F	VF	XF
ND(1663)	ND	43.25	70.00	120	250	—

KM# 32 200 REIS
Silver **Countermark:** Type IV **Note:** Countermarked on Portugal 1 Tostao.

CM Date	Host Date	Good	VG	F	VF	XF
ND(1663)	ND	50.00	85.00	145	325	—

KM# 33.1 250 REIS
Silver **Countermark:** Type IV **Note:** Countermarked on Portugal-Evora Mint 200 Reis, KM#51. (Value 5 as 5).

CM Date	Host Date	Good	VG	F	VF	XF
ND(1663)	ND	290	475	750	1,100	—

KM# 33.2 250 REIS
Silver **Countermark:** Type IV **Note:** Countermarked on Portugal-Lisbon Mint 200 Reis, KM#49.

CM Date	Host Date	Good	VG	F	VF	XF
ND(1663)	ND	350	600	950	—	—

KM# 33.3 250 REIS
Silver **Countermark:** Type IV **Note:** Countermarked on Portugal-Porto Mint 200 Reis, KM#50.

CM Date	Host Date	Good	VG	F	VF	XF
ND(1663)	ND	215	350	575	875	—

KM# 35 300 REIS
Silver **Countermark:** Type IV **Note:** Countermarked on Portugal 200 Reis.

CM Date	Host Date	Good	VG	F	VF	XF
ND(1663)	ND	110	215	350	575	—

KM# 37 500 REIS
Silver **Countermark:** Type IV **Note:** Countermarked on Portugal 1 Cruzado.

CM Date	Host Date	Good	VG	F	VF	XF
ND(1663)	ND	300	425	900	1,450	—

KM# 36 500 REIS
Silver **Countermark:** Type IV **Note:** Countermarked on Portugal 400 Reis.

CM Date	Host Date	Good	VG	F	VF	XF
ND(1663)	ND	150	210	425	725	—

KM# 38 600 REIS
Silver **Countermark:** Type IV **Note:** Countermarked on Portugal 400 Reis.

CM Date	Host Date	Good	VG	F	VF	XF
ND(1663)	ND	175	290	600	1,000	—

COUNTERMARKED COINAGE

Type VI

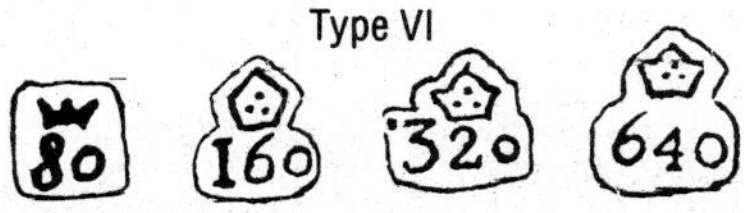

c/m: Crowned 80, 160, 320, or 640 in contoured frame. Authorized by Provision of March 23, 1679 on Spanish Colonial 1, 2, 4, and 8 Reales cob coins.

KM# 50 80 REIS
3.3800 g., Silver **Countermark:** Type VI **Note:** Countermarked on Spanish Colonial 1 Real.

CM Date	Host Date	Good	VG	F	VF	XF
ND(1679)	ND Rare	—	—	—	—	—

KM# 51 160 REIS
6.7700 g., Silver **Countermark:** Type VI **Note:** Countermarked on Spanish Colonial 2 Reales.

CM Date	Host Date	Good	VG	F	VF	XF
ND(1679)	ND Rare	—	—	—	—	—

KM# 52 320 REIS
13.5400 g., Silver **Countermark:** Type VI **Note:** Countermarked on Spanish Colonial 4 Reales.

CM Date	Host Date	Good	VG	F	VF	XF
ND(1679)	ND Rare	—	—	—	—	—

KM# 53 640 REIS
27.0700 g., Silver **Countermark:** Type VI **Note:** Countermarked on Spanish Colonial 8 Reales.

CM Date	Host Date	Good	VG	F	VF	XF
ND(1679)	ND Rare	—	—	—	—	—

COUNTERMARKED COINAGE

Type VIII

c/m: Crowned globe. Authorized by Royal charter of March 17, 1688 on Portuguese Tostaos or Spanish Colonial 4 and 8 Reales cob coins. Often found with additional countermarks.

KM# 63.1 200 REIS
Silver **Countermark:** Type VIII **Note:** Countermarked on Portugal 1 Tostao.

CM Date	Host Date	Good	VG	F	VF	XF
ND(1688)	ND	90.00	165	165	500	—

KM# 63.2 200 REIS
Silver **Countermark:** Type VIII **Note:** Countermarked on Brazil 200 Reis, KM#32.

CM Date	Host Date	Good	VG	F	VF	XF
ND(1688)	ND	180	350	575	—	—

KM# 64.1 300 REIS
13.5400 g., Silver **Countermark:** Type VIII **Note:** Countermarked on Spanish Colonial 4 Reales.

CM Date	Host Date	Good	VG	F	VF	XF
ND(1688)	ND	110	220	350	575	—

KM# 64.2 300 REIS
13.5400 g., Silver **Countermark:** Type VIII **Note:** Countermarked on Bolivia 4 Reales, KM#18.3.

CM Date	Host Date	Good	VG	F	VF	XF
ND(1688)	1660	195	350	575	925	—

KM# 65 600 REIS
27.0700 g., Silver **Countermark:** Type VIII **Note:** Countermarked on Spanish Colonial 8 Reales.

CM Date	Host Date	Good	VG	F	VF	XF
ND(1688)	ND	220	450	725	1,200	—

MILLED COINAGE

KM# 74 20 REIS
0.5600 g., 0.9170 Silver 0.0165 oz. ASW **Obv:** Narrow crown on shield of arms

Date	Mintage	VG	F	VF	XF	Unc
ND(1695-1698)	—	155	235	675	975	—

KM# 73 20 REIS
0.5600 g., 0.9170 Silver 0.0165 oz. ASW **Obv:** Large crown on shield of arms **Obv. Legend:** PETRVS. II. D. G. P. REX. R. D **Rev:** Globe on cross, rosettes in angles **Note:** Struck at Bahia.

Date	Mintage	VG	F	VF	XF	Unc
ND(1695) Unique	—	—	—	—	—	—

KM# 85.1 20 REIS
0.5600 g., 0.9170 Silver 0.0165 oz. ASW **Obv:** Crowned arms **Note:** Struck at Rio de Janeiro.

Date	Mintage	VG	F	VF	XF	Unc
ND(1699)	—	90.00	150	350	600	—

KM# 85.2 20 REIS
Silver **Ruler:** Pedro **Obv:** Crowned arms **Rev:** Globe on cross, rosettes in angles

Date	Mintage	VG	F	VF	XF	Unc
ND(1700-1702) P	—	60.00	145	350	600	—

KM# 76 40 REIS
1.1200 g., 0.9170 Silver 0.0330 oz. ASW **Obv:** Wide, low crown on shield of arms

Date	Mintage	Good	VG	F	VF	XF
ND(1695-98)	—	80.00	115	265	450	—

KM# 75 40 REIS
1.1200 g., 0.9170 Silver 0.0330 oz. ASW **Obv:** Large high crown on shield of arms **Obv. Legend:** PETRVS. II. D. G. P. REX. R. D **Note:** Struck at Bahia.

Date	Mintage	Good	VG	F	VF	XF
ND(1695) Unique	—	—	—	—	—	—

KM# 86.1 40 REIS
1.1200 g., 0.9170 Silver 0.0330 oz. ASW **Obv:** Crowned arms **Note:** Struck at Rio de Janiero.

Date	Mintage	Good	VG	F	VF	XF
ND(1699)	—	80.00	115	265	450	—

KM# 86.2 40 REIS
Silver **Ruler:** Pedro **Obv:** Crowned arms **Obv. Legend:** PETRVS • II • D • G • P • R • E • B • D • **Rev:** Sash crosses globe on cross, thin straight parallels **Rev. Legend:** SIGN NATA STAB SVBQ **Note:** Varieties exist.

Date	Mintage	Good	VG	F	VF	XF
ND(1700-02)P	—	80.00	115	265	450	—

KM# 78 80 REIS
2.2400 g., 0.9170 Silver 0.0660 oz. ASW **Obv:** Narrow crown above shield of arms

Date	Mintage	Good	VG	F	VF	XF
1695	—	32.50	46.75	90.00	135	—
1696	—	32.50	46.75	90.00	135	—
1697	—	55.00	110	270	600	—

KM# 77 80 REIS
2.2400 g., 0.9170 Silver 0.0660 oz. ASW **Obv:** Large crown above shield of arms, value at left, date divided near top **Obv. Legend:** PETRVS. II. D. G. PORT. REX. B. D **Rev:** Globe on cross **Note:** Struck at Bahia.

Date	Mintage	Good	VG	F	VF	XF
1695	—	45.50	90.00	210	375	—

KM# 87.1 80 REIS
2.2648 g., 0.9170 Silver 0.0668 oz. ASW **Obv:** Crowned arms divide date, value at left **Note:** Struck at Rio de Janeiro

Date	Mintage	Good	VG	F	VF	XF
1699	—	22.50	45.50	90.00	135	—
1700	—	30.00	60.00	175	350	—

KM# 87.2 80 REIS
2.2400 g., 0.9170 Silver 0.0660 oz. ASW **Ruler:** Pedro **Obv:** Crowned arms **Obv. Legend:** PETRVS • II • D • G • ... **Rev:** Globe on cross with "P" at center **Rev. Legend:** SIGN NATA STAB SVBQ **Note:** Varieties exist.

Date	Mintage	Good	VG	F	VF	XF
1700P	—	50.00	105	240	525	—

KM# 79.2 160 REIS
4.4800 g., 0.9170 Silver 0.1321 oz. ASW **Rev:** Without punctuation

Date	Mintage	Good	VG	F	VF	XF
1695	—	45.50	90.00	220	425	—

KM# 80 160 REIS
4.4800 g., 0.9170 Silver 0.1321 oz. ASW **Obv:** Narrow crown above shield of arms

Date	Mintage	Good	VG	F	VF	XF
1695	—	32.50	55.00	100	150	—
1696	—	32.50	55.00	100	150	—
1697	—	100	190	400	675	—

KM# 79.1 160 REIS
4.4800 g., 0.9170 Silver 0.1321 oz. ASW **Obv:** Large crown above shield of arms, value at left, date divided near top **Obv. Legend:** PETRVS. II. D. G. PORT. REX. E. B. D **Rev:** Globe on cross **Note:** Struck at Bahia.

Date	Mintage	Good	VG	F	VF	XF
1695	—	32.50	45.50	90.00	135	—

KM# 88.1 160 REIS
4.4800 g., 0.9170 Silver 0.1321 oz. ASW **Obv:** Crowned arms divide date, value at left **Note:** Struck at Rio de Janiero.

Date	Mintage	Good	VG	F	VF	XF
1699	—	32.50	55.00	90.00	150	—
1700	—	45.50	90.00	220	425	—

KM# 88.2 160 REIS
Silver **Ruler:** Pedro **Obv:** Crowned arms divide value at left from crosses at right **Obv. Legend:** PETRVS • II • D • G • P • R • E .... **Rev:** Globe on cross with "P" at center **Rev. Legend:** SIGN NATA STAB SVBQ **Note:** Varieties exist.

Date	Mintage	Good	VG	F	VF	XF
1700P	—	100	190	400	675	—

KM# 81.2 320 REIS
8.9600 g., 0.9170 Silver 0.2641 oz. ASW **Rev:** Round globe on cross **Note:** Struck at Bahia

Date	Mintage	VG	F	VF	XF	Unc
1695	—	22.50	45.00	90.00	185	—
1695 PETRS	—	60.00	110	215	425	—

KM# 82 320 REIS
8.9600 g., 0.9170 Silver 0.2641 oz. ASW **Obv:** Narrow crown above shield of arms **Note:** Struck at Bahia, varieties exist.

Date	Mintage	VG	F	VF	XF	Unc
1695	—	30.00	55.00	120	225	—
1696	—	30.00	55.00	120	225	—
1697	—	90.00	150	350	675	—
1698	—	190	375	800	1,450	—

KM# 81.1 320 REIS
8.9600 g., 0.9170 Silver 0.2641 oz. ASW **Obv:** Large crown above shield of arms, value at left, date divided near top **Obv. Legend:** PETRVS. II. D. G. PORT. REX. E. BRAS. D **Rev:** Oval globe on cross **Note:** Struck at Bahia.

Date	Mintage	VG	F	VF	XF	Unc
1695	—	42.25	80.00	205	400	—

KM# 89.1 320 REIS
8.9600 g., 0.9170 Silver 0.2641 oz. ASW **Note:** Struck at Rio de Janeiro, varieties exist.

Date	Mintage	VG	F	VF	XF	Unc
1699	—	30.00	55.00	120	225	—

KM# 89.2 320 REIS
8.9600 g., 0.9170 Silver 0.2641 oz. ASW **Ruler:** Pedro **Obv:** Crowned arms divide date, value at left **Obv. Legend:** PETRVS • II • D • G • PORT • .... **Rev:** Round globe on cross **Rev. Legend:** SIGN • NATA STAB • SVBQ

Date	Mintage	VG	F	VF	XF	Unc
1700P	—	16.00	22.50	55.00	135	—

KM# 83.1 640 REIS
17.9200 g., 0.9170 Silver 0.5283 oz. ASW **Obv:** Large crown above shield of arms, value at left, date divided near top **Obv. Legend:** PETRVS. II. D. G. PORT. REX. ET. BRAS. D.. **Rev:** Globe on cross

Date	Mintage	VG	F	VF	XF	Unc
1695	—	65.00	110	220	350	—

KM# 83.2 640 REIS
17.9200 g., 0.9170 Silver 0.5283 oz. ASW **Rev:** Without punctuation

Date	Mintage	VG	F	VF	XF	Unc
1695	—	90.00	155	375	600	—

KM# 84 640 REIS
17.9200 g., 0.9170 Silver 0.5283 oz. ASW **Obv:** Narrow crown above shield of arms, value at left, date divided near top **Rev:** Globe on cross **Note:** Varieties exist.

Date	Mintage	VG	F	VF	XF	Unc
1695	—	32.50	55.00	120	225	—
1696	—	32.50	55.00	120	225	—
1697	—	39.00	70.00	135	265	—
1698	—	39.00	70.00	135	265	—

KM# 90.1 640 REIS
17.9200 g., 0.9170 Silver 0.5283 oz. ASW **Note:** Varieties exist.

Date	Mintage	VG	F	VF	XF	Unc
1699	—	39.00	65.00	130	250	—
1700	—	45.50	85.00	150	300	—

KM# 90.2 640 REIS
17.9200 g., 0.9170 Silver 0.5283 oz. ASW **Ruler:** Pedro **Obv:** Crowned arms divide date above and value at left from florals at right **Obv. Legend:** PETRVS • II • D G • PORT • REX • ET • BRAS

• DN • **Rev:** Globe on cross, thick, curved parallels **Rev. Legend:** SVBQ SIGN. NATA STAB.

Date	Mintage	VG	F	VF	XF	Unc
1700P	—	65.00	115	225	450	—

KM# 87 1000 REIS

2.0400 g., 0.9170 Gold 0.0601 oz. AGW **Obv:** Crowned arms, value at side **Rev:** Cross in quatrefoil, date above **Note:** Struck at Bahia.

Date	Mintage	VG	F	VF	XF	Unc
1696 Unique	—	—	—	—	—	—

KM# 96 1000 REIS

2.0400 g., 0.9170 Gold 0.0601 oz. AGW **Note:** Struck at Rio de Janeiro; legend varieties exist.

Date	Mintage	VG	F	VF	XF	Unc
1699	—	100	145	275	500	—
1700	—	100	145	275	500	—

KM# 85 2000 REIS

4.0800 g., 0.9170 Gold 0.1203 oz. AGW **Obv:** Crowned arms, value at side **Rev. Legend:** Cross in quatrefoil, date above **Note:** Struck at Bahia.

Date	Mintage	VG	F	VF	XF	Unc
1695	—	650	1,300	2,650	4,600	—

KM# 88 2000 REIS

4.0800 g., 0.9170 Gold 0.1203 oz. AGW **Obv:** Smaller crown above arms

Date	Mintage	VG	F	VF	XF	Unc
1696	—	210	330	600	900	—
1697	—	200	300	550	850	—

KM# 97 2000 REIS

4.0800 g., 0.9170 Gold 0.1203 oz. AGW **Note:** Legend varieties exist; Struck at Rio De Janero.

Date	Mintage	VG	F	VF	XF	Unc
1699	—	200	300	500	800	—
1700	—	210	320	660	850	—

KM# 86 4000 REIS

8.1600 g., 0.9170 Gold 0.2406 oz. AGW **Obv:** Crowned arms, value at side **Rev:** Cross in quatrefoil, date above **Note:** Struck at Bahia.

Date	Mintage	VG	F	VF	XF	Unc
1695	—	450	850	400	2,750	—

KM# 89 4000 REIS

8.1600 g., 0.9170 Gold 0.2406 oz. AGW **Obv:** Taller crown above arms **Note:** Struck at Bahia.

Date	Mintage	VG	F	VF	XF	Unc
1696	—	425	825	1,250	1,850	—
1697	—	425	825	1,250	1,850	—
1698	—	425	825	1,250	1,850	—

KM# 98 4000 REIS

8.1600 g., 0.9170 Gold 0.2406 oz. AGW **Note:** Legend and punctuation varieties exist.

Date	Mintage	VG	F	VF	XF	Unc
1699/8	—	400	500	800	1,500	—
1699	—	400	500	800	1,500	—
1700	—	400	500	800	1,500	—

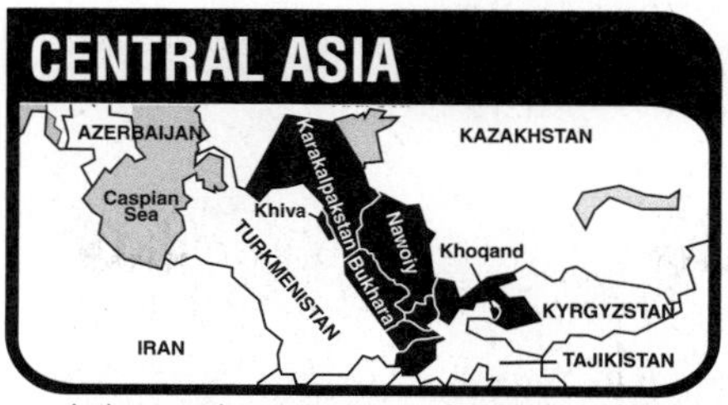

In the several centuries prior to 1500 which witnessed the breakup of the Mongol Empire and the subsequent rise of smaller successor states, no single power or dynasty was able to control the vast expanses of Western and Central Asia. The region known previously as Transoxiana, the land beyond the Oxus River (modern Amu Darya), became the domain of the Shaybanids, then the Janids. The territory ruled by these dynasties had no set borders, which rather expanded and contracted as the fortunes of the rulers ebbed and flowed. At their greatest extent, the khanate took in parts of what are now northern Iran and Afghanistan, as well as part or all of modern Turkmenistan, Uzbekistan, Kazakhstan, Tadzhikistan and Kyrgyzstan. Coins are known to have been struck by virtually every ruler, but some are quite scarce owing to short reigns or the ever-changing political and economic situation.

MINTS

Abivard
Akhshi/Akhshikath
Andigan/Andijan
Asfarayin/Isfarayin
Astarabad
Awbah
Badakhshan
Balkh
Bistam
Bukhara
Damghan
Herat
Hisar
Karmin
Kish
Kufan/Kufin
Langar
Marw
Mashhad
Nasaf
Nimruz
Nisa
Qarshi (copper only)
Qayin
Qunduz
Sabzavar
Samarqand
Tashkand (Tashkent)
Termez
Tun
Turbat
Urdu (camp mint)
Yazur

JANID

The Janids were the successors to the Shaybanid dynasty and they maintained coinage traditions similar to those of their predecessors. Janid silver coins are almost invariably poorly struck, rarely showing either mint or date. After about AH1090/1679AD, the alloy became increasingly debased and was mostly copper after the early AH1100s/1670s AD. By contrast, the gold coins of the Janids are found to be of high quality and alloy. The original silver tanka conformed to the 4.7 gram weight inherited from the Shaybanids, but sank to below 4 grams by the end of the dynasty. Mint names, when they are visible on the silver coins, have only been recorded for Balkh, Bukhara and Samarqand.

The dates of rule given for the Janid khans are rather tentative. The standard lists in the genealogical references to not agree with the dates found on the coins in all cases.

During the rule of the last Janid, Abu'l-Ghazi Khan in the late $13^{th}/18^{th}$ century, the territory was split into three smaller principalities: Bukhara, Khiva and Khoqand, which see.

RULERS

Yar Muhammad Khan, ca AH1007-08/1598-99AD
Jani Muhammad Khan, AH1007-10/1598-1601AD
Baqi Muhammad Khan, AH1010-14/1601-05AD
Wali Muhammad Khan, AH1014-27/1605-18AD
Imam Quli Khan, AH1027-54/1618-44AD
Nadr Muhammad Khan, AH1054-57/1644-47AD
Occupation by Mughal Shah Jahan I, at Balkh AH1056-57/1647AD
'Abd al-'Aziz Khan, AH1057-91/1647-80AD
Subhan Quli Khan, AH1091-1114/1680-1702AD
'Ubayd Allah Khan I, AH1114-17/1702-05AD
Abu'l-Fayz Khan, AH1117-60/1705-47AD
'Abd al-Mu'min Khan, AH1160-64/1747-51AD
Muhammad Rahim, AH1167-71/1753-58AD
'Abu'l-Ghazi Khan, AH1171-1200/1758-85AD

KHANATE

Yar Muhammad Khan

AH1007-1008

HAMMERED COINAGE

Balkh

MB# 3.1 TANKA

4.7000 g., Silver

Date	Mintage	Good	VG	F	VF	XF
ND(1599)	—	—	55.00	80.00	110	155

Bukhara

MB# 3.2 TANKA

4.7000 g., Silver

Date	Mintage	Good	VG	F	VF	XF
ND(1599)	—	—	50.00	80.00	115	155

Samarqand

MB# 3.3 TANKA

4.7000 g., Silver

Date	Mintage	Good	VG	F	VF	XF
AH1008	—	—	70.00	100	135	185
ND(1600)	—	—	50.00	80.00	115	155

Jani Muhammad Khan

AH1007-1010

HAMMERED COINAGE

Balkh

MB# 5.1 TANKA

4.6000 g., Silver

Date	Mintage	Good	VG	F	VF	XF
AH1008	—	—	30.00	50.00	80.00	125
ND(1601)	—	—	20.00	30.00	50.00	85.00

Bukhara

MB# 5.2 TANKA

4.6000 g., Silver

Date	Mintage	Good	VG	F	VF	XF
AH1009	—	—	40.00	60.00	100	150
ND(1601)	—	—	30.00	45.00	70.00	110

MB# 5.4 TANKA

4.6000 g., Silver

Date	Mintage	Good	VG	F	VF	XF
ND(1601)	—	—	20.00	35.00	60.00	95.00

Samarqand

MB# 5.3 TANKA

4.6000 g., Silver

Date	Mintage	Good	VG	F	VF	XF
AH1010	—	—	40.00	60.00	100	150
ND(1601)	—	—	30.00	50.00	85.00	125

Baqi Muhammad Khan

AH1010-1014

HAMMERED COINAGE

Balkh

KM# 7.1 TANKA

4.6000 g., Silver **Obv:** Ruler's names in cartouche, titles, mint and date around **Rev:** Kalima in cartouche

Date	Mintage	Good	VG	F	VF	XF
AH1011	—	—	35.00	50.00	85.00	125
ND	—	—	18.00	30.00	45.00	70.00

Bukhara

KM# 7.2 TANKA
4.6000 g., Silver **Obv:** Ruler's names in cartouche, titles, mint and date around **Rev:** Kalima in cartouche

Date	Mintage	Good	VG	F	VF	XF
AH1011	—	—	30.00	50.00	100	165
AH1012	—	—	30.00	50.00	100	165
AH1014	—	—	20.00	40.00	75.00	110

KM# 7.4 TANKA
4.6000 g., Silver **Obv:** Ruler's names in cartouche, titles, mint and date around **Rev:** Kalima in cartouche

Date	Mintage	Good	VG	F	VF	XF
AH1011	—	—	20.00	40.00	70.00	110
AH1013	—	—	20.00	40.00	70.00	110
ND	—	—	12.00	25.00	45.00	75.00

Samarqand

KM# 7.3 TANKA
4.6000 g., Silver **Obv:** Ruler's names in cartouche, titles, mint and date around **Rev:** Kalima in cartouche

Date	Mintage	Good	VG	F	VF	XF
AH1011	—	—	30.00	50.00	100	140
ND	—	—	20.00	40.00	70.00	110

Wali Muhammad Khan
AH1014-1027
HAMMERED COINAGE

Balkh

KM# 9.1 TANKA
4.5300 g., Silver **Obv:** Ruler's name in cartouche, titles around **Rev:** Kalima in cartouche

Date	Mintage	Good	VG	F	VF	XF
AH1014	—	—	35.00	50.00	80.00	125
ND(1618)	—	—	20.00	30.00	60.00	100

Bukhara

KM# 9.2 TANKA
4.5300 g., Silver **Obv:** Ruler's name in cartouche, titles around **Rev:** Kalima in cartouche

Date	Mintage	Good	VG	F	VF	XF
ND(1618)	—	—	17.50	35.00	60.00	100

KM# 9.4 TANKA
4.5300 g., Silver **Obv:** Ruler's names and titles in cartouche **Rev:** Kalima in cartouche

Date	Mintage	Good	VG	F	VF	XF
ND(1618)	—	—	20.00	30.00	60.00	100

Samarqand

KM# 9.3 TANKA
4.5300 g., Silver **Obv:** Ruler's name in cartouche, titles around **Rev:** Kalima in cartouche

Date	Mintage	Good	VG	F	VF	XF
AH1014	—	—	40.00	60.00	95.00	140
AH1015	—	—	40.00	60.00	95.00	140
AH1020	—	—	40.00	60.00	95.00	140
ND	—	—	17.50	35.00	60.00	100

Imam Quli Khan
AH1027-1054
HAMMERED COINAGE

Balkh

KM# 11.1 TANKA
4.2500 g., Silver **Obv:** Ruler's names in cartouche, titles, mint and date around **Rev:** Kalima in cartouche

Date	Mintage	Good	VG	F	VF	XF
ND(1644) Balkh	—	—	25.00	45.00	70.00	115

Bukhara

KM# 11.2 TANKA
4.2500 g., Silver **Obv:** Ruler's names in cartouche, titles, mint and date around **Rev:** Kalima in cartouche

Date	Mintage	Good	VG	F	VF	XF
ND(1644)	—	—	25.00	45.00	75.00	115

KM# 11.3 TANKA
4.2500 g., Silver **Obv:** Ruler's names in cartouche, titles, mint and date around **Rev:** Kalima in cartouche

Date	Mintage	Good	VG	F	VF	XF
AH1033	—	—	30.00	50.00	85.00	135
ND(1644)	—	—	12.00	25.00	45.00	70.00

Nadr Muhammad Khan
AH1054-1057
HAMMERED COINAGE

KM# 12 DANGI (PUL)
Copper wt. 3.38-4.51g

Date	Mintage	Good	VG	F	VF	XF
ND(1650) No Mint	—	—	—	—	—	—

Balkh

KM# 13.1 TANKA
4.2500 g., Silver

Date	Mintage	Good	VG	F	VF	XF
AH1053	—	—	40.00	70.00	110	165
AH1055	—	—	40.00	70.00	110	165
ND(1647)	—	—	25.00	45.00	70.00	110

Bukhara

KM# 13.2 TANKA
4.2500 g., Silver

Date	Mintage	Good	VG	F	VF	XF
ND(1647)	—	—	25.00	45.00	75.00	110

KM# 13.3 TANKA
4.2500 g., Silver

Date	Mintage	Good	VG	F	VF	XF
AH1054	—	—	25.00	45.00	70.00	110
AH1055	—	—	25.00	45.00	70.00	110
ND(1647)	—	—	20.00	30.00	50.00	85.00

Shah Jahan I (Mughal)
AH1056-1057
HAMMERED COINAGE

KM# 15 TANKA
4.2500 g., Silver **Obv:** Emperor's name in cartouche **Rev:** Kalima in cartouche **Note:** All coins of this type struck at Balkh, but mint name almost never visible.

Date	Mintage	Good	VG	F	VF	XF
AH1057 Balkh	—	—	200	325	475	725
AH1057	—	—	175	250	375	600
ND(1647)	—	—	90.00	150	250	500

Balkh

KM# 18 MOHUR
Gold 10.8-11g **Obv:** Legend within square, with knots at corners; "Shah Jahan Bad Shah Ghazi," titles, mint and date around **Rev:** Kalima in cartouche **Note:** Listed under Mughal India as KM# 260.16. Weight varies.

Date	Mintage	Good	VG	F	VF	XF
AH1056//1057	—	—	400	650	900	1,450
AH1057	—	—	400	650	900	1,450

'Abd al-'Aziz Khan
AH1057-1091
HAMMERED COINAGE

KM# 19 DANGI (PUL)
4.5000 g., Copper

Date	Mintage	Good	VG	F	VF	XF
ND(1660) No Mint	—	—	—	—	—	—

Balkh

KM# 20.1 TANKA
4.2500 g., Silver

Date	Mintage	Good	VG	F	VF	XF
AH1060	—	—	40.00	70.00	100	165
AH1062	—	—	40.00	70.00	100	165
ND(1680)	—	—	20.00	40.00	65.00	100

Bukhara

KM# 20.2 TANKA
4.2500 g., Silver

Date	Mintage	Good	VG	F	VF	XF
ND(1680)	—	—	20.00	40.00	70.00	110

KM# 20.3 TANKA
4.2500 g., Silver

Date	Mintage	Good	VG	F	VF	XF
AH1058	—	—	17.50	35.00	60.00	100
AH1077	—	—	17.50	35.00	60.00	100
ND(1680)	—	—	12.00	25.00	45.00	70.00

KM# 22 TANKA
4.2500 g., Silver **Countermark:** 'abd al-'aziz bahadur khan **Obv:** Countermarked with name of ruler in crescent moon on earlier issues

Date	Mintage	Good	VG	F	VF	XF
ND(1680)	—	—	50.00	75.00	110	165

Subhan Quli Khan
AH1091-1114
HAMMERED COINAGE

KM# 23 DANGI (PUL)
4.1000 g., Copper

Date	Mintage	Good	VG	F	VF	XF
ND(1685)	—	—	—	—	—	—

Balkh

KM# 25 TANKA
4.2500 g., Silver **Countermark:** "balkh"

Date	Mintage	Good	VG	F	VF	XF
ND(1685)	—	—	45.00	75.00	115	175

KM# 24 TANKA
4.2500 g., Billon **Note:** All specimens lack mint in the dies.

Date	Mintage	Good	VG	F	VF	XF
ND(1685)	—	25.00	50.00	75.00	110	165

SHAYBANID

The Shaybanids, an Uzbek dynasty which ruled from Samarqand and Bukhara, derived their name from a possible genealogical connection to the early Islamic Shaybanid Arabs. Their coinage closely follows Timurid prototypes and retains the silver tanka denomination. The only gold coins produced in sufficient numbers for circulation is only found issued by 'Abd Allah II and 'Abd al-Mu'min. Only those of the former are at all common.

The earliest Shaybanid silver tankas weighted one mithqal, then reckoned as 4.78 grams. From AH913-19/1507-13AD, the tanka was 1/12 heavier and so weighted about 5.15 grams, but the mithqal weight was restored by AH924/1513AD. The mithqal fell gradually during the $10^{th}/16^{th}$ century to about 4.6 grams by the time the Janid dynasty replaced the Shaybanids.

Many of the rulers produced countermarked coins, mostly anonymously and thus not always readily assigned to an individual reign. The only listed countermarks are those which have been attributed to a ruler with any certainty.

The mint names on most Shaybanid coins are prefixed with the expression shirmard, roughly translatable as "lion-hearted." The term is not an epithet for the mint, but rather the name of the currency, just as bih bud had previously been the name of the currency of the Timurid Sultan Husayn.

Types of Shaybanid silver coins are characterized by their obverse and reverse cartouches. However, the listings here will give generic types for each reign, with various mint and date combinations noted.

RULERS

Muhammad Shaybani, AH905-16/1500-10AD
Kuchkunji, AH916-37/1510-31AD
Abu Sa'id, AH937-40/1531-34AD
Abu'l-Ghazi 'Ubayd Allah, AH940-46/1534-39AD
'Abd Allah I, AH946-47/1539-40AD
'Abd al-Latif, AH947-59/1540-52AD
Nawruz Ahmad, AH959-63/1552-56AD
Pir Muhammad I, AH963-68/1556-61AD
Iskandar, AH968-91/1561-83AD
'Abd Allah II, AH991-1006/1583-98AD
'Abd al-Mu'min, AH1006-07/1598AD
Pir Muhammad II, AH1007/1598AD
'Abd al-Amin, AH1007/1598-99AD

LOCAL RULERS

Timur Muhammad, contender at Heart AH918-19/1512-13AD
Yar Muhammad I, at Bukhara ca AH957-59/1550-52AD
Burhan Sayyid, at Bukhara ca AH958-64/1551-57AD
Timur Ahmad, at Tashkent ca AH963-64/1556-57AD
Din Muhammad, at Marw and other places
AH968 and 974-80/1560 and 1566-72AD
Sultan Sa'id, at Samarqand and Andigan ca AH975-80/1567-72AD
Darwish Ahmad, at Balkh and Bukhara ca AH981-87/1573-79AD
Bahadur Khan, perhaps at Bukhara and Tashkent ca AH1000/1592AD
Kildi Muhammad Khan, at Tashkent ca AH1000s/1590s AD
Muhammad Ibrahim, at Balkh AH1008-09/1599-1600AD

KHANATE

Muhammad Ibrahim

Local ruler at Balkh

HAMMERED COINAGE

Balkh

MB# 61 TANKA

4.7000 g., Silver **Note:** Sometimes dated on both sides

Date	Mintage	Good	VG	F	VF	XF
AH1008	—	—	50.00	75.00	110	170
AH1008//1009	—	—	70.00	100	145	215
ND	—	—	25.00	45.00	80.00	125

CEYLON

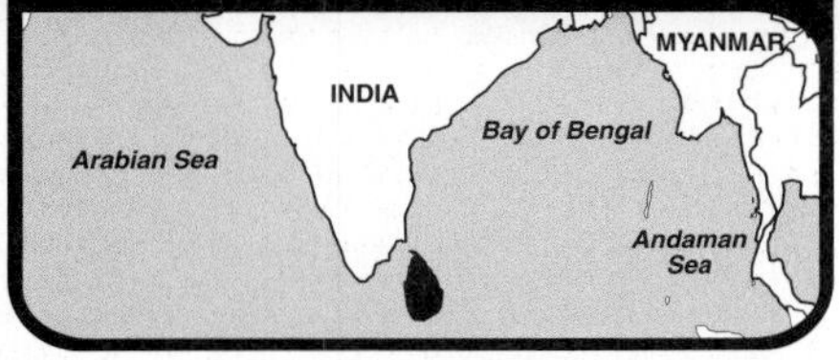

The earliest known inhabitants of Ceylon, the Veddahs, were subjugated by the Sinhalese from northern India in the 6th century B.C. Sinhalese rule was maintained until 1408, after which the island was controlled by China for 30 years. The Portuguese came to Ceylon in 1505 and maintained control of the coastal area for 150 years. The Dutch supplanted them in 1658, which were in turn supplanted by the British who seized the Dutch colonies in 1796, and made them a Crown Colony in 1802.

PORTUGUESE COLONY

Portuguese ships appeared off India in 1498. By 1505 their first governor was installed and was looking forward to settlement and trade expansion, especially the latter. Through his son he made a contact with the king of Ceylon that involved the paying of tribute to the Portuguese.

All of the early trade in Ceylon used local or the home coins of Portugal. The first coins made in Ceylon were not produced until the reign of Philip II, 1598-1621. He claimed Ceylon as a possession even though the kings of Kandy ruled the interior. Coins were made intermittently until 1645. After 1642, however, most of the silver was produced at Goa.

The last Portuguese fortress fell into Dutch hands in 1655.

OCCUPATION COINAGE

KM# 1 1/4 BAZARUCO

1.2000 g., Copper **Obv:** Cross in circle **Rev:** Globe

Date	Mintage	Good	VG	F	VF	XF
ND(1597-1655)	—	37.50	75.00	150	275	—

KM# 2 1/4 BAZARUCO

1.3000 g., Copper **Obv:** Circle in cross **Rev:** Cross - L monogram in circle

Date	Mintage	Good	VG	F	VF	XF
ND(1597-1655)	—	37.50	75.00	150	275	—

KM# 3 1/4 BAZARUCO

1.3000 g., Copper **Rev:** Cross - L monogram retrograde

Date	Mintage	Good	VG	F	VF	XF
ND(1597-1655)	—	37.50	75.00	150	275	—

KM# 4 BAZARUCO

2.7000 g., Copper **Obv:** Crowned arms in circle **Rev:** Globe

Date	Mintage	Good	VG	F	VF	XF
ND(1597-1655)	—	37.50	75.00	150	275	—

KM# 5 BAZARUCO

3.0000 g., Tin **Obv:** Globe **Rev:** Gridiron of St. Lawrence

Date	Mintage	Good	VG	F	VF	XF
ND(1621-40)	—	35.00	70.00	145	250	—

KM# 6 TANGA

2.6600 g., Silver **Obv:** Crowned arms divide D T in circle **Rev:** A over T in circle

Date	Mintage	Good	VG	F	VF	XF
ND(1598-1621)	—	75.00	150	325	500	—

KM# 7 TANGA

2.6400 g., Silver **Obv:** Crowned arms in circle **Rev:** T A monogram in circle

Date	Mintage	Good	VG	F	VF	XF
ND(1598-1621)	—	65.00	125	250	450	—

KM# 8 TANGA

2.6200 g., Silver **Rev:** Gridiron of St. Lawrence in circle

Date	Mintage	Good	VG	F	VF	XF
ND(1598-1621)	—	45.00	95.00	160	285	—

KM# 9.1 TANGA

2.3600 g., Silver **Obv:** Crowned arms **Rev:** Gridiron of St. Lawrence divides S-F

Date	Mintage	Good	VG	F	VF	XF
ND(1621-40)	—	32.00	65.00	100	175	—
1631	—	32.00	65.00	100	175	—

KM# 9.2 TANGA

2.3700 g., Silver **Obv:** Crowned arms divide C Lo, in circle **Rev:** Gridiron of St. Lawrence divides date, crown below

Date	Mintage	Good	VG	F	VF	XF
1640	—	42.00	80.00	160	325	—

KM# 10 TANGA

2.2000 g., Silver **Obv:** Crowned arms divide G A in circle **Rev:** TA monogram divides D S, date below

Date	Mintage	Good	VG	F	VF	XF
1642	—	16.00	32.00	65.00	125	—
1643	—	20.00	37.50	75.00	150	—
1647	—	17.00	35.00	70.00	140	—

KM# 12 TANGA

1.9600 g., Silver **Obv:** Crowned arms divide C Lo in circle

Date	Mintage	Good	VG	F	VF	XF
1644	—	145	270	550	900	—

KM# 11 TANGA

2.1000 g., Silver **Rev:** Gridiron of St. Lawrence divides date, crown below

Date	Mintage	Good	VG	F	VF	XF
1645	—	32.00	65.00	135	250	—
1646	—	32.00	65.00	135	250	—

KM# 13 TANGA

1.9600 g., Silver **Obv:** Crowned arms divide A G

Date	Mintage	Good	VG	F	VF	XF
1646	—	37.50	75.00	150	300	—

KM# 14 2 TANGAS

4.3700 g., Silver **Obv:** Crowned arms divide G A in circle **Rev:** T A monogram divides D S, date below

Date	Mintage	Good	VG	F	VF	XF
1642	—	42.00	80.00	170	325	—
1643	—	25.00	50.00	100	200	—
1644	—	27.50	55.00	110	225	—
1649	—	60.00	120	240	450	—

KM# 15 2 TANGAS

4.3100 g., Silver **Rev:** Gridiron of St. Lawrence divides date, crown below

Date	Mintage	Good	VG	F	VF	XF
1645	—	50.00	100	220	425	—

DUTCH COLONY

The Dutch first sighted Ceylon in 1602. They made a treaty with the king of Kandy for trading rights and the Dutch would have to expel the Portuguese. Between 1638 and 1658 the Dutch had accomplished their purpose. The Portuguese were gone from Ceylon.

As the Dutch trade with Ceylon prospered the coins in use were local coins and countermarked coins of the Portuguese colonies. It was not until sometime after 1660 that the Dutch began striking anonymous copper coins.

In the second third of the 1700's, copper duits of the Netherlands provinces were sent to the East and used widely there. The VOC monogram on these coins became a familiar sight to the merchants of the sub-continent and the East Indies.

Local coinage started again in 1783.

Netherlands United East India Company

MONETARY SYSTEM

4 Duiten = 1 Stuiver
4 Stuivers = 1 Fanam
4-1/2 Stuivers = 1 Shahi
9-1/2 Stuivers = 1 Larin

OCCUPATION COINAGE

KM# 16 1/8 STUIVER

Copper **Obv:** Value in wreath **Rev:** Value in wreath

Date	Mintage	Good	VG	F	VF	XF
ND(1660-1720)	—	30.00	42.00	75.00	125	—

KM# 17 1/4 STUIVER

Copper **Obv:** Value in wreath **Rev:** Value in wreath

Date	Mintage	Good	VG	F	VF	XF
ND(1660-1720)	—	25.00	30.00	60.00	90.00	—

KM# 18.1 1/2 STUIVER

Copper **Obv:** Value in wreath **Rev:** Value in wreath

Date	Mintage	Good	VG	F	VF	XF
ND(1660-1720)	—	15.00	27.50	50.00	80.00	—

KM# 18.2 1/2 STUIVER

Copper **Obv:** Small value in wreath **Rev:** Small value in wreath

Date	Mintage	Good	VG	F	VF	XF
ND(1660-1720)	—	15.00	27.50	50.00	80.00	—

KM# 19.3 STUIVER

Copper **Obv:** Value "1 St" in wreath of small leaves (thorns) **Rev:** Value "1 St" in wreath of small leaves (thorns)

Date	Mintage	Good	VG	F	VF	XF
ND(1660-1720)	—	25.00	42.00	75.00	110	—

KM# 19.2 STUIVER

Copper **Obv:** Value "1 St" in wreath of 2 branches **Rev:** Value "1 St" in wreath of 2 branches

Date	Mintage	Good	VG	F	VF	XF
ND(ca. 1675)	—	27.50	45.00	85.00	120	—

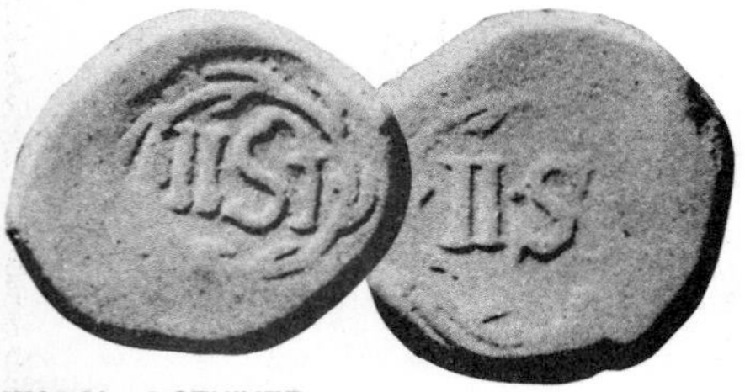

KM# 20 2 STUIVER

Copper **Obv:** Value "11 St" in wreath **Rev:** Value "11 St" in wreath

Date	Mintage	Good	VG	F	VF	XF
ND(1660-1720)	—	16.50	25.00	45.00	75.00	—

BRITISH COMMONWEALTH

COUNTERMARKED COINAGE

Type I

Type II

Type III

KM# 52 TANGA

Silver **Series:** Galle **Countermark:** G/LL **Note:** Type II countermark on Tanga of Colombo.

CM Date	Host Date	Good	VG	F	VF	XF
ND(c.1680)	1631	130	260	450	650	—

KM# 53 TANGA

Silver **Series:** Galle **Countermark:** G/LL **Note:** Type II countermark on Tanga of Malacca.

CM Date	Host Date	Good	VG	F	VF	XF
ND(c.1680)	1631	150	300	500	750	—
ND(c.1680)	1632	150	300	500	750	—

KM# 54 TANGA

Silver **Series:** Galle **Countermark:** G/LL **Note:** Type II countermark on Tanga of Colombo.

CM Date	Host Date	Good	VG	F	VF	XF
ND(c.1680)	1640	130	260	435	650	—

KM# 39 TANGA

Silver **Series:** Colombo **Countermark:** C/VOC **Note:** Type I countermark on India-Portuguese Tanga of Goa.

CM Date	Host Date	Good	VG	F	VF	XF
ND(c.1680)	164x	100	200	350	500	—

KM# 38 TANGA

Silver **Series:** Colombo **Countermark:** C/VOC **Note:** Type I countermark on India-Portuguese Tanga of Goa.

CM Date	Host Date	Good	VG	F	VF	XF
ND(c.1680)	1645	100	160	225	350	—
ND(c.1680)	1649	100	200	350	500	—

KM# 59 2 TANGAS

Silver **Series:** Jaffna **Countermark:** I/VOC **Note:** Type III countermark on India-Portuguese 2 Tangas of Goa.

CM Date	Host Date	Good	VG	F	VF	XF
ND(c.1680)	1640	150	300	500	750	—
ND(c.1680)	1642	150	300	500	750	—
ND(c.1680)	16xx	150	300	500	750	—

KM# 55 2 TANGAS

Silver **Series:** Galle **Countermark:** G/LL **Note:** Type II countermark on India-Portuguese 2 Tangas of Goa.

CM Date	Host Date	Good	VG	F	VF	XF
ND(c.1680)	164x	100	200	275	450	—
ND(c.1680)	1642	100	200	275	450	—

KM# 40 2 TANGAS

Silver **Series:** Colombo **Countermark:** C/VOC **Note:** Type I countermark on India-Portuguese 2 Tangas of Goa, KM#68.

CM Date	Host Date	Good	VG	F	VF	XF
ND(c.1680)	1642	130	260	435	650	—

KM# 60 2 TANGAS

Silver **Series:** Jaffna **Countermark:** I/VOC **Note:** Type III countermark on India-Portuguese 2 Tangas of Goa.

CM Date	Host Date	Good	VG	F	VF	XF
ND(c.1680)	1645	150	300	500	750	—

KM# 41 2 TANGAS

Silver **Series:** Colombo **Countermark:** C/VOC **Note:** Type I countermark on India-Portuguese 2 Tangas of Chaul-Bassein.

CM Date	Host Date	Good	VG	F	VF	XF
ND(c.1680)	1646	150	300	500	750	—

KM# 56 2 TANGAS

Silver **Series:** Galle **Countermark:** G/LL **Note:** Type II countermark on India-Portuguese 2 Tangas of Goa.

CM Date	Host Date	Good	VG	F	VF	XF
ND(c.1680)	1650	100	200	350	500	—
ND(c.1680)	1651	100	200	350	500	—
ND(c.1680)	1652	100	200	350	500	—

KM# 42 2 TANGAS

Silver **Series:** Colombo **Countermark:** C/VOC **Note:** Type I countermark on India-Portuguese 2 Tangas of Diu.

CM Date	Host Date	Good	VG	F	VF	XF
ND(c.1680)	1655	100	200	350	500	—

KM# 43 2 TANGAS

Silver **Series:** Colombo **Countermark:** C/VOC **Note:** Type I countermark on India-Portuguese 2 Tangas of Goa.

CM Date	Host Date	Good	VG	F	VF	XF
ND(c.1680)	1656	100	200	350	500	—

KM# 46 1/2 ABBASI (Mahmudi or 2 Shahis)

3.6900 g., Silver **Countermark:** C/VOC **Note:** Type I countermark on Iranian 1/2 Abbasi of Safi I.

CM Date	Host Date	Good	VG	F	VF	XF
ND(c.1680)	ND(AH1039-52)	42.00	70.00	125	185	—

KM# 47 1/2 ABBASI (Mahmudi or 2 Shahis)

3.6900 g., Silver **Countermark:** C/VOC **Note:** Type I countermark on Iranian 1/2 Abbasi of Abbas II.

CM Date	Host Date	Good	VG	F	VF	XF
ND(c.1680)	ND(AH1052-77)	42.00	70.00	125	185	—

KM# 48 1/2 ABBASI (Mahmudi or 2 Shahis)

3.6900 g., Silver **Countermark:** C/VOC **Note:** Type I countermark on Iranian 1/2 Abbasi of Sulaiman I.

CM Date	Host Date	Good	VG	F	VF	XF
ND(c.1680)	ND(AH1080-92) Date off flan	40.00	70.00	120	180	—
ND(c.1680)	AH1080	40.00	70.00	120	180	—
ND(c.1680)	AH1085	40.00	70.00	120	180	—
ND(c.1680)	AH1086	40.00	70.00	120	180	—
ND(c.1680)	AH1088	40.00	70.00	120	180	—
ND(c.1680)	AH1089	40.00	70.00	120	180	—
ND(c.1680)	AH1091	40.00	70.00	120	180	—
ND(c.1680)	AH1092	40.00	70.00	120	180	—

KM# 49 ABBASI (4 Shahis)

7.3900 g., Silver **Countermark:** C/VOC **Note:** Type I countermark on Iranian Abbasi of Abbas II.

CM Date	Host Date	Good	VG	F	VF	XF
ND(c.1680)	AH1065	50.00	85.00	140	220	—

KM# 50 ABBASI (4 Shahis)

7.3900 g., Silver **Countermark:** C/VOC **Note:** Type I countermark on Iranian Abbasi of Sulaiman I.

CM Date	Host Date	Good	VG	F	VF	XF
ND(c.1680)	AH1078	50.00	85.00	140	220	—
	ND(AH1080-92) //(c.1680) Date off flan	50.00	85.00	140	220	—

KM# 51 LARGE ABBASI (5 Shahis)

9.2300 g., Silver **Countermark:** C/VOC **Note:** Type I countermark on Iranian 5 Shahi of Abbas II.

CM Date	Host Date	Good	VG	F	VF	XF
ND(c.1680)	ND(AH1052-77)	100	160	250	350	—

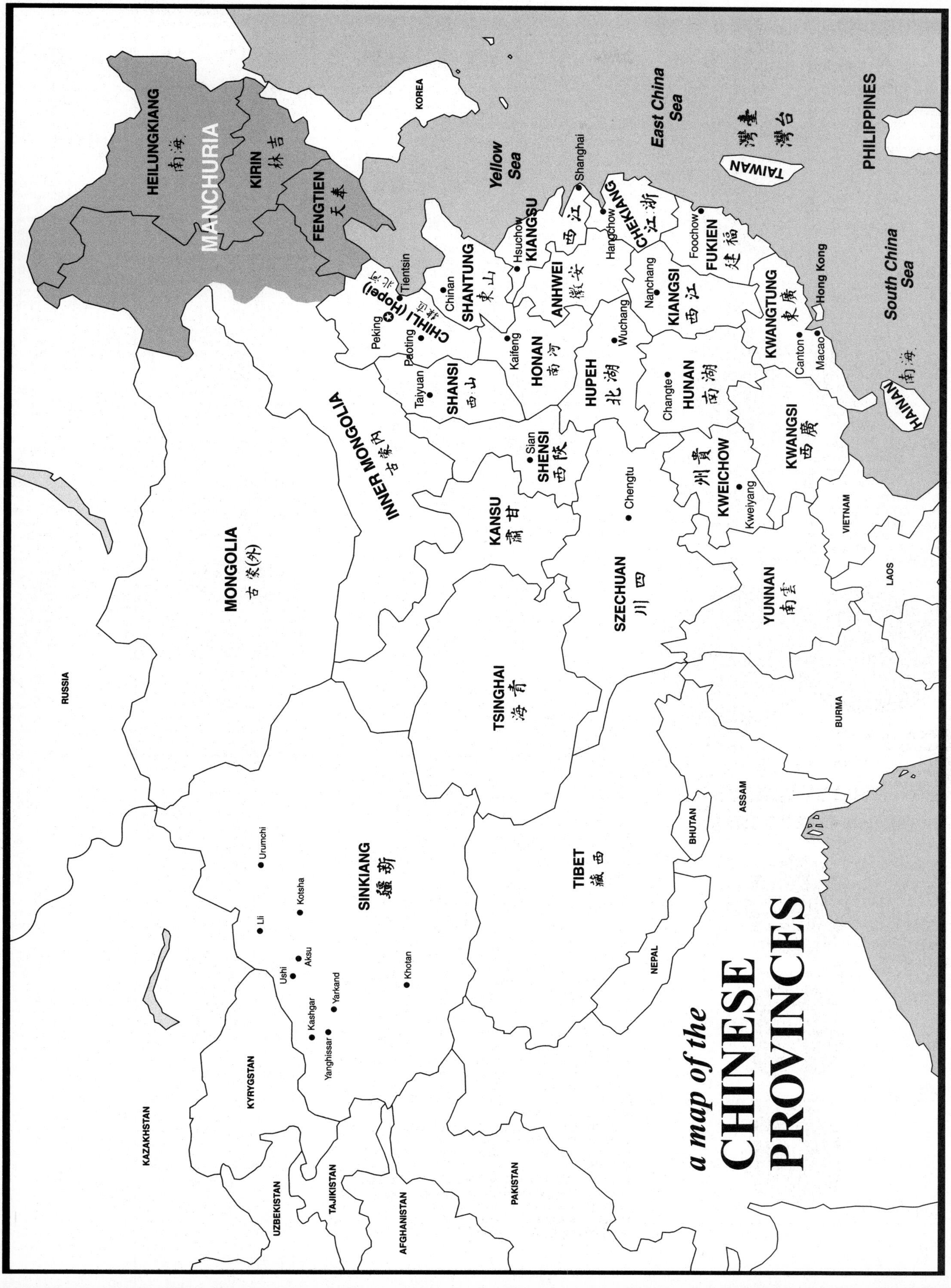
a map of the
CHINESE
PROVINCES
MANCHURIA
HEILUNGKIANG
KIRIN
FENGTIEN
KOREA
Yellow Sea
East China Sea
TAIWAN
PHILIPPINES
South China Sea
HAINAN
Shanghai
CHEKIANG
Hangchow
KIANGSU
Hsuchow
SHANTUNG
Chinan
Tientsin
CHIHLI (Hopei)
Peking
Paoting
ANHWEI
FUKIEN
Foochow
KIANGSI
Nanchang
Hong Kong
KWANGTUNG
Canton
Macao
HONAN
Kaifeng
HUPEH
Wuchang
SHANSI
Taiyuan
HUNAN
Changte
KWANGSI
KWEICHOW
Kweiyang
SHENSI
Sian
INNER MONGOLIA
KANSU
SZECHUAN
Chengtu
YUNNAN
VIETNAM
LAOS
BURMA
MONGOLIA
RUSSIA
TSINGHAI
TIBET
ASSAM
BHUTAN
NEPAL
SINKIANG
Urumchi
Kotsha
Li
Aksu
Ushi
Khotan
Yarkand
Kashgar
Yanghissar
KAZAKHSTAN
KYRYGSTAN
UZBEKISTAN
TAJIKISTAN
AFGHANISTAN
PAKISTAN

EMPIRE

EMPERORS

MING DYNASTY

During the reign of Wan-li (Shen Tsung), the Board of Revenue and Board of Works were ordered to produce the *Wan-li T'ung-pao* cash pieces in 1576AD. The reverses of these cash pieces include: dot, crescent, *Kung* (two types), *Cheng, T'ien, Fen, Li* and muled obverses. Subsequently, due to large scales of war and famine, military authorities, provinces, and private sources minted similar coins in large quantities, including 2, 5, and 10 cash, 1 Fen and 1 Tael pieces. It is interesting to note that even the palace eunuch produced small silver coins during later years of Wan-li.

萬 曆

Wan li (Shen Tsung)
1573-1619AD

萬 曆 通 寶

Wan-li T'ung-pao

泰 昌

T'ai-ch'ang (Kwang Tsung)
1620AD

泰 昌 通 寶

T'ai-ch'ang T'ung-pao

天 啓

T'ien-chi (Hsi Tsung)
1621-1627AD

天 啓 通 寶

T'ien-ch'i T'ung-pao

崇 禎

Ch'ung-chên (Chuang Lieh)
1628-1644AD

崇 禎 通 寶

Ch'ung-chên T'ung-pao

NOTE: The character *chen* is written 禎 or 禎

The minting of the Ch'ung-chên T'ung-pao pieces started in the first year of Ch'ung-chên (1628). There are many varieties in lettering on the obverse. The reverses include: mints, areas, years, worth and events.

MING-CH'ING REBEL ERA

大 明

Ta-ming (Ming Prince of Lu)

大 明 通 寶

Ta-ming T'ung-pao

弘 光 福 王

Hung-kuang (Prince of Fu; Fu King; Fu Wang)

弘 光 通 寶

Hung-kuang T'ung-pao

隆 武 唐 王

Lung-wu (Prince of T'ang, Foochow; T'ang King, T'ang Wang)

隆 武 通 寶

Lung'wu T'ung-pao

永 曆

Yung-li (Prince Yung-ming, 'Chao-ch'ing Fu', Kwangtung)
1647-1662AD

永 曆 通 寶

Yung-li T'ung-pao

永 昌 李 自 成

Yung-ch'ang (Li Tzu-ch'eng 'Hsi-an Fu')
1606-1645AD

永 昌 通 寶

Yung-ch'ang T'ung-pao

大 順 張 獻 忠

Ta-shun (Chang Hsien-chung 'Ch'eng-tu')

大 順 通 寶

Ta-shun T'ung-pao

興 朝 孫 可 望

Hsing-ch'ao (Sun K'o-wang 'Kuei-yang')

興 朝 通 寶

Hsing-chao T'ung-pao

利 用 吳 三 桂

Li-yung (Wu San-kuel)

利 用 通 寶

Li-yung T'ung-pao

昭 武 平 西 王

Chao-wu (P'ing-hsi Wang, Yunnan)

昭 武 通 寶

Chao-wu T'ung-pao

洪 化 吳 世 璠

Hung-hua (Wu Shih-fan)

洪 化 通 寶

Hung-hua T'ung-pao

裕 民 耿 精 忠

Yü-min (Keng Ching-chung)

裕 民 通 寶

Yü-min T'ung-pao

CH'ING DYNASTY

1644-1911AD

天 命

T'ien-ming (T'ai Tsu)
1616-1627AD

天 命 通 寶

T'ien-ming T'ung-pao

順 治

Shun-chih (Shih Tsu)
1644-1661AD (Peking)

順 治 通 寶

Shun-chih T'ung-pao

康 熙

K'ang-hsi (Sheng Tsu)
(Kangxi) 1662-1722AD

康 熙 通 寶

K'ang-hsi T'ung-pao

CHARACTERS

一	I, YI	士	Shih I	心	Hsin
二	Erh	合	Ho	宇	Yu
三	San	工	Kung	宙	Chou
四	Szu	主	Chu	來	Lai
五	Wu	川	Ch'uan	往	Wang
六	Liu	之	Chih	晋	Chin
七	Ch'i	正	Cheng	村	Ts'un
八	Pa	又	Yu	日	Jih
九	Chiu	山	Shan	列	Lieh
十	Shih	大	Ta	仁	Jen
主	Chung	中	Feng	手	Shang
順	Shun	云	Yun	手	Shou
天	T'ien	利	Li	穴	Kung
分	Fen				

SYCEE (INGOTS)

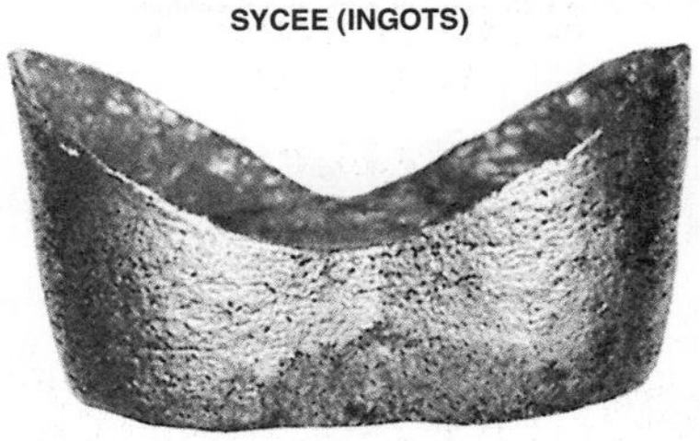

Prior to 1889 the general coinage issued by the Chinese government was the copper-alloy cash coin. Despite occasional short-lived experiments with silver and gold coinage, and disregarding paper money which tended to be unreliable, the government expected the people to get by solely with cash coins. This system worked well for individuals making purchases for themselves, but was unsatisfactory for trade and large business transactions, since a dollar's worth of cash coins weighed about four pounds. As a result, a private currency consisting of silver ingots, usually stamped by the firm which made them, came into use. These were the sycee ingots.

It is not known when these ingots first came into use. Some sources date them to the Yuan (Mongol) dynasty but they are certainly much older. Examples are known from as far back as the Han dynasty (206 BC - 220 AD) but prior to the Sung era (960 - 1280AD) they were used mainly for hoarding wealth. The development of commerce by the Sung dynasty, however, required the use of silver or gold to pay for large purchases. By the Mongol period (1280-1368) silver ingots and paper money had become the dominant currencies, especially for trade. The western explorers who traveled to China during this period (such as Marco Polo) mention both paper money and sycee but not a single one refers to cash coins.

During the Ming dynasty (1368-1644) trade fell off and the use of silver decreased. But toward the end of that dynasty, Dutch and British ships began a new China trade and sycee once again became common

The word sycee (pronounced "sigh - see") is a western corruption of the Chinese word hsi-szu ("fine silk") or hsi yin ("fine silver") and is first known to have appeared in the English language in the late 1600's. By the early 1700's the word appeared regularly in the records of the British East India Company. Westerners also called these ingots "boat money" or "shoe money" owing to the fact that the most common type of ingot resembles a Chinese shoe. The Chinese, however, called the ingots by a variety of names, the most common of which were yuan pao, wen-yin (fine silver) and yin-ting (silver ingot).

The ingots were cast in molds (giving them their characteristic shapes) and while the metal was still semi-liquid, the inscription was impressed. It was due to this procedure that the sides of some sycee are higher than the center. The manufacturers were usually silver firms, often referred to as lu fang's, and after the sycee was finished it was occasionally tested and marked by the kung ku (public assayer).

Sycee were not circulated as we understand it. One didn't usually carry a sycee to market and spend it. Usually the ingots were used as a means of carrying a large amount of money on trips (as we would carry $100 bills instead of $5 bills) or for storing wealth. Large transactions between merchants or banks were paid by means of crates of sycee - each containing 60 fifty tael ingots.

Sycee are known in a variety of shapes the most common of which are the shoe or boat shaped, drum shaped, and loaf shaped (rectangular or hourglass-shaped, with a generally flat surface). Other shapes include one that resembles a double headed axe (this is the oldest type known), one that is square and flat, and others that are "fancy" (in the form of fish, butterflies, leaves, etc.).

Sycee have no denominations as they were simply ingots that passed by weight. Most are in more or less standard weights, however, the most common being 1, 5, 10 and 50 taels. Other weights known include 1/10, 1/5, 1/4, 1/3, 1/2, 2/3, 72/100 (this is the weight of a dollar), 3/4, 2, 3, 4, 6, 7, 8 and 25 taels. Most of the pieces weighing less than 5 taels were used as gifts or souvenirs.

The actual weight of any given value of sycee varied considerably due to the fact that the tael was not a single weight but a general term for a wide range of local weight standards. The weight of the tael varied depending upon location and type of tael in question. For example in one town, the weight of a tael of rice, of silver and of stones may each be different. In addition, the fineness of silver also varied depending upon location and type of tael in question. It was not true, as westerners often wrote, that sycee were made of pure silver. For most purposes, a weight of 37 grams may be used for the tael.

Weights and Current Market Value of Sycee (Weights are approximate)

1/2 Tael	17-19 grams	26.00
72/100 Tael	25-27 grams	36.00
1 Tael	35-38 grams	46.00
2 Taels	70-75 grams	70.00
3 Taels	100-140 grams	85.00
5 Taels	175-190 grams	110.00
7 Taels	240-260 grams	125.00
10 Taels	350-380 grams	250.00
25 Taels	895-925 grams	3500.
50 Taels	1790-1850 grams	2000.
50 Taels, square	1790-1850 grams	1600.

REFERENCE

Catalog reference Schjöth #: *Chinese Currency* by Fredrik Schjöth ©1965 by Virgil Hancock, published by Krause Publications, Iola, Wisconsin, U.S.A.

MING DYNASTY
1368 - 1644

Wan-li
Wanli, Shen Tsung

CAST COINAGE

KM# 1.1 CASH

Cast Bronze **Obv. Inscription:** "Wan-li T'ung-pao" **Rev:** Plain **Mint:** Hu-pu Board of Revenue **Note:** Size varies: 24-26mm. Schjöth #1185.

Date	Mintage	Good	VG	F	VF	XF
ND(1573-1619)	—	1.00	2.00	3.00	4.50	—

Note: Previously listed KM#1.1a with a diameter of 87mm is a special issue not intended for circulation

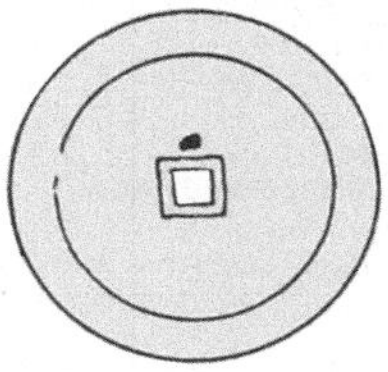

KM# 1.2 CASH

Cast Bronze **Obv. Inscription:** "Wan-li T'ung-pao" **Rev:** Small dot above **Mint:** Hu-pu Board of Revenue **Note:** Size varies: 24-26mm. Schjöth #1186.

Date	Mintage	Good	VG	F	VF	XF
ND(1573-1619)	—	4.50	7.50	11.00	15.00	—

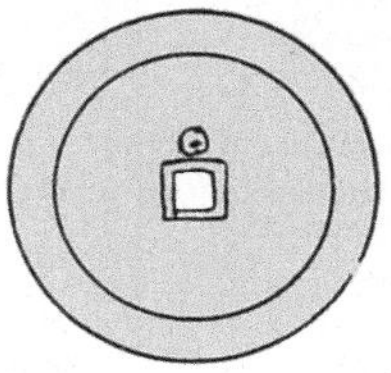

KM# 1.3 CASH

Cast Bronze **Obv. Inscription:** "Wan-li T'ung-pao" **Rev:** Small circle above **Mint:** Hu-pu Board of Revenue **Note:** Size varies: 24-26mm. Schjöth #1187.

Date	Mintage	Good	VG	F	VF	XF
ND(1573-1619)	—	15.00	25.00	35.00	50.00	—

KM# 1.4 CASH

Cast Bronze **Obv. Inscription:** "Wan-li T'ung-pao" **Rev:** Crescent above **Mint:** Hu-pu Board of Revenue **Note:** Size varies: 24-26mm.

Date	Mintage	Good	VG	F	VF	XF
ND(1573-1619)	—	25.00	35.00	50.00	72.50	—

KM# 1.5 CASH

Cast Bronze **Obv. Inscription:** Wan-li T'ung-pao **Rev:** Crescent with dot above **Mint:** Hu-pu Board of Revenue **Note:** Size varies: 24-26mm.

Date	Mintage	Good	VG	F	VF	XF
ND(1573-1619)	—	50.00	70.00	100	140	—

KM# 2.1 CASH

Cast Bronze **Obv. Inscription:** "Wan-li T'ung-pao" **Rev:** Small "Kung" above **Mint:** Kung-pu Board of Public Works **Note:** Size varies: 24-26mm. Schjöth #1188.

Date	Mintage	Good	VG	F	VF	XF
ND(1573-1619)	—	15.00	25.00	35.00	50.00	—

KM# 2.2 CASH

Cast Bronze **Obv. Inscription:** "Wan-li T'ung-pao" **Rev:** Large "Kung" above **Mint:** Kung-pu Board of Public Works **Note:** Size varies: 24-26mm.

Date	Mintage	Good	VG	F	VF	XF
ND(1573-1619)	—	15.00	25.00	35.00	—	—

KM# 2.3 CASH

Cast Bronze **Obv. Inscription:** Wan-li T'ung-pao **Rev:** "Kung" sideways at left. **Mint:** Kung-pu Board of Public Works **Note:** Size varies: 24-26mm.

Date	Mintage	Good	VG	F	VF	XF
ND(1573-1619)	—	25.00	35.00	50.00	72.50	—

KM# 2.4 CASH

Cast Bronze, 24-26 mm. **Obv. Inscription:** Wan-li T'ung-pao **Rev:** Inverted "Kung" at bottom **Mint:** Kung-pu Board of Public Works **Note:** Size varies.

Date	Mintage	Good	VG	F	VF	XF
ND(1573-1619)	—	10.00	15.00	21.50	30.00	—

KM# 3.1 CASH

Cast Bronze, 24-26 mm. **Obv. Inscription:** "Wan-li T'ung-pao" **Rev:** Small "Kung" above **Mint:** Kung-pu Board of Public Works **Note:** Size varies. Schjöth #1189.

Date	Mintage	Good	VG	F	VF	XF
ND(1573-1619)	—	8.50	12.50	17.50	25.00	—

KM# 3.2 CASH

Cast Bronze, 24-26 mm. **Obv. Inscription:** Wan-li T'ung-pao **Rev:** Medium "Kung" above **Mint:** Kung-pu Board of Public Works **Note:** Size varies.

Date	Mintage	Good	VG	F	VF	XF
ND(1573-1619)	—	7.00	10.00	15.00	20.00	—

KM# 3.3 CASH

Cast Bronze, 24-26 mm. **Obv. Inscription:** Wan-li T'ung-pao **Rev:** Large "Kung" above **Mint:** Kung-pu Board of Public Works **Note:** Size varies.

Date	Mintage	Good	VG	F	VF	XF
ND(1573-1619)	—	14.00	20.00	30.00	42.50	—

KM# A4 CASH

Cast Bronze, 24-26 mm. **Obv. Inscription:** "Wan-li T'ung-pao" **Rev:** "Ho" sideways above crescent at lower left **Note:** Prev. KM#4.1 Size varies.

Date	Mintage	Good	VG	F	VF	XF
ND(1573-1619)	—	175	250	350	500	—

KM# 4.1 CASH

Cast Bronze, 24-26 mm. **Obv. Inscription:** Wan-li T'ung-pao **Rev:** Small "T'ien" above **Note:** Size varies.

Date	Mintage	Good	VG	F	VF	XF
ND(1573-1619)	—	10.00	14.00	20.00	30.00	—

KM# 4.2 CASH

Cast Bronze, 24-26 mm. **Obv. Inscription:** "Wan-li T'ung-pao" **Rev:** Large "T'ien" above **Note:** Size varies.

Date	Mintage	Good	VG	F	VF	XF
ND(1573-1619)	—	8.50	12.50	17.50	25.00	—

KM# 5.1 CASH

Cast Bronze, 24-26 mm. **Obv. Inscription:** "Wan-li T'ung-pao" **Rev:** Small "Chêng" above **Note:** Size varies. Prev. KM#5.

Date	Mintage	Good	VG	F	VF	XF
ND(1573-1619)	—	37.50	55.00	90.00	130	—

KM# 5.2 CASH

Cast Bronze, 24-26 mm. **Obv. Inscription:** Wan-li T'ung-pao **Rev:** Large "Chêng" above **Mint:** Kung-pu Board of Public Works **Note:** Size varies.

Date	Mintage	Good	VG	F	VF	XF
ND(1573-1619)	—	35.00	50.00	70.00	100	—

KM# 6 CASH

Cast Bronze, 20-22 mm. **Obv. Inscription:** "Wan-li T'ung-pao" **Rev:** Plain **Note:** Reduced size. Size varies. Schjöth #1190.

Date	Mintage	Good	VG	F	VF	XF
ND(1573-1619)	—	1.00	2.00	3.00	4.00	—

厘 

KM# 7.1 CASH

Cast Bronze **Obv. Inscription:** "Wan-li T'ung-pao" **Rev:** "Li" at right **Note:** Schjöth #1191. "Li" = 1/1000 of a Tael. Prev. KM#7.

Date	Mintage	Good	VG	F	VF	XF
ND(1573-1619)	—	15.00	25.00	35.00	—	—

KM# 7.2 CASH

Cast Bronze **Obv. Inscription:** Wan-li T'ung-pao **Rev:** "Li" at right, "Erh" sideways at left

Date	Mintage	Good	VG	F	VF	XF
ND(1573-1619)	—	70.00	100	150	225	—

KM# 8 CASH

Cast Bronze, 24-26 mm. **Obv. Inscription:** "Wan-li T'ung-pao" **Rev:** "Li" and "Ts'ai" **Note:** Size varies.

Date	Mintage	Good	VG	F	VF	XF
ND(1573-1619)	—	12.00	20.00	—	—	—

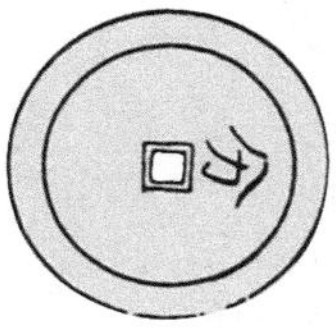

KM# 9 CASH

Cast Bronze, 24-26 mm. **Obv. Inscription:** "Wan-li T'ung-pao" **Rev:** "Fen" sideways at right **Note:** Size varies. Schjöth #1192.

Date	Mintage	Good	VG	F	VF	XF
ND(1573-1619)	—	6.00	8.50	12.50	18.50	—

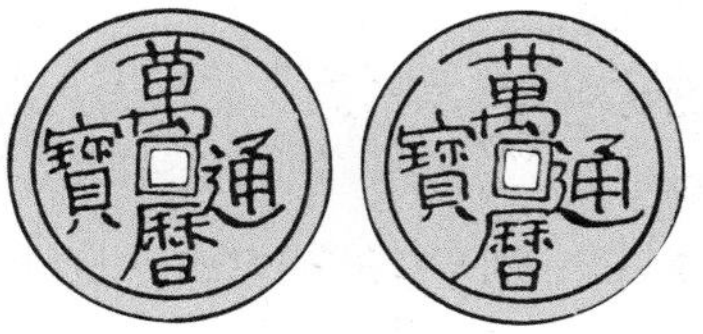

KM# 10 CASH

Cast Bronze, 24-26 mm. **Obv. Inscription:** "Wan-li T'ung-pao" **Note:** Schjöth #1198. Muled obverses, (error). Size varies.

Date	Mintage	Good	VG	F	VF	XF
ND(1573-1619)	—	15.00	25.00	35.00	50.00	—

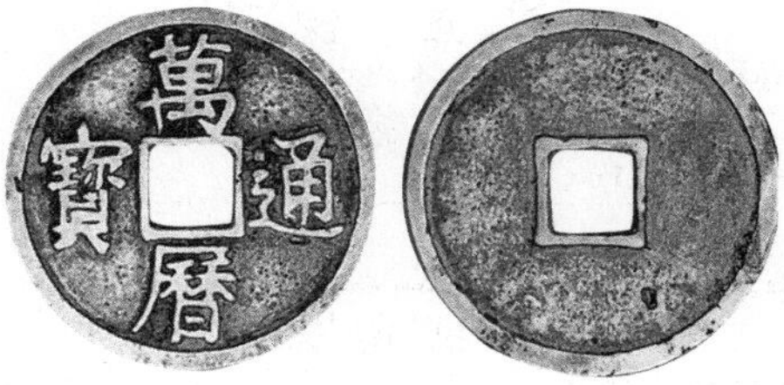

KM# 13.1 2 CASH

Cast Bronze, 27-29 mm. **Obv. Inscription:** "Wan-li T'ung-pao" **Rev:** Plain **Note:** Size varies. Schjöth #1193.

Date	Mintage	Good	VG	F	VF	XF
ND(1573-1619)	—	10.00	17.50	25.00	37.50	—

KM# 13.2 2 CASH

Cast Bronze, 27-29 mm. **Obv. Inscription:** "Wan-li T'ung-pao" **Rev:** Dot in crescent above **Note:** Size varies.

Date	Mintage	Good	VG	F	VF	XF
ND(1573-1619)	—	20.00	30.00	45.00	62.50	—

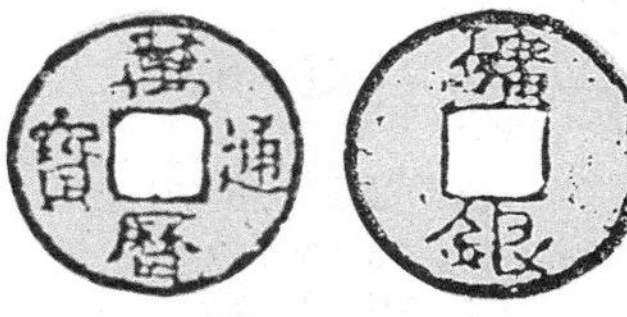

KM# 14 MACE

Cast Silver, 20 mm. **Obv. Inscription:** "Wan-li T'ung-pao" **Rev:** "K'uang-yin" **Note:** Prev. KM#A13.

Date	Mintage	Good	VG	F	VF	XF
ND(1573-1619)	—	275	385	550	800	—

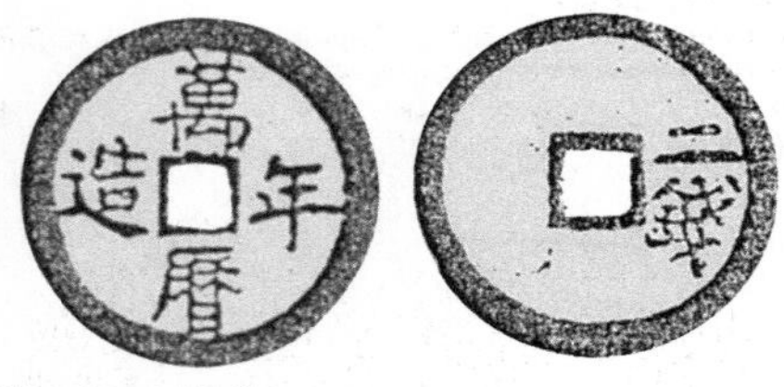

KM# 15 2 MACE
Cast Silver, 26 mm. **Obv. Inscription:** "Wan-li Nien-tsao" **Rev:** "Erh (2) Mace" at right **Note:** Prev. KM#14.

Date	Mintage	Good	VG	F	VF	XF
ND(1573-1619)	—	1,400	2,000	3,500	5,000	—

KM# 16 4 MACE
Cast Silver, 31 mm. **Obv. Inscription:** "Wan-li T'ung-pao" **Rev. Inscription:** "K'uang-yin Szu (4)-Mace"

Date	Mintage	Good	VG	F	VF	XF
ND(1573-1619)	—	4,000	6,000	8,500	12,500	—

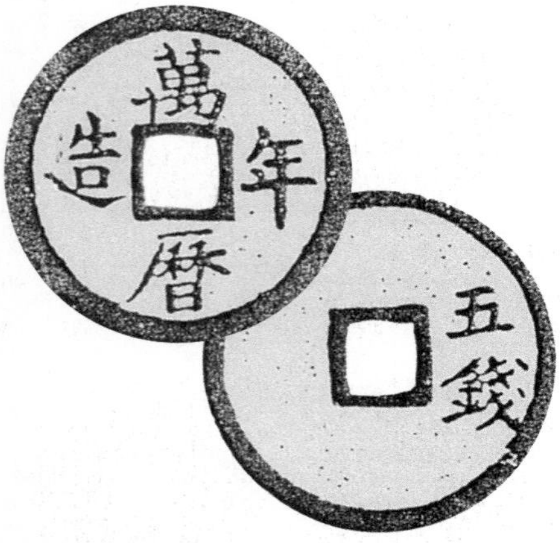

KM# 17 5 MACE
Cast Silver, 37 mm. **Obv. Inscription:** "Wan-li Nien-tsao" **Rev:** Wu (5) Mace at right

Date	Mintage	Good	VG	F	VF	XF
ND(1573-1619)	—	6,000	8,500	12,500	18,000	—

T'ai-ch'ang
Kwang Tsung
CAST COINAGE

KM# 20.1 CASH
Cast Copper **Obv. Inscription:** "Tai-ch'ang T'ung-pao" **Rev:** Plain **Note:** Schjöth #1199.

Date	Mintage	Good	VG	F	VF	XF
ND(1620)	—	6.00	10.00	15.00	22.50	—

KM# 20.x CASH
Cast Copper **Obv:** Lower part of T'ai composed differently: hsin instead of shui **Note:** The "hsin-tai" is getting close to too rare to list.

Date	Mintage	Good	VG	F	VF	XF
ND(1620)	—	—	130	190	250	—

KM# 20.2 CASH
Cast Copper **Obv. Inscription:** "Tai-ch'ang T'ung-pao" **Rev:** Dot above **Note:** Schjöth #1200.

Date	Mintage	Good	VG	F	VF	XF
ND(1620)	—	8.00	14.00	20.00	28.50	—

KM# 20.3 CASH
Cast Copper **Obv. Inscription:** "Tai-ch'ang T'ung-pao" **Rev:** Crescent above

Date	Mintage	Good	VG	F	VF	XF
ND(1620)	—	15.00	25.00	35.00	50.00	—

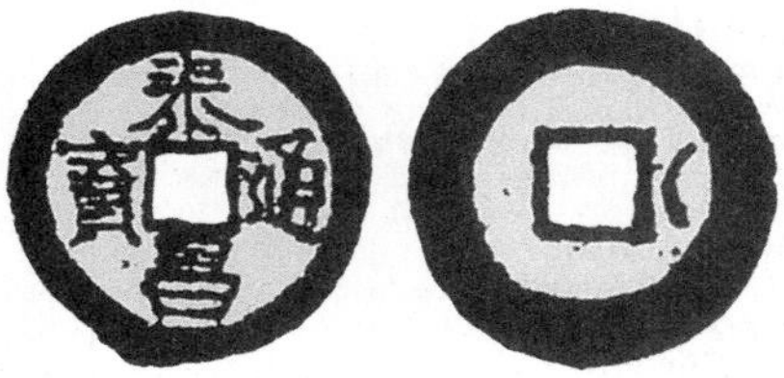

KM# 20.4 CASH
Cast Copper **Obv. Inscription:** "Tai-ch'ang T'ung-pao" **Rev:** Crescent at right

Date	Mintage	Good	VG	F	VF	XF
ND(1620)	—	15.00	25.00	35.00	50.00	—

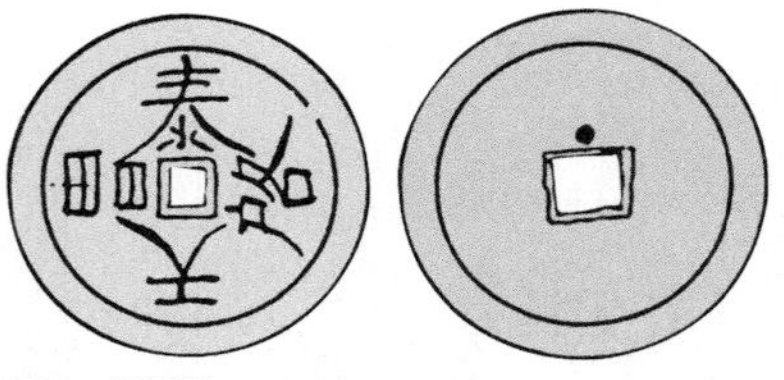

KM# 21 CASH
Cast Copper **Obv. Inscription:** "Tai-ch'ang T'ien-ch'i" **Rev:** Dot above **Note:** Schjöth #1201.

Date	Mintage	Good	VG	F	VF	XF
ND(1620)	—	25.00	40.00	60.00	85.00	—

T'ien-ch'i
Tianqi, Hsi Tsung
CAST COINAGE

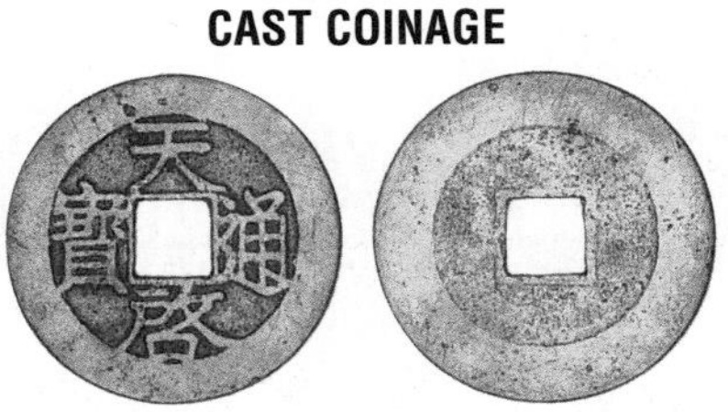

KM# 25.1 CASH
Cast Bronze **Obv. Inscription:** "T'ien-ch'i T'ung-pao" **Rev:** Plain **Note:** Schjöth #1202.

Date	Mintage	Good	VG	F	VF	XF
ND(1621-27)	—	2.25	3.75	5.50	7.50	—

KM# 25.2 CASH
Cast Bronze **Obv. Inscription:** "T'ien-ch'i T'ung-pao" **Rev:** Crescent below **Note:** Schjöth #1203.

Date	Mintage	Good	VG	F	VF	XF
ND(1621-27)	—	2.25	3.75	5.50	7.50	—

KM# 25.3 CASH
Cast Bronze **Obv. Inscription:** "T'ien-ch'i T'ung-pao" **Rev:** Dot above

Date	Mintage	Good	VG	F	VF	XF
ND(1621-27)	—	2.25	3.75	5.50	7.50	—

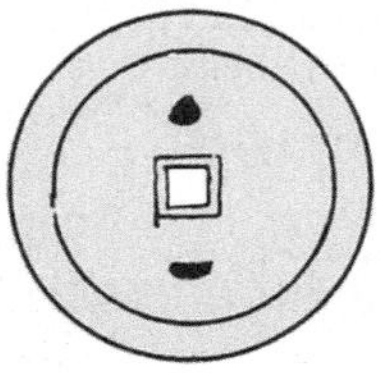

KM# 25.4 CASH
Cast Bronze **Obv. Inscription:** "T'ien-ch'i T'ung-pao" **Rev:** Dot above, crescent below **Note:** Schjöth #1204.

Date	Mintage	Good	VG	F	VF	XF
ND(1621-27)	—	6.00	10.00	15.00	20.00	—

KM# 25.5 CASH
Cast Bronze **Obv. Inscription:** "T'ien-ch'i T'ung-pao" **Rev:** Dot below **Note:** Schjöth #1205.

Date	Mintage	Good	VG	F	VF	XF
ND(1621-27)	—	2.25	3.75	5.50	7.50	—

KM# 25.6 CASH
Cast Bronze **Obv. Inscription:** "T'ien-ch'i T'ung-pao" **Rev:** Dot at right

Date	Mintage	Good	VG	F	VF	XF
ND(1621-27)	—	3.00	5.00	7.50	10.00	—

KM# 25.7 CASH
Cast Bronze **Obv. Inscription:** "T'ien-ch'i T'ung-pao" **Rev:** Circle at right **Note:** Schjöth #1206.

Date	Mintage	Good	VG	F	VF	XF
ND(1621-27)	—	2.25	3.75	5.50	7.50	—

KM# 26 CASH
Cast Bronze **Obv. Inscription:** "T'ien-ch'i T'ung-pao" **Rev:** "Hu" above **Mint:** Hu-pu Board of Revenue **Note:** Schjöth #1207-08.

Date	Mintage	Good	VG	F	VF	XF
ND(1621-27)	—	3.00	5.00	7.50	10.00	—

KM# 27 CASH
Cast Bronze **Obv. Inscription:** "T'ien-ch'i T'ung-pao" **Rev:** "Kung" above **Mint:** Kung-pu Board of Public Works **Note:** Schjöth #1209.

Date	Mintage	Good	VG	F	VF	XF
ND(1621-27)	—	3.00	5.00	7.50	10.00	—

Note: See also Sch.#1210

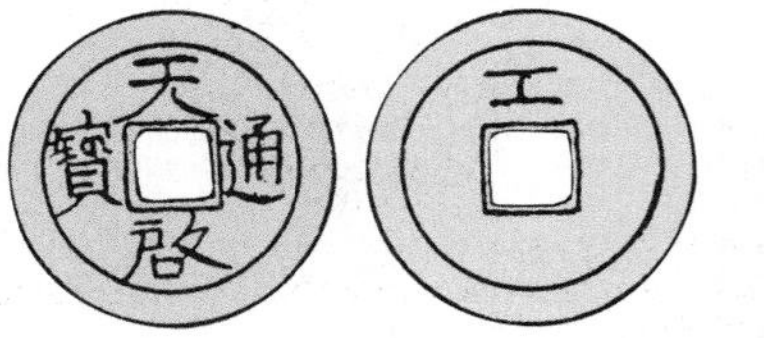

KM# 30.1 CASH
Cast Bronze, 21-23 mm. **Obv. Inscription:** "T'ien-ch'i T'ung-

pao" **Rev:** "Kung" above **Mint:** Kung-pu Board of Public Works **Note:** Schjöth #1210. Reduced size.

Date	Mintage	Good	VG	F	VF	XF
ND(1621-27)	—	3.00	5.00	7.50	10.00	—

Note: See also Sch.#1209

KM# 30.2 CASH
Cast Bronze **Obv. Inscription:** "T'ien-ch'i T'ung-pao" **Rev:** "Kung" below **Mint:** Kung-pu Board of Public Works **Note:** Schjöth #1211.

Date	Mintage	Good	VG	F	VF	XF
ND(1621-27)	—	3.00	5.00	7.50	12.50	—

新

一分

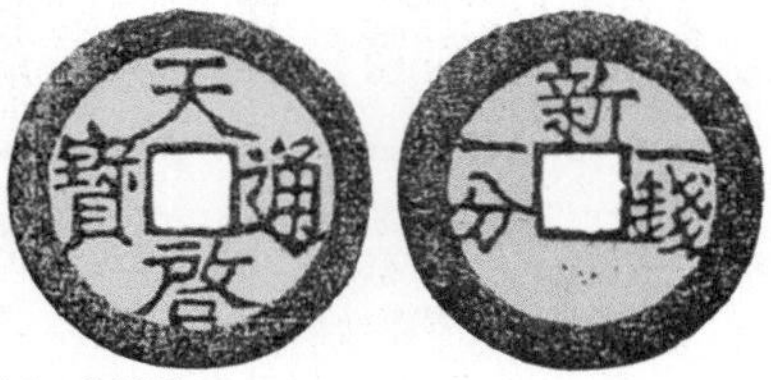

KM# 31.1 CASH
Cast Bronze **Obv. Inscription:** "T'ien-ch'i T'ung-pao" **Rev:** "Kung" below **Rev. Legend:** "Hsin yi-ch'ien yi-fen" **Mint:** Kung-pu Board of Public Works **Note:** Schjöth #1212.

Date	Mintage	Good	VG	F	VF	XF
ND(1621-27)	—	25.00	42.50	60.00	80.00	—

京

KM# 31.2 CASH
Cast Bronze **Obv. Inscription:** "T'ien-ch'i T'ung-pao" **Rev:** "Ching" above **Mint:** Ching

Date	Mintage	Good	VG	F	VF	XF
ND(1621-27)	—	40.00	70.00	150	225	—

密

KM# 31.3 CASH
Cast Bronze **Obv. Inscription:** "T'ien-ch'i T'ung-pao" **Rev:** "Mi" above **Mint:** Miyün

Date	Mintage	Good	VG	F	VF	XF
ND(1621-27)	—	30.00	50.00	100	140	—

新

KM# 31.4 CASH
Cast Bronze **Obv. Inscription:** "T'ien-ch'i T'ung-pao" **Rev:** "Hsin" above

Date	Mintage	Good	VG	F	VF	XF
ND(1621-27)	—	—	—	—	—	—

上日

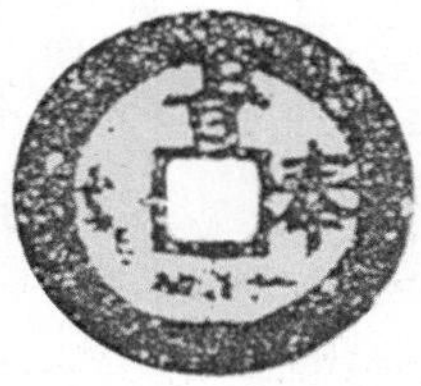

KM# 31.5 CASH
Cast Bronze **Obv. Inscription:** "T'ien-ch'i T'ung-pao" **Rev:** "Chih" above and "Feng" right

Date	Mintage	Good	VG	F	VF	XF
ND(1621-27)	—	—	—	—	—	—

錢

KM# 31.6 CASH
Cast Bronze **Obv. Inscription:** "T'ien-ch'i T'ung-pao" **Rev:** "Ch'ien" left and "Yi" right

Date	Mintage	Good	VG	F	VF	XF
ND(1621-27)	—	25.00	45.00	75.00	—	—

一錢

KM# 31.7 CASH
Cast Bronze **Obv. Inscription:** "T'ien-ch'i T'ung-pao" **Rev:** "Yi Ch'ien" right

Date	Mintage	Good	VG	F	VF	XF
ND(1621-27)	—	20.00	40.00	75.00	—	—

禾

KM# 31.8 CASH
Cast Bronze **Obv. Inscription:** "T'ien-ch'i T'ung-pao" **Rev:** "Yi" above "Ch'ien" below

Date	Mintage	Good	VG	F	VF	XF
ND(1621-27)	—	—	—	—	—	—

一禾

KM# 31.9 CASH
Cast Bronze **Obv. Inscription:** "T'ien-ch'i T'ung-pao" **Rev:** "Yi Ch'ien" left

Date	Mintage	Good	VG	F	VF	XF
ND(1621-27)	—	—	—	—	—	—

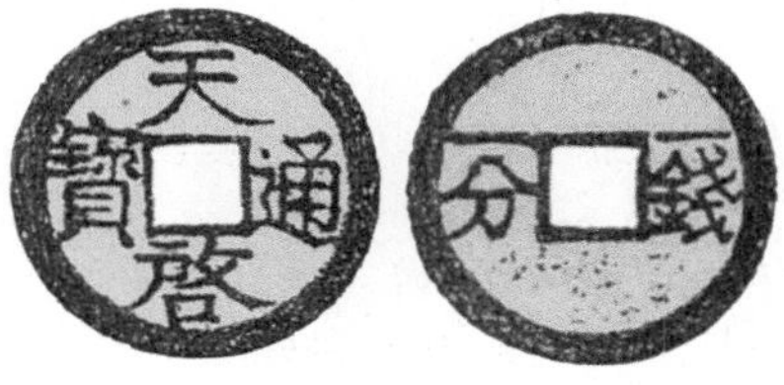

一分 一錢

KM# 31.10 CASH
Cast Bronze **Obv. Inscription:** "T'ien-ch'i T'ung-pao" **Rev:** "Yi Fen" left, "Yi Ch'ien" right

Date	Mintage	Good	VG	F	VF	XF
ND(1621-27)	—	25.00	45.00	75.00	110	—

二分 一錢

KM# 31.11 CASH
Cast Bronze **Obv. Inscription:** "T'ien-ch'i T'ung-pao" **Rev:** "Erh Fen" left, "Yi Ch'ien" right

Date	Mintage	Good	VG	F	VF	XF
ND(1621-27)	—	25.00	45.00	75.00	110	—

KM# 35 CASH
Cast Bronze **Obv. Inscription:** "T'ien-ch'i T'ung-pao" **Rev:** "Chê" above **Mint:** Chêkiang **Note:** Schjöth #1213.

Date	Mintage	Good	VG	F	VF	XF
ND(1621-27)	—	10.00	15.00	22.50	30.00	—

Note: Also see Sch.#1213A

KM# 36 CASH
Cast Bronze **Obv. Inscription:** "T'ien-ch'i T'ung-pao" **Rev:** "Yün" above **Mint:** Yünnan Fu **Note:** Schjöth #1214.

Date	Mintage	Good	VG	F	VF	XF
ND(1621-27)	—	4.50	7.50	11.00	15.00	—

KM# 36A CASH
Cast Bronze **Obv. Inscription:** "T'ien-ch'i T'ung-pao" **Rev:** "Yün" above **Mint:** Yünnan Fu **Note:** Schjöth #1214A.

Date	Mintage	Good	VG	F	VF	XF
ND(1621-27)	—	—	—	—	—	—

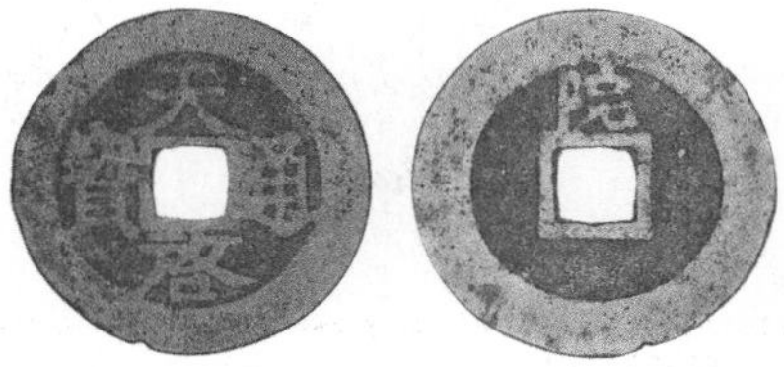

KM# 37.1 CASH
Cast Bronze **Obv. Inscription:** "T'ien-ch'i T'ung-pao" **Rev:** Narrow (5mm) "Yüan" above **Note:** Schjöth #1215.

Date	Mintage	Good	VG	F	VF	XF
ND(1621-27)	—	10.00	17.50	25.00	35.00	—

KM# 37.2 CASH
Cast Bronze **Obv. Inscription:** "T'ien-ch'i T'ung-pao" **Rev:** Wide (7mm) "Yüan" above **Note:** Schjöth #1215.

Date	Mintage	Good	VG	F	VF	XF
ND(1621-27)	—	10.00	17.50	25.00	35.00	—

KM# 25.8 CASH
Cast Bronze **Obv. Inscription:** T'ien-Ch'i T'ung-pao **Rev:** Circle at right, crescnet below

Date	Mintage	Good	VG	F	VF	XF
ND(1621-27)	—	2.25	3.75	5.50	7.50	—

KM# 32 CASH
Bronze, 23 mm. **Obv. Inscription:** T'ien-ch'i T'ung-pao **Rev. Inscription:** Yi Ch'ien

Date	Mintage	Good	VG	F	VF	XF
ND(1621-27)	—	3.00	7.00	12.00	26.00	—

一夊

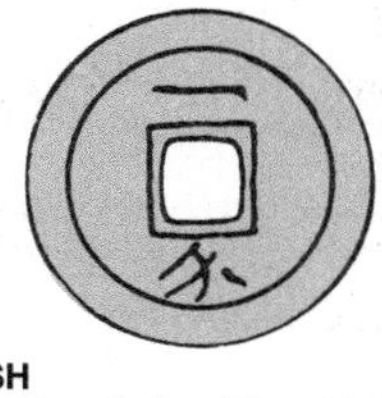

KM# 38 CASH
Cast Bronze **Obv. Inscription:** "T'ien-ch'i T'ung-pao" **Rev:** "Yi Ch'ien" (1 Cash) **Note:** Schjöth #1216.

Date	Mintage	Good	VG	F	VF	XF
ND(1621-27)	—	13.00	21.00	30.00	40.00	—

KM# 39 CASH
Cast Bronze **Obv. Inscription:** "T'ien-ch'i T'ung-pao" **Rev:** "Chên" above

Date	Mintage	Good	VG	F	VF	XF
ND(1621-27)	—	25.00	42.50	60.00	85.00	—

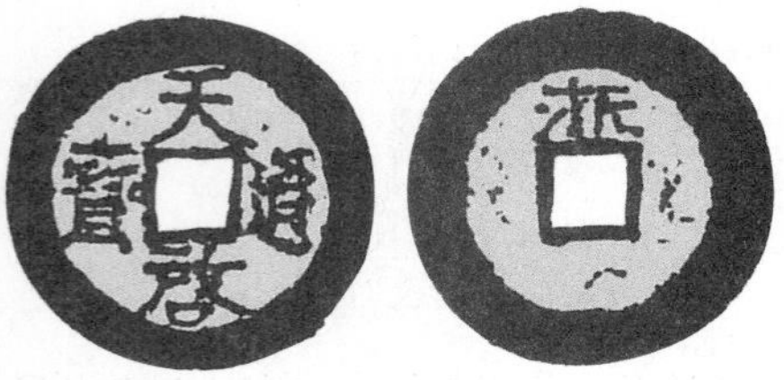

KM# 28 2 CASH
Cast Bronze **Obv. Inscription:** "T'ien-ch'i T'ung-pao" **Rev:** "Chê" above **Mint:** Chê **Note:** Schjöth #1213A.

Date	Mintage	Good	VG	F	VF	XF
ND(1621-27) Rare	—	—	—	—	—	—

Note: See also Schjöth #1213

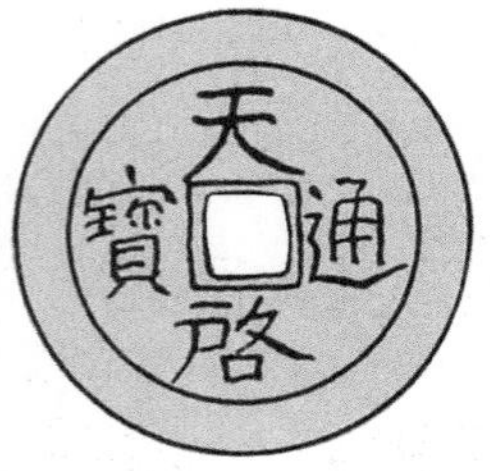

KM# 41 2 CASH
Cast Bronze, 30-32 mm. **Obv. Inscription:** "T'ien-ch'i T'ung-pao" **Rev:** Blank without rim **Note:** Schjöth #1217. Size varies.

Date	Mintage	Good	VG	F	VF	XF
ND(1621-27)	—	7.50	10.00	15.00	20.00	—

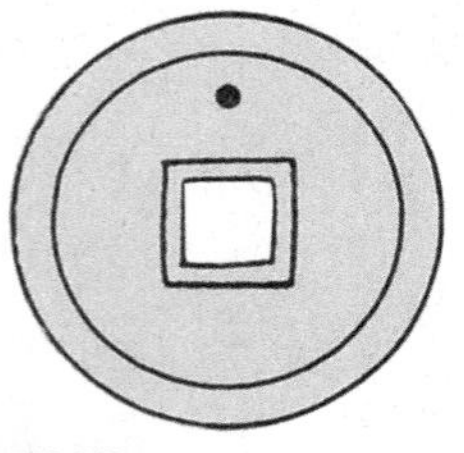

KM# 42.1 2 CASH
Cast Bronze **Obv. Inscription:** "T'ien-ch'i T'ung-pao" **Rev:** Dot above **Note:** Schjöth #1218.

Date	Mintage	Good	VG	F	VF	XF
ND(1621-27)	—	10.00	15.00	20.00	30.00	—

KM# 42.2 2 CASH
Cast Bronze **Obv. Inscription:** "T'ien-ch'i T'ung-pao" **Rev:** Dot below

Date	Mintage	Good	VG	F	VF	XF
ND(1621-27)	—	10.00	15.00	20.00	30.00	—

KM# 42.3 2 CASH
Cast Bronze **Obv. Inscription:** "T'ien-ch'i T'ung-pao" **Rev:** Dot right

Date	Mintage	Good	VG	F	VF	XF
ND(1621-27)	—	10.00	15.00	20.00	30.00	—

KM# A43 2 CASH
Cast Bronze **Obv. Inscription:** "T'ien-ch'i T'ung-pao" **Note:** Muled obverses, error. Schjöth #1219.

Date	Mintage	Good	VG	F	VF	XF
ND(1621-27)	—	—	—	—	—	—

KM# 43 2 CASH
Cast Bronze **Obv. Inscription:** "T'ien-ch'i T'ung-pao" **Rev:** "Erh" (two) above, dot below

Date	Mintage	Good	VG	F	VF	XF
ND(1621-27)	—	25.00	45.00	85.00	—	—

KM# 45 10 CASH
Cast Brass **Obv. Inscription:** "T'ien-ch'i T'ung-pao" **Rev:** Plain **Note:** Schjöth #1220.

Date	Mintage	Good	VG	F	VF	XF
ND(1621-27)	—	10.00	15.00	25.00	40.00	—

KM# A46 10 CASH
Cast Brass **Obv. Inscription:** "T'ien-ch'i T'ung-pao" **Rev. Inscription:** "T'ien-ch'i T'ung-pao" **Note:** Mule. Two obverses of KM#45.

Date	Mintage	Good	VG	F	VF	XF
ND(1621-27)	—	—	—	—	—	—

KM# 46 10 CASH
Cast Brass **Obv. Inscription:** "T'ien-ch'i T'ung-pao" **Rev:** "Shih" (ten) above **Mint:** Chê **Note:** Schjöth #1221.

Date	Mintage	Good	VG	F	VF	XF
ND(1621-27)	—	10.00	17.50	28.00	45.00	—

KM# 47 10 CASH
Cast Brass **Obv. Inscription:** "T'ien-ch'i T'ung-pao" **Rev:** "Shih" (ten) above, dot below **Mint:** Chê **Note:** Schjöth #1222.

Date	Mintage	Good	VG	F	VF	XF
ND(1621-27)	—	12.50	22.50	32.50	50.00	—

KM# 48 10 CASH
Cast Brass **Obv. Inscription:** "T'ien-ch'i T'ung-pao" **Rev:** "Shih" (ten) below

Date	Mintage	Good	VG	F	VF	XF
ND(1621-27)	—	12.50	22.50	40.00	65.00	—

KM# 49.1 10 CASH
Cast Brass **Obv. Inscription:** "T'ien-ch'i T'ung-pao" **Rev:** "Shih" (ten) above, "Yi-liang" (one tael) at right **Mint:** Chê **Note:** Schjöth #1223. Rim size and character varieties exist.

Date	Mintage	Good	VG	F	VF	XF
ND(1621-27)	—	10.00	15.00	40.00	65.00	—

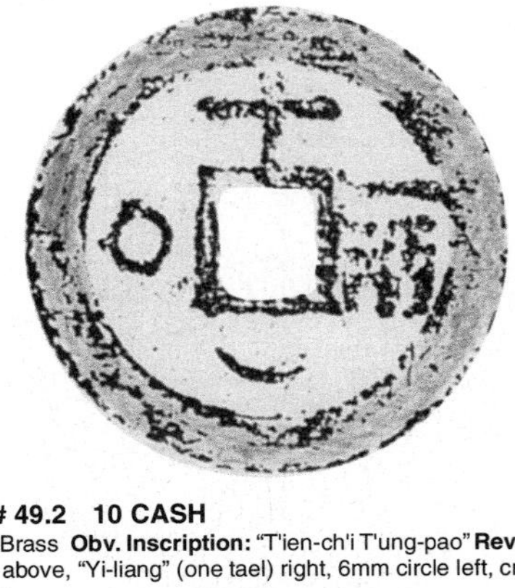

KM# 49.2 10 CASH
Cast Brass **Obv. Inscription:** "T'ien-ch'i T'ung-pao" **Rev:** "Shih" (ten) above, "Yi-liang" (one tael) right, 6mm circle left, crescent below

Date	Mintage	Good	VG	F	VF	XF
ND(1621-27)	—	15.00	30.00	60.00	100	—

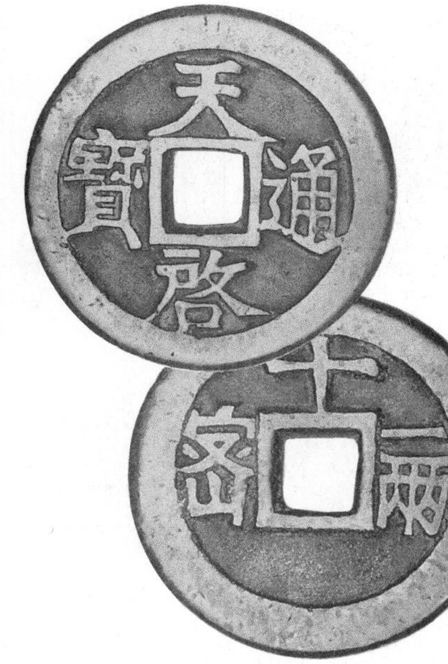

KM# 49.3 10 CASH

Cast Brass **Obv. Inscription:** "T'ien-ch'i T'ung-pao" **Rev:** "Shih" (ten) above, "Yi-liang" (one tael) at right, 6mm circle left, crescent below **Rev. Inscription:** Shih, Yi-liang, Mi **Mint:** Miyün

Date	Mintage	Good	VG	F	VF	XF
ND(1621-27)	—	150	300	450	—	—

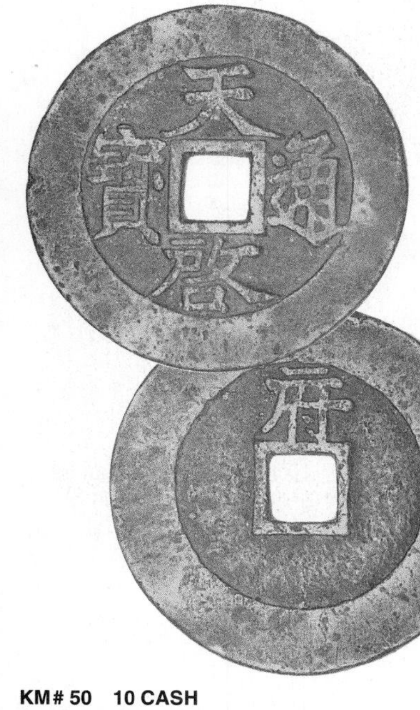

KM# 50 10 CASH

Cast Brass **Obv. Inscription:** "T'ien-ch'i T'ung-pao" **Rev:** "Fu" above **Mint:** Fu **Note:** Schjöth #1224.

Date	Mintage	Good	VG	F	VF	XF
ND(1621-27)	—	100	200	350	600	—

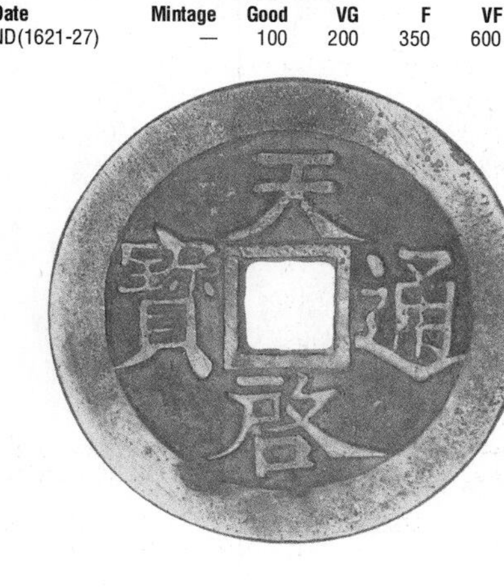

KM# 51 10 CASH

Cast Brass **Obv. Inscription:** "T'ien-ch'i T'ung-pao" **Rev:** "Chên" above, "Shih" (ten) below **Mint:** Chênting **Note:** Schjöth #1225.

Date	Mintage	Good	VG	F	VF	XF
ND(1621-27)	—	100	200	350	600	—

Ch'ung-chên

Chongzhen, Chuang Lieh

CAST COINAGE

KM# 53 CASH

Cast Bronze **Obv. Inscription:** "Ch'ung-chên T'ung-pao" **Rev:** Plain **Note:** Schjöth #1226.

Date	Mintage	Good	VG	F	VF	XF
ND(1628-44)	—	1.50	3.00	5.50	8.00	—

KM# 54 CASH

Cast Bronze **Obv:** Characters deviating in style **Obv. Inscription:** "Ch'ung-chên T'ung-pao" **Note:** Schjöth #1227.

Date	Mintage	Good	VG	F	VF	XF
ND(1628-44)	—	2.50	3.00	5.50	8.00	—

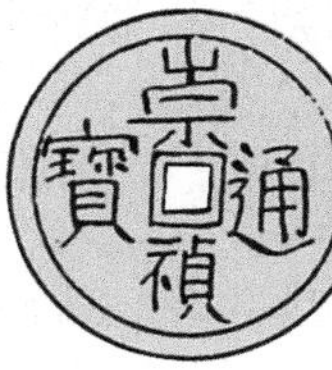

KM# 55.2 CASH

Cast Bronze **Obv:** Larger characters **Obv. Inscription:** "Ch'ung-chên T'ung-pao" **Note:** Schjöth #1229.

Date	Mintage	Good	VG	F	VF	XF
ND(1628-44)	—	1.50	4.00	5.50	8.00	—

KM# 57 CASH

Cast Bronze **Obv. Inscription:** "Ch'ung-chên T'ung-pao" **Rev:** Concave border around center hole **Note:** Schjöth #1230.

Date	Mintage	Good	VG	F	VF	XF
ND(1628-44)	—	1.50	4.00	5.50	8.00	—

KM# 58.1 CASH

Cast Bronze **Obv. Inscription:** "Ch'ung-chên T'ung-pao" **Rev:** Dot above **Note:** Schjöth #1231-32.

Date	Mintage	Good	VG	F	VF	XF
ND(1628-44)	—	2.50	5.00	6.50	10.00	—

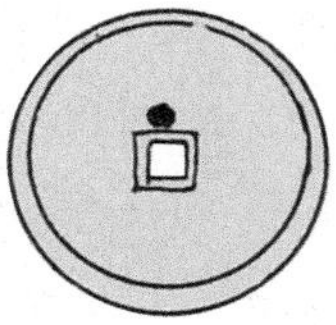

KM# 58.2 CASH

Cast Bronze **Obv. Inscription:** "Ch'ung-chên T'ung-pao" **Rev:** Dot above near square hole **Note:** Schjöth #1233.

Date	Mintage	Good	VG	F	VF	XF
ND(1628-44)	—	2.50	5.00	6.50	10.00	—

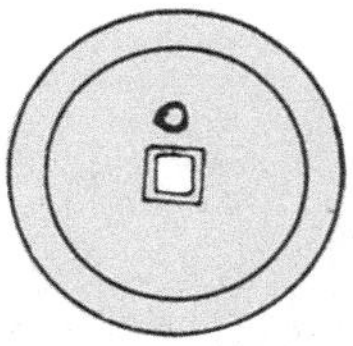

KM# 58.3 CASH

Cast Bronze **Obv. Inscription:** "Ch'ung-chên T'ung-pao" **Rev:** Circle above **Note:** Schjöth #1234.

Date	Mintage	Good	VG	F	VF	XF
ND(1628-44)	—	3.00	10.00	15.00	20.00	—

KM# 58.4 CASH

Cast Bronze **Obv. Inscription:** "Ch'ung-chên T'ung-pao" **Rev:** Dot in circle below **Note:** Schjöth #1235.

Date	Mintage	Good	VG	F	VF	XF
ND(1628-44)	—	5.50	12.00	18.00	25.00	—

KM# 58.5 CASH

Cast Bronze **Obv. Inscription:** "Ch'ung-chên T'ung-pao" **Rev:** Dot in circle above

Date	Mintage	Good	VG	F	VF	XF
ND(1628-44)	—	6.00	10.00	15.00	20.00	—

KM# 59 CASH

Cast Bronze **Obv. Inscription:** "Ch'ung-chên T'ung-pao" **Rev:** Cyclical date "Chia" above **Note:** Schjöth #1236.

Date	Mintage	Good	VG	F	VF	XF
ND(1634-35)	—	10.00	20.00	30.00	40.00	—

KM# 60 CASH

Cast Bronze **Obv. Inscription:** "Ch'ung-chên T'ung-pao" **Rev:** Cyclical date "Yi" above **Note:** Schjöth #1237.

Date	Mintage	Good	VG	F	VF	XF
ND(1636-36)	—	7.50	12.00	15.00	25.00	—

KM# 61 CASH

Cast Bronze **Obv. Inscription:** "Ch'ung-chên T'ung-pao" **Rev:** Cyclical date "Ping" above **Note:** Schjöth #1238.

Date	Mintage	Good	VG	F	VF	XF
ND(1636-37)	—	15.00	25.00	35.00	50.00	—

KM# A62 CASH

Cast Bronze **Obv. Inscription:** "Ch'ung-chên T'ung-pao" **Rev:** Cyclical date "Ting" above

Date	Mintage	Good	VG	F	VF	XF
ND(1637-38)	—	15.00	20.00	30.00	40.00	—

KM# 62 CASH

Cast Bronze **Obv. Inscription:** "Ch'ung-chên T'ung-pao" **Rev:** Cyclical date "Wu" above **Note:** Schjöth #1239.

Date	Mintage	Good	VG	F	VF	XF
ND(1638-39)	—	10.00	20.00	30.00	40.00	—

KM# 63 CASH

Cast Bronze **Obv. Inscription:** "Ch'ung-chên T'ung-pao" **Rev:** Cyclical date "Chi" above **Note:** Schjöth #1240.

Date	Mintage	Good	VG	F	VF	XF
ND(1639-40)	—	15.00	20.00	30.00	40.00	—

KM# A64 CASH

Cast Bronze **Obv. Inscription:** "Ch'ung-chên T'ung-pao" **Rev:** Cyclical date "Keng" above

Date	Mintage	Good	VG	F	VF	XF
ND(1640-41)	—	15.00	20.00	30.00	40.00	—

KM# 64 CASH

Cast Bronze **Obv. Inscription:** "Ch'ung-chên T'ung-pao" **Rev:** "Yi" above, "Ch'ien" below **Note:** Schjöth #1241.

Date	Mintage	Good	VG	F	VF	XF
ND(1628-44)	—	10.00	17.50	25.00	35.00	—

KM# 65 CASH

Cast Bronze **Obv. Inscription:** "Ch'ung-chên T'ung-pao" **Rev:** "Yi-ch'ien" at right **Note:** Schjöth #1242.

Date	Mintage	Good	VG	F	VF	XF
ND(1628-44)	—	10.00	14.00	20.00	28.00	—

KM# 66 CASH

Cast Bronze **Obv. Inscription:** "Ch'ung-chên T'ung-pao" **Rev:** "Yi Ch'ien" at right, dot below **Note:** Schjöth #1243.

Date	Mintage	Good	VG	F	VF	XF
ND(1628-44)	—	6.00	10.00	15.00	20.00	—

KM# 67 CASH

Cast Bronze **Obv. Inscription:** "Ch'ung-chên T'ung-pao" **Rev:** "Pa (eight) Ch'ien" at right **Note:** Schjöth #1244.

Date	Mintage	Good	VG	F	VF	XF
ND(1628-44)	—	10.00	17.50	25.00	35.00	—

KM# 68.1 CASH

Cast Bronze **Obv. Inscription:** "Ch'ung-chên T'ung-pao" **Rev:** "Pa" (eight) below **Note:** Schjöth #1245.

Date	Mintage	Good	VG	F	VF	XF
ND(1628-44)	—	6.00	10.00	15.00	20.00	—

KM# 68.2 CASH

Cast Bronze **Obv. Inscription:** "Ch'ung-chên T'ung-pao" **Rev:** Dot above, "Pa" (eight) below **Note:** Schjöth #1246.

Date	Mintage	Good	VG	F	VF	XF
ND(1628-44)	—	10.00	17.50	25.00	35.00	—

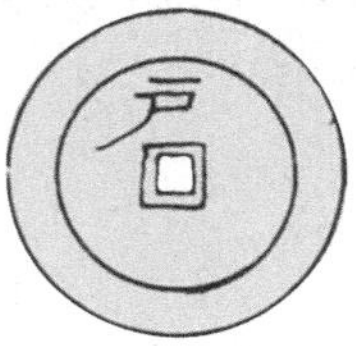

KM# 69 CASH

Cast Bronze **Obv. Inscription:** "Ch'ung-chên T'ung-pao" **Rev:** "Hu" above **Mint:** Hu-pu Board of Revenue **Note:** Schjöth #1247-48.

Date	Mintage	Good	VG	F	VF	XF
ND(1628-44)	—	6.00	10.00	15.00	20.00	—

KM# 70 CASH

Cast Bronze **Obv. Inscription:** "Ch'ung-chên T'ung-pao" **Rev:** "Hu" below **Mint:** Hu-pu Board of Revenue **Note:** Schjöth #1249.

Date	Mintage	Good	VG	F	VF	XF
ND(1628-44)	—	5.50	9.00	13.00	18.00	—

KM# 71 CASH

Cast Bronze **Obv. Inscription:** "Ch'ung-chên T'ung-pao" **Rev:** "Hu" above, "Chiu" below **Mint:** Hu-pu Board of Revenue **Note:** Schjöth #1250.

Date	Mintage	Good	VG	F	VF	XF
ND(1628-44)	—	10.00	17.50	25.00	35.00	—

KM# 72.1 CASH

Cast Bronze, 23 mm. **Obv. Inscription:** "Ch'ung-chên T'ung-pao" **Rev:** "Kung" above **Mint:** Kung-pu Board of Public Works **Note:** Schjöth #1251.

Date	Mintage	Good	VG	F	VF	XF
ND(1628-44)	—	6.00	10.00	15.00	20.00	—

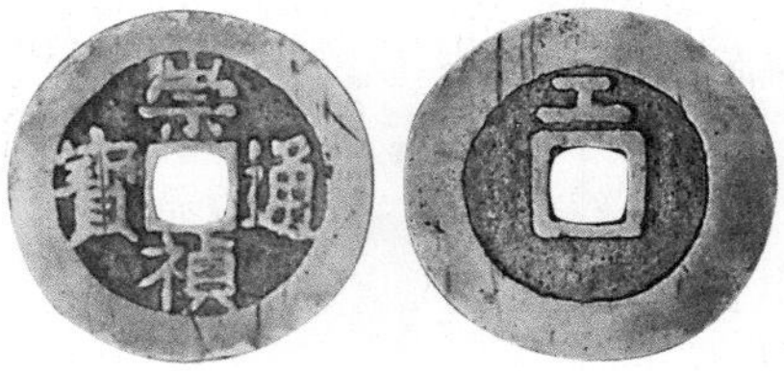

KM# 72.2 CASH

Cast Bronze, 26 mm. **Obv. Inscription:** "Ch'ung-chên T'ung-pao" **Rev:** "Kung" above **Mint:** Kung-pu Board of Public Works

Date	Mintage	Good	VG	F	VF	XF
ND(1628-44)	—	6.00	10.00	15.00	20.00	—

KM# 73.1 CASH

Cast Bronze **Obv. Inscription:** "Ch'ung-chên T'ung-pao" **Rev:** "Kung" below **Mint:** Kung-pu Board of Public Works **Note:** Schjöth #1252.

Date	Mintage	Good	VG	F	VF	XF
ND(1628-44)	—	6.00	10.00	15.00	20.00	—

工

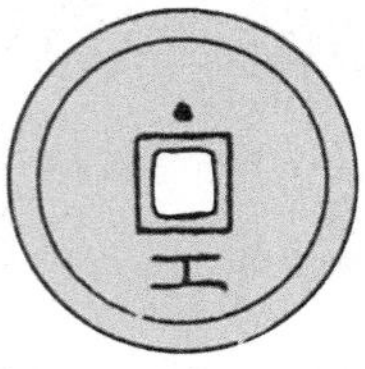

KM# 73.2 CASH

Cast Bronze **Obv. Inscription:** "Ch'ung-chên T'ung-pao" **Rev:** Dot above, "Kung" below **Mint:** Kung-pu Board of Public Works **Note:** Schjöth #1253.

Date	Mintage	Good	VG	F	VF	XF
ND(1628-44)	—	8.50	14.00	20.00	28.00	—

KM# 74 CASH

Cast Bronze **Obv. Inscription:** "Ch'ung-chên T'ung-pao" **Rev:** "Chü" above **Note:** Schjöth #1254.

Date	Mintage	Good	VG	F	VF	XF
ND(1628-44)	—	8.50	14.00	20.00	28.00	—

官

KM# 75.1 CASH

Cast Bronze **Obv. Inscription:** "Ch'ung-chên T'ung-pao" **Rev:** "Kuan" above **Note:** Schjöth #1255.

Date	Mintage	Good	VG	F	VF	XF
ND(1628-44)	—	9.00	15.00	21.00	30.00	—

KM# 75.2 CASH

Cast Bronze **Obv. Inscription:** "Ch'ung-chên T'ung-pao" **Rev:** "Kuan" above, crescent below **Note:** Schjöth #1256.

Date	Mintage	Good	VG	F	VF	XF
ND(1628-44)	—	9.00	15.00	21.00	30.00	—

KM# 76 CASH

Cast Bronze **Obv. Inscription:** "Ch'ung-chên T'ung-pao" **Rev:** "Hsin" above **Note:** Schjöth #1257.

Date	Mintage	Good	VG	F	VF	XF
ND(1628-44)	—	8.00	13.00	16.00	26.00	—

KM# 77 CASH

Cast Bronze **Obv. Inscription:** "Ch'ung-chên T'ung-pao" **Rev:** "Chiang" above **Mint:** Chiangning **Note:** Schjöth #1258.

Date	Mintage	Good	VG	F	VF	XF
ND(1628-44)	—	8.00	13.00	16.00	26.00	—

KM# 78 CASH

Cast Bronze **Obv. Inscription:** "Ch'ung-chên T'ung-pao" **Rev:** "Yü" above **Mint:** Yülin **Note:** Schjöth #1259.

Date	Mintage	Good	VG	F	VF	XF
ND(1628-44)	—	15.00	20.00	30.00	40.00	—

重

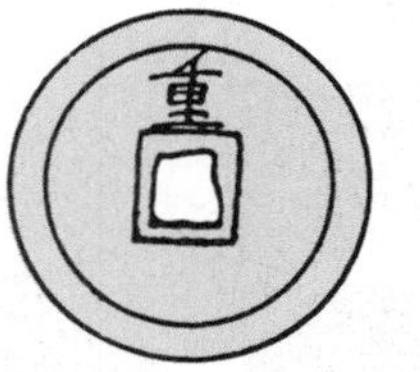

KM# 79.1 CASH

Cast Bronze **Obv. Inscription:** "Ch'ung-chên T'ung-pao" **Rev:** "Ch'ung" above **Mint:** Ch'ungch'ing **Note:** Schjöth #1260.

Date	Mintage	Good	VG	F	VF	XF
ND(1628-44)	—	6.00	10.00	15.00	20.00	—

重

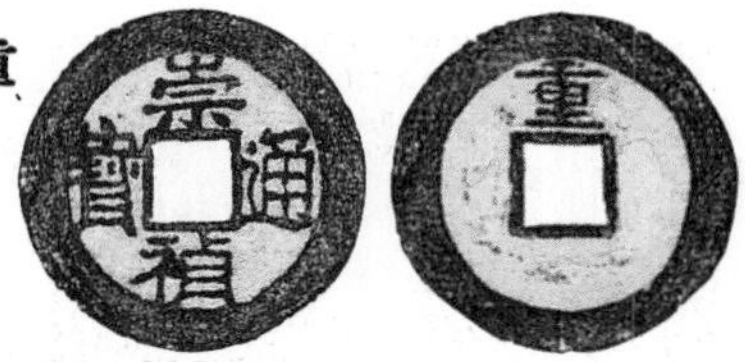

KM# 79.2 CASH

Cast Bronze **Obv. Inscription:** "Ch'ung-chên T'ung-pao" **Rev:** "Ch'ung" above deviating in style **Mint:** Ch'ungch'ing **Note:** Schjöth #1261.

Date	Mintage	Good	VG	F	VF	XF
ND(1628-44)	—	6.00	10.00	15.00	20.00	—

KM# 79.3 CASH

Cast Bronze **Obv. Inscription:** "Ch'ung-chên T'ung-pao" **Rev:** "Ch'ung" above, dot below **Mint:** Ch'ungch'ing

Date	Mintage	Good	VG	F	VF	XF
ND(1628-44)	—	6.00	10.00	15.00	20.00	—

KM# 79.4 CASH

Cast Bronze **Obv. Inscription:** "Ch'ung-chên T'ung-pao" **Rev:** "Ch'ung" above, crescent below **Mint:** Ch'ungch'ing

Date	Mintage	Good	VG	F	VF	XF
ND(1628-44)	—	6.00	10.00	15.00	20.00	—

KM# 79.5 CASH

Cast Bronze **Obv. Inscription:** "Ch'ung-chên T'ung-pao" **Rev:** "Ch'ung" above, "Yi-Ch'ien" right, crescent below **Mint:** Ch'ungch'ing

Date	Mintage	Good	VG	F	VF	XF
ND(1628-44)	—	10.00	15.00	25.00	—	—

加

KM# 80.1 CASH

Cast Bronze **Obv. Inscription:** "Ch'ung-chên T'ung-pao" **Rev:** "Chia" above **Mint:** Chiating Fu **Note:** Schjöth #1262.

Date	Mintage	Good	VG	F	VF	XF
ND(1628-44)	—	8.50	14.00	20.00	28.00	—

KM# 80.2 CASH

Cast Bronze **Obv. Inscription:** "Ch'ung-chên T'ung-pao" **Rev:** Dot above, "Chia" below **Mint:** Chiating Fu

Date	Mintage	Good	VG	F	VF	XF
ND(1628-44)	—	20.00	30.00	40.00	—	—

KM# 81 CASH

Cast Bronze **Obv. Inscription:** "Ch'ung-chên T'ung-pao" **Rev:** "Lü" above **Mint:** Lüchou **Note:** Schjöth #1263.

Date	Mintage	Good	VG	F	VF	XF
ND(1628-44)	—	6.00	10.00	15.00	20.00	—

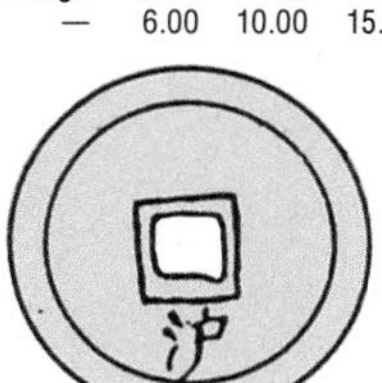

KM# 82.1 CASH

Cast Bronze **Obv. Inscription:** "Ch'ung-chên T'ung-pao" **Rev:** "Lü" below **Mint:** Lüchou **Note:** Schjöth #1264.

Date	Mintage	Good	VG	F	VF	XF
ND(1628-44)	—	8.50	14.00	20.00	28.00	—

KM# 82.2 CASH

Cast Bronze **Obv. Inscription:** "Ch'ung-chên T'ung-pao" **Rev:** Dot above, "Lü" below **Mint:** Lüchou **Note:** Schjöth #1265.

Date	Mintage	Good	VG	F	VF	XF
ND(1628-44)	—	8.50	14.00	20.00	28.00	—

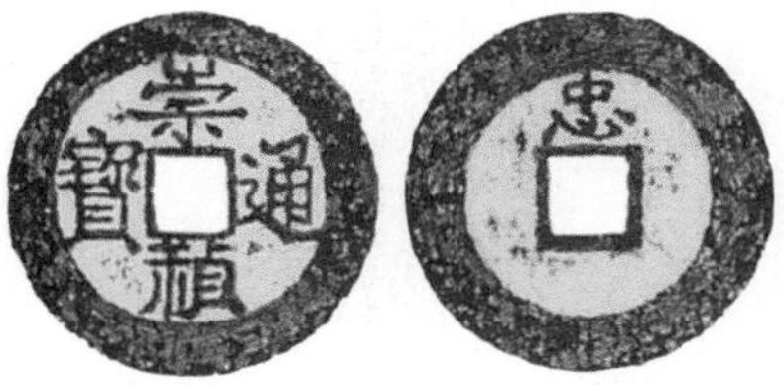

KM# 83 CASH

Cast Bronze **Obv. Inscription:** "Ch'ung-chên T'ung-pao" **Rev:** "Chung" above **Mint:** Chungchou **Note:** Schjöth #1266.

Date	Mintage	Good	VG	F	VF	XF
ND(1628-44)	—	15.00	25.00	35.00	50.00	—

KM# 84 CASH

Cast Bronze **Obv. Inscription:** "Ch'ung-chên T'ung-pao" **Rev:** "Ying" above **Mint:** Yingt'ien **Note:** Schjöth #1267.

Date	Mintage	Good	VG	F	VF	XF
ND(1628-44)	—	9.00	15.00	21.00	30.00	—

青

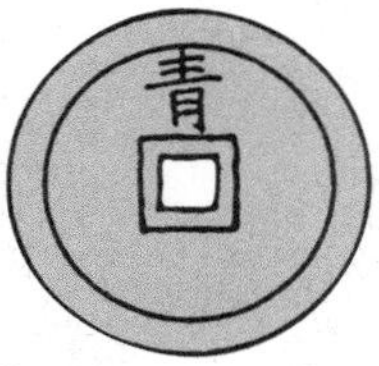

KM# 85 CASH

Cast Bronze **Obv. Inscription:** "Ch'ung-chên T'ung-pao" **Rev:** "Ch'ing" above **Mint:** Chingchou **Note:** Schjöth #1268.

Date	Mintage	Good	VG	F	VF	XF
ND(1628-44)	—	9.00	15.00	21.00	30.00	—

KM# 86 CASH

Cast Bronze **Obv. Inscription:** "Ch'ung-chên T'ung-pao" **Rev:** "Ch'ing" below **Mint:** Chingchou

Date	Mintage	Good	VG	F	VF	XF
ND(1628-44)	—	8.50	14.00	20.00	28.00	—

KM# 87.1 CASH

Cast Bronze **Obv. Inscription:** "Ch'ung-chên T'ung-pao" **Rev:** "Kuei" above **Mint:** Kueichou **Note:** Schjöth #1269.

Date	Mintage	Good	VG	F	VF	XF
ND(1628-44)	—	3.25	5.50	7.50	12.00	—

KM# 88.1 CASH

Cast Bronze **Obv. Inscription:** "Ch'ung-chên T'ung-pao" **Rev:** "Kuang" above **Mint:** Kuangchou Fu **Note:** Schjöth #1270.

Date	Mintage	Good	VG	F	VF	XF
ND(1628-44)	—	7.50	12.50	18.00	25.00	—

KM# 89 CASH
Cast Bronze **Obv. Inscription:** "Ch'ung-chên T'ung-pao" **Rev:** "T'ai" above, "P'ing" below **Mint:** T'ai-p'ing Fu **Note:** Schjöth #1271.

Date	Mintage	Good	VG	F	VF	XF
ND(1628-44)	—	10.00	15.00	20.00	30.00	—

KM# 90 CASH
Cast Bronze **Obv. Inscription:** "Ch'ung-chên T'ung-pao" **Rev:** "Fu" above **Mint:** Hsüan "fu" Ch'êng **Note:** Schjöth #1272.

Date	Mintage	Good	VG	F	VF	XF
ND(1628-44)	—	10.00	15.00	20.00	30.00	—

KM# 88.2 CASH
Cast Copper **Obv. Inscription:** "Ch'ung-chên T'ung-pao" **Rev:** Kuang below **Mint:** Kuangchou Fu **Note:** Schjöth #1270.

Date	Mintage	Good	VG	F	VF	XF
ND(1628-44)	—	20.00	35.00	50.00	70.00	—

KM# 55.1 CASH
Cast Bronze **Obv:** Characters deviating in style **Obv. Inscription:** "Ch'ung-chên T'ung-pao" **Rev:** Plain **Mint:** Board of Public Works **Note:** Schjöth #1228.

Date	Mintage	Good	VG	F	VF	XF
ND(1628-44)	—	1.50	4.00	5.50	8.00	—

舊

KM# A94 CASH
Cast Bronze **Obv. Inscription:** Ch'ung-chên T'ung-pao **Rev:** Chiu above **Mint:** Board of Revenue **Note:** H20.268.

Date	Mintage	Good	VG	F	VF	XF
ND(1628-44)	—	40.00	80.00	135	—	—

KM# 87.2 CASH
Cast Bronze **Obv. Inscription:** Ch'ung-chên T'ung-pao **Rev:** Kuei above, dot below **Mint:** Kueichou **Note:** Schjöth #1269.

Date	Mintage	Good	VG	F	VF	XF
ND(1628-44)	—	10.00	20.00	35.00	50.00	—

KM# 91 CASH
Cast Bronze **Obv. Inscription:** "Ch'ung-chên T'ung-pao" **Rev:** "Ch'ing" above, "Chung" below **Note:** Schjöth #1273.

Date	Mintage	Good	VG	F	VF	XF
ND(1628-44)	—	15.00	25.00	30.00	50.00	—

KM# 92 CASH
Cast Bronze **Obv. Inscription:** "Ch'ung-chên T'ung-pao" **Rev:** "Chi" above **Mint:** Board of Public Works **Note:** Schjöth #1274.

Date	Mintage	Good	VG	F	VF	XF
ND(1628-44)	—	10.00	15.00	20.00	30.00	—

KM# 93 CASH
Cast Bronze **Obv. Inscription:** "Ch'ung-chên T'ung-pao" **Rev:** "Chi" below **Note:** Schjöth #1275.

Date	Mintage	Good	VG	F	VF	XF
ND(1628-44)	—	7.50	12.50	15.00	25.00	—

共

KM# 94 CASH
Cast Bronze **Obv. Inscription:** "Ch'ung-chên T'ung-pao" **Rev:** "Kung" below **Mint:** Kungch'êng **Note:** Schjöth #1276.

Date	Mintage	Good	VG	F	VF	XF
ND(1628-44)	—	10.00	17.50	25.00	35.00	—

KM# A95 CASH
Cast Bronze **Obv. Inscription:** "Ch'ung-chên T'ung-pao" **Rev:** "Ping" (meaning unknown)

Date	Mintage	Good	VG	F	VF	XF
ND(1628-44)	—	25.00	35.00	50.00	—	—

KM# 95.1 CASH
Cast Bronze, 23 mm. **Obv. Inscription:** "Ch'ung-chên T'ung-pao" **Rev:** Galloping horse below **Note:** Schjöth #1277.

Date	Mintage	Good	VG	F	VF	XF
ND(1628-44)	—	20.00	32.50	45.00	60.00	—

KM# 95.2 CASH
Cast Bronze, 26 mm. **Obv. Inscription:** "Ch'ung-chên T'ung-pao" **Rev:** Galloping horse left deviating in style below **Note:** Schjöth #1278. Privately made amulet.

Date	Mintage	Good	VG	F	VF	XF
ND(1628-44)	—	20.00	32.50	45.00	60.00	—

KM# 95.3 CASH
Cast Bronze **Obv. Inscription:** "Ch'ung-chên T'ung-pao" **Rev:** Horse right above and horse left below

Date	Mintage	Good	VG	F	VF	XF
ND(1628-44)	—	40.00	70.00	100	—	—

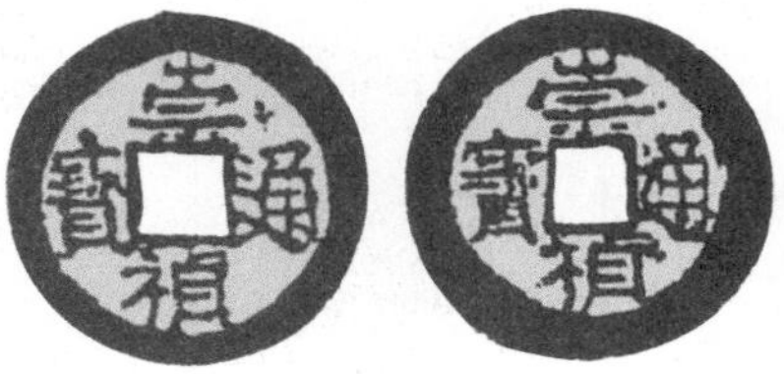

KM# 96 CASH
Cast Bronze **Obv. Inscription:** "Ch'ung-chên T'ung-pao" **Rev:** Rabbit below

Date	Mintage	Good	VG	F	VF	XF
ND(1628-44)	—	—	—	—	—	—

KM# 97 CASH
Cast Bronze **Obv. Inscription:** "Ch'ung-chên T'ung-pao" **Rev. Inscription:** Ch'ung-chên T'ung-pao **Note:** Muled obverses (error).

Date	Mintage	Good	VG	F	VF	XF
ND(1628-44)	—	32.50	52.50	75.00	100	—

KM# A98 CASH
Cast Bronze, 25 mm. **Rev. Inscription:** "Chih" above

Date	Mintage	Good	VG	F	VF	XF
ND(1628-44)	—	60.00	100	140	200	—

KM# A99 2 CASH
Cast Bronze, 25 mm. **Rev. Inscription:** "Erh" (two) below

Date	Mintage	Good	VG	F	VF	XF
ND(1628-44)	—	1.75	3.00	4.75	6.00	—

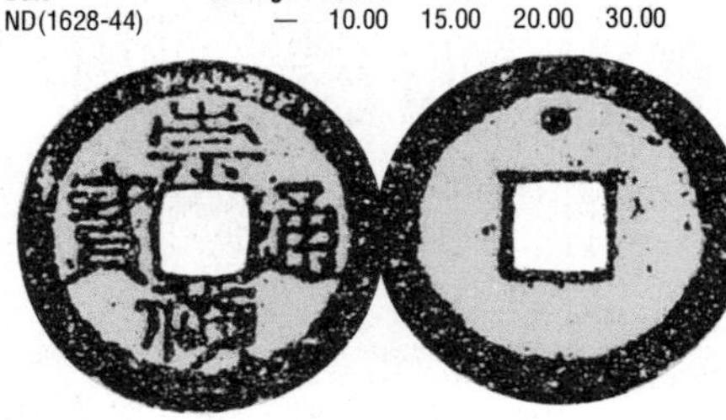

KM# 99 2 CASH
Cast Bronze **Obv. Inscription:** "Ch'ung-chên T'ung-pao" **Rev:** "Êrh" (two) at right **Note:** Schjöth #1282.

Date	Mintage	Good	VG	F	VF	XF
ND(1628-44)	—	10.00	15.00	20.00	30.00	—

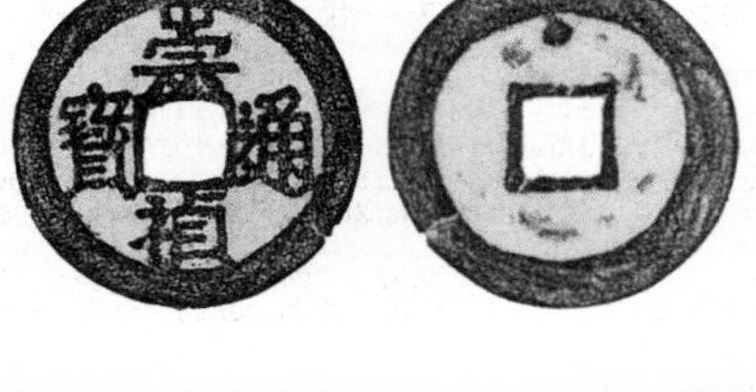

KM# 100 2 CASH
Cast Bronze **Obv. Inscription:** "Ch'ung-chên T'ung-pao" **Rev:** "Êrh" (two) at right, small dot below **Note:** Schjöth #1283.

Date	Mintage	Good	VG	F	VF	XF
ND(1628-44)	—	4.00	7.00	10.00	15.00	—

Note: The illustrations for Schjöth's #1282 and 1283 were misleading while the descriptive text was correct

KM# A101 2 CASH
Cast Bronze **Obv. Inscription:** "Ch'ung-chên T'ung-pao" **Rev:** Dot above only

Date	Mintage	Good	VG	F	VF	XF
ND(1628-44)	—	5.00	10.00	15.00	20.00	—

KM# 101 2 CASH
Cast Bronze **Obv. Inscription:** "Ch'ung-chên T'ung-pao" **Rev:** "Hu" above, "Êrh" (two) below **Mint:** Hu-pu Board of Revenue **Note:** Schjöth #1279.

Date	Mintage	Good	VG	F	VF	XF
ND(1628-44)	—	16.00	25.00	35.00	50.00	—

KM# A102 2 CASH
Cast Bronze **Obv. Inscription:** "Ch'ung-chên T'ung-pao" **Rev:** "Êrh" left, "Chu" right

Date	Mintage	Good	VG	F	VF	XF
ND(1628-44)	—	35.00	55.00	75.00	—	—

KM# B102 2 CASH
Cast Bronze **Obv. Inscription:** "Ch'ung-chên T'ung-pao" **Rev:** "Chih" above, "Feng" right

Date	Mintage	Good	VG	F	VF	XF
ND(1628-44)	—	22.00	37.50	50.00	—	—

KM# 102 2 CASH
Cast Bronze **Obv. Inscription:** "Ch'ung-chên T'ung-pao" **Rev:** "Hu" at right, "Êrh" (two) sideways at left **Mint:** Hu-pu Board of Revenue **Note:** Schjöth #1280.

Date	Mintage	Good	VG	F	VF	XF
ND(1628-44)	—	10.00	15.00	21.50	30.00	—

KM# A103 2 CASH
Cast Bronze, 25 mm. **Rev. Inscription:** "Erh" (two) at right, "Hu" at left

Date	Mintage	Good	VG	F	VF	XF
ND(1628-44)	—	1.50	2.50	3.50	5.00	—

KM# 103 2 CASH
Cast Bronze **Obv. Inscription:** "Ch'ung-chên T'ung-pao" **Rev:** "Kung" above, "Êrh" (two) below **Mint:** Kung-pu Board of Public Works **Note:** Schjöth #1281.

Date	Mintage	Good	VG	F	VF	XF
ND(1628-44)	—	10.00	17.50	25.00	35.00	—

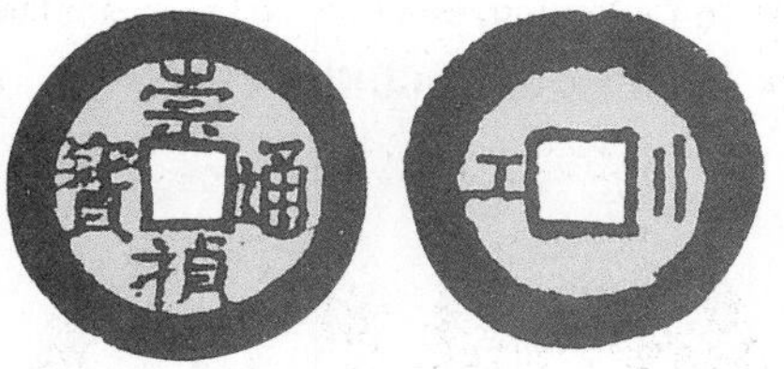

KM# 104.1 2 CASH
Cast Bronze **Obv. Inscription:** "Ch'ung-chên T'ung-pao" **Rev:** "Êrh" (two) at right, "Kung" at left **Mint:** Kung-pu Board of Public Works

Date	Mintage	Good	VG	F	VF	XF
ND(1628-44)	—	15.00	25.00	37.50	50.00	—

KM# 104.2 2 CASH
Cast Bronze **Obv:** Characters deviating in style **Obv. Inscription:** "Ch'ung-chên T'ung-pao" **Rev:** "Êrh" (two) at right, "Kung" at left **Mint:** Kung-pu Board of Public Works

Date	Mintage	Good	VG	F	VF	XF
ND(1628-44)	—	10.00	17.50	25.00	35.00	—

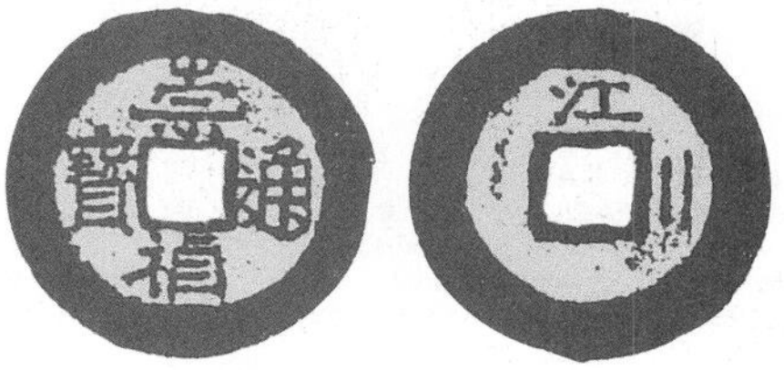

KM# 105 2 CASH
Cast Bronze **Obv. Inscription:** "Ch'ung-chên T'ung-pao" **Rev:** "Chiang" above, "Êrh" (two) sideways at right

Date	Mintage	Good	VG	F	VF	XF
ND(1628-44)	—	20.00	35.00	47.50	70.00	—

KM# 106 2 CASH
Cast Bronze **Obv. Inscription:** "Ch'ung-chên T'ung-pao" **Rev:** "Chi" at right, "Êrh" (two) at left **Mint:** Board of Public Works

Date	Mintage	Good	VG	F	VF	XF
ND(1628-44)	—	100	200	300	400	—

KM# 107 2 CASH
Cast Bronze, 25 mm. **Rev. Inscription:** "Chü" at right, "Chü" at left

Date	Mintage	Good	VG	F	VF	XF
ND(1628-44)	—	25.00	40.00	65.00	90.00	—

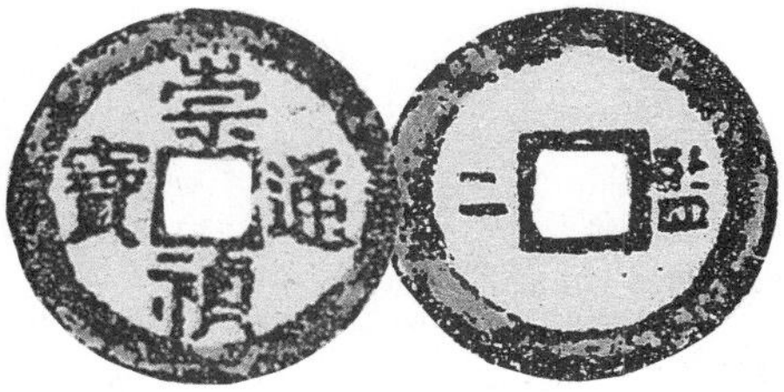

KM# 108 2 CASH
Cast Bronze, 29 mm. **Rev. Inscription:** "Chien" at right, "Erh" (two) at left

Date	Mintage	Good	VG	F	VF	XF
ND(1628-44)	—	25.00	40.00	65.00	90.00	—

KM# 109 5 CASH
Cast Bronze **Obv. Inscription:** "Ch'ung-chên T'ung-pao" **Rev:** "Hu" at right, "Wu" (five) at left **Mint:** Hu-pu Board of Revenue

Date	Mintage	Good	VG	F	VF	XF
ND(1628-44)	—	20.00	35.00	47.50	70.00	—

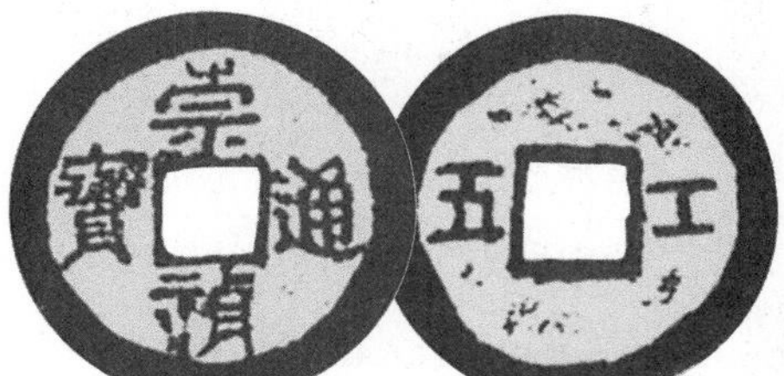

KM# 110 5 CASH
Cast Bronze **Obv. Inscription:** "Ch'ung-chên T'ung-pao" **Rev:** "Kung" at right, "Wu" (five) at left **Mint:** Kung-pu Board of Public Works

Date	Mintage	Good	VG	F	VF	XF
ND(1628-44)	—	25.00	42.50	60.00	85.00	—

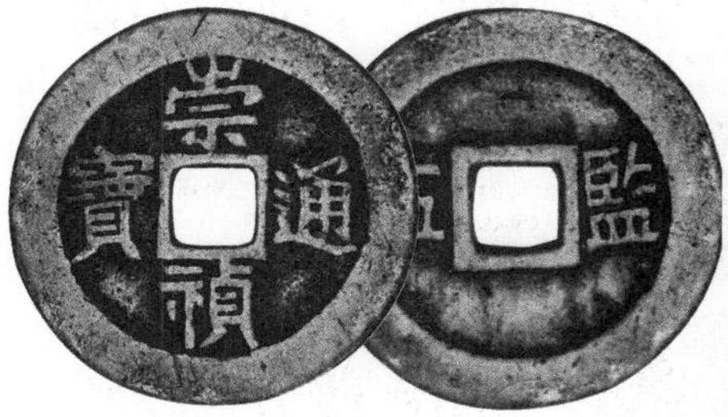

KM# 111 5 CASH
Cast Bronze **Obv. Inscription:** "Ch'ung-chên T'ung-pao" **Rev:** "Chien" at right, "Wu" (five) at left **Note:** Schjöth #1284.

Date	Mintage	Good	VG	F	VF	XF
ND(1628-44)	—	18.00	30.00	45.00	65.00	—

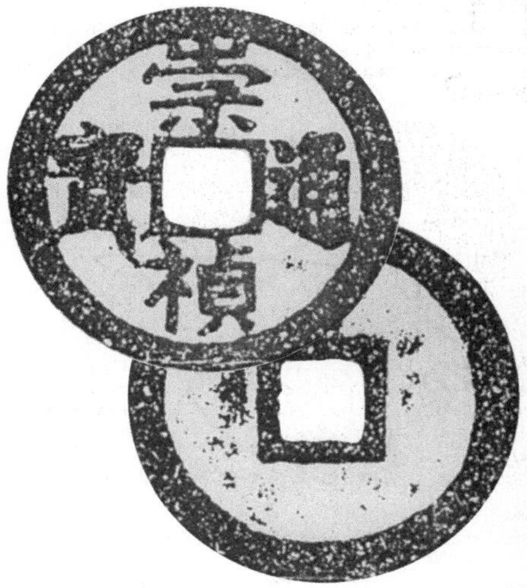

KM# 112 10 CASH
Cast Bronze **Obv. Inscription:** "Ch'ung-chên T'ung-pao" **Rev:** Plain

Date	Mintage	Good	VG	F	VF	XF
ND(1628-44)	—	125	250	350	500	—

MING-CH'ING REBEL ERA

Issued during the years of the revolt to overthrow the Ming Dynasty by the Manchu's, while the Manchus (Ch'ing Dynasty) were consolidating their control over all of China. Thus classed as "rebel coinage" as issued by the Manchu's in the Ming Era.

Ta-ming

Ming Prince of Lu

CAST COINAGE

KM# 115 CASH

Cast Bronze **Obv. Inscription:** "Ta-ming T'ung-pao" **Rev:** Plain **Note:** Schjöth #1285.

Date	Mintage	Good	VG	F	VF	XF
ND(1628-44)	—	20.00	30.00	45.00	65.00	—

KM# 116 CASH

Cast Bronze **Rev:** "Hu" above **Note:** Schjöth #1286.

Date	Mintage	Good	VG	F	VF	XF
ND(1628-44)	—	20.00	30.00	45.00	65.00	—

KM# A117.1 CASH

Cast Bronze **Obv. Inscription:** "Ta-ming T'ung-pao" **Rev:** "Shuai" above

Date	Mintage	Good	VG	F	VF	XF
ND(1628-44)	—	20.00	30.00	45.00	65.00	—

KM# A117.2 CASH

Cast Bronze **Obv. Inscription:** "Ta-ming T'ung-pao" **Rev:** "Shuai" right

Date	Mintage	Good	VG	F	VF	XF
ND(1628-44)	—	20.00	30.00	45.00	65.00	—

KM# 117 CASH

Cast Bronze **Obv. Inscription:** "Ta-ming T'ung-pao" **Rev:** "Kung" above

Date	Mintage	Good	VG	F	VF	XF
ND(1628-44)	—	18.00	30.00	45.00	65.00	—

Hung-kuang

Prince of Fu; Fu King; Fu Wang

CAST COINAGE

KM# 118.1 CASH

Cast Bronze **Obv. Inscription:** "Hung-kuang T'ung-pao" **Rev:** Plain **Note:** Schjöth #1287.

Date	Mintage	Good	VG	F	VF	XF
ND(1644)	—	3.50	6.00	8.50	12.00	—

KM# 118.2 CASH

Cast Bronze **Obv. Inscription:** "Hung-kuang T'ung-pao" **Rev:** Dot above **Note:** Schjöth #1288.

Date	Mintage	Good	VG	F	VF	XF
ND(1644)	—	4.50	7.50	11.00	15.00	—

KM# 119 CASH

Cast Bronze **Obv. Inscription:** "Hung-kuang T'ung-pao" **Rev:** "Feng" above **Mint:** Fengyang Fu **Note:** Schjöth #1289.

Date	Mintage	Good	VG	F	VF	XF
ND(1644)	—	35.00	55.00	90.00	125	—

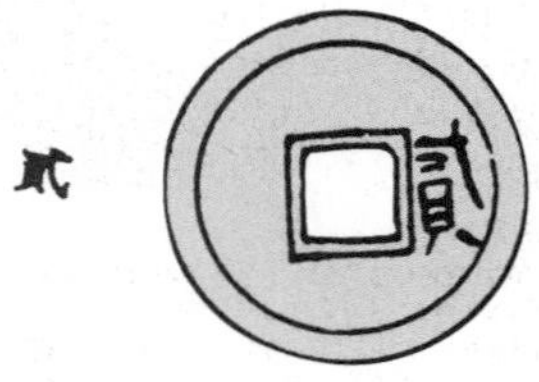

KM# 120 2 CASH

Cast Bronze **Obv. Inscription:** "Hung-kuang T'ung-pao" **Rev:** Official "Êrh" (two) at right **Note:** Schjöth #1290.

Date	Mintage	Good	VG	F	VF	XF
ND(1644)	—	30.00	60.00	120	150	—

Lung-wu

Prince of T'ang

CAST COINAGE

KM# 122.1 CASH

Cast Bronze, 24-26 mm. **Obv. Inscription:** "Lung-wu T'ung-pao" **Rev:** Plain **Note:** Size varies. Schjöth #1291.

Date	Mintage	Good	VG	F	VF	XF
ND(1645)	—	5.00	8.50	12.00	16.00	—

KM# 122.2 CASH

Cast Bronze **Obv. Inscription:** "Lung-wu T'ung-pao" **Rev:** Dot above **Note:** Schjöth #1292.

Date	Mintage	Good	VG	F	VF	XF
ND(1645)	—	6.00	10.00	15.00	20.00	—

KM# 122.3 CASH

Cast Bronze **Obv:** Character "Lung" written differently **Obv. Inscription:** "Lung-wu T'ung-pao" **Rev:** Plain **Mint:** Foochou

Date	Mintage	Good	VG	F	VF	XF
ND(1645)	—	—	—	—	—	—

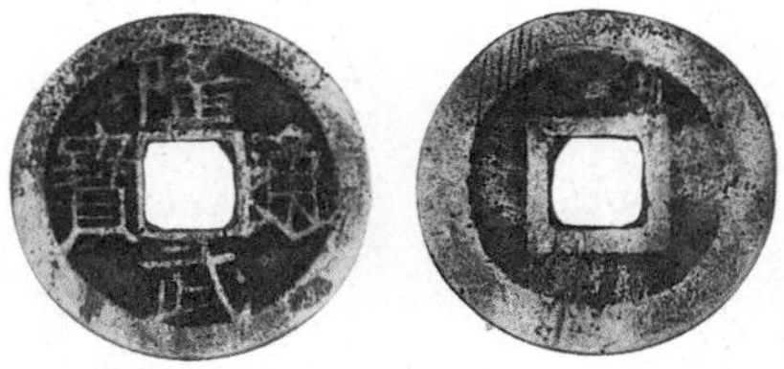

KM# A123 CASH

Cast Bronze **Obv:** Different style "lung" in legend **Obv. Legend:** "Lung-wu T'ung-pao" **Rev:** Plain

Date	Mintage	Good	VG	F	VF	XF
ND(1645)	—	—	—	—	—	—

KM# B123 CASH

Cast Bronze **Obv:** Different style "lung" in legend **Obv. Legend:** "Lung-wu T'ung-pao" **Rev:** Plain

Date	Mintage	Good	VG	F	VF	XF
ND(1645)	—	—	—	—	—	—

KM# 123 CASH

Cast Bronze **Obv. Inscription:** "Lung-wu T'ung-pao" **Rev:** "Hu" above **Note:** Schjöth #1293.

Date	Mintage	Good	VG	F	VF	XF
ND(1645)	—	8.00	12.00	16.00	24.00	—

KM# 124 CASH

Cast Bronze **Obv. Inscription:** "Lung-wu T'ung-pao" **Rev:** "Kung" above **Note:** Schjöth #1294.

Date	Mintage	Good	VG	F	VF	XF
ND(1645)	—	8.00	12.00	16.00	24.00	—

KM# A125 CASH

Iron, 22 mm. **Obv. Inscription:** "Lung-wu T'ung-pao" **Rev:** Plain

Date	Mintage	Good	VG	F	VF	XF
ND(1645)	—	30.00	60.00	90.00	125	—

KM# 126 2 CASH

Cast Bronze **Obv. Legend:** "Lung-wu T'ung-pao" **Rev:** Plain **Note:** Schjöth #1295.

Date	Mintage	Good	VG	F	VF	XF
ND(1645)	—	8.50	14.00	20.00	30.00	—

Yung-ch'ang

Li Tzu'ch'eng, Hsi'au Fu

CAST COINAGE

KM# 161 CASH

Cast Bronze, 23-25 mm. **Obv. Inscription:** "Yung-ch'ang T'ung-pao" **Rev:** Plain **Note:** Schjöth #1323. Size varies.

Date	Mintage	Good	VG	F	VF	XF
ND(1644)	—	12.50	17.50	27.50	40.00	—

KM# 162 CASH

Cast Bronze **Obv. Inscription:** Yung-ch'ang T'ung-pao **Rev:** "Yi" above **Note:** Schjöth #1324

Date	Mintage	Good	VG	F	VF	XF
ND(1644)	—	—	—	—	—	—

KM# 165 5 CASH

Cast Bronze, 36-38 mm. **Obv. Inscription:** "Yung-ch'ang T'ung-pao" **Rev:** Plain **Note:** Schjöth #1325. Size varies: 36-38 millimeters.

Date	Mintage	Good	VG	F	VF	XF
ND(1644)	—	12.00	21.00	30.00	45.00	—

Yung-li

Prince Yung-ming, Chao-ch'ing Fu, Kwangtung

CAST COINAGE

KM# 128.1 CASH
Cast Bronze **Obv. Inscription:** "Yung-li T'ung-pao" **Rev:** Plain **Note:** Schjöth #1296.

Date	Mintage	Good	VG	F	VF	XF
ND(1647-62)	—	2.00	3.50	5.00	7.50	—

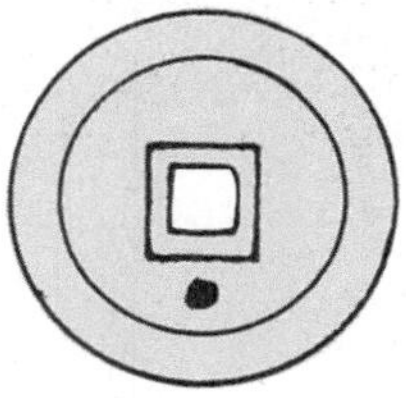

KM# 128.2 CASH
Cast Bronze **Obv. Inscription:** "Yung-li T'ung-pao" **Rev:** Dot below **Note:** Schjöth #1297.

Date	Mintage	Good	VG	F	VF	XF
ND(1647-62)	—	4.00	7.00	10.00	15.00	—

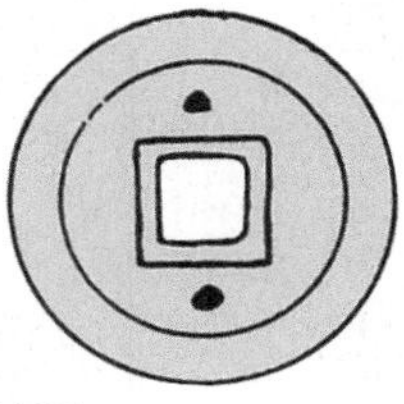

KM# 128.3 CASH
Cast Bronze **Obv. Inscription:** "Yung-li T'ung-pao" **Rev:** Dot above and below **Note:** Schjöth #1298.

Date	Mintage	Good	VG	F	VF	XF
ND(1647-62)	—	6.00	10.00	15.00	20.00	—

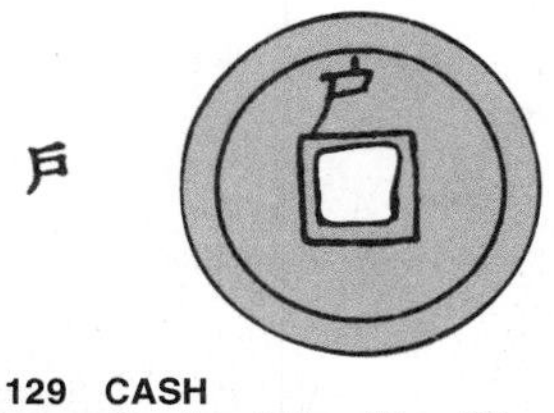

KM# 129 CASH
Cast Bronze **Obv. Inscription:** "Yung-li T'ung-pao" **Rev:** Large "Hu" above **Note:** Schjöth #1299.

Date	Mintage	Good	VG	F	VF	XF
ND(1647-62)	—	3.00	6.00	10.00	15.00	—

KM# 130 CASH
Cast Bronze **Obv. Inscription:** "Yung-li T'ung-pao" **Rev:** "Yu" above **Note:** Schjöth #1300.

Date	Mintage	Good	VG	F	VF	XF
ND(1647-62)	—	30.00	45.00	60.00	90.00	—

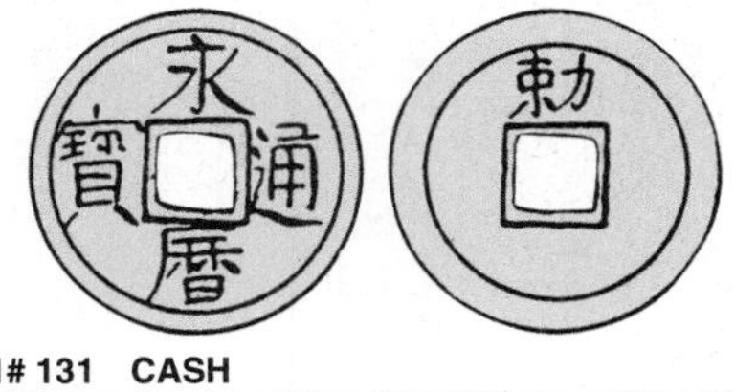

KM# 131 CASH
Cast Bronze **Obv. Inscription:** "Yung-li T'ung-pao" **Rev:** "Ch'ih" **Note:** Schjöth #1301.

Date	Mintage	Good	VG	F	VF	XF
ND(1647-62)	—	40.00	65.00	90.00	125	—

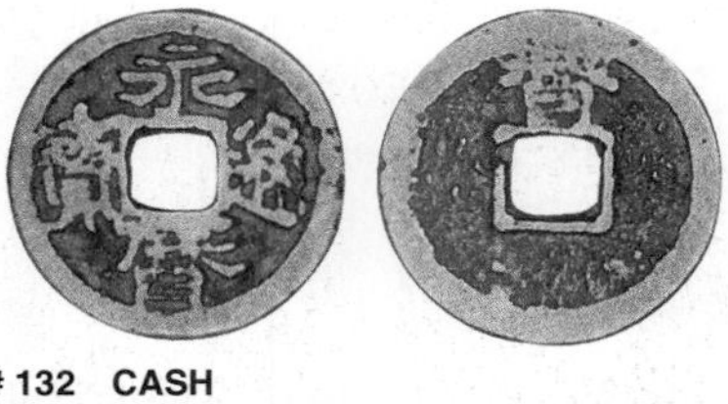

KM# 132 CASH
Cast Bronze **Obv. Inscription:** "Yung-li T'ung-pao" **Rev:** "Tu" above **Note:** Schjöth #1302-03.

Date	Mintage	Good	VG	F	VF	XF
ND(1647-62)	—	—	—	—	—	—

Note: The illustrations for Schjöth #1302 and #1303 were misleading while the descriptive text was correct

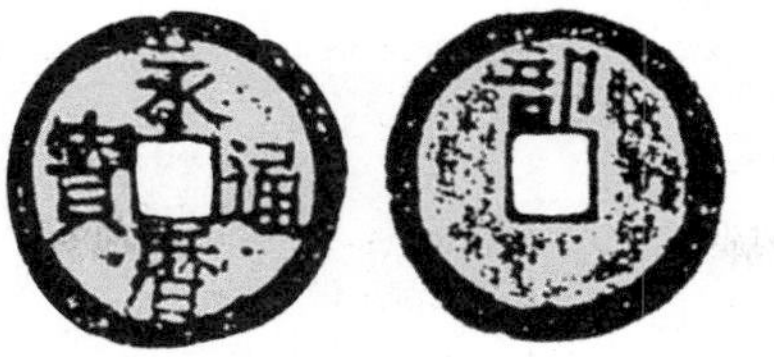

KM# 133 CASH
Cast Bronze **Obv. Inscription:** "Yung-li T'ung-pao" **Rev:** "Pu" above

Date	Mintage	Good	VG	F	VF	XF
ND(1647-62)	—	90.00	160	225	335	—

KM# 134 CASH
Cast Bronze **Obv. Inscription:** "Yung-li T'ung-pao" **Rev:** "Tao" above **Note:** Schjöth #1304.

Date	Mintage	Good	VG	F	VF	XF
ND(1647-62)	—	60.00	100	200	300	—

KM# 135 CASH
Cast Bronze **Obv. Inscription:** "Yung-li T'ung-pao" **Rev:** "Liu" above **Note:** Schjöth #1305.

Date	Mintage	Good	VG	F	VF	XF
ND(1647-62)	—	10.00	15.00	25.00	40.00	—

KM# 136 CASH
Cast Bronze **Obv. Inscription:** "Yung-li T'ung-pao" **Rev:** "Yüeh" **Note:** Schjöth #1306.

Date	Mintage	Good	VG	F	VF	XF
ND(1647-62)	—	16.00	28.00	40.00	50.00	—

KM# A137 CASH
Cast Bronze **Obv. Inscription:** "Yung-li T'ung-pao" **Rev:** Small "Fu" above

Date	Mintage	Good	VG	F	VF	XF
ND(1647-62)	—	10.00	15.00	25.00	40.00	—

KM# 137 CASH
Cast Bronze **Obv. Inscription:** "Yung-li T'ung-pao" **Rev:** Large "Fu" above **Note:** Schjöth #1307.

Date	Mintage	Good	VG	F	VF	XF
ND(1647-62)	—	12.00	20.00	28.00	40.00	—

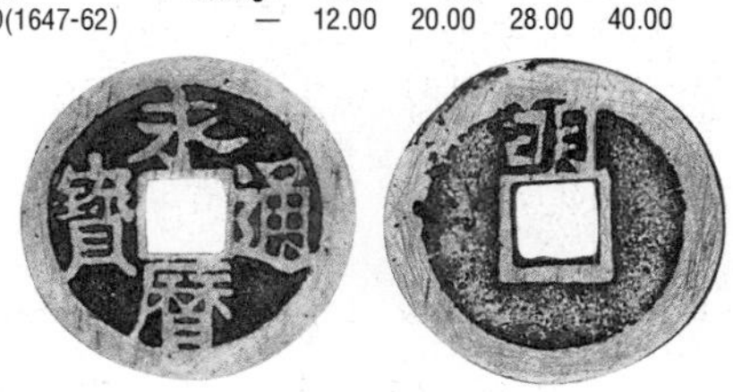

KM# 138 CASH
Cast Bronze **Obv. Inscription:** "Yung-li T'ung-pao" **Rev:** "Ming" above **Note:** Schjöth #1308.

Date	Mintage	Good	VG	F	VF	XF
ND(1647-62)	—	12.00	20.00	25.00	35.00	—

KM# A139 CASH
Cast Bronze **Obv. Inscription:** "Yung-li T'ung-pao" **Rev:** Small "T'ing" above **Note:** Schjöth #1308.

Date	Mintage	Good	VG	F	VF	XF
ND(1647-62)	1,647	150	250	400	500	—

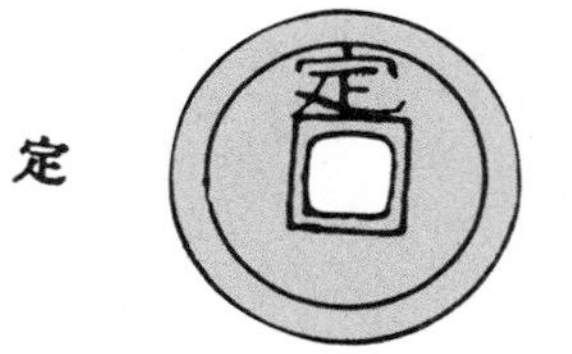

KM# 139 CASH
Cast Bronze **Obv. Inscription:** "Yung-li T'ung-pao" **Rev:** "T'ing" above **Note:** Schjöth #1309.

Date	Mintage	Good	VG	F	VF	XF
ND(1647-62)	—	12.00	20.00	25.00	35.00	—

KM# 140 CASH
Cast Bronze **Obv. Inscription:** "Yung-li T'ung-pao" **Rev:** "Kuo" above **Note:** Schjöth #1310.

Date	Mintage	Good	VG	F	VF	XF
ND(1647-62)	—	35.00	60.00	100	250	—

KM# 141 CASH
Cast Bronze **Obv. Inscription:** "Yung-li T'ung-pao" **Rev:** "Kung" above **Mint:** Kung-pu Board of Public Works **Note:** Schjöth #1311.

Date	Mintage	Good	VG	F	VF	XF
ND(1647-62)	—	6.00	10.00	15.00	20.00	—

KM# 142 CASH
Cast Bronze **Obv. Inscription:** "Yung-li T'ung-pao" **Rev:** "Kung" below **Mint:** Kung-pu Board of Public Works **Note:** Schjöth #1312.

Date	Mintage	Good	VG	F	VF	XF
ND(1647-62)	—	6.00	10.00	15.00	20.00	—

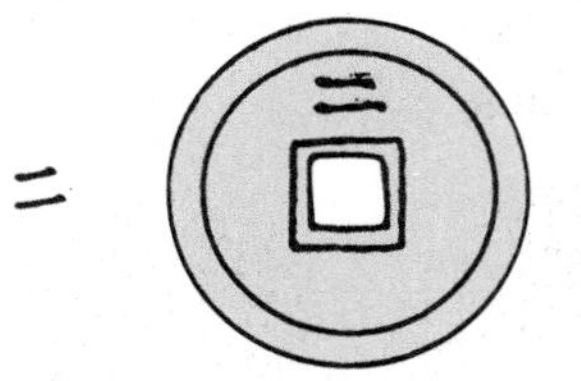

KM# 145 2 CASH
Cast Bronze **Obv. Inscription:** Yung-li T'ung-pao **Rev:** "Erh" (two) above **Note:** Schjöth #1313.

Date	Mintage	Good	VG	F	VF	XF
ND(1647-62)	—	10.00	17.50	25.00	35.00	—

KM# 146 2 CASH
Cast Bronze **Obv. Inscription:** "Yung-li T'ung-pao" **Rev:** "Êrh" (two) above, "Li" below **Note:** Schjöth #1314.

Date	Mintage	Good	VG	F	VF	XF
ND(1647-62)	—	12.50	20.00	32.50	45.00	—

KM# 147 2 CASH
Cast Bronze, 26-28 mm. **Obv:** Legend in seal script **Obv. Inscription:** "Yung-li T'ung-pao" **Note:** Schjöth #1315. Size varies.

Date	Mintage	Good	VG	F	VF	XF
ND(1647-62)	—	20.00	35.00	55.00	90.00	—

KM# 148 2 CASH
Cast Bronze **Obv:** Legend in "running hand" **Obv. Inscription:** "Yung-li T'ung-pao" **Note:** Schjöth #1316.

Date	Mintage	Good	VG	F	VF	XF
ND(1647-62)	—	20.00	35.00	55.00	90.00	—

KM# 149 2 CASH
Cast Bronze **Obv:** Legend in "grass characters" **Obv. Inscription:** "Yung-li T'ung-pao" **Note:** Schjöth #1317.

Date	Mintage	Good	VG	F	VF	XF
ND(1647-62)	—	20.00	35.00	55.00	90.00	—

KM# 150 2 CASH
Cast Bronze, 31-33 mm. **Obv. Inscription:** "Yung-li T'ung-pao" **Note:** Schjöth #1318. Size varies.

Date	Mintage	Good	VG	F	VF	XF
ND(1647-62)	—	17.50	27.50	37.50	50.00	—

KM# 153 5 CASH
Cast Bronze, 31-33 mm. **Obv. Inscription:** Yung-li T'ung-pao **Rev:** "Wu" (five) above, "Li" below **Note:** Schjöth #1319. Size varies.

Date	Mintage	Good	VG	F	VF	XF
ND(1647-62)	—	12.00	20.00	28.00	40.00	—

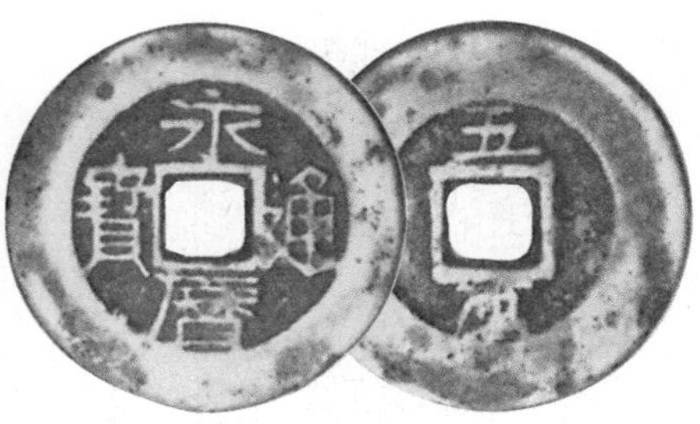

KM# 154 5 CASH
Cast Bronze, 34-36 mm. **Rev:** "Wu" (five) above, "Li" below **Note:** Schjöth #1320. Size varies.

Date	Mintage	Good	VG	F	VF	XF
ND(1647-62)	—	12.50	18.50	22.50	30.00	—

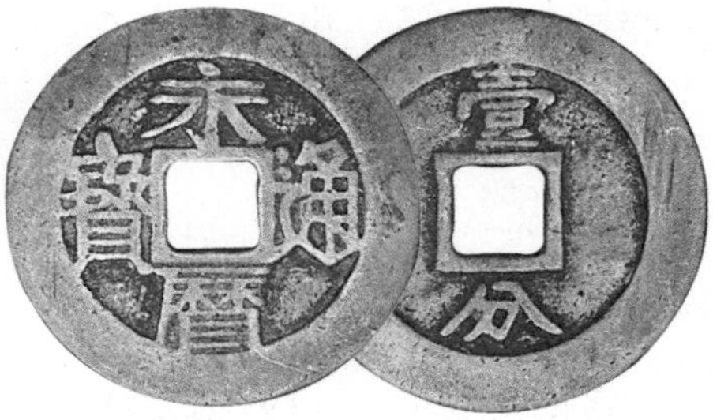

KM# 157 FEN
Cast Bronze **Obv. Inscription:** "Yung-li T'ung-pao" **Rev:** "Yi" (one) above, "Fen" (candareen) below **Note:** Schjöth #1321. Size varies: 34-36 millimeters.

Date	Mintage	Good	VG	F	VF	XF
ND(1647-62)	—	12.00	20.00	28.00	40.00	—

KM# 158 FEN
Cast Bronze, 45-47 mm. **Obv. Inscription:** Large "Yung-li T'ung-pao" **Rev:** Large "Yi" (one) above, "Fen" (candareen) below **Note:** Schjöth #1322. Size varies.

Date	Mintage	Good	VG	F	VF	XF
ND(1647-62)	—	18.00	30.00	42.00	65.00	—

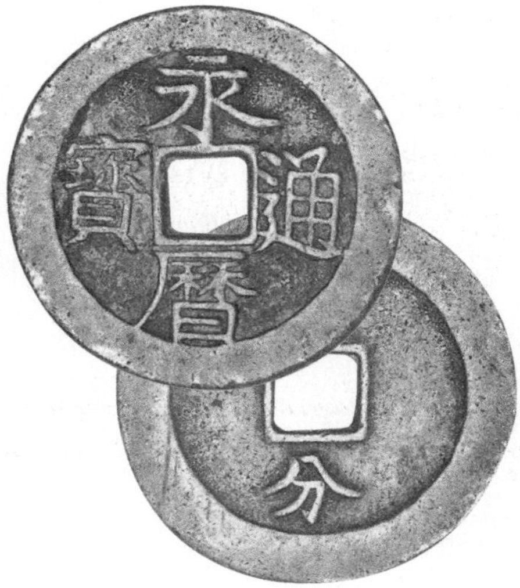

KM# 159 FEN
Cast Bronze, 45-47 mm. **Obv. Inscription:** Small "Yung-li T'ung-pao" **Rev:** Small "Yi" (one) above, "Fen" (candareen) below **Note:** Size varies.

Date	Mintage	Good	VG	F	VF	XF
ND(1647-62)	—	18.00	30.00	42.00	65.00	—

Ta-shun

Chang Hsien-chung

CAST COINAGE

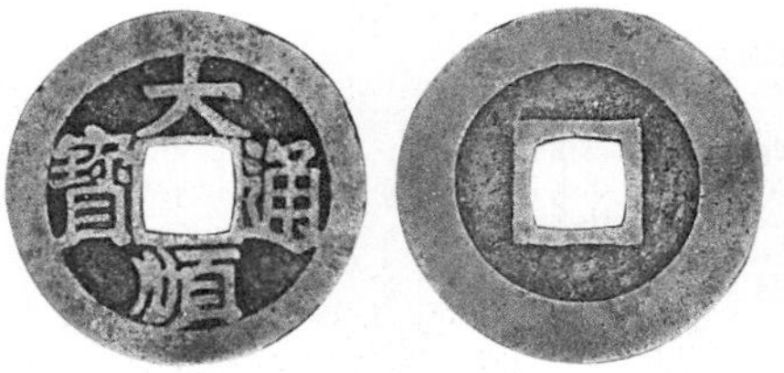

KM# 168 CASH
Cast Bronze **Obv. Inscription:** "Ta-shun T'ung-pao" **Rev:** Plain **Note:** Schjöth #1326.

Date	Mintage	Good	VG	F	VF	XF
ND(1644)	—	7.50	12.50	17.50	25.00	—

KM# 169 CASH
Cast Bronze **Obv. Inscription:** "Ta-shun T'ung-pao" **Rev:** "Hu" below **Note:** Schjöth #1327.

Date	Mintage	Good	VG	F	VF	XF
ND(1644)	—	12.00	21.00	30.00	45.00	—

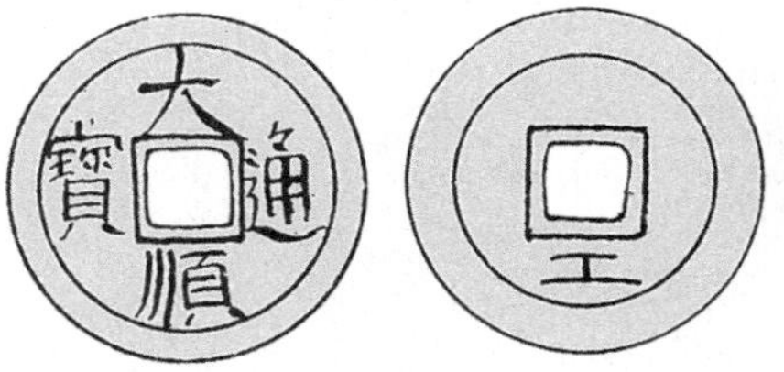

KM# 170 CASH
Cast Bronze **Obv. Inscription:** "Ta-shun T'ung-pao" **Rev:** "Kung" below **Note:** Schjöth #1328.

Date	Mintage	Good	VG	F	VF	XF
ND(1644)	—	7.50	12.50	17.50	25.00	—

Hsing-ch'ao

Sun K'o-wang

CAST COINAGE

KM# 173 CASH
Cast Bronze, 22-24 mm. **Obv. Inscription:** "Hsing-Ch'ao T'ung-pao" **Rev:** "Kung" below **Note:** Schjöth #1329. Size varies.

Date	Mintage	Good	VG	F	VF	XF
ND(1644)	—	12.50	17.50	27.50	40.00	—

KM# 174 CASH
Cast Bronze, 26-28 mm. **Obv. Inscription:** "Hsing-ch'ao T'ung-pao" **Rev:** "Kung" below **Note:** Schjöth #1330. Size varies.

Date	Mintage	Good	VG	F	VF	XF
ND(1644)	—	5.00	8.50	12.00	15.00	—

五
厘

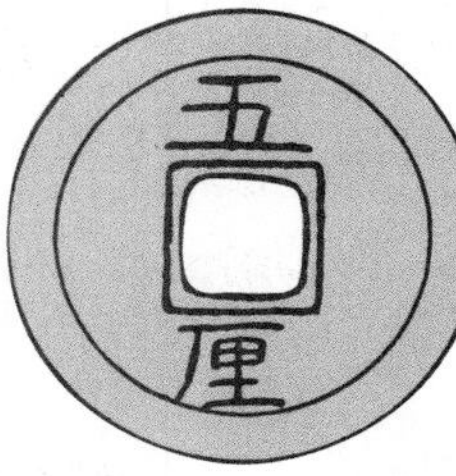

KM# 177.1 5 CASH
Cast Bronze, 30-32 mm. **Obv. Inscription:** "Hsing-ch'ao T'ung-pao" **Rev:** "Wu" (five) above, "Li" below **Note:** Schjöth #1331. Size varies.

Date	Mintage	Good	VG	F	VF	XF
ND(1644)	—	12.50	17.50	22.50	30.00	—

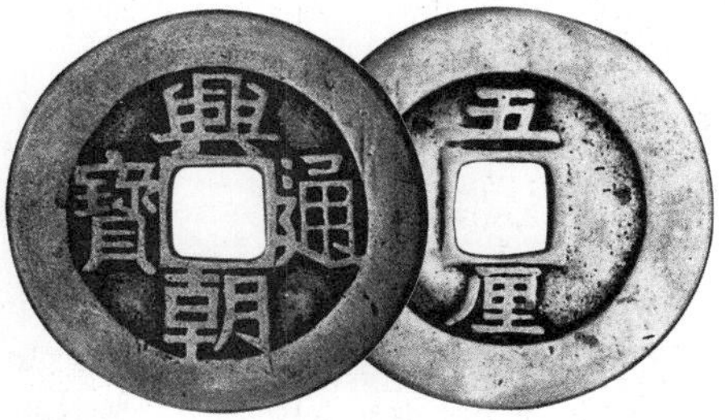

KM# 177.2 5 CASH
Cast Bronze, 32-36 mm. **Obv. Inscription:** "Hsing-ch'ao T'ung-pao" **Rev:** "Wu" (five) above, "Li" below **Note:** Schjöth #1332. Size varies.

Date	Mintage	Good	VG	F	VF	XF
ND(1644)	—	10.00	15.00	20.00	25.00	—

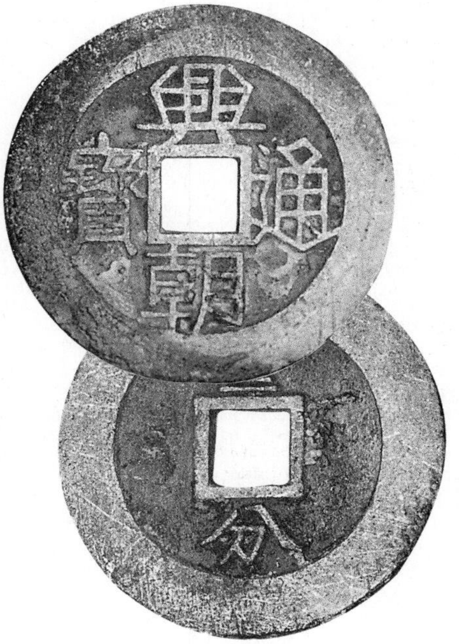

KM# 181 FEN
Cast Bronze, 48-50 mm. **Obv. Inscription:** "Hsing-ch'ao T'ung-pao" **Rev:** "Yi" (one) above, "Fen" (candareen) below **Note:** Schjöth #1333. Size varies.

Date	Mintage	Good	VG	F	VF	XF
ND(1644)	—	20.00	30.00	50.00	70.00	—

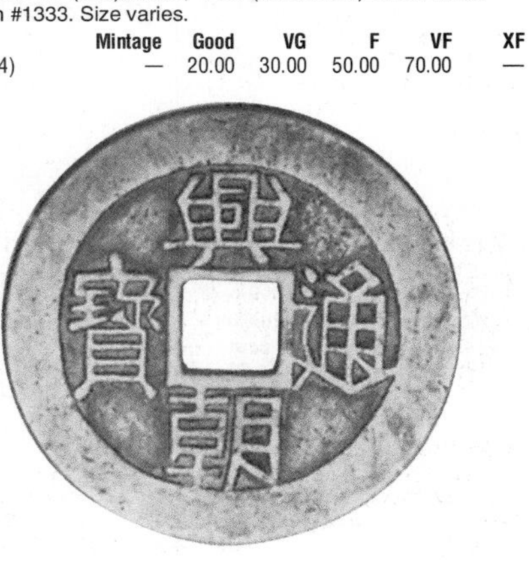

KM# 182 FEN
Cast Bronze, 44-46 mm. **Obv. Inscription:** "Hsing-ch'ao T'ung-pao" **Rev:** "Yi" (one) above, "Fen" (candareen) below **Note:** Schjöth #1334. Reduced size.

Date	Mintage	Good	VG	F	VF	XF
ND(1644)	—	15.00	25.00	40.00	60.00	—

Li-yung
Wu San-kuei

CAST COINAGE

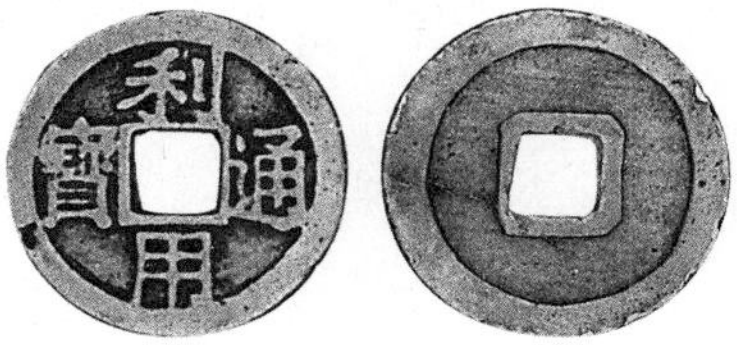

KM# 185 CASH
Cast Bronze, 22-24 mm. **Obv. Inscription:** "Li-yung T'ung-pao" **Rev:** Plain **Note:** Schjöth #1335. Size varies.

Date	Mintage	Good	VG	F	VF	XF
ND(1674)	—	1.50	2.50	3.50	5.00	—

KM# 186.1 CASH
Cast Bronze **Obv. Inscription:** "Li-yung T'ung-pao" **Rev:** Small-sized "Li" at right **Note:** Schjöth #1336.

Date	Mintage	Good	VG	F	VF	XF
ND(1674)	—	3.00	5.00	8.00	10.00	—

KM# 186.2 CASH
Cast Bronze **Obv. Inscription:** "Li-yung T'ung-pao" **Rev:** Small "Li" at left

Date	Mintage	Good	VG	F	VF	XF
ND(1674)	—	—	—	—	—	—

KM# 186.3 CASH
Cast Bronze **Obv. Inscription:** "Li-yung T'ung-pao" **Rev:** Large "Li" at right

Date	Mintage	Good	VG	F	VF	XF
ND(1674)	—	—	—	—	—	—

KM# 187 CASH
Cast Bronze **Obv. Inscription:** "Li-yung T'ung-pao" **Rev:** "Kuei" above **Mint:** Kueichow Fu **Note:** Schjöth #1337.

Date	Mintage	Good	VG	F	VF	XF
ND(1674)	—	3.00	5.00	8.00	10.00	—

KM# 188 CASH
Cast Bronze **Obv. Inscription:** "Li-yung T'ung-pao" **Rev:** Yün" at right **Mint:** Yünnan Fu **Note:** Schjöth #1338.

Date	Mintage	Good	VG	F	VF	XF
ND(1674)	—	5.50	9.00	14.00	18.00	—

KM# 190 2 CASH
Cast Bronze, 25-27 mm. **Obv. Inscription:** "Li-yung T'ung-pao" **Rev:** Plain **Note:** Size varies.

Date	Mintage	Good	VG	F	VF	XF
ND(1674)	—	5.50	9.00	14.00	18.00	—

KM# 191 2 CASH
Cast Bronze **Obv. Inscription:** "Li-yung T'ung-pao" **Rev:** Yün" at right **Mint:** Yün **Note:** Schjöth #1339.

Date	Mintage	Good	VG	F	VF	XF
ND(1674)	—	6.50	11.00	16.00	22.00	—

KM# 192 2 CASH
Cast Bronze **Obv. Inscription:** "Li-yung T'ung-pao" **Rev:** "Êrh" (two) at right, "Li" at left **Note:** Schjöth #1340.

Date	Mintage	Good	VG	F	VF	XF
ND(1674)	—	5.50	9.00	14.00	18.00	—

KM# 195 5 CASH
Cast Bronze **Obv. Inscription:** "Li-yung T'ung-pao" **Rev:** "Wu" (five) above, "Li" below **Note:** Schjöth #1341.

Date	Mintage	Good	VG	F	VF	XF
ND(1674)	—	8.00	10.00	18.00	20.00	—

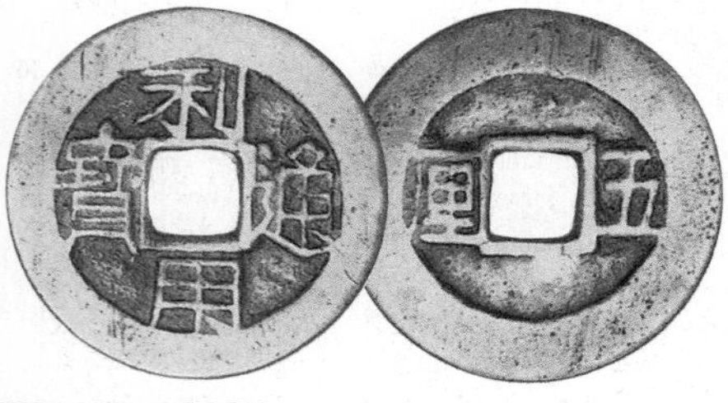

KM# 196 5 CASH

Cast Bronze **Obv. Inscription:** "Li-yung T'ung-pao" **Rev:** "Wu" (five) at right, "Li" at left

Date	Mintage	Good	VG	F	VF	XF
ND(1674)	—	9.00	12.00	18.00	25.00	—

KM# 197 FEN

Cast Bronze, 39-41 mm. **Obv:** Large inscription **Obv. Inscription:** "Li-yung T'ung-pao" **Rev:** "Yi" (one) at right, "Fen" (candareen) at left **Note:** Schjöth #1342. Size varies.

Date	Mintage	Good	VG	F	VF	XF
ND(1674)	—	15.00	25.00	37.50	55.00	—

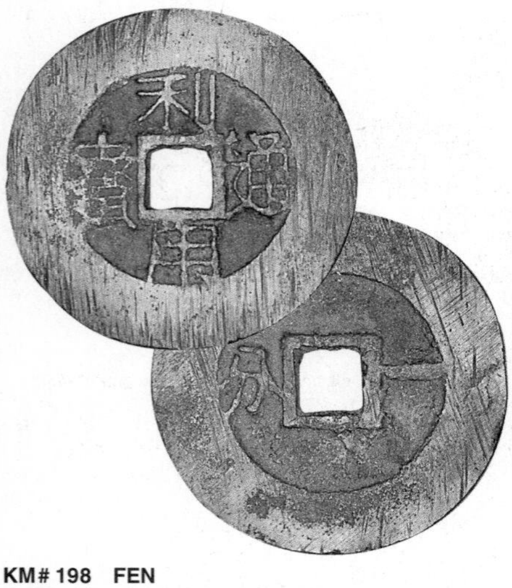

KM# 198 FEN

Cast Bronze **Obv:** Small inscription **Obv. Inscription:** "Li-yung T'ung-pao" **Rev:** Small "Yi" (one) at right, "Fen" (candareen) at left

Date	Mintage	Good	VG	F	VF	XF
ND(1674)	—	15.00	25.00	37.50	55.00	—

KM# 199 FEN

Cast Bronze **Obv:** Large inscription **Obv. Inscription:** "Li-yung T'ung-pao" **Rev:** Large "Yi" (one) above, "Fen" (candareen) below **Note:** Sch.#1343.

Date	Mintage	Good	VG	F	VF	XF
ND(1674)	—	25.00	37.50	52.50	75.00	—

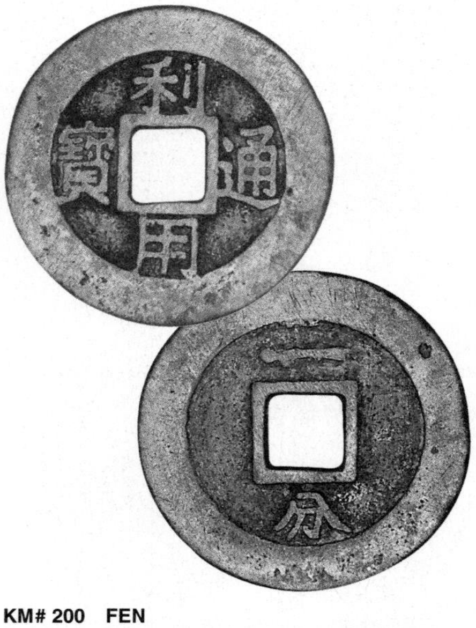

KM# 200 FEN

Cast Bronze, 38-40 mm. **Obv:** Small inscription **Obv. Inscription:** "Li-yung T'ung-pao" **Rev:** Small "Yi" (one) above, "Fen" (candareen) below **Note:** Reduced size.

Date	Mintage	Good	VG	F	VF	XF
ND(1674)	—	20.00	25.00	35.00	50.00	—

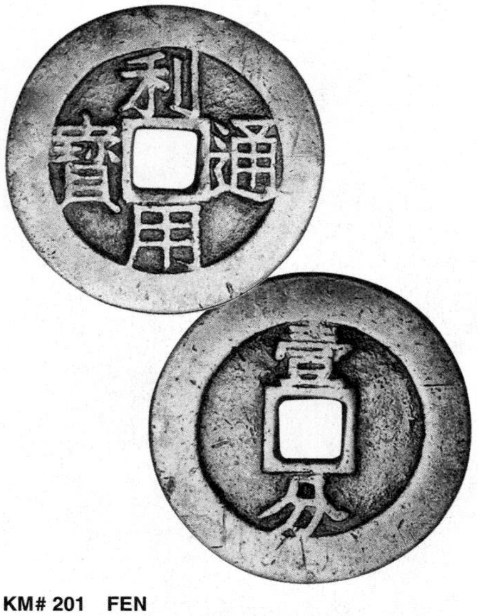

KM# 201 FEN

Cast Bronze **Obv. Inscription:** "Li-yung T'ung-pao" **Rev:** Official "Yi" (one) above, "Fen" (candareen) below

Date	Mintage	Good	VG	F	VF	XF
ND(1674)	—	30.00	45.00	60.00	90.00	—

Chao-wu

P'ing-hsi Wang

CAST COINAGE

KM# 203 CASH

Cast Bronze, 23-25 mm. **Obv:** Seal script characters **Obv. Inscription:** "Chao-wu T'ung-pao" **Rev:** Plain **Note:** Size varies.

Date	Mintage	Good	VG	F	VF	XF
ND(1678)	—	15.00	25.00	35.00	50.00	—

KM# 204.1 CASH

Cast Bronze **Obv:** Orthodox **Obv. Inscription:** "Chao-wu T'ung-pao" **Rev:** Plain **Note:** Schjöth #1345. Prev. KM#204.

Date	Mintage	Good	VG	F	VF	XF
ND(1678)	—	0.75	1.50	3.00	5.00	—

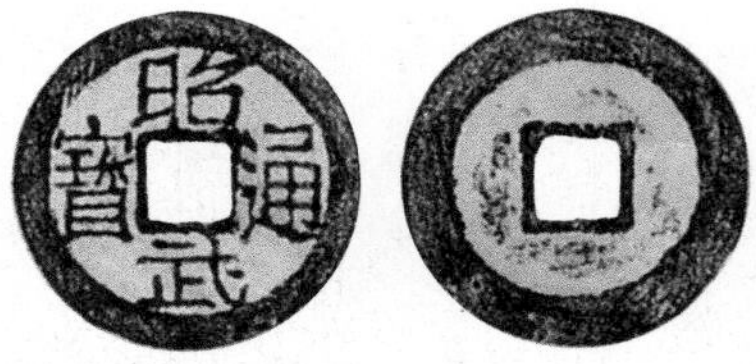

KM# 204.2 CASH

Cast Bronze **Obv:** Head of t'ung is open rectangle **Obv. Inscription:** "Chao-wu T'ung-pao" **Rev:** Plain

Date	Mintage	Good	VG	F	VF	XF
ND(1678)	—	26.50	32.50	40.00	50.00	—

KM# 205 CASH

Cast Bronze **Obv:** Orthodox characters **Obv. Inscription:** "Chao-wu T'ung-pao" **Rev:** "Kung" below **Mint:** Kung-pu Board of Public Works **Note:** Schjöth #1346.

Date	Mintage	Good	VG	F	VF	XF
ND(1678)	—	2.00	3.00	4.50	6.00	—

KM# 208 FEN

Cast Bronze **Obv:** Seal script characters **Obv. Inscription:** "Chao-wu T'ung-pao" **Rev:** Seal script characters **Rev. Legend:** "Yi" (one), "Fen" (candareen) **Note:** Schjöth #1347.

Date	Mintage	Good	VG	F	VF	XF
ND(1678)	—	20.00	30.00	45.00	65.00	—

Hung-hua
Wu Shih-fan

CAST COINAGE

KM# 211 CASH
Cast Bronze **Obv. Inscription:** "Hung-hua T'ung-pao" **Rev:** Plain **Note:** Schjöth #1348. Size varies: 23-25 millimeters.

Date	Mintage	Good	VG	F	VF	XF
ND(ca.1679)	—	1.00	1.50	2.00	3.00	—

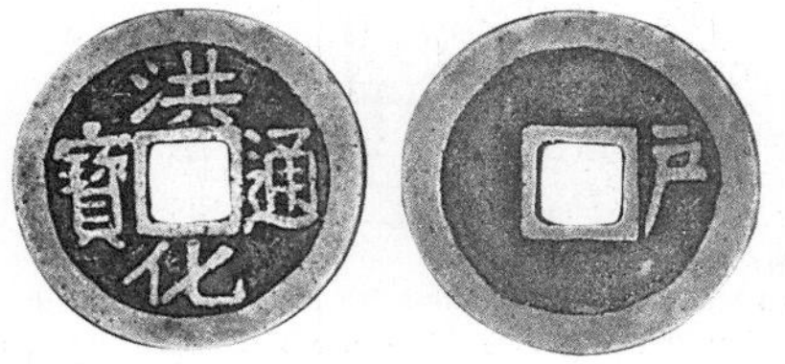

KM# 212 CASH
Cast Bronze **Obv. Inscription:** "Hung-hua T'ung-pao" **Rev:** "Hu" at right **Mint:** Hu-pu Board of Revenue **Note:** Schjöth #1349.

Date	Mintage	Good	VG	F	VF	XF
ND(ca.1679)	—	1.75	2.50	3.50	5.00	—

KM# 213 CASH
Cast Bronze **Obv. Inscription:** "Hung-hua T'ung-pao" **Rev:** "Kung" at right **Mint:** Kung-pu Board of Public Works **Note:** Schjöth #1350.

Date	Mintage	Good	VG	F	VF	XF
ND(ca.1679)	—	2.25	3.00	4.50	6.00	—

Yü-min
Keng Ching-chung

CAST COINAGE

KM# 217.1 CASH
Cast Bronze, 22-24 mm. **Obv. Inscription:** "Yü-min T'ung-pao" **Rev:** Plain **Mint:** Fukien **Note:** Schjöth #1351. Size varies.

Date	Mintage	Good	VG	F	VF	XF
ND(1674)	—	—	—	—	—	—

KM# 217.2 CASH
Cast Bronze **Obv:** Inscription deviating style **Obv. Inscription:** "Yü-min T'ung-pao" **Rev:** Plain **Mint:** Fukien **Note:** Schjöth #1352.

Date	Mintage	Good	VG	F	VF	XF
ND(1674)	—	6.00	10.00	15.00	20.00	—

KM# 220 FEN
Cast Bronze, 25-27 mm. **Obv. Inscription:** "Yü-min T'ung-pao" **Rev:** "Yi" (one) "Fen" (candareen) at right **Mint:** Fukien **Note:** Schjöth #1353. Size varies.

Date	Mintage	Good	VG	F	VF	XF
ND(1674)	—	7.50	12.50	20.00	30.00	—

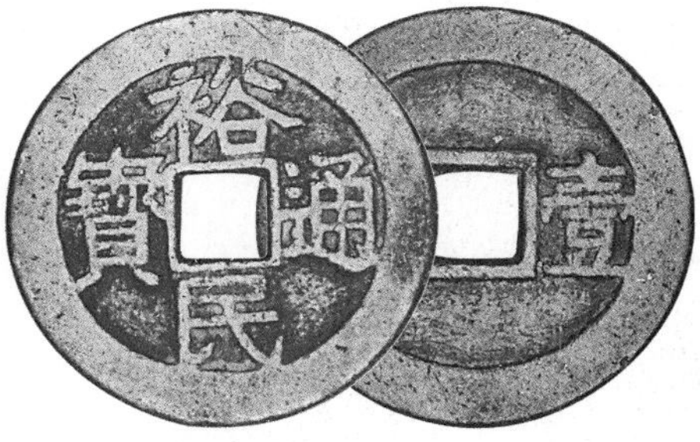

KM# 223 MACE
Cast Bronze, 37-39 mm. **Obv. Inscription:** "Yü-min T'ung-pao" **Rev:** "Yi" (one) at right, "Ch'ien" (mace) at left **Mint:** Fukien **Note:** Schjöth #1354. Size varies.

Date	Mintage	Good	VG	F	VF	XF
ND(1674)	—	25.00	35.00	50.00	70.00	—

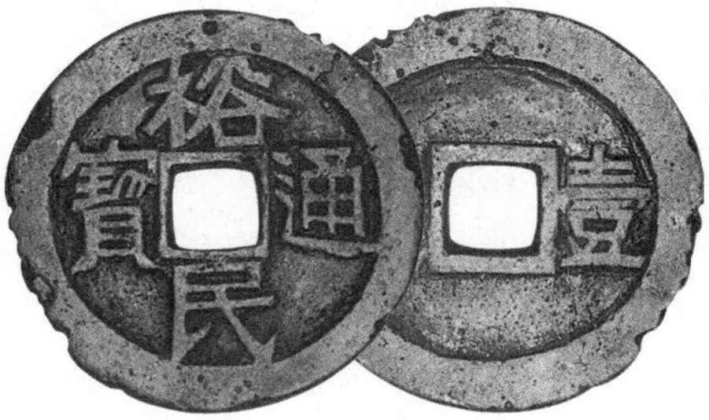

KM# 224 MACE
Cast Bronze **Obv. Inscription:** "Yü-min T'ung-pao" **Rev:** "Chê" at right, "Ch'ien" (mace) at left **Mint:** Fukien

Date	Mintage	Good	VG	F	VF	XF
ND(1674)	—	50.00	90.00	130	180	—

CH'ING DYNASTY
Manchu, 1644 - 1911

Shun-chih
Shunzhi

CAST COINAGE

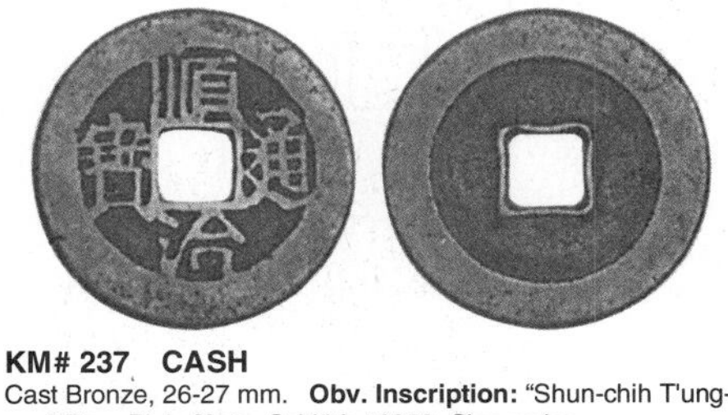

KM# 237 CASH
Cast Bronze, 26-27 mm. **Obv. Inscription:** "Shun-chih T'ung-pao" **Rev:** Plain **Note:** Schjöth #1359. Size varies.

Date	Mintage	Good	VG	F	VF	XF
ND(1644-61)	—	1.50	2.50	4.00	6.00	—

工

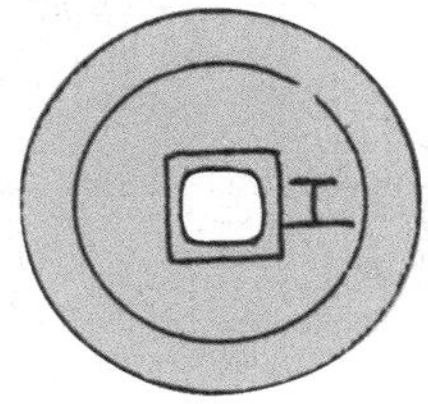

KM# 238 CASH
Cast Bronze **Obv. Inscription:** "Shun-chih T'ung-pao" **Rev:** "Kung" at right **Mint:** Kung-pu Board of Public Works **Note:** Schjöth #1360.

Date	Mintage	Good	VG	F	VF	XF
ND(1644-61)	—	2.50	4.00	6.50	8.00	—

工

KM# 239 CASH
Cast Bronze **Obv. Inscription:** "Shun-chih T'ung-pao" **Rev:** "Kung" above **Mint:** Kung-pu Board of Public Works

Date	Mintage	Good	VG	F	VF	XF
ND(1644-61)	—	50.00	85.00	150	250	—

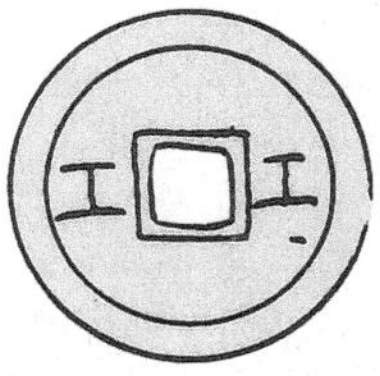

KM# 240 CASH
Cast Bronze **Obv. Inscription:** "Shun-chih T'ung-pao" **Rev:** "Kung" at left and right **Mint:** Kung-pu Board of Public Works **Note:** Schjöth #1361.

Date	Mintage	Good	VG	F	VF	XF
ND(1644-61)	—	—	—	—	—	—

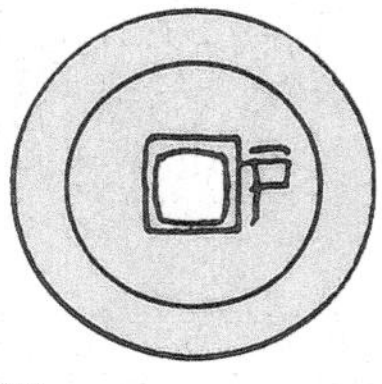

KM# 241 CASH
Cast Bronze **Obv. Inscription:** "Shun-chih T'ung-pao" **Rev:** "Hu" at right **Mint:** Hu-pu Board of Revenue **Note:** Schjöth #1362.

Date	Mintage	Good	VG	F	VF	XF
ND(1644-61)	—	1.50	2.50	4.00	6.00	—

戶

KM# 242 CASH
Cast Bronze **Obv. Inscription:** "Shun-chih T'ung-pao" **Rev:** "Hu" above **Mint:** Hu-pu Board of Revenue

Date	Mintage	Good	VG	F	VF	XF
ND(1644-61)	—	85.00	115	165	225	—

KM# 243 CASH
Cast Bronze **Obv. Inscription:** "Shun-chih T'ung-pao" **Rev:** "Ho" at right **Mint:** Honan **Note:** Schjöth #1363.

Date	Mintage	Good	VG	F	VF	XF
ND(1644-61)	—	5.00	8.00	15.00	20.00	—

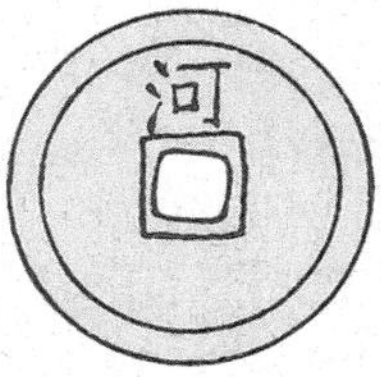

KM# 244 CASH

Cast Bronze **Obv. Inscription:** "Shun-chih T'ung-pao" **Rev:** "Ho" above **Mint:** Honan **Note:** Schjöth #1364.

Date	Mintage	Good	VG	F	VF	XF
ND(1644-61)	—	5.00	8.00	15.00	20.00	—

KM# 245 CASH

Cast Bronze **Obv. Inscription:** "Shun-chih T'ung-pao" **Rev:** "Lin" at right **Mint:** Linching **Note:** Schjöth #1365.

Date	Mintage	Good	VG	F	VF	XF
ND(1647-50)	—	10.00	15.00	20.00	25.00	—

KM# 247 CASH

Cast Bronze **Obv. Inscription:** "Shun-chih T'ung-pao" **Rev:** "Hsüan" at right **Mint:** Hsüan Prefecture **Note:** Schjöth #1367.

Date	Mintage	Good	VG	F	VF	XF
ND(1644-61)	—	10.00	15.00	20.00	25.00	—

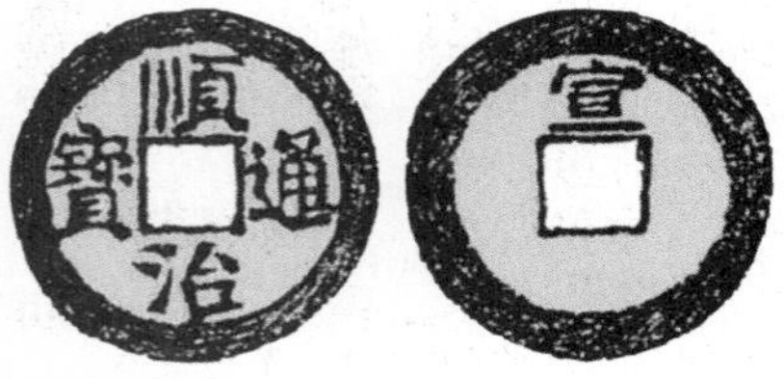

KM# 248 CASH

Cast Bronze **Obv. Inscription:** "Shun-chih T'ung-pao" **Rev:** "Hsüan" above **Mint:** Hsüan Prefecture **Note:** Schjöth #1368.

Date	Mintage	Good	VG	F	VF	XF
ND(1644-61)	—	100	160	225	325	—

薊

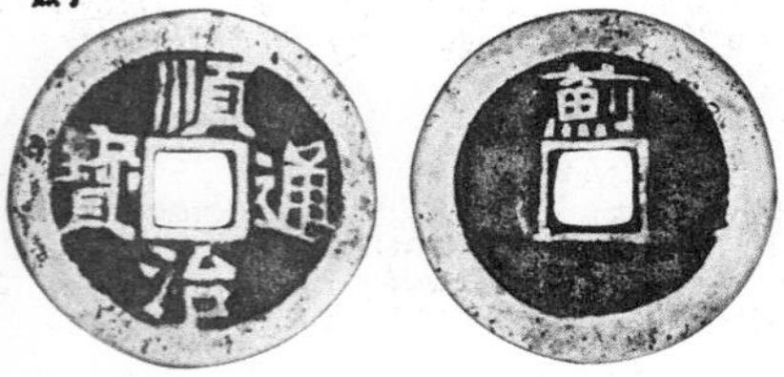

KM# A249 CASH

Cast Bronze **Obv. Inscription:** "Shun-chih T'ung-pao" **Rev:** "Chi" above **Mint:** Chichou

Date	Mintage	Good	VG	F	VF	XF
ND(1644-61)	—	75.00	125	175	250	—

薊

KM# 249 CASH

Cast Bronze **Obv. Inscription:** "Shun-chih T'ung-pao" **Rev:** "Chi" at right **Mint:** Chichou **Note:** Schjöth #1369.

Date	Mintage	Good	VG	F	VF	XF
ND(1644-61)	—	22.50	35.00	50.00	75.00	—

原

KM# 250 CASH

Cast Bronze **Obv. Inscription:** "Shun-chih T'ung-pao" **Rev:** "Yüan" at right **Mint:** T'aiyüan Fu **Note:** Schjöth #1370.

Date	Mintage	Good	VG	F	VF	XF
ND(1644-61)	—	7.50	12.50	20.00	—	—

KM# 251 CASH

Cast Bronze **Obv. Inscription:** "Shun-chih T'ung-pao" **Rev:** "Yüan" above **Mint:** T'aiyüan Fu **Note:** Schjöth #1371.

Date	Mintage	Good	VG	F	VF	XF
ND(1644-61)	—	10.00	17.50	25.00	—	—

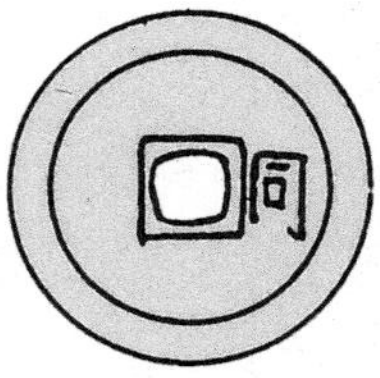

KM# 252 CASH

Cast Bronze **Obv. Inscription:** "Shun-chih T'ung-pao" **Rev:** "T'ung" at right **Mint:** Tat'ung **Note:** Schjöth #1372.

Date	Mintage	Good	VG	F	VF	XF
ND(1644-61)	—	5.50	9.00	15.00	—	—

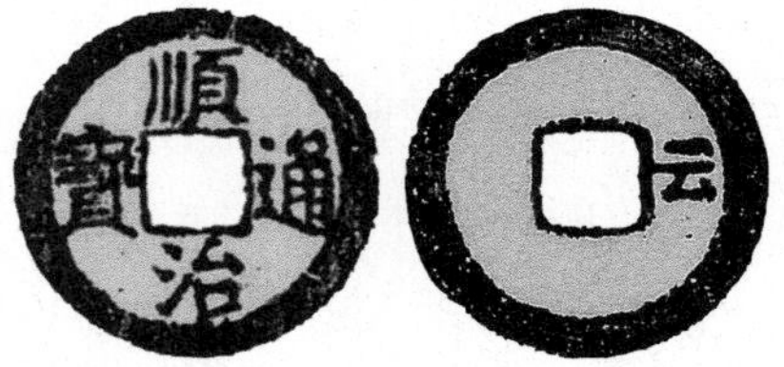

KM# 253 CASH

Cast Bronze **Obv. Inscription:** "Shun-chih T'ung-pao" **Rev:** "Yün" at right **Mint:** Miyün **Note:** Schjöth #1373.

Date	Mintage	Good	VG	F	VF	XF
ND(1644-61)	—	10.00	20.00	35.00	—	—

荆

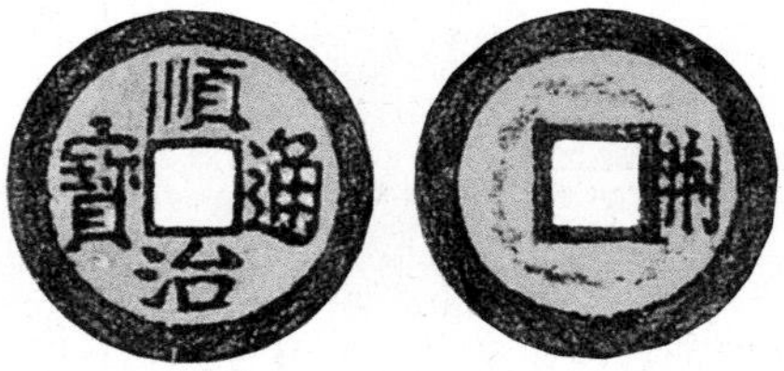

KM# 254 CASH

Cast Bronze **Obv. Inscription:** "Shun-chih T'ung-pao" **Rev:** "Ching" at right **Mint:** Chingchou **Note:** Schjöth #1374.

Date	Mintage	Good	VG	F	VF	XF
ND(1644-61)	—	75.00	125	175	250	—

寧

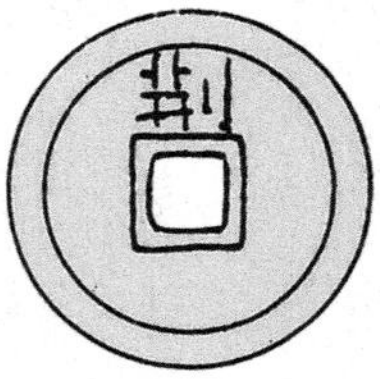

KM# 255 CASH

Cast Bronze **Obv. Inscription:** "Shun-chih T'ung-pao" **Rev:** "Ching" above **Mint:** Chingchou **Note:** Schjöth #1375.

Date	Mintage	Good	VG	F	VF	XF
ND(1644-61)	—	35.00	75.00	110	150	—

KM# 256 CASH

Cast Bronze **Obv. Inscription:** "Shun-chih T'ung-pao" **Rev:** "Ch'ang" above **Mint:** Wuch'ang **Note:** Schjöth #1376.

Date	Mintage	Good	VG	F	VF	XF
ND(1644-61)	—	5.50	9.00	15.00	—	—

KM# 257 CASH

Cast Bronze **Obv. Inscription:** "Shun-chih T'ung-pao" **Rev:** "Ning" above **Mint:** Chiangning **Note:** Schjöth #1377.

Date	Mintage	Good	VG	F	VF	XF
ND(1644-61)	—	5.50	9.00	15.00	—	—

Note: Attributed to Ninghsia Mint by some authorities

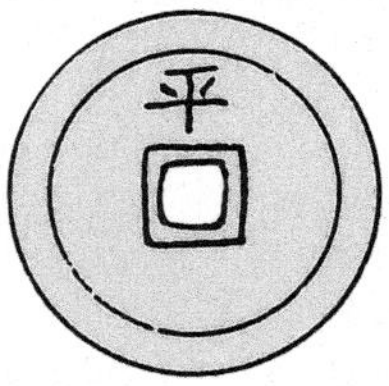

KM# 267 CASH

Cast Bronze **Obv. Inscription:** "Shun-chih T'ung-pao" **Rev:** "P'ing" above **Mint:** T'aiping Fu **Note:** Schjöth #1387.

Date	Mintage	Good	VG	F	VF	XF
ND(1644-61)	—	—	—	—	—	—

KM# A269 CASH

Cast Bronze **Obv. Inscription:** "Shun-chih T'ung-pao" **Rev:** "Yen" at top **Mint:** Yensui

Date	Mintage	Good	VG	F	VF	XF
ND(1644-61)	—	100	175	300	500	—

延

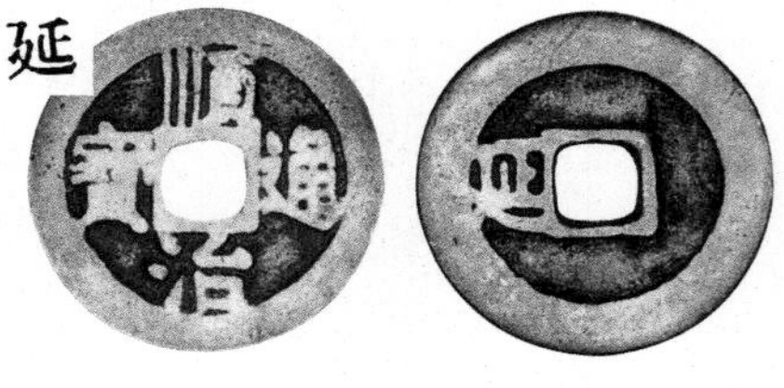

KM# 269 CASH

Cast Bronze **Obv. Inscription:** "Shun-chih T'ung-pao" **Rev:** "Yen" at left **Mint:** Yensui

Date	Mintage	Good	VG	F	VF	XF
ND(1646)	—	45.00	75.00	150	300	—

KM# 271 CASH

Cast Bronze **Obv. Inscription:** "Shun-chih T'ung-pao" **Rev:** Inverted crescent above

Date	Mintage	Good	VG	F	VF	XF
ND(1644-61)	—	5.50	9.00	15.00	25.00	—

KM# 272 CASH

Cast Bronze, 23 mm. **Obv. Inscription:** "Shun-chih T'ung-pao" **Rev:** Small circle above **Note:** Schjöth #1389. Reduced size.

Date	Mintage	Good	VG	F	VF	XF
ND(1644-61)	—	15.00	25.00	35.00	—	—

KM# 273 CASH

Cast Bronze, 26 mm. **Obv. Inscription:** "Shun-chih T'ung-pao" **Rev:** "Yi" (one) at right

Date	Mintage	Good	VG	F	VF	XF
ND(1644-61)	—	7.50	15.00	22.50	30.00	—

Note: Believed to be a trial issue

KM# 278 CASH

Cast Bronze **Obv. Inscription:** "Shun-chih T'ung-pao" **Rev:** "Yi (one) Li" at left, "Chê" at right **Mint:** Chêkiang **Note:** Schjöth #1393.

Date	Mintage	Good	VG	F	VF	XF
ND(1644-61)	—	8.00	10.00	15.00	20.00	—

KM# 279 CASH

Cast Bronze **Obv. Inscription:** "Shun-chih T'ung-pao" **Rev:** "Yi (one) Li" at left, "Fukien" at right **Mint:** Fuchou **Note:** Schjöth #1394.

Date	Mintage	Good	VG	F	VF	XF
ND(1644-61)	—	12.00	20.00	30.00	40.00	—

KM# 280 CASH

Cast Bronze **Obv. Inscription:** "Shun-chih T'ung-pao" **Rev:** "Yi (one) Li" at left, "Tung" at right **Mint:** Shantung **Note:** Schjöth #1395.

Date	Mintage	Good	VG	F	VF	XF
ND(1644-61)	—	5.00	8.00	10.00	15.00	—

臨

KM# 281 CASH

Cast Bronze **Obv. Inscription:** "Shun-chih T'ung-pao" **Rev:** "Yi (one) Li" at left, "Lin" at right **Mint:** Linch'ing **Note:** Schjöth #1396.

Date	Mintage	Good	VG	F	VF	XF
ND(1644-61)	—	5.50	9.00	15.00	20.00	—

KM# 274 CASH

Cast Bronze **Obv. Inscription:** "Shun-chih T'ung-pao" **Rev:** "?rh" (two) at right

Date	Mintage	Good	VG	F	VF	XF
ND	—	100	200	400	750	—

Note: These were once found to be all circulating forgeries with 'kung' at right cut away to erh, to make a 2 cash piece; Now there are numismatic fakes being made starting with existing cash altered to make a mother cash; This will usually be a larger plain reverse piece which only needs 'erh' to be added; Above is one made from a Nurhaci large cash; No genuine 2 cash exists

KM# 270 CASH

Cast Bronze, 25 mm. **Obv. Inscription:** "Shun-chih T'ung-pao" **Rev:** Small circle above **Note:** Schjöth #1388.

Date	Mintage	Good	VG	F	VF	XF
ND(1644)	—	5.50	9.90	15.00	22.00	—

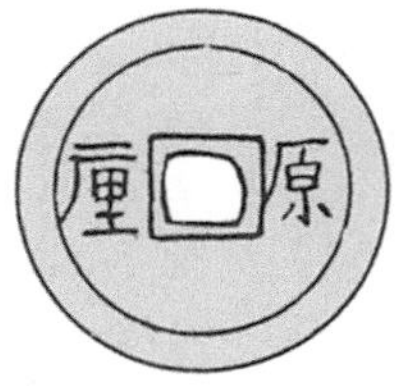

KM# A282 CASH

Cast Bronze **Obv. Inscription:** "Shun-chih T'ung-pao" **Rev:** "Yi (one) Li" at left, "Yüan" at right **Mint:** T'aiyüan Fu **Note:** Schjöth #1397. Prev. KM#281A.

Date	Mintage	Good	VG	F	VF	XF
ND(1644-61)	—	6.00	10.00	14.00	20.00	—

KM# 282 CASH

Cast Bronze **Obv. Inscription:** "Shun-chih T'ung-pao" **Rev:** "Yi (one) Li" at left, "Yang" at right **Mint:** Yangho **Note:** Schjöth #1398.

Date	Mintage	Good	VG	F	VF	XF
ND(1644-61)	—	15.00	20.00	25.00	30.00	—

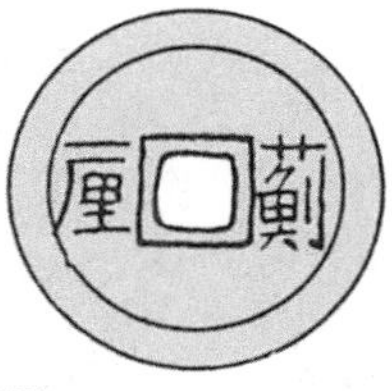

KM# 283 CASH

Cast Bronze **Obv. Inscription:** "Shun-chih T'ung-pao" **Rev:** "Yi (one) Li" at left, "Chi" at right **Mint:** Chichou **Note:** Schjöth #1399.

Date	Mintage	Good	VG	F	VF	XF
ND(1644-61)	—	5.50	9.00	15.00	20.00	—

KM# 268 CASH

Cast Bronze **Obv. Inscription:** "Shun-chih T'ung-pao" **Rev:** "Yen" at right **Mint:** Yensui

Date	Mintage	Good	VG	F	VF	XF
ND(1647-48)	—	45.00	75.00	150	300	—

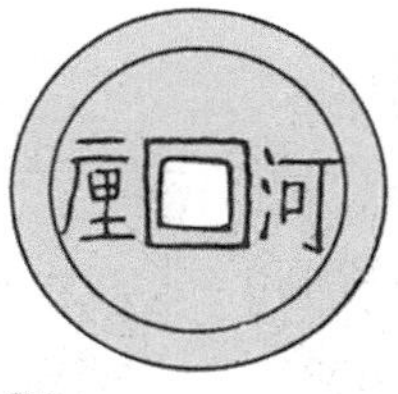

KM# 284 CASH

Cast Bronze **Obv. Inscription:** "Shun-chih T'ung-pao" **Rev:** "Yi (one) Li" at left, "Ho" at right **Mint:** Honan **Note:** Schjöth #1400.

Date	Mintage	Good	VG	F	VF	XF
ND(1644-61)	—	5.50	9.00	15.00	20.00	—

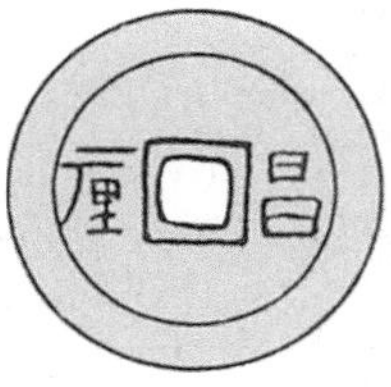

KM# 285 CASH

Cast Bronze **Obv. Inscription:** "Shun-chih T'ung-pao" **Rev:** "Yi (one) Li" at left, "Ch'ang" at right **Mint:** Wuch'ang **Note:** Schjöth #1401.

Date	Mintage	Good	VG	F	VF	XF
ND(1644-61)	—	5.50	9.00	15.00	20.00	—

陽

KM# 263 CASH

Cast Bronze **Obv. Inscription:** "Shun-chih T'ung-pao" **Rev:** "Yang" at right **Mint:** Yangho **Note:** Schjöth #1383.

Date	Mintage	Good	VG	F	VF	XF
ND(1649-50)	—	10.00	25.00	50.00	100	—

東

KM# 260 CASH

Cast Bronze **Obv. Inscription:** "Shun-chih T'ung-pao" **Rev:** "Tung" at right **Mint:** Shantung **Note:** Schjöth #1380.

Date	Mintage	Good	VG	F	VF	XF
ND(1649-50)	—	1.50	3.00	6.00	—	—

浙

KM# 258 CASH

Cast Bronze **Obv. Inscription:** "Shun-chih T'ung-pao" **Rev:** "Chê" at right **Mint:** Chêkiang **Note:** Schjöth #1378.

Date	Mintage	Good	VG	F	VF	XF
ND(1649-50)	—	1.50	3.00	6.00	—	—

KM# 286 CASH

Cast Bronze **Obv. Inscription:** "Shun-chih T'ung-pao" **Rev:** "Yi (one) Li" at left, "Shan" at right **Mint:** Shansi **Note:** Schjöth #1402.

Date	Mintage	Good	VG	F	VF	XF
ND(1644-61)	—	5.50	9.00	15.00	20.00	—

KM# 287 CASH

Cast Bronze **Obv. Inscription:** "Shun-chih T'ung-pao" **Rev:** "Yi (one) Li" at left, "Ning" at right **Mint:** Chiangning **Note:** Schjöth #1403.

Date	Mintage	Good	VG	F	VF	XF
ND(1644-61)	—	5.50	9.00	15.00	20.00	—

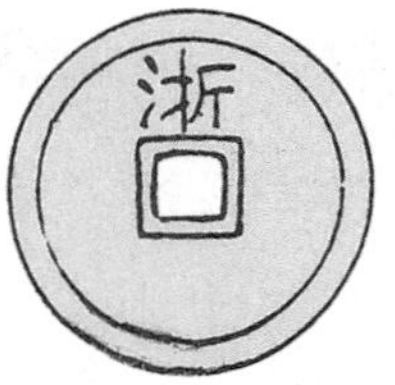

KM# 259 CASH

Cast Bronze **Obv. Inscription:** "Shun-chih T'ung-pao" **Rev:** "Chê" above **Mint:** Chêkiang **Note:** Schjöth #1379.

Date	Mintage	Good	VG	F	VF	XF
ND(1651-52)	—	2.50	5.00	10.00	—	—

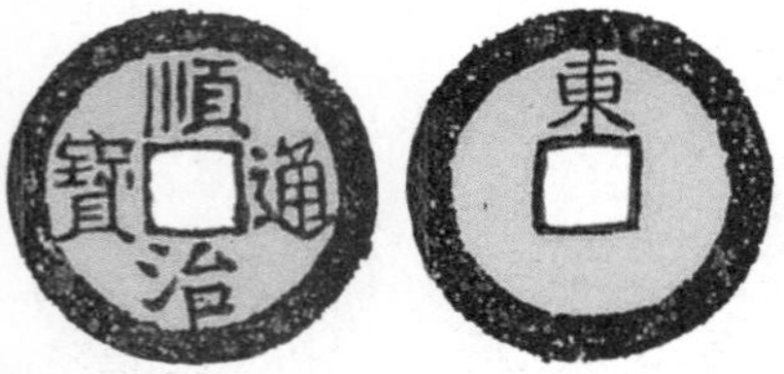

KM# 261 CASH

Cast Bronze **Obv. Inscription:** "Shun-chih T'ung-pao" **Rev:** "Tung" above **Mint:** Shantung **Note:** Schjöth #1381.

Date	Mintage	Good	VG	F	VF	XF
ND(1651-52)	—	1.50	3.00	6.00	—	—

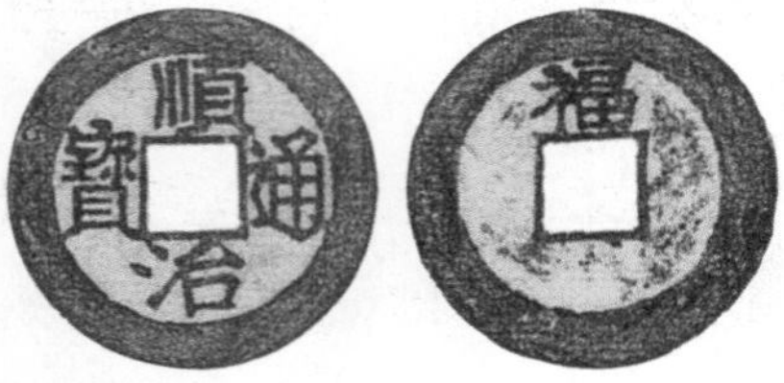

KM# 262 CASH

Cast Bronze **Obv. Inscription:** "Shun-chih T'ung-pao" **Rev:** "Fu" above **Mint:** Fuchow **Note:** Schjöth #1382.

Date	Mintage	Good	VG	F	VF	XF
ND(1651-52)	—	8.50	14.00	20.00	35.00	—

KM# 264 CASH

Cast Bronze **Obv. Inscription:** "Shun-chih T'ung-pao" **Rev:** "Yang" above **Mint:** Yangho **Note:** Schjöth #1384.

Date	Mintage	Good	VG	F	VF	XF
ND(1651)	—	18.00	30.00	65.00	120	—

襄

KM# 265 CASH

Cast Bronze **Obv. Inscription:** "Shun-chih T'ung-pao" **Rev:** "Hsiang" above **Mint:** Hsiangyang **Note:** Schjöth #1385.

Date	Mintage	Good	VG	F	VF	XF
ND(1651)	—	20.00	35.00	75.00	150	—

Note: Records indicate some mints were to be casting in the period of single character reverse marks, but whose cash have never been found; In many works they are noted to exist regardless; In Ting Fu-pao they are even drawn in by pen, without notation of that fact; These are: shen above & right, tung & kiang above, and ning, kuang, chang, & fu at right

臨

KM# 246 CASH

Cast Bronze **Obv. Inscription:** "Shun-chih T'ung-pao" **Rev:** "Lin" above **Mint:** Linching **Note:** Schjöth #1366.

Date	Mintage	Good	VG	F	VF	XF
ND(1651)	—	20.00	30.00	35.00	40.00	—

KM# 288 CASH

Cast Bronze **Obv. Inscription:** "Shun-chih T'ung-pao" **Rev:** "Yi (one) Li" at left, "Yün" at right **Mint:** Miyün **Note:** Schjöth #1404.

Date	Mintage	Good	VG	F	VF	XF
ND(1644-61)	—	5.50	9.00	15.00	20.00	—

戶

KM# 275 CASH

Cast Bronze **Obv. Inscription:** "Shun-chih T'ung-pao" **Rev:** "Yi (one) Li" at left, "Hu" at right **Mint:** Hu-pu Board of Revenue **Note:** Schjöth #1390.

Date	Mintage	Good	VG	F	VF	XF
ND(1653-56)	—	1.75	3.50	5.00	7.00	—

KM# 276 CASH

Cast Bronze **Obv. Inscription:** "Shun-chih T'ung-pao" **Rev:** "Yi (one) Li" at left, "Kung" at right **Mint:** Kung-pu Board of Public Works **Note:** Schjöth #1391.

Date	Mintage	Good	VG	F	VF	XF
ND(1653-56)	—	1.75	3.50	5.00	7.00	—

KM# 289 CASH

Cast Bronze **Obv. Inscription:** "Shun-chih T'ung-pao" **Rev:** "Yi (one) Li" at left, "T'ung" at right **Mint:** Tat'ung

Date	Mintage	Good	VG	F	VF	XF
ND(1644-61)	—	30.00	50.00	70.00	100	—

KM# 290 CASH

Cast Bronze **Obv. Inscription:** "Shun-chih T'ung-pao" **Rev:** "Yi (one) Li" at left, "Hsüan" at right **Mint:** Hsüanfu

Date	Mintage	Good	VG	F	VF	XF
ND(1644-61)	—	4.50	7.00	11.00	15.00	—

KM# 291 CASH

Cast Bronze **Obv. Inscription:** "Shun-chih T'ung-pao" **Rev. Inscription:** "Shun-chih T'ung-pao" **Note:** Muling of 2 obverses.

Date	Mintage	Good	VG	F	VF	XF
ND(1644-61)	—	7.00	12.00	20.00	35.00	—

KM# 277 CASH

Cast Bronze **Obv. Inscription:** "Shun-chih T'ung-pao" **Rev:** "Yi (one) Li" at left, "Chiang" at right **Mint:** Chiangning **Note:** Schjöth #1392.

Date	Mintage	Good	VG	F	VF	XF
ND(1655-56)	—	10.00	15.00	20.00	25.00	—

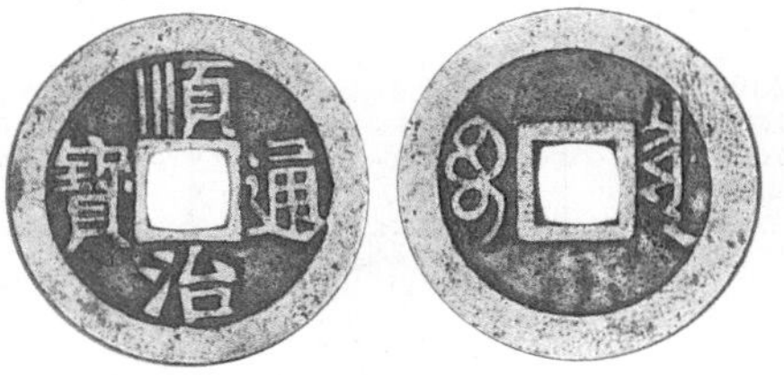

KM# 293 CASH

Cast Bronze, 26-27 mm. **Obv. Inscription:** "Shun-chih T'ung-pao" **Rev:** Manchu "Boo-Ciowan" **Mint:** Hu-pu Board of Revenue **Note:** Size varies.

Date	Mintage	Good	VG	F	VF	XF
ND(1694)	—	0.75	1.25	2.00	3.00	—

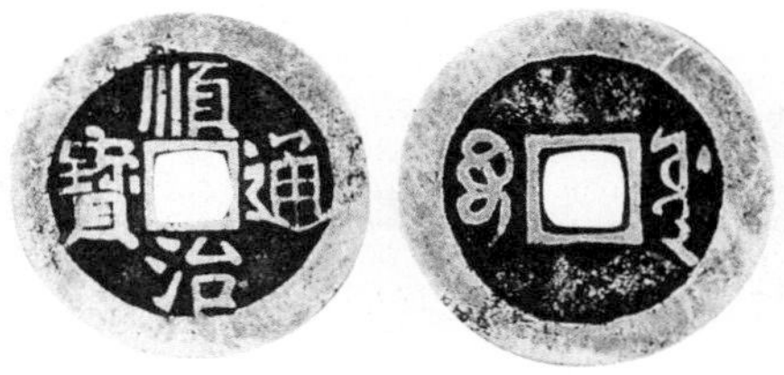

KM# 294 CASH

Cast Bronze **Obv. Inscription:** "Shun-chih T'ung-pao" **Rev:** Manchu "Boo-yuwan" **Mint:** Kung-pu Board of Public Works **Note:** Schjöth #1406.

Date	Mintage	Good	VG	F	VF	XF
ND1644	—	0.75	1.25	2.00	3.00	—

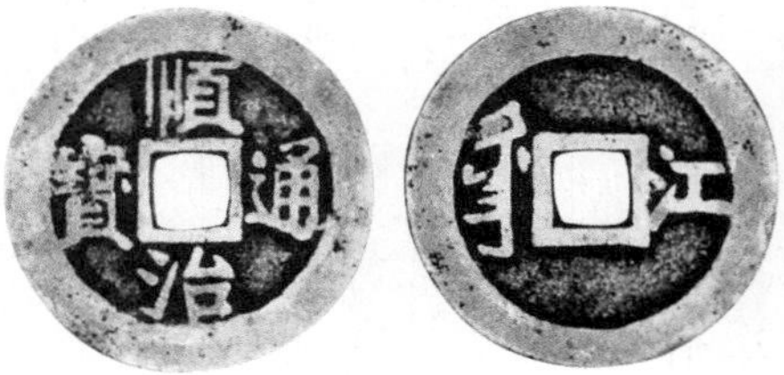

KM# 295 CASH

Cast Bronze **Obv. Inscription:** "Shun-chih T'ung-pao" **Rev:** Manchu "Giyang" at left, Chinese "Chiang" at right **Mint:** Chiangning **Note:** Schjöth #1407.

Date	Mintage	Good	VG	F	VF	XF
ND(1644-61)	—	1.50	3.00	5.00	7.00	—

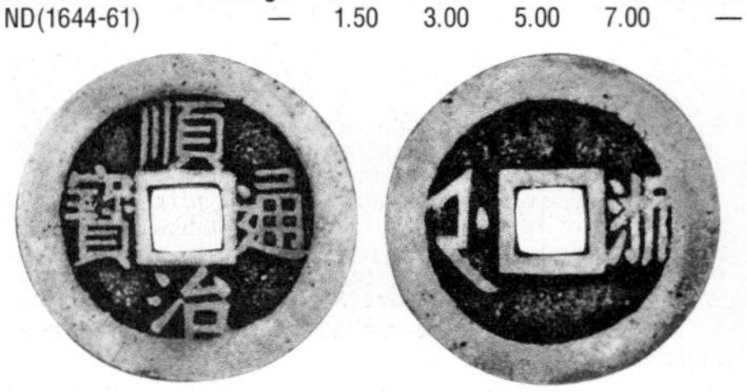

KM# 296 CASH

Cast Bronze **Obv. Inscription:** "Shun-chih T'ung-pao" **Rev:**

Manchu "Je" at left, Chinese "Chê" at right **Mint:** Chêkiang **Note:** Schjöth #1408.

Date	Mintage	Good	VG	F	VF	XF
ND(1644-61)	—	1.00	2.00	3.00	5.00	—

KM# 297 CASH

Cast Bronze **Obv. Inscription:** "Shun-chih T'ung-pao" **Rev:** Manchu "Dung" at left, Chinese "Tung" at right **Mint:** Shantung **Note:** Schjöth #1409.

Date	Mintage	Good	VG	F	VF	XF
ND(1644-61)	—	0.75	1.25	2.00	3.00	—

KM# 298 CASH

Cast Bronze **Obv. Inscription:** "Shun-chih T'ung-pao" **Rev:** Manchu "Lin"(?) at left, Chinese "Lin" at right **Mint:** Linch'ing **Note:** Schjöth #1410.

Date	Mintage	Good	VG	F	VF	XF
ND(1644-61)	—	1.00	2.00	3.00	5.00	—

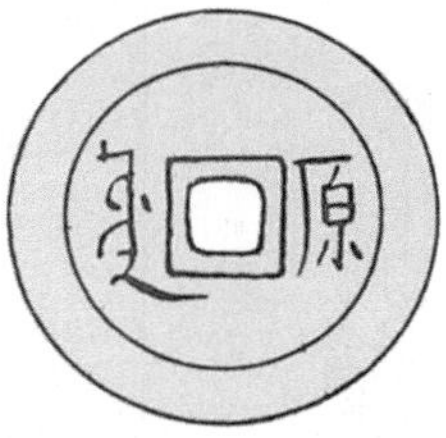

KM# 299 CASH

Cast Bronze **Obv. Inscription:** "Shun-chih T'ung-pao" **Rev:** Manchu "Yuwan" at left, Chinese "Yüan" at right **Mint:** T'aiyüan Fu **Note:** Schjöth #1411.

Date	Mintage	Good	VG	F	VF	XF
ND(1644-61)	—	3.00	6.00	10.00	15.00	—

KM# 300 CASH

Cast Bronze **Obv. Inscription:** "Shun-chih T'ung-pao" **Rev:** Manchu "Siowan" at left, Chinese "Hsüan" at right **Mint:** Hsüanfu **Note:** Schjöth #1412.

Date	Mintage	Good	VG	F	VF	XF
ND(1644-61)	—	0.75	1.25	2.00	3.00	—

KM# 301 CASH

Cast Bronze **Obv. Inscription:** "Shun-chih T'ung-pao" **Rev:** Manchu "Gi" at left, Chinese "Chi" at right **Mint:** Chichou **Note:** Schjöth #1413.

Date	Mintage	Good	VG	F	VF	XF
ND(1644-61)	—	1.00	2.00	3.00	5.00	—

KM# 302 CASH

Cast Bronze **Obv. Inscription:** "Shun-chih T'ung-pao" **Rev:** Manchu "Ho" at left, Chinese "Ho" at right **Mint:** Honan **Note:** Schjöth #1414.

Date	Mintage	Good	VG	F	VF	XF
ND(1644-61)	—	1.00	2.00	3.00	5.00	—

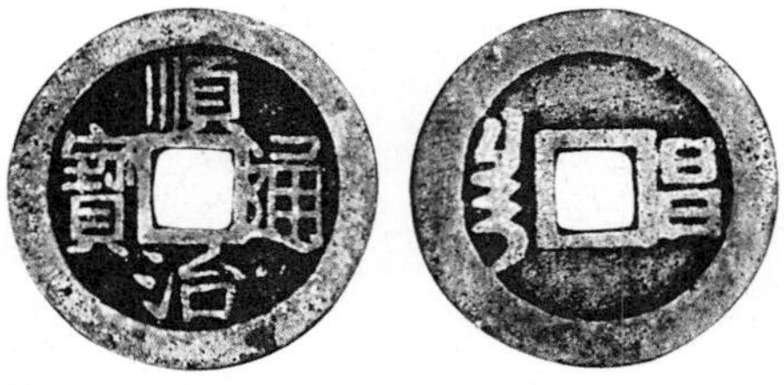

KM# 303 CASH

Cast Bronze **Obv. Inscription:** "Shun-chih T'ung-pao" **Rev:** Manchu "Cang" at left, Chinese "Ch'ang" at right **Mint:** Wuch'ang **Note:** Schjöth #1415.

Date	Mintage	Good	VG	F	VF	XF
ND(1644-61)	—	1.00	2.00	3.00	5.00	—

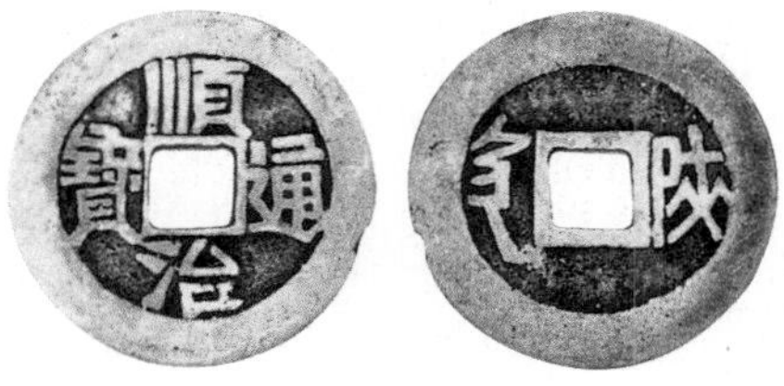

KM# 304 CASH

Cast Bronze **Obv. Inscription:** "Shun-chih T'ung-pao" **Rev:** Manchu "San" at left, Chinese "Shen" at right **Mint:** Shensi **Note:** Schjöth #1416.

Date	Mintage	Good	VG	F	VF	XF
ND(1644-61)	—	1.50	3.00	5.00	7.00	—

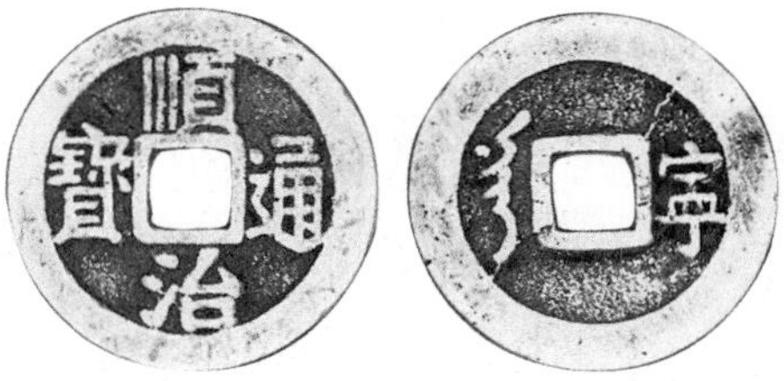

KM# 305 CASH

Cast Bronze **Rev:** Manchu "Ning"(?) at left, Chinese "Ning" at right **Rev. Inscription:** "Shun-chih T'ung-pao" **Mint:** Kiangning **Note:** Schjöth #1417.

Date	Mintage	Good	VG	F	VF	XF
ND(1644-61)	—	1.00	2.00	3.00	5.00	—

KM# 306 CASH

Cast Bronze **Obv. Inscription:** "Shun-chih T'ung-pao" **Rev:** Manchu "Tung" at left, Chinese "T'ung" at right **Mint:** Tat'ung **Note:** Schjöth #1418.

Date	Mintage	Good	VG	F	VF	XF
ND(1644-61)	—	1.00	2.00	3.00	5.00	—

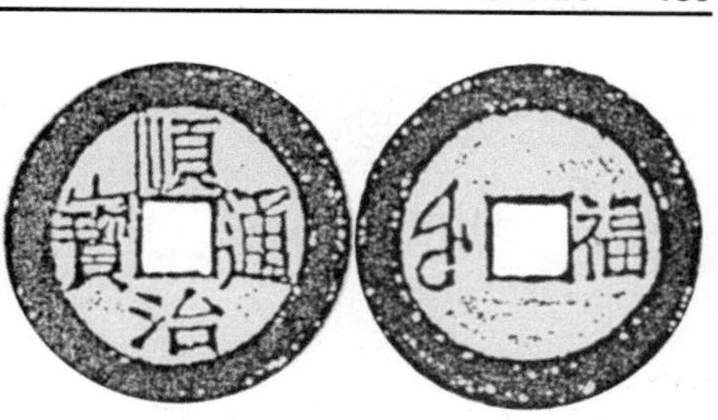

KM# 307 CASH

Cast Bronze **Obv. Inscription:** "Shun-chih T'ung-pao" **Rev:** Manchu "Fu" at left, Chinese "Fu" at right **Mint:** Fuchou

Date	Mintage	Good	VG	F	VF	XF
ND(1644-61)	—	50.00	100	150	200	—

K'ang-hsi

1662-1722, Kangxi

CAST COINAGE

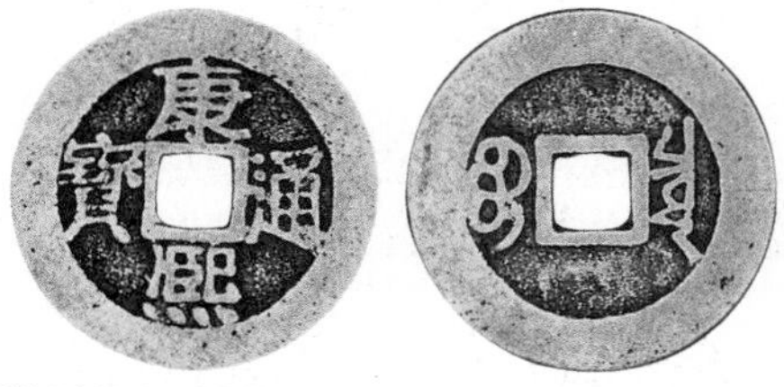

KM# 311.1 CASH

Cast Bronze, 25-27 mm. **Obv. Inscription:** "K'ang-hsi T'ung-pao" with open "hsi" **Rev:** Manchu "Boo-ciowan". **Mint:** Hu-pu Board of Revenue **Note:** Size varies. Schjöth #1419.

Date	Mintage	Good	VG	F	VF	XF
ND(1662-1722)	—	0.50	0.70	1.00	1.50	—

KM# 311.1a CASH

Cast Bronze, 25-27 mm. **Obv:** Wide rims **Obv. Inscription:** "K'ang-hsi T'ung-pao" with open "hsi" **Rev:** Manchu "Boo-ciowan" **Mint:** Hu-pu Board of Revenue **Note:** Size varies. Schjöth #1419. Prev. KM#311.1s.

Date	Mintage	Good	VG	F	VF	XF
ND(1662-1722)	—	0.50	0.70	1.00	1.50	—

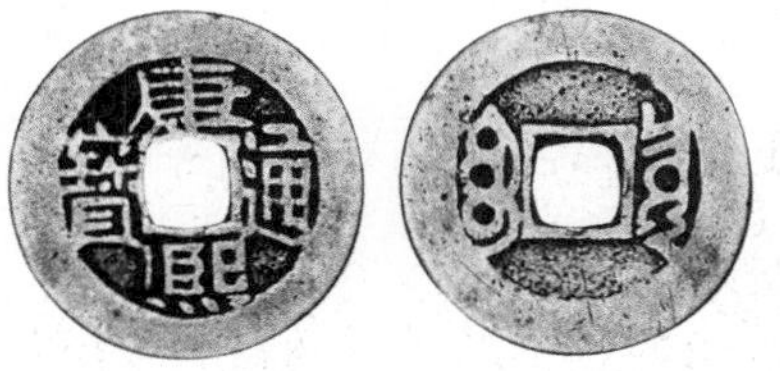

KM# 311.1b CASH

Cast Bronze, 24 mm. **Obv. Inscription:** K'ang-hsi T'ung-pao. **Rev:** Manchu "Boo-ciowan". **Mint:** Hu-pu Board of Revenue **Note:** Wide rims. Prev. KM#311.2s.

Date	Mintage	Good	VG	F	VF	XF
ND(1662-1722)	—	0.50	0.70	1.00	1.50	—

KM# 311.2 CASH

Cast Bronze **Obv. Inscription:** K'ang-hsi T'ung-pao **Rev:** Manchu "Boo-ciowan" with dot above **Mint:** Hu-pu Board of Revenue **Note:** Schjöth #1420.

Date	Mintage	Good	VG	F	VF	XF
ND(1662-1722)	—	14.00	20.00	28.50	40.00	—

KM# 312.1 CASH

Cast Bronze, 25-26 mm. **Obv:** One dot "T'ung" at right **Obv. Inscription:** K'ang-hsi T'ung-pao **Rev:** Manchu "Boo-Yuwan" **Mint:** Kung-pu Board of Public Works **Note:** Size varies. Narrow rims. Schjöth #1421.

Date	Mintage	Good	VG	F	VF	XF
ND(1662-1722)	—	0.20	0.50	0.80	2.00	—

KM# 312.2 CASH

Cast Bronze, 25-26 mm. **Obv:** 2 dot "T'ung" at right **Obv. Inscription:** K'ang-hsi T'ung-pao **Rev:** Manchu "Boo-Yuwan" **Mint:** Kung-pu Board of Public Works **Note:** Size varies. Wide rims.

Date	Mintage	Good	VG	F	VF	XF
ND(1662-1722)	—	0.20	0.50	0.80	1.50	—

KM# 312a CASH

Cast Bronze, 23-25 mm. **Obv. Inscription:** K'ang-hsi T'ung-pao **Mint:** Kung-pu Board of Public Works **Note:** Reduced size. Schjöth #1422. Prev. KM#313.

Date	Mintage	Good	VG	F	VF	XF
ND(1662-1722)	—	0.50	0.70	1.00	1.50	—

KM# 314 CASH

Cast Bronze, 25 mm. **Obv. Inscription:** K'ang-hsi T'ung-pao **Rev:** Manchu "Boo" at left, Chinese "Ho" (Honan) at right **Mint:** Honan

Date	Mintage	Good	VG	F	VF	XF
ND(1662-1722)	—	5.00	7.00	10.00	15.00	—

KM# 315 CASH

Cast Bronze **Rev:** Manchu "Gung" at left, Chinese "Kung" **Mint:** Kungch'ang

Date	Mintage	Good	VG	F	VF	XF
ND(1670)	—	400	600	850	1,200	—

同

KM# 318 CASH

Cast Bronze **Series:** Talisman (Poem Cash) **Obv. Inscription:** K'ang-hsi T'ung-pao **Rev:** Manchu "Tung" at left, Chinese "T'ung at right **Mint:** Tat'ung **Note:** Schjöth #1423.

Date	Mintage	Good	VG	F	VF	XF
ND(1662-1722)	—	1.50	2.25	3.50	5.00	—

福

KM# 319 CASH

Cast Bronze **Series:** Talisman (Poem Cash) **Obv. Inscription:** K'ang-hsi T'ung-pao **Rev:** Manchu "Fu" at left, Chinese "Fu" at right **Mint:** Fuchou **Note:** Schjöth #1424.

Date	Mintage	Good	VG	F	VF	XF
ND(1662-1722)	—	1.50	2.25	3.50	5.00	—

臨

KM# 320.1 CASH

Cast Bronze **Series:** Talisman (Poem Cash) **Obv. Inscription:** K'ang-hsi T'ung-pao **Rev:** Manchu "Lin" at left, Chinese "Lin" at right **Mint:** Linch'ing **Note:** Schjöth #1425.

Date	Mintage	Good	VG	F	VF	XF
ND(1662-1722)	—	1.50	2.25	3.50	5.00	—

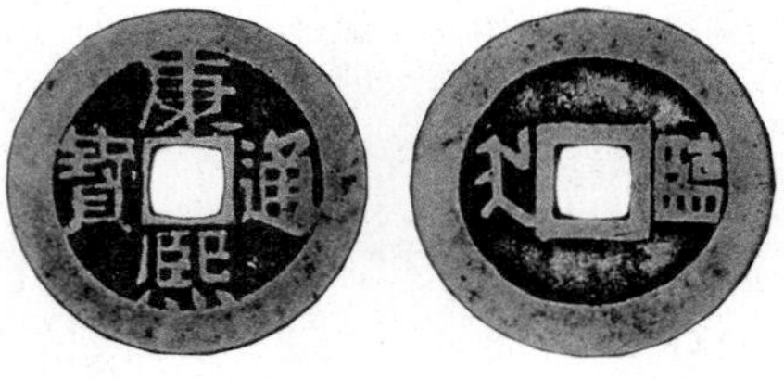

KM# 320.2 CASH

Cast Bronze **Series:** Talisman (Poem Cash) **Obv. Inscription:** K'ang-hsi T'ung-pao **Rev:** Manchu "Lin" at left, Chinese "Lin" at right deviating in style **Mint:** Linch'ing

Date	Mintage	Good	VG	F	VF	XF
ND(1662-1722)	—	1.50	2.25	3.50	5.00	—

東

KM# 321 CASH

Cast Bronze **Series:** Talisman (Poem Cash) **Obv. Inscription:** K'ang-hsi T'ung-pao **Rev:** Manchu "Dung" at left, Chinese "Tung" at right **Mint:** Shantung **Note:** Schjöth #1426.

Date	Mintage	Good	VG	F	VF	XF
ND(1662-1722)	—	1.50	2.25	3.50	5.00	—

江

KM# 322 CASH

Cast Bronze **Series:** Talisman (Poem Cash) **Obv. Inscription:** K'ang-hsi T'ung-pao **Rev:** Manchu "Giyang" at left, Chinese "Chiang" at right **Mint:** Chiangning **Note:** Schjöth #1427.

Date	Mintage	Good	VG	F	VF	XF
ND(1622-1722)	—	1.50	2.25	3.50	5.00	—

宣

KM# 323 CASH

Cast Bronze **Series:** Talisman (Poem Cash) **Obv. Inscription:** K'ang-hsi T'ung-pao **Rev:** Manchu "Siowan" at left, Chinese "Hsüan" at right **Mint:** Hsüanhua **Note:** Schjöth #1428.

Date	Mintage	Good	VG	F	VF	XF
ND(1622-1722)	—	1.50	2.25	3.50	5.00	—

原

KM# 324 CASH

Cast Bronze **Series:** Talisman (Poem Cash) **Obv. Inscription:** K'ang-hsi T'ung-pao **Rev:** Manchu "Yuwan" at left, Chinese "Yuan" at right **Mint:** T'aiyüan Fu **Note:** Schjöth #1429.

Date	Mintage	Good	VG	F	VF	XF
ND(1662-1722)	—	1.50	2.25	3.50	5.00	—

蘇

KM# 325 CASH

Cast Bronze **Series:** Talisman (Poem Cash) **Obv. Inscription:** K'ang-hsi T'ung-pao **Rev:** Manchu "Su" at left, Chinese "Su" at right **Mint:** Soochou **Note:** Schjöth #1430.

Date	Mintage	Good	VG	F	VF	XF
ND(1662-1722)	—	1.50	2.25	3.50	5.00	—

薊

KM# 326 CASH

Cast Bronze **Series:** Talisman (Poem Cash) **Obv. Inscription:** K'ang-hsi T'ung-pao **Rev:** Manchu "Gi" at left, Chinese "Chi" at right **Mint:** Chichou **Note:** Schjöth #1431.

Date	Mintage	Good	VG	F	VF	XF
ND(1662-1722)	—	1.50	2.25	3.50	5.00	—

昌

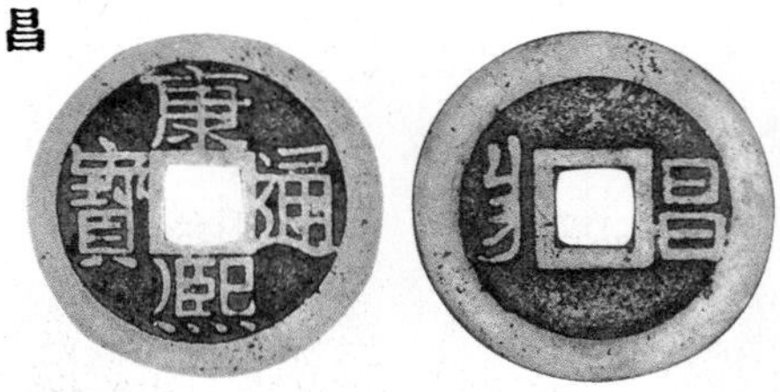

KM# 327 CASH

Cast Bronze **Series:** Talisman (Poem Cash) **Obv. Inscription:** K'ang-hsi T'ung-pao **Rev:** Manchu "Cang" at left, Chinese "Ch'ang" at right **Mint:** Wuch'ang **Note:** Schjöth #1432.

Date	Mintage	Good	VG	F	VF	XF
ND(1662-1722)	—	1.50	2.25	3.50	5.00	—

寧

KM# 328 CASH

Cast Bronze **Series:** Talisman (Poem Cash) **Obv. Inscription:** K'ang-hsi T'ung-pao **Rev:** Manchu "Ning" at left, Chinese "Ning" at right **Mint:** Ningpo **Note:** Schjöth #1433.

Date	Mintage	Good	VG	F	VF	XF
ND(1662-1722)	—	1.50	2.25	3.50	5.00	—

河

KM# 329 CASH

Cast Bronze, 39 mm. **Series:** Talisman (Poem Cash) **Obv. Inscription:** K'ang-hsi T'ung-pao **Rev:** Manchu "Ho" at left, Chinese "Ho" at right **Mint:** K'aifeng **Note:** Schjöth #1434.

Date	Mintage	Good	VG	F	VF	XF
ND(1662-1722)	—	1.50	2.25	3.50	5.50	—

南

KM# 330.1 CASH

Cast Bronze, 27 mm. **Series:** Talisman (Poem Cash) **Obv. Inscription:** K'ang-hsi T'ung-pao **Rev:** Manchu "Nan" at left, Chinese "Nan" at right **Mint:** Ch'angsha **Note:** Schjöth #1435.

Date	Mintage	Good	VG	F	VF	XF
ND(1662-1722)	—	12.50	17.50	25.00	35.00	—

KM# 330.2 CASH

Cast Bronze, 25 mm. **Series:** Talisman (Poem Cash) **Obv. Inscription:** "K'ang-hsi T'ung-pao" **Rev:** Manchu "Nan" at left, Chinese "Nan" at right **Mint:** Ch'angsha

Date	Mintage	Good	VG	F	VF	XF
ND(1662-1722)	—	3.00	5.00	7.00	10.00	—

Note: The larger 27mm examples were cast during later reigns

廣

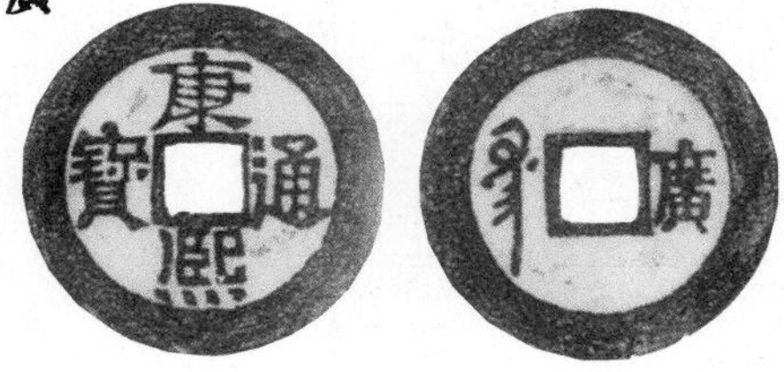

KM# 331.1 CASH

Cast Bronze, 24 mm. **Series:** Talisman (Poem Cash) **Obv. Inscription:** K'ang-hsi T'ung-pao **Rev:** Manchu "Guwang" at left, Chinese "Kuang" at right **Mint:** Kuangchou **Note:** Schjöth #1436.

Date	Mintage	Good	VG	F	VF	XF
ND(1662-1722)	—	0.70	1.00	1.40	2.00	—

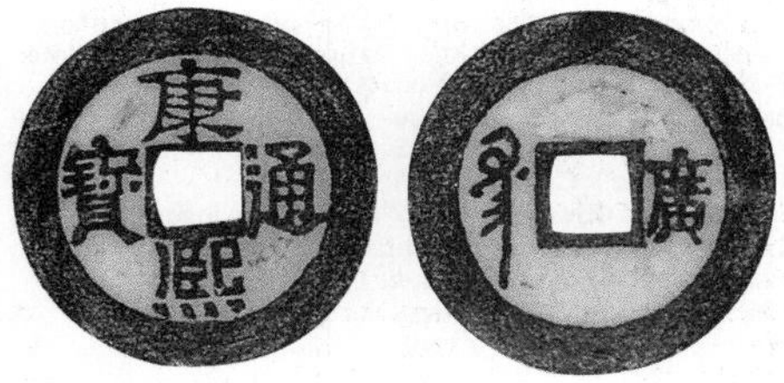

KM# 331.2 CASH

Cast Bronze, 27 mm. **Series:** Talisman (Poem Cash) **Obv. Inscription:** K'ang-hsi T'ung-pao **Rev:** Large Manchu "Guwang" at left, Chinese "Kuang" at right **Mint:** Kuangchou **Note:** Schjöth #1436.

Date	Mintage	Good	VG	F	VF	XF
ND(1662-1722)	—	70.00	100	140	200	—

Note: The larger 27mm examples were cast during later reigns

浙

KM# 332 CASH

Cast Bronze, 25 mm. **Series:** Talisman (Poem Cash) **Obv. Inscription:** K'ang-hsi T'ung-pao. **Rev:** Manchu "Je" at left, Chinese "Chê" at right **Mint:** Chêkiang **Note:** Schjöth #1437.

Date	Mintage	Good	VG	F	VF	XF
ND(1662-1722)	—	1.50	2.25	3.50	5.00	—

KM# 332a CASH

Cast Bronze, 22 mm. **Series:** Talisman (Poem Cash) **Obv. Inscription:** K'ang-hsi T'ung-pao **Rev:** Small Manchu "Je" at left, Chinese "Chê" at right **Mint:** Chêkiang **Note:** Schjöth #1437.

Date	Mintage	Good	VG	F	VF	XF
ND(1696-1699)	—	1.50	2.25	3.50	5.00	—

臺

KM# 333.1 CASH

Cast Bronze, 24 mm. **Series:** Talisman (Poem Cash) **Obv. Inscription:** "K'ang-hsi T'ung-pao" **Rev:** Manchu "Tai" at left, Chinese "Tai" at right **Mint:** T'aiwan **Note:** Schjöth #1438.

Date	Mintage	Good	VG	F	VF	XF
ND(1662-1722)	—	5.00	7.00	10.00	15.00	—

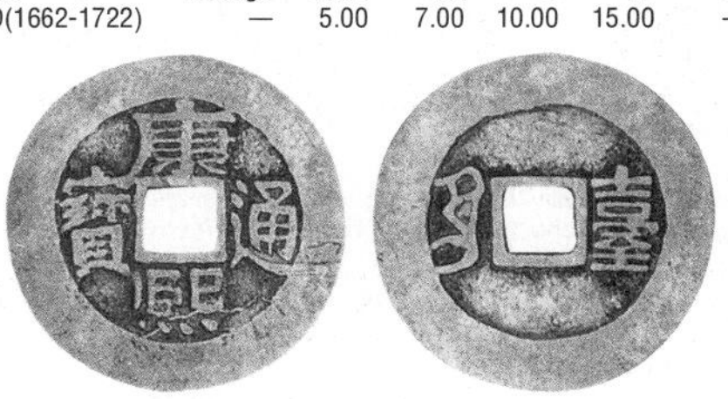

KM# 333.2 CASH

Cast Bronze, 27 mm. **Series:** Talisman (Poem Cash) **Obv. Inscription:** "K'ang-hsi T'ung-pao" **Rev:** Manchu "Tai" at left, Chinese "Tai" at right **Mint:** T'aiwan **Note:** Schjöth #1438. Varieties exist.

Date	Mintage	Good	VG	F	VF	XF
ND(1662-1722)	—	20.00	50.00	80.00	100	—

桂

KM# 334 CASH

Cast Bronze **Series:** Talisman (Poem Cash) **Obv. Inscription:** K'ang-hsi T'ung-pao **Rev:** Manchu "Guway" at left, Chinese "Kuei" at right **Mint:** Kuelin **Note:** Schjöth #1439.

Date	Mintage	Good	VG	F	VF	XF
ND(1662-1722)	—	3.00	5.00	7.00	10.00	—

陝

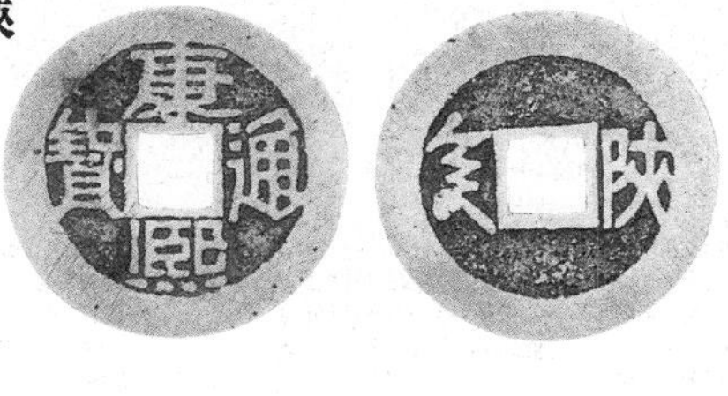

KM# 335.1 CASH

Cast Bronze, 27 mm. **Series:** Talisman (Poem Cash) **Obv. Inscription:** K'ang-hsi T'ung-pao with open "hsi" **Rev:** Manchu "San" at left, Chinese "Shan" at right **Mint:** Sian **Note:** Schjöth #1440.

Date	Mintage	Good	VG	F	VF	XF
ND(1662-1722)	—	1.50	2.25	3.50	5.00	—

KM# 335.2 CASH

Cast Bronze, 27 mm. **Series:** Talisman (Poem Cash) **Obv. Inscription:** K'ang-hsi T'ung-pao **Rev:** Manchu "San" at left with extra dot, Chinese "Shan" at right **Mint:** Sian **Note:** Schjöth #1440.

Date	Mintage	Good	VG	F	VF	XF
ND(1662-1722)	—	1.50	2.25	3.50	5.00	—

雲

KM# 336 CASH

Cast Bronze, 27 mm. **Series:** Talisman (Poem Cash) **Obv. Inscription:** "K'ang-hsi T'ung-pao" **Rev:** Manchu "Yôn" at left, Chinese "Yün" at right **Mint:** Yünnan Fu **Note:** Schjöth #1441.

Date	Mintage	Good	VG	F	VF	XF
ND(1662-1722)	—	1.50	2.25	3.50	5.00	—

漳

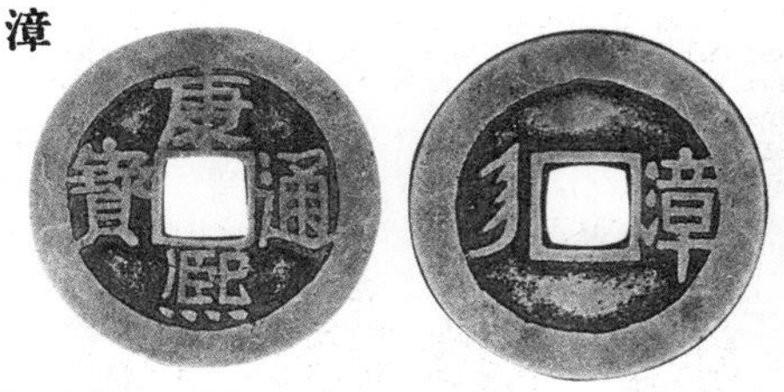

KM# 337 CASH

Cast Bronze **Series:** Talisman (Poem Cash) **Obv. Inscription:** "K'ang-hsi T'ung-pao" **Rev:** Manchu "Jiyang" (?) at left, Chinese "Chang" at right **Mint:** Changchou **Note:** Schjöth #1442. See also KM#342.

Date	Mintage	Good	VG	F	VF	XF
ND(1662-1722)	—	1.50	2.25	3.50	5.00	—

KM# A338 CASH

Cast Bronze **Series:** Talisman (Poem Cash) **Obv. Inscription:** K'ang-hsi T'ung-pao **Rev:** Manchu "Tung" at left, Chinese "T'ung" at right **Mint:** T'ung **Note:** Schjöth #1423.

Date	Mintage	Good	VG	F	VF	XF
ND(1662-1722)	—	0.70	1.00	1.40	2.00	—

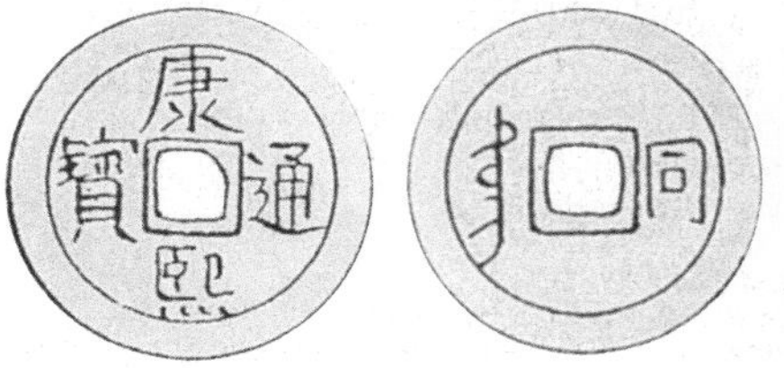

KM# 338 CASH

Cast Bronze **Series:** "Lo-han" **Obv. Inscription:** K'ang-hsi T'ung-pao **Rev:** Manchu "Tung" at left, Chinese "T'ung" at right **Mint:** T'ung **Note:** Similar to KM#318. Schjöth #1444.

Date	Mintage	Good	VG	F	VF	XF
ND(1662-1722)	—	5.00	7.00	10.00	15.00	—

KM# 339 CASH

Cast Bronze **Series:** "Lo-han" **Obv. Inscription:** K'ang-hsi T'ung-pao **Rev:** Manchu "Fu" at left, Chinese "Fu" at right **Mint:** Fuchou **Note:** Similar to KM#319.

Date	Mintage	Good	VG	F	VF	XF
ND(1662-1722)	—	5.00	7.00	10.00	15.00	—

KM# 340 CASH

Cast Brass **Series:** Lo-han **Obv. Inscription:** "K'ang-hsi T'ung-pao" with closed "hsi" **Rev:** Manchu "Boo-ciowan" **Mint:** Hu-pu Board of Revenue **Note:** Schjöth #1443.

Date	Mintage	Good	VG	F	VF	XF
ND(1662-1722)	—	5.00	7.00	10.00	15.00	—

河

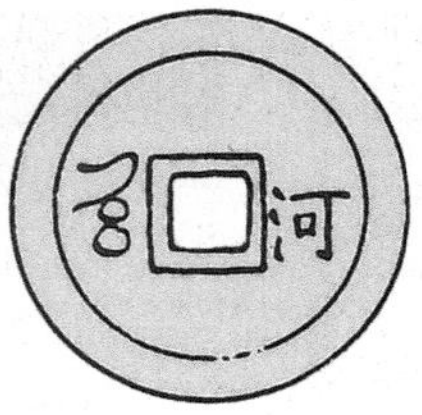

KM# 341 CASH

Cast Brass **Series:** Talisman (Poem Cash) **Obv. Inscription:** "K'ang-hsi T'ung-pao" with closed "hsi" **Rev:** Manchu "Ho" at left, Chinese "Ho" at right **Mint:** Honan **Note:** Schjöth #1444.

Date	Mintage	Good	VG	F	VF	XF
ND(1662-1722)	—	5.00	7.00	10.00	15.00	—

漳

KM# 342 CASH

Cast Brass **Series:** Lo-han **Obv. Inscription:** "K'ang-hsi T'ung-pao" with closed "hsi" **Rev:** Manchu "Jiyang Chang" at left, Chinese "Chang" at right **Mint:** Changchou **Note:** Schjöth #1445. See also KM#337.

Date	Mintage	Good	VG	F	VF	XF
ND(1662-1722)	—	5.00	7.00	10.00	15.00	—

南

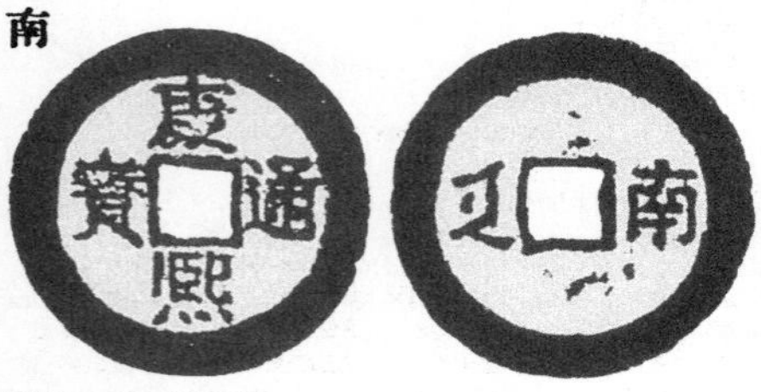

KM# 345 CASH

Cast Bronze, 28 mm. **Obv. Inscription:** K'ang-hsi T'ung-pao with open "hsi" **Rev:** Manchu "Nan" at left, Chinese "Nan" at right **Mint:** Hunan

Date	Mintage	Good	VG	F	VF	XF
ND(1662-1722)	—	85.00	150	220	300	—

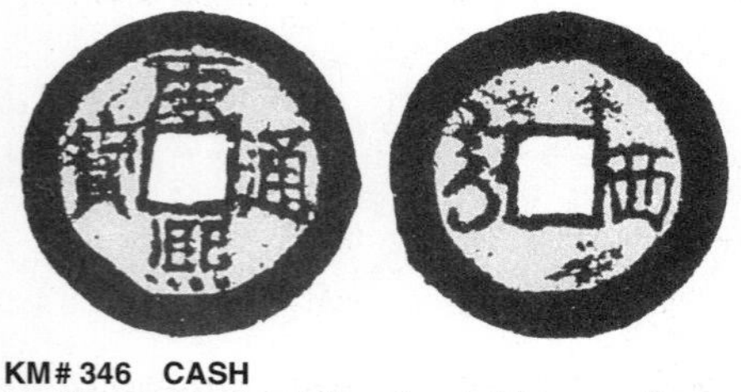

KM# 346 CASH

Cast Bronze **Obv. Inscription:** K'ang-hsi T'ung-pao with open "hsi" **Rev:** Manchu "Si" at left, Chinese "Hsi" at right **Mint:** Jungho

Date	Mintage	Good	VG	F	VF	XF
ND(1662-1722)	—	300	600	900	1,200	—

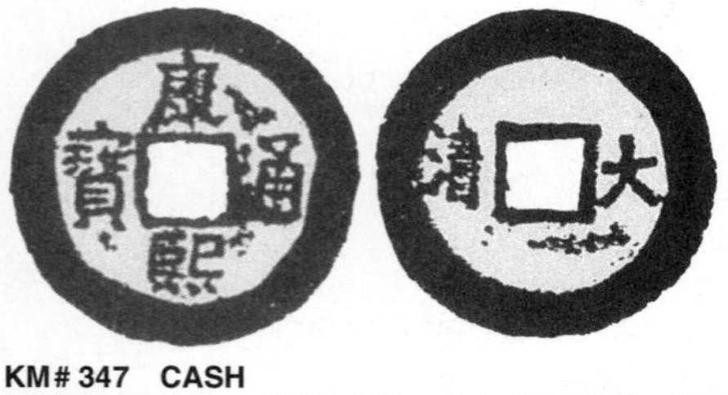

KM# 347 CASH

Cast Bronze, 27 mm. **Subject:** K'ang-hsi's 60th Birthday **Obv. Inscription:** K'ang-hsi T'ung-pao with open "hsi" **Rev:** Chinese "ching" at left, "Ta" at right **Mint:** Fuchou

Date	Mintage	Good	VG	F	VF	XF
ND(1662-1722)	—	65.00	100	140	200	—

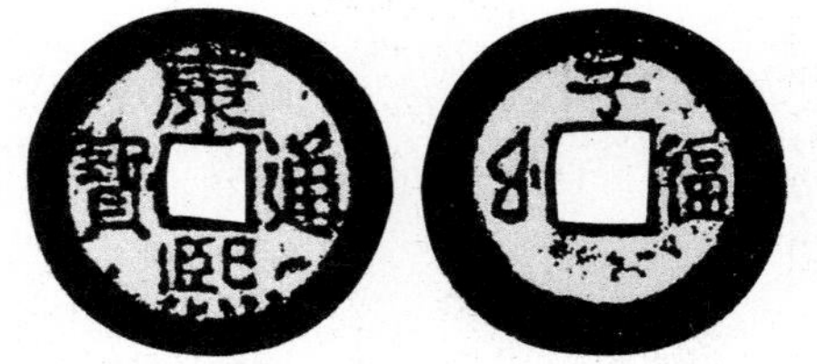

KM# 348.1 CASH

Cast Bronze, 26 mm. **Obv. Inscription:** K'ang-hsi T'ung-pao with open "hsi" **Rev:** Manchu "Fu" at left, Chinese "Fu" at right, "Tzu" (first) above **Mint:** Fuchou

Date	Mintage	Good	VG	F	VF	XF
ND(1662-1722)	—	200	400	600	800	—

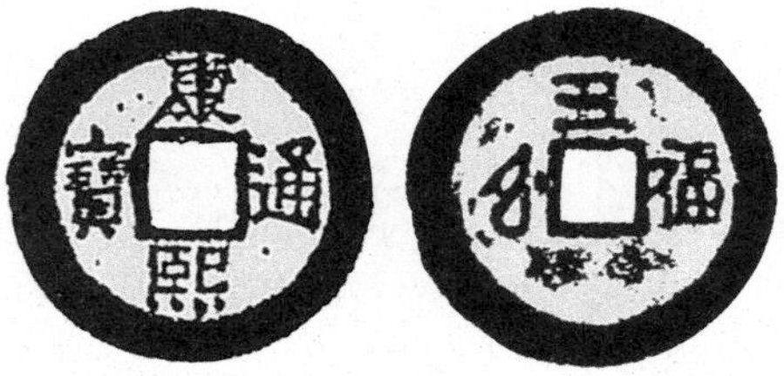

KM# 348.2 CASH

Cast Bronze **Obv. Inscription:** K'ang-hsi T'ung-pao with open "hsi" **Rev:** Manchu "Fu" at left, Chinese "Fu" at right, "Chou" (2nd) above **Mint:** Fuchou

Date	Mintage	Good	VG	F	VF	XF
ND(1662-1722)	—	200	400	600	800	—

KM# 348.3 CASH

Cast Bronze **Obv. Inscription:** K'ang-hsi T'ung-pao with open "hsi" **Rev:** Manchu "Fu" at left, Chinese "Yin" (3rd) above **Mint:** Fuchou

Date	Mintage	Good	VG	F	VF	XF
ND(1662-1722)	—	200	400	600	800	—

KM# 348.4 CASH

Cast Bronze **Obv. Inscription:** K'ang-hsi T'ung-pao with open "hsi" **Rev:** Manchu "Fu" at left, Chinese "Si" (6th) above **Mint:** Fuchou

Date	Mintage	Good	VG	F	VF	XF
ND(1662-1722)	—	200	400	600	800	—

KM# 348.7 CASH

Cast Bronze **Obv. Inscription:** K'ang-hsi T'ung-pao with open "hsi" **Rev:** Manchu "Fu" at left, Chinese "Shen" (9th) above **Mint:** Fuchou

Date	Mintage	Good	VG	F	VF	XF
ND(1662-1722)	—	200	400	600	800	—

KM# 348.8 CASH

Cast Bronze **Obv. Inscription:** K'ang-hsi T'ung-pao with open "hsi" **Rev:** Manchu "Fu" at left, Chinese "Yu" (10th) above **Mint:** Fuchou

Date	Mintage	Good	VG	F	VF	XF
ND(1662-1722)	—	200	400	600	800	—

KM# 348.9 CASH

Cast Bronze **Obv. Inscription:** K'ang-hsi T'ung-pao with open "hsi" **Rev:** Manchu "Fu" at left, Chinese "Hai" (12th) above **Mint:** Fuchou

Date	Mintage	Good	VG	F	VF	XF
ND(1662-1722)	—	250	500	750	1,000	—

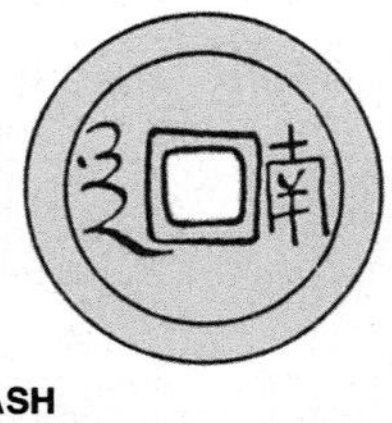

KM# 351 CASH

Red Copper, 23-24 mm. **Series:** Talisman (Poem Cash) **Obv. Inscription:** "K'ang-hsi T'ung-pao" with open "hsi" **Rev:** Manchu "Nan" at left, Chinese "Nan" at right **Mint:** Ch'angsha **Note:** Size varies. Schjöth #1446.

Date	Mintage	Good	VG	F	VF	XF
ND(1662-1722)	—	12.50	17.50	25.00	35.00	—

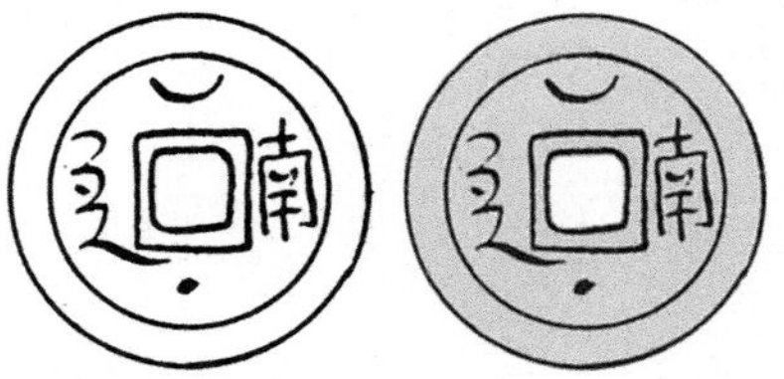

KM# 352 CASH

Red Copper **Obv. Inscription:** "K'ang-hsi T'ung-pao" with open "hsi" **Rev:** Manchu "Nan" at left, Chinese "Nan" at right, crescent above, dot below **Mint:** Ch'angsha **Note:** Schjöth #1447.

Date	Mintage	Good	VG	F	VF	XF
ND(1662-1722)	—	42.50	70.00	100	150	—

KM# 353 CASH

Red Copper **Obv. Inscription:** "K'ang-hsi T'ung-pao" with open "hsi" **Rev:** Manchu "Cang" at left, Chinese "Ch'ang" at right **Mint:** Wuch'ang **Note:** Schjöth #1448.

Date	Mintage	Good	VG	F	VF	XF
ND(1662-1722)	—	1.50	2.25	3.50	5.00	—

廣

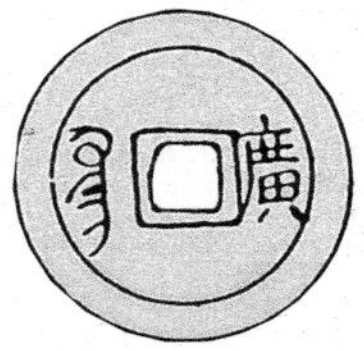

KM# 354 CASH

Red Copper **Obv. Inscription:** "K'ang-hsi T'ung-pao" with open "hsi" **Rev:** Rotated reverse; Manchu "Guwang" at left, Chinese "Kuang" at right **Mint:** Kuangtung **Note:** Schjöth #1449.

Date	Mintage	Good	VG	F	VF	XF
ND(1662-1722)	—	1.50	2.25	3.50	5.00	—

KM# 355 CASH

Red Copper **Obv. Inscription:** "K'ang-hsi T'ung-pao" with open "si" **Rev. Inscription:** "K'ang-hsi T'ung-pao" **Note:** Muling. Schjöth #1450.

Date	Mintage	Good	VG	F	VF	XF
ND(1662-1722)	—	17.50	25.00	35.00	50.00	—

KM# 356 CASH

Red Copper **Obv. Inscription:** "K'ang-hsi T'ung-pao" with open "hsi" **Rev:** Manchu "Boo-yuwan" **Mint:** Kung-pu Board of Public Works **Note:** Schjöth #1451.

Date	Mintage	Good	VG	F	VF	XF
ND(1662-1722)	—	1.50	2.25	3.50	5.00	—

KM# 357 CASH

Red Copper, 19 mm. **Obv. Inscription:** K'ang-hsi T'ung-pao with open "hsi" **Rev:** Manchu "Boo-kuei" **Mint:** Kueilin **Note:** Reduced size. Schjöth #1451.

Date	Mintage	Good	VG	F	VF	XF
ND(1662-1722)	—	1.50	2.25	3.50	5.00	—

KM# 312.1a CASH

Cast Bronze **Obv:** One dot "T'ung" at right **Rev. Inscription:** Manchu Boo-Yuwan **Mint:** Kung-pu Board of Public Works **Note:** Reduced size, corrupt mint product.

Date	Mintage	Good	VG	F	VF	XF
ND(1662-1722)	—	0.15	0.35	0.55	1.00	—

KM# 312.2a CASH

Cast Bronze **Obv:** 2 dot "T'ung" at right **Rev. Inscription:** Manchu Boo-Yuwan **Mint:** Kung-pu Board of Public Works **Note:** Reduced size, corrupt mint product.

Date	Mintage	Good	VG	F	VF	XF
ND(1662-1722)	—	0.15	0.35	0.55	1.00	—

通

KM# 312.3 CASH

Cast Bronze, 26 mm. **Obv. Inscription:** "K'ang-hsi Tung-pao" with one dot T'ung **Rev:** Manchu "Boo-Yuwan" **Note:** Wide rims.

Date	Mintage	Good	VG	F	VF	XF
ND(1662-1722)	—	3.00	6.00	10.00	17.50	—

KM# A340 CASH

Cast Bronze **Series:** "Lo-han" **Obv. Inscription:** K'ang-hsi T'ung-pao **Rev:** Manchu "Yuwan" at left, Chinese "Yüan" at right **Mint:** T'aiyüan-fu **Note:** Similar to KM#324.

Date	Mintage	Good	VG	F	VF	XF
ND(1662-1722)	—	5.00	7.00	10.00	15.00	—

KM# B340 CASH

Cast Bronze **Series:** "Lo-han" **Obv. Inscription:** K'ang-hsi T'ung-pao **Rev:** Manchu "Su" at left, Chinese "Su" at right **Mint:** Soochou **Note:** Similar to KM#325.

Date	Mintage	Good	VG	F	VF	XF
ND(1662-1722)	—	5.00	7.00	10.00	15.00	—

KM# C340 CASH

Cast Bronze **Series:** "Lo-han" **Obv. Inscription:** K'ang-hsi T'ung-pao **Rev:** Manchu "Gi" at left, chinese "Chi" at right **Mint:** Chichou **Note:** Similar to KM#326.

Date	Mintage	Good	VG	F	VF	XF
ND(1662-1722)	—	5.00	7.00	10.00	15.00	—

KM# D340 CASH

Cast Bronze **Series:** "Lo-han" **Obv. Inscription:** K'ang-hsi T'ung-pao **Rev:** Manchu "Ning" at left, Chinese "Ning" at right **Mint:** Ningpo **Note:** Similar to KM#328.

Date	Mintage	Good	VG	F	VF	XF
ND(1662-1722)	—	5.00	7.00	10.00	15.00	—

KM# E340 CASH

Cast Bronze **Series:** "Lo-han" **Obv. Inscription:** K'ang-hsi T'ung-pao **Rev:** Manchu "Nan" at left, Chinese "Nan" at right **Mint:** Ch'angsha **Note:** Similar to KM#330.

Date	Mintage	Good	VG	F	VF	XF
ND(1662-1722)	—	5.00	7.00	10.00	15.00	—

KM# F340 CASH

Cast Bronze **Series:** "Lo-han" **Obv. Inscription:** K'ang-hsi T'ung-pao **Rev:** Manchu "Guwang" at left, Chinese "Kuang" at right **Mint:** Kuangchou **Note:** Similar to KM#331.

Date	Mintage	Good	VG	F	VF	XF
ND(1662-1722)	—	1.00	1.40	2.00	3.00	—

T"ien-ming

T'ai Tsu

CAST COINAGE

KM# 228 CASH

Cast Bronze, 25-26 mm. **Obv. Inscription:** Manchu "Abkai fulingga han juha" (Imperial coin Heavenly Mandate) **Rev:** Plain **Note:** Schjöth #1355. Size varies.

Date	Mintage	Good	VG	F	VF	XF
ND(1616-27)	—	10.00	20.00	40.00	80.00	—

KM# 229 CASH

Cast Bronze **Obv. Inscription:** "T'ien-ming T'ung-pao" **Rev:** Plain **Note:** Schjöth #1356.

Date	Mintage	Good	VG	F	VF	XF
ND(1616-27)	—	40.00	60.00	75.00	120	—

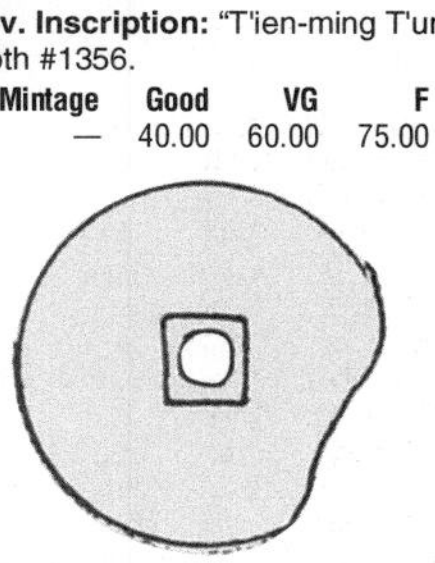

KM# 230 CASH

Cast Bronze, 23 mm. **Obv:** Inscription in different style **Obv. Inscription:** "T'ien-ming T'ung-pao" **Note:** Reduced size.

Date	Mintage	Good	VG	F	VF	XF
ND(1616-27)	—	300	600	900	1,200	—

PATTERNS

Including off metal castings

KM#	Date	Mintage	Identification	Mkt Val
Pn1	ND(1628)	—	Cash. Cast Bronze.	225
Pn3	ND(1644)	—	Cash. Cast Bronze. "Nan".	3,750
Pn4	ND(1644)	—	2 Cash. Cast Bronze. "Boo-ciowan".	2,250
Pn5	ND(1644)	—	Cash. Cast Bronze. "Boo-han".	650
Pn6	ND(1644)	—	Cash. Cast Bronze. Manchu and Chinese "Fu".	650
Pn7	ND(1644)	—	Tael. Cast Bronze. "Shih" above "Yi Tael" at right.	3,000
Pn8	ND(1662)	—	Cash. Cast Bronze. "Boo-Fu".	850
Pn9	ND(1662)	—	Cash. Cast Bronze. Manchu and Chinese "Guwang-kuang".	500
Pn10	ND(1662)	—	Cash. Cast Bronze. Manchu and Chinese "Guwang-kuang".	500
Pn11	ND(1662)	—	Cash. Cast Bronze. Manchu and Chinese "Yun".	500
Pn12	ND(1662)	—	Cash. Cast Bronze. Manchu and Chinese "Tai".	500
Pn13	ND(1662)	—	2 Cash. Cast Bronze. "Boo-yuwan".	3,200
Pn14	ND(1662)	—	10 Cash. Cast Bronze. "Boo-yuwan".	2,800

SINKIANG PROVINCE

Hsinkiang, Xinjiang
"New Dominion"

An autonomous region in western China, often referred to as Chinese Turkestan. High mountains surround 2000 ft. tableland on three sides with a large desert in center of this province. Many salt lakes, mining and some farming and oil. Inhabited by early man and was referred to as the "Silk Route" to the West. Sinkiang (Xinjiang) has been historically under the control of many factions, including Genghis Khan. It became a province in 1884. China has made claim to Sinkiang (Xinjiang) for many, many years. This rule has been more nominal than actual. Sinkiang (Xinjiang) had eight imperial mints, only three of which were in operation toward the end of the reign of Kuang Hsü

MONETARY SYSTEM

2 Pul = 1 Cash
2 Cash = 5 Li
4 Cash = 10 Li = 1 Fen
25 Cash = 10 Fen = 1 Miscal = 1 Ch'ien, Mace, Tanga
10 Miscals (Mace) = 1 Liang (Tael or Sar)
20 Miscals (Tangas) = 1 Tilla

LOCAL MINT NAMES AND MARKS

MINT CHINESE MANCHU UYGHUR

Yarkand, now Shache (Yarkant)

EMPIRE

Tsewang Arabtan

1697-1727

CAST TRIBAL COINAGE

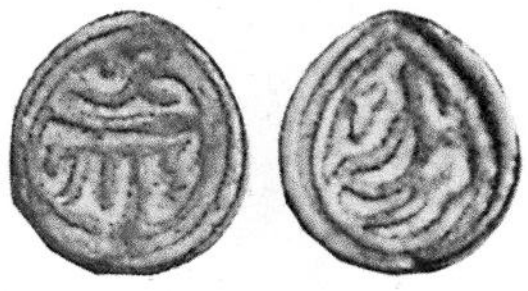

KM# 360 PUL

Cast Copper **Obv. Inscription:** Tsewang **Rev. Inscription:** Zarb Yarkand **Mint:** Yarkand **Note:** Turki inscriptions. Prev. C36-7.1.

Date	Mintage	Good	VG	F	VF	XF
ND(1697-1727)	—	30.00	50.00	80.00	140	—

COLOMBIA

The Republic of Colombia, in the northwestern corner of South America, has an area of 440,831 sq. mi. (1,138,910 sq. km

The northern coast of present Colombia was one of the first parts of the American continent to be visited by Spanish navigators. At Darien in Panama is the site of the first permanent European settlement on the American mainland in 1510. New Granada, as Colombia was known until 1861, stemmed from the settlement of Santa Marta in 1525. New Granada was established as a Spanish colony in 1549. Independence was declared in 1810, and secured in 1819 when Simon Bolivar united Colombia, Venezuela, Panama and Ecuador as the Republic of Gran Colombia. Venezuela withdrew from the Republic in 1829; Ecuador in 1830; and Panama in 1903.

RULER

Spanish, until 1819

MINT MARKS

C, NER, NR, NRE, R, RN, S - Cartagena
B, F, FS, N, NR, S, SF - Nuevo Reino (Bogota)
A, M - Medellin (capital), Antioquia (state)
(m) - Medellin, w/o mint mark
NR – Nueva Reino
P, PN, Pn, POPAYAN - Popayan
SM – Santa Marta
caduceus - Bogota
floral spray - Popayan

ASSAYERS' INITIALS

Bogota and Popayan Mints

Initials	Date	Name
A	1622-26	Inigo de Alvis
A	1632-42	Alonso de Anuncibay
A, ARC, ARCE, VA	1692-1721	Buena Ventura de Arce
G, P, PG	1678-92	Pedro Garcia de Villanueva
OLM, OLMS	1676	Jose de Olmos (silver only)
P	1627-32	Miguel Pinto Camargo
POR, PORAM, PORAMS, PORAS, PORM, PORMS, PORMOS, PORNS, PORS, PRS, R, RMS	1651-76	Pedro Ramos (pillars & waves)
R	1642-76	Pedro Ramos (Hapsburg shield)
SM	1677-78	Jose Silvestre de Soto Maldonado (gold only)
T	1627	Alonso Turrillo de Yebra

SYMBOLS

Symbol	Date	Name
	1697	Sebastian de Chavarria
	1649-51	Juan Rodrigues de Roas
	1618	Baltasar Ramos Leceta
	1636-40	Pedro Trevino
	1640-43	Pedro Trevino
	1643-48	Pedro Trevino
	1684-97	Pedro de Villar

Cartagena Mint

Initial	Date	Name
A	1622-28	Inigo de Alvis or Martin de Arbustante
E	1622	Jacobo Emayr (unconfirmed)
E	1626-35	Echeverria (unconfirmed)
H	1622	Juan de la Hera
S	1653-55	Unknown

MONETARY SYSTEM

16 Reales = 1 Escudo

COLONIAL

COB COINAGE

Note: Values given for dated cobs are representative of average strikes with the last two digits of the date discernible. The esthetic appearance, quality of strike, and presence of date, mint mark and assayer initials all have an effect on the value of cobs.

Note: Colombian cob 1/4 Reales, which are all very rare, did not bear dates in their design, but can be dated at least approximately by virtue of the fact that the castle on the obverse and the lion on the reverse match exactly with the castles and lions in the shield of the 8 Reales struck in the same year or period.

NOTE: The cob 1/2 Reales of Colombia are distinguishable from other mints cob 1/2 Reales by virtue of the fact that the P and the S of the PHILIPPVS monogram touch at the top

KM# 1.1 1/4 REAL

2.3000 g., Billon **Ruler:** Philip IV **Obv:** Arms **Rev:** Pomegranate between pillars, crown above **Note:** Struck at Santa Fe de Bogota. These coins were struck using one part 0.930 fine silver to four parts copper making a total silver fineness of 0.186g. Surviving examples are well under the regulatory weight. Prev. KM#1.

Date	Mintage	Good	VG	F	VF	XF
ND(1622) A Rare	—	—	—	—	—	—

KM# 1.2 1/4 REAL

2.3000 g., Billon **Ruler:** Philip IV **Obv:** Arms **Rev:** Mintmark to left of pillars, crown above **Note:** Struck at Cartagena. These coins were struck using one part 0.930 fine silver to four parts copper making a total silver fineness of 0.186g.

Date	Mintage	Good	VG	F	VF	XF
ND(1622) RN Rare	—	—	—	—	—	—

KM# C7 1/4 REAL

0.8600 g., 0.9310 Silver 0.0257 oz. ASW **Obv:** Castle in rectangle **Rev:** Cross with castles and lions **Note:** Possibly struck at Cartagena

Date	Mintage	Good	VG	F	VF	XF
ND(1622-55) Unique	—	—	—	—	—	—

Note: Attribution tentative

KM# A7 1/4 REAL

0.8600 g., 0.9310 Silver 0.0257 oz. ASW **Obv:** Castle **Rev:** Lion

Date	Mintage	Good	VG	F	VF	XF
ND(1651)	—	200	250	400	650	—
ND(1652)	—	200	250	400	650	—
ND(1657) Unique	—	—	—	—	—	—

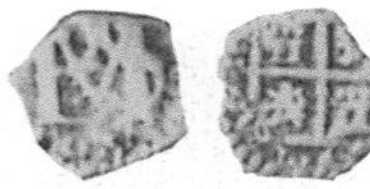

KM# 8 1/2 REAL

1.6917 g., 0.9310 Silver 0.0506 oz. ASW **Obv:** Crowned monogram **Rev:** Cross, castles, and lions in angles

Date	Mintage	Good	VG	F	VF	XF
ND(1622-66) Date off flan	—	100	140	250	350	—
1627 P Rare	—	—	—	—	—	—
1630 P Rare	—	—	—	—	—	—
1633 A Rare	—	—	—	—	—	—
1652 R Rare	—	—	—	—	—	—
1653 R Rare	—	—	—	—	—	—
1656 R Rare	—	—	—	—	—	—
1657 Rare	—	—	—	—	—	—
1658 Rare	—	—	—	—	—	—
1662 R Rare	—	—	—	—	—	—
1665 R Rare	—	—	—	—	—	—

KM# D8 1/2 REAL

1.6917 g., 0.9310 Silver 0.0506 oz. ASW **Obv:** Crowned monogram **Rev:** Cross, castles, and lions in angles **Note:** Struck at the Cartagena Mint.

Date	Mintage	Good	VG	F	VF	XF
ND(1653-55)C S Unique	—	—	—	—	—	—
ND(1653-55)NR E Unique	—	—	—	—	—	—
ND(1653-55)C E Unique	—	—	—	—	—	—

KM# A8 1/2 REAL

1.6917 g., 0.9310 Silver 0.0506 oz. ASW **Obv:** Monogram of Philip IV, legend of Charles II 1673 **Note:** Struck at the Bogota Mint.

Date	Mintage	Good	VG	F	VF	XF
ND Date off flan	—	90.00	125	200	325	—
1666 R Rare	—	—	—	—	—	—
1667/6 R Rare	—	—	—	—	—	—
1667 R Rare	—	—	—	—	—	—
1673 R Rare	—	—	—	—	—	—

KM# 5 REAL

3.3834 g., 0.9310 Silver 0.1013 oz. ASW **Obv:** Hapsburg shield **Rev:** Cross of Jerusalem, lions, and castles in quarters **Note:** Struck at the Bogota Mint.

Date	Mintage	Good	VG	F	VF	XF
ND(1627-50) Date off flan	—	100	150	250	400	—
1627 P Rare	—	—	—	—	—	—
1628 P Rare	—	—	—	—	—	—
1629 P Rare	—	—	—	—	—	—
1633 A Rare	—	—	—	—	—	—
1650 R Rare	—	—	—	—	—	—

KM# A5 REAL

3.3834 g., 0.9310 Silver 0.1013 oz. ASW **Obv:** Hapsburg shield **Obv. Legend:** PHILIPPVS IIII.. **Rev:** Cross of Jerusalem, lions, and castles in quarters **Note:** Struck at the Cartagena Mint.

Date	Mintage	Good	VG	F	VF	XF
162xRN H Rare	—	—	—	—	—	—
ND(1627-29)NR E Date off flan	—	100	150	250	400	—
ND(1627-29)RN E Date off flan	—	100	150	250	400	—
1633C E Rare	—	—	—	—	—	—

KM# 9 REAL

3.3834 g., 0.9310 Silver 0.1013 oz. ASW **Obv:** Lions and castles **Rev:** Pillars and waves **Note:** Struck at the Bogota Mint.

Date	Mintage	Good	VG	F	VF	XF
ND(1651-53) Date off flan	—	165	275	400	575	—
1651 R	—	200	400	750	1,000	—
1652 R	—	200	400	750	1,000	—
1653 R	—	200	400	750	1,000	—

KM# A9 REAL

3.3834 g., 0.9310 Silver 0.1013 oz. ASW **Obv:** Hapsburg shield **Rev:** Pillars and waves **Note:** Mule. Struck at the Bogota Mint.

Date	Mintage	Good	VG	F	VF	XF
1653 R Rare	—	—	—	—	—	—

KM# A15 REAL

3.3834 g., 0.9310 Silver 0.1013 oz. ASW **Obv:** Castles and lions in quartered shield **Rev:** Pillars and waves **Note:** Struck at the Cartagena Mint.

Date	Mintage	Good	VG	F	VF	XF
ND(1655) S Unique	—	—	—	—	—	—

KM# 15 REAL

3.3834 g., 0.9310 Silver 0.1013 oz. ASW **Obv:** Lions and castles **Rev:** Pillars **Note:** Struck at the Bogota Mint

Date	Mintage	Good	VG	F	VF	XF
ND(1665-76) PoR, PoRS Rare	—	—	—	—	—	—
ND(1666-1702) Date off flan; Rare	—	—	—	—	—	—
1676 OLM Rare	—	—	—	—	—	—
ND(1678-92) PG Rare	—	—	—	—	—	—
ND(1692-1702) VA Rare	—	—	—	—	—	—

KM# A6.1 2 REALES

6.7668 g., 0.9310 Silver 0.2025 oz. ASW **Obv:** Hapsburg shield with Portuguese escutcheon, denomination right of shield **Obv. Legend:** PHILIPPVS III.. **Rev:** Castles and lions **Note:** Struck at the Cartagena Mint.

Date	Mintage	Good	VG	F	VF	XF
1622S F	—	—	—	—	—	—

Note: Only two examples known

KM# A6.2 2 REALES

6.7668 g., 0.9310 Silver 0.2025 oz. ASW **Obv:** Arms without Portuguese escutcheon, without denomination right of shield **Note:** Struck at the Cartagena Mint.

Date	Mintage	Good	VG	F	VF	XF
1622 RN E	—	—	—	—	—	—

KM# A6.3 2 REALES

6.7668 g., 0.9310 Silver 0.2025 oz. ASW **Obv:** Without denomination right of shield **Obv. Legend:** PHILIPVS IIII.. **Note:** Struck at the Cartagena Mint.

Date	Mintage	Good	VG	F	VF	XF
1627 RN E	—	400	600	1,000	2,000	—
1628 RN E Rare	—	—	—	—	—	—
ND(1627-29) R E Date off flan	—	150	260	325	500	—
1629 RN E Rare	—	—	—	—	—	—
ND(1627-29) RN E Date off flan	—	150	250	325	500	—
ND(1627-29) NR E Date off flan	—	150	250	325	500	—
1630 CE E	—	350	550	950	1,500	—
1631 CE E	—	350	550	950	1,500	—
1632 CE E	—	350	550	950	1,500	—
1633 CE E	—	350	550	950	1,500	—
1634 CE E	—	350	550	950	1,500	—
ND(1630-34) CE E Date off flan	—	150	250	325	500	—

KM# 6.1 2 REALES

6.7668 g., 0.9310 Silver 0.2025 oz. ASW **Obv:** Hapsburg shield **Rev:** Castles and lions **Note:** Struck at the Bogota Mint.

Date	Mintage	Good	VG	F	VF	XF
1627 P	—	400	600	1,000	1,500	—
1628 P	—	350	550	950	1,500	—
1630 P	—	350	550	950	1,500	—
ND(1627-30) P Date off flan	—	150	250	325	500	—
ND(1632-42) A Date off flan	—	150	250	325	500	—
1647 R	—	400	600	1,000	1,500	—
ND(1647) R Date off flan	—	150	250	325	500	—

KM# 6.2 2 REALES
6.7668 g., 0.9310 Silver 0.2025 oz. ASW **Rev:** Pillars and waves **Note:** Mule. Struck at the Bogota Mint.

Date	Mintage	Good	VG	F	VF	XF
1652 R Rare	—	—	—	—	—	—

KM# 6.3 2 REALES
6.7668 g., 0.9310 Silver 0.2025 oz. ASW **Obv:** Lions and castles **Note:** Varieties in shield and denomination exist. Struck at the Bogota Mint. Prev. KM#6.2.

Date	Mintage	Good	VG	F	VF	XF
ND(1652-65) Date off flan	—	175	275	375	575	—
1652 R	—	300	500	900	1,350	—
1659 POR	—	350	550	950	1,500	—
1662 POR	—	350	550	950	1,500	—
1664 POR	—	350	550	950	1,500	—
1665 P.oS	—	350	550	950	1,500	—

KM# 6.4 2 REALES
6.7668 g., 0.9310 Silver 0.2025 oz. ASW **Obv:** Lions and castles **Rev:** Pillars and waves **Note:** Struck at the Cartagena Mint. Prev. KM#6.3.

Date	Mintage	Good	VG	F	VF	XF
ND(1655) C-S Rare	—	—	—	—	—	—

KM# 16 2 REALES
6.7668 g., 0.9310 Silver 0.2025 oz. ASW **Obv:** Legend of Charles II **Rev:** Pillars and waves, PLVS VLTRA within **Note:** Struck at the Bogota Mint.

Date	Mintage	Good	VG	F	VF	XF
ND(1665-76) R	—	200	300	450	1,000	—
1676 O.L.M. Rare	—	—	—	—	—	—
1688 P Rare	—	—	—	—	—	—
1690 PG Rare	—	—	—	—	—	—
ND(1678-92) PG	—	250	350	500	1,000	—
1693 ARC	—	400	575	1,000	1,750	—

KM# 2.1 4 REALES
13.5337 g., 0.9310 Silver 0.4051 oz. ASW **Obv:** Arms with Portuguese escutcheon, legend around **Rev:** Lions and castles in quarters **Note:** Struck at the Bogota Mint.

Date	Mintage	Good	VG	F	VF	XF
1622 S A Rare	—	—	—	—	—	—

KM# 2.3 4 REALES
13.5337 g., 0.9310 Silver 0.4051 oz. ASW **Obv:** Arms with Portuguese escutcheon **Note:** Struck at the Cartagena Mint.

Date	Mintage	Good	VG	F	VF	XF
ND(1622)RN A Rare	—	—	—	—	—	—
Note: Denomination below A						
ND(1662)RN A Rare	—	—	—	—	—	—
Note: Denomination above A						

KM# 2.2 4 REALES
13.5337 g., 0.9310 Silver 0.4051 oz. ASW **Obv:** Arms without Portuguese escutcheon **Note:** Struck at the Bogota Mint.

Date	Mintage	Good	VG	F	VF	XF
ND(1627-51) Date off flan	—	700	1,200	1,500	2,000	—
1627 T Rare	—	—	—	—	—	—
1627 P Rare	—	—	—	—	—	—
1628 P Rare	—	—	—	—	—	—
1631 P Rare	—	—	—	—	—	—
ND(1632-42) A Rare	—	—	—	—	—	—
1643 R Rare	—	—	—	—	—	—
1644 R Rare	—	—	—	—	—	—
1650 R Rare	—	—	—	—	—	—
1651 R Rare	—	—	—	—	—	—
ND(1628-33) R	—	700	1,200	1,500	2,000	—

KM# 2.4 4 REALES
13.5337 g., 0.9310 Silver 0.4051 oz. ASW **Obv:** Arms without Portuguese escutcheon **Note:** Struck at the Cartagena Mint.

Date	Mintage	Good	VG	F	VF	XF
ND(1628-33) Date off flan	—	700	1,200	1,500	2,000	—
1628 E Rare	—	—	—	—	—	—
1630RN E Rare	—	—	—	—	—	—
1632C E Rare	—	—	—	—	—	—
1633C E Rare	—	—	—	—	—	—

KM# 10.1 4 REALES
13.5337 g., 0.9310 Silver 0.4051 oz. ASW **Obv:** Arms with lions and castles quartered, value at right **Obv. Legend:** PHILIPPVS IV.. **Rev:** Pillars, PLVS VLTRA, mint mark within, date vertical **Note:** Struck at the Bogota Mint.

Date	Mintage	Good	VG	F	VF	XF
1651 PoR	—	1,750	2,750	3,750	5,000	—
ND(1651-65) Date off flan	—	700	1,200	1,500	2,000	—
1653	—	1,750	2,750	3,750	5,000	—
1653 POR	—	1,750	2,750	3,750	5,000	—
1654 POR	—	1,750	2,750	3,750	5,000	—
1657 POR	—	1,750	2,750	3,750	5,000	—
1658 PRS	—	1,750	2,750	3,750	5,000	—
1661 PORS	—	1,750	2,750	3,750	5,000	—
1662 P.oR	—	1,750	2,750	3,750	5,000	—
1662 P.oRS	—	1,750	2,750	3,750	5,000	—
1662 POR	—	1,750	2,750	3,750	5,000	—
1662 PORS	—	1,750	2,750	3,750	5,000	—
1664 PoRS	—	1,750	2,750	3,750	5,000	—
1665 PoR	—	1,750	2,750	3,750	5,000	—

KM# 10.2 4 REALES
13.5337 g., 0.9310 Silver 0.4051 oz. ASW **Obv:** Castles and lions in shield **Rev:** Pillars and waves, stars in field **Note:** Struck at the Cartagena Mint.

Date	Mintage	Good	VG	F	VF	XF
ND(1655)C S Rare	—	—	—	—	—	—

KM# 11 4 REALES
13.5337 g., 0.9310 Silver 0.4051 oz. ASW **Obv:** Lions and castles, legend of Charles II **Rev:** Pillars and waves, PLVS VLTRA and mint mark within **Note:** Struck at the Bogota Mint.

Date	Mintage	Good	VG	F	VF	XF
ND(1666-1701) Date off flan	—	900	1,500	2,500	3,750	—
1666 PoR Rare	—	—	—	—	—	—
1667 P. oR Rare	—	—	—	—	—	—
1668 PoRS Rare	—	—	—	—	—	—
1669/6 PRS Rare	—	—	—	—	—	—
1676 O.L.M. Rare	—	—	—	—	—	—
1680 PoGA Rare	—	—	—	—	—	—
1690 PG Rare	—	—	—	—	—	—
1693 VA Rare	—	—	—	—	—	—

KM# 3.2 8 REALES
27.0674 g., 0.9310 Silver 0.8102 oz. ASW **Note:** Struck at the Cartagena Mint.

Date	Mintage	Good	VG	F	VF	XF
1621RN A Rare	—	—	—	—	—	—
1622RN A Rare	—	—	—	—	—	—

KM# 3.1 8 REALES
27.0674 g., 0.9310 Silver 0.8102 oz. ASW **Obv:** Arms with Portuguese escutcheon, legend of Philip III **Rev:** Cross with lions and castles in quarters **Note:** Struck at the Bogota Mint.

Date	Mintage	Good	VG	F	VF	XF
1622 S A Rare	—	—	—	—	—	—

KM# 3.4 8 REALES

27.0674 g., 0.9310 Silver 0.8102 oz. ASW **Note:** Struck at the Cartagena Mint. Prev. KM#3.3.

Date	Mintage	Good	VG	F	VF	XF
ND(1626-34) Date off flan	—	750	1,250	1,750	2,500	—
1626 NER Rare	—	—	—	—	—	—
1628 E Rare	—	—	—	—	—	—
1629NRE /NER Rare	—	—	—	—	—	—
1630RN E Rare	—	—	—	—	—	—
1633RN E Rare	—	—	—	—	—	—
1633C E Rare	—	—	—	—	—	—
1634C E Rare	—	—	—	—	—	—

Note: Cartagena 8 Reales from 1627 to 1630 show mint mark assayers as RNE, NRE, or NER. Two are known with NER to left and small RN to right

KM# 3.3 8 REALES

27.0674 g., 0.9310 Silver 0.8102 oz. ASW **Obv:** Arms without Portuguese escutcheon, VIII at right **Obv. Legend:** PHILIPPVS IIII D G **Rev:** Lions and castles in quarters **Note:** Struck at the Bogota Mint.

Date	Mintage	Good	VG	F	VF	XF
ND(1627-51) P	—	750	1,250	1,750	2,500	—
1627 P Rare	—	—	—	—	—	—
1628 P	—	1,500	2,500	3,500	5,000	—
1629 P	—	1,500	2,500	3,500	5,000	—
1633 A	—	1,500	2,500	3,500	5,000	—
1634 A	—	1,500	2,500	3,500	5,000	—

KM# 7.1 8 REALES

27.0674 g., 0.9310 Silver 0.8102 oz. ASW **Obv:** Pillars and waves **Note:** Struck at the Bogota Mint.

Date	Mintage	Good	VG	F	VF	XF
ND(1651-65) Date off flan	—	700	1,000	1,250	1,500	—
1651 P. oRMS	—	1,000	2,000	3,000	4,000	—
1651 RMS	—	1,000	2,000	3,000	4,000	—
1651 PoRAM	—	1,000	2,000	3,000	4,000	—
1651 PoRAMS	—	1,000	2,000	3,000	4,000	—
1651 PoRMOS	—	1,000	2,000	3,000	4,000	—
1652 P. oRAS	—	1,000	2,000	3,000	4,000	—
1652 PoRMS	—	1,000	2,000	3,000	4,000	—
1653 P oRMS	—	1,000	2,000	3,000	4,000	—
1653 P oRAS	—	1,000	2,000	3,000	4,000	—
1653 P oRS	—	1,000	2,000	3,000	4,000	—
1653 P. oMS Rare	—	—	—	—	—	—
1654 P. oRS	—	1,000	2,000	3,000	4,000	—
1655 P. ORS	—	1,000	2,000	3,000	4,000	—
1656 P. oRS	—	1,000	2,000	3,000	4,000	—
1657 P. oRM Rare	—	—	—	—	—	—
1657 P. oRS	—	1,000	2,000	3,000	4,000	—
1658 P. oRS Rare	—	—	—	—	—	—
1659 P. oRS Rare	—	—	—	—	—	—
1659 P. oRAS Rare	—	—	—	—	—	—
166Z P. oRS	—	1,000	2,000	3,000	4,000	—
1662 PoR Rare	—	—	—	—	—	—
1663 PoR	—	1,000	2,000	3,000	4,000	—
1663 PRS	—	1,000	2,000	3,000	4,000	—
1663 P. oRS	—	1,000	2,000	3,000	4,000	—
1664 P. oRS	—	1,000	2,000	3,000	4,000	—
1665 P. oRS	—	1,000	2,000	3,000	4,000	—

KM# 7.2 8 REALES

27.0674 g., 0.9310 Silver 0.8102 oz. ASW **Rev:** Pillars and waves, stars in field **Note:** Struck at the Cartagena Mint.

Date	Mintage	Good	VG	F	VF	XF
1655 C-S Rare	—	—	—	—	—	—

KM# 12 8 REALES

27.0674 g., 0.9310 Silver 0.8102 oz. ASW **Ruler:** Philip V **Obv:** Arms within beaded circle, legend of Charles II **Rev:** Pillars, "PLVS VLTRA" and "MM" between

Date	Mintage	Good	VG	F	VF	XF
ND(1667-1703) Date off flan	—	1,000	1,750	2,500	3,250	—
1667 P. oRS Rare	—	—	—	—	—	—
1668 P. oRS VIII at left, Rare	—	—	—	—	—	—
1668 P. oRS VIII at right, Rare	—	—	—	—	—	—
1669 P. oRS Rare	—	—	—	—	—	—
1670 P. oRS Rare	—	—	—	—	—	—
1671 P. oRS Rare	—	—	—	—	—	—
1676 OLMS Rare	—	—	—	—	—	—
1680 PoGA Rare	—	—	—	—	—	—
1687 JEMI Unique	—	—	—	—	—	—
1688 PG Rare	—	—	—	—	—	—
1690 PG Rare	—	—	—	—	—	—
1691 PG Rare	—	—	—	—	—	—
1692 ARC Rare	—	—	—	—	—	—
1693 VA Rare	—	—	—	—	—	—

KM# A13 ESCUDO

3.3834 g., 0.9170 Gold 0.0997 oz. AGW **Ruler:** Philip IV **Obv:** Arms **Rev:** Cross of Jerusalem **Note:** Struck at the Bogota Mint.

Date	Mintage	F	VF	XF	Unc	BU
ND(1627-29)NR A Rare	—	—	—	—	—	—

KM# 13 ESCUDO

3.3834 g., 0.9170 Gold 0.0997 oz. AGW **Ruler:** Philip V **Obv:** Arms **Rev:** Cross of Jerusalem

Date	Mintage	F	VF	XF	Unc	BU
ND(1666-1715) Date off flan	—	1,750	2,000	—	—	—
1672 R Rare	—	—	—	—	—	—
1687 G Rare	—	—	—	—	—	—

KM# B13 ESCUDO

3.3834 g., 0.9170 Gold 0.0997 oz. AGW **Ruler:** Philip IV **Obv:** Lions and castles **Rev:** Cross of Jerusalem **Note:** Struck at the Bogota Mint.

Date	Mintage	F	VF	XF	Unc	BU
ND Unique, date off flan	—	—	—	—	—	—

KM# 4.3 2 ESCUDOS

6.7668 g., 0.9170 Gold 0.1995 oz. AGW **Ruler:** Ferdinand VI **Obv:** Legends of Philip III **Note:** Struck at the Cartagena Mint.

Date	Mintage	F	VF	XF	Unc	BU
1622S F Rare	—	—	—	—	—	—

Note: Swiss Bank Ortiz sale No. 27 1-91, XF realized $27,200; Spink America Norweb sale 3-97, XF realized $35,200

KM# 4.4 2 ESCUDOS

6.7668 g., 0.9170 Gold 0.1995 oz. AGW **Ruler:** Ferdinand VI **Obv:** Legends of Philip IV **Note:** Struck at the Cartagena Mint.

Date	Mintage	F	VF	XF	Unc	BU
ND(1627-29)NR E Date off flan	—	1,400	1,700	2,000	—	—
ND(1627-29)R E Date off flan	—	1,400	1,700	2,000	—	—
ND(1627-29)RN E Date off flan	—	1,400	1,700	2,000	—	—
1627R E Rare	—	—	—	—	—	—
1628RN E Rare	—	—	—	—	—	—
1629R E Rare	—	—	—	—	—	—
ND(1630-35)C E Rare	—	1,300	1,650	2,000	—	—
1630C E Rare	—	—	—	—	—	—
1631C E Rare	—	—	—	—	—	—
1632C E Rare	—	—	—	—	—	—
1633C E Rare	—	—	—	—	—	—
1634C E Rare	—	—	—	—	—	—
1635C E Rare	—	—	—	—	—	—

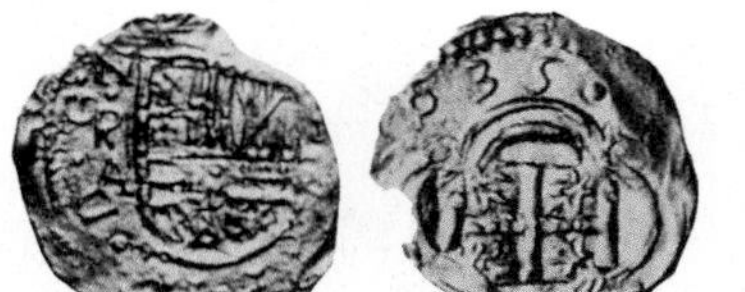

KM# 4.1 2 ESCUDOS

6.7668 g., 0.9170 Gold 0.1995 oz. AGW **Ruler:** Philip IV **Note:** Struck at the Bogota Mint.

Date	Mintage	F	VF	XF	Unc	BU
ND(1627-29)NR A	—	1,500	1,750	2,000	—	—

Note: This issue is distinguishable from the contemporaneous assayer A cobs of Cartagena by the inclusion of a pomegranate (dot) at the bottom and transpositions of lions and castles in the shield

Date	Mintage	F	VF	XF	Unc	BU
1628NR A Rare	—	—	—	—	—	—
ND(1628-55) Date off flan	—	1,250	1,650	2,000	—	—
1628NR P Rare	—	—	—	—	—	—
1629RN P Rare	—	—	—	—	—	—

Date	Mintage	F	VF	XF	Unc	BU
1632NR A Rare	—	—	—	—	—	—
1633NR A	—	1,500	1,950	2,500	3,000	—
1634NR A	—	1,500	1,950	2,500	3,000	—
1635NR A	—	1,500	1,950	2,500	3,000	—
1636NR A	—	1,500	1,950	2,500	3,000	—
1637NR A Rare	—	—	—	—	—	—
1638NR A Rare	—	—	—	—	—	—
1639NR A Rare	—	—	—	—	—	—
1640NR A Rare	—	—	—	—	—	—
1641NR A Rare	—	—	—	—	—	—
1642NR R Rare	—	—	—	—	—	—
1643NR R Rare	—	—	—	—	—	—
1644NR R Rare	—	—	—	—	—	—
1645NR R Rare	—	—	—	—	—	—
1646NR R Rare	—	—	—	—	—	—
1647NR R Rare	—	—	—	—	—	—
1648NR R Rare	—	—	—	—	—	—
1649NR R Rare	—	—	—	—	—	—
1650NR R Rare	—	—	—	—	—	—
1651NR R	—	1,500	1,950	2,500	3,000	—
1652NR R	—	1,500	1,950	2,500	3,000	—
1653NR R	—	1,500	1,950	2,500	3,000	—
1654NR R	—	1,500	1,950	2,500	3,000	—
1655NR R	—	1,500	1,950	2,500	3,000	—
1656NR R Rare	—	—	—	—	—	—
1657NR R Rare	—	—	—	—	—	—
1658NR R Rare	—	—	—	—	—	—
1659NR R Rare	—	—	—	—	—	—
1660NR R Rare	—	—	—	—	—	—
1661NR R Rare	—	—	—	—	—	—
1662NR R Rare	—	—	—	—	—	—
1663NR R Rare	—	—	—	—	—	—
1664NR R Rare	—	—	—	—	—	—
1665NR R Rare	—	—	—	—	—	—

KM# 14.1 2 ESCUDOS

6.7668 g., 0.9170 Gold 0.1995 oz. AGW **Ruler:** Charles II **Obv:** Arms **Rev:** Cross of Jerusalem, lions and castles in quarters **Note:** Struck at the Bogota Mint.

Date	Mintage	F	VF	XF	Unc	BU
ND(1667-93) Date off flan	—	1,000	1,200	2,000	—	—
1667NR R Rare	—	—	—	—	—	—
1668NR R Rare	—	—	—	—	—	—
1669NR R Rare	—	—	—	—	—	—
1670NR R Rare	—	—	—	—	—	—
1671NR R Rare	—	—	—	—	—	—
1672NR R Rare	—	—	—	—	—	—
1673NR R Rare	—	—	—	—	—	—
1674NR R Rare	—	—	—	—	—	—
1675NR R Rare	—	—	—	—	—	—
1676NR R Rare	—	—	—	—	—	—
ND(1677-78)NR SM 3 known	—	—	—	—	—	—
1678NR G, P Rare	—	—	—	—	—	—
1679NR G, P Rare	—	—	—	—	—	—
1680NR G, P Rare	—	—	—	—	—	—
1681NR G, P Rare	—	—	—	—	—	—
1682NR G, P Rare	—	—	—	—	—	—
1683NR G, P Rare	—	—	—	—	—	—
1684NR G, P Rare	—	—	—	—	—	—
1685NR G, P Rare	—	—	—	—	—	—
1686NR G, P Rare	—	—	—	—	—	—
1687NR G, P Rare	—	—	—	—	—	—
1688NR G, P Rare	—	—	—	—	—	—
1689NR G, P Rare	—	—	—	—	—	—
1690NR G, P Rare	—	—	—	—	—	—
1691NR G, P Rare	—	—	—	—	—	—
1692NR G, P Rare	—	—	—	—	—	—
1692NR A	—	1,750	2,250	2,750	—	—
1693NR A	—	1,750	2,250	2,750	—	—

KM# 14.2 2 ESCUDOS

6.7682 g., 0.9170 Gold 0.1995 oz. AGW **Ruler:** Philip V **Note:** No mint mark.

Date	Mintage	F	VF	XF	Unc	BU
ND(1694-1713) Date off flan	—	1,400	1,850	2,250	3,000	—
1694 ARCE	—	1,500	2,000	2,500	3,000	—
1695 ARCE	—	1,500	2,000	2,500	3,000	—
1696 ARCE	—	1,500	2,000	2,500	3,000	—
1697 ARCE	—	1,500	2,000	2,500	3,000	—
1698 ARCE	—	1,500	2,000	2,500	3,000	—
1699 ARCE	—	1,500	2,000	2,500	3,000	—
1700 ARCE	—	1,500	2,000	2,500	3,000	—

COURLAND

The people of Courland are of Aryan descent primarily from the German Order of Livonian Knights. They were nomadic tribesmen who settled along the Baltic prior to the 13th century. Ideally situated as a trade route and lacking a central government, they were conquered in 1561 by Poland and Sweden.

When the Livonian Order was dissolved in 1561 the then Master of the Order, Gotthard Kettler was made Duke of Courland. During the 17th century, Courland remained part of Poland, but went under Russia after Poland's division. When the Kettler line became extinct in 1737 Courland was awarded to Ernst Johann Biron, chief advisor and lover of Empress Anna of Russia. After her death he was exiled but returned in 1763. He abdicated in favor of his son Peter in 1769.

RULERS

Frederic & Guillaume Kettler, 1589-1639
Jacob Kettler, 1639-82
Friedrich Casimir Kettler, 1682-98

DUCHY

STANDARD COINAGE

KM# 3 SOLIDUS

Silver **Ruler:** Frederic & Guillaume Kettler **Obv:** S on shield below crown that divides legend **Obv. Legend:** SIGIS III D G REX POL and L - SOLIDVS DVCVM CVRLAS **Rev:** Lion of Courland within circle **Note:** Obverse legend varieties exist.

Date	Mintage	VG	F	VF	XF	Unc
1600	—	30.00	50.00	90.00	190	—
1601	—	30.00	50.00	90.00	190	—
1602	—	30.00	50.00	90.00	190	—
1604	—	30.00	50.00	90.00	190	—
1605	—	30.00	50.00	90.00	190	—
1606	—	30.00	50.00	90.00	190	—
1607	—	30.00	50.00	90.00	190	—
1610	—	30.00	50.00	90.00	190	—
1611	—	30.00	50.00	90.00	190	—

KM# 6 SOLIDUS

Silver **Ruler:** Jacob Kettler **Obv:** Eagle with shield on breast within circle **Obv. Legend:** SOLIDVS D G IACOB (date) - CVRL ET SEMOE DVX **Rev:** Crowned III within circle **Note:** Obverse legend varieties exist.

Date	Mintage	VG	F	VF	XF	Unc
ND	—	35.00	60.00	110	200	—
1646	—	35.00	60.00	110	200	—
1662	—	35.00	60.00	110	200	—

KM# 14.1 SOLIDUS

Bronze **Ruler:** Friedrich Casimir Kettler **Obv:** Armored bust right **Obv. Legend:** FRID CASIN L C S DVX - SOLIDVS CVRLANDIAE **Rev:** Eagle with square-topped divided shield of Courland and Semgal on breast, lion and elk at bottom

Date	Mintage	VG	F	VF	XF	Unc
1696	—	25.00	45.00	85.00	165	—

KM# 14.2 SOLIDUS

Bronze **Ruler:** Friedrich Casimir Kettler **Obv:** Crowned FC monogram **Note:** Legend varieties exist.

Date	Mintage	VG	F	VF	XF	Unc
ND	—	—	—	—	—	—

KM# 9 3 POLCHER (1/2 Grosz - 1/24 Thaler)

Silver **Ruler:** Friedrich Casimir Kettler **Obv:** Square shield, divided at bottom, arms of Kettler in crown above **Rev:** 24 in orb, cross above divides legend **Note:** Legend varieties exist.

Date	Mintage	VG	F	VF	XF	Unc
1687	—	50.00	100	200	350	—
1689	—	50.00	100	200	350	—
1695	—	50.00	100	200	350	—

KM# 13 3 POLCHER (1/2 Grosz - 1/24 Thaler)

Silver **Ruler:** Friedrich Casimir Kettler **Obv:** Crowned divided shield within circle **Rev:** Ornate cross above orb with 24 **Note:** Legend varieties exist.

Date	Mintage	VG	F	VF	XF	Unc
1695	—	40.00	80.00	160	285	—
1696	—	40.00	80.00	160	285	—

KM# 4 3 GROSZY

Silver **Ruler:** Frederic & Guillaume Kettler **Obv:** Bust right **Rev:** III above arms dividing eagle and horse and rider, legend and date below **Note:** Legend varieties exist.

Date	Mintage	VG	F	VF	XF	Unc
1604	—	400	800	1,600	2,850	—
1606	—	400	800	1,600	2,850	—
ND	—	400	800	1,600	2,850	—

KM# 11 6 GROSZY

Silver **Ruler:** Friedrich Casimir Kettler

Date	Mintage	VG	F	VF	XF	Unc
1687	—	—	—	—	—	—
1689	—	—	—	—	—	—
1694 4CVR	—	60.00	120	225	400	—
1695	—	60.00	120	225	400	—
1696	—	60.00	120	225	400	—

KM# 12 ORT (18 Grozy - 1 Timf)

Silver **Ruler:** Friedrich Casimir Kettler

Date	Mintage	VG	F	VF	XF	Unc
1689	—	—	—	—	—	—
1694	—	100	200	350	700	—

KM# 5.1 THALER

Silver **Ruler:** Jacob Kettler **Obv:** Large ornate armor plated bust of Jacob Kettler right **Rev:** Eagle and horse and rider in geometric outline, date in legend **Note:** Dav. #4348.

Date	Mintage	VG	F	VF	XF	Unc
1643	—	—	—	—	—	—

Note: Reported, not confirmed

Date	Mintage	VG	F	VF	XF	Unc
1644 Rare	—	—	—	—	—	—

Note: WAG Auction 46, 2-08, VF realized approximately $22,470.

KM# 5.2 THALER

Silver **Ruler:** Jacob Kettler **Obv:** Small bust **Note:** Dav. #4349. Punctuation varieties exist in legends of Dav. #4348 and Dav. #4349.

Date	Mintage	VG	F	VF	XF	Unc
1645	—	1,500	3,000	5,500	9,500	—

Note: WAG, Auction 36, 2-06, Unc realized approximately $16,680.

Date	Mintage	VG	F	VF	XF	Unc
1646 Reported, not confirmed	—	—	—	—	—	—

TRADE COINAGE

KM# 7 DUCAT

3.5000 g., 0.9860 Gold 0.1109 oz. AGW **Ruler:** Jacob Kettler **Rev:** Shield

Date	Mintage	VG	F	VF	XF	Unc
1644	—	4,500	9,000	17,500	25,000	—
1645	—	4,500	9,000	17,500	25,000	—
1646	—	4,500	9,000	17,500	25,000	—

KM# 10 DUCAT

3.5000 g., 0.9860 Gold 0.1109 oz. AGW **Ruler:** Friedrich Casimir Kettler **Obv:** Bust of Friedrich Casimir right **Rev:** Crowned eagle with arms of Courland and Semgal on chest, last 2 digits of date between wings and neck

Date	Mintage	VG	F	VF	XF	Unc
1689	—	3,000	6,000	12,000	17,000	—

KM# 8 10 DUCAT

35.0000 g., 0.9860 Gold 1.1095 oz. AGW **Ruler:** Jacob Kettler

Date	Mintage	VG	F	VF	XF	Unc
1644 Rare	—	—	—	—	—	—

CRIMEA (KRIM)

The Crimea (ancient Tauris or Tauric Chersonese, Turkish Kirim or Krim, Russian Krym) is a peninsula of southern Russia extending into the Black Sea southwest of the Sea of Azov.

In ancient times, The Crimea was inhabited by the Goths and Scythians, was colonized by the Greeks, and ranked, in part, as a tributary state of Rome. During the succeeding centuries, the Goths, Huns, Khazars, Byzantine Greeks, Kipchak Turks, and the Tatars of Batu Khan who founded the Tatar Khanate in Russia known as the Empire of the Golden Horde overran the Crimea. After the destruction of the Golden Horde by Tamerlane (Timur) in 1395, the Crimean Taters founded an independent khanate under Haji Ghirai, which reigned first at Solkhat (Eski Kirim or Stary Krym). The Crimean khans ruled as tributary princes of the Ottoman Empire from 1478 to 1777, when they became dependent upon Russia.

RULERS

Ghazi Giray II, AH996-1017 / 1588-1608AD
Salamat Giray I, AH1017-1019 / 1608-1610AD
Jani Beg Giray, 1st reign, AH1019-1032 / 1610-1623AD
Jani Beg Giray, 2nd reign, AH1036-1044 / 1627-1635AD
'Inayat Giray, AH1044-1046 / 1635-1637AD
Bahadur Giray, AH1046-1051 / 1637-1641AD
Islam Giray III, AH1054-1064 / 1644-1654AD
Muhammad Giray IV, 2nd reign, AH1064-1076 / 1654-1666AD
'Adil Giray, AH1076-1082 / 1666-1671AD
Selim Giray I, 1st reign, AH1082-1089 / 1671-1678AD
Murad Giray, AH1089-1094 / 1678-1683AD
Selim Giray I, 2nd reign, AH1095-1103 / 1684-1691AD
Sa'adat Giray II, AH1103 / 1691AD
Safa Giray, AH1103-1104 / 1691-1692AD
Selim Giray I, 3rd reign, AH1104-1110 / 1692-1699AD
Dawlat Giray II, 1st reign, AH1110-1114 / 1699-1702AD

MINT MARKS

باغجه سراي

Bagchih-Serai

كفه

Kaffa

MONETARY SYSTEM

3 Manghir (Agcheh, Asper) – 1 Para
2 Para = 1 Ikilik
2-1/2 Ikilik = 1 Beshlik
2 Beshlik = 1 Onlik
2 Onlik = 1 Yirmilik = 1/2 Kurus
2 Yirmilik = 1 Kurus
1-1/2 Kurus = 1 Altmishlik

Russian Names	Turkish Names
2 Polushka = 1 Denga	= 2 Akche
2 Denga = 1 Kopek	= 3 Akche
5 Kopecks = 1 Kyrmis	= 15 Akche
2 Kyrmis = 1 Ishal (Tschal)	= 25 Akche

From AH1017-1169/1608-1756AD silver coins (akeches) and copper coins were struck in the names of 24 Khanate rulers. They are all very similar to the coin illustrated as C#125, usually with the obverse showing the ruler's and his father's names and the reverse with a toughra above *duribe* and the mintname.

Dawlat Giray I

HAMMERED COINAGE

MB# 5 AKCE

Billon Weight varies: 0.35-0.61g **Obv:** Ruler's name and titles **Rev:** Tamgha in center, mint and date around

Date	Mintage	Good	VG	F	VF	XF
ND(date missing)	—	15.00	30.00	40.00	55.00	—

Muhammad Giray II

MB# 6 AKCE

Billon Weight varies: 0.45-0.69g **Obv:** Ruler's name and titles **Rev:** Tamgha in center, mint and date around

Date	Mintage	Good	VG	F	VF	XF
AH985	—	20.00	35.00	45.00	70.00	—
ND(date missing)	—	15.00	30.00	40.00	55.00	—

Islam Giray II

MB# 7.2 AKCE

Billon Weight varies: 0.52-0.54g **Obv:** Ruler's name and titles **Rev:** Tamgha in center, date in margin

Date	Mintage	Good	VG	F	VF	XF
AH990	—	40.00	65.00	85.00	115	—

MB# 7.1 AKCE

Billon Weight varies: 0.52-0.54g **Obv:** Ruler's name and titles **Rev:** Tamgha in center, mint and date around

Date	Mintage	Good	VG	F	VF	XF
AH992	—	50.00	75.00	100	135	—
ND(date missing)	—	25.00	45.00	65.00	90.00	—

Ghazi Giray II

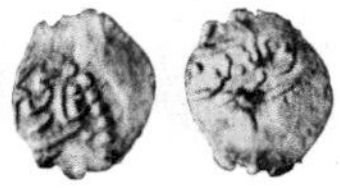

MB# 8 AKCE

Billon Weight varies: 0.28-0.38g **Obv:** Ruler's name and titles **Rev:** Mint and date

Date	Mintage	Good	VG	F	VF	XF
AH996	—	20.00	35.00	45.00	60.00	—
ND(date missing)	—	10.00	17.00	25.00	40.00	—

Salamat Giray I

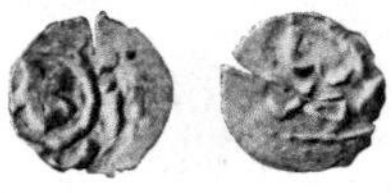

KM# 1 AKCE

Silver Weight varies: 0.28-0.30g **Obv:** Ruler's name and titles **Rev:** Mint and date

Date	Mintage	Good	VG	F	VF	XF
AH1017	—	20.00	35.00	50.00	70.00	—
ND(date missing)	—	15.00	30.00	40.00	55.00	—

Jani Beg Giray

KM# 2 AKCE

Silver Weight varies: 0.28-0.33g **Obv:** Ruler's name and titles **Rev:** Mint and date

Date	Mintage	Good	VG	F	VF	XF
AH1019	—	20.00	30.00	40.00	55.00	—
ND(date missing)	—	12.00	20.00	30.00	45.00	—

KM# 3.1 AKCE

Silver 0.28-0.33 **Obv:** Ruler's name and titles **Rev:** Mint and date **Note:** Weight varies.

Date	Mintage	Good	VG	F	VF	XF
AH[1036]	—	20.00	35.00	45.00	60.00	—
ND(date missing)	—	15.00	25.00	35.00	50.00	—

KM# 3.2 AKCE

Silver 0.29-0.33 **Obv:** Ruler's name and titles **Rev:** Date **Note:** Weight varies.

Date	Mintage	Good	VG	F	VF	XF
AH1036	—	18.00	28.00	40.00	55.00	—

'Inayat Giray

KM# 4 AKCE

0.3000 g., Silver **Obv:** Ruler's name and titles **Rev:** Tamgha in center, date below

Date	Mintage	Good	VG	F	VF	XF
AH1044	—	45.00	60.00	75.00	125	—

Bahadur Giray

KM# A5 AKCE

0.3000 g., Silver **Obv:** Ruler's name and titles **Rev:** Tamgha in center, date below

Date	Mintage	Good	VG	F	VF	XF
AH1046	—	45.00	60.00	75.00	125	—
ND(date missing)	—	35.00	45.00	60.00	95.00	—

Islam Giray III

KM# 5 AKCE

Silver 0.24-0.25 **Obv:** Ruler's name and titles **Rev:** Tamgha above mint and date **Note:** Weight varies.

Date	Mintage	Good	VG	F	VF	XF
AH1054	—	30.00	45.00	60.00	75.00	—
ND(date missing)	—	15.00	25.00	35.00	50.00	—

Muhammad Giray IV

KM# 6 AKCE

0.2800 g., Silver **Obv:** "Muhammad" in circle, titles around **Rev:** Tamgha above mint and date

Date	Mintage	Good	VG	F	VF	XF
AH1064	—	25.00	40.00	50.00	65.00	—
ND(date missing)	—	20.00	35.00	45.00	60.00	—

KM# 7 BESHLIK

Silver 1.34-1.36 **Obv:** Ruler's name and titles **Rev:** "zarb" in cartouche, tamgha above, mint and date below **Note:** Weight varies.

Date	Mintage	Good	VG	F	VF	XF
AH1064	—	30.00	45.00	60.00	85.00	—
ND(date missing)	—	20.00	35.00	45.00	65.00	—

'Adil Giray

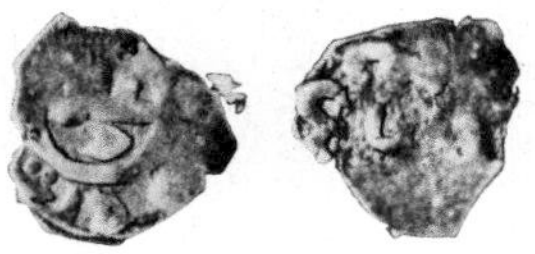

KM# 8 BESHLIK

Silver 1.35-1.39 **Obv:** "'Adil" in circle, titles around **Rev:** Tamgha in center, mint and date around **Note:** Weight varies.

Date	Mintage	Good	VG	F	VF	XF
AH1076	—	30.00	45.00	60.00	85.00	—
ND(date missing)	—	20.00	35.00	45.00	65.00	—

Selim Giray I

KM# 9 BESHLIK

Silver 1.40-1.85 **Obv:** Ruler's name and titles **Rev:** Tamgha above mint and date **Note:** Weight varies.

Date	Mintage	Good	VG	F	VF	XF
AH1082	—	50.00	65.00	85.00	125	—
AH1085	—	50.00	65.00	85.00	125	—
ND(date missing)	—	40.00	50.00	70.00	95.00	—

Murad Giray

KM# 10 BESHLIK

Silver 0.98-1.35 **Obv:** Ruler's name and titles **Rev:** Tamgha in circle, mint and date around **Note:** Weight varies.

Date	Mintage	Good	VG	F	VF	XF
AH1089	—	50.00	65.00	85.00	125	—
ND(date missing)	—	40.00	50.00	70.00	95.00	—

Selim Giray I

KM# 11 BESHLIK

Silver Weight varies: 1.20-1.30g **Obv:** Ruler's name and titles **Rev:** Tamgha above mint and date

Date	Mintage	Good	VG	F	VF	XF
AH1095	—	50.00	65.00	85.00	115	—
ND(date missing)	—	40.00	50.00	65.00	90.00	—

KM# 11A PARA

0.6000 g., Silver **Obv:** Ruler's name and titles **Rev:** Tamgha above mint and date

Date	Mintage	Good	VG	F	VF	XF
AH1095	—	60.00	70.00	90.00	135	—
ND(date missing)	—	40.00	50.00	70.00	95.00	—

KM# 11B AKCE

0.2500 g., Silver **Obv:** Ruler's name and titles **Rev:** Tamgha above mint and date

Date	Mintage	Good	VG	F	VF	XF
AH1095	—	50.00	65.00	85.00	125	—
ND(date missing)	—	40.00	50.00	70.00	95.00	—

Sa'adat Giray II

KM# A12 BESHLIK

1.2500 g., Silver **Obv:** Ruler's name and titles **Rev:** Tamgha in center divides mintname, date below

Date	Mintage	Good	VG	F	VF	XF
AH1102 (error for 1103)	—	55.00	70.00	90.00	125	—

Safa Giray

KM# 12 BESHLIK

Silver 1.03-1.30 **Obv:** Ruler's name and titles **Rev:** Tamgha above mint and date **Note:** Weight varies.

Date	Mintage	Good	VG	F	VF	XF
AH1103	—	50.00	65.00	85.00	125	—
ND(date missing)	—	40.00	50.00	70.00	95.00	—

Selim Giray I

KM# 13 BESHLIK

Silver 0.76-0.97 **Obv:** Ruler's name and titles **Rev:** Tamgha above mint and date **Note:** Weight varies.

Date	Mintage	Good	VG	F	VF	XF
AH1108	—	50.00	65.00	85.00	110	—
ND(date missing)	—	40.00	50.00	70.00	95.00	—

Dawlat Giray II

KM# A14 AKCE

0.2000 g., Silver **Obv:** Ruler's name and titles **Rev:** Tamgha above mint and date

Date	Mintage	Good	VG	F	VF	XF
AH1111	—	65.00	75.00	90.00	130	—

KM# 14 BESHLIK

Silver 0.96-1.05 **Obv:** Ruler's name and titles **Rev:** Tamgha above mint and date **Note:** Weight varies.

Date	Mintage	Good	VG	F	VF	XF
AH1111	—	35.00	45.00	60.00	75.00	—

DENMARK

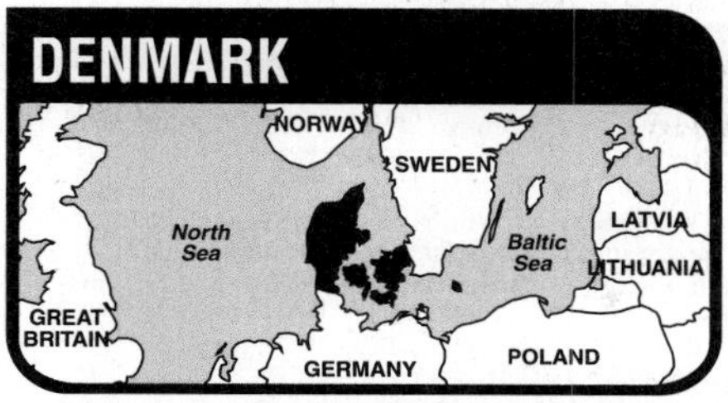

The Kingdom of Denmark (Danmark), is located at the mouth of the Baltic Sea.

Denmark, a great power during the Viking period of the 9th-11th centuries, conducted raids on western Europe and England, and in the 11th century united England, Denmark and Norway under the rule of King Canute. Despite a struggle between the crown and the nobility (13th-14th centuries) which forced the King to grant a written constitution, Queen Margaret (Margrethe) (1387-1412) succeeded in uniting Denmark, Norway, Sweden, Finland and Greenland under the Danish crown, placing all of Scandinavia under the rule of Denmark. An unwise alliance with Napoleon contributed to the dismembering of the empire and fostered a liberal movement which succeeded in making Denmark a constitutional monarchy in 1849.

RULERS

Christian IV, 1588-1648
Frederik III, 1648-1670
Christian V, 1670-1699
Frederik IV, 1699-1730

MINT MARKS

Copenhagen

Mark		Date	Name
(a)		1596-1628	Nicolaus Schwabe
BZ		1627-28	Nicolaus Schwabe
(b)		1610-14	Hans Fleming
(c)		1614-21	Johan Post
(d)		1614-15	Casper Fleming
(s)		1620	?
(o)		1621-23	Johan Engelbrecht
(e)		1628-29	Peder Gruner
(f)		1630-43	Peder Gruner
(g)		1629	Mathias Clausen
(h)		1644-62	Henrik Køhler
(i)		1662-63	Johan Stichman
(j)		1663-64	Casper Herbach
(k)		1664-70	Frederik Casper Herbach
(l)		1664-70	Gottfried Kruger
GK and		1670-80	Gottfried Kruger
Heart		1690-	Christian Winnecke

Elsinore

Mark		Date	Name
(m)		1607-10	Hans Fleming

Frederiksborg

Mark		Date	Name
(n)		1621-23	Johan Engelbrecht

Gluckstadt

Mark		Date	Name
(p)		1640-43	Simon Timpf
(q)		1644-48 1657-60 1664-96	Jacob Schiegelt
IW		1664-79	Johan Woltereck
CW		1679-1718	Christopher Woltereck

Unknown

Mark		Date	Name
(r)		1620-23	?
(t)			?

(c) - Copenhagen (Kobenhavn), crown
(h) - Copenhagen, heart
(o) - Altona, orb, 1842-63
KM - Copenhagen
S – Rendsborg, 1716-20

NOTE: (ch) - crossed hammers - Kongsberg.

MINT OFFICIALS' INITIALS

Copenhagen

Initial	Date	Name
	1602-29	Nikolaus Schwabe
P	1614-22	Johan Post
	1620-24	Michael Wile
	1620-22	Johan Engelbrecht
NS	1624-27	Nicolaus Schwabe
BZ	1627	Balthazar Zwierner
G	1628-43	Peter Gruner
	1629	Mathius Clauesen
HK or ligate HK	1644-62	Hendrik Kohler
IS	1644-48	Jacob Schiegelt
IL	1645-46	?
IS	1662-63	Johan Stichmann
CH	1663-64	Casper Herbach
FCH	1664-71	Frederik Casper Herbach, Jr.
GK	1665-80	Gottfried Kruger
GS	1680-90	Gregorius Streseman
CW	1690-1700	Christian Winnecke, Sr.
AMB	1692-	Anton Maybusch, die-cutter

NOTE: The letter P was only used on Danish West Indies coins.

Frederiksborg

Initial	Date	Name
	1622-23	Paul Golden and Johan Engelbrecht

Gluckstadt

Initial	Date	Name
	1616-31	Albert Dionis
Feather w/ligate TS	1640-43	Simon Timpf
I, crossed halberds, W		Johan Woltereck

NOTE: This mint was temporarily closed from 1631 to 1640.

Helsinger

Initial	Date	Name
	1607-14	Hans Flemming
	1614-15	Casper Flemming

Lyngby

Initial	Date	Name
FCH	1668-70	F.C.

MONETARY SYSTEM

(Until 1813)

4 Penning = 1 Huid = 1/4 Skilling
6 Penning = 1 Sosling = 1/2 Skilling
16 Skillings = 1 Mark
64 Skilling Danske = 4 Mark = 1 Krone
96 Skilling Danske = 6 Mark = 1 Daler Specie
12 Mark = 1 Ducat
10 Ducat = 1 Portugaloser

KINGDOM

WIRE MONEY

KM# 62 DENNING

5.8000 g., 0.8880 Silver 0.1656 oz. ASW **Ruler:** Christian IV **Obv:** Ruler on horse. Below horse the letter P **Rev:** Titles of Russian czar Mikhail Fjodorovitsj Romanov **Note:** Issued for the Petsora Company, for use in trade with Russia. Strikes with a "P" below the horse on the obverse were minted in Copenhagen. Those strikes with an "M", or no letter at all, were minted in Gluckstadt. Varieties exist. Prev. KM#62.2.

Date	Mintage	Good	VG	F	VF	XF
ND(1619) P Rare	Est. 72,000	—	—	—	—	—

STANDARD COINAGE

Through 1813

KM# 6 PENNING

0.5850 g., Copper **Obv:** Date within crowned C, 1C602 **Note:** Uniface.

Date	Mintage	Good	VG	F	VF	XF
1602	—	300	600	1,200	2,000	—

KM# 5 PENNING

0.5850 g., Copper **Obv:** Date within crowned C, 1C602 **Rev. Legend:** PEN/NING **Note:** Varieties exist with line below crown, presumably a die break.

Date	Mintage	Good	VG	F	VF	XF
1602	—	1,000	1,500	2,500	4,000	—

KM# 7 2 PENNING

0.5850 g., Copper **Obv:** Date within crowned C, 1C602 **Rev:** I*I/ PEN/ NING

Date	Mintage	Good	VG	F	VF	XF
1602	—	300	500	900	1,400	—

KM# 8 HVID

0.7130 g., 0.0930 Silver 0.0021 oz. ASW, 17 mm. **Obv:** Long cross on oval design divides date **Obv. Legend:** CHRISTIANVS IIII • D: G • DANI • **Rev:** Crowned C, date partially within as 1C602 **Rev. Legend:** NORVEGI: VANDA: GOT • Q • REX (clover)

Date	Mintage	Good	VG	F	VF	XF
1602	—	500	900	1,500	2,000	—

KM# 9 HVID

0.7130 g., 0.0930 Silver 0.0021 oz. ASW, 15 mm. **Obv:** Short cross on oval design **Obv. Legend:** CHRISTIANVS III D G DAN • **Rev:** Crowned C, date within C602 **Rev. Legend:** NORVEGI • VANDA • GOT • Q • REX (clover)

Date	Mintage	Good	VG	F	VF	XF
1602	—	30.00	60.00	140	300	—

KM# 34 HVID

0.7130 g., 0.0930 Silver 0.0021 oz. ASW **Obv:** Crowned C within circle **Obv. Legend:** CHRISTIANVS • IIII • D: G: DAN: **Rev:** Short cross with ornaments within circle, mintmaster mark at top **Rev. Legend:** NOR: VAN: GOT: Q: REX • 1607

Date	Mintage	Good	VG	F	VF	XF
1607(m) Unique	—	—	—	—	—	—

KM# 54 HVID

0.7130 g., 0.0930 Silver 0.0021 oz. ASW **Obv:** Short cross on oval design **Obv. Legend:** CHRISTIAN III D G DAN • (clover) **Rev:** Crowned C, date within C **Rev. Legend:** NOR: VAN: GOT • REX

Date	Mintage	Good	VG	F	VF	XF
1613	—	400	700	1,000	—	—
1614	—	75.00	150	300	700	—

KM# 63.1 HVID

0.5640 g., 0.0930 Silver 0.0017 oz. ASW, 13-14 mm. **Obv:** Long cross and ornaments **Obv. Legend:** CHRISTIAN 4 D G D • **Rev:** Crowned C4, date in legend **Rev. Legend:** NOR VAN GOT REX •

Date	Mintage	Good	VG	F	VF	XF
ND1618-19(a) on obverse	—	400	700	1,000	1,500	—
ND1618-19(a) on reverse	—	25.00	50.00	115	250	—
ND1618-19(c) on obverse	—	30.00	55.00	115	380	—
1619(c)	—	40.00	70.00	200	425	—

KM# 63.2 HVID

0.5640 g., 0.0930 Silver 0.0017 oz. ASW, 15 mm. **Obv:** Long cross and ornaments **Obv. Legend:** CHRISTIAN 4 D G D **Rev:** Crowned C4 **Rev. Legend:** NOR VAN GOT REX •

Date	Mintage	Good	VG	F	VF	XF
ND1618-19	—	200	375	650	1,000	—

KM# 63.3 HVID

0.5640 g., 0.0930 Silver 0.0017 oz. ASW, 12 mm. **Obv:** Long cross and ornaments **Obv. Legend:** CHRISTIAN 4 DA **Rev:** Crowned C4 **Rev. Legend:** NOR • VAN • GOT • REX

Date	Mintage	Good	VG	F	VF	XF
ND(1618-19)	—	40.00	90.00	225	650	—

KM# 86 HVID

Silver **Obv:** Long cross on oval shield **Rev:** Crowned C4 monogram in pellet border, legend around

Date	Mintage	Good	VG	F	VF	XF
1624	—	25.00	50.00	110	240	—
1625	—	25.00	50.00	120	270	—

KM# 175 HVID

Copper **Obv:** Crowned F3 monogram **Rev:** Date quartered by long cross

Date	Mintage	Good	VG	F	VF	XF
1651	—	40.00	80.00	180	475	—

KM# 380.1 HVID

0.5570 g., 0.1250 Silver 0.0022 oz. ASW **Obv:** Crowned C5 monogram **Rev:** Value and date, "DANSK"

Date	Mintage	Good	VG	F	VF	XF
1686	—	25.00	50.00	100	200	—

KM# 380.2 HVID

0.5570 g., 0.1250 Silver 0.0022 oz. ASW **Rev:** "DANS"

Date	Mintage	Good	VG	F	VF	XF
1686	—	40.00	70.00	150	380	—

KM# 10 SøSLING (1/2 Skilling)

1.0630 g., 0.1250 Silver 0.0043 oz. ASW, 19 mm. **Obv:** Crowned shield with lions on forked crossarms, breaks legend at top **Obv. Legend:** CHRISTIANVS IIII D G DANI **Rev:** Crowned bust of Christian IV right within legend **Rev. Legend:** NORVEGI: VANDA: GOTH: Q · REX **Note:** Milled.

Date	Mintage	Good	VG	F	VF	XF
ND(1602)	—	100	200	600	1,100	—

KM# 22.1 SøSLING (1/2 Skilling)

1.0170 g., 0.1250 Silver 0.0041 oz. ASW, 17 mm. **Obv:** Crowned bust of Christian IV facing right with low collar, breaks legend at bottom **Obv. Legend:** CHRISTIAN • IIII • D: G • DAN **Rev:** Crowned shield with lions on forked crossarms, breaks legend at top **Rev. Legend:** NOR VAND GOTO REX **Note:** Milled.

Date	Mintage	Good	VG	F	VF	XF
ND(1604)	—	20.00	40.00	100	190	—

KM# 22.2 SøSLING (1/2 Skilling)

1.0170 g., 0.1250 Silver 0.0041 oz. ASW, 17 mm. **Obv:** Crowned bust of Christian IV facing right with low collar, breaks legend at bottom **Obv. Legend:** CHRISTIAN · IIII · D: G · DAN **Rev:** Crowned shield with beaded border, lions on forked crossarms, breaks legend at top **Rev. Legend:** NOR VAND GOTO REX

Date	Mintage	Good	VG	F	VF	XF
ND(1604)	—	25.00	50.00	115	210	—

KM# 40.1 SøSLING (1/2 Skilling)

1.0170 g., 0.1250 Silver 0.0041 oz. ASW, 16.5 mm. **Obv:** Crowned bust of Christian IV facing right with high collar, breaks legend at bottom **Obv. Legend:** CHRISTIAN: IIII • D: G • DA **Rev:** Crowned shield with lions on forked crossarms, within beaded border, breaks legend at top **Rev. Legend:** NOR VAN GOT REX

Date	Mintage	Good	VG	F	VF	XF
ND(1607-09)(a)	—	25.00	50.00	90.00	150	—

KM# 40.2 SøSLING (1/2 Skilling)

1.0630 g., 0.1250 Silver 0.0043 oz. ASW, 16.5 mm. **Obv:** Crowned bust of Christian IV facing right with high collar, breaks legend at bottom **Obv. Legend:** CHRISTIAN: IIII · D: G · DA **Rev:** Crowned shield with lebards and hearts, beaded border, breaks legend at top **Rev. Legend:** NOR VAN GOT REX **Note:** Without mint mark

Date	Mintage	Good	VG	F	VF	XF
ND(1607-09)	—	35.00	70.00	120	200	—

KM# 40.3 SøSLING (1/2 Skilling)

1.0170 g., 0.1250 Silver 0.0041 oz. ASW, 16.5 mm. **Obv:** Crowned bust of Christian IV facing right with high collar, breaks legend at bottom **Obv. Legend:** CHRISTIAN: IIII · D: G · DA **Rev:** Crowned shield with lions on forked crossarms, breaks legend at top **Rev. Legend:** NOR VAN GOT REX

Date	Mintage	Good	VG	F	VF	XF
ND(1607-09)	—	25.00	50.00	95.00	160	—

KM# 40.4 SøSLING (1/2 Skilling)

1.0170 g., 0.1250 Silver 0.0041 oz. ASW, 16.5 mm. **Obv:** Crowned bust of Christian IV facing right with high collar, breaks legend at top **Obv. Legend:** CHRISTIAN: IIII · D: G · DA **Rev:** Crowned shield with lions on forked crossarms, beaded border, breaks legend at top **Rev. Legend:** NOR VAN GOT REX

Date	Mintage	Good	VG	F	VF	XF
ND(1607-09)	—	30.00	80.00	200	325	—

KM# 47.1 SøSLING (1/2 Skilling)

1.0170 g., 0.1250 Silver 0.0041 oz. ASW, 16 mm. **Obv:** Crowned bust of Christian IV facing right with ruffled collar, breaks legend at bottom **Obv. Legend:** CHRISTIAN IIII · D G DA **Rev:** Crowned shield with lebards on forked crossarms, breaks legend at top **Rev. Legend:** NOR VAN GOT REX

Date	Mintage	Good	VG	F	VF	XF
ND(1611)	—	—	150	300	675	—

KM# 47.2 SøSLING (1/2 Skilling)

1.0170 g., 0.1250 Silver 0.0041 oz. ASW, 16 mm. **Obv:** Crowned bust of Christian IV facing right with ruffled collar, breaks legend at bottom **Obv. Legend:** CHRISTIAN IIII • D G DA **Rev:** Crowned shield with forked crossarms, breaks legend at top **Rev. Legend:** NOR VAN GOT REX

Date	Mintage	Good	VG	F	VF	XF
ND(1611) Rare	—	—	—	—	—	—

KM# 47.3 SøSLING (1/2 Skilling)

1.0170 g., 0.1250 Silver 0.0041 oz. ASW **Obv:** Crowned bust of Christian IV facing right with ruffled collar, breaks legend at top **Obv. Legend:** CHRISTIAN IIII·D G DA **Rev:** Crowned shield with hearts surrounding lebards, breaks legend at top **Rev. Legend:** NOR VAN GOT REX

Date	Mintage	Good	VG	F	VF	XF
ND(1611) Rare	—	—	—	—	—	—

KM# 48.1 SøSLING (1/2 Skilling)

1.0170 g., 0.1250 Silver 0.0041 oz. ASW, 16 mm. **Obv:** Crowned bust of Christian IV facing right with ruffled collar, breaks legend at top **Obv. Legend:** CHRISTIAN IIII D G DA **Rev:** Crowned shield with lions and hearts on crossarms with straight cut ends, breaks legend at top

Date	Mintage	Good	VG	F	VF	XF
ND(1614)(a)	—	100	190	410	800	—

KM# 48.2 SøSLING (1/2 Skilling)

1.0170 g., 0.1250 Silver 0.0041 oz. ASW, 16 mm. **Obv:** Crowned bust of Christian IV facing right with ruffled collar, breaks legend at top **Obv. Legend:** CHRISTIAN IIII D G DA **Rev:** Crowned shield with lions and hearts on crossarms with straight cut ends, breaks legend at top

Date	Mintage	Good	VG	F	VF	XF
ND(1614)	—	60.00	140	320	700	—

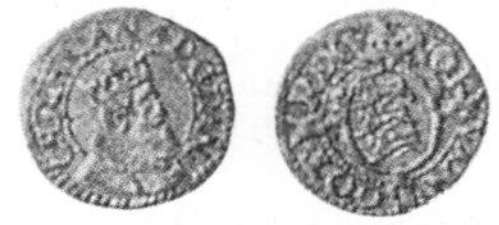

KM# 45 SøSLING (1/2 Skilling)

0.5300 g., Silver **Obv:** Crowned bust of Christian IV right, breaks legend at bottom **Obv. Legend:** CHRISTIAN 4 D G DAN **Rev:** Crowned shield on forked crossarms, breaks legend at top **Rev. Legend:** NOR VAN GOT REX

Date	Mintage	Good	VG	F	VF	XF
ND(1622)	—	55.00	110	200	400	—

KM# 87 SøSLING (1/2 Skilling)

Copper **Obv:** Crowned bust right breaks circle at bottom **Rev:** Value and date within oval shield

Date	Mintage	Good	VG	F	VF	XF
1624(a)	—	30.00	60.00	200	550	—

KM# 123 SøSLING (1/2 Skilling)

Silver **Obv:** Crowned bust right without circle **Rev:** Value and date within ornate oval shield

Date	Mintage	Good	VG	F	VF	XF
1631(a)	—	200	400	850	1,650	—

KM# 176 SøSLING (1/2 Skilling)

Copper **Obv:** Crowned F3 monogram **Rev:** Value and date

Date	Mintage	Good	VG	F	VF	XF
1651(h)	—	15.00	30.00	80.00	200	—

KM# 177 SøSLING (1/2 Skilling)

Copper **Obv:** Crowned oval shield **Rev:** Value and date within fancy border

Date	Mintage	Good	VG	F	VF	XF
1651 Unique	—	—	—	—	—	—

KM# 381 1/2 SKILLING

0.6680 g., 0.1560 Silver 0.0034 oz. ASW **Obv:** Crowned double C5 monogram **Rev:** Value and date

Date	Mintage	Good	VG	F	VF	XF
1686	—	25.00	45.00	90.00	225	—

KM# 421.1 1/2 SKILLING

3.6540 g., Copper **Obv:** Armored bust right **Rev:** Crown dividing value

Date	Mintage	Good	VG	F	VF	XF
1693	—	12.50	22.50	75.00	150	—
1694	—	10.00	17.50	45.00	125	—
1696	—	25.00	45.00	95.00	240	—

KM# 421.2 1/2 SKILLING

3.6540 g., Copper **Obv:** Armored bust right **Rev:** Without value

Date	Mintage	Good	VG	F	VF	XF
1693	—	1,500	2,000	2,750	3,250	—
1694 Unique	—	—	—	—	—	—

KM# 29.1 SKILLING

1.6020 g., 0.1710 Silver 0.0088 oz. ASW **Obv:** Crowned oval shield on long cross **Rev:** Value and date within central legend

Date	Mintage	Good	VG	F	VF	XF
1605(a)	—	20.00	35.00	65.00	120	—
1613(a)	—	225	475	925	1,250	—
1614(a)	—	20.00	40.00	75.00	175	—
1615(a)	—	20.00	40.00	75.00	175	—
1616(a)	—	35.00	70.00	140	300	—

KM# 29.2 SKILLING

1.6020 g., 0.1710 Silver 0.0088 oz. ASW **Obv:** Oval shield **Rev:** Date in outer legend **Note:** Varieties exist

Date	Mintage	Good	VG	F	VF	XF
1615(c)	—	30.00	60.00	130	325	—
1617(a)	—	27.50	55.00	115	300	—
1618(a)	—	28.00	57.50	120	310	—
1619(c)	—	32.50	70.00	140	390	—
1619(a)	—	125	220	600	—	—

KM# 39 SKILLING

1.6020 g., 0.1710 Silver 0.0088 oz. ASW **Obv:** Crowned flat-topped shield on long cross **Rev:** Date in central legend

Date	Mintage	Good	VG	F	VF	XF
1608	—	125	225	325	800	—

KM# A40.1 SKILLING

1.6020 g., 0.1710 Silver 0.0088 oz. ASW **Obv:** Crowned notched oval shield on long cross **Note:** Varieties exist. Prev. KM#40.1.

Date	Mintage	Good	VG	F	VF	XF
1608(m)	—	25.00	50.00	90.00	220	—
1609(m)	—	25.00	50.00	90.00	220	—
1611(m)	—	20.00	40.00	60.00	130	—
1612(m)	—	25.00	50.00	90.00	220	—
1613(m)	—	22.50	45.00	85.00	190	—
1614(d)	—	30.00	60.00	115	230	—
1615(d)	—	25.00	50.00	90.00	220	—

KM# A40.2 SKILLING

1.6020 g., 0.1710 Silver 0.0088 oz. ASW **Obv:** Shield in case at center **Rev:** Date in outer legend **Note:** Prev. KM#40.2.

Date	Mintage	Good	VG	F	VF	XF
1615(c) Rare	—	—	—	—	—	—

KM# 67 SKILLING

0.5320 g., 0.3120 Silver 0.0053 oz. ASW **Obv:** Crowned C4 monogram **Note:** Varieties exist.

Date	Mintage	Good	VG	F	VF	XF
1619(c)	—	75.00	140	310	775	—
1620(a)	—	20.00	40.00	75.00	170	—
1620(o)	—	20.00	40.00	75.00	170	—
1620(r)	—	20.00	40.00	75.00	170	—
1621(a)	—	20.00	40.00	75.00	170	—
1621(o)	—	20.00	40.00	75.00	170	—
1621(r)	—	20.00	40.00	75.00	170	—
1622(a)	—	20.00	45.00	100	200	—
1622(o)	—	20.00	140	280	580	—
1622(r)	—	30.00	55.00	120	325	—
1622 Unique	—	—	—	—	—	—
1623(r)	—	30.00	55.00	120	350	—

KM# 65 SKILLING

0.8590 Silver **Obv:** Crowned C4 monogram **Rev:** Value above, 96 in circle dividing date

Date	Mintage	Good	VG	F	VF	XF
1619(a)	—	175	375	900	2,000	—
1619(c) Rare	—	—	—	—	—	—

KM# 66.1 SKILLING

0.5320 g., 0.3120 Silver 0.0053 oz. ASW **Obv:** Crown within legend **Rev:** Value and date

Date	Mintage	Good	VG	F	VF	XF
1619(a)	—	150	250	600	1,250	—

KM# 66.2 SKILLING

0.5320 g., 0.3120 Silver 0.0053 oz. ASW **Obv:** No inner circle **Rev:** Value and date

Date	Mintage	Good	VG	F	VF	XF
1619(a)	—	150	250	600	1,250	—

KM# 88 SKILLING

0.5320 g., 0.3120 Silver 0.0053 oz. ASW **Obv:** Crowned oval shield on long cross **Rev:** Value within legend and date

Date	Mintage	Good	VG	F	VF	XF
1624(a) closed crown	—	20.00	45.00	90.00	165	—
1624(a) open crown	—	75.00	125	260	400	—

KM# 113.1 SKILLING

0.2920 g., 0.8750 Silver 0.0082 oz. ASW **Obv:** Crowned C4 monogram dividing date, 1S **Note:** Bracteate

Date	Mintage	Good	VG	F	VF	XF
(16)29(e)	—	115	175	325	825	—

KM# 113.2 SKILLING

0.2920 g., 0.8750 Silver 0.0082 oz. ASW **Obv:** Without 1S **Note:** Bracteate

Date	Mintage	Good	VG	F	VF	XF
(16)29(e)	—	70.00	125	300	700	—

KM# 131 SKILLING

0.2920 g., 0.8750 Silver 0.0082 oz. ASW **Obv:** Crowned oval arms on long cross **Rev:** Value within legend and date

Date	Mintage	Good	VG	F	VF	XF
1644	—	20.00	65.00	135	220	—
1648(h)	—	20.00	50.00	115	190	—
1648(h) Rare	—	—	—	—	—	—

KM# 156.1 SKILLING

0.2920 g., 0.8750 Silver 0.0082 oz. ASW **Obv. Legend:** FRIDERIC • 9 • III • D • G • DAN • **Rev. Legend:** NOR • VAN • GOTO • ELEC • R •

Date	Mintage	Good	VG	F	VF	XF
1648(h)	—	25.00	75.00	200	400	—
1648(h) Rare; Two knobs on shield	—	—	—	—	—	—

KM# 156.2 SKILLING

0.2920 g., 0.8750 Silver 0.0082 oz. ASW **Rev:** Legend without ELEC • R •

Date	Mintage	Good	VG	F	VF	XF
1648(h)	—	35.00	80.00	210	420	—
1649(h)	—	25.00	50.00	110	225	—
1650(h)	—	30.00	55.00	130	300	—
1652(h) Four points on each shield side	—	20.00	40.00	70.00	200	—
1652(h) Three points on each shield side	—	15.00	25.00	60.00	140	—
1653(h) Three points on each shield side	—	20.00	40.00	75.00	200	—

KM# A157 SKILLING

0.2920 g., 0.8750 Silver 0.0082 oz. ASW **Obv:** KM#156.2, 1650 **Rev:** KM#184.1, 1655

Date	Mintage	Good	VG	F	VF	XF
1650/55(h)	—	150	200	250	—	—

KM# 184.1 SKILLING

0.2920 g., 0.8750 Silver 0.0082 oz. ASW **Obv. Legend:** FRIDERIC • 3 • D • G • D • **Rev:** Cross arms on side of shield **Rev. Legend:** NOR • VAN • G • R •

Date	Mintage	Good	VG	F	VF	XF
1652(h) Convex-topped shield	—	25.00	50.00	120	285	—
1652(h) Rare; Round-topped shield	—	—	—	—	—	—
1653(h)	—	25.00	50.00	120	285	—
1654(h) Round-topped shield	—	20.00	45.00	70.00	190	—
1654(h) Without cross arms	—	22.50	55.00	140	320	—
1654(h) Rare; Convex-topped shield	—	—	—	—	—	—
1655(h) Rare	—	—	—	—	—	—

KM# 184.2 SKILLING

0.2920 g., 0.8750 Silver 0.0082 oz. ASW **Obv. Legend:** FRIDERIC • III • D • G • D • **Rev. Legend:** NOR • VAN • G • REX •

Date	Mintage	Good	VG	F	VF	XF
1655(h) Dots flank shield	—	50.00	100	260	400	—
1655(h) Without dots; Rare	—	—	—	—	—	—

KM# 184.3 SKILLING

0.2920 g., 0.8750 Silver 0.0082 oz. ASW **Obv. Legend:** FRIDERIC • 3 D • G • DAN • **Rev. Legend:** NOR • VAN • GOT • REX •

Date	Mintage	Good	VG	F	VF	XF
1665(h) Second circle under shield	—	50.00	100	210	525	—
1665(h) Without second circle	—	25.00	55.00	120	290	—

KM# A185 SKILLING

0.2920 g., 0.8750 Silver 0.0082 oz. ASW **Obv:** Shield divides date **Obv. Legend:** FRIDERIC • III • D • G • DAN • **Rev. Legend:** NOR • VAN • GOT • REX •

Date	Mintage	Good	VG	F	VF	XF
1661(h)	—	25.00	50.00	125	290	—

KM# 254 SKILLING

0.2920 g., 0.8750 Silver 0.0082 oz. ASW **Obv:** Hearts in shield **Obv. Legend:** FRIDERIC • 3 • D • G • DAN • **Rev. Legend:** NOR • VAN • GOT • REX •

Date	Mintage	Good	VG	F	VF	XF
1665(k)	—	700	1,100	1,650	—	—
1667(k)	—	25.00	50.00	100	210	—
1667(l)	—	30.00	60.00	115	290	—
1668(k) 1 known	—	—	—	1,500	—	—

KM# 357 SKILLING

0.2920 g., 0.8750 Silver 0.0082 oz. ASW **Obv:** Crowned shield, titles of Christian V **Note:** Varieties exist.

Date	Mintage	Good	VG	F	VF	XF
1676(k)	—	6.00	12.00	30.00	60.00	—
1677	—	12.50	25.00	65.00	140	—
1680(l)	—	6.00	12.00	35.00	70.00	—
1681(l) GS	—	12.50	25.00	65.00	140	—

KM# 382 SKILLING

1.1140 g., 0.1870 Silver 0.0067 oz. ASW **Obv:** Crowned double C5 monogram

Date	Mintage	VG	F	VF	XF	Unc
1686GS	—	40.00	110	275	700	—

KM# 16.1 2 SKILLING

Silver **Obv:** Crowned shield on long cross **Rev:** Value and date within central legend **Note:** Varieties exist.

Date	Mintage	Good	VG	F	VF	XF
1603(a)	—	15.00	30.00	60.00	140	—
1604(a)	—	15.00	30.00	60.00	140	—
1605(a)	—	25.00	50.00	120	320	—
1607(a)	—	30.00	60.00	150	330	—
1607(m)	—	45.00	90.00	200	400	—
1608(a)	—	25.00	50.00	120	320	—
1608(m)	—	32.50	65.00	125	300	—
1609(a)	—	30.00	60.00	145	350	—
1611(a)	—	30.00	60.00	145	350	—
1613(a)	—	30.00	60.00	145	350	—

KM# 16.2 2 SKILLING

Silver **Rev:** Date in outer legend

Date	Mintage	Good	VG	F	VF	XF
1618(c)	—	25.00	50.00	120	320	—
1618(a)	—	200	300	500	800	—

KM# 68 2 SKILLING

0.7870 g., 0.8590 Silver 0.0217 oz. ASW **Obv:** Date above crown **Rev:** Value, 48 in oval, legend **Note:** Varieties exist.

Date	Mintage	Good	VG	F	VF	XF
1619(a)	—	110	180	425	950	—
1619(c)	—	140	280	600	1,050	—

KM# 69 2 SKILLING

0.5250 g., 0.8590 Silver 0.0145 oz. ASW **Obv:** Crown **Rev:** Value and date

Date	Mintage	Good	VG	F	VF	XF
1619(c)	—	50.00	120	260	600	—
1620(r)	—	45.00	100	250	550	—
1621(c) Rare	—	—	—	—	—	—

KM# 80.1 2 SKILLING

0.5250 g., 0.8590 Silver 0.0145 oz. ASW **Obv:** Crown within pellet circle **Rev:** Value, 72 in oval

Date	Mintage	Good	VG	F	VF	XF
1620	—	60.00	120	290	700	—

KM# 80.2 2 SKILLING

0.5250 g., 0.8590 Silver 0.0145 oz. ASW **Obv:** Without pellet circle

Date	Mintage	Good	VG	F	VF	XF
1620 Unique	—	—	—	—	—	—

KM# 89 2 SKILLING

1.2990 g., 0.2810 Silver 0.0117 oz. ASW **Obv:** Crowned shield on long cross **Rev:** Value in circle, date in legend **Note:** Varieties exist.

Date	Mintage	Good	VG	F	VF	XF
1624(a)	—	10.00	20.00	40.00	90.00	—
1625(a)	—	10.00	20.00	40.00	90.00	—
1626(a)	—	20.00	40.00	70.00	150	—
1627(a)	—	10.00	20.00	45.00	70.00	—
1629(e)	—	20.00	40.00	70.00	150	—

KM# 120 2 SKILLING

0.5250 g., 0.8590 Silver 0.0145 oz. ASW **Obv:** Crowned shield **Rev:** Value and date

Date	Mintage	Good	VG	F	VF	XF
1630(e)	—	20.00	65.00	130	380	—
1632(f)	—	18.00	55.00	110	320	—

KM# 132 2 SKILLING

0.5250 g., 0.8590 Silver 0.0145 oz. ASW **Obv:** Crowned oval arms on long cross **Rev:** Value in circle, date in legend **Note:** Varieties exist.

Date	Mintage	Good	VG	F	VF	XF
1644(h)	—	10.00	20.00	40.00	80.00	—
1645(h)	—	10.00	20.00	40.00	80.00	—
1648(h)	—	10.00	20.00	40.00	80.00	—

KM# 157 2 SKILLING

0.5250 g., 0.8590 Silver 0.0145 oz. ASW **Obv:** Crowned oval shield **Obv. Legend:** FRIDERIC • 9 • III • D • G • DAN • **Rev:** Value at center II/ SKIL/ DANS **Rev. Legend:** NOR • VAN • GOTO • ELEC: R:

Date	Mintage	Good	VG	F	VF	XF
1648(h) Date in obverse legend	—	40.00	70.00	160	270	—
1648(h) Oval shield divides date	—	25.00	45.00	100	200	—
1648(h) Shield with concave sides	—	20.00	30.00	50.00	120	—
1649(h)	—	75.00	125	200	350	—

KM# 158 2 SKILLING

0.5250 g., 0.8590 Silver 0.0145 oz. ASW **Rev:** Value in center: II/ SKIL/ NGDA/ NSK **Rev. Legend:** NOR • VAN • GOTO • Q • REX •

Date	Mintage	Good	VG	F	VF	XF
1648(h) Closed notches on shield	—	10.00	20.00	50.00	90.00	—
1649(h)	—	8.00	17.50	35.00	70.00	—
1650(h)	—	22.50	45.00	85.00	170	—
1650(h) Lower notches open	—	8.00	17.50	35.00	70.00	—
1650(h) All notches open	—	50.00	100	210	390	—
1650(h) Without notches	—	8.00	17.50	35.00	70.00	—
1651(h)	—	10.00	20.00	50.00	90.00	—

KM# A159 2 SKILLING

1.2990 g., 0.2810 Silver 0.0117 oz. ASW **Obv:** Obverse of KM#158, 1651 **Rev:** Reverse of KM#178, 1651, date below denomination

Date	Mintage	Good	VG	F	VF	XF
1651//1651(h) Rare	—	—	—	—	—	—

KM# 178 2 SKILLING

1.2990 g., 0.2810 Silver 0.0117 oz. ASW **Obv. Legend:** FRIDERIC • 9 • 3 • D • G • DAN **Rev:** Value in center: II/ SKIL/ DANS **Rev. Legend:** NOR • VAN • GOTO • Q • REX •

Date	Mintage	Good	VG	F	VF	XF
ND(1651)(h)	—	75.00	120	200	400	—
1651(h) Date below denomination	—	22.50	60.00	125	350	—
1651(h) Date in outer legend	—	10.00	20.00	50.00	90.00	—

KM# 189.1 2 SKILLING

1.2990 g., 0.2810 Silver 0.0117 oz. ASW **Obv:** Shield on second inner circle **Obv. Legend:** NOR • V • G • REX: **Rev. Legend:** FRIDERIC • 3 • D • G • D •

Date	Mintage	Good	VG	F	VF	XF
1653(h)	—	75.00	125	210	340	—

KM# 189.2 2 SKILLING

1.2990 g., 0.2810 Silver 0.0117 oz. ASW **Obv:** Without second circle **Rev. Legend:** FRIDERIC • 3 • D • G • D •

Date	Mintage	Good	VG	F	VF	XF
1653(h)	—	8.00	15.00	35.00	70.00	—
1654(h)	—	8.00	15.00	35.00	70.00	—
1655(h)	—	10.00	20.00	45.00	75.00	—

KM# A190 2 SKILLING

1.2990 g., 0.2810 Silver 0.0117 oz. ASW **Obv:** Crown above shield

Date	Mintage	Good	VG	F	VF	XF
1654 Flat-topped shield, emperor's crown	—	30.00	60.00	140	300	—
1654 Ellipse-shaped shield, king's crown	—	60.00	120	240	400	—
1654 Rare; Oval-shaped shield, king's crown	—	200	300	500	1,000	—
1655 Ellipse-shaped shield, king's crown	—	60.00	120	240	400	—
1655 Oval-shaped shield, king's crown	—	12.50	25.00	50.00	100	—

KM# 209 2 SKILLING

1.2990 g., 0.2810 Silver 0.0117 oz. ASW **Obv:** Crowned shield with ornamented sides **Obv. Legend:** FRIDERIC: III: D: G: DA **Rev. Legend:** NOR • VAN • GOT • REX •

Date	Mintage	Good	VG	F	VF	XF
1657(h) Rare; Long ornamentation	—	—	—	—	—	—
1657(h) Short ornamentation	—	12.50	25.00	50.00	110	—
1657(h) Bottom of ornamentation curls in	—	17.50	35.00	60.00	130	—
1658(h)	—	17.50	35.00	60.00	130	—
1658(h) Long ornamentation	—	15.00	30.00	55.00	110	—
1658(h) Bottom of ornamentation curls out	—	35.00	65.00	150	325	—
1659(h) Long ornamentation	—	10.00	20.00	40.00	90.00	—
1660(h)	—	10.00	20.00	40.00	90.00	—
1661(h)	—	9.00	17.50	35.00	80.00	—
1662(h)	—	10.00	20.00	40.00	85.00	—
1662(i)	—	10.00	20.00	40.00	85.00	—
1663(j)	—	20.00	45.00	90.00	170	—
1663(i)	—	10.00	20.00	40.00	85.00	—
1664(j)	—	12.00	20.00	45.00	90.00	—

KM# A210.1 2 SKILLING

1.2990 g., 0.2810 Silver 0.0117 oz. ASW **Obv:** Crowned shield in inner circle **Obv. Legend:** FRIDERIC • 3 • D • G • DAN •

Date	Mintage	Good	VG	F	VF	XF
1664(k)	—	17.50	35.00	65.00	135	—
1665(k)	—	15.00	30.00	60.00	130	—

KM# A210.2 2 SKILLING

1.2990 g., 0.2810 Silver 0.0117 oz. ASW **Obv:** Without inner circle **Rev. Legend:** FRIDERIC • 3 • D • G • DAN •

Date	Mintage	Good	VG	F	VF	XF
1664(k)	—	15.00	30.00	60.00	130	—
1665(k)	—	125	200	300	600	—

KM# 249.1 2 SKILLING

1.2990 g., 0.2810 Silver 0.0117 oz. ASW **Obv:** Crowned shield in inner circle with shield-like ornamentation on sides

Date	Mintage	Good	VG	F	VF	XF
1665(k)	—	10.00	20.00	40.00	90.00	—
1666(k)	—	650	1,000	1,500	—	—
1667(k)	—	100	200	300	—	—

KM# 249.2 2 SKILLING

1.2990 g., 0.2810 Silver 0.0117 oz. ASW **Obv:** Without inner circle **Note:** Varieties exist.

Date	Mintage	Good	VG	F	VF	XF
1664(k)	—	15.00	30.00	60.00	120	—
1665(k)	—	30.00	65.00	150	325	—
1666(k)	—	17.50	35.00	65.00	125	—
1667(k)	—	20.00	45.00	70.00	140	—
1667(l)	—	15.00	32.50	60.00	120	—

KM# 256 2 SKILLING

1.2990 g., 0.2810 Silver 0.0117 oz. ASW **Obv:** Crowned F3 monogram **Obv. Legend:** DOMINUS • PROVIDEBIT • **Rev:** Value: II/ SKILLING/ DANSKE/ 1665 **Note:** Directions of obverse legend inidcated after date.

Date	Mintage	Good	VG	F	VF	XF
1665(k) Clockwise from bottom	—	30.00	60.00	140	340	—
1665 GK Counterclockwise from top	—	30.00	60.00	140	340	—
1665 GK Clockwise from bottom	—	30.00	60.00	140	340	—
1665(k) Clockwise from top	—	140	225	550	800	—
1666(k) Clockwise from bottom	—	140	225	550	800	—
1666(k) Clockwise from top	—	140	225	550	800	—

KM# 281 2 SKILLING

1.2990 g., 0.2810 Silver 0.0117 oz. ASW **Obv:** Crowned, fancy shield **Obv. Legend:** FRIDERIC • III • D • G • DAN • **Rev:** Value: II/ SKILLI/ NGDA/ NSK **Rev. Legend:** NOR • VAN • GOT • REX •

Date	Mintage	Good	VG	F	VF	XF
1667(k) Rare; mint mark in outer legend	—	—	—	—	—	—
1667(l)	—	40.00	75.00	160	350	—
1667(l) Mintmark in center legend	—	50.00	100	200	400	—

KM# 282.1 2 SKILLING

1.2990 g., 0.2810 Silver 0.0117 oz. ASW **Obv. Legend:** FRIDERIC • III • D • G • DAN **Rev:** Value: II/ SKILL/ DANS after legend, date **Rev. Legend:** NOR • VAN • GOT • REX •

Date	Mintage	Good	VG	F	VF	XF
1667(l) Rare	—	—	—	—	—	—
Note: Shield bottom pointed; mint mark in outer legend						
1668(l)	—	15.00	30.00	60.00	120	—
Note: Mint mark in center field						
1669 GK	—	40.00	70.00	160	300	—
Note: Shield bottom round						

KM# 282.2 2 SKILLING

1.2990 g., 0.2810 Silver 0.0117 oz. ASW **Obv:** Shield with flat top

Date	Mintage	Good	VG	F	VF	XF
1667(l) Mint mark in center field	—	10.00	20.00	45.00	75.00	—
1667(l) Mint mark in outer legend	—	10.00	20.00	45.00	80.00	—
1667(k) Mint mark in outer legend	—	15.00	30.00	60.00	120	—
1668(k) Mint mark in outer legend	—	10.00	20.00	40.00	70.00	—
1668(l) Rare; Mint mark in outer legend	—	—	—	—	—	—
1669(k) Mint mark in outer legend	—	15.00	30.00	55.00	100	—
1670(k)	—	40.00	80.00	160	310	—

KM# 358 2 SKILLING

1.2990 g., 0.2810 Silver 0.0117 oz. ASW **Obv:** Titles of Christian V **Note:** Varieties exist.

Date	Mintage	Good	VG	F	VF	XF
1676(l)	—	8.00	17.50	35.00	75.00	—
1677(l)	—	5.00	12.00	30.00	55.00	—
1680(l)	—	8.00	17.50	35.00	75.00	—
1681(l)	—	6.00	14.00	32.50	65.00	—
1861(l) Error	—	55.00	110	220	480	—

KM# 383.1 2 SKILLING

1.2990 g., 0.2810 Silver 0.0117 oz. ASW **Obv:** Crowned double C5 monogram, crown 11mm wide **Rev:** Value and date

Date	Mintage	Good	VG	F	VF	XF
1686 GS	—	15.00	32.50	60.00	140	—

KM# 383.2 2 SKILLING

1.2990 g., 0.2810 Silver 0.0117 oz. ASW **Obv:** Crown 13mm wide

Date	Mintage	Good	VG	F	VF	XF
1686 GS	—	15.00	32.50	60.00	140	—

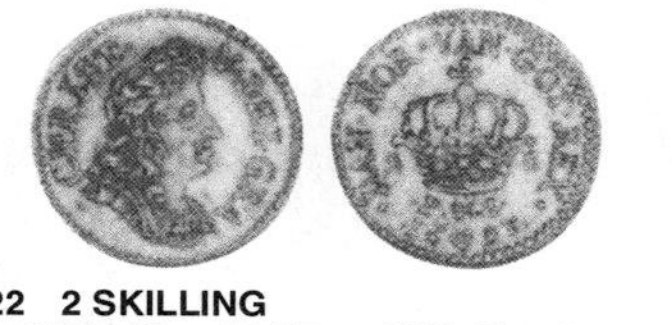

KM# 422 2 SKILLING

0.9130 g., 0.5000 Silver 0.0147 oz. ASW **Obv:** Armored bust right **Rev:** Large crown dividing value, date below

Date	Mintage	Good	VG	F	VF	XF
1693	—	40.00	80.00	200	420	—

KM# 11 4 SKILLING

1.4620 g., 0.4530 Silver 0.0213 oz. ASW **Obv:** Crowned oval shield on long cross **Rev:** Value, date in legend

Date	Mintage	Good	VG	F	VF	XF
1602(a)	—	300	500	800	1,400	—
1604(a)	—	225	350	600	1,100	—
1609(a) Oval shield	—	250	400	725	1,200	—
1609(m) Flat-topped shield	—	600	900	1,400	2,000	—

KM# 30 4 SKILLING

1.4620 g., 0.8880 Silver 0.0417 oz. ASW **Obv:** Crowned bust right **Rev:** Value above oval shield

Date	Mintage	Good	VG	F	VF	XF
1606(a)	—	650	1,200	2,000	3,200	—
1608(a)	—	300	500	1,000	2,750	—

KM# 41 4 SKILLING

1.4620 g., 0.8880 Silver 0.0417 oz. ASW **Obv:** Crowned 1/2-length figure right **Rev:** Value above square-topped shield

Date	Mintage	Good	VG	F	VF	XF
1608(m)	—	140	220	350	550	—
1609(m)	—	175	270	400	800	—

KM# 55.1 4 SKILLING

1.4620 g., 0.4370 Silver 0.0205 oz. ASW **Obv:** Oval shield on long cross **Rev:** Value, date in legend

Date	Mintage	Good	VG	F	VF	XF
1616(a)	—	40.00	95.00	190	375	—
1617(a)	—	150	350	600	1,100	—
1618(a)	—	45.00	110	190	375	—
1619(a)	—	40.00	95.00	190	375	—

KM# 55.2 4 SKILLING

1.4620 g., 0.4370 Silver 0.0205 oz. ASW **Obv:** Crowned square-topped shield on long cross **Note:** Varieties exist.

Date	Mintage	Good	VG	F	VF	XF
1616(c)	—	40.00	95.00	190	375	—
1617(c)	—	75.00	135	350	600	—
1618(c)	—	42.50	100	200	400	—
1619(c)	—	75.00	135	400	750	—

KM# 70.1 4 SKILLING

1.4620 g., 0.4370 Silver 0.0205 oz. ASW **Obv:** Crown intersects legend **Rev:** Value and 24 in oval, date in legend **Note:** Varieties exist.

Date	Mintage	Good	VG	F	VF	XF
1619(a)	—	75.00	150	400	950	—
Note: Mint master mark on reverse						
1619(c)	—	400	900	1,500	—	—

KM# 70.2 4 SKILLING

1.4620 g., 0.4370 Silver 0.0205 oz. ASW **Obv:** Date added above crown

Date	Mintage	Good	VG	F	VF	XF
1619(c) Rare; Mintmark on reverse	—	—	—	—	—	—
1619 Unique; no mintmark	—	—	—	—	—	—

KM# A71 4 SKILLING

1.4620 g., 0.4370 Silver 0.0205 oz. ASW **Obv:** 1 Skilling, KM#40.1 **Rev:** 4 Skilling, KM#70.2 **Note:** Mule.

Date	Mintage	Good	VG	F	VF	XF
1619 Unique	—	—	—	—	—	—

KM# 81 4 SKILLING

1.4620 g., 0.4370 Silver 0.0205 oz. ASW **Obv:** Crown **Rev:** Value, 36 in oval in inner circle, date in legend **Note:** Varieties exist.

Date	Mintage	Good	VG	F	VF	XF
1620(a) Mintmark on reverse	—	30.00	55.00	110	290	—
1620(c) Mintmark on obverse	—	300	800	1,500	—	—
1620(r)	—	50.00	100	200	400	—
1620(n)	—	125	225	550	900	—
1621(a) Mintmark on reverse	—	200	400	600	—	—
1621(r) Mintmark on obverse	—	30.00	60.00	140	225	—
1621(n)	—	60.00	120	275	650	—

KM# 121 4 SKILLING

1.1810 g., 0.8750 Silver 0.0332 oz. ASW **Obv:** Crowned bust right **Rev:** Value, date in legend

Date	Mintage	Good	VG	F	VF	XF
1630(f)	—	17.50	35.00	80.00	220	—
163Z(f)	—	20.00	40.00	100	260	—

KM# 133.1 4 SKILLING

1.9490 g., 0.2500 Silver 0.0157 oz. ASW **Obv:** Crowned C4 monogram, value in legend **Rev:** Hebrew letters between IUSTUS above and IUDEX below. Date at bottom.

Date	Mintage	Good	VG	F	VF	XF
1644(h)	—	25.00	55.00	110	300	—
1645(h)	—	17.50	30.00	80.00	260	—

KM# 133.2 4 SKILLING

1.9490 g., 0.2500 Silver 0.0157 oz. ASW **Rev:** Date at top

Date	Mintage	Good	VG	F	VF	XF
1644(h)	—	200	—	450	600	1,000

KM# 257.1 4 SKILLING

1.9490 g., 0.2500 Silver 0.0157 oz. ASW **Obv:** Crowned F3 monogram, legend reads counterclockwise from top **Rev:** Value and date **Note:** Varieties exist.

Date	Mintage	Good	VG	F	VF	XF
1665	—	25.00	50.00	120	400	—

KM# 257.2 4 SKILLING

1.9490 g., 0.2500 Silver 0.0157 oz. ASW **Obv:** Legend reads clockwise from bottom **Rev:** Value and date

Date	Mintage	Good	VG	F	VF	XF
1665	—	100	175	325	775	—

KM# 283.1 4 SKILLING

1.9490 g., 0.2500 Silver 0.0157 oz. ASW **Obv:** Crowned shield

Date	Mintage	Good	VG	F	VF	XF
1667	—	25.00	50.00	115	350	—

KM# 283.2 4 SKILLING

1.9490 g., 0.2500 Silver 0.0157 oz. ASW **Obv:** Shield variety with pointed bottom

Date	Mintage	Good	VG	F	VF	XF
1669	—	30.00	60.00	1,510	400	—

KM# 440 4 SKILLING

1.9490 g., 0.2500 Silver 0.0157 oz. ASW **Obv:** Laureate bust right **Rev:** Crown divides 4S, date below

Date	Mintage	Good	VG	F	VF	XF
1696	—	500	1,000	1,500	2,000	—

KM# 83 6 SKILLING

Silver **Obv:** Crowned oval shield **Rev:** Crowned C4 monogram divides value, date below

Date	Mintage	Good	VG	F	VF	XF
1622	—	175	475	1,150	2,100	—

KM# 109 6 SKILLING

11.7110 g., 0.7810 Silver 0.2940 oz. ASW **Obv:** Crowned oval arms **Rev:** Value and date **Note:** Varieties exist

Date	Mintage	Good	VG	F	VF	XF
1627(a) Mint mark at top	—	150	350	800	1,500	—
1628(a) Mint mark at top	—	225	300	400	600	—
1628(a) Mint mark at bottom	—	25.00	40.00	65.00	150	—
1628(e)	—	30.00	45.00	95.00	200	—
1629(e)	—	20.00	35.00	60.00	140	—

KM# 110 6 SKILLING

11.7110 g., 0.7810 Silver 0.2940 oz. ASW **Obv:** Crowned bust right **Rev:** Value and date **Note:** Varieties exist

Date	Mintage	Good	VG	F	VF	XF
1628 RD	—	27.50	45.00	115	200	—
1629 RD	—	250	325	500	700	—
1629(g)	—	22.50	40.00	90.00	180	—

KM# 32 8 SKILLING

2.9230 g., 0.8880 Silver 0.0834 oz. ASW **Obv:** Crowned bust right, date below **Rev:** Value above oval arms

Date	Mintage	Good	VG	F	VF	XF
ND	—	100	200	600	1,000	—
1606	—	20.00	37.50	80.00	200	—
1607	—	20.00	37.50	80.00	200	—
1608	—	17.50	35.00	65.00	160	—

KM# 32.1 8 SKILLING

2.9230 g., 0.8880 Silver 0.0834 oz. ASW **Obv:** Crowned oval shield on cross within legend **Obv. Legend:** CHRISTIANVS III. D:G.DANI **Rev:** Value and date in center within circle and legend; value reads: VIII SKILLINCK DANS **Rev. Legend:** NORVE. VANDA. GOTHO:REX (clover) **Note:** Prev. KM#31.

Date	Mintage	Good	VG	F	VF	XF
1606	—	900	1,500	4,000	7,500	—
ND Unique	—	—	—	—	—	—

KM# 32.2 8 SKILLING

2.9230 g., 0.8880 Silver 0.0834 oz. ASW **Obv. Legend:** CHRISTIANVS IIII. D:G.DANI **Obv. Designer:** Crowned bust right, date below **Rev. Legend:** NORVEGI. VANDA. GOTHORVM. REX (clover) **Rev. Designer:** Value above oval arms on crossarms within continuous legend, value reads: VIII SKILLIK DANS

Date	Mintage	Good	VG	F	VF	XF
1606	—	25.00	45.00	125	280	—
1607	—	25.00	45.00	125	280	—
1608	—	100	350	700	1,000	—

KM# 32.3 8 SKILLING

2.9230 g., 0.8880 Silver 0.0834 oz. ASW **Obv. Legend:** CHRISTIANVS IIII. D:G.DANI **Obv. Designer:** Crowned bust right, date below **Rev. Legend:** NORVEGI:VAN DALO:GOTO:REX (clover) **Rev. Designer:** Value above oval arms on cross arms, value reads: VIII DANSKE SKILLING, shield separates legend at bottom

Date	Mintage	Good	VG	F	VF	XF
ND	—	200	400	800	1,000	—
1608	—	22.50	40.00	110	260	—

KM# 32.4 8 SKILLING

2.9230 g., 0.8880 Silver 0.0834 oz. ASW **Obv:** Crowned 1/2-length figure right, date in legend **Obv. Legend:** CHRISTIANVS IIII. D:G:DAN: **Rev:** Value above flat-topped shield on cross arms; value reads: VIII SKILLIN K DANSK **Rev. Legend:** NORVE: VAND: GOTO: Q: REX (clover) **Note:** Prev. KM#42.

Date	Mintage	Good	VG	F	VF	XF
1608	—	30.00	60.00	160	360	—

KM# 32.5 8 SKILLING

2.9230 g., 0.8880 Silver 0.0834 oz. ASW **Obv:** Crowned bust right, date in legend **Obv. Legend:** CHRISTIANVS IIII. D:G.DANI **Rev:** Value above oval arms on cross arms, value reads: VIII DANSKE SKILLING, shield sepaarates legend at bottom **Rev. Legend:** NORVEGI: VANDA: GOTO: REX (clover)

Date	Mintage	Good	VG	F	VF	XF
1609	—	180	200	400	800	—

KM# 32.6 8 SKILLING

2.9230 g., 0.8880 Silver 0.0834 oz. ASW **Obv:** Crowned bust right, date in legend **Obv. Legend:** CHRISTIANVS IIII. D:G.DANI **Rev:** Value above oval arms, no cross arms; value reads: VIII DANKSE SKILLING, shield separates legend at bottom **Rev. Legend:** NORVEGI: VAN DA: GOTO: REX (clover)

Date	Mintage	Good	VG	F	VF	XF
1609	—	275	400	600	1,000	—

KM# 71.1 8 SKILLING

0.8590 Silver **Obv:** Date above crown **Rev:** Date, value and 12 in oval within legend **Note:** Varieties exist.

Date	Mintage	Good	VG	F	VF	XF
1619(c)	—	1,000	200	3,500	5,500	—

KM# 71.2 8 SKILLING

0.8590 Silver **Rev:** Without date in legend

Date	Mintage	Good	VG	F	VF	XF
1619(c)	—	1,500	2,250	4,500	7,000	—

KM# 82 8 SKILLING

0.8590 Silver **Obv:** Crown **Rev:** Value and 18 in oval, date in legend **Note:** Varieties exist.

Date	Mintage	Good	VG	F	VF	XF
1620(a)	—	60.00	1,200	250	550	—
1620(c)	—	750	1,000	1,500	2,500	—
1620(s)	—	800	1,100	2,000	3,500	—
1620(n)	—	50.00	100	210	500	—
1620(r)	—	50.00	100	210	500	—
1621(a)	—	65.00	125	275	700	—
1621(n)	—	60.00	120	250	550	—
1621(r)	—	65.00	120	365	575	—

KM# 84 8 SKILLING

0.8880 Silver **Obv:** Crowned C4 monogram **Rev:** Value and date

Date	Mintage	Good	VG	F	VF	XF
1622	—	25.00	50.00	105	260	—
1623	—	30.00	60.00	125	290	—

KM# 90 8 SKILLING

0.8590 Silver **Obv:** Crowned C4 monogram, mint mark at right **Rev:** Value and date

Date	Mintage	Good	VG	F	VF	XF
1624 No mintmark	—	200	300	500	800	—
1624(a)	—	22.50	45.00	80.00	190	—
1625(a)	—	25.00	50.00	95.00	210	—

KM# 122 8 SKILLING

2.3860 g., 0.8750 Silver 0.0671 oz. ASW **Obv:** Crowned 1/2-length figure right **Rev:** Value within circle, date in legend

Date	Mintage	Good	VG	F	VF	XF
1630(f)	—	35.00	70.00	180	450	—

KM# 305.1 8 SKILLING

2.7840 g., 0.6710 Silver 0.0601 oz. ASW, 21 mm. **Obv:** Crowned and draped bust right of Frederick III **Rev:** Crown above three shields **Note:** Varieties exist.

Date	Mintage	Good	VG	F	VF	XF
1669(k)	—	100	200	400	900	—

KM# 305.2 8 SKILLING

2.7840 g., 0.6710 Silver 0.0601 oz. ASW, 23 mm.

Date	Mintage	Good	VG	F	VF	XF
1669 No mintmark	—	100	200	400	900	—

KM# 341 8 SKILLING

2.7840 g., 0.6710 Silver 0.0601 oz. ASW **Obv:** Crowned C5 monogram **Rev:** Value and date

Date	Mintage	Good	VG	F	VF	XF
1672 Value: VIII	—	60.00	125	300	625	—
1672 Value: Viii	—	150	300	600	900	—

KM# 423 8 SKILLING

2.2400 g., 0.8330 Silver 0.0600 oz. ASW **Obv:** Armored bust of Christian V right **Rev:** Large crown, date below

Date	Mintage	Good	VG	F	VF	XF
1693	—	900	1,500	2,250	3,000	—

KM# 465 8 SKILLING

2.2400 g., 0.8330 Silver 0.0600 oz. ASW **Obv. Legend:** Christ V - DEI GRA(T) **Rev:** Denomination flanks crown

Date	Mintage	Good	VG	F	VF	XF
1695 DEI GRA	—	20.00	35.00	80.00	200	—
1695 DEI GRAT	—	200	400	600	800	—

KM# 470 8 SKILLING

3.0570 g., 0.5620 Silver 0.0552 oz. ASW **Ruler:** Frederik IV **Obv:** Armored bust right **Obv. Legend:** FRID • IIII • DEI • GRAT • **Rev:** Large crown divides value, heart divides date in legend below **Rev. Legend:** DAN • NOR • VAN • GOT • REX •

Date	Mintage	VG	F	VF	XF	Unc
1700	—	25.00	50.00	140	380	—

KM# 85 12 SKILLING

3.0240 g., 0.8880 Silver 0.0863 oz. ASW **Obv:** Crowned oval shield **Rev:** Crowned C4 monogram, value below

Date	Mintage	Good	VG	F	VF	XF
1622	—	30.00	55.00	90.00	240	—
1623	—	35.00	60.00	100	270	—
16xx	—	10.00	20.00	40.00	75.00	—

KM# 91 12 SKILLING

3.0770 g., 0.8590 Silver 0.0850 oz. ASW **Obv:** Crowned C4 monogram **Rev:** Value and date

Date	Mintage	Good	VG	F	VF	XF
1624(a)	—	25.00	50.00	115	310	—
1625(a)	—	27.50	55.00	125	335	—

KM# 92 16 SKILLING

0.8590 Silver **Obv:** Crowned oval shield **Rev:** Value and date

Date	Mintage	Good	VG	F	VF	XF
1624(a)	—	45.00	90.00	190	300	—
1625(a)	—	60.00	140	280	550	—

KM# 107 16 SKILLING

0.8590 Silver **Obv:** Crowned shield w/crowned C4 monogram dividing date **Rev:** Value

Date	Mintage	Good	VG	F	VF	XF
1625(a) Rare	—	—	—	—	—	—

KM# 136.1 16 SKILLING

5.5680 g., 0.5930 Silver 0.1062 oz. ASW **Obv:** Date in legend **Rev:** Hebrew inscription and mint mark

Date	Mintage	Good	VG	F	VF	XF
1644(h) Mint mark at bottom	—	45.00	90.00	160	350	—
1644(h) Mint mark at top	—	125	200	350	500	—

KM# 136.2 16 SKILLING

5.5680 g., 0.5930 Silver 0.1062 oz. ASW **Rev:** Date

Date	Mintage	Good	VG	F	VF	XF
1645(h)	—	60.00	120	210	425	—
1646(h)	—	150	325	700	2,000	—

KM# 93 24 SKILLING

6.0500 g., Silver **Obv:** Crowned oval shield on long cross **Rev:** Value and date within legend

Date	Mintage	Good	VG	F	VF	XF
16Z4(a)	—	140	280	600	1,200	—

KM# 12 MARK

9.4110 g., 0.5930 Silver 0.1794 oz. ASW **Obv:** Crowned oval shield on long cross **Rev:** Value and date within legend

Date	Mintage	Good	VG	F	VF	XF
1602	—	140	225	550	1,100	—
1604	—	130	210	525	1,000	—

KM# 12a MARK

6.1540 g., 0.8880 Silver 0.1757 oz. ASW **Obv:** Crowned oval shield on long corss **Rev:** Value and date within legend

Date	Mintage	Good	VG	F	VF	XF
1606(a)	—	100	200	400	800	—

KM# 33.1 MARK

6.1540 g., 0.8880 Silver 0.1757 oz. ASW **Obv:** Crown above bust right breaking circle at bottom **Rev:** Oval arms dividing date, value above

Date	Mintage	Good	VG	F	VF	XF
1606(a)	—	125	250	600	1,300	—

KM# 33.2 MARK

6.1540 g., 0.8880 Silver 0.1757 oz. ASW **Obv:** Crown above bust right within circle **Rev:** Oval arms dividing date, value above

Date	Mintage	Good	VG	F	VF	XF
1607(a)	—	110	220	550	1,100	—

KM# 36 MARK

6.1540 g., 0.8880 Silver 0.1757 oz. ASW **Obv:** Crowned 1/2-length figure right, date in legend **Rev:** Value above flat-top shield between branches

Date	Mintage	Good	VG	F	VF	XF
1607(m)	—	35.00	65.00	150	350	—
Note: Coins dated 1607 exist with ornamentation						
1608(m)	—	30.00	60.00	115	280	—
1609(m)	—	100	200	575	1,100	—

KM# 37 MARK

9.3540 g., 0.5930 Silver 0.1783 oz. ASW **Rev:** Value above shield on long cross

Date	Mintage	Good	VG	F	VF	XF
1607(m) Rare	—	—	—	—	—	—
1609(m)	—	650	1,000	1,500	—	—

KM# 52 MARK

8.6610 g., 0.5930 Silver 0.1651 oz. ASW **Rev:** Value above oval shield on long cross **Note:** Varieties exist

Date	Mintage	Good	VG	F	VF	XF
1612(b)	—	60.00	110	225	425	—
1613(b)	—	50.00	100	180	400	—
1614(a)	—	225	450	775	1,100	—
1614(b)	—	35.00	65.00	140	340	—
1614(c)	—	50.00	100	180	400	—
1614(d)	—	90.00	180	350	625	—
1615(a)	—	30.00	65.00	125	275	—
1615(c)	—	75.00	150	300	800	—
1616(a)	—	50.00	100	180	400	—
1616(c)	—	40.00	70.00	195	290	—
1617(a)	—	35.00	65.00	140	340	—
1617(c)	—	40.00	70.00	180	375	—
1618(a)	—	70.00	140	280	575	—
1618(c)	—	80.00	160	300	650	—

KM# 266 MARK

5.5680 g., 0.5930 Silver 0.1062 oz. ASW **Obv:** Draped bust of Frederik III

Date	Mintage	Good	VG	F	VF	XF
1666	—	120	180	300	600	—

KM# 297 MARK

5.5680 g., 0.5930 Silver 0.1062 oz. ASW **Obv:** Crowned F3 monogram **Rev:** Crowned shield on short cross

Date	Mintage	Good	VG	F	VF	XF
1668	—	250	500	100	2,100	—

KM# 342.1 MARK

5.5680 g., 0.6710 Silver 0.1201 oz. ASW **Obv:** Crowned C5 monogram, end of C free of 5 **Rev:** Value and date

Date	Mintage	Good	VG	F	VF	XF
1672	—	35.00	65.00	160	350	—
1676	—	50.00	90.00	200	45.00	—

KM# 342.2 MARK

5.5680 g., 0.6710 Silver 0.1201 oz. ASW **Obv:** End of C entwines 5 **Rev:** Value and date

Date	Mintage	Good	VG	F	VF	XF
1676	—	30.00	60.00	130	300	—

KM# 350 MARK

5.5680 g., 0.6710 Silver 0.1201 oz. ASW **Obv:** Crowned fancy double C5 monogram

Date	Mintage	Good	VG	F	VF	XF
1675	—	22.50	60.00	180	380	—

KM# 379 MARK

5.5680 g., 0.6710 Silver 0.1201 oz. ASW **Obv:** Crowned double C5 monogram **Rev:** Value and date on crowned shield on short cross

Date	Mintage	Good	VG	F	VF	XF
1685	—	55.00	110	200	425	—

KM# 404.1 MARK

5.5680 g., 0.6710 Silver 0.1201 oz. ASW **Obv:** Crowned fancy double C5 monogram, no legend **Rev:** Crowned shield divide horizontal date above 1-M **Rev. Legend:** D • G • REX • DA • NO • V • G • **Note:** Varieties exist

Date	Mintage	Good	VG	F	VF	XF
1691CW	—	60.00	100	200	450	—

KM# 404.2 MARK

5.5680 g., 0.6710 Silver 0.1201 oz. ASW **Obv:** Crowned fancy double C5 monogram, no legend **Rev:** Crowned shield divide curved date above 1-M **Rev. Legend:** D • G • REX • DA • NO • V • G •

Date	Mintage	Good	VG	F	VF	XF
1691CW	—	70.00	110	220	500	—

KM# 404.3 MARK

5.5680 g., 0.6710 Silver 0.1201 oz. ASW **Obv:** Crowned fancy double C5 monogram, no legend **Rev:** Crowned shield divide horizontal date, shield without value **Rev. Legend:** D • G • REX • DA • NO • V • G •

Date	Mintage	Good	VG	F	VF	XF
1691CW Rare	—	—	—	—	—	—

KM# 404.4 MARK

5.5680 g., 0.6710 Silver 0.1201 oz. ASW **Obv:** Crowned fancy double C5 monogram, no legend **Rev:** Date in legend **Rev. Legend:** D • G • REX • DA • NO • V • G • **Note:** Size of 8 Skilling, KM 427 but double thickness. No indication of value.

Date	Mintage	Good	VG	F	VF	XF
1692CW	—	70.00	140	260	525	—
1693	—	—	—	—	—	—

KM# 424.1 MARK

5.5680 g., 0.6710 Silver 0.1201 oz. ASW **Obv:** Armored bust right **Rev:** Large crown dividing value, date below

Date	Mintage	Good	VG	F	VF	XF
1693	—	35.00	65.00	160	400	—
1694	—	40.00	70.00	180	410	—

KM# 424.2 MARK

5.5680 g., 0.6710 Silver 0.1201 oz. ASW **Rev:** Large crown, date below, no value

Date	Mintage	Good	VG	F	VF	XF
1693	—	650	1,150	1,600	2,200	—
1696	—	600	1,000	1,500	2,000	—

KM# 23 2 MARK

16.5800 g., 0.6460 Silver 0.3443 oz. ASW **Obv:** Crowned oval arms on long cross **Obv. Legend:** CHRISTIAN IV **Rev:** Value and date within circle, legend

Date	Mintage	Good	VG	F	VF	XF
1604	—	300	750	1,500	3,300	—

KM# 137 2 MARK
11.1360 g., 0.5930 Silver 0.2123 oz. ASW

Date	Mintage	Good	VG	F	VF	XF
1644(h)	—	60.00	120	250	410	—
1645(h)	—	70.00	140	300	480	—
1646(h)	—	100	200	400	800	—

KM# 185 2 MARK
11.1360 g., 0.6710 Silver 0.2402 oz. ASW **Obv:** Crowned F3 monogram **Rev:** Crowned shield on long cross, date in legend

Date	Mintage	Good	VG	F	VF	XF
165Z(h)	—	140	250	500	1,100	—

KM# 190 2 MARK
11.1360 g., 0.6710 Silver 0.2402 oz. ASW **Obv:** Crowned F3 monogram, date in legend **Rev:** Shield with round top

Date	Mintage	Good	VG	F	VF	XF
1653(h)	—	150	250	500	1,000	—

KM# 191.1 2 MARK
11.1360 g., 0.6710 Silver 0.2402 oz. ASW **Obv:** Crowned F3 monogram **Rev:** Crowned, encircled flat-top shield on short cross, wtihout pellets

Date	Mintage	Good	VG	F	VF	XF
1653(h)	—	300	600	1,000	1,500	—

KM# 191.2 2 MARK
11.1360 g., 0.6710 Silver 0.2402 oz. ASW **Obv:** Crowned F3 monogram **Rev:** Without circle around shield

Date	Mintage	Good	VG	F	VF	XF
1653(h)	—	200	400	700	1,100	—
1654(h)	—	300	500	800	1,200	—
1655(h)	—	175	350	600	1,000	—
1657(h)	—	200	400	800	1,200	—

KM# A191 2 MARK
11.1360 g., 0.6710 Silver 0.2402 oz. ASW **Obv:** KM#185 **Rev:** KM#190 **Note:** Mule.

Date	Mintage	Good	VG	F	VF	XF
ND Rare	—	—	—	—	—	—

KM# 218 2 MARK
11.1360 g., 0.6710 Silver 0.2402 oz. ASW **Obv:** Crowned F3 monogram, legend, value, and date **Rev:** Crowned shield on short cross within pellet border

Date	Mintage	Good	VG	F	VF	XF
1658	—	100	200	450	900	—
1659	—	120	225	475	950	—
1660	—	200	400	600	1,000	—
1661	—	400	600	1,000	1,600	—

KM# 259.1 2 MARK
11.1360 g., 0.6710 Silver 0.2402 oz. ASW **Obv:** Laureate bust of Frederik III right **Obv. Legend:** FRIDERICVS • III • D • G • DA • NOR • **Rev:** Crown above motto in script, date in legend **Rev. Legend:** VAN • DALORVM • GOTHORVM • QVE • REX •

Date	Mintage	Good	VG	F	VF	XF
1666	—	300	500	900	1,200	—
1666 GK	—	50.00	110	280	550	—
1667 GK	—	50.00	180	380	750	—

KM# 259.2 2 MARK
11.1360 g., 0.6710 Silver 0.2402 oz. ASW **Obv:** No circle around bust **Rev:** Motto in print

Date	Mintage	Good	VG	F	VF	XF
1665 GK	—	90.00	170	340	750	—
1666(k) Unique	—	—	—	—	—	—
1666 GK	—	90.00	170	340	750	—

KM# 259.3 2 MARK
11.1360 g., 0.6710 Silver 0.2402 oz. ASW **Obv:** Bust in inner circle

Date	Mintage	Good	VG	F	VF	XF
1666 GK Rare	—	600	1,000	1,500	2,000	—

KM# 267.1 2 MARK
11.1360 g., 0.6710 Silver 0.2402 oz. ASW **Obv:** Laureate bust of Frederik III right **Obv. Legend:** FRID • III • D • G • DAN • NOR • VAN • GO • REX • **Rev:** Date above crown **Rev. Legend:** DVS • SLESVHOLS • STORM • DITM • COM • IN • OL & DE •

Date	Mintage	Good	VG	F	VF	XF
1666 GK	—	800	1,100	1,500	2,000	—

KM# 267.2 2 MARK
11.1360 g., 0.6710 Silver 0.2402 oz. ASW **Obv:** Laureate bust of Frederik III right **Obv. Legend:** FRID • III • D • G • DAN • NOR • VAN • GO • REX • **Rev:** Date below crown **Rev. Legend:** DVS • SLESVHOLS • STORM • DITM • COM • IN • OL & DE •

Date	Mintage	Good	VG	F	VF	XF
1666 GK	—	120	220	450	950	—

KM# 268 2 MARK
11.1360 g., 0.6710 Silver 0.2402 oz. ASW **Obv. Legend:** FRIDERICVS • III • D • G • DAN • NORV • **Rev. Legend:** GOTHO • Q • VE • REX / II • MARCK • DANSKA • 1666

Date	Mintage	Good	VG	F	VF	XF
1666	—	210	375	600	1,000	—

KM# 269.1 2 MARK
11.1360 g., 0.6710 Silver 0.2402 oz. ASW **Obv. Legend:** FRIDERIC • 3 • D • G • DAN • NORVAN • GOT • REX • **Rev:** Crown 18 mm in size **Rev. Legend:** II • MARK • DANSKE • Ao • 1666

Date	Mintage	Good	VG	F	VF	XF
1666(k)	—	275	500	850	1,200	—

KM# 269.2 2 MARK
11.1360 g., 0.6710 Silver 0.2402 oz. ASW **Obv:** Bust in inner circle **Rev:** Crown 23 mm in size; DOMINUS PROVIDEBIT in print

Date	Mintage	Good	VG	F	VF	XF
1666(k)	—	125	225	475	1,000	—

KM# 269.3 2 MARK
11.1360 g., 0.6710 Silver 0.2402 oz. ASW **Obv:** Bust in inner circle **Rev:** Crown in 23 mm size; DOMINUS PROVIDEBIT in script

Date	Mintage	Good	VG	F	VF	XF
1666(k)	—	125	225	475	1,000	—

KM# 284 2 MARK
11.1360 g., 0.6710 Silver 0.2402 oz. ASW **Obv:** Crowned F3 monogram **Note:** Legends face outward, counter clockwise from upper left.

Date	Mintage	Good	VG	F	VF	XF
1667	—	125	250	425	850	—
1668	—	120	225	400	825	—

KM# 298 2 MARK
11.1360 g., 0.6710 Silver 0.2402 oz. ASW **Obv:** Crowned F3 monogram. **Note:** Legends face outward, clockwise from upper right.

Date	Mintage	Good	VG	F	VF	XF
1668	—	95.00	150	300	625	—
1669	—	100	200	425	800	—

KM# 329.1 2 MARK
11.1360 g., 0.6710 Silver 0.2402 oz. ASW **Obv:** Fancy crowned C5 monogram, legends face outward

Date	Mintage	Good	VG	F	VF	XF
1671	—	100	225	450	900	—

KM# 329.2 2 MARK
11.1360 g., 0.6710 Silver 0.2402 oz. ASW **Obv:** Plain monogram of Christian 5

Date	Mintage	Good	VG	F	VF	XF
1671	—	100	225	450	900	—

KM# 369 2 MARK
11.1360 g., 0.6710 Silver 0.2402 oz. ASW **Obv:** Legends face inward **Rev:** Legends face inward

Date	Mintage	Good	VG	F	VF	XF
1681 GS	—	100	175	350	600	—
1682 GS	—	115	190	400	700	—

KM# 377.1 2 MARK
11.1360 g., 0.6710 Silver 0.2402 oz. ASW **Obv:** Crowned double C5 monogram **Rev:** Value and date on crowned shield on short cross

Date	Mintage	Good	VG	F	VF	XF
1684 GS	—	75.00	150	300	650	—
1685 GS	—	75.00	150	350	650	—

KM# 377.2 2 MARK
11.1360 g., 0.6710 Silver 0.2402 oz. ASW **Obv:** Crowned double C5 monogram **Rev:** Wider shield

Date	Mintage	Good	VG	F	VF	XF
1685 GS	—	80.00	160	360	700	—

KM# 385 2 MARK
11.1360 g., 0.6710 Silver 0.2402 oz. ASW **Obv:** Crowned ornate double C5 monogram, legend around

Date	Mintage	Good	VG	F	VF	XF
1686 GS	—	100	200	400	800	—

KM# 385a 2 MARK
11.1360 g., 0.5930 Silver 0.2123 oz. ASW

Date	Mintage	Good	VG	F	VF	XF
1689 GS	—	130	260	500	900	—

KM# 403 2 MARK
11.1360 g., 0.5930 Silver 0.2123 oz. ASW **Obv:** Half-length bust in armor right **Rev:** Crowned oval shield dividing value and date

Date	Mintage	Good	VG	F	VF	XF
1690 CW	—	200	400	800	1,600	—

KM# 406.1 2 MARK
11.1360 g., 0.5930 Silver 0.2123 oz. ASW **Obv:** Crowned double C5 monogram within legend; legend reads clockwise from top **Obv. Legend:** D • G • REX • DAN • NOR • VAN • GOT **Rev:** Crowned arms divide horizontal date above 2-M; legend reads clockwise from the top **Rev. Legend:** PIETATE ET IVSTITIA

Date	Mintage	Good	VG	F	VF	XF
1691 CW	—	—	150	300	600	—

KM# 406.2 2 MARK
11.1360 g., 0.5930 Silver 0.2123 oz. ASW **Obv:** Crowned double C5 monogram within legend; legend reads clockwise from top **Obv. Legend:** D • G • REX • DAN • NOR • VAN • GOT **Rev:** Crowned arms divide curved date above 2-M; legend reads clockwise from the top **Rev. Legend:** PIETATE ET IVSTITIA **Note:** Varieties exist.

Date	Mintage	Good	VG	F	VF	XF
1691 CW	—	—	200	400	700	—

KM# 406.3 2 MARK
11.1360 g., 0.5930 Silver 0.2123 oz. ASW **Obv:** Crowned double C5 monogram within legend; legend reads clockwise from top **Obv. Legend:** D • G • REX • DAN • NOR • VAN • GOT **Rev:** Date in legend **Rev. Legend:** PIETATE ET IVSTITIA

Date	Mintage	Good	VG	F	VF	XF
1692 CW	—	—	250	450	800	—

KM# 426 2 MARK
11.1360 g., 0.5930 Silver 0.2123 oz. ASW **Obv:** Armored bust right **Rev:** Large crown, value and date below **Note:** Similar to 1 Mark, KM#424, but double thickness.

Date	Mintage	Good	VG	F	VF	XF
1693 Rare	—	—	—	—	—	—
1696 Rare	—	—	—	—	—	—

KM# 427 2 MARK
11.1360 g., 0.5930 Silver 0.2123 oz. ASW **Rev:** Large crown, date below **Note:** Size of 8 Skilling, KM 423 but four times thickness. No indication of value.

Date	Mintage	Good	VG	F	VF	XF
1693	—	—	—	—	—	—

KM# 56 1/8 KRONE
2.2380 g., 0.8590 Silver 0.0618 oz. ASW **Obv:** Crowned King standing with scepter **Obv. Legend:** CHRISTIAN IIII D G DANI **Rev:** Date above, R.F.P. below crown **Rev. Legend:** NORV: VAND: GOTO: Q: REX

Date	Mintage	Good	VG	F	VF	XF
1618(c)	—	700	1,400	2,800	—	—

KM# 57 1/4 KRONE
4.4970 g., 0.8590 Silver 0.1242 oz. ASW **Obv:** Crowned King standing with scepter **Obv. Legend:** CHRISTIAN IIII • D: G: DAN • **Rev:** Date above, R.F.P. below crown **Rev. Legend:** NORVE: VANDA: GOTO: REX **Note:** Varieties exist.

Date	Mintage	Good	VG	F	VF	XF
1618(a)	—	175	350	1,000	2,000	—
1618(c)	—	200	400	1,100	2,100	—

KM# 58 1/2 KRONE
9.3010 g., 0.8590 Silver 0.2569 oz. ASW **Obv:** Crowned king standing, scepter upright **Obv. Legend:** CHRISTIANVS IIII • D: G • DANI **Rev:** Date above, R.F.P. below crown **Rev. Legend:** NORVEG: VANDAL: GOTO: Q • REX

Date	Mintage	Good	VG	F	VF	XF
1618(a)	—	100	200	500	1,000	—
1618(c)	—	150	300	600	1,150	—

KM# 58a 1/2 KRONE
9.4550 g., 0.8590 Silver 0.2611 oz. ASW **Note:** Varieties exist.

Date	Mintage	Good	VG	F	VF	XF
1619(a)	—	160	290	575	1,100	—
1619(c)	—	160	290	575	1,100	—
16Z0(a)	—	160	290	575	1,100	—
1620(c) Rare	—	160	290	575	100	—
1620(r)	—	180	325	700	1,250	—
16Z1(a)	—	175	350	700	1,250	—
1621(r)	—	175	350	700	1,250	—

KM# 94 1/2 KRONE
9.4550 g., 0.8590 Silver 0.2611 oz. ASW, 30 mm. **Obv:** Crowned king standing, scepter horizontal **Obv. Legend:** CHRISTIAVS IIII • D: G: DANI **Rev:** Date above, R.F.P. below open crown **Rev. Legend:** NORVEG: VANDALO: GOTORU Q • REX

Date	Mintage	Good	VG	F	VF	XF
16Z4(a)	—	—	2,250	5,000	—	—

KM# 95.1 1/2 KRONE
9.4550 g., 0.8590 Silver 0.2611 oz. ASW, 26 mm. **Obv:** Crowned bust of Christian IV right, breaking legend at top and bottom **Obv. Legend:** CHRISTIAN IIII D: G **Rev:** Letters R.F.P. below large crown within circle, date in legend **Rev. Legend:** DANI • NOR • VAN • GOT • Q • REX

Date	Mintage	Good	VG	F	VF	XF
16Z4(a)	—	—	110	180	525	—

KM# 95.2 1/2 KRONE
9.4550 g., 0.8590 Silver 0.2611 oz. ASW, 23-25 mm. **Obv:** Crowned bust of Christian IV right, breaking legend at top and bottom **Obv. Legend:** CHRISTIAN IIII D: G **Rev:** Letters R.F.P. below large crown within smaller circle, date in legend **Rev. Legend:** DANI • NOR • VAN • GOT • Q • REX **Note:** Size varies.

Date	Mintage	Good	VG	F	VF	XF
16Z4(a)	—	—	90.00	150	425	—
16Z5(a)	—	—	100	165	500	—

KM# 95.3 1/2 KRONE
9.4550 g., 0.8590 Silver 0.2611 oz. ASW, 23-25 mm. **Obv:** Crowned bust of Christian IV right, breaking legend at top and bottom **Obv. Legend:** CHRISTIAN IIII D: G **Rev:** Letters R.F.P. below large crown within smaller circle, date in legend **Rev. Legend:** DANI • NOR • VAN • GOT • Q • REX **Note:** Size varies.

Date	Mintage	Good	VG	F	VF	XF
16Z4(a)	—	100	200	400	—	—

KM# 179 1/2 KRONE
9.4550 g., 0.8590 Silver 0.2611 oz. ASW **Obv:** Crowned bust of Frederik right dividing date **Rev:** Large crown within legend

Date	Mintage	VG	F	VF	XF	Unc
1651(h)	—	450	900	1,800	3,000	—

KM# 258 1/2 KRONE
0.7910 Silver **Obv:** Crowned figure of Frederik III standing right **Rev:** Crown and motto within circle, date in legend

Date	Mintage	VG	F	VF	XF	Unc
1665 GK	—	450	900	1,800	3,000	—

KM# 59 KRONE (4 Mark)
18.7660 g., 0.8590 Silver 0.5182 oz. ASW **Obv:** Crowned king standing with scepter and orb **Obv. Legend:** CHRISTIANVS IIII D: G: DANIA • **Rev:** Date above, R.F.P. below 5-pointed crown **Note:** Dav. #3517.

Date	Mintage	Good	VG	F	VF	XF
1618(a)	—	100	200	425	800	—
1618(c)	—	100	200	425	800	—

KM# 59.1 KRONE (4 Mark)
18.7660 g., 0.8590 Silver 0.5182 oz. ASW **Obv:** Crowned king standing with scepter and orb **Obv. Legend:** CHRISTIANVS IIII D: G: DANIA • **Rev:** Date above, R.F.P. below 3-pointed crown

Date	Mintage	Good	VG	F	VF	XF
1618(c)	—	125	250	500	1,000	—

KM# 59a KRONE (4 Mark)
18.9090 g., 0.8590 Silver 0.5222 oz. ASW **Obv:** Crowned king standing with scepter and orb **Obv. Legend:** CHRISTIANVS IIII D: G: DANIA • **Rev:** Date above, R.F.P. below 5-pointed crown

Date	Mintage	Good	VG	F	VF	XF
1619(a)	—	100	200	400	800	—
1619(c)	—	115	230	450	925	—
16Z0(a)	—	100	200	400	800	—
1620(c)	—	200	425	650	1,150	—
1620(s) Rare	—	—	—	—	—	—
1620(r)	—	100	200	400	800	—
16Z1(a)	—	100	200	400	800	—
1621(r)	—	110	225	450	950	—
1622(a) Unique	—	—	—	—	—	—

KM# 96 KRONE (4 Mark)
18.9090 g., 0.8590 Silver 0.5222 oz. ASW **Obv:** Crowned standing figure of Christian IV, numerals IIII left of King's feet **Rev:** Open crown **Note:** Dav. #3519.

Date	Mintage	Good	VG	F	VF	XF
1624(a)	—	400	750	1,800	3,800	—

KM# 97 KRONE (4 Mark)
18.9090 g., 0.8590 Silver 0.5222 oz. ASW **Obv:** Numeral IIII at left of King's feet, smaller and thicker planchet **Rev:** Closed Crown **Note:** Dav. #3519A. Size of 1/2 Krone but double thickness.

Date	Mintage	Good	VG	F	VF	XF
16Z4(a)	—	50.00	110	270	550	—
1625(a)	—	50.00	110	250	525	—

KM# 180 KRONE (4 Mark)
18.9090 g., 0.8590 Silver 0.5222 oz. ASW **Obv:** Crowned bust right **Rev:** Crown with DOMINUS PROVIDEBIT around bottom, reading clockwise from right **Note:** Dav. #3567.

Date	Mintage	Good	VG	F	VF	XF
1651(h)	—	125	250	500	1,000	—
1652(h)	—	150	275	550	1,100	—

KM# 181 KRONE (4 Mark)

18.9090 g., 0.8590 Silver 0.5222 oz. ASW **Rev:** Motto reading counterclockwise **Note:** Dav. #3567A.

Date	Mintage	Good	VG	F	VF	XF
1651	—	250	500	1,000	1,500	—

KM# 182 KRONE (4 Mark)

18.9090 g., 0.8590 Silver 0.5222 oz. ASW **Rev:** Motto DOMIN: PROVID: reading clockwise **Note:** Dav. #3567B.

Date	Mintage	Good	VG	F	VF	XF
1651(h)	—	130	260	525	1,050	—
165Z(h)	—	130	260	525	1,050	—

KM# 186.1 KRONE (4 Mark)

22.2720 g., 0.6710 Silver 0.4805 oz. ASW **Obv:** Crowned F3 monogram within beaded border **Rev:** Crowned shield on long cross, hearts on sheild, no mintmaster mark **Note:** Dav. #3569. Prev. KM#186.

Date	Mintage	Good	VG	F	VF	XF
165Z	—	100	200	350	600	—

KM# 186.2 KRONE (4 Mark)

22.2720 g., 0.6710 Silver 0.4805 oz. ASW **Obv:** Crowned F3 monogram within beaded border **Rev:** Crowned shield on long cross, beaded border, no hearts on shield **Note:** Dav. #3569A. Prev. KM#187.

Date	Mintage	Good	VG	F	VF	XF
165Z	—	90.00	160	315	550	—
1653	—	200	400	800	1,600	—

KM# 186.3 KRONE (4 Mark)

22.2720 g., 0.6710 Silver 0.4805 oz. ASW **Ruler:** Frederik III **Rev:** Crowned shield on long cross, no beaded border, hearts on shield, mintmaster mark left of crown

Date	Mintage	Good	VG	F	VF	XF
1633(h) error date for 1653	—	200	300	500	900	—

Note: This 1633 error date coin belongs to a group of foreign produced kroner of Frederik 3 and Christian 5 called "mysteriekroner"; They are basicly copies (counterfeits) of the Danish versions with similar finess, and they circulated alongside with the Danish produced kroner, and are dificult to distinguish from these; Known dates range from 1653 (33) to 1679

Date	Mintage	Good	VG	F	VF	XF
165Z(h) Rare	—	—	—	—	—	—
1653(h)	—	100	200	350	600	—

KM# 192.1 KRONE (4 Mark)

22.2720 g., 0.6710 Silver 0.4805 oz. ASW **Obv:** Crowned F3 monogram within chain of Order of St. Michael, date in legend **Rev:** Crowned flat-top shield on cross within chair of Order of St. Michael **Note:** Dav. #3570. Prev. KM#192. The Order of St. Michael is a French Order.

Date	Mintage	Good	VG	F	VF	XF
1653	—	1,000	1,500	2,500	4,000	—

KM# 192.2 KRONE (4 Mark)

22.2720 g., 0.6710 Silver 0.4805 oz. ASW **Obv:** KM#192.1 **Rev:** KM#186.3 **Note:** Mule. Prev. KM#A193

Date	Mintage	Good	VG	F	VF	XF
1653(h)	—	500	1,000	2,000	3,250	—

KM# 192.3 KRONE (4 Mark)

22.2720 g., 0.6710 Silver 0.4805 oz. ASW **Obv:** KM#186.3 **Rev:** KM#192.1 **Note:** Mule. Prev. KM#B193.

Date	Mintage	Good	VG	F	VF	XF
1653	—	750	1,250	2,250	3,500	—

KM# 194.1 KRONE (4 Mark)

22.2720 g., 0.6710 Silver 0.4805 oz. ASW **Ruler:** Frederik III **Obv:** Crowned F3 monogram within beaded border with III MARCK DANSKE (date) in legend **Rev:** Crowned flat-top shield on short cross, cross arms within rounded ends, mintmaster mark to right of crown **Rev. Legend:** DOMINVS PROVIDEBIT **Note:** Dav. #3574. Prev. KM#194.

Date	Mintage	Good	VG	F	VF	XF
1653(h)	—	90.00	180	350	600	—
1654(h)	—	120	240	370	700	—

KM# 194.1a KRONE (4 Mark)

22.2720 g., 0.6710 Silver 0.4805 oz. ASW **Ruler:** Frederik III **Rev:** As KM#194.1, mintmaster mark to left of crown **Rev. Legend:** DOMINVS PROVIDEBIT

Date	Mintage	Good	VG	F	VF	XF
1653(h) Rare	—	—	—	—	—	—

KM# 194.1b KRONE (4 Mark)

22.2720 g., 0.6710 Silver 0.4805 oz. ASW **Ruler:** Frederik III **Rev:** As KM#194.1 but without mintmaster mark

Date	Mintage	Good	VG	F	VF	XF
1654	—	125	270	450	750	—

KM# 194.2 KRONE (4 Mark)

22.2720 g., 0.6710 Silver 0.4805 oz. ASW **Ruler:** Frederik III **Obv:** Crowned F3 monogram within beaded border, legend **Obv. Legend:** IIII MARCK DANSKE • (date) **Rev:** Crowned flat-top shield on short cross; crossarms with forked ends, mintmaster mark to left of crown **Rev. Legend:** DOMINVS PROVIDEBIT

Date	Mintage	Good	VG	F	VF	XF
1654(h)	—	115	225	360	625	—
1655(h)	—	115	225	360	625	—

KM# 194.2a KRONE (4 Mark)

22.2720 g., 0.6710 Silver 0.4805 oz. ASW **Ruler:** Frederik III **Obv:** As KM#194.2 but different style lettering **Rev:** Legend reads: DOMINUS PROUIDEBIT, no mintmaster mark

Date	Mintage	Good	VG	F	VF	XF
1655 Rare	—	—	—	—	—	—
1656	—	400	900	1,400	2,100	—
1657 Rare	—	—	—	—	—	—
1658	—	125	270	450	800	—

KM# 194.2b KRONE (4 Mark)

22.2720 g., 0.6710 Silver 0.4805 oz. ASW **Obv:** Crowned F3 monogram **Rev:** Shield without beaded border. Legend: DOMINVS PROVIDEBIT and mintmaster mark **Note:** Dav. #3574A. Prev. KM#203.

Date	Mintage	Good	VG	F	VF	XF
1655(h)	—	115	225	360	625	—
1656(h) Rare	—	—	—	—	—	—
1657(h)	—	140	300	500	900	—

KM# 194.3 KRONE (4 Mark)

22.2720 g., 0.6710 Silver 0.4805 oz. ASW **Obv:** Crowned F3 monogram within beaded border, legend **Obv. Legend:** IIII: MARCK: DANSKE • (date) **Rev:** Crowned fancy shield on short cross, legend **Rev. Legend:** DOMINUS PROVIDEBIT **Note:** Dav. #3572. Prev. KM#193.

Date	Mintage	Good	VG	F	VF	XF
1653 error date for 1657, rare	—	—	—	—	—	—
1655 error date for 1657, unique	—	—	—	—	—	—
1657(h)	—	125	270	450	800	—

KM# 194.3a KRONE (4 Mark)

22.2720 g., 0.6710 Silver 0.4805 oz. ASW **Ruler:** Frederik III **Obv:** Crowned F3 monogram within beaded border, within legend **Obv. Legend:** IIII MARCK DANSKE • (date) **Rev:** Crowned fancy shield on short cross within circle, legend, crossarms with straight-sided triangular ends, mintmaster mark to right of crown **Rev. Legend:** DOMINUS PROVIDEBIT

Date	Mintage	Good	VG	F	VF	XF
1657(h)	—	125	270	450	750	—
1658(h)	—	125	270	450	750	—

KM# 194.4 KRONE (4 Mark)

22.2720 g., 0.6710 Silver 0.4805 oz. ASW **Ruler:** Frederik III **Obv:** Crowned F3 monogram within beaded border, within legend **Obv. Legend:** IIII MARCK DANSKE • (date) **Rev:** Crowned flat-top shield on short cross within circle, legend, crossarms with straight-sided triangular ends, mintmaster mark to right of crown **Rev. Legend:** DOMINUS PROVIDEBIT

Date	Mintage	Good	VG	F	VF	XF
1658(h)	—	115	225	360	675	—

KM# 194.4a KRONE (4 Mark)

22.2720 g., 0.6710 Silver 0.4805 oz. ASW **Ruler:** Frederik III **Obv:** Crowned F3 monogram within beaded border, within legend **Obv. Legend:** IIII MARCK DANSKE • (date) **Rev:** Crowned flat-top shield on short cross, shield breaks circle at bottom, crossarms with straight-sided triangular ends, no mintmaster mark **Rev. Legend:** DOMINUS PROVIDEBIT

Date	Mintage	Good	VG	F	VF	XF
1658	—	90.00	160	310	525	—
1659	—	90.00	160	310	525	—

KM# 194.5 KRONE (4 Mark)

22.2720 g., 0.6710 Silver 0.4805 oz. ASW **Ruler:** Frederik III **Obv:** Crowned F3 monogram within beaded border **Obv. Legend:** IIII MARCK DANSKE • (date) **Rev:** Crowned flat-top shield on short cross, crossarms with flat ends, no mintmaster mark **Rev. Legend:** DOMINVS PROVIDEBIT

Date	Mintage	Good	VG	F	VF	XF
1659	—	80.00	150	270	500	—
1660	—	80.00	150	270	500	—
1661	—	4,540	750	1,250	2,000	—

KM# 221 KRONE (4 Mark)

0.6710 Silver **Obv:** Crowned F3 monogram, EBEN-EZER at sides, mound breaks circle **Obv. Legend:** IIII MARK DANSKE **Rev:** Arm with sword from cloud cuts hand reaching for crown **Note:** Dav. #3576.

Date	Mintage	Good	VG	F	VF	XF
1659	—	400	850	1,400	2,750	—

KM# 222 KRONE (4 Mark)

0.6710 Silver **Obv:** Crowned F3 monogram, mound between EBEN-EZER within circle **Obv. Legend:** IIII MARK DANSKE **Note:** Dav. #3576A.

Date	Mintage	Good	VG	F	VF	XF
1659	—	500	1,000	1,600	2,850	—
1660	—	600	1,150	1,750	3,000	—

KM# 223 KRONE (4 Mark)

0.6710 Silver **Obv:** Crowned F3 monogram - EBEN-EZER **Obv. Legend:** *DOMINVS * PROVIDEBIT * **Rev:** Small crown, hand open **Rev. Legend:** * SOLI * DEO - * GLORIA **Note:** Dav. #3578. The listing formerly 223.2 is PN15.

Date	Mintage	Good	VG	F	VF	XF
1659	—	400	850	1,400	2,750	—

KM# A224 KRONE (4 Mark)

0.6710 Silver **Obv:** KM#194.5, EBEN-EZER **Rev:** KM#223 **Note:** Mule.

Date	Mintage	Good	VG	F	VF	XF
1660 Unique	—	—	—	—	—	—

KM# 331 KRONE (4 Mark)

18.9090 g., 0.6710 Silver 0.4079 oz. ASW **Obv:** King standing **Rev:** Crown **Note:** Size of 1/2 Krone, but double thickness.

Date	Mintage	Good	VG	F	VF	XF
1665	—	300	625	1,000	2,750	—

KM# 270 KRONE (4 Mark)

22.2720 g., 0.6710 Silver 0.4805 oz. ASW **Obv:** Armored bust right **Rev:** Date above crown, G-K, DOMINUS PROVIDEBIT below **Note:** Dav. #3579.

Date	Mintage	Good	VG	F	VF	XF
1666 GK	—	110	220	500	1,000	—

KM# 271 KRONE (4 Mark)

22.2720 g., 0.6710 Silver 0.4805 oz. ASW **Obv:** King in Roman outfit **Rev:** Date above large crown **Note:** Dav. #3579A.

Date	Mintage	Good	VG	F	VF	XF
1666	—	400	800	1,100	2,000	—

KM# 272 KRONE (4 Mark)

22.2720 g., 0.6710 Silver 0.4805 oz. ASW **Obv:** Crowned F3 monogram in print, legend reads counterclockwise from upper left **Rev:** Crowned arms divide G-K, legend reads counterclockwise from upper left **Note:** Dav. #3580.

Date	Mintage	Good	VG	F	VF	XF
1666	—	300	650	1,000	1,750	—

KM# 273.1 KRONE (4 Mark)

22.2720 g., 0.6710 Silver 0.4805 oz. ASW **Obv:** Crowned F3 monogram in print; legends reads clockwise from upper right **Rev:** Legends reads clockwise from upper left **Note:** Dav. #3580A.

Date	Mintage	Good	VG	F	VF	XF
1666	—	300	650	1,000	1,750	—

KM# 273.2 KRONE (4 Mark)

22.2720 g., 0.6710 Silver 0.4805 oz. ASW **Obv:** Crowned F3 monogram in print, legend reads counterclockwise from upper right **Rev:** Legends reads counterclockwise from upper left

Date	Mintage	Good	VG	F	VF	XF
1667 Unique	—	—	—	—	—	—

KM# 274 KRONE (4 Mark)

22.2720 g., 0.6710 Silver 0.4805 oz. ASW **Obv:** Script monogram, legend reading left to right **Note:** Dav. #3581.

Date	Mintage	Good	VG	F	VF	XF
1666	—	80.00	150	300	600	—
1667	—	65.00	125	260	500	—
1668	—	65.00	125	260	500	—
1669	—	65.00	125	260	500	—

KM# 275 KRONE (4 Mark)

22.2720 g., 0.6710 Silver 0.4805 oz. ASW **Obv. Legend:** Legend reading right to left **Note:** Dav. #3581A.

Date	Mintage	Good	VG	F	VF	XF
1666	—	65.00	125	260	500	—
1668	—	250	375	550	950	—

KM# 276 KRONE (4 Mark)

22.2720 g., 0.6710 Silver 0.4805 oz. ASW **Obv. Legend:** IIII MARCK... **Rev. Legend:** DOMINUS - PROVIDEBIT **Note:** Dav. #3582.

Date	Mintage	Good	VG	F	VF	XF
1666	—	100	200	300	675	—
1667	—	190	300	500	900	—
1668	—	125	250	400	800	—
1669	—	115	160	350	725	—
1670	—	240	495	800	1,150	—

KM# 285 KRONE (4 Mark)

22.2720 g., 0.6710 Silver 0.4805 oz. ASW **Obv:** Crowned F3 monogram in script **Rev:** Without G-K at sides of arms, legends reading left to right **Note:** Dav. #3581B.

Date	Mintage	Good	VG	F	VF	XF
1667	—	190	300	500	900	—
1669	—	250	475	800	1,200	—

KM# 299.1 KRONE (4 Mark)

22.2720 g., 0.6710 Silver 0.4805 oz. ASW **Obv. Legend:** DOMINVS. PROVIDEBIT **Rev:** Legend reads right to left **Rev. Legend:** IIII MARCK... **Note:** Dav. #3583.

Date	Mintage	Good	VG	F	VF	XF
1668	—	100	200	400	800	—

KM# 299.2 KRONE (4 Mark)

22.2720 g., 0.6710 Silver 0.4805 oz. ASW **Obv:** Legend reads left to right

Date	Mintage	Good	VG	F	VF	XF
1668	—	100	200	400	800	—

KM# 306 KRONE (4 Mark)

22.2720 g., 0.6710 Silver 0.4805 oz. ASW **Obv:** Four rosettes in legend **Note:** Dav. #3584.

Date	Mintage	Good	VG	F	VF	XF
1669 Rare	—	—	—	—	—	—
1669(a)	—	125	250	450	900	—

KM# 320 KRONE (4 Mark)

22.2720 g., 0.6710 Silver 0.4805 oz. ASW **Obv:** Three crowned F3 monograms **Rev:** Three crowned shields in frame **Note:** Dav. #3585.

Date	Mintage	Good	VG	F	VF	XF
1670 Rare	—	—	3,500	5,750	8,500	12,000

KM# 330 KRONE (4 Mark)

22.2720 g., 0.6710 Silver 0.4805 oz. ASW **Obv:** Crowned ornate C5 monogram **Rev:** Crowned Danish arms **Note:** Dav. #3633.

Date	Mintage	Good	VG	F	VF	XF
1671 G-K	—	40.00	70.00	150	375	—
1672 G-K	—	40.00	70.00	160	400	—
1673 G-K	—	—	—	—	—	—
Note: Strike mark left and right of shield						
1673 G-K	—	—	—	—	—	—
Note: Strike mark below shield						
1677 G-K Rare	—	—	—	—	—	—
1680 G-K Rare	—	—	—	—	—	—

KM# 343 KRONE (4 Mark)

22.2720 g., 0.6710 Silver 0.4805 oz. ASW **Obv:** Crowned plain C5 monogram **Note:** Dav. #3633A.

Date	Mintage	Good	VG	F	VF	XF
1671	—	40.00	70.00	180	380	—
1672	—	40.00	70.00	190	400	—
1674 Rare	—	—	—	—	—	—

KM# 359 KRONE (4 Mark)

22.2720 g., 0.6710 Silver 0.4805 oz. ASW **Obv:** Without inner circle **Rev:** Arms divide G-K, without inner circle **Note:** Dav. #3635.

Date	Mintage	Good	VG	F	VF	XF
1676	—	65.00	130	300	550	—
1677	—	225	500	800	1,050	—
1678 Rare	—	—	—	—	—	—

KM# 366 KRONE (4 Mark)

22.2720 g., 0.6710 Silver 0.4805 oz. ASW **Note:** Size as 1/2 Krone, but double thickness.

Date	Mintage	Good	VG	F	VF	XF
1680 GS	—	175	350	750	1,500	—

KM# 367.1 KRONE (4 Mark)

22.2720 g., 0.6710 Silver 0.4805 oz. ASW **Obv:** Bust of King right on pedestal **Rev:** Crowned arms, narrow cross superimposed **Note:** Dav. #3636.

Date	Mintage	Good	VG	F	VF	XF
1680	—	225	400	850	1,750	—

KM# 367.2 KRONE (4 Mark)

22.2720 g., 0.6710 Silver 0.4805 oz. ASW **Rev:** Wide cross superimposed

Date	Mintage	Good	VG	F	VF	XF
1680	—	225	400	850	1,750	—

KM# 365 KRONE (4 Mark)

22.2720 g., 0.6710 Silver 0.4805 oz. ASW **Obv:** Standing figure of king **Rev:** Crowned arms **Note:** Size as a 1/2 Krone, but double thickness

Date	Mintage	Good	VG	F	VF	XF
1680 GS	—	200	400	800	1,600	—

KM# 370 KRONE (4 Mark)

22.2720 g., 0.6710 Silver 0.4805 oz. ASW **Obv:** Crowned C5 monogram **Rev:** Crowned Danish arms on cross, G-S below **Note:** Dav. #3637.

Date	Mintage	Good	VG	F	VF	XF
1681 GS	—	45.00	80.00	200	400	—
1682 GS	—	45.00	80.00	200	400	—

KM# 378 KRONE (4 Mark)

22.2720 g., 0.6710 Silver 0.4805 oz. ASW **Obv:** Crowned double C5 monogram **Rev:** Crowned shield with text over cross inscription **Rev. Legend:** IIII/ MARCK/ DANSKE/ date/ G.S. **Note:** Dav. #3638. Varieties exist.

Date	Mintage	Good	VG	F	VF	XF
1684 GS	—	90.00	180	375	625	—
1685 GS	—	85.00	160	325	550	—

KM# 386.1 KRONE (4 Mark)
22.2720 g., 0.6710 Silver 0.4805 oz. ASW **Obv:** Small thin crowned C5 double monogram with many flourishes **Rev:** Crowned ornate arms, draped, G-S below **Note:** Dav. #3639. Varieties exist.

Date	Mintage	Good	VG	F	VF	XF
1686 GS	—	55.00	110	200	420	—
1689 GS	—	60.00	120	220	500	—

KM# 386.2 KRONE (4 Mark)
22.2720 g., 0.6710 Silver 0.4805 oz. ASW **Obv:** Thin monogram **Rev:** Undraped shield

Date	Mintage	Good	VG	F	VF	XF
1686 GS	—	60.00	120	220	475	—
1689 GS	—	60.00	120	220	475	—

KM# 386.3 KRONE (4 Mark)
22.2720 g., 0.6710 Silver 0.4805 oz. ASW **Obv:** Large monograms **Rev:** Draped arms, G-S below **Note:** Dav. #3639A.

Date	Mintage	Good	VG	F	VF	XF
1689 GS	—	90.00	180	350	575	—

KM# 386.4 KRONE (4 Mark)
22.2720 g., 0.6710 Silver 0.4805 oz. ASW **Obv:** Thick monogram **Rev:** Undraped shield

Date	Mintage	Good	VG	F	VF	XF
1689 GS	—	80.00	140	280	540	—

KM# 400 KRONE (4 Mark)
22.2720 g., 0.6710 Silver 0.4805 oz. ASW **Obv:** Half-length bust in armor right **Rev:** Crowned arms divide date and 4-M, C-W below **Note:** Dav. #3640.

Date	Mintage	Good	VG	F	VF	XF
1690 CW	—	300	600	1,200	2,000	—

KM# 401.1 KRONE (4 Mark)
22.2720 g., 0.6710 Silver 0.4805 oz. ASW **Obv:** Crowned double C5 monogram within legend, legend reads clockwise from bottom **Obv. Legend:** DEI GR REX DAN • NOR • V • G **Rev:** Crowned arms divide horizontal date and 4-M above, CW below, legend reads clockwise from top **Rev. Legend:** PIETATE ET IVSTITIA **Note:** Dav. #3642.

Date	Mintage	Good	VG	F	VF	XF
1690 CW	—	—	200	500	900	—

KM# 401.2 KRONE (4 Mark)
22.2720 g., 0.6710 Silver 0.4805 oz. ASW **Obv:** Crowned double C5 monogram within legend, legend reads clockwise from top **Obv. Legend:** D.G.REX.DAN.NOR VAN GOT **Rev:** Crowned arms divide horizontal date above 4-M, CW below, legend reads clockwise from upper right **Rev. Legend:** PIETATE ET IVSTITIA **Note:** Dav. #3643.

Date	Mintage	Good	VG	F	VF	XF
1691 CW	—	—	120	240	500	—
1692 CW	—	—	125	260	550	—

KM# 401.3 KRONE (4 Mark)
Silver **Obv:** Crowned double C5 monogram within legend, legend reads clockwise from bottom **Obv. Legend:** DEI GR REX DAN • NOR • V • G **Rev:** Crowned arms divide curved date and 4-M above, CW below, legend reads clockwise from top **Rev. Legend:** PIETATE ET IUSTITIA

Date	Mintage	Good	VG	F	VF	XF
1691 CW	—	—	150	300	600	—

KM# 401.4 KRONE (4 Mark)
22.2720 g., 0.6710 Silver 0.4805 oz. ASW **Obv:** Crowned double C5 monograms **Rev:** Crowned arms divide 4-M and C-W, date in legend **Rev. Legend:** PIETATE ET IVSTITIA **Note:** Dav. #3645.

Date	Mintage	VG	F	VF	XF	Unc
1692 CW	—	125	260	550	—	—

KM# 407 KRONE (4 Mark)
22.2720 g., 0.6710 Silver 0.4805 oz. ASW **Obv:** Bust right **Rev:** Crowned arms divide date, 4-M and C-W **Note:** Dav. #3644.

Date	Mintage	VG	F	VF	XF	Unc
1691 CW Unique	—	—	—	—	—	—

KM# 428.1 KRONE (4 Mark)
17.9880 g., 0.8330 Silver 0.4817 oz. ASW **Rev:** Crown above PIET • IVST, date divided by heart **Note:** Dav. #3648.

Date	Mintage	VG	F	VF	XF	Unc
1693	—	100	220	480	900	—
1694	—	100	220	480	900	—
1695	—	125	280	575	1,100	—
1696	—	125	280	575	1,100	—
1699	—	500	800	1,200	—	—

KM# 428.2 KRONE (4 Mark)
17.9880 g., 0.8330 Silver 0.4817 oz. ASW **Obv:** AMB. F. below bust **Note:** Dav. #3648A.

Date	Mintage	VG	F	VF	XF	Unc
1693	—	250	500	1,000	2,000	—

KM# 428.4 KRONE (4 Mark)
17.9880 g., 0.8330 Silver 0.4817 oz. ASW **Rev:** Ring around crown **Note:** Dav. #3648C.

Date	Mintage	VG	F	VF	XF	Unc
1693	—	600	1,150	1,600	2,250	—

KM# 428.5 KRONE (4 Mark)
17.9880 g., 0.8330 Silver 0.4817 oz. ASW **Obv:** Armored bust right **Rev:** Large crown **Note:** Date in Roman numerals.

Date	Mintage	VG	F	VF	XF	Unc
1693 (MDCXCIII)	—	—	—	—	—	—

KM# 448 KRONE (4 Mark)
17.9880 g., 0.8330 Silver 0.4817 oz. ASW **Ruler:** Frederik IV **Obv:** Bust right **Obv. Legend:** FRID • IIII • D • G • DAN • NOR • VA • GO • RE... **Rev:** Three crowned double "F4" monograms, arms between **Rev. Legend:** DOMINUS • MI HI • ADIUTOR • **Note:** Dav. #A1287.

Date	Mintage	VG	F	VF	XF	Unc
1699	—	375	750	1,550	2,250	—
1700	—	315	675	1,400	2,100	—

KM# 60.1 2 KRONE
37.8190 g., 0.8590 Silver 1.0444 oz. ASW **Obv:** Crowned King standing right with scepter, star in legend at left foot **Obv. Legend:** CHRISTIANUS IIII D: G • DANIA **Rev:** R.F.P. above, CORONA DANICA below crown, within legend **Rev. Legend:** NORVEG: VANDALO: GOTOR: Q: REX **Note:** Dav. #3516 & 3516B.

Date	Mintage	Good	VG	F	VF	XF
1618(a)	—	180	375	750	1,500	—

KM# 60.2 2 KRONE
37.8190 g., 0.8590 Silver 1.0444 oz. ASW **Obv:** Crowned King standing right with scepter **Obv. Legend:** CHRISTIANUS IIII D: G • DANIA **Rev:** R.F.P. above, CORONA DANICA below crown, within legend **Rev. Legend:** NORVEG: VANDALO: GOTOR: Q: REX **Note:** Dav. #3516A.

Date	Mintage	Good	VG	F	VF	XF
1618(a)	—	250	575	1,000	1,750	—
1618(c)	—	280	650	1,200	2,000	—
1619(a)	—	280	650	1,200	2,000	—
1619(c)	—	280	650	1,200	2,000	—

KM# 60.3 2 KRONE
37.8190 g., 0.8590 Silver 1.0444 oz. ASW **Obv:** Crowned King standing right with scepter, star in legend at left foot **Obv. Legend:** CHRISTIANUS IIII D:G.DANIA **Rev:** R.F.P. missing above crown, CORONA DANICA below crown, within legend **Rev. Legend:** NORVEG:VANDALO:GOTOR:Q:REX

Date	Mintage	Good	VG	F	VF	XF
1618(a)	—	600	1,000	1,900	3,600	—

KM# 60.4 2 KRONE
37.8190 g., 0.8590 Silver 1.0444 oz. ASW **Obv:** Crowned King standing right with scepter, star in legend at left foot **Obv. Legend:** CHRISTIANZVS IIII D: G • DANIÆ **Rev:** *R*F*P* above, CORONA DANICA below crown, within legend **Rev. Legend:** NORVEG: VANDALO: GOTOR: Q: REX **Note:** Dav. #3516C.

Date	Mintage	Good	VG	F	VF	XF
1619(c)	—	280	650	1,200	2,000	—

KM# 61.1 2 KRONE
37.8190 g., 0.8590 Silver 1.0444 oz. ASW **Obv:** Without star in legend **Rev:** R • F • P • above crown **Note:** Dav. #3516A.

Date	Mintage	Good	VG	F	VF	XF
1618	—	250	575	1,000	1,750	—

KM# 61.2 2 KRONE

37.8190 g., 0.8590 Silver 1.0444 oz. ASW **Obv:** Crowned King standing right without scepter **Rev:** R. F. P. above crown **Note:** Dav. #3516B.

Date	Mintage	Good	VG	F	VF	XF
1618(c)	—	280	650	1,200	2,000	—

KM# 61.3 2 KRONE

37.8190 g., 0.8590 Silver 1.0444 oz. ASW **Rev:** *R * F * P * above crown **Note:** Dav. #3516C.

Date	Mintage	Good	VG	F	VF	XF
1618	—	250	575	1,000	1,750	—

KM# 99 2 KRONE

37.8190 g., 0.8590 Silver 1.0444 oz. ASW **Obv:** King with lowered scepter **Rev:** New crown **Note:** Dav. #3518.

Date	Mintage	Good	VG	F	VF	XF
1624(a)	—	350	625	1,750	3,750	—

KM# 183 2 KRONE

37.8190 g., 0.8590 Silver 1.0444 oz. ASW **Note:** Similar to 1 Krone, KM#180, but double thickness. Dav. #3566.

Date	Mintage	Good	VG	F	VF	XF
1651(h)	—	2,000	3,000	5,500	7,000	—

KM# 195 2 KRONE

44.5440 g., 0.6710 Silver 0.9609 oz. ASW **Note:** Similar to 1 Krone, KM#186, but double thickness. Dav. #3568.

Date	Mintage	Good	VG	F	VF	XF
1653	—	3,000	4,000	5,500	7,000	—

KM# 210 2 KRONE

44.5440 g., 0.6710 Silver 0.9609 oz. ASW **Note:** Similar to 1 Krone, KM#194.2b, but double thickness. Dav. #3573.

Date	Mintage	Good	VG	F	VF	XF
1655	—	1,700	2,400	3,750	5,000	—

KM# 211 2 KRONE

44.5440 g., 0.6710 Silver 0.9609 oz. ASW **Note:** Similar to 1 Krone, KM#194.3, but double thickness. Dav. #3571.

Date	Mintage	Good	VG	F	VF	XF
1657 Rare	—	1,600	2,300	3,500	4,750	—

KM# 224 2 KRONE

44.5440 g., 0.6710 Silver 0.9609 oz. ASW **Note:** Similar to 1 Krone, KM#221, but double thickness. Dav. #3575.

Date	Mintage	Good	VG	F	VF	XF
1659 Rare	—	—	—	—	—	—

KM# 225 2 KRONE

44.5440 g., 0.6710 Silver 0.9609 oz. ASW **Note:** Dav. #3577. Similar to KM#223.1.

Date	Mintage	Good	VG	F	VF	XF
1659	—	600	1,100	3,500	5,500	—

KM# A226 2 KRONE

44.5440 g., 0.6710 Silver 0.9609 oz. ASW **Note:** Similar to 1 Krone, KM#270, but double thickness.

Date	Mintage	Good	VG	F	VF	XF
1666 Unique	—	—	—	—	—	—

KM# 351.1 2 KRONE

39.0020 g., 0.7670 Silver 0.9617 oz. ASW **Obv:** King on horseback **Rev:** Crowned Danish arms **Note:** Dav. #3634. 8 Mark.

Date	Mintage	Good	VG	F	VF	XF
1675	—	100	180	380	760	—

KM# 351.2 2 KRONE

39.0020 g., 0.7670 Silver 0.9617 oz. ASW **Obv:** Horse walking on grass **Note:** 8 Mark

Date	Mintage	Good	VG	F	VF	XF
1675	—	130	280	550	1,000	—

KM# 408 2 KRONE

44.5440 g., 0.6710 Silver 0.9609 oz. ASW **Obv:** Crowned double C5 monograms **Rev:** Crowned arms divide date and 4-M at sides, date below **Note:** Dav. #3641. Similar to KM#401.3.

Date	Mintage	VG	F	VF	XF	Unc
1691	—	—	—	10,000	15,000	—

KM# 409 2 KRONE

44.5440 g., 0.6710 Silver 0.9609 oz. ASW **Obv:** King on horseback right **Rev:** Crowned arms divide date C-W, date in legend **Note:** Dav. #A3644. 8 Mark.

Date	Mintage	VG	F	VF	XF	Unc
1691 Unique	—	—	—	—	—	—

KM# 429 2 KRONE

35.9770 g., 0.8330 Silver 0.9635 oz. ASW **Note:** Dav. #A3647. Similar to 1 Krone, KM#428.1, but double thickness.

Date	Mintage	VG	F	VF	XF	Unc
1693	—	—	1,500	3,250	5,000	—
1694	—	—	1,500	3,250	5,000	—
1695	—	—	2,000	4,000	8,000	—
1696 Unique	—	—	—	—	—	—

KM# A430 2 KRONE

35.9770 g., 0.8330 Silver 0.9635 oz. ASW **Note:** Similar to 1 Mark, KM#424, but eight times in thickness.

Date	Mintage	VG	F	VF	XF	Unc
1693	—	800	1,800	4,000	6,500	—
1696 Rare	—	—	—	—	—	—

KM# 410 3 KRONE

66.8150 g., 0.8330 Silver 1.7893 oz. ASW **Obv:** Crowned double C5 monograms **Rev:** Crowned arms divide date and 4-M, date below **Note:** Dav. #A3641. Similar to KM#401.3 but three times thickness.

Date	Mintage	VG	F	VF	XF	Unc
1691 Rare	—	—	—	—	—	—

KM# 430 3 KRONE

53.9660 g., 0.8330 Silver 1.4452 oz. ASW **Note:** Dav. #3646. Similar to KM#428.1 but three times thickness.

Date	Mintage	VG	F	VF	XF	Unc
1693	—	—	3,500	5,750	9,000	—
1694	—	—	3,000	5,000	8,000	—
1695 Rare	—	—	—	—	—	—
1696 Rare	—	—	—	—	—	—

KM# 449 3 KRONE

45.2870 g., 0.9330 Silver 1.3584 oz. ASW **Subject:** Death of Christian V and Accession of Frederik IV **Note:** Dav. #A3649.

Date	Mintage	VG	F	VF	XF	Unc
1699	—	—	3,000	5,500	8,000	—

KM# 431 4 KRONE

71.9550 g., 0.8830 Silver 2.0427 oz. ASW **Note:** Dav. #3646A. Similar to 1 Krone, KM#428.1, but four times thickness.

Date	Mintage	VG	F	VF	XF	Unc
1693 Unique	—	—	—	—	—	—

KM# 432 6 KRONE

107.9320 g., 0.8830 Silver 3.0640 oz. ASW **Note:** Dav. #3646B. Similar to 1 Krone, KM#428.1, but six times thickness.

Date	Mintage	VG	F	VF	XF	Unc
1693 Unique	—	—	—	—	—	—

KM# 72 1/2 GOLD KRONE

1.4610 g., 0.9170 Gold 0.0431 oz. AGW **Obv:** Crowned arms mounted on cross in inner circle **Rev:** Large crown in circle, date in legend

Date	Mintage	VG	F	VF	XF	Unc
1619	—	2,000	3,000	4,000	5,500	—

KM# 73 GOLD KRONE

2.9730 g., 0.9170 Gold 0.0876 oz. AGW **Obv:** Crowned arms mounted on cross in inner circle **Rev:** Date above large crown in inner circle

Date	Mintage	VG	F	VF	XF	Unc
1619(a) Rare	—	—	—	—	—	—
1619(c)	—	5,000	9,000	13,000	19,000	—

KM# 206.1 GOLD KRONE

2.9730 g., 0.9170 Gold 0.0876 oz. AGW **Rev:** Large crown with legend below in inner circle, date at top

Date	Mintage	VG	F	VF	XF	Unc
1655	—	8,000	11,000	15,000	—	—

KM# 206.2 GOLD KRONE

2.9730 g., 0.9170 Gold 0.0876 oz. AGW **Obv:** Date below shield

Date	Mintage	VG	F	VF	XF	Unc
1655 Rare	—	—	—	—	—	—

KM# 278 GOLD KRONE

2.9730 g., 0.9170 Gold 0.0876 oz. AGW **Obv:** Laureate bust of Frederik III right

Date	Mintage	VG	F	VF	XF	Unc
1666	—	8,000	11,000	15,000	20,000	—

KM# 303 GOLD KRONE

2.9730 g., 0.9170 Gold 0.0876 oz. AGW **Rev:** Large crown with legend above, value: 18 MARK, date below

Date	Mintage	VG	F	VF	XF	Unc
1668 GK	—	—	7,000	10,000	15,000	—

KM# 74.1 2 GOLD KRONE

5.9960 g., 0.9170 Gold 0.1768 oz. AGW **Obv:** Crowned arms mounted on cross in inner circle **Rev:** Date above large crown in inner circle

Date	Mintage	VG	F	VF	XF	Unc
1619(c)	—	8,000	11,000	15,000	20,000	—
1621(r) Rare	—	—	—	—	—	—

KM# 74.2 2 GOLD KRONE

5.9960 g., 0.9170 Gold 0.1768 oz. AGW **Rev:** Date in legend

Date	Mintage	VG	F	VF	XF	Unc
1619(a) Unique	—	—	—	—	—	—
1626(a) Rare	—	—	—	—	—	—
1628(e)	—	8,000	11,000	15,000	20,000	—
1628(f) Rare	—	—	—	—	—	—
1630(f) Rare	—	—	—	—	—	—
1633(f) Rare	—	—	—	—	—	—
1635(f) Unique	—	—	—	—	—	—
1637(f)	—	8,000	11,000	15,000	20,000	—
1648(h)	—	6,000	10,000	14,000	19,000	—

KM# 111 2 GOLD KRONE

5.9960 g., 0.9170 Gold 0.1768 oz. AGW **Obv:** Crowned bust of Christian IV right in inner circle **Rev:** Large crown in inner circle, date in legend

Date	Mintage	VG	F	VF	XF	Unc
1628 RD	—	8,000	11,000	15,000	20,000	—
1629 RD Rare	—	—	—	—	—	—

KM# 279 2 GOLD KRONE

5.9960 g., 0.9170 Gold 0.1768 oz. AGW **Obv:** Laureate bust of Frederik III right **Rev:** Large crown with date above and legend below in inner circle

Date	Mintage	VG	F	VF	XF	Unc
1666 Unique	—	—	—	—	—	—

KM# 286 1/8 SPECIEDALER

3.5960 g., 0.8750 Silver 0.1012 oz. ASW **Obv:** Laureate and draped bust of Frederik III right **Rev:** Crowned shield

Date	Mintage	Good	VG	F	VF	XF
1667 Rare	—	—	—	—	—	—

KM# 13 1/4 SPECIEDALER

7.3080 g., 0.8880 Silver 0.2086 oz. ASW **Subject:** Christian IV **Obv:** Crown above oval shield on long cross, oval shield in each angle **Rev:** Cross in central oval shield, seven oval shields around

Date	Mintage	Good	VG	F	VF	XF
1602 Rare	—	—	—	—	—	—

KM# 100 1/2 SPECIEDALER

14.6160 g., 0.8810 Silver 0.4140 oz. ASW **Obv:** Crowned bust of Christian IV right **Rev:** Crown above circle of 13 oval shields, large oval shield in center

Date	Mintage	Good	VG	F	VF	XF
1624 NS	—	500	900	1,900	4,100	—
1627 NS	—	475	850	1,750	3,900	—
1628 NS	—	500	900	1,900	4,100	—
1631 PG Rare	—	—	—	—	—	—
1632 PG	—	2,000	3,000	4,750	7,000	—
1634 PG	—	1,500	2,500	4,250	6,000	—
1646 HK	—	500	1,000	2,000	3,750	—

KM# 260 1/2 SPECIEDALER

14.3870 g., 0.8750 Silver 0.4047 oz. ASW **Obv:** Laureate and draped bust of Frederik III right **Rev:** Crowned arms

Date	Mintage	Good	VG	F	VF	XF
1665 GK Rare	—	—	—	—	—	—

KM# 17 SPECIEDALER

29.2320 g., 0.8880 Silver 0.8345 oz. ASW **Obv:** King sitting on throne, date beside pillars **Rev:** Crowned arms **Note:** Dav. #3511.

Date	Mintage	Good	VG	F	VF	XF
1603 Rare	—	—	—	—	—	—

KM# 18 SPECIEDALER

29.2320 g., 0.8880 Silver 0.8345 oz. ASW **Obv:** King on throne, date at side of pillars **Rev:** Large cross within 2 legends in 2 circles, date in Roman numerals in inner circle. **Note:** Dav. #A3512.

Date	Mintage	Good	VG	F	VF	XF
1603 Unique	—	—	—	—	—	—

KM# 19 SPECIEDALER

29.2320 g., 0.8880 Silver 0.8345 oz. ASW **Obv:** Crowned arms **Rev:** Cross **Note:** Dav. #3512. Mule of reverses of KM#17 and 18. Date in Roman numerals.

Date	Mintage	Good	VG	F	VF	XF
1603	—	8,000	12,000	16,000	22,000	—

KM# 144 SPECIEDALER

29.2320 g., 0.8750 Silver 0.8223 oz. ASW **Note:** Similar to 2 Daler, KM#147. Dav. #3537. Breddaler.

Date	Mintage	Good	VG	F	VF	XF
ND(1607-14) Unique	—	—	—	—	—	—

KM# 145 SPECIEDALER

29.2320 g., 0.8750 Silver 0.8223 oz. ASW **Obv:** Half figure of King **Rev:** King on horseback **Note:** Dav. #3538. Breddaler.

Date	Mintage	Good	VG	F	VF	XF
ND(ca.1611) Unique	—	—	—	—	—	—

KM# 43 SPECIEDALER

29.2320 g., 0.8750 Silver 0.8223 oz. ASW **Obv:** Crowned King standing right with scepter, orb and sword divides date **Rev:** Crown above arms on cross, nine shields around **Note:** Dav. #3513.

Date	Mintage	Good	VG	F	VF	XF
1608(a)	—	700	1,100	1,800	2,900	—
1609(a)	—	600	1,000	1,700	2,800	—

KM# 44 SPECIEDALER

29.2320 g., 0.8750 Silver 0.8223 oz. ASW **Note:** Dav. #3514.

Date	Mintage	Good	VG	F	VF	XF
1608(b) Rare	—	—	—	—	—	—
1609(b)	—	2,000	3,000	4,000	6,000	—
1610(b)	—	800	1,500	2,250	4,500	—
1618(a)	—	1,000	1,600	2,500	4,750	—
1619(a)	—	1,000	1,600	2,500	4,750	—
1620(a)	—	1,000	1,600	2,500	4,750	—
1621(a) Rare	—	—	—	—	—	—

KM# 53 SPECIEDALER

29.2320 g., 0.8750 Silver 0.8223 oz. ASW **Obv:** Redesigned crowned King, without scepter and orb **Rev:** Crowned oval shield at center, 13 shields around **Note:** Dav. #A3516.

Date	Mintage	Good	VG	F	VF	XF
1612 Unique	—	—	—	—	—	—

KM# 101 SPECIEDALER

29.2320 g., 0.8750 Silver 0.8223 oz. ASW **Obv:** Crowned half bust right, inscription in ornate shield, date below **Rev:** Crown above oval arms on cross, 13 shields around **Note:** Dav. #3524.

Date	Mintage	Good	VG	F	VF	XF
16Z4 NS	—	250	525	875	1,900	—
16Z5 NS	—	300	600	1,000	2,250	—
16Z6 NS	—	250	525	900	2,000	—
16Z7 BZ	—	800	1,300	2,200	5,250	—
16Z7 NS	—	200	475	800	1,850	—
16Z8 NS	—	200	475	800	1,850	—
1631 PG	—	550	1,000	1,500	2,750	—
1632 PG	—	400	700	1,200	7,500	—
1634 PG	—	400	700	1,200	2,500	—

KM# 102 SPECIEDALER

29.2320 g., 0.8750 Silver 0.8223 oz. ASW **Rev:** Fancy-shaped shields **Note:** Dav. #3526.

Date	Mintage	Good	VG	F	VF	XF
1624	—	2,500	4,750	8,000	15,000	—

KM# 103 SPECIEDALER

29.2320 g., 0.8750 Silver 0.8223 oz. ASW **Rev:** Short cross at center, flat-top shields around **Note:** Dav. #3528.

Date	Mintage	Good	VG	F	VF	XF
1624 Unique	—	—	—	—	—	—

KM# 142 SPECIEDALER

29.2320 g., 0.8750 Silver 0.8223 oz. ASW **Obv:** New small bust of King, legend by date inside frame **Rev:** Smaller crown, larger center shield **Note:** Dav. #3536.

Date	Mintage	Good	VG	F	VF	XF
1646 *HK CHRITIANUS	—	450	700	1,150	2,250	—
1646 *HK	—	400	600	1,000	2,100	—

KM# 143 SPECIEDALER

29.2320 g., 0.8750 Silver 0.8223 oz. ASW **Obv:** New larger bust, legend ends above date **Note:** Dav. #3536A.

Date	Mintage	Good	VG	F	VF	XF
1647 H-K	—	350	550	900	2,000	—

KM# 168 SPECIEDALER

29.2320 g., 0.8750 Silver 0.8223 oz. ASW **Obv:** Crowned bust right **Rev:** Crown above center shield on cross, 11 shields around, date in legend **Note:** Dav. #3540.

Date	Mintage	Good	VG	F	VF	XF
1649 HK	—	350	700	1,350	2,500	—
1650 HK	—	300	600	1,150	2,250	—
1651 HK Rare	—	—	—	—	—	12,000

KM# 169 SPECIEDALER

29.2320 g., 0.8750 Silver 0.8223 oz. ASW **Obv:** Crowned armored bust right **Obv. Legend:** FRIDERICVS III D • G • DAN • NOR • VAN • GOT • REX **Rev:** Crown divides date, 13 shields around center shield **Rev. Legend:** DOMINUS PROVIDENT • **Note:** Dav. #3540A.

Date	Mintage	Good	VG	F	VF	XF
1649	—	450	775	1,400	3,000	—

KM# A170.1 SPECIEDALER

28.7750 g., 0.8750 Silver 0.8095 oz. ASW **Rev:** Flat-topped inner shield on small cross in inner circle

Date	Mintage	Good	VG	F	VF	XF
1653 HK Rare	—	—	—	—	—	—

KM# A170.2 SPECIEDALER

28.7750 g., 0.8750 Silver 0.8095 oz. ASW **Rev:** Round-top inner shield

Date	Mintage	Good	VG	F	VF	XF
1653 HK Unique	—	—	—	—	—	—

KM# 204 SPECIEDALER

28.7750 g., 0.8750 Silver 0.8095 oz. ASW **Obv:** Fuller large head **Rev:** Oval center arms, flat-top shields around **Note:** Dav. #3544.

Date	Mintage	Good	VG	F	VF	XF
1655 HK	—	700	1,200	2,250	4,000	—
1656 HK	—	900	1,500	2,750	5,000	—

KM# 207 SPECIEDALER

28.7750 g., 0.8750 Silver 0.8095 oz. ASW **Rev:** Oval center arms, oval provincial shields around **Note:** Dav. #3544A.

Date	Mintage	Good	VG	F	VF	XF
1656 HK	—	—	—	—	6,000	—

KM# 212 SPECIEDALER

28.7750 g., 0.8750 Silver 0.8095 oz. ASW **Obv:** Crowned bust right barely breaking upper inner circle **Rev:** Small crown above oblong arms, shields around **Note:** Dav. #3546.

Date	Mintage	Good	VG	F	VF	XF
1657 HK	—	500	1,000	2,000	4,500	—
1661 HK	—	500	1,000	2,000	4,500	—

KM# 238 SPECIEDALER

28.7750 g., 0.8750 Silver 0.8095 oz. ASW **Obv:** Crown separates legend at top **Note:** Dav. #3546A.

Date	Mintage	Good	VG	F	VF	XF
1661 HK	—	500	1,000	2,000	4,000	—
1662 IS Rare	—	—	—	—	—	—

KM# 240 SPECIEDALER

28.7750 g., 0.8750 Silver 0.8095 oz. ASW **Obv:** Crowned bust right **Rev:** Crowned arms on cross divides date and I-S **Note:** Dav. #3548.

Date	Mintage	Good	VG	F	VF	XF
1662 Unique	—	—	—	—	—	—
1663	—	—	—	14,000	20,000	—

KM# 248 SPECIEDALER

28.7750 g., 0.8750 Silver 0.8095 oz. ASW **Obv:** Crown above crossed scepter and sword, orb below **Rev:** Repeated cypher of F3 in center on cross with four crowns in angles **Note:** Dav. #3549.

Date	Mintage	VG	F	VF	XF	Unc
1663 Rare	—	—	—	—	—	—

KM# 250 SPECIEDALER

28.7750 g., 0.8750 Silver 0.8095 oz. ASW **Obv:** Crown above bust right **Rev:** Crowned arms in sprays, crown divides date **Note:** Dav. #3550.

Date	Mintage	VG	F	VF	XF	Unc
1664 CH	—	2,000	3,500	6,000	10,000	—

KM# 251 SPECIEDALER

28.7750 g., 0.8750 Silver 0.8095 oz. ASW **Rev:** Date beside arms **Note:** Dav. #3550A.

Date	Mintage	VG	F	VF	XF	Unc
1664 CH Rare	—	—	—	—	—	—

KM# 261 SPECIEDALER

28.7750 g., 0.8750 Silver 0.8095 oz. ASW **Obv:** Laureate bust breaks upper legend **Rev:** Date left of crown, FCH below **Note:** Dav. #3551.

Date	Mintage	VG	F	VF	XF	Unc
1665 Rare	—	—	—	—	—	—

KM# 262 SPECIEDALER

28.7750 g., 0.8750 Silver 0.8095 oz. ASW **Obv:** Crown above smaller arms on cross, date divided at top and FC-H at bottom **Note:** Dav. #3553.

Date	Mintage	VG	F	VF	XF	Unc
1665	—	1,750	3,000	5,000	8,000	—
1666 Rare	—	—	—	—	—	—

KM# 277 SPECIEDALER

28.7750 g., 0.8750 Silver 0.8095 oz. ASW **Obv:** Laureate bust without inner circle **Rev:** Crowned arms dividing G-K, date below, without inner circle **Note:** Dav. #3554.

Date	Mintage	VG	F	VF	XF	Unc
1665 Rare	—	—	—	—	—	—

KM# 288 SPECIEDALER

28.7750 g., 0.8750 Silver 0.8095 oz. ASW **Obv:** Laureate bust in arms facing right without circle **Obv. Legend:** FRID • III • D • G • DAN • NOR • VAN • GOT • REX • **Rev:** Crowned national arms on shield with flat top, GK flanking. **Rev. Legend:** DUX • SL • HO • STO • CO • OL & DEL • **Note:** Dav. #3555.

Date	Mintage	VG	F	VF	XF	Unc
1667 GK	—	—	—	3,500	6,500	10,000

KM# 289 SPECIEDALER

28.7750 g., 0.8750 Silver 0.8095 oz. ASW **Ruler:** Frederik III **Obv:** Laureate bust facing right without circle, wearing robe with lion's head on shoulder **Obv. Legend:** FRID • III • D • G • DAN • NOR • VAN • GOT • REX • **Rev:** Crowned national arms in four sections separated by a cross, small center shield on shield with flat top, GK flanking **Rev. Legend:** DUX • SL • HO • STO • CO • OL & DEL • **Note:** Dav. #3555A.

Date	Mintage	VG	F	VF	XF	Unc
1667 GK Rare	—	—	—	—	—	—

KM# 290 SPECIEDALER

28.7750 g., 0.8750 Silver 0.8095 oz. ASW **Obv:** Laureate bust in armor and pellet circle breaks upper legend **Obv. Legend:** FRIDERICVS • 3 • D • G • DAN • NOR • VAN • GOT • REX • **Rev:** Crowned national arms in three sections in round ornamented shield on cross, FCH below **Rev. Legend:** DOMIN NUS * PROVIDE BIT • 1667 **Note:** Dav. #3556.

Date	Mintage	VG	F	VF	XF	Unc
1667 FCH	—	—	—	8,000	12,500	—

KM# 292 SPECIEDALER

28.7750 g., 0.8750 Silver 0.8095 oz. ASW **Obv:** Laureate bust in arms facing right with lion head on shoulder. Breaks circle at top **Obv. Legend:** FRIDERICVS • 3 • D • G • DAN • NOR • VAN • GOT • REX • **Rev:** Crowned national arms on small ornamented shield on cross, within wide bayberry branch wreath **Rev. Legend:** *DOMINUS * * PROVIDEBIT * **Note:** Dav. #3557.

Date	Mintage	VG	F	VF	XF	Unc
1667 FCH Rare	—	—	—	3,000	5,000	—
ND FCH Unique	—	—	—	—	—	—

KM# 287 SPECIEDALER

28.7750 g., 0.8750 Silver 0.8095 oz. ASW **Obv:** Laureat bust in armor right draped with lion head on shoulder, breaks circle at top **Obv. Legend:** FRIDERICVS • 3 • D • G • DAN • NOR • VAN • GOT • REX • **Rev:** Crowned national arms in three sections, in small round shield in bayberry branch wreath without berries on cross **Rev. Legend:** *DOMINUS* PROVIDEBIT* **Note:** Dav. #3553A.

Date	Mintage	VG	F	VF	XF	Unc
1667 FCH Rare	—	—	—	—	—	—

KM# 291 SPECIEDALER

28.7750 g., 0.8750 Silver 0.8095 oz. ASW **Obv:** Laureate bust breaks legend at bottom **Obv. Legend:** FRID • III • D • G • DAN • NOR • VAN • GOT • REX • **Rev:** Crowned national arms on round ornamented shield on cross, within wide bayberry wreath with berries **Rev. Legend:** *DOMINUS * PROVIDEBIT * **Note:** Dav. #A3557.

Date	Mintage	VG	F	VF	XF	Unc
1667 FCH Unique	—	—	—	—	—	—

KM# 300 SPECIEDALER

28.7750 g., 0.8750 Silver 0.8095 oz. ASW **Obv:** Laureate bust divides legend at bottom **Rev:** Crowned arms on cross, 15 shields around, date divided at sides **Note:** Dav. #3559.

Date	Mintage	VG	F	VF	XF	Unc
1668	—	900	1,800	3,000	4,500	—
1669 Rare	—	—	—	—	—	—

KM# 301 SPECIEDALER

28.7750 g., 0.8750 Silver 0.8095 oz. ASW **Obv:** Bust right without inner circle, continuous legend **Rev:** Three oval shields in center crowned, 15 shields around, date in Roman numerals on edge **Note:** Dav. #3560.

Date	Mintage	VG	F	VF	XF	Unc
1668	—	1,750	2,500	4,250	6,500	—
ND	—	1,250	2,500	4,250	6,500	—

KM# 307 SPECIEDALER

28.7750 g., 0.8750 Silver 0.8095 oz. ASW **Obv:** Laureate bust divides legend at top **Rev:** Three oval shields in center crowned, 15 shields around, date in Roman numerals on edge **Note:** Dav. #3561.

Date	Mintage	VG	F	VF	XF	Unc
1669	—	1,750	3,000	5,000	8,000	—

KM# 308 SPECIEDALER

28.7750 g., 0.8750 Silver 0.8095 oz. ASW **Obv:** Laureate bust divides legend at bottom **Rev:** Date divided at sides of arms **Rev. Legend:** DOM - INVS - PROVI - DEBIT **Note:** Dav. #3563.

Date	Mintage	VG	F	VF	XF	Unc
1669 Rare	—	—	—	—	—	—

KM# 309 SPECIEDALER

28.7750 g., 0.8750 Silver 0.8095 oz. ASW **Note:** Similar to 2 Daler, KM#311. Dav. #3565.

Date	Mintage	VG	F	VF	XF	Unc
ND	—	—	2,250	5,000	7,500	—

KM# 321 SPECIEDALER

28.7750 g., 0.8750 Silver 0.8095 oz. ASW **Obv:** Bust of Christian V right **Rev:** Bust of Frederik III right **Note:** Dav. #3628.

Date	Mintage	VG	F	VF	XF	Unc
ND(1670)	—	—	—	12,500	19,000	—

KM# 322 SPECIEDALER

28.7750 g., 0.8750 Silver 0.8095 oz. ASW **Rev:** Three arms crowned in wreath, 15 shields around, date on edge **Note:** Dav. #3629.

Date	Mintage	VG	F	VF	XF	Unc
ND	—	1,000	2,850	5,500	8,500	—
1670	—	1,500	3,000	6,000	9,000	—

KM# 349 SPECIEDALER

28.7750 g., 0.8750 Silver 0.8095 oz. ASW **Obv:** Date below bust **Obv. Legend:** CHRIST. V. D. G... **Note:** Dav. #3630.

Date	Mintage	VG	F	VF	XF	Unc
1674	—	1,200	2,400	4,500	7,000	10,000

KM# 352 SPECIEDALER

28.7750 g., 0.8750 Silver 0.8095 oz. ASW **Obv:** Crowned bust with scepter and globe **Rev:** Three crowned C5 monograms **Note:** Dav. #3631.

Date	Mintage	VG	F	VF	XF	Unc
1675	—	1,000	2,250	5,000	6,500	—

KM# 411 SPECIEDALER

28.7750 g., 0.8750 Silver 0.8095 oz. ASW **Obv:** Bust right **Rev:** Crowned arms on cross, 15 crowned shields around, date below **Note:** Dav. #3632.

Date	Mintage	VG	F	VF	XF	Unc
1691 Rare	—	—	—	—	—	—

KM# 154 1-1/2 SPECIEDALER

Silver **Note:** Similar to 2 Speciedaler, KM#147. Dav. #3537A. Breddaler.

Date	Mintage	Good	VG	F	VF	XF
ND(1607-14) Rare	—	—	—	—	—	—

KM# 155 1-1/2 SPECIEDALER

Silver **Obv:** 1/2-figure of king **Rev:** King on horseback **Note:** Dav. #3538A. Breddaler.

Date	Mintage	Good	VG	F	VF	XF
ND(ca.1611) Rare	—	—	—	—	—	—

KM# 20 2 SPECIEDALER

58.4640 g., 0.8880 Silver 1.6691 oz. ASW **Obv:** Crowned arms **Rev:** Cross **Note:** Similar to 1 Speciedaler, KM318. Dav. #3512A. Date in Roman numerals.

Date	Mintage	Good	VG	F	VF	XF
1603 Unique	—	—	—	—	—	—

KM# 147 2 SPECIEDALER

58.4640 g., 0.8880 Silver 1.6691 oz. ASW **Ruler:** Christian IV **Obv. Legend:** • CHRISTIANVS • - IIII • D: - G • DA: NO • VA • G: Q • REX - X • **Rev. Legend:** REGNA • FIR - MAT • ... **Note:** Dav. #3537B. Breddaler.

Date	Mintage	Good	VG	F	VF	XF
ND(1607-14)	—	2,000	4,000	9,000	14,000	—

KM# 148 2 SPECIEDALER

58.4640 g., 0.8880 Silver 1.6691 oz. ASW **Obv:** 1/2-figure of king **Rev:** King on horseback **Note:** Dav. #3538B. Breddaler.

Date	Mintage	Good	VG	F	VF	XF
ND(ca,1611)	—	3,000	5,500	11,500	17,500	—

KM# 105 2 SPECIEDALER

58.4640 g., 0.8880 Silver 1.6691 oz. ASW **Rev:** Fancy shaped shields **Note:** Similar to 1 Speciedaler, KM#102. Dav. #3525.

Date	Mintage	Good	VG	F	VF	XF
1624	—	4,000	8,000	12,000	17,000	—

KM# 106 2 SPECIEDALER

58.4640 g., 0.8880 Silver 1.6691 oz. ASW **Obv:** Crowned 1/2-bust above framed inscription **Rev:** Crown above oval arms on cross, 13 flat-top shields around **Note:** Similar to 1 Speciedaler, KM#103. Dav. #3527.

Date	Mintage	Good	VG	F	VF	XF
1624 Rare	—	—	—	—	—	—

KM# 104 2 SPECIEDALER

58.4640 g., 0.8880 Silver 1.6691 oz. ASW **Obv:** Crowned 1/2-bust above framed inscription **Rev:** Crown above oval arms on cross, 13 shields around **Note:** Dav. #3523.

Date	Mintage	Good	VG	F	VF	XF
1624 NS	—	900	1,500	2,750	6,000	—
1626 NS	—	1,000	1,600	3,000	6,500	—
1627 BZ	—	1,100	1,750	3,250	7,000	—
1627 NS	—	1,000	1,600	3,000	6,500	—
1628 NS	—	1,000	1,600	3,000	6,500	—
1631 PG	—	1,300	2,000	3,500	7,500	—
1632 PG Rare	—	—	—	—	—	—
1634 PG Rare	—	—	—	—	—	—

KM# 146 2 SPECIEDALER

58.4640 g., 0.8880 Silver 1.6691 oz. ASW **Obv:** Crowned 1/2-bust above framed inscription **Rev:** Crown above oval arms on cross, 13 shields around **Note:** Similar to 1 Speciedaler, KM#142. Dav. #3535.

Date	Mintage	Good	VG	F	VF	XF
1647 Rare	—	—	—	—	—	—

KM# 170 2 SPECIEDALER

58.4640 g., 0.8880 Silver 1.6691 oz. ASW **Note:** Similar to 1 Speciedaler, KM#168. Dav. #3539.

Date	Mintage	VG	F	VF	XF	Unc
1649	—	7,500	12,500	19,000	—	—
1650 Rare	—	—	—	—	—	—

KM# 196.1 2 SPECIEDALER

57.5500 g., 0.8750 Silver 1.6189 oz. ASW **Obv:** Large crowned head right **Rev:** Center shield with flat top **Note:** Dav. #3541.

Date	Mintage	VG	F	VF	XF	Unc
1653	—	2,750	4,750	8,500	11,000	—

KM# 196.2 2 SPECIEDALER

57.5500 g., 0.8750 Silver 1.6189 oz. ASW **Obv:** Large crowned head right **Rev:** Center shield with rounded top **Note:** Dav. #3541

Date	Mintage	Good	VG	F	VF	XF
1653 Rare	—	—	—	—	—	—

KM# 205 2 SPECIEDALER

57.5500 g., 0.8750 Silver 1.6189 oz. ASW **Obv:** Large crowned had right **Rev:** Center shield with flat top **Note:** Dav. #3543. Similar to 1 Speciedaler, KM#204.

Date	Mintage	VG	F	VF	XF	Unc
1655	—	—	4,500	8,000	12,000	—
1656	—	—	5,500	10,000	15,000	—

KM# 208 2 SPECIEDALER

57.5500 g., 0.8750 Silver 1.6189 oz. ASW **Obv:** Bust right without inner circle, legend breaks at bottom **Rev:** Oval center arms with flat-top provincial shields around **Note:** Dav. #A3545. Similar to 1 Speciedaler, KM#207.

Date	Mintage	VG	F	VF	XF	Unc
1656 Rare	—	—	—	—	—	—

KM# 213 2 SPECIEDALER

57.5500 g., 0.8750 Silver 1.6189 oz. ASW **Note:** Similar to 1 Speciedaler, KM#212. Dav. #3545.

Date	Mintage	VG	F	VF	XF	Unc
1657 HK	—	3,250	6,500	11,000	15,000	—
1661 HK	—	3,250	6,500	11,000	15,000	—

KM# 239 2 SPECIEDALER

57.5500 g., 0.8750 Silver 1.6189 oz. ASW **Note:** Similar to 1 Speciedaler, KM#238. Dav. #3545A.

Date	Mintage	VG	F	VF	XF	Unc
1661 HK	—	2,000	3,000	4,750	6,750	—

KM# 241 2 SPECIEDALER

57.5500 g., 0.8750 Silver 1.6189 oz. ASW **Note:** Similar to 1 Speciedaler, KM#240. Dav. #3547.

Date	Mintage	VG	F	VF	XF	Unc
1662 IS Unique	—	—	—	—	—	—
1663 IS	—	5,000	10,000	15,000	22,000	—
1664 CH Rare	—	—	—	—	—	—

KM# 263 2 SPECIEDALER

57.5500 g., 0.8750 Silver 1.6189 oz. ASW **Obv:** Laureate bust breaks upper legend **Rev:** Crown above small arms on cross, date divided at top, FC-H at bottom **Note:** Similar to 1 Speciedaler, KM#262. Dav. #3552.

Date	Mintage	VG	F	VF	XF	Unc
1665 Rare	—	—	—	—	—	—
1666 Unique	—	—	—	—	—	—

KM# 302 2 SPECIEDALER

57.5500 g., 0.8750 Silver 1.6189 oz. ASW **Obv:** Laureate bust divides legend at bottom, circle around bust **Rev:** Crowned arms on cross, 15 shields around one center shield, date divided at sides **Note:** Similar to 1 Speciedaler, KM#300. Dav. #3558.

Date	Mintage	VG	F	VF	XF	Unc
1668 Rare	—	—	—	—	—	—
1669 Rare	—	—	—	—	—	—

KM# 310 2 SPECIEDALER

57.5500 g., 0.8750 Silver 1.6189 oz. ASW **Rev:** Date divided at sides of arms **Rev. Legend:** DOM - INVS - PROVI - DEBIT **Note:** Similar to 1 Speciedaler, KM#308. Dav. #3562.

Date	Mintage	VG	F	VF	XF	Unc
1669	—	2,000	4,000	6,000	—	—

KM# 311 2 SPECIEDALER

57.5500 g., 0.8750 Silver 1.6189 oz. ASW **Note:** Similar to 1 Speciedaler, KM#309. Dav. #3564.

Date	Mintage	VG	F	VF	XF	Unc
ND Rare	—	—	—	—	—	—
1669 Date on edge	—	1,500	2,500	4,000	6,000	—

KM# 324 2 SPECIEDALER

57.5500 g., 0.8750 Silver 1.6189 oz. ASW **Note:** Similar to 1 Speciedaler, KM#322. Dav. #3629A.

Date	Mintage	VG	F	VF	XF	Unc
ND Rare	—	—	—	—	—	—

KM# 24 3 SPECIEDALER

Gold **Obv:** Crowned bust of Christian IV right in inner circle **Rev:** Value and date in circle **Note:** Klippe.

Date	Mintage	VG	F	VF	XF	Unc
1604 Unique	61	—	—	—	—	—

KM# 77 3 SPECIEDALER

Silver **Note:** Similar to 2 Speciedaler, KM#147. Dav. #3537C. Breddaler.

Date	Mintage	VG	F	VF	XF	Unc
ND(1607-14) Rare	—	—	—	—	—	—

KM# 78 3 SPECIEDALER

Silver **Obv:** 1/2-figure of king **Rev:** King on horseback **Note:** Dav. #3538C. Breddaler.

Date	Mintage	VG	F	VF	XF	Unc
ND(ca.1611) Rare	—	—	—	—	—	—

KM# 76 3 SPECIEDALER

Silver **Rev:** Fancy shaped shields **Note:** Similar to Speciedaler, KM#102. Dav. #A3525.

Date	Mintage	VG	F	VF	XF	Unc
1624 Rare	—	—	—	—	—	—

KM# 75 3 SPECIEDALER

Silver **Note:** Similar to Speciedaler, KM#104. Dav. #3622.

Date	Mintage	VG	F	VF	XF	Unc
1624	—	10,000	20,000	30,000	—	—
1627 Unique	—	—	—	—	—	—
1628 Unique	—	—	—	—	—	—

KM# 230 3 SPECIEDALER

Silver **Note:** Similar to 1 Speciedaler, KM#212. Dav. #3545B.

Date	Mintage	VG	F	VF	XF	Unc
1661 HK	—	10,000	20,000	30,000	—	—

KM# 231 3 SPECIEDALER

Silver **Note:** Similar to 1 Speciedaler, KM#240. Dav. #A3547.

Date	Mintage	VG	F	VF	XF	Unc
1662 IS Rare	—	—	—	—	—	—

KM# 232 3 SPECIEDALER

Silver **Obv:** Laureate bust breaks upper legend **Rev:** Crown above smaller arms on cross, date divided at top, FC-H at bottom **Note:** Dav. #3552A.

Date	Mintage	VG	F	VF	XF	Unc
1665 Unique	—	—	—	—	—	—

KM# 233 3 SPECIEDALER

86.3250 g., 0.8750 Silver 2.4284 oz. ASW **Obv:** Laureate bust breaks legend at bottom **Rev:** Small crowned arms on cross, divided date above, FC-H below **Note:** Dav. #B3557.

Date	Mintage	VG	F	VF	XF	Unc
1668 Unique	—	—	—	—	—	—

KM# 25 4 SPECIEDALER

9.7440 g., 0.8330 Gold 0.2609 oz. AGW **Note:** Klippe. 21 x 21 mm.

Date	Mintage	VG	F	VF	XF	Unc
1604 Diamond	588	10,000	15,000	25,000	—	—
1604 Square; rare	Inc. above	—	—	—	—	—

KM# 115 4 SPECIEDALER

Silver **Note:** Similar to 2 Specidaler, KM#147. Dav. #3537D. Breddaler.

Date	Mintage	VG	F	VF	XF	Unc
ND(1607-14) Rare	—	—	—	—	—	—

KM# 79 4 SPECIEDALER

Silver **Note:** Dav. #3521.

Date	Mintage	VG	F	VF	XF	Unc
1624	—	13,500	21,500	32,500	—	—
1627 Unique	—	—	—	—	—	—

KM# 234 4 SPECIEDALER

115.1000 g., 0.8750 Silver 3.2378 oz. ASW **Note:** Similar to 1 Specidaler, KM#212. Dav. #3545C.

Date	Mintage	VG	F	VF	XF	Unc
1661 HK Unique	—	—	—	—	—	—

KM# 315 4 SPECIEDALER

115.1000 g., 0.8750 Silver 3.2378 oz. ASW **Note:** Similar to 1 Specidaler, KM#240. Dav. #B3547.

Date	Mintage	VG	F	VF	XF	Unc
1662 IS Unique	—	—	—	—	—	—

KM# 316 4 SPECIEDALER

115.1000 g., 0.8750 Silver 3.2378 oz. ASW **Note:** Similar to 2 Specidaler, KM#311. Dav. #3564A.

Date	Mintage	VG	F	VF	XF	Unc
ND Unique	—	—	—	—	—	—

KM# 26 6 SPECIEDALER

13.1750 g., 0.9230 Gold 0.3910 oz. AGW **Obv:** Crowned bust of Christian IV right in inner circle **Rev:** Value and date in circle **Note:** Klippe.

Date	Mintage	VG	F	VF	XF	Unc
1604 Diamond	425	—	—	45,000	—	—
1604 Square; rare	Inc. above	—	—	—	—	—

KM# 116 6 SPECIEDALER

Silver **Note:** Similar to 2 Specidaler, KM#147. Dav. #3537E.

Date	Mintage	VG	F	VF	XF	Unc
ND(1607-14) Unique	—	—	—	—	—	—

KM# 27 8 SPECIEDALER

17.6490 g., 0.9370 Gold 0.5317 oz. AGW **Obv:** Crowned bust of Christian IV right in inner circle **Rev:** Value and date in circle **Note:** Klippe.

Date	Mintage	VG	F	VF	XF	Unc
1604 Rare	409	—	—	—	—	—

KM# 50.1 1/2 ROSENOBEL

4.4970 g., 0.8330 Gold 0.1204 oz. AGW, 28 mm. **Obv:** Crowned Christian IV right in inner circle, continuous legend **Rev:** Elephant left with crowned initial on side cloth

Date	Mintage	VG	F	VF	XF	Unc
1611	—	—	—	—	65,000	—

KM# 50.2 1/2 ROSENOBEL

4.4970 g., 0.8330 Gold 0.1204 oz. AGW, 24 mm. **Obv:** Crown breaks legend

Date	Mintage	VG	F	VF	XF	Unc
1611 Rare	—	—	—	—	—	—

KM# 51 ROSENOBEL

8.9940 g., 0.8330 Gold 0.2409 oz. AGW **Obv:** Crowned Christian IV right in inner circle **Rev:** Elephant left with crowned initial on side cloth

Date	Mintage	VG	F	VF	XF	Unc
1611	—	14,000	20,000	25,000	37,500	—
1612	—	11,000	16,000	23,000	35,000	—
1613	—	—	—	27,500	40,000	—
1627	—	—	—	32,500	5,000	—
1629 Rare	—	—	—	—	—	—

KM# B45 GUILDER (Hungarian Guilder)

3.4900 g., 0.9720 Gold 0.1091 oz. AGW **Obv:** King standing **Rev:** Large shield, date in legend

Date	Mintage	VG	F	VF	XF	Unc
1607 Rare	—	—	—	—	—	—
1608 Unique	—	—	—	—	—	—

KM# A45 GUILDER (Hungarian Guilder)

3.4900 g., 0.9720 Gold 0.1091 oz. AGW **Rev:** Shield of three lions mounted on cross **Note:** Prev. KM#45.

Date	Mintage	VG	F	VF	XF	Unc
1608 Rare	—	—	—	—	—	—
1611	—	4,000	7,000	11,000	15,000	—

KM# 108 GUILDER (Rhinish Guilder)

3.2490 g., 0.7600 Gold 0.0794 oz. AGW **Obv:** Crowned bust of Christian IV right in inner circle **Rev:** Crowned arms mounted on cross in inner circle **Note:** Minted for paying Danish troops during part of the "30 Years War".

Date	Mintage	Good	VG	F	VF	XF
1625	29,000	—	2,000	3,000	6,000	9,000
1627	2,168	—	2,000	3,000	6,000	9,000
1628	—	—	3,000	4,500	7,000	11,000
1632	2,570	—	2,500	3,500	6,500	10,000

KM# 46 2 GUILDER (2 Hungarian Guilder)

6.9800 g., 0.9720 Gold 0.2181 oz. AGW **Obv:** Christian IV standing right in inner circle **Rev:** Crowned arms mounted on cross in circle of 13 shields of arms

Date	Mintage	VG	F	VF	XF	Unc
1608 Rare	—	—	—	—	—	—

KM# A47 3 GUILDER (3 Hungarian Guilder/Sovereign)

Gold **Obv:** Standing King Christian IV divides date **Note:** Similar to 2 Guilder, KM#46.

Date	Mintage	VG	F	VF	XF	Unc
1608	—	—	—	—	100,000	—

KM# 114 1/4 PORTUGALOSER (2-1/2 Ducat)

8.6610 g., 0.9790 Gold 0.2726 oz. AGW **Obv:** Cross in inner circle, date at top **Rev:** Crowned heart in inner circle, radiant Jehovah in Hebrew at top

Date	Mintage	VG	F	VF	XF	Unc
1629 Unique	—	—	—	—	—	—

FR# 68 PORTUGALOSER (10 Ducat)

34.6450 g., 0.9790 Gold 1.0904 oz. AGW **Obv:** Equestrian figure of Christian IV right in cartouche **Obv. Legend:** :CHRISTIANVS: IIII: D: G: DAN: NO • VA • G • REX **Rev:** Crowned arms within legend **Rev. Legend:** DUX • SCL • HOL • ST • • DIT • COM • IN • OL • ETZ

Date	Mintage	VG	F	VF	XF	Unc
ND(1610)	—	—	—	75,000	100,000	—

KM# 174 1/16 DUCAT

Gold **Ruler:** Frederik III **Obv:** Crowned F3 monogram within legend **Obv. Legend:** DOMINUS PROVIDEBIT **Note:** Brakteate striking

Date	Mintage	VG	F	VF	XF	Unc
ND	—	600	1,000	—	—	—

KM# A143 1/4 DUCAT

0.8730 g., 0.9790 Gold 0.0275 oz. AGW **Obv:** Christian IV standing right **Rev:** Three-line inscription (one in Hebrew) above date **Note:** Prev. KM#143.

Date	Mintage	VG	F	VF	XF	Unc
1646	—	900	1,500	3,750	5,500	—
1647	—	1,250	2,000	4,250	6,500	—
1648 Unique	—	—	—	—	—	—

KM# 149 1/4 DUCAT

0.8730 g., 0.9790 Gold 0.0275 oz. AGW **Obv:** Crowned C4 monogram divides date **Rev:** Eyeglasses above two-line inscription **Rev. Legend:** VIDE MIRA DOMI

Date	Mintage	VG	F	VF	XF	Unc
1647 Rare	—	—	—	—	—	—

KM# 150 1/4 DUCAT

0.8730 g., 0.9790 Gold 0.0275 oz. AGW **Obv:** Christian IV standing right **Rev:** Eyeglasses above two-line inscription

Date	Mintage	VG	F	VF	XF	Unc
ND Rare	—	—	—	—	—	—

KM# 235 1/4 DUCAT

0.8730 g., 0.9790 Gold 0.0275 oz. AGW **Obv:** Frederik III **Rev:** Crowned cruciform double F monograms with 3 at center

Date	Mintage	VG	F	VF	XF	Unc
1660(h)	—	1,000	1,500	2,500	4,000	—
1664(a)	—	1,400	2,000	3,000	5,000	—

KM# 264.1 1/4 DUCAT

0.8730 g., 0.9790 Gold 0.0275 oz. AGW **Obv:** Crowned F3 monogram, legend reads clockwise from top **Rev:** Value and date

Date	Mintage	VG	F	VF	XF	Unc
1665(k)	—	500	1,000	2,000	3,100	—
1668(k)	—	550	1,100	2,250	3,250	—

KM# 264.2 1/4 DUCAT

0.8730 g., 0.9790 Gold 0.0275 oz. AGW **Obv:** Crowned F3 monogram, legend reads counterclockwise from top

Date	Mintage	VG	F	VF	XF	Unc
1665(k) Unique	—	—	—	—	15,000	—
1665 GK	—	—	—	6,000	10,000	—

KM# 325 1/4 DUCAT

0.8730 g., 0.9790 Gold 0.0275 oz. AGW **Obv:** Two crowned F3 monograms **Note:** 3 Mark

Date	Mintage	VG	F	VF	XF	Unc
1670 GK	—	800	1,500	2,500	3,500	—

KM# 353 1/4 DUCAT

0.8730 g., 0.9790 Gold 0.0275 oz. AGW **Obv:** Crowned C5 monograms **Rev:** Value and date **Note:** 3 Mark

Date	Mintage	VG	F	VF	XF	Unc
1675	—	1,000	1,500	2,500	4,000	—

KM# 360 1/4 DUCAT

0.8730 g., 0.9790 Gold 0.0275 oz. AGW **Obv:** Laureate bust of Christian V right **Note:** 3 Mark

Date	Mintage	VG	F	VF	XF	Unc
1676	—	1,350	1,800	3,000	5,000	—

KM# 436 1/4 DUCAT

0.8730 g., 0.9790 Gold 0.0275 oz. AGW **Obv:** Older bust of Christian V right **Rev:** Large crown above date **Note:** Similar to 1/2 Ducat, KM#437.

Date	Mintage	VG	F	VF	XF	Unc
1694 Unique	—	—	—	—	—	—

KM# 138 1/2 DUCAT

1.7450 g., 0.9790 Gold 0.0549 oz. AGW **Obv:** Christian IV standing right in inner circle **Rev:** Three-line inscription (1 in Hebrew) above date

Date	Mintage	VG	F	VF	XF	Unc
1644	—	800	1,500	3,750	5,000	—
1645	—	1,000	2,000	4,000	5,250	—
1646	—	1,000	2,000	4,000	5,250	—

KM# 151 1/2 DUCAT

1.7450 g., 0.9790 Gold 0.0549 oz. AGW **Obv:** Crowned C4 monogram **Rev:** Eyeglasses above two-line inscription and date

Date	Mintage	VG	F	VF	XF	Unc
1647	—	5,000	10,000	16,000	24,000	—

KM# 152 1/2 DUCAT

1.7450 g., 0.9790 Gold 0.0549 oz. AGW **Obv:** Christian IV standing right in inner circle **Rev:** Eyeglasses above inscription and date

Date	Mintage	VG	F	VF	XF	Unc
1647	—	4,500	9,000	14,500	20,000	—

KM# 188 1/2 DUCAT

1.7450 g., 0.9790 Gold 0.0549 oz. AGW **Obv:** Laureate bust of Frederik III in inner circle **Rev:** Three-line inscription and date in inner circle

Date	Mintage	VG	F	VF	XF	Unc
1652(h)	—	—	—	—	5,000	—

KM# 229 1/2 DUCAT

1.7450 g., 0.9790 Gold 0.0549 oz. AGW **Obv:** Frederik III **Rev:** Crowned cruciform double F monograms with 3 at center

Date	Mintage	VG	F	VF	XF	Unc
1659	—	600	1,200	2,750	4,250	—
1664	—	750	1,500	3,000	4,500	—

KM# 312 1/2 DUCAT

1.7450 g., 0.9790 Gold 0.0549 oz. AGW **Obv:** Crowned F3 monogram in inner circle **Rev:** Value and date

Date	Mintage	VG	F	VF	XF	Unc
1669	—	2,250	3,750	5,750	—	—

KM# 354 1/2 DUCAT

1.7450 g., 0.9790 Gold 0.0549 oz. AGW **Obv:** Laureate bust of Christian V right **Rev:** Crowned C5 monograms divide date

Date	Mintage	VG	F	VF	XF	Unc
1675GK	—	—	1,450	2,400	3,500	—

KM# 355 1/2 DUCAT

1.7450 g., 0.9790 Gold 0.0549 oz. AGW **Obv:** Equestrian figure of Christian V right **Rev:** Three crowned C5 monograms entwined

Date	Mintage	VG	F	VF	XF	Unc
ND(1685) Rare	—	—	—	10,000	—	—

KM# 356 1/2 DUCAT

1.7450 g., 0.9790 Gold 0.0549 oz. AGW **Obv:** Equestrian figure left

Date	Mintage	VG	F	VF	XF	Unc
ND(1685) Unique	—	—	—	—	—	—

KM# 437 1/2 DUCAT

1.7450 g., 0.9790 Gold 0.0549 oz. AGW **Obv:** Older bust of Christian V **Rev:** Large crown, date below **Note:** Size as 1/4 Ducat KM#436 but double thickness.

Date	Mintage	VG	F	VF	XF	Unc
1694	—	600	1,300	2,750	4,000	—
1696	—	1,100	2,000	3,250	4,250	—

KM# 441 1/2 DUCAT

1.7450 g., 0.9790 Gold 0.0549 oz. AGW **Obv:** Equestrian figure of Christian V, city view behind horse walking **Rev:** Crowned oval arms mounted above cross, date below

Date	Mintage	VG	F	VF	XF	Unc
1696	—	2,000	3,000	6,000	9,000	—

KM# 442 1/2 DUCAT

1.7450 g., 0.9790 Gold 0.0549 oz. AGW **Obv:** Equestrian figure of Christian V, horse prancing **Rev:** Crowned oval arms without drapery, mounted above cross

Date	Mintage	VG	F	VF	XF	Unc
ND	—	800	1,500	2,500	3,500	—

KM# 124 DUCAT

3.4900 g., 0.9790 Gold 0.1098 oz. AGW **Obv:** Christian IV standing right in inner circle **Rev:** Crowned arms in inner circle, date in legend

Date	Mintage	VG	F	VF	XF	Unc
1637 Rare	—	—	—	—	—	—

KM# 141 DUCAT

3.4900 g., 0.9790 Gold 0.1098 oz. AGW **Obv:** Standing figure of King with scepter and orb **Rev:** Hebrew text in center

Date	Mintage	VG	F	VF	XF	Unc
1644(h)	—	1,500	2,750	5,500	7,000	—
Note: Flower between King's feet						
1644(h) No flower, unique	—	—	—	—	—	—
1645	—	1,000	1,900	4,000	6,500	—
1646	—	1,250	2,250	4,200	7,000	—
1647	—	1,250	2,250	4,200	7,000	—
1648	—	1,250	2,250	4,200	7,000	—

KM# 153 DUCAT

3.4900 g., 0.9790 Gold 0.1098 oz. AGW **Obv:** Crowned C4 monogram divides date **Rev:** Eyeglasses above two-line inscription

Date	Mintage	VG	F	VF	XF	Unc
1647 Unique	—	—	—	—	—	—

KM# 171 DUCAT

3.4900 g., 0.9790 Gold 0.1098 oz. AGW **Ruler:** Frederik III **Obv:** Laureate head of Frederik III right wtih date below in inner circle

Date	Mintage	VG	F	VF	XF	Unc
1649(h)	—	2,000	3,000	4,750	6,500	—
1650(h) Rare	—	2,500	3,500	5,500	7,250	—
1651(h)	—	2,000	3,000	4,750	6,500	—

KM# 197 DUCAT

3.4900 g., 0.9790 Gold 0.1098 oz. AGW **Obv:** Crowned bust of Frederik III right, date below **Rev:** Inscription in 3 lines in center. **Rev. Legend:** DOMINUS PROVIDEBIT

Date	Mintage	VG	F	VF	XF	Unc
1653 Rare	—	—	—	—	—	—

KM# 198 DUCAT

3.4900 g., 0.9790 Gold 0.1098 oz. AGW **Obv:** Bust, date below. No motto. **Rev:** Crowned cruciform double F monograms with 3 at center

Date	Mintage	VG	F	VF	XF	Unc
1653 Rare	—	—	3,250	5,000	7,000	—

KM# 199 DUCAT

3.4900 g., 0.9790 Gold 0.1098 oz. AGW **Rev:** Motto in script writing joins crowns of cross, within legend

Date	Mintage	VG	F	VF	XF	Unc
1653 Unique	—	—	—	—	—	—

KM# 215 DUCAT

3.4900 g., 0.9790 Gold 0.1098 oz. AGW **Obv:** Smaller crowned bust of Frederik III right with date above **Rev:** Script writing removed

Date	Mintage	VG	F	VF	XF	Unc
1657	—	2,250	4,250	6,000	8,200	—

KM# 236 DUCAT

3.4900 g., 0.9790 Gold 0.1098 oz. AGW **Obv:** Bust of Frederik III right, within legend **Rev:** Crowned cruciform double F monograms with 3 at center

Date	Mintage	VG	F	VF	XF	Unc
1660(h)	—	2,000	3,000	4,000	5,000	—
1661(h)	—	2,250	3,250	4,500	5,750	—
1662(i)	—	2,000	3,000	4,000	5,000	—
ND(h)	—	2,000	3,000	4,000	5,000	—

KM# 242 DUCAT

3.4900 g., 0.9790 Gold 0.1098 oz. AGW **Obv:** Crowned bust extends to top edge **Rev:** Crowned cruciform double F monograms with 3 at center

Date	Mintage	VG	F	VF	XF	Unc
1662 Rare	—	—	—	—	—	—
1662(i) Rare	—	—	—	—	—	—
1663(i) Rare	—	—	—	—	—	—
1664(j)	—	2,000	3,000	4,000	5,000	—

KM# 252 DUCAT

3.4900 g., 0.9790 Gold 0.1098 oz. AGW **Obv:** Laureate head of Frederik III right

Date	Mintage	VG	F	VF	XF	Unc
1664(j) Rare	—	—	—	—	—	—

KM# 265.1 DUCAT

3.4900 g., 0.9790 Gold 0.1098 oz. AGW **Obv:** Crowned bust of Frederik III right within legend clockwise from upper right **Rev:** Crowned cruciform double F monograms with 3 at center

Date	Mintage	VG	F	VF	XF	Unc
1665 Rare	—	—	—	—	—	—
1666 Rare	—	—	—	—	—	—

KM# 265.2 DUCAT

3.4900 g., 0.9790 Gold 0.1098 oz. AGW **Obv:** Bust, legend clockwise from lower left

Date	Mintage	VG	F	VF	XF	Unc
1665 Rare	—	—	—	—	—	—

KM# 294 DUCAT

3.4900 g., 0.9790 Gold 0.1098 oz. AGW **Obv:** Laureate bust extends to lower edge, legend clockwise from lower left

Date	Mintage	VG	F	VF	XF	Unc
1667 Rare	—	—	—	—	—	—
1667(a) Rare	—	—	—	—	—	—

KM# 304 DUCAT

3.4900 g., 0.9790 Gold 0.1098 oz. AGW **Obv:** Frederik III within circle **Rev:** Crowned arms, date below within circle

Date	Mintage	VG	F	VF	XF	Unc
1667 GK	—	2,500	4,250	6,500	9,000	—
1668 GK	—	2,000	4,000	6,000	8,500	—

KM# 313 DUCAT

3.4900 g., 0.9790 Gold 0.1098 oz. AGW **Obv:** Crowned bust of Frederik III right **Rev:** Crown above three arms - two above one, date divided by lower shield

Date	Mintage	VG	F	VF	XF	Unc
1669 GK Rare	—	—	—	—	—	—
1670 GK	—	1,750	2,750	4,500	6,500	—

KM# 340.1 DUCAT

3.4900 g., 0.9790 Gold 0.1098 oz. AGW **Obv:** Laureate bust right **Obv. Legend:** CHRIST(IAN)-V **Note:** Broad flan

Date	Mintage	VG	F	VF	XF	Unc
1671/69	—	1,500	2,500	4,000	6,000	—
1672	—	1,500	2,500	4,000	6,000	—
1674 Rare	—	—	—	—	—	—

KM# 340.2 DUCAT

3.4900 g., 0.9790 Gold 0.1098 oz. AGW **Obv. Legend:** CHRIST • 5...

Date	Mintage	VG	F	VF	XF	Unc
1672	—	600	1,000	1,750	2,500	—

KM# 445 DUCAT

3.4900 g., 0.9790 Gold 0.1098 oz. AGW **Obv:** Christian V on horseback facing right **Obv. Legend:** PIETATE ET IUSTITIA **Rev:** Crowned monogram **Note:** Small, thick planchet. Size of 1/2 Ducat.

Date	Mintage	VG	F	VF	XF	Unc
ND(1675)	—	2,250	3,500	5,000	7,000	—

KM# 371 DUCAT

3.4900 g., 0.9790 Gold 0.1098 oz. AGW **Obv:** Bust of Christian V right **Rev:** Crowned arms in inner circle

Date	Mintage	VG	F	VF	XF	Unc
1681 Rare	—	—	—	—	—	—
1683	—	1,600	2,750	5,000	—	—

KM# 372 DUCAT

3.4900 g., 0.9790 Gold 0.1098 oz. AGW **Rev:** Model of Frederiksborg fortress in Guinea

Date	Mintage	VG	F	VF	XF	Unc
1682	—	2,750	5,000	9,000	14,000	—

KM# 374.1 DUCAT

3.4900 g., 0.9790 Gold 0.1098 oz. AGW **Obv:** Equestrian figure of Christian V right, baton points backwards **Rev:** Three crowned C5 monograms entwined **Note:** Small, thick planchet.

Date	Mintage	VG	F	VF	XF	Unc
ND(1685)	—	1,250	2,000	3,000	4,750	—

KM# 375 DUCAT

3.4900 g., 0.9790 Gold 0.1098 oz. AGW **Obv:** Equestrian figure of Christian V left, amongst trees **Rev:** Three entwined crowned C5 monograms **Note:** Small, thick planchet

Date	Mintage	VG	F	VF	XF	Unc
ND(1685)	—	1,400	2,250	3,250	5,000	—

KM# 374.2 DUCAT

3.4900 g., 0.9790 Gold Small, thick planchet 0.1098 oz. AGW **Obv:** Equistrian figure of Christian V right, baton points forward **Rev:** Three crowned C5 monograms entwined

Date	Mintage	VG	F	VF	XF	Unc
ND(1685)	—	1,000	1,650	2,500	4,750	—

KM# 376 DUCAT

3.4900 g., 0.9790 Gold 0.1098 oz. AGW **Obv:** Armored bust of Christian V right **Rev:** Three entwined crowned C5 monograms

Date	Mintage	VG	F	VF	XF	Unc
ND(1687) Unique	—	—	—	—	—	—

KM# 387 DUCAT

3.4900 g., 0.9790 Gold 0.1098 oz. AGW **Obv:** Bust within legend **Rev:** Crowned arms within elephant order, surrounded by 15 small arms, date at top, GS at bottom

Date	Mintage	VG	F	VF	XF	Unc
1687 GS	—	3,500	7,000	13,000	20,000	—
ND	—	3,500	7,000	13,000	20,000	—

KM# 394 DUCAT

3.4900 g., 0.9790 Gold 0.1098 oz. AGW **Obv:** Draped bust of Christian V right in elaborate hat **Rev:** View of Christiansborg fortress in Guinea in inner circle

Date	Mintage	VG	F	VF	XF	Unc
1688 Rare	—	4,000	6,000	8,000	12,000	—

KM# 388 DUCAT

3.4900 g., 0.9790 Gold 0.1098 oz. AGW **Obv:** Older head of Christian V right **Rev:** Arms at center surrounded by 15 small arms

Date	Mintage	VG	F	VF	XF	Unc
ND(1690)	—	3,000	5,000	7,250	10,000	—

KM# 389 DUCAT

3.4900 g., 0.9790 Gold 0.1098 oz. AGW **Rev:** Three crowned C5 monograms entwined

Date	Mintage	VG	F	VF	XF	Unc
ND(1690) Rare	—	—	—	—	—	—

KM# 412.1 DUCAT

3.4900 g., 0.9790 Gold 0.1098 oz. AGW **Obv:** Draped bust of Christian V right **Obv. Legend:** PIETATE ET INSTITIA **Rev:** Crowned oval arms divide date

Date	Mintage	VG	F	VF	XF	Unc
1691 Unique	—	—	—	—	—	—

KM# 413 DUCAT

3.4900 g., 0.9790 Gold 0.1098 oz. AGW **Obv:** Smaller draped bust of Christian V right

Date	Mintage	VG	F	VF	XF	Unc
1691	—	4,500	7,000	10,000	14,000	—
1692 Unique	—	—	—	—	—	—

KM# 415.1 DUCAT

3.4900 g., 0.9790 Gold 0.1098 oz. AGW **Obv:** Bust of Christian V right, breaks legend at top

Date	Mintage	VG	F	VF	XF	Unc
1691	—	2,000	3,500	5,000	7,500	—
1692	—	2,000	3,500	5,000	7,500	—

KM# 415.2 DUCAT

3.4900 g., 0.9790 Gold 0.1098 oz. AGW **Obv:** Bust of Christian V, breaks legend at bottom

Date	Mintage	VG	F	VF	XF	Unc
1691	—	900	1,400	2,250	4,500	—

KM# 412.2 DUCAT

3.4900 g., 0.9790 Gold 0.1098 oz. AGW **Obv:** Laureate bust of Christian V right **Rev:** Crowned oval arms, date in legend

Date	Mintage	VG	F	VF	XF	Unc
1692	—	1,500	3,000	6,000	8,000	—

KM# 414 DUCAT

3.4900 g., 0.9790 Gold 0.1098 oz. AGW **Obv:** Crowned double C5 monograms **Rev:** Crowned arms divide date

Date	Mintage	VG	F	VF	XF	Unc
1691 CW	—	800	1,750	3,000	4,250	—

KM# 418 DUCAT

3.4900 g., 0.9790 Gold 0.1098 oz. AGW **Obv:** Bust of Christian V left on rearing horse

Date	Mintage	VG	F	VF	XF	Unc
1692	—	1,000	1,750	2,750	4,250	—

KM# A433 DUCAT

3.4900 g., 0.9790 Gold 0.1098 oz. AGW **Rev:** Crown above date **Note:** Large planchet

Date	Mintage	VG	F	VF	XF	Unc
1693	—	1,000	2,000	3,100	5,500	—

KM# 415.3 DUCAT

3.4900 g., 0.9790 Gold 0.1098 oz. AGW **Obv:** Bust of Christian V right, breaks legend at top and bottom **Note:** Prev. KM#415.2.

Date	Mintage	VG	F	VF	XF	Unc
1693	—	900	1,400	2,250	4,500	—
1696	—	1,000	1,850	3,000	5,000	—

KM# 438 DUCAT

3.4900 g., 0.9790 Gold 0.1098 oz. AGW **Obv:** Christian V **Rev:** Triple monogram

Date	Mintage	VG	F	VF	XF	Unc
1694	—	1,000	2,000	3,000	4,250	—

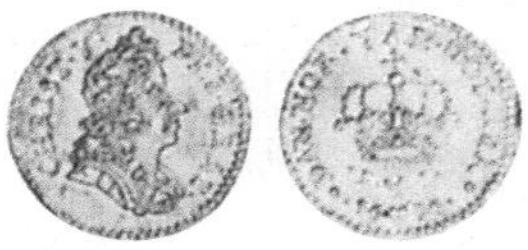

KM# 433 DUCAT

3.4900 g., 0.9790 Gold 0.1098 oz. AGW **Rev:** Crown above date **Note:** Small, thick planchet. Size as 1/4 Ducat, but 4 times thickness.

Date	Mintage	VG	F	VF	XF	Unc
1694	—	1,000	2,000	3,000	5,000	—
1696	—	900	1,800	2,750	4,250	—

KM# 443 DUCAT

3.4900 g., 0.9790 Gold 0.1098 oz. AGW **Obv:** Christian V on horseback facing right, city view in background **Rev:** Crowned arms **Note:** Size as 1/2 Ducat but double thikness.

Date	Mintage	VG	F	VF	XF	Unc
1696	—	2,000	3,000	4,000	6,000	—

KM# 444 DUCAT

3.4900 g., 0.9790 Gold 0.1098 oz. AGW **Obv:** Christian V on rearing horse, no drapery **Rev:** Crowned arms **Note:** Size as 1/2 Ducat but double thickness.

Date	Mintage	VG	F	VF	XF	Unc
ND(1696)	—	1,000	1,500	2,000	3,000	—

KM# B445 DUCAT

3.4900 g., 0.9790 Gold 0.1098 oz. AGW **Obv:** Christian V on horseback, left **Rev:** Crowned double monogram **Note:** Size as 1/2 Ducat but double thickness.

Date	Mintage	VG	F	VF	XF	Unc
ND(1696)	—	3,000	4,000	6,500	10,000	—

KM# A445 DUCAT

3.4900 g., 0.9790 Gold 0.1098 oz. AGW **Obv:** Christian V on horseback right **Rev:** Draped crowned oval arms **Note:** Size as 1/2 Ducat but double thickness.

Date	Mintage	VG	F	VF	XF	Unc
ND(1696)	—	2,000	3,000	4,500	6,000	—

KM# 453 DUCAT

3.4900 g., 0.9790 Gold 0.1098 oz. AGW **Obv:** Bust of Christian V right **Rev:** Ship

Date	Mintage	VG	F	VF	XF	Unc
1699	—	1,750	3,000	4,500	7,500	—

KM# 454 DUCAT

3.4900 g., 0.9790 Gold 0.1098 oz. AGW **Subject:** Death of the King **Obv:** Monogram on pyramid with base, winds of heaven blowing from above **Obv. Legend:** NEC • VI • NEC • METU **Rev:** Ships in harbor of Copenhagen, motto above

Date	Mintage	VG	F	VF	XF	Unc
ND(1699)	—	1,000	2,000	3,000	4,500	—

KM# 455 DUCAT

3.4900 g., 0.9790 Gold 0.1098 oz. AGW **Subject:** Death of the King **Obv:** Without base on pyramid **Rev:** Motto in banner above city

Date	Mintage	VG	F	VF	XF	Unc
ND(1699)	—	1,000	2,000	3,250	5,500	—

KM# 456 DUCAT

3.4900 g., 0.9790 Gold 0.1098 oz. AGW **Subject:** Coronation of King Frederik IV **Obv:** Frederik IV **Rev:** Christian V

Date	Mintage	VG	F	VF	XF	Unc
ND(1699)	—	1,000	2,000	3,000	5,000	—

KM# 471 DUCAT

3.4900 g., 0.9790 Gold 0.1098 oz. AGW **Rev:** Crowned double F4 monograms, date below

Date	Mintage	VG	F	VF	XF	Unc
1700	—	1,000	2,000	3,000	5,000	—

KM# 139 2 DUCAT

6.9800 g., 0.9790 Gold 0.2197 oz. AGW **Obv:** Christian IV standing right in inner circle **Rev:** Three-line inscription (one in Hebrew) above date in starry border

Date	Mintage	VG	F	VF	XF	Unc
1644(h) Rare	—	—	—	8,000	12,000	—

KM# 140 2 DUCAT

6.9800 g., 0.9790 Gold 0.2197 oz. AGW **Rev:** Without starry border

Date	Mintage	VG	F	VF	XF	Unc
1644(h) Unique	—	—	—	—	—	—
1645(h)	—	2,500	4,000	6,000	—	—
1646(h)	—	2,000	2,800	5,000	9,000	—
1648(h)	—	1,800	2,600	4,750	9,000	—

KM# 200 2 DUCAT

6.9800 g., 0.9790 Gold 0.2197 oz. AGW **Obv:** Crowned bust of Frederik III right, date below **Rev:** Crowned cruciform double F monograms wtih 3 at center

Date	Mintage	VG	F	VF	XF	Unc
1653 Rare	—	—	—	—	—	—

KM# 216.1 2 DUCAT

6.9800 g., 0.9790 Gold 0.2197 oz. AGW **Ruler:** Frederik III **Obv:** Crowned bust to right **Obv. Legend:** FRIDERICUS: III: D: G: DANIA: NORWEGIÆ. **Rev:** Sailing ship, date in exergue **Rev. Legend:** VANDALOR: GOTHOR: Q: REX •.

Date	Mintage	VG	F	VF	XF	Unc
1657	95	3,000	4,500	6,750	10,000	—
1658	100	3,000	4,500	6,750	10,000	—

KM# 216.2 2 DUCAT

6.9800 g., 0.9790 Gold 0.2197 oz. AGW **Rev:** Sailing ship, date in exergue **Rev. Legend:** DOMINVS • PROVIDEBIT **Note:** Varieties exist.

Date	Mintage	VG	F	VF	XF	Unc
1664	—	3,000	4,500	6,750	10,000	—
1666 Unique	—	—	—	—	—	—
1667 Unique	—	—	—	—	—	—

KM# 244 2 DUCAT

6.9800 g., 0.9790 Gold 0.2197 oz. AGW **Obv:** Crowned bust of Frederik III right in inner circle **Rev:** Crowned arms mounted on cross divides date in inner circle

Date	Mintage	VG	F	VF	XF	Unc
1662(I)	—	2,500	4,000	7,000	10,000	—
1663(I)	—	3,000	4,500	7,250	11,000	—

KM# 243 2 DUCAT

6.9800 g., 0.9790 Gold 0.2197 oz. AGW **Rev:** Crowned cruziform double F3 monogram, 3 in center

Date	Mintage	VG	F	VF	XF	Unc
1662(I) Rare	—	—	—	—	—	—

KM# 295 2 DUCAT

6.9800 g., 0.9790 Gold 0.2197 oz. AGW **Obv:** Laureate bust of Frederik III right without inner circle **Rev:** Sailing ship, date in exergue

Date	Mintage	VG	F	VF	XF	Unc
1667	—	3,250	5,000	8,000	12,000	—

KM# 326 2 DUCAT

6.9800 g., 0.9790 Gold 0.2197 oz. AGW **Obv:** Laureate head of Frederik III right **Rev:** Crowned cruciform double F3 monogram, date

Date	Mintage	VG	F	VF	XF	Unc
1670	—	4,000	7,000	10,000	14,000	—

KM# 328 2 DUCAT

6.9800 g., 0.9790 Gold 0.2197 oz. AGW **Obv:** Laureate bust of Christian V right **Rev:** Crowned double C5 monogram, date in legend

Date	Mintage	VG	F	VF	XF	Unc
1670	—	—	—	—	15,000	—

KM# 346 2 DUCAT

6.9800 g., 0.9790 Gold 0.2197 oz. AGW **Obv:** Crowned C5 monogram **Rev:** Elephant

Date	Mintage	VG	F	VF	XF	Unc
1673	—	3,000	5,000	8,000	12,000	—

KM# 347 2 DUCAT

6.9800 g., 0.9790 Gold 0.2197 oz. AGW **Obv:** Christian V **Note:** Size as a 1/2 Ducat, but planchet is four times as thick.

Date	Mintage	VG	F	VF	XF	Unc
ND(1675)	—	1,250	2,000	3,000	5,000	—

KM# 348 2 DUCAT

6.9800 g., 0.9790 Gold 0.2197 oz. AGW **Obv:** Christian V right on rearing horse **Rev:** Three crowned C5 monograms entwined **Note:** Size as 1/2 Ducat, 4 times thickness

Date	Mintage	VG	F	VF	XF	Unc
ND(1685) Unique	—	—	—	—	—	—

KM# 390 2 DUCAT

6.9800 g., 0.9790 Gold 0.2197 oz. AGW **Obv:** Bust of Christian V right **Rev:** Crowned round arms in circle of 15 shields, date divided near top

Date	Mintage	VG	F	VF	XF	Unc
1687	—	12,000	18,000	25,000	35,000	—

KM# 395.1 2 DUCAT

6.9800 g., 0.9790 Gold 0.2197 oz. AGW **Obv:** Draped bust of Christian V right, wearing elaborate hat **Rev:** View of Christiansborg fortress in Guinea in inner circle **Edge:** Lettered

Date	Mintage	VG	F	VF	XF	Unc
1688 Unique	—	—	—	—	—	—

KM# 395.2 2 DUCAT

6.9800 g., 0.9790 Gold 0.2197 oz. AGW **Obv:** Draped bust of Christian V right, wearing elaborate hat **Rev:** View of Christiansborg fortress in Guinea in inner circle **Edge:** Plain

Date	Mintage	VG	F	VF	XF	Unc
1688	—	5,000	9,000	14,000	20,000	—

KM# 416.1 2 DUCAT

6.9800 g., 0.9790 Gold 0.2197 oz. AGW **Obv:** Wide draped bust of Christian V right **Rev:** Crowned oval arms divide date

Date	Mintage	VG	F	VF	XF	Unc
1691	—	3,000	6,000	10,000	15,000	—

KM# 416.2 2 DUCAT

6.9800 g., 0.9790 Gold 0.2197 oz. AGW **Obv:** Slender draped bust of Christian V right **Rev:** Crowned oval arms, date surrounding shield

Date	Mintage	VG	F	VF	XF	Unc
1691	—	3,000	5,000	8,500	11,500	—

KM# 419 2 DUCAT

6.9800 g., 0.9790 Gold 0.2197 oz. AGW **Obv:** Laureate bust of Christian V right, legend below **Obv. Legend:** A. MEIBUS F. **Rev:** Three crowned C5 monograms surround radiant triangle

Date	Mintage	VG	F	VF	XF	Unc
1692 Rare	—	—	—	—	—	—

KM# 439 2 DUCAT

6.9800 g., 0.9790 Gold 0.2197 oz. AGW **Obv:** Plain bust of Christian V right **Rev:** Large crown **Note:** Minted from same dies as 2 Krone, KM#429.

Date	Mintage	VG	F	VF	XF	Unc
1693 Rare	—	—	—	—	—	—

KM# 434 2 DUCAT

6.9800 g., 0.9790 Gold 0.2197 oz. AGW **Rev:** Large crown above date **Note:** Size as 1/4 Ducat, planchet eight times as thick

Date	Mintage	VG	F	VF	XF	Unc
1694	—	5,000	8,000	12,000	18,000	—
1696	—	5,500	9,000	1,350	20,000	—

KM# 446 2 DUCAT

6.9800 g., 0.9790 Gold 0.2197 oz. AGW **Obv:** Christian V right on prancing horse **Rev:** Crowned round arms mounted on cross, date divided below

Date	Mintage	VG	F	VF	XF	Unc
1696 Rare	—	—	—	—	—	—

KM# 447 2 DUCAT

6.9800 g., 0.9790 Gold 0.2197 oz. AGW **Obv:** Christian V right on rearing horse **Rev:** Crowned oval arms with drapery **Note:** Similar to KM#A445.

Date	Mintage	VG	F	VF	XF	Unc
ND Rare	—	—	—	—	—	—

KM# A447 2 DUCAT

6.9800 g., 0.9790 Gold 0.2197 oz. AGW **Rev:** Arms without drapery **Note:** Similar to 1 Ducat, KM#444.

Date	Mintage	VG	F	VF	XF	Unc
ND Rare	—	—	—	—	—	—

KM# 457 2 DUCAT

6.9800 g., 0.9790 Gold 0.2197 oz. AGW **Obv:** Bust of Christian V right **Rev:** Three-masted ship in harbor of Christiansborg fortress

Date	Mintage	VG	F	VF	XF	Unc
1699	—	3,000	6,000	10,000	15,000	—

KM# 458 2 DUCAT

6.9800 g., 0.9790 Gold 0.2197 oz. AGW **Subject:** Death of the King **Obv:** Monogram on pyramid with base, winds of heaven blowing from above **Rev:** Ships in harbor of Copenhagen, motto above **Rev. Legend:** HAFNIA DANUIÆ

Date	Mintage	VG	F	VF	XF	Unc
ND(1699)	—	3,000	6,000	10,000	14,000	—

KM# 459 2 DUCAT

6.9800 g., 0.9790 Gold 0.2197 oz. AGW **Subject:** Death of the King **Obv:** Without base on pyramid **Obv. Legend:** HAFNIA DANUIÆ **Rev:** Motto above city in banner

Date	Mintage	VG	F	VF	XF	Unc
ND(1699) Unique	—	—	—	—	—	—

KM# 460 2 DUCAT

6.9800 g., 0.9790 Gold 0.2197 oz. AGW **Obv:** Smoke and flames from center point **Rev:** Group of weapons, banner and battle trophies

Date	Mintage	VG	F	VF	XF	Unc
ND(1699)	—	—	—	—	4,000	6,500	—

KM# 461 2 DUCAT

6.9800 g., 0.9790 Gold 0.2197 oz. AGW **Subject:** Coronation of Frederik IV **Obv:** Bust of Frederik IV right **Rev:** Bust of Christian V right

Date	Mintage	VG	F	VF	XF	Unc
ND(1699) Rare	—	—	—	—	—	—

KM# 245 3 DUCAT

10.4710 g., 0.9790 Gold 0.3296 oz. AGW **Rev:** Crowned cruciform double F monograms with 3 at center

Date	Mintage	VG	F	VF	XF	Unc
1662(I) Unique	—	—	—	—	—	—

KM# 246 3 DUCAT

10.4710 g., 0.9790 Gold 0.3296 oz. AGW **Obv:** Crowned bust extends to top edge

Date	Mintage	VG	F	VF	XF	Unc
1662(I) Unique	—	—	—	—	—	—

KM# 280 3 DUCAT

10.4710 g., 0.9790 Gold 0.3296 oz. AGW **Obv:** Crowned bust of Frederik III right in inner circle **Rev:** Ship with date in exergue

Date	Mintage	VG	F	VF	XF	Unc
1666 Unique	—	—	—	—	—	—

KM# 296 3 DUCAT

10.4710 g., 0.9790 Gold 0.3296 oz. AGW **Obv:** Laureate bust of Frederik III right **Rev:** Ship

Date	Mintage	VG	F	VF	XF	Unc
1667 Unique	—	—	—	—	—	—

KM# 391 3 DUCAT

10.4710 g., 0.9790 Gold 0.3296 oz. AGW **Obv:** Bust of Christian V right **Rev:** Crowned round arms in circle of 15 shields, date divided near top

Date	Mintage	VG	F	VF	XF	Unc
1687 Unique	—	—	—	—	—	—

KM# 462 3 DUCAT

10.4710 g., 0.9790 Gold 0.3296 oz. AGW, 28 mm. **Subject:** Coronation of Frederik IV **Obv:** Bust of Frederik IV right **Rev:** Bust of Christian V right, A. Meibus F. below

Date	Mintage	VG	F	VF	XF	Unc
ND(1699) Unique	—	—	—	—	—	—

KM# 463 3 DUCAT

10.4710 g., 0.9790 Gold 0.3296 oz. AGW, 21 mm. **Subject:** Coronation of Frederik IV **Obv:** Bust right of Frederik IV **Rev:** Bust right of Christian V

Date	Mintage	VG	F	VF	XF	Unc
ND(1699) Rare	—	—	—	—	—	—

KM# 472 3 DUCAT

10.4710 g., 0.9790 Gold 0.3296 oz. AGW **Rev:** Crowned double F4 monograms, date below

Date	Mintage	VG	F	VF	XF	Unc
1700 Unique	—	—	—	—	—	—

KM# 217.1 4 DUCAT

13.9610 g., 0.9790 Gold 0.4394 oz. AGW **Obv:** Frederik III **Rev:** Ship **Rev. Legend:** VANDALOR: GOTHOR: Q: REX • **Note:** Size as 2 Ducat KM#216.1 but double thickness

Date	Mintage	VG	F	VF	XF	Unc
1657	—	6,000	10,000	15,000	20,000	—
1658 Unique	—	—	—	—	—	—

KM# 217.2 4 DUCAT

13.9610 g., 0.9790 Gold 0.4394 oz. AGW **Rev:** Ship **Rev. Legend:** DOMINVS • PROVIDEBIT

Date	Mintage	VG	F	VF	XF	Unc
1664 Rare	—	—	—	—	—	—

KM# 435 4 DUCAT

13.9610 g., 0.9790 Gold 0.4394 oz. AGW **Obv:** Crowned C5 monogram **Rev:** Elephant with litter on back, date in exergue

Date	Mintage	VG	F	VF	XF	Unc
1683 Unique	—	—	—	—	—	—

KM# 396 4 DUCAT

13.9610 g., 0.9790 Gold 0.4394 oz. AGW **Obv:** Draped bust of Christian V right in elaborate hat **Rev:** View of Christiansborg fortress in Guinea in inner circle

Date	Mintage	VG	F	VF	XF	Unc
1688 Rare	—	—	—	—	—	—

KM# 464 4 DUCAT

13.9610 g., 0.9790 Gold 0.4394 oz. AGW **Subject:** Coronation of Frederik IV **Obv:** Bust of Frederik IV right **Rev:** Bust of Christian V right **Note:** Similar to 1 Ducat, KM#456.

Date	Mintage	VG	F	VF	XF	Unc
ND(1699) Unique	—	—	—	—	—	—

KM# 219 5 DUCAT

17.4520 g., 0.9790 Gold 0.5493 oz. AGW **Obv:** Crowned arms divide date in inner circle **Rev:** Crowned F3 monogram above Norwegian arms in palms in inner circle

Date	Mintage	VG	F	VF	XF	Unc
1658 Unique	—	—	—	—	—	—

KM# 201 5 DUCAT

17.4520 g., 0.9790 Gold 0.5493 oz. AGW **Obv:** Crowned bust extends to top edge **Note:** Similar to KM#244, but 2-1/2 times thickness.

Date	Mintage	VG	F	VF	XF	Unc
1662 Unique	—	—	—	—	—	—

KM# 247 5 DUCAT

17.4520 g., 0.9790 Gold 0.5493 oz. AGW **Obv:** Crowned bust of Frederik III right in inner circle **Rev:** Crowned arms mounted on cross divides date in inner circle **Note:** Size of 1 Ducat but 5 times thickness.

Date	Mintage	VG	F	VF	XF	Unc
1662 Unique	—	—	—	—	—	—

KM# 253 5 DUCAT

17.4520 g., 0.9790 Gold 0.5493 oz. AGW **Obv:** Draped bust of Frederik III, right **Rev:** Crowned arms within legend and date **Note:** Similar to KM#260.

Date	Mintage	VG	F	VF	XF	Unc
1665 GK Rare	—	—	—	—	—	—

KM# 392 5 DUCAT

17.4520 g., 0.9790 Gold 0.5493 oz. AGW **Obv:** Bust of Christian V right **Rev:** Crowned round arms in circle of 15 shields, date divided near top

Date	Mintage	VG	F	VF	XF	Unc
1687 Unique	—	—	—	—	—	—

KM# 420 5 DUCAT

17.4520 g., 0.9790 Gold 0.5493 oz. AGW **Obv:** Laureate bust of Christian V right **Rev:** Three crowned C5 monograms surround radiant triangle

Date	Mintage	VG	F	VF	XF	Unc
1692 Unique	—	—	—	—	—	—

KM# 314 10 DUCAT

34.9040 g., 0.9790 Gold 1.0986 oz. AGW **Obv:** Draped and laureate bust of Federik III right **Rev:** Crown above three shields in circle of 15 shields **Edge Lettering:** DOMINVS PROVEDEBIT.ANNO.MDCLXIX

Date	Mintage	VG	F	VF	XF	Unc
1669 Unique	—	—	—	—	—	—

KM# A315 10 DUCAT

34.9040 g., 0.9790 Gold 1.0986 oz. AGW **Note:** Similar to 1 Krone, KM#428.1. Prev. KM#315.

Date	Mintage	VG	F	VF	XF	Unc
1693 Unique	—	—	—	—	—	—
1696 Unique	—	—	—	—	—	—

KM# 4 LION DALER

Silver **Obv:** King standing behind arms **Rev:** Norwegian arms within legend **Note:** Dav. #3515.

Date	Mintage	VG	F	VF	XF	Unc
1608	—	—	—	—	—	—

LARGESSE COINAGE

Largesse is defined as a generous giving. It became the practice to throw coins to the people at coronations and royal funerals, while more important persons were presented with medals to commemorate the occasion.

KM# 14 4 SOLIDI (4 Skilling)

Silver **Obv:** Elephant left **Rev:** Value and date within legend

Date	Mintage	Good	VG	F	VF	XF
1603	—	150	300	600	1,500	2,250

KM# 15 8 SOLIDI (8 skilling)

Silver **Obv:** Elephant left **Rev:** Value and date within legend

Date	Mintage	Good	VG	F	VF	XF
1603	—	250	500	1,000	2,250	3,250

KM# 159 1/12 SPECIE DALER

0.8810 Silver **Obv:** Frederik III **Rev:** Incense vase **Note:** Klippe.

Date	Mintage	Good	VG	F	VF	XF
1648	—	70.00	140	300	575	1,000

KM# 160 1/6 SPECIEDALER

0.8810 Silver **Obv:** Laureate bust of Frederik III right **Rev:** Vase with incence **Note:** Klippe.

Date	Mintage	Good	VG	F	VF	XF
1648	—	80.00	175	350	775	1,200

KM# 161 1/4 SPECIEDALER

9.3080 g., Silver **Obv:** Laureate bust of Frederik III right **Obv. Legend:** Jug **Rev:** Vase with incense **Note:** Klippe.

Date	Mintage	Good	VG	F	VF	XF
1648	—	120	270	525	1,000	1,800

KM# 162 1/2 DUCAT

1.7450 g., 0.9790 Gold 0.0549 oz. AGW **Obv:** Frederik III **Rev:** Vase with incense **Note:** Klippe

Date	Mintage	VG	F	VF	XF	Unc
1648	—	1,000	1,800	3,500	5,000	—

KM# 163.1 DUCAT

3.4900 g., 0.9790 Gold 0.1098 oz. AGW **Obv:** Frederik III, small bust **Rev:** Vase with incense **Note:** Klippe

Date	Mintage	VG	F	VF	XF	Unc
1648	—	1,450	2,850	4,250	6,250	—

KM# 163.2 DUCAT

3.4900 g., 0.9790 Gold 0.1098 oz. AGW **Obv:** Frederik III, large bust **Rev:** Vase with incense **Note:** Klippe.

Date	Mintage	VG	F	VF	XF	Unc
1648	—	1,450	2,850	4,750	6,250	—

KM# 164 2 DUCAT

6.9800 g., 0.9790 Gold 0.2197 oz. AGW **Obv:** Laureate head of Frederik III right, date below **Rev:** Vase with incense **Note:** Klippe.

Date	Mintage	VG	F	VF	XF	Unc
1648	5	6,000	8,000	12,500	—	—

KM# 165 3 DUCAT

10.4710 g., 0.9790 Gold 0.3296 oz. AGW **Obv:** Laureate head of Frederik III right, date below **Rev:** Vase with incense **Note:** Klippe. Size as 2 Ducat, KM#164, but 1-1/2 times thickness.

Date	Mintage	VG	F	VF	XF	Unc
1648 Unique	5	—	—	—	—	—

KM# 166 4 DUCAT

13.9610 g., 0.9790 Gold 0.4394 oz. AGW **Obv:** Laureate head of Frederik III right, date below **Rev:** Vase with incense **Note:** Klippe. Size as 2 Ducat, KM#164, but twice thickness.

Date	Mintage	VG	F	VF	XF	Unc
1648 Unique	5	—	—	—	—	—

KM# 167 5 DUCAT

17.4520 g., 0.9790 Gold 0.5493 oz. AGW **Obv:** Laurreate head of Frederik III right, date below **Rev:** Vase with incense **Note:** Klippe. Size as 2 Ducat, KM#164. Planchet 2-1/2 times thickness.

Date	Mintage	VG	F	VF	XF	Unc
1648 Unique	5	—	—	—	—	—

TRADE COINAGE

Danish East India Co.

D.O.C. - Dansk Ostindisk Compagni

Originally formed in 1616 to develop trade and colonization in Asia and the East Indies under the protection of Christian IV. It was dissolved in 1634 and later reorganized in 1670 lasting until 1729 when it was closed due to its debts.

A few years later the company reorganized under the name, Danish Asiatic Company - D.A.C. Coins bearing these initials can be found listed under Tranquebar.

KM# 117 PIASTRE

27.1910 g., 0.9160 Silver 0.8007 oz. ASW **Obv:** Shield of arms on cross **Rev:** • R • F • P • above crown, date below

Date	Mintage	VG	F	VF	XF	Unc
1624 7 known	—	—	—	—	—	—

Note: Hoiland sale, 5-2006 realized $60,000.

KM# 317 SPECIEDALER

28.8930 g., 0.8750 Silver 0.8128 oz. ASW **Obv:** Armored bust with knot at shoulder, six laurel leaves **Rev:** Crowned C5 over crowned DOC monogram **Edge:** Plain **Note:** Dav. #409.

Date	Mintage	VG	F	VF	XF	Unc
1671 GK	—	—	4,000	8,000	12,000	—

KM# 318 SPECIEDALER

28.8930 g., 0.8750 Silver 0.8128 oz. ASW **Edge Lettering:** .PIETATE. ET. IUSTITIA. ANNO. MDCLXXI. **Note:** Dav. #409B.

Date	Mintage	VG	F	VF	XF	Unc
MDCLXXI (1671) GK 6 known	—	—	—	8,000	12,000	—

KM# 362 SPECIEDALER

28.8930 g., 0.8750 Silver 0.8128 oz. ASW **Obv:** Armored bust wearing Order of the Elephant **Note:** Dav. #410.

Date	Mintage	VG	F	VF	XF	Unc
1672 GK 10 known	—	—	—	7,500	11,000	—

KM# 319 SPECIEDALER

28.8930 g., 0.8750 Silver 0.8128 oz. ASW **Obv:** Modified armored bust with broach at shoulder, seven laurel leaves **Note:** Dav. #409A.

Date	Mintage	VG	F	VF	XF	Unc
1672 GK 5-6 known	—	—	—	7,500	11,000	—

KM# 363 2 SPECIEDALER

57.5500 g., 0.8750 Silver 1.6189 oz. ASW **Note:** Dav. #408. Similar to 1 Specidaler, KM#317.

Date	Mintage	VG	F	VF	XF	Unc
1671 Rare	—	—	—	—	—	—

PATTERNS

Including off metal strikes

KM#	Date	Mintage	Identification	Mkt Val
Pn1	ND(1606)	—	8 Skilling. Gold. 4.6500 g. off metal strike in gold	—
Pn2	ND	—	Mark. Gold. 10.7500 g. off metal strike in gold	—
PnA2	ND(1610)	—	Portugaloser. Silver. Prev. FR68a.	—
Pn3	ND	—	Mark. Gold. 8.0800 g. off metal strike in gold	—
Pn4	ND	—	1/2 Speciedaler. Gold. 22.6400 g. off metal strike in gold	—
Pn5	1608	—	Sovereign. 10.0000 g.	—
PnA5	1619	—	Hvid. Copper. Crowned C4. Value and date within square border. Prev. Km#64.	—
Pn6	1629	—	Rosenobel. Silver. KM#51.	—
Pn7	1629	—	1/4 Portugaloser. Silver. KM#114	—
Pn8	ND	—	2 Ducat. Silver. KM#327	—
PnA8	1644	—	20 Skilling. Silver.	4,000
PnB8	1644	—	20 Skilling. Silver. Without value.	—
Pn10	1653	—	5 Ducat. Gold. 17.0000 g.	—
Pn11	1653	—	10 Ducat. Gold. 34.0000 g.	—
Pn13	1655	—	5 Ducat. Gold. 17.0000 g. KM#204	—
Pn14	1656	—	5 Ducat. Gold. 17.0000 g. KM#204	—
Pn15	1659	—	Krone. Silver.	3,200
Pn16	1664	—	1/4 Ducat. Silver. KM#235	—
PnA16	1659	—	3 Ducat. Gold. KM#221	—
PnB16	1659	—	3 Ducat. Gold. KM#223	—
PnC16	1659	—	4 Ducat. Gold. KM#221	—
PnD16	1659	—	4 Ducat. Gold. KM#223	—
PnE16	1659	—	6 Ducat. Gold. KM#221	—
PnF16	1659	—	6 Ducat. Gold. KM#223	—
PnG16	1659	—	5 Ducat. Gold. KM#223	—
PnH16	1659	—	10 Ducat. Gold. KM#223	—
PnI16	1659	—	20 Ducat. Gold. KM#223	—
PnJ16	1659	—	5 Ducat. Gold. KM#221	—
Pn17	1665	—	1/2 Ducat. Silver. 1.4700 g.	—
PnA17	1619	—	Hvid. Copper. Like KM#64.	—
Pn18	1669	—	10 Ducat. Silver. KM#314	—
Pn19	ND	—	10 Ducat. Silver. KM#314	—
Pn20	1670	—	Ducat. Silver. KM#313	—
Pn21	1672	—	Ducat. Silver. KM#340	—
Pn22	ND	—	Ducat. Silver. Equestrian figure of Christian V right.	—
Pn23	ND	—	Ducat. Silver. Equestrian figure of Christian V left.	—
Pn24	1673	—	2 Ducat. Silver. KM#346	—
Pn25	ND	—	2 Ducat. Silver. KM#347	—
Pn26	ND	—	Ducat. Silver. KM#445	—
Pn27	ND	—	Ducat. Silver. KM#454	—
Pn28	1683	—	4 Ducat. Silver. KM#453	—
Pn29	1687	—	2 Ducat. Silver. KM#390	—
Pn30	1689	—	Krone. Gold. 34.7000 g.	—
Pn31	1691	—	Ducat. Copper.	—
Pn32	1693	—	Krone. Silver. KM#428.2; Roman numeral date.	—
Pn33	1696	—	Ducat. Silver. KM#433	—
Pn34	1696	—	Ducat. Silver. Equestrian figure of Christian V left.	—
Pn35	ND	—	1/2 Ducat. Silver. KM#454	—
Pn36	ND(1699)	—	Ducat. Silver. KM#456	—
Pn37	ND(1699)	—	3 Ducat. Silver. KM#462	—
Pn38	1699	—	Krone. Gold. 17.0000 g. KM#448	40,000
Pn39	1699	—	Krone. Gold. 34.0000 g. KM#448	—
Pn40	1700	—	Krone. Gold. 17.0000 g. KM#448	—
Pn41	1700	—	Ducat. Silver. KM#471	—

GLUCKSTADT

DUCHY

WIRE MONEY COINAGE

Authorized by Christian IV in 1619, the denning was to be used for trade in the Petsori River region of Russia by the Petsori Company. Fashioned after Russian silver wire-kopeks, dennings may have been considered counterfeits.

KM# 5.1 DENNING

0.8880 Silver **Ruler:** Christian IV **Obv:** King on horseback, M below **Rev:** Titles of czar Mikhail Fjodorovitsj Romanov **Note:** Weight varies: .470-.510 grams. Actual silver weight varies: .0134-.0146.

Date	Mintage	Good	VG	F	VF	XF
ND(1619) Rare	—	—	—	—	—	—

KM# 5.2 DENNING

0.8880 Silver **Ruler:** Christian IV **Obv:** HCPI below horse **Note:** Weight varies: .470-.510 grams. Actual silver weight varies: .0134-.0146.

Date	Mintage	Good	VG	F	VF	XF
ND(c.1620) Rare	—	—	—	—	—	—

KM# 5.3 DENNING

0.8880 Silver **Ruler:** Christian IV **Rev:** Titles of czar Vasilij Ivanovitsj Shuskij **Note:** Weight varies: .470-.510 grams. Actual silver weight varies: .0134-.0146.

Date	Mintage	Good	VG	F	VF	XF
ND(c.1620) Rare	—	—	—	—	—	—

KM# 5.4 DENNING

0.8880 Silver **Ruler:** Christian IV **Rev:** Titles of czar Boris Fjodorovitsj Gudonov **Note:** Weight varies: .470-.510 grams. Actual silver weight varies: .0134-.0146.

Date	Mintage	Good	VG	F	VF	XF
ND(c.1620) Rare	—	—	—	—	—	—

KM# 5.5 DENNING

0.8880 Silver **Ruler:** Christian IV **Rev:** Titles of (imposter) czar Dimitri Ivanovitsj **Note:** Weight varies: .470-.510 grams. Actual silver weight varies: .0134-.0146.

Date	Mintage	Good	VG	F	VF	XF
ND(c.1620) Rare	—	—	—	—	—	—

KM# 6.1 DENNING

0.8880 Silver **Ruler:** Christian IV **Obv:** King on horseback, M below **Rev:** Titles of Christian IV in German **Note:** Weight varies: .470-.510 grams. Actual silver weight varies: .0134-.0146.

Date	Mintage	Good	VG	F	VF	XF
ND(c.1620) Rare	—	—	—	—	—	—

KM# 6.2 DENNING

0.8880 Silver **Ruler:** Christian IV **Obv:** Without M below horse **Note:** Weight varies: .470-.510 grams. Actual silver weight varies: .0134-.0146.

Date	Mintage	Good	VG	F	VF	XF
ND(c.1620) Rare	—	—	—	—	—	—

KM# 7 DENNING
0.8880 Silver **Ruler:** Christian IV **Obv:** King on horseback, M below **Rev:** Titles of Christian IV in Russian **Note:** Weight varies: .470-.510 grams. Actual silver weight varies: .0134-.0146.

Date	Mintage	Good	VG	F	VF	XF
ND(c.1620) Rare	—	—	—	—	—	—

KM# 8.1 2 SKILLING LYBSK (4 Skilling Dansk)
1.0080 g., 0.8880 Silver 0.0288 oz. ASW **Ruler:** Christian IV **Obv:** King on galloping horse right, open crown; value below: IISL **Rev:** Six-line inscription **Note:** Wire money.

Date	Mintage	Good	VG	F	VF	XF
ND(1620-23)	—	50.00	100	250	575	—

KM# 8.2 2 SKILLING LYBSK (4 Skilling Dansk)
1.0080 g., 0.8880 Silver 0.0288 oz. ASW **Ruler:** Christian IV **Obv:** Value as: 2SL **Note:** Wire money.

Date	Mintage	Good	VG	F	VF	XF
ND(1620-23)	—	32.50	65.00	150	300	—

KM# 8.3 2 SKILLING LYBSK (4 Skilling Dansk)
1.0080 g., 0.8880 Silver 0.0288 oz. ASW **Ruler:** Christian IV **Obv:** King on jumping horse, value as 2SL • **Note:** Wire money.

Date	Mintage	Good	VG	F	VF	XF
ND(1620-23)	—	30.00	60.00	140	340	—

KM# 8.4 2 SKILLING LYBSK (4 Skilling Dansk)
1.0080 g., 0.8880 Silver 0.0288 oz. ASW **Ruler:** Christian IV **Obv:** Value: • 2SL **Note:** Wire money.

Date	Mintage	Good	VG	F	VF	XF
ND(1620-23)	—	80.00	140	340	—	—

KM# 8.5 2 SKILLING LYBSK (4 Skilling Dansk)
1.0080 g., 0.8880 Silver 0.0288 oz. ASW **Ruler:** Christian IV **Obv:** King on horseback right, no crown, value as 2SL: **Note:** Wire money.

Date	Mintage	Good	VG	F	VF	XF
ND(1620-23)	—	45.00	90.00	270	—	—

KM# 8.6 2 SKILLING LYBSK (4 Skilling Dansk)
1.0080 g., 0.8880 Silver 0.0288 oz. ASW **Ruler:** Christian IV **Obv:** Value: ZSL **Note:** Wire money.

Date	Mintage	Good	VG	F	VF	XF
ND(1624-30)	—	20.00	40.00	80.00	220	—

KM# 9.1 4 SKILLING LYBSK
2.0160 g., 0.8880 Silver 0.0576 oz. ASW **Ruler:** Christian IV **Obv:** King on horseback right, open crown, value below as: 4 SL: **Rev:** Six-line inscription **Note:** Wire money.

Date	Mintage	Good	VG	F	VF	XF
ND(1620-23)	—	75.00	150	350	—	—

KM# 9.2 4 SKILLING LYBSK
2.0160 g., 0.8880 Silver 0.0576 oz. ASW **Ruler:** Christian IV **Obv:** King on horseback, closed crown, value 4 SL **Note:** Wire money.

Date	Mintage	Good	VG	F	VF	XF
ND(1624-30)	—	35.00	65.00	175	425	—

STANDARD COINAGE

KM# 10 SøSLING LYBSK
0.0630 g., 0.3310 Silver 0.0007 oz. ASW **Ruler:** Christian IV **Obv:** Crowned C4 monogram **Rev:** Value in four lines

Date	Mintage	Good	VG	F	VF	XF
(16)Z3	—	45.00	90.00	180	350	—
(16)Z4	—	15.00	30.00	60.00	120	—
(16)Z5	—	20.00	45.00	70.00	130	—
ND	—	90.00	150	300	550	—

KM# 25 SøSLING LYBSK
0.7040 g., 0.3120 Silver 0.0071 oz. ASW **Ruler:** Christian IV **Obv:** Crowned C4 monogram, titles of Christian IV in legend **Rev:** Value in three lines, legend, date **Rev. Legend:** G: DAN: N: V: G: Q: REX:

Date	Mintage	Good	VG	F	VF	XF
1640(p) SOESLIN	—	80.00	250	500	900	—
1641(p) SOESLIN	—	200	400	700	1,100	—
1641(p) SECHSLIN	—	50.00	100	275	550	—
1642(p) SECHSLIN	—	50.00	100	275	550	—
1643(p) SOESLIN	—	80.00	250	550	900	—
1643(p) SECHSLIN	—	50.00	100	275	550	—
1644(q) SOESLIN	—	45.00	50.00	240	480	—
1645(q) SOESLIN	—	50.00	90.00	240	480	—
1646(q) SOESLIN	—	40.00	80.00	220	440	—
1647(q) SOESLIN	—	40.00	80.00	220	440	—
1647(q) SECHSLIN	—	—	—	—	—	—
1648(q) SOESLIN; Unique	—	—	—	—	—	—

KM# 41 SøSLING LYBSK
0.7040 g., 0.3120 Silver 0.0071 oz. ASW **Ruler:** Frederik III **Obv:** Crowned F3 monogram, titles of Frederic III in legend

Date	Mintage	Good	VG	F	VF	XF
1658(q)	—	35.00	70.00	180	400	—
1659(q)	—	30.00	60.00	140	350	—
1660(q)	—	27.50	22.00	120	335	—

KM# 81 SKILLING DANSKE (Sosling Libsk)
0.6830 g., 0.3050 Silver 0.0067 oz. ASW **Ruler:** Christian V **Obv:** Crowned F5 monogram divides date **Rev:** Value in three lines: I/SKILLING/DANSKE

Date	Mintage	Good	VG	F	VF	XF
1694(q)	—	90.00	180	360	750	—

KM# 19 2 SKILLING DANSKE (Skilling Lybsk)
1.2990 g., 0.2800 Silver 0.0117 oz. ASW **Ruler:** Christian IV **Obv:** Crowned shield, titles of Christian IV in legend **Rev:** Value in four lines: II/SKILI/NG DA/NS:, date in legend

Date	Mintage	Good	VG	F	VF	XF
1627	—	275	475	1,000	1,750	—

KM# 71 2 SKILLING DANSKE (Skilling Lybsk)
1.2990 g., 0.2800 Silver 0.0117 oz. ASW **Obv:** Titles of Christian V in legend

Date	Mintage	Good	VG	F	VF	XF
1681(q)	—	25.00	55.00	100	240	—

KM# 78 2 SKILLING DANSKE (Skilling Lybsk)
1.2240 g., 0.3430 Silver 0.0135 oz. ASW **Obv:** Crowned C5 monogram divides date **Rev:** Value in three lines: II/ SKILLING/ DANSKE

Date	Mintage	Good	VG	F	VF	XF
1693	—	12.50	25.00	60.00	140	—
1694	—	9.00	20.00	50.00	110	—

KM# 79 4 SKILLING DANSKE (2 Skilling Lybsk)
1.9510 g., 0.4370 Silver 0.0274 oz. ASW **Obv:** Crowned C5 monogram divides date **Rev:** Crowned, ornamented oval arms, value in legend: IIII • SKILLING • DANSKE •

Date	Mintage	Good	VG	F	VF	XF
1693	—	6.00	12.00	30.00	80.00	—
1694	—	9.00	18.00	37.50	110	—

KM# 82.1 8 SKILLING DANSKE (4 Skilling Lybsk)
3.0570 g., 0.5620 Silver 0.0552 oz. ASW **Obv:** Crowned C5 monogram, legend reads counterclockwise from top **Obv. Legend:** PIETATE IVSTITIA **Rev:** Value in three lines: VIII/ SKILLING/ DANSKE, date below

Date	Mintage	Good	VG	F	VF	XF
1694	—	100	200	325	500	—

KM# 82.2 8 SKILLING DANSKE (4 Skilling Lybsk)
3.0570 g., 0.5620 Silver 0.0552 oz. ASW **Obv:** Legend reads clockwise from top **Obv. Legend:** PIETATE IVSTITIA

Date	Mintage	Good	VG	F	VF	XF
1694	—	8.00	20.00	50.00	100	—
1695	—	8.00	20.00	50.00	100	—
1697	—	25.00	55.00	100	210	—

KM# 31 3 SKILLING LYBSK
1.7850 g., 0.8120 Silver 0.0466 oz. ASW **Ruler:** Christian IV **Rev:** III/SCHIL/LING/L:G in circle

Date	Mintage	Good	VG	F	VF	XF
1644(q)	—	25.00	50.00	110	260	—

KM# 18 6 SKILLING LYBSK
2.9230 g., 0.8880 Silver 0.0834 oz. ASW **Ruler:** Christian IV **Obv:** Crowned C4 monogram **Rev:** Value, date

Date	Mintage	Good	VG	F	VF	XF
1625	—	200	425	775	1,500	—

KM# 30.1 8 SKILLING LYBSK (Mark Dansk)
4.8720 g., 0.8120 Silver 0.1272 oz. ASW **Ruler:** Christian IV **Obv:** Crowned bust right, curved shield below **Rev:** Fortuna standing on globe with banner divides date

Date	Mintage	Good	VG	F	VF	XF
1641 (p)	—	130	275	650	1,250	—
1642 (p)	—	140	300	700	1,350	—
1645 (q)	—	900	1,400	2,250	3,500	—

KM# 30.2 8 SKILLING LYBSK (Mark Dansk)
4.8720 g., 0.8120 Silver 0.1272 oz. ASW **Ruler:** Christian IV **Obv:** Shield with flat top and straight sides

Date	Mintage	Good	VG	F	VF	XF
1642	—	125	225	600	950	—

KM# A4 MARK DANSKE (8 Skilling Lybsk)
8.3520 g., 0.5900 Silver 0.1584 oz. ASW **Obv:** 1/2 figure of Christian IV right, date in legend **Rev:** Value: • I • /MARCK/ DANSKE above shield in inner circle

Date	Mintage	Good	VG	F	VF	XF
1617 Rare	—	—	—	—	—	—
1627	—	200	350	550	1,100	—
1628	—	180	325	525	900	—
1629	—	250	550	900	1,400	—

KM# 32 2 MARK DANSKE
11.1360 g., 0.5930 Silver 0.2123 oz. ASW **Ruler:** Christian IV **Obv:** Crowned C4 monogram **Rev:** Three-line Hebrew inscription

Date	Mintage	Good	VG	F	VF	XF
1645(q)	—	100	200	380	600	—

KM# 65 2 MARK DANSKE
11.1360 g., 0.6710 Silver 0.2402 oz. ASW **Ruler:** Christian V **Obv:** Crowned C5 monogram **Rev:** Crowned shield on cross, value and date in outer legend

Date	Mintage	Good	VG	F	VF	XF
1679(q)	—	200	300,450	425	750	—
1680(q)	—	300	550	800	1,200	—
1681(q)	—	190	325	600	900	—
1682(q)	—	190	325	600	900	—

KM# 80.1 2 MARK DANSKE
11.1360 g., 0.6710 Silver 0.2402 oz. ASW **Ruler:** Christian V **Obv:** Crowned double C5 monogram in palm leaves **Rev:** Crowned, ornamented oval shield on cross divides date below, value: II • MARCK • DANSKE in legend

Date	Mintage	Good	VG	F	VF	XF
1693CW	—	90.00	150	300	550	—
1694CW	—	120	220	400	800	—

KM# 80.2 2 MARK DANSKE
11.1360 g., 0.6710 Silver 0.2402 oz. ASW **Ruler:** Christian V **Obv:** Smaller monogram with laurel branches

Date	Mintage	Good	VG	F	VF	XF
1694CW	—	80.00	160	290	620	—
1696CW	—	110	190	375	775	—

KM# A43 4 MARK DANSKE (Krone)
Silver **Ruler:** Frederik III **Obv:** Crowned F3 monogram **Rev:** Crowned arms divide date

Date	Mintage	Good	VG	F	VF	XF
1659IW Rare	—	—	—	—	—	—
1660IW	—	85.00	150	275	500	—

KM# B43 4 MARK DANSKE (Krone)
Silver **Ruler:** Frederik III **Obv:** Crowned F 3 monogram **Rev:** Crowned arms, date in legend

Date	Mintage	Good	VG	F	VF	XF
1659IW	—	50.00	100	170	260	—
1660IW	—	60.00	115	190	285	—

KM# 63 4 MARK DANSKE (Krone)
22.2720 g., 0.6710 Silver 0.4805 oz. ASW **Ruler:** Christian V **Obv:** Crowned C5 monogram, king's motto in legend **Rev:** Crowned shield on cross, date and value in legend **Note:** Dav. #3678.

Date	Mintage	Good	VG	F	VF	XF
1671	—	75.00	125	250	550	—
1672	—	65.00	110	220	475	—
1673	—	45.00	90.00	180	380	—
1677	—	70.00	120	240	525	—
1679	—	65.00	110	220	475	—
1680	—	75.00	125	250	550	—
1681	—	75.00	125	250	550	—
1682	—	65.00	110	220	475	—

KM# 77.1 4 MARK DANSKE (Krone)
22.2720 g., 0.6710 Silver 0.4805 oz. ASW **Ruler:** Christian V **Obv:** Crowned double C5 monogram in palm leaves **Rev:** Crowned, ornamented oval shield on cross with Order of the Elephant sash, value and date in legend **Note:** Dav. #3679.

Date	Mintage	Good	VG	F	VF	XF
1692	—	70.00	140	275	550	—
1693	—	65.00	110	220	475	—
1694	—	65.00	110	220	475	—

KM# 77.2 4 MARK DANSKE (Krone)
22.2720 g., 0.6710 Silver 0.4805 oz. ASW **Ruler:** Christian V **Rev:** Crowned, ornamented oval shield on cross with Order of the Elephant sash, date below shield

Date	Mintage	Good	VG	F	VF	XF
1693	—	60.00	120	270	500	—

KM# 80 4 MARK DANSKE (Krone)
22.2720 g., 0.6710 Silver 0.4805 oz. ASW **Ruler:** Christian V **Obv:** Crowned double C5 monogram in laurel branches **Rev:** Crowned, cartouched, oval shield on cross with Order of the Elephant, value and date in legend **Note:** Dav. #3680.

Date	Mintage	Good	VG	F	VF	XF
1694	—	90.00	160	300	550	—
1695	—	95.00	170	320	595	—
1696	—	90.00	150	280	525	—

KM# 11 1/16 SPECIEDALER (3 Skilling Lybsk)

1.4610 g., 0.8880 Silver 0.0417 oz. ASW **Ruler:** Christian IV **Obv:** Crowned C4 monogram, 16 in cartouche **Rev:** Fortuna standing on globe, holding banner

Date	Mintage	Good	VG	F	VF	XF
ND	—	50.00	100	200	4,000	—
1623	—	22.50	45.00	90.00	180	—
1624	—	25.00	50.00	100	200	—
1625	—	25.00	50.00	100	200	—

KM# 26 1/16 SPECIEDALER (3 Skilling Lybsk)

1.7850 g., 0.8120 Silver 0.0466 oz. ASW **Ruler:** Christian IV **Obv:** Crowned bust right **Rev:** Value within legend **Rev. Legend:** MON NOV GLUCKST (1641-47);DAN.NO. V. G. Q. REX (1640-41) **Note:** Varieties exist.

Date	Mintage	Good	VG	F	VF	XF
1640(p) Legend A	—	45.00	95.00	220	440	—
1641(q) Legend A	—	42.50	90.00	210	425	—
1641(p) Legend B	—	25.00	50.00	100	220	—
1642(p) Legend B	—	25.00	50.00	100	220	—
1643(q) Legend B	—	20.00	35.00	60.00	180	—
1645(q) Legend B	—	25.00	50.00	80.00	200	—
1646(q) Legend B	—	22.50	55.00	90.00	220	—
1647(q) Legend B	—	30.00	60.00	140	380	—

KM# 42.1 1/16 SPECIEDALER (3 Skilling Lybsk)

1.7850 g., 0.8120 Silver 0.0466 oz. ASW **Ruler:** Frederik III **Obv:** Elongated crowned bust right of Frederick III **Obv. Legend:** FRIDERIC • 3...

Date	Mintage	Good	VG	F	VF	XF
1658	—	25.00	50.00	100	280	—
1659	—	20.00	40.00	85.00	240	—

KM# 42.2 1/16 SPECIEDALER (3 Skilling Lybsk)

1.7850 g., 0.8120 Silver 0.0466 oz. ASW **Ruler:** Frederik III **Obv:** Wide bust, crown suspended above head

Date	Mintage	Good	VG	F	VF	XF
1658	—	25.00	55.00	120	300	—

KM# 42.3 1/16 SPECIEDALER (3 Skilling Lybsk)

1.7850 g., 0.8120 Silver 0.0466 oz. ASW **Ruler:** Frederik III **Obv:** Small bust, crown on head

Date	Mintage	Good	VG	F	VF	XF
1658	—	40.00	80.00	160	375	—

KM# 42.4 1/16 SPECIEDALER (3 Skilling Lybsk)

1.7850 g., 0.8120 Silver 0.0466 oz. ASW **Ruler:** Frederik III **Obv:** Large bust **Obv. Legend:** FRIDERIC • III •...

Date	Mintage	Good	VG	F	VF	XF
1660 Rare	—	—	—	—	—	—

KM# 54.1 1/16 SPECIEDALER (3 Skilling Lybsk)

1.7850 g., 0.8120 Silver 0.0466 oz. ASW **Obv:** Realistic crowned bust right **Rev:** Value: XVI/ E • REIC/ HS • THA

Date	Mintage	Good	VG	F	VF	XF
1665	—	15.00	32.50	62.50	150	—
1666	—	10.00	20.00	40.00	85.00	—
1667	—	17.50	40.00	100	250	—
1669 Rare	—	—	—	—	—	—

KM# 54.2 1/16 SPECIEDALER (3 Skilling Lybsk)

1.7850 g., 0.8120 Silver 0.0466 oz. ASW **Rev:** Value: • XVI/ • E: REIC/HS • DAL

Date	Mintage	Good	VG	F	VF	XF
1665	—	12.50	25.00	40.00	140	—

KM# 57 1/16 SPECIEDALER (3 Skilling Lybsk)

1.7850 g., 0.8120 Silver 0.0466 oz. ASW **Ruler:** Frederik III **Obv:** Armored bust of Frederic III **Rev:** Date in center legend

Date	Mintage	Good	VG	F	VF	XF
1667	—	10.00	20.00	40.00	110	—
1668	—	10.00	20.00	40.00	110	—
1669	—	15.00	27.50	55.00	140	—
1670	—	125	250	450	700	—

KM# 69 1/16 SPECIEDALER (3 Skilling Lybsk)

1.7850 g., 0.8120 Silver 0.0466 oz. ASW **Ruler:** Christian V **Obv:** Crowned bust of Christian right

Date	Mintage	Good	VG	F	VF	XF
1680	—	1,000	1,500	2,000	4,000	—

KM# 12 1/8 SPECIEDALER

Silver **Ruler:** Christian IV **Obv:** Crowned C4 monogram **Rev:** Fortuna standing on globe, holding banner

Date	Mintage	Good	VG	F	VF	XF
1623 Rare	—	—	—	—	—	—

KM# 55 1/8 SPECIEDALER

3.5700 g., 0.8120 Silver 0.0932 oz. ASW **Obv:** Crowned bust right **Rev:** Value: • VIII • / EINEN / REICHS / DALER • in inner circle, date below

Date	Mintage	Good	VG	F	VF	XF
1665	—	200	475	110	2,800	—

KM# 13 1/4 SPECIEDALER

Silver **Ruler:** Christian IV **Obv:** Crowned C4 monogram **Rev:** Fortuna standing on globe, holding banner

Date	Mintage	Good	VG	F	VF	XF
1623	—	1,000	1,600	3,000	5,000	—

KM# 33 1/4 SPECIEDALER

Silver **Ruler:** Christian IV **Obv:** Crowned bust right above square-topped shield **Rev:** Fortuna

Date	Mintage	Good	VG	F	VF	XF
1645	—	1,750	3,000	5,000	7,000	—

KM# 14 1/2 SPECIEDALER

0.8880 Silver **Ruler:** Christian IV **Obv:** Standing Fortuna right behind crowned shield **Rev:** Fortuna standing on globe, holding banner

Date	Mintage	Good	VG	F	VF	XF
(1)6Z3	—	500	1,000	2,000	4,250	—
(1)6Z5	—	1,500	2,500	4,500	6,500	—
(16)Z7 Unique	—	—	—	—	—	—

KM# 34 1/2 SPECIEDALER

0.8880 Silver **Ruler:** Christian IV **Obv:** Crowned bust right above square-topped shield

Date	Mintage	Good	VG	F	VF	XF
1645 IS	—	1,250	2,250	4,000	6,000	—
1646 IS	—	2,000	3,000	4,500	7,000	—

KM# 15 SPECIEDALER

Silver **Ruler:** Christian IV **Obv:** Lions in shield face right **Note:** Dav. #3668. Legend varieties exist.

Date	Mintage	Good	VG	F	VF	XF
16Z3	—	450	900	1,800	3,600	—
16Z4	—	500	900	1,800	3,600	—
16Z5	—	500	1,000	2,000	4,000	—
16Z7 Rare	—	—	—	—	—	—

KM# 20 SPECIEDALER

Silver **Ruler:** Christian IV **Obv:** Lions in shield face left **Note:** Dav. #3668D.

Date	Mintage	Good	VG	F	VF	XF
16Z9 Rare	—	—	—	—	—	—
1630 Unique	—	—	—	—	—	—

KM# 27 SPECIEDALER

Silver **Ruler:** Christian IV **Obv:** Crowned bust of King above Danish arms **Rev:** Fortuna with banner at left **Note:** Dav. #3670.

Date	Mintage	VG	F	VF	XF	Unc
1640(p) IS	—	1,500	3,000	6,000	10,000	—
1641(p) IS	—	1,750	3,500	7,000	11,000	—
1642(p) IS	—	1,500	3,000	6,000	10,000	—
1644(q) IS Rare	—	—	—	—	—	—
1645(q) IS	—	1,500	3,000	5,500	9,000	—
1646(q) IS	—	1,000	1,900	4,750	7,000	—
1647(q) IS	—	1,500	3,000	6,000	10,000	—
1648(q) IS Unique	—	—	—	—	—	—

KM# 43.1 SPECIEDALER

Silver **Ruler:** Frederik III **Obv:** King's bust divides legend at top **Rev:** Fortuna in laurel wreath **Note:** Dav. #3671. Prev. KM#43.

Date	Mintage	VG	F	VF	XF	Unc
1659 Unique	—	—	—	—	—	—

KM# 44 SPECIEDALER

Silver **Ruler:** Frederik III **Obv:** Inner circle unbroken **Rev:** Inner circle unbroken **Note:** Dav. #3672.

Date	Mintage	VG	F	VF	XF	Unc
1659 Unique	—	—	—	—	—	—

KM# 43.2 SPECIEDALER

Silver **Ruler:** Frederik III **Obv:** Inner circle unbroken **Rev:** Fortuna in laurel wreath **Note:** Dav. #3672a. Prev. KM#45.

Date	Mintage	VG	F	VF	XF	Unc
1659 Unique	—	—	—	—	—	—

KM# 51 SPECIEDALER

Silver **Ruler:** Frederik III **Obv:** Inner circle broken above and below **Rev:** Fortuna in laurel wreath **Note:** Dav. #3673.

Date	Mintage	VG	F	VF	XF	Unc
1664	—	3,750	6,250	9,500	—	—
1666 Rare	—	—	—	—	—	—

KM# 74.1 SPECIEDALER

Silver **Ruler:** Christian V **Obv:** Standing Christian V with scepter and globe **Rev:** Crowned double C5 monogram **Note:** Dav. #3676.

Date	Mintage	VG	F	VF	XF	Unc
ND(1682) Unique	—	—	—	—	—	—

KM# 74.2 SPECIEDALER

Silver **Ruler:** Christian V **Edge:** With inscription

Date	Mintage	VG	F	VF	XF	Unc
ND(1682)	—	2,000	4,000	8,000	12,000	—

KM# 73 SPECIEDALER

Silver **Ruler:** Christian V **Obv:** Bust of Christian V right **Rev:** Three crowned C5 monograms **Edge Lettering:** PIETATE-ET-JUSTITIA-ANNO-MDCLXXXIII - CW **Note:** Dav. #3677.

Date	Mintage	VG	F	VF	XF	Unc
MDCLXXXIII (1683)	—	3,000	6,000	10,000	15,000	—

KM# 16 2 SPECIEDALER

Silver **Ruler:** Christian IV **Note:** Similar to 1 Thaler, KM#15. Dav. #3667. Planchet is twice as thick.

Date	Mintage	Good	VG	F	VF	XF
1623	—	3,500	6,000	10,000	15,000	—

KM# 28 2 SPECIEDALER

Silver **Ruler:** Christian IV **Obv:** Crowned bust of King above Danish arms **Rev:** Fortuna with banner at left **Note:** Dav. #3669. Planchet is twice as thick.

Date	Mintage	Good	VG	F	VF	XF
1640 Rare	—	—	—	—	—	—
1641	—	2,000	3,500	5,000	8,000	—

KM# 17 3 SPECIEDALER

Silver **Ruler:** Christian IV **Note:** Similar to 1 Thaler, KM#15. Dav. #A3667. Planchet three times as thick.

Date	Mintage	Good	VG	F	VF	XF
1623 Unique	—	—	—	—	—	—

KM# 35 1/2 DUCAT

1.7450 g., 0.9790 Gold 0.0549 oz. AGW **Ruler:** Christian IV **Obv:** Christian IV standing right in inner circle **Rev:** Three-line inscription (one in Hebrew) above date

Date	Mintage	VG	F	VF	XF	Unc
1645 (q) Rare	—	—	—	—	—	—
1646 (q) Rare	—	—	—	—	—	—

KM# 29 DUCAT

3.5000 g., 0.9860 Gold 0.1109 oz. AGW **Ruler:** Christian IV **Obv:** Christian IV standing with scepter and orb **Rev:** Four-line inscription in tablet, date below

Date	Mintage	VG	F	VF	XF	Unc
1640(p) Rare	—	—	—	—	—	—
1642(p) Unique	2,341	—	—	—	—	—
1646(q) IS	—	8,000	12,000	19,000	—	—

KM# 36 DUCAT

3.5000 g., 0.9860 Gold 0.1109 oz. AGW **Ruler:** Christian IV **Rev:** Three-line inscription (one in Hebrew) above date

Date	Mintage	VG	F	VF	XF	Unc
1645(q)	—	3,000	5,000	8,000	—	—
1645(q) Note: "4" between feet	—	—	—	—	—	—
1646(q) Unique	—	—	—	—	—	—

KM# 50 DUCAT

3.5000 g., 0.9860 Gold 0.1109 oz. AGW **Ruler:** Frederik III **Obv:** Laureate head of Frederik III right, date below head in inner circle **Rev:** Figure of fortune in branches

Date	Mintage	VG	F	VF	XF	Unc
1660 IS Rare	—	—	—	—	—	—

KM# 52 DUCAT

3.5000 g., 0.9860 Gold 0.1109 oz. AGW **Obv:** Crowned head of Frederic III right in inner circle **Rev:** Figure of fortune in branches, date in legend

Date	Mintage	VG	F	VF	XF	Unc
1664 Unique	—	—	—	—	—	—

KM# 56 DUCAT
3.5000 g., 0.9860 Gold 0.1109 oz. AGW **Obv:** Crowned head of Frederic III right in inner circle **Rev:** Date at bottom

Date	Mintage	VG	F	VF	XF	Unc
1666(q) IW	—	2,000	3,000	6,000	12,000	—
1667(q) IW	—	2,600	4,500	7,000	13,000	—
1668(q) IW	—	3,250	5,500	8,000	14,000	—
1669(q) IW	—	2,600	4,500	7,000	13,000	—

KM# 64.1 DUCAT
3.5000 g., 0.9860 Gold 0.1109 oz. AGW **Obv:** Crowned bust of Christian V right, legend begins at lower left **Rev:** Three crowned C5 monograms entwined

Date	Mintage	VG	F	VF	XF	Unc
1672IW	—	1,250	2,400	3,250	5,000	—
1673IW	—	1,250	2,400	3,250	5,000	—
1674IW	—	1,000	2,000	2,800	4,000	—
1676IW	—	1,100	2,200	3,000	4,500	—

KM# 64.2 DUCAT
3.5000 g., 0.9860 Gold 0.1109 oz. AGW **Obv:** Legend begins at upper right

Date	Mintage	VG	F	VF	XF	Unc
1672 Rare	—	—	—	—	—	—
1673 Rare	—	—	—	—	—	—

KM# 66 DUCAT
3.5000 g., 0.9860 Gold 0.1109 oz. AGW **Obv:** Laureate bust of Christian V right

Date	Mintage	VG	F	VF	XF	Unc
1679 Rare	—	—	—	—	30,000	—

KM# 70.1 DUCAT
3.5000 g., 0.9860 Gold 0.1109 oz. AGW **Obv:** Smaller, draped bust of Christian V to right

Date	Mintage	VG	F	VF	XF	Unc
1680	—	1,400	2,500	4,000	6,500	—
1685	—	1,800	3,000	4,500	7,000	—

KM# 70.2 DUCAT
3.5000 g., 0.9860 Gold 0.1109 oz. AGW **Obv:** Neck bare on draped bust

Date	Mintage	VG	F	VF	XF	Unc
1680	—	1,400	2,500	4,000	6,500	10,000

KM# 72 DUCAT
3.5000 g., 0.9860 Gold 0.1109 oz. AGW **Obv:** Christian V standing right **Rev:** Figure of Fortuna in branches

Date	Mintage	VG	F	VF	XF	Unc
1682IW	—	2,500	4,500	8,000	12,500	—

KM# 40.1 GOLD KRONE
2.9730 g., 0.9170 Gold 0.0876 oz. AGW **Ruler:** Frederik III **Obv:** Crowned, ornamented oval shield on cross, titles of Frederic III in legend **Rev:** Crown divides date in inner circle, motto: DOMINUS PROVIDEBIT below, legend reads clockwise from lower left

Date	Mintage	VG	F	VF	XF	Unc
1657(q) Rare	—	—	—	—	—	—
1659(q) Rare	—	—	—	—	—	—
1660(q)	—	4,000	7,500	10,000	—	—

KM# 40.2 GOLD KRONE
2.9730 g., 0.9170 Gold 0.0876 oz. AGW **Ruler:** Frederik III **Obv:** Crowned, ornamented oval shield on cross **Rev:** Crown divides date in inner circle, legend reads counterclockwise from upper right

Date	Mintage	VG	F	VF	XF	Unc
1660	—	2,000	5,000	8,000	—	—

PATTERNS

Including off metal strikes

KM#	Date	Mintage	Identification	Mkt Val
Pn1	1623	—	1/2 Speciedaler. Silver. 40 mm. Klippe, square.	—
Pn2	1623	—	Speciedaler. Silver. 47 mm. KM#15, square.	—
Pn3	1623	—	Speciedaler. Silver. 43 mm. KM#15, square.	—
Pn4	1624	—	Speciedaler. Silver. 48 mm. KM#15, square.	—
Pn5	1624	—	Speciedaler. Silver. 45 mm. KM#15, hexagonal.	—
Pn6	1624	—	Speciedaler. Silver. 47mm. KM#15, hexagonal.	—
Pn7	1624	—	Speciedaler. Silver. 48mm. KM#15, octagonal.	—

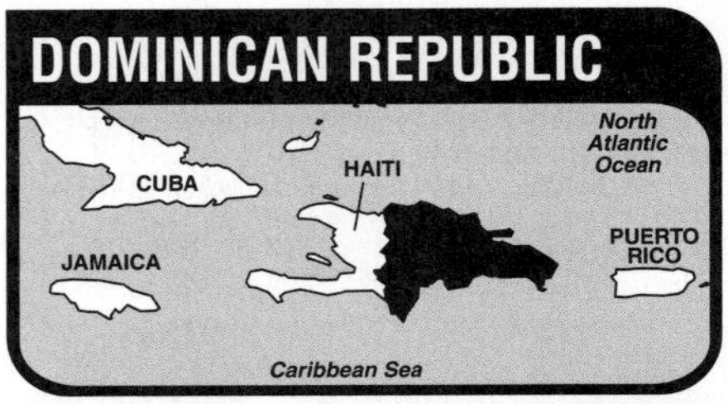

SANTO DOMINGO

(Hispaniola – Española)

The first coinage for circulation in Santo Domingo and other possessions in the New World was ordered by Fernando the Catholic on April 15, 1505 to be acquired from the Seville Mint. A second issue was acquired from the Burgos Mint.

RULERS
Ferdinand II & Elizabeth, 1479-1504
Charles & Johanna, 1516-1556
Philip II, 1556-1598
Philip III, 1598-1621
Philip IV, 1621-1665

MINT MARKS
B – Burgos
B-B – Burgos
S-S – Seville
SDo monogram – Santo Domingo

SPANISH COLONIAL

COUNTERMARKED COINAGE

ca. 1651-52

The debasement of 4 and 8 Reales at the Potosi mint during 1625-1648 led to an investigation and the installation of new mint officials. The coinage that followed during 1649-1651 fell a little short of the required fineness and was recalled and given various countermarks, primarily done at Potosi.

KM# 1 7-1/2 REALES
27.0674 g., 0.8590 Silver 0.7475 oz. ASW **Ruler:** Philip IV **Countermark:** Crowned S*D **Note:** Countermark in beaded circle on Potosi 8 Reales, KM#19.1b.

CM Date	Host Date	Good	VG	F	VF	XF
ND	ND(1649-51) o Rare	—	—	—	—	—

DUTCH GUIANA

Dutch Guiana, located on the north central coast of South America between Guyana and French Guiana has an area of 63,037 sq. mi. (163,270 sq. km.). The country is rich in minerals and forests, and self-sufficient in rice, the staple food crop.

Lieutenants of Amerigo Vespucci sighted the Guiana coast in 1499. Spanish explorers of the 16th century, disappointed at finding no gold, departed leaving the area to be settled by the British in 1652. The colony prospered and the Netherlands acquired it in 1667 in exchange for the Dutch rights in Nieuw Nederland (state of New York).

RULER
Dutch, until 1975

COLONY

TOKEN COINAGE

KM# 1 DUIT
Copper, 20 mm. **Obv:** Parrot on branch with one leaf, "1" above, date below **Rev:** Ornamental tree

Date	Mintage	Good	VG	F	VF	XF
1679	—	—	150	250	400	800

KM# 2 DUIT
Copper, 20 mm. **Obv:** Parrot on branch with one leaf, "1" above, date below **Note:** Uniface.

Date	Mintage	Good	VG	F	VF	XF
1679	—	—	75.00	150	250	400

KM# 3 2 DUIT (Oord)
Copper, 20 mm. **Obv:** Parrot on branch with two leaves, "2" above, date below **Rev:** Ornamental tree

Date	Mintage	Good	VG	F	VF	XF
1679	—	—	150	275	500	1,100

KM# 4 2 DUIT (Oord)
Copper, 20 mm. **Obv:** Parrot on branch with two leaves, "2" above, date below **Rev:** Ornamental tree **Note:** Uniface.

Date	Mintage	Good	VG	F	VF	XF
1679	—	—	100	200	300	600

KM# 5 4 DUIT (1/2 Stuiver)
Copper, 20 mm. **Obv:** Parrot on branch with four leaves, "4" above, date below **Rev:** Ornamental tree

Date	Mintage	Good	VG	F	VF	XF
1679	—	—	150	300	600	1,250

KM# 6 4 DUIT (1/2 Stuiver)
Copper, 20 mm. **Obv:** Parrot on branch with three leaves, "4" above, date below **Rev:** Ornamental tree

Date	Mintage	Good	VG	F	VF	XF
1679	—	—	150	300	550	1,150

KM# 7 4 DUIT (1/2 Stuiver)
Copper, 20 mm. **Obv:** Parrot on branch with three leaves, "4" above, date below **Note:** Uniface.

Date	Mintage	Good	VG	F	VF	XF
1679	—	—	150	250	450	900

KM# 8 4 DUIT (1/2 Stuiver)
Copper, 20 mm. **Obv:** Parrot on branch with four leaves, "4" above, date below **Note:** Uniface.

Date	Mintage	Good	VG	F	VF	XF
1679	—	—	—	700	1,200	2,000

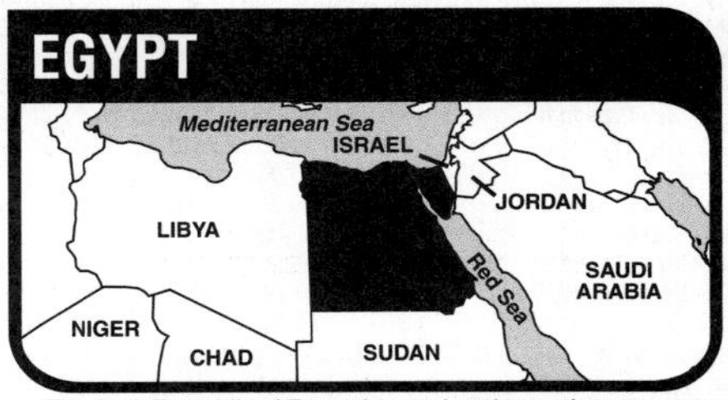

The Arab Republic of Egypt, located on the northeastern corner of Africa, has an area of 385,229 sq. mi. (1,1001,450 sq. km.). Although Egypt is an almost rainless expanse of desert, its economy is predominantly agricultural.

Egyptian history dates back to about 3000 B.C. when the empire was established by uniting the upper and lower kingdoms. Following its 'Golden Age' (16th to 13th centuries B.C.), Egypt was conquered by Persia (525 B.C.) and Alexander the Great (332 B.C.). The Ptolemies, descended from one of Alexander's generals, ruled until the suicide of Cleopatra (30 B.C.) when Egypt became the private domain of the Roman emperor, and subsequently part of the Byzantine world. Various Muslim dynasties ruled Egypt from 641 on, including Ayyubid Sultans to 1250 and Mamluks to 1517. It was then conquered by the Ottoman Turks, interrupted by the occupation of Napoleon (1798-1801). A semi-independent dynasty was founded by Muhammad Ali in 1805 which lasted until 1952

RULER
Ottoman, until 1882

MONETARY SYSTEM
40 Paras = 1 Qirsh (Piastre)

MINT MARKS

Egyptian coins issued prior to the advent of the British Protectorate series of Sultan Hussein Kamil introduced in 1916 were very similar to Turkish coins of the same period. They can best be distinguished by the presence of the Arabic word *Misr* Egypt) on the reverse, which generally appears immediately above the Muslim accession date of the ruler, which is presented in Arabic numerals. Each coin is individually dated according to the regnal years.

INITIAL LETTERS

Letters, symbols and numerals were placed on coins during the reigns of Mustafa II (1695) until Selim III (1789). They have been observed in various positions but the most common position being over *bin* in the third row of the obverse. In Egypt these letters and others used on the Paras (Medins) above the word *duribe* on the reverse during this period.

INITIAL LETTERS, NUMERALS

Alif	ba	ha	ha	dal
ا	ب	ح	ح	د
i	ii	iii	iv	v
ra	sin	sad	(?) sm	ta
ر	س	ص	صم	ط
vi	vii	viii	ix	x
tha	'ain	(hamza)	kaf	mim
ظ	ع	ء	ق	م
xi	xii	xiii	xiv	xv

INITIAL LETTERS, NUMERALS				
noon	noon w/o dot	ha	(?) ra	ah
ن	ں	هو	ر	اح
xvi	xvii	xviii	xix	xx
es	ba	bkr	ha	raa
اس	با	بكر	حا	را
xxi	xxii	xxiii	xxiv	xxv
ragib	sma	msi	'aa	gha
راغب	سا	صسى	عا	غا
xxvi	xxvii	xxviii	xxvix	xxx
'ab	'abd	'ad	'an	md
عب	عبد	عد	عن	مد
xxxi	xxxii	xxxiii	xxxiv	xxxv
mr	mk	mdm	mha	ha
مر	مط	مصر	مها	ده
xxxvi	xxxvii	xxxviii	xxxix	xl
ya	42a	md6	6md	6mdm
يا	١٣٤	٦ملا	٦مد	٦مصر
xli	xlii	xliii	xliv	xlv

OTTOMAN EMPIRE
1595 - 1914AD

Ahmed I
AH1012-1026/1603-1617AD
HAMMERED COINAGE

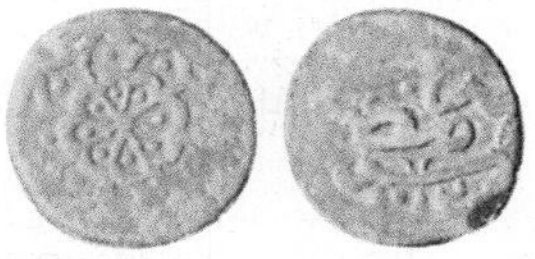

KM# 8 MANGIR
Copper **Mint:** Misr

Date	Mintage	Good	VG	F	VF	XF
AH1012	—	—	—	—	—	—

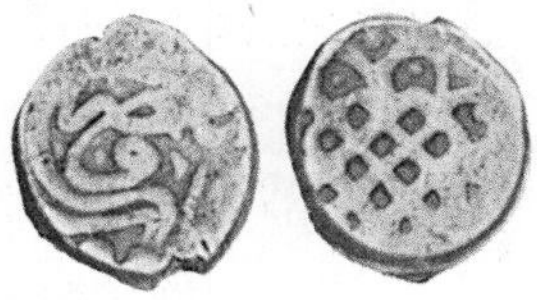

KM# 9 MANGIR
Copper **Mint:** Misr

Date	Mintage	Good	VG	F	VF	XF
AH1012	—	8.00	20.00	30.00	50.00	—
AH1013 Rare	—	—	—	—	—	—

KM# 12 AKCE
0.5000 g., Silver **Mint:** Misr

Date	Mintage	VG	F	VF	XF	Unc
AH1012	—	4.00	10.00	35.00	60.00	—

KM# 15 MEDIN
Silver, 14-17 mm. **Mint:** Misr **Note:** Size varies. Weight varies: 0.83-1.00 grams.

Date	Mintage	VG	F	VF	XF	Unc
AH1012	—	10.00	20.00	30.00	50.00	—

KM# 18 ALTIN
Gold **Mint:** Misr **Note:** Weight varies: 3.45-3.50 grams.

Date	Mintage	VG	F	VF	XF	Unc
AH1012	—	BV	175	275	450	—
AH1013	—	BV	175	275	450	—
AH1014	—	BV	175	275	450	—
AH1015	—	BV	175	275	450	—

Mustafa I
First Reign, AH1026-1027/1617-1618AD
HAMMERED COINAGE

KM# 28 ALTIN
Gold **Obv:** Large legend **Rev:** Large legend **Mint:** Misr **Note:** Weight varies: 3.20-3.45 grams.

Date	Mintage	VG	F	VF	XF	Unc
AH1026	—	750	1,500	3,000	5,000	—

Osman II
AH1027-1031/1618-1622AD
HAMMERED COINAGE

KM# 31 AKCE
Silver **Mint:** Misr **Note:** Weight varies: 0.28-0.36 grams.

Date	Mintage	F	VF	XF	Unc	BU
AH1027	—	25.00	45.00	75.00	—	—

KM# 32 MEDIN
0.9200 g., Silver **Mint:** Misr

Date	Mintage	VG	F	VF	XF	Unc
AH1027	—	15.00	25.00	35.00	60.00	—

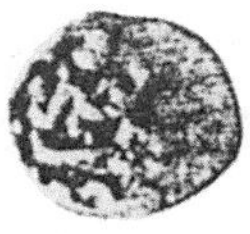

KM# 33 MEDIN
0.9200 g., Silver **Obv:** KM#32 **Rev:** KM#15 **Mint:** Misr **Note:** Weight varies: 0.80-0.98 grams. Mule.

Date	Mintage	VG	F	VF	XF	Unc
AH1012 (sic 1618)	—	15.00	25.00	35.00	60.00	—

KM# 34 ALTIN
3.5000 g., Gold **Mint:** Misr

Date	Mintage	VG	F	VF	XF	Unc
AH1027	—	300	1,000	1,500	2,000	—

Mustafa I
Second Reign, AH1031-1032/1622-1623AD
HAMMERED COINAGE

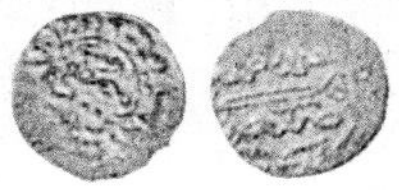

KM# 21 AKCE
0.3200 g., Silver **Mint:** Misr

Date	Mintage	VG	F	VF	XF	Unc
AH1031	—	15.00	25.00	40.00	65.00	—

KM# 26 MEDIN
Silver, 14 mm. **Mint:** Misr **Note:** Weight varies: 0.80-0.96 grams.

Date	Mintage	VG	F	VF	XF	Unc
AH1031	—	20.00	30.00	50.00	80.00	—
AH1032 (sic)	—	—	—	—	—	—

KM# 29 ALTIN
Gold **Obv:** Small legend **Rev:** Small legend **Mint:** Misr **Note:** Weight varies: 3.20-3.45 grams.

Date	Mintage	VG	F	VF	XF	Unc
AH1031	—	400	1,000	2,000	3,000	—

Murad IV
AH1032-49/1623-1640AD
HAMMERED COINAGE

KM# 36 AKCE
0.3500 g., Silver **Mint:** Misr

Date	Mintage	VG	F	VF	XF	Unc
AH1032	—	10.00	20.00	30.00	50.00	—

KM# 38 MEDIN
0.8500 g., Silver **Mint:** Misr

Date	Mintage	VG	F	VF	XF	Unc
AH1031 (sic)	—	—	—	—	—	—
AH1032	—	10.00	20.00	35.00	60.00	—

KM# 40 ALTIN
3.2000 g., Gold **Mint:** Misr

Date	Mintage	VG	F	VF	XF	Unc
AH1032	—	BV	200	400	600	—

Ibrahim
AH1049-1058/1640-1648AD
HAMMERED COINAGE

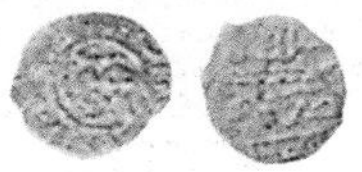

KM# 42 AKCE
Silver **Mint:** Misr **Note:** Weight varies: 0.18-0.32 grams.

Date	Mintage	VG	F	VF	XF	Unc
AH1049	—	15.00	25.00	35.00	55.00	—

KM# 48 ONLUK
2.9800 g., Silver **Mint:** Misr

Date	Mintage	VG	F	VF	XF	Unc
AH1058	—	35.00	80.00	150	250	—

KM# 43 MEDIN
2.9800 g., Silver **Mint:** Misr **Note:** Weight varies: 0.68-0.75 grams.

Date	Mintage	VG	F	VF	XF	Unc
AH1049	—	15.00	25.00	35.00	55.00	—

KM# 44 ALTIN
3.4500 g., Gold **Mint:** Misr

Date	Mintage	VG	F	VF	XF	Unc
AH1049	—	150	250	400	600	—

Mehmed IV
AH1058-1099/1648-1687AD
HAMMERED COINAGE

KM# 46 AKCE
0.3100 g., Silver, 13 mm. **Mint:** Misr

Date	Mintage	VG	F	VF	XF	Unc
AH1058	—	15.00	25.00	40.00	65.00	—

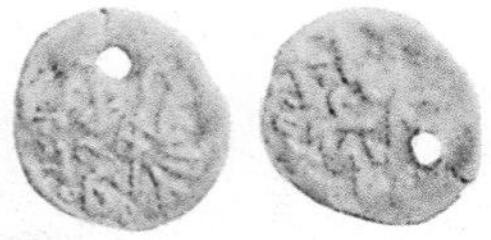

KM# 47 MEDIN
Silver **Mint:** Misr **Note:** Weight varies: 0.58-0.78 grams.

Date	Mintage	VG	F	VF	XF	Unc
AH1058	—	10.00	15.00	25.00	40.00	—

KM# 49 ALTIN
3.5000 g., Gold **Mint:** Misr

Date	Mintage	VG	F	VF	XF	Unc
AH1058	—	BV	175	400	600	—

Suleyman II
AH1099-1102/1687-1691AD
HAMMERED COINAGE

KM# 51 MEDIN
0.6900 g., Silver **Mint:** Misr

Date	Mintage	VG	F	VF	XF	Unc
AH1099	—	—	—	—	—	—

KM# 53 SHERIFI ALTIN
3.4000 g., Gold **Mint:** Misr

Date	Mintage	VG	F	VF	XF	Unc
AH1099	—	BV	180	400	750	—

Ahmed II
AH1102-1106/1691-1695AD
HAMMERED COINAGE

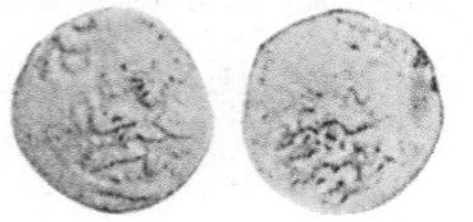

KM# 55 MEDIN
0.5700 g., Silver **Mint:** Misr

Date	Mintage	VG	F	VF	XF	Unc
AH1102	—	15.00	25.00	40.00	75.00	—

KM# 57 SHERIFI ALTIN
3.4000 g., Gold **Mint:** Misr

Date	Mintage	VG	F	VF	XF	Unc
AH1102	—	BV	250	500	800	—

Mustafa II
AH1106-15/1695-1703AD
HAMMERED COINAGE

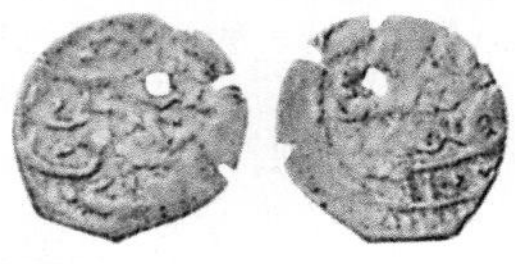

KM# 60 PARA
0.6500 g., Silver **Mint:** Misr

Date	Mintage	VG	F	VF	XF	Unc
AH1106	—	12.00	25.00	40.00	65.00	—

KM# 62 SHERIFI ALTIN
3.2000 g., Gold **Mint:** Misr

Date	Mintage	VG	F	VF	XF	Unc
AH1106	—	BV	250	400	600	—

KM# 63 JEDID ESHREFI ALTIN
3.2500 g., Gold, 17-20 mm. **Obv:** Tughra **Rev:** Mint name **Mint:** Misr **Note:** Size varies.

Date	Mintage	VG	F	VF	XF	Unc
AH1109	—	BV	180	300	500	—

ESTONIA

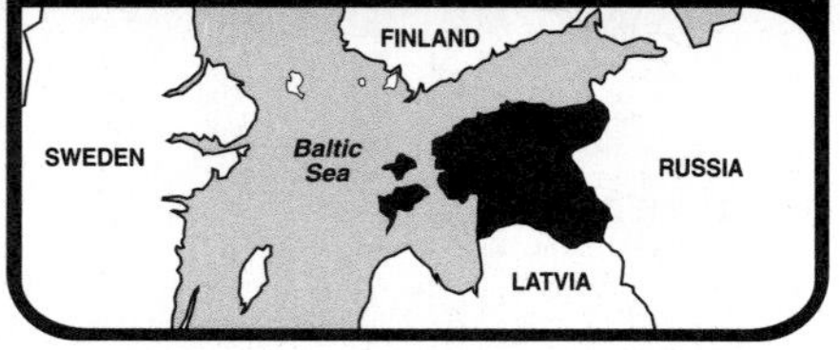

This small and ancient Baltic state had enjoyed but two decades of independence since the 13th century until the present time. After having been conquered by the Danes, the Livonian Knights, the Teutonic Knights of Germany (who reduced the people to serfdom), the Swedes, the Poles and Russia, Estonia declared itself an independent republic on Feb. 24, 1918 but was not freed until Feb. 1919. The peace treaty was signed Feb. 2, 1920. Shortly after the start of World War II, it was again occupied by Russia and incorporated as the 16th state of the U.S.S.R Germany occupied the tiny state from 1941 to 1944, after which it was retaken by Russia. Most of the nations of the world, including the United States and Great Britain, did not recognize Estonia's incorporation into the Soviet Union.

The coinage, issued during the country's brief independence, is obsolete.

NARVA

This city was founded by the Danes in 1223. It was a center for the Livonian knights and a member of the Hanseatic League. Captured by the Swedes in 1581, and then recaptured by the Russians in 1704, it was ceded to them by the Treaty of Nystad in 1721. Narva continues to be an important industrial center.

RULERS
Swedish

MONEYERS' INITIALS

Initial	Date	Name
LN	1670-72	Lewin von Numers

SWEDISH ADMINISTRATION
STANDARD COINAGE

KM# 1 ORE
Silver **Obv:** Crowned CXI monogram in wreath **Rev:** Crowned arms divide date and value, palm branches and script LN below arms

Date	Mintage	VG	F	VF	XF	Unc
1670 LN	—	25.00	45.00	100	220	—
1671 LN	—	20.00	35.00	70.00	170	—

KM# 2.1 ORE
Silver **Rev:** Without palm branches below arms

Date	Mintage	VG	F	VF	XF	Unc
1670	—	35.00	75.00	150	300	—

KM# 2.2 ORE
Silver **Rev:** Script LN below arms

Date	Mintage	VG	F	VF	XF	Unc
1670 LN	—	20.00	32.00	70.00	170	—
1671 LN	—	20.00	32.00	70.00	170	—

KM# 2.3 ORE
Silver **Rev:** Small LN below arms

Date	Mintage	VG	F	VF	XF	Unc
1671 LN	—	17.00	32.00	70.00	170	—

KM# 2.4 ORE
Silver **Rev:** Small LN divided by arms at bottom

Date	Mintage	VG	F	VF	XF	Unc
1671 LN	—	20.00	32.00	70.00	170	—
1672 LN	—	30.00	55.00	120	275	—

KM# 3.1 2 ORE
Silver **Obv:** Crowned CRS monogram in wreath **Rev:** Crowned arms divide date and value, palm branches and script LN below arms

Date	Mintage	VG	F	VF	XF	Unc
1670 LN	—	25.00	45.00	100	220	—
1671 LN	—	25.00	45.00	100	220	—

KM# 3.2 2 ORE
Silver **Rev:** Small LN below arms

Date	Mintage	VG	F	VF	XF	Unc
1670 LN	—	30.00	55.00	120	275	—
1671 LN	—	25.00	45.00	100	220	—

KM# 5.1 2 ORE
Silver **Rev:** Small LN below arms, without palm branches

Date	Mintage	VG	F	VF	XF	Unc
1671 LN	—	40.00	80.00	170	400	—

KM# 5.2 2 ORE
Silver **Rev:** Arms divide LN at bottom

Date	Mintage	VG	F	VF	XF	Unc
1671 LN	—	30.00	60.00	130	300	—

KM# 4.1 4 ORE
Silver **Obv:** Crowned C in inner circle **Rev:** Crowned arms divide value in inner circle, date in legend

Date	Mintage	VG	F	VF	XF	Unc
1670	—	45.00	110	220	475	—
1671 Rare	—	—	—	—	—	—
1672	—	70.00	150	300	700	—

KM# 4.2 4 ORE
Silver **Rev:** Script LN mintmaster's initials in legend below arms

Date	Mintage	VG	F	VF	XF	Unc
1670 LN	—	32.00	70.00	145	325	—
1671 LN	—	32.00	70.00	145	325	—

KM# 4.3 4 ORE
Silver **Rev:** Arms divide value and mintmaster's initials

Date	Mintage	VG	F	VF	XF	Unc
1670 LN	—	55.00	120	240	550	—
1671 LN	—	30.00	60.00	120	275	—
1672 LN	—	55.00	120	240	550	—

KM# 6 4 ORE
Silver **Obv:** Without inner circle

Date	Mintage	VG	F	VF	XF	Unc
1671 LN	—	—	—	—	—	—

KM# 7 4 ORE

Silver **Rev:** Without inner circle, small LN below arms

Date	Mintage	VG	F	VF	XF	Unc
1671 LN	—	30.00	60.00	110	230	—

KM# 8 4 ORE

Silver **Obv:** Without inner circle **Rev:** Arms divide value and mintmaster's initials

Date	Mintage	VG	F	VF	XF	Unc
1671 LN	—	30.00	60.00	110	230	—

KM# 9.1 4 ORE

Silver **Obv:** With inner circle **Rev:** Without outer legend, small LN below arms

Date	Mintage	VG	F	VF	XF	Unc
1671 LN	—	32.00	70.00	145	325	—

KM# 9.2 4 ORE

Silver **Rev:** Script LN mintmaster's initials below arms

Date	Mintage	VG	F	VF	XF	Unc
1671 LN Rare	—	—	—	—	—	—

KM# 4.4 4 ORE

Silver **Rev:** Small LN below arms in legend

Date	Mintage	VG	F	VF	XF	Unc
1672 LN	—	125	250	450	750	—

KM# 10 DUCAT

3.5000 g., 0.9860 Gold 0.1109 oz. AGW **Obv:** Bust of Charles left **Rev:** Crowned arms, date in legend

Date	Mintage	VG	F	VF	XF	Unc
1671 LN Rare	—	—	—	—	—	—

KM# 11 DUCAT

3.5000 g., 0.9860 Gold 0.1109 oz. AGW **Obv:** Crowned C in inner circle

Date	Mintage	VG	F	VF	XF	Unc
1671 LN Rare	—	—	—	—	—	—

PATTERNS

Including off metal strikes

KM#	Date	Mintage	Identification	Mkt Val
Pn1	(1)671	—	Ducat. Silver. KM#11.	—

REVAL

This old city is the present city of Tallinn in Estonia on the Gulf of Finland. It was founded by the Danes about 1219 and became an important Baltic port and a member of the Hanseatic League. It passed to Sweden in 1561 after dissolution of the Teutonic Knights. Occupied by the Russians in 1710, it was ceded to them in 1721.

RULER

Swedish

MONEYERS' INITIALS

Initial	Date	Name
FL	1675-81	Friedrich Lembkens
GP	1648-52	Gerhard Philip
(a) Asterisk		?
(b) Crossed Battle-axes		?
(c) Crossed cannons		?
(f) Fleur de lis	1625-27	Friedrich Ulmer
(m) Maltese Cross		?
(s) Shamrock	1620-23	Cyriacus Klein
(st) Star of David		?
W/o mm	1663-75	Michael Paulsen

REFERENCE

S = Hugo Frhr. Von Saurma-Jeltsch, ***Die Saurmasche Münzsammlung deutscher, schweizerischer und polnischer Gepräge von etwa dem Beginn der Groschenzeit bis zur Kipperperiode***, Berlin, 1892.

SWEDISH ADMINISTRATION

STANDARD COINAGE

KM# 1 ORE

Silver **Obv:** Sheaf divides G R, A above in inner circle **Obv. Legend:** MONETA (date) NOVA **Rev:** Crowned shield of 3 leopards in inner circle **Note:** Legend varieties exist.

Date	Mintage	VG	F	VF	XF	Unc
1620 Rare	—	—	—	—	—	—
1621 (s)	—	10.00	20.00	47.00	90.00	—
1621	—	10.00	20.00	47.00	90.00	—

KM# 2 ORE

Silver **Obv. Legend:** MONETA NOVA (date) **Note:** Legend varieties exist.

Date	Mintage	VG	F	VF	XF	Unc
1620 Rare	—	—	—	—	—	—
1621 Rare	—	—	—	—	—	—
1622 (s)	—	10.00	20.00	45.00	90.00	—
1622	—	14.00	27.50	60.00	115	—
1623 (a)	—	10.00	20.00	45.00	90.00	—
16Z3 (b)	—	55.00	100	170	230	—
1623 (m)	—	10.00	20.00	45.00	90.00	—
1623 (s)	—	20.00	42.00	90.00	175	—
1623	—	10.00	20.00	45.00	90.00	—
1624 (a)	—	10.00	20.00	45.00	90.00	—
1624 (c)	—	20.00	42.00	90.00	175	—
1624 (st)	—	10.00	20.00	45.00	90.00	—
1624	—	10.00	20.00	45.00	90.00	—
1625 (a)/(b)	—	20.00	35.00	75.00	145	—
1625 (b)	—	15.00	30.00	60.00	115	—
1625 (f) Rare	—	—	—	—	—	—
1625 (s + battle axe) Rare	—	—	—	—	—	—
1625 (st)	—	20.00	42.00	90.00	175	—
1626 (b) Rare	—	—	—	—	—	—
1628 (b)	—	20.00	42.00	90.00	175	—
1629	—	—	—	—	—	—

KM# 3 ORE

Silver **Note:** Klippe.

Date	Mintage	VG	F	VF	XF	Unc
1622 Rare	—	—	—	—	—	—

KM# 4 ORE

Silver **Rev:** 3 leopards in inner circle without shield

Date	Mintage	VG	F	VF	XF	Unc
1622 (s)	—	35.00	70.00	145	285	—

KM# 6 ORE

Silver **Obv:** Crowned Vasa arms divide date in inner circle **Rev:** Crowned Reval arms divide value in inner circle **Note:** Legend varieties exist.

Date	Mintage	VG	F	VF	XF	Unc
1648	—	15.00	30.00	60.00	145	—
1649	—	17.00	35.00	75.00	175	—
1650	—	17.00	35.00	75.00	175	—
1651	—	17.00	35.00	75.00	175	—

KM# 9.1 ORE

Silver **Obv:** Crowned arms (rampant lion left) divide date in inner circle **Rev:** Crowned Reval arms divide value in inner circle **Note:** Varieties exist.

Date	Mintage	VG	F	VF	XF	Unc
ND Rare	—	—	—	—	—	—
1663 Rare	—	—	—	—	—	—
1664	—	35.00	70.00	145	285	—
1665	—	15.00	30.00	60.00	115	—
1666	—	15.00	30.00	60.00	115	—
1667	—	17.00	35.00	75.00	145	—

KM# 9.2 ORE

Silver **Rev:** 1-R of value lying on side

Date	Mintage	VG	F	VF	XF	Unc
1665	—	15.00	30.00	60.00	115	—

KM# 9.3 ORE

Silver **Obv:** Denomination **Rev:** Date

Date	Mintage	VG	F	VF	XF	Unc
1666	—	35.00	70.00	145	285	—

KM# 10.1 ORE

Silver **Obv:** Rampant lion right in crowned arms

Date	Mintage	VG	F	VF	XF	Unc
1664	—	35.00	70.00	145	285	—

KM# 10.2 ORE

Silver **Rev:** Value 1 OR

Date	Mintage	VG	F	VF	XF	Unc
1664	—	35.00	70.00	145	285	—

KM# 23 ORE

Silver **Obv:** Crowned C R S **Rev:** Crowned arms in branches divide date and value

Date	Mintage	VG	F	VF	XF	Unc
1665	—	30.00	55.00	115	230	—

KM# 24.1 ORE

Silver **Obv:** Rampant lion left in crowned arms without inner circle

Date	Mintage	VG	F	VF	XF	Unc
1666	—	30.00	55.00	115	230	—

KM# 24.2 ORE

Silver **Obv:** Without inner circle **Rev:** Without inner circle

Date	Mintage	VG	F	VF	XF	Unc
1666	—	17.00	35.00	75.00	145	—
1668 Rare	—	—	—	—	—	—

KM# 27 ORE

Silver **Obv:** Crowned CXI monogram in branches **Rev:** Crowned arms divide value in inner circle

Date	Mintage	VG	F	VF	XF	Unc
ND Rare	—	—	—	—	—	—

KM# 28 ORE

Silver **Rev:** Crowned arms divide date, without branches, outer legend OR value

Date	Mintage	VG	F	VF	XF	Unc
1668	—	20.00	42.00	90.00	175	—

KM# 35 ORE

Silver **Rev:** Crowned arms in branches divide date and value

Date	Mintage	VG	F	VF	XF	Unc
1669	—	15.00	30.00	60.00	115	—
1670	—	15.00	30.00	60.00	115	—

KM# 45 ORE

Silver

Date	Mintage	VG	F	VF	XF	Unc
1672	—	17.00	35.00	75.00	145	—
1673	—	17.00	35.00	75.00	145	—
1674	—	25.00	42.00	90.00	175	—

KM# 47 ORE

Silver **Rev:** With value, without branches

Date	Mintage	VG	F	VF	XF	Unc
1673	—	17.00	35.00	75.00	145	—
1674	—	17.00	35.00	75.00	145	—

KM# 11 2 ORE

Silver **Obv:** Crowned C R S in laurel wreath **Rev:** Crowned oval arms divide date and value

Date	Mintage	VG	F	VF	XF	Unc
1664 Rare	—	—	—	—	—	—

KM# 12 2 ORE

Silver **Rev:** Crowned spade arms in branches divide date and value **Note:** Varieties exist.

Date	Mintage	VG	F	VF	XF	Unc
1664	—	20.00	42.00	95.00	180	—
1665	—	20.00	42.00	95.00	180	—
1666	—	15.00	30.00	65.00	120	—
1667	—	15.00	30.00	65.00	120	—
1668	—	15.00	30.00	65.00	120	—
1669	—	40.00	80.00	160	310	—

KM# A29 2 ORE

Silver **Obv:** Crowned CRS in palm branches

Date	Mintage	VG	F	VF	XF	Unc
1668	—	30.00	55.00	120	235	—

KM# 40 2 ORE

Silver **Obv:** Crowned CRS in laurel wreath **Rev:** Without branches below arms

Date	Mintage	VG	F	VF	XF	Unc
1671 Rare	—	—	—	—	—	—

KM# 25 4 ORE

Silver **Obv:** Crowned C in inner circle **Rev:** Crowned arms divide value, date in legend

Date	Mintage	VG	F	VF	XF	Unc
1667	—	35.00	70.00	150	290	—
667	—	20.00	42.00	95.00	180	—
1668	—	20.00	42.00	95.00	180	—
668	—	20.00	42.00	95.00	180	—
1669	—	35.00	70.00	150	290	—

KM# 30 4 ORE

Silver **Obv:** Crowned CRS in laurel wreath **Rev:** Crowned arms in branches divide date and value

Date	Mintage	VG	F	VF	XF	Unc
1668	—	25.00	50.00	110	210	—
1669	—	20.00	42.00	95.00	180	—
1670	—	20.00	42.00	95.00	180	—

KM# 37 4 ORE

Silver **Obv:** Crowned C in laurel wreath

Date	Mintage	VG	F	VF	XF	Unc
1670	—	27.50	55.00	120	235	—

KM# 41 4 ORE

Silver **Obv:** Crowned C in inner circle

Date	Mintage	VG	F	VF	XF	Unc
1671	—	20.00	42.00	95.00	180	—
1673	—	35.00	70.00	150	290	—
1674	—	75.00	145	260	500	—

KM# 13 MARK

Silver **Obv:** Bust of Charles XI left **Rev:** Crowned oval arms in cartouche, date in legend

Date	Mintage	VG	F	VF	XF	Unc
1664 Rare	—	—	—	—	—	—

KM# 14 2 MARK
Silver **Obv:** Draped bust of Charles XI left **Rev:** Crowned arms in cartouche, date in legend, crown divides value

Date	Mintage	VG	F	VF	XF	Unc
1664	—	1,000	1,750	3,000	6,000	—

KM# 15 2 MARK
Silver **Obv:** Draped bust of Charles XI right in inner circle

Date	Mintage	VG	F	VF	XF	Unc
1664 Rare	—	—	—	—	—	—

KM# 16 2 MARK
Silver **Rev:** Helmeted arms divide value in inner circle, date in legend

Date	Mintage	VG	F	VF	XF	Unc
1664 Rare	—	—	—	—	—	—

KM# 26 2 MARK
Silver **Obv:** Draped bust of Charles XI left **Rev:** Crowned spade arms divide date and value

Date	Mintage	VG	F	VF	XF	Unc
1667 Rare	—	—	—	—	—	—
1668 Unique	—	—	—	—	—	—

KM# 42 2 MARK
Silver **Obv:** Without lettering below bust

Date	Mintage	VG	F	VF	XF	Unc
1671	—	750	1,250	2,500	5,000	—

KM# 5.1 4 MARK
Silver **Obv:** 1/2 figure of Gustav II Adolf right with scepter and orb in inner circle **Rev:** Crowned arms divide date in inner circle **Note:** Prev. KM#5.

Date	Mintage	VG	F	VF	XF	Unc
1623 Rare	—	—	—	—	—	—

KM# 5.3 4 MARK
Silver **Note:** Triple thickness - struck to weight of 12 mark, 56.4 grams. Dav. #4583.

Date	Mintage	VG	F	VF	XF	Unc
1623 Rare	—	—	—	—	—	—

KM# 5.2 4 MARK
Silver **Note:** 2-1/2 thickness - struck to weight of 10 mark, 47 grams. Dav. #4584.

Date	Mintage	VG	F	VF	XF	Unc
1623	—	—	—	—	—	—

KM# 17.1 4 MARK
Silver **Obv:** Draped bust of Charles XI left in inner circle **Rev:** Crowned oval arms divide value in inner circle, large cross below arms

Date	Mintage	VG	F	VF	XF	Unc
1664 Rare	—	—	—	—	—	—

KM# 17.2 4 MARK
Silver **Rev:** Small cross below arms

Date	Mintage	VG	F	VF	XF	Unc
1664	—	1,250	2,500	5,000	9,000	—

KM# 18.1 4 MARK
Silver **Rev:** Helmeted straight shield, helmet divides value, shield divides date in inner circle

Date	Mintage	VG	F	VF	XF	Unc
1664 Rare	—	—	—	—	—	—

KM# 18.2 4 MARK
Silver **Rev:** Numerals of date inverted

Date	Mintage	VG	F	VF	XF	Unc
1664	—	1,200	2,250	4,500	8,500	—
ND Rare	—	—	—	—	—	—

KM# 49 10 MARK
Silver **Obv:** 1/2 figure right **Rev:** Crowned arms divide date **Note:** Dav. #4584.

Date	Mintage	VG	F	VF	XF	Unc
1623 Rare	—	—	—	—	—	—

KM# 50 12 MARK
Silver **Note:** Similar to 10 Mark, KM#49.

Date	Mintage	VG	F	VF	XF	Unc
1623 Rare	—	—	—	—	—	—

KM# 8.1 RIKSDALER
Silver **Obv:** Crowned bust of Christian right in inner circle **Rev:** Crowned oval arms divide date in inner circle, GP below arms **Note:** Dav. #4585.

Date	Mintage	VG	F	VF	XF	Unc
1652 GP	—	7,000	9,000	15,000	22,500	—

KM# 8.2 RIKSDALER
Silver **Rev:** Crowned oval arms divide date in GP in inner circle **Note:** Dav. 4585A.

Date	Mintage	VG	F	VF	XF	Unc
1652 GP Rare	—	—	—	—	—	—

KM# 19 RIKSDALER
Silver **Obv:** Draped bust of Charles XI left in inner circle **Rev:** Helmeted arms in inner circle

Date	Mintage	VG	F	VF	XF	Unc
1664 Unique	—	—	—	—	—	—

TRADE COINAGE

KM# 7.1 DUCAT
3.5000 g., 0.9860 Gold 0.1109 oz. AGW **Obv:** Bust of Christina left **Rev:** GP below arms

Date	Mintage	VG	F	VF	XF	Unc
1650 GP Rare	—	—	—	—	—	—

Note: Künker Auction 185, 3-11, SF realized approx. $19,500

KM# 7.2 DUCAT
3.5000 g., 0.9860 Gold 0.1109 oz. AGW **Rev:** GP at sides of arms

Date	Mintage	VG	F	VF	XF	Unc
1650 GP	—	—	—	—	—	—

KM# 20 DUCAT
3.5000 g., 0.9860 Gold 0.1109 oz. AGW **Obv:** Laureate bust of Charles right **Rev:** Crowned arms, date in legend

Date	Mintage	VG	F	VF	XF	Unc
1664 Rare	—	—	—	—	—	—
1665 Rare	—	—	—	—	—	—
1666 Rare	—	—	—	—	—	—

Note: Künker Auction 185, 3-11, XF realized approx. $44,550

KM# 31 DUCAT
3.5000 g., 0.9860 Gold 0.1109 oz. AGW **Obv:** Laureate bust of Charles left **Rev:** Crowned arms in straight sided shield divides date

Date	Mintage	VG	F	VF	XF	Unc
1668 Rare	—	—	—	—	—	—

KM# 36 DUCAT
3.5000 g., 0.9860 Gold 0.1109 oz. AGW **Rev:** Crowned arms in oval shield, date in legend

Date	Mintage	VG	F	VF	XF	Unc
1669 Rare	—	—	—	—	—	—

KM# 38 DUCAT
3.5000 g., 0.9860 Gold 0.1109 oz. AGW **Obv:** Laureate bust of Charles left with small shoulder drape **Rev:** Crowned arms in straight-sided shield divides date

Date	Mintage	VG	F	VF	XF	Unc
1670 Rare	—	—	—	—	—	—
1671 Rare	—	—	—	—	—	—

KM# 43 DUCAT
3.5000 g., 0.9860 Gold 0.1109 oz. AGW **Rev:** Date in legend

Date	Mintage	VG	F	VF	XF	Unc
1671 Rare	—	—	—	—	—	—

KM# 48 DUCAT
3.5000 g., 0.9860 Gold 0.1109 oz. AGW **Obv:** Laureate bust of Charles right **Rev:** Crowned arms, shield with various side ornaments

Date	Mintage	VG	F	VF	XF	Unc
1675 Rare	—	—	—	—	—	—
1676 Rare	—	—	—	—	—	—
1677 Rare	—	—	—	—	—	—
1681 Rare	—	—	—	—	—	—

KM# 21 2 DUCAT
7.0000 g., 0.9860 Gold 0.2219 oz. AGW **Obv:** Large bust of Charles right **Rev:** Crowned oval arms, date in legend

Date	Mintage	VG	F	VF	XF	Unc
1664 Unique	—	—	—	—	—	—

KM# 22 2 DUCAT
7.0000 g., 0.9860 Gold 0.2219 oz. AGW **Obv:** Small bust of Charles right

Date	Mintage	VG	F	VF	XF	Unc
1664 Rare	—	—	—	—	—	—

KM# 32 2 DUCAT
7.0000 g., 0.9860 Gold 0.2219 oz. AGW **Obv:** Large bust of Charles left **Rev:** Crowned arms in straight-sided shield divides date

Date	Mintage	VG	F	VF	XF	Unc
1668 Rare	—	—	—	—	—	—

KM# 39 2 DUCAT
7.0000 g., 0.9860 Gold 0.2219 oz. AGW **Obv:** Small bust of Charles left

Date	Mintage	VG	F	VF	XF	Unc
1670 Rare	—	—	—	—	—	—

KM# 44 2 DUCAT
7.0000 g., 0.9860 Gold 0.2219 oz. AGW **Rev:** Date in legend **Note:** Legend varieties exist.

Date	Mintage	VG	F	VF	XF	Unc
1671 Rare	—	—	—	—	—	—

KM# 33 4 DUCAT
14.0000 g., 0.9860 Gold 0.4438 oz. AGW **Obv:** Laureate bust of Charles left **Rev:** Crowned arms in straight-sided shield divides date

Date	Mintage	VG	F	VF	XF	Unc
1668 Unique	—	—	—	—	—	—

KM# 34 5 DUCAT
17.5000 g., 0.9860 Gold 0.5547 oz. AGW **Obv:** Laureate bust of Charles left **Rev:** Crowned arms in straight-sided shield divides date

Date	Mintage	VG	F	VF	XF	Unc
1668 Rare	—	—	—	—	—	—

KM# 46 5 DUCAT
17.5000 g., 0.9860 Gold 0.5547 oz. AGW **Obv:** Laureate bust of Charles left **Rev:** Crowned arms divide value, date in legend

Date	Mintage	VG	F	VF	XF	Unc
1672 Rare	—	—	—	—	—	—

PATTERNS

Including off metal strikes

KM#	Date	Mintage	Identification	Mkt Val
Pn1	1648	—	Ore. Gold. KM#6, weight of 1 Ducat.	—
Pn2	1665	—	2 Ore. Gold. KM#12.	—
Pn3	671	—	2 Ducat. Silver. KM#44.	—
Pn4	1673	—	2 Mark. Copper. KM#42.	—

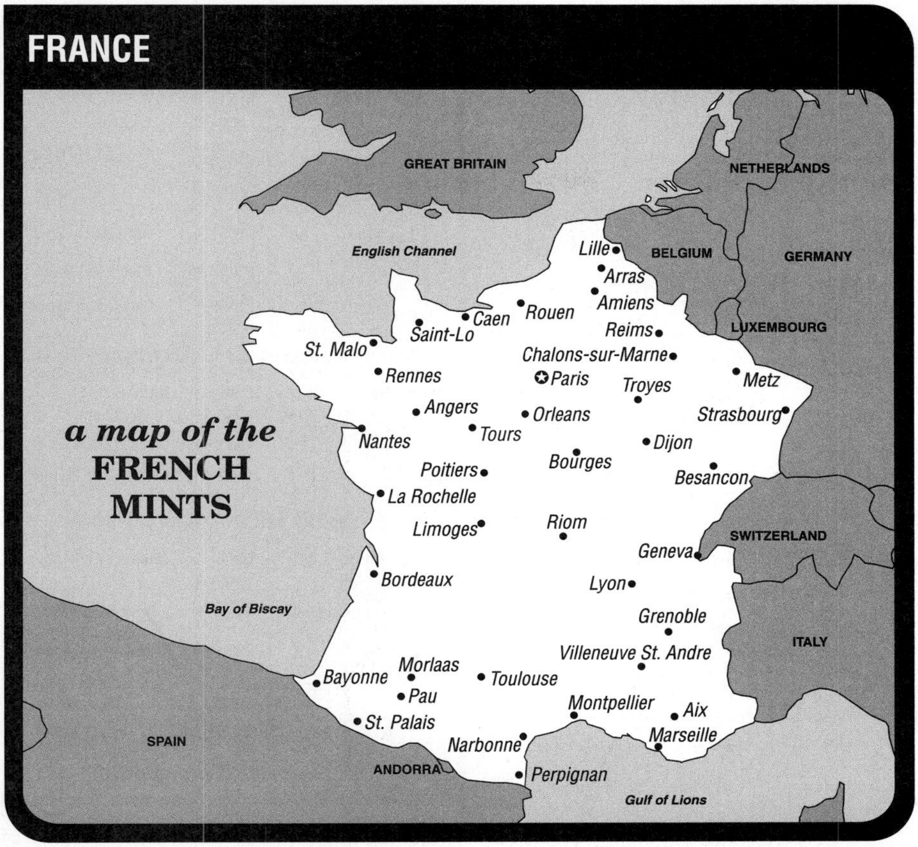

France, the Gaul of ancient times, emerged from the Renaissance as a modern centralized national state which reached its zenith during the reign of Louis XIV (1643-1715) when it became an absolute monarchy and the foremost power in Europe. Although his reign marks the golden age of French culture, the domestic abuses and extravagance of Louis XIV plunged France into a series of costly wars. This, along with a system of special privileges granted the nobility and other favored groups, weakened the monarchy and brought France to bankruptcy. This laid the way for the French Revolution of 1789-99 that shook Europe and affected the whole world.

RULERS

Henry IV, 1589-1610
Louis XIII, 1610-1643
Louis XIV, 1643-1715

MINT MARKS AND PRIVY MARKS

In addition to the date and mint mark which are customary on western civilization coinage, most coins manufactured by the French Mints contain two or three small 'Marks or Differents' as the French call them. These privy marks represent the men responsible for the dies which struck the coins. One privy mark is sometimes for the Engraver General (since 1880 the title is Chief Engraver). The other privy mark is the signature of the Mint Director of each mint; another one is the different' of the local engraver. Three other marks appeared at the end of Louis XIV's reign: one for the Director General of Mints, one for the General Engineer of Mechanical edge-marking, one identifying over struck coins in 1690-1705 and in 1715-1723. Equally amazing and unique is that sometimes the local assayer's or Judge-custody's 'different' or 'secret pellet' appears. Since 1880 this privy mark has represented the office rather than the personage of both the Administration of Coins & Medals and the Mint Director, and a standard privy mark has been used (cornucopia).

For most dates these privy marks are important though minor features for advanced collectors or local researchers. During some issue dates, however, the marks changed. To be even more accurate sometimes the marks changed when the date didn't, even though it should have. These coins can be attributed to the proper mintage report only by considering the privy marks. Previous references (before G. Sobin and F. Droulers) have by and large ignored these privy marks. It is entirely possible that unattributed varieties may exist for any privy mark transition. All transition years which may have two or three varieties or combinations of privy marks have the known attribution indicated after the date (if it has been confirmed).

MONETARY SYSTEM

1641-1689

3 Livres = 1 Silver Ecu
3-1/3 Ecus = 1 Louis d'or
1 Louis d'or = 10 Livres

1690-1725

Very unstable rates period.
1 Livre = 20 Sols
1 Sol = 12 Deniers
1 Liard = 3 Deniers

Engraver Generals' Privy Marks

Mark	Desc.	Date	Name
		1623-25	Nicolas Briot
		1625-31	Pierre Regnier
		1630-46	Johan Darmand Lorfelin
	Rose (on silver only)	1641-45	
•		1643-72	Jean Warin
	Castle tower	1662-73	Jean Baptiste du Four (assistant)
	Sun (usually or none)	1682-1703	Joseph Roettiers

Local Engravers' Privy Marks

Engraver Generals' and local engravers' privy marks may appear on coins of mints which are dated as follows:

A – Paris

Mark	Desc.	Date	Name
	4 pellets around fleur de lis	1644-48	Unknown
	Circle in triangle	1651-53	Francois Biaru
	Clover	1676	Pierre Rousseau
	Crescent	1679-93	Nicolas Aury
	Double triangle	1693-94	J. Mauger & J. Roussel
		1694-1703	Joseph Roettiers

AA – Metz

Mark	Desc.	Date	Name
	Crowned M	1690-93	Unknown
	Inflamed heart or none	1690-93	Etienne Rade
	Pierced heart	1693-94	Etienne Rade
	Hermine between 2 pellets	1694-1700	Unknown

B – Rouen

Mark	Desc.	Date	Name
	Star	1654-61	Nicolas Droux I
	Bee hive	1662-65	Nicolas Droux II
	Bee	1679-84	Nicolas Droux III
		1690-99	Nicolas Droux III
		1699-1700	Pierre Racine

BB – Strasbourg

Mark	Desc.	Date	Name
	Eagle's head	1694-99	Unknown

C – Saint Lo

Mark	Desc.	Date	Name
	Crescent	1625-28	Johan Euldes
	Star	1646-51	Israel Dubosc
	Star	1651-53	Michael Dupin
	Scallop	1653-57	Israel Dubosc

C – Caen

Mark	Desc.	Date	Name
		1693-1703	Thomas Bernard III

D – Lyon

Mark	Desc	Date	Name
	Three pellets	1643	Claude Warin
	Rose	1644-45	Jean Warin
	Star	1648-5	Claude Warin
	Eagle's head	1675-1709	Clair Jacquemin I

E - Tours

Mark	Desc.	Date	Name
	Cross	1656-80	Charles Thomas I
	Cross	1699-1722	Charles Thomas II

F – Angers

Mark	Desc.	Date	Name
	Clover	1611-32	Jean Boyoin
	Trefoil	1643-54	Unknown
	Palm	1655	Unknown
	Acorn	1656	Unknown
	Crescented cross	1658-59	Unknown
	Crossed 4 figure	1659-60	Rene Fauvel

G – Poitiers

Mark	Desc.	Date	Name
	Heart	1642-57	Rene Herpin
	Bird	1659-60	Rene Herpin
	Heart	1660	Rene Herpin
	Besant or none	1690-93	Unknown
	Heart	1693-98	Unknown

H – La Rochelle

Mark	Desc.	Date	Name
	Heart	1647-56	Abraham Desbo...
	Triangle	1658-61	Abraham Desbordes
	Rose	1690-92	Michel Brioshe
	Clover	1694-97	Gilles Nassivet I
	Acorn	1697-1704	Jacques Biollay

I – Limoges

Mark	Desc.	Date	Name
	Tear drop	1650-56	Unknown
	Rowel	1656-60	Unknown

	Tower	1660-80	Pierre Guybuert
	Carrick-bend?	1680-81	Unknown
	Tower	1690-92	Michel Briosne
	Latin cross	1693-1725	Francois Ponroy

K - Bordeaux

Mark	Desc.	Date	Name
	Nought	1620-46	
		1640-42	Pierre Prevost
		1643-44	Julien Noblet
		1645-46	Geoffrey Assore
	Fleur-de-lis	1646-47	Christophe Compuest
	Star	1660-84	Christophe Compuest
	Tower	1693-95 and 1708-09	Unknown
	Fleur-de-lis	1696-1715	Jacques Petit I

Crowned L - Lille

L - Bayonne

Mark	Desc.	Date	Name
	Cross	1652-53	Guillaume Fons
		1659-72	Leon Boisnet
	Running dog right	1672-74	Joseph Boisnet
	Star	1675-80	Jean Boisnet
	Palm	1682-94	
	Natural rose	1695-1735	Leon Mousset

M - Toulouse

Mark	Desc.	Date	Name
	Scallop	1648-53	Jean Favre I
	Flower	1691-94	Guillaume Favre III
	Scallop	1695	

Crowned M - Metz

N - Montpellier

Mark	Desc.	Date	Name
	Clover	1647-1694	Antoine Gautron
	Clover flanked by pellets	1679	
	Clover	1690-1700	Jacques Baudau

O - Riom

Mark	Desc.	Date	Name
	Rosette	1651-53	Unknown
	Clover	1691-92	Joseph Socke
	Clover	1697-1744	Jean Villa

P - Dijon

Mark	Desc.	Date	Name
	Clover	1637-1736	Guillaume Desvarennes
		1691-1738	Simon Roger

Q - Narbonne

R – Villeneuve St. André
Crowned S - Troyes

S - Reims

Mark	Desc.	Date	Name
	Rooster	1680-84	Claude Hardy
	Square	1693-1701	Pierre Delahaye

T - Nantes

Mark	Desc.	Date	Name
	Triangle	1642-56	Guillaume Langlois
	Globe	1654	
	Cross	1693-97	Pierre de la Croix
	Cross	1698-1709	Jean Beranger

V - Troyes

Mark	Desc.	Date	Name
	Double ring	1690-1710	Paul Rondot

W - Lille

Mark	Desc.	Date	Name
	Rosette	1693-1699	Claude Hardy
	Duckling	1700-02	Claude Hardy

X - Amiens

Mark	Desc.	Date	Name
	Crossed orb	1653-58	Jean Verdeloche
	Clover	1685-86	Claude Hardy
	Heart	1690-97	Michel Molard
	Star	1699-1703	Pierre-Gabriel Lemoyne

Y - Bourges

Mark	Desc.	Date	Name
	Arches	1690-92	Mathieu Malherbe des Portes
	Paddle-wheel (2 in 1703-05)	1692-1704	Francois Delobel

(2 back-to-back C's) - Besancon

Mark	Desc.	Date	Name
	Rowel	1694-99	Charles Louis Durand
	Swan	1699-1704	Bon-Anatole Nicole

& - Aix

Mark	Desc.	Date	Name
	Feather or none	1634-39	Johan Leger
	Diamond	1647-67	Jacques Cabassol I
	Diamond	1656-64	Jacques Cabassol II
	Small Diamond	1664-1708	Jean Joseph Cabassol

9 – Rennes

Mark	Desc.	Date	Name
	Acorn	1647-98	Jehan Noblet
	Crescent	1649-52	Denis Mathias
	Castle tower	1676-92	Jean Bedard
	Flower	1690-91	
	Heart	1692-1704	Rene Mathias

Legend DD or/and (cow) - Pau

Mark	Desc	Date	Name
	Intertwined olive branches	1650-51	Richard Lemy
	Various collections of pellets and stars	1651-56	Richard ?
	Dog running right	1663-83	Jacques de Soubiran
	Star	1683-91	Pierre de Loyard
	Heart	1691	Jacques de Soubiran
	Star	1692-96	Pierre de Loyard
	Heart	1696-1702	Jacques de Soubiran

Legend BD - Morlaas

Mark	Desc.	Date	Name
	1-3 stars	1637-49	Richard Lemy
	2 intertwined olive branches	1650-59	Richard Lemy
	Pellet	1660	Bertrand de Beaumont

Legend REX – Saint Palais

Mark	Desc.	Date	Name
	None	1646-49	
	Inverted heart	1650-58	Simon d'Armagnac
	Clover	1659-61	Pierre d'Armagnac
	$	1662-65	Jacques de Soubiran

Mint Directors' Privy Marks

A – Paris, Central Mint

Some modern coins struck from dies produced at the Paris Mint have the A mint mark. In the absence of a mint mark, the cornucopia privy mark serves to attribute a coin to Paris design.

Mark	Desc.	Date	Name
	Crossed palm	1630	Jean-Gabriel Fustel and Francois Ravel
	Pellet above crossed palm	1631	Francois Guibert
	Rose	1633-35	Gabriel Davin
	Forked cross	1635-42	Louis de la Croix
	Lily	1648	Jean Racle
	Marigold	1648	Jean Bouin
	Marigold	1649-53	Jean Racle
	Grape cluster	1653-55	Claude Monchallon
	Leaf	1656-57	Claude Banat
	Hermine	1657-58	Pierre Briot
	Crescent		Michel Fournier
	Lily w/stem	1662	Michel Magnier
	Lily w/stem	1662	Alexander Viollet
	Leopard right	1663	Unknown
	Inverted small heart	1663-65	Unknown
	Dove	1666	Unknown
	Sun w/human mask	1666-72	Pierre Cheval
	Cormorant	1672-74	Vincent Forher
	Laurel crown	1675-76	Jean Hindret
	Palm	1677-79	Jean Hindret
	Palm	1680-89	Pierre Batillie
	Sun	1684-85	Pierre Rouseau
	Sun	1685-88	Melchior Villain
	Sun	1688-89	Pierre Rousseau
	Sun	1689-	Jean Castagny
	Sun	1690-96	Hierosme de la Guerre

	Scallop	1699-1700	Nicolas de Saint Paul

A – Paris, Louvre Office

Mark	Desc.	Date	Name
	Rose or pellet or none (on the gold)	1640-46	Jean Warin
	Heart	1646-48	Louis Le Bicheur

A – Paris, Matignon Office

Mark	Desc.	Date	Name
	Rose between 2 pellets, 2 pellets or 1 pellet	1642-46	Isaac Briot & Jean Racle

AA - Metz

Mark	Desc.	Date	Name
	Grain ear in a crescent	1690-91	Antoine Talon
	Bomb	1692-97	Claude-Nicolas Boulard d'Ingonville
	Rose	1698-1700	Michel Rabigueau de Montelon

AR - Arras

Mark	Desc.	Date	Name
	Rat	1641-56	Artus (or Arthur) Aymond (or Emond) Jean-Jacques Morodet (1645)

B - Rouen

Mark	Desc	Date	Name
	Crown	1616-19	
	Hand	1633	
	Flower	1647-53	Pierre Cheval
	Cap	1664-65	

BB - Strasbourg

Mark	Desc.	Date	Name
	Flower	1694	

C – Saint Lo

Mark	Desc.	Date	Name
	Cross	1615	

D - Lyon

Mark	Desc.	Date	Name
	Star or none	1643-45	Jean Warin
	Crescent	1649-52	Andre Peyron
	VA monogram	1652-58	Jean Claudron
	Orb	1666-67	Isaac Estoille
	Rock pile	1669-71	Nicolas Simon
	Lion rampant or none	1681-88	Jean-Rene Dervieux
	Crescent	1690-93	Jean-Pierre Dervieux

E - Tours

Mark	Desc.	Date	Name
	Spread bird	1679	

F - Angers

Mark	Desc.	Date	Name
	Sheaf	1658-59	Matharin Haudoin
	Clover	1660	Francois de la Pierre
	Clover	1660	Nicolas Ruellan
	Torch	1660-61	Michel Garrot

G - Poitiers

Mark	Desc.	Date	Name
	Holy Spirit's dove	1647-53	Samuel Massonneau
	None	(1692-1700)	
	Latin cross	1692-1706	Gaspard Perrin

H – La Rochelle

Mark	Desc.	Date	Name
	Diamond	1647-53	Samuel Massonneau
	Diamond	1690-97	Germain and Francois Fodere
	Arrow	1697-1723	Jean Donat

I - Limoges

Mark	Desc.	Date	Name
	She-duckling	1619-22	Etienne Pinchault
	Crucifix	1650-54	Francois Malbay
	Sceptre	1679-81	Francois-Martin de la Bashide
	Kid left	1693-97	Joseph Chevreau Dumesmil
	Hound left	1697	Martin Courant
	Harp	1698-1725	Pierre David de la Vergne

K - Bordeaux

Mark	Desc.	Date	Name
	Bald head	1647	Jehan Luppe
	Bald head	1647-54	Jean de la Vaud
	Fleur-de-lis	1679-84	Jean-Baptiste Barlet
	Flower bud on stem	1694-96	Andre Langlois de Vaurain
	None	1697-1705	Bernard la Molire

L - Bayonne

Mark	Desc.	Date	Name
	LB monogram	1643-56	Martin de la Borde
	Heart	1662-66	Louis Martin
	Crown	1666-68	Joachim Gaillard
	Rose	1673-74	Etienne Verdoye
	Clover	1675-83	Michel Porchery
	Hermine	1679-83	Unknown
	Clover	1684-89	Michel Porchery

M - Toulouse

Mark	Desc.	Date	Name
	Heart	1648-49	
	Wing	1652-53	
	Fleur-de-lis	1691	

N - Montpellier

Mark	Desc.	Date	Name
	Star	1646-48	Laurent Mottry
	Tower	1666-69	Michel Porchery
	Pellets flanking star	1679-80	Francois Parent
	Lion's head (facing 1693-98)	1690-98	Pierre Berthelet

O - Clermont

O - Riom

Mark	Desc.	Date	Name
	Acorn on branch	1652	

P - Semur

P - Dijon

Mark	Desc.	Date	Name
	Fleur-de-lis	1652-53	Claude Burgat
	Arrow in quiver	1690-93	Melchior Villain
	Arrow in quiver	1693	Cezar d'Hubinet
	Arrow in quiver	1693-95	Jean-Nicolas Lancelot

Q - Narbonne

Mark	Desc.	Date	Name
	Holy spirit dove	1644-46	Tristan Brueys (1649) Claude Aubert (1645-46)
	Crescent	1650	Christophe de Jouy
	Flying angel holding crown	1650-52	Antoinne de Peyras
	Flying angel holding crown	1653	Jean Bacarisse

R – Villenueve Saint Andre

Mark	Desc.	Date	Name
	Unknown	1644-46	Charles Le Fresne
	Crescent	1660	Louis Martin
	Crescent	1661-62	Unknown

Crowned S – Troyes

(1690-93)
(See also V)

Mark	Desc.	Date	Name
	3 Cabochon's ring slantwise	1690-91	Pierre Paillot
	Heart	1691-93	Francois Boula

S - Reims

Mark	Desc.	Date	Name
	Holy Spirit dove	1680-83	Cezar Maniquet
	Clover	1690-95	Jean Hindret
	Acorn	1696-1705	Jacques Lagoille

T - Nantes

Mark	Desc.	Date	Name
	Holy Spirit dove	1646-53	Jehan Demarques
	Marigold	1653-55	Vincent Jourdain
	Hermine	1659-62	Andre Borgault

V – Troyes

(See also S)

Mark	Desc.	Date	Name
	Scallop	1694-97	Jean Baptiste de Mallerois
	Greek cross	1697-1700	Jean Sauvayre

X - Amiens

Mark	Desc.	Date	Name
	Hermine	1652-55	Nicolas Cezard
	Heart	1690-97	Louis Euldes

Y - Bourges

Mark	Desc.	Date	Name
	Sprig w/2 leaves	1694	Pierre Mace de Ballereau
	Crossed globe	1695-1700	Jules de la Planche de Coco

9 - Rennes

Mark	Desc.	Date	Name
	Rose	1651-53	Jehan Demarques
	Rose	1653-54	Vincent Jourdain
	Rose	1655	Rene Le Tellin
	Rose	1656-59	Mathieu Desrieux
	Star	1662-63	Jean Boulanger
	Star	1663-64	Claude Richard
	Star	1664-66	Jacques Nodain
	Hermine	1666-75	Marcel Memissin de Launoy
	Acorn	1673	Kin to Memissin de Launoy
	Palm	1675-77	Unknown
	Sunburst	1678-82	Marcel Memissin de Launoy
	Sunburst	1682-83	Jean-Jacques Baraly
	Orb	1684-86	Jean-Jacques Baraly
	Lion rampant	1693-1709	Jean-Jacques Baraly

& - Aix

Mark	Desc.	Date	Name
	Facing lion's head	1646-59	Laurent Motry
	Facing lion's head	1659-61	Pierre Nicolay
	Pierced star	1666-72	Pierre Desmaratz
	Olive branch	1679-84	Nicolas Simon
	Sunburst or none	1687-91	Francois Bouchaud
	None	1692-1703	Marc Pielat du Pignet

2 back to back C's - Besancon

Mark	Desc.	Date	Name
	Uprooted conifers	1694-97	Nicolas charles Nyele
	Uprooted conifers	1697-1700	Claude Francois Arbilleur

Crowned M – Metz

(1690-93 only)
From 1693, see also AA

Mark	Desc.	Date	Name
	Sprig in crescent	1690-91	Antoine Talon
	Comet	1692-97	Claude-Nicolas Boulard d'Ingonville

Legend ending NARE and/or Cow - Pau

Mark	Desc.	Date	Name
	Crossed olive	1650-51	Richard Lamy
F	Letter F alternatively w/2 or 4 stars	1651-53	Pierre Du Four
F	Letter F alternatively w/2 or 4 stars	1653-60	Robert Fisson
G	Letter G	1652	Bertrandlalande de Gayon
	Letter P	1653	Pierre de Niert
V	Letter V	1652	Etienne Du Verger
	Wood pigeon	1663-65	Reiset Du Verger
	Crescent	1663-64 and 1666-71	Louis allerie
	Blown rose	1672-75	Jean d'Azmagnan
	Clover	1673-75	
	Lily flanked by 2 pellets	1675-79	Unknown
	Orb	1685-89	Louis Allorie
	Orb	1690-95	Francois de La Serre
	Harpoon	1696-98	Rene Rousseau de Vilmor
	Hunting dog right	1698-1700 and 1708	Martin Courant

Legend ending NA, RE. DB and/or Letter M in 1652-62 only - Morlaas

Mark	Desc.	Date	Name
	Letter Z	1652-54	Bertrand La Lande de Gayon
R A	Letters A or R	1654-58	Martin d'Arretche or Robert Fisson alternatively
	Thistle flower	1659	Unknown
	Buffoon's crown	1659-60	Unknown
	She-goose	1660	Etienne Verdoya
	Buffoon's crown	1661-62	Unknown

Arms of France-Navarra – Saint Palais

Mark	Desc.	Date	Name
	W w/2 stars	1650-59	Etienne Verdoye
	2 stars under bust	1659-60	Unknown
	Tower	1665	Unknown
	Heart	1666-69	Jean d'Armagnan
		1670-72	Francois LeNoir

Feurs

Mark	Desc.	Date	Name
	1 pellet	1637-43	

Lay

Mark	Desc.	Date	Name
	2 pellets	1637-43	

Macon

(never open)

Mark	Desc.	Date	Name
	3 pellets	1637-43	

Maromme

Mark	Desc.	Date	Name
	Cross of 5 pellets	1637-43	

Roquemaure

Mark	Desc.	Date	Name
	4 pellets	1637-43	

Troyes

Mark	Desc.	Date	Name
	Starburst	1637-43	

Valence

Mark	Desc.	Date	Name
	Star	1637-43	

KINGDOM

MILLED COINAGE

KM# 15 DENIER TOURNOIS

Copper **Ruler:** Henri IV **Obv:** Laureate bust right **Rev:** 2 fleur-de-lis, mint mark **Mint:** Paris

Date	Mintage	VG	F	VF	XF	Unc
1603A	—	12.50	25.00	50.00	110	—
1604A	—	12.50	25.00	50.00	110	—
1605/4A	—	12.50	25.00	50.00	110	—
1606A	—	12.50	25.00	50.00	110	—
1607A	—	12.50	25.00	50.00	110	—
1608/7A	—	12.50	25.00	50.00	110	—

KM# 32 DENIER TOURNOIS

Copper **Ruler:** Henri IV **Rev:** Quartered shield for France and Dauphine **Mint:** Grenoble

Date	Mintage	VG	F	VF	XF	Unc
1607Z	—	—	—	—	—	—
1608Z	—	—	—	—	—	—

KM# 42.1 DENIER TOURNOIS

Copper **Ruler:** Louis XIII **Obv:** Infant bust right in shirt **Rev:** 2 fleur-de-lis, mint mark below **Mint:** Paris

Date	Mintage	VG	F	VF	XF	Unc
1611A	—	5.00	12.00	30.00	90.00	—
1612A	—	5.00	12.00	30.00	90.00	—
1613A	—	5.00	12.00	30.00	90.00	—
1614A	—	5.00	12.00	30.00	85.00	—
1615A	—	5.00	12.00	30.00	85.00	—
1616A	—	5.00	12.00	30.00	85.00	—
1617A	—	5.00	12.00	30.00	85.00	—
1618A	—	5.00	12.00	30.00	85.00	—
1620A	—	6.00	13.00	32.00	110	—
1621A	—	7.00	15.00	40.00	145	—

KM# 42.2 DENIER TOURNOIS

Copper **Ruler:** Louis XIII **Mint:** Lyon

Date	Mintage	VG	F	VF	XF	Unc
1611D	—	6.00	13.00	32.00	110	—
1613D	—	7.00	15.00	40.00	145	—
1615D	—	5.00	12.00	30.00	95.00	—
1617D	—	7.00	15.00	40.00	145	—
1618D	—	6.00	13.00	32.00	110	—

KM# 42.3 DENIER TOURNOIS

Copper **Ruler:** Louis XIII **Mint:** Poitiers

Date	Mintage	VG	F	VF	XF	Unc
1619G	—	7.00	15.00	40.00	145	—

KM# 42.4 DENIER TOURNOIS

Copper **Ruler:** Louis XIII **Mint:** Bordeaux

Date	Mintage	VG	F	VF	XF	Unc
1610K	—	—	—	—	—	—
1611K	—	—	—	—	—	—
1612K	—	7.00	15.00	40.00	145	—
1613K	—	—	—	—	—	—
1614K	—	—	—	—	—	—
1617K	—	—	—	—	—	—
1618K	—	7.00	15.00	40.00	145	—

KM# 42.5 DENIER TOURNOIS

Copper **Ruler:** Louis XIII **Mint:** Toulouse

Date	Mintage	VG	F	VF	XF	Unc
1611M	—	7.00	15.00	40.00	145	—
1612M	—	7.00	15.00	40.00	145	—

KM# 42.6 DENIER TOURNOIS

Copper **Ruler:** Louis XIII **Mint:** Villeneuve St. André

Date	Mintage	VG	F	VF	XF	Unc
1617R	—	9.00	18.00	45.00	160	—
1618R	—	6.00	12.00	30.00	100	—

KM# 42.7 DENIER TOURNOIS

Copper **Ruler:** Louis XIII **Mint:** Nantes

Date	Mintage	VG	F	VF	XF	Unc
1610T	—	7.00	15.00	40.00	145	—
1611T	—	7.00	15.00	40.00	145	—
1613T	—	7.00	15.00	40.00	145	—
1616T	—	7.00	15.00	40.00	145	—

KM# 42.8 DENIER TOURNOIS

Copper **Ruler:** Louis XIII **Mint:** Amiens

Date	Mintage	VG	F	VF	XF	Unc
1614X	—	6.00	13.00	32.00	110	—
1615X	—	7.00	15.00	40.00	145	—
1616X	—	7.00	15.00	40.00	145	—

KM# 70.1 DENIER TOURNOIS

Copper **Ruler:** Louis XIII **Obv:** Laureate youthful bust right in shirt **Mint:** Paris

Date	Mintage	VG	F	VF	XF	Unc
1620A	—	6.00	13.00	32.00	110	—
1621A	—	6.00	13.00	32.00	110	—
1622A	—	6.00	13.00	32.00	110	—
1625A	—	6.00	13.00	32.00	110	—
1626A	—	6.00	13.00	32.00	110	—
1627A	—	6.00	13.00	32.00	110	—
1628A	—	6.00	13.00	32.00	110	—
1629A	—	6.00	13.00	32.00	110	—

KM# 70.2 DENIER TOURNOIS

Copper **Ruler:** Louis XIII **Mint:** Lyon

Date	Mintage	VG	F	VF	XF	Unc
1624D	—	—	—	—	—	—

KM# 70.3 DENIER TOURNOIS

Copper **Ruler:** Louis XIII **Mint:** Poitiers

Date	Mintage	VG	F	VF	XF	Unc
1618G	—	—	—	—	—	—
1619G	—	6.00	13.00	32.00	110	—
1620G	—	6.00	13.00	32.00	110	—
1621G	—	6.00	13.00	32.00	110	—
1622G	—	6.00	13.00	32.00	110	—
1624G	—	6.00	13.00	32.00	110	—

KM# 70.4 DENIER TOURNOIS

Copper **Ruler:** Louis XIII **Mint:** La Rochelle

Date	Mintage	VG	F	VF	XF	Unc
1619H	—	—	—	—	—	—

KM# 70.5 DENIER TOURNOIS

Copper **Ruler:** Louis XIII **Mint:** Bordeaux

Date	Mintage	VG	F	VF	XF	Unc
1618K	—	6.00	13.00	32.00	110	—
1619K	—	—	—	—	—	—
1620K	—	—	—	—	—	—
1621K	—	—	—	—	—	—

KM# 70.6 DENIER TOURNOIS

Copper **Ruler:** Louis XIII **Mint:** Villeneuve St. André

Date	Mintage	VG	F	VF	XF	Unc
1621R	—	6.00	13.00	32.00	110	—
1622R	—	—	—	—	—	—
1625R	—	—	—	—	—	—

KM# 79.1 DENIER TOURNOIS

Copper **Ruler:** Louis XIII **Obv:** Older bust right in ruffled collar **Mint:** Paris

Date	Mintage	VG	F	VF	XF	Unc
1629A	—	10.00	20.00	50.00	180	—
1630A	—	10.00	20.00	50.00	180	—
1631A	—	10.00	20.00	50.00	180	—
1632A	—	10.00	20.00	50.00	180	—

KM# 79.2 DENIER TOURNOIS

Copper **Ruler:** Louis XIII **Mint:** Lyon

Date	Mintage	VG	F	VF	XF	Unc
1627D	—	10.00	20.00	50.00	180	—
1628D	—	10.00	20.00	50.00	180	—
1632D	—	10.00	20.00	50.00	180	—

KM# 79.3 DENIER TOURNOIS

Copper **Ruler:** Louis XIII **Mint:** Tours

Date	Mintage	VG	F	VF	XF	Unc
1632E	—	10.00	20.00	50.00	180	—
1633E	—	12.00	25.00	60.00	215	—
1634E	—	12.00	25.00	60.00	215	—
1635E	—	15.00	30.00	70.00	240	—

KM# 79.4 DENIER TOURNOIS

Copper **Ruler:** Louis XIII **Mint:** Poitiers

Date	Mintage	VG	F	VF	XF	Unc
1626G	—	10.00	20.00	50.00	180	—
1627G	—	10.00	20.00	50.00	180	—

KM# 79.5 DENIER TOURNOIS

Copper **Ruler:** Louis XIII **Mint:** La Rochelle

Date	Mintage	VG	F	VF	XF	Unc
1631H	—	—	—	—	—	—
1632H	—	—	—	—	—	—

KM# 79.6 DENIER TOURNOIS

Copper **Ruler:** Louis XIII **Mint:** Bordeaux

Date	Mintage	VG	F	VF	XF	Unc
1627K	—	—	—	—	—	—
1628K	—	10.00	20.00	50.00	180	—
1633K	—	10.00	20.00	50.00	180	—

KM# 79.7 DENIER TOURNOIS

Copper **Ruler:** Louis XIII **Mint:** Riom

Date	Mintage	VG	F	VF	XF	Unc
1624O	—	10.00	20.00	50.00	180	—
1625O	—	—	—	—	—	—
1626O	—	10.00	20.00	50.00	180	—

KM# 89 DENIER TOURNOIS

Copper **Ruler:** Louis XIII **Obv:** Older bust right **Rev:** 2 fleur-de-lis, shield below **Mint:** Saint Palais **Note:** Mint mark: shield.

Date	Mintage	VG	F	VF	XF	Unc
1634	—	35.00	65.00	175	500	—
1635	—	25.00	45.00	125	450	—

KM# 167 DENIER TOURNOIS

Copper **Ruler:** Louis XIV **Obv:** Laureate head right **Rev:** 2 fleur-de-lis, mint mark below **Mint:** Paris

Date	Mintage	VG	F	VF	XF	Unc
1648A	—	10.00	20.00	60.00	210	—
1649A	—	8.00	16.00	40.00	145	—

KM# 16.1 DOUBLE TOURNOIS

Copper **Ruler:** Henri IV **Obv:** Laureate, armored bust right **Mint:** Paris

Date	Mintage	VG	F	VF	XF	Unc
1603A	—	20.00	40.00	90.00	235	—
1604A	—	20.00	40.00	90.00	235	—
1605/4A	—	20.00	40.00	90.00	235	—
1606A	—	20.00	40.00	90.00	235	—
1607A	—	20.00	40.00	90.00	235	—
1608A	—	20.00	40.00	90.00	235	—
1609A	—	20.00	40.00	90.00	235	—
1610A	—	20.00	40.00	90.00	235	—

KM# 16.2 DOUBLE TOURNOIS

2.8000 g., Copper, 20.3 mm. **Ruler:** Henri IV **Subject:** Henry IV **Obv:** Portrait within legend **Rev:** Three fleur-de-lis within legend **Edge:** Plain **Mint:** Lyon

Date	Mintage	F	VF	XF	Unc	BU
1608D	—	40.00	90.00	175	—	—

KM# 33 DOUBLE TOURNOIS

Copper **Ruler:** Henri IV **Rev:** Quartered shield of France and Dauphine **Mint:** Grenoble

Date	Mintage	VG	F	VF	XF	Unc
1608Z	—	—	—	—	—	—

KM# 43.1 DOUBLE TOURNOIS

Copper **Ruler:** Louis XIII **Obv:** Juvenile bust right in shirt **Rev:** 3 fleur-de-lis **Mint:** Paris

Date	Mintage	VG	F	VF	XF	Unc
1611A	—	5.00	12.00	35.00	110	—
1612A	—	5.00	12.00	35.00	110	—
1613A	—	5.00	12.00	35.00	110	—
1614A	—	5.00	12.00	35.00	110	—
1615A	—	7.00	15.00	45.00	150	—
1616A	—	6.00	13.00	38.00	130	—
1617A	—	5.00	12.00	35.00	110	—
1618A	—	5.00	12.00	35.00	110	—

KM# 43.2 DOUBLE TOURNOIS

Copper **Ruler:** Louis XIII **Mint:** Lyon

Date	Mintage	VG	F	VF	XF	Unc
1611D	—	7.00	15.00	45.00	160	—
1613D	—	7.00	15.00	45.00	160	—
1614D	—	7.00	15.00	45.00	160	—
1615D	—	7.00	15.00	45.00	160	—
1618D	—	7.00	15.00	45.00	160	—

KM# 43.3 DOUBLE TOURNOIS

Copper **Ruler:** Louis XIII **Mint:** Poitiers

Date	Mintage	VG	F	VF	XF	Unc
1617G	—	7.00	15.00	45.00	160	—
1618G	—	7.00	15.00	45.00	160	—
1619G	—	7.00	15.00	45.00	160	—
1620G	—	5.00	12.00	35.00	110	—
1621G	—	6.00	13.00	38.00	130	—

KM# 43.4 DOUBLE TOURNOIS

Copper **Ruler:** Louis XIII **Mint:** Bordeaux

Date	Mintage	VG	F	VF	XF	Unc
1610K	—	8.00	17.00	50.00	180	—
1611K	—	5.00	12.00	35.00	110	—
1612K	—	5.00	12.00	35.00	110	—
1613K	—	8.00	17.00	50.00	180	—
1614K	—	8.00	17.00	50.00	180	—
1616K	—	8.00	17.00	50.00	180	—
1617K	—	8.00	17.00	50.00	180	—
1618K	—	7.00	15.00	45.00	160	—
1620K	—	8.00	17.00	50.00	180	—

KM# 43.5 DOUBLE TOURNOIS

Copper **Ruler:** Louis XIII **Mint:** Toulouse

Date	Mintage	VG	F	VF	XF	Unc
1611M	—	—	—	—	—	—
1612M	—	7.00	15.00	45.00	160	—

KM# 43.6 DOUBLE TOURNOIS

Copper **Ruler:** Louis XIII **Mint:** Villeneuve St. André

Date	Mintage	VG	F	VF	XF	Unc
1616R	—	7.00	15.00	45.00	160	—
1617R	—	7.00	15.00	45.00	160	—
1618R	—	7.00	15.00	45.00	160	—
1620R	—	10.00	20.00	65.00	230	—
1621R	—	7.00	15.00	45.00	160	—
1622R	—	8.00	17.00	50.00	180	—

KM# 43.7 DOUBLE TOURNOIS

Copper **Ruler:** Louis XIII **Mint:** Nantes

Date	Mintage	VG	F	VF	XF	Unc
1611T	—	8.00	17.00	50.00	180	—
1613T	—	7.00	15.00	45.00	160	—
1614T	—	7.00	15.00	45.00	160	—
1615T	—	7.00	15.00	45.00	160	—
1616T	—	6.00	12.00	35.00	130	—

KM# 43.8 DOUBLE TOURNOIS

Copper **Ruler:** Louis XIII **Mint:** Amiens

Date	Mintage	VG	F	VF	XF	Unc
1612X	—	7.00	15.00	45.00	160	—
1614X	—	7.00	15.00	45.00	160	—
1615X	—	6.00	12.00	40.00	145	—
1616X	—	7.00	15.00	45.00	160	—

KM# 43.9 DOUBLE TOURNOIS

Copper **Ruler:** Louis XIII **Mint:** Aix **Note:** Mint mark: Ampersand.

Date	Mintage	VG	F	VF	XF	Unc
1612	—	—	—	—	—	—
1613	—	7.00	15.00	45.00	160	—
1614	—	8.00	17.00	50.00	180	—

KM# 59.1 DOUBLE TOURNOIS

Copper **Ruler:** Louis XIII **Obv:** Laarger, youthful bust right in ruffled collar **Mint:** Paris

Date	Mintage	VG	F	VF	XF	Unc
1618A	—	10.00	20.00	60.00	215	—

KM# 59.2 DOUBLE TOURNOIS

Copper **Ruler:** Louis XIII **Mint:** Lyon

Date	Mintage	VG	F	VF	XF	Unc
1611D	—	6.00	12.00	35.00	130	—
1612D	—	8.00	17.00	50.00	180	—
1613D	—	6.00	12.00	35.00	130	—
1614D	—	10.00	20.00	60.00	215	—
1615D	—	6.00	12.00	35.00	130	—
1617D	—	7.00	15.00	45.00	160	—

KM# 59.3 DOUBLE TOURNOIS

Copper **Ruler:** Louis XIII **Mint:** Bordeaux

Date	Mintage	VG	F	VF	XF	Unc
1611K	—	7.00	15.00	45.00	160	—
1612K	—	7.00	15.00	45.00	160	—
1613K	—	8.00	17.00	50.00	180	—
1614K	—	10.00	20.00	60.00	215	—

KM# 59.4 DOUBLE TOURNOIS

Copper **Ruler:** Louis XIII **Mint:** Toulouse

Date	Mintage	VG	F	VF	XF	Unc
1611M	—	7.00	15.00	45.00	160	—
1612M	—	7.00	15.00	45.00	160	—

KM# 59.5 DOUBLE TOURNOIS

Copper **Ruler:** Louis XIII **Mint:** Nantes

Date	Mintage	VG	F	VF	XF	Unc
1610T	—	6.00	12.00	35.00	130	—
1611T	—	8.00	17.00	50.00	180	—
1612T	—	8.00	17.00	50.00	180	—
1613T	—	7.00	15.00	45.00	160	—
1614T	—	10.00	20.00	60.00	215	—
1616T	—	8.00	17.00	50.00	180	—

KM# 59.6 DOUBLE TOURNOIS

Copper **Ruler:** Louis XIII **Mint:** Aix **Note:** Mint mark: Ampersand.

Date	Mintage	VG	F	VF	XF	Unc
1612	—	7.00	15.00	45.00	160	—
1613	—	8.00	17.00	50.00	180	—
1614	—	10.00	20.00	65.00	230	—
1616	—	—	—	—	—	—

KM# 60 DOUBLE TOURNOIS

Copper **Ruler:** Louis XIII **Obv:** Large youthful mailed bust right **Mint:** Amiens

Date	Mintage	VG	F	VF	XF	Unc
1614X	—	8.00	17.00	50.00	180	—
1615X	—	7.00	15.00	45.00	160	—
1616X	—	8.00	17.00	50.00	180	—

KM# 61.1 DOUBLE TOURNOIS

Copper **Ruler:** Louis XIII **Obv:** Middle-aged laureate bust right in shirt **Mint:** Paris

Date	Mintage	VG	F	VF	XF	Unc
1620A	—	7.00	15.00	45.00	160	—
1621A	—	6.00	12.00	35.00	130	—
1622A	—	8.00	17.00	50.00	180	—
1625A	—	6.00	12.00	35.00	130	—
1626A	—	6.00	12.00	35.00	130	—
1627A	—	7.00	15.00	45.00	160	—
1628A	—	6.00	12.00	35.00	130	—
1629A	—	7.00	15.00	45.00	160	—

KM# 61.2 DOUBLE TOURNOIS

Copper **Ruler:** Louis XIII **Mint:** Lyon

Date	Mintage	VG	F	VF	XF	Unc
1624D	—	—	—	—	—	—
1625D	—	8.00	17.00	50.00	180	—

Date	Mintage	VG	F	VF	XF	Unc
1626D	—	—	—	—	—	—
1627D	—	8.00	17.00	50.00	180	—
1628D	—	6.00	12.00	35.00	130	—
1629D	—	6.00	12.00	35.00	130	—

KM# 61.3 DOUBLE TOURNOIS

Copper **Ruler:** Louis XIII **Mint:** Poitiers

Date	Mintage	VG	F	VF	XF	Unc
1619G	1,086,000	7.00	15.00	45.00	160	—
1621G	—	10.00	20.00	60.00	215	—
1622G	—	10.00	20.00	60.00	215	—
1624G	—	—	—	—	—	—
1626G	—	8.00	17.00	50.00	180	—
1627G	—	6.00	12.00	35.00	130	—
1628G	—	10.00	20.00	60.00	215	—

KM# 61.4 DOUBLE TOURNOIS

Copper **Ruler:** Louis XIII **Mint:** La Rochelle

Date	Mintage	VG	F	VF	XF	Unc
1619H	—	—	—	—	—	—

KM# 61.5 DOUBLE TOURNOIS

Copper **Ruler:** Louis XIII **Mint:** Bordeaux

Date	Mintage	VG	F	VF	XF	Unc
1619K	—	8.00	17.00	50.00	180	—
1620K	—	7.00	15.00	45.00	160	—
1621K	—	—	—	—	—	—
1623K	—	10.00	20.00	60.00	215	—
1627K	—	7.00	15.00	45.00	160	—
1628K	—	10.00	20.00	60.00	215	—
1629K	—	8.00	17.00	50.00	180	—

KM# 61.6 DOUBLE TOURNOIS

Copper **Ruler:** Louis XIII **Mint:** Riom

Date	Mintage	VG	F	VF	XF	Unc
16220	—	—	—	—	—	—
Note: Reported, not confirmed						
16230	—	10.00	20.00	60.00	180	—
16240	—	7.00	15.00	45.00	135	—
16250	—	8.00	17.00	50.00	150	—
16260	—	8.00	17.00	50.00	150	—

KM# 61.7 DOUBLE TOURNOIS

Copper **Ruler:** Louis XIII **Mint:** Villeneuve St. André

Date	Mintage	VG	F	VF	XF	Unc
1621R	—	7.00	15.00	45.00	160	—
1622R	—	8.00	17.00	50.00	180	—
1625R	—	—	—	—	—	—
1626R	—	8.00	17.00	50.00	180	—
1627R	—	7.00	15.00	45.00	160	—

KM# 72.1 DOUBLE TOURNOIS

Copper **Ruler:** Louis XIII **Obv:** Older bust right in ruffled collar **Mint:** Paris

Date	Mintage	VG	F	VF	XF	Unc
1627A	—	7.00	15.00	45.00	160	—
1628A	—	6.00	12.00	35.00	130	—
1629A	—	6.00	12.00	35.00	130	—
1630A	—	7.00	15.00	45.00	160	—
1631A	—	8.00	17.00	50.00	180	—
1632A	—	8.00	17.00	50.00	180	—
1633A	—	8.00	17.00	50.00	180	—
1635A	—	6.00	12.00	35.00	130	—

KM# 72.2 DOUBLE TOURNOIS

Copper **Ruler:** Louis XIII **Mint:** Lyon

Date	Mintage	VG	F	VF	XF	Unc
1627D	—	8.00	17.00	50.00	180	—
1628D	—	6.00	12.00	35.00	130	—
1629D	—	6.00	12.00	35.00	130	—
1630D	—	7.00	15.00	45.00	160	—
1631D	—	6.00	12.00	35.00	130	—
1632D	—	8.00	17.00	50.00	180	—
1633D	—	6.00	12.00	35.00	130	—
1634D	—	7.00	15.00	45.00	160	—
1635D	—	8.00	17.00	50.00	180	—

KM# 72.3 DOUBLE TOURNOIS

Copper **Ruler:** Louis XIII **Mint:** Tours

Date	Mintage	VG	F	VF	XF	Unc
1629E	—	10.00	20.00	60.00	215	—
1631E	—	8.00	17.00	50.00	180	—
1632E	—	8.00	17.00	50.00	180	—
1633E	—	6.00	12.00	35.00	130	—
1634E	—	8.00	17.00	50.00	180	—
1635E	—	8.00	17.00	50.00	180	—

KM# 72.4 DOUBLE TOURNOIS

Copper **Ruler:** Louis XIII **Mint:** Poitiers

Date	Mintage	VG	F	VF	XF	Unc
1627G	—	6.00	12.00	35.00	130	—
1628G	—	10.00	20.00	60.00	215	—
1633G	—	—	—	—	—	—

KM# 72.5 DOUBLE TOURNOIS

Copper **Ruler:** Louis XIII **Mint:** La Rochelle

Date	Mintage	VG	F	VF	XF	Unc
1631H	—	7.00	15.00	45.00	160	—
1632H	—	8.00	17.00	50.00	180	—
1633H	—	8.00	17.00	50.00	180	—
1634H	—	8.00	17.00	50.00	180	—

KM# 72.6 DOUBLE TOURNOIS

Copper **Ruler:** Louis XIII **Mint:** Bordeaux

Date	Mintage	VG	F	VF	XF	Unc
1627K	—	8.00	18.00	55.00	160	—
1628K	—	12.00	25.00	70.00	215	—
1631K	—	—	—	—	—	—
1632K	—	10.00	20.00	60.00	180	—
1633K	—	10.00	20.00	60.00	180	—
1635K	—	—	—	—	—	—

KM# 72.7 DOUBLE TOURNOIS

Copper **Ruler:** Louis XIII **Mint:** Villeneuve St. André

Date	Mintage	VG	F	VF	XF	Unc
1634R	—	—	—	—	—	—

KM# 85 DOUBLE TOURNOIS

Copper **Ruler:** Louis XIII **Obv:** Navarre shield below bust **Mint:** Saint Palais

Date	Mintage	VG	F	VF	XF	Unc
1632	—	20.00	40.00	125	450	—
1633	—	25.00	50.00	150	550	—
1635	—	20.00	40.00	125	450	—
1636	—	20.00	40.00	125	450	—
1638	—	25.00	50.00	150	550	—
1639	—	25.00	50.00	150	550	—
1643	—	25.00	50.00	150	550	—

KM# 86.1 DOUBLE TOURNOIS

Copper **Ruler:** Louis XIII **Obv:** Laureate and draped large bust right **Rev:** Three fleur-de-lis **Mint:** Paris

Date	Mintage	VG	F	VF	XF	Unc
1628A	—	—	—	—	—	—
1629A	—	10.00	18.00	50.00	180	—
1630A	—	8.00	14.00	35.00	130	—
1637A	—	8.00	14.00	35.00	130	—
1638A	—	10.00	18.00	50.00	180	—

KM# 86.2 DOUBLE TOURNOIS

Copper **Ruler:** Louis XIII **Mint:** Rouen

Date	Mintage	VG	F	VF	XF	Unc
1637B	—	9.00	16.00	45.00	160	—
1638B	—	10.00	18.00	50.00	180	—
1639B	—	10.00	18.00	50.00	180	—
1640B	—	10.00	18.00	50.00	180	—

KM# 86.3 DOUBLE TOURNOIS

Copper **Ruler:** Louis XIII **Mint:** Lyon

Date	Mintage	VG	F	VF	XF	Unc
1628D	—	—	—	—	—	—
1630D	—	8.00	14.00	35.00	130	—
1631D	—	10.00	18.00	50.00	180	—
1632D	—	10.00	18.00	50.00	180	—
1637D	—	9.00	16.00	45.00	160	—
1638D	—	10.00	18.00	50.00	180	—
1639D	—	—	—	—	—	—
1640D	—	10.00	18.00	50.00	180	—

KM# 86.4 DOUBLE TOURNOIS

Copper **Ruler:** Louis XIII **Mint:** Tours

Date	Mintage	VG	F	VF	XF	Unc
1637E	—	8.00	14.00	35.00	130	—
1638E	—	10.00	18.00	50.00	180	—
1639E	—	10.00	18.00	50.00	180	—
1640E	—	10.00	18.00	50.00	180	—

KM# 86.5 DOUBLE TOURNOIS

Copper **Ruler:** Louis XIII **Mint:** La Rochelle

Date	Mintage	VG	F	VF	XF	Unc
1638H	—	10.00	18.00	50.00	180	—
1639H	—	9.00	16.00	45.00	160	—
1640H	—	9.00	16.00	45.00	160	—

KM# 86.6 DOUBLE TOURNOIS

Copper **Ruler:** Louis XIII **Mint:** Bordeaux

Date	Mintage	VG	F	VF	XF	Unc
1637K	—	8.00	14.00	35.00	130	—
1638K	—	10.00	18.00	50.00	180	—
1639K	—	9.00	16.00	45.00	160	—
1640K	—	10.00	18.00	50.00	180	—

KM# 86.7 DOUBLE TOURNOIS

Copper **Ruler:** Louis XIII **Mint:** Feurs **Note:** Strike mark: 1 pellet.

Date	Mintage	VG	F	VF	XF	Unc
1636	—	10.00	18.00	50.00	180	—
1637	—	10.00	18.00	50.00	180	—
1638	—	10.00	18.00	50.00	180	—
1639	—	10.00	18.00	50.00	180	—
1640	—	10.00	18.00	50.00	180	—

KM# 86.8 DOUBLE TOURNOIS

Copper **Ruler:** Louis XIII **Mint:** Lay **Note:** Strike mark: 2 pellets.

Date	Mintage	VG	F	VF	XF	Unc
1637	—	10.00	18.00	50.00	180	—
1638	—	10.00	18.00	50.00	180	—
1639	—	10.00	18.00	50.00	180	—
1640	—	10.00	18.00	50.00	180	—

KM# 86.9 DOUBLE TOURNOIS

Copper **Ruler:** Louis XIII **Mint:** Macon **Note:** Strike mark: 3 pellets.

Date	Mintage	VG	F	VF	XF	Unc
1637	—	10.00	18.00	50.00	180	—
1638	—	10.00	18.00	50.00	180	—
1640	—	10.00	18.00	50.00	180	—

KM# 86.10 DOUBLE TOURNOIS

Copper **Ruler:** Louis XIII **Mint:** Maromme **Note:** Strike mark: Cross of 5 pellets.

Date	Mintage	VG	F	VF	XF	Unc
1637	—	10.00	18.00	50.00	180	—
1639	—	10.00	18.00	50.00	180	—
1640	—	10.00	18.00	50.00	180	—

KM# 86.11 DOUBLE TOURNOIS

Copper **Ruler:** Louis XIII **Mint:** Roquemaure **Note:** Mint mark: 4 pellets.

Date	Mintage	VG	F	VF	XF	Unc
1637	—	10.00	18.00	50.00	180	—
1638	—	10.00	18.00	50.00	180	—
1639	—	10.00	18.00	50.00	180	—
1640	—	10.00	18.00	50.00	180	—

KM# 86.12 DOUBLE TOURNOIS

Copper **Ruler:** Louis XIII **Mint:** Troyes **Note:** Strike mark: Starburst.

Date	Mintage	VG	F	VF	XF	Unc
1637	—	10.00	18.00	50.00	180	—
1638	—	10.00	18.00	50.00	180	—

KM# 86.13 DOUBLE TOURNOIS

Copper **Ruler:** Louis XIII **Mint:** Valence **Note:** Strike mark: Star.

Date	Mintage	VG	F	VF	XF	Unc
1638	—	10.00	18.00	50.00	180	—
1639	—	10.00	18.00	50.00	180	—
1640	—	10.00	18.00	50.00	180	—

KM# 86.14 DOUBLE TOURNOIS

Copper **Ruler:** Louis XIII **Mint:** Vienne **Note:** Strike mark: Crescent.

Date	Mintage	VG	F	VF	XF	Unc
1638	—	10.00	18.00	50.00	180	—
1639	—	10.00	18.00	50.00	180	—
1640	—	10.00	18.00	50.00	180	—

KM# 127.1 DOUBLE TOURNOIS

Copper **Ruler:** Louis XIII **Obv:** Laureate head left **Obv. Legend:** LOVIS XIII R.D. FRAN ET NA... **Mint:** Paris

Date	Mintage	VG	F	VF	XF	Unc
1642A	—	6.00	12.00	35.00	130	—
1643A	—	6.00	12.00	35.00	130	—

KM# 127.2 DOUBLE TOURNOIS
Copper **Ruler:** Louis XIII **Mint:** Rouen

Date	Mintage	VG	F	VF	XF	Unc
1643B	—	9.00	18.00	50.00	180	—

KM# 127.3 DOUBLE TOURNOIS
Copper **Ruler:** Louis XIII **Mint:** Lyon

Date	Mintage	VG	F	VF	XF	Unc
1643D	—	9.00	18.00	50.00	180	—

KM# 127.4 DOUBLE TOURNOIS
Copper **Ruler:** Louis XIII **Mint:** Tours

Date	Mintage	VG	F	VF	XF	Unc
1643E	—	8.00	15.00	45.00	160	—

KM# 127.5 DOUBLE TOURNOIS
Copper **Ruler:** Louis XIII **Mint:** Angers

Date	Mintage	VG	F	VF	XF	Unc
1643F	—	8.00	15.00	45.00	160	—

KM# 127.6 DOUBLE TOURNOIS
Copper **Ruler:** Louis XIII **Mint:** La Rochelle

Date	Mintage	VG	F	VF	XF	Unc
1642H	—	8.00	12.00	35.00	130	—
1643H	—	8.00	12.00	35.00	130	—

KM# 127.7 DOUBLE TOURNOIS
Copper **Ruler:** Louis XIII **Mint:** Bordeaux

Date	Mintage	VG	F	VF	XF	Unc
1642K	—	8.00	12.00	35.00	130	—
1643K	—	8.00	12.00	35.00	130	—

KM# 127.8 DOUBLE TOURNOIS
Copper **Ruler:** Louis XIII **Mint:** Feurs **Note:** Strike mark: Pellet.

Date	Mintage	VG	F	VF	XF	Unc
1642	—	9.00	18.00	50.00	180	—
1643	—	9.00	18.00	50.00	180	—

KM# 127.9 DOUBLE TOURNOIS
Copper **Ruler:** Louis XIII **Mint:** Lay **Note:** Strike mark: 2 pellets.

Date	Mintage	VG	F	VF	XF	Unc
1642	—	9.00	18.00	50.00	180	—
1643	—	9.00	18.00	50.00	180	—

KM# 127.10 DOUBLE TOURNOIS
Copper **Ruler:** Louis XIII **Mint:** Macon **Note:** Strike mark: 3 pellets.

Date	Mintage	VG	F	VF	XF	Unc
1643	—	10.00	20.00	65.00	230	—

KM# 127.11 DOUBLE TOURNOIS
Copper **Ruler:** Louis XIII **Mint:** Roquemaure **Note:** Strike mark: 4 pellets.

Date	Mintage	VG	F	VF	XF	Unc
1643	—	12.00	20.00	75.00	240	—

KM# 127.12 DOUBLE TOURNOIS
Copper **Ruler:** Louis XIII **Mint:** Vienne **Note:** Strike mark: Crescent.

Date	Mintage	VG	F	VF	XF	Unc
1643	—	12.00	20.00	65.00	230	—

KM# 151 DOUBLE TOURNOIS
Copper **Ruler:** Louis XIV **Obv:** Laureate head right **Rev:** Crosses flanking crowned fleur-de-lis **Mint:** Paris

Date	Mintage	VG	F	VF	XF	Unc
1644A	—	100	225	350	900	—
1647A	—	125	250	400	1,000	—

KM# 193 DOUBLE TOURNOIS
Billon **Ruler:** Louis XIV **Obv:** Cross with fluer-de-lis at ends **Rev:** Three fleur-de-lis, crow above

Date	Mintage	VG	F	VF	XF	Unc
1656	—	25.00	50.00	170	550	—

KM# 87 DOUBLE LORRAIN
Copper **Ruler:** Louis XIII **Obv:** Laureate bust right **Rev:** Three fleur-de-lis **Mint:** Stenay

Date	Mintage	VG	F	VF	XF	Unc
1633	—	12.00	25.00	65.00	230	—
1636	—	12.00	25.00	65.00	230	—
1637	—	12.00	25.00	65.00	230	—
1638	—	12.00	25.00	65.00	230	—
1639	—	12.00	25.00	65.00	230	—
1640	—	12.00	25.00	65.00	230	—

KM# 90 DOUBLE LORRAIN
Copper **Ruler:** Louis XIII **Obv:** Bust right in shirt

Date	Mintage	VG	F	VF	XF	Unc
1635	—	15.00	30.00	75.00	240	—

KM# 91 DOUBLE LORRAIN
Copper **Ruler:** Louis XIII **Obv:** Laureate bust

Date	Mintage	VG	F	VF	XF	Unc
1635	—	20.00	40.00	125	400	—

KM# 128 DOUBLE LORRAIN
Copper **Ruler:** Louis XIII **Obv:** Laureate head

Date	Mintage	VG	F	VF	XF	Unc
1642	—	25.00	50.00	150	475	—

KM# 50 VACQUETTE
Billon **Ruler:** Louis XIII **Obv:** Quartered shield, cow and crowned L's **Rev:** Cross in quatrefoil **Mint:** Morlaas

Date	Mintage	VG	F	VF	XF	Unc
1612	—	30.00	80.00	225	700	—
1613	473,000	30.00	80.00	250	750	—
1614	291,000	—	—	—	—	—
1615	120,000	—	—	—	—	—
1619	312,000	30.00	80.00	270	725	—
1642	—	30.00	80.00	225	700	—
ND	—	25.00	70.00	200	650	—

KM# 63 DOUBLE VACQUETTE
Billon **Ruler:** Louis XIII **Obv:** Quartered shield of Bearn **Rev:** Cross in quatrefoil, date in angles **Mint:** Morlaas

Date	Mintage	VG	F	VF	XF	Unc
1619	—	65.00	125	300	750	—
1642	—	—	—	—	—	—

Note: Reported, not confirmed

KM# 78.1 SIZAIN
Billon **Ruler:** Louis XIII **Obv:** Crowned shield of France **Rev:** Cross with fleur-de-lis in angles **Mint:** Uncertain Mint

Date	Mintage	VG	F	VF	XF	Unc
1628 Rare	—	—	—	—	—	—
1629 Rare	—	—	—	—	—	—

KM# 78.2 SIZAIN
Billon **Ruler:** Louis XIII **Mint:** Paris

Date	Mintage	VG	F	VF	XF	Unc
1642A	—	200	400	800	1,600	—

KM# 198 SIZAIN
Billon **Ruler:** Louis XIV **Obv:** Crowned shield of France, small crowned L's at sides **Rev:** Cross with fleur-de-lis in angles

Date	Mintage	VG	F	VF	XF	Unc
1658	—	400	1,000	2,000	4,000	—

KM# 196 6 BLANCS
Billon **Ruler:** Louis XIV **Obv:** Laureate, draped and mailed bust right **Rev:** Crown above three fleur-de-lis, value in exergue **Mint:** Bordeaux

Date	Mintage	VG	F	VF	XF	Unc
1657K	—	350	750	1,450	3,600	—

KM# 58.1 DOUZAIN
Billon **Ruler:** Louis XIII **Obv:** Crowned shield of France **Rev:** Cross with crown or L's in angles **Mint:** Paris

Date	Mintage	VG	F	VF	XF	Unc
1617A	—	45.00	90.00	175	550	—
1618A	—	40.00	80.00	165	500	—

KM# 58.2 DOUZAIN
Billon **Ruler:** Louis XIII **Mint:** La Rochelle

Date	Mintage	VG	F	VF	XF	Unc
1616H	—	30.00	65.00	125	400	—
1620H	—	30.00	65.00	125	400	—
1625H	—	30.00	65.00	125	400	—
1626H	—	30.00	65.00	125	400	—
1628H	—	30.00	65.00	125	400	—

KM# 58.2a DOUZAIN
0.6000 g., 0.8780 Silver 0.0169 oz. ASW **Ruler:** Louis XIII **Rev:** Cross with crown or fleur-de-lis in angles **Mint:** Paris

Date	Mintage	VG	F	VF	XF	Unc
1625A	7,803	100	300	650	1,500	—

KM# 58.3 DOUZAIN
Billon **Ruler:** Louis XIII **Mint:** Toulouse

Date	Mintage	VG	F	VF	XF	Unc
1611M	—	50.00	100	200	600	—

KM# 58.4 DOUZAIN
Billon **Ruler:** Louis XIII **Mint:** Montpellier

Date	Mintage	VG	F	VF	XF	Unc
1621N	—	30.00	65.00	125	400	—
1622N	—	30.00	65.00	125	400	—
1628N	—	50.00	100	200	600	—
1629N	—	60.00	120	225	650	—

KM# 197 DOUZAIN
Billon **Ruler:** Louis XIV **Obv:** Crowned shield of France, small crowned L's flanking **Rev:** Cross with fleur-de-lis in angles

Date	Mintage	VG	F	VF	XF	Unc
1658	—	500	1,000	2,000	4,000	—

KM# 5 LIARD
Billon **Ruler:** Henri IV **Obv:** Crowned H, three fleur-de-lis around **Rev:** Short cross with fleur-de-lis at ends **Mint:** Uncertain Mint

Date	Mintage	VG	F	VF	XF	Unc
1601	—	—	—	—	—	—

KM# 34 LIARD
Billon **Ruler:** Henri IV **Obv:** Cross with cows and crowned H in angles **Rev:** Cross in quatre lobe **Mint:** Bearn

Date	Mintage	VG	F	VF	XF	Unc
1609	—	—	—	—	—	—

KM# 191.1 LIARD
Copper **Ruler:** Louis XIV **Obv:** Young bust in robe right **Rev:** Large crowned L, divide fleur-de-lis **Mint:** Paris

Date	Mintage	VG	F	VF	XF	Unc
1654A	—	100	200	325	775	—

KM# 191.2 LIARD
Copper **Ruler:** Louis XIV **Mint:** Bordeaux

Date	Mintage	VG	F	VF	XF	Unc
1656K	—	125	250	400	850	—

KM# 189 LIARD
Billon **Ruler:** Louis XIV **Obv:** Crowned shield of France **Rev:** Cross with fleur-de-lis in angles

Date	Mintage	VG	F	VF	XF	Unc
1655	—	65.00	125	250	650	—

KM# 190 LIARD
Billon **Ruler:** Louis XIV **Rev:** Maltese cross

Date	Mintage	VG	F	VF	XF	Unc
1655	—	65.00	125	250	650	—

KM# 192.1 LIARD
Copper **Ruler:** Louis XIV **Rev:** Value above three fleur-de-lis, mint mark within **Mint:** Paris

Date	Mintage	VG	F	VF	XF	Unc
1655A	—	8.00	16.00	45.00	180	—
1656A	—	10.00	18.00	50.00	190	—
1657A	—	12.00	24.00	55.00	210	—

KM# 192.2 LIARD
Copper **Ruler:** Louis XIV **Mint:** Rouen

Date	Mintage	VG	F	VF	XF	Unc
1655B	—	8.00	18.00	45.00	175	—
1656B	—	9.00	20.00	50.00	180	—
1657B	—	12.00	30.00	75.00	270	—
1658B	—	20.00	50.00	125	425	—

KM# 192.3 LIARD
Copper **Ruler:** Louis XIV **Note:** Strike mark: B*.

Date	Mintage	VG	F	VF	XF	Unc
1655	—	8.00	18.00	45.00	175	—
1656	—	10.00	25.00	60.00	215	—

KM# 192.4 LIARD

Copper **Ruler:** Louis XIV **Mint:** Saint Lô

Date	Mintage	VG	F	VF	XF	Unc
1655C	—	8.00	18.00	45.00	175	—
1656C	—	12.00	30.00	75.00	270	—
1657C	—	10.00	25.00	60.00	215	—

KM# 192.5 LIARD

Copper **Ruler:** Louis XIV **Mint:** Lyon

Date	Mintage	VG	F	VF	XF	Unc
1655D	—	7.00	16.00	45.00	180	—
1656D	—	10.00	25.00	75.00	240	—
1657D	—	8.00	18.00	55.00	190	—

KM# 192.6 LIARD

Copper **Ruler:** Louis XIV **Mint:** Tours

Date	Mintage	VG	F	VF	XF	Unc
1655E	—	9.00	20.00	50.00	160	—
1656E	—	9.00	20.00	50.00	160	—
1657E	—	9.00	20.00	50.00	160	—
1658E	—	20.00	50.00	125	360	—

KM# 192.7 LIARD

Copper **Ruler:** Louis XIV **Mint:** Poitiers

Date	Mintage	VG	F	VF	XF	Unc
1655G	—	9.00	20.00	50.00	190	—
1656G	—	25.00	60.00	150	500	—
1657G	—	12.00	30.00	75.00	270	—

KM# 192.8 LIARD

Copper **Ruler:** Louis XIV **Mint:** Poitiers

Date	Mintage	VG	F	VF	XF	Unc
1657G	—	12.00	30.00	75.00	300	—
1658G	—	17.00	40.00	100	400	—

KM# 192.9 LIARD

Copper **Ruler:** Louis XIV **Mint:** Limoges

Date	Mintage	VG	F	VF	XF	Unc
1655I	—	—	—	125	475	—
1656I	—	10.00	28.00	70.00	290	—
1657I	—	9.00	25.00	60.00	240	—
1658I	—	20.00	50.00	125	475	—

KM# 192.10 LIARD

Copper **Ruler:** Louis XIV **Mint:** Bordeaux

Date	Mintage	VG	F	VF	XF	Unc
1655K	—	12.00	30.00	75.00	300	—
1656K	—	10.00	28.00	70.00	290	—
1657K	—	12.00	30.00	75.00	300	—

KM# 192.11 LIARD

Copper **Ruler:** Louis XIV **Mint:** Villeneuve St. André

Date	Mintage	VG	F	VF	XF	Unc
1655R	—	12.00	30.00	75.00	300	—
1656R	—	10.00	28.00	70.00	290	—
1657R	—	12.00	30.00	75.00	300	—

KM# 284.1 LIARD

Copper **Ruler:** Louis XIV **Obv:** Older mailed bust right **Mint:** Paris

Date	Mintage	VG	F	VF	XF	Unc
1693A	1,291,000	9.00	25.00	60.00	240	—
1694A	—	9.00	25.00	60.00	240	—
1696A	—	9.00	25.00	60.00	240	—
1697A	—	8.00	20.00	50.00	210	—
1698A	—	8.00	20.00	50.00	210	—
1699A	—	10.00	28.00	70.00	300	—

KM# 284.2 LIARD

Copper **Ruler:** Louis XIV **Mint:** Metz

Date	Mintage	VG	F	VF	XF	Unc
1694AA	—	15.00	35.00	80.00	325	—
1697AA	—	15.00	35.00	80.00	325	—

KM# 284.3 LIARD

Copper **Ruler:** Louis XIV **Mint:** Rouen

Date	Mintage	VG	F	VF	XF	Unc
1693B	—	9.00	25.00	60.00	240	—
1694B	—	15.00	35.00	80.00	325	—
1695B	—	15.00	35.00	80.00	325	—
1697B	—	15.00	35.00	80.00	325	—
1698B	—	15.00	35.00	80.00	325	—
1699B	—	10.00	28.00	70.00	300	—
1700B	—	18.00	40.00	100	425	—

KM# 284.4 LIARD

Copper **Ruler:** Louis XIV **Mint:** Lyon

Date	Mintage	VG	F	VF	XF	Unc
1693D	2,063,000	8.00	20.00	50.00	210	—
1694D	602,000	18.00	40.00	100	425	—
1695D	2,850,000	8.00	20.00	50.00	210	—
1696D	39,000	15.00	35.00	80.00	325	—
1697D	—	—	—	—	—	—
1699D	3,876,000	9.00	25.00	60.00	240	—

KM# 284.5 LIARD

Copper **Ruler:** Louis XIV **Mint:** Tours

Date	Mintage	VG	F	VF	XF	Unc
1693E	—	15.00	35.00	80.00	325	—
1696E	317,000	—	—	—	—	—
1697E	213,000	15.00	35.00	80.00	325	—
1698E	—	10.00	28.00	70.00	300	—
1699E	—	9.00	25.00	60.00	240	—

KM# 284.6 LIARD

Copper **Ruler:** Louis XIV **Mint:** Poitiers

Date	Mintage	VG	F	VF	XF	Unc
1696G	—	10.00	28.00	70.00	300	—
1697G	—	17.00	40.00	100	425	—

KM# 284.7 LIARD

Copper **Ruler:** Louis XIV **Mint:** La Rochelle

Date	Mintage	VG	F	VF	XF	Unc
1695H	—	15.00	35.00	80.00	325	—
1696H	—	9.00	25.00	60.00	240	—
1698H	—	15.00	35.00	80.00	325	—
1699H	—	10.00	28.00	70.00	300	—

KM# 284.8 LIARD

Copper **Ruler:** Louis XIV **Mint:** Bordeaux

Date	Mintage	VG	F	VF	XF	Unc
1693K	—	10.00	28.00	70.00	300	—
1696K	—	15.00	35.00	80.00	325	—
1698K	—	10.00	28.00	70.00	300	—

KM# 284.9 LIARD

Copper **Ruler:** Louis XIV **Mint:** Bayonne

Date	Mintage	VG	F	VF	XF	Unc
1695L	—	9.00	25.00	60.00	240	—
1696L	—	15.00	35.00	80.00	325	—
1697L	—	15.00	35.00	80.00	325	—
1698L	—	15.00	35.00	80.00	325	—
1699L	—	9.00	25.00	60.00	240	—

KM# 284.10 LIARD

Copper **Ruler:** Louis XIV **Mint:** Toulouse

Date	Mintage	VG	F	VF	XF	Unc
1693	49,000	17.00	50.00	150	475	—
1694	—	—	—	—	—	—
1695	—	15.00	35.00	80.00	325	—
1697	—	10.00	28.00	70.00	300	—

KM# 284.11 LIARD

Copper **Ruler:** Louis XIV **Mint:** Montpellier

Date	Mintage	VG	F	VF	XF	Unc
1693N	768,000	15.00	35.00	80.00	325	—
1694N	—	17.00	40.00	100	425	—
1695N	—	10.00	28.00	70.00	300	—
1696N	79,000	—	—	—	—	—
1697N	3,097,000	9.00	25.00	60.00	240	—
1699N	—	15.00	35.00	80.00	325	—

KM# 284.12 LIARD

Copper **Ruler:** Louis XIV **Mint:** Riom

Date	Mintage	VG	F	VF	XF	Unc
1693O	75,000	20.00	50.00	125	475	—
1695O	—	15.00	35.00	80.00	325	—
1698O	—	15.00	35.00	80.00	325	—
1699O	—	10.00	28.00	70.00	300	—

KM# 284.13 LIARD

Copper **Ruler:** Louis XIV **Mint:** Dijon

Date	Mintage	VG	F	VF	XF	Unc
1693P	26,000	—	—	—	—	—
1695P	105,000	15.00	35.00	80.00	325	—
1697P	123,000	15.00	35.00	80.00	325	—
1698P	3,626,000	8.00	20.00	50.00	210	—

KM# 284.14 LIARD

Copper **Ruler:** Louis XIV **Mint:** Reims

Date	Mintage	VG	F	VF	XF	Unc
1693S	—	15.00	35.00	80.00	325	—
1696S	—	15.00	35.00	80.00	325	—
1697S	—	8.00	20.00	50.00	210	—
1698S	—	15.00	35.00	80.00	325	—

KM# 284.15 LIARD

Copper **Ruler:** Louis XIV **Mint:** Nantes

Date	Mintage	VG	F	VF	XF	Unc
1697T	—	9.00	25.00	60.00	240	—

KM# 284.16 LIARD

Copper **Ruler:** Louis XIV **Mint:** Troyes

Date	Mintage	VG	F	VF	XF	Unc
1693V	274,000	15.00	35.00	80.00	325	—
1695V	—	15.00	35.00	80.00	325	—
1697V	Est. 1,600,000	9.00	25.00	60.00	240	
1698V	2,888,000	9.00	25.00	60.00	240	—

KM# 284.18 LIARD

Copper **Ruler:** Louis XIV **Mint:** Amiens

Date	Mintage	VG	F	VF	XF	Unc
1693X	—	15.00	35.00	80.00	325	—
1695X	—	15.00	35.00	80.00	325	—
1696X	—	9.00	25.00	60.00	240	—
1697X	—	9.00	25.00	60.00	240	—
1698X	—	9.00	25.00	60.00	240	—
1699X	—	10.00	28.00	70.00	300	—

KM# 284.19 LIARD

Copper **Ruler:** Louis XIV **Mint:** Bourges

Date	Mintage	VG	F	VF	XF	Unc
1693Y	—	15.00	35.00	80.00	325	—
1695Y	—	15.00	35.00	80.00	325	—
1698Y	—	15.00	35.00	80.00	325	—
1699Y	—	15.00	35.00	80.00	325	—

KM# 284.20 LIARD

Copper **Ruler:** Louis XIV **Mint:** Rennes **Note:** Mint mark: Numeral 9.

Date	Mintage	VG	F	VF	XF	Unc
1693	—	15.00	35.00	80.00	325	—
1694	—	15.00	35.00	80.00	325	—
1697	—	10.00	28.00	70.00	300	—

KM# 284.21 LIARD

Copper **Ruler:** Louis XIV **Mint:** Aix **Note:** Mint mark: Ampersand.

Date	Mintage	VG	F	VF	XF	Unc
1693	—	15.00	35.00	80.00	325	—
1694	—	17.00	40.00	100	425	—
1698	—	15.00	35.00	80.00	325	—
1699	—	8.00	20.00	50.00	210	—

KM# 284.22 LIARD

Copper **Ruler:** Louis XIV **Mint:** Lille **Note:** Mint mark: Crowned L.

Date	Mintage	VG	F	VF	XF	Unc
1693	1,649,000	9.00	25.00	60.00	240	—
1694	—	15.00	35.00	80.00	325	—
1695	—	15.00	35.00	80.00	325	—
1696	2,907,000	8.00	20.00	50.00	210	—
1697	1,753,000	10.00	28.00	70.00	300	—
1698	—	10.00	28.00	70.00	300	—
1699	845,000	15.00	35.00	80.00	325	—
1700	—	17.00	40.00	100	350	—

KM# 284.23 LIARD

Copper **Ruler:** Louis XIV **Mint:** Metz **Note:** Mint mark: Crowned M.

Date	Mintage	VG	F	VF	XF	Unc
1693	—	20.00	45.00	100	425	—

KM# 284.24 LIARD

Copper **Ruler:** Louis XIV **Mint:** Troyes **Note:** Mint mark: Crowned S.

Date	Mintage	VG	F	VF	XF	Unc
1693	—	20.00	40.00	85.00	350	—
1695	—	20.00	40.00	85.00	350	—

KM# 284.25 LIARD

Copper **Ruler:** Louis XIV **Mint:** Besançon **Note:** Mint mark: Monogram of two back-to-back C's.

Date	Mintage	VG	F	VF	XF	Unc
1698	3,636,000	10.00	22.00	55.00	220	—

KM# 304 LIARD

Copper **Ruler:** Louis XIV **Obv:** Bust right **Mint:** Pau **Note:** Mint mark: Cow.

Date	Mintage	VG	F	VF	XF	Unc
1694	—	20.00	45.00	120	450	—
1695	—	20.00	45.00	120	450	—
1696	273,000	20.00	45.00	120	450	—
1697	—	20.00	45.00	120	450	—
1698	—	20.00	45.00	120	450	—

KM# 309 2 DENIERS

Copper **Ruler:** Louis XIV **Rev:** Crown above 3 fleur-de-lis **Mint:** Strasbourg

Date	Mintage	VG	F	VF	XF	Unc
1695BB	331,000	—	—	—	—	—
1696BB	—	8.00	20.00	40.00	150	—
1697BB	1,157,000	10.00	25.00	50.00	180	—
1698BB	—	8.00	20.00	40.00	150	—
1699BB	—	8.00	20.00	40.00	150	—
1700BB	—	10.00	25.00	50.00	180	—

KM# 137 3 DENIERS (Liard)

Copper **Ruler:** Louis XIV **Obv:** Laureate head right **Rev:** Crown above fleur-de-lis dividing 3D **Mint:** Paris

Date	Mintage	VG	F	VF	XF	Unc
1643A	—	60.00	125	250	575	—
1644A	—	60.00	125	250	575	—
1647A	—	60.00	125	250	575	—
1648A	—	60.00	125	250	575	—
NDA	—	60.00	125	250	575	—

KM# 170 3 DENIERS (Liard)

Copper **Ruler:** Louis XIV **Rev:** Crown above large L, dividing fleur-de-lis, denomination in exergue, 3 DENIERS **Mint:** Paris

Date	Mintage	VG	F	VF	XF	Unc
1649A	—	50.00	100	200	500	—

KM# 171 3 DENIERS (Liard)

Copper **Ruler:** Louis XIV **Rev:** Denomination in exergue as III DEN **Mint:** Paris

Date	Mintage	VG	F	VF	XF	Unc
1649A	—	75.00	150	350	775	—

KM# 310 4 DENIERS

Copper **Ruler:** Louis XIV **Obv:** Armored bust right **Rev:** Crown above 3 fleur-de-lis **Mint:** Strasbourg

Date	Mintage	VG	F	VF	XF	Unc
1696BB	2,731,000	8.00	20.00	55.00	175	—
1697BB	1,257,000	8.00	20.00	55.00	175	—
1698BB	1,872,000	8.00	20.00	55.00	175	—
1699BB	Inc. above	8.00	20.00	55.00	175	—
1700BB	—	—	—	—	—	—

KM# 116 15 DENIERS

Billon **Ruler:** Louis XIII **Obv:** Crowned shield, fleur-de-lis counterstamp above **Rev:** Cross, fleur-de-lis in angles and as counterstamp at center **Mint:** Paris

Date	Mintage	VG	F	VF	XF	Unc
1641A	—	500	1,000	2,000	—	—

KM# 285.1 15 DENIERS

Billon **Ruler:** Louis XIV **Obv:** Eight crowned back-to-back L's **Rev:** Crowned shield of France **Mint:** Paris

Date	Mintage	VG	F	VF	XF	Unc
1693A	—	8.00	20.00	40.00	150	—
1695A	—	8.00	20.00	40.00	150	—
1696A	—	—	—	—	—	—
1700A	—	—	—	—	—	—

KM# 285.2 15 DENIERS

Billon **Ruler:** Louis XIV **Mint:** Metz

Date	Mintage	VG	F	VF	XF	Unc
1697AA	—	12.00	30.00	60.00	220	—
1698AA	—	12.00	30.00	60.00	220	—

KM# 285.3 15 DENIERS

Billon **Ruler:** Louis XIV **Mint:** Rouen

Date	Mintage	VG	F	VF	XF	Unc
1692B	—	9.00	22.00	45.00	160	—
1693B	—	9.00	22.00	45.00	160	—
1695B	—	—	—	—	—	—
1696B	—	—	—	—	—	—
1698B	—	—	—	—	—	—
1700B	—	—	—	—	—	—

KM# 285.4 15 DENIERS

Billon **Ruler:** Louis XIV **Mint:** Caen

Date	Mintage	VG	F	VF	XF	Unc
1697C	—	—	—	—	—	—

KM# 285.5 15 DENIERS

Billon **Ruler:** Louis XIV **Mint:** Lyon

Date	Mintage	VG	F	VF	XF	Unc
1692D	—	—	—	—	—	—
1693D	—	9.00	22.00	45.00	160	—
1694D	—	9.00	22.00	45.00	160	—
1695D	—	9.00	22.00	45.00	160	—
1696D	—	9.00	22.00	45.00	160	—
1698D	—	—	—	—	—	—
1699D	—	—	—	—	—	—
1700D	—	—	—	—	—	—

KM# 285.6 15 DENIERS

Billon **Ruler:** Louis XIV **Mint:** Tours

Date	Mintage	VG	F	VF	XF	Unc
1693E	—	9.00	22.00	45.00	160	—
1694E	—	9.00	22.00	45.00	160	—
1695E	—	9.00	22.00	45.00	160	—
1697E	—	10.00	25.00	50.00	180	—

KM# 285.7 15 DENIERS

Billon **Ruler:** Louis XIV **Mint:** Poitiers

Date	Mintage	VG	F	VF	XF	Unc
1693G	—	9.00	22.00	45.00	160	—
1695G	—	—	—	—	—	—
1696G	—	—	—	—	—	—

KM# 285.8 15 DENIERS

Billon **Ruler:** Louis XIV **Mint:** La Rochelle

Date	Mintage	VG	F	VF	XF	Unc
1693H	—	10.00	25.00	50.00	180	—
1700H	—	—	—	—	—	—

KM# 285.9 15 DENIERS

Billon **Ruler:** Louis XIV **Mint:** Limoges

Date	Mintage	VG	F	VF	XF	Unc
1695I	—	—	—	—	—	—
1696I	—	—	—	—	—	—

KM# 285.10 15 DENIERS

Billon **Ruler:** Louis XIV **Mint:** Bayonne

Date	Mintage	VG	F	VF	XF	Unc
1693L	—	10.00	25.00	50.00	180	—

KM# 285.11 15 DENIERS

Billon **Ruler:** Louis XIV **Mint:** Toulouse

Date	Mintage	VG	F	VF	XF	Unc
1692M	—	9.00	22.00	45.00	160	—
1693M	—	9.00	22.00	45.00	160	—
1694M	—	—	—	—	—	—
1695M	—	—	—	—	—	—
1696M	—	—	—	—	—	—
1698M	—	—	—	—	—	—

KM# 285.12 15 DENIERS

Billon **Ruler:** Louis XIV **Mint:** Montpellier

Date	Mintage	VG	F	VF	XF	Unc
1692N	—	9.00	22.00	45.00	160	—
1693N	—	9.00	22.00	45.00	160	—
1694N	—	10.00	25.00	50.00	180	—
1695N	—	—	—	—	—	—
1696N	—	10.00	25.00	50.00	180	—
1697N	—	12.00	30.00	60.00	220	—
1698N	—	—	—	—	—	—
1700N	—	—	—	—	—	—

KM# 285.13 15 DENIERS

Billon **Ruler:** Louis XIV **Mint:** Riom

Date	Mintage	VG	F	VF	XF	Unc
1692O	—	—	—	—	—	—
1693O	—	—	—	—	—	—
1695O	—	—	—	—	—	—
1696O	—	—	—	—	—	—
1697O	—	—	—	—	—	—

KM# 285.14 15 DENIERS

Billon **Ruler:** Louis XIV **Mint:** Dijon

Date	Mintage	VG	F	VF	XF	Unc
1693P	—	9.00	22.00	45.00	160	—
1694P	—	—	—	—	—	—
1695P	—	9.00	22.00	45.00	160	—
1696P	—	—	—	—	—	—
1697P	—	20.00	40.00	100	350	—
1698P	—	20.00	40.00	100	350	—

KM# 285.15 15 DENIERS

Billon **Ruler:** Louis XIV **Mint:** Reims

Date	Mintage	VG	F	VF	XF	Unc
1693S	—	—	—	—	—	—
1694S	—	9.00	22.00	45.00	160	—
1695S	—	—	—	—	—	—
1696S	—	—	—	—	—	—
1699S	—	—	—	—	—	—

KM# 285.16 15 DENIERS

Billon **Ruler:** Louis XIV **Mint:** Nantes

Date	Mintage	VG	F	VF	XF	Unc
1695T	—	9.00	22.00	45.00	160	—
1698T	—	—	—	—	—	—

KM# 285.17 15 DENIERS

Billon **Ruler:** Louis XIV **Mint:** Troyes

Date	Mintage	VG	F	VF	XF	Unc
1695V	—	12.00	30.00	60.00	220	—

KM# 285.18 15 DENIERS

Billon **Ruler:** Louis XIV **Mint:** Amiens

Date	Mintage	VG	F	VF	XF	Unc
1693X	—	—	—	—	—	—
1695X	—	—	—	—	—	—

KM# 285.19 15 DENIERS

Billon **Ruler:** Louis XIV **Mint:** Bourges

Date	Mintage	VG	F	VF	XF	Unc
1692Y	—	—	—	—	—	—
1693Y	—	—	—	—	—	—
1695Y	—	—	—	—	—	—
1698Y	—	—	—	—	—	—

KM# 285.20 15 DENIERS

Billon **Ruler:** Louis XIV **Mint:** Aix **Note:** Mint mark: Ampersand.

Date	Mintage	VG	F	VF	XF	Unc
1693	—	9.00	22.00	45.00	160	—
1694	—	9.00	22.00	45.00	160	—
1695	—	9.00	22.00	45.00	160	—
1696	—	10.00	25.00	50.00	180	—
1700	—	—	—	—	—	—

KM# 285.22 15 DENIERS

Billon **Ruler:** Louis XIV **Obv:** Crowned double monograms form cross with fleur-de-lis at angles **Rev:** Crowned shield **Mint:** Lille **Note:** Mint mark: Crowned L.

Date	Mintage	VG	F	VF	XF	Unc
1693	—	—	—	—	—	—
1696	—	—	—	—	—	—
1697	—	10.00	25.00	50.00	180	—
1698	—	—	—	—	—	—
1699	—	10.00	25.00	50.00	180	—
1700	—	15.00	35.00	75.00	265	—

KM# 285.23 15 DENIERS

Billon **Ruler:** Louis XIV **Mint:** Troyes **Note:** Mint mark: Crowned S.

Date	Mintage	VG	F	VF	XF	Unc
1692	—	10.00	25.00	50.00	180	—
1693	—	15.00	35.00	75.00	265	—

KM# 285.24 15 DENIERS

Billon **Ruler:** Louis XIV **Mint:** Besançon **Note:** Mint mark: Monogram of two back-to-back C's.

Date	Mintage	VG	F	VF	XF	Unc
1695	—	—	—	—	—	—
1696	—	9.00	22.00	45.00	160	—
1697	—	—	—	—	—	—
1698	—	20.00	40.00	100	350	—
1699	—	—	—	—	—	—

KM# 286.1 15 DENIERS

Billon **Ruler:** Louis XIV **Mint:** Paris **Note:** Smaller, new design overstruck on old flans.

Date	Mintage	VG	F	VF	XF	Unc
1693A	—	7.00	15.00	25.00	65.00	—

KM# 286.2 15 DENIERS

Billon **Ruler:** Louis XIV **Mint:** Lyon

Date	Mintage	VG	F	VF	XF	Unc
1693D	—	7.00	15.00	25.00	65.00	—
1694D	—	7.00	15.00	25.00	65.00	—
1695D	—	7.00	15.00	25.00	65.00	—
1696D	—	7.00	15.00	25.00	65.00	—
1698D	—	7.00	15.00	25.00	65.00	—

KM# 286.3 15 DENIERS

Billon **Ruler:** Louis XIV **Mint:** Tours

Date	Mintage	VG	F	VF	XF	Unc
1693E	—	7.00	15.00	25.00	65.00	—
1694E	—	7.00	15.00	25.00	65.00	—
1695E	—	7.00	15.00	25.00	65.00	—
1696E	—	7.00	15.00	25.00	65.00	—
1697E	—	7.00	15.00	25.00	65.00	—

KM# 286.4 15 DENIERS

Billon **Ruler:** Louis XIV **Mint:** La Rochelle

Date	Mintage	VG	F	VF	XF	Unc
1694H	—	7.00	15.00	28.00	70.00	—
1697H	—	7.00	15.00	28.00	70.00	—

KM# 286.5 15 DENIERS

Billon **Ruler:** Louis XIV **Mint:** Bayonne

Date	Mintage	VG	F	VF	XF	Unc
1695L	—	7.00	15.00	25.00	65.00	—

KM# 286.6 15 DENIERS

Billon **Ruler:** Louis XIV **Mint:** Toulouse

Date	Mintage	VG	F	VF	XF	Unc
1692M	—	7.00	15.00	25.00	65.00	—

KM# 286.7 15 DENIERS

Billon **Ruler:** Louis XIV **Mint:** Riom

Date	Mintage	VG	F	VF	XF	Unc
1695O	—	8.00	16.00	30.00	80.00	—

KM# 286.8 15 DENIERS

Billon **Ruler:** Louis XIV **Mint:** Dijon

Date	Mintage	VG	F	VF	XF	Unc
1694P	—	7.00	15.00	25.00	65.00	—
1695P	—	7.00	15.00	25.00	65.00	—

KM# 286.9 15 DENIERS

Billon **Ruler:** Louis XIV **Mint:** Rennes **Note:** Mint mark: Numeral 9.

Date	Mintage	VG	F	VF	XF	Unc
1695	—	7.00	15.00	25.00	65.00	—
1697	—	7.00	15.00	25.00	65.00	—

KM# 288 15 DENIERS

Billon **Ruler:** Louis XIV **Obv:** Eight crowned L' back-to-back **Rev:** Crowned shield of France and Navarre

Date	Mintage	VG	F	VF	XF	Unc
ND	—	65.00	135	250	—	—

KM# 289 15 DENIERS

Billon **Ruler:** Louis XIV **Rev:** Crowned shield of France, Navarre and Bearn

Date	Mintage	VG	F	VF	XF	Unc
1692	—	22.00	60.00	110	350	—
1693	—	22.00	60.00	110	350	—
1694	—	25.00	65.00	120	375	—
1695	25,000	25.00	65.00	130	400	—
1696	134,000	22.00	60.00	110	350	—
1697	—	22.00	60.00	110	350	—
1698	6,828	—	—	—	—	—
1699	3,626	25.00	65.00	120	375	—
1700	692	—	—	—	—	—

KM# 287.1 15 DENIERS

Billon **Ruler:** Louis XIV **Mint:** Lyon

Date	Mintage	VG	F	VF	XF	Unc
1693D	—	7.00	15.00	25.00	65.00	—
1694D	—	7.00	15.00	25.00	65.00	—
1696D	—	7.00	15.00	25.00	65.00	—

KM# 287.2 15 DENIERS

Billon **Ruler:** Louis XIV **Mint:** Tours **Note:** Counterstamp: Fleur-de-lis.

Date	Mintage	VG	F	VF	XF	Unc
1692E	—	7.00	15.00	25.00	65.00	—
1693E	—	7.00	15.00	25.00	65.00	—
1694E	—	7.00	15.00	25.00	65.00	—

KM# 287.3 15 DENIERS

Billon **Ruler:** Louis XIV **Mint:** La Rochelle

Date	Mintage	VG	F	VF	XF	Unc
1694H	—	7.00	15.00	25.00	65.00	—

KM# 287.4 15 DENIERS

Billon **Ruler:** Louis XIV **Mint:** Toulouse

Date	Mintage	VG	F	VF	XF	Unc
1694M	—	7.00	15.00	25.00	65.00	—

KM# 287.5 15 DENIERS

Billon **Ruler:** Louis XIV **Mint:** Montpellier

Date	Mintage	VG	F	VF	XF	Unc
1694N	—	7.00	15.00	25.00	65.00	—

KM# 287.6 15 DENIERS
Billon **Ruler:** Louis XIV **Mint:** Dijon

Date	Mintage	VG	F	VF	XF	Unc
1693P	—	7.00	15.00	25.00	65.00	—

KM# 287.7 15 DENIERS
Billon **Ruler:** Louis XIV **Mint:** Aix **Note:** Mint mark: Ampersand.

Date	Mintage	VG	F	VF	XF	Unc
1692	—	7.00	15.00	30.00	70.00	—

KM# 287.8 15 DENIERS
Billon **Ruler:** Louis XIV **Mint:** Rennes **Note:** Mint mark: Numeral 9.

Date	Mintage	VG	F	VF	XF	Unc
1697	—	7.00	15.00	25.00	65.00	—

KM# 195 5 LIARDS
Billon **Ruler:** Louis XIV **Rev:** Crown above 3 fleur-de-lis, date and value **Mint:** Bordeaux

Date	Mintage	VG	F	VF	XF	Unc
1657K	—	250	600	1,250	2,900	—

KM# 311 16 DENIERS
Billon **Ruler:** Louis XIV **Obv:** Crowned shield of France dividing value **Rev:** Fleur-de-lis at ends of outlined cross **Mint:** Strasbourg

Date	Mintage	VG	F	VF	XF	Unc
1696BB	2,084,000	9.00	22.00	45.00	160	—
1697BB	292,000	12.00	30.00	70.00	250	—
1698BB	71,000	—	—	—	—	—
1699BB	65,000	15.00	40.00	80.00	270	—
1700BB	731,000	—	—	—	—	—

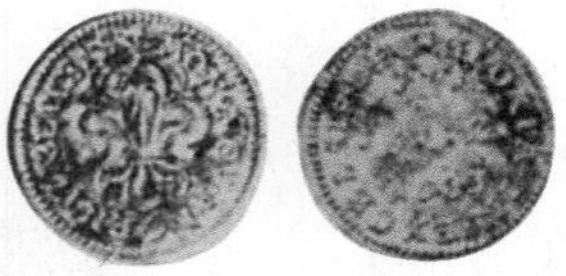

KM# 245 SOL
0.5110 g., 0.8330 Silver 0.0137 oz. ASW **Ruler:** Louis XIV **Obv:** Large fleur-de-lis **Rev:** Value and date within legend **Mint:** Strasbourg

Date	Mintage	VG	F	VF	XF	Unc
1682	—	20.00	50.00	110	325	—
1683	—	25.00	60.00	125	350	—
1684	—	30.00	75.00	150	450	—
1685	—	—	—	—	—	—
1686	—	—	—	—	—	—
1687	—	—	—	—	—	—
1688	—	—	—	—	—	—

KM# 231 2 SOLS
0.8150 g., 0.7980 Silver 0.0209 oz. ASW **Ruler:** Louis XIV **Obv:** Laureate and draped bust right **Rev:** Crown above two fleur-de-lis, mint mark below

Date	Mintage	VG	F	VF	XF	Unc
1674A	—	30.00	75.00	145	425	—
1675A	—	25.00	65.00	135	400	—
1676A	—	30.00	75.00	145	425	—
1677A	—	40.00	90.00	175	500	—

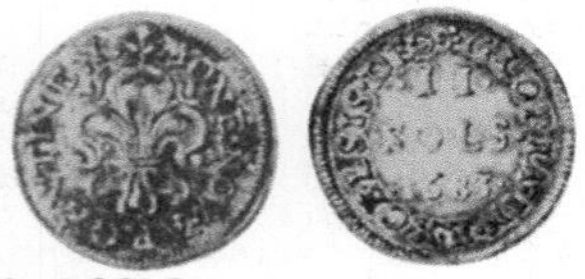

KM# 246 2 SOLS
1.0220 g., 0.7980 Silver 0.0262 oz. ASW **Ruler:** Louis XIV **Obv:** Large fleur-de-lis **Rev:** Value and date within legend

Date	Mintage	VG	F	VF	XF	Unc
1682	—	15.00	35.00	95.00	240	—
1683	—	15.00	35.00	95.00	240	—
1684	—	15.00	35.00	95.00	240	—
1687	—	15.00	35.00	95.00	240	—

KM# 232.1 4 SOLS
1.8090 g., 0.7980 Silver 0.0464 oz. ASW **Ruler:** Louis XIV **Obv:** Draped bust right **Rev:** Crown above fleur-de-lis cross **Mint:** Paris

Date	Mintage	VG	F	VF	XF	Unc
1674A	—	8.00	20.00	45.00	160	—
1675A	—	7.00	18.00	40.00	145	—
1676A	—	7.00	18.00	40.00	145	—
1677A	—	7.00	18.00	40.00	145	—
1679A	—	15.00	40.00	85.00	270	—

KM# 232.2 4 SOLS
1.8090 g., 0.7980 Silver 0.0464 oz. ASW **Ruler:** Louis XIV **Mint:** Lyon

Date	Mintage	VG	F	VF	XF	Unc
1674D	Est. 370,000	8.00	20.00	45.00	160	—
1675D	Est. 3,689,000	7.00	18.00	40.00	145	—
1676D	Est. 4,186,000	7.00	18.00	40.00	145	—
1677D	Est. 4,507,000	7.00	18.00	40.00	145	—

KM# 247 4 SOLS
2.0440 g., 0.8330 Silver 0.0547 oz. ASW **Ruler:** Louis XIV **Obv:** Large fleur-de-lis **Rev:** Value and date within legend **Mint:** Strasbourg

Date	Mintage	VG	F	VF	XF	Unc
1682	91,000	70.00	150	300	725	—

KM# 281.1 4 SOLS 2 DENIERS
1.8090 g., 0.7980 Silver 0.0464 oz. ASW **Ruler:** Louis XIV **Obv:** Draped bust right **Rev:** Crowned double L monogram **Mint:** Paris

Date	Mintage	VG	F	VF	XF	Unc
1691A	—	6.00	15.00	30.00	85.00	—
1692A	—	6.00	15.00	30.00	85.00	—
1693A	—	6.00	16.00	32.00	95.00	—
1695A	—	7.00	17.00	35.00	110	—

KM# 281.2 4 SOLS 2 DENIERS
1.8090 g., 0.7980 Silver 0.0464 oz. ASW **Ruler:** Louis XIV **Mint:** Rouen

Date	Mintage	VG	F	VF	XF	Unc
1691B	—	6.00	16.00	32.00	95.00	—
1692B	—	7.00	17.00	35.00	110	—

KM# 281.3 4 SOLS 2 DENIERS
1.8090 g., 0.7980 Silver 0.0464 oz. ASW **Ruler:** Louis XIV **Mint:** Caen

Date	Mintage	VG	F	VF	XF	Unc
1696C	—	8.00	20.00	40.00	120	—
1697C	69,000	—	—	—	—	—

KM# 281.4 4 SOLS 2 DENIERS
1.8090 g., 0.7980 Silver 0.0464 oz. ASW **Ruler:** Louis XIV **Mint:** Lyon

Date	Mintage	VG	F	VF	XF	Unc
1691D	2,812,000	6.00	15.00	30.00	85.00	—
1692D	5,544,000	6.00	15.00	30.00	90.00	—
1693D	1,491,000	6.00	15.00	30.00	90.00	—
1694D	770,000	6.00	15.00	30.00	90.00	—
1695D	456,000	6.00	15.00	30.00	90.00	—
1696D	281,000	7.00	17.00	35.00	110	—
1697D	149,000	—	—	—	—	—
1698D	70,000	—	—	—	—	—
1699D	53,000	9.00	22.00	45.00	130	—
1700D	5,259	—	—	—	—	—

KM# 281.5 4 SOLS 2 DENIERS
1.8090 g., 0.7980 Silver 0.0464 oz. ASW **Ruler:** Louis XIV **Mint:** Tours

Date	Mintage	VG	F	VF	XF	Unc
1691E	—	6.00	15.00	30.00	90.00	—
1692E	—	6.00	15.00	30.00	90.00	—
1693E	—	7.00	17.00	35.00	110	—
1694E	—	7.00	17.00	35.00	110	—

KM# 281.6 4 SOLS 2 DENIERS
1.8090 g., 0.7980 Silver 0.0464 oz. ASW **Ruler:** Louis XIV **Mint:** La Rochelle

Date	Mintage	VG	F	VF	XF	Unc
1691H	—	6.00	15.00	30.00	90.00	—
1692H	—	8.00	20.00	40.00	120	—
1700H	—	18.00	35.00	65.00	215	—

KM# 281.7 4 SOLS 2 DENIERS
1.8090 g., 0.7980 Silver 0.0464 oz. ASW **Ruler:** Louis XIV **Mint:** Bordeaux

Date	Mintage	VG	F	VF	XF	Unc
1691K	—	6.00	16.00	32.00	95.00	—
1692K	—	6.00	15.00	30.00	90.00	—
1693K	—	6.00	16.00	32.00	95.00	—

KM# 281.8 4 SOLS 2 DENIERS
1.8090 g., 0.7980 Silver 0.0464 oz. ASW **Ruler:** Louis XIV **Mint:** Bayonne **Note:** Mint mark: Crowned L.

Date	Mintage	VG	F	VF	XF	Unc
1691	Est. 272,000	8.00	20.00	40.00	120	—
1692L	—	—	—	—	—	—

KM# 281.9 4 SOLS 2 DENIERS
1.8090 g., 0.7980 Silver 0.0464 oz. ASW **Ruler:** Louis XIV **Mint:** Toulouse

Date	Mintage	VG	F	VF	XF	Unc
1691M	—	6.00	16.00	32.00	95.00	—
1692M	—	6.00	15.00	30.00	90.00	—
1693M	—	6.00	15.00	30.00	90.00	—
1694M	—	6.00	16.00	32.00	95.00	—

KM# 281.10 4 SOLS 2 DENIERS
1.8090 g., 0.7980 Silver 0.0464 oz. ASW **Ruler:** Louis XIV **Mint:** Montpellier

Date	Mintage	VG	F	VF	XF	Unc
1691N	Est. 1,084,000	6.00	15.00	30.00	90.00	—
1692N	2,113,000	6.00	15.00	30.00	85.00	—
1693N	289,000	7.00	17.00	35.00	110	—
1694N	196,000	—	—	—	—	—
1695N	112,000	—	—	—	—	—
1696N	63,000	8.00	20.00	40.00	120	—
1697N	40,000	—	—	—	—	—
1698N	11,000	—	—	—	—	—
1699N	17,000	—	—	—	—	—
1700N	1,000	—	—	—	—	—

KM# 281.11 4 SOLS 2 DENIERS
1.8090 g., 0.7980 Silver 0.0464 oz. ASW **Ruler:** Louis XIV **Mint:** Riom

Date	Mintage	VG	F	VF	XF	Unc
16910	—	8.00	20.00	40.00	120	—

KM# 281.12 4 SOLS 2 DENIERS
1.8090 g., 0.7980 Silver 0.0464 oz. ASW **Ruler:** Louis XIV **Mint:** Dijon

Date	Mintage	VG	F	VF	XF	Unc
1691P	300,000	6.00	16.00	35.00	100	—
1692P	—	6.00	15.00	32.00	95.00	—
1693P	—	6.00	16.00	35.00	100	—

KM# 281.13 4 SOLS 2 DENIERS
1.8090 g., 0.7980 Silver 0.0464 oz. ASW **Ruler:** Louis XIV **Mint:** Troyes

Date	Mintage	VG	F	VF	XF	Unc
1691S	—	7.00	17.00	35.00	110	—
1692S	—	6.00	16.00	32.00	95.00	—
1694S	—	8.00	20.00	40.00	120	—

KM# 281.14 4 SOLS 2 DENIERS
1.8090 g., 0.7980 Silver 0.0464 oz. ASW **Ruler:** Louis XIV **Mint:** Nantes

Date	Mintage	VG	F	VF	XF	Unc
1698T	—	—	—	—	—	—

KM# 281.15 4 SOLS 2 DENIERS
1.8090 g., 0.7980 Silver 0.0464 oz. ASW **Ruler:** Louis XIV **Mint:** Troyes

Date	Mintage	VG	F	VF	XF	Unc
1692V	—	7.00	17.00	35.00	110	—
1694V	—	—	—	—	—	—
1695V	—	—	—	—	—	—
1696V	—	—	—	—	—	—
1697V	—	—	—	—	—	—
1698V	—	—	—	—	—	—
1699V	—	—	—	—	—	—

KM# 281.16 4 SOLS 2 DENIERS
1.8090 g., 0.7980 Silver 0.0464 oz. ASW **Ruler:** Louis XIV **Mint:** Lille

Date	Mintage	VG	F	VF	XF	Unc
1693W	—	6.00	16.00	32.00	95.00	—
1694W	—	6.00	16.00	32.00	95.00	—
1696W	45,000	—	—	—	—	—
1697W	45,000	—	—	—	—	—
1699W	30,000	—	—	—	—	—

KM# 281.17 4 SOLS 2 DENIERS
1.8090 g., 0.7980 Silver 0.0464 oz. ASW **Ruler:** Louis XIV **Mint:** Amiens

Date	Mintage	VG	F	VF	XF	Unc
1691X	—	8.00	20.00	40.00	120	—

KM# 281.18 4 SOLS 2 DENIERS
1.8090 g., 0.7980 Silver 0.0464 oz. ASW **Ruler:** Louis XIV **Mint:** Bourges

Date	Mintage	VG	F	VF	XF	Unc
1691Y	1,015,000	6.00	16.00	32.00	95.00	—
1692Y	—	7.00	17.00	35.00	110	—
1693Y	136,000	7.00	17.00	35.00	110	—
1694Y	11,000	—	—	—	—	—

KM# 281.19 4 SOLS 2 DENIERS
1.8090 g., 0.7980 Silver 0.0464 oz. ASW **Ruler:** Louis XIV **Mint:** Aix **Note:** Mint mark: Ampersand.

Date	Mintage	VG	F	VF	XF	Unc
1691	—	—	—	30.00	—	—
1692	—	6.00	16.00	32.00	95.00	—
1693	—	7.00	17.00	35.00	110	—
1694	—	7.00	17.00	35.00	110	—
1696	—	7.00	17.00	40.00	110	—
1697	—	8.00	20.00	45.00	120	—

KM# 281.20 4 SOLS 2 DENIERS
1.8090 g., 0.7980 Silver 0.0464 oz. ASW **Ruler:** Louis XIV **Mint:** Rennes **Note:** Mint mark: Numeral 9.

Date	Mintage	VG	F	VF	XF	Unc
1691	—	7.00	17.00	35.00	110	—
1692	—	6.00	15.00	30.00	85.00	—
1693	—	6.00	16.00	32.00	95.00	—
1694	—	7.00	17.00	35.00	110	—
1695	—	7.00	17.00	35.00	110	—

KM# 281.21 4 SOLS 2 DENIERS

1.8090 g., 0.7980 Silver 0.0464 oz. ASW **Ruler:** Louis XIV **Mint:** Metz **Note:** Mint mark: Crowned M.

Date	Mintage	VG	F	VF	XF	Unc
1691	—	6.00	16.00	32.00	95.00	—

KM# 281.22 4 SOLS 2 DENIERS

1.8090 g., 0.7980 Silver 0.0464 oz. ASW **Ruler:** Louis XIV **Mint:** Troyes **Note:** Mint mark: Crowned S.

Date	Mintage	VG	F	VF	XF	Unc
1691	500,000	6.00	16.00	32.00	95.00	—
1692	—	6.00	16.00	32.00	95.00	—
1693	—	6.00	16.00	32.00	95.00	—

KM# 283 4 SOLS 2 DENIERS

1.8090 g., 0.7980 Silver 0.0464 oz. ASW **Ruler:** Louis XIV **Mint:** Pau

Date	Mintage	VG	F	VF	XF	Unc
1692	—	20.00	40.00	80.00	240	—
1693	—	25.00	50.00	100	300	—
1696	14,000	—	—	—	—	—
1697	7,572	—	—	—	—	—
1698	4,248	—	—	—	—	—
1699	304	—	—	—	—	—

KM# 248 10 SOLS

5.0750 g., 0.8330 Silver 0.1359 oz. ASW **Ruler:** Louis XIV **Obv:** Large fleur-de-lis **Rev:** Value and date within legend **Mint:** Strasbourg

Date	Mintage	VG	F	VF	XF	Unc
1682BB	—	150	300	500	1,100	—

KM# 249 15 SOLS (1/8 ECU)

7.6670 g., 0.8330 Silver 0.2053 oz. ASW **Ruler:** Louis XIV **Obv:** Large fleur-de-lis **Rev:** Value and date within legend **Mint:** Strasbourg

Date	Mintage	VG	F	VF	XF	Unc
1682	—	250	500	1,100	3,000	—
1685	—	—	—	—	—	—
1689	—	—	—	—	—	—

KM# 194 20 SOLS (Lis d'Argent)

8.0070 g., 0.9580 Silver 0.2466 oz. ASW **Ruler:** Louis XIV **Obv:** Laureate and draped bust right **Rev:** Cross of 8 crowned L's back to back **Mint:** Paris

Date	Mintage	VG	F	VF	XF	Unc
1656A	—	800	1,750	3,500	7,200	—

KM# 263 30 SOLS (1/2 ECU)

15.3340 g., 0.8330 Silver 0.4107 oz. ASW **Ruler:** Louis XIV **Obv:** Large fleur-de-lis **Rev:** Value and date within legend **Mint:** Strasbourg

Date	Mintage	VG	F	VF	XF	Unc
1682BB	—	100	200	325	650	—
1683BB	—	125	250	400	775	—
1684BB	—	100	200	350	725	—
1685BB	—	100	200	325	650	—
1687BB	—	125	250	400	800	—
1688BB	—	100	200	325	650	—
1689BB	—	100	200	325	650	—

KM# 156 1/2 LOUIS D'OR

3.3500 g., 0.9170 Gold 0.0988 oz. AGW **Ruler:** Louis XIV **Obv:** Laureate child head of Louis XIV, with long curl at right **Mint:** Rouen

Date	Mintage	VG	F	VF	XF	Unc
1649B	—	400	750	1,500	3,000	—

KM# 13 1/4 FRANC

Billon **Ruler:** Henri IV **Obv:** Laureate, armored bust right **Rev:** Cross fleuree, H at center **Mint:** Bordeaux

Date	Mintage	VG	F	VF	XF	Unc
1602K	—	150	275	450	1,000	—

KM# 17.1 1/4 FRANC

Billon **Ruler:** Henri IV **Mint:** Poitiers

Date	Mintage	VG	F	VF	XF	Unc
1603G	—	150	275	450	1,000	—

KM# 17.2 1/4 FRANC

Billon **Ruler:** Henri IV **Obv:** Laureate, armored bust right, fleur-de-lis behind head **Mint:** Villeneuve St. André

Date	Mintage	VG	F	VF	XF	Unc
1603R	—	150	275	450	1,000	—

KM# 18 1/4 FRANC

Billon **Ruler:** Henri IV **Rev:** Cross fleuree, H at center, Dauphine and fleur-de-lis in angles

Date	Mintage	VG	F	VF	XF	Unc
1603	—	—	—	—	—	—

KM# 52.1 1/4 FRANC

3.5470 g., 0.8330 Silver 0.0950 oz. ASW **Ruler:** Louis XIII **Obv:** Laureate bust right in ruffled collar **Rev:** Cross fleuree with L at center **Mint:** Paris

Date	Mintage	VG	F	VF	XF	Unc
1614A	—	—	—	—	—	—
1625A	—	50.00	120	235	725	—

KM# 52.2 1/4 FRANC

3.5470 g., 0.8330 Silver 0.0950 oz. ASW **Ruler:** Louis XIII **Mint:** Rouen

Date	Mintage	VG	F	VF	XF	Unc
1612B	—	50.00	120	235	725	—
1614B	—	50.00	120	235	725	—
1615B	—	50.00	120	235	725	—

KM# 52.3 1/4 FRANC

3.5470 g., 0.8330 Silver 0.0950 oz. ASW **Ruler:** Louis XIII **Mint:** Lyon

Date	Mintage	VG	F	VF	XF	Unc
1615D	—	50.00	120	235	725	—

KM# 52.4 1/4 FRANC

3.5470 g., 0.8330 Silver 0.0950 oz. ASW **Ruler:** Louis XIII **Mint:** Toulouse

Date	Mintage	VG	F	VF	XF	Unc
1615M	—	50.00	120	235	725	—
1622M	—	50.00	120	235	725	—

KM# 52.5 1/4 FRANC

3.5470 g., 0.8330 Silver 0.0950 oz. ASW **Ruler:** Louis XIII **Mint:** Amiens

Date	Mintage	VG	F	VF	XF	Unc
1615X	—	—	—	—	—	—
1617X	—	—	—	—	—	—

KM# 53.1 1/4 FRANC

3.5470 g., 0.8330 Silver 0.0950 oz. ASW **Ruler:** Louis XIII **Obv:** Bust right in ruffled collar **Mint:** Paris

Date	Mintage	VG	F	VF	XF	Unc
1615A	—	50.00	120	235	725	—
1618A	—	—	—	—	—	—

KM# 53.2 1/4 FRANC

3.5470 g., 0.8330 Silver 0.0950 oz. ASW **Ruler:** Louis XIII **Mint:** Rouen

Date	Mintage	VG	F	VF	XF	Unc
1615B	—	50.00	120	235	725	—
1623B	—	50.00	120	235	725	—
1625B	—	50.00	120	235	725	—

KM# 53.3 1/4 FRANC

3.5470 g., 0.8330 Silver 0.0950 oz. ASW **Ruler:** Louis XIII **Mint:** Saint Lô

Date	Mintage	VG	F	VF	XF	Unc
1617C	—	—	—	—	—	—
1625C	—	—	—	—	—	—

KM# 53.4 1/4 FRANC

3.5470 g., 0.8330 Silver 0.0950 oz. ASW **Ruler:** Louis XIII **Mint:** Troyes

Date	Mintage	VG	F	VF	XF	Unc
1615S	—	50.00	120	235	725	—
1618S	4,279	50.00	120	235	725	—
1626S	5,708	50.00	120	235	725	—

KM# 93.1 1/4 FRANC

3.5470 g., 0.8330 Silver 0.0950 oz. ASW **Ruler:** Louis XIII **Obv:** Laureate bust right in shirt collar **Mint:** Bordeaux

Date	Mintage	VG	F	VF	XF	Unc
1640K	—	50.00	120	235	725	—

KM# 93.2 1/4 FRANC

3.5470 g., 0.8330 Silver 0.0950 oz. ASW **Ruler:** Louis XIII **Mint:** Bayonne

Date	Mintage	VG	F	VF	XF	Unc
1641L	—	—	—	—	—	—

KM# 93.3 1/4 FRANC

3.5470 g., 0.8330 Silver 0.0950 oz. ASW **Ruler:** Louis XIII **Mint:** Toulouse

Date	Mintage	VG	F	VF	XF	Unc
1631M	—	—	—	—	—	—
1633M	—	—	—	—	—	—
1634M	—	—	—	—	—	—
1635M	—	50.00	120	235	725	—
1636M	—	50.00	120	235	725	—
1637M	—	—	—	—	—	—
1638M	—	50.00	120	235	725	—
1639M	—	50.00	120	235	725	—
1640M	—	—	—	—	—	—
1641M	—	50.00	120	235	725	—

KM# 93.4 1/4 FRANC

3.5470 g., 0.8330 Silver 0.0950 oz. ASW **Ruler:** Louis XIII **Mint:** Montpellier

Date	Mintage	VG	F	VF	XF	Unc
1641N	—	85.00	165	300	925	—

KM# 93.5 1/4 FRANC

3.5470 g., 0.8330 Silver 0.0950 oz. ASW **Ruler:** Louis XIII **Mint:** Troyes

Date	Mintage	VG	F	VF	XF	Unc
1631S	2,233	85.00	165	300	925	—
1632S	—	—	—	—	—	—
1634S	—	—	—	—	—	—
1635S	—	—	—	—	—	—

KM# 93.6 1/4 FRANC

3.5470 g., 0.8330 Silver 0.0950 oz. ASW **Ruler:** Louis XIII **Mint:** Grenoble

Date	Mintage	VG	F	VF	XF	Unc
1641Z	—	85.00	165	300	925	—

KM# 93.7 1/4 FRANC

3.5470 g., 0.8330 Silver 0.0950 oz. ASW **Ruler:** Louis XIII **Mint:** Amiens

Date	Mintage	VG	F	VF	XF	Unc
1636X	—	—	—	—	—	—

KM# 94.1 1/4 FRANC

3.5470 g., 0.8330 Silver 0.0950 oz. ASW **Ruler:** Louis XIII **Obv:** Laureate bust right in larger shirt collar **Mint:** Amiens

Date	Mintage	VG	F	VF	XF	Unc
1638	—	60.00	125	250	750	—

KM# 94.2 1/4 FRANC

3.5470 g., 0.8330 Silver 0.0950 oz. ASW **Ruler:** Louis XIII **Mint:** Montpellier

Date	Mintage	VG	F	VF	XF	Unc
1636N	—	—	—	—	—	—
1638N	—	60.00	125	250	750	—

KM# 94.3 1/4 FRANC

3.5470 g., 0.8330 Silver 0.0950 oz. ASW **Ruler:** Louis XIII **Mint:** Villeneuve St. André

Date	Mintage	VG	F	VF	XF	Unc
1638R	—	—	—	—	—	—

KM# 94.4 1/4 FRANC

3.5470 g., 0.8330 Silver 0.0950 oz. ASW **Ruler:** Louis XIII **Mint:** Aix **Note:** Mint mark: Ampersand.

Date	Mintage	VG	F	VF	XF	Unc
1636	—	—	—	—	—	—

KM# 14.1 1/2 FRANC

Silver **Ruler:** Henri IV **Obv:** Laureate, armored bust right **Rev:** Cross fleuree, H in center **Mint:** Paris

Date	Mintage	VG	F	VF	XF	Unc
1602A	—	125	250	425	850	—
1604A	—	150	300	500	950	—

KM# 14.2 1/2 FRANC

Silver **Ruler:** Henri IV **Mint:** Lyon

Date	Mintage	VG	F	VF	XF	Unc
1602D	—	125	250	425	850	—
1603D	—	125	250	425	850	—
1604D	—	125	250	425	850	—
1605D	—	125	250	425	850	—

KM# 14.3 1/2 FRANC

Silver **Ruler:** Henri IV **Mint:** Angers

Date	Mintage	VG	F	VF	XF	Unc
1604F	—	125	250	425	850	—

KM# 14.4 1/2 FRANC

Silver **Ruler:** Henri IV **Mint:** Poitiers

Date	Mintage	VG	F	VF	XF	Unc
1603G	—	125	250	425	700	—

KM# 19 1/2 FRANC

Silver **Ruler:** Henri IV **Obv:** Laureate, armored bust right, fleur-de-lis behind head **Mint:** Villeneuve St. André

Date	Mintage	VG	F	VF	XF	Unc
1602R	—	125	250	425	850	—
1603R	—	125	250	425	850	—
1606R	—	125	250	425	850	—
1607R	—	125	250	425	850	—

KM# 76 1/2 FRANC

0.8330 Silver **Ruler:** Louis XIII **Obv:** Armored laureate bust right in ruffled collar **Mint:** Toulouse

Date	Mintage	VG	F	VF	XF	Unc
1610M	—	55.00	140	310	850	—
1611M	—	40.00	100	200	600	—
1612M	—	—	—	—	—	—
1615M	—	30.00	80.00	165	500	—
1616M	—	30.00	80.00	165	500	—
1617M	—	30.00	80.00	165	500	—
1618M	—	30.00	80.00	165	500	—
1619M	—	—	—	—	—	—
1620M	—	40.00	100	200	600	—
1621M	—	40.00	100	200	600	—
1622M	—	40.00	100	200	600	—
1623M	—	40.00	100	200	600	—
1624M	—	40.00	100	200	600	—
1625M	—	30.00	80.00	165	500	—
1626M	—	30.00	80.00	165	500	—
1627M	—	30.00	80.00	165	500	—

KM# 74 1/2 FRANC

0.8330 Silver **Ruler:** Louis XIII **Obv:** Large laureate bust in ruffled collar, legend begins at 12 o'clock **Mint:** Saint Lô

Date	Mintage	VG	F	VF	XF	Unc
1611C	—	—	—	—	—	—
1614C	—	35.00	90.00	175	550	—
1615C	—	25.00	60.00	120	400	—

KM# 73.1 1/2 FRANC

Silver **Ruler:** Louis XIII **Obv:** Laureate bust right in ruffled collar, mint mark below **Rev:** Cross fleuree with L at center **Mint:** Paris

Date	Mintage	VG	F	VF	XF	Unc
1627A	—	50.00	120	235	725	—

KM# 73.2 1/2 FRANC

0.8330 Silver **Ruler:** Louis XIII **Mint:** Rouen

Date	Mintage	VG	F	VF	XF	Unc
1611B	—	35.00	90.00	175	550	—
1612B	—	35.00	90.00	175	550	—
1613B	—	35.00	90.00	175	550	—
1614B	—	35.00	90.00	175	550	—
1615B	—	30.00	75.00	145	475	—
1616B	—	35.00	90.00	175	550	—
1617B	—	30.00	75.00	145	475	—
1619B	—	35.00	90.00	175	550	—
1626B	—	—	—	—	—	—
1627B	—	—	—	—	—	—

KM# 73.3 1/2 FRANC

Silver **Ruler:** Louis XIII **Mint:** Saint Lô

Date	Mintage	VG	F	VF	XF	Unc
1616C	—	35.00	90.00	175	550	—
1617C	—	35.00	90.00	175	550	—
1618C	—	—	—	—	—	—
1621C	—	—	—	—	—	—
1622C	—	—	—	—	—	—
1623C	—	—	—	—	—	—
1625C	—	—	—	—	—	—
1626C	—	—	—	—	—	—
1627C	—	—	—	—	—	—
1630C	—	—	—	—	—	—

KM# 73.4 1/2 FRANC

Silver **Ruler:** Louis XIII **Mint:** Tours

Date	Mintage	VG	F	VF	XF	Unc
1615E	—	35.00	90.00	175	550	—

KM# 73.5 1/2 FRANC

Silver **Ruler:** Louis XIII **Mint:** Angers

Date	Mintage	VG	F	VF	XF	Unc
1623F	—	35.00	90.00	185	550	—
1624F	—	—	—	—	—	—
1625F	—	35.00	90.00	185	550	—

KM# 73.6 1/2 FRANC

Silver **Ruler:** Louis XIII **Mint:** Troyes

Date	Mintage	VG	F	VF	XF	Unc
1615S	—	30.00	75.00	145	475	—

KM# 75 1/2 FRANC

0.8330 Silver **Ruler:** Louis XIII **Obv:** Legend begins at 7 o'clock **Mint:** Limoges

Date	Mintage	VG	F	VF	XF	Unc
1613I	—	30.00	80.00	165	500	—
1614I	—	40.00	100	200	600	—
1615I	—	30.00	80.00	165	500	—
1620I	—	35.00	90.00	175	550	—
1621I	—	40.00	100	200	600	—
1622I	—	40.00	100	200	600	—
1626I	—	40.00	100	200	600	—
1630I	—	40.00	100	200	600	—

KM# 77.1 1/2 FRANC

0.8330 Silver **Ruler:** Louis XIII **Obv:** Large young bust right in ruffled collar **Mint:** Paris

Date	Mintage	VG	F	VF	XF	Unc
1615A	—	40.00	100	215	650	—
1616A	—	40.00	100	215	650	—
1617A	—	60.00	150	285	900	—
1618A	—	60.00	150	285	900	—
1620A	—	40.00	100	215	650	—
1622A	—	80.00	200	400	1,300	—
1623A	—	—	—	—	—	—
1624A	—	—	—	—	—	—
1625A	—	—	—	—	—	—

KM# 77.2 1/2 FRANC

0.8330 Silver **Ruler:** Louis XIII **Mint:** Saint Lô

Date	Mintage	VG	F	VF	XF	Unc
1616C	—	50.00	125	235	775	—
1617C	—	—	—	—	—	—
1618C	—	55.00	140	245	800	—
1619C	—	60.00	150	275	900	—
1620C	—	60.00	150	275	900	—
1623C	—	—	—	—	—	—

KM# 77.3 1/2 FRANC

0.8330 Silver **Ruler:** Louis XIII **Mint:** Lyon

Date	Mintage	VG	F	VF	XF	Unc
1615D	—	40.00	100	200	600	—

KM# 77.4 1/2 FRANC

0.8330 Silver **Ruler:** Louis XIII **Mint:** Tours

Date	Mintage	VG	F	VF	XF	Unc
1618E	—	55.00	140	275	800	—
1619E	—	—	—	—	—	—

KM# 77.5 1/2 FRANC

0.8330 Silver **Ruler:** Louis XIII **Mint:** Troyes

Date	Mintage	VG	F	VF	XF	Unc
1611S	—	40.00	100	200	600	—
1615S	—	30.00	75.00	150	475	—
1616S	—	40.00	100	200	600	—
1617S	—	40.00	100	200	600	—
1618S	—	—	—	—	—	—
1620S	—	—	—	—	—	—
1626S	—	—	—	—	—	—

KM# 77.6 1/2 FRANC

0.8330 Silver **Ruler:** Louis XIII **Mint:** Amiens

Date	Mintage	VG	F	VF	XF	Unc
1615X	—	40.00	100	200	600	—
1616X	—	70.00	175	350	1,000	—
1617X	—	70.00	175	350	1,000	—

KM# 77.7 1/2 FRANC

0.8330 Silver **Ruler:** Louis XIII **Mint:** Rennes **Note:** Mint mark: Numeral 9.

Date	Mintage	VG	F	VF	XF	Unc
1615	—	40.00	100	200	600	—
1617	—	—	—	—	—	—
1619	—	—	—	—	—	—
1620	—	70.00	175	350	1,000	—

KM# 117.1 1/2 FRANC

0.8330 Silver **Ruler:** Louis XIII **Obv:** Large laureate bust right in shirt collar **Mint:** Rouen

Date	Mintage	VG	F	VF	XF	Unc
1641B	—	40.00	100	200	600	—

KM# 117.2 1/2 FRANC

0.8330 Silver **Ruler:** Louis XIII **Mint:** Saint Lô

Date	Mintage	VG	F	VF	XF	Unc
1632C	—	80.00	200	400	1,150	—
1636C	—	45.00	110	225	650	—
1637C	—	45.00	110	225	650	—
1640C	—	—	—	—	—	—
1641C	—	—	—	—	—	—

KM# 117.3 1/2 FRANC

0.8330 Silver **Ruler:** Louis XIII **Mint:** Lyon

Date	Mintage	VG	F	VF	XF	Unc
1632D	—	40.00	100	200	600	—
1641D	—	—	—	—	—	—

KM# 117.4 1/2 FRANC

0.8330 Silver **Ruler:** Louis XIII **Mint:** La Rochelle

Date	Mintage	VG	F	VF	XF	Unc
1641H	—	—	—	—	—	—

KM# 117.5 1/2 FRANC

0.8330 Silver **Ruler:** Louis XIII **Mint:** Limoges

Date	Mintage	VG	F	VF	XF	Unc
1630I	—	75.00	185	375	1,100	—
1631I	—	—	—	—	—	—
1632I	—	—	—	—	—	—

KM# 117.6 1/2 FRANC

0.8330 Silver **Ruler:** Louis XIII **Mint:** Bordeaux

Date	Mintage	VG	F	VF	XF	Unc
1638K	—	90.00	225	450	1,300	—
1639K	—	75.00	185	375	1,100	—

KM# 117.7 1/2 FRANC

0.8330 Silver **Ruler:** Louis XIII **Mint:** Bayonne

Date	Mintage	VG	F	VF	XF	Unc
1629L	—	40.00	100	200	600	—

KM# 117.8 1/2 FRANC

0.8330 Silver **Ruler:** Louis XIII **Mint:** Toulouse

Date	Mintage	VG	F	VF	XF	Unc
1627M	—	40.00	100	200	600	—
1628M	—	40.00	100	200	600	—
1629M	—	40.00	100	200	600	—
1630M	—	40.00	100	200	600	—
1631M	—	—	—	—	—	—
1632M	—	40.00	100	220	650	—
1633M	—	40.00	100	220	650	—
1634M	—	40.00	100	220	650	—
1635M	—	40.00	100	220	650	—
1636M	—	40.00	100	220	650	—
1637M	—	40.00	100	200	600	—
1638M	—	40.00	100	200	600	—
1639M	—	35.00	85.00	175	550	—
1640M	—	35.00	85.00	175	550	—
1641M	—	35.00	85.00	175	550	—

KM# 117.9 1/2 FRANC

0.8330 Silver **Ruler:** Louis XIII **Mint:** Dijon

Date	Mintage	VG	F	VF	XF	Unc
1637P	—	—	—	—	—	—
1638P	—	—	—	—	—	—

KM# 117.10 1/2 FRANC

0.8330 Silver **Ruler:** Louis XIII **Mint:** Troyes

Date	Mintage	VG	F	VF	XF	Unc
1631	—	75.00	185	375	1,100	—
1632	—	—	—	—	—	—
1634	—	—	—	—	—	—
1635	—	—	—	—	—	—
1637	—	45.00	110	225	650	—
1638	—	45.00	110	225	650	—
1639	—	45.00	110	225	650	—
1640	—	—	—	—	—	—
1641	—	—	—	—	—	—

KM# 117.11 1/2 FRANC

0.8330 Silver **Ruler:** Louis XIII **Mint:** Amiens

Date	Mintage	VG	F	VF	XF	Unc
1632X	—	—	—	—	—	—
1636X	—	90.00	225	450	1,200	—

KM# 117.12 1/2 FRANC

0.8330 Silver **Ruler:** Louis XIII **Mint:** Bourges

Date	Mintage	VG	F	VF	XF	Unc
1640Y	—	—	—	—	—	—

KM# 118.1 1/2 FRANC

0.8330 Silver **Ruler:** Louis XIII **Obv:** Tall laureate bust right in cloak **Mint:** Saint Lô

Date	Mintage	VG	F	VF	XF	Unc
1638C	—	90.00	225	450	1,200	—
1639C	—	90.00	225	450	1,200	—

KM# 118.2 1/2 FRANC

0.8330 Silver **Ruler:** Louis XIII **Mint:** Montpellier

Date	Mintage	VG	F	VF	XF	Unc
1633N	—	—	—	—	—	—
1636N	—	—	—	—	—	—
1637N	—	55.00	140	275	800	—
1638N	—	75.00	185	375	1,100	—
1639N	—	80.00	200	400	1,150	—
1640N	—	75.00	185	375	1,100	—
1641N	—	55.00	140	275	800	—

KM# 118.3 1/2 FRANC
0.8330 Silver **Ruler:** Louis XIII **Mint:** Aix **Note:** Mint mark: Ampersand.

Date	Mintage	VG	F	VF	XF	Unc
1635	—	70.00	175	350	1,000	—
1636	—	70.00	175	350	1,000	—
1637	—	70.00	175	350	1,000	—
1638	—	45.00	110	225	650	—
1639	—	75.00	185	375	1,100	—
1640	—	70.00	175	350	1,000	—
1641	—	50.00	125	250	750	—

KM# 119.1 1/2 FRANC
0.8330 Silver **Ruler:** Louis XIII **Obv:** Tall laureate draped bust right **Mint:** Arras

Date	Mintage	VG	F	VF	XF	Unc
1641AR	—	150	300	500	1,100	—
1642AR	—	—	—	—	—	—

KM# 119.2 1/2 FRANC
0.8330 Silver **Ruler:** Louis XIII **Mint:** Grenoble

Date	Mintage	VG	F	VF	XF	Unc
1641Z	—	275	500	850	1,900	—

ECU COINAGE

KM# 130 1/48 ECU
0.5600 g., 0.9170 Silver 0.0165 oz. ASW **Ruler:** Louis XIII **Obv:** Laureate and draped bust right **Rev:** Crowned shield **Mint:** Paris

Date	Mintage	VG	F	VF	XF	Unc
1642A	—	350	600	1,100	2,000	—
1643A	—	350	600	1,100	2,000	—

KM# 152 1/48 ECU
0.5650 g., 0.9170 Silver 0.0167 oz. ASW **Ruler:** Louis XIV **Obv:** Small laureate and draped bust right **Rev:** Crowned shield of France, long legends

Date	Mintage	VG	F	VF	XF	Unc
1644	—	300	550	950	2,500	—

KM# 153 1/48 ECU
0.5650 g., 0.9170 Silver 0.0167 oz. ASW **Ruler:** Louis XIV **Obv:** Large laureate and draped bust right **Rev:** Legends are abbreviated

Date	Mintage	VG	F	VF	XF	Unc
1644A	—	85.00	180	350	900	—

KM# 138 1/24 ECU
1.1200 g., 0.9170 Silver 0.0330 oz. ASW **Ruler:** Louis XIII **Obv:** Laureate and draped bust right **Rev:** Crowned shield **Mint:** Paris

Date	Mintage	VG	F	VF	XF	Unc
1643A Point	—	275	500	900	2,150	—

KM# 139 1/24 ECU
1.1300 g., 0.9170 Silver 0.0333 oz. ASW **Ruler:** Louis XIV **Obv:** Laureate, draped and mailed bust right, long legend **Rev:** Crowned shield of France

Date	Mintage	VG	F	VF	XF	Unc
1643	—	200	400	700	1,750	—
1644	—	200	400	700	1,750	—

KM# 154 1/24 ECU
1.1300 g., 0.9170 Silver 0.0333 oz. ASW, 15 mm. **Ruler:** Louis XIV **Obv:** Laureate and draped bust right, abbreviated legend

Date	Mintage	VG	F	VF	XF	Unc
1644A	—	125	250	425	950	—

KM# 258.1 1/16 ECU
2.3300 g., 0.8220 Silver 0.0616 oz. ASW **Ruler:** Louis XIV **Obv:** Draped bust right **Rev:** Crowned quartered shield of France, Navarre, Old and New Burgundy **Mint:** Lille

Date	Mintage	VG	F	VF	XF	Unc
1686LL	—	—	—	—	—	—

KM# 258.2 1/16 ECU
2.3300 g., 0.8220 Silver 0.0616 oz. ASW **Ruler:** Louis XIV **Mint:** Lille **Note:** Mint mark: Crowned L.

Date	Mintage	VG	F	VF	XF	Unc
1686	—	40.00	100	225	550	—
1687	—	50.00	125	250	600	—
1688	—	60.00	150	300	725	—

KM# 305 1/16 ECU
2.3500 g., 0.8570 Silver 0.0647 oz. ASW **Ruler:** Louis XIV **Rev:** Palms at sides of crowned quartered shield **Mint:** Lille

Date	Mintage	VG	F	VF	XF	Unc
1694W	—	225	550	1,150	2,200	—
1695W	—	—	—	—	—	—
1696W	—	300	750	1,600	3,000	—
1697W	—	300	750	1,600	3,000	—
1698W	—	250	675	1,450	2,700	—
1699W	—	—	—	—	—	—

KM# 131 1/12 ECU (10 Sols)
2.2400 g., 0.9170 Silver 0.0660 oz. ASW **Ruler:** Louis XIII **Obv:** Laureate, draped bust right **Rev:** Crowned shield **Mint:** Paris

Date	Mintage	VG	F	VF	XF	Unc
1641A Point	—	200	400	600	1,100	—
1642A Rose	107,000	100	200	425	775	—
1642A Point	Inc. above	85.00	175	350	625	—
1642A 2 points	Inc. above	100	200	425	775	—

KM# 132.1 1/12 ECU (10 Sols)
2.2400 g., 0.9170 Silver 0.0660 oz. ASW **Ruler:** Louis XIII **Obv:** Laureate, draped and mailed bust right

Date	Mintage	VG	F	VF	XF	Unc
1642 Rose	571,000	75.00	165	325	650	—
1642 Point	Inc. above	65.00	150	300	600	—
1643 Rose	13,995,000	15.00	35.00	65.00	170	—
1643 Point	31,237,000	15.00	30.00	60.00	155	—

KM# 132.2 1/12 ECU (10 Sols)
2.2400 g., 0.9170 Silver 0.0660 oz. ASW **Ruler:** Louis XIII **Mint:** Lyon

Date	Mintage	VG	F	VF	XF	Unc
1643D 3 points	Est. 125,000	175	375	750	1,450	—

KM# 140.1 1/12 ECU (10 Sols)
2.2610 g., 0.9170 Silver 0.0667 oz. ASW **Ruler:** Louis XIV **Obv:** Laureate, draped and mailed bust right, short hair curl before ear **Rev:** Crowned shield of France **Mint:** Paris

Date	Mintage	VG	F	VF	XF	Unc
1643A Rose	—	20.00	50.00	100	300	—
1643A Point	—	12.00	32.00	65.00	190	—
1644A Rose	—	12.00	32.00	65.00	190	—
1644A Point	—	12.00	32.00	65.00	210	—
1644A Rose and 2 points	—	16.00	40.00	80.00	240	—
1645A Rose	—	16.00	40.00	80.00	240	—
1645A Point	—	20.00	50.00	100	300	—

KM# 140.2 1/12 ECU (10 Sols)
2.2610 g., 0.9170 Silver 0.0667 oz. ASW **Ruler:** Louis XIV **Mint:** Lyon

Date	Mintage	VG	F	VF	XF	Unc
1644D	—	20.00	50.00	100	300	—
1645D	—	—	—	—	—	—
1648D	—	—	—	—	—	—
1649D	—	60.00	125	225	725	—
1650D	—	—	—	—	—	—
1652D	—	—	—	—	—	—
1653D	—	—	—	—	—	—

KM# 166.1 1/12 ECU (10 Sols)
2.2610 g., 0.9170 Silver 0.0667 oz. ASW **Ruler:** Louis XIV **Obv:** Larger bust, long hair curl before ear **Mint:** Paris

Date	Mintage	VG	F	VF	XF	Unc
1646A Rose	—	—	—	—	—	—
1646A Point	—	10.00	22.00	40.00	120	—
1647A	—	10.00	22.00	40.00	120	—
1648A Fleur	—	20.00	50.00	100	325	—
1648A Point	—	—	—	—	—	—
1649A	—	20.00	50.00	100	325	—
1650A	—	—	—	—	—	—
1651A	—	25.00	65.00	125	450	—
1652A	—	10.00	22.00	50.00	160	—
1653A	—	10.00	22.00	45.00	145	—
1654A	—	10.00	25.00	55.00	180	—
1655A	—	12.00	30.00	65.00	210	—
1657A	—	—	—	—	—	—
1658A	—	—	—	—	—	—

KM# 166.2 1/12 ECU (10 Sols)
2.2610 g., 0.9170 Silver 0.0667 oz. ASW **Ruler:** Louis XIV **Mint:** Rouen

Date	Mintage	VG	F	VF	XF	Unc
1649B	—	—	—	—	—	—
1650B	—	—	—	—	—	—
1652B	—	—	—	—	—	—
1653B	—	10.00	22.00	45.00	145	—
1654B	—	12.00	30.00	65.00	210	—
1659B	—	20.00	50.00	110	350	—

KM# 166.3 1/12 ECU (10 Sols)
2.2610 g., 0.9170 Silver 0.0667 oz. ASW **Ruler:** Louis XIV **Mint:** Saint Lô

Date	Mintage	VG	F	VF	XF	Unc
1650C	—	30.00	75.00	150	475	—
1651C	—	—	—	—	—	—
1653C	—	—	—	—	—	—
1654C	—	—	—	—	—	—

KM# 166.4 1/12 ECU (10 Sols)
2.2610 g., 0.9170 Silver 0.0667 oz. ASW **Ruler:** Louis XIV **Mint:** Lyon

Date	Mintage	VG	F	VF	XF	Unc
1657D	—	35.00	85.00	165	550	—
1658D	—	10.00	20.00	55.00	180	—
1659D	—	10.00	22.00	45.00	145	—
1660D	—	10.00	22.00	40.00	120	—
1661D	—	10.00	22.00	40.00	120	—

KM# 166.5 1/12 ECU (10 Sols)
2.2610 g., 0.9170 Silver 0.0667 oz. ASW **Ruler:** Louis XIV **Mint:** Tours

Date	Mintage	VG	F	VF	XF	Unc
1652E	—	35.00	85.00	165	550	—
1653E	—	—	—	—	—	—
1656E	—	40.00	100	200	650	—
1659E	—	35.00	85.00	165	550	—
1660E	—	35.00	90.00	175	550	—

KM# 166.6 1/12 ECU (10 Sols)
2.2610 g., 0.9170 Silver 0.0667 oz. ASW **Ruler:** Louis XIV **Mint:** Angers

Date	Mintage	VG	F	VF	XF	Unc
1647F	—	—	—	—	—	—
1648F	—	—	—	—	—	—
1649F	—	—	—	—	—	—
1650F	—	25.00	60.00	120	400	—
1651F	—	—	—	—	—	—
1654F	—	—	—	—	—	—
1658F	—	—	—	—	—	—
1659F	—	35.00	85.00	165	550	—
1660F	—	35.00	85.00	165	550	—

KM# 166.7 1/12 ECU (10 Sols)
2.2610 g., 0.9170 Silver 0.0667 oz. ASW **Ruler:** Louis XIV **Mint:** Poitiers

Date	Mintage	VG	F	VF	XF	Unc
1650G	—	—	—	—	—	—

KM# 166.8 1/12 ECU (10 Sols)
2.2610 g., 0.9170 Silver 0.0667 oz. ASW **Ruler:** Louis XIV **Mint:** La Rochelle

Date	Mintage	VG	F	VF	XF	Unc
1648H	—	—	—	—	—	—
1649H	—	—	—	—	—	—
1650H	—	—	—	—	—	—
1651H	—	45.00	120	225	725	—
1652H	—	50.00	130	260	850	—
1653H	—	50.00	130	260	850	—
1654H	—	—	—	—	—	—
1655H	—	—	—	—	—	—
1656H	—	—	—	—	—	—

KM# 166.9 1/12 ECU (10 Sols)
2.2610 g., 0.9170 Silver 0.0667 oz. ASW **Ruler:** Louis XIV **Mint:** Limoges

Date	Mintage	VG	F	VF	XF	Unc
1649I	—	—	—	—	—	—
1650I	—	—	—	—	—	—
1651I	—	50.00	125	250	775	—
1652I	—	—	—	—	—	—
1653I	—	—	—	—	—	—
1654I	—	—	—	—	—	—
1657I	—	35.00	85.00	165	550	—
1659I	—	30.00	75.00	150	475	—
1660I	—	30.00	75.00	150	475	—

KM# 166.10 1/12 ECU (10 Sols)
2.2610 g., 0.9170 Silver 0.0667 oz. ASW **Ruler:** Louis XIV **Mint:** Bordeaux

Date	Mintage	VG	F	VF	XF	Unc
1647K	—	—	—	—	—	—
1648K	—	15.00	40.00	80.00	240	—
1649K	—	30.00	75.00	150	475	—
1650K	—	—	—	—	—	—
1651K	—	—	—	—	—	—
1652K	—	35.00	90.00	175	550	—
1653K	—	35.00	90.00	175	550	—

Date	Mintage	VG	F	VF	XF	Unc
1654K	—	—	—	—	—	—
1655K	—	—	—	—	—	—
1656K	—	—	—	—	—	—
1657K	—	—	—	—	—	—
1658K	—	30.00	75.00	150	475	—
1659K	—	30.00	75.00	150	475	—
1660K	—	—	—	—	—	—

KM# 166.11 1/12 ECU (10 Sols)
2.2610 g., 0.9170 Silver 0.0667 oz. ASW **Ruler:** Louis XIV **Mint:** Bayonne

Date	Mintage	VG	F	VF	XF	Unc
1650L	—	—	—	—	—	—
1651L	—	—	—	—	—	—
1652L	—	—	—	—	—	—
1653L	—	30.00	75.00	160	500	—
1654L	—	—	—	—	—	—
1655L	—	—	—	—	—	—
1656L	—	—	—	—	—	—
1657L	—	—	—	—	—	—
1658L	—	—	—	—	—	—
1659L	—	—	—	—	—	—
1660L	—	—	—	—	—	—

KM# 166.12 1/12 ECU (10 Sols)
2.2610 g., 0.9170 Silver 0.0667 oz. ASW **Ruler:** Louis XIV **Mint:** Toulouse

Date	Mintage	VG	F	VF	XF	Unc
1647M	—	25.00	65.00	135	450	—
1648M	—	—	—	—	—	—
1649M	—	—	—	—	—	—
1650M	—	—	—	—	—	—
1653M	—	35.00	90.00	175	550	—
1655M	—	—	—	—	—	—
1658M	—	30.00	75.00	150	475	—
1659M	—	—	—	—	—	—
1661M	—	—	—	—	—	—
1662M	—	—	—	—	—	—

KM# 166.13 1/12 ECU (10 Sols)
2.2610 g., 0.9170 Silver 0.0667 oz. ASW **Ruler:** Louis XIV **Mint:** Montpellier

Date	Mintage	VG	F	VF	XF	Unc
1647N	—	—	—	—	—	—
1648N	—	20.00	50.00	100	325	—
1649N	—	10.00	25.00	55.00	180	—
1650N	—	12.00	30.00	65.00	210	—
1651N	—	12.00	30.00	65.00	210	—
1652N	—	12.00	30.00	65.00	210	—
1653N	—	15.00	40.00	80.00	240	—
1658N	—	10.00	25.00	55.00	180	—
1659N	—	10.00	25.00	55.00	180	—

KM# 166.14 1/12 ECU (10 Sols)
2.2610 g., 0.9170 Silver 0.0667 oz. ASW **Ruler:** Louis XIV **Mint:** Riom

Date	Mintage	VG	F	VF	XF	Unc
1652O	—	—	—	—	—	—
1653O	—	—	—	—	—	—

KM# 166.15 1/12 ECU (10 Sols)
2.2610 g., 0.9170 Silver 0.0667 oz. ASW **Ruler:** Louis XIV **Mint:** Dijon

Date	Mintage	VG	F	VF	XF	Unc
1652P	—	—	—	—	—	—
1653P	—	—	—	—	—	—

KM# 166.16 1/12 ECU (10 Sols)
2.2610 g., 0.9170 Silver 0.0667 oz. ASW **Ruler:** Louis XIV **Mint:** Narbonne

Date	Mintage	VG	F	VF	XF	Unc
1650Q	—	—	—	—	—	—
1651Q	—	40.00	100	220	650	—
1652Q	—	—	—	—	—	—
1653Q	—	—	—	—	—	—

KM# 166.17 1/12 ECU (10 Sols)
2.2610 g., 0.9170 Silver 0.0667 oz. ASW **Ruler:** Louis XIV **Mint:** Troyes

Date	Mintage	VG	F	VF	XF	Unc
1651S	—	35.00	85.00	175	550	—
1652S	—	—	—	—	—	—
1653S	—	30.00	75.00	150	475	—
1654S	—	—	—	—	—	—

KM# 166.18 1/12 ECU (10 Sols)
2.2610 g., 0.9170 Silver 0.0667 oz. ASW **Ruler:** Louis XIV **Mint:** Nantes

Date	Mintage	VG	F	VF	XF	Unc
1647T	—	—	—	—	—	—
1648T	—	—	—	—	—	—
1659T	—	—	—	—	—	—
1660T	—	—	—	—	—	—

KM# 166.19 1/12 ECU (10 Sols)
2.2610 g., 0.9170 Silver 0.0667 oz. ASW **Ruler:** Louis XIV **Mint:** Amiens

Date	Mintage	VG	F	VF	XF	Unc
1653X	—	30.00	75.00	150	475	—
1655X	—	30.00	75.00	150	475	—
1658X	—	—	—	—	—	—
1660X	—	—	—	—	—	—

KM# 166.20 1/12 ECU (10 Sols)
2.2610 g., 0.9170 Silver 0.0667 oz. ASW **Ruler:** Louis XIV **Mint:** Bourges

Date	Mintage	VG	F	VF	XF	Unc
1648Y	—	—	—	—	—	—
1649Y	—	—	—	—	—	—
1650Y	—	25.00	60.00	120	325	—
1653Y	—	30.00	75.00	150	400	—
1654Y	—	35.00	85.00	175	450	—
1655Y	—	30.00	75.00	150	400	—
1656Y	—	35.00	85.00	175	450	—

KM# 166.21 1/12 ECU (10 Sols)
2.2610 g., 0.9170 Silver 0.0667 oz. ASW **Ruler:** Louis XIV **Mint:** Arras

Date	Mintage	VG	F	VF	XF	Unc
1652AR	—	35.00	85.00	175	550	—
1653AR	—	35.00	85.00	175	550	—

KM# 166.22 1/12 ECU (10 Sols)
2.2610 g., 0.9170 Silver 0.0667 oz. ASW **Ruler:** Louis XIV **Mint:** Aix **Note:** Mint mark: Ampersand.

Date	Mintage	VG	F	VF	XF	Unc
1647	—	25.00	65.00	125	450	—
1648	—	25.00	65.00	125	450	—
1649	—	20.00	50.00	100	325	—
1651	—	35.00	85.00	175	550	—
1652	—	20.00	50.00	100	325	—
1653	—	15.00	40.00	80.00	240	—
1654	—	30.00	75.00	150	475	—
1656	—	—	—	—	—	—
1657	—	20.00	50.00	100	325	—
1658	—	12.00	30.00	65.00	210	—
1659	—	12.00	30.00	65.00	210	—
1660	—	—	—	—	—	—
1661	—	—	—	—	—	—
1663	—	35.00	85.00	175	550	—

KM# 166.23 1/12 ECU (10 Sols)
2.2610 g., 0.9170 Silver 0.0667 oz. ASW **Ruler:** Louis XIV **Mint:** Rennes **Note:** Mint mark: Numeral 9.

Date	Mintage	VG	F	VF	XF	Unc
1647	—	—	—	—	—	—
1648	—	—	—	—	—	—
1649	—	—	—	—	—	—
1653	—	—	—	—	—	—
1654	—	—	—	—	—	—
1655	—	—	—	—	—	—
1657	—	—	—	—	—	—
1658	—	—	—	—	—	—
1659	—	—	—	—	—	—
1662	—	30.00	75.00	150	475	—

KM# 182.1 1/12 ECU (10 Sols)
2.2610 g., 0.9170 Silver 0.0667 oz. ASW **Ruler:** Louis XIV **Rev:** Crowned shield of France, Navarre and Bearn **Mint:** Pau

Date	Mintage	VG	F	VF	XF	Unc
1650 Leaves	—	175	300	650	1,800	—
1651 Leaves	—	175	300	650	1,800	—
1652 * F *	—	175	300	650	1,800	—
1653 * F *	—	175	300	650	1,800	—
1655 * F *	—	175	300	650	1,800	—
1675	—	200	400	750	2,000	—
1676	—	200	400	750	2,000	—
1679	—	200	400	750	2,000	—

KM# 182.2 1/12 ECU (10 Sols)
2.2610 g., 0.9170 Silver 0.0667 oz. ASW **Ruler:** Louis XIV **Mint:** Morlaas

Date	Mintage	VG	F	VF	XF	Unc
1653 * G *	—	175	300	650	1,800	—
1660	—	175	300	650	1,800	—
1661	—	175	300	650	1,800	—

KM# 181 1/12 ECU (10 Sols)
2.2610 g., 0.9170 Silver 0.0667 oz. ASW **Ruler:** Louis XIV **Obv:** Large laureate draped, mailed bust right **Rev:** Crowned shield of France and Navarre **Mint:** Saint Palais

Date	Mintage	VG	F	VF	XF	Unc
1651 * V *	—	200	400	750	2,400	—
1653 * V *	—	200	400	750	2,400	—
1654 * V *	—	225	450	825	2,650	—
1655 * V *	—	225	450	825	2,650	—
1656 * V *	—	250	500	900	2,900	—
1658 * V *	—	250	500	900	2,900	—
1660 * V *	—	250	500	900	2,900	—
1661 * V *	—	250	500	900	2,900	—

KM# 199.1 1/12 ECU (10 Sols)
2.2610 g., 0.9170 Silver 0.0667 oz. ASW **Ruler:** Louis XIV **Rev:** Crowned shield of France **Mint:** Paris

Date	Mintage	VG	F	VF	XF	Unc
1658A	—	15.00	35.00	75.00	270	—
1659A	—	7.00	16.00	35.00	110	—
1660A	—	7.00	16.00	35.00	110	—
1661A	—	8.00	20.00	45.00	130	—
1662A	—	7.00	16.00	35.00	110	—
1663A	—	8.00	20.00	45.00	130	—
1664A	—	8.00	20.00	45.00	130	—
1665A	—	25.00	60.00	120	425	—
1667A	—	30.00	75.00	150	500	—
1669A	—	30.00	75.00	150	500	—
1670A	—	37.50	95.00	185	650	—

KM# 199.2 1/12 ECU (10 Sols)
2.2610 g., 0.9170 Silver 0.0667 oz. ASW **Ruler:** Louis XIV **Mint:** Rouen

Date	Mintage	VG	F	VF	XF	Unc
1659B	—	20.00	50.00	110	350	—
1660B	—	8.00	20.00	45.00	130	—
1661B	—	30.00	75.00	150	500	—
1662B	—	16.00	40.00	85.00	300	—
1664B	—	16.00	40.00	85.00	300	—

KM# 199.3 1/12 ECU (10 Sols)
2.2610 g., 0.9170 Silver 0.0667 oz. ASW **Ruler:** Louis XIV **Mint:** Lyon

Date	Mintage	VG	F	VF	XF	Unc
1660D	—	7.00	16.00	35.00	110	—
1661D	—	7.00	16.00	35.00	110	—
1662D	—	7.00	16.00	35.00	110	—
1663D	—	7.00	16.00	35.00	110	—
1664D	—	8.00	20.00	45.00	140	—
1665D	—	12.00	30.00	75.00	250	—
1666D	—	—	—	—	—	—
1668D	—	—	—	—	—	—
1669D	—	—	—	—	—	—
1670D	—	—	—	—	—	—
1671D	—	—	—	—	—	—
1673D	—	—	—	—	—	—

KM# 199.4 1/12 ECU (10 Sols)
2.2610 g., 0.9170 Silver 0.0667 oz. ASW **Ruler:** Louis XIV **Mint:** La Rochelle

Date	Mintage	VG	F	VF	XF	Unc
1661H	—	30.00	75.00	150	500	—
1662H	—	—	—	—	—	—

KM# 199.5 1/12 ECU (10 Sols)
2.2610 g., 0.9170 Silver 0.0667 oz. ASW **Ruler:** Louis XIV **Mint:** Limoges

Date	Mintage	VG	F	VF	XF	Unc
1659I	—	25.00	60.00	125	425	—
1660I	—	30.00	75.00	150	500	—
1661I	—	20.00	50.00	110	350	—
1662I	—	35.00	80.00	165	550	—
1663I	—	30.00	75.00	150	500	—

KM# 199.6 1/12 ECU (10 Sols)
2.2610 g., 0.9170 Silver 0.0667 oz. ASW **Ruler:** Louis XIV **Mint:** Bordeaux

Date	Mintage	VG	F	VF	XF	Unc
1660K	—	30.00	75.00	150	500	—
1662K	—	30.00	75.00	150	500	—

KM# 199.7 1/12 ECU (10 Sols)
2.2610 g., 0.9170 Silver 0.0667 oz. ASW **Ruler:** Louis XIV **Mint:** Bayonne

Date	Mintage	VG	F	VF	XF	Unc
1660L	—	30.00	75.00	150	500	—
1661L	—	—	—	—	—	—
1662L	—	—	—	—	—	—
1663L	—	—	—	—	—	—
1664L	—	20.00	50.00	110	350	—
1665L	—	—	—	—	—	—
1666L	—	—	—	—	—	—
1667L	—	—	—	—	—	—
1668L	—	—	—	—	—	—
1672L	—	—	—	—	—	—

KM# 199.8 1/12 ECU (10 Sols)
2.2610 g., 0.9170 Silver 0.0667 oz. ASW **Ruler:** Louis XIV **Mint:** Toulouse

Date	Mintage	VG	F	VF	XF	Unc
1661M	—	15.00	35.00	80.00	270	—
1662M	—	15.00	35.00	80.00	270	—
1666M	—	—	—	—	—	—
1671M	—	—	—	—	—	—

KM# 199.9 1/12 ECU (10 Sols)
2.2610 g., 0.9170 Silver 0.0667 oz. ASW **Ruler:** Louis XIV **Mint:** Montpellier

Date	Mintage	VG	F	VF	XF	Unc
1659N	—	15.00	35.00	80.00	270	—
1660N	—	20.00	50.00	110	350	—

Date	Mintage	VG	F	VF	XF	Unc
1661N	—	20.00	50.00	110	350	—
1662N	—	25.00	60.00	125	425	—

KM# 199.10 1/12 ECU (10 Sols)
2.2610 g., 0.9170 Silver 0.0667 oz. ASW **Ruler:** Louis XIV **Mint:** Dijon

Date	Mintage	VG	F	VF	XF	Unc
1661P	—	—	—	—	—	—

KM# 199.11 1/12 ECU (10 Sols)
2.2610 g., 0.9170 Silver 0.0667 oz. ASW **Ruler:** Louis XIV **Mint:** Villeneuve St. André

Date	Mintage	VG	F	VF	XF	Unc
1660R	—	—	—	—	—	—
1661R	—	15.00	35.00	80.00	270	—
1662R	—	20.00	50.00	110	350	—

KM# 199.12 1/12 ECU (10 Sols)
2.2610 g., 0.9170 Silver 0.0667 oz. ASW **Ruler:** Louis XIV **Mint:** Nantes

Date	Mintage	VG	F	VF	XF	Unc
1660T	—	40.00	100	200	650	—
1661T	—	8.00	20.00	45.00	130	—
1662T	—	—	—	—	—	—

KM# 199.13 1/12 ECU (10 Sols)
2.2610 g., 0.9170 Silver 0.0667 oz. ASW **Ruler:** Louis XIV **Mint:** Amiens

Date	Mintage	VG	F	VF	XF	Unc
1659X	—	30.00	75.00	160	550	—
1660X	—	—	—	—	—	—

KM# 199.14 1/12 ECU (10 Sols)
2.2610 g., 0.9170 Silver 0.0667 oz. ASW **Ruler:** Louis XIV **Mint:** Aix **Note:** Mint mark: Ampersand.

Date	Mintage	VG	F	VF	XF	Unc
1658	—	15.00	35.00	80.00	270	—
1659	—	12.00	30.00	70.00	240	—
1660	—	20.00	50.00	110	350	—
1661	—	15.00	35.00	80.00	270	—
1662	—	12.00	30.00	70.00	240	—
1663	—	12.00	30.00	70.00	240	—
1664	—	12.00	30.00	70.00	240	—
1665	—	12.00	30.00	70.00	240	—
1666	—	40.00	100	220	650	—
1667	—	30.00	75.00	150	500	—
1668	—	—	—	—	—	—
1669	—	35.00	80.00	165	550	—
1670	—	—	—	—	—	—
1671	—	—	—	—	—	—
1672	—	—	—	—	—	—

KM# 210 1/12 ECU (10 Sols)
2.2610 g., 0.9170 Silver 0.0667 oz. ASW **Ruler:** Louis XIV **Obv:** Juvenile bust right **Rev:** Crowned quartered shield of Dauphine **Mint:** Grenoble

Date	Mintage	VG	F	VF	XF	Unc
1660Z	—	100	200	400	950	—
1661Z	—	125	250	500	1,200	—
1662Z	—	165	325	650	1,500	—

KM# 235.1 1/12 ECU (10 Sols)
2.2610 g., 0.9170 Silver 0.0667 oz. ASW **Ruler:** Louis XIV **Subject:** Parliament **Obv:** Armored bust right **Rev:** Crowned shield of France **Mint:** Paris

Date	Mintage	VG	F	VF	XF	Unc
1679A	—	150	300	600	1,450	—
1680A	—	150	300	600	1,450	—
1681A	—	125	250	500	1,200	—
1682A	—	150	300	600	1,450	—
1683A	—	500	750	1,200	—	—

Note: Type au jabot

KM# 235.2 1/12 ECU (10 Sols)
2.2610 g., 0.9170 Silver 0.0667 oz. ASW **Ruler:** Louis XIV **Mint:** Aix **Note:** Mint mark: Ampersand.

Date	Mintage	VG	F	VF	XF	Unc
1679	—	150	300	600	1,450	—
1680	—	150	300	600	1,450	—
1681	—	—	—	—	—	—
1682	—	175	350	700	1,800	—

KM# 282.1 1/12 ECU (10 Sols)
2.2610 g., 0.9170 Silver 0.0667 oz. ASW **Ruler:** Louis XIV **Obv:** Draped bust right **Rev:** Eight crowned L's, cruciform, fleur-de-lis in angles **Mint:** Paris

Date	Mintage	VG	F	VF	XF	Unc
1691A	—	50.00	100	200	500	—

KM# 282.2 1/12 ECU (10 Sols)
2.2610 g., 0.9170 Silver 0.0667 oz. ASW **Ruler:** Louis XIV **Mint:** Lille **Note:** Mint mark: Crowned L.

Date	Mintage	VG	F	VF	XF	Unc
1691	—	75.00	150	300	750	—

KM# 282.3 1/12 ECU (10 Sols)
2.2610 g., 0.9170 Silver 0.0667 oz. ASW **Ruler:** Louis XIV **Mint:** Metz **Note:** Mint mark: Crowned M.

Date	Mintage	VG	F	VF	XF	Unc
1691	—	75.00	150	300	750	—

KM# 290.1 1/12 ECU (10 Sols)
2.2610 g., 0.9170 Silver 0.0667 oz. ASW **Ruler:** Louis XIV **Obv:** Mailed bust right **Rev:** Palm branches below crowned circular shield of France **Mint:** Paris

Date	Mintage	VG	F	VF	XF	Unc
1693A	—	50.00	125	250	625	—
1694A	—	35.00	85.00	165	425	—
1695A	—	40.00	100	200	500	—

KM# 290.2 1/12 ECU (10 Sols)
2.2610 g., 0.9170 Silver 0.0667 oz. ASW **Ruler:** Louis XIV **Mint:** Caen

Date	Mintage	VG	F	VF	XF	Unc
1694C	—	45.00	110	225	575	—
1697C	50,000	50.00	125	250	625	—

KM# 290.3 1/12 ECU (10 Sols)
2.2610 g., 0.9170 Silver 0.0667 oz. ASW **Ruler:** Louis XIV **Mint:** Lyon

Date	Mintage	VG	F	VF	XF	Unc
1694D	644,000	40.00	100	200	500	—
1695D	318,000	—	—	—	—	—
1696D	181,000	55.00	130	260	650	—
1697D	72,000	60.00	140	275	700	—
1698D	24,000	—	—	—	—	—
1699D	22,000	—	—	—	—	—
1700D	3,000	—	—	—	—	—

KM# 290.4 1/12 ECU (10 Sols)
2.2610 g., 0.9170 Silver 0.0667 oz. ASW **Ruler:** Louis XIV **Mint:** Tours

Date	Mintage	VG	F	VF	XF	Unc
1695E	—	50.00	125	250	625	—
1697E	—	65.00	150	300	750	—

KM# 290.5 1/12 ECU (10 Sols)
2.2610 g., 0.9170 Silver 0.0667 oz. ASW **Ruler:** Louis XIV **Mint:** Poitiers

Date	Mintage	VG	F	VF	XF	Unc
1694G	—	45.00	110	225	575	—
1696G	24,000	—	—	—	—	—

KM# 290.6 1/12 ECU (10 Sols)
2.2610 g., 0.9170 Silver 0.0667 oz. ASW **Ruler:** Louis XIV **Mint:** La Rochelle

Date	Mintage	VG	F	VF	XF	Unc
1694H	—	50.00	125	250	625	—
1695H	—	—	—	—	—	—
1696H	—	65.00	150	300	750	—

KM# 290.7 1/12 ECU (10 Sols)
2.2610 g., 0.9170 Silver 0.0667 oz. ASW **Ruler:** Louis XIV **Mint:** Toulouse

Date	Mintage	VG	F	VF	XF	Unc
1695M	—	50.00	125	250	625	—
1697M	—	60.00	145	275	700	—

KM# 290.19 1/12 ECU (10 Sols)
2.2610 g., 0.9170 Silver 0.0667 oz. ASW **Ruler:** Louis XIV **Obv:** Mailed bust right **Rev:** Palm branches below crowned circular shield of France **Mint:** Besançon **Note:** Mint mark: Back-to-back C's.

Date	Mintage	VG	F	VF	XF	Unc
1694	11,000	—	—	—	—	—
1695	5,187	—	—	—	—	—
1696	—	60.00	140	275	700	—
1697	3,516	—	—	—	—	—
1698	1,083	—	—	—	—	—
1699	759	—	—	—	—	—

KM# 290.8 1/12 ECU (10 Sols)
2.2610 g., 0.9170 Silver 0.0667 oz. ASW **Ruler:** Louis XIV **Mint:** Montpellier

Date	Mintage	VG	F	VF	XF	Unc
1694N	108,000	45.00	110	225	575	—
1695N	126,000	45.00	110	225	575	—
1696N	52,000	50.00	125	250	625	—
1697N	24,000	65.00	150	300	750	—
1698N	9,350	—	—	—	—	—
1699N	6,137	—	—	—	—	—

KM# 290.9 1/12 ECU (10 Sols)
2.2610 g., 0.9170 Silver 0.0667 oz. ASW **Ruler:** Louis XIV **Mint:** Riom

Date	Mintage	VG	F	VF	XF	Unc
1694O	—	50.00	125	250	625	—

KM# 290.10 1/12 ECU (10 Sols)
2.2610 g., 0.9170 Silver 0.0667 oz. ASW **Ruler:** Louis XIV **Mint:** Dijon

Date	Mintage	VG	F	VF	XF	Unc
1694P	111,000	50.00	125	250	625	—
1695P	48,000	—	—	—	—	—
1697P	5,989	—	—	—	—	—

KM# 290.11 1/12 ECU (10 Sols)
2.2610 g., 0.9170 Silver 0.0667 oz. ASW **Ruler:** Louis XIV **Mint:** Reims

Date	Mintage	VG	F	VF	XF	Unc
1694S	—	50.00	125	250	625	—

KM# 290.12 1/12 ECU (10 Sols)
2.2610 g., 0.9170 Silver 0.0667 oz. ASW **Ruler:** Louis XIV **Mint:** Nantes

Date	Mintage	VG	F	VF	XF	Unc
1694T	—	50.00	125	250	625	—
1698T	—	60.00	140	275	700	—

KM# 290.13 1/12 ECU (10 Sols)
2.2610 g., 0.9170 Silver 0.0667 oz. ASW **Ruler:** Louis XIV **Mint:** Troyes

Date	Mintage	VG	F	VF	XF	Unc
1694V	—	—	—	—	—	—
1695V	—	—	—	—	—	—
1696V	—	—	—	—	—	—
1697V	—	60.00	140	285	750	—
1698V	—	—	—	—	—	—
1699V	—	—	—	—	—	—

KM# 290.14 1/12 ECU (10 Sols)
2.2610 g., 0.9170 Silver 0.0667 oz. ASW **Ruler:** Louis XIV **Mint:** Lille

Date	Mintage	VG	F	VF	XF	Unc
1697W	12,000	—	—	—	—	—
1699W	53,000	—	—	—	—	—
1700W	—	100	200	425	1,050	—

KM# 290.15 1/12 ECU (10 Sols)
2.2610 g., 0.9170 Silver 0.0667 oz. ASW **Ruler:** Louis XIV **Mint:** Amiens

Date	Mintage	VG	F	VF	XF	Unc
1695X	—	50.00	125	250	625	—
1697X	—	60.00	140	275	700	—

KM# 290.16 1/12 ECU (10 Sols)
2.2610 g., 0.9170 Silver 0.0667 oz. ASW **Ruler:** Louis XIV **Mint:** Bourges

Date	Mintage	VG	F	VF	XF	Unc
1696Y	—	65.00	150	300	750	—

KM# 290.17 1/12 ECU (10 Sols)
2.2610 g., 0.9170 Silver 0.0667 oz. ASW **Ruler:** Louis XIV **Mint:** Rennes **Note:** Mint mark: Numeral 9.

Date	Mintage	VG	F	VF	XF	Unc
1694	—	50.00	125	250	625	—
1695	—	50.00	125	250	625	—

KM# 290.18 1/12 ECU (10 Sols)
2.2610 g., 0.9170 Silver 0.0667 oz. ASW **Ruler:** Louis XIV **Mint:** Aix **Note:** Mint mark: Ampersand.

Date	Mintage	VG	F	VF	XF	Unc
1694	—	50.00	125	250	625	—
1695	—	45.00	110	225	575	—

KM# 291 1/12 ECU (10 Sols)
2.2610 g., 0.9170 Silver 0.0667 oz. ASW **Ruler:** Louis XIV **Rev:** Palm branches below crowned circular shield of France, Navarre and Bearn **Mint:** Pau **Note:** Mint mark: Cow.

Date	Mintage	VG	F	VF	XF	Unc
1693	—	400	800	1,650	3,900	—
1694	—	400	800	1,650	3,900	—
1697	—	450	900	1,750	4,200	—
1698	912	—	—	—	—	—
1699	516	500	1,000	2,000	4,800	—

KM# 21 1/8 ECU
Silver **Ruler:** Henri IV **Rev:** Cross with crown at ends **Mint:** Saint Lô

Date	Mintage	VG	F	VF	XF	Unc
ND	—	20.00	50.00	145	350	—

KM# 25 1/8 ECU
Silver **Ruler:** Henri IV **Obv:** Without value

Date	Mintage	VG	F	VF	XF	Unc
1601	—	25.00	60.00	150	375	—
1604	—	25.00	60.00	150	375	—

KM# 2.1 1/8 ECU
Silver **Ruler:** Henri IV **Obv:** Fleur-de-lis cross **Obv. Legend:** HENRICVS•IIII•D•G•FRANC•ET•NA(VA)•REX•BD **Rev:** Crowned arms of France, Navarre and Béarn **Rev. Legend:** GRATIA•DEI•SVM•Q(•D);SVM **Mint:** Morlaas **Note:** Previous KM#26.1.

Date	Mintage	Good	VG	F	VF	XF
1602	—	—	—	—	—	—
1604	—	8.00	25.00	65.00	175	400
1607	—	10.00	30.00	70.00	—	—
1608	—	10.00	30.00	70.00	—	—
1609	—	10.00	30.00	70.00	—	—

KM# 2.2 1/8 ECU
Silver **Ruler:** Henri IV **Obv:** Fleur-de-lis cross **Obv. Legend:** HENRICVS•IIII (or 4)•D•G• FRANC•ET•NAVA•REX• BD **Rev:** Crowned arms of France, Navarre and Béarn **Rev. Legend:** GRATIA•DEI•SVM•Q•D; SVM **Mint:** Pau

Date	Mintage	Good	VG	F	VF	XF
1605	—	20.00	50.00	150	—	—
1606	—	20.00	50.00	150	—	—
1608	—	—	—	—	—	—

KM# 22.1 1/8 ECU
Silver **Ruler:** Henri IV **Rev:** Cross fleuree, fleur-de-lis in angle **Mint:** Toulouse

Date	Mintage	VG	F	VF	XF	Unc
1602M	—	20.00	50.00	145	350	—

KM# 22.2 1/8 ECU
Silver **Ruler:** Henri IV **Mint:** Villeneuve St. André

Date	Mintage	VG	F	VF	XF	Unc
1607R	—	20.00	50.00	145	475	—

KM# 22.3 1/8 ECU
Silver **Ruler:** Henri IV **Mint:** Nantes

Date	Mintage	VG	F	VF	XF	Unc
1603T	—	20.00	50.00	145	350	—
1604T	—	20.00	50.00	145	350	—

KM# 22.4 1/8 ECU

Silver **Ruler:** Henri IV **Note:** Mint is uncertain.

Date	Mintage	VG	F	VF	XF	Unc
1603	—	20.00	50.00	145	350	—

KM# 23 1/8 ECU

Silver **Ruler:** Henri IV **Obv:** Crowned shield of Dauphine **Mint:** Grenoble

Date	Mintage	VG	F	VF	XF	Unc
1603Z	—	—	—	—	—	—

KM# 24 1/8 ECU

Silver **Ruler:** Henri IV **Obv:** Fleur-de-lis cross dividing value **Rev:** Crowned shield of France and Navarre **Mint:** Grenoble

Date	Mintage	VG	F	VF	XF	Unc
1604	—	30.00	75.00	145	350	—

KM# 20 1/8 ECU

Silver **Ruler:** Henri IV **Obv:** Crowned shield of France **Rev:** Cross with fleur-de-lis at ends **Mint:** Paris

Date	Mintage	VG	F	VF	XF	Unc
1607A	—	20.00	50.00	145	475	—

KM# 44.1 1/8 ECU

4.7800 g., 0.9170 Silver 0.1409 oz. ASW **Ruler:** Louis XIII **Obv:** Cross with fleur-de-lis at ends **Rev:** Crowned shield of France **Mint:** Paris

Date	Mintage	VG	F	VF	XF	Unc
1611A	—	—	—	—	—	—
1612A	—	—	—	—	—	—
1625A	—	—	—	—	—	—
1628A	—	—	—	—	—	—
1631A	—	—	—	—	—	—
1634A	—	—	—	—	—	—

KM# 44.2 1/8 ECU

4.7800 g., 0.9170 Silver 0.1409 oz. ASW **Ruler:** Louis XIII **Mint:** Rouen

Date	Mintage	VG	F	VF	XF	Unc
1615B	—	20.00	50.00	125	400	—
1635B	—	—	—	—	—	—

KM# 44.3 1/8 ECU

4.7800 g., 0.9170 Silver 0.1409 oz. ASW **Ruler:** Louis XIII **Mint:** Saint Lô

Date	Mintage	VG	F	VF	XF	Unc
1612C	—	22.00	55.00	135	425	—
1613C	—	30.00	70.00	175	500	—
1614C	—	30.00	70.00	175	500	—
1615C	—	65.00	160	400	1,150	—
1625C	—	—	—	—	—	—
1627C	—	—	—	—	—	—
1634C	—	—	—	—	—	—
1640C	—	45.00	120	275	800	—
1642C	—	22.00	55.00	135	425	—
1643C	—	30.00	70.00	175	500	—

KM# 44.4 1/8 ECU

4.7800 g., 0.9170 Silver 0.1409 oz. ASW **Ruler:** Louis XIII **Mint:** Lyon

Date	Mintage	VG	F	VF	XF	Unc
1621D	—	—	—	—	—	—
1622D	—	—	—	—	—	—
1625D	—	—	—	—	—	—
1643D	—	—	—	—	—	—

KM# 44.5 1/8 ECU

4.7800 g., 0.9170 Silver 0.1409 oz. ASW **Ruler:** Louis XIII **Mint:** Tours

Date	Mintage	VG	F	VF	XF	Unc
1618E	—	—	—	—	—	—
1643E	—	35.00	80.00	200	575	—

KM# 44.6 1/8 ECU

4.7800 g., 0.9170 Silver 0.1409 oz. ASW **Ruler:** Louis XIII **Mint:** Angers

Date	Mintage	VG	F	VF	XF	Unc
1611F	—	—	—	—	—	—
1612F	—	—	—	—	—	—
1613F	—	30.00	70.00	175	500	—
1625F	—	—	—	—	—	—
1642F	—	30.00	70.00	175	500	—
1643F	—	30.00	70.00	175	500	—

KM# 44.7 1/8 ECU

4.7800 g., 0.9170 Silver 0.1409 oz. ASW **Ruler:** Louis XIII **Mint:** Poitiers

Date	Mintage	VG	F	VF	XF	Unc
1643G	—	22.00	55.00	135	425	—

KM# 44.8 1/8 ECU

4.7800 g., 0.9170 Silver 0.1409 oz. ASW **Ruler:** Louis XIII **Mint:** La Rochelle

Date	Mintage	VG	F	VF	XF	Unc
1616H	—	—	—	—	—	—
1617H	—	—	—	—	—	—
1618H	—	—	—	—	—	—

KM# 44.9 1/8 ECU

4.7800 g., 0.9170 Silver 0.1409 oz. ASW **Ruler:** Louis XIII **Mint:** Limoges

Date	Mintage	VG	F	VF	XF	Unc
1612I	—	25.00	65.00	150	425	—
1642I	—	—	—	—	—	—

KM# 44.10 1/8 ECU

4.7800 g., 0.9170 Silver 0.1409 oz. ASW **Ruler:** Louis XIII **Mint:** Bordeaux

Date	Mintage	VG	F	VF	XF	Unc
1610K	—	—	—	—	—	—
1611K	—	22.00	55.00	135	500	—
1616K	—	22.00	55.00	135	500	—
1629K	—	—	—	—	—	—
1630K	—	—	—	—	—	—
1631K	—	—	—	—	—	—
1640K	—	45.00	120	275	1,000	—
1642K	—	22.00	55.00	135	500	—
1643K	—	22.00	55.00	135	500	—

KM# 44.11 1/8 ECU

4.7800 g., 0.9170 Silver 0.1409 oz. ASW **Ruler:** Louis XIII **Mint:** Bayonne

Date	Mintage	VG	F	VF	XF	Unc
1611L	—	22.00	55.00	135	425	—
1612L	—	—	—	—	—	—
1613L	—	—	—	—	—	—
1614L	—	22.00	55.00	135	425	—
1615L	—	—	—	—	—	—
1616L	—	22.00	55.00	135	425	—
1617L	—	—	—	—	—	—
1618L	—	22.00	55.00	135	425	—
1619L	—	22.00	55.00	135	425	—
1621L	—	—	—	—	—	—
1622L	—	35.00	80.00	200	575	—
1623L	—	—	—	—	—	—
1624L	—	—	—	—	—	—
1626L	—	35.00	80.00	200	575	—
1627L	—	30.00	70.00	175	500	—
1628L	—	30.00	70.00	175	500	—
1629L	—	30.00	70.00	175	500	—
1630L	—	35.00	80.00	200	575	—
1631L	—	—	—	—	—	—
1632L	—	—	—	—	—	—
1633L	—	—	—	—	—	—
1637L	—	—	—	—	—	—
1640L	—	—	—	—	—	—
1641L	—	—	—	—	—	—
1642L	—	22.00	55.00	135	425	—

KM# 44.12 1/8 ECU

4.7800 g., 0.9170 Silver 0.1409 oz. ASW **Ruler:** Louis XIII **Mint:** Toulouse

Date	Mintage	VG	F	VF	XF	Unc
1616M	—	22.00	55.00	135	425	—
1642M	—	—	—	—	—	—

KM# 44.13 1/8 ECU

4.7800 g., 0.9170 Silver 0.1409 oz. ASW **Ruler:** Louis XIII **Mint:** Nantes

Date	Mintage	VG	F	VF	XF	Unc
1610T	—	—	—	—	—	—
1611T	—	—	—	—	—	—
1612T	—	—	—	—	—	—
1613T	—	—	—	—	—	—
1614T	—	—	—	—	—	—
1615T	—	—	—	—	—	—
1616T	—	30.00	70.00	175	500	—
1617T	—	30.00	70.00	175	500	—
1618T	—	30.00	70.00	175	500	—
1619T	—	—	—	—	—	—
1620T	—	—	—	—	—	—
1621T	—	—	—	—	—	—
1622T	—	—	—	—	—	—
1623T	—	—	—	—	—	—
1624T	—	—	—	—	—	—
1625T	—	—	—	—	—	—
1628T	—	35.00	80.00	200	575	—
1642T	—	30.00	70.00	175	500	—
1643T	—	22.00	55.00	135	425	—

KM# 44.14 1/8 ECU

4.7800 g., 0.9170 Silver 0.1409 oz. ASW **Ruler:** Louis XIII **Mint:** Amiens

Date	Mintage	VG	F	VF	XF	Unc
1642X	—	22.00	55.00	135	425	—
1643X	—	—	—	—	—	—

KM# 44.15 1/8 ECU

4.7800 g., 0.9170 Silver 0.1409 oz. ASW **Ruler:** Louis XIII **Mint:** Bourges

Date	Mintage	VG	F	VF	XF	Unc
1640Y	—	—	—	—	—	—
1642Y	—	—	—	—	—	—
1643Y	—	—	—	—	—	—

KM# 44.16 1/8 ECU

4.7800 g., 0.9170 Silver 0.1409 oz. ASW **Ruler:** Louis XIII **Mint:** Grenoble

Date	Mintage	VG	F	VF	XF	Unc
1642Z	—	35.00	80.00	200	575	—

KM# 44.17 1/8 ECU

4.7800 g., 0.9170 Silver 0.1409 oz. ASW **Ruler:** Louis XIII **Mint:** Rennes **Note:** Mint mark: Numeral 9.

Date	Mintage	VG	F	VF	XF	Unc
1611	—	22.00	55.00	135	425	—
1612	—	22.00	55.00	135	425	—
1613	—	22.00	55.00	135	425	—
1614	—	—	—	—	—	—
1615	—	22.00	55.00	135	425	—
1616	—	22.00	55.00	135	425	—
1617	—	30.00	70.00	175	500	—
1618	—	—	—	—	—	—
1619	—	—	—	—	—	—
1620	—	—	—	—	—	—
1621	—	—	—	—	—	—
1623	—	—	—	—	—	—
1624	—	35.00	80.00	200	575	—
1625	—	—	—	—	—	—
1627	—	—	—	—	—	—
1628	—	—	—	—	—	—
1629	—	35.00	80.00	200	575	—
1642	—	30.00	70.00	175	500	—
1643	—	22.00	55.00	135	425	—

KM# 44.18 1/8 ECU

4.7800 g., 0.9170 Silver 0.1409 oz. ASW **Ruler:** Louis XIII **Mint:** Arras

Date	Mintage	VG	F	VF	XF	Unc
1641AR	—	40.00	100	250	600	—
1642AR	—	30.00	80.00	200	475	—
1646AR	—	40.00	100	250	600	—

KM# 46 1/8 ECU

4.7800 g., 0.9170 Silver 0.1409 oz. ASW **Ruler:** Louis XIII **Rev:** Crowned shield of France, Navarre and Bearne **Mint:** Pau **Note:** Mint mark: Cow.

Date	Mintage	VG	F	VF	XF	Unc
1610	—	28.00	70.00	165	450	—
1612	—	28.00	70.00	165	450	—
1613	—	28.00	70.00	165	450	—
1614	—	28.00	70.00	165	450	—
1617	—	28.00	70.00	165	450	—
1620	—	28.00	70.00	165	450	—
1623	—	28.00	70.00	165	450	—
1625	—	28.00	70.00	165	450	—
1631	—	28.00	70.00	165	450	—
1643	—	30.00	80.00	200	600	—

KM# 45 1/8 ECU

4.7800 g., 0.9170 Silver 0.1409 oz. ASW **Ruler:** Louis XIII **Rev:** Crowned shield of France and Navarre **Mint:** Saint Palais

Date	Mintage	VG	F	VF	XF	Unc
1611C	—	25.00	60.00	150	425	—
1612M	—	30.00	80.00	200	600	—
1613M	—	25.00	60.00	150	425	—
1614M	—	25.00	60.00	150	425	—
1615M	—	25.00	60.00	150	425	—
1616M	—	25.00	60.00	150	425	—
1617M	—	25.00	60.00	150	425	—
1618M	—	25.00	60.00	150	425	—
1619M	—	28.00	70.00	165	450	—
1620M	—	25.00	60.00	150	425	—
1621F	—	28.00	70.00	165	450	—
1623F	—	25.00	60.00	150	425	—
1629F	—	25.00	60.00	150	425	—

KM# 141.1 1/8 ECU

4.7800 g., 0.9170 Silver 0.1409 oz. ASW **Ruler:** Louis XIV **Obv:** Cross fleuree **Rev:** Crowned shield of France dividing value, VIII **Mint:** Paris

Date	Mintage	VG	F	VF	XF	Unc
1643A	—	20.00	50.00	125	325	—
1644A	—	—	—	—	—	—

KM# 141.2 1/8 ECU

4.7800 g., 0.9170 Silver 0.1409 oz. ASW **Ruler:** Louis XIV **Mint:** Rouen

Date	Mintage	VG	F	VF	XF	Unc
1644B	—	—	—	—	—	—

KM# 141.3 1/8 ECU

4.7800 g., 0.9170 Silver 0.1409 oz. ASW **Ruler:** Louis XIV **Mint:** Saint Lô

Date	Mintage	VG	F	VF	XF	Unc
1643C	—	30.00	75.00	165	450	—
1644C	—	30.00	75.00	165	450	—
1646C	—	30.00	75.00	165	450	—

KM# A141.3 1/8 ECU

4.7800 g., 0.9170 Silver 0.1409 oz. ASW **Ruler:** Louis XIV **Mint:** Angers

Date	Mintage	VG	F	VF	XF	Unc
1643F	—	30.00	75.00	165	450	—
1644F	—	20.00	50.00	125	325	—
1645F	—	25.00	65.00	150	425	—

KM# 141.4 1/8 ECU
4.7800 g., 0.9170 Silver 0.1409 oz. ASW **Ruler:** Louis XIV **Mint:** Poitiers

Date	Mintage	VG	F	VF	XF	Unc
1644G	—	—	—	—	—	—
1645G	—	30.00	75.00	165	450	—
1646G	2,722	35.00	90.00	200	550	—

KM# 141.5 1/8 ECU
4.7800 g., 0.9170 Silver 0.1409 oz. ASW **Ruler:** Louis XIV **Mint:** La Rochelle

Date	Mintage	VG	F	VF	XF	Unc
1644H	—	25.00	65.00	150	425	—

KM# 141.6 1/8 ECU
4.7800 g., 0.9170 Silver 0.1409 oz. ASW **Ruler:** Louis XIV **Mint:** Limoges

Date	Mintage	VG	F	VF	XF	Unc
1644I	—	—	—	—	—	—

KM# 141.7 1/8 ECU
4.7800 g., 0.9170 Silver 0.1409 oz. ASW **Ruler:** Louis XIV **Mint:** Bordeaux

Date	Mintage	VG	F	VF	XF	Unc
1644K	—	25.00	65.00	150	425	—
1645K	—	25.00	65.00	150	425	—

KM# 141.8 1/8 ECU
4.7800 g., 0.9170 Silver 0.1409 oz. ASW **Ruler:** Louis XIV **Mint:** Bayonne

Date	Mintage	VG	F	VF	XF	Unc
1645L	—	30.00	75.00	165	450	—
1646L	—	25.00	65.00	150	425	—
1647L	—	25.00	65.00	150	425	—
1648L	11,000	—	—	—	—	—
1649L	6,350	—	—	—	—	—

KM# 141.9 1/8 ECU
4.7800 g., 0.9170 Silver 0.1409 oz. ASW **Ruler:** Louis XIV **Mint:** Toulouse

Date	Mintage	VG	F	VF	XF	Unc
1644M	—	25.00	65.00	150	425	—
1645M	—	25.00	65.00	150	425	—
1647M	3,629	25.00	65.00	150	425	—

KM# 141.10 1/8 ECU
4.7800 g., 0.9170 Silver 0.1409 oz. ASW **Ruler:** Louis XIV **Mint:** Montpellier

Date	Mintage	VG	F	VF	XF	Unc
1644N	—	25.00	65.00	150	425	—
1645N	—	30.00	75.00	165	450	—

KM# 141.11 1/8 ECU
4.7800 g., 0.9170 Silver 0.1409 oz. ASW **Ruler:** Louis XIV **Mint:** Amiens

Date	Mintage	VG	F	VF	XF	Unc
1645X	—	25.00	65.00	150	425	—
1649X	—	35.00	90.00	200	550	—

KM# 141.12 1/8 ECU
4.7800 g., 0.9170 Silver 0.1409 oz. ASW **Ruler:** Louis XIV **Mint:** Bourges

Date	Mintage	VG	F	VF	XF	Unc
1648Y	—	32.00	80.00	175	475	—

KM# 141.13 1/8 ECU
4.7800 g., 0.9170 Silver 0.1409 oz. ASW **Ruler:** Louis XIV **Mint:** Aix **Note:** Mint mark: Ampersand.

Date	Mintage	VG	F	VF	XF	Unc
1646	—	—	—	—	—	—

KM# 141.14 1/8 ECU
4.7800 g., 0.9170 Silver 0.1409 oz. ASW **Ruler:** Louis XIV **Mint:** Rennes **Note:** Mint mark: Numeral 9.

Date	Mintage	VG	F	VF	XF	Unc
1645	210,000	25.00	75.00	165	450	—
1646	73,000	20.00	50.00	125	325	—
1647	3,629	30.00	75.00	165	450	—

KM# 141.15 1/8 ECU
4.7800 g., 0.9170 Silver 0.1409 oz. ASW **Ruler:** Louis XIV **Mint:** Besançon **Note:** Mint mark: Two back-to-back C's monogram.

Date	Mintage	VG	F	VF	XF	Unc
1645	—	30.00	75.00	165	450	—
1646	—	—	—	—	—	—

KM# 165 1/8 ECU
4.7800 g., 0.9170 Silver 0.1409 oz. ASW **Ruler:** Louis XIV **Mint:** Arras

Date	Mintage	VG	F	VF	XF	Unc
1644AR	—	50.00	100	200	600	—
1645AR	—	50.00	100	200	600	—
1646AR	—	50.00	100	200	600	—

KM# 168 1/8 ECU
4.7800 g., 0.9170 Silver 0.1409 oz. ASW **Ruler:** Louis XIV **Rev. Legend:** Crowned shield of France and Navarre **Mint:** Saint Palais

Date	Mintage	VG	F	VF	XF	Unc
1648	—	40.00	90.00	185	575	—
1649	—	40.00	90.00	185	575	—
1650	—	40.00	90.00	185	575	—

KM# 169 1/8 ECU
4.7800 g., 0.9170 Silver 0.1409 oz. ASW **Ruler:** Louis XIV **Rev:** Crowned shield of France, Navarre and Bearn **Mint:** Morlaas

Date	Mintage	VG	F	VF	XF	Unc
1648P B**	—	65.00	125	250	775	—

KM# 259.1 1/8 ECU
4.7000 g., 0.8570 Silver 0.1295 oz. ASW **Ruler:** Louis XIV **Obv:** Draped bust right **Rev:** Crowned quartered shield of France, Old and New Burgundy **Mint:** Lille

Date	Mintage	VG	F	VF	XF	Unc
1686LL	Est. 98,000	90.00	200	425	1,400	—

KM# 259.2 1/8 ECU
4.7000 g., 0.8570 Silver 0.1295 oz. ASW **Ruler:** Louis XIV **Mint:** Lille **Note:** Mint mark: Crowned L.

Date	Mintage	VG	F	VF	XF	Unc
1686	209,000	75.00	170	375	1,200	—
1687	77,000	90.00	200	450	1,500	—
1688	64,000	100	225	500	1,600	—

KM# 292 1/8 ECU
4.7000 g., 0.8570 Silver 0.1295 oz. ASW **Ruler:** Louis XIV **Rev:** Crowned quartered circular shield of France, Old and New Burgundy dividing palms **Mint:** Lille

Date	Mintage	VG	F	VF	XF	Unc
1693W	—	200	450	1,000	2,400	—
1694W	—	200	450	1,000	2,400	—
1695W	—	200	450	1,000	2,400	—
1696W	18,000	—	—	—	—	—
1697W	10,000	200	450	1,000	2,400	—
1698W	—	250	550	1,250	3,000	—
1699W Rare	800	—	—	—	—	—
1700W	—	250	550	1,250	3,000	—

KM# 1.1 1/4 ECU
Silver **Ruler:** Henri IV **Obv:** Cross with lis **Obv. Legend:** HENRICVS•IIII•D•G•FRANC•ET•NA(VA)•REX• BD **Rev:** Crowned arms of France, Navarre and Béarn **Rev. Legend:** GRATIA•DEI•SVM•Q(•D) (or IDQ)•SVM **Mint:** Pau

Date	Mintage	Good	VG	F	VF	XF
1601	—	—	—	—	—	—
1602	—	—	—	—	—	—
1603	—	30.00	60.00	100	—	—
1604	—	30.00	60.00	100	—	—
1605	—	30.00	60.00	100	—	—
1606	—	30.00	60.00	100	—	—
1607	—	30.00	60.00	100	—	—
1608	—	30.00	60.00	100	—	—
1609	—	30.00	60.00	100	—	—
1610	—	30.00	60.00	100	—	—

KM# 1.2 1/4 ECU
Silver **Ruler:** Henri IV **Obv:** Fleur-de-lis cross **Obv. Legend:** HENRICVS•IIII•D•G•FRANC•ET • NA(VA)•REX• BD **Rev:** Crowned arms of France, Navarre and Béarn **Rev. Legend:** GRATIA•BEI•SVM•Q(•D) or (IDQ)•SVM **Mint:** Morlaas

Date	Mintage	Good	VG	F	VF	XF
1601	—	30.00	60.00	100	—	—
1602	—	30.00	60.00	100	—	—
1603	—	30.00	60.00	100	—	—
1604	—	30.00	60.00	100	—	—
1605	—	30.00	60.00	100	—	—
1606	—	30.00	60.00	100	—	—
1607	—	30.00	60.00	100	—	—
1608	—	30.00	60.00	100	—	—
1609	—	30.00	60.00	100	—	—
1610	—	30.00	60.00	100	—	—

KM# 30 1/4 ECU
Silver **Ruler:** Henri IV **Rev:** Crowned shield of Dauphine **Mint:** Grenoble

Date	Mintage	VG	F	VF	XF	Unc
1601Z	—	70.00	175	350	725	—
1602Z	—	50.00	125	250	625	—
1603Z	—	60.00	150	300	725	—
1604Z	—	50.00	125	250	625	—
1605Z	—	50.00	125	250	625	—

KM# 31 1/4 ECU
Silver **Ruler:** Henri IV **Rev:** Crowned shield of France and Navarre **Mint:** Saint Palais

Date	Mintage	VG	F	VF	XF	Unc
1601	—	40.00	100	250	625	—
1602	—	40.00	100	250	625	—
1603	—	40.00	100	250	625	—
1604	—	40.00	100	250	625	—
1605	—	40.00	100	250	625	—
1606	—	40.00	100	250	625	—
1607	—	40.00	100	250	625	—
1608	—	40.00	100	250	625	—
1609	—	40.00	100	250	625	—
1610F	—	40.00	100	250	625	—

KM# 27.1 1/4 ECU
Silver **Ruler:** Henri IV **Obv:** Crowned shield of France **Rev:** Cross with fleur-de-lis at ends **Mint:** Paris

Date	Mintage	VG	F	VF	XF	Unc
1607	—	35.00	90.00	225	500	—

KM# 27.3 1/4 ECU
Silver **Ruler:** Henri IV **Mint:** La Rochelle

Date	Mintage	VG	F	VF	XF	Unc
1606H	—	45.00	100	250	650	—
1607H	—	45.00	100	250	—	—
1608H	—	45.00	100	250	—	—

KM# 27.4 1/4 ECU
Silver **Ruler:** Henri IV **Mint:** Villeneuve St. André

Date	Mintage	VG	F	VF	XF	Unc
1603R	—	35.00	90.00	225	600	—
1606R	—	35.00	90.00	225	—	—
1607R	—	35.00	90.00	225	—	—

KM# 27.5 1/4 ECU
Silver **Ruler:** Henri IV

Date	Mintage	VG	F	VF	XF	Unc
1601F	—	40.00	100	250	—	—
1602F	—	40.00	100	250	525	—

KM# 29 1/4 ECU
Silver **Ruler:** Henri IV **Obv:** Cross fleuree **Mint:** Aix **Note:** Mint mark: Ampersand.

Date	Mintage	VG	F	VF	XF	Unc
1603	—	35.00	90.00	225	600	—

KM# A29 1/4 ECU
Silver **Ruler:** Henri IV **Obv:** Crowned shield of France divides "V" and "III" **Obv. Legend:** HENRICVS 4 D.G. **Rev:** Cross fleuree **Mint:** Bordeaux

Date	Mintage	VG	F	VF	XF	Unc
1603K	—	—	—	—	—	—

KM# 28 1/4 ECU
Silver **Ruler:** Henri IV **Rev:** Cross with crown at ends **Mint:** Saint Lô

Date	Mintage	VG	F	VF	XF	Unc
1603C	—	35.00	90.00	225	600	—
1607C	—	35.00	90.00	225	600	—

KM# 47.1 1/4 ECU
6.4400 g., 0.9170 Silver 0.1899 oz. ASW **Ruler:** Louis XIII **Obv:** Cross with fleur-de-lis at ends **Rev:** Crowned shield of France **Mint:** Paris

Date	Mintage	VG	F	VF	XF	Unc
1611A	—	—	—	—	—	—
1612A	—	—	—	—	—	—
1620A	—	—	—	—	—	—
1624A	—	—	—	—	—	—
1625A	—	40.00	100	225	600	—
1628A	—	—	—	—	—	—
1631A	—	—	—	—	—	—
1634A	—	—	—	—	—	—
1636A	—	35.00	90.00	200	550	—
1637A	—	—	—	—	—	—
1639A	—	—	—	—	—	—
1641A	—	28.00	65.00	150	400	—
1642A	—	22.00	55.00	125	325	—
1643A	—	20.00	45.00	100	270	—

KM# 47.2 1/4 ECU
6.4400 g., 0.9170 Silver 0.1899 oz. ASW **Ruler:** Louis XIII **Mint:** Rouen

Date	Mintage	VG	F	VF	XF	Unc
1611B	—	20.00	45.00	100	220	—
1614B	—	—	—	—	—	—
1615B	—	20.00	40.00	90.00	200	—
1622B	—	—	—	—	—	—
1623B	—	—	—	—	—	—
1624B	—	—	—	—	—	—
1626B	—	—	—	—	—	—
1628B	—	—	—	—	—	—
1629B	—	—	—	—	—	—
1632B	—	28.00	65.00	150	400	—
1636B	—	—	—	—	—	—
1637B	—	—	—	—	—	—

Date	Mintage	VG	F	VF	XF	Unc
1640B	—	22.00	55.00	125	325	—
1642B	—	—	—	—	—	—

KM# 47.3 1/4 ECU

6.4400 g., 0.9170 Silver 0.1899 oz. ASW **Ruler:** Louis XIII **Mint:** Saint Lô

Date	Mintage	VG	F	VF	XF	Unc
1611C	—	—	—	—	—	—
1612C	—	22.00	50.00	110	270	—
1613C	—	22.00	50.00	110	270	—
1614C	—	22.00	50.00	110	270	—
1615C	—	22.00	50.00	110	270	—
1616C	—	28.00	65.00	160	400	—
1617C	—	35.00	90.00	200	550	—
1623C	—	—	—	—	—	—
1624C	—	35.00	90.00	200	550	—
1625C	—	—	—	—	—	—
1627C	—	90.00	200	400	1,100	—
1628C	—	—	—	—	—	—
1630C	—	40.00	100	225	600	—
1633C	—	—	—	—	—	—
1634C	—	40.00	100	225	600	—
1642C	—	22.00	50.00	110	270	—
1643C	—	25.00	65.00	140	350	—

KM# 47.4 1/4 ECU

6.4400 g., 0.9170 Silver 0.1899 oz. ASW **Ruler:** Louis XIII **Mint:** Lyon

Date	Mintage	VG	F	VF	XF	Unc
1621D	—	—	—	—	—	—
1622D	—	—	—	—	—	—
1624D	—	—	—	—	—	—
1625D	—	—	—	—	—	—
1633D	—	—	—	—	—	—
1642D	—	20.00	40.00	90.00	200	—
1643D	—	—	—	—	—	—

KM# 47.5 1/4 ECU

6.4400 g., 0.9170 Silver 0.1899 oz. ASW **Ruler:** Louis XIII **Mint:** Tours

Date	Mintage	VG	F	VF	XF	Unc
1617E	—	20.00	40.00	90.00	220	—
1618E	—	—	—	—	—	—
1642E	—	22.00	50.00	110	270	—
1643E	—	25.00	65.00	140	350	—

KM# 47.6 1/4 ECU

6.4400 g., 0.9170 Silver 0.1899 oz. ASW **Ruler:** Louis XIII **Mint:** Angers

Date	Mintage	VG	F	VF	XF	Unc
1611F	—	—	—	—	—	—
1612F	—	—	—	—	—	—
1613F	—	22.00	55.00	125	325	—
1614F	—	—	—	—	—	—
1615F	—	20.00	40.00	90.00	200	—
1616F	—	22.00	55.00	125	325	—
1617F	—	20.00	40.00	90.00	220	—
1618F	—	20.00	55.00	125	325	—
1621F	—	—	—	—	—	—
1623F	—	—	—	—	—	—
1625F	—	—	—	—	—	—
1642F	—	25.00	65.00	145	350	—
1643F	—	25.00	65.00	145	350	—
1644F	—	32.00	80.00	185	475	—
1645F	—	32.00	80.00	185	475	—

KM# 47.7 1/4 ECU

6.4400 g., 0.9170 Silver 0.1899 oz. ASW **Ruler:** Louis XIII **Mint:** Poitiers

Date	Mintage	VG	F	VF	XF	Unc
1642G	—	35.00	90.00	210	550	—
1643G	—	22.00	55.00	130	325	—

KM# 47.8 1/4 ECU

6.4400 g., 0.9170 Silver 0.1899 oz. ASW **Ruler:** Louis XIII **Mint:** La Rochelle

Date	Mintage	VG	F	VF	XF	Unc
1615H	—	—	—	—	—	—
1616H	—	22.00	50.00	110	270	—
1617H	—	20.00	40.00	90.00	220	—

Date	Mintage	VG	F	VF	XF	Unc
1618H	—	—	—	—	—	—
1627H	—	35.00	90.00	200	550	—
1640H	—	35.00	90.00	200	550	—
1641H	—	—	—	—	—	—
1642H	—	28.00	65.00	150	400	—
1643H	—	—	—	—	—	—

KM# 47.9 1/4 ECU

6.4400 g., 0.9170 Silver 0.1899 oz. ASW **Ruler:** Louis XIII **Mint:** Limoges

Date	Mintage	VG	F	VF	XF	Unc
1611I	—	20.00	40.00	90.00	200	—
1612I	—	—	—	—	—	—
1613I	—	22.00	55.00	125	325	—
1615I	—	20.00	40.00	90.00	200	—
1617I	—	20.00	40.00	90.00	210	—
1642I	—	22.00	55.00	125	325	—

KM# 47.10 1/4 ECU

6.4400 g., 0.9170 Silver 0.1899 oz. ASW **Ruler:** Louis XIII **Mint:** Bordeaux

Date	Mintage	VG	F	VF	XF	Unc
1611K	—	20.00	40.00	90.00	200	—
1612K	—	22.00	50.00	110	270	—
1613K	—	—	—	—	—	—
1615K	—	22.00	55.00	125	325	—
1616K	—	22.00	55.00	125	325	—
1618K	—	—	—	—	—	—
1629K	—	—	—	—	—	—
1630K	—	—	—	—	—	—
1631K	—	—	—	—	—	—
1632K	—	—	—	—	—	—
1639K	—	35.00	90.00	200	550	—
1640K	—	22.00	55.00	125	325	—
1642K	—	22.00	50.00	110	270	—
1643K	—	22.00	50.00	110	270	—

KM# 47.11 1/4 ECU

6.4400 g., 0.9170 Silver 0.1899 oz. ASW **Ruler:** Louis XIII **Mint:** Bayonne

Date	Mintage	VG	F	VF	XF	Unc
1610L	—	—	—	—	—	—
1611L	—	20.00	40.00	90.00	210	—
1612L	—	20.00	40.00	90.00	210	—
1613L	—	20.00	40.00	90.00	210	—
1614L	—	22.00	45.00	100	220	—
1615L	—	20.00	40.00	90.00	210	—
1616L	—	22.00	45.00	100	220	—
1617L	—	22.00	45.00	100	220	—
1618L	—	22.00	45.00	100	220	—
1619L	—	30.00	65.00	150	400	—
1621L	—	22.00	45.00	100	220	—
1622L	—	22.00	45.00	100	220	—
1623L	—	22.00	45.00	100	220	—
1624L	—	22.00	50.00	110	270	—
1626L	—	22.00	50.00	110	270	—
1627L	—	20.00	40.00	90.00	210	—
1628L	—	20.00	40.00	90.00	210	—
1629L	—	20.00	40.00	90.00	210	—
1630L	—	—	—	—	—	—
1631L	—	25.00	55.00	125	325	—
1632L	—	22.00	50.00	110	270	—
1633L	—	35.00	90.00	200	550	—
1637L	—	—	—	—	—	—
1640L	—	40.00	100	225	600	—
1641L	—	28.00	65.00	150	400	—
1642L	—	25.00	55.00	125	325	—
1643L	—	25.00	55.00	125	325	—

KM# 47.12 1/4 ECU

6.4400 g., 0.9170 Silver 0.1899 oz. ASW **Ruler:** Louis XIII **Mint:** Toulouse

Date	Mintage	VG	F	VF	XF	Unc
1613M	—	20.00	40.00	90.00	200	—
1619M	—	25.00	55.00	125	325	—
1642M	—	35.00	90.00	200	550	—
1643M	—	20.00	40.00	90.00	200	—

KM# 47.13 1/4 ECU

6.4400 g., 0.9170 Silver 0.1899 oz. ASW **Ruler:** Louis XIII **Mint:** Montpellier

Date	Mintage	VG	F	VF	XF	Unc
1642N	—	22.00	50.00	110	350	—
1643N	—	25.00	55.00	125	400	—

KM# 47.14 1/4 ECU

6.4400 g., 0.9170 Silver 0.1899 oz. ASW **Ruler:** Louis XIII **Mint:** Dijon

Date	Mintage	VG	F	VF	XF	Unc
1638P	—	35.00	90.00	200	550	—
1639P	—	35.00	90.00	200	550	—
1640P	—	—	—	—	—	—

KM# 47.15 1/4 ECU

6.4400 g., 0.9170 Silver 0.1899 oz. ASW **Ruler:** Louis XIII **Mint:** Perpignan

Date	Mintage	VG	F	VF	XF	Unc
1645Q	—	35.00	90.00	200	550	—

KM# 47.16 1/4 ECU

6.4400 g., 0.9170 Silver 0.1899 oz. ASW **Ruler:** Louis XIII **Mint:** Nantes

Date	Mintage	VG	F	VF	XF	Unc
1610T	—	22.00	45.00	100	220	—
1611T	—	20.00	40.00	90.00	200	—
1612T	—	20.00	40.00	90.00	200	—
1613T	—	22.00	45.00	110	270	—
1614T	—	22.00	45.00	110	270	—
1615T	—	20.00	40.00	90.00	200	—
1616T	—	22.00	45.00	100	220	—
1617T	—	20.00	40.00	90.00	200	—
1618T	—	20.00	40.00	90.00	200	—
1619T	—	—	—	—	—	—
1620T	—	—	—	—	—	—
1622T	—	—	—	—	—	—
1623T	—	20.00	40.00	90.00	200	—
1624T	—	22.00	45.00	110	270	—
1625T	—	22.00	45.00	110	270	—
1626T	—	—	—	—	—	—
1642T	—	22.00	45.00	110	270	—
1643T	—	25.00	55.00	125	325	—

KM# 47.17 1/4 ECU

6.4400 g., 0.9170 Silver 0.1899 oz. ASW **Ruler:** Louis XIII **Mint:** Amiens

Date	Mintage	VG	F	VF	XF	Unc
1636X	—	—	—	—	—	—
1641X	—	—	—	—	—	—
1642X	—	25.00	55.00	125	325	—
1643X	—	28.00	65.00	150	400	—

KM# 47.18 1/4 ECU

6.4400 g., 0.9170 Silver 0.1899 oz. ASW **Ruler:** Louis XIII **Mint:** Bourges

Date	Mintage	VG	F	VF	XF	Unc
1640Y	—	—	—	—	—	—
1642Y	—	35.00	90.00	200	550	—

KM# 47.19 1/4 ECU

6.4400 g., 0.9170 Silver 0.1899 oz. ASW **Ruler:** Louis XIII **Mint:** Grenoble

Date	Mintage	VG	F	VF	XF	Unc
1641Z	—	—	—	—	—	—
1642Z	—	28.00	65.00	150	400	—
1643Z	—	25.00	55.00	125	325	—

KM# 47.20 1/4 ECU

6.4400 g., 0.9170 Silver 0.1899 oz. ASW **Ruler:** Louis XIII **Mint:** Aix **Note:** Mint mark: Ampersand.

Date	Mintage	VG	F	VF	XF	Unc
1642	—	—	—	—	—	—
1643	—	22.00	55.00	125	325	—

KM# 47.21 1/4 ECU

6.4400 g., 0.9170 Silver 0.1899 oz. ASW **Ruler:** Louis XIII **Mint:** Rennes **Note:** Mint mark: Numeral 9.

Date	Mintage	VG	F	VF	XF	Unc
1611	—	20.00	40.00	90.00	200	—
1612	—	20.00	40.00	90.00	200	—
1613	—	20.00	40.00	90.00	200	—
1614	—	22.00	45.00	110	270	—
1615	—	20.00	40.00	90.00	200	—
1616	—	20.00	40.00	90.00	200	—
1617	—	20.00	40.00	90.00	200	—
1618	—	20.00	40.00	90.00	200	—
1620	—	25.00	55.00	125	325	—
1623	—	—	—	—	—	—
1624	—	20.00	40.00	90.00	200	—
1625	—	25.00	55.00	125	325	—
1642	—	—	—	—	—	—
1643	—	25.00	55.00	125	325	—

KM# 47.22 1/4 ECU

6.4400 g., 0.9170 Silver 0.1899 oz. ASW **Ruler:** Louis XIII **Mint:** Arras

Date	Mintage	VG	F	VF	XF	Unc
1624AR	—	28.00	65.00	150	400	—
1641AR	1,121	70.00	175	350	900	—
1642AR	153,000	20.00	40.00	90.00	210	—
1643AR	86,000	22.00	45.00	110	270	—

KM# 48 1/4 ECU

6.4400 g., 0.9170 Silver 0.1899 oz. ASW **Ruler:** Louis XIII **Rev:** Crowned shield of France and Navarre **Mint:** Saint Palais

Date	Mintage	VG	F	VF	XF	Unc
1610C	—	30.00	60.00	150	300	—
1611C	—	30.00	60.00	150	300	—
1612M	65,000	30.00	60.00	150	300	—

Date	Mintage	VG	F	VF	XF	Unc
1613M	81,000	30.00	60.00	150	300	—
1614M	69,000	30.00	60.00	150	300	—
1615M	—	30.00	60.00	150	300	—
1616M	53,000	30.00	60.00	150	300	—
1617M	—	30.00	60.00	150	300	—
1618M	—	30.00	60.00	150	300	—
1619F	51,000	30.00	60.00	150	300	—
1619M	Inc. above	30.00	60.00	150	300	—
1620F	—	30.00	60.00	150	300	—
1620M	—	30.00	60.00	150	300	—
1621F	—	30.00	60.00	150	300	—
1623F	92,000	30.00	60.00	150	300	—
1625F	—	30.00	60.00	150	300	—
1626F	—	30.00	60.00	150	300	—
1627F	—	30.00	60.00	150	300	—
1629F	—	30.00	60.00	150	300	—
1631F	99,000	30.00	60.00	150	300	—

KM# 49.1 1/4 ECU
6.4400 g., 0.9170 Silver 0.1899 oz. ASW **Ruler:** Louis XIII **Rev:** Crowned shield of France, Navarre and Bearn **Mint:** Pau

Date	Mintage	VG	F	VF	XF	Unc
1610	—	28.00	65.00	150	300	—
1612	64,000	35.00	75.00	165	325	—
1613	54,000	35.00	75.00	165	325	—
1614	42,000	35.00	75.00	165	325	—
1615	—	35.00	75.00	165	325	—
1617	—	40.00	85.00	185	350	—
1618	—	40.00	85.00	185	350	—
1619	—	35.00	75.00	165	325	—
1621	—	35.00	75.00	165	325	—
1622	64,000	40.00	85.00	185	350	—
1623	—	35.00	75.00	165	325	—
1625	—	—	—	—	—	—
1626	—	35.00	75.00	165	325	—
1627	—	35.00	75.00	165	325	—
1628	—	35.00	75.00	165	325	—
1629	—	28.00	65.00	150	300	—
1630	—	35.00	75.00	165	325	—
1631	21,000	—	—	—	—	—
1639	—	40.00	85.00	185	350	—
1643	—	40.00	85.00	185	350	—

KM# 49.2 1/4 ECU
6.4400 g., 0.9170 Silver 0.1899 oz. ASW **Ruler:** Louis XIII **Mint:** Morlaas **Note:** Mint mark: Star or * and letter.

Date	Mintage	VG	F	VF	XF	Unc
1610	—	60.00	160	350	700	—
1611	—	35.00	75.00	165	325	—
1612	115,000	35.00	75.00	165	325	—
1613	72,000	35.00	75.00	165	325	—
1614	68,000	35.00	75.00	165	325	—
1615	—	40.00	85.00	185	350	—
1616	—	35.00	75.00	165	325	—
1617	—	35.00	75.00	165	325	—
1618	—	28.00	65.00	150	300	—
1619	—	35.00	75.00	165	325	—
1620	—	35.00	75.00	165	325	—
1622	—	—	—	—	—	—
1624	—	35.00	75.00	165	325	—
1625	—	35.00	75.00	165	325	—
1626	—	35.00	75.00	165	325	—
1627	—	35.00	75.00	165	325	—
1628	—	35.00	75.00	165	325	—
1629	99,000	35.00	75.00	165	325	—
1630	—	—	—	—	—	—
1631	—	35.00	75.00	165	325	—

KM# 133 1/4 ECU
6.7460 g., 0.9170 Silver 0.1989 oz. ASW **Ruler:** Louis XIII **Obv:** Laureate mailed bust right **Mint:** Paris

Date	Mintage	VG	F	VF	XF	Unc
1642A Rose	625,000	125	300	625	1,200	—
1642A Point	—	110	275	575	1,150	—
1642A 2 points	—	110	275	575	1,150	—
1642A 2 points and 1 below bust	—	125	300	625	1,200	—

KM# 134.1 1/4 ECU
6.7460 g., 0.9170 Silver 0.1989 oz. ASW **Ruler:** Louis XIII **Obv:** Laureate, draped and mailed bust right **Mint:** Paris

Date	Mintage	VG	F	VF	XF	Unc
1642 Rose	647,000	90.00	220	450	875	—
1642 Point	—	90.00	220	450	875	—
1642 2 points	—	90.00	220	450	875	—
1643 Rose	Est. 3,089,000	80.00	200	425	850	—
1643 Point	—	65.00	165	350	700	—
1643 2 points	Est. 4,626,000	65.00	165	350	700	—

KM# 134.2 1/4 ECU
6.7460 g., 0.9170 Silver 0.1989 oz. ASW **Ruler:** Louis XIII **Mint:** Lyon

Date	Mintage	VG	F	VF	XF	Unc
1643D 3 points	Est. 17,000	175	425	825	1,600	—

KM# 142.1 1/4 ECU
6.4400 g., 0.9170 Silver 0.1899 oz. ASW **Ruler:** Louis XIV **Obv:** Outlined cross with fleur-de-lis at ends **Rev:** Crowned shield of France **Mint:** Paris

Date	Mintage	VG	F	VF	XF	Unc
1643A	—	20.00	45.00	100	270	—
1644A	—	—	—	—	—	—

KM# 142.2 1/4 ECU
6.4400 g., 0.9170 Silver 0.1899 oz. ASW **Ruler:** Louis XIII **Mint:** Rouen

Date	Mintage	VG	F	VF	XF	Unc
1644B	—	25.00	60.00	135	350	—
1645B	—	35.00	90.00	200	550	—

KM# 142.3 1/4 ECU
6.4400 g., 0.9170 Silver 0.1899 oz. ASW **Ruler:** Louis XIV **Mint:** Saint Lô

Date	Mintage	VG	F	VF	XF	Unc
1643C	—	28.00	65.00	150	400	—
1644C	—	20.00	50.00	120	325	—
1645C	—	25.00	60.00	135	350	—
1646C	—	28.00	65.00	150	400	—
1647C	—	—	—	—	—	—

KM# 142.4 1/4 ECU
6.4400 g., 0.9170 Silver 0.1899 oz. ASW **Ruler:** Louis XIV **Mint:** Tours

Date	Mintage	VG	F	VF	XF	Unc
1643E	—	32.00	80.00	175	475	—

KM# 142.5 1/4 ECU
6.4400 g., 0.9170 Silver 0.1899 oz. ASW **Ruler:** Louis XIV **Mint:** Angers

Date	Mintage	VG	F	VF	XF	Unc
1643F	—	28.00	65.00	150	400	—
1644F	—	20.00	50.00	120	325	—
1645F	—	28.00	65.00	150	400	—
1646F	—	28.00	65.00	150	400	—

KM# 142.6 1/4 ECU
6.4400 g., 0.9170 Silver 0.1899 oz. ASW **Ruler:** Louis XIV **Mint:** Poitiers

Date	Mintage	VG	F	VF	XF	Unc
1644G	—	35.00	90.00	200	550	—
1645G	—	35.00	90.00	200	550	—
1646G	—	35.00	90.00	200	550	—

KM# 142.7 1/4 ECU
6.4400 g., 0.9170 Silver 0.1899 oz. ASW **Ruler:** Louis XIV **Mint:** La Rochelle

Date	Mintage	VG	F	VF	XF	Unc
1643H	—	—	—	—	—	—
1644H	—	32.00	80.00	175	475	—
1645H	—	35.00	90.00	200	550	—
1646H	—	—	—	—	—	—

KM# 142.8 1/4 ECU
6.4400 g., 0.9170 Silver 0.1899 oz. ASW **Ruler:** Louis XIV **Mint:** Limoges

Date	Mintage	VG	F	VF	XF	Unc
1644I	—	32.00	80.00	175	475	—
1645I	—	32.00	80.00	175	475	—

KM# 142.9 1/4 ECU
6.4400 g., 0.9170 Silver 0.1899 oz. ASW **Ruler:** Louis XIV **Mint:** Bordeaux

Date	Mintage	VG	F	VF	XF	Unc
1643K	—	28.00	65.00	150	400	—
1644K	—	25.00	60.00	135	350	—
1645K	—	25.00	60.00	135	350	—
1646K	—	28.00	65.00	150	400	—
1647K	—	40.00	100	225	600	—

KM# 142.10 1/4 ECU
6.4400 g., 0.9170 Silver 0.1899 oz. ASW **Ruler:** Louis XIV **Mint:** Bayonne

Date	Mintage	VG	F	VF	XF	Unc
1643L	—	32.00	80.00	175	475	—
1644L	—	30.00	75.00	165	450	—
1645L	—	25.00	60.00	135	350	—
1646L	—	20.00	50.00	120	325	—
1647L	—	25.00	60.00	135	350	—
1648L	—	25.00	60.00	135	350	—
1649L	—	25.00	60.00	135	350	—

KM# 142.11 1/4 ECU
6.4400 g., 0.9170 Silver 0.1899 oz. ASW **Ruler:** Louis XIV **Mint:** Toulouse

Date	Mintage	VG	F	VF	XF	Unc
1644M	—	20.00	50.00	120	325	—
1645M	—	20.00	50.00	120	325	—
1646M	—	25.00	60.00	135	350	—
1647M	17,000	—	—	—	—	—

KM# 142.12 1/4 ECU
6.4400 g., 0.9170 Silver 0.1899 oz. ASW **Ruler:** Louis XIV **Mint:** Montpellier

Date	Mintage	VG	F	VF	XF	Unc
1644N	—	25.00	60.00	135	350	—
1645N	—	30.00	75.00	165	450	—
1646N	—	28.00	65.00	150	400	—

KM# 142.13 1/4 ECU
6.4400 g., 0.9170 Silver 0.1899 oz. ASW **Ruler:** Louis XIV **Mint:** Narbonne

Date	Mintage	VG	F	VF	XF	Unc
1645Q	16,000	32.00	80.00	175	475	—
1646Q	—	35.00	90.00	200	550	—

KM# 142.14 1/4 ECU
6.4400 g., 0.9170 Silver 0.1899 oz. ASW **Ruler:** Louis XIV **Mint:** Villeneuve St. André

Date	Mintage	VG	F	VF	XF	Unc
1643R	—	28.00	65.00	150	400	—
1644R	—	35.00	90.00	200	550	—
1645R	—	—	—	—	—	—
1646R	—	—	—	—	—	—

KM# 142.15 1/4 ECU
6.4400 g., 0.9170 Silver 0.1899 oz. ASW **Ruler:** Louis XIV **Mint:** Nantes

Date	Mintage	VG	F	VF	XF	Unc
1644T	—	25.00	60.00	135	350	—
1645T	—	25.00	60.00	135	350	—
1646T	—	20.00	50.00	120	325	—
1647T	—	30.00	75.00	165	450	—

KM# 142.16 1/4 ECU
6.4400 g., 0.9170 Silver 0.1899 oz. ASW **Ruler:** Louis XIV **Mint:** Amiens

Date	Mintage	VG	F	VF	XF	Unc
1644X	—	32.00	80.00	175	475	—
1645X	—	25.00	60.00	135	350	—
1646X	—	—	—	—	—	—

KM# 142.17 1/4 ECU
6.4400 g., 0.9170 Silver 0.1899 oz. ASW **Ruler:** Louis XIV **Mint:** Bourges

Date	Mintage	VG	F	VF	XF	Unc
1643Y	—	32.00	80.00	175	475	—
1644Y	—	—	—	—	—	—

KM# 142.18 1/4 ECU
6.4400 g., 0.9170 Silver 0.1899 oz. ASW **Ruler:** Louis XIV **Mint:** Grenoble

Date	Mintage	VG	F	VF	XF	Unc
1644Z	—	—	—	—	—	—

KM# 142.19 1/4 ECU
6.4400 g., 0.9170 Silver 0.1899 oz. ASW **Ruler:** Louis XIV **Mint:** Rennes **Note:** Mint mark: Numeral 9.

Date	Mintage	VG	F	VF	XF	Unc
1644	—	20.00	50.00	120	325	—
1645	—	20.00	45.00	100	270	—
1646	—	28.00	65.00	150	400	—
1647	—	25.00	60.00	135	350	—

KM# 142.20 1/4 ECU
6.4400 g., 0.9170 Silver 0.1899 oz. ASW **Ruler:** Louis XIV **Mint:** Aix **Note:** Mint mark: Ampersand.

Date	Mintage	VG	F	VF	XF	Unc
1643	—	25.00	60.00	135	350	—
1644	—	20.00	65.00	150	400	—
1645	—	—	—	—	—	—
1646	—	35.00	90.00	200	550	—

KM# 142.21 1/4 ECU
6.4400 g., 0.9170 Silver 0.1899 oz. ASW **Ruler:** Louis XIV **Mint:** Marseille **Note:** Mint mark: AV monogram

Date	Mintage	VG	F	VF	XF	Unc
1644	—	32.00	80.00	175	400	—
1645	—	35.00	90.00	200	450	—
1646	—	—	—	—	—	—

KM# 160.1 1/4 ECU

6.4400 g., 0.9170 Silver 0.1899 oz. ASW **Ruler:** Louis XIV **Rev:** Crowned shield of France, Navarre and Bearn **Mint:** Morlaas

Date	Mintage	VG	F	VF	XF	Unc
1643B	—	30.00	75.00	185	425	—
1644B	—	30.00	75.00	185	425	—
1645B	—	32.00	80.00	200	475	—
1646B	—	35.00	90.00	220	550	—
1647B	—	32.00	80.00	200	475	—
1648B	—	—	—	—	—	—

KM# 160.2 1/4 ECU

6.4400 g., 0.9170 Silver 0.1899 oz. ASW **Ruler:** Louis XIV **Note:** Without mint mark.

Date	Mintage	VG	F	VF	XF	Unc
1649	—	35.00	90.00	250	550	—

KM# 160.3 1/4 ECU

6.4400 g., 0.9170 Silver 0.1899 oz. ASW **Ruler:** Louis XIV **Mint:** Pau **Note:** Mint mark: Crossed palms.

Date	Mintage	VG	F	VF	XF	Unc
1650	—	40.00	100	235	600	—
1652	—	40.00	100	235	600	—

KM# 161.1 1/4 ECU

6.4400 g., 0.9170 Silver 0.1899 oz. ASW **Ruler:** Louis XIV **Obv:** Laureate, draped and mailed youthful bust right, short hair before ear **Rev:** Crowned shield of France **Mint:** Paris

Date	Mintage	VG	F	VF	XF	Unc
1643A Point	—	40.00	100	235	600	—
1643A Rose	—	45.00	110	250	650	—
1644A Point	—	40.00	90.00	220	550	—
1644A Rose	—	30.00	75.00	185	450	—
1644A 2 points and rose	—	50.00	135	300	800	—
1645A Point	—	40.00	90.00	220	550	—
1645A Rose	—	40.00	90.00	220	550	—
1645A 2 points and rose	—	50.00	135	300	800	—

KM# 161.2 1/4 ECU

6.4400 g., 0.9170 Silver 0.1899 oz. ASW **Ruler:** Louis XIV **Mint:** Lyon

Date	Mintage	VG	F	VF	XF	Unc
1644D	—	65.00	165	345	900	—
1645D	—	65.00	165	345	900	—
1648D	—	90.00	200	420	1,100	—
1649D	—	90.00	200	420	1,100	—
1650D	—	—	—	—	—	—
1651D	—	—	—	—	—	—

KM# 143 1/4 ECU

6.4400 g., 0.9170 Silver 0.1899 oz. ASW **Ruler:** Louis XIV **Obv:** Crowned shield of France **Rev:** Outlined cross, fleur-de-lis at ends **Mint:** Arras

Date	Mintage	VG	F	VF	XF	Unc
1643AR	—	30.00	75.00	165	450	—
1644AR	—	32.00	80.00	175	475	—
1645AR	—	32.00	80.00	175	475	—
1646AR	—	35.00	90.00	200	550	—

KM# 162.1 1/4 ECU

6.4400 g., 0.9170 Silver 0.1899 oz. ASW **Ruler:** Louis XIV **Obv:** Long hair curl before ear **Mint:** Paris

Date	Mintage	VG	F	VF	XF	Unc
1646A	—	60.00	150	325	875	—
1647A	—	35.00	90.00	200	550	—
1648A	—	45.00	110	245	650	—
1649A	—	50.00	120	275	750	—
1650A	—	35.00	90.00	200	550	—
1651A	—	50.00	120	275	750	—
1652A	—	32.00	80.00	180	500	—
1653A	—	35.00	90.00	200	550	—
1654A	—	50.00	120	275	750	—
1655A	—	50.00	120	275	750	—
1657A	—	—	—	—	—	—

KM# 162.2 1/4 ECU

6.4400 g., 0.9170 Silver 0.1899 oz. ASW **Ruler:** Louis XIV **Mint:** Arras

Date	Mintage	VG	F	VF	XF	Unc
1647AR	—	75.00	175	350	925	—
1652AR	—	50.00	120	275	750	—
1655AR	—	50.00	135	300	800	—

KM# 162.3 1/4 ECU

6.4400 g., 0.9170 Silver 0.1899 oz. ASW **Ruler:** Louis XIV **Mint:** Rouen

Date	Mintage	VG	F	VF	XF	Unc
1649B	—	50.00	120	275	750	—
1650B	—	50.00	135	300	800	—
1652B	—	50.00	135	300	750	—
1653B	—	50.00	135	300	750	—
1654B	—	60.00	150	325	875	—
1655B	—	—	—	—	—	—

KM# 162.4 1/4 ECU

6.4400 g., 0.9170 Silver 0.1899 oz. ASW **Ruler:** Louis XIV **Mint:** Saint Lô

Date	Mintage	VG	F	VF	XF	Unc
1649C	—	—	—	—	—	—
1650C	—	50.00	135	300	800	—
1651C	—	75.00	175	350	925	—
1652C	—	50.00	120	275	750	—
1653C	—	—	—	—	—	—
1655C	—	—	—	—	—	—

KM# 162.5 1/4 ECU

6.4400 g., 0.9170 Silver 0.1899 oz. ASW **Ruler:** Louis XIV **Mint:** Lyon

Date	Mintage	VG	F	VF	XF	Unc
1652D	—	50.00	120	275	750	—
1653D	—	50.00	120	275	750	—
1654D	—	—	—	—	—	—
1657D	—	—	—	—	—	—
1658D	—	—	—	—	—	—

KM# 162.6 1/4 ECU

6.4400 g., 0.9170 Silver 0.1899 oz. ASW **Ruler:** Louis XIV **Mint:** Tours

Date	Mintage	VG	F	VF	XF	Unc
1652E	—	—	—	—	—	—
1653E	—	—	—	—	—	—
1654E	—	—	—	—	—	—
1655E	—	—	—	—	—	—

KM# 162.7 1/4 ECU

6.4400 g., 0.9170 Silver 0.1899 oz. ASW **Ruler:** Louis XIV **Mint:** Angers

Date	Mintage	VG	F	VF	XF	Unc
1646F	—	75.00	175	350	925	—
1647F	—	—	—	—	—	—
1648F	—	50.00	120	275	750	—
1649F	—	—	—	—	—	—
1650F	—	50.00	120	275	750	—
1651F	—	—	—	—	—	—
1652F	—	—	—	—	—	—
1653F	—	75.00	175	350	925	—
1654F	—	—	—	—	—	—
1656F	—	—	—	—	—	—

KM# 162.8 1/4 ECU

6.4400 g., 0.9170 Silver 0.1899 oz. ASW **Ruler:** Louis XIV **Mint:** Poitiers

Date	Mintage	VG	F	VF	XF	Unc
1648G	—	—	—	—	—	—
1649G	—	—	—	—	—	—
1650G	—	—	—	—	—	—
1652G	—	—	—	—	—	—
1653G	—	—	—	—	—	—

KM# 162.9 1/4 ECU

6.4400 g., 0.9170 Silver 0.1899 oz. ASW **Ruler:** Louis XIV **Mint:** La Rochelle

Date	Mintage	VG	F	VF	XF	Unc
1646H	—	—	—	—	—	—
1648H	—	—	—	—	—	—
1649H	—	—	—	—	—	—
1650H	—	90.00	200	400	1,100	—
1651H	—	—	—	—	—	—
1652H	—	—	—	—	—	—
1653H	—	—	—	—	—	—
1654H	—	—	—	—	—	—
1655H	—	—	—	—	—	—
1656H	—	—	—	—	—	—

KM# 162.10 1/4 ECU

6.4400 g., 0.9170 Silver 0.1899 oz. ASW **Ruler:** Louis XIV **Mint:** Limoges

Date	Mintage	VG	F	VF	XF	Unc
1649I	—	—	—	—	—	—
1650I	—	—	—	—	—	—
1651I	—	—	—	—	—	—
1652I	—	—	—	—	—	—
1653I	—	—	—	—	—	—
1654I	—	—	—	—	—	—

KM# 162.11 1/4 ECU

6.4400 g., 0.9170 Silver 0.1899 oz. ASW **Ruler:** Louis XIV **Mint:** Bordeaux

Date	Mintage	VG	F	VF	XF	Unc
1647K	—	40.00	100	225	600	—
1648K	—	50.00	120	275	750	—
1649K	—	50.00	120	275	750	—
1650K	—	50.00	120	275	750	—
1651K	—	—	—	—	—	—
1652K	—	—	—	—	—	—
1653K	—	—	—	—	—	—
1654K	—	—	—	—	—	—
1655K	—	—	—	—	—	—
1656K	—	—	—	—	—	—
1657K	—	—	—	—	—	—
1660K	—	90.00	200	400	1,100	—

KM# 162.12 1/4 ECU

6.4400 g., 0.9170 Silver 0.1899 oz. ASW **Ruler:** Louis XIV **Mint:** Bayonne

Date	Mintage	VG	F	VF	XF	Unc
1650L	—	50.00	135	300	800	—
1651L	—	50.00	120	275	750	—
1652L	—	—	—	—	—	—
1653L	—	50.00	120	275	750	—
1654L	—	—	—	—	—	—
1655L	—	40.00	100	225	600	—
1656L	—	—	—	—	—	—
1657L	—	—	—	—	—	—
1658L	—	—	—	—	—	—
1659L	—	—	—	—	—	—
1660L	—	—	—	—	—	—
1661L	—	—	—	—	—	—

KM# 162.13 1/4 ECU

6.4400 g., 0.9170 Silver 0.1899 oz. ASW **Ruler:** Louis XIV **Mint:** Toulouse

Date	Mintage	VG	F	VF	XF	Unc
1648M	—	90.00	200	400	1,100	—
1649M	—	50.00	120	275	750	—
1650M	—	—	—	—	—	—
1651M	—	—	—	—	—	—
1653M	—	—	—	—	—	—
1654M	—	—	—	—	—	—
1655M	—	—	—	—	—	—
1656M	—	—	—	—	—	—
1659M	—	—	—	—	—	—

KM# 162.14 1/4 ECU

6.4400 g., 0.9170 Silver 0.1899 oz. ASW **Ruler:** Louis XIV **Mint:** Montpellier

Date	Mintage	VG	F	VF	XF	Unc
1646N	—	50.00	135	300	800	—
1647N	—	50.00	120	275	750	—
1648N	—	—	—	—	—	—
1649N	—	—	—	—	—	—
1650N	—	—	—	—	—	—
1651N	—	—	—	—	—	—
1652N	—	—	—	—	—	—
1653N	—	—	—	—	—	—
1659N	—	—	—	—	—	—
1660N	—	—	—	—	—	—

KM# 162.15 1/4 ECU

6.4400 g., 0.9170 Silver 0.1899 oz. ASW **Ruler:** Louis XIV **Mint:** Riom

Date	Mintage	VG	F	VF	XF	Unc
16520	—	—	—	—	—	—
16530	—	—	—	—	—	—

KM# 162.16 1/4 ECU

6.4400 g., 0.9170 Silver 0.1899 oz. ASW **Ruler:** Louis XIV **Mint:** Dijon

Date	Mintage	VG	F	VF	XF	Unc
1652P	—	—	—	—	—	—
1653P	—	50.00	135	300	800	—

KM# 162.17 1/4 ECU
6.4400 g., 0.9170 Silver 0.1899 oz. ASW **Ruler:** Louis XIV **Mint:** Narbonne

Date	Mintage	VG	F	VF	XF	Unc
1650Q	—	—	—	—	—	—
1651Q	—	—	—	—	—	—
1652Q	—	—	—	—	—	—
1653Q	—	75.00	175	350	925	—

KM# 162.18 1/4 ECU
6.4400 g., 0.9170 Silver 0.1899 oz. ASW **Ruler:** Louis XIV **Mint:** Troyes

Date	Mintage	VG	F	VF	XF	Unc
1650S	—	—	—	—	—	—
1651S	—	75.00	175	350	925	—
1652S	—	—	—	—	—	—
1653S	—	—	—	—	—	—
1654S	—	75.00	175	350	925	—
1655S	—	50.00	135	300	800	—
1656S	—	—	—	—	—	—

KM# 162.19 1/4 ECU
6.4400 g., 0.9170 Silver 0.1899 oz. ASW **Ruler:** Louis XIV **Mint:** Nantes

Date	Mintage	VG	F	VF	XF	Unc
1647T	—	—	—	—	—	—
1648T	—	—	—	—	—	—
1649T	—	50.00	135	300	800	—
1650T	—	75.00	175	350	925	—
1653T	—	45.00	110	245	650	—
1654T	—	—	—	—	—	—
1655T	—	—	—	—	—	—
1656T	—	—	—	—	—	—
1659T	—	—	—	—	—	—
1660T	—	—	—	—	—	—

KM# 162.20 1/4 ECU
6.4400 g., 0.9170 Silver 0.1899 oz. ASW **Ruler:** Louis XIV **Mint:** Amiens

Date	Mintage	VG	F	VF	XF	Unc
1652X	—	—	—	—	—	—
1653X	—	—	—	—	—	—
1655X	—	50.00	120	275	750	—

KM# 162.21 1/4 ECU
6.4400 g., 0.9170 Silver 0.1899 oz. ASW **Ruler:** Louis XIV **Mint:** Bourges

Date	Mintage	VG	F	VF	XF	Unc
1648Y	—	50.00	135	300	800	—
1649Y	—	—	—	—	—	—
1650Y	—	—	—	—	—	—
1653Y	—	75.00	175	350	925	—
1654Y	—	—	—	—	—	—
1655Y	—	—	—	—	—	—

KM# 162.22 1/4 ECU
6.4400 g., 0.9170 Silver 0.1899 oz. ASW **Ruler:** Louis XIV **Mint:** Aix **Note:** Mint mark: Ampersand.

Date	Mintage	VG	F	VF	XF	Unc
1646	—	50.00	120	275	750	—
1647	—	—	—	—	—	—
1648	—	—	—	—	—	—
1649	—	50.00	120	275	750	—
1651	—	—	—	—	—	—
1652	—	—	—	—	—	—
1653	—	50.00	120	275	750	—
1654	—	—	—	—	—	—
1656	—	—	—	—	—	—
1657	—	—	—	—	—	—
1658	—	—	—	—	—	—
1659	—	—	—	—	—	—
1660	—	—	—	—	—	—
1661	—	—	—	—	—	—
1662	—	—	—	—	—	—

KM# 162.23 1/4 ECU
6.4400 g., 0.9170 Silver 0.1899 oz. ASW **Ruler:** Louis XIV **Mint:** Rennes **Note:** Mint mark: Numeral 9.

Date	Mintage	VG	F	VF	XF	Unc
1648	—	—	—	—	—	—
1649	—	50.00	120	275	750	—
1650	—	50.00	120	275	750	—
1651	—	40.00	100	225	600	—
1652	—	—	—	—	—	—
1653	—	40.00	100	225	600	—
1654	—	35.00	90.00	200	550	—
1655	—	40.00	100	225	600	—
1656	—	30.00	75.00	165	450	—
1657	—	—	—	—	—	—
1659	—	—	—	—	—	—

KM# 159 1/4 ECU
6.4400 g., 0.9170 Silver 0.1899 oz. ASW **Ruler:** Louis XIV **Rev:** Crowned shield of Navarre and France **Mint:** Saint Palais

Date	Mintage	VG	F	VF	XF	Unc
1647	—	32.00	80.00	175	475	—
1648	—	32.00	80.00	175	475	—
1649	—	32.00	80.00	175	475	—
1650	—	32.00	80.00	175	475	—
1651	—	32.00	80.00	175	475	—

KM# 187.1 1/4 ECU
6.4400 g., 0.9170 Silver 0.1899 oz. ASW **Ruler:** Louis XIV **Rev:** Crowned shield of France, Navarre and Bearn **Mint:** Pau **Note:** Mint mark: Crossed palms.

Date	Mintage	VG	F	VF	XF	Unc
1651	—	300	750	1,500	3,200	—

KM# 187.2 1/4 ECU
6.4400 g., 0.9170 Silver 0.1899 oz. ASW **Ruler:** Louis XIV **Mint:** Pau **Note:** Mint mark: *F*.

Date	Mintage	VG	F	VF	XF	Unc
1655	—	300	750	1,500	3,200	—
1657	—	300	750	1,500	3,200	—
1658	—	300	750	1,500	3,200	—

KM# 187.3 1/4 ECU
6.4400 g., 0.9170 Silver 0.1899 oz. ASW **Ruler:** Louis XIV **Mint:** Morlaas **Note:** Mint mark: *G*.

Date	Mintage	VG	F	VF	XF	Unc
1653	—	300	750	1,500	3,200	—

KM# 188 1/4 ECU
6.4400 g., 0.9170 Silver 0.1899 oz. ASW **Ruler:** Louis XIV **Rev:** Crowned shield of Dauphine **Mint:** Grenoble

Date	Mintage	VG	F	VF	XF	Unc
1653Z	—	—	—	—	—	—

KM# 186.1 1/4 ECU
6.4400 g., 0.9170 Silver 0.1899 oz. ASW **Ruler:** Louis XIV **Obv:** Laureate, draped and mailed bust right **Rev:** Crowned shield of France and Navarre **Mint:** Troyes

Date	Mintage	VG	F	VF	XF	Unc
1654 V*	—	250	650	1,500	3,200	—
1655 V*	—	250	650	1,500	3,200	—
1656 V*	—	250	650	1,500	3,200	—
1662 V*	—	250	650	1,500	3,200	—

KM# 186.2 1/4 ECU
6.4400 g., 0.9170 Silver 0.1899 oz. ASW **Ruler:** Louis XIV **Mint:** Besançon **Note:** Mint mark: Back-to-back C's.

Date	Mintage	VG	F	VF	XF	Unc
1662	—	300	750	1,500	3,200	—

KM# 213.1 1/4 ECU
6.4400 g., 0.9170 Silver 0.1899 oz. ASW **Ruler:** Louis XIV **Obv:** Laurreate, draped older bust right **Rev:** Crowned shield of France **Mint:** Paris

Date	Mintage	VG	F	VF	XF	Unc
1664A	—	100	250	550	1,150	—
1666A	—	80.00	200	450	950	—
1667A	—	120	300	650	1,350	—
1668A	—	120	300	650	1,350	—
1674A	—	150	350	800	1,750	—

KM# 213.2 1/4 ECU
6.4400 g., 0.9170 Silver 0.1899 oz. ASW **Ruler:** Louis XIV **Mint:** Lyon

Date	Mintage	VG	F	VF	XF	Unc
1667D	—	—	—	—	—	—
1668D	—	—	—	—	—	—
1669D	—	—	—	—	—	—
1670D	—	—	—	—	—	—
1671D	—	—	—	—	—	—

KM# 213.3 1/4 ECU
6.4400 g., 0.9170 Silver 0.1899 oz. ASW **Ruler:** Louis XIV **Mint:** Bayonne

Date	Mintage	VG	F	VF	XF	Unc
1663L	—	120	300	650	1,350	—
1664L	—	—	—	—	—	—
1666L	—	—	—	—	—	—
1668L	—	—	—	—	—	—
1669L	—	—	—	—	—	—
1670L	—	—	—	—	—	—
1672L	—	—	—	—	—	—

KM# 213.4 1/4 ECU
6.4400 g., 0.9170 Silver 0.1899 oz. ASW **Ruler:** Louis XIV **Mint:** Toulouse

Date	Mintage	VG	F	VF	XF	Unc
1672M	—	—	—	—	—	—

KM# 213.5 1/4 ECU
6.4400 g., 0.9170 Silver 0.1899 oz. ASW **Ruler:** Louis XIV **Mint:** Montpellier

Date	Mintage	VG	F	VF	XF	Unc
1666N	—	—	—	—	—	—
1667N	—	100	250	550	1,150	—
1668N	—	150	350	850	1,750	—

KM# 213.6 1/4 ECU
6.4400 g., 0.9170 Silver 0.1899 oz. ASW **Ruler:** Louis XIV **Mint:** Aix **Note:** Mint mark: Ampersand.

Date	Mintage	VG	F	VF	XF	Unc
1665	—	135	325	750	1,600	—
1666	—	100	250	550	1,150	—
1667	—	135	325	750	1,600	—
1669	—	—	—	—	—	—
1670	—	135	325	750	1,600	—
1671	—	120	300	650	1,350	—
1672	—	—	—	—	—	—

KM# 213.7 1/4 ECU
6.4400 g., 0.9170 Silver 0.1899 oz. ASW **Ruler:** Louis XIV **Mint:** Rennes **Note:** Mint mark: Numeral 9.

Date	Mintage	VG	F	VF	XF	Unc
1661	—	120	300	650	1,350	—
1667	—	100	250	550	1,150	—
1668	—	100	250	550	1,150	—
1669	—	—	—	—	—	—
1670	—	120	300	650	1,350	—
1671	—	—	—	—	—	—
1672	—	—	—	—	—	—
1673	—	120	300	650	1,350	—

KM# 233 1/4 ECU
6.4400 g., 0.9170 Silver 0.1899 oz. ASW **Ruler:** Louis XIV **Rev:** Crowned shield of France, Navarre and Bearn **Mint:** Pau

Date	Mintage	VG	F	VF	XF	Unc
1674	—	500	1,250	2,850	5,500	—
1675	—	500	1,250	2,850	5,500	—

KM# 234.1 1/4 ECU
6.4400 g., 0.9170 Silver 0.1899 oz. ASW **Ruler:** Louis XIV **Obv:** Older bust in court dress right **Rev:** Crowned shield of France **Mint:** Paris

Date	Mintage	VG	F	VF	XF	Unc
1676A	—	650	1,400	3,000	—	—
1679A	—	650	1,400	3,000	—	—
1680A	—	700	1,500	3,300	—	—
1681A	—	—	—	—	—	—
1682A	—	650	1,400	3,000	6,250	—
1683A	—	—	—	—	—	—

KM# 234.2 1/4 ECU
6.4400 g., 0.9170 Silver 0.1899 oz. ASW **Ruler:** Louis XIV **Mint:** Bayonne

Date	Mintage	VG	F	VF	XF	Unc
1677L Juvenile	—	400	800	1,200	—	—
1678L	—	—	—	—	—	—
1681L	—	—	—	—	—	—
1682L Cravate	—	800	1,600	3,200	—	—

KM# 234.3 1/4 ECU
6.4400 g., 0.9170 Silver 0.1899 oz. ASW **Ruler:** Louis XIV **Mint:** Montpellier

Date	Mintage	VG	F	VF	XF	Unc
1679N	—	500	1,150	2,350	5,200	—

KM# 234.4 1/4 ECU
6.4400 g., 0.9170 Silver 0.1899 oz. ASW **Ruler:** Louis XIV **Mint:** Aix **Note:** Mint mark: Ampersand.

Date	Mintage	VG	F	VF	XF	Unc
1679	—	350	850	1,800	4,200	—
1680	—	450	1,100	2,350	5,200	—
1681	—	500	1,200	2,650	5,500	—
1683	—	—	—	—	—	—

KM# 234.5 1/4 ECU
6.4400 g., 0.9170 Silver 0.1899 oz. ASW **Ruler:** Louis XIV **Mint:** Rennes **Note:** Mint mark: Numeral 9.

Date	Mintage	VG	F	VF	XF	Unc
1677	—	—	—	—	—	—
1678	—	—	—	—	—	—
1679	—	700	1,600	3,500	—	—
1680	—	—	—	—	—	—
1682	—	—	—	—	—	—
1683	—	—	—	—	—	—

KM# 254 1/4 ECU
6.4400 g., 0.9170 Silver 0.1899 oz. ASW **Ruler:** Louis XIV **Obv:** Modified bust

Date	Mintage	VG	F	VF	XF	Unc
1684 Rare, jabot	—	7,000	12,000	20,000	—	—

KM# 260.1 1/4 ECU
6.4400 g., 0.9170 Silver 0.1899 oz. ASW **Ruler:** Louis XIV **Obv:** Draped bust right **Rev:** Crowned, quartered shield of France, Old and New Burgundy **Mint:** Lille

Date	Mintage	VG	F	VF	XF	Unc
1686IL	373,000	150	350	700	1,550	—

KM# 260.2 1/4 ECU
6.4400 g., 0.9170 Silver 0.1899 oz. ASW **Ruler:** Louis XIV **Mint:** Lille **Note:** Mint mark: Crowned L.

Date	Mintage	VG	F	VF	XF	Unc
1686	—	165	375	750	1,650	—
1687	751,000	180	400	850	1,800	—
1688	139,000	165	375	750	1,650	—

KM# 270.1 1/4 ECU
6.4400 g., 0.9170 Silver 0.1899 oz. ASW **Ruler:** Louis XIV **Obv:** Draped bust right **Rev:** Eight crowned L's back to back **Mint:** Paris

Date	Mintage	VG	F	VF	XF	Unc
1690A	—	50.00	120	275	620	—
1691A	—	45.00	110	250	575	—

KM# 270.2 1/4 ECU
6.4400 g., 0.9170 Silver 0.1899 oz. ASW **Ruler:** Louis XIV **Mint:** Rouen

Date	Mintage	VG	F	VF	XF	Unc
1690B	—	50.00	135	300	675	—
1691B	—	50.00	120	275	625	—

KM# 270.3 1/4 ECU
6.4400 g., 0.9170 Silver 0.1899 oz. ASW **Ruler:** Louis XIV **Mint:** Lyon

Date	Mintage	VG	F	VF	XF	Unc
1690D	170,000	50.00	135	300	675	—
1691D	730,000	45.00	110	250	565	—
1692D	159,000	60.00	150	325	725	—
1693D	23,000	60.00	150	325	725	—

KM# 270.9 1/4 ECU
6.4400 g., 0.9170 Silver 0.1899 oz. ASW **Ruler:** Louis XIV **Mint:** Montpellier

Date	Mintage	VG	F	VF	XF	Unc
1690N	90,000	60.00	150	325	725	—
1691N	224,000	50.00	120	275	625	—
1692N	33,000	75.00	175	350	775	—
1693N	6,315	—	—	—	—	—

KM# 270.10 1/4 ECU
6.4400 g., 0.9170 Silver 0.1899 oz. ASW **Ruler:** Louis XIV **Mint:** Riom

Date	Mintage	VG	F	VF	XF	Unc
1691O	16,000	—	—	—	—	—
1693O	—	—	—	—	—	—

KM# 270.11 1/4 ECU
6.4400 g., 0.9170 Silver 0.1899 oz. ASW **Ruler:** Louis XIV **Mint:** Dijon

Date	Mintage	VG	F	VF	XF	Unc
1690P	7,172	50.00	135	300	675	—
1691P	—	50.00	135	300	675	—
1693P	—	—	—	—	—	—

KM# 270.12 1/4 ECU
6.4400 g., 0.9170 Silver 0.1899 oz. ASW **Ruler:** Louis XIV **Mint:** Reims

Date	Mintage	VG	F	VF	XF	Unc
1691S	—	50.00	135	300	675	—
1692S	—	—	—	—	—	—

KM# 270.13 1/4 ECU
6.4400 g., 0.9170 Silver 0.1899 oz. ASW **Ruler:** Louis XIV **Mint:** Amiens

Date	Mintage	VG	F	VF	XF	Unc
1690X	—	75.00	175	350	725	—
1692X	14,000	75.00	175	350	725	—

KM# 270.14 1/4 ECU
6.4400 g., 0.9170 Silver 0.1899 oz. ASW **Ruler:** Louis XIV **Mint:** Bourges

Date	Mintage	VG	F	VF	XF	Unc
1691Y	37,000	50.00	120	275	625	—
1692Y	—	75.00	175	350	775	—
1693Y	8,228	—	—	—	—	—

KM# 270.17 1/4 ECU
6.4400 g., 0.9170 Silver 0.1899 oz. ASW **Ruler:** Louis XIV **Mint:** Lille **Note:** Mint mark: Crowned L.

Date	Mintage	VG	F	VF	XF	Unc
1690	—	50.00	135	300	675	—

KM# 271 1/4 ECU
6.4400 g., 0.9170 Silver 0.1899 oz. ASW **Ruler:** Louis XIV **Obv:** Draped bust right **Rev:** Eight crowned L's back to back, fleur-de-lis in angles **Mint:** Pau

Date	Mintage	VG	F	VF	XF	Unc
1690	—	100	250	800	2,500	—
1691	—	100	250	800	2,500	—

KM# 272 1/4 ECU
6.4400 g., 0.9170 Silver 0.1899 oz. ASW **Ruler:** Louis XIV **Obv:** Laureate draped bust right **Mint:** Reims

Date	Mintage	VG	F	VF	XF	Unc
1690S	—	—	—	—	—	—

KM# 270.4 1/4 ECU
6.4400 g., 0.9170 Silver 0.1899 oz. ASW **Ruler:** Louis XIV **Mint:** Tours

Date	Mintage	VG	F	VF	XF	Unc
1691E	—	50.00	120	275	625	—

KM# 270.5 1/4 ECU
6.4400 g., 0.9170 Silver 0.1899 oz. ASW **Ruler:** Louis XIV **Mint:** Poitiers

Date	Mintage	VG	F	VF	XF	Unc
1691G	265	175	350	700	2,000	—

KM# 270.6 1/4 ECU
6.4400 g., 0.9170 Silver 0.1899 oz. ASW **Ruler:** Louis XIV **Mint:** La Rochelle

Date	Mintage	VG	F	VF	XF	Unc
1691H	—	50.00	135	300	675	—
1693H	—	50.00	135	300	675	—

KM# 270.7 1/4 ECU
6.4400 g., 0.9170 Silver 0.1899 oz. ASW **Ruler:** Louis XIV **Mint:** Limoges

Date	Mintage	VG	F	VF	XF	Unc
1691I	—	50.00	135	300	675	—
1692I	—	50.00	120	275	625	—

KM# 270.8 1/4 ECU
6.4400 g., 0.9170 Silver 0.1899 oz. ASW **Ruler:** Louis XIV **Mint:** Toulouse

Date	Mintage	VG	F	VF	XF	Unc
1691M	382,000	45.00	110	250	565	—

KM# 270.18 1/4 ECU
6.4400 g., 0.9170 Silver 0.1899 oz. ASW **Ruler:** Louis XIV **Mint:** Troyes **Note:** Mint mark: Crowned S.

Date	Mintage	VG	F	VF	XF	Unc
1691	—	50.00	120	275	625	—
1693	—	—	—	—	—	—

KM# 270.15 1/4 ECU
6.4400 g., 0.9170 Silver 0.1899 oz. ASW **Ruler:** Louis XIV **Mint:** Rennes **Note:** Mint mark: Numeral 9.

Date	Mintage	VG	F	VF	XF	Unc
1691	—	50.00	135	300	675	—
1692	—	80.00	185	375	800	—

KM# 270.16 1/4 ECU
6.4400 g., 0.9170 Silver 0.1899 oz. ASW **Ruler:** Louis XIV **Mint:** Aix **Note:** Mint mark: Ampersand.

Date	Mintage	VG	F	VF	XF	Unc
1691	—	50.00	120	275	625	—

KM# 294 1/4 ECU
6.4400 g., 0.9170 Silver 0.1899 oz. ASW **Ruler:** Louis XIV **Obv:** Mailed bust right **Rev:** Crowned circular shield of France, Navarre and Bearn **Mint:** Pau

Date	Mintage	VG	F	VF	XF	Unc
1693	—	—	—	—	—	—
1694	—	750	1,500	2,750	5,000	—
1695	—	750	1,500	2,750	5,000	—
1696	1,063	—	—	—	—	—
1697	258	—	—	—	—	—
1698	476	—	—	—	—	—
1699	360	—	—	—	—	—
1700	28	—	—	—	—	—

KM# 293.1 1/4 ECU
6.4400 g., 0.9170 Silver 0.1899 oz. ASW **Ruler:** Louis XIV **Obv:** Mailed bust right **Rev:** Crowned circular shield of France dividing palms **Mint:** Paris

Date	Mintage	VG	F	VF	XF	Unc
1693A	—	50.00	120	275	625	—
1694A	—	45.00	110	250	565	—
1697A	—	60.00	150	325	725	—
1698A	—	90.00	200	400	900	—

KM# 293.2 1/4 ECU
6.4400 g., 0.9170 Silver 0.1899 oz. ASW **Ruler:** Louis XIV **Mint:** Metz

Date	Mintage	VG	F	VF	XF	Unc
1693AA	—	90.00	200	400	900	—

KM# 293.3 1/4 ECU
6.4400 g., 0.9170 Silver 0.1899 oz. ASW **Ruler:** Louis XIV **Mint:** Rouen

Date	Mintage	VG	F	VF	XF	Unc
1693B	—	60.00	150	325	725	—
1694B	—	60.00	150	325	725	—
1696B	—	50.00	135	300	675	—

KM# 293.4 1/4 ECU
6.4400 g., 0.9170 Silver 0.1899 oz. ASW **Ruler:** Louis XIV **Mint:** Strasbourg

Date	Mintage	VG	F	VF	XF	Unc
1694BB	—	75.00	175	350	775	—

KM# 293.5 1/4 ECU
6.4400 g., 0.9170 Silver 0.1899 oz. ASW **Ruler:** Louis XIV **Mint:** Caen

Date	Mintage	VG	F	VF	XF	Unc
1697C	—	75.00	175	350	900	—

KM# 293.6 1/4 ECU
6.4400 g., 0.9170 Silver 0.1899 oz. ASW **Ruler:** Louis XIV **Mint:** Lyon

Date	Mintage	VG	F	VF	XF	Unc
1693D	57,000	50.00	135	300	675	—
1694D	440,000	50.00	120	275	625	—
1695D	176,000	50.00	135	300	675	—
1696D	89,000	60.00	150	325	725	—
1697D	18,000	—	—	—	—	—
1698D	6,251	75.00	175	350	775	—
1699D	6,272	—	—	—	—	—
1700D	2,020	—	—	—	—	—

KM# 293.7 1/4 ECU
6.4400 g., 0.9170 Silver 0.1899 oz. ASW **Ruler:** Louis XIV **Mint:** Tours

Date	Mintage	VG	F	VF	XF	Unc
1693E	—	50.00	120	275	625	—
1695E	—	75.00	175	350	775	—

KM# 293.9 1/4 ECU
6.4400 g., 0.9170 Silver 0.1899 oz. ASW **Ruler:** Louis XIV **Mint:** Poitiers

Date	Mintage	VG	F	VF	XF	Unc
1696G	11,000	—	—	—	—	—

KM# 293.10 1/4 ECU
6.4400 g., 0.9170 Silver 0.1899 oz. ASW **Ruler:** Louis XIV **Mint:** La Rochelle

Date	Mintage	VG	F	VF	XF	Unc
1693H	—	60.00	150	325	725	—
1694H	—	60.00	150	325	725	—

KM# 293.11 1/4 ECU
6.4400 g., 0.9170 Silver 0.1899 oz. ASW **Ruler:** Louis XIV **Mint:** Limoges

Date	Mintage	VG	F	VF	XF	Unc
1694I	—	50.00	135	325	700	—
1695I	—	50.00	135	300	675	—
1696I	—	70.00	170	330	750	—
1697I	—	75.00	175	350	775	—

KM# 293.12 1/4 ECU
6.4400 g., 0.9170 Silver 0.1899 oz. ASW **Ruler:** Louis XIV **Mint:** Bordeaux

Date	Mintage	VG	F	VF	XF	Unc
1694K	—	50.00	135	300	675	—
1696K	—	75.00	175	350	775	—

KM# 293.13 1/4 ECU
6.4400 g., 0.9170 Silver 0.1899 oz. ASW **Ruler:** Louis XIV **Mint:** Toulouse

Date	Mintage	VG	F	VF	XF	Unc
1693M	—	75.00	175	350	775	—
1694M	—	60.00	150	325	725	—

KM# 293.14 1/4 ECU
6.4400 g., 0.9170 Silver 0.1899 oz. ASW **Ruler:** Louis XIV **Mint:** Montpellier

Date	Mintage	VG	F	VF	XF	Unc
1693N	40,000	60.00	150	325	725	—
1694N	261,000	50.00	120	275	625	—
1695N	37,000	—	—	—	—	—
1696N	11,000	—	—	—	—	—
1697N	8,200	—	—	—	—	—
1698N	1,265	—	—	—	—	—
1699N	992	—	—	—	—	—
1700N	186	—	—	—	—	—

KM# 293.15 1/4 ECU
6.4400 g., 0.9170 Silver 0.1899 oz. ASW **Ruler:** Louis XIV **Mint:** Riom

Date	Mintage	VG	F	VF	XF	Unc
1693O	4,487	—	—	—	—	—
1694O	—	90.00	200	400	900	—
1697O	—	50.00	135	300	675	—

KM# 293.16 1/4 ECU
6.4400 g., 0.9170 Silver 0.1899 oz. ASW **Ruler:** Louis XIV **Mint:** Dijon

Date	Mintage	VG	F	VF	XF	Unc
1693P	28,000	—	—	—	—	—
1694P	247,000	50.00	120	275	625	—
1695P	24,000	—	—	—	—	—
1697P	4,373	—	—	—	—	—

KM# 293.17 1/4 ECU
6.4400 g., 0.9170 Silver 0.1899 oz. ASW **Ruler:** Louis XIV **Mint:** Reims

Date	Mintage	VG	F	VF	XF	Unc
1693S	—	75.00	175	350	775	—
1697S	—	—	—	—	—	—

KM# 293.18 1/4 ECU
6.4400 g., 0.9170 Silver 0.1899 oz. ASW **Ruler:** Louis XIV **Mint:** Nantes

Date	Mintage	VG	F	VF	XF	Unc
1694T	—	75.00	175	350	775	—
1697T	—	75.00	175	350	775	—

KM# 293.19 1/4 ECU
6.4400 g., 0.9170 Silver 0.1899 oz. ASW **Ruler:** Louis XIV **Mint:** Troyes

Date	Mintage	VG	F	VF	XF	Unc
1693V	—	—	—	—	—	—
1694V	150,000	50.00	135	300	675	—
1695V	—	—	—	—	—	—
1696V	—	75.00	175	350	775	—
1697V	—	—	—	—	—	—
1698V	—	—	—	—	—	—
1699V	—	—	—	—	—	—

KM# 293.20 1/4 ECU
6.4400 g., 0.9170 Silver 0.1899 oz. ASW **Ruler:** Louis XIV **Mint:** Lille

Date	Mintage	VG	F	VF	XF	Unc
1693W	—	60.00	150	325	725	—
1694W	—	50.00	135	300	675	—
1695W	—	75.00	175	350	775	—
1697W	6,000	—	—	—	—	—
1699W	5,400	—	—	—	—	—

KM# 293.21 1/4 ECU
6.4400 g., 0.9170 Silver 0.1899 oz. ASW **Ruler:** Louis XIV **Mint:** Amiens

Date	Mintage	VG	F	VF	XF	Unc
1693X	—	60.00	150	325	725	—
1694X	—	60.00	150	325	725	—
1695X	—	60.00	150	325	725	—

KM# 293.22 1/4 ECU
6.4400 g., 0.9170 Silver 0.1899 oz. ASW **Ruler:** Louis XIV **Mint:** Bourges

Date	Mintage	VG	F	VF	XF	Unc
1693Y	50,000	75.00	175	350	775	—
1694Y	—	60.00	150	325	725	—

KM# 293.23 1/4 ECU
6.4400 g., 0.9170 Silver 0.1899 oz. ASW **Ruler:** Louis XIV **Mint:** Aix **Note:** Mint mark: Ampersand.

Date	Mintage	VG	F	VF	XF	Unc
1693	—	75.00	175	350	775	—
1694	—	50.00	135	300	675	—
1695	—	75.00	175	350	775	—

KM# 293.24 1/4 ECU
6.4400 g., 0.9170 Silver 0.1899 oz. ASW **Ruler:** Louis XIV **Mint:** Rennes **Note:** Mint mark: Numeral 9.

Date	Mintage	VG	F	VF	XF	Unc
1693	—	—	—	—	—	—
1694	—	60.00	150	325	725	—
1695	—	50.00	135	300	675	—
1696	—	75.00	175	350	775	—

KM# 293.25 1/4 ECU
6.4400 g., 0.9170 Silver 0.1899 oz. ASW **Ruler:** Louis XIV **Mint:** Besançon **Note:** Mint mark: Two back-to-back C's monogram.

Date	Mintage	VG	F	VF	XF	Unc
1694	38,000	60.00	150	325	725	—
1695	18,000	—	—	—	—	—
1697	1,705	—	—	—	—	—
1698	908	—	—	—	—	—
1699	697	—	—	—	—	—

KM# 306 1/4 ECU
6.4400 g., 0.8570 Silver 0.1774 oz. ASW **Ruler:** Louis XIV **Obv:** Mailed bust right **Rev:** Crowned circular quartered shield of France, Navarre, Old and New Burgundy **Mint:** Lille

Date	Mintage	VG	F	VF	XF	Unc
1694W	—	400	800	1,450	2,750	—
1695W	—	475	950	1,750	3,250	—
1696W	13,000	—	—	—	—	—
1697W	12,000	475	950	1,750	3,250	—
1699W	1,800	—	—	—	—	—

KM# 307 1/4 ECU
6.7460 g., 0.9170 Silver 0.1989 oz. ASW **Ruler:** Louis XIV **Obv:** Large fleur-de-lis **Rev:** Crowned circular shield of France dividing palms **Mint:** Strasbourg

Date	Mintage	VG	F	VF	XF	Unc
1694BB	—	350	750	1,400	2,500	—
1695BB	—	300	600	1,250	2,250	—
1696BB	—	350	750	1,400	2,500	—
1699BB	—	400	850	1,600	2,800	—

KM# 121 1/2 ECU
13.5440 g., 0.9170 Silver 0.3993 oz. ASW **Ruler:** Louis XIII **Obv:** Laureate and draped bust right **Rev:** Crowned shield **Mint:** Paris

Date	Mintage	VG	F	VF	XF	Unc
1641A Rose	—	600	1,000	1,700	3,000	—
1642A Rose	—	325	675	1,500	2,500	—
1642A Rose/2 points	—	300	625	1,350	2,350	—
1642A Rose/2 points	—	300	625	1,350	2,350	—

KM# 135.1 1/2 ECU
13.5440 g., 0.9170 Silver 0.3993 oz. ASW **Ruler:** Louis XIII **Obv:** Laureate, draped and mailed bust right

Date	Mintage	VG	F	VF	XF	Unc
1642 Rose	—	275	550	1,000	1,650	—
1642 1 or 2 points	—	275	550	1,000	1,650	—
1643 Rose	—	275	550	1,000	1,650	—
1643	—	300	625	1,150	2,100	—
1643 Point	—	275	550	1,000	1,650	—

KM# 135.2 1/2 ECU
13.5440 g., 0.9170 Silver 0.3993 oz. ASW **Ruler:** Louis XIII **Mint:** Lyon

Date	Mintage	VG	F	VF	XF	Unc
1643D	—	400	800	1,750	3,000	—

KM# 163.1 1/2 ECU
13.5440 g., 0.9170 Silver 0.3993 oz. ASW **Ruler:** Louis XIV **Obv:** Laureate, draped and mailed bust right, short hair before ear **Rev:** Crowned shield of France **Mint:** Paris

Date	Mintage	VG	F	VF	XF	Unc
1643A Point	—	60.00	150	325	725	—
1643A Rose	—	65.00	160	350	775	—
1644A Point	—	60.00	150	325	725	—
1644A Rose	—	50.00	125	275	625	—
1644A Rose and 2 points	—	50.00	125	275	625	—
1645A Point	—	45.00	110	250	600	—
1645A Rose and 2 points	—	70.00	170	375	825	—
1645A Rose	—	60.00	150	325	725	—

KM# 163.2 1/2 ECU
13.5440 g., 0.9170 Silver 0.3993 oz. ASW **Ruler:** Louis XIV **Mint:** Lyon

Date	Mintage	VG	F	VF	XF	Unc
1644D	—	75.00	200	425	1,050	—
1645D	—	75.00	200	425	1,050	—
1648D	—	90.00	225	500	1,250	—
1649D	—	90.00	225	500	1,250	—
1650D	—	100	250	550	1,400	—
1651D	—	80.00	215	475	1,200	—
1652D	—	75.00	200	425	1,050	—

KM# 164.1 1/2 ECU
13.5440 g., 0.9170 Silver 0.3993 oz. ASW **Ruler:** Louis XIV **Obv:** Long hair before ear **Mint:** Paris

Date	Mintage	VG	F	VF	XF	Unc
1646A	—	45.00	90.00	160	350	—
1647A	—	30.00	65.00	130	300	—
1648A	—	28.00	55.00	125	300	—
1649A	—	28.00	55.00	125	300	—
1650A	—	28.00	55.00	125	300	—
1651A	—	30.00	65.00	130	350	—
1652A	—	28.00	55.00	125	300	—
1653A	—	30.00	65.00	130	350	—
1654A	—	28.00	55.00	125	300	—
1655A	—	28.00	55.00	125	300	—
1658A	—	—	—	—	—	—
1659A	Est. 66,000	—	—	—	—	—

KM# 164.2 1/2 ECU
13.5440 g., 0.9170 Silver 0.3993 oz. ASW **Ruler:** Louis XIV **Mint:** Arras

Date	Mintage	VG	F	VF	XF	Unc
1646AR	—	35.00	90.00	200	550	—
1647AR	—	50.00	120	275	750	—
1648AR	—	50.00	115	250	650	—
1649AR	—	—	—	—	—	—
1650AR	—	55.00	135	300	800	—
1651AR	—	45.00	100	225	600	—
1652AR	—	28.00	60.00	135	350	—
1653AR	—	28.00	60.00	135	350	—
1655AR	—	50.00	120	275	750	—
1656AR	—	150	325	650	—	—

KM# 164.3 1/2 ECU
13.5440 g., 0.9170 Silver 0.3993 oz. ASW **Ruler:** Louis XIV **Mint:** Rouen

Date	Mintage	VG	F	VF	XF	Unc
1646B	—	28.00	60.00	140	350	—
1647B	—	25.00	55.00	125	325	—
1648B	—	25.00	55.00	125	325	—
1649B	—	25.00	50.00	120	290	—
1650B	—	25.00	55.00	125	325	—
1651B	—	25.00	50.00	120	300	—
1652B	—	25.00	50.00	120	300	—
1653B	—	25.00	50.00	120	300	—
1654B	—	35.00	75.00	165	450	—
1655B	—	25.00	50.00	120	300	—
1657B	—	—	—	—	—	—
1658B	—	75.00	175	350	925	—

KM# 164.4 1/2 ECU
13.5440 g., 0.9170 Silver 0.3993 oz. ASW **Ruler:** Louis XIV **Mint:** Saint Lô

Date	Mintage	VG	F	VF	XF	Unc
1647C	—	28.00	60.00	140	350	—
1648C	—	28.00	60.00	140	350	—
1649C	—	28.00	60.00	140	350	—
1650C	—	28.00	60.00	140	350	—
1651C	—	25.00	55.00	125	325	—
1652C	—	25.00	50.00	120	300	—
1653C	—	25.00	55.00	125	325	—
1654C	—	30.00	65.00	150	400	—
1655C	—	30.00	65.00	150	400	—
1656C	—	—	—	—	—	—

KM# 164.5 1/2 ECU
13.5440 g., 0.9170 Silver 0.3993 oz. ASW **Ruler:** Louis XIV **Mint:** Lyon

Date	Mintage	VG	F	VF	XF	Unc
1652D	—	40.00	95.00	200	550	—
1653D	—	25.00	55.00	125	325	—
1654D	—	35.00	75.00	165	450	—
1657D	—	45.00	100	225	600	—
1658D	—	55.00	135	300	800	—
1659D	—	40.00	95.00	200	550	—

KM# 164.6 1/2 ECU
13.5440 g., 0.9170 Silver 0.3993 oz. ASW **Ruler:** Louis XIV **Mint:** Tours

Date	Mintage	VG	F	VF	XF	Unc
1649E	—	30.00	65.00	150	400	—
1651E	—	40.00	95.00	200	550	—
1652E	—	25.00	50.00	120	300	—
1653E	—	28.00	60.00	140	350	—
1654E	—	—	—	—	—	—
1656E	—	35.00	75.00	165	450	—
1657E	—	40.00	95.00	200	550	—
1658E	—	40.00	95.00	200	550	—
1659E	—	55.00	125	275	750	—
1660E	—	55.00	125	275	750	—

KM# 164.7 1/2 ECU
13.5440 g., 0.9170 Silver 0.3993 oz. ASW **Ruler:** Louis XIV **Mint:** Angers

Date	Mintage	VG	F	VF	XF	Unc
1647F	—	—	—	—	—	—
1648F	—	—	—	—	—	—
1649F	—	35.00	75.00	165	450	—
1650F	—	30.00	65.00	150	400	—
1651F	—	40.00	95.00	200	550	—
1652F	—	25.00	50.00	120	300	—
1653F	—	28.00	55.00	125	300	—

Date	Mintage	VG	F	VF	XF	Unc
1654F	—	—	—	—	—	—
1655F	—	30.00	65.00	150	400	—
1656F	—	28.00	55.00	125	325	—
1658F	—	—	—	—	—	—
1659F	—	40.00	95.00	200	550	—
1660F	—	45.00	100	225	600	—

KM# 164.8 1/2 ECU
13.5440 g., 0.9170 Silver 0.3993 oz. ASW **Ruler:** Louis XIV
Mint: Poitiers

Date	Mintage	VG	F	VF	XF	Unc
1647G	—	165	325	650	—	—
1648G	—	—	—	—	—	—
1649G	—	25.00	50.00	120	300	—
1650G	—	25.00	50.00	120	300	—
1651G	—	25.00	50.00	120	300	—
1652G	—	25.00	50.00	120	300	—
1653G	—	25.00	50.00	120	300	—
1655G	—	45.00	100	225	600	—
1656G	—	—	—	—	—	—
1657G	—	35.00	85.00	180	475	—
1659G	—	45.00	100	225	600	—
1660G	—	55.00	125	275	750	—

KM# 164.9 1/2 ECU
13.5440 g., 0.9170 Silver 0.3993 oz. ASW **Ruler:** Louis XIV
Mint: La Rochelle

Date	Mintage	VG	F	VF	XF	Unc
1646H	—	40.00	95.00	200	550	—
1647H	—	30.00	65.00	140	350	—
1648H	—	55.00	125	275	750	—
1649H	—	55.00	125	275	750	—
1650H	—	40.00	95.00	200	550	—
1651H	—	40.00	95.00	200	550	—
1652H	—	55.00	125	275	750	—
1653H	—	35.00	75.00	165	450	—
1654H	—	30.00	65.00	150	400	—
1655H	—	25.00	55.00	130	325	—
1656H	—	35.00	75.00	165	450	—
1658H	—	40.00	95.00	200	550	—
1659H	—	45.00	100	225	600	—
1660H	—	—	—	—	—	—

KM# 164.10 1/2 ECU
13.5440 g., 0.9170 Silver 0.3993 oz. ASW **Ruler:** Louis XIV
Mint: Limoges

Date	Mintage	VG	F	VF	XF	Unc
1650I	—	40.00	95.00	200	550	—
1651I	—	40.00	95.00	200	550	—
1652I	—	55.00	125	275	750	—
1653I	—	—	—	—	—	—
1654I	—	110	210	440	1,000	—
1655I	—	35.00	80.00	175	475	—
1656I	—	30.00	65.00	150	400	—
1657I	—	40.00	95.00	200	550	—
1658I	—	—	—	—	—	—
1659I	—	45.00	100	225	600	—
1660I	—	55.00	125	275	750	—

KM# 164.11 1/2 ECU
13.5440 g., 0.9170 Silver 0.3993 oz. ASW **Ruler:** Louis XIV
Mint: Bordeaux

Date	Mintage	VG	F	VF	XF	Unc
1647K	—	30.00	65.00	140	350	—
1648K	—	30.00	70.00	150	400	—
1649K	—	30.00	70.00	150	400	—
1650K	—	30.00	70.00	150	400	—
1651K	—	30.00	70.00	150	400	—
1652K	—	30.00	70.00	150	400	—
1653K	—	—	—	—	—	—
1654K	—	—	—	—	—	—
1655K	—	30.00	70.00	150	400	—
1656K	—	30.00	70.00	150	400	—
1657K	—	35.00	80.00	175	475	—
1659K	—	45.00	100	225	600	—
1660K	—	40.00	95.00	200	550	—

KM# 164.12 1/2 ECU
13.5440 g., 0.9170 Silver 0.3993 oz. ASW **Ruler:** Louis XIV
Mint: Bayonne

Date	Mintage	VG	F	VF	XF	Unc
1650L	—	25.00	55.00	125	325	—
1651L	—	25.00	55.00	125	325	—
1652L	—	25.00	50.00	120	300	—
1653L	—	25.00	55.00	125	325	—
1654L	—	30.00	65.00	150	400	—
1655L	—	25.00	55.00	125	325	—
1656L	—	35.00	75.00	165	450	—
1657L	—	35.00	75.00	165	450	—
1658L	—	45.00	100	225	600	—
1659L	—	35.00	75.00	165	450	—
1660L	—	35.00	75.00	165	450	—

KM# 164.13 1/2 ECU
13.5440 g., 0.9170 Silver 0.3993 oz. ASW **Ruler:** Louis XIV
Mint: Toulouse

Date	Mintage	VG	F	VF	XF	Unc
1647M	—	55.00	125	275	750	—
1648M	—	35.00	75.00	165	450	—
1649M	—	40.00	95.00	200	550	—
1650M	—	30.00	65.00	140	350	—
1651M	—	30.00	65.00	140	350	—
1652M	—	30.00	65.00	140	350	—
1653M	—	45.00	100	225	600	—
1654M	—	35.00	75.00	165	450	—
1655M	—	25.00	55.00	125	325	—
1656M	—	—	—	—	—	—
1659M	—	40.00	95.00	200	550	—
1660M	—	—	—	—	—	—
1661M	—	—	—	—	—	—

KM# 164.14 1/2 ECU
13.5440 g., 0.9170 Silver 0.3993 oz. ASW **Ruler:** Louis XIV
Mint: Montpellier

Date	Mintage	VG	F	VF	XF	Unc
1646N	—	40.00	95.00	200	550	—
1647N	—	40.00	95.00	200	550	—
1648N	—	30.00	65.00	140	350	—
1649N	—	—	—	—	—	—
1650N	—	25.00	55.00	125	325	—
1651N	—	30.00	65.00	140	350	—
1652N	—	25.00	55.00	125	325	—
1653N	—	35.00	75.00	165	450	—
1656N	—	65.00	150	325	875	—
1657N	—	65.00	150	325	875	—
1658N	—	55.00	125	275	750	—
1659N	—	—	—	—	—	—

KM# 164.15 1/2 ECU
13.5440 g., 0.9170 Silver 0.3993 oz. ASW **Ruler:** Louis XIV
Mint: Riom

Date	Mintage	VG	F	VF	XF	Unc
1652O	—	55.00	125	275	750	—
1653O	—	—	—	—	—	—

KM# 164.16 1/2 ECU
13.5440 g., 0.9170 Silver 0.3993 oz. ASW **Ruler:** Louis XIV
Mint: Dijon

Date	Mintage	VG	F	VF	XF	Unc
1646P	—	—	—	—	—	—
1647P	—	—	—	—	—	—
1651P	—	—	—	—	—	—
1652P	—	25.00	55.00	125	325	—
1653P	—	25.00	55.00	125	325	—
1654P	—	—	—	—	—	—
1655P	—	45.00	100	225	600	—
1657P	—	—	—	—	—	—

KM# 164.17 1/2 ECU
13.5440 g., 0.9170 Silver 0.3993 oz. ASW **Ruler:** Louis XIV
Mint: Perpignan

Date	Mintage	VG	F	VF	XF	Unc
1650Q	—	30.00	65.00	140	350	—
1651Q	—	30.00	65.00	140	350	—
1652Q	—	35.00	75.00	165	450	—
1653Q	—	35.00	75.00	165	450	—
1654Q	—	45.00	100	225	600	—

KM# 164.18 1/2 ECU
13.5440 g., 0.9170 Silver 0.3993 oz. ASW **Ruler:** Louis XIV
Mint: Villeneuve St. André

Date	Mintage	VG	F	VF	XF	Unc
1661R	—	—	—	—	—	—
1662R	—	—	—	—	—	—

KM# 164.19 1/2 ECU
13.5440 g., 0.9170 Silver 0.3993 oz. ASW **Ruler:** Louis XIV
Mint: Troyes

Date	Mintage	VG	F	VF	XF	Unc
1649S	—	—	—	—	—	—
1650S	—	—	—	—	—	—
1651S	—	25.00	55.00	150	400	—
1652S	—	—	—	—	—	—
1653S	—	30.00	65.00	150	500	—
1654S	—	35.00	75.00	165	550	—
1655S	—	40.00	95.00	200	650	—

KM# 164.20 1/2 ECU
13.5440 g., 0.9170 Silver 0.3993 oz. ASW **Ruler:** Louis XIV
Mint: Nantes

Date	Mintage	VG	F	VF	XF	Unc
1647T	—	50.00	115	250	650	—
1648T	—	—	—	—	—	—
1649T	—	30.00	65.00	150	400	—
1650T	—	25.00	55.00	125	325	—
1651T	—	55.00	125	275	750	—
1652T	—	25.00	50.00	120	300	—
1653T	—	30.00	65.00	150	400	—
1654T	—	25.00	50.00	120	300	—
1655T	—	25.00	55.00	125	325	—
1656T	—	30.00	65.00	150	425	—
1659T	—	—	—	—	—	—

KM# 164.21 1/2 ECU
13.5440 g., 0.9170 Silver 0.3993 oz. ASW **Ruler:** Louis XIV
Mint: Bourges

Date	Mintage	VG	F	VF	XF	Unc
1648Y	—	125	275	525	—	—
1649Y	—	30.00	65.00	150	400	—
1650Y	—	40.00	95.00	200	550	—
1651Y	—	30.00	65.00	140	350	—
1652Y	—	25.00	50.00	120	300	—
1653Y	—	35.00	75.00	165	450	—
1654Y	—	35.00	75.00	165	450	—
1655Y	—	40.00	95.00	200	550	—
1656Y	—	40.00	95.00	200	550	—

KM# 164.22 1/2 ECU
13.5440 g., 0.9170 Silver 0.3993 oz. ASW **Ruler:** Louis XIV
Mint: Amiens

Date	Mintage	VG	F	VF	XF	Unc
1650X	—	—	—	—	—	—
1651X	—	—	—	—	—	—
1652X	—	25.00	55.00	125	325	—
1653X	—	25.00	50.00	120	300	—
1654X	—	30.00	65.00	150	400	—
1655X	—	25.00	50.00	120	300	—
1658X	—	—	—	—	—	—
1659X	—	—	—	—	—	—
1660X	—	—	—	—	—	—

KM# 164.23 1/2 ECU
13.5440 g., 0.9170 Silver 0.3993 oz. ASW **Ruler:** Louis XIV
Mint: Aix **Note:** Mint mark: Ampersand.

Date	Mintage	VG	F	VF	XF	Unc
1646	—	25.00	55.00	125	325	—
1647	—	25.00	50.00	120	300	—
1648	—	30.00	65.00	140	350	—
1649	—	30.00	65.00	140	350	—
1650	—	40.00	95.00	200	550	—
1651	—	30.00	65.00	150	400	—
1652	—	25.00	55.00	125	325	—
1653	—	35.00	75.00	165	450	—
1656	—	30.00	65.00	150	400	—
1657	—	30.00	65.00	140	350	—
1658	—	—	—	—	—	—
1659	—	45.00	100	225	600	—

KM# 164.24 1/2 ECU
13.5440 g., 0.9170 Silver 0.3993 oz. ASW **Ruler:** Louis XIV
Mint: Rennes **Note:** Mint mark: Numeral 9.

Date	Mintage	VG	F	VF	XF	Unc
1648	—	30.00	65.00	140	350	—
1649	—	25.00	50.00	120	300	—
1650	—	25.00	50.00	120	300	—
1651	—	25.00	50.00	120	300	—

Date	Mintage	VG	F	VF	XF	Unc
1652	—	25.00	50.00	120	300	—
1653	—	25.00	50.00	120	300	—
1654	—	35.00	75.00	165	450	—
1655	—	25.00	55.00	125	325	—
1656	—	25.00	50.00	120	300	—
1657	—	30.00	65.00	150	400	—
1658	—	30.00	65.00	150	400	—
1659	—	45.00	100	225	600	—

KM# 183 1/2 ECU
13.5440 g., 0.9170 Silver 0.3993 oz. ASW **Ruler:** Louis XIV
Obv: Laureate draped and mailed bust right, long hair before ear **Rev:** Crowned shield of France and Navarre **Mint:** Saint Palais **Note:** Strike mark: * V *.

Date	Mintage	VG	F	VF	XF	Unc
1652	—	200	400	825	1,600	—
1653	—	200	400	825	1,600	—
1654	—	200	400	825	1,600	—
1655	—	200	400	825	1,600	—
1656	—	175	350	750	1,400	—
1658	—	185	375	775	1,500	—
1659 No V	—	250	500	900	1,800	—
1662	—	350	700	1,200	2,800	—

KM# 185 1/2 ECU
13.5440 g., 0.9170 Silver 0.3993 oz. ASW **Ruler:** Louis XIV
Rev: Crowned shield of Dauphine **Mint:** Grenoble

Date	Mintage	VG	F	VF	XF	Unc
1653Z	—	—	—	—	—	—

KM# 184.1 1/2 ECU
13.5440 g., 0.9170 Silver 0.3993 oz. ASW **Ruler:** Louis XIV
Mint: Pau **Note:** Strike mark: Palm.

Date	Mintage	VG	F	VF	XF	Unc
1650	—	300	600	1,000	2,500	—
1651	—	300	600	1,000	2,500	—

KM# 184.2 1/2 ECU
13.5440 g., 0.9170 Silver 0.3993 oz. ASW **Ruler:** Louis XIV
Mint: Pau **Note:** Strike mark: * F *.

Date	Mintage	VG	F	VF	XF	Unc
1653	—	250	500	900	1,800	—
1654	—	250	500	900	1,800	—
1655	—	220	450	850	1,700	—
1656	—	220	450	850	1,700	—

KM# 184.3 1/2 ECU
13.5440 g., 0.9170 Silver 0.3993 oz. ASW **Ruler:** Louis XIV
Mint: Morlaas **Note:** Strike mark: * G *.

Date	Mintage	VG	F	VF	XF	Unc
1653	—	275	550	1,000	2,000	—

KM# 184.4 1/2 ECU
13.5440 g., 0.9170 Silver 0.3993 oz. ASW **Ruler:** Louis XIV
Mint: Morlaas **Note:** Strike mark: M.

Date	Mintage	VG	F	VF	XF	Unc
1662	—	275	550	1,000	2,000	—

KM# 200 1/2 ECU
13.5440 g., 0.9170 Silver 0.3993 oz. ASW **Ruler:** Louis XIV
Obv: Laureate, draped and mailed bust right **Mint:** Bourges **Note:** Hybrid design.

Date	Mintage	VG	F	VF	XF	Unc
1658Y	—	200	425	825	1,650	—
1659Y	—	200	425	825	1,650	—
1660Y	—	200	425	825	1,650	—
1661Y	—	200	425	825	1,650	—
1662Y	—	200	425	825	1,650	—

KM# 202.1 1/2 ECU
13.5440 g., 0.9170 Silver 0.3993 oz. ASW **Ruler:** Louis XIV
Obv: Youthful laureate, draped and mailed bust right **Rev:** Crowned French shield **Mint:** Paris

Date	Mintage	VG	F	VF	XF	Unc
1659A	—	65.00	130	325	550	—
1661A	—	—	—	—	—	—
1662A	—	60.00	125	300	525	—
1664A	—	—	—	—	—	—
1666A	—	60.00	125	300	525	—

Date	Mintage	VG	F	VF	XF	Unc
1667A	—	55.00	115	275	475	—
1668A	—	55.00	115	275	475	—
1669A	—	60.00	125	300	525	—

KM# 202.2 1/2 ECU
13.5440 g., 0.9170 Silver 0.3993 oz. ASW **Ruler:** Louis XIV
Mint: Rouen

Date	Mintage	VG	F	VF	XF	Unc
1659B	—	100	200	485	900	—
1660B	—	—	—	—	—	—
1662B	—	50.00	110	250	425	—
1663B	—	—	—	—	—	—
1664B	—	—	—	—	—	—

KM# 202.3 1/2 ECU
13.5440 g., 0.9170 Silver 0.3993 oz. ASW **Ruler:** Louis XIV
Mint: Lyon

Date	Mintage	VG	F	VF	XF	Unc
1660D	—	85.00	175	425	750	—
1663D	—	—	—	—	—	—
1664D	—	85.00	175	425	750	—
1665D	—	60.00	125	300	525	—
1666D	—	60.00	125	300	525	—
1667D	—	60.00	125	300	525	—
1668D	—	—	—	—	—	—
1669D	—	—	—	—	—	—
1670D	—	—	—	—	—	—
1671D	—	—	—	—	—	—
1672D	—	75.00	150	375	650	—
1673D	—	75.00	150	375	650	—

KM# 202.4 1/2 ECU
13.5440 g., 0.9170 Silver 0.3993 oz. ASW **Ruler:** Louis XIV
Mint: Tours

Date	Mintage	VG	F	VF	XF	Unc
1660E	—	100	200	475	825	—
1661E	—	100	200	475	825	—
1662E	—	85.00	175	425	750	—

KM# 202.5 1/2 ECU
13.5440 g., 0.9170 Silver 0.3993 oz. ASW **Ruler:** Louis XIV
Mint: Angers

Date	Mintage	VG	F	VF	XF	Unc
1660F	—	85.00	175	425	750	—
1661F	—	—	—	—	—	—

KM# 202.6 1/2 ECU
13.5440 g., 0.9170 Silver 0.3993 oz. ASW **Ruler:** Louis XIV
Mint: La Rochelle

Date	Mintage	VG	F	VF	XF	Unc
1661H	—	85.00	175	425	750	—

KM# 202.7 1/2 ECU
13.5440 g., 0.9170 Silver 0.3993 oz. ASW **Ruler:** Louis XIV
Mint: Limoges

Date	Mintage	VG	F	VF	XF	Unc
1661I	—	85.00	175	425	750	—
1662I	—	150	300	700	1,250	—
1664I	—	85.00	175	425	750	—

KM# 202.8 1/2 ECU
13.5440 g., 0.9170 Silver 0.3993 oz. ASW **Ruler:** Louis XIV
Mint: Bordeaux

Date	Mintage	VG	F	VF	XF	Unc
1660K	—	60.00	125	300	525	—
1661K	—	85.00	175	425	750	—

KM# 202.9 1/2 ECU
13.5440 g., 0.9170 Silver 0.3993 oz. ASW **Ruler:** Louis XIV
Mint: Bayonne

Date	Mintage	VG	F	VF	XF	Unc
1659L	—	70.00	140	350	600	—
1660L	—	60.00	125	300	525	—
1661L	—	60.00	125	300	525	—
1662L	—	75.00	150	375	650	—
1663L	—	75.00	150	375	650	—
1664L	—	75.00	150	375	650	—
1665L	—	70.00	140	350	600	—

Date	Mintage	VG	F	VF	XF	Unc
1666L	—	—	—	—	—	—
1667L	—	75.00	150	375	650	—
1668L	—	—	—	—	—	—
1669L	—	85.00	175	425	750	—
1670L	—	100	200	500	850	—
1671L	—	—	—	—	—	—
1672L	—	85.00	175	425	750	—

KM# 202.10 1/2 ECU
13.5440 g., 0.9170 Silver 0.3993 oz. ASW **Ruler:** Louis XIV
Mint: Toulouse

Date	Mintage	VG	F	VF	XF	Unc
1662M	—	—	—	—	—	—
1663M	—	75.00	145	360	625	—
1666M	—	70.00	140	350	600	—
1667M	—	70.00	140	350	600	—
1668M	—	70.00	140	350	600	—
1669M	—	—	—	—	—	—
1670M	—	—	—	—	—	—
1671M	—	85.00	175	425	750	—

KM# 202.11 1/2 ECU
13.5440 g., 0.9170 Silver 0.3993 oz. ASW **Ruler:** Louis XIV
Mint: Montpellier

Date	Mintage	VG	F	VF	XF	Unc
1660N	—	—	—	—	—	—
1661N	—	—	—	—	—	—
1662N	—	—	—	—	—	—
1666N	—	55.00	115	275	475	—
1667N	—	70.00	140	350	600	—
1668N	—	85.00	175	425	750	—

KM# 202.13 1/2 ECU
13.5440 g., 0.9170 Silver 0.3993 oz. ASW **Ruler:** Louis XIV
Mint: Nantes

Date	Mintage	VG	F	VF	XF	Unc
1659T	—	85.00	175	425	750	—
1660T	—	85.00	175	425	750	—
1661T	—	—	—	—	—	—
1662T	—	60.00	125	300	525	—
1663T	—	70.00	140	350	600	—
1665T	—	70.00	140	350	600	—
1667T	—	70.00	140	350	600	—
1670T	—	85.00	175	425	750	—

KM# 202.14 1/2 ECU
13.5440 g., 0.9170 Silver 0.3993 oz. ASW **Ruler:** Louis XIV
Mint: Amiens

Date	Mintage	VG	F	VF	XF	Unc
1660X	—	—	—	—	—	—

KM# 202.15 1/2 ECU
13.5440 g., 0.9170 Silver 0.3993 oz. ASW **Ruler:** Louis XIV
Mint: Aix **Note:** Mint mark: Ampersand.

Date	Mintage	VG	F	VF	XF	Unc
1660	—	—	—	—	—	—
1661	—	—	—	—	—	—
1662	—	—	—	—	—	—
1665	—	85.00	175	425	750	—
1666	—	60.00	125	300	525	—
1667	—	70.00	140	350	600	—
1669	—	—	—	—	—	—
1670	—	100	200	500	850	—
1671	—	100	200	475	825	—
1672	—	100	200	475	825	—

KM# 202.16 1/2 ECU
13.5440 g., 0.9170 Silver 0.3993 oz. ASW **Ruler:** Louis XIV
Mint: Rennes **Note:** Mint mark: Numeral 9.

Date	Mintage	VG	F	VF	XF	Unc
1659	—	85.00	175	425	750	—
1660	—	70.00	140	350	600	—
1661	—	60.00	125	300	525	—
1662	—	50.00	115	275	475	—
1663	—	60.00	125	300	525	—
1664	—	60.00	125	300	525	—

Date	Mintage	VG	F	VF	XF	Unc
1665	—	85.00	175	425	750	—
1667	—	65.00	130	325	550	—
1668	—	60.00	125	300	525	—
1669	—	—	—	—	—	—
1670	—	60.00	125	300	525	—
1671	—	—	—	—	—	—
1672	—	90.00	185	450	775	—

KM# 229 1/2 ECU

13.5440 g., 0.9170 Silver 0.3993 oz. ASW **Ruler:** Louis XIV **Obv:** Crowned shield of Dauphine **Mint:** Grenoble

Date	Mintage	VG	F	VF	XF	Unc
1660Z Rare	642	—	—	—	—	—

KM# 228 1/2 ECU

13.5440 g., 0.9170 Silver 0.3993 oz. ASW **Ruler:** Louis XIV **Rev:** Crowned shield of French, Navarre and Bearn **Mint:** Pau

Date	Mintage	VG	F	VF	XF	Unc
1667	—	300	750	1,500	3,250	—
1674	—	275	675	1,350	3,000	—
1675	—	275	675	1,350	3,000	—
1676	—	275	675	1,350	3,000	—
1677	—	275	675	1,350	3,000	—
1678	—	325	825	1,650	3,750	—
1679	—	325	825	1,650	3,750	—
1680	—	400	1,000	2,200	4,500	—

KM# 225.1 1/2 ECU

13.5440 g., 0.9170 Silver 0.3993 oz. ASW **Ruler:** Louis XIV **Obv:** Laureate, draped bust right **Mint:** Paris

Date	Mintage	VG	F	VF	XF	Unc
1670A	—	60.00	125	300	625	—
1671A	—	70.00	140	350	725	—
1672A	—	55.00	115	275	575	—
1673A	—	—	—	—	—	—

KM# 225.3 1/2 ECU

13.5440 g., 0.9170 Silver 0.3993 oz. ASW **Ruler:** Louis XIV **Mint:** Rennes **Note:** Mint mark: Numeral 9.

Date	Mintage	VG	F	VF	XF	Unc
1673	—	70.00	140	350	725	—
1674	—	100	200	500	1,000	—
1675	—	—	—	—	—	—
1676	—	100	200	475	1,000	—
1677	—	150	300	700	1,500	—
1678	—	—	—	—	—	—
1679	—	55.00	115	275	600	—
1680	—	150	300	700	1,500	—

KM# 230.1 1/2 ECU

13.5440 g., 0.9170 Silver 0.3993 oz. ASW **Ruler:** Louis XIV **Subject:** Parliament **Obv:** Draped armored bust right **Rev:** Crowned shield of France **Mint:** Paris

Date	Mintage	VG	F	VF	XF	Unc
1674A	—	125	325	825	1,450	—
1676A	—	165	400	1,000	1,750	—
1678A	—	—	—	—	—	—
1679A	—	110	275	675	1,200	—
1680A	—	125	325	825	1,450	—
1681A	—	125	325	825	1,450	—
1682A	—	145	375	950	1,650	—
1683A	—	135	350	850	1,475	—

KM# 230.2 1/2 ECU

13.5440 g., 0.9170 Silver 0.3993 oz. ASW **Ruler:** Louis XIV **Mint:** Rouen

Date	Mintage	VG	F	VF	XF	Unc
1679B	—	125	325	825	1,450	—
1680B	—	140	365	900	1,550	—
1681B	—	165	400	1,000	1,750	—
1683B	—	—	—	—	—	—

KM# 230.3 1/2 ECU

13.5440 g., 0.9170 Silver 0.3993 oz. ASW **Ruler:** Louis XIV **Mint:** Lyon

Date	Mintage	VG	F	VF	XF	Unc
1678D	—	180	450	1,100	1,950	—
1679D	—	140	365	900	1,550	—
1680D	—	140	365	900	1,550	—
1681D	—	—	—	—	—	—
1682D	—	180	450	1,100	1,950	—

KM# 230.4 1/2 ECU

13.5440 g., 0.9170 Silver 0.3993 oz. ASW **Ruler:** Louis XIV **Mint:** La Rochelle

Date	Mintage	VG	F	VF	XF	Unc
1679H	—	140	365	900	1,550	—
1680H	—	—	—	—	—	—

KM# 230.5 1/2 ECU

13.5440 g., 0.9170 Silver 0.3993 oz. ASW **Ruler:** Louis XIV **Mint:** Bordeaux

Date	Mintage	VG	F	VF	XF	Unc
1680K	—	—	—	—	—	—
1681K	—	—	—	—	—	—
1682K	—	—	—	—	—	—
1683K	—	145	370	925	1,600	—

KM# 230.6 1/2 ECU

13.5440 g., 0.9170 Silver 0.3993 oz. ASW **Ruler:** Louis XIV **Mint:** Bayonne

Date	Mintage	VG	F	VF	XF	Unc
1673L	—	—	—	—	—	—
1674L	—	125	325	825	1,450	—
1675L	—	140	365	900	1,550	—
1676L	—	140	365	900	1,550	—
1677L	—	165	400	1,000	1,750	—
1678L	—	—	—	—	—	—
1679L	—	140	365	900	1,550	—
1680L	—	—	—	—	—	—
1681L	—	140	365	900	1,550	—
1682L	—	—	—	—	—	—
1683L	—	145	370	925	1,600	—

KM# 230.7 1/2 ECU

13.5440 g., 0.9170 Silver 0.3993 oz. ASW **Ruler:** Louis XIV **Mint:** Montpellier

Date	Mintage	VG	F	VF	XF	Unc
1679N	—	140	365	900	1,550	—
1680N	—	225	550	1,350	2,350	—

KM# 230.8 1/2 ECU

13.5440 g., 0.9170 Silver 0.3993 oz. ASW **Ruler:** Louis XIV **Mint:** Reims

Date	Mintage	VG	F	VF	XF	Unc
1680	—	—	—	—	—	—
1681	—	—	—	—	—	—
1682	—	180	450	1,100	2,000	—

KM# 230.9 1/2 ECU

13.5440 g., 0.9170 Silver 0.3993 oz. ASW **Ruler:** Louis XIV **Mint:** Aix **Note:** Mint mark: Ampersand.

Date	Mintage	VG	F	VF	XF	Unc
1679	—	140	365	900	1,550	—
1680	—	180	450	1,100	1,950	—
1681	—	—	—	—	—	—
1682	—	140	365	900	1,550	—
1683	—	—	—	—	—	—
1684	—	200	475	1,200	2,150	—

KM# 230.10 1/2 ECU

13.5440 g., 0.9170 Silver 0.3993 oz. ASW **Ruler:** Louis XIV **Mint:** Rennes **Note:** Mint mark: Numeral 9.

Date	Mintage	VG	F	VF	XF	Unc
1680	—	135	350	850	1,475	—
1681	—	—	—	—	—	—
1682	—	180	450	1,100	1,950	—
1683	—	180	450	1,100	1,950	—

KM# 251 1/2 ECU

13.5440 g., 0.9170 Silver 0.3993 oz. ASW **Ruler:** Louis XIV **Rev:** Crowned shield of France, Navarre and Bearn **Mint:** Pau

Date	Mintage	VG	F	VF	XF	Unc
1680	—	1,000	2,000	3,500	7,000	—
1681	—	1,000	2,000	3,500	7,000	—
1682	—	1,000	2,000	3,500	7,000	—
1685	—	1,000	2,000	3,500	7,000	—
1686	—	1,000	2,000	3,500	7,000	—

KM# 250.1 1/2 ECU

13.5440 g., 0.9170 Silver 0.3993 oz. ASW **Ruler:** Louis XIV **Subject:** Parliament **Obv:** Older draped bust right, palm above head **Rev:** Crowned shield of France **Mint:** Paris **Note:** Type au Jabot

Date	Mintage	VG	F	VF	XF	Unc
1683A Jabot	—	550	1,350	2,700	4,500	—
1684A Jabot	—	550	1,350	2,700	4,500	—

KM# 250.2 1/2 ECU

13.5440 g., 0.9170 Silver 0.3993 oz. ASW **Ruler:** Louis XIV **Mint:** Rouen

Date	Mintage	VG	F	VF	XF	Unc
1684B Parlement	—	—	—	—	—	—

KM# 250.3 1/2 ECU

13.5440 g., 0.9170 Silver 0.3993 oz. ASW **Ruler:** Louis XIV **Mint:** Lyon

Date	Mintage	VG	F	VF	XF	Unc
1684D Jabot	—	975	2,500	5,000	8,300	—
1685D Jabot	—	975	2,500	5,000	8,300	—

KM# 250.4 1/2 ECU

13.5440 g., 0.9170 Silver 0.3993 oz. ASW **Ruler:** Louis XIV **Mint:** Bordeaux

Date	Mintage	VG	F	VF	XF	Unc
1684K Parlement	—	975	2,500	5,000	8,300	—
1685K Parlement	—	—	—	—	—	—

KM# 250.5 1/2 ECU

13.5440 g., 0.9170 Silver 0.3993 oz. ASW **Ruler:** Louis XIV **Mint:** Bayonne

Date	Mintage	VG	F	VF	XF	Unc
1684L Parlement	—	975	2,500	5,000	8,300	—
1685L Parlement	—	—	—	—	—	—

KM# 250.6 1/2 ECU

13.5440 g., 0.9170 Silver 0.3993 oz. ASW **Ruler:** Louis XIV **Mint:** Troyes

Date	Mintage	VG	F	VF	XF	Unc
1684S	—	—	—	—	—	—

KM# 250.7 1/2 ECU

13.5440 g., 0.9170 Silver 0.3993 oz. ASW **Ruler:** Louis XIV **Mint:** Aix **Note:** Mint mark: Ampersand.

Date	Mintage	VG	F	VF	XF	Unc
1684 Parlement	—	975	2,500	5,000	8,300	—
1685 Parlement	—	900	2,250	5,000	7,500	—
1686 Parlement	—	975	2,500	5,000	8,300	—

KM# 250.8 1/2 ECU

13.5440 g., 0.9170 Silver 0.3993 oz. ASW **Ruler:** Louis XIV **Mint:** Rennes **Note:** Mint mark: Numeral 9.

Date	Mintage	VG	F	VF	XF	Unc
1683 Jabot	—	2,500	4,000	5,500	—	—
1684	—	—	—	—	—	—
1685 Jabot	—	2,500	4,000	5,500	—	—
1686	—	—	—	—	—	—

KM# 261.1 1/2 ECU

13.5440 g., 0.9170 Silver 0.3993 oz. ASW **Ruler:** Louis XIV **Obv:** Draped bust right **Rev:** Crowned shield of France **Edge Lettering:** DOMINE SALVUM FAC REGEM **Mint:** Paris

Date	Mintage	VG	F	VF	XF	Unc
1686A	—	2,000	4,000	8,000	12,000	—
1687A	—	2,000	4,000	8,000	12,000	—
1688A	—	3,000	5,000	9,500	—	—
1689A	—	—	—	—	—	—

KM# 261.2 1/2 ECU

13.5440 g., 0.9170 Silver 0.3993 oz. ASW **Ruler:** Louis XIV **Mint:** Lyon

Date	Mintage	VG	F	VF	XF	Unc
1686D	—	—	—	—	—	—
1687D	—	2,250	4,500	8,500	—	—
1688D	—	2,250	4,500	8,500	12,500	—
1689D	—	2,400	5,500	10,000	—	—

KM# 261.3 1/2 ECU

13.5440 g., 0.9170 Silver 0.3993 oz. ASW **Ruler:** Louis XIV **Mint:** Bordeaux

Date	Mintage	VG	F	VF	XF	Unc
1686K	—	—	—	—	—	—
1687K	—	—	—	—	—	—
1688K	—	—	—	—	—	—

KM# 261.4 1/2 ECU

13.5440 g., 0.9170 Silver 0.3993 oz. ASW **Ruler:** Louis XIV **Mint:** Bayonne

Date	Mintage	VG	F	VF	XF	Unc
1686L	—	—	—	—	—	—
1687L	—	2,400	5,500	10,000	—	—
1688L	—	—	—	—	—	—
1689L	—	—	—	—	—	—

KM# 261.5 1/2 ECU

13.5440 g., 0.9170 Silver 0.3993 oz. ASW **Ruler:** Louis XIV **Mint:** Rennes **Note:** Mint mark: Numeral 9.

Date	Mintage	VG	F	VF	XF	Unc
1687	—	2,000	5,000	9,500	—	—
1688	—	2,000	5,000	9,500	—	—
1689	—	—	—	—	—	—

KM# 261.6 1/2 ECU

13.5440 g., 0.9170 Silver 0.3993 oz. ASW **Ruler:** Louis XIV **Mint:** Aix **Note:** Mint mark: Ampersand.

Date	Mintage	VG	F	VF	XF	Unc
1689	—	2,500	5,000	9,000	13,500	—

KM# 262.1 1/2 ECU
13.5440 g., 0.9170 Silver 0.3993 oz. ASW **Ruler:** Louis XIV
Obv: Draped bust right **Rev:** Crowned quartered shield of Frand and New and Old Burgundy **Edge Lettering:** DOMINE SALVUM FAC REGEM CHRISTIANISSIMVM **Mint:** Paris

Date	Mintage	VG	F	VF	XF	Unc
1685A	—	275	675	1,350	2,250	—
1686A	—	300	750	1,500	2,500	—

KM# 262.2 1/2 ECU
13.5440 g., 0.9170 Silver 0.3993 oz. ASW **Ruler:** Louis XIV
Mint: Lille

Date	Mintage	VG	F	VF	XF	Unc
1686IL	—	275	675	1,350	2,250	—

KM# 262.3 1/2 ECU
13.5440 g., 0.9170 Silver 0.3993 oz. ASW **Ruler:** Louis XIV
Mint: Amiens

Date	Mintage	VG	F	VF	XF	Unc
1685X	—	300	750	1,500	2,500	—
1686X	—	300	750	1,500	2,500	—

KM# 262.4 1/2 ECU
13.5440 g., 0.9170 Silver 0.3993 oz. ASW **Ruler:** Louis XIV
Mint: Lille **Note:** Mint mark: Crowned L.

Date	Mintage	VG	F	VF	XF	Unc
1686	—	300	750	1,500	2,500	—
1687	—	275	675	1,350	2,250	—
1688	—	325	825	1,650	2,750	—
1689	94,000	—	—	—	—	—

KM# 273.1 1/2 ECU
13.5440 g., 0.9170 Silver 0.3993 oz. ASW **Ruler:** Louis XIV
Obv: Draped bust right **Rev:** Cruciform eight L's with crown at each end, fleur-de-lis in angles **Mint:** Paris

Date	Mintage	VG	F	VF	XF	Unc
1690A	—	35.00	90.00	200	450	—
1691A	—	35.00	90.00	200	450	—
1692A	—	50.00	135	300	675	—
1693A	—	50.00	135	300	675	—

KM# 273.2 1/2 ECU
13.5440 g., 0.9170 Silver 0.3993 oz. ASW **Ruler:** Louis XIV
Mint: Rouen

Date	Mintage	VG	F	VF	XF	Unc
1690B	—	40.00	100	225	500	—
1691B	—	45.00	110	250	550	—

KM# 273.3 1/2 ECU
13.5440 g., 0.9170 Silver 0.3993 oz. ASW **Ruler:** Louis XIV
Mint: Lyon

Date	Mintage	VG	F	VF	XF	Unc
1690D	—	40.00	100	225	500	—
1691D	—	45.00	110	250	550	—
1692D	—	—	—	—	—	—
1693D	—	—	—	—	—	—

KM# 273.4 1/2 ECU
13.5440 g., 0.9170 Silver 0.3993 oz. ASW **Ruler:** Louis XIV
Mint: Tours

Date	Mintage	VG	F	VF	XF	Unc
1690E	—	45.00	110	250	550	—
1691E	—	45.00	110	250	550	—

KM# 273.5 1/2 ECU
13.5440 g., 0.9170 Silver 0.3993 oz. ASW **Ruler:** Louis XIV
Mint: Poitiers

Date	Mintage	VG	F	VF	XF	Unc
1690G	—	60.00	150	325	725	—
1691G	—	100	200	420	950	—
1692G	—	60.00	150	325	725	—

KM# 273.6 1/2 ECU
13.5440 g., 0.9170 Silver 0.3993 oz. ASW **Ruler:** Louis XIV
Mint: La Rochelle

Date	Mintage	VG	F	VF	XF	Unc
1690H	—	60.00	150	325	725	—
1691H	—	60.00	150	325	725	—
1692H	—	60.00	150	325	725	—

KM# 273.7 1/2 ECU
13.5440 g., 0.9170 Silver 0.3993 oz. ASW **Ruler:** Louis XIV
Mint: Limoges

Date	Mintage	VG	F	VF	XF	Unc
1690I	—	60.00	150	325	725	—
1691I	—	45.00	110	250	550	—
1693I	—	—	—	—	—	—

KM# 273.8 1/2 ECU
13.5440 g., 0.9170 Silver 0.3993 oz. ASW **Ruler:** Louis XIV
Mint: Bordeaux

Date	Mintage	VG	F	VF	XF	Unc
1690K	—	60.00	150	325	725	—
1691K	—	45.00	110	250	550	—
1692K	—	60.00	150	325	725	—

KM# 273.9 1/2 ECU
13.5440 g., 0.9170 Silver 0.3993 oz. ASW **Ruler:** Louis XIV
Mint: Bayonne

Date	Mintage	VG	F	VF	XF	Unc
1690L	—	85.00	185	385	800	—
1691L	—	60.00	150	325	725	—

KM# 273.10 1/2 ECU
13.5440 g., 0.9170 Silver 0.3993 oz. ASW **Ruler:** Louis XIV
Mint: Toulouse

Date	Mintage	VG	F	VF	XF	Unc
1690M	—	60.00	150	325	725	—
1691M	—	35.00	90.00	200	450	—
1693M	—	60.00	150	325	725	—

KM# 273.11 1/2 ECU
13.5440 g., 0.9170 Silver 0.3993 oz. ASW **Ruler:** Louis XIV
Mint: Montpellier

Date	Mintage	VG	F	VF	XF	Unc
1690N	—	50.00	135	300	675	—
1691N	—	45.00	110	250	550	—
1692N	—	60.00	150	325	725	—
1693N	—	—	—	—	—	—

KM# 273.12 1/2 ECU
13.5440 g., 0.9170 Silver 0.3993 oz. ASW **Ruler:** Louis XIV
Mint: Riom

Date	Mintage	VG	F	VF	XF	Unc
1690O	—	—	—	—	—	—
1691O	—	50.00	135	300	675	—
1692O	—	60.00	150	325	725	—
1693O	—	—	—	—	—	—

KM# 273.13 1/2 ECU
13.5440 g., 0.9170 Silver 0.3993 oz. ASW **Ruler:** Louis XIV
Mint: Dijon

Date	Mintage	VG	F	VF	XF	Unc
1690P	—	60.00	150	325	725	—
1691P	—	60.00	150	325	725	—
1692P	—	60.00	150	325	725	—
1693P	—	—	—	—	—	—

KM# 273.14 1/2 ECU
13.5440 g., 0.9170 Silver 0.3993 oz. ASW **Ruler:** Louis XIV
Mint: Troyes

Date	Mintage	VG	F	VF	XF	Unc
1690S	—	60.00	150	325	725	—
1691S	—	60.00	150	325	725	—

KM# 273.15 1/2 ECU
13.5440 g., 0.9170 Silver 0.3993 oz. ASW **Ruler:** Louis XIV
Mint: Amiens

Date	Mintage	VG	F	VF	XF	Unc
1690X	—	60.00	150	325	725	—
1691X	—	50.00	135	300	675	—
1692X	—	60.00	150	325	725	—
1693X	—	60.00	150	325	725	—

KM# 273.16 1/2 ECU
13.5440 g., 0.9170 Silver 0.3993 oz. ASW **Ruler:** Louis XIV
Mint: Bourges

Date	Mintage	VG	F	VF	XF	Unc
1690Y	—	60.00	150	325	725	—
1691Y	—	60.00	150	325	725	—
1692Y	—	—	—	—	—	—
1693Y	—	—	—	—	—	—

KM# 273.17 1/2 ECU
13.5440 g., 0.9170 Silver 0.3993 oz. ASW **Ruler:** Louis XIV
Mint: Rennes **Note:** Mint mark: Numeral 9.

Date	Mintage	VG	F	VF	XF	Unc
1690	—	50.00	135	300	675	—
1691	—	40.00	110	245	550	—
1692	—	60.00	150	325	725	—

KM# 273.18 1/2 ECU
13.5440 g., 0.9170 Silver 0.3993 oz. ASW **Ruler:** Louis XIV
Mint: Aix **Note:** Mint mark: Ampersand.

Date	Mintage	VG	F	VF	XF	Unc
1690	—	45.00	110	250	600	—
1691	—	60.00	150	325	750	—

KM# 273.19 1/2 ECU
13.5440 g., 0.9170 Silver 0.3993 oz. ASW **Ruler:** Louis XIV
Mint: Lille **Note:** Mint mark: Crowned L.

Date	Mintage	VG	F	VF	XF	Unc
1690	—	40.00	100	235	550	—
1691	—	50.00	135	300	675	—
1692	—	—	—	—	—	—
1693	—	75.00	175	350	775	—

KM# 273.20 1/2 ECU
13.5440 g., 0.9170 Silver 0.3993 oz. ASW **Ruler:** Louis XIV
Mint: Toulouse **Note:** Mint mark: Crowned M.

Date	Mintage	VG	F	VF	XF	Unc
1691	—	60.00	150	325	725	—

KM# 273.21 1/2 ECU
13.5440 g., 0.9170 Silver 0.3993 oz. ASW **Ruler:** Louis XIV
Mint: Troyes **Note:** Mint mark: Crowned S.

Date	Mintage	VG	F	VF	XF	Unc
1690	—	60.00	150	325	725	—
1691	—	45.00	110	250	600	—
1692	—	60.00	150	325	725	—
1693	—	60.00	150	325	725	—

KM# 274 1/2 ECU
13.5440 g., 0.9170 Silver 0.3993 oz. ASW **Ruler:** Louis XIV
Mint: Pau

Date	Mintage	VG	F	VF	XF	Unc
1690	—	120	550	1,100	2,000	—
1691	—	120	550	1,100	2,100	—
1692	—	120	550	1,200	2,300	—

KM# 295.1 1/2 ECU
13.5440 g., 0.9170 Silver 0.3993 oz. ASW **Ruler:** Louis XIV
Obv: Mailed bust right **Rev:** Crowned circular shield of France dividing palm branches **Mint:** Paris

Date	Mintage	VG	F	VF	XF	Unc
1693A	—	35.00	90.00	200	450	—
1694A	—	40.00	100	225	500	—
1695A	—	30.00	75.00	200	400	—
1696A	—	40.00	100	225	500	—
1697A	—	45.00	110	250	550	—
1698A	—	—	—	—	—	—

KM# 295.2 1/2 ECU
13.5440 g., 0.9170 Silver 0.3993 oz. ASW **Ruler:** Louis XIV
Mint: Metz

Date	Mintage	VG	F	VF	XF	Unc
1693AA	—	75.00	175	350	775	—
1694AA	—	100	215	475	1,000	—
1695AA	—	50.00	135	300	675	—
1699AA	—	100	215	475	1,000	—

KM# 295.3 1/2 ECU
13.5440 g., 0.9170 Silver 0.3993 oz. ASW **Ruler:** Louis XIV
Mint: Rouen

Date	Mintage	VG	F	VF	XF	Unc
1693B	—	45.00	110	250	550	—
1694B	—	45.00	110	250	550	—
1697B	—	50.00	135	300	675	—
1698B	—	60.00	150	325	725	—

KM# 295.4 1/2 ECU
13.5440 g., 0.9170 Silver 0.3993 oz. ASW **Ruler:** Louis XIV
Mint: Strasbourg

Date	Mintage	VG	F	VF	XF	Unc
1694BB	—	60.00	150	325	725	—
1695BB	—	60.00	150	325	725	—

KM# 295.5 1/2 ECU
13.5440 g., 0.9170 Silver 0.3993 oz. ASW **Ruler:** Louis XIV
Mint: Caen

Date	Mintage	VG	F	VF	XF	Unc
1695C	—	60.00	150	325	725	—
1697C	—	—	—	—	—	—

KM# 295.6 1/2 ECU
13.5440 g., 0.9170 Silver 0.3993 oz. ASW **Ruler:** Louis XIV
Mint: Lyon

Date	Mintage	VG	F	VF	XF	Unc
1693D	—	40.00	100	225	500	—
1694D	—	30.00	75.00	165	450	—
1695D	—	45.00	110	250	550	—
1696D	—	—	—	—	—	—
1697D	—	—	—	—	—	—
1699D	—	—	—	—	—	—
1700D	—	—	—	—	—	—

KM# 295.7 1/2 ECU
13.5440 g., 0.9170 Silver 0.3993 oz. ASW **Ruler:** Louis XIV
Mint: Tours

Date	Mintage	VG	F	VF	XF	Unc
1694E	—	40.00	100	225	500	—
1695E	—	45.00	110	250	550	—
1696E	—	45.00	110	250	550	—
1697E	—	60.00	150	325	725	—

KM# 295.8 1/2 ECU
13.5440 g., 0.9170 Silver 0.3993 oz. ASW **Ruler:** Louis XIV
Mint: Poitiers

Date	Mintage	VG	F	VF	XF	Unc
1693G	—	50.00	135	300	675	—
1694G	—	50.00	135	300	675	—
1695G	—	45.00	110	250	550	—
1696G	—	60.00	150	325	725	—
1699G	—	60.00	150	325	725	—

KM# 295.9 1/2 ECU
13.5440 g., 0.9170 Silver 0.3993 oz. ASW **Ruler:** Louis XIV
Mint: La Rochelle

Date	Mintage	VG	F	VF	XF	Unc
1693H	—	40.00	100	225	500	—
1694H	—	45.00	110	250	550	—
1695H	—	45.00	110	250	550	—
1697H	—	60.00	150	325	725	—
1698H	—	60.00	150	325	725	—
1699H	—	70.00	200	380	900	—

KM# 295.10 1/2 ECU
13.5440 g., 0.9170 Silver 0.3993 oz. ASW **Ruler:** Louis XIV
Mint: Limoges

Date	Mintage	VG	F	VF	XF	Unc
1694I	—	60.00	150	325	725	—
1695I	—	125	300	700	1,500	—
1696I	—	60.00	150	325	725	—

KM# 295.11 1/2 ECU
13.5440 g., 0.9170 Silver 0.3993 oz. ASW **Ruler:** Louis XIV **Mint:** Bordeaux

Date	Mintage	VG	F	VF	XF	Unc
1693K	—	40.00	100	225	500	—
1694K	—	45.00	110	250	550	—
1695K	—	45.00	110	250	550	—
1697K	—	45.00	110	250	550	—
1698K	—	60.00	150	325	725	—

KM# 295.12 1/2 ECU
13.5440 g., 0.9170 Silver 0.3993 oz. ASW **Ruler:** Louis XIV **Mint:** Bayonne

Date	Mintage	VG	F	VF	XF	Unc
1694L	—	50.00	135	300	675	—
1700L	—	—	—	—	—	—

KM# 295.13 1/2 ECU
13.5440 g., 0.9170 Silver 0.3993 oz. ASW **Ruler:** Louis XIV **Mint:** Toulouse

Date	Mintage	VG	F	VF	XF	Unc
1694M	—	45.00	110	250	550	—
1695M	—	45.00	110	250	550	—
1696M	—	45.00	110	250	550	—

KM# 295.14 1/2 ECU
13.5440 g., 0.9170 Silver 0.3993 oz. ASW **Ruler:** Louis XIV **Mint:** Montpellier

Date	Mintage	VG	F	VF	XF	Unc
1693N	—	40.00	100	225	500	—
1694N	—	40.00	100	225	500	—
1695N	—	45.00	110	250	550	—
1696N	—	—	—	—	—	—
1697N	—	—	—	—	—	—
1699N	—	—	—	—	—	—

KM# 295.15 1/2 ECU
13.5440 g., 0.9170 Silver 0.3993 oz. ASW **Ruler:** Louis XIV **Mint:** Riom

Date	Mintage	VG	F	VF	XF	Unc
1693O	—	45.00	110	250	550	—
1694O	—	45.00	110	250	550	—
1697O	—	—	—	—	—	—

KM# 295.16 1/2 ECU
13.5440 g., 0.9170 Silver 0.3993 oz. ASW **Ruler:** Louis XIV **Mint:** Dijon

Date	Mintage	VG	F	VF	XF	Unc
1693P	—	40.00	100	225	500	—
1694P	—	40.00	100	225	500	—
1695P	—	40.00	100	225	500	—
1697P	—	—	—	—	—	—
1700P	—	—	—	—	—	—

KM# 295.18 1/2 ECU
13.5440 g., 0.9170 Silver 0.3993 oz. ASW **Ruler:** Louis XIV **Mint:** Troyes

Date	Mintage	VG	F	VF	XF	Unc
1693S	—	35.00	90.00	200	450	—
1694S	—	40.00	100	225	500	—
1697S	—	60.00	150	325	725	—

KM# 295.19 1/2 ECU
13.5440 g., 0.9170 Silver 0.3993 oz. ASW **Ruler:** Louis XIV **Mint:** Nantes

Date	Mintage	VG	F	VF	XF	Unc
1693T	—	45.00	110	250	550	—
1694T	—	40.00	100	225	500	—
1695T	—	45.00	110	250	550	—
1696T	—	45.00	110	250	550	—
1697T	—	45.00	110	250	550	—
1698T	—	50.00	135	300	675	—

KM# 295.20 1/2 ECU
13.5440 g., 0.9170 Silver 0.3993 oz. ASW **Ruler:** Louis XIV **Mint:** Troyes

Date	Mintage	VG	F	VF	XF	Unc
1693V	—	50.00	135	300	675	—
1694V	—	40.00	100	225	500	—
1695V	—	—	—	—	—	—
1696V	—	50.00	135	300	675	—
1697V	—	60.00	150	325	725	—
1698V	—	—	—	—	—	—
1699V	—	75.00	175	350	775	—

KM# 295.21 1/2 ECU
13.5440 g., 0.9170 Silver 0.3993 oz. ASW **Ruler:** Louis XIV **Mint:** Lille

Date	Mintage	VG	F	VF	XF	Unc
1693W	—	40.00	100	225	550	—
1694W	—	40.00	100	225	550	—
1695W	—	40.00	100	225	550	—
1696W	—	—	—	—	—	—
1697W	—	—	—	—	—	—
1698W	—	—	—	—	—	—
1699W	—	60.00	150	325	725	—
1700W	—	80.00	200	500	1,800	—

KM# 295.22 1/2 ECU
13.5440 g., 0.9170 Silver 0.3993 oz. ASW **Ruler:** Louis XIV **Mint:** Amiens

Date	Mintage	VG	F	VF	XF	Unc
1693X	—	40.00	100	225	500	—
1694X	—	40.00	100	225	500	—
1695X	—	40.00	100	230	520	—
1696X	—	50.00	135	300	675	—

KM# 295.23 1/2 ECU
13.5440 g., 0.9170 Silver 0.3993 oz. ASW **Ruler:** Louis XIV **Mint:** Bourges

Date	Mintage	VG	F	VF	XF	Unc
1693Y	—	50.00	135	300	675	—
1694Y	—	50.00	135	300	675	—
1699Y	—	60.00	150	325	725	—

KM# 295.24 1/2 ECU
13.5440 g., 0.9170 Silver 0.3993 oz. ASW **Ruler:** Louis XIV **Mint:** Aix **Note:** Mint mark: Ampersand.

Date	Mintage	VG	F	VF	XF	Unc
1693	—	50.00	135	300	675	—
1694	—	40.00	100	225	500	—

KM# 295.25 1/2 ECU
13.5440 g., 0.9170 Silver 0.3993 oz. ASW **Ruler:** Louis XIV **Mint:** Rennes **Note:** Mint mark: Numeral 9.

Date	Mintage	VG	F	VF	XF	Unc
1693	—	45.00	110	250	550	—
1694	—	40.00	100	225	500	—
1695	—	35.00	90.00	200	450	—
1696	—	60.00	150	325	725	—

KM# 295.26 1/2 ECU
13.5440 g., 0.9170 Silver 0.3993 oz. ASW **Ruler:** Louis XIV **Mint:** Metz **Note:** Mint mark: Crowned M.

Date	Mintage	VG	F	VF	XF	Unc
1693	—	40.00	100	225	500	—

KM# 295.27 1/2 ECU
13.5440 g., 0.9170 Silver 0.3993 oz. ASW **Ruler:** Louis XIV **Mint:** Troyes **Note:** Mint mark: Crowned S.

Date	Mintage	VG	F	VF	XF	Unc
1693	—	100	200	450	1,000	—

KM# 295.28 1/2 ECU
13.5440 g., 0.9170 Silver 0.3993 oz. ASW **Ruler:** Louis XIV **Mint:** Besançon **Note:** Mint mark: Back-to-back C's.

Date	Mintage	VG	F	VF	XF	Unc
1694	—	45.00	110	250	550	—
1695	—	60.00	150	325	725	—
1696	—	—	—	—	—	—
1697	—	—	—	—	—	—
1698	—	—	—	—	—	—
1699	—	60.00	150	325	725	—

KM# 296 1/2 ECU
13.5440 g., 0.9170 Silver 0.3993 oz. ASW **Ruler:** Louis XIV **Rev:** Crowned circular shield of France, Navarre and Berne between palm branches **Mint:** Pau

Date	Mintage	VG	F	VF	XF	Unc
1693	—	1,050	1,900	3,150	5,600	—
1694	—	1,050	1,900	3,150	5,600	—
1695	—	1,050	1,900	3,150	5,600	—
1696	—	—	—	—	—	—
1697	—	1,050	1,900	3,150	5,600	—
1698	—	—	—	—	—	—
1700	—	—	—	—	—	—

KM# 297 1/2 ECU
13.5440 g., 0.9170 Silver 0.3993 oz. ASW **Ruler:** Louis XIV **Rev:** Crowned quartered shield of France, Navarre and Old and New Burgundy between palm branches **Mint:** Lille

Date	Mintage	VG	F	VF	XF	Unc
1693W	—	225	575	1,450	2,500	—
1694W	—	200	475	1,250	2,250	—
1695W	—	275	650	1,650	2,750	—
1696W	—	275	650	1,650	2,750	—
1697W	—	—	—	—	—	—
1699W	—	350	850	2,000	3,250	—

KM# 308 1/2 ECU
15.3340 g., 0.8330 Silver 0.4107 oz. ASW **Ruler:** Louis XIV **Obv:** Large fleur-de-lis **Rev:** Crowned shield of France **Mint:** Strasbourg

Date	Mintage	VG	F	VF	XF	Unc
1694BB	—	65.00	130	325	550	—
1695BB	—	80.00	160	400	700	—
1696BB	—	85.00	175	425	750	—
1697BB	—	100	220	490	850	—

KM# 120.1 ECU
Silver **Ruler:** Louis XIII **Obv:** Bust with bare neck **Rev:** Rose above crown **Mint:** Paris **Note:** Dav. #3796.

Date	Mintage	VG	F	VF	XF	Unc
1641A	—	3,000	5,000	9,000	15,000	—
1642A	—	850	2,000	4,000	8,000	—

KM# 120.2 ECU
Silver **Ruler:** Louis XIII **Rev:** Rose flanked by points above crown

Date	Mintage	VG	F	VF	XF	Unc
1642	—	850	2,000	4,000	8,000	—

KM# 120.3 ECU
Silver **Ruler:** Louis XIII **Rev:** Point above crown

Date	Mintage	VG	F	VF	XF	Unc
1642	—	850	2,000	4,000	8,000	—

KM# 129.1 ECU
Silver **Ruler:** Louis XIII **Obv:** Draped bust **Rev:** Point above crown **Note:** Dav. #3797.

Date	Mintage	VG	F	VF	XF	Unc
1642	—	500	1,000	2,400	4,500	—
1643	—	400	800	1,900	3,500	—

KM# 129.2 ECU
Silver **Ruler:** Louis XIII **Rev:** Rose above crown

Date	Mintage	VG	F	VF	XF	Unc
1643	—	400	800	1,900	3,500	—

KM# 129.3 ECU
Silver **Ruler:** Louis XIII **Rev:** Three points above crown **Mint:** Lyon

Date	Mintage	VG	F	VF	XF	Unc
1643D	—	700	1,350	2,750	4,500	—
1643D With reverse mint mark	—	750	1,500	3,000	5,000	—

KM# 144.1 ECU
Silver **Ruler:** Louis XIV **Obv:** Bust with short curl **Rev:** Rose above crown **Mint:** Paris

Date	Mintage	VG	F	VF	XF	Unc
1643A	—	125	250	500	950	—
1644A	—	100	225	450	900	—
1645A	—	150	325	650	1,200	—

KM# 144.2 ECU
Silver **Ruler:** Louis XIV **Rev:** Rose flanked by points above crown **Mint:** Paris

Date	Mintage	VG	F	VF	XF	Unc
1644A	—	125	250	500	950	—
1645A	—	135	275	550	1,000	—

KM# 144.3 ECU

Silver **Ruler:** Louis XIV **Rev:** Point above crown **Mint:** Paris

Date	Mintage	VG	F	VF	XF	Unc
1643A	—	135	275	650	1,000	—
1644A	—	125	250	600	1,000	—
1645A	—	100	200	400	900	—

KM# 144.4 ECU

Silver **Ruler:** Louis XIV **Mint:** Lyon

Date	Mintage	VG	F	VF	XF	Unc
1643D	—	—	—	—	—	—
1644D	—	225	450	850	1,600	—
1645D	—	250	500	950	1,750	—

KM# 155.1 ECU

Silver **Ruler:** Louis XIV **Obv:** Bust with long curl **Mint:** Paris **Note:** Dav. #3799.

Date	Mintage	VG	F	VF	XF	Unc
1646A	—	75.00	150	300	725	—
1647A	—	250	450	800	1,800	—
1648A	—	—	—	—	—	—
1649A	—	60.00	125	250	575	—
1651A	—	50.00	100	200	550	—
1652A	—	40.00	80.00	165	500	—
1653A	—	50.00	100	200	550	—

KM# 155.2 ECU

Silver **Ruler:** Louis XIV **Mint:** Rouen

Date	Mintage	VG	F	VF	XF	Unc
1646B	—	65.00	135	275	625	—
1647B	—	60.00	125	250	575	—
1648B	—	55.00	115	225	550	—
1651B	—	50.00	100	200	500	—
1652B	—	50.00	100	200	500	—
1653B	—	60.00	125	250	575	—

KM# 155.3 ECU

Silver **Ruler:** Louis XIV **Mint:** Saint Lô

Date	Mintage	VG	F	VF	XF	Unc
1648C Rare	—	—	—	—	—	—
1651C Rare	—	—	—	—	—	—

KM# 155.4 ECU

Silver **Ruler:** Louis XIV **Mint:** Lyon

Date	Mintage	VG	F	VF	XF	Unc
1652D	—	65.00	135	275	625	—

KM# 155.5 ECU

Silver **Ruler:** Louis XIV **Mint:** Angers

Date	Mintage	VG	F	VF	XF	Unc
1647F	—	85.00	175	350	775	—
1648F	—	65.00	135	275	625	—
1649F	—	275	500	1,100	2,150	—
1653F	—	180	325	625	1,450	—

KM# 155.6 ECU

Silver **Ruler:** Louis XIV **Mint:** Poitiers

Date	Mintage	VG	F	VF	XF	Unc
1647G	—	85.00	175	350	725	—
1648G	—	85.00	175	350	725	—
1649G	—	85.00	175	350	725	—
1650G	—	85.00	175	350	725	—

KM# 155.7 ECU

Silver **Ruler:** Louis XIV **Mint:** La Rochelle

Date	Mintage	VG	F	VF	XF	Unc
1646H	—	85.00	175	350	750	—
1647H	—	65.00	135	275	625	—
1648H	—	85.00	175	350	750	—
1649H	—	65.00	135	275	625	—

KM# 155.8 ECU

Silver **Ruler:** Louis XIV **Mint:** Limoges

Date	Mintage	VG	F	VF	XF	Unc
1652I	—	65.00	135	275	625	—
1653I	—	65.00	135	275	625	—

KM# 155.9 ECU

Silver **Ruler:** Louis XIV **Mint:** Bordeaux

Date	Mintage	VG	F	VF	XF	Unc
1647K	—	65.00	135	275	625	—
1648K	—	75.00	150	300	700	—
1649K	—	65.00	135	275	625	—
1650K	—	250	450	800	1,800	—
1651K	—	85.00	175	350	750	—
1652K	—	65.00	135	275	625	—
1653K	—	90.00	185	375	850	—
1654K	—	250	450	800	1,800	—

KM# 155.10 ECU

Silver **Ruler:** Louis XIV **Mint:** Bayonne

Date	Mintage	VG	F	VF	XF	Unc
1652L	—	65.00	135	275	625	—
1653L	—	65.00	135	275	625	—
1654L	—	200	375	675	1,600	—
1659L	—	85.00	175	350	750	—

KM# 155.11 ECU

Silver **Ruler:** Louis XIV **Mint:** Toulouse

Date	Mintage	VG	F	VF	XF	Unc
1647M	—	65.00	135	275	625	—
1648M	—	60.00	125	250	575	—
1649M	—	250	450	825	1,850	—
1651M	—	250	450	800	1,800	—
1652M	—	65.00	135	275	625	—
1653M	—	65.00	135	275	625	—
1654M	—	250	450	825	1,850	—

KM# 155.12 ECU

Silver **Ruler:** Louis XIV **Mint:** Montpellier

Date	Mintage	VG	F	VF	XF	Unc
1647	—	180	325	750	1,450	—
1648	—	65.00	135	275	650	—
1649	—	65.00	135	275	650	—
1650	—	250	450	800	1,800	—
1651	—	—	—	—	—	—
1652	—	—	—	—	—	—
1652	—	90.00	185	375	850	—

KM# 155.13 ECU

Silver **Ruler:** Louis XIV **Mint:** Riom

Date	Mintage	VG	F	VF	XF	Unc
1652O	—	250	450	800	1,800	—
1653O	—	250	450	800	1,800	—

KM# 155.14 ECU

Silver **Ruler:** Louis XIV **Mint:** Dijon

Date	Mintage	VG	F	VF	XF	Unc
1651P	—	275	500	900	2,100	—
1652P	—	60.00	125	250	575	—
1653P	—	85.00	175	350	750	—

KM# 155.15 ECU

Silver **Ruler:** Louis XIV **Mint:** Troyes

Date	Mintage	VG	F	VF	XF	Unc
1651S	—	85.00	175	350	750	—
1652S	—	60.00	125	250	575	—
1653S	—	65.00	135	275	625	—

KM# 155.16 ECU

Silver **Ruler:** Louis XIV **Mint:** Nantes

Date	Mintage	VG	F	VF	XF	Unc
1647T	—	85.00	175	350	750	—
1648T	—	65.00	135	275	625	—
1649T	—	60.00	125	250	575	—
1650T	—	550	950	1,800	3,800	—
1651T	—	—	—	—	—	—
1652T	—	65.00	135	275	625	—
1653T	—	85.00	175	350	750	—

KM# 155.17 ECU

Silver **Ruler:** Louis XIV **Mint:** Amiens

Date	Mintage	VG	F	VF	XF	Unc
1652X	—	60.00	125	250	575	—
1653X	—	65.00	135	275	625	—

KM# 155.18 ECU

Silver **Ruler:** Louis XIV **Mint:** Aix **Note:** Mint mark: Ampersand.

Date	Mintage	VG	F	VF	XF	Unc
1647	—	250	450	800	1,800	—
1648	—	65.00	135	275	625	—
1649	—	65.00	135	275	625	—
1652	—	65.00	135	275	625	—
1653	—	65.00	135	275	625	—
1654	—	—	—	—	—	—

KM# 155.19 ECU

Silver **Ruler:** Louis XIV **Mint:** Rennes **Note:** Mint mark: Numeral 9.

Date	Mintage	VG	F	VF	XF	Unc
1648	—	65.00	135	275	625	—
1652	—	60.00	125	250	575	—
1653	—	55.00	120	225	500	—

KM# 181.1 ECU

Silver **Ruler:** Louis XIV **Rev:** Crowned arms of France, Navarre and Bearn **Mint:** Pau **Note:** Dav. #3801.

Date	Mintage	VG	F	VF	XF	Unc
1650	—	225	400	875	2,700	—
1651	—	225	400	875	2,700	—
1652	—	225	400	875	2,700	—
1653	—	225	400	875	2,700	—
1654	—	275	475	1,050	3,300	—
1655	—	275	475	1,050	3,300	—
1656	—	275	475	1,050	3,300	—
1657	—	300	500	1,150	3,500	—
1658	—	300	500	1,150	3,500	—
1660	—	275	475	1,050	3,300	—
1662	—	300	500	1,150	3,500	—

KM# 181.2 ECU

Silver **Ruler:** Louis XIV **Mint:** Saint Palais

Date	Mintage	VG	F	VF	XF	Unc
1652	—	300	500	1,400	4,500	—

KM# 181.3 ECU

Silver **Ruler:** Louis XIV **Mint:** Toulouse

Date	Mintage	VG	F	VF	XF	Unc
1652M	—	275	425	1,200	3,900	—
1653M	—	275	425	1,200	3,900	—
1654M	—	275	475	1,250	4,100	—
1655M	—	275	425	1,200	3,900	—
1656M	—	250	425	1,150	3,600	—
1657M	—	275	425	1,200	3,900	—
1658M	—	275	475	1,250	4,100	—
1659M	—	275	425	1,200	3,900	—
1660M	—	275	425	1,200	3,900	—
1661M	—	275	425	1,200	3,900	—
1662M	—	275	425	1,200	3,900	—

KM# 180 ECU

Silver **Ruler:** Louis XIV **Rev:** Crowned arms of France and Navarre **Mint:** Saint Palais **Note:** Issued for Navarre. Dav. #3800.

Date	Mintage	VG	F	VF	XF	Unc
1652	—	270	475	850	1,600	—
1653	—	270	475	850	1,600	—
1654	—	300	500	900	1,750	—
1655	—	270	475	850	1,600	—
1656	—	300	500	900	1,750	—
1657	—	270	475	850	1,600	—
1658	—	300	500	900	1,750	—
1659	—	325	550	950	1,850	—
1660	—	300	500	900	1,750	—
1661	—	300	500	900	1,750	—
1662	—	350	600	1,000	2,000	—

KM# 211.1 ECU

Silver **Ruler:** Louis XIV **Obv:** Draped bust **Rev:** Crowned arms of France **Mint:** Paris **Note:** Dav. #3802.

Date	Mintage	VG	F	VF	XF	Unc
1662A	—	155	295	575	1,050	—
1663A	—	130	260	525	975	—
1664A	—	155	295	575	1,050	—
1665A	—	200	300	600	—	—
1666A	—	130	260	525	975	—
1670A	—	130	260	525	975	—
1672A	—	130	260	525	975	—

KM# 211.2 ECU

Silver **Ruler:** Louis XIV **Mint:** Rouen

Date	Mintage	VG	F	VF	XF	Unc
1664B	—	145	270	550	1,200	—

KM# 211.3 ECU

Silver **Ruler:** Louis XIV **Mint:** Bayonne

Date	Mintage	VG	F	VF	XF	Unc
1663L	—	120	240	475	975	—
1664L	—	120	240	475	975	—

KM# 211.4 ECU

Silver **Ruler:** Louis XIV **Mint:** Nantes

Date	Mintage	VG	F	VF	XF	Unc
1663T	—	—	—	—	—	—

KM# 211.5 ECU

Silver **Ruler:** Louis XIV **Mint:** Rennes **Note:** Mint marl: Numeral 9.

Date	Mintage	VG	F	VF	XF	Unc
1663	—	185	350	650	1,250	—
1664	—	90.00	185	375	700	—
1665	—	120	225	450	900	—

KM# 216 ECU

Silver **Ruler:** Louis XIV **Rev:** Crowned arms of France, Navarre and Bearn **Mint:** Pau **Note:** Dav. #3804.

Date	Mintage	VG	F	VF	XF	Unc
1663	—	300	525	1,450	3,500	—
1664	—	265	450	1,250	3,000	—
1665	—	265	450	1,250	3,000	—
1666	—	300	525	1,450	3,500	—
1667	—	225	425	1,150	2,700	—
1668	—	300	525	1,450	3,500	—
1669	—	300	525	1,450	3,500	—
1670	—	425	675	1,800	4,700	—
1671	—	425	675	1,800	4,700	—
1672	—	425	675	1,800	4,700	—
1673	—	375	650	1,750	4,400	—
1674	—	225	425	1,150	2,700	—
1675	—	225	425	1,150	2,700	—
1676	—	350	600	1,600	4,100	—
1679	—	265	450	1,250	3,000	—
1680	—	425	675	1,800	4,700	—

KM# 215 ECU

Silver **Ruler:** Louis XIV **Rev:** Crowned arms of France and Navarre **Mint:** Saint Palais **Note:** Dav. #3803.

Date	Mintage	VG	F	VF	XF	Unc
1664	—	650	1,100	1,950	3,750	—
1665	—	650	1,000	1,800	3,550	—
1666	—	—	—	—	—	—
1667	—	650	1,100	1,800	3,750	—
1668	—	650	1,100	1,800	3,750	—
1669	—	700	1,200	2,500	4,800	—
1670	—	650	1,100	1,800	3,750	—
1671	—	650	1,000	1,800	3,550	—

KM# 214.1 ECU

Silver **Ruler:** Louis XIV **Obv:** Modified draped bust **Mint:** Rouen **Note:** Dav. #3802A.

Date	Mintage	VG	F	VF	XF	Unc
1665B	—	125	275	1,000	1,500	—

KM# 214.2 ECU

Silver **Ruler:** Louis XIV **Mint:** Bayonne

Date	Mintage	VG	F	VF	XF	Unc
1665L	—	90.00	185	375	700	—
1666L	—	100	200	400	750	—
1667L	—	100	200	400	750	—
1668L	—	100	200	400	750	—
1669L	—	100	200	400	750	—
1670L	—	100	200	400	750	—
1671L	—	120	225	450	800	—
1672L	—	90.00	185	375	650	—

KM# 214.3 ECU

Silver **Ruler:** Louis XIV **Mint:** Aix **Note:** Mint mark: Ampersand.

Date	Mintage	VG	F	VF	XF	Unc
1666	—	120	225	450	800	—
1667	—	90.00	185	375	650	—
1668	—	120	225	475	850	—
1669	—	90.00	185	375	650	—
1670	—	120	225	450	800	—
1671	—	125	250	500	900	—
1672	—	180	325	625	1,200	—

KM# 214.4 ECU

Silver **Ruler:** Louis XIV **Mint:** Rennes **Note:** Mint mark: Numeral 9.

Date	Mintage	VG	F	VF	XF	Unc
1665	—	90.00	185	375	650	—
1666	—	120	225	450	800	—
1667	—	100	200	400	750	—
1668	—	75.00	150	300	600	—
1669	—	120	225	450	800	—
1670	—	75.00	150	300	600	—
1671	—	90.00	185	375	650	—
1672	—	120	225	450	800	—
1673	—	150	275	500	900	—
1674	—	—	—	—	—	—
1675	—	—	—	—	—	—
1676	—	180	325	625	1,150	—

KM# 226.1 ECU

Silver **Ruler:** Louis XIV **Obv:** "Parliamentary" bust in armor **Rev:** Crowned arms of France **Mint:** Paris **Note:** Dav. #3805.

Date	Mintage	VG	F	VF	XF	Unc
1672A	—	250	450	1,450	2,700	—
1673A	—	100	200	400	1,000	—
1674A	—	—	—	—	—	—
1675A	—	225	400	700	1,550	—
1676A	—	180	325	625	1,450	—
1677A	—	250	450	1,450	2,700	—
1678A	—	250	450	1,100	2,200	—
1679A	—	100	200	400	1,000	—
1680A	—	180	325	625	1,450	—
1682A	—	180	325	625	1,450	—
1683A	—	250	450	1,200	2,400	—

KM# 226.2 ECU

Silver **Ruler:** Louis XIV **Mint:** Rouen

Date	Mintage	VG	F	VF	XF	Unc
1679B	—	250	425	750	1,800	—
1680B	—	225	400	700	1,650	—
1682B	—	—	—	—	—	—
1683B	—	275	500	900	2,200	—

KM# 226.3 ECU

Silver **Ruler:** Louis XIV **Mint:** Lyon

Date	Mintage	VG	F	VF	XF	Unc
1676D	—	—	—	—	—	—
1681D	—	—	—	—	—	—

KM# 226.4 ECU

Silver **Ruler:** Louis XIV **Mint:** Tours

Date	Mintage	VG	F	VF	XF	Unc
1679E	—	180	325	700	1,650	—
1680E	—	225	400	700	1,650	—

KM# 226.5 ECU

Silver **Ruler:** Louis XIV **Mint:** La Rochelle

Date	Mintage	VG	F	VF	XF	Unc
1680H	—	225	400	700	1,750	—

KM# 226.6 ECU

Silver **Ruler:** Louis XIV **Mint:** Limoges

Date	Mintage	VG	F	VF	XF	Unc
1679I	—	225	400	700	1,650	—
1680I	—	250	450	800	1,950	—
1681I	—	250	450	800	1,950	—

KM# 226.7 ECU

Silver **Ruler:** Louis XIV **Mint:** Bordeaux

Date	Mintage	VG	F	VF	XF	Unc
1679K	—	180	325	625	1,450	—
1680K	—	225	400	700	1,650	—
1681K	—	225	400	700	1,650	—
1682K	—	225	400	700	1,650	—
1683K	—	180	325	625	1,450	—

KM# 226.8 ECU

Silver **Ruler:** Louis XIV **Mint:** Bayonne

Date	Mintage	VG	F	VF	XF	Unc
1673L	—	180	325	625	1,450	—
1674L	—	250	450	800	2,000	—
1675L	—	225	400	700	1,650	—
1676L	—	180	325	625	1,450	—
1677L	—	250	425	750	1,750	—
1678L	—	225	400	700	1,650	—
1679L	—	135	275	550	1,250	—
1680L	—	135	275	550	1,250	—
1681L	—	135	275	550	1,250	—
1682L	—	135	275	550	1,250	—
1683L	—	135	275	550	1,250	—
1684L	—	225	400	700	1,650	—

KM# 226.9 ECU

Silver **Ruler:** Louis XIV **Mint:** Montpellier

Date	Mintage	VG	F	VF	XF	Unc
1680N	—	250	600	1,400	2,800	—

KM# 226.10 ECU

Silver **Ruler:** Louis XIV **Mint:** Reims

Date	Mintage	VG	F	VF	XF	Unc
1680S	—	250	450	900	2,100	—
1681S	—	225	400	800	1,750	—
1682S	—	—	—	—	—	—
1683S	—	250	450	800	1,950	—

KM# 226.11 ECU

Silver **Ruler:** Louis XIV **Mint:** Amiens

Date	Mintage	VG	F	VF	XF	Unc
1679X	—	180	325	625	1,450	—
1680X	—	225	400	700	1,700	—
1681X	—	135	275	550	1,250	—
1682X	—	300	625	1,150	2,700	—
1683X	—	—	—	—	—	—

KM# 226.12 ECU

Silver **Ruler:** Louis XIV **Mint:** Aix **Note:** Mint mark: Ampersand.

Date	Mintage	VG	F	VF	XF	Unc
1679	—	180	325	625	1,450	—
1680	—	180	325	625	1,450	—
1681	—	225	400	700	1,650	—
1683	—	225	400	700	1,650	—

KM# 226.13 ECU

Silver **Ruler:** Louis XIV **Mint:** Rennes **Note:** Mint mark: Numeral 9.

Date	Mintage	VG	F	VF	XF	Unc
1673	—	135	275	550	1,250	—
1677	—	—	—	—	—	—
1679	—	135	275	550	1,250	—
1680	—	135	275	550	1,250	—
1681	—	225	400	700	1,650	—
1682	—	125	250	500	1,150	—
1683	—	135	275	550	1,250	—

KM# 227 ECU

Silver **Ruler:** Louis XIV **Obv:** "Parliamentary" bust in armor **Rev:** Crowned arms of France and Navarre **Mint:** Saint Palais **Note:** Dav. #3806.

Date	Mintage	VG	F	VF	XF	Unc
1672 Rare	—	—	10,000	22,000	33,000	—

KM# 252 ECU

Silver **Ruler:** Louis XIV **Obv:** Older bust **Rev:** Crowned arms of France, Navarre and Bearn **Mint:** Pau **Note:** Dav. #3807.

Date	Mintage	VG	F	VF	XF	Unc
1680	—	500	950	3,500	9,000	—
1681	—	450	850	3,250	9,000	—
1682	—	450	850	3,250	9,000	—
1683	—	450	850	3,250	9,000	—
1684	—	800	1,500	5,000	12,000	—
1685	—	800	1,500	5,000	12,000	—
1686	—	850	1,800	6,000	14,000	—

KM# 253.1 ECU

Silver **Ruler:** Louis XIV **Obv:** Older, heavier bust right **Rev:** Crowned French arms **Mint:** Paris **Note:** Dav. #3808.

Date	Mintage	VG	F	VF	XF	Unc
1683A	—	350	775	1,800	4,200	—
1684A	—	450	1,000	1,950	4,500	—

KM# 253.3 ECU

Silver **Ruler:** Louis XIV **Mint:** Bordeaux

Date	Mintage	VG	F	VF	XF	Unc
1684K	—	—	—	—	—	—

KM# 253.4 ECU

Silver **Ruler:** Louis XIV **Mint:** Aix **Note:** Mint mark: Ampersand.

Date	Mintage	VG	F	VF	XF	Unc
1684	—	—	—	—	—	—

KM# 253.5 ECU

Silver **Ruler:** Louis XIV **Mint:** Rennes **Note:** Mint mark: Numeral 9.

Date	Mintage	VG	F	VF	XF	Unc
1683	—	350	775	1,500	3,200	—
1684	—	350	775	1,500	3,200	—
1685	—	400	900	1,700	3,600	—

KM# 255.1 ECU

Silver **Ruler:** Louis XIV **Obv:** Bust right with open throat and less draping **Mint:** Paris **Note:** Dav. #3809.

Date	Mintage	VG	F	VF	XF	Unc
1684A	—	1,050	1,950	3,600	6,200	—
1685A	—	975	1,750	3,300	5,500	—
1686A	—	725	1,300	2,600	4,900	—
1687A	—	1,050	1,950	3,600	6,200	—
1688A	—	—	—	—	—	—
1689A	—	1,050	1,950	3,600	6,200	—

KM# 255.2 ECU

Silver **Ruler:** Louis XIV **Mint:** Lyon

Date	Mintage	VG	F	VF	XF	Unc
1689D	—	1,150	2,150	4,100	6,800	—

KM# 255.3 ECU

Silver **Ruler:** Louis XIV **Mint:** Bordeaux

Date	Mintage	VG	F	VF	XF	Unc
1685K	—	—	—	—	—	—
1686K	—	—	—	—	—	—
1687K	—	—	—	—	—	—
1688K	—	1,150	2,150	4,100	6,800	—

KM# 255.4 ECU

Silver **Ruler:** Louis XIV **Mint:** Bayonne

Date	Mintage	VG	F	VF	XF	Unc
1685L	—	725	1,300	2,600	4,900	—
1686L	—	1,050	1,950	3,600	6,200	—
1687L	—	—	—	—	—	—
1688L	—	1,200	2,500	4,500	7,500	—
1689L	—	1,050	1,950	3,600	6,200	—

KM# 255.5 ECU

Silver **Ruler:** Louis XIV **Mint:** Amiens

Date	Mintage	VG	F	VF	XF	Unc
1685X	—	1,300	3,000	5,700	10,000	—

KM# 255.6 ECU

Silver **Ruler:** Louis XIV **Mint:** Aix **Note:** Mint mark: Ampersand.

Date	Mintage	VG	F	VF	XF	Unc
1687	—	—	—	—	—	—
1688	—	—	—	—	—	—
1689	—	1,350	2,550	4,700	8,100	—

KM# 255.7 ECU

Silver **Ruler:** Louis XIV **Mint:** Rennes **Note:** Mint mark: Numeral 9.

Date	Mintage	VG	F	VF	XF	Unc
1685	—	—	—	—	—	—
1686	—	1,050	1,950	3,600	6,200	—
1687	—	725	1,300	2,600	4,900	—
1688	—	—	—	—	—	—
1689	—	1,050	1,950	3,600	6,200	—

KM# 257.1 ECU

Silver **Ruler:** Louis XIV **Rev:** Crowned shield with arms of France and Old and New Burgundy **Mint:** Paris **Note:** Dav. #3810.

Date	Mintage	VG	F	VF	XF	Unc
1685A	—	650	1,250	2,500	5,000	—

KM# 257.2 ECU

Silver **Ruler:** Louis XIV **Mint:** Lille

Date	Mintage	VG	F	VF	XF	Unc
1686IL	—	650	1,250	3,000	6,200	—

KM# 257.3 ECU

Silver **Ruler:** Louis XIV **Mint:** Amiens

Date	Mintage	VG	F	VF	XF	Unc
1685X	—	1,000	2,500	4,500	8,000	—

KM# 275.1 ECU

Silver **Ruler:** Louis XIV **Obv:** Date below bust **Rev:** PD in center **Mint:** Paris **Note:** Values given for the Dav. #3811 issues are for examples struck over recalled Ecus. Clear examples of the new planchets command an average 20-30% premium. Dav. #3811.

Date	Mintage	VG	F	VF	XF	Unc
1690A	—	50.00	100	200	450	—
1691A	—	50.00	100	200	450	—
1692A	—	60.00	125	250	575	—
1693A	—	55.00	115	225	500	—

KM# 275.2 ECU

Silver **Ruler:** Louis XIV **Mint:** Rouen

Date	Mintage	VG	F	VF	XF	Unc
1690B	—	75.00	150	300	700	—
1691B	—	60.00	125	300	600	—
1692B	—	75.00	150	300	700	—
1693B	—	90.00	185	375	825	—

KM# 275.3 ECU

Silver **Ruler:** Louis XIV **Mint:** Lyon

Date	Mintage	VG	F	VF	XF	Unc
1690D	—	75.00	150	300	700	—
1691D	—	55.00	115	250	600	—
1692D	—	60.00	125	250	575	—
1693D	—	80.00	160	325	725	—

KM# 275.4 ECU

Silver **Ruler:** Louis XIV **Mint:** Tours

Date	Mintage	VG	F	VF	XF	Unc
1690E	—	55.00	115	225	500	—
1691E	—	60.00	125	250	525	—
1692E	—	75.00	150	300	575	—
1693E	—	—	—	—	—	—

KM# 275.5 ECU

Silver **Ruler:** Louis XIV **Mint:** Poitiers

Date	Mintage	VG	F	VF	XF	Unc
1690G	—	90.00	185	375	825	—
1691G	—	60.00	125	250	575	—
1692G	—	90.00	190	385	875	—

KM# 275.6 ECU

Silver **Ruler:** Louis XIV **Mint:** La Rochelle

Date	Mintage	VG	F	VF	XF	Unc
1690H	—	90.00	185	375	825	—
1691H	—	60.00	125	250	575	—
1692H	—	65.00	135	275	625	—
1693H	—	75.00	150	300	700	—

KM# 275.7 ECU

Silver **Ruler:** Louis XIV **Mint:** Limoges

Date	Mintage	VG	F	VF	XF	Unc
1690I	—	90.00	190	385	875	—
1691I	—	75.00	150	300	700	—
1692I	—	60.00	125	250	575	—
1693I	—	—	—	—	—	—

KM# 275.8 ECU

Silver **Ruler:** Louis XIV **Mint:** Bordeaux

Date	Mintage	VG	F	VF	XF	Unc
1690K	—	60.00	125	250	575	—
1691K	—	75.00	150	300	700	—
1692K	—	65.00	135	275	625	—
1693K	—	80.00	160	325	725	—

KM# 275.9 ECU

Silver **Ruler:** Louis XIV **Mint:** Bayonne

Date	Mintage	VG	F	VF	XF	Unc
1690L	—	60.00	125	250	575	—
1691L	—	75.00	150	300	700	—
1692L	—	90.00	190	385	875	—

KM# 275.10 ECU

Silver **Ruler:** Louis XIV **Mint:** Toulouse

Date	Mintage	VG	F	VF	XF	Unc
1690M	—	65.00	135	275	625	—
1691M	—	60.00	125	250	575	—
1692M	—	80.00	160	325	725	—
1693M	—	75.00	150	300	700	—

KM# 275.11 ECU

Silver **Ruler:** Louis XIV **Mint:** Montpellier

Date	Mintage	VG	F	VF	XF	Unc
1690N	—	60.00	125	250	575	—
1691N	—	55.00	115	225	500	—
1692N	—	75.00	150	300	700	—
1693N	—	90.00	190	385	875	—

KM# 275.12 ECU

Silver **Ruler:** Louis XIV **Mint:** Riom

Date	Mintage	VG	F	VF	XF	Unc
1691O	—	80.00	150	310	700	—
1692O	—	80.00	160	325	725	—
1693O	—	—	—	—	—	—

KM# 275.13 ECU

Silver **Ruler:** Louis XIV **Mint:** Dijon

Date	Mintage	VG	F	VF	XF	Unc
1690P	—	75.00	150	300	700	—
1691P	—	60.00	125	250	575	—
1692P	—	75.00	150	300	700	—
1693P	—	90.00	190	350	875	—

KM# 275.14 ECU

Silver **Ruler:** Louis XIV **Mint:** Reims

Date	Mintage	VG	F	VF	XF	Unc
1690S	—	55.00	115	225	500	—
1691S	—	55.00	115	225	500	—
1692S	—	75.00	150	300	700	—
1693S	—	—	—	—	—	—

KM# 275.15 ECU

Silver **Ruler:** Louis XIV **Mint:** Amiens

Date	Mintage	VG	F	VF	XF	Unc
1690X	—	50.00	100	200	450	—
1691X	—	55.00	115	225	500	—
1692X	—	65.00	135	275	625	—
1693X	—	75.00	150	300	700	—

KM# 275.16 ECU
Silver **Ruler:** Louis XIV **Mint:** Bourges

Date	Mintage	VG	F	VF	XF	Unc
1690Y	—	65.00	135	275	700	—
1691Y	—	75.00	150	300	750	—
1692Y	—	60.00	125	250	600	—
1693Y	—	75.00	150	300	750	—

KM# 275.17 ECU
Silver **Ruler:** Louis XIV **Mint:** Bayonne **Note:** Mint mark: Crowned L.

Date	Mintage	VG	F	VF	XF	Unc
1690	—	65.00	135	275	625	—
1691	—	65.00	135	275	625	—
1692	—	90.00	190	385	875	—

KM# 275.18 ECU
Silver **Ruler:** Louis XIV **Mint:** Metz **Note:** Mint mark: Crowned M.

Date	Mintage	VG	F	VF	XF	Unc
1690	—	65.00	135	275	625	—
1691	—	60.00	125	250	575	—
1693	—	90.00	190	385	875	—

KM# 275.19 ECU
Silver **Ruler:** Louis XIV **Mint:** Troyes **Note:** Mint mark: Crowned S.

Date	Mintage	VG	F	VF	XF	Unc
1690	—	60.00	125	250	575	—
1691	—	75.00	150	300	700	—

KM# 275.20 ECU
Silver **Ruler:** Louis XIV **Mint:** Aix **Note:** Mint mark: Ampersand.

Date	Mintage	VG	F	VF	XF	Unc
1690	—	60.00	125	250	575	—
1691	—	60.00	125	250	575	—
1692	—	65.00	135	275	625	—
1693	—	80.00	160	325	725	—

KM# 275.21 ECU
Silver **Ruler:** Louis XIV **Mint:** Rennes **Note:** Mint mark: Numeral 9.

Date	Mintage	VG	F	VF	XF	Unc
1690	—	55.00	115	225	500	—
1691	—	50.00	100	200	450	—
1692	—	60.00	125	250	575	—

KM# 276 ECU
Silver **Ruler:** Louis XIV **Mint:** Pau **Note:** Dav. #3812.

Date	Mintage	VG	F	VF	XF	Unc
1690	—	100	250	950	1,600	—
1691	—	125	300	1,050	1,800	—

KM# 298.1 ECU
Silver **Ruler:** Louis XIV **Obv:** Bust with square neckline **Rev:** Crowned round arms in palm sprays **Mint:** Paris **Note:** Values given for the KM#298 issues are for examples struck over recalled ECU. Clear examples struck on new planchets command an average 20-30% premium. Dav. #3813.

Date	Mintage	VG	F	VF	XF	Unc
1693A	—	45.00	90.00	175	375	—
1694A	—	45.00	90.00	175	375	—
1695A	—	45.00	90.00	175	375	—
1696A	—	75.00	150	300	700	—
1697A	—	50.00	100	200	450	—
1698A	—	55.00	115	225	500	—
1699A	—	—	—	—	—	—
1700A	—	—	—	—	—	—

KM# 298.2 ECU
Silver **Ruler:** Louis XIV **Mint:** Metz

Date	Mintage	VG	F	VF	XF	Unc
1693AA	—	75.00	150	300	700	—
1694AA	—	55.00	115	225	500	—
1695AA	—	75.00	150	300	700	—
1696AA	—	—	—	—	—	—
1697AA	—	100	200	375	825	—
1699AA	—	—	—	—	—	—

KM# 298.3 ECU
Silver **Ruler:** Louis XIV **Mint:** Rouen

Date	Mintage	VG	F	VF	XF	Unc
1693B	—	75.00	150	300	700	—
1694B	—	55.00	115	225	500	—
1695B	—	75.00	150	300	700	—
1696B	—	75.00	150	300	700	—
1697B	—	90.00	185	375	825	—
1698B	—	65.00	135	275	625	—
1699B	—	75.00	150	300	700	—
1700B	—	—	—	—	—	—

KM# 298.4 ECU
Silver **Ruler:** Louis XIV **Mint:** Strasbourg

Date	Mintage	VG	F	VF	XF	Unc
1694BB	—	65.00	135	275	625	—
1695BB	—	90.00	185	375	825	—
1697BB	—	—	—	—	—	—

KM# 298.5 ECU
Silver **Ruler:** Louis XIV **Mint:** Caen

Date	Mintage	VG	F	VF	XF	Unc
1694C	—	75.00	150	300	875	—
1695C	—	100	225	425	1,200	—
1696C	—	—	—	—	—	—
1697C	—	75.00	150	300	875	—
1700C	—	—	—	—	—	—

KM# 298.7 ECU
Silver **Ruler:** Louis XIV **Mint:** Tours

Date	Mintage	VG	F	VF	XF	Unc
1693E	—	90.00	185	375	775	—
1694E	—	60.00	125	250	550	—
1695E	—	90.00	185	375	775	—
1696E	—	90.00	190	385	850	—
1698E	—	—	—	—	—	—
1699E	—	150	275	450	950	—

KM# 298.8 ECU
Silver **Ruler:** Louis XIV **Mint:** Poitiers

Date	Mintage	VG	F	VF	XF	Unc
1693G	—	75.00	150	300	700	—
1694G	—	75.00	150	300	700	—
1695G	—	90.00	185	375	825	—
1696G	—	75.00	150	300	700	—
1697G	—	175	325	550	1,150	—
1698G	—	125	250	450	1,000	—

KM# 298.10 ECU
Silver **Ruler:** Louis XIV **Mint:** Limoges

Date	Mintage	VG	F	VF	XF	Unc
1693I	—	65.00	135	275	625	—
1694I	—	75.00	150	300	700	—
1695I	—	75.00	150	300	700	—
1696I	—	125	250	450	1,100	—
1697I	—	—	—	—	—	—
1698I	—	90.00	190	385	875	—
1699I	—	—	—	—	—	—

KM# 298.11 ECU
Silver **Ruler:** Louis XIV **Mint:** Bordeaux

Date	Mintage	VG	F	VF	XF	Unc
1693K	—	75.00	150	300	700	—
1694K	—	55.00	115	225	500	—
1695K	—	75.00	150	300	700	—
1696K	—	90.00	185	375	825	—
1697K	—	100	225	425	950	—
1698K	—	55.00	115	225	500	—
1699K	—	90.00	190	385	875	—

KM# 298.14 ECU
Silver **Ruler:** Louis XIV **Mint:** Montpellier

Date	Mintage	VG	F	VF	XF	Unc
1693N	—	55.00	115	225	500	—
1694N	—	50.00	100	200	450	—
1695N	—	65.00	135	275	625	—
1696N	—	75.00	150	300	700	—
1697N	—	90.00	185	375	825	—
1698N	—	—	—	—	—	—
1699N	—	—	—	—	—	—

KM# 298.15 ECU
Silver **Ruler:** Louis XIV **Mint:** Riom

Date	Mintage	VG	F	VF	XF	Unc
1693O	—	65.00	135	275	625	—
1694O	—	75.00	150	300	700	—
1695O	—	90.00	185	375	825	—
1696O	—	90.00	190	385	875	—
1697O	—	125	250	450	1,000	—
1698O	—	—	—	—	—	—
1700O	—	—	—	—	—	—

KM# 298.16 ECU
Silver **Ruler:** Louis XIV **Mint:** Dijon

Date	Mintage	VG	F	VF	XF	Unc
1693P	—	60.00	125	250	575	—
1694P	—	60.00	125	250	575	—
1695P	—	90.00	185	400	1,000	—
1696P	—	—	—	—	—	—
1697P	—	90.00	190	385	875	—
1698P	—	—	—	—	—	—
1699P	—	—	—	—	—	—

KM# 298.17 ECU
Silver **Ruler:** Louis XIV **Mint:** Troyes

Date	Mintage	VG	F	VF	XF	Unc
1693S	—	60.00	125	250	575	—
1694S	—	65.00	135	275	625	—
1695S	—	90.00	185	375	825	—
1696S	—	100	225	425	950	—
1697S	—	—	—	—	—	—
1698S	—	—	—	—	—	—
1699S	—	—	—	—	—	—

KM# 298.18 ECU
Silver **Ruler:** Louis XIV **Mint:** Nantes

Date	Mintage	VG	F	VF	XF	Unc
1693T	—	—	—	—	—	—
1694T	—	65.00	135	275	625	—
1695T	—	75.00	150	300	700	—
1696T	—	100	225	425	950	—
1697T	—	90.00	185	375	825	—
1698T	—	65.00	135	275	625	—
1699T	—	125	250	450	1,000	—

KM# 298.19 ECU
Silver **Ruler:** Louis XIV **Mint:** Troyes

Date	Mintage	VG	F	VF	XF	Unc
1693V	—	65.00	135	275	625	—
1694V	—	60.00	125	250	575	—
1695V	—	90.00	185	375	825	—
1696V	—	90.00	185	375	825	—

KM# 298.20 ECU
Silver **Ruler:** Louis XIV **Mint:** Lille

Date	Mintage	VG	F	VF	XF	Unc
1693W	—	60.00	125	250	575	—
1694W	—	55.00	115	225	500	—
1695W	—	65.00	135	275	625	—
1696W	—	75.00	150	300	700	—
1697W	—	75.00	150	300	700	—
1698W	—	90.00	190	385	875	—
1699W	—	90.00	190	385	875	—

KM# 298.21 ECU

Silver **Ruler:** Louis XIV **Mint:** Amiens

Date	Mintage	VG	F	VF	XF	Unc
1693X	—	75.00	150	300	700	—
1694X	—	65.00	135	275	625	—
1695X	—	60.00	125	250	575	—
1696X	—	90.00	185	375	825	—
1697X	—	90.00	185	375	825	—
1698X	—	—	—	—	—	—
1699X	—	125	250	450	1,000	—
1700X	—	—	—	—	—	—

KM# 298.22 ECU

Silver **Ruler:** Louis XIV **Mint:** Bourges

Date	Mintage	VG	F	VF	XF	Unc
1693Y	—	65.00	135	275	625	—
1694Y	—	75.00	150	300	700	—
1695Y	—	90.00	190	385	875	—
1696Y	—	90.00	185	375	825	—
1697Y	—	—	—	—	—	—
1698Y	—	—	—	—	—	—
1699Y	—	—	—	—	—	—

KM# 298.24 ECU

Silver **Ruler:** Louis XIV **Mint:** Rennes **Note:** Mint mark: Numeral 9.

Date	Mintage	VG	F	VF	XF	Unc
1693	—	60.00	125	250	575	—
1694	—	55.00	115	225	500	—
1695	—	60.00	125	250	575	—
1696	—	65.00	135	275	625	—
1697	—	60.00	125	250	575	—
1698	—	65.00	135	275	625	—
1699	—	—	—	—	—	—
1700	—	—	—	—	—	—

KM# 298.25 ECU

Silver **Ruler:** Louis XIV **Mint:** Metz **Note:** Mint mark: Crowned M.

Date	Mintage	VG	F	VF	XF	Unc
1693	—	90.00	185	375	825	—

KM# 298.26 ECU

Silver **Ruler:** Louis XIV **Mint:** Besançon **Note:** Mint mark: Back-to-back C's.

Date	Mintage	VG	F	VF	XF	Unc
1694	—	60.00	125	250	450	—
1695	—	90.00	190	385	700	—
1696	—	90.00	210	420	920	—
1697	—	100	300	550	1,100	—
1698	—	—	—	—	—	—
1699	—	—	—	—	—	—

KM# 299 ECU

Silver **Ruler:** Louis XIV **Rev:** Crowned round arms of France, Navarre and Bearn in palm sprays **Mint:** Pau **Note:** Dav. #3814.

Date	Mintage	VG	F	VF	XF	Unc
1693	—	900	2,000	5,500	10,000	—
1694	—	900	2,000	5,500	10,000	—
1695	—	1,200	2,600	6,000	11,500	—
1696	—	1,350	3,000	6,500	12,500	—
1697	—	—	—	—	—	—
1698	—	—	—	—	—	—
1699	—	—	—	—	—	—
1700	—	—	—	—	—	—

KM# 300 ECU

Silver **Ruler:** Louis XIV **Rev:** Crowned round arms of France, Navarre and Old and New Burgundy **Mint:** Lille **Note:** Dav. #3815.

Date	Mintage	VG	F	VF	XF	Unc
1693W	—	900	1,650	2,750	—	—
1694W	—	800	1,500	2,500	—	—
1695W	—	1,200	2,250	3,750	—	—
1696W	—	1,500	2,750	4,500	—	—
1697W	—	1,650	3,000	5,000	—	—
1698W	—	2,000	3,500	5,500	—	—
1699W	—	2,250	4,000	6,500	—	—
1700W	—	2,500	4,250	7,000	—	—

KM# 6.2 1/2 ECU D'OR

1.6750 g., 0.9580 Gold 0.0516 oz. AGW **Ruler:** Henri IV **Obv:** Crowned arms within inner beaded circle **Obv. Legend:** HENRICVS • IIII • D : G • FRAN • ET • NAVA • REX **Rev:** Cross fleuree in inner beaded circle **Rev. Legend:** + CHRS • VINCIT• CHRS • REGNAT • CHRS • IMP • **Edge:** Plain **Mint:** Saint Lô **Note:** Fr. #397.

Date	Mintage	Good	VG	F	VF	XF
1601C Rare	—	—	—	—	—	—
1603C Rare	—	—	—	—	—	—

KM# 7.5 1/2 ECU D'OR

1.6750 g., 0.9580 Gold 0.0516 oz. AGW **Ruler:** Henri IV **Obv:** Crowned arms; legend begins at upper right **Obv. Legend:** * HENRICVS • IIII • D • G • FRAM • ET • NA • REX **Rev:** Cross fleuree with H below each lis **Rev. Legend:** Latin cross CHRISTVS • REGNAT • VINCIT • ET • IMPERAT • **Edge:** Plain **Mint:** Rennes **Note:** Mint mark is "9".

Date	Mintage	Good	VG	F	VF	XF
1601	—	—	600	1,100	1,800	5,000
1602	—	—	600	1,100	1,800	5,000
1603	—	—	600	1,100	1,800	5,000

KM# 7.4 1/2 ECU D'OR

1.6750 g., 0.9580 Gold 0.0516 oz. AGW **Ruler:** Henri IV **Obv:** Crowned arms; legend begins at upper right **Obv. Legend:** * HENRICVS • IIII • D • G • FRAM • ET • NA • REX **Rev:** Cross fleuree with H below each lis **Rev. Legend:** + CHRISTVS • REGNAT • VINCIT • ET • IMPERAT • **Edge:** Plain **Mint:** Troyes

Date	Mintage	Good	VG	F	VF	XF
1603V	—	—	—	—	—	—

Note: Reported, not confirmed

KM# 8.1 1/2 ECU D'OR

1.6750 g., 0.9580 Gold 0.0516 oz. AGW **Ruler:** Henri IV **Obv:** Crowned arms; legend begins at lower left **Obv. Legend:** * HENRICVS • IIII • D • G • FRAN • ET • NA • REX **Rev:** Lobed, floriated cross **Rev. Legend:** + CHRISTVS • REGNAT • VINCIT • ET • IMPERAT • **Edge:** Plain **Mint:** Paris

Date	Mintage	Good	VG	F	VF	XF
1601A	—	—	600	1,000	1,500	3,200
1602A	—	—	600	1,000	1,500	3,200
1603A	—	—	600	1,000	1,500	3,200
1604A	—	—	600	1,000	1,500	3,200
1605A	—	—	600	1,000	1,500	3,200
1606A	—	—	600	1,000	1,500	3,200
1607A	—	—	600	1,000	1,500	3,200
1608A	—	—	600	1,000	1,500	3,200
1609A	—	—	600	1,000	1,500	3,200
1610A	—	—	600	1,000	1,500	3,200

KM# 8.2 1/2 ECU D'OR

1.6750 g., 0.9580 Gold 0.0516 oz. AGW **Ruler:** Henri IV **Obv:** Crowned arms; legend begins at lower left **Obv. Legend:** * HENRICVS • IIII • D • G • FRAN • ET • NA • REX **Rev:** Lobed, floriated cross **Rev. Legend:** + CHRISTVS • REGNAT • VINCIT • ET • IMPERAT • **Edge:** Plain **Mint:** Rouen

Date	Mintage	Good	VG	F	VF	XF
1607B	—	—	600	1,000	1,500	3,200
1608B	—	—	600	1,000	1,500	3,200
1609B	—	—	600	1,000	1,500	3,200
1610B	—	—	600	1,000	1,500	3,200

KM# 8.5 1/2 ECU D'OR

1.6750 g., 0.9580 Gold 0.0516 oz. AGW **Ruler:** Henri IV **Obv:** Crowned arms; legend begins at lower left **Obv. Legend:** * HENRICVS • IIII • D • G • FRAN • ET • NA • REX **Rev:** Lobed, floriated cross **Rev. Legend:** + CHRISTVS • REGNAT • VINCIT • ET • IMPERAT • **Edge:** Plain **Mint:** La Rochelle

Date	Mintage	Good	VG	F	VF	XF
1605H	—	—	600	1,000	1,500	3,200

KM# 8.6 1/2 ECU D'OR

1.6750 g., 0.9580 Gold 0.0516 oz. AGW **Ruler:** Henri IV **Obv:** Crowned arms; legend begins at lower left **Obv. Legend:** * HENRICVS • IIII • D • G • FRAN • ET • NA • REX **Rev:** Lobed, floriated cross **Rev. Legend:** Latin cross CHRISTVS • REGNAT • VINCIT • ET • IMPERAT • **Edge:** Plain **Mint:** Bordeaux

Date	Mintage	Good	VG	F	VF	XF
1607K	—	—	—	—	—	—

KM# 8.10 1/2 ECU D'OR

1.6750 g., 0.9580 Gold 0.0516 oz. AGW **Ruler:** Henri IV **Obv:** Crowned arms; legend begins at lower left **Obv. Legend:** * HENRICVS • IIII • D • G • FRAN • ET • NA • REX **Rev:** Lobed, floriated cross **Rev. Legend:** + CHRISTVS • REGNAT • VINCIT • ET • IMPERAT • **Edge:** Plain **Mint:** Amiens

Date	Mintage	Good	VG	F	VF	XF
1604X	—	—	600	1,000	1,500	3,200

KM# 40.1 1/2 ECU D'OR

1.6700 g., 0.9580 Gold 0.0514 oz. AGW **Ruler:** Louis XIII **Obv:** Legend around border, starting at upper right **Obv. Legend:** LVDOVICVS XIII... **Mint:** Paris

Date	Mintage	VG	F	VF	XF	Unc
1610A	—	—	—	—	—	—
1611A	—	—	—	—	—	—
1613A	—	600	1,100	2,000	4,200	—
1614A	—	550	900	1,900	4,200	—
1615A	—	550	900	1,900	4,200	—
1618A	—	—	—	—	—	—
1619A	—	600	1,100	2,000	4,200	—
1620A	—	600	1,100	2,000	4,200	—
1621A	—	600	1,100	2,000	4,200	—
1622A	—	600	1,100	2,000	4,200	—
1623A	—	600	1,100	2,000	4,200	—
1624A	—	600	1,100	2,000	4,200	—
1625A	—	600	1,100	2,000	4,200	—
1626A	—	600	1,100	2,000	4,200	—
1627A	—	600	1,100	2,000	4,200	—
1628A	—	600	1,100	2,000	4,200	—
1629A	—	600	1,100	2,000	4,200	—
1630A	—	600	1,100	2,000	4,200	—
1631A	—	—	—	—	—	—
1632A	—	—	—	—	—	—
1633A	—	600	1,100	2,000	4,200	—
1634A	—	—	—	—	—	—
1635A	—	—	—	—	—	—
1636A	—	—	—	—	—	—
1637A	—	—	—	—	—	—
1638A	—	600	1,100	2,000	4,200	—
1643A	—	—	—	—	—	—

KM# 40.2 1/2 ECU D'OR

1.6700 g., 0.9580 Gold 0.0514 oz. AGW **Ruler:** Louis XIII **Mint:** Arras

Date	Mintage	VG	F	VF	XF	Unc
1641AR Rare	—	—	—	—	—	—
1642AR Rare	—	—	—	—	—	—
1643AR Rare	—	—	—	—	—	—

KM# 40.3 1/2 ECU D'OR

1.6700 g., 0.9580 Gold 0.0514 oz. AGW **Ruler:** Louis XIII **Mint:** Rouen

Date	Mintage	VG	F	VF	XF	Unc
1612B Rare	—	—	—	—	—	—
1613B Rare	—	—	—	—	—	—
1614B Rare	—	—	—	—	—	—
1615B	—	550	900	1,900	4,000	—
1616B	—	600	1,100	2,000	4,000	—
1619B Rare	—	—	—	—	—	—
1624B Rare	—	—	—	—	—	—
1627B Rare	—	—	—	—	—	—
1628B Rare	—	—	—	—	—	—
1632B	—	600	1,100	2,000	4,000	—
1634B Rare	—	—	—	—	—	—
1635B Rare	—	—	—	—	—	—

KM# 40.4 1/2 ECU D'OR
1.6700 g., 0.9580 Gold 0.0514 oz. AGW **Ruler:** Louis XIII **Mint:** Saint Lô

Date	Mintage	VG	F	VF	XF	Unc
1615C Rare	—	—	—	—	—	—
1616C Rare	—	—	—	—	—	—
1628C Rare	—	—	—	—	—	—
1635C Rare	—	—	—	—	—	—

KM# 40.5 1/2 ECU D'OR
1.6700 g., 0.9580 Gold 0.0514 oz. AGW **Ruler:** Louis XIII **Mint:** Lyon

Date	Mintage	VG	F	VF	XF	Unc
1625D Rare	—	—	—	—	—	—
1629D	—	600	1,100	2,000	4,000	—
1630D	—	600	1,100	2,000	4,000	—
1632D Rare	—	—	—	—	—	—
1638D Rare	—	—	—	—	—	—

KM# 40.6 1/2 ECU D'OR
1.6700 g., 0.9580 Gold 0.0514 oz. AGW **Ruler:** Louis XIII **Mint:** Tours

Date	Mintage	VG	F	VF	XF	Unc
1616E	—	600	1,100	2,000	4,000	—

KM# 40.7 1/2 ECU D'OR
1.6700 g., 0.9580 Gold 0.0514 oz. AGW **Ruler:** Louis XIII **Mint:** Angers

Date	Mintage	VG	F	VF	XF	Unc
1631F Rare	—	—	—	—	—	—

KM# 40.8 1/2 ECU D'OR
1.6700 g., 0.9580 Gold 0.0514 oz. AGW **Ruler:** Louis XIII **Mint:** La Rochelle

Date	Mintage	VG	F	VF	XF	Unc
1633H	—	600	1,100	2,000	4,000	—
1637H	—	600	1,100	2,000	4,000	—

KM# 40.9 1/2 ECU D'OR
1.6700 g., 0.9580 Gold 0.0514 oz. AGW **Ruler:** Louis XIII **Mint:** Limoges

Date	Mintage	VG	F	VF	XF	Unc
1632I Rare	—	—	—	—	—	—
1642I Rare	—	—	—	—	—	—

KM# 40.10 1/2 ECU D'OR
1.6700 g., 0.9580 Gold 0.0514 oz. AGW **Ruler:** Louis XIII **Mint:** Bordeaux

Date	Mintage	VG	F	VF	XF	Unc
1611K	—	600	1,100	2,000	4,000	—
1629K Rare	—	—	—	—	—	—
1630K	—	600	1,100	2,000	4,000	—
Note: 1630 dates exist with inner circle on both sides						
1633K Rare	—	—	—	—	—	—
1638K Rare	—	—	—	—	—	—

KM# 40.11 1/2 ECU D'OR
1.6700 g., 0.9580 Gold 0.0514 oz. AGW **Ruler:** Louis XIII **Mint:** Toulouse

Date	Mintage	VG	F	VF	XF	Unc
1614M	—	600	1,100	2,000	4,000	—
1632M Rare	—	—	—	—	—	—
1633M	—	600	1,100	2,000	4,000	—
1634M Rare	—	—	—	—	—	—
1635M Rare	—	—	—	—	—	—
1636M Rare	—	—	—	—	—	—
1637M Rare	—	—	—	—	—	—
1640M Rare	—	—	—	—	—	—
1642M Rare	—	—	—	—	—	—
1643M	—	600	1,100	2,000	4,000	—

KM# 40.12 1/2 ECU D'OR
1.6700 g., 0.9580 Gold 0.0514 oz. AGW **Ruler:** Louis XIII **Mint:** Montpellier

Date	Mintage	VG	F	VF	XF	Unc
1636N	—	600	1,100	2,000	4,000	—
1639N	—	600	1,100	2,000	4,000	—
1640N Rare	—	—	—	—	—	—

KM# 40.13 1/2 ECU D'OR
1.6700 g., 0.9580 Gold 0.0514 oz. AGW **Ruler:** Louis XIII **Mint:** Dijon

Date	Mintage	VG	F	VF	XF	Unc
1637P Rare	—	—	—	—	—	—
1639P Rare	—	—	—	—	—	—
1640P Rare	—	—	—	—	—	—

KM# 40.14 1/2 ECU D'OR
1.6700 g., 0.9580 Gold 0.0514 oz. AGW **Ruler:** Louis XIII **Mint:** Troyes

Date	Mintage	VG	F	VF	XF	Unc
1613S	—	600	1,100	2,000	4,000	—
1615S	—	600	1,100	2,000	4,000	—
1631S	—	600	1,100	2,000	4,000	—
1635S	—	600	1,100	2,000	4,000	—

KM# 40.15 1/2 ECU D'OR
1.6700 g., 0.9580 Gold 0.0514 oz. AGW **Ruler:** Louis XIII **Mint:** Amiens

Date	Mintage	VG	F	VF	XF	Unc
1615X	—	600	1,100	2,000	4,000	—
1631X Rare	—	—	—	—	—	—
1633X	—	600	1,100	2,000	4,000	—
1634X	—	600	1,100	2,000	4,000	—
1635X	—	550	900	1,900	4,000	—
1636X	—	600	1,100	2,000	4,000	—
1637X	—	550	900	1,900	4,000	—
1638X	—	600	1,100	2,000	4,000	—
1640X	—	600	1,100	2,000	4,000	—
1641X	—	600	1,100	2,000	4,000	—
1642X Rare	—	—	—	—	—	—
1643X Rare	—	—	—	—	—	—

KM# 40.16 1/2 ECU D'OR
1.6700 g., 0.9580 Gold 0.0514 oz. AGW **Ruler:** Louis XIII **Mint:** Aix **Note:** Mint mark: Ampersand.

Date	Mintage	VG	F	VF	XF	Unc
1637 Rare	—	—	—	—	—	—
1638 Rare	—	—	—	—	—	—

KM# 54 1/2 ECU D'OR
1.6700 g., 0.9580 Gold 0.0514 oz. AGW **Ruler:** Louis XIII **Obv:** Legend begins at lower left **Mint:** Rouen **Note:** Inner beaded circle on both sides

Date	Mintage	VG	F	VF	XF	Unc
1615B	—	—	—	—	—	—

KM# 56 1/2 ECU D'OR
1.6700 g., 0.9580 Gold 0.0514 oz. AGW **Ruler:** Louis XIII **Obv:** Legend begins at lower left **Mint:** Paris

Date	Mintage	VG	F	VF	XF	Unc
1616A	—	600	1,100	2,000	4,000	—

KM# 62 1/2 ECU D'OR
1.6700 g., 0.9580 Gold 0.0514 oz. AGW **Ruler:** Louis XIII **Obv:** Mint mark below arms **Rev:** Dot at center of cross **Mint:** Amiens

Date	Mintage	VG	F	VF	XF	Unc
1618X	—	600	1,100	2,000	4,000	—

KM# 122 1/2 ECU D'OR
1.6700 g., 0.9580 Gold 0.0514 oz. AGW **Ruler:** Louis XIII **Obv:** Arms of France and Dauphine in inner circle **Note:** Mint mark: Anchor.

Date	Mintage	VG	F	VF	XF	Unc
1641	—	3,000	7,000	12,000	22,000	—

KM# 145.1 1/2 ECU D'OR
1.6700 g., 0.9580 Gold 0.0514 oz. AGW **Ruler:** Louis XIV **Obv:** Crowned arms around border starting at upper right **Obv. Legend:** LVDOVICVS XIIII... **Rev:** Ornamented and lobed cross, mint mark at center, legend around border **Mint:** Paris

Date	Mintage	VG	F	VF	XF	Unc
1643A	—	2,000	3,500	4,500	8,000	—
1645A	—	2,000	3,500	4,500	8,000	—
1647A Rare	—	—	—	—	—	—
1648A Rare	—	—	—	—	—	—
1650A Rare	—	—	—	—	—	—
1654A Rare	—	—	—	—	—	—

KM# 145.2 1/2 ECU D'OR
1.6700 g., 0.9580 Gold 0.0514 oz. AGW **Ruler:** Louis XIV **Mint:** Arras

Date	Mintage	VG	F	VF	XF	Unc
1644AR Rare	—	—	—	—	—	—

KM# 145.3 1/2 ECU D'OR
1.6700 g., 0.9580 Gold 0.0514 oz. AGW **Ruler:** Louis XIV **Mint:** Bordeaux

Date	Mintage	VG	F	VF	XF	Unc
1644K Rare	—	—	—	—	—	—
1645K Rare	—	—	—	—	—	—

KM# 145.4 1/2 ECU D'OR
1.6700 g., 0.9580 Gold 0.0514 oz. AGW **Ruler:** Louis XIV **Mint:** Toulouse

Date	Mintage	VG	F	VF	XF	Unc
1644M Rare	—	—	—	—	—	—
1646M Rare	—	—	—	—	—	—

KM# 145.5 1/2 ECU D'OR
1.6700 g., 0.9580 Gold 0.0514 oz. AGW **Ruler:** Louis XIV **Mint:** Amiens

Date	Mintage	VG	F	VF	XF	Unc
1644X Rare	—	—	—	—	—	—
1645X Rare	—	—	—	—	—	—
1647X	—	1,500	3,100	3,700	6,800	—

KM# 9.2 ECU D'OR
3.3500 g., 0.9580 Gold 0.1032 oz. AGW **Ruler:** Henri IV **Obv:** Crowned arms within inner beaded circle **Obv. Legend:** HENRICVS • IIII • D : G • FRAN • ET • NAVA • REX **Rev:** Cross fleuree in inner beaded circle **Rev. Legend:** + CHRS • VINCIT • CHRS • REGNAT • CHRS • IMP • **Edge:** Plain **Mint:** Saint Lô **Note:** Fr. #396.

Date	Mintage	Good	VG	F	VF	XF
1601C	—	—	1,500	2,800	4,500	7,500
1602C	—	—	1,500	2,800	4,500	7,500
1603C	—	—	1,500	2,800	4,500	7,500
1610C	—	—	1,500	2,800	4,500	7,500

KM# 10.2 ECU D'OR
3.3500 g., 0.9580 Gold 0.1032 oz. AGW **Ruler:** Henri IV **Obv:** Crowned arms; legend begins at upper right **Obv. Legend:** * HENRICVS • IIII • D • G • FRAN • ET • NA • REX **Rev:** Cross fleuree with H below each lis **Rev. Legend:** + CHRISTVS • REGNAT • VINCIT • ET • IMPERAT • **Edge:** Plain **Mint:** Tours

Date	Mintage	Good	VG	F	VF	XF
1602E	—	—	900	1,650	3,000	5,300
1604E	—	—	900	1,650	3,000	5,300

KM# 10.4 ECU D'OR
3.3500 g., 0.9580 Gold 0.1032 oz. AGW **Ruler:** Henri IV **Obv:** Crowned arms; legend begins at upper right **Obv. Legend:** * HENRICVS • IIII • D • G • FRAN • ET • NA • REX **Rev:** Cross fleuree with H below each lis **Rev. Legend:** + CHRISTVS • REGNAT • VINCIT • ET • IMPERAT • **Edge:** Plain **Mint:** Troyes

Date	Mintage	Good	VG	F	VF	XF
1601V	—	—	900	1,650	3,000	4,800
1602V	—	—	900	1,650	3,000	4,800
1603V	—	—	900	1,650	3,000	4,800

KM# 10.5 ECU D'OR
3.3500 g., 0.9580 Gold 0.1032 oz. AGW **Ruler:** Henri IV **Obv:** Crowned arms; legend begins at upper right **Obv. Legend:** * HENRICVS • IIII • D • G • FRAN • ET • NA • REX **Rev:** Cross fleuree with H below each lis **Rev. Legend:** + CHRISTVS • REGNAT • VINCIT • ET • IMPERAT • **Edge:** Plain **Mint:** Rennes **Note:** Mint mark "9" (for Rennes mint).

Date	Mintage	Good	VG	F	VF	XF
1601	—	—	900	1,650	3,000	5,300
1602	—	—	900	1,650	3,000	5,300
1603	—	—	900	1,650	3,000	5,300

KM# 10.7 ECU D'OR
3.3500 g., 0.9580 Gold 0.1032 oz. AGW **Ruler:** Henri IV **Obv:** Legend around crowned arms **Obv. Legend:** HENRICVS... **Rev:** Cross fleuree with H below each lis

Date	Mintage	VG	F	VF	XF	Unc
1601-03	—	900	1,650	3,000	4,800	—

KM# 11 ECU D'OR
3.3500 g., 0.9580 Gold 0.1032 oz. AGW **Ruler:** Louis XIII **Obv:** Legend around crowned arms at lower left **Obv. Legend:** HENRICVS... **Rev:** Lobed and cross fleuree

Date	Mintage	VG	F	VF	XF	Unc
1601-10	—	550	900	1,400	3,000	—

KM# 11.1 ECU D'OR
3.3500 g., 0.9580 Gold 0.1032 oz. AGW **Ruler:** Henri IV **Obv:** Crowned arms; legend begins at lower left **Obv. Legend:** * HENRICVS • IIII • D • G • FRAN • ET • NA • REX **Rev:** Lobed, floriated cross **Rev. Legend:** + CHRISTVS • REGNAT • VINCIT • ET • IMPERAT • **Edge:** Plain **Mint:** Paris **Note:** Fr. #392.

Date	Mintage	Good	VG	F	VF	XF
1601A	—	—	825	1,350	2,100	4,200
1602A	—	—	825	1,350	2,100	4,200
1603A	—	—	825	1,350	2,100	4,200
1604A	—	—	825	1,350	2,100	4,200
1605A	—	—	825	1,350	2,100	4,200
1606A	—	—	825	1,350	2,100	4,200
1607A	—	—	825	1,350	2,100	4,200
1608A	—	—	825	1,350	2,100	4,200
1609A	—	—	825	1,350	2,100	4,200
1610A	—	—	825	1,350	2,100	4,200

KM# 11.2 ECU D'OR
3.3500 g., 0.9580 Gold 0.1032 oz. AGW **Ruler:** Henri IV **Obv:** Crowned arms; legend begins at lower left **Obv. Legend:** * HENRICVS • IIII • D • G • FRAN • ET • NA • REX **Rev:** Lobed, floriated cross **Rev. Legend:** + CHRISTVS • REGNAT • VINCIT • ET • IMPERAT • **Edge:** Plain **Mint:** Rouen

Date	Mintage	Good	VG	F	VF	XF
1607B	—	—	825	1,350	2,100	4,200
1608B	—	—	825	1,350	2,100	4,200
1609B	—	—	825	1,350	2,100	4,200
1610B	—	—	825	1,350	2,100	4,200

KM# 11.5 ECU D'OR
3.3500 g., 0.9580 Gold 0.1032 oz. AGW **Ruler:** Henri IV **Obv:** Crowned arms; legend begins at lower left **Obv. Legend:** * HENRICVS • IIII • D • G • FRAN • ET • NA • REX **Rev:** Lobed, floriated cross **Rev. Legend:** + CHRISTVS • REGNAT • VINCIT • ET • IMPERAT • **Edge:** Plain **Mint:** La Rochelle

Date	Mintage	Good	VG	F	VF	XF
1601H	—	—	825	1,350	2,100	4,200
1605H	—	—	825	1,350	2,100	4,200

KM# 11.7 ECU D'OR
3.3500 g., 0.9580 Gold 0.1032 oz. AGW **Ruler:** Henri IV **Obv:** Crowned arms; legend begins at lower left **Obv. Legend:** * HENRICVS • IIII • D • G • FRAN • ET • NA • REX **Rev:** Lobed, floriated cross **Rev. Legend:** + CHRISTVS • REGNAT • VINCIT • ET • IMPERAT • **Edge:** Plain **Mint:** Bordeaux

Date	Mintage	Good	VG	F	VF	XF
1602K	—	—	825	1,350	2,100	4,200
1607K	—	—	825	1,350	2,100	4,200

KM# 11.11 ECU D'OR

3.3500 g., 0.9580 Gold 0.1032 oz. AGW **Ruler:** Henri IV **Obv:** Crowned arms; legend begins at lower left **Obv. Legend:** * HENRICVS • IIII • D • G • FRAN • ET • NA • REX **Rev:** Lobed, floriated cross **Rev. Legend:** + CHRISTVS • REGNAT • VINCIT • ET • IMPERAT • **Edge:** Plain **Mint:** Amiens

Date	Mintage	Good	VG	F	VF	XF
1604X	—	—	825	1,350	2,100	4,200

KM# 12 ECU D'OR

3.3500 g., 0.9580 Gold 0.1032 oz. AGW **Ruler:** Louis XIII **Obv:** Legend at upper right **Obv. Legend:** HENRICVS...

Date	Mintage	VG	F	VF	XF	Unc
1601-10	—	825	1,350	2,100	4,200	—

KM# 41.1 ECU D'OR

3.3500 g., 0.9580 Gold 0.1032 oz. AGW **Ruler:** Louis XIII **Obv:** Legend at upper right **Obv. Legend:** LVDOVICVS XIII... **Mint:** Paris

Date	Mintage	VG	F	VF	XF	Unc
1610A	—	300	525	675	1,350	—
1611A	—	300	525	675	1,350	—
1612A	—	300	525	675	1,350	—
1613A	—	300	525	675	1,350	—
1614A	—	300	525	675	1,350	—
1615A	—	300	525	675	1,350	—
1616A	—	300	525	675	1,350	—
1617A	—	300	525	675	1,350	—
1618A Rare	—	—	—	—	—	—
1619A Rare	—	—	—	—	—	—
1620A Rare	—	—	—	—	—	—
1621A	—	325	550	725	1,400	—
1622A Rare	—	—	—	—	—	—
1623A	—	300	525	675	1,350	—
1624A Rare	—	—	—	—	—	—
1625A	—	300	525	675	1,350	—
1626A	—	300	525	675	1,350	—
1627A	—	300	525	675	1,350	—
1628A	—	300	525	675	1,350	—
1629A	—	300	525	675	1,350	—
1630A	—	300	525	675	1,350	—
1631A	—	300	525	675	1,350	—
1632A Rare	—	—	—	—	—	—
1633A	—	300	525	675	1,350	—
1634A	—	300	525	675	1,350	—
1635A	—	300	525	675	1,350	—
1636A	—	300	525	675	1,350	—
1637A	—	300	525	675	1,350	—
1638A	—	300	525	675	1,350	—
1639A	—	300	525	675	1,350	—
1640A	—	350	600	825	1,450	—
1641A	—	350	600	825	1,450	—
1642A	—	300	525	675	1,350	—
1643A	—	300	525	675	1,350	—

KM# 41.2 ECU D'OR

3.3500 g., 0.9580 Gold 0.1032 oz. AGW **Ruler:** Louis XIII **Mint:** Arras

Date	Mintage	VG	F	VF	XF	Unc
1641AR	—	375	650	1,150	1,950	—
1642AR Rare	—	—	—	—	—	—
1643AR Rare	—	—	—	—	—	—
1644AR engraving error	—	450	725	1,300	2,100	—
1645AR engraving error	—	450	725	1,300	2,100	—

KM# 41.3 ECU D'OR

3.3500 g., 0.9580 Gold 0.1032 oz. AGW **Ruler:** Louis XIII **Mint:** Saint Lô

Date	Mintage	VG	F	VF	XF	Unc
1610C Rare	—	—	—	—	—	—
1612C Rare	—	—	—	—	—	—
1613C Rare	—	—	—	—	—	—
1615C	—	425	600	900	1,500	—
1616C Rare	—	—	—	—	—	—
1618C Rare	—	—	—	—	—	—
1620C Rare	—	—	—	—	—	—
1628C Rare	—	—	—	—	—	—
1632C Rare	—	—	—	—	—	—
1633C Rare	—	—	—	—	—	—
1634C Rare	—	—	—	—	—	—
1635C	—	350	600	825	1,450	—
1636C Rare	—	—	—	—	—	—
1637C	—	300	525	675	1,350	—
1638C	—	300	525	675	1,350	—
1639C Rare	—	—	—	—	—	—
1640C Rare	—	—	—	—	—	—
1641C	—	350	600	825	1,450	—
1642C Rare	—	—	—	—	—	—
1643C Rare	—	—	—	—	—	—

KM# 41.4 ECU D'OR

3.3500 g., 0.9580 Gold 0.1032 oz. AGW **Ruler:** Louis XIII **Mint:** Lyon

Date	Mintage	VG	F	VF	XF	Unc
1616D	—	300	525	675	1,400	—
1624D Rare	—	—	—	—	—	—
1627D Rare	—	—	—	—	—	—
1629D	—	300	525	675	1,400	—
1630D Rare	—	—	—	—	—	—
1631D Rare	—	—	—	—	—	—
1632D Rare	—	—	—	—	—	—
1633D Rare	—	—	—	—	—	—
1635D Rare	—	—	—	—	—	—
1636D Rare	—	—	—	—	—	—
1637D	—	300	525	675	1,400	—
1638D	—	300	525	675	1,400	—
1639D	—	300	525	675	1,400	—
1640D	—	300	525	675	1,400	—
1641D	—	300	525	725	1,500	—
1642D Rare	—	—	—	—	—	—
1643D Rare	—	—	—	—	—	—

KM# 41.5 ECU D'OR

3.3500 g., 0.9580 Gold 0.1032 oz. AGW **Ruler:** Louis XIII **Mint:** Tours

Date	Mintage	VG	F	VF	XF	Unc
1615E Rare	4,078	—	—	—	—	—
1618E Rare	—	—	—	—	—	—
1619E Rare	—	—	—	—	—	—
1641E Rare	—	—	—	—	—	—
1642E Rare	—	—	—	—	—	—
1643E Rare	—	—	—	—	—	—

KM# 41.6 ECU D'OR

3.3500 g., 0.9580 Gold 0.1032 oz. AGW **Ruler:** Louis XIII **Mint:** Angers

Date	Mintage	VG	F	VF	XF	Unc
1631F Rare	—	—	—	—	—	—
1632F Rare	—	—	—	—	—	—
1641F Rare	—	—	—	—	—	—
1642F Rare	—	—	—	—	—	—
1643F Rare	—	—	—	—	—	—

KM# 41.7 ECU D'OR

3.3500 g., 0.9580 Gold 0.1032 oz. AGW **Ruler:** Louis XIII **Mint:** Poitiers

Date	Mintage	VG	F	VF	XF	Unc
1642G	—	350	600	825	1,450	—
1643G Rare	—	—	—	—	—	—

KM# 41.8 ECU D'OR

3.3500 g., 0.9580 Gold 0.1032 oz. AGW **Ruler:** Louis XIII **Mint:** La Rochelle

Date	Mintage	VG	F	VF	XF	Unc
1641H	—	350	600	825	1,450	—
1642H Rare	—	—	—	—	—	—
1643H Rare	—	—	—	—	—	—

KM# 41.9 ECU D'OR

3.3500 g., 0.9580 Gold 0.1032 oz. AGW **Ruler:** Louis XIII **Mint:** Limoges

Date	Mintage	VG	F	VF	XF	Unc
1630I Rare	—	—	—	—	—	—
1631I	—	375	650	900	1,500	—
1632I Rare	—	—	—	—	—	—
1641I Rare	—	—	—	—	—	—
1642I Rare	—	—	—	—	—	—
1643I Rare	—	—	—	—	—	—

KM# 41.10 ECU D'OR

3.3500 g., 0.9580 Gold 0.1032 oz. AGW **Ruler:** Louis XIII **Mint:** Bordeaux

Date	Mintage	VG	F	VF	XF	Unc
1611	—	—	—	—	—	—
1630	—	—	—	—	—	—
1631K Rare	—	—	—	—	—	—
1632K Rare	1,500	—	—	—	—	—
1633K Rare	—	—	—	—	—	—
1638K Rare	—	—	—	—	—	—
1639K	—	300	575	750	1,450	—
1640K	—	300	525	675	1,350	—
1642K	—	350	600	825	1,450	—
1643K	—	350	600	825	1,450	—

KM# 41.11 ECU D'OR

3.3500 g., 0.9580 Gold 0.1032 oz. AGW **Ruler:** Louis XIII **Mint:** Bayonne

Date	Mintage	VG	F	VF	XF	Unc
1632L	—	450	725	975	1,650	—
1633L	—	350	600	825	1,450	—
1635L Rare	—	—	—	—	—	—
1636L Rare	—	—	—	—	—	—
1637L	—	300	525	675	1,350	—
1642L Rare	—	—	—	—	—	—
1643L Rare	—	—	—	—	—	—

KM# 41.12 ECU D'OR

3.3500 g., 0.9580 Gold 0.1032 oz. AGW **Ruler:** Louis XIII **Mint:** Toulouse

Date	Mintage	VG	F	VF	XF	Unc
1632M	—	—	—	—	—	—
1633M	—	—	—	—	—	—
1634M	—	300	525	675	1,350	—
1635M	—	—	—	—	—	—
1636M Rare	—	—	—	—	—	—
1637M Rare	—	—	—	—	—	—
1638M Rare	—	—	—	—	—	—
1639M Rare	—	—	—	—	—	—
1640M Rare	—	—	—	—	—	—
1641M	—	350	600	825	1,450	—
1642M Rare	—	—	—	—	—	—
1643M	—	350	600	825	1,450	—

KM# 41.13 ECU D'OR

3.3500 g., 0.9580 Gold 0.1032 oz. AGW **Ruler:** Louis XIII **Mint:** Montpellier

Date	Mintage	VG	F	VF	XF	Unc
1629N	—	350	600	825	1,450	—
1635N	—	350	600	825	1,450	—
1636N Rare	—	—	—	—	—	—
1637N Rare	—	—	—	—	—	—
Note: 1637 dates exist with inner circle on both sides						
1638N Rare	—	—	—	—	—	—
1639N Rare	—	—	—	—	—	—
1640N	—	300	525	675	1,350	—
1641N	—	300	525	675	1,350	—
1642N Rare	—	—	—	—	—	—
1643N	—	350	600	825	1,450	—

KM# 41.14 ECU D'OR

3.3500 g., 0.9580 Gold 0.1032 oz. AGW **Ruler:** Louis XIII **Mint:** Dijon

Date	Mintage	VG	F	VF	XF	Unc
1615P	—	300	525	675	1,350	—
1637P Rare	—	—	—	—	—	—
1638P Rare	—	—	—	—	—	—
1639P Rare	—	—	—	—	—	—
1640P Rare	—	—	—	—	—	—

KM# 41.15 ECU D'OR

3.3500 g., 0.9580 Gold 0.1032 oz. AGW **Ruler:** Louis XIII **Mint:** Troyes

Date	Mintage	VG	F	VF	XF	Unc
1615S	—	300	525	675	1,350	—
1631S	—	350	600	825	1,450	—
1632S Rare	—	—	—	—	—	—
1634S	—	375	675	975	1,800	—
1635S	—	350	600	825	1,450	—
1637S	—	300	525	675	1,350	—
1638S	—	300	525	675	1,350	—
1639S	—	300	525	675	1,350	—
1640S Rare	—	—	—	—	—	—
1641S Rare	—	—	—	—	—	—

KM# 41.16 ECU D'OR

3.3500 g., 0.9580 Gold 0.1032 oz. AGW **Ruler:** Louis XIII **Mint:** Nantes

Date	Mintage	VG	F	VF	XF	Unc
1615T	—	300	525	675	1,350	—
1616T	—	350	600	825	1,450	—
1617T	—	300	525	675	1,350	—
1625T	—	350	600	825	1,450	—
1642T	—	350	600	825	1,450	—
1643T Rare	—	—	—	—	—	—

KM# 41.17 ECU D'OR

3.3500 g., 0.9580 Gold 0.1032 oz. AGW **Ruler:** Louis XIII **Mint:** Amiens

Date	Mintage	VG	F	VF	XF	Unc
1615X Rare	—	—	—	—	—	—
1616X	—	300	525	675	1,350	—
1617X Rare	—	—	—	—	—	—
1631X	—	300	525	675	1,350	—
1632X Rare	—	—	—	—	—	—
1633X Rare	—	—	—	—	—	—
1634X	—	375	600	750	1,500	—
1635X	—	300	525	675	1,350	—
1636X	—	300	525	675	1,350	—
1637X	—	300	525	675	1,350	—
1638X	—	300	525	675	1,350	—
1639X	—	300	525	675	1,350	—
1640X	—	300	525	675	1,350	—
1641X	—	300	525	675	1,350	—
1642X	—	300	525	675	1,350	—
1643X Rare	—	—	—	—	—	—

KM# 41.18 ECU D'OR

3.3500 g., 0.9580 Gold 0.1032 oz. AGW **Ruler:** Louis XIII **Mint:** Bourges

Date	Mintage	VG	F	VF	XF	Unc
1627Y Rare	—	—	—	—	—	—
1628Y Rare	—	—	—	—	—	—
1629Y Rare	—	—	—	—	—	—
1639Y	—	375	650	900	1,500	—
1640Y Rare	—	—	—	—	—	—
1641Y	—	350	600	825	1,450	—
1642Y Rare	—	—	—	—	—	—
1643Y	—	350	600	825	1,450	—

KM# 41.19 ECU D'OR

3.3500 g., 0.9580 Gold 0.1032 oz. AGW **Ruler:** Louis XIII **Mint:** Rennes **Note:** Mint mark: Numeral 9.

Date	Mintage	VG	F	VF	XF	Unc
1614 Rare	—	—	—	—	—	—
1642 Rare	—	—	—	—	—	—
1643 Rare	—	—	—	—	—	—

KM# 41.20 ECU D'OR

3.3500 g., 0.9580 Gold 0.1032 oz. AGW **Ruler:** Louis XIII **Mint:** Aix **Note:** Mint mark: Ampersand.

Date	Mintage	VG	F	VF	XF	Unc
1634 Rare	—	—	—	—	—	—
1635	—	300	525	675	1,350	—
1637	—	300	525	675	1,350	—
1638 Rare	—	—	—	—	—	—
1639	—	350	600	825	1,450	—
1640	—	300	525	675	1,350	—
1641	—	300	525	675	1,350	—
1642	—	350	675	1,050	1,500	—
1643 Rare	—	—	—	—	—	—

KM# 51 ECU D'OR

3.3500 g., 0.9580 Gold 0.1032 oz. AGW **Ruler:** Louis XIII **Obv:** Legend begins at lower left **Mint:** Rouen

Date	Mintage	VG	F	VF	XF	Unc
1612B	—	350	600	825	1,450	—
1616B	—	350	600	825	1,450	—
1617B	—	350	600	825	1,450	—
1619B	—	350	600	825	1,450	—
1626B	—	350	600	825	1,450	—
1632B	—	300	525	675	1,350	—
1633B	—	300	525	675	1,350	—
1634B	—	300	525	675	1,350	—
1635B	—	300	525	675	1,350	—
1636B	—	300	525	675	1,350	—
1637B	—	300	525	675	1,350	—
1638B	—	300	525	675	1,350	—
1641B Rare	—	—	—	—	—	—
1642B	—	—	—	—	—	—
1643B	—	350	600	825	1,450	—

KM# 55 ECU D'OR

3.3500 g., 0.9580 Gold 0.1032 oz. AGW **Ruler:** Louis XIII **Obv:** Crowned arms in denticled inner circle, date in legend **Rev:** Cross fleuree in denticled circle **Mint:** Saint Lô

Date	Mintage	VG	F	VF	XF	Unc
1615C	—	250	400	550	1,000	—

KM# 57 ECU D'OR

3.3500 g., 0.9580 Gold 0.1032 oz. AGW **Ruler:** Louis XIII **Obv:** Crowned arms in inner circle, date in legend **Rev:** Ornamented and lobed cross in inner circle, mint mark at center **Mint:** Lyon

Date	Mintage	VG	F	VF	XF	Unc
1616D	—	300	450	650	1,300	—

KM# 88 ECU D'OR

3.3500 g., 0.9580 Gold 0.1032 oz. AGW **Ruler:** Louis XIII **Obv:** Legend begins at lower left **Mint:** Rouen

Date	Mintage	VG	F	VF	XF	Unc
1633B	—	250	400	550	1,100	—

KM# 92 ECU D'OR

3.3500 g., 0.9580 Gold 0.1032 oz. AGW **Ruler:** Louis XIII **Obv:** Mint mark below arms **Rev:** Dot at center of cross **Mint:** Amiens

Date	Mintage	VG	F	VF	XF	Unc
1638X	—	250	400	550	950	—

KM# 100 ECU D'OR

3.3500 g., 0.9580 Gold 0.1032 oz. AGW **Ruler:** Louis XIII **Obv:** Plain inner circle surrounds major devices, legend begins at lower left **Rev:** Plain inner circle surrounds major devices **Mint:** Montpellier

Date	Mintage	VG	F	VF	XF	Unc
1640N	—	250	400	550	1,100	—

KM# 124 ECU D'OR

3.3500 g., 0.9580 Gold 0.1032 oz. AGW **Ruler:** Louis XIII **Obv:** Arms of France and Dauphine **Mint:** Grenoble

Date	Mintage	VG	F	VF	XF	Unc
1641Z	—	1,500	4,000	8,000	15,000	—
1642Z	—	1,500	4,000	8,000	15,000	—

KM# 123 ECU D'OR

3.3500 g., 0.9580 Gold 0.1032 oz. AGW **Ruler:** Louis XIII **Mint:** Paris **Note:** Reduced size, finer style.

Date	Mintage	VG	F	VF	XF	Unc
1641A	—	400	650	1,100	2,000	—

KM# 146.1 ECU D'OR

3.3500 g., 0.9580 Gold 0.1032 oz. AGW **Ruler:** Louis XIV **Obv:** Legend at upper right **Obv. Legend:** LVDOVICVS XIIII... **Mint:** Paris

Date	Mintage	VG	F	VF	XF	Unc
1643A	—	250	450	650	1,000	—
1644A	—	250	450	650	1,000	—
1645A	—	250	450	650	1,000	—
1646A	—	250	450	650	1,000	—
1647A	—	250	450	650	1,000	—
1648A Rare	—	—	—	—	—	—
1649A	—	250	450	650	1,000	—
1650A Rare	—	—	—	—	—	—
1651A	—	—	—	—	—	—
1652A	—	400	700	1,000	1,600	—
1653A Rare	—	—	—	—	—	—
1654A Rare	—	—	—	—	—	—

KM# 146.2 ECU D'OR

3.3500 g., 0.9580 Gold 0.1032 oz. AGW **Ruler:** Louis XIV **Mint:** Arras

Date	Mintage	VG	F	VF	XF	Unc
1644AR	—	400	700	1,000	1,600	—
1645AR Rare	—	—	—	—	—	—
1646AR Rare	—	—	—	—	—	—

KM# 146.3 ECU D'OR

3.3500 g., 0.9580 Gold 0.1032 oz. AGW **Ruler:** Louis XIV **Mint:** Rouen

Date	Mintage	VG	F	VF	XF	Unc
1644B	—	250	450	650	1,000	—
1645B Rare	—	—	—	—	—	—

KM# 146.4 ECU D'OR

3.3500 g., 0.9580 Gold 0.1032 oz. AGW **Ruler:** Louis XIV **Mint:** Saint Lô

Date	Mintage	VG	F	VF	XF	Unc
1641C	—	500	900	1,400	2,600	—
1643C Rare	—	—	—	—	—	—
1644C	—	400	700	1,200	1,950	—
1645C Rare	—	—	—	—	—	—
1646C Rare	—	—	—	—	—	—
1647C Rare	—	—	—	—	—	—

KM# 146.5 ECU D'OR

3.3500 g., 0.9580 Gold 0.1032 oz. AGW **Ruler:** Louis XIV **Mint:** Lyon

Date	Mintage	VG	F	VF	XF	Unc
1643D Rare	—	—	—	—	—	—
1644D Rare	—	—	—	—	—	—
1645D	—	250	450	650	1,100	—

KM# 146.6 ECU D'OR

3.3500 g., 0.9580 Gold 0.1032 oz. AGW **Ruler:** Louis XIV **Mint:** La Rochelle

Date	Mintage	VG	F	VF	XF	Unc
1644H Rare	—	—	—	—	—	—
1645H	—	400	700	1,000	1,600	—
1646H Rare	—	—	—	—	—	—

KM# 146.7 ECU D'OR

3.3500 g., 0.9580 Gold 0.1032 oz. AGW **Ruler:** Louis XIV **Mint:** Limoges

Date	Mintage	VG	F	VF	XF	Unc
1644I Rare	—	—	—	—	—	—
1645I	—	400	700	1,000	1,600	—
1646I Rare	—	—	—	—	—	—
1647I	—	400	700	1,000	1,600	—
1648I Rare	—	—	—	—	—	—

KM# 146.8 ECU D'OR

3.3500 g., 0.9580 Gold 0.1032 oz. AGW **Ruler:** Louis XIV **Mint:** Bordeaux

Date	Mintage	VG	F	VF	XF	Unc
1644K Rare	—	—	—	—	—	—
1645K	—	500	800	1,100	1,600	—
1646K Rare	—	—	—	—	—	—

KM# 146.9 ECU D'OR

3.3500 g., 0.9580 Gold 0.1032 oz. AGW **Ruler:** Louis XIV **Mint:** Toulouse

Date	Mintage	VG	F	VF	XF	Unc
1644M Rare	—	—	—	—	—	—
1645M Rare	—	—	—	—	—	—
1646M Rare	—	—	—	—	—	—

KM# 146.10 ECU D'OR

3.3500 g., 0.9580 Gold 0.1032 oz. AGW **Ruler:** Louis XIV **Mint:** Montpellier

Date	Mintage	VG	F	VF	XF	Unc
1644N Rare	—	—	—	—	—	—
1646N Rare	—	—	—	—	—	—
1647N Rare	—	—	—	—	—	—

KM# 146.11 ECU D'OR

3.3500 g., 0.9580 Gold 0.1032 oz. AGW **Ruler:** Louis XIV **Mint:** Narbonne

Date	Mintage	VG	F	VF	XF	Unc
1645Q Rare	—	—	—	—	—	—
1646Q Rare	—	—	—	—	—	—

KM# 146.12 ECU D'OR

3.3500 g., 0.9580 Gold 0.1032 oz. AGW **Ruler:** Louis XIV **Mint:** Nantes

Date	Mintage	VG	F	VF	XF	Unc
1644T Rare	—	—	—	—	—	—
1645T Rare	—	—	—	—	—	—
1646T Rare	—	—	—	—	—	—

KM# 146.13 ECU D'OR

3.3500 g., 0.9580 Gold 0.1032 oz. AGW **Ruler:** Louis XIV **Mint:** Amiens

Date	Mintage	VG	F	VF	XF	Unc
1643X	—	250	450	650	1,100	—
1644X	—	250	450	650	1,100	—
1645X	—	250	450	650	1,100	—
1646X	—	250	450	650	1,100	—
1647X	—	250	450	650	1,100	—
1648X	—	250	450	650	1,100	—

KM# 146.14 ECU D'OR

3.3500 g., 0.9580 Gold 0.1032 oz. AGW **Ruler:** Louis XIV **Mint:** Aix **Note:** Mint mark: Ampersand.

Date	Mintage	VG	F	VF	XF	Unc
1643	—	250	450	650	1,100	—
1644	—	250	450	650	1,100	—
1645 Rare	—	—	—	—	—	—
1646	—	400	700	1,000	1,750	—

KM# 146.15 ECU D'OR

3.3500 g., 0.9580 Gold 0.1032 oz. AGW **Ruler:** Louis XIV **Note:** Mint mark: MA monogram.

Date	Mintage	VG	F	VF	XF	Unc
1644	—	400	700	1,000	1,600	—
1645 Rare	—	—	—	—	—	—
1646 Rare	—	—	—	—	—	—

KM# 217 LIS D'OR

3.9800 g., 0.9580 Gold 0.1226 oz. AGW **Ruler:** Louis XIV **Mint:** Paris

Date	Mintage	VG	F	VF	XF	Unc
1656A	—	1,000	2,500	6,000	10,000	—
1657A	—	2,000	3,500	8,500	13,000	—

KM# 101 1/2 LOUIS D'OR

3.3400 g., 0.9170 Gold 0.0985 oz. AGW **Ruler:** Louis XIII **Obv:** Loius XIII **Rev. Legend:** • CHRS • REGN • • VINC • • IMP • **Mint:** Paris

Date	Mintage	VG	F	VF	XF	Unc
1640A	—	200	400	700	1,250	—
1641A	—	200	400	700	1,250	—
1642A	—	200	400	700	1,250	—
1643A	—	200	400	700	1,250	—

KM# 102 1/2 LOUIS D'OR

3.3400 g., 0.9170 Gold 0.0985 oz. AGW **Ruler:** Louis XIII **Obv:** Large head of Loius XIII right, D • G • in legend at right of head **Mint:** Paris

Date	Mintage	VG	F	VF	XF	Unc
1640A	—	600	1,000	2,000	3,000	—

KM# 103 1/2 LOUIS D'OR
3.3400 g., 0.9170 Gold 0.0985 oz. AGW **Ruler:** Louis XIII **Obv. Legend:** • LVDO • XIII • D • G •... **Mint:** Paris

Date	Mintage	VG	F	VF	XF	Unc
1640A	—	450	800	1,400	2,500	—

KM# 125 1/2 LOUIS D'OR
3.3400 g., 0.9170 Gold 0.0985 oz. AGW **Ruler:** Louis XIII **Obv:** Long curl on Louis XIII **Rev:** Star after legend **Mint:** Paris

Date	Mintage	VG	F	VF	XF	Unc
1641A	—	200	350	650	1,100	—
1642A	—	200	350	650	1,100	—
1643A	—	200	350	650	1,100	—

KM# 126 1/2 LOUIS D'OR
3.3400 g., 0.9170 Gold 0.0985 oz. AGW **Ruler:** Louis XIII **Obv:** Large head **Rev:** Cross after legend **Mint:** Paris

Date	Mintage	VG	F	VF	XF	Unc
1641A	—	1,000	1,500	3,250	5,500	—

KM# 147 1/2 LOUIS D'OR
3.3400 g., 0.9170 Gold 0.0985 oz. AGW **Ruler:** Louis XIII **Obv. Legend:** • LUD • XIII • D • G •... **Mint:** Lyon

Date	Mintage	VG	F	VF	XF	Unc
1643D	—	400	750	1,250	2,250	—

KM# 148.1 1/2 LOUIS D'OR
3.3500 g., 0.9170 Gold 0.0988 oz. AGW **Ruler:** Louis XIV **Obv:** Laureate child head of Louis XIV, with short curl at right **Rev:** Eight L's cruciform with crown at end of each arm, mint mark at center **Mint:** Paris

Date	Mintage	VG	F	VF	XF	Unc
1643A	—	900	1,800	2,650	5,200	—
1644A	—	650	1,300	2,100	3,900	—
1645A	—	650	1,300	2,100	3,900	—

KM# 148.2 1/2 LOUIS D'OR
3.3500 g., 0.9170 Gold 0.0988 oz. AGW **Ruler:** Louis XIV **Mint:** Lyon

Date	Mintage	VG	F	VF	XF	Unc
1643D	—	900	1,800	2,650	4,300	—
1644D	—	650	1,300	2,350	3,600	—
1645D	—	900	1,800	2,650	4,300	—
1646D Rare	—	—	—	—	—	—
1649D	—	1,000	2,050	2,950	4,700	—
1650D	—	1,000	2,050	2,950	4,700	—
1652D Rare	—	—	—	—	—	—

KM# 156.1 1/2 LOUIS D'OR
3.3500 g., 0.9170 Gold 0.0988 oz. AGW **Ruler:** Louis XIV **Obv:** Laureate child head of Louis XIV, with long curl at right **Mint:** Paris

Date	Mintage	VG	F	VF	XF	Unc
1646A	—	350	650	1,300	2,900	—
1647	—	350	650	1,300	2,900	—
1648A	—	400	725	1,450	3,000	—
1649A Rare	—	—	—	—	—	—
1650A	—	400	725	1,450	3,000	—
1651A	—	425	775	1,600	3,200	—
1652A	—	350	650	1,300	2,900	—
1653A	—	425	775	1,600	3,300	—
1654A Rare	—	—	—	—	—	—
1657A Rare	—	—	—	—	—	—

KM# 156.2 1/2 LOUIS D'OR
3.3500 g., 0.9170 Gold 0.0988 oz. AGW **Ruler:** Louis XIV **Mint:** Arras

Date	Mintage	VG	F	VF	XF	Unc
1652AR	—	425	775	1,600	3,200	—

KM# 156.3 1/2 LOUIS D'OR
3.3500 g., 0.9170 Gold 0.0988 oz. AGW **Ruler:** Louis XIV **Mint:** Saint Lô

Date	Mintage	VG	F	VF	XF	Unc
1649C Rare	—	—	—	—	—	—

KM# 156.4 1/2 LOUIS D'OR
3.3500 g., 0.9170 Gold 0.0988 oz. AGW **Ruler:** Louis XIV **Mint:** Lyon

Date	Mintage	VG	F	VF	XF	Unc
1653D Rare	—	—	—	—	—	—
1659D Rare	—	—	—	—	—	—
1661D Rare	—	—	—	—	—	—

KM# 156.5 1/2 LOUIS D'OR
3.3500 g., 0.9170 Gold 0.0988 oz. AGW **Ruler:** Louis XIV **Mint:** Angers

Date	Mintage	VG	F	VF	XF	Unc
1648F	—	700	1,200	1,800	3,000	—
1650F Rare	—	—	—	—	—	—

KM# 156.6 1/2 LOUIS D'OR
3.3500 g., 0.9170 Gold 0.0988 oz. AGW **Ruler:** Louis XIV **Mint:** La Rochelle

Date	Mintage	VG	F	VF	XF	Unc
1648H Rare	—	—	—	—	—	—
1649H Rare	—	—	—	—	—	—
1650H Rare	—	—	—	—	—	—
1651H Rare	—	—	—	—	—	—
1652H	—	600	1,200	1,800	3,000	—
1653H Rare	—	—	—	—	—	—
1654H Rare	—	—	—	—	—	—

KM# 156.7 1/2 LOUIS D'OR
3.3500 g., 0.9170 Gold 0.0988 oz. AGW **Ruler:** Louis XIV **Mint:** Limoges

Date	Mintage	VG	F	VF	XF	Unc
1652I Rare	—	—	—	—	—	—
1653I Rare	—	—	—	—	—	—
1655I Rare	—	—	—	—	—	—

KM# 156.8 1/2 LOUIS D'OR
3.3500 g., 0.9170 Gold 0.0988 oz. AGW **Ruler:** Louis XIV **Mint:** Bordeaux

Date	Mintage	VG	F	VF	XF	Unc
1648K Rare	—	—	—	—	—	—

KM# 156.9 1/2 LOUIS D'OR
3.3500 g., 0.9170 Gold 0.0988 oz. AGW **Ruler:** Louis XIV **Mint:** Toulouse

Date	Mintage	VG	F	VF	XF	Unc
1648M Rare	—	—	—	—	—	—

KM# 156.10 1/2 LOUIS D'OR
3.3500 g., 0.9170 Gold 0.0988 oz. AGW **Ruler:** Louis XIV **Mint:** Montpellier

Date	Mintage	VG	F	VF	XF	Unc
1646N Rare	—	—	—	—	—	—
1647N Rare	—	—	—	—	—	—
1652N Rare	—	—	—	—	—	—
1653N Rare	—	—	—	—	—	—

KM# 156.11 1/2 LOUIS D'OR
3.3500 g., 0.9170 Gold 0.0988 oz. AGW **Ruler:** Louis XIV **Mint:** Riom

Date	Mintage	VG	F	VF	XF	Unc
1651O Rare	—	—	—	—	—	—
1652O Rare	—	—	—	—	—	—
1653O	—	350	750	1,500	3,000	—

KM# 156.12 1/2 LOUIS D'OR
3.3500 g., 0.9170 Gold 0.0988 oz. AGW **Ruler:** Louis XIV **Mint:** Dijon

Date	Mintage	VG	F	VF	XF	Unc
1652P Rare	—	—	—	—	—	—

KM# 156.13 1/2 LOUIS D'OR
3.3500 g., 0.9170 Gold 0.0988 oz. AGW **Ruler:** Louis XIV **Mint:** Nantes

Date	Mintage	VG	F	VF	XF	Unc
1649T Rare	—	—	—	—	—	—

KM# 156.14 1/2 LOUIS D'OR
3.3500 g., 0.9170 Gold 0.0988 oz. AGW **Ruler:** Louis XIV **Mint:** Bourges

Date	Mintage	VG	F	VF	XF	Unc
1648Y Rare	—	—	—	—	—	—
1650Y Rare	—	—	—	—	—	—

KM# 212 1/2 LOUIS D'OR
3.3500 g., 0.9170 Gold 0.0988 oz. AGW **Ruler:** Louis XIV **Obv:** Laureate juvenile bust of Louis XIV right, date below **Mint:** Paris

Date	Mintage	VG	F	VF	XF	Unc
1661A	—	—	—	—	—	—
Note: Reported, not confirmed						
1663A	—	—	—	—	—	—
Note: Reported, not confirmed						
1668A	—	—	—	—	—	—
Note: Reported, not confirmed						

KM# 218.1 1/2 LOUIS D'OR
3.3500 g., 0.9170 Gold 0.0988 oz. AGW **Ruler:** Louis XIV **Obv:** New juvenile head of Louis XIV right, date below **Mint:** Paris

Date	Mintage	VG	F	VF	XF	Unc
1668A	—	1,450	2,700	4,550	9,000	—
1669A	—	1,450	2,700	4,550	9,000	—
1670A	—	1,450	2,700	4,550	9,000	—
1671A Rare	—	—	—	—	—	—
1674A Rare	—	—	—	—	—	—
1677A	—	1,450	2,700	4,550	9,000	—
1678A Rare	—	—	—	—	—	—
1679A	—	1,450	2,700	4,550	9,000	—
1680A Rare	—	—	—	—	—	—
1682A Rare	—	—	—	—	—	—
1683A Rare	—	—	—	—	—	—
1684A Large head	400	1,450	3,000	5,000	11,000	—

KM# 218.2 1/2 LOUIS D'OR
3.3500 g., 0.9170 Gold 0.0988 oz. AGW **Ruler:** Louis XIV **Mint:** Rennes **Note:** Mint mark: Numeral 9.

Date	Mintage	VG	F	VF	XF	Unc
1679 Rare	—	—	—	—	—	—
1680 Rare	—	—	—	—	—	—
1681 Rare	—	—	—	—	—	—

KM# 264 1/2 LOUIS D'OR
3.3500 g., 0.9170 Gold 0.0988 oz. AGW **Ruler:** Louis XIV **Obv:** Laureate juvenile head of Louis XIV right, date below **Mint:** Lyon

Date	Mintage	VG	F	VF	XF	Unc
1687D Large head	—	1,300	2,700	4,600	9,000	—
1688D	—	1,300	2,700	4,600	9,000	—
1689D	—	1,300	2,700	4,600	9,000	—

KM# 277.1 1/2 LOUIS D'OR
3.3500 g., 0.9170 Gold 0.0988 oz. AGW **Ruler:** Louis XIV **Obv:** Older laureate head of Louis XIV right **Rev:** Crowned arms, mint mark above, date in legend **Mint:** Paris

Date	Mintage	VG	F	VF	XF	Unc
1690A	—	300	500	750	1,650	—
1691A	—	300	500	750	1,650	—
1693A	—	300	500	750	1,650	—

KM# 277.2 1/2 LOUIS D'OR
3.3500 g., 0.9170 Gold 0.0988 oz. AGW **Ruler:** Louis XIV **Mint:** Rouen

Date	Mintage	VG	F	VF	XF	Unc
1690B	—	300	500	750	1,750	—
1691B	—	300	500	750	1,750	—
1692B	—	300	500	750	1,750	—

KM# 277.3 1/2 LOUIS D'OR
3.3500 g., 0.9170 Gold 0.0988 oz. AGW **Ruler:** Louis XIV **Mint:** Lyon

Date	Mintage	VG	F	VF	XF	Unc
1690D	—	300	500	750	1,650	—
1691D	—	300	500	750	1,650	—
1692D Rare	—	—	—	—	—	—

KM# 277.4 1/2 LOUIS D'OR
3.3500 g., 0.9170 Gold 0.0988 oz. AGW **Ruler:** Louis XIV **Mint:** Tours

Date	Mintage	VG	F	VF	XF	Unc
1691E	—	300	500	750	1,650	—
1692E	—	300	500	750	1,650	—
1693E	—	300	500	750	1,650	—

KM# 277.5 1/2 LOUIS D'OR
3.3500 g., 0.9170 Gold 0.0988 oz. AGW **Ruler:** Louis XIV **Mint:** Poitiers

Date	Mintage	VG	F	VF	XF	Unc
1690G	—	350	600	900	1,950	—
1691G	—	325	550	800	1,750	—
1692G Rare	—	—	—	—	—	—

KM# 277.6 1/2 LOUIS D'OR
3.3500 g., 0.9170 Gold 0.0988 oz. AGW **Ruler:** Louis XIV **Mint:** La Rochelle

Date	Mintage	VG	F	VF	XF	Unc
1693H	—	300	500	750	1,400	—

KM# 277.7 1/2 LOUIS D'OR
3.3500 g., 0.9170 Gold 0.0988 oz. AGW **Ruler:** Louis XIV **Mint:** Limoges

Date	Mintage	VG	F	VF	XF	Unc
1690I	—	300	500	750	1,400	—
1691I	—	300	500	750	1,400	—
1692I Rare	—	—	—	—	—	—

KM# 277.8 1/2 LOUIS D'OR
3.3500 g., 0.9170 Gold 0.0988 oz. AGW **Ruler:** Louis XIV **Mint:** Bordeaux

Date	Mintage	VG	F	VF	XF	Unc
1690K	—	300	500	750	1,650	—

KM# 277.9 1/2 LOUIS D'OR
3.3500 g., 0.9170 Gold 0.0988 oz. AGW **Ruler:** Louis XIV **Mint:** Bayonne

Date	Mintage	VG	F	VF	XF	Unc
1690L	—	550	750	1,200	3,200	—
1691L	—	300	550	800	1,600	—

KM# 277.10 1/2 LOUIS D'OR
3.3500 g., 0.9170 Gold 0.0988 oz. AGW **Ruler:** Louis XIV **Mint:** Toulouse

Date	Mintage	VG	F	VF	XF	Unc
1690M	—	300	500	750	2,000	—
1691M	—	300	500	750	2,000	—

KM# 277.11 1/2 LOUIS D'OR
3.3500 g., 0.9170 Gold 0.0988 oz. AGW **Ruler:** Louis XIV **Mint:** Montpellier

Date	Mintage	VG	F	VF	XF	Unc
1690N Rare	—	—	—	—	—	—
1691N Rare	—	—	—	—	—	—

KM# 277.12 1/2 LOUIS D'OR
3.3500 g., 0.9170 Gold 0.0988 oz. AGW **Ruler:** Louis XIV **Mint:** Riom

Date	Mintage	VG	F	VF	XF	Unc
1691O	—	300	500	750	1,650	—
1693O Rare	—	—	—	—	—	—

KM# 277.13 1/2 LOUIS D'OR
3.3500 g., 0.9170 Gold 0.0988 oz. AGW **Ruler:** Louis XIV **Mint:** Dijon

Date	Mintage	VG	F	VF	XF	Unc
1690P	—	300	500	750	1,650	—
1691P	—	250	400	550	1,400	—
1692P	—	300	500	750	1,650	—
1693P Rare	—	—	—	—	—	—

KM# 277.14 1/2 LOUIS D'OR
3.3500 g., 0.9170 Gold 0.0988 oz. AGW **Ruler:** Louis XIV **Mint:** Amiens

Date	Mintage	VG	F	VF	XF	Unc
1691X	—	325	550	800	1,950	—

KM# 277.15 1/2 LOUIS D'OR
3.3500 g., 0.9170 Gold 0.0988 oz. AGW **Ruler:** Louis XIV **Mint:** Bourges

Date	Mintage	VG	F	VF	XF	Unc
1691Y	4,596	300	500	750	1,750	—
1692Y Rare	—	—	—	—	—	—

KM# 277.16 1/2 LOUIS D'OR
3.3500 g., 0.9170 Gold 0.0988 oz. AGW **Ruler:** Louis XIV **Mint:** Aix **Note:** Mint mark: Ampersand.

Date	Mintage	VG	F	VF	XF	Unc
1690	—	300	500	750	1,650	—
1692	—	300	500	750	1,650	—

KM# 277.17 1/2 LOUIS D'OR
3.3500 g., 0.9170 Gold 0.0988 oz. AGW **Ruler:** Louis XIV **Mint:** Rennes **Note:** Mint mark: Numeral 9.

Date	Mintage	VG	F	VF	XF	Unc
1690	—	300	500	750	1,650	—
1691	—	300	500	750	1,650	—

KM# 277.18 1/2 LOUIS D'OR
3.3500 g., 0.9170 Gold 0.0988 oz. AGW **Ruler:** Louis XIV **Mint:** Bayonne **Note:** Mint mark: Crowned L.

Date	Mintage	VG	F	VF	XF	Unc
1690	—	300	500	750	1,400	—
1691	—	300	500	750	1,400	—
1692	—	300	500	750	1,400	—

KM# 301.1 1/2 LOUIS D'OR
3.3500 g., 0.9170 Gold 0.0988 oz. AGW **Ruler:** Louis XIV **Obv:** Older laureate head of Louis XIV **Mint:** Paris

Date	Mintage	VG	F	VF	XF	Unc
1693A	—	250	400	600	1,400	—
1694A	—	250	400	600	1,400	—
1695A	—	250	400	600	1,400	—
1697A	—	250	400	600	1,400	—
1700A	—	400	600	900	2,200	—

KM# 301.2 1/2 LOUIS D'OR
3.3500 g., 0.9170 Gold 0.0988 oz. AGW **Ruler:** Louis XIV **Mint:** Rouen

Date	Mintage	VG	F	VF	XF	Unc
1694B	—	250	400	600	1,400	—
1695B	—	350	500	800	2,050	—

KM# 301.3 1/2 LOUIS D'OR
3.3500 g., 0.9170 Gold 0.0988 oz. AGW **Ruler:** Louis XIV **Mint:** Strasbourg

Date	Mintage	VG	F	VF	XF	Unc
1694BB	—	250	400	600	1,650	—
1695BB	—	250	400	600	1,650	—

KM# 301.4 1/2 LOUIS D'OR
3.3500 g., 0.9170 Gold 0.0988 oz. AGW **Ruler:** Louis XIV **Mint:** Caen

Date	Mintage	VG	F	VF	XF	Unc
1694C	—	250	400	600	1,400	—
1696C	—	250	400	600	1,400	—

KM# 301.5 1/2 LOUIS D'OR
3.3500 g., 0.9170 Gold 0.0988 oz. AGW **Ruler:** Louis XIV **Mint:** Lyon

Date	Mintage	VG	F	VF	XF	Unc
1693D Rare	—	—	—	—	—	—
1694D	—	225	375	500	1,250	—
1695D	—	250	400	600	1,400	—
1696D	—	250	400	600	1,400	—
1697D	—	300	450	700	1,500	—
1698D Rare	—	—	—	—	—	—

KM# 301.6 1/2 LOUIS D'OR
3.3500 g., 0.9170 Gold 0.0988 oz. AGW **Ruler:** Louis XIV **Mint:** Tours

Date	Mintage	VG	F	VF	XF	Unc
1694E	—	250	400	600	1,400	—
1696E	—	250	400	600	1,400	—

KM# 301.7 1/2 LOUIS D'OR
3.3500 g., 0.9170 Gold 0.0988 oz. AGW **Ruler:** Louis XIV **Mint:** Poitiers

Date	Mintage	VG	F	VF	XF	Unc
1694G	—	250	400	600	1,400	—

KM# 301.8 1/2 LOUIS D'OR
3.3500 g., 0.9170 Gold 0.0988 oz. AGW **Ruler:** Louis XIV **Mint:** La Rochelle

Date	Mintage	VG	F	VF	XF	Unc
1693H	—	250	400	600	1,400	—
1694H	—	300	450	700	1,500	—

KM# 301.9 1/2 LOUIS D'OR
3.3500 g., 0.9170 Gold 0.0988 oz. AGW **Ruler:** Louis XIV **Mint:** Limoges

Date	Mintage	VG	F	VF	XF	Unc
1693I	—	250	400	600	1,400	—
1694I	—	250	400	600	1,400	—
1696I	—	250	400	600	1,400	—

KM# 301.10 1/2 LOUIS D'OR
3.3500 g., 0.9170 Gold 0.0988 oz. AGW **Ruler:** Louis XIV **Mint:** Bayonne

Date	Mintage	VG	F	VF	XF	Unc
1694L	—	250	400	600	1,400	—

KM# 301.11 1/2 LOUIS D'OR
3.3500 g., 0.9170 Gold 0.0988 oz. AGW **Ruler:** Louis XIV **Mint:** Toulouse

Date	Mintage	VG	F	VF	XF	Unc
1693M	—	250	400	600	1,400	—
1694M	—	250	400	600	1,400	—
1695M	—	250	400	600	1,400	—

KM# 301.12 1/2 LOUIS D'OR
3.3500 g., 0.9170 Gold 0.0988 oz. AGW **Ruler:** Louis XIV **Mint:** Montpellier

Date	Mintage	VG	F	VF	XF	Unc
1693N	—	250	400	600	1,400	—
1694N	—	250	400	600	1,400	—
1695N	—	250	400	600	1,400	—
1696N Rare	—	—	—	—	—	—
1697N Rare	—	—	—	—	—	—
1698N Rare	—	—	—	—	—	—

KM# 301.13 1/2 LOUIS D'OR
3.3500 g., 0.9170 Gold 0.0988 oz. AGW **Ruler:** Louis XIV **Mint:** Riom

Date	Mintage	VG	F	VF	XF	Unc
1693O Rare	—	—	—	—	—	—
1694O	—	250	400	600	1,400	—
1695O	—	250	400	600	1,400	—
1697O Rare	—	—	—	—	—	—

KM# 301.14 1/2 LOUIS D'OR
3.3500 g., 0.9170 Gold 0.0988 oz. AGW **Ruler:** Louis XIV **Mint:** Dijon

Date	Mintage	VG	F	VF	XF	Unc
1693P	—	250	400	600	1,400	—
1694P Rare	—	—	—	—	—	—
1697P Rare	—	—	—	—	—	—
1698P Rare	—	—	—	—	—	—

KM# 301.15 1/2 LOUIS D'OR
3.3500 g., 0.9170 Gold 0.0988 oz. AGW **Ruler:** Louis XIV **Mint:** Reims

Date	Mintage	VG	F	VF	XF	Unc
1693S	—	250	400	600	1,400	—
1698S Rare	—	—	—	—	—	—

KM# 301.16 1/2 LOUIS D'OR
3.3500 g., 0.9170 Gold 0.0988 oz. AGW **Ruler:** Louis XIV **Mint:** Troyes

Date	Mintage	VG	F	VF	XF	Unc
1694V	—	350	550	800	1,650	—
1700V	—	400	600	900	2,200	—

KM# 301.17 1/2 LOUIS D'OR
3.3500 g., 0.9170 Gold 0.0988 oz. AGW **Ruler:** Louis XIV **Mint:** Lille

Date	Mintage	VG	F	VF	XF	Unc
1693W	—	250	400	600	1,400	—
1694W	—	250	400	600	1,400	—

KM# 301.18 1/2 LOUIS D'OR
3.3500 g., 0.9170 Gold 0.0988 oz. AGW **Ruler:** Louis XIV **Mint:** Amiens

Date	Mintage	VG	F	VF	XF	Unc
1695X	—	250	400	700	1,400	—

KM# 301.19 1/2 LOUIS D'OR
3.3500 g., 0.9170 Gold 0.0988 oz. AGW **Ruler:** Louis XIV **Mint:** Bourges

Date	Mintage	VG	F	VF	XF	Unc
1694Y	—	250	400	600	1,400	—
1698Y Rare	—	—	—	—	—	—

KM# 301.20 1/2 LOUIS D'OR
3.3500 g., 0.9170 Gold 0.0988 oz. AGW **Ruler:** Louis XIV **Mint:** Aix **Note:** Mint mark: &.

Date	Mintage	VG	F	VF	XF	Unc
1694	—	250	400	700	1,400	—

KM# 301.21 1/2 LOUIS D'OR
3.3500 g., 0.9170 Gold 0.0988 oz. AGW **Ruler:** Louis XIV **Mint:** Rennes **Note:** Mint mark: Numeral 9.

Date	Mintage	VG	F	VF	XF	Unc
1694 Rare	—	—	—	—	—	—

KM# 301.22 1/2 LOUIS D'OR
3.3500 g., 0.9170 Gold 0.0988 oz. AGW **Ruler:** Louis XIV **Mint:** Pau **Note:** Mint mark: Cow.

Date	Mintage	VG	F	VF	XF	Unc
1694	—	250	400	600	1,400	—
1696 Rare	—	—	—	—	—	—
1698 Rare	—	—	—	—	—	—

KM# 104 LOUIS D'OR
6.6900 g., 0.9170 Gold 0.1972 oz. AGW **Ruler:** Louis XIII **Obv:** Laureate head with long curl **Rev. Legend:** • CHRS • • REGN • • VINC • • IMP • **Mint:** Paris

Date	Mintage	VG	F	VF	XF	Unc
1640A	—	350	700	1,000	1,650	3,250
1641A	—	350	700	1,000	1,650	3,250
1642A	—	350	700	1,000	1,650	3,250
1643A	—	350	700	1,000	1,850	3,750

KM# 105 LOUIS D'OR
6.6900 g., 0.9170 Gold 0.1972 oz. AGW **Ruler:** Louis XIII **Obv:** Laureate head with short curl

Date	Mintage	VG	F	VF	XF	Unc
1640A	—	350	700	1,450	2,400	—
1641A	—	350	700	1,200	2,100	—

KM# 106 LOUIS D'OR
6.6900 g., 0.9170 Gold 0.1972 oz. AGW **Ruler:** Louis XIII **Obv:** Large head **Rev:** Legend begins in lower right quarter and ends... • IMPE •

Date	Mintage	VG	F	VF	XF	Unc
1640A	—	1,200	2,100	3,600	6,600	—

KM# 107 LOUIS D'OR
6.6900 g., 0.9170 Gold 0.1972 oz. AGW **Ruler:** Louis XIII **Obv:** Large head with legend **Obv. Legend:** • LVDO • XIII • D • G •... **Rev. Legend:** ...• IMPE •

Date	Mintage	VG	F	VF	XF	Unc
1640A	—	1,500	2,400	4,200	6,000	—

KM# 136.1 LOUIS D'OR
6.6900 g., 0.9170 Gold 0.1972 oz. AGW **Ruler:** Louis XIII **Obv:** Older head **Rev:** Legend begins in upper left quarter

Date	Mintage	VG	F	VF	XF	Unc
1642A	—	350	700	1,300	2,400	—
1643A	—	375	750	1,300	2,400	—

KM# 136.2 LOUIS D'OR
6.6900 g., 0.9170 Gold 0.1972 oz. AGW **Ruler:** Louis XIII **Mint:** Lyon

Date	Mintage	VG	F	VF	XF	Unc
1643D	—	775	1,500	2,400	3,600	—

KM# 149.1 LOUIS D'OR
6.6900 g., 0.9170 Gold 0.1972 oz. AGW **Ruler:** Louis XIV **Obv:** Laureate child head of Louis XIV, with short curl **Mint:** Paris

Date	Mintage	VG	F	VF	XF	Unc
1643A	—	375	650	1,100	2,150	—
1644A	—	375	650	1,100	2,150	—
1645A	—	375	650	1,100	2,150	—
1646A Rare	—	—	—	—	—	—

KM# 149.2 LOUIS D'OR
6.6900 g., 0.9170 Gold 0.1972 oz. AGW **Ruler:** Louis XIV **Mint:** Lyon

Date	Mintage	VG	F	VF	XF	Unc
1644D	—	375	650	1,050	2,100	—
1645D	—	375	725	1,100	2,150	—

Date	Mintage	VG	F	VF	XF	Unc
1648D	—	375	725	1,100	2,150	—
1649D	—	375	725	1,100	2,150	—
1650D	—	475	925	1,300	2,600	—
1651D	—	375	725	1,100	2,150	—
1652D Tower	—	475	925	1,300	2,600	—
1652D Crescent	—	475	925	1,300	2,600	—
1656D	—	525	1,050	1,650	2,900	—

KM# 157.1 LOUIS D'OR

6.6900 g., 0.9170 Gold 0.1972 oz. AGW **Ruler:** Louis XIV **Obv:** Head with long curl **Mint:** Paris

Date	Mintage	VG	F	VF	XF	Unc
1646A	—	295	525	800	1,350	2,750
1647A	—	295	525	800	1,350	2,750
1648A	—	295	525	800	1,350	2,750
1649A	—	295	525	800	1,350	2,750
1650A	—	295	525	800	1,350	2,750
1651A	—	295	525	800	1,350	2,750
1652A	—	295	525	800	1,350	2,750
1653A	—	295	525	800	1,350	2,750
1654A	—	295	525	800	1,350	2,750
1655A	—	295	525	800	1,350	2,750
1657A	—	295	525	800	1,350	2,750
1658A Rare	—	—	—	—	—	—
1659A	600,000	325	600	925	1,450	3,000

KM# 157.2 LOUIS D'OR

6.6900 g., 0.9170 Gold 0.1972 oz. AGW **Ruler:** Louis XIV **Mint:** Arras

Date	Mintage	VG	F	VF	XF	Unc
1646AR	200	600	1,200	1,650	3,500	—
1648AR	—	375	650	1,050	1,750	—
1649AR Rare	—	—	—	—	—	—
1650AR	—	375	650	1,050	1,750	—
1651AR	—	375	650	1,050	1,750	—
1652AR	—	375	650	1,050	1,750	—
1653AR	—	375	650	1,050	1,750	—
1655AR	—	375	650	1,050	1,750	—
1656AR	—	375	650	1,050	1,750	—
1657AR	—	375	650	1,050	1,750	—

KM# 157.3 LOUIS D'OR

6.6900 g., 0.9170 Gold 0.1972 oz. AGW **Ruler:** Louis XIV **Mint:** Rouen

Date	Mintage	VG	F	VF	XF	Unc
1646B	—	375	650	1,050	1,750	3,500
1647B	—	375	650	1,050	1,750	3,500
1648B Rare	—	—	—	—	—	—
1649B Rare	—	—	—	—	—	—
1650B	—	375	650	1,050	1,750	3,500
1651B	—	375	650	1,050	1,750	3,500
1652B	—	375	650	1,050	1,750	3,500
1653B	—	375	650	1,050	1,750	3,500
1655B Rare	—	—	—	—	—	—
1657B Rare	—	—	—	—	—	—
1658B	200	475	925	1,300	2,650	5,250
1659B Rare	—	—	—	—	—	—

KM# 157.4 LOUIS D'OR

6.6900 g., 0.9170 Gold 0.1972 oz. AGW **Ruler:** Louis XIV **Mint:** Saint Lô

Date	Mintage	VG	F	VF	XF	Unc
1647C	—	375	650	1,050	1,750	3,500
1648C	—	375	650	1,050	1,750	3,500
1649C	—	375	650	1,050	1,750	3,500
1650C	—	375	650	1,050	1,750	3,500
1651C	—	375	650	1,050	1,750	3,500
1652C	—	375	650	1,050	1,750	3,500
1653C	2,049	375	650	1,050	1,750	3,500
1654C	—	375	650	1,050	1,750	3,500
1655C Rare	—	—	—	—	—	—

KM# 157.5 LOUIS D'OR

6.6900 g., 0.9170 Gold 0.1972 oz. AGW **Ruler:** Louis XIV **Mint:** Lyon

Date	Mintage	VG	F	VF	XF	Unc
1652D	—	295	525	800	1,300	2,750
1653D	—	295	525	800	1,300	2,750
1654D Rare	—	—	—	—	—	—
1657D	—	375	650	1,050	1,750	3,500
1658D	—	375	650	1,050	1,750	3,500
1659D Rare	—	—	—	—	—	—

KM# 157.6 LOUIS D'OR

6.6900 g., 0.9170 Gold 0.1972 oz. AGW **Ruler:** Louis XIV **Mint:** Tours

Date	Mintage	VG	F	VF	XF	Unc
1652E	—	325	600	925	1,450	3,000
1653E	—	295	525	800	1,300	2,750
1654E Rare	—	—	—	—	—	—

KM# 157.7 LOUIS D'OR

6.6900 g., 0.9170 Gold 0.1972 oz. AGW **Ruler:** Louis XIV **Mint:** Angers

Date	Mintage	VG	F	VF	XF	Unc
1647F Rare	—	—	—	—	—	—
1648F	—	375	650	1,050	1,750	3,500
1649F	—	375	650	1,050	1,750	3,500
1650F	—	375	650	1,050	1,750	3,500
1651F	—	525	1,050	1,600	2,450	5,000
1652F	—	375	650	1,050	1,750	3,500
1653F Rare	—	—	—	—	—	—
1654F	—	375	650	1,050	1,750	3,500
1655F Rare	—	—	—	—	—	—
1656F Rare	—	—	—	—	—	—

KM# 157.8 LOUIS D'OR

6.6900 g., 0.9170 Gold 0.1972 oz. AGW **Ruler:** Louis XIV **Mint:** Poitiers

Date	Mintage	VG	F	VF	XF	Unc
1650G Rare	—	—	—	—	—	—

KM# 157.9 LOUIS D'OR

6.6900 g., 0.9170 Gold 0.1972 oz. AGW **Ruler:** Louis XIV **Mint:** La Rochelle

Date	Mintage	VG	F	VF	XF	Unc
1646H	—	375	650	1,050	1,750	3,500
1647H Rare	—	—	—	—	—	—
1648H Rare	—	—	—	—	—	—
1649H	—	375	650	1,050	1,750	3,500
1650H	—	375	650	1,050	1,750	3,500
1651H	—	375	650	1,050	1,750	3,500
1652H Rare	—	—	—	—	—	—
1653H	—	375	650	1,050	1,750	3,500
1654H Rare	—	—	—	—	—	—
1655H Rare	—	—	—	—	—	—

KM# 157.10 LOUIS D'OR

6.6900 g., 0.9170 Gold 0.1972 oz. AGW **Ruler:** Louis XIV **Mint:** Limoges

Date	Mintage	VG	F	VF	XF	Unc
1648I Rare	—	—	—	—	—	—
1650I Rare	—	—	—	—	—	—
1651I	2,377	375	650	1,050	1,750	3,500
1652I	—	325	600	925	1,450	3,000
1653I	—	325	600	925	1,450	3,000
1654I Rare	—	—	—	—	—	—
1655I Rare	—	—	—	—	—	—
1656I Rare	—	—	—	—	—	—
1657I Rare	—	—	—	—	—	—
1659I	—	375	650	1,050	1,750	3,500

KM# 157.11 LOUIS D'OR

6.6900 g., 0.9170 Gold 0.1972 oz. AGW **Ruler:** Louis XIV **Mint:** Bordeaux

Date	Mintage	VG	F	VF	XF	Unc
1647K Rare	—	—	—	—	—	—
1648K Rare	—	—	—	—	—	—
1649K Rare	—	—	—	—	—	—
1650K	1,858	375	650	1,050	1,750	3,500
1651K Rare	—	—	—	—	—	—
1652K Rare	—	—	—	—	—	—
1653K Rare	—	—	—	—	—	—
1654K Rare	—	—	—	—	—	—
1655K Rare	—	—	—	—	—	—
1656K	—	325	600	925	1,450	3,000
1657K Rare	—	—	—	—	—	—

KM# 157.12 LOUIS D'OR

6.6900 g., 0.9170 Gold 0.1972 oz. AGW **Ruler:** Louis XIV **Mint:** Toulouse

Date	Mintage	VG	F	VF	XF	Unc
1647M	—	375	650	1,050	1,750	3,500
1648M Rare	—	—	—	—	—	—
1651M Rare	—	—	—	—	—	—
1652M	—	325	600	925	1,450	3,000
1653M	—	325	600	925	1,450	3,000
1654M Rare	—	—	—	—	—	—
1655M Rare	—	—	—	—	—	—
1656M Rare	—	—	—	—	—	—
1659M Rare	—	—	—	—	—	—

KM# 157.13 LOUIS D'OR

6.6900 g., 0.9170 Gold 0.1972 oz. AGW **Ruler:** Louis XIV **Mint:** Montpellier

Date	Mintage	VG	F	VF	XF	Unc
1646N Rare	—	—	—	—	—	—
1647N Rare	—	—	—	—	—	—
1648N Rare	—	—	—	—	—	—
1649N	—	295	525	800	1,300	2,750
1650N	—	295	525	800	1,300	2,750
1651N	—	295	525	800	1,300	2,750
1652N	—	295	525	800	1,300	2,750
1653N Rare	—	—	—	—	—	—
1656N	—	295	525	800	1,300	2,750
1657N	—	295	525	800	1,300	2,750
1658N Rare	—	—	—	—	—	—
1659N Rare	—	—	—	—	—	—

KM# 157.14 LOUIS D'OR

6.6900 g., 0.9170 Gold 0.1972 oz. AGW **Ruler:** Louis XIV **Mint:** Riom

Date	Mintage	VG	F	VF	XF	Unc
1652O Rare	—	—	—	—	—	—
1653O	—	325	600	925	1,450	3,000

KM# 157.15 LOUIS D'OR

6.6900 g., 0.9170 Gold 0.1972 oz. AGW **Ruler:** Louis XIV **Mint:** Dijon

Date	Mintage	VG	F	VF	XF	Unc
1646P	—	350	600	950	1,450	3,500
1650P Rare	—	—	—	—	—	—
1651P	775	425	700	1,100	1,700	4,000
1653P	—	350	600	950	1,450	3,500

KM# 157.16 LOUIS D'OR

6.6900 g., 0.9170 Gold 0.1972 oz. AGW **Ruler:** Louis XIV **Mint:** Narbonne

Date	Mintage	VG	F	VF	XF	Unc
1651Q	—	325	600	925	1,450	3,000
1652Q	—	375	650	1,050	1,750	3,500
1653Q Rare	—	—	—	—	—	—

KM# 157.17 LOUIS D'OR

6.6900 g., 0.9170 Gold 0.1972 oz. AGW **Ruler:** Louis XIV **Mint:** Villeneuve St. André

Date	Mintage	VG	F	VF	XF	Unc
1651R	—	325	600	925	1,450	3,000

KM# 157.18 LOUIS D'OR

6.6900 g., 0.9170 Gold 0.1972 oz. AGW **Ruler:** Louis XIV **Mint:** Troyes

Date	Mintage	VG	F	VF	XF	Unc
1651S	—	325	600	925	1,450	3,000
1652S	—	325	600	925	1,450	3,000
1653S	—	325	600	925	1,450	3,000
1654S Rare	—	—	—	—	—	—
1655S Rare	—	—	—	—	—	—

KM# 157.19 LOUIS D'OR

6.6900 g., 0.9170 Gold 0.1972 oz. AGW **Ruler:** Louis XIV **Mint:** Nantes

Date	Mintage	VG	F	VF	XF	Unc
1647T Rare	—	—	—	—	—	—
1649T Rare	—	—	—	—	—	—
1650T	—	375	650	1,050	1,750	3,500
1651T	—	375	650	1,050	1,750	3,500
1652T	—	375	650	1,050	1,750	3,500
1653T Rare	—	—	—	—	—	—
1654T	—	375	650	1,050	1,750	3,500
1655T Rare	—	—	—	—	—	—
1656T Rare	—	—	—	—	—	—

KM# 157.20 LOUIS D'OR

6.6900 g., 0.9170 Gold 0.1972 oz. AGW **Ruler:** Louis XIV **Mint:** Amiens

Date	Mintage	VG	F	VF	XF	Unc
1650X	—	295	525	800	1,300	2,750
1651X	—	295	525	800	1,300	2,750
1652X	—	295	525	800	1,300	2,750
1653X	—	295	525	800	1,300	2,750
1654X Rare	—	—	—	—	—	—
1655X Rare	—	—	—	—	—	—
1659X Rare	—	—	—	—	—	—

KM# 157.21 LOUIS D'OR

6.6900 g., 0.9170 Gold 0.1972 oz. AGW **Ruler:** Louis XIV **Mint:** Bourges

Date	Mintage	VG	F	VF	XF	Unc
1653Y	—	325	600	925	1,450	3,000
1654Y	—	325	600	925	1,450	3,000
1655Y	—	375	650	1,050	1,750	3,500
1656Y Rare	—	—	—	—	—	—

KM# 157.22 LOUIS D'OR

6.6900 g., 0.9170 Gold 0.1972 oz. AGW **Ruler:** Louis XIV **Mint:** Aix **Note:** Mint mark: &.

Date	Mintage	VG	F	VF	XF	Unc
1646 Rare	—	—	—	—	—	—
1647 Rare	—	—	—	—	—	—
1648	—	295	525	800	1,300	2,750
1649 Rare	—	—	—	—	—	—
1651	—	295	525	800	1,300	2,750
1652	—	295	525	800	1,300	2,750
1653	—	295	525	800	1,300	2,750
1654	—	295	525	800	1,300	2,750
1656 Rare	—	—	—	—	—	—
1657 Rare	—	—	—	—	—	—
1658 Rare	—	—	—	—	—	—
1659 Rare	—	—	—	—	—	—

KM# 200.1 LOUIS D'OR
6.6900 g., 0.9170 Gold 0.1972 oz. AGW **Ruler:** Louis XIV **Obv:** Laureate juvenile head of Louis XIV **Mint:** Paris

Date	Mintage	VG	F	VF	XF	Unc
1658A	—	325	600	925	1,800	3,600
1659A	—	325	600	925	1,800	3,600
1660A	—	325	600	925	1,800	3,600
1661A	—	325	600	925	1,800	3,600
1662A	—	325	600	925	1,800	3,600
1663A	—	325	600	925	1,800	3,600
1664A	—	325	600	925	1,800	3,600
1665A	—	325	600	925	1,800	3,600
1666A	—	325	600	925	1,800	3,600
1667A	—	325	600	925	1,800	3,600
1668A	—	325	600	925	1,800	3,600

KM# 200.2 LOUIS D'OR
6.6900 g., 0.9170 Gold 0.1972 oz. AGW **Ruler:** Louis XIV **Mint:** Rouen

Date	Mintage	VG	F	VF	XF	Unc
1660B	—	375	650	1,100	2,100	4,250
1661B Rare	—	—	—	—	—	—
1662B	—	375	650	1,100	2,100	4,250

KM# 200.3 LOUIS D'OR
6.6900 g., 0.9170 Gold 0.1972 oz. AGW **Ruler:** Louis XIV **Mint:** Lyon

Date	Mintage	VG	F	VF	XF	Unc
1661D	—	325	600	1,050	2,050	4,200
1662D	—	325	600	1,050	2,050	4,200
1663D	—	325	600	1,050	2,050	4,200
1664D	—	325	600	1,050	2,050	4,200
1665D	—	325	600	1,050	2,050	4,200
1666D Rare	—	—	—	—	—	—
1667D Rare	—	—	—	—	—	—
1668D	—	325	600	1,050	2,050	4,200
1669D	—	325	600	1,050	2,050	4,200
1670D	—	325	600	1,050	2,050	4,200

KM# 200.4 LOUIS D'OR
6.6900 g., 0.9170 Gold 0.1972 oz. AGW **Ruler:** Louis XIV **Mint:** Limoges

Date	Mintage	VG	F	VF	XF	Unc
1662I	—	375	650	1,100	2,100	4,250

KM# 200.5 LOUIS D'OR
6.6900 g., 0.9170 Gold 0.1972 oz. AGW **Ruler:** Louis XIV **Mint:** Bordeaux

Date	Mintage	VG	F	VF	XF	Unc
1660K	9,091	325	600	1,000	1,900	3,850
1661K Rare	—	—	—	—	—	—

KM# 200.6 LOUIS D'OR
6.6900 g., 0.9170 Gold 0.1972 oz. AGW **Ruler:** Louis XIV **Mint:** Bayonne

Date	Mintage	VG	F	VF	XF	Unc
1662L Rare	—	—	—	—	—	—
1663L	—	375	650	1,100	2,100	4,250
1664L Rare	—	—	—	—	—	—
1668L	—	325	600	1,000	1,900	3,850
1669L	—	325	600	1,000	1,900	3,850
1670L	—	325	600	925	1,850	3,750
1671L	—	325	600	925	1,850	3,750
1672L	—	325	600	925	1,850	3,750

KM# 200.7 LOUIS D'OR
6.6900 g., 0.9170 Gold 0.1972 oz. AGW **Ruler:** Louis XIV **Mint:** Montpellier

Date	Mintage	VG	F	VF	XF	Unc
1660N	1,600	375	650	1,100	2,100	7,250
1662N	—	375	650	1,100	2,100	4,250
1666N Rare	—	—	—	—	—	—
1667N	—	325	600	925	1,800	3,600
1668N Rare	—	—	—	—	—	—

KM# 200.8 LOUIS D'OR
6.6900 g., 0.9170 Gold 0.1972 oz. AGW **Ruler:** Louis XIV **Mint:** Amiens

Date	Mintage	VG	F	VF	XF	Unc
1659X	—	325	600	1,000	2,000	4,400
1660X Rare	—	—	—	—	—	—
1661X	1,000	—	—	—	—	—

KM# 200.9 LOUIS D'OR
6.6900 g., 0.9170 Gold 0.1972 oz. AGW **Ruler:** Louis XIV **Mint:** Bourges

Date	Mintage	VG	F	VF	XF	Unc
1660Y	219	650	1,200	1,650	3,600	7,250

KM# 200.10 LOUIS D'OR
6.6900 g., 0.9170 Gold 0.1972 oz. AGW **Ruler:** Louis XIV **Mint:** Aix **Note:** Mint mark: &.

Date	Mintage	VG	F	VF	XF	Unc
1660	1,124	375	650	1,100	2,100	4,250
1661	1,740	375	650	1,100	2,100	4,250
1662	—	375	650	1,100	2,100	4,250
1663 Rare	—	—	—	—	—	—
1664 Rare	—	—	—	—	—	—
1665 Rare	—	—	—	—	—	—
1666 Rare	—	—	—	—	—	—
1667	—	375	650	1,100	2,100	4,250
1668 Rare	—	—	—	—	—	—
1669	—	—	—	—	—	—
1670 Rare	—	—	—	—	—	—
1671 Rare	—	—	—	—	—	—
1672	—	375	650	1,100	2,100	4,250

KM# 200.11 LOUIS D'OR
6.6900 g., 0.9170 Gold 0.1972 oz. AGW **Ruler:** Louis XIV **Mint:** Pau **Note:** Mint mark: Cow.

Date	Mintage	VG	F	VF	XF	Unc
1665	—	1,200	2,700	3,900	7,900	—
1668	—	1,200	2,700	3,900	7,900	—
1674	—	1,200	2,700	3,900	7,900	—
1679	—	1,200	2,700	3,900	7,900	—

KM# 200.12 LOUIS D'OR
6.6900 g., 0.9170 Gold 0.1972 oz. AGW **Ruler:** Louis XIV **Mint:** Villeneuve St. André

Date	Mintage	VG	F	VF	XF	Unc
1660R	—	800	1,500	3,300	5,500	—

KM# 219.1 LOUIS D'OR
6.6900 g., 0.9170 Gold 0.1972 oz. AGW **Ruler:** Louis XIV **Obv:** New juvenile head of Louis XIV **Mint:** Paris

Date	Mintage	VG	F	VF	XF	Unc
1668A	—	325	600	925	1,450	3,000
1669A	—	325	600	925	1,450	3,000
1670A	—	325	600	925	1,450	3,000
1671A	—	325	600	925	1,450	3,000
1672A	—	325	600	925	1,450	3,000
1673A	—	325	600	925	1,450	3,000
1674A	—	325	600	925	1,450	3,000
1675A	—	325	600	925	1,450	3,000
1676A	—	325	600	925	1,450	3,000
1677A	—	325	600	925	1,450	3,000
1678A	—	325	600	925	1,450	3,000

KM# 219.2 LOUIS D'OR
6.6900 g., 0.9170 Gold 0.1972 oz. AGW **Ruler:** Louis XIV **Mint:** Rouen

Date	Mintage	VG	F	VF	XF	Unc
1679B Rare	—	—	—	—	—	—
1680B	—	375	650	1,050	1,550	3,150

KM# 219.3 LOUIS D'OR
6.6900 g., 0.9170 Gold 0.1972 oz. AGW **Ruler:** Louis XIV **Mint:** Lyon

Date	Mintage	VG	F	VF	XF	Unc
1669D	—	375	650	1,050	1,550	3,150
1670D	—	375	650	1,050	1,550	3,150
1671D	—	375	650	1,050	1,550	3,150
1672D	—	375	650	1,050	1,550	3,150
1673D	—	375	650	1,050	1,550	3,150
1674D	—	375	650	1,050	1,550	3,150
1675D	—	375	650	1,100	1,750	3,500
1677D	—	375	650	1,100	1,750	3,500
1678D Rare	—	—	—	—	—	—
1679D	—	375	650	1,050	1,550	3,150
1680D	—	375	650	1,050	1,550	3,150
1681D	—	375	650	1,050	1,550	3,150
1682D	—	375	650	1,050	1,550	3,150
1683D	—	375	650	1,050	1,550	3,150

KM# 219.4 LOUIS D'OR
6.6900 g., 0.9170 Gold 0.1972 oz. AGW **Ruler:** Louis XIV **Mint:** Tours

Date	Mintage	VG	F	VF	XF	Unc
1680E Rare	—	—	—	—	—	—

KM# 219.5 LOUIS D'OR
6.6900 g., 0.9170 Gold 0.1972 oz. AGW **Ruler:** Louis XIV **Mint:** Limoges

Date	Mintage	VG	F	VF	XF	Unc
1679I Rare	—	—	—	—	—	—
1680I	—	375	650	1,050	1,550	3,150

KM# 219.6 LOUIS D'OR
6.6900 g., 0.9170 Gold 0.1972 oz. AGW **Ruler:** Louis XIV **Mint:** Bordeaux

Date	Mintage	VG	F	VF	XF	Unc
1679K Rare	—	—	—	—	—	—

KM# 219.7 LOUIS D'OR
6.6900 g., 0.9170 Gold 0.1972 oz. AGW **Ruler:** Louis XIV **Mint:** Bayonne

Date	Mintage	VG	F	VF	XF	Unc
1672L	—	325	600	925	1,450	3,000
1673L	—	325	600	925	1,450	3,000
1674L	—	325	600	925	1,450	3,000
1675L	—	350	650	1,000	1,550	—
1676L	220,000	325	600	925	1,450	3,000
1677L Rare	—	—	—	—	—	—
1678L Rare	—	—	—	—	—	—
1679L	—	325	600	925	1,450	3,000
1680L	—	325	600	925	1,450	3,000
1681L	—	325	600	925	1,450	3,000
1682L	—	325	600	925	1,450	3,000
1683L Rare	—	—	—	—	—	—
1684L Rare	—	—	—	—	—	—

KM# 219.8 LOUIS D'OR
6.6900 g., 0.9170 Gold 0.1972 oz. AGW **Ruler:** Louis XIV **Mint:** Montpellier

Date	Mintage	VG	F	VF	XF	Unc
1679N Rare	—	—	—	—	—	—
1680N	—	400	800	1,200	1,550	—

KM# 219.9 LOUIS D'OR
6.6900 g., 0.9170 Gold 0.1972 oz. AGW **Ruler:** Louis XIV **Mint:** Troyes

Date	Mintage	VG	F	VF	XF	Unc
1680S Rare	—	—	—	—	—	—
1681S Rare	—	—	—	—	—	—
1682S	—	375	650	1,100	1,750	3,500
1683S Rare	—	—	—	—	—	—
1684S Rare	—	—	—	—	—	—

KM# 219.10 LOUIS D'OR
6.6900 g., 0.9170 Gold 0.1972 oz. AGW **Ruler:** Louis XIV **Mint:** Amiens

Date	Mintage	VG	F	VF	XF	Unc
1679X Rare	—	—	—	—	—	—
1681X Rare	—	—	—	—	—	—

KM# 219.11 LOUIS D'OR
6.6900 g., 0.9170 Gold 0.1972 oz. AGW **Ruler:** Louis XIV **Mint:** Aix **Note:** Mint mark: Ampersand.

Date	Mintage	VG	F	VF	XF	Unc
1679 Rare	—	—	—	—	—	—
1680 Rare	—	—	—	—	—	—

KM# 219.12 LOUIS D'OR
6.6900 g., 0.9170 Gold 0.1972 oz. AGW **Ruler:** Louis XIV **Mint:** Rennes **Note:** Mint mark: Numeral 9.

Date	Mintage	VG	F	VF	XF	Unc
1679 Rare	—	—	—	—	—	—
1680 Rare	—	—	—	—	—	—
1681 Rare	—	—	—	—	—	—
1682 Rare	—	—	—	—	—	—
1683 Rare	—	—	—	—	—	—

KM# 236.1 LOUIS D'OR
6.6900 g., 0.9170 Gold 0.1972 oz. AGW **Ruler:** Louis XIV **Obv:** Older head of Louis XIV **Mint:** Paris

Date	Mintage	VG	F	VF	XF	Unc
1679A	—	450	825	1,950	3,600	7,250
1680A	—	450	825	1,950	3,600	7,250
1681A	—	450	825	1,950	3,600	7,250
1682A	—	450	825	1,950	3,600	7,250
1683A	470,000	450	825	1,950	3,600	7,250

KM# 236.2 LOUIS D'OR
6.6900 g., 0.9170 Gold 0.1972 oz. AGW **Ruler:** Louis XIV **Mint:** Rouen

Date	Mintage	VG	F	VF	XF	Unc
1681B	—	475	850	1,950	3,600	7,250
1682B Rare	—	—	—	—	—	—
1683B Rare	—	—	—	—	—	—
1684B Rare	—	—	—	—	—	—

KM# 236.3 LOUIS D'OR
6.6900 g., 0.9170 Gold 0.1972 oz. AGW **Ruler:** Louis XIV **Mint:** Bordeaux

Date	Mintage	VG	F	VF	XF	Unc
1680K	—	500	900	1,550	2,400	4,750
1682K Rare	—	—	—	—	—	—
1683K Rare	—	—	—	—	—	—
1684K Rare	—	—	—	—	—	—

KM# 236.4 LOUIS D'OR
6.6900 g., 0.9170 Gold 0.1972 oz. AGW **Ruler:** Louis XIV **Mint:** Amiens

Date	Mintage	VG	F	VF	XF	Unc
1679X	—	475	850	2,000	3,700	7,500

Date	Mintage	VG	F	VF	XF	Unc
1680X	—	475	850	2,000	3,700	7,500
1681X Rare	—	—	—	—	—	—

KM# 236.5 LOUIS D'OR
6.6900 g., 0.9170 Gold 0.1972 oz. AGW **Ruler:** Louis XIV **Mint:** Aix **Note:** Mint mark: Ampersand.

Date	Mintage	VG	F	VF	XF	Unc
1681 Rare	—	—	—	—	—	—
1682	—	475	850	1,950	3,600	7,250
1683	—	475	850	1,950	3,600	7,250

KM# 236.6 LOUIS D'OR
6.6900 g., 0.9170 Gold 0.1972 oz. AGW **Ruler:** Louis XIV **Mint:** Pau **Note:** Mint mark: Cow.

Date	Mintage	VG	F	VF	XF	Unc
1681	—	1,100	2,200	3,850	6,100	—
1683	—	1,100	2,200	3,850	6,100	—
1687 Rare	—	—	—	—	—	—
1688	—	1,100	2,200	3,850	6,100	—

KM# 256.1 LOUIS D'OR
6.6900 g., 0.9170 Gold 0.1972 oz. AGW **Ruler:** Louis XIV **Obv:** Large laureate head of Louis XIV **Mint:** Paris

Date	Mintage	VG	F	VF	XF	Unc
1684A	—	725	1,150	1,850	7,000	—
1685A	—	725	1,150	1,850	7,000	—
1686A	—	725	1,150	1,850	7,000	—
1687A	—	725	1,150	1,850	7,000	—
1688A	—	725	1,150	1,850	7,000	—
1689A	—	725	1,150	1,850	7,000	—

KM# 256.2 LOUIS D'OR
6.6900 g., 0.9170 Gold 0.1972 oz. AGW **Ruler:** Louis XIV **Mint:** Lyon

Date	Mintage	VG	F	VF	XF	Unc
1683D	—	725	1,150	1,850	7,000	—
1684D	—	725	1,150	1,850	7,000	—
1685D	—	725	1,150	1,850	7,000	—
1686D	—	725	1,150	1,850	7,000	—
1687D	—	725	1,150	1,850	7,000	—
1688D	—	725	1,150	1,850	7,000	—
1689D	—	725	1,150	1,850	7,000	—

KM# 256.3 LOUIS D'OR
6.6900 g., 0.9170 Gold 0.1972 oz. AGW **Ruler:** Louis XIV **Mint:** Bordeaux

Date	Mintage	VG	F	VF	XF	Unc
1685K	—	675	1,150	1,800	7,000	—
1686K Rare	—	—	—	—	—	—
1687K	—	675	1,150	1,800	7,000	—
1688K Rare	—	—	—	—	—	—

KM# 256.4 LOUIS D'OR
6.6900 g., 0.9170 Gold 0.1972 oz. AGW **Ruler:** Louis XIV **Mint:** Bayonne

Date	Mintage	VG	F	VF	XF	Unc
1685L Rare	—	—	—	—	—	—
1686L Rare	—	—	—	—	—	—
1687L	—	775	1,300	2,150	4,500	—
1688L Rare	—	—	—	—	—	—
1689L Rare	—	—	—	—	—	—

KM# 256.6 LOUIS D'OR
6.6900 g., 0.9170 Gold 0.1972 oz. AGW **Ruler:** Louis XIV **Mint:** Amiens

Date	Mintage	VG	F	VF	XF	Unc
1685X Rare	—	—	—	—	—	—

KM# 256.7 LOUIS D'OR
6.6900 g., 0.9170 Gold 0.1972 oz. AGW **Ruler:** Louis XIV **Mint:** Aix **Note:** Mint mark: Ampersand.

Date	Mintage	VG	F	VF	XF	Unc
1684	—	725	1,150	1,850	7,000	—
1685 Rare	—	—	—	—	—	—
1686 Rare	—	—	—	—	—	—
1687	—	725	1,150	1,850	7,000	—
1688 Rare	—	—	—	—	—	—
1689	5,851	725	1,150	1,850	7,000	—

KM# 256.8 LOUIS D'OR
6.6900 g., 0.9170 Gold 0.1972 oz. AGW **Ruler:** Louis XIV **Mint:** Rennes **Note:** Mint mark: Numeral 9.

Date	Mintage	VG	F	VF	XF	Unc
1684	—	725	1,150	1,850	7,000	—
1685 Rare	—	—	—	—	—	—
1686 Rare	—	—	—	—	—	—
1687 Rare	—	—	—	—	—	—

Date	Mintage	VG	F	VF	XF	Unc
1688 Rare	—	—	—	—	—	—
1689 Rare	—	—	—	—	—	—

KM# 256.9 LOUIS D'OR
6.6900 g., 0.9170 Gold 0.1972 oz. AGW **Ruler:** Louis XIV **Mint:** Lille **Note:** Mint mark: Crowned L.

Date	Mintage	VG	F	VF	XF	Unc
1686 Rare	—	—	—	—	—	—
1687	—	725	1,150	2,150	3,900	—
1688 Rare	—	—	—	—	—	—
1689 Rare	—	—	—	—	—	—

KM# 278.1 LOUIS D'OR
6.6900 g., 0.9170 Gold 0.1972 oz. AGW **Ruler:** Louis XIV **Obv:** Old laureate head of Louis XIV **Mint:** Paris

Date	Mintage	VG	F	VF	XF	Unc
1690A	—	295	500	775	1,450	3,000
1691A	—	295	500	775	1,450	3,000
1692A	—	325	550	875	1,750	3,500
1693A	—	325	550	875	1,750	3,500

KM# 278.2 LOUIS D'OR
6.6900 g., 0.9170 Gold 0.1972 oz. AGW **Ruler:** Louis XIV **Mint:** Rouen

Date	Mintage	VG	F	VF	XF	Unc
1690B	—	295	500	775	1,450	3,000
1691B	—	295	500	775	1,450	3,000

KM# 278.3 LOUIS D'OR
6.6900 g., 0.9170 Gold 0.1972 oz. AGW **Ruler:** Louis XIV **Mint:** Lyon

Date	Mintage	VG	F	VF	XF	Unc
1690D	—	295	500	775	1,450	3,000
1691D	—	295	500	775	1,450	3,000
1692D	—	295	500	875	2,050	4,000
1693D Rare	—	—	—	—	—	—

KM# 278.4 LOUIS D'OR
6.6900 g., 0.9170 Gold 0.1972 oz. AGW **Ruler:** Louis XIV **Mint:** Tours

Date	Mintage	VG	F	VF	XF	Unc
1691E	—	325	550	875	1,550	—
1692E	—	325	550	925	1,750	—
1693E Rare	—	—	—	—	—	—

KM# 278.5 LOUIS D'OR
6.6900 g., 0.9170 Gold 0.1972 oz. AGW **Ruler:** Louis XIV **Mint:** Poitiers

Date	Mintage	VG	F	VF	XF	Unc
1690G	—	325	550	925	1,750	3,500
1691G	—	295	500	875	1,550	3,150
1692G Rare	—	—	—	—	—	—

KM# 278.6 LOUIS D'OR
6.6900 g., 0.9170 Gold 0.1972 oz. AGW **Ruler:** Louis XIV **Mint:** La Rochelle

Date	Mintage	VG	F	VF	XF	Unc
1692H Rare	—	—	—	—	—	—
1693H Rare	—	—	—	—	—	—

KM# 278.7 LOUIS D'OR
6.6900 g., 0.9170 Gold 0.1972 oz. AGW **Ruler:** Louis XIV **Mint:** Limoges

Date	Mintage	VG	F	VF	XF	Unc
1690I	—	295	500	775	1,450	3,000
1691I	—	295	500	775	1,450	3,000
1692I Rare	—	—	—	—	—	—
1693I Rare	—	—	—	—	—	—

KM# 278.8 LOUIS D'OR
6.6900 g., 0.9170 Gold 0.1972 oz. AGW **Ruler:** Louis XIV **Mint:** Bordeaux

Date	Mintage	VG	F	VF	XF	Unc
1690K	—	295	500	775	1,450	3,000
1691K	—	295	500	775	1,450	3,000
1692K	—	295	500	775	1,450	3,000

KM# 278.9 LOUIS D'OR
6.6900 g., 0.9170 Gold 0.1972 oz. AGW **Ruler:** Louis XIV **Mint:** Bayonne

Date	Mintage	VG	F	VF	XF	Unc
1690L Rare	—	—	—	—	—	—
1691L	—	295	500	775	1,550	3,150
1692L Rare	—	—	—	—	—	—
1693L Rare	—	—	—	—	—	—

KM# 278.10 LOUIS D'OR
6.6900 g., 0.9170 Gold 0.1972 oz. AGW **Ruler:** Louis XIV **Mint:** Toulouse

Date	Mintage	VG	F	VF	XF	Unc
1690M	—	325	550	925	1,750	3,500
1691M	—	295	500	775	1,450	3,000

KM# 278.11 LOUIS D'OR
6.6900 g., 0.9170 Gold 0.1972 oz. AGW **Ruler:** Louis XIV **Mint:** Montpellier

Date	Mintage	VG	F	VF	XF	Unc
1690N	—	295	500	775	1,450	3,000
1691N	—	295	500	775	1,450	3,000
1693N Rare	—	—	—	—	—	—

KM# 278.12 LOUIS D'OR
6.6900 g., 0.9170 Gold 0.1972 oz. AGW **Ruler:** Louis XIV **Mint:** Riom

Date	Mintage	VG	F	VF	XF	Unc
1690O	—	325	550	875	1,750	3,500
1691O Rare	—	—	—	—	—	—
1692O	—	325	550	875	1,750	3,500
1693O Rare	—	—	—	—	—	—

KM# 278.13 LOUIS D'OR
6.6900 g., 0.9170 Gold 0.1972 oz. AGW **Ruler:** Louis XIV **Mint:** Dijon

Date	Mintage	VG	F	VF	XF	Unc
1690P	—	295	500	775	1,450	3,000
1691P	—	295	500	775	1,450	3,000
1692P Rare	—	—	—	—	—	—
1693P	—	325	550	1,000	1,850	3,750

KM# 278.15 LOUIS D'OR
6.6900 g., 0.9170 Gold 0.1972 oz. AGW **Ruler:** Louis XIV **Mint:** Reims

Date	Mintage	VG	F	VF	XF	Unc
1690S	—	295	500	775	1,450	3,000
1691S	—	295	500	775	1,450	3,000
1692S Rare	—	—	—	—	—	—
1693S	—	325	550	875	1,700	3,350

KM# 278.16 LOUIS D'OR
6.6900 g., 0.9170 Gold 0.1972 oz. AGW **Ruler:** Louis XIV **Mint:** Amiens

Date	Mintage	VG	F	VF	XF	Unc
1690X	—	325	550	875	1,700	3,350
1691X Rare	—	—	—	—	—	—
1692X	—	325	550	1,000	1,850	3,750
1693X Rare	—	—	—	—	—	—

KM# 278.17 LOUIS D'OR
6.6900 g., 0.9170 Gold 0.1972 oz. AGW **Ruler:** Louis XIV **Mint:** Bourges

Date	Mintage	VG	F	VF	XF	Unc
1690Y	—	295	500	775	1,450	3,000
1691Y	—	325	550	875	1,750	3,500
1692Y	—	325	550	875	1,750	3,500
1693Y Rare	—	—	—	—	—	—

KM# 278.18 LOUIS D'OR
6.6900 g., 0.9170 Gold 0.1972 oz. AGW **Ruler:** Louis XIV **Mint:** Aix **Note:** Mint mark: &.

Date	Mintage	VG	F	VF	XF	Unc
1690	—	295	500	775	1,450	3,000
1691 Rare	—	—	—	—	—	—

KM# 278.19 LOUIS D'OR
6.6900 g., 0.9170 Gold 0.1972 oz. AGW **Ruler:** Louis XIV **Mint:** Rennes **Note:** Mint mark: Numeral 9.

Date	Mintage	VG	F	VF	XF	Unc
1690	—	295	500	775	1,450	3,000
1691	—	325	550	875	1,550	3,150
1692	—	325	550	875	1,550	3,150
1693	—	325	550	925	1,750	3,500

KM# 278.20 LOUIS D'OR
6.6900 g., 0.9170 Gold 0.1972 oz. AGW **Ruler:** Louis XIV **Mint:** Lille **Note:** Mint mark: Crowned L.

Date	Mintage	VG	F	VF	XF	Unc
1690	—	295	500	775	1,550	3,150
1691 Rare	—	—	—	—	—	—
1692 Rare	—	—	—	—	—	—
1693 Rare	—	—	—	—	—	—

KM# 278.21 LOUIS D'OR
6.6900 g., 0.9170 Gold 0.1972 oz. AGW **Ruler:** Louis XIV **Mint:** Metz **Note:** Mint mark: Crowned M.

Date	Mintage	VG	F	VF	XF	Unc
1690	—	295	500	775	1,450	3,000
1691	—	295	500	775	1,450	3,000

KM# 278.22 LOUIS D'OR

6.6900 g., 0.9170 Gold 0.1972 oz. AGW **Ruler:** Louis XIV **Mint:** Troyes **Note:** Mint mark: Crowned S.

Date	Mintage	VG	F	VF	XF	Unc
1690	—	325	550	925	1,550	3,150
1691 Rare	—	—	—	—	—	—
1692 Rare	—	—	—	—	—	—

KM# 279 LOUIS D'OR

6.6900 g., 0.9170 Gold 0.1972 oz. AGW **Ruler:** Louis XIV **Rev:** Arms of France and Navarre Bearn **Mint:** Pau

Date	Mintage	VG	F	VF	XF	Unc
1690	—	1,500	3,000	4,000	7,500	—
1691	—	1,750	3,750	5,500	9,000	—
1692	—	2,500	4,250	6,500	11,000	—
1693	—	3,500	6,000	9,000	14,000	—

KM# 302.1 LOUIS D'OR

6.6900 g., 0.9170 Gold 0.1972 oz. AGW **Ruler:** Louis XIV **Obv:** Old laureate head of Louis XIV **Mint:** Paris

Date	Mintage	VG	F	VF	XF	Unc
1693A	—	285	350	600	1,600	3,200
1694A	—	285	350	600	1,600	3,200
1695A	—	285	350	600	1,600	3,200
1696A	—	285	350	600	1,600	3,200
1697A	—	285	350	600	1,600	3,200
1698A	—	285	350	600	1,600	3,200
1699A	—	285	350	600	1,600	3,200
1700A	—	285	350	600	1,600	3,200

KM# 302.2 LOUIS D'OR

6.6900 g., 0.9170 Gold 0.1972 oz. AGW **Ruler:** Louis XIV **Mint:** Metz

Date	Mintage	VG	F	VF	XF	Unc
1693AA Rare	—	—	—	—	—	—
1694AA	—	285	350	600	1,600	3,500
1695AA	—	285	350	600	1,600	3,500
1696AA	—	285	350	600	1,600	3,500
1699AA Rare	—	—	—	—	—	—

KM# 302.3 LOUIS D'OR

6.6900 g., 0.9170 Gold 0.1972 oz. AGW **Ruler:** Louis XIV **Mint:** Rouen

Date	Mintage	VG	F	VF	XF	Unc
1693B	—	285	350	600	1,600	3,500
1694B	—	285	350	600	1,600	3,500
1695B	—	285	350	600	1,600	3,500
1696B	—	285	350	600	1,600	3,500
1699B Rare	—	—	—	—	—	—
1700B Rare	—	—	—	—	—	—

KM# 302.4 LOUIS D'OR

6.6900 g., 0.9170 Gold 0.1972 oz. AGW **Ruler:** Louis XIV **Obv:** Older laureate head of Lois XIV **Rev:** 4 L's around mint mark **Mint:** Strasbourg

Date	Mintage	VG	F	VF	XF	Unc
1694BB	—	285	350	600	1,600	3,500
1695BB	—	285	350	600	1,600	3,500
1696BB	—	285	350	600	1,600	3,500
1697BB	—	285	350	600	1,600	3,500
1700BB Rare	—	—	—	—	—	—

KM# 302.5 LOUIS D'OR

6.6900 g., 0.9170 Gold 0.1972 oz. AGW **Ruler:** Louis XIV **Mint:** Caen

Date	Mintage	VG	F	VF	XF	Unc
1694C	—	285	350	600	1,450	—
1695C	—	285	350	600	1,450	—
1696C	—	285	350	600	1,450	—
1697C Rare	—	—	—	—	—	—

KM# 302.6 LOUIS D'OR

6.6900 g., 0.9170 Gold 0.1972 oz. AGW **Ruler:** Louis XIV **Mint:** Lyon

Date	Mintage	VG	F	VF	XF	Unc
1693D	—	300	475	725	1,700	3,750
1694D	—	285	350	600	1,600	3,500
1695D	—	285	350	600	1,600	3,500
1696D	—	285	350	600	1,600	3,500
1697D	—	285	350	600	1,600	3,500
1698D Rare	—	—	—	—	—	—
1699D Rare	—	—	—	—	—	—
1700D	—	285	350	600	1,600	3,500

KM# 302.7 LOUIS D'OR

6.6900 g., 0.9170 Gold 0.1972 oz. AGW **Ruler:** Louis XIV **Mint:** Tours

Date	Mintage	VG	F	VF	XF	Unc
1693E	—	285	350	600	1,300	3,000
1694E	—	285	350	600	1,300	3,000
1695E Rare	—	—	—	—	—	—
1696E Rare	—	—	—	—	—	—
1697E	—	285	350	600	1,300	3,000
1698E Rare	—	—	—	—	—	—
1699E Rare	—	—	—	—	—	—

KM# 302.8 LOUIS D'OR

6.6900 g., 0.9170 Gold 0.1972 oz. AGW **Ruler:** Louis XIV **Mint:** Poitiers

Date	Mintage	VG	F	VF	XF	Unc
1693G	—	285	350	600	1,600	3,500
1694G	—	285	350	600	1,600	3,500
1695G	—	285	350	600	1,600	3,500
1697G Rare	—	—	—	—	—	—
1699G Rare	—	—	—	—	—	—

KM# 302.9 LOUIS D'OR

6.6900 g., 0.9170 Gold 0.1972 oz. AGW **Ruler:** Louis XIV **Mint:** La Rochelle

Date	Mintage	VG	F	VF	XF	Unc
1693H Rare	—	—	—	—	—	—
1694H	—	285	350	600	1,600	3,500
1695H	—	285	350	600	1,600	3,500
1698H	—	300	475	725	1,700	3,750
1699H	—	285	350	600	1,600	3,500
1700H Rare	—	—	—	—	—	—

KM# 302.10 LOUIS D'OR

6.6900 g., 0.9170 Gold 0.1972 oz. AGW **Ruler:** Louis XIV **Mint:** Limoges

Date	Mintage	VG	F	VF	XF	Unc
1693I	—	300	475	800	1,700	—
1694I	—	300	475	800	1,700	—
1696I	—	300	475	800	1,700	—

KM# 302.11 LOUIS D'OR

6.6900 g., 0.9170 Gold 0.1972 oz. AGW **Ruler:** Louis XIV **Mint:** Bordeaux

Date	Mintage	VG	F	VF	XF	Unc
1693K	—	285	350	600	1,600	3,500
1694K Rare	—	—	—	—	—	—
1695K	—	285	350	600	1,600	3,500
1696K	—	285	350	600	1,600	3,500
1698K Rare	—	—	—	—	—	—
1699K Rare	—	—	—	—	—	—
1700K Rare	—	—	—	—	—	—

KM# 302.12 LOUIS D'OR

6.6900 g., 0.9170 Gold 0.1972 oz. AGW **Ruler:** Louis XIV **Mint:** Bayonne

Date	Mintage	VG	F	VF	XF	Unc
1693L Rare	—	—	—	—	—	—
1694L	—	285	350	600	1,600	3,500
1696L	—	285	350	600	1,600	3,500
1700L Rare	—	—	—	—	—	—

KM# 302.13 LOUIS D'OR

6.6900 g., 0.9170 Gold 0.1972 oz. AGW **Ruler:** Louis XIV **Mint:** Toulouse

Date	Mintage	VG	F	VF	XF	Unc
1693M	—	285	350	600	1,600	3,500
1694M	—	285	350	600	1,600	3,500
1695M	—	285	350	600	1,600	3,500
1696M	—	285	475	725	1,700	3,750

KM# 302.14 LOUIS D'OR

6.6900 g., 0.9170 Gold 0.1972 oz. AGW **Ruler:** Louis XIV **Mint:** Montpellier

Date	Mintage	VG	F	VF	XF	Unc
1693N	—	285	350	600	1,600	3,500
1694N	—	285	350	600	1,600	3,500
1695N Rare	—	—	—	—	—	—
1696N Rare	—	—	—	—	—	—
1697N Rare	—	—	—	—	—	—
1698N Rare	—	—	—	—	—	—
1699N Rare	—	—	—	—	—	—
1700N Rare	—	—	—	—	—	—

KM# 302.15 LOUIS D'OR

6.6900 g., 0.9170 Gold 0.1972 oz. AGW **Ruler:** Louis XIV **Mint:** Riom

Date	Mintage	VG	F	VF	XF	Unc
1693O	—	285	350	600	1,600	3,500
1694O	—	285	350	600	1,600	3,500
1695O	—	285	350	600	1,600	3,500
1696O	—	285	350	600	1,600	3,500
1697O Rare	—	—	—	—	—	—
1698O Rare	—	—	—	—	—	—
1700O Rare	—	—	—	—	—	—

KM# 302.16 LOUIS D'OR

6.6900 g., 0.9170 Gold 0.1972 oz. AGW **Ruler:** Louis XIV **Mint:** Dijon

Date	Mintage	VG	F	VF	XF	Unc
1693P	—	285	350	600	1,300	3,000
1694P	—	285	350	600	1,300	3,000
1695P Rare	—	—	—	—	—	—
1697P Rare	—	—	—	—	—	—
1698P	—	285	350	600	1,300	3,000
1700P Rare	—	—	—	—	—	—

KM# 302.17 LOUIS D'OR

6.6900 g., 0.9170 Gold 0.1972 oz. AGW **Ruler:** Louis XIV **Mint:** Reims

Date	Mintage	VG	F	VF	XF	Unc
1693S	—	295	400	600	1,450	3,150
1695S	—	BV	300	500	1,300	3,000
1696S	—	BV	300	500	1,300	3,000
1697S Rare	—	—	—	—	—	—
1699S Rare	—	—	—	—	—	—
1700S Rare	—	—	—	—	—	—

KM# 302.18 LOUIS D'OR

6.6900 g., 0.9170 Gold 0.1972 oz. AGW **Ruler:** Louis XIV **Mint:** Nantes

Date	Mintage	VG	F	VF	XF	Unc
1693T	—	285	350	600	1,600	3,500
1694T	—	285	350	600	1,600	3,500
1695T	—	285	350	600	1,600	3,500
1696T	—	285	350	600	1,600	3,500
1698T	—	300	475	725	1,700	3,750
1699T	—	285	350	600	1,600	3,500

KM# 302.19 LOUIS D'OR

6.6900 g., 0.9170 Gold 0.1972 oz. AGW **Ruler:** Louis XIV **Mint:** Troyes

Date	Mintage	VG	F	VF	XF	Unc
1693V Rare	—	—	—	—	—	—
1694V	—	285	350	600	1,600	3,500
1697V	—	300	475	725	1,700	3,500
1699V Rare	—	—	—	—	—	—

KM# 302.20 LOUIS D'OR

6.6900 g., 0.9170 Gold 0.1972 oz. AGW **Ruler:** Louis XIV **Mint:** Lille

Date	Mintage	VG	F	VF	XF	Unc
1693W	—	285	350	600	1,600	3,500
1694W	—	285	350	600	1,600	3,500
1695W	—	285	350	600	1,600	3,500
1696W	—	285	350	600	1,600	3,500
1697W Rare	—	—	—	—	—	—
1698W Rare	—	—	—	—	—	—
1699W	—	285	350	600	1,600	3,500
1700W	—	285	350	600	1,600	3,500

KM# 302.21 LOUIS D'OR

6.6900 g., 0.9170 Gold 0.1972 oz. AGW **Ruler:** Louis XIV **Mint:** Amiens

Date	Mintage	VG	F	VF	XF	Unc
1693X Rare	—	—	—	—	—	—
1694X	—	285	350	600	1,600	3,500
1695X	—	285	350	600	1,600	3,500
1696X	—	285	350	600	1,600	3,500
1697X Rare	—	—	—	—	—	—

KM# 302.22 LOUIS D'OR

6.6900 g., 0.9170 Gold 0.1972 oz. AGW **Ruler:** Louis XIV **Mint:** Bourges

Date	Mintage	VG	F	VF	XF	Unc
1693Y	—	285	350	600	1,600	3,500
1694Y	—	300	475	725	1,700	3,750
1696Y	—	285	350	600	1,600	3,500
1698Y Rare	—	—	—	—	—	—

KM# 302.23 LOUIS D'OR

6.6900 g., 0.9170 Gold 0.1972 oz. AGW **Ruler:** Louis XIV **Mint:** Aix **Note:** Mint mark: &.

Date	Mintage	VG	F	VF	XF	Unc
1693	—	285	350	600	1,600	3,200
1694	—	285	350	600	1,600	3,200
1695	—	285	350	600	1,600	3,200
1696 Rare	—	—	—	—	—	—
1698 Rare	—	—	—	—	—	—
1700 Rare	—	—	—	—	—	—

KM# 302.24 LOUIS D'OR

6.6900 g., 0.9170 Gold 0.1972 oz. AGW **Ruler:** Louis XIV **Mint:** Rennes **Note:** Mint mark: 9.

Date	Mintage	VG	F	VF	XF	Unc
1693	—	285	350	600	1,600	3,200
1694	—	285	350	600	1,600	3,200
1695	—	285	350	600	1,600	3,200
1696	—	300	475	725	1,700	3,400
1697	—	300	475	725	1,700	3,400
1700	—	285	350	600	1,600	3,200

KM# 302.25 LOUIS D'OR

6.6900 g., 0.9170 Gold 0.1972 oz. AGW **Ruler:** Louis XIV **Mint:** Pau **Note:** Mint mark: Cow.

Date	Mintage	VG	F	VF	XF	Unc
1693	—	425	650	1,100	2,350	4,750
1694	—	425	650	1,100	2,350	4,750
1695	—	425	650	1,100	2,350	4,750
1696 Rare	—	—	—	—	—	—
1697	—	425	650	1,150	2,550	5,000
1698 Rare	—	—	—	—	—	—
1699 Rare	—	—	—	—	—	—
1700 Rare	—	—	—	—	—	—

KM# 302.26 LOUIS D'OR

6.6900 g., 0.9170 Gold 0.1972 oz. AGW **Ruler:** Louis XIV **Mint:** Besançon **Note:** Mint mark: Back-to-back C's.

Date	Mintage	VG	F	VF	XF	Unc
1694	—	320	550	900	2,000	4,350
1695	—	320	550	900	2,000	4,350

Date	Mintage	VG	F	VF	XF	Unc
1697 Rare	—	—	—	—	—	—
1698 Rare	—	—	—	—	—	—
1699 Rare	—	—	—	—	—	—

KM# 334.1 LOUIS D'OR
6.6900 g., 0.9170 Gold 0.1972 oz. AGW **Ruler:** Louis XIV **Obv:** Laureate head right **Obv. Legend:** LVD • XIIII • D • G FR • ET • NAV • REX • **Rev:** Crowned back to back L's, Hand of Justice and sceptre cross at center **Rev. Legend:** CHRS • REGN • VINC • IMP **Mint:** Paris

Date	Mintage	VG	F	VF	XF	Unc
1700A	—	295	425	650	1,500	3,300

KM# 108 2 LOUIS D'OR
13.3900 g., 0.9170 Gold 0.3948 oz. AGW **Ruler:** Louis XIII **Rev. Legend:** • CHRS • • REGN • • VINC • • IMP • **Mint:** Paris

Date	Mintage	VG	F	VF	XF	Unc
1640A	432,000	1,000	2,500	4,250	7,500	—
1641A	72,000	1,500	3,250	5,500	9,500	—
1642A Rare	894	—	—	—	—	—
1643A Rare	—	—	—	—	—	—

KM# 109 2 LOUIS D'OR
13.3900 g., 0.9170 Gold 0.3948 oz. AGW **Ruler:** Louis XIII **Obv:** Large head **Obv. Legend:** • LVDO • XIII • D • G •... **Rev. Legend:** ...IMPE •

Date	Mintage	VG	F	VF	XF	Unc
1640	—	2,000	3,500	6,750	11,000	—

KM# 110.1 2 LOUIS D'OR
13.3900 g., 0.9170 Gold 0.3948 oz. AGW **Ruler:** Louis XIII **Rev:** Cross at end of legend **Mint:** Paris

Date	Mintage	VG	F	VF	XF	Unc
1640	—	2,500	4,500	9,500	15,000	—
1641	—	2,500	4,500	9,500	15,000	—

KM# 110.2 2 LOUIS D'OR
13.3900 g., 0.9170 Gold 0.3948 oz. AGW **Ruler:** Louis XIII **Mint:** Lyon

Date	Mintage	VG	F	VF	XF	Unc
1643D	13,000	2,000	4,000	7,500	10,000	—

KM# 150.1 2 LOUIS D'OR
13.3900 g., 0.9170 Gold 0.3948 oz. AGW **Ruler:** Louis XIV **Obv:** Laureate child head of Louis XIV right with short curl **Mint:** Paris

Date	Mintage	VG	F	VF	XF	Unc
1643A Rare	200	—	—	—	—	—
1644A Rare	—	—	—	—	—	—

KM# 150.2 2 LOUIS D'OR
13.3900 g., 0.9170 Gold 0.3948 oz. AGW **Ruler:** Louis XIV **Mint:** Lyon

Date	Mintage	VG	F	VF	XF	Unc
1644D Rare	7,000	—	—	—	—	—
1645D Rare	1,160	—	—	—	—	—
1648D	1,582	5,000	9,500	15,000	30,000	—

KM# 158.1 2 LOUIS D'OR
13.3900 g., 0.9170 Gold 0.3948 oz. AGW **Ruler:** Louis XIV **Obv:** Head with long curl **Mint:** Paris

Date	Mintage	VG	F	VF	XF	Unc
1646A Rare	—	—	—	—	—	—
1650A Rare	13,000	—	—	—	—	—

KM# 158.2 2 LOUIS D'OR
13.3900 g., 0.9170 Gold 0.3948 oz. AGW **Ruler:** Louis XIV **Mint:** Rouen

Date	Mintage	VG	F	VF	XF	Unc
1647B Rare	—	—	—	—	—	—

KM# 158.3 2 LOUIS D'OR
13.3900 g., 0.9170 Gold 0.3948 oz. AGW **Ruler:** Louis XIV **Mint:** Angers

Date	Mintage	VG	F	VF	XF	Unc
1647F	362	2,100	4,900	8,400	14,000	—
1648F Rare	725	—	—	—	—	—

KM# 158.4 2 LOUIS D'OR
13.3900 g., 0.9170 Gold 0.3948 oz. AGW **Ruler:** Louis XIV **Mint:** La Rochelle

Date	Mintage	VG	F	VF	XF	Unc
1646H Rare	—	—	—	—	—	—
1647H	2,400	1,250	3,100	7,000	14,000	—
1648H	120	2,400	5,600	9,100	17,000	—
1649H	—	1,250	3,100	7,000	14,000	—

KM# 158.5 2 LOUIS D'OR
13.3900 g., 0.9170 Gold 0.3948 oz. AGW **Ruler:** Louis XIV **Mint:** Bordeaux

Date	Mintage	VG	F	VF	XF	Unc
1648K	1,522	1,400	3,500	7,000	14,000	—
1649K	—	1,400	3,500	7,000	14,000	—
1650K Rare	600	—	—	—	—	—

KM# 158.6 2 LOUIS D'OR
13.3900 g., 0.9170 Gold 0.3948 oz. AGW **Ruler:** Louis XIV **Mint:** Toulouse

Date	Mintage	VG	F	VF	XF	Unc
1647M	600	1,400	3,500	7,000	14,000	—
1648M	1,112	1,400	3,500	7,000	14,000	—

KM# 158.7 2 LOUIS D'OR
13.3900 g., 0.9170 Gold 0.3948 oz. AGW **Ruler:** Louis XIV **Mint:** Montpellier

Date	Mintage	VG	F	VF	XF	Unc
1646N Rare	—	—	—	—	—	—
1647N Rare	471	—	—	—	—	—
1648N	526	2,000	4,250	8,500	15,000	—
1649N Rare	363	—	—	—	—	—
1651N Rare	892	—	—	—	—	—
1652N Rare	1,319	—	—	—	—	—

KM# 158.8 2 LOUIS D'OR
13.3900 g., 0.9170 Gold 0.3948 oz. AGW **Ruler:** Louis XIV **Mint:** Dijon

Date	Mintage	VG	F	VF	XF	Unc
1646P	120	—	—	8,400	17,000	—
1651P Rare	1,660	—	—	—	—	—
1652P	2,127	1,050	2,800	6,300	12,500	—

KM# 158.9 2 LOUIS D'OR
13.3900 g., 0.9170 Gold 0.3948 oz. AGW **Ruler:** Louis XIV **Mint:** Aix **Note:** Mint mark: Ampersand.

Date	Mintage	VG	F	VF	XF	Unc
1646 Rare	—	—	—	—	—	—
1647 Rare	—	—	—	—	—	—

KM# 280.1 2 LOUIS D'OR
13.3900 g., 0.9170 Gold 0.3948 oz. AGW **Ruler:** Louis XIV **Obv:** Laureate older head of Louis XIV **Mint:** Paris

Date	Mintage	VG	F	VF	XF	Unc
1690A	—	600	1,150	2,350	5,500	—
1691A	—	900	1,500	2,950	6,900	—
1692A	—	900	1,500	2,950	6,900	—
1693A	—	900	1,500	3,000	7,000	—

KM# 280.2 2 LOUIS D'OR
13.3900 g., 0.9170 Gold 0.3948 oz. AGW **Ruler:** Louis XIV **Mint:** Rouen

Date	Mintage	VG	F	VF	XF	Unc
1690B	—	900	1,500	2,950	6,900	—
1691B Rare	—	—	—	—	—	—
1692B	—	900	1,500	2,950	6,900	—
1693B Rare	—	—	—	—	—	—

KM# 280.3 2 LOUIS D'OR
13.3900 g., 0.9170 Gold 0.3948 oz. AGW **Ruler:** Louis XIV **Mint:** Lyon

Date	Mintage	VG	F	VF	XF	Unc
1690D	295,000	900	1,500	2,950	6,900	—
1691D Rare	—	—	—	—	—	—
1692D Rare	—	—	—	—	—	—

KM# 280.4 2 LOUIS D'OR
13.3900 g., 0.9170 Gold 0.3948 oz. AGW **Ruler:** Louis XIV **Mint:** Tours

Date	Mintage	VG	F	VF	XF	Unc
1690E	—	900	1,500	2,950	6,900	—

KM# 280.5 2 LOUIS D'OR
13.3900 g., 0.9170 Gold 0.3948 oz. AGW **Ruler:** Louis XIV **Mint:** Poitiers

Date	Mintage	VG	F	VF	XF	Unc
1690G	—	900	1,650	3,250	7,800	—
1691G	—	900	1,500	2,950	6,900	—
1692G Rare	—	—	—	—	—	—
1693G Rare	—	—	—	—	—	—

KM# 280.6 2 LOUIS D'OR
13.3900 g., 0.9170 Gold 0.3948 oz. AGW **Ruler:** Louis XIV **Mint:** La Rochelle

Date	Mintage	VG	F	VF	XF	Unc
1691H	—	900	1,500	2,950	6,900	—
1692H Rare	—	—	—	—	—	—

KM# 280.7 2 LOUIS D'OR
13.3900 g., 0.9170 Gold 0.3948 oz. AGW **Ruler:** Louis XIV **Mint:** Limoges

Date	Mintage	VG	F	VF	XF	Unc
1690I Rare	—	—	—	—	—	—
1692I Rare	—	—	—	—	—	—
1693I Rare	—	—	—	—	—	—

KM# 280.8 2 LOUIS D'OR
13.3900 g., 0.9170 Gold 0.3948 oz. AGW **Ruler:** Louis XIV **Mint:** Bordeaux

Date	Mintage	VG	F	VF	XF	Unc
1690K	—	900	1,650	3,250	7,800	—

KM# 280.9 2 LOUIS D'OR
13.3900 g., 0.9170 Gold 0.3948 oz. AGW **Ruler:** Louis XIV **Mint:** Toulouse

Date	Mintage	VG	F	VF	XF	Unc
1691M	—	900	1,500	2,950	6,900	—
1692M Rare	—	—	—	—	—	—
1693M Rare	—	—	—	—	—	—

KM# 280.10 2 LOUIS D'OR
13.3900 g., 0.9170 Gold 0.3948 oz. AGW **Ruler:** Louis XIV **Mint:** Montpellier

Date	Mintage	VG	F	VF	XF	Unc
1690N	1,235	1,200	1,750	3,600	8,600	—

KM# 280.11 2 LOUIS D'OR
13.3900 g., 0.9170 Gold 0.3948 oz. AGW **Ruler:** Louis XIV **Mint:** Riom

Date	Mintage	VG	F	VF	XF	Unc
1691O Rare	—	—	—	—	—	—

KM# 280.12 2 LOUIS D'OR
13.3900 g., 0.9170 Gold 0.3948 oz. AGW **Ruler:** Louis XIV **Mint:** Dijon

Date	Mintage	VG	F	VF	XF	Unc
1691P	3,145	1,200	1,750	3,600	8,600	—
1693P Rare	—	—	—	—	—	—

KM# 280.13 2 LOUIS D'OR
13.3900 g., 0.9170 Gold 0.3948 oz. AGW **Ruler:** Louis XIV **Mint:** Amiens

Date	Mintage	VG	F	VF	XF	Unc
1690X	5,200	1,200	1,750	3,600	8,600	—
1691X	—	900	1,500	2,950	6,900	—
1692X Rare	—	—	—	—	—	—

KM# 280.14 2 LOUIS D'OR
13.3900 g., 0.9170 Gold 0.3948 oz. AGW **Ruler:** Louis XIV **Mint:** Bourges

Date	Mintage	VG	F	VF	XF	Unc
1690Y Rare	—	—	—	—	—	—
1691Y Rare	—	—	—	—	—	—
1692Y Rare	—	—	—	—	—	—
1693Y Rare	—	—	—	—	—	—

KM# 280.15 2 LOUIS D'OR
13.3900 g., 0.9170 Gold 0.3948 oz. AGW **Ruler:** Louis XIV **Mint:** Aix **Note:** Mint mark: Ampersand.

Date	Mintage	VG	F	VF	XF	Unc
1690	—	900	1,500	2,950	6,900	—
1691 Rare	—	—	—	—	—	—
1692 Rare	—	—	—	—	—	—

KM# 280.16 2 LOUIS D'OR
13.3900 g., 0.9170 Gold 0.3948 oz. AGW **Ruler:** Louis XIV **Mint:** Rennes **Note:** Mint mark: Numeral 9.

Date	Mintage	VG	F	VF	XF	Unc
1690	—	900	1,500	2,950	6,900	—
1691	—	900	1,500	2,950	6,900	—
1692 Rare	—	—	—	—	—	—
1693 Rare	—	—	—	—	—	—

KM# 280.17 2 LOUIS D'OR
13.3900 g., 0.9170 Gold 0.3948 oz. AGW **Ruler:** Louis XIV **Mint:** Lille **Note:** Mint mark: Crowned L.

Date	Mintage	VG	F	VF	XF	Unc
1692 Rare	—	—	—	—	—	—

KM# 280.18 2 LOUIS D'OR
13.3900 g., 0.9170 Gold 0.3948 oz. AGW **Ruler:** Louis XIV **Mint:** Metz **Note:** Mint mark: Crowned M.

Date	Mintage	VG	F	VF	XF	Unc
1691	—	900	1,650	3,250	7,800	—

KM# 280.19 2 LOUIS D'OR
13.3900 g., 0.9170 Gold 0.3948 oz. AGW **Ruler:** Louis XIV **Mint:** Troyes **Note:** Mint mark: Crowned S.

Date	Mintage	VG	F	VF	XF	Unc
1690	—	1,200	1,750	3,600	8,600	—
1691 Rare	—	—	—	—	—	—
1692 Rare	—	—	—	—	—	—

KM# 303.1 2 LOUIS D'OR

13.3900 g., 0.9170 Gold 0.3948 oz. AGW **Ruler:** Louis XIV **Obv:** Older laureate head of Louis XIV **Mint:** Paris

Date	Mintage	VG	F	VF	XF	Unc
1693A	—	600	1,100	2,400	4,500	—
1694A	—	600	1,100	2,400	4,500	—
1695A	—	600	1,100	2,400	4,500	—
1696A	—	600	1,100	2,400	4,500	—
1697A	—	600	1,100	2,400	4,500	—
1698A	—	600	1,100	2,400	4,500	—
1699A	—	600	1,100	2,400	4,500	—
1700A	—	600	1,100	2,400	4,500	—

KM# 303.2 2 LOUIS D'OR

13.3900 g., 0.9170 Gold 0.3948 oz. AGW **Ruler:** Louis XIV **Mint:** Metz

Date	Mintage	VG	F	VF	XF	Unc
1693AA Rare	—	—	—	—	—	—
1694AA	—	600	1,100	2,400	4,500	—
1695AA	—	600	1,100	2,400	4,500	—
1696AA Rare	—	—	—	—	—	—
1697AA	—	600	1,100	2,400	4,500	—
1699AA	—	600	1,100	2,400	4,500	—

KM# 303.3 2 LOUIS D'OR

13.3900 g., 0.9170 Gold 0.3948 oz. AGW **Ruler:** Louis XIV **Mint:** Rouen

Date	Mintage	VG	F	VF	XF	Unc
1693B	—	600	1,200	2,700	5,300	—
1694B Rare	—	—	—	—	—	—
1695B Rare	—	—	—	—	—	—
1696B Rare	—	—	—	—	—	—
1697B Rare	—	—	—	—	—	—
1698B Rare	—	—	—	—	—	—
1700B Rare	—	—	—	—	—	—

KM# 303.4 2 LOUIS D'OR

13.3900 g., 0.9170 Gold 0.3948 oz. AGW **Ruler:** Louis XIV **Mint:** Strasbourg

Date	Mintage	VG	F	VF	XF	Unc
1694BB	—	600	1,100	2,400	4,850	—
1695BB	—	600	1,100	2,400	4,850	—
1696BB	—	600	1,100	2,400	4,850	—
1697BB Rare	—	—	—	—	—	—
1698BB Rare	—	—	—	—	—	—
1699BB Rare	—	—	—	—	—	—
1700BB	—	650	1,600	3,000	5,800	—

KM# 303.5 2 LOUIS D'OR

13.3900 g., 0.9170 Gold 0.3948 oz. AGW **Ruler:** Louis XIV **Mint:** Caen

Date	Mintage	VG	F	VF	XF	Unc
1695C	—	600	1,100	2,400	4,850	—
1696C Rare	—	—	—	—	—	—
1697C Rare	—	—	—	—	—	—
1700C Rare	—	—	—	—	—	—

KM# 303.6 2 LOUIS D'OR

13.3900 g., 0.9170 Gold 0.3948 oz. AGW **Ruler:** Louis XIV **Mint:** Lyon

Date	Mintage	VG	F	VF	XF	Unc
1693D	—	600	1,200	2,700	5,300	—
1694D	—	600	1,200	2,700	5,300	—
1695D	—	600	1,200	2,700	5,300	—
1696D Rare	—	—	—	—	—	—
1697D Rare	—	—	—	—	—	—
1698D Rare	—	—	—	—	—	—
1699D Rare	—	—	—	—	—	—
1700D Rare	—	—	—	—	—	—

KM# 303.7 2 LOUIS D'OR

13.3900 g., 0.9170 Gold 0.3948 oz. AGW **Ruler:** Louis XIV **Mint:** Tours

Date	Mintage	VG	F	VF	XF	Unc
1696E	—	600	1,100	2,400	4,850	—

KM# 303.9 2 LOUIS D'OR

13.3900 g., 0.9170 Gold 0.3948 oz. AGW **Ruler:** Louis XIV **Mint:** Poitiers

Date	Mintage	VG	F	VF	XF	Unc
1694G Rare	—	—	—	—	—	—
1695G Rare	—	—	—	—	—	—
1696G	—	725	1,300	2,950	6,900	—
1697G Rare	—	—	—	—	—	—
1698G Rare	—	—	—	—	—	—

KM# 303.10 2 LOUIS D'OR

13.3900 g., 0.9170 Gold 0.3948 oz. AGW **Ruler:** Louis XIV **Mint:** La Rochelle

Date	Mintage	VG	F	VF	XF	Unc
1694H	—	625	1,150	2,650	6,300	—
1695H Rare	—	—	—	—	—	—
1696H	—	600	1,100	2,400	4,850	—
1697H Rare	—	—	—	—	—	—
1698H Rare	—	—	—	—	—	—
1699H Rare	—	—	—	—	—	—
1700H Rare	—	—	—	—	—	—

KM# 303.11 2 LOUIS D'OR

13.3900 g., 0.9170 Gold 0.3948 oz. AGW **Ruler:** Louis XIV **Mint:** Limoges

Date	Mintage	VG	F	VF	XF	Unc
1694I Rare	—	—	—	—	—	—
1695I Rare	—	—	—	—	—	—
1696I	—	600	1,100	2,400	4,850	—
1697I	—	775	2,150	4,200	6,900	—
1699I Rare	—	—	—	—	—	—

KM# 303.12 2 LOUIS D'OR

13.3900 g., 0.9170 Gold 0.3948 oz. AGW **Ruler:** Louis XIV **Mint:** Bordeaux

Date	Mintage	VG	F	VF	XF	Unc
1697K Rare	—	—	—	—	—	—
1698K Rare	—	—	—	—	—	—
1699K Rare	—	—	—	—	—	—

KM# 303.13 2 LOUIS D'OR

13.3900 g., 0.9170 Gold 0.3948 oz. AGW **Ruler:** Louis XIV **Mint:** Bayonne

Date	Mintage	VG	F	VF	XF	Unc
1694L Rare	—	—	—	—	—	—
1695L	—	600	1,100	2,400	4,850	—
1696L	—	600	1,100	2,400	4,850	—
1697L	—	600	1,100	2,400	4,850	—
1698L Rare	—	—	—	—	—	—
1699L Rare	—	—	—	—	—	—
1700L Rare	—	—	—	—	—	—

KM# 303.14 2 LOUIS D'OR

13.3900 g., 0.9170 Gold 0.3948 oz. AGW **Ruler:** Louis XIV **Mint:** Toulouse

Date	Mintage	VG	F	VF	XF	Unc
1694M	—	600	1,100	2,400	4,850	—
1695M	—	650	1,200	2,700	4,850	—
1696M Rare	—	—	—	—	—	—
1697M	—	600	1,100	2,400	4,850	—
1698M Rare	—	—	—	—	—	—
1699M Rare	—	—	—	—	—	—
1700M Rare	—	—	—	—	—	—

KM# 303.15 2 LOUIS D'OR

13.3900 g., 0.9170 Gold 0.3948 oz. AGW **Ruler:** Louis XIV **Mint:** Montpellier

Date	Mintage	VG	F	VF	XF	Unc
1693N Rare	—	—	—	—	—	—
1694N Rare	—	—	—	—	—	—
1695N Rare	—	—	—	—	—	—
1696N	—	775	2,100	4,800	9,000	—
1697N Rare	—	—	—	—	—	—
1698N Rare	—	—	—	—	—	—
1699N Rare	—	—	—	—	—	—
1700N Rare	—	—	—	—	—	—

KM# 303.16 2 LOUIS D'OR

13.3900 g., 0.9170 Gold 0.3948 oz. AGW **Ruler:** Louis XIV **Mint:** Riom

Date	Mintage	VG	F	VF	XF	Unc
1693O Rare	—	—	—	—	—	—
1694O Rare	—	—	—	—	—	—
1695O Rare	—	—	—	—	—	—
1696O	—	650	1,200	3,000	6,200	—
1698O Rare	—	—	—	—	—	—

KM# 303.17 2 LOUIS D'OR

13.3900 g., 0.9170 Gold 0.3948 oz. AGW **Ruler:** Louis XIV **Mint:** Dijon

Date	Mintage	VG	F	VF	XF	Unc
1693P	6,025	650	1,200	3,000	6,200	—
1694P	7,917	650	1,200	3,000	6,200	—
1695P Rare	—	—	—	—	—	—
1696P	—	650	1,200	3,000	6,200	—
1697P Rare	—	—	—	—	—	—
1698P Rare	—	—	—	—	—	—
1699P	—	650	1,200	3,000	6,200	—
1700P Rare	—	—	—	—	—	—

KM# 303.18 2 LOUIS D'OR

13.3900 g., 0.9170 Gold 0.3948 oz. AGW **Ruler:** Louis XIV **Mint:** Reims

Date	Mintage	VG	F	VF	XF	Unc
1695S	—	600	1,100	2,400	4,850	—
1696S Rare	—	—	—	—	—	—
1697S Rare	—	—	—	—	—	—

KM# 303.19 2 LOUIS D'OR

13.3900 g., 0.9170 Gold 0.3948 oz. AGW **Ruler:** Louis XIV **Mint:** Nantes

Date	Mintage	VG	F	VF	XF	Unc
1695T	—	600	1,100	2,400	4,850	—
1696T Rare	—	—	—	—	—	—
1697T Rare	—	—	—	—	—	—
1698T Rare	—	—	—	—	—	—
1699T	—	650	1,200	2,700	5,300	—

KM# 303.20 2 LOUIS D'OR

13.3900 g., 0.9170 Gold 0.3948 oz. AGW **Ruler:** Louis XIV **Mint:** Troyes

Date	Mintage	VG	F	VF	XF	Unc
1694V Rare	—	—	—	—	—	—
1695V Rare	—	—	—	—	—	—
1696V Rare	—	—	—	—	—	—
1699V Rare	—	—	—	—	—	—

KM# 303.21 2 LOUIS D'OR

13.3900 g., 0.9170 Gold 0.3948 oz. AGW **Ruler:** Louis XIV **Mint:** Lille

Date	Mintage	VG	F	VF	XF	Unc
1693W	—	600	1,100	2,400	4,850	—
1699W Rare	—	—	—	—	—	—

KM# 303.22 2 LOUIS D'OR

13.3900 g., 0.9170 Gold 0.3948 oz. AGW **Ruler:** Louis XIV **Mint:** Amiens

Date	Mintage	VG	F	VF	XF	Unc
1698X Rare	—	—	—	—	—	—
1699X Rare	—	—	—	—	—	—

KM# 303.23 2 LOUIS D'OR

13.3900 g., 0.9170 Gold 0.3948 oz. AGW **Ruler:** Louis XIV **Mint:** Bourges

Date	Mintage	VG	F	VF	XF	Unc
1694Y	—	650	1,200	2,700	5,800	—
1695Y Rare	—	—	—	—	—	—
1696Y Rare	—	—	—	—	—	—
1697Y	—	650	1,200	2,700	5,800	—
1698Y Rare	—	—	—	—	—	—

KM# 303.24 2 LOUIS D'OR

13.3900 g., 0.9170 Gold 0.3948 oz. AGW **Ruler:** Louis XIV **Mint:** Rennes **Note:** Mint mark: Numeral 9.

Date	Mintage	VG	F	VF	XF	Unc
1693	—	600	1,100	2,400	4,850	—
1695 Rare	—	—	—	—	—	—
1696 Rare	—	—	—	—	—	—
1697 Rare	—	—	—	—	—	—
1698 Rare	—	—	—	—	—	—
1699 Rare	—	—	—	—	—	—

KM# 303.25 2 LOUIS D'OR

13.3900 g., 0.9170 Gold 0.3948 oz. AGW **Ruler:** Louis XIV **Mint:** Aix **Note:** Mint mark: Ampersand.

Date	Mintage	VG	F	VF	XF	Unc
1694 Rare	—	—	—	—	—	—
1695 Rare	—	—	—	—	—	—
1696 Rare	—	—	—	—	—	—
1699 Rare	—	—	—	—	—	—

KM# 303.26 2 LOUIS D'OR

13.3900 g., 0.9170 Gold 0.3948 oz. AGW **Ruler:** Louis XIV **Mint:** Besançon **Note:** Mint mark: Back-to-back C's.

Date	Mintage	VG	F	VF	XF	Unc
1694 Rare	—	—	—	—	—	—
1695	—	600	1,100	2,400	4,850	—
1696	—	650	1,200	3,000	5,400	—
1697 Rare	—	—	—	—	—	—
1698 Rare	—	—	—	—	—	—
1699 Rare	—	—	—	—	—	—

KM# 303.27 2 LOUIS D'OR

13.3900 g., 0.9170 Gold 0.3948 oz. AGW **Ruler:** Louis XIV **Mint:** Pau **Note:** Mint mark: Cow.

Date	Mintage	VG	F	VF	XF	Unc
1695	—	750	1,500	3,000	6,300	—
1696 Rare	—	—	—	—	—	—
1697	—	750	1,500	3,000	6,300	—
1698 Rare	—	—	—	—	—	—
1699 Rare	—	—	—	—	—	—

KM# 335.1 2 LOUIS D'OR

13.3900 g., 0.9170 Gold 0.3948 oz. AGW **Ruler:** Louis XIV **Obv:** Laureate head right **Obv. Legend:** LVD • XIIII • D • G FR • ET • NAV • REX **Rev:** Crowned back to back L's with sceptre and hand of Justice crossed at center behind circle **Rev. Legend:** CHRS REGN VINC IMP **Mint:** Paris

Date	Mintage	VG	F	VF	XF	Unc
1700A	—	700	1,400	2,500	5,500	—

KM# 111 4 LOUIS D'OR

26.7700 g., 0.9170 Gold 0.7892 oz. AGW **Ruler:** Louis XIII **Obv:** Laureate head of Louis XIII right, date below **Rev:** Eight L's back-to-back forming cross with crown at end of each arm, mint mark at center **Mint:** Paris

Date	Mintage	VG	F	VF	XF	Unc
1640A	—	—	55,000	100,000	160,000	—

KM# 112 8 LOUIS D'OR

53.5400 g., 0.9170 Gold 1.5784 oz. AGW **Ruler:** Louis XIII **Obv:** Laureate head of Louis XIII right, date below **Rev:** Eight L's back-to-back forming cross with crown at end of each arm, mint mark at center **Rev. Legend:** CHRISTUS • REGNAT • VINCIT • ET • IMPERAT **Mint:** Paris

Date	Mintage	VG	F	VF	XF	Unc
1640A	—	—	55,000	90,000	130,000	—

KM# 113 8 LOUIS D'OR
53.5400 g., 0.9170 Gold 1.5784 oz. AGW **Ruler:** Louis XIII **Rev. Legend:** CHRS • REGN • VINC • IMP •

Date	Mintage	VG	F	VF	XF	Unc
1640	—	—	60,000	95,000	140,000	—

KM# 114 10 LOUIS D'OR
66.9200 g., 0.9170 Gold 1.9729 oz. AGW **Ruler:** Louis XIII **Mint:** Paris

Date	Mintage	VG	F	VF	XF	Unc
1640A	—	—	50,000	85,000	150,000	—

KM# 115 10 LOUIS D'OR
66.9200 g., 0.9170 Gold 1.9729 oz. AGW **Ruler:** Louis XIII **Obv:** Laureate and draped bust of Louis XIII right

Date	Mintage	VG	F	VF	XF	Unc
1640A	—	—	—	—	250,000	—

ESSAIS

Standard metals unless otherwise noted

KM#	Date	Mintage	Identification	Mkt Val
E1	1634	—	1/2 Ecu D'Or. Gold. 1.3500 g.	9,000
E2	1634	—	Ecu D'Or. Gold.	12,000
AE3	1642	—	Sizain. Gold. 4.5700 g.	—

PATTERNS

KM#	Date	Mintage	Identification	Mkt Val
Pn1	1602	—	4 Sols.	—
Pn2	1602	—	6 Sols.	—
Pn3	1604A	—	Double Tournois. Silver. Ciani #1579	1,000
Pn4	1607A	—	Douzain.	1,000

KM#	Date	Mintage	Identification	Mkt Val
Pn5	1607A	—	1/4 Franc. Silver. Ciani #1552	4,000
Pn6	1607A	—	1/2 Franc. Silver.	4,000

KM#	Date	Mintage	Identification	Mkt Val
Pn7	1607A	—	Franc. Silver.	6,000
Pn8	ND	—	Liard. Silver. of Bearn	—
Pn9	1613D	—	Denier Tournois. Silver.	1,150

KM#	Date	Mintage	Identification	Mkt Val
Pn10	1616A NB	—	Franc. 0.8330 Silver. 14.1880 g. Nicolas Briot	1,200
Pn11	1618A	—	Franc. Silver.	—

KM#	Date	Mintage	Identification	Mkt Val
PnA11	1618A	—	1/4 Franc. Silver.	4,500
PnA12	1620G	—	Denier Tournois. Silver.	—

KM#	Date	Mintage	Identification	Mkt Val
PnB12	1625	—	1/2 Franc. Silver.	3,750
PnC12	1629A	—	Double Tournois. Silver.	—
PnD12	1648A	—	Denier Tournois. Silver.	—
PnE12	1639	—	Douzain. Silver.	—
PnF12	1642A	—	2 Sols 6 Deniers. Silver.	1,650

PIEFORTS

Standard metals unless otherwise noted

KM#	Date	Mintage	Identification	Mkt Val
P5	1607	—	1/4 Ecu. PARIS	2,500
P6	1607	—	1/8 Ecu. PARIS	2,000

KM#	Date	Mintage	Identification	Mkt Val
P7	1607A	—	Franc. Lettered edge. 56.13 grams.	6,500

KM#	Date	Mintage	Identification	Mkt Val
P8	1607A	—	1/2 Franc. Lettered edge. 28.26 grams. Quadruple thickness.	5,000
P9	1607A	—	1/4 Franc.	4,500
P10	ND	—	Double Tournois.	500
PA10	1607A	—	Ecu D'Or. Gold. 13.3500 g. KM#11	7,500
PB10	1607A	—	1/2 Ecu D'Or. Gold. 6.5500 g. KM#8	4,500
PC10	1607A	—	Ecu D'Or. Gold. KM#11. Weight varies: 5.70-6.75 grams.	—
PD10	1607A	—	1/2 Ecu D'Or. Gold. 3.2700 g. KM#8	800
PE10	1607A	—	Douzain. Quadruple thickness.	900
PF10	1607	—	Double Tournois.	750
P11	ND	—	Denier Tournois.	500
P20	1618A	—	Douzain. Silver.	650
P21	1618A	—	1/8 Ecu. Striated edge.	—
P22	1618A	—	1/8 Ecu. Lettered edge.	2,000
P23	1618A	—	1/4 Ecu. Lettered edge.	2,500

KM#	Date	Mintage	Identification	Mkt Val
P24	1618A	—	1/4 Franc. Lettered edge.	3,500

KM#	Date	Mintage	Identification	Mkt Val
P25	1618A	—	1/2 Franc. Lettered edge. Quadruple thickness. 28.02 grams.	6,500
P26	1618A	—	1/2 Franc. Striated edge.	2,500
P27	1618A	—	Franc. Briot lettered edge.	8,500
P28	1618A	—	1/2 Ecu D'Or. Striated edge.	6,500
P40	1643A	—	1/12 Ecu. Lettered edge. Quadruple thickness. 9.11 grams.	3,000

KM#	Date	Mintage	Identification	Mkt Val
P41	1643A	—	1/12 Ecu. Lettered edge. Quadruple thickness.	1,200
P43	1643A	—	1/4 Ecu. Lettered edge. Quadruple thickness. 27.40 grams.	8,500
P44	1643A	—	1/2 Ecu. Lettered edge. Quadruple thickness. 54.78 grams.	6,500
P45	1643A	—	1/2 Ecu. Lettered edge. Quadruple thickness. 54.93 grams.	7,000
P46	1643A	—	Ecu. Lettered edge. Quadruple thickness.	5,000

KM#	Date	Mintage	Identification	Mkt Val
P47	1643A	—	Ecu. Lettered edge. Quadruple thickness. 109.86 grams.	12,500
P48	1643A	—	Ecu D'Or. Lettered edge. Quadruple thickness.	8,000
P49	1643A	—	Ecu D'Or. Striated edge.	5,500
P50	1643A	—	Louis D'Or. Lettered edge. Quadruple thickness.	10,000
P51	1643A	—	Double Louis D'Or. Lettered edge. Quadruple thickness.	15,000
P60	1644A	—	1/12 Ecu. Lettered edge. Quadruple thickness.	2,500
P61	1644A	—	1/4 Ecu. Lettered edge. Quadruple thickness.	3,500
P62	1644A	—	1/2 Ecu. Lettered edge. Quadruple thickness. 5474 grams.	4,500

KM#	Date	Mintage	Identification	Mkt Val
P63	1644A	—	Ecu. Lettered edge. Quadruple thickness. 109.77 grams.	10,000
P64	1644A	—	1/2 Louis D'Or. Lettered edge. Quadruple thickness. 13.43 grams.	13,500

FRENCH STATES

AIRE

(Aire-sur-la-lys, Artois)

A town in north France on the Lys, lies in a low and marshy area at the junction of 3. canals

In the middle ages, Aire belonged to the counts of Flanders and a charter of 1188 is still extant. It was given to France by the Peace of Utrecht in 1713. In World War I, it was one of the headquarters of the British Army Expeditionary Forces.

NOTE: See also Spanish Netherlands-Artois.

COUNTY

SIEGE COINAGE

1641

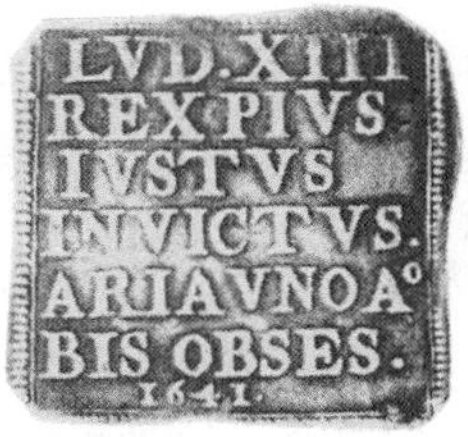

KM# 13 4 GRAMMES 70

Silver **Obv:** Legend in seven lines - LVD XIII/REX PIVS/JVSTYS/INVICTVS/ARIA ANO A /BIS OBES/1641 **Note:** Uniface.

Date	Mintage	VG	F	VF	XF	Unc
1641	—	1,900	2,350	3,100	4,000	—

KM# 14 9 GRAMMES 80

Silver **Obv:** Legend in seven lines - LVD XIII/REX PIVS/JVSTYS/INVICTVS/ARIA ANO A /BIS OBES/1641 **Note:** Uniface.

Date	Mintage	VG	F	VF	XF	Unc
1641	—	1,750	2,350	3,350	4,750	—

BOISBELLE & HENRICHEMONT

A principality located 22 miles east of Vierzon, Cher Department, northwest of Bourges.

RULERS
Maximilian I of Bethune, 1597-1641
Maximilian III, 1641-1661

PRINCIPALITY

STANDARD COINAGE

KM# 3 DOUBLE TOURNOIS

Copper **Obv. Legend:** MAX • D • BETHVNE • P • S • DENRIC **Rev:** Lis around shield **Rev. Legend:** DOVBLE • TOVRNOIS

Date	Mintage	VG	F	VF	XF	Unc
1636	—	18.00	35.00	75.00	150	—

KM# 4 DOUBLE TOURNOIS

Copper **Obv. Legend:** MAXI. P. BET. P. S. DENRIC ET BB

Date	Mintage	VG	F	VF	XF	Unc
1636	—	18.00	40.00	90.00	175	—

KM# 5 DOUBLE TOURNOIS

2.7700 g., Copper, 20.6 mm. **Ruler:** Maximilien I of Bethune **Obv:** Bust right **Obv. Legend:** MAX. D. BETH. NE. P. S. DHENRIC. **Rev:** Arms in circle of fleur-de-lis **Rev. Legend:** DOVBLE TOVRNOIS 1637L **Edge:** Plain

Date	Mintage	F	VF	XF	Unc	BU
1637L	—	50.00	100	200	—	—

KM# 6 DOUBLE TOURNOIS

Copper **Obv. Legend:** MAX D BETHVNE P S DHEN

Date	Mintage	VG	F	VF	XF	Unc
1641	—	18.00	40.00	90.00	175	—

KM# 15 DOUBLE TOURNOIS

Copper **Obv:** Bust **Obv. Legend:** M. D. BETHVNE P. S. DENRICHE.

Date	Mintage	VG	F	VF	XF	Unc
1642 H	—	20.00	45.00	100	200	—

KM# 10 1/2 FRANC

7.0800 g., Silver **Obv. Legend:** MAXI. D BETHVNE. P. S... **Rev:** M on floral cross

Date	Mintage	VG	F	VF	XF	Unc
1637	—	650	1,250	2,000	3,000	—

PATTERNS

Including off metal strikes

KM#	Date	Mintage	Identification	Mkt Val
Pn1	1636	—	Double Tournois. Silver. 2.6000 g.	750

PIEFORTS

KM#	Date	Mintage	Identification	Mkt Val
P1	1637	—	1/2 Franc. Silver. 14.0000 g.	2,000

BOUILLON & SEDAN

Small duchy located in the southeastern Province of Luxembourg in Belgium and also in the Sedan of northern France. Sold by Godfrey V in 1098 to Bishopric of Liege to finance his activities in the crusades. It came under the French in 1678 and later became a part of the Netherlands in 1815.

RULERS
Henri de la Tour, 1591-1623
Frederick Maurice, 1623-1652
Geoffrey Maurice, 1652-1671

MONETARY SYSTEM
3 Deniers = 1 Liard
4 Liards = 1 Sol
20 Sols = 1 Livre
6 Livres = 1 Ecu

DUCHY

STANDARD COINAGE

KM# 9 2 TOURNOIS

Copper **Obv:** Henri de la Tour **Rev:** Crowned arms **Rev. Legend:** DOVBLE TOVRNOIS

Date	Mintage	Good	VG	F	VF	XF
1614	—	5.00	10.00	20.00	60.00	200

KM# 14.1 2 TOURNOIS

Copper **Obv:** Bust right **Obv. Legend:** F. MAVRICE. DE. LATOVR. P. S. D. S. **Rev:** Tower with fleur-de-lis **Rev. Legend:** DOVBLE TOVRNOIS

Date	Mintage	Good	VG	F	VF	XF
1632	—	5.00	10.00	20.00	60.00	200
1633	—	5.00	10.00	20.00	60.00	200

KM# 14.2 2 TOURNOIS

Copper **Obv:** Bust right **Obv. Legend:** F. M. D. L. TOVR. DVC. D. BVILLON **Rev:** Tower with fleur-de-lis, and date **Rev. Legend:** DOVBLE. DE. SEDAN

Date	Mintage	Good	VG	F	VF	XF
1635	—	5.00	10.00	20.00	60.00	200
1636	—	5.00	10.00	20.00	60.00	200
1637	—	5.00	10.00	20.00	60.00	200
1638	—	5.00	10.00	20.00	60.00	200

KM# 14.3 2 TOURNOIS

Copper **Obv:** Bust right **Obv. Legend:** F. M. D. L. TOVR. DVC. D. BVILLON **Rev:** Three fleur-de-lis around tower **Rev. Legend:** DOVBLE. DE. SEDAN

Date	Mintage	Good	VG	F	VF	XF
1641	—	6.00	12.00	25.00	65.00	225
1642	—	6.00	12.00	25.00	65.00	225
1643	—	6.00	12.50	25.00	65.00	225

KM# 5 LIARD

Copper **Rev:** Fleur-de-lis **Rev. Legend:** LIARD TOVRNOIS

Date	Mintage	Good	VG	F	VF	XF
1614	—	70.00	150	300	550	1,000

KM# 40 LIARD

Copper **Obv:** Frederic Maurice **Rev:** Fleur-de-lis

Date	Mintage	Good	VG	F	VF	XF
1642	—	8.00	12.00	25.00	75.00	250

KM# 42 LIARD

Copper **Obv:** Crowned arms **Obv. Legend:** GODF. F. MAV. D. G. DVX. BVLLIONEVS. **Rev:** LIARD DE BOVILLON 1681, with fleur-de-lis between towers

Date	Mintage	Good	VG	F	VF	XF
1681	—	5.00	10.00	20.00	60.00	200

KM# 12.1 2 LIARDS

Copper **Obv. Legend:** HENR • DE • LA • TPVR • D • BVLLIONAEVS **Rev:** Crowned arms **Rev. Legend:** ...SEDANENSIS

Date	Mintage	Good	VG	F	VF	XF
1613	—	6.50	12.50	25.00	55.00	—
1614	—	6.50	12.50	25.00	50.00	—

KM# 12.2 2 LIARDS

Copper **Rev. Legend:** ...BVLLIONEVS

Date	Mintage	Good	VG	F	VF	XF
1613	—	7.00	13.50	27.50	60.00	—

KM# 12.3 2 LIARDS

Copper **Rev. Legend:** ...SEDANI ET RAV

Date	Mintage	Good	VG	F	VF	XF
1614	—	5.00	10.00	22.00	50.00	—

KM# 12.4 2 LIARDS

Copper **Rev. Legend:** ...SEDANI ET RAVC

Date	Mintage	Good	VG	F	VF	XF
1614	—	5.00	10.00	22.00	50.00	—

KM# 13 2 LIARDS

Copper **Obv:** Large bust

Date	Mintage	Good	VG	F	VF	XF
ND	—	6.00	12.50	30.00	60.00	—

KM# 43 2 LIARDS

3.5500 g., Copper, 23.9 mm. **Ruler:** Geoffrey Maurice **Obv:** Bust right **Obv. Legend:** BVLLIONEUS. GOD. EF. FD. G. DUX **Rev:** DOVBLE DE BOVILLON in three lines above a fleur-de-lis between two towers **Edge:** Plain

Date	Mintage	F	VF	XF	Unc	BU
ND(circa 1681)	—	35.00	70.00	—	—	—

KM# 15 5 SOLS

Copper **Obv. Legend:** HENR DE L D BVLLINAEVS **Rev:** Crowned arms **Rev. Legend:** MONET. ARC. NOVA. SEDAN.

Date	Mintage	Good	VG	F	VF	XF
ND	—	275	550	875	—	1,500

KM# 45 5 SOLS

Copper **Obv:** Geoffrey Maurice **Rev:** Crowned arms

Date	Mintage	Good	VG	F	VF	XF
1684	—	—	—	40.00	75.00	200

Note: Restrike c.1845-60

KM# 16 1/2 ECU

9.9500 g., Silver **Obv:** Date at lower left, value "XV" at lower right below eagle's talons **Obv. Legend:** HENRICVS. DE... **Rev:** Crowned arms

Date	Mintage	Good	VG	F	VF	XF
1613	—	350	700	1,250	2,150	4,000
1614	—	350	700	1,250	2,150	4,000

KM# 19 ECU (30 Sous)

Silver **Obv:** Date at left, XXX at right below eagle's talons **Obv. Legend:** * HENRICVS. DE. LA. TOVR. **Note:** Dav. #3816.

Date	Mintage	VG	F	VF	XF	Unc
1613	—	95.00	180	325	550	—
1614	—	95.00	180	325	550	—

KM# 21 ECU (30 Sous)

Silver **Rev:** Similar to KM#19 with Bouillon arms in fourth quarter **Note:** Dav. #3817.

Date	Mintage	VG	F	VF	XF	Unc
1613	—	115	230	400	750	1,600
1614	—	115	230	400	750	1,600

KM# 22 ECU (30 Sous)

Silver **Obv:** Similar to KM#19 with date at lower right, value "XXX" at lower left below eagle's talons **Rev:** Similar to KM#19 with Turenne arms in second and third quarters **Note:** Dav. #3818.

Date	Mintage	VG	F	VF	XF	Unc
1613 Rare	—	—	—	—	—	—
1614 Rare	—	—	—	—	—	—

KM# 24 ECU (45 Sous)

Silver **Obv:** Legend around bust with .XLV. below **Obv. Legend:** * HENRICVS. DE. LA. - TOVR. DVX. BVLLIONII **Note:** Dav. #3819.

Date	Mintage	VG	F	VF	XF	Unc
1614 Rare	—	—	—	—	—	—

KM# 25 ECU (45 Sous)

Silver **Obv:** Similar to KM#24 with legend beginning at lower left **Rev:** Modified frame for arms **Note:** Dav. #3820.

Date	Mintage	VG	F	VF	XF	Unc
1614	—	775	1,550	2,650	4,500	—

KM# 28 ECU (45 Sous)

Silver **Obv:** Similar to KM#27 with date below smaller bust **Rev. Legend:** SVPREMVS. PRINCEPS. SEDANI... **Note:** Dav. #3821.

Date	Mintage	VG	F	VF	XF	Unc
1614 Rare	—	—	—	—	—	—

KM# 26 ECU (45 Sous)

Silver **Obv:** Similar to KM#25 without • XLV • below bust **Rev:** Similar to KM#25 **Note:** Dav. #A3821.

Date	Mintage	VG	F	VF	XF	Unc
1614 Rare	—	—	—	—	—	—

KM# 27 ECU (45 Sous)

Silver **Obv:** Date below bust **Note:** Dav. #B3821.

Date	Mintage	VG	F	VF	XF	Unc
1614 Rare	—	—	—	—	—	—

KM# 29 ECU (45 Sous)

Silver **Obv. Legend:** *HENRICVS + DE + LA * TOVR... **Rev. Legend:** SVP. PRINCEPS. SEDANI. ET RAVCVRT. **Note:** Dav. #3822.

Date	Mintage	VG	F	VF	XF	Unc
1615	—	775	1,550	2,650	4,500	—
1616	—	775	1,550	2,650	4,500	—

KM# 35 ECU (45 Sous)

Silver **Obv:** Legend around cuirassed knight over lion arms **Obv. Legend:** * FRED. MAVRIT * - * D. G. PRIN. AVR * **Rev:** Rampant lion left **Rev. Legend:** * CONFIDENS * DNO * NON * MOVETVR * 1634 **Note:** Dav. #3823.

Date	Mintage	VG	F	VF	XF	Unc
1634	—	800	1,650	2,850	4,750	—

KM# 3 ECU D'OR

3.3600 g., 0.9520 Gold 0.1028 oz. AGW **Obv:** Crowned arms in inner circle **Rev:** Cross in inner circle

Date	Mintage	VG	F	VF	XF	Unc
1610	—	325	725	1,200	2,000	—
ND	—	325	725	1,200	2,000	—

KM# 30 ECU D'OR

3.3600 g., 0.9520 Gold 0.1028 oz. AGW **Obv:** Bust of Henri right in inner circle **Rev:** Crowned arms

Date	Mintage	VG	F	VF	XF	Unc
1614	—	750	1,650	3,000	5,500	—

KM# 4 2 ECU D'OR

6.7200 g., 0.9520 Gold 0.2057 oz. AGW **Obv:** Crowned arms in inner circle **Rev:** Cross in inner circle

Date	Mintage	VG	F	VF	XF	Unc
1610	—	925	1,950	3,250	5,200	—
1614	—	1,350	2,850	5,500	7,500	—
ND	—	925	1,950	3,250	5,200	—

BURGUNDY

(Dole)

City in eastern France 25 miles southeast of Dijon. Roman ruins show early settlement in the area. Later used as a Burgundian mint by the Spanish kings.

RULERS

Spanish

MINT MARKS

(c) – crosslet

r - rosette

(s) - star

SPANISH RULE

STANDARD COINAGE

KM# 10 3 PATARDS

Silver **Ruler:** Philip IV **Obv:** Floriate cross **Obv. Legend:** PHIL ✠ IIII • D • G • REX • HISP • **Rev:** Crowned arms **Rev. Legend:** ARCHID •

Date	Mintage	VG	F	VF	XF	Unc
1624	—	85.00	175	250	400	—

KM# 14 1/2 PATAGON

Silver **Ruler:** Philip IV **Obv:** St. Andrew's cross with crown above divides date **Obv. Legend:** PHIL. IIII. D. G. HISP. ET. INDIAR. REX **Rev:** Crowned arms **Rev. Legend:** ARCHID ? AVST (RIE) ? (DVX) ? ET ? COM ? BVRG ? Zc

Date	Mintage	VG	F	VF	XF	Unc
1625	—	—	—	—	—	—
1626	—	—	—	—	—	—

Date	Mintage	VG	F	VF	XF	Unc
1627	—	—	—	—	—	—
1634	—	—	—	—	—	—
1635	—	—	—	—	—	—
1636	—	—	—	—	—	—
1638	—	—	—	—	—	—

KM# 15 PATAGON

Silver **Ruler:** Philip IV **Obv:** St. Andrew's cross with crown above divides date **Obv. Legend:** ✠ • PHIL • IIII • D • G • REX • HISP • INDIAR **Rev:** Crowned arms in Order chain **Rev. Legend:** ARCHID • AVST(RIE) • (DVX) • ET • COM • BVRG • Zc **Note:** Dav.#4472.

Date	Mintage	Good	VG	F	VF	XF
1622(c)	—	45.00	90.00	165	285	500
1622(r)	—	45.00	90.00	165	285	500
1623(r)	—	45.00	90.00	165	285	500
1624(r)	—	45.00	90.00	165	285	500
1625(r)	—	45.00	90.00	165	285	500
1625(s)	—	45.00	90.00	165	285	500
1626(r)	—	45.00	90.00	165	285	500
1626(s)	—	45.00	90.00	165	285	500
1627(s)	—	45.00	90.00	165	285	500
1628(s)	—	45.00	90.00	165	285	500
1634(s)	—	45.00	90.00	165	285	500
1635(s)	—	45.00	90.00	165	285	500
1636(s)	—	45.00	90.00	165	285	500
1639(s)	—	45.00	90.00	165	285	500

KM# 16 2 PATAGON

Silver **Ruler:** Philip IV **Obv:** St. Andrew's cross divides date, crown above **Obv. Legend:** ✠ • PHIL • IIII • D • G • REX • HISP • INDIAR **Rev:** Crowned arms in Order chain **Rev. Legend:** ARCHID • AVST(RIE) • (DVX) • ET • COM • BVRG • Zc **Note:** Dav.#4471.

Date	Mintage	Good	VG	F	VF	XF
1622 Rare	—	—	—	—	—	—
1633(s) Rare	—	—	—	—	—	—

KM# 13 1/4 DUCATON

Silver **Ruler:** Philip IV **Obv:** Bust right **Obv. Legend:** PHIL ? IIII ? D ? G ? REX ? HISP ? INDIAR ? Zc **Rev:** Crowned arms in Order collar **Rev. Legend:** ARCH ? AVST ? DVX ? ET ? COM ? BVRG ? Zc

Date	Mintage	VG	F	VF	XF	Unc
1622	—	—	—	—	—	—
1632	—	—	—	—	—	—
1634	—	—	—	—	—	—
1635	—	—	—	—	—	—
1647	—	—	—	—	—	—

TRADE COINAGE

KM# 17 CORONA

3.3800 g., 0.9170 Gold 0.0996 oz. AGW **Ruler:** Philip IV **Obv:** St. Andrew's cross with crown above, date in legend **Rev:** Crowned arms between two crowned steels **Note:** Fr. #118.

Date	Mintage	VG	F	VF	XF	Unc
1632 Rare	—	—	—	—	—	—

CHATEAU-RENAUD

A small city in northern France near the Belgian border. Francois de Bourbon, Prince Conti acquired the city when he married Louise Marguerite of Lorraine in 1605. After his death in 1614 Louise Marguerite ruled until she ceded the property to Louis XIII of France in 1629.

RULERS

Francois and Louise Marguerite, 1605-1614

Louise Marguerite, alone 1614-1631

PRINCIPALITY

STANDARD COINAGE

KM# 5 2 DENIERS (Tournois)

Copper **Obv:** Bust **Obv. Legend:** F • DE • BOVRBON • P • DE • CONTI **Rev:** Fleur-de-lis **Rev. Legend:** DOVBLE TOVRNOIS **Note:** Varieties exist.

Date	Mintage	VG	F	VF	XF	Unc
ND(1603-05)	—	7.00	15.00	30.00	60.00	—

KM# 25 LIARD

Copper **Obv:** Bust **Obv. Legend:** FRANCOIS DE BOYRBON **Rev:** Crowned arms **Rev. Legend:** PRINCE. DE. CONTI. SOVER.

Date	Mintage	VG	F	VF	XF	Unc
1613	—	10.00	20.00	40.00	80.00	—

KM# 26.1 LIARD

Copper **Obv:** Large bust right **Obv. Legend:** FRANCOIS. DE. BOVRBON. **Rev:** Crowned arms **Rev. Legend:** P. DE. CONTI. S. DE. CH. RENAV.

Date	Mintage	VG	F	VF	XF	Unc
1613	—	10.00	15.00	40.00	80.00	—
1614	—	10.00	18.00	45.00	85.00	—

KM# 26.2 LIARD

Copper **Obv:** Small bust right **Obv. Legend:** FRANCOIS. DE. BOVRBON. **Rev:** Crowned arms **Rev. Legend:** P. DE. CONTI. S. DE. CH. RENAV.

Date	Mintage	VG	F	VF	XF	Unc
1613	—	8.00	14.00	35.00	75.00	—
1614	—	8.00	16.00	40.00	85.00	—

KM# 7 2 KREUTZERS (Douzain)

Billon **Obv:** Crowned arms **Rev:** Cross with two crowns and two lis in angles

Date	Mintage	VG	F	VF	XF	Unc
ND(1605-14)	—	125	225	450	750	—

KM# 30 2 KREUTZERS (Douzain)

Billon **Obv:** Crowned arms **Obv. Legend:** MONETA NOVA ARGEN. CH. **Rev:** Eagle **Rev. Legend:** SVB. VMBRA ALARVM TVARVM

Date	Mintage	VG	F	VF	XF	Unc
1619	—	125	225	450	750	—

KM# 35.1 GROS

Billon **Obv:** Crowned arms **Obv. Legend:** LVDOVICA. MARGAR. LOT **Rev:** Crowned eagle **Rev. Legend:** IN. OMNEM. TERR. SONVS. EOR.

Date	Mintage	VG	F	VF	XF	Unc
ND(1614)	—	100	200	375	675	—

KM# 35.2 GROS

Billon **Obv:** Crowned arms **Obv. Legend:** LVD MARGARETA A LO **Rev. Legend:** IN OMNEM. TER. SONVS EOR.

Date	Mintage	VG	F	VF	XF	Unc
ND(1614-31)	—	125	250	475	750	—

KM# 39 ESCALIN

Silver **Ruler:** Louise Marguerite, alone **Obv:** Ornate crowned arms **Obv. Legend:** MONETA ⁜ NOVA ⁜ ARGENT ⁜ L **Rev:** Crowned imperial eagle with orb on chest

Date	Mintage	Good	VG	F	VF	XF
ND(1614-29)	—	65.00	125	200	350	—

KM# 37 ESCALIN

4.9000 g., Silver **Obv:** Crowned arms **Obv. Legend:** MARG. A. LOTH. D. G... **Rev:** Crowned St. Andrew's cross **Rev. Legend:** MONETA ARGENTEA. CASTRO. REGINAL. CV.

Date	Mintage	VG	F	VF	XF	Unc
ND(1614-31)	—	250	450	800	—	—

KM# 38 ESCALIN

4.9000 g., Silver **Obv:** Crowned arms **Obv. Legend:** With: LVD

Date	Mintage	VG	F	VF	XF	Unc
ND(1614-31)	—	250	450	800	—	—

KM# 40 ESCALIN

4.9000 g., Silver **Obv:** Crowned arms on St. Andrew's cross **Obv. Legend:** MONETA NOVA ARGENT-IA CHA **Rev:** Crowned imperial eagle **Rev. Legend:** SIT • NOMEN • DOMINI • BENEDICTVM

Date	Mintage	VG	F	VF	XF	Unc
ND(1614-31)	—	150	300	550	850	—

KM# 41 ESCALIN

4.9000 g., Silver **Obv:** Date in legend

Date	Mintage	VG	F	VF	XF	Unc
1617	—	175	350	600	900	—

KM# 59 ESCALIN

4.9000 g., Silver **Obv:** Crowned and feathered arms **Obv. Legend:** MONE • NOVA • ARGENTCHA **Rev:** Crowned imperial eagle **Rev. Legend:** DA. PACEM. DOMINE. IN. DIEBVS. NOS. **Note:** Imitation of 5 Stuber from East Friesland.

Date	Mintage	VG	F	VF	XF	Unc
ND(1625)	—	150	300	550	850	—

KM# 45 1/4 ECU

Silver **Obv:** Crowned arms **Obv. Legend:** F. BOVRB. LVD MARGAR. LOT. **Rev:** Cross, fleur-de-lis **Rev. Legend:** IN OMNEM. TERRAM.

Date	Mintage	VG	F	VF	XF	Unc
ND(1605-14)	—	750	1,250	1,850	2,750	—

KM# 52 ECU (30 Sous)

Silver **Obv:** Legend around chateau surmounted by three towers with lion above **Obv. Legend:** MONETA. NOVA. ARGENTIA * PRINCIP: CHA. R. **Rev:** Legend around crowned double eagle **Rev. Legend:** DILIGITE. IVSTICIA. QUI. IVDICATIS. TERRAM **Note:** Dav. #A3828.

Date	Mintage	VG	F	VF	XF	Unc
1612 (7?) Rare	—	—	—	—	—	—

KM# 50 ECU (30 Sous)

Silver **Obv. Legend:** * F. BOVRBONIVS. L. MARGARETA. A. LOTARINGIA. **Rev. Legend:** IN. OMNEM. TERRAM. SONVS. EORVM. **Note:** Dav. #3824.

Date	Mintage	VG	F	VF	XF	Unc
1614	—	2,000	3,500	6,500	—	—

KM# 51 ECU (30 Sous)

Silver **Obv:** Legend around bust **Obv. Legend:** .FR. BOVRBONIVS. LVD. MARGARETA. A LOTHARIN **Rev:** Similar to KM#50 **Note:** Dav. #3825.

Date	Mintage	VG	F	VF	XF	Unc
ND	—	2,150	4,000	7,000	—	—

KM# 53 PATAGON

Silver **Obv. Legend:** LVD MARG. A LODH. D G. SVP. PR. C. REGI. **Rev. Legend:** ...CAS. TRO. REGINALDI. **Note:** Dav. #3826.

Date	Mintage	VG	F	VF	XF	Unc
ND CV Rare	—	—	—	—	—	—

KM# 56 PATAGON

Silver **Rev. Legend:** ...CAST. REGI. CVSA + **Note:** Dav. #3827.

Date	Mintage	VG	F	VF	XF	Unc
ND Rare	—	—	—	—	—	—

KM# 63 PATAGON

Silver **Obv:** Similar to KM#53 **Obv. Legend:** DEI. GR. **Rev:** Eagle arms in center and below **Rev. Legend:** MON. NOVA. ARGENTEA. CAST. REG. CVSA **Note:** Dav. #3828.

Date	Mintage	VG	F	VF	XF	Unc
1626 Rare	—	—	—	—	—	—

KM# 64 PATAGON

Silver **Obv:** Similar to KM#53 **Rev:** Similar to KM#53 but date divided by cross **Note:** Dav. #3829.

Date	Mintage	VG	F	VF	XF	Unc
1628 Rare	—	—	—	—	—	—

KM# 17 FLORIN D'OR

3.5000 g., 0.9860 Gold 0.1109 oz. AGW **Obv:** Bust of Francois, legend begins at lower left **Rev:** Crowned arms with cross of Lorraine on each side **Note:** Fr.#114.

Date	Mintage	VG	F	VF	XF	Unc
ND	—	475	950	1,500	2,350	—

KM# 18 FLORIN D'OR

3.5000 g., 0.9860 Gold 0.1109 oz. AGW **Rev:** Without crosses of Lorraine

Date	Mintage	VG	F	VF	XF	Unc
ND	—	400	875	1,450	2,150	—

KM# 19 FLORIN D'OR

3.5000 g., 0.9860 Gold 0.1109 oz. AGW **Rev:** Legend begins at lower left

Date	Mintage	VG	F	VF	XF	Unc
ND	—	400	875	1,450	2,150	—

KM# 20 FLORIN D'OR

3.5000 g., 0.9860 Gold 0.1109 oz. AGW

Date	Mintage	VG	F	VF	XF	Unc
ND	—	400	875	1,450	2,150	—

KM# 70 ECU D'OR

3.3600 g., 0.9520 Gold 0.1028 oz. AGW **Obv:** Crowned arms with Jerusalem cross on each side **Rev:** Cross **Note:** Fr.#115.

Date	Mintage	VG	F	VF	XF	Unc
ND	—	800	1,750	3,000	4,250	—

DOMBES

Region in eastern France near the Swiss border. Purchased by the Duke of Bourbon in 1402. Briefly in the royal domains from 1527 to 1560. Granted at that time to the Duke of Bourbon-Montpensier. The brother of Louis XIII married a Dombes heiress in 1626. After the death of their daughter, Dombes was once again annexed to France.

RULERS
Henri II de Montpensier, 1592-1608
Marie de Montpensier, 1608-1626
Gaston de Orleans and Marie, 1626-1627
Gaston de Orleans, 1627-1650
Anne Marie Louise de Orleans, 1650-1693

DUCHY

STANDARD COINAGE

KM# 16 LIARD

Billon **Ruler:** Henri II de Montpensier **Obv:** Crowned H within three fleur-de-lis **Obv. Legend:** H. P. DOMBAR. D. MONTISP. M. **Rev:** Cross of the Order of Saint-Esprit **Rev. Legend:** DNS. ADIVTOR. MEVS.

Date	Mintage	VG	F	VF	XF	Unc
1606	—	10.00	20.00	42.00	85.00	—
1609	—	10.00	20.00	42.00	85.00	—

KM# A22 LIARD

Billon **Obv:** Crowned M within 3 fleur-de-lis, legend around **Obv. Legend:** MAR... BARD • MONTISP... **Rev:** Maltese cross **Rev. Legend:** DNS • ADIVTOR....

Date	Mintage	VG	F	VF	XF	Unc
1615	—	10.00	20.00	42.00	85.00	—

KM# 25 LIARD

Billon **Ruler:** Gaston de Orleans and Marie **Obv:** Crowned GM monogram within 3 fleur-de-lis **Obv. Legend:** GAST.ET.M.SOVV.D.D.DOMB **Rev:** Cross of the Order of Saint-Esprit **Rev. Legend:** DNS.ADIVTOR.MEVS.

Date	Mintage	VG	F	VF	XF	Unc
ND	—	18.00	36.00	70.00	120	—
1628	—	18.00	36.00	70.00	120	—
1629	—	18.00	36.00	70.00	120	—

KM# 26 LIARD

Billon **Ruler:** Gaston de Orleans **Obv:** Crowned G within three fleur-de-lis **Obv. Legend:** GASTON. VS. D. L. SOV. DOMB. **Rev:** Cross fo the Order of Saint-Esprit, date **Rev. Legend:** DNS. ADIVTOR. MEVS.

Date	Mintage	VG	F	VF	XF	Unc
1639	—	8.00	18.00	37.50	80.00	—

KM# 22 DENIER TOURNOIS

Copper **Ruler:** Marie de Montpensier **Obv:** Bust left **Obv. Legend:** MARIE. SOVVE. DE. DOMBES **Rev:** M with two fleur-de-lis above, date **Rev. Legend:** DENIER TOVRNOIS

Date	Mintage	VG	F	VF	XF	Unc
1624	—	15.00	30.00	55.00	110	—

KM# 28 DENIER TOURNOIS

Copper **Ruler:** Gaston de Orleans **Obv:** Bust right **Obv. Legend:** GAST. PAT. R. VSVFR. PR. DOM **Rev:** Three fleur-de-lis, date **Rev. Legend:** DENIER. TOVRNOIS.

Date	Mintage	VG	F	VF	XF	Unc
1644	—	12.00	25.00	48.00	95.00	—
1649	—	12.00	25.00	48.00	95.00	—

KM# 29 DENIER TOURNOIS

Copper **Ruler:** Gaston de Orleans **Obv:** Bust right **Obv. Legend:** GASTON. V. F. P. D. **Rev:** Two fleur-de-lis, date **Rev. Legend:** DENIER. TOVRNOIS.

Date	Mintage	VG	F	VF	XF	Unc
1649 Small bust	—	12.00	25.00	48.00	95.00	—
1650A	—	12.00	25.00	48.00	95.00	—
1651A Large bust	—	12.00	25.00	48.00	95.00	—
1652	—	12.00	25.00	48.00	95.00	—
1654A	—	12.00	25.00	48.00	95.00	—

KM# 24 DOUBLE TOURNOIS

Copper **Ruler:** Marie de Montpensier **Obv:** Bust left **Obv. Legend:** MARIE. SOVVER. DE. DOMBES. B. **Rev:** Three fleur-de-lis, date **Rev. Legend:** DOVBLE. TOVRNOIS.

Date	Mintage	VG	F	VF	XF	Unc
1620	—	12.00	27.50	50.00	100	—
1621	—	12.00	27.50	50.00	100	—
1622	—	12.00	25.00	48.00	95.00	—
1624	—	12.00	25.00	48.00	95.00	—
1626	—	12.00	25.00	48.00	95.00	—
1627	—	12.00	27.50	50.00	100	—

KM# 32 DOUBLE TOURNOIS

Copper, 22.5 mm. **Ruler:** Gaston de Orleans **Obv:** Bust right **Obv. Legend:** GASTON. VSV. F. DE. LA. SOV. DOM. **Rev:** Three fleur-de-lis, date **Rev. Legend:** DOVBLE. TOVRNOIS.

Date	Mintage	VG	F	VF	XF	Unc
1629	—	12.00	25.00	48.00	95.00	—
1635	—	12.00	25.00	48.00	95.00	—
1636	—	12.00	25.00	48.00	95.00	—

Note: Minor legend varieties exist

Date	Mintage	VG	F	VF	XF	Unc
1637	—	12.00	25.00	48.00	95.00	—
1642	—	12.00	25.00	48.00	95.00	—
1643	—	12.00	25.00	48.00	95.00	—

KM# 34 DOUBLE TOURNOIS
Copper **Obv:** Bust right **Obv. Legend:** GASTON. VSV. D. LA. SOV. DOM. G. **Rev:** Three fleur-de-lis, date **Rev. Legend:** DOVBLE. TOVRNOIS.

Date	Mintage	VG	F	VF	XF	Unc
1640	—	12.00	25.00	48.00	95.00	—
1641	—	12.00	25.00	48.00	95.00	—
1643	—	12.00	25.00	48.00	95.00	—

KM# 40 1/12 ECU
13.5500 g., Silver **Ruler:** Anne Marie Louise de Orleans **Obv:** Bust right **Obv. Legend:** AN • MA • LOV • PRINC • SOVV • DE • DOM **Rev:** Crowned arms divides date **Rev. Legend:** DNS • ADIVTOR • ET • REDEM • MEVS

Date	Mintage	Good	VG	F	VF	XF
1664	—	25.00	65.00	125	250	450
1665	—	25.00	65.00	125	250	450

KM# 41 1/12 ECU
13.5500 g., Silver, 21 mm. **Ruler:** Anne Marie Louise de Orleans **Obv:** Bust right **Obv. Legend:** AN • MA • LOV • DE • BOVRBON **Rev:** Crowned arms divides date **Rev. Legend:** PRINC + SOVV DE + DOMBES

Date	Mintage	Good	VG	F	VF	XF
1668	—	25.00	65.00	125	250	450

KM# 18 1/2 TESTON
4.6800 g., Silver **Ruler:** Henri II de Montpensier **Obv:** Bust left, date **Obv. Legend:** HENRIC. P. DOMBAR. D. MONTISP. R. **Rev:** Crowned arms between crowned H's, date **Rev. Legend:** DNS. ADIVTOR. ET. REDEM. MEVS.

Date	Mintage	Good	VG	F	VF	XF
16xx	—	35.00	75.00	145	275	450

KM# 20 TESTON
8.1600 g., Silver **Ruler:** Henri II de Montpensier **Obv:** Bust right **Obv. Legend:** HENRIC. P. DOMBAR. D. MONTISP. R. **Rev:** Crowned arms between crowned H's, date **Rev. Legend:** DNS. ADIVTOR. ET. REDEM. MEVS.

Date	Mintage	Good	VG	F	VF	XF
1605	—	18.00	42.00	80.00	160	300
1606	—	18.00	42.00	80.00	160	300

KM# 21 TESTON
8.1600 g., Silver **Ruler:** Henri II de Montpensier **Obv:** Bust of Henry II left **Obv. Legend:** ✠ HENRIC • P • DOMBAR • D • MONTISP • R **Rev:** Crowned arms between crowned H's **Rev. Legend:** ✠ DNS • ADIVTOR • ET • REDEM • MEVS •

Date	Mintage	Good	VG	F	VF	XF
1606/5	—	20.00	45.00	100	165	300

KM# 45 1/2 ECU (30 Sols)
13.5500 g., Silver **Ruler:** Anne Marie Louise de Orleans **Obv:** Bust right **Obv. Legend:** AN • MA • LVD • PRINC • SVPRE • DOMBA **Rev:** Crowned arms **Rev. Legend:** * DOMINVS * ADIVTOR • • ET REDE • MEVS **Note:** Prev. KM#39.

Date	Mintage	Good	VG	F	VF	XF
1673A	—	650	1,250	2,500	4,500	7,500

DAV# 3830 ECU
Silver **Ruler:** Gaston de Orleans **Obv:** Armored bust right **Obv. Legend:** GASTON • VS • P DOMBARVM **Rev:** Crowned arms **Rev. Legend:** DOMINVS. ADIVTOR. ET. REDE. MEVS.

Date	Mintage	VG	F	VF	XF	Unc
1652	—	1,450	2,850	4,800	7,800	—

DAV# 3831 ECU
Silver **Ruler:** Anne Marie Louise de Orleans **Obv:** Bust right **Obv. Legend:** AN. MA. LVD. PRIN. SVPRE. DOMBAR. **Rev:** Crowned arms **Rev. Legend:** DOMINVS * ADVITOR * * ET • REDE • MEVS

Date	Mintage	VG	F	VF	XF	Unc
1673A	—	1,500	3,000	5,000	8,500	—

FR# 126 1/2 ECU D'OR
1.7100 g., 0.9520 Gold 0.0523 oz. AGW **Ruler:** Marie de Montpensier **Obv:** Crowned arms **Rev:** Ornamental cross, date in legend

Date	Mintage	VG	F	VF	XF	Unc
1614 Unique	—	—	—	—	—	—

FR# 125 ECU D'OR
3.3600 g., 0.9520 Gold 0.1028 oz. AGW **Ruler:** Marie de Montpensier **Obv:** Crowned arms **Rev:** Ornamental cross of palms, date in legend

Date	Mintage	VG	F	VF	XF	Unc
1618 Unique	—	—	—	—	—	—

FR# 127 ECU D'OR
3.2700 g., 0.9520 Gold 0.1001 oz. AGW **Ruler:** Gaston de Orleans and Marie **Obv:** Crowned arms **Rev:** Ornamental lobed cross with fleurs de lis at end of each arm, date in legend

Date	Mintage	VG	F	VF	XF	Unc
1627 Unique	—	—	—	—	—	—

FR# 129 ECU D'OR
3.3600 g., 0.9520 Gold 0.1028 oz. AGW **Ruler:** Gaston de Orleans **Obv:** Crowned arms **Rev:** Ornamental lobed cross with fleurs de lis at end of each arm, date in legend

Date	Mintage	VG	F	VF	XF	Unc
1639 Unique	—	—	—	—	—	—
1640	—	850	1,700	2,800	5,000	—
1641	—	850	1,700	2,800	5,000	—

FR# 128 2 ECU D'OR
6.6000 g., 0.9520 Gold 0.2020 oz. AGW **Ruler:** Gaston de Orleans **Obv:** Crowned arms **Rev:** Ornamental lobed cross with lis at end of each arm, date in legend

Date	Mintage	VG	F	VF	XF	Unc
1640	—	1,150	2,200	4,500	7,500	—

Date	Mintage	VG	F	VF	XF	Unc
1641	—	1,150	2,200	4,500	7,500	—
1642	—	1,150	2,200	4,500	7,500	—

FR# 131 LOUIS D'OR
6.7100 g., 0.9170 Gold 0.1978 oz. AGW **Ruler:** Gaston de Orleans **Obv:** Laureate bust right, date below **Rev:** Cross of eight L's with crown at end of each arm, fleur de lis in angles **Note:** Posthumous issue.

Date	Mintage	VG	F	VF	XF	Unc
1652	—	4,500	6,000	8,000	12,000	—

FR# 130 2 LOUIS D'OR
13.3800 g., 0.9170 Gold 0.3945 oz. AGW **Ruler:** Gaston de Orleans **Obv:** Laureate bust of Gaston right, date below **Rev:** Cross of 8 L's with crown at end of each arm, fleur de lis in angles **Note:** Posthumous issue.

Date	Mintage	VG	F	VF	XF	Unc
1652A	—	6,000	7,500	11,500	17,000	—

TRADE COINAGE

FR# 132 DUCAT
3.5000 g., 0.9860 Gold 0.1109 oz. AGW **Ruler:** Anne Marie Louise de Orleans **Obv:** Ruler by standing saint **Rev:** Standing figure of Christ

Date	Mintage	VG	F	VF	XF	Unc
ND	—	550	1,100	2,200	3,850	—

PATTERNS

Including off metal strikes

KM#	Date	Mintage	Identification	Mkt Val
Pn1	1620	—	Liard. Silver.	—

NEVERS & RETHEL

The county of Nevers, located in central France, and the duchy of Rethel established in 1581 located in northern France near the Belgian border were united when a Rethel heiress married the son of the Duke of Mantua, Louis Gonzaga. Their great-grandson, Charles III (1637-1665) was active as Duke of Mantua and sold Rethel and all the rest of his French possessions to Cardinal Mazarin in 1663.

RULERS
Charles of Gonzaga, 1601-1637
Charles II of Gonzaga, 1637-1659

DUCHY

STANDARD COINAGE

KM# 9 DENIER TOURNOIS
Copper **Ruler:** Charles of Gonzaga **Obv:** Charles **Rev:** Crowned arms

Date	Mintage	VG	F	VF	XF	Unc
1609	—	25.00	45.00	85.00	175	—

KM# 47 DENIER TOURNOIS
Copper **Rev:** Two fluer-de-lis **Note:** Varieties exist.

Date	Mintage	VG	F	VF	XF	Unc
1652A	—	9.00	18.00	35.00	75.00	—
1653	—	—	—	—	—	—
1653A	—	9.00	18.00	35.00	75.00	—

KM# 1 DOUBLE TOURNOIS
Copper **Obv:** Bust right **Obv. Legend:** CH. D. GONZ. D. DE. NEVERS. **Rev:** Crowned arms **Rev. Legend:** DOUBLE. TOVRNOIS.

Date	Mintage	VG	F	VF	XF	Unc
1608	—	10.00	20.00	40.00	80.00	—
1610	—	10.00	20.00	40.00	80.00	—
1611	—	10.00	20.00	40.00	80.00	—

KM# 3 DOUBLE TOURNOIS

Copper **Ruler:** Charles of G... Bust **Rev:** Fleur-de-lis **Rev. Legend:** DOVBL... **Note:** Varieties exist.

Date	Mintage	VG	F	VF	XF	Unc
1634			35.00	70.00	150	—

KM# 5 DOUBLE TOURNOIS

Copper **Obv:** Charles I, like KM-3 **Rev. Legend:** like KM-50 **Note:** Similar to KM#3.

Date	Mintage	VG	F	VF	XF	Unc
1635	—	10.00	20.00	40.00	85.00	—
1636	—	10.00	20.00	40.00	85.00	—
1637	—	10.00	20.00	40.00	85.00	—

KM# 50 DOUBLE TOURNOIS

Copper **Obv:** Bust right Charles II **Obv. Legend:** CHARLES. II. BVC. D. MANT. S. DAR. **Rev:** Three fleur-de-lis and date **Rev. Legend:** DOVBLE D. LA. SOV. DAR.

Date	Mintage	VG	F	VF	XF	Unc
1639	—	9.00	18.00	35.00	75.00	—
1640	—	9.00	18.00	35.00	75.00	—
1642	—	9.00	18.00	35.00	75.00	—
1645	—	9.00	18.00	35.00	75.00	—

KM# 2 LIARD

Copper **Ruler:** Charles of Gonzaga **Obv:** Crowned bust of Charles left **Obv. Legend:** KARO • DVX • NIV • ET • RETH • S • PR • ARCH **Rev:** Crowned five-fold arms between K's **Rev. Legend:** * MEI • DEVS • SIGNACVLVM • CORDIS

Date	Mintage	Good	VG	F	VF	XF
1607	—	20.00	42.50	75.00	125	200

KM# 53 LIARD

Copper **Obv:** Charles II **Obv. Legend:** CHARLES II: D. D. MANOV. **Rev:** Three lis **Rev. Legend:** LIARD DE FRANC • C • **Note:** Struck in imitation of liards of Louis XIV.

Date	Mintage	VG	F	VF	XF	Unc
1655A	—	15.00	25.00	50.00	100	—

KM# 12.1 2 LIARD

Copper **Obv:** Bust **Obv. Legend:** CAR • GONZ • D • NIV • ET • RETH **Rev:** Crowned arms **Rev. Legend:** SVP • PRINCEPS • ARCHENSIS

Date	Mintage	VG	F	VF	XF	Unc
1608	—	12.00	25.00	48.00	100	—
1609	—	12.00	25.00	48.00	100	—
1610	—	12.00	25.00	48.00	100	—
1611	—	12.00	25.00	48.00	100	—
1613	—	12.00	25.00	48.00	100	—

KM# 12.3 2 LIARD

Copper, 23-24 mm. **Ruler:** Charles of Gonzaga **Obv:** Bust to left, date in exergue **Obv. Legend:** CAR. DVX. NIVERNENS. ET. RETH. **Rev:** Crowned shield of 4-fold arms with quartered central shield **Rev. Legend:** DEI. GR. PRINCEPS. ARCHENSIS.

Date	Mintage	VG	F	VF	XF	Unc
1613	—	12.00	25.00	45.00	85.00	—

KM# 12.2 2 LIARD

Copper **Obv:** Bust right **Rev:** Crowned arms **Rev. Legend:** SVP•PRINCEPS•ARCHENSIS **Note:** Variation in obverse legend.

Date	Mintage	VG	F	VF	XF	Unc
1614	—	12.00	25.00	48.00	100	—

KM# 15 1/2 ESCALIN

Silver **Obv:** Floral cross **Obv. Legend:** CAROLVS • GONZ • D • NIVERN • ET • RETH **Rev:** Crowned arms **Rev. Legend:** SVP • PRINCEPS • ARCHENSIS

Date	Mintage	VG	F	VF	XF	Unc
1609	—	275	450	700	1,150	—

KM# 21 1/2 ECU

Silver **Obv:** Crowned arms **Obv. Legend:** CAROLVS • I • D.G. • MAN • MONF • NIV • MA • I • RET • DVX... **Rev:** St. Louis of Gonzaque

Date	Mintage	VG	F	VF	XF	Unc
ND	—	950	1,500	—	—	—

KM# 28 ECU OF 30 SOUS

Silver **Obv:** Without value **Obv. Legend:** CAROLVS • DVX •... **Note:** Dav. #3834.

Date	Mintage	VG	F	VF	XF	Unc
ND Rare	—	—	—	—	—	—

KM# 24 ECU OF 30 SOUS

Silver **Obv:** Date at left, "XXX" at right below eagle's talons **Obv. Legend:** CAROLVS. GONZAGA. DVX. NIVERN. ET. RETH. **Note:** Dav. #3832.

Date	Mintage	VG	F	VF	XF	Unc
1610	—	120	240	425	725	—

KM# 25 ECU OF 30 SOUS

Silver **Obv:** With • XXX • at left, date at right below eagle's talons **Note:** Dav. #3832A.

Date	Mintage	VG	F	VF	XF	Unc
1611	—	120	240	425	950	2,000

KM# 26 ECU OF 30 SOUS

Silver **Obv:** With XXX at left, date at right below eagle's talons **Obv. Legend:** CAROLVS • DVX • NIVERNENS (IS) • RETHELENSIS **Note:** Dav. #3833.

Date	Mintage	VG	F	VF	XF	Unc
1613	—	120	240	425	950	2,000

KM# 27 ECU OF 30 SOUS

Silver **Obv:** With date at left, XXX at right below eagle's talons **Note:** Dav. #3833A.

Date	Mintage	VG	F	VF	XF	Unc
1614	—	140	275	465	975	—

KM# 31 ECU

Silver **Obv. Legend:** CAR. GONZ. D. NIV. ET. RET. DEI. GRA. ... **Note:** Dav. #3837.

Date	Mintage	VG	F	VF	XF	Unc
ND	—	1,650	2,750	4,200	—	—

KM# 32 ECU

Silver **Obv. Legend:** S • IMP • PRINC **Note:** Dav. #3838.

Date	Mintage	VG	F	VF	XF	Unc
ND	—	1,650	2,750	4,200	—	—

KM# 33 ECU

Silver **Obv. Legend:** CAROLVS. I. DE. G. DVX. MANTVAE. VIII. ET. MON. FER. VI. **Note:** Dav. #3839.

Date	Mintage	VG	F	VF	XF	Unc
ND	—	1,650	2,750	4,200	6,250	—

KM# 34 ECU

Silver **Obv. Legend:** ...DEI. GRATIA. DVX. MANTVAE. BIII. ET. **Rev. Legend:** .MONTIS * FERRATI. VI * SVP. PRIN... **Note:** Dav. #3840.

Date	Mintage	VG	F	VF	XF	Unc
ND	—	1,650	2,750	4,200	—	—

KM# 29 ECU

Silver **Obv. Legend:** .CAR. GONZ. ET. CLEVEN. D. NIV. ET. RETH **Note:** Dav. #3835.

Date	Mintage	VG	F	VF	XF	Unc
1611 Rare	—	—	—	—	—	—

KM# 30 ECU

Silver **Obv. Legend:** CAROLVS. DVX. NIVERNENSIS... **Note:** Dav. #3836.

Date	Mintage	VG	F	VF	XF	Unc
1614	—	650	1,250	2,500	4,500	—

KM# 38 GOLD ECU

3.3600 g., 0.9520 Gold 0.1028 oz. AGW **Obv:** Bust of Charles of Gonzaga right, date below **Rev:** Crowned arms in inner circle

Date	Mintage	VG	F	VF	XF	Unc
1608	—	2,500	4,500	7,000	10,000	—

KM# 60 PATAGON

Silver **Obv:** Legend around crowned arms in Order collar **Obv. Legend:** .CAROLVS. II. D. G. DVX. MANT. MONT. ET. AR. P. **Rev:** Legend around crowned Burgundian cross with crowned monograms at side, mint mark below **Rev. Legend:** .SIT. NOMEN. DOMINI. BENEDICTVM. **Note:** Dav. #3841.

Date	Mintage	VG	F	VF	XF	Unc
ND(1637-59) Rare	—	—	—	—	—	—

KM# 39 FLORIN

3.5000 g., 0.9860 Gold 0.1109 oz. AGW **Obv:** Charles of Gonzaga standing in nner circle **Rev:** Crowned arms in inner circle

Date	Mintage	VG	F	VF	XF	Unc
ND(1601-37)	—	600	1,200	2,000	3,000	—

KM# 40 FLORIN

3.5000 g., 0.9860 Gold 0.1109 oz. AGW **Obv:** Legend in cartouche

Date	Mintage	VG	F	VF	XF	Unc
ND(1601-37)	—	500	1,000	1,800	2,750	—

KM# 42 FLORIN

3.5000 g., 0.9860 Gold 0.1109 oz. AGW **Obv:** Arms in inner circle **Rev:** Crowned imperial eagle in inner circle

Date	Mintage	VG	F	VF	XF	Unc
ND Rare	—	—	—	—	—	—

KM# 43 FLORIN

3.5000 g., 0.9860 Gold 0.1109 oz. AGW **Obv:** Crowned arms in inner circle **Rev:** Jerusalem cross in inner circle

Date	Mintage	VG	F	VF	XF	Unc
160[illegible]	—	—	—	—	—	—

[illegible]ANGE

Principality in sou[illegible] being 18 miles north of Av[illegible] during the time of Charlemag[illegible] Baux and Chalon. In 1530 Rene [illegible] with the town of Orange the ruler and then William the Silent ([illegible] became of importance founder of the Dutch Republic. William [illegible] last ruler of Orange. William's attention was [illegible] the houses of [illegible]erlands and in 1672 the troops of Louis XIV occupie[illegible] came it was incorporated into France (though actual title did [illegible] until 1713). William became King of England in 1689.

RULERS

Philip William, 1584-1618
Maurice, 1618-1625
Frederick Henry, 1625-1647
William IX of Nassau, 1647-1650
William Henry of Nassau, 1650-1702

MONETARY SYSTEM

3 Deniers = 1 Liard
4 Liards = 1 Sol
20 Sols = 1 Livre
6 Livres = 1 Ecu
4 Ecus = 1 D'or

PRINCIPALITY

STANDARD COINAGE

KM# 54 OBOL

Billon **Note:** Similar to 1 Denier, KM#58.

Date	Mintage	VG	F	VF	XF	Unc
ND(1625-47)	—	25.00	50.00	100	—	—

KM# 58 DENIER TOURNOIS

Billon **Obv:** Cornet divides F-H

Date	Mintage	VG	F	VF	XF	Unc
ND(1625-47)	—	15.00	30.00	60.00	125	—

KM# 81 DENIER TOURNOIS

Copper **Obv:** Bust **Obv. Legend:** GVILLEM. D. G. PRI. AVR **Rev:** Three lis **Rev. Legend:** DENIER TOURNOIS

Date	Mintage	VG	F	VF	XF	Unc
1650	—	12.50	25.00	50.00	100	—

KM# 109 DENIER TOURNOIS

Copper **Obv:** Similar to KM#107 **Rev:** Cornet and three lis

Date	Mintage	VG	F	VF	XF	Unc
ND(1650-1702)	—	12.50	25.00	50.00	100	—

KM# 111 DENIER TOURNOIS

Copper **Obv:** Later bust

Date	Mintage	VG	F	VF	XF	Unc
ND(1650-1702)	—	12.50	25.00	50.00	100	—

KM# 107 DENIER TOURNOIS

Copper **Obv:** Bust **Rev:** Three lis

Date	Mintage	VG	F	VF	XF	Unc
1651	—	12.50	25.00	50.00	100	—
1652	—	12.50	25.00	50.00	100	—
1653/2	—	12.50	25.00	50.00	100	—
1653	—	12.50	25.00	50.00	100	—
1654	—	12.50	25.00	50.00	100	—

KM# 38 LIARD

Billon **Obv:** Crowned M **Rev:** Cross

Date	Mintage	VG	F	VF	XF	Unc
ND(1618-25)	—	12.50	25.00	50.00	100	—

KM# 59 DOUBLE TOURNOIS

Copper **Ruler:** Frederick Henry **Obv:** Bust **Rev:** 3 lis

Date	Mintage	VG	F	VF	XF	Unc
ND	—	12.50	25.00	55.00	110	—
1637	—	12.50	25.00	55.00	110	—
1640	—	12.50	25.00	55.00	110	—

Date	Mintage	VG	F	VF	XF	Unc
1641	—	12.50	25.00	55.00	110	—
1642	—	12.50	25.00	55.00	110	—

KM# 112 DOUBLE TOURNOIS

Copper **Ruler:** William Henry of Nassau **Obv:** Bust **Rev:** 3 lis

Date	Mintage	VG	F	VF	XF	Unc
1659	—	15.00	30.00	65.00	125	—

KM# 86 1/12 ECU (5 Sols)

2.2500 g., Silver **Obv:** Small long bust **Obv. Legend:** GVILLEMVS. D. G. PRIN. AVR. **Rev:** Crowned arms **Rev. Legend:** SOLI • DEO • HONOR...

Date	Mintage	VG	F	VF	XF	Unc
1650	—	35.00	75.00	145	250	—

KM# 115 1/12 ECU (5 Sols)

2.2500 g., Silver **Obv:** Young bust **Obv. Legend:** GVIL. HNR. D. G. PRI. AV. **Rev:** Crowned arms, three lis

Date	Mintage	VG	F	VF	XF	Unc
1661	—	35.00	75.00	145	250	—

KM# 118 1/12 ECU (5 Sols)

2.2500 g., Silver **Obv:** Young bust **Obv. Legend:** GVIL. HNR. D. G. PRI. AVR. **Rev:** Lions in crowned arms **Rev. Legend:** SOLI. DEO. HONOR. ET. GLO.

Date	Mintage	VG	F	VF	XF	Unc
1667	—	35.00	75.00	145	250	—

KM# 90 1/12 ECU (5 Sols)

2.2500 g., Silver **Obv:** Large bust **Obv. Legend:** GVIL. HNR. D. G. PRI. AV. **Rev:** Crowned arms, date divided by crown

Date	Mintage	VG	F	VF	XF	Unc
1657	—	35.00	75.00	145	300	—
1661	—	35.00	75.00	145	300	—
1665	—	35.00	75.00	145	300	—

KM# 20 1/2 FRANC

6.8700 g., Silver **Obv:** Bust of Philip William **Obv. Legend:** PHIL. G. I. D. G. PRIN. AVR. COM. NAS. **Rev:** Floral cross with fleur-de-lis

Date	Mintage	VG	F	VF	XF	Unc
1617	—	75.00	150	325	450	—

KM# 43.1 1/2 FRANC

6.8700 g., Silver **Ruler:** Maurice **Obv:** Bust of Maurice right **Rev:** Floreate cross **Note:** Prev. KM#43.

Date	Mintage	VG	F	VF	XF	Unc
1619	—	60.00	120	250	375	—
1621	—	60.00	120	250	375	—

KM# 43.2 1/2 FRANC

6.8700 g., Silver **Ruler:** Maurice **Obv:** Bust of Maurice right in inner circle

Date	Mintage	VG	F	VF	XF	Unc
1621	—	60.00	120	250	375	—

KM# 63.1 1/2 FRANC

6.8700 g., Silver **Obv:** Bust of Frederick Henry **Obv. Legend:** ...CO. NAS. **Rev:** H in floral cross

Date	Mintage	VG	F	VF	XF	Unc
1641	—	50.00	100	225	350	—

KM# 63.2 1/2 FRANC

6.8700 g., Silver **Obv. Legend:** ...COM. NASS.

Date	Mintage	VG	F	VF	XF	Unc
1642	—	50.00	100	225	400	—

KM# 15 TESTON

9.2700 g., Silver **Obv:** Bust of Philip William **Obv. Legend:** PHILIP. G. I. D. G... **Rev:** Crowned arms

Date	Mintage	VG	F	VF	XF	Unc
1607	—	75.00	150	325	500	—

KM# 68 TESTON

9.2700 g., Silver **Obv:** Bust of Frederick Henry right **Rev:** Crowned arms within inner circle

Date	Mintage	VG	F	VF	XF	Unc
ND(1625-47)	—	45.00	90.00	200	300	—

KM# 69 TESTON

9.2700 g., Silver **Obv:** Bust of Frederick Henry **Rev:** Crowned arms separate legend

Date	Mintage	VG	F	VF	XF	Unc
ND(1625-47)	—	60.00	120	225	350	—

KM# 95 1/2 ECU

13.5900 g., Silver **Obv:** Bust **Obv. Legend:** GVILLELMVS. D. G. PRINC. AVR. **Rev:** Crowned arms

Date	Mintage	VG	F	VF	XF	Unc
1649	—	200	375	650	1,000	—

KM# 25 ECU

Silver **Obv. Legend:** MAVRITIVS. I. D. G. PRIN. ABR. COM. NA(SS). **Rev:** Legend around **Rev. Legend:** SOLI DEO. HONOR. ET. GLORI **Note:** Dav. #3843.

Date	Mintage	VG	F	VF	XF	Unc
1618	—	1,400	2,800	4,500	6,500	—
1622	—	1,400	2,800	4,500	6,500	—

KM# 98 ECU

Silver **Ruler:** William IX of Nassau **Note:** Dav. #3844.

Date	Mintage	VG	F	VF	XF	Unc
1649	—	1,750	3,500	5,500	—	—
1650	—	1,750	3,500	5,500	—	—

KM# 99 ECU

Silver **Ruler:** William Henry of Nassau **Note:** Dav. #3845.

Date	Mintage	VG	F	VF	XF	Unc
1652 Retrograde 2; rare	—	—	—	—	—	—

KM# 30 1/2 PISTOLE

3.3500 g., Gold **Obv:** Bust of Philip William right **Rev:** Crowned arms

Date	Mintage	VG	F	VF	XF	Unc
1617 Rare	—	—	—	—	—	—

KM# 32 PISTOLE

6.6200 g., Gold **Obv:** Bust of Philip William right **Rev:** Crowned arms

Date	Mintage	VG	F	VF	XF	Unc
ND	—	1,750	3,500	5,500	9,500	—
1617	—	1,750	3,500	5,500	9,500	—

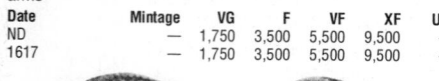

KM# 72 PISTOLE

6.6200 g., Gold **Obv:** Bust of Frederick Henry right in inner circle **Rev:** Crowned arms in inner circle, date in legend

Date	Mintage	VG	F	VF	XF	Unc
ND	—	750	1,650	3,250	5,500	—
1640	—	750	1,650	3,250	5,500	—

KM# 75 PISTOLE

6.6200 g., Gold **Obv:** Old bust of Frederick Henry

Date	Mintage	VG	F	VF	XF	Unc
1643	—	750	1,650	2,750	5,000	—

KM# 101 PISTOLE

6.6200 g., Gold **Obv:** Armored bust of William right **Rev:** Crowned arms, date in legend

Date	Mintage	VG	F	VF	XF	Unc
1649 Rare	—	—	—	—	—	—

KM# 34 2 PISTOLE

13.0900 g., Gold **Obv:** Bust of Philip William right **Rev:** Crowned arms, date above crown

Date	Mintage	VG	F	VF	XF	Unc
1616	—	2,000	4,000	7,000	11,500	—

KM# 49 2 PISTOLE

13.0900 g., Gold **Obv:** Bust of Maurice right **Rev:** Crowned arms in inner circle

Date	Mintage	VG	F	VF	XF	Unc
1618 Rare	—	—	—	—	—	—
1619 Rare	—	—	—	—	—	—

KM# 73 2 PISTOLE

13.0900 g., Gold **Obv:** Frederick Henry **Rev:** Crowned arms in inner circle, date in legend

Date	Mintage	VG	F	VF	XF	Unc
ND	—	850	1,850	3,500	5,500	—
1641	—	850	1,850	3,500	5,500	—

KM# 76 2 PISTOLE

13.0900 g., Gold **Obv:** Old bust of Frederick Henry

Date	Mintage	VG	F	VF	XF	Unc
1645	—	725	1,550	2,750	5,000	—

KM# 102 2 PISTOLE

13.0900 g., Gold **Obv:** Armored bust of William right **Rev:** Crowned arms, date in legend

Date	Mintage	VG	F	VF	XF	Unc
1649 Rare	—	—	—	—	—	—

TRADE COINAGE

KM# 74 DUCAT

3.5000 g., 0.9860 Gold 0.1109 oz. AGW

Date	Mintage	VG	F	VF	XF	Unc
1645	—	450	1,000	2,000	3,250	—

KM# 125 ZECCHINO

3.5000 g., 0.9860 Gold 0.1109 oz. AGW **Obv:** Prince kneeling before Christ **Rev:** Madonna in oval shield

Date	Mintage	VG	F	VF	XF	Unc
ND(1650-1702)	—	450	1,000	1,850	3,000	—

VERDUN

(Verdun-sur-Meuse)

Town, dating to Roman times, in northeastern France 35 miles west of Metz. A bishopric founded here in the 3rd century. City destroyed during Barbarian invasions and took until the end of the 5th century to recover. Site of signing of famous treaty in 843. Part of German empire until taken by Henry II of France in 1552 and officially recognized by the Treaty of Westphalia in 1648. Pivotal locale during the Franco-Prussian War and in World War I.

RULERS

Eric of Lorraine-Vaudemont, 1593-1611
Charles of Lorraine-Chaligny, 1611-1622

BISHOPRIC

STANDARD COINAGE

KM# 13 GROS

Billon **Ruler:** Charles **Obv:** Crowned eagle **Obv. Legend:** CAROLVS. A. LOTHARINGIA. EPIS. **Rev:** Crowned paired shields **Rev. Legend:** ET. COMES. VIR. JVS. PRS. IMPE.

Date	Mintage	VG	F	VF	XF	Unc
ND(1611-22)	—	85.00	165	300	550	—

KM# 5 1/8 TESTON

Billon **Ruler:** Eric **Obv:** Bust **Obv. Legend:** ERRIC. A. LOTH. EPS. ET. CO. VIR. **Rev:** Crowned arms of Lorraine, mitre

Date	Mintage	VG	F	VF	XF	Unc
1608	—	900	1,750	—	—	—

KM# 17 1/8 TESTON

Billon **Ruler:** Eric **Obv:** Bust **Obv. Legend:** CAROLVS... **Rev:** Crowned arms, mitre **Rev. Legend:** MONET. NO. AN.

Date	Mintage	VG	F	VF	XF	Unc
1610	—	800	1,650	—	—	—

KM# 8 TESTON

8.3800 g., Silver **Ruler:** Eric **Obv:** Eric left **Rev:** Crowned arms

Date	Mintage	VG	F	VF	XF	Unc
1608	—	800	1,500	—	—	—

KM# 20 TESTON

8.3800 g., Silver **Ruler:** Charles **Obv:** Charles right **Rev:** Crowned arms

Date	Mintage	VG	F	VF	XF	Unc
ND(1617)	—	700	1,150	—	—	—

KM# 24 THALER

Silver **Ruler:** Charles **Rev. Legend:** ...VIRDVNENSIS. PRS. IMP. -* **Note:** Dav. #5911.

Date	Mintage	VG	F	VF	XF	Unc
ND	—	1,650	2,750	4,500	—	—

KM# 25 THALER

Silver **Ruler:** Charles **Rev:** Crowned arms decorated **Rev. Legend:** ...PRS. STI. IMPERii **Note:** Dav. #5912.

Date	Mintage	VG	F	VF	XF	Unc
ND	—	1,650	2,750	4,500	—	—

KM# 26 THALER

Silver **Ruler:** Charles **Rev:** Crowned arms **Rev. Legend:** ...PRS. SRI. IMPERIi (IMPERIii) **Note:** Dav. #5913

Date	Mintage	VG	F	VF	XF	Unc
ND	—	1,250	2,250	4,000	—	—

KM# 11 FLORIN D'OR

3.5000 g., 0.9860 Gold 0.1109 oz. AGW **Ruler:** Eric

Date	Mintage	VG	F	VF	XF	Unc
1608	—	750	1,650	3,200	5,500	—
1610	—	750	1,650	3,200	5,500	—
1611	—	750	1,650	3,200	5,500	—

KM# 30 FLORIN D'OR

3.5000 g., 0.9860 Gold 0.1109 oz. AGW **Ruler:** Charles

Date	Mintage	VG	F	VF	XF	Unc
1612	—	650	1,450	3,000	5,000	—

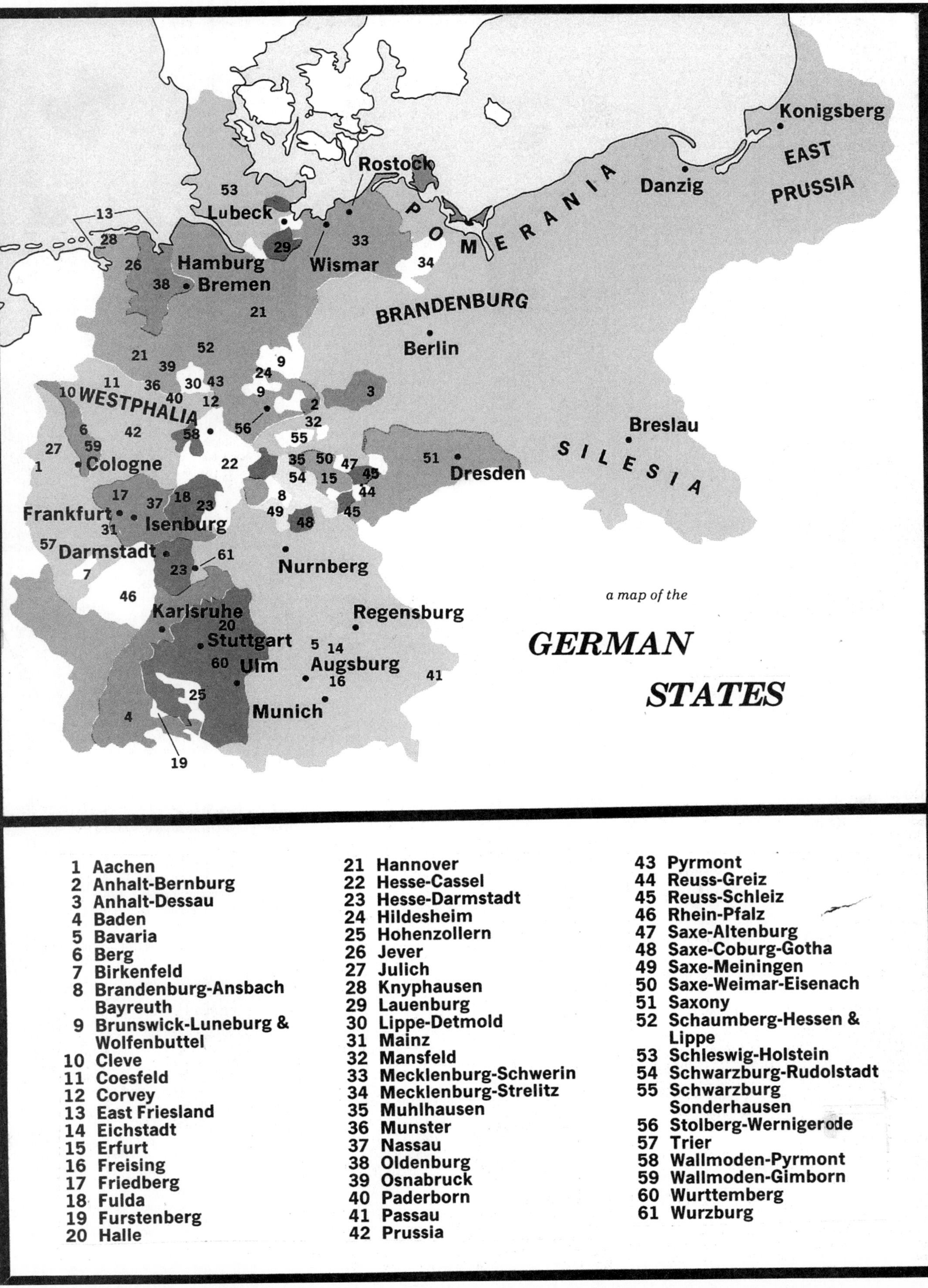

1 Aachen
2 Anhalt-Bernburg
3 Anhalt-Dessau
4 Baden
5 Bavaria
6 Berg
7 Birkenfeld
8 Brandenburg-Ansbach Bayreuth
9 Brunswick-Luneburg & Wolfenbuttel
10 Cleve
11 Coesfeld
12 Corvey
13 East Friesland
14 Eichstadt
15 Erfurt
16 Freising
17 Friedberg
18 Fulda
19 Furstenberg
20 Halle
21 Hannover
22 Hesse-Cassel
23 Hesse-Darmstadt
24 Hildesheim
25 Hohenzollern
26 Jever
27 Julich
28 Knyphausen
29 Lauenburg
30 Lippe-Detmold
31 Mainz
32 Mansfeld
33 Mecklenburg-Schwerin
34 Mecklenburg-Strelitz
35 Muhlhausen
36 Munster
37 Nassau
38 Oldenburg
39 Osnabruck
40 Paderborn
41 Passau
42 Prussia
43 Pyrmont
44 Reuss-Greiz
45 Reuss-Schleiz
46 Rhein-Pfalz
47 Saxe-Altenburg
48 Saxe-Coburg-Gotha
49 Saxe-Meiningen
50 Saxe-Weimar-Eisenach
51 Saxony
52 Schaumberg-Hessen & Lippe
53 Schleswig-Holstein
54 Schwarzburg-Rudolstadt
55 Schwarzburg Sonderhausen
56 Stolberg-Wernigerode
57 Trier
58 Wallmoden-Pyrmont
59 Wallmoden-Gimborn
60 Wurttemberg
61 Wurzburg

Although the origin of the German Empire can be traced to the Treaty of Verdun that ceded Charlemagne's lands east of the Rhine to German Prince Louis, it was for centuries little more than a geographic expression, consisting of hundreds of effectively autonomous big and little states. Nominally the states owed their allegiance to the Holy Roman Emperor, who was also a German king, but as the Emperors exhibited less and less concern for Germany the actual power devolved on the lords of the individual states. The fragmentation of the empire climaxed with the tragic denouement of the Thirty Years War, 1618-48, which devastated much of Germany, destroyed its agriculture and medieval commercial eminence and ended the attempt of the Hapsburgs to unify Germany. Deprived of administrative capacity by a lack of resources, the imperial authority became utterly powerless. At this time Germany contained an estimated 1,800 individual states, some with a population of as little as 300. The German Empire of recent history (the creation of Bismarck) was formed on April 14, 1871, when the king of Prussia became German Emperor William I. The new empire comprised 4 kingdoms, 6 grand duchies, 12 duchies and principalities, 3 free cities and the non-autonomous province of Alsace-Lorraine. The states had the right to issue gold and silver coins of higher value than 1 Mark; coins of 1 Mark and under were general issues of the empire.

MONETARY SYSTEM

Until 1871 the Mark (Marck) was a measure of weight.

North German States until 1837

2 Heller = 1 Pfennig
8 Pfennige = 1 Mariengroschen
12 Pfennige = 1 Groschen
24 Groschen = 1 Thaler
2 Gulden = 1-1/3 Reichsthaler
1 Speciesthaler (before 1753)

South German States until 1837

8 Heller = 4 Pfennige = 1 Kreuzer
24 Kreuzer Landmunze = 20 Kreuzer Convention Munze
120 Convention Kreuzer = 2 Convention Gulden = 1 Convention Thaler

AACHEN

(Achen, Urbs Aquensis, Aquis Grani)

FREE CITY

STANDARD COINAGE

KM# 1 HELLER

Copper **Obv:** Eagle **Rev:** Value "I" divides date in wreath

Date	Mintage	Good	VG	F	VF	XF
(1)604	15,000	55.00	100	200	400	775

KM# 4 2 HELLER

Copper **Obv:** Eagle in shield divides date **Rev:** Value "II" in center

Date	Mintage	Good	VG	F	VF	XF
(1)6(0)5	20,000	45.00	90.00	150	300	600

KM# 14 2 HELLER

Copper **Obv:** Eagle, date divided by tail **Rev:** Value in center

Date	Mintage	Good	VG	F	VF	XF
(16)22	—	35.00	50.00	100	200	350
(16)38	—	35.00	50.00	100	200	350

KM# 2 3 HELLER

Copper **Obv:** Eagle **Rev:** Value "III" in center

Date	Mintage	Good	VG	F	VF	XF
(1604/5) Rare	—	—	—	—	—	—

KM# 3 4 HELLER

Copper **Obv:** Eagle divides date **Rev:** Value "IIII" in center

Date	Mintage	Good	VG	F	VF	XF
1604	30,000	35.00	75.00	140	275	—
(1)605	30,000	35.00	75.00	140	275	—
1619	80,000	15.00	32.00	65.00	135	—
1621	40,000	20.00	40.00	85.00	170	—
1624	40,000	20.00	40.00	85.00	170	—
1625	—	—	—	—	—	—
Note: Reported, not confirmed						
1634	140,000	8.00	15.00	30.00	60.00	—
(16)38	600,000	8.00	15.00	30.00	60.00	—
(16)43	200,000	8.00	15.00	30.00	60.00	—
(16)55	200,000	8.00	15.00	30.00	60.00	—
(16)6- Rare	—	—	—	—	—	—

KM# 5 4 HELLER

Copper **Obv:** Eagle divides date, legend around **Rev:** Value "IIII" in wreath

Date	Mintage	Good	VG	F	VF	XF
1614	60,000	27.00	55.00	100	190	—
1615	60,000	27.00	55.00	100	190	—
1616	100,000	27.00	55.00	100	190	—

KM# 30 4 HELLER

Copper **Obv:** Eagle divides date **Rev. Inscription:** AQVIS / GRANVM / IIII

Date	Mintage	Good	VG	F	VF	XF
(16)56	—	—	—	—	—	—
Note: Reported, not confirmed						
(16)58	500,000	8.00	15.00	30.00	60.00	—

KM# 31 4 HELLER

Copper **Obv:** Arms divide date **Rev:** Legend above value **Rev. Inscription:** REICHS / STAT. ACH / IIII

Date	Mintage	VG	F	VF	XF	Unc
(16)70	150,000	10.00	20.00	40.00	85.00	—
(16)71	80,000	10.00	20.00	40.00	85.00	—
(16)74	—	10.00	20.00	40.00	85.00	—
(16)76	150,000	10.00	20.00	40.00	85.00	—
(16)78	60,000	10.00	20.00	40.00	85.00	—
(16)81	60,000	10.00	20.00	40.00	85.00	—
(16)85	100,000	10.00	20.00	40.00	85.00	—
(16)86	60,000	10.00	20.00	40.00	85.00	—
(16)87	20,000	10.00	20.00	40.00	85.00	—
(16)88	200,000	10.00	20.00	40.00	85.00	—
(16)90	50,000	10.00	20.00	40.00	85.00	—
(16)91	30,000	10.00	20.00	40.00	85.00	—
(16)93	—	10.00	20.00	40.00	85.00	—
(16)96	—	10.00	20.00	40.00	85.00	—

KM# 7 MARCK

Silver **Obv:** Imperial eagle, titles of Matthias **Rev:** 1/2-length figure of Charlemagne above arms, date

Date	Mintage	VG	F	VF	XF	Unc
1616	—	110	175	250	450	—

KM# 10 MARCK

Silver **Obv:** 1/2-length figure of Charlemagne above arms **Rev:** Value, date in center, legend **Note:** Kipper Marck.

Date	Mintage	VG	F	VF	XF	Unc
1619	—	40.00	75.00	135	275	—
1620	—	40.00	75.00	135	275	—

KM# 16 MARCK

Silver **Obv:** 1/2-length figure of Charlemagne above arms, date **Rev:** Imperial eagle, titles of Ferdinand II

Date	Mintage	VG	F	VF	XF	Unc
1631	—	85.00	140	200	350	—
(16)31	—	85.00	140	200	350	—
1633	—	85.00	140	200	350	—

KM# 23 MARCK

Silver **Obv:** 1/2-length figure of Charlemagne above arms **Rev:** Value, date

Date	Mintage	VG	F	VF	XF	Unc
1643 Rare	—	—	—	—	—	—

KM# 6 2 MARCK

Silver **Obv:** 1/2-length figure of Charlemagne above arms, date **Rev:** Imperial eagle, titles of Matthias

Date	Mintage	VG	F	VF	XF	Unc
1615 Rare	—	—	—	—	—	—
1616 Rare	—	—	—	—	—	—

KM# 19 2 MARCK

Silver **Rev:** Imperial eagle with 2 on breast, titles of Ferdinand III

Date	Mintage	VG	F	VF	XF	Unc
(16)39	—	50.00	100	200	400	—
(16)46	—	50.00	100	200	400	—
ND	—	50.00	100	200	400	—

KM# 29 2 MARCK

Silver **Rev:** Value **Rev. Legend:** II/MARCK/ACH

Date	Mintage	VG	F	VF	XF	Unc
1649 Rare	—	—	—	—	—	—

KM# 11 3 MARCK

Silver **Obv:** 1/2-length figure of Charlemagne above arms **Rev:** Value, date in center, inscription around **Note:** Kipper 3 Marck.

Date	Mintage	VG	F	VF	XF	Unc
1619	—	80.00	160	325	650	—

KM# 15 3 MARCK

Silver **Obv:** 1/2-length figure of Charlemagne, date **Rev:** Value in center, titles of Ferdinand II

Date	Mintage	VG	F	VF	XF	Unc
(16)26	—	75.00	150	300	600	—
(16)31	—	75.00	150	300	600	—
(16)34	—	75.00	150	300	600	—

KM# 20 3 MARCK

Silver **Rev:** Titles of Ferdinand III

Date	Mintage	VG	F	VF	XF	Unc
(16)39	—	60.00	120	250	425	—
(16)40	—	60.00	120	250	425	—
(16)41	—	60.00	120	250	425	—

KM# 21 4 MARCK

Silver **Obv:** 1/2-length figure of Charlemagne divides date **Rev:** Value in rhombus, titles of Ferdinand III

Date	Mintage	VG	F	VF	XF	Unc
(16)3-	—	225	450	900	1,800	—
(16)42	—	225	450	900	1,800	—
(16)44	—	225	450	900	1,800	—
(16)45	—	225	450	900	1,800	—
(16)46	—	225	450	900	1,800	—

KM# 26 4 MARCK

Silver **Rev:** Value in baroque frame, date in legend

Date	Mintage	VG	F	VF	XF	Unc
1646	—	225	450	900	1,800	—
1647	—	225	450	900	1,800	—
1648	—	225	450	900	1,800	—

KM# 27 4 MARCK

Silver **Obv:** KM#21, 1/2-length figure of Charlemagne divides date **Rev:** KM#26, Value in baroque frame, date in legend **Note:** Mule.

Date	Mintage	VG	F	VF	XF	Unc
1646/1647	—	250	550	1,100	2,200	—

KM# 12 6 MARCK

Silver **Obv:** 1/2-length figure of Charlemagne above arms **Rev:** Value, date in center, inscription around **Note:** Kipper 6 Marck.

Date	Mintage	VG	F	VF	XF	Unc
1619	—	250	525	1,050	2,100	—
1620	—	250	525	1,050	2,100	—
1621	—	300	600	1,200	2,400	—

KM# 13 6 MARCK

Silver **Rev:** Value and date in cartouche

Date	Mintage	VG	F	VF	XF	Unc
1620	—	250	525	1,050	2,100	—

KM# 8 THALER

Silver **Obv:** Imperial eagle, titles of Matthias **Rev:** Charlemagne seated above city arms, divides date **Note:** Dav. #5002.

Date	Mintage	VG	F	VF	XF	Unc
1616 Rare	—	—	—	—	—	—

KM# 24 THALER

Silver **Obv:** Titles of Ferdinand III **Rev:** Smaller figure of Charlemagne **Rev. Legend:** MON. NOVA. REGIAE.. **Note:** Dav. #5004

Date	Mintage	VG	F	VF	XF	Unc
1643 Rare	—	—	—	—	—	—

KM# 40 THALER

Silver **Rev. Legend:** MON. NOVA. REGNE.. **Note:** Dav. #5005.

Date	Mintage	VG	F	VF	XF	Unc
1644 Rare	—	—	—	—	—	—

KM# 53 THALER

Silver **Rev:** Wildman with crowned helmet, surmounted by eagle holding flags, standing behind city arms **Note:** Dav. #5007.

Date	Mintage	VG	F	VF	XF	Unc
ND Rare	—	—	—	—	—	—

KM# 9 2 THALER

Silver **Obv:** Imperial eagle, titles of Matthias **Rev:** Charlemagne seated above city arms divides date **Note:** Thick flan. Dav. #5001.

Date	Mintage	VG	F	VF	XF	Unc
1616 Rare	—	—	—	—	—	—

KM# 25 2 THALER

Silver **Obv:** Titles of Ferdinand III **Rev:** Smaller figure of CHarlemagne **Note:** Dav. #5003.

Date	Mintage	VG	F	VF	XF	Unc
1643 Rare	—	—	—	—	—	—

KM# 54 2 THALER
Silver **Obv:** Wildman with crowned helmet, surmounted by eagle holding flags, standing behind city arms **Rev:** Crowned imperial eagle with orb on breast **Note:** Dav. #5006.

Date	Mintage	VG	F	VF	XF	Unc
ND Rare	—	—	—	—	—	—

TRADE COINAGE

KM# 17 GOLDGULDEN
3.5000 g., 0.9860 Gold 0.1109 oz. AGW **Obv:** Charlemagne seated facing **Rev:** Imperial eagle, titles of Ferdinand II **Note:** Fr. #6.

Date	Mintage	VG	F	VF	XF	Unc
1634	—	2,000	4,000	7,000	12,000	—

KM# 18 GOLDGULDEN
3.5000 g., 0.9860 Gold 0.1109 oz. AGW **Obv:** Charlemagne seated **Rev:** Eagle with titles of Ferdinand II **Note:** Klippe. Fr. #7.

Date	Mintage	VG	F	VF	XF	Unc
1634 Rare	—	—	—	—	—	—

KM# 46 DUCAT
3.5000 g., 0.9860 Gold 0.1109 oz. AGW **Obv:** Madonna standing **Rev:** Value in tablet

Date	Mintage	VG	F	VF	XF	Unc
ND(1640) Unique	—	—	—	15,000	—	—

KM# 22 DUCAT
3.5000 g., 0.9860 Gold 0.1109 oz. AGW **Obv:** Ferdinand III standing **Rev:** Bust of Charlemagne **Note:** Fr. #8.

Date	Mintage	VG	F	VF	XF	Unc
1641	—	1,600	3,200	6,500	11,500	—
1643	—	1,600	3,200	6,500	11,500	—
1645	—	1,600	3,200	6,500	11,500	—

KM# 28 DUCAT
3.5000 g., 0.9860 Gold 0.1109 oz. AGW **Obv:** Ferdinand III standing **Rev:** Value and date in tablet **Note:** Fr. #9.

Date	Mintage	VG	F	VF	XF	Unc
1646	—	600	1,250	2,850	4,500	—

KM# 45 DUCAT
3.5000 g., 0.9860 Gold 0.1109 oz. AGW **Obv:** Bust of Charlemagne **Rev:** Madonna standing **Note:** Fr. #10.

Date	Mintage	VG	F	VF	XF	Unc
ND Rare	—	—	—	—	—	—

AHLEN

(Alen)

A city in Westphalia, 18 miles southeast of Munster, the center for the manufacture of shoes and enamelware. Coal mining is also done in the area. Issued copper coins in 1584, 1610 and 1616.

ARMS
Crowned and winged eel

CROSS REFERENCE
F = Gisela Förschner, ***Deutsche Münzen Mittelalter bis Neuzeit***, v. 1 – ***Aachen bis Augsburg***, Melsungen, 1984.

PROVINCIAL TOWN

REGULAR COINAGE

KM# 1 2 PFENNINGE
Copper **Obv:** Arms in center, legend, date **Obv. Legend:** STADT ALEN **Rev:** Value: II in center

Date	Mintage	Good	VG	F	VF	XF
1610	—	80.00	150	325	650	—

KM# 2 3 PFENNINGE
Copper **Obv:** Arms in center, legend, date **Obv. Legend:** STADT ALEN **Rev:** Value: III in center

Date	Mintage	Good	VG	F	VF	XF
1610	—	80.00	150	325	650	—

KM# 3 6 PFENNINGE
Copper **Obv:** Arms in center, legend, date **Obv. Legend:** STADT ALEN **Rev:** Value: VI in center

Date	Mintage	Good	VG	F	VF	XF
1610	—	100	185	375	750	—

KM# 4 12 PFENNINGE
Copper **Obv:** Arms in center, legend, date **Obv. Legend:** STADT ALEN **Rev:** Value: XII in center

Date	Mintage	Good	VG	F	VF	XF
1610	—	150	300	600	1,150	2,600
1616 Rare	—	—	—	—	—	—

ALSACE

An old German area located in northeastern France between the Rhine River and Vosges Mountains which later became a French province.

Ruled by Rome, gradually being penetrated by the Germanic peoples. Belonged to the Holy Roman Empire 870-1648 while being united to the duchy of Swabia in 925. Later broken up into feudal principalities controlled chiefly by the Bishop of Strasbourg and Hapsburg family in the 14th century. Upper Alsace was given to Burgundy in 1469, but soon broke free. Occupied by French in Thirty Years' War and linked with France by means of Louis XIV's "Chambers of Reunion" 1680. Ceded to Germany by the Treaty of Frankfurt 1871 and under the German Empire 1871-1918. It was subject to unsuccessful attempts to Germanize between 1880-1910 and was restored to France by the Treaty of Versailles in 1919. In World War II held by Germany 1940-44; retaken by French and American armies and again restored to France.

RULERS
Rudolf II, 1603-1612
Maximilian, 1613-1618
Ferdinand II, 1619-1623
Leopold of Austria,
As Bishop of Strasbourg, 1620-
As Landgrave of Alsace, -1632

ENSISHEIM MINT

Coat of arms usually at bottom left or right section of extensive crowned arms or in legend.

MINT OFFICIALS' INITIALS

Initials	Date	Name
B, PB	1601-29	Peter Balde

MONETARY SYSTEM
8 Heller = 4 Pfennig = 1 Kreuzer
60 Kreuzer = 1 Florin Gulden
120 Kreuzer = 1 Thaler

LANDGRAVIATE

STANDARD COINAGE

KM# 238 4 HELLER
Silver **Ruler:** Rudolf II **Obv:** Crowned pointed-top oval arms **Rev:** Cross **Mint:** Ensisheim

Date	Mintage	VG	F	VF	XF	Unc
ND(1602-12)	—	—	—	—	—	—

KM# 239 4 HELLER
Silver **Ruler:** Rudolf II **Obv:** Crowned square-topped arms **Mint:** Ensisheim

Date	Mintage	VG	F	VF	XF	Unc
ND(1602-12)	—	—	—	—	—	—

KM# 275 4 HELLER
Silver **Ruler:** Maximilian **Obv:** Coat of arms **Rev:** Cruciform

Date	Mintage	VG	F	VF	XF	Unc
ND(1612-18)	—	100	200	400	700	—

KM# 240 3 KREUZER
Silver **Ruler:** Rudolf II **Obv:** Bust of Rudolph right **Rev:** Three shields **Mint:** Ensisheim

Date	Mintage	VG	F	VF	XF	Unc
1602	—	35.00	75.00	150	325	—
1603	—	35.00	75.00	150	325	—
1604	—	35.00	75.00	150	325	—
1605	—	35.00	75.00	150	325	—
1606	—	35.00	75.00	150	325	—
1607	—	35.00	75.00	150	325	—
ND	—	35.00	75.00	150	325	—

KM# 241 6 KREUZER
Silver **Ruler:** Rudolf II **Obv:** Bust of Rudolph right **Rev:** Crowned arms **Mint:** Ensisheim

Date	Mintage	VG	F	VF	XF	Unc
ND(1602-12)	—	60.00	125	210	435	—

KM# 242 10 KREUZER
Silver **Ruler:** Rudolf II **Obv:** Bust of Rudolph II right **Rev:** Crowned arms in Order chain **Mint:** Ensisheim

Date	Mintage	VG	F	VF	XF	Unc
ND(1602-12)	—	75.00	150	300	600	—

KM# 276 10 KREUZER
Silver **Ruler:** Maximilian **Obv:** Bust right

Date	Mintage	VG	F	VF	XF	Unc
ND(1612)	—	120	190	350	725	—

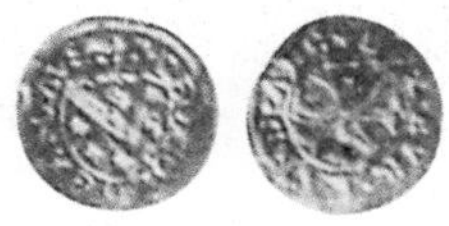

KM# 250 VIERER
Silver **Obv:** Crowned arms **Rev:** Round cruciform

Date	Mintage	VG	F	VF	XF	Unc
ND(1619)	—	22.00	45.00	90.00	185	—
1623	—	22.00	45.00	90.00	185	—
1624	—	22.00	45.00	90.00	185	—

KM# 251 PLAPPERT (Schilling)
Silver **Obv:** Crowned arms **Rev:** Short cross

Date	Mintage	VG	F	VF	XF	Unc
ND(1619)	—	35.00	70.00	130	265	—
1623	—	35.00	70.00	130	265	—
1624	—	35.00	70.00	130	265	—

KM# 252 DUPLEX (Schilling)
Silver **Ruler:** Leopold V **Obv:** Crowned arms **Rev:** Short cross **Mint:** Ensisheim

Date	Mintage	VG	F	VF	XF	Unc
ND(1621-25)	—	55.00	110	225	450	—

KM# 262 DUPLEX (Schilling)
Silver **Ruler:** Leopold V **Obv:** Crowned ornate arms **Rev:** Short cross **Mint:** Ensisheim

Date	Mintage	VG	F	VF	XF	Unc
1623	—	45.00	90.00	160	325	—
1624	—	45.00	90.00	160	325	—

KM# A282 DUPLEX (2 Schilling)
Silver **Ruler:** Leopold V **Obv:** Crowned two-fold arms of Alsace and Pfirt, date divided at top, titles of Archduke Leopold **Rev:** Floriated cross, "2" in circle in center, titles continued **Mint:** Ensisheim **Note:** Ref. M#76.

Date	Mintage	VG	F	VF	XF	Unc
1634	—	—	—	—	—	—

KM# 253 24 KREUZER (Sechsbätzner)
Silver **Obv:** Crowned armored bust of Leopold holding scepter right **Rev:** Crowned circular arms

Date	Mintage	VG	F	VF	XF	Unc
ND(1630-32)	—	100	200	350	650	—

KM# 243 1/4 THALER
Silver **Ruler:** Rudolf II **Obv:** Bust of Rudolph II right **Rev:** Crowned arms in Order chain **Mint:** Ensisheim

Date	Mintage	VG	F	VF	XF	Unc
ND(1602-12)	—	75.00	150	300	600	—

KM# 277 1/4 THALER
Silver **Ruler:** Maximilian **Note:** Similar to 1/4 Thaler, KM#243.

Date	Mintage	VG	F	VF	XF	Unc
ND(1612)	—	75.00	150	275	550	—

KM# 254.1 1/4 THALER
Silver **Ruler:** Leopold V **Obv:** Draped bust of Leopold right **Rev:** Crowned arms **Mint:** Ensisheim

Date	Mintage	VG	F	VF	XF	Unc
ND(1630-32)	—	75.00	150	275	550	—

KM# 254.2 1/4 THALER
Silver **Ruler:** Leopold V **Obv:** Crowned half-length bust of Leopold in plain armor holding scepter right **Rev:** Crowned arms **Mint:** Ensisheim

Date	Mintage	VG	F	VF	XF	Unc
ND(1619)	—	75.00	150	275	550	—

KM# 254.3 1/4 THALER
Silver **Ruler:** Leopold V **Obv:** Crowned half-length bust of Leopold in ornate armor holding scepter right **Rev:** Crowned arms **Mint:** Ensisheim

Date	Mintage	VG	F	VF	XF	Unc
ND(1627-30)	—	75.00	150	275	550	—

KM# 244 1/2 THALER
Silver **Ruler:** Rudolf II **Obv:** Bust of Rudolph II right **Rev:** Crowned arms in Order chain **Mint:** Ensisheim

Date	Mintage	VG	F	VF	XF	Unc
ND(1602-12)	—	55.00	115	235	475	—

KM# 278 1/2 THALER
Silver **Ruler:** Maximilian **Obv:** Similar to 2 Thaler, KM#280

Date	Mintage	VG	F	VF	XF	Unc
ND(1612)	—	55.00	115	235	475	—

KM# 259 1/2 THALER
Silver **Ruler:** Leopold V **Obv:** Draped bust of Leopold right **Rev:** Crowned arms **Mint:** Ensisheim

Date	Mintage	VG	F	VF	XF	Unc
ND(1621-25)	—	55.00	115	235	475	—

KM# 264 1/2 THALER
Silver **Ruler:** Leopold V **Obv:** Crowned half-length bust of Leopold in plain armor holding scepter right **Rev:** Crowned arms **Mint:** Ensisheim

Date	Mintage	VG	F	VF	XF	Unc
ND(1625-26)	—	55.00	115	235	475	—

KM# 266 1/2 THALER
Silver **Ruler:** Leopold V **Obv:** Crowned half-length bust of Leopold in ornate armor holding scepter right **Rev:** Crowned arms **Mint:** Ensisheim

Date	Mintage	VG	F	VF	XF	Unc
ND(1627-30)	—	55.00	115	235	475	—

KM# 269 1/2 THALER
Silver **Ruler:** Leopold V **Obv:** Bust of Leopold right **Rev:** Crowned arms **Mint:** Ensisheim

Date	Mintage	VG	F	VF	XF	Unc
ND(1631)	—	55.00	115	235	475	—

KM# 270 1/2 THALER
Silver **Ruler:** Leopold V **Mint:** Ensisheim **Note:** Klippe

Date	Mintage	VG	F	VF	XF	Unc
ND(1631) Rare	—	—	—	—	—	—

KM# 246.1 THALER
Silver **Ruler:** Rudolf II **Obv:** Large bust of Rudolf II right **Obv. Legend:** RVDOLPHVS. II. D. G. RO: IM. SEM. AVG. HVN. BO(H). REX **Rev. Legend:** NEC NON ARCHIDVCES. AVS. D. BVR. LANDG. ALS CO FE(R). **Mint:** Ensisheim **Note:** Dav. #3032.

Date	Mintage	VG	F	VF	XF	Unc
ND	—	100	200	325	550	—

KM# 246.2 THALER
Silver **Ruler:** Rudolf II **Obv:** Date below shoulder **Mint:** Ensisheim **Note:** Dav. #3033.

Date	Mintage	VG	F	VF	XF	Unc
1603	—	100	200	325	550	—
1603 PB	—	100	200	325	550	—
1605	—	100	200	325	550	—
1608	—	100	200	325	550	—

KM# 246.3 THALER
Silver **Ruler:** Rudolf II **Obv:** Date below shoulder **Rev:** Crown divides legend, larger arms in Order chain **Mint:** Ensisheim **Note:** Dav. #3034.

Date	Mintage	VG	F	VF	XF	Unc
1603 B	—	125	250	400	700	—
1605 B	—	125	250	400	700	—
1606	—	125	250	400	700	—
1610	—	125	250	400	700	—

KM# 246.4 THALER

Silver **Ruler:** Rudolf II **Obv:** Date in field behind collar **Mint:** Ensisheim

Date	Mintage	VG	F	VF	XF	Unc
1607	—	150	300	450	775	—

KM# 247.1 THALER

Silver **Ruler:** Rudolf II **Obv:** Large bust of Rudolph II right, lion's head on shoulder, date reads inward **Mint:** Ensisheim **Note:** Dav. #3035.

Date	Mintage	VG	F	VF	XF	Unc
1606	—	150	300	450	775	—

KM# 245 THALER

Silver **Ruler:** Rudolf II **Obv:** Small bust of Rudolph II right with lion's head on shoulder **Obv. Legend:** + RVDOLPHVS • II • D: G • RO •... **Rev:** Crowned arms in Order chain **Rev. Legend:** NEC NON ARCHIDVCES... **Mint:** Ensisheim **Note:** Dav. #A3033.

Date	Mintage	VG	F	VF	XF	Unc
1606	—	125	250	400	700	—

KM# 247.2 THALER

Silver **Ruler:** Rudolf II **Obv:** Small bust of Rudolf II right **Mint:** Ensisheim **Note:** Dav. #A3035.

Date	Mintage	VG	F	VF	XF	Unc
1606	—	150	300	450	775	—

KM# 247.3 THALER

Silver **Ruler:** Rudolf II **Obv:** Without lion's head on shoulder, date reads outward **Mint:** Ensisheim **Note:** Dav. #B3035. Varieties exist.

Date	Mintage	VG	F	VF	XF	Unc
1608	—	150	300	450	775	—
1609	—	150	300	450	775	—
1610	—	150	300	450	775	—
1611	—	150	300	450	775	—
1612	—	150	300	450	775	—

KM# 247.4 THALER

Silver **Ruler:** Rudolf II **Obv:** With lion's head on shoulder, date reads outward **Mint:** Ensisheim

Date	Mintage	VG	F	VF	XF	Unc
1609	—	150	300	475	800	—

KM# 247.5 THALER

Silver **Ruler:** Rudolf II **Rev. Legend:** NEC NON ARCHDUSES... **Mint:** Ensisheim **Note:** Dav. #3035A.

Date	Mintage	VG	F	VF	XF	Unc
1612	—	—	—	—	—	—
1613	—	150	300	475	800	—

KM# 279.1 THALER

Silver **Ruler:** Maximilian **Obv:** Draped bust, date in front **Note:** Dav. #3326.

Date	Mintage	VG	F	VF	XF	Unc
ND(1612)	—	120	240	400	650	—
1614	—	120	240	400	650	—
1615	—	120	240	400	650	—

KM# 279.2 THALER

Silver **Ruler:** Maximilian **Obv:** Armored bust with lion's face in shoulder drapery, date in front

Date	Mintage	VG	F	VF	XF	Unc
1616	—	120	240	400	650	—
1617	—	120	240	400	650	—

KM# 279.3 THALER

Silver **Ruler:** Maximilian **Obv:** Armored bust with lion's face sideways in shoulder drapery, date below **Note:** Dav. #3327.

Date	Mintage	VG	F	VF	XF	Unc
1617	—	145	290	450	725	—
1618	—	145	290	450	725	—

KM# 279.4 THALER

Silver **Ruler:** Maximilian **Obv:** Bust barely touches legend at "G" **Rev:** Without inner circle **Note:** Dav. #3327A.

Date	Mintage	VG	F	VF	XF	Unc
1618	—	70.00	145	270	475	—

KM# 279.5 THALER

Silver **Ruler:** Maximilian **Obv:** Similar to KM#279.3 but date in front **Note:** Dav. #3327B. Struck posthumously.

Date	Mintage	VG	F	VF	XF	Unc
1619	—	70.00	145	270	475	—

KM# 256.1 THALER

Silver **Ruler:** Leopold V **Obv:** Bust of Leopold right, date in front **Rev:** Crowned arms with two shields at left and right **Rev. Legend:** ET - STIR.CARIN: - CARN:LAND: - ALS **Mint:** Ensisheim **Note:** Dav. #3340.

Date	Mintage	VG	F	VF	XF	Unc
16Z0	—	55.00	110	215	350	—

KM# 256.2 THALER

Silver **Ruler:** Leopold V **Obv:** Bust of Leopold right, date below bust **Obv. Legend:** D: G: LEOPOL:... **Mint:** Ensisheim **Note:** Dav. #3341.

Date	Mintage	VG	F	VF	XF	Unc
16Z0	—	55.00	110	215	350	—

KM# 256.3 THALER

Silver **Ruler:** Leopold V **Obv. Legend:** LEOPOLDVS. D: G. ET... **Mint:** Ensisheim **Note:** Dav. #3342.

Date	Mintage	VG	F	VF	XF	Unc
16Z0	—	55.00	110	215	350	1,500

KM# 256.4 THALER
Silver **Ruler:** Leopold V **Obv. Legend:** LEOPOLD: D: G: ET •... **Mint:** Ensisheim **Note:** Dav. #3343.

Date	Mintage	VG	F	VF	XF	Unc
16Z0	—	55.00	110	215	350	—

KM# 256.5 THALER
Silver **Ruler:** Leopold V **Obv:** Bust divides date **Obv. Legend:** + LEOPOL: D: G: ET. AR - CHIDVCES... **Mint:** Ensisheim **Note:** Dav. #3344.

Date	Mintage	VG	F	VF	XF	Unc
16Z0	—	55.00	110	215	350	—

KM# A257 THALER
27.9200 g., Silver **Ruler:** Ferdinand II **Obv:** Date before bust **Note:** Dav. #3168.

Date	Mintage	VG	F	VF	XF	Unc
1621	—	90.00	180	325	600	—

KM# B257.1 THALER
Silver **Ruler:** Ferdinand II **Obv:** Date behind bust with straight ruffled collar **Note:** Dav. #3169.

Date	Mintage	VG	F	VF	XF	Unc
1621	—	90.00	180	325	600	—

KM# A270 THALER
Silver **Ruler:** Ferdinand II **Obv:** Date below bust **Note:** Dav. #3170.

Date	Mintage	VG	F	VF	XF	Unc
1621	—	90.00	180	325	600	—
1623	—	90.00	180	325	600	—

KM# 257.1 THALER
Silver **Ruler:** Leopold V **Obv:** Bust of Leopold right **Obv. Legend:** + LEOPOLD: D: G. ARCHIDVX:... **Rev:** Crowned arms **Rev. Legend:** + RELIZ: ARCHID: GVBERNAT: PLEN: ET. COM: TIR: LAND. ALS **Mint:** Ensisheim **Note:** Varieties exist. Dav. #3345.

Date	Mintage	VG	F	VF	XF	Unc
1621	—	42.00	95.00	180	325	—
1622	—	42.00	95.00	180	325	—
1623	—	42.00	95.00	180	325	—
1624	—	42.00	95.00	180	325	—

KM# 257.2 THALER
Silver **Ruler:** Leopold V **Obv:** Bust divides date **Mint:** Ensisheim **Note:** Varieties exist. Dav. #3346.

Date	Mintage	VG	F	VF	XF	Unc
1621	—	42.00	95.00	180	325	—
1624	—	42.00	95.00	180	325	—

KM# 257.3 THALER
Silver **Ruler:** Leopold V **Obv. Legend:** LEOPOLDVS. AVS... **Mint:** Ensisheim **Note:** Varieties exist. Dav. #3346A.

Date	Mintage	VG	F	VF	XF	Unc
1625	—	42.00	85.00	145	240	425

KM# B257.2 THALER
Silver **Ruler:** Ferdinand II **Obv:** Date behind bust with curved ruffled collar

Date	Mintage	VG	F	VF	XF	Unc
1622	—	90.00	180	325	600	—

KM# A265 THALER
Silver **Ruler:** Ferdinand II **Note:** Dav. #3170A. Klippe.

Date	Mintage	VG	F	VF	XF	Unc
1623 Rare	—	—	—	—	—	—

KM# 260 THALER
Silver **Ruler:** Leopold V **Obv:** Date behind bust **Mint:** Ensisheim **Note:** Dav. #3347.

Date	Mintage	VG	F	VF	XF	Unc
16ZZ	—	55.00	110	210	350	—

KM# 261 THALER
Silver **Ruler:** Leopold V **Obv:** Date in front of bust **Mint:** Ensisheim **Note:** Dav. #3348.

Date	Mintage	VG	F	VF	XF	Unc
16Z3	—	48.00	100	200	325	—
16ZZ	—	48.00	100	200	325	—

KM# 265.1 THALER

Silver **Ruler:** Leopold V **Obv:** 1/2-length bust right with scepter, date in front **Rev:** Crowned arms with Alsace as central arms **Mint:** Ensisheim **Note:** Dav. #3350.

Date	Mintage	VG	F	VF	XF	Unc
1626	—	60.00	120	220	425	1,000

KM# 265.2 THALER

Silver **Ruler:** Leopold V **Obv:** Thinner modified bust **Mint:** Ensisheim **Note:** Dav. #3350A.

Date	Mintage	VG	F	VF	XF	Unc
1626	—	60.00	120	220	425	—

KM# 267.1 THALER

Silver **Ruler:** Leopold V **Obv:** Bust breaking legend at bottom **Mint:** Ensisheim **Note:** Dav. #3351.

Date	Mintage	VG	F	VF	XF	Unc
1627	—	60.00	120	220	425	1,000

KM# 267.2 THALER

Silver **Ruler:** Leopold V **Obv:** Small bust with cloak over left shoulder **Mint:** Ensisheim **Note:** Dav. #3352.

Date	Mintage	VG	F	VF	XF	Unc
1627	—	95.00	180	325	600	—

KM# 267.3 THALER

Silver **Ruler:** Leopold V **Obv:** Large bust with cloak over left shoulder **Mint:** Ensisheim **Note:** Dav. #3352.

Date	Mintage	VG	F	VF	XF	Unc
1627	—	95.00	180	325	600	—

KM# 267.4 THALER

Silver **Ruler:** Leopold V **Obv:** Bust right with date in front **Mint:** Ensisheim **Note:** Varieties exist. Dav. #3353.

Date	Mintage	VG	F	VF	XF	Unc
1627	—	60.00	120	220	425	850
1628	—	60.00	120	220	425	850
1629	—	60.00	120	220	425	850
1630	—	60.00	120	220	425	850

KM# 268 THALER

Silver **Ruler:** Leopold V **Mint:** Ensisheim **Note:** Klippe. Dav. #3353A.

Date	Mintage	VG	F	VF	XF	Unc
1630 Rare	—	—	—	—	—	—

KM# 272 THALER

Silver **Ruler:** Leopold V **Obv:** Bust without cloak **Rev:** Crowned arms in Order chain with two small shields at sides **Mint:** Ensisheim **Note:** Dav. #3355.

Date	Mintage	VG	F	VF	XF	Unc
1631	—	60.00	120	220	425	850
1632	—	60.00	120	220	425	850

KM# 273 THALER

Silver **Ruler:** Leopold V **Mint:** Ensisheim **Note:** Klippe. Dav. #3355A.

Date	Mintage	VG	F	VF	XF	Unc
1632 Rare	—	—	—	—	—	—
ND Rare	—	—	—	—	—	—

KM# 248 2 THALER

Silver **Ruler:** Rudolf II **Obv:** Bust of Rudolf II right **Obv. Legend:** + RVDOLPHVS: II: DG: ROM: IM: SE: AV: GE: HV: BO: REX **Rev:** Crowned ornate rounded arms **Rev. Legend:** NEC NON ARCHIDVCESA... **Mint:** Ensisheim **Note:** Dav. #3031.

Date	Mintage	VG	F	VF	XF	Unc
1603	—	850	1,450	2,650	4,800	—
1604	—	850	1,450	2,650	4,800	—
1607	—	850	1,450	2,650	4,800	—
1609	—	850	1,450	2,650	4,800	—

KM# 280 2 THALER

Silver **Ruler:** Maximilian **Obv:** Armored bust of Maximilian right **Obv. Legend:** + MAXIMILIANVS D: G ++ ARCH: AVST: DVX: BVR: STIR: CARIN(T) **Rev:** Crowned arms with shields at left and right **Rev. Legend:** (:)ET: CARN: MAG: PRVSS: ADML: LAND: ALS: COM: FER. **Note:** Dav. #3325.

Date	Mintage	VG	F	VF	XF	Unc
1614	—	475	950	1,750	3,250	—
1619	—	475	950	1,750	3,250	—

KM# 281 2 THALER

Silver

Date	Mintage	VG	F	VF	XF	Unc
1617	—	600	1,200	2,200	3,600	—

KM# 284 2 THALER

Silver **Ruler:** Leopold

Date	Mintage	VG	F	VF	XF	Unc
ND(1620)	—	475	1,000	1,800	3,350	—

KM# 258 2 THALER
Silver **Ruler:** Leopold V **Obv:** Bust of Leopold right, legend **Obv. Legend:** LEOPOLDVS D G... **Rev:** Crowned arms shield at left and right **Rev. Legend:** .STIRIAE. CARINT - CARN: LAND: ALS **Mint:** Ensisheim **Note:** Dav. #3339.

Date	Mintage	VG	F	VF	XF	Unc
ND(1621)	—	650	1,300	2,400	4,200	—

KM# 271 2 THALER
Silver **Ruler:** Leopold V **Obv:** Crowned half-length bust of Leopold with scepter **Rev:** Crowned arms **Rev. Legend:** SAC: CAES: MA: ANTER: PROVINC. PLEN. GVB. **Mint:** Ensisheim **Note:** Dav. #3349.

Date	Mintage	VG	F	VF	XF	Unc
ND(1627)	—	550	1,150	2,150	3,600	—

KM# 274 2 THALER
Silver **Ruler:** Leopold V **Rev:** Crowned arms in Order chain with shields at left and right **Rev. Legend:** DVX. - DURG. LAND, ALS. - FER. **Mint:** Ensisheim **Note:** Dav. #3354.

Date	Mintage	VG	F	VF	XF	Unc
ND(1631) Rare	—	—	—	—	—	—

TRADE COINAGE

KM# 283 DUCAT
3.5000 g., 0.9860 Gold 0.1109 oz. AGW **Ruler:** Leopold V **Obv:** Arms of Alsace in Order chain within circle, legend surrounds **Obv. Legend:** LEOPOLDVS. D-G:... **Rev:** St. Leopold standing facing with banner, holding church model in left hand **Mint:** Ensisheim **Note:** Posthumous issue. Fr. #119a.

Date	Mintage	VG	F	VF	XF	Unc
ND(1631-34) Rare	—	—	—	—	—	—

KM# A276 6-1/2 DUCAT
22.7500 g., 0.9860 Gold 0.7212 oz. AGW **Ruler:** Rudolf II **Obv:** Laureate bust of Rudolph II right **Rev:** Crowned arms **Mint:** Ensisheim **Note:** Struck with 1 Thaler dies, KM#247.3.

Date	Mintage	VG	F	VF	XF	Unc
1611 Rare	—	—	—	—	—	—

ANHALT

The Principality of Anhalt in Central Germany, surrounded by Brandenburg, Brunswick and Saxony, had its origins in the same Ascanian family from which descended the margraves of Brandenburg and the dukes of Saxony. The nucleus of the Anhalt domains was the countship of Ballenstädt, whose first recorded ruler, Albrecht I, was in control there during the late 10th century. Albrecht's great-great-grandson, Albrecht III the Bear, ruled in Anhalt until 1170 and was also the margrave of Brandenburg until his death, as well as duke of Saxony until 1153. The patrimony was divided in 1170 and Albrecht III's third son, Bernhard, ruled in Anhalt and began a line of descendants, which lasted into the 20th century.

Various divisions occurred during the ensuing centuries, but the ruling princes often struck joint coinages. At the death of Georg I of Dessau and Köthen in 1474, his five surviving sons ruled together. Only two of them had any male children and they ruled separately in Dessau and Köthen until the latter fell extinct in 1566, at which time that branch reverted to Dessau. Meanwhile, Dessau had been divided in 1516 into Dessau, Plötzkau and Zerbst, but all reverted to Zerbst after a generation. One of the Zerbst princes succeeded in reuniting all the Anhalt lands in 1570 and his sons ruled jointly until the great division of 1603.

RULERS

After the division of 1603, the princes of Anhalt continued to issue joint coinage in many denominations. As some members of one generation died, their places were taken by their sons and various combinations of brothers, uncles, nephews and cousins are represented on the coins, either with their full or abbreviated names or simply as "brothers and fathers - princes of Anhalt". There are 4 distinct periods of joint coinage, 3 of which follow one upon the other and a later period separated from the first 3 by forty years.

Period I, 1603-1618
Johann Georg I von Dessau
Christian I von Bernburg
Augustus von Plötzkau
Rudolf von Zerbst
Ludwig von Köthen

Period II, 1618-1621
Christian I von Bernburg
Augustus von Plötzkau
Rudolf von Zerbst
Ludwig von Köthen
Johann Kasimir von Dessau
Georg Aribert von Dessau

Period III, 1621-1630
Christian I von Bernburg
Augustus von Plötzkau
Ludwig von Köthen
Johann Kasimir von Dessau
Georg Aribert von Dessau
Johann von Zerbst

Period IV, 1670-1693
Johann Georg II von Dessau (d.1693)
Victor Amadeus von Bernburg (d.1718)
Wilhelm von Harzgerode (d.1709)
Carl Wilhelm von Zerbst (d.1718)
Emanuel Lebrecht von Köthen (d. 1704)

MINT OFFICIALS' INITIALS

Initials	Date	Name
CP	1674-90	Christoph Pflug
DH		?
EI		Erik Jäger
GK		?
HB		?
HF		?
HI, II	1614-18	Johann (Hans) Jakob
HS	1622-24	Heinrich Schultze
IA	1666-76	Johann Arendsberg der Jünger in Zerbst and Reinstein
IS		?
IW		?
K		?
SK		?
SV		?

ARMS

Anhalt – two-fold divided vertically, ½ eagle on left, 8 (or more) horizontal bars on right, alternately shaded, sometimes with opened crown laid across diagonally (ducal Saxony). The two sides are often reversed in early issues.

Ascanian dynasty – crowned bear standing (early), crowned bear on wall (later).

Aschersleben – checkerboard.

CROSS REFERENCE

M = Julius Mann, *Anhaltische Münzen und Medaillen vom Ende des XV. Jahrhunderts bis 1906*, Hannover, 1907.

PRINCIPALITY

JOINT COINAGE

KM# 15 HELLER
Billon **Obv:** Two-fold arms separate two-digit date or date above **Note:** Uniface. Varieties exist.

Date	Mintage	Good	VG	F	VF	XF
1619	—	25.00	45.00	75.00	135	250
(16)20	—	25.00	45.00	75.00	135	250
1621	—	25.00	45.00	75.00	135	250
(16)21	—	25.00	45.00	75.00	135	250
(16)22	—	25.00	45.00	75.00	135	250
ND	—	25.00	45.00	75.00	135	250

KM# 21 HELLER
Billon, 14 mm. **Obv:** Two-fold arms, date **Note:** Varieties exist.

Date	Mintage	Good	VG	F	VF	XF
1621	—	22.00	40.00	65.00	125	210

KM# 20 HELLER
Billon **Obv:** Two-fold arms, date above **Rev:** Two-fold arms

Date	Mintage	Good	VG	F	VF	XF
(16)21	—	22.00	40.00	65.00	125	210

KM# 22 HELLER
Billon **Obv:** Two-fold arms, one above **Rev:** Imperial orb divides date

Date	Mintage	Good	VG	F	VF	XF
1621	—	30.00	50.00	75.00	135	250
(16)21	—	27.00	45.00	65.00	110	210

KM# 23 HELLER
Billon **Obv:** Two-fold arms **Rev:** Bear right on wall

Date	Mintage	Good	VG	F	VF	XF
ND	—	35.00	65.00	110	165	325

KM# 19 HELLER
Billon **Note:** Bear on wall with gate.

Date	Mintage	Good	VG	F	VF	XF
ND Rare	—	—	—	—	—	—

KM# 25 PFENNIG
Billon **Rev:** Gate with three towers divides date

Date	Mintage	Good	VG	F	VF	XF
1621 Rare	—	—	—	—	—	—

KM# 24 PFENNIG
Billon **Obv:** Two-fold arms **Rev:** Bear right on wall, date in legend **Note:** Kipper Pfennig.

Date	Mintage	Good	VG	F	VF	XF
1621 Rare	—	—	—	—	—	—

KM# 26 2 PFENNIG
Billon **Obv:** Two-fold arms, date above **Rev:** II/PFEN/GE **Note:** Kipper 2 Pfennig.

Date	Mintage	Good	VG	F	VF	XF
(16)21 Rare	—	—	—	—	—	—

KM# 27 3 PFENNIG (Dreier)
Billon **Obv:** Two-fold arms, date above **Rev:** Imperial orb with 3 **Note:** Kipper 3 Pfennig. Varieties exist.

Date	Mintage	Good	VG	F	VF	XF
1621 GK	—	11.00	20.00	35.00	65.00	125
1621 SK	—	11.00	20.00	35.00	65.00	125
(16)21	—	11.00	20.00	35.00	65.00	125

KM# 28 3 PFENNIG (Dreier)
Billon **Rev:** Heart-shaped shield and date **Note:** Varieties exist.

Date	Mintage	Good	VG	F	VF	XF
(16)21	—	12.00	20.00	30.00	65.00	110

KM# 29 3 PFENNIG (Dreier)
Billon **Rev:** Imperial orb in rhombus

Date	Mintage	Good	VG	F	VF	XF
1621	—	15.00	25.00	40.00	75.00	150
(16)21	—	15.00	25.00	40.00	75.00	150

KM# 30 3 PFENNIG (Dreier)
Billon **Obv:** Oval shield

Date	Mintage	Good	VG	F	VF	XF
(16)21	—	15.00	25.00	40.00	75.00	150

KM# 53 3 PFENNIG (Dreier)
Silver **Obv:** Two-fold arms, date above **Rev:** Imperial orb with 3 in lower half divides date

Date	Mintage	Good	VG	F	VF	XF
(16)22	—	17.00	32.00	65.00	120	200

KM# 48 3 PFENNIG (Dreier)
Billon **Obv:** Two-fold arms in round or oval shield **Rev:** Imperial orb with 3 in lower half divides date **Note:** Varieties exist.

Date	Mintage	Good	VG	F	VF	XF
(16)22	—	9.00	15.00	30.00	50.00	100
ND	—	9.00	15.00	30.00	50.00	100
ND V	—	9.00	15.00	30.00	50.00	100
ND SV	—	9.00	15.00	30.00	50.00	100

KM# 49 3 PFENNIG (Dreier)
Billon **Obv:** Square or rectangular shield, pointed or rounded bottom **Note:** Varieties exist.

Date	Mintage	Good	VG	F	VF	XF
(16)22	—	9.00	15.00	30.00	50.00	100
ND	—	—	—	—	—	—

KM# 50 3 PFENNIG (Dreier)
Billon **Obv:** Heart-shaped shield **Rev:** Orb in rhombus **Note:** Varieties exist.

Date	Mintage	Good	VG	F	VF	XF
(16)22	—	15.00	22.00	35.00	60.00	120

KM# 51 3 PFENNIG (Dreier)
Billon **Obv:** Large B **Rev:** Lion left, value III above **Note:** Varieties exist.

Date	Mintage	Good	VG	F	VF	XF
ND Rare	—	—	—	—	—	—

KM# 52 3 PFENNIG (Dreier)
Billon **Obv:** Large B between two flowers **Rev:** 3 in heart-shaped cartouche **Note:** Varieties exist.

Date	Mintage	Good	VG	F	VF	XF
ND Rare	—	—	—	—	—	—

KM# 54 3 PFENNIG (Dreier)
Silver **Obv:** Two-fold arms in square or rectangular shield **Note:** Varieties exist.

Date	Mintage	Good	VG	F	VF	XF
1622 HB	—	15.00	30.00	60.00	115	230
1622 SV	—	15.00	30.00	60.00	115	230
1622	—	15.00	30.00	60.00	115	230
(16)22	—	15.00	30.00	60.00	115	230

KM# 55 3 PFENNIG (Dreier)
Silver **Obv:** Two-fold arms in round or oval shield **Note:** Varieties exist.

Date	Mintage	Good	VG	F	VF	XF
(16)22	—	10.00	20.00	40.00	75.00	150
ND SV	—	10.00	20.00	40.00	75.00	150

KM# 57 4 PFENNIG
Silver **Obv:** Date added

Date	Mintage	Good	VG	F	VF	XF
1622 Rare	—	—	—	—	—	—

KM# 56 4 PFENNIG
Silver **Obv:** Two-fold arms in oval shield **Rev:** Square with value IIII, date **Note:** Kipper 4 Pfennig. Varieties exist.

Date	Mintage	Good	VG	F	VF	XF
1622	—	20.00	40.00	65.00	120	240

KM# 18 2 SCHILLING
Silver **Obv:** Crowned two-fold arms **Rev:** DS monogram, date either split above and below or all below **Note:** Kipper 2 Schilling. Varieties exist.

Date	Mintage	VG	F	VF	XF	Unc
1620	—	20.00	40.00	75.00	150	275
1621	—	20.00	40.00	75.00	150	275
ND	—	20.00	40.00	75.00	150	275

KM# 42 12 KREUZER
Silver **Obv:** Angel above two-fold arms **Rev:** Imperial eagle with value 12 on breast **Note:** Kipper 12 Kreuzer. Varieties exist.

Date	Mintage	VG	F	VF	XF	Unc
ND Rare	—	—	—	—	—	—

KM# 43 12 KREUZER
Silver **Rev:** Three shields, one above two, value 12 in legend at bottom **Note:** Varieties exist.

Date	Mintage	VG	F	VF	XF	Unc
ND HW Rare	—	—	—	—	—	—

KM# 44 12 KREUZER
Silver **Obv:** Crowned two-fold arms **Rev:** Three shields, two above one, one below divides date **Note:** Varieties exist.

Date	Mintage	VG	F	VF	XF	Unc
1621	—	55.00	150	275	550	—
1621 DH	—	55.00	150	275	550	—

KM# 73 12 KREUZER
Silver **Obv:** Small angel's head above heart-shaped two-fold arms **Rev:** Imperial eagle with value 12 on breast, date

Date	Mintage	VG	F	VF	XF	Unc
1622 IW	—	55.00	150	275	550	—

KM# 45 24 KREUZER
Silver **Obv:** Angel above two-fold arms, date **Rev:** Imperial eagle with value 24 on breast **Note:** Kipper 24 Kreuzer. Varieties exist.

Date	Mintage	VG	F	VF	XF	Unc
1621	—	70.00	140	275	550	—
ND	—	70.00	140	275	550	—

KM# 46 24 KREUZER
Silver **Obv:** Two-fold arms

Date	Mintage	VG	F	VF	XF	Unc
1621 DH	—	70.00	140	275	550	—
ND	—	70.00	140	275	550	—

KM# 47 24 KREUZER
Silver **Obv:** Crowned two-fold arms **Rev:** One shield above divides date, two shields below, value 24 in legend at bottom **Note:** Varieties exist.

Date	Mintage	VG	F	VF	XF	Unc
ND K	—	70.00	140	275	550	—
ND	—	70.00	140	275	550	—

KM# 74 24 KREUZER
Silver **Obv:** Angel above two-fold arms, date **Rev:** Imperial eagle with 24 on breast, date

Date	Mintage	VG	F	VF	XF	Unc
1622	—	70.00	140	275	550	—

KM# 11 4 GROSCHEN
Silver **Obv:** Heart-shaped two-fold arms, date **Rev:** Three shields, one above, two below; value 4 in lower legend

Date	Mintage	VG	F	VF	XF	Unc
1616 Rare	—	—	—	—	—	—

KM# 38 4 GROSCHEN
Silver **Rev:** Without date **Note:** Varieties exist.

Date	Mintage	VG	F	VF	XF	Unc
1620	—	50.00	85.00	130	240	—
1621	—	50.00	85.00	130	240	—
ND	—	50.00	85.00	130	240	—

KM# 39 4 GROSCHEN
Silver **Obv:** Crowned two-fold arms **Rev:** Three shields, one above divides date, two below without value **Note:** Varieties exist.

Date	Mintage	VG	F	VF	XF	Unc
1621	—	45.00	80.00	125	250	—
1621 HW	—	50.00	85.00	140	250	—
ND	—	45.00	80.00	125	250	—

KM# 33 4 GROSCHEN
Silver **Obv:** Angel above two-fold arms **Rev:** Three shields, two above, one below divides date, value 4 in center **Note:** Kipper 4 Groschen.

Date	Mintage	VG	F	VF	XF	Unc
1621	—	55.00	95.00	150	300	—

KM# 34 4 GROSCHEN
Silver **Rev:** One shield above, two below, value 4 between lower two **Note:** Varieties exist.

Date	Mintage	VG	F	VF	XF	Unc
ND	—	55.00	95.00	140	250	—

KM# 35 4 GROSCHEN
Silver **Obv:** Two-fold arms **Rev:** 4 in circle at bottom **Note:** Varieties exist.

Date	Mintage	VG	F	VF	XF	Unc
1621	—	50.00	95.00	135	275	—
ND	—	50.00	95.00	135	275	—

KM# 36 4 GROSCHEN
Silver **Obv:** Crowned two-fold arms **Rev:** One shield above divides date, two shields below, value 4 in circle in lower legend **Note:** Varieties exist.

Date	Mintage	VG	F	VF	XF	Unc
(16)21	—	55.00	95.00	150	300	—

KM# 37 4 GROSCHEN
Silver **Obv:** Two-fold arms **Rev:** Three shields, two above, one below divides date, value IIII in circle at bottom **Note:** Varieties exist.

Date	Mintage	VG	F	VF	XF	Unc
ND	—	55.00	95.00	150	300	—

KM# 40 8 GROSCHEN
Silver **Obv:** Angel above two-fold arms **Rev:** Three shields, two above, one below divides date, value 8 in legend at bottom **Note:** Kipper 8 Groschen.

Date	Mintage	VG	F	VF	XF	Unc
1621	—	60.00	100	170	275	—
ND HW	—	60.00	100	170	275	—

KM# 41 8 GROSCHEN
Silver **Obv:** Crowned two-fold arms **Rev:** Three shields, one above divides date, two below **Note:** Varieties exist.

Date	Mintage	VG	F	VF	XF	Unc
1621	—	55.00	95.00	150	300	—
(16)21	—	55.00	95.00	150	300	—
ND	—	55.00	95.00	150	300	—
ND K	—	55.00	95.00	150	300	—

KM# 83 8 GROSCHEN
Silver **Obv:** Crowned nine-fold arms **Rev:** Value, date **Note:** Gute 8 Groschen. Varieties exist.

Date	Mintage	VG	F	VF	XF	Unc
1669	—	35.00	65.00	120	225	—

KM# 90 8 GROSCHEN
Silver **Obv:** Crowned nine-fold arms in wreath

Date	Mintage	VG	F	VF	XF	Unc
1689 CP	—	35.00	65.00	120	225	—

KM# 88 16 GROSCHEN
Silver **Obv:** Crowned 9-fold arms in wreath **Rev:** 6-line inscription **Note:** Varieties exist.

Date	Mintage	VG	F	VF	XF	Unc
1683 CP	—	50.00	95.00	145	275	—
1684 CP	—	50.00	95.00	145	275	—
1685 CP	—	50.00	95.00	145	275	—
1686 CP	—	50.00	95.00	145	275	—
1689 CP	—	50.00	95.00	145	275	—

KM# 59 1/84 THALER (6 Pfennig - Kortling)
Billon **Obv:** Two-fold arms **Rev:** Orb in rhombus

Date	Mintage	Good	VG	F	VF	XF
1622	—	22.00	45.00	85.00	165	325

KM# 60 1/84 THALER (6 Pfennig - Kortling)
Billon **Obv:** Arms of Aschersleben (checkerboard) **Rev:** Imperial orb with value 84 divides date

Date	Mintage	Good	VG	F	VF	XF
(16)22 Rare	—	—	—	—	—	—

KM# 58 1/84 THALER (6 Pfennig - Kortling)
Billon **Obv:** Two-fold arms in ornate frame **Rev:** Imperial orb with value 84 divides date **Note:** Kipper 1/84 Thaler. Varieties exist.

Date	Mintage	Good	VG	F	VF	XF
1622	—	17.00	33.00	75.00	150	300

KM# 1 1/24 THALER (Groschen)
Silver **Obv:** Four-fold arms in heart-shaped shield, legend **Rev:** Imperial orb with 24 divides date, legend **Note:** Varieties exist.

Date	Mintage	VG	F	VF	XF	Unc
1614 II	—	15.00	27.00	55.00	100	200
1615	—	15.00	27.00	55.00	100	200
1615 II	—	15.00	27.00	55.00	100	200

KM# 7 1/24 THALER (Groschen)
Silver **Rev:** Crowned two-fold arms in oval shield, date **Note:** Varieties exist.

Date	Mintage	VG	F	VF	XF	Unc
1615	—	15.00	27.00	55.00	100	200
1616	—	15.00	27.00	55.00	100	200
1617	—	15.00	27.00	55.00	100	200

KM# 8 1/24 THALER (Groschen)
Silver **Obv:** Crowned 2-fold arms in oval shield, date **Note:** Klippe. Varieties exist.

Date	Mintage	VG	F	VF	XF	Unc
1615	—	35.00	60.00	110	225	—
1617	—	25.00	45.00	80.00	165	—

KM# 14 1/24 THALER (Groschen)
Silver, 20 mm. **Obv:** Square-topped shield **Note:** Varieties exist.

Date	Mintage	VG	F	VF	XF	Unc
1617	—	13.00	25.00	50.00	100	—
1618	—	13.00	25.00	50.00	100	—

KM# 16 1/24 THALER (Groschen)
Silver **Obv:** Crowned two-fold arms **Rev:** Imperial orb with 24, date in legend **Note:** Kipper 1/24 Thaler. Varieties exist.

Date	Mintage	VG	F	VF	XF	Unc
1619	—	13.00	25.00	50.00	100	—
1620	—	13.00	25.00	50.00	100	—
(16)20	—	13.00	25.00	50.00	100	—
1621	—	13.00	25.00	50.00	100	—
ND	—	13.00	25.00	50.00	100	—

KM# 17 1/24 THALER (Groschen)
Silver **Obv:** Crowned 2-fold arms **Rev:** Imperial orb with 24, date in legend **Note:** Klippe.

Date	Mintage	VG	F	VF	XF	Unc
1619	—	35.00	70.00	110	225	—
1620	—	35.00	70.00	110	225	—

KM# 31 1/24 THALER (Groschen)
Silver **Obv:** Bear right on wall **Rev:** Imperial orb with 24, date

Date	Mintage	VG	F	VF	XF	Unc
1621 Rare	—	—	—	—	—	—

KM# 32 1/24 THALER (Groschen)
Billon **Obv:** Crowned two-fold arms **Rev:** Imperial orb with 24, date in legend

Date	Mintage	VG	F	VF	XF	Unc
1621	—	15.00	27.00	55.00	100	200

KM# 63 1/24 THALER (Groschen)
Silver **Rev:** Small orb with 24 above two shields, date

Date	Mintage	VG	F	VF	XF	Unc
1622 HB	—	15.00	30.00	60.00	125	—

KM# 61 1/24 THALER (Groschen)
Silver, 22-24 mm. **Obv:** Helmeted two-fold arms **Rev:** Imperial orb with 24, date **Note:** Size varies. Varieties exist.

Date	Mintage	VG	F	VF	XF	Unc
1622	—	13.00	25.00	50.00	100	—
1623	—	13.00	25.00	50.00	100	—

KM# 72 1/24 THALER (Groschen)
Silver **Obv:** Four-fold arms **Rev:** Imperial orb with 24, date **Note:** Klippe.

Date	Mintage	VG	F	VF	XF	Unc
1622 IS Rare	—	—	—	—	—	—

KM# 64 1/24 THALER (Groschen)
Silver, 14-17 mm. **Obv:** Oval two-fold arms **Rev:** Imperial orb with 24, date **Note:** Size varies. Varieties exist.

Date	Mintage	VG	F	VF	XF	Unc
1622	—	13.00	25.00	50.00	100	—
1622 HB	—	13.00	25.00	50.00	100	—
ND	—	13.00	25.00	50.00	100	—

KM# 65 1/24 THALER (Groschen)
Silver **Note:** Klippe. Varieties exist.

Date	Mintage	VG	F	VF	XF	Unc
ND	—	27.00	50.00	95.00	185	—

KM# 66 1/24 THALER (Groschen)
Silver **Obv:** Bear on wall right

Date	Mintage	VG	F	VF	XF	Unc
(16)22 Rare	—	—	—	—	—	—

KM# 67 1/24 THALER (Groschen)
Silver **Obv:** Two-fold arms with straight-sided shield with pointed or rounded bottom **Note:** Varieties exist.

Date	Mintage	VG	F	VF	XF	Unc
ND	—	16.00	35.00	65.00	130	—

KM# 68 1/24 THALER (Groschen)
Silver **Obv:** Two shields above one shield **Rev:** Imperial orb with 24

Date	Mintage	VG	F	VF	XF	Unc
ND	—	16.00	35.00	65.00	130	—

KM# 69 1/24 THALER (Groschen)
Silver **Obv:** Bear on wall right

Date	Mintage	VG	F	VF	XF	Unc
ND	—	16.00	35.00	65.00	130	—

KM# 70 1/24 THALER (Groschen)
Silver **Obv:** Arms of Aschersleben (checkerborad)

Date	Mintage	VG	F	VF	XF	Unc
ND	—	20.00	35.00	75.00	155	—

KM# 71 1/24 THALER (Groschen)
Silver, 22-24 mm. **Obv:** Angel's head and wings above two-fold arms **Note:** Size varies.

Date	Mintage	VG	F	VF	XF	Unc
ND	—	20.00	35.00	65.00	120	—

KM# 62 1/24 THALER (Groschen)
Silver **Note:** Klippe.

Date	Mintage	VG	F	VF	XF	Unc
1623	—	35.00	70.00	120	200	—

KM# 87 1/24 THALER (Groschen)
Silver **Obv:** Crowned 9-fold arms in wreath **Rev:** Value, date **Rev. Legend:** 24 EINEN ... **Note:** Varieties exist.

Date	Mintage	VG	F	VF	XF	Unc
1683 CP	—	20.00	40.00	80.00	175	—
1684 CP	—	20.00	40.00	80.00	175	—

KM# 89 1/12 THALER
Silver **Obv:** Crowned 9-fold arms in wreath **Rev:** Value **Rev. Legend:** 12 EINEN... **Note:** Varieties exist.

Date	Mintage	VG	F	VF	XF	Unc
1684 CP	—	16.00	35.00	75.00	130	—
1686 CP	—	16.00	35.00	75.00	130	—
1688 CP	—	16.00	35.00	75.00	130	—
1689 CP	—	16.00	35.00	75.00	130	—

KM# 79 1/4 THALER
Silver **Obv:** Helmeted nine-fold arms **Rev:** Crowned imperial eagle with orb and VI on breast, date

Date	Mintage	VG	F	VF	XF	Unc
1624 HS Rare	—	—	—	—	—	—

KM# 84 1/3 THALER
Silver **Obv:** Crowned nine-fold arms **Rev:** Crowned, erect bear walking left, value, date **Note:** Varieties exist.

Date	Mintage	VG	F	VF	XF	Unc
1669 IA	—	60.00	120	235	475	—
1670 IA	—	60.00	120	235	475	—

KM# 85 1/3 THALER
Silver **Obv:** Value below arms

Date	Mintage	VG	F	VF	XF	Unc
1670 IA	—	100	200	325	550	—

KM# 2 1/2 THALER
Silver **Obv:** 2 conjoined busts facing right, another bust facing left **Rev:** 2 busts facing

Date	Mintage	VG	F	VF	XF	Unc
1614 II Rare	—	—	—	—	—	—

KM# 75 1/2 THALER
Silver **Obv:** Nine-fold arms **Rev:** Crowned imperial eagle with orb and 12 on breast, date

Date	Mintage	VG	F	VF	XF	Unc
1622 HS Rare	—	—	—	—	—	—

KM# 77 1/2 THALER
Silver **Obv:** Shield of arms **Rev:** Double-headed eagle, value in orb on breast

Date	Mintage	VG	F	VF	XF	Unc
1623 HS	—	600	1,000	1,600	2,750	—
1624 HS	—	600	1,000	1,600	2,750	—

KM# 78 1/2 THALER
Silver **Obv:** 9-fold arms **Rev:** Crowned imperial eagle, orb with 12 on breast, date **Note:** Klippe.

Date	Mintage	VG	F	VF	XF	Unc
1623 HS Rare	—	—	—	—	—	—

KM# 80.1 1/2 THALER
Silver, 31 mm. **Obv:** Shield of arms **Obv. Legend:** PRI. ANH. COM. - ASC. FRA. E. PAT. **Rev:** Crowned imperial eagle, 1Z in orb on breast, date divided by crown at top **Rev. Legend:** MONETA. NOVA. - ARGENTEA. AN: **Note:** Ref. Mann 188a. Varieties exist.

Date	Mintage	VG	F	VF	XF	Unc
16Z4 HS	—	235	475	950	—	—
1625 EI	—	300	600	1,200	—	—

KM# 80.2 1/2 THALER
Silver, 32 mm. **Obv:** Spanish shield of 9-fold arms, 3 ornate helmets above **Obv. Legend:** PRIN. ANHAL. COMI. ASC. FRA. ET. PAT. **Rev:** Crowned imperial eagle, 1Z in orb on breast, date divided by crown above **Rev. Legend:** MONETA. NOUA. ARGENTEA. **Note:** Ref. Mann 188b.

Date	Mintage	VG	F	VF	XF	Unc
16Z4 HS	—	—	—	—	—	—

KM# 80.3 1/2 THALER
Silver, 32 mm. **Obv:** Spanish shield of 9-fold arms, 3 ornate helmets above **Obv. Legend:** PRINC. ANHAL. COM. ASC. FRA. E. PA. **Rev:** Crowned imperial eagle, 1Z in orb on breast, date divided by crown at top, tail of eagle divides SER - VES **Rev. Legend:** MONETA. NOUA. ARGENTEA. **Note:** Ref. Mann 188c.

Date	Mintage	VG	F	VF	XF	Unc
16Z4	—	—	—	—	—	—

KM# 86.1 2/3 THALER
Silver **Obv:** Capped nine-fold arms **Obv. Legend:** MONETA • NOVA • PRINC • ANHALT **Rev:** Crowned, erect bear left, value below divides date **Note:** Varieties exist.

Date	Mintage	VG	F	VF	XF	Unc
1670	—	90.00	145	275	550	—
1670 IA	—	90.00	145	275	550	—

KM# 86.2 2/3 THALER
Silver **Obv:** Capped 9-fold arms in inner circle **Obv. Legend:** *MONETA • NOVA • PRINC • ANHALTINOR **Rev:** Crowned erect bear left in inner circle, date at right of value below **Rev. Legend:** IN • DOMINO • FIDUCIA • NOSTRA

Date	Mintage	VG	F	VF	XF	Unc
1670 IA	—	90.00	145	275	550	—

KM# 3 THALER

Silver **Note:** Dav. #6002.

Date	Mintage	VG	F	VF	XF	Unc
1614 II	—	400	800	1,650	2,750	—
1615 HI	—	400	800	1,650	2,750	—
1616 HI	—	400	800	1,650	2,750	—
1617 HI	—	400	800	1,650	2,750	—
1618 HI	—	400	800	1,650	2,750	—

KM# 9 THALER

Silver **Obv:** 2 conjoined bust facing right, another bust facing left **Rev:** 2 busts facing each other **Note:** Klippe. Dav. #6002A.

Date	Mintage	VG	F	VF	XF	Unc
1615 HI Rare	—	—	—	—	—	—
1616 HI Rare	—	—	—	—	—	—

KM# 76.2 THALER

Silver **Rev:** Date divided by crown **Note:** Varieties exist. Dav. #6003.

Date	Mintage	VG	F	VF	XF	Unc
1622 HS	—	175	350	700	1,350	—
1623 HS	—	175	350	700	1,350	—
1624 HS	—	175	350	700	1,350	—

KM# 76.1 THALER

Silver **Note:** Dav. #6003A.

Date	Mintage	VG	F	VF	XF	Unc
1622	—	200	375	750	1,450	—

KM# 81 THALER

Silver **Obv:** Shield of arms **Rev:** Double-headed eagle with value in orb on breast **Note:** Varieties exist. Dav. #6005.

Date	Mintage	VG	F	VF	XF	Unc
1624	—	175	325	650	1,150	1,850
1624 EI	—	175	350	700	1,350	—
1625 EI	—	175	350	700	1,350	—

KM# 4 2 THALER

60.0000 g., Silver **Obv:** 2 conjoined 1/2-length busts facing left, another bust facing right **Rev:** 2 busts facing each other **Note:** Thick flan. Dav. #6001.

Date	Mintage	VG	F	VF	XF	Unc
1614 II Rare	—	—	—	—	—	—
1615 HI Rare	—	—	—	—	—	—
1618 HI Rare	—	—	—	—	—	—

KM# 82 2 THALER

70.0000 g., Silver **Obv:** Shield of arms breaks inner circle at bottom **Rev:** Double-headed eagle with value on breast **Note:** Thick flan. Varieties exist. Dav. #6004.

Date	Mintage	VG	F	VF	XF	Unc
1624 EI Rare	—	—	—	—	—	—
1624 EI/HS Rare	—	—	—	—	—	—
1625 EI Rare	—	—	—	—	—	—

TRADE COINAGE

KM# 12 1/2 DUCAT

1.7500 g., 0.9860 Gold 0.0555 oz. AGW **Obv:** Three tournament helmets **Rev:** Helmeted arms

Date	Mintage	VG	F	VF	XF	Unc
1616	—	450	1,150	2,750	6,500	—
1618	—	450	1,150	2,750	6,500	—

KM# 13 1/2 DUCAT

1.7500 g., 0.9860 Gold 0.0555 oz. AGW **Obv:** Crowned arms **Rev:** Crowned imperial eagle **Note:** Klippe.

Date	Mintage	VG	F	VF	XF	Unc
1616 Rare	—	—	—	—	—	—

KM# 10 DUCAT

3.5000 g., 0.9860 Gold 0.1109 oz. AGW **Obv:** Three tournament helmets **Rev:** Crowned arms

Date	Mintage	VG	F	VF	XF	Unc
1615	—	750	1,450	3,850	8,250	—
1616	—	750	1,450	3,850	8,250	—
1617	—	750	1,450	3,850	8,250	—
1618	—	750	1,450	3,850	8,250	—
ND	—	750	1,450	3,850	8,250	—

KM# 5 3 DUCAT

10.5000 g., 0.9860 Gold 0.3328 oz. AGW **Obv:** Facing busts of Johann Georg and Christian in inner circle **Rev:** Busts of August and Rudolf facing Ludwig in inner circle

Date	Mintage	VG	F	VF	XF	Unc
1614 II Rare	—	—	—	—	—	—
1616 HI Rare	—	—	—	—	—	—

KM# 6 4 DUCAT

14.0000 g., 0.9860 Gold 0.4438 oz. AGW **Obv:** Facing busts of Johann Georg and Christian in inner circle **Rev:** Busts of August and Rudolf facing Ludwig in inner circle

Date	Mintage	VG	F	VF	XF	Unc
1614 Rare	—	—	—	—	—	—

PATTERNS

Including off metal strikes

KM#	Date	Mintage	Identification	Mkt Val
Pn1	1615 HI	—	3 Ducat. Silver. KM#5	—
Pn2	1615 HI	—	3 Ducat. Silver. 17.1200 g. Klippe, KM#5.	—

ANHALT-BERNBURG

Located in north-central Germany. Appeared as part of the patrimony of Albrecht the Bear of Brandenburg in 1170. Bracteates were first made in the 12th century. It was originally in the inheritance of Heinrich the Fat in 1252 and became extinct in 1468. The division of 1603, among the sons of Joachim Ernst, revitalized Anhalt-Bernburg. Bernburg passed to Dessau after the death of Alexander Carl in 1863.

RULERS

Christian I, 1603-1630
Christian II, 1630-1656
Viktor I Amadeus, 1656-1718

PRINCIPALITY

REGULAR COINAGE

KM# 1 THALER

Silver **Ruler:** Christian II **Obv:** Bust of Christian II right divides date **Obv. Legend:** D: G: CHRISTIANVS. PR. ANHALD... **Rev:** Crowned imperial eagle **Rev. Legend:** FERDINANDVS. II. D: G: ROMANORVM... **Note:** Dav. #6006.

Date	Mintage	VG	F	VF	XF	Unc
1635	—	700	1,150	1,800	2,700	—

KM# 2 THALER

Silver **Ruler:** Christian II **Obv:** Similar to KM#1 **Rev:** Helmeted arms **Rev. Legend:** *ASTRA PETIT VIRTVS **Note:** Dav. #6007.

Date	Mintage	VG	F	VF	XF	Unc
1636	—	145	325	650	1,450	4,300
1640	—	145	325	650	1,450	4,300
1643	—	145	325	650	1,450	4,300
1644	—	145	325	650	1,450	4,300
1645	—	145	325	650	1,450	4,300

ANHALT-DESSAU

Dessau was part of the 1252 division that included Zerbst and Cothen. In 1396 Zerbst divided into Zerbst and Dessau. In 1508 Zerbst was absorbed into Dessau. Dessau was given to the eldest son of Joachim Ernst in the division of 1603. As other lines became extinct, they fell to Dessau, which united all branches in 1863.

RULERS

Johann Georg I, 1603-1618
Johann Kasimir, 1618-1660
Johann Georg II, 1660-1693
Leopold I, 1693-1747

MINT OFFICIALS' INITIALS

Initials	Date	Name
AB	1657-64	Adrian Becker, warden in Berlin
ABK-APK	1667-80	Anton Bernhard Koburger in Mansfeld-Eisleben
CM	1693-94	Christoph Muller
FCV	1674-76	Franc Carl Uhle
IEG	1692-93	Johann Ernst Graul

PRINCIPALITY

REGULAR COINAGE

KM# 1 GROSCHEN

Silver **Ruler:** Johann Kasimir **Subject:** Death of Johann Kasimir **Obv:** Crowned 9-fold arms **Rev:** 12-line inscription **Note:** Varieties exist.

Date	Mintage	VG	F	VF	XF	Unc
MDCLX (1660) AB	—	40.00	85.00	175	350	—

KM# 8 1/12 THALER

Silver **Ruler:** Johann Georg II **Obv:** Crowned 2-fold arms **Rev:** Value, date **Note:** Varieties exist.

Date	Mintage	VG	F	VF	XF	Unc
1693 IEG	—	35.00	75.00	150	300	—

KM# 4 1/3 THALER

Silver **Ruler:** Johann Georg II **Note:** Similar to 2/3 Thaler, KM#5. Varieties exist.

Date	Mintage	VG	F	VF	XF	Unc
1674 ABK	—	55.00	110	225	450	—
1674 APK	—	55.00	110	225	450	—
1676 FCV	—	55.00	110	225	450	—

KM# 9 1/3 THALER

Silver **Ruler:** Johann Georg II **Note:** Similar to 2/3 Thaler, KM#5. Varieties exist.

Date	Mintage	VG	F	VF	XF	Unc
1693 IEG	—	45.00	85.00	175	350	—

KM# 10 1/3 THALER

Silver **Ruler:** Johann Georg II **Obv:** Similar to 2/3 Thaler, KM#6 but bust left **Note:** Varieties exist.

Date	Mintage	VG	F	VF	XF	Unc
1693 Rare	—	—	—	—	—	—

KM# 2 2/3 THALER

Silver **Ruler:** Johann Kasimir **Subject:** Death of Johann Kasimir **Obv:** Helmeted 9-fold arms **Rev:** 12-line inscription

Date	Mintage	VG	F	VF	XF	Unc
MDCLX (1660) AB	—	—	230	460	925	—

KM# 5.1 2/3 THALER

Silver **Ruler:** Johann Georg II **Obv:** Bust of Johann George II right **Rev:** Large date in legend at 10 o'clock; crowned arms

Date	Mintage	VG	F	VF	XF	Unc
1674 APK	—	40.00	65.00	175	350	—
1674 ABK	—	55.00	100	200	425	—

KM# 5.2 2/3 THALER

Silver **Ruler:** Johann Georg II **Rev:** Small date in a legend at 10 o'clock

Date	Mintage	VG	F	VF	XF	Unc
1674 APK	—	55.00	100	200	425	—
1675	—	55.00	100	200	425	—
1675 FCV	—	55.00	100	200	425	—
1676 FCV	—	55.00	100	200	425	—

KM# 5.3 2/3 THALER

Silver **Ruler:** Johann Georg II **Rev:** Oval arms within palm branches

Date	Mintage	VG	F	VF	XF	Unc
1674	—	55.00	100	200	425	—
1674 APK	—	55.00	100	200	425	—
1675 FCV	—	55.00	100	200	425	—
1676 FCV	—	55.00	100	200	425	—

KM# 5.4 2/3 THALER

Silver **Ruler:** Johann Georg II **Rev:** Date divided by denomination at bottom **Note:** Varieties exist.

Date	Mintage	VG	F	VF	XF	Unc
1676 FCV	—	55.00	100	200	425	—

KM# 6.2 2/3 THALER

Silver **Ruler:** Johann Georg II **Rev:** Arms divide IE-G, shorter palm branches **Note:** Varieties exist.

Date	Mintage	VG	F	VF	XF	Unc
1692 IEG	—	135	275	575	1,150	—
1693 IEG	—	100	200	400	800	—

KM# 6.1 2/3 THALER

Silver **Ruler:** Johann Georg II **Obv:** Bust of Johann George II right **Rev:** Crowned arms in sprays

Date	Mintage	VG	F	VF	XF	Unc
1692 IEG	—	140	275	575	1,150	—
1693 IEG	—	140	275	575	1,150	—

KM# 12 2/3 THALER

Silver **Ruler:** Leopold I **Note:** Similar to KM#6.

Date	Mintage	VG	F	VF	XF	Unc
1694 CM Rare	—	—	—	—	—	—

KM# 3 THALER

Silver **Ruler:** Johann Kasimir **Subject:** Death of Johann Kasimir **Obv:** Helmeted 9-fold arms **Obv. Legend:** D. G. IOHAN: CASIMER: PRINCEPS ANHALT:... **Rev:** 12-line inscription **Note:** Varieties exist. Dav. #6008.

Date	Mintage	VG	F	VF	XF	Unc
MDCLX (1660) AB	—	425	825	1,800	4,150	9,400

KM# 7.1 THALER

Silver **Ruler:** Johann Georg II **Obv:** Bust of Johann George II right **Obv. Legend:** IOH.GEORG.D. - G.PR.ANHALT **Rev:** Crowned arms divide date

Date	Mintage	VG	F	VF	XF	Unc
1692	—	500	925	1,950	4,400	—

KM# 7.2 THALER

Silver **Ruler:** Johann Georg II **Rev:** Crowned arms divide date and I.E. - G. **Note:** Dav. #6010. Varieties exist.

Date	Mintage	VG	F	VF	XF	Unc
1692 IEG	—	375	725	1,400	3,300	7,700
1693 IEG	—	375	725	1,400	3,300	7,700

KM# 11 THALER

Silver **Ruler:** Johann Georg II **Subject:** Death of Johann Georg II **Obv:** Bust of Johann Georg II right **Obv. Legend:** IOH. GEORG. D-G. PR. ANHALT **Rev:** 18-line inscription, date **Note:** Dav. #6011. Varieties exist.

Date	Mintage	VG	F	VF	XF	Unc
1693 Rare	—	—	—	—	—	—

PATTERNS

Including off metal strikes

KM#	Date	Mintage	Identification	Mkt Val
PnA1	1660 AB	—	Groschen. Gold. KM1.	6,500
PnB1	1660 AB	—	2/3 Thaler. Gold. KM2.	—

ANHALT-HARZGERODE

Established as a colateral line from Anhalt-Bernburg in 1630. When it became extinct in 1709, title reverted to Bernburg.

RULERS

Friedrich, 1630-1670
Wilhelm, 1670-1709

MINT OFFICIALS' INITIALS

Initials	Date	Name
AF	?	
BA	1679-80	Bastian Altmann in Plotzkau
CF	1678-86	Christoph Fischer in Dresden
CP	1674-90	Christoph Pflug in Zerbst
E	?	
HF	?	
SD	1675-76, 1669-75, 1678-80	Simon (Siegmund) Dannes in Reuss-Schleiz
TF	1695-96	Thomas Fischer

PRINCIPALITY

REGULAR COINAGE

KM# 2 6 PFENNIG

Silver **Ruler:** Wilhelm **Obv:** Crowned W **Rev:** Value, date

Date	Mintage	VG	F	VF	XF	Unc
1694	—	35.00	60.00	120	240	—

KM# 1.1 2/3 THALER

Silver **Ruler:** Wilhelm **Obv:** Legend above portrait with loose hair curls

Date	Mintage	VG	F	VF	XF	Unc
ND	—	60.00	120	235	475	—
ND BA	—	60.00	120	235	475	—
1675 SD	—	60.00	120	235	475	—
1675 CP	—	60.00	120	235	475	—
1676 SD	—	60.00	120	235	475	—
1679 BA Date above initials	—	60.00	120	235	475	—
1679 BA Date below initials	—	60.00	120	235	475	—
1679	—	60.00	120	235	475	—

KM# 1.2 2/3 THALER

Silver **Ruler:** Wilhelm **Rev:** Vertical date divided by arms

Date	Mintage	VG	F	VF	XF	Unc
1675	—	60.00	120	235	475	—

KM# 1.3 2/3 THALER

Silver **Ruler:** Wilhelm **Obv:** Small portrait with loose curls

Date	Mintage	VG	F	VF	XF	Unc
1675 CP	—	60.00	120	235	475	—

KM# 1.4 2/3 THALER

Silver **Ruler:** Wilhelm **Obv:** Crude portrait, tight curls, unbroken legend above

Date	Mintage	VG	F	VF	XF	Unc
1676 AF	—	60.00	120	235	475	—
1676 SD	—	60.00	120	235	475	—
1677 AF	—	60.00	120	235	475	—
1679 SD	—	60.00	120	235	475	—

KM# 1.5 2/3 THALER

Silver **Ruler:** Wilhelm **Obv:** Tight curls break legend at top

Date	Mintage	VG	F	VF	XF	Unc
1676 AF	—	60.00	120	235	475	—

KM# 5 2/3 THALER

Silver **Ruler:** Wilhelm **Rev:** Value divides date **Rev. Legend:** NACH/DEN/LEIPZIGER/FUS

Date	Mintage	VG	F	VF	XF	Unc
1695	—	90.00	150	275	575	—

KM# 1.6 2/3 THALER

Silver **Ruler:** Wilhelm **Obv:** Refined older portrait **Note:** Varieties exist.

Date	Mintage	VG	F	VF	XF	Unc
1695 TF	—	60.00	120	235	475	—
1696 TF	—	60.00	120	235	475	—

KM# 3 THALER

Silver **Ruler:** Wilhelm **Obv:** Helmeted ornate arms **Rev:** Five-line inscription with date **Note:** Dav. #6012.

Date	Mintage	VG	F	VF	XF	Unc
1694 Rare	—	—	—	—	—	—

KM# 4 THALER

Silver **Ruler:** Wilhelm **Obv:** Half-length bust right **Rev:** Five-line inscription with date in circle **Note:** Dav. #6013.

Date	Mintage	VG	F	VF	XF	Unc
1694 E	—	650	1,350	2,750	4,700	—

KM# 6 THALER

Silver **Ruler:** Wilhelm **Rev:** Helmeted arms, date **Note:** Dav. #6014.

Date	Mintage	VG	F	VF	XF	Unc
1695 TF	—	750	1,600	3,300	5,500	—
1696 TF	—	750	1,600	3,300	5,500	—

KM# 7 THALER

Silver **Ruler:** Wilhelm **Obv:** Three-line inscription AUS/BEU. THE/THAL surrounded by mining tools **Rev:** Fourteen-line inscription with date **Note:** Mining Thaler. Dav. #6015.

Date	Mintage	VG	F	VF	XF	Unc
1698 Rare	—	—	—	—	—	—

ANHALT-KOTHEN

Köthen has a checkered history after the patrimony of Heinrich the Fat in 1252. It was often ruled with other segments of the House of Anhalt. Founded as a separate line in 1603, became extinct in 1665 and passed to Plötzkau which changed the name to Köthen. It passed to Dessau after the death of Heinrich in 1847.

RULERS

Ludwig, 1603-1650
Wilhelm Ludwig, 1650-1665
Lebrecht von Plötzkau, 1665-1669
Emanuel von Plötzkau, 1669-1670
Emanuel Lebrecht, 1671-1704

PRINCIPALITY

REGULAR COINAGE

KM# 15 1/8 THALER

Silver **Ruler:** Wilhelm Ludwig **Subject:** Death of Wilhelm Ludwig **Obv:** Helmeted 9-fold arms, date **Obv. Legend:** 9-line inscription

Date	Mintage	VG	F	VF	XF	Unc
1665 HPK	—	—	450	950	1,850	—

KM# 1 1/3 THALER

Silver **Ruler:** Ludwig **Subject:** Death of Ludwig's Son, Ludwig **Obv:** Crowned 9-fold arms **Obv. Legend:** 9-line inscription, date in Roman numerals

Date	Mintage	VG	F	VF	XF	Unc
1624	—	450	850	1,600	3,000	—

KM# 7 1/3 THALER

Silver **Ruler:** Ludwig **Subject:** Death of Ludwig's Daughter, Louise Amona **Obv:** 9-fold arms **Obv. Legend:** 12-line inscription

Date	Mintage	VG	F	VF	XF	Unc
1625 AK	—	450	850	1,600	3,000	—

KM# 12 1/3 THALER

Silver **Ruler:** Ludwig **Subject:** Death of Ludwig **Obv:** Helmeted 9-fold arms **Obv. Legend:** 7-line inscription, date in Roman numerals

Date	Mintage	VG	F	VF	XF	Unc
1650 HPK	—	375	750	1,400	2,650	—

KM# 16 1/3 THALER

Silver **Ruler:** Wilhelm Ludwig **Subject:** Death of Wilhelm Ludwig **Obv:** Helmeted 9-fold arms, date **Obv. Legend:** 9-line inscription

Date	Mintage	VG	F	VF	XF	Unc
1665 HPK	—	450	850	1,600	3,000	—

KM# A13 1/2 THALER
14.4100 g., Silver **Ruler:** Ludwig **Subject:** Death of Ludwig **Obv:** Helmeted 9-fold arms **Rev:** 9-line inscription

Date	Mintage	VG	F	VF	XF	Unc
MDCL (1650) HPK	—	750	1,300	2,300	4,200	—

KM# 17 1/2 THALER
Silver **Ruler:** Wilhelm Ludwig **Subject:** Death of Wilhelm Ludwig **Note:** Similar to 1 Thaler, KM#19.

Date	Mintage	VG	F	VF	XF	Unc
1665 HPK	—	700	1,200	2,200	4,000	—

KM# 2 2/3 THALER
Silver **Ruler:** Ludwig **Subject:** Death of Ludwig's Son, Ludwig **Obv:** Helmeted 9-fold arms, date below **Obv. Legend:** 10-line inscription

Date	Mintage	VG	F	VF	XF	Unc
1624 Rare	—	—	—	—	—	—

KM# 3 2/3 THALER
Silver **Ruler:** Ludwig **Obv. Legend:** Imperial eagle with 12 in orb on breast, date

Date	Mintage	VG	F	VF	XF	Unc
1624 HS Rare	—	—	—	—	—	—

KM# 8 2/3 THALER
Silver **Ruler:** Ludwig **Subject:** Death of Ludwig's Daughter, Louise Amona **Obv:** Helmeted 9-fold arms **Obv. Legend:** 12-line inscription

Date	Mintage	VG	F	VF	XF	Unc
MDCXXV (1625) AK Rare	—	—	—	—	—	—

KM# 9 2/3 THALER
Silver **Ruler:** Ludwig **Subject:** Death of Ludwig's Wife, Amona Amalia von Bentheim **Obv:** Crowned arms of Bentheim-Tecklenburg and Anhalt **Rev. Legend:** 13-line inscription

Date	Mintage	VG	F	VF	XF	Unc
MDCXXV (1625)	—	—	—	2,500	4,250	—

KM# 13 2/3 THALER
Silver **Ruler:** Ludwig **Subject:** Death of Ludwig **Obv:** Helmeted ornate 9-fold arms **Obv. Legend:** AUF DEINEN WEGEN LEIT ... **Rev. Inscription:** LUDOVICUS • / SENIOR • DG: PRIN / ... **Note:** Similar to 1 Thaler, KM#14. Varieties exist.

Date	Mintage	VG	F	VF	XF	Unc
1650 HPK Rare	—	—	—	—	—	—

KM# 18 2/3 THALER
Silver **Ruler:** Wilhelm Ludwig **Subject:** Death of Wilhelm Ludwig **Obv:** Crowned supported arms **Obv. Legend:** D. G. AVGVSTVS LVDOVICVS PRINCEPS ANHALT **Rev:** Bear holding shield **Note:** Similar to 1 Thaler, KM#19.

Date	Mintage	VG	F	VF	XF	Unc
1665 HPK Rare	—	—	—	—	—	—

KM# 4 THALER
Silver **Ruler:** Ludwig **Subject:** Death of Ludwig's Son, Ludwig **Obv:** Helmeted nine-fold arms **Obv. Legend:** • MEIN • END • UND • LEBEN • **Rev. Inscription:** ...HO • XVI • REQIE • IN/SP(E)RE • MOR • **Note:** Dav. #6016. Varieties exist.

Date	Mintage	VG	F	VF	XF	Unc
1624	—	450	875	2,200	3,750	—

KM# 6 THALER
Silver **Ruler:** Ludwig **Obv:** Helmeted 9-fold arms **Rev:** Crowned imperial eagle with 24 in orb on breast, date **Note:** Dav. #6017.

Date	Mintage	VG	F	VF	XF	Unc
1624 HS Rare	—	—	—	—	—	—

KM# 5 THALER
Silver **Ruler:** Ludwig **Subject:** Death of Ludwig's son **Obv:** Helmeted 9-fold arms **Rev:** 10-line inscription **Note:** Klippe. Dav. #6016A.

Date	Mintage	VG	F	VF	XF	Unc
1624 Rare	—	—	—	—	—	—

KM# 10 THALER
Silver **Ruler:** Ludwig **Subject:** Death of Ludwig's Daughter, Louise Amona **Obv:** Helmeted 9-fold arms **Rev:** 12-line inscription **Note:** Dav. #6018. Varieties exist.

Date	Mintage	VG	F	VF	XF	Unc
MDCXXV (1625) AK Rare	—	—	—	—	—	—

KM# 11 THALER
Silver **Ruler:** Ludwig **Subject:** Death of Ludwig's Wife, Amona Amalia von Bentheim **Obv:** Crowned arms of Bentheim-Tecklenburg and Anhalt **Rev:** 13-line inscription **Note:** Dav. #6019. Varieties exist.

Date	Mintage	VG	F	VF	XF	Unc
MDCXXV (1625)	—	210	425	950	2,000	—

KM# 14 THALER
Silver **Ruler:** Ludwig **Subject:** Death of Ludwig **Obv:** Helmeted ornate nine-fold arms **Obv. Legend:** AUF DEINEN WEGEN LEIT;... **Rev. Inscription:** LUDOVICUS • / SENIOR • D G : PRIN/... **Note:** Dav. #6020. Varieties exist.

Date	Mintage	VG	F	VF	XF	Unc
MDCL (1650) HPK	—	180	350	850	1,800	3,000

KM# 19 THALER
Silver **Ruler:** Wilhelm Ludwig **Subject:** Death of Wilhelm Ludwig **Obv:** Helmeted ornate nine-fold arms **Obv. Legend:** LEHRE MICH DEIN WORT MEINER... **Rev. Inscription:** WILHELMUS / LUDOVICVS DG • PRIN / ... **Note:** Dav. #6022.

Date	Mintage	VG	F	VF	XF	Unc
1665 HPK	—	300	775	1,200	2,200	—

KM# 21 THALER
Silver **Ruler:** Emanuel Lebrecht **Subject:** Founding of the Lutheran Church **Obv:** Bust right wtih two-fold arms below **Rev:** Leaping horse right **Note:** Dav. #6024. Varieties exist.

Date	Mintage	VG	F	VF	XF	Unc
1694	—	900	2,000	3,900	6,600	—

KM# 20 2 THALER
Silver **Ruler:** Wilhelm Ludwig **Subject:** Death of Wilhelm Ludwig **Obv:** Helmeted ornate nine-fold arms **Obv. Legend:** LEHRE MICH DEIN WORT MEINER... **Rev. Inscription:** WILHELMUS / LUDOVICVS D G • PRIN / ... **Note:** Dav. #6021. Varieties exist.

Date	Mintage	VG	F	VF	XF	Unc
1665 HPK	—	1,150	1,800	3,000	5,400	—

KM# 22 2 THALER
Silver **Ruler:** Emanuel Lebrecht **Subject:** Founding of the Lutheran Church **Obv:** Bust right with two-fold arms below **Rev:** Leaping horse right **Note:** Dav. #6023.

Date	Mintage	VG	F	VF	XF	Unc
1694 Rare	—	—	—	—	—	—

PATTERNS

Including off metal strikes

KM#	Date	Mintage	Identification	Mkt Val
Pn1	1650 HPK	—	1/3 Thaler. Gold. KM#12.	—

ANHALT-PLOTZKAU

Main Plötzkau line founded during the new division of the Anhalt properties in 1603. Continued until 1665 when it inherited Köthen. Hereafter this branch known as Anhalt-Köthen.

RULERS
August, 1603-1653
Lebrecht, 1653-1665

MINT OFFICIALS' INITIALS

Initials	Date	Name
PS	1622	Peter Schroder

PRINCIPALITY

REGULAR COINAGE

KM# 4 DREIER (3 Pfennig)
1.0000 g., Silver, 17.7 mm. **Ruler:** August **Obv:** Helmet **Rev:** Imperial orb with value 3 divides date **Note:** Kipper Dreier. Varieties exist.

Date	Mintage	VG	F	VF	XF	Unc
1622 PS	—	55.00	110	225	425	—

KM# 5 GULDEN (2/3 Thaler)
Silver **Ruler:** August **Obv:** Half-length bust right **Rev:** Helmeted nine-fold arms, date

Date	Mintage	VG	F	VF	XF	Unc
1625 Rare	—	—	—	—	—	—
ND Rare	—	—	—	—	—	—

TRADE COINAGE

KM# 1 GOLDGULDEN
3.5000 g., 0.9860 Gold 0.1109 oz. AGW **Ruler:** August **Obv:** Phoenix rising from altar **Rev:** Fountain

Date	Mintage	VG	F	VF	XF	Unc
1615	—	—	1,250	2,750	6,500	—
1617	—	—	1,250	2,750	6,500	—
1620	—	—	1,250	2,750	6,500	—

KM# 2 2 GOLDGULDEN
7.0000 g., 0.9860 Gold 0.2219 oz. AGW **Ruler:** August **Obv:** Phoenix rising from altar **Rev:** Fountain

Date	Mintage	VG	F	VF	XF	Unc
1620	—	—	—	6,000	9,500	—

KM# 3 3 GOLDGULDEN
10.5000 g., 0.9860 Gold 0.3328 oz. AGW **Ruler:** August **Obv:** Phoenix rising from altar **Rev:** Fountain below portico, lamb with banner

Date	Mintage	VG	F	VF	XF	Unc
1620 Rare	—	—	—	—	—	—

Note: USB Auction 76, 1-08, XF realized $13,580

PATTERNS

Including off metal strikes

KM#	Date	Mintage	Identification	Mkt Val
Pn2	ND	—	Gulden. Gold. KM#5	—
Pn1	1625	—	Gulden. Gold. KM#5	—

Note: Dr. Busso Peus Auction 397, 11-08, XF realized $25,940

ANHALT-ZERBST

Zerbst was one of the major parts of the division of 1252. It was divided into Zerbst and Dessau in 1396 and absorbed Bernburg in 1486. Zerbst ceded to Dessau in 1508 and was given to the 4th son of Joachim Ernst in the division of 1603. It became extinct in 1793 and was divided between Dessau, Bernburg and Cothen.

RULERS
Rudolf III, 1603-1621
Johann VI, 1621-1667
Carl Wilhelm, 1667-1718

MINT OFFICIALS' INITIALS

Initials	Date	Name
AF	?	
CP	1674-90	Christoph Pflug
GW	1701	
IB	Ca.1664	Johann Bostelmann
IO	1663	Johann Otto
PS	1622	Peter Schroder in Köthen
SD	1675-76	Simon (Siegmund) Dannes in Harzgerode

PRINCIPALITY

REGULAR COINAGE

KM# 9 PFENNING
Silver **Ruler:** Johann VI **Obv:** 2-fold arms, date above **Note:** Uniface. Varieties exist.

Date	Mintage	Good	VG	F	VF	XF
1663 IO	—	20.00	35.00	65.00	130	265

KM# 10 3 PFENNIG (Dreier)
Silver **Ruler:** Johann VI **Obv:** Helmet **Rev:** Imperial orb with 3 divides date **Note:** Varieties exist.

Date	Mintage	Good	VG	F	VF	XF
1663 IO	—	16.00	35.00	55.00	110	175

KM# 24 3 PFENNIG (Dreier)
Silver **Ruler:** Carl Wilhelm **Rev:** Imperial orb with 3 divides date

Date	Mintage	VG	F	VF	XF	Unc
1676 AF	—	16.00	35.00	70.00	140	—
1676 CP	—	16.00	35.00	70.00	140	—

KM# 23 3 PFENNIG (Dreier)
Silver **Ruler:** Carl Wilhelm **Obv:** Oval 2-fold arms **Rev:** 2 branches form wreath with 3 that divides date **Note:** Varieties exist.

Date	Mintage	VG	F	VF	XF	Unc
1676 SD	—	20.00	40.00	70.00	140	—

KM# 5 GROSCHEN
Silver **Ruler:** Johann VI **Subject:** Under Regency of August von Plotzkau **Obv:** Helmeted 2-fold arms **Rev:** Imperial orb with 24, date **Note:** Kipper Groschen. Varieties exist.

Date	Mintage	VG	F	VF	XF	Unc
1622 PS	—	15.00	32.00	65.00	130	—

KM# 11 GROSCHEN
Silver **Ruler:** Johann VI **Obv:** Helmeted 2-fold arms **Rev:** Imperial orb with 24, date **Note:** Varieties exist.

Date	Mintage	VG	F	VF	XF	Unc
1663 IO	—	15.00	32.00	65.00	130	—
1664 IB	—	15.00	32.00	65.00	130	—

KM# 12 GROSCHEN
Silver **Ruler:** Johann VI **Subject:** Death of Johann **Obv:** Bust right **Rev:** Crowned arms, date **Note:** Varieties exist.

Date	Mintage	VG	F	VF	XF	Unc
1667	—	—	—	—	—	—

KM# 22 GROSCHEN
Silver **Ruler:** Carl Wilhelm **Obv:** Crowned arms **Rev:** Imperial orb with 3 divides date **Note:** Varieties exist.

Date	Mintage	VG	F	VF	XF	Unc
1675 CP	—	16.00	35.00	75.00	150	—
1676 CP	—	16.00	35.00	75.00	150	—
1676 SD	—	16.00	35.00	75.00	150	—
1677 CP	—	16.00	35.00	75.00	150	—
1677 SD	—	16.00	35.00	75.00	150	—

KM# 2 1/2 GULDEN (1/3 Thaler)
Silver **Ruler:** Rudolf III **Subject:** Death of Rudolf **Obv:** Angel holding crowned heart-shaped 2-fold arms **Rev:** 10-line inscription

Date	Mintage	VG	F	VF	XF	Unc
MDCXXI (1621) Rare	—	—	—	—	—	—

KM# 6 1/2 GULDEN (1/3 Thaler)
Silver **Ruler:** Johann VI **Subject:** Death of Johann's sister, Elisabeth **Obv:** 8-line inscription **Rev:** 8-line inscription, date in Roman numerals

Date	Mintage	VG	F	VF	XF	Unc
1639 Rare	—	—	—	—	—	—

KM# 28 GULDEN (2/3 Thaler)
Silver **Ruler:** Carl Wilhelm **Subject:** Death of Karl Wilhelm's mother, Sophie Auguste von Holstein-Gottorp **Note:** Similar to 1 Thaler, KM#29 but 10 line inscription. Varieties exist.

Date	Mintage	VG	F	VF	XF	Unc
1680 Rare	—	—	—	—	—	—

KM# 26 1/192 THALER
Silver **Ruler:** Carl Wilhelm **Obv:** 2-fold arms **Rev:** Value 192 in center, date

Date	Mintage	VG	F	VF	XF	Unc
(16)77	—	—	—	—	—	—

KM# 20 1/16 THALER
Silver **Ruler:** Carl Wilhelm **Obv:** Bust right in circle **Obv. Legend:** CARL WIL. P. A. C. A. D. S. B. I & K. **Rev:** Denomination in circle **Rev. Legend:** IN. DOMIN: FIDUCIA. HOSTRA. **Note:** Varieties exist.

Date	Mintage	VG	F	VF	XF	Unc
ND	—	65.00	125	225	425	—

KM# 13 1/4 THALER
Silver **Ruler:** Johann VI **Subject:** Death of Johann **Obv:** 1/2-length bust right **Rev:** Crowned arms, date

Date	Mintage	VG	F	VF	XF	Unc
1667	—	—	—	—	—	—

KM# 17 1/3 THALER
Silver **Ruler:** Carl Wilhelm **Note:** Varieties exist.

Date	Mintage	VG	F	VF	XF	Unc
1674 CP	—	500	900	1,600	3,200	—
1675 CP	—	500	900	1,600	3,200	—

KM# 14 1/2 THALER
Silver **Ruler:** Carl Wilhelm **Obv:** 1/2-length bust right **Rev:** Crowned arms, date

Date	Mintage	VG	F	VF	XF	Unc
1667 CP	—	—	—	—	—	—

KM# 18 2/3 THALER

Silver **Ruler:** Carl Wilhelm **Obv:** Bust right within inner circle, legend around **Rev:** Crowned 12-fold arms divide date, value below in circle, legend around

Date	Mintage	VG	F	VF	XF	Unc
1674 CP	—	55.00	100	200	400	—
1675 CP	—	55.00	100	200	400	—

KM# 19.1 2/3 THALER

Silver **Ruler:** Carl Wilhelm **Obv:** Portrait in inner circle **Rev:** Vertical date divided by arms

Date	Mintage	VG	F	VF	XF	Unc
1674 CP	—	70.00	120	235	475	—

KM# 19.2 2/3 THALER

Silver **Ruler:** Carl Wilhelm **Rev:** Date in legend divided by crown

Date	Mintage	VG	F	VF	XF	Unc
1674 CP	—	80.00	160	325	650	—

KM# 19.3 2/3 THALER

Silver **Ruler:** Carl Wilhelm **Obv:** Portrait divides legend at bottom, without inner circle, date in legend at 10 o'clock

Date	Mintage	VG	F	VF	XF	Unc
1675 CP	—	50.00	85.00	175	375	775

KM# 19.4 2/3 THALER

Silver **Ruler:** Carl Wilhelm **Rev:** Misaligned date divided by arms

Date	Mintage	VG	F	VF	XF	Unc
1676 CP	—	60.00	100	200	425	—

KM# 19.5 2/3 THALER

Silver **Ruler:** Carl Wilhelm **Rev:** Horizontal date divided by straight-sided arms

Date	Mintage	VG	F	VF	XF	Unc
1676 CP	—	60.00	100	200	425	—

KM# 19.6 2/3 THALER

Silver **Ruler:** Carl Wilhelm **Rev:** Horizontal date divided by concave-sided arms

Date	Mintage	VG	F	VF	XF	Unc
1677 CP	—	60.00	100	200	425	650
1678 CP	—	45.00	90.00	180	400	600
1679 CP	—	45.00	90.00	180	400	600

KM# 19.7 2/3 THALER

Silver **Ruler:** Carl Wilhelm **Rev:** Date divided by ornamented coat of arms **Note:** Varieties exist.

Date	Mintage	VG	F	VF	XF	Unc
1678 CP	—	45.00	90.00	180	400	600

KM# 1 THALER

Silver **Ruler:** Rudolf III **Obv:** Bust right **Rev:** Crowned 9-fold arms, date **Note:** Dav. #6025.

Date	Mintage	VG	F	VF	XF	Unc
1605 Rare	—	—	—	—	—	—

KM# 4 THALER

Silver **Ruler:** Rudolf III **Rev:** 10-line inscription **Note:** Dav. #6027.

Date	Mintage	VG	F	VF	XF	Unc
1621	—	325	775	1,550	2,600	—

KM# 3 THALER

Silver **Ruler:** Rudolf III **Subject:** Death of Rudolf **Note:** Similar to KM#4 but inscription ends: HOR: 13 1/2, date. Dav. #6026.

Date	Mintage	VG	F	VF	XF	Unc
1621	—	875	1,750	3,450	5,800	—

KM# 7 THALER

Silver **Ruler:** Johann VI **Subject:** Death of Johann's sister, Elisabeth **Obv:** 8-line inscription **Rev:** 8-line inscription **Note:** Dav. #6029.

Date	Mintage	VG	F	VF	XF	Unc
MDCXXXIX (1639) Rare	—	—	—	—	—	—

KM# 15 THALER

Silver **Ruler:** Johann VI **Subject:** Death of Johann **Note:** Dav. #6031. Varieties exist.

Date	Mintage	VG	F	VF	XF	Unc
MDCLXVII (1667)	200	575	1,400	2,900	4,600	—

KM# 25 THALER

Silver **Ruler:** Carl Wilhelm **Note:** Dav. #6032.

Date	Mintage	VG	F	VF	XF	Unc
1676 CP	—	1,150	2,300	4,600	7,800	—
ND Rare	—	—	—	—	—	—

KM# 27 THALER

Silver **Ruler:** Carl Wilhelm **Note:** Dav. #6033. Varieties exist.

Date	Mintage	VG	F	VF	XF	Unc
1677 CP	—	1,150	2,300	4,600	7,800	—
1678 CP	—	1,150	2,300	4,600	7,800	—

KM# 29 THALER

Silver **Ruler:** Carl Wilhelm **Subject:** Death of Karl Wilhelm's mother, Sophie Auguste von Holstein-Gottorp **Note:** Dav. #A6035. Varieties exist.

Date	Mintage	VG	F	VF	XF	Unc
1680	—	575	1,400	2,900	4,600	—

KM# 8 2 THALER

Silver **Ruler:** Johann VI **Subject:** Death of Johann's sister, Elisabeth **Obv:** 8-line inscription **Rev:** 8-line inscription **Note:** Dav. #6028.

Date	Mintage	VG	F	VF	XF	Unc
MDCXXXIX (1639) Rare	—	—	—	—	—	—

KM# 16 2 THALER

Silver **Ruler:** Johann VI **Subject:** Death of Johann **Obv:** Bust of Johann VI right in inner circle **Rev:** Helmeted arms **Note:** Dav. #6030.

Date	Mintage	VG	F	VF	XF	Unc
1667	—	900	1,800	3,600	6,000	—

TRADE COINAGE

KM# A21 4 DUCAT

14.0000 g., 0.9860 Gold 0.4438 oz. AGW **Ruler:** Carl Wilhelm **Obv:** Bust of Carl Wilhelm right **Rev:** Crowned arms divide date **Note:** Struck with 1/3 Thaler dies.

Date	Mintage	F	VF	XF	Unc	BU
1676 CP Rare	—	—	—	—	—	—

PATTERNS

Including off metal strikes

KM#	Date	Mintage	Identification	Mkt Val
Pn1	1667	—	Groschen. Gold. KM#12.	—
Pn2	1667	—	1/2 Thaler. Gold. KM#14.	—
Pn3	1674 CP	—	2/3 Thaler. Tin. KM#18.	400

ANHOLT

A town in Westphalia, Anholt is 7 miles (12km) west of Bocholt and very near the border with the Netherlands. It had early been the seat of a lordship, later a county, which passed into the possession of the Bronkhorst-Batenburg dynasty. A few coins were struck for local use in the late 16th century and again about the time of the Peace of Westphalia (1648-50).

RULERS

Dietrick V von Bronckhorst-Batenburg, 1585-1637

Leopold Philipp von Salm, 1637-1663

LORDSHIP

REGULAR COINAGE

KM# 1 STUBER

Copper **Ruler:** Leopold Philipp **Obv:** Crowned four-fold arms divide value 1-S, titles of Leopold Philipp **Rev:** Ornate cross **Note:** Varieties exist.

Date	Mintage	Good	VG	F	VF	XF
ND	—	50.00	95.00	190	375	600

KM# 2 6 STUBER

Copper **Ruler:** Leopold Philipp **Obv:** Crowned eight-fold arms divide value 6-S, titles of Leopold Philipp **Rev:** Rampant lion left holding sword and shield with Anholt arms (crowned column)

Date	Mintage	Good	VG	F	VF	XF
ND	—	250	450	850	1,600	—

TOWN

The town of Anholt in the lordship issued some coppers in the early 17th century.

REGULAR COINAGE

KM# 6 1/4 STUBER

Copper **Ruler:** Leopold Philipp **Obv:** Crowned rampant lion left in crowned shield between branches **Rev:** CI/VITAS/ANH in wreath

Date	Mintage	Good	VG	F	VF	XF
ND	—	60.00	120	275	500	—

KM# 7 1/4 STUBER

Copper **Ruler:** Leopold Philipp **Obv:** Lion right **Rev:** CVS/ANH in wreath

Date	Mintage	Good	VG	F	VF	XF
ND	—	35.00	75.00	150	325	—

PATTERNS

Including off metal strikes

KM#	Date	Mintage	Identification	Mkt Val
Pn1	ND	—	Stuber. Silver. KM#1	—

ANKLAM

Anklam was a town in the duchy of Pomerania (Pommern) situated on the Peene River, 5 miles (8 kilometers) from the Baltic Sea coast and 27 miles (45 kilometers) northeast of Neubrandenburg. It was founded as a fortress by the Slavs, but gained rights as an important town and became a member of the Hanseatic League. Anklam bought the right to produce its own coinage from the duke in 1325 and began striking a series of small silver coins. After the dissolution of the Pomeranian provincial diet in 1622, during the Kipper Period of the Thirty Years' War, Anklam countermarked the minor silver coinage which circulated from other nearby states in its local region. The town came under Swedish rule in 1648, but was taken by Brandenburg-Prussia in 1676. Except for a short period in the early 18th century, it remained part of Prussia.

ARMS

Arrowhead pointing upwards

REFERENCE

F = Gisela Föschner, ***Deutsche Münzen: Mittelalter bis Neuzeit, vol. I,*** Melsungen, 1984.

PROVINCIAL TOWN

COUNTERMARKED COINAGE

Countermark types:

Countermark #1: Arrowhead (city arms) divides 'A - 3' (=3 sundische Schilling)

Countermark #2: Arrowhead (city arms) only

KM# 5 3 SCHILLING (Sundische)

Silver **Note:** Countermark 1 on Pomerania-Wolgast 2 Schilling, KM#5. F#8.

CM Date	Host Date	Good	VG	F	VF	XF
ND(1622)	1609	40.00	80.00	160	325	—
ND(1622)	1610	40.00	80.00	160	325	—
ND(1622)	1611	40.00	80.00	160	325	—
ND(1622)	161Z	40.00	80.00	160	325	—
ND(1622)	1613	40.00	80.00	160	325	—
ND(1622)	1614	40.00	80.00	160	325	—
ND(1622)	1615	40.00	80.00	160	325	—
ND(1622)	1616	40.00	80.00	160	325	—
ND(1622)	1617	40.00	80.00	160	325	—
ND(1622)	1618	40.00	80.00	160	325	—
ND(1622)	1619	40.00	80.00	160	325	—
ND(1622)	16Z0	40.00	80.00	160	325	—
ND(1622)	16Z1	40.00	80.00	160	325	—

KM# 4 3 SCHILLING (Sundische)

Silver **Note:** Countermark 1 on Pomerania-Stettin 2 Schilling, KM#6.

CM Date	Host Date	Good	VG	F	VF	XF
ND(1622)	1618	40.00	80.00	160	325	—
ND(1622)	1619	40.00	80.00	160	325	—
ND(1622)	16Z0	40.00	80.00	160	325	—

KM# 6 3 SCHILLING (Sundische)

Silver, 23 mm. **Note:** Countermark 1 on Schaumburg-Pinneberg 1/16 Thaler, KM#100.

CM Date	Host Date	Good	VG	F	VF	XF
	(1)6Z0	—	—	—	—	—

KM# 1 3 SCHILLING (Sundische)

Silver **Note:** Countermark 1 on Brunswick-Harburg 1/16 Thaler, KM#14.1. F#9. Known also with additional countermark of Hamburg (city).

CM Date	Host Date	Good	VG	F	VF	XF
ND(1622)	16Z0	45.00	95.00	175	350	—
ND(1622)	16Z1	45.00	95.00	175	350	—
ND(1622)	ND(1620-1)	45.00	95.00	175	350	—

KM# 2 3 SCHILLING (Sundische)

Silver **Note:** Countermark 1 on Pomerania-Stettin 2 Schilling, KM#95. F#6.

CM Date	Host Date	Good	VG	F	VF	XF
ND(1622)	16Z1	40.00	80.00	160	325	—
ND(1622)	16ZZ	40.00	80.00	160	325	—
ND(1622)	16Z3	40.00	80.00	160	325	—
ND(1622)	16Z4	40.00	80.00	160	325	—
ND(1622)	16Z5	40.00	80.00	160	325	—
ND(1622)	16Z8	40.00	80.00	160	325	—
ND(1622)	16Z9	40.00	80.00	160	325	—

ARENBERG

A small principality with lands between the present-day Belgian border and the Rhine, west of Koblenz. The earliest lords of Arenberg are mentioned in the 12th century. The title and lands passed in marriage to the countship of Mark from where a new line of Arenberg lords began in the 14th century. At the end of the 15th century branch lines were founded in Sedan, Lumain and Roche-- fort. The male line of Arenberg became extinct in 1541 and passed by marriage to Ligne-Barbancon in 1547. The new line was raised to the rank of count in 1549, to prince in 1576 and to that of duke in 1644. The right to mint coins was granted in 1570. Philipp Franz issued Arenberg's only 17th century thaler. The lands on the left bank of the Rhine were lost to France in 1801 and the remaining possessions were mediatized in 1810.

RULERS

Karl, 1568-1616, prince 1576

Philipp Karl, 1616-1640

Philipp Franz, 1640-1674, duke 1644

Karl Eugen, 1674-1681

Philipp Karl Franz, 1681-1691

Leopold Philipp Karl, 1691-1754

Under regency of Maria Henrietta, 1691-1706

Alone, 1706-1754

MINTOFFICIALS' INITIALS

Initials	Date	Name
NL	Ca. 1668-80	Nikolaus Longerich in Dortmund

PRINCIPALITY

REGULAR COINAGE

KM# 4 8 HELLER
Silver **Ruler:** Karl Eugen **Obv:** Crowned arms **Rev:** Value in center, date in legend

Date	Mintage	VG	F	VF	XF	Unc
1676 NL	—	275	400	650	1,200	—

KM# 5 2 ALBUS
Silver **Ruler:** Karl Eugen **Obv:** Crowned arms **Rev:** 2/ALBVS/COLSCH/date **Note:** Varieties exist.

Date	Mintage	VG	F	VF	XF	Unc
1676	—	60.00	125	235	475	950
1676 NL	—	60.00	125	235	475	950
1677 NL	—	60.00	125	235	475	950

KM# 1 1/20 THALER
Silver **Ruler:** Karl **Obv:** Arms in ornately-shaped shield **Rev:** Christ child with imperial orb within sun with wavy rays, date between rays

Date	Mintage	VG	F	VF	XF	Unc
1601 Rare	—	—	—	—	—	—

KM# 3.1 2/3 THALER
Silver **Ruler:** Philipp Franz **Obv:** Crowned supported arms with value 2/3 below **Rev:** Eagle standing on rocks with wings spread looking over left wing at sun, date

Date	Mintage	VG	F	VF	XF	Unc
1670	—	—	—	—	—	—
Note: Reported, not confirmed						
1676 NL	—	—	—	—	—	—

KM# 3.2 2/3 THALER
Silver **Ruler:** Karl Eugen **Obv:** Value 60 below arms

Date	Mintage	VG	F	VF	XF	Unc
1676 NL Rare	—	—	—	—	—	—

KM# 6 2/3 THALER
Silver **Ruler:** Karl Eugen **Obv:** Bust right **Rev:** Crowned and supported arms, value 2/3 below, date

Date	Mintage	VG	F	VF	XF	Unc
1676 NL	—	475	850	1,500	2,400	—

KM# 2 THALER
Silver **Ruler:** Philipp Franz **Obv:** Crowned, helmeted and supported arms with date divided above **Rev:** Christ child seated with imperial orb in sun with rays **Note:** Dav. #6035.

Date	Mintage	VG	F	VF	XF	Unc
1641 Rare	—	—	—	—	—	—

AUGSBURG

Founded in the late 9th century in the city of Augsburg, the bishopric eventually extended as far as the Bavarian frontier on the north and east, to Tyrol on the south and to Upper Swabia on the west. The earliest episcopal coinage dates from the mid-10th century and issues continued through each of the next eight and one-half centuries. The bishopric was secularized in 1803 and was absorbed by Bavaria.

RULERS
Heinrich V von Knöringen, 1598-1646
Gustavus Adolphus, King of Sweden, 1632-1634
Sigmund Franz, Grossherzog von Österreich, 1646-1665
Johann Christof von Freiberg, 1665-1690
Alexander Sigismund von Pfalz-Neuburg,1690-1737

MINT OFFICIALS' INITIALS

Initials	Date	Name
2 horseshoes	1688-97	Johann Christoph Holeisen

REFERENCE
F = Gisela Förschner, ***Deutsche Münzen Mittelalter bis Neuzeit, v. 1 – Aachen bis Augsburg,*** Melsungen, 1984

BISHOPRIC

REGULAR COINAGE

KM# 7 1/2 KREUZER
Silver **Ruler:** Heinrich V **Obv:** Arms in baroque frame divide date, value 240 (1/240th Thaler) above **Note:** Kipper issue, uniface.

Date	Mintage	VG	F	VF	XF	Unc
1623	—	125	200	350	650	—

KM# 2 KREUZER
Copper **Ruler:** Heinrich V **Obv:** Arms divide date, HEA above **Note:** Kipper issue, uniface. Varieties exist.

Date	Mintage	Good	VG	F	VF	XF
1621	—	25.00	50.00	85.00	165	300
1622	—	25.00	50.00	85.00	165	300

KM# A1 KREUZER
Copper **Ruler:** Heinrich V **Obv:** Monogram HAE above arms divides value 1-20, (1/120th Thaler), date above **Note:** Kipper issue, uniface.

Date	Mintage	Good	VG	F	VF	XF
1621	—	25.00	50.00	85.00	165	300

KM# 3 KREUZER
Copper **Ruler:** Heinrich V **Obv:** Round arms wtih date above, all in wreath **Rev:** Value in 3 lines within wreath **Rev. Inscription:** I / KREIT / ZER **Note:** Kipper issue.

Date	Mintage	Good	VG	F	VF	XF
1622	—	16.00	35.00	65.00	130	250

KM# 4 KREUZER
Copper **Ruler:** Heinrich V **Obv:** Ornately-shaped arms, date above **Rev:** Value in 3-line inscription **Rev. Inscription:** I / KREIT / ZER **Note:** Kipper issue. Varieties exist.

Date	Mintage	Good	VG	F	VF	XF
1622	—	16.00	35.00	65.00	130	250

KM# 10 2 KREUZER
Silver **Ruler:** Johann Christof **Obv:** Two oval arms in baroque frame, date above **Rev:** Imperial eagle, orb with 2 on breast

Date	Mintage	VG	F	VF	XF	Unc
1681	—	—	—	—	—	—

KM# 12 2 KREUZER
Silver **Ruler:** Alexander Sigismund **Obv:** Crowned arms **Rev:** Oval shield with 2 in center, mitre above divides date

Date	Mintage	VG	F	VF	XF	Unc
1694	—	—	—	—	—	—

KM# 5 24 KREUZER
Silver **Ruler:** Heinrich V **Obv:** Arms in baroque frame, date **Rev:** Imperial eagle with 24 on breast **Note:** Kipper issue.

Date	Mintage	VG	F	VF	XF	Unc
1622	—	200	300	550	1,000	—

KM# 13 1/2 THALER
Silver **Ruler:** Alexander Sigismund **Obv:** Bust to right **Obv. Legend:** ALEX. SIG. D. G. - EPISC. AVGVST. **Rev:** Large crown above 2 adjacent oval arms in baroque frame, date below **Rev. Legend:** COM. PAL. RH. BA. CL. ET. MONT. DVX.

Date	Mintage	VG	F	VF	XF	Unc
1694 PHM	—	500	900	1,500	2,900	—

KM# 6 THALER
Silver **Ruler:** Heinrich V **Obv:** Madonna and child above oval 4-fold arms in baroque frame, date at end of legend **Obv. Legend:** + SVB + TVVM + PRÆSIDIVM + CONFVGIMVS + **Rev:** Crowned imperial eagle, shield of arms on breast **Rev. Legend:** FERDINANDVS + II + ROM ‡ IMP ‡ SEMP ‡ AVG ‡ **Note:** Dav. #5008.

Date	Mintage	VG	F	VF	XF	Unc
1622 Rare	—	—	—	—	—	—

KM# 11 THALER
Silver **Ruler:** Johann Christof **Obv:** Oval shield of 4-fold arms in baroque frame, mitre, crozier and sword handle above divide date **Obv. Legend:** + IOANN : CHRISTOPH : D: G: EPISCOP. AVGVSTAN9 S. R. I. PRINCEPS **Rev:** Madonna and child on crescent, surrounded by flames **Rev. Legend:** PVLCHRA VT LVNA + ELECTA VT SOL. **Note:** Dav. #5009.

Date	Mintage	VG	F	VF	XF	Unc
1681 PHM Rare	—	—	—	—	—	—

KM# 14 THALER
Silver **Ruler:** Alexander Sigismund **Obv:** Bust to right **Obv. Legend:** ALEX + SIG + D + G + - EPISC + AVGVST. **Rev:** Crown

above 2 adjacent oval shields of arms in baroque frame, date divided at bottom **Rev. Legend:** + COM + PAL + RH + BA + IV + CL + ET + MONT + DVX & + **Note:** Dav. #5010.

Date	Mintage	VG	F	VF	XF	Unc
1694 PHM	—	220	500	1,000	1,650	—

FREE CITY

Founded by the Romans about 15 B.C. and named Augusta Vindelicorum in honor of the Emperor Augustus, the city was the site of a German imperial mint for several centuries from about the year 1000. In 1276, Augsburg was made a free imperial city, but did not receive the right to strike its own coins until 1521. Earlier date issues were produced under the office of the Imperial Chamberlain, as listed above. Augsburg's coinage came to an end in 1805 and the city followed the bishopric into Bavarian envelopment in the following year.

MINT OFFICIALS' INITIALS

Initials	Date	Name
BS, or 3 corn ears	1630-38	Balthasar Schmidt
PHM, M, or *	1677-1718	Philipp Heinrich Muller, die-cutter
1 horseshoe	1638-68	Johann Bartholomaus Holeisen der Ältere
2 horseshoe	1668-97	Johann Christoph Holeisen
3 horseshoes	1639-68	Johann Bartholomaus Holeisen der Jüngere, assistant mintmaster

REFERENCE

F = Albert von Forster, ***Die Erzeugnisse der Stempelschneidekunst in Augsburg und Ph. H. Müller's nach meiner Sammlung beschrieben und die Augsburger Stadtmünzen,*** Leipzig, 1910.

REGULAR COINAGE

KM# 1 HELLER

Copper **Obv:** Pine cone divides date within wreath **Rev:** CCCC/XX (1/420th of a gulden) **Note:** Varieties exist.

Date	Mintage	Good	VG	F	VF	XF
1608	—	10.00	20.00	40.00	80.00	—
1609	—	10.00	20.00	40.00	80.00	—
1610	—	10.00	20.00	40.00	80.00	—
1612	—	10.00	20.00	40.00	80.00	—
1614	—	10.00	20.00	40.00	80.00	—
1615	—	10.00	20.00	40.00	80.00	—
1617	—	10.00	20.00	40.00	80.00	—
1620	—	10.00	20.00	40.00	80.00	—
1621	—	10.00	20.00	40.00	80.00	—
1622	—	10.00	20.00	40.00	80.00	—

KM# A23 HELLER

Copper **Obv:** Pine cone in cartouche divides date **Rev:** Cross in quatrefoil **Note:** Struck on rhomboid flan. Varieties exist.

Date	Mintage	VG	F	VF	XF	Unc
1624	—	6.00	20.00	40.00	80.00	—
1626	—	6.00	20.00	40.00	80.00	—
1629	—	6.00	20.00	40.00	80.00	—
1630	—	6.00	20.00	40.00	80.00	—
1631	—	6.00	20.00	40.00	80.00	—
1632	—	6.00	20.00	40.00	80.00	—
1633	—	6.00	20.00	40.00	80.00	—
1636	—	6.00	20.00	40.00	80.00	—
1645	—	6.00	20.00	40.00	80.00	—
1659	—	6.00	20.00	40.00	80.00	—
1660	—	6.00	20.00	40.00	80.00	—
1661	—	6.00	20.00	40.00	80.00	—
1664	—	6.00	20.00	40.00	80.00	—
1665	—	6.00	20.00	40.00	80.00	—
1666	—	6.00	20.00	40.00	80.00	—
1668	—	6.00	20.00	40.00	80.00	—
1669	—	6.00	20.00	40.00	80.00	—
1670	—	6.00	20.00	40.00	80.00	—
1671	—	6.00	20.00	40.00	80.00	—
1672	—	6.00	20.00	40.00	80.00	—
1673	—	6.00	20.00	40.00	80.00	—
1674	—	6.00	20.00	40.00	80.00	—
1676	—	6.00	20.00	40.00	80.00	—
1677	—	6.00	20.00	40.00	80.00	—
1678	—	6.00	20.00	40.00	80.00	—
1680	—	6.00	20.00	40.00	80.00	—
1681	—	6.00	20.00	40.00	80.00	—
1682	—	6.00	20.00	40.00	80.00	—
1683	—	6.00	20.00	40.00	80.00	—
1684	—	6.00	20.00	40.00	80.00	—
1685	—	6.00	20.00	40.00	80.00	—
1686	—	6.00	20.00	40.00	80.00	—
1687	—	6.00	20.00	40.00	80.00	—
1689	—	6.00	20.00	40.00	80.00	—
1690	—	6.00	20.00	40.00	80.00	—
1691	—	6.00	20.00	40.00	80.00	—
1692	—	6.00	20.00	40.00	80.00	—
1693	—	6.00	20.00	40.00	80.00	—
1694	—	6.00	20.00	40.00	80.00	—
1695	—	6.00	20.00	40.00	80.00	—
1697	—	6.00	20.00	40.00	80.00	—
1699	—	6.00	20.00	40.00	80.00	—
1700	—	6.00	20.00	40.00	80.00	—

KM# A7 2 HELLER

Copper **Obv:** Large A divides date within circle **Rev:** CC/X (1/210th of a gulden) in circle **Note:** Struck on square flan.

Date	Mintage	Good	VG	F	VF	XF
1621	—	9.00	16.00	35.00	70.00	140
1622	—	9.00	16.00	35.00	70.00	140

KM# A14 PFENNIG

Silver **Obv:** Letter A in circle **Rev:** Date in circle **Note:** Struck on square flan.

Date	Mintage	Good	VG	F	VF	XF
1623	—	10.00	18.00	35.00	65.00	130

KM# A24 PFENNIG

Silver **Obv:** Letter A in circle **Rev:** Date in clover shape **Note:** Klippe.

Date	Mintage	Good	VG	F	VF	XF
1624	—	14.00	27.00	55.00	110	225

KM# 9 1/2 KREUZER

Copper **Rev:** HALB/KREITZER in wreath

Date	Mintage	Good	VG	F	VF	XF
1621	—	12.00	20.00	40.00	80.00	150

KM# 8 1/2 KREUZER

Copper **Obv:** Pinecone divides date within wreath **Rev:** HALB/KREITZ/ER in wreath **Note:** Kipper 1/2 Kreuzer. Varieties exist.

Date	Mintage	Good	VG	F	VF	XF
1621	—	12.00	20.00	40.00	80.00	150

KM# A25 1/2 KREUZER

Silver **Note:** Uniface. Pinecone divides 1/2-K in trefoil, date divided by upper lobe of trefoil.

Date	Mintage	Good	VG	F	VF	XF
(16)24	—	12.00	20.00	40.00	80.00	150
(16)25	—	12.00	20.00	40.00	80.00	150

KM# 81 1/2 KREUZER

Silver **Obv:** Pine cone divides date within ornamented trefoil **Note:** Uniface. Varieties exist.

Date	Mintage	Good	VG	F	VF	XF
1643	—	12.00	20.00	40.00	80.00	150
1644	—	15.00	27.00	55.00	110	170
1651	—	12.00	20.00	40.00	80.00	150
1677	—	12.00	20.00	40.00	80.00	150
1696	—	12.00	20.00	40.00	80.00	150

KM# 111 1/2 KREUZER

Silver **Obv:** Pine cone divides date, branch on either side **Note:** Uniface.

Date	Mintage	Good	VG	F	VF	XF
1697	—	12.00	20.00	40.00	80.00	150

KM# 78 KREUZER

Silver **Rev:** Titles of Ferdinand III **Note:** Varieties exist.

Date	Mintage	Good	VG	F	VF	XF
1640	—	12.00	20.00	40.00	80.00	150
1641	—	12.00	20.00	40.00	80.00	150
1642	—	12.00	20.00	40.00	80.00	150
1643	—	12.00	20.00	40.00	80.00	150
1644	—	12.00	20.00	40.00	80.00	150
1645	—	12.00	20.00	40.00	80.00	150
1651	—	12.00	20.00	40.00	80.00	150

KM# 109 KREUZER

Silver **Obv:** Pine cone divides date within circle **Rev:** Crowned imperial eagle with 1 in orb circle, titles of Leopold **Note:** Varieties exist.

Date	Mintage	VG	F	VF	XF	Unc
1695	—	12.00	20.00	40.00	80.00	150
1696	—	12.00	20.00	40.00	80.00	150
1697	—	12.00	20.00	40.00	80.00	150

KM# A10 KREUZER

Silver **Obv:** Pine cone divides date within wreath **Rev:** I/KRE/ZER in wreath

Date	Mintage	Good	VG	F	VF	XF
1622	—	15.00	25.00	50.00	100	—

KM# A15 KREUZER

Copper **Obv:** Pine cone divides date within circle **Rev:** Crowned imperial eagle with 1 in orb on breast, titles of Ferdinand II **Note:** Varieties exist.

Date	Mintage	Good	VG	F	VF	XF
1623	—	8.00	15.00	35.00	75.00	—
1624	—	8.00	15.00	35.00	75.00	—
1625	—	8.00	15.00	35.00	75.00	—

KM# A5 2 KREUZER (1/2 Batzen)

Silver **Obv:** Pine cone divides date within circle **Rev:** Crowned imperial eagle with II in orb on breast, titles of Fedinand II

Date	Mintage	VG	F	VF	XF	Unc
1620	—	—	—	—	—	—

KM# A16 2 KREUZER (1/2 Batzen)

Silver **Obv:** Pine cone divides date within circle **Rev:** Crowned imperial eagle with 2 in orb on breast, titles of Ferdinand II **Note:** Varieties exist.

Date	Mintage	Good	VG	F	VF	XF
1623	—	14.00	30.00	60.00	85.00	125
1624	—	14.00	30.00	60.00	85.00	125
1625	—	14.00	30.00	60.00	85.00	125
1635	—	14.00	30.00	60.00	85.00	125
1636	—	14.00	30.00	60.00	85.00	125
1637	—	14.00	30.00	60.00	85.00	125

KM# A28 2 KREUZER (1/2 Batzen)

Silver **Obv:** Pine cone in cartouche divides date within circle **Rev:** Crowned imperial eagle with 2 in orb on breast, titles of Ferdinand II

Date	Mintage	VG	F	VF	XF	Unc
1625	—	16.00	35.00	65.00	130	—

KM# 72 2 KREUZER (1/2 Batzen)

Silver **Obv:** Pine cone divides date within circle **Rev:** Crowned imperial eagle with 2 in orb on breast, titles of Ferdinand III

Date	Mintage	VG	F	VF	XF	Unc
1637	—	—	—	—	—	—

KM# 88 2 KREUZER (1/2 Batzen)

Silver **Obv:** Pine cone divides date within circle **Rev:** Crowned imperial eagle with 2 in orb on breast, titles of Leopold I **Note:** Varieties exist.

Date	Mintage	VG	F	VF	XF	Unc
1660	—	16.00	30.00	65.00	130	—
1661	—	16.00	30.00	65.00	130	—
1665	—	16.00	30.00	65.00	130	—
1680	—	16.00	30.00	65.00	130	—
1681	—	16.00	30.00	65.00	130	—
1692	—	16.00	30.00	65.00	130	—
1694	—	16.00	30.00	65.00	130	—
1695	—	16.00	30.00	65.00	130	—

KM# 95 2 KREUZER (1/2 Batzen)

Silver **Obv:** Pine cone in oval shield **Rev:** STADT/MINTZ/date in circle

Date	Mintage	VG	F	VF	XF	Unc
1687	—	—	—	—	—	—

KM# 102 4 KREUZER (Batzen)

Silver **Obv:** Pine cone in oval baroque frame, date above **Rev:** Crowned imperial eagle, 4 in orb on breast, titles of Leopold I **Note:** Varieties exist.

Date	Mintage	VG	F	VF	XF	Unc
1694	—	16.00	35.00	70.00	140	—
1695	—	32.00	65.00	130	260	—

KM# A6 6 KREUZER

Silver **Obv:** Pine cone between two branches within circle, date in Roman numerals **Rev:** Crowned imperial eagle, VI in orb on breast, titles of Ferdinand II **Note:** Kipper issue.

Date	Mintage	VG	F	VF	XF	Unc
1620	—	—	—	—	—	—

KM# 11.1 6 KREUZER

Silver **Obv:** Pine cone in oval baroque frame divides date **Rev:** VI/STADT/MINTZ

Date	Mintage	VG	F	VF	XF	Unc
1622	—	—	—	—	—	—

KM# 11.2 6 KREUZER

Silver **Rev:** VI:K/STADT/MINTZ

Date	Mintage	VG	F	VF	XF	Unc
1622	—	80.00	160	325	650	—

KM# 12.1 15 KREUZER

Silver **Obv:** Pine cone divides date within oval baroque frame **Rev:** 3-line inscription **Rev. Inscription:** XV/STADT/MINTZ **Note:** Kipper issue.

Date	Mintage	VG	F	VF	XF	Unc
1622	—	—	—	—	—	—

KM# 12.2 15 KREUZER

Silver **Obv:** Pine cone divides date within oval baroque frame **Rev:** 3-line inscription **Rev. Inscription:** XV:K/STADT/MINTZ **Note:** Kipper issue.

Date	Mintage	VG	F	VF	XF	Unc
1622	—	—	—	—	—	—

KM# A13 30 KREUZER

Silver **Obv:** Pine cone divides date within oval baroque frame **Rev:** XXX/STADT/MINTZ

Date	Mintage	VG	F	VF	XF	Unc
1622	—	—	—	—	—	—

KM# A17 1/9 THALER

Silver **Obv:** Pine cone in cartouche, date in Roman numerals in margin **Rev:** Crowned imperial eagle, '1/9' in shield on breast, titles of Ferdinand II **Note:** Varieties exist.

Date	Mintage	Good	VG	F	VF	XF
1623	—	65.00	135	275	550	—
1624	—	65.00	135	275	550	—
1625	—	65.00	135	275	550	—

KM# 35 1/9 THALER

Silver **Obv:** Pine cone in oval baroque frame, date above **Rev:** Crowned eagle with wings spread, perched on shield with '1/9'

Date	Mintage	VG	F	VF	XF	Unc
1626	—	120	200	300	600	—

KM# 46 1/9 THALER

Silver **Obv:** Large pine cone above city view, Roman numeral date in cartouche below **Rev:** Crowned eagle with wings spread, value '1/9' on breast, titles of Ferdinand II

Date	Mintage	VG	F	VF	XF	Unc
MDCXXVII (1627)	—	60.00	120	235	475	—

KM# 57 1/9 THALER

Silver **Obv:** Large pine cone above city view, Roman numeral date in cartouche below **Rev:** Crowned imperial eagle with orb on breast, value '1/9' in oval below, titles of Ferdinand II **Note:** Similar to 1/6 Thaler, KM#58 but 1/9 on reverse.

Date	Mintage	VG	F	VF	XF	Unc
MDCXXVIII (1628)	—	75.00	150	275	550	—

KM# A18 1/6 THALER

Silver **Obv:** Pine cone between 2 branches within circle, date in Roman numerals in margin **Rev:** Crowned imperial eagle with '1/6' in oval on breast, titles of Ferdinand II **Note:** Varieties exist.

Date	Mintage	VG	F	VF	XF	Unc
MDCXXIII (1623)	—	120	235	475	—	—
MDCXXIIII (1624)	—	120	235	475	—	—
MDCXXV (1625)	—	120	235	475	—	—

KM# 36 1/6 THALER

Silver **Obv:** Pine cone in oval baroque frame, date above **Rev:** Crowned imperial eagle with wings spread, perched on shield with value 1/6, titles of Ferdinand II

Date	Mintage	VG	F	VF	XF	Unc
1626	—	—	—	—	—	—

KM# 47 1/6 THALER

Silver **Note:** Similar to 1/3 Thaler, KM#37, but value 1/6 on reverse.

Date	Mintage	VG	F	VF	XF	Unc
1627	—	80.00	160	325	650	—

KM# 58 1/6 THALER

Silver **Obv:** Large pine cone above city view, Roman numeral date in cartouche below **Rev:** Crowned imperial eagle with orb on breast, value '1/6' in small shield below, titles of Ferdinand II

Date	Mintage	VG	F	VF	XF	Unc
MDCXXVIII (1628)	—	65.00	135	275	550	—

KM# 59 1/6 THALER

Silver **Obv:** Pine cone within wreath held by hand above, rays from clouds, date **Rev:** Crowned imperial eagle with orb on breast, value '1/6' in small shield below, titles of Ferdinand II

Date	Mintage	VG	F	VF	XF	Unc
1628	—	150	225	375	775	—

KM# A19 1/4 THALER

Silver **Obv:** Pine cone in baroque frame, Roman numeral date in legend **Rev:** Crowned imperial eagle, value '1/4' in shield on breast, titles of Ferdinand II **Note:** Varieties exist.

Date	Mintage	VG	F	VF	XF	Unc
MDCXXIII (1623)	—	—	—	—	—	—

KM# 103 1/4 THALER

Silver **Obv:** Large pine cone on pedestal in oval baroque frame, Roman numeral date in margin at top **Rev:** Crowned imperial eagle, value '1/4' in shield on breast, titles of Leopold I

Date	Mintage	VG	F	VF	XF	Unc
MDCXCIV (1694)	—	65.00	135	275	550	—

KM# 112 1/4 THALER

Silver **Obv:** Pine cone on pedestal between two river gods, date below **Rev:** Bust of Leopold I to right

Date	Mintage	VG	F	VF	XF	Unc
1700	—	—	—	—	—	—

KM# 37 1/3 THALER

Silver **Obv:** Pine cone above city view, Roman numeral date in cartouche below **Rev:** Crowned eagle with spread wings, shield with '1/3' on breast, titles of Ferdinand II

Date	Mintage	VG	F	VF	XF	Unc
MDCXXVI (1626)	—	100	175	275	575	—

KM# 38 1/3 THALER

Silver **Obv:** Pine cone above city view, Roman numeral date in cartouche below **Rev:** Crowned eagle with spread wings, titles of Ferdinand II

Date	Mintage	VG	F	VF	XF	Unc
MDCXXVI (1626)	—	750	1,500	3,000	6,000	—

KM# 60 1/3 THALER

Silver **Obv:** Pine cone above city view, Roman numeral date in cartouche below **Rev:** Crowned eagle with spread wings, shield with '1/3' on breast, titles of Ferdinand II

Date	Mintage	VG	F	VF	XF	Unc
MDCXXVIII (1628)	—	—	—	—	—	—

KM# 82 1/3 THALER

Silver **Obv:** Pine cone above city view, date in cartouche below **Rev:** Crowned imperial eagle, shield with '1/3' on breast, titles of Ferdinand II

Date	Mintage	VG	F	VF	XF	Unc
1643	—	90.00	150	300	600	—

KM# A20 1/2 THALER

Silver **Obv:** Pine cone between two river gods, Roman numeral date below **Rev:** Bust of Ferdinand II to left above eagle

Date	Mintage	VG	F	VF	XF	Unc
MDCXXIII (1623)	—	525	950	1,600	3,000	—

KM# 48 1/2 THALER

Silver **Obv:** Pine cone held by angels above city view, Roman numeral date below in cartouche **Rev:** Crowned eagle with spread wings, titles of Ferdinand II

Date	Mintage	VG	F	VF	XF	Unc
MDCXXVII (1627)	—	200	325	600	1,150	—

KM# 64 1/2 THALER

Silver **Obv:** Pine cone within wreath held by hand above, rays from clouds **Rev:** Crowned imperial eagle, date divided by crown above, no indication of value

Date	Mintage	VG	F	VF	XF	Unc
1629	—	—	—	—	—	—

KM# 79 1/2 THALER

Silver **Obv:** Large pine cone in front of city view, on pedestal which divides date **Rev:** Armored bust to right, titles of Ferdinand III

Date	Mintage	VG	F	VF	XF	Unc
1640	—	125	200	325	650	—
1641	—	125	200	325	650	—
1643	—	60.00	100	190	385	—

KM# 104 1/2 THALER

Silver **Obv:** Pine cone on pedestal in oval baroque frame, Roman numeral date divided above **Rev:** Crowned imperial eagle, orb on breast, titles of Leopold I

Date	Mintage	VG	F	VF	XF	Unc
MDCLXXXXIV (1694)	—	100	200	360	725	—

KM# 39 2/3 THALER

Silver **Obv:** Pine cone in oval baroque frame, date above **Rev:** Crowned eagle with 2/3 in shield on breast, titles of Ferdinand II **Note:** Dav. 234.

Date	Mintage	VG	F	VF	XF	Unc
1626	—	—	—	—	—	—

KM# 40 2/3 THALER

Silver **Obv:** Pine cone in oval baroque frame, Roman numeral date above **Rev:** Crowned eagle with 2/3 in shield on breast, titles of Ferdinand II **Note:** Dav. 235.

Date	Mintage	VG	F	VF	XF	Unc
MDCXXVI (1626)	—	175	325	750	1,500	—
MDCXXVII (1627)	—	175	325	750	1,500	—
MDCXXVIII (1628)	—	175	325	750	1,500	—

KM# 49 2/3 THALER

Silver **Obv:** City view, pine cone above, Roman numeral date below **Rev:** Crowned eagle with 2/3 in shield on breast, titles of Ferdinand II **Note:** Dav. 236.

Date	Mintage	VG	F	VF	XF	Unc
MDCXXVII (1627)	—	200	375	775	1,550	—

KM# A21 THALER

Silver **Obv:** Pine cone between two river gods, Roman numeral date in cartouche below **Rev:** Half-length figure turned 3/4 to left above eagle with spread wings, titles of Ferdinand II **Note:** Varieties exist. Dav. #5011.

Date	Mintage	VG	F	VF	XF	Unc
MDCXXIII (1623)	—	500	925	1,500	—	—
MDCXXIV (1624)	—	500	925	1,500	—	—

KM# 26.1 THALER

Silver **Obv:** Enthroned Augusta holding pine cone and lance, Roman numeral date below **Rev:** Eagle with spread wings and open tail holding imperial orb and scepter, titles of Ferdinand II **Note:** Varieties exist. Dav. #5012.

Date	Mintage	VG	F	VF	XF	Unc
MDCXXIV (1624)	—	165	325	550	1,000	—

KM# 26.2 THALER

Silver **Obv:** Enthroned Augusta holding pine cone and lance, date in Roman numerals below in cartouche **Rev:** Eagle with spread wings and closed tail holding imperial orb and scepter, titles of Ferdinand II **Note:** Dav. #5013.

Date	Mintage	VG	F	VF	XF	Unc
MDCXXIV (1624)	—	165	325	550	1,000	—

KM# 27.1 THALER

Silver **Obv:** Large pine cone held by 2 angels above city view, Roman numeral date in cartouche below **Rev:** Crowned eagle with spread wings holding orb, sword and scepter in claws, titles of Ferdinand II **Note:** Dav. #5014.

Date	Mintage	VG	F	VF	XF	Unc
MDCXXIV (1624)	—	90.00	180	425	775	—
MDCXXV (1625)	—	90.00	180	425	775	—

KM# 29 THALER

Silver **Obv:** Small pine cone held by 2 angels above city view, Roman numeral date below in cartouche **Rev:** Crowned eagle with spread wings, holding orb, sword and scepter in claws, titles of Ferdinand II **Note:** Dav. #5017.

Date	Mintage	VG	F	VF	XF	Unc
MDCXXV (1625)	—	—	—	—	—	—

Rare

KM# 30.1 THALER

Silver **Obv:** St. Ulrich behind pine cone in oval baroque frame dividing date **Rev:** Crowned imperial eagle with orb on breast, titles of Ferdinand II **Note:** Dav. #5019.

Date	Mintage	VG	F	VF	XF	Unc
1625	—	95.00	195	450	825	—

KM# 30.2 THALER

Silver **Obv:** St. Ulrich behind pine cone in oval baroque frame dividing date, crozier breaks legend at ...ANV - S **Rev:** Crowned imperial eagle, orb on breast, titles of Ferdinand II **Note:** Dav. #5019A.

Date	Mintage	VG	F	VF	XF	Unc
1625	—	95.00	195	450	825	—

KM# 27.2 THALER

Silver **Obv:** Large pine cone held by 2 angels above city view, flower garlands below angels, Roman numeral date in cartouche at bottom **Rev:** Crowned eagle with spread wings, holding sword and scepter in claws, titles of Ferdinand II **Note:** Dav. #5024.

Date	Mintage	VG	F	VF	XF	Unc
MDCXXVI (1626)	—	95.00	195	450	825	1,950

KM# 27.3 THALER

Silver **Obv:** Large pine cone held by 2 angels above city view,

Roman numeral date in cartouche below **Rev:** Crowned eagle with spread wings, holding sword and scepter, titles of Ferdinand II **Note:** Dav. #5024A.

Date	Mintage	VG	F	VF	XF	Unc
MDCXXVI (1626)	—	95.00	195	450	825	1,950

KM# 41 THALER

Silver **Obv:** Pine cone in oval baroque frame, date divided at top **Rev:** Crowned eagle with spread wings, holding orb, sword and scepter in claws, titles of Ferdinand II **Note:** Dav. #5021.

Date	Mintage	VG	F	VF	XF	Unc
1626	—	85.00	165	350	650	—

KM# 27.4 THALER

Silver **Obv:** Large pine cone held by 2 angels above city view, Roman numeral date in cartouche below **Rev:** Crowned eagle with spread wings, holding sword and scepter, all in circle, titles of Ferdinand II **Note:** Dav. #5026.

Date	Mintage	VG	F	VF	XF	Unc
MDCXXVII (1627)	—	110	220	500	875	—

KM# 50 THALER

Silver **Obv:** Small pine cone held by 2 angels with garlands underneath, all above city view, Roman numeral date below in cartouche **Rev:** Crowned imperial eagle with orb on breast in circle, titles of Ferdinand II **Note:** Dav. #5028.

Date	Mintage	VG	F	VF	XF	Unc
MDCXXVII (1627)	—	100	200	450	825	—
MDCXXVIII (1628)	—	100	200	450	825	—

KM# 51 THALER

Silver **Obv:** Large pine cone in oval baroque frame, Roman numeral date in upper part of frame **Rev:** Crowned eagle with spread wing, holding orb, sword and scepter, no circle around, titles of Ferdinand II **Note:** Dav. #5029.

Date	Mintage	VG	F	VF	XF	Unc
MDCXXVII (1627)	—	110	240	525	925	—

KM# 52 THALER

Silver **Obv:** Large pine cone in oval baroque frame, Roman numeral date divided at top **Rev:** Crowned imperial eagle, orb on breast, titles of Ferdinand II **Note:** Dav. #5031.

Date	Mintage	VG	F	VF	XF	Unc
MDCXXVII (1627)	—	110	240	525	925	—

KM# 61 THALER

Silver **Obv:** Large pine cone in laurel and palm wreath held by hand from above right **Rev:** Crowned imperial eagle, orb on breast, date divided at top, titles of Ferdinand II **Note:** Varieties exist. Dav. #5035.

Date	Mintage	VG	F	VF	XF	Unc
1628	—	85.00	165	450	1,100	2,200
1629	—	85.00	165	450	1,100	2,200
1635	—	85.00	165	450	1,100	2,200

KM# A68 THALER

Silver **Ruler:** Gustavus Adolphus **Obv:** Armored bust turned 3/4 to right **Rev:** Crowned oval 4-fold arms with small central shield, in baroque frame, small pine cone arms below, date divided at top **Note:** Swedish occupation. Varieties exist. Dav. #4543.

Date	Mintage	VG	F	VF	XF	Unc
1632	—	195	350	600	1,050	—

KM# 74 THALER

Silver **Obv:** Large pine cone in laurel and palm wreath held by hand from upper right **Rev:** Crowned imperial eagle, orb on breast, date divided at top, titles of Ferdinand III **Note:** Dav. #5037.

Date	Mintage	VG	F	VF	XF	Unc
1638	—	165	325	550	1,000	—

KM# 77 THALER

Silver **Obv:** City view with large pine cone in center, divided date in cartouche below **Rev:** Laureate armored bust to right, titles of Ferdinand III **Note:** Dav. #5039.

Date	Mintage	VG	F	VF	XF	Unc
1639	—	70.00	140	275	500	1,000
1640	—	70.00	140	275	500	1,000
1641	—	70.00	140	275	500	1,000
1642	—	70.00	140	275	500	1,000
1643	—	70.00	140	275	500	1,000
1645	—	70.00	140	275	500	1,000

KM# 76 THALER

Silver **Obv:** City view with large pine cone in center, divided date in cartouche below **Rev:** Bust turned 3/4 to right, titles of Ferdinand III **Note:** Dav. #5038.

Date	Mintage	VG	F	VF	XF	Unc
1639	—	220	450	650	1,100	—

KM# 86 THALER

Silver **Obv:** City view with large pine cone in center, divided date in cartouche below **Rev:** Laureate armored bust to right, titles of Leopold I **Note:** Dav. #5040.

Date	Mintage	VG	F	VF	XF	Unc
1658	—	450	775	1,300	2,200	—

KM# 91.1 THALER

Silver **Obv:** Crowned imperial eagle, oval shield of arms on breast, small pine cone below tail, date at end of legend to left of crown **Obv. Legend:** MONETA. CAMBII. BONA - REIP. AVG. VINDELIC. **Rev:** Laureate armored bust to right **Rev. Legend:** IMP. CAES. LEOPOLDVS. P. F. GER. HVN. BOH. REX. **Note:** Dav. #5041.

Date	Mintage	VG	F	VF	XF	Unc
1676	—	775	1,300	2,200	3,850	—

KM# 91.2 THALER

Silver **Obv:** Crowned imperial eagle, oval shield of arms on breast, small pine cone below tail, date divided by crown at top **Obv. Legend:** AVGVSTA - VINDELICORVM. **Rev:** Small laureate armored bust to right **Rev. Legend:** IMP. CAES. LEOPOLDVS. P. F. GER. HVN. BOH. REX. **Note:** Dav. #5042.

Date	Mintage	VG	F	VF	XF	Unc
1676 Rare	—	—	—	—	—	—

KM# 91.3 THALER

Silver **Obv:** Crowned imperial eagle, oval shield of arms on breast, small pine cone below tail, date divided by crown at top **Obv. Legend:** AVGVSTA - VINDELICORVM. **Rev:** Large laureate armored bust to right **Rev. Legend:** IMP. CAES. LEOPOLDVS. P. F. GER. HVN. BOH. REX. **Note:** Dav. #5044.

Date	Mintage	VG	F	VF	XF	Unc
1681 Rare	—	—	—	—	—	—

KM# 96 THALER

Silver **Obv:** Pine cone on pedestal between palm and laurel branches, rays shining down, date at top **Obv. Legend:** AVGVSTA VIN - DELICORVM. **Rev:** Large laureate armored bust to right in double circle **Rev. Legend:** IMP. CAES. LEOPOLDVS. P. F. GER. HVN. BOH. REX. **Note:** Dav. #5045.

Date	Mintage	VG	F	VF	XF	Unc
1689 Rare	—	—	—	—	—	—

KM# 105.1 THALER

Silver **Obv:** Large pine cone on pedestal, 2 river gods at left and right, Roman numeral date in cartouche below **Obv. Legend:** AVGVSTA VINDELICORVM. **Rev:** Crowned imperial eagle, orb on breast **Rev. Legend:** LEOPOLDVS D. G. - ROM. IMP. S. AVG. **Note:** Dav. #5047.

Date	Mintage	VG	F	VF	XF	Unc
MDCXCIV (1694)	—	120	240	500	800	1,200

KM# 105.2 THALER

Silver **Obv:** Large pine cone on pedestal, 2 river gods at left and right, Neptune at left, Roman numeral date in cartouche below **Obv. Legend:** AVGVSTA VINDELICORVM. **Rev:** Crowned imperial eagle, orb on breast **Rev. Legend:** LEOPOLDVS D. G. - ROM. IMP. S. AVG. **Note:** Varieties exist. Dav. #5048.

Date	Mintage	VG	F	VF	XF	Unc
MDCXCIV (1694)	—	120	240	500	800	1,200

KM# 106 THALER

Silver **Obv:** Large pine cone in oval baroque frame, Roman numeral date divided above **Obv. Legend:** AVGVSTA VIN - DELICORVM. **Rev:** Crowned imperial eagle, orb on breast **Rev. Legend:** LEOPOLDVS D.G. ROM. IMP. S. AVG. **Note:** Dav. #5049.

Date	Mintage	VG	F	VF	XF	Unc
MDCXCIV (1694)	—	120	240	500	800	1,200

KM# 107 THALER

Silver **Obv:** Large pine cone on pedestal between laurel branches, Roman numeral date at end of legend **Obv. Legend:** AVGVSTA VINDELICORVM. **Rev:** Crowned imperial eagle, orb on breast **Rev. Legend:** LEOPOLDVS D.G. ROM. IMP. S. AVG. **Note:** Dav. #5050.

Date	Mintage	VG	F	VF	XF	Unc
MDCXCIV (1694) Rare	—	—	—	—	—	—

KM# 31 2 THALER

Silver **Obv:** Pine cone held by 2 angels above city view, Roman numeral date below **Rev:** Crowned eagle with spread wings, holding sword and scepter in claws, titles of Ferdinand II **Note:** Dav. #5016.

Date	Mintage	VG	F	VF	XF	Unc
MDCXXV (1625) Rare	—	—	—	—	—	—
MDCXXVI (1626) Rare	—	—	—	—	—	—

KM# 32.1 2 THALER

Silver **Obv:** Large pine cone held by 2 angels above city view, Roman numeral date in cartouche below **Rev:** Crowned eagle with spread wings, holding sword and scepter, titles of Ferdinand II **Note:** Dav. #5018.

Date	Mintage	VG	F	VF	XF	Unc
MDCXXV (1625)	—	2,000	3,300	4,500	7,800	—

KM# 32.2 2 THALER

Silver **Obv:** Large pine cone held by 2 angels above city view, Left angel holding lightning bolt, right angel holding laurel wreath, Roman numeral date in cartouche below **Rev:** Crowned eagle with spread wings, holding sword and scepter, titles of Ferdinand II **Note:** Dav. #A5023.

Date	Mintage	VG	F	VF	XF	Unc
MDCXXVI (1626)	—	2,000	3,300	4,500	7,800	—

KM# 42 2 THALER

Silver **Obv:** Large pine cone in oval baroque frame, date divided at top **Rev:** Crowned eagle with spread wings, holding orb, sword and scepter, titles of Ferdinand II **Note:** Dav. #5020.

Date	Mintage	VG	F	VF	XF	Unc
1626	—	1,800	3,000	4,200	7,200	—

KM# 32.3 2 THALER

Silver **Obv:** Pine cone held by 2 angels above city view, Roman numeral date in cartouche below **Rev:** Crowned eagle with spread wings, holding sword and scepter in claws, titles of Ferdinand II **Note:** Dav. #A5025.

Date	Mintage	VG	F	VF	XF	Unc
MDCXXVII (1627) Rare	—	—	—	—	—	—

KM# 53 2 THALER

Silver **Obv:** Pine cone held by 2 angels above city view, Roman numeral date in cartouche below **Rev:** Crowned imperial eagle, orb on breast, titles of Ferdinand II **Note:** Dav. #5027.

Date	Mintage	VG	F	VF	XF	Unc
MDCXXVII (1627)	—	1,800	3,000	4,200	7,200	—

KM# 54 2 THALER

Silver **Obv:** Large pine cone on pedestal in oval baroque frame, date divided at top **Rev:** Crowned imperial eagle, orb on breast, titles of Ferdinand II **Note:** Dav. #5030.

Date	Mintage	VG	F	VF	XF	Unc
1627	—	1,800	3,000	4,200	7,200	—

KM# 62 2 THALER

Silver **Obv:** Pine cone held by 2 angels above city view, Roman numeral date in cartouche below **Rev:** Crowned imperial eagle, titles of Ferdinand II **Note:** Dav. #5032.

Date	Mintage	VG	F	VF	XF	Unc
MDCXXVIII (1628) Rare	—	—	—	—	—	—

KM# 63 2 THALER

Silver **Obv:** Large pine cone on pedestal in oval baroque frame, Roman numeral date divided at top **Rev:** Crowned imperial eagle, orb on breast, titles of Ferdinand II **Note:** Dav. #5034.

Date	Mintage	VG	F	VF	XF	Unc
MDCXXVIII (1628)	—	1,200	2,100	3,300	5,400	—
MDCXXIX (1629)	—	1,200	2,100	3,300	5,400	—

KM# B68 2 THALER

Silver **Obv:** Bust of Gustav Adolph II right **Rev:** Similar to 1 thaler, KM#A68 **Note:** Swedish issue. Dav. #4542.

Date	Mintage	VG	F	VF	XF	Unc
1632 Unique	—	—	—	—	—	—

KM# 94 2 THALER

Silver **Obv:** Crowned imperial eagle, orb above oval shield of arms on breast, small pine cone below, crown divides date at top **Rev:** Laureate armored bust to right, titles of Leopold I **Note:** Dav. #5043.

Date	Mintage	VG	F	VF	XF	Unc
1681 Rare	—	—	—	—	—	—

KM# 108 2 THALER

Silver **Obv:** Large pine cone on pedestal supported by river gods, Roman numeral date in cartouche below **Rev:** Crowned imperial eagle, orb on breast, titles of Leopold I **Note:** Dav. #5046.

Date	Mintage	VG	F	VF	XF	Unc
MDCXCIV (1694) Rare	—	—	—	—	—	—

KM# 33 3 THALER

Silver **Obv:** Small pine cone held by 2 angels above large city view, Roman numeral date in cartouche below **Rev:** Crowned eagle with spread wings, holding sword and scepter in claws, titles of Ferdinand II **Note:** Dav. #A5015.

Date	Mintage	VG	F	VF	XF	Unc
MDCXXV (1625) Rare	—	—	—	—	—	—

KM# 43 3 THALER

Silver **Obv:** Large pine cone in oval baroque frame, date divided above **Rev:** Crowned eagle with spread wings, holding orb, sword and scepter in claws, titles of Ferdinand II **Note:** Dav. #5020.

Date	Mintage	VG	F	VF	XF	Unc
1626 Rare	—	—	—	—	—	—

KM# 55 3 THALER

Silver **Obv:** Large pine cone held by 2 angels above small city view, Roman numeral date in cartouche below **Rev:** Crowned eagle with spread wings, holding sword and scepter in claws, titles of Ferdinand II **Note:** Dav. #5025.

Date	Mintage	VG	F	VF	XF	Unc
MDCXXVII (1627) Rare	—	—	—	—	—	—

KM# 65 3 THALER

Silver **Obv:** Large pine cone in oval baroque frame, Roman numeral date divided above **Rev:** Crowned imperial eagle, orb on breast, titles of Ferdinand II **Note:** Dav. #5033.

Date	Mintage	VG	F	VF	XF	Unc
MDCXXIX (1629) Rare	—	—	—	—	—	—

KM# C68 3 THALER

Silver **Obv:** Bust of Gustav Adolph II right **Rev:** Similar to 1 Thaler, KM#A68

Date	Mintage	VG	F	VF	XF	Unc
1632 Unique	—	—	—	—	—	—

KM# 34 4 THALER

Silver **Obv:** Small pine cone held by 2 angels above large city view, Roman numeral date in cartouche below **Rev:** CRowned eagle with spread wings, holding sword and scepter in claws, titles of Ferdinand II **Note:** Dav. #5015.

Date	Mintage	VG	F	VF	XF	Unc
MDCXXV (1625) Rare	—	—	—	—	—	—
MDCXXVI (1626) Rare	—	—	—	—	—	—

KM# 44 4 THALER

Silver **Obv:** Large pine cone held by 2 angels above large city view, Roman numeral date in cartouche below **Rev:** Crowned eagle with spread wings, holding sword and scepter in claws, titles of Ferdinand II **Note:** Dav. #5023.

Date	Mintage	VG	F	VF	XF	Unc
MDCXXVI (1626) Rare	—	—	—	—	—	—

TRADE COINAGE

KM# A2 GOLDGULDEN

3.5000 g., 0.9860 Gold 0.1109 oz. AGW **Obv:** Pine cone on pedestal within circle, Roman numeral date in exergue **Obv. Legend:** AVGVSTA. VINDELIC. **Rev:** Crowned imperial eagle within circle with shield of arms on breast **Rev. Legend:** RVDOLPHVS. II. - ROM. IMP. P. F. AVG. **Note:** Fr. 48.

Date	Mintage	VG	F	VF	XF	Unc
MDCIX (1609)	—	1,750	3,500	5,500	10,000	—

KM# A3 GOLDGULDEN

3.5000 g., 0.9860 Gold 0.1109 oz. AGW **Obv:** Seated female figure left **Rev:** Crowned imperial eagle, titles of Matthias II **Note:** Fr. 50.

Date	Mintage	VG	F	VF	XF	Unc
1613	—	750	1,500	3,000	5,500	—

KM# A4 GOLDGULDEN

3.5000 g., 0.9860 Gold 0.1109 oz. AGW **Obv:** Pine cone within circle **Rev:** Crowned bust of Ferdinand II to right **Note:** Fr. 51.

Date	Mintage	VG	F	VF	XF	Unc
1619	—	1,500	3,500	7,000	12,500	—

KM# A22 GOLDGULDEN

3.5000 g., 0.9860 Gold 0.1109 oz. AGW **Obv:** Pine cone in cartouche **Rev:** Crowned imperial eagle within circle, titles of Ferdinand II **Note:** Fr. 52.

Date	Mintage	VG	F	VF	XF	Unc
1623	—	1,150	2,250	4,500	7,500	—
1628	—	1,150	2,250	4,500	7,500	—

KM# 56 GOLDGULDEN

3.5000 g., 0.9860 Gold 0.1109 oz. AGW **Obv:** St. Afra and St. Ulric standing **Rev:** Crowned imperial eagle, titles of Ferdinand II **Note:** Fr. 56.

Date	Mintage	VG	F	VF	XF	Unc
1627	—	1,750	3,500	5,500	10,000	—
1628	—	1,750	3,500	5,500	10,000	—

KM# 66 DUCAT

3.5000 g., 0.9860 Gold 0.1109 oz. AGW **Obv:** Full-length facing figure of St. Afra, large pine cone at right **Obv. Legend:** S. AFRAE. PROTECT. - AVGVSTA. VINDEL. **Rev:** Crowned imperial eagle, shield of arms on breast, date at end of legend **Rev. Legend:** FERDINAND. II. D.G. ROM. IMP. S. AVG. P. F. **Note:** Fr. 59.

Date	Mintage	VG	F	VF	XF	Unc
1629	—	200	300	675	1,650	—
1630 BS	—	200	300	675	1,650	—
1631	—	200	300	675	1,650	—
1634	—	200	300	675	1,650	—
1635 BS	—	200	300	675	1,650	—
1636 BS	—	200	300	675	1,650	—
1637 BS	—	200	300	675	1,650	—

KM# 68 DUCAT

3.5000 g., 0.9860 Gold 0.1109 oz. AGW **Obv:** Bust of Gustuvus Adolphus turned 3/4 to right **Rev:** Crowned shield of oval 4-fold arms,with central shield, in baroque frame, date divided by bottom of crown **Note:** Fr. 112.

Date	Mintage	VG	F	VF	XF	Unc
1632	—	1,000	2,000	4,000	6,500	—
1633	—	1,000	2,000	4,000	6,500	—

KM# 71 DUCAT

3.5000 g., 0.9860 Gold 0.1109 oz. AGW **Obv:** Bust of Gustavus Adolphus to right **Rev:** Crowned shield of oval 4-fold arms,with central shield, in baroque frame, date divided by bottom of crown **Note:** Fr. 113.

Date	Mintage	VG	F	VF	XF	Unc
1634	—	350	650	1,650	3,000	—
1635	—	350	650	1,650	3,000	—

KM# 73 DUCAT

3.5000 g., 0.9860 Gold 0.1109 oz. AGW **Obv:** Pine cone in oval baroque frame, date divided above **Obv. Legend:** AVGVSTA. VIN - DELICORVM **Rev:** Bust turned 3/4 to right **Rev. Legend:** FERDINAND. III. D.G. R. I. S. A. P. F. **Note:** Fr. 61.

Date	Mintage	VG	F	VF	XF	Unc
1637	—	225	325	700	1,750	—
1638	—	225	325	700	1,750	—
1639	—	225	325	700	1,750	—
1640	—	225	325	700	1,750	—
1641	—	225	325	700	1,750	—
1642	—	225	325	700	1,750	—
1643	—	225	325	700	1,750	—

KM# 75 DUCAT

3.5000 g., 0.9860 Gold 0.1109 oz. AGW **Obv:** Full-length facing figure of St. Afra, pine cone at right **Obv. Legend:** S. AFRA. PROTECT. - AVGVSTA. VINDEL. **Rev:** Crowned imperial eagle, shield of arms on breast, date at end of legend **Rev. Legend:** FERDINAND. III. D.G. ROM. IMP. S. AVG. P. F. **Note:** Fr. 63.

Date	Mintage	VG	F	VF	XF	Unc
1637	—	275	375	725	1,850	—
1638	—	275	375	725	1,850	—
1639	—	275	375	725	1,850	—
1642	—	275	375	725	1,850	—

KM# 83 DUCAT

3.5000 g., 0.9860 Gold 0.1109 oz. AGW **Obv:** Pine cone in oval baroque frame, date divided at top **Obv. Legend:** AVGVSTA. VIN - DELICORVM. **Rev:** Laureate armored bust to right **Rev. Legend:** FERDINAND. III. D.G. R. I. S. A. P. F. **Note:** Fr. 61.

Date	Mintage	VG	F	VF	XF	Unc
1645	—	225	325	775	1,400	2,750
1646	—	225	325	775	1,400	2,750

Date	Mintage	VG	F	VF	XF	Unc
1647	—	225	325	775	1,400	2,750
1648	—	225	325	775	1,400	2,750
1649	—	225	325	775	1,400	2,750
1650	—	225	325	775	1,400	2,750
1651	—	225	325	775	1,400	2,750
1652	—	225	325	775	1,400	2,750
1653	—	225	325	775	1,400	2,750
1654	—	225	325	775	1,400	2,750
1655	—	225	325	775	1,400	2,750
1656	—	225	325	775	1,400	2,750
1657	—	225	325	775	1,400	2,750

KM# 84 DUCAT

3.5000 g., 0.9860 Gold 0.1109 oz. AGW **Subject:** Coronation of Ferdinand IV as King of the Romans in Augsburg **Obv:** Eight-line inscription with date in wreath **Rev:** Crowned imperial eagle on column, trophies below **Note:** Fr. 64.

Date	Mintage	VG	F	VF	XF	Unc
1653	—	325	525	825	2,000	—

KM# 87 DUCAT

3.5000 g., 0.9860 Gold 0.1109 oz. AGW **Obv:** Pine cone in oval baroque frame, date divided at top **Obv. Legend:** AVGVSTA. VIN - DELICORVM. **Rev:** Laureate armored bust to right **Rev. Legend:** LEOPOLD(9)(VS). D.G. R. I. S. A. P. F. **Note:** Fr. 67. Varieties exist.

Date	Mintage	VG	F	VF	XF	Unc
1658	—	325	450	825	1,750	—
1659	—	325	450	825	1,750	—
1660	—	325	450	825	1,750	—
1661	—	325	450	825	1,750	—
1662	—	325	450	825	1,750	—
1663	—	325	450	825	1,750	—
1664	—	325	450	825	1,750	—
1667	—	325	450	825	1,750	—
1669	—	325	450	825	1,750	—
1671	—	325	450	825	1,750	—
1672	—	325	450	825	1,750	—
1673	—	325	450	825	1,750	—
1675	—	325	450	825	1,750	—
1677	—	325	450	825	1,750	—

KM# 92 DUCAT

3.5000 g., 0.9860 Gold 0.1109 oz. AGW **Obv:** Pine cone on pedestal in wreath, date at end of legend **Obv. Legend:** AVGVSTA. VINDELICORVM. **Rev:** Laureate armored bust to right **Rev. Legend:** LEOPOLDVS. D.G. R. I. S. A. P. F. **Note:** Fr. 68.

Date	Mintage	VG	F	VF	XF	Unc
1677	—	325	550	850	1,950	—
1681	—	325	550	850	1,950	—
1682	—	325	550	850	1,950	—
1684	—	325	550	850	1,950	—
1685	—	325	550	850	1,950	—
1686	—	325	550	850	1,950	—
1687	—	325	550	850	1,950	—
1688	—	325	550	850	1,950	—
1689	—	325	550	850	1,950	—
1691	—	325	550	850	1,950	—
1692	—	325	550	850	1,950	—

KM# 97 DUCAT

3.5000 g., 0.9860 Gold 0.1109 oz. AGW **Obv:** Laureate armored bust to right, small pine cone flanked by two horseshoes at bottom **Obv. Legend:** LEOPOLDVS. AVG. - IMP. CÆSAR. P. F. **Rev:** Bust of Eleonora Magdalene to left **Note:** Fr. 71.

Date	Mintage	VG	F	VF	XF	Unc
1689	—	275	400	700	1,800	—

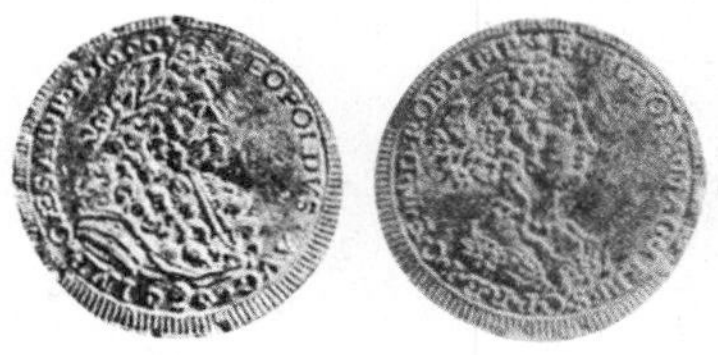

KM# 98 DUCAT

3.5000 g., 0.9860 Gold 0.1109 oz. AGW **Obv:** Laureate armored bust to right, small pine cone flanked by two horseshoes at bottom **Obv. Legend:** LEOPOLDVS. AVG. - IMP. CÆSAR. P. F. **Rev:** Bust of Eleonora Magdalene to right **Note:** Fr. 71.

Date	Mintage	VG	F	VF	XF	Unc
1690	—	275	400	700	1,800	—

KM# 99 DUCAT

3.5000 g., 0.9860 Gold 0.1109 oz. AGW **Subject:** Coronation of Josef (I) as King of Hungary **Obv:** Hungarian crown between 2 branches, 3-line inscription with Roman numeral date below, small pine cone between 2 horseshoes at bottom **Obv. Inscription:** CORONAT. / XXVI IANV / MDCXC. **Rev:** Bust to right **Note:** Fr. 78.

Date	Mintage	VG	F	VF	XF	Unc
MDCXC (1690)	—	375	600	900	2,150	—

KM# 110 DUCAT

3.5000 g., 0.9860 Gold 0.1109 oz. AGW **Obv:** Pine cone between river gods, date divided at bottom **Obv. Legend:** AVGVSTA VINDELICOR. **Rev:** Bust to right **Rev. Legend:** LEOPOLDVS - D.G. R. I. S. A. P. **Note:** Fr. 75.

Date	Mintage	VG	F	VF	XF	Unc
1695	—	325	550	950	2,250	—
1697	—	325	550	950	2,250	—
1699	—	325	550	950	2,250	—

KM# 45 2 DUCAT

7.0000 g., 0.9860 Gold 0.2219 oz. AGW **Obv:** St. Afra and St. Ulric standing **Rev:** Crowned imperial eagle in inner circle, titles of Ferdinand II

Date	Mintage	VG	F	VF	XF	Unc
1626	—	2,500	4,500	8,500	14,500	—

KM# 69 2 DUCAT

7.0000 g., 0.9860 Gold 0.2219 oz. AGW **Obv:** Conjoined busts of Gustavus Adolphus and Maria Eleonora right

Date	Mintage	VG	F	VF	XF	Unc
1632	—	1,500	3,000	6,500	11,500	—

KM# 80 2 DUCAT

7.0000 g., 0.9860 Gold 0.2219 oz. AGW **Obv:** Pine cone in oval baroque frame, date divided at top **Rev:** Laureate armored bust to right, titles of Ferdinand III **Note:** Fr. 60.

Date	Mintage	VG	F	VF	XF	Unc
1641	—	750	1,800	3,500	8,000	—
1643	—	750	1,800	3,500	8,000	—

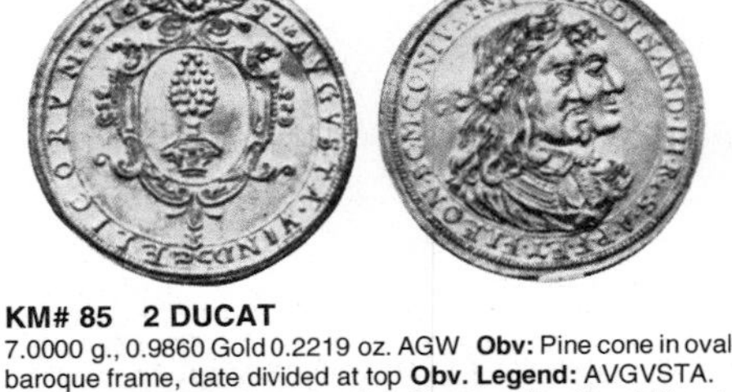

KM# 85 2 DUCAT

7.0000 g., 0.9860 Gold 0.2219 oz. AGW **Obv:** Pine cone in oval baroque frame, date divided at top **Obv. Legend:** AVGVSTA. VIND - ELICORVM. **Rev:** Accolated busts of Ferdinand III and Eleanor to right **Rev. Legend:** FERDINAND. III. R. I. S. A. P. F. ET. ELEON. E. C. M. CONIVA. IMP. **Note:** Fr. 62.

Date	Mintage	VG	F	VF	XF	Unc
1657	—	700	1,500	3,000	6,750	—

KM# 89 2 DUCAT

7.0000 g., 0.9860 Gold 0.2219 oz. AGW **Obv:** Pine cone in oval baroque frame, date divided at upper left and right in margin **Obv. Legend:** AVGVSTA. VIN - DELICORVM. **Rev:** Accolated busts of Leopold and Margaret to left **Rev. Legend:** LEOPOLDVS. D.G. R. I. S. A. MARGARETA. IMPERATRIX. **Note:** Fr. 70.

Date	Mintage	VG	F	VF	XF	Unc
1672	—	650	1,250	2,500	4,500	7,750

KM# 100 2 DUCAT

7.0000 g., 0.9860 Gold 0.2219 oz. AGW **Obv:** Pine cone in oval baroque frame, date divided above **Rev:** Accolated busts of Leopold and Eleanor to right **Note:** Fr. 73.

Date	Mintage	VG	F	VF	XF	Unc
1691	—	1,250	2,500	5,000	8,500	—

KM# 113 2 DUCAT

7.0000 g., 0.9860 Gold 0.2219 oz. AGW **Obv:** Pine cone between 2 river gods **Rev:** Laureate bust of Leopold to right **Note:** Fr. 74.

Date	Mintage	VG	F	VF	XF	Unc
1700 Rare	—	—	—	—	—	—

KM# 70 3 DUCAT

10.5000 g., 0.9860 Gold 0.3328 oz. AGW **Obv:** Accolated busts of Gustav Adolphus and Maria Eleanore to right **Rev:** Crown above 2 oval shields of arms in baroque frame, date in cartouche below **Note:** Fr. 110.

Date	Mintage	VG	F	VF	XF	Unc
1632 Rare	—	—	—	—	—	—

KM# 90 3 DUCAT

10.5000 g., 0.9860 Gold 0.3328 oz. AGW **Obv:** Pine cone in cartouche, date above **Rev:** Accolated busts of Leopold I and Margaret to right **Note:** Fr. 69.

Date	Mintage	VG	F	VF	XF	Unc
1672	—	—	—	12,500	20,000	—

KM# 101 3 DUCAT

10.5000 g., 0.9860 Gold 0.3328 oz. AGW **Obv:** Pine cone in baroque frame, date above **Rev:** Accolated busts of Leopold I and Eleanore to right **Note:** Fr. 72.

Date	Mintage	VG	F	VF	XF	Unc
1691	—	—	—	12,500	20,000	—

KM# 67 4 DUCAT

14.0000 g., 0.9860 Gold 0.4438 oz. AGW **Obv:** Full-length facing figure of St. Afra, large pine cone at right **Rev:** Crowned imperial eagle, titles of Ferdinand II **Note:** Fr. 57.

Date	Mintage	VG	F	VF	XF	Unc
1630 Rare	—	—	—	—	—	—

KM# A33 10 DUCAT

35.0000 g., 0.9860 Gold 1.1095 oz. AGW **Obv:** City view, date below **Rev:** Crowned imperial eagle holding sword and scepter **Note:** Fr. 53.

Date	Mintage	VG	F	VF	XF	Unc
1625 Rare	—	—	—	—	—	—

KM# A64 10 DUCAT

35.0000 g., 0.9860 Gold 1.1095 oz. AGW **Obv:** Large pine cone in laurel and palm wreath held by hand from upper right **Obv. Legend:** AVGVSTA. VIN - DELICORVM. **Rev:** Crowned imperial eagle, orb on breast, date divided at top **Rev. Legend:** IMP. CÆS. FERD. II. P. F. GER. HVN. BOH. REX. **Note:** Struck with Thaler dies, KM#61. Fr. 55.

Date	Mintage	VG	F	VF	XF	Unc
1629 Rare	—	—	—	—	—	—

PATTERNS

Including off metal strikes

KM#	Date	Mintage	Identification	Mkt Val
PnA1	1608	—	Heller. Silver. KM#1	—
Pn2	1608	—	Heller. Gold. KM#1	—
Pn3	1609	—	Heller. Silver. KM#1	—
Pn4	1615	—	Heller. Silver. KM#1	—
Pn5	1621	—	2 Heller. Silver. KM#7	—
Pn6	1653	—	Ducat. Silver. KM#84	—
Pn7	1690	—	Ducat. Silver. KM#99	—

BADEN

The earliest rulers of Baden, in the southwestern part of Germany along the Rhine, descended from the dukes of Zähringen in the late 11th century. The first division of the territory occurred in 1190, when separate lines of margraves were established in Baden and in Hachberg. Immediately prior to its extinction in 1418, Hachberg was sold back to Baden, which underwent several minor divisions itself during the next century. Baden acquired most of the Countship of Sponheim from Electoral Pfalz near the end of the 15th century. In 1515, the most significant division of the patrimony took place, in which the Baden-Baden and Baden-(Pforzheim) Durlach lines were established.

ARMS

Baden – diagonal bar from upper left to lower right
Sponheim – checkerboard

The usual arrangement is 4-fold arms of Baden quartered with Sponheim.

REFERENCE

W = Friedrich Wielandt, ***Badische Münzen- und Geldgeschichte***, 3rd edn., Karlsruhe, 1979.

BADEN-BADEN LINE

Margraviate

Established in 1515 by Christoph I's eldest son, Bernhard III. This branch was often at odds with the rulers of the younger Baden-Durlach line because of religious differences resulting from the Protestant Reformation. When Baden-Baden finally became extinct in 1771, all lands and titles reverted to Baden-Durlach and all of Baden was reunited after a split of more than 250 years.

RULERS

Wilhelm, 1622-1677
Ludwig Wilhelm, 1677-1707

ARMS

Baden – diagonal bar from upper left to lower right
The usual arrangement is shield of 4-fold arms of Baden quartered with Sponheim

MINT OFFICIALS' INITIALS

Initials	Date	Name
GC	1624-29	Georg Cramer

REGULAR COINAGE

KM# 2 PFENNIG

Silver **Ruler:** Wilhelm **Note:** Uniface. Four-fold arms divide W-M, date above. Varieties exist.

Date	Mintage	Good	VG	F	VF	XF
1624	—	40.00	80.00	175	325	—
1626	—	40.00	80.00	175	325	—

KM# 9 PFENNIG

Silver **Ruler:** Wilhelm **Note:** Four-fold arms, WM above date.

Date	Mintage	Good	VG	F	VF	XF
ND	—	40.00	80.00	175	325	—

KM# 17 PFENNIG

Silver **Ruler:** Wilhelm **Note:** Klippe. Four-fold arms divide W-M, date above.

Date	Mintage	Good	VG	F	VF	XF
1676 Rare	—	—	—	—	—	—

KM# 5 ALBUS

Silver **Obv:** Four-fold arms in baroque frame **Rev:** Crowned imperial eagle with 2 in orb on breast, date **Note:** Varieties exist.

Date	Mintage	Good	VG	F	VF	XF
1625	—	60.00	110	190	350	—
1636	—	60.00	110	190	350	—
1637	—	60.00	110	190	350	—

KM# 4 12 KREUZER (3 Batzen)

Silver **Obv:** Bust with wide collar right **Rev:** Manifold arms, date above, value XII at top **Note:** Varieties exist.

Date	Mintage	Good	VG	F	VF	XF
1624	—	65.00	130	200	400	—
1625	—	65.00	130	200	400	—
1626	—	65.00	130	200	400	—

KM# 7 12 KREUZER (3 Batzen)

Silver **Note:** Klippe.

Date	Mintage	Good	VG	F	VF	XF
1626 Rare	—	—	—	—	—	—

KM# 3 GROSCHEN

Silver **Obv:** Four-fold arms, date above **Rev:** Crowned imperial eagle with 3 in orb on breast **Note:** Varieties exist.

Date	Mintage	Good	VG	F	VF	XF
1624	—	60.00	125	200	425	—

KM# 14 1/18 THALER

Silver **Obv:** Half-length bust in mantle right **Rev:** Manifold arms in baroque frame, date above, value 18.ST.FVR. 1/.R. DALER below

Date	Mintage	VG	F	VF	XF	Unc
1638	—	85.00	175	350	—	—

KM# 15 1/6 THALER

Silver **Obv:** Half-length bust in mantle right **Rev:** Manifold arms in baroque frame, date above, value 6.ST.FVR. 1.R. THALER

Date	Mintage	VG	F	VF	XF	Unc
1638	—	400	800	1,500	—	—

KM# 10 1/2 THALER

Silver **Ruler:** Wilhelm **Obv:** Half-length bust right **Rev:** Eight shields around central shield which divides date

Date	Mintage	VG	F	VF	XF	Unc
1629 GC	—	—	—	—	—	—

KM# 6.1 THALER

Silver **Obv. Legend:** GVILHELM'D + G + MAR + BAD + ET + HACH: **Note:** Dav. #6036.

Date	Mintage	VG	F	VF	XF	Unc
1624	—	650	1,150	2,100	3,600	—

KM# 6.2 THALER

Silver **Obv:** Different bust from KM#6.1 **Obv. Legend:** GVILHELMVS. D. G. MARCHIO... **Note:** Dav. #6038.

Date	Mintage	VG	F	VF	XF	Unc
1625	—	400	725	1,500	2,700	—
1626	—	400	725	1,500	2,700	—
1627	—	400	725	1,500	2,700	—

KM# 11 THALER

Silver **Ruler:** Wilhelm **Obv:** Half-length bust right **Rev:** Eight shields around central shield **Note:** Dav. #6040.

Date	Mintage	VG	F	VF	XF	Unc
ND(1629) GC	—	1,950	3,050	5,500	8,300	—

KM# 8 2 THALER

Silver **Note:** Similar to 1 Thaler, KM#6.2. Dav. #6037.

Date	Mintage	VG	F	VF	XF	Unc
1627 Rare	—	—	—	—	—	—

KM# 12 2 THALER

Silver **Obv:** Half-length bust right **Rev:** Eight shields around central shield **Note:** Dav. #6039.

Date	Mintage	VG	F	VF	XF	Unc
ND(1629) GC Rare	—	—	—	—	—	—

TRADE COINAGE

KM# 13 3 GOLDGULDEN

10.5000 g., 0.9860 Gold 0.3328 oz. AGW **Obv:** St. George and the dragon in inner circle **Rev:** Eight shields in a circle with Baden shield in center of inner circle

Date	Mintage	VG	F	VF	XF	Unc
ND(1629) GC Rare	—	—	—	—	—	—

KM# 16 DUCAT

3.5000 g., 0.9860 Gold 0.1109 oz. AGW **Obv:** Wilhelm

Date	Mintage	VG	F	VF	XF	Unc
1674	—	—	—	7,500	11,500	—

BADEN-DURLACH LINE

Grand Duchy

Although Baden-Durlach was founded upon the division of Baden in 1515, the youngest son of Christoph I did not begin ruling in his own right until the demise of his father. This part of Baden was called Pforzheim until 1565, when the margrave moved his seat from the former to Durlach, located to the west and nearer the Rhine. After the male line of Baden-Baden failed in 1771 and the two parts of Baden were reunited, the fortunes of the margraviate continued to grow. Karlsruhe, near Durlach, was developed into a well-planned capital city. The ruler was given the rank of elector in 1803, only to be raised to grand duke three years later. The monarchy came to an end in 1918, but had by this time become one of the largest states in Germany.

RULERS

Georg Friedrich, 1604-1622
Friedrich V, 1622-1659
Friedrich VI, 1659-1677
Friedrich VII Magnus, 1677-1709

MINT OFFICIALS' INITIALS

Initials	Date	Name
D	1622-23	David Niederlander in Pforzheim
	1621-23	And Daniel Weber, warden
I	1626	Karl Junginger (Junzinger)
IPL	?	?
MS	Ca. 1625-28	Moritz Salander, die-cutter in Tubingen
P	1623-30	Peter Marzolf Pfeiffer in Pforzheim
PI	Ca. 1623-25	Johann Pfister, die-cutter in Tubingen

REGULAR COINAGE

KM# A9 PFENNIG

Silver **Note:** Uniface. Schussel type. Arms divide Z-B, GFM above. Previous KM#9.

Date	Mintage	Good	VG	F	VF	XF
ND(1610)	—	30.00	60.00	100	200	—

KM# A12 PFENNIG

Silver **Obv:** Arms divide date. GFM above, D below **Note:** Previous KM#12.

Date	Mintage	Good	VG	F	VF	XF
1621 D	—	30.00	60.00	100	200	—

KM# 29 PFENNIG

Silver **Obv:** Arms divide Z-B, FM above, date below **Note:** Schussel type.

Date	Mintage	Good	VG	F	VF	XF
1623	—	30.00	60.00	100	200	350
1624	—	30.00	60.00	100	200	350

KM# A5 2 PFENNIGE (1/84 Gulden)

Silver **Obv:** Ornately-shaped arms divide Z-B, GFM above **Rev:** Imperial orb with 84 divides date **Note:** Klippe. Prev. KM#5.

Date	Mintage	Good	VG	F	VF	XF
1609	—	35.00	65.00	110	210	—
1610	—	35.00	65.00	110	210	—

KM# A10 6 PFENNIGE (1/28 Gulden)

Silver **Obv:** Four-fold arms with central shield, value 6 at top **Rev:** Imperial orb with 28, cross on top divides date **Note:** Klippe. Previous KM#10.

Date	Mintage	Good	VG	F	VF	XF
1610	—	45.00	90.00	150	300	—

KM# A18 8 PFENNIGE

Silver **Obv:** Bust of Georg Friedrich right **Rev:** Eight-fold arms with VIII above, date in legend **Note:** Prev. KM#18.

Date	Mintage	Good	VG	F	VF	XF
1622	—	45.00	80.00	140	275	—

KM# A20 8 PFENNIGE

Silver **Obv:** Bust of Friedrich V right **Rev:** Eight-fold arms with VIII above **Note:** Prev. KM#20.

Date	Mintage	Good	VG	F	VF	XF
ND(1622-23)	—	45.00	80.00	140	275	—

KM# A19 8 PFENNIGE

Silver **Obv:** Helmeted and mantled triangular arms, titles of Friedrich V **Rev:** Value VIII in center, date in legend **Note:** Varieties exist. Prev. KM#19.

Date	Mintage	Good	VG	F	VF	XF
1622	—	45.00	80.00	140	275	—

KM# 30 KREUZER

Silver **Obv:** Bust of Friedrich V right **Rev:** Arms with value (1) above, date in legend

Date	Mintage	Good	VG	F	VF	XF
1623	—	45.00	80.00	140	275	—

KM# 31 KREUZER

Silver **Obv:** Value (1) below bust **Note:** Varieties exist.

Date	Mintage	Good	VG	F	VF	XF
1623	—	45.00	80.00	140	275	—
1624	—	45.00	80.00	140	225	—

KM# 32 2 KREUZER (1/2 Batzen)

Silver **Ruler:** Ernst Friedrich **Obv:** Bust right, value (2) below **Rev:** Eight-fold arms, date in legend

Date	Mintage	Good	VG	F	VF	XF
1623	—	60.00	100	175	310	—
1624	—	60.00	100	175	310	—

KM# 57 2 KREUZER (1/2 Batzen)

Silver **Ruler:** Friedrich V **Obv:** Eight-fold arms **Rev:** Imperial orb with 2, date divided at top

Date	Mintage	Good	VG	F	VF	XF
1633	—	40.00	80.00	150	300	—
1634	—	40.00	80.00	150	300	—
1637	—	45.00	85.00	160	300	—

KM# 58 2 KREUZER (1/2 Batzen)

Silver **Ruler:** Friedrich V **Obv:** Crown with horns above mantled arms, titles of Friedrich VII **Rev:** Three shields, two slanted above one, value below

Date	Mintage	Good	VG	F	VF	XF
ND	—	35.00	70.00	140	275	—

KM# 59 3 KREUZER (1 Groschen)

Silver **Obv:** Bust of Friedrich VII right **Rev:** Crowned arms between two branches, value 3 below

Date	Mintage	VG	F	VF	XF	Unc
ND	—	—	—	—	—	—

KM# 47 6 KREUZER (1/15 Thaler)

Silver **Obv:** Half-length armored figure right, value 1/15 in oval below **Rev:** Eight-fold arms, value 6.K above. date in legend

Date	Mintage	Good	VG	F	VF	XF
1626	—	60.00	110	190	350	—

KM# 60 6 KREUZER (1/15 Thaler)

Silver **Obv:** Bust of Friedrich VII right **Rev:** Crowned arms between two branches, value 6 below

Date	Mintage	Good	VG	F	VF	XF
ND	—	40.00	80.00	140	275	—

KM# A13 12 KREUZER (3 Batzen)

Silver **Obv:** Bust right **Rev:** Eight-fold arms divide date, value (12) above **Note:** Prev. KM#13.

Date	Mintage	Good	VG	F	VF	XF
1621	—	60.00	110	190	350	—

KM# 21 12 KREUZER (Kipper)

Silver **Obv:** Bust of Friedrich V right divides date **Rev:** Eight-fold arms with value 12 above

Date	Mintage	Good	VG	F	VF	XF
1622	—	60.00	110	190	350	—

KM# 33 12 KREUZER (Kipper)

Silver **Obv:** Bust of Friedrich V right **Rev:** Eight-fold arms, date above, without value

Date	Mintage	Good	VG	F	VF	XF
1623	—	60.00	110	190	350	—

KM# 61 12 KREUZER (Kipper)

Silver **Obv:** Bust of Friedrich VII right **Rev:** Crowned eight-fold arms, value (12) above

Date	Mintage	Good	VG	F	VF	XF
ND	—	40.00	80.00	140	275	—

KM# A15 24 KREUZER (6 Batzen)

Silver **Rev:** 10-fold arms and value (24) below **Note:** Klippe. Prev. KM#15.

Date	Mintage	VG	F	VF	XF	Unc
1621 Rare	—	—	—	—	—	—

KM# A14 24 KREUZER (6 Batzen)

Silver **Obv:** Bust right **Rev:** Eight-fold arms divide date, value (24) above **Note:** Prev. KM#14.

Date	Mintage	VG	F	VF	XF	Unc
1621	—	—	—	—	—	—

KM# A17 24 KREUZER (Kipper)

Silver **Obv:** 1/2-length figure of Georg Friedrich right, date divided by head **Rev:** Eight-fold arms, without value **Note:** Varieties exist. Prev. KM#17.

Date	Mintage	Good	VG	F	VF	XF
1621	—	65.00	125	225	450	—
1622	—	65.00	125	225	450	—
1622 D-PI	—	65.00	125	225	450	—
ND	—	65.00	125	225	450	—
ND D	—	65.00	125	225	450	—
ND D-PI	—	65.00	125	225	450	—
ND IPL	—	65.00	125	225	450	—
ND PI	—	65.00	125	225	450	—

KM# A16 24 KREUZER (Kipper)

Silver **Obv:** Bust of Georg Friedrich right **Rev:** Eight-fold arms, date above, without value **Note:** Varieties exist. Prev. KM#16.

Date	Mintage	VG	F	VF	XF	Unc
1621	—	—	—	—	—	—

KM# 23 24 KREUZER (Kipper)

Silver **Obv:** Bust of Friedrich V right, head divides date **Rev:** Eight-fold arms, value 24 above

Date	Mintage	Good	VG	F	VF	XF
1622	—	—	—	—	—	—
1623	—	—	—	—	—	—

KM# 22 24 KREUZER (Kipper)

Silver **Note:** Klippe. Varieties exist.

Date	Mintage	Good	VG	F	VF	XF
1622 D	—	—	—	—	—	—
ND D	—	—	—	—	—	—

KM# 35 24 KREUZER (Kipper)

Silver **Obv:** Bust of Friedrich V right **Rev:** Eight-fold arms, without value **Note:** Varieties exist.

Date	Mintage	Good	VG	F	VF	XF
ND	—	—	—	—	—	—
ND PI	—	—	—	—	—	—

KM# 36 24 KREUZER (Kipper)

Silver **Obv:** 1/2-length figure of Friedrich V right **Note:** Varieties exist.

Date	Mintage	Good	VG	F	VF	XF
ND	—	50.00	100	200	395	—
ND PI	—	50.00	100	200	395	—

KM# 34 24 KREUZER (Kipper)

Silver **Note:** Klippe.

Date	Mintage	Good	VG	F	VF	XF
1623 Rare	—	—	—	—	—	—

KM# 37 24 KREUZER (Kipper)

Silver **Note:** Klippe.

Date	Mintage	Good	VG	F	VF	XF
ND Rare	—	—	—	—	—	—

KM# 39 1/4 THALER

Silver **Obv:** 1/2-length figure right, value (1/4) below **Rev:** Eight-fold arms in ornate frame, date above

Date	Mintage	Good	VG	F	VF	XF
1624	—	—	—	—	—	—

KM# 40 1/4 THALER

Silver **Note:** Klippe.

Date	Mintage	Good	VG	F	VF	XF
1624 Rare	—	—	—	—	—	—

KM# 49 1/4 THALER

Silver **Rev:** Ornamented square arms with curved bottom, without value, floral ornaments in each corner **Note:** Klippe.

Date	Mintage	Good	VG	F	VF	XF
1626 Rare	—	—	—	—	—	—

KM# 48 1/4 THALER

Silver **Obv:** 1/2-length figure right **Rev:** Eight-fold arms in oval baroque frame, surmounted by angel's head, value (1/4) above, date divided below

Date	Mintage	Good	VG	F	VF	XF
1626 I	—	—	—	—	—	—

KM# 41 1/2 THALER

Silver **Obv:** 1/2-length figure right, value (1/2) below **Rev:** Eight-fold arms in ornate frame, date above

Date	Mintage	Good	VG	F	VF	XF
1624	—	—	—	—	—	—

KM# 42 1/2 THALER

Silver **Note:** Klippe.

Date	Mintage	Good	VG	F	VF	XF
1624 Rare	—	—	—	—	—	—

KM# 50 1/2 THALER

Silver **Obv:** 1/2-length figure right **Rev:** Ornamented square arms with curved bottom, without value, floral ornaments in each corner **Note:** Klippe.

Date	Mintage	Good	VG	F	VF	XF
1626 Rare	—	—	—	—	—	—

KM# 53 1/2 THALER

Silver **Rev:** Oval eight-fold arms in baroque frame, date in legend

Date	Mintage	Good	VG	F	VF	XF
1628 MS-I	—	—	—	—	—	—

KM# 54 1/2 THALER

Silver **Rev:** Date divided below arms

Date	Mintage	Good	VG	F	VF	XF
1629 P	—	—	—	—	—	—

KM# A6.1 THALER

Silver **Note:** Similar to KM#6.2 but arms at top in V-shape. Previous KM#6.1. Dav. 6042.

Date	Mintage	VG	F	VF	XF	Unc
1609	—	1,000	2,000	3,500	6,500	—

KM# A6.2 THALER

Silver **Note:** Previous KM#6.2. Dav. 6043.

Date	Mintage	VG	F	VF	XF	Unc
1610	—	1,250	2,500	4,000	7,000	—

KM# 25 THALER

Silver **Note:** Klippe. Dav. #6045A.

Date	Mintage	VG	F	VF	XF	Unc
1622 Rare	—	—	—	—	—	—

KM# 24 THALER

Silver **Obv:** Georg Friedrich **Note:** Dav. #6045.

Date	Mintage	VG	F	VF	XF	Unc
1622	—	425	850	1,650	2,850	—

KM# 26 THALER

Silver **Note:** Dav. #6046.

Date	Mintage	VG	F	VF	XF	Unc
1622	—	425	850	1,650	2,850	—

KM# 38.1 THALER

Silver **Note:** Similar to KM#43 but date divided above arms, P-I below. Dav. #6047.

Date	Mintage	VG	F	VF	XF	Unc
1623 PI	—	500	900	1,750	3,000	—

KM# 44 THALER

Silver **Note:** Klippe. Dav. #6048A.

Date	Mintage	VG	F	VF	XF	Unc
1624 Rare	—	—	—	—	—	—

KM# 43 THALER
Silver **Note:** Dav. #6048.

Date	Mintage	VG	F	VF	XF	Unc
1624	—	375	750	1,500	2,700	—

KM# 45 THALER
Silver **Rev:** Date arranged differently **Note:** Dav. #6049.

Date	Mintage	VG	F	VF	XF	Unc
1624	—	375	750	1,500	2,700	—
1625	—	375	750	1,500	2,700	—

KM# 46 THALER
Silver **Rev:** Date below arms **Note:** Dav. #6050.

Date	Mintage	VG	F	VF	XF	Unc
1625	—	400	800	1,600	2,800	—

KM# 51.1 THALER
Silver **Note:** Dav. #6052.

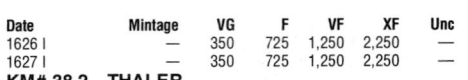

Date	Mintage	VG	F	VF	XF	Unc
1626 I	—	350	725	1,250	2,250	—
1627 I	—	350	725	1,250	2,250	—

KM# 38.2 THALER
Silver **Rev:** Date above arms, P-I divided below **Note:** Dav. #6053.

Date	Mintage	VG	F	VF	XF	Unc
1626 PI	—	350	725	1,250	2,250	—

KM# 51.2 THALER
Silver **Obv. Legend:** ...MAR. Z. BAD. V. H. A. L. Z. S. G. Z. SP. **Note:** Dav. #6055.

Date	Mintage	VG	F	VF	XF	Unc
1628 I	—	350	725	1,250	2,250	—

KM# 55.1 THALER
Silver **Rev:** Date divided 16-29 by lower half of arms, P below **Note:** Dav. #6056.

Date	Mintage	VG	F	VF	XF	Unc
1629 P	—	400	800	1,600	2,800	—

KM# 56 THALER
Silver **Ruler:** Friedrich V **Rev:** Helmeted arms, date above **Note:** Dav. #6057.

Date	Mintage	VG	F	VF	XF	Unc
1629 P	—	850	1,500	2,500	4,500	—

KM# 55.2 THALER
Silver **Obv. Legend:** ...M. Z: BA. V: HA: L. Z. SAV... **Note:** Dav. #6058.

Date	Mintage	VG	F	VF	XF	Unc
1634 P Rare	—	—	—	—	—	—

KM# 62 THALER
Silver **Obv:** Bust right **Rev:** Eight-fold arms, crown above divides date **Note:** Dav. #6059.

Date	Mintage	VG	F	VF	XF	Unc
1681 Rare	—	—	—	—	—	—

KM# A7 2 THALER
28.6000 g., 0.8330 Silver 0.7659 oz. ASW **Note:** Similar to 1 Thaler, KM#A6.1. Prev. KM#7. Dav. 6041.

Date	Mintage	VG	F	VF	XF	Unc
1609 Rare	—	—	—	—	—	—

KM# 27 2 THALER
Silver **Note:** Klippe. Similar to 1 Thaler, KM#24. Dav. #6044.

Date	Mintage	VG	F	VF	XF	Unc
1622 Rare	—	—	—	—	—	—

KM# 52.1 2 THALER
Silver **Note:** Similar to 1 Thaler, KM#51.1. Dav. #6051.

Date	Mintage	VG	F	VF	XF	Unc
1626 Rare	—	—	—	—	—	—

KM# 52.2 2 THALER
Silver **Obv. Legend:** MAR • Z • BAD. V. H. L. Z. S. G. Z. SP. **Note:** Dav. #6054.

Date	Mintage	VG	F	VF	XF	Unc
1628 I Rare	—	—	—	—	—	—

TRADE COINAGE

KM# A8 GOLDGULDEN
3.5000 g., 0.9860 Gold 0.1109 oz. AGW **Obv:** Bust of Georg Friedrich right divides date in inner circle **Rev:** Ornate cross with arms in angles, Baden shield at center in inner circle

Date	Mintage	VG	F	VF	XF	Unc
1609 Rare	—	—	—	—	—	—

KM# 28 DUCAT
3.5000 g., 0.9860 Gold 0.1109 oz. AGW **Obv:** Georg Friedrich standing right divides date in inner circle **Rev:** Square arms within inner circle

Date	Mintage	VG	F	VF	XF	Unc
1622	—	—	—	—	—	—

KM# A11 2 DUCAT
7.0000 g., 0.9860 Gold 0.2219 oz. AGW **Obv:** Large bust of Georg Friedrich right divides date in inner circle **Rev:** Ornate cross with arms in angles, Baden shield in center of inner circle

Date	Mintage	VG	F	VF	XF	Unc
1610 Rare	—	—	—	—	—	—

KM# B12 6 DUCAT
21.0000 g., 0.9860 Gold 0.6657 oz. AGW **Obv:** 1/2-length bust Georg Friedrich right divides date in inner circle **Note:** Struck with 1 Thaler dies, KM#6.2.

Date	Mintage	VG	F	VF	XF	Unc
1610 Rare	—	—	—	—	—	—

LOCAL COINAGE

KM# B10 RAPPEN
Silver **Issuer:** Hachberg, Struck on Swiss Standard **Note:** Uniface. Plain arms in circle within circle of pellets. Varieties exist. Previous KM#10.

Date	Mintage	VG	F	VF	XF	Unc
ND	—	50.00	100	210	—	—

KM# A6 2 PFENNIG (Kipper)
Silver **Obv:** Arms in circle of pellets, value and date in legend **Rev:** Arms of Usenberg (wings), around H. LANDSWEHRUNG **Note:** Previous KM#6.

Date	Mintage	VG	F	VF	XF	Unc
1622	—	50.00	100	200	360	725

KM# B11 2 PFENNIG (Kipper)
Silver **Obv:** Value around arms within wreath **Note:** Previous KM#11.

Date	Mintage	VG	F	VF	XF	Unc
ND	—	25.00	45.00	90.00	180	—

KM# C12 2 PFENNIG (Kipper)
Silver **Obv:** Arms in circle of dots, value around **Rev:** Three small shields, one above two **Rev. Legend:** H. LANDSWEHRVNG **Note:** Previous KM#12.

Date	Mintage	VG	F	VF	XF	Unc
ND	—	15.00	30.00	60.00	120	—

KM# B13 2 PFENNIG (Kipper)
Silver **Rev:** Arms of Usenberg **Rev. Legend:** H. LANDSWEHRUNG **Note:** Previous KM#13.

Date	Mintage	VG	F	VF	XF	Unc
ND	—	15.00	30.00	60.00	120	—

KM# B14 4 PFENNIG
Silver **Obv:** Arms in circle of dots, value IIII around **Rev:** Three small shields, one above two **Rev. Legend:** H. LANDSWEHRVNG **Note:** Previous KM#14.

Date	Mintage	VG	F	VF	XF	Unc
ND	—	30.00	60.00	100	180	—

KM# B15 5 PFENNIG
Silver **Obv:** Arms in notched shield between two rosettes **Rev:** Usenberg arms, around V. PF. HACB. L. WEHRUNG **Note:** Previous KM#15.

Date	Mintage	VG	F	VF	XF	Unc
ND	—	—	—	—	—	—

KM# B7 8 PFENNIG (Kipper)
Silver **Obv:** Arms, date **Rev:** Usenberg arms **Rev. Legend:** HACHBERGENSIS **Note:** Previous KM#7.

Date	Mintage	VG	F	VF	XF	Unc
1622	—	75.00	150	300	—	—
1623	—	75.00	150	300	—	—

KM# B16 9 KREUZER (1/12 Thaler)
Silver **Obv:** Arms, titles of Friedrich VII **Rev:** Usenberg arms, IX above, 1/12 in oval cartouche below **Note:** Previous KM#16.

Date	Mintage	VG	F	VF	XF	Unc
ND	—	—	—	—	—	—

KM# B17 12 KREUZER (3 Batzen)
Silver **Obv:** Crown with horns above mantles arms, titles of Friedrich VII **Rev:** Three shields, one above two, crown above, value XII in legend at top **Note:** Previous KM#17.

Date	Mintage	VG	F	VF	XF	Unc
ND	—	100	200	425	850	—

KM# B8 12 KREUZER (3 Batzen)
Silver **Obv:** Bust of Georg Friedrich right **Rev:** Four-fold arms (Baden and Usenberg), value 12 above, date in legend **Note:** Previous KM#8.

Date	Mintage	VG	F	VF	XF	Unc
1622	—	—	—	—	—	—

KM# B5 24 KREUZER (6 Batzen)
Silver **Obv:** Bust of Georg Friedrich right **Rev:** Four-fold arms(Baden and Usenberg), value 24 above, date in legend **Note:** Varieties exist. Previous KM#5.

Date	Mintage	VG	F	VF	XF	Unc
16Z1	—	275	550	1,000	1,800	—
16ZZ	—	275	550	1,000	1,800	—

KM# B18 15 BATZEN (60 Kreuzer)
Silver **Obv:** Bust of Friedrich VII right **Rev:** Value in four lines **Note:** Previous KM#18.

Date	Mintage	VG	F	VF	XF	Unc
ND	—	3,000	5,000	9,000	—	—

KM# B18a 15 BATZEN (60 Kreuzer)
Lead **Note:** Previous KM#18a.

Date	Mintage	VG	F	VF	XF	Unc
ND	—	—	—	—	—	—

KM# B19 15 BATZEN (60 Kreuzer)
Silver **Rev:** Three shields, one above two, crown above, value XV BAZEN in legend at top **Note:** Previous KM#19.

Date	Mintage	VG	F	VF	XF	Unc
ND	—	—	—	—	—	—

KM# B20 16 BATZEN
Silver **Obv:** Bust of Friedrich VII right **Rev:** Value XVI. BZ. **Note:** Previous KM#20.

Date	Mintage	VG	F	VF	XF	Unc
ND	—	3,500	6,000	11,500	—	—

KM# A21 GULDEN
Silver **Obv:** Crowned and supported arms, titles of Friedrich VII **Rev:** Three shields, one above two, value LX. K. above **Note:** Prev. KM#21.

Date	Mintage	VG	F	VF	XF	Unc
ND Rare	—	—	—	—	—	—

PATTERNS

Including off metal strikes

KM#	Date	Mintage	Identification	Mkt Val
Pn1	1624	—	Thaler. Lead. KM#6.	—
PnA2	1610	—	2 Ducat. Silver. KM#11.	—
Pn2	1627	—	Thaler. Lead. KM#6.	—
PnA3	1622	—	Thaler. Lead. KM#24.	—

BAMBERG

The bishopric was founded in 1007 by Emperor Heinrich II (1002-24) in the town of Bamberg, 32 miles (53 kilometers) north-northwest of Nürnberg. The bishops began issuing their own coinage almost from the beginning and were given the rank of Prince of the Empire by the emperor about 1250. The bishopric was secularized in 1801 and was incorporated into Bavaria the following year.

RULERS
Johann Philipp von Gebsattel, 1599-1609
Johann Gottfried von Aschhausen, 1609-1622
Johann Georg II, Fuchs von Dornheim, 1622-1633
Franz, Graf von Hatzfeld, 1633-1642
Melchior Otto, Voigt von Salzburg, 1642-1653
Philipp Valentin, Voigt von Rieneck, 1653-1672
Peter Philipp von Dernbach, 1672-1683
Marquard Sebastian, Schenk von Staufenberg, 1683-1693
Lothar Franz, Freiherr von Schönborn, 1693-1729

ARMS: Lion rampant left over which superimposed a diagonal band from upper left to lower right.

MINT MARKS
B - Bamberg Mint
F - Fürth Mint

MINT OFFICIALS' INITIALS

Initials	Date	Name
A		
AL	1678-83	Adam Longerich in Koblenz
CB	1683-96	Conrad Bechtmann in Aschaffenburg
CS	1622-54	Conrad Stutz, die-cutter in Fürth and mintmaster of the Franconian Circle
GFN or +	1682-1724	Georg Friedrich Nurnberger, die-cutter and mintmaster in Nurnberg
MF	1681-82	Jakob Merkel, die-cutter in Bamberg
VBW	1685, 1695-1729	Ulrich Buckhard Wildering in Mainz

BISHOPRIC

REGULAR COINAGE

KM# 11 HELLER
Copper **Note:** Uniface. Arms of Bamberg divide date, value I above.

Date	Mintage	Good	VG	F	VF	XF
1622	—	13.00	27.00	45.00	85.00	—

KM# 12 2 HELLER
Copper **Note:** Uniface. Arms of Bamberg divide date, value II above.

Date	Mintage	Good	VG	F	VF	XF
1622	—	13.00	27.00	45.00	85.00	—

KM# 13 3 HELLER
Copper **Obv:** Arms with date divided by B above **Rev:** Value III in wreath

Date	Mintage	Good	VG	F	VF	XF
1622 B	—	13.00	27.00	45.00	85.00	—
ND B	—	13.00	27.00	45.00	85.00	—

KM# 25 3 HELLER
Billon **Note:** Uniface. Two shields with arms of Bamberg and Dornheim divide date, value III above.

Date	Mintage	Good	VG	F	VF	XF
1629 F	—	17.00	27.00	50.00	85.00	—

KM# 34 3 HELLER
Copper **Obv:** Arms with date divided by B above **Rev:** Value III in wreath

Date	Mintage	Good	VG	F	VF	XF
1649	—	17.00	27.00	50.00	85.00	—

KM# 35 3 HELLER
Billon **Obv:** Two shields with arms, crown above divides date, value III h1 below **Rev:** Value III h1

Date	Mintage	Good	VG	F	VF	XF
1649	—	17.00	27.00	50.00	85.00	—

KM# 53 3 HELLER
Billon **Note:** Uniface. Crowned triple arms in trefoil, date above.

Date	Mintage	Good	VG	F	VF	XF
1676	—	14.00	25.00	45.00	80.00	150
1677	—	14.00	25.00	45.00	80.00	150
1681	—	14.00	25.00	45.00	80.00	150
1683	—	14.00	25.00	45.00	80.00	150
ND	—	14.00	25.00	45.00	80.00	150

KM# 70 3 HELLER
Copper **Obv:** Crowned double arms, date **Rev:** Value III h1. in wreath

Date	Mintage	VG	F	VF	XF	Unc
1683 AL	—	16.00	30.00	60.00	125	225
1685 ++	—	16.00	30.00	60.00	125	225
1686 ++	—	16.00	30.00	60.00	125	225
1687 ++	—	16.00	30.00	60.00	125	225
1688 ++	—	16.00	30.00	60.00	125	225
1689 ++	—	16.00	30.00	60.00	125	225
1690 ++	—	16.00	30.00	60.00	125	225

KM# 10 PFENNIG
Silver **Ruler:** Johann Georg II **Obv:** Two shields with arms of Bamberg and Dornheim **Note:** Uniface.

Date	Mintage	VG	F	VF	XF	Unc
1620 F	—	50.00	100	210	425	—
1627 F	—	50.00	100	210	425	—
16Z9 F	—	50.00	100	210	425	—

KM# 18 PFENNIG
Silver **Note:** Arms with date above.

Date	Mintage	VG	F	VF	XF	Unc
1624	—	13.00	27.00	50.00	100	—

KM# 19 PFENNIG
Silver **Note:** Hohlpfennig. Bamberg arms divide date.

Date	Mintage	VG	F	VF	XF	Unc
1624	—	13.00	27.00	50.00	100	—

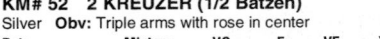

KM# 37 PFENNIG
Silver **Note:** Two shields with arms, crown divides date above, value 1 below.

Date	Mintage	VG	F	VF	XF	Unc
1649	—	13.00	27.00	50.00	100	—

KM# 36 PFENNIG
Silver **Note:** Arms divide date.

Date	Mintage	VG	F	VF	XF	Unc
1649	—	13.00	27.00	50.00	100	—

KM# 56 PFENNIG
Silver **Obv:** Crowned triple arms in trefoil, date above, value 1 below.

Date	Mintage	VG	F	VF	XF	Unc
1677	—	13.00	27.00	50.00	100	—

KM# 57 PFENNIG
Silver **Note:** Without date or value.

Date	Mintage	VG	F	VF	XF	Unc
ND	—	13.00	27.00	50.00	100	165

KM# 77 PFENNIG
Silver **Obv:** Crowned double arms of Bamberg and Staufenberg, date above.

Date	Mintage	VG	F	VF	XF	Unc
1685	—	10.00	20.00	40.00	80.00	165
1687	—	10.00	20.00	40.00	80.00	165
1690	—	10.00	20.00	40.00	80.00	165
ND	—	10.00	20.00	40.00	80.00	165

KM# 97 PFENNIG
Silver **Ruler:** Lother Franz **Obv:** Three shields of arms, lower one divides date, value 1 above **Note:** Uniface.

Date	Mintage	VG	F	VF	XF	Unc
1700	—	10.00	22.00	45.00	90.00	—

KM# 14 KREUZER
Copper

Date	Mintage	Good	VG	F	VF	XF
1622 B	—	13.00	27.00	50.00	100	—

KM# 22 2 KREUZER (1/2 Batzen)
Silver **Obv:** Crowned arms, date above **Rev:** Bust of St. Heinrich holding scepter and imperial orb with value 2

Date	Mintage	Good	VG	F	VF	XF
1627 F	—	13.00	27.00	50.00	100	—
1629 F	—	13.00	27.00	50.00	100	—
ND	—	13.00	27.00	50.00	100	—

KM# 39 2 KREUZER (1/2 Batzen)
Silver **Obv:** Crowned double arms, date below

Date	Mintage	Good	VG	F	VF	XF
1649	—	13.00	27.00	50.00	100	—

KM# 51 2 KREUZER (1/2 Batzen)
Silver **Obv:** Crowned triple arms in trefoil **Rev:** Bust of Heinrich holding orb with 2, date divided to either side

Date	Mintage	VG	F	VF	XF	Unc
1673	—	13.00	27.00	50.00	100	—
1676	—	13.00	27.00	50.00	100	—
1677	—	13.00	27.00	50.00	100	—
1678	—	13.00	27.00	50.00	100	—
1683	—	13.00	27.00	50.00	100	—

KM# 52 2 KREUZER (1/2 Batzen)
Silver **Obv:** Triple arms with rose in center

Date	Mintage	VG	F	VF	XF	Unc
ND	—	13.00	27.00	50.00	100	—

KM# 88 2 KREUZER (1/2 Batzen)
Silver **Note:** Similar to 4 Kreuzer, KM#85 but with value 2.

Date	Mintage	VG	F	VF	XF	Unc
1696 GFN	756,000	13.00	27.00	50.00	100	—

KM# 42 3 KREUZER
Silver **Subject:** Death of Melchior Otto **Obv:** Crowned four-fold arms **Rev:** Seven-line inscription with date, imperial orb with 3

Date	Mintage	VG	F	VF	XF	Unc
1653	2,440	—	120	235	475	—

KM# 47 3 KREUZER
Silver **Subject:** Death of Philipp Valentin

Date	Mintage	VG	F	VF	XF	Unc
1672	4,000	—	100	200	400	—

KM# 81 3 KREUZER
Silver **Subject:** Death of Marquard Sebastian **Obv:** Crowned double arms, supported by two lions, between branches **Rev:** Eight-line inscription with date, imperial orb with 3 below

Date	Mintage	VG	F	VF	XF	Unc
1693 GFN	—	—	100	200	400	—

KM# 23 4 KREUZER (Batzen)
Silver **Obv:** Crowned arms, date above **Rev:** Bust of St. Heinrich holding scepter and imperial orb with value 4

Date	Mintage	VG	F	VF	XF	Unc
1627 F	—	20.00	40.00	75.00	155	—
1628 F	—	20.00	40.00	75.00	155	—
1629 F	—	20.00	40.00	75.00	155	—
1630 F	—	20.00	40.00	75.00	155	—

KM# 31 4 KREUZER (Batzen)
Silver **Obv:** Crowned triple arms in form of trefoil, date below **Rev:** Bust of St. Heinrich holding imperial orb with value 4

Date	Mintage	VG	F	VF	XF	Unc
1635	—	20.00	40.00	75.00	155	325

KM# 40 4 KREUZER (Batzen)
Silver **Obv:** Crowned double arms, date above

Date	Mintage	VG	F	VF	XF	Unc
1649	—	20.00	40.00	75.00	155	—

KM# 59 4 KREUZER (Batzen)
Silver **Obv:** Crowned triple arms in trefoil **Rev:** Date divided to either side

Date	Mintage	VG	F	VF	XF	Unc
1680	—	20.00	40.00	57.00	155	—

KM# 60 4 KREUZER (Batzen)
Silver **Obv:** Crowned four-fold arms, central shield of Dernbach arms **Note:** Varieties exist.

Date	Mintage	VG	F	VF	XF	Unc
1680	—	45.00	90.00	160	325	—

KM# 85 4 KREUZER (Batzen)
Silver, 23 mm. **Ruler:** Lother Franz **Obv:** Crowned oval 6-fold arms with central shield of Bamberg, superimposed on crossed sword and crozier, between 2 palm branches, date divided at top **Obv. Legend:** LOTHAR. FRANC. D. G. A. & E. M. E. BAMB. **Rev:** Facing 1/3-length crowned and robed figure of St. Heinrich holding scepter and orb with value 4 **Rev. Legend:** S. HEINRICVS. IMPERATOR.

Date	Mintage	VG	F	VF	XF	Unc
1696 GFN	891,000	16.00	35.00	75.00	155	—
1698 GFN	1,382,000	16.00	35.00	75.00	155	—
1700 GFN	1,093,000	16.00	35.00	75.00	155	—

KM# 61 6 KREUZER
Silver **Obv:** Four-fold arms with central shield of Dernbach arms divide date, value VI:K: above **Rev:** Bust of bishop

Date	Mintage	VG	F	VF	XF	Unc
1680 Rare	—	—	—	—	—	—

KM# 15 GROSCHEN (3 Kreuzer)
Silver **Subject:** Death of Johann Gottfried **Obv:** Crowned and helmeted arms **Rev:** Inscription with date above imperial orb with B

Date	Mintage	VG	F	VF	XF	Unc
1622	—	—	—	—	—	—

KM# 29 GROSCHEN (3 Kreuzer)
Silver **Subject:** Death of Franz von Hatzfeld **Obv:** Crowned and helmeted four-fold arms with central shield of Hatzfeld **Rev:** Six-line inscription with dates, small imperial orb below, B at bottom

Date	Mintage	VG	F	VF	XF	Unc
1642	—	—	—	—	—	—

KM# 20.1 1/84 THALER (3 Pfennig)
Silver, 16 mm. **Ruler:** Johann Georg II **Obv:** Two ornate adjacent shields with arms of Bamberg and Dornheim, date above **Rev:** Imperial orb with 84 in ornamented rhombus

Date	Mintage	Good	VG	F	VF	XF
16Z4	—	12.00	20.00	35.00	65.00	130

KM# 20.2 1/84 THALER (3 Pfennig)
Silver, 16 mm. **Ruler:** Johann Georg II **Obv:** Two ornate adjacent shields with arms of Bamberg and Dornheim, cross and crozier crossed behind, crown above, mintmark below **Rev:** Imperial orb with 84 divides date within ornamented rhombus
Mint: Fürth

Date	Mintage	VG	F	VF	XF	Unc
16Z9F	—	20.00	35.00	65.00	130	—

KM# 30 1/84 THALER (3 Pfennig)
Silver **Obv:** Three arms in form of trefoil, date below

Date	Mintage	Good	VG	F	VF	XF
1635	—	12.00	20.00	35.00	75.00	—

KM# 38 1/84 THALER (3 Pfennig)
Silver **Obv:** Crowned double arms, date below

Date	Mintage	Good	VG	F	VF	XF
1649	—	10.00	16.00	35.00	75.00	150
1652	—	10.00	16.00	35.00	75.00	150

KM# 54 1/84 THALER (3 Pfennig)
Silver **Obv:** Triple arms **Rev:** Imperial orb with 84 divides date

Date	Mintage	Good	VG	F	VF	XF
1676	—	10.00	16.00	35.00	75.00	150
1678	—	10.00	16.00	35.00	75.00	150
1680	—	10.00	16.00	35.00	75.00	150

Date	Mintage	Good	VG	F	VF	XF
1681	—	10.00	16.00	35.00	75.00	150
1682	—	10.00	16.00	35.00	75.00	150

KM# 55 1/84 THALER (3 Pfennig)

Silver **Obv:** Triple arms, F in center, date below **Rev:** Imperial orb with 84

Date	Mintage	Good	VG	F	VF	XF
1676 F	—	10.00	16.00	35.00	75.00	150
1677 F	—	10.00	16.00	35.00	75.00	150
1682 F	—	10.00	16.00	35.00	75.00	150
ND F	—	10.00	16.00	35.00	75.00	150

KM# 58 1/84 THALER (3 Pfennig)

Silver **Obv:** Triple arms in trefoil divide date

Date	Mintage	Good	VG	F	VF	XF
1679	—	12.00	25.00	50.00	100	200

KM# 75 1/84 THALER (3 Pfennig)

Silver, 16 mm. **Ruler:** Marquard Sebastian **Obv:** Two adjacent shields of arms, Bamberg on left and Staufenberg on right, cross and crozier behind shields, crown above, mintmark below in center, where present **Rev:** Imperial orb with 84 divides date, MS - EB divided by top of cross

Date	Mintage	VG	F	VF	XF	Unc
1684 A	—	15.00	30.00	60.00	120	240
1684	—	15.00	30.00	60.00	120	240
1685 A	—	15.00	30.00	60.00	120	240
1686 A	—	15.00	30.00	60.00	120	240
1686	—	15.00	30.00	60.00	120	240
1687 A	—	15.00	30.00	60.00	120	240
1690 A	—	15.00	30.00	60.00	120	240
1691 A	—	15.00	30.00	60.00	120	240

KM# 69 1/24 THALER (Groschen)

Silver **Obv:** Triple arms in trefoil **Rev:** Imperial orb with 24, date divided above

Date	Mintage	Good	VG	F	VF	XF
1682 MF	—	—	—	—	—	—

KM# 72 1/24 THALER (Groschen)

Silver **Subject:** Death of Peter Philipp **Obv:** Crowned four-fold arms, central shield of Dernbach arms

Date	Mintage	VG	F	VF	XF	Unc
1683	—	50.00	100	200	400	—

KM# 71 1/24 THALER (Groschen)

Silver **Obv:** Crowned triple arms **Note:** Varieties exist.

Date	Mintage	VG	F	VF	XF	Unc
1683 AL	—	12.00	25.00	50.00	100	200
1683 MF	—	12.00	25.00	50.00	100	200

KM# 76 1/24 THALER (Groschen)

1.6000 g., Silver, 20.8 mm. **Obv:** Crowned double arms **Rev:** Imperial orb with 24 divides date

Date	Mintage	VG	F	VF	XF	Unc
1684 AL	—	15.00	30.00	60.00	120	—
1684 VBW	—	15.00	30.00	60.00	120	—
1685 VBW	—	15.00	30.00	60.00	120	—
1685	—	15.00	30.00	60.00	120	—

KM# 62 1/4 THALER

Silver **Obv:** Bust of bishop **Rev:** Crowned four-fold arms, central shield of Dernbach arms, value 1/4 below divides date

Date	Mintage	VG	F	VF	XF	Unc
1680 Rare	—	—	—	—	—	—

KM# 63 1/4 THALER

Silver **Obv:** Bust right, value 1/2 below **Rev:** Crowned four-fold arms, central shield of Dernbach arms, date above

Date	Mintage	VG	F	VF	XF	Unc
1680 Rare	—	—	—	—	—	—

KM# 66 1/4 THALER

Silver **Rev:** Date below arms

Date	Mintage	VG	F	VF	XF	Unc
1681 Rare	—	—	—	—	—	—

KM# 86 1/4 THALER

Silver **Obv:** Bust right **Rev:** Crowned and helmeted four-fold arms, date below

Date	Mintage	VG	F	VF	XF	Unc
1694 GFN	640	—	—	—	—	—

KM# 8 THALER

Silver **Obv:** Facing bust, four arms in legend with IOANNES.CHRISTOPH.NEVSTETTER.D.STVRMER. **Rev:** Crown in clouds above figure of man, PRAEPOS. ET. SEN. BAMB. CVSTOS. MOGVNT. CAN. HERB. P. S. C. M. A. CO. **Note:** Issued by Johann Christoph Neustaedter, Provost of the Cathedral, 1610-38.

Date	Mintage	VG	F	VF	XF	Unc
ND(ca.1610) Rare	—	—	—	—	—	—

KM# 16 THALER

Silver **Obv:** Johann Georg II **Rev:** SS. Heinrich and Kunigunda **Note:** Dav. #5051.

Date	Mintage	VG	F	VF	XF	Unc
ND(1622) CS	—	400	750	1,100	2,000	—

KM# 26 THALER

Silver **Obv:** Crowned four-fold arms with arms of Hatzfeld in center **Rev:** Crowned imperial eagle with orb on breast, titles of Ferdinand II **Note:** Dav. #5053.

Date	Mintage	VG	F	VF	XF	Unc
ND(1632) Rare	—	—	—	—	—	—

KM# 41 THALER

Silver **Note:** Dav. #5054.

Date	Mintage	VG	F	VF	XF	Unc
1649	—	850	1,750	3,500	7,000	—

KM# 45 THALER

Silver **Note:** Dav. #5055.

Date	Mintage	VG	F	VF	XF	Unc
1657	—	1,200	2,250	4,500	8,000	—

KM# 64.1 THALER

Silver **Obv:** Bust right **Obv. Legend:** PETRVS... **Rev:** Crowned four-fold arms, central shield of Dernbach arms, all in baroque frame, date divided to lower left and right **Note:** Dav. #5056.

Date	Mintage	VG	F	VF	XF	Unc
1680	—	2,500	4,500	7,500	12,000	—

KM# 65 THALER

Silver **Rev:** Date divided at top **Note:** Dav. #5058.

Date	Mintage	VG	F	VF	XF	Unc
1680	—	2,500	4,500	7,500	12,000	—

KM# 64.2 THALER

Silver **Obv. Legend:** PETR... **Note:** Varieties exist. Dav. #5057.

Date	Mintage	VG	F	VF	XF	Unc
1680	—	2,500	4,500	7,500	12,000	—

KM# 67.1 THALER

Silver **Rev:** Smaller arms between two branches, date at bottom **Note:** Dav. #5059.

Date	Mintage	VG	F	VF	XF	Unc
1681	—	2,500	4,500	7,500	12,000	—

KM# 67.2 THALER

Silver **Rev:** Crowned arms divide date **Note:** Dav. #5060.

Date	Mintage	VG	F	VF	XF	Unc
1681	—	2,500	4,500	7,500	12,000	—

KM# 68 THALER

Silver **Rev:** Four-fold arms, central shield of Dernbach arms, supported by two lions, all between two branches **Note:** Dav. #5061.

Date	Mintage	VG	F	VF	XF	Unc
ND	—	—	—	—	—	—

KM# 78 THALER

Silver **Rev:** Crowned four-fold arms in baroque frame, date above **Note:** Dav. #5062.

Date	Mintage	VG	F	VF	XF	Unc
1687	—	2,000	3,500	6,500	10,000	—

KM# 80 THALER

Silver **Obv:** Sts. Heinrich and Kunigunda **Rev:** Madonna **Note:** Dav. #5063.

Date	Mintage	VG	F	VF	XF	Unc
1690 GFN	—	200	350	750	1,500	2,500
1691	—	200	350	750	1,500	2,500

KM# 82 THALER

Silver **Rev:** Emperor Heinrich II **Note:** Sede Vacante. Dav. #5064.

Date	Mintage	VG	F	VF	XF	Unc
1693 GFN	—	250	500	1,150	2,500	—

KM# 87 THALER

Silver **Ruler:** Lother Franz **Obv:** Bust right **Obv. Legend:** LOTHAR•FRANC•D.G.•EPIS-BAMB•S•R•I•PRINC• **Rev:** Crowned and helmeted four-fold arms, date below **Note:** Dav. #5065.

Date	Mintage	VG	F	VF	XF	Unc
1694 GFN	13,000	175	350	650	1,200	—

KM# 89 THALER

Silver **Note:** Dav. #5066.

Date	Mintage	VG	F	VF	XF	Unc
1696 GFN	53,000	175	350	650	1,200	4,500
1696 CB	Inc. above	175	350	650	1,200	—

KM# 95 THALER

Silver **Obv:** Oval arms, angel's head and wings below **Note:** Dav. #5067.

Date	Mintage	VG	F	VF	XF	Unc
1697 GFN	Inc. above	240	425	725	1,250	—

KM# 27 2 THALER

Silver **Obv:** Crowned four-fold arms with arms of Hatzfeld in center **Rev:** Crowned imperial eagle with orb on breast, titles of Ferdinand II **Note:** Dav. #5052.

Date	Mintage	VG	F	VF	XF	Unc
ND(1632) Rare	—	—	—	—	—	—

KM# 96 3 THALER

Silver **Note:** Similar to 1 Thaler, KM#89, but oval arms, angel head, wings below arms. Dav. #A5057.

Date	Mintage	VG	F	VF	XF	Unc
1697 GFN Rare	—	—	—	—	—	—

TRADE COINAGE

KM# 17 GOLDGULDEN

3.5000 g., 0.9860 Gold 0.1109 oz. AGW **Subject:** Death of the Bishop **Obv:** Crowned arms **Rev:** Inscription

Date	Mintage	VG	F	VF	XF	Unc
1622	—	—	—	—	—	—

KM# 21 GOLDGULDEN

3.5000 g., 0.9860 Gold 0.1109 oz. AGW **Obv:** Bust of Johann Georg facing 1/2 right in inner circle **Rev:** Two saints holding church, two shields of arms below **Note:** Fr.#161.

Date	Mintage	VG	F	VF	XF	Unc
1624	—	2,000	4,000	7,000	15,000	—
1628	—	1,200	2,500	5,000	9,000	—

KM# 6 DUCAT

3.5000 g., 0.9860 Gold 0.1109 oz. AGW **Obv:** Two saints holding church, arms below in inner circle **Rev:** Two shields of arms below crown in inner circle **Note:** Fr#160.

Date	Mintage	VG	F	VF	XF	Unc
1601	—	1,250	2,500	5,500	9,000	—
1602	—	1,250	2,500	5,500	9,000	—

KM# 24 DUCAT

3.5000 g., 0.9860 Gold 0.1109 oz. AGW **Obv:** Bust of Johann Georg facing 1/2 right in inner circle **Rev:** Two saints holding church, two shields of arms below **Note:** Fr.#162.

Date	Mintage	VG	F	VF	XF	Unc
1628 CS	—	1,150	2,400	5,000	8,000	—
1631 CS	—	1,150	2,400	5,000	8,000	—

KM# 32 DUCAT

3.5000 g., 0.9860 Gold 0.1109 oz. AGW **Note:** Fr.#164.

Date	Mintage	VG	F	VF	XF	Unc
1635	—	300	650	1,100	2,100	—
1637	—	300	650	1,100	2,100	—
1638	—	300	650	1,100	2,100	—
1640	—	300	650	1,100	2,100	—

KM# 33 DUCAT

3.5000 g., 0.9860 Gold 0.1109 oz. AGW **Obv:** Bust of Melchoir Otto right **Rev:** Crowned arms divide date **Note:** Fr. #165.

Date	Mintage	VG	F	VF	XF	Unc
1647	—	800	1,800	3,000	6,000	—

KM# 46 DUCAT

3.5000 g., 0.9860 Gold 0.1109 oz. AGW **Obv:** Bust of Philip Valentin right **Rev:** Two shields of arms below crown, date below **Note:** Fr. #167.

Date	Mintage	VG	F	VF	XF	Unc
1657	—	700	1,650	2,750	5,700	—

KM# 79 DUCAT

3.5000 g., 0.9860 Gold 0.1109 oz. AGW **Obv:** Bust right **Rev:** Crowned four-fold arms in baroque frame, date above

Date	Mintage	VG	F	VF	XF	Unc
1687 Rare	—	—	—	—	—	—

KM# 90 DUCAT

3.5000 g., 0.9860 Gold 0.1109 oz. AGW **Subject:** Peace of Ryswick **Obv:** Crowned and mantled six-fold arms, date below **Rev:** Altar divides EIN-DVC

Date	Mintage	VG	F	VF	XF	Unc
1696 GFN	—	—	—	1,000	2,000	—

KM# 91 DUCAT

3.5000 g., 0.9860 Gold 0.1109 oz. AGW **Rev:** Minerva standing with olive branch and shield, FAVENTE NVMINE

Date	Mintage	VG	F	VF	XF	Unc
1696 GFN	—	—	—	—	—	—

KM# 92 DUCAT

3.5000 g., 0.9860 Gold 0.1109 oz. AGW **Rev:** Female seated left, CONCORDIA below

Date	Mintage	VG	F	VF	XF	Unc
ND(1696) GFN	—	—	450	750	1,900	—

KM# 7 2 DUCAT
7.0000 g., 0.9860 Gold 0.2219 oz. AGW **Obv:** Two saints holding church, arms below in inner circle **Rev:** Two shield of arms below crown in inner circle **Note:** Fr. #159.

Date	Mintage	VG	F	VF	XF	Unc
1601 Rare	—	—	—	—	—	—

KM# 93 2 DUCAT
7.0000 g., 0.9860 Gold 0.2219 oz. AGW **Obv:** Crowned and mantled six-fold arms, date below **Rev:** Altar divides Ein-Duc **Note:** Struck with Ducat dies but double in weight.

Date	Mintage	VG	F	VF	XF	Unc
1696 Rare	838	—	—	—	—	—

KM# 94 2 DUCAT
7.0000 g., 0.9860 Gold 0.2219 oz. AGW **Rev:** Minerva standing with olive branch and shield, FAVENTE NVMINE.

Date	Mintage	VG	F	VF	XF	Unc
1696	1,441	—	—	3,500	5,500	—

KM# A47 5 DUCAT
17.5000 g., 0.9860 Gold 0.5547 oz. AGW **Obv:** Bust of Philipp Valentin right **Rev:** Two ornate shields below crown

Date	Mintage	F	VF	XF	Unc	BU
1657 Rare	—	—	—	—	—	—

KM# A97 5 DUCAT
17.5000 g., 0.9860 Gold 0.5547 oz. AGW **Obv:** Bust of Lothar Franz right **Rev:** Arms

Date	Mintage	F	VF	XF	Unc	BU
1697 Rare	—	—	—	—	—	—

KM# A80 10 DUCAT
35.0000 g., 0.9860 Gold 1.1095 oz. AGW **Obv:** Bust right **Rev:** Crowned 4-fold arms in baroque frame, date above **Note:** Struck with 1 Thaler dies, KM#78.

Date	Mintage	F	VF	XF	Unc	BU
1687 Rare	—	—	—	—	—	—

KM# B97 10 DUCAT
35.0000 g., 0.9860 Gold 1.1095 oz. AGW **Obv:** Oval arms, angel's head and wings below **Note:** Struck with 1 Thaler dies, KM#95.

Date	Mintage	F	VF	XF	Unc	BU
1697 GFN Rare	—	—	—	—	—	—

PATTERNS

Including off metal strikes

KM#	Date	Mintage	Identification	Mkt Val
Pn2	1698 GFN	—	4 Kreuzers. Copper. KM#85	—
Pn3	1700 GFN	—	4 Kreuzers. Copper. KM#85	—

BARBY

A small lordship located near the junction of the Elbe and Saale Rivers, about midway between Magdeburg and Dessau, founded in the early 13th century. The lord of Barby was a vassal of Saxony and was raised to the rank of count in 1497. The countship was divided in 1565, but only the main line of Barby and its successor in 1617, Barby-Mühlingen, issued any coinage. Barby became extinct in 1659 and its lands passed to Anhalt and Saxe-Weissenfels.

RULERS

Wolfgang II, 1565-1615
Wolfgang Friedrich, 1615-1617
Albrecht Friedrich, 1617-1641
and Jost Günther, 1617-1651
August Ludwig, 1641-1659

MINT OFFICIALS' INITIALS

Initials	Date	Name
(a)=  or HM	1611-1615	Heinrich Meyer, mintmaster
	1612-?	Georg Krell, warden
(b)=  or CG	1616-1618	Casper Gieseler, mintmaster
	1618 (January-April)	Heinrich Westermann, mintmaster
(c)= 	1618 (June)-1619 (Spring)	Heinrich Oppermann, mintmaster
	1620 (January)-1621 (March)	Hans Jacob, mint contractor
	1621 (January)-1622	Johann Schmeidler, mint admin.
	1621	Johann Kaulitz & Peter Eulenbeck,mint contractors

ARMS

4-fold with crowned displayed eagle in upper left and lower right, open rose in upper right and lower left.

REFERENCE

M = Manfred Mehl, **Die Münzen der Grafen von Barby und Mühlingen**, Hamburg, 1998.

COUNTSHIP

REGULAR COINAGE

KM# 52 PFENNIG
Copper Weight varies: 0.36-0.49g., 12 mm. **Ruler:** Albrecht Friedrich and Jost Günther **Obv:** Crowned Spanish shield, with concave sides, of rose arms divides date **Note:** Ref. M-132. Uniface.

Date	Mintage	Good	VG	F	VF	XF
(16)21	—	—	—	—	—	—

KM# 53 PFENNIG
0.3300 g., Copper, 11 mm. **Ruler:** Albrecht Friedrich and Jost Günther **Obv:** Crowned Spanish shield of rose arms divides date **Note:** Ref. M-133. Uniface. Prev. KM#19.

Date	Mintage	Good	VG	F	VF	XF
(16)21	—	10.00	20.00	35.00	75.00	—

KM# 54 PFENNIG
0.2500 g., Copper, 11 mm. **Ruler:** Albrecht Friedrich and Jost Günther **Obv:** Spanish shield, with concave sides, of rose arms divides date **Note:** Ref. M-134. Uniface.

Date	Mintage	Good	VG	F	VF	XF
(16)21	—	—	—	—	—	—

KM# 55 PFENNIG
0.1900 g., Copper, 11.5-12 mm. **Ruler:** Albrecht Friedrich and Jost Günther **Obv:** Round 4-fold arms in circle of pellets **Note:** Ref. M-140. Uniface.

Date	Mintage	Good	VG	F	VF	XF
ND(1621)	—	—	—	—	—	—

KM# 57 3 FLITTER
Copper Weight varies: 0.50-1.54g., 15 mm. **Ruler:** Albrecht Friedrich and Jost Günther **Obv:** Crowned ornate shield of 4-fold arms **Rev:** 4-line inscription with date **Rev. Inscription:** .III. / FLITT / REN / (date) **Note:** Ref. M-130. Prev. KM#21. Kipper coinage. Varieties exist.

Date	Mintage	Good	VG	F	VF	XF
(1)6Z1	—	40.00	75.00	150	300	—
(1)621	—	40.00	75.00	150	300	—
1621	—	40.00	75.00	150	300	—

KM# 58 3 FLITTER
0.6300 g., Copper, 15 mm. **Ruler:** Albrecht Friedrich and Jost Günther **Obv:** Crowned ornate shield of rose arms **Rev:** 4-line inscription with date **Rev. Inscription:** .III. / FLITT / REN / (date) **Note:** Ref. M-131. Kipper coinage.

Date	Mintage	Good	VG	F	VF	XF
(1)6Z1	—	—	—	—	—	—

KM# 59 3 FLITTER
Copper, 16 mm. **Ruler:** Albrecht Friedrich and Jost Günther **Obv:** Round 4-fold arms **Rev:** Value 111 above 5-petaled flower divides D - E? in circle of pellets **Note:** Kipper coinage.

Date	Mintage	Good	VG	F	VF	XF
ND(1621-2)	—	100	200	300	475	—

KM# 60 3 FLITTER
0.9300 g., Copper, 16 mm. **Ruler:** Albrecht Friedrich and Jost Günther **Obv:** Round 4-fold arms **Rev:** Small crown in center, 111 above, curved around bottom from right to left FLITTER **Note:** Ref. M-139. Kipper coinage.

Date	Mintage	Good	VG	F	VF	XF
ND(1621)	—	—	—	—	—	—

KM# 62 3 PFENNIG
Copper Weight varies: 0.77-0.80g., 16 mm. **Ruler:** Albrecht Friedrich and Jost Günther **Obv:** Crowned Spanish shield of 4-fold arms **Rev:** Imperial orb with 3 divides date **Note:** Ref. M-123. Kipper coinage.

Date	Mintage	Good	VG	F	VF	XF
(16)Z1	—	—	—	—	—	—

KM# 63 3 PFENNIG
0.6300 g., Copper, 16 mm. **Ruler:** Albrecht Friedrich and Jost Günther **Obv:** Crowned ornate shield of 4-fold arms **Rev:** Imperial orb with 3 divides date **Note:** Ref. M-124. Kipper Coinage.

Date	Mintage	Good	VG	F	VF	XF
(16)Z1	—	—	—	—	—	—

KM# 64 3 PFENNIG
0.4300 g., Copper, 15 mm. **Ruler:** Albrecht Friedrich and Jost Günther **Obv:** Crowned Spanish shield, with concave sides, of 4-fold arms **Rev:** Imperial orb with 3 divides date in ornamented rhombus **Note:** Ref. M-125. Kipper coinage.

Date	Mintage	Good	VG	F	VF	XF
16Z1	—	—	—	—	—	—

KM# 65 3 PFENNIG
0.4000 g., Copper, 15 mm. **Ruler:** Albrecht Friedrich and Jost Günther **Obv:** Round 4-fold arms **Rev:** Small crown in center, EIN. DREIE above, date below, all in circle **Note:** Ref. M-126. Kipper coinage.

Date	Mintage	Good	VG	F	VF	XF
1621	—	—	—	—	—	—

KM# 66 3 PFENNIG
Copper Weight varies: 0.41-1.24g., 15-16 mm. **Ruler:** Albrecht Friedrich and Jost Günther **Obv:** Crowned Spanish shield of 4-fold arms **Rev:** In ornamented rhombus, value 3 with date divided above **Note:** Ref. M-127, 129. Kipper coinage. Prev. KM#20.

Date	Mintage	Good	VG	F	VF	XF
16Z1	—	32.00	65.00	135	275	—

KM# 67 3 PFENNIG
0.8600 g., Copper, 15 mm. **Ruler:** Albrecht Friedrich and Jost Günther **Obv:** Crowned Spanish shield with rose arms **Rev:** Imperial orb with 3 divides date in ornamented rhombus **Note:** Ref. M-128. Kipper coinage.

Date	Mintage	Good	VG	F	VF	XF
16Z1	—	—	—	—	—	—

KM# 68 3 PFENNIG
Copper Weight varies: 0.56-1.18g., 16 mm. **Ruler:** Albrecht Friedrich and Jost Günther **Obv:** Crowned Spanish shield of 4-fold arms **Rev:** Imperial orb with 3, annulet at left and right **Note:** Ref. M#135-37.

Date	Mintage	Good	VG	F	VF	XF
ND(1621)	—	—	—	—	—	—

KM# 69 3 PFENNIG
0.5600 g., Copper, 15 mm. **Ruler:** Albrecht Friedrich and Jost Günther **Obv:** Round 4-fold arms **Rev:** Imperial orb with 3 in ornamented rhombus **Note:** Ref. M-138.

Date	Mintage	Good	VG	F	VF	XF
ND(1621)	—	—	—	—	—	—

KM# 73 3 PFENNIG
0.6800 g., Copper, 16 mm. **Ruler:** Albrecht Friedrich and Jost Günther **Obv:** Crowned ornate shield of 4-fold arms **Rev:** Imperial orb with 3 divides date **Note:** Ref. M-141.

Date	Mintage	Good	VG	F	VF	XF
(16)22	—	—	—	—	—	—

KM# 74 3 PFENNIG
Copper, 15 mm. **Ruler:** Albrecht Friedrich and Jost Günther **Obv:** Crowned ornate shield of 4-fold arms **Rev:** Imperial orb with 3 divides date in ornamented rhombus **Note:** Ref. M-142.

Date	Mintage	Good	VG	F	VF	XF
16ZZ	—	—	—	—	—	—

KM# 75 3 PFENNIG
Silver Weight varies: 0.64-0.83g., 16-17 mm. **Ruler:** Albrecht Friedrich and Jost Günther **Obv:** Spanish shield of 4-fold arms in baroque frame **Rev:** Imperial orb with 3 divides date **Note:** Ref. M-143.

Date	Mintage	Good	VG	F	VF	XF
16ZZ	—	—	—	—	—	—

KM# 2 1/21 GULDEN (Groschen)
1.6100 g., Silver, 21 mm. **Ruler:** Wolfgang II **Obv:** Spanish shield of 4-fold arms **Obv. Legend:** MON. NO. COM(IT). BARB. ET. MVL. **Rev:** Imperial orb with Z1 divides date **Rev. Legend:** RVD. II. D. G. ROM. IMP. S. AV. **Note:** Ref. M-8, 9. Varieties exist.

Date	Mintage	VG	F	VF	XF	Unc
1611 (a)	—	70.00	125	225	300	—

KM# 3 1/21 GULDEN (Groschen)
Silver Weight varies: 1.31-1.85g., 20-21 mm. **Ruler:** Wolfgang II **Obv:** Spanish shield of 4-fold arms **Obv. Legend:** MON. NO(V). COMIT. BARB. E(T). MVL. **Rev:** Imperial orb with Z1, date divided by top of cross in margin **Rev. Legend:** RVD. II. D. G. RO. IMP. S. AVG. **Note:** Ref. M-10, 11. Varieties exist.

Date	Mintage	VG	F	VF	XF	Unc
1611 (a)	—	—	—	—	—	—

KM# 4 1/21 GULDEN (Groschen)
1.7400 g., Silver, 20 mm. **Ruler:** Wolfgang II **Obv:** Spanish shield, with concave sides, of 4-fold arms **Obv. Legend:** MON. NO. COM. BARB. ET. MVL. **Rev:** Imperial orb with Z1 divides mintmaster's initials, date divided by top of cross in margin **Rev. Legend:** RVD. II. ROM. IMP. S. AVG. **Note:** Ref. M-12.

Date	Mintage	VG	F	VF	XF	Unc
1611 HM(a)	—	—	—	—	—	—

KM# 6 1/24 THALER (Groschen)
Silver Weight varies: 1.09-2.36g., 20-21 mm. **Ruler:** Wolfgang II **Obv:** Spanish shield of 4-fold arms, often in baroque frame **Obv. Legend:** MO(N). NO(V)(A). COMI(T). (T) BARB(I). E(T). M(VL)(L) **Rev:** Imperial orb with Z4, date divided by top of cross in margin **Rev. Legend:** RVD(OL)(P). II. RO(M). I(M)(P). S. A(V)(G). **Note:** Ref. M-13, 23, 31, 32, 36-39, 44-46, 54, 55. Prev. KM#5. Varieties exist.

Date	Mintage	VG	F	VF	XF	Unc
1610	—	50.00	90.00	200	350	—
1611	—	40.00	80.00	175	300	—
1611 (a)	—	40.00	80.00	175	300	—
161Z	—	40.00	80.00	175	300	—
161Z (a)	—	40.00	80.00	175	300	—
1613 (a)	—	40.00	80.00	175	300	—

KM# 8 1/24 THALER (Groschen)
Silver Weight varies: 1.16-2.20g., 19-21 mm. **Ruler:** Wolfgang II **Obv:** Spanish shield of 4-fold arms in baroque frame **Obv. Legend:** MO(N)(.) NO(V)(A). COM(IT). BARB(I). E(T). M(VL)(L)(I). **Rev:** Imperial orb with Z4, date divided above orb by base of cross **Rev. Legend:** RVD(OL)(P). II. (D.G.) RO(M)(A). IMP. S. A(V)(G)(VS). **Note:** Ref. M-16-19, 21, 49-52, 56. Varieties exist.

Date	Mintage	VG	F	VF	XF	Unc
1611 (a)	—	35.00	75.00	120	225	—
(1)611 (a)	—	35.00	75.00	120	225	—
161Z (a)	—	35.00	75.00	120	225	—
1613 (a)	—	35.00	75.00	120	225	—

KM# 10 1/24 THALER (Groschen)
Silver Weight varies: 1.56-1.77g., 20 mm. **Ruler:** Wolfgang II **Obv:** Spanish shield, with concave sides, of 4-fold arms **Obv. Legend:** MON. NO. COM(IT). BARB. ET. M(VL). **Rev:** Imperial orb with Z4, date divided above orb by base of cross **Rev. Legend:** RVD(OLP). II. RO. IMP. S. AV(G). **Note:** Ref. M-20, 34, 35. Varieties exist.

Date	Mintage	VG	F	VF	XF	Unc
1611 (a)	—	—	—	—	—	—
161Z	—	—	—	—	—	—

KM# 7 1/24 THALER (Groschen)
Silver Weight varies: 1.29-1.73g., 20 mm. **Ruler:** Wolfgang II **Obv:** Spanish shield of 4-fold arms, often in baroque frame **Obv. Legend:** MO. NO. COMIT. BARB(I). E(T). MVLL. **Rev:** Imperial orb with Z4, date at end of legend **Rev. Legend:** RVD. II. RO. IM. S. AV. **Note:** Ref. M-14, 15. Varieties exist.

Date	Mintage	VG	F	VF	XF	Unc
1611	—	—	—	—	—	—

KM# 9 1/24 THALER (Groschen)
Silver Weight varies: 1.53-1.72g., 20-21 mm. **Ruler:** Wolfgang II **Obv:** Spanish shield of 4-fold arms, usually in baroque frame **Obv. Legend:** MO(N). NO(V)(A). COM(IT). BARB. E. M(VL)(I). **Rev:** Imperial orb with Z4 divides mintmaster's initials, date divided by top of cross in margin **Rev. Legend:** RVD. II. ROM. IMP. S(EMP). AV(G)(VS). **Note:** Ref. M#24-28. Varieties exist.

Date	Mintage	VG	F	VF	XF	Unc
1611 HM	—	—	—	—	—	—
1611 HM(a)	—	—	—	—	—	—

KM# 11 1/24 THALER (Groschen)
Silver, 20 mm. **Ruler:** Wolfgang II **Obv:** Ornately shaped shield of 4-fold arms **Obv. Legend:** MON. NOVA. COMIT. BARB. ET. M. **Rev:** Imperial orb with Z4, date divided by top of cross in margin **Rev. Legend:** RVD. II. RO. IM. S. AVG. **Note:** Ref. M-22.

Date	Mintage	VG	F	VF	XF	Unc
(1)611	—	—	—	—	—	—

KM# 12 1/24 THALER (Groschen)
Silver Weight varies: 1.40-1.54g., 20.5-21 mm. **Ruler:** Wolfgang II **Obv:** Spanish shield of 4-fold arms **Obv. Legend:** MO. NO. COMIT. BARB(I). E(T). MVLL. **Rev:** Imperial orb with Z4 **Rev. Legend:** RVDOL. II. RO. IM. S. AV. **Note:** Ref. M-29, 30. Varieties exist

Date	Mintage	VG	F	VF	XF	Unc
ND(1611-12) (a)	—	—	—	—	—	—

KM# 13 1/24 THALER (Groschen)
Silver Weight varies: 1.29-1.66g., 19-20 mm. **Ruler:** Wolfgang II **Obv:** Spanish shield of 4-fold arms, often in baroque frame **Obv. Legend:** MO. NO. CO. BARB. ET. M. **Rev:** Imperial orb with Z4, date divided by tope of cross in margin **Rev. Legend:** MATI. D. G. RO. I. S. A. **Note:** Ref. M-53, 80. Varieties exist.

Date	Mintage	VG	F	VF	XF	Unc
161Z (a)	—	—	—	—	—	—
1615 (a)	—	—	—	—	—	—

KM# 14 1/24 THALER (Groschen)
Silver Weight varies: 1.36-1.91g., 20-21 mm. **Ruler:** Wolfgang II **Obv:** Spanish shield, with concave sides, of 4-fold arms **Obv. Legend:** MON. NO(V). COM(IT). BARB(IE). ET. M(VL). **Rev:** Imperial orb with Z4, date divided by top of cross in margin **Rev. Legend:** RVD(OLP). II. RO(M). I(MP). S(E). A(V). **Note:** Ref. M#40-43. Varieties exist.

Date	Mintage	VG	F	VF	XF	Unc
161Z (a)	—	—	—	—	—	—
(1)61Z (a)	—	—	—	—	—	—

KM# 15 1/24 THALER (Groschen)
1.5400 g., Silver, 21 mm. **Ruler:** Wolfgang II **Obv:** Oval shield of 4-fold arms in baroque frame **Obv. Legend:** MON. NO. COMIT. BARB. ET. MVL. **Rev:** Imperial orb with Z4, date divided by tope of cross in margin **Rev. Legend:** RVDOLP. II. RO. I. S. AV. **Note:** Ref. M-33, 47.

Date	Mintage	VG	F	VF	XF	Unc
161Z	—	—	—	—	—	—
161Z (a)	—	—	—	—	—	—

KM# 16 1/24 THALER (Groschen)
1.7400 g., Silver, 21 mm. **Ruler:** Wolfgang II **Obv:** Oval shield of 4-fold arms in baroque frame **Obv. Legend:** MON. NO. COMIT. BARB. ET. MVL. **Rev:** Imperial orb with Z4, date divided above orb by base of cross **Rev. Legend:** RVDOLP. II. RO. IMP. S. AV. **Note:** Ref. M-48.

Date	Mintage	VG	F	VF	XF	Unc
161Z (a)	—	—	—	—	—	—

KM# 18 1/24 THALER (Groschen)
Silver Weight varies: 1.04-1.68g., 20 mm. **Ruler:** Wolfgang II **Obv:** Spanish shield of 4-fold arms, usually in baroque frame **Obv. Legend:** M(O)N. NO(VA). COMIT. BARB. ET. M. **Rev:** Imperial orb with Z4 divides mintmaster's initials, date divided by top of cross in margin **Rev. Legend:** M(A)(T)I. (I.) D. G. RO(M). (IM.) SEM. A(V). **Note:** Ref. M#59-71, 75, 79. Prev. KM#6. Varieties exist.

Date	Mintage	VG	F	VF	XF	Unc
1613 HM	—	30.00	60.00	120	240	—
1613 HM(a)	—	30.00	60.00	120	240	—
1614 HM	—	30.00	60.00	120	240	—
1614 HM(a)	—	30.00	60.00	120	240	—
1615 HM	—	30.00	60.00	120	240	—
1615 HM(a)	—	30.00	60.00	120	240	—
1617	—	30.00	60.00	120	240	—

KM# 17 1/24 THALER (Groschen)
Silver Weight varies: 1.49-1.65g., 20 mm. **Ruler:** Wolfgang II **Obv:** Spanish shield of 4-fold arms in baroque frame **Obv. Legend:** MON. NOVA.COMIT. BARB. ET. M. **Rev:** Imperial orb with Z4, date divided above orb by base of cross **Rev. Legend:** MATI. D. G. RO. IM. SEM. AV. **Note:** Ref. M-57, 58. Varieties exist.

Date	Mintage	VG	F	VF	XF	Unc
1613	—	—	—	—	—	—

KM# 20 1/24 THALER (Groschen)
1.5000 g., Silver, 20 mm. **Ruler:** Wolfgang II **Obv:** Spanish shield, with concave sides, of 4-fold arms, in baroque frame **Obv. Legend:** MO. NO. CO. BARBE. ET. M. **Rev:** Imperial orb with Z4, date divided by top of cross in margin **Rev. Legend:** MATT. DG. RO. IM. **Note:** Ref. M-81.

Date	Mintage	VG	F	VF	XF	Unc
1615 (a)	—	—	—	—	—	—

KM# 21 1/24 THALER (Groschen)
Silver Weight varies: 1.19-1.29g., 20-21 mm. **Ruler:** Wolfgang II **Obv:** Spanish shield, with concave sides, of 4-fold arms **Obv. Legend:** MON. NOVA. COMIT. BARB. ET. M. **Rev:** Imperial orb with Z4 divides mintmaster's initials, date divided by top of cross in margin **Rev. Legend:** MAT. II. D. G. RO. IM. SEM. A. **Note:** Ref. M-76, 77. Varieties exist.

Date	Mintage	VG	F	VF	XF	Unc
1615 HM	—	—	—	—	—	—

KM# 22 1/24 THALER (Groschen)
Silver Weight varies: 1.35-1.61g., 20 mm. **Ruler:** Wolfgang II **Obv:** Spanish shield of 4-fold arms in baroque frame, mintmaster's initials in ligature at end of legend **Obv. Legend:** MO. NO. CO. BARBE. ET. M. **Rev:** Imperial orb with Z4, date divided by tope of cross in margin **Rev. Legend:** MAT(T)(I). D. G. RO. I(M). (S.) (A.) **Note:** Ref. M-78.

Date	Mintage	VG	F	VF	XF	Unc
1615 HM(a)	—	—	—	—	—	—

KM# 23 1/24 THALER (Groschen)
Silver, 20 mm. **Ruler:** Wolfgang II **Obv:** Spanish shield, with concave sides, of 4-fold arms in baroque frame, rosette at left and right **Obv. Legend:** MN. NOVA. COMIT. BARB. ET. M. **Rev:** Imperial orb with Z4, date divided by top of cross in margin **Rev. Legend:** MATI. DG. RO. I. S. A.

Date	Mintage	VG	F	VF	XF	Unc
1615	—	35.00	80.00	125	210	—

KM# 36 1/24 THALER (Groschen)
Silver Weight varies: 1.01-1.58g., 19-20 mm. **Ruler:** Wolfgang Friedrich **Obv:** Crowned Spanish shield of 4-fold arms, usually in baroque frame **Obv. Legend:** MO. NO. CO. BARB(E). ET. M. **Rev:** Imperial orb with Z4, date divided by top of cross in margin, mintmaster's symbol at end of legend **Rev. Legend:** MATI. D. G. RO. I. S. (A.) **Note:** Ref. M#91, 95-100, 102, 103. Varieties exist.

Date	Mintage	VG	F	VF	XF	Unc
1616 (b)	—	20.00	40.00	70.00	130	—
1617 (b)	—	20.00	40.00	70.00	130	—

KM# 35 1/24 THALER (Groschen)
Silver Weight varies: 1.15-1.52g., 20 mm. **Ruler:** Wolfgang Friedrich **Obv:** Spanish shield of 4-fold arms, usually in baroque frame **Obv. Legend:** MO. NO. CO. BARBE. ET. M. **Rev:** Imperial orb with Z4, date divided by top of cross in margin, mintmaster's symbol at end of legend **Rev. Legend:** MATI. D. G. RO. I. S. A. **Note:** Ref. M-93, 94, 101.

Date	Mintage	VG	F	VF	XF	Unc
1616 (b)	—	20.00	40.00	70.00	130	—
1617 (b)	—	20.00	40.00	70.00	130	—

KM# 28 1/24 THALER (Groschen)
1.3700 g., Silver, 20 mm. **Ruler:** Wolfgang Friedrich **Obv:** Spanish shield of 4-fold arms in baroque frame **Rev:** Imperial orb with Z4 divides date **Note:** Ref. M-89.

Date	Mintage	VG	F	VF	XF	Unc
1616 (a)	—	—	—	—	—	—

KM# 29 1/24 THALER (Groschen)
Silver Weight varies: 1.04-1.55g., 20 mm. **Ruler:** Wolfgang Friedrich **Obv:** Spanish shield of 4-fold arms in baroque frame **Obv. Legend:** MO. NO. CO. BARBE. ET. M. **Rev:** Imperial orb with Z4, date divided by top of cross in margin **Rev. Legend:** MATI. D. G. RO. I(M). S. A(V). **Note:** Ref. M-84, 85.

Date	Mintage	VG	F	VF	XF	Unc
1616 (a)	—	—	—	—	—	—

KM# 30 1/24 THALER (Groschen)
1.3100 g., Silver, 20 mm. **Ruler:** Wolfgang Friedrich **Obv:** Spanish shield of 4-fold arms in baroque frame, mintmaster's initials in ligature at end of legend **Obv. Legend:** M. NO. CO. BARBE. ET. M. **Rev:** Imperial orb with Z4, date divided by top of cross in margin **Rev. Legend:** MATT. D.G. RO. IM. **Note:** Ref. M-82.

Date	Mintage	VG	F	VF	XF	Unc
1616 HM(a)	—	—	—	—	—	—

KM# 31 1/24 THALER (Groschen)
Silver Weight varies: 1.38-1.55g., 20 mm. **Ruler:** Wolfgang Friedrich **Obv:** Spanish shield, with concave sides, of 4-fold arms in baroque frame **Obv. Legend:** MO. NO. CO. BARBE. ET. M. **Rev:** Imperial orb with Z4, date divided by top of cross in margin **Rev. Legend:** MATT. D.G. RO. IM. **Note:** Ref. M-86.

Date	Mintage	VG	F	VF	XF	Unc
1616 (a)	—	—	—	—	—	—

KM# 32 1/24 THALER (Groschen)
Silver Weight varies: 1.06-1.54g., 20 mm. **Ruler:** Wolfgang Friedrich **Obv:** Crowned Spanish shield of 4-fold arms in baroque frame **Obv. Legend:** MO. NO. CO. BARBE. ET. M. **Rev:** Imperial orb with Z4, date divided by top of cross in margin **Rev. Legend:** MATI. D. G. RO. I(M). S. A(V). **Note:** Ref. M-83.

Date	Mintage	VG	F	VF	XF	Unc
1616 (a)	—	20.00	40.00	65.00	100	—

KM# 33 1/24 THALER (Groschen)
1.5500 g., Silver, 19-20 mm. **Ruler:** Wolfgang Friedrich **Obv:** Crowned oval shield of 4-fold arms in baroque frame **Obv. Legend:** MO. NO. CO. BARBE. ET. M. **Rev:** Imperial orb with Z4, date divided by top of cross in margin **Rev. Legend:** MATI. D.G. RO. I. S. A. **Note:** Ref. M-87, 88.

Date	Mintage	VG	F	VF	XF	Unc
1616 (a)	—	—	—	—	—	—

KM# 34 1/24 THALER (Groschen)
1.4800 g., Silver, 20 mm. **Ruler:** Wolfgang Friedrich **Obv:** Spanish shield of 4-fold arms, usually in baroque frame **Obv. Legend:** MO. NO. CO. BARB(E). ET. M. **Rev:** Imperial orb with Z4, date divided by top of cross in margin, mintmaster's symbol at beginning of legend **Rev. Legend:** MATI. D. G. RO. I. S. A. **Note:** Ref. M-92.

Date	Mintage	VG	F	VF	XF	Unc
1616 (b)	—	—	—	—	—	—

KM# 37 1/24 THALER (Groschen)

1.4000 g., Silver, 20 mm. **Ruler:** Wolfgang Friedrich **Obv:** Spanish shield of 4-fold arms, usually in baroque frame **Rev:** Imperial orb with Z4, date divided by top of cross in margin, mintmaster's initials at end of legend **Note:** Ref. M-90.

Date	Mintage	VG	F	VF	XF	Unc
1616 CG	—	—	—	—	—	—

KM# 39 1/24 THALER (Groschen)

Silver Weight varies: 1.20-1.67g., 19-20 mm. **Ruler:** Albrecht Friedrich and Jost Günther **Obv:** Crowned Spanish shield of four-fold arms in baroque frame **Obv. Legend:** MO. NO. CO. BARB. ET. M. **Rev:** Imperial orb with 24, date divided by top of cross in margin **Rev. Legend:** MAT. D.G. RO. I(M). S. A. **Note:** Ref. M#104-6. Prev. KM#15. Varieties exist.

Date	Mintage	VG	F	VF	XF	Unc
1618	—	25.00	40.00	80.00	155	—
1618 (c)	—	25.00	40.00	80.00	155	—

KM# 40 1/24 THALER (Groschen)

Silver, 20x21 mm. **Ruler:** Albrecht Friedrich and Jost Günther **Obv:** Crowned Spanish shield of 4-fold arms in baroque frame **Obv. Legend:** MO. NO. CO. BARB. ET. M. **Rev:** Imperial orb with 24, date divided by top of cross in margin **Rev. Legend:** MAT. D. G. RO. I. S. A. **Note:** Ref. M-105a. Klippe.

Date	Mintage	VG	F	VF	XF	Unc
1618 (c)	—	—	—	—	—	—

KM# 42 1/24 THALER (Groschen)

Silver Weight varies: 0.83-1.41g., 17-18 mm. **Ruler:** Albrecht Friedrich and Jost Günther **Obv:** Crowned Spanish shield of 4-fld arms, often in baroque frame **Obv. Legend:** MO. NO(V). CO. BAR(B). E(T). M. **Rev:** Imperial orb with Z4 or 24, date divided by top of cross in margin **Rev. Legend:** MAT. D. G. R(O). I. S. A. **Note:** Ref. M#107-112. Kipper coinage. Varieties exist.

Date	Mintage	VG	F	VF	XF	Unc
1619	—	25.00	60.00	100	165	—
1619 (c)	—	35.00	80.00	125	210	—

KM# 44 1/24 THALER (Groschen)

Silver Weight varies: 0.89-1.19g., 16-17 mm. **Ruler:** Albrecht Friedrich and Jost Günther **Obv:** Crowned Spanish shield of 4-fold arms **Obv. Legend:** MO. NO. CO. BAR. ET. M. **Rev:** Imperial orb with 24, date divided by top of cross in margin **Rev. Legend:** FER. II. D. G. RO. I. S. A. **Note:** Ref. M-113. Kipper coinage.

Date	Mintage	VG	F	VF	XF	Unc
(16)20	—	—	—	—	—	—

KM# 45 1/24 THALER (Groschen)

Silver Weigh varies: 0.67-1.06g., 16-17 mm. **Ruler:** Albrecht Friedrich and Jost Günther **Obv:** Crowned Spanish shield of four-fold arms **Obv. Legend:** MO. NO. CO. BAR. E(T). M. **Rev:** Imperial orb with 24 **Rev. Legend:** FER. II. D. G. RO. I. S. A(V). **Note:** Ref. M-121, 122. Prev. KM#16. Kipper coinage.

Date	Mintage	VG	F	VF	XF	Unc
ND(1620-1)	—	15.00	30.00	60.00	120	—

KM# 47 4 GROSCHEN

Silver Weight varies: 1.84-2.05g., 24 mm. **Ruler:** Albrecht Friedrich and Jost Günther **Obv:** Crowned Spanish shield of 4-fold arms in baroque frame **Obv. Legend:** COMIT. BARBI. ET. MUHL(I)(N). **Rev:** Crowned imperial eagle, 4 in orb on breast **Rev. Legend:** FER. II. D. G. ROM. IMP. SEM. A(U)(V)(G). **Note:** Ref. M-114. Kipper coinage.

Date	Mintage	VG	F	VF	XF	Unc
ND(1620-1)	—	—	—	—	—	—

KM# 48 12 KREUZER

Silver Weight varies: 1.61-2.11g., 25 mm. **Ruler:** Albrecht Friedrich and Jost Günther **Obv:** Crowned Spanish shield of 4-fold arms in baroque frame **Obv. Legend:** COMIT. BARB(I). ET. MUHLI(N). **Rev:** Crowned imperial eagle, 12 in orb on breast **Rev. Legend:** FER. II. D. G. ROM. IM. SEM. A(U)(V)(G). **Note:** Ref. M-115. Kipper coinage.

Date	Mintage	VG	F	VF	XF	Unc
ND(1620-1)	—	—	—	—	—	—

KM# 49 2 SCHILLING

Silver Weight varies: 0.73-1.09g., 17-20 mm. **Ruler:** Albrecht Friedrich and Jost Günther **Obv:** Round 4-fold arms **Obv. Legend:** COM. BARB. ET. MU(H)(L). **Rev:** Large intertwined DS in circle **Rev. Legend:** MO(N). NO. ARGENT(E)(A). **Note:** Ref. M-117, 119. Kipper coinage. Doppelschilling. Prev. KM#18.

Date	Mintage	VG	F	VF	XF	Unc
ND(1620-1)	—	—	—	—	—	—

KM# 50 2 SCHILLING

Silver Weight varies: 1.00-1.40g., 19-21 mm. **Ruler:** Albrecht Friedrich and Jost Günther **Obv:** Ornate shield of 4-fold arms in circle **Obv. Legend:** COMI. BARB. ET. M(I)(U)H(L)(I). **Rev:** Large intertwined DS in circle **Rev. Legend:** MON. NOU. ARGENTEA. **Note:** Ref. M-118, 120. Kipper coinage. Doppelschilling. Prev. KM#17. Varieties exist.

Date	Mintage	VG	F	VF	XF	Unc
ND(1620-1)	—	—	—	—	—	—

KM# 71 2 SCHILLING

Silver, 21 mm. **Ruler:** Albrecht Friedrich and Jost Günther **Obv:** Ornate shield of 4-fold arms in circle **Obv. Legend:** COMI. BARB. ET. MUHL. **Rev:** Large intertwined DS in circle, date divided above and below **Rev. Legend:** MON. NOU. ARGENTEA. **Note:** Ref. M-116. Kipper coinage. Doppelschilling.

Date	Mintage	VG	F	VF	XF	Unc
(1)6Z1	—	—	—	—	—	—

KM# 24 THALER

28.4500 g., Silver, 45 mm. **Ruler:** Wolfgang II **Obv:** Spanish shield of 4-fold arms in baroque frame, 2 ornate helmets above, mintmaster's initials between crests, date divided 1-6 by helmets, 1-5 by bottom of arms **Obv. Legend:** WOLFGANG. COMES. BARBYENSIS. ET. MVLINGENS. **Rev:** Half-length armored figure to right holding baton, helmet at far right, 2-line inscription in exergue, legend divided by four small shields of arms **Rev. Legend:** ZV. GOTT - ALLEIN - DIE. HOFF - NVNG. MEIN. **Rev. Inscription:** TRAV. SCHAV / .WEHM. **Note:** Ref. M-72; Dav. 6060. Prev. KM#10.

Date	Mintage	VG	F	VF	XF	Unc
1615 HM(a) Rare	—	—	—	—	—	—

KM# 25 THALER

29.0500 g., Silver, 44 mm. **Ruler:** Wolfgang II **Subject:** Death of Wolfgang II **Obv:** Spanish shield of 4-fold arms in baroque frame, 2 ornate helmets above, mintmaster's initials between crests, date divided 1-6 by helmets, 1-5 by bottom of arms **Obv. Legend:** WOLFGANG. COMES. BARBYENSIS. ET. MVLINGENS. **Rev:** 9-line inscription with Roman numeral date **Rev. Inscription:** OBIIT / XXIII. MAR / A. MDCXV CVM / SINCERVS CHRI / STI. ET STRENVVS / PATRIÆ VIXIS / SET MILES / ANNOS XXCIII / .MIII . DVII. **Note:** Ref. M-74; Dav. 6062. Prev. KM#11.

Date	Mintage	VG	F	VF	XF	Unc
1615 HM(a) Rare	—	—	—	—	—	—

KM# 26 2 THALER

57.9100 g., Silver, 45 mm. **Ruler:** Wolfgang II **Subject:** Death of Wolfgang II **Obv:** Spanish shield of 4-fold arms in baroque frame, 2 ornate helmets above, mintmaster's initials between crests, date divided 1-6 by helmets, 1-5 by bottom of arms **Obv. Legend:** WOLFGANG. COMES. BARBYENSIS. ET. MVLINGENS. **Rev:** 9-line inscription with Roman numeral date **Rev. Inscription:** OBIIT / XXIII. MAR / A. MDCXV CVM / SINCERVS CHRI / STI. ET STRENVVS / PATRIÆ VIXIS / SET MILES / ANNOS XXCIII / .MIII . DVII. **Note:** Ref. M-73; Dav. 6061. Prev. KM#12. Struck from Thaler dies, KM#25.

Date	Mintage	VG	F	VF	XF	Unc
1615 HM(a) Rare	—	—	—	—	—	—

BAVARIA

(Bayern)

One of the largest states in Germany, Bavaria was a duchy from earliest times, ruled by the Agilholfingen dynasty from 553 until it was suppressed by Charlemagne in 788. Bavaria remained a territory of the Carolingian Empire from that time until 911, when the son of the Count of Scheyern was made duke and began a new line of rulers there. A number of dukes during the next century and a half were elected emperor, but when the mail line became extinct, Empress Agnes gave Bavaria to the Counts of Nordheim in 1061. His descendant, Heinrich XII the Lion, fell out of favor with the emperor and was deposed. The duchy was then entrusted to Otto VI von Wittelsbach, Count of Scheyern and descendant of the counts who had ruled from the early 10th century. Duke Otto I, as he was known from 1180 on, was the ancestor of the dynasty which ruled in Bavaria until 1918 and, from the late 13th century, in the Rhine Palatinate as well (see Electoral Pfalz). The first of several divisions took place in 1255 when lines in Upper and Lower Bavaria were established. The line in Lower Bavaria became extinct in 1340 and the territory reverted to Upper Bavaria. Meanwhile, the division of Upper Bavaria and the Palatinate took place and was confirmed by treaty in 1329, although the electoral vote residing with the Wittelsbachs was to be held jointly by the two branches. In 1347, Bavaria and all other holdings of the family in Brandenburg, the Tyrol and Holland were divided among six brothers. Munich had become the chief city of the duchy by this time. In 1475, Duke Stephen I, who had reunited most of the family's holdings in Bavaria, died and left three sons who promptly divided their patrimony once again. The lines of Ingolstadt, Landshut and Munich were founded, but as the other lines died out, the one seated in Munich regained control of all of Bavaria. Duke Albrecht IV instituted primogeniture in 1506 and from that time on, Bavaria remained united. When Elector Friedrich V of the Palatinate (Pfalz) was elected King of Bohemia in 1618, an event which helped precipitate the Thirty Years' War, Duke Maximilian I of Bavaria sided with the emperor against his kinsman. The electoral dignity had been given to the Pfalz branch of the Wittelsbachs by the Golden Bull of 1356, a fact which was a source of contention with the Bavarian branch of the family. With the ouster of Friedrich V, Maximilian I obtained the electoral right and control of the Palatinate in 1623, then also ruled over the Upper Palatinate (Oberpfalz) from 1628 until the conclusion of the war and the Peace of Westphalia. The Bavarian Wittelsbachs became extinct in 1777 and the line in Electoral Pfalz acquired Bavaria, thus uniting the two main territories of the dynasty under a single ruler for the first time since the early 14th century. When Napoleon abolished the Holy Roman Empire in 1806, bringing an end to the electoral system, the ruler of Bavaria was raised to the rank of king. The 19th century saw tragedy upon tragedy visit the royal family. Because of his opposition to the parliamentary reform movement, Ludwig I was forced to abdicate in 1848. His grandson, Ludwig II, inspired by his upbringing to spend his fortune building the fairy tale castle of Neuschwanstein, was forcibly removed by court nobles and died under mysterious circumstances in 1886. His younger brother, Otto, was declared insane and the kingdom was ruled by his uncle, the beloved Prince Luitpold, as prince regent. Ludwig II, the last King of Bavaria, was forced to abdicate at the end of World War I.

RULERS

Maximilian I, 1598-1651
Ferdinand Maria, 1651-1679
Maximilian II, Emanuel, 1679-1726

MINT OFFICIALS' INITIALS

Amberg Mint

Initials or marks	Date	Name
(a)= ☿ NF	1621-22	Nicholas Fischer, mintmaster
(b)= ☾	1621-22	Johann Rentsch and Jonas Riedl, mintmasters
(c)= ♀ and/or ♅	1622	Georg Kellner and Neuberger, mintmasters
(d)= ✳	1622-23	Christoph Hegner, mintmaster and Georg Kellner
	1622-23	Michael Liedl, mintmaster
	1623	Barthel Simon, warden
(e)= ☾ or G	1624-26	Hans Christoph Geissler
	1624-26	Georg Thomas Paur, die-cutter
	1626-27	Claus Oppermann, mintmaster
	1627	Johann Weber, warden

Heidelberg Mint

Initials or mark	Date	Name
	1620-24	Johann Ludwig Eichelstein, mintmaster
GC	1624-28	Georg Crämer, mint director

Kemnath Mint

Initial or mark	Date	Name
(f)= ✳	1623	Andreas Liebholz (Liebholdt) aand Georg Kellner, mintmasters

Munich Mint

Initials	Date	Name
	1586-1615	Kaspar Lechner, die-cutter
	1596-1620	Balthasar Hitschler (Hutschler), warden
	1596-1601	Paulus van Vianen, goldsmith
	1600-34	Eberl Christoph Ulrich, die-cutter and medailleur
	Ca. 1618-23	Hans Pernegger, warden
	Ca. 1618-20	Hans Georg Vollmann, goldsmith and die-cutter
	1618-26	Isaak Zeggin, goldsmith
	1620-25	Paul Krieger, mint director
	Ca. 1620	Maximilian Jungholzer, warden
	1620	Zacharias Hülz, comptroller
	Ca. 1620	Andreas Pfundtmaier, comptroller
	1621	Saulus Beringer, mint director
	Ca. 1623-66	Paul Zeggin, medailleur
	1625	Martin Ziegler, mint contractor
	1625-32	Martin Hollmayr, warden
	Ca. 1631	Hans Jakob Perschl, die-cutter
	Ca. 1631	Georg Schultes, die-cutter in Augsburg
	Ca. 1632-35	Martin Holmayr, mintmaster
	Ca. 1635-65	Philipp Paul, mint contractor
	1637	Christoph Früchtinger, warden
	1641	Christoph Fichner, warden
	1642-50	Balthasar Müller, goldsmith
	1647-69	Johann Schändl, warden
	1651	Hans Diener, warden
	1651-62	Christoph Wascher, goldsmith
	1652-61	Johann Benno Hözer, die-cutter
	Ca. 1654	Georg Jungholzer, warden
	1661	Johann Jakob Hözer, die-cutter
	Ca. 1665-68	Franz Friesshamer, mint inspector
CZ	1666-1713	Kaspar Zeggin, die-cutter
	1669	Kaspar Preiss, goldsmith
	1673	Christian Sayler, goldsmith

	1675	Albrecht Johann Philipp Jakob Oberleitner, warden
	1677-1705	Moritz Angermayr, warden
MB	Ca. 1680-1725	Martin Brunner, medailleur in Nürnberg
	1681-82	Sebastian Wendl, goldsmith
	1681-1702	Hans Georg Schmidt, goldsmith
	1682	Johann Karl Renner, die-cutter
	Ca. 1687-1718	Johann Christoph Packhenreiter, mint director
	1690	Johann Jakob Langebein, die-cutter
	1691-1700	Johann Gottlieb Stotz, warden
	1692	Franz Karl Angermayr, warden
	1697	Johann Strobl, goldsmith

Neumarkt Mint

Initial	Date	Name
(g)= or	1623-26	Hans Zissler, mintmaster

ARMS

Wittelsbach and Bavaria – field of lozenges (diamond shapes); Pfalz – rampant lion, usually to the left

MINT MARKS

A – Amberg, 1763-95

M - Munich

DUCHY

REGULAR COINAGE

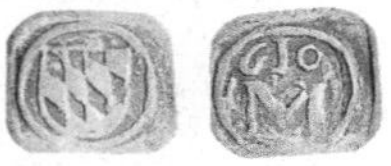

KM# 5 PFENNIG

0.2500 g., Silver, 11-12 mm. **Ruler:** Maximilian I **Obv:** Shield of Wittelsbach arms in circle **Rev:** 'M' below date in circle **Mint:** Munich **Note:** Ref. H#57; JB#832-36. Struck on squarish flans. (Schwarzpfennig). Varieties exist.

Date	Mintage	VG	F	VF	XF	Unc
1606	—	8.00	15.00	35.00	75.00	—
1607	—	8.00	15.00	35.00	75.00	—
(1)608	—	8.00	15.00	35.00	75.00	—
(1)609	—	8.00	15.00	35.00	75.00	—
(1)610	—	8.00	15.00	35.00	75.00	—
(1)611	—	8.00	15.00	35.00	75.00	—
(1)61Z	—	8.00	15.00	35.00	75.00	—
(1)613	—	8.00	15.00	35.00	75.00	—
(1)614	—	8.00	15.00	35.00	75.00	—
(1)615	—	8.00	15.00	35.00	75.00	—
(1)616	—	8.00	15.00	35.00	75.00	—
(1)617	—	8.00	15.00	35.00	75.00	—
(1)618	—	8.00	15.00	35.00	75.00	—
(1)6Z0	—	8.00	15.00	35.00	75.00	—
(1)6Z1	—	8.00	15.00	35.00	75.00	—

KM# 12 PFENNIG (Kipper)

Copper, 12 mm. **Ruler:** Maximilian I **Obv:** Shield of Wittelsbach arms in circle **Rev:** Value • I • in circle **Mint:** Munich **Note:** Ref. H#64; JB-862. Prev. KM#6. Struck on squarish flan.

Date	Mintage	VG	F	VF	XF	Unc
ND(1621-23)	—	16.00	32.00	65.00	130	—

KM# 48 PFENNIG (Kipper)

Silver, 12 mm. **Ruler:** Maximilian I **Obv:** Crowned Pfalz lion to left holding imperial orb, 'P' at right **Mint:** Amberg **Note:** Uniface. Ref. G#96; H-79. Oberpfalz issue.

Date	Mintage	VG	F	VF	XF	Unc
ND(1621-23)	—	55.00	120	175	300	—

KM# 49 PFENNIG (Kipper)

Silver **Ruler:** Maximilian I **Obv:** Crowned Pfalz lion to right holding imperial orb, 'P' at left **Mint:** Amberg **Note:** Uniface. Ref. G#97; H-97. Oberpfalz issue.

Date	Mintage	VG	F	VF	XF	Unc
ND(1621-23)	—	—	—	—	—	—

KM# 8 2 PFENNIG

Copper, 15 mm. **Ruler:** Maximilian I **Obv:** Shield of Wittelsbach arms in circle **Rev:** Value I•I in circle **Mint:** Munich **Note:** Ref. H#65; JB-861. Kipper. Prev. KM#23.

Date	Mintage	VG	F	VF	XF	Unc
ND(1621-23)	—	15.00	30.00	60.00	125	—

KM# 15 2 PFENNIG

Copper, 11-12 mm. **Ruler:** Maximilian I **Obv:** Shield of Wittelsbach arms in circle **Rev:** Large '2' in circle **Mint:** Munich **Note:** Ref. H#66. Prev. KM#24. Struck on squarish flans.

Date	Mintage	VG	F	VF	XF	Unc
ND(1621-23)	—	15.00	30.00	60.00	125	—

KM# 51 4 PFENNIG (Kipper)

Silver **Ruler:** Maximilian I **Obv:** 2 ornate adjacent shields of arms, Pfalz at left and Bavaria at right, imperial orb below **Rev:** 2-line inscription in laurel wreath **Rev. Inscription:** • IIII • / • PFE • **Mint:** Amberg **Note:** Ref. G#94; JB-961; H-80. Oberpfalz issue. Varieties exist.

Date	Mintage	VG	F	VF	XF	Unc
ND(1621-23)	—	—	—	—	—	—

KM# 10 4 PFENNIG (Kipper)

Copper **Ruler:** Maximilian I **Obv:** Bavarian arms in wreath **Rev:** Value 'IIII' in wreath **Mint:** Munich **Note:** Ref. H#67. Prev. KM#26.

Date	Mintage	VG	F	VF	XF	Unc
ND(1621-22)	—	8.00	15.00	30.00	60.00	—

KM# 18 4 PFENNIG (Kipper)

Copper **Ruler:** Maximilian I **Obv:** Bavarian arms in circle **Rev:** Cross in circle **Mint:** Munich **Note:** Ref. H#69. Prev. KM#28.

Date	Mintage	VG	F	VF	XF	Unc
ND(1621-22)	—	16.00	32.00	65.00	135	—

KM# 17 KREUZER (Kipper)

Copper **Ruler:** Maximilian I **Obv:** Bavarian arms in circle **Rev:** 'K' in circle **Mint:** Munich **Note:** Octagonal planchet. Ref. H#68. Prev. KM#27.

Date	Mintage	VG	F	VF	XF	Unc
ND(1621-22)	—	16.00	32.00	65.00	135	—

KM# 81 KREUZER (Kipper)

0.7900 g., Copper, 17.5 mm. **Ruler:** Maximilian I **Obv:** 2 ornate adjacent shields of arms, Pfalz on left, Bavaria on right, imperial orb below **Rev:** 4-line inscription with date **Rev. Inscription:** (rosette) I (rosette) / KREVT / • ZER • / (date) **Mint:** Amberg **Note:** Ref. G#95; JB-962; H-81. Oberpfalz issue.

Date	Mintage	VG	F	VF	XF	Unc
1622	—	35.00	70.00	115	200	—

KM# 82 KREUZER (Kipper)

Copper, 17.5 mm. **Ruler:** Maximilian I **Obv:** 2 ornate adjacent shields of arms, Pfalz on left, Bavaria on right, imperial orb below **Rev:** 4-line inscription with date **Rev. Inscription:** • I • / KREVTZ / • ER • / (date) **Mint:** Amberg **Note:** Ref. H#81; Kraaz 544. Oberpfalz issue.

Date	Mintage	VG	F	VF	XF	Unc
1622	—	25.00	45.00	85.00	160	—

KM# 128.2 2 KREUZER (1/2 Batzen)

Silver **Ruler:** Maximilian I **Obv:** Shield of Wittelsbach arms with scalloped sides in circle **Obv. Legend:** M. C. P. R. V. B. D. S. R. I. A. E. **Rev:** Imperial orb with value 'Z' in circle **Rev. Legend:** SOLI. DEO GLORIA. **Mint:** Munich **Note:** Ref. JB#929. Prev. KM#30.

Date	Mintage	VG	F	VF	XF	Unc
ND(1623-37)	—	8.00	16.00	35.00	75.00	—

KM# 38.1 3 KREUZER (Groschen)

1.5000 g., Silver, 20-21 mm. **Ruler:** Maximilian I **Obv:** Shield of Wittelsbach arms, with scalloped sides, in circle **Obv. Legend:** + GROSSVS NOVVS BAVARICVS. **Rev:** Rampant lion of Pfalz to left in circle, value (3) in oval below **Rev. Legend:** + SOLI DEO - GLORIA. **Mint:** Munich **Note:** Ref. H#58; JB-830. Prev. KM#116.

Date	Mintage	VG	F	VF	XF	Unc
ND(1620)	290,000	75.00	150	300	600	—

KM# 38.2 3 KREUZER (Groschen)

1.6800 g., Silver, 20-21 mm. **Ruler:** Maximilian I **Obv:** Ornamented round shield of Wittelsbach arms **Obv. Legend:** GROSS(VS). NOVVS. BAVARICVS. **Rev:** Pfalz lion rampant to left in circle, value (3) in oval below **Rev. Legend:** SOLI(.) DEO - GLORIA. **Mint:** Munich **Note:** Ref. H#58; JB-831.

Date	Mintage	VG	F	VF	XF	Unc
ND(1620)	Inc. above	75.00	150	300	600	—

KM# 84 6 KREUZER (Kipper)

Silver, 21-22 mm. **Ruler:** Maximilian I **Obv:** Oval shield of Wittelsbach arms in baroque frame **Obv. Legend:** SOLI. EO. GLORIA. **Rev:** 4-line inscription with date **Rev. Inscription:** (date) / LANDT / MYNZ / VI. **Mint:** Munich **Note:** Ref. H#70; BJ-853. Prev. KM#17.

Date	Mintage	VG	F	VF	XF	Unc
1622	—	13.00	27.00	45.00	90.00	—

KM# 86 15 KREUZER (1/4 Gulden)

Silver, 27 mm. **Ruler:** Maximilian I **Obv:** Oval shield of Wittelsbach arms in baroque frame **Obv. Legend:** SIT. NOMEN. DNI. BENEDTM. **Rev:** 3-line inscription in cartouche, date above **Rev. Inscription:** LANDT / MYNZ / XV. **Mint:** Munich **Note:** Ref. H#71; JB-852. Prev. KM#18. Varieties exist.

Date	Mintage	VG	F	VF	XF	Unc
1622	—	30.00	60.00	125	250	—

KM# 40 24 KREUZER (Kipper)

0.6900 Silver Weight varies: 6.68-7.6g., 29 mm. **Ruler:** Maximilian I **Obv:** Wittelsbach arms in oval baroque frame **Obv. Legend:** MONETA NOVVA BAVARICA. **Rev:** Crowned Pfalz lion to left in oval baroque frame **Rev. Legend:** SIT. NOMEN. DNI: BENEDTM: **Mint:** Munich **Note:** Ref. H#59; JB-829. Prev. KM#11.

Date	Mintage	VG	F	VF	XF	Unc
ND(1620)	1,013,000	130	250	470	925	—

KM# 53.1 24 KREUZER (Kipper)

6.0500 g., Silver, 30 mm. **Ruler:** Maximilian I **Obv:** Ornate 3-fold arms of Pfalz, Bavaria and imperial orb, electoral hat above **Obv. Legend:** ★ MONET ★ ARGE ★ SVPERI ★ PALA ★ BAVAR (or variant) **Rev:** Crowned Pfalz lion to left in baroque frame, value (24) at top **Rev. Legend:** ADIVTOR ★ NOST ★ IN ★ NOMIN ★ DOMI (or variant) **Mint:** Amberg **Note:** Ref. G#66. Prev. Pfalz-Simmern KM#45. Oberpfalz issue.

Date	Mintage	VG	F	VF	XF	Unc
ND(1621)	—	60.00	125	250	500	—

KM# 53.2 24 KREUZER (Kipper)
4.1800 g., Silver, 30 mm. **Ruler:** Maximilian I **Obv:** Ornate 3-fold arms of Pfalz, Bavaria and imperial orb, electoral hat above, date at end of legend **Obv. Legend:** MONET. ARGE. SVPER. PALA. BAVA. **Rev:** Crowned Pfalz lion to left in baroque frame, value (24) at top **Rev. Legend:** ADIVTOR. NOS. IN. NOMIN. DOMIN. **Mint:** Amberg **Note:** Ref. G#72. Prev. Pfalz-Simmern KM#45. Oberpfalz issue.

Date	Mintage	VG	F	VF	XF	Unc
1621 (a)	—	60.00	125	250	500	—

KM# 53.3 24 KREUZER (Kipper)
Silver, 31 mm. **Ruler:** Maximilian I **Obv:** Ornate 3-fold arms of Pfalz, Bavaria and imperial orb, electoral hat and value above, date at end of legend **Obv. Legend:** MONET. ARGE. SVPERI. PALA. BAVA. **Rev:** Crowned Pfalz lion to left in baroque frame **Rev. Legend:** ADIVTOR. NOS. IN. NOMIN. DOMINI. NE. **Mint:** Amberg **Note:** Ref. G#75. Prev. Pfalz-Simmern KM#45. Oberpfalz issue.

Date	Mintage	VG	F	VF	XF	Unc
1621 (a) NF	—	60.00	125	250	500	—

KM# 54.1 24 KREUZER (Kipper)
Silver Weight varies: 3.53-4.53g., 30-32 mm. **Ruler:** Maximilian I **Obv:** Crowned Pfalz lion to left in baroque frame **Obv. Legend:** MONET • ARGE ★ SVPERI ★PALA • BAVAR • 24 **Rev:** Ornate 3-fold arms of Pfalz, Bavaria and imperial orb, electoral hat above, date at end of legend **Rev. Legend:** • ADIVTOR ★ NOST ★ IN ★ NOMIN • DOMIN **Mint:** Amberg **Note:** Ref. G#71, 73, 76, 78-80; JB-949, 951. Prev. Pfalz-Simmern KM#45. Oberpfalz issue. Varieties exist.

Date	Mintage	VG	F	VF	XF	Unc
1621 (a)	—	60.00	125	250	500	—
1621 (b)	—	60.00	125	250	500	—
1622 (b)	—	60.00	125	250	500	—

KM# 54.2 24 KREUZER (Kipper)
4.2600 g., Silver, 31 mm. **Ruler:** Maximilian I **Obv:** Crowned Pfalz lion to left in baroque frame, date at end of legend **Obv. Legend:** MONET ★ ARGE ★ SVPER ★ PALA ★ BAVA ★ **Rev:** Ornate 3-fold arms of Pfalz, Bavaria and imperial orb, electoral hat and value (24) above **Rev. Legend:** ADIVTOR NOSTR ★ IN NOMIN • DOMIN . **Mint:** Amberg **Note:** Ref. G#74.

Date	Mintage	VG	F	VF	XF	Unc
1621 (a)	—	60.00	125	250	500	—

KM# 54.3 24 KREUZER (Kipper)
5.1300 g., Silver, 29-31 mm. **Ruler:** Maximilian I **Obv:** Ornate 3-fold arms of Pfalz, Bavaria and imperial orb with value '24,' electoral hat above **Obv. Legend:** MONET. ARGEN. SVPERI. PALA. BAVARI. **Rev:** Crowned Pfalz lion to left in baroque frame, date at end of legend **Rev. Legend:** ADIVTOR. NOST. IN. NOMIN. DOMIN. **Mint:** Amberg **Note:** Ref. G#77; JB-950; H-82. Prev. Pfalz-Simmern KM#45. Oberpfalz issue.

Date	Mintage	VG	F	VF	XF	Unc
1621 (b)	—	60.00	125	250	500	—

KM# 57.1 24 KREUZER (Kipper)
5.0300 g., Silver, 30 mm. **Ruler:** Maximilian I **Obv:** Ornate 3-fold arms of Pfalz, Bavaria and imperial orb, electoral hat above **Obv. Legend:** + MONET. ARGE. SVPER. PAL. BAVAR. **Rev:** Bust TO right in circle, date at end of legend **Rev. Legend:** ADIVTOR. NOSTR. IN. NOM. DOM. **Mint:** Amberg **Note:** Ref. G#67. Prev. Pfalz-Simmern KM#45. Oberpfalz issue.

Date	Mintage	VG	F	VF	XF	Unc
1621 (a)	—	60.00	125	250	500	—

KM# 57.2 24 KREUZER (Kipper)
Silver, 31 mm. **Ruler:** Maximilian I **Obv:** Ornate 3-fold arms of Pfalz, Bavaria and imperial orb, electoral hat and value (24) at top **Obv. Legend:** + MONET. ARGE. SVPERI. PALA. BAVAR. **Rev:** Bust right in circle, date at end of legend **Rev. Legend:** ADIVTOR. NOS(TR). IN. NOMIN(e). DOM(IN). **Mint:** Amberg **Note:** Ref. G#69-70. Prev. Pfalz-Simmern KM#45. Oberpfalz issue. Varieties exist.

Date	Mintage	VG	F	VF	XF	Unc
1621	—	60.00	125	250	500	—

KM# 56.2 24 KREUZER (Kipper)
3.7000 g., Silver, 29-32 mm. **Ruler:** Maximilian I **Obv:** 2 adjacent shields of arms, imperial orb below, value (24) at top **Obv. Legend:** MONET(A). ARGE(N)(T). SVPER(I). PALA. BAVA ★ **Rev:** Crowned Pfalz lion to left in baroque frame, date at end of legend **Rev. Legend:** ADIVTO(R). NOST. IN. NOMI(N)(E). D(O)(MI)(N)(I). **Mint:** Amberg **Note:** Ref. G#85, 87, 88-93; JB#955-60. Prev. Pfalz-Simmern KM#45. Oberpfalz issue. Varieties exist.

Date	Mintage	VG	F	VF	XF	Unc
1622	—	—	—	—	—	—
1622 (d)	—	—	—	—	—	—
1623 (d)	—	—	—	—	—	—

KM# 53.4 24 KREUZER (Kipper)
Silver Weight varies: 3.19-3.47g., 30-31 mm. **Ruler:** Maximilian I **Obv:** Ornate 3-fold arms of Pfalz, Bavaria and imperial orb, electoral hat and value above **Obv. Legend:** MONET. ARGEN. SVPERI. PALA. BAV. **Rev:** Crowned Pfalz lion to left in baroque frame, date at end of legend **Rev. Legend:** ADIVTOR. NOST. IN. NOMIN. DOMINI. **Mint:** Amberg **Note:** Ref. G#82-83; JB-953. Prev. Pfalz-Simmern KM#45. Oberpfalz issue. Varieties exist.

Date	Mintage	VG	F	VF	XF	Unc
1622 (c)	—	—	—	—	—	—

KM# 55 24 KREUZER (Kipper)
Silver Weight varies: 3.07-3.59g., 29-31 mm. **Ruler:** Maximilian I **Obv:** Crowned Pfalz lion to left in baroque frame, date at top **Obv. Legend:** MONET. ARGEN (.) SVPERI. PAL(A) (*) BA(VA). **Rev:** 2 ornate adjacent shields of arms, Pfalz at left, Bavaria at right, imperial orb between 2 arms below, electoral hat above **Rev. Legend:** ADIVTOR (*) NOST(R) (*) IN (*) OM(I) * DOMI. **Mint:** Amberg **Note:** Ref. G#81, 86; JB-954; H-84. Prev. Pfalz-Simmern KM#45. Oberpfalz issue. Varieties exist.

Date	Mintage	VG	F	VF	XF	Unc
1622	—	—	—	—	—	—

KM# 56.1 24 KREUZER (Kipper)
Silver, 29 mm. **Ruler:** Maximilian I **Obv:** Ornate 3-fold arms of Pfalz, Bavaria and imperial orb, electoral hat and date above **Obv. Legend:** MONET. ARGEN. SVPERI. PALA. BAVA. **Rev:** 2 adjacent shields of arms with imperial orb between and below **Rev. Legend:** ADIVTOR. NOST. IN. NOMIN. DOMINI. **Mint:** Amberg **Note:** Ref. G#84; JB-952. Prev. Pfalz-Simmern KM#45. Oberpfalz issue.

Date	Mintage	VG	F	VF	XF	Unc
1622 (c)	—	—	—	—	—	—

KM# 56.3 24 KREUZER (Kipper)
Silver, 30 mm. **Ruler:** Maximilian I **Obv:** 2 adjacent shields of arms, imperial orb below, electoral hat and value (24) at top **Obv. Legend:** MONET. ARGE. SVPER. PALA. BA* **Rev:** Crowned Pfalz lion to left in baroque frame, date at end of legend **Rev. Legend:** ADIVTOR. NOT. IN. NOMI. DMI. **Mint:** Kemnath **Note:** Ref. G#111. Prev. Pfalz-Simmern KM#45. Oberpfalz issue.

Date	Mintage	VG	F	VF	XF	Unc
1623 (f)	—	400	900	1,500	2,500	—

KM# 95 30 KREUZER (Kipper)
Silver Weight varies: 3.20-3.60g., 30 mm. **Ruler:** Maximilian I **Obv:** Oval shield of Wittelsbach arms in baroque frame **Obv. Legend:** SIT. NOMEN. DNI. BENEDTM. **Rev:** 3-line inscription in cartouche, date above **Rev. Inscription:** LANDT / MYNZ / XXX **Mint:** Munich **Note:** Ref. H#72; JB-851. Prev. KM#19. 1/4 Thaler.

Date	Mintage	VG	F	VF	XF	Unc
1622	—	50.00	100	175	350	—

KM# 96 30 KREUZER (Kipper)
Silver, 30-31 mm. **Ruler:** Maximilian I **Obv:** Oval 4-fold arms of Bavaria and Pfalz, ducal cap above, Order of Golden Fleece around **Obv. Legend:** MONETA. NOVA(.) - BAVARICA. **Rev:** Facing seated lion, paws on horizontal bars, with oval in center containing value '30,' resting on pedestal, date divided to left and right of hind paws **Rev. Legend:** SIT. NOMEN. DNI: BENEDTM. **Mint:** Munich **Note:** Ref. H#73; JB-850. Prev. KM#20. (1/4 Thaler).

Date	Mintage	VG	F	VF	XF	Unc
1622	—	50.00	100	175	350	—

KM# 65.2 48 KREUZER
Silver Weight varies: 10.50-13.50g., 35 mm. **Ruler:** Maximilian I **Obv:** 4-fold arms of Bavaria and Pfalz in Spanish shield, ducal cap above, Order of Golden Fleece around **Obv. Legend:** MONET(A). NOV(-)A. (-) BAVARICA. **Rev:** Lion seated at right, holding ornate frame at left in which value '48,' all in single linear circle **Rev. Legend:** SIT. NOMEN. DNI. BENEDTM. **Mint:** Munich **Note:** Ref. H#74; JB-849. Prev. KM#152.2. Varieties exist.

Date	Mintage	VG	F	VF	XF	Unc
ND(1621-23)	—	100	200	450	800	—

KM# 65.1 48 KREUZER (Kipper)
Silver Weight varies: 10.50-13.50g., 35 mm. **Ruler:** Maximilian I **Obv:** 4-fold arms of Bavaria and Pfalz in Spanish shield, ducal cap above, Order of the Golden Fleece around **Obv. Legend:** MONETA. NOVA - .BAVARICA. **Rev:** Lion seated at right, holding ornate frame at left in which value '48,' all in double linear circles **Rev. Legend:** SIT. NOMEN. DNI: BENEDTM. **Mint:** Munich **Note:** Ref. H#74; JB-849. Prev. KM#152.1. Varieties exist.

Date	Mintage	VG	F	VF	XF	Unc
ND(1621-23)	—	100	200	450	800	—

KM# 65.3 48 KREUZER (Kipper)
8.7900 g., Silver, 35 mm. **Ruler:** Maximilian I **Obv:** Oval shield of 4-fold arms of Bavaria and Pfalz, ducal cap above, Order of Golden Fleece around, all in single linear circle **Obv. Legend:** MONETA NOVA - BAVARICA. **Rev:** Lion seated at right, holding ornate frame at left in which value '48,' all in single linear circle **Rev. Legend:** SIT. NOMEN. DNI: BENEDTM. **Mint:** Munich **Note:** Muling of an obverse die of 60 Kreuzer, KM#44.2 with reverse of 48 Kreuzer, KM#65.2.

Date	Mintage	VG	F	VF	XF	Unc
ND(1621-23)	—	200	375	600	1,000	—

KM# 44.2 60 KREUZER
Silver, 36 mm. **Ruler:** Maximilian I **Obv:** Oval shield of 4-fold arms of Bavaria and Pfalz, ducal hat above, Order of Golden Fleece around, all in single linear circle **Obv. Legend:** MONETA. NOVA. BAVARICA. **Rev:** Facing seated lion, paws on horizontal bars, with oval in center containing value '60,' resting on pedestal, date divided to left and right of hind paws, all in single linear circle **Rev. Legend:** SIT. NOMEN. DNI: BENEDTM: **Mint:** Munich **Note:** Ref. H#76. Prev. KM#12.2.

Date	Mintage	VG	F	VF	XF	Unc
1621	—	185	350	650	1,200	—
1622	—	185	350	650	1,200	—
1623	—	185	350	650	1,200	—

KM# 69.1 60 KREUZER

Silver, 36 mm. **Ruler:** Maximilian I **Obv:** 4-fold arms of Bavaria and Pfalz in Spanish shield, ducal cap above, Order of Golden Fleece around sides and bottom, all in double linear circles **Obv. Legend:** MONETA. NOVA - BAVARICA. **Rev:** Facing seated lion, paws on horizontal bars, with oval in center containing value '60,' resting on pedestal, date divided to left and right of hind paws, all in double linear circles **Rev. Legend:** SIT. NOMEN. DNI: BENEDTM. **Mint:** Munich **Note:** Ref. H#75; JB-846. Prev. KM#13.1.

Date	Mintage	VG	F	VF	XF	Unc
1621	—	220	400	650	1,200	—

KM# 69.2 60 KREUZER

Silver, 36 mm. **Ruler:** Maximilian I **Obv:** 4-fold arms of Bavaria and Pfalz in Spanish shield, ducal cap above, Order of Golden Fleece around sides and bottom, all in single linear circle **Obv. Legend:** .MONETA. NOVA - BAVARICA. **Rev:** Facing seated lion, paws on horizontal bars, with oval in center containing value '60,' resting on pedestal, date divided to left and right of hind paws, all in single linear circle **Rev. Legend:** SIT. NOMEN. DNI: BENEDTM. **Mint:** Munich **Note:** Ref. H#75. Prev. KM#13.2.

Date	Mintage	VG	F	VF	XF	Unc
1623	—	220	400	650	1,200	—

KM# 44.1 60 KREUZER (Kipper)

Silver, 36 mm. **Ruler:** Maximilian I **Obv:** Oval shield of 4-fold arms of Bavaria and Pfalz, ducal cap above, Order of Golden Fleece around, in double linear circles **Obv. Legend:** MONETA.(.) NOVA (-) (.)BAVARICA. **Rev:** Facing seated lion, paws on horizontal bars, with oval in center containing value '60,' resting on pedestal, date divided to left and right of hind paws, all in double linear circles **Rev. Legend:** SIT. NOMEN. DNI: BENEDTM: **Mint:** Munich **Note:** Ref. H#76, 76a; JB#842-845.Prev. KM#12.1. Varieties exist.

Date	Mintage	VG	F	VF	XF	Unc
ND(1621)	—	220	400	650	1,200	—
1621	—	220	400	650	1,200	—
1622	—	220	400	650	1,200	—
Note: Example in aXF realized approximately $1,450 in June 2009 Künker auction.						
1623	—	220	400	650	1,200	—

KM# 74 120 KREUZER

24.1800 g., Silver, 40-42 mm. **Ruler:** Maximilian I **Obv:** Oval shield of 4-fold arms of Bavaria and Pfalz, ducal cap above, Order of Golden Fleece around **Obv. Legend:** MONETA NOVA(.) - BAVARICA. **Rev:** Facing seated lion, paws on horizontal bars, with oval in center containing value '120,' resting on pedestal, date divided to left and right of hind paws **Rev. Legend:** SIT. NOMEN. DNI: BENEDTM. **Mint:** Munich **Note:** Ref. H#78; JB-839, 841. Prev. KM#16.

Date	Mintage	VG	F	VF	XF	Unc
1621	—	425	850	1,700	3,250	—
1622	—	425	850	1,700	3,250	—

KM# 73 120 KREUZER (Kipper)

Silver, 40-42 mm. **Ruler:** Maximilian I **Obv:** Oval shield of 4-fold arms of Bavaria and Pfalz, ducal cap above, Order of Golden Fleece around **Obv. Legend:** MONE(T)A NOVA(:) - BAVARICA(:) **Rev:** Facing seated lion, paws holding oval cartouche containing value '120,' date divided to left and right of center **Rev. Legend:** SIT. NOMEN. D(O)NI: BENEDTM: **Mint:** Munich **Note:** Ref. H#78; JB-837, 838. Prev. KM#15. Varieties exist.

Date	Mintage	VG	F	VF	XF	Unc
1621	—	260	475	925	1,700	—

KM# 149 1/4 THALER

Silver, 30 mm. **Ruler:** Maximilian I **Obv:** Crowned oval shield of 4-fold arms of Bavaria and Pfalz in baroque frame, Order of Golden Fleece suspended below, date at top in margin **Obv. Legend:** MAXIMIL. D. G. COM. PAL. RH. VT. BAV. DVX. **Rev:** Facing Madonna with Child, clouds below, rays around, in circle **Rev. Legend:** CLYPEVS OMNIBVS IN TE SPERANTIBVS. **Mint:** Munich **Note:** Ref. H#60. Prev. KM#36.

Date	Mintage	VG	F	VF	XF	Unc
1623	—	50.00	100	200	360	—

KM# 100 1/2 THALER

Silver, 35 mm. **Ruler:** Maximilian I **Obv:** Crowned oval shield of 4-fold arms of Bavaria and Pfalz, supported by two lions at left and right, date in cartouche below **Obv. Legend:** MAXIMILIANVS. D:G: COM: PAL: RHE: VTRQ: BOIARIÆ. DVX. **Rev:** Seated facing Madonna with Child surrounded by rays **Rev. Legend:** CLYPES OMNIBVS. IN TE SPERANTIBVS. **Mint:** Munich **Note:** Ref. H#61; JB-828. Prev. KM#21.

Date	Mintage	VG	F	VF	XF	Unc
1622	—	150	300	600	1,150	—

KM# 30 THALER

Silver, 41 mm. **Ruler:** Maximilian I **Obv:** Heart-shaped shield of 4-fold arms of Bavaria and Pfalz, supported by 2 lions, ducal cap above, Order of Golden Fleece suspended below, R.N. date at end of legend **Obv. Legend:** MAXIMILIANVS. D: G: COM: PAL: RHE: VTRQ. BOIARIÆ. DVX. **Rev:** Seated Madonna with Child, surrounded by rays **Rev. Legend:** CLYPEVS OMNIBVS IN TE SPERANTIBVS. **Mint:** Munich **Note:** Ref. H#62; JB-822. Dav. #6063. Varieties exist.

Date	Mintage	VG	F	VF	XF	Unc
MDCVIII (1618)	—	300	550	1,150	2,000	—

KM# 31.1 THALER

Silver, 41-42 mm. **Ruler:** Maximilian I **Obv:** Oval shield of 4-fold arms of Bavaria and Pfalz, supported by 2 lions, ducal cap above, Order of Golden Fleece suspended below, R.N. date at end of legend **Obv. Legend:** MAXIMILIANVS. D. G. COM. PAL. RHE. VTRQ. BOIARIÆ. DVX. **Rev:** Seated Madonna with Child, surrounded by rays **Rev. Legend:** CLYPEVS OMNIBVS IN TE SPERANTIBVS. **Mint:** Munich **Note:** Ref. H#62a; JB-823, 824. Dav. #6064. Prev. KM#9.1.

Date	Mintage	VG	F	VF	XF	Unc
MDCXVIII (1618)	—	205	425	900	1,500	—
MDCXX (1620)	41,000	205	425	900	1,500	—

KM# 31.2 THALER

Silver, 41-42 mm. **Ruler:** Maximilian I **Obv:** Oval shield of 4-fold arms of Bavaria and Pfalz, supported by 2 lions, ducal cap above,

Order of Golden Fleece suspended below, Arabic date at end of legend **Obv. Legend:** MAXIMILIANS. D. G. COM. PAL. RHE. VTRQ. BOIARIÆ. DVX. **Rev:** Seated Madonna with Child, surrounded by rays **Rev. Legend:** CLYPEVS OMNIBVS IN TE SPERANTIBVS. **Mint:** Munich **Note:** Ref. H#62a; JB-825. Dav. #6065. Prev. KM#9.2.

Date	Mintage	VG	F	VF	XF	Unc
1622	—	270	575	1,150	—	—

KM# 31.3 THALER

Silver, 41-42 mm. **Ruler:** Maximilian I **Obv:** Oval shield of 4-fold arms of Bavaria and Pfalz, supported by 2 lions, ducal cap above, Order of Golden Fleece suspended below, date divided below arms **Obv. Legend:** MAXIMILIANVS. D. G. COM. PAL. RHE. VT(.)R Q: BOIARIÆ. DVX. **Rev:** Seated Madonna with Child, surrounded by rays **Rev. Legend:** CLYPEVS OMNIBVS IN TE SPERANTIBVS. **Mint:** Munich **Note:** Ref. H#62a; JB-826, 827. Varieties exist.

Date	Mintage	VG	F	VF	XF	Unc
1623	1,623	150	400	775	1,200	—

TRADE COINAGE

KM# 33 2 DUCAT

7.0000 g., 0.9860 Gold 0.2219 oz. AGW, 27 mm. **Ruler:** Maximilian I **Obv:** Oval shield of 4-fold arms of Bavaria and Pfalz, supported by 2 lions, ducal cap above, Order of Golden Fleece suspended below, R.N. date at end of legend **Obv. Legend:** MAXIMILIANVS D: G: CO: PA: RHE: VTRQ: BOIARIÆ DVX. **Rev:** Seated Madonna with Child, feet on upturned crescent, rays around **Rev. Legend:** VITA DVLCEDO ET SPES NOSTRA. **Mint:** Munich **Note:** Ref. H#63; JB-821. Fr. #191. Prev. KM#10.

Date	Mintage	VG	F	VF	XF	Unc
MDCXVIII (1618)	—	375	850	1,550	3,250	—

KM# 27 4 DUCAT

14.0000 g., 0.9860 Gold 0.4438 oz. AGW, 35 mm. **Ruler:** Maximilian I **Obv:** Full-length facing armored figure of duke, supported at right by pedestal on which 4-fold arms of Bavaria and Pfalz with ducal cap above, recumbent lion at his feet, R.N. date in exergue **Obv. Legend:** MAXIMILIANVS. I. COM. PAL. RHE. DVX. BAVARIÆ. **Rev:** Madonna and Child in clouds above view of Munich **Rev. Legend:** SVB. HOC. PRAESIDIO. **Mint:** Munich **Note:** Ref. JB-779. Fr.#189. Prev. KM#7.

Date	Mintage	VG	F	VF	XF	Unc
MDCX (1610) Rare	—	—	—	—	—	—

ELECTORATE

REGULAR COINAGE

KM# 106 PFENNIG

0.2200 g., Silver, 11-12 mm. **Ruler:** Maximilian I **Obv:** Shield of Wittelsbach arms in circle **Rev:** 'M' below date in circle **Mint:** Munich **Note:** Ref. H#86; JB#940-943. Struck on squarish flans. (Schwarzpfennig). Varieties exist.

Date	Mintage	VG	F	VF	XF	Unc
16Z3	—	8.00	16.00	32.00	65.00	—
16Z4	—	8.00	16.00	32.00	65.00	—
16Z5	—	8.00	16.00	32.00	65.00	—
16Z6	—	8.00	16.00	32.00	65.00	—
16Z7	—	8.00	16.00	32.00	65.00	—
1631	—	8.00	16.00	32.00	65.00	—

KM# 107 PFENNIG

Silver **Ruler:** Maximilian I **Obv:** 3-fold arms of Pfalz, Bavaria and imperial orb, legend above **Obv. Legend:** M.P.C. **Mint:** Kemnath **Note:** Uniface. Ref. #G116; JB-987; H-126. Prev. Pfalz-Simmern KM#8. Oberpfalz issue.

Date	Mintage	VG	F	VF	XF	Unc
ND(1623)	—	30.00	60.00	120	240	—

KM# 108 PFENNIG

Silver **Ruler:** Maximilian I **Obv:** 3-fold arms, legend above **Obv. Legend:** M.D.E. **Mint:** Kemnath **Note:** Uniface. Ref. #G123-124; JB-985-6; H-127. Prev. Pfalz-Simmern KM#7. Oberpfalz issue.

Date	Mintage	VG	F	VF	XF	Unc
ND(1623)	—	30.00	60.00	120	240	—
ND(1623) (f)	—	30.00	60.00	120	240	—

KM# 163 PFENNIG

Copper **Ruler:** Maximilian I **Obv:** Bavaria arms in Spanish shield within circle of pellets **Mint:** Heidelberg **Note:** Uniface hohl-type. Ref. JB#1008. Rheinpfalz issue.

Date	Mintage	VG	F	VF	XF	Unc
ND(ca.1624-28)	—	—	—	—	—	—

KM# 242 PFENNIG

Billon, 12 mm. **Ruler:** Maximilian I **Obv:** Shield of Wittelsbach arms divides date, +C+ above **Mint:** Munich **Note:** Ref. H#87; JB#944-48. Uniface. Prev. KM#51. Varieties exist.

Date	Mintage	VG	F	VF	XF	Unc
1630	—	7.00	14.00	28.00	55.00	—
1631	187,000	7.00	14.00	28.00	55.00	—
1632	—	7.00	14.00	28.00	55.00	—
1633	—	7.00	14.00	28.00	55.00	—
1634	—	7.00	14.00	28.00	55.00	—
1635	—	7.00	14.00	28.00	55.00	—
1638	—	7.00	14.00	28.00	55.00	—
1639	—	7.00	14.00	28.00	55.00	—
1640	—	7.00	14.00	28.00	55.00	—
1642	—	7.00	14.00	28.00	55.00	—
1643	—	7.00	14.00	28.00	55.00	—
1644	—	7.00	14.00	28.00	55.00	—
1645	—	7.00	14.00	28.00	55.00	—
1646	—	7.00	14.00	28.00	55.00	—
1647	—	7.00	14.00	28.00	55.00	—
1648	—	7.00	14.00	28.00	55.00	—
1649	—	7.00	14.00	28.00	55.00	—

KM# 251 PFENNIG

Billon, 10-11 mm. **Ruler:** Maximilian I **Obv:** Shield of Wittelsbach arms, 'C' divides date above **Mint:** Munich **Note:** Ref. H#88; JB-944a. Uniface. Prev. KM#54.

Date	Mintage	VG	F	VF	XF	Unc
1634	—	7.00	14.00	28.00	55.00	—

KM# 286 PFENNIG

Billon, 11 mm. **Ruler:** Ferdinand Maria **Obv:** Ornately shaped shield of Wittelsbach arms divides date, +C+ above **Note:** Ref. H#159; JB#1419-24. Uniface. Prev. KM#77.

Date	Mintage	VG	F	VF	XF	Unc
1653	—	7.00	14.00	28.00	55.00	—
1654	—	7.00	14.00	28.00	55.00	—
1655	—	7.00	14.00	28.00	55.00	—
1660	—	7.00	14.00	28.00	55.00	—
1661	—	7.00	14.00	28.00	55.00	—
1662	—	7.00	14.00	28.00	55.00	—
1663	—	7.00	14.00	28.00	55.00	—
1664	—	7.00	14.00	28.00	55.00	—
1665	—	7.00	14.00	28.00	55.00	—
1666	—	7.00	14.00	28.00	55.00	—
1667	—	7.00	14.00	28.00	55.00	—
1672	—	7.00	14.00	28.00	55.00	—
1673	—	7.00	14.00	28.00	55.00	—
1675	—	7.00	14.00	28.00	55.00	—

KM# 331 PFENNIG

Billon, 10 mm. **Ruler:** Ferdinand Maria **Obv:** Shield of Wittelsbach arms, 'C' divides date above **Mint:** Munich **Note:** Ref. H#160; JB-1425. Uniface. Prev. KM#104.

Date	Mintage	VG	F	VF	XF	Unc
1677	—	7.00	14.00	28.00	55.00	—
1678	—	7.00	14.00	28.00	55.00	—
1679	—	7.00	14.00	28.00	55.00	—

KM# 335 PFENNIG

Billon, 10-11 mm. **Ruler:** Maximilian II, Emanuel **Obv:** Shield of Wittelsbach arms between palm branches, date divided by 'C' above **Mint:** Munich **Note:** Ref. H#182; JB-1703. Uniface. Prev. KM#112.

Date	Mintage	VG	F	VF	XF	Unc
1680	—	10.00	20.00	35.00	75.00	—
1681	—	10.00	20.00	35.00	75.00	—
1682	—	10.00	20.00	35.00	75.00	—
1683	—	10.00	20.00	35.00	75.00	—
1684	—	10.00	20.00	35.00	75.00	—
1685	—	10.00	20.00	35.00	75.00	—
1686	—	10.00	20.00	35.00	75.00	—
1688	—	10.00	20.00	35.00	75.00	—
1690	—	10.00	20.00	35.00	75.00	—
1693	—	10.00	20.00	35.00	75.00	—
1695	—	10.00	20.00	35.00	75.00	—
1696	—	10.00	20.00	35.00	75.00	—
1697	—	10.00	20.00	35.00	75.00	—
1699	—	10.00	20.00	35.00	75.00	—
1700	—	10.00	20.00	35.00	75.00	—

KM# 110 2 PFENNIG

0.5000 g., Silver, 15 mm. **Ruler:** Maximilian I **Obv:** 3 small shields of arms, 2 above 1, in trefoil, value II above, date divided by lower arms **Mint:** Kemnath **Note:** Uniface. Ref. #G122; JB-984; H-128. Prev. Pfalz-Simmern KM#57. Oberpfalz issue.

Date	Mintage	VG	F	VF	XF	Unc
1623	—	25.00	50.00	100	200	—

KM# 114 3 PFENNIG (Dreier)

0.8000 g., Silver, 16-18 mm. **Ruler:** Maximilian I **Obv:** 3-fold arms of Pfalz, Bavaria and imperial orb, legend above **Obv. Legend:** • M • D • E • **Rev:** Imperial orb with III divides date **Mint:** Kemnath **Note:** Ref. #G115, 121; JB-983; H-129. Prev. Pfalz-Simmern KM#58. Oberpfalz Issue. Varieties exist.

Date	Mintage	VG	F	VF	XF	Unc
1623	—	30.00	60.00	120	240	—
1623 (f)	—	30.00	60.00	120	240	—

KM# 338.1 5 PFENNIG

Silver, 15-16 mm. **Ruler:** Maximilian II, Emanuel **Obv:** Crowned Spanish shield of Wittelsbach arms, with central shield of imperial orb, between 2 palm branches **Rev:** 4-line inscription with date divided by value in first line, mintmaster's initials in last line **Rev. Inscription:** V / PF. EN / (=)ING / CZ **Mint:** Munich **Note:** Ref. H#186; JB-1697, 1698. Prev. KM#110. Varieties exist. 1/2 Landmünze or 1-1/4 Kreuzer.

Date	Mintage	VG	F	VF	XF	Unc
1683 CZ	—	35.00	75.00	150	300	—
1684 CZ	—	35.00	75.00	150	300	—

KM# 338.2 5 PFENNIG

Silver, 15-16 mm. **Ruler:** Maximilian II, Emanuel **Obv:** Crowned Spanish shield of Wittelsbach arms, with central shield of imperial orb, between 2 palm branches **Rev:** 4-line inscription, date divides mintmaster's initials in last line **Rev. Inscription:** V / PF. EN / ING / C (date) Z **Mint:** Munich **Note:** Ref. H#186; JB-1697. Prev. KM#110. 1/2 Landmünze or 1-1/4 Kreuzer.

Date	Mintage	VG	F	VF	XF	Unc
1683 CZ	—	35.00	75.00	150	300	—

KM# 338.3 5 PFENNIG

Silver, 15-16 mm. **Ruler:** Maximilian II, Emanuel **Obv:** Crowned Spanish shield of Wittelsbach arms, with central shield of imperial orb, between 2 palm branches, date divided by 'C' above **Rev:** 4-line inscription with mintmaster's initials in last line **Rev. Inscription:** V / PF. EN / ING / CZ **Mint:** Munich **Note:** Ref. H#186; JB-1697. Prev. KM#110. 1/2 Landmünze or 1-1/4 Kreuzer.

Date	Mintage	VG	F	VF	XF	Unc
1683 CZ	—	35.00	75.00	150	300	—
1684 CZ	—	35.00	75.00	150	300	—

KM# 334 10 PFENNIG

Silver, 19 mm. **Ruler:** Maximilian II, Emanuel **Obv:** Crowned shield of Wittelsbach arms with central shield of imperial orb **Rev:** 3-line inscription with date, mint official's initials below or to sides of date **Rev. Inscription:** LAND / MINZ / (date) **Mint:** Munich **Note:** Ref. H#187; JB-1694, 1694. Prev. KM#111. Landmünze or 2-1/2 Kreuzer. Varieties exist.

Date	Mintage	VG	F	VF	XF	Unc
1679 CZ	—	10.00	20.00	40.00	80.00	—
1680 CZ	—	10.00	20.00	40.00	80.00	—
1681 CZ	—	10.00	20.00	40.00	80.00	—

KM# 336 10 PFENNIG

Silver, 18-19 mm. **Ruler:** Maximilian II, Emanuel **Obv:** Crowned shield of Wittelsbach arms, with central shield of imperial orb, between 2 palm branches, no legend **Rev:** 3-line inscription with date, mint official's initials and symbol below **Rev. Inscription:** LAND / MINZ / (date) **Mint:** Munich **Note:** Ref. H#188; JB-1695, 1696. Varieties exist. Prev. KM#113. Landmünze or 2-1/2 Kreuzer.

Date	Mintage	VG	F	VF	XF	Unc
1681 CZ	—	10.00	20.00	40.00	80.00	—
1682 CZ	—	10.00	20.00	40.00	80.00	—
1683 CZ	—	10.00	20.00	40.00	80.00	—
1684 CZ	—	10.00	20.00	40.00	80.00	—
1685 CZ	—	10.00	20.00	40.00	80.00	—
1686 CZ	—	10.00	20.00	40.00	80.00	—
1687 CZ	—	10.00	20.00	40.00	80.00	—
1688 CZ	—	10.00	20.00	40.00	80.00	—
1689 CZ	—	10.00	20.00	40.00	80.00	—
1690 CZ	—	10.00	20.00	40.00	80.00	—

KM# 117 1/2 KREUZER

0.5000 g., Silver, 14 mm. **Ruler:** Maximilian I **Obv:** Ornamented Spanish shield of Wittelsbach arms, value (1/2) divides date above **Mint:** Munich **Note:** Ref. H#89; JB-934. Uniface. Prev. KM#25.

Date	Mintage	VG	F	VF	XF	Unc
1623	—	10.00	20.00	40.00	80.00	—
1624	—	10.00	20.00	40.00	80.00	—
1625	—	10.00	20.00	40.00	80.00	—
1626	—	10.00	20.00	40.00	80.00	—
1627	—	10.00	20.00	40.00	80.00	—

KM# 220 1/2 KREUZER

0.5000 g., Silver, 14 mm. **Ruler:** Maximilian I **Obv:** Ornamented shield of Wittelsbach arms with scalloped sides divides date, value (1/2) in oval flanked by various ornaments above **Mint:** Munich **Note:** Ref. H#90; JB#935-9. Uniface. Prev. KM#47. Varieties exist.

Date	Mintage	VG	F	VF	XF	Unc
1627	—	10.00	20.00	40.00	80.00	—
1631	—	10.00	20.00	40.00	80.00	—
1632	—	10.00	20.00	40.00	80.00	—
1635	—	10.00	20.00	40.00	80.00	—
1638	—	10.00	20.00	40.00	80.00	—
1639	—	10.00	20.00	40.00	80.00	—
1640	—	10.00	20.00	40.00	80.00	—
1642	—	10.00	20.00	40.00	80.00	—
1646	—	10.00	20.00	40.00	80.00	—
1647	—	10.00	20.00	40.00	80.00	—
1649	—	10.00	20.00	40.00	80.00	—
1651	—	10.00	20.00	40.00	80.00	—

KM# 283 1/2 KREUZER

0.5000 g., Silver, 12 mm. **Ruler:** Ferdinand Maria **Obv:** Ornamented shield of Wittelsbach arms with scalloped sides divides date, value (1/2) in oval flanked by various ornaments above **Mint:** Munich **Note:** Ref. H#161; JB#1414-17. Uniface. Prev. KM#75. Varieties exist.

Date	Mintage	VG	F	VF	XF	Unc
1652	—	10.00	20.00	40.00	80.00	—
1661	—	10.00	20.00	40.00	80.00	—
1666	—	10.00	20.00	40.00	80.00	—
1668	—	10.00	20.00	40.00	80.00	—
1671	—	10.00	20.00	40.00	80.00	—

KM# 327 1/2 KREUZER

0.5000 g., Silver, 12 mm. **Ruler:** Ferdinand Maria **Obv:** Ornate shield of Wittelsbach arms, value (1/2) divides date above **Mint:** Munich **Note:** Ref. H#162; JB-1418. Uniface. Prev. KM#101.

Date	Mintage	VG	F	VF	XF	Unc
1676	—	10.00	20.00	40.00	80.00	—

KM# 121 KREUZER

Silver **Ruler:** Maximilian I **Obv:** 3-fold arms of Pfalz, Bavaria and imperial orb, electoral hat above **Obv. Legend:** MAX C. P. R. V. B. D. S. R. I. A. ET. EL* **Rev:** Crowned imperial eagle, I in orb on breast **Rev. Legend:** FER. D. II. ROMAN. IMPERATOR. **Mint:** Amberg **Note:** Ref. G#101; JB-979; H-130. Prev. Pfalz-Simmern KM#59. Oberpfalz issue.

Date	Mintage	VG	F	VF	XF	Unc
ND(1623) (d)	—	30.00	65.00	135	275	—

KM# 122 KREUZER

Silver **Ruler:** Maximilian I **Obv:** 3 small shields of arms, 2 above 1, value 'I' between 2 upper arms, lower shield divides date, legend above **Obv. Legend:** • M • D • E • **Rev:** Maltese cross in circle of pellets **Rev. Legend:** FERD. II. ROM. IMPERA. **Mint:** Amberg **Note:** Ref. G#102, 103; JB-981, 982; H-132. Prev. Pfalz-Simmern KM#61. Oberpfalz issue.

Date	Mintage	VG	F	VF	XF	Unc
1623 (d)	—	30.00	65.00	135	275	—
1624 (d)	—	30.00	65.00	135	275	—

KM# 123 KREUZER

Silver **Ruler:** Maximilian I **Obv:** Imperial orb with 'I' divides date **Obv. Legend:** MAX. C. P. R. V. B. D. S. R. I. EL. **Rev:** Crowned imperial eagle in circle of pellets **Rev. Legend:** FERDI. II. ROMA. IMPER. **Mint:** Kemnath **Note:** Ref. G#120; JB-980; H-131. Prev. Pfalz-Simmern KM#60. Oberpfalz issue.

Date	Mintage	VG	F	VF	XF	Unc
1623	—	30.00	65.00	135	275	—

KM# 120 KREUZER

0.8000 g., Silver, 16 mm. **Ruler:** Maximilian I **Obv:** Shield of Wittelsbach arms, with scalloped sides, in circle **Obv. Legend:** M. C. P. R. V. B. D. S. R. I. A. E. E. **Rev:** Small shield with value '1' superimposed on double-cross in circle, date at top in margin **Rev. Legend:** SOLI. DEO. GLORIA. **Mint:** Munich **Note:** Ref. H#91; JB#930-33. Prev. KM#29. Varieties exist.

Date	Mintage	VG	F	VF	XF	Unc
1623	—	10.00	20.00	40.00	80.00	—
1624	—	10.00	20.00	40.00	80.00	—
1625	—	10.00	20.00	40.00	80.00	—
1630	—	10.00	20.00	40.00	80.00	—
1631	—	10.00	20.00	40.00	80.00	—
1635	—	10.00	20.00	40.00	80.00	—
1638	—	10.00	20.00	40.00	80.00	—
1640	—	10.00	20.00	40.00	80.00	—
1644	—	10.00	20.00	40.00	80.00	—
1646	—	10.00	20.00	40.00	80.00	—
1648	—	10.00	20.00	40.00	80.00	—
1650	—	10.00	20.00	40.00	80.00	—
1651	—	10.00	20.00	40.00	80.00	—
1652	—	10.00	20.00	40.00	80.00	—
1653	—	10.00	20.00	40.00	80.00	—
1654	—	10.00	20.00	40.00	80.00	—

KM# 165 KREUZER

Silver **Ruler:** Maximilian I **Obv:** Bavaria arms in Spanish shield **Obv. Legend:** MAX • D • G (• C)(O) • P • R • V • BA • D • S • R • I • E(L) **Rev:** Imperial orb with 'I' divides date **Rev. Legend:** FER • II • ROM • IMP • SEMP • A(V)(GV) • **Mint:** Heidelberg **Note:** Ref. JB#1004-06. Prev. Pfalz-Simmern KM#63. Rheinpfalz issue. Legend varieties exist.

Date	Mintage	VG	F	VF	XF	Unc
1624	—	35.00	75.00	150	300	—
1625	—	35.00	75.00	150	300	—

KM# 248 KREUZER

1.8000 g., Silver, 25x25 mm. **Ruler:** Maximilian I **Obv:** Shield of Wittelsbach arms superimposed on cross **Obv. Legend:** MAX. D G. C. P. R. V. BA. D S R I. E. **Rev:** Imperial orb with '1' divides date at cross **Rev. Legend:** FER. II. ROM. IMP. SEM. AV. **Mint:** Heidelberg **Note:** Klippe. Ref. JB#1007. Prev. Pfalz-Simmern KM#85. Rheinpfalz issue.

Date	Mintage	VG	F	VF	XF	Unc
1633	—	—	—	—	—	—

KM# 247 KREUZER

Silver **Ruler:** Maximilian I **Obv:** Shield of Wittelsbach arms superimposed on cross **Obv. Legend:** MAX. D.G. C. P. R. BAV. D. S. R. I. E. **Rev:** Imperial orb with value '1' divides date at cross **Rev. Legend:** FER. II. ROM. IMP. SEM. AV. **Mint:** Heidelberg **Note:** Ref. H-150.

Date	Mintage	VG	F	VF	XF	Unc
1633	—	40.00	90.00	160	325	—

KM# 288 KREUZER

0.7000 g., Silver, 16 mm. **Ruler:** Ferdinand Maria **Obv:** Ornate shield of Wittelsbach arms **Obv. Legend:** F. M. C. P. R. V. B. D. S. R. I. A. (E. E.) L. L. **Rev:** Small shield with value '1' superimposed on double-cross in circle, date at top in margin **Rev. Legend:** SOLI. DEO. GLORIA. **Mint:** Munich **Note:** Ref. H#163; JB-1412, 1413. Prev. KM#78.

Date	Mintage	VG	F	VF	XF	Unc
1653	—	15.00	35.00	75.00	155	—
1654	—	22.00	35.00	75.00	155	—
1656	—	22.00	35.00	75.00	155	—

KM# 352 KREUZER

Silver, 15 mm. **Ruler:** Maximilian II, Emanuel **Obv:** Draped bust to right, die-cutter's initial below, where present **Obv. Legend:** MAX. EM. - H. I. B. C. &. **Rev:** Crowned oval shield of Wittelsbach arms, with central shield of imperial orb, in baroque frame, value '1' in cartouche at bottom, date divided to left and right, no legend **Mint:** Munich **Note:** Ref. H#184; JB-1699. Prev. KM#120.

Date	Mintage	VG	F	VF	XF	Unc
1692 Z	—	18.00	30.00	45.00	90.00	—
1692	—	12.00	25.00	35.00	75.00	—

KM# 366 KREUZER

Silver, 15 mm. **Ruler:** Maximilian II, Emanuel **Obv:** Draped bust to right **Obv. Legend:** MAX. EM. - H. I. B. C. &. **Rev:** Crowned oval shield of Wittelsbach arms, with central shield of imperial orb, in baroque frame, value '1' in cartouche at bottom, date in legend **Rev. Legend:** ANN(O) - (date) **Mint:** Munich **Note:** Ref. H#184; JB-1700. Prev. KM#120. Varieties exist.

Date	Mintage	VG	F	VF	XF	Unc
1695	—	10.00	20.00	35.00	75.00	—
1696	—	10.00	20.00	35.00	75.00	—
1697	—	10.00	20.00	35.00	75.00	—
1698	—	10.00	20.00	35.00	75.00	—
1699	—	10.00	20.00	35.00	75.00	—
1700	—	10.00	20.00	35.00	75.00	—

KM# 128.1 2 KREUZER (1/2 Batzen)

Silver Weight varlies: 1.10-1.15g. **Ruler:** Maximilian I **Obv:** Shield of Wittelsbach arms with scalloped sides **Obv. Legend:** M. C. P. R. V. B. D. S. R. I. A. E. E. **Rev:** Imperial orb with value '2,' date divided by cross at top **Rev. Legend:** SOLI. DEO GLORIA. **Mint:** Munich **Note:** Ref. JB#923-7. Prev. KM#31.

Date	Mintage	VG	F	VF	XF	Unc
1623	—	10.00	25.00	50.00	90.00	125
1624	—	10.00	25.00	50.00	90.00	125
1625	—	10.00	25.00	50.00	90.00	125
1626	—	10.00	25.00	50.00	90.00	125
1628	—	10.00	25.00	50.00	90.00	125
1629	—	10.00	25.00	50.00	90.00	125
1630	—	10.00	25.00	50.00	90.00	125
1631	20,000	10.00	25.00	50.00	90.00	125
1632	—	10.00	25.00	50.00	90.00	125
1635	—	10.00	25.00	50.00	90.00	125
1636	—	10.00	25.00	50.00	90.00	125
1637	—	10.00	25.00	50.00	90.00	125

KM# 129 2 KREUZER (1/2 Batzen)

Silver, 18.5 mm. **Ruler:** Maximilian I **Obv:** 3-fold arms of Pfalz, Bavaria and imperial orb, electoral hat above **Obv. Legend:** *MAX. C. P. R. V. B. D. S. R. I. A. E. T. E. L. **Rev:** Crowned imperial eagle, '2' in orb on breast **Rev. Legend:** FERD II ROMAN IMPERATOR. **Mint:** Amberg **Note:** Ref. G#100; H-133. Oberpfalz issue.

Date	Mintage	VG	F	VF	XF	Unc
ND(1623) (d)	—	—	—	—	—	—

KM# 130 2 KREUZER (1/2 Batzen)

Silver, 19-20 mm. **Ruler:** Maximilian I **Obv:** Imperial orb with Z or 2 **Obv. Legend:** *MAX. C. P. R. V. B. D. S. R. I. A. ET. EL. **Rev:** Crowned imperial eagle **Rev. Legend:** FERD. II. ROMA IMPERA. **Mint:** Kemnath **Note:** Ref. G#117. Oberpfalz issue.

Date	Mintage	VG	F	VF	XF	Unc
ND(1623) (f)	—	—	—	—	—	—

KM# 131 2 KREUZER (1/2 Batzen)

Silver, 19 mm. **Ruler:** Maximilian I **Obv:** Imperial orb with Z or 2 divides date **Obv. Legend:** *MAX. C. P. R. V. B. D. S. R. I. A. ET. E(L). **Rev:** Crowned imperial eagle **Rev. Legend:** FERD(I). II. ROMA(N). IMPERA(ATO)(R). **Mint:** Kemnath **Note:** Ref. G#118-19; JB-977; H-135. Oberpfalz issue. Varieties exist.

Date	Mintage	VG	F	VF	XF	Unc
1623 (f)	—	—	—	—	—	—

KM# 132 2 KREUZER (1/2 Batzen)
Silver, 19 mm. **Ruler:** Maximilian I **Obv:** Imperial orb with Z or 2 **Obv. Legend:** MAX. C. P. R. V. B. D. S. R. I. A. E. **Rev:** Crowned imperial eagle **Rev. Legend:** FERD(I). II. RO(M). IMPER(A). **Mint:** Neumarkt **Note:** Ref. G#172; JB-975; H-134. Oberpfalz issue.

Date	Mintage	VG	F	VF	XF	Unc
ND(1623-26) (g)	—	—	—	—	—	—

KM# 133 2 KREUZER (1/2 Batzen)
Silver, 19 mm. **Ruler:** Maximilian I **Obv:** Imperial orb with Z or 2 divides date **Obv. Legend:** MAX. C. P. R. V. B. D. S. R. I. A. EL. **Rev:** Crowned imperial eagle **Rev. Legend:** FERDINAN. II. D. G. ROM. IMP. **Mint:** Neumarkt **Note:** Ref. G#174; JB-976. Oberpfalz issue.

Date	Mintage	VG	F	VF	XF	Unc
1623 (g)	—	—	—	—	—	—

KM# 168 2 KREUZER (1/2 Batzen)
Silver, 18-20 mm. **Ruler:** Maximilian I **Obv:** Imperial orb with Z or 2 **Obv. Legend:** MAX. C. P. R. V. B. D. S. R. I. A. E. **Rev:** Crowned imperial eagle **Rev. Legend:** FERDINAN. II. D. G. ROM. IMPE. **Mint:** Amberg **Note:** Ref. G#104, 105; H-135. Oberpfalz issue.

Date	Mintage	VG	F	VF	XF	Unc
ND(1624-26) (e)	—	—	—	—	—	—
ND(1624-26) G	—	—	—	—	—	—

KM# 169 2 KREUZER (1/2 Batzen)
Silver, 19 mm. **Ruler:** Maximilian I **Obv:** Imperial orb with Z or 2 divides date **Obv. Legend:** MAX. C. P. R. V. B. D. S. R. I. A. E. **Rev:** Crowned imperial eagle **Rev. Legend:** FERDINAN. II - D. G. ROM. IMP(E). **Mint:** Amberg **Note:** Ref. G#106-09; JB-978; H-135. Oberpfalz issue. Varieties exist.

Date	Mintage	VG	F	VF	XF	Unc
1624	—	—	—	—	—	—
1624 (e)	—	—	—	—	—	—
1625	—	—	—	—	—	—
1625 (e)	—	—	—	—	—	—

KM# 170.2 2 KREUZER (1/2 Batzen)
Silver **Ruler:** Maximilian I **Obv:** Bavaria arms in ornamented Spanish shield **Obv. Legend:** MAX • D • G • CO • P • R • V • BA • D • S • R • **Rev:** Imperial orb divides date **Rev. Legend:** FERD • II • ROM • IMP • SEMP • AVG • **Mint:** Heidelberg **Note:** Ref. JB#999-1003. Prev. Pfalz-Simmern KM#64. Rheinpfalz issue. Varieties exist.

Date	Mintage	VG	F	VF	XF	Unc
1624	—	40.00	75.00	150	300	—
1625	—	40.00	75.00	150	300	—
1626	—	40.00	75.00	150	300	—
1632	—	40.00	75.00	150	300	—
1633	—	40.00	75.00	150	300	—

KM# 170.1 2 KREUZER (1/2 Batzen)
Silver **Ruler:** Maximilian I **Obv:** Bavaria arms in ornamented Spanish shield, date above **Obv. Legend:** MAX. D. G. CO. P. R. V. BA. D. S. R. **Rev:** Imperial orb with Z **Rev. Legend:** FERD. II. ROM. IMP. SEMP. AVG. **Mint:** Heidelberg **Note:** Ref. JB#998. Prev. Pfalz-Simmern KM#64. Rheinpfalz issue.

Date	Mintage	VG	F	VF	XF	Unc
1624	—	25.00	55.00	110	230	—

KM# 170.3 2 KREUZER (1/2 Batzen)
Silver **Ruler:** Maximilian I **Obv:** Wittelsbach arms in Spanish shield ornamented on top and sides **Obv. Legend:** MAX. D. G. CO. P. R. V. BA. D. S. R. I. E. **Rev:** Imperial orb with value 'Z' divides date, countermarked with crowned lion of Pfalz **Rev. Legend:** FERD. II. ROM. IMP. SEMP. AV. **Mint:** Heidelberg **Note:** Ref. JB#1000. Prev. Pfalz-Simmern KM#70. Rheinpfalz issue.

Date	Mintage	VG	F	VF	XF	Unc
1625	—	—	—	—	—	—

KM# 205 2 KREUZER (1/2 Batzen)
Silver, 19 mm. **Ruler:** Maximilian I **Obv:** Imperial orb with Z or 2, cross at top of orb divides date **Obv. Legend:** MAX. C. P. R. V. B. D. S. R. I. A. E. **Rev:** Crowned imperial eagle **Rev. Legend:** FERDINANI. - 1. DG. RM IMP. **Mint:** Amberg **Note:** Ref. G#110; JB-978a; H-135. Oberpfalz issue.

Date	Mintage	VG	F	VF	XF	Unc
1626 (e)	—	—	—	—	—	—

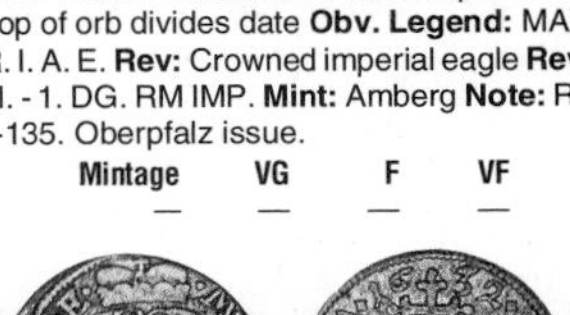

KM# 244.1 2 KREUZER (1/2 Batzen)
Silver **Ruler:** Maximilian I **Obv:** Ornately-shaped shield of Wittelsbach arms, electoral hat above **Obv. Legend:** M. C. P. R. V. B. D. S. R. I. A. E. E. **Rev:** Imperial orb with value '2,' date divided by cross at top **Rev. Legend:** SOLI. DEO. GLORIA. **Mint:** Munich **Note:** Ref. JB#928. Prev. KM#52.1.

Date	Mintage	VG	F	VF	XF	Unc
1632	—	15.00	30.00	60.00	120	—

KM# 244.2 2 KREUZER (1/2 Batzen)
Silver, 17.5 mm. **Ruler:** Maximilian I **Obv:** Shield of Wittelsbach arms, with scalloped sides, in circle **Obv. Legend:** M. C. P. R. V. B. D. S. R. I. A. E. E. **Rev:** Imperial orb with 2, date divided in margin at top **Rev. Legend:** SOLI. DEO. GLORIA. **Mint:** Munich **Note:** Prev. KM#52.2.

Date	Mintage	VG	F	VF	XF	Unc
1635	—	15.00	30.00	60.00	120	—

KM# 304 2 KREUZER (1/2 Batzen)
Silver, 18 mm. **Ruler:** Ferdinand Maria **Obv:** Shield of Wittelsbach arms, with scalloped sides, in circle **Obv. Legend:** F. M. V. B. & P. S. D. C. P. R. S. R. I. A. & E. L. L. **Rev:** Imperial orb with 2, date divided in margin at top **Rev. Legend:** SOLI. DEO. GLORIA. **Mint:** Munich **Note:** Ref. H#164; JB-1405, 1406. Prev. KM#88. Varieties exist.

Date	Mintage	VG	F	VF	XF	Unc
1660	—	15.00	30.00	60.00	120	—

KM# 308 2 KREUZER (1/2 Batzen)
Silver, 18 mm. **Ruler:** Ferdinand Maria **Obv:** Crowned shield of Wittelsbach arms with scalloped sides **Obv. Legend:** F. M. V. B & P. S. D. C. P. R. S. R. I. A. & E. L. L. **Rev:** Imperial orb with 2, date divided by top of cross on orb **Rev. Legend:** SOLI. DEO. GLORIA. **Mint:** Munich **Note:** Ref. H#165; JB#1407-11. Prev. KM#90. Varieties exist.

Date	Mintage	VG	F	VF	XF	Unc
1661	—	15.00	30.00	60.00	120	—
1665	—	15.00	30.00	60.00	120	—
1666	—	15.00	30.00	60.00	120	—
1667	—	15.00	30.00	60.00	120	—
1669	—	15.00	30.00	60.00	120	—
1671	—	15.00	30.00	60.00	120	—
1672	—	15.00	30.00	60.00	120	—
1676	—	15.00	30.00	60.00	120	—

KM# 134 3 KREUZER (Groschen)
Billon, 21-22 mm. **Ruler:** Maximilian I **Obv:** Oval 4-fold arms of Bavaria and Pfalz, Order of Golden Fleece around, electoral hat above **Obv. Legend:** MAX. C. P. R. H. V. - B. D. S. R. I. A. EL. **Rev:** Imperial orb with 3 divides date, titles of Ferdinand II **Rev. Legend:** FERDINAN. II. ROMA. IMPERAT. **Mint:** Kemnath **Note:** Ref. G#114; JB-974; H-136.. Prev. Pfalz-Simmern KM#62. Oberpfalz issue.

Date	Mintage	VG	F	VF	XF	Unc
1623	—	60.00	120	235	475	—

KM# 347 3 KREUZER (Groschen)
Silver, 20 mm. **Ruler:** Maximilian II, Emanuel **Obv:** Armored and draped bust to right **Obv. Legend:** MAX. EM(AN). H. I. B. C. &. **Rev:** Crowned oval shield of 4-fold arms of Bavaria and Pfalz, with central shield of imperial orb, in baroque frame, value (3) in cartouche below divides date **Rev. Legend:** LAND - GROSCH. **Mint:** Munich **Note:** Ref. H#189; JB#1682-4. Prev. KM#117. Varieties exist.

Date	Mintage	VG	F	VF	XF	Unc
1690	—	15.00	30.00	65.00	170	—
1690 CZ	—	15.00	30.00	65.00	170	—
1691	—	15.00	30.00	65.00	170	—
1692	—	15.00	30.00	65.00	170	—
1693	—	15.00	30.00	65.00	170	—
1694	—	15.00	30.00	65.00	170	—

KM# 367 3 KREUZER (Groschen)
Silver, 20 mm. **Ruler:** Maximilian II, Emanuel **Obv:** Small draped bust to right in partial circle **Obv. Legend:** MAX. EM(AN). (-) H. I. B. C. &. **Rev:** Crowned oval shield of 4-fold arms of Bavaria and Pfalz, with central shield of imperial orb, in baroque frame, within circle, value (3) in cartouche below divides date **Rev. Legend:** LAND - GROSCH. **Mint:** Munich **Note:** Ref. H#189; JB#1684-6. Prev. KM#128. Varieties exist.

Date	Mintage	VG	F	VF	XF	Unc
1695	—	15.00	30.00	65.00	130	—
1696	—	15.00	30.00	65.00	130	—
1697	—	15.00	30.00	65.00	130	—
1698	—	15.00	30.00	65.00	130	—

KM# 348 15 KREUZER (1/4 Gulden)
Silver, 29 mm. **Ruler:** Maximilian II, Emanuel **Obv:** Armored and draped bust to right **Obv. Legend:** MAX. EM(AN). - H. I. B. C. &. (c.) **Rev:** Crowned oval shield of 4-fold arms of Bavaria and Pfalz, with central shield of imperial orb, in baroque frame, value (XV) in cartouche divides date below **Rev. Legend:** LAND - MINZ. **Mint:** Munich **Note:** Ref. H#191; JB#1660-4. Prev. KM#118. Varieties exist.

Date	Mintage	VG	F	VF	XF	Unc
1691	—	30.00	60.00	120	240	—
1691 CZ	—	30.00	60.00	120	240	—
1692	—	30.00	60.00	120	240	—
1692 CZ	—	30.00	60.00	120	240	—
1692 CZ Retrograde Z	—	30.00	60.00	120	240	—

KM# 353.1 15 KREUZER (1/4 Gulden)
Silver, 29 mm. **Ruler:** Maximilian II, Emanuel **Obv:** Draped bust to right **Obv. Legend:** MAX. EM. - H. I. B. C. &. **Rev:** Crowned oval shield of 4-fold arms of Bavaria and Pfalz, with central shield of imperial orb, in baroque frame, value (XV) in cartouche divides date below **Rev. Legend:** LAND - MINZ. **Mint:** Munich **Note:** Ref. H#192; JB#1665-7. Prev. KM#121.1. Varieties exist.

Date	Mintage	VG	F	VF	XF	Unc
1692	—	35.00	70.00	140	285	—
1692 CZ	—	35.00	70.00	140	285	—
1692 +C+Z+	—	35.00	70.00	140	285	—
1692 C+Z	—	35.00	70.00	140	285	—
1693 C+Z	—	35.00	70.00	140	285	—
1693 +C+Z+	—	35.00	70.00	140	285	—

KM# 353.2 15 KREUZER (1/4 Gulden)
Silver, 29 mm. **Ruler:** Maximilian II, Emanuel **Obv:** Draped bust with flat bottom to right **Obv. Legend:** MAX. EM. - H. I. B. C. &. **Rev:** Crowned oval shield of 4-fold arms of Bavaria and Pfalz, with central shield of imperial orb, in baroque frame, value (XV) in cartouche divides date below **Rev. Legend:** LAND - MINZ. **Mint:** Munich **Note:** Ref. H#192; JB#1668-71. Prev. KM#121.2.

Date	Mintage	VG	F	VF	XF	Unc
1694	—	35.00	70.00	140	285	—
1695	—	35.00	70.00	140	285	—
1696	—	35.00	70.00	140	285	—

KM# 369.1 15 KREUZER (1/4 Gulden)

Silver, 29 mm. **Ruler:** Maximilian II, Emanuel **Obv:** Draped bust to right in partial linear circle **Obv. Legend:** MAX. EM. - H. I. B. C. &. **Rev:** Crowned oval shield of 4-fold arms of Bavaria and Pfalz, with central shield of imperial orb, in baroque frame, all in partial linear circle, value (XV) in cartouche divides date below **Rev. Legend:** LAND - MINZ. **Mint:** Munich **Note:** Ref. H#192; JB-1672. Prev. KM#129.1.

Date	Mintage	VG	F	VF	XF	Unc
1696	—	30.00	60.00	120	240	—
1697	—	30.00	60.00	120	240	—

KM# 369.2 15 KREUZER (1/4 Gulden)

Silver, 29 mm. **Ruler:** Maximilian II, Emanuel **Obv:** Draped bust to right in partial beaded circle **Obv. Legend:** MAX. EM. - H. I. B. C. &. **Rev:** Crowned oval shield of 4-fold arms of Bavaria and Pfalz, with central shield of imperial orb, in baroque frame, in partial beaded circle, value (XV) in cartouche divides date below **Rev. Legend:** LAND - MINZ. **Mint:** Munich **Note:** Ref. H#192; JB#1673-7. Prev. KM#129.2. Varieties exist.

Date	Mintage	VG	F	VF	XF	Unc
1697	—	35.00	70.00	140	285	—
1698	—	35.00	70.00	140	285	—
1699	—	35.00	70.00	140	285	—
1700	—	35.00	70.00	140	285	—

KM# 356 30 KREUZER (1/2 Gulden)

Silver, 34 mm. **Ruler:** Maximilian II, Emanuel **Obv:** Draped bust in antique style to right **Obv. Legend:** MAX. EM. - H. I. B. C. &. **Rev:** Crowned oval shield of 4-fold arms of Bavaria and Pfalz, with central shield of imperial orb, in baroque frame, value (30) in cartouche divides date below **Rev. Legend:** LAND - MINZ. **Mint:** Munich **Note:** Ref. H#195; JB#1651-3. Prev. KM#123. Varieties exist.

Date	Mintage	VG	F	VF	XF	Unc
1692 +C+Z+	—	40.00	80.00	160	325	—
1693 +C+Z+	—	40.00	80.00	160	325	—

KM# 355 30 KREUZER (1/2 Gulden)

Silver, 33 mm. **Ruler:** Maximilian II, Emanuel **Obv:** Draped bust to right **Obv. Legend:** MAX. EM. - H. I. B. C &. **Rev:** Crowned oval shield of 4-fold arms of Bavaria and Pfalz, with central shield of imperial orb, in baroque frame, value (30) in cartouche divides date below **Rev. Legend:** LAND - MINZ. **Mint:** Munich **Note:** Ref. H#194; JB#1649-50. Prev. KM#122.

Date	Mintage	VG	F	VF	XF	Unc
1692 +C+Z+	—	40.00	80.00	140	285	—

KM# 142 1/24 THALER (Groschen)

1.6000 g., Silver, 22 mm. **Ruler:** Maximilian I **Obv:** 4-fold arms of Bavaria and Pfalz with central shield of imperial orb, surrounded by Order of the Golden Fleece, electoral hat above **Obv. Legend:** MAX. C. P. RH - V. B. D. S. R. I. A. **Rev:** Imperial orb with 24 divides date **Rev. Legend:** FERD. II. ROM. IMPERAT. **Mint:** Kemnath **Note:** Ref. G#113. Oberpfalz issue.

Date	Mintage	VG	F	VF	XF	Unc
1623	—	—	—	—	—	—

KM# 145 1/9 THALER

3.7500 g., Silver, 23-24 mm. **Ruler:** Maximilian I **Obv:** Crowned oval shield of 4-fold arms of Bavaria and Pfalz, with central shield of imperial orb, in baroque frame, Order of Golden Fleece around, value (1/9) in oval below **Obv. Legend:** MAX. CO. P. R. V. BA. D. - S. R. I. ARCHID. ET. EL. **Rev:** Madonna standing with Child and holding scepter in circle, date divided above Madonna's shoulders **Rev. Legend:** CLYPEVS OMNIBVS IN TE SPERANTIBVS. **Mint:** Munich **Note:** Ref. H#96; JB-921. Prev. KM#33.

Date	Mintage	VG	F	VF	XF	Unc
1623	—	20.00	40.00	85.00	175	—
1640	—	20.00	40.00	85.00	175	—

KM# 144 1/9 THALER

3.7500 g., Silver, 23-24 mm. **Ruler:** Maximilian I **Obv:** Crowned oval shield of 4-fold arms of Bavaria and Pfalz, with central shield of imperial orb, in baroque frame, Order of Golden Fleece around, value (1/9) in oval below **Obv. Legend:** MAX. CO. P. R. V. BA. D. (-) S. (-) R. I. ARCHID. ET. EL. **Rev:** Madonna standing with Child and holding scepter in circle **Rev. Legend:** CLYPEVS OMNIBVS IN TE SPERANTIBVS. **Mint:** Munich **Note:** Ref. H#95; JB-918. Prev. KM#32. Varieties exist.

Date	Mintage	VG	F	VF	XF	Unc
ND(1623)	—	50.00	100	200	400	—

KM# 254 1/9 THALER

3.7500 g., Silver, 23-24 mm. **Ruler:** Maximilian I **Obv:** Crowned oval shield of 4-fold arms of Bavaria and Pfalz, with central shield of imperial orb, in baroque frame, Order of Golden Fleece around, value (1/9) in oval below date divided at top **Obv. Legend:** MAX. CO. P. R. V. BA. D(.) (-) S. (-) R. I. ARCHID. ET. EL. **Rev:** Madonna standing with Child and holding scepter in circle **Rev. Legend:** CLYPEVS OMNIBVS IN TE SPERANTIBVS. **Mint:** Munich **Note:** Ref. H#97; JB-919, 920. Prev. KM#55. Varieties exist.

Date	Mintage	VG	F	VF	XF	Unc
(16)38	—	22.00	45.00	90.00	180	—
1640	—	22.00	45.00	90.00	180	—

KM# 293 1/9 THALER

3.1500 g., Silver, 23-24 mm. **Ruler:** Ferdinand Maria **Obv:** Crowned oval shiield of 4-fold arms of Bavaria and Pfalz, with central shield of imperial orb, in baroque frame, date divided near bottom of arms, all in circle, value (1/9) in oval below **Obv. Legend:** .F. M. V. B. & P. S. D. C. P. R. S. - R. I. A. R. EL. & VIC. L. L. **Rev:** Half-length facing Madonna with Child, clouds below, rays around **Rev. Legend:** CLYPEVS OMNIBVS IN TE SPERANTIBVS. **Mint:** Munich **Note:** Vicariat issue. Ref. H#175; JB-1403. Prev. KM#81.

Date	Mintage	VG	F	VF	XF	Unc
1657	—	325	600	1,100	2,100	—

KM# 294 1/9 THALER

3.1500 g., Silver, 23-24 mm. **Ruler:** Ferdinand Maria **Obv:** Crowned round shield of 4-fold arms of Bavaria-Pfalz, in baroque frame, divides date, value (1/9) in oval below **Obv. Legend:** F. M. V. B & P. S. D. C. P. R - S. R. I. AR. EL & VIC. L. L. **Rev:** Half-length facing Madonna with Child, clouds below, rays around **Rev. Legend:** CLYPEVS OMNIBVS IN TE SPERANTIBVS. **Mint:** Munich **Note:** Vicariat issue. Ref. H#176; JB-1402. Prev. KM#82.

Date	Mintage	VG	F	VF	XF	Unc
1657	—	325	600	1,100	2,100	—

KM# 147 1/6 THALER

4.7000 g., Silver, 26 mm. **Ruler:** Maximilian I **Obv:** Crowned oval shield of 4-fold arms of Bavaria and Pfalz, with central shield of imperial orb, in baroque frame, Order of Golden Fleece around, all in circle, value (1/6) in oval below **Obv. Legend:** MAX. CO. P. R. V. BA. D. S. - R. I. ARCHID. ET. ELE. **Rev:** Facing Madonna with Child, clouds below, rays around, date divided above Madonna's shoulders **Rev. Legend:** CLYPEVS OMNIBVS IN TE SPERANTIBVS. **Mint:** Munich **Note:** Ref. H#99; JB-915. Prev. KM#35.

Date	Mintage	VG	F	VF	XF	Unc
1623	—	50.00	100	200	400	—
1624	—	50.00	100	200	400	—

KM# 146 1/6 THALER

4.7000 g., Silver, 27-28 mm. **Ruler:** Maximilian I **Obv:** Crowned oval shield of 4-fold arms of Bavaria and Pfalz, with central shield of imperial orb, in baroque frame, Order of Golden Fleece around, all in circle, value '1/6' in oval below **Obv. Legend:** MAX(IM). CO. P(A). R(H). V(T). BA. (-) D(VX). S. (-) R. I. ARCHI(D). ET. ELE(C). **Rev:** Seated Madonna with Child, turned slightly to left, clouds below, surrounded by rays, in circle **Rev. Legend:** CLYPEVS OMNIBVS IN TE SPERANTIBVS. **Mint:** Munich **Note:** Ref. H#98; JB-914. Prev. KM#34. Varieties exist.

Date	Mintage	VG	F	VF	XF	Unc
ND(1623)	—	50.00	100	200	400	—

KM# 190 1/6 THALER

4.7000 g., Silver, 27 mm. **Ruler:** Maximilian I **Obv:** Crowned oval shield of 4-fold arms of Bavaria and Pfalz, with central shield of imperial orb, in baroque frame, Order of Golden Fleece around, all in circle, date divided at top, value (1/6) in oval below **Obv. Legend:** MAX. CO. P. R. V. BA. D. S. - R. I. ARCHID. ET. EL. **Rev:** Facing Madonna with Child, clouds below, rays around, in circle **Rev. Legend:** CLYPEVS OMNIBVS IN TE SPERANTIBVS. **Mint:** Munich **Note:** Ref. H#100; JB-916, 917. Prev. KM#38.

Date	Mintage	VG	F	VF	XF	Unc
1625	—	35.00	75.00	150	300	—
1626	—	35.00	75.00	150	300	—
1638	—	35.00	75.00	150	300	—

KM# 295 1/6 THALER

4.7500 g., Silver, 27.5 mm. **Ruler:** Ferdinand Maria **Obv:** Crowned oval shield of 4-fold arms of Bavaria and Pfalz, with central shield of imperial orb, in baroque frame, date divided near bottom, value (1/6) in oval below **Obv. Legend:** F. M. V. B. & P. S. D. C. P. R. S. - R. I. AR. EL & VIC. L. L. **Rev:** Facing Madonna with Child, clouds below, rays around, in circle **Rev. Legend:**

CLYPEVS. OMNIBVS. IN. TE. SPERANTIBVS. **Mint:** Munich **Note:** Vicariat issue. Ref. H#177; JB-1401. Prev. KM#83.

Date	Mintage	VG	F	VF	XF	Unc
1657	—	425	825	1,500	2,600	—

KM# 150 1/4 THALER

Silver, 33-34 mm. **Ruler:** Maximilian I **Obv:** 2 ornately shaped shield of arms of Pfalz on left and Bavaria on right, small Spanish shield of imperial orb between, electoral hat above, Order of Golden Fleece underneath all **Obv. Legend:** MAXI. D G. C. P. R. H - V. B. D. S. R. I. AR. E. EL. **Rev:** Crowned imperial eagle **Rev. Legend:** FERDI. II. ROMANORVM. IMPERAT. **Mint:** Neumarkt **Note:** Ref. G#171; JB-973. Prev. Pfalz-Simmern KM#27. Oberpfalz issue.

Date	Mintage	VG	F	VF	XF	Unc
ND(1623-26) (g)	—	—	—	—	—	—

KM# 151 1/4 THALER

Silver, 32 mm. **Ruler:** Maximilian I **Obv:** 2 ornately shaped shield of arms of Pfalz on left and Bavaria on right, small Spanish shield of imperial orb between divides date, electoral hat above, Order of Golden Fleece underneath all **Obv. Legend:** MAXI. D. G. C. P. R. V. - B. D. S. R. I. AR. ET. EL. **Rev:** Crowned imperial eagle **Rev. Legend:** FERDI. II. ROMANORVM. IMPERAT. **Mint:** Neumarkt **Note:** Ref. G#173; JB-972a; H-138. Oberpfalz issue.

Date	Mintage	VG	F	VF	XF	Unc
(16)23 (g)	—	—	—	—	—	—

KM# 261 1/3 THALER

10.0000 g., Silver, 32 mm. **Ruler:** Maximilian I **Obv:** Crowned oval shield of 4-fold arms of Bavaria ad Pfalz, with central shield of imperial orb, in baroque frame, Order of Golden Fleece around, value (1/3) in oval below **Obv. Legend:** MAXIM. CO. PA. RH. VT. BAV - DVX. S. R. I. ARCHID. ET. ELE. **Rev:** Madonna seated with Child on upturned crescent, holding scepter in right hand, clouds below, rays around, all in circle **Rev. Legend:** CLYPEVS OMNIBVS IN TE SPERANTIBVS. **Mint:** Munich **Note:** Ref. H#101; JB-912. Prev. KM#59.

Date	Mintage	VG	F	VF	XF	Unc
ND(1625)	—	550	1,000	1,800	3,250	—

KM# 264 1/3 THALER

Silver, 31-32 mm. **Ruler:** Maximilian I **Obv:** Crowned oval shield of 4-fold arms of Bavaria and Pfalz, with central shield of imperial orb, in baroque frame, Order of Golden Fleece around, date divided at upper left and right, value (1/3) in oval below **Obv. Legend:** MAXIM. CO. PA. RH. VT. BAV. - DVX. S. R. I ARCHID. ET. ELE. **Rev:** Madonna seated with Child on upturned crescent, holding scepter in left hand, clouds below, rays around, all in circle **Rev. Legend:** CLYPEVS OMNIBVS IN TE SPERANTIBVS. **Mint:** Munich **Note:** Ref. H#102; JB-913. Prev. KM#60.

Date	Mintage	VG	F	VF	XF	Unc
1640	—	425	800	1,500	2,600	—

KM# 297 1/3 THALER

8.7500 g., Silver, 30 mm. **Ruler:** Ferdinand Maria **Obv:** Crowned oval shield of 4-fold arms of Bavaria and Pfalz, with central shield of imperial orb, in baroque frame, divides date, Order of Golden Fleece suspended below, value (1/3) in circle at bottom **Obv. Legend:** + FER. MAR. V. B & P. S. DVX. C. - P. R. S. R. I. AR. EL & VIC. L. L. **Rev:** Madonna seated with Child on upturned crescent, holding scepter in left hand, rays around, all in circle **Rev. Legend:** + CLYPEVS OMNIBVS IN TE SPERANTIBVS. **Mint:** Munich **Note:** Vicariat issue. Ref. H#178; JB-1400. Prev. KM#84.

Date	Mintage	VG	F	VF	XF	Unc
1657	—	550	1,000	1,800	3,250	—

KM# 224 1/2 THALER

Silver, 39 mm. **Ruler:** Maximilian I **Obv:** Oval shield of 4-fold arms of Bavaria and Pfalz, with central shield of imperial orb, supported by 2 lions, Order of Golden Fleece around crown divides date above **Obv. Legend:** MAXIMIL. COM. PAL. RH. VT. BAV. DVX. S. R. I. ARCHIDAP. ET. ELECT. **Rev:** Madonna seated with Child, clouds below, rays around **Rev. Legend:** CLYPEVS OMNIBVS IN TE SPERANTIBVS. **Mint:** Munich **Note:** Ref. H#104; JB-910. Prev. KM#49.

Date	Mintage	VG	F	VF	XF	Unc
1627	—	125	250	500	1,000	—
1638	—	125	250	500	1,000	—

KM# 223 1/2 THALER

Silver, 36 mm. **Ruler:** Maximilian I **Obv:** Crowned oval shield of 4-fold arms of Bavaria and Pfalz, with central shield of imperial orb, supported by 2 lions, Order of Golden Fleece suspended underneath, date below **Obv. Legend:** MAXIMIL. COM. PAL. RH. VT. BAV. DVX. S. R. I. ARCHIDAP. ET. ELECT. **Rev:** Madonna seated with Child on upturned crescent, holding scepter in right hand, clouds below, rays around, all in circle **Rev. Legend:** CLYPEVS OMNIBVS IN TE SPERANTIBVS. **Mint:** Munich **Note:** Ref. H#103; JB-911. Prev. KM#48.

Date	Mintage	VG	F	VF	XF	Unc
1627	—	190	350	650	1,250	—
1627/3	—	350	650	1,250	2,100	—

KM# 225 1/2 THALER

Silver **Ruler:** Maximilian I **Obv:** Oval 4-fold arms of Bavaria and Pfalz in baroque frame, electoral hat above, Order of Golden Fleece below **Obv. Legend:** MAXI. D. G. COM. P. RHE. V. - BA. DVX. S. R. I. A. ET. EL. **Rev:** Crowned imperial eagle, date divided below **Rev. Legend:** FERDINAND. II. D. G. ROM. IMPER. SEMP. AVG. **Mint:** Heidelberg **Note:** Ref. JB#997. Rheinpfalz issue.

Date	Mintage	VG	F	VF	XF	Unc
(16)27 GC	—	—	—	—	—	—

KM# 360 1/2 THALER

Silver, 36 mm. **Ruler:** Maximilian II, Emanuel **Obv:** Crowned oval shield of 4-fold arms of Bavaria and Pfalz, with central shield of imperial orb, Order of Golden Fleece around, date at end of legend **Obv. Legend:** MAX. EM. V. B & P. S. D. C. P. R. - S. R. I. A & EL. L. L. **Rev:** Seated Madonna with Child, holding scepter in right hand, upturned crescent below, rays and clouds around **Rev. Legend:** CLYPEVS OMNIBVS IN TE SPERANTIBVS. **Mint:** Munich **Note:** Ref. H#197; JB-1648. Prev. KM#124.

Date	Mintage	VG	F	VF	XF	Unc
1694	—	350	650	1,250	2,100	—

KM# 361 1/2 THALER

Silver, 35 mm. **Ruler:** Maximilian II, Emanuel **Obv:** Draped bust to right **Obv. Legend:** MAX. EMANVEL. D. G. V. B & P. S. D. C. P. R. S. R. I. A. D & E. L. L. **Rev:** Seated Madonna with Child, holding scepter in right hand, upturned crescent below right foot, crowned oval shield of 4-fold arms of Bavaria and Pfalz, with central shield of imperial orb, Order of Golden Fleece around, at lower right, date at end of **Rev. Legend:** * CLYPEVS OMNIBVS IN TE SPERANTIBVS * **Mint:** Munich **Note:** Ref. H#198; JB-1647. Prev. KM#125.

Date	Mintage	VG	F	VF	XF	Unc
1694	—	350	650	1,250	2,100	—

KM# 31.4 THALER

Silver, 43 mm. **Ruler:** Maximilian I **Obv:** Oval shield of 4-fold arms of Bavaria and Pfalz, supported by 2 lions, ducal cap above, Order of Golden Fleece suspended below, date at end of legend **Obv. Legend:** MAXIMIL: COM: PAL: RH: VT: BAV: DVX. S. R. I. ARCHIDAP. ET. ELECT. **Rev:** Seated Madonna with Child, surrounded by rays **Rev. Legend:** CLYPEVS OMNIBVS IN TE SPERANTIBVS. **Mint:** Munich **Note:** Dav. #6066. Prev. KM#9.3.

Date	Mintage	VG	F	VF	XF	Unc
1623	—	145	375	750	1,150	—

KM# 156 THALER

Silver, 40 mm. **Ruler:** Maximilian I **Obv:** Crowned oval shield of 4-fold arms of Bavaria and Pfalz in baroque frame, with central shield of imperial orb, date divided to lower left and right, Order of Gold Fleece suspended below **Obv. Legend:** MAXIMIL COM. PAL. RH. VT. BAV. DVX. S. R. I. ARCHIDAP. ET. ELECTOR. **Rev:** Madonna seated facing with Child, feet resting on upturned crescent moon, clouds below, rays around **Rev. Legend:** CLYPEVS OMNIBVS IN TE SPERANTIBVS. **Mint:** Munich **Note:** Dav. #6067; JB#883-4; H-105. Prev. KM#37.

Date	Mintage	VG	F	VF	XF	Unc
1623	—	100	200	400	750	1,450
1624	—	100	200	400	750	1,450

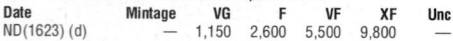

KM# 157 THALER

Silver, 42 mm. **Ruler:** Maximilian I **Obv:** 4-fold arms of Bavaria and Pfalz, with central shield, in oval baroque frame, electoral hat above, Order of Golden Fleece curved below **Obv. Legend:** MAX: COM: P: RHE. VT. B (-) A (-) V. DUX. S. R. I. AR. ET. EL. **Rev:** Crowned imperial eagle in circle **Rev. Legend:** FERDINANDVS • II • ROMANORVM • IMPERATOR * **Mint:** Amberg **Note:** Dav. #6083; G#98-99; JB#968-9; H-141, 142. Prev. Pfalz-Simmern KM#49. Oberpfalz issue.

Date	Mintage	VG	F	VF	XF	Unc
ND(1623) (d)	—	1,150	2,600	5,500	9,800	—

KM# 158 THALER

Silver, 42 mm. **Ruler:** Maximilian I **Obv:** Oval shield of 4-fold arms of Bavaria and Pfalz, with central shield, supported by 2 lions, electoral hat above, Order of Golden Fleece curved below **Obv. Legend:** MAXIMIL. D G. COMPAL. RH. V. BA. D. G. R. I. ARCHI (ET. EL). **Rev:** Crowned imperial eagle in circle **Rev. Legend:** FERDINANVS. II. ROMANORVM. IMPERATORVM. **Mint:** Kemnath **Note:** Dav. #6084; G#112; H-142. Prev. Pfalz-Simmern KM#50. Oberpfalz issue.

Date	Mintage	VG	F	VF	XF	Unc
ND(1623)	—	1,400	2,900	5,800	—	—

KM# 159 THALER

Silver, 42 mm. **Ruler:** Maximilian I **Obv:** 4-fold arms of Bavaria and Pfalz, with central shield, in ornamented Spanish shield, electoral cap above, Order of Golden Fleece curved along sides and below **Obv. Legend:** MAXIMIL • DG • COM • P - AL • RH • V • B • D • S • R • I • A • ET • E • **Rev:** Crowned imperial eagle in circle **Rev. Legend:** FERDINAN • II • ROMANORVM • IMPERATOR **Mint:** Neumarkt **Note:** Dav. #6086; G#170; JB-963; H-143. Prev. Pfalz-Simmern KM#51. Oberpfalz issue.

Date	Mintage	VG	F	VF	XF	Unc
ND(1623-26) (g)	—	1,400	2,900	5,800	—	—

KM# 175.2 THALER

Silver, 43 mm. **Ruler:** Maximilian I **Obv:** Crowned Spanish shield of 4-fold arms of Bavaria and Pfalz, with central shield of imperial orb, in baroque frame, Order of Golden Fleece around **Obv. Legend:** MAXIMIL • DG • COM • P - AL • RH • V • B • D • S • R • I • A • ET • E • **Rev:** Crowned imperial eagle, date divided below legs **Rev. Legend:** FERDINANDVS • II • ROMANORVM • IMPERATOR • **Mint:** Neumarkt **Note:** Dav. #6089. Ref. JB-964, 966; H#144. Prev. Pfalz-Simmern KM#65. Oberpfalz issue.

Date	Mintage	VG	F	VF	XF	Unc
1624 (g)	—	750	1,450	2,900	—	—

KM# 178.1 THALER

Silver, 40-41 mm. **Ruler:** Maximilian I **Obv:** 4-fold arms of Bavaria and Pfalz, with central shield, in oval baroque frame, date divided below, electoral hat above, Order of Golden Fleece curved beneath **Obv. Legend:** • MAXI: D:G: COM: P: RH: V. - BA. DVX. S. R. I. AR. ET. EL. **Rev:** Crowned imperial eagle in circle **Rev. Legend:** FERDINAND: II • D:G: ROMA: IMPER: SEMP: AVGV • **Mint:** Heidelberg **Note:** Dav. #6090; JB-989; H-153. Prev. Pfalz-Simmern KM#66.1. Rheinpfalz issue.

Date	Mintage	VG	F	VF	XF	Unc
1624	—	1,150	2,300	4,050	—	—
1626 Rare	—	—	—	—	—	—

KM# 175.1 THALER

Silver, 42-43 mm. **Ruler:** Maximilian I **Obv:** Ornately shaped shield of 4-fold arms of Bavaria and Pfalz, with central shield, electoral hat above, Order of Golden Fleece curved below **Obv. Legend:** MAXIMIL • DG • COM • P - AL • RH • V • B • D • S • R • I • ET • E • **Rev:** Crowned imperial eagle in circle, date divided to left and right below wings **Rev. Legend:** FERDINANDVS • II • ROMANORVM • IMPERATOR • **Mint:** Neumarkt **Note:** Dav. #6089; G#177; JB-965; H-144. Prev. Pfalz-Simmern KM#65. Oberpfalz issue.

Date	Mintage	VG	F	VF	XF	Unc
1624 (g)	—	875	1,750	3,450	—	—

KM# 176 THALER

Silver, 43-44 mm. **Ruler:** Maximilian I **Obv:** Ornately shaped shield of 4-fold arms of Bavaria and Pfalz, with central shield, electoral hat above, Order of Golden Fleece curved below **Obv. Legend:** MAXIMIL • DG • COM • P - AL • RH • V • B • D • S • R • I • A • ET • E • **Rev:** Crowned imperial eagle, large date divided by bottom of tail **Rev. Legend:** FERDINANDVS • II • ROMANORVM • **Mint:** Neumarkt **Note:** Ref. G#178; JB-964. Oberpfalz issue.

Date	Mintage	VG	F	VF	XF	Unc
1624	—	1,400	2,900	4,600	—	—

KM# 177 THALER

Silver, 43 mm. **Ruler:** Maximilian I **Obv:** Ornately shaped shield of 4-fold arms of Bavaria and Pfalz, with central shield, electoral hat above, Order of Golden Fleece curved below **Obv. Legend:** MAXIMIL • DG • COM • P - AL • RH • V • B • D • S • R • I • A • ET • E • **Rev:** Crowned imperial eagle, small date below eagle's legs **Rev. Legend:** FERDINANDVS • II • ROMANORVM • IMPERATOR • **Mint:** Neumarkt **Note:** Ref. G#179; JB-966. Oberpfalz issue.

Date	Mintage	VG	F	VF	XF	Unc
1624 (g)	—	1,400	2,900	4,600	—	—

KM# 178.2 THALER

Silver, 40-41 mm. **Ruler:** Maximilian I **Obv:** 4-fold arms of Bavaria and Pfalz, with central shield, in oval baroque frame, date divided below, electoral hat above, Order of Golden Fleece curved beneath **Obv. Legend:** MAXI. D. G. COM. P. RH. V. - BA. DVX. S. R. I. AR. ET. EL. **Rev:** Crowned imperial eagle in circle **Rev. Legend:** MAXIMILIAN. D. G. ROMANORVM. IMPRAT. **Mint:** Heidelberg **Note:** Ref. Dav. #6090A; JB-990. Rheinpfalz issue.

Date	Mintage	VG	F	VF	XF	Unc
1624	—	—	—	—	—	—

KM# 194 THALER

Silver, 42 mm. **Ruler:** Maximilian I **Obv:** Crowned oval shield of 4-fold arms of Bavaria and Pfalz in baroque frame, with central shield of imperial orb, date divided at left and right, lions' head at left and right of crown, Order of Golden Fleece suspended below **Obv. Legend:** MAXIMIL COM. PAL. RH. VT. BAV. D - VX. S. R. I. ARCHIDAP. ET. ELECTOR. **Rev:** Madonna seated facing with Child, feet resting on upturned crescent moon, clouds below, rays around **Rev. Legend:** CLYPEVS OMNIBVS IN TE SPERANTIBVS. **Mint:** Munich **Note:** Dav. #6069; H-106. Prev. KM#39.

Date	Mintage	VG	F	VF	XF	Unc
1625	—	100	175	400	1,050	2,000

KM# 195 THALER

Silver, 40-42 mm. **Ruler:** Maximilian I **Obv:** Crowned oval shield of 4-fold arms of Bavaria and Pfalz in baroque frame, with central shield of imperial orb, date divided by lions' heads at left and right of crown, Order of Golden Fleece suspended below **Obv. Legend:** MAXIML COM. PAL. RH. VT. BAV. DVX. S. R. I. ARCHIDAP. ET. ELECTO. **Rev:** Madonna seated facing with Child, feet resting on upturned crescent moon, clouds below, rays around **Rev. Legend:** CLYPEVS OMNIBVS IN TE SPERANTIBVS. **Mint:** Munich **Note:** Dav. #6070; JB-886, 891; H-107. Prev. KM#40.

Date	Mintage	VG	F	VF	XF	Unc
16Z5	—	100	175	400	1,050	2,000
1626	—	100	175	400	1,050	2,000

KM# 196 THALER

Silver, 42 mm. **Ruler:** Maximilian I **Obv:** Crowned oval shield of 4-fold arms of Bavaria and Pfalz, with central shield of imperial orb, supported by 2 lions, Order of Golden Fleece suspended below, date in cartouche at bottom **Obv. Legend:** MAXIMIL COM. PAL. RH. VT. BAV. DVX. S. R. I. ARCHIDAP. ET. ELECT. **Rev:** Madonna seated facing with Child, feet resting on upturned crescent moon, clouds below, rays around **Rev. Legend:** CLYPEVS OMNIBVS IN TE SPERANTIBVS. **Mint:** Munich **Note:** Dav. #6071; JB-889; H-109. Prev. KM#41.

Date	Mintage	VG	F	VF	XF	Unc
1625	—	100	175	375	875	—

KM# 197 THALER

Silver, 42 mm. **Ruler:** Maximilian I **Obv:** Crowned oval shield of 4-fold arms of Bavaria and Pfalz, with central shield of imperial orb, supported by 2 lions, Order of Golden Fleece suspended below, date in cartouche at bottom **Obv. Legend:** MAXIMIL COM. PAL. RH. VT. BAV. DVX. S. R. I. ARCHIDAP. ET. ELECT. **Rev:** Madonna seated with Child, turned slightly to left, feet resting on upturned crescent moon, clouds below, rays around **Rev. Legend:** CLYPEVS OMNIBVS IN TE SPERANTIBVS. **Mint:** Munich **Note:** Dav. #6071A. Prev. KM#42.

Date	Mintage	VG	F	VF	XF	Unc
1625	—	105	190	400	925	—

KM# 208 THALER

Silver, 44-45 mm. **Ruler:** Maximilian I **Obv:** Crowned oval shield of 4-fold arms of Bavaria and Pfalz, with central shield of imperial orb, supported by 2 lions, Order of Golden Fleece suspended below, date in cartouche at bottom **Obv. Legend:** MAXIMIL. COM. PAL. RH. VT. BAV. DVX. S. R. I. ARCHIDAP. ET. ELECT. **Rev:** Facing seated Madonna with Child, feet resting on upturned crescent moon, clouds below, all within an arc of flames **Rev. Legend:** CLYPEVS OMNIBVS IN TE SPERANTIBVS. **Mint:** Munich **Note:** Dav. #6073; JB-892, 893, 896; H-108. Prev. KM#45. Varieties exist.

Date	Mintage	VG	F	VF	XF	Unc
1626	—	100	175	350	700	—
1627/6	—	100	175	350	700	—
1627	—	100	175	350	700	—

KM# 209 THALER

Silver, 43-44 mm. **Ruler:** Maximilian I **Obv:** Crowned oval shield of 4-fold arms of Bavaria and Pfalz, with central shield of imperial orb, supported by 2 lions, Order of Golden Fleece suspended below, date divided in cartouche at bottom **Obv. Legend:** MAXIMIL. COM. PAL. RH. VT. BAV. DVX. S. R. I. ARCHIDAP. ET. ELECT. **Rev:** Facing seated Madonna on clouds, holding Child at left, radiant beams behind **Rev. Legend:** CLYPEVS OMNIBVS IN TE SPERANTIBVS. **Mint:** Munich **Note:** Dav. #6074; JB-894, 895; H-110. Prev. KM#A50.

Date	Mintage	VG	F	VF	XF	Unc
1626	—	100	175	375	750	1,750
1627	—	100	175	375	750	1,750

KM# 210 THALER

Silver, 42 mm. **Ruler:** Maximilian I **Obv:** 4-fold arms of Bavaria and Pfalz, with central shield, in oval baroque frame, date divided to upper left and right, electoral hat above, Order of Golden Fleece curved below **Obv. Legend:** MAXI. D. G. COM. P. R(H). V. - BA. DVX. S. R. I. A(R). ET. EL. **Rev:** Crowned imperial eagle in circle **Rev. Legend:** FERDINAND. II. D. G. ROM. IMPER. SEMP. AVGV. **Mint:** Heidelberg **Note:** Dav. #6092; JB-991, 992; H-153. Prev. Pfalz-Simmern KM#72. Rheinpfalz issue. Varieties exist.

Date	Mintage	VG	F	VF	XF	Unc
1626 GC Rare	—	—	—	—	—	—

KM# 227.1 THALER

Silver, 43-44 mm. **Ruler:** Maximilian I **Obv:** Crowned oval shield of 4-fold arms of Bavaria and Pfalz, with central shield of imperial orb, supported by 2 lions, Order of Golden Fleece suspended below, date in cartouche at bottom **Obv. Legend:** MAXIMIL. COM. PAL. RH. VT. BAV. DVX. S. R. I. ARCHIDAP. ET. ELECT. **Rev:** Facing seated Madonna holding Child at left, clouds below, rays around arcing overhead **Rev. Legend:** CLYPEVS OMNIBVS IN TE SPERANTIBVS. **Mint:** Munich **Note:** Dav. #6075; JB#897-900, 903; H-111. Prev. KM#50.1.

Date	Mintage	VG	F	VF	XF	Unc
1627	—	95.00	165	300	600	1,400
1628/7	—	95.00	165	300	600	1,400
1628	—	95.00	165	300	600	1,400
1629	—	95.00	165	300	600	1,400

Date	Mintage	VG	F	VF	XF	Unc
1631	1,352	95.00	165	300	600	1,400
1637	—	95.00	165	300	600	1,400

KM# 228 THALER
Silver, 38-40 mm. **Ruler:** Maximilian I **Obv:** 4-fold arms of Bavaria and Pfalz, with central shield, in oval baroque frame, date divided to upper left and right, electoral hat above, Order of Golden Fleece curved below **Obv. Legend:** MAXI. D. G. COM. P(A). RH(E). V - BA. DVX. . R. I. A(R). E(T). (P.) E(LE). **Rev:** Crowned imperial eagle in circle **Rev. Legend:** FERDINAND. II D. G. ROMA. IMPER. SEMP. AVG(V). **Mint:** Heidelberg **Note:** Dav. #6093; JB#994-6; H-154. Prev. Pfalz-Simmern KM#75. Rheinpfalz issue. Varieties exist.

Date	Mintage	VG	F	VF	XF	Unc
1627 GC	—	3,300	6,600	11,500	—	—

KM# 229 THALER
Silver, 41 mm. **Ruler:** Maximilian I **Obv:** Armored and draped bust to right **Obv. Legend:** MAXIMILIANVS: D:G: COM: PAL: RHENI. VTRI: BAVARIÆ • DVX • **Rev:** Oval shield of 4-fold arms of Bavaria and Pfalz, with central shield, supported by 2 lions, electoral hat flanked by 2 ornate helmets above, Order of Golden Fleece curved below, date divided by mintmaster's initials at bottom **Rev. Legend:** SACRI • ROM • IMP • ARCHIDAPIFER • ET • PRINCEPS • ELECTOR **Mint:** Heidelberg **Note:** Dav. #6096; B-993; H-154. Prev. Pfalz-Simmern KM#76. Rheinpfalz issue.

Date	Mintage	VG	F	VF	XF	Unc
1627 GC Rare	—	—	—	—	—	—

Note: US Auction 65 9-06, VF realized approximately $15,460

KM# 227.2 THALER
29.1500 g., Silver, 39 mm. **Ruler:** Maximilian I **Obv:** Crowned oval shield of 4-fold arms of Bavaria and Pfalz, with central shield of imperial orb, supported by 2 lions, Order of Golden Fleece suspended below, date in cartouche at bottom, all in circle **Obv. Legend:** MAXIMIL. COM. PAL. RH. VT. BAV. DVX. S. R. I. ARCHIDAP. ET. ELECT. **Rev:** Facing seated Madonna holding Child at left, clouds below, rays around arcing overhead, all in circle **Rev. Legend:** CLYPEVS OMNIBVS IN TE SPERANTIBVS. **Mint:** Munich **Note:** Dav. #6076; JB-901, 902; H-111. Prev. KM#50.2. Varieties exist.

Date	Mintage	VG	F	VF	XF	Unc
1632	—	220	400	825	1,550	—

KM# 227.3 THALER
Silver, 45 mm. **Ruler:** Maximilian I **Obv:** Crowned oval shield of 4-fold arms of Bavaria and Pfalz, with central shield of imperial orb, supported by 2 lions, Order of Golden Fleece suspended below, Roman numeral date in two lines in cartouche at bottom **Obv. Legend:** MAXIMIL. COM PA(L). - RH. VT. BAV. DVX. S. R. I. AR - CHIDAP. ET. ELECT. **Rev:** Facing seated Madonna holding Child at left, clouds below, rays around behind **Rev. Legend:** CLYPEVS OMNIBVS IN TE SPERANTIBVS. **Mint:** Munich **Note:** Dav. #6078; JB-904; H-111. Prev. KM#50.3.

Date	Mintage	VG	F	VF	XF	Unc
MDCXXXVIII (1638)	—	125	250	500	1,000	2,050

KM# 263.1 THALER
Silver, 46-47 mm. **Ruler:** Maximilian I **Obv:** Crowned oval shield of 4-fold arms of Bavaria and Pfalz, with central shield of imperial orb, supported by 2 lions, Order of Golden Fleece suspended below, date divided in cartouche at bottom **Obv. Legend:** MAXIMIL. COM. PA. - RH. VT. BAV. DVX. S. R. - I. ARCHIDAP. ET. EL. **Rev:** Facing seated Madonna, holding Child at left, upturned crescent moon below, flames around, all in beaded circle **Rev. Legend:** CLYPEVS OMNIBVS IN TE SPERANTIBVS. **Mint:** Munich **Note:** Dav. #6079; JP-906; H-112. Prev. KM#58.1.

Date	Mintage	VG	F	VF	XF	Unc
1639 Rare	—	—	—	—	—	—

KM# 263.2 THALER
Silver, 45 mm. **Ruler:** Maximilian I **Obv:** Crowned oval shield of 4-fold arms of Bavaria and Pfalz, with central shield of imperial orb, supported by 2 lions, Order of Golden Fleece suspended underneath, Roman numeral date curved below **Obv. Legend:** MAXIMIL. COM. PA. - RH. VT. BAV. DVX. S. R. - I. ARCHIDAP. ET. EL. **Rev:** Facing seated Madonna, holding Child at left, upturned crescent below, flames around, all in beaded circle **Rev. Legend:** CLYPEVS OMNIBVS IN TE SPERANTIBVS. **Mint:** Munich **Note:** Dav. #6080; JB-907; H-112. Prev. KM#58.2.

Date	Mintage	VG	F	VF	XF	Unc
MDCXXXX (1640)	—	155	325	625	1,150	2,150

KM# 263.3 THALER
Silver, 43-44 mm. **Ruler:** Maximilian I **Obv:** Crowned oval shield of 4-fold arms of Bavaria and Pfalz, with central shield of imperial orb, supported by 2 lions, Order of Golden Fleece suspended underneath, Arabic date below **Obv. Legend:** MAXIMIL. COM. PAL. - RH. VT. BAV. DVX. S. R. I. AR - CHIDAP. ET. ELECT. **Rev:** Facing seated Madonna, holding Child at left, upturned crescent moon below, flames around, all in beaded circle **Rev. Legend:** CLYPEVS OMNIBVS IN TE SPERANTIBVS. **Mint:** Munich **Note:** Dav. #6081; JB-908; H-112. Prev. KM#58.3.

Date	Mintage	VG	F	VF	XF	Unc
1641	—	115	230	450	925	1,900

KM# 276 THALER
Silver, 40-41 mm. **Ruler:** Maximilian I **Obv:** Crowned oval shield of 4-fold arms of Bavaria and Pfalz, with central shield of imperial orb, Order of Golden Fleece around, date divided below **Obv.**

Legend: +MAXIM. CO. PA. RH. VT. BAV. DVX. S. R. I. ARCHID. ET. ELE. **Rev:** Facing seated Madonna, holding Child at right, upturned crescent moon below, flames around, all in circle **Rev. Legend:** CLYPEVS OMNIBVS IN TE SPERANTIBVS. **Mint:** Munich **Note:** Dav. #6082; JB-909; H-113. Prev. KM#65.

Date	Mintage	VG	F	VF	XF	Unc
1643	—	650	1,300	2,700	4,500	—

KM# 299 THALER

Silver, 40-41 mm. **Ruler:** Ferdinand Maria **Obv:** Crowned oval shield of 4-fold arms of Bavaria and Pfalz, with central shield of imperial orb, in baroque frame, crown above divides date **Obv. Legend:** FER. MAR. V. B & P. S. DVX. CO. P. R. S. R. I. AR. EL & VIC. L. L. **Rev:** Facing seated Madonna, holding Child at right, upturned crescent moon below, flames around, all in circle **Rev. Legend:** CLYPEVS. OMNIBVS. IN. TE. SPERANTIBVS. **Mint:** Munich **Note:** Vicariat issue. Dav. #6098; JB-1399; H-179. Prev. KM#85.

Date	Mintage	VG	F	VF	XF	Unc
1657	—	1,000	2,100	4,200	7,200	—

KM# 300 THALER

Silver, 40-41 mm. **Ruler:** Ferdinand Maria **Obv:** 10-line inscription **Obv. Inscription:** D. G. / FERDINANDVS. / MARIA SVP: ET INF. / BAV: ACSVP: PAL: DVX. / CO: PAL: RHE: S: R: IMP: / ARCHID: ET. ELECT: ATQ. / POST. EXCESS: DIVI. / FERDI: III. IMP. AVG: / VICARIVS. LAND: / LEICHT: ETC. **Rev:** Madonna with Child seated at left, elector at right, kneeling to left, holding orb in right hand, crowned oval shield of 4-fold arms of Bavaria and Pfalz, with central shield of imperial orb, at bottom center divides date **Rev. Legend:** O. MARIA. ORA. - PRO. ME. **Mint:** Munich **Note:** Vicariat issue. Dav. #6097; JB-1398; H-180. Prev. KM#86.

Date	Mintage	VG	F	VF	XF	Unc
1657	—	950	2,000	3,900	6,600	—

KM# 363.1 THALER

Silver, 42-43 mm. **Ruler:** Maximilian II, Emanuel **Obv:** Armored and draped bust to right **Obv. Legend:** MAX. EMANVEL. D. G. V. B & P. S. D. C. P. R. S. R. I. A. D & E. L. L. **Rev:** Seated Madonna, head turned slightly to right, with Child, small crowned oval shield of 4-fold arms of Bavaria and Pfalz, with central shield of imperial orb, Order of Golden Fleece around, at lower right, date at end of legend **Rev. Legend:** CLYPEVS OMNIBVS IN TE SPERANTIBVS. **Mint:** Munich **Note:** Dav. #6099; JB-1645; H-199. Prev. KM#126.1.

Date	Mintage	VG	F	VF	XF	Unc
1694	—	85.00	175	325	575	1,450

KM# 363.2 THALER

Silver, 42-43 mm. **Ruler:** Maximilian II, Emanuel **Obv:** Armored and draped bust, with high, curly wig, to right **Obv. Legend:** MAX. EMANVEL. D. G. V. B & P. S. D. C. P. R. S. R. I. A. D & E. L. L. **Rev:** Seated Madonna, head turned slightly to right, with Child, small crowned oval shield of 4-fold arms of Bavaria and Pfalz, with central shield of imperial orb, Order of Golden Fleece around, at lower right, date at end of legend **Rev. Legend:** CLYPEVS OMNIBVS IN TE SPERANTIBVS. **Mint:** Munich **Note:** Dav. #6099A; H-199. Prev. KM#126.2.

Date	Mintage	VG	F	VF	XF	Unc
1694	—	75.00	145	290	450	1,050

KM# 365.1 THALER

Silver, 43-44 mm. **Ruler:** Maximilian II, Emanuel **Obv:** Armored and draped bust to right, small lettering in legend **Obv. Legend:** MAX. EMANVEL. D. G. V. B & P. S. D. C. P. R. S. R. I. A. D & E. L. L. **Rev:** Seated Madonna, heard turned slightly to left, with Child, small crowned oval shield of 4-fold arms of Bavaria and Pfalz, with central shield of imperial orb, Order of Golden Fleece around, at lower right, date at end of legend, which is in small let **Rev. Legend:** CLYPEVS OMNIBVS IN TE SPERANTIBVS. **Mint:** Munich **Note:** Dav. #6100; H-199. Prev. KM#127.1.

Date	Mintage	VG	F	VF	XF	Unc
1694	—	75.00	175	350	575	1,300

KM# 365.2 THALER

Silver, 43 mm. **Ruler:** Maximilian II, Emanuel **Obv:** Armored and draped bust to right, legend in large letters **Obv. Legend:** MAX. EMANVEL. D. G. V. B & P. S. D. C. P. R. S. R. I. A. D & E. L. L. **Rev:** Seated Madonna, heard turned slightly to left, with Child, small crowned oval shield of 4-fold arms of Bavaria and Pfalz, with central shield of imperial orb, Order of Golden Fleece around, at lower right, 6-pointed star before date at end of legend, **Rev. Legend:** CLYPEVS OMNIBVS IN TE SPERANTIBVS * **Mint:** Munich **Note:** Dav. #6101; JB-1646; H-199. Prev. KM#127.2.

Date	Mintage	VG	F	VF	XF	Unc
1695	—	75.00	175	350	575	1,300

KM# 231 1-1/2 THALER

Silver, 41 mm. **Ruler:** Maximilian I **Obv:** Armored and draped bust to right **Obv. Legend:** MAXIMILIANVS. D. G. COM. PAL. RHENI. VTRI. BAVARIÆ. DVX. **Rev:** Oval shield of 4-fold arms of Bavaria and Pfalz, with central shield, supported by 2 lions, electoral hat flanked by 2 ornate helmets above, Order of Golden Fleece curved below, date divided by mintmaster's initials at bottom **Rev. Legend:** SACRI. ROM. IMP. ARCHIDAMPIFER. ET. PRINCEPS. ELECTOR. **Mint:** Heidelberg **Note:** Dav. #6095; JB-993; H-155. Prev. Pfalz-Simmern KM#77. Rheinpfalz issue.

Date	Mintage	VG	F	VF	XF	Unc
1627 CG Rare	—	—	—	—	—	—

KM# 161 2 THALER

Silver, 43 mm. **Ruler:** Maximilian I **Obv:** 4-fold arms of Bavaria and Pfalz, with central shield, in oval baroque frame, electoral hat above, Order of Golden Fleece curved below **Obv. Legend:** MAXIMILIAN • DG • CO - M • PAL • R • V • B • D • S • R • I • A • ET E • **Rev:** Crowned imperial eagle in circle **Rev. Legend:** FERDINANDVS II ROMANORVM • IMPERATOR • **Mint:** Neumarkt **Note:** Dav. #6085; G-169; H-145. Prev. Pfalz-Simmern KM#30. Oberpfalz issue.

Date	Mintage	VG	F	VF	XF	Unc
ND(1623-26) (g) Rare	—	—	—	—	—	—

KM# 184 2 THALER

Silver, 41-43 mm. **Ruler:** Maximilian I **Obv:** 4-fold arms of Bavaria and Pfalz, with central shield, in ornamented Spanish shield, electoral hat above, Order of Golden Fleece curved below **Obv. Legend:** MAXIMIL(IA). D G. CO(-)M. P(-)AL. R(H). V. B. D. S. R. I. A. ET. E. **Rev:** Crowned imperial eagle, date above or below legs **Rev. Legend:** FERDINANDVS II ROMANORVM(.) IMPERATOR. **Mint:** Neumarkt **Note:** Dav. #6088; G-175, 180; JB-970; H-146. Prev. Pfalz-Simmern KM#69. Oberpfalz issue. Varieties exist.

Date	Mintage	VG	F	VF	XF	Unc
1624 (g) Rare	—	—	—	—	—	—
1626 (g) Rare	—	—	—	—	—	—

KM# 183 2 THALER

Silver, 42-43 mm. **Ruler:** Maximilian I **Obv:** 4-fold arms of Bavaria and Pfalz, with central shield, in oval baroque frame, electoral hat above, Order of Golden Fleece curved below **Obv. Legend:** MAXIMIL. DG. COM. PA - RH V B D. S. R I. AR ET EL **Rev:** Crowned imperial eagle, date divided by tail **Rev. Legend:** FERDINANDVS II ROMANORVM • IMPERATOR • **Mint:** Neumarkt **Note:** Dav. #6087; G-176; JB-967; H-147. Prev. Pfalz-Simmern KM#68. Oberpfalz issue.

Date	Mintage	VG	F	VF	XF	Unc
1624 (g) Rare	—	—	—	—	—	—

KM# 200 2 THALER

Silver, 43-45 mm. **Ruler:** Maximilian I **Obv:** Crowned oval shield of 4-fold arms of Bavaria and Pfalz in baroque frame, with central shield of imperial orb, date divided at left and right, lions' heads to left and right of crown, Order of Golden Fleece suspended below **Obv. Legend:** MAXIMIL COM. PAL. RH. VT. BAV. D - VX. S. R. I. ARCHIDAP. ET. ELECTOR. **Rev:** Madonna seated facing with Child, feet resting on upturned crescent moon, clouds below, rays around **Rev. Legend:** CLYPEVS OMNIBVS IN TE SPERANTIBVS. **Mint:** Munich **Note:** Dav. #6068; H-114. Prev. KM#43.

Date	Mintage	VG	F	VF	XF	Unc
1625	—	425	1,000	2,100	3,000	—

KM# 215 2 THALER

Silver, 44-45 mm. **Ruler:** Maximilian I **Obv:** Crowned oval shield of 4-fold arms of Bavaria and Pfalz, with central shield of imperial orb, supported by 2 lions, Order of Golden Fleece suspended below, date in cartouche at bottom **Obv. Legend:** MAXIMIL. COM. PAL. RH. VT. BAV. DVX. S. R. I. ARCHIDAP. ET. ELECT. **Rev:** Facing seated Madonna with Child, feet resting on upturned crescent moon, clouds below, all within an arc of flames **Rev. Legend:** CLYPEVS OMNIBVS IN TE SPERANTIBVS. **Mint:** Munich **Note:** Dav. #6072; JB-892;; H-115. Prev. KM#46.

Date	Mintage	VG	F	VF	XF	Unc
1626	—	350	900	1,800	2,700	—

KM# 216 2 THALER

Silver, 40-41 mm. **Ruler:** Maximilian I **Obv:** 4-fold arms of Bavaria and Pfalz, with central shield, in oval baroque frame, date divided below, electoral cap above, Order of Golden Fleece curved below **Obv. Legend:** MAXIMILIAN • DG • CO - M • PAL • R • V • B • D • S • R • I • A • ET • E • **Rev:** Crowned imperial eagle in circle **Rev. Legend:** FERDINANDVS • II • ROMANORVM • IMPERATOR • **Mint:** Heidelberg **Note:** Dav. #A6090. Prev. Pfalz-Simmern KM#73. Rheinpfalz issue.

Date	Mintage	VG	F	VF	XF	Unc
1626 Rare	—	—	—	—	—	—

KM# 217 2 THALER

Silver, 42 mm. **Ruler:** Maximilian I **Obv:** 4-fold arms of Bavaria and Pfalz, with central shield, in oval baroque frame, date divided to upper left and right, electoral hat above, Order of Golden Fleece curved below **Obv. Legend:** MAXI. D. G. COM. P. R(H). V. - BA. DVX. S. R. I. A(R). ET. EL. **Rev:** Crowned imperial eagle in circle **Rev. Legend:** FERDINAND. II. D. G. ROM. IMPER. SEMP. AVGV. **Mint:** Heidelberg **Note:** Dav. 6091; JB-991; H-156. Prev. Pfalz-Simmern KM#74. Rheinpfalz issue. Varieties exist.

Date	Mintage	VG	F	VF	XF	Unc
1626 GC Rare	—	—	—	—	—	—

KM# 236 2 THALER

Silver, 41 mm. **Ruler:** Maximilian I **Obv:** Armored and draped bust to right **Obv. Legend:** MAXIMILIANVS • D:G: COM: PAL: RHENI. VTRI: BAVARIÆ • DVX • **Rev:** Oval shield of 4-fold arms of Bavaria and Pfalz, with central shield, supported by 2 lions, electoral hat flanked by 2 ornate helmets above, Order of Golden Fleece below, date divided by mintmaster's initials at bottom **Rev. Legend:** SACRI • ROM • IMP • ARCHIDAPIFER • ET • PRINCEPS • ELECTOR **Mint:** Heidelberg **Note:** Dav. #6094; JB-993; H-157. Prev. Pfalz-Simmern KM#78. Rheinpfalz issue.

Date	Mintage	VG	F	VF	XF	Unc
1627 GC Rare	—	—	—	—	—	—

KM# 257 2 THALER

Silver, 45 mm. **Ruler:** Maximilian I **Obv:** Crowned oval shield of 4-fold arms of Bavaria and Pfalz, with central shield of imperial orb, supported by 2 lions, Order of Golden Fleece suspended below, Roman numeral date in 2 lines in cartouche at bottom **Obv. Legend:** MAXIMIL. COM. PAL. - RH. VT. BAV. DVX. S. R. I. AR - CHIDAP. ET. ELECT. **Rev:** Facing seated Madonna holding Child at left, clouds below, rays around arcing over head **Rev. Legend:** CLYPEVS OMNIBVS IN TE SPERANTIBVS. **Mint:** Munich **Note:** Dav. #6077; JB-904; H-116. Prev. KM#56.

Date	Mintage	VG	F	VF	XF	Unc
MDCXXXVIII (1638)	—	350	900	1,800	2,700	—

KM# 257A 2 THALER

Silver **Ruler:** Maximilian I **Obv:** Crowned oval shield of 4-fold arms of Bavaria and Pfalz, with central shield of imperial orb, supported by 2 lions, Order of Golden Fleece suspended below, Roman numeral date in 2 lines in cartouche at bottom **Obv. Legend:** MAXIMIL. COM. PAL. - RH. VT. BAV. DVX. S. R. I. AR - CHIDAP. ET. ELECT. **Rev:** Facing seated Madonna holding Child at left, clouds below, rays around arcing over head **Rev. Legend:** CLYPEVS OMNIBVS IN TE SPERANTIBVS. **Mint:** Munich **Note:** Dav. #6077A; JB-904. Klippe

Date	Mintage	VG	F	VF	XF	Unc
MDCXXXVIII (1638) Rare	—	—	—	—	—	—

TRADE COINAGE

KM# 202 GOLDGULDEN

3.5000 g., 0.9860 Gold 0.1109 oz. AGW **Ruler:** Maximilian I **Obv:** Crowned arms with lion supporters in inner circle **Rev:** Radiant Madonna and child in inner circle **Mint:** Munich **Note:** Prev. KM#44.

Date	Mintage	VG	F	VF	XF	Unc
(16)25	—	650	1,300	2,500	4,150	—

KM# 203 GOLDGULDEN

Gold, 22 mm. **Ruler:** Maximilian I **Obv:** Oval 4-fold arms of Bavaria and Pfalz, with central shield of imperial orb, Order of Golden Fleece around **Obv. Legend:** MAX. D. G. C. P. R. V. - BA. D. S. R. I. AR. E. E. **Rev:** Crowned imperial eagle, date divided near claws **Rev. Legend:** FERD. II. D. G. ROM. IMP. SEMP. AVG. **Mint:** Heidelberg **Note:** Fr. #192; JB-988; H-158. Rheinpfalz issue. Prev. Pfalz-Simmern KM#71.

Date	Mintage	VG	F	VF	XF	Unc
1625	—	825	1,650	3,300	5,500	—

KM# 325 GOLDGULDEN

3.5000 g., 0.9860 Gold 0.1109 oz. AGW **Ruler:** Ferdinand Maria **Obv:** Armored bust of Ferdinand Maria right **Rev:** Madonna and child above crowned arms divide date **Note:** Fr. #210. Prev. KM#100.

Date	Mintage	VG	F	VF	XF	Unc
1674CZ	—	230	450	925	1,650	—
1675CZ	—	175	290	450	1,050	—
1676CZ	—	175	350	575	1,250	—
1677CZ	—	230	400	700	1,400	—
1678CZ	—	230	450	925	1,650	—
1679CZ	—	175	350	575	1,250	—

KM# 350 GOLDGULDEN

3.5000 g., 0.9860 Gold 0.1109 oz. AGW **Ruler:** Maximilian III, Josef **Obv:** Draped bust right **Rev:** Date divided by Madonna and child above and arms below **Note:** First reign. Fr. #219/220. Prev. KM#119.

Date	Mintage	VG	F	VF	XF	Unc
1691	—	550	1,000	1,750	2,650	—
1697	—	450	875	1,300	2,200	—
1698	—	450	875	1,300	2,200	—
1699	—	450	875	1,300	2,200	—
1700	—	450	875	1,300	2,200	—

KM# 317 1/4 DUCAT

0.8750 g., 0.9860 Gold 0.0277 oz. AGW **Ruler:** Ferdinand Maria **Obv:** Bust of Ferdinand Maria right, continuous legend **Rev:** Capped arms, value below, cap divides date without legend **Mint:** Munich **Note:** Vicariat issue. Fr. #212. Prev. KM#96.

Date	Mintage	VG	F	VF	XF	Unc
1672	—	250	650	1,100	1,650	—

KM# 321 1/4 DUCAT

0.8750 g., 0.9860 Gold 0.0277 oz. AGW **Ruler:** Ferdinand Maria **Obv:** Divided legend **Rev:** Continuous legend **Note:** Fr. #212. Prev. KM#98.

Date	Mintage	VG	F	VF	XF	Unc
1673	—	250	650	1,100	1,650	—

KM# 329 1/4 DUCAT

0.8750 g., 0.9860 Gold 0.0277 oz. AGW **Ruler:** Ferdinand Maria **Obv:** Bust of Ferdinand Maria right in inner circle **Rev:** Capped arms in inner circle, value below, cap divides date **Note:** Fr. #212. Prev. KM#102.

Date	Mintage	VG	F	VF	XF	Unc
1676	—	250	650	1,100	1,650	—

KM# 309 1/2 DUCAT

1.7500 g., 0.9860 Gold 0.0555 oz. AGW **Ruler:** Ferdinand Maria **Subject:** Birth of Maximilian Emanuel **Obv:** Crowned arms **Rev:** Madonna and child seated facing **Note:** Fr. #204. Prev. KM#91.

Date	Mintage	VG	F	VF	XF	Unc
1662	—	475	1,200	2,000	2,950	—

KM# 319 1/2 DUCAT

1.7500 g., 0.9860 Gold 0.0555 oz. AGW **Ruler:** Ferdinand Maria **Obv:** Bust of Ferdinand Maria right in inner circle **Rev:** Crowned arms in inner circle, value below **Mint:** Munich **Note:** Fr. #211. Prev. KM#97.

Date	Mintage	VG	F	VF	XF	Unc
1672	—	550	1,200	2,400	4,250	—
1678	—	550	1,200	2,400	4,250	—

KM# 246 DUCAT

3.4900 g., 0.9860 Gold 0.1106 oz. AGW **Ruler:** Maximilian I **Obv:** Capped arms in Order collar, cap divides date **Rev:** Radiant Madonna and child **Mint:** Munich **Note:** Fr. #193. Prev. KM#53.

Date	Mintage	VG	F	VF	XF	Unc
1632	—	450	1,100	2,000	3,100	—
1640	—	450	1,100	2,000	3,100	—

KM# 259 DUCAT

3.4900 g., 0.9860 Gold 0.1106 oz. AGW **Ruler:** Maximilian I **Obv:** Elector kneeling before Madonna and child in inner circle **Note:** Fr. #195. Prev. KM#57.

Date	Mintage	VG	F	VF	XF	Unc
1638	—	325	725	1,400	2,400	—

KM# 274 DUCAT

3.4900 g., 0.9860 Gold 0.1106 oz. AGW **Ruler:** Maximilian I **Obv:** Without inner circle **Note:** Fr. #195. Prev. KM#63.

Date	Mintage	VG	F	VF	XF	Unc
1642	—	275	650	1,300	2,200	—
1643	—	275	650	1,300	2,200	—
1644	—	275	650	1,300	2,200	—
1645	—	275	650	1,300	2,200	—
1646	—	500	1,100	1,750	2,650	—
1647	—	275	650	1,300	2,200	—

KM# 277 DUCAT

3.4900 g., 0.9860 Gold 0.1106 oz. AGW **Ruler:** Maximilian I **Obv:** Elector standing facing 1/2 right **Rev:** Madonna and child seated facing **Note:** Fr. #199. Prev. KM#66.

Date	Mintage	VG	F	VF	XF	Unc
1644	—	650	1,650	3,300	6,600	—
1645	—	650	1,650	3,300	6,600	—
1646	—	650	1,650	3,300	6,600	—

KM# 278 DUCAT

3.4900 g., 0.9860 Gold 0.1106 oz. AGW **Ruler:** Maximilian I **Obv:** Elector standing facing 1/2 right, pedestal with arms on front holds orb **Rev:** City view of Munich **Note:** Fr. #197. Prev. KM#67.

Date	Mintage	VG	F	VF	XF	Unc
1645	—	550	1,250	2,500	4,950	—

KM# 279 DUCAT

3.4900 g., 0.9860 Gold 0.1106 oz. AGW **Ruler:** Maximilian I **Obv:** Without arms on side of table **Note:** Prev. KM#68.

Date	Mintage	VG	F	VF	XF	Unc
1645	—	550	1,250	2,500	4,950	—

KM# 290 DUCAT

3.4900 g., 0.9860 Gold 0.1106 oz. AGW **Ruler:** Ferdinand Maria **Obv:** Elector Ferdinand Maria standing near table at right which holds an orb **Rev:** Madonna and child above capped arms, date divided at sides **Note:** Prev. KM#79.

Date	Mintage	VG	F	VF	XF	Unc
1655	—	825	2,050	3,600	6,100	—

KM# 291 DUCAT

3.4900 g., 0.9860 Gold 0.1106 oz. AGW **Ruler:** Ferdinand Maria **Obv:** Elector standing facing with left hand on helmet on pedestal **Rev:** Madonna and child with shield of arms **Note:** Fr. #202. Prev. KM#80.

Date	Mintage	VG	F	VF	XF	Unc
1655	—	700	1,800	3,150	4,950	—
1660	—	700	1,800	3,150	4,950	—
1667	—	700	1,800	3,150	4,950	—
1671	—	700	1,800	3,150	4,950	—

KM# 302 DUCAT

3.4900 g., 0.9860 Gold 0.1106 oz. AGW **Ruler:** Ferdinand Maria **Note:** Vicariat issue. Fr. #201. Prev. KM#87.

Date	Mintage	VG	F	VF	XF	Unc
1657	—	825	2,000	4,150	5,800	—

KM# 306 DUCAT

3.4900 g., 0.9860 Gold 0.1106 oz. AGW **Ruler:** Ferdinand Maria **Obv:** Bust of Ferdinand Maria right **Note:** Prev. KM#89.

Date	Mintage	VG	F	VF	XF	Unc
1660 Rare	—	—	—	—	—	—
1678 Rare	—	—	—	—	—	—

KM# 311 DUCAT

3.4900 g., 0.9860 Gold 0.1106 oz. AGW **Ruler:** Ferdinand Maria **Subject:** Birth of Princess Louise **Obv:** Bust of Adelaide facing 1/2 right **Rev:** Arms in cartouche divides date **Note:** Fr. #205. Prev. KM#92.

Date	Mintage	VG	F	VF	XF	Unc
1663	—	825	1,650	2,750	4,150	—

KM# 316 DUCAT

3.4900 g., 0.9860 Gold 0.1106 oz. AGW **Ruler:** Ferdinand Maria **Subject:** Birth of Joseph Clemens **Obv:** Arms topped by three cherubs divides date **Rev:** St. Nicholas seated facing **Note:** Fr. #208. Prev. KM#95.

Date	Mintage	VG	F	VF	XF	Unc
1671	—	800	1,750	3,150	4,950	—

KM# 330 DUCAT

3.4900 g., 0.9860 Gold 0.1106 oz. AGW **Ruler:** Ferdinand Maria **Obv:** Elector standing facing with left hand on helmet on pedestal **Rev:** Madonna and child with angels above view of Munich in inner circle **Note:** Fr. #213. Prev. KM#103.

Date	Mintage	VG	F	VF	XF	Unc
1676	—	1,100	2,650	4,600	6,600	—
1677	—	1,100	2,650	4,600	6,600	—
1678	—	1,100	2,650	4,600	6,600	—

KM# 345 DUCAT

3.4900 g., 0.9860 Gold 0.1106 oz. AGW **Ruler:** Maximilian II, Emanuel **Obv:** Maximilian Emanuel **Note:** Fr. #217. Prev. KM#115.

Date	Mintage	VG	F	VF	XF	Unc
1687	—	875	2,000	3,500	5,500	—
1697	—	875	2,000	3,500	5,500	—

KM# 275 2 DUCAT
7.0000 g., 0.9860 Gold 0.2219 oz. AGW **Ruler:** Maximilian I **Subject:** Maximilian I as Elector **Obv:** Elector kneeling before Madonna and child **Note:** Fr. #194. Prev. KM#64.

Date	Mintage	VG	F	VF	XF	Unc
1642	—	375	750	1,150	2,750	—
1644	—	375	750	1,150	2,750	—
1645	—	375	750	1,150	2,750	—
1647	—	375	750	1,150	2,750	—

KM# 281 2 DUCAT
7.0000 g., 0.9860 Gold 0.2219 oz. AGW **Ruler:** Maximilian I **Note:** Fr. #198. Prev. KM#69.

Date	Mintage	VG	F	VF	XF	Unc
1645	—	1,100	2,200	4,450	7,200	—

KM# 314 2 DUCAT
7.0000 g., 0.9860 Gold 0.2219 oz. AGW **Ruler:** Ferdinand Maria **Subject:** Birth of Prince Cajetan Maria **Obv:** Sun and moon above globe **Rev:** Three shields of arms **Note:** Fr. #207. Prev. KM#94.

Date	Mintage	VG	F	VF	XF	Unc
1670	—	1,800	3,600	6,600	10,000	—

KM# 323 2 DUCAT
7.0000 g., 0.9860 Gold 0.2219 oz. AGW **Ruler:** Ferdinand Maria **Subject:** Birth of Princess Violanta Beatrix **Obv:** Crowned and mantled arms, two above one, date below **Rev:** Column with orb on top in inner circle **Note:** Fr. #209. Prev. KM#99.

Date	Mintage	VG	F	VF	XF	Unc
1673	—	1,400	2,700	4,500	9,000	—

KM# 339 2 DUCAT
7.0000 g., 0.9860 Gold 0.2219 oz. AGW **Ruler:** Maximilian II, Emanuel **Obv:** Armored bust of Maximilian Emanuel, date below **Rev:** Madonna standing with crowned shield of arms **Note:** Fr. #216. Prev. KM#114.

Date	Mintage	VG	F	VF	XF	Unc
1685	—	1,700	3,350	6,400	10,000	—
1687	—	1,700	3,350	6,400	10,000	—

KM# 371 2 DUCAT
7.0000 g., 0.9860 Gold 0.2219 oz. AGW **Ruler:** Maximilian II, Emanuel **Subject:** Birth of Prince Karl Albert **Note:** Fr. #221. Prev. KM#130.

Date	Mintage	VG	F	VF	XF	Unc
1697	—	725	1,450	2,700	5,800	—

KM# 372 2 DUCAT
7.0000 g., 0.9860 Gold 0.2219 oz. AGW **Ruler:** Maximilian II, Emanuel **Subject:** Birth of Prince Ferdinand Maria **Note:** Fr. #222. Prev. KM#131.

Date	Mintage	VG	F	VF	XF	Unc
1699	—	475	1,100	2,100	5,000	—

KM# 285 3 DUCAT
10.5000 g., 0.9860 Gold 0.3328 oz. AGW **Ruler:** Ferdinand Maria **Subject:** Wedding of Ferdinand Maria and Adelaide **Obv:** Ferdinand Maria and Adelaide **Note:** Fr. #200. Prev. KM#76.

Date	Mintage	VG	F	VF	XF	Unc
1652	—	2,650	5,400	8,400	14,000	—

KM# 312 4 DUCAT
14.0000 g., 0.9860 Gold 0.4438 oz. AGW **Ruler:** Ferdinand Maria **Subject:** Birth of Prince Louis Amadeus **Obv:** Crowned double shield with initialled medallions at sides **Rev:** Family kneeling before new prince, angel with palm and wreath above **Note:** Fr. #206. Prev. KM#93.

Date	Mintage	VG	F	VF	XF	Unc
1665	—	4,300	7,300	11,500	20,000	—

KM# 240 5 DUCAT
Gold **Ruler:** Maximilian I **Subject:** Maximilian I as Duke **Obv:** Crowned arms **Rev:** Madonna with child **Mint:** Heidelberg **Note:** Fr. #190. Rheinpfalz issue. Prev. KM#A11.

Date	Mintage	VG	F	VF	XF	Unc
1627 Rare	—	—	—	—	—	—

KM# 268 5 DUCAT
17.5000 g., 0.9860 Gold 0.5547 oz. AGW **Ruler:** Maximilian I **Rev:** New fortifications of Munich, date at top **Note:** Fr.#196. Prev. KM#61.

Date	Mintage	VG	F	VF	XF	Unc
1640	—	—	1,500	3,000	5,700	—

KM# 269 5 DUCAT
17.5000 g., 0.9860 Gold 0.5547 oz. AGW **Ruler:** Maximilian I **Rev:** New fortifications of Munich, date divided by city view **Note:** Fr.#196. Prev. KM#62.

Date	Mintage	VG	F	VF	XF	Unc
1640	—	—	2,350	4,300	9,400	—

KM# 307 5 DUCAT
17.3500 g., Gold, 34 mm. **Ruler:** Ferdinand Maria **Subject:** Birth of Princess Maria Anna **Obv:** Busts of Ferdinand Maria and Henriette Adelheid to right **Obv. Legend:** VT VIDEANT FILIOS FILIORVM SVORVM PACEM SVPER IPSOS. PS. 127. **Rev:** Ornamented shield of Wittelsbach arms, angel head and wings above, legend with date in chronogram **Mint:** Munich **Note:** Fr. #203; JB-1361. Prev. KM#A90.

Date	Mintage	VG	F	VF	XF	Unc
1660	—	2,400	4,800	7,200	12,000	—

KM# 341 5 DUCAT
17.4000 g., Gold, 35 mm. **Ruler:** Maximilian II, Emanuel **Subject:** Marriage of Maximilian II Emanuel and Maria Antonie von Habsburg **Obv:** 2 busts facing one another within palm and laurel branches **Obv. Legend:** QVOS DEVS CONIVNXIT EOSDEM IN OMNE ÆVVM BENEDICAT DEVS. **Rev:** 2 adjacent oval shields, crowned arms of Austria on left, 4-fold arms of Bavaria and Pfalz, with central shield of imperial orb, electoral hat above, on right, all within palm and laurel branches **Rev. Legend:** VT VIDEANT FILIOS FILIORVM ET PACEM SVPER IPSOS. **Mint:** Munich **Note:** Fr.#214; JB-1468. Prev. KM#A115.

Date	Mintage	VG	F	VF	XF	Unc
ND(1685) CZ	—	—	4,200	7,200	11,500	—

KM# 342 5 DUCAT
17.3500 g., Gold, 35 mm. **Ruler:** Maximilian II, Emanuel **Subject:** Homage of Cities for Marriage of Maximilian II Emanuel and Maria Antonie von Habsburg **Obv:** 2 accolated busts to right **Obv. Legend:** A DEO PACIS BELLIQUE TEMPORE PERENIS FELICITAS **Rev:** Shield of Bavaria arms hanging from garland, arms of Munich, Landshut, Burghausen and Straubing around, angel above **Rev. Legend:** + ITA VOVENTIBVS VTRIVSQVE BAVARIÆ STATIBVS DEVOTISSIMIS. **Mint:** Munich **Note:** Fr. #215; JB-1472. Prev. KM#B115.

Date	Mintage	VG	F	VF	XF	Unc
ND(1685)	—	—	4,200	7,200	11,500	—

KM# 357 5 DUCAT
17.4000 g., Gold, 33 mm. **Ruler:** Maximilian II, Emanuel **Subject:** Birth of Prince Josef Ferdinand **Obv:** Young prince among arms of Austria and Bavaria, imperial orb on pedestal, on which 3-line inscription with date **Obv. Inscription:** IOS: FERD: / LEOPOLDO. / NATO: 28. OCT. 1692. **Rev:** Imperial orb on globe, above triangle with Eye of God, rays streaming down **Rev. Legend:** EX PARVO SPES - MAXIMA MVNDI. **Mint:** Munich **Note:** Fr. #218; JB-1518. Prev. KM#A124.

Date	Mintage	VG	F	VF	XF	Unc
1692	—	2,400	6,000	9,600	—	—

BECKUM

A small provincial city in Westphalia located about 20 miles southeast of Münster, founded in 1139. It had a local copper coinage in the late 16th and early 17th centuries.

REFERENCE

W = Joseph Weingärtner, ***Die Bremischen Münzen – Beschreibung der Kupfermünzen Westfalens nebst historischen Nachrichten,*** 2 vols., Paderborn, 1872-81.

PROVINCIAL TOWN

REGULAR COINAGE

KM# 7 2 PFENNIG
Copper **Obv:** Arms (three wavy bends), STADT BE-KEM **Rev:** Value II and date in ornamented square

Date	Mintage	Good	VG	F	VF	XF
1622 Rare	—	—	—	—	—	—

KM# 8 3 PFENNIG
Copper **Obv:** Arms, STADT BEKEM **Rev:** Value interspersed with date in ornamented square

Date	Mintage	Good	VG	F	VF	XF
1622	—	45.00	90.00	150	250	—

KM# 5 6 PFENNIG
Copper **Obv:** Arms, STADT BEKEM, date **Rev:** Value VI in ornamented square

Date	Mintage	Good	VG	F	VF	XF
1609	—	50.00	100	200	400	—

KM# 9 6 PFENNIG
Copper **Obv:** Arms, STADT BEKEM **Rev:** Value interspersed with date

Date	Mintage	Good	VG	F	VF	XF
1622	—	50.00	100	200	400	—

KM# 6 12 PFENNIG
Copper **Obv:** Arms, STADT BEKEM **Rev:** Date interspersed with value XII

Date	Mintage	Good	VG	F	VF	XF
1609	—	150	225	350	700	—
1622	—	135	200	325	650	—

BEESKOW

A provincial town on the River Spree in Brandenburg-Prussia, about 43 miles southeast of Berlin. Beeskow is mentioned as early as 1185 and came under the control of the lords of Strele in the second half of the 13th century. It passed through the possession of several local noble families before its final acquisition by Brandenburg in 1571. The Elector of Brandenburg permitted a local copper coinage during the inflationary period at the beginning of the Thirty Years' War.

PROVINCIAL TOWN

REGULAR COINAGE

KM# 1 PFENNIG (Kipper)
Copper, 13 mm. **Obv:** Arms of Biberstein (stag antler) and of Strele (3 scythe blades), date above, letter B below. **Note:** Uniface.

Date	Mintage	Good	VG	F	VF	XF
1621	—	27.00	55.00	110	225	—

BENTHEIM-BENTHEIM

The countship of Bentheim was located on both sides of the Vechte River along the border between the Netherlands and Westphalia. The lords of Bentheim were descended from an eleventh-century marriage alliance of the countships of Holland and Nordheim. Tecklenburg was obtained through marriage in the middle of the 13th century with a separate line being founded in 1269. In 1454, Bentheim was divided into the lines of Bentheim-Bentheim and Bentheim-Steinfurt. The latter was a territory located about midway between the county of Bentheim and the city of Münster in Westphalia. The various divisions were reunited by marriage during the 16th century only to be divided again into five lines in 1606. By family agreement (1691), the heirs to the two lines of Bentheim-Bentheim and Bentheim-Steinfurt exchanged their counties and titles in 1693. Bentheim-Bentheim became extinct in 1803, when the last count died, but he had already ceded Bentheim to Hannover in 1753. It passed to Berg in 1806 and then to Prussia in 1813. Bentheim-Steinfurt was mediatized in 1806, but the count was raised to the rank of prince in 1817. The counts of Bentheim-Steinfurt did not issue any coinage, rather allowing that of Bentheim-Bentheim to circulate in their territory.

RULERS
Arnold Jobst, 1606-1643
Ernst Wilhelm, 1643-1693
Arnold Moritz Wilhelm, 1693-1701

MINT OFFICIALS' INITIALS

Initials	Date	Name
JO	1692-96	Johann Odendahl in Munster
LK	Ca. 1659-64	Johann Longerich, warden
	1659-62	Engelbert Kettler, mintmaster

COUNTY

REGULAR COINAGE

KM# 2.1 DEUT (2 Pfennig - 1/8 Stüber)
Copper **Ruler:** Ernest Wilhelm **Obv:** Crowned double EC monogram between two branches **Rev:** Between two branches DVTT/PENT/HEIM/date

Date	Mintage	Good	VG	F	VF	XF
1654	—	10.00	20.00	40.00	80.00	—

KM# 2.2 DEUT (2 Pfennig - 1/8 Stüber)
Copper **Ruler:** Ernest Wilhelm **Obv:** Crowned double EC monogram between 2 laurel branches. **Rev:** DVTT/BENT/HEIM

Date	Mintage	Good	VG	F	VF	XF
1662	—	90.00	100	200	400	—
1664	—	90.00	100	200	400	—

KM# 16 DEUT (2 Pfennig - 1/8 Stüber)
Copper **Ruler:** Ernest Wilhelm **Obv:** Without branches

Date	Mintage	Good	VG	F	VF	XF
1662	—	50.00	100	210	425	—

KM# 17 STUBER
Silver **Ruler:** Ernest Wilhelm **Obv:** Bentheim arms in baroque frame, date above in margin. **Rev:** Crowned imperial eagle, value 'I' in circle on breast. **Note:** Kennepohl 15.

Date	Mintage	VG	F	VF	XF	Unc
1662	—	25.00	55.00	115	230	—

KM# 15 2 STUBER
Silver **Ruler:** Ernest Wilhelm **Obv:** Bentheim arms, date above **Rev:** Crowned imperial eagle with 2 on breast

Date	Mintage	VG	F	VF	XF	Unc
1660	—	25.00	55.00	115	230	—
1662	—	25.00	55.00	115	230	—
1663	—	25.00	55.00	115	230	—

KM# 3 6 STUBER (Blamüser)
Silver **Ruler:** Ernest Wilhelm **Obv:** Crowned manifold arms in baroque frame, date divided above **Rev:** Crowned imperial eagle

Date	Mintage	VG	F	VF	XF	Unc
1659 LK	—	75.00	150	300	600	—
1662 LK	—	50.00	100	200	425	—

KM# 20 1/8 THALER
Silver **Ruler:** Ernest Wilhelm **Obv:** Crowned arms between two branches **Rev:** VIII/EINEN/REICHES/THALER in center, date in legend

Date	Mintage	VG	F	VF	XF	Unc
1673	—	—	—	—	—	—

KM# 25 1/2 THALER
Silver **Ruler:** Arnold Moritz Wilhelm **Obv:** Bust right **Rev:** Helmeted arms, date

Date	Mintage	VG	F	VF	XF	Unc
1695 JO	—	—	—	—	—	—

KM# 4 THALER
Silver **Ruler:** Ernest Wilhelm **Note:** Dav. #6104.

Date	Mintage	VG	F	VF	XF	Unc
1659 LK	—	1,150	1,950	3,150	5,200	—
1660 LK	—	1,150	1,950	3,150	5,200	—

KM# 26 THALER
Silver **Ruler:** Arnold Moritz Wilhelm **Obv:** Bust right **Rev:** Helmeted arms, date **Note:** Dav. #6105.

Date	Mintage	VG	F	VF	XF	Unc
1696 JO Rare	—	—	—	—	—	—

KM# 5 1-1/2 THALER
Silver **Ruler:** Ernest Wilhelm **Note:** Dav. #6103.

Date	Mintage	VG	F	VF	XF	Unc
1659 LK Rare	—	—	—	—	—	—

KM# 6 2 THALER
Silver **Ruler:** Ernest Wilhelm **Note:** Similar to 1 Thaler, KM#4. Dav. #6102.

Date	Mintage	VG	F	VF	XF	Unc
1659 LK Rare	—	—	—	—	—	—
1660 LK Rare	—	—	—	—	—	—

TRADE COINAGE

KM# 7 DUCAT
3.5000 g., 0.9860 Gold 0.1109 oz. AGW **Ruler:** Ernest Wilhelm **Obv:** Crowned arms **Rev:** Three-line inscription with date below

Date	Mintage	VG	F	VF	XF	Unc
1659 LK	—	3,500	5,500	9,000	14,500	—

KM# 8 2 DUCAT
7.0000 g., 0.9860 Gold 0.2219 oz. AGW **Ruler:** Ernest Wilhelm **Obv:** Crowned arms **Rev:** Three-line inscription with date below

Date	Mintage	VG	F	VF	XF	Unc
1659 LK Rare	—	—	—	—	—	—

KM# 9 2 DUCAT
7.0000 g., 0.9860 Gold 0.2219 oz. AGW **Ruler:** Ernest Wilhelm **Note:** Klippe.

Date	Mintage	VG	F	VF	XF	Unc
1659 LK Rare	—	—	—	—	—	—

LOCAL COINAGE

Helfenstein

Coinage struck for the Lordship of Helfenstein (Helpenstein)

KM# 32 GROSCHEN (1/24 Thaler)
Silver **Ruler:** Arnold Moritz Wilhelm **Obv:** Lion right, ARNO: DO: IN: HELFEN: **Rev:** Imperial eagle with 24 on breast, titles of Ferdinand II **Note:** Kipper Groschen.

Date	Mintage	VG	F	VF	XF	Unc
ND Rare	—	—	—	—	—	—

BENTHEIM-TECKLENBURG-RHEDA

The countship of Tecklenburg was located about halfway between the cities of Münster and Osnabrück in Westphalia and was acquired by Bentheim through marriage during the first half of the 13th century and the separate line of Bentheim-Tecklenburg was founded in 1269. The lordship of Rheda, to the southeast of Tecklenburg, was acquired by marriage in the mid-14th century. After the reunification of the 16th century, a new line of Bentheim-Tecklenburg-Rheda was founded in 1606. The county of Tecklenburg was lost to Solms in 1696, then sold to Prussia in 1707. Rheda was mediatized in 1805.

RULERS
Adolf, 1606-1623
Moritz, 1623-1674
Johann Adolf, 1674-1701

MINT OFFICIALS' INITIALS

Initials	Date	Name
ILC		Johann Schitzkey of Liegnitz, die-cutter for Cologne, initials read "Johann Liegnitz Coloniensis"
IS, JS		Johann (Wilhelm) Salter

COUNTY / LORDSHIP

REGULAR COINAGE

KM# 106 PFENNIG

Copper **Obv:** 4-fold arms with central shield of Rheda arms between two branches, date above **Rev:** I/G. T. P. between two branches

Date	Mintage	VG	F	VF	XF	Unc
1685	—	13.00	27.00	50.00	100	—

Note: G.T.P. = Graflich Tecklenburgische Pfennige

KM# 107 1-1/2 PFENNIG

Copper **Obv:** 4-fold arms with central shield of Rheda arms between two branches, date above **Rev:** Value between two branches

Date	Mintage	VG	F	VF	XF	Unc
1685	—	17.00	35.00	75.00	150	—

KM# 108 2 PFENNIG

Copper **Obv:** 4-fold arms with central shield of Rheda arms between two branches, date above **Rev:** Value I.I. between two branches

Date	Mintage	VG	F	VF	XF	Unc
1685	—	13.00	27.00	50.00	100	—

KM# 32 3 PFENNING

Copper **Obv:** 4-fold arms, TEKELNBVRGK in legend **Rev:** Value III surrounded by ornaments within circle, outer border of 16 lilies **Note:** Kipper 3 Pfennig.

Date	Mintage	Good	VG	F	VF	XF
ND(1622-23)	—	20.00	40.00	85.00	175	—

KM# 34 3 PFENNING (Dreier)

Billon **Obv:** Crowned arms of Tecklenburg and Rheda in heart-shaped shield, divide ADO-G. Z. B.

Date	Mintage	VG	F	VF	XF	Unc
1622	—	—	—	—	—	—

KM# 35 3 PFENNING (Dreier)

Billon **Ruler:** Adolf **Obv:** Helmeted arms of Hoya divide inscription. **Obv. Legend:** ADOL - G. Z. B. T. **Rev:** Imperial orb with '3' divides date.

Date	Mintage	VG	F	VF	XF	Unc
16ZZ	—	—	—	—	—	—

KM# 36 3 PFENNING (Dreier)

Billon **Obv:** Helmeted arms of Linden divide ADOLF. G.- Z. B. V. TEC.

Date	Mintage	VG	F	VF	XF	Unc
1622	—	—	—	—	—	—

Note: Hoya and Lingen were counties belonging to Bentheim

KM# 33 3 PFENNING (Dreier)

Billon **Obv:** 4-fold arms, central shield of Rheda arms, all in ornamented shield **Rev:** Imperial orb with 3 divides date **Note:** Kipper 3 Pfennig

Date	Mintage	VG	F	VF	XF	Unc
1622	—	—	—	—	—	—

KM# 109 3 PFENNING (Dreier)

Copper **Obv:** 4-fold arms with central shield of Rheda arms between two branches, date above **Rev:** Value I. I. I. between two branches

Date	Mintage	VG	F	VF	XF	Unc
1685	—	17.00	35.00	75.00	150	—

KM# 110 4 PFENNIG

Copper **Ruler:** Johann Adolf **Obv:** 4-fold arms with central shield of Rheda arms between two branches, date above. **Rev:** 2-line inscription with value between 2 branches. **Rev. Inscription:** IIII/G.T.P. **Mint:** Tecklenburg **Note:** Kennepohl 130.

Date	Mintage	VG	F	VF	XF	Unc
1685	—	20.00	40.00	85.00	175	—

KM# 89 4-1/2 PFENNIG

Copper **Obv:** 4-fold arms, central shield of Rheda arms, date above **Rev. Inscription:** 4 1/2 / PFENN / TECL

Date	Mintage	VG	F	VF	XF	Unc
1674	—	500	1,000	2,000	—	—

KM# 90 5 PFENNIG

Billon **Obv:** Helmet in wreath **Rev. Inscription:** Date / V / G. T. P.

Date	Mintage	VG	F	VF	XF	Unc
1674	—	60.00	110	190	275	—

KM# 95 5 PFENNIG

Billon **Obv:** Helmet between two palm branches

Date	Mintage	VG	F	VF	XF	Unc
1677	—	60.00	110	200	385	—

KM# 91 6 PFENNING (1/42 Thaler)

Billon **Ruler:** Moritz **Obv:** Crowned M in wreath **Rev:** 4-line inscription with date, value '42' in oval below. **Rev. Inscription:** 1674 / VI / PFENN / TECL. **Mint:** Kirchstapel **Note:** Kennepohl 117.

Date	Mintage	VG	F	VF	XF	Unc
1674	—	25.00	45.00	80.00	150	—

KM# 96 6 PFENNING (1/42 Thaler)

Billon **Obv:** Crowned 4-fold arms, central shield of Rheda arms date divided to either side **Rev. Inscription:** VI / PFENN / TECL / 42

Date	Mintage	VG	F	VF	XF	Unc
1677	—	38.00	75.00	140	275	—

KM# 105 6 PFENNING (1/42 Thaler)

Billon **Obv:** Crowned JA monogram between two palm branches **Rev. Inscription:** Date / VI / PFENNI / TECLB / 42

Date	Mintage	VG	F	VF	XF	Unc
1683	—	38.00	75.00	140	275	—

KM# 16 8 PFENNIG (Fürstengroschen)

Silver **Obv:** 4-fold arms, central shield of Rheda arms **Obv. Legend:** TECKELNB.LANDMVNTZ **Rev:** Crowned imperial eagle, orb on breast **Rev. Legend:** VIII SVVER PFENNINGE **Note:** Kipper 8 Pfennig. Valued at 8 heavy Pfennig, the standard for the Furstengroschen was usually 9 heavy Pfennig in Westphalia.

Date	Mintage	VG	F	VF	XF	Unc
ND(1620)	—	75.00	150	300	600	—

KM# 37 MARIENGROSCHEN (1/36 Thaler)

Billon **Obv:** 4-fold arms, central shield of Rheda arms in ornamented shield, ADOL. C. B... around **Rev:** Madonna, MARIA.-GROSS., date

Date	Mintage	VG	F	VF	XF	Unc
1622	—	—	—	—	—	—

KM# 44 MARIENGROSCHEN (1/36 Thaler)

Billon **Obv:** Crowned lion left (Rheda) holding Tecklenburg arms, date in legend **Rev:** Madonna with rays on either side

Date	Mintage	VG	F	VF	XF	Unc
1623	—	—	—	—	—	—

Note: These mariengroschen were struck to the equivalent of a Tecklenburger half-schilling

KM# 56 2 MARIENGROSCHEN

Silver **Obv:** Crowned 4-fold arms **Rev:** Date in legend **Rev. Inscription:** II / MARI / GRO

Date	Mintage	VG	F	VF	XF	Unc
1656	—	—	—	—	—	—

KM# 57 4 MARIENGROSCHEN

Silver **Obv:** Crowned 4-fold arms **Rev:** Date in legend **Rev. Inscription:** IIII / MARIE / GRO

Date	Mintage	VG	F	VF	XF	Unc
1656	—	—	—	—	—	—

KM# 82 6 MARIENGROSCHEN

Silver **Obv:** Crowned 4-fold arms, central shield of Rheda arms **Rev:** Date in legend **Rev. Inscription:** VI / MARIE / GROS

Date	Mintage	VG	F	VF	XF	Unc
1671	—	65.00	135	275	550	—

KM# 86 6 MARIENGROSCHEN

Silver **Obv:** Helmeted arms, date in legend

Date	Mintage	VG	F	VF	XF	Unc
1672	—	60.00	120	235	475	—

KM# 87 6 MARIENGROSCHEN

Silver **Rev:** Date below value in center

Date	Mintage	VG	F	VF	XF	Unc
1672	—	60.00	120	235	475	—
1673	—	60.00	120	235	475	—

KM# 81 12 MARIENGROSCHEN (1/3 Thaler)

Silver **Ruler:** Moritz **Obv:** Crowned 4-fold arms with central shield in circle. **Obv. Legend:** MAUR. C. I. B. TEC. S. ET L. D. I. R. W. HL. AH. **Rev:** 3-line inscription in circle, date at end of legend. **Rev. Legend:** VON FEINEM SILBER. **Rev. Inscription:** XII / MARIEN / GROS. **Note:** Varieties exist.

Date	Mintage	VG	F	VF	XF	Unc
1670	—	60.00	125	235	475	—
1671 MAVRITZ	—	100	200	400	775	—
1671 MAUR	—	50.00	100	200	425	—
1672	—	60.00	125	235	475	—

KM# 92 12 MARIENGROSCHEN (1/3 Thaler)

Silver **Obv:** Crowned 4-fold arms with central shield in circle **Obv. Legend:** MAUR. C. I. B. TEC. S. ETL. D. I. R. W. HL. AH. **Rev:** 3-line inscription in circle, date at end of legend **Rev. Legend:** VON FEINEM SILBER **Rev. Inscription:** XII / MARIEN / GROS,

Date	Mintage	VG	F	VF	XF	Unc
1675	—	65.00	125	235	475	—

KM# 94 12 MARIENGROSCHEN (1/3 Thaler)

Silver **Obv:** Helmet above arms

Date	Mintage	VG	F	VF	XF	Unc
1676	—	65.00	125	235	475	—

KM# 93 24 MARIENGROSCHEN (2/3 Thaler)

Silver **Ruler:** Johann Adolf **Obv:** Ornate helmet. **Obv. Legend:** I. ADOLF. C. I. B. TEC. SI. ET L. D. I. R. W. HL. A. H. **Rev:** 3-line inscription in circle, date at end of legend. **Rev. Legend:** MONETA NOVA ARGENTEA. **Rev. Inscription:** XXIIII / MARIEN / GROS. **Note:** Dav. #1019. Varieties exist.

Date	Mintage	VG	F	VF	XF	Unc
1675	—	90.00	180	360	725	—
1676	—	90.00	180	360	725	—
1677	—	90.00	180	360	725	—

KM# 19 12 KREUZER (Schreckenberger)

Silver **Rev:** Helmeted 4-fold arms, central shield of Rheda

Date	Mintage	VG	F	VF	XF	Unc
ND(1620-22)	—	50.00	90.00	180	325	—

KM# 20 12 KREUZER (Schreckenberger)

Silver **Ruler:** Adolf **Rev:** Helmeted Tecklenburg arms, A. G. Z...

Date	Mintage	VG	F	VF	XF	Unc
ND(1620-22)	—	50.00	90.00	180	325	—

KM# 21 12 KREUZER (Schreckenberger)

Silver **Rev:** Helmeted Rheda arms

Date	Mintage	VG	F	VF	XF	Unc
ND(1620-22)	—	50.00	90.00	180	325	—

KM# 18 12 KREUZER (Schreckenberger)

Silver **Ruler:** Adolf **Obv:** Helmeted 4-fold arms without central shield. **Obv. Legend:** ADOLF. COM. TECKLENBVRG. **Rev:** Crowned imperial eagle, '1Z' in circle on breast. **Rev. Legend:** FERDINAN. II. D.G. R. I. S. AV. **Mint:** Freudenberg **Note:** Kennepohl 50a.

Date	Mintage	VG	F	VF	XF	Unc
ND(1620-22)	—	50.00	90.00	180	325	—

KM# 17 12 KREUZER (Schreckenberger)

Silver **Obv:** 4-fold arms, central shield of Rheda arms **Obv. Legend:** TECKELNB.LANDMUNTZ **Rev:** Crowned imperial eagle, orb on breast with 12, titles of Ferdinand II **Note:** Kipper 12 Kreuzer.

Date	Mintage	VG	F	VF	XF	Unc
ND(1620-22)	—	50.00	90.00	180	325	—

KM# 27 12 KREUZER (Schreckenberger)

Silver **Rev:** Helmet divides date

Date	Mintage	VG	F	VF	XF	Unc
1621	—	50.00	90.00	180	325	—

KM# 11 5 STUBER

Silver **Rev:** Helmeted arms with central shield of Rheda arms

Date	Mintage	VG	F	VF	XF	Unc
ND(1619-22)	—	60.00	125	275	550	—

KM# 8 5 STUBER

Silver **Obv:** Crowned imperial eagle, titles of Matthias **Rev:** Helmeted arms of Rheda (lion left) **Rev. Legend:** PIETATE. ET. IUSTICIA. U. S. **Note:** Kipper 5 Stuber.

Date	Mintage	VG	F	VF	XF	Unc
ND(1619)	—	60.00	125	275	550	—

KM# 13 5 STUBER

Silver **Ruler:** Adolf **Obv:** Ornate helmet above 4-fold arms with central shield. **Obv. Legend:** MO. NO. ADOLF. CO. ET DO. TECKLEBVR. **Rev:** Crowned imperial eagle in circle. **Rev. Legend:** PIETATE. ET. IVSTITIA. V. B. **Mint:** Freudenberg **Note:** Kipper 6 Stüber. Varieties exist.

Date	Mintage	VG	F	VF	XF	Unc
ND(1619-22)	—	60.00	125	275	550	—

KM# 10 5 STUBER

Silver **Note:** Klippe.

Date	Mintage	VG	F	VF	XF	Unc
ND(1619-22) Rare	—	—	—	—	—	—

KM# 12 5 STUBER

Silver **Note:** Klippe.

Date	Mintage	VG	F	VF	XF	Unc
ND(1619-22) Rare	—	—	—	—	—	—

KM# 14 5 STUBER

Silver **Note:** Klippe.

Date	Mintage	VG	F	VF	XF	Unc
ND(1619-22) Rare	—	—	—	—	—	—

KM# 9 5 STUBER

Silver **Obv. Legend:** DEVS. PROVIDEBIT. V. ST. **Rev:** Helmeted 4-fold arms **Note:** Varieties exist.

Date	Mintage	VG	F	VF	XF	Unc
ND(1619-22)	—	65.00	135	275	550	—

KM# 15 6 STUBER

Silver **Ruler:** Adolf **Obv:** Crowned 6-fold arms in circle. **Obv. Legend:** MO. NO. ADOLF. CO. ET DO. TECLEBVRG. **Rev:** Crowned imperial eagle in circle. **Rev. Legend:** MATH. D.G. EL. RO. IMP. SEM. AVG. **Note:** Kipper 6 Stüber. Varieties exist.

Date	Mintage	VG	F	VF	XF	Unc
ND(1619)	—	70.00	150	300	600	—

KM# 58 1/28 THALER (Fürstengroschen)

Silver **Obv:** Crowned imperial eagle, orb on breast with 28, titles of Ferdinand III **Rev:** Crowned 4-fold arms, central shield of Rheda arms, date in legend

Date	Mintage	VG	F	VF	XF	Unc
1656	—	75.00	150	300	600	—
1657	—	90.00	180	360	725	—

KM# 59 1/28 THALER (Fürstengroschen)

Silver **Obv:** Value (28) at bottom

Date	Mintage	VG	F	VF	XF	Unc
1656	—	—	—	—	—	—

KM# 5 1/24 THALER (1 Groschen)

Silver **Obv:** Imperial orb with 24, date divided at top, titles of Matthias **Rev:** Helmeted 4-fold arms, central shield of Rheda arms **Note:** Varieties exist.

Date	Mintage	VG	F	VF	XF	Unc
1618	—	45.00	95.00	190	385	—
1619	—	45.00	95.00	190	385	—

KM# 24 1/24 THALER (1 Groschen)

Silver **Obv:** Imperial orb with 24, date in legend, titles of Ferdinand II **Rev:** Helmeted 4-fold arms **Note:** Small module. Varieties exist.

Date	Mintage	VG	F	VF	XF	Unc
(1)620	—	75.00	150	300	600	—
(16)20	—	75.00	150	300	600	—
(16)02 Error for 1620	—	75.00	150	300	600	—

KM# 38 1/24 THALER (1 Groschen)

Silver **Obv:** Imperial orb with 24, date divided at top, titles of Ferdinand II **Rev:** Helmeted 4-fold arms, central shield of Rheda arms

Date	Mintage	VG	F	VF	XF	Unc
1622	—	—	—	—	—	—

KM# 39 1/24 THALER (1 Groschen)

Silver **Obv:** Date divided by orb **Rev:** Crowned 4-fold arms

Date	Mintage	VG	F	VF	XF	Unc
1622	—	—	—	—	—	—

KM# 22 1/21 THALER (1 Schilling)

Silver **Obv:** Crowned imperial eagle, orb on breast, titles of Ferdinand II **Rev:** 4-fold arms, central shield of Rheda arms, LANTMVNTZ XXI. ZVM. DALER

Date	Mintage	VG	F	VF	XF	Unc
ND(1620)	—	—	—	—	—	—

KM# 23 1/21 THALER (1 Schilling)

Silver **Obv:** Helmeted 4-fold arms **Obv. Legend:** MO. NO. ADOL... **Rev:** Crowned imperial eagle, 21 in orb on breast, date **Rev. Legend:** LANDT. MVNTZ XXI. Z. THATL. **Note:** This Tecklenburg schilling equalled 1-1/2 schilling on the Westphalian standard.

Date	Mintage	VG	F	VF	XF	Unc
1620	—	135	275	450	925	—
(1)620	—	135	275	450	925	—
1621	—	135	275	450	925	—
(1)621	—	135	275	450	925	—
(16)21	—	135	275	450	925	—

KM# 6 1/16 THALER (2 Schilling)

Silver **Obv:** Crowned imperial eagle, orb with 16 on breast, titles of Matthias and date in legend **Rev:** 4-fold arms, three helmets above

Date	Mintage	VG	F	VF	XF	Unc
1618	—	175	375	775	—	—
1619	—	175	375	775	—	—

KM# 25 1/16 THALER (2 Schilling)

Silver **Obv:** Eagle's tail divides value 1-6, titles of Ferdinand II **Rev:** Single helmet

Date	Mintage	VG	F	VF	XF	Unc
1620	—	—	—	—	—	—

KM# 98 1/16 THALER (2 Schilling)

Silver **Obv:** Crowned 4-fold arms, central shield of Rheda arms

Date	Mintage	VG	F	VF	XF	Unc
1677	—	45.00	90.00	175	350	—

KM# 97 1/16 THALER (2 Schilling)

Silver **Ruler:** Johann Adolf **Obv:** Bust right in circle. **Obv. Legend:** ADOLF. C. I. B. TEC. Si. E. L. **Rev:** 4-line inscription with date in circle. **Rev. Legend:** MONETA. NOVA. ARGENTEA. **Rev. Inscription:** XVI / REICHS / THAL / 1677. **Mint:** Kirchstapel **Note:** Kennepohl 125.

Date	Mintage	VG	F	VF	XF	Unc
1677	—	80.00	160	325	650	—

KM# 60 1/14 THALER (2 Fürstengroschen)

Silver **Obv:** Crowned imperial eagle, 14 in orb on breast, titles of Ferdinand III, date in legend **Rev:** Helmeted 4-fold arms, central shield of Rheda arms

Date	Mintage	VG	F	VF	XF	Unc
1656	—	—	—	—	—	—

KM# 84 1/14 THALER (2 Fürstengroschen)

Silver **Rev:** Crowned arms

Date	Mintage	VG	F	VF	XF	Unc
1671	—	80.00	160	325	650	—

KM# 83 1/14 THALER (2 Fürstengroschen)

Silver **Obv:** Titles of Leopold **Rev:** Date in legend **Note:** Varieties exist.

Date	Mintage	VG	F	VF	XF	Unc
1671	—	70.00	135	275	550	—
1672	—	70.00	135	275	550	—
1673	—	70.00	135	275	550	—

KM# 85 1/8 THALER (Blamüser)

Silver **Ruler:** Moritz **Obv:** Crowned 4-fold arms in ornamented frame with central shield. **Obv. Legend:** M. C. IN B. TEC. SI. ET L. D. R. WH. A. H. **Rev:** 4-line inscription in circle, small imperial orb at bottom, date at end of legend. **Rev. Legend:** MONETA NOVA - ARGENTEA. **Rev. Inscription:** VIII / EINEN / REICHS / THAL. **Note:** Kennepohl 111. Varieties exist.

Date	Mintage	VG	F	VF	XF	Unc
1671	—	65.00	135	275	550	—
1672	—	65.00	135	275	550	—
1673	—	65.00	135	275	550	—

KM# 26 1/2 THALER

Silver **Obv:** Arms with three helmets above **Rev:** Helmeted arms of Nassau **Note:** Klippe.

Date	Mintage	VG	F	VF	XF	Unc
ND(1621) Rare	—	—	—	—	—	—

KM# 88 2/3 THALER

Silver **Obv:** Crowned 4-fold arms, central shield of Rheda arms, branch on each side, value in oval below, date in legend **Rev:** Helmet of Tecklenburg

Date	Mintage	VG	F	VF	XF	Unc
1673	—	—	—	—	—	—

KM# 7 THALER

Silver **Obv:** Crowned imperial eagle divides date, titles of Matthias II **Rev:** Bust of Adolf right **Note:** Dav. #7801.

Date	Mintage	VG	F	VF	XF	Unc
1618 Rare	—	—	—	—	—	—
ND Rare	—	—	—	—	—	—

KM# 62 THALER

Silver **Note:** Klippe. Dav. #7801A.

Date	Mintage	VG	F	VF	XF	Unc
ND Rare	—	—	—	—	—	—

KM# 63 THALER

Silver **Note:** Similar to KM#64. Dav. #7803.

Date	Mintage	VG	F	VF	XF	Unc
ND Rare	—	—	—	—	—	—

KM# 64 THALER

Silver **Note:** Dav. #7804.

Date	Mintage	VG	F	VF	XF	Unc
1657 ILC	—	2,100	4,200	7,200	10,000	—

KM# 66 1-1/2 THALER

Silver **Obv:** Crowned imperial eagle, titles of Matthias II **Rev:** Bust of Adolf right **Note:** Klippe.

Date	Mintage	VG	F	VF	XF	Unc
ND Rare	—	—	—	—	—	—

KM# 30 3 THALER

Silver **Obv:** Crowned imperial eagle divides date left and right of heads and feet, titles of Ferdinand II **Rev:** Arms with three helmets above **Note:** Dav. #7802.

Date	Mintage	VG	F	VF	XF	Unc
1621 Rare	—	—	—	—	—	—

TRADE COINAGE

KM# 31 GOLDGULDEN

Gold **Obv:** Tecklenburg arms with helmet of Limburg above **Rev:** Nassau arms and helmet

Date	Mintage	VG	F	VF	XF	Unc
ND(1621) Rare	—	—	—	—	—	—

KM# 61 DUCAT

3.5000 g., 0.9860 Gold 0.1109 oz. AGW **Obv:** Bust of Moritz right **Rev:** Crowned arms

Date	Mintage	VG	F	VF	XF	Unc
1656	—	4,000	6,000	10,000	17,000	—

KM# 65 DUCAT

3.5000 g., 0.9860 Gold 0.1109 oz. AGW **Obv:** Without circles **Rev:** Without circles

Date	Mintage	VG	F	VF	XF	Unc
1657	—	—	—	—	—	—

LOCAL COINAGE

Rheda

Special Coinage for the Lordship of Rheda

KM# 40 HELLER

Copper **Obv:** Crowned rampant lion left (Rheda arms), REDE in legend **Rev:** 1 in circle, border of 12 lilies

Date	Mintage	Good	VG	F	VF	XF
ND(pre-1623)	—	55.00	100	210	425	—

KM# 41.1 PFENNIG

Copper **Obv:** Crowned rampant lion left, REDE in legend **Rev:** I in circle, border of 12 lilies

Date	Mintage	Good	VG	F	VF	XF
ND(pre-1623)	—	50.00	100	200	400	—

KM# 41.2 PFENNIG

Copper **Obv:** RHEDA in legend

Date	Mintage	Good	VG	F	VF	XF
ND(pre-1623)	—	50.00	100	200	400	—

KM# 52 PFENNIG

Copper **Obv:** Similar to 5 Pfennig, KM#69 **Note:** Varieties exist.

Date	Mintage	Good	VG	F	VF	XF
1655	—	40.00	65.00	125	250	—
1659	—	45.00	70.00	135	275	—

KM# 51 1-1/2 PFENNIG

Copper **Obv:** Similar to 5 Pfennig, KM#69 **Rev:** I I **Note:** Varieties exist.

Date	Mintage	Good	VG	F	VF	XF
ND	—	35.00	55.00	110	225	—
1655	—	35.00	55.00	110	225	—
1659	—	35.00	55.00	110	225	—

KM# 53 2 PFENNIG

Copper **Obv:** Similar to 5 Pfennig, KM#69 **Rev:** II in circle of 12 lilies **Note:** Varieties exist.

Date	Mintage	Good	VG	F	VF	XF
1655	—	20.00	40.00	85.00	170	—
1659	—	25.00	50.00	100	200	—

KM# 42 3 PFENNIG

Copper **Obv:** Rheda arms **Rev:** III in ornamented square

Date	Mintage	Good	VG	F	VF	XF
ND(pre-1623)	—	90.00	175	325	650	—

KM# 43 3 PFENNIG

Copper **Obv:** Crowned rampant lion left, REDE in legend **Rev:** Value III in ornamented circle

Date	Mintage	Good	VG	F	VF	XF
ND(pre-1623)	—	75.00	150	300	600	—

KM# 54 3 PFENNIG

Copper **Ruler:** Moritz **Note:** Kennepohl 95. Varieties exist.

Date	Mintage	Good	VG	F	VF	XF
1655	—	25.00	50.00	100	200	—
1659	—	15.00	30.00	60.00	125	350

KM# 67 3 PFENNIG

Copper **Obv:** Lion right

Date	Mintage	Good	VG	F	VF	XF
1659	—	60.00	120	225	450	—

KM# 55.1 4 PFENNIG

Copper **Obv:** Similar to 5 Pfennig, KM#69. **Rev:** IIII in circle, border of 12 lilies

Date	Mintage	Good	VG	F	VF	XF
1655	—	25.00	50.00	100	200	—
1659	—	13.00	27.00	55.00	110	—

KM# 68 4 PFENNIG

Copper **Obv:** Lion right

Date	Mintage	Good	VG	F	VF	XF
1659	—	32.00	65.00	135	270	—

KM# 55.2 4 PFENNIG

Copper **Ruler:** Moritz **Rev:** Border of dots **Note:** Kennepohl 93. Additional varieties exist.

Date	Mintage	Good	VG	F	VF	XF
1659	—	13.00	27.00	55.00	110	—

KM# 71 5 PFENNIG

Copper **Obv:** DE/RANG/D in circle

Date	Mintage	Good	VG	F	VF	XF
1659 Rare	—	—	—	—	—	—

KM# 69 5 PFENNIG

Copper **Ruler:** Moritz **Note:** Varieties exist.

Date	Mintage	Good	VG	F	VF	XF
1659	—	15.00	32.00	65.00	135	—
1669	—	15.00	32.00	65.00	135	—

KM# 70 5 PFENNIG

Copper **Obv:** Lion right **Note:** Varieties exist.

Date	Mintage	Good	VG	F	VF	XF
1659	—	45.00	95.00	190	380	—

KM# 72 6 PFENNIG

Copper **Obv:** Similar to 5 Pfennig, KM#69. **Rev:** Value VI **Note:** Varieties exist.

Date	Mintage	Good	VG	F	VF	XF
1659	—	20.00	40.00	80.00	160	—

BERLIN

Located on the River Spree, Berlin was settled in the 12th century. It grew to become a major city and the capital of the margraviate and electorate of Brandenburg (see). It later was capital of the Kingdom of Prussia and finally, of the German Empire of 1871-1918 and the German Republic until 1945. Local coinage was struck for Berlin in the early period of the Thirty Years' War.

CITY

REGULAR COINAGE

KM# 1 SCHERF (1/2 Pfennig)
Copper **Note:** 1/2 Pfennig kipper. Uniface. Bear left in oval frame, date curved.

Date	Mintage	Good	VG	F	VF	XF
1621	—	50.00	100	200	400	—

KM# 3 SCHERF (1/2 Pfennig)
Copper **Note:** Date divided by frame, 1-6 above 2-1.

Date	Mintage	Good	VG	F	VF	XF
1621	—	50.00	100	200	400	—

KM# 2 SCHERF (1/2 Pfennig)
Copper **Note:** Date in straight line.

Date	Mintage	Good	VG	F	VF	XF
1621	—	50.00	100	200	400	—

BERLIN & KOLLN

During the early part of the Thirty Years' War, a joint coinage was issued for Berlin and Kolln, a city on the Spree just southeast of Berlin. Kolln was also the site of a mint for the electors of Brandenburg.

CITY

REGULAR COINAGE

KM# 3 PFENNIG
Copper **Note:** Frames connected by loop at top.

Date	Mintage	Good	VG	F	VF	XF
1621	—	55.00	110	225	450	—

KM# 1 PFENNIG
Copper **Obv:** Arms of Berlin (bear left) and Kolln (eagle) in adjoining oval frames, date below. **Note:** Kipper Pfennig. Uniface.

Date	Mintage	Good	VG	F	VF	XF
1621	—	55.00	110	225	450	—

KM# 2 PFENNIG
Copper **Note:** Oval frames connected by arch at top.

Date	Mintage	Good	VG	F	VF	XF
1621	—	55.00	110	225	450	—

BESANCON

Besançon is located in Franche-Comté, 70 miles (116 kilometers) southwest of Mühlhausen in Alsace and almost the same distance west-northwest of Bern, Switzerland. This city was well known in Roman times as Vesontio and was first occupied by Julius Caesar in 58 B.C. An archbishopric was founded here in the 2nd century. The archbishops became princes of the empire ca.1288.

The city became a free imperial city in 1184 and soon came under the influence of the dukes of Burgundy, then of the imperial Hapsburgs and later within the Spanish sphere of influence after the abdication of Emperor Charles V in 1556. In 1678 it was formally ceded to France by the Peace of Nijmegen.

The normal devices employed on the city coinage are the city arms and a bust or figure of Emperor Charles V, even long after his death, because it was he who gave Besançon the mint right in 1526 and renewed it in 1534.

ARMS
Eagle, head to left, between two columns.

FREE CITY

STANDARD COINAGE

KM# 3 KREUZER
0.7500 g., Silver **Obv:** Ornate shield of city arms in circle, date at end of legend **Obv. Legend:** MONETA. BISVNTINÆ. **Rev:** Crowned bust to left in circle **Rev. Legend:** +CAROLVS. V. IMPERATOR.

Date	Mintage	VG	F	VF	XF	Unc
1605	—	40.00	80.00	125	210	—

KM# 7 CAROLUS
Silver, 18-19 mm. **Obv:** Shield of city arms, date above, in circle **Obv. Legend:** +MONET. CIVI. BISVNTINE. **Rev:** Crowned bust to right in circle **Rev. Legend:** +CAROLVS. V. IMPERATOR. **Note:** Saurma 1831.

Date	Mintage	VG	F	VF	XF	Unc
1616	—	10.00	20.00	40.00	85.00	—
1619	—	10.00	20.00	40.00	85.00	—

KM# 10 CAROLUS
1.4600 g., Billon **Obv:** Ornate shield of city arms in circle **Obv. Legend:** MONE. CIVI. BISVNTINAE **Rev:** Crowned bust to left divides date in circle **Rev. Legend:** CAROLVS: V: IMPERATOR.

Date	Mintage	VG	F	VF	XF	Unc
1622	—	25.00	50.00	100	200	—

KM# 15 GROSCHEN
Billon Weight varies: 2.09-2.10g., 23 mm. **Obv:** Crowned B between columns divides date in circle **Obv. Legend:** MONETA. CIV. IMP. BISONT. **Rev:** Laureate bust to left in circle **Rev. Legend:** +CAROLVS.V.IMPERATOR

Date	Mintage	VG	F	VF	XF	Unc
1622	—	40.00	80.00	160	325	—
1623	—	45.00	90.00	190	350	—

KM# 20 2 GROSCHEN (1/4 Teston)
Billon, 29 mm. **Obv:** City arms in circle **Obv. Legend:** +MONETA. CIV. IMP. BISONT. **Rev:** Laureatee bust to left divides date in circle, value (2) in oval cartouche below **Rev. Legend:** +CAROLVS. V. IMPERATOR.

Date	Mintage	VG	F	VF	XF	Unc
1623	—	65.00	125	250	500	—
1624	—	65.00	125	250	500	—

KM# 25 8 GROS (Teston)
Silver Weight varies: 8.11-8.28g., 29-30 mm. **Obv:** Shield of city arms, date above **Obv. Legend:** +MONETA. CIV. IMP. BISONT. **Rev:** Laureate bust to left i circle, value (8) in oval below **Rev. Legend:** +CAROLVS. V. - IMPERATOR.

Date	Mintage	Good	VG	F	VF	XF
1623	—	50.00	100	200	400	725
1624	—	35.00	75.00	150	300	600

KM# 33 8 GROS (Teston)
7.8700 g., Silver, 29 mm. **Obv:** Shield of city arms, date above **Obv. Legend:** +MONETA. CIV. IMP. BISONT. **Rev:** Laureate bust to left in circle, star in oval below **Rev. Legend:** +CAROLVS. V. - IMPERATOR.

Date	Mintage	VG	F	VF	XF	Unc
1639	—	—	—	—	—	—

KM# 28 1/2 THALER (16 Gros)
Silver Weight varies: 13.27-14.14g., 35 mm. **Obv:** City arms in circle, date at end of legend **Obv. Legend:** +MONETA: CIVI: IMP: BISVNTINÆ. **Rev:** Laureate bust to left in circle **Rev. Legend:** +CAROLVS. V. IMPERATOR.

Date	Mintage	VG	F	VF	XF	Unc
1642	—	125	225	450	900	—
1643	—	200	400	750	1,500	—
1644	—	125	225	450	900	—
1645	—	225	350	650	1,300	—

KM# 27 THALER (32 Gros)
27.6700 g., Silver, 45 mm. **Obv:** City arms in circle, date at end of legend **Obv. Legend:** +MONETA: CIVI: IMP: BISVNTINÆ. **Rev:** Laureate draped bust to left in circle, value (32) in cartouche below **Rev. Legend:** +CAROLVS: V: - IMPERATOR. **Note:** Dav. 5068.

Date	Mintage	VG	F	VF	XF	Unc
1624	—	425	850	1,450	2,500	—
1625	—	425	850	1,450	2,500	—

KM# 37 THALER (32 Gros)
Silver Weight varies: 27.84-28.02g., 42 mm. **Obv:** City arms in circle, date at end of legend **Obv. Legend:** +MONETA: CIVI: IMP: BISVNTINÆ. **Rev:** Laureate draped bust to left in circle **Rev. Legend:** +CAROLVS: V. IMPERATOR **Note:** Dav. 5069.

Date	Mintage	VG	F	VF	XF	Unc
1640	—	525	1,100	1,850	3,450	—
1641	—	525	1,100	1,850	3,450	—

KM# 48 THALER (32 Gros)
Silver Weight varlies: 27.46-28.25g., 41-45 mm. **Obv:** Crowned imperial eagle, shield of city arms on breast **Obv. Legend:** MONETA. CIVIT. IMP(ER). (I.) BISVNTINÆ. **Rev:** Full-length crowned and armored figure of Karl V, turned slightly to right, holding scepter and orb, divides date **Rev. Legend:** CAROLVS. QVINT - ROM. IMPERATOR. **Note:** Dav. 5070.

Date	Mintage	VG	F	VF	XF	Unc
1658	—	230	500	700	950	—
1659	—	175	325	525	750	—
1660	15,356	175	325	525	750	—
1661	—	175	325	525	750	—
1663	—	350	625	875	1,150	—
1664	—	200	375	625	875	—
1666	—	175	325	525	750	—
1667	—	175	325	525	750	—

KM# 52 PISTOLET
6.9200 g., Gold, 27 mm. **Obv:** Crowned imperial eagle with shield of city arms on breast **Obv. Legend:** MONETA. CIVIT. IMP. BISVNTINAE. **Rev:** Crowned and armored full-length figure of Karl V, holding orb and scepter, turned to right, divides date **Rev. Legend:** CAROLVS. QVINT - ROM. IMPERAT. **Note:** Fr. 76.

Date	Mintage	VG	F	VF	XF	Unc
1662	—	1,200	3,000	5,100	9,000	—
1664	—	1,200	3,000	5,100	9,000	—
1666	—	1,200	3,000	5,100	9,000	—
1667	—	1,200	3,000	5,100	9,000	—

KM# 57 PISTOLET
6.6100 g., Gold, 25 mm. **Obv:** Imperial eagle with shield of city arms on breast, date at end of legend **Obv. Legend:** +MONETA. CIVIT. IMP. BISVNTINAE. **Rev:** Laureate bust to right **Rev. Legend:** CAROLVS. QVINT. ROM. IMPERATOR. **Note:** Fr. 74.

Date	Mintage	VG	F	VF	XF	Unc
1667	—	1,150	2,700	4,500	7,800	—
1673	—	1,150	2,700	4,500	7,800	—

KM# 54 2 PISTOLET
Gold **Obv:** 3-line inscription, date in chronogram **Rev:** Laureate bust of Philip IV of Spain right **Note:** Fr. 80.

Date	Mintage	VG	F	VF	XF	Unc
1664 Rare	—	—	—	—	—	—

TRADE COINAGE

KM# 35 1/2 PISTOLET
Gold, 23 mm. **Obv:** Imperial eagle with shield of city arms on breast, in circle, date at end of legend **Obv. Legend:** +MONE. AVREA. CIVI. BISVNTINÆ. **Rev:** Laureate head to left in circle **Rev. Legend:** +CAROLVS. V. IMPERATOR. **Note:** Fr. 75.

Date	Mintage	VG	F	VF	XF	Unc
1639	—	1,850	2,500	3,000	4,250	—

KM# 43 1/2 PISTOLET
Gold Weight varies: 3.27-3.32g., 23 mm. **Obv:** Imperial eagle, shield of city arms on breast, in circle, date at end of legend **Obv. Legend:** MON. AVR. CIVIT. IMP. BISVNTINÆ. **Rev:** Laureate head to right in circle **Rev. Legend:** CAROLVS. V. - IMPERATOR. AVG. **Note:** Fr. 75.

Date	Mintage	VG	F	VF	XF	Unc
1653	—	1,400	1,850	2,500	4,200	—
1654	—	1,600	2,250	3,000	4,800	—

KM# 56 2 PISTOLET
Gold, 33 mm. **Obv:** Crowned imperial eagle with shield of city arms on breast **Obv. Legend:** MONETA. CIVIT. IMP. BISVNTINAE. **Rev:** Crowned and armored full-length figure, holding orb and scepter, turned to right, divides date **Rev. Legend:** CAROLVS. QVINT - ROM. IMPERAT. **Note:** Fr. 75a.

Date	Mintage	VG	F	VF	XF	Unc
1666	—	2,200	2,750	4,000	6,000	—

KM# 45 1/2 DUCAT
1.7500 g., 0.9860 Gold Weight varies: 1.70-1.74g. 0.0555 oz. AGW, 17 mm. **Obv:** Five-line inscription with date in ornamented square **Obv. Inscription:** DVCATVS / .CIVIT. / BISVNT / AD. LEG. / IMP. (date) **Rev:** Full-length crowned and armored figure turned to right, holding orb and scepter **Rev. Legend:** CAROLVS. V. - IMPERATOR. **Note:** Fr. 79.

Date	Mintage	VG	F	VF	XF	Unc
1655	—	300	500	1,000	2,000	—

KM# 39 DUCAT
3.5000 g., 0.9860 Gold Weight varies: 3.23-3.43g. 0.1109 oz. AGW, 24 mm. **Obv:** 5-line inscription with date in ornamented tablet **Rev:** Full-length crowned and armored figure turned to right, holding orb and scepter **Rev. Legend:** CAROLVS. V. - IMPERATOR. **Rev. Inscription:** DVCATVS / CIVIT. / BISVNT / AD. LEG. / IMP. (date) **Note:** Fr. 78.

Date	Mintage	VG	F	VF	XF	Unc
1642	—	—	—	—	—	—
1649	—	750	1,100	1,500	2,750	—
1655 Rare	—	—	—	—	—	—
1656	—	1,350	1,800	2,500	4,000	—

KM# 40 2 DUCAT
Gold Weight varies: 6.92-6.99g., 28 mm. **Obv:** Imperial eagle with shield of city arms on breast in oval, large crown above, 7 ornate shields of arms around in circle, no legend **Rev:** Laureate bust to right **Rev. Legend:** FERDINAND. III. D. G. RO. IMP. S. A. ET.

Date	Mintage	VG	F	VF	XF	Unc
ND(1641-64) 3 known	—	—	—	—	—	—

Note: An example in XF-AU realized approximately $18,400 in the Hess-Divo sale of April 2008.

KM# 41 2 DUCAT
7.0000 g., 0.9860 Gold 0.2219 oz. AGW, 27 mm. **Obv:** 5-line inscription with date in ornamented square **Rev:** Full-length crowned and armored figure turned to right, holding orb and scepter **Rev. Legend:** CAROLVS. V. - IMPERATOR. **Rev. Inscription:** DVCATVS / .CIVIT. / BISVNT / AD. LEG. / IMP. (date) **Note:** Fr. 77.

Date	Mintage	VG	F	VF	XF	Unc
1642	—	—	—	—	—	—
1654	—	—	—	—	—	—

BIBERACH

Located in Württemberg 22 miles to the southwest of Ulm, Biberach became a free imperial city in 1312. The city came under the control of Baden in 1803 and then of Württemberg in 1806.

FREE CITY

REGULAR COINAGE

KM# 5 1/2 BATZEN (2 Kreuzer)
Silver **Obv:** Crowned beaver (arms) right **Rev:** Crowned imperial eagle, titles of Ferdinand II **Note:** Kipper 1/2 Batzen.

Date	Mintage	VG	F	VF	XF	Unc
ND(1619-22) Rare	—	—	—	—	—	—

KM# 7 3 BATZEN (12 Kreuzer)
Silver **Countermark:** Crowned beaver left in oval, 12 below **Note:** Countermark on Pfalz-Neuburg 6 Batzen.

Date	Mintage	VG	F	VF	XF	Unc
ND(1619-22) Rare	—	—	—	—	—	—

KM# 6 3 BATZEN (12 Kreuzer)
Silver **Obv:** Crowned beaver right **Rev:** Crowned imperial eagle with 12 on breast **Note:** Kipper 3 Batzen.

Date	Mintage	VG	F	VF	XF	Unc
ND(1619-22) Rare	—	—	—	—	—	—

BOCHOLT

This provincial town in the bishopric of Munster is located near the Dutch border. It had a local copper coinage from 1615-1762. Bocholt passed to Salm-Salm in 1803 and later went to Prussia.

MONETARY SYSTEM
21 Heller = 6 Pfennig = 1/60 Thaler

PROVINCIAL TOWN

REGULAR COINAGE

KM# 5 10-1/2 HELLER
Copper **Obv:** City arms, STADT BOCHOLT, date **Rev:** Value X in ornamented border **Note:** Varieties exist.

Date	Mintage	Good	VG	F	VF	XF
1616	—	22.00	45.00	90.00	180	—
1690	—	50.00	100	225	550	—

KM# 6.1 15-1/2 HELLER
Copper **Obv:** City arms, STADT BOCHOLT, date **Rev:** Value X.V. in ornamented border

Date	Mintage	Good	VG	F	VF	XF
1616	—	50.00	100	225	550	—

KM# 6.2 15-1/2 HELLER
Copper **Rev:** Value X.V.

Date	Mintage	Good	VG	F	VF	XF
1689	—	20.00	40.00	85.00	170	—

KM# 7 21 HELLER
Copper **Obv:** City arms, STADT BOCHOLT, date **Rev:** Value XXI in ornamented border

Date	Mintage	Good	VG	F	VF	XF
1616	—	35.00	75.00	150	300	750

KM# 15 21 HELLER
Copper **Rev:** Angel head and wings above value in center, 60 EININ REICHSTALER in legend

Date	Mintage	Good	VG	F	VF	XF
1670	—	20.00	40.00	85.00	175	—

KM# 20 21 HELLER

Copper **Rev:** Angel head and wings above city arms, arms dividing I-S (1Stuber) **Note:** Varieties exist.

Date	Mintage	VG	F	VF	XF	Unc
1689	—	18.00	37.00	75.00	150	—
1690	—	18.00	37.00	75.00	150	—

KM# 8 2 PFENNIG

Copper **Obv:** City arms, STADT BOCHOLT, date **Rev:** Value II in ornamented border

Date	Mintage	Good	VG	F	VF	XF
1616	—	45.00	95.00	185	375	—

KM# 9 3 PFENNIG

Copper **Obv:** City arms, STADT BOCHOLT, date **Rev:** Value III in ornamented border

Date	Mintage	Good	VG	F	VF	XF
1616	—	27.00	55.00	110	225	500

KM# 10 4 PFENNIG

Copper **Obv:** City arms, STADT BOCHOLT, date **Rev:** Value IIII in ornamented border

Date	Mintage	Good	VG	F	VF	XF
1616	—	30.00	60.00	125	250	500

KM# 11 12 PFENNIG

Copper **Obv:** City arms, STADT BOCHOLT, date **Rev:** Value XII in ornamented square

Date	Mintage	Good	VG	F	VF	XF
1617	—	35.00	75.00	150	300	—

BRANDENBURG CITY ISSUES

A city in the old margraviate of Brandenburg, originally the capital of the local pre-Christian Slavic tribe of the area. It is located on the Havel River 35 miles west-southwest of Berlin. It was the capital of the margraviate prior to Berlin. Some copper coins were issued during the early part of the Thirty Years' War for the Altstadt and Neustadt (old and new divisions of the city).

ALTSTADT

STANDARD COINAGE

KM# 1 SCHERF (1/2 Pfennig)

Copper **Obv:** City gate, ASB above (Alt-Stadt-Brandenburg) **Note:** Kipper. Uniface.

Date	Mintage	Good	VG	F	VF	XF
ND(1621)	—	60.00	120	250	475	—

NEUSTADT

STANDARD COINAGE

KM# 2 SCHERF (1/2 Pfennig)

Copper **Obv:** Knight w/eagle shield in arch of city gate, date above **Note:** Kipper. Uniface.

Date	Mintage	Good	VG	F	VF	XF
(1)621	—	50.00	100	210	425	—
1621	—	50.00	100	210	425	—

KM# 3 PFENNIG

Copper **Obv:** Knight w/eagle shield in arch of city gate, NSB above (Neu-Stadt Brandenburg) **Note:** Kipper. Uniface.

Date	Mintage	Good	VG	F	VF	XF
ND(1621)	—	65.00	135	275	550	—

KM# 4 PFENNIG

Copper **Obv:** Knight w/eagle shield in arch of city gate, date above **Note:** Kipper. Uniface.

Date	Mintage	Good	VG	F	VF	XF
1621	—	65.00	135	275	550	—

BRANDENBURG

(Brandenburg-Prussia)

The territory which was to become Brandenburg was inhabited by various Slavic tribes in the early Middle Ages. Charlemagne managed to diminish their power to some extent, but they regained their control after his passing. The Slav capital at Brennibor was captured by Emperor Heinrich I (918-36) and from that place Brandenburg takes its name. A series of margraves more or less continued to press the Slav tribes, but some were so ineffectual that the Slavs regained much of their former domains, especially after the death of Emperor Otto I (973). The early 12th century saw the return to active warfare against the Slavs. In 1134, the conquered lands were divided into the Altmark (Old or North Mark), west of the Elbe River, the Mittelmark (Middle Mark), between the Elbe and the Oder, and the Neumark (New Mark), east of the Oder River. Duke Lothar of Saxony appointed Albrecht the Bear of Ballenstädt as Margrave of the Nordmark (Altmark) and his long reign until 1170 brought stability to the lands under his control. The Ascanian rulers consolidated their power in Brandenburg and eventually obtained the electoral dignity in the 13th century. When the dynasty in Brandenburg became extinct, title passed to Emperor Ludwig III of Bavaria (1314-47), who made his eldest son ruler there. The margraviate continued to be ruled by members of the various imperial families or their appointees until the early 15th century. The Hohenzollerns of Swabia, who had been hereditary burgraves of Nürnberg since the late 12th century, acquired a mortgage on Brandenburg from the perpetually impecunious Emperor. In a stroke, Friedrich VI of Nürnberg became Elector Friedrich I of Brandenburg in 1415, thus placing the family into position to become rulers of the future most powerful state of the Empire.

Several of the Electors' sons ruled in the Hohenzollern possessions of Franconia (see Brandenburg in Franconia) and two founded the lines of Brandenburg-Ansbach and Brandenburg-Bayreuth (which see). Elector Johann Sigismund inherited the Duchy of Prussia in 1618 and the electorate was known henceforth as Brandenburg-Prussia. The Electorate sided with the Protestant cause during the Thirty Years' War, having submitted to the Reformation in 1539. The lessons of the war brought about the build-up of military power and territorial expansion under Friedrich Wilhelm, the Great Elector, which formed the basis of the Hohenzollerns' rise as a leading power in Europe. Johann Sigismund's great grandson assumed the title of King in Prussia in 1701 and the old margraviate of Brandenburg became just a province of the Kingdom. See Prussia for subsequent history and coin issues.

RULERS

Joachim Friedrich, 1598-1608
Johann Sigismund, 1608-1619
Georg Wilhelm, 1619-1640
Friedrich Wilhelm, 1640-1688
Friedrich III, 1688-1701

MINT OFFICIALS' INITIALS

Berlin/Kölln

Initial	Date	Name
AB	1642-44	Adrian Berlin
AB	1658-64	Andreas Becker, warden
CS	1675-1701	Christoph Stricker, warden
CT	1645-58	Carl Thauer, as mintmaster and warden
GL	1667-83	Gottfried Leygebe, die-cutter
IBS, IS, S	1681-97	Johann Bernhard Schultz, die-cutter
IL	1664-75	Jobst Liebmann, warden
IP	1625-27	Jacob Panckaert
LCS	1682-1701	Lorenz Christoph Schneider
LM, M	1620-42	Liborius Müller
RF	1688-1703	Raimund Faltz, die-cutter

Driesen

Initial	Date	Name
HL	1607-15	Heinrich Laffert

Emmerich

See Cleves listings.

Halberstadt

Initial	Date	Name
LCS	1679-82	Lorenz Christoph Schneider

Kölln an der Spree

Initial	Date	Name
HVR (swan)	1584-1604	Heinrich von Rehnen
MH	1589-1604	Melchior Hoffman as warden
	1604-20	As mintmaster

Konigsberg

Initial	Date	Name
BA	1685-87	Bastian Altmann
CG, G	1664-78	Caspar Geelhaar, the Elder as warden
CG	1699-1728	Caspar Geelhaar, the Younger
CM	1646-60	Christoph Melchior as warden
(q) = Cross on heart	1619-39	Ernst Pfaler as warden
CV	1672-74	Christoph Varenhorst
DK	1627-51, 56	David Koch
DS	1667-91	David Schirmer as warden
GR	1684	Unknown die-cutter
HM, HM monogram	1660-63	Hans Muller
HS	1674-77, 79-85, 87-94	Heinrich Sievertz
MK	1624-27	Marcus Koch
NB	1624-59	Noah Brettschneider, die-cutter
SD	1695-99	Siegmund Dannies
SI	?-1624	Simon Jansen
TT	1669-72	Thomas Timpf
(e)= UM with 3 stars	1653-60	Jonas Kasimir von Eulenburg

Krossen

Initial	Date	Name
GF	1668-74	Gottfried Frommholdt
IPE	1667-68	Julius Philipp Eisendracht

Magdeburg

Initial	Date	Name
HFH	1698-1719	Heinrich Friedrich Halter
ICS	1683-90	Johann Christoph Seehie, as warden
	1690-95	As mintmaster
IE	1683-90	Johann Ehlers

Minden

Initial	Date	Name
AVH	1674-79	Arnold Vahrenholtz
AVH	1674-79	August von Hakeberg as warden
BH	1682-1713	Bastian Hille
GDZ	1674-78	Georg David Ziegenhom
GM	1689-1711	Gottfried Metelles as die-cutter
HB	1652, 69-73	Heinrich Bonhorst
IW	1671-73	Johann Willemsen
SD	1682-85	Siegmund Dannies

Regenstein

Initial	Date	Name
IA	1674-77	Johann Arendsburg

Stargard

Initial	Date	Name
SD	1689-92	Siegmund Dannies

NOTE: All issues of Joachim Friedrich were struck in Kölln.

References: B = Emil Bahrfeldt, ***Das Münzwesen der Mark Brandenburg unter den Hohenzollern bis zum grossen Kurfürsten, von 1415 bis 1640,*** Berlin 1895.

D = Kurt Dost, ***Münzen im Preussenland – Herzogtum Preussen und Provinz Ostpreussen im Königreich 1525-1821***, Essen, 1990.

N = Erich Neumann, ***Münzeprägungen des Kurfürstentums Brandenburg und des Königreichs Preussen,*** 1. Band, ***Hohenzollern 1415-1701, Cologne, 1998. Die Münzen des Kurfürstentums Brandenburg unter der Herrschaft der Hozenzollern 1415-1701***, Cologne, 1998.

ELECTORATE AND MARGRAVIATE

REGULAR COINAGE

KM# 481 MATTHIER

Silver **Obv:** Crowned scepter divides date **Rev. Inscription:** EIN / MATIER / MIND. **Mint:** Minden

Date	Mintage	VG	F	VF	XF	Unc
1679	—	90.00	180	360	—	—

KM# 514 MATTHIER

Silver **Rev:** Date moved to fourth line

Date	Mintage	VG	F	VF	XF	Unc
1684	—	120	250	475	—	—

KM# 260 PFENNIG

Silver **Obv:** Inscription, date **Obv. Inscription:** I / PF. BR / LANDES / MVNZ **Mint:** Kölln **Note:** Uniface. Varieties exist.

Date	Mintage	VG	F	VF	XF	Unc
1653	117,000	60.00	120	235	475	—
1657	Inc. above	60.00	120	235	475	—
ND	Inc. above	60.00	120	235	475	—
1663	—	60.00	120	235	475	—

KM# 321 PFENNIG

Silver, 12.5 mm. **Ruler:** Friedrich Wilhelm **Obv:** Crowned scepter divides date turned on side and mintmaster's initials **Mint:** Berlin **Note:** Ref. S-1529. Uniface.

Date	Mintage	VG	F	VF	XF	Unc
1662 AB	163,458	65.00	135	275	550	—

KM# 384 PFENNIG

Silver **Obv:** Crowned scepter divides 1 - PF and date, palm branches below **Mint:** Berlin **Note:** Uniface.

Date	Mintage	VG	F	VF	XF	Unc
1669	—	65.00	135	275	550	—

KM# 405 PFENNIG

Silver **Note:** Crowned scepter, three small leaves on both sides.

Date	Mintage	VG	F	VF	XF	Unc
ND(1670)	—	45.00	90.00	190	385	—

KM# 438 PFENNIG

Silver **Obv:** Crowned scepter arms divide mintmaster's initials **Rev:** 1/PFEN/date

Date	Mintage	VG	F	VF	XF	Unc
1675 IL	—	65.00	135	275	550	—

KM# 439 PFENNIG

Silver **Ruler:** Friedrich Wilhelm **Obv:** Ornamented oval arms **Mint:** Berlin

Date	Mintage	VG	F	VF	XF	Unc
1675 CS	—	65.00	135	275	550	—

KM# 462 PFENNIG

Silver **Ruler:** Friedrich Wilhelm **Obv:** Crowned scepter divides date **Rev:** I/PF: BR / LANDT / MVNZ / C.S. **Mint:** Berlin

Date	Mintage	VG	F	VF	XF	Unc
1676 CS	—	40.00	100	225	450	—
1679 CS	—	40.00	100	225	450	—

KM# 463 PFENNIG

Silver **Obv:** Crowned scepter arms **Rev:** I / PF. BR / LAND. M / date / C.S. **Mint:** Berlin

Date	Mintage	VG	F	VF	XF	Unc
1676 CS	—	60.00	120	235	475	—

KM# 517 PFENNIG

Silver **Ruler:** Friedrich Wilhelm **Obv:** Crowned scepter arms between two palm branches **Rev. Inscription:** I / PF. BR / LANDT / MVNZ / date **Mint:** Halberstadt

Date	Mintage	VG	F	VF	XF	Unc
1685 LCS	—	60.00	120	235	475	—

KM# 537 PFENNIG

Silver **Mint:** Minden

Date	Mintage	VG	F	VF	XF	Unc
ND(1688-1701) BH	—	60.00	120	235	475	—

KM# 536 PFENNIG

Silver **Ruler:** Friedrich III **Obv:** Scepter between palm branches **Note:** Uniface.

Date	Mintage	VG	F	VF	XF	Unc
ND(1688-1701)	—	45.00	90.00	190	385	—

KM# 565 PFENNIG

Silver **Ruler:** Friedrich III **Obv:** Crowned scepter arms between two palm branches **Rev. Inscription:** 1 / PF.BR / LANDT / MVNZ / date **Mint:** Stargard **Note:** Varieties exist.

Date	Mintage	VG	F	VF	XF	Unc
1690 SD	—	60.00	120	235	475	—
1692 SD	—	60.00	120	235	475	—

KM# 597 PFENNIG

Silver **Ruler:** Friedrich III **Obv:** Inscription, date **Obv. Inscription:** I / PF:BR / L: MVNZ **Mint:** Berlin **Note:** Uniface.

Date	Mintage	VG	F	VF	XF	Unc
1695 LCS	1,062,000	45.00	90.00	190	385	—

KM# 239 2 PFENNIG

Silver **Obv:** Crowned oval scepter arms divide date **Rev. Inscription:** II / PF. BR / LANDES / MUNZ (or MVNZ) **Mint:** Kölln **Note:** Varieties exist.

Date	Mintage	VG	F	VF	XF	Unc
1651	749,000	65.00	135	275	550	—
1653	Inc. above	65.00	135	275	550	—
1654	Inc. above	65.00	135	275	550	—
1656	Inc. above	65.00	135	275	550	—
1657	Inc. above	65.00	135	275	550	—
1658	Inc. above	65.00	135	275	550	—
1659	Inc. above	65.00	135	275	550	—
1660	Inc. above	65.00	135	275	550	—
1666	—	65.00	135	275	550	—

KM# 261 2 PFENNIG

Silver **Rev:** Date also at bottom

Date	Mintage	VG	F	VF	XF	Unc
1653	Inc. above	65.00	135	275	550	—

KM# 367 2 PFENNIG

Silver **Obv:** Crowned scepter arms between palm branches **Rev:** Inscription in cartouche, date above **Rev. Inscription:** II/PFEN **Mint:** Berlin

Date	Mintage	VG	F	VF	XF	Unc
1668 IL	—	65.00	135	275	550	—

KM# 428 2 PFENNIG

Silver **Rev:** Without cartouche, leaf on each side of II

Date	Mintage	VG	F	VF	XF	Unc
1674 IL	—	65.00	135	275	550	—

KM# 464 2 PFENNIG

Silver **Obv:** Crowned scepter arms divide date **Rev. Inscription:** II / PF.BR / LANDT / MVNZ

Date	Mintage	VG	F	VF	XF	Unc
1676 CS	—	65.00	135	275	550	—
1684 LCS	—	65.00	135	275	550	—
1685 LCS	—	65.00	135	275	550	—

KM# 566 2 PFENNIG

Silver **Mint:** Magdeburg

Date	Mintage	VG	F	VF	XF	Unc
1690 ICS	—	45.00	90.00	190	385	—
1692 ICS	—	45.00	90.00	190	385	—
1700 HFH	—	45.00	90.00	190	385	—

KM# 567 2 PFENNIG

Silver **Obv:** Crowned scepter arms divide date **Rev. Inscription:** II / PF.BR / LANDT / MVNZ **Mint:** Stargard

Date	Mintage	VG	F	VF	XF	Unc
1690 SD	—	45.00	90.00	190	385	—
1692 SD	—	45.00	90.00	190	385	—

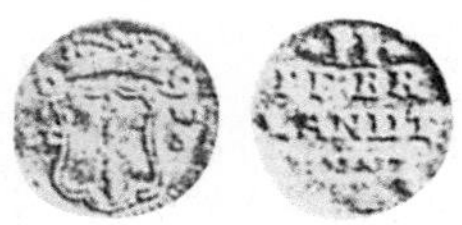

KM# 598 2 PFENNIG

Silver **Mint:** Berlin

Date	Mintage	VG	F	VF	XF	Unc
1695 LCS	636,000	40.00	80.00	160	325	—
1700 LCS	—	40.00	80.00	160	325	—

KM# 599 2 PFENNIG

Silver **Mint:** Minden

Date	Mintage	VG	F	VF	XF	Unc
1695 BH	—	65.00	100	225	450	—
ND BH	—	65.00	100	225	450	—

KM# 7 3 PFENNIG (Dreier)

Silver **Ruler:** Joachim Friedrich **Obv:** 4-fold arms with scepter shield in center **Mint:** Kölln **Note:** Ref. B#519-521.

Date	Mintage	VG	F	VF	XF	Unc
1601 (e)	—	125	240	425	775	—

KM# 60 3 PFENNIG (Dreier)

Silver **Obv:** Eagle arms **Rev:** Scepter divides date **Mint:** Berlin **Note:** Kipper. Varieties exist.

Date	Mintage	VG	F	VF	XF	Unc
16Z0	—	16.00	35.00	65.00	130	—

KM# 82 3 PFENNIG (Dreier)

Silver **Obv:** Eagle's head in shield **Note:** Varieties exist.

Date	Mintage	VG	F	VF	XF	Unc
16Z1	—	16.00	35.00	65.00	130	—
16ZZ	—	16.00	35.00	65.00	130	—

KM# 81 3 PFENNIG (Dreier)

Silver **Obv:** Eagle not in shield

Date	Mintage	VG	F	VF	XF	Unc
16Z1	—	16.00	35.00	65.00	130	—

KM# 83 3 PFENNIG (Dreier)

Silver **Obv:** Imperial orb with value 3 in circle **Rev:** Scepter divides date in circle

Date	Mintage	VG	F	VF	XF	Unc
16Z1	—	16.00	35.00	65.00	130	—

KM# 262 3 PFENNIG (Dreier)

Silver **Obv:** Crowned eagle, scepter arms on breast **Rev:** Inscription, date **Rev. Inscription:** 3 / PF. BR / LANDES / MUNZ / **Mint:** Kölln

Date	Mintage	VG	F	VF	XF	Unc
1653	898,000	13.00	27.00	55.00	110	—
1654	Inc. above	13.00	27.00	55.00	110	—
1657	Inc. above	13.00	27.00	55.00	110	—
1658	Inc. above	13.00	27.00	55.00	110	—
1659	Inc. above	13.00	27.00	55.00	110	—
1660	Inc. above	13.00	27.00	55.00	110	—

KM# 326 3 PFENNIG (Dreier)

Silver **Ruler:** Friedrich Wilhelm **Obv:** Crowned eagle with scepter arms **Rev:** Imperial orb with value 3 divides date **Mint:** Berlin

Date	Mintage	VG	F	VF	XF	Unc
1663 AB	39,708	16.00	33.00	65.00	130	—

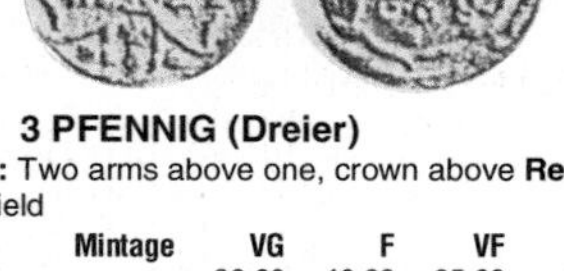

KM# 368 3 PFENNIG (Dreier)

Silver **Obv:** Two arms above one, crown above **Rev:** Value 3/date in shield

Date	Mintage	VG	F	VF	XF	Unc
1668	—	20.00	40.00	65.00	130	—

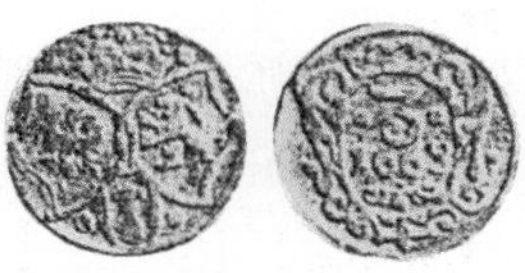

KM# 369 3 PFENNIG (Dreier)
Silver **Rev:** Value and date in ornamented oval shield

Date	Mintage	VG	F	VF	XF	Unc
1668	—	20.00	40.00	65.00	130	—

KM# 370 3 PFENNIG (Dreier)
Silver **Obv:** Crowned 4-fold arms **Rev:** 3/PFEN in two palm branches, date above

Date	Mintage	VG	F	VF	XF	Unc
1668 IL	—	20.00	40.00	65.00	130	—

KM# 371 3 PFENNIG (Dreier)
Silver **Rev:** Imperial orb with 3 divides date **Note:** Varieties exist.

Date	Mintage	VG	F	VF	XF	Unc
1668 IL	—	20.00	40.00	65.00	130	—
1669 IL	—	20.00	40.00	65.00	130	—
1669	—	20.00	40.00	65.00	130	—
1673 IL	—	20.00	40.00	65.00	130	—
1675 CS	—	20.00	40.00	65.00	130	—

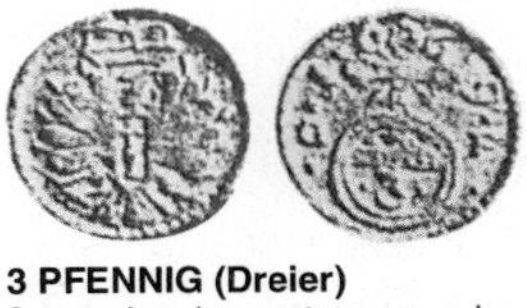

KM# 385 3 PFENNIG (Dreier)
Silver **Obv:** Crowned eagle, scepter arms on breast **Rev:** Imperial orb with 3 divides date **Mint:** Krossen

Date	Mintage	VG	F	VF	XF	Unc
1669 GF	—	20.00	40.00	75.00	155	—
1670 GF	—	20.00	40.00	75.00	155	—

KM# 418 3 PFENNIG (Dreier)
Silver **Obv:** Without scepter on eagle's breast **Rev:** Inscription, date **Rev. Inscription:** 3 / PF. BR / LANDES / MVNZ / **Mint:** Minden

Date	Mintage	VG	F	VF	XF	Unc
1671 IW	—	20.00	40.00	75.00	155	—

KM# 465 3 PFENNIG (Dreier)
Silver **Obv:** Scepter on eagle's breast **Mint:** Berlin **Note:** Varieties exist.

Date	Mintage	VG	F	VF	XF	Unc
1676 CS	—	10.00	20.00	40.00	80.00	—
1679 CS	—	10.00	20.00	40.00	80.00	—
1683 LCS	—	10.00	20.00	40.00	80.00	—
1684 LCS	—	10.00	20.00	40.00	80.00	—
1685 LCS	—	10.00	20.00	40.00	80.00	—
1686 LCS	—	10.00	20.00	40.00	80.00	—
1687 LCS	357,000	10.00	20.00	40.00	80.00	—

KM# 547 3 PFENNIG (Dreier)
Silver **Mint:** Stargard **Note:** Varieties exist.

Date	Mintage	VG	F	VF	XF	Unc
1689 SD	—	12.00	25.00	50.00	100	—
1690 SD	—	12.00	25.00	50.00	100	—
1691 SD	—	12.00	25.00	50.00	100	—
1692 SD	—	12.00	25.00	50.00	100	—

KM# 546 3 PFENNIG (Dreier)
Silver **Rev. Inscription:** LANDT/MVNTZ **Mint:** Magdeburg

Date	Mintage	VG	F	VF	XF	Unc
1689 IE	—	10.00	20.00	40.00	80.00	—
1690 ICS	—	10.00	20.00	40.00	80.00	—
1691 ICS	—	10.00	20.00	40.00	80.00	—
1692 ICS	—	10.00	20.00	40.00	80.00	—
1695 ICS	—	10.00	20.00	40.00	80.00	—
1700 HFH	—	10.00	20.00	40.00	80.00	—

KM# 600 3 PFENNIG (Dreier)
Silver **Rev. Inscription:** LANDT / MVNZ **Mint:** Berlin

Date	Mintage	VG	F	VF	XF	Unc
1695 LCS	651,000	10.00	20.00	40.00	80.00	—

KM# 601 3 PFENNIG (Dreier)
Silver **Rev. Inscription:** LANDT / MVNTZ **Mint:** Minden

Date	Mintage	VG	F	VF	XF	Unc
1695 BH	—	27.00	45.00	90.00	180	—

KM# 625 3 PFENNIG (Dreier)
Silver **Obv:** Crowned 4-fold arms **Rev:** Imperial orb with 3 divides date **Mint:** Berlin

Date	Mintage	VG	F	VF	XF	Unc
1700 LCS	—	10.00	20.00	40.00	80.00	—

KM# 386 KORTLING (1/84 Taler)
Silver **Obv:** 6-fold arms **Rev:** Imperial orb with 6 **Mint:** Minden

Date	Mintage	VG	F	VF	XF	Unc
ND(ca.1669-73)	—	12.00	25.00	50.00	100	—

KM# 466 4 PFENNIG
Silver **Obv:** Crowned oval scepter arms **Rev:** Inscription, date **Rev. Inscription:** IIII / PFEN. BRA / DEB. LAND / MVNTZ / **Mint:** Berlin **Note:** Varieties exist.

Date	Mintage	VG	F	VF	XF	Unc
1676 CS	—	15.00	30.00	65.00	130	—
1684 LCS	—	15.00	30.00	65.00	130	—
1685 LCS	—	15.00	30.00	65.00	130	—
1686 LCS	—	15.00	30.00	65.00	130	—
1687 LCS	144,000	15.00	30.00	65.00	130	—

KM# 548 4 PFENNIG
Silver **Obv:** Oval arms in baroque cartouche **Mint:** Stargard **Note:** Varieties exist.

Date	Mintage	VG	F	VF	XF	Unc
1689 SD	—	20.00	45.00	90.00	185	—
1690 SD	—	20.00	45.00	90.00	185	—
1691 SD	—	20.00	45.00	90.00	185	—
1692 SD	—	20.00	45.00	90.00	185	—

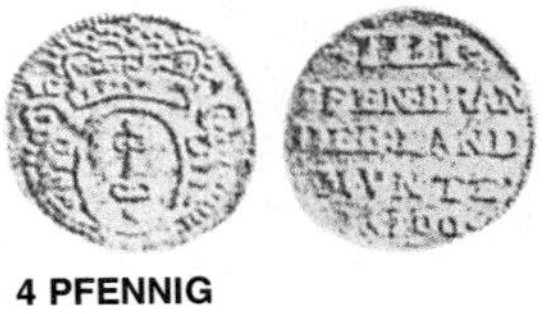

KM# 626 4 PFENNIG
Silver **Mint:** Berlin

Date	Mintage	VG	F	VF	XF	Unc
1700 LCS	—	50.00	100	210	425	—

KM# 627 4 PFENNIG
Silver **Obv:** Different cartouche and small crown **Mint:** Magdeburg

Date	Mintage	VG	F	VF	XF	Unc
1700 HFH	—	50.00	100	210	425	—

KM# 56.1 DREIPöLKER
(3 Baltic Schilling, 1 1/2 Polish Groschen)
Silver **Ruler:** Johann Sigismund **Obv:** Imperial orb with Z4 divides date **Obv. Legend:** IO. SI. MAR. BRA. S. R. I. EL. P. D. **Rev:** Electoral hat above three-fold arms, value '3' in frame at bottom **Rev. Legend:** PRO LEGE & PR. GREGE. **Mint:** Königsberg **Note:** Ref. D#300-11.

Date	Mintage	VG	F	VF	XF	Unc
(16)19 (q)	3,373,404	60.00	120	—	—	—
(16)Z0 (q)	4,795,972	50.00	90.00	180	—	—

KM# 56.2 DREIPöLKER
(3 Baltic Schilling, 1 1/2 Polish Groschen)
Silver **Ruler:** Georg Wilhelm **Mint:** Königsberg

Date	Mintage	VG	F	VF	XF	Unc
1619	3,373,000	9.00	20.00	33.00	65.00	—
1620	4,796,000	9.00	20.00	33.00	65.00	—
1621	2,560,000	9.00	20.00	33.00	65.00	—
1622	5,198,000	9.00	20.00	33.00	65.00	—
1623	4,452,000	9.00	20.00	33.00	65.00	—
1624	1,084,000	9.00	20.00	33.00	65.00	—
1624 MK	6,479,000	9.00	20.00	33.00	65.00	—
1625	5,459,000	9.00	20.00	33.00	65.00	—
1626	10,901,000	9.00	20.00	33.00	65.00	—
1627	2,380,000	9.00	20.00	33.00	65.00	—
1628	258,000	9.00	20.00	33.00	65.00	—
1633	151,000	9.00	20.00	33.00	65.00	—
1634	157,000	9.00	20.00	33.00	65.00	—
1635	Inc. above	9.00	20.00	33.00	65.00	—

KM# 56.3 DREIPöLKER
(3 Baltic Schilling, 1 1/2 Polish Groschen)
Silver **Ruler:** Georg Wilhelm **Obv:** Imperial orb with 24 divides date, titles of Georg Wilhelm **Rev:** Crowned 4-fold arms with scepter shield in center, value "3" below **Rev. Legend:** DIEV & MON. DROICT **Mint:** Königsberg **Note:** Ref. N#10.110. Varieties exist.

Date	Mintage	VG	F	VF	XF	Unc
(16)1Z (q) Error	Inc. above	8.00	16.00	30.00	60.00	—
(16)Z1 (q)	2,560,000	8.00	16.00	30.00	60.00	—
(16)ZZ (q)	5,198,000	8.00	16.00	30.00	60.00	—
(16)22 (q)	Inc. above	8.00	16.00	30.00	60.00	—
(16)23 (q)	4,452,000	8.00	16.00	30.00	60.00	—
1624 (q)	1,084,000	8.00	16.00	30.00	60.00	—

KM# 56.4 DREIPöLKER
(3 Baltic Schilling, 1 1/2 Polish Groschen)
Silver **Ruler:** Georg Wilhelm **Mint:** Königsberg **Note:** Ref. N#10.110a. Similar to KM#56.2 but titles of Georg Wilhelm on both sides. Varieties exist.

Date	Mintage	VG	F	VF	XF	Unc
(16)24 (q)	Inc. above	—	—	—	—	—

KM# 56.5 DREIPÖLKER
(3 Baltic Schilling, 1 1/2 Polish Groschen)
Silver **Ruler:** Georg Wilhelm **Obv:** Crowned 4-fold arms with scepter shield in center, value (3) below **Obv. Legend:** GE. WI. MAR. BR. S. R. I. EL. **Rev:** Imperial orb with 24 divides date **Rev. Legend:** MONE. NO(VA). DVC. PRVS. **Mint:** Königsberg **Note:** Ref. N#10.111, 10.112; D#367-88. Varieties exist.

Date	Mintage	VG	F	VF	XF	Unc
(16)24 (q)	6,478,892	8.00	16.00	30.00	60.00	—
(16)25 (q)	5,458,762	8.00	16.00	30.00	60.00	—
(16)26 (q)	10,901,000	8.00	16.00	30.00	60.00	—
(16)Z7 (q)	2,380,457	8.00	16.00	30.00	60.00	—
(16)Z8 (q)	257,932	15.00	35.00	75.00	150	—
(16)33 (q)	151,400	15.00	35.00	75.00	150	—

KM# 515 DREIPöLKER
(3 Baltic Schilling, 1 1/2 Polish Groschen)
Silver **Mint:** Berlin **Note:** Coinage for Province of Russia.

Date	Mintage	VG	F	VF	XF	Unc
1684	480,000	—	—	—	—	—

KM# 518 DREIPöLKER
(3 Baltic Schilling, 1 1/2 Polish Groschen)
Silver **Ruler:** Friedrich Wilhelm **Obv:** 5-fold arms, value 3 below **Rev:** Imperial orb with 24 divides date to upper left and right **Mint:** Königsberg

Date	Mintage	VG	F	VF	XF	Unc
(16)85	480,000	35.00	75.00	150	—	—

KM# 240 6 PFENNIG
Silver **Obv:** Crowned oval scepter arms **Rev:** Inscription, date **Rev. Inscription:** 6 / PFENN (or PFENNIG) / BRANDENB / LANDES / MUNZ (or MVNZ) / **Mint:** Kölln **Note:** Varieties exist.

Date	Mintage	VG	F	VF	XF	Unc
1651	486,000	16.00	33.00	65.00	130	—
1652	Inc. above	16.00	33.00	65.00	130	—
1653	Inc. above	16.00	33.00	65.00	130	—
1656	Inc. above	16.00	33.00	65.00	130	—
1657	Inc. above	16.00	33.00	65.00	130	—
1658	Inc. above	16.00	33.00	65.00	130	—
1659	Inc. above	16.00	33.00	65.00	130	—

KM# 406 6 PFENNIG
Silver **Obv:** Crowned scepter arms between palm branches **Rev:** Inscription, date **Mint:** Berlin

Date	Mintage	VG	F	VF	XF	Unc
1670 IL	—	35.00	75.00	150	300	—

KM# 467 6 PFENNIG

Silver **Note:** Varieties exist.

Date	Mintage	VG	F	VF	XF	Unc
1676 CS	—	10.00	20.00	40.00	85.00	—
1678 CS	—	10.00	20.00	40.00	85.00	—
1682 LCS	—	10.00	20.00	40.00	85.00	—
1683 LCS	—	10.00	20.00	40.00	85.00	—
1684 LCS	—	10.00	20.00	40.00	85.00	—
1685 LCS	—	10.00	20.00	40.00	85.00	—
1686 LCS	—	10.00	20.00	40.00	85.00	—
1687 LCS	—	10.00	20.00	40.00	85.00	—

KM# 513 6 PFENNIG

Silver **Rev. Inscription:** 6 / PF.BRAN / DEB... **Mint:** Magdeburg **Note:** Varieties exist.

Date	Mintage	VG	F	VF	XF	Unc
1684 IE	—	10.00	20.00	40.00	85.00	—
1685 IE	—	10.00	20.00	40.00	85.00	—
1686 IE	—	10.00	20.00	40.00	85.00	—
1687 IE	—	10.00	20.00	40.00	85.00	—
1688 ICS	—	10.00	20.00	40.00	85.00	—

KM# 569 6 PFENNIG

Silver **Mint:** Minden **Note:** Varieties exist.

Date	Mintage	VG	F	VF	XF	Unc
1690 BH	—	20.00	40.00	100	200	550
1693 BH	—	20.00	40.00	100	200	550
1695 BH	—	20.00	40.00	100	200	550

KM# 568 6 PFENNIG

Silver **Mint:** Magdeburg

Date	Mintage	VG	F	VF	XF	Unc
1690 IE	—	10.00	20.00	40.00	85.00	—
1691 ICS	—	10.00	20.00	40.00	85.00	—
1692 ICS	—	10.00	20.00	40.00	85.00	—
1693 ICS	—	10.00	20.00	40.00	85.00	—
1694 ICS	—	10.00	20.00	40.00	85.00	—
1695 ICS	—	10.00	20.00	40.00	85.00	—
1700 HFH	—	10.00	20.00	40.00	85.00	—

KM# 592 6 PFENNIG

Silver **Mint:** Berlin

Date	Mintage	VG	F	VF	XF	Unc
1694 LCS	1,048,000	10.00	20.00	40.00	80.00	—
1700 LCS	—	10.00	20.00	40.00	80.00	—

KM# 343 KREUZER

Silver **Obv:** Bust right, value (1) below **Rev:** Silesian eagle, date in legend **Mint:** Krossen

Date	Mintage	VG	F	VF	XF	Unc
1666	—	25.00	55.00	110	—	—

KM# 84 8 PFENNIG

Silver **Obv:** Scepter arms, date above **Rev:** Inscription in circle **Mint:** Berlin

Date	Mintage	VG	F	VF	XF	Unc
16Z0 Rare	—	—	—	—	—	—

KM# 40 3 KREUZER (Groschen)

Silver **Obv:** Crowned eagle with shield on breast divides date **Rev:** Six shields surround Hohenzollern arms **Mint:** Kölln

Date	Mintage	VG	F	VF	XF	Unc
1611	—	—	—	—	—	—
161Z Rare	—	—	—	—	—	—
ND(1612) Rare	—	—	—	—	—	—

KM# 344 3 KREUZER (Groschen)

Silver **Obv:** Bust right, value (3) below **Rev:** Silesian eagle, date in legend **Mint:** Krossen

Date	Mintage	VG	F	VF	XF	Unc
1666	—	50.00	100	175	—	—
1667	—	50.00	100	175	—	—

KM# 113 SOLIDUS (Schilling)

Silver, 16 mm. **Ruler:** Georg Wilhelm **Obv:** Crowned Prussian eagle with 'S' on breast **Obv. Legend:** GOERG WILH. MAR. BR. S. R. I. ELE. **Rev:** GW monogram in circle, date at end of legend **Rev. Legend:** SOLIDVS PRVSSIAE. **Mint:** Königsberg **Note:** Ref. N-10.113; D#314-31.

Date	Mintage	VG	F	VF	XF	Unc
1623 (a)	—	16.00	33.00	65.00	130	—
1624 (a)	44,138	16.00	33.00	65.00	130	—
1625 (a)	2,092,661	10.00	20.00	40.00	85.00	—
1626 (a)	1,119,626	10.00	20.00	40.00	85.00	—
1627 (a)	6,970,425	10.00	20.00	40.00	85.00	—
1628 (a)	4,990,050	10.00	20.00	40.00	85.00	—
1629 (a)	8,586,150	10.00	20.00	40.00	85.00	—
1630 (a)	6,000,000	10.00	20.00	40.00	85.00	—
1631 (a)	—	10.00	20.00	40.00	85.00	—
1633 (a)	7,043,467	10.00	20.00	40.00	85.00	—
1633/23 (a)	Inc. above	—	—	—	—	—

KM# A119 GROSCHEN

Silver **Ruler:** Georg Wilhelm **Obv:** Crowned bust right, titles of Georg Wilhelm **Rev:** Eagle with "S" on breast in circle, date in legend **Rev. Legend:** GROSS. DUC. PRVSSIAE **Mint:** Königsberg **Note:** Ref. N#10.108.

Date	Mintage	VG	F	VF	XF	Unc
1625 (q)	35,000	250	500	1,000	2,000	—

KM# A150 GROSCHEN

Silver **Ruler:** Georg Wilhelm **Obv:** Scepter shield, titles of Georg Wilhelm **Rev:** Eagle with crowend "GV" on breast, small shield of Hohenzollern arms below, date in legend **Mint:** Königsberg **Note:** Ref. N#10.109.

Date	Mintage	VG	F	VF	XF	Unc
1633 (q)	—	—	—	—	—	—

KM# 241 GROSCHEN

Silver **Ruler:** Friedrich Wilhelm **Obv:** Crowned 5-fold arms **Rev. Inscription:** I / GROSCH / BRANDENB / LANDES / MUNZ / date **Mint:** Berlin **Note:** Varieties exist.

Date	Mintage	VG	F	VF	XF	Unc
1651	1,884,000	13.00	27.00	45.00	90.00	—
1652	Inc. above	13.00	27.00	45.00	90.00	—
1653	Inc. above	13.00	27.00	45.00	90.00	—
1659	Inc. above	13.00	27.00	45.00	90.00	—

KM# 616 GROSCHEN

Silver **Ruler:** Friedrich III **Obv:** Crowned scepter arms between palm branches, date divided above **Rev:** Value in four lines **Mint:** Königsberg

Date	Mintage	VG	F	VF	XF	Unc
1699 SD	150,000	25.00	45.00	90.00	185	—

KM# 628 GROSCHEN

Silver **Ruler:** Friedrich III **Rev:** Date at bottom **Mint:** Königsberg

Date	Mintage	VG	F	VF	XF	Unc
1700 CG	100,000	25.00	45.00	90.00	185	—

KM# 6 1/24 THALER (Groschen)

Silver **Ruler:** Joachim Friedrich **Obv:** Ornate 4-fold arms with scepter shield in center, titles of Joachim Friedrich **Rev:** Imperial orb with 24 in baroque frame, date in legend **Mint:** Kölln **Note:** Ref. B#522-525. Varieties exist.

Date	Mintage	VG	F	VF	XF	Unc
1601 (e)	—	375	750	1,500	2,750	—

KM# 20 1/24 THALER (Groschen)

Silver **Ruler:** Joachim Friedrich **Rev:** Imperial orb with 24 in baroque frame divides date **Mint:** Kölln **Note:** Ref. B#526-27. Similar to KM#6.

Date	Mintage	VG	F	VF	XF	Unc
1604 MH	22,000	—	—	—	—	—
1606 MH	—	—	—	—	—	—
1607	—	—	—	—	—	—

KM# A43 1/24 THALER (Groschen)

Silver **Ruler:** Johann Sigismund **Mint:** Driesen **Note:** Ref. B#593, 595. Klippe.

Date	Mintage	VG	F	VF	XF	Unc
161Z HL	—	—	—	—	—	—
1614 HL	—	—	—	—	—	—

KM# 42 1/24 THALER (Groschen)

Silver **Obv:** Imperial orb with 24 divides date **Rev:** 5-fold arms **Mint:** Driesen **Note:** Varieties exist.

Date	Mintage	VG	F	VF	XF	Unc
161Z HL	—	20.00	45.00	75.00	155	—
1613 HL	—	20.00	45.00	75.00	155	—
1614 HL	—	20.00	45.00	75.00	155	—
1615 HL	—	20.00	45.00	75.00	155	—
ND HL	—	20.00	45.00	75.00	155	—

KM# 41 1/24 THALER (Groschen)

Silver **Obv:** Eagle with arms on breast **Rev:** Imperial orb with 24 divides date **Mint:** Kölln

Date	Mintage	VG	F	VF	XF	Unc
1612 MH	530,000	16.00	33.00	60.00	120	—
1613 MH	Inc. above	16.00	33.00	60.00	120	—
1614 MH	325,000	16.00	33.00	60.00	120	—
1615 MH	Inc. above	16.00	33.00	60.00	120	—
1616 MH	466,000	16.00	33.00	60.00	120	—
1617 MH	Inc. above	16.00	33.00	60.00	120	—
1618 MH	—	16.00	33.00	60.00	120	—
1619 MH	—	16.00	33.00	60.00	120	—

KM# 65 1/24 THALER (Groschen)

Silver **Obv:** Imperial orb with 24 **Rev:** 4-fold arms in cruciform **Mint:** Berlin **Note:** Kipper 1/24 Thaler.

Date	Mintage	VG	F	VF	XF	Unc
ND(ca.1620) LM	—	25.00	45.00	85.00	165	—

KM# 104 1/24 THALER (Groschen)

Silver **Rev:** Crowned scepter arms **Mint:** Kölln **Note:** Kipper 1/24 Thaler.

Date	Mintage	VG	F	VF	XF	Unc
ND(1622/23)	—	25.00	40.00	85.00	165	—

KM# 106 1/24 THALER (Groschen)

Silver **Obv:** Imperial orb with 24 divides date **Rev:** Crowned scepter arms **Mint:** Krossen **Note:** Kipper 1/24 Thaler.

Date	Mintage	VG	F	VF	XF	Unc
1622	317,000	20.00	40.00	80.00	160	—
1623	131,000	20.00	40.00	80.00	160	—
ND	—	—	—	—	—	—

KM# 105 1/24 THALER (Groschen)

Silver **Obv:** Crowned scepter arms **Rev:** Imperial orb with 24

Date	Mintage	VG	F	VF	XF	Unc
ND(1622/23)	—	20.00	40.00	80.00	165	—

KM# 109 1/24 THALER (Groschen)

Silver **Obv:** Five small arms around scepter arms in center **Rev:** Imperial orb with 24, cross divides date, all in shield frame **Mint:** Kölln

Date	Mintage	VG	F	VF	XF	Unc
1623 LM	—	27.00	60.00	115	230	—

KM# 110 1/24 THALER (Groschen)

Silver **Ruler:** Georg Wilhelm **Rev:** Orb in oval frame divides date **Mint:** Berlin

Date	Mintage	VG	F	VF	XF	Unc
1623 LM	—	25.00	50.00	100	200	—

KM# 111 1/24 THALER (Groschen)

Silver **Ruler:** Georg Wilhelm **Obv:** 5-fold arms **Rev:** Imperial orb with 24, cross divides date, all in shield frame **Mint:** Berlin

Date	Mintage	VG	F	VF	XF	Unc
16Z3 LM	—	16.00	33.00	75.00	155	—

KM# 115 1/24 THALER (Groschen)

Silver **Ruler:** Georg Wilhelm **Rev:** Date divided outside shield frame **Mint:** Kölln

Date	Mintage	VG	F	VF	XF	Unc
1624 LM	423,000	16.00	32.00	65.00	130	—
1628 LM	79,000	16.00	32.00	65.00	130	—
1631 LM	—	16.00	32.00	65.00	130	—

KM# 116.1 1/24 THALER (Groschen)
Silver **Mint:** Königsberg

Date	Mintage	VG	F	VF	XF	Unc
1624	35,000	16.00	35.00	75.00	155	—
1625	—	16.00	35.00	75.00	155	—
1626	—	16.00	35.00	75.00	155	—

KM# 119 1/24 THALER (Groschen)
Silver **Mint:** Kölln

Date	Mintage	VG	F	VF	XF	Unc
1625 IP	480,000	16.00	35.00	75.00	155	—
1627 IP	117,000	20.00	45.00	95.00	195	—

KM# 140 1/24 THALER (Groschen)
Silver **Obv:** Imperial orb with 24 **Rev:** 5-fold arms, date above **Mint:** Berlin

Date	Mintage	VG	F	VF	XF	Unc
1631 LM	—	22.00	45.00	90.00	185	—
1632 LM	—	22.00	45.00	90.00	185	—
1633 LM	—	22.00	45.00	90.00	185	—
1634 LM	—	22.00	45.00	90.00	185	—
1635 LM	—	22.00	45.00	90.00	185	—
1636 LM	—	22.00	45.00	90.00	185	—

KM# 116.2 1/24 THALER (Groschen)
Silver

Date	Mintage	VG	F	VF	XF	Unc
1634	33,000	16.00	35.00	75.00	155	—
1635	Inc. above	—	—	—	—	—

KM# 244 1/24 THALER (Groschen)
Silver **Ruler:** Friedrich Wilhelm **Obv:** Bust with large head right **Rev:** Scepter arms in baroque frame, value Z-4 in two ovals below divide date **Mint:** Halberstadt

Date	Mintage	VG	F	VF	XF	Unc
1651	100,539	25.00	50.00	100	200	—

KM# 245 1/24 THALER (Groschen)
1.7600 g., Silver, 22-23 mm. **Ruler:** Friedrich Wilhelm **Obv:** Smaller head **Rev:** Value 24 in oval divides date **Mint:** Halberstadt **Note:** Varieties exist.

Date	Mintage	VG	F	VF	XF	Unc
1651	Inc. above	20.00	40.00	85.00	175	—
1656	1,246,459	20.00	40.00	85.00	175	—
1657	1,134,300	20.00	40.00	85.00	175	—
1658	907,867	20.00	40.00	85.00	175	—
1659	958,034	20.00	40.00	85.00	175	—
1660	366,975	20.00	40.00	85.00	175	—

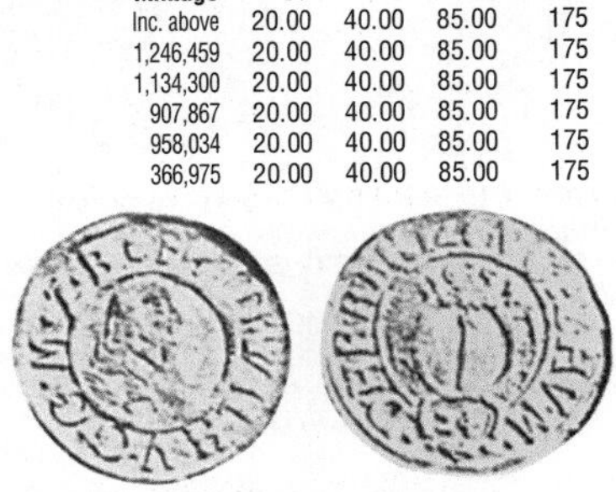

KM# 246 1/24 THALER (Groschen)
Silver **Ruler:** Friedrich Wilhelm **Rev:** Date above arms **Mint:** Halberstadt **Note:** Varieties exist.

Date	Mintage	VG	F	VF	XF	Unc
1651	Inc. above	20.00	40.00	85.00	175	—
1652	—	20.00	40.00	85.00	175	—
1653	300,000	20.00	40.00	85.00	175	—

KM# 264 1/24 THALER (Groschen)
Silver **Ruler:** Friedrich Wilhelm **Rev:** Date divided below value **Mint:** Halberstadt **Note:** Varieties exist.

Date	Mintage	VG	F	VF	XF	Unc
1653	Inc. above	15.00	30.00	60.00	125	—
1654	450,000	15.00	30.00	60.00	125	—
1655	600,000	15.00	30.00	60.00	125	—
1656	Inc. above	15.00	30.00	60.00	125	—
1658	Inc. above	15.00	30.00	60.00	125	—
1659	Inc. above	15.00	30.00	60.00	125	—
1660	Inc. above	15.00	30.00	60.00	125	—
1661	118,857	15.00	30.00	60.00	125	—

KM# 265 1/24 THALER (Groschen)
Silver **Obv:** Eagle with oval scepter arms on breast **Rev:** Inscription, date in legend **Rev. Inscription:** HALBER / STETISCHE / LANDMVNZ / Z4

Date	Mintage	VG	F	VF	XF	Unc
1653	Inc. above	—	—	—	—	—

KM# 319 1/24 THALER (Groschen)
Silver **Obv:** Eagle, scepter arms on breast **Rev:** Imperial orb with 24 divides date **Mint:** Berlin

Date	Mintage	VG	F	VF	XF	Unc
1661 AB	371,571	15.00	30.00	60.00	125	—
1662 AB	671,829	15.00	30.00	60.00	125	—
1663 AB	124,153	15.00	30.00	60.00	125	—
1664 AB	83,258	15.00	30.00	60.00	125	—

KM# 337 1/24 THALER (Groschen)
Silver **Obv:** Bust right **Rev:** Eagle, scepter arms on breast, divides date at bottom

Date	Mintage	VG	F	VF	XF	Unc
1665	—	15.00	30.00	60.00	125	—
1666	—	15.00	30.00	60.00	125	—

KM# 346 1/24 THALER (Groschen)
Silver **Ruler:** Friedrich Wilhelm **Rev:** 24 on eagle's breast **Mint:** Berlin

Date	Mintage	VG	F	VF	XF	Unc
1666	—	12.00	27.00	55.00	115	—
1666 IL	—	12.00	27.00	55.00	115	—
1667 IL	—	12.00	27.00	55.00	115	—

KM# 349 1/24 THALER (Groschen)
Silver **Ruler:** Friedrich Wilhelm **Obv:** Crowned 5-fold arms **Rev. Inscription:** 24 / EINEN / REICHS / THALER / date **Mint:** Berlin

Date	Mintage	VG	F	VF	XF	Unc
1667 IL	—	9.00	20.00	40.00	85.00	—
1668 IL	—	9.00	20.00	40.00	85.00	—

KM# 350 1/24 THALER (Groschen)
Silver **Ruler:** Friedrich Wilhelm **Obv:** Date divided by crown at top **Mint:** Berlin

Date	Mintage	VG	F	VF	XF	Unc
1667 IL	—	9.00	20.00	40.00	85.00	—

KM# 351 1/24 THALER (Groschen)
Silver **Ruler:** Friedrich Wilhelm **Rev:** Date also at bottom **Mint:** Berlin **Note:** Varieties exist.

Date	Mintage	VG	F	VF	XF	Unc
1667 IL	—	10.00	20.00	40.00	85.00	—
1667/8 IL	—	10.00	20.00	40.00	85.00	—
1668 IL	—	10.00	20.00	40.00	85.00	—

KM# 352 1/24 THALER (Groschen)
Silver **Obv:** Crowned 5-fold arms, crown divides date **Mint:** Krossen **Note:** Varieties exist.

Date	Mintage	VG	F	VF	XF	Unc
1667 IPE	—	10.00	20.00	40.00	85.00	—
1667 GF	—	10.00	20.00	40.00	85.00	—
1668 GF	—	10.00	20.00	40.00	85.00	—

KM# 372 1/24 THALER (Groschen)
Silver **Ruler:** Friedrich Wilhelm **Obv:** Crowned 5-fold arms **Rev:** Imperial orb with 24 divides date at top **Mint:** Krossen **Note:** Varieties exist.

Date	Mintage	VG	F	VF	XF	Unc
1668 GF	—	10.00	20.00	40.00	85.00	—
1669 GF	—	10.00	20.00	40.00	85.00	—
1670 GF	—	10.00	20.00	40.00	85.00	—
1671 GF	—	10.00	20.00	40.00	85.00	—
1672 GF	—	10.00	20.00	40.00	85.00	—
1674 GF	—	10.00	20.00	40.00	85.00	—

KM# 374 1/24 THALER (Groschen)
Silver **Ruler:** Friedrich Wilhelm **Rev:** Imperial orb with 24 divides date **Mint:** Berlin **Note:** Varieties exist.

Date	Mintage	VG	F	VF	XF	Unc
1668 IL	—	10.00	20.00	40.00	85.00	—
1669 IL	—	10.00	20.00	40.00	85.00	—
1670 IL	—	10.00	20.00	40.00	85.00	—
1671 IL	—	10.00	20.00	40.00	85.00	—
1672 IL	—	10.00	20.00	40.00	85.00	—
1673 IL	—	10.00	20.00	40.00	85.00	—
1674 IL	—	10.00	20.00	40.00	85.00	—
1675 CS	—	10.00	20.00	40.00	85.00	—

KM# 373 1/24 THALER (Groschen)
Silver **Rev. Inscription:** 24 / 1.R / THAL / date **Mint:** Berlin

Date	Mintage	VG	F	VF	XF	Unc
1668 IL	—	27.00	55.00	115	230	—

KM# 388 1/24 THALER (Groschen)
Silver **Ruler:** Friedrich Wilhelm **Rev. Inscription:** 24 / 1.R. / THALER / date **Mint:** Berlin / Kölln

Date	Mintage	VG	F	VF	XF	Unc
1668 IL	—	27.00	55.00	115	230	—
1669 IL	—	27.00	55.00	115	230	—

KM# 389 1/24 THALER (Groschen)
Silver **Ruler:** Friedrich Wilhelm **Obv:** Arms **Rev:** Value **Mint:** Minden

Date	Mintage	VG	F	VF	XF	Unc
1669 HB	—	13.00	32.00	65.00	130	—
1670 HB	—	13.00	32.00	65.00	130	—
1671 IW	—	13.00	32.00	65.00	130	—
1672 IW	—	13.00	32.00	65.00	130	—
1679 AVH	—	13.00	32.00	65.00	130	—
1683 BH	—	13.00	32.00	65.00	130	—

KM# 442 1/24 THALER (Groschen)
Silver **Ruler:** Friedrich Wilhelm **Obv:** Imperial orb with 24, date in legend **Mint:** Berlin

Date	Mintage	VG	F	VF	XF	Unc
1675 CS	—	13.00	30.00	60.00	120	—

KM# 483 1/24 THALER (Groschen)

Silver **Ruler:** Friedrich Wilhelm **Obv:** Shield of arms **Rev:** 5-line inscription within inner circle **Mint:** Halberstadt

Date	Mintage	VG	F	VF	XF	Unc
1679 LCS	—	12.00	25.00	50.00	100	—

KM# 484 1/24 THALER (Groschen)

Silver **Ruler:** Friedrich Wilhelm **Obv:** Bust **Rev:** Value **Mint:** Minden

Date	Mintage	VG	F	VF	XF	Unc
1679 AVH	—	30.00	75.00	150	300	—

KM# 482 1/24 THALER (Groschen)

Silver **Rev. Inscription:** 24 / EINEN / REICHS / THALER / date **Note:** Varieties exist.

Date	Mintage	VG	F	VF	XF	Unc
1679 CS	—	10.00	20.00	40.00	85.00	—
1684 LCS	—	10.00	20.00	40.00	85.00	—
1685 LCS	—	10.00	20.00	40.00	85.00	—

KM# 485 1/24 THALER (Groschen)

Silver **Ruler:** Friedrich Wilhelm **Obv:** Crowned 5-fold arms **Rev:** Imperial orb with 24 **Mint:** Minden **Note:** Varieties exist.

Date	Mintage	VG	F	VF	XF	Unc
1679	—	16.00	32.00	65.00	130	—
1679 AVH	—	16.00	32.00	65.00	130	—
1683 BH	—	16.00	32.00	65.00	130	—

KM# 503 1/24 THALER (Groschen)

Silver **Ruler:** Friedrich Wilhelm **Obv:** Date in legend **Mint:** Berlin **Note:** Varieties exist.

Date	Mintage	VG	F	VF	XF	Unc
1682 LCS	—	10.00	20.00	40.00	85.00	—
1683 LCS	—	10.00	20.00	40.00	85.00	—

KM# 505 1/24 THALER (Groschen)

Silver **Ruler:** Friedrich Wilhelm **Obv:** Crowned 5-fold arms **Rev. Inscription:** 24 / EINEN / REICHS / THALER / date **Mint:** Magdeburg **Note:** Varieties exist.

Date	Mintage	VG	F	VF	XF	Unc
1683 IE	—	—	—	—	—	—
1685 IE	—	—	—	—	—	—
1687 IE	—	—	—	—	—	—

KM# 549 1/24 THALER (Groschen)

Silver **Ruler:** Friedrich III **Obv:** Arms divide date **Mint:** Berlin **Note:** Varieties exist.

Date	Mintage	VG	F	VF	XF	Unc
1689 LCS	103,000	20.00	40.00	80.00	165	—

KM# 345 6 KREUZER

Silver **Obv:** Crowned bust right **Rev:** Crowned triple arms, date in legend **Mint:** Krossen

Date	Mintage	VG	F	VF	XF	Unc
1666	—	250	500	950	—	—
(16)66	—	250	500	950	—	—

KM# 263 SCHILLING (1/32 Thaler)

Silver **Obv:** Crowned eagle, value 1 on breast **Rev:** FW monogram, date in legend

Date	Mintage	VG	F	VF	XF	Unc
1653	3,783,000	12.00	25.00	50.00	100	—
1654	5,595,000	12.00	25.00	50.00	100	—
1655	1,693,000	12.00	25.00	50.00	100	—

KM# 288 SCHILLING (1/32 Thaler)

Silver **Obv:** FWC monogram divides date **Rev:** Value in three lines

Date	Mintage	VG	F	VF	XF	Unc
1657	1,080,000	13.00	27.00	50.00	100	—
1657	Inc. above	13.00	27.00	50.00	100	—
1658	—	13.00	27.00	50.00	100	—
1658	Inc. above	13.00	27.00	50.00	100	—
1659	—	—	—	—	—	—
1659	47,000	13.00	27.00	50.00	100	—

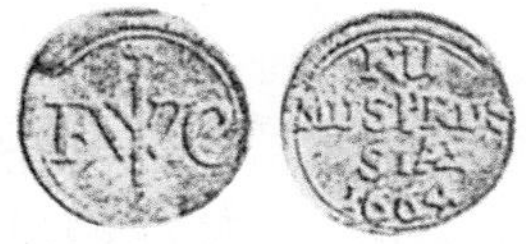

KM# 330 SCHILLING (1/32 Thaler)

Silver **Obv:** FWC monogram behind scepter **Rev. Inscription:** NU / MUS. PRUS / SIAE / date

Date	Mintage	VG	F	VF	XF	Unc
1664	997,000	27.00	55.00	110	220	—
1665	Inc. above	27.00	55.00	110	220	—

KM# 387 SCHILLING (1/32 Thaler)

Silver **Obv:** Crowned FWC monogram **Rev:** Value, date in four lines

Date	Mintage	VG	F	VF	XF	Unc
1669	2,141,000	13.00	27.00	55.00	110	—
1670	7,830,000	13.00	27.00	55.00	110	—
1671	Inc. above	13.00	27.00	55.00	110	—

KM# 590 SCHILLING (1/32 Thaler)

Silver **Ruler:** Friedrich III **Obv:** Crowned FC III monogram **Rev:** Value, date in four lines **Mint:** Königsberg

Date	Mintage	VG	F	VF	XF	Unc
1693 HS	4,340,091	10.00	20.00	40.00	85.00	—
1694 HS	760,839	10.00	20.00	40.00	85.00	—
1695 SD	612,000	10.00	20.00	40.00	85.00	—
1697 SD	737,000	10.00	20.00	40.00	85.00	—
1698 SD	1,473,000	10.00	20.00	40.00	85.00	—
1699 SD	737,000	10.00	20.00	40.00	85.00	—
1700 CG	300,000	10.00	20.00	40.00	85.00	—

KM# A56 2 SCHILLING (1/16 Thaler)

Silver **Ruler:** Georg Wilhelm **Obv:** Eagle, scepter shield on breast, titles of Georg Wilhelm **Rev:** Intertwined "DS", date below, titles continuous **Mint:** Berlin **Note:** Ref. B#612-13. Kipper 2 Schilling.

Date	Mintage	VG	F	VF	XF	Unc
16Z1 LM	—	—	—	—	—	—
16Z1	—	—	—	—	—	—

KM# 93 2 SCHILLING (1/16 Thaler)

Silver **Obv:** Eagle, scepter arms on breast **Rev:** Imperial orb without value **Mint:** Berlin

Date	Mintage	VG	F	VF	XF	Unc
1622	—	—	—	—	—	—

KM# 94 2 GROSCHEN (1/12 Thaler)

Silver **Ruler:** Georg Wilhelm **Obv:** Bust right, value 2 below **Rev:** Oval scepter arms in baroque frame **Mint:** Krossen

Date	Mintage	VG	F	VF	XF	Unc
ND(1622/23)	9,880	—	—	—	—	—

KM# 95 2 GROSCHEN (1/12 Thaler)

Silver **Ruler:** Georg Wilhelm **Obv:** Value II

Date	Mintage	VG	F	VF	XF	Unc
ND(1622/23)	Inc. above	—	—	—	—	—

KM# 149 2 GROSCHEN (1/12 Thaler)

Silver **Ruler:** Georg Wilhelm **Mint:** Königsberg

Date	Mintage	VG	F	VF	XF	Unc
1634	—	—	—	—	—	—

KM# 242 2 GROSCHEN (1/12 Thaler)

Silver **Ruler:** Friedrich Wilhelm **Obv:** Crowned 5-fold arms **Rev. Inscription:** II / GROSCH / BRANDENB / LANDES / MUNZ / date **Mint:** Kölln **Note:** Varieties exist.

Date	Mintage	VG	F	VF	XF	Unc
1651	16,051,000	20.00	40.00	85.00	170	—
1652	Inc. above	20.00	40.00	85.00	170	—
1653	Inc. above	20.00	40.00	85.00	170	—
1654	Inc. above	20.00	40.00	85.00	170	—
1655	Inc. above	20.00	40.00	85.00	170	—
1656	Inc. above	20.00	40.00	85.00	170	—
1657	Inc. above	20.00	40.00	85.00	170	—
1658	Inc. above	20.00	40.00	85.00	170	—
1659	Inc. above	20.00	40.00	85.00	170	—
1660	Inc. above	20.00	40.00	85.00	170	—

KM# A149 1/12 THALER (Doppelgroschen)

Silver **Ruler:** Georg Wilhelm **Obv:** Crowned bust right, titles of Georg Wilhelm **Rev:** Legend, date **Rev. Legend:** ✠MONE. NOV. ARG. DVCIS. PRVSS. **Rev. Inscription:** XII / EINEN / REICHS / TALER / ✠ **Mint:** Königsberg **Note:** Ref. D#602.

Date	Mintage	VG	F	VF	XF	Unc
1634	—	—	—	—	—	—

KM# B149 1/12 THALER (Doppelgroschen)

Silver **Ruler:** Georg Wilhelm **Obv:** Crowned bust right, titles of Georg Wilhellm **Rev. Inscription:** MONE: / NOVA • ARG: / DVC • PRVSSIAE / +XII+ / EINEN • REICHS / • THALER • / • date• **Mint:** Königsberg **Note:** Ref. D#603.

Date	Mintage	VG	F	VF	XF	Unc
1634	—	—	—	—	—	—

Note: The above coin is possibly a pattern

KM# 486 1/12 THALER (Doppelgroschen)

Silver **Ruler:** Friedrich Wilhelm **Mint:** Berlin **Note:** Varieties exist.

Date	Mintage	VG	F	VF	XF	Unc
1679 CS	—	16.00	35.00	75.00	150	—
1683 IL	—	16.00	35.00	75.00	150	—
1683 LCS	—	16.00	35.00	75.00	150	—
1684 LCS	—	16.00	35.00	75.00	150	—
1685 LCS	—	16.00	35.00	75.00	150	—
1686 LCS	—	16.00	35.00	75.00	150	—
1687 LCS	2,674,000	16.00	35.00	75.00	150	—
1688 LCS	Inc. above	16.00	35.00	75.00	150	—

KM# 487 1/12 THALER (Doppelgroschen)

Silver **Ruler:** Friedrich Wilhelm **Obv:** Crowned 5-fold arms **Rev. Inscription:** 12 / EINEN / REICHS / THALER / date **Mint:** Halberstadt

Date	Mintage	VG	F	VF	XF	Unc
1679 LCS	—	—	—	—	—	—

KM# 507 1/12 THALER (Doppelgroschen)

Silver **Ruler:** Friedrich Wilhelm **Mint:** Minden

Date	Mintage	VG	F	VF	XF	Unc
1683 BH	—	15.00	32.00	65.00	130	—
1684 BH	—	15.00	32.00	65.00	130	—
1685 BH	—	15.00	32.00	65.00	130	—
1686 SD	—	15.00	32.00	65.00	130	—

KM# 506 1/12 THALER (Doppelgroschen)

Silver **Ruler:** Friedrich III **Mint:** Magdeburg **Note:** Varieties exist.

Date	Mintage	VG	F	VF	XF	Unc
1683 IE	—	20.00	35.00	75.00	155	—
1684 IE	—	20.00	35.00	75.00	155	—

Date	Mintage	VG	F	VF	XF	Unc
1685 IE	—	20.00	35.00	75.00	155	—
1686 IE	—	20.00	35.00	75.00	155	—
1687 IE	—	20.00	35.00	75.00	155	—
1689 IE	—	20.00	35.00	75.00	155	—

KM# 533 1/12 THALER (Doppelgroschen)
Silver **Ruler:** Friedrich Wilhelm **Rev:** 5-line inscription **Rev. Inscription:** 12 / EINEN / REICHS / THAL / date **Mint:** Magdeburg **Note:** Varieties exist.

Date	Mintage	VG	F	VF	XF	Unc
1687 IE	—	25.00	40.00	80.00	165	—
1688 IE	—	25.00	40.00	80.00	165	—
1688 ICS	—	25.00	40.00	80.00	165	—

KM# 532 1/12 THALER (Doppelgroschen)
34.0000 g., Copper, 31 mm. **Ruler:** Friedrich Wilhelm **Mint:** Magdeburg **Note:** Klippe.

Date	Mintage	VG	F	VF	XF	Unc
1687 IS	—	—	100	200	400	—

KM# 550 1/12 THALER (Doppelgroschen)
Silver **Ruler:** Friedrich III **Mint:** Berlin **Note:** Varieties exist.

Date	Mintage	VG	F	VF	XF	Unc
1689 LCS	681,000	16.00	35.00	75.00	155	—
1692 LCS	Inc. above	16.00	35.00	75.00	155	—

KM# 551 1/12 THALER (Doppelgroschen)
Silver **Ruler:** Friedrich III **Obv:** Arms divide date **Mint:** Halberstadt **Note:** Varieties exist.

Date	Mintage	VG	F	VF	XF	Unc
1689 LCS	Inc. above	16.00	35.00	75.00	155	—
1690 LCS	2,653,000	16.00	35.00	75.00	155	—
1691 LCS	4,903,000	16.00	35.00	75.00	155	—
1692 LCS	Inc. above	16.00	35.00	75.00	155	—

KM# 552 1/12 THALER (Doppelgroschen)
Silver **Ruler:** Friedrich III **Mint:** Stargard

Date	Mintage	VG	F	VF	XF	Unc
1689 SD	—	15.00	30.00	60.00	120	—
1690 SD	—	15.00	30.00	60.00	120	—
1691 SD	—	15.00	30.00	60.00	120	—

KM# 553 1/12 THALER (Doppelgroschen)
Silver **Ruler:** Friedrich III **Obv:** Crowned oval arms **Rev. Inscription:** 12 / EINEN / REICHS / THALE / date **Mint:** Minden

Date	Mintage	VG	F	VF	XF	Unc
1689 BH	—	15.00	30.00	60.00	120	—
1690 BH	—	15.00	30.00	60.00	120	—
1691 BH	—	15.00	30.00	60.00	120	—
1693 BH	—	15.00	30.00	60.00	120	—
1695 BH	—	15.00	30.00	60.00	120	—

KM# 571 1/12 THALER (Doppelgroschen)
Silver **Ruler:** Friedrich III **Mint:** Magdeburg

Date	Mintage	VG	F	VF	XF	Unc
1690 IE	—	15.00	30.00	60.00	120	—
1691 ICS	—	15.00	30.00	60.00	120	—
1692 ICS	—	15.00	30.00	60.00	120	—
1693 ICS	—	15.00	30.00	60.00	120	—

Date	Mintage	VG	F	VF	XF	Unc
1699 HFH	—	15.00	30.00	60.00	120	—
1700 HFH	—	15.00	30.00	60.00	120	—

KM# 572 1/12 THALER (Doppelgroschen)
Silver **Ruler:** Friedrich III **Mint:** Stargard

Date	Mintage	VG	F	VF	XF	Unc
1690 SD	—	15.00	30.00	60.00	120	—

KM# 580 1/12 THALER (Doppelgroschen)
3.4000 g., Silver, 25.8 mm. **Ruler:** Friedrich III **Mint:** Berlin

Date	Mintage	VG	F	VF	XF	Unc
1692 LCS	Inc. above	15.00	30.00	60.00	120	—
1693 LCS	5,489,000	15.00	30.00	60.00	120	—
1699 LCS	204,000	15.00	30.00	60.00	120	—
1700 LCS	993,000	15.00	30.00	60.00	120	—

KM# 581 1/12 THALER (Doppelgroschen)
Silver **Ruler:** Friedrich III **Mint:** Stargard

Date	Mintage	VG	F	VF	XF	Unc
1692 SD	—	—	—	—	—	—

KM# 582 1/12 THALER (Doppelgroschen)
Silver **Ruler:** Friedrich III **Mint:** Magdeburg

Date	Mintage	VG	F	VF	XF	Unc
1692 ICS	—	15.00	30.00	60.00	120	—
1693 ICS	—	15.00	30.00	60.00	120	—
1698 HFH	—	15.00	30.00	60.00	120	—
1699 HFH	—	15.00	30.00	60.00	120	—
1700 HFH	—	15.00	30.00	60.00	120	—

KM# 338 24 PFENNIG
Silver **Obv:** Bust right **Rev:** Silesian eagle, value (XXIIII) below, date in legend **Mint:** Krossen

Date	Mintage	VG	F	VF	XF	Unc
1665	—	—	—	—	—	—

KM# 339 15 KREUZER (1/6 Taler)
Silver **Obv:** Bust right, value XV below **Rev:** Silesian eagle (crescent and cross on breast), date in legend **Mint:** Krossen

Date	Mintage	VG	F	VF	XF	Unc
1665	—	—	—	—	—	—

KM# 531 15 KREUZER (1/6 Taler)
Silver **Mint:** Berlin **Note:** Coinage for District of Krossen.

Date	Mintage	VG	F	VF	XF	Unc
1687 LCS	255,000	30.00	65.00	125	230	—

KM# 92 24 KREUZER
Silver **Obv:** Bust right, balue 24 below **Rev:** Crowned eagle with scepter arms on breast **Mint:** Krossen **Note:** Kipper.

Date	Mintage	VG	F	VF	XF	Unc
ND(1622)	3,734	—	—	—	—	—

KM# 617 2 GROSCHEN
Silver **Ruler:** Friedrich III **Obv:** Crowned eagle **Rev:** Value, date in six lines **Mint:** Königsberg

Date	Mintage	VG	F	VF	XF	Unc
1699 SD	75,000	13.00	27.00	55.00	110	—
1700 CG	50,000	13.00	27.00	55.00	110	—

KM# 97 3 GROSCHEN
Silver **Obv:** Bust right, value III below **Rev:** Crowned eagle with scepter arms on breast divides date **Mint:** Krossen

Date	Mintage	VG	F	VF	XF	Unc
1622	97,000	25.00	50.00	100	200	—

KM# 98 3 GROSCHEN
Silver **Obv:** Without crown above eagle

Date	Mintage	VG	F	VF	XF	Unc
1622	Inc. above	20.00	40.00	80.00	160	—
(16)22	Inc. above	20.00	40.00	80.00	160	—
1623	2,851,000	20.00	40.00	80.00	160	—

KM# 96 3 GROSCHEN
Silver **Obv:** Eagle with scepter arms on breast **Rev:** Imperial orb with value 3 G **Mint:** Kölln **Note:** Kipper 3 Groschen.

Date	Mintage	VG	F	VF	XF	Unc
ND(1622/23)	—	20.00	40.00	80.00	160	—

KM# 602 3 GROSCHEN
Silver **Ruler:** Friedrich III **Mint:** Königsberg **Note:** Varieties exist.

Date	Mintage	VG	F	VF	XF	Unc
1695 SD	1,384,000	10.00	20.00	55.00	110	—
1696 SD	2,800,000	10.00	20.00	55.00	110	—
1697 SD	650,000	10.00	20.00	55.00	110	—
1698 SD	5,850,000	10.00	20.00	55.00	110	—
1699 SD	Inc. above	10.00	20.00	55.00	110	—
1700 CG	360,000	10.00	20.00	55.00	110	—

KM# 61 4 GROSCHEN
Silver **Obv:** Bust right **Rev:** Four oval arms in cartouche, one at top divides date, value IIII / GROS in center **Mint:** Berlin

Date	Mintage	VG	F	VF	XF	Unc
16Z0 LM	—	25.00	45.00	90.00	185	—

KM# 62 4 GROSCHEN
Silver **Rev:** Value in center IIII only

Date	Mintage	VG	F	VF	XF	Unc
16Z0 LM	—	25.00	45.00	90.00	185	—
16Z1 LM	—	25.00	45.00	90.00	185	—

KM# 63 6 GROSCHEN
Silver, 27 mm. **Ruler:** Georg Wilhelm **Obv:** Armored bust to right **Obv. Legend:** GEORG. WILHELM. V. G. G. M. Z. BRAND. **Rev:** Eagle with scepter shield on breast divides date, VI below in margin **Rev. Legend:** D. H. R. R. ERTZC. V. - CHVRF. I. P. Z. G. C. B. **Mint:** Berlin **Note:** Ref. B-619-22. Kipper issue. Varieties exist.

Date	Mintage	VG	F	VF	XF	Unc
16Z0 LM	—	175	375	750	1,500	—
16Z1	—	175	375	750	1,500	—
16Z1 LM	—	175	375	750	1,500	—

KM# 101 6 GROSCHEN
Silver **Rev:** Date divided below arms

Date	Mintage	VG	F	VF	XF	Unc
1622	Inc. above	35.00	65.00	130	265	—
1623	129,000	35.00	65.00	130	265	—

KM# 99 6 GROSCHEN
Silver **Obv:** Eagle with scepter arms on breast **Rev:** Imperial orb with 6 G **Mint:** Kölln **Note:** Kipper 6 Groschen.

Date	Mintage	VG	F	VF	XF	Unc
ND(1622/23)	—	16.00	33.00	60.00	120	—

KM# 100 6 GROSCHEN
Silver **Obv:** Bust right, value VI below **Rev:** Oval scepter arms in baroque frame, imperial orb with 6 above divides date **Mint:** Krossen **Note:** Kipper 6 Groschen.

Date	Mintage	VG	F	VF	XF	Unc
1622	151,000	27.00	45.00	90.00	185	—

KM# 297 6 GROSCHEN

Silver **Ruler:** Friedrich Wilhelm **Obv:** Crowned bust right **Mint:** Königsberg

Date	Mintage	VG	F	VF	XF	Unc
1658 (r)	288,000	20.00	40.00	80.00	160	—
1659 (r)	288,000	20.00	40.00	80.00	160	—

KM# 429 6 GROSCHEN

Silver **Note:** Varieties exist.

Date	Mintage	VG	F	VF	XF	Unc
1674 CV	104,000	30.00	55.00	90.00	185	—
1679 HS	1,114,000	16.00	33.00	55.00	115	175
1680 HS	Inc. above	16.00	33.00	55.00	115	175
1681 HS	1,650,000	16.00	33.00	55.00	115	175
1682 HS	4,400,000	16.00	33.00	55.00	115	175
1683 HS	3,367,000	16.00	33.00	55.00	115	175
1684 HS	4,193,000	16.00	33.00	55.00	115	175
1685 HS	1,043,000	16.00	33.00	55.00	115	175
1685 BA	Inc. above	16.00	33.00	55.00	115	175
1686 BA	Inc. above	16.00	33.00	55.00	115	175
1687 HS	480,000	16.00	33.00	55.00	115	175
1688 HS	Inc. above	16.00	33.00	55.00	115	175

KM# 519 6 GROSCHEN

Silver **Obv:** Laureate bust right **Rev:** Crowned triple arms, date divided below, value VI **Mint:** Berlin **Note:** Coinage for Province of Prussia.

Date	Mintage	VG	F	VF	XF	Unc
1685 LCS	866,000	20.00	40.00	80.00	160	—

KM# 610 6 GROSCHEN

Silver **Note:** Varieties exist.

Date	Mintage	VG	F	VF	XF	Unc
1698 SD	1,528,972	16.00	33.00	55.00	115	—
1699 SD	Inc. above	16.00	33.00	55.00	115	—
1700 CG	273,500	16.00	33.00	55.00	115	—

KM# 64 8 GROSCHEN

Silver **Ruler:** Georg Wilhelm **Obv:** Bust right **Rev:** Scepter arms in ornamented frame divide date, value VIII below in legend **Mint:** Berlin **Note:** Varieties exist.

Date	Mintage	VG	F	VF	XF	Unc
1620 LM	—	65.00	130	275	550	—
16Z1 LM	—	65.00	130	275	550	—
16Z1	—	65.00	130	275	550	—
162Z	—	65.00	130	275	550	—

KM# 85 12 GROSCHEN

Silver **Obv:** Eagle with scepter arms on breast divides date, value XII below **Rev:** Imperial orb and seven small shields around center in which value "1Z G" appears **Mint:** Berlin

Date	Mintage	VG	F	VF	XF	Unc
1621	—	—	—	—	—	—

KM# 102 12 GROSCHEN

Silver **Obv:** Bust right, value XII below **Rev:** Eagle with scepter arms on breast, date divided below **Mint:** Krossen **Note:** Kipper 12 Groschen.

Date	Mintage	VG	F	VF	XF	Unc
1622	33,000	40.00	65.00	130	260	—

KM# 103 12 GROSCHEN

Silver **Rev:** Crown above eagle **Note:** Kipper 12 Groschen.

Date	Mintage	VG	F	VF	XF	Unc
1622	Inc. above	55.00	100	200	400	—
1623	12,000	55.00	100	200	400	—
ND	Inc. above	55.00	100	200	400	—

KM# 243 18 GROSCHEN (1/5 Thaler)

Silver **Obv:** Crowned half-length figure right **Rev:** 5-fold arms divide 18 and mintmaster's initials (or only 18 and initials), crown above dvides date **Mint:** Königsberg

Date	Mintage	VG	F	VF	XF	Unc
1651 CM	53,000	32.00	65.00	130	260	—
1652 CM	27,000	45.00	90.00	180	360	—
1655 CM	80,000	25.00	55.00	115	230	—
1656	Inc. above	25.00	55.00	115	230	—
1656 CM	318,000	25.00	55.00	115	230	—
1656 DK	Inc. above	25.00	55.00	115	230	—
1657 CM	—	25.00	55.00	115	230	—
1657 DK	265,000	25.00	55.00	115	230	—
1657 NB	Inc. above	25.00	55.00	115	230	—
1658 NB	53,000	32.00	65.00	130	265	—

KM# 311 18 GROSCHEN (1/5 Thaler)

Silver **Ruler:** Friedrich Wilhelm **Obv:** Bust right **Rev:** Eagle divides value 1-8 **Mint:** Königsberg

Date	Mintage	VG	F	VF	XF	Unc
MDCLX (1660) HM	162,827	32.00	65.00	130	265	—

KM# 318 18 GROSCHEN (1/5 Thaler)

Silver **Ruler:** Friedrich Wilhelm **Rev:** Arabic date **Mint:** Königsberg

Date	Mintage	VG	F	VF	XF	Unc
1661 HM	148,717	32.00	65.00	130	265	—
1662 HM	144,029	32.00	65.00	130	265	—
1663 HM	95,977	32.00	65.00	130	265	—

KM# 331 18 GROSCHEN (1/5 Thaler)

Silver **Ruler:** Friedrich Wilhelm **Rev:** Without value, date in legend **Mint:** Königsberg

Date	Mintage	VG	F	VF	XF	Unc
1664	27,133	27.00	50.00	100	210	—

KM# 336 18 GROSCHEN (1/5 Thaler)

Silver **Ruler:** Friedrich Wilhelm **Rev:** Arms divide value 1-8 **Mint:** Königsberg

Date	Mintage	VG	F	VF	XF	Unc
1665	122,200	27.00	50.00	100	210	—
1666	69,365	27.00	55.00	110	220	—
1667	30,037	27.00	55.00	110	220	—

KM# 431 18 GROSCHEN (1/5 Thaler)

Silver **Ruler:** Friedrich Wilhelm **Obv:** Head right **Rev:** Crowned 5-fold arms divide 1-8, date in legend

Date	Mintage	VG	F	VF	XF	Unc
1674 CV	30,000	27.00	55.00	110	220	—
1674 HS	369,380	27.00	55.00	110	220	—

KM# 440 18 GROSCHEN (1/5 Thaler)

Silver **Ruler:** Friedrich Wilhelm **Obv:** Laureate bust right

Date	Mintage	VG	F	VF	XF	Unc
1675 HS	106,000	27.00	50.00	100	210	—

KM# 441 18 GROSCHEN (1/5 Thaler)

Silver **Obv:** Crowned bust right **Rev:** Crowned eagle divides 1-8

Date	Mintage	VG	F	VF	XF	Unc
MDCLXXV (1675) HS	Inc. above	27.00	50.00	100	210	—
MDCLXXVI (1676) HS	158,000	27.00	50.00	100	210	—

KM# 468 18 GROSCHEN (1/5 Thaler)

6.5000 g., Silver, 29.1 mm.

Date	Mintage	VG	F	VF	XF	Unc
1676 HS	Inc. above	16.00	35.00	75.00	155	—
1679 HS	120,000	16.00	35.00	75.00	155	—
1680 HS	Inc. above	16.00	35.00	75.00	155	—
1681 HS	178,000	16.00	35.00	75.00	155	—
1682 HS	474,000	16.00	35.00	75.00	155	—
1683 HS	364,000	16.00	35.00	75.00	155	—
1684 HS	1,109,000	16.00	35.00	75.00	155	—
1685 HS	3,316,000	16.00	35.00	75.00	155	—
1685 BA	337,000	16.00	35.00	75.00	155	—
1686 BA	Inc. above	16.00	35.00	75.00	155	—
1687 BA	—	16.00	35.00	75.00	155	—
1687 HS	41,000	27.00	55.00	100	170	—
1688 AB	—	16.00	35.00	75.00	155	—
1689 HS	—	16.00	35.00	75.00	155	—

KM# 520 18 GROSCHEN (1/5 Thaler)
Silver **Ruler:** Friedrich Wilhelm **Obv:** Laureate bust right **Rev:** Crowned oval 5-fold arms divide value 1 - 8, date in legend **Mint:** Berlin **Note:** Coinage for the Province of Prussia.

Date	Mintage	VG	F	VF	XF	Unc
1685 LCS	68,810	25.00	50.00	100	210	—
1686 LCS	—	25.00	50.00	100	210	—

KM# 611 18 GROSCHEN (1/5 Thaler)
Silver, 28.6 mm. **Ruler:** Friedrich III **Obv:** Crowned bust with sword right **Rev:** Crowned imperial eagle **Mint:** Königsberg **Note:** Varieties exist.

Date	Mintage	VG	F	VF	XF	Unc
1698 SD	5,904,000	16.00	35.00	75.00	155	—
1699 SD	Inc. above	16.00	35.00	100	200	—
1700 CG	83,500	25.00	50.00	100	200	—

KM# 108 1/96 THALER
Silver **Obv:** Eagle with scepter arms in baroque frame **Rev:** Imperial orb with 96, date above, all in shield frame **Mint:** Kölln **Note:** Dreier 1/96 Thaler.

Date	Mintage	VG	F	VF	XF	Unc
1623 LM	—	16.00	35.00	75.00	155	—

KM# 114 1/96 THALER
Silver **Obv:** Eagle in squared shield frame **Rev:** Date divided outside frame

Date	Mintage	VG	F	VF	XF	Unc
1624 LM	1,275,000	10.00	20.00	40.00	80.00	—

KM# 118 1/96 THALER
Silver **Obv:** Eagle not enclosed in frame **Rev:** Imperial orb with 96, not enclosed in frame **Note:** Varieties exist.

Date	Mintage	VG	F	VF	XF	Unc
1625	480,000	17.00	35.00	75.00	155	—

KM# 407 1/48 THALER (1/2 Groschen)
Billon **Obv:** Crowned 5-fold arms **Rev. Inscription:** 48 / EINEN / REICHS / THALER / date **Mint:** Berlin

Date	Mintage	VG	F	VF	XF	Unc
1670 IL	—	25.00	45.00	90.00	185	—

KM# 408 1/36 THALER
Silver **Obv:** Crowned 5-fold arms **Rev. Inscription:** 36 / EINEN / REICHS / THALER / date

Date	Mintage	VG	F	VF	XF	Unc
1670 IL	—	—	—	—	—	—

KM# 87 1/16 THALER
Silver **Ruler:** Georg Wilhelm **Obv:** Eagle, scepter arms on breast **Rev:** DS (= Doppelschilling), imperial orb with 16 above, date below **Mint:** Berlin

Date	Mintage	VG	F	VF	XF	Unc
1621 Rare	—	—	—	—	—	—

KM# 209 1/8 THALER (Blamüser)
Silver **Ruler:** Friedrich Wilhelm **Mint:** Berlin

Date	Mintage	VG	F	VF	XF	Unc
1643 AB	—	—	—	—	—	—
1648 CT	—	—	—	—	—	—

KM# 274 1/8 THALER (Blamüser)
Silver **Ruler:** Friedrich Wilhelm **Subject:** Birthday of Friedrich Wilhelm and Birth of Prince Karl Emil **Obv:** Crowned 1/2-length facing bust **Rev:** 7-line inscription, date

Date	Mintage	VG	F	VF	XF	Unc
1655	—	—	—	—	—	—

KM# 275 1/8 THALER (Blamüser)
Silver **Ruler:** Friedrich Wilhelm **Obv:** Uncrowned bust

Date	Mintage	VG	F	VF	XF	Unc
1655	—	—	—	—	—	—

KM# 276 1/8 THALER (Blamüser)
Silver **Ruler:** Friedrich Wilhelm **Obv:** 7-line inscription, floral decoration above **Mint:** Berlin / Kölln

Date	Mintage	VG	F	VF	XF	Unc
1655 CT	—	—	—	—	—	—

KM# 353 1/8 THALER (Blamüser)
Silver **Ruler:** Friedrich Wilhelm **Subject:** Death of Friedrich Wilhelm's Wife, Luise Henriette von Nassau-Oranien **Obv:** Crowned CL monogram **Rev:** 7-line inscription with date **Mint:** Berlin / Kölln

Date	Mintage	VG	F	VF	XF	Unc
1667 IL	—	—	—	—	—	—

KM# 354 1/8 THALER (Blamüser)
Silver **Ruler:** Friedrich Wilhelm **Obv:** Crowned arms **Rev:** 7-line inscription with date, laurel spray above **Mint:** Berlin / Kölln

Date	Mintage	VG	F	VF	XF	Unc
1667 IL	—	33.00	75.00	150	300	—

KM# 355 1/8 THALER (Blamüser)
Silver **Ruler:** Friedrich Wilhelm **Rev:** Eight-line inscription with date, without spray above **Mint:** Berlin / Kölln

Date	Mintage	VG	F	VF	XF	Unc
1667 IL	—	33.00	75.00	150	300	—

KM# 409 1/8 THALER (Blamüser)
Silver **Ruler:** Friedrich Wilhelm **Obv:** Head right **Rev:** 10-fold arms, crown above divides date, value 1/8 below **Mint:** Minden

Date	Mintage	VG	F	VF	XF	Unc
1670 HB	—	85.00	175	350	650	—

KM# 419 1/8 THALER (Blamüser)
Silver **Ruler:** Friedrich Wilhelm **Mint:** Minden

Date	Mintage	VG	F	VF	XF	Unc
1670 HB	—	85.00	175	350	650	—
1671 HB	—	85.00	175	350	650	—
1671 IW	—	85.00	175	350	650	—
1672 IW	—	85.00	175	350	650	—
1676 GDZ	—	85.00	175	350	650	—
1676 AVH	—	85.00	175	350	650	—

KM# 302 1/6 THALER (1/4 Gulden)
Silver **Ruler:** Friedrich Wilhelm **Subject:** Death of Princess Anna Sophie **Obv:** Crowned arms in wreath **Rev:** 11-line inscription with date, value 1/6 in circle below **Mint:** Berlin

Date	Mintage	VG	F	VF	XF	Unc
1659 AB	—	—	—	—	—	—

KM# 312 1/6 THALER (1/4 Gulden)
Silver **Ruler:** Friedrich Wilhelm **Subject:** Death of Friedrich Wilhelm's Mother, Elisabet Charlotte **Obv:** 17-line inscription **Rev:** 12-line inscription with date **Mint:** Berlin / Kölln

Date	Mintage	VG	F	VF	XF	Unc
1660 AB	—	—	—	—	—	—

KM# 322 1/6 THALER (1/4 Gulden)
Silver **Ruler:** Friedrich Wilhelm **Obv:** Crowned FWC monogram **Rev. Inscription:** VI / EINEN REICHS / THALER / Ao date **Mint:** Berlin

Date	Mintage	VG	F	VF	XF	Unc
1662 AB	13,679	190	385	775	—	—
1663 AB	36,340	190	385	775	—	—
1664 AB	7,684	190	385	775	—	—

KM# 356 1/6 THALER (1/4 Gulden)
Silver **Ruler:** Friedrich Wilhelm **Obv:** Bust right **Rev:** Crowned arms divide date, value (1/6) below **Mint:** Berlin / Kölln

Date	Mintage	VG	F	VF	XF	Unc
1667 IL	—	100	210	425	850	—
1668 IL	—	100	210	425	850	—

KM# 375 1/6 THALER (1/4 Gulden)
Silver **Ruler:** Friedrich Wilhelm **Obv:** Bust right **Rev:** Crowned ornate 5-fold arms, value 1/6 below **Mint:** Berlin / Kölln **Note:** Varieties exist.

Date	Mintage	VG	F	VF	XF	Unc
1668 IL	—	110	225	450	900	—
1669 IL	—	110	225	450	900	—
1673 IL	—	110	225	450	900	—
1674 IL	—	110	225	450	900	—

KM# 430 1/6 THALER (1/4 Gulden)
Silver **Ruler:** Friedrich Wilhelm **Rev:** Date in legend **Mint:** Berlin / Kölln

Date	Mintage	VG	F	VF	XF	Unc
1674 IL	—	40.00	90.00	180	360	—
1675 IL	—	40.00	90.00	180	360	—

KM# 17 1/4 THALER
Silver **Ruler:** Joachim Friedrich **Obv:** 1/2-length bust right **Rev:** 7-fold arms, date in legend **Mint:** Königsberg

Date	Mintage	VG	F	VF	XF	Unc
1602 (e)	—	—	—	—	—	—

KM# 21 1/4 THALER
Silver **Ruler:** Joachim Friedrich **Rev:** 7-fold arms divide date **Mint:** Kolln an der Spree

Date	Mintage	VG	F	VF	XF	Unc
1604 MH	—	—	—	—	—	—

KM# 43 1/4 THALER
Silver **Ruler:** Johann Sigismund **Obv:** 1/2-length bust right, date below **Rev:** 12-fold arms **Mint:** Kolln an der Spree

Date	Mintage	VG	F	VF	XF	Unc
1612 MH	—	—	—	—	—	—

KM# 86.2 1/4 THALER
Silver **Ruler:** Georg Wilhelm **Obv:** 1/2-length armored figure right, scepter on shoulder, date to right of figure, titles of Georg Wilhelm **Rev:** Crowned 4-fold arms, scepter shield in center, all in baroque frame, titles continuous **Mint:** Königsberg **Note:** Ref. N#96.

Date	Mintage	VG	F	VF	XF	Unc
16Z1 (q)	Inc. above	75.00	150	300	600	—

KM# 86.3 1/4 THALER
Silver **Ruler:** Georg Wilhelm **Obv:** 1/2-length armored figure right, scepter on shoulder, date below figure and helmet to right, titles of Georg Wilhelm **Rev:** Crowned 4-fold arms, scepter shield in center, all in baroque frame, titles continuous **Mint:** Königsberg **Note:** Ref. N#97. Varieties exist.

Date	Mintage	VG	F	VF	XF	Unc
16Z1	Inc. above	25.00	50.00	100	200	—
16Z1 (q)	Inc. above	25.00	50.00	100	200	—
16ZZ (q)	1,588,751	25.00	50.00	100	200	—
16ZZ	Inc. above	25.00	50.00	100	200	—

KM# 86.1 1/4 THALER
Silver, 29 mm. **Ruler:** Georg Wilhelm **Obv:** 1/2-length armored figure right, scepter on shoulder, divides date **Obv. Legend:** GEORG WILHELMVS V. G. G. M. Z. BRAN. **Rev:** Crowned 4-fold arms, scepter shield in center, all in baroque frame, titles continued **Rev. Legend:** D. H. R. R. ERT. C. V. CHVRF. I. P. Z. G. C. B. H. **Mint:** Königsberg **Note:** Ref. N-10.95.

Date	Mintage	VG	F	VF	XF	Unc
16Z1 (q)	585,448	27.00	50.00	100	210	—

KM# 86.4 1/4 THALER
Silver **Ruler:** Georg Wilhelm **Obv:** 1/2-length armored figure right, scepter on shoulder, titles of Georg Wilhelm **Rev:** Date divided by arms **Mint:** Königsberg **Note:** Ref. N#98.

Date	Mintage	VG	F	VF	XF	Unc
16ZZ (q)	Inc. above	27.00	50.00	100	210	—
(16)ZZ (q)	Inc. above	27.00	50.00	100	210	—

KM# 86.5 1/4 THALER
Silver **Ruler:** Georg Wilhelm **Obv:** 1/2-length figure with large ruffled collar right, scepter on shoulder, titles of Georg Wilhelm **Rev:** Crowned 4-fold arms, scepter shield in center, all in baroque frame **Mint:** Königsberg **Note:** Ref. N#99.

Date	Mintage	VG	F	VF	XF	Unc
(16)ZZ (q)	Inc. above	27.00	50.00	100	210	—

KM# 86.7 1/4 THALER
6.6000 g., Silver, 30 mm. **Ruler:** Georg Wilhelm **Obv:** 1/2-length figure in electoral robe right, scepter on shoulder **Obv. Legend:** GEORG WILHELM V. G. G. M. Z. BRAN(D). **Rev:** Crowned Spanish shield of 4-fold arms, scepter shield in center **Rev. Legend:** D. H. R. R. ERT(Z). C. V. CHVRF. I. P. Z. G. C. B. H. **Mint:** Königsberg **Note:** Ref. N-10.101. Varieties exist. Prev. KM#86.2.

Date	Mintage	VG	F	VF	XF	Unc
(16)ZZ (q)	Inc. above	20.00	45.00	90.00	180	—
(16)22 (q)	Inc. above	20.00	45.00	90.00	180	—
(16)23 (q)	1,055,347	20.00	45.00	90.00	180	—
(16)24 (q)	2,334,429	20.00	45.00	90.00	180	—

KM# 86.6 1/4 THALER
Silver **Ruler:** Georg Wilhelm **Obv:** 1/2-length figure with crown and no helmet right, titles of Georg Wilhelm **Rev:** Crowned 4-fold arms, scepter shield in center, all in baroque frame **Mint:** Königsberg **Note:** Ref. N#100.

Date	Mintage	VG	F	VF	XF	Unc
(16)ZZ (q)	Inc. above	—	—	—	—	—

KM# 86a 1/4 THALER
Silver **Ruler:** Georg Wilhelm **Obv:** 1/2-length figure wears ermine robe, scepter on shoulder, titles of Georg Wilhelm **Rev:** Crowned 4-fold arms, scepter shield in center, all in baroque frame **Mint:** Königsberg **Note:** Ref. N#102. Kipper 1/4 Thaler. approximate weight: 3.5 grams.

Date	Mintage	VG	F	VF	XF	Unc
(16)23 (q)	—	27.00	50.00	100	210	—

KM# 86.8 1/4 THALER
Silver, 30.2 mm. **Ruler:** Georg Wilhelm **Obv:** Crowned bust right **Rev:** Large crown above arms and "S" on breast of eagle in upper left quarter **Mint:** Königsberg **Note:** Ref. N#103.

Date	Mintage	VG	F	VF	XF	Unc
(16)24 (q)	Inc. above	30.00	55.00	110	225	—

KM# 86.9 1/4 THALER
Silver **Ruler:** Georg Wilhelm **Obv:** 1/2-length uncrowned figure right, scepter on shoulder, titles of Georg Wilhelm **Rev:** Crowned 4-fold arms divide date **Mint:** Königsberg **Note:** Ref. N#104.

Date	Mintage	VG	F	VF	XF	Unc
(16)24 (q)	Inc. above	30.00	55.00	110	225	—
16Z4 (q)	Inc. above	30.00	55.00	110	225	—

KM# 86.10 1/4 THALER
Silver **Ruler:** Georg Wilhelm **Obv:** Eagle with "S" on breast in circle **Obv. Legend:** MONETA. NOVA. **Rev:** Shield of Hohenzollern arms in baroque frame, date **Rev. Legend:** DVCIS IN BORVSSIA • • A • **Mint:** Königsberg **Note:** Ref. D#600. Possibly a pattern.

Date	Mintage	VG	F	VF	XF	Unc
16Z4	—	30.00	55.00	110	225	—

KM# 86.11 1/4 THALER
Silver **Ruler:** Georg Wilhelm **Obv:** Eagle with 'S' on breast in circle **Obv. Legend:** MONETA. NOVA. **Rev:** ANNI/date in circle **Rev. Legend:** DVCIS. IN . BORVSSIA. **Mint:** Königsberg **Note:** Ref. D#601. Possibly a pattern.

Date	Mintage	VG	F	VF	XF	Unc
16Z4	Inc. above	30.00	55.00	110	225	—

KM# 86.12 1/4 THALER
Silver **Ruler:** Georg Wilhelm **Obv:** 1/2-length figure wears ermine robe, scepter on shoulder, titles of Georg Wilhelm **Rev:** Large crown above arms without 'S' on breast of eagle in upper left quarter **Mint:** Königsberg **Note:** Ref. N#105.

Date	Mintage	VG	F	VF	XF	Unc
(16)25/4 (q)	—	30.00	55.00	110	225	—

KM# 86.13 1/4 THALER
Silver **Ruler:** Georg Wilhelm **Obv:** 1/2-length figure right, scepter on shoulder, titles of Georg Wilhelm **Rev:** Large crown above arms, 'S' on breast of eagle in lower right quarter **Mint:** Königsberg **Note:** Ref. N#106.

Date	Mintage	VG	F	VF	XF	Unc
(16)25 (q)	353,429	30.00	55.00	110	225	—

KM# 86.14 1/4 THALER
Silver **Ruler:** Georg Wilhelm **Obv:** 1/2-length figure right, scepter on shoulder, titles of Georg Wilhelm **Obv. Legend:** GEORGWILHD • G • MARCHIO • BRAND **Rev:** Mintmaster's symbol in cartouche below arms **Mint:** Königsberg **Note:** Ref. N#107.

Date	Mintage	VG	F	VF	XF	Unc
(16)25 (q)	Inc. above	27.00	45.00	90.00	190	—
(16)26 (q)	55,629	—	—	—	—	—

KM# 86.15 1/4 THALER
Silver **Ruler:** Georg Wilhelm **Obv:** 1/2-length figure right, scepter on shoulder, titles of Georg Wilhelm **Rev:** 11-fold arms with scepter shield in center, date above, titles continuous in legend **Mint:** Berlin / Kölln **Note:** Ref. N#40.

Date	Mintage	VG	F	VF	XF	Unc
1633 LM Rare	—	—	—	—	—	—

KM# 124.2 1/4 THALER
Silver **Ruler:** Georg Wilhelm **Obv:** 1/2-length armored figure to right, scepter over shoulder, titles of Georg Wilhelm **Rev:** 7-fold arms with central shield, electoral hat above, date divided at top **Rev. Legend:** ANFANG BEDENCK DAS END (or variant) **Mint:** Königsberg **Note:** Ref. N#38b.

Date	Mintage	VG	F	VF	XF	Unc
1634 (q)	—	—	—	—	—	—

KM# 175 1/4 THALER
Silver **Ruler:** Georg Wilhelm **Subject:** Death of Georg Wilhelm **Obv:** In ornamented shield with electoral hat above, 8-fold arms with scepter shield in center, titles of Georg Wilhelm **Rev:** 6-line inscription with R.N. dates **Mint:** Königsberg **Note:** Ref. D#619.

Date	Mintage	VG	F	VF	XF	Unc
1640 (MDCXL) DK	—	—	—	3,800	7,200	—

KM# 182 1/4 THALER
Silver **Ruler:** Friedrich Wilhelm **Obv:** Crowned and robed elector holding scepter on horse rearing to right **Rev:** Scepter arms in center of large rose, 23 small oval arms around

Date	Mintage	VG	F	VF	XF	Unc
ND(1641/3)	—	—	—	—	—	—

KM# 210 1/4 THALER
Silver **Ruler:** Friedrich Wilhelm **Obv:** Crowned and robed half-length figure right **Rev:** 5-fold arms, date above **Mint:** Berlin / Kölln

Date	Mintage	VG	F	VF	XF	Unc
1643 AB	—	—	—	—	—	—
1648 CT	—	—	—	—	—	—

KM# 277 1/4 THALER
Silver **Ruler:** Friedrich Wilhelm **Subject:** Birthday of Friedrich Wilhelm and Birth of Prince Karl Emil **Mint:** Berlin / Kölln

Date	Mintage	VG	F	VF	XF	Unc
1655 AB	—	—	—	—	—	—
1655 CT	—	325	625	1,200	—	—

KM# 303 1/4 THALER
Silver **Ruler:** Friedrich Wilhelm **Subject:** Death of Princess Anna Sophia **Obv:** Crowned arms in wreath **Rev:** 11-line inscription with date in circle below **Mint:** Berlin / Kölln

Date	Mintage	VG	F	VF	XF	Unc
1659 AB	—	—	—	—	—	—

KM# 313 1/4 THALER
Silver **Ruler:** Friedrich Wilhelm **Subject:** Death of Friedrich Wilhelm's Mother, Elisabet Charlotte **Obv:** 14-line inscription **Rev:** 14-line inscription with date **Mint:** Berlin / Kölln

Date	Mintage	VG	F	VF	XF	Unc
1660 AB	—	—	—	—	—	—

KM# 357 1/4 THALER
Silver **Ruler:** Friedrich Wilhelm **Subject:** Death of Friedrich

Wilhelm's Wife, Luise Henriette von Nassau-Oranien **Obv:** Crowned arms in laurel wreath **Rev:** Seven-line inscription with date, imperial orb in laurel spray above **Mint:** Berlin / Kölln

Date	Mintage	VG	F	VF	XF	Unc
1667 IL	—	—	—	—	—	—

KM# 358 1/4 THALER
Silver **Ruler:** Friedrich Wilhelm **Obv:** Crowned CL monogram, figure of Genius holding a live branch at right **Rev:** 7-line inscription with date in frame, imperial orb between two laurel sprays above **Mint:** Berlin / Kölln

Date	Mintage	VG	F	VF	XF	Unc
1667 IL-GL	—	—	—	—	—	—

KM# A509 1/4 THALER
Silver **Ruler:** Friedrich Wilhelm **Subject:** Death of Wilhelm (III)'s wife, Elisabeth Henriette von Hessen-Kassel **Obv:** Bust right **Rev:** Crowned tablet with 8-line inscrption and dates, skull and crossbones below

Date	Mintage	VG	F	VF	XF	Unc
1683	—	—	—	—	—	—

KM# 538 1/4 THALER
Silver **Ruler:** Friedrich Wilhelm **Subject:** Homage of County of Mark

Date	Mintage	VG	F	VF	XF	Unc
1688	—	33.00	80.00	160	325	—

KM# 539 1/4 THALER
Silver **Ruler:** Friedrich Wilhelm **Subject:** Death of Friedrich Wilhelm **Obv:** Bust right, two legend inscription around **Rev:** Eagle on palm tree above trophies

Date	Mintage	VG	F	VF	XF	Unc
1688 Schultz	—	—	—	—	—	—

KM# 323 1/3 THALER (1/2 Gulden)
Silver **Ruler:** Friedrich Wilhelm **Obv:** Crowned FWC monogram **Rev. Inscription:** III / EINEN REICHS / THALER / Ao date **Mint:** Berlin

Date	Mintage	VG	F	VF	XF	Unc
1662 AB	18,214	225	450	900	1,800	—
1664 AB	2,188	250	500	1,000	2,000	—

KM# 359 1/3 THALER (1/2 Gulden)
Silver **Ruler:** Friedrich Wilhelm **Obv:** Bust right **Rev:** Crowned arms divide date, value (1/3) below **Mint:** Berlin / Kölln

Date	Mintage	VG	F	VF	XF	Unc
1667 IL	—	33.00	75.00	150	300	—
1668 IL	—	33.00	75.00	150	300	—

KM# 360.2 1/3 THALER (1/2 Gulden)
Silver **Ruler:** Friedrich Wilhelm **Obv:** Inner circle, modified designs **Rev:** Inner circle, modified designs **Mint:** Krossen

Date	Mintage	VG	F	VF	XF	Unc
1667 GF	—	50.00	100	190	380	—

KM# 360.1 1/3 THALER (1/2 Gulden)
Silver **Ruler:** Friedrich Wilhelm **Obv:** without inner circle **Rev:** without inner circle **Mint:** Krossen **Note:** Varieties exist.

Date	Mintage	VG	F	VF	XF	Unc
1667 IPE	—	45.00	90.00	180	360	—
1667 GF	—	45.00	90.00	180	360	—
1668 GF	—	45.00	90.00	180	360	—
1669 GF	—	45.00	90.00	180	360	—
1670 GF	—	45.00	90.00	180	360	—

KM# 376.1 1/3 THALER (1/2 Gulden)
Silver **Ruler:** Friedrich Wilhelm **Obv:** Bust right, date below bust **Rev:** Value below crowned arms **Mint:** Berlin / Kölln **Note:** Varieties exist.

Date	Mintage	VG	F	VF	XF	Unc
1668 IL	—	33.00	75.00	150	300	—
1669 IL	—	33.00	75.00	150	300	—
1670 IL	—	33.00	75.00	150	300	—
1671 IL	—	33.00	75.00	150	300	—
1672 IL	—	33.00	75.00	150	300	—
1673 IL	—	33.00	75.00	150	300	—
1674 IL	—	33.00	75.00	150	300	—
1675 IL	—	33.00	75.00	150	300	—

KM# 377 1/3 THALER (1/2 Gulden)
Silver **Ruler:** Friedrich Wilhelm **Rev:** Arms between two palm branches **Mint:** Berlin / Kölln **Note:** Varieties exist.

Date	Mintage	VG	F	VF	XF	Unc
1668 IL	—	33.00	75.00	150	300	—
1669 IL	—	33.00	75.00	150	300	—

KM# 378 1/3 THALER (1/2 Gulden)
Silver **Ruler:** Friedrich Wilhelm **Mint:** Krossen **Note:** Varieties exist.

Date	Mintage	VG	F	VF	XF	Unc
1668 GF	—	33.00	75.00	150	300	—
1670 GF	—	33.00	75.00	150	300	—
1671 GF	—	33.00	75.00	150	300	—
1672 GF	—	33.00	75.00	150	300	—
1673 GF	—	33.00	75.00	150	300	—
1674 GF	—	33.00	75.00	150	300	—
ND(1675) GF	—	33.00	75.00	150	300	—

KM# 379 1/3 THALER (1/2 Gulden)
Silver **Ruler:** Friedrich Wilhelm **Obv:** Bust laureate and drapeped right **Mint:** Königsberg **Note:** Varieties exist.

Date	Mintage	VG	F	VF	XF	Unc
1668 G-DS	100,000	—	—	—	—	—
1668 CG-DS	Inc. above	—	—	—	—	—
ND1669 CG-SD	150,000	—	—	—	—	—
1669 TT	278,000	55.00	100	200	425	—
1670 TT	1,055,000	40.00	75.00	150	300	—
1671 TT	833,000	40.00	80.00	200	425	—
1672 TT	865,000	40.00	80.00	200	425	—
1672 CV	Inc. above	40.00	80.00	200	425	—
1673 CV	638,000	55.00	100	200	425	—
1674 CV	736,000	55.00	100	200	425	—
1675 HS	1,407,000	33.00	60.00	120	240	—

KM# 390 1/3 THALER (1/2 Gulden)
Silver **Ruler:** Friedrich Wilhelm **Obv:** Head laureate right **Mint:** Königsberg

Date	Mintage	VG	F	VF	XF	Unc
ND1669 CG-DS	Inc. above	55.00	100	200	425	—
ND1669 TT-DS	Inc. above	55.00	100	200	425	—
1674 HS	Inc. above	55.00	100	200	425	—

KM# 391 1/3 THALER (1/2 Gulden)
Silver **Ruler:** Friedrich Wilhelm **Rev:** Complete date left of crown **Mint:** Königsberg

Date	Mintage	VG	F	VF	XF	Unc
1669 DS-TT	Inc. above	55.00	100	200	425	—
1669 TT	Inc. above	55.00	100	200	425	—
1670 TT	Inc. above	55.00	100	200	425	—
1675 HS	Inc. above	55.00	100	200	425	—
1676 HS	17,000	55.00	100	200	425	—

KM# 392 1/3 THALER (1/2 Gulden)
Silver **Ruler:** Friedrich Wilhelm **Mint:** Minden

Date	Mintage	VG	F	VF	XF	Unc
1669 HB	—	200	400	800	1,550	—
1670 HB	—	200	400	800	1,550	—

KM# 410 1/3 THALER (1/2 Gulden)
Silver **Ruler:** Friedrich Wilhelm **Obv:** 1/3 on label at shoulder **Mint:** Minden

Date	Mintage	VG	F	VF	XF	Unc
1670 HB	—	100	200	350	650	—
1671 HB	—	100	200	350	650	—
1671 IW	—	75.00	150	285	550	—
1672 IW	—	75.00	150	285	550	—
1673 IW	—	70.00	140	250	550	—

KM# 421 1/3 THALER (1/2 Gulden)
Silver **Ruler:** Friedrich Wilhelm **Obv:** Bust right, value 1/3 below **Rev:** Crowned arms, 1/3 below **Mint:** Berlin

Date	Mintage	VG	F	VF	XF	Unc
ND(1672) IL	—	45.00	80.00	160	325	—

KM# 433 1/3 THALER (1/2 Gulden)
Silver **Ruler:** Friedrich Wilhelm **Obv:** Bust right **Rev:** 10-fold arms, crown above divides date, value 1/3 below **Mint:** Regenstein

Date	Mintage	VG	F	VF	XF	Unc
1674 IA	—	80.00	165	335	675	—
1675 IA	—	80.00	165	335	675	—

KM# 434 1/3 THALER (1/2 Gulden)
Silver **Ruler:** Friedrich Wilhelm **Rev:** Complete date left of crown **Mint:** Minden

Date	Mintage	VG	F	VF	XF	Unc
1674 GDZ	—	45.00	80.00	160	325	—
1674 AVH	—	45.00	80.00	160	325	—
1675 GDZ	—	45.00	80.00	160	325	—
1679 AVH	—	45.00	80.00	160	325	—
1683 BH	—	45.00	80.00	160	325	—

KM# 432 1/3 THALER (1/2 Gulden)
Silver **Ruler:** Friedrich Wilhelm **Obv:** Bust right **Rev:** Value below crowned arms, date in legend **Mint:** Berlin / Kölln **Note:** Varieties exist.

Date	Mintage	VG	F	VF	XF	Unc
1674 IL	—	40.00	75.00	150	300	—
1675 IL	—	40.00	75.00	150	300	—
1687 LCS	—	40.00	75.00	150	300	—
1688 LCS	—	40.00	75.00	150	300	—

KM# 376.2 1/3 THALER (1/2 Gulden)
Silver **Ruler:** Friedrich Wilhelm **Obv:** CS below bust **Rev:** Date in legend **Mint:** Berlin / Kölln **Note:** Varieties exist.

Date	Mintage	VG	F	VF	XF	Unc
1675 CS	—	75.00	150	300	600	—

KM# 469 1/3 THALER (1/2 Gulden)
Silver **Ruler:** Friedrich Wilhelm **Obv:** Date in legend divided by bust **Mint:** Regenstein

Date	Mintage	VG	F	VF	XF	Unc
1676 IA	—	80.00	165	335	675	—

KM# 470 1/3 THALER (1/2 Gulden)
Silver **Ruler:** Friedrich Wilhelm **Obv:** Date in legend divided by bust **Rev:** 10-fold arms, crown above divides date, value 1/3 below **Mint:** Regenstein

Date	Mintage	VG	F	VF	XF	Unc
1676/1675 IA	—	80.00	165	335	675	—

KM# 508 1/3 THALER (1/2 Gulden)
Silver **Ruler:** Friedrich Wilhelm **Obv:** Bust right **Rev:** 10-fold arms, crown above divides date, value 1/3 below **Mint:** Magdeburg

Date	Mintage	VG	F	VF	XF	Unc
1683 IE	—	85.00	175	375	775	—
1686 IE	—	85.00	175	375	775	—

KM# 524 1/3 THALER (1/2 Gulden)
Silver **Ruler:** Friedrich Wilhelm **Mint:** Berlin

Date	Mintage	VG	F	VF	XF	Unc
1686 LCS	—	45.00	75.00	150	300	—

KM# 554 1/3 THALER (1/2 Gulden)
Silver **Ruler:** Friedrich III **Mint:** Stargard **Note:** Similar to KM#573.

Date	Mintage	VG	F	VF	XF	Unc
1689 SD	—	125	250	500	1,000	—
1690 SD	—	125	250	500	1,000	—

KM# 573 1/3 THALER (1/2 Gulden)
Silver **Ruler:** Friedrich III **Mint:** Berlin **Note:** Varieties exist.

Date	Mintage	VG	F	VF	XF	Unc
1690 LCS	—	40.00	95.00	190	385	—
1691 LCS	—	80.00	175	375	775	—
1692 LCS	—	80.00	175	375	775	—
1693 LCS	—	80.00	175	375	775	—
1698 LCS	19,000	80.00	175	375	775	—
1699 LCS	18,000	80.00	175	375	775	—
1700 LCS	8,000	125	250	500	1,000	—

KM# 583 1/3 THALER (1/2 Gulden)
Silver **Ruler:** Friedrich III **Obv:** Bust right **Rev:** Arms **Mint:** Minden

Date	Mintage	VG	F	VF	XF	Unc
1692 BH	—	125	200	425	850	—
1693 BH	—	125	200	425	850	—

KM# 593 1/3 THALER (1/2 Gulden)
Silver **Ruler:** Friedrich III **Mint:** Magdeburg **Note:** Similar to KM#573.

Date	Mintage	VG	F	VF	XF	Unc
1694 ICS	—	125	250	475	950	—
1695 ICS	—	150	300	600	1,200	—
1700 HFH	—	115	220	435	875	—

KM# 18 1/2 THALER
Silver **Ruler:** Joachim Friedrich **Obv:** Half-length bust right divides date **Rev:** 7-fold arms **Mint:** Königsberg

Date	Mintage	VG	F	VF	XF	Unc
1602 (e)	—	—	—	—	—	—

KM# 22 1/2 THALER
Silver **Ruler:** Joachim Friedrich **Rev:** Date in legend **Mint:** Kolln an der Spree

Date	Mintage	VG	F	VF	XF	Unc
1604 MH	—	—	—	—	—	—
1605 MH	—	—	—	—	—	—

KM# 44 1/2 THALER
Silver **Ruler:** Johann Sigismund **Obv:** Half-length bust right, date below **Rev:** 12-fold arms **Mint:** Kolln an der Spree

Date	Mintage	VG	F	VF	XF	Unc
1612 MH	—	2,000	3,250	5,000	7,750	—

KM# 66 1/2 THALER
Silver **Ruler:** Georg Wilhelm **Obv:** 3/4-length figure right, holding baton and helmet **Rev:** Crowned 12-fold arms in baroque frame **Mint:** Berlin

Date	Mintage	VG	F	VF	XF	Unc
ND(1620/21) LM	—	—	—	—	—	—

KM# 124.1 1/2 THALER
Silver **Ruler:** Georg Wilhelm **Obv:** 1/2-length armored figure to right, scepter over shoulder, titles of Georg Wilhelm **Rev:** 23-fold arms with scepter shield in center, electoral hat above, date divided at top **Rev. Legend:** ANFANG BEDENCK DAS END (or variant) **Mint:** Königsberg **Note:** Ref. N#38a. Prev. KM#124.

Date	Mintage	VG	F	VF	XF	Unc
16Z7 (q)	2,179	325	600	1,100	1,950	—
16Z8 (q)	5,425	325	600	1,100	1,950	—
16Z9 (q)	11,000	325	600	1,100	1,950	—
1634 (q)	—	—	—	—	—	—

KM# 127 1/2 THALER
Silver **Ruler:** Georg Wilhelm **Rev:** Crowned 12-fold arms, date in legend **Mint:** Kölln

Date	Mintage	VG	F	VF	XF	Unc
1628 LM	—	250	500	950	1,800	—
1631 LM	—	250	500	950	1,800	—
1636 LM	—	250	500	950	1,800	—
1637 LM	—	250	500	950	1,800	—

KM# 150.2 1/2 THALER
Silver **Ruler:** Georg Wilhelm **Obv:** 1/2-length armored figure to right, scepter over shoulder, titles of Georg Wilhelm **Rev:** 7-fold arms with central shield, legend and date above crown **Rev. Legend:** MONETA. NOVA. ARGENTEA DVCIS PRVSSIÆ **Mint:** Königsberg **Note:** Ref. N#39. Varieties exist.

Date	Mintage	VG	F	VF	XF	Unc
1635 DK (q)	—	350	650	1,100	—	—
1636 DK (q)	—	350	650	1,100	—	—
1637 DK (q)	—	350	650	1,100	—	—
1638 DK (q)	—	350	650	1,100	—	—

KM# 150.1 1/2 THALER

Silver **Ruler:** Georg Wilhelm **Obv:** 1/2-length figure right with helmet **Rev:** 8-fold arms with scepter shield in center, electoral hat above, date divided at top **Mint:** Königsberg **Note:** Ref. N#38c. Prev. KM#150.

Date	Mintage	VG	F	VF	XF	Unc
1636 DK (q)	—	350	650	1,200	—	—
1639 DK	—	350	650	1,200	—	—

Note: Some coins dated 1639 were struck from Thaler dies of KM#160.2 on thin, broad flans

KM# 162 1/2 THALER

Silver **Ruler:** Georg Wilhelm **Obv:** Crowned half-length bust right **Mint:** Kölln

Date	Mintage	VG	F	VF	XF	Unc
1637 LM	—	750	1,400	—	—	—
1638 LM	—	750	1,400	—	—	—
1639 LM	—	750	1,400	—	—	—

KM# 176 1/2 THALER

Silver **Ruler:** Georg Wilhelm **Rev:** Without crown above arms, only date **Mint:** Kölln

Date	Mintage	VG	F	VF	XF	Unc
1640 LM	—	1,200	2,400	—	—	—

KM# 183 1/2 THALER

Silver **Ruler:** Friedrich Wilhelm **Obv:** Crowned and robed half-length figure **Rev:** Arms in rhombus divides date at top **Mint:** Berlin

Date	Mintage	VG	F	VF	XF	Unc
1641 LM	—	—	—	—	—	—

KM# 186 1/2 THALER

Silver **Ruler:** Friedrich Wilhelm **Obv:** Bust entirely within circle **Mint:** Königsberg

Date	Mintage	VG	F	VF	XF	Unc
ND(1641/3) DK	—	—	—	—	—	—

KM# 184 1/2 THALER

Silver **Ruler:** Friedrich Wilhelm **Obv:** Crowned and robed half-length figure in wreath **Rev:** Arms in wreath, date in legend **Mint:** Kölln **Note:** Varieties exist.

Date	Mintage	VG	F	VF	XF	Unc
1641 LM	—	1,750	3,000	—	—	—
1642 LM	—	1,750	3,000	—	—	—

KM# 185 1/2 THALER

Silver **Ruler:** Friedrich Wilhelm **Obv:** Half-length bust 3/4 right breaks circle at top **Rev:** Plumed helmet, ARMAT ET ORNAT on band below, surrounded by 23 small oval arms **Mint:** Königsberg **Note:** Varieties exist.

Date	Mintage	VG	F	VF	XF	Unc
ND(1641/3) DK	—	—	—	—	—	—

KM# 204 1/2 THALER

Silver **Ruler:** Friedrich Wilhelm **Obv:** Half-length figure right with helmet **Rev:** Crowned ornate 9-fold arms, date divided in upper left and right **Mint:** Königsberg

Date	Mintage	VG	F	VF	XF	Unc
1642 DK	—	—	—	—	—	—

KM# 211 1/2 THALER

Silver **Ruler:** Friedrich Wilhelm **Obv:** 1/2-length figure with cap right **Rev:** Arms with 12 fields **Mint:** Berlin

Date	Mintage	VG	F	VF	XF	Unc
1643 AB	—	1,800	3,300	—	—	—
1644 AB	—	1,800	3,300	—	—	—
1647 CT	—	.1,800	3,300	—	—	—

KM# 247 1/2 THALER

Silver **Ruler:** Friedrich Wilhelm **Obv:** Bust right in circle **Rev:** Helmeted arms **Mint:** Königsberg

Date	Mintage	VG	F	VF	XF	Unc
ND(1651-6) CM Rare	—	—	—	—	—	—

KM# 279 1/2 THALER

Silver **Ruler:** Friedrich Wilhelm **Obv:** Elector standing 3/4 right, helmet on table at right **Rev:** Square arms, crown above divides date **Mint:** Kölln

Date	Mintage	VG	F	VF	XF	Unc
1655 CT	—	—	—	—	—	—
1657 CT	—	—	—	—	—	—

KM# 278 1/2 THALER

Silver **Ruler:** Friedrich Wilhelm **Subject:** Birthday of Friedrich Wilhelm and Birth of Prince Karl Emil **Obv:** Facing half-length bust **Rev:** Crowned six-line inscription, date **Mint:** Berlin **Note:** Struck on thick flan with 1/4 Thaler dies.

Date	Mintage	VG	F	VF	XF	Unc
1655 AB	—	—	—	—	—	—
1655 CT	—	—	—	—	—	—

KM# 298 1/2 THALER

Silver **Ruler:** Friedrich Wilhelm **Subject:** Attainment of Sovereignty over East Prussia **Obv:** Elector on horse galloping right, town below hoofs, date at bottom **Rev:** Eight-line inscription **Mint:** Kölln

Date	Mintage	VG	F	VF	XF	Unc
1658 CT	—	650	1,300	2,300	4,500	—

KM# 299 1/2 THALER

Silver **Ruler:** Friedrich Wilhelm **Rev:** Nine-line inscription **Mint:** Kölln

Date	Mintage	VG	F	VF	XF	Unc
1658 AB	—	650	1,300	2,300	4,500	—

KM# 314 1/2 THALER

Silver **Ruler:** Friedrich Wilhelm **Subject:** Death of Friedrich Wilhelm's Mother, Elisabet Charlotte **Obv:** 17-line inscription **Rev:** 12-line inscription with date **Mint:** Kölln

Date	Mintage	VG	F	VF	XF	Unc
1660 AB	—	—	—	—	—	—

KM# 332 1/2 THALER

Silver **Ruler:** Friedrich Wilhelm **Obv:** Elector standing 3/4 right, helmet on table at right **Rev:** Crowned arms divide date **Mint:** Kölln

Date	Mintage	VG	F	VF	XF	Unc
1664 AB	425	—	—	—	—	—

KM# 361 1/2 THALER

Silver **Ruler:** Friedrich Wilhelm **Subject:** Death of Friedrich Wilhelm's Wife, Luise Henriette von Nassau-Oranien **Obv:** Facing bust of Luise Henriette **Rev:** Nine-line inscription, date

Date	Mintage	VG	F	VF	XF	Unc
1667	—	800	1,450	2,700	4,800	—

KM# 362 1/2 THALER

Silver **Ruler:** Friedrich Wilhelm **Obv:** Bust of Luise Henriette left **Rev:** Six-line inscription with date in ornamented square **Mint:** Kölln

Date	Mintage	VG	F	VF	XF	Unc
1667 GL-IL	—	750	1,500	3,000	—	—

KM# 584 1/2 THALER

Silver **Ruler:** Friedrich III **Mint:** Minden

Date	Mintage	VG	F	VF	XF	Unc
1692 BH	—	—	—	—	—	—

KM# 420 2/3 THALER (Gulden)

Silver **Ruler:** Friedrich Wilhelm **Obv:** Laureate bust right **Rev:** Crowned ornate arms, value 2/3 below, date in legend **Mint:** Königsberg

Date	Mintage	VG	F	VF	XF	Unc
1671 TT	56,000	175	350	675	1,150	—
1672 TT	56,000	175	350	675	1,150	—
1675 HS	54,000	175	350	675	1,150	—
1676 HS	25,000	175	350	675	1,150	—

KM# 422 2/3 THALER (Gulden)
Silver **Ruler:** Friedrich Wilhelm **Rev:** Arms between palm branches **Mint:** Berlin

Date	Mintage	VG	F	VF	XF	Unc
1672 IL	—	100	200	335	675	—
1673 IL	—	100	200	335	675	—

KM# 423 2/3 THALER (Gulden)
Silver **Ruler:** Friedrich Wilhelm **Rev:** 2/3 below arms, date divided at top **Mint:** Minden

Date	Mintage	VG	F	VF	XF	Unc
1672 IW	—	250	475	775	1,300	—

KM# 437 2/3 THALER (Gulden)
Silver **Ruler:** Friedrich Wilhelm **Rev:** Date divided at top by crown **Mint:** Regenstein

Date	Mintage	VG	F	VF	XF	Unc
1674 IA	—	80.00	140	250	475	—
1647 IA Rare; error	—	—	—	—	—	—

KM# 435 2/3 THALER (Gulden)
Silver **Ruler:** Friedrich Wilhelm **Obv:** Bust right, date below **Obv. Legend:** FRID: WILH: D:G: M • BR • S • R • I • ARCH(1C): & EL(EC) • **Rev:** Crowned arms, value below **Rev. Legend:** MONETA NOVA - ARGENTIA **Mint:** Berlin **Note:** Dav.#244.

Date	Mintage	VG	F	VF	XF	Unc
1674 IL	—	80.00	160	300	625	—
1675 IL	—	80.00	160	300	625	—
ND IL	—	80.00	160	300	625	—
1675 CS	—	80.00	160	300	625	—

KM# 436 2/3 THALER (Gulden)
Silver **Ruler:** Friedrich Wilhelm **Obv. Legend:** FRID: WILH: D:G: M ? BR ? S ? R ? I ? ... **Rev:** Crowned arms, date at upper left, value below **Rev. Legend:** MONETA NOVA - ARGENT: **Mint:** Berlin **Note:** Dav. #245.

Date	Mintage	VG	F	VF	XF	Unc
1674 IL	—	90.00	165	300	625	—
1675 IL	—	90.00	165	300	625	—

KM# 445.1 2/3 THALER (Gulden)
Silver **Ruler:** Friedrich Wilhelm **Obv:** Bust right, value 2/3 on shoulder **Obv. Legend:** FRID: WILH: D • G • M • BR: & ELEC **Rev:** Crowned arms, crown divides date, arms divide initials. **Rev. Legend:** MONETA • NOVA • ARGENTEA • **Mint:** Minden **Note:** Varieties exist. Dav.#261A.

Date	Mintage	VG	F	VF	XF	Unc
1675 GD-Z	—	80.00	140	275	550	—
1676 GD-Z	—	80.00	140	275	550	—

KM# 443 2/3 THALER (Gulden)
Silver **Ruler:** Friedrich Wilhelm **Obv:** Bust right, CS below **Obv. Legend:** FRID: WILH: D:G: M: BR • SRI ARC & EL(E) • **Rev:** Crowned arms, date at upper left, value below **Rev. Legend:** MONETA • NOVA - ARGENT: **Mint:** Berlin **Note:** Dav.#246.

Date	Mintage	VG	F	VF	XF	Unc
1675 CS	—	45.00	100	175	350	—
1676 CS	—	45.00	100	175	350	—

KM# 444 2/3 THALER (Gulden)
Silver **Ruler:** Friedrich Wilhelm **Obv:** Bust of Friedrich Wilhelm right **Obv. Legend:** FRID. WILH. D.G.M. BR. & ELEC. **Rev:** Crowned arms with initials above, value 2/3 below **Rev. Legend:** 1.6.75. MONETA NO. (VA). ARGENTIA **Mint:** Minden **Note:** Dav.#260.

Date	Mintage	VG	F	VF	XF	Unc
1.6.75. GD-Z	—	110	200	350	650	—

KM# 445.2 2/3 THALER (Gulden)
Silver **Ruler:** Friedrich Wilhelm **Mint:** Minden **Note:** Dav.#261B.

Date	Mintage	VG	F	VF	XF	Unc
1675 A-VH	—	80.00	140	275	550	—
1676 A-VH	—	80.00	140	275	550	—

KM# 445.3 2/3 THALER (Gulden)
Silver **Ruler:** Friedrich Wilhelm **Rev:** Date at upper left **Mint:** Minden **Note:** Dav.#261C.

Date	Mintage	VG	F	VF	XF	Unc
1675 GD-Z	—	80.00	140	275	550	—
1676 GD-Z	—	80.00	140	275	550	—
1678 GD-Z	—	80.00	140	275	550	—
1679 GD-Z	—	80.00	140	275	550	—

KM# 447 2/3 THALER (Gulden)
Silver **Ruler:** Friedrich Wilhelm **Obv:** Bust right divides date at bottom **Obv. Legend:** FRID: WILH: D: G: M: B: ELEC **Rev:** Crowned arms, value below **Rev. Legend:** MONETA • NO • ARG: REINS **Mint:** Regenstein **Note:** Varieties exist. Dav.#267.

Date	Mintage	VG	F	VF	XF	Unc
1675 IA	—	60.00	120	240	475	—
1676 IA	—	60.00	120	240	475	—
1677 IA	—	60.00	120	240	475	—

KM# 445.4 2/3 THALER (Gulden)
Silver **Ruler:** Friedrich Wilhelm **Rev:** Two sets of initials **Mint:** Minden **Note:** Dav.#261D.

Date	Mintage	VG	F	VF	XF	Unc
1676 GD-Z/A-VH	—	80.00	140	275	550	—

KM# 480 2/3 THALER (Gulden)
Silver **Ruler:** Friedrich Wilhelm **Obv:** Value 2/3 below bust **Mint:** Berlin

Date	Mintage	VG	F	VF	XF	Unc
1678 CS	—	100	200	325	650	—
1679 CS	—	100	200	325	650	—
1680 CS	—	100	200	325	650	—
1682 LCS	—	100	200	325	650	—

KM# 488 2/3 THALER (Gulden)
Silver **Ruler:** Friedrich Wilhelm **Obv:** Bust right in circle, date divided below **Rev:** Crowned arms in circle, value 2/3 below **Mint:** Halberstadt

Date	Mintage	VG	F	VF	XF	Unc
1679 LCS	—	125	250	500	950	—

KM# 509.1 2/3 THALER (Gulden)
Silver **Ruler:** Friedrich Wilhelm **Mint:** Berlin

Date	Mintage	VG	F	VF	XF	Unc
1683 LCS	—	100	200	350	725	—
1685 LCS	—	100	200	350	725	—

KM# 509.2 2/3 THALER (Gulden)
Silver **Ruler:** Friedrich Wilhelm **Mint:** Berlin / Kölln

Date	Mintage	VG	F	VF	XF	Unc
1683 LCS	—	100	200	335	675	—

KM# 510 2/3 THALER (Gulden)
Silver **Ruler:** Friedrich Wilhelm **Rev:** Crowned arms, value 2/3 below, date divided in legend at top **Mint:** Magdeburg

Date	Mintage	VG	F	VF	XF	Unc
1683 IE	—	45.00	100	200	385	—

KM# 445.5 2/3 THALER (Gulden)
Silver **Ruler:** Friedrich Wilhelm **Mint:** Minden **Note:** Dav.#261E.

Date	Mintage	VG	F	VF	XF	Unc
1683 B H	—	80.00	140	275	550	—

KM# A446 2/3 THALER (Gulden)
Silver **Ruler:** Friedrich Wilhelm **Rev:** Crowned arms divide date. **Mint:** Minden **Note:** Dav.#262.

Date	Mintage	VG	F	VF	XF	Unc
1683 B H	—	80.00	140	275	550	—

KM# 446 2/3 THALER (Gulden)
Silver **Ruler:** Friedrich Wilhelm **Rev:** Large crowned arms, date in legend at upper left, arms divide initials **Mint:** Minden **Note:** Varieties exist. Dav.#263.

Date	Mintage	VG	F	VF	XF	Unc
1683 B-H	—	175	375	650	1,150	—

KM# 511 2/3 THALER (Gulden)
Silver **Ruler:** Friedrich Wilhelm **Mint:** Minden **Note:** Varieties exist.

Date	Mintage	VG	F	VF	XF	Unc
1683 BH	—	55.00	125	240	475	—
1684 BH	—	55.00	125	240	475	—

KM# 525 2/3 THALER (Gulden)
Silver **Ruler:** Friedrich Wilhelm **Obv:** Bust right in circle **Rev:** Crowned arms, date above, value below **Mint:** Berlin

Date	Mintage	VG	F	VF	XF	Unc
1686 LCS	—	100	200	360	725	—

KM# 526 2/3 THALER (Gulden)
Silver **Ruler:** Friedrich Wilhelm **Rev:** Arms between two palm branches and date in legend **Mint:** Berlin

Date	Mintage	VG	F	VF	XF	Unc
1686 LCS	—	100	200	360	725	—
1687 LCS	1,459,000	100	200	360	725	—

KM# 534.1 2/3 THALER (Gulden)
Silver **Ruler:** Friedrich Wilhelm **Rev:** Crowned arms divide mintmaster's initials, date in legend, value 2/3 below **Mint:** Berlin **Note:** Varieties exist.

Date	Mintage	VG	F	VF	XF	Unc
1687 LCS	Inc. above	30.00	65.00	130	260	—
1688 LCS	Inc. above	30.00	65.00	130	260	—

KM# A541 2/3 THALER (Gulden)
Silver **Ruler:** Friedrich Wilhelm **Obv:** Bust of Friedrich Wilhelm right in inner circle **Obv. Legend:** FRID. WILH: D:G. M. B. S. R. I. ARC & EL **Rev:** Crown arms, value 2/3 below **Rev. Legend:** CHVRF. BRAND LANDMVNZ **Mint:** Berlin **Note:** Dav. #252.

Date	Mintage	VG	F	VF	XF	Unc
1688 LCS	—	45.00	90.00	180	360	—

KM# B541 2/3 THALER (Gulden)
Silver **Ruler:** Friedrich Wilhelm **Obv:** Bust of Friedrich Wilhelm right in inner circle **Obv. Legend:** FRID. WILH: D:G. M. B. S. R. I. ARC & EL **Rev:** Crowned arms in inner circle, value 2/3 below **Rev. Legend:** CHVRF: BRAND LANDMVNZ **Mint:** Berlin **Note:** Dav. #253.

Date	Mintage	VG	F	VF	XF	Unc
1688 LCS	—	45.00	90.00	180	360	—

KM# 534.2 2/3 THALER (Gulden)
Silver **Ruler:** Friedrich Wilhelm **Mint:** Berlin / Kölln

Date	Mintage	VG	F	VF	XF	Unc
1688 LCS	Inc. above	30.00	65.00	130	260	—

KM# 540 2/3 THALER (Gulden)
Silver **Ruler:** Friedrich Wilhelm **Mint:** Magdeburg

Date	Mintage	VG	F	VF	XF	Unc
1688 ICS	—	80.00	140	275	550	—

KM# 555 2/3 THALER (Gulden)
Silver **Ruler:** Friedrich III **Rev:** Crowned arms divide date **Mint:** Berlin

Date	Mintage	VG	F	VF	XF	Unc
1689 LCS	2,216,000	45.00	90.00	180	360	—

KM# 557 2/3 THALER (Gulden)
Silver **Ruler:** Friedrich III **Mint:** Magdeburg

Date	Mintage	VG	F	VF	XF	Unc
1689 IE	—	40.00	80.00	160	325	—
1690 IE	—	40.00	80.00	160	325	—
1690 ICS	—	40.00	80.00	160	325	—
1691 ICS	—	40.00	80.00	160	325	—
1692 ICS	—	40.00	80.00	160	325	—
1693 ICS	—	40.00	80.00	160	325	—
1694 ICS	—	40.00	80.00	160	325	—
1695 ICS	—	40.00	80.00	160	325	—

KM# 558 2/3 THALER (Gulden)
Silver **Ruler:** Friedrich Wilhelm **Mint:** Minden

Date	Mintage	VG	F	VF	XF	Unc
1689	—	55.00	110	240	450	—
1690	—	55.00	110	240	450	—
1690 BH	—	55.00	110	240	450	—
1691 BH	—	55.00	110	240	450	—
1693 BH	—	55.00	110	240	450	—
1694 BH	—	55.00	110	240	450	—

KM# 559 2/3 THALER (Gulden)
Silver **Ruler:** Friedrich III **Mint:** Minden

Date	Mintage	VG	F	VF	XF	Unc
1689 BH	—	65.00	140	250	475	—
1689 BH-GM	—	65.00	140	250	475	—

KM# 560 2/3 THALER (Gulden)
Silver **Ruler:** Friedrich III **Mint:** Stargard **Note:** Varieties exist.

Date	Mintage	VG	F	VF	XF	Unc
1689 SD	—	80.00	140	250	475	—
1690 SD	—	55.00	100	200	450	—
1691 SD	—	55.00	100	200	450	—

KM# 556 2/3 THALER (Gulden)
Silver **Ruler:** Friedrich III **Mint:** Berlin **Note:** Many varieties exist.

Date	Mintage	VG	F	VF	XF	Unc
1689 LCS	Inc. above	40.00	80.00	160	325	—
1690 LCS	4,743,000	40.00	80.00	160	325	—
1691 LCS	2,101,000	40.00	80.00	160	325	—
1692 LCS	Inc. above	40.00	80.00	160	325	—
1693 LCS	1,472,000	40.00	80.00	160	325	—
1695 LCS	Inc. above	40.00	80.00	160	325	—

KM# 576 2/3 THALER (Gulden)

Silver **Ruler:** Friedrich III **Mint:** Minden **Note:** Varieties exist.

Date	Mintage	VG	F	VF	XF	Unc
1691 BH	—	45.00	100	200	425	—
1692 BH	—	45.00	100	200	425	—
1693 BH	—	45.00	100	200	425	—
1694 BH	—	45.00	100	200	425	—

KM# 594 2/3 THALER (Gulden)

Silver **Ruler:** Friedrich III **Mint:** Magdeburg

Date	Mintage	VG	F	VF	XF	Unc
1694 ICS	—	75.00	150	300	625	—
1695 ICS	—	75.00	150	300	625	—

KM# 612 2/3 THALER (Gulden)

Silver **Ruler:** Friedrich III **Rev:** Shield more ornately shaped **Mint:** Berlin

Date	Mintage	VG	F	VF	XF	Unc
1698 LCS	240,000	75.00	150	300	625	—
1699 LCS	168,000	75.00	150	300	625	—
1700 LCS	75,000	75.00	150	300	625	—

KM# 613 2/3 THALER (Gulden)

Silver **Ruler:** Friedrich III **Mint:** Magdeburg

Date	Mintage	VG	F	VF	XF	Unc
1698 HFH	—	75.00	150	300	625	—
1699 HFH	—	75.00	150	300	625	—
1700 HFH	—	75.00	150	300	625	—

KM# 618 2/3 THALER (Gulden)

Silver **Ruler:** Friedrich III **Mint:** Magdeburg

Date	Mintage	VG	F	VF	XF	Unc
1699 HFH	—	75.00	150	300	625	—
1700 HFH	—	75.00	150	300	625	—

KM# 448 3/4 THALER

Silver **Ruler:** Friedrich Wilhelm **Subject:** Victory at Battle of Fehrbellin **Obv:** Elector on horse galloping right **Rev:** 14-line inscription with date **Mint:** Berlin

Date	Mintage	VG	F	VF	XF	Unc
1675	—	—	—	—	—	—

KM# 19 THALER

Silver **Ruler:** Joachim Friedrich **Obv:** Half-length bust right divides date **Rev:** Helmeted 16-fold arms **Mint:** Kölln **Note:** Dav. #6112.

Date	Mintage	VG	F	VF	XF	Unc
1602 (e)	1,355	3,000	4,800	8,400	12,000	—
1604 MH	—	3,000	4,800	8,400	12,000	—

KM# 23 THALER

Silver **Ruler:** Joachim Friedrich **Rev:** 17-fold arms **Note:** Dav. #6113.

Date	Mintage	VG	F	VF	XF	Unc
1604	—	3,000	4,800	9,000	14,000	—

KM# 25 THALER

Silver **Ruler:** Joachim Friedrich **Rev:** Date in legend **Mint:** Kolln an der Spree **Note:** Dav. #6114.

Date	Mintage	VG	F	VF	XF	Unc
1605 MH Rare	—	—	—	—	—	—

KM# 26.1 THALER

Silver **Ruler:** Joachim Friedrich **Rev:** Arms divide date **Rev. Legend:** IMP: ARCHI. CA... **Mint:** Kolln an der Spree **Note:** Dav. #6116.

Date	Mintage	VG	F	VF	XF	Unc
1605 MH Rare	—	—	—	—	—	—

KM# 26.2 THALER

Silver **Ruler:** Joachim Friedrich **Rev. Legend:** ROM. IMP. ARC... **Mint:** Kolln an der Spree **Note:** Dav. #6117.

Date	Mintage	VG	F	VF	XF	Unc
ND MH Rare	—	—	—	—	—	—

KM# 35.1 THALER

Silver **Ruler:** Johann Sigismund **Obv:** Half-length bust, date below **Obv. Legend:** IOH. SIGISM... **Rev:** Helmeted manifold arms **Mint:** Kolln an der Spree **Note:** Dav. #6119.

Date	Mintage	VG	F	VF	XF	Unc
1611	—	2,700	4,500	7,800	12,000	—
1611 MH	—	2,700	4,500	7,800	12,000	—
1614 MH	—	2,700	4,500	7,800	12,000	—

KM# 36 THALER

Silver **Ruler:** Johann Sigismund **Obv:** Facing half-length bust, date below **Rev:** Cross, arms in center and in border at end of each arm **Note:** Dav. #6120.

Date	Mintage	VG	F	VF	XF	Unc
1611	—	3,000	4,800	9,000	14,000	—

KM# 45 THALER

Silver **Ruler:** Johann Sigismund **Rev:** Helmeted manifold arms **Mint:** Kolln ande Spree/Driesen **Note:** Dav. #6121.

Date	Mintage	VG	F	VF	XF	Unc
ND MH	—	2,700	4,800	8,400	14,000	—
1612 MH	—	2,700	4,800	8,400	14,000	—
1612 HL	—	2,700	4,500	7,800	12,000	—

KM# 47 THALER

Silver **Ruler:** Johann Sigismund **Mint:** Kölln **Note:** Dav. #6123.

Date	Mintage	VG	F	VF	XF	Unc
ND(1612/13) MH	—	3,000	5,400	9,000	15,000	—

KM# 35.2 THALER

Silver **Ruler:** Johann Sigismund **Obv. Legend:** IOH. SIGIS... **Mint:** Kolln an der Spree **Note:** Dav. #6124.

Date	Mintage	VG	F	VF	XF	Unc
1615 MH Rare	—	—	—	—	—	—

KM# 35.3 THALER

Silver **Ruler:** Johann Sigismund **Obv. Legend:** IOH. SIGISM ... ROM ... E. E. L. **Mint:** Berlin / Kölln **Note:** Dav. #6125.

Date	Mintage	VG	F	VF	XF	Unc
1617 MH	—	3,000	5,400	9,000	—	—
1617 HL	—	3,000	5,400	9,000	—	—
ND HL	—	3,000	5,400	9,000	—	—

KM# 54 THALER

Silver **Ruler:** Johann Sigismund **Rev:** Arms divide date **Mint:** Berlin / Kölln

Date	Mintage	VG	F	VF	XF	Unc
1617 MH Rare	—	—	—	—	—	—

KM# 46 THALER

Silver **Ruler:** Johann Sigismund **Mint:** Driesen **Note:** Dav. #6122.

Date	Mintage	VG	F	VF	XF	Unc
ND(1619)	—	3,000	4,800	9,000	14,000	—

KM# 67 THALER

Silver **Ruler:** Georg Wilhelm **Subject:** Union of Brandenburg With Prussia **Obv:** 3/4-length figure right **Rev:** Eagle, heart-shaped shield with SA on breast divides date **Mint:** Berlin **Note:** Dav. #6126.

Date	Mintage	VG	F	VF	XF	Unc
1620 LM	—	900	1,800	3,600	6,000	—

KM# 68 THALER

Silver **Ruler:** Georg Wilhelm **Obv:** Bust right **Rev:** Scepter arms in ornamented frame divide date, value below in legend **Mint:** Berlin / Kölln **Note:** Dav. #6127.

Date	Mintage	VG	F	VF	XF	Unc
1620 LM	—	900	1,800	3,600	6,000	—

KM# 69 THALER

Silver **Ruler:** Georg Wilhelm **Mint:** Berlin / Kölln **Note:** Dav. #6128.

Date	Mintage	VG	F	VF	XF	Unc
1620 LM	—	550	1,800	3,600	6,000	—

KM# 70 THALER

Silver **Ruler:** Georg Wilhelm **Obv:** Bust right holding sceptre **Rev:** Eagle with outspread wings **Mint:** Berlin / Kölln **Note:** Dav. #6129.

Date	Mintage	VG	F	VF	XF	Unc
1620 LM	—	1,000	2,000	3,900	6,600	—

KM# 71 THALER

Silver **Ruler:** Georg Wilhelm **Obv:** Bust right holding sceptre in inner circle **Rev:** Helmeted 25-fold arms, date divided at top by initials **Mint:** Berlin / Kölln **Note:** Dav. #6130.

Date	Mintage	VG	F	VF	XF	Unc
1620 LM	—	1,000	2,000	3,900	6,600	—

KM# 72 THALER

Silver **Ruler:** Georg Wilhelm **Rev:** Date divides initials at top **Mint:** Berlin / Kölln **Note:** Dav. #6131.

Date	Mintage	VG	F	VF	XF	Unc
1620 LM	—	1,000	2,000	3,900	6,600	—

KM# 73 THALER

Silver **Ruler:** Georg Wilhelm **Obv:** Bust of Georg Wilhelm right holding sceptre **Rev:** Eagle with wings spread in inner circle, no arms on wings **Mint:** Berlin / Kölln **Note:** Dav. #6132.

Date	Mintage	VG	F	VF	XF	Unc
1620 LM	—	1,000	2,000	3,900	6,600	—

KM# 74 THALER

Silver **Ruler:** Georg Wilhelm **Mint:** Berlin **Note:** Dav. #6134.

Date	Mintage	VG	F	VF	XF	Unc
1620 LM	—	1,000	2,000	3,900	6,600	—

KM# 88 THALER

Silver **Ruler:** Georg Wilhelm **Obv:** Half-length figure right, date below **Rev:** Arms **Mint:** Berlin **Note:** Dav. #6135.

Date	Mintage	VG	F	VF	XF	Unc
1621 Rare	—	—	—	—	—	—

KM# 89 THALER

Silver **Ruler:** Georg Wilhelm **Obv:** 1/2-length figure right, date below **Rev:** Mint mark of Ernst Pfaler at end inscription **Mint:** Königsberg

Date	Mintage	VG	F	VF	XF	Unc
1621 (a) Rare	—	—	—	—	—	—

KM# 117 THALER

Silver **Ruler:** Georg Wilhelm **Obv:** Crowned bust right **Rev:** Arms, crown above divides date **Mint:** Kölln **Note:** Dav. #6138.

Date	Mintage	VG	F	VF	XF	Unc
1624 LM Rare	—	—	—	—	—	—

KM# 125 THALER

Silver **Ruler:** Georg Wilhelm **Mint:** Königsberg **Note:** Dav. #6141.

Date	Mintage	VG	F	VF	XF	Unc
16Z7 (a)	7,318	500	1,000	1,950	3,850	—
16Z8 (a)	11,000	500	1,000	1,950	3,850	—
16Z9 (a)	15,000	500	1,000	1,950	3,850	—
1630 (a)	20,000	500	1,000	1,950	3,850	—
1631 (a)	4,000	500	1,000	1,950	3,850	—
1632 (a)	—	500	1,000	1,950	3,850	—
1633 (a)	34,000	500	1,000	1,950	3,850	—
1634 (a)	Inc. above	500	1,000	1,950	3,850	—
1635 (a)	Inc. above	500	1,000	1,950	3,850	—

KM# 128 THALER

Silver **Ruler:** Georg Wilhelm **Obv:** Half-length figure right **Rev:** Helmeted arms, date above **Mint:** Kölln **Note:** Dav. #6143.

Date	Mintage	VG	F	VF	XF	Unc
1628 LM	—	1,200	2,400	4,800	7,800	—
1631 LM	—	1,200	2,400	4,800	7,800	—
1632 LM	—	1,200	2,400	4,800	7,800	—
1633 LM	—	1,200	2,400	4,800	7,800	—

KM# A143 THALER

Silver **Ruler:** Georg Wilhelm **Obv:** 1/2-length figure of Georg Wilhelm right, scepter on shoulder **Rev:** Shield of arms **Mint:** Königsberg **Note:** Ref. Dost #608-11. Struck from 2 Thaler dies, KM#143.

Date	Mintage	VG	F	VF	XF	Unc
1630 (q)	—	1,200	2,400	4,800	7,800	—
1631	—	1,200	2,400	4,800	7,800	—

KM# 141.1 THALER

Silver **Ruler:** Georg Wilhelm **Rev:** Different arms divide L-M **Mint:** Berlin **Note:** Dav. #6146.

Date	Mintage	VG	F	VF	XF	Unc
1631 LM	—	725	1,400	2,200	3,850	—
1633 LM	—	725	1,400	2,200	3,850	—

KM# 145.1 THALER

Silver **Ruler:** Georg Wilhelm **Rev:** Mintmaster's initials and date in legend **Mint:** Berlin **Note:** Dav. #6147.

Date	Mintage	VG	F	VF	XF	Unc
1632 LM	—	825	1,650	3,300	5,500	—
1633 LM	—	825	1,650	3,300	5,500	—
1635 LM	—	825	1,650	3,300	5,500	—

KM# 145.2 THALER

Silver **Ruler:** Georg Wilhelm **Rev:** Larger cap on arms **Mint:** Berlin **Note:** Dav. #6149.

Date	Mintage	VG	F	VF	XF	Unc
1633 LM	—	825	1,650	3,300	3,650	—
1636 LM	—	825	1,650	3,300	3,650	—

KM# 146 THALER

Silver **Ruler:** Georg Wilhelm **Rev:** Cap above arms divides mintmaster's initials **Mint:** Berlin **Note:** Dav. #6150.

Date	Mintage	VG	F	VF	XF	Unc
1633 LM	—	350	725	1,400	2,500	—

KM# 147.1 THALER

Silver **Ruler:** Georg Wilhelm **Obv. Legend:** GEORG. WILH... **Rev:** Arms divide mintmaster's initials, **Rev. Legend:** PRVS. IVL... **Mint:** Berlin **Note:** Dav. #6154.

Date	Mintage	VG	F	VF	XF	Unc
1633 LM	—	1,450	2,400	3,600	6,000	—
1637 LM	—	1,450	2,400	3,600	6,000	—

KM# 156 THALER

Silver **Ruler:** Georg Wilhelm **Mint:** Königsberg **Note:** Dav. #6151.

Date	Mintage	VG	F	VF	XF	Unc
1635 DK (a)	Inc. above	375	750	1,500	3,050	—
1636 DK (a)	17,000	375	750	1,500	3,050	7,200
1637 DK (a)	3,428	450	775	1,650	3,300	—
1638 DK (a)	5,556	450	775	1,650	3,300	7,200
1639 DK	3,000	450	775	1,650	3,300	—

KM# 160.1 THALER

Silver **Ruler:** Georg Wilhelm **Obv:** Heavier figure **Rev:** Date divided by large crown **Rev. Legend:** ANFANG ... **Mint:** Königsberg **Note:** Dav. #6152.

Date	Mintage	VG	F	VF	XF	Unc
1636 DK (a)	Inc. above	475	800	1,650	3,300	—

KM# 163 THALER

Silver **Ruler:** Georg Wilhelm **Obv:** 3/4-length figure right holding sceptre over right shoulder **Rev:** Small crown above arms divides mintmaster's initials **Mint:** Berlin **Note:** Dav. #6155.

Date	Mintage	VG	F	VF	XF	Unc
1637 LM	—	1,450	2,400	3,600	6,000	—
1638 LM	—	1,450	2,400	3,600	6,000	—
1639 LM	—	1,450	2,400	4,200	7,200	—

KM# 147.2 THALER

Silver **Ruler:** Georg Wilhelm **Obv. Legend:** GEORG. WILHEL... **Rev. Legend:** ET. EL. PR... **Mint:** Berlin **Note:** Dav. #6156.

Date	Mintage	VG	F	VF	XF	Unc
1639 LM	—	1,450	2,400	3,600	6,000	—

KM# 166.1 THALER

Silver **Ruler:** Georg Wilhelm **Obv:** 3/4-length figure right holding sword over right shoulder **Rev:** Crowned arms **Rev. Legend:** PRVS. IVL... **Mint:** Berlin **Note:** Dav. #6157.

Date	Mintage	VG	F	VF	XF	Unc
1639 LM Rare	—	—	—	—	—	—

KM# 167 THALER

Silver **Ruler:** Georg Wilhelm **Obv:** Half-length figure 3/4 to left. **Rev:** Shield of arms **Mint:** Königsberg **Note:** Dav. #6158.

Date	Mintage	VG	F	VF	XF	Unc
1639 DK Rare	Inc. above	—	—	—	—	—

KM# 166.2 THALER

Silver **Obv:** 3/4-length figure right **Rev:** Crowned arms **Rev. Legend:** EL. PRV. GV. CL... **Note:** Dav. #6159.

Date	Mintage	VG	F	VF	XF	Unc
1639 Rare	—	—	—	—	—	—

KM# 160.2 THALER

Silver **Ruler:** Georg Wilhelm **Obv:** Different bust with short wig **Rev. Legend:** ANFANCK...ENDE. **Mint:** Königsberg **Note:** Dav. #6160. Varieties exist.

Date	Mintage	VG	F	VF	XF	Unc
1639 DK	Inc. above	1,500	3,000	5,400	9,000	—

KM# 160.3 THALER

28.7800 g., Silver, 44 mm. **Ruler:** Georg Wilhelm **Obv:** Half-length armored figure to right, holding scepter over right shoulder, helmet at right **Obv. Legend:** GEORG: WILH: D:G: MARCHI: BRAN: SAC: ROM: IMP: ARCHIO: & EL: D: PRUS:. **Rev:** Ornately shaped shield of 7-fold arms, with central shield of scepter arms, large electoral hat above divides date, mintmaster's initials divided at bottom **Rev. Legend:** MONETA NOVA ARGENTEA DUCIS PRUSSIÆ: **Mint:** Königsberg

Date	Mintage	VG	F	VF	XF	Unc
1639 DK Rare	—	—	—	—	—	—

Note: A VF-XF example realized approximately $21,800 in a March 2010 Künker auction.

KM# A181 THALER

Silver **Ruler:** Friedrich Wilhelm **Mint:** Königsberg **Note:** Ref. Dost #556. Similar to 2 Thaler, KM#181.

Date	Mintage	VG	F	VF	XF	Unc
1640 DK	—	—	—	—	—	—

KM# 166.3 THALER

Silver **Ruler:** Georg Wilhelm **Mint:** Berlin **Note:** Dav. #6161.

Date	Mintage	VG	F	VF	XF	Unc
1640 LM	—	725	1,400	2,200	3,900	—

KM# 141.2 THALER
Silver **Ruler:** Georg Wilhelm **Mint:** Berlin **Note:** Dav. #6163.

Date	Mintage	VG	F	VF	XF	Unc
1640 LM	—	725	1,400	2,200	3,900	—

KM# 177 THALER
Silver **Ruler:** Friedrich Wilhelm **Rev:** Similar to KM#166, but date divided below arms **Mint:** Berlin **Note:** Dav. #6165.

Date	Mintage	VG	F	VF	XF	Unc
1640 LM	—	725	1,400	2,200	3,900	—

KM# 178 THALER
Silver **Ruler:** Friedrich Wilhelm **Subject:** Death of Georg Wilhelm **Obv:** Facing bust, two circular inscriptions **Rev:** 11-line inscription with R.N. date in border of 24 small arms **Mint:** Königsberg **Note:** Dav. #6166.

Date	Mintage	VG	F	VF	XF	Unc
MDCXL (1640) DK	3,000	—	—	13,500	18,500	—

Note: Künker Auction 165, 3-10, VF-XF realized approximately $14,975.

KM# 187 THALER
Silver **Ruler:** Friedrich Wilhelm **Mint:** Berlin **Note:** Dav. #6167.

Date	Mintage	VG	F	VF	XF	Unc
1641 LM	—	825	1,650	3,300	5,500	—

KM# 188 THALER
Silver **Ruler:** Friedrich Wilhelm **Obv:** Larger figure lower on die **Mint:** Berlin **Note:** Dav. #6168.

Date	Mintage	VG	F	VF	XF	Unc
1641 LM	—	825	1,300	2,500	4,150	—

KM# 189 THALER
Silver **Ruler:** Friedrich Wilhelm **Obv:** Larger figure extends to lower edge of flan **Mint:** Berlin **Note:** Dav. #6169.

Date	Mintage	VG	F	VF	XF	Unc
1641 LM	—	850	1,750	3,400	5,700	—
164Z LM	—	850	1,750	3,400	5,700	—
1642	—	850	1,750	3,400	5,700	—

KM# 190 THALER
Silver **Ruler:** Friedrich Wilhelm **Obv:** Crowned bust right **Rev:** Crowned arms **Mint:** Königsberg **Note:** Dav. #6171.

Date	Mintage	VG	F	VF	XF	Unc
ND(1641) Rare	—	—	—	—	—	—

KM# 191 THALER
Silver **Ruler:** Friedrich Wilhelm **Mint:** Königsberg **Note:** Dav. #6172.

Date	Mintage	VG	F	VF	XF	Unc
1641 DK	—	1,400	2,750	4,700	7,700	—

KM# 192 THALER
Silver **Ruler:** Friedrich Wilhelm **Rev:** Scepter arms in center of large rose, 23 small oval arms around

Date	Mintage	VG	F	VF	XF	Unc
ND(1641/3)	—	1,800	3,600	6,100	—	—

KM# 206 THALER

Silver **Ruler:** Friedrich Wilhelm **Mint:** Königsberg **Note:** Dav. #6173.

Date	Mintage	VG	F	VF	XF	Unc
1642 DK Rare	—	—	—	—	—	—

Note: WAG Auction 49, 2-09, VF-XF realized approx. $13,495.

KM# 205 THALER

Silver **Ruler:** Friedrich Wilhelm **Rev:** Without wreath **Note:** Dav. #6170.

Date	Mintage	VG	F	VF	XF	Unc
ND(1642/3)	—	825	1,650	3,300	5,500	—

KM# 212.1 THALER

Silver **Ruler:** Friedrich Wilhelm **Rev:** Similar to KM#212.2 but different shield decorations. **Mint:** Berlin **Note:** Dav. #6174.

Date	Mintage	VG	F	VF	XF	Unc
1643 AB Rare	—	—	—	—	—	—

KM# 212.2 THALER

Silver **Ruler:** Friedrich Wilhelm **Mint:** Berlin **Note:** Dav. #6178.

Date	Mintage	VG	F	VF	XF	Unc
1643 AB	—	900	1,800	3,600	6,100	—
1644 AB	—	900	1,800	3,600	6,100	—
1645 CT	—	900	1,800	3,600	6,100	—

KM# 212.3 THALER

Silver **Ruler:** Friedrich Wilhelm **Obv:** Broader bust **Rev:** Date above complicated arms **Mint:** Berlin **Note:** Dav. #6180. Varieties exist.

Date	Mintage	VG	F	VF	XF	Unc
1645 CT	—	975	1,950	3,850	6,600	—
1647 CT	—	975	1,950	3,850	6,600	—

KM# 220 THALER

Silver **Ruler:** Friedrich Wilhelm **Mint:** Berlin **Note:** Dav. #6182.

Date	Mintage	VG	F	VF	XF	Unc
1645 CT	—	650	1,300	2,750	5,500	—
1646 CT	—	650	1,300	2,750	5,500	—
1647 CT	—	650	1,300	2,750	5,500	—
1648 CT	—	650	1,300	2,750	5,500	—
1649 CT	—	650	1,300	2,750	5,500	—
1650 CT	—	650	1,300	2,750	5,500	8,800

KM# 235.1 THALER

Silver **Ruler:** Friedrich Wilhelm **Rev:** Helmeted and supported arms **Rev. Legend:** MADG. PR… **Mint:** Berlin **Note:** Dav. #6183.

Date	Mintage	VG	F	VF	XF	Unc
1650 CT	—	550	1,050	2,050	5,500	—

KM# 235.2 THALER

Silver **Ruler:** Friedrich Wilhelm **Rev. Legend:** C. U. I. N. S. C. C… **Note:** Dav. #6184.

Date	Mintage	VG	F	VF	XF	Unc
ND(1651)	—	725	1,400	2,750	6,300	—

KM# 249 THALER

Silver **Ruler:** Friedrich Wilhelm **Obv. Legend:** BR.S.-R. I. ARCHIC. ET. ELECT. **Mint:** Berlin **Note:** Dav. #6185.

Date	Mintage	VG	F	VF	XF	Unc
1651 CT	—	—	—	—	—	—
1653 CT Rare	—	—	—	—	—	—

Note: Künker Auction 81, 3-03, XF realized approximately $23,145

KM# 248 THALER
Silver **Ruler:** Friedrich Wilhelm **Obv:** Elector standing 3/4 to right **Obv. Legend:** BR:-SAC. R. I. ARC: C. ET EL :. **Rev:** Date divided left and right **Mint:** Berlin **Note:** Dav. #6185A.

Date	Mintage	VG	F	VF	XF	Unc
1651 CT Rare	—	—	—	—	—	—

KM# 250 THALER
Silver **Ruler:** Friedrich Wilhelm **Obv:** Bust right in circle **Rev:** Helmeted arms **Mint:** Königsberg **Note:** Struck from 1/2 Thaler dies.

Date	Mintage	VG	F	VF	XF	Unc
ND(1651-6) CM Rare	—	—	—	—	—	—

KM# 257 THALER
Silver **Ruler:** Friedrich Wilhelm **Obv:** Half-length figure 3/4 to right **Rev:** Helmeted and supported arms, date divided below **Mint:** Königsberg **Note:** Dav. #6186.

Date	Mintage	VG	F	VF	XF	Unc
1652 CM	—	1,450	2,400	4,150	7,200	—

KM# 290 THALER
Silver **Ruler:** Friedrich Wilhelm **Obv:** Eagle below forelegs of horse **Mint:** Berlin **Note:** Dav. #6187.

Date	Mintage	VG	F	VF	XF	Unc
1657 AB	—	550	1,100	2,200	4,150	—
1657 CT	—	550	1,100	2,200	4,150	—

KM# 289 THALER
Silver **Ruler:** Friedrich Wilhelm **Subject:** Attainment of Sovereignty over East Prussia **Obv:** Town below forelegs of horse **Mint:** Berlin **Note:** Dav. #6188.

Date	Mintage	VG	F	VF	XF	Unc
1657 CT	—	775	1,650	3,300	5,500	—

KM# 315 THALER
Silver **Ruler:** Friedrich Wilhelm **Subject:** Death of Friedrich Wilhelm's Mother, Elisabet Charlotte **Mint:** Berlin **Note:** Dav. #6191.

Date	Mintage	VG	F	VF	XF	Unc
1660 AB	—	650	1,300	2,750	4,950	—

KM# 324 THALER
Silver **Ruler:** Friedrich Wilhelm **Obv:** Half-length bust right **Rev:** Helmeted and supported arms divide date **Mint:** Berlin **Note:** Dav. #6192.

Date	Mintage	VG	F	VF	XF	Unc
1662 AB	940	1,950	3,300	6,100	8,800	—

KM# 327 THALER
Silver **Ruler:** Friedrich Wilhelm **Obv:** Friedrich mounted on horse right **Rev:** Helmeted arms **Mint:** Berlin **Note:** Dav. #6193.

Date	Mintage	VG	F	VF	XF	Unc
1663 AB	2,193	1,000	2,000	3,850	7,200	—

KM# 328 THALER
Silver **Ruler:** Friedrich Wilhelm **Obv:** Friedrich mounted on prancing horse right **Rev:** Helmeted arms **Mint:** Berlin **Note:** Klippe. Dav. #A6193.

Date	Mintage	VG	F	VF	XF	Unc
1663 AB Rare	Inc. above	—	—	—	—	—

KM# 333 THALER
Silver **Ruler:** Friedrich Wilhelm **Mint:** Berlin **Note:** Dav. #6194.

Date	Mintage	VG	F	VF	XF	Unc
1664 AB	2,972	650	1,400	2,750	6,100	9,400
1664 IL	Inc. above	775	1,650	3,300	6,600	9,400
1665 IL	Inc. above	775	1,650	3,300	6,600	9,400

KM# 363 THALER
Silver **Ruler:** Friedrich Wilhelm **Subject:** Death of Friedrich Wilhelm's Wife, Luise Henriette von Nassau-Oranien **Obv:** Facing bust of Luise Henriette **Rev:** Ten-line inscription with date **Mint:** Berlin **Note:** Dav. #6195.

Date	Mintage	VG	F	VF	XF	Unc
1667 IL	—	1,650	3,300	6,100	9,900	—

KM# 364 THALER
Silver **Ruler:** Friedrich Wilhelm **Obv:** Facing bust of Henriette

von Nassau-Oranien **Rev:** Crowned frame with five-line inscription **Mint:** Berlin **Note:** Dav. #6196.

Date	Mintage	VG	F	VF	XF	Unc
1667 IL-GL Rare	—	—	—	—	—	—

KM# 365 THALER

Silver **Ruler:** Friedrich Wilhelm **Obv:** Bust of Luise Henriette left **Mint:** Berlin **Note:** Dav. #6197.

Date	Mintage	VG	F	VF	XF	Unc
1667 IL-GL Rare	—	—	—	—	—	—

Note: WAG Auction 47, 6-08, XF realized approximately $15,750, Peus Auction 391, 5-07, XF realized approximately $10,875.

KM# 411 THALER

Silver **Ruler:** Friedrich Wilhelm **Obv:** Bust right, date below **Rev:** Crowned arms between two palm branches **Mint:** Berlin **Note:** Dav. #6198.

Date	Mintage	VG	F	VF	XF	Unc
1670 IL Rare	—	—	—	—	—	—
1673 IL Rare	—	—	—	—	—	—

KM# 424 THALER

Silver **Ruler:** Friedrich Wilhelm **Obv:** Laureate bust right **Rev:** Helmeted and supported arms, date in legend **Mint:** Königsberg **Note:** Dav. #6199.

Date	Mintage	VG	F	VF	XF	Unc
1672 TT	5,400	1,550	2,600	4,700	7,700	—
1677 HS	1,000	1,650	2,750	5,200	8,800	—

KM# 449 THALER

Silver **Ruler:** Friedrich Wilhelm **Subject:** Victory at Battle of Fehrbellin **Mint:** Berlin **Note:** Dav. #6200.

Date	Mintage	VG	F	VF	XF	Unc
1675	—	750	1,500	3,050	5,200	—

KM# 452 THALER

Silver **Ruler:** Friedrich Wilhelm **Rev:** LINVM. 18 IVN, date below figure **Note:** Dav. #6201.

Date	Mintage	VG	F	VF	XF	Unc
1675	—	650	1,300	2,750	4,950	—

KM# 451 THALER

Silver **Ruler:** Friedrich Wilhelm **Rev:** Inscription, date below figure **Rev. Inscription:** F. BELLIN VM. 18 IVN/ **Note:** Dav. #6201A.

Date	Mintage	VG	F	VF	XF	Unc
1675	—	600	1,200	2,500	4,700	—

KM# 453 THALER

Silver **Ruler:** Friedrich Wilhelm **Rev:** Figure without helmet looking right **Note:** Dav. #6201B.

Date	Mintage	VG	F	VF	XF	Unc
1675	—	875	1,800	3,600	6,100	—

KM# 454 THALER

Silver **Ruler:** Friedrich Wilhelm **Obv:** Elector on horse galloping left **Note:** Dav. #6202.

Date	Mintage	VG	F	VF	XF	Unc
1675	—	825	1,650	3,300	—	—

KM# 450 THALER

Silver **Ruler:** Friedrich Wilhelm **Rev:** 14-line inscription

Date	Mintage	VG	F	VF	XF	Unc
1675	—	650	1,400	2,750	—	—

KM# 472 THALER

Silver **Ruler:** Friedrich Wilhelm **Obv:** Half-length figure right with helmet, date in lower left **Rev:** Crowned eagle, scepter arms on breast, 25 small shields on wings **Mint:** Berlin **Note:** Dav. #6203.

Date	Mintage	VG	F	VF	XF	Unc
1677 CS Rare	—	—	—	—	—	—

KM# 473.1 THALER

Silver **Ruler:** Friedrich Wilhelm **Obv:** Draped bust right **Rev:** Helmeted arms **Mint:** Berlin **Note:** Dav. #6204.

Date	Mintage	VG	F	VF	XF	Unc
1677 CS	—	1,500	3,050	4,950	7,700	—
1678 CS	—	1,500	3,050	4,950	7,700	—

KM# 474 THALER

Silver **Ruler:** Friedrich Wilhelm **Rev:** Date divided by arms **Mint:** Berlin **Note:** Dav. #6205.

Date	Mintage	VG	F	VF	XF	Unc
1677 CS Rare	—	—	—	—	—	—
1678 CS Rare	—	—	—	—	—	—

Note: Künker Auction 134, 1-08, XF realized approximately, $13,685

KM# 473.2 THALER

Silver **Ruler:** Friedrich Wilhelm **Rev:** Shield different shape **Mint:** Berlin **Note:** Dav. #6206.

Date	Mintage	VG	F	VF	XF	Unc
1678 CS	—	1,450	2,400	4,150	6,600	—
1679 CS	—	1,300	2,200	3,600	6,100	—

KM# 489 THALER

Silver **Ruler:** Friedrich Wilhelm **Subject:** Victory Against Sweden for Pomerania **Obv:** Elector on horse galloping right, date below **Rev:** Helmeted and supported arms **Mint:** Berlin **Note:** Dav. #6207.

Date	Mintage	VG	F	VF	XF	Unc
1679 CS-GL Rare	—	—	—	—	—	—

Note: Künker Auction 81, 3-03, VF-XF realized approximately $10,195

KM# 490 THALER

Silver **Ruler:** Friedrich Wilhelm **Mint:** Berlin **Note:** Dav. #6208.

Date	Mintage	VG	F	VF	XF	Unc
1679 CS	—	—	4,800	7,800	12,000	—

Note: Künker Auction 81, 3-03, XF-Unc realized approximately $16,530

KM# 473.3 THALER

Silver **Ruler:** Friedrich Wilhelm **Obv. Legend:** ... A. RC. & EL & **Mint:** Berlin **Note:** Dav. #6209. Varieties exist.

Date	Mintage	VG	F	VF	XF	Unc
1680 CS	—	1,150	1,900	3,600	6,000	—

KM# 500 THALER

Silver **Ruler:** Friedrich Wilhelm **Obv:** Bust right, date divided to lower sides **Rev:** Helmeted arms divide mintmaster's initials **Mint:** Halberstadt **Note:** Dav. #6210.

Date	Mintage	VG	F	VF	XF	Unc
1680 LCS	—	2,400	4,200	7,800	12,000	—

KM# 501 THALER

Silver **Ruler:** Friedrich Wilhelm **Subject:** Homage of the City of Madgeburg, 30 May 1681 **Obv:** Bust of elector right in oval frame linked to clouds and to city of Madgeburg by three chains **Rev:** Maiden kneeling right in landscape, sun, eagle and cornucopia in clouds above, date below **Mint:** Magdeburg

Date	Mintage	VG	F	VF	XF	Unc
1681 IE Rare	—	—	—	—	—	—

KM# 516 THALER

Silver **Ruler:** Friedrich Wilhelm **Mint:** Berlin **Note:** Dav. #6211.

Date	Mintage	VG	F	VF	XF	Unc
1684 IE	—	1,950	3,150	6,100	9,600	—
1686 IE	—	1,950	3,150	6,100	9,600	—

KM# 521 THALER

Silver **Ruler:** Friedrich Wilhelm **Obv:** Bust right in circle **Rev:** Crowned eagle, scepter arms on breast, eight shields on wings, date divided at lower left and right **Mint:** Berlin **Note:** Dav. #6212.

Date	Mintage	VG	F	VF	XF	Unc
1685 LCS	—	1,400	2,750	4,600	7,700	—

KM# 527 THALER

Silver **Ruler:** Friedrich Wilhelm **Mint:** Berlin **Note:** Dav. #6213.

Date	Mintage	VG	F	VF	XF	Unc
1686 LCS	—	1,500	3,050	4,950	8,300	—

KM# 577 THALER

Silver **Ruler:** Friedrich III **Obv:** Bust right **Rev:** Large crowned ornate arms, date divided to lower left and right **Mint:** Magdeburg **Note:** Dav. #6214.

Date	Mintage	VG	F	VF	XF	Unc
1691 ICS	—	1,300	2,400	4,150	6,600	—

KM# 585 THALER
Silver **Ruler:** Friedrich III **Rev:** Arms divide date **Mint:** Minden **Note:** Dav. #6215.

Date	Mintage	VG	F	VF	XF	Unc
1692 BH Rare	—	—	—	—	—	—

KM# 586.1 THALER
Silver **Ruler:** Friedrich III **Mint:** Berlin **Note:** Dav. #6217.

Date	Mintage	VG	F	VF	XF	Unc
1692 LCS-IBS	500,000	1,300	2,400	4,150	6,600	—

KM# 586.2 THALER
Silver **Ruler:** Friedrich III **Obv:** Side and back view of bust **Mint:** Berlin **Note:** Dav. #6218. Varieties exist.

Date	Mintage	VG	F	VF	XF	Unc
1692 LCS-IBS	Inc. above	1,450	2,550	4,250	6,900	—

KM# 591 THALER
Silver **Ruler:** Friedrich III **Obv:** Bust right **Rev:** Crown divides date above arms **Mint:** Berlin **Note:** Dav. #6219.

Date	Mintage	VG	F	VF	XF	Unc
1693 LCS-IBS	Inc. above	1,450	2,550	4,250	6,900	—

KM# 603 THALER
Silver **Ruler:** Friedrich III **Rev:** Larger crown and arms **Mint:** Berlin **Note:** Dav. #6220.

Date	Mintage	VG	F	VF	XF	Unc
ND1695 LCS-IBS	—	1,450	2,550	4,250	6,900	—

KM# 604.2 THALER
Silver **Ruler:** Friedrich Wilhelm **Mint:** Magdeburg **Note:** Dav. #6222.

Date	Mintage	VG	F	VF	XF	Unc
1695 ICS	—	275	475	825	1,400	—

KM# 605.2 THALER
Silver **Ruler:** Friedrich III **Mint:** Magdeburg

Date	Mintage	VG	F	VF	XF	Unc
1695 ICS	—	300	500	850	1,650	—

KM# 605.1 THALER
Silver **Ruler:** Friedrich III **Rev:** Without legend **Mint:** Berlin **Note:** Dav. #6222.

Date	Mintage	VG	F	VF	XF	Unc
1695 LCS	—	275	400	650	1,000	—

KM# 604.1 THALER
Silver **Ruler:** Friedrich Wilhelm **Mint:** Berlin **Note:** Albertus Thaler. Dav. #6221.

Date	Mintage	VG	F	VF	XF	Unc
1695 LCS	—	200	350	575	950	—
1696 LCS	—	225	400	650	1,000	—

KM# 604.3 THALER
Silver **Ruler:** Friedrich III **Mint:** Minden **Note:** Dav. #6222.

Date	Mintage	VG	F	VF	XF	Unc
1696 BH	—	300	500	850	1,650	—

KM# 10 2 THALER
Silver **Ruler:** Joachim Friedrich **Obv:** Half-length bust right **Rev:** Helmeted 15-fold arms, date in legend **Mint:** Kölln **Note:** Dav. #6111.

Date	Mintage	VG	F	VF	XF	Unc
1602/0 (e) Rare	—	—	—	—	—	—

KM# 27 2 THALER
Silver **Ruler:** Joachim Friedrich **Obv:** Half-length bust of Joachim right divides date **Rev:** Helmeted 16-fold arms divide date **Mint:** Kolln an der Spree **Note:** Dav. #6115.

Date	Mintage	VG	F	VF	XF	Unc
1605 MH Rare	—	—	—	—	—	—

KM# 37 2 THALER
Silver **Ruler:** Johann Sigismund **Obv:** Half-length bust of Johann, date below **Rev:** Helmeted mani-fold arms **Mint:** Kolln an der Spree **Note:** Dav. #6118.

Date	Mintage	VG	F	VF	XF	Unc
1611	—	3,000	4,800	7,800	12,000	—
1611 MH	—	3,000	4,800	7,800	12,000	—
1614 MH	—	3,000	4,800	7,800	12,000	—

KM# 75 2 THALER
Silver **Ruler:** Georg Wilhelm **Mint:** Berlin **Note:** Dav. #6133.

Date	Mintage	VG	F	VF	XF	Unc
1620 LM Rare	—	—	—	—	—	—

KM# 112.1 2 THALER

Silver **Ruler:** Georg Wilhelm **Obv:** Crowned half-length figure right **Obv. Legend:** GEORG: WILHELM :V:: G: G: **Rev:** Helmeted arms, date above **Mint:** Königsberg **Note:** Dav. #6136.

Date	Mintage	VG	F	VF	XF	Unc
1623	300	2,100	3,600	6,000	9,600	—

KM# 112.2 2 THALER

Silver **Ruler:** Georg Wilhelm **Obv. Legend:** GEORG. WILHEL: V: G: G: MARC... **Note:** Dav. #6137.

Date	Mintage	VG	F	VF	XF	Unc
1623	Inc. above	2,400	4,200	6,600	11,000	—

KM# 133 2 THALER

Silver **Ruler:** Georg Wilhelm **Note:** Dav. #6140.

Date	Mintage	VG	F	VF	XF	Unc
1629	—	1,550	2,650	4,500	7,200	—
1630	3,000	1,550	2,650	4,500	7,200	—
1635	—	1,550	2,650	4,500	7,200	—

KM# 143 2 THALER

Silver **Ruler:** Georg Wilhelm **Obv:** 1/2-length figure right **Rev:** Helmeted arms **Mint:** Königsberg **Note:** Dav. #6144.

Date	Mintage	VG	F	VF	XF	Unc
1630 (a)	—	1,550	2,650	4,500	7,200	—
1631	—	1,550	2,650	4,500	7,200	—

KM# 142 2 THALER

Silver **Ruler:** Georg Wilhelm **Obv:** Half-length figure right **Rev:** Helmeted arms, date above **Mint:** Berlin **Note:** Dav. #6142.

Date	Mintage	VG	F	VF	XF	Unc
1631 LM	—	1,850	3,000	5,400	8,400	—

KM# 164 2 THALER

Silver **Ruler:** Georg Wilhelm **Obv. Legend:** GEORG. WILH ... **Rev:** Arms divide mintmaster's initials **Rev. Legend:** PRVS. IVL ... **Mint:** Berlin **Note:** Dav. #6153.

Date	Mintage	VG	F	VF	XF	Unc
1633 LM Rare	—	—	—	—	—	—
1635 LM Rare	—	—	—	—	—	—
1636 LM Rare	—	—	—	—	—	—
1637 LM Rare	—	—	—	—	—	—

KM# 151 2 THALER

Silver **Ruler:** Georg Wilhelm **Obv:** 3/4-length figure right **Rev:** Crowned arms, date and mintmaster's initials in legend **Mint:** Berlin **Note:** Dav. #6148.

Date	Mintage	VG	F	VF	XF	Unc
1634 LM Rare	—	—	—	—	—	—
1635 LM Rare	—	—	—	—	—	—
1636 LM Rare	—	—	—	—	—	—

KM# 179 2 THALER

Silver **Ruler:** Georg Wilhelm **Obv:** 1/2-length figure right **Rev:** Crowned arms **Mint:** Berlin **Note:** Dav. #6162.

Date	Mintage	VG	F	VF	XF	Unc
1640 LM Rare	—	—	—	—	—	—

KM# 180 2 THALER

Silver **Ruler:** Georg Wilhelm **Rev:** Date divided below arms **Mint:** Berlin **Note:** Dav. #6164.

Date	Mintage	VG	F	VF	XF	Unc
1640 LM Rare	—	—	—	—	—	—

KM# 181 2 THALER

Silver **Ruler:** Georg Wilhelm **Mint:** Königsberg **Note:** Dav. #LS256.

Date	Mintage	VG	F	VF	XF	Unc
1640 DK	—	2,900	5,000	8,300	13,000	—

KM# 193 2 THALER

Silver **Ruler:** Friedrich Wilhelm **Rev:** Scepter arms in center of large rose, 23 interlinked small oval arms around **Note:** Dav. #LS258.

Date	Mintage	VG	F	VF	XF	Unc
ND(1641/3)	—	2,200	3,600	6,500	10,000	—

KM# 213 2 THALER

Silver **Ruler:** Friedrich Wilhelm **Mint:** Berlin **Note:** Dav. #6177.

Date	Mintage	VG	F	VF	XF	Unc
1643 AB	—	1,800	3,100	5,200	8,200	—
1644 AB	—	1,800	3,100	5,200	8,200	—
1645 CT	—	1,800	3,100	5,200	8,200	—

KM# 221 2 THALER

Silver **Ruler:** Friedrich Wilhelm **Mint:** Berlin **Note:** Similar to 1 Thaler, KM#220. Dav. #6181.

Date	Mintage	VG	F	VF	XF	Unc
1645 CT	—	1,800	3,100	5,000	7,900	—
1646 CT	—	1,800	3,100	5,000	7,900	—
1648 CT	—	1,800	3,100	5,000	7,900	—

KM# 236 2 THALER

Silver **Ruler:** Friedrich Wilhelm **Rev:** Helmeted and supported arms **Mint:** Berlin **Note:** Dav. #A6183.

Date	Mintage	VG	F	VF	XF	Unc
1650 CT	—	1,850	3,200	5,200	8,200	—

KM# 266 2 THALER

Silver **Ruler:** Friedrich Wilhelm **Obv. Legend:** BR. S. - R. I. ARCHIC. ET. ELECT. **Mint:** Berlin **Note:** Similar to 1 Thaler, KM#249.

Date	Mintage	VG	F	VF	XF	Unc
1653 CT	—	2,150	3,500	6,000	9,600	—

KM# 267 2 THALER

Silver **Ruler:** Friedrich Wilhelm **Mint:** Königsberg **Note:** Dav. #LS260.

Date	Mintage	VG	F	VF	XF	Unc
1653 CM	—	2,900	5,000	8,300	13,000	—

KM# 292 2 THALER

Silver **Ruler:** Friedrich Wilhelm **Subject:** Attainment of Sovereignty over East Prussia **Obv:** Town below forelegs of horse **Rev:** 9-line inscription **Mint:** Berlin

Date	Mintage	VG	F	VF	XF	Unc
1657 CT	—	2,100	3,500	5,800	9,400	—

KM# 455 2 THALER

Silver **Ruler:** Friedrich Wilhelm **Subject:** Victory at Battle of Fehrbellin **Obv:** Elector mounted on rearing horse right with town below forelegs **Rev:** 13-line inscription

Date	Mintage	VG	F	VF	XF	Unc
1675	—	1,850	3,200	5,200	8,200	—

KM# 456 2 THALER

Silver **Ruler:** Friedrich Wilhelm **Rev:** Inscription below figure **Rev. Inscription:** F. BELLIN VM. 18 IVN / date

Date	Mintage	VG	F	VF	XF	Unc
1675	—	1,850	3,200	5,200	8,200	—

KM# 587 2 THALER

Silver **Ruler:** Friedrich III **Obv:** Back and side view of bust **Mint:** Berlin **Note:** Dav. #6216.

Date	Mintage	VG	F	VF	XF	Unc
ND1692 LCS-IBS Rare	—	—	—	—	—	—

KM# A118 3 THALER

Silver **Ruler:** Georg Wilhelm **Obv:** Armored bust right, wide band with 19 small shields of arms around **Rev:** 4-fold arms with scepter shield in center, within ornamented shield, date divided near bottom, electoral hat above, all in circle, three circles of legends with name and titles of Georg Wilhelm **Mint:** Königsberg **Note:** Ref. Dost #604.

Date	Mintage	VG	F	VF	XF	Unc
1624 MK-NB	—	—	—	—	—	—

KM# 217 3 THALER

Silver **Ruler:** Friedrich Wilhelm **Mint:** Berlin **Note:** Similar to 1 Thaler, KM#212. Dav. #6176.

Date	Mintage	VG	F	VF	XF	Unc
1644 AB Rare	—	—	—	—	—	—

KM# 222 3 THALER

Silver **Ruler:** Friedrich Wilhelm **Mint:** Berlin **Note:** Similar to 1 Thaler, KM#220.

Date	Mintage	VG	F	VF	XF	Unc
1645 CT Rare	—	—	—	—	—	—

KM# 457 3 THALER

Silver **Ruler:** Friedrich Wilhelm **Subject:** Victory at Battle of Fehrbellin **Note:** Similar to 1 Thaler, KM#449

Date	Mintage	VG	F	VF	XF	Unc
1675 Rare	—	—	—	—	—	—

KM# 129 4 THALER

Silver **Ruler:** Georg Wilhelm **Mint:** Königsberg **Note:** Dav. #6139. Similar to 1 Thaler, KM#125.

Date	Mintage	VG	F	VF	XF	Unc
1628 (a) Rare	—	—	—	—	—	—

KM# A139 4 THALER

Silver **Ruler:** Georg Wilhelm **Obv:** 1/2-length bust of Georg Wilhelm right, scepter on shoulder **Rev:** Shield of arms **Mint:** Königsberg **Note:** Ref. Dost #607. Struck from 2 Thaler dies, KM#143.

Date	Mintage	VG	F	VF	XF	Unc
1630 (q)	—	—	—	—	—	—

KM# 218 4 THALER

Silver **Ruler:** Friedrich Wilhelm **Mint:** Berlin **Note:** Similar to 1 Thaler, KM#212. Dav. #6175.

Date	Mintage	VG	F	VF	XF	Unc
1644 AB Rare	—	—	—	—	—	—

KM# 223 4 THALER

Silver **Ruler:** Friedrich Wilhelm **Mint:** Berlin **Note:** Similar to 1 Thaler, KM#220. Dav. #6179.

Date	Mintage	VG	F	VF	XF	Unc
1645 CT Rare	—	—	—	—	—	—

TRADE COINAGE

KM# 51 GOLDGULDEN
3.5000 g., 0.9860 Gold 0.1109 oz. AGW **Ruler:** Johann Sigismund **Obv:** Facing bust of Johann Sigismund **Rev:** Crowned arms in inner circle **Mint:** Kölln **Note:** Fr.#2145.

Date	Mintage	VG	F	VF	XF	Unc
1614	1,314	1,500	3,300	6,600	11,000	—
1615	Inc. above	1,500	3,300	6,600	11,000	—
1617	1,296	1,500	3,300	6,600	11,000	—

KM# 52 GOLDGULDEN
3.5000 g., 0.9860 Gold 0.1109 oz. AGW **Ruler:** Johann Sigismund **Obv:** Bust of Johann Sigismund to right **Note:** Fr.#2144.

Date	Mintage	VG	F	VF	XF	Unc
1615	Inc. above	2,800	6,000	11,500	17,000	—

KM# 55 GOLDGULDEN
3.5000 g., 0.9860 Gold 0.1109 oz. AGW **Ruler:** Johann Sigismund **Obv:** Half figure of Johann Sigismund right **Note:** Fr.#2146.

Date	Mintage	VG	F	VF	XF	Unc
1617	Inc. above	1,700	3,850	7,300	11,000	—

KM# 76 GOLDGULDEN
3.5000 g., 0.9860 Gold 0.1109 oz. AGW **Ruler:** Georg Wilhelm **Obv:** Bust of George Wilhelm right **Rev:** Crowned sceptre shield in inner circle **Mint:** Berlin

Date	Mintage	VG	F	VF	XF	Unc
1620 LM Rare	—	—	—	—	—	—

KM# 107 GOLDGULDEN
3.5000 g., 0.9860 Gold 0.1109 oz. AGW **Ruler:** Georg Wilhelm **Obv:** Laureate bust right, titles of Georg Wilhelm **Rev:** 6-fold arms with scepter shield in center, date above, titles continuous **Note:** Fr. #2155.

Date	Mintage	VG	F	VF	XF	Unc
16ZZ Rare	—	—	—	—	—	—

KM# 130 GOLDGULDEN
3.5000 g., 0.9860 Gold 0.1109 oz. AGW **Ruler:** Georg Wilhelm **Obv:** Armored bust of George Wilhelm right holding scepter **Rev:** Crowned arms in inner circle **Mint:** Kölln

Date	Mintage	VG	F	VF	XF	Unc
1628 LM	—	900	2,000	4,000	6,750	—

KM# 131 GOLDGULDEN
3.5000 g., 0.9860 Gold 0.1109 oz. AGW **Ruler:** Georg Wilhelm **Obv:** Bust of Georg Wilhelm right in elector's attire **Mint:** Kölln

Date	Mintage	VG	F	VF	XF	Unc
1628 LM	—	1,200	2,700	5,200	7,800	—

KM# 90 2 GOLDGULDEN
7.0000 g., 0.9860 Gold 0.2219 oz. AGW **Ruler:** Georg Wilhelm **Obv:** Bust of Georg Wilhelm right **Rev:** Twelve-fold arms in inner circle **Mint:** Berlin

Date	Mintage	VG	F	VF	XF	Unc
1621 Rare	—	—	—	—	—	—

KM# 132.2 2 GOLDGULDEN
Silver **Ruler:** Georg Wilhelm **Obv:** Bust of Georg Wilhelm right in elector's costume holding scepter **Rev:** 12-fold arms **Mint:** Kölln **Note:** Fr. #2159.

Date	Mintage	VG	F	VF	XF	Unc
ND LM	—	1,650	3,850	6,500	10,000	—

KM# 132.1 2 GOLDGULDEN
7.0000 g., 0.9860 Gold 0.2219 oz. AGW **Ruler:** Georg Wilhelm **Obv:** Bust of Georg Wilhelm right in elector's attire holding scepter **Rev:** Twelve-fold arms topped by elector's cap **Mint:** Kölln **Note:** Prev. KM#132.

Date	Mintage	VG	F	VF	XF	Unc
1628 LM Rare	—	—	—	—	—	—

KM# 380 1/4 DUCAT
0.8750 g., 0.9860 Gold 0.0277 oz. AGW **Ruler:** Friedrich Wilhelm **Obv:** Bust of Friedrich Wilhelm right in laureated helmet **Rev:** Crown above displayed eagle **Mint:** Berlin

Date	Mintage	VG	F	VF	XF	Unc
1668 IL	—	500	1,250	2,250	3,500	—

KM# 458 1/4 DUCAT
0.8750 g., 0.9860 Gold 0.0277 oz. AGW **Ruler:** Friedrich Wilhelm **Obv:** Bust of Friedrich Wilhelm right **Mint:** Berlin

Date	Mintage	VG	F	VF	XF	Unc
1675 IL	—	500	1,250	2,250	3,500	—

KM# 273 1/2 DUCAT
0.8750 g., 0.9860 Gold 0.0277 oz. AGW **Ruler:** Friedrich Wilhelm **Obv:** Bust of Friedrich Wilhelm right in elector's attire in inner circle **Rev:** Crowned scepter shield in palm branches **Mint:** Berlin

Date	Mintage	VG	F	VF	XF	Unc
ND	—	650	1,600	3,200	5,500	—

KM# 281 1/2 DUCAT
0.8750 g., 0.9860 Gold 0.0277 oz. AGW **Ruler:** Friedrich Wilhelm **Rev:** Capped complex arms in inner circle, arms divide date **Mint:** Berlin

Date	Mintage	VG	F	VF	XF	Unc
1655 CT	—	425	950	1,850	3,500	—

KM# 381 1/2 DUCAT
0.8750 g., 0.9860 Gold 0.0277 oz. AGW **Ruler:** Friedrich Wilhelm **Obv:** Bust of Friedrich Wilhelm to right in laureated helmet **Rev:** Crown above displayed eagle **Mint:** Berlin

Date	Mintage	VG	F	VF	XF	Unc
1668 IL	—	475	1,100	2,050	3,750	—

KM# 412 1/2 DUCAT
0.8750 g., 0.9860 Gold 0.0277 oz. AGW **Ruler:** Friedrich Wilhelm **Obv:** Laureate bust of Friedrich Wilhelm right **Rev:** Crowned displayed eagle divides date **Mint:** Königsberg **Note:** Varieties exist.

Date	Mintage	VG	F	VF	XF	Unc
1670 TT	—	300	575	1,000	1,850	—
1671 TT	—	300	575	1,000	1,850	—
1685 HS	400	300	575	1,000	1,850	—

KM# 475 1/2 DUCAT
0.8750 g., 0.9860 Gold 0.0277 oz. AGW **Ruler:** Friedrich Wilhelm **Subject:** The Conquest of Stettin **Obv:** Equestrian figure of Friedrich Wilhelm right **Rev:** Five-line inscription **Mint:** Berlin **Note:** Varieties exist.

Date	Mintage	VG	F	VF	XF	Unc
1677	—	350	800	1,450	2,500	—

KM# 606 1/2 DUCAT
0.8750 g., 0.9860 Gold 0.0277 oz. AGW **Ruler:** Friedrich III **Obv:** Laureate bust of Friedrich III **Rev:** Crowned scepter shield **Mint:** Minden

Date	Mintage	VG	F	VF	XF	Unc
1695 BH	—	1,250	2,150	4,250	8,500	—

KM# 629 1/2 DUCAT
0.8750 g., 0.9860 Gold 0.0277 oz. AGW **Ruler:** Friedrich III **Obv:** Laureate head of Friedrich III right **Rev:** Crowned displayed eagle with date at bottom **Mint:** Königsberg

Date	Mintage	VG	F	VF	XF	Unc
1700 CG	400	575	1,200	2,250	3,750	—

KM# 286 3/4 DUCAT
2.6250 g., 0.9860 Gold 0.0832 oz. AGW **Ruler:** Friedrich Wilhelm **Obv:** Facing bust of Friedrich Wilhelm in elector's costume in inner circle **Rev:** Capped scepter shield divides date with value below in inner circle **Mint:** Berlin

Date	Mintage	VG	F	VF	XF	Unc
1656 CT	—	1,100	2,850	5,500	10,000	—

KM# 28 DUCAT
3.5000 g., 0.9860 Gold 0.1109 oz. AGW **Ruler:** Joachim Friedrich **Obv:** Joachim Friedrich standing in inner circle **Rev:** Eagle in inner circle, arms on breast **Mint:** Kölln **Note:** Fr. #2142.

Date	Mintage	VG	F	VF	XF	Unc
1605	—	1,300	2,900	5,500	8,750	—
1606	—	1,300	2,900	5,500	8,750	—

KM# 31 DUCAT
3.5000 g., 0.9860 Gold 0.1109 oz. AGW **Ruler:** Johann Sigismund **Obv:** Bust of Johann Sigismund right in inner circle **Rev:** Crowned arms in inner circle **Note:** Fr. #2147.

Date	Mintage	VG	F	VF	XF	Unc
ND	—	2,500	5,000	9,500	14,500	—

KM# 38 DUCAT
3.5000 g., 0.9860 Gold 0.1109 oz. AGW **Ruler:** Johann Sigismund **Obv:** Johann Sigismund standing in inner circle **Rev:** Eagle in inner circle **Note:** Fr. #2148.

Date	Mintage	VG	F	VF	XF	Unc
1610	—	1,300	2,650	5,000	9,000	—
1611	—	1,300	2,650	5,000	9,000	—
1612	—	1,300	2,650	5,000	9,000	—
1614	1,206	1,300	2,650	5,000	9,000	—

KM# 77 DUCAT
3.5000 g., 0.9860 Gold 0.1109 oz. AGW **Ruler:** Georg Wilhelm **Obv:** George Wilhelm standing beside table holding helmet **Rev:** Five shields of arms **Mint:** Berlin

Date	Mintage	VG	F	VF	XF	Unc
1620 LM Rare	—	—	—	—	—	—

KM# 121 DUCAT
3.5000 g., 0.9860 Gold 0.1109 oz. AGW **Ruler:** Georg Wilhelm **Obv:** Bust of George Wilhelm right in elector's attire **Rev:** Twelve-fold arms in inner circle **Mint:** Berlin / Kölln

Date	Mintage	VG	F	VF	XF	Unc
1626 IP	—	1,250	2,750	5,000	9,000	—

KM# 126 DUCAT
3.5000 g., 0.9860 Gold 0.1109 oz. AGW **Ruler:** Georg Wilhelm **Obv:** Full-length armored figure to right, titles of Georg Wilhelm **Rev:** 12-fold arms, date **Rev. Legend:** MONE. NOVA. AVREA. DVCA. PRVSSIAE **Mint:** Königsberg **Note:** Fr. #2179.

Date	Mintage	VG	F	VF	XF	Unc
1627 (q)	—	1,250	2,750	5,000	9,000	—

KM# 144 DUCAT
3.5000 g., 0.9860 Gold 0.1109 oz. AGW **Ruler:** Georg Wilhelm **Obv:** Full-length armored figure right, titles of Georg Wilhelm **Rev:** Electoral hat above 12-fold arms **Rev. Legend:** MONE. NOVA. AVREA. DVCA. PRVSSI? **Mint:** Königsberg **Note:** Fr. #2180.

Date	Mintage	VG	F	VF	XF	Unc
1631	—	1,250	2,750	5,000	9,000	—
1632	—	1,250	2,750	5,000	9,000	—

KM# 148 DUCAT
3.5000 g., 0.9860 Gold 0.1109 oz. AGW **Ruler:** Georg Wilhelm **Obv:** Crowned bust right, titles of Georg Wilhelm **Rev:** 4-fold arms with scepter shield in center divide date, electoral hat above **Rev. Legend:** MONE. NOVA ... **Mint:** Königsberg **Note:** Fr. #2182, 2183.

Date	Mintage	VG	F	VF	XF	Unc
1632	—	850	1,700	3,150	5,500	—
1633 DK	—	850	1,700	3,150	5,500	—
1634 DK (q)	—	850	1,700	3,150	5,500	—
1635 DK	—	850	1,700	3,150	5,500	—
1635 DK (q)	—	850	1,700	3,150	5,500	—
1636 DK (q)	—	850	1,700	3,150	5,500	—
1637 DK (q)	—	850	1,700	3,150	5,500	—
1638 DK	—	850	1,700	3,150	5,500	—
1638 DK (q)	—	850	1,700	3,150	5,500	—
1639 DK	—	850	1,700	3,150	5,500	—
1640 DK	—	850	1,700	3,150	5,500	—

KM# A148 DUCAT
Gold **Ruler:** Georg Wilhelm **Obv:** Full-length armored figure right, titles of Georg Wilhelm **Rev:** 4-fold arms with scepter shield in center divide date, electoral hat above **Rev. Legend:** MONE. NOVA ... **Mint:** Königsberg **Note:** Ref. Dost #569, Neumann #10.13.

Date	Mintage	VG	F	VF	XF	Unc
1633 (q)	—	1,200	2,400	4,800	8,000	—

KM# 158 DUCAT
3.5000 g., 0.9860 Gold 0.1109 oz. AGW **Ruler:** Georg Wilhelm **Obv:** Bust of Georg Wilhelm facing right, in elector's cap **Rev:** Capped arms of 5 fiefs divides date in inner circle **Mint:** Königsberg

Date	Mintage	VG	F	VF	XF	Unc
1635 DK	—	550	1,300	2,350	3,750	—
1637 DK	—	550	1,300	2,350	3,750	—

Date	Mintage	VG	F	VF	XF	Unc
1639 DK	—	550	1,300	2,350	3,750	—
1640 DK	—	550	1,300	2,350	3,750	—

KM# 157 DUCAT

3.5000 g., 0.9860 Gold 0.1109 oz. AGW **Ruler:** Georg Wilhelm **Obv:** Crowned bust right, titles of Georg Wilhelm **Rev:** 8-fold arms with central shield divide date **Mint:** Königsberg **Note:** Fr. #2185.

Date	Mintage	VG	F	VF	XF	Unc
1635 DK (q)	3,898	550	1,300	2,350	3,750	—
1638 DK (q)	2,947	550	1,300	2,350	3,750	—
1639 DK	—	550	1,300	2,350	3,750	—

KM# A166 DUCAT

3.5000 g., 0.9860 Gold 0.1109 oz. AGW **Ruler:** Georg Wilhelm **Obv:** Bust right, titles of Georg Wilhelm **Rev:** 8-fold arms with central shield divide date **Mint:** Königsberg **Note:** Fr. #2186.

Date	Mintage	VG	F	VF	XF	Unc
1639 DK	—	875	1,750	3,850	6,750	—

KM# 168 DUCAT

3.5000 g., 0.9860 Gold 0.1109 oz. AGW **Ruler:** Georg Wilhelm **Obv:** Georg Wilhelm standing in inner circle **Rev:** Scepter within circle of shields of arms in inner circle **Mint:** Kölln

Date	Mintage	VG	F	VF	XF	Unc
1639 LM	—	600	1,450	2,500	4,000	—

KM# 169 DUCAT

3.5000 g., 0.9860 Gold 0.1109 oz. AGW **Ruler:** Georg Wilhelm **Obv:** Bust of Georg Wilhelm right in inner circle **Rev:** Capped arms of nine fiefs in inner circle **Mint:** Königsberg

Date	Mintage	VG	F	VF	XF	Unc
1639 DK	—	500	1,200	2,250	3,750	—

KM# 194 DUCAT

3.5000 g., 0.9860 Gold 0.1109 oz. AGW **Ruler:** Friedrich Wilhelm **Obv:** Friedrich Wilhelm standing to right by table **Rev:** Scepter within circle of six shields of arms in inner circle **Mint:** Berlin

Date	Mintage	VG	F	VF	XF	Unc
1641 LM	—	550	1,300	2,400	4,000	—

KM# 195 DUCAT

3.5000 g., 0.9860 Gold 0.1109 oz. AGW **Ruler:** Friedrich Wilhelm **Rev:** Elaborate arms of nine fiefs **Mint:** Berlin

Date	Mintage	VG	F	VF	XF	Unc
1641 LM	—	475	1,100	2,100	3,500	—

KM# 196 DUCAT

3.5000 g., 0.9860 Gold 0.1109 oz. AGW **Ruler:** Friedrich Wilhelm **Obv:** Crowned bust of Friedrich Wilhelm right in inner circle **Rev:** Capped arms divides date in inner circle **Mint:** Königsberg

Date	Mintage	VG	F	VF	XF	Unc
1641 DK	—	425	1,100	2,100	3,500	—
1648 DK	—	425	1,100	2,100	3,500	—
1649 DK	—	425	1,100	2,100	3,500	—

KM# 214 DUCAT

3.5000 g., 0.9860 Gold 0.1109 oz. AGW **Ruler:** Friedrich Wilhelm **Obv:** Friedrich Wilhelm standing to right by table in inner circle **Rev:** Elaborate arms of twelve fiefs, date bove in inner circle **Mint:** Berlin

Date	Mintage	VG	F	VF	XF	Unc
1643 AB	—	550	1,200	2,200	3,600	—

KM# 215 DUCAT

3.5000 g., 0.9860 Gold 0.1109 oz. AGW **Ruler:** Friedrich Wilhelm **Obv:** Facing bust of Friedrich Wilhelm in inner circle **Rev:** Capped arms divide date in inner circle **Mint:** Königsberg

Date	Mintage	VG	F	VF	XF	Unc
1643 DK	—	1,050	2,400	4,500	7,000	—

KM# 224 DUCAT

3.5000 g., 0.9860 Gold 0.1109 oz. AGW **Ruler:** Friedrich Wilhelm **Subject:** For Prussia **Obv:** Bust of Friedrich Wilhelm right in elector's attire in inner circle **Mint:** Berlin

Date	Mintage	VG	F	VF	XF	Unc
1646 CT	—	625	1,400	2,750	4,250	—

KM# 229 DUCAT

3.5000 g., 0.9860 Gold 0.1109 oz. AGW **Ruler:** Friedrich Wilhelm **Obv:** Bust of Friedrich Wilhelm right in elector's costume in inner circle **Rev:** Capped arms of six fiefs in inner circle **Mint:** Bielefeld

Date	Mintage	VG	F	VF	XF	Unc
1648 Rare	—	—	—	—	—	—

KM# 251 DUCAT

3.5000 g., 0.9860 Gold 0.1109 oz. AGW **Ruler:** Friedrich Wilhelm **Obv:** Bust of Friedrich Wilhelm standing facing in inner circle **Rev:** Capped arms in inner circle, cap divides date **Mint:** Berlin

Date	Mintage	VG	F	VF	XF	Unc
1651 CT	—	1,100	2,400	4,600	6,750	—

KM# 252 DUCAT

3.5000 g., 0.9860 Gold 0.1109 oz. AGW **Ruler:** Friedrich Wilhelm **Obv:** Bust of Friedrich Wilhelm right in inner circle **Rev:** Capped arms divide date in inner circle **Mint:** Königsberg

Date	Mintage	VG	F	VF	XF	Unc
1651 CM	—	425	1,100	2,100	3,500	—
1657 DK	2,400	425	1,100	2,100	3,500	—
1660/57 DK	—	425	1,100	2,100	3,500	—

KM# 258 DUCAT

3.5000 g., 0.9860 Gold 0.1109 oz. AGW **Ruler:** Friedrich Wilhelm **Obv:** Small bust of Friedrich Wilhelm right in elector's attire in crenellated circle **Rev:** Capped arms 26 fiefs, date at bottom **Mint:** Minden

Date	Mintage	VG	F	VF	XF	Unc
1652 HB	—	1,650	3,650	6,900	10,000	—

KM# 270 DUCAT

3.5000 g., 0.9860 Gold 0.1109 oz. AGW **Ruler:** Friedrich Wilhelm **Obv:** 3/4 figure of Friedrich Wilhelm right in inner circle **Rev:** Capped arms in inner circle **Mint:** Berlin

Date	Mintage	VG	F	VF	XF	Unc
1654 CT	—	650	1,500	2,800	4,500	—
1656 CT	—	650	1,500	2,800	4,500	—

KM# 293 DUCAT

3.5000 g., 0.9860 Gold 0.1109 oz. AGW **Ruler:** Friedrich Wilhelm **Obv:** Bust right of Friedrich Wilhelm **Rev:** Capped arms in inner circle **Mint:** Königsberg

Date	Mintage	VG	F	VF	XF	Unc
1657 NB	—	1,050	2,100	3,950	6,750	—
1658	3,600	1,050	2,100	3,950	6,750	—

KM# 320 DUCAT

3.5000 g., 0.9860 Gold 0.1109 oz. AGW **Ruler:** Friedrich Wilhelm **Obv:** Bust of Friedrich right **Rev:** Capped arms in inner circle, mintmaster's initials at bottom **Mint:** Königsberg

Date	Mintage	VG	F	VF	XF	Unc
1661 HM	14,000	1,000	2,150	3,900	6,750	—
1662 HM	Inc. above	1,000	2,150	3,900	6,750	—
1663 HM	Inc. above	1,000	2,150	3,900	6,750	—

KM# 325 DUCAT

3.5000 g., 0.9860 Gold 0.1109 oz. AGW **Ruler:** Friedrich Wilhelm **Obv:** Friedrich Wilhelm **Rev:** Crowned arms divide date and mintmaster's initials **Mint:** Berlin

Date	Mintage	VG	F	VF	XF	Unc
1662 AB	456	1,900	4,150	8,000	11,500	—
1665 IL	—	2,650	5,800	11,000	16,000	—
1666 IL	—	2,650	5,800	11,000	16,000	—

KM# 335 DUCAT

3.5000 g., 0.9860 Gold 0.1109 oz. AGW **Ruler:** Friedrich Wilhelm **Obv:** Bust of Friedrich right in inner circle **Rev:** Shield of arms in inncer circle **Mint:** Königsberg **Note:** Varieties exist.

Date	Mintage	VG	F	VF	XF	Unc
1664	6,781	550	1,200	2,300	3,750	—
1665	Inc. above	550	1,200	2,300	3,750	—
1666	3,626	550	1,200	2,300	3,750	—
1667 CG	3,500	550	1,200	2,300	3,750	—

KM# 340 DUCAT

3.5000 g., 0.9860 Gold 0.1109 oz. AGW **Ruler:** Friedrich Wilhelm **Obv:** 3/4 figure of Friedrich Wilhelm right in inner circle **Rev:** Crowned arms divide date in inner circle **Mint:** Berlin **Note:** For Prussia.

Date	Mintage	VG	F	VF	XF	Unc
1665 IL	—	825	1,800	3,600	5,750	—

KM# 341 DUCAT

3.5000 g., 0.9860 Gold 0.1109 oz. AGW **Ruler:** Friedrich Wilhelm **Obv:** Bust of Friedrich Wilhelm right in inner circle **Mint:** Berlin

Date	Mintage	VG	F	VF	XF	Unc
1665 IL	—	2,400	5,300	10,500	16,500	—

KM# A366 DUCAT

3.5000 g., 0.9860 Gold 0.1109 oz. AGW **Ruler:** Friedrich Wilhelm **Obv:** 1/2-length bust Friedrich Wilhelm right holding sword **Rev:** 5-fold arms, on ornamented shield

Date	Mintage	VG	F	VF	XF	Unc
1666	—	1,900	4,150	8,000	11,500	—

KM# 366 DUCAT

3.5000 g., 0.9860 Gold 0.1109 oz. AGW **Ruler:** Friedrich Wilhelm **Obv:** Bust right **Rev:** Small capped scepter shield and date surrounded by 13 shields of arms **Mint:** Berlin

Date	Mintage	VG	F	VF	XF	Unc
1667 IL	—	550	1,200	2,300	3,500	—

KM# 382 DUCAT

3.5000 g., 0.9860 Gold 0.1109 oz. AGW **Ruler:** Friedrich Wilhelm **Obv:** Laureate bust of Friedrich Wilhelm right **Rev:** Crowned displayed eagle, crown divides date **Mint:** Königsberg

Date	Mintage	VG	F	VF	XF	Unc
1668 CG	4,500	1,000	2,200	4,200	6,000	—
1668 DS	Inc. above	1,000	2,200	4,200	6,000	—
1673 CV	—	1,250	2,750	5,300	7,750	—
1674 CV	—	1,250	2,750	5,300	7,750	—

KM# 383 DUCAT

3.5000 g., 0.9860 Gold 0.1109 oz. AGW **Ruler:** Friedrich Wilhelm **Obv:** Bust of Friedrich Wilhelm right **Rev:** Crowned scepter shield in garter oval in palm branches, date **Mint:** Berlin

Date	Mintage	VG	F	VF	XF	Unc
1668 IL	—	575	1,450	2,600	4,250	—
1673 IL	—	575	1,450	2,600	4,250	—
1674 IL	—	575	1,450	2,600	4,250	—
1675 CS	—	575	1,450	2,600	4,250	—
1677 CS	—	575	1,450	2,600	4,250	—

KM# 393 DUCAT

3.5000 g., 0.9860 Gold 0.1109 oz. AGW **Obv:** Friedrich Wilhelm **Mint:** Königsberg

Date	Mintage	VG	F	VF	XF	Unc
1669 CG/DS	—	1,500	3,200	6,000	9,000	—

KM# 394 DUCAT

3.5000 g., 0.9860 Gold 0.1109 oz. AGW **Ruler:** Friedrich Wilhelm **Obv:** Bust of Friedrich Wilhelm right, date below **Rev:** Crown scepter shield in garter oval in branches **Mint:** Berlin

Date	Mintage	VG	F	VF	XF	Unc
1669 IL	—	950	2,400	4,500	7,000	—
1670 IL	—	950	2,400	4,500	7,000	—
1671 IL	—	950	2,400	4,500	7,000	—
1672 IL	—	950	2,400	4,500	7,000	—

KM# 413 DUCAT

3.5000 g., 0.9860 Gold 0.1109 oz. AGW **Ruler:** Friedrich Wilhelm **Obv:** Bust of Friedrich Wilhelm right **Rev:** Crowned arms, crown divides date **Mint:** Minden

Date	Mintage	VG	F	VF	XF	Unc
1670 HB	—	2,000	4,000	8,500	15,000	—

KM# 414 DUCAT

3.5000 g., 0.9860 Gold 0.1109 oz. AGW **Ruler:** Friedrich Wilhelm **Obv:** Laureate bust of Friedrich Wilhelm right **Mint:** Königsberg

Date	Mintage	VG	F	VF	XF	Unc
1670 TT	—	1,100	2,350	4,500	8,500	—
1671 TT	—	1,100	2,350	4,500	8,500	—
1672 TT	—	1,100	2,350	4,500	8,500	—
1679 HS	400	775	1,750	3,300	6,000	—
1681 HS	—	775	1,750	3,300	6,000	—
1682 HS	200	775	1,750	3,300	6,000	—

KM# 471 DUCAT

3.5000 g., 0.9860 Gold 0.1109 oz. AGW **Ruler:** Friedrich Wilhelm **Rev:** Crowned round arms, crown divides date **Mint:** Königsberg

Date	Mintage	VG	F	VF	XF	Unc
1676 HS	200	725	1,550	3,000	5,500	—
1683 HS	200	725	1,550	3,000	5,500	—
1684 HS	600	725	1,550	3,000	5,500	—
1686 BA	1,000	725	1,550	3,000	5,500	—

KM# 491 DUCAT

3.5000 g., 0.9860 Gold 0.1109 oz. AGW **Ruler:** Friedrich Wilhelm **Obv:** Bust of Friedrich Wilhelm right in inner circle, date below **Rev:** Scepter in branches in inner circle **Mint:** Halberstadt

Date	Mintage	VG	F	VF	XF	Unc
1679 LCS	—	2,650	5,600	9,900	16,500	—

KM# 492 DUCAT

3.5000 g., 0.9860 Gold 0.1109 oz. AGW **Ruler:** Friedrich Wilhelm **Obv:** Bust of Friedrich Wilhelm right **Rev:** Crowned scepter shield in garter oval in palm branches **Mint:** Berlin

Date	Mintage	VG	F	VF	XF	Unc
1679 CS	—	1,150	2,500	4,900	7,750	—
1680 CS	—	1,150	2,500	4,900	7,750	—
1681 CS	—	1,150	2,500	4,900	7,750	—
1682 CS	—	1,150	2,500	4,900	7,750	—
1683 LCS	—	1,150	2,500	4,900	7,750	—
1684 LCS	—	1,150	2,500	4,900	7,750	—
1685 LCS	—	1,150	2,500	4,900	7,750	—
1686 LCS	—	1,150	2,500	4,900	7,750	—

KM# 504 DUCAT

3.5000 g., 0.9860 Gold 0.1109 oz. AGW **Ruler:** Friedrich Wilhelm **Obv:** Bust of Friedrich Wilhelm right **Rev:** Sailing ship on rough water **Mint:** Berlin **Note:** Trade coin for the Guinea Coast of Africa.

Date	Mintage	VG	F	VF	XF	Unc
1682 CS	—	1,150	2,650	5,200	9,500	—
1682 LCS	—	1,150	2,650	5,200	9,500	—
1683 LCS	—	1,150	2,650	5,200	9,500	—
1685 LCS	—	1,150	2,650	5,200	9,500	—
1686 LCS	—	1,150	2,650	5,200	9,500	—

KM# 522.1 DUCAT

3.5000 g., 0.9860 Gold 0.1109 oz. AGW **Ruler:** Friedrich Wilhelm **Rev:** Crowned round scepter shield in garter in palm branches **Mint:** Berlin

Date	Mintage	VG	F	VF	XF	Unc
1685 LCS	—	1,150	2,500	5,000	9,750	—

KM# 522.2 DUCAT

3.5000 g., 0.9860 Gold 0.1109 oz. AGW **Ruler:** Friedrich Wilhelm **Obv:** Different armor **Mint:** Berlin

Date	Mintage	VG	F	VF	XF	Unc
1686 LCS	—	1,150	2,500	5,000	9,750	—

KM# 528 DUCAT

3.5000 g., 0.9860 Gold 0.1109 oz. AGW **Ruler:** Friedrich Wilhelm **Obv:** Half figure of Friedrich Wilhelm right **Mint:** Berlin

Date	Mintage	VG	F	VF	XF	Unc
1686 LCS	—	1,150	2,650	5,200	9,500	—
1687 LCS	—	1,150	2,650	5,200	9,500	—
1688 LCS	—	1,150	2,650	5,200	9,500	—

KM# 529 DUCAT

3.5000 g., 0.9860 Gold 0.1109 oz. AGW **Ruler:** Friedrich Wilhelm **Obv:** Armored half figure of Friedrich Wilhelm **Rev:** Sailing ship right, date in legend **Mint:** Berlin **Note:** Trade coin for the Guinea Coast of Africa.

Date	Mintage	VG	F	VF	XF	Unc
1686 LCS	—	1,150	2,650	5,200	9,500	—
1687 LCS	—	1,150	2,650	5,200	9,500	—
1688 LCS	—	1,150	2,650	5,200	9,500	—

KM# 535 DUCAT

3.5000 g., 0.9860 Gold 0.1109 oz. AGW **Ruler:** Friedrich Wilhelm **Obv:** Laureate bust of Friedrich Wilhelm **Rev:** Crowned round arms, crown divides date **Mint:** Königsberg

Date	Mintage	VG	F	VF	XF	Unc
1687 HS	200	825	1,800	3,600	7,500	—

KM# 541 DUCAT

3.5000 g., 0.9860 Gold 0.1109 oz. AGW **Ruler:** Friedrich III **Obv:** Bust of Friedrich III **Rev:** Cruciform crowned F III monogram **Mint:** Berlin

Date	Mintage	VG	F	VF	XF	Unc
1688	—	1,300	2,850	5,600	10,000	—

KM# 543 DUCAT
3.5000 g., 0.9860 Gold 0.1109 oz. AGW **Ruler:** Friedrich III
Obv: Bust right **Rev:** Brandenburg flag at stern **Mint:** Berlin

Date	Mintage	VG	F	VF	XF	Unc
1688 LCS	—	1,150	2,650	5,200	9,500	—
1690 LCS	—	1,150	2,650	5,200	9,500	—

KM# 542 DUCAT
3.5000 g., 0.9860 Gold 0.1109 oz. AGW **Ruler:** Friedrich III
Obv: Draped bust of Friedrich III right **Rev:** Sailing ship right, date in legend **Mint:** Berlin **Note:** Trade coin for the Guinea Coast of Africa.

Date	Mintage	VG	F	VF	XF	Unc
1688 LCS	—	1,150	2,650	5,200	9,500	—

KM# 561 DUCAT
3.5000 g., 0.9860 Gold 0.1109 oz. AGW **Ruler:** Friedrich III
Obv: Bust of Friedrich III right **Rev:** Crowned oval scepter shield in palm branches **Mint:** Berlin **Note:** Varieties exist.

Date	Mintage	VG	F	VF	XF	Unc
1689 LCS	—	1,150	2,550	5,000	9,000	—
1690 LCS	—	1,150	2,550	5,000	9,000	—

KM# 574 DUCAT
3.5000 g., 0.9860 Gold 0.1109 oz. AGW **Ruler:** Friedrich III
Subject: Homage **Obv:** Crown over 8-line inscription

Date	Mintage	VG	F	VF	XF	Unc
1690 Rare	—	—	—	—	—	—

KM# 578 DUCAT
3.5000 g., 0.9860 Gold 0.1109 oz. AGW **Ruler:** Friedrich III **Rev:** Crowned arms divide date **Mint:** Minden

Date	Mintage	VG	F	VF	XF	Unc
1691 BH Rare	—	—	—	—	—	—

KM# 579 DUCAT
3.5000 g., 0.9860 Gold 0.1109 oz. AGW **Ruler:** Friedrich III
Obv: Laureate and draped bust of Friedrich III right **Rev:** Crowned oval arms in cartouche, crown divides date **Mint:** Königsberg

Date	Mintage	VG	F	VF	XF	Unc
1691 HS	400	900	1,900	3,750	7,500	—
1693 HS	200	900	1,900	3,750	7,500	—
1695 SD	200	900	1,900	3,750	7,500	—
1697 SD	200	900	1,900	3,750	7,500	—
1700 CG	—	900	2,500	3,750	7,500	—

KM# 588 DUCAT
3.5000 g., 0.9860 Gold 0.1109 oz. AGW **Ruler:** Friedrich III
Obv: Bust of Friedrich III right **Rev:** Crowned scepter shield **Mint:** Magdeburg

Date	Mintage	VG	F	VF	XF	Unc
1692 ICS	—	2,250	4,950	9,800	16,500	—

KM# 589 DUCAT
3.5000 g., 0.9860 Gold 0.1109 oz. AGW **Ruler:** Friedrich III
Obv: Bust right **Obv. Legend:** FRID. III. D.G. M. B. S. R. I. A. C. E **Rev:** Sailing ship divides date **Rev. Legend:** DEO DUCE **Mint:** Berlin

Date	Mintage	VG	F	VF	XF	Unc
169Z S//LCS	—	1,200	2,500	5,000	8,500	—
1694 S//LCS	—	1,200	2,500	5,000	8,500	—
1695 S//LCS	—	1,200	2,500	5,000	8,500	—
1696 S//LCS	—	1,200	2,500	5,000	8,500	—

KM# 595 DUCAT
3.5000 g., 0.9860 Gold 0.1109 oz. AGW **Ruler:** Friedrich III
Subject: Founding of University of Halle an der Saale

Date	Mintage	VG	F	VF	XF	Unc
1694	—	—	—	—	—	—

KM# 607 DUCAT
3.5000 g., 0.9860 Gold 0.1109 oz. AGW **Ruler:** Friedrich III **Rev:** Crowned eagle above arms divides date **Mint:** Minden

Date	Mintage	VG	F	VF	XF	Unc
1695 BH Rare	—	—	—	—	—	—

KM# 608 DUCAT
3.5000 g., 0.9860 Gold 0.1109 oz. AGW **Ruler:** Friedrich III
Obv: Draped bust of Friedrich III right **Rev:** Crowned scepter shield in garter in palm branches **Mint:** Berlin

Date	Mintage	VG	F	VF	XF	Unc
1696 LCS	—	850	1,750	3,500	7,000	—

KM# 609 DUCAT
3.5000 g., 0.9860 Gold 0.1109 oz. AGW **Ruler:** Friedrich III **Rev:** Scepter shield in garter within cruciform crowned F III monograms, date at top **Mint:** Berlin

Date	Mintage	VG	F	VF	XF	Unc
1697 RF//LCS	—	850	1,800	3,650	7,000	—

KM# 614.1 DUCAT
3.5000 g., 0.9860 Gold 0.1109 oz. AGW **Ruler:** Friedrich III
Obv: Small head of Friedrich III **Mint:** Berlin

Date	Mintage	VG	F	VF	XF	Unc
1697 FR//LCS	—	850	1,800	3,650	7,000	—

KM# 614.2 DUCAT
3.5000 g., 0.9860 Gold 0.1109 oz. AGW **Ruler:** Friedrich III
Obv: Large head of Friedrich III **Mint:** Berlin

Date	Mintage	VG	F	VF	XF	Unc
1698 RF//LCS	—	625	1,400	2,950	6,300	—
1699 RF//LCS	—	625	1,400	2,950	6,300	—

KM# 24 2 DUCAT
7.0000 g., 0.9860 Gold 0.2219 oz. AGW **Ruler:** Joachim Friedrich **Obv:** Half-length bust right **Rev:** 7-fold arms, date in legend **Mint:** Kolln an der Spree

Date	Mintage	VG	F	VF	XF	Unc
1604 MH Rare	—	—	—	—	—	—

KM# 30 2 DUCAT
7.0000 g., 0.9860 Gold 0.2219 oz. AGW **Ruler:** Joachim Friedrich **Obv:** Joachim Friedrich standing in inner circle **Rev:** Eagle in inner circle, arms on breast **Note:** Fr.#2141.

Date	Mintage	VG	F	VF	XF	Unc
1606 Rare	—	—	—	—	—	—

KM# 48 2 DUCAT
7.0000 g., 0.9860 Gold 0.2219 oz. AGW **Ruler:** Johann Sigismund **Obv:** Half-length bust right, date below **Rev:** Arms in ornamented shield **Mint:** Kolln an der Spree

Date	Mintage	VG	F	VF	XF	Unc
1612 MH Rare	—	—	—	—	—	—

KM# 53 2 DUCAT
7.0000 g., 0.9860 Gold 0.2219 oz. AGW **Ruler:** Johann Sigismund **Obv:** Johann Sigismund standing in inner circle **Rev:** Crowned arms in inner circle **Note:** Fr.#2149.

Date	Mintage	VG	F	VF	XF	Unc
1615 Rare	—	—	—	—	—	—

KM# 78 2 DUCAT
7.0000 g., 0.9860 Gold 0.2219 oz. AGW **Ruler:** Georg Wilhelm
Obv: George Wilhelm standing by table with helmet **Rev:** Scepter surrounded by eight shields of arms **Mint:** Berlin

Date	Mintage	VG	F	VF	XF	Unc
1620 LM	—	1,500	2,950	5,500	9,000	—

KM# 79 2 DUCAT
7.0000 g., 0.9860 Gold 0.2219 oz. AGW **Ruler:** Georg Wilhelm
Rev: Crowned arms in inner circle **Mint:** Berlin

Date	Mintage	VG	F	VF	XF	Unc
ND(1620-21) LM	—	2,050	4,250	7,750	11,500	—

KM# B56 2 DUCAT
7.0000 g., 0.9860 Gold 0.2219 oz. AGW **Ruler:** Georg Wilhelm
Mint: Berlin **Note:** Ref. Neumann #10.41. Struck with 12 Gröscher dies, KM#85.

Date	Mintage	VG	F	VF	XF	Unc
16Z1	—	—	—	—	—	—

KM# 122 2 DUCAT
7.0000 g., 0.9860 Gold 0.2219 oz. AGW **Ruler:** Georg Wilhelm
Obv: Bust of Georg Wilhelm right in elector's costume **Rev:** Crowned arms of 12 fiefs in inner circle **Mint:** Berlin / Kölln **Note:** Struck from Ducat dies.

Date	Mintage	VG	F	VF	XF	Unc
1626 IP Rare	—	—	—	—	—	—

KM# 152 2 DUCAT
7.0000 g., 0.9860 Gold 0.2219 oz. AGW **Ruler:** Georg Wilhelm
Obv: Bust of Georg Wilhelm right with elector's cap **Rev:** Capped arms of five fiefs **Mint:** Königsberg **Note:** Fr. #2181.

Date	Mintage	VG	F	VF	XF	Unc
1634 DK (a)	—	1,600	3,300	6,000	9,000	—

KM# 153 2 DUCAT
7.0000 g., 0.9860 Gold 0.2219 oz. AGW **Ruler:** Georg Wilhelm
Obv: Georg Wilhelm standing by table with helmet **Rev:** 12-fold arms in inner circle **Mint:** Kölln

Date	Mintage	VG	F	VF	XF	Unc
1634 LM	—	1,200	2,400	4,250	7,500	—
1636 LM	—	1,100	2,400	4,250	—	—

KM# 159 2 DUCAT
7.0000 g., 0.9860 Gold 0.2219 oz. AGW **Ruler:** Georg Wilhelm
Rev: Crowned oval arms in inner circle **Mint:** Berlin

Date	Mintage	VG	F	VF	XF	Unc
1635 LM	—	1,200	2,400	4,550	7,750	—

KM# 165 2 DUCAT
7.0000 g., 0.9860 Gold 0.2219 oz. AGW **Ruler:** Georg Wilhelm
Obv: Standing Georg Wilhelm half facing right **Rev:** Crowned eagle with 12 small shields of arms on breast and wings **Mint:** Berlin

Date	Mintage	VG	F	VF	XF	Unc
1637 LM	—	1,200	2,400	4,250	7,000	—
1638 LM	—	1,200	2,400	4,250	7,000	—
1640 LM	—	1,200	2,400	4,250	7,000	—

KM# 197 2 DUCAT
7.0000 g., 0.9860 Gold 0.2219 oz. AGW **Ruler:** Friedrich Wilhelm **Obv:** Standing figure of Friedrich Wilhelm right **Mint:** Berlin

Date	Mintage	VG	F	VF	XF	Unc
1641 LM	—	1,200	2,800	4,850	8,000	—

KM# 198 2 DUCAT
7.0000 g., 0.9860 Gold 0.2219 oz. AGW **Ruler:** Friedrich Wilhelm **Obv:** Friedrich Wilhelm standing in floral arch, date below **Rev:** Arms in floral wreath **Mint:** Berlin

Date	Mintage	VG	F	VF	XF	Unc
1641	—	1,200	2,800	4,850	8,000	—
1641 LM	—	1,200	2,800	4,850	8,000	—

KM# 199 2 DUCAT
7.0000 g., 0.9860 Gold 0.2219 oz. AGW **Ruler:** Friedrich Wilhelm **Obv:** Crowned and robed elector holding scepter on horse rearing to right **Rev:** Scepter arms in center of large rose, 23 small oval arms around **Mint:** Königsberg

Date	Mintage	VG	F	VF	XF	Unc
ND(1641-43)	—	1,500	3,150	5,500	9,000	—

KM# 216 2 DUCAT
7.0000 g., 0.9860 Gold 0.2219 oz. AGW **Ruler:** Friedrich Wilhelm **Obv:** Friedrich Wilhelm standing with left hand and helmet on table **Rev:** Elaborate arms in inner circle **Mint:** Berlin

Date	Mintage	VG	F	VF	XF	Unc
1643 AB	—	1,200	2,400	4,250	7,500	—
1644 AB	—	1,200	2,400	4,250	7,500	—
1646 CT	—	1,200	2,400	4,250	7,500	—

KM# 237 2 DUCAT
7.0000 g., 0.9860 Gold 0.2219 oz. AGW **Ruler:** Friedrich Wilhelm **Rev:** Crowned arms in inner circle, date above crown **Mint:** Berlin

Date	Mintage	VG	F	VF	XF	Unc
1650 CT	—	1,500	3,150	5,500	9,000	—
1654 CT	—	1,500	3,150	5,500	9,000	—

KM# 271 2 DUCAT
7.0000 g., 0.9860 Gold 0.2219 oz. AGW **Ruler:** Friedrich Wilhelm **Obv:** Armored bust of Friedrich Wilhelm in inner circle **Rev:** Crowned arms in inner circle, crown divides date **Mint:** Berlin

Date	Mintage	VG	F	VF	XF	Unc
1654 CT	—	2,000	4,600	7,500	11,500	—
1665 IL	—	2,000	4,600	7,500	11,500	—

KM# 282 2 DUCAT
7.0000 g., 0.9860 Gold 0.2219 oz. AGW **Ruler:** Friedrich Wilhelm **Subject:** 35th Birthday of Friedrich Wilhelm and Birth of Prince Karl Emil

Date	Mintage	VG	F	VF	XF	Unc
1655	—	1,450	2,900	5,000	7,500	—

KM# 283 2 DUCAT
7.0000 g., 0.9860 Gold 0.2219 oz. AGW **Ruler:** Friedrich Wilhelm **Rev:** Cap above inscription

Date	Mintage	VG	F	VF	XF	Unc
1655	—	1,450	2,900	5,000	7,500	—

KM# 287 2 DUCAT
7.0000 g., 0.9860 Gold 0.2219 oz. AGW **Ruler:** Friedrich Wilhelm **Obv:** 3/4 figure of Friedrich Wilhelm right in inner circle **Rev:** Capped arms in inner circle **Mint:** Berlin **Note:** Struck from 1 Ducat dies, KM#270.

Date	Mintage	VG	F	VF	XF	Unc
1656 CT	—	2,000	4,600	7,500	11,500	—

KM# 342 2 DUCAT
7.0000 g., 0.9860 Gold 0.2219 oz. AGW **Ruler:** Friedrich Wilhelm **Obv:** Half-length figure to right **Rev:** Crown above square 25-fold arms divides date **Mint:** Berlin

Date	Mintage	VG	F	VF	XF	Unc
1665 IL	—	2,000	4,600	7,500	11,500	—

KM# 395 2 DUCAT
7.0000 g., 0.9860 Gold 0.2219 oz. AGW **Ruler:** Friedrich Wilhelm **Obv:** Draped bust of Friedrich Wilhelm **Rev:** Crowned arms in palm branches

Date	Mintage	VG	F	VF	XF	Unc
1669	—	2,000	4,600	7,500	11,500	—

KM# 396 2 DUCAT
7.0000 g., 0.9860 Gold 0.2219 oz. AGW **Ruler:** Friedrich Wilhelm **Subject:** 14th Birthday of Prince Karl Emil **Obv:** Bust of Friedrich Wilhelm right **Rev:** Bust of Prince Karl Emil right **Mint:** Königsberg

Date	Mintage	VG	F	VF	XF	Unc
1669 CG Rare	—	—	—	—	—	—

KM# 415 2 DUCAT
7.0000 g., 0.9860 Gold 0.2219 oz. AGW **Ruler:** Friedrich Wilhelm **Obv:** Bust of Friedrich Wilhelm right in elector's cap and atire **Rev:** Crowned arms in palm branches **Mint:** Berlin

Date	Mintage	VG	F	VF	XF	Unc
1670	—	2,100	4,800	7,600	12,000	—

KM# 416.1 2 DUCAT
7.0000 g., 0.9860 Gold 0.2219 oz. AGW **Ruler:** Friedrich Wilhelm **Obv:** Laureate bust of Friedrich Wilhelm right **Mint:** Königsberg

Date	Mintage	VG	F	VF	XF	Unc
1670 TT	—	1,300	3,000	5,900	10,000	—
1671 TT	—	1,300	3,000	5,900	10,000	—
1672 TT	—	1,300	3,000	5,900	10,000	—
1673 CV	—	1,200	2,700	5,400	9,000	—
1674 CV	—	1,200	2,700	5,400	9,000	—

KM# 416.2 2 DUCAT
7.0000 g., 0.9860 Gold 0.2219 oz. AGW **Ruler:** Friedrich Wilhelm **Obv:** Bust right **Rev:** Florals at sides of arms **Mint:** Königsberg

Date	Mintage	VG	F	VF	XF	Unc
1675 HS	—	1,200	2,700	5,400	9,000	—
1679 HS	—	1,200	2,700	5,400	9,000	—
1682 HS	—	1,200	2,700	5,400	9,000	—
1683 HS	—	1,200	2,700	5,400	9,000	—
1684 HS	—	1,200	2,700	5,400	9,000	—
1686 BA	—	1,450	3,250	6,500	11,000	—

KM# 476.2 2 DUCAT
7.0000 g., 0.9860 Gold 0.2219 oz. AGW **Ruler:** Friedrich Wilhelm **Obv:** Bust of Friedrich Wilhelm right **Rev:** City view **Note:** Finer style than 476.1.

Date	Mintage	VG	F	VF	XF	Unc
1677 IH	—	1,200	2,400	4,200	7,500	—

KM# 476.1 2 DUCAT
7.0000 g., 0.9860 Gold 0.2219 oz. AGW **Ruler:** Friedrich Wilhelm **Subject:** Conquest of Stettin **Obv:** Laureate bust right **Rev:** Eagle and griffin holding scepter above city view **Mint:** Berlin

Date	Mintage	VG	F	VF	XF	Unc
1677 CS	—	1,200	2,400	4,200	7,500	—

KM# 477 2 DUCAT
7.0000 g., 0.9860 Gold 0.2219 oz. AGW **Ruler:** Friedrich Wilhelm **Obv:** Bust right **Rev:** City view with sun shining at right **Mint:** Berlin

Date	Mintage	VG	F	VF	XF	Unc
1677 CS	—	1,200	2,400	4,200	7,500	—

KM# 478.1 2 DUCAT
7.0000 g., 0.9860 Gold 0.2219 oz. AGW **Ruler:** Friedrich Wilhelm **Obv:** Bust right **Rev:** Sun shining at left of city view **Mint:** Berlin

Date	Mintage	VG	F	VF	XF	Unc
1677 IH	—	1,200	2,400	4,200	7,500	—

KM# 478.2 2 DUCAT
7.0000 g., 0.9860 Gold 0.2219 oz. AGW **Ruler:** Friedrich Wilhelm **Obv:** Bust right **Rev:** Modified city view, face in sun **Mint:** Berlin

Date	Mintage	VG	F	VF	XF	Unc
1677 CS	—	1,200	2,400	4,200	7,500	—

KM# B509 2 DUCAT
7.0000 g., 0.9860 Gold 0.2219 oz. AGW **Ruler:** Friedrich Wilhelm **Subject:** Death of Wilhelm (III)'s wife, Elisabeth Henriette von Hessen-Kassel **Obv:** Bust right **Rev:** Crowned tablet with 8-line inscription and dates, skull and crossbones below **Note:** Struck with 1/4 Thaler dies, KM#A509.

Date	Mintage	VG	F	VF	XF	Unc
1683	—	—	—	—	—	—

KM# 544 2 DUCAT
7.0000 g., 0.9860 Gold 0.2219 oz. AGW **Ruler:** Friedrich III **Subject:** Homage of County of Mark

Date	Mintage	VG	F	VF	XF	Unc
1688	—	—	—	—	—	—

KM# 575 2 DUCAT
7.0000 g., 0.9860 Gold 0.2219 oz. AGW **Ruler:** Friedrich III **Subject:** Homage

Date	Mintage	VG	F	VF	XF	Unc
1690	—	—	—	—	—	—

KM# 615 2 DUCAT
7.0000 g., 0.9860 Gold 0.2219 oz. AGW **Ruler:** Friedrich III **Obv:** Head of Friedrich III right **Rev:** Scepter shield in garter within cruciform crowned F III monogram, date at top **Mint:** Berlin

Date	Mintage	VG	F	VF	XF	Unc
1698 RF/LCS Rare	—	—	—	—	—	—
1699 RF/LCS Rare	—	—	—	—	—	—
1700 RF/LCS Rare	—	—	—	—	—	—

KM# A160 3 DUCAT
10.5000 g., 0.9860 Gold 0.3328 oz. AGW **Ruler:** Georg Wilhelm **Obv:** 1/2-length armored figure to right, scepter over shoulder, helmet at right, titles of Georg Wilhelm **Rev:** 8-fold arms with scepter shield in center within ornamented frame, electoral hat above divides date **Rev. Legend:** ANFANCK. BEDENCK... **Mint:** Königsberg **Note:** Fr. #2177.

Date	Mintage	VG	F	VF	XF	Unc
1635 DK (q)	—	—	—	—	—	—

KM# 200 3 DUCAT
10.5000 g., 0.9860 Gold 0.3328 oz. AGW **Ruler:** Friedrich Wilhelm **Obv:** Crowned and robed elector holding scepter on horse rearing to right **Rev:** Scepter arms in center of large rose, 23 small oval arms around **Mint:** Königsberg **Note:** Struck from 1/4 Thaler dies.

Date	Mintage	VG	F	VF	XF	Unc
ND(1641/3)	—	—	—	12,000	20,000	—

KM# 284 3 DUCAT
10.5000 g., 0.9860 Gold 0.3328 oz. AGW **Ruler:** Friedrich Wilhelm **Subject:** Birthday of Friedrich Wilhelm and Birth of Prince Karl Emil **Rev:** Crowned 6-line inscription **Mint:** Berlin **Note:** Struck from 1/4 Thaler dies.

Date	Mintage	VG	F	VF	XF	Unc
1655 CT Rare	—	—	—	—	—	—

KM# 329 3 DUCAT
10.5000 g., 0.9860 Gold 0.3328 oz. AGW **Ruler:** Friedrich Wilhelm **Subject:** Homage of Konigsberg **Rev:** 9-line inscription

Date	Mintage	VG	F	VF	XF	Unc
1663	—	—	—	7,000	10,000	—

KM# 417 3 DUCAT
10.5000 g., 0.9860 Gold 0.3328 oz. AGW **Ruler:** Friedrich Wilhelm **Obv:** Bust right, date below **Rev:** Crowned arms above crossed palm branches

Date	Mintage	VG	F	VF	XF	Unc
1670	—	—	—	—	—	—

KM# 545 3 DUCAT
10.5000 g., 0.9860 Gold 0.3328 oz. AGW **Subject:** Death of Friedrich Wilhelm **Obv:** Bust right, two legends around **Rev:** Eagle on palm tree above trophies

Date	Mintage	VG	F	VF	XF	Unc
1688	—	—	—	—	—	—

KM# 596 3 DUCAT
10.5000 g., 0.9860 Gold 0.3328 oz. AGW **Ruler:** Friedrich III **Subject:** Founding of University of Halle an der Saale

Date	Mintage	VG	F	VF	XF	Unc
1694	—	—	—	—	—	—

KM# 123 4 DUCAT
14.0000 g., 0.9860 Gold 0.4438 oz. AGW **Ruler:** Georg Wilhelm **Obv:** Bust of Georg Wilhelm right in elector's costume **Rev:** Crowned twelve-fold arms in inner circle **Mint:** Kölln

Date	Mintage	VG	F	VF	XF	Unc
1626 IP Rare	4	—	—	—	—	—

KM# 225 4 DUCAT
14.0000 g., 0.9860 Gold 0.4438 oz. AGW **Ruler:** Friedrich Wilhelm **Obv:** 1/2-length figure with cap right **Rev:** Arms w/12 shields **Mint:** Berlin **Note:** Struck with 1/2 Thaler dies KM#211a.

Date	Mintage	VG	F	VF	XF	Unc
1647 CT Rare	—	—	—	—	—	—

KM# 285 4 DUCAT
14.0000 g., 0.9860 Gold 0.4438 oz. AGW **Ruler:** Friedrich Wilhelm **Subject:** Birthday of Friedrich Wilhelm and Birth of Prince Karl Friedrich **Rev:** Crowned six-line inscription and value 4 punched in **Mint:** Berlin

Date	Mintage	VG	F	VF	XF	Unc
1655 AB Rare	—	—	—	—	—	—

KM# 294 4 DUCAT
14.0000 g., 0.9860 Gold 0.4438 oz. AGW **Ruler:** Friedrich Wilhelm **Obv:** Bust of Friedrich Wilhelm right in inner circle **Rev:** Capped arms in inner circle **Mint:** Königsberg

Date	Mintage	VG	F	VF	XF	Unc
ND(1657) Rare	—	—	—	—	—	—

KM# 347 4 DUCAT
14.0000 g., 0.9860 Gold 0.4438 oz. AGW **Ruler:** Friedrich Wilhelm **Obv:** Elector standing 3/4 right, helmet on table at right **Rev:** Crowned arms divide altered date **Mint:** Berlin

Date	Mintage	VG	F	VF	XF	Unc
1666/64 IL/AB Rare	—	—	—	—	—	—

KM# 39 5 DUCAT (1/2 Portugalöser)
14.0000 g., 0.9860 Gold 0.4438 oz. AGW **Ruler:** Johann Sigismund **Obv:** Bust right **Rev:** Cross, arms in center, shield at end of each arm **Mint:** Kölln **Note:** Fr. #2151.

Date	Mintage	VG	F	VF	XF	Unc
ND(1611) Rare	—	—	—	—	—	—
1613 Rare	—	—	—	—	—	—
1614 Rare	—	—	—	—	—	—

KM# 49 5 DUCAT (1/2 Portugalöser)
14.0000 g., 0.9860 Gold 0.4438 oz. AGW **Ruler:** Johann Sigismund **Obv:** 1/2-length bust right, date below **Rev:** Arms in ornamented shield **Mint:** Kolln an der Spree

Date	Mintage	VG	F	VF	XF	Unc
1612 MH	—	—	—	—	—	—

KM# A127 5 DUCAT (1/2 Portugalöser)
17.5000 g., 0.9860 Gold 0.5547 oz. AGW **Ruler:** Georg Wilhelm **Obv:** 1/2-length armored figure to right, titles of Georg Wilhelm **Rev:** 12-fold arms in ornamented frame, electoral hat above divides date, titles continuous **Mint:** Königsberg **Note:** Struck from dies intended for 1/2 Thaler.

Date	Mintage	VG	F	VF	XF	Unc
1627 (q)	—	—	—	—	—	—

KM# B143 5 DUCAT (1/2 Portugalöser)
17.5000 g., 0.9860 Gold 0.5547 oz. AGW **Ruler:** Georg Wilhelm **Obv:** 1/2-length figure right, scepter on shoulder **Rev:** Crowned shield of arms **Mint:** Königsberg **Note:** Struck from Thaler dies, KM#125.

Date	Mintage	VG	F	VF	XF	Unc
1630 (q)	—	—	—	—	—	—

KM# 154 5 DUCAT (1/2 Portugalöser)
14.0000 g., 0.9860 Gold 0.4438 oz. AGW **Ruler:** Georg Wilhelm **Obv:** Elector on horse rearing to right **Rev:** Eagle with arms on breast and small shields on wings, date divided by legs below **Mint:** Berlin

Date	Mintage	VG	F	VF	XF	Unc
1634 LM Rare	—	—	—	—	—	—

KM# 161 5 DUCAT (1/2 Portugalöser)
14.0000 g., 0.9860 Gold 0.4438 oz. AGW **Ruler:** Georg Wilhelm **Obv:** 1/2-length figure right with helmet **Rev:** Crowned arms, date divided above **Mint:** Königsberg **Note:** Fr. #2176. Struck with 1/2 Thaler dies, KM#150.1.

Date	Mintage	VG	F	VF	XF	Unc
1636 DK Rare	—	—	—	—	—	—

KM# 201 5 DUCAT (1/2 Portugalöser)
14.0000 g., 0.9860 Gold 0.4438 oz. AGW **Ruler:** Friedrich Wilhelm **Obv:** 1/2-length bust 3/4 right breaks circle at top **Rev:** Plumed helmet, ARMAT ET ORNAT on band below, surrounded by 23 small oval arms **Note:** Struck with 1/2 Thaler dies.

Date	Mintage	VG	F	VF	XF	Unc
ND(1641-43) Rare	—	—	—	—	—	—

KM# 219 5 DUCAT (1/2 Portugalöser)
14.0000 g., 0.9860 Gold 0.4438 oz. AGW **Ruler:** Friedrich Wilhelm **Mint:** Berlin **Note:** Struck with 1/2 Thaler dies.

Date	Mintage	VG	F	VF	XF	Unc
1644 AB Rare	—	—	—	—	—	—

KM# 226 5 DUCAT (1/2 Portugalöser)
14.0000 g., 0.9860 Gold 0.4438 oz. AGW **Ruler:** Friedrich Wilhelm **Rev:** Helmeted and supported arms **Mint:** Berlin **Note:** Struck with 1 Thaler dies, KM#235.

Date	Mintage	VG	F	VF	XF	Unc
1647 CT	—	—	—	—	—	—

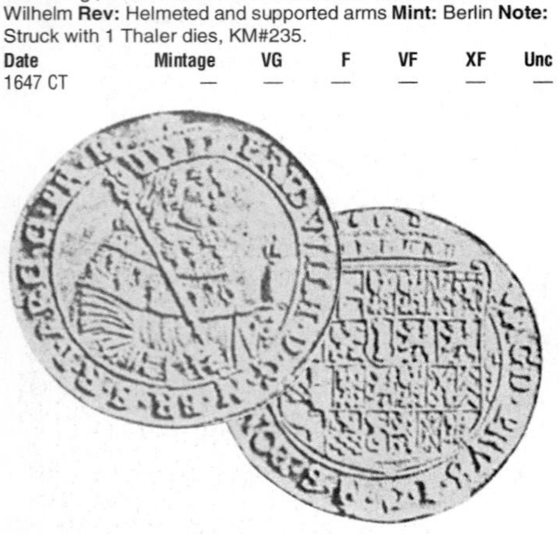

KM# 238 5 DUCAT (1/2 Portugalöser)
14.0000 g., 0.9860 Gold 0.4438 oz. AGW **Ruler:** Friedrich Wilhelm **Obv:** 1/2-figure of Friedrich Wilhelm right in elector's costume in inner circle **Rev:** Capped arms in inner circle, date in legend **Mint:** Berlin

Date	Mintage	VG	F	VF	XF	Unc
1650 CT Rare	—	—	—	—	—	—

KM# 253 5 DUCAT (1/2 Portugalöser)
14.0000 g., 0.9860 Gold 0.4438 oz. AGW **Ruler:** Friedrich Wilhelm **Rev:** Helmeted and supported arms **Note:** Struck with 1 Thaler dies, KM#235.1.

Date	Mintage	VG	F	VF	XF	Unc
ND(1651)	—	—	—	—	—	—

KM# 254 5 DUCAT (1/2 Portugalöser)
14.0000 g., 0.9860 Gold 0.4438 oz. AGW **Ruler:** Friedrich Wilhelm **Obv:** Bust right in circle **Rev:** Helmeted arms **Mint:** Königsberg **Note:** Struck with 1/2 Thaler dies, KM#247.

Date	Mintage	VG	F	VF	XF	Unc
ND(1651-61) CM Rare	—	—	—	—	—	—

KM# 259 5 DUCAT (1/2 Portugalöser)
14.0000 g., 0.9860 Gold 0.4438 oz. AGW **Ruler:** Friedrich Wilhelm **Obv:** Friedrich Wilhelm standing by table with helmet **Rev:** Capped arms in inner circle, date divided at top **Mint:** Berlin

Date	Mintage	VG	F	VF	XF	Unc
1652 CT Rare	—	—	—	—	—	—
1653 CT Rare	—	—	—	—	—	—
1655 CT Rare	—	—	—	—	—	—
1657 CT Rare	—	—	—	—	—	—

KM# 268 5 DUCAT (1/2 Portugalöser)
14.0000 g., 0.9860 Gold 0.4438 oz. AGW **Ruler:** Friedrich Wilhelm **Obv:** Friedrich Wilhelm **Mint:** Berlin

Date	Mintage	VG	F	VF	XF	Unc
1653 CT Rare	—	—	—	—	—	—

KM# 272 5 DUCAT (1/2 Portugalöser)
14.0000 g., 0.9860 Gold 0.4438 oz. AGW **Ruler:** Friedrich Wilhelm **Obv:** 3/4 figure of Friedrich Wilhelm right in inner circle **Rev:** Capped arms in inner circle **Note:** Thick planchet, from Ducat dies, KM#270.

Date	Mintage	VG	F	VF	XF	Unc
1654 Rare	—	—	—	—	—	—

KM# 295 5 DUCAT (1/2 Portugalöser)
14.0000 g., 0.9860 Gold 0.4438 oz. AGW **Ruler:** Friedrich Wilhelm **Obv:** Bust of Friedrich Wilhelm right in inner circle **Mint:** Königsberg

Date	Mintage	VG	F	VF	XF	Unc
ND(1657) Rare	—	—	—	—	—	—

KM# 300 5 DUCAT (1/2 Portugalöser)
14.0000 g., 0.9860 Gold 0.4438 oz. AGW **Ruler:** Friedrich Wilhelm **Subject:** Attainment of Sovereignty over East Prussia **Obv:** Elector on horse galloping right, town below hoofs, date at bottom **Rev:** Eight-line inscription **Mint:** Berlin

Date	Mintage	VG	F	VF	XF	Unc
1658 CT	—	—	—	—	—	—

KM# 301 5 DUCAT (1/2 Portugalöser)
14.0000 g., 0.9860 Gold 0.4438 oz. AGW **Ruler:** Friedrich Wilhelm **Rev:** 9-line inscription **Mint:** Berlin

Date	Mintage	VG	F	VF	XF	Unc
1658 AB	—	—	—	—	—	—

KM# 348 5 DUCAT (1/2 Portugalöser)
14.0000 g., 0.9860 Gold 0.4438 oz. AGW **Ruler:** Friedrich Wilhelm **Rev:** Crowned arms divide date in inner circle **Mint:** Berlin

Date	Mintage	VG	F	VF	XF	Unc
1664 AB	—	—	—	—	—	—
1666/64 IL/AB Rare	—	—	—	—	—	—

KM# 425 5 DUCAT (1/2 Portugalöser)
14.0000 g., 0.9860 Gold 0.4438 oz. AGW **Ruler:** Friedrich Wilhelm **Obv:** Laureate bust right **Rev:** Helmeted and supported arms, date in legend **Mint:** Königsberg **Note:** Struck with 1 Thaler dies.

Date	Mintage	VG	F	VF	XF	Unc
1672 TT	—	—	—	—	—	—

KM# 493 5 DUCAT (1/2 Portugalöser)
14.0000 g., 0.9860 Gold 0.4438 oz. AGW **Ruler:** Friedrich Wilhelm **Mint:** Berlin **Note:** Struck with 1 Thaler dies KM#490.

Date	Mintage	VG	F	VF	XF	Unc
1679 CS	—	—	—	—	—	—

KM# 512 5 DUCAT (1/2 Portugalöser)
14.0000 g., 0.9860 Gold 0.4438 oz. AGW **Ruler:** Friedrich Wilhelm **Obv:** Armored bust of Friedrich Wilhelm right, date in legend **Rev:** Capped arms **Mint:** Magdeburg

Date	Mintage	VG	F	VF	XF	Unc
1683 IE Rare	—	—	—	—	—	—

KM# 523 5 DUCAT (1/2 Portugalöser)
14.0000 g., 0.9860 Gold 0.4438 oz. AGW **Ruler:** Friedrich Wilhelm **Obv:** Bust right in circle **Rev:** Crowned eagle, scepter arms on breast, eight shields on wings, date divided at lower left and right **Mint:** Berlin **Note:** Struck with 1 Thaler dies, KM#521.

Date	Mintage	VG	F	VF	XF	Unc
1685 LCS	—	—	—	—	—	—

KM# 91 6 DUCAT
21.0000 g., 0.9860 Gold 0.6657 oz. AGW **Ruler:** Georg Wilhelm **Obv:** 1/2-length figure right, date below **Rev:** Arms, mint mark of Ernst Pfaler at end of reverse legend **Mint:** Königsberg **Note:** Similar to 1 Thaler, KM#88.

Date	Mintage	VG	F	VF	XF	Unc
1621 (a) Unique	—	—	—	—	—	—

KM# 227 6 DUCAT
21.0000 g., 0.9860 Gold 0.6657 oz. AGW **Ruler:** Friedrich Wilhelm **Obv:** 1/2-length figure with cap right **Rev:** Arms with 12 fields **Mint:** Berlin **Note:** Struck with 1/2 Thaler dies, KM#211.

Date	Mintage	VG	F	VF	XF	Unc
1647 CT Rare	—	—	—	—	—	—

KM# 479 6 DUCAT
21.0000 g., 0.9860 Gold 0.6657 oz. AGW **Ruler:** Friedrich Wilhelm **Obv:** Laureate bust right **Rev:** Helmeted and supported arms, date in legend **Mint:** Königsberg **Note:** Struck with 1 Thaler dies.

Date	Mintage	VG	F	VF	XF	Unc
1677 HS	—	—	—	—	—	—

KM# 530 6 DUCAT
21.0000 g., 0.9860 Gold 0.6657 oz. AGW **Ruler:** Friedrich Wilhelm **Mint:** Berlin **Note:** Struck with 1 Thaler dies, KM#527.

Date	Mintage	VG	F	VF	XF	Unc
1686 LCS Rare	—	—	—	—	—	—

KM# B127 8 DUCAT
28.0000 g., 0.9860 Gold 0.8876 oz. AGW **Ruler:** Georg Wilhelm **Obv:** 1/2-length figure right **Rev:** Crowned shield of arms **Mint:** Königsberg **Note:** Fr. #2175. Struck from Thaler dies, KM#125.

Date	Mintage	VG	F	VF	XF	Unc
16Z7 (q)	—	—	—	—	—	—

KM# 459 8 DUCAT
28.0000 g., 0.9860 Gold 0.8876 oz. AGW **Ruler:** Friedrich Wilhelm **Subject:** Victory at Battle of Fehrbellin **Mint:** Berlin **Note:** Struck with 1 Thaler dies, KM#449.

Date	Mintage	VG	F	VF	XF	Unc
1675 Rare	—	—	—	—	—	—

Note: Tempelhofer Auction 2-83 XF realized $19,500

KM# 29 10 DUCAT (Portugalöser)
35.0000 g., 0.9860 Gold 1.1095 oz. AGW **Ruler:** Joachim Friedrich **Obv:** Half-length bust right holding scepter and helmet **Rev:** Ornate cross, date at bottom arm, surrounded by 17 small shields **Mint:** Kölln **Note:** Fr. #2143.

Date	Mintage	VG	F	VF	XF	Unc
1605 Rare	—	—	—	—	—	—

KM# 50 10 DUCAT (Portugalöser)
35.0000 g., 0.9860 Gold 1.1095 oz. AGW **Ruler:** Johann Sigismund **Obv:** Bust right **Rev:** Cross, arms in center, shield at end of each arm **Note:** Fr. #2150.

Date	Mintage	VG	F	VF	XF	Unc
ND(1611) Rare	—	—	—	—	—	—
1612 Rare	—	—	—	—	—	—
1613 Rare	—	—	—	—	—	—
1614 Rare	—	—	—	—	—	—

KM# 80 10 DUCAT (Portugalöser)
35.0000 g., 0.9860 Gold 1.1095 oz. AGW **Ruler:** Georg Wilhelm **Obv:** Elector on horse galloping right **Mint:** Berlin **Note:** Struck with 1 Thaler dies, KM#74.

Date	Mintage	VG	F	VF	XF	Unc
1620 LM Rare	—	—	—	—	—	—

KM# A100 10 DUCAT (Portugalöser)
35.0000 g., 0.9860 Gold 1.1095 oz. AGW **Ruler:** Georg Wilhelm **Obv:** Crowned 1/2-length figure right **Obv. Legend:** GEORG: WILHELM: V: G: G: **Rev:** Helmeted arms, date above **Mint:** Königsberg **Note:** Ref. Dost #558. Struck from 1 Thaler dies, KM#112.1.

Date	Mintage	VG	F	VF	XF	Unc
1623 Rare	—	—	—	—	—	—

KM# C143 10 DUCAT (Portugalöser)
35.0000 g., 0.9860 Gold 1.1095 oz. AGW **Ruler:** Georg Wilhelm **Obv:** 1/2-length figure right, scepter on shoulder **Rev:** Shield of arms **Mint:** Königsberg **Note:** Fr. #2174. Struck from 2 Thaler dies, KM#143.

Date	Mintage	VG	F	VF	XF	Unc
1630 (q) Rare	—	—	—	—	—	—

KM# 155 10 DUCAT (Portugalöser)
35.0000 g., 0.9860 Gold 1.1095 oz. AGW **Ruler:** Georg Wilhelm **Obv:** Elector on horse rearing to right **Rev:** Eagle with arms on breast and small shields on wings, date divided by legs below **Mint:** Berlin **Note:** Struck with 5 Ducat dies, KM#154.

Date	Mintage	VG	F	VF	XF	Unc
1634 LM Rare	—	—	—	—	—	—

KM# 202 10 DUCAT (Portugalöser)
35.0000 g., 0.9860 Gold 1.1095 oz. AGW **Ruler:** Friedrich Wilhelm **Obv:** Crowned and robed half-length figure right **Rev:** Scepter arms in center of large rose, 23 small oval arms around **Mint:** Königsberg

Date	Mintage	VG	F	VF	XF	Unc
ND(1641-3) Rare	—	—	—	—	—	—

KM# 208 10 DUCAT (Portugalöser)
35.0000 g., 0.9860 Gold 1.1095 oz. AGW **Ruler:** Friedrich Wilhelm **Obv:** Bust right, helmet at right **Rev:** Helmeted arms divide date **Mint:** Königsberg **Note:** Struck with 1 Thaler dies, KM#206.

Date	Mintage	VG	F	VF	XF	Unc
1642 DK	—	—	—	—	—	—

KM# 255 10 DUCAT (Portugalöser)
35.0000 g., 0.9860 Gold 1.1095 oz. AGW **Ruler:** Friedrich Wilhelm **Obv:** Friedrich Wilhelm standing in ornamental inner circle **Rev:** Seven helmeted arms with knight supporters, date divided near center **Mint:** Berlin

Date	Mintage	VG	F	VF	XF	Unc
1651 CT Rare	—	—	—	—	—	—

KM# 256 10 DUCAT (Portugalöser)
35.0000 g., 0.9860 Gold 1.1095 oz. AGW **Ruler:** Friedrich Wilhelm **Obv:** Capped bust right with sword and sceptre **Rev:** Helmeted and supported arms

Date	Mintage	VG	F	VF	XF	Unc
ND(1651) Unique	—	—	—	—	—	—

Note: Hess Auction 3-83 XF realized $25,000

KM# 269 10 DUCAT (Portugalöser)
35.0000 g., 0.9860 Gold 1.1095 oz. AGW **Ruler:** Friedrich Wilhelm **Obv:** Elector standing 3/4 to right **Obv. Legend:** BR. S.-R. I. ARCHIC. ET. ELECT. **Rev:** Helmeted arms **Mint:** Berlin **Note:** Struck with 1 Thaler dies, KM#249.

Date	Mintage	VG	F	VF	XF	Unc
1653 CT	—	—	—	—	—	—

KM# 296 10 DUCAT (Portugalöser)
35.0000 g., 0.9860 Gold 1.1095 oz. AGW **Ruler:** Friedrich Wilhelm **Subject:** Attainment of Sovereignty over East Prussia **Obv:** Town below forelegs of horse **Mint:** Berlin **Note:** Struck with 1 Thaler dies, KM#249.

Date	Mintage	VG	F	VF	XF	Unc
1657 CT Rare	—	—	—	—	—	—

KM# 397 10 DUCAT (Portugalöser)
35.0000 g., 0.9860 Gold 1.1095 oz. AGW **Ruler:** Friedrich Wilhelm **Subject:** Return of Elector to Prussia in 1669 **Obv:** Crowned and robed figure of elector holding scepter on horse rearing right on carpet, date below **Rev:** Figure of Brandenburgia in landscape with child on knee, eagle with laruel wreath in beak above **Mint:** Berlin

Date	Mintage	VG	F	VF	XF	Unc
1669 GL Rare	—	—	—	—	—	—

KM# 426 10 DUCAT (Portugalöser)
35.0000 g., 0.9860 Gold 1.1095 oz. AGW **Ruler:** Friedrich Wilhelm **Obv:** Laureate bust right **Rev:** Helmeted and supported arms, date in legend **Mint:** Königsberg **Note:** Struck with 1 Thaler dies, KM#424.

Date	Mintage	VG	F	VF	XF	Unc
1672 TT Rare	—	—	—	—	—	—

KM# 460 10 DUCAT (Portugalöser)
35.0000 g., 0.9860 Gold 1.1095 oz. AGW **Ruler:** Friedrich Wilhelm **Subject:** Victory at Battle of Fehrbellin **Mint:** Berlin **Note:** Struck with 1 Thaler dies, similar to KM#449.

Date	Mintage	VG	F	VF	XF	Unc
1675 Rare	—	—	—	—	—	—

KM# 502 10 DUCAT (Portugalöser)
35.0000 g., 0.9860 Gold 1.1095 oz. AGW **Ruler:** Friedrich Wilhelm **Subject:** Homage of the City of Magdeburg, 30 May 1681 **Obv:** Bust of elector right in oval frame linked to clouds and to city of Magdeburg by three chains **Rev:** Maiden kneeling right in landscape, sun, eagle and cornucopia in clouds above, date below **Mint:** Magdeburg **Note:** Struck with 1 Thaler dies, KM#501.

Date	Mintage	VG	F	VF	XF	Unc
1681 IE Rare	—	—	—	—	—	—

KM# B100 15 DUCAT
52.5000 g., 0.9860 Gold 1.6642 oz. AGW **Ruler:** Georg Wilhelm **Obv:** Crowned 1/2-length figure right **Obv. Legend:** GEORG: WILHELM: V: G: G **Rev:** Helmeted arms, date above **Mint:** Königsberg **Note:** Struck from 2 Thaler dies, KM#112.1.

Date	Mintage	VG	F	VF	XF	Unc
1623 Rare	—	—	—	—	—	—

KM# 203 15 DUCAT
52.5000 g., 0.9860 Gold 1.6642 oz. AGW **Ruler:** Friedrich Wilhelm **Obv:** 1/2-length bust 3/4 to right **Rev:** Scepter arms in center of large rose, 23 small oval arms around **Mint:** Königsberg **Note:** Struck with 1 Thaler dies, KM#192.

Date	Mintage	VG	F	VF	XF	Unc
ND(1641-3) Rare	—	—	—	—	—	—

KM# 461 20 DUCAT

70.0000 g., 0.9860 Gold 2.2190 oz. AGW **Ruler:** Friedrich Wilhelm **Subject:** Victory at Battle of Fehrbellin **Mint:** Berlin **Note:** Struck with 1 Thaler dies, KM#449.

Date	Mintage	VG	F	VF	XF	Unc
1675 Rare	—	—	—	—	—	—

KM# B119 50 DUCAT

175.0000 g., 0.9860 Gold 5.5474 oz. AGW **Ruler:** Georg Wilhelm **Obv:** Armored bust right, wide band with 19 small shields of arms around **Rev:** 4-fold arms with scepter shield in center, within ornamented shield, date divided near bottom, electoral hat above, all in circle, 3 circles of legends with name and titles of Georg Wilhelm **Mint:** Königsberg **Note:** Fr. #2173. Struck from 3 Thaler dies, KM#A118.

Date	Mintage	VG	F	VF	XF	Unc
1624 MK-NB Rare	—	—	—	—	—	—

PATTERNS

Including off metal strikes

KM#	Date	Mintage	Identification	Mkt Val
Pn1	1668 IL	—	Ducat. Silver. KM#394	150
PnA2	1677 CS	—	2 Ducat. Silver. KM#476.1	300
Pn2	1677 CS	—	2 Ducat. Silver. KM#477	240
PnA3	1677 CS	—	2 Ducat. Silver. KM#478.2	300
Pn3	1688	—	2 Ducat. Silver. KM#544. County of Mark.	160
Pn4	1690	—	Ducat. Silver. KM#574. Homage.	180
Pn5	1690	—	2 Ducat. Silver. KM#575. Homage.	240
Pn6	1694	—	Ducat. Silver. KM#595. University of Halle an der Salle.	210
Pn7	1694	—	3 Ducat. Silver. KM#596. University of Halle an der Salle.	145
Pn8	1699 RF/LCS	—	2 Ducat. Silver. KM#619. Struck on octagonal flan.	—

BRANDENBURG-ANSBACH

Located in northern Bavaria. The first coins appeared ca. 1150. This area was given and sold to many individuals, usually with some relationship to the elector of Brandenburg. It was sold to Prussia in 1791 and was ceded to Bavaria in 1806.

RULERS

Joachim Ernst, 1603-1625
Friedrich II, Albrecht and Christian, 1625-1634
Albrecht III, 1634-1667
Johann Friedrich, 1667-1686
Christian Albrecht, 1686-1692
Georg Friedrich II, 1692-1703

MINT MARKS

(c) - Crailsheim, pot hook
(d) - Dachsbach, lily
F - Furth
(f) - Furth, cloverleaf
(k) - Kitzingen, crenellated tower top
O - Onolzbach (Ansbach)
(r) - Roth, rosette
R - Roth
(s) - Schwabach, four-petaled flower
S - Schwabach

MINT OFFICIALS' INITIALS

Initial	Date	Name
(a) 2 horseshoes	1668-97	Johann Christoph Holeisen in Augsburgi
CG	Ca.1622-25	Christian Goebel
CS	1622-54	Conrad Stutz, die-cutter in Furth, mintmaster of the Franconian Circle
GH	1683-1711	Georg Hautsch, die-cutter in Nürnberg
GL	1621-22	Georg Lesse in Roth
IR	Ca.1624	Unknown
PG		Unknown

MARGRAVIATE

REGULAR COINAGE

KM# 130 HELLER

Copper **Ruler:** Georg Friedrich II **Obv:** Crowned arms **Rev:** 1/HEL/LER/date

Date	Mintage	VG	F	VF	XF	Unc
1699	—	9.00	16.00	32.00	65.00	—
1700	—	9.00	16.00	32.00	65.00	—

KM# 18 PFENNING

Copper **Ruler:** Joachim Ernst **Obv:** Arms divide I-E, value above **Note:** Kipper issue. Uniface.

Date	Mintage	VG	F	VF	XF	Unc
1622	—	27.00	55.00	85.00	190	—

KM# 55 PFENNING

Copper **Ruler:** Albrecht III **Obv:** Shield of Hohenzollern arms, B. O. above. **Note:** Uniface.

Date	Mintage	VG	F	VF	XF	Unc
ND(1639-67)	—	—	—	—	—	—

KM# 129 PFENNING

Billon **Ruler:** Georg Friedrich II **Obv:** Two adjacent oval shields of arms, value 1 divides date above **Note:** Uniface.

Date	Mintage	VG	F	VF	XF	Unc
1697	—	16.00	25.00	60.00	125	—
1698	—	16.00	25.00	60.00	125	—
1700	—	16.00	25.00	60.00	125	—

KM# 19 2 PFENNING

Copper **Ruler:** Joachim Ernst **Obv:** Arms divide value II and date **Note:** Kipper issue. Uniface.

Date	Mintage	VG	F	VF	XF	Unc
1622	—	27.00	55.00	110	225	—

KM# 34 2 PFENNING

Billon **Ruler:** Joachim Ernst **Obv:** Two shields of arms, I.E.M.B. above, mintmark below **Rev:** 4-line inscription with date **Mint:** Fürth

Date	Mintage	VG	F	VF	XF	Unc
1623 F	—	—	—	—	—	—

KM# 20 3 PFENNIG

Copper **Ruler:** Joachim Ernst **Obv:** Arms divide date, I.E.M.Z.B. above **Rev:** FC (Frankischer Creis) above 3 **Note:** Kipper issue.

Date	Mintage	VG	F	VF	XF	Unc
1622	—	25.00	45.00	85.00	190	—

KM# 21 3 PFENNIG (Dreier)

Billon **Ruler:** Joachim Ernst **Obv:** Eagle **Rev:** Imperial orb with value 3, date

Date	Mintage	VG	F	VF	XF	Unc
1622	—	—	—	—	—	—

KM# 22 4 PFENNING

Copper **Ruler:** Joachim Ernst **Note:** Kipper issue.

Date	Mintage	VG	F	VF	XF	Unc
1622	—	22.00	45.00	90.00	175	—

KM# 23 KREUZER (4 Pfennig)

Silver **Ruler:** Joachim Ernst **Obv:** Oval shield of Hohenzollern arms, I.E.M.Z.B. above **Rev:** 5-line inscription with date and mintmark **Rev. Inscription:** I / KREVTZ / ER / (date) / F **Mint:** Fürth

Date	Mintage	VG	F	VF	XF	Unc
1622F	—	10.00	20.00	40.00	80.00	—
1623F	—	10.00	20.00	40.00	80.00	—

KM# 35 KREUZER (4 Pfennig)

Silver **Ruler:** Joachim Ernst **Obv:** Three arms

Date	Mintage	VG	F	VF	XF	Unc
1623	—	—	—	—	—	—

KM# 43 KREUZER (4 Pfennig)

Silver **Ruler:** Joachim Ernst **Obv:** Oval shield of arms in baroque frame, I.E.M.Z.B. above **Rev:** 4-line inscription with date, mintmark below **Rev. Inscription:** I / KREVTZ / ER / (date) **Mint:** Roth

Date	Mintage	VG	F	VF	XF	Unc
1624 R	—	75.00	150	300	600	—

KM# 100 KREUZER (4 Pfennig)

Silver **Ruler:** Johann Friedrich

Date	Mintage	VG	F	VF	XF	Unc
1683	—	12.00	25.00	55.00	110	—
1685	—	12.00	25.00	55.00	110	—

KM# 105 KREUZER (4 Pfennig)

Silver **Ruler:** Johann Friedrich **Obv:** Bust right **Rev:** Crowned eagle with I on breast, date divided above

Date	Mintage	VG	F	VF	XF	Unc
1686	—	20.00	40.00	80.00	165	—

KM# 115 KREUZER (4 Pfennig)

Silver **Ruler:** Georg Friedrich II **Obv:** Monogram **Rev:** Arms, date

Date	Mintage	VG	F	VF	XF	Unc
1693	—	15.00	30.00	65.00	130	—

KM# 116 KREUZER (4 Pfennig)

Silver **Ruler:** Georg Friedrich II **Obv:** Bust right **Rev:** Crowned eagle with I on breast, date divided above **Note:** Similar to KM#136.

Date	Mintage	VG	F	VF	XF	Unc
1693	—	10.00	20.00	40.00	80.00	—
1694	—	10.00	20.00	40.00	80.00	—
1695	—	10.00	20.00	40.00	80.00	—
1696	—	10.00	20.00	40.00	80.00	—
1697	—	10.00	20.00	40.00	80.00	—
1698	—	10.00	20.00	40.00	80.00	—
1699	—	10.00	20.00	40.00	80.00	—
1700	—	10.00	20.00	40.00	80.00	—

KM# A23 2 KREUZER (1/2 Batzen)

Silver **Ruler:** Joachim Ernst **Obv:** Eagle **Rev:** Imperial orb with value 2, date **Mint:** Roth

Date	Mintage	VG	F	VF	XF	Unc
1622 R	—	27.00	55.00	90.00	185	—

KM# 36 2 KREUZER (1/2 Batzen)

Silver **Ruler:** Joachim Ernst **Obv:** Two shields of arms, value II above, mintmark below **Rev:** Eagle **Mint:** Fürth

Date	Mintage	VG	F	VF	XF	Unc
1623 F	—	27.00	55.00	90.00	185	—

KM# 101 2 KREUZER (1/2 Batzen)

Silver **Ruler:** Johann Friedrich **Obv:** Bust right **Rev:** Imperial orb with value 2, date

Date	Mintage	VG	F	VF	XF	Unc
1683	—	27.00	55.00	90.00	185	—
1686	—	27.00	55.00	90.00	185	—

KM# 117 2 KREUZER (1/2 Batzen)

Silver **Ruler:** Georg Friedrich II **Obv:** Bust right **Rev:** Imperial orb with value 2, date

Date	Mintage	VG	F	VF	XF	Unc
1693	—	27.00	55.00	90.00	185	—
1694	—	27.00	55.00	90.00	185	—
1695	—	27.00	55.00	90.00	185	—
1696	—	27.00	55.00	90.00	185	—

KM# 118 2 KREUZER (1/2 Batzen)

Silver **Ruler:** Georg Friedrich II **Obv:** Four arms **Rev:** Imperial orb with value 2, date

Date	Mintage	VG	F	VF	XF	Unc
1694	—	20.00	40.00	65.00	130	—

KM# 27 3 KREUZER (Groschen)

Silver **Ruler:** Joachim Ernst **Obv:** Eagle with arms on breast, date in legend **Rev:** Imperial orb with value 3

Date	Mintage	VG	F	VF	XF	Unc
1622 IR	—	15.00	30.00	65.00	130	—
1623 IR	—	15.00	30.00	65.00	130	—
1624 IR	—	15.00	30.00	65.00	130	—
1625 IR	—	15.00	30.00	65.00	130	—

KM# 44 3 KREUZER (Groschen)
Silver **Ruler:** Joachim Ernst **Obv:** Eagle with arms on breast, date in legend **Rev:** Imperial orb with value 3 **Note:** Klippe.

Date	Mintage	VG	F	VF	XF	Unc
1624	—	80.00	175	275	575	—

KM# 61 3 KREUZER (Groschen)
Silver **Ruler:** Albrecht III **Obv:** Arms **Rev:** Imperial orb with value 3, date

Date	Mintage	VG	F	VF	XF	Unc
1652	—	—	—	—	—	—

KM# 24 4 KREUZER (Batzen)
Silver **Ruler:** Joachim Ernst **Obv:** Two arms, value IIII K above, F below, date in legend **Rev:** Eagle **Mint:** Fürth **Note:** Varieties exist.

Date	Mintage	VG	F	VF	XF	Unc
1622 F	—	20.00	40.00	80.00	160	—
1623 F	—	20.00	40.00	80.00	160	—
1624 F	—	20.00	40.00	80.00	160	—
1625 F	—	20.00	40.00	80.00	160	—

KM# 102 4 KREUZER (Batzen)
Silver **Ruler:** Johann Friedrich **Obv:** Arms **Rev:** Value, date

Date	Mintage	VG	F	VF	XF	Unc
1683	—	75.00	125	225	450	—

KM# 124 4 KREUZER (Batzen)
Silver **Ruler:** Georg Friedrich II **Obv:** 2 arms in inner circle **Rev:** Crowned imperial eagle, 4 in orb on breast

Date	Mintage	VG	F	VF	XF	Unc
1695	—	10.00	25.00	55.00	110	—
1696	—	10.00	25.00	55.00	110	—

KM# 37 6 KREUZER
Silver **Ruler:** Joachim Ernst **Obv:** Two shields of arms, value VI K above, mintmark below **Rev:** Eagle, date **Mint:** Fürth

Date	Mintage	VG	F	VF	XF	Unc
1623 F	—	60.00	120	240	425	—

KM# 45 6 KREUZER
Silver **Ruler:** Joachim Ernst **Subject:** Death of Joachim Ernst **Obv:** Bust **Rev:** Inscription with date, value below VI. K. **Mint:** Fürth

Date	Mintage	VG	F	VF	XF	Unc
1625 F	—	45.00	120	200	360	—

KM# 46 6 KREUZER
Silver **Ruler:** Joachim Ernst **Rev:** Without indication of value

Date	Mintage	VG	F	VF	XF	Unc
1625	—	55.00	115	200	400	—

KM# 83 6 KREUZER
Silver **Ruler:** Johann Friedrich **Obv:** Bust, value 6 below **Rev:** Arms, date

Date	Mintage	VG	F	VF	XF	Unc
1677	—	55.00	115	200	400	—
1678	—	55.00	115	200	400	—

KM# 103 6 KREUZER
Silver **Ruler:** Johann Friedrich **Obv:** Two arms, value above **Rev:** Eagle, date

Date	Mintage	VG	F	VF	XF	Unc
1683	—	55.00	115	200	400	—
1684	—	55.00	115	200	400	—

KM# 11A 12 KREUZER
2.8700 g., Silver, 25 mm. **Ruler:** Joachim Ernst **Obv:** Ornately-shaped shield of Hohenzollern arms in circle, date at end of legend **Obv. Legend:** IOA. ER. D. G. MAR. BRAN. PRUSSIAE. **Rev:** Crowned imperial eagle, 1Z in orb on breast **Rev. Legend:** ST. PO. CA. V. CR. IA. D. BVR. I. NVR. PR. RV. **Mint:** Fürth **Note:** Kipper issue.

Date	Mintage	VG	F	VF	XF	Unc
(16)21 Rare	—	—	—	—	—	—

Note: An example in VF realized approximately $2,600 in a Peus auction of November 2008.

KM# 16 24 KREUZER
Silver **Ruler:** Joachim Ernst **Obv:** Facing bust **Rev:** Value 24 between shields

Date	Mintage	VG	F	VF	XF	Unc
1621 CS	—	85.00	170	340	675	—

KM# 13 24 KREUZER
Silver **Ruler:** Joachim Ernst **Obv:** Bust right, date in legend **Rev:** Eagle with 24 in orb on breast **Note:** Kipper 24 Kreuzer. Varieties exist.

Date	Mintage	VG	F	VF	XF	Unc
1621	—	75.00	150	300	600	—
1621 (f)	—	75.00	150	300	600	—
1621 (k)	—	75.00	150	300	600	—
1622	—	75.00	150	300	600	—
1622 (d)	—	75.00	150	300	600	—
1622 (f)	—	75.00	150	300	600	—
1622 (k)	—	75.00	150	300	600	—
1622 0	—	75.00	150	300	600	—
1622 (r)	—	75.00	150	300	600	—
1622 (s)	—	75.00	150	300	600	—

KM# 14 24 KREUZER
Silver **Ruler:** Joachim Ernst **Obv:** Bust right, date in legend **Rev:** Eagle with 24 in orb on breast **Note:** Klippe.

Date	Mintage	VG	F	VF	XF	Unc
1621 (k)	—	—	—	—	—	—

KM# 15 24 KREUZER
Silver **Ruler:** Joachim Ernst **Obv:** 4-fold arms, central shield of Nuremberg burgraviate (lion rampant left), date **Note:** Varieties exist.

Date	Mintage	VG	F	VF	XF	Unc
1621	—	75.00	150	300	600	—
1621 (d)	—	75.00	150	300	600	—
1621 GL	—	75.00	150	300	600	—
1622 (f)	—	75.00	150	300	600	—

KM# 25.1 24 KREUZER
Silver **Ruler:** Joachim Ernst **Obv:** Bust right divides date **Rev:** Eagle with 24 in orb on breast **Mint:** Crailsheim

Date	Mintage	VG	F	VF	XF	Unc
1622 (c)	—	80.00	165	335	675	—

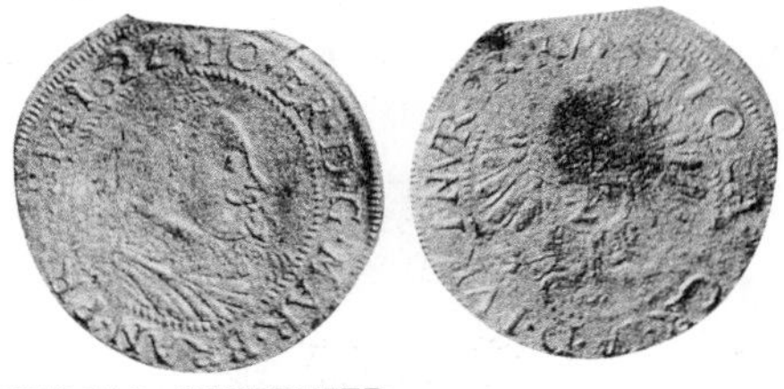

KM# 25.2 24 KREUZER
Silver **Ruler:** Joachim Ernst **Obv:** Bust right, date in legend **Mint:** Crailsheim

Date	Mintage	VG	F	VF	XF	Unc
1622 (c)	—	80.00	165	335	675	—

KM# 26 48 KREUZER (Kippergulden)
Silver **Ruler:** Joachim Ernst **Obv:** Bust 3/4 to right, date in legend **Rev:** Eagle wtih 48 in orb on breast **Mint:** Dachsbach **Note:** Kipper issue.

Date	Mintage	VG	F	VF	XF	Unc
1622 (d)	—	250	425	750	1,300	—

KM# 67 GROSCHEN (1/24 Thaler)
2.3000 g., Silver, 22.2 mm. **Ruler:** Albrecht III **Subject:** Death of Albrecht III **Obv:** Facing bust **Rev:** Inscription with date

Date	Mintage	VG	F	VF	XF	Unc
1667	—	—	—	—	—	—

KM# 99 GROSCHEN (1/24 Thaler)
Silver **Ruler:** Johann Friedrich **Obv:** Arms **Rev:** Value as GG(Guter Groschen), date

Date	Mintage	VG	F	VF	XF	Unc
1682	—	—	—	—	—	—

KM# 106 GROSCHEN (1/24 Thaler)
Silver **Ruler:** Johann Friedrich **Subject:** Death of Johann Friedrich **Obv:** Bust right **Rev:** Inscription with date

Date	Mintage	VG	F	VF	XF	Unc
1686	—	—	—	—	—	—

KM# 107 2 GROSCHEN (1/12 Thaler)
Silver **Ruler:** Johann Friedrich **Subject:** Death of Johann Friedrich **Obv:** Bust right **Rev:** Inscription with date

Date	Mintage	VG	F	VF	XF	Unc
1686	—	—	—	—	—	—

KM# 17 1/24 THALER (Groschen)
Silver **Ruler:** Joachim Ernst **Obv:** Eagle, date in legend **Rev:** Imperial orb with value 24

Date	Mintage	VG	F	VF	XF	Unc
1621	—	16.00	33.00	60.00	110	—

KM# 81 1/24 THALER (Groschen)
Silver **Ruler:** Johann Friedrich **Rev:** Imperial orb with value 24, date

Date	Mintage	VG	F	VF	XF	Unc
1676	—	10.00	25.00	55.00	110	—
1682	—	10.00	25.00	55.00	110	—
1683	—	10.00	25.00	55.00	110	—
1684	—	10.00	25.00	55.00	110	—

KM# 28 1/8 THALER
Silver **Ruler:** Joachim Ernst **Obv:** Bust 3/4 right divides date **Rev:** 4-fold arms in baroque frame

Date	Mintage	VG	F	VF	XF	Unc
1622	—	—	—	—	—	—

KM# 68 1/8 THALER
Silver **Ruler:** Albrecht III **Subject:** Death of Albrecht III **Obv:** Facing bust **Rev:** Inscription with date

Date	Mintage	VG	F	VF	XF	Unc
1667	—	—	—	—	—	—

KM# 38 1/6 THALER (1/4 Gulden)
Silver **Ruler:** Joachim Ernst **Obv:** Eagle with 6 on breast **Rev:** Three arms in cartouche, one above 2 with top one dividing date **Mint:** Fürth

Date	Mintage	VG	F	VF	XF	Unc
1623 F	—	—	—	—	—	—

KM# 82 1/6 THALER (1/4 Gulden)
Silver **Ruler:** Johann Friedrich

Date	Mintage	VG	F	VF	XF	Unc
1676	—	16.00	35.00	75.00	150	—
1677	—	16.00	35.00	75.00	150	—

Date	Mintage	VG	F	VF	XF	Unc
1678	—	20.00	35.00	75.00	150	—
1679	—	16.00	35.00	75.00	150	—

KM# 84 1/6 THALER (1/4 Gulden)

Silver **Ruler:** Johann Friedrich **Obv:** Bust right **Rev:** Piety and Justice standing

Date	Mintage	VG	F	VF	XF	Unc
1679	—	—	—	—	—	—

KM# 56 1/3 THALER (1/2 Gulden)

Silver **Ruler:** Johann Friedrich **Obv:** Bust right **Rev:** Crowned arms between palm branches, date divides value below

Date	Mintage	VG	F	VF	XF	Unc
1676	—	325	600	1,100	2,000	—

KM# 29 1/2 THALER

Silver **Ruler:** Joachim Ernst

Date	Mintage	VG	F	VF	XF	Unc
1622	—	—	—	—	—	—

KM# 39 1/2 THALER

Silver **Ruler:** Joachim Ernst **Obv:** Half-length bust 3/4 right **Rev:** 4-fold arms, central shield of Nuremberg burgraviate, divide date

Date	Mintage	VG	F	VF	XF	Unc
1623 CS	—	—	—	—	—	—

KM# 47 1/2 THALER

Silver **Ruler:** Joachim Ernst **Subject:** Death of Joachim Ernst **Rev:** 7-line inscription, date

Date	Mintage	VG	F	VF	XF	Unc
1625	—	—	—	—	—	—

KM# 51 1/2 THALER

Silver **Ruler:** Friedrich II, Albrecht and Christian

Date	Mintage	VG	F	VF	XF	Unc
1628	—	—	—	—	—	—
1629	—	—	—	—	—	—

KM# 108 1/2 THALER

Silver **Ruler:** Johann Friedrich **Subject:** Death of Johann Friedrich

Date	Mintage	VG	F	VF	XF	Unc
1686	—	500	900	1,700	3,200	—

KM# 79 2/3 THALER (Gulden)

Silver **Ruler:** Johann Friedrich

Date	Mintage	VG	F	VF	XF	Unc
1675	—	60.00	120	235	475	—
1676	—	60.00	120	235	475	—
1677	—	60.00	120	235	475	—
1679	—	60.00	120	235	475	—

KM# 80 2/3 THALER (Gulden)

Silver **Ruler:** Johann Friedrich **Rev:** Arms between palm sprays

Date	Mintage	VG	F	VF	XF	Unc
1675	—	55.00	110	200	425	—
1676	—	55.00	110	200	425	—
1677	—	55.00	110	200	425	—
1679	—	55.00	110	200	425	—

KM# 85 2/3 THALER (Gulden)

Silver **Ruler:** Johann Friedrich **Obv:** Crowned oval arms in baroque frame, value divides date below **Rev:** Arm from clouds holds crown above heart on altar

Date	Mintage	VG	F	VF	XF	Unc
1679	—	—	—	—	—	—

KM# 86 2/3 THALER (Gulden)

Silver **Ruler:** Johann Friedrich **Obv:** Bust right **Rev:** Table with cross, scales, branches, value divides date below

Date	Mintage	VG	F	VF	XF	Unc
1679	—	—	—	—	—	—

KM# 87 2/3 THALER (Gulden)

Silver **Ruler:** Johann Friedrich **Obv:** Bust right **Rev:** Piety and Justice, value divides date

Date	Mintage	VG	F	VF	XF	Unc
1679	—	—	—	—	—	—

KM# 5 THALER

Silver **Ruler:** Joachim Ernst **Note:** Dav. 6226.

Date	Mintage	VG	F	VF	XF	Unc
1609	—	775	1,500	2,700	4,500	—
1619	—	205	350	650	1,200	—
1620	—	205	350	650	1,200	—

KM# 11 THALER

Silver **Ruler:** Joachim Ernst **Note:** Dav. #6227.

Date	Mintage	VG	F	VF	XF	Unc
1620	—	210	400	775	1,500	—

KM# 12 THALER

Silver **Ruler:** Joachim Ernst **Obv:** Smaller bust holding baton **Note:** Dav. #6228.

Date	Mintage	VG	F	VF	XF	Unc
1620	—	240	450	725	1,500	3,900
1621	—	300	575	1,150	2,100	—

KM# 30 THALER

Silver **Ruler:** Joachim Ernst **Obv:** Bust 3/4 to left **Rev:** Squared 12-fold arms in baroque frame, date divided above **Note:** Dav. 6229.

Date	Mintage	VG	F	VF	XF	Unc
1622 Rare	—	—	—	—	—	—

KM# 31 THALER

Silver **Ruler:** Joachim Ernst **Note:** Dav. 6230.

Date	Mintage	VG	F	VF	XF	Unc
1622 CG	—	240	550	1,150	2,200	—
1625 CG	—	240	475	950	1,900	—

KM# 40 THALER

Silver **Ruler:** Joachim Ernst **Obv:** Similar to KM#41 **Obv. Legend:** ...RVG **Rev:** Oval 4-fold arms, central shield of Nuremberg lion, all in baroque frame whtich divides date **Note:** Dav. 6231.

Date	Mintage	VG	F	VF	XF	Unc
1623 CS	—	475	950	1,900	3,900	—

KM# 41 THALER

Silver **Ruler:** Joachim Ernst **Obv:** Larger bust **Obv. Legend:** ...RV **Rev:** Larger arms **Note:** Dav. 6232.

Date	Mintage	VG	F	VF	XF	Unc
1623 CS	—	325	625	1,200	2,050	5,000

KM# 42 THALER

Silver **Ruler:** Joachim Ernst **Obv:** Bust divides date in inner circle **Rev:** Arms **Note:** Dav. 6233.

Date	Mintage	VG	F	VF	XF	Unc
1623	—	475	950	1,900	3,750	9,100

KM# 48.1 THALER

Silver **Ruler:** Joachim Ernst **Subject:** Death of Joachim Ernst **Obv:** Facing bust holding baton **Rev:** 8-line inscription **Note:** Dav. #6234.

Date	Mintage	VG	F	VF	XF	Unc
1625	—	575	1,150	2,050	3,450	—

KM# 48.2 THALER

Silver **Ruler:** Joachim Ernst **Subject:** Death of Joachim Ernst **Obv:** Facing bust holding baton and helmet **Note:** Varieties exist. Dav. 6235.

Date	Mintage	VG	F	VF	XF	Unc
1625	—	625	1,250	2,250	4,050	—

KM# 50.1 THALER

Silver **Ruler:** Friedrich II, Albrecht and Christian **Obv:** Three facing half figures, shield dividing date below **Rev:** Helmeted arms **Note:** Dav. 6236. Two varieties exist.

Date	Mintage	VG	F	VF	XF	Unc
1626	—	90.00	180	350	800	—

KM# 50.2 THALER

Silver **Ruler:** Friedrich II, Albrecht and Christian **Obv:** Slightly changed design **Rev:** Longer shield **Note:** Dav. 6237.

Date	Mintage	VG	F	VF	XF	Unc
1627	—	60.00	120	270	650	1,400
1628/7	—	70.00	150	350	775	—
1628	—	60.00	120	270	650	—
1629/8	—	70.00	150	350	775	—

KM# 50.3 THALER

Silver **Ruler:** Friedrich II, Albrecht and Christian **Obv:** Ornate oval shield below figures **Note:** Varieties exist. Dav. 6238.

Date	Mintage	VG	F	VF	XF	Unc
1629	—	70.00	145	300	600	1,400
1630	—	80.00	150	425	900	1,800
1631	—	90.00	180	475	1,100	2,700

KM# 69.1 THALER

Silver **Ruler:** Albrecht III **Subject:** Death of Albrecht III **Obv:** Facing bust **Obv. Legend:** ALBERTVS. MARCH. BRAN. **Rev:** 7-line inscription **Rev. Legend:** VAND. IN. SILES. CROS. ET. TAG. **Note:** Dav. 6239.

Date	Mintage	VG	F	VF	XF	Unc
1667	—	1,500	2,500	4,400	8,100	—

KM# 69.2 THALER

Silver **Ruler:** Albrecht III **Subject:** Death of Albrecht III **Obv. Legend:** ALBERT. MRCH: BRAND... **Rev. Legend:** VAND: IN SIL: CROS: & IAGER... **Note:** Dav. 6240.

Date	Mintage	VG	F	VF	XF	Unc
1667	—	1,250	2,200	4,050	7,500	—

KM# 88 THALER

Silver **Ruler:** Johann Friedrich **Obv:** Helmeted arms, date divided below **Rev:** Three standing figures, column at right, value on edge **Note:** Dav. 6242.

Date	Mintage	VG	F	VF	XF	Unc
1679 Rare	—	—	—	—	—	—

Note: UBS Auction 53, 1-02, VF-XF realized approx. $8,785

KM# 95 THALER

Silver **Ruler:** Johann Friedrich **Obv:** Oval arms **Note:** Dav. 6243.

Date	Mintage	VG	F	VF	XF	Unc
1680 Rare	—	—	—	—	—	—

KM# 96 THALER

Silver **Ruler:** Johann Friedrich **Note:** Dav. 6245.

Date	Mintage	VG	F	VF	XF	Unc
1680	—	1,500	2,500	5,000	8,100	—
1684	—	1,900	3,150	5,600	8,800	—
1685	—	1,900	3,150	5,600	8,800	—

KM# 109.1 THALER

Silver **Ruler:** Johann Friedrich **Subject:** Death of Johann Friedrich **Note:** Dav. #6246.

Date	Mintage	VG	F	VF	XF	Unc
1686	—	1,900	3,150	5,300	8,500	—

KM# 109.2 THALER

Silver **Ruler:** Johann Friedrich **Subject:** Death of Johann Friedrich **Rev. Legend:** STET. POM. VAND. I. SIL... **Note:** Dav. #6247.

Date	Mintage	VG	F	VF	XF	Unc
1686	—	3,150	5,600	9,400	15,000	—

KM# 119 THALER
Silver **Ruler:** Georg Friedrich II **Note:** Dav. #6249.

Date	Mintage	VG	F	VF	XF	Unc
1694	—	2,050	3,450	5,900	9,400	—

KM# 121 THALER
Silver **Ruler:** Georg Friedrich II **Rev:** Arms flanked by palm branches **Note:** Dav. #6251.

Date	Mintage	VG	F	VF	XF	Unc
1694 GH Rare	—	—	—	—	—	—

KM# 122 THALER
Silver **Ruler:** Georg Friedrich II **Obv:** Bust right **Rev:** Crowned arms, date divided below **Note:** Dav. #6252.

Date	Mintage	VG	F	VF	XF	Unc
1694 Rare	—	—	—	—	—	—

KM# 120.2 THALER
Silver **Ruler:** Georg Friedrich II **Note:** Dav. #6253.

Date	Mintage	VG	F	VF	XF	Unc
1694 PHM-(a)	—	625	1,100	2,000	3,300	—
1695 PHM	—	625	1,100	2,000	3,300	—
1695 PHM-PG	—	625	1,100	2,000	3,300	—

KM# 120.1 THALER
Silver **Ruler:** Georg Friedrich II **Note:** Similar to KM#120.2 but without initials below bust. Dav. #6250.

Date	Mintage	VG	F	VF	XF	Unc
1694	—	1,000	1,600	2,700	4,800	—
1695	—	1,000	1,600	2,700	4,800	—

KM# 125 THALER
Silver **Ruler:** Georg Friedrich II **Obv:** Bust right **Rev:** Similar to KM#126 obverse **Note:** Dav. #6255.

Date	Mintage	VG	F	VF	XF	Unc
1696 Rare	—	—	—	—	—	—

KM# 127 THALER
Silver **Ruler:** Georg Friedrich II **Note:** Dav. #6257.

Date	Mintage	VG	F	VF	XF	Unc
1696 PHM-PG	—	1,250	2,500	4,700	8,100	—

KM# 126 THALER
Silver **Ruler:** Georg Friedrich II **Obv:** Reverse of KM#125 **Rev:** Reverse of KM#119 **Note:** Mule. Dav. #6256.

Date	Mintage	VG	F	VF	XF	Unc
1696//1694 Rare	—	—	—	—	—	—

KM# 89 2 THALER
Silver **Ruler:** Johann Friedrich **Obv:** Helmeted ornate arms, date divided below **Rev:** Three standing figures, column at right, value on edge **Note:** Dav. 6241.

Date	Mintage	VG	F	VF	XF	Unc
1679 Rare	—	—	—	—	—	—

KM# 97 2 THALER
Silver **Ruler:** Johann Friedrich **Obv:** Bust right **Rev:** Helmeted ornate arms, date divided below **Note:** Dav. 6244.

Date	Mintage	VG	F	VF	XF	Unc
1680 Rare	—	—	—	—	—	—

KM# 123 2 THALER
Silver **Ruler:** Georg Friedrich II **Note:** Similar to Thaler, KM#119. Dav. 6248.

Date	Mintage	VG	F	VF	XF	Unc
1694 Rare	—	—	—	—	—	—

KM# 128 2 THALER
Silver **Ruler:** Georg Friedrich II **Note:** Dav. #6254.

Date	Mintage	VG	F	VF	XF	Unc
1696 PHM Rare	—	—	—	—	—	—

TRADE COINAGE

KM# 10 GOLDGULDEN
3.5000 g., 0.9860 Gold 0.1109 oz. AGW **Ruler:** Joachim Ernst **Obv:** Facing armored half-length figure **Rev:** Ornate shield of 4-fold arms with central shield of Nürnberg

Date	Mintage	VG	F	VF	XF	Unc
1610	—	240	600	1,100	2,000	—
1611	—	240	600	1,100	2,000	—
1619	—	240	600	1,100	2,000	2,700
1620	—	240	600	1,100	2,000	—
1621	—	240	600	1,100	2,000	—
1623	—	240	600	1,100	2,000	—
1624	—	240	600	1,100	2,000	—

KM# 75 CAROLIN
10.5000 g., 0.9860 Gold 0.3328 oz. AGW **Ruler:** Johann Friedrich **Obv:** Bust to right in circle **Rev:** Shield of arms in circle

Date	Mintage	VG	F	VF	XF	Unc
1672 Rare	—	—	—	—	—	—

KM# 98 1/4 DUCAT
0.8750 g., 0.9860 Gold 0.0277 oz. AGW **Ruler:** Johann Friedrich **Rev:** Figures of Piety and Justice

Date	Mintage	VG	F	VF	XF	Unc
1680	—	120	210	350	725	—
1684	—	120	210	350	725	1,200

KM# 6 DUCAT
3.5000 g., 0.9860 Gold 0.1109 oz. AGW **Ruler:** Joachim Ernst **Obv:** Standing facing armored figure in inner circle **Rev:** Shield of manifold arms divides date in inner circle

Date	Mintage	VG	F	VF	XF	Unc
1609	—	300	450	900	1,900	—
1619	—	300	450	900	1,900	—
1620	—	300	450	900	1,900	—
1623	—	300	450	900	1,900	—
1624	—	300	450	900	1,900	—

KM# 49 DUCAT
3.5000 g., 0.9860 Gold 0.1109 oz. AGW **Ruler:** Friedrich II, Albrecht and Christian **Obv:** 3 facing half-length armored figures, date divided in exergue by small shield **Rev:** Oval shield of manifold arms

Date	Mintage	VG	F	VF	XF	Unc
1625	—	240	350	725	1,750	—
1626	—	240	350	725	1,750	—
1627	—	240	350	725	1,750	—
1628	—	240	350	725	1,750	—
1629	—	240	350	725	1,750	—
1630	—	240	350	725	1,750	—
1632	—	240	350	725	1,750	—

KM# 60 DUCAT
3.5000 g., 0.9860 Gold 0.1109 oz. AGW **Ruler:** Albrecht III

Date	Mintage	VG	F	VF	XF	Unc
1651	—	325	725	1,450	2,700	—
1652	—	325	725	1,450	2,700	—
1663	—	425	900	1,800	3,000	—

KM# 66 DUCAT
3.5000 g., 0.9860 Gold 0.1109 oz. AGW **Ruler:** Albrecht III **Obv:** Bust to right **Rev:** Cruciform monogram

Date	Mintage	VG	F	VF	XF	Unc
1664 Rare	—	—	—	—	—	—

KM# 76.1 DUCAT
3.5000 g., 0.9860 Gold 0.1109 oz. AGW **Ruler:** Johann Friedrich **Note:** Fr. 333.

Date	Mintage	VG	F	VF	XF	Unc
1672	—	825	1,800	3,500	6,100	—

KM# 76.2 DUCAT
3.5000 g., 0.9860 Gold 0.1109 oz. AGW **Ruler:** Johann Friedrich **Obv:** Armored bust to right **Obv. Legend:** IOHANNES. FR. - D. G. MAR. BRAND. **Rev:** Crowned oval shield of manifold arms in baroque frame, date divided below **Rev. Legend:** PIETATE - ET - IVSTITIA **Note:** Fr. 334.

Date	Mintage	VG	F	VF	XF	Unc
1680	—	775	1,600	2,750	5,200	—
1683	—	775	1,600	2,750	5,200	—

KM# 78 1-1/4 DUCAT
4.3750 g., 0.9860 Gold 0.1387 oz. AGW **Ruler:** Johann Friedrich **Obv:** Crowned arms **Rev:** Piety and Justice standing

Date	Mintage	VG	F	VF	XF	Unc
1674	—	325	550	1,100	2,200	—

KM# 32 2 DUCAT
7.0000 g., 0.9860 Gold 0.2219 oz. AGW **Ruler:** Joachim Ernst **Obv:** Joachim Ernst standing facing in inner circle **Rev:** Complex arms divide date in inner circle

Date	Mintage	VG	F	VF	XF	Unc
1622 Rare	—	—	—	—	—	—

KM# 65 2 DUCAT
7.0000 g., 0.9860 Gold 0.2219 oz. AGW **Ruler:** Albrecht III **Obv:** Bust to right in circle **Rev:** Shield of arms in circle

Date	Mintage	VG	F	VF	XF	Unc
1660 Rare	—	—	—	—	—	—

KM# 77 2 DUCAT
7.0000 g., 0.9860 Gold 0.2219 oz. AGW **Ruler:** Johann Friedrich **Obv:** Bust to right in circle

Date	Mintage	VG	F	VF	XF	Unc
1672	—	775	1,750	3,600	7,200	—
1677	—	775	1,750	3,600	7,200	—
1683	—	775	1,750	3,600	7,200	—

KM# 104 2 DUCAT
7.0000 g., 0.9860 Gold 0.2219 oz. AGW **Ruler:** Johann Friedrich **Obv:** Crowned arms **Rev:** Piety and Justice standing

Date	Mintage	VG	F	VF	XF	Unc
1683 Rare	—	—	—	—	—	—

KM# 54 3 DUCAT
10.5000 g., 0.9860 Gold 0.3328 oz. AGW **Ruler:** Friedrich II, Albrecht and Christian **Note:** Similar to 1 Ducat, KM#49.

Date	Mintage	VG	F	VF	XF	Unc
1630 Rare	—	—	—	—	—	—

KM# A77 3 DUCAT
10.5000 g., 0.9860 Gold 0.3328 oz. AGW **Ruler:** Johann Friedrich **Obv:** Draped bust to right **Rev:** Crowned shield of manifold arms divides date

Date	Mintage	VG	F	VF	XF	Unc
1672 Rare	—	—	—	—	—	—

KM# 33 4 DUCAT
14.0000 g., 0.9860 Gold 0.4438 oz. AGW **Ruler:** Joachim Ernst **Obv:** Armored figure standing facing in inner circle **Rev:** Shield of manifold arms divides date in inner circle

Date	Mintage	VG	F	VF	XF	Unc
1622 Rare	—	—	—	—	—	—

KM# A50 4 DUCAT
14.0000 g., 0.9860 Gold 0.4438 oz. AGW **Ruler:** Friedrich II, Albrecht and Christian **Note:** Similar to 1 Ducat, KM#49.

Date	Mintage	VG	F	VF	XF	Unc
1626 Rare	—	—	—	—	—	—
1628 Rare	—	—	—	—	—	—
1629 Rare	—	—	—	—	—	—

KM# A55 5 DUCAT (1/2 Portugalöser)
17.5000 g., 0.9860 Gold 0.5547 oz. AGW **Ruler:** Friedrich II, Albrecht and Christian **Note:** Similar to 1 Ducat, KM#49.

Date	Mintage	VG	F	VF	XF	Unc
1631 Rare	—	—	—	—	—	—

KM# 53 6 DUCAT
21.0000 g., 0.9860 Gold 0.6657 oz. AGW **Ruler:** Friedrich II, Albrecht and Christian **Note:** Similar to 1 Ducat, KM#49.

Date	Mintage	VG	F	VF	XF	Unc
1629 Rare	—	—	—	—	—	—

KM# 52 10 DUCAT (Portugalöser)
35.0000 g., 0.9860 Gold 1.1095 oz. AGW **Ruler:** Friedrich II, Albrecht and Christian **Note:** Struck with Thaler dies, KM#50.2.

Date	Mintage	VG	F	VF	XF	Unc
1628 Rare	—	—	—	—	—	—

PATTERNS

Including off metal strikes

KM#	Date	Mintage	Identification	Mkt Val
Pn1	1675	—	2/3 Thaler. Lead. KM#79	—

BRANDENBURG-BAYREUTH

Located in northern Bavaria. Became the property of the first Hohenzollern Elector of Brandenburg, Friedrich I. Bayreuth, passed to several individuals and became extinct in 1769 with the lands passing to Ansbach.

RULERS
Christian, 1603-1655
Christian Ernst, 1655-1712

MINT MARKS
B - Bayersdorf
(b) - Bayreuth
C,(c), (cu) - heart, (K) - Kulmbach
(cr) urn - Creussen
(d) bee - Dachsbach
(e) half-moon - Erlangen
F - Furth

MINT OFFICIALS' INITIALS

Initial	Date	Name
(ba) arrow	1622	Christoph Niedermann in Bayreuth
CA	1622	Christof Arnold in Kulmbach
CO	1613-23	Claus Oppermann in Bayreuth
CS	1622-54	Conrad Stutz, die-cutter in Furth and mintmaster of the Franconian Circle
(el) cross	1621	Johann Creitz in Hof
(er) flower	1621	Heinrich Oppermann in Hof
GFN	1682-1724	Georg Friedrich Nurnberger, die-cutter and mintmaster in Nüremberg
	1682-1710	Mintmaster of the Franconian Circle
H	1622	Michael Junghannss in Hof
HDE	1614-24	Hans David Emmert in Kulmbach
HR	1621	Hans Rentsch in Neustadt/Aisch
HR-IR	1621	Hans Rentsch and Jonas Ruedel, joint mintmasters in Kulmbach
HS	1622-23	Heinrich Straub in Nüremberg
HZ		Unknown
IAP	1695-1718	Johann Adam Poppendick, mintmaster in Bayreuth
ICF		Unknown
IR	1621	Jonas Ruedel in Bayreuth
L, LS	1622	Hans Luders in Pegnitz
(n) acorn	1622	Stefan Peckstein in Neustadt/Culm
(S) (s) letter s in stirrup	1622	Joachim Freundt in Schauenstein
SK		Unknown
SS	1622	Peter Steininger in Wunsiedel
VW	1622	Valentin Wolffram in Schauenstein
(w) millwheel	1622	Andreas Muller in Weissenstadt
(wu)	1622	H. Preussinger and D. Zetzner, mintmasters in Wunsiedel

MARGRAVIATE

REGULAR COINAGE

KM# 58 HELLER
Silver **Ruler:** Christian **Obv:** Four arms in cruciform, in angles value I and divided date **Note:** Uniface.

Date	Mintage	VG	F	VF	XF	Unc
1637 Rare	—	—	—	—	—	—

KM# 100 HELLER
Silver **Ruler:** Christian Ernst **Obv:** Crowned CE monogram between branches **Rev:** Arms, date above, value in legend

Date	Mintage	VG	F	VF	XF	Unc
1693	—	10.00	20.00	40.00	80.00	—
1696	—	10.00	20.00	40.00	80.00	—
ND	—	10.00	20.00	40.00	80.00	—

KM# 108 HELLER
Silver **Ruler:** Christian Ernst **Obv:** Crowned CE monogram divides date **Rev. Inscription:** BAY / REUTH / ER HEL / LER

Date	Mintage	VG	F	VF	XF	Unc
1697	—	25.00	60.00	120	240	—
1698	—	25.00	60.00	120	240	—

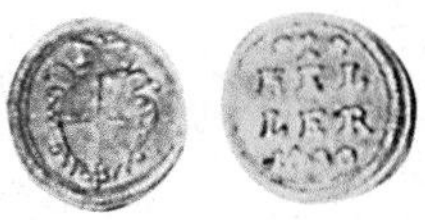

KM# 109 HELLER
Copper **Ruler:** Christian Ernst **Obv:** Crowned oval Hohenzollern arms in baroque frame **Rev. Inscription:** 1 / HEL / LER / date

Date	Mintage	VG	F	VF	XF	Unc
1698	—	10.00	20.00	40.00	80.00	—
1699	—	10.00	20.00	40.00	80.00	—
1700	—	10.00	20.00	40.00	80.00	—

KM# 44 3 HELLER (1-1/2 Pfennig)
Silver **Ruler:** Christian **Obv:** Eagle **Rev. Inscription:** ++ / III h1 / date

Date	Mintage	VG	F	VF	XF	Unc
1624	—	90.00	185	375	775	—
1650	—	150	300	600	1,200	—

KM# 19 PFENNIG
Billon **Ruler:** Christian **Obv:** Two shields of arms, date above, HZ below **Note:** Uniface. Kipper issue.

Date	Mintage	VG	F	VF	XF	Unc
1622	—	22.00	45.00	85.00	160	—

KM# 37 PFENNIG
Billon **Ruler:** Christian **Note:** Hohl type. Two arms, date above, HS below.

Date	Mintage	VG	F	VF	XF	Unc
1623	—	22.00	45.00	85.00	110	—

KM# 36 PFENNIG
Billon **Ruler:** Christian **Obv:** 3 arms, HS below **Note:** Uniface.

Date	Mintage	VG	F	VF	XF	Unc
1623	—	32.00	60.00	115	225	—

KM# 45 PFENNIG
Billon **Ruler:** Christian **Obv:** Three arms, date

Date	Mintage	VG	F	VF	XF	Unc
1624	—	22.00	45.00	90.00	190	—
1625	—	22.00	45.00	90.00	190	—

KM# 66 PFENNIG
Silver **Ruler:** Christian **Obv:** Shield of Hohenzollern arms, date divided above **Note:** Uniface.

Date	Mintage	VG	F	VF	XF	Unc
1650	—	15.00	30.00	60.00	120	—

KM# 101 PFENNIG
Billon **Ruler:** Christian Ernst **Obv:** Crowned and mantled arms **Rev:** Crowned eagle divides date

Date	Mintage	VG	F	VF	XF	Unc
1693	—	10.00	20.00	40.00	85.00	—

KM# 13 3 PFENNIG (Dreier)
Billon **Ruler:** Christian **Obv:** Eagle, value 3 on breast **Rev:** Shield of Hohenzollern arms, date above **Note:** Kipper 3 Pfennig.

Date	Mintage	VG	F	VF	XF	Unc
1621 (e)	—	—	—	—	—	—

KM# 20 3 PFENNIG (Dreier)
Silver **Ruler:** Christian **Obv:** Shield of Hohenzollern arms, date in legend **Rev:** Imperial orb with value 3 **Note:** Kipper 3 Pfennig.

Date	Mintage	VG	F	VF	XF	Unc
1622	—	16.00	32.00	65.00	130	—
1623	—	16.00	32.00	65.00	130	—

KM# 83 3 PFENNIG (Dreier)
Billon **Ruler:** Christian Ernst **Rev:** Arms

Date	Mintage	VG	F	VF	XF	Unc
1678	—	15.00	32.00	65.00	130	—
1686	—	15.00	32.00	65.00	130	—

KM# 95 6 PFENNIG
Silver **Ruler:** Christian Ernst **Obv:** Arms **Rev:** Imperial orb with value 6

Date	Mintage	VG	F	VF	XF	Unc
1688	—	18.00	37.00	75.00	150	—
1689	—	18.00	37.00	75.00	150	—
1690	—	18.00	37.00	75.00	150	—
1691	—	18.00	37.00	75.00	150	—
1695	—	18.00	37.00	75.00	150	—
1696	—	18.00	37.00	75.00	150	—

KM# 21 KREUZER
Copper **Ruler:** Christian **Obv:** Eagle **Rev:** Value **Note:** Kipper issue.

Date	Mintage	VG	F	VF	XF	Unc
1622	—	—	—	—	—	—

KM# 22.1 KREUZER
Copper, 16 mm. **Ruler:** Christian **Obv:** Shield of Hohenzollern arms in baroque frame **Rev:** 4-line inscription with date **Rev. Inscription:** I / KREVT / ZER / (date) **Note:** Kipper issue.

Date	Mintage	Good	VG	F	VF	XF
1622	—	55.00	100	150	275	—

KM# 22.2 KREUZER

Copper **Ruler:** Christian **Obv:** Shield of Hohenzoller arms in ornamented shield **Rev:** 4-line inscription with date **Rev. Inscription:** I / KREVT / ZER / (date) **Mint:** Kulmbach **Note:** Kipper issue.

Date	Mintage	VG	F	VF	XF	Unc
1622C	—	120	250	475	—	—

KM# 38 KREUZER

Copper **Ruler:** Christian **Obv:** Eagle **Rev:** Imperial orb with value I, date

Date	Mintage	VG	F	VF	XF	Unc
1623	—	27.00	40.00	80.00	165	—

KM# 59 KREUZER

Copper **Ruler:** Christian **Obv:** Four arms in cruciform date **Rev:** Double cross (*)

Date	Mintage	VG	F	VF	XF	Unc
1637	—	27.00	40.00	80.00	165	—

KM# 67 KREUZER

Copper **Ruler:** Christian **Obv:** Hohenzollern arms **Rev:** Eagle with value 1 on breast, date

Date	Mintage	VG	F	VF	XF	Unc
1650	—	27.00	40.00	80.00	165	—

KM# 115 KREUZER

Silver **Ruler:** Christian Ernst **Obv:** Bust right **Obv. Legend:** EINEN CREVZER **Rev:** Crowned eagle, Hohenzollern arms on breast, date in legend

Date	Mintage	VG	F	VF	XF	Unc
1697	—	16.00	32.00	65.00	130	—
1700	—	16.00	32.00	65.00	130	—

KM# 46 2 KREUZER (1/2 Batzen)

Silver **Ruler:** Christian

Date	Mintage	VG	F	VF	XF	Unc
1624	—	10.00	22.00	45.00	90.00	—
1637	—	10.00	22.00	45.00	90.00	—
1651	—	10.00	22.00	45.00	90.00	—

KM# 56 2 KREUZER (1/2 Batzen)

Silver **Ruler:** Christian

Date	Mintage	VG	F	VF	XF	Unc
1631	—	13.00	27.00	55.00	115	—
1650	—	13.00	27.00	55.00	115	—

KM# 75 3 KREUZER

Silver **Ruler:** Christian Ernst **Obv:** Arms **Rev:** Imperial orb with value 3

Date	Mintage	VG	F	VF	XF	Unc
1662	—	15.00	30.00	60.00	120	—

KM# 39 4 KREUZER (Batzen)

Silver **Ruler:** Christian

Date	Mintage	VG	F	VF	XF	Unc
1623 (b)	—	20.00	40.00	85.00	175	—
1623 (k)	—	20.00	40.00	85.00	175	—
1624 (k)	—	20.00	40.00	85.00	175	—
1630	—	20.00	40.00	85.00	175	—
1630 F	—	20.00	40.00	85.00	175	—
1632 F	—	20.00	40.00	85.00	175	—
1633 F	—	20.00	40.00	85.00	175	—

KM# 47 4 KREUZER (Batzen)

Silver **Ruler:** Christian **Obv:** Arms **Rev:** Value

Date	Mintage	VG	F	VF	XF	Unc
1624	—	—	—	—	—	—

KM# 51 4 KREUZER (Batzen)

Silver **Ruler:** Christian **Obv:** Four arms in cruciform, date **Rev:** Crowned imperial eagle

Date	Mintage	VG	F	VF	XF	Unc
1625	—	—	—	—	—	—

KM# A11 12 KREUZER

Silver **Ruler:** Christian **Obv:** Oval 4-fold arms with central shield divides date **Rev:** Eagle, orb with 12 on breast **Note:** Kipper 12 Kreuzer.

Date	Mintage	VG	F	VF	XF	Unc
1620	—	100	200	400	775	—

KM# 10 12 KREUZER

Silver **Ruler:** Christian **Obv:** 4-fold arms with central shield divide C-O, date above **Rev:** Eagle, orb with 12 on breast **Note:** Kipper issue.

Date	Mintage	VG	F	VF	XF	Unc
1620 CO	—	100	200	400	775	—

KM# 107.1 15 KREUZER

Silver, 26 mm. **Ruler:** Christian Ernst **Obv:** Armored bust to right, value (XV) below **Obv. Legend:** CHRISTIAN. ERNST. D: G: M: BRANDENB. **Rev:** Brandenburg eagle, oval shield of Hohenzollern arms on breast, neck divides date, legs divide mintmaster's initials **Rev. Legend:** NACH. CHVR. SACHS. V: BRAND. KORN: V: SCHROT.

Date	Mintage	VG	F	VF	XF	Unc
1696 IAP	—	950	1,700	2,900	4,250	—

KM# 107.2 15 KREUZER

Silver, 26 mm. **Ruler:** Christian Ernst **Obv:** Armored bust to right in circle, (XV) below **Obv. Legend:** CHRISTIAN. ERNST. D: G: M: BRANDENB. **Rev:** Brandenburg eagle, oval shield of Hohenzollern arms on breast, neck divides date, legs divide mintmaster's initials, all in circle **Rev. Legend:** NACH. CHVR. SACHS. V: BRAND. KORN: V: SCHROT. **Mint:** Bayreuth

Date	Mintage	VG	F	VF	XF	Unc
1696 IAP	—	950	1,700	2,900	4,250	—

KM# 11 24 KREUZER (6 Batzen)

Silver **Ruler:** Christian **Obv:** Arms of Nuremberg burgraviate in ornamented frame, date above **Rev:** Eagle, value (24) above **Note:** Kipper issue.

Date	Mintage	VG	F	VF	XF	Unc
1620 (b)	—	80.00	125	220	425	—
1621	—	80.00	125	220	425	—

KM# 16 24 KREUZER (6 Batzen)

Silver **Ruler:** Christian **Obv:** 4-fold arms, date above **Rev:** Eagle, orb with 24 on breast **Note:** Kipper issue.

Date	Mintage	VG	F	VF	XF	Unc
1621 (c)	—	80.00	135	200	385	—
1621 HR-IR	—	80.00	135	200	385	—

KM# 14 24 KREUZER (6 Batzen)

Silver **Ruler:** Christian **Note:** Kipper issue. Varieties exist.

Date	Mintage	VG	F	VF	XF	Unc
1621 (b)	—	65.00	100	175	325	—
1621 (e)	—	65.00	100	175	325	—
1621 (el)	—	65.00	100	175	325	—
1621 (er)	—	65.00	100	175	325	—
1621 IR	—	65.00	100	175	325	—

KM# 17 24 KREUZER (6 Batzen)

Silver **Ruler:** Christian **Obv:** Arms **Rev:** Eagle, orb with 24 on breast, tail divides date **Note:** Kipper issue. Varieties exist.

Date	Mintage	VG	F	VF	XF	Unc
1621	—	65.00	100	175	325	—
1622 (ba)	—	65.00	100	175	325	—
1622 CA	—	65.00	100	175	325	—
1622 (cu)	—	65.00	100	175	325	—
1622 H	—	65.00	100	175	325	—
1622 (w)	—	65.00	100	175	325	—
ND	—	65.00	100	175	325	—
ND (d)	—	65.00	100	175	325	—
ND (e)	—	65.00	100	175	325	—
ND (w)	—	65.00	100	175	325	—

KM# 15 24 KREUZER (6 Batzen)

Silver **Ruler:** Christian **Obv:** Eagle **Rev:** Date divided above arms **Note:** Kipper issue. Varieties exist.

Date	Mintage	VG	F	VF	XF	Unc
1621 HR	—	85.00	140	235	475	—

KM# 23 24 KREUZER (6 Batzen)

Silver **Ruler:** Christian **Note:** Klippe.

Date	Mintage	VG	F	VF	XF	Unc
1622 (w)	—	100	200	400	800	—

KM# A29 24 KREUZER (6 Batzen)

Silver **Ruler:** Christian **Obv:** Arms of Nuremberg burgraviate in baroque frame, date at end of legend **Obv. Legend:** ST • PO • CA • V • CR • IAD • BVRG: I • NV • P. R. **Rev:** Displayed eagle, '24' in orb on breast, mint symbol at top in margin **Rev. Legend:** CHRISTIAN • D.G. MAR • BRAN • PRVSSI • **Mint:** Schauenstein **Note:** Kipper issue.

Date	Mintage	F	VF	XF	Unc	BU
16ZZ (s)	—	—	—	—	—	—

KM# 24 24 KREUZER (6 Batzen)

Silver **Ruler:** Christian **Obv:** Bust right, date in legend **Rev:** Eagle, orb with 24 on breast **Note:** Kipper issue.

Date	Mintage	VG	F	VF	XF	Unc
1622 (cr)	—	85.00	140	235	475	—

KM# 25 24 KREUZER (6 Batzen)
Silver **Ruler:** Christian **Rev:** Date in legend **Note:** Kipper issue.

Date	Mintage	VG	F	VF	XF	Unc
1622	—	65.00	100	165	325	—

KM# 26 24 KREUZER (6 Batzen)
Silver **Ruler:** Christian **Rev:** Eagle's tail divides date **Mint:** Erlangen **Note:** Kipper issue.

Date	Mintage	VG	F	VF	XF	Unc
1622 (e)	—	85.00	140	235	475	—

KM# 27 24 KREUZER (6 Batzen)
Silver **Ruler:** Christian **Obv:** Arms of Nuremberg burgraviate in ornamented frame **Rev:** Eagle, orb with 24 on breast, tail divides date **Mint:** Neustadt/Culm **Note:** Kipper issue.

Date	Mintage	VG	F	VF	XF	Unc
1622 (n)	—	65.00	100	165	325	—

KM# 28 24 KREUZER (6 Batzen)
Silver **Ruler:** Christian **Obv:** Oval arms of Nuremberg in baroque frame, date divided above **Rev:** Eagle, orb with 24 on breast **Note:** Kipper issue.

Date	Mintage	VG	F	VF	XF	Unc
1622 L	—	75.00	125	190	360	—
1622 LS	—	75.00	125	190	360	—
ND (S)	—	75.00	125	190	360	—

KM# 29 24 KREUZER (6 Batzen)
Silver **Ruler:** Christian **Obv:** Arms of Nuremberg burgraviate in ornamented frame **Rev:** Date in legend **Note:** Kipper issue.

Date	Mintage	VG	F	VF	XF	Unc
1622	—	100	200	400	800	—
ND (S)	—	100	200	400	800	—

KM# 30 24 KREUZER (6 Batzen)
Silver **Ruler:** Christian **Obv:** Oval arms of Nuremberg in baroque frame, date in legend **Rev:** Eagle, orb with 24 on breast **Note:** Kipper issue.

Date	Mintage	VG	F	VF	XF	Unc
1622 VW-(s)	—	75.00	125	190	360	—
1622 (S)	—	75.00	125	190	360	—
1622 SS	—	75.00	125	190	360	—

KM# 31 24 KREUZER (6 Batzen)
Silver **Ruler:** Christian **Obv:** Arms of Nuremberg burgraviate in ornamented frame **Rev:** Eagle, orb with 24 on breast, tail divides date **Note:** Kipper issue.

Date	Mintage	VG	F	VF	XF	Unc
1622 (wu)	—	80.00	120	200	385	—

KM# 32 24 KREUZER (6 Batzen)
Silver **Ruler:** Christian **Rev:** Tail of eagle divides date, orb with 24 on breast **Note:** Kipper issue.

Date	Mintage	VG	F	VF	XF	Unc
1622	—	80.00	120	200	385	—

KM# 48 SCHILLING (1/28 Gulden)
Silver **Ruler:** Christian **Obv:** Four arms in cruciform date **Rev:** Crowned imperial eagle, value 28 in orb on breast

Date	Mintage	VG	F	VF	XF	Unc
1624 Rare	—	—	—	—	—	—

KM# 69 GROSCHEN (1/24 Thaler)
Silver **Ruler:** Christian **Subject:** Death of Christian **Obv:** Bust right **Rev:** Inscription with date

Date	Mintage	VG	F	VF	XF	Unc
1655	—	40.00	85.00	150	300	—

KM# 81 GROSCHEN (1/24 Thaler)
Silver **Ruler:** Christian Ernst **Obv:** Bust right **Rev:** Arms

Date	Mintage	VG	F	VF	XF	Unc
1676	—	—	—	—	—	—

KM# 34 1/24 THALER (Groschen)
Silver **Ruler:** Christian **Rev:** Nuremberg burgraviatre arms **Note:** Large module.

Date	Mintage	VG	F	VF	XF	Unc
ND(1622)	—	—	—	—	—	—

KM# 35 1/24 THALER (Groschen)
Silver **Ruler:** Christian **Note:** Similar to KM#33.

Date	Mintage	VG	F	VF	XF	Unc
1622	—	11.00	25.00	50.00	100	—
1623	—	11.00	25.00	50.00	100	—
1624	—	11.00	25.00	50.00	100	—
1650	—	11.00	25.00	50.00	100	—

KM# 33 1/24 THALER (Groschen)
Silver **Ruler:** Christian **Obv:** Imperial orb with value 24 **Rev:** Hohenzollern arms, date **Note:** small module.

Date	Mintage	VG	F	VF	XF	Unc
1622	—	13.00	27.00	55.00	110	—

KM# 90 1/24 THALER (Groschen)
Silver **Ruler:** Christian Ernst **Obv:** Orb with value within inner circle, legend surrounds **Rev:** Eagle with shield on breast within inner circle **Note:** Similar to KM#125.

Date	Mintage	VG	F	VF	XF	Unc
1680	—	16.00	32.00	65.00	130	—
1684	—	16.00	32.00	65.00	130	—
1695	—	16.00	32.00	65.00	130	—
1696	—	16.00	32.00	65.00	130	—

KM# 91 1/12 THALER (2 Groschen)
Silver **Ruler:** Christian Ernst **Obv:** Crowned shield of arms **Rev:** Imperial orb with value 12

Date	Mintage	VG	F	VF	XF	Unc
1680	—	16.00	33.00	65.00	130	—
1685	—	16.00	33.00	65.00	130	—

KM# 103 1/12 THALER (2 Groschen)
Silver **Ruler:** Christian Ernst **Obv:** Crowned two oval arms in baroque frame **Rev:** 12/EINEN/THAL/ date

Date	Mintage	VG	F	VF	XF	Unc
1695	—	16.00	33.00	65.00	130	—
1696	—	16.00	33.00	65.00	130	—

KM# 70 1/4 THALER
Silver **Ruler:** Christian **Subject:** Death of Christian

Date	Mintage	VG	F	VF	XF	Unc
1655	—	250	450	900	1,550	—

KM# 104 1/4 THALER
Silver **Ruler:** Christian Ernst **Obv:** Bust right **Rev:** Crowned oval arms in baroque frame divide date, value 1/4 below

Date	Mintage	VG	F	VF	XF	Unc
1695 IAP	—	—	—	—	—	—

KM# 49 1/2 THALER
Silver **Ruler:** Christian **Obv:** 1/2-length bust right **Rev:** 12-fold arms

Date	Mintage	VG	F	VF	XF	Unc
1624 HDE	—	250	500	1,000	1,800	—
1624/7	—	250	500	1,000	1,800	—

KM# 93 1/2 THALER
Silver **Ruler:** Christian Ernst **Obv:** Bust right **Rev:** Crowned oval arms between two branches, date below

Date	Mintage	VG	F	VF	XF	Unc
1683	—	—	—	—	—	—

KM# 12 2/3 THALER (Gulden)
Silver **Ruler:** Christian **Rev:** Date in legend **Note:** Klippe. Dav. #6259.

Date	Mintage	VG	F	VF	XF	Unc
1620 Rare	—	—	—	—	—	—

KM# 18 2/3 THALER (Gulden)
Silver **Ruler:** Christian **Obv:** Date in legend **Rev:** Helmeted arms **Note:** Dav. #6260.

Date	Mintage	VG	F	VF	XF	Unc
1621 CO	—	800	1,400	2,600	4,500	—

KM# 82 2/3 THALER (Gulden)
Silver **Ruler:** Christian Ernst

Date	Mintage	VG	F	VF	XF	Unc
1677 Rare	—	—	—	—	—	—

KM# 102 2/3 THALER (Gulden)
Silver **Ruler:** Christian Ernst **Obv:** Bust right **Rev:** Helmeted arms between crossed palm branches, date in legend **Note:** Dav. #6278.

Date	Mintage	VG	F	VF	XF	Unc
1693 ICF Rare	—	—	—	—	—	—

KM# 105 2/3 THALER (Gulden)
Silver **Ruler:** Christian Ernst **Note:** Similar to KM#102 but date and IAP below crossed palm branches. Dav. #6279.

Date	Mintage	VG	F	VF	XF	Unc
1695 IAP Rare	—	—	—	—	—	—

KM# 5 THALER
Silver, 39 mm. **Ruler:** Christian **Obv:** Armored and mantled bust to right, small Nuremberg burgraviate arms below **Obv. Legend:** CHRISTIAN. D. G. MAR - CH* BRAND* PRVSSIÆ. **Rev:** Oval shield of manifold arms in baroque frame divide date **Rev. Legend:** ST. POM. CAS. VAN. CR. IAG. DVX. BVRG. IN NVR. PR. RV. **Note:** Dav. #6258.

Date	Mintage	VG	F	VF	XF	Unc
1609	—	925	1,450	2,750	4,350	—

KM# 40 THALER
Silver **Ruler:** Christian **Obv:** Margrave on horse rearing right **Obv. Legend:** CHRISTIANVS: D:G: MARCHIO: BRANDEN: PRVSSIAE. **Rev:** Oval 4-fold arms with central shield divides date **Rev. Legend:** STE: POM: CAS: VAN: CRO: IAG: DUX: BVR: I: NVR: PR: RV. **Note:** Dav. #6261.

Date	Mintage	VG	F	VF	XF	Unc
1623 CO Rare	—	—	—	—	—	—

KM# 41 THALER
Silver **Ruler:** Christian **Obv:** Armored bust to right **Obv. Legend:** CHRISTIAN. D. G. MARCHI. BRANDENB. PRUSSIAE. **Rev:** Arms, date above **Rev. Legend:** ST. PO. CA. VA. CR. I. DUX. BUR. IN. NUR. **Note:** Dav. #6262.

Date	Mintage	VG	F	VF	XF	Unc
1623 HS Rare	—	—	—	—	—	—

KM# 42.1 THALER
Silver **Ruler:** Christian **Note:** Dav. #6263.

Date	Mintage	VG	F	VF	XF	Unc
1623 Rare	—	—	—	—	—	—

KM# 42.2 THALER
Silver **Ruler:** Christian **Obv:** 1/2-length bust right holding baton **Rev:** 12-fold arms **Note:** Dav. #6265.

Date	Mintage	VG	F	VF	XF	Unc
1623 HDE	—	400	700	1,150	1,850	—
1624 HDE	—	400	700	1,150	1,850	—

KM# 50 THALER
Silver **Ruler:** Christian **Obv:** Bust right, small Nuremberg burgraviate arms below **Rev:** Helmeted complex arms in baroque frame, date in legend **Note:** Dav. #6266.

Date	Mintage	VG	F	VF	XF	Unc
1624 CS	—	400	700	1,150	1,850	—

KM# 52.1 THALER
Silver **Ruler:** Christian **Obv:** Armored half-length figure to right, legend divided by 3 small shield of arms **Obv. Legend:** CHRISTIAN. - D. G. MARC. - BRANDEN. - PRUSSIAE. **Rev:** Large shield of manifold arms in baroque frame, 3 ornate helmets above, date at end of legend **Rev. Legend:** ST. P. CA. V. CR. IA. - D. BURG. I. NURNB. **Note:** Dav. #6267.

Date	Mintage	VG	F	VF	XF	Unc
1627	—	400	700	1,150	1,850	—
1630	—	400	700	1,150	1,850	—

KM# 53 THALER
Silver **Ruler:** Christian **Obv:** Armored bust to right, small shield of Nürnberg arms below **Obv. Legend:** CHRISTIANUS. D. G. MARCH - IO. BRANDENBURG. PRUSS. **Rev:** Large shield of manifold arms in baroque frame, 3 ornate helmets above, date divided at lower left and right of shield **Rev. Legend:** ST. PO. CA. VA. CR. IA. - D. BURG. I. NURNB. **Note:** Dav. #6268.

Date	Mintage	VG	F	VF	XF	Unc
1628	—	400	700	1,150	1,850	—
1629	—	400	700	1,150	1,850	—

KM# 55 THALER
Silver **Ruler:** Christian **Obv:** Bust 3/4 rigjt, small shield below **Rev:** Similar to KM#42 but date in reverse legend **Note:** Dav. #6269.

Date	Mintage	VG	F	VF	XF	Unc
1630 Rare	—	—	—	—	—	—

KM# 52.2 THALER
Silver **Ruler:** Christian **Obv:** Armored half-length figure to right, legend divided by 3 small shield of arms **Obv. Legend:** CHRISTIAN. - D. G. MARC. - BRANDEN. - PRUSSIAE. **Rev:** Large shield of manifold arms in baroque frame, 3 ornate helmets above, date divided between crests of helmets **Rev. Legend:** ST. PO. CA. VA. CR. IA. - D. BURG. I. NURNB. **Note:** Dav. #6267A.

Date	Mintage	VG	F	VF	XF	Unc
1636	—	400	700	1,150	1,850	—
1638	—	400	700	1,150	1,850	—
1641	—	400	700	1,150	1,850	—
1644	—	400	700	1,150	1,850	—

KM# 71 THALER
Silver **Ruler:** Christian **Subject:** Death of Christian **Obv:** Armored and draped bust to left **Obv. Legend:** + CHRISTIANUS. MAR. BRAND. DUX. MAGD. PRUSS. STET. POMER. **Rev:** 8-line inscription with dates **Rev. Legend:** + CAS. VAND. IN. SIL. CROS. & IAGER. BURG. NORIMB. PR. HALB. & MIN. **Rev. Inscription:** NAT9 / COLONIÆ AD / SUEVUM 30. IANU. / 1581. DENATUS / BARUTHI 30. MAI. / 1655. Ao. REGIMIN. / 52. ÆT. 74. & 4. / MENS. **Note:** Dav. #6270.

Date	Mintage	VG	F	VF	XF	Unc
1655	—	750	1,300	2,050	3,800	—

KM# 77 THALER
Silver **Ruler:** Christian Ernst **Note:** Dav. #6271.

Date	Mintage	VG	F	VF	XF	Unc
1662	—	575	875	1,450	2,550	—

KM# 78 THALER
Silver **Ruler:** Christian Ernst **Subject:** Election of Christian Ernst as Captain of Franconian Circle **Note:** Dav. #6272.

Date	Mintage	VG	F	VF	XF	Unc
1664	—	450	800	1,250	2,400	3,800

KM# 80 THALER
Silver **Ruler:** Christian Ernst **Subject:** Marriage of Christian Ernst to Sophie Luisa von Wurttemberg **Note:** Dav. #6273.

Date	Mintage	F	VF	XF	Unc	BU
1671	—	600	925	1,750	3,150	—

KM# 84 THALER
Silver **Ruler:** Christian Ernst **Subject:** Christian Ernst's Name Day **Note:** Dav. #6274.

Date	Mintage	F	VF	XF	Unc	BU
1679 Rare	—	—	—	—	—	—

KM# 85 THALER
Silver **Ruler:** Christian Ernst **Subject:** Birth of Prince Georg Wilhelm **Note:** Dav. #6275.

Date	Mintage	F	VF	XF	Unc	BU
1679 Rare	—	—	—	—	—	—

KM# 87 THALER
Silver **Ruler:** Christian Ernst **Rev:** Without four words next to tree **Note:** Dav. #6276A.

Date	Mintage	F	VF	XF	Unc	BU
1679	—	725	1,200	2,150	3,700	—

KM# 86 THALER
Silver **Ruler:** Christian Ernst **Subject:** Pregnancy of Sophie Luisa **Obv:** Crowned column in garden **Rev:** Palm tree, sun above, crowned hearts on either side, date **Note:** Dav. #6276.

Date	Mintage	VG	F	VF	XF	Unc
1679	—	—	725	1,200	2,150	3,350

KM# 92 THALER
Silver **Ruler:** Christian Ernst **Note:** Dav. 6277.

Date	Mintage	VG	F	VF	XF	Unc
1680 Rare	—	—	—	—	—	—
1681 Rare	—	—	—	—	—	—
1683 Rare	—	—	—	—	—	—

KM# 43 2 THALER
Silver **Ruler:** Christian **Note:** Similar to 1 Thaler, KM#42. Dav. #6264.

Date	Mintage	VG	F	VF	XF	Unc
1623 HDE Rare	—	—	—	—	—	—
1624 HDE Rare	—	—	—	—	—	—

TRADE COINAGE

KM# 94 1/2 DUCAT
1.7500 g., 0.9860 Gold 0.0555 oz. AGW **Ruler:** Christian Ernst **Obv:** Bust to right **Rev:** Arms

Date	Mintage	VG	F	VF	XF	Unc
1685	—	220	450	925	1,950	—

KM# 6 DUCAT
3.5000 g., 0.9860 Gold 0.1109 oz. AGW **Ruler:** Christian **Obv:** Armored full-length facing figure **Rev:** Arms in inner circle

Date	Mintage	VG	F	VF	XF	Unc
1609	—	205	350	825	1,600	—
1628	—	205	350	825	1,600	—
1629	—	205	350	825	1,600	—
1630	—	205	350	825	1,600	—
1631	—	205	350	825	1,600	—
1632	—	205	350	825	1,600	—

KM# 57 DUCAT
3.5000 g., 0.9860 Gold 0.1109 oz. AGW **Ruler:** Christian **Obv:** Armored bust to right **Rev:** Oval shield of 4-foldarms in inner circle, date divided at upper left and right

Date	Mintage	VG	F	VF	XF	Unc
1631	—	165	325	725	1,300	—
1641	—	165	325	725	1,300	—
1642	—	165	325	725	1,300	—
1644	—	165	325	725	1,300	—
ND	—	165	325	725	1,300	—

KM# 68 DUCAT
3.5000 g., 0.9860 Gold 0.1109 oz. AGW **Ruler:** Christian **Subject:** 50th Year of Reign

Date	Mintage	VG	F	VF	XF	Unc
1653 Rare	—	—	—	—	—	—

KM# 72 DUCAT
3.5000 g., 0.9860 Gold 0.1109 oz. AGW **Ruler:** Christian Ernst **Obv:** Bust right **Rev:** Arms in inner circle

Date	Mintage	VG	F	VF	XF	Unc
1659	—	1,000	2,000	3,500	6,500	—
1662	—	1,000	2,000	3,500	6,500	—
1677	—	1,000	2,000	3,500	6,500	—
1694	—	1,000	2,000	3,500	6,500	—

KM# 7 2 DUCAT
7.0000 g., 0.9860 Gold 0.2219 oz. AGW **Ruler:** Christian **Obv:** Armored full-length facing figure **Rev:** Arms in inner circle

Date	Mintage	VG	F	VF	XF	Unc
1609	—	1,200	2,650	4,600	7,400	—

KM# 106 2 DUCAT
7.0000 g., 0.9860 Gold 0.2219 oz. AGW **Ruler:** Christian Ernst **Obv:** Conjoined busts of Christian Ernst and Louisa right, date below **Rev:** View of Cronach mine with sun chariot in sky above

Date	Mintage	VG	F	VF	XF	Unc
1695 Rare	—	—	—	—	—	—

KM# 8 4 DUCAT
14.0000 g., 0.9860 Gold 0.4438 oz. AGW **Ruler:** Christian **Obv:** Armored full-length facing figure **Rev:** Arms in inner circle

Date	Mintage	VG	F	VF	XF	Unc
1609	—	2,750	4,950	7,700	14,000	—

KM# A81 5 DUCAT (1/2 Portugalöser)
17.5000 g., 0.9860 Gold 0.5547 oz. AGW **Ruler:** Christian Ernst **Subject:** Marriage of Christian Ernst to Sophia Luisa von Wurttemberg **Note:** Similar to Thaler, KM#80.

Date	Mintage	VG	F	VF	XF	Unc
1671 Rare	—	—	—	—	—	—

KM# A79 6 DUCAT
21.0000 g., 0.9860 Gold 0.6657 oz. AGW **Ruler:** Christian Ernst **Subject:** Election of Christian Ernst as Captain of Franconian Circle **Note:** Similar to Thaler, KM#78.

Date	Mintage	VG	F	VF	XF	Unc
1664 Rare	—	—	—	—	—	—

KM# A72 8 DUCAT
28.0000 g., 0.9860 Gold 0.8876 oz. AGW **Ruler:** Christian **Subject:** Death of Christian **Note:** Struck with Thaler dies, KM#71.

Date	Mintage	VG	F	VF	XF	Unc
1655 Rare	—	—	—	—	—	—

KM# A56 10 DUCAT (Portugalöser)
35.0000 g., 0.9860 Gold 1.1095 oz. AGW **Ruler:** Christian **Note:** Struck with Thaler dies, KM#55.

Date	Mintage	VG	F	VF	XF	Unc
1630 Rare	—	—	—	—	—	—

PATTERNS

Including off metal strikes

KM#	Date	Mintage	Identification	Mkt Val
Pn1	1630	—	4 Kreuzer. Tin. KM#39	—
Pn2	1676	—	Groschen. Lead. KM#81	—
Pn3	1691	—	6 Pfennig. Copper. KM#95	—

BRANDENBURG-FRANCONIA

(Brandenburg in Franken)

The Hohenzollerns of Swabia established their power as Burgraves of Nürnberg in the early 13th century. They soon acquired first Ansbach, then Bayreuth through marriage, becoming the most influential family in East Franconia, territories which extended from southwest to northeast between Swabia and Meissen. Various sons of the Brandenburg electors ruled portions of the Franconian holdings during the 15th century. Friedrich I, the younger brother of Elector Johann II Cicero (1486-99) established a permanent presence in Franconia in the late 15th century, becoming sole ruler there when Sigmund of Bayreuth and Kulmbach died in 1495. Friedrich I's descendants ruled jointly or separately during all of the 16th century, as well as supplying the Dukes of Prussia for much of the same period. When Friedrich I's grandson, Georg Friedrich, died childless in 1603, two younger sons of Elector Johann Georg were sent to rule as Margraves of Brandenburg-Ansbach and Brandenburg-Bayreuth. Georg Friedrich was Duke of Jägerndorf from 1543 and Administrator of Prussia from 1578. Coinage in his name for those places are listed therein.

RULERS
Georg Friedrich I, 1543-1603

ARMS
Brandenburg – eagle
Hohenzollern – shield quartered, 2 opposite quarters usually shaded
Nürnberg, Burgraves – crowned lion rampant left in checkered boarder

REFERENCE
S = Friedrich von Schrötter, **Brandenburg-Fränkisches Münzwesen**, Part I – ***Das Münzwesen der hohenzollernschen Burggrafen von Nürnberg und der Markgrafen von Brandenburg in Franken, 1350-1515***; Part II – ***Das Münzenwesen der hohenzollernschen Burggrafen von Nürnberg und der Markgrafen von Brandenburg in Franken, 1515-1603***, Halle (Saale), 1927-29.

MARGRAVIATE

REGULAR COINAGE

KM# 5 1/8 THALER
Silver **Subject:** Death of Georg Friedrich I **Obv:** Half-length armored figure to right, titles of Georg Friedrich I **Rev:** Five-line inscription with date **Rev. Inscription:** IST GOTT MIT VNS... **Mint:** Nürnberg

Date	Mintage	VG	F	VF	XF	Unc
1603	—	100	175	325	650	—

KM# 16 1/8 THALER
Silver **Subject:** Death of Georg Friedrich I's Wife, Sophia of Brunswick-Lüneburg **Obv:** Two adjacent oval shields of arms, four-fold arms of Brandenburg on left, five-fold of Brunswick on right, crown above, titles of Sophia **Rev:** Ten-line inscription with dates **Mint:** Nürnberg

Date	Mintage	VG	F	VF	XF	Unc
1639	—	—	—	—	—	—

KM# 6 1/4 THALER
Silver **Subject:** Death of Georg Friedrich I **Obv:** Similar to MB#42 **Rev:** Five-line inscription with dates **Rev. Inscription:** IST GOTT MIT VNS... **Mint:** Nürnberg

Date	Mintage	VG	F	VF	XF	Unc
1603	—	—	250	350	550	—

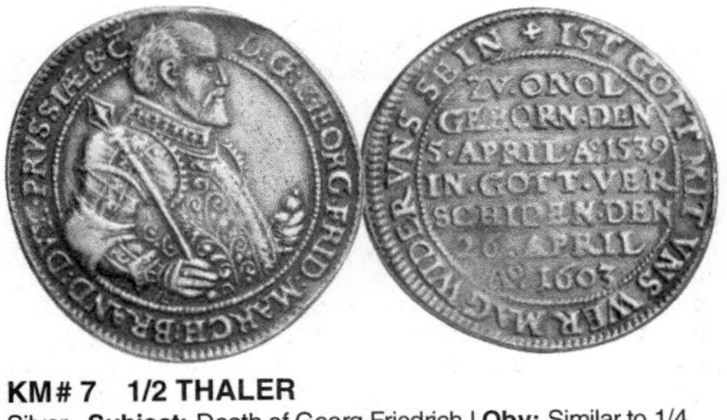

KM# 7 1/2 THALER
Silver **Subject:** Death of Georg Friedrich I **Obv:** Similar to 1/4 Thaler, KM#6 **Rev:** Seven-line inscription with dates **Mint:** Nürnberg

Date	Mintage	VG	F	VF	XF	Unc
1603	—	200	400	775	—	—

KM# 17 1/2 THALER
Silver **Subject:** Death of Georg Friedrich I's Wife, Sophia of Brunswick-Lüneburg **Obv:** Similar to 1/8 Thaler, KM#6 **Mint:** Nürnberg

Date	Mintage	VG	F	VF	XF	Unc
1639	—	—	—	—	—	—

KM# 8 THALER
Silver **Subject:** Death of Georg Friedrich **Obv:** Half figure right **Rev:** Seven-line inscription **Note:** Dav.#6224.

Date	Mintage	VG	F	VF	XF	Unc
1603	—	725	1,250	2,300	3,750	—

KM# 18 THALER
Silver **Subject:** Death of Georg Friedrich I's Wife, Sophia of Brunswick-Lüneburg **Obv:** Similar to 1/8 Thaler, KM#16 **Mint:** Schwabach

Date	Mintage	VG	F	VF	XF	Unc
1639	—	—	—	—	—	—

KM# 9 2 THALER
Silver **Subject:** Death of Georg Friedrich **Note:** Similar to 1 Thaler, KM#8. Dav.#6223.

Date	Mintage	VG	F	VF	XF	Unc
1603 Rare	—	—	—	—	—	—

JOINT COINAGE

KM# 12 THALER
Silver **Obv:** Facing busts of Christian and Joachim, date below **Rev:** Oval arms **Note:** Dav.#6225.

Date	Mintage	VG	F	VF	XF	Unc
1609	—	850	1,700	2,700	4,500	—

TRADE COINAGE

KM# 19 2 DUCAT
7.0000 g., 0.9860 Gold 0.2219 oz. AGW **Subject:** Death of Georg Friedrich I's Wife, Sophia of Brunswick-Lüneburg **Obv:** 2 adjacent oval shields of arms, 4-fold of Brandenburg on left, 5-fold of Brunswick on right, crown above, titles of Sophia **Rev:** 10-line inscription with dates **Note:** Struck with 1/8 Thaler dies, KM#16.

Date	Mintage	VG	F	VF	XF	Unc
1639 Rare	—	—	—	—	—	—

KM# 13 10 DUCAT (Portugalöser)
35.0000 g., 0.9860 Gold 1.1095 oz. AGW **Note:** Struck with 1 Thaler dies, KM#12. Fr. #316.

Date	Mintage	VG	F	VF	XF	Unc
1609 Rare	—	—	—	—	—	—

BREISACH

(Breysach, Brisach)

The city of Breisach, located on the Rhine about 12.5 miles (21km) west-northwest of Freiburg, has been an inhabited place since ancient times. It was a Roman fortified town and was of such importance that the surrounding territory became known as the Breisgau. Acquired by Emperor Otto I in 939, Breisach was later the site of an imperial mint and became an imperial town in 1275. Breisach issued its own coinage from about the mid-14th until the late 16th centuries. However, a series of emergency coins were struck during the Thirty Years' War, when the imperial garrison was besieged by the Swedish army in 1633. The French ended up in possession of Breisach at the end of the war in 1648 and it was taken and retaken by them all during the latter half of the 17th century. The city was reunited to the Empire in 1697 and so remained until 1801, when Breisach and all of the Breisgau were acquired by the Duke of Modena. Breisach finally passed to Baden in 1805.

ARMS

Six hills arranged in two rows of three each, one behind the other, sometimes with cross above.

REFERENCES

S = Hugo Frhr. Von Saurma-Jeltsch, ***Die Saurmasche Münzsammlung deutscher, schweizerischer und polnischer Gepräge von etwa dem Beginn der Groschenzeit bis zur Kipperperiode***, Berlin, 1892.

Sch = Wolfgang Schulten, ***Deutsche Münzen aus der Zeit Karls V.***, Frankfurt am Main, 1974.

CITY

SIEGE COINAGE

1633

KM# 1 KREUZER
3.6200 g., Silver **Note:** Klippe.

Date	Mintage	VG	F	VF	XF	Unc
1633	—	350	450	650	900	—

KM# 2 24 KREUZER (Sechsbätzner)
8.0000 g., Silver **Rev:** Date above 3 shields, lower shield divides value: XX-IIII **Note:** Klippe.

Date	Mintage	VG	F	VF	XF	Unc
1633	—	450	525	650	1,250	—

KM# 3.1 48 KREUZER (Zwolfbätzner)
16.4000 g., Silver **Rev:** Date above 3 shields, lower shield divides value: XL-VIII **Note:** Klippe.

Date	Mintage	VG	F	VF	XF	Unc
1633	—	375	475	525	1,100	—

KM# 3.2 48 KREUZER (Zwolfbätzner)
16.4000 g., Silver **Obv:** Legend **Rev:** Date above three ornate arms

Date	Mintage	F	VF	XF	Unc	BU
1633	—	475	595	1,150	—	—

KM# 5 THALER
Silver **Note:** Klippe.

Date	Mintage	VG	F	VF	XF	Unc
1633	—	—	—	12,500	17,500	—

Note: Kunker Auction 154, 6-09, XF realized approx. $16,655; Grun Auction 50, 11-08, VF-XF realized approx. $10,870

KM# 4 DUCAT
3.5000 g., 0.9860 Gold 0.1109 oz. AGW **Note:** Klippe.

Date	Mintage	VG	F	VF	XF	Unc
1633	—	3,000	5,000	9,500	13,500	—

SIEGE COINAGE

1648

KM# 7 48 KREUZER (Zwolfbätzner)
Silver **Obv:** Shield of city arms in circle, value XLVIII in exergue **Obv. Legend:** MONETA. NOVA. BRISACENSIS. **Note:** Uniface klippe.

Date	Mintage	VG	F	VF	XF	Unc
ND(1648)	—	525	825	1,625	—	—

TRADE COINAGE

KM# 6 DUCAT
3.5000 g., 0.9860 Gold 0.1109 oz. AGW **Subject:** Capitulation of City to French and Protestant Forces **Obv:** City arms **Rev:** 6-line inscription with date **Note:** FR. #396.

Date	Mintage	VG	F	VF	XF	Unc
1638	—	3,500	6,000	10,000	15,000	—

BREMEN

Established at about the same time as the bishopric in 787, Bremen was under the control of the bishops and archbishops until joining the Hanseatic League in 1276. Archbishop Albrecht II granted the mint right to the city in 1369, but this was not formalized by imperial decree until 1541. In 1646, Bremen was raised to free imperial status and continued to strike its own coins into the early 20th century. The city lost its free imperial status in 1803 and was controlled by France from 1806 until 1813. Regaining it independence in 1815, Bremen joined the North German Confederation in 1867 and the German Empire in 1871. Since 1369, there was practically continuous coinage until 1907.

MINT OFFICIALS' INITIALS

Initial or marks	Date	Name
	1572-1604	Alrich Koldewehr
	1603-28	Heinrich (Johann?) Klamp, warden
	1613-16	Ippo Ritzema
	1617-24	Johann Wientjes
	1624-34	Gerhard (Gerdt) Dreyer
	1634-69	Thomas Isenbein
	1634	Johann Caulitz, warden
	1674-84	Ernst Krulle, warden and mintmaster
	1687-97	Otto Krulle

ARMS

Key, often in shield

ARCHBISHOPRIC

A bishopric was established at the present site of Bremen by St. Wilhad in 787. When the Norse destroyed Hamburg in 848, the archbishop of that city transferred his see to Bremen. Eventually, the connection between the two waned and Bremen remained the seat of an archbishop, which obtained the mint right as early as 888. During the 11th century, this right was extended to allow mints to be established in various towns under Bremen's control. The Protestant Reformation overtook Bremen in 1522, although Catholic episcopal princes attempted to maintain Rome's influence there. At the start of the Thirty Years' War in 1618, however, Protestantism was firmly entrenched in Bremen. The last archbishop was driven from his see by the Swedes in 1644 and Bremen was joined to Verden as a secular duchy (see Bremen and Verden). This arrangement was confirmed by the Peace of Westphalia in 1648.

RULERS

Johann III Rode von Wale, 1496-1511
Christoph, Herzog von Braunschweig-Lüneburg, 1511-1558, Administrator, 1511-1514
Georg, Herzog von Braunschweig-Lüneburg, 1558-1566
Heinrich III, Herzog von Sachsen-Lauenburg, 1567-1585
Johann Adolf, Herzog von Holstein-Gottorp, 1585-1596
Johann Friedrich, Herzog von Holstein-Gottorp, 1585-1634
Friedrich II, Prince of Denmark, 1634-44 (1648)

MINT OFFICIALS' INITIALS

Initials	Date	Name
HR	1615-18	Hans Rücke
PT	1641-43	Peter Timpf

ARMS

Key at angle to upper left or right, sometimes 2 crossed keys (representing dual sees of Bremen and Hamburg.

REFERENCE

J = Hermann Jungk, Die Bremischen Münzen – Münzen und Medaillen des Erzbisthums und der Stadt Bremen, Bremen, 1875.

REGULAR COINAGE

KM# 35 SECHSLING (1/2 Schilling)

0.7040 g., 0.3120 Silver 0.0071 oz. ASW **Ruler:** Friedrich II **Obv:** 2 crossed keys (aarms) **Obv. Legend:** FRID: D:G: A: E: EP: BARE: E: VER: **Rev:** Denomination in center **Rev. Legend:** C: H: H: N: D: S: H: S: D: C: O: E: D: 1641 **Rev. Inscription:** I / SECH / S. LIN **Mint:** Bremervörde

Date	Mintage	VG	F	VF	XF	Unc
1641 PT	—	110	225	460	925	—

KM# 16 2 GROTE (12 Pfennig)

Silver **Ruler:** Johann Friedrich **Obv:** Helmeted 8-fold arms **Rev:** Crossed keys in ornately-shaped shield, date in legend

Date	Mintage	VG	F	VF	XF	Unc
1611	—	—	—	—	—	—

KM# A40 1/2 REICHSORT (1/8 Thaler)

Silver **Ruler:** Friedrich II **Obv:** Bust right, titles in legend **Obv. Legend:** FRID. D: G: A: E: EP: BR: E: V. **Rev:** Denomination in center within legend around **Rev. Legend:** C: H: H: N: D: S: H: S: D: C: O: E: D: 1642 PT **Rev. Inscription:** I / HALB / REICHS / ORT **Mint:** Bremervörde

Date	Mintage	VG	F	VF	XF	Unc
1642 PT Unique	—	—	—	—	—	—

Note: Westfalische Munzauktion No. 13, 9-98, VF realized $8300.

KM# 17 MARK (32 Grote)

Silver **Ruler:** Johann Friedrich **Obv:** Helmeted 8-fold arms **Rev:** Crossed keys divide 3Z GRO and date in legend

Date	Mintage	VG	F	VF	XF	Unc
1611	—	—	—	—	—	—

KM# 7 4 GROSCHEN

Silver **Ruler:** Johann Friedrich **Obv:** Bust right **Rev:** 8-fold arms

Date	Mintage	VG	F	VF	XF	Unc
ND	—	300	500	950	1,800	—

KM# 8 4 GROSCHEN

Silver **Ruler:** Johann Friedrich **Obv:** Bust right in inner circle **Rev:** Value above arms **Rev. Inscription:** 4 GROS

Date	Mintage	VG	F	VF	XF	Unc
ND	—	300	500	950	1,800	—

KM# 4 2 SCHILLING / 1/16 THALER (Dütchen)

Silver **Ruler:** Johann Friedrich **Obv:** Horseman right, crossed keys at upper right, Holstein arms (nettle) upper left, value 2 SL below **Rev:** 5-line inscription with titles of Johann Friedrich **Note:** Struck in style of Russian wire Kopek.

Date	Mintage	VG	F	VF	XF	Unc
ND	—	27.00	45.00	90.00	185	—

KM# 36 2 SCHILLING / 1/16 THALER (Dütchen)

Silver **Ruler:** Friedrich II **Obv:** Crossed keys **Rev. Inscription:** II / SCHIL / LING

Date	Mintage	VG	F	VF	XF	Unc
1641 PT	—	400	700	1,250	2,000	—
1643 PT	—	400	700	1,250	2,000	—

KM# 6 4 SCHILLING

Silver **Ruler:** Johann Friedrich **Obv:** Horseman left **Rev:** 5-line inscription

Date	Mintage	VG	F	VF	XF	Unc
ND	—	40.00	85.00	170	340	—

KM# 5 4 SCHILLING

Silver **Ruler:** Johann Friedrich **Obv:** Horseman right, crossed keys at upper right, Holstein arms (nettle) upper left, value 4 SL below **Rev:** 5-line inscription with titles of Johann Friedrich **Note:** Struck in style of Russian wire Kopeks.

Date	Mintage	VG	F	VF	XF	Unc
ND	—	40.00	80.00	160	325	—

KM# 24 1/24 THALER (1 Groschen)

Silver **Ruler:** Johann Friedrich **Obv:** 8-fold arms **Rev:** Imperial orb with Z4 divides date, titles of Matthias

Date	Mintage	VG	F	VF	XF	Unc
(1)619	—	40.00	85.00	160	325	—

KM# 25 1/24 THALER (1 Groschen)

Silver **Ruler:** Johann Friedrich **Obv:** 8-fold arms **Rev:** Imperial orb with Z4 divides date, titles of Matthias **Note:** Klippe.

Date	Mintage	VG	F	VF	XF	Unc
(16)19 Rare	—	—	—	—	—	—

KM# 31 1/24 THALER (1 Groschen)

Silver **Ruler:** Johann Friedrich **Obv:** Imperial orb with 24, date in legend, titles of Ferdinand II **Rev:** 3-fold arms **Note:** Small module.

Date	Mintage	VG	F	VF	XF	Unc
(1)621	—	45.00	100	180	360	—
(16)21	—	45.00	100	180	360	—

KM# 15 1/16 THALER (Dütchen)

Silver **Ruler:** Johann Friedrich **Obv:** Helmeted 8-fold arms **Rev:** Crowned imperial eagle, crossed keys on breast, necks divide value 1-6, date in legend, titles of Rudolf II **Note:** Normal style.

Date	Mintage	VG	F	VF	XF	Unc
1611	—	33.00	60.00	120	240	—

KM# 18 1/16 THALER (Dütchen)

Silver **Ruler:** Johann Friedrich **Obv:** 8-fold arms **Rev:** 3 helmets, value 1-6 below date in legend

Date	Mintage	VG	F	VF	XF	Unc
1612	—	25.00	45.00	95.00	190	—
1613	—	25.00	45.00	95.00	190	—
1614	—	25.00	45.00	95.00	190	—
1615	—	25.00	45.00	95.00	190	—
1616	—	25.00	45.00	95.00	190	—

KM# 22 1/16 THALER (Dütchen)

Silver **Ruler:** Johann Friedrich **Obv:** Helmeted 8-fold arms **Rev:** Crowned imperial eagle, crossed keys on breast, necks divide value 1-6, date in legend, titles of Matthias **Note:** Varieties exist.

Date	Mintage	VG	F	VF	XF	Unc
1613	—	25.00	55.00	110	225	—
1614	—	25.00	55.00	110	225	—
1615 HR	—	25.00	55.00	110	225	—
1616	—	25.00	55.00	110	225	—
1616 HR	—	25.00	55.00	110	225	—
1617	—	25.00	55.00	110	225	—
1618	—	25.00	55.00	110	225	—
1619	—	25.00	55.00	110	225	—

KM# 30 1/16 THALER (Dütchen)

Silver **Ruler:** Johann Friedrich **Obv:** Titles of Ferdinand II without indication of value **Note:** Kipper.

Date	Mintage	VG	F	VF	XF	Unc
1620	—	40.00	80.00	160	300	—

KM# 37.1 1/16 THALER (Dütchen)

1.7850 g., 0.8120 Silver 0.0466 oz. ASW **Ruler:** Friedrich II **Obv:** Bust right **Obv. Legend:** FRID: D: G: A: E: EP: BR: E: VE: **Rev:** Value in center, date in legend **Rev. Legend:** C: H: H: N: D: S: H: S: D: C: O: E: D: **Rev. Inscription:** XVI / E. REIC / HSDA **Mint:** Bremervörde **Note:** Varieties exist.

Date	Mintage	VG	F	VF	XF	Unc
1641	—	25.00	50.00	100	210	—
1642	—	25.00	50.00	100	210	—
1643	—	25.00	50.00	100	210	—

KM# 37.2 1/16 THALER (Dütchen)

1.7850 g., 0.8120 Silver 0.0466 oz. ASW **Ruler:** Friedrich II **Obv:** Bust of Archbishop Friedrich within inner circle **Obv. Legend:** FREDERICVS. D. G. A. EP. BR. E. VERD: **Rev:** Value in center, date in legend **Rev. Legend:** C. H. H. N. D. S. H. S. D. C. O. E. D. **Rev. Inscription:** XVI / E. REIC / HSDA **Mint:** Bremervörde **Note:** Kipper. Legend varieties exist.

Date	Mintage	VG	F	VF	XF	Unc
1642	—	100	200	400	650	—
1643 Unique	—	—	—	—	—	—

KM# 40 1/2 THALER

14.6100 g., 0.8880 Silver 0.4171 oz. ASW **Ruler:** Friedrich II **Obv:** Bust of Archbishop Frederik and motto within inner circle and legend **Obv. Legend:** FRIDERICVS. D: G: ARCH: EPISC: BREM: VERDEN: **Rev:** Crowned arms, date divided below **Rev. Legend:** C. HALV. HAE. NOR. D. SLE. HOLS. STO. DIT. C. O. E. D.

Date	Mintage	VG	F	VF	XF	Unc
1642 PT Rare	—	—	—	—	—	—

KM# 9 THALER
29.2300 g., 0.8880 Silver 0.8345 oz. ASW **Ruler:** Johann Friedrich **Obv:** Bust right **Rev:** Helmeted arms **Note:** Dav. #5071.

Date	Mintage	VG	F	VF	XF	Unc
ND(1611) Rare	—	—	—	—	—	—

KM# 19.1 THALER
29.2300 g., 0.8880 Silver 0.8345 oz. ASW **Ruler:** Johann Friedrich **Rev:** Helmeted 8-fold arms, legend and date **Rev. Legend:** HER: NORW ...

Date	Mintage	VG	F	VF	XF	Unc
1612 Rare	—	—	—	—	—	—

KM# 19.2 THALER
29.2300 g., 0.8880 Silver 0.8345 oz. ASW **Rev. Legend:** HER: NORWEG: DVX: SLES: **Note:** Dav. #5074.

Date	Mintage	VG	F	VF	XF	Unc
1616 HR Rare	—	—	—	—	—	—

KM# 19.3 THALER
29.2300 g., 0.8880 Silver 0.8345 oz. ASW **Ruler:** Johann Friedrich **Rev. Legend:** HER: NORWEG: DVX: SLESW: ET: HOL: **Note:** Dav. #5075.

Date	Mintage	VG	F	VF	XF	Unc
1618 Rare	—	—	—	—	—	—

KM# 19.4 THALER
Silver **Ruler:** Johann Friedrich **Rev. Legend:** HER: NOR: DUX - SLES: E: HOL: **Note:** Dav. #5076. Varieties exist.

Date	Mintage	VG	F	VF	XF	Unc
1622	—	1,200	2,400	4,500	7,500	—

KM# 38 THALER
29.2300 g., 0.8880 Silver 0.8345 oz. ASW **Ruler:** Friedrich II **Obv:** Bust of Archbishop Friedrich II right and motto within inner circle and legend **Obv. Legend:** FRIDERICVS: D: G: ARCH: &. EPISC: BREM: &. VERDEN: **Rev:** Crowned oval arms, date divided above **Rev. Legend:** C: HALB: HÆ: NOR: D: SLE: HOLS: STO: DIT: C: O: E: D: **Mint:** Bremervörde **Note:** Dav. #5078.

Date	Mintage	VG	F	VF	XF	Unc
1641 PT	—	2,400	4,200	7,800	11,500	—

KM# 20 2 THALER
58.4600 g., 0.8880 Silver 1.6690 oz. ASW **Ruler:** Johann Friedrich **Obv:** Bust right **Rev:** Helmeted 8-fold arms, date in legend **Note:** Dav. #5072.

Date	Mintage	VG	F	VF	XF	Unc
1612 Rare	—	—	—	—	—	—

KM# 39 2 THALER
58.4600 g., 0.8880 Silver 1.6690 oz. ASW **Ruler:** Friedrich II **Obv:** Bust of Archbishop Friedrich II right and motto within inner circle and legend **Obv. Legend:** FRIDERICUS: D: G. ARCH: & EPISC: BREM: &. VERDEN: **Rev:** Crowned oval arms, date divided above **Rev. Legend:** C: HALBBB: HÆ: NOR: D: SLE: HOLS: STO: DIT: C: O: E: D: **Mint:** Bremervörde **Note:** Dav. #5077.

Date	Mintage	VG	F	VF	XF	Unc
1641 PT	—	5,400	9,000	16,000	27,000	—

TRADE COINAGE

KM# 21 GOLDGULDEN
3.5000 g., 0.9860 Gold 0.1109 oz. AGW **Ruler:** Johann Friedrich **Obv:** Arms topped by 3 helmets **Rev:** St. Peter standing holding key and book, date in exergue

Date	Mintage	VG	F	VF	XF	Unc
1612 Rare	—	—	—	—	—	—

KM# 23 GOLDGULDEN
3.5000 g., 0.9860 Gold 0.1109 oz. AGW **Ruler:** Johann Friedrich **Obv:** Arms of Holstein joined with those of Bremen

Date	Mintage	VG	F	VF	XF	Unc
1618 Rare	—	—	—	—	—	—

KM# 10 10 DUCAT (Portugalöser)
Gold **Obv:** Bust right, margin of 8 small oval arms **Rev:** Cross in center, 3 circular legends

Date	Mintage	VG	F	VF	XF	Unc
ND Rare	—	—	—	—	—	—

FREE CITY

Established at about the same time as the bishopric in 787, Bremen was under the control of the bishops and archbishops until joining the Hanseatic League in 1276. Archbishop Albrecht II granted the mint right to the city in 1369, but this was not formalized by imperial decree until 1541. In 1646, Bremen was raised to free imperial status and continued to strike its own coins into the early 20th century. The city lost its free imperial status in 1803 and was controlled by France from 1806 until 1813. Regaining it independence in 1815, Bremen joined the North German Confederation in 1867 and the German Empire in 1871.

MINT OFFICIALS' INITIALS

Initials	Date	Name
(c) = 	1572-1604	Alrich Koldewehr
	1603-28	Heinrich (Johann?) Klamp, warden
(d) = 	1613-16	Ippo Ritzema
(e) = 	1617-24	Johann Wientjes
(f) =	1624-34	Gerhard (Gerdt) Dreyer
TI	1634-69	Thomas Isenbein
	1634	Johann Caulitz, warden
HL	1670-73	Hermann Luders
	1674-84	Ernst Krulle, warden and mintmaster
	1687-97	Otto Krulle

ARMS
Key, often in shield

REGULAR COINAGE

KM# 145 SCHWAREN
Billon **Obv:** Key in circle **Rev:** St. Peter in circle

Date	Mintage	VG	F	VF	XF	Unc
ND(1671) HL	103,000	35.00	65.00	140	250	—

KM# 151 SCHWAREN
Billon **Obv:** Key divides date in circle

Date	Mintage	VG	F	VF	XF	Unc
1676	143,000	25.00	55.00	110	200	—

KM# 155 SCHWAREN
Billon **Obv:** Key with date in legend **Rev:** St. Peter in circle

Date	Mintage	VG	F	VF	XF	Unc
1687	144,000	15.00	35.00	75.00	150	—
1690	—	15.00	35.00	75.00	150	—
1697	180,000	15.00	30.00	75.00	150	—
1698	—	15.00	30.00	75.00	150	—

KM# 50 1/2 GROTEN
Billon **Obv:** Key in shield in circle **Rev:** Cross in circle

Date	Mintage	VG	F	VF	XF	Unc
ND(ca.1602-13)	—	20.00	40.00	80.00	160	—

KM# 82 1/2 GROTEN
Billon **Obv:** Key in circle

Date	Mintage	VG	F	VF	XF	Unc
ND(ca.1624-34)	36,000	15.00	30.00	60.00	125	—

KM# 100.1 1/2 GROTEN
Billon **Obv:** Key divides date in circle **Rev:** Cross in circle **Note:** Varieties exist.

Date	Mintage	VG	F	VF	XF	Unc
1640	90,000	10.00	20.00	37.00	75.00	—
1659	17,000	10.00	20.00	37.00	75.00	—
1664	—	—	—	3,500	—	—
1672	—	10.00	20.00	37.00	75.00	—
1688	—	10.00	20.00	37.00	75.00	—

KM# 64 GROTEN
Silver **Obv:** Key in shield within pointed trilobe, date in legend **Rev:** Imperial eagle, titles of Matthias

Date	Mintage	VG	F	VF	XF	Unc
1614 (d)	—	—	—	—	—	—

KM# 78 GROTEN
Silver **Obv:** Imperial eagle, titles of Ferdinand II **Rev:** Key in shield in circle, date in legend

Date	Mintage	VG	F	VF	XF	Unc
1623	2,448,000	10.00	25.00	50.00	100	—
1626	—	10.00	25.00	50.00	100	—
1627	—	10.00	25.00	50.00	100	—

KM# 150 GROTEN
Silver **Obv:** Crowned imperial eagle, titles of Leopold

Date	Mintage	VG	F	VF	XF	Unc
1674	376,000	20.00	40.00	80.00	160	—

KM# A4 1 1/2 GROTEN (Schilling; 1/36 Thaler)
Silver **Obv:** City arms in oval baroque frame, date at end of legend **Obv. Legend:** MON. NOU. REIP. BREMENS. **Rev:** Crowned imperial eagle, 36 in orb on breast, titles of Rudolf II **Note:** J-855.

Date	Mintage	VG	F	VF	XF	Unc
1603	—	—	—	—	—	—

KM# 53 2 GROTE (1/27 Thaler)
Silver **Obv:** Arms in oval baroque frame, date in legend **Obv. Legend:** MON. NOU... **Rev:** Crowned imperial eagle, 27 in orb on breast, titles of Rudolf II

Date	Mintage	VG	F	VF	XF	Unc
1603	—	—	—	—	—	—

KM# 86 2 GROTE (1/27 Thaler)
Silver **Obv:** Imperial eagle, titles of Ferdinand II **Rev:** Key in circle, date in legend

Date	Mintage	VG	F	VF	XF	Unc
1625	—	—	—	—	—	—

KM# 106 2 GROTE (1/36 Thaler)
Silver **Obv:** Key divides date in circle, 2 in circle in legend **Rev:** Imperial eagle, 36 in circle above

Date	Mintage	VG	F	VF	XF	Unc
1641	114,000	22.00	45.00	90.00	180	—
1642	86,000	30.00	60.00	120	240	—
1646	290,000	15.00	30.00	60.00	120	—

KM# 110 2 GROTE (1/36 Thaler)
Silver **Rev:** 36 not in circle above

Date	Mintage	VG	F	VF	XF	Unc
1646	Inc. above	15.00	30.00	60.00	120	—

KM# 130 2 GROTE (1/36 Thaler)
Silver **Obv:** Key divides date in circle **Rev:** Crowned imperial eagle, 36 on breast, titles of Leopold

Date	Mintage	VG	F	VF	XF	Unc
1660	—	15.00	32.00	65.00	110	—
1671	199,000	15.00	32.00	65.00	110	650

KM# 54 3 GROTE (1/18 Thaler; 2 Schilling)
Silver **Obv:** Arms in ornamented oval shield, date in legend **Rev:** Crowned imperial eagle, 18 on breast, titles of Rudolf II

Date	Mintage	VG	F	VF	XF	Unc
1603	—	—	—	—	—	—
1608	—	—	—	—	—	—

KM# 65 3 GROTE (1/18 Thaler; 2 Schilling)
Silver **Rev:** Titles of Matthias

Date	Mintage	VG	F	VF	XF	Unc
1614 (d)	—	33.00	55.00	115	230	—
1615 (d)	—	33.00	55.00	115	230	—

KM# 88 3 GROTE (1/24 Thaler)
Silver **Obv:** Arms, date divided partly inside and outside shield **Rev:** Crowned imperial eagle, 24 in orb on breast, titles of Ferdinand II

Date	Mintage	VG	F	VF	XF	Unc
1629 (f)	—	25.00	45.00	90.00	185	—

KM# 90 3 GROTE (1/24 Thaler)
Silver **Obv:** Without value in orb **Rev:** Arms divide date in ornamented shield

Date	Mintage	VG	F	VF	XF	Unc
1634 (f)	61,000	10.00	20.00	45.00	95.00	—
1635 (g)	90,000	10.00	20.00	45.00	95.00	—
1636 (g)	101,000	10.00	20.00	45.00	95.00	—
1637 (g)	101,000	10.00	20.00	45.00	95.00	—

KM# 147 3 GROTE (1/24 Thaler)
Silver **Obv:** Crowned arms in baroque shield divide date, value III GROT below **Rev:** Crowned imperial eagle, 24 in orb on breast, titles of Leopold

Date	Mintage	VG	F	VF	XF	Unc
1672 HL	—	17.00	35.00	70.00	140	—

KM# 108 4 GROTE (Flinderken)
Silver **Rev:** Crowned imperial eagle, titles of Ferdinand III

Date	Mintage	VG	F	VF	XF	Unc
1646 (g)	48,000	17.00	35.00	75.00	155	—
1647 (g)	12,000	17.00	35.00	75.00	155	—
1649 (g)	197,000	17.00	35.00	75.00	155	—

KM# 131 4 GROTE (Flinderken)
Silver, 28 mm. **Obv:** Key divides date in ornamented circle superimposed on cross **Obv. Legend:** BRE - MER - STAT - GELT. **Rev:** Crowned imperial eagle, 4 in orb on breast **Rev. Legend:** LEOP. D. G. ROM. IMP. SE. AU(G).

Date	Mintage	VG	F	VF	XF	Unc
1660	66,000	22.00	45.00	80.00	160	—

KM# 146 4 GROTE (Flinderken)
Silver **Rev:** 18 in orb on breast

Date	Mintage	VG	F	VF	XF	Unc
1671	22,000	16.00	35.00	75.00	155	—

KM# 148 6 GROTE / 1/12 THALER
Silver

Date	Mintage	VG	F	VF	XF	Unc
1672 HL	—	16.00	35.00	75.00	155	—

KM# 68 12 GROTE (1/6 Thaler)
Silver **Obv:** Supported oval arms in shield, crown above **Rev:** Crowned imperial eagle, date and titles of Matthias in legend

Date	Mintage	VG	F	VF	XF	Unc
1617	—	—	—	—	—	—

KM# 79 12 GROTE (1/6 Thaler)
3.6000 g., Silver, 26 mm. **Obv:** Helmeted and supported arms **Obv. Legend:** MO: NO - R - E - . BREM. **Rev:** Crowned imperial eagle, date divided above **Rev. Legend:** FER. II. D. G. RO. IM. SE. AU. **Note:** Ref. J#611-13.

Date	Mintage	VG	F	VF	XF	Unc
16Z3 (e)	—	200	400	700	1,100	—

KM# 121 12 GROTE (1/6 Thaler)
Silver **Obv:** Crowned oval arms divide date in baroque frame, value (XII) below in legend **Rev:** Crowned imperial eagle, titles of Ferdinand III

Date	Mintage	VG	F	VF	XF	Unc
1653	15,000	25.00	45.00	90.00	185	—

KM# 122 12 GROTE (1/6 Thaler)
Silver

Date	Mintage	VG	F	VF	XF	Unc
1654	127,000	16.00	33.00	75.00	155	—
1657	141,000	16.00	33.00	75.00	155	—

KM# 123 12 GROTE (1/6 Thaler)
Silver **Rev:** Titles of Leopold **Note:** Varieties exist.

Date	Mintage	VG	F	VF	XF	Unc
1658	140,000	27.00	35.00	70.00	140	—
1659	411,000	27.00	35.00	70.00	140	—
1664	69,000	27.00	35.00	70.00	140	—
1666	88,000	27.00	35.00	70.00	140	—
1667	145,000	27.00	35.00	70.00	140	—
1672 HL	—	27.00	35.00	70.00	140	—

KM# 124.1 24 GROTE (1/3 Thaler)
Silver **Obv:** Vertical date divided by arms **Note:** Varieties exist.

Date	Mintage	VG	F	VF	XF	Unc
1658	35,000	45.00	90.00	180	360	—
1659	54,000	45.00	90.00	180	360	—
1660	34,000	45.00	90.00	180	360	—
1664	9,000	45.00	90.00	180	360	—
1666	39,000	45.00	90.00	180	360	—
1672	—	45.00	90.00	180	360	—

KM# 124.2 24 GROTE (1/3 Thaler)
Silver **Obv:** Horizontal date divided by arms

Date	Mintage	VG	F	VF	XF	Unc
1672 HL	—	50.00	1,000	200	400	—

KM# 66 32 GROTE (Mark)
Silver **Obv:** Supported oval arms, 1 MARCK below, date in legend **Rev:** Crowned imperial eagle, 32 in orb on breast, titles of Matthias **Note:** Dav. #319.

Date	Mintage	VG	F	VF	XF	Unc
1614 (d)	—	—	2,650	5,000	8,500	—

KM# 69 32 GROTE (Mark)
Silver **Obv:** Crown above supported oval arms in ornamented shield, date above crown **Note:** Dav. #A319.

Date	Mintage	VG	F	VF	XF	Unc
1617 (e)	—	—	1,000	1,800	3,250	—

KM# 70 32 GROTE (Mark)

Silver Weight varies: 29.00-29.03g., 40x40 mm. **Obv:** Oval shield of city arms supported by 2 lions within crowned and ornamented Spanish shield, date divided above **Obv. Legend:** MONE. NOVA. REIPVB. BREMENS. **Rev:** Crowned imperial eagle, 32 - GR - OT divided by tail and right claw **Rev. Legend:** MATTH. D. G. RO. IMPER. SEMP. AUG. **Note:** Ref. J-536. Klippe.

Date	Mintage	VG	F	VF	XF	Unc
1617 (e) Rare	—	—	—	—	—	—

Note: An example in VF-XF realized approximately $11,800 in a September 2009 WAG auction.

KM# 135 48 GROTE (2/3 Thaler)

Silver **Obv:** Crowned arms divide date 48 GROT in border **Rev:** Crowned imperial eagle, titles of Leopold **Note:** Dav. #320.

Date	Mintage	VG	F	VF	XF	Unc
1666	—	—	—	—	—	—

KM# 67 GROSCHEN / 1/24 THALER

Silver **Obv:** Arms in oval baroque frame **Rev:** Imperial orb with 24 divides date, titles of Matthias

Date	Mintage	VG	F	VF	XF	Unc
1616 (d)	—	35.00	75.00	150	300	—

KM# 60 GROSCHEN / 1/24 THALER

Silver **Obv:** Helmeted and supported oval arms **Rev:** Imperial orb with 24, titles of Matthias

Date	Mintage	VG	F	VF	XF	Unc
ND(1617-19) (e)	—	30.00	60.00	120	240	—

KM# 71 1/16 THALER (Dütchen)

Silver **Obv:** Helmeted and supported oval arms **Rev:** Crowned imperial eagle, value 16 in orb on breast, date and titlews of Matthias in legend

Date	Mintage	VG	F	VF	XF	Unc
ND(1617-19) (e)	—	60.00	120	240	—	—

Note: Some pieces exist with a key countermark (VF $250)

Date	Mintage	VG	F	VF	XF	Unc
1617	—	75.00	150	300	—	—

KM# 72 1/16 THALER (Dütchen)

Silver **Obv:** Helmeted and supported oval arms **Rev:** Crowned imperial eagle, value 16 in orb on breast, date and titles of Matthias in legend **Note:** Klippe.

Date	Mintage	VG	F	VF	XF	Unc
1617 (e)	—	—	—	—	—	—

KM# 55 1/4 THALER

Silver **Obv:** Supported arms in oval baroque frame, date divided above **Rev:** Crowned imperial eagle, titles of Rudolf II

Date	Mintage	VG	F	VF	XF	Unc
1603 Rare	—	—	—	—	—	—

KM# 119 1/4 THALER

Silver **Obv:** Crowned and supported oval arms, date below, 1/4 in orb above **Rev:** Titles of Ferdinand III

Date	Mintage	VG	F	VF	XF	Unc
1651 TI NOVA.	732	200	350	600	1,150	—
1651 TI NOVA:	—	225	375	700	1,300	—

KM# 51 1/2 THALER

Silver **Obv:** Supported oval arms, date above **Rev:** Titles of Rudolf II

Date	Mintage	VG	F	VF	XF	Unc
1602	—	900	1,600	3,000	6,000	—

KM# 107 1/2 THALER

Silver

Date	Mintage	VG	F	VF	XF	Unc
1643 TI	—	425	750	1,200	2,200	—

KM# 115 1/2 THALER

Silver **Obv:** Crown above arms, date below

Date	Mintage	VG	F	VF	XF	Unc
1650 TI	—	575	925	1,700	3,250	—

KM# 134 1/2 THALER

Silver **Rev:** Titles of Leopold

Date	Mintage	VG	F	VF	XF	Unc
1661 TI	—	250	400	700	1,150	—

KM# 136 1/2 THALER

Silver **Obv:** Crowned and supported oval arms **Rev:** 1/2-length figure of Leopold left, holding orb and sword

Date	Mintage	VG	F	VF	XF	Unc
ND(1666)	—	2,300	4,500	7,500	—	—

KM# 137 1/2 THALER

Silver **Rev:** Crowned imperial eagle, titles of Leopold

Date	Mintage	VG	F	VF	XF	Unc
ND(1666)	—	—	—	—	—	—

KM# 52.1 THALER

Silver **Obv:** Supported oval arms, date divided above **Rev:** Crowned imperial eagle, titles of Rudolf II **Note:** Dav. #5080.

Date	Mintage	VG	F	VF	XF	Unc
1602	—	1,500	3,025	6,050	10,450	—

Note: Wag Auction 31, 5-05, XF-Unc realized approximately $19,550

Date	Mintage	VG	F	VF	XF	Unc
1603	—	1,500	3,025	6,050	10,450	—

KM# 52.2 THALER

Silver **Note:** Thick flan. Dav. #5080A.

Date	Mintage	VG	F	VF	XF	Unc
1602 Rare	—	—	—	—	—	—

KM# 61 THALER

Silver **Rev:** Titles of Matthias **Note:** Dav. #5082.

Date	Mintage	VG	F	VF	XF	Unc
1613 (d) Rare	—	—	—	—	—	—

KM# 73 THALER

Silver **Obv:** Supported oval arms in larger shield with ornate helmet above, date divided above **Note:** Dav. #5084.

Date	Mintage	VG	F	VF	XF	Unc
1617 (e)	—	4,950	9,350	16,500	—	—

Note: Wag Auction 31, 5-05, F realized approximately $11,915

KM# 76 THALER

Silver **Obv:** Helmeted and supported arms **Rev:** Titles of Ferdinand II and date in legend **Note:** Dav. #5086.

Date	Mintage	VG	F	VF	XF	Unc
1621	—	1,500	3,025	6,050	10,450	—
1622	—	1,500	3,025	6,050	10,450	—
16ZZ	—	1,500	3,025	6,050	10,450	—

KM# 77 THALER

Silver **Obv:** Helmeted and supported arms **Rev:** Crowned imperial eagle, titles of Ferdinand II, date in legend **Note:** Klippe. Dav. #5085.

Date	Mintage	F	VF	XF	Unc	BU
1621 Rare	—	—	—	—	—	—

KM# 81 THALER

Silver **Rev:** Date divided by eagle's tail **Note:** Klippe. Dav. #5085.

Date	Mintage	F	VF	XF	Unc	BU
1623 Rare	—	—	—	—	—	—
1624 Rare	—	—	—	—	—	—

KM# 80 THALER

Silver **Rev:** Date divided by eagle's tail **Note:** Dav. #5089.

Date	Mintage	VG	F	VF	XF	Unc
1623 (e)	—	1,275	2,475	4,950	8,250	—
1624 (e)	49,000	1,275	2,475	4,950	8,250	—

KM# 83 THALER

Silver **Obv:** Large key, date in legend **Note:** Dav. #5090.

Date	Mintage	VG	F	VF	XF	Unc
1624	Inc. above	2,050	3,850	7,150	12,625	—

Note: Künlear Auction 105, 5-05, XF realized approx. $12,935

KM# 84 THALER

Silver **Obv:** Lion supported oval arms in ornamented frame, date divided above **Note:** Dav. #5091.

Date	Mintage	VG	F	VF	XF	Unc
1624	Inc. above	1,500	3,025	6,050	10,450	—

KM# 91.1 THALER

Silver **Obv:** Supported arms in ornately-shaped frame, date **Note:** Dav. #5093.

Date	Mintage	VG	F	VF	XF	Unc
1634 TI	2,988	375	600	1,020	1,800	—

KM# 91.2 THALER

Silver **Obv:** T - I separated by support arms **Note:** Dav. #5094.

Date	Mintage	VG	F	VF	XF	Unc
1634 TI	Inc. above	400	780	1,500	3,125	—

KM# 91.3 THALER

Silver **Obv:** T - I divided below by bottom of frame **Note:** Varieties exist. Dav. #5096.

Date	Mintage	VG	F	VF	XF	Unc
1635 TI	748	375	720	1,440	3,000	—

KM# 101.1 THALER

Silver **Obv:** Arms with lion supporters **Obv. Legend:** MON. NOVA... **Rev:** Crowned imperial eagle **Note:** Similar to KM#101.2. Dav. #5098.

Date	Mintage	VG	F	VF	XF	Unc
1640 TI	946	525	1,025	2,100	3,600	—

KM# 101.2 THALER

Silver **Obv:** Arms with lion supporters **Rev:** Crowned imperial eagle **Note:** Varieties exist. Dav. #5100.

Date	Mintage	VG	F	VF	XF	Unc
1641 TI	Inc. above	375	720	1,400	2,400	—
1642 TI	—	375	720	1,400	2,400	—
1644 TI	—	375	1,100	1,925	3,375	—

Note: Wag Auction 48, 9-08, XF+ realized approx. $13,250

KM# 116.1 THALER

Silver **Note:** Dav. #5102.

Date	Mintage	VG	F	VF	XF	Unc
1650 TI	1,627	375	725	1,450	2,700	—

KM# 116.2 THALER

Silver **Obv:** Lion supporters looking outward **Note:** Dav. #5104.

Date	Mintage	VG	F	VF	XF	Unc
1657 TI	378	450	900	1,800	3,300	6,075

KM# 116.3 THALER

Silver **Obv:** Different lions **Obv. Legend:** MON: NOVA: ARG. **Note:** Varieties exist. Dav. #5105.

Date	Mintage	VG	F	VF	XF	Unc
1657 TI	Inc. above	—	—	3,850	6,050	—

KM# 132.2 THALER

Silver **Rev. Legend:** ...AUGUS: **Note:** Dav. #5107.

Date	Mintage	VG	F	VF	XF	Unc
1660 TI	3,942	360	600	900	1,700	2,500
1666 TI	—	360	600	900	1,700	2,500

KM# 132.1 THALER

Silver **Rev. Legend:** ...AUGUST: **Note:** Dav. #5107A.

Date	Mintage	VG	F	VF	XF	Unc
1660 TI	—	360	600	900	1,680	—

KM# 132.3 THALER

Silver **Obv. Legend:** MONETA NOVA REIPUBLICAE... **Note:** Varieties exist. Dav. #5110.

Date	Mintage	VG	F	VF	XF	Unc
1668	—	770	1,650	3,300	5,500	—

KM# A77 1-1/2 THALER

Silver Weight varies: 39-50-43.85g., 42x42 mm. **Obv:** Spanish shield of city arms supported by 2 lions, ornate helmet above with lion crest **Obv. Legend:** MONE. NOVA. - RE - IP - VB. BREMENSIS. **Rev:** Crowned imperial eagle, orb on breast, date at end of legend **Rev. Legend:** FERDI. II. D. G. ROMAN. IMPER. SEMPER. AU. **Note:** Ref. J-456; Dav. 5085. Klippe.

Date	Mintage	VG	F	VF	XF	Unc
16Z1 Rare	—	—	—	—	—	—

Note: An example in VF-XF realized approximately $22,100 in a September 2009 WAG auction.

KM# 56 2 THALER

Silver **Obv:** Supported oval arms, date divided above **Rev:** Crowned imperial eagle, titles of Rudolf II **Note:** Dav. #5079.

Date	Mintage	F	VF	XF	Unc	BU
1603 Rare	—	—	—	—	—	—

KM# 62 2 THALER

Silver **Rev:** Titles of Matthias **Note:** Dav. #5081.

Date	Mintage	F	VF	XF	Unc	BU
1613 Rare	—	—	—	—	—	—

KM# 74 2 THALER

Silver **Obv:** Supported oval arms in larger shield with ornate helnet above, date divided above **Note:** Dav. #5083.

Date	Mintage	VG	F	VF	XF	Unc
1617 Rare	—	—	—	—	—	—

KM# 85 2 THALER

Silver **Obv:** Helmeted and supported arms **Rev:** Titles of Ferdinand II, date divided by eagle's tail **Note:** Dav. #5087.

Date	Mintage	VG	F	VF	XF	Unc
1624 Rare	—	—	—	—	—	—

KM# 92.1 2 THALER

Silver **Obv:** Supported arms in ornately-shaped frame, date above, .T. .I. below **Note:** Dav. #5092.

Date	Mintage	VG	F	VF	XF	Unc
1634 TI Rare	—	—	—	—	—	—

KM# 92.2 2 THALER

Silver **Obv:** .T. .I. divided below by bottom of frame **Note:** Varieties exist. Dav. #5095.

Date	Mintage	VG	F	VF	XF	Unc
1635 TI Rare	—	—	—	—	—	—

KM# 102.1 2 THALER

Silver **Obv. Legend:** .MON. NOVA. ARG... **Note:** Similar to KM#102.2 but different obverse legend. Dav. #5097.

Date	Mintage	VG	F	VF	XF	Unc
1640 TI Rare	—	—	—	—	—	—

KM# 102.2 2 THALER

Silver **Note:** Varieties exist. Dav. #5099.

Date	Mintage	VG	F	VF	XF	Unc
1641 TI Rare	—	—	—	—	—	—

Note: Westfälische Auktionsgesellschaft, Auction 46, 2-08, XF+ realized approximately $22,108.

Date	Mintage	VG	F	VF	XF	Unc
164Z TI Rare	—	—	—	—	—	—

KM# 117.1 2 THALER

Silver **Note:** Dav. #5101A.

Date	Mintage	VG	F	VF	XF	Unc
1650 TI	—	1,450	2,400	4,200	7,200	—

KM# 117.2 2 THALER

Silver **Obv:** Lion supporters looking outward **Note:** Dav. #5103.

Date	Mintage	VG	F	VF	XF	Unc
1657 TI	—	2,150	4,200	9,000	15,000	—

KM# 133.1 2 THALER

Silver **Obv:** Lion supporters looking inward **Rev. Legend:** LEOPOLD: D: G:... **Note:** Dav. #5106.

Date	Mintage	VG	F	VF	XF	Unc
1660 TI Rare	—	—	—	—	—	—
1666 TI	—	2,175	4,200	9,000	15,000	—

KM# 133.3 2 THALER

Silver **Rev. Legend:** LEOPOLDUS... **Note:** Dav. #5109A.

Date	Mintage	VG	F	VF	XF	Unc
1666	—	750	1,500	2,800	5,000	—
1668	—	750	1,500	2,800	5,000	—

KM# 133.2 2 THALER

Silver, 45 mm. **Obv:** Lion supporters looking outward **Obv. Legend:** MONETA NOVA REIPUBLICÆ BREMENSIS. **Rev. Legend:** LEOPOLD: D: G: ROM: IMP: SEM: AUGUS: **Note:** Ref. J-503; Dav. 5109.

Date	Mintage	VG	F	VF	XF	Unc
1666	—	900	1,800	3,275	6,000	—
1668/6	—	900	1,800	3,275	6,000	—

KM# 118 3 THALER

Silver **Note:** Similar to 1 Thaler KM#116. Dav. #5101.

Date	Mintage	VG	F	VF	XF	Unc
1650 TI	—	1,625	2,700	4,500	7,800	—

KM# 138 3 THALER

Silver **Note:** Similar to 1 Thaler KM#132. Dav. #A5108.

Date	Mintage	VG	F	VF	XF	Unc
1668 Rare	—	—	—	—	—	—

KM# 139 4 THALER

Silver **Note:** Similar to 1 Thaler KM#132. Dav. #5108.

Date	Mintage	VG	F	VF	XF	Unc
1668 Rare	—	—	—	—	—	—

COUNTERMARKED COINAGE

1620-1621

A countermark of the city arms - a key - was used to identify some coins which circulated in the city. The precise reason for the use of this countermark is not known, but it is interesting to note that it occurs on double-schilling type coins during the very early period of the Thirty Years' War. Its use may be related to a new monetary ordinance agreed to among the cities of Bremen, Hamburg, Lubeck, and the duchies of Mecklenburg-Schwerin and Mecklenburg-Strelitz dated 20 April 1620.

KM# A75 4 SKILLING

Silver **Countermark:** Key **Note:** Countermark on Denmark 4 Skilling, KM#55.2.

CM Date	Host Date	Good	VG	F	VF	XF
ND(c.1620-21)	1616 (c)	28.50	47.50	95.00	175	—
ND(ca.1620-21)	1617 (c)	28.50	47.50	95.00	175	—
ND(ca.1620-21)	1618 (c)	28.50	47.50	95.00	175	—
ND(ca.1620-21)	1619 (c)	28.50	47.50	95.00	175	—

KM# C75.6 2 SCHILLING

Silver **Countermark:** Key **Note:** Countermark on Mecklenburg-Schwerin 2 Schilling, KM#22.

CM Date	Host Date	Good	VG	F	VF	XF
ND(ca.1620-21)	1612	27.50	45.00	90.00	165	—
ND(ca.1620-21)	1614 (b)	27.50	45.00	90.00	165	—
ND(ca.1620-21)	1615 (b)	27.50	45.00	90.00	165	—
ND(ca.1620-21)	(16)15 (b)	27.50	45.00	90.00	165	—
ND(ca.1620-21)	1616 (b)	27.50	45.00	90.00	165	—

KM# C75.4 2 SCHILLING

Silver **Countermark:** Key **Note:** Countermark on Mecklenburg-Schwerin 2 Schilling, KM#19.

CM Date	Host Date	Good	VG	F	VF	XF
ND(ca.1620-21)	1613 (b)	45.00	75.00	150	260	—
ND(ca.1620-21)	(16)15 (b)	45.00	75.00	150	260	—

KM# C75.5 2 SCHILLING

Silver **Countermark:** Key **Note:** Countermark on Mecklenburg-Schwerin 2 Schilling, KM#20.

CM Date	Host Date	Good	VG	F	VF	XF
ND(ca.1620-21)	1613 (b)	40.00	65.00	130	240	—
ND(ca.1620-21)	(1)613 (b)	40.00	65.00	130	240	—
ND(ca.1620-21)	1614 (b)	40.00	65.00	130	240	—
ND(ca.1620-21)	(1)614 (b)	40.00	65.00	130	240	—
ND(ca.1620-21)	(16)14 (b)	40.00	65.00	130	240	—
ND(ca.1620-21)	(16)15 (b)	40.00	65.00	130	240	—

KM# C75.3 2 SCHILLING

Silver **Countermark:** Key **Note:** Countermark on Mecklenburg-Güstrow 2 Schilling, KM#20.

CM Date	Host Date	Good	VG	F	VF	XF
ND(ca.1620-21)	1614	40.00	65.00	130	240	—
ND(ca.1620-21)	1615 (b)	40.00	65.00	130	240	—
ND(ca.1620-21)	1615	40.00	65.00	130	240	—
ND(ca.1620-21)	1616 (b)	40.00	65.00	130	240	—
ND(ca.1620-21)	1616	40.00	65.00	130	240	—
ND(ca.1620-21)	1617 (b)	40.00	65.00	130	240	—
ND(ca.1620-21)	1617	40.00	65.00	130	240	—
ND(ca.1620-21)	1618	40.00	65.00	130	240	—
ND(ca.1620-21)	ND(1614-18) (b)	40.00	65.00	130	240	—

KM# C75.8 2 SCHILLING

Silver **Countermark:** Key **Note:** Countermark on Pomerania-Wolgast 2 Schilling.

CM Date	Host Date	Good	VG	F	VF	XF
ND(ca.1620-21)	1615	20.00	32.50	65.00	115	—

KM# C75.1 2 SCHILLING

Silver **Countermark:** Key **Note:** Countermark on Holstein-Gottorp 2 Schilling.

CM Date	Host Date	Good	VG	F	VF	XF
ND(ca.1620-21)	1615	32.50	55.00	110	195	—

KM# C75.7 2 SCHILLING

Silver **Countermark:** Key **Note:** Countermark on Mecklenburg-Schwerin 2 Schilling, KM#33.

CM Date	Host Date	Good	VG	F	VF	XF
ND(ca.1620-21)	1616 (b)	27.50	45.00	90.00	165	—
ND(ca.1620-21)	(16)16 (b)	27.50	45.00	90.00	165	—
ND(ca.1620-21)	1617 (b)	27.50	45.00	90.00	165	—
ND(ca.1620-21)	(1)6(1)7 (b)	27.50	45.00	90.00	165	—
ND(ca.1620-21)	ND(1618) (b)	27.50	45.00	90.00	165	—

KM# C75.2 2 SCHILLING

Silver **Countermark:** Key **Note:** Countermark on Holstein-Gottorp 2 Schilling.

CM Date	Host Date	Good	VG	F	VF	XF
ND(ca.1620-21)	1617	32.50	55.00	110	195	—
ND(ca.1620-21)	1618	32.50	55.00	110	195	—

KM# B75 1/18-1/2 THALER

Silver **Countermark:** Key **Note:** Countermark on Schaumburg-Pinneberg 1/18-1/2 Thaler, KM#72.

CM Date	Host Date	Good	VG	F	VF	XF
ND(ca.1620-21)	(1)613 (q)	40.00	65.00	130	230	—
ND(ca.1620-21)	(1)614 (q)	40.00	65.00	130	230	—
ND(ca.1620-21)	(1)615 (q)	40.00	65.00	130	230	—
ND(ca.1620-21)	(1)616 (q)	40.00	65.00	130	230	—

KM# 75.2 1/16 THALER

Silver **Countermark:** Key **Note:** Countermark on Bremen and Verden 1/16 Thaler, KM#18.

CM Date	Host Date	Good	VG	F	VF	XF
ND(ca.1620-21)	161Z	16.50	27.50	55.00	100	—
ND(ca.1620-21)	1613	16.50	27.50	55.00	100	—
ND(ca.1620-21)	1614	16.50	27.50	55.00	100	—
ND(ca.1620-21)	1615	16.50	27.50	55.00	100	—
ND(ca.1620-21)	1616	16.50	27.50	55.00	100	—

KM# 75.3 1/16 THALER

Silver **Countermark:** Key **Note:** Countermark on Bremen and Verden 1/16 Thaler, KM#22.

CM Date	Host Date	Good	VG	F	VF	XF
ND(ca.1620-21)	1613	16.50	27.50	55.00	100	—
ND(ca.1620-21)	1614	16.50	27.50	55.00	100	—
ND(ca.1620-21)	1615 HR	16.50	27.50	55.00	100	—
ND(ca.1620-21)	1616	16.50	27.50	55.00	100	—
ND(ca.1620-21)	1616 HR	16.50	27.50	55.00	100	—
ND(ca.1620-21)	1617	16.50	27.50	55.00	100	—
ND(ca.1620-21)	1618	16.50	27.50	55.00	100	—
ND(ca.1620-21)	1619	16.50	27.50	55.00	100	—

KM# 75.12 1/16 THALER

Silver **Countermark:** Key **Note:** Countermark on Wismar 1/16 Thaler.

CM Date	Host Date	Good	VG	F	VF	XF
ND(ca.1620-21)	1613	30.00	50.00	100	180	—
ND(ca.1620-21)	1614	30.00	50.00	100	180	—
ND(ca.1620-21)	1615	30.00	50.00	100	180	—
ND(ca.1620-21)	1616	30.00	50.00	100	180	—
ND(ca.1620-21)	1617	30.00	50.00	100	180	—
ND(ca.1620-21)	1618	30.00	50.00	100	180	—
ND(ca.1620-21)	1619	30.00	50.00	100	180	—

KM# 75.5 1/16 THALER

Silver **Countermark:** Key **Note:** Countermark on Hamburg-City 1/16 Thaler, KM#29.

CM Date	Host Date	Good	VG	F	VF	XF
ND(ca.1620-21)	1614	37.50	65.00	120	225	—
ND(ca.1620-21)	1615	37.50	65.00	120	225	—
ND(ca.1620-21)	1616	37.50	65.00	120	225	—
ND(ca.1620-21)	1617	37.50	65.00	120	225	—

KM# 75.11 1/16 THALER

Silver **Countermark:** Key **Note:** Countermark on Stade 1/16 Thaler.

CM Date	Host Date	Good	VG	F	VF	XF
ND(ca.1620-21)	1615	32.50	55.00	110	195	—
ND(ca.1620-21)	1616	32.50	55.00	110	195	—
ND(ca.1620-21)	1617	32.50	55.00	110	195	—
ND(ca.1620-21)	1618	32.50	55.00	110	195	—
ND(ca.1620-21)	1619	32.50	55.00	110	195	—

KM# 75.4 1/16 THALER

Silver **Countermark:** Key **Note:** Countermark on Brunswick-Lüneburg-Harburg 1/16 Thaler, KM#7.

CM Date	Host Date	Good	VG	F	VF	XF
ND(ca.1620-21)	1616	60.00	100	200	350	—
ND(ca.1620-21)	1617	60.00	100	200	350	—
ND(ca.1620-21)	1618	60.00	100	200	350	—
ND(ca.1620-21)	1619	60.00	100	200	350	—
ND(ca.1620-21)	ND(1616-19)	60.00	100	200	350	—

KM# 75.7 1/16 THALER

Silver **Countermark:** Key **Note:** Countermark on Schaumburg-Pinneberg 1/16 Thaler, KM#77. Also found with countermark of Hamburg.

CM Date	Host Date	Good	VG	F	VF	XF
ND(ca.1620-21)	(1)616 (f)	37.50	62.50	120	230	—
ND(ca.1620-21)	(1)617 (f)	37.50	62.50	120	230	—
ND(ca.1620-21)	(1)617 (q)	37.50	62.50	120	230	—
ND(ca.1620-21)	(1)618 (t)	37.50	62.50	120	230	—
ND(ca.1620-21)	(1)619 (t)	37.50	62.50	120	230	—
ND(ca.1620-21)	(1)6Z0 (t)	37.50	62.50	120	230	—

KM# 75.6 1/16 THALER

Silver **Countermark:** Key **Note:** Countermark on Ratzeburg 1/16 Thaler.

CM Date	Host Date	Good	VG	F	VF	XF
ND(ca.1620-21)	1617	30.00	50.00	100	180	—
ND(ca.1620-21)	1618	30.00	50.00	100	180	—

KM# 75.1 1/16 THALER

Silver **Countermark:** Key **Note:** Countermark on Bentheim-Tecklenburg-Rheda 1/16 Thaler, KM#6.

CM Date	Host Date	Good	VG	F	VF	XF
ND(ca.1620-21)	1618	75.00	125	240	450	—
ND(ca.1620-21)	1619	75.00	125	240	450	—

KM# 75.8 1/16 THALER

Silver **Countermark:** Key **Note:** Countermark on Schaumburg-Pinneberg 1/16 Thaler, KM#100.

CM Date	Host Date	Good	VG	F	VF	XF
ND(ca.1620-21)	(1)6Z0	30.00	50.00	100	180	—
ND(ca.1620-21)	(1)6Z0 (b)	30.00	50.00	100	180	—
ND(ca.1620-21)	(1)6Z1 (i)	30.00	50.00	100	180	—

KM# 75.9 1/16 THALER

Silver **Countermark:** Key **Note:** Countermark on Schaumburg-Pinneberg 1/16 Thaler, KM#118.

CM Date	Host Date	Good	VG	F	VF	XF
ND(ca.1620-21)	16Z1(p)//16Z1 (h)	30.00	50.00	100	180	—

KM# 75.10 1/16 THALER

Silver **Countermark:** Key **Note:** Countermark on Schaumberg-Pinneberg 1/16 Thaler, KM#122.

CM Date	Host Date	Good	VG	F	VF	XF
ND(ca.1620-21)	16Z1 (h)	27.50	45.00	90.00	165	—
ND(ca.1620-21)	ND(1621) (h)	27.50	45.00	90.00	165	—

TRADE COINAGE

KM# 63 GOLDGULDEN

3.5000 g., 0.9860 Gold 0.1109 oz. AGW **Obv:** Bremen arms, date divided at bottom in inner circle **Rev:** Crowned imperial eagle in inner circle, titles of Matthias **Note:** Fr. #398.

Date	Mintage	VG	F	VF	XF	Unc
1613 (d)	—	2,750	5,500	10,000	17,500	—

KM# 87 GOLDGULDEN

3.5000 g., 0.9860 Gold 0.1109 oz. AGW **Obv:** Bremen arms in inner circle, date in legend **Rev:** Crowned imperial eagle in inner circle, titles of Ferdinand II **Note:** Fr. 400. Varieties exist.

Date	Mintage	VG	F	VF	XF	Unc
1627 (f)	—	1,000	2,000	3,500	6,500	—
1635 TI	1,121	1,000	2,000	3,500	6,500	—

KM# 93 GOLDGULDEN

3.5000 g., 0.9860 Gold 0.1109 oz. AGW **Obv:** Bremen arms with supporters, date above in inner circle **Note:** Fr. #399. Varieties exist.

Date	Mintage	VG	F	VF	XF	Unc
1635 (g)	Inc. above	1,000	2,000	3,500	6,500	—
1637 (g)	—	1,000	2,000	3,500	6,500	—

KM# 94 GOLDGULDEN

3.5000 g., 0.9860 Gold 0.1109 oz. AGW **Obv:** Date divided below arms

Date	Mintage	VG	F	VF	XF	Unc
1637 (g)	—	—	—	—	—	—

KM# 103 GOLDGULDEN

3.5000 g., 0.9860 Gold 0.1109 oz. AGW **Rev:** Crowned imperial eagle in inner circle, titles of Ferdinand III **Note:** Fr. 404.

Date	Mintage	VG	F	VF	XF	Unc
1640 TI	—	750	1,500	3,000	5,500	—

KM# 109 2 GOLDGULDEN

7.0000 g., 0.9860 Gold 0.2219 oz. AGW **Obv:** Bremen arms with lion supporters, date above in inner circle **Rev:** Crowned imperial eagle in inner circle, titles of Ferdinand III **Note:** Fr. #403.

Date	Mintage	VG	F	VF	XF	Unc
1649 Rare	—	—	—	—	—	—

KM# 104 DUCAT

3.5000 g., 0.9860 Gold 0.1109 oz. AGW **Obv:** Ferdinand II standing divides date in inner circle **Rev:** Bremen arms with lion supporters in inner circle **Note:** Fr. #402.

Date	Mintage	VG	F	VF	XF	Unc
1640	116	400	900	1,750	3,500	—
1640 TI	Inc. above	400	900	1,750	3,500	—
1641	Inc. above	400	900	1,750	3,500	—
1641 TI	Inc. above	400	900	1,750	3,500	—
1642 TI	—	400	900	1,750	3,500	—
1652 TI	—	600	1,200	2,250	4,000	—

KM# 125 DUCAT

3.5000 g., 0.9860 Gold 0.1109 oz. AGW **Obv:** Leopold standing divides date in inner circle **Rev:** Crowned arms with lion supporters in inner circle **Note:** Fr. #412.

Date	Mintage	VG	F	VF	XF	Unc
1659 TI	—	600	1,200	2,250	4,000	—
1667 TI	—	600	1,200	2,250	4,000	—

KM# 149 DUCAT

3.5000 g., 0.9860 Gold 0.1109 oz. AGW **Note:** Fr. #413.

Date	Mintage	VG	F	VF	XF	Unc
167Z HL	—	650	1,500	2,500	5,250	—

KM# 105 2 DUCAT

7.0000 g., 0.9860 Gold 0.2219 oz. AGW **Obv:** Ferdinand III standing divides date in inner circle **Rev:** Crowned arms with lion supporters in inner circle **Note:** Fr. #401, 405.

Date	Mintage	VG	F	VF	XF	Unc
1640 TI	—	2,500	5,000	9,500	17,500	—
1652 TI	—	2,500	5,000	9,500	17,500	—

KM# 126 2 DUCAT

7.0000 g., 0.9860 Gold 0.2219 oz. AGW **Obv:** Leopold standing divides date in inner circle **Note:** Fr. 411.

Date	Mintage	VG	F	VF	XF	Unc
1659 TI	—	1,500	3,000	6,000	11,000	—
1667 TI	—	1,500	3,000	6,000	11,000	—

KM# 120 3 DUCAT

10.5000 g., 0.9860 Gold 0.3328 oz. AGW **Obv:** Ferdinand III standing divides date in inner circle **Rev:** Crowned arms with lion supporters in inner circle **Note:** Fr. #410.

Date	Mintage	VG	F	VF	XF	Unc
1659 TI Rare	—	—	—	—	—	—

PATTERNS

Including off metal strikes

KM#	Date	Mintage	Identification	Mkt Val
Pn1	1613	—	Thaler. Gold. KM#61	—
Pn2	1614	—	3 Grote. Gold. KM#65	—
Pn3	1617	—	12 Grote. Gold. KM#68	—
Pn4	1666	—	48 Grote. Gold. KM#135	—
Pn5	ND(1666)	—	1/12 Thaler. Gold. KM#136	—
Pn6	ND(1666)	—	1/12 Thaler. Gold. KM#137	—
Pn7	1666 TI	—	Thaler. Gold. KM#132	—
Pn8	1668	—	Thaler. Gold. KM#132	—
Pn9	ND(1671) HL	—	Schwaren. Gold. KM#145	—
Pn10	1671	—	2 Grote. Gold. KM#130	—
Pn11	1671 HL	—	4 Grote. Gold. KM#146	—
Pn12	1697	—	Schwaren. Gold. KM#155	2,000

BREMEN & VERDEN

The Archbishopric of Bremen and the Bishopric of Verden (which see) were taken by Sweden during the Thirty Years' War and joined together as a secular duchy. This action by Sweden was confirmed as part of the Peace of Westphalia which brought an end to the war in 1648. The King of Sweden was also entitled as Duke of Bremen and Verden. Except for a brief period of Danish rule (1702-04), Sweden continued its rule over the duchy until 1719, at which time it was transferred to the Electorate of Hannover.

RULERS

Johann Friedrich of Holstein-Gottorp, 1596-1634

SWEDISH RULERS

Queen Christina, 1648-54
Karl X Gustaf, 1654-60
Karl XI, 1660-97
Karl XII, 1697-1718

MINT OFFICIALS' INITIALS

Initial	Date	Name
AH	1670-76	Andreas Hille
HR	1615-18	Hans Rucke
ICA	1691-93	Julius Christian Arensburg
IS	1680-85	Jacob Schroeder
LM	1695-98	Lambert Marinus
MM	1659-60, 1666-70	Michael Moller
PT	1641-43, 49-50	Peter Timpf

DUCHY

REGULAR COINAGE

KM# 84 SECHSLING (1/2 Schilling; 1/96 Thaler)

Silver **Ruler:** Karl XI

Date	Mintage	VG	F	VF	XF	Unc
1674 AH	—	10.00	25.00	50.00	100	—
1675 AH	—	10.00	25.00	50.00	100	—
1676 AH	—	10.00	25.00	50.00	100	—
1680 IS	288,000	10.00	25.00	50.00	100	—
1681 IS	336,000	10.00	25.00	50.00	100	—
1682 IS	288,000	10.00	25.00	50.00	100	—
1683 IS	576,000	10.00	25.00	50.00	100	—
1684 IS	288,000	10.00	25.00	50.00	100	—
1685 IS	48,000	10.00	25.00	50.00	100	—

KM# 110 SECHSLING (1/2 Schilling; 1/96 Thaler)

Silver **Ruler:** Karl XI

Date	Mintage	VG	F	VF	XF	Unc
1691 ICS	82,000	13.00	27.00	55.00	110	—
1696 LM	145,000	13.00	27.00	55.00	110	—
1697 LM	177,000	13.00	27.00	55.00	110	—

KM# 50 2 SCHILLING

Silver **Ruler:** Queen Christina **Obv:** Crossed keys above cross (arms of Bremen & Verden) **Rev. Inscription:** II / SCHIL / LING / date

Date	Mintage	VG	F	VF	XF	Unc
(1)650 PT	3,000	45.00	90.00	165	325	—

KM# 75 1/48 THALER (Schilling)

Silver **Ruler:** Karl XI **Obv:** Crowned arms **Rev. Inscription:** 48 / REICHS / DALER / date

Date	Mintage	VG	F	VF	XF	Unc
1670	—	35.00	75.00	150	300	600
1671	—	35.00	75.00	150	300	600
1672	—	35.00	75.00	150	300	600

KM# 90 1/48 THALER (Schilling)

Silver **Ruler:** Karl XI **Rev. Inscription:** 48 / REICHS / DALER **Note:** Similar to 1/24 Thaler (KM#91).

Date	Mintage	VG	F	VF	XF	Unc
1676 AH	—	15.00	30.00	60.00	120	—
1685 IS	48,000	15.00	30.00	60.00	120	—

KM# 111 1/48 THALER (Schilling)

Silver **Ruler:** Karl XI **Obv:** Crowned C monogram **Rev. Inscription:** 48 / EIN / REICHS / THAL.

Date	Mintage	VG	F	VF	XF	Unc
1691 ICA	73,000	15.00	30.00	60.00	120	—

KM# 114 1/48 THALER (Schilling)

Silver **Ruler:** Karl XI **Obv:** Crowned C monogram **Rev. Inscription:** 48 EIN. R.D.

Date	Mintage	VG	F	VF	XF	Unc
1696 LM	83,000	15.00	30.00	60.00	120	—
1697 LM	144,000	15.00	30.00	60.00	120	—

KM# 60 1/24 THALER (Groschen; 2 Schilling)

Silver **Ruler:** Karl XI **Obv:** Crowned arms **Rev. Inscription:** 24 / E. REICHS / DALER / date

Date	Mintage	VG	F	VF	XF	Unc
1660 MM	—	33.00	65.00	115	230	—
1666 MM	—	33.00	65.00	115	230	—
1667 MM	—	33.00	65.00	115	230	—

KM# 65 1/24 THALER (Groschen; 2 Schilling)

Silver **Ruler:** Karl XI **Rev. Inscription:** 24 / I REICH / S DALER

Date	Mintage	VG	F	VF	XF	Unc
1668 MM	—	33.00	65.00	115	230	—

KM# 66 1/24 THALER (Groschen; 2 Schilling)

Silver **Ruler:** Karl XI **Rev. Inscription:** 24 / I REICH / S TALER

Date	Mintage	VG	F	VF	XF	Unc
1668 MM	—	33.00	65.00	115	230	—
1669 MM	—	33.00	65.00	115	230	—

KM# 76 1/24 THALER (Groschen; 2 Schilling)

Silver **Ruler:** Karl XI **Rev. Inscription:** 24 / I REICH / S DALER **Note:** Varieties exist.

Date	Mintage	VG	F	VF	XF	Unc
1670 AH	—	33.00	65.00	115	230	—
1671 AH	—	33.00	65.00	115	230	—
1672 AH	—	33.00	65.00	115	230	—
1673 AH	—	33.00	65.00	115	230	—

KM# 80 1/24 THALER (Groschen; 2 Schilling)

Silver **Ruler:** Karl XI **Obv:** Crowned script CRS monogram in circle **Rev. Inscription:** 24 / E RT / date

Date	Mintage	VG	F	VF	XF	Unc
1673 AH	—	45.00	90.00	180	—	—

KM# 81 1/24 THALER (Groschen; 2 Schilling)

Silver **Ruler:** Karl XI **Obv:** Monogram not in circle

Date	Mintage	VG	F	VF	XF	Unc
1673 AH	—	60.00	120	240	—	—

KM# 91 1/24 THALER (Groschen; 2 Schilling)

Silver **Ruler:** Karl XI **Rev. Inscription:** 24 / REICHS / DALER

Date	Mintage	VG	F	VF	XF	Unc
1676 AH	—	15.00	30.00	60.00	120	—
1682 IS	60,000	15.00	30.00	60.00	120	—

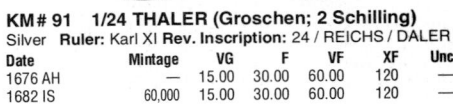

Date	Mintage	VG	F	VF	XF	Unc
1683 IS	48,000	15.00	30.00	60.00	120	—
1684 IS	60,000	15.00	30.00	60.00	120	—

KM# 100 1/24 THALER (Groschen; 2 Schilling)
Silver **Ruler:** Karl XI **Obv:** Crowned C monogram **Rev:** 3 sections - arms of Bremen, arms of Verden and value, and IS

Date	Mintage	VG	F	VF	XF	Unc
1682 IS Rare	—	—	—	—	—	—

KM# 112 1/24 THALER (Groschen; 2 Schilling)
Silver **Ruler:** Karl XI **Rev. Inscription:** 24 / EIN: / REICHS / THAL:

Date	Mintage	VG	F	VF	XF	Unc
1691 ICA	89,000	10.00	20.00	40.00	85.00	—
1692 ICA	94,000	10.00	20.00	40.00	85.00	—

KM# 115 1/24 THALER (Groschen; 2 Schilling)
Silver **Ruler:** Karl XI **Obv:** Crowned C monogram

Date	Mintage	VG	F	VF	XF	Unc
1696 LM	149,000	15.00	30.00	65.00	130	—
1697 LM	124,000	15.00	30.00	65.00	130	—

KM# 41 1/16 THALER (Dütchen; 3 Schilling)
Silver **Ruler:** Queen Christina **Obv:** Laureate bust of Queen Christina right **Rev. Inscription:** XVI / I REICH / DALER / date **Note:** Varieties exist.

Date	Mintage	VG	F	VF	XF	Unc
(1)649 PT	96,000	40.00	65.00	120	240	—
(1)650 PT	Inc. above	40.00	65.00	120	240	—

KM# 51 1/16 THALER (Dütchen; 3 Schilling)
Silver **Ruler:** Queen Christina **Obv:** Small bust

Date	Mintage	VG	F	VF	XF	Unc
1650 PT	—	30.00	60.00	120	240	—

KM# 62 1/16 THALER (Dütchen; 3 Schilling)
1.7500 g., Silver, 21 mm. **Ruler:** Karl XI **Obv:** Laureate bust of Karl XI right **Obv. Legend:** MON: NO: DUC. BREM. ET. VERD: **Rev. Inscription:** XVI / I REIC / HS DA / date **Note:** Ref. B-12a.

Date	Mintage	VG	F	VF	XF	Unc
1666 MM	—	45.00	90.00	180	360	—

KM# 63 1/16 THALER (Dütchen; 3 Schilling)
1.7500 g., Silver, 21 mm. **Ruler:** Karl XI **Obv:** Bust right in inner circle **Rev. Inscription:** XVI / I REIC(HS) / (HS) T(A)(H)(LER) / (date) **Note:** Ref. B-12b, 15, 19, 21. Varieties exist.

Date	Mintage	VG	F	VF	XF	Unc
1666 MM	—	33.00	60.00	120	240	—
1667 MM	—	33.00	60.00	120	240	—
1668 MM	—	33.00	60.00	120	240	—
1669 MM	—	33.00	60.00	120	240	—

KM# 67 1/16 THALER (Dütchen; 3 Schilling)
Silver **Ruler:** Karl XI **Obv:** Plain bust

Date	Mintage	VG	F	VF	XF	Unc
1668 MM Rare	—	—	—	—	—	—

KM# 77 1/16 THALER (Dütchen; 3 Schilling)
Silver **Ruler:** Karl XI **Obv:** Bust right in inner circle **Rev. Inscription:** SVI / REICHS / DALAR / date

Date	Mintage	VG	F	VF	XF	Unc
1670 AH	—	33.00	60.00	120	240	—

KM# 82 1/16 THALER (Dütchen; 3 Schilling)
Silver **Ruler:** Karl XI **Obv:** Crowned script CRS monogram **Rev. Inscription:** 16 / E R T / date **Note:** Varieties exist.

Date	Mintage	VG	F	VF	XF	Unc
1673 AH	—	75.00	150	300	—	—

KM# 101 1/12 THALER (4 Schilling)
Silver **Ruler:** Karl XI **Obv:** Crowned C monogram

Date	Mintage	VG	F	VF	XF	Unc
1682 IS	12,000	15.00	30.00	60.00	120	—

KM# 102 1/12 THALER (4 Schilling)
Silver **Ruler:** Karl XI **Obv:** Crowned C monogram **Note:** Klippe. Weight of 1/2 Thaler.

Date	Mintage	VG	F	VF	XF	Unc
1682 IS Rare	—	—	—	—	—	—

KM# 116 1/12 THALER (4 Schilling)
Silver **Ruler:** Karl XI **Rev. Inscription:** 12 / EIN R D. **Note:** Similar to 1/24 Thaler (KM#115).

Date	Mintage	VG	F	VF	XF	Unc
1696 LM	49,000	15.00	30.00	65.00	130	—
1697 LM	25,000	15.00	30.00	65.00	130	—

KM# 85 1/6 THALER (4 Groschen; 1/2 Mark)
Silver **Ruler:** Karl XI **Obv:** Bust of Karl XI right

Date	Mintage	VG	F	VF	XF	Unc
1674 AH	—	65.00	125	270	—	—
1675 AH	—	65.00	125	270	—	—

KM# 117 1/6 THALER (4 Groschen; 1/2 Mark)
Silver **Ruler:** Karl XII **Obv:** Bust right **Rev:** 2 crossed keys at left, cross at right

Date	Mintage	VG	F	VF	XF	Unc
1697 LM	9,194	60.00	120	240	—	—

KM# 86 1/3 THALER (1/2 Gulden; Mark)
Silver **Ruler:** Karl XI **Obv:** Bust of Karl XI right **Rev:** 2 crossed keys at left, cross at right

Date	Mintage	VG	F	VF	XF	Unc
1674 AH	—	450	700	1,300	2,200	—
1675 AH	—	325	500	800	1,450	—

KM# 118 1/3 THALER (1/2 Gulden; Mark)
Silver **Ruler:** Karl XII **Obv:** Older, larger bust

Date	Mintage	VG	F	VF	XF	Unc
1697 LM	5,000	—	—	—	—	—

KM# 119 1/3 THALER (1/2 Gulden; Mark)
Silver **Ruler:** Karl XII **Note:** Similar to 2/3 Thaler (KM#121).

Date	Mintage	VG	F	VF	XF	Unc
1697 LM	Inc. above	600	1,100	1,800	3,500	—

KM# 68 2 MARK
Silver **Ruler:** Karl XI **Obv:** Bust within inner circle **Rev:** Small crown

Date	Mintage	VG	F	VF	XF	Unc
1668	—	175	375	750	1,500	—

KM# 69 2 MARK
Silver **Ruler:** Karl XI **Note:** Similar to 4 Marks (KM#70)

Date	Mintage	VG	F	VF	XF	Unc
1668 MM	—	175	375	750	1,500	—
1670 AH	—	175	375	750	1,500	—

KM# 78 2 MARK
Silver **Ruler:** Karl XI **Note:** Similar to 4 Marks (KM#79).

Date	Mintage	VG	F	VF	XF	Unc
1670 (c)	—	375	750	1,500	3,000	—

KM# 87 2/3 THALER (Gulden; 2 Mark)
Silver **Ruler:** Karl XI **Obv:** Bust of Karl XI right **Rev:** 2 crossed keys at left, cross at right

Date	Mintage	VG	F	VF	XF	Unc
1674 AH	—	100	210	425	850	—
1675 AH	—	100	210	425	850	—

KM# 89 2/3 THALER (Gulden; 2 Mark)
Silver **Ruler:** Karl XI **Obv:** Bust without drapery

Date	Mintage	VG	F	VF	XF	Unc
1675 AH	—	150	250	425	850	—

KM# 120 2/3 THALER (Gulden; 2 Mark)
Silver **Ruler:** Karl XI **Obv:** Older, larger bust

Date	Mintage	VG	F	VF	XF	Unc
1697 LM	—	200	350	600	1,100	—

KM# 121 2/3 THALER (Gulden; 2 Mark)
Silver **Ruler:** Karl XII **Obv:** Bust right **Rev:** 2 crossed keys at left, cross at right

Date	Mintage	VG	F	VF	XF	Unc
1697 LM	5,000	325	450	800	1,550	—
1698/7 LM	30,000	200	350	625	1,100	—

KM# 42 THALER
Silver **Ruler:** Queen Christina **Obv:** Laureate bust of Christina right **Rev:** Crowned and supported arms, date divided below **Note:** Dav. #6280.

Date	Mintage	VG	F	VF	XF	Unc
1649 PT Unique	—	—	—	—	—	—

KM# 83 THALER
Silver **Ruler:** Karl XI **Obv:** Small bust of Karl XI right **Rev:** Crossed keys at left, cross at right **Note:** Dav. #6282.

Date	Mintage	VG	F	VF	XF	Unc
1673 AH	—	950	1,775	3,525	6,050	—
1674 AH	—	950	1,775	3,525	6,050	—

KM# 113 THALER
Silver **Ruler:** Karl XI **Obv:** Bust right **Rev:** Crowned and supported arms, date in legend **Note:** Dav. #6283.

Date	Mintage	VG	F	VF	XF	Unc
1692 ICA	6,111	1,000	1,875	3,700	6,325	—

KM# 61 4 MARK
Silver **Ruler:** Karl X Gustaf **Obv:** Script CGRS monogram **Note:** Varieties exist.

Date	Mintage	VG	F	VF	XF	Unc
1660 MM	—	400	775	1,375	2,200	—

KM# 64 4 MARK
Silver **Ruler:** Karl XI **Obv:** Crowned CRS monogram **Rev:** Crowned arms divide value 4 - M

Date	Mintage	VG	F	VF	XF	Unc
1666 MM	—	—	—	—	—	—
1667 MM	—	660	1,325	2,200	4,250	—
ND MM	—	660	1,325	2,200	4,250	—

KM# 70 4 MARK
Silver **Ruler:** Karl XI **Obv:** Crown above date, initials below

Date	Mintage	VG	F	VF	XF	Unc
1668 MM	—	225	500	880	1,375	—

KM# 79 4 MARK
Silver **Ruler:** Karl XI **Obv:** Bust within inner circle

Date	Mintage	VG	F	VF	XF	Unc
1670 AH	—	225	500	900	1,375	—

KM# 88 2 THALER
Silver **Ruler:** Karl XI **Obv:** Bust of Karl XI right **Rev:** 2 crossed keys at left, cross at right **Note:** Dav. #6281.

Date	Mintage	VG	F	VF	XF	Unc
1674 AH Rare	—	—	—	—	—	—

TRADE COINAGE

KM# 92 DUCAT
3.5000 g., 0.9860 Gold 0.1109 oz. AGW **Ruler:** Karl XI **Obv:** Laureate head of Karl XI right **Rev:** Entwined C's monogram with date above

Date	Mintage	VG	F	VF	XF	Unc
1676 AH Rare	—	—	—	—	—	—

KM# 52 5 DUCAT (1/2 Portugalöser)
17.5000 g., 0.9860 Gold 0.5547 oz. AGW **Ruler:** Queen Christina **Obv:** Laureate bust of Christina right in inner circle **Rev:** Crowned arms in inner circle, date below

Date	Mintage	VG	F	VF	XF	Unc
1650 PT Rare	—	—	—	—	—	—

KM# 53 10 DUCAT (Portugalöser)
35.0000 g., 0.9860 Gold 1.1095 oz. AGW **Ruler:** Queen Christina **Obv:** Laureate bust of Christina right in inner circle **Rev:** Crowned arms in inner circle, date below

Date	Mintage	VG	F	VF	XF	Unc
1650 PT Rare	—	—	—	—	—	—

BRESLAU

One of the chief cities of Silesia, Breslau is the present day Wroclaw in Poland, 135 miles (225 kilometers) east of Dresden and 200 miles (330 kilometers) southwest of Warsaw. The site was settled in the early 10th century and a bishopric was soon established in close proximity to the town. The bishop was made a Prince of the Empire in 1290 and he obtained the right to coin money at the same time. The fortunes of the bishopric closely followed those of the city. The portion of territory which came into the possession of Prussia was secularized in 1810.

RULERS
Johann VI of Sitsch, 1600-1608
Karl, Erzherzog of Österreich, 1608-1624
Karl Ferdinand, Prinz von Polen, 1625-1655
Leopold Wilhelm, Erzherzog of Österreich, 1655-1662
Karl Josef, Erzherzog of Österreich, 1662-1664
Sebastian of Rostock, 1664-1671
Friedrich, Landgraf of Hessen-Darmstadt, 1671-1682
Wolfgang Georg of Pfalz, elected 1682, not seated
Franz Ludwig, Pfalzgraf of Neuburg, 1683-1732

MINT OFFICIALS' INITIALS

Initial or marks	Date	Name
(a)=	1614-?	Valentin Jahn (Janus)
HR (b)= and/or	1612-53	Jans Rieger (Johann Rüger) der Ältere, warden and die-cutter
HR	1653-60	Han Rieger der Jüngere, warden
(c)= ✡	1618-20	Unknown
BZ	1620-24	Balthasar Zwirner (Zwürner), contractor
(d)=	1621-36	Johann Hans Riedel
(e)=	1624-27	Johann Jakob Huser, contractor
(f)= LPH/ЯH =	1678-1701	Leonhard Paul Haller, warden and mintmaster
(g)=	Ca. 1693	Unknown

ARMS
Breslau/Neisse – one to six lilies
Austria – horizontal shaded bar across middle of shield
Silesia – eagle, crescent moon on breast

NOTE: The arms of Neisse, a principality acquired by the bishops, are usually found on the episcopal coinage of Breslau, being practically identical one with the other.

REFERENCES

F/S = Ferdinand Friedensburg and Hans Seger, ***Schlesiens Münzen und Medaillen der neueren Zeit***, Breslau, 1901 (reprint Frankfurt/Main, 1976.

J/M = Norbert Jaschke and Fritz P. Maercker, ***Schlesische Münzen und Medaillen,*** Ihringen, 1985.

S = Hugo Frhr. Von Saurma-Jeltsch, ***Die Saurmasche Münzsammlung Deutscher, Schweizeerischer und Polnischer Gepräge von etwa dem Beginn der Groschenzeit bis zur Kipperperiode***, Berlin, 1892.

S/S = Hugo Frhr. Von Saurma-Jeltsch, ***Schlesische Münzen und Medaillen***, Breslau, 1883.

Sch = Wolfgangg Schulten, ***Deutsche Münzen aus der Zeit Karls V***, Frankfurt am Main, 1974.

BISHOPRIC

REGULAR COINAGE

KM# 45 3 HELLER
Copper **Ruler:** Karl **Obv:** Crowned shield of Austria divides date, value 'III H' in exergue **Note:** Ref. F/S#2642. Uniface.

Date	Mintage	VG	F	VF	XF	Unc
1622	—	8.00	15.00	35.00	70.00	—

KM# 46 4 HELLER (Kipper)
Copper **Ruler:** Karl **Obv:** Crowned shield of Austria-Burgundy arms **Rev:** Crowned 'N' divides date, IIII • H in exergue **Note:** Ref. F/S#2623, 2640.

Date	Mintage	VG	F	VF	XF	Unc
ND	—	8.00	15.00	35.00	70.00	—
16ZZ	—	8.00	15.00	35.00	70.00	—

KM# 47 4 HELLER (Kipper)
0.9100 g., Copper, 15 mm. **Ruler:** Karl **Obv:** Crowned shield of Austrian arms in ornamented frame **Rev:** 'N' divides date, IIII - H in exergue **Mint:** Neisse **Note:** Ref. F/S#2641.

Date	Mintage	VG	F	VF	XF	Unc
1622	—	8.00	15.00	35.00	70.00	—
16ZZ	—	8.00	15.00	35.00	70.00	—

KM# 179 GRöSCHL (Dreier; 3 Pfennig)

Silver **Ruler:** Franz Ludwig **Obv:** Oval 8-fold arms with central shield of Pfalz in baroque frame, miter above divides date **Rev:** Silesian eagle in oval baroque frame, crossed palm and laurel branches below **Note:** Ref. F/S#2737.

Date	Mintage	VG	F	VF	XF	Unc
1693 LPH	—	12.00	25.00	45.00	90.00	—

KM# 187 GRöSCHL (Dreier; 3 Pfennig)

Silver **Ruler:** Franz Ludwig **Obv:** Spanish shield in which 8-fold arms with central shield of Pfalz divide date, miter and electoral crown above **Rev:** Silesian eagle, crown above **Note:** Ref. F/S#2743, 2748.

Date	Mintage	VG	F	VF	XF	Unc
1699 LPH	—	12.00	28.00	40.00	85.00	—
1700 LPH	—	12.00	28.00	40.00	85.00	—

KM# 152 1/2 KREUZER

Silver **Ruler:** Friedrich **Obv:** Silesian eagle divides date above 2 small shields of arms, in left mintmaster's symbol, in right '1/2' **Note:** Ref. F/S#2673, 2702. Uniface.

Date	Mintage	VG	F	VF	XF	Unc
1678 (f)	—	8.00	16.00	35.00	75.00	—
1679 (f)	—	8.00	16.00	35.00	75.00	—

KM# 161 1/2 KREUZER

Silver **Ruler:** Friedrich **Obv:** Hessian lion rampant left in oval baroque frame, value '1/2' in oval below, date divided above arms, cardinal's hat at top **Note:** Ref. F/S#2716, 2721. Uniface.

Date	Mintage	VG	F	VF	XF	Unc
1680	—	8.00	16.00	35.00	75.00	—
1681	—	8.00	16.00	35.00	75.00	—
1681 LPH	—	8.00	16.00	35.00	75.00	—

KM# 168 1/2 KREUZER

Silver **Ruler:** Friedrich **Obv:** 4-fold arms divide date near bottom, cardinal's hat above **Rev:** Silesian eagle in laurel wreath **Note:** Ref. F/S#2725-26.

Date	Mintage	VG	F	VF	XF	Unc
1682	—	8.00	16.00	35.00	75.00	—
1682 LPH	—	8.00	16.00	35.00	75.00	—

KM# 169 1/2 KREUZER

Silver, 15.6 mm. **Ruler:** Friedrich **Obv:** 4-fold arms, date above **Rev:** Silesian eagle in laurel wreath **Note:** Ref. F/S#2727.

Date	Mintage	VG	F	VF	XF	Unc
1682	—	14.00	30.00	45.00	90.00	—

KM# 180 1/2 KREUZER

Silver **Ruler:** Franz Ludwig **Obv:** Oval 6-fold arms with central shield of Pfalz, '1/2' in small oval in lower half, all in baroque frame, miter above divides date **Note:** Ref. F/S#2738, 2753. Uniface.

Date	Mintage	VG	F	VF	XF	Unc
1693	—	12.00	28.00	40.00	85.00	175

KM# 162 KREUZER

Silver, 16 mm. **Ruler:** Friedrich **Obv:** Bust right in circle, value 'I' in small shield below **Obv. Legend:** FRID. S. R. E. C. LAN - HAS. EP. WRAT. **Rev:** Silesian eagle in circle, date at top **Rev. Legend:** PRO. DEO. ET - ECCLESIA. **Mint:** Breslau **Note:** Ref. F/S#2715, 2719-19a.

Date	Mintage	VG	F	VF	XF	Unc
1680 LPH (f)	—	15.00	30.00	50.00	100	165
1681 LPH (f)	—	15.00	30.00	50.00	100	165

KM# 165 KREUZER

Silver **Ruler:** Friedrich **Obv:** Bust right in circle, value '1' below, titles of Friedrich **Rev:** Silesian eagle in circle, date at top, value at bottom **Note:** Ref. F/S#2720.

Date	Mintage	VG	F	VF	XF	Unc
1681 LPH	—	20.00	40.00	70.00	145	—

KM# 184 KREUZER

Silver **Ruler:** Franz Ludwig **Obv:** Bust right, value '1' in oval below, titles of Franz Ludwig **Rev:** Oval 8-fold arms with central shield of Pfalz in baroque frame, miter above divides date, titles cont. **Note:** Ref. F/S#2741.

Date	Mintage	VG	F	VF	XF	Unc
1694 LPH	—	20.00	40.00	70.00	145	—

KM# 192 KREUZER

Silver **Ruler:** Franz Ludwig **Obv:** Bust right, value '1' in oval below, titles of Franz Ludwig **Rev:** Spanish shield with 8-fold arms with central shield of Pfalz, crown above divides date, titles cont. **Note:** Ref. F/S#2745.

Date	Mintage	VG	F	VF	XF	Unc
1700 LPH	—	12.00	28.00	40.00	85.00	—

KM# 191 KREUZER

Silver, 16 mm. **Ruler:** Franz Ludwig **Obv:** Bust right, value '1' in oval below, titles of Franz Ludwig **Rev:** Spanish shield in which 8-fold arms with central shield of Pfalz divides date, crown above, titles cont. **Note:** Ref. F/S#2746-47, 2751.

Date	Mintage	VG	F	VF	XF	Unc
1700 LPH	—	12.00	28.00	40.00	85.00	—

KM# 193 KREUZER

Silver **Ruler:** Franz Ludwig **Obv:** Bust right, value '1' in oval below, titles of Franz Ludwig **Rev:** Spanish shield with 8-fold arms with central shield of Pfalz, crown above round arms divides date, titles cont. **Note:** Ref. J/M#202.

Date	Mintage	VG	F	VF	XF	Unc
1700 LPH	—	12.00	28.00	40.00	85.00	—

KM# 19 3 KREUZER (Groschen)

Silver **Ruler:** Karl **Obv:** Bust right, value '3' in oval below, titles of Karl **Rev:** 3 small shields of arms, 1 above 2, titles cont. and date **Note:** Ref. F/S#2594, 2598, 2601-02, 2612-15, 2629-30. Varieties exist.

Date	Mintage	VG	F	VF	XF	Unc
1614 (a)	—	22.00	45.00	75.00	150	—
1615 (a)	—	22.00	45.00	75.00	125	—
1616 (a)	—	22.00	45.00	75.00	125	—
1617 (a)	—	22.00	45.00	75.00	150	—
1618 (a)	—	22.00	45.00	75.00	150	—
1618 (c)	—	22.00	45.00	75.00	150	—
1619 (c)	—	22.00	45.00	75.00	150	—
1620 (c)	—	22.00	45.00	75.00	150	—
1621 (c)	—	22.00	45.00	75.00	125	—
1621 (d)	—	22.00	45.00	75.00	125	—

KM# 49 3 KREUZER (Groschen)

Silver **Ruler:** Karl **Obv:** Bust right, value '3' in oval below, titles of Karl **Rev:** 3 small shields of arms, 1 above 2, titles cont. and date, small module and low-grade silver **Note:** Ref. F/S#2635-36. Kipper 3 Kreuzer.

Date	Mintage	VG	F	VF	XF	Unc
16ZZ	—	32.00	70.00	110	200	—
16ZZ (d)	—	32.00	70.00	110	200	—

KM# 50 3 KREUZER (Groschen)

Silver **Ruler:** Karl **Obv:** Bust right, value '3' in oval below, titles of Karl **Rev:** Eagle with arms of Austria on breast, titles cont. and date **Note:** Ref. F/S#2637.

Date	Mintage	VG	F	VF	XF	Unc
16ZZ	—	25.00	50.00	100	200	—

KM# 51 3 KREUZER (Groschen)

Silver **Ruler:** Karl **Obv:** Bust right, value '3' in oval below, titles of Karl **Rev:** Crowned arms of Austria in ornamented frame, titles cont. and date **Note:** Ref. F/S#2638.

Date	Mintage	VG	F	VF	XF	Unc
16ZZ	—	25.00	50.00	95.00	125	—

KM# 52 3 KREUZER (Groschen)

Silver **Ruler:** Karl **Obv:** Eagle of Silesia in circle, value '3' below, titles of Karl **Rev:** Crowned arms of Austria in ornamented frame, titles cont. and date **Note:** Ref. F/S#2639.

Date	Mintage	VG	F	VF	XF	Unc
16ZZ	—	25.00	50.00	100	200	—

KM# 125 3 KREUZER (Groschen)

Silver **Ruler:** Karl Ferdinand **Obv:** Bust right in circle, titles of Karl Ferdinand **Rev:** Crowned 4-fold arms with central shield in ornamented frame, '3' in oval below, titles cont. and date **Note:** Ref. S/S#152.

Date	Mintage	VG	F	VF	XF	Unc
1654	—	—	—	—	—	—

KM# 154 3 KREUZER (Groschen)

Silver **Ruler:** Friedrich **Obv:** Bust right in circle, value '3' in oval below, titles of Friedrich **Rev:** 4-fold arms with 4-fold central shield, cardinal's hat above divides date **Rev. Legend:** PRO. DEO ... **Note:** Ref. F/S#2701, 2714.

Date	Mintage	VG	F	VF	XF	Unc
1679 LPH (f)	—	17.00	35.00	75.00	155	—
1680 LPH (f)	—	17.00	35.00	75.00	155	—

KM# 181 3 KREUZER (Groschen)

Silver **Ruler:** Franz Ludwig **Obv:** Bust right, value '3' in oval below, titles of Franz Ludwig **Rev:** Oval 8-fold arms with central shield of Pfalz in baroque frame, miter above divides date, titles cont. **Note:** Ref. F/S#2736.

Date	Mintage	VG	F	VF	XF	Unc
1693 LPH (g)	—	—	—	—	—	—

KM# 155 6 KREUZER

Silver **Ruler:** Friedrich **Obv:** Bust right in circle, value VI in oval below, titles of Friedrich **Rev:** 4-fold arms with 4-fold central shield, cardinal's hat above divides date **Rev. Legend:** PRO. DEO ... **Note:** Ref. F/S#2699-2700, 2713.

Date	Mintage	VG	F	VF	XF	Unc
1679 (f)	—	—	—	—	—	—
1679 LPH (f)	—	20.00	40.00	80.00	160	—
1680 LPH (f)	—	20.00	40.00	80.00	160	—

KM# 182 6 KREUZER

Silver **Ruler:** Franz Ludwig **Obv:** Bust right, value VI in oval below, titles of Franz Ludwig **Rev:** Oval 8-fold arms with central shield of Pfalz in baroque frame, miter above divides date, titles cont. **Note:** Ref. F/S#2735, 2735a.

Date	Mintage	VG	F	VF	XF	Unc
1693 LPH (f)	—	15.00	35.00	75.00	150	—
1693 LPH (g)	—	15.00	35.00	75.00	150	—

KM# 53 12 KREUZER (Schreckenberger)

Silver **Ruler:** Karl **Obv:** Bust right in circle, titles of Karl **Rev:** 3 small shields of arms, 1 above 2, value '1Z' below, titles cont. and date **Note:** Ref. F/S#2634. Kipper 12 Kreuzer.

Date	Mintage	VG	F	VF	XF	Unc
1622	—	—	—	—	—	—

KM# 156 15 KREUZER (1/4 Gulden; 1/6 Thaler)

5.6600 g., Silver, 29.9 mm. **Ruler:** Friedrich **Obv:** Bust right in circle, value 'XV' in oval below, titles of Friedrich **Rev:** 4-fold arms with 4-fold central shield, cardinal's hat above divides date **Rev. Legend:** PRO. DEO ... **Edge:** Plain **Note:** Ref. F/S#2697-98, 2710-12. Prev. KM#401. Varieties exist.

Date	Mintage	VG	F	VF	XF	Unc
1679 ( )H (f)	—	—	—	—	—	—
1679 LPH (f)	—	25.00	50.00	100	200	—
1680 LPH (f)	—	25.00	50.00	100	200	—

KM# 183 15 KREUZER (1/4 Gulden; 1/6 Thaler)
6.3000 g., Silver, 30 mm. **Ruler:** Franz Ludwig **Obv:** Bust right, value 'XV' in oval below, titles of Franz Ludwig **Rev:** Oval 8-fold arms with central shield of Pfalz in baroque frame, miter above divides date, titles cont. **Note:** Ref. F/S#2733-34, 2740.

Date	Mintage	VG	F	VF	XF	Unc
1693 LPH (f)	—	20.00	45.00	80.00	160	—
1694 LPH (f)	—	20.00	45.00	80.00	160	—

KM# 41 24 KREUZER (Doppelschreckenberger)
Silver **Ruler:** Karl **Obv:** Bust right in circle, value 'Z4' below, titles of Karl **Rev:** Crowned manifold arms with central shield of Silisian eagle in ornamented frame, titles cont. **Note:** Ref. F/S#2621. Kipper 24 Kreuzer.

Date	Mintage	VG	F	VF	XF	Unc
ND(1621-22)	—	—	—	—	—	—

KM# 42 24 KREUZER (Doppelschreckenberger)
Silver **Ruler:** Karl **Obv:** Bust right in circle, value 'Z4' below, titles of Karl **Rev:** Small shield of Silesian eagle superimposed on floriated cross in ornamened shield, crown above, titles cont. **Note:** Ref. F/S#2622. Kipper 24 Kreuzer.

Date	Mintage	VG	F	VF	XF	Unc
ND(1621-22)	—	—	—	—	—	—

KM# 43 24 KREUZER (Doppelschreckenberger)
Silver **Ruler:** Karl **Obv:** Bust right in circle, value 'Z4' and date below, titles of Karl **Rev:** Crowned manifold arms with central shield of Silesian eagle in ornamented frame, titles cont. **Note:** Ref. F/S#2627, 2632. Kipper 24 Kreuzer. Varieties exist.

Date	Mintage	VG	F	VF	XF	Unc
16Z1	—	100	200	350	700	1,150
16ZZ	—	100	200	350	700	1,150

KM# 44 24 KREUZER (Doppelschreckenberger)
Silver **Ruler:** Karl **Obv:** Bust right in circle, value 'Z4' and date below, titles of Karl **Rev:** 2 small oval arms, miter on top of each to left and right of large crowned arms **Note:** Ref. F/S#2628. Kipper 24 Kreuzer.

Date	Mintage	VG	F	VF	XF	Unc
16Z1	—	95.00	180	360	—	—

KM# 54 24 KREUZER (Doppelschreckenberger)
Silver **Ruler:** Karl **Obv:** Bust right in circle, value 'Z4' below, titles of Karl **Rev:** Eagle with Austrian arms on breast, tail divides date where present **Note:** Ref. F/S#2620, 2633. Kipper 24 Kreuzer.

Date	Mintage	VG	F	VF	XF	Unc
16ZZ	—	20.00	45.00	90.00	—	—
ND	—	15.00	30.00	60.00	—	—

KM# 65 1/4 THALER
Silver **Ruler:** Karl Ferdinand **Obv:** Bust right, titles of Karl Ferdinand **Rev:** 2 adjacent shields of arms in baroque frames, miter above, date at bottom, titles cont. **Note:** Ref. F/S#2660. Hexagonal Klippe.

Date	Mintage	VG	F	VF	XF	Unc
163Z Rare	—	—	—	—	—	—

KM# 32 1/2 THALER
Silver **Ruler:** Karl **Obv:** Bust right in circle, titles of Karl **Rev:** Crowned ornate manifold arms, 2 small 4-fold arms with miter above to left and right, titles cont. and date **Note:** Ref. F/S#2600. Klippe.

Date	Mintage	VG	F	VF	XF	Unc
1616 (a + b) Rare	—	—	—	—	—	—

KM# 35 1/2 THALER
Silver **Ruler:** Karl **Obv:** Bust right in circle, titles of Karl **Rev:** Crowned ornate manifold arms, 2 small 4-fold arms with miter above to left and right, titles cont. and date **Note:** Ref. F/S#2611.

Date	Mintage	VG	F	VF	XF	Unc
1618 (a + b) Rare	—	—	—	—	—	—

KM# 55 1/2 THALER
Silver **Ruler:** Karl **Obv:** Bust right in circle, titles of Karl **Rev:** Crowned manifold arms with central shield of Silesian eagle in ornamented frame, date below arms, titles cont. **Note:** Ref. F/S#2631. Klippe.

Date	Mintage	VG	F	VF	XF	Unc
1622 (b) Rare	—	—	—	—	—	—

KM# 66 1/2 THALER
Silver **Ruler:** Karl Ferdinand **Obv:** Bust right in circle, titles of Karl **Rev:** Crowned ornate manifold arms, 2 small 4-fold arms with miter above to left and right, titles cont. and date **Note:** Ref. F/S#2657. Klippe.

Date	Mintage	VG	F	VF	XF	Unc
163Z Rare	—	—	—	—	—	—

KM# 67 1/2 THALER
Silver **Ruler:** Karl Ferdinand **Obv:** Bust right in circle, titles of Karl **Rev:** Crowned ornate manifold arms, 2 small 4-fold arms with miter above to left and right, titles cont. and date **Note:** Ref. F/S#2658. Octagonal Klippe.

Date	Mintage	VG	F	VF	XF	Unc
163Z Rare	—	—	—	—	—	—

KM# 68 1/2 THALER
Silver **Ruler:** Karl Ferdinand **Obv:** Bust right in circle, titles of Karl **Rev:** Crowned ornate manifold arms, 2 small 4-fold arms with miter above to left and right, titles cont. and date **Note:** Ref. F/S#2659. Hexagonal Klippe. Struck from same dies as 1/4 Thaler, KM#32, on thick flan.

Date	Mintage	VG	F	VF	XF	Unc
163Z Rare	—	—	—	—	—	—

KM# 98 1/2 THALER
Silver **Ruler:** Karl Ferdinand **Obv:** Bust right, titles of Karl Ferdinand **Rev:** 2 small oval arms, crossed crozier and scepter between, Eye of God above with rays streaming down, date at bottom **Rev. Legend:** OMNIS POTESTAS A DEO EST **Note:** Ref. F/S#2682. Octagonal Klippe.

Date	Mintage	VG	F	VF	XF	Unc
164Z HR Rare	—	—	—	—	—	—

KM# 112 1/2 THALER
Silver **Ruler:** Karl Ferdinand **Obv:** Bust left in circle, titles of Karl Ferdinand **Rev:** Crowned 4-fold arms with central shield divide date, titles cont. **Note:** Ref. S/S#146. Octagonal Klippe.

Date	Mintage	VG	F	VF	XF	Unc
1653 Rare	—	—	—	—	—	—

KM# 136 1/2 THALER
Silver **Ruler:** Karl Josef **Obv:** 4-fold arms with oval 4-fold inner arms and central shield in ornamented frame, miter above, titles of Sebastian **Rev:** Full-length figure of St. John the Baptist holding lamb divides date **Rev. Legend:** MUNIA ... **Note:** Ref. F/S#2686.

Date	Mintage	VG	F	VF	XF	Unc
1665	—	900	1,500	2,500	3,800	—

KM# 20 THALER
Silver **Ruler:** Karl **Obv:** Bust right in circle, titles of Karl **Rev:** Crowned ornate manifold arms, 2 small 4-fold arms with miter above to left and right, titles cont. and date **Note:** Ref. F/S#2593, 2597, 2610.

Date	Mintage	VG	F	VF	XF	Unc
1614 (a + b) Rare	—	—	—	—	—	—
1615 (a) Rare	—	—	—	—	—	—
1618 (a + b) Rare	—	—	—	—	—	—

KM# 56 THALER
Silver **Ruler:** Karl **Obv:** Bust right in circle, titles of Karl **Rev:** Crowned ornate manifold arms, 2 small 4-fold arms with miter above to left and right, titles cont. and date **Note:** Ref. J/M#183-84. Klippe.

Date	Mintage	VG	F	VF	XF	Unc
16ZZ Rare	—	—	—	—	—	—
ND(1623-24) BZ Rare	—	—	—	—	—	—

KM# 69 THALER
Silver **Ruler:** Karl Ferdinand **Obv:** Bust right, titles of Karl Ferdinand **Rev:** 2 adjacent shields of arms in baroque frames, miter above, date at bottom, titles cont. **Note:** Ref. F/S#2654.

Date	Mintage	VG	F	VF	XF	Unc
163Z	—	—	—	—	—	—

KM# 70 THALER
Silver **Ruler:** Karl Ferdinand **Obv:** Bust right, titles of Karl Ferdinand **Rev:** 2 adjacent shields of arms in baroque frames, miter above, date at bottom, titles cont. **Note:** Ref. F/S#2655. Dav. 5111. Octagonal Klippe.

Date	Mintage	VG	F	VF	XF	Unc
163Z	—	1,800	3,375	6,000	—	—

KM# 71 THALER
Silver **Ruler:** Karl Ferdinand **Obv:** Bust right, titles of Karl Ferdinand **Rev:** 2 adjacent shields of arms in baroque frames, miter above, date at bottom, titles cont. **Note:** Ref. F/S#2656. Hexagonal Klippe.

Date	Mintage	VG	F	VF	XF	Unc
163Z	—	—	—	—	—	—

KM# 88 THALER
Silver **Ruler:** Karl Ferdinand **Obv:** 3/4 facing bust **Obv. Legend:** KAR+FERD+PP+... **Rev:** Two oval shields with crossed Bishop's rod and staff, eye of God above **Rev. Legend:** OMNIS POTESTAS... **Note:** Dav. 5114.

Date	Mintage	VG	F	VF	XF	Unc
1639	—	1,025	1,980	3,600	6,480	—

KM# 89 THALER
Silver **Ruler:** Karl Ferdinand **Obv:** 3/4 facing bust **Obv. Legend:** KAR + FERD + ... **Rev:** 2 oval shields with crossed Bishop's rod and staff, eye of God above **Rev. Legend:** OMNIS POTESTAS ... **Note:** Octagonal klippe. Dav. 5114A.

Date	Mintage	VG	F	VF	XF	Unc
1639 Rare	—	—	—	—	—	—

KM# 90 THALER
Silver **Ruler:** Karl Ferdinand **Obv:** 3/4 facing bust **Obv. Legend:** KAR + FERD + PP + **Rev:** 2 oval shields with crossed Bishop's rod and staff, eye of God above **Rev. Legend:** OMNIS POTESTAS ... **Note:** Oval flan. Dav. 5114B.

Date	Mintage	VG	F	VF	XF	Unc
1639 Rare	—	—	—	—	—	—

KM# 100 THALER
Silver **Ruler:** Karl Ferdinand **Obv:** Bust right, titles of Karl Ferdinand **Rev:** 2 adjacent shields of arms in baroque frames, miter above, date at bottom, titles cont. **Note:** Dav.#5116A. Ref. F/S#2681. Klippe.

Date	Mintage	VG	F	VF	XF	Unc
164Z HR Rare	—	—	—	—	—	—

KM# 99 THALER
Silver **Ruler:** Karl Ferdinand **Obv:** Bust right **Obv. Legend:** CAROLVS•FERDINAN: D: G:... **Rev:** 2 oval shields with crossed Bishop's rod and staff, eye of God above **Rev. Legend:** OMNIS POTESTAS ... **Note:** Dav. 5116.

Date	Mintage	VG	F	VF	XF	Unc
1642	—	1,200	2,350	4,325	7,200	—

KM# 137 THALER
Silver **Ruler:** Sebastian **Obv:** 4-fold arms with oval 4-fold inner arms and central shield in ornamented frame, miter above, titles of Sebastian **Rev:** Full-length figure of St. John the Baptist holding lamb, divides date **Rev. Legend:** MUNUS ... **Note:** Ref. F/S#2685. Struck on 1/2 Thaler, KM#136 thick flan, same dies.

Date	Mintage	VG	F	VF	XF	Unc
1665	—	—	—	—	—	—

KM# 144 THALER

Silver **Ruler:** Sebastian **Obv:** Mitered ornamented shield **Obv. Legend:** SEBASTIANVS... **Rev:** St. John standing divides date **Rev. Legend:** MVNVS. CAESAR: - MAXIMILIANI. I: **Note:** Ausbeute Thaler. Dav. 5120.

Date	Mintage	VG	F	VF	XF	Unc
1667	—	1,050	2,475	5,500	9,900	16,500

KM# 157 THALER

Silver, 45 mm. **Ruler:** Friedrich **Obv:** Bust to right wearing cardinal's robes and skullcap **Obv. Legend:** FRIDERICVS. S. R. E. CARD. PNPS. LANDG. HASS. EPS. VRATISL. **Rev:** Shield of manifold arms in baroque frame, cardinal's hat above, Roman numeral date at end of legend **Rev. Legend:** * PRO * DEO * ET * ECCLES - IA * ANNO * **Note:** Dav. 5121.

Date	Mintage	VG	F	VF	XF	Unc
MDCLXXIX (1679)	—	550	1,100	2,200	4,675	8,650
MDCLXXX (1680)	—	550	1,100	2,200	4,675	8,650

KM# 185 THALER

Silver **Ruler:** Franz Ludwig **Obv:** Bust right **Obv. Legend:** FRANC. LUDOV. D. G... **Rev:** Capped ornamental shield **Rev. Legend:** COM. PALAT. RHENI ... **Note:** Dav. 5122.

Date	Mintage	VG	F	VF	XF	Unc
1694	—	600	1,150	2,150	3,575	—

KM# 21 2 THALER

Silver **Ruler:** Karl **Obv:** Bust right, titles of Karl **Rev:** Crowned ornate manifold arms, 2 small 4-fold arms with miter above to left and right, titles cont. and date **Note:** Ref. F/S#2592, 2609. Struck from same dies as Thaler, KM#20.

Date	Mintage	VG	F	VF	XF	Unc
1614 (a + b) Rare	—	—	—	—	—	—
1618 (a + b) Rare	—	—	—	—	—	—

KM# 60 2 THALER

Silver **Ruler:** Karl Ferdinand **Obv:** Bust of Karl right, date below **Obv. Legend:** CAR • FERD • P • P • ET • S • EPS • WRAT **Rev:** Bishop's hat above arms in cartouche **Rev. Legend:** A • IOVA • PRINCIPIVM **Note:** Dav. 5111. Klippe.

Date	Mintage	VG	F	VF	XF	Unc
1631	—	3,600	6,375	10,800	—	—

KM# 72 2 THALER

Silver **Ruler:** Karl Ferdinand **Obv:** Bust right, titles of Karl Ferdinand **Rev:** 2 adjacent shields of arms in baroque frames, miter above, date at bottom, titles cont. **Note:** Ref. F/S#2652.

Date	Mintage	VG	F	VF	XF	Unc
163Z Rare	—	—	—	—	—	—

KM# 73 2 THALER

Silver **Ruler:** Karl Ferdinand **Obv:** Bust right, titles of Karl Ferdinand **Rev:** 2 adjacent shields of arms in baroque frames, miter above, date at bottom, titles cont. **Note:** Ref. F/S#2653. Klippe.

Date	Mintage	VG	F	VF	XF	Unc
163Z Rare	—	—	—	—	—	—

KM# 93 2 THALER

Silver **Ruler:** Karl Ferdinand **Obv:** 3/4 facing bust **Obv. Legend:** KAR + FERD + PP + **Rev:** 2 oval shields with crossed Bishop's rod and staff, eye of God above **Rev. Legend:** OMNIS POTESTAS ... **Note:** Octagonal klippe. Dav. 5113A.

Date	Mintage	VG	F	VF	XF	Unc
1639 Rare	—	—	—	—	—	—

KM# 92 2 THALER

Silver **Ruler:** Karl Ferdinand **Obv:** 3/4 facing bust **Obv. Legend:** KAR + FERD + PP + **Rev:** 2 oval shields with crossed Bishop's rod and staff, eye of God above **Rev. Legend:** OMNIS POTESTAS ... **Note:** Dav. 5113.

Date	Mintage	VG	F	VF	XF	Unc
1639	—	2,700	4,875	8,175	13,800	—

KM# 101 2 THALER

Silver **Ruler:** Karl Ferdinand **Obv:** Bust right **Obv. Legend:** CAROLVS • FERDINAN: D: G: ... **Rev:** 2 oval shields with crossed Bishop's rod and staff, eye of God above **Rev. Legend:** OMNIS POTESTAS ... **Note:** Dav. 5115.

Date	Mintage	VG	F	VF	XF	Unc
1642	—	3,000	5,100	8,400	—	—

KM# 103 2 THALER

Silver **Ruler:** Karl Ferdinand **Obv:** Bust right **Obv. Legend:** CAROLVS • FERDINAN: D: G: **Rev:** 2 oval shields with crossed Bishop's rod and staff, eye of God above **Rev. Legend:** OMNIS POTESTAS ... **Note:** Hexagonal flan. Dav. 5115B.

Date	Mintage	VG	F	VF	XF	Unc
1642 Rare	—	—	—	—	—	—

KM# 104 2 THALER

Silver **Ruler:** Karl Ferdinand **Obv:** Bust left **Obv. Legend:** CAROLVS • FERDINAN: D: G: **Rev:** 2 oval shields with crossed Bishop's rod and staff, eye of God above **Rev. Legend:** OMNIS POTESTAS ... **Note:** Octagonal flan. Dav. 5115C.

Date	Mintage	VG	F	VF	XF	Unc
1642 Rare	—	—	—	—	—	—

KM# 102 2 THALER

Silver **Ruler:** Karl Ferdinand **Obv:** Bust right **Obv. Legend:** CAROLVS • FERDINAN: D: G: ... **Rev:** 2 oval shields with crossed Bishop's rod and staff, eye of God above **Rev. Legend:** OMNIS POTESTAS ... **Note:** Oval flan. Dav. 5115A.

Date	Mintage	VG	F	VF	XF	Unc
1642 Rare	—	—	—	—	—	—

KM# 105 2-1/2 THALER

Silver **Ruler:** Karl Ferdinand **Obv:** Bust right **Obv. Legend:** CAROLVS • FERDINAN: D: G: **Rev:** 2 oval shields with crossed Bishop's rod and staff, eye of God above **Rev. Legend:** OMNIS POTESTAS ... **Note:** Dav. 5115D.

Date	Mintage	VG	F	VF	XF	Unc
1642 Rare	—	—	—	—	—	—

KM# 106 2-1/2 THALER

Silver **Ruler:** Karl Ferdinand **Obv:** Bust right **Obv. Legend:** CAROLVS • FERDINAN: D: G: • **Rev:** 2 oval shields with crossed Bishop's rod and staff, eye of God above **Rev. Legend:** OMNIS POTESTAS ... **Note:** Hexagonal klippe. Dav. 5115E.

Date	Mintage	VG	F	VF	XF	Unc
1642 Rare	—	—	—	—	—	—

KM# 22 3 THALER

Silver **Ruler:** Karl **Obv:** Bust right in circle, titles of Karl **Rev:** Crowned ornate manifold arms, 2 small 4-fold arms with miter above to left and right, titles cont. and date **Note:** Ref. F/S#2591. Struck with same dies as Thaler, KM#20.

Date	Mintage	VG	F	VF	XF	Unc
1614 (a + b) Rare	—	—	—	—	—	—

KM# 94 3 THALER

Silver **Ruler:** Karl Ferdinand **Obv:** 3/4 facing bust **Obv. Legend:** KAR + FERD + PP + ... **Rev:** 2 oval shields with crossed Bishop's rod and staff, eye of God above **Rev. Legend:** OMNIS POTESTAS ... **Note:** Dav. 5113B.

Date	Mintage	VG	F	VF	XF	Unc
1639 Rare	—	—	—	—	—	—

KM# 107 3 THALER

Ruler: Karl Ferdinand **Obv:** Bust right, titles of Karl Ferdinand **Rev:** 2 adjacent shields of arms in baroque frames, miter above, date at bottom, titles cont. **Note:** Dav. #5115F. Ref. F/S#2673.

Date	Mintage	VG	F	VF	XF	Unc
164Z HR Rare	—	—	—	—	—	—

KM# 23 4 THALER

Silver **Ruler:** Karl **Obv:** Bust right in circle, titles of Karl **Rev:** Crowned ornate manifold arms, 2 small 4-fold arms with miter above to left and right, titles cont. and date **Note:** Ref. F/S#2590. Struck from same dies as Thaler, KM#20.

Date	Mintage	VG	F	VF	XF	Unc
1614 (a + b) Rare	—	—	—	—	—	—

KM# 95 4 THALER

Silver **Ruler:** Karl Ferdinand **Obv:** 3/4 facing bust **Obv. Legend:** KAR + FERD + PP + ... **Rev:** 2 oval shields with crossed Bishop's rod and staff, eye of God above **Rev. Legend:** OMNIS POTESTAS ... **Note:** Dav. 5113C.

Date	Mintage	VG	F	VF	XF	Unc
1639 Rare	—	—	—	—	—	—

TRADE COINAGE

KM# 174 1/6 DUCAT

0.5833 g., 0.9860 Gold 0.0185 oz. AGW **Ruler:** Franz Ludwig **Obv:** Bust of Franz Ludwig right **Rev:** Arms **Note:** Fr. 526.

Date	Mintage	VG	F	VF	XF	Unc
ND(1683-1732)	—	150	300	600	1,000	—

KM# 173 1/6 DUCAT

Gold **Ruler:** Franz Ludwig **Obv:** Bust right, value 1/6 in oval below bust, titles of Franz Ludwig **Rev:** Oval 8-fold arms with central shield of Pfalz in baroque frame, miter above divides date, titles cont. **Note:** Ref. F/S#2729; S/S#192, 194.

Date	Mintage	VG	F	VF	XF	Unc
1686	—	—	—	—	—	—
ND	—	—	—	—	—	—

KM# 36 1/2 DUCAT

1.7500 g., 0.9860 Gold 0.0555 oz. AGW **Ruler:** Karl **Obv:** Bust of Karl right in circle, date below in exergue, titles of Karl **Rev:** 3 small shields of arms, bottoms to center in trefoil style, titles cont. **Note:** Ref. F/S#2608; J/M#181a. Fr. 498. Varieties exist.

Date	Mintage	VG	F	VF	XF	Unc
1618	—	400	800	1,400	3,000	—

KM# 3 DUCAT

3.5000 g., 0.9860 Gold 0.1109 oz. AGW **Ruler:** Johann VI **Obv:** 4-fold arms with central shield of Sitsch (horizontal bar), miter above, titles of Johann VI **Rev:** Standing figure of St. John the Baptist **Note:** Fr. 484.

Date	Mintage	VG	F	VF	XF	Unc
ND(1600-08)	—	400	900	1,750	3,000	—

KM# 9 DUCAT

Gold **Ruler:** Karl **Obv:** Bust right in circle, titles of Karl **Rev:** Small shield of Silesian eagle superimposed on floriated cross in ornamented shield, crown above, titles cont. **Note:** Fr. #501. Ref. F/S#2619.

Date	Mintage	VG	F	VF	XF	Unc
ND(1608-24) Rare	—	—	—	—	—	—

KM# 14 DUCAT

3.5000 g., 0.9860 Gold 0.1109 oz. AGW **Ruler:** Karl **Obv:** Bust of Karl right **Rev:** Two shields of arms topped by crown and mitre **Note:** Fr. 486.

Date	Mintage	VG	F	VF	XF	Unc
1611	—	750	1,500	2,400	4,500	—
1612	—	750	1,500	2,400	4,500	—

KM# 15 DUCAT

3.5000 g., 0.9860 Gold 0.1109 oz. AGW **Ruler:** Karl **Subject:** Shooting Festival **Obv:** Two shields of arms topped by crown and mitre **Rev:** Five-line inscription with date above **Note:** Fr. 489.

Date	Mintage	VG	F	VF	XF	Unc
1612	—	675	1,350	2,100	4,150	—

KM# 25 DUCAT

3.5000 g., 0.9860 Gold 0.1109 oz. AGW **Ruler:** Karl **Obv:** Bust right in circle, titles of Karl **Rev:** 3 small shields of arms, 1 above 2, titles cont. and date **Note:** Fr. 496. Ref. F/S#2588.

Date	Mintage	VG	F	VF	XF	Unc
1614 (a)	—	675	1,450	2,250	4,350	—

KM# 26 DUCAT

Gold **Ruler:** Karl **Obv:** Bust right in circle, titles of Karl **Rev:** 3 small shields of arms, 1 above 2, date below, titles cont. **Note:** Ref. F/S#2589.

Date	Mintage	VG	F	VF	XF	Unc
1614 HR, (a)	—	950	1,850	3,750	6,250	—

KM# 37 DUCAT

3.5000 g., 0.9860 Gold 0.1109 oz. AGW **Ruler:** Karl **Obv:** Bust right in circle, titles of Karl **Rev:** Crowned manifold arms, titles cont. and date **Note:** Fr. 497. Ref. F/S#2607.

Date	Mintage	VG	F	VF	XF	Unc
1618	—	2,000	3,500	6,000	9,500	—

KM# 139 DUCAT

3.5000 g., 0.9860 Gold 0.1109 oz. AGW **Ruler:** Sebastian **Obv:** 4-fold arms with oval 4-fold inner arms and central shield in ornamented frame, miter above, titles of Sebastian **Rev:** Full-length figure of St. John the Baptist holding lamb, divides date **Rev. Legend:** MUNUS ... **Note:** Fr. 515. Ref. F/S#2684.

Date	Mintage	VG	F	VF	XF	Unc
1665 Rare	—	—	—	—	—	—

KM# A157 DUCAT

3.5000 g., 0.9860 Gold 0.1109 oz. AGW **Ruler:** Friedrich **Obv:** Bust of Frederich right **Rev:** Arms with cherub head above **Note:** Fr. 518.

Date	Mintage	VG	F	VF	XF	Unc
1679	—	700	1,600	2,500	4,500	—
1680	—	700	1,600	2,500	4,500	—
1681	—	700	1,600	2,500	4,500	—
1682	—	700	1,600	2,500	4,500	—

KM# 158 DUCAT

Gold **Ruler:** Friedrich **Obv:** Bust right in circle, titles of Friedrich **Rev:** 4-fold arms with 4-fold central shield, cardinal's hat above divides date **Rev. Legend:** PRO. DEO ... **Note:** Fr. #518. Ref. F/S#2695, 2708, 2718, 2724.

Date	Mintage	VG	F	VF	XF	Unc
1679 LPH (f)	—	700	1,600	2,500	4,500	—
1680 LPH (f)	—	700	1,600	2,500	4,500	—
1681 LPH (f)	—	700	1,600	2,500	4,500	—
1682 LPH (f)	—	700	1,600	2,500	4,500	—

KM# 175 DUCAT

3.5000 g., 0.9860 Gold 0.1109 oz. AGW **Ruler:** Franz Ludwig **Obv:** Bust right, titles of Franz Ludwig **Rev:** 4-fold arms in oval, slightly heart-shaped baroque frame, 4-fold central shield with inner shield of Pfalz, miter above divides date **Note:** Fr. 523. Ref. F/S#2730, 2732.

Date	Mintage	VG	F	VF	XF	Unc
1686	—	725	1,600	2,700	5,200	—
1688	—	725	1,600	2,700	5,200	—
1691	—	725	1,600	2,700	5,200	—
1693	—	725	1,600	2,700	5,200	—
1696	—	725	1,600	2,700	5,200	—
1700	—	725	1,600	2,700	5,200	—

KM# 189 DUCAT

Gold **Ruler:** Franz Ludwig **Obv:** Bust right, date below, titles of Franz Ludwig **Rev:** Crowned 8-fold arms with central shield of Pfalz, 4 small shield of arms around in cruciform **Note:** Fr. #524. Ref. F/S#2742, 2750.

Date	Mintage	VG	F	VF	XF	Unc
1699 LPH	—	2,000	3,500	6,000	10,000	—

KM# 5 2 DUCAT

7.0000 g., 0.9860 Gold 0.2219 oz. AGW **Ruler:** Johann VI **Obv:** Arms topped by mitre **Rev:** St. John standing **Note:** Fr. 483.

Date	Mintage	VG	F	VF	XF	Unc
1603	—	2,000	4,000	7,500	12,500	—

KM# 6 2 DUCAT

7.0000 g., 0.9860 Gold 0.2219 oz. AGW **Ruler:** Johann VI **Obv:** 4-fold arms with central shield of Sitsch (horizontal bar), miter above, titles of Johann VI **Rev:** 1/2-length figure of St. John the Baptist turned slightly to left, date in exergue **Rev. Legend:** MVNVS ... **Note:** Fr. 483a. Ref. F/S#2577.

Date	Mintage	VG	F	VF	XF	Unc
1603 Rare	—	—	—	—	—	—

KM# 10 2 DUCAT

7.0000 g., 0.9860 Gold 0.2219 oz. AGW **Ruler:** Karl **Obv:** Bust of Karl right **Rev:** Three shields abreast in inner circle

Date	Mintage	VG	F	VF	XF	Unc
ND(1608-24)	—	1,850	3,500	6,500	10,000	—

KM# 12 2 DUCAT

Gold **Ruler:** Karl **Obv:** Bust right in circle, titles of Karl **Rev:** 2 small oval arms, miter on top of each to left and right of large arms, titles cont. **Note:** Ref. F/S#2617. Struck on thick flan, probably from dies intended for Ducat, although not known for that denomination.

Date	Mintage	VG	F	VF	XF	Unc
ND(1608-24) Rare	—	—	—	—	—	—

KM# 11 2 DUCAT

Gold **Ruler:** Karl **Obv:** Bust right in circle, titles of Karl **Rev:** Small shield of Silesian eagle superimposed on floriated cross in ornamented shield, crown above, titles cont. **Note:** Ref. F/S#2618. Struck on thick flan from same dies as Ducat, KM#9.

Date	Mintage	VG	F	VF	XF	Unc
ND(1608-24)	—	2,000	4,000	8,000	15,000	—

KM# 16 2 DUCAT

7.0000 g., 0.9860 Gold 0.2219 oz. AGW **Ruler:** Karl **Subject:** Shooting Festival **Obv:** Two shields of armor topped by crown and mitre **Rev:** Five-line inscription with date above **Note:** Fr. 488.

Date	Mintage	VG	F	VF	XF	Unc
1612	—	1,250	2,250	4,250	7,500	—

KM# 75 2 DUCAT

7.0000 g., 0.9860 Gold 0.2219 oz. AGW **Ruler:** Karl Ferdinand **Obv:** Bust of Karl Ferdinand right **Rev:** Two shields of arms topped by mitre **Note:** Fr. 511.

Date	Mintage	VG	F	VF	XF	Unc
1632	—	1,750	3,250	6,500	10,000	—

KM# 76 2 DUCAT

7.0000 g., 0.9860 Gold 0.2219 oz. AGW **Ruler:** Karl Ferdinand **Obv:** Bust of Karl Ferdinand right **Rev:** 2 shields of arms topped by mitre **Note:** Octagonal klippe. Fr. 512.

Date	Mintage	VG	F	VF	XF	Unc
1632 Rare	—	—	—	—	—	—

KM# 131 2 DUCAT

Gold **Ruler:** Karl Ferdinand **Obv:** Bust right **Obv. Legend:** CAROLUS FERDINANDUS ... **Rev:** Crowned oval 4-fold arms, date in legend **Note:** Ref. S/S#149.

Date	Mintage	VG	F	VF	XF	Unc
1654 Rare	—	—	—	—	—	—

KM# 141 2 DUCAT

7.0000 g., 0.9860 Gold 0.2219 oz. AGW **Ruler:** Sebastian **Obv:** Bust to right **Rev:** Arms **Note:** Fr. 514.

Date	Mintage	VG	F	VF	XF	Unc
1665 Rare	—	—	—	—	—	—

KM# 142 2 DUCAT

7.0000 g., 0.9860 Gold 0.2219 oz. AGW **Ruler:** Sebastian **Obv:** 4-fold arms with oval 4-fold inner arms and central shield in ornamented frame, miter above, titles of Sebastian **Rev:** Full-length figure of St. John the Baptist holding lamb divides date **Rev. Legend:** MUNUS CAESAR MAXIMILIANI I **Note:** Fr. 515a. Ref. F/S#2683.

Date	Mintage	VG	F	VF	XF	Unc
1665	—	3,560	7,000	11,500	20,000	—

KM# 159 2 DUCAT

7.0000 g., 0.9860 Gold 0.2219 oz. AGW **Ruler:** Friedrich **Obv:** Facing enthroned figure of St. Wenzel holding imperial orb and flag, titles of Friedrich **Rev:** Ornate manifold arms under cardinal's hat, date divided at top **Rev. Legend:** PRO DEO ... **Note:** Ref. J/M#198.

Date	Mintage	VG	F	VF	XF	Unc
1679 Rare	—	—	—	—	—	—

KM# 160 2 DUCAT

Gold **Ruler:** Friedrich **Obv:** Bust right in circle, titles of Friedrich **Rev:** 4-fold arms with 4-fold central shield, cardinal's hat above divides date **Rev. Legend:** PRO DEO ... **Note:** Fr. #517. Ref. F/S#2694, 2706, 2727, 2723.

Date	Mintage	VG	F	VF	XF	Unc
1679 LPH (f)	—	1,750	3,500	6,500	10,000	—
1680 LPH (f)	—	1,750	3,500	6,500	10,000	—
1681 LPH (f)	—	1,750	3,500	6,500	10,000	—
1682 LPH (f)	—	1,750	3,500	6,500	10,000	—

KM# 164 2 DUCAT

Gold **Ruler:** Friedrich **Obv:** Facing bust in circle, titles of Friedrich **Rev:** 4-fold arms with 4-fold central shield, angel's head and wings above, sunface below **Note:** Ref. F/S#2707.

Date	Mintage	VG	F	VF	XF	Unc
1680 LPH Rare	—	—	—	—	—	—

KM# 166 2 DUCAT

Gold **Ruler:** Friedrich **Obv:** Bust right in circle, titles of Friedrich **Rev:** 4-fold arms with 4-fold central shield, angel's head and wings above arms and sunface below

Date	Mintage	VG	F	VF	XF	Unc
1681 LPH Rare	—	—	—	—	—	—

KM# 172 2 DUCAT

7.0000 g., 0.9860 Gold 0.2219 oz. AGW **Ruler:** Friedrich **Obv:** Bust right, titles of Friedrich **Rev:** Small oval arms in baroque frame, angel's head and wings above arms and sunface below **Note:** Fr. 517a. Ref. F/S#2722.

Date	Mintage	VG	F	VF	XF	Unc
1682 LPH Rare	—	—	—	—	—	—

KM# 177 2 DUCAT

7.0000 g., 0.9860 Gold 0.2219 oz. AGW **Ruler:** Franz Ludwig **Obv:** Bust to right **Rev:** Shield of manifold arms, mitre above divides date **Note:** Fr. 522.

Date	Mintage	VG	F	VF	XF	Unc
1690	—	1,350	2,750	5,500	9,500	—
1693	—	1,350	2,750	5,500	9,500	—

KM# 7 3 DUCAT

10.5000 g., 0.9860 Gold 0.3328 oz. AGW **Ruler:** Johann VI **Obv:** 4-fold arms with central shield of Sitsch (horizontal bar), mitr above, titles of Johann VI **Rev:** 1/2-length figure of St. John the Baptist turned slightly to left, date in exergue **Rev. Legend:** MVNVS ... **Note:** Klippe. Fr. 482. Ref. F/S#2576. Struck on square flan from same dies as 2 Ducat, KM#6.

Date	Mintage	VG	F	VF	XF	Unc
1603 Rare	—	—	—	—	—	—

KM# 17 3 DUCAT

10.5000 g., 0.9860 Gold 0.3328 oz. AGW **Ruler:** Karl **Subject:** Shooting Festival **Obv:** Two shields of arms topped by crown and mitre **Rev:** Five-line inscription with date above **Note:** Fr. 487.

Date	Mintage	VG	F	VF	XF	Unc
1612 Rare	—	—	—	—	—	—

KM# 27 3 DUCAT

10.5000 g., 0.9860 Gold 0.3328 oz. AGW **Ruler:** Karl **Obv:** Large bust right beaks circle at top, titles of Karl **Rev:** Crowned ornate manifold arms, 2 small 4-fold arms with miter above to left and right, titles cont. and date **Note:** Fr. 495. Ref. F/S#2587. Varieties exist.

Date	Mintage	VG	F	VF	XF	Unc
1614 (a) Rare	—	—	—	—	—	—
1618 (a + b) Rare	—	—	—	—	—	—

KM# 77 3 DUCAT
10.5000 g., 0.9860 Gold 0.3328 oz. AGW, 30 mm. **Ruler:** Karl Ferdinand **Obv:** Bust to right **Obv. Legend:** CAR: FERDINAND. D.G. PR. POL: ET SVEC: **Rev:** Two adjacent ornately-shaped shields of 4-fold arms with central shields, mitre above, date at bottom **Rev. Legend:** EPISCOPVS. WRATISLAVIENSIS. **Mint:** Breslau **Note:** Fr. 509; F/S 2651.

Date	Mintage	VG	F	VF	XF	Unc
1632	—	2,500	5,000	9,000	16,500	—

Note: An example in VF realized approximately $7,000 in May 2009 Hess-Divo auction. Künker Auction 171, VF-XF realized approximately $15,970

KM# 78 3 DUCAT
10.5000 g., 0.9860 Gold 0.3328 oz. AGW **Ruler:** Karl Ferdinand **Obv:** Bust of Karl Ferdinand right **Rev:** 2 shields of arms topped by mitre **Note:** Klippe. Fr. 510.

Date	Mintage	VG	F	VF	XF	Unc
1632 Rare	—	—	—	—	—	—

KM# 133 3 DUCAT
Gold **Ruler:** Karl Ferdinand **Obv:** Bust right in inner circle **Obv. Legend:** CAROLUS FERDINANDUS ... **Rev:** 4-fold arms, date in legend **Note:** Ref. S/S#148. Klippe.

Date	Mintage	VG	F	VF	XF	Unc
1654 Rare	—	—	—	—	—	—

KM# 150 3 DUCAT
10.5000 g., 0.9860 Gold 0.3328 oz. AGW **Ruler:** Friedrich **Obv:** Bust right in circle, titles of Friedrich **Rev:** Squarish 4-fold arms with crowned 4-fold central shield divide date near bottom, miter and electoral hat above, cardinal's hat over all **Rev. Legend:** PRO. DEO ... **Note:** Fr. 516. Ref. F/S#2689.

Date	Mintage	VG	F	VF	XF	Unc
1674 Rare	—	—	—	—	—	—

KM# 38 4 DUCAT
14.0000 g., 0.9860 Gold 0.4438 oz. AGW **Ruler:** Karl **Obv:** Bust right in circle, titles of Karl **Rev:** Crowned ornate manifold arms, 2 small 4-fold arms with miter above to left and right, titles cont. and date **Note:** Fr. 494. Ref. F/S#2605.

Date	Mintage	VG	F	VF	XF	Unc
1618 (a + b) Rare	—	—	—	—	—	—

KM# 79 4 DUCAT
14.0000 g., 0.9860 Gold 0.4438 oz. AGW **Ruler:** Karl Ferdinand **Obv:** Bust to right **Rev:** Crowned arms **Note:** Fr. 508.

Date	Mintage	VG	F	VF	XF	Unc
1632 Rare	—	—	—	—	—	—

KM# 121 4 DUCAT
Gold **Ruler:** Karl Ferdinand **Obv:** Bust left in circle, titles of Karl Ferdinand **Rev:** Crowned 4-fold arms with central shield divide date, titles cont. **Note:** Ref. S/S#143. Klippe

Date	Mintage	VG	F	VF	XF	Unc
1653 Rare	—	—	—	—	—	—

KM# 134 4 DUCAT
Gold **Ruler:** Balthasar **Obv:** Bust right **Obv. Legend:** CAROLUS FERDINANDUS ... **Rev:** Crowned oval 4-fold arms, date in legend **Note:** Ref. S/S#147. Octagonal Klippe.

Date	Mintage	VG	F	VF	XF	Unc
1654 Rare	—	—	—	—	—	—

KM# 33 5 DUCAT (1/2 Portugalöser)
Gold **Ruler:** Karl **Obv:** Bust right in circle, titles of Karl **Rev:** Crowned ornate manifold arms, 2 small 4-fold arms with miter above to left and right, titles cont. and date **Note:** Fr. #493. Ref. F/S#2599, 2616. Varieties exist.

Date	Mintage	VG	F	VF	XF	Unc
1616 (a + b)	—	—	—	—	—	—
ND BZ	—	—	—	—	—	—

KM# 80 5 DUCAT (1/2 Portugalöser)
17.5000 g., 0.9860 Gold 0.5547 oz. AGW **Ruler:** Karl Ferdinand **Obv:** Bust to right **Rev:** Crowned arms **Note:** Fr. 506.

Date	Mintage	VG	F	VF	XF	Unc
1632 Rare	—	—	—	—	—	—
1639 Rare	—	—	—	—	—	—

KM# 81 5 DUCAT (1/2 Portugalöser)
17.5000 g., 0.9860 Gold 0.5547 oz. AGW **Ruler:** Karl Ferdinand **Obv:** Bust of Karl Ferdinand right **Rev:** Crowned arms **Note:** Klippe. Fr. 507.

Date	Mintage	VG	F	VF	XF	Unc
1632 Rare	—	—	—	—	—	—

KM# 28 6 DUCAT
Gold **Ruler:** Karl **Obv:** Large bust right breaks circle at top, titles of Karl **Rev:** Crowned ornate manifold arms, 2 small 4-fold arms with miter above to left and right, titles cont. and date **Note:** Fr. #492. Ref. F/S#2586.

Date	Mintage	VG	F	VF	XF	Unc
1614 (a + b) Rare	—	—	—	—	—	—

KM# 82 6 DUCAT
21.0000 g., 0.9860 Gold 0.6657 oz. AGW **Ruler:** Karl Ferdinand **Obv:** Bust to right **Note:** Fr. 504.

Date	Mintage	VG	F	VF	XF	Unc
1632 Rare	—	—	—	—	—	—
1639 Rare	—	—	—	—	—	—

KM# 83 6 DUCAT
21.0000 g., 0.9860 Gold 0.6657 oz. AGW **Ruler:** Karl Ferdinand **Obv:** Bust of Karl Ferdinand right **Note:** Klippe. Fr. 505.

Date	Mintage	VG	F	VF	XF	Unc
1632 Rare	—	—	—	—	—	—

KM# 29 7 DUCAT
Gold **Ruler:** Karl **Obv:** Bust right in circle, titles of Karl **Rev:** Crowned ornate manifold arms, 2 small 4-fold arms with miter above to left and right, titles cont. and date **Note:** Ref. J/M#180a. Struck from same dies as Thaler, KM#20.

Date	Mintage	VG	F	VF	XF	Unc
1614 (a + b) Rare	—	—	—	—	—	—

KM# 39 7 DUCAT
Gold **Ruler:** Karl **Obv:** Large bust right breaks circle at top, titles of Karl **Rev:** Crowned ornate manifold arms, 2 small 4-fold arms with miter above to left and right, titles cont. and date **Note:** Fr. #491. Ref. F/S#2604.

Date	Mintage	VG	F	VF	XF	Unc
1618 (a + b) Rare	—	—	—	—	—	—

KM# 146 9 DUCAT
Gold **Ruler:** Sebastian **Obv:** Mitred ornamented shield **Obv. Legend:** SEBASTIANVS ... **Rev:** St. John standing divides date **Rev. Legend:** MVNVS. CAESAR: - MAXIMILIANI. I" **Note:** Fr. 513. Ref. F/S#2687. Struck with Thaler dies, KM #144.

Date	Mintage	VG	F	VF	XF	Unc
1667 Rare	—	—	—	—	—	—

KM# 31 10 DUCAT (Portugalöser)
Gold **Ruler:** Karl **Obv:** Bust right in circle, titles of Karl **Rev:** Crowned ornate manifold arms, 2 small 4-fold arms with miter above to left and right, titles cont. and date **Note:** Fr. #490. Ref. F/S#2596, 2603. Struck from same dies as Thaler, KM#20.

Date	Mintage	VG	F	VF	XF	Unc
1615 (a + b) Rare	—	—	—	—	—	—
1618 (a + b) Rare	—	—	—	—	—	—

KM# 62 10 DUCAT (Portugalöser)
Gold **Ruler:** Karl Ferdinand **Obv:** Bust of Karl right, date below **Obv. Legend:** CAR • FERD • P • P • ET • S • EPS • WRAT **Rev:** Bishop's hat above arms in cartouche **Rev. Legend:** A • IOVA • PRINCIPIVM. **Note:** Ref. S/S#123; J/M#192-93. Struck from same dies as 2 Thaler, KM#60.

Date	Mintage	VG	F	VF	XF	Unc
1631 Rare	—	—	—	—	—	—
1631 CVB (e) Rare	—	—	—	—	—	—

KM# 86 10 DUCAT (Portugalöser)
Gold **Ruler:** Karl Ferdinand **Obv:** Bust right in circle, titles of Karl Ferdinand **Rev:** 2 oval shields with crossed Bishop's rod and staff, eye of God above **Rev. Legend:** OMNIS POTESTAS ... **Note:** Ref. F/S#2661.

Date	Mintage	VG	F	VF	XF	Unc
1638 Rare	—	—	—	—	—	—

KM# 85 10 DUCAT (Portugalöser)
35.0000 g., 0.9860 Gold 1.1095 oz. AGW **Ruler:** Karl Ferdinand **Obv:** Bust to right **Rev:** Arms **Note:** Fr. 503.

Date	Mintage	VG	F	VF	XF	Unc
1638 Rare	—	—	—	—	—	—

KM# 96 10 DUCAT (Portugalöser)
35.0000 g., 0.9860 Gold 1.1095 oz. AGW **Ruler:** Karl Ferdinand **Obv:** 3/4 facing bust **Obv. Legend:** KAR + FERD + PP + **Rev:** 2 oval shields with crossed Bishop's rod and staff, eye of God above **Rev. Legend:** OMNIS POTESTAS ... **Note:** Fr. 503a. Struck with Thaler dies, KM #88.

Date	Mintage	VG	F	VF	XF	Unc
1639 Rare	—	—	—	—	—	—

Note: Heritage NY Signature Sale 2008, 1-10, XF realized $22,655

KM# 110 10 DUCAT (Portugalöser)
35.0000 g., 0.9860 Gold 1.1095 oz. AGW **Ruler:** Karl Ferdinand **Obv:** Bust right **Obv. Legend:** CAROLVS • FERDINAN: D: G: ... **Rev:** 2 oval shields with crossed Bishop's rod and staff, eye of God above **Rev. Legend:** OMNIS POTESTAS ... **Note:** Fr. 503b. Struck with Thaler dies, KM #99.

Date	Mintage	VG	F	VF	XF	Unc
1642 Rare	—	—	—	—	—	—

KM# 109 10 DUCAT (Portugalöser)
Gold **Ruler:** Karl Ferdinand **Obv:** Bust right **Obv. Legend:** CAROLVS • FERDINAN: D: G: ... **Rev:** 2 oval shields with crossed Bishop's rod and staff, eye of God above **Rev. Legend:** OMNIS POTESTAS ... **Note:** Ref. F/S#2672. Struck from same dies as Thaler, KM#99.

Date	Mintage	VG	F	VF	XF	Unc
164Z Rare	—	—	—	—	—	—

KM# 123 10 DUCAT (Portugalöser)
Gold **Ruler:** Karl Ferdinand **Obv:** Bust left in circle, titles of Karl Ferdinand **Rev:** Crowned 4-fold arms with central shield divide date, titles cont. **Note:** Ref. S/S#140. Struck from same dies as Thaler, KM#113.

Date	Mintage	VG	F	VF	XF	Unc
1653 Rare	—	—	—	16,500	28,000	—

KM# 63 15 DUCAT
Gold **Ruler:** Karl Ferdinand **Obv:** Bust of Karl right, date below **Obv. Legend:** CAR • FERD • P • P • ET • S • EPS • WRAT. **Rev:** Bishop's hat above arms in cartouche **Rev. Legend:** A • IOVA • PRINCIPIVM **Note:** Struck from same dies as 2 Thaler, KM#60.

Date	Mintage	VG	F	VF	XF	Unc
1631 CVB (e) Rare	—	—	—	—	—	—

KM# 84 15 DUCAT
52.5000 g., 0.9860 Gold 1.6642 oz. AGW **Ruler:** Karl Ferdinand **Obv:** Bust right, titles of Karl Ferdinand **Rev:** 2 adjacent shields of arms in baroque frames, miter above, date at bottom, titles cont. **Note:** Fr. 502. Ref. F/S#2645. Struck from same dies as Thaler, KM#69.

Date	Mintage	VG	F	VF	XF	Unc
163Z Rare	—	—	—	—	—	—

CITY

After its founding in the early 10th century, Breslau was subject to Poland until it became the capital of the Duchy of Middle Silesia in 1163. Duke Heinrich VI gave the already semi-autonomous city the mint right in 1318. Breslau came under the rule of Bohemia in 1360 and for most of the time up until 1526 maintained some semblance of independence. In that year, all of Bohemia and Silesia became Habsburg domains, but as a result of a war with Prussia, Breslau was ceded to the latter in 1741. A city coinage was struck until about the early 18th century, and a Prussian mint operated in Breslau from about 1750 until the late 19th century.

MINT OFFICIALS' INITIALS

Initial	Date	Name
HR (sometimes in ligature)	1622-36	Hans Riedel (Rüdel)

REFERENCES

F/S = Ferdinand Friedensburg and Hans Seger, ***Schlesiens Münzen und Medaillen der neueren Zeit***, Breslau, 1901 (reprint Frankfurt/Main, 1976.

J/M = Norbert Jaschke and Fritz P. Maercker, ***Schlesische Münzen und Medaillen,*** Ihringen, 1985.

S = Hugo Frhr. Von Saurma-Jeltsch, ***Die Saurmasche Münzsammlung Deutscher, Schweizerischer und Polnischer Gepräge von etwa dem Beginn der Groschenzeit bis zur Kipperperiode***, Berlin, 1892.

S/S = Hugo Frhr. Von Saurma-Jeltsch, ***Schlesische Münzen und Medaillen***, Breslau, 1883.

Sch = Wolfgang Schulten, ***Deutsche Münzen aus der Zeit Karls V,*** Frankfurt am Main, 1974.

REGULAR COINAGE

KM# 276 HELLER
Copper, 11-12 mm. **Obv:** Date above large 'W' **Rev:** Crowned 'F' in circle within wreath **Note:** F/S-3473, 3488. Kipper issue.

Date	Mintage	VG	F	VF	XF	Unc
16Z1	—	30.00	60.00	125	250	—
16ZZ	—	—	—	—	—	—

KM# 280 HELLER
Copper **Obv:** Crowned 'W' divides date **Note:** Ref. S/S#114. Uniface. Kipper Heller.

Date	Mintage	VG	F	VF	XF	Unc
1622	—	14.00	22.00	45.00	90.00	—

KM# 281 3 HELLER

Copper **Obv:** Trefoil divides date, Bohemian lion in upper arch, Silesian eagle to lower left, 'W' lower right **Note:** Ref. S/S#115-16. Uniface. Kipper 3 Heller.

Date	Mintage	VG	F	VF	XF	Unc
1622 HR	—	18.00	35.00	75.00	150	—
1623 HR	—	18.00	35.00	75.00	150	—

KM# 277 3 KREUZER (Groschen)

Silver **Obv:** 4-fold arms with central shield, date at end of legend **Obv. Legend:** MONETA. S. P. Q. WRATISL. **Rev:** Silesian eagle, value '3' in oval below, titles of Ferdinand II **Note:** Fr. #3472, 3485-86.

Date	Mintage	VG	F	VF	XF	Unc
1621 HR	—	35.00	75.00	125	240	—
1622 HR	—	35.00	75.00	125	240	—

KM# 278 24 KREUZER (Doppelschreckenberger)

Silver **Obv:** 4-fold arms with central shield in ornamented frame **Obv. Legend:** MONETA. S. P. Q. WRATISLAVIENSIS. **Rev:** Silesian eagle in circle, value 'Z4' below, titles of Ferdinand II and date **Note:** Fr. #3471, 3481.

Date	Mintage	VG	F	VF	XF	Unc
16Z1	—	50.00	90.00	150	310	—
16ZZ	—	50.00	90.00	150	310	—

KM# 282 24 KREUZER (Doppelschreckenberger)

Silver **Obv:** 4-fold arms with central shield in ornamented frame **Obv. Legend:** MONETA. S.P.Q. WRATISLAVIENSIS. **Rev:** High collared bust right in circle, value 'Z4' below, titles of Ferdinand II and date **Note:** Fr. #3482, 3484.

Date	Mintage	VG	F	VF	XF	Unc
16ZZ HR	—	50.00	90.00	160	300	—
ND	—	50.00	90.00	160	300	—

KM# 283 24 KREUZER (Doppelschreckenberger)

Silver **Obv:** 4-fold arms with central shield in ornamented frame **Obv. Legend:** MONETA. S.P.Q. WRATISLAVIENSIS. **Rev:** High collared bust right in circle, value Z4 below, titles of Ferdinand II and date **Note:** Fr. #3483. Klippe.

Date	Mintage	VG	F	VF	XF	Unc
16ZZ HR	—	—	—	—	—	—

KM# 301 1/4 THALER

Silver **Obv:** Oval 4-fold arms with central shield in baroque frame, ornate helmet above, date at end of legend **Obv. Legend:** MON. NOV. ... **Rev:** Laureate armored bust right, titles of Leopold I **Note:** Fr. #3501.

Date	Mintage	VG	F	VF	XF	Unc
1662	—	1,100	2,000	3,750	6,500	—

KM# 284 1/2 THALER

Silver **Obv:** 4-fold arms with central shield, ornate helmet above divides date at top **Obv. Legend:** MONETA ... **Rev:** Laureate high collared bust right, titles of Ferdinand II **Note:** Ref. S/S#106.

Date	Mintage	VG	F	VF	XF	Unc
1622 HR	—	—	—	—	—	—

KM# 297 1/2 THALER

Silver **Obv:** 4-fold arms with central shield, ornate helmet aabove divides date **Obv. Legend:** PRÆMIVM. DILIGENTIÆ. PRO. SCHOLIS. S. P. Q. WRAT. **Rev:** Crowned bust right, titles of Ferdinand III **Note:** Ref. F/S#3515, 3517.

Date	Mintage	VG	F	VF	XF	Unc
1643	—	—	—	—	—	—
1646	—	1,900	3,600	6,800	—	—

KM# 302 1/2 THALER

Silver **Obv:** Oval 4-fold arms with central shield in baroque frame, ornate helmet above, date at end of legend **Obv. Legend:** MON. NOV. ... **Rev:** Laureate armored bust right, titles of Leopold I **Note:** Ref. F/S#3500.

Date	Mintage	VG	F	VF	XF	Unc
1662 Rare	—	—	—	—	—	—

KM# 286 THALER

Silver **Obv:** Bust right in inner circle **Obv. Legend:** FERDINA • D:G • RO ... **Rev:** Helmeted arms **Rev. Legend:** MONETA • S • P.Q. WRATISLAVIENS **Note:** Dav. #5123A. Ref. F/S#3480. Klippe.

Date	Mintage	VG	F	VF	XF	Unc
16ZZ HR Rare	—	—	—	—	—	—

KM# 285 THALER

Silver **Obv:** Helmeted arms **Obv. Legend:** MONETA • S • P. Q. WRATISLAVIENS **Rev:** Bust of Ferdinand II to right **Rev. Legend:** FERDINA • D: G • RO... **Note:** Dav. 5123.

Date	Mintage	VG	F	VF	XF	Unc
16ZZ	—	805	1,700	3,450	6,325	—

KM# 298 THALER

Silver **Subject:** Scholastic Prize **Obv:** 4-fold arms with central shield, ornate helmet above divides date **Obv. Legend:** PRÆMIVM. DILIGENTIÆ. PRO. SCHOLIS. S. P. Q. WRAT. **Rev:** Crowned bust right, titles of Ferdinand III **Note:** Ref. F/S#3514, 3516.

Date	Mintage	VG	F	VF	XF	Unc
1643	—	1,380	2,875	5,750	9,200	—
1646	—	—	—	—	—	—

KM# 303 THALER

Silver **Obv:** Helmeted arms **Obv. Legend:** MON. NOV... WRATISLAV **Rev:** Bust of Leopold I to right **Rev. Legend:** LEOPOLD. D. G. R... **Note:** Dav. 5124.

Date	Mintage	VG	F	VF	XF	Unc
1662	—	975	2,025	3,750	7,475	—

KM# 309 THALER

Silver **Obv:** 4-fold arms with central shield in baroque frame, date at end of legend **Obv. Legend:** MONETA NOVA ... **Rev:** Laureate bust right, titles of Leopold I **Note:** Ref. F/S#3504.

Date	Mintage	VG	F	VF	XF	Unc
1670 Rare	—	—	—	—	—	—

Note: Künker Auction 135, 1-08, XF realized approximately $10,360

TRADE COINAGE

KM# 271 1/2 DUCAT

Gold **Subject:** Coronation of Friedrich von der Pfalz **Obv:** Crowned 'F' in wreath **Rev:** Intertwined double 'W' in wreath **Note:** Ref. J/M#379.

Date	Mintage	VG	F	VF	XF	Unc
ND(1619)	—	—	—	—	—	—

KM# 288 1/2 DUCAT

1.7500 g., 0.9860 Gold 0.0555 oz. AGW **Obv:** Crowned arms **Rev:** Crowned bust of Ferdinand II to right **Note:** Fr. 469.

Date	Mintage	VG	F	VF	XF	Unc
1622	—	375	750	1,500	2,800	—

KM# 295 1/2 DUCAT

1.7500 g., 0.9860 Gold 0.0555 oz. AGW **Ruler:** Karl Ferdinand **Obv:** Crowned imperial eagle, shield of arms on breast, date at end of legend **Rev:** Crowned bust of Ferdinand III to right in circle **Note:** Previous KM #95.

Date	Mintage	VG	F	VF	XF	Unc
1642	—	450	900	1,800	3,500	—

KM# 305 1/2 DUCAT
Gold **Obv:** Oval 4-fold arms with central shield in baroque frame, ornate helmet above, date at end of legend **Obv. Legend:** MON. NOV. ... **Rev:** Laureate armored bust right, titles of Leopold I **Note:** Ref. S/S#129.

Date	Mintage	VG	F	VF	XF	Unc
1662	—	—	—	—	—	—

KM# 250 DUCAT
3.5000 g., 0.9860 Gold 0.1109 oz. AGW **Obv:** Shield of 4-fold arms, with central shield, in circle, date at end of legend **Rev:** Crowned bust of Matthias II to right **Note:** Fr. 457.

Date	Mintage	VG	F	VF	XF	Unc
1611	—	475	950	1,800	3,200	—
1612	—	475	950	1,800	3,200	—
1613	—	475	950	1,800	3,200	—

KM# 261 DUCAT
3.5000 g., 0.9860 Gold 0.1109 oz. AGW **Subject:** Shooting Festival **Rev:** 6-line inscription with date **Note:** Fr. 461.

Date	Mintage	VG	F	VF	XF	Unc
1614	—	650	1,150	2,400	4,750	—

KM# 267 DUCAT
3.5000 g., 0.9860 Gold 0.1109 oz. AGW **Rev:** Crowned bust of Matthias to right in circle **Note:** Fr. 464.

Date	Mintage	VG	F	VF	XF	Unc
1617	—	550	1,100	2,000	3,750	—

KM# 273 DUCAT
3.5000 g., 0.9860 Gold 0.1109 oz. AGW **Obv:** Crowned Bohemian lion left above 4-fold arms with central shield of Electoral Pfalz superimposed on lion, date at end of legend **Obv. Legend:** MONE. AVRE ... **Rev:** Crowned bust right, titles of Friedrich **Note:** Fr. 466.

Date	Mintage	VG	F	VF	XF	Unc
1620 Rare	—	—	—	—	—	—

Note: Fritz Rudolf Künker Münzenhandlung Auction 140, 6-08, nearly XF realized approximately $17,050.

KM# 289 DUCAT
3.5000 g., 0.9860 Gold 0.1109 oz. AGW **Obv:** Crowned bust of Ferdinand II to right **Rev:** Crowned arms **Note:** Fr. 468.

Date	Mintage	VG	F	VF	XF	Unc
1622	—	1,000	2,000	3,500	6,500	—

KM# 292 DUCAT
3.5000 g., 0.9860 Gold 0.1109 oz. AGW **Obv:** Christ on cross, balance scale over date divided by arms **Rev:** Crowned bust of Ferdinand III to right in circle **Note:** Fr. 471.

Date	Mintage	VG	F	VF	XF	Unc
1630	—	425	850	1,550	2,900	—

KM# 299 DUCAT
3.5000 g., 0.9860 Gold 0.1109 oz. AGW **Obv:** Crowned arms **Rev:** Crowned bust of Ferdinand III to right **Note:** Previous KM #110.

Date	Mintage	VG	F	VF	XF	Unc
1646	—	750	1,500	2,900	5,600	—

KM# 306 DUCAT
Gold **Obv:** Oval 4-fold arms with central shield in baroque frame, ornate helmet above, date at end of legend **Obv. Legend:** MON. NOV. ... **Rev:** Laureate armored bust right, titles of Leopold I **Note:** Ref. S/S#128.

Date	Mintage	VG	F	VF	XF	Unc
1662 Rare	—	—	—	—	—	—

KM# 251 2 DUCAT
7.0000 g., 0.9860 Gold 0.2219 oz. AGW **Obv:** Ornate helmet divides date above shield of 4-fold arms with central shield **Rev:** Large crowned bust of Matthias II to right **Note:** Fr. 455.1.

Date	Mintage	VG	F	VF	XF	Unc
1611	—	800	1,600	3,600	7,000	—

KM# 252 2 DUCAT
7.0000 g., 0.9860 Gold 0.2219 oz. AGW **Obv:** Ornate helmet divides date above shield of 4-fold arms with central shield **Rev:** Small crowned bust of Matthias to right in circle **Note:** Fr. 455.2.

Date	Mintage	VG	F	VF	XF	Unc
1612	—	1,250	2,500	5,000	10,000	—

KM# 254 2 DUCAT
7.0000 g., 0.9860 Gold 0.2219 oz. AGW **Obv:** Crowned bust of Matthias II right **Rev:** Arms in inner circle **Note:** Fr. 456. Klippe. Struck with Ducat dies, KM #250.

Date	Mintage	VG	F	VF	XF	Unc
1612 Rare	—	—	—	—	—	—

KM# 253 2 DUCAT
Gold **Note:** Ref. J/M#377a. Similar to KM#252 (Fr.#455), but dated 1612 below arms and 1613 divided by crest on helmet

Date	Mintage	VG	F	VF	XF	Unc
1612-1613	—	800	1,450	3,200	5,750	—

KM# 263 2 DUCAT
Gold **Subject:** Shooting Festival **Obv:** Helmeted arms of Breslau **Rev:** 5-line inscription with date above **Note:** Fr. #460a. Ref. F/S#3464. Klippe.

Date	Mintage	VG	F	VF	XF	Unc
1614	—	—	—	—	—	—

KM# 262 2 DUCAT
7.0000 g., 0.9860 Gold 0.2219 oz. AGW **Subject:** Shooting Festival **Obv:** Helmeted arms of Breslau **Rev:** Five-line inscription with date above **Note:** Fr. 460.

Date	Mintage	VG	F	VF	XF	Unc
1614	—	1,200	2,400	4,800	8,500	—

KM# 268 2 DUCAT
7.0000 g., 0.9860 Gold 0.2219 oz. AGW **Obv:** Crowned F, inscription over arms **Rev:** Crowned bust of Matthias to right **Note:** Fr. 462.

Date	Mintage	VG	F	VF	XF	Unc
1617	—	500	1,150	2,500	4,750	—

KM# 269 2 DUCAT
7.0000 g., 0.9860 Gold 0.2219 oz. AGW **Obv:** Crowned arms **Rev:** Bust right **Note:** Fr. 463. Klippe. Struck with Ducat dies, KM #267.

Date	Mintage	VG	F	VF	XF	Unc
1617	—	775	1,850	3,750	7,500	—

KM# 274 2 DUCAT
7.0000 g., 0.9860 Gold 0.2219 oz. AGW **Obv:** 4-fold arms with central shield, ornate helmet above, crest of helmet divides date **Obv. Legend:** MONETA. AVREA ... **Rev:** Crowned bust right within double legend with titles of Friedrich **Note:** Fr. 465. Ref. F/S#3469.

Date	Mintage	VG	F	VF	XF	Unc
1620 Rare	—	—	—	—	—	—

Note: Fritz Rudolf Künker Münzenhandlung Auction 140, 6-08, VF realized approximately $17,050.

KM# 293 2 DUCAT
7.0000 g., 0.9860 Gold 0.2219 oz. AGW **Obv:** Christ on cross, balance scale over date divided by arms **Note:** Fr. 470.

Date	Mintage	VG	F	VF	XF	Unc
1630	—	525	1,150	2,650	5,000	—

KM# 307 2 DUCAT
Gold **Obv:** Oval 4-fold arms with central shield in baroque frame, ornate helmet above, date at end of legend **Obv. Legend:** MON. NOV. ... **Rev:** Laureate armored bust right, titles of Leopold I **Note:** Ref. S/S#127.

Date	Mintage	VG	F	VF	XF	Unc
1662	—	—	—	—	—	—

KM# 255 3 DUCAT
10.5000 g., 0.9860 Gold 0.3328 oz. AGW **Obv:** Shield of arms in circle **Rev:** Crowned bust of Matthias to right **Note:** Fr. 453.

Date	Mintage	VG	F	VF	XF	Unc
1612	—	1,500	3,000	6,000	10,000	—

KM# 256 3 DUCAT
10.5000 g., 0.9860 Gold 0.3328 oz. AGW **Obv:** Crowned bust of Matthias II right **Rev:** Arms in inner circle **Note:** Klippe. Fr. 454.

Date	Mintage	VG	F	VF	XF	Unc
1612 Rare	—	—	—	—	—	—

KM# 264 3 DUCAT
10.5000 g., 0.9860 Gold 0.3328 oz. AGW **Subject:** Shooting Festival **Obv:** Helmeted arms of Breslau **Rev:** 5-line inscription with date above **Note:** Klippe. Fr. 459.

Date	Mintage	VG	F	VF	XF	Unc
1614	—	—	8,250	12,625	18,700	—

KM# 265 3 DUCAT
10.5000 g., 0.9860 Gold 0.3328 oz. AGW **Subject:** Shooting Festival **Obv:** Helmeted arms of Breslau **Rev:** 6-line inscription with date **Note:** Fr. 458.

Date	Mintage	VG	F	VF	XF	Unc
1614 Rare	—	2,200	4,400	8,250	12,625	—

KM# 290 3 DUCAT
10.5000 g., 0.9860 Gold 0.3328 oz. AGW **Obv:** Crowned shield of arms **Rev:** Crowned bust of Ferdinand II to right **Note:** Klippe. Fr. 467.

Date	Mintage	VG	F	VF	XF	Unc
1622	—	—	6,600	11,000	18,700	—

KM# 257 4 DUCAT
14.0000 g., 0.9860 Gold 0.4438 oz. AGW **Obv:** Crowned shield of arms **Rev:** Crowned bust of Matthias to right **Note:** Fr. 452.

Date	Mintage	VG	F	VF	XF	Unc
1612 Rare	—	—	—	—	—	—

KM# 258 5 DUCAT (1/2 Portugalöser)
17.5000 g., 0.9860 Gold 0.5547 oz. AGW **Obv:** Crowned shield of arms **Rev:** Crowned bust of Matthias to right **Note:** Fr. 450.

Date	Mintage	VG	F	VF	XF	Unc
1612 Rare	—	—	—	—	—	—

KM# 259 5 DUCAT (1/2 Portugalöser)
17.5000 g., 0.9860 Gold 0.5547 oz. AGW **Obv:** Crowned shield of arms **Rev:** Crowned bust of Matthias to right **Note:** Klippe. Fr. 451.

Date	Mintage	VG	F	VF	XF	Unc
1612 Rare	—	—	—	—	—	—

PATTERNS
Including off metal strikes

KM#	Date	Mintage	Identification	Mkt Val
Pn3	1613	—	2 Ducat. Lead. Ref. J/M#377. Klippe. KM#254 (Fr#456).	—
Pn4	MDCLXX VI (1676	—	1/2 Thaler. Copper. Bust right, titles of Friedrich. Capped arms. * PRO * DEOTCCLES .... Ref. J/M#197b. Sim. to Thaler, KM#58. (Dav. #5121.)	—

KM#	Date	Mintage	Identification	Mkt Val
Pn5	MDCLXX VI (1676)	—	Ducat. Silver. Bust right in circle, titles of Friedrich. 4-fold arms with 4-fold central shield, cardinal's hat above, no value or R.N. date in upper left. Ref. S/S#164. Similar to 3 Kreuzer, KM#154.	—
Pn6	MDCLXX VI (1676)	—	Ducat. Copper. Bust right in circle, titles of Friedrich. 4-fold arms with 4-fold central shield, cardinal's hat above, no value or date. Ref. F/S#2690. KM#154.	—

BRUNSWICK

FREE CITY

The city of Brunswick (German: Braunschweig) is located on the Oker River in northern Germany, 37 miles (62 kilometers) southeast of Hannover and 53 miles (88 kilometers) northwest of Magdeburg. Founded about 861 by Bruno of Saxony, the town became an important place in the late Middle Ages and was an early member of the Hanseatic League. The dukes of Brunswick made the city their early capital and never relinquished their control completely. The city was granted the right to produce its own coins, however, first in 1296 and reiterated in 1345. The municipal coinage was produced in considerable quantities during the 16th and most of the 17th centuries. Brunswick became a Protestant enclave during the Reformation and suffered during the Thirty Years' War. It was included in the Kingdom of Westphalia from 1807 until 1813. In 1834, Brunswick gained its independence from the duke and enjoyed self-rule from that point onwards into the modern age.

MINT OFFICIALS' MARKS & INITIALS

Mark	Desc.	Date	Name
		1599-1600, 1606-09	Peter Schrader (or Schröder)
(b) =  or 		1620-48	Paul Becker
(c) =  or HB		1648-67	Hans Becker
	B/IGB	1675-85	Johann Georg Breuer
	BH	1675-76	Bastian Hille

ARMS

Rampant lion to left

Patron saint – St. Author

REGULAR COINAGE

KM# 15.1 FLITTER

Copper Weight varies: 0.57-0.66g., 13-14 mm. **Obv:** Rampant lion to left, B between forepaws, in wreath **Rev:** 4-line inscription with date, where present, in wreath **Rev. Inscription:** I / FLIT / TER / (date) **Note:** Ref. J-94, 96, 98. Kipper issue.

Date	Mintage	VG	F	VF	XF	Unc
(1)6Z0	—	22.00	40.00	85.00	170	—
(1)6Z1	—	22.00	40.00	85.00	170	—
ND1621-2)	—	22.00	40.00	85.00	170	—

KM# 15.2 FLITTER

Copper Weight varies: 0.73-1.02g., 13-14 mm. **Obv:** Rampant lion to left in wreath **Rev:** 4-line inscription with date in wreath **Rev. Inscription:** I / FLIT / TER / (date) **Note:** Ref. J-95. Kipper issue.

Date	Mintage	VG	F	VF	XF	Unc
16Z0	—	22.00	40.00	85.00	170	—

KM# 15.3 FLITTER

Copper Weight varies: 0.50-0.53g., 13-14 mm. **Obv:** Rampant lion left, B below **Rev:** 4-line inscription with date, where present **Rev. Inscription:** I / FLIT / TER / (date) **Note:** Ref. J-96a, 97. Kipper issue.

Date	Mintage	VG	F	VF	XF	Unc
(1)6Z1	—	22.00	40.00	85.00	170	—
ND(1621-2)	—	22.00	40.00	85.00	170	—

KM# 16 3 FLITTER

0.6000 g., Copper, 15 mm. **Obv:** Large 'B' between 4 annulets **Rev:** City arms without shield, value III above **Note:** Ref. J-99. Kipper issue.

Date	Mintage	VG	F	VF	XF	Unc
ND(1620-22)	—	—	—	—	—	—

KM# A17 3 FLITTER

Copper, 15 mm. **Obv:** Rampant lion right **Rev:** 4-line inscription with date **Rev. Inscription:** III / FLIT / TER / (date) **Note:** Kipper issue.

Date	Mintage	VG	F	VF	XF	Unc
16Z1	—	22.00	45.00	90.00	185	—

KM# 32 PFENNIG

Silver Weight varies: 0.33-0.40g., 8x10 mm. **Obv:** Rampant lion to left, B below, date divided above 1-62-5 **Note:** Ref. J-229. Uniface. Klippe.

Date	Mintage	VG	F	VF	XF	Unc
1625	—	—	—	—	—	—

KM# 34 PFENNIG

Silver Weight varies: 0.40-0.57g., 20 mm. **Obv:** Rampant lion left in center of cup-shaped depression, date below on rim divided by B **Note:** Ref. J#254-65. Uniface hohlpfennig type.

Date	Mintage	VG	F	VF	XF	Unc
1627	—	13.00	27.00	55.00	110	—
1632	—	13.00	27.00	55.00	110	—
1635	—	13.00	27.00	55.00	110	—
1637	—	13.00	27.00	55.00	110	—
1638	—	13.00	27.00	55.00	110	—
1641	—	13.00	27.00	55.00	110	—
1644	—	13.00	27.00	55.00	110	—
1649	—	—	—	—	—	—
Note: Reported, not confirmed.						
1650	—	13.00	27.00	55.00	110	—
1653	—	13.00	27.00	55.00	110	—
1655	—	—	—	—	—	—
Note: Reported, not confirmed.						
1657	—	13.00	27.00	55.00	110	—

KM# 36 PFENNIG

Silver Weight varies: 0.22-0.42g., 13-14 mm. **Obv:** Rampant lion to left, B divides date below **Note:** Ref. J#230-53, 301. Uniface.

Date	Mintage	VG	F	VF	XF	Unc
1628	—	11.00	22.00	45.00	90.00	—
1629	—	11.00	22.00	45.00	90.00	—
1630	—	11.00	22.00	45.00	90.00	—
1631	—	11.00	22.00	45.00	90.00	—
1633	—	11.00	22.00	45.00	90.00	—
1634	—	11.00	22.00	45.00	90.00	—
1635	—	11.00	22.00	45.00	90.00	—
1636	—	—	—	—	—	—
Note: Reported, not confirmed.						
1637	—	10.00	22.00	45.00	90.00	—
1638	—	10.00	22.00	45.00	90.00	—
1640	—	10.00	22.00	45.00	90.00	—
1641	—	10.00	22.00	45.00	90.00	—
1642	—	10.00	22.00	45.00	90.00	—
1644	—	10.00	22.00	45.00	90.00	—
1645	—	10.00	22.00	45.00	90.00	—
1646	—	10.00	22.00	45.00	90.00	—
1647	—	10.00	22.00	45.00	90.00	—
1648	—	10.00	22.00	45.00	90.00	—
1649	—	10.00	22.00	45.00	90.00	—
1652	—	10.00	22.00	45.00	90.00	—
1653	—	10.00	22.00	45.00	90.00	—
1657	—	10.00	22.00	45.00	90.00	—
1658	—	—	—	—	—	—
Note: Reported, not confirmed.						
1659	—	10.00	22.00	45.00	90.00	—
1660	—	—	—	—	—	—
Note: Reported, not confirmed.						
1678	—	10.00	22.00	45.00	90.00	—

KM# 70 2 PFENNIG

0.3500 g., Silver, 14 mm. **Obv:** 4-line inscription with date and mintmaster's initial **Obv. Inscription:** 2 / PENN / (date) / (initial) **Rev:** 3-line inscription **Rev. Inscription:** BR / STAT / GEL **Note:** Ref. J-294.

Date	Mintage	VG	F	VF	XF	Unc
1676 B	—	30.00	60.00	110	220	—

KM# 11 3 PFENNIG (Dreier)

Silver Weight varies: 0.82-0.88g., 17 mm. **Obv:** Rampant lion left in ornamented shield **Rev:** Imperial orb with 3 divides date **Note:** Ref. J-90, 217. Varieties exist.

Date	Mintage	VG	F	VF	XF	Unc
1608	—	20.00	33.00	75.00	155	—
16Z3	—	20.00	33.00	75.00	155	—

KM# 22 3 PFENNIG (Dreier)

Silver Weight varies: 0.55-0.83g., 16-17 mm. **Obv:** Ornamented shield of city arms **Obv. Legend:** MO. NO - BR(U)(V)N(S). **Rev:** Imperial orb with 3 divides date **Note:** Ref. J#216, 218-28. Varieties exist.

Date	Mintage	VG	F	VF	XF	Unc
16ZZ (b)	—	18.00	32.00	60.00	120	—
1623 (b)	—	18.00	32.00	60.00	120	—
1633 (b)	—	18.00	32.00	60.00	120	—
1634 (b)	—	18.00	32.00	60.00	120	—
1635 (b)	—	18.00	32.00	60.00	120	—
1637 (b)	—	18.00	32.00	60.00	120	—
1638 (b)	—	18.00	32.00	60.00	120	—
1641 (b)	—	18.00	32.00	60.00	120	—
1642 (b)	—	18.00	32.00	60.00	120	—
1644 (b)	—	18.00	32.00	60.00	120	—
1645 (b)	—	18.00	32.00	60.00	120	—
1646 (b)	—	18.00	32.00	60.00	120	—
1648 (b)	—	—	—	—	—	—
Note: Reported, not confirmed.						

KM# 71 3 PFENNIG (Dreier)

0.5800 g., Silver, 15 mm. **Obv:** Crowned script B divides STAT-GELT, mintmaster's initial below **Rev:** Imperial orb with 3 divides date **Note:** Ref. J-291.

Date	Mintage	VG	F	VF	XF	Unc
1676 B	—	35.00	65.00	130	265	—

KM# 72 3 PFENNIG (Dreier)

Silver Weight varies: 0.50-0.57g., 15 mm. **Obv:** Crowned rampant lion to left **Obv. Legend:** BR. ST - GELT. **Rev:** Imperial orb with 3 divides date **Note:** Ref. J-292.

Date	Mintage	VG	F	VF	XF	Unc
1676 B	—	27.00	55.00	110	220	—

KM# 73 4 PFENNIG

Silver Weight varies: 0.55-0.79g., 16-17 mm. **Obv:** Crowned rampant lion to left **Obv. Legend:** BRVNS(V). STAT. GELT. **Rev:** 4-line inscription with date, where present **Rev. Inscription:** IIII / GVTE / P(F)EN(N) / (date) **Note:** Ref. J#288-90. Varieties exist. The mintmaster's initial is found either at the top, center or bottom of the reverse.

Date	Mintage	VG	F	VF	XF	Unc
1676 B	—	30.00	65.00	135	270	—
ND B	—	27.00	60.00	120	240	—

KM# 80 4-1/2 PFENNIG

0.8400 g., Silver, 18 mm. **Obv:** Rampant lion to left in circle **Obv. Legend:** BRAUNSC(H)WEIGISC. **Rev:** 2-line inscription, date at end of legend **Rev. Legend:** STADGELDT. **Rev. Inscription:** 4 1/2 / PFEN **Note:** Ref. J-302.

Date	Mintage	VG	F	VF	XF	Unc
1680	—	—	—	—	—	—

KM# 47 MATTHIER

Silver Weight varies: 1.06-1.17g., 18 mm. **Obv:** Rampant lion to left in circle **Obv. Legend:** BRAUNSCHWEIGIS. **Rev:** 3-line inscription, date at end of legend **Rev. Legend:** STADTGELDT. **Rev. Inscription:** I / MAT / TIR **Note:** Ref. J-214.

Date	Mintage	VG	F	VF	XF	Unc
1647	—	—	—	—	—	—

KM# 24 MARIENGROSCHEN (1/36 Thaler)

Silver Weight varies: 1.05-1.87g., 21 mm. **Obv:** City arms in circle, date at end of legend **Obv. Legend:** MONE(TA). NOVA. BRUN(SV). **Rev:** Madonna with Child surrounded by flames **Rev. Legend:** MARIA. MA - TER. DOM(I)(NI). **Note:** Ref. J#206-210. Varieties exist.

Date	Mintage	VG	F	VF	XF	Unc
1622 (b)	—	20.00	40.00	80.00	160	—
1623 (b)	—	20.00	40.00	80.00	160	—
1625 (b)	—	20.00	40.00	80.00	160	—
1627 (b)	—	20.00	40.00	80.00	160	—
1653 HB	—	20.00	40.00	80.00	160	—

KM# 25 MARIENGROSCHEN (1/36 Thaler)

Silver Weight varies: 4.65-4.95g., 24X24 mm. **Obv:** City arms in circle, date at end of legend **Obv. Legend:** MONE. NOVA. BRUN. **Rev:** Madonna with Child, surrounded by flames **Rev. Legend:** MARIA. MA - TER. DOM. **Note:** Klippe, 4.65-4.95g. Weight of 1/6 Thaler.

Date	Mintage	VG	F	VF	XF	Unc
1622 (b)	—	105	150	300	600	—

KM# 76 1/96 THALER (3 Pfennig)

Silver Weight varies: 0.45-0.67g., 15 mm. **Obv:** Rampant lion left **Obv. Legend:** MONE. NOVA. ARGEN. **Rev:** Value 96 in center, date at end of legend **Rev. Legend:** BR. STAT. GELT. **Note:** Ref. J-293.

Date	Mintage	VG	F	VF	XF	Unc
1676 B	—	35.00	65.00	130	265	—

KM# 33 1/64 THALER
Silver Weight varies: 0.85-1.04g., 20 mm. **Obv:** Rampant lion left in circle **Obv. Legend:** BRAUNSCHWEIGISC. **Rev:** Imperial orb with 64 in circle, date at end of legend **Rev. Legend:** STADTGELDT. **Note:** Ref. 211-13.

Date	Mintage	VG	F	VF	XF	Unc
1625 (b)	—	—	—	—	—	—
1644 (b)	—	—	—	—	—	—
1645 (b)	—	—	—	—	—	—

KM# 8 1/24 THALER (Groschen)
Silver Weight varies: 1.73-2.07g., 21 mm. **Obv:** Rampant lion to left in circle **Obv. Legend:** MO. NO. ARG. REIP. BRUNS. **Rev:** Imperial orb with 24 divides date **Rev. Legend:** RVD. II. RO. IMP. SEM. AV. **Note:** Ref. J-86.

Date	Mintage	VG	F	VF	XF	Unc
1606	—	30.00	60.00	120	—	—

KM# 9 1/24 THALER (Groschen)
Silver Weight varies: 1.67-2.00g., 22 mm. **Obv:** Rampant lion to left in circle **Obv. Legend:** MO. NO. REIP. ARG. BRVNS. **Rev:** Imperial orb with 24, date divided in margin at top **Rev. Legend:** RUD. II. RO. IMP. S. AU. **Note:** Ref. J-87.

Date	Mintage	VG	F	VF	XF	Unc
1606	—	30.00	60.00	120	—	—

KM# 10 1/24 THALER (Groschen)
4.1800 g., Silver, 24x24 mm. **Obv:** Rampant lion to left in circle **Obv. Legend:** MO. NO. REIP. AR. BRVNS. **Rev:** Imperial orb with 24, date divided in margin at top **Rev. Legend:** RUD. II. RO. IMP. S. AU. **Note:** Ref. J-87a. Klippe.

Date	Mintage	VG	F	VF	XF	Unc
1606	—	—	—	—	—	—

KM# 18 1/24 THALER (Groschen)
1.0000 g., Silver, 18.5 mm. **Obv:** Shield of city arms, ornate helmet above **Obv. Legend:** MO. NO. RE - IP. BRUN. **Rev:** Imperial orb with Z4, date divided at top **Rev. Legend:** FER. D. G. RO. I. S. A. **Note:** Ref. J-91.Kipper issue, small module.

Date	Mintage	VG	F	VF	XF	Unc
1620	—	22.00	42.00	80.00	160	—

KM# 23 1/24 THALER (Groschen)
1.8700 g., Silver, 21 mm. **Obv:** Shield of city arms, ornate helmet above **Obv. Legend:** MO. NO. RE - IP. BRUNSV. **Rev:** Imperial orb wtih 24 divides date **Rev. Legend:** FERDI. II. D. G. ROM. IMP. SE. AU. **Note:** Ref. J-203, 204.

Date	Mintage	VG	F	VF	XF	Unc
1622 (b)	—	22.00	42.00	80.00	160	—
1625 (b)	—	—	—	—	—	—

Note: Reported, not confirmed.

KM# 46 1/24 THALER (Groschen)
Silver, 21 mm. **Obv:** Shield of city arms, ornate helmet above **Obv. Legend:** MO. NO. RE - IP. BRUNSV. **Rev:** Imperial orb with 24 divides date **Rev. Legend:** FERD. III. D. G. ROM. IMP. SE. AU. **Note:** Ref. J-205.

Date	Mintage	VG	F	VF	XF	Unc
1642 (b)	—	—	—	—	—	—

Note: Reported, not confirmed.

KM# 74 1/24 THALER (Groschen)
1.6700 g., Silver, 22 mm. **Obv:** Crowned shield of city arms **Obv. Legend:** BRVN - SVIC. **Rev:** Imperial orb with 24, date at end of legend **Rev. Legend:** MONETA. NOVA. **Note:** Ref. J-299.

Date	Mintage	VG	F	VF	XF	Unc
1676	—	20.00	35.00	75.00	155	—

KM# 19 2 SCHILLING (1/16 Thaler or Dütchen)
Silver Weight varies: 1.32-1.90g., 25 mm. **Obv:** Shield of city arms in ornamented frame **Obv. Legend:** MON. NO. REIPUB. BRUN. **Rev:** Crowned imperial eagle, 16 in orb on breast, date at end of legend **Rev. Legend:** FERDI. II. D. G. RO. I. S. A. **Note:** Ref. J-92.

Date	Mintage	VG	F	VF	XF	Unc
(1)6Z0	—	—	—	—	—	—

KM# 65 2 SCHILLING (1/16 Thaler or Dütchen)
Silver Weight varies: 1.60-1.65g., 20 mm. **Obv:** 4-line inscription with mintmaster's initials, date at end of legend legend **Obv. Legend:** MONETA. NOVA. ARGENT. **Obv. Inscription:** XVI / REICHS / THALE / (initials) **Rev:** Bust of Duke Rudolf August to right in circle **Rev. Legend:** RV. AVGVSTVS. HERZ. Z. B. V. L. **Note:** Ref. J-286, 287.

Date	Mintage	VG	F	VF	XF	Unc
1675 GB	—	40.00	80.00	150	300	—
1676 GB	—	40.00	80.00	150	300	—
1676	—	40.00	80.00	150	300	—

KM# 78 2 SCHILLING (1/16 Thaler or Dütchen)
Silver Weight varies: 1.60-1.70g., 20 mm. **Obv:** 4-line inscription with date **Obv. Legend:** MONETA. NOVA. ARGENT. **Obv. Inscription:** XVI / RECH / TALE / (date) **Rev:** Bust of Duke Rudolf August to right **Rev. Legend:** RV. AVGVSTVS. HERZ. Z. B. V. L. **Note:** Ref. J-298.

Date	Mintage	VG	F	VF	XF	Unc
1677	—	—	—	—	—	—

KM# 20.1 12 KREUZER
Silver, 30 mm. **Obv:** Shield of city arms, ornate helmet above **Obv. Legend:** MO. NO. RE - IP. BRUNS. **Rev:** Crowned imperial eagle, 1Z in orb on breast, all in circle, date at end of legend **Rev. Legend:** FERDIN. II. D. G. RO. IM. SE. A. **Note:** Ref. J-93. Kipper issue.

Date	Mintage	VG	F	VF	XF	Unc
(16)Z1	—	85.00	145	275	550	—

KM# 20.2 12 KREUZER
5.5000 g., Silver **Obv:** Shield of city arms, ornate helmet above **Obv. Legend:** MO. NO. RE - IP. BRUNS. **Rev:** Crowned imperial eagle, 1Z in orb on breast, all in circle, date at end of legend **Rev. Legend:** FERDIN. II. D. G. RO. IM. SE. A. **Note:** Ref. J-93a. Klippe.

Date	Mintage	VG	F	VF	XF	Unc
(16)Z1	—	—	—	—	—	—

KM# 21 12 KREUZER
5.6300 g., Silver, 27x28 mm. **Obv:** Shield of city arms, ornate helmet above **Obv. Legend:** MO. NO. REI - PUB. BRUNS. **Rev:** Crowned imperial eagle, 1Z in orb on breast, all in circle, date divided by crown at top **Rev. Legend:** FERDI. II. D. G. RO. I. S. A. **Note:** Ref. J-93a. Klippe in fine style.

Date	Mintage	VG	F	VF	XF	Unc
1621 Rare	—	—	—	—	—	—

KM# 27 1/8 THALER (1/2 Reichsort=3 Groschen)
Silver Weight varies: 3.16-3.47g., 26 mm. **Obv:** City arms in circle, date at end of legend **Obv. Legend:** MONETA NOV REIP BRUNSVIC. **Rev:** Crowned imperial eagle, 3 in orb on breast **Rev. Legend:** FERDINAND. 2. D. G. ROM. IMP. S. A. **Note:** Ref. J-200, 201.

Date	Mintage	VG	F	VF	XF	Unc
1624 (b)	—	—	—	—	—	—
1628 (b)	—	—	—	—	—	—

Note: Reported, not confirmed.

KM# 43 1/8 THALER (1/2 Reichsort=3 Groschen)
Silver, 26 mm. **Obv:** City arms in circle, date at end of legend **Obv. Legend:** MONETA NOV REIP BRUNSVIC. **Rev:** Crowned imperial eagle, 3 in orb on breast **Rev. Legend:** FERDINAND. III. D. G. ROM. IMP. S. A.

Date	Mintage	VG	F	VF	XF	Unc
1638 (b)	—	—	—	—	—	—

Note: Reported, not confirmed.

KM# 57 6 MARIENGROSCHEN (1/4 Gulden)
5.4500 g., Silver, 26-27 mm. **Obv:** City arms in circle **Obv. Legend:** BRUNSCHWIGISCH. **Rev:** 3-line inscription, date at end of legend **Rev. Legend:** STADT GELDT. **Rev. Inscription:** VI / MARIEN / GROS. **Note:** Ref. J-268, 269. Prev. KM#55.

Date	Mintage	VG	F	VF	XF	Unc
1669	—	35.00	65.00	130	260	—
1671	—	35.00	65.00	130	260	—
1671/69	—	35.00	65.00	130	260	—

KM# 61 6 MARIENGROSCHEN (1/4 Gulden)
3.8400 g., Silver, 27 mm. **Obv:** 4-line inscription with date, no legend **Obv. Inscription:** VI / MARIEN / GROSCH / (date) **Rev:** Bust of Duke Rudolf August right **Rev. Legend:** RVD. A. - D. B. E. L. **Note:** Ref. J-280.

Date	Mintage	VG	F	VF	XF	Unc
1675 B	—	35.00	65.00	130	260	—

KM# 28 1/4 THALER (6 Groschen)
Silver Weight varies: 6.65-7.25g., 30 mm. **Obv:** City arms in circle **Obv. Legend:** MON(ETA). NOV(A). REIP. BR(U)(V) NSVIC(EN). **Rev:** Imperial eagle, 6 in orb on breast, crown above divides date **Rev. Legend:** FER(DI)(N)(AN). II. D. G. RO(M). I(M). S(E). (A)(U)(G). **Note:** Ref. J#182-90. Varieties exist.

Date	Mintage	VG	F	VF	XF	Unc
1624 (b)	—	325	600	1,100	2,200	—
1625 (b)	—	325	600	1,100	2,200	—
1627 (b)	—	325	600	1,100	2,200	—
1628 (b)	—	325	600	1,100	2,200	—
1629 (b)	—	325	600	1,100	2,200	—
1630 (b)	—	325	—	1,100	2,200	—
1631 (b)	—	325	600	1,100	2,200	—
1632 (b)	—	325	600	1,100	2,200	—
1633 (b)	—	325	600	1,100	2,200	—
1636 (b)	—	325	600	1,100	2,200	—

KM# 44 1/4 THALER (6 Groschen)
Silver Weight varies: 7.07-7.41g. **Obv:** City arms in circle **Obv. Legend:** MONE(TA). NOV(A). REIP. BRUNS(V)(U)I(C). **Rev:** Imperial eagle, 6 in orb on breast, crown above divides date **Rev. Legend:** FERDI. III. D. G. RO. IM. SE. AU. **Note:** Ref. J#191-98. Varieties exist.

Date	Mintage	VG	F	VF	XF	Unc
1638 (b)	—	325	600	1,100	2,200	—
1639 (b)	—	325	600	1,100	2,200	—
1641 (b)	—	325	600	1,100	2,200	—
1643 (b)	—	325	600	1,100	2,200	—
1646 (b)	—	325	600	1,100	2,200	—
1647 (b)	—	325	600	1,100	2,200	—
1648 (b)	—	325	600	1,100	2,200	—
1657 (c)	—	325	600	1,100	2,200	—

KM# 45 1/4 THALER (6 Groschen)
10.1500 g., Silver **Obv:** City arms in circle **Obv. Legend:** MONETA. NOV. REIP. BRUNSVIC. **Rev:** Imperial eagle, 6 in orb on breast, crown above divides date **Rev. Legend:** FERDI. III. D. G. RO. IM. SE. AU. **Note:** Ref. J-193. Klippe.

Date	Mintage	VG	F	VF	XF	Unc
1641 (b)	—	—	—	—	—	—

KM# 60 1/4 THALER (6 Groschen)
Silver, 30 mm. **Obv:** City arms in circle **Obv. Legend:** MONE. NOVA. REIP. BRUNSVIC. **Rev:** Imperial eagle, 6 in orb on breast, crown above divides date **Rev. Legend:** LEOPOLD. I. D. G. RO IM. S. AU. **Note:** Ref. J-199.

Date	Mintage	VG	F	VF	XF	Unc
1670 (c) Rare	—	—	—	—	—	—

KM# 58 12 MARIENGROSCHEN (1/2 Gulden)
9.9500 g., Silver, 32-34 mm. **Obv:** City arms in circle **Obv. Legend:** BRUNSCHWIGISCH. **Rev:** 4-line inscription, date at end of legend **Rev. Legend:** STADT GELDT. **Rev. Inscription:** XII / MARIEN / GROSCH / EN **Note:** Ref. J-266, 267. Prev. KM#56.

Date	Mintage	VG	F	VF	XF	Unc
1669	—	60.00	105	210	425	—
1671	—	60.00	105	210	425	—

KM# 62 12 MARIENGROSCHEN (1/2 Gulden)
Silver Weight varies: 8.22-8.25g., 30-31 mm. **Obv:** 4-line inscription with date **Obv. Legend:** MONETA. NOVA. ARGENT. **Obv. Inscription:** 12 / MARIEN / GROSCH / (date) **Rev:** Bust of Duke Rudolf August to right **Rev. Legend:** R. AVG. D. - B. E. LVN. **Note:** Ref. J-278.

Date	Mintage	VG	F	VF	XF	Unc
1675 B	—	60.00	110	225	450	—

KM# 63 12 MARIENGROSCHEN (1/2 Gulden)
8.2500 g., Silver, 30 mm. **Obv:** 4-line inscription with date **Obv. Legend:** MONETA. NOVA. BRVNSV. **Obv. Inscription:** 12 / MARIEN / GROSCH / (date) **Rev:** Rampant lion to left, large crown above **Rev. Legend:** RVD. AVG. D. G. E. LVN. **Note:** Ref. J-279.

Date	Mintage	VG	F	VF	XF	Unc
1675 B	—	60.00	110	225	450	—

KM# 29 1/2 THALER (12 Groschen)
Silver Weight varies: 13.87-14.75g., 36-37 mm. **Obv:** City arms in circle **Obv. Legend:** MONETA. NOVA. REIP. BRUNSVICEN. **Rev:** Imperial eagle, 12 in orb on breast, crown above divides date **Rev. Legend:** FERDINAND. II. D. G. ROM. IM. S. A. **Note:** Ref. J#164-72.

Date	Mintage	VG	F	VF	XF	Unc
1624 (b)	—	170	325	625	1,150	—
1627 (b)	—	170	325	625	1,150	—
1628 (b)	—	170	325	625	1,150	—
1629 (b)	—	170	325	625	1,150	—
1630 (b)	—	170	325	625	1,150	—
1631 (b)	—	170	325	625	1,150	—
1632 (b)	—	170	325	625	1,150	—
1633 (b)	—	170	325	625	1,150	—
1637 (b)	—	170	325	625	1,150	—

KM# 40 1/2 THALER (12 Groschen)
Silver Weight varies: 13.55-14.54g., 36-37 mm. **Obv:** City arms in circle **Obv. Legend:** MONETA. NOVA. REIP. BRUNSVICEN. **Rev:** Imperial eagle, 6 in orb on breast, crown above divides date **Rev. Legend:** FERDI. III. D. G. ROM. IM. S. A. **Note:** Ref. J#172-79.

Date	Mintage	VG	F	VF	XF	Unc
1637 (b)	—	170	325	625	1,150	—
1638 (b)	—	170	325	625	1,150	—
1639 (b)	—	170	325	625	1,150	—
1641 (b)	—	170	325	625	1,150	—
1642 (b)	—	170	325	625	1,150	—
1643 (b)	—	170	325	625	1,150	—
1645 (b)	—	170	325	625	1,150	—
1657 (c)	—	170	325	625	1,150	—

KM# 41 1/2 THALER (12 Groschen)
Silver Weight varies: 15.30-19.00g., 39x40 mm. **Obv:** City arms in circle **Obv. Legend:** MONETA. NOVA. REIP. BRUNSVICEN. **Rev:** Imperial eagle, 12 in orb on breast, crown above divides date **Rev. Legend:** FERDI. III. D. G. ROM. IM. S. A. **Note:** Ref. J-172, 176. Klippe.

Date	Mintage	VG	F	VF	XF	Unc
1637 (b)	—	—	—	—	—	—
1642 (b)	—	—	—	—	—	—

KM# 50 1/2 THALER (12 Groschen)
Silver Weight varies: 14.44-14.50g., 40x40 mm. **Obv:** City arms in circle **Obv. Legend:** MONETA. NOVA. REIP. BRUNSVICEN. **Rev:** Imperial eagle 12 in orb on breast, crown above divides date **Rev. Legend:** LEOPOLD. I. D. G. ROM. IMP. SEM. AU. **Note:** Ref. J-180, 181.

Date	Mintage	VG	F	VF	XF	Unc
1658 (c)	—	—	—	—	—	—
1670 (c) Rare	—	—	—	—	—	—

KM# 64 24 MARIENGROSCHEN (Gulden)
Silver Weight varies: 16.38-16.75g., 36-37 mm. **Obv:** Oval city arms, within frame of 2 tied palm fronds, divide 2-line inscription, large crown above, value XXIIII at top, date divided at bottom **Obv. Inscription:** MAR - IEN / GRO - SCH. **Rev:** Armored bust of Duke Rudolf August to right **Rev. Legend:** RVD. AVG. D. - B. E. LVNEB. **Note:** Ref. J-277.

Date	Mintage	VG	F	VF	XF	Unc
1675 B	—	100	180	325	650	—

KM# 75 24 MARIENGROSCHEN (Gulden)
Silver Weight varies: 16.44-16.80g., 36 mm. **Obv:** 3-line inscription, date below **Obv. Legend:** MONETA. NOVA. ARGENTEA. **Obv. Inscription:** XXIIII / MARIEN. / GROSCH. **Rev:** Armored and draped bust of Duke Rudolf August to right **Rev. Legend:** RVD. AVG. D. - B. E. LVNEB. **Note:** Ref. J-285.

Date	Mintage	VG	F	VF	XF	Unc
1676 B	—	100	190	325	650	—

KM# 77 24 MARIENGROSCHEN (Gulden)
16.3000 g., Silver, 37 mm. **Obv:** 3-line inscription, date in margin at top **Obv. Legend:** MONETA. NOVA. ARGENTA. **Obv. Inscription:** XXIIII / MARIEN. / GROSC. **Rev:** Armored and draped bust of Duke Rudolf August to right **Rev. Legend:** RVD. AVG. D. - B. E. LVNEB. **Note:** Ref. J-300.

Date	Mintage	VG	F	VF	XF	Unc
1677	—	100	175	325	650	—

KM# 66.2 2/3 THALER (Gulden)
Silver Weight varies: 14.35-17.25g., 36-40 mm. **Obv:** Rampant lion to left on wall between 2 towers connected by arch over lion, legend begins at lower left, value (2/3) divides date in exergue **Obv. Legend:** MONETA. - BRVNSV. **Rev:** Large armored and draped bust of Duke Rudolf August to right **Rev. Legend:** RVD. AVG. D. - B. E. LVNEB. **Note:** Ref. J-271, 281; Dav. 451.

Date	Mintage	VG	F	VF	XF	Unc
1675 IGB	—	85.00	150	275	575	—
1676 IGB	—	85.00	150	275	575	—

KM# 66.1 2/3 THALER (Gulden)
Silver Weight varies: 16.05-16.75g., 36 mm. **Obv:** Rampant lion to left on wall between 2 towers, legend begins at lower left, value (2/3) divides date in exergue **Obv. Legend:** MONETA. - BRVNSV. **Rev:** Armored and draped bust of Duke Rudolf August to right **Rev. Legend:** RVD. AVG. D. - B. E. LVNEB. **Note:** Ref. J-270; Dav. 450.

Date	Mintage	VG	F	VF	XF	Unc
1675 IGB	—	85.00	150	275	575	—

KM# 66.3 2/3 THALER (Gulden)
Silver Weight varies: 16.03-16.85g., 36 mm. **Obv:** Rampant lion to left between 2 towers on wall that does not extend to edge of design, ornate arch above lion and connecting the towers, legend begins at lower left, value (2/3) in exergue **Obv. Legend:** MONETA. - BRVNSV. **Rev:** Armored and draped bust of Duke Rudolf August to right **Rev. Legend:** RVD. AVG. D. - B. E. LVNEB. **Note:** Ref. J-272; Dav. 452.

Date	Mintage	VG	F	VF	XF	Unc
1675 IGB	—	85.00	150	275	575	—

KM# 66.4 2/3 THALER (Gulden)
Silver Weight varies: 15.83-16.67g., 35-37 mm. **Obv:** Rampant lion to left on wall between 2 towers, legend begins at lower left, value (2/3) divides date in exergue **Obv. Legend:** MONETA. - ARGENT. **Rev:** Armored and draped bust of Duke Rudolf August to right, legend begins at lower left, value (2/3) in exergue **Rev. Legend:** RVD. AVG. D. - B. E. LVNEB. **Note:** Ref. J#275-75, 282-84; Dav. 457. Varieties exist.

Date	Mintage	VG	F	VF	XF	Unc
1675 B	—	85.00	150	275	575	—
1676 B	—	85.00	150	275	575	—
1676	—	85.00	150	275	575	—

KM# 68.1 2/3 THALER (Gulden)
Silver Weight varies: 12.90-16.40g., 39 mm. **Obv:** Rampant lion to left on high city wall between 2 towers with tall points, value (2/3) in oval below gate divides date **Obv. Legend:** MONETA - BR(V)(U)NSV. **Rev:** Large armored bust of Duke Rudolf August to right **Rev. Legend:** RUD. AUG. (-) D. (-) B. E. LUNEB. **Note:** Ref. J-295, 296; Dav. 454. Varieties exist.

Date	Mintage	VG	F	VF	XF	Unc
1675 BH	—	105	165	325	650	—

KM# 68.2 2/3 THALER (Gulden)
Silver, 39 mm. **Obv:** Rampant lion to left on high city wall between 2 towers with tall points, value (2/3) in oval below gate divides date **Obv. Legend:** MONETA - ARGENT. **Rev:** Armored bust of Duke Rudolf August to right **Rev. Legend:** RVD. AVG. D. - B. E. LVNEB. **Note:** Ref. J-276; Dav. 456.

Date	Mintage	VG	F	VF	XF	Unc
1675	—	105	165	325	650	—

KM# 67 2/3 THALER (Gulden)
Silver Weight varies: 16.70-17.35g., 36 mm. **Obv:** Rampant lion to left between 2 large towers, ornamented arch above, date divided at top, value (2/3) in oval below, legend begins at upper right **Obv. Legend:** MONETA - BRVNSV. **Rev:** Armored bust of Duke Rudolf August to right **Rev. Legend:** RVD. AVG. - D. BR. ET. L. **Note:** Ref. J-273; Dav. 453.

Date	Mintage	VG	F	VF	XF	Unc
1675 IGB	—	105	170	300	625	—

KM# 69 2/3 THALER (Gulden)
Silver Weight varies: 15.30-16.68g., 39 mm. **Obv:** Large crowned Spanish shield of city arms with concave sides, value (2/3) in oval divides date below **Obv. Legend:** MONETA - BRUNSV. **Rev:** Armored bust of Duke Rudolf August to right **Rev. Legend:** RUD. AUG. D. G. DUX B. E. LUNEB. **Note:** Ref. J-297; Dav. 455.

Date	Mintage	VG	F	VF	XF	Unc
1675 BH	—	95.00	170	300	600	—

KM# 30.2 THALER (24 Groschen)
Silver Weight varies: 28.12-29.37g., 43-44 mm. **Obv:** Spanish shield of city arms in ornamented frame, ornate helmet above **Obv. Legend:** MON(E). NOV(A). REIP. - BR(U)(V)NS(V)(U)ICENS(IS). **Rev:** Crowned imperial eagle, 24 in orb on breast, date divided at top **Rev. Legend:** FERDINAND. II. D. . ROM. IMP. S(E)(M). A(U)(V)(G)(U)(V)(S). **Note:** Ref. J#132-38, 141; Dav. 5127.

Date	Mintage	VG	F	VF	XF	Unc
1624 (b)	Inc. above	110	220	450	825	—
1625 (b)	—	110	220	450	825	—
1626 (b)	—	110	220	450	825	—
1627 (b)	—	110	220	450	825	—
1628 (b)	—	110	220	450	825	—
1629 (b)	—	110	220	450	825	—
1630 (b)	—	110	220	450	825	—

KM# 30.1 THALER (24 Groschen)
28.9200 g., Silver, 44 mm. **Obv:** Spanish shield of city arms in ornamented frame, ornate helmet above **Obv. Legend:** MONETA. NOVA - BRUNSVICENSI(S). **Rev:** Crowned imperial eagle, 24 in orb on breast, date divided at top **Rev. Legend:** FERDINAND(9). II. D. G. ROM. IMP. S. AU(GUS). **Note:** Ref. J-132; Dav. 5125.

Date	Mintage	VG	F	VF	XF	Unc
1624 (b)	64,902	110	220	450	825	—

KM# 30.3 THALER (24 Groschen)
Silver Weight varies: 28.45-29.37g., 42 mm. **Obv:** Spanish shield of city arms in ornamented frame, ornate helmet above **Obv. Legend:** MONE. NOVA. REIP. - BRVNVICENS(IS). **Rev:** Crowned imperial eagle, 24 in orb on breast, date dividd at top **Rev. Legend:** FERDINAND. II. D. G. ROM. IMP. SEM. AUGUS. **Note:** Ref. J#139-44; Dav. 5128.

Date	Mintage	VG	F	VF	XF	Unc
1631 (b)	—	110	220	450	825	—
1632 (b)	—	110	220	450	825	—
1633 (b)	—	110	220	450	825	—
1634 (b)	—	110	220	450	825	—
1635 (b)	—	110	220	450	825	—
1636 (b)	—	110	220	450	825	—

KM# 42 THALER (24 Groschen)
Silver Weight varies: 28.50-29.33g., 42 mm. **Obv:** Spanish shield of city arms in ornamented frame, ornate helmet above **Obv. Legend:** MONE. NOVA. REIP. - BRVNSVICENSIS. **Rev:** Crowned imperial eagle, 24 in orb on breast, date divided at top **Rev. Legend:** FERDINAN(D). III. D. G. ROM. IMP. SEM. AU(G)(US). **Note:** Ref. S#145-60; Dav. 5129.

Date	Mintage	VG	F	VF	XF	Unc
1637 (b)	—	250	525	1,050	1,950	—
1638 (b)	—	250	525	1,050	1,950	—
1639 (b)	—	250	525	1,050	1,950	—

Date	Mintage	VG	F	VF	XF	Unc
1640 (b)	—	250	525	1,050	1,950	—
1641 (b)	—	250	525	1,050	1,950	—
1642 (b)	—	250	525	1,050	1,950	—
1643 (b)	—	250	525	1,050	1,950	—
1644 (b)	—	250	525	1,050	1,950	—
1645 (b)	—	250	525	1,050	1,950	—
1646 (b)	—	250	525	1,050	1,950	—
1647 (b)	—	250	525	1,050	1,950	—
1648 (b)	—	250	525	1,050	1,950	—
1651 (c)	—	250	525	1,050	1,950	—
1653 (c)	—	250	525	1,050	1,950	—
1655 (c)	—	250	525	1,050	1,950	—
1657 (c)	—	250	525	1,050	1,950	—

KM# 51 THALER (24 Groschen)

Silver Weight varies: 27.93-28.95g., 44-46.5 mm. **Obv:** Spanish shield of city arms in ornamented frame, ornate helmet above **Obv. Legend:** MON(E). NOVA. REIP. - R(V)(U)NS(V) (U)ICENS(IS). **Rev:** Crowned imperial eagle, 24 in orb on breast, date divided at top **Rev. Legend:** LEOPOLD(US). I. D. G. ROM. IMP. SEM(P). AUGUS. **Note:** Ref. J#161-63; Dav. 5130.

Date	Mintage	VG	F	VF	XF	Unc
1658 (c)	—	800	1,750	3,450	6,300	—
1659 (c)	—	800	1,750	3,450	6,300	—
1660 (c)	—	800	1,750	3,450	6,300	—
1670 (c)	—	700	1,400	2,900	5,800	9,800

KM# 52 1-1/4 THALER

Silver Weight varies: 35.40-35.88g., 53 mm. **Obv:** Shield of city arms, oval with value 1-1/4 in base, either punched or engraved in die, ornate helmet above **Obv. Legend:** MON. NOV. REIP. - BRUNSVICENSIS. **Rev:** Imperial eagle with orb on breast, crown above divides date **Rev. Legend:** LEOPOLDUS. I. D. G. ROM. IMP. SEM. AUGU. **Note:** Ref. J-130, 131; Dav. LS265.

Date	Mintage	VG	F	VF	XF	Unc
1659 (c)	—	725	1,200	1,900	2,650	—

KM# 53 1-1/2 THALER

Silver Weight varies: 43.30-43.32g., 53 mm. **Obv:** Shield of city arms, oval with value 1-1/2 in base punched in, ornate helmet above **Obv. Legend:** MON. NOV. REIP. - BRUNSVICENSIS. **Rev:** Imperial eagle with orb on breast, crown above divides date **Rev. Legend:** LEOPOLDUS. I. D. G. ROM. IIMP. SEM. AUGU. **Note:** Ref. J-129; Dav. LS264.

Date	Mintage	VG	F	VF	XF	Unc
1659 (c)	—	850	1,450	2,400	4,200	—

KM# 31 2 THALER

Silver, 44 mm. **Obv:** Spanish shield of city arms in ornamented frame, ornate helmet above **Obv. Legend:** MON. NOV. REIP. - BRUNSVICENSIS. **Rev:** Crowned imperial eagle, orb on breast, date divided at top **Rev. Legend:** FERDINAN. II. D. G ROM. IMP. S. AUGUS. **Note:** Dav. 5126.

Date	Mintage	VG	F	VF	XF	Unc
1624 (b) Rare	—	—	—	—	—	—
1628 (b) Rare	—	—	—	—	—	—

KM# 54 2-1/4 THALER

57.5500 g., Silver, 53 mm. **Obv:** Shield of city arms, oval with value 2-1/4 in base punched in, ornate helmet above **Obv. Legend:** MON. NOV. REIP. - BRUNSVICENSIS. **Rev:** Imperial eagle with orb on breast, crown above divides date **Rev. Legend:** LEOPOLDUS. I. D. G. ROM. IMP. SEM. AUGU. **Note:** Ref. J-128.

Date	Mintage	VG	F	VF	XF	Unc
1659 (c) Rare	—	—	—	—	—	—

TRADE COINAGE

KM# 26.2 GOLDGULDEN

3.2535 g., 0.7710 Gold Weight varies: 3.08-3.25g. 0.0806 oz. AGW, 23-24 mm. **Obv:** City arms in ornamented circle, date at end of legend **Obv. Legend:** MO. NO. AUR. REIP. BR(U)(V)NSV(I). **Rev:** Crowned imperial eagle, orb on breast **Rev. Legend:** FERDIN. II. D. G. ROM. IM. SE. AU. **Note:** Ref. J#101-107; Fr. 533.

Date	Mintage	VG	F	VF	XF	Unc
1622 (b)	—	950	2,250	3,300	6,000	—
1627 (b)	—	950	2,250	3,300	6,000	—
1628 (b)	—	950	2,250	3,300	6,000	—
1629 (b)	—	950	2,250	3,300	6,000	—
1630 (b)	—	950	2,250	3,300	6,000	—
1631 (b)	—	950	2,250	3,300	6,000	—
1632 (b)	—	950	2,250	3,300	6,000	—
1633 (b)	—	950	2,250	3,300	6,000	—

KM# 26.1 GOLDGULDEN

3.2500 g., 0.7710 Gold Weight varies: 3.20-3.23g. 0.0806 oz. AGW, 23 mm. **Obv:** City arms in circle, date at end of legend **Obv. Legend:** MO. NO. AUR. REIP. BRUNSV. **Rev:** Crowned imperial eagle, orb on breast **Rev. Legend:** FERDIN. II. D.G. ROM. IMP. SE. A. **Note:** Ref. J-100; Fr. 533.

Date	Mintage	VG	F	VF	XF	Unc
1622 (b)	603	950	2,250	3,300	6,000	—

KM# 26.3 GOLDGULDEN

3.2500 g., 0.7710 Gold Weight varies: 3.15-3.25g. 0.0806 oz. AGW, 23-24 mm. **Obv:** City arms in ornamented circle, date at end of legend **Obv. Legend:** MO. NO. AVRI. REIP. BRVNSVI. **Rev:** Crowned imperial eagle, orb on breast **Rev. Legend:** FERDIN. II. D. G. ROM. IM. SE. AV. **Note:** Ref. J#108-110; Fr. 533.

Date	Mintage	VG	F	VF	XF	Unc
1634 (b)	—	625	1,500	2,200	4,000	—
1635 (b)	—	625	1,500	2,200	4,000	—
1636 (b)	—	625	1,500	2,200	4,000	—

KM# 35 DUCAT

3.5000 g., 0.9860 Gold Weight varies: 3.29-3.50g. 0.1109 oz. AGW, 21-22 mm. **Obv:** 5-line inscription in ornamented square **Obv. Inscription:** DUCATUS / NOVUS: / REIPUBL / BRUNSUI / CENSIS: **Rev:** Crowned imperial eagle in oval baroque frame, date at end of legend **Rev. Legend:** FERDINAN. III. D. G. ROM. IMP. SEM. AU. **Note:** Ref. J#111-20; Fr. 534. Some variants have V's in place of the V's.

Date	Mintage	VG	F	VF	XF	Unc
1638 (b)	—	875	1,900	2,850	5,300	—
1639 (b)	—	875	1,900	2,850	5,300	—
1640 (b)	—	875	1,900	2,850	5,300	—
1641 (b)	—	875	1,900	2,850	5,300	—
1642 (b)	—	875	1,900	2,850	5,300	—
1643 (b)	—	875	1,900	2,850	5,300	—
1646 (b)	—	1,150	2,500	3,800	7,000	—
1647 (b)	—	1,150	2,500	3,800	7,000	—
1648 HB	—	1,150	2,500	3,800	7,000	—
1649 HB	—	1,150	2,500	3,800	7,000	—

KM# 48 DUCAT

3.5000 g., 0.9860 Gold Weight varies: 3.37-3.51g. 0.1109 oz. AGW, 22-23 mm. **Obv:** 5-line inscription in ornamented square, date divided below **Obv. Inscription:** DVCATVS / NOVVS / REIPVBL / BRVNSVI / CENSIS **Rev:** Crowned imperial eagle in oval baroque frame **Rev. Legend:** FERDINAN. III. D. G. ROM. IMP. SEM. AV(G). **Note:** Ref. J#21-123; Fr. 534.

Date	Mintage	VG	F	VF	XF	Unc
1650 HB	—	575	1,250	1,900	3,500	—
1654 HB	—	575	1,250	1,900	3,500	—
1656 HB	—	575	1,250	1,900	3,500	—

KM# 49 DUCAT

3.5000 g., 0.9860 Gold Weight varies: 3.38-3.47g. 0.1109 oz. AGW, 23 mm. **Obv:** 5-line inscription in ornamented square, date divided below **Obv. Inscription:** DVCATVS. / NOUUS: / REIPUBL / BRUNSUI / CENSIS. **Rev:** Crowned imperial eagle, orb on breast, in circle **Rev. Legend:** LEOPOLD. D. G. ROM. IMP. SEM. AVG. **Note:** Ref. J-124, 125; Fr. 535.

Date	Mintage	VG	F	VF	XF	Unc
1658 HB	—	575	1,250	1,900	3,500	—
1659 HB	—	575	1,250	1,900	3,500	—

KM# 55 DUCAT

3.5000 g., 0.9860 Gold Weight varies: 3.41-3.46g. 0.1109 oz. AGW, 26 mm. **Obv:** 5-line inscription in ornamented square, date divided below, where present **Obv. Inscription:** DVCATVS / NOVVS / REIPVBL / BRVNSVI / CENSIS. **Rev:** Crowned imperial eagle in oval baroque frame **Rev. Legend:** LEOPOLDUS. I. D. G. ROM. IMP. SEM. AUGUS. **Note:** Ref. J-126, 127; Fr. 536.

Date	Mintage	VG	F	VF	XF	Unc
1660	—	575	1,250	1,900	3,500	—
ND(1660+)	—	575	1,250	1,900	3,500	—

BRUNSWICK DUCHIES

Braunschweig

The earliest rulers of Brunswick, in north-central Germany, were the Brunon dukes of Saxony, who controlled the territory from about 1000AD. By 1137, the dynasty died out in the male line and Brunswick passed in marriage to the Welf Duke of Bavaria, Heinrich I the Proud (1136-39). His son, Heinrich II the Lion (1139-95), ruled all of Bavaria, Saxony and Brunswick, but lost control of all his territories except Brunswick in 1180. This, then was the beginning of the rule of the Welf dynasty over the lands of Brunswick which would last until 1918. Over the centuries, many acquisitions and divisions of territory took place and one branch of the dynasty even became kings of Great Britain.

ARMS

Brunswick – 2 leopards passant left, one above the other

Lüneburg – lion rampant left, often surrounded by many small hearts

Unter-Diepholz – heraldic eagle, head left, wings spread

NOTE: Additionally, the symbol for all Welf lands, invoking the memory of the dynasty's rule over Lower Saxony, was the leaping Saxon horse, usually found as a crest above helmets and shields of arms.

REFERENCE

W = Gerhard Welter, ***Die Münzen der Welfen seit Heinrich dem Löwen***, 3 v., Braunschweig: Klinkhardt & Biermann, 1971-78.

BRUNSWICK-BEVERN

Branch of the house of Brunswick founded in 1666 by Ferdinand Albrecht I, son of August II of Brunswick-Dannenberg. At the death of Ferdinand Albrecht II in 1735, his eldest son maintained the Wolfenbüttel line and a younger son maintained the Bevern line. After 1735 Bevern was closely associated with Prussian policy. With the extinction of the line in 1809 properties reverted to Brunswick-Wolfenbüttel.

RULERS

Ferdinand Albrecht I, 1666-1687

MINT OFFICIALS' INITIALS

Initial	Date	Name
RB	1676-1711	Rudolf Bornemann in Zellerfeld

REFERENCE

W = Gerhard Welter, ***Die Münzen der Welfen seit Heinrich dem Löwen***, 3 v., Braunschweig: Klinkhardt & Biermann, 1971-78.

DUCHY

REGULAR COINAGE

KM# 7 THALER

28.6000 g., Silver, 47 mm. **Ruler:** Ferdinand Albrecht I **Subject:** Death of Ferdinand Albrecht **Obv:** Spanish shield of 11-fold arms, 5 ornate helmets above **Obv. Legend:** FERDINAND ALBERT D. G. DUX BRUNS. & LUN. **Rev:** 12-line inscription with Roman numeral dates **Rev. Inscription:** NATUS / XI. CALEND. IUN: / M.DCXXXVI / PER LUSTR. EUROP. UNIV. / VAR. EXOR NAT. LITER / SUSCEPT. E. CHRISTINA / HASS. PRINCIE / PROL. NUMEROS / PIUS PRUD. PLAC. / OBIIT BEVER / VIII. CAL. MAI. / MDCL.XXXVII. **Mint:** Zellerfeld **Note:** Ref. W-1878; Dav. 6399.

Date	Mintage	VG	F	VF	XF	Unc
MDCLXXXVII (1687) RB	—	650	1,150	1,850	3,000	—

TRADE COINAGE

KM# 6 DUCAT

3.5000 g., 0.9860 Gold 0.1109 oz. AGW, 23 mm. **Ruler:** Ferdinand Albrecht I **Obv:** Facing mantled bust with long hair, turned slightly to right **Rev:** Crowned shield of 11-fold arms in laurel wreath **Mint:** Zellerfeld **Note:** Ref. W-1877; Fr. 663.

Date	Mintage	VG	F	VF	XF	Unc
1680	—	2,500	4,500	8,000	12,500	—

KM# 5 2 DUCAT

7.0000 g., 0.9860 Gold 0.2219 oz. AGW, 29.5 mm. **Ruler:** Ferdinand Albrecht I **Obv:** Facing mantled bust with long hair, turned slightly to right **Obv. Legend:** FERDINAND. ALBRECHT. HERZOG. Z. BRV. JVNÆB - NOS. G. G. **Rev:** Crowned shield of 11-fold arms in laurel wreath, date below **Rev. Legend:** MEDIIS. TRAN - QVILLVS. IN. VNDIS. **Mint:** Zellerfeld **Note:** Ref. W-1876; Fr. 662.

Date	Mintage	VG	F	VF	XF	Unc
1678 Rare	—	—	—	—	—	—

PATTERNS

Including off metal strikes

KM#	Date	Mintage	Identification	Mkt Val
Pn1	1680	—	Ducat. Silver. KM#6.	650

BRUNSWICK-DANNENBERG

Established upon the division of Brunswick-Lüneburg-Celle in 1559, but only remained a separate entity for two generations. Upon the death of Julius Ernst in 1636, it was joined by his son with the domains of Hitzacker and Wolfenbüttel to form a much enlarged Brunswick-Wolfenbüttel.

RULERS

Julius Ernst, 1598-1636
August II the Younger, in district of Hitzacker, 1604-1635

MINT OFFICIALS' MARKS & INITIALS

Mark or Initial	Date	Name
HL	1617	Henning Loehr mintmaster in Osterode
(d)= 	1617-21	Georg Krukenberg, mintmaster in Hitzacker
(a)= 	1619-25	Bartold Bartels in Dannenberg
	1623-25	In Scharnebeck
(b)= 	Ca.1623	Unknown in Scharnebeck
HGM	1619-21	Hans Georg Meinhard in Winseln
	1622-?	In Moisburg
(c)= M	Ca.1623	Unknown in Scharnebeck
HMG	Ca.1623	Unknown in Scharnebeck
HKW or W	Ca.1624	Unknown in Scharnebeck

DUCHY

REGULAR COINAGE

KM# 22 6 PFENNIG

Copper, 17 mm. **Ruler:** Julius Ernst **Obv:** Shield of Brunswick arms **Obv. Legend:** IUL: ERN: D: G: D: B: ET L: **Rev:** 4-line inscription with date **Rev. Inscription:** VI / PEN / NING / (date) **Note:** W-717.

Date	Mintage	VG	F	VF	XF	Unc
1621	—	150	300	650	—	—

KM# 13 3 KREUZER (Groschen)

Silver, 18 mm. **Ruler:** Julius Ernst **Obv:** Shield of 4-fold arms **Obv. Legend:** ORA. ET. LABORA. **Rev:** Crowned imperial eagle, 3 in circle on breast, date at end of legend **Rev. Legend:** MA - R. **Note:** W-716. Kipper issue.

Date	Mintage	VG	F	VF	XF	Unc
16Z0	—	—	—	—	—	—

KM# 15 1/24 THALER (Groschen)

0.8000 g., Silver, 16 mm. **Ruler:** Julius Ernst **Obv:** Shield of arms of Unter-Diepholz **Obv. Legend:** DURAT - VIRTVS. **Rev:** Imperial orb with Z4 **Rev. Legend:** FER. II. D. G. R. I. S. AV. **Mint:** Dannenberg **Note:** Ref. W-714.

Date	Mintage	VG	F	VF	XF	Unc
ND(1619-25) (a)	—	300	600	1,200	—	—

KM# 16 2 SCHILLING (Doppelschilling = 1/16 Taler)

Silver Weight varies: 1.50-2.00g., 21-23.5 mm. **Ruler:** Julius Ernst **Obv:** Shield of 4-fold arms **Obv. Legend:** IULIUS. ERNESTUS. (D.G.) **Rev:** Intertwined DS in center, small imperial orb above **Rev. Legend:** (D.G.) DVX. BRVNS. E(T). LUN(Æ)(B). **Mint:** Dannenberg **Note:** Ref. W-712B. Kipper issue. Varieties exist.

Date	Mintage	VG	F	VF	XF	Unc
ND(1619) (a)	—	100	225	450	900	—
1620 (a)	—	100	225	450	900	—

KM# 7 2 SCHILLING (Doppelschilling = 1/16 Taler)

1.8000 g., Silver, 22 mm. **Ruler:** Julius Ernst **Obv:** Shield of 4-fold arms **Obv. Legend:** IULIUS. ERNES: D: G: D: B: E: L: **Rev:** Intertwined DS in center, small imperial orb above **Rev. Legend:** MATTHIAS. D:G. RO. IM. . AU. **Mint:** Dannenberg **Note:** Ref. W-711, 712C. Varieties exist. Kipper issue.

Date	Mintage	VG	F	VF	XF	Unc
ND(1619) (a)	—	125	275	500	1,025	—

KM# 8 2 SCHILLING (Doppelschilling = 1/16 Taler)

1.9000 g., Silver, 22.5 mm. **Ruler:** Julius Ernst **Obv:** Shield of 4-fold arms, 3 helmets above **Obv. Legend:** IULI(U). ER(N). (D.G.) **Rev:** Intertwined DS in center, small imperial orb above **Rev. Legend:** DUX. BRUNS. ET. LUNÆBU. **Note:** W-712A. Kipper issue. Varieties exist.

Date	Mintage	VG	F	VF	XF	Unc
ND(1619-21)	—	100	225	450	900	—

KM# 28 2 SCHILLING (Doppelschilling = 1/16 Taler)

Silver **Ruler:** Julius Ernst **Obv:** Shield of 4-fold arms **Rev:** 4-line inscription with date **Rev. Legend:** NACH REICHS. SCHROT. U. KORN. **Rev. Inscription:** II / SCHIL / LING / (date) **Mint:** Dannenberg **Note:** Ref. W-713.

Date	Mintage	VG	F	VF	XF	Unc
1624 (a)	—	—	—	—	—	—

KM# 6 1/16 THALER

Silver **Ruler:** Julius Ernst **Obv:** Shield of 4-fold arms, 3 helmets above **Obv. Legend:** IULI: - ERN: **Rev:** Crowned imperial eagle, 16 in orb on breast **Rev. Legend:** MATTIAS. D. G. RO: IM: S: AU: **Note:** W-712D. Kipper issue.

Date	Mintage	VG	F	VF	XF	Unc
ND(1619)	—	—	—	—	—	—

KM# 17 1/16 THALER

2.1500 g., Silver, 23 mm. **Ruler:** Julius Ernst **Obv:** Shield of 8-fold arms, 3 helmets above **Obv. Legend:** IU. ER: D - G. D. B. E. L. **Rev:** Crowned imperial eagle, 16 in orb on breast, date at end of legend **Rev. Legend:** MATTHIAS. D. G. R. IM. S. A. **Mint:** Dannenberg **Note:** W-710. Kipper issue.

Date	Mintage	VG	F	VF	XF	Unc
1619 (a)	—	—	—	—	—	—

KM# 18 1/8 THALER (1/2 Reichsort)

Silver, 29 mm. **Ruler:** Julius Ernst **Subject:** Death of Julius Ernst's Mother, Ursula of Saxe-Lauenburg **Obv:** Armored bust to right **Obv. Legend:** IULIUS. ERNEST. D. G. DUX. BRUN. E. LU. **Rev:** Six-line inscription with date **Rev. Inscription:** V. G. G. / URSULA. G. / Z. S. E. U. W. H. Z. B. / U. L. WITWE: / OBIIT. 1Z. OCT. / AN: 16Z0. **Mint:** Dannenberg **Note:** Ref. W-719.

Date	Mintage	VG	F	VF	XF	Unc
16Z0 (a)	—	—	—	—	—	—

KM# 24 1/8 THALER (1/2 Reichsort)

Silver Weigh varies: 3.00-3.50g., 24-25 mm. **Ruler:** Julius Ernst **Obv:** Armored bust to right, date at end of legend **Obv. Legend:** U. G. G. IULI. ER. H. Z. B. UL. **Rev:** 5-line inscription with date **Rev. Inscription:** I / HALBER / REICHES / ORDT / (date) **Mint:** Scharnebeck **Note:** Ref. W-708.

Date	Mintage	VG	F	VF	XF	Unc
(1)6Z3//16Z3 HMG	—	90.00	150	300	600	—

KM# 29 1/8 THALER (1/2 Reichsort)

Silver, 27 mm. **Ruler:** Julius Ernst **Obv:** Armored bust to right **Obv. Legend:** V. G. G. IULIUS. ERNESTUS. H. Z. BRUN. U. L. **Rev:** 4-line inscription, date at end of legend **Rev. Legend:** TIME DEUM. HONO: CÆSAR. **Rev. Inscription:** EIN. / HALB. / REICHS / ORT. **Mint:** Dannenberg **Note:** Ref. W-709.

Date	Mintage	VG	F	VF	XF	Unc
16Z4 (a)	—	90.00	150	300	600	—

KM# 14 4 GROSCHEN (1/6 Taler)

Silver, 23 mm. **Ruler:** Julius Ernst **Obv:** Crowned shield of 4-fold arms **Obv. Legend:** CONVERTE. ME. DOMINE. **Rev:** Crowned imperial eagle, '4G' in orb on breast **Rev. Legend:** FERDINAN. D. G. R. IM. S. AV. **Note:** Ref. W-715. Kipper issue.

Date	Mintage	VG	F	VF	XF	Unc
ND(1619-21)	—	—	—	—	—	—

KM# 25 1/4 THALER

6.7000 g., Silver, 28.5 mm. **Ruler:** Julius Ernst **Obv:** Armored bust to right, date at end of legend **Obv. Legend:** U. G. G. IULIUS. ER. H. Z. B. U. L. **Rev:** Shield of 8-fold arms **Rev. Legend:** TIME. DEUM. HONORA. CE-H. **Mint:** Scharnebeck **Note:** Ref. W-707A.

Date	Mintage	VG	F	VF	XF	Unc
(1)6Z3 (b)	—	125	275	500	1,025	—
(1)6Z3 HMG	—	125	275	500	1,025	—

KM# 30.1 1/4 THALER

Silver Weight varies: 7.00-7.10g., 29-30 mm. **Ruler:** Julius Ernst **Obv:** Armored bust to right, date at end of legend **Obv. Legend:** V. G. G. IULIUS. ERNESTUS. H. Z. BR. U. L. **Rev:** Shield of 8-fold arms, 3 ornate helmets above **Rev. Legend:** TIM. DEU. HON. CÆS. **Mint:** Dannenberg **Note:** Ref. W-707.

Date	Mintage	VG	F	VF	XF	Unc
(1)6Z4 (a)	—	125	275	500	1,025	—
ND(1624) (a)	—	125	275	500	1,025	—

KM# 30.2 1/4 THALER

7.0000 g., Silver, 29 mm. **Ruler:** Julius Ernst **Obv:** Armored bust to right, date at end of legend **Obv. Legend:** V. G. G. IVLIVS. ERNES. H. Z. BR. V. LV. **Rev:** Shield of 8-fold arms, 3 ornate helmets above **Rev. Legend:** TIM. DEV - HON. CÆ. **Mint:** Winsen **Note:** Ref. W-707.

Date	Mintage	VG	F	VF	XF	Unc
(1)6Z4 WHK	—	125	275	500	1,025	—

KM# 19 1/2 THALER

14.6500 g., Silver, 29 mm. **Ruler:** Julius Ernst **Subject:** Death of Julius Ernst's Mother, Ursula of Saxe-Lauenburg **Obv:** Armored bust to right **Obv. Legend:** IULIUS. ERNEST. D. G. DUX. BRUN. E. LU. **Rev:** 6-line inscription with date **Rev. Inscription:** V. G. G. / URSULA. G. / Z. S. E. U. W. H. Z. B. / U. L. WITWE / OBIIT. 1Z. OCT. / AN: 16Z0. **Mint:** Dannenberg **Note:** Ref. W-718A. Struck on thick flan from 1/8 Thaler dies, KM#18.

Date	Mintage	VG	F	VF	XF	Unc
16Z0 (a)	—	—	—	—	—	—

KM# 31.1 1/2 THALER

14.3000 g., Silver, 34-35 mm. **Ruler:** Julius Ernst **Obv:** Armored bust to right **Obv. Legend:** V. G. G. IULIUS. ERNESTUS. H. Z. BRUN. U. LU. **Rev:** Shield of 8-fold arms, 3 helmets above, date divided among helmets **Rev. Legend:** TIM. DEU. HON. CÆS. **Mint:** Scharnebeck **Note:** Ref. W-706.

Date	Mintage	VG	F	VF	XF	Unc
16Z3 (c)	—	1,100	2,600	5,000	9,000	—

KM# 31.2 1/2 THALER
14.3000 g., Silver, 34-35 mm. **Ruler:** Julius Ernst **Obv:** Armored bust to right **Obv. Legend:** V: G: G: IULIUS. ERNESTUS. H. Z. BRUN. U. LU. **Rev:** Shield of 8-fold arms, 3 helmets above, date divided among helmets **Rev. Legend:** TIM(E). DEU(M). (-) HO(-)N(O)(R). CÆS(A)(R). **Mint:** Dannenberg **Note:** Ref. W-706. Varieties exist.

Date	Mintage	VG	F	VF	XF	Unc
(1)6Z4 (a)	—	1,100	2,600	5,000	9,000	—
16Z4 (a)	—	1,100	2,600	5,000	9,000	—
16Z5 (a)	—	1,100	2,600	5,000	9,000	—

KM# 20 1/2 THALER
14.3000 g., Silver, 36 mm. **Ruler:** Julius Ernst **Obv:** Armored bust to right **Obv. Legend:** IULIUS. ERNESTUS. D. G. DUX. BRUN. E. LUN. **Rev:** Shield of 8-fold arms, 3 helmets above, date divided among helmets **Rev. Legend:** TIM. DEU. HO - NOR. CÆS. **Mint:** Winsen **Note:** Ref. W-705.

Date	Mintage	VG	F	VF	XF	Unc
ND(1624)	—	900	1,800	3,500	6,500	—
ND(1624) W	—	900	1,800	3,500	6,500	—

KM# 5.2 THALER
27.6000 g., Silver, 41 mm. **Ruler:** Julius Ernst **Obv:** 2 busts facing each other **Obv. Legend:** D. G. IULI, ERNEST, AUGUST, DUCES. BR. ET. LU. **Rev:** Shield of 8-fold arms, 3 ornate helmets above, date at end of legend **Rev. Legend:** CONCORDIA. DITAT. ANNO. **Mint:** Clausthal **Note:** Ref. W-720. Dav. 6416.

Date	Mintage	VG	F	VF	XF	Unc
1617 (d) Rare	—	—	—	—	—	—

KM# 5.1 THALER
29.0000 g., Silver, 42 mm. **Ruler:** Julius Ernst **Obv:** Two busts facing each other **Obv. Legend:** D. G. IULI, ERNEST, AUGUST, DUCES. BR. ET. LU. **Rev:** Shield of 8-fold arms, 3 ornate helmets above, date at end of legend **Rev. Legend:** CONCORDIA. DITAT. ANNO. **Mint:** Osterode **Note:** Ref. W-720; Dav. 6415.

Date	Mintage	VG	F	VF	XF	Unc
1617 HL Rare	—	—	—	—	—	—

KM# 9 THALER
29.0000 g., Silver, 42-43 mm. **Ruler:** Julius Ernst **Obv:** Armored bust to right **Obv. Legend:** IULIUS. ERNESTUS. D: G: DUX. B: ET: LUNÆB **Rev:** Shield of 8-fold arms, 3 ornate helmets above, date divided among helmets **Rev. Legend:** RECTE. FACIENDO. - NEMINEM. TIMEAS. **Mint:** Dannenberg **Note:** Ref. W-701; Dav. 6418.

Date	Mintage	VG	F	VF	XF	Unc
1619 (a)	—	750	1,250	2,200	—	—
16Z0 (a)	—	750	1,250	2,200	—	—

KM# 21 THALER
29.0000 g., Silver, 42 mm. **Ruler:** Julius Ernst **Subject:** Death of Julius Ernst's Mother, Ursula of Saxe-Lauenburg **Obv:** Armored bust to right **Obv. Legend:** IULIUS. ERNESTUS D. G. DUX. B. ET. LUNÆB. **Rev:** 8-line inscription with date **Rev. Inscription:** V. G. G. / URSULA. G. / Z. S. E. U. W. H. Z. B. U. / L. WITTIBE. IM. / LXVII. IAHR. / IHRES. ALTERS. / OBIIT. 1Z. OCT / A. 16Z0. **Mint:** Dannenberg **Note:** Ref. W-718; Dav. 6428.

Date	Mintage	VG	F	VF	XF	Unc
16Z0 (a) Rare	—	—	—	—	—	—

KM# 10 THALER
29.0000 g., Silver, 41-42 mm. **Ruler:** Julius Ernst **Obv:** Armored bust to right **Obv. Legend:** IULIUS. ERNESTUS. D. G. DUX. BRUN. E. LUNÆ. **Rev:** Crowned imperial eagle, 3Z in orb on breast **Rev. Legend:** FERDINANDVS. II. D. G. ROM(A). IM. SE(M). AU. **Mint:** Dannenberg **Note:** Ref. W-702; Dav. 6419. 32 Schilling. Varieties exist.

Date	Mintage	VG	F	VF	XF	Unc
ND(1621) (a)	—	700	1,200	2,000	—	—

KM# 23.1 THALER
29.0000 g., Silver, 42 mm. **Ruler:** Julius Ernst **Obv:** Armored bust to right **Obv. Legend:** IULIUS. ERNESTUS. D. G. DUX. BRUN. E. LUNÆ. **Rev:** Shield of 8-fold arms, 3 ornate helmets above, date in margin at top **Rev. Legend:** TIME. DEUM. - HONO. CÆSA. **Mint:** Dannenberg **Note:** Ref. W-703A. Dav. 6420.

Date	Mintage	VG	F	VF	XF	Unc
16ZZ (a)	—	375	750	1,200	2,000	—
16Z3 (a)	—	375	750	1,200	2,000	—
ND(1623) (a)	—	375	750	1,200	2,000	—

KM# 26.1 THALER
29.0000 g., Silver, 41 mm. **Ruler:** Julius Ernst **Obv:** Armored bust to right **Obv. Legend:** IULIUS. ERNESTUS. D. G. DUX. B: ET: LUNÆB. **Rev:** Shield of 8-fold arms, date divided among 3 ornate helmets above **Rev. Legend:** TIME. DEUM. - HONO. CAESA. **Mint:** Scharnebeck **Note:** Ref. W-703B; Dav. 6421.

Date	Mintage	VG	F	VF	XF	Unc
16Z3 (c)	—	900	1,650	2,750	—	—

KM# 27.1 THALER
29.0000 g., Silver, 41 mm. **Ruler:** Julius Ernst **Obv:** Armored bust to right **Obv. Legend:** U. G. G. IULIUS. ERNESTUS. H. Z. BR. U. LU. **Rev:** Shield of 8-fold arms, date divided among 3 ornate helmets above **Rev. Legend:** TIME. DEUM. - HONO. CÆSA. **Mint:** Scharnebeck **Note:** Ref. W-703B; Dav. 6422.

Date	Mintage	VG	F	VF	XF	Unc
16Z3 (c)//HMG	—	300	600	975	1,650	—

KM# 27.2 THALER
29.0000 g., Silver, 41 mm. **Ruler:** Julius Ernst **Obv:** Armored bust to right **Obv. Legend:** U. G. G. IULIUS. ERNESTUS. H. Z. BR. U. LU. **Rev:** Shield of 8-fold arms, date divided among 3 ornate helmets above **Rev. Legend:** TIME. DEUM. - HONO. CÆSA. **Mint:** Scharnebeck **Note:** Ref. Dav. 6422A.

Date	Mintage	VG	F	VF	XF	Unc
16Z3 (c)	—	300	600	975	1,750	—

KM# 32 THALER
29.0000 g., Silver, 41 mm. **Ruler:** Julius Ernst **Obv:** Armored bust to right **Obv. Legend:** V. G. G. IULIUS. ERNESTUS. H. Z. BRUN. U. LUN. **Rev:** Ornate shield of 8-fold arms, 3 ornate helmets above, date divided in margin at top **Rev. Legend:** TIME. DEUM. (-) HO(-)NOR(A). CÆSA(R)(E)(M). **Mint:** Dannenberg **Note:** Ref. W-704; Dav. 6427. Varieties exist.

Date	Mintage	VG	F	VF	XF	Unc
16Z4 (a)	—	280	550	900	1,650	—
16Z5 (a)	—	280	550	900	1,650	—

KM# 27.4 THALER
Silver Weight varies: 28.65-29.10g., 42 mm. **Ruler:** Julius Ernst **Obv:** Armored bust to right **Obv. Legend:** V: G: G: IULIUS. ERNESTUS. H. Z. BRUN. U. LUN. **Rev:** Ornate shield of 8-fold arms in baroque frame, date divided among 3 ornate helmets above **Rev. Legend:** TIME. DEUM. HO - NORA. CÆSAREM. **Mint:** Dannenberg **Note:** Ref. W-704; Dav. 6426.

Date	Mintage	VG	F	VF	XF	Unc
16Z4 (a)	—	280	550	950	1,650	—
16Z5 (a)	—	300	600	950	1,750	—

KM# 23.2 THALER
29.0000 g., Silver, 42-43 mm. **Ruler:** Julius Ernst **Obv:** Armored bust to right **Obv. Legend:** IULIUS. ERNESTUS. D. G. DUX. BRUN. E. LUNÆ. **Rev:** Ornate shield of 8-fold arms in baroque frame, 3 ornate helmets above, date divided in margin at top **Rev. Legend:** TIME. DEUM. HO(-)N(-)ORA. CÆSAR. **Mint:** Dannenberg **Note:** Ref. W-703A; Dav. 6423. Varieties exist.

Date	Mintage	VG	F	VF	XF	Unc
16Z4 (a)	—	1,000	2,000	4,000	6,500	—

KM# 26.2 THALER

29.0000 g., Silver, 43 mm. **Ruler:** Julius Ernst **Obv:** Armored bust to right **Obv. Legend:** IULIUS. ERNESTUS. D. G. DUX. BRUN: E: LUN. **Rev:** Shield of 8-fold arms, date divided among 3 ornate helmets above **Rev. Legend:** TIME. DEUM. HON - ORA. CAESAREM. **Note:** Ref. W-703B; Dav. 6424.

Date	Mintage	VG	F	VF	XF	Unc
16Z4	—	475	950	1,750	3,000	—

KM# 27.3 THALER

29.0000 g., Silver, 43-44 mm. **Ruler:** Julius Ernst **Obv:** Armored bust to right **Obv. Legend:** V.G.G. IVLIVS. ERNESTVS. H. Z. BRVN. V. L. **Rev:** Shield of 8-fold arms, date divided among 3 ornate helmets above **Rev. Legend:** TIME. DEVM. - HONO. CAESA. **Mint:** Winsen **Note:** Ref. W-703B; Dav. 6425.

Date	Mintage	VG	F	VF	XF	Unc
16Z4 HKW	—	500	1,000	2,000	—	—

KM# 27.5 THALER

29.0000 g., Silver, 42 mm. **Ruler:** Julius Ernst **Obv:** Armored bust to right **Obv. Legend:** V. G. G. IULIUS. ERNESTUS. H. Z. BRUN. U. LUN. **Rev:** Ornate shield of 8-fold arms in baroque frame, date divided among 3 ornate helmets above **Rev. Legend:** TIME. DEUM. HONO.C(Æ)(AE)SA. **Mint:** Dannenberg **Note:** Ref. W-704; Dav. 6426A.

Date	Mintage	VG	F	VF	XF	Unc
16Z4 (a)	—	275	475	825	1,700	—

KM# 27.6 THALER

29.0000 g., Silver, 42 mm. **Ruler:** Julius Ernst **Obv:** Armored bust to right **Obv. Legend:** V. G. G. IULIUS. ERNESTUS. H. Z. BRUN. U. LUN. **Rev:** Ornate shield of 8-fold arms in baroque frame, date divided among 3 ornate helmets above **Rev. Legend:** TIME. DEUM. HONO. CÆSAR. **Note:** Ref. W-704; Dav. 6426B. Varieties exist.

Date	Mintage	VG	F	VF	XF	Unc
16Z5 (a)	—	275	425	750	1,650	—

KM# 11 2 THALER

58.0000 g., Silver, 41-42 mm. **Ruler:** Julius Ernst **Obv:** Armored bust to right **Obv. Legend:** IULIUS. ERNESTUS. D. G. DUX. B. ET. LUNÆB. **Rev:** Shield of 8-fold arms divides date, 3 ornate helmets above **Rev. Legend:** RECTE. FACIENDO. - NEMINEM. TIMEAS. **Mint:** Dannenberg **Note:** Ref. W-700; Dav. 6417.

Date	Mintage	VG	F	VF	XF	Unc
1619 (a)	—	5,400	9,000	15,000	—	—

TRADE COINAGE

KM# 12 GOLDGULDEN

3.2500 g., Gold, 23 mm. **Ruler:** Julius Ernst **Obv:** Armored bust to right **Obv. Legend:** IVLIVS. ERNESTVS. D. G. D. B. E. L. **Rev:** Shield of 8-fold arms, 3 ornate helmets above, date at end of legend **Rev. Legend:** REC. FAC. NE. TI. **Mint:** Dannenberg **Note:** Ref. W-698; Fr. 539.

Date	Mintage	VG	F	VF	XF	Unc
1619 (a) Rare	—	—	—	—	—	—

KM# 33 DUCAT

3.5000 g., 0.9860 Gold Weight varies: 3.30-3.49g. 0.1109 oz. AGW, 22.5 mm. **Ruler:** Julius Ernst **Obv:** Bust to right **Obv. Legend:** V. G. G. IUL. ERNES. H. Z. BR. U. L. **Rev:** Shield of 8-fold arms, 3 ornate helmets above, date at end of legend **Rev. Legend:** T. D. H. CÆS. **Mint:** Dannenberg **Note:** Ref. W-699; Fr. 540.

Date	Mintage	VG	F	VF	XF	Unc
(1)6Z5 (a) Rare	—	—	—	—	—	—

BRUNSWICK-HARBURG

Harburg, a city on the Elbe just south of Hamburg and about 22 miles northwest of the city of Lüneburg, was the seat of a branch line of dukes founded from Brunswick-Lüneburg in 1521. This line became extinct and the territory went to Brunswick-Lüneburg-Celle in 1642.

RULERS

Otto I der Ältere, 1521-1549
Otto II der Jüngere, 1549-1603
Christoph, 1603-1606
Otto III, 1603-41
Johann Friedrich, 1603-1619
Wilhelm VI August, 1603-1642

MINT OFFICIALS' INITIALS

Initial	Date	Name
(t)= 	1615-19	Thomas Timpf the Elder
(h)= 	1618-24	Thomas Timpf the Younger
(b)= 	1619-25	Barthold Bartels in Dannenberg
	1625	In Scharnebeck
	1630-31	In Harburg
GM= 	1622	Hans Georg Meinhard in Moisburg
HS	1622-40	Henning Schreiber in Clausthal
HR	1622-27	Hans Rücke in Harburg
	1622-26	In Moisburg
CH	1625-26	Lazarus Christian Hopfgarten in Harburg
(q)= 	1627-29	Wilhelm Quensel in Harburg and Moisburg

DUCHY

REGULAR COINAGE

KM# A21 WITTEN (1/96 Thaler)

Silver, 16 mm. **Ruler:** Otto III **Obv:** Lüneburg arms **Rev:** Cross divides value 9 - 6 **Note:** Ref. W#742B.

Date	Mintage	VG	F	VF	XF	Unc
16ZZ	—	—	—	—	—	—

KM# 6 PFENNIG

Silver **Ruler:** Wilhelm VI August **Note:** 4-fold arms. Varieties exist.

Date	Mintage	VG	F	VF	XF	Unc
ND(ca-1610)	—	85.00	175	375	775	—

KM# 5 PFENNIG

Silver **Ruler:** Wilhelm VI August **Note:** Uniface. Hohlpfennig type. 6-fold arms, W above, no legend.

Date	Mintage	VG	F	VF	XF	Unc
ND(ca-1610)	—	85.00	175	375	775	—

KM# 20 3 PFENNIG

Silver **Ruler:** Wilhelm VI August **Obv:** Brunswick helmet with horse crest **Rev:** Imperial orb with 3

Date	Mintage	VG	F	VF	XF	Unc
1622	—	30.00	60.00	120	—	—

KM# A20 3 PFENNIG

Silver **Ruler:** Otto III **Obv:** Ornamented shield of Lüneburg arms, W.D.B.E.L. above **Rev:** Value in 4 lines **Note:** Ref. W#743B.

Date	Mintage	VG	F	VF	XF	Unc
ND(1622-23)	—	30.00	60.00	120	—	—

KM# 27 3 PFENNIG

Copper **Ruler:** Wilhelm VI August **Obv:** Lüneburg arms **Rev:** Value, date in 4 lines

Date	Mintage	VG	F	VF	XF	Unc
1623	—	30.00	60.00	120	—	—

KM# A23 3 PFENNIG

Silver **Ruler:** Otto III **Obv:** Lüneburg arms in oval shield (lion with 8 hearts around) **Rev:** Value and date in 4 lines **Note:** Ref. W#743A.

Date	Mintage	VG	F	VF	XF	Unc
16Z3	—	30.00	60.00	120	—	—

KM# 18 12 KREUZER

Silver **Ruler:** Wilhelm VI August **Obv:** Crowned imperial eagle, 12 in orb on breast, titles of Ferdinand II **Rev:** Crowned 12-fold arms **Note:** Kipper 12 Kreuzer.

Date	Mintage	VG	F	VF	XF	Unc
(1621/2)	—	45.00	85.00	165	325	—

KM# 42 2 MARIENGROSCHEN

Silver **Ruler:** Wilhelm VI August **Obv:** Brunswick helmet with horse **Rev:** Value II, date in 4 lines

Date	Mintage	VG	F	VF	XF	Unc
1638 HS	—	35.00	65.00	110	230	—
1639 HS	—	35.00	65.00	110	230	—
1640 HS	—	35.00	65.00	110	230	—
1642 HS	—	35.00	65.00	110	230	—
ND HS	—	35.00	65.00	110	230	—

KM# 19 4 GROSCHEN (1/6 Thaler)

Silver **Ruler:** Wilhelm VI August **Obv:** Crowned imperial eagle, 4G in orb on breast, titles of Ferdinand II **Rev:** Crowned 6-fold arms **Note:** Kipper 4 Groschen.

Date	Mintage	VG	F	VF	XF	Unc
1621	—	—	—	—	—	—

KM# 11 1/24 THALER

Silver **Ruler:** Wilhelm VI August **Obv:** Imperial orb with 24, titles of Matthias **Rev:** Ornamented 4-fold arms **Note:** Varieties exist.

Date	Mintage	VG	F	VF	XF	Unc
1618	—	17.00	33.00	60.00	120	—
1619	—	17.00	33.00	60.00	120	—

KM# B12 1/24 THALER

Silver **Ruler:** Wilhelm VI August **Obv:** Imperial orb with 24, titles of Matthias **Rev:** Helmet above 2 shields with 2 leopards and lion rampant left between hearts **Note:** Prev. KM#51.

Date	Mintage	VG	F	VF	XF	Unc
1619	—	150	300	600	1,200	—

KM# 13 1/24 THALER

Silver **Ruler:** Wilhelm VI August **Obv:** Titles of Ferdinand II

Date	Mintage	VG	F	VF	XF	Unc
1620	—	20.00	42.00	70.00	140	—
1621	—	20.00	42.00	70.00	140	—
ND	—	20.00	42.00	70.00	140	—

KM# 23 1/24 THALER

Silver **Ruler:** Wilhelm VI August **Rev:** Brunswick helmet with horse

Date	Mintage	VG	F	VF	XF	Unc
1622	—	20.00	42.00	70.00	140	—

KM# 7 1/16 THALER

Silver **Ruler:** Wilhelm VI August **Obv:** Crowned imperial eagle, 16 in orb on breast, date in legend, titles of Matthias **Rev:** Helmeted 6-fold arms

Date	Mintage	VG	F	VF	XF	Unc
1616	—	32.00	60.00	120	240	—
1617	—	32.00	60.00	120	240	—
1618	—	32.00	60.00	120	240	—
(16)19	—	32.00	60.00	120	240	—
ND	—	32.00	60.00	120	240	—
1619	—	32.00	60.00	120	240	—

KM# 12 1/16 THALER

Silver **Ruler:** Wilhelm VI August **Rev:** Crowned 6-fold arms

Date	Mintage	VG	F	VF	XF	Unc
1619	—	35.00	65.00	130	265	—

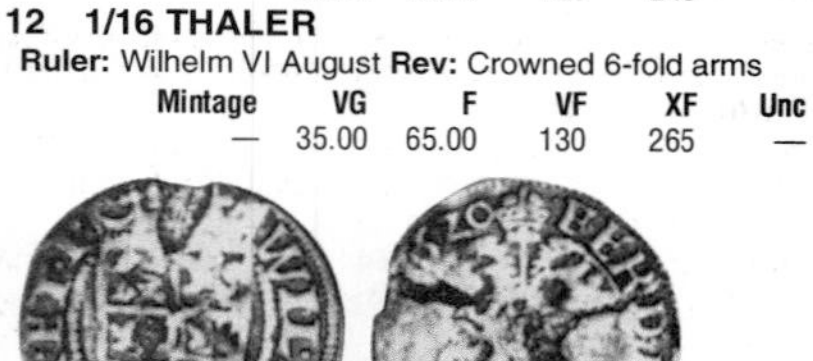

KM# 14.1 1/16 THALER

Silver **Ruler:** Wilhelm VI August **Obv:** Titles of Ferdinand II

Date	Mintage	VG	F	VF	XF	Unc
1620	—	60.00	120	190	380	—
1621	—	60.00	120	190	380	—
ND	—	60.00	120	190	380	—

KM# 14.2 1/16 THALER

Silver **Ruler:** Wilhelm VI August **Obv:** 4-fold arms with 3 helmets above

Date	Mintage	VG	F	VF	XF	Unc
16Z0	—	60.00	120	190	380	—

KM# 22 1/2 REICHSORT (= 1/8 Thaler)

Silver **Ruler:** Wilhelm VI August **Note:** Klippe.

Date	Mintage	VG	F	VF	XF	Unc
1622 (h)	—	—	—	—	—	—
1622 HR	—	—	—	—	—	—

KM# 21 1/2 REICHSORT (= 1/8 Thaler)

Silver **Ruler:** Wilhelm VI August **Note:** Varieties exist.

Date	Mintage	VG	F	VF	XF	Unc
1622	—	80.00	160	300	500	—
1622 (h)	—	80.00	160	300	500	—
1622 HR	—	80.00	160	300	500	—
1623 (h)	—	80.00	160	300	500	—
1624 (h)	—	80.00	160	300	500	—
1627 HR	—	80.00	160	300	500	—

KM# 24 1/8 THALER

Silver **Ruler:** Wilhelm VI August **Obv:** Bust right **Rev:** Helmeted 6-fold arms

Date	Mintage	VG	F	VF	XF	Unc
1622	—	225	425	750	1,400	—

KM# 30 1/8 THALER

Silver **Ruler:** Wilhelm VI August **Rev:** Value in 4 lines

Date	Mintage	VG	F	VF	XF	Unc
1625 CH	—	225	425	750	1,400	—

KM# 31 1/8 THALER

Silver **Ruler:** Wilhelm VI August **Obv:** 6-fold arms, small imperial orb **Rev. Legend:** VIII/EINEN/REICHS/DALER

Date	Mintage	VG	F	VF	XF	Unc
1625 CH	—	225	425	750	1,400	—

KM# 32 1/8 THALER

Silver **Ruler:** Wilhelm VI August **Subject:** Death of Wilhelm August's 7th Son, Johannes **Obv:** 7-fold arms **Rev:** 8-line inscription

Date	Mintage	VG	F	VF	XF	Unc
1628 HS	—	100	190	325	675	—

KM# 36 1/8 THALER

Silver **Ruler:** Wilhelm VI August **Subject:** Death of Wilhelm August's 5th Son, Magnus **Obv:** Crowned 7-fold arms **Rev:** Crown above 6-line inscription with date

Date	Mintage	VG	F	VF	XF	Unc
1632 HS	—	100	190	325	675	—

KM# 43 1/8 THALER

Silver **Ruler:** Wilhelm VI August **Subject:** Death of Wilhelm August **Obv:** Crowned 11-fold arms **Rev:** 9-line inscription with date

Date	Mintage	VG	F	VF	XF	Unc
1642 HS	—	100	190	325	675	—

KM# 25 1/4 THALER

Silver **Ruler:** Wilhelm VI August **Obv:** Bust right **Rev:** Helmeted oval 6-fold arms, date divided at top **Note:** Varieties exist.

Date	Mintage	VG	F	VF	XF	Unc
1622 HR	—	350	700	1,400	2,400	—
1623	—	750	1,500	3,000	—	—
1624 HR	—	350	700	1,400	2,400	—
1627 HR	—	350	700	1,400	2,400	—
1630	—	350	700	1,400	2,400	—
1630 (b)	—	350	700	1,400	2,400	—
1631 (b)	—	350	700	1,400	2,400	—
ND (h)	—	350	700	1,400	2,400	—
ND HR	—	350	700	1,400	2,400	—

KM# 33 1/4 THALER

Silver **Ruler:** Wilhelm VI August **Subject:** Death of Wilhelm August's 7th Son, Johannes **Obv:** 7-fold arms **Rev:** 8-line inscription

Date	Mintage	VG	F	VF	XF	Unc
1628 HS	—	175	375	675	1,150	—

KM# 37 1/4 THALER

Silver **Ruler:** Wilhelm VI August **Subject:** Death of Wilhelm August's 5th Son, Magnus **Obv:** Crowned 7-fold arms **Rev:** Crown above 6-line inscription

Date	Mintage	VG	F	VF	XF	Unc
1632 HS	—	175	375	675	1,150	—

KM# 44 1/4 THALER

Silver **Ruler:** Wilhelm VI August **Subject:** Death of Wilhelm August **Obv:** Crowned 11-fold arms **Rev:** 9-line inscription with date

Date	Mintage	VG	F	VF	XF	Unc
1642 HS	—	175	375	675	1,150	—

KM# 47 1/4 THALER

Silver **Ruler:** Wilhelm VI August **Subject:** Death of Wilhelm August's Sister, Catherine Sophie, Countess of Schaumburg-Saxonhagen **Obv:** Crowned 12-fold arms **Rev:** 8-line inscription with date

Date	Mintage	VG	F	VF	XF	Unc
1665	—	175	375	675	1,150	—

KM# 15 1/2 THALER

Silver **Ruler:** Wilhelm VI August **Obv:** Bust right **Rev:** Helmeted oval 6-fold arms, date divided at top **Note:** Varieties exist.

Date	Mintage	VG	F	VF	XF	Unc
1620 (h)	—	650	1,300	2,400	—	—
1622 HR	—	650	1,300	2,400	—	—
1622	—	650	1,300	2,400	—	—
1623 (h)	—	650	1,300	2,400	—	—
1623	—	650	1,300	2,400	—	—
1624 HR	—	650	1,300	2,400	—	—
1625 CH	—	650	1,300	2,400	—	—
1627	—	650	1,300	2,400	—	—
1630 (b)	—	650	1,300	2,400	—	—

KM# 34 1/2 THALER

Silver **Ruler:** Wilhelm VI August **Subject:** Death of Wilhelm August's 7th Son, Johannes **Obv:** 7-fold arms **Rev:** 8-line inscription

Date	Mintage	VG	F	VF	XF	Unc
1628 HS	—	290	500	875	1,700	—

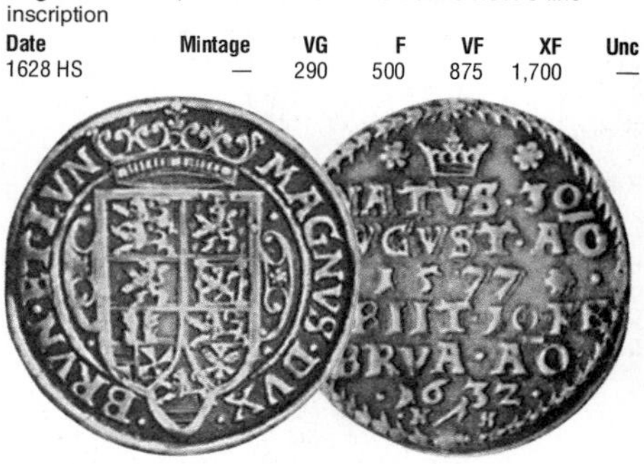

KM# 38 1/2 THALER

Silver **Ruler:** Wilhelm VI August **Subject:** Death of Wilhelm August's 5th Son, Magnus **Obv:** Crowned 7-fold arms **Rev:** Crown above 6-line inscription

Date	Mintage	VG	F	VF	XF	Unc
1632 HS	—	290	500	875	1,700	—

KM# 45 1/2 THALER

Silver **Ruler:** Wilhelm VI August **Subject:** Death of Wilhelm August **Obv:** Facing bust **Rev:** 9-line inscription with date

Date	Mintage	VG	F	VF	XF	Unc
1642 HS	—	290	500	875	1,700	—

KM# 48 1/2 THALER

Silver **Ruler:** Wilhelm VI August **Subject:** Death of Wilhelm August's Sister, Catherine Sophie, Countess of Schaumburg-Saxonhagen **Obv:** Crowned 12-fold arms **Rev:** 8-line inscription with date

Date	Mintage	VG	F	VF	XF	Unc
1665	—	290	500	875	1,700	—

KM# 8 THALER

Silver **Ruler:** Wilhelm VI August **Obv:** Bust right, date in field to right **Rev:** Triple-helmeted 6-fold arms **Note:** Dav. #6402.

Date	Mintage	VG	F	VF	XF	Unc
1617	—	350	625	1,000	1,600	—

KM# 9 THALER

Silver **Ruler:** Wilhelm VI August **Obv:** Similar to KM#16 **Rev:** Date at top **Note:** Dav. #6403.

Date	Mintage	VG	F	VF	XF	Unc
1617	—	350	625	1,000	1,600	—

KM# 16 THALER

Silver **Ruler:** Wilhelm VI August **Obv:** Bust right **Rev:** Triple-helmeted 6-fold arms, date divided at top **Note:** Varieties exist. Dav. #6405.

Date	Mintage	VG	F	VF	XF	Unc
1620 (h)	—	150	300	500	1,000	—
1622 (h)	—	150	300	500	1,000	—
1622 HR	—	150	300	500	1,000	—
1622	—	150	300	500	1,000	—
1623 (h)	—	150	300	500	1,000	—
1623 HR	—	150	300	500	1,000	—
1623	—	150	300	500	1,000	—
1624 (h)	—	150	300	500	1,000	—
1624 HR	—	150	300	500	1,000	—
1625 CH	—	150	300	500	1,000	—
1625 HR	—	150	300	500	1,000	—
1627 HR	—	150	300	500	1,000	—
1627 (q)	—	150	300	500	1,000	—
1630 (b)	—	150	300	500	1,000	—
1631 (b)	—	150	300	500	1,000	—
ND HR	—	150	300	500	1,000	—

KM# 26 THALER

Silver **Ruler:** Wilhelm VI August **Note:** Klippe. Dav. #6405A.

Date	Mintage	VG	F	VF	XF	Unc
1622 (h) GM Rare	—	—	—	—	—	—
1624 (h) Rare	—	—	—	—	—	—

KM# 28 THALER

Silver **Ruler:** Wilhelm VI August **Rev:** Date divided below arms **Note:** Dav. #6406.

Date	Mintage	VG	F	VF	XF	Unc
1623 HR	—	350	625	1,000	1,600	—

KM# 29 THALER

Silver **Ruler:** Wilhelm VI August **Rev:** Date divided between helmets **Note:** Dav. #6406A.

Date	Mintage	VG	F	VF	XF	Unc
1623 HR	—	350	625	1,000	1,600	—

KM# 35 THALER

Silver **Ruler:** Wilhelm VI August **Subject:** Death of Wilhelm August's 7th Son, Johannes **Note:** Dav. #6656.

Date	Mintage	VG	F	VF	XF	Unc
16Z8 HS	—	350	725	1,400	2,600	—

KM# 39 THALER

Silver **Ruler:** Wilhelm VI August **Subject:** Death of Wilhelm August's 5th Son, Magnus **Obv:** Crowned 7-fold arms **Rev:** Crown above 6-line inscription **Note:** Dav. #6657.

Date	Mintage	VG	F	VF	XF	Unc
1632 HS	—	350	725	1,400	2,600	—

KM# 40.1 THALER

Silver **Ruler:** Wilhelm VI August **Obv:** Facing 1/2-length figure **Obv. Legend:** WILHELMUS.D:G. DUX.BRUNS.ET.LUNEB **Rev:** 5 helmets above 11-fold arms, date in legend **Note:** Dav. #6407.

Date	Mintage	VG	F	VF	XF	Unc
1636 HS	—	150	300	550	950	—

KM# 40.2 THALER

Silver **Ruler:** Wilhelm VI August **Obv. Legend:** BRUNSUIC. ET. LUNEB **Note:** Dav. #6408.

Date	Mintage	VG	F	VF	XF	Unc
1637 HS	—	150	300	550	950	—
1638 HS	—	150	300	550	950	—

KM# 40.3 THALER

Silver **Ruler:** Wilhelm VI August **Rev:** Date right of plume above helmets **Note:** Dav. #6409.

Date	Mintage	VG	F	VF	XF	Unc
1638 HS	—	150	300	550	950	—

KM# 40.5 THALER

Silver **Ruler:** Wilhelm VI August **Obv:** Head to outer edge **Rev:** Helmeted arms to edge at top **Note:** Dav. #6411.

Date	Mintage	VG	F	VF	XF	Unc
1639 HS	—	125	265	425	750	—

KM# 40.4 THALER

Silver **Ruler:** Wilhelm VI August **Obv. Legend:** ...LUNE **Rev:** Date **Rev. Legend:** ...PROUI--DEBIT-ANO **Note:** Varieties exist. Dav. #6410.

Date	Mintage	VG	F	VF	XF	Unc
1639 HS	—	125	265	425	750	—

KM# 40.6 THALER

Silver **Ruler:** Wilhelm VI August **Rev:** Legend without ANO or AO **Note:** Varieties exist. Dav. #6412.

Date	Mintage	VG	F	VF	XF	Unc
1640 HS	—	125	265	425	750	—
1641 HS	—	125	265	425	750	—
1642 HS	—	125	265	425	750	—

KM# 46 THALER

Silver **Ruler:** Wilhelm VI August **Subject:** Death of Wilhelm August **Obv:** Facing 1/2-length figure **Rev:** 10-line inscription with date **Note:** Dav. #6413.

Date	Mintage	VG	F	VF	XF	Unc
1642 HS	—	150	300	550	950	—

KM# 49 THALER

Silver **Subject:** Death of Wilhelm August's Sister, Catherine Sophie, Countess of Schaumburg-Saxonhagen **Obv:** Crowned 12-fold arms **Rev:** 9-line inscription with date **Note:** Dav. #6414.

Date	Mintage	VG	F	VF	XF	Unc
1665 Rare	—	—	—	—	—	—

KM# A12 1-1/2 THALER
44.7000 g., Silver **Ruler:** Wilhelm VI August **Obv:** 1/2-length figure towards helmet on table right **Rev:** Triple-helmeted 6-fold arms **Note:** Dav. #LS248. Prev. KM#50.

Date	Mintage	VG	F	VF	XF	Unc
ND(ca.l1618) Rare	—	—	—	—	—	—

KM# 10 2 THALER
Silver **Ruler:** Wilhelm VI August **Obv:** Bust right, date in field to right **Rev:** Triple-helmeted 6-fold arms **Note:** Dav. #6401.

Date	Mintage	VG	F	VF	XF	Unc
1617 Rare	—	—	—	—	—	—

KM# 17 2 THALER
Silver **Ruler:** Wilhelm VI August **Obv:** Bust right **Rev:** Triple-helmeted 6-fold arms, date divided at top **Note:** Dav. #6404.

Date	Mintage	VG	F	VF	XF	Unc
1620 (h) Rare	—	—	—	—	—	—

BRUNSWICK-HITZACKER

This subdivision of Brunswick-Dannenberg, centered on the town of the same name located on the Elbe Riveer just 4 miles (7 km) north-northwest of Dannenberg, was administered separately by one ruler in the early 17th century. It returned to the general governance of Dannenberg a year before the latter was united to Brunswick-Wolfenbüttel.

RULER
August II der Jüngere, 1604-1635

REFERENCE
W = Gerhard Welter, ***Die Münzen der Welfen seit Heinrich dem Löwen***, 3 v., Braunschweig: Klinkhardt & Biermann, 1971-78.

DUCHY

REGULAR COINAGE

KM# 54 1/96 THALER (Sechsling)
Silver **Ruler:** August II **Obv:** Imperial orb with 96, titles of Ferdinand II, date in legend **Rev:** Lion rampant left

Date	Mintage	VG	F	VF	XF	Unc
1622	—	—	—	—	—	—

KM# 46 1/24 THALER (Groschen)
Silver **Ruler:** August II **Obv:** 2-fold arms divided vertically, Brunswick on left, Luneburg on right, titles of August II **Rev:** Imperial orb with Z4, titles of Ferdinand II, date in margin **Note:** W#761.

Date	Mintage	VG	F	VF	XF	Unc
1620	—	175	320	600	1,100	—
1621	—	175	320	600	1,100	—
16ZZ	—	175	320	600	1,100	—

KM# 40 1/16 THALER (Doppelschilling)
Silver **Ruler:** August II **Obv:** Five-fold arms, titles of August II **Rev:** DS in imperial orb, date in margin **Note:** W#757A.

Date	Mintage	VG	F	VF	XF	Unc
(1)618	—	—	—	—	—	—

KM# 42.2 1/16 THALER (Doppelschilling)
Silver **Ruler:** August II **Obv:** Crowned arms of lion rampant right, surrounded by small hearts (Luneburg) **Rev:** DS in circle, date in margin

Date	Mintage	VG	F	VF	XF	Unc
1619	—	—	—	—	—	—

KM# 41 1/16 THALER (Doppelschilling)
Silver **Ruler:** August II **Obv:** Lion rampant to right, date in margin **Rev:** DS in circle **Note:** Kipper. W#755.

Date	Mintage	VG	F	VF	XF	Unc
1619	—	—	—	—	—	—
ND	—	—	—	—	—	—

KM# 42.1 1/16 THALER (Doppelschilling)
Silver **Ruler:** August II **Obv:** Lion rampant right **Rev:** 'DS' in circle, date in margin **Note:** Ref. W#755.

Date	Mintage	VG	F	VF	XF	Unc
1619	—	—	—	—	—	—

KM# 49 1/16 THALER (Doppelschilling)
Silver **Ruler:** August II **Obv:** H.Z. BRUN. U LUN. in margin, date **Note:** Similar to KM#48. W#757.

Date	Mintage	VG	F	VF	XF	Unc
1619	—	75.00	150	250	500	—
16Z0	—	75.00	150	250	500	—

KM# 42.3 1/16 THALER (Doppelschilling)
Silver **Ruler:** August II **Rev:** DS in Spanish shield **Note:** W#755B.

Date	Mintage	VG	F	VF	XF	Unc
1619	—	—	—	—	—	—

KM# 43 1/16 THALER (Doppelschilling)
Silver **Ruler:** August II **Obv:** 4-fold arms, titles of August II **Rev:** DS in circle, small imperial orb above, date in margin **Note:** W#756.

Date	Mintage	VG	F	VF	XF	Unc
1619	—	75.00	150	275	500	—
16Z0	—	75.00	150	275	500	—

KM# 48 1/16 THALER (Doppelschilling)
Silver **Ruler:** August II **Obv:** DS in circle, date in margin **Rev:** Crowned imperial eagle, 16 in orb on breast, titles of Ferdinand II **Note:** W#757.

Date	Mintage	VG	F	VF	XF	Unc
(16)Z0	—	75.00	150	275	500	—

KM# 50 1/16 THALER (Doppelschilling)
1.6000 g., Silver, 21.8 mm. **Ruler:** August II **Obv:** Four-fold arms, AUGUSTUS... **Rev:** DS is circle, margin AUGUSTUS..., date **Note:** W#759.

Date	Mintage	VG	F	VF	XF	Unc
(16)Z0	—	85.00	165	285	550	—

KM# 51 1/16 THALER (Doppelschilling)
Silver **Ruler:** August II **Obv:** DS in circle **Rev:** Imperial eagle, 16 in orb on breast **Note:** W#760.

Date	Mintage	VG	F	VF	XF	Unc
16Z0	—	75.00	150	275	475	—

KM# 55 1/4 THALER
Silver **Ruler:** August II **Note:** W#754.

Date	Mintage	VG	F	VF	XF	Unc
16ZZ	—	—	—	—	—	—
1623 (t)	—	—	—	—	—	—

KM# 56 1/2 THALER
Silver **Ruler:** August II **Note:** W#753.

Date	Mintage	VG	F	VF	XF	Unc
ND (h)	—	2,400	4,000	6,800	—	—

KM# 57 1/2 THALER
Silver **Ruler:** August II **Subject:** Death of August's First Wife, Clara Maria von Pommern **Obv:** 11-fold arms **Rev:** 6-line inscription with date

Date	Mintage	VG	F	VF	XF	Unc
1623	—	—	—	—	—	—

KM# 45 THALER
Silver **Ruler:** August II **Note:** Dav. #6329. Klippe.

Date	Mintage	VG	F	VF	XF	Unc
1619 Rare	—	—	—	—	—	—

KM# 44.1 THALER
Silver **Ruler:** August II **Obv:** Bust right **Rev:** Helmeted 11-fold arms, date divided above **Note:** Dav. #6332.

Date	Mintage	VG	F	VF	XF	Unc
1619 Rare	—	—	—	—	—	—
1623 Rare	—	—	—	—	—	—
1624 Rare	—	—	—	—	—	—

KM# 52 THALER
Silver **Ruler:** August II **Obv:** Helmeted eleven-fold arms **Rev:** Arm from cloud holding trowel above unfinished pyramid, date in legend **Note:** Dav. #6331.

Date	Mintage	VG	F	VF	XF	Unc
1621 Rare	—	—	—	—	—	—

KM# 53 THALER
Silver **Ruler:** August II **Obv:** Crowned imperial eagle, titles of Ferdinand II **Note:** Dav. #6334. Kipper.

Date	Mintage	VG	F	VF	XF	Unc
ND Rare	—	—	—	—	—	—

KM# 44.2 THALER
Silver **Ruler:** August II **Rev:** Without date **Note:** Dav. #6330.

Date	Mintage	VG	F	VF	XF	Unc
ND	—	3,050	5,800	9,600	—	—

KM# 58 THALER
Silver **Ruler:** August II **Subject:** Death of August's First Wife, Clara Maria von Pommern **Obv:** 7-line inscription with date, baroque scroll above and below **Rev:** Panel with 5-line inscription in center, skull and hourglass above, dates in legend **Note:** Dav. #6333. Kipper.

Date	Mintage	VG	F	VF	XF	Unc
1623	—	1,650	3,050	5,200	8,800	—

BRUNSWICK-LUNEBURG-CALENBERG

The duchy of Brunswick-Lüneburg-Calenberg was established as a division of Brunswick-New-Lüneburg in 1636. It was further divided into Brunswick-Lüneburg-Calenberg and Brunswick-Lüneburg-Celle in 1648. In 1692 the duke was raised to the rank of elector and the principality became known as the Electorate of Brunswick-Lüneburg-Calenberg-Hannover. After the Napoleonic Wars, Hannover became a kingdom in 1814 and passed to Prussia in 1866.

RULERS
Georg I, 1636-1641
Christian Ludwig, 1641-1648
Georg II Wilhelm, 1648-1665
Johann Friedrich, 1665-1679
Ernst August, 1679-1698

MINT OFFICIALS' INITIALS

Initial	Date	Name
CH	-	?
HB	1675-1711	Heinrich Bonhorst in Clausthal
HIF	Ca.1678	?
HS (w/ or w/o crossed keys)	1626-72	Henning Schluter in Goslar and Zellerfeld
IES	1676-84	Johann Erich Schidt in Hannover
IH	Ca.1638	Unknown die-cutter
IPE	1672-75	Julius Philipp Eisendrath in Goslar and Zellerfeld
LW	1640-75	Lippold Weber (Weffer, Wepper) in Clausthal
RB	1673-76	Rudolf Bornemann in Hannover
	1676-1711	In Zellerfeld
	1685-1704	In Goslar
(b) ligate backward B and H		Bastian Hille

REFERENCE
W = Gerhard Welter, ***Die Münzen der Welfen seit Heinrich dem Löwen***, 3 v., Braunschweig: Klinkhardt & Biermann, 1971-78.

DUCHY

REGULAR COINAGE

KM# 43 PFENNIG
0.5000 g., Silver, 12.9 mm. **Obv:** Crowned CL monogram, date. **Note:** Uniface. Hohlpfennig type.

Date	Mintage	VG	F	VF	XF	Unc
1642 LW	—	50.00	85.00	160	325	—
1647	—	50.00	85.00	160	325	—
1648	—	50.00	85.00	160	325	—

KM# 59 PFENNIG

Silver **Obv:** Crowned GW monogram divides date **Note:** Uniface, Hohlpfennig type.

Date	Mintage	VG	F	VF	XF	Unc
1659	—	50.00	85.00	160	325	—
1663 HS	—	50.00	85.00	160	325	—
ND	—	50.00	85.00	160	325	—

KM# 86 PFENNIG

Silver **Note:** Crowned script JF monogram, date.

Date	Mintage	VG	F	VF	XF	Unc
1665 HS	—	45.00	80.00	150	300	—
1667 HS	—	45.00	80.00	150	300	—
1668 HS	—	45.00	80.00	150	300	—
1669 HS	—	45.00	80.00	150	300	—
1671 HS	—	45.00	80.00	150	300	—
1672 HS	—	45.00	80.00	150	300	—
1672 IPE	—	45.00	80.00	150	300	—
1675 IPE	—	45.00	80.00	150	300	—
1677 RB	—	45.00	80.00	150	300	—
1678 RB	—	45.00	80.00	150	300	—
1679 RB	—	45.00	80.00	150	300	—

KM# 91 PFENNIG

Silver **Obv:** Crowned JF monogram, date. **Note:** Hohlpfennig type.

Date	Mintage	VG	F	VF	XF	Unc
1666 LW	—	37.00	75.00	130	265	—
1667 LW	—	37.00	75.00	130	265	—
1668 LW	—	37.00	75.00	130	265	—
1670 LW	—	37.00	75.00	130	265	—
1671 LW	—	37.00	75.00	130	265	—
1672 LW	—	37.00	75.00	130	265	—
1673 LW	—	37.00	75.00	130	265	—
1675	—	37.00	75.00	130	265	—
1677	—	37.00	75.00	130	265	—
1679	—	37.00	75.00	130	265	—

KM# 92 PFENNIG

Silver **Note:** St. Andrew with cross divides date.

Date	Mintage	VG	F	VF	XF	Unc
1666 LW	—	50.00	100	180	360	—
1667 LW	—	50.00	100	180	360	—

KM# 193 PFENNIG

Silver **Obv:** Crowned script JF monogram **Rev. Inscription:** * / EX / DURIS / GLORIA / *

Date	Mintage	VG	F	VF	XF	Unc
1677	—	—	—	—	—	—

KM# 255 PFENNIG

Silver **Obv:** Crowned EA monogram divides date. **Note:** Uniface hohlpfennig type. Varieties exist.

Date	Mintage	VG	F	VF	XF	Unc
1680 RB	—	32.00	50.00	100	200	—
1681 RB	—	32.00	50.00	100	200	—
1684 RB	—	32.00	50.00	100	200	—
1685 RB	—	32.00	50.00	100	200	—
1687 RB	—	32.00	50.00	100	200	—
1690 RB	—	32.00	50.00	100	200	—
1693 RB	—	32.00	50.00	100	200	—
1694 RB	—	32.00	50.00	100	200	—
1697 RB	—	32.00	50.00	100	200	—

KM# 289 PFENNIG

Silver **Mint:** Clausthal **Note:** Without mintmaster's initials. Varieties exist.

Date	Mintage	VG	F	VF	XF	Unc
1682	—	22.00	37.00	65.00	130	—
1683	—	22.00	37.00	65.00	130	—
1690	—	22.00	37.00	65.00	130	—

KM# 352 PFENNIG

Copper **Obv:** Crowned script EA monogram **Rev:** Value, date

Date	Mintage	VG	F	VF	XF	Unc
1691	—	12.00	25.00	50.00	100	—
1692	—	12.00	25.00	50.00	100	—

KM# 386 PFENNIG

Copper **Obv:** Plain script monogram

Date	Mintage	VG	F	VF	XF	Unc
1694	—	12.00	25.00	50.00	100	—

KM# 387 PFENNIG

Silver **Obv:** Horse leaping left, date below **Note:** Uniface. Hohlpfennig type.

Date	Mintage	VG	F	VF	XF	Unc
1694	—	30.00	60.00	120	200	—
1697	—	30.00	60.00	120	200	—
1698	—	30.00	60.00	120	200	—

KM# 296 1-1/2 PFENNIG

Silver **Obv:** Crowned EA monogram **Rev:** Value, date in two lines

Date	Mintage	VG	F	VF	XF	Unc
1680	—	40.00	85.00	170	—	—
1683	—	40.00	85.00	170	—	—
1686	—	40.00	85.00	170	—	—

KM# 297 1-1/2 PFENNIG

Silver **Rev:** Value, date in three lines **Note:** Gute 1-1/2 Pfennig.

Date	Mintage	VG	F	VF	XF	Unc
1683	—	—	—	—	—	—

KM# 353 1-1/2 PFENNIG

Copper **Obv:** Crowned script EA monogram **Rev:** Value, date in five lines

Date	Mintage	VG	F	VF	XF	Unc
1691	—	—	—	—	—	—

KM# 178 2 PFENNIG

Silver **Obv:** Crowned script JF monogram dividing date **Rev:** Value in four lines

Date	Mintage	VG	F	VF	XF	Unc
1676	—	35.00	75.00	150	—	—
1679	—	35.00	75.00	150	—	—

KM# 298 2 PFENNIG

Silver **Obv:** Crowned intertwined script EA monogram **Rev:** Value

Date	Mintage	VG	F	VF	XF	Unc
1683	—	35.00	75.00	150	—	—

KM# 307 2 PFENNIG

Silver **Obv:** Monogram in block letters

Date	Mintage	VG	F	VF	XF	Unc
1684	—	35.00	75.00	150	—	—

KM# 58 3 PFENNIG

Silver **Obv:** Crowned GW monogram divides date **Rev:** Imperial orb with 3 **Note:** Dreier 3 Pfennig.

Date	Mintage	VG	F	VF	XF	Unc
1657 HS	—	22.00	42.00	85.00	170	—
1662 HS	—	22.00	42.00	85.00	170	—
1665 HS	—	22.00	42.00	85.00	170	—

KM# 93 3 PFENNIG

Silver **Obv:** Crowned script JF monogram

Date	Mintage	VG	F	VF	XF	Unc
1666 LW	—	20.00	40.00	80.00	165	—
1667 LW	—	20.00	40.00	80.00	165	—
1668 LW	—	20.00	40.00	80.00	165	—
1670 LW	—	20.00	40.00	80.00	165	—
1671 HS	—	20.00	40.00	80.00	165	—
1673 IPE	—	30.00	60.00	110	215	—
1675	—	20.00	40.00	80.00	165	—
1677 RB	—	20.00	40.00	80.00	165	—
1678 RB	—	20.00	40.00	80.00	165	—

KM# 103 3 PFENNIG

Silver **Obv:** St. Andrew with cross

Date	Mintage	VG	F	VF	XF	Unc
1667 LW	—	22.00	42.00	85.00	170	—
1673 LW	—	22.00	42.00	85.00	170	—
1674 LW	—	22.00	42.00	85.00	170	—

KM# 274 3 PFENNIG

Silver **Obv:** Crowned script EA monogram divides date **Note:** Varieties exist.

Date	Mintage	VG	F	VF	XF	Unc
1681 HB	—	20.00	40.00	85.00	170	—
1682 HB	—	20.00	40.00	85.00	170	—
1683 HB	—	20.00	40.00	85.00	170	—
1683	—	20.00	40.00	85.00	170	—
1684	—	20.00	40.00	85.00	170	—
1692 RB	—	20.00	40.00	85.00	170	—

KM# 308 3 PFENNIG

Silver **Obv:** Intertwined monogram

Date	Mintage	VG	F	VF	XF	Unc
1684 HB	—	25.00	50.00	100	—	—

KM# 160 4 PFENNIG

Silver **Obv:** Crowned script JF monogram **Rev:** Value in three or four lines

Date	Mintage	VG	F	VF	XF	Unc
1675	—	55.00	110	225	450	—
1677	—	55.00	110	225	450	—

KM# 161 4 PFENNIG

Silver **Obv:** Crowned monogram **Rev:** Value 4 **Note:** Gute 4 Pfennig.

Date	Mintage	VG	F	VF	XF	Unc
1675	—	55.00	110	225	450	—
1677 RB	—	55.00	110	225	450	—
1678	—	55.00	110	225	450	—
1679	—	55.00	110	225	450	—

KM# 194 4 PFENNIG

Silver **Rev:** Value IIII in three lines **Note:** Gute 4 Pfennig.

Date	Mintage	VG	F	VF	XF	Unc
1677	—	65.00	135	275	550	—
1679	—	65.00	135	275	550	—

KM# 275 4 PFENNIG

Silver **Obv:** Crowned EA monogram divides date **Rev:** Value 4 **Note:** Gute 4 Pfennig.

Date	Mintage	VG	F	VF	XF	Unc
1681 RB	—	32.50	65.00	135	275	—
1682 RB	—	32.50	65.00	135	275	—

KM# 290 4 PFENNIG

Silver **Obv:** Crowned script EA monogram **Rev:** Value IIII, date

Date	Mintage	VG	F	VF	XF	Unc
1682 HB	—	32.50	65.00	135	275	—
1687 HB	—	32.50	65.00	135	275	—

KM# 299 4 PFENNIG

Silver **Obv:** Crowned EA monogram divides date **Rev:** Value IIII **Note:** Gute 4 Pfennig.

Date	Mintage	VG	F	VF	XF	Unc
1683	—	32.50	65.00	135	275	—

KM# 309 4 PFENNIG

Silver **Obv:** EA monogram, legend **Obv. Legend:** SOLA BOMA... **Rev:** Value IIII, date

Date	Mintage	VG	F	VF	XF	Unc
1684	—	32.50	65.00	135	275	—

KM# 330 4 PFENNIG

Silver **Obv:** Crowned EA monogram divides date **Rev:** Value IIII LANDMUNTZ... **Note:** Varieties exist.

Date	Mintage	VG	F	VF	XF	Unc
1686 HB	—	32.50	65.00	135	275	—
1688 HB	—	32.50	65.00	135	275	—

KM# 332 4 PFENNIG

Silver **Obv:** Crowned script EA monogram divides date **Rev:** Value IIII, date

Date	Mintage	VG	F	VF	XF	Unc
1688 HB	—	32.50	65.00	135	275	—

KM# 354 4 PFENNIG

Silver **Note:** Date on obverse only.

Date	Mintage	VG	F	VF	XF	Unc
1691	—	32.50	65.00	135	275	—

KM# 361 4 PFENNIG

Silver **Obv:** Crowned EA monogram divides mintmaster's initials **Rev:** Value 4 in center, date in legend **Note:** Gute 4 Pfennig.

Date	Mintage	VG	F	VF	XF	Unc
1692 RB	—	32.50	65.00	135	275	—

KM# 371 4 PFENNIG

Silver **Obv:** Crowned script monogram **Rev:** Value IIII, date in four lines

Date	Mintage	VG	F	VF	XF	Unc
1693	—	32.50	65.00	135	275	—
1694	—	32.50	65.00	135	275	—
1695	—	32.50	65.00	135	275	—
1697	—	32.50	65.00	135	275	—

KM# 162 MATTIER (= 4 Pfennig)

Silver **Obv:** Crowned JF monogram **Rev:** Value in three lines

Date	Mintage	VG	F	VF	XF	Unc
1675	—	45.00	90.00	180	—	—
1676	—	45.00	90.00	180	—	—

KM# 301 4-1/2 PFENNIG

Silver **Rev:** Value without GUTE

Date	Mintage	VG	F	VF	XF	Unc
1683	—	—	—	—	—	—

KM# 300 4-1/2 PFENNIG

Silver **Obv:** Crowned EA monogram **Rev:** Value, date **Note:** Gute 4-1/2 Pfennig.

Date	Mintage	VG	F	VF	XF	Unc
1683	—	—	—	—	—	—

KM# 302 6 PFENNIG

Silver **Obv:** Crowned EA monogram divides date **Rev:** Imperial orb with 6

Date	Mintage	VG	F	VF	XF	Unc
1683	—	20.00	45.00	90.00	180	—
1684	—	20.00	45.00	90.00	180	—
1685	—	20.00	45.00	90.00	180	—

KM# 17 MARIENGROSCHEN (1/36 Thaler)

Silver **Obv:** Helmet with horse **Rev:** Value in three lines

Date	Mintage	VG	F	VF	XF	Unc
ND(ca.1636) HS	—	10.00	20.00	40.00	80.00	—

KM# 56 MARIENGROSCHEN (1/36 Thaler)
Silver **Obv:** Crowned GW monogram

Date	Mintage	VG	F	VF	XF	Unc
1652	—	15.00	30.00	65.00	130	—
1655	—	15.00	30.00	65.00	130	—
1656	—	15.00	30.00	65.00	130	—
1657	—	15.00	30.00	65.00	130	—

KM# 104 MARIENGROSCHEN (1/36 Thaler)
Silver **Obv:** Crowned script JF monogram, date in legend

Date	Mintage	VG	F	VF	XF	Unc
1667	—	15.00	30.00	65.00	130	—
1673	—	15.00	30.00	65.00	130	—

KM# 141 MARIENGROSCHEN (1/36 Thaler)
Silver **Obv:** Wildman, tree in right hand

Date	Mintage	VG	F	VF	XF	Unc
1673	—	15.00	30.00	65.00	130	—
1674	—	15.00	30.00	65.00	130	—
1675	—	15.00	30.00	65.00	130	—
1676	—	15.00	30.00	65.00	130	—
1677	—	15.00	30.00	65.00	130	—
1678	—	15.00	30.00	65.00	130	—
1679	—	15.00	30.00	65.00	130	—

KM# 163 MARIENGROSCHEN (1/36 Thaler)
Silver **Obv:** Horse leaping left **Rev:** Madonna, value in legend

Date	Mintage	VG	F	VF	XF	Unc
1675	—	18.00	36.00	70.00	140	—

KM# 164 MARIENGROSCHEN (1/36 Thaler)
Silver **Rev:** Value in three lines

Date	Mintage	VG	F	VF	XF	Unc
1675	—	15.00	30.00	65.00	130	—

KM# 165 MARIENGROSCHEN (1/36 Thaler)
Silver **Obv:** Crowned script JF monogram **Rev:** Madonna

Date	Mintage	VG	F	VF	XF	Unc
1675	—	13.00	27.00	55.00	110	—
1679	—	13.00	27.00	55.00	110	—

KM# 166 MARIENGROSCHEN (1/36 Thaler)
Silver **Obv:** Value in three lines

Date	Mintage	VG	F	VF	XF	Unc
ND(ca.1675)	—	11.00	22.00	45.00	75.00	125

KM# 291 MARIENGROSCHEN (1/36 Thaler)
Silver **Obv:** Widlman, tree in right hand **Rev:** Value, date

Date	Mintage	VG	F	VF	XF	Unc
1682	—	12.00	25.00	50.00	100	—
1683	—	12.00	25.00	50.00	100	—
1684	—	12.00	25.00	50.00	100	—
1685	—	12.00	25.00	50.00	100	—
1686	—	12.00	25.00	50.00	100	—
1687	—	12.00	25.00	50.00	100	—
1688	—	12.00	25.00	50.00	100	—

KM# 292 MARIENGROSCHEN (1/36 Thaler)
Silver **Obv:** Value in three lines **Rev:** Madonna divides date

Date	Mintage	VG	F	VF	XF	Unc
1682	—	12.00	22.00	45.00	70.00	100
1683 HB	—	12.00	22.00	45.00	70.00	100

KM# 303 MARIENGROSCHEN (1/36 Thaler)
Silver **Obv:** Crowned script EA monogram **Rev:** Value, date

Date	Mintage	VG	F	VF	XF	Unc
1683	—	22.00	35.00	75.00	155	—
1684	—	22.00	35.00	75.00	155	—
1685	—	22.00	35.00	75.00	155	—
1691 HB	—	22.00	35.00	75.00	155	—

KM# 310 MARIENGROSCHEN (1/36 Thaler)
Silver **Obv:** Intertwined script EA monogram

Date	Mintage	VG	F	VF	XF	Unc
1684	—	22.00	35.00	75.00	155	—

KM# 333 MARIENGROSCHEN (1/36 Thaler)
Silver **Obv:** KM#291 **Rev:** Type of Rudolf August, with REMIGIO ALTISSIMI UNI, date **Note:** Mule.

Date	Mintage	VG	F	VF	XF	Unc
1688	—	—	—	—	—	—

KM# 355 MARIENGROSCHEN (1/36 Thaler)
Silver **Obv:** Value, date in four lines **Obv. Legend:** FURSTL... **Rev:** Madonna

Date	Mintage	VG	F	VF	XF	Unc
1691 HB	—	—	—	—	—	—
1697 HB	—	—	—	—	—	—

KM# 356 MARIENGROSCHEN (1/36 Thaler)
Silver **Obv. Legend:** ERNEST: AUG:

Date	Mintage	VG	F	VF	XF	Unc
1691	—	—	—	—	—	—

KM# 357 MARIENGROSCHEN (1/36 Thaler)
Silver **Obv. Legend:** FR. BR. LUNE...

Date	Mintage	VG	F	VF	XF	Unc
1691 HB	—	25.00	45.00	90.00	180	—
1692 HB	—	25.00	45.00	90.00	180	—
1695 HB	—	25.00	45.00	90.00	180	—
1697 HB	—	25.00	45.00	90.00	180	—

KM# 372 MARIENGROSCHEN (1/36 Thaler)
Silver **Obv. Legend:** C. B. LVNEB...

Date	Mintage	VG	F	VF	XF	Unc
1693 HB	—	25.00	45.00	90.00	180	—
1695 HB	—	25.00	45.00	90.00	180	—
1697 HB	—	25.00	45.00	90.00	180	—

KM# 23.2 2 MARIENGROSCHEN
1.3200 g., Silver, 19.7 mm. **Ruler:** Georg I **Obv:** Horse ornamented helmet **Rev:** Denomination as "MARIE GROS" and radiant sun at top **Edge:** Plain

Date	Mintage	F	VF	XF	Unc	BU
1638HS	—	20.00	40.00	85.00	170	—

KM# 23 2 MARIENGROSCHEN
Silver **Obv:** Helmet with horse **Rev:** Value in three lines, date divided by II

Date	Mintage	VG	F	VF	XF	Unc
1638 HS	—	14.00	28.00	55.00	115	—
1639 HS	—	14.00	28.00	55.00	115	—
1640 HS	—	14.00	28.00	55.00	115	—
1641 HS	—	14.00	28.00	55.00	115	—
1642 HS Error	—	14.00	28.00	55.00	115	—
ND	—	14.00	28.00	55.00	115	—

KM# 44 2 MARIENGROSCHEN
Silver

Date	Mintage	VG	F	VF	XF	Unc
1642 HS	—	11.00	22.00	40.00	85.00	—
1643 HS	—	11.00	22.00	40.00	85.00	—
1644 HS	—	11.00	22.00	40.00	85.00	—
1645 HS	—	11.00	22.00	40.00	85.00	—
1646 HS	—	11.00	22.00	40.00	85.00	—

KM# 45 2 MARIENGROSCHEN
Silver **Obv:** Crowned CL monogram **Rev:** Value in three lines

Date	Mintage	VG	F	VF	XF	Unc
1642	—	11.00	22.00	40.00	85.00	—
1645	—	11.00	22.00	40.00	85.00	—
1646	—	11.00	22.00	40.00	85.00	—
1647	—	11.00	22.00	40.00	85.00	—
1648	—	11.00	22.00	40.00	85.00	—

KM# 51 2 MARIENGROSCHEN
Silver **Obv:** Crowned GW monogram

Date	Mintage	VG	F	VF	XF	Unc
1649	—	11.00	22.00	35.00	70.00	—
1650	—	11.00	22.00	35.00	70.00	—
1651	—	11.00	22.00	35.00	70.00	—
1652	—	11.00	22.00	35.00	70.00	—
1653	—	11.00	22.00	35.00	70.00	—
1654	—	11.00	22.00	35.00	70.00	—
1655	—	11.00	22.00	35.00	70.00	—
1656	—	11.00	22.00	35.00	70.00	—
1657	—	11.00	22.00	35.00	70.00	—
1659	—	11.00	22.00	35.00	70.00	—
1661	—	11.00	22.00	35.00	70.00	—

KM# 105 2 MARIENGROSCHEN
Silver **Obv:** Wildman, tree in right hand

Date	Mintage	VG	F	VF	XF	Unc
1667	—	10.00	20.00	40.00	80.00	—
1673	—	10.00	20.00	40.00	80.00	—
1675	—	10.00	20.00	40.00	80.00	—
1676 GROS	—	10.00	20.00	40.00	80.00	—
1677 GORS Error	—	10.00	20.00	40.00	80.00	—
1678	—	10.00	20.00	40.00	80.00	—
1679	—	10.00	20.00	40.00	80.00	—

KM# 107 2 MARIENGROSCHEN
Silver **Obv:** Crowned IF monogram, date in legend

Date	Mintage	VG	F	VF	XF	Unc
1667	—	14.00	28.00	55.00	110	—

KM# 106 2 MARIENGROSCHEN
Silver **Obv:** Horse leaping left **Note:** Varieties exist.

Date	Mintage	VG	F	VF	XF	Unc
1667	—	—	—	—	—	—
1673	—	—	—	—	—	—
1675	—	—	—	—	—	—

KM# 179 2 MARIENGROSCHEN
Silver **Obv:** Value in three lines **Rev:** Madonna

Date	Mintage	VG	F	VF	XF	Unc
1676	—	—	—	—	—	—

KM# 256 2 MARIENGROSCHEN
Silver **Obv:** Wildman, tree in right hand, title as duke **Rev:** Value in three lines, date in legend

Date	Mintage	VG	F	VF	XF	Unc
1680	—	13.00	27.00	55.00	110	—
1682	—	13.00	27.00	55.00	110	—
1683	—	13.00	27.00	55.00	110	—
1684	—	13.00	27.00	55.00	110	—
1688 BEL Error	—	13.00	27.00	55.00	110	—
1689 B & L	—	13.00	27.00	55.00	110	—
1690 BEL Error	—	13.00	27.00	55.00	110	—

KM# 257 2 MARIENGROSCHEN
Silver **Obv:** Value, date in four lines **Rev:** Horse leaping left

Date	Mintage	VG	F	VF	XF	Unc
1680 HB	—	—	—	—	—	—

KM# 276 2 MARIENGROSCHEN
Silver **Obv:** Date in legend

Date	Mintage	VG	F	VF	XF	Unc
1681 HB	—	10.00	25.00	50.00	100	—
1684 HB	—	10.00	25.00	50.00	100	—
1685 HB	—	10.00	25.00	50.00	100	—
1688	—	10.00	25.00	50.00	100	—

KM# 311 2 MARIENGROSCHEN
Silver **Obv:** Value in three line, date in legends **Rev:** St. Andrew with cross

Date	Mintage	VG	F	VF	XF	Unc
1684 HB	—	—	—	—	—	—

KM# 336 2 MARIENGROSCHEN
Silver **Obv:** Crowned script EA monogram **Rev:** Value in three lines, date in legend

Date	Mintage	VG	F	VF	XF	Unc
1689 HB	—	12.00	20.00	45.00	90.00	—
1697 HB	—	12.00	20.00	45.00	90.00	—

KM# 362 2 MARIENGROSCHEN
Silver **Obv:** Date divided by monogram

Date	Mintage	VG	F	VF	XF	Unc
1692 HB	—	9.00	17.00	35.00	75.00	—
1693 HB	—	9.00	17.00	35.00	75.00	—

KM# 373 2 MARIENGROSCHEN
Silver **Obv:** Wildman, tree in right hand, title as elector **Rev:** Value in three lines, date in legend

Date	Mintage	VG	F	VF	XF	Unc
1693	—	15.00	30.00	60.00	120	—
1694	—	15.00	30.00	60.00	120	—
1695	—	15.00	30.00	60.00	120	—
1696	—	15.00	30.00	60.00	120	—
1697	—	15.00	30.00	60.00	120	—

KM# 363 3 MARIENGROSCHEN (= 1/12 Thaler)
Silver **Obv:** Value in four lines **Rev:** Horse leaping left

Date	Mintage	VG	F	VF	XF	Unc
1692	—	—	—	—	—	—

KM# 87 4 MARIENGROSCHEN
Silver **Obv:** Horse leaping left **Rev:** Value in four lines **Note:** Varieties exist.

Date	Mintage	VG	F	VF	XF	Unc
1665	—	10.00	20.00	40.00	80.00	—
1667	—	10.00	20.00	40.00	80.00	—
1668	—	10.00	20.00	40.00	80.00	—
1669	—	10.00	20.00	40.00	80.00	—
1670	—	10.00	20.00	40.00	80.00	—
1671	—	10.00	20.00	40.00	80.00	—
1672	—	10.00	20.00	40.00	80.00	—
1673	—	10.00	20.00	40.00	80.00	—

KM# 108 4 MARIENGROSCHEN
Silver **Obv:** Wildman, tree in right hand **Rev:** Value in three lines, date in legend

Date	Mintage	VG	F	VF	XF	Unc
1667	—	10.00	20.00	40.00	80.00	—
1668	—	10.00	20.00	40.00	80.00	—
1669	—	10.00	20.00	40.00	80.00	—
1673	—	10.00	20.00	40.00	80.00	—

KM# 109 4 MARIENGROSCHEN
Silver **Obv:** Crowned script JF monogram, date in legend **Rev:** Value in four lines

Date	Mintage	VG	F	VF	XF	Unc
1667	—	15.00	30.00	50.00	100	—

KM# 142 4 MARIENGROSCHEN
Silver **Obv:** Horse leaping left **Rev:** St. Andrew with cross

Date	Mintage	VG	F	VF	XF	Unc
1673	—	13.00	27.00	55.00	110	—

KM# 143 4 MARIENGROSCHEN
Silver **Obv:** Value in five lines **Rev:** St. Andrew with cross, date in legend **Rev. Legend:** S. ANDREASBERG * ANNO

Date	Mintage	VG	F	VF	XF	Unc
1673	—	13.00	27.00	55.00	110	—

KM# 154 4 MARIENGROSCHEN
Silver **Obv:** Wildman with tree in right hand, 4 at right **Rev:** Value in three lines, date in legend

Date	Mintage	VG	F	VF	XF	Unc
1674	—	12.00	22.00	45.00	80.00	—
1675	—	12.00	22.00	45.00	80.00	—
1676	—	12.00	22.00	45.00	80.00	—
1677	—	12.00	22.00	45.00	80.00	—
1678	—	12.00	22.00	45.00	80.00	—
1679	—	12.00	22.00	45.00	80.00	—

KM# 180 4 MARIENGROSCHEN
Silver

Date	Mintage	VG	F	VF	XF	Unc
1676	—	22.00	45.00	90.00	180	—

KM# 210 4 MARIENGROSCHEN
Silver **Obv:** Value in five lines **Rev:** St. Andrew with cross **Rev. Legend:** ST. ANDREAS * REVIVISCENS

Date	Mintage	VG	F	VF	XF	Unc
1679	—	14.00	27.00	55.00	110	—

KM# 277 4 MARIENGROSCHEN
Silver **Rev:** Horse leaping left, date at bottom

Date	Mintage	VG	F	VF	XF	Unc
1681 HB	—	10.00	20.00	40.00	85.00	—
1686 HB	—	10.00	20.00	40.00	85.00	—

KM# 304 4 MARIENGROSCHEN
Silver **Obv:** Wildman with tree in right hand, title as duke **Rev:** Value in three lines, date in legend

Date	Mintage	VG	F	VF	XF	Unc
1683	—	10.00	22.00	45.00	90.00	—
1687	—	10.00	22.00	45.00	90.00	—
1688	—	10.00	22.00	45.00	90.00	—
1689	—	10.00	22.00	45.00	90.00	—

KM# 338 4 MARIENGROSCHEN
Silver **Rev:** Arabic date at bottom

Date	Mintage	VG	F	VF	XF	Unc
1689 HB	—	10.00	20.00	40.00	80.00	—
1690 HB	—	10.00	20.00	40.00	80.00	—
1692	—	10.00	20.00	40.00	80.00	—

KM# 337 4 MARIENGROSCHEN
Silver **Note:** Similar to KM#338 but Roman numeral date.

Date	Mintage	VG	F	VF	XF	Unc
1689 HB	—	—	—	—	—	—

KM# 364 4 MARIENGROSCHEN
Silver

Date	Mintage	VG	F	VF	XF	Unc
1692 HB	—	10.00	20.00	40.00	70.00	—
1694 HB	—	10.00	20.00	40.00	70.00	—
1696 HB	—	10.00	20.00	40.00	70.00	—

KM# 374 4 MARIENGROSCHEN
Silver **Obv:** Wildman with tree in right hand, title as elector **Rev:** Value in three lines, date in legend

Date	Mintage	VG	F	VF	XF	Unc
1693	—	10.00	20.00	40.00	80.00	—
1694	—	10.00	20.00	40.00	80.00	—
1695	—	10.00	20.00	40.00	80.00	—
1697	—	10.00	20.00	40.00	80.00	—

KM# 120.1 6 MARIENGROSCHEN (= 1/6 Thaler)
Silver **Obv:** Wildman with tree in right hand, 6 at right **Rev:** Value in three lines

Date	Mintage	VG	F	VF	XF	Unc
1668	—	15.00	30.00	65.00	130	—
1669	—	15.00	30.00	65.00	130	—
1671	—	15.00	30.00	65.00	130	—
1673	—	15.00	30.00	65.00	130	—
1674	—	15.00	30.00	65.00	130	—
1675	—	15.00	30.00	65.00	130	—
1676	—	15.00	30.00	65.00	130	—
1677	—	15.00	30.00	65.00	130	—
1678	—	15.00	30.00	65.00	130	—
1679	—	15.00	30.00	65.00	130	—

KM# 120.2 6 MARIENGROSCHEN (= 1/6 Thaler)
Silver **Obv:** Without 6 at right of wildman

Date	Mintage	VG	F	VF	XF	Unc
1668	—	—	—	—	—	—

KM# 121 6 MARIENGROSCHEN (= 1/6 Thaler)
Silver **Obv:** Horse leaping left **Rev:** Value in four lines

Date	Mintage	VG	F	VF	XF	Unc
1668	—	15.00	35.00	70.00	145	—

KM# 258 6 MARIENGROSCHEN (= 1/6 Thaler)
Silver **Obv:** Wildman with tree in right hand, title as duke **Rev:** Value in three lines, date in legend

Date	Mintage	VG	F	VF	XF	Unc
1680	—	15.00	30.00	65.00	130	—
1681	—	15.00	30.00	65.00	130	—
1682	—	15.00	30.00	65.00	130	—
1683	—	15.00	30.00	65.00	130	—
1687	—	15.00	30.00	65.00	130	—
1688	—	15.00	30.00	65.00	130	—
1689	—	15.00	30.00	65.00	130	—

KM# 334 6 MARIENGROSCHEN (= 1/6 Thaler)
Silver **Obv:** Title as duke

Date	Mintage	VG	F	VF	XF	Unc
1688 HB	—	11.00	27.00	55.00	110	—
1689 HB	—	11.00	27.00	55.00	110	—
1690 HB	—	11.00	27.00	55.00	110	—
1692 HB	—	11.00	27.00	55.00	110	—

KM# 375 6 MARIENGROSCHEN (= 1/6 Thaler)
Silver **Obv:** Wildman with tree in right hand, title as elector **Rev:** Value in three lines, date in legend

Date	Mintage	VG	F	VF	XF	Unc
1693	—	14.00	32.00	65.00	130	—
1694	—	14.00	32.00	65.00	130	—
1695	—	14.00	32.00	65.00	130	—
1696	—	14.00	32.00	65.00	130	—
1697	—	14.00	32.00	65.00	130	—
1698	—	14.00	32.00	65.00	130	—

KM# 376 6 MARIENGROSCHEN (= 1/6 Thaler)
Silver **Obv:** Value, date in four lines, titles as elector **Rev:** Horse leaping left

Date	Mintage	VG	F	VF	XF	Unc
1693 HB	—	11.00	27.00	55.00	115	—
1694 HB	—	11.00	27.00	55.00	115	—
1696 HB	—	11.00	27.00	55.00	115	—
1697 HB	—	11.00	27.00	55.00	115	—

KM# 122 12 MARIENGROSCHEN (= 1/3 Thaler)
Silver **Note:** Similar to KM#136 but without 12 at right of wildman.

Date	Mintage	VG	F	VF	XF	Unc
1668	—	22.00	40.00	85.00	170	—
1669	—	22.00	40.00	85.00	170	—
1670	—	22.00	40.00	85.00	170	—
1673	—	22.00	40.00	85.00	170	—
1674	—	22.00	40.00	85.00	170	—

KM# 123 12 MARIENGROSCHEN (= 1/3 Thaler)
Silver **Note:** Varieties exist.

Date	Mintage	VG	F	VF	XF	Unc
1668	—	22.00	40.00	85.00	175	—
1669	—	22.00	40.00	85.00	175	—
1670	—	22.00	40.00	85.00	175	—
1671	—	22.00	40.00	85.00	175	—
1672	—	22.00	40.00	85.00	175	—
1673	—	22.00	40.00	85.00	175	—

KM# 136 12 MARIENGROSCHEN (= 1/3 Thaler)
Silver

Date	Mintage	VG	F	VF	XF	Unc
1669	—	—	—	—	—	—
1671	—	22.00	40.00	85.00	170	—
1672	—	22.00	40.00	85.00	170	—
1627 Error, 27 instead of 72	—	—	—	—	—	—

Date	Mintage	VG	F	VF	XF	Unc
1675	—	22.00	40.00	85.00	170	—
1676	—	22.00	40.00	85.00	170	—
1677	—	22.00	40.00	85.00	170	—
1678	—	22.00	40.00	85.00	170	—
1679	—	22.00	40.00	85.00	170	—
1970 date error	—	—	—	—	—	—

KM# 137 12 MARIENGROSCHEN (= 1/3 Thaler)
Silver **Obv:** Similar to KM#123 **Rev:** St. Andrew with cross

Date	Mintage	VG	F	VF	XF	Unc
1672	—	—	—	—	—	—

KM# 138 12 MARIENGROSCHEN (= 1/3 Thaler)
Silver **Obv:** Value in five lines

Date	Mintage	VG	F	VF	XF	Unc
1672	—	—	—	—	—	—

KM# 167 12 MARIENGROSCHEN (= 1/3 Thaler)
Silver **Note:** Similar to KM#123 but struck on smaller, thicker flan (27mm).

Date	Mintage	VG	F	VF	XF	Unc
1675	—	45.00	80.00	160	325	—

KM# 259 12 MARIENGROSCHEN (= 1/3 Thaler)
Silver **Obv:** Title as Duke

Date	Mintage	VG	F	VF	XF	Unc
1680	—	20.00	33.00	75.00	155	—
1681	—	20.00	33.00	75.00	155	—
1682	—	20.00	33.00	75.00	155	—
1683	—	—	—	—	—	—
1684	—	20.00	33.00	75.00	155	—
1686	—	20.00	33.00	75.00	155	—
1687	—	20.00	33.00	75.00	155	—
1688	—	20.00	33.00	75.00	155	—
1689	—	20.00	33.00	75.00	155	—
1690	—	20.00	33.00	75.00	155	—
1691	—	20.00	33.00	75.00	155	—
1692	—	20.00	33.00	75.00	155	—

KM# 377 12 MARIENGROSCHEN (= 1/3 Thaler)
Silver **Obv:** Title as elector

Date	Mintage	VG	F	VF	XF	Unc
1693	—	25.00	50.00	100	200	—
1694	—	25.00	50.00	100	200	—
1695	—	25.00	50.00	100	200	—
1696	—	25.00	50.00	100	200	—
1697	—	25.00	50.00	100	200	—
1698	—	25.00	50.00	100	200	—

KM# 139 24 MARIENGROSCHEN (= 2/3 Thaler)
Silver, 36 mm. **Obv:** Horse leaping left **Rev:** Value 24, date in four lines

Date	Mintage	VG	F	VF	XF	Unc
1672	—	27.00	55.00	115	230	—
1673	—	27.00	55.00	115	230	—
1674	—	27.00	55.00	115	230	—

KM# 140 24 MARIENGROSCHEN (= 2/3 Thaler)
Silver **Obv:** Value (XXIIII), date in four lines **Rev:** St. Andrew with cross **Note:** Thick flan (30mm).

Date	Mintage	VG	F	VF	XF	Unc
1672	—	110	210	320	600	—
1675	—	110	210	320	600	—

KM# 158 24 MARIENGROSCHEN (= 2/3 Thaler)
Silver **Note:** Smaller, thicker flan (30mm), value XXIIII.

Date	Mintage	VG	F	VF	XF	Unc
1674	—	110	190	275	475	—
1675	—	110	190	275	475	—

KM# 155 24 MARIENGROSCHEN (= 2/3 Thaler)
Silver **Obv:** Bust right **Rev:** Value, date in four lines

Date	Mintage	VG	F	VF	XF	Unc
1674	—	—	—	—	—	—
1676	—	—	—	—	—	—

KM# 156 24 MARIENGROSCHEN (= 2/3 Thaler)
Silver **Obv:** Wildman, tree in right hand, 24 at right **Rev:** Value in three lines, date in legend

Date	Mintage	VG	F	VF	XF	Unc
1674	—	—	—	—	—	—

KM# 157 24 MARIENGROSCHEN (= 2/3 Thaler)
Silver **Obv:** Horse leaping left **Rev:** Value and date in six lines

Date	Mintage	VG	F	VF	XF	Unc
1674	—	27.00	50.00	100	210	—
1675	—	27.00	50.00	100	210	—
1676	—	27.00	50.00	100	210	—

KM# 168 24 MARIENGROSCHEN (= 2/3 Thaler)
Silver

Date	Mintage	VG	F	VF	XF	Unc
1675 RB	—	60.00	115	200	400	—

KM# 169 24 MARIENGROSCHEN (= 2/3 Thaler)
Silver **Rev:** Large ship right of palm

Date	Mintage	VG	F	VF	XF	Unc
1675 RB	—	60.00	115	200	400	—

KM# 195 24 MARIENGROSCHEN (= 2/3 Thaler)
Silver **Obv:** Wildman with tree in right hand, 24 at right **Rev:** Value in four lines with V. FEIN. SILB.

Date	Mintage	VG	F	VF	XF	Unc
1677	—	45.00	85.00	175	375	—
1678	—	45.00	85.00	175	375	—
1679	—	45.00	85.00	175	375	—
1680	—	45.00	85.00	175	375	—

KM# 260 24 MARIENGROSCHEN (= 2/3 Thaler)
Silver **Obv:** Crowned 12-fold arms, date above **Rev:** Horse leaping left, value in legend

Date	Mintage	VG	F	VF	XF	Unc
1680 IES	—	—	—	—	—	—

KM# 378 24 MARIENGROSCHEN (= 2/3 Thaler)
Silver **Note:** Similar to 12 Mariengroschen KM#377, but 24 at right of wildman on obverse, value in four lines on reverse.

Date	Mintage	VG	F	VF	XF	Unc
1693	—	45.00	80.00	175	375	—
1694	—	45.00	80.00	175	375	—
1695	—	45.00	80.00	175	375	—
1696	—	45.00	80.00	175	375	—
1697	—	45.00	80.00	175	375	—
1698	—	45.00	80.00	175	375	—

KM# 5 1/28 THALER
Silver **Obv:** Crowned 4-fold arms **Rev:** Crowned imperial eagle, orb on breast with 28, titles of Ferdinand II

Date	Mintage	VG	F	VF	XF	Unc
ND(1619)	—	—	—	—	—	—

KM# 13 1/24 THALER (Groschen)
Silver **Obv:** Helmet with horse above shield with lion left **Rev:** Imperial orb with 24, date divided by cross above

Date	Mintage	VG	F	VF	XF	Unc
1635 CH	—	11.00	25.00	40.00	85.00	—
1636 CH	—	11.00	25.00	40.00	85.00	—
1637 CH	—	11.00	25.00	40.00	85.00	—

KM# 94 1/24 THALER (Groschen)
Silver **Obv:** Imperial orb with 24 **Rev:** St. Andrew with cross

Date	Mintage	VG	F	VF	XF	Unc
1666 LW	—	35.00	70.00	140	285	—
1667 LW	—	35.00	70.00	140	285	—

KM# 95 1/24 THALER (Groschen)
Silver **Rev:** Horse leaping left

Date	Mintage	VG	F	VF	XF	Unc
1666 LW	—	35.00	70.00	140	285	—

KM# 211 1/24 THALER (Groschen)
Silver **Obv:** Crowned script JF monogram, date in legend **Rev:** Imperial orb with 24

Date	Mintage	VG	F	VF	XF	Unc
1679	—	—	—	—	—	—

KM# 212 1/24 THALER (Groschen)
Silver **Subject:** Death of Johann Friedrich **Rev:** 11-line inscription

Date	Mintage	VG	F	VF	XF	Unc
1679 RB	—	33.00	55.00	100	200	—

KM# 213 1/24 THALER (Groschen)
Silver **Rev:** 12-line inscription

Date	Mintage	VG	F	VF	XF	Unc
1679 HB	—	35.00	60.00	110	225	—

KM# 181 1/16 THALER
Silver **Obv:** Bust left **Rev:** Value in four lines, date in legend **Note:** Varieties exist.

Date	Mintage	VG	F	VF	XF	Unc
1676	—	—	—	—	—	—
1676 TAHL Error	—	—	—	—	—	—
1677	—	—	—	—	—	—

KM# 214 1/16 THALER
Silver **Subject:** Death of Johann Friedrich **Obv:** Imperial orb with 1/16 **Rev:** 11-line inscription with date

Date	Mintage	VG	F	VF	XF	Unc
1679 RB	—	35.00	70.00	135	275	—

KM# 215 1/16 THALER
Silver **Rev:** 12-line inscription with date

Date	Mintage	VG	F	VF	XF	Unc
1679 HB	—	35.00	70.00	135	275	—

KM# 35 1/8 THALER
Silver **Obv:** Crowned 11-fold arms **Rev:** Wildman, tree in right hand, date

Date	Mintage	VG	F	VF	XF	Unc
1640 HS	—	—	—	—	—	—
1641 HS	—	—	—	—	—	—

KM# 36 1/8 THALER
Silver **Subject:** Death of Georg **Obv:** Bust left **Rev:** 12-line inscription

Date	Mintage	VG	F	VF	XF	Unc
MDCXXXXI (1641)	—	300	550	1,000	1,750	—

KM# 37 1/8 THALER
Silver **Rev:** 13-line inscription

Date	Mintage	VG	F	VF	XF	Unc
1641 HS	—	300	550	1,000	1,750	—

KM# 60 1/8 THALER
3.5000 g., Silver **Subject:** Death of Ann Eleonora, Wife of Georg **Note:** Similar to 1 Thaler, KM#64.

Date	Mintage	VG	F	VF	XF	Unc
1659 HS	—	300	475	750	1,300	—

KM# 80 1/8 THALER
Silver **Obv:** Crowned 12-fold arms **Rev:** Wildman, tree in right hand

Date	Mintage	VG	F	VF	XF	Unc
1664 HS	—	—	—	—	—	—

KM# 96.1 1/8 THALER
Silver **Rev:** St. Andrew with cross, date in legend

Date	Mintage	VG	F	VF	XF	Unc
1666 LW	—	—	—	—	—	—

KM# 96.2 1/8 THALER
Silver **Ruler:** Johann Friedrich **Obv:** Crowned 12-fold arms, titles of Johann Friedrich in German **Rev:** Wildman holding tree branch in his right hand

Date	Mintage	VG	F	VF	XF	Unc
1667	—	—	—	—	—	—

KM# 217 1/8 THALER
Silver **Note:** Similar to KM#216 but 25.8mm.

Date	Mintage	VG	F	VF	XF	Unc
1679 HB	—	75.00	130	215	425	—

KM# 216 1/8 THALER
Silver, 29 mm. **Subject:** Death of Johann Friedrich

Date	Mintage	VG	F	VF	XF	Unc
MDCLXXIX (1679) RB	—	80.00	160	275	550	—

KM# A365 1/8 THALER
Silver **Obv:** Helmeted 12-fold arms **Rev:** Wildman with tree in right hand

Date	Mintage	VG	F	VF	XF	Unc
1692	—	—	—	—	—	—

KM# 365 1/8 THALER
Silver **Obv:** Bust right **Rev:** Crowned 12-fold arms

Date	Mintage	VG	F	VF	XF	Unc
1692 HB	—	70.00	135	215	425	—

KM# 408 1/8 THALER
Silver **Subject:** Death of Ernest August **Rev:** Nine-line inscription with date

Date	Mintage	VG	F	VF	XF	Unc
1698	—	85.00	145	215	425	—

KM# 24 1/4 THALER
Silver **Obv:** Crowned 11-fold arms **Rev:** Wildman, tree in right hand, date

Date	Mintage	VG	F	VF	XF	Unc
1638 HS	—	—	—	—	—	—

KM# 38 1/4 THALER
Silver **Subject:** Death of Georg **Obv:** Crowned 11-fold arms **Rev:** 11-line inscription, date in roman numerals

Date	Mintage	VG	F	VF	XF	Unc
1641 HS	—	65.00	120	180	425	—

KM# 48 1/4 THALER
Silver **Obv:** Bust right **Rev:** Crowned 12-fold arms, date in legend

Date	Mintage	VG	F	VF	XF	Unc
1646 HS	—	—	—	—	—	—

KM# 55 1/4 THALER
Silver **Obv:** Crowned 12-fold arms **Rev:** Wildman, tree in right hand, date in legend

Date	Mintage	VG	F	VF	XF	Unc
1650 HS	—	30.00	65.00	130	265	—
1651 HS	—	30.00	65.00	130	265	—
1653 HS	—	30.00	65.00	130	265	—

KM# 61 1/4 THALER
Silver **Subject:** Death of Ann Eleanora, Wife of Georg **Note:** Similar to 1 Thaler, KM#64.

Date	Mintage	VG	F	VF	XF	Unc
1659 HS	—	85.00	165	300	600	—

KM# 81 1/4 THALER
Silver **Obv:** Similar to KM#97 **Rev:** Wildman, tree in both hands on right side

Date	Mintage	VG	F	VF	XF	Unc
1664 HS	—	—	—	—	—	—

KM# 97 1/4 THALER
Silver

Date	Mintage	VG	F	VF	XF	Unc
1666 LW	—	160	320	600	1,100	—
1671 LW	—	160	320	600	1,100	—

KM# 110 1/4 THALER
Silver **Obv:** Title: DUX **Rev:** Wildman, tree in right hand, date in legend

Date	Mintage	VG	F	VF	XF	Unc
1667 HS	—	—	—	—	—	—

KM# 111 1/4 THALER
Silver **Obv:** Title: HERTZOG

Date	Mintage	VG	F	VF	XF	Unc
1667 HS	—	—	—	—	—	—

KM# 130 1/4 THALER
Silver **Obv:** Horse leaping left **Rev:** Palm tree on stone

Date	Mintage	VG	F	VF	XF	Unc
1670	—	—	—	—	—	—

KM# 145 1/4 THALER
Silver **Obv:** Head right

Date	Mintage	VG	F	VF	XF	Unc
1673	—	—	—	—	—	—

KM# 144 1/4 THALER
Silver **Note:** Similar to 1/3 Thaler, KM#146.

Date	Mintage	VG	F	VF	XF	Unc
1673	—	—	—	—	—	—

KM# 182 1/4 THALER
Silver **Obv:** Bust right **Rev:** Crowned 12-fold arms

Date	Mintage	VG	F	VF	XF	Unc
1676 HB	—	—	—	—	—	—

KM# 218 1/4 THALER
Silver, 30 mm. **Subject:** Death of Johann Friedrich **Obv:** Helmeted 12-fold arms **Rev:** 13-line inscription with date **Note:** Varieties exist.

Date	Mintage	VG	F	VF	XF	Unc
1679 RB	—	90.00	170	300	600	—
1679 HB	—	90.00	170	300	600	—

KM# 261 1/4 THALER
Silver **Obv:** Crowned 12-fold arms **Rev:** Horse leaping left **Note:** Posthumous issue for Johann Friedrich.

Date	Mintage	VG	F	VF	XF	Unc
1680 HB	—	—	—	—	—	—

KM# 331 1/4 THALER
Silver **Obv:** Helmeted 12-fold arms

Date	Mintage	VG	F	VF	XF	Unc
1686 HB	—	625	1,000	1,700	2,750	—

KM# 345 1/4 THALER
Silver **Obv:** Crowned 12-fold arms **Rev:** St. Andrew with cross

Date	Mintage	VG	F	VF	XF	Unc
1690 HB	—	—	—	—	—	—

KM# 366 1/4 THALER
Silver **Obv:** Bust right **Rev:** Helmeted 12-fold arms

Date	Mintage	VG	F	VF	XF	Unc
1692 HB	—	—	—	—	—	—

KM# 367 1/4 THALER

Silver **Obv:** Crowned 12-fold arms **Rev:** Wildman, tree in right hand

Date	Mintage	VG	F	VF	XF	Unc
1692 RB	—	—	—	—	—	—

KM# 409 1/4 THALER

Silver **Subject:** Death of Ernest August **Obv:** Bust right **Rev:** 11-line inscription with date

Date	Mintage	VG	F	VF	XF	Unc
1698	—	—	—	—	—	—

KM# 146 1/3 THALER

Silver **Obv:** Bust right **Rev:** Island palm tree, value in orb divides date below

Date	Mintage	VG	F	VF	XF	Unc
1673	—	60.00	95.00	175	350	—

KM# 147.1 1/3 THALER

Silver

Date	Mintage	VG	F	VF	XF	Unc
1673	—	45.00	85.00	140	275	—

KM# 147.2 1/3 THALER

7.2000 g., Silver **Obv:** Wide portrait and cloak **Rev:** FEIN SILB and Arabic date in exergue

Date	Mintage	VG	F	VF	XF	Unc
1676	—	45.00	85.00	140	275	—

KM# 183 1/3 THALER

Silver, 28 mm. **Obv:** Bust left **Rev:** Island palm tree, value in orb divides date below

Date	Mintage	VG	F	VF	XF	Unc
1676	—	65.00	115	225	450	—
ND	—	65.00	115	225	450	—

KM# 184 1/3 THALER

Silver **Obv:** Horse leaping left, value divided date below **Rev:** St. Andrew with cross

Date	Mintage	VG	F	VF	XF	Unc
1676	—	130	210	320	625	—
1677	—	130	210	320	625	—
1678	—	130	210	320	625	—

KM# 185 1/3 THALER

Silver **Obv:** Horse leaping left **Rev:** 1/3 in inner circle, legend around

Date	Mintage	VG	F	VF	XF	Unc
ND(1678)	—	100	200	300	550	—

KM# 219 1/3 THALER

Silver **Obv:** Small bust right in inner circle **Rev:** Island palm tree, value in orb divides date below

Date	Mintage	VG	F	VF	XF	Unc
MDCLXXIX (1679) HB	—	70.00	125	250	500	—

KM# 220 1/3 THALER

7.2000 g., Silver **Subject:** Death of Johann Friedrich

Date	Mintage	VG	F	VF	XF	Unc
1679 RB	—	125	250	500	900	—

KM# 147.3 1/3 THALER

Silver **Obv:** Thin portrait and cloak

Date	Mintage	VG	F	VF	XF	Unc
1679 HB	—	45.00	85.00	130	265	—

KM# 278 1/3 THALER

Silver **Obv:** Crowned 12-fold arms **Rev:** Horse leaping left, value 1/3 below divides date **Note:** Varieties exist.

Date	Mintage	VG	F	VF	XF	Unc
1681 HB	—	75.00	150	300	—	—
1684 HB	—	75.00	150	300	—	—
1686 HB	—	75.00	150	300	—	—

KM# 305 1/3 THALER

Silver **Note:** Varieties exist.

Date	Mintage	VG	F	VF	XF	Unc
MDCLXXXIII (1683) HB	—	60.00	125	210	425	—
MDCLXXXVI (1686) HB	—	60.00	125	210	425	—
MDCLXXXVII (1687) HB	—	60.00	125	210	425	—
MDCLXXXVIII (1688) HB	—	60.00	125	210	425	—

KM# 346 1/3 THALER

Silver **Rev:** St. Andrew with cross, date in legend

Date	Mintage	VG	F	VF	XF	Unc
1690 HB	—	27.00	55.00	110	220	—
1692 HB	—	27.00	55.00	110	220	—

KM# 388 1/3 THALER

Silver **Obv:** Crowned script EA monogram **Rev:** St. Andrew with cross

Date	Mintage	VG	F	VF	XF	Unc
MDCXCIV (1694) HB	—	30.00	65.00	130	265	—
MDCVC (1695) HB	—	30.00	65.00	130	265	—

KM# 393 1/3 THALER

Silver **Obv:** KM#388 **Rev:** KM#392 **Note:** Mule.

Date	Mintage	VG	F	VF	XF	Unc
1694/1695 HB	—	60.00	125	250	525	—

KM# 392 1/3 THALER

Silver **Rev:** Arabic year divided near bottom

Date	Mintage	VG	F	VF	XF	Unc
1695 HB	—	30.00	65.00	130	265	—

KM# 404 1/3 THALER

Silver **Obv:** Arabic date divided by monogram

Date	Mintage	VG	F	VF	XF	Unc
1696 HB	—	30.00	60.00	120	240	—
1697 HB	—	30.00	60.00	120	240	—

KM# 19 1/2 THALER

Silver **Obv:** Half-length figure left **Rev:** Crowned 11-fold arms, date in legend

Date	Mintage	VG	F	VF	XF	Unc
1637 HS	—	65.00	130	235	475	—
1638 HS	—	65.00	130	235	475	—
1639 HS	—	65.00	130	235	475	—
1640 HS	—	65.00	130	235	475	—
1641 HS	—	65.00	130	235	475	—

KM# 39 1/2 THALER

Silver **Subject:** Death of George **Rev:** 13-line inscription

Date	Mintage	VG	F	VF	XF	Unc
MDCXLI (1641) HS	—	165	300	550	1,000	—

KM# 50 1/2 THALER

Silver **Obv:** Crowned 12-fold arms **Rev:** Wildman, tree in right hand

Date	Mintage	VG	F	VF	XF	Unc
1647 HS	—	—	—	—	—	—

KM# 62 1/2 THALER

Silver **Obv:** Crowned 12-fold arms **Rev:** Wildman, tree in both hands on right side

Date	Mintage	VG	F	VF	XF	Unc
1659 HS	—	150	275	500	900	—
1660 HS	—	150	275	500	900	—

KM# 63 1/2 THALER

Silver **Subject:** Death of Anna Eleonora, Wife of Georg **Note:** Similar to 1 thaler, KM#64.

Date	Mintage	VG	F	VF	XF	Unc
1659 HS	—	150	300	550	1,000	—

KM# 100 1/2 THALER

Silver **Note:** Varieties exist.

Date	Mintage	VG	F	VF	XF	Unc
1666 HS	—	90.00	185	345	675	—

Date	Mintage	VG	F	VF	XF	Unc
1667 HS	—	90.00	185	345	675	—
1679 RB	—	90.00	185	345	675	—

KM# 99 1/2 THALER
Silver **Note:** Klippe.

Date	Mintage	VG	F	VF	XF	Unc
1666 LW	—	—	—	—	—	—

KM# 98 1/2 THALER
Silver

Date	Mintage	VG	F	VF	XF	Unc
1666 LW	—	100	190	300	500	—
1671 LW	—	100	190	300	500	—

KM# 186 1/2 THALER
Silver **Obv:** Bust right **Rev:** Crowned 12-fold arms

Date	Mintage	VG	F	VF	XF	Unc
1676 HB	—	—	—	—	—	—

KM# 201 1/2 THALER
Silver **Obv:** Helmeted 12-fold arms **Rev:** 13-line inscription with date

Date	Mintage	VG	F	VF	XF	Unc
1678 HB	—	—	—	—	—	—

KM# 221 1/2 THALER
Silver **Rev:** Roman numeral date in legend

Date	Mintage	VG	F	VF	XF	Unc
1679 HB	—	200	350	700	1,200	—

KM# 222 1/2 THALER
Silver **Obv:** Bust right **Rev:** Horse leaping left

Date	Mintage	VG	F	VF	XF	Unc
1679	—	135	275	550	1,000	—

KM# 223 1/2 THALER
Silver **Subject:** Death of Johann Friedrich **Obv:** Helmeted 12-fold arms **Rev:** 13-line inscription

Date	Mintage	VG	F	VF	XF	Unc
MDCXXIX (1679) HB	—	175	350	700	1,200	—
MDCXXIX (1679) RB	—	175	350	700	1,200	—
MDCXXIX (1679)	—	175	350	700	1,200	—

KM# 321 1/2 THALER
Silver **Obv:** Bust right **Rev:** Helmeted 12-fold arms

Date	Mintage	VG	F	VF	XF	Unc
MDCLXXXV (1685)	—	—	—	—	—	—

KM# 339 1/2 THALER
Silver **Rev:** Arabic date in legend

Date	Mintage	VG	F	VF	XF	Unc
1689 HB	—	—	—	—	—	—

KM# 368 1/2 THALER
7.3000 g., Silver, 28.4 mm. **Rev:** Value as R.T. (Reichstaler)

Date	Mintage	VG	F	VF	XF	Unc
1692 HB	—	—	—	—	—	—

KM# 410 1/2 THALER
Silver **Subject:** Death of Ernst August **Rev:** 12-line inscription with date

Date	Mintage	VG	F	VF	XF	Unc
1698	—	150	200	300	550	—

KM# 148 2/3 THALER
Silver **Note:** Similar to KM#187 but without V. FEIN SILB.

Date	Mintage	VG	F	VF	XF	Unc
1673	—	65.00	135	275	525	—
1674	—	65.00	135	275	525	—
1676	—	65.00	135	275	525	—
1677	—	65.00	135	275	525	—
1678	—	65.00	135	275	525	—

KM# 170 2/3 THALER
Silver **Rev:** Large 2/3, date in legend

Date	Mintage	VG	F	VF	XF	Unc
1675 RB	—	250	475	900	1,750	—

KM# 171 2/3 THALER
Silver

Date	Mintage	VG	F	VF	XF	Unc
1675 RB	—	50.00	100	210	425	—
1676 RB	—	50.00	100	210	425	—

KM# 172 2/3 THALER
Silver

Date	Mintage	VG	F	VF	XF	Unc
1675 RB	—	45.00	85.00	175	375	800
1676	—	45.00	85.00	175	375	800
1676 RB	—	45.00	85.00	175	375	800
1677	—	45.00	85.00	175	375	800
1678	—	45.00	85.00	175	375	800
ND	—	45.00	85.00	175	375	800

KM# 188.1 2/3 THALER
Silver

Date	Mintage	VG	F	VF	XF	Unc
1676	—	50.00	100	210	425	850

KM# 187 2/3 THALER
Silver **Note:** Varieties exist.

Date	Mintage	VG	F	VF	XF	Unc
1676	—	45.00	95.00	190	385	800
1677	—	45.00	95.00	190	385	800
1678	—	45.00	95.00	190	385	800
1679 HB	—	45.00	95.00	190	385	800

KM# 188.2 2/3 THALER
Silver

Date	Mintage	VG	F	VF	XF	Unc
1677	—	85.00	175	375	750	—

KM# A224 2/3 THALER
Silver **Obv:** Bust right **Rev:** Two ships "keeling" left, flanking island palm

Date	Mintage	VG	F	VF	XF	Unc
1677	—	85.00	175	375	750	—

KM# B224 2/3 THALER
Silver **Rev:** Ships upright

Date	Mintage	VG	F	VF	XF	Unc
1677	—	85.00	175	350	650	—

KM# 188.3 2/3 THALER
Silver

Date	Mintage	VG	F	VF	XF	Unc
1678	—	75.00	150	300	600	—

KM# 202 2/3 THALER
Silver

Date	Mintage	VG	F	VF	XF	Unc
1678	—	110	220	325	650	—

KM# 204 2/3 THALER
Silver, 30.5 mm.

Date	Mintage	VG	F	VF	XF	Unc
ND	—	60.00	125	250	525	—

KM# 203 2/3 THALER

Silver **Note:** Similar to KM#204 but 34mm and value in wreath.

Date	Mintage	VG	F	VF	XF	Unc
ND	—	—	—	—	—	—

KM# C224 2/3 THALER

Silver **Rev:** Island with four rocks

Date	Mintage	VG	F	VF	XF	Unc
1679 HB	—	80.00	160	325	650	—

KM# D224 2/3 THALER

Silver **Rev:** Island with six rocks

Date	Mintage	VG	F	VF	XF	Unc
1679 HB	—	80.00	160	325	650	—

KM# E224 2/3 THALER

Silver **Rev:** Island rock cluster

Date	Mintage	VG	F	VF	XF	Unc
1679 HB	—	80.00	160	325	650	—

KM# F224 2/3 THALER

14.5000 g., Silver, 34 mm. **Rev:** Roman numeral date in legend

Date	Mintage	VG	F	VF	XF	Unc
1679 HB	—	75.00	150	300	600	—

KM# 224 2/3 THALER

Silver

Date	Mintage	VG	F	VF	XF	Unc
1679 HB	—	75.00	150	300	600	—

KM# 225 2/3 THALER

Silver **Subject:** Death of Johann Friedrich

Date	Mintage	VG	F	VF	XF	Unc
1679 RB	—	—	—	—	—	—

KM# 262.1 2/3 THALER

Silver **Rev:** Trees behind wildman

Date	Mintage	VG	F	VF	XF	Unc
1680	—	45.00	90.00	180	360	—
1681	—	45.00	90.00	180	360	—
1682	—	45.00	90.00	180	360	—
1683	—	45.00	90.00	180	360	—
1684	—	45.00	90.00	180	360	—
1685	—	45.00	90.00	180	360	—
1686	—	45.00	90.00	180	360	—
1687	—	45.00	90.00	180	360	—
1688	—	45.00	90.00	180	360	—
1689	—	45.00	90.00	180	360	—
1690	—	45.00	90.00	180	360	—
1691	—	45.00	90.00	180	360	—
1692	—	45.00	90.00	180	360	—
1693	—	45.00	90.00	180	360	—
1693 RB	—	45.00	90.00	180	360	—

KM# 263 2/3 THALER

Silver, 35 mm. **Obv. Legend:** SOLA BONA QUAE HONESTA: FEIN (2/3) SILB **Rev:** Horse leaping left in circle, value 2/3 below **Rev. Legend:** ERN:AUG:D . G. E. O. D. B. & L. **Note:** Varieties exist.

Date	Mintage	VG	F	VF	XF	Unc
1680 HB	—	50.00	100	200	400	—
1681 HB	—	50.00	100	200	400	—
1682 HB	—	50.00	100	200	400	—
1683 HB	—	50.00	100	200	400	—
1683 IES	—	50.00	100	200	400	—
1684 HB	—	50.00	100	200	400	—

KM# A264 2/3 THALER

Silver **Obv:** Date above crowned shield **Rev:** Leaping horse

Date	Mintage	VG	F	VF	XF	Unc
1680 IES	—	—	—	—	—	—

KM# B264 2/3 THALER

Silver **Obv:** Crowned shield divides date and initials **Rev:** Value below horse

Date	Mintage	VG	F	VF	XF	Unc
1680 HB	—	55.00	110	225	—	—
1681 HB	—	55.00	110	225	—	—
1682 HB	—	55.00	110	225	—	—
1683 HB	—	55.00	110	225	—	—

KM# 264 2/3 THALER

Silver **Obv:** Larger arms with sprays **Rev:** Date divided by value at bottom

Date	Mintage	VG	F	VF	XF	Unc
1680 IES	—	45.00	85.00	180	360	—

KM# A312 2/3 THALER

16.8000 g., Silver, 37 mm. **Rev:** Initials

Date	Mintage	VG	F	VF	XF	Unc
1683 IES	—	45.00	85.00	180	360	—

KM# B312 2/3 THALER

16.5000 g., Silver **Obv:** Initials

Date	Mintage	VG	F	VF	XF	Unc
MDCLXXXIII (1683) IES	—	65.00	125	240	—	—
MDCLXXXIV (1684) IES	—	65.00	125	240	—	—

KM# 312 2/3 THALER

16.5000 g., Silver **Obv:** Helmeted 12-fold arms divide date **Rev:** Horse leaping left

Date	Mintage	VG	F	VF	XF	Unc
1684 HB	—	70.00	135	235	475	—

KM# 314 2/3 THALER

Silver **Rev:** Horse in wreath

Date	Mintage	VG	F	VF	XF	Unc
1684 IES	—	70.00	135	240	480	—

KM# 313 2/3 THALER

Silver **Note:** Similar to KM#315 but 2/3 divides date below.

Date	Mintage	VG	F	VF	XF	Unc
1684 IES	—	70.00	135	240	480	—

KM# 315 2/3 THALER

Silver **Note:** Varieties exist.

Date	Mintage	VG	F	VF	XF	Unc
MDCLXXXV (1685) HB	—	60.00	110	230	475	—
MDCLXXXVI (1686) HB	—	60.00	110	230	475	—
MDCLXXXVII (1687) HB	—	60.00	110	230	475	—
MDCLXXXVII (1687) HB Error "DUAE"	—	60.00	110	230	475	—
MDCLXXXVIII (1688) HB	—	60.00	110	230	475	—

KM# 340 2/3 THALER

Silver **Rev:** 2/3 below divides date and FEIN-SILB

Date	Mintage	VG	F	VF	XF	Unc
1689 HB	—	45.00	90.00	160	300	—
1690 HB	—	45.00	90.00	160	300	—
1691 HB	—	45.00	90.00	160	300	—
1692 HB	—	45.00	90.00	160	300	—
1693 HB	—	45.00	90.00	160	300	—

KM# 347 2/3 THALER

Silver **Rev:** Without wreath and without FEIN-SILB

Date	Mintage	VG	F	VF	XF	Unc
1690 IES	—	40.00	65.00	110	225	—
1690 Stars	—	40.00	65.00	110	225	—
1691 Stars	—	40.00	65.00	110	225	—
1692 Stars	—	40.00	65.00	110	225	—

KM# 348 2/3 THALER

Silver **Rev:** FEIN-SILB divided by value

Date	Mintage	VG	F	VF	XF	Unc
1690	—	45.00	85.00	145	275	—
1692	—	45.00	85.00	145	275	—

KM# 269 2/3 THALER

15.4000 g., Silver, 34.8 mm. **Ruler:** Ernst August **Obv:** Crowned arms in center circle divide stars **Rev:** Horse jumping left in inner circle above denomination which divides the date in the legend **Edge:** Plain

Date	Mintage	F	VF	XF	Unc	BU
1690	—	—	—	—	—	—

KM# 262.2 2/3 THALER
Silver **Obv:** Stars above date **Rev:** Grass under wildman

Date	Mintage	VG	F	VF	XF	Unc
1690	—	45.00	90.00	180	360	—
1693	—	45.00	90.00	180	360	—

KM# 379 2/3 THALER
Silver

Date	Mintage	VG	F	VF	XF	Unc
1693	—	45.00	90.00	180	360	—
1694	—	45.00	90.00	180	360	—

KM# 380 2/3 THALER
Silver **Rev:** Large crown above horse leaping left, value 2/3 below, date in legend

Date	Mintage	VG	F	VF	XF	Unc
1693	—	—	—	—	—	—

KM# 10 THALER
Silver **Obv:** Half-length figure right, date **Rev:** Female figure of Concord between figures of four dukes

Date	Mintage	VG	F	VF	XF	Unc
1634 HS	—	—	—	—	—	—

KM# 14 THALER
Silver **Obv:** Bust right **Rev:** Helmeted arms, date in legend **Note:** Dav. #6502.

Date	Mintage	VG	F	VF	XF	Unc
1635	—	400	800	1,500	2,500	—
1636	—	400	800	1,500	2,500	—

KM# 18 THALER
Silver **Rev:** Date divided at top in legend **Note:** Dav. #6503.

Date	Mintage	VG	F	VF	XF	Unc
1636	—	400	800	1,500	2,500	—

KM# 20 THALER
Silver **Rev:** Similar to KM#21 but larger arms, date in upper right legend **Note:** Dav. #6504.

Date	Mintage	VG	F	VF	XF	Unc
1637 HS	—	130	250	450	750	—
1638 HS	—	130	250	450	750	—

KM# 21 THALER
Silver **Note:** Dav. #6505.

Date	Mintage	VG	F	VF	XF	Unc
1637 HS	—	130	250	450	750	—
1638 HS	—	130	250	450	750	—
1639 HS	—	130	250	450	750	—

KM# 22.1 THALER
Silver **Rev:** Wildman facing forward, legend, date **Rev. Legend:** TRAWE ICH ANNO **Note:** Dav. #6507.

Date	Mintage	VG	F	VF	XF	Unc
1637 HS	—	90.00	170	300	550	—
1638 HS	—	90.00	170	300	550	—
1639 HS	—	90.00	170	300	550	—

KM# 30 THALER
Silver **Note:** Dav. #6506.

Date	Mintage	VG	F	VF	XF	Unc
1639 HS	—	130	250	450	750	—
1640 HS	—	130	250	450	750	—
1641 HS	—	130	250	450	750	—
1642 HS	—	130	250	450	750	—

KM# 22.2 THALER
Silver **Note:** Varieties exist. Dav. #6508.

Date	Mintage	VG	F	VF	XF	Unc
1639 HS	—	90.00	170	300	550	—
1640 HS	—	90.00	170	300	550	—
1641 HS	—	90.00	170	300	550	—
1642 HS	—	90.00	170	300	550	—

KM# 40 THALER
Silver **Subject:** Death of Georg **Obv:** 1/2-length figure left **Rev:** 11-line inscription **Note:** Dav. #6510.

Date	Mintage	VG	F	VF	XF	Unc
1641 HS	—	400	650	1,200	2,000	—

KM# 41 THALER
Silver **Obv:** 1/2-length figure left **Rev:** 10-line inscription, date in Roman numerals **Note:** Dav. #6510A.

Date	Mintage	VG	F	VF	XF	Unc
1641 HS	—	400	650	1,200	2,000	—

KM# 47.1 THALER
Silver **Obv:** Helmeted 12-fold arms dividing H S **Obv. Legend:** C RIS: LUD: HERTZ. Z. G: L. **Rev:** Wildman with tree in right hand **Note:** Dav. #6515.

Date	Mintage	VG	F	VF	XF	Unc
1643 HS	—	90.00	170	300	550	—

KM# 47.2 THALER
Silver **Obv. Legend:** CHRISTI: LUD: D. G. DUX. BR: E: L: **Note:** Dav. #6516.

Date	Mintage	VG	F	VF	XF	Unc
1643 HS	—	90.00	170	300	550	—

KM# 47.3 THALER
Silver **Obv. Legend:** CHRISTI: LUD: H. Z: B: L: **Note:** Dav. #6517.

Date	Mintage	VG	F	VF	XF	Unc
1643 HS	—	90.00	170	300	550	—
1646 HS	—	90.00	170	300	550	—
1648	—	90.00	170	300	550	—
1648 HS	—	90.00	170	300	550	—
1649	—	90.00	170	300	550	—
1649 HS	—	90.00	170	300	550	—
1650	—	90.00	170	300	550	—
1650 HS	—	90.00	170	300	550	—
1652	—	90.00	170	300	550	—
1652 HS	—	90.00	170	300	550	—

KM# 47.4 THALER
Silver **Rev:** H mint mark, S in legend **Note:** Dav. #6517B.

Date	Mintage	VG	F	VF	XF	Unc
1643	—	90.00	170	300	550	—
1648	—	90.00	170	300	550	—
1652	—	90.00	170	300	550	—
1653	—	90.00	170	300	550	—
1655	—	90.00	170	300	550	—
1657	—	90.00	170	300	550	—
1663	—	90.00	170	300	550	—
1664	—	90.00	170	300	550	—
1665	—	90.00	170	300	550	—

KM# 46.1 THALER
Silver **Obv:** 3/4-length bust right, baton in left hand **Rev:** Helmeted 12-fold arms, date in legend **Note:** Dav. #6512.

Date	Mintage	VG	F	VF	XF	Unc
1643 HS	—	240	450	800	1,500	—
1644	—	240	450	800	1,500	—
1645	—	240	450	800	1,500	—

KM# 46.2 THALER
Silver **Obv:** 3/4-length bust right, baton in right hand **Note:** Dav. #6513.

Date	Mintage	VG	F	VF	XF	Unc
1645	—	240	450	800	1,500	—
1645 HS	—	240	450	800	1,500	—
1646	—	240	450	800	1,500	—
1646 HS	—	240	450	800	1,500	—
1647	—	240	450	800	1,500	—
1647 HS	—	240	450	800	1,500	—

KM# 46.3 THALER

Silver **Obv:** 3/4-length bust right, raised baton in left hand **Note:** Dav. #6514.

Date	Mintage	VG	F	VF	XF	Unc
1647	—	240	450	800	1,500	—
1648 HS	—	240	450	800	1,500	—
1649	—	240	450	800	1,500	—

KM# 52.1 THALER

Silver **Obv. Legend:** V. G. G. GEORG. WILH: HERTZ:... **Note:** Dav. #6526.

Date	Mintage	VG	F	VF	XF	Unc
1649	—	90.00	170	300	550	—

KM# 52.2 THALER

Silver **Note:** Dav. #6527.

Date	Mintage	VG	F	VF	XF	Unc
1649 HS	—	90.00	170	300	550	—
1650 HS	—	90.00	170	300	550	—
1651 HS	—	90.00	170	300	550	—
1652	—	90.00	170	300	550	—
1652 HS	—	90.00	170	300	550	—
1653 HS	—	90.00	170	300	550	—

KM# 57.1 THALER

Silver **Note:** Dav. #6528.

Date	Mintage	VG	F	VF	XF	Unc
1654 HS	—	90.00	170	300	550	—
1655 HS	—	90.00	170	300	550	—
1656 HS	—	90.00	170	300	550	—
1657 HS	—	90.00	170	300	550	—
1658 HS	—	90.00	170	300	550	—
1659 HS	—	90.00	170	300	550	—
1660 HS	—	90.00	170	300	550	—
1661 HS	—	90.00	170	300	550	—
1662 HS	—	90.00	170	300	550	—
1663 HS	—	90.00	170	300	550	—
1664 HS	—	90.00	170	300	550	—

KM# 64 THALER

Silver **Subject:** Death of Eleanora, Wife of Georg **Note:** Dav. #6511.

Date	Mintage	VG	F	VF	XF	Unc
1659 HS Rare	—	—	—	—	—	—

KM# 73 THALER

Silver **Obv:** Bust right in circle of fourteen small shields, date divided below **Rev:** Figures of Piety and Justice below tree, arm from heaven with wreath **Note:** Dav. #6532.

Date	Mintage	VG	F	VF	XF	Unc
1661 HS	—	350	600	1,000	1,850	—
1662 HS	—	350	600	1,000	1,850	—

KM# 79 THALER

Silver **Obv:** Bust right **Rev:** Helmeted 12-fold arms, date in legend **Note:** Dav. #6535.

Date	Mintage	VG	F	VF	XF	Unc
1662	—	500	700	1,200	2,000	—
1664 HS	—	500	700	1,200	2,000	—
1665	—	500	700	1,200	2,000	—

KM# 88 THALER

Silver **Obv:** Bust left **Rev:** Helmeted 12-fold arms, date in legend **Note:** Dav. #6536.

Date	Mintage	VG	F	VF	XF	Unc
1664 LW	—	90.00	170	300	550	—
1665 Rare	—	—	—	—	—	—
1665 HS Rare	—	—	—	—	—	—

KM# 57.2 THALER

Silver **Obv:** Legend continuous from left to right **Note:** Dav. #6529.

Date	Mintage	VG	F	VF	XF	Unc
1664 HS	—	90.00	170	300	550	—
1665 HS	—	90.00	170	300	550	—
1666 HS	—	90.00	170	300	550	—

KM# 89 THALER

Silver **Note:** Dav. #6544.

Date	Mintage	VG	F	VF	XF	Unc
1665 HS	—	100	200	400	1,000	—
1666 HS	—	100	200	400	1,000	—
1667 HS	—	100	200	400	1,000	—

KM# 82 THALER

Silver **Rev:** Date, prancing horse left **Rev. Legend:** ANNO **Note:** Dav. #6549.

Date	Mintage	VG	F	VF	XF	Unc
1665 LW	—	90.00	170	300	550	—
1667 LW	—	90.00	170	300	550	—
1668 LW	—	90.00	170	300	550	—
1669 LW	—	90.00	170	300	550	—
1670 LW	—	90.00	170	300	550	—
1671 LW	—	90.00	170	300	550	—
1672 LW	—	90.00	170	300	550	—
1673 LW	—	90.00	170	300	550	—

KM# 101 THALER

Silver **Obv:** Similar to KM#216 **Rev:** St. Andrew with cross, date in legend **Note:** Dav. #6557.

Date	Mintage	VG	F	VF	XF	Unc
1666 LW	—	240	450	800	1,500	—
1667 LW	—	240	450	800	1,500	—
1669 LW	—	240	450	800	1,500	—

KM# 102 THALER

Silver **Note:** Dav. #6569.

Date	Mintage	VG	F	VF	XF	Unc
1666	—	400	650	1,100	2,000	—
1667	—	400	650	1,100	2,000	—
1668	—	400	650	1,100	2,000	—
1669	—	400	650	1,100	2,000	—
1670	—	400	650	1,100	2,000	—
1671	—	400	650	1,100	2,000	—

KM# 114 THALER

Silver **Rev:** Legend, date, prancing horse left **Rev. Legend:** EX DURIS GLORIA * ANNO * **Note:** Dav. #6550.

Date	Mintage	VG	F	VF	XF	Unc
1667 LW	—	90.00	170	300	550	—
1673 LW	—	90.00	170	300	550	—

KM# 115 THALER

Silver **Note:** Dav. #6551.

Date	Mintage	VG	F	VF	XF	Unc
1667 LW	—	200	400	750	1,250	—
1668 LW	—	200	400	750	1,250	—
1669 LW	—	200	400	750	1,250	—
1670 LW	—	200	400	750	1,250	—
1671 LW	—	200	400	750	1,250	—
1673 LW	—	200	400	750	1,250	—
1674 LW	—	200	400	750	1,250	—
1675 HB	—	200	400	750	1,250	—

KM# 113.1 THALER

Silver **Obv. Legend:** IOHAN FRIEDRICH: D: G DUX BR: ET LUNEB **Note:** Dav. #6546.

Date	Mintage	VG	F	VF	XF	Unc
1667 HS	—	90.00	170	300	550	—
1668 HS	—	90.00	170	300	550	—
1669 HS	—	90.00	170	300	550	—

KM# 116 THALER

Silver **Obv:** Bust left **Rev:** Horse leaping left in empty field

Date	Mintage	VG	F	VF	XF	Unc
1667	—	—	—	—	—	—
1670	—	—	—	—	—	—

KM# 112 THALER

Silver **Note:** Similar to KM#89 but EX DVRIS GLORIA added to reverse legend. Dav. #6545.

Date	Mintage	VG	F	VF	XF	Unc
1667 HS	—	90.00	170	300	550	—

KM# 124.1 THALER

Silver **Rev:** Helmeted 12-fold arms, date in legend **Note:** Dav. #6578.

Date	Mintage	VG	F	VF	XF	Unc
1668 LW Rare	—	—	—	—	—	—

KM# 124.2 THALER

Silver **Rev:** Legend, date **Rev. Legend:** EX DVRIS GLORIA ANNO **Note:** Dav. #6579.

Date	Mintage	VG	F	VF	XF	Unc
1669	—	500	900	1,400	2,500	—
1670	—	500	900	1,400	2,500	—
1671	—	500	900	1,400	2,500	—

KM# 124.3 THALER

Silver **Obv:** C below bust **Note:** Dav. #6579A.

Date	Mintage	VG	F	VF	XF	Unc
1670 C	—	500	900	1,400	2,500	—

KM# 113.2 THALER

Silver **Obv. Legend:** ...BRUNS: ET LUN: **Rev:** Initials by tree **Note:** Dav. #6547.

Date	Mintage	VG	F	VF	XF	Unc
1670 HS	—	90.00	170	300	550	—
1671 HS	—	90.00	170	300	550	—
1672 HS	—	90.00	170	300	550	—
1673 IPE	—	90.00	170	300	550	—
1675 IPE	—	90.00	170	300	550	—

KM# 149.1 THALER

Silver **Obv:** Bust right with short hair **Note:** Dav. #6570.

Date	Mintage	VG	F	VF	XF	Unc
1673	—	600	1,000	1,750	3,000	—

KM# 150 THALER

Silver **Note:** Helmeted 12-fold arms, date divided near bottom. Dav. #6580.

Date	Mintage	VG	F	VF	XF	Unc
1673 HB Rare	—	—	—	—	—	—
1676 HB Rare	—	—	—	—	—	—
1677 HB Rare	—	—	—	—	—	—

KM# 159 THALER
Silver **Note:** Dav. #6558.

Date	Mintage	VG	F	VF	XF	Unc
1674	—	700	1,100	1,800	3,000	—

KM# 173 THALER
Silver **Rev:** Horse on hilly ground **Note:** Dav. #6552.

Date	Mintage	VG	F	VF	XF	Unc
1675 HB Rare	—	—	—	—	—	—
1677 HB Rare	—	—	—	—	—	—

KM# 149.2 THALER
Silver **Obv:** Bust right with long hair **Note:** Dav. #6573.

Date	Mintage	VG	F	VF	XF	Unc
1675	—	400	650	1,100	2,000	—
1676	—	400	650	1,100	2,000	—

KM# 174 THALER
Silver **Note:** Similar to KM#227. Dav. #6560.

Date	Mintage	VG	F	VF	XF	Unc
1675 HB	—	500	900	1,400	2,500	—
1678 HB	—	500	900	1,400	2,500	—
1679 HB	—	500	900	1,400	2,500	—

KM# 189 THALER
Silver **Subject:** 100th Anniversary - University of Helmstedt **Obv:** 16-line inscription **Rev:** Fountain between two palm trees **Note:** Dav. #6588.

Date	Mintage	VG	F	VF	XF	Unc
1676 HB	—	1,900	3,100	5,200	9,500	—

KM# 113.3 THALER
Silver **Obv. Legend:** ...FRIDER...LUNAE **Note:** Dav. #6548.

Date	Mintage	VG	F	VF	XF	Unc
1677 RB	—	180	350	700	1,200	—
1678 RB	—	180	350	700	1,200	—
1679 RB	—	180	350	700	1,200	—

KM# 206.2 THALER
Silver **Obv:** Taller shield **Obv. Legend:** DUX BR. EL. **Note:** Dav. #6555.

Date	Mintage	VG	F	VF	XF	Unc
1678 HB Rare	—	—	—	—	—	—

KM# 208.1 THALER
Silver **Obv:** Small bust right **Rev:** Helmeted 12-fold arms, divided near top **Note:** Dav. #6581.

Date	Mintage	VG	F	VF	XF	Unc
1678 HB Rare	—	—	—	—	—	—

KM# 206.1 THALER
Silver **Note:** Similar to KM#115, but date at reverse bottom. Dav. #6554.

Date	Mintage	VG	F	VF	XF	Unc
1678 HB Rare	—	—	—	—	—	—

KM# 205 THALER
Silver **Note:** Similar to KM#115, but date divided by arms. Dav. #6553.

Date	Mintage	VG	F	VF	XF	Unc
1678 HB Rare	—	—	—	—	—	—

KM# 207 THALER
Silver **Note:** Hybrid Thaler. Similar to KM#227. Dav. #6561.

Date	Mintage	VG	F	VF	XF	Unc
1678 HB	—	500	900	1,400	2,500	—

KM# 226 THALER
Silver **Note:** Similar to KM#115, but horse in circle. Dav. #6556.

Date	Mintage	VG	F	VF	XF	Unc
MDCLXXIX (1679) HB Rare	—	—	—	—	—	—

KM# 232 THALER
Silver **Obv:** Small bust right in laurel wreath **Rev:** Helmeted 12-fold arms, date divided near top **Note:** Dav. #6582.

Date	Mintage	VG	F	VF	XF	Unc
1679 HB Rare	—	—	—	—	—	—

KM# 233 THALER
Silver **Note:** Dav. #6583.

Date	Mintage	VG	F	VF	XF	Unc
1679 HB Rare	—	—	—	—	—	—

KM# 208.2 THALER
Silver **Rev:** Date divided at top, arms dividing H-B **Note:** Dav. #6584.

Date	Mintage	VG	F	VF	XF	Unc
1679 HB Rare	—	—	—	—	—	—

KM# 229 THALER
Silver **Note:** Dav. #6575.

Date	Mintage	VG	F	VF	XF	Unc
1679 RB	—	400	650	1,100	2,000	—

KM# 230 THALER
Silver **Note:** Dav. #6576.

Date	Mintage	VG	F	VF	XF	Unc
1679 RB	—	400	650	1,100	2,000	—

KM# 231 THALER
Silver **Rev:** Sea and ships added **Note:** Dav. #6577.

Date	Mintage	VG	F	VF	XF	Unc
1679 RB Rare	—	—	—	—	—	—

KM# 234 THALER
Silver **Subject:** Death of Joahnn Friedrich **Note:** Dav. #6589.

Date	Mintage	VG	F	VF	XF	Unc
1679	—	350	600	1,000	1,800	—

KM# 235 THALER
Silver **Note:** Dav. #6590.

Date	Mintage	VG	F	VF	XF	Unc
1679 HB	—	300	550	900	1,500	—

KM# 227.1 THALER
Silver **Rev:** St. Andrew holdign cross, date in Roman numerals **Note:** Dav. #6562.

Date	Mintage	VG	F	VF	XF	Unc
MDCLXIX (1679) HB	—	500	900	1,400	2,500	—

KM# 228 THALER
Silver **Obv:** Date in top legend **Note:** Dav. #6563.

Date	Mintage	VG	F	VF	XF	Unc
1679 HB Rare	—	—	—	—	—	—

KM# 227.2 THALER
Silver **Obv. Legend:** IOANNES. FRIDER-ICVS... **Note:** Dav. #6564.

Date	Mintage	VG	F	VF	XF	Unc
1679 Rare	—	—	—	—	—	—

KM# 227.3 THALER
Silver **Obv:** Helmeted arms divide HB **Obv. Legend:** IOAN. FRIDER-D. G. **Note:** Dav. #6565.

Date	Mintage	VG	F	VF	XF	Unc
1679 HB Rare	—	—	—	—	—	—

KM# 265.1 THALER
Silver **Obv:** Titles of Ernst August **Note:** Dav. #6591.

Date	Mintage	VG	F	VF	XF	Unc
1680 RB	—	100	200	350	600	—
1681 RB	—	100	200	350	600	—
1683 RB	—	100	200	350	600	—
1686 RB	—	100	200	350	600	—
1687 RB	—	100	200	350	600	—

KM# 266 THALER
Silver **Rev:** Horse leaping left in circle, date in legend **Note:** Dav. #6602.

Date	Mintage	VG	F	VF	XF	Unc
1680 HB	—	200	400	700	1,200	—

KM# 267.1 THALER
Silver **Obv. Legend:** ERNEST: AUG: D. G. -EP: OSN: DUX+.L. **Note:** Dav. #6603.

Date	Mintage	VG	F	VF	XF	Unc
MDCLXXX (1680) HB	—	200	400	700	1,200	—

KM# 267.2 THALER
Silver **Obv. Legend:** ...D: G: EPISC. -OSN: DUX BR: ET LUN: **Note:** Dav. #6604.

Date	Mintage	VG	F	VF	XF	Unc
1680 HB	—	200	400	700	1,200	—
1681 HB	—	200	400	700	1,200	—

KM# 279 THALER
Silver **Note:** Dav. #6592.

Date	Mintage	VG	F	VF	XF	Unc
1681 RB	—	100	200	350	650	—
1686 RB	—	100	200	350	650	—
1687 RB	—	100	200	350	650	—

KM# 280 THALER
Silver **Note:** Similar to KM#293 but arms divide date. Dav. #6629.

Date	Mintage	VG	F	VF	XF	Unc
1681 HB	—	400	700	1,200	2,200	—
1682 HB	—	400	700	1,200	2,200	—

KM# 293 THALER
Silver **Note:** Dav. #6630.

Date	Mintage	VG	F	VF	XF	Unc
1682 RB	—	400	700	1,200	2,200	—
1685 RB	—	400	700	1,200	2,200	—
1687 RB	—	400	700	1,200	2,200	—

KM# 294 THALER
Silver **Ruler:** Ernst August **Obv:** Bust of Ernst facing 3/4 right **Note:** Dav. #6631.

Date	Mintage	VG	F	VF	XF	Unc
1682 HB	—	500	900	1,400	2,500	—

KM# A294 THALER

Silver **Note:** Dav. #A6631.

Date	Mintage	VG	F	VF	XF	Unc
1682 HB	—	500	900	1,400	2,500	—

KM# 295 THALER

Silver **Obv:** Bust right within full circle continuous legend **Rev:** Helmeted arms divide date near bottom **Note:** Dav. #A6632.

Date	Mintage	VG	F	VF	XF	Unc
1682 HB	—	500	900	1,400	2,500	—

KM# 267.3 THALER

Silver **Obv. Legend:** ERN: AUG: D. G. EP: O. D. B. +L. **Note:** Dav. #6605.

Date	Mintage	VG	F	VF	XF	Unc
1682 HB Rare	—	—	—	—	—	—

KM# 267.4 THALER

Silver **Obv. Legend:** ...E. O. D. BR. +LUN: **Note:** Dav. #6606.

Date	Mintage	VG	F	VF	XF	Unc
1683 HB Rare	—	—	—	—	—	—

KM# 306 THALER

Silver **Note:** Dav. #6612.

Date	Mintage	VG	F	VF	XF	Unc
1683 HB	—	350	600	1,000	1,850	—
1685 HB	—	350	600	1,000	1,850	—
1686 HB	—	350	600	1,000	1,850	—
1687 HB	—	350	600	1,000	1,850	—

KM# 267.5 THALER

Silver **Obv:** Legend on band **Obv. Legend:** ERNEST: AUG: D. G. EP. EP. OSN. D. B. ++ L **Note:** Dav. #6607.

Date	Mintage	VG	F	VF	XF	Unc
1684 HB Rare	—	—	—	—	—	—

KM# 316 THALER

Silver **Note:** Dav. #6593.

Date	Mintage	VG	F	VF	XF	Unc
1684 RB	—	100	180	350	600	—
1685 RB	—	100	180	350	600	—

KM# 318 THALER

Silver **Obv:** Bust right splits circle at top and bottom **Rev:** Helmeted arms divide date near top **Note:** Dav. #6632.

Date	Mintage	VG	F	VF	XF	Unc
1684 HB	—	450	800	1,300	2,250	—

KM# 319 THALER

Silver **Obv:** Bust right **Rev:** Horse leaping left **Note:** Dav. #6634.

Date	Mintage	VG	F	VF	XF	Unc
MDCLXXXIV (1684)	—	450	800	1,300	2,250	—

KM# 320.1 THALER

Silver **Rev:** Arabic date **Note:** Dav. #6633.

Date	Mintage	VG	F	VF	XF	Unc
1684 HB	—	450	800	1,300	2,250	—

KM# 317.1 THALER

Silver **Rev:** Horse leaping left in laurel wreath **Note:** Dav. #6608.

Date	Mintage	VG	F	VF	XF	Unc
1684 HB Rare	—	—	—	—	—	—

KM# 317.2 THALER

Silver **Obv. Legend:** ERNESTUS. AUGUSTUS.-...+LUNB. **Note:** Dav. #6610.

Date	Mintage	VG	F	VF	XF	Unc
1685 HB	—	550	950	1,500	2,750	—
1686 HB	—	550	950	1,500	2,750	—

KM# 320.2 THALER

Silver **Obv:** Without inner circle **Rev:** Inner circle at top **Note:** Dav. #6640.

Date	Mintage	VG	F	VF	XF	Unc
1687 HB	—	450	800	1,300	2,250	—
1688 HB	—	350	600	1,000	1,850	—
1689 HB	—	350	600	1,000	1,850	—

KM# 317.3 THALER

Silver **Obv. Legend:** Ends:...ET. L. **Note:** Dav. #6611.

Date	Mintage	VG	F	VF	XF	Unc
1686 HB	—	550	950	1,500	2,750	—

KM# 320.3 THALER

Silver **Rev:** Large legends, small date **Note:** Dav. #6642.

Date	Mintage	VG	F	VF	XF	Unc
1690 HB	—	350	600	1,000	1,850	—

KM# 320.4 THALER

Silver **Note:** Dav. #6645.

Date	Mintage	VG	F	VF	XF	Unc
1691 HB	—	350	600	1,000	1,850	—

KM# 323 THALER

Silver **Obv:** Bust left **Rev:** Helmeted arms, date in legend **Note:** Dav. #6635.

Date	Mintage	VG	F	VF	XF	Unc
1685 RB Rare	—	—	—	—	—	—

KM# 324 THALER

Silver **Note:** Similar to KM#320 but date divided above. Dav. #6636.

Date	Mintage	VG	F	VF	XF	Unc
1685 HB	—	450	800	1,300	2,250	—

KM# 322 THALER

Silver **Obv:** Helmeted 12-fold arms **Rev:** Horse leaping left in laurel wreath, edge inscription **Note:** Mining Thaler. Dav. #6609.

Date	Mintage	VG	F	VF	XF	Unc
1685 HB	—	550	950	1,500	2,750	—
1686 HB Rare	—	—	—	—	—	—

KM# 325.1 THALER

Silver **Note:** Similar to KM#320 but Roman numeral in legend. Dav. #6637.

Date	Mintage	VG	F	VF	XF	Unc
MDCLXXXV (1685) HB	—	350	600	1,000	1,850	—
MDCLXXXVI (1686) HB	—	350	600	1,000	1,850	—

KM# 325.2 THALER

Silver **Obv. Legend:** ERN. AUG. D. G.-EP. OSN. D. BR. ET LUN. **Rev. Legend:** ...HO-NESTA. ANNO... **Note:** Dav. #6638.

Date	Mintage	VG	F	VF	XF	Unc
1687 HB	—	350	600	1,000	1,850	—

KM# 325.3 THALER

Silver **Obv. Legend:** ERNST: AUG:-D. G. EP. O. D. B. ET L. **Note:** Dav. #6641.

Date	Mintage	VG	F	VF	XF	Unc
1690 HB	—	350	600	1,000	1,850	—

KM# 325.4 THALER

Silver **Obv. Legend:** ERNST: AUGUST:-D. G. EP. OSN: D. BR: +LU: **Note:** Dav. #6643.

Date	Mintage	VG	F	VF	XF	Unc
1690 HB	—	350	600	1,000	1,850	—

KM# 325.5 THALER

Silver **Obv. Legend:** ERN: AUG: D. G.-EP: O. D. B. ET LU: **Note:** Dav. #6644.

Date	Mintage	VG	F	VF	XF	Unc
1691 HB	—	350	600	1,000	1,850	—

KM# 325.6 THALER

Silver **Obv. Legend:** ERN: AUG:-D. G... **Note:** Dav. #6646.

Date	Mintage	VG	F	VF	XF	Unc
1692 HB	—	350	600	1,000	1,850	—

KM# 325.7 THALER

Silver **Obv. Legend:** ERNEST: AUG:... **Note:** Dav. #6647.

Date	Mintage	F	VF	XF	Unc	BU
1692 HB	—	350	600	1,000	1,850	—

KM# 335.1 THALER
Silver **Obv:** Helmeted arms **Rev:** St. Andrew with cross **Note:** Dav. #6621.

Date	Mintage	VG	F	VF	XF	Unc
MDCLXXXVIII (1688) HB	—	200	400	700	1,250	—

KM# 335.2 THALER
Silver **Obv:** Without inner circle **Note:** Dav. #6623.

Date	Mintage	VG	F	VF	XF	Unc
MDCLXXXVIII (1688) HB	—	200	400	700	1,250	—

KM# 265.2 THALER
Silver **Obv. Legend:** ERNEST: AVG: D: G. EPISC OSN: DVX BR: + LU **Note:** Dav. #6594.

Date	Mintage	VG	F	VF	XF	Unc
1689 RB	—	100	200	350	600	—
1692 RB	—	100	200	350	600	—

KM# 351.1 THALER
Silver **Obv:** Helmeted plain shield **Note:** Dav. #6624.

Date	Mintage	VG	F	VF	XF	Unc
1690 HB	—	180	350	650	1,100	—

KM# 349 THALER
Silver **Obv:** Helmeted 12-fold arms divide date **Rev:** Horse leaping left in open field **Note:** Dav. #6613.

Date	Mintage	VG	F	VF	XF	Unc
1690 HB	—	350	600	1,000	1,850	—

KM# 350 THALER
Silver **Note:** With edge inscription. Mining Thaler. Dav. #6615.

Date	Mintage	VG	F	VF	XF	Unc
1690 HB	—	350	600	1,000	1,850	—
1692 HB	—	350	600	1,000	1,850	—

KM# 359 THALER
Silver **Note:** Similar to KM#351 but date in legend. Dav. #6625.

Date	Mintage	VG	F	VF	XF	Unc
1691 HB	—	180	350	650	1,100	—

KM# 360 THALER
Silver **Obv:** Bust right **Rev:** Roman arms and trophies **Rev. Legend:** EN. LABOR... **Note:** Dav. #6650.

Date	Mintage	VG	F	VF	XF	Unc
ND(1691-92)	—	700	1,200	2,000	3,500	—

KM# 358 THALER
Silver **Obv:** Helmeted 12-fold arms, date in legend **Rev:** Horse leaping left in open field **Note:** Dav. #6614.

Date	Mintage	VG	F	VF	XF	Unc
1691 HB	—	350	600	1,000	1,850	—

KM# 265.3 THALER
Silver **Obv. Legend:** ...AUG:...DUX BR: + LUN: **Note:** Dav. #6595.

Date	Mintage	VG	F	VF	XF	Unc
1691 RB	—	100	200	350	600	—

KM# 351.2 THALER
Silver **Obv:** Helmeted curved shield **Note:** Dav. #6626.

Date	Mintage	VG	F	VF	XF	Unc
1692 HB	—	180	350	650	1,100	—

KM# 370 THALER
Silver **Note:** Similar to KM#320, but date is on edge. Dav. #6648.

Date	Mintage	VG	F	VF	XF	Unc
1692 HB Rare	—	—	—	—	—	—

KM# 369 THALER
Silver **Note:** Similar to KM#265, but arms divide date on obverse. Dav. #6596.

Date	Mintage	VG	F	VF	XF	Unc
1692 RB	—	120	220	400	750	—
1693 RB	—	—	—	—	—	—

KM# 385 THALER
Silver **Obv:** KM#384 reverse **Rev:** KM#383 **Note:** Mule.

Date	Mintage	VG	F	VF	XF	Unc
1693 HB-H Rare	—	—	—	—	—	—

KM# 384 THALER
Silver **Note:** Varieties exist. Dav. #6649.

Date	Mintage	VG	F	VF	XF	Unc
1693 HB	—	260	450	800	1,300	—
1694 HB	—	260	450	800	1,300	—
1695 HB	—	260	450	800	1,300	—
1696 HB	—	260	450	800	1,300	—
1697 HB	—	260	450	800	1,300	—

KM# 383 THALER
Silver **Obv:** Crowned 15-fold arms **Rev:** Horse leaping left above Roman numeral date **Note:** Dav. #6616.

Date	Mintage	VG	F	VF	XF	Unc
1693 HB	—	450	800	1,300	2,250	—

KM# 382.1 THALER
Silver **Note:** Similar to KM#382.2, but different scrollwork below wildman. Dav. #6597.

Date	Mintage	VG	F	VF	XF	Unc
1693 RB	—	120	220	400	750	—

KM# 382.2 THALER
Silver **Note:** Dav. #6598.

Date	Mintage	VG	F	VF	XF	Unc
1694 RB	—	120	220	400	750	—
1695 RB	—	120	220	400	750	—
1696 RB	—	120	220	400	750	—

KM# 382.3 THALER
Silver **Rev:** Without scrollwork below wildman, R. B at right **Note:** Dav. #6599.

Date	Mintage	VG	F	VF	XF	Unc
1696 RB	—	120	220	400	750	—

KM# 382.4 THALER
Silver **Obv:** Very small date **Note:** Dav. #6600.

Date	Mintage	VG	F	VF	XF	Unc
1696 RB	—	120	220	400	750	—

KM# 382.5 THALER
Silver **Obv:** Smaller letters, different cartouche **Note:** Dav. #6601.

Date	Mintage	VG	F	VF	XF	Unc
1697 RB	—	120	220	400	750	—
1698 RB	—	120	220	400	750	—

KM# 394.1 THALER
Silver **Note:** Dav. #6627.

Date	Mintage	VG	F	VF	XF	Unc
1695 HB	—	130	250	450	800	—
1697 HB	—	130	250	450	800	—

KM# 394.2 THALER
Silver **Obv:** Crowned arms rounded at top **Note:** Dav. #6628.

Date	Mintage	VG	F	VF	XF	Unc
1697	—	180	350	650	1,100	—

KM# 405.1 THALER
Silver **Obv:** Crowned 15-fold arms **Obv. Legend:** ...EL: EP: O: **Rev:** Horse leaping left above Arabic date **Note:** Dav. #6617.

Date	Mintage	VG	F	VF	XF	Unc
1696 HB	—	450	800	1,300	2,250	—
1697 HB	—	450	800	1,300	2,250	—

KM# 405.2 THALER
Silver **Obv. Legend:** ...ELECT: EP: OSN: **Note:** Dav. #6618.

Date	Mintage	VG	F	VF	XF	Unc
1696 HB	—	450	800	1,300	2,250	—

KM# 406 THALER
Silver **Obv:** Arms divide date **Note:** Dav. #6620.

Date	Mintage	VG	F	VF	XF	Unc
1697 HB	—	450	800	1,300	2,250	—

KM# 411 THALER
Silver **Subject:** Death of Earnest August **Obv:** Bust right **Rev:** 12-line inscription with Roman numeral date **Note:** Dav. #6651.

Date	Mintage	VG	F	VF	XF	Unc
1698	—	300	550	900	1,500	—

KM# 75 1-1/4 THALER
35.8000 g., Silver **Rev:** Without value stamped in **Note:** Dav. #6531B.

Date	Mintage	VG	F	VF	XF	Unc
1661 HS	—	450	800	1,550	2,900	—

KM# 74.1 1-1/4 THALER
35.8000 g., Silver **Rev:** Stamped with value 1-1/4 **Note:** Dav. #6531. Illustration reduced.

Date	Mintage	VG	F	VF	XF	Unc
1661 HS	—	400	725	1,400	2,700	—
1662 HS	—	400	725	1,400	2,700	—

KM# 74.2 1-1/4 THALER
35.8000 g., Silver **Rev:** Stamped with value 5/4 **Note:** Dav. #6531A.

Date	Mintage	VG	F	VF	XF	Unc
1661 HS	—	450	800	1,550	2,900	—
1662 HS	—	450	800	1,550	2,900	—

KM# 83 1-1/4 THALER
35.8000 g., Silver **Note:** Dav. #6534.

Date	Mintage	VG	F	VF	XF	Unc
1664 HS	—	350	600	1,150	2,100	—

KM# 117 1-1/4 THALER
35.8000 g., Silver **Note:** Similar to 1 Thaler, KM#102, but 1-1/4 stamped in. Dav. #6568.

Date	Mintage	VG	F	VF	XF	Unc
1667	—	400	725	1,400	2,500	—
1668	—	400	725	1,400	2,500	—
1669	—	400	725	1,400	2,500	—
1671	—	400	725	1,400	2,500	—

KM# 175 1-1/4 THALER
35.8000 g., Silver **Note:** Similar to 1 Thaler, KM#149. Dav. #6572.

Date	Mintage	VG	F	VF	XF	Unc
1675	—	400	725	1,400	2,500	—

KM# 236 1-1/4 THALER
35.8000 g., Silver **Note:** Similar to 1 Thaler, KM#229. Dav. #6574.

Date	Mintage	VG	F	VF	XF	Unc
1679 RB	—	400	725	1,400	2,500	—

KM# 268 1-1/4 THALER
36.1000 g., Silver **Obv:** Helmeted arms **Rev:** Wildman, tree in right hand, date in legend, value in oval at bottom in die **Note:** Dav. #LS235.

Date	Mintage	VG	F	VF	XF	Unc
1680	—	1,550	2,700	5,000	8,800	—

KM# 11 1-1/2 THALER
Silver **Obv:** Half-length figure right, date **Rev:** Female figure of Concord between figures of four dukes **Note:** Dav. #LS137.

Date	Mintage	VG	F	VF	XF	Unc
1634 HS	—	3,200	5,400	8,500	—	—

KM# 84 1-1/2 THALER
Silver **Note:** Similar to 1-1/4 Thaler, KM#83, but 1-1/2 stamped in. Dav. #6533.

Date	Mintage	VG	F	VF	XF	Unc
1664 HS	—	325	600	1,150	2,100	—

KM# 131.1 1-1/2 THALER
42.0000 g., Silver **Obv:** Crowned script JF monogram surrounded by 14 small shields, date in legend, 1-1/2 stamped in **Rev:** Horse leaping left above mining scene **Note:** Dav. #LS202.

Date	Mintage	VG	F	VF	XF	Unc
1670 LW	—	625	1,100	1,800	2,800	—

KM# 131.2 1-1/2 THALER
42.0000 g., Silver **Note:** Dav. #LS204.

Date	Mintage	VG	F	VF	XF	Unc
1671 LW	—	625	1,100	1,800	2,800	—

KM# 131.3 1-1/2 THALER
42.0000 g., Silver **Note:** Dav. #LS206.

Date	Mintage	VG	F	VF	XF	Unc
1672 LW	—	625	1,100	1,800	2,800	—

KM# 131.4 1-1/2 THALER
42.0000 g., Silver **Note:** Dav. #LS208. Illustration reduced.

Date	Mintage	VG	F	VF	XF	Unc
1672 RB	—	625	1,100	1,800	2,800	—

KM# 176 1-1/2 THALER
Silver **Note:** Varieties exist. Similar to 1 Thaler, KM#227, but 1-1/2 stamped in. Dav. #6559.

Date	Mintage	VG	F	VF	XF	Unc
1675 HB	—	625	1,150	2,150	3,600	—

KM# 190 1-1/2 THALER
Silver **Subject:** 100th Anniversary - University of Helmstedt **Obv:** 16-line inscription **Rev:** Fountain between two palm trees **Note:** Dav. #6587.

Date	Mintage	VG	F	VF	XF	Unc
1676 Rare	—	—	—	—	—	—

KM# 237 1-1/2 THALER
42.8000 g., Silver, 64 mm. **Subject:** Death of Johann Friedrich **Note:** Dav. #LS223. Illustration reduced.

Date	Mintage	VG	F	VF	XF	Unc
1679 RB	—	625	1,250	2,350	4,100	—

KM# 281.1 1-1/2 THALER
42.0000 g., Silver, 63 mm. **Note:** Illustration reduced. Dav. #LS240.

Date	Mintage	VG	F	VF	XF	Unc
1681 RB	—	775	1,550	2,800	4,700	—

KM# 281.2 1-1/2 THALER
43.4000 g., Silver **Note:** Dav. #LS245. Illustration reduced.

Date	Mintage	VG	F	VF	XF	Unc
1688 RB	—	600	1,150	2,150	3,600	—

KM# 196 1-3/4 THALER
50.0000 g., Silver **Obv:** Crowned script JF monogram surrounded by 14 small shields, date in legend **Rev:** Horse leaping left above mining scene

Date	Mintage	VG	F	VF	XF	Unc
1677 HB	—	—	—	—	—	—

KM# 407 1-3/4 THALER
52.0000 g., Silver **Obv:** Bust right **Rev:** Crowned oval 15-fold arms, without value stated

Date	Mintage	VG	F	VF	XF	Unc
1697 HB	—	—	—	—	—	—

KM# 12 2 THALER
Silver **Obv:** Half-lentgh figure right, date **Rev:** Female figure of Concord between figures of four ducks **Note:** Dav. #LS136.

Date	Mintage	VG	F	VF	XF	Unc
1634 HS	—	5,500	7,800	11,000	—	—

KM# 42 2 THALER
Silver **Subject:** Death of Georg **Obv:** Half-length figure left **Rev:** 10-line inscription **Note:** Dav. #6509.

Date	Mintage	VG	F	VF	XF	Unc
MDCXLI (1641) HS Rare	—	—	—	—	—	—

KM# 76 2 THALER
Silver **Obv:** Bust right in circle of 14 small shields, date divided below **Rev:** Figures of Piety and Justice below tree, arm from heaven with wreath, 2 punched in **Note:** Dav. #6530.

Date	Mintage	VG	F	VF	XF	Unc
1661 HS	—	775	1,500	2,750	4,300	—

KM# 118 2 THALER
Silver **Note:** Similar to 1 Thaler, KM#102. Dav. #6567.

Date	Mintage	VG	F	VF	XF	Unc
1667	—	625	1,150	2,100	3,550	—
1669	—	625	1,150	2,100	3,550	—
1670	—	625	1,150	2,100	3,550	—

KM# 132.1 2 THALER
57.3000 g., Silver, 66 mm. **Note:** Illustration reduced. Dav. #LS201.

Date	Mintage	VG	F	VF	XF	Unc
1670 LW	—	700	1,300	2,350	3,900	—

KM# 132.2 2 THALER

57.3000 g., Silver **Note:** Dav. #LS203. Illustration reduced.

Date	Mintage	VG	F	VF	XF	Unc
1671 LW	—	700	1,300	2,350	3,900	—

KM# 132.3 2 THALER

57.3000 g., Silver **Note:** Dav. #LS205.

Date	Mintage	VG	F	VF	XF	Unc
1672 LW	—	700	1,300	2,350	3,900	—

KM# 132.4 2 THALER

57.3000 g., Silver **Note:** Dav. #LS207.

Date	Mintage	VG	F	VF	XF	Unc
1672 RB	—	700	1,300	2,350	3,900	—

KM# 132.5 2 THALER

57.3000 g., Silver **Note:** Dav. #LS213.

Date	Mintage	VG	F	VF	XF	Unc
1677 RB	—	700	1,300	2,350	3,900	—
1677 HB	—	700	1,300	2,350	3,900	—

KM# 192 2 THALER

Silver **Subject:** 100th Anniversary of the University of Helmstedt **Obv:** 16-line inscription **Rev:** Fountain between two palm trees **Note:** Dav. #6586.

Date	Mintage	VG	F	VF	XF	Unc
1676 Rare	—	—	—	—	—	—

KM# 191 2 THALER

Silver **Note:** Similar to 1 Thaler, KM#149. Dav. #6571.

Date	Mintage	VG	F	VF	XF	Unc
1676	—	625	1,150	2,100	3,550	—

KM# 209 2 THALER

Silver **Obv:** Bust right in circle **Rev:** Mining scene, Roman numeral date in legend **Note:** Mining Thaler. Dav. #6585.

Date	Mintage	VG	F	VF	XF	Unc
1678 HIF	—	1,000	2,000	3,550	5,900	—

KM# 239 2 THALER

50.6000 g., Silver, 64 mm. **Obv:** Crowned script JF monogram in wreath, 2 punched in at bottom **Rev:** 20-line inscription **Note:** Illustration reduced. Dav.#LS226.

Date	Mintage	VG	F	VF	XF	Unc
1679	—	6,200	10,000	14,000	—	—

KM# 238 2 THALER

56.6000 g., Silver, 64 mm. **Subject:** Death of Friedrich **Note:** Dav. #LS222. Illustration reduced.

Date	Mintage	VG	F	VF	XF	Unc
1679	—	650	1,300	2,450	4,350	—

KM# A269 2 THALER

52.3000 g., Silver, 65 mm. **Note:** Illustration reduced. Dav. #LS233.

Date	Mintage	VG	F	VF	XF	Unc
1680 RB	—	—	775	1,300	—	—

KM# 282.1 2 THALER

57.0000 g., Silver **Note:** Similar to 1-1/2 thalers, KM#281. Dav. #LS239.

Date	Mintage	VG	F	VF	XF	Unc
1681 RB	—	1,150	2,350	4,300	7,100	—

KM# 326 2 THALER

59.3000 g., Silver **Obv:** Helmeted arms, date at bottom, value punched in at left **Rev:** Lute player standing on snail, panoramic view of countryside behind **Note:** Dav.#LS243.

Date	Mintage	VG	F	VF	XF	Unc
1685 RB	—	1,550	2,750	4,300	6,200	—

KM# 282.2 2 THALER

59.3000 g., Silver **Note:** Dav. #LS244. Illustration reduced.

Date	Mintage	VG	F	VF	XF	Unc
1688 RB	—	875	1,750	3,100	5,100	—

KM# 197 2-1/4 THALER

67.5000 g., Silver **Obv:** Crowned script JF monogram surrounded by 14 small shields, date in legend **Rev:** Horse leaping left above mining scene **Note:** Dav. #LS210A.

Date	Mintage	VG	F	VF	XF	Unc
1677 HB	—	—	—	—	—	—

KM# 283 2-1/2 THALER

Silver **Obv:** Intertwined crowned script EA monogram in wreath surrounded by 15 small crowned arms, date at lower right in legend, 2-1/2 punched in at bottom **Rev:** Horse leaping left above mining scene **Note:** Dav. #LS239.

Date	Mintage	VG	F	VF	XF	Unc
1681 RB	—	—	—	—	—	—

KM# 119 3 THALER

Silver **Note:** Similar to 1 Thaler, KM#102. Dav. #6566.

Date	Mintage	VG	F	VF	XF	Unc
1667 Rare	—	—	—	—	—	—

KM# 133.1 3 THALER

86.2000 g., Silver, 73 mm. **Obv:** Crowned script JF monogram surrounded by 14 small shields, date in legend, 3 punched in **Note:** Illustration reduced. Dav. #LS200.

Date	Mintage	VG	F	VF	XF	Unc
1670 LW	—	925	1,750	3,100	5,500	—

KM# 133.2 3 THALER

86.2000 g., Silver **Note:** Dav. #LS212.

Date	Mintage	VG	F	VF	XF	Unc
1677 RB	—	925	1,750	3,100	5,500	—

KM# 240 3 THALER

83.7000 g., Silver, 78 mm. **Subject:** Death of Johann Friedrich **Obv:** 3 punched in **Rev:** 21-line inscription **Note:** Dav. #LS221. Illustration reduced.

Date	Mintage	VG	F	VF	XF	Unc
1679	—	1,550	3,100	5,900	10,000	—

KM# 270 3 THALER

Silver **Obv:** Bust right in circle **Rev:** Arms of Osnabruck in lower foreground, palm tree at left, sailing ship in background, rock at right, sun above, date below **Note:** Dav. #LS232. Illustration reduced.

Date	Mintage	VG	F	VF	XF	Unc
1680 RB Rare	—	—	—	—	—	—

KM# 271 3 THALER

86.6000 g., Silver **Obv:** Helmeted arms **Rev:** Wildman, tree in right hand, date in legend, 3 punched in over die-struck 1-1/4 **Note:** Dav. #LS234.

Date	Mintage	VG	F	VF	XF	Unc
1680	—	3,100	5,500	9,400	—	—

KM# 284 3 THALER

86.6000 g., Silver **Obv:** Intertwined crowned script EA monogram in wreath surrounded by 15 small crowned arms, date at lower right in legend, 3 punched in at bottom **Rev:** Horse leaping left above mining scene **Note:** Dav. #LS238. Illustration reduced.

Date	Mintage	VG	F	VF	XF	Unc
1681 RB	—	775	1,550	2,950	5,200	—

KM# 327 3 THALER

77.7000 g., Silver, 75 mm. **Obv:** Hlemeted arms, date divided at bottom, 3 punched in at left **Rev:** Lute player standing on snail, panoramic view of countryside behind **Note:** Illustration reduced. Dav. #LS242.

Date	Mintage	VG	F	VF	XF	Unc
1685 RB	—	2,100	3,550	5,500	7,800	—

KM# 328 3-1/2 THALER

103.5000 g., Silver, 72 mm. **Obv:** Helmeted arms, date divided at bottom **Rev:** Lute player standing on snail, panoramic view of countryside behing **Note:** Dav. #LS241A.

Date	Mintage	VG	F	VF	XF	Unc
1685 RB Rare	—	—	—	—	—	—

KM# 25 4 THALER

Silver **Obv:** Duke on horse left **Rev:** Helmeted 12-fold arms, supported by two wildmen, date in Roman numerals **Note:** Varieties exist. Dav. #LS242.

Date	Mintage	VG	F	VF	XF	Unc
1638 HS-IH Rare	—	—	—	—	—	—

KM# 70 4 THALER

Silver, 87 mm. **Note:** Illustration reduced. Dav. #LS195.

Date	Mintage	VG	F	VF	XF	Unc
1660 HS	—	900	1,750	3,250	5,200	—

KM# 77 4 THALER

Silver **Note:** Similar to KM#70, but bust right and 4 punched in. Dav. #LS196.

Date	Mintage	VG	F	VF	XF	Unc
1661 HS	—	—	—	—	—	—

KM# 134 4 THALER

115.2000 g., Silver **Obv:** Crowned script JF monogram surrounded by 14 small shields, date in legend, 4 punched in **Rev:** Horse leaping left above mining scene **Note:** Dav. #LS199. Illustration reduced.

Date	Mintage	VG	F	VF	XF	Unc
1670 LW	—	1,850	3,100	5,500	9,400	—

KM# 198 4 THALER

Silver **Obv:** 4 punched in or omitted **Note:** Dav. #LS211

Date	Mintage	VG	F	VF	XF	Unc
1677 RB	—	2,350	3,900	6,200	10,000	—

KM# 242 4 THALER

Silver **Obv:** Crowned script JF monogram in laurel wreath, 4 punched in **Rev:** Death cutting numbered branches off palm tree, four-line inscription **Note:** Dav. #LS218.

Date	Mintage	VG	F	VF	XF	Unc
1679	—	2,350	3,900	6,200	10,000	—

KM# 241 4 THALER

Silver **Subject:** Death of Johann Friedrich **Note:** Similar to 1 Thaler, KM#235, but 4 punched in. Dav. #LS220

Date	Mintage	VG	F	VF	XF	Unc
1679	—	1,100	2,100	3,900	6,200	—

KM# 272 4 THALER

Silver **Obv:** Bust right in circle, 4 punched in below bust **Rev:** Arms of Osnabruck in lower foreground, palm tree at left, sailing ship in background, rock at right, sun above, date below **Note:** Dav. #LS231.

Date	Mintage	VG	F	VF	XF	Unc
1680 RB	—	2,350	3,900	6,200	10,000	—

KM# 285 4 THALER

Silver **Obv:** Intertwined crowned script EA monogram in wreath, surrounded by 15 small crowned arms, date at lower right in legend, 4 punched at bottom **Rev:** Horse leaping left above mining scene **Note:** Dav. #LS237. Illustration reduced.

Date	Mintage	VG	F	VF	XF	Unc
1681 RB	—	2,350	3,900	6,200	10,000	—

KM# 329 4 THALER

101.6000 g., Silver, 75 mm. **Obv:** Helmeted arms, date divided at bottom, 4 punched in at left **Rev:** Lute player, standing on snail, panoramic view of countryside behind **Note:** Illustration reduced. Dav. #LS241.

Date	Mintage	VG	F	VF	XF	Unc
1685 RB	—	2,800	4,700	7,100	10,000	—

KM# 26 5 THALER

Silver, 87 mm. **Obv:** Duke on horse left **Rev:** Helmeted 12-fold arms, supported by two wildmen, date in Roman numerals **Note:** Varieties exist. Dav. #LS141.

Date	Mintage	VG	F	VF	XF	Unc
1638 HS-IH Rare	—	—	—	—	—	—

Note: Spink Taisei Zurich Milas sale 4-92 XF realized $15,075

KM# 71 5 THALER

143.5000 g., Silver, 82 mm. **Ruler:** Georg II Wilhelm **Note:** Sumilar to 4 Thalers, KM#70, but 5 punched in. Dav. #LS194.

Date	Mintage	VG	F	VF	XF	Unc
1660 HS Rare	—	—	—	—	—	—

Note: Spink Taisei Zurich Milas sale 4-92 XF realized $12,060

KM# 78 5 THALER

Silver **Note:** Sumilar to KM#71, but bust right. Dav. #LS196.

Date	Mintage	VG	F	VF	XF	Unc
1661 HS Rare	—	—	—	—	—	—

KM# 135 5 THALER

Silver **Obv:** Crowned script JF monogram surrounded by 14 small shields, date in margin, 5 punched in **Rev:** Horse leaping left above mining scene **Note:** Dav. #LS198.

Date	Mintage	VG	F	VF	XF	Unc
1670 LW Rare	—	—	—	—	—	—

KM# 199.1 5 THALER

Silver **Obv:** Without value shown **Note:** Dav. #LS209.

Date	Mintage	VG	F	VF	XF	Unc
1677 RB Rare	—	—	—	—	—	—

KM# 199.2 5 THALER

Silver **Note:** Dav. #LS210.

Date	Mintage	VG	F	VF	XF	Unc
1677 HB Rare	—	—	—	—	—	—

KM# 243 5 THALER

Silver **Subject:** Death of Johann Friedrich **Note:** Similar to 1 Thaler, KM#235, but 5 punched in. Dav. #LS219.

Date	Mintage	VG	F	VF	XF	Unc
1679 Rare	—	—	—	—	—	—

KM# 286 5 THALER

Silver **Obv:** Intertwined crowned script EA monogram in wreath, surrounded by 15 small crowned arms, date at lower right in legend, 5 punched in at bottom **Rev:** Horse leaping left above mining scene **Note:** Dav. #LS236.

Date	Mintage	VG	F	VF	XF	Unc
1681 RB Rare	—	—	—	—	—	—

KM# 27 6 THALER

Silver **Obv:** Duke on horse left **Rev:** Helmeted 12-fold arms, supported by two wildmen, date in Roman numerals **Note:** Dav. #LS140.

Date	Mintage	VG	F	VF	XF	Unc
1638 HS-IH Rare	—	—	—	—	—	—

KM# 72 6 THALER

172.5000 g., Silver, 85 mm. **Obv:** Bust 3/4 left in circle of 14 small shields, date divided below, 6 punched in **Rev:** Figures of Piety and Justice below tree, arm from heaven with wreath **Note:** Illustration reduced. Dav. #LS193.

Date	Mintage	VG	F	VF	XF	Unc
1660 HS Rare	—	—	—	—	—	—

Note: Spink Taisei Zurich Milas sale 4-92 VF-XF realized $12,060

KM# 200 6 THALER

Silver **Obv:** Crowned script JF monogram surrounded by 14 small shields, date in legend, 6 punched in **Rev:** Horse leaping left above mining scene **Note:** Cross-reference number Dav. #LS210B.

Date	Mintage	VG	F	VF	XF	Unc
1677 RB Rare	—	—	—	—	—	—

KM# 246 6 THALER

Silver **Rev:** Dates in Arabic numerals

Date	Mintage	VG	F	VF	XF	Unc
1679 Rare	—	—	—	—	—	—

KM# 244 6 THALER

Silver **Subject:** Death of Johann Friedrich **Obv:** Crowned script JF monogram in laurel wreath, 6 punched in **Rev:** Death, cutting numbered branches off palm tree, four-line inscription **Note:** Dav. #LS217.

Date	Mintage	VG	F	VF	XF	Unc
1679 Rare	—	—	—	—	—	—

KM# 245 6 THALER

Silver **Rev:** 18-line inscription with Roman numeral dates **Note:** Dav. #LS225.

Date	Mintage	VG	F	VF	XF	Unc
1679 Rare	—	—	—	—	—	—

KM# 28 8 THALER

Silver, 91 mm. **Note:** Illustration reduced. Dav. #LS139.

Date	Mintage	VG	F	VF	XF	Unc
1638 HS-IH Rare	—	—	—	—	—	—

KM# 248 8 THALER

Silver **Rev:** 18-line inscription

Date	Mintage	VG	F	VF	XF	Unc
MDCXXIX (1679) Rare	—	—	—	—	—	—

KM# 247 8 THALER

Silver **Subject:** Death of Johann Friedrich **Obv:** Crowned script JF monogram in laurel wreath, 8 punched in **Rev:** Death cutting numbered branches off palm tree, 4-line inscription **Note:** Dav. #LS216.

Date	Mintage	VG	F	VF	XF	Unc
1679 Rare	—	—	—	—	—	—

KM# 29 10 THALER

Silver **Obv:** Duke on horse left **Rev:** Helmeted 12-fold arms supported by two wildmen **Note:** Dav. #LS138.

Date	Mintage	VG	F	VF	XF	Unc
MDCXXXVIII (1638) HS-IH Rare	—	—	—	—	—	—

KM# 249 10 THALER

Silver **Subject:** Death of Johann Friedrich **Obv:** Crowned script JF monogram in laurel wreath, 10 punched in **Rev:** Death cutting numbered branches off palm tree, 4-line inscription **Note:** Dav. #LS215.

Date	Mintage	VG	F	VF	XF	Unc
1679 Rare	—	—	—	—	—	—

KM# 250 10 THALER

Silver **Rev:** 18-line inscription with Roman numeral dates **Note:** Dav. #LS224.

Date	Mintage	VG	F	VF	XF	Unc
1679 Rare	—	—	—	—	—	—

KM# 251 12 THALER
Silver **Obv:** Crowned script JF monogram in laurel wreath, 12 punched in **Rev:** Death cutting numbered branches off palm tree, 4-line inscription **Note:** Dav. #LS214. Illustration reduced.

Date	Mintage	VG	F	VF	XF	Unc
1679 Rare	—	—	—	—	—	—

TRADE COINAGE

KM# 15 GOLDGULDEN
3.5000 g., 0.9860 Gold 0.1109 oz. AGW **Obv:** Crowned arms in inner circle **Rev:** Orb in inner circle

Date	Mintage	VG	F	VF	XF	Unc
1635	—	800	1,800	3,500	5,500	—

KM# 395 1/4 DUCAT
0.8750 g., 0.9860 Gold 0.0277 oz. AGW **Obv:** Bust right, value 1/4 below **Rev:** Horse leaping left

Date	Mintage	VG	F	VF	XF	Unc
1695	—	125	190	500	1,000	—

KM# 396 1/4 DUCAT
0.8750 g., 0.9860 Gold 0.0277 oz. AGW **Obv:** Ernst August

Date	Mintage	VG	F	VF	XF	Unc
1695	—	—	—	—	—	—

KM# 397 1/2 DUCAT
1.7500 g., 0.9860 Gold 0.0555 oz. AGW **Obv:** Bust right, value 1/2 below **Rev:** Horse leaping left

Date	Mintage	VG	F	VF	XF	Unc
1695	—	150	300	650	1,300	—

KM# 398 1/2 DUCAT
1.7500 g., 0.9860 Gold 0.0555 oz. AGW **Obv:** Bust of Ernst August right

Date	Mintage	VG	F	VF	XF	Unc
1695	—	—	—	—	—	—

KM# 16 DUCAT
3.5000 g., 0.9860 Gold 0.1109 oz. AGW **Obv:** Armored bust of Georg left holding scepter in inner circle **Rev:** Crowned arms in inner circle

Date	Mintage	VG	F	VF	XF	Unc
1635 HS	—	500	1,150	2,100	3,600	—
1636 HS	—	500	1,150	2,100	3,600	—
1637 HS	—	500	1,150	2,100	3,600	—
1638 HS	—	500	1,150	2,100	3,600	—
ND HS	—	500	1,150	2,100	3,600	—

KM# 49 DUCAT
3.5000 g., 0.9860 Gold 0.1109 oz. AGW **Obv:** Bust of Christian Ludwig right in inner circle

Date	Mintage	VG	F	VF	XF	Unc
1646 HS	—	650	1,500	2,900	4,550	—

KM# 85 DUCAT
3.5000 g., 0.9860 Gold 0.1109 oz. AGW **Obv:** Bust right **Rev:** Crowned 12-fold arms, date in legend

Date	Mintage	VG	F	VF	XF	Unc
1664 HS	—	575	1,300	2,300	3,900	—

KM# 125 DUCAT
3.5000 g., 0.9860 Gold 0.1109 oz. AGW **Rev:** Palm on rock in sea

Date	Mintage	VG	F	VF	XF	Unc
1668	—	475	1,050	1,850	3,100	—

KM# 126 DUCAT
3.5000 g., 0.9860 Gold 0.1109 oz. AGW **Obv:** Bust left **Rev:** Crowned 12-fold arms

Date	Mintage	VG	F	VF	XF	Unc
1669 HB	—	475	1,050	1,850	3,100	—
ND LW	—	475	1,050	1,850	3,100	—

KM# 151 DUCAT
3.5000 g., 0.9860 Gold 0.1109 oz. AGW **Rev:** Palm tree on rockyisland, ships at sides in inner circle, Roman numeral date

Date	Mintage	VG	F	VF	XF	Unc
1673	—	375	925	1,650	2,850	—
1679 HB	—	375	925	1,650	2,850	—

KM# 177 DUCAT
3.5000 g., 0.9860 Gold 0.1109 oz. AGW **Obv:** Bust of Johann Friedrich right

Date	Mintage	VG	F	VF	XF	Unc
1675	—	375	925	1,650	2,850	—

KM# 287 DUCAT
3.5000 g., 0.9860 Gold 0.1109 oz. AGW **Obv:** Bust of Ernst August right **Rev:** Crowned arms divide date

Date	Mintage	VG	F	VF	XF	Unc
1681 RB	—	650	1,300	2,900	4,250	—
1685	—	650	1,300	2,900	4,250	—
1694 HB	—	650	1,300	2,900	4,250	—
1698 HB	—	650	1,300	2,900	4,250	—

KM# 389 DUCAT
3.5000 g., 0.9860 Gold 0.1109 oz. AGW **Obv:** Capped arms divides date

Date	Mintage	VG	F	VF	XF	Unc
1694	—	425	900	1,650	3,300	—
1698	—	425	900	1,650	3,300	—

KM# 399 DUCAT
3.5000 g., 0.9860 Gold 0.1109 oz. AGW **Obv:** Bust right **Rev:** Horse leaping left

Date	Mintage	VG	F	VF	XF	Unc
1695	—	775	1,500	3,050	5,500	—

KM# 400 DUCAT
3.5000 g., 0.9860 Gold 0.1109 oz. AGW **Rev:** Rearing horse, date in exergue

Date	Mintage	VG	F	VF	XF	Unc
1695	—	550	1,200	2,200	4,400	—
1698	—	550	1,200	2,200	4,400	—

KM# 412 DUCAT
3.5000 g., 0.9860 Gold 0.1109 oz. AGW **Subject:** Death of the Duke

Date	Mintage	VG	F	VF	XF	Unc
1698	—	375	925	1,850	3,100	—

KM# 152 2 DUCAT
7.0000 g., 0.9860 Gold 0.2219 oz. AGW **Obv:** Johann Friedrich

Date	Mintage	VG	F	VF	XF	Unc
1673	—	2,300	4,600	8,900	16,500	—

KM# 390 2 DUCAT
7.0000 g., 0.9860 Gold 0.2219 oz. AGW **Obv:** Bust right **Rev:** Crowned 15-fold arms, date below

Date	Mintage	VG	F	VF	XF	Unc
1694 HB	—	1,500	3,350	7,000	11,500	—

KM# 391 2 DUCAT
7.0000 g., 0.9860 Gold 0.2219 oz. AGW **Obv:** Bust of Ernst August right **Rev:** Capped arms divides date

Date	Mintage	VG	F	VF	XF	Unc
1694	—	1,500	3,350	7,000	11,500	—
1695	—	1,500	3,350	7,000	11,500	—

KM# 401 2 DUCAT
7.0000 g., 0.9860 Gold 0.2219 oz. AGW **Rev:** Horse leaping left

Date	Mintage	VG	F	VF	XF	Unc
1695	—	1,150	2,550	5,800	9,800	—

KM# 402 2 DUCAT
7.0000 g., 0.9860 Gold 0.2219 oz. AGW **Rev:** Rearing horse, date in exergue

Date	Mintage	VG	F	VF	XF	Unc
1695	—	1,500	2,750	7,000	11,500	—

KM# 153 4 DUCAT
14.0000 g., 0.9860 Gold 0.4438 oz. AGW **Obv:** Bust of Johann Friedrich right **Rev:** Palm tree on rocky island, ships at sides in inner circle

Date	Mintage	VG	F	VF	XF	Unc
1673 Rare	—	—	—	—	—	—

KM# 90 10 DUCAT (Portugalöser)
35.0000 g., 0.9860 Gold 1.1095 oz. AGW **Obv:** Bust left **Rev:** Helmeted 12-fold arms, date in legend **Note:** Struck with 1 Thaler dies, KM#88.

Date	Mintage	VG	F	VF	XF	Unc
1665 Rare	—	—	—	—	—	—

KM# 129 10 DUCAT (Portugalöser)
33.6900 g., 0.9860 Gold 1.0679 oz. AGW

Date	Mintage	VG	F	VF	XF	Unc
1670 Unique	—	—	—	—	—	—

Note: Bowers and Merena Guia sale 3-88, XF realized $16,500

KM# 288 10 DUCAT (Portugalöser)
35.0000 g., 0.9860 Gold 1.1095 oz. AGW **Obv:** Bust right in circle **Rev:** Crowned arms divide date **Note:** Similar to 1 thaler, KM#293 but arms divide date.

Date	Mintage	VG	F	VF	XF	Unc
1681 HB Rare	—	—	—	—	—	—

KM# A333 10 DUCAT (Portugalöser)
35.0000 g., 0.9860 Gold 1.1095 oz. AGW **Obv:** Bust of Ernst August **Rev:** Arms

Date	Mintage	VG	F	VF	XF	Unc
1685 Rare	—	—	—	—	—	—

KM# 403 10 DUCAT (Portugalöser)
35.0000 g., 0.9860 Gold 1.1095 oz. AGW **Note:** Similar to 1 Thaler, KM#394.

Date	Mintage	VG	F	VF	XF	Unc
1695 HB Rare	—	—	—	—	—	—

KM# 273 20 DUCAT (Doppelportugalöser)
70.0000 g., 0.9860 Gold 2.2190 oz. AGW **Obv:** Bust right **Rev:** Arms of Osnabruck (wheel) in front of seascape

Date	Mintage	VG	F	VF	XF	Unc
1680 RB Rare	—	—	—	—	—	—

BRUNSWICK-LUNEBURG-CALENBERG-HANNOVER

Located in north-central Germany. The first duke began his rule in 1235. The first coinage appeared c. 1175. There was considerable shuffling of territory until 1692 when Ernst August became the elector of Hannover. George Ludwig became George I of England in 1714. There was separate coinage for Luneburg until during the reign of George III. The name was changed to Hannover in 1814.

RULERS
Georg Ludwig (George I of England), 1698-1727

BRUNSWICK MINTS AND MINT OFFICIALS' INITIALS

Celle Mint

Initial	Date	Name
III	1687-1705	Jobst Jakob Janisch

Clausthal Mint

Initial	Date	Name
HB	1675-1711	Heinrich Bonhorst

Zellerfeld Mint

Initial	Date	Name
RB	1676-1711	Rudolf Bornemann
***	1698-1715	Used instead of initials during this period

REFERENCE
W = Gerhard Welter, ***Die Münzen der Welfen seit Heinrich dem Löwen***, 3 v., Braunschweig: Klinkhardt & Biermann, 1971-78.

ELECTORATE

REGULAR COINAGE

KM# 5 PFENNING
Silver **Ruler:** George Ludwig **Obv:** Horse leaping left, date below **Note:** Uniface, hohl-type.

Date	Mintage	VG	F	VF	XF	Unc
1698	—	5.00	9.00	15.00	33.00	—
1700	—	5.00	9.00	15.00	33.00	—

KM# 24 PFENNING

Copper **Ruler:** George Ludwig **Obv:** Crowned GLC monogram **Rev:** Value, date

Date	Mintage	VG	F	VF	XF	Unc
1699	—	10.00	17.00	35.00	75.00	—

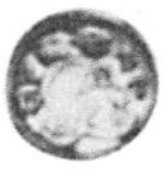

KM# 30 PFENNING

Silver **Ruler:** George Ludwig **Obv:** Crowned monogram, date **Note:** Uniface. hohl-type.

Date	Mintage	VG	F	VF	XF	Unc
1700 RB	—	7.00	15.00	35.00	70.00	—

KM# 25 4 PFENNING

Billon **Ruler:** George Ludwig **Obv:** Horse leaping left **Rev:** Value, date **Note:** Varieties exist.

Date	Mintage	VG	F	VF	XF	Unc
1699	—	12.00	25.00	50.00	100	—
1700 HB	—	12.00	25.00	50.00	100	—

KM# 26.1 MARIENGROSCHEN

Silver, 17 mm. **Ruler:** George Ludwig **Obv:** 4-line inscription with date, mintmaster's initials below **Obv. Legend:** C. F. BR. LUN. LAND MUNTZ. **Obv. Inscription:** I / MARIEN / GROS: / (date) **Rev:** Full-length standing figure of Madonna holding Child in frame with rays around **Mint:** Clausthal

Date	Mintage	VG	F	VF	XF	Unc
1699 HB	—	8.00	15.00	35.00	70.00	—
1700 HB	—	8.00	15.00	35.00	70.00	—

KM# 6 2 MARIENGROSCHEN

Silver **Ruler:** George Ludwig **Obv:** Value in 3 lines, date in legend **Rev:** Wildman, tree in right hand

Date	Mintage	VG	F	VF	XF	Unc
1698 ***	—	8.00	16.00	33.00	75.00	—
1700 ***	—	8.00	16.00	33.00	75.00	—

KM# 7 2 MARIENGROSCHEN

Silver **Ruler:** George Ludwig **Obv:** Wildman, tree in right hand **Rev:** Value, date

Date	Mintage	VG	F	VF	XF	Unc
1698 ***	—	12.00	25.00	50.00	100	—
1699 ***	—	12.00	25.00	50.00	100	—

KM# 31 2 MARIENGROSCHEN

Silver **Ruler:** George Ludwig **Obv:** Value and date within inner circle **Rev:** Horse leaping left within inner circle

Date	Mintage	VG	F	VF	XF	Unc
1700	—	8.00	17.00	35.00	75.00	—

KM# 8 4 MARIENGROSCHEN

Silver **Obv:** Crowned GLC monogram **Rev:** Value, date

Date	Mintage	VG	F	VF	XF	Unc
1698 HB	—	15.00	35.00	70.00	145	—

KM# 9 4 MARIENGROSCHEN

Silver **Obv:** Wildman, tree in right hand **Rev:** Value, date

Date	Mintage	VG	F	VF	XF	Unc
1698 ***	—	16.00	35.00	70.00	145	—

KM# 33 4 MARIENGROSCHEN

2.0600 g., Silver Clausthal Mint - 1705, Zellerfeld Mint 1712-14., 21.17 mm. **Ruler:** George Ludwig **Obv:** Value in 4 lines **Obv. Legend:** GEORG: LVD: D•G•D•B•&•L•S•R•I•A•T•&•E* **Rev:** Horse leaping left, date below **Rev. Legend:** IN RECTO DECUS **Edge:** Plain **Note:** Varieties exist.

Date	Mintage	VG	F	VF	XF	Unc
1700	—	10.00	20.00	40.00	85.00	—

KM# 32 4 MARIENGROSCHEN

Silver **Ruler:** George Ludwig **Obv:** Value in 3 lines, date in legend **Rev:** Wildman, tree in right hand

Date	Mintage	VG	F	VF	XF	Unc
1700 ***	—	13.00	27.00	55.00	110	—

KM# 10 6 MARIENGROSCHEN

Silver **Obv:** Wildman, tree in right hand **Rev:** Value, date

Date	Mintage	VG	F	VF	XF	Unc
1698 ***	—	16.00	35.00	75.00	150	—
1699 ***	—	16.00	35.00	75.00	150	—

KM# 11 6 MARIENGROSCHEN

Silver **Ruler:** George Ludwig **Obv:** Value, date **Rev:** Wildman, tree in right hand

Date	Mintage	VG	F	VF	XF	Unc
1699 ***	—	16.00	35.00	75.00	150	—
1700 ***	—	16.00	35.00	75.00	150	—

KM# 12 6 MARIENGROSCHEN (1/6 Thaler)

Silver **Ruler:** George Ludwig **Obv:** Value VI..., date in circle **Rev:** Horse leaping left, value Y6 below in circle

Date	Mintage	VG	F	VF	XF	Unc
1698 HB	—	20.00	40.00	80.00	160	—
1700 HB	—	20.00	40.00	80.00	160	—

KM# 13 12 MARIENGROSCHEN

Silver **Obv:** Similar to 24 Mariengroschen, KM#14 but 12 to right **Rev:** XII... in three lines, date in legend

Date	Mintage	VG	F	VF	XF	Unc
1698 ***	—	30.00	65.00	130	265	—

KM# 34 12 MARIENGROSCHEN

Silver **Ruler:** George Ludwig **Obv:** Value XII... in 3 lines, date in legend **Obv. Legend:** * GEORG: LUD: D: G: D: BR: & L: S: R: I: EL: **Rev:** Wildman, tree in right hand, 12 to right **Rev. Legend:** IN RECTO DECUS.

Date	Mintage	VG	F	VF	XF	Unc
1700 ***	—	27.00	55.00	110	220	—

KM# 15 24 MARIENGROSCHEN (Gulden)

Silver **Ruler:** George Ludwig **Obv:** Value, date in legend **Obv. Legend:** GEORG: LUD: D: G: D: BR: & L: S: R: I: ELECT: **Rev:** Wildman with tree in right hand, 24 at right **Rev. Legend:** IN RECTO DECUS

Date	Mintage	VG	F	VF	XF	Unc
1698 ***	—	50.00	100	210	425	—
1699 ***	—	50.00	100	210	425	—
1700 ***	—	50.00	100	210	425	—

KM# 14 24 MARIENGROSCHEN (Gulden)

Silver

Date	Mintage	VG	F	VF	XF	Unc
1698 ***	—	35.00	75.00	150	300	—
1699 ***	—	35.00	75.00	150	300	—

KM# 27 1/3 THALER

Silver

Date	Mintage	VG	F	VF	XF	Unc
1699 HB	—	65.00	100	210	425	—
1700 HB	—	65.00	100	210	425	—

KM# A17 2/3 THALER (Gulden)

Silver **Ruler:** Ernst August **Obv:** Bust right **Rev:** Leaping horse left, value divides date below **Note:** Prev. Bruns.-Lune-Calenberg 2/3 Thaler, KM#381.

Date	Mintage	VG	F	VF	XF	Unc
1693	—	60.00	125	250	500	—
1693 HB	—	60.00	125	250	500	—
1694 HB	—	60.00	125	250	500	—
1695 HB	—	60.00	125	250	500	—
1696 HB	—	60.00	125	250	500	—
1697 HB	—	60.00	125	250	500	—

KM# 17 2/3 THALER (Gulden)

Silver **Ruler:** George Ludwig **Obv:** Crowned complex arms divide date **Rev:** Horse leaping left, value below

Date	Mintage	VG	F	VF	XF	Unc
1698 HB	—	40.00	80.00	150	300	—
1699 HB	—	40.00	80.00	150	300	—
1700 HB	—	40.00	80.00	150	300	—

KM# 16 2/3 THALER (Gulden)

Silver **Obv:** Crowned arms divide date **Rev:** Column, 2/3 on base, IN RECTO DECUS on band behind

Date	Mintage	VG	F	VF	XF	Unc
1698 HB	—	110	225	450	900	—

KM# 18 THALER
Silver **Obv:** Crowned arms divide date to lower left and right **Rev:** Wildman, tree in right hand **Note:** Dav. #6652.

Date	Mintage	F	VF	XF	Unc	BU
1698 RB	—	150	265	500	—	—
1699 RB	—	150	265	500	—	—

KM# 19 THALER
Silver **Ruler:** George Ludwig **Note:** Dav. #6654 and #2057.

Date	Mintage	F	VF	XF	Unc	BU
1698 HB	—	125	225	375	800	—
1699 HB	—	125	225	375	800	—
1700 HB	—	125	225	375	800	—

KM# 20 THALER
Silver **Ruler:** George Ludwig **Note:** Dav. #6655 and #2061.

Date	Mintage	F	VF	XF	Unc	BU
1698 HB	—	125	225	400	850	—
1699 HB	—	125	225	400	850	—
1700 HB	—	125	225	400	850	—

KM# 35 THALER
Silver **Ruler:** George Ludwig **Obv:** Crowned complex arms within ornate frame **Obv. Legend:** GEORG: LUD: D: G: D: BR: & L: S: R: I: EL **Rev:** Wildman with tree in right hand, RB at right **Rev. Legend:** IN RECTO DECUS **Note:** Dav. #6653 and #2065.

Date	Mintage	F	VF	XF	Unc	BU
1700 RB	—	120	250	450	900	—

TRADE COINAGE

KM# 21 DUCAT
3.5000 g., 0.9860 Gold 0.1109 oz. AGW **Ruler:** George Ludwig **Obv:** Crowned arms **Rev:** Horse leaping left

Date	Mintage	VG	F	VF	XF	Unc
1698	—	650	1,150	2,200	4,150	—
1700	—	650	1,150	2,200	4,150	—

KM# 22 2 DUCAT
7.0000 g., 0.9860 Gold 0.2219 oz. AGW **Obv:** Laureate bust of George I left **Rev:** Capped arms, date in legend

Date	Mintage	VG	F	VF	XF	Unc
1698 HB	—	1,150	2,900	6,400	12,000	—

BRUNSWICK-LUNEBURG-CELLE

When Heinrich (VII) der Mittlere abdicated in 1520, his three sons soon divided the duchy, establishing the lines of Brunswick-Lüneburg-Celle, Brunswick-Gifhorn and Brunswick-Harburg. Celle was further divided in 1559 into Brunswick-Lüneburg-Celle and Brunswick-Dannenberg, but had been effectively ruled as two separate territories from 1546. The seat of the duchy was the town of Celle (Zelle), located about 20 miles (33 kilometers) northeast of Hannover. When the line fell extinct in 1705, Celle passed to Brunswick-Lüneburg-Calenberg-Hannover.

RULERS
Ernst V, 1592-1611
Christian, 1611-1633
August I the Elder, 1633-1636
Friedrich V, 1636-1648
Christian Ludwig, 1648-1665
Georg II Wilhelm, 1665-1705

MINT MARKS
N - Nienburg Mint
- Zellerfeld Mint, 1698-1715

MINT OFFICIALS' INITIALS

Initial	Date	Name
CD	1622	Cord Delbruge die-cutter in Celle
GM/HGM	1619-21	Hans Georg Meinhard
(h)	1622	Henning Hans in Winsen
HB	1675-1711	Heinrich Bonhorst in Clausthal
HHO	1625	Henning Oppermann in Catlenburg
HL	1617	Heinrich Leohr in Clausthal and Hitzacker
HL	1622-25	Henning Loehr in Goslar, Osterode and Zellerfeld
HP	1623-29	Heinrich Pechstein in andreasberg
HR	Ca.1647	Unknown die-cutter
HS (usually w/ingot hook)	1622-40	Henning Schreiber in Clausthal
	1621-24	In Lauterberg
	1619-21	In Osterode
HS(w/ or w/o crossed keys)	1626-72	Henning Schluter in Goslar and Zellerfeld
HVE	1619	Hans von Ecke in Andreasberg
	1621-23	In Catlenburg
	1622-25	In Osterode
Iii/III/JJJ	1687-1705	Jobst Jakob Janisch in Celle
IR	-	Unknown
(k) or variant	1617-21	Georg Krukenberg in Clausthal
LW	1640-75	Lippold Weber (Wefer) in Clausthal
+M+	Ca.1635	Unknown
NZ	Ca.1635	Unknown
RD	1673-86	Rudolf Dornstrauch in Celle
VF	1623-24	Urban Feigenhauer in Catlenburg
(w)	1622	Hans Heine in Winsen

REFERENCE
W = Gerhard Welter, ***Die Münzen der Welfen seit Heinrich dem Löwen***, 3 v., Braunschweig: Klinkhardt & Biermann, 1971-78.

DUCHY

REGULAR COINAGE

KM# 21 PFENNIG
Copper **Ruler:** Christian **Rev:** GUTER added to value **Note:** Guter Pfennig.

Date	Mintage	VG	F	VF	XF	Unc
1620	—	22.00	45.00	90.00	180	—
1621	—	22.00	45.00	90.00	180	—

KM# 20 PFENNIG
Copper **Ruler:** Christian **Obv:** Lion rampant left **Rev:** Value, date in 4 lines

Date	Mintage	VG	F	VF	XF	Unc
1620	—	20.00	45.00	90.00	180	—

KM# 22 PFENNIG
Copper **Rev:** Value in 2 lines

Date	Mintage	VG	F	VF	XF	Unc
ND(1620/1)	—	30.00	60.00	125	250	—

KM# 58 PFENNIG
Silver **Ruler:** Christian **Obv:** St. Andrew with cross, date **Note:** Uniface.

Date	Mintage	VG	F	VF	XF	Unc
1623 HP	—	—	—	—	—	—

KM# 59 PFENNIG
Silver **Ruler:** Christian **Obv:** Crowned initials C, date. **Note:** Uniface. Hohlpfennig type.

Date	Mintage	VG	F	VF	XF	Unc
1623 VF	—	33.00	55.00	100	210	—
1624 VF	—	33.00	55.00	100	210	—
1624 HS	—	33.00	55.00	100	210	—
1625 VF	—	33.00	55.00	100	210	—
1633 HSA	—	33.00	55.00	100	210	—

KM# 148 PFENNIG
Silver **Ruler:** Friedrich V **Obv:** Crowned F monogram, date. **Note:** Uniface. Hohlpfennig type.

Date	Mintage	VG	F	VF	XF	Unc
1638 HS	—	33.00	55.00	100	210	—
1642 LW	—	33.00	55.00	100	210	—
1647 LW	—	33.00	55.00	100	210	—
1648 LW	—	33.00	55.00	100	210	—

KM# 214 PFENNIG
Silver **Ruler:** Christian Ludwig **Obv:** Crowned CL monogram, date **Note:** Uniface. Hohlpfennig type.

Date	Mintage	VG	F	VF	XF	Unc
1650 LW	—	27.00	45.00	90.00	180	—
1651 LW	—	27.00	45.00	90.00	180	—
1655 LW	—	27.00	45.00	90.00	180	—
1656 LW	—	27.00	45.00	90.00	180	—
1657 LW	—	27.00	45.00	90.00	180	—
1657 SW Error	—	27.00	45.00	90.00	180	—
1659 LW	—	27.00	45.00	90.00	180	—
1660 LW	—	27.00	45.00	90.00	180	—
1663 HST	—	27.00	45.00	90.00	180	—
1663 LW	—	27.00	45.00	90.00	180	—
1664 LW	—	27.00	45.00	90.00	180	—
1665 LW	—	27.00	45.00	90.00	180	—
1665 HS	—	27.00	45.00	90.00	180	—

KM# 318 PFENNIG
Copper **Ruler:** Georg II Wilhelm **Obv:** Horse rearing left **Rev:** Value I PFEN

Date	Mintage	VG	F	VF	XF	Unc
1686	—	10.00	20.00	45.00	85.00	—
1687/6	—	11.00	27.00	55.00	110	—
1687	—	10.00	25.00	50.00	105	—

KM# 319 PFENNIG
Copper **Ruler:** Georg II Wilhelm **Obv:** Horse left, date below **Rev:** Value **Rev. Inscription:** 1-1/2 / PFEN

Date	Mintage	VG	F	VF	XF	Unc
1687	—	10.00	20.00	40.00	80.00	—

KM# 320 PFENNIG

Copper

Date	Mintage	VG	F	VF	XF	Unc
1687	—	10.00	20.00	40.00	80.00	—
1688	—	10.00	20.00	40.00	80.00	—
1689	—	10.00	20.00	40.00	80.00	—

KM# 336 PFENNIG

Copper

Date	Mintage	VG	F	VF	XF	Unc
1691 GW	—	8.00	16.00	32.00	65.00	—
1694	—	8.00	16.00	32.00	65.00	—
1695	—	8.00	16.00	32.00	65.00	—
1696	—	8.00	16.00	32.00	65.00	—
1697	—	8.00	16.00	32.00	65.00	—
1698	—	8.00	16.00	32.00	65.00	—
1699	—	8.00	16.00	32.00	65.00	—

KM# 351 PFENNIG

Silver **Ruler:** Georg II Wilhelm **Obv:** Horse leaping left, date below **Note:** Uniface.

Date	Mintage	VG	F	VF	XF	Unc
1694	—	—	—	—	—	—

KM# 353 PFENNIG

Copper **Ruler:** Georg II Wilhelm **Obv:** Crowned 'GW' monogram **Rev:** Value

Date	Mintage	VG	F	VF	XF	Unc
1698	—	8.00	16.00	32.00	65.00	—

KM# 321 1-1/2 PFENNIG

Copper **Ruler:** Georg II Wilhelm **Obv:** Horse leaping left, 'GW' monogram above right, date below **Rev:** Value

Date	Mintage	VG	F	VF	XF	Unc
1687	—	8.00	16.00	32.00	65.00	—
1688	—	8.00	16.00	32.00	65.00	—
1689	—	8.00	16.00	32.00	65.00	—

KM# 337 1-1/2 PFENNIG

Copper **Ruler:** Georg II Wilhelm **Obv:** Crowned 'GW' monogram **Rev:** Value, date in 5 lines

Date	Mintage	VG	F	VF	XF	Unc
1691	—	7.00	15.00	30.00	60.00	—
1699	—	7.00	15.00	30.00	60.00	—
ND	—	7.00	15.00	30.00	60.00	—

KM# 354 1-1/2 PFENNIG

Copper **Ruler:** Georg II Wilhelm **Obv:** Crowned 'GW' monogram **Rev:** Value, date in 5 lines

Date	Mintage	VG	F	VF	XF	Unc
1698	—	8.00	16.00	32.00	65.00	—
1699	—	8.00	16.00	32.00	65.00	—
ND	—	8.00	16.00	32.00	65.00	—

KM# 23 2 GUTE PFENNIG

Copper **Obv:** Lion rampant left **Rev:** Value with GUTE and date in 2 or 3 lines

Date	Mintage	VG	F	VF	XF	Unc
1620	—	17.00	35.00	75.00	150	—
1620 GM	—	17.00	35.00	75.00	150	—
1621 GM	—	17.00	35.00	75.00	150	—
ND CD	—	17.00	35.00	75.00	150	—

KM# 186 2 GUTE PFENNIG

Silver **Obv:** Crowned F monogram **Rev:** Value, date in 3 lines

Date	Mintage	VG	F	VF	XF	Unc
1648 LW	—	50.00	100	210	425	—

KM# 215 2 GUTE PFENNIG

Silver **Obv:** Crowned CL monogram **Rev:** Value in 3 lines

Date	Mintage	VG	F	VF	XF	Unc
1650 LW	—	275	450	900	—	—
1653 LW	—	275	450	900	—	—
1654 LW	—	275	450	900	—	—
1658 LW	—	250	450	900	—	—

KM# 25.1 3 PFENNIG

Copper **Obv:** Lion rampant left **Rev:** Value GUTER III **Note:** Gute 3 Pfennig.

Date	Mintage	VG	F	VF	XF	Unc
1620 GM	—	20.00	40.00	80.00	165	—
1621 GM	—	20.00	40.00	80.00	165	—
1622 (h)	—	20.00	40.00	80.00	165	—
1622 GM	—	—	—	—	—	—

KM# 30 3 PFENNIG

Copper **Ruler:** Christian **Obv:** Lion rampant left **Rev:** Without 'GUTER' in value **Note:** Varieties exist.

Date	Mintage	VG	F	VF	XF	Unc
1621	—	15.00	30.00	60.00	125	—

KM# 31 3 PFENNIG

Copper **Obv:** Lion rampant left **Rev:** Imperial orb with 3

Date	Mintage	VG	F	VF	XF	Unc
1621	—	18.00	37.00	75.00	150	—
1622	—	18.00	37.00	75.00	150	—

KM# 51 3 PFENNIG

Copper **Obv:** Titles in 4 lines, crown above **Rev:** Imperial orb with 3

Date	Mintage	VG	F	VF	XF	Unc
1622	—	18.00	37.00	75.00	150	—

KM# 52 3 PFENNIG

Copper **Rev:** Orb in rhombus

Date	Mintage	VG	F	VF	XF	Unc
1622	—	18.00	37.00	75.00	150	—

KM# 53 3 PFENNIG

Copper **Obv:** Lion rampant left in shield **Rev:** Value with GUTE in 2 lines

Date	Mintage	VG	F	VF	XF	Unc
1622	—	18.00	37.00	75.00	150	—

KM# 25.2 3 PFENNIG

Copper **Rev:** Value III GP

Date	Mintage	VG	F	VF	XF	Unc
ND CD	—	18.00	37.00	75.00	150	—

KM# 96 3 PFENNIG

Silver **Ruler:** Christian **Obv:** Lion rampant left **Rev:** Value with GUTE in 3 lines, date in legend **Mint:** Goslar **Note:** Gute 3 Pfennig.

Date	Mintage	VG	F	VF	XF	Unc
1630 HS	—	16.00	35.00	75.00	150	—

KM# 140 3 PFENNIG

Silver **Rev:** Imperial orb with 3

Date	Mintage	VG	F	VF	XF	Unc
1637 HS	—	16.00	35.00	75.00	150	—
1638 HS	—	16.00	35.00	75.00	150	—
1639 HS	—	16.00	35.00	75.00	150	—
1642 LW	—	16.00	35.00	75.00	150	—
1643 LW	—	16.00	35.00	75.00	150	—
1644 LW	—	16.00	35.00	75.00	150	—
1645 LW	—	16.00	35.00	75.00	150	—
1646 LW	—	16.00	35.00	75.00	150	—
1647 LW	—	16.00	35.00	75.00	150	—
1648 LW	—	16.00	35.00	75.00	150	—

KM# 201 3 PFENNIG

Silver **Ruler:** Christian Ludwig **Obv:** Crowned CL monogram **Mint:** Goslar

Date	Mintage	VG	F	VF	XF	Unc
1649 HS	—	35.00	75.00	150	300	—
1650 HS	—	35.00	75.00	150	300	—

KM# 216 3 PFENNIG

Silver **Obv:** Crowned CL monogram

Date	Mintage	VG	F	VF	XF	Unc
1650 LW	—	16.00	35.00	75.00	150	—
1653 LW	—	16.00	35.00	75.00	150	—
1656 LW	—	16.00	35.00	75.00	150	—

KM# 239 3 PFENNIG

Silver **Ruler:** Christian Ludwig **Rev. Legend:** H.Z. - M.B

Date	Mintage	VG	F	VF	XF	Unc
1656	—	16.00	35.00	65.00	150	—

KM# 275 3 PFENNIG

Silver **Obv:** Crowned GW monogram, date in legend **Rev:** Imperial orb with 3

Date	Mintage	VG	F	VF	XF	Unc
1673 RD	—	16.00	32.00	65.00	135	—
1674 RD	—	16.00	32.00	65.00	135	—
1675 RD	—	16.00	32.00	65.00	135	—
1677 RD	—	16.00	32.00	65.00	135	—

KM# 276 3 PFENNIG

Silver **Obv:** Crowned GW monogram **Rev:** Value in 3 lines, date in legend

Date	Mintage	VG	F	VF	XF	Unc
1673 RD	—	16.00	32.00	65.00	135	—

KM# 307 3 PFENNIG

Silver **Obv:** Crowned GW monogram **Rev:** Imperial orb with 3, date

Date	Mintage	VG	F	VF	XF	Unc
1683 III	—	17.00	35.00	70.00	140	—
1696 iii	—	17.00	35.00	70.00	140	—

KM# 329 3 PFENNIG

Silver **Ruler:** Georg II Wilhelm **Obv:** Crowned GW monogram divides date **Rev:** Imperial orb with 3

Date	Mintage	VG	F	VF	XF	Unc
1690 iii	—	10.00	25.00	50.00	100	—

KM# 60 3 PFENNIG (Dreiling)

Silver **Ruler:** Christian **Obv:** St. Andrew with cross **Rev:** Imperial orb with 3 **Mint:** Andreasberg

Date	Mintage	VG	F	VF	XF	Unc
1623 HP	—	—	—	—	—	—

KM# 26 WITTEN (4 Pfennig)

Copper **Obv:** Lion rampant left **Rev:** Value in 3 lines

Date	Mintage	VG	F	VF	XF	Unc
1620 GM	—	—	—	—	—	—
1621 GM	—	—	—	—	—	—

KM# 187 4 GUTE PFENNIG

Silver **Obv:** Crowned F monogram **Rev:** Value in 3 lines

Date	Mintage	VG	F	VF	XF	Unc
1648 LW	—	35.00	80.00	165	360	—

KM# 217 4 GUTE PFENNIG

Silver **Obv:** Crowned CL monogram

Date	Mintage	VG	F	VF	XF	Unc
1650 LW	—	35.00	75.00	150	300	—
1653 LW	—	35.00	75.00	150	300	—
1656 LW	—	35.00	75.00	150	300	—

KM# 277 4 GUTE PFENNIG

Silver **Obv:** Crowned GW monogram, date in legend **Rev:** Value in 4 lines

Date	Mintage	VG	F	VF	XF	Unc
1673 RD	—	27.00	55.00	110	225	—
1677 RD	—	27.00	55.00	110	225	—

KM# 171 6 PFENNIG

Silver **Obv:** Lion rampant left in circle of hearts **Rev:** Imperial orb with 6

Date	Mintage	VG	F	VF	XF	Unc
1645 LW	—	45.00	90.00	180	—	—
1647 LW	—	45.00	90.00	180	—	—

KM# 218 6 PFENNIG

Silver **Obv:** Lion rampant left in circle **Rev:** Imperial orb with 6 divides date

Date	Mintage	VG	F	VF	XF	Unc
1650 LW	—	50.00	100	210	—	—
1653 LW	—	50.00	100	210	—	—
1655 LW	—	50.00	100	210	—	—

KM# 308 6 PFENNIG

Silver **Obv:** Crowned GW monogram **Rev:** Imperial orb with 6

Date	Mintage	VG	F	VF	XF	Unc
1684	—	50.00	100	210	—	—
1685	—	50.00	100	210	—	—

KM# 27 SESLING (6 Pfennig)

Copper **Obv:** Lion rampant left **Rev:** Value in 4 lines

Date	Mintage	VG	F	VF	XF	Unc
(1)620 GM	—	—	—	—	—	—

KM# 32 1/2 SILBERGROSCHEN

Silver **Obv:** 4-fold arms with central shield of Minden arms (crossed keys) **Rev:** Value in 4 lines, small imperial orb below with value 48

Date	Mintage	VG	F	VF	XF	Unc
1621	—	80.00	165	335	—	—

KM# 33 SILBERGROSCHEN
Silver **Obv:** Lion rampant right in circle of hearts **Rev:** Value in 4 lines

Date	Mintage	VG	F	VF	XF	Unc
1621	—	50.00	100	210	—	—

KM# 34 SILBERGROSCHEN
Silver **Obv:** 4-fold arms **Rev:** Value in 4 lines

Date	Mintage	VG	F	VF	XF	Unc
1621	—	75.00	150	300	—	—

KM# 35 SILBERGROSCHEN
Silver **Rev:** Small imperial orb with 24 at bottom

Date	Mintage	VG	F	VF	XF	Unc
1621	—	60.00	120	240	—	—

KM# 36 SILBERGROSCHEN
Silver **Rev:** Arms in circle and 32 in orb

Date	Mintage	VG	F	VF	XF	Unc
1621	—	—	—	—	—	—

KM# 120 MARIENGROSCHEN
Silver **Obv:** Brunswick helmet with horse **Rev:** Value, date in 4 lines

Date	Mintage	VG	F	VF	XF	Unc
ND(1636-40) HS	—	—	—	—	—	—

KM# 188 MARIENGROSCHEN
Silver **Note:** Similar to 2 Mariengroschen, KM#202.

Date	Mintage	VG	F	VF	XF	Unc
1648	—	13.00	27.00	55.00	110	—
1653	—	13.00	27.00	55.00	110	—
1662	—	13.00	27.00	55.00	110	—

KM# 278 MARIENGROSCHEN
Silver **Obv:** Crowned GW monogram, date in legend **Rev:** Value in 4 lines **Rev. Legend:** VON REICHSTAL.SILB

Date	Mintage	VG	F	VF	XF	Unc
1673 RB	—	17.00	35.00	70.00	140	—

KM# 279 MARIENGROSCHEN
Silver **Rev. Legend:** N.REICHS.SCHROUT U.KORN

Date	Mintage	VG	F	VF	XF	Unc
1673 RD	—	17.00	35.00	70.00	140	—

KM# 292 MARIENGROSCHEN
Silver **Rev:** Value in 4 lines

Date	Mintage	VG	F	VF	XF	Unc
1675 RD	—	17.00	35.00	70.00	145	—

KM# 299 MARIENGROSCHEN
Silver **Obv:** Value, date in 4 lines **Rev:** Madonna and child

Date	Mintage	VG	F	VF	XF	Unc
1676	—	13.00	27.00	55.00	110	—
1683	—	13.00	27.00	55.00	110	—
1684	—	13.00	27.00	55.00	110	—
1685	—	13.00	27.00	55.00	110	—

KM# 304 MARIENGROSCHEN
Silver **Obv:** Date in legend

Date	Mintage	VG	F	VF	XF	Unc
1677	—	15.00	30.00	60.00	120	—
1680	—	15.00	30.00	60.00	120	—

KM# 339 MARIENGROSCHEN
Silver **Obv:** Value, date in 4 lines **Obv. Legend:** FURST:BR:LUN:LANDTMUNTZ

Date	Mintage	VG	F	VF	XF	Unc
1691	—	13.00	30.00	60.00	120	—
1697 iii	—	13.00	30.00	60.00	120	—

KM# 338.1 MARIENGROSCHEN
Silver **Ruler:** Georg II Wilhelm **Obv:** Value in 4 lines, date **Obv. Legend:** F: BR: L: LANDTMUNTZ **Rev:** Madonna and child

Date	Mintage	VG	F	VF	XF	Unc
1691 RD	—	10.00	30.00	60.00	120	—
1697 JJJ	—	10.00	30.00	60.00	120	—

KM# 141 2 MARIENGROSCHEN
Silver **Obv:** Brunswick helmet with horse **Rev:** Value, date in 4 lines

Date	Mintage	VG	F	VF	XF	Unc
1637 HS	—	16.00	32.00	65.00	130	—
1638 HS	—	16.00	32.00	65.00	130	—
1639 HS	—	16.00	32.00	65.00	130	—
1640 HS	—	16.00	32.00	65.00	130	—
ND HS	—	16.00	32.00	65.00	130	—
1647 HS	—	16.00	32.00	65.00	130	—

KM# 202 2 MARIENGROSCHEN
Silver

Date	Mintage	VG	F	VF	XF	Unc
1649	—	13.00	27.00	55.00	110	—
1650	—	13.00	27.00	55.00	110	—
1651	—	13.00	27.00	55.00	110	—
1652	—	13.00	27.00	55.00	110	—
1653	—	13.00	27.00	55.00	110	—
1654	—	13.00	27.00	55.00	110	—
1655	—	13.00	27.00	55.00	110	—
1656	—	13.00	27.00	55.00	110	—
1659	—	13.00	27.00	55.00	110	—

KM# 271 2 MARIENGROSCHEN
Silver **Obv:** Crowned GW monogram **Rev:** Value in 3 lines

Date	Mintage	VG	F	VF	XF	Unc
1667	—	13.00	30.00	60.00	120	—
1680	—	13.00	30.00	60.00	120	—
1681	—	13.00	30.00	60.00	120	—
1681/71	—	13.00	30.00	60.00	120	—

KM# 280 2 MARIENGROSCHEN
Silver **Obv:** Crowned GW monogram, date in legend

Date	Mintage	VG	F	VF	XF	Unc
1673 RD	—	—	—	—	—	—

KM# 322 2 MARIENGROSCHEN
Silver **Ruler:** Georg II Wilhelm **Obv:** Crowned GW monogram, date in legend **Rev:** Value in 4 lines

Date	Mintage	VG	F	VF	XF	Unc
1687	—	13.00	30.00	60.00	120	—
1687 ***	—	13.00	30.00	60.00	120	—
1687 iii	—	13.00	30.00	60.00	120	—
1697 JJJ	—	13.00	30.00	60.00	120	—
1698 JJJ	—	13.00	30.00	60.00	120	—

KM# 355 2 MARIENGROSCHEN
Silver **Obv:** Monogram in ornate letters

Date	Mintage	VG	F	VF	XF	Unc
1698 JJJ	—	16.00	35.00	70.00	140	—

KM# 37 4 GROSCHEN
Silver **Obv:** Crowned 4-fold arms **Rev:** Crowned imperial eagle, value 4 G in orb on breast, titles of Ferdinand II **Note:** Kipper 4 Groschen.

Date	Mintage	VG	F	VF	XF	Unc
ND(1621/2)	—	—	—	—	—	—

KM# 270 4 MARIENGROSCHEN
Silver **Obv:** Crowned GW monogram, date in legend **Rev:** Value in 3 lines

Date	Mintage	VG	F	VF	XF	Unc
1666 JJJ	—	13.00	30.00	60.00	120	—
1667	—	13.00	30.00	60.00	120	—

KM# 327 6 MARIENGROSCHEN
Silver **Obv:** Value in 4 lines **Rev:** Horse leaping left

Date	Mintage	VG	F	VF	XF	Unc
1689 JJJ	—	16.00	35.00	70.00	140	—

KM# 352 8 GUTE GROSCHEN (1/3 Thaler)
Silver **Note:** Similar to 16 Gute Groschen, KM#347 but value VIII.

Date	Mintage	VG	F	VF	XF	Unc
1694 JJJ	—	33.00	65.00	110	225	—
1698 JJJ	—	33.00	65.00	110	225	—

KM# 347.1 16 GUTE GROSCHEN (2/3 Thaler)
Silver

Date	Mintage	VG	F	VF	XF	Unc
1693 JJJ	—	70.00	100	150	265	—
1694 JJJ	—	70.00	100	150	265	—

KM# 347.2 16 GUTE GROSCHEN (2/3 Thaler)
Silver

Date	Mintage	VG	F	VF	XF	Unc
1698 JJJ	—	60.00	125	210	425	—

KM# 288 24 MARIENGROSCHEN (2/3 Thaler)
Silver **Obv:** Date in circle **Obv. Legend:** 24/MARIEN/GROSCH **Rev:** Horse leaping left

Date	Mintage	VG	F	VF	XF	Unc
1674	—	40.00	80.00	135	275	—
1674 RD	—	40.00	80.00	135	275	—
1675	—	40.00	80.00	135	275	—
1675 RD	—	40.00	80.00	135	275	—
1676	—	40.00	80.00	135	275	—
1676 RD	—	40.00	80.00	135	275	—

KM# 293 24 MARIENGROSCHEN (2/3 Thaler)
Silver **Obv:** XXIIII, date in wreath

Date	Mintage	VG	F	VF	XF	Unc
1675 RD	—	45.00	85.00	150	300	—
1677	—	45.00	85.00	150	300	—

KM# 300 24 MARIENGROSCHEN (2/3 Thaler)
Silver **Obv:** Bust right, value 60 below **Rev:** XXIIII and date without wreath

Date	Mintage	VG	F	VF	XF	Unc
1676	—	—	—	—	—	—

KM# 330 24 MARIENGROSCHEN (2/3 Thaler)
Silver **Obv:** Value in 3 lines **Rev:** Horse leaping left, date below

Date	Mintage	VG	F	VF	XF	Unc
1690 JJJ	—	27.00	55.00	110	225	—
1691 JJJ	—	27.00	55.00	110	225	—

KM# 12 2 SCHILLING
Silver **Obv:** 4-fold arms **Rev:** Intertwined DS, date in legend

Date	Mintage	VG	F	VF	XF	Unc
1619 GM	—	—	—	—	—	—
1621 GM	—	—	—	—	—	—
ND GM	—	—	—	—	—	—

KM# 13 2 SCHILLING
Silver **Obv:** Helmeted 4-fold arms

Date	Mintage	VG	F	VF	XF	Unc
1619 GM	—	—	—	—	—	—
1620 GM	—	—	—	—	—	—
ND GM	—	—	—	—	—	—

KM# 14 2 SCHILLING
Silver **Rev:** Date 1-9 divided by DS, 16 below

Date	Mintage	VG	F	VF	XF	Unc
1619 GM	—	—	—	—	—	—

KM# 38 2 SCHILLING
Silver **Obv:** 5-line inscription **Rev:** Helmet with horse, value Z S below

Date	Mintage	VG	F	VF	XF	Unc
1621	—	—	—	—	—	—

KM# 54 2 SCHILLING
Silver **Obv:** Four-fold arms **Rev:** Value in four lines **Note:** Varieties exist.

Date	Mintage	VG	F	VF	XF	Unc
(1)6ZZ	—	35.00	75.00	150	300	—
(1)6Z3	—	35.00	75.00	150	300	—

KM# 19 12 KREUZER (Dreibätzner; Schreckenberger)
Silver **Obv:** Crowned Luneburg lion rampant left **Obv. Legend:** IN MANV... **Rev:** Crowned imperial eagle, 12 in orb on breast, titles of Ferdinand II, date in legend **Note:** Kipper 12 Kreuzer.

Date	Mintage	VG	F	VF	XF	Unc
1621	—	100	200	375	725	—

KM# 39 12 KREUZER (Dreibätzner; Schreckenberger)
Silver **Obv:** Crowned arms of Luttenberg, lion left above 6 bars **Obv. Legend:** MONETA DVCAT.GRVBENHA **Rev:** Crowned imperial eagle with 12 in orb on breast, titles of Ferdinand II **Note:** Kipper Coinage for Grubenhagen.

Date	Mintage	VG	F	VF	XF	Unc
1621	—	100	200	375	725	—

KM# 24 12 KREUZER (Dreibätzner; Schreckenberger)
Silver **Obv:** Crowned Luneburg lion rampant right, titles of Christian **Rev:** Crowned imperial eagle, 1Z in orb on breast, titles of Ferdinand II, date in legend **Note:** Varieties exist.

Date	Mintage	VG	F	VF	XF	Unc
16Z1	—	100	200	375	725	—

KM# 40 24 KREUZER
Silver **Obv:** Crowned lion rampant right **Rev:** Crowned imperial eagle, 24 in orb on breast, titles of Ferdinand II **Note:** Kipper 24 Kreuzer.

Date	Mintage	VG	F	VF	XF	Unc
1621	—	150	325	575	1,100	—

KM# 43 HALB ORT HALB (1/4 Ort; 1/16 Thaler)
Silver **Obv:** Crowned imperial eagle wtih 16 in orb on breast, titles of Ferdinand II **Rev:** 4-fold arms with central shield of Minden (crossed keys) **Note:** Kipper Halb Ort Halb.

Date	Mintage	VG	F	VF	XF	Unc
1621	—	—	—	—	—	—

KM# 56 HALB ORT HALB (1/4 Ort; 1/16 Thaler)
Silver **Obv:** Bust right **Rev:** Value in 4 lines **Note:** Kipper Halb Ort Halb.

Date	Mintage	VG	F	VF	XF	Unc
1622	—	—	—	—	—	—

KM# 70 HALB ORT HALB (1/4 Ort; 1/16 Thaler)
Silver **Obv:** Crowned 8-fold arms **Rev:** Value in 4 lines **Rev. Legend:** IN.SPE.ET.SILENTIO

Date	Mintage	VG	F	VF	XF	Unc
1624 HS	—	30.00	65.00	130	265	—
1627 HS	—	30.00	65.00	130	265	—

KM# 84 HALB ORT HALB (1/4 Ort; 1/16 Thaler)
Silver **Obv:** Crowned 9-fold arms **Rev. Legend:** DANTE. DEO. VIRTUTE. DUCE

Date	Mintage	VG	F	VF	XF	Unc
1626 HS	—	30.00	65.00	130	265	—
1627 HS	—	30.00	65.00	130	265	—

KM# 85 HALB ORT HALB (1/4 Ort; 1/16 Thaler)
Silver **Obv:** Ornamented 9-fold arms **Rev:** Value in 5 lines

Date	Mintage	VG	F	VF	XF	Unc
1626 HS	—	—	—	—	—	—

KM# 118 HALB ORT HALB (1/4 Ort; 1/16 Thaler)
Silver **Obv:** Crowned 7-fold arms with central shield of Ratzeburg arms (mitre above castle tower) **Rev:** Date in legend **Rev. Legend:** I/HALB/ORT/HALB

Date	Mintage	VG	F	VF	XF	Unc
1635 HS	—	—	—	—	—	—

KM# 175 HALB ORT HALB (1/4 Ort; 1/16 Thaler)
Silver **Obv:** Crowned F monogram **Rev:** Value in 5 lines

Date	Mintage	VG	F	VF	XF	Unc
1647 LW	—	30.00	60.00	110	225	—
1648 LW	—	30.00	60.00	110	225	—

KM# 248 HALB ORT HALB (1/4 Ort; 1/16 Thaler)
Silver **Obv:** Crowned CL monogram above date in laurel wreath **Rev:** Horse leaping left, 16 in field

Date	Mintage	VG	F	VF	XF	Unc
1659 LW	—	20.00	40.00	80.00	160	—
1661 LW	—	20.00	40.00	80.00	160	—
1663 LW	—	20.00	40.00	80.00	160	—
1665 LW	—	20.00	40.00	80.00	160	—

KM# 47 HALB REICHSORT (1/8 Thaler)
Silver

Date	Mintage	VG	F	VF	XF	Unc
1621	—	45.00	95.00	190	385	—
1624 HS	—	45.00	95.00	190	385	—
1625 HS	—	45.00	95.00	190	385	—
1626 HS	—	45.00	95.00	190	385	—
1627 HS	—	45.00	95.00	190	385	—
1628 HS	—	45.00	95.00	190	385	—

KM# 71 HALB REICHSORT (1/8 Thaler)
Silver **Obv:** Value in 3 lines **Rev:** 10-fold arms

Date	Mintage	VG	F	VF	XF	Unc
1624	—	45.00	95.00	190	385	—

KM# 72 HALB REICHSORT (1/8 Thaler)
Silver **Obv:** St. Andrew with cross **Rev:** Crowned 8-fold arms, date divided at bottom

Date	Mintage	VG	F	VF	XF	Unc
1624 HP	—	—	—	—	—	—

KM# 88 HALB REICHSORT (1/8 Thaler)
Silver **Obv:** Crowned 9-fold arms **Rev:** Value in 5 lines

Date	Mintage	VG	F	VF	XF	Unc
1629 HS	—	80.00	170	300	625	—
1630 HS	—	80.00	170	300	625	—
1631 HS	—	80.00	170	300	625	—
1632 HS	—	80.00	170	300	625	—
1633 HS	—	80.00	170	300	625	—

KM# 103 HALB REICHSORT (1/8 Thaler)
Silver **Obv:** St. Andrew with cross **Rev:** Crowned 9-fold arms, divided at bottom

Date	Mintage	VG	F	VF	XF	Unc
1633 HS	—	—	—	—	—	—

KM# 104 HALB REICHSORT (1/8 Thaler)
Silver **Subject:** Death of Christian **Obv:** Crowned 9-fold arms **Rev:** 9-line inscription with date

Date	Mintage	VG	F	VF	XF	Unc
1633	—	—	—	—	—	—

KM# 113 HALB REICHSORT (1/8 Thaler)
Silver **Obv:** Crowned 9-fold arms with central shield of Ratzeburg arms **Rev:** Date in legend **Rev. Legend:** I/HALB/REICHS/ORT

Date	Mintage	VG	F	VF	XF	Unc
1634 HS	—	100	175	350	700	—
1635 HS	—	100	175	350	700	—
1636 HS	—	100	175	350	700	—

KM# 123 HALB REICHSORT (1/8 Thaler)
Silver **Obv:** Crowned 11-fold arms with central shield **Rev:** Wildman, tree in right hand

Date	Mintage	VG	F	VF	XF	Unc
1636 HS	—	—	—	—	—	—

KM# 124 HALB REICHSORT (1/8 Thaler)
Silver **Subject:** Death of August I **Rev:** 9-line inscription with date

Date	Mintage	VG	F	VF	XF	Unc
1636 HS	—	175	375	725	—	—

KM# 125 HALB REICHSORT (1/8 Thaler)
Silver **Obv:** Crowned 7-fold arms with central shield

Date	Mintage	VG	F	VF	XF	Unc
1636 HS	—	—	—	—	—	—

KM# 149 HALB REICHSORT (1/8 Thaler)
Silver **Obv:** Crowned 11-fold arms

Date	Mintage	VG	F	VF	XF	Unc
1638 HS	—	25.00	50.00	90.00	185	—
1639 HS	—	25.00	50.00	90.00	185	—
1640 HS	—	25.00	50.00	90.00	185	—
1640 LW	—	25.00	50.00	90.00	185	—
1642 LW	—	25.00	50.00	90.00	185	—

KM# 162 HALB REICHSORT (1/8 Thaler)
Silver **Subject:** Death of Friedrich's Sister, Margarethe, Wife of Johann Casimir of Saxe-Coburg **Obv:** Helmeted 12-fold arms **Rev:** 10-line inscription with date

Date	Mintage	VG	F	VF	XF	Unc
1643 LW	—	—	—	—	—	—

KM# 161 HALB REICHSORT (1/8 Thaler)
Silver **Obv:** Crowned 12-fold arms **Note:** Varieties exist.

Date	Mintage	VG	F	VF	XF	Unc
1643 LW	—	55.00	110	175	325	—
1644 LW	—	55.00	110	175	325	—
1645 LW	—	55.00	110	175	325	—
ND LW	—	55.00	110	175	325	—

KM# 172.1 HALB REICHSORT (1/8 Thaler)
Silver **Note:** Varieties exist with and without bow at shoulder.

Date	Mintage	VG	F	VF	XF	Unc
1645 LW	—	55.00	110	175	325	—
1646 LW	—	55.00	110	175	325	—
1647 LW	—	55.00	110	175	325	—
1648 LW	—	55.00	110	175	325	—

KM# 173 HALB REICHSORT (1/8 Thaler)
Silver **Rev:** Similar to KM#149

Date	Mintage	VG	F	VF	XF	Unc
1646	—	—	—	—	—	—

KM# 189 HALB REICHSORT (1/8 Thaler)
Silver **Subject:** Death of Friedrich V **Rev:** 9-line inscription with date

Date	Mintage	VG	F	VF	XF	Unc
1648 LW	—	—	—	—	—	—

KM# 204 HALB REICHSORT (1/8 Thaler)
Silver **Obv:** 12-fold arms in circle, date divided 1-6/4-8, titles of Friedrich V **Rev:** Horse leaping left in circle, date **Rev. Legend:** *SINCERE **Note:** Mule.

Date	Mintage	VG	F	VF	XF	Unc
1648/1649 LW Rare	—	—	—	—	—	—

KM# 172.2 HALB REICHSORT (1/8 Thaler)
Silver

Date	Mintage	VG	F	VF	XF	Unc
ND LW	—	55.00	110	175	325	—

KM# 203 HALB REICHSORT (1/8 Thaler)
Silver **Obv:** 12-fold arms, small crown in legend **Rev:** Horse leaping left

Date	Mintage	VG	F	VF	XF	Unc
1649 LW	—	55.00	110	175	325	—
1650 LW	—	55.00	110	175	325	—

KM# 220 HALB REICHSORT (1/8 Thaler)
Silver **Obv:** Large crown above arms

Date	Mintage	VG	F	VF	XF	Unc
1650 LW	—	55.00	110	175	325	—
1653 LW	—	55.00	110	175	325	—
1654 LW	—	55.00	110	175	325	—
1655 LW	—	55.00	110	175	325	—
1657 LW	—	55.00	110	175	325	—
1659 LW	—	55.00	110	175	325	—
1660 LW	—	55.00	110	175	325	—
1662 LW	—	55.00	110	175	325	—
1663 LW	—	55.00	110	175	325	—
1664 LW	—	55.00	110	175	325	—
1665 LW	—	55.00	110	175	325	—

KM# 265 HALB REICHSORT (1/8 Thaler)
3.6000 g., Silver, 27.7 mm. **Subject:** Death of Christian Ludwig **Obv:** 12-fold arms, small crown in legend **Rev:** 10-line inscription with date

Date	Mintage	VG	F	VF	XF	Unc
1665 LW	—	—	—	—	—	—

KM# 282 HALB REICHSORT (1/8 Thaler)
Silver **Obv:** Horse leaping left **Rev:** Crowned 12-fold arms

Date	Mintage	VG	F	VF	XF	Unc
1673 RD	—	—	—	—	—	—

KM# 348 1/96 THALER
Silver **Obv:** Value 96 in palm wreath **Rev:** Horse leaping left

Date	Mintage	VG	F	VF	XF	Unc
1693 iii	—	27.00	45.00	80.00	160	—

KM# 323 1/48 THALER (1/2 Groschen)
Silver **Ruler:** Georg II Wilhelm **Obv:** Crowned GW monogram **Rev:** Value, date **Rev. Legend:** F. BR. LANTMUNTZ

Date	Mintage	VG	F	VF	XF	Unc
1687 III	—	12.00	25.00	50.00	100	—
1688 III	—	12.00	25.00	50.00	100	—
1688 iii	—	12.00	25.00	50.00	100	—
1690 III	—	12.00	25.00	50.00	100	—
1690 iii	—	12.00	25.00	50.00	100	—
1691 iii	—	12.00	25.00	50.00	100	—
1694 iii	—	12.00	25.00	50.00	100	—
1695 III	—	12.00	25.00	50.00	100	—
1695 iii	—	12.00	25.00	50.00	100	—
1696 iii	—	12.00	25.00	50.00	100	—
1699 III	—	12.00	25.00	50.00	100	—

KM# 356 1/48 THALER (1/2 Groschen)
Silver **Ruler:** Georg II Wilhelm **Obv:** Monogram of ornate letters **Rev:** Value within orb

Date	Mintage	VG	F	VF	XF	Unc
1698 III	—	12.00	25.00	50.00	100	—

KM# 5 1/24 THALER (Groschen)
Silver **Obv:** Imperial orb with 24, titles of Matthias **Rev:** Helmeted 4-fold arms

Date	Mintage	VG	F	VF	XF	Unc
1617	—	20.00	35.00	70.00	140	—
1619	—	20.00	35.00	70.00	140	—

KM# 10 1/24 THALER (Groschen)
Silver **Obv:** Lion rampant right **Rev:** Imperial orb wtih 24

Date	Mintage	VG	F	VF	XF	Unc
1618 (k)	—	27.00	55.00	100	165	—

KM# 11 1/24 THALER (Groschen)
Silver **Obv:** Lion rampant left **Rev:** Imperial orb with 24 **Rev. Legend:** IUSTITIA.ET.CONCOR

Date	Mintage	VG	F	VF	XF	Unc
1618 (k)	—	20.00	45.00	90.00	185	—
1619 (k)	—	20.00	45.00	90.00	185	—

KM# 15 1/24 THALER (Groschen)
Silver **Obv:** Lion rampant right

Date	Mintage	VG	F	VF	XF	Unc
1619 (k)	—	27.00	55.00	110	225	—

KM# 41 1/24 THALER (Groschen)
Silver **Obv:** Lion rampant left **Obv. Legend:** C. D. G. E. E. M. D BEL **Rev:** Imperial orb with 24 **Rev. Legend:** NACH. R. SCHROT. V. KORN

Date	Mintage	VG	F	VF	XF	Unc
1621	—	27.00	55.00	110	225	—

KM# 42 1/24 THALER (Groschen)
Silver **Subject:** Coinage for Grubenhagen **Obv:** Imperial orb with 24, titles of Ferdinand II **Rev:** Round Lutterberg arms (lion left above 6 bars) **Rev. Legend:** MONE-DVC.GRVBENH

Date	Mintage	VG	F	VF	XF	Unc
1621	—	—	—	—	—	—

KM# 55 1/24 THALER (Groschen)
Silver **Obv:** Arms of Lutterberg **Rev:** Imperial orb with 24 **Rev. Legend:** NACH.R.SCHROT.V.KORN

Date	Mintage	VG	F	VF	XF	Unc
1622 HS	—	13.00	27.00	55.00	110	—
1623 HS	—	13.00	27.00	55.00	110	—
1624 HS	—	13.00	27.00	55.00	110	—
1628 HS	—	13.00	27.00	55.00	110	—
1629 HS	—	13.00	27.00	55.00	110	—
1631 HS	—	13.00	27.00	55.00	110	—
1632 HS	—	13.00	27.00	55.00	110	—
1633 HS	—	13.00	27.00	55.00	110	—

KM# 61 1/24 THALER (Groschen)
Silver **Obv:** St. Andrew with cross divides date

Date	Mintage	VG	F	VF	XF	Unc
1623 HP	—	25.00	50.00	100	—	—
1624 HP	—	25.00	50.00	100	—	—

KM# 63 1/24 THALER (Groschen)
Silver **Rev. Legend:** NACH.A.SCHROT.V.K.16.23

Date	Mintage	VG	F	VF	XF	Unc
1623 HP	—	25.00	50.00	100	—	—

KM# 64 1/24 THALER (Groschen)
Silver **Obv:** Crowned arms **Rev:** St. Andrew with cross

Date	Mintage	VG	F	VF	XF	Unc
1623 HP	—	25.00	50.00	100	—	—

KM# 65 1/24 THALER (Groschen)
Silver **Obv:** Imperial orb with 24

Date	Mintage	VG	F	VF	XF	Unc
1623	—	15.00	35.00	70.00	140	—
1624	—	15.00	35.00	70.00	140	—
1624 HP	—	15.00	35.00	70.00	140	—

KM# 62 1/24 THALER (Groschen)
Silver **Note:** Klippe.

Date	Mintage	VG	F	VF	XF	Unc
1623 HP	—	—	—	—	—	—

KM# 68 1/24 THALER (Groschen)
Silver **Obv. Legend:** CHRIST.D.G **Rev. Legend:** CHRISTIAN D.G

Date	Mintage	VG	F	VF	XF	Unc
1624	—	—	—	—	—	—

KM# 69 1/24 THALER (Groschen)
Silver **Obv:** Crowned 8-fold arms **Rev:** Imperial orb with 24 **Rev. Legend:** NACH.R.SCHROT.V K 16-24

Date	Mintage	VG	F	VF	XF	Unc
1624 HS	—	33.00	55.00	110	225	—

KM# 112 1/24 THALER (Groschen)
Silver **Obv:** Lutterberg arms **Rev:** Imperial orb with 24

Date	Mintage	VG	F	VF	XF	Unc
1634 HS	—	15.00	35.00	70.00	140	—
1635 HS	—	15.00	35.00	70.00	140	—
1636 HS	—	15.00	35.00	70.00	140	—

KM# 122 1/24 THALER (Groschen)
Silver **Obv:** Crowned Lutterberg-Scharzfeld arms

Date	Mintage	VG	F	VF	XF	Unc
1635 HS Error	—	25.00	50.00	100	200	—
1637 HS	—	25.00	50.00	100	200	—
1638 HS	—	25.00	50.00	100	200	—
1641 LW	—	25.00	50.00	100	200	—
1642 LW	—	25.00	50.00	100	200	—
1643 LW	—	25.00	50.00	100	200	—
1644 LW	—	25.00	50.00	100	200	—
1647 LW	—	25.00	50.00	100	200	—
1648 LW	—	25.00	50.00	100	200	—

KM# 121 1/24 THALER (Groschen)
Silver **Obv:** Brunswick helmet with horse **Note:** Varieties exist (mintmasters initials on either obverse or reverse).

Date	Mintage	VG	F	VF	XF	Unc
1636 HS	—	—	—	—	—	—

KM# 219 1/24 THALER (Groschen)
Silver **Obv:** Crowned Lutterberg arms (wtih 5 bars)

Date	Mintage	VG	F	VF	XF	Unc
1650 LW	—	25.00	50.00	100	200	—
1651 LW	—	25.00	50.00	100	200	—
1655 LW	—	25.00	50.00	100	200	—
1657 LW	—	25.00	50.00	100	200	—

KM# 228 1/24 THALER (Groschen)
Silver **Subject:** Death of Sybilla, 2nd Wife of Julius Ernst zu Dannenberg **Obv:** Crowned 12-fold arms, value 24 sideways on left **Rev:** 9-line inscription with date

Date	Mintage	VG	F	VF	XF	Unc
1652	—	—	—	—	—	—

KM# 246 1/24 THALER (Groschen)
Silver **Subject:** Death of Christian Ernst's Aunt Clara **Obv:** Horse leaping left, 24 in oval below **Rev:** 10-line inscription with date

Date	Mintage	VG	F	VF	XF	Unc
1658 LW	—	27.00	55.00	90.00	185	—

KM# 255 1/24 THALER (Groschen)

Silver **Obv:** Imperial orb wtih 24 in circle **Rev:** Horse leaping left in circle

Date	Mintage	VG	F	VF	XF	Unc
1661 LW	—	15.00	30.00	60.00	120	—
1662 LW	—	15.00	30.00	60.00	120	—
1663 LW	—	15.00	30.00	60.00	120	—
1665 LW	—	15.00	30.00	60.00	120	—

KM# 264 1/24 THALER (Groschen)

Silver **Subject:** Death of Christian Ludwig

Date	Mintage	VG	F	VF	XF	Unc
1665 LW	—	40.00	80.00	165	230	—

KM# 281 1/24 THALER (Groschen)

Silver **Obv:** Crowned GW monogram, date in legend **Rev:** Imperial orb with 24 **Rev. Legend:** REICHSTHALER SILBER

Date	Mintage	VG	F	VF	XF	Unc
1673 RD	—	20.00	45.00	90.00	185	—

KM# A279 1/24 THALER (Groschen)

Silver **Rev. Legend:** F.BR.LUNEB.LANDTMUNTZ

Date	Mintage	VG	F	VF	XF	Unc
1674 RD	—	16.00	35.00	75.00	155	—
1675 RD	—	16.00	35.00	75.00	155	—
1688 iii	—	16.00	35.00	75.00	155	—
1690 iii	—	16.00	35.00	75.00	155	—
1691 iii	—	16.00	35.00	75.00	155	—

KM# 301 1/24 THALER (Groschen)

Silver **Obv:** Horse leaping left, German titles **Rev:** Imperial orb with 24, date

Date	Mintage	VG	F	VF	XF	Unc
1676 RD	—	15.00	30.00	60.00	120	—
1677 RD	—	15.00	30.00	60.00	120	—
1678 RD	—	15.00	30.00	60.00	120	—
1680 RD	—	15.00	30.00	60.00	120	—

KM# 309 1/24 THALER (Groschen)

Silver **Rev. Legend:** MONETA NOVA ARGENTEA

Date	Mintage	VG	F	VF	XF	Unc
1684 IT	—	13.00	27.00	55.00	110	—

KM# 324 1/24 THALER (Groschen)

Silver **Obv:** GW monogram above horse

Date	Mintage	VG	F	VF	XF	Unc
1687 III	—	13.00	27.00	55.00	110	—
1688 iii	—	13.00	27.00	55.00	110	—

KM# 349 1/24 THALER (Groschen)

Silver **Ruler:** Georg II Wilhelm **Obv:** Latin titles and date below horse **Rev:** Imperial orb with 24

Date	Mintage	VG	F	VF	XF	Unc
1693 III	—	11.00	27.00	55.00	110	—
1693 iii	—	11.00	27.00	55.00	110	—
1694 III	—	11.00	27.00	55.00	110	—
1694 iii	—	11.00	27.00	55.00	110	—
1695 III	—	11.00	27.00	55.00	110	—
1695 iii	—	11.00	27.00	55.00	110	—
1696 III	—	11.00	27.00	55.00	110	—
1696 iii	—	11.00	27.00	55.00	110	—

KM# 236 1/16 THALER

Silver **Obv:** Crowned CL monogram in wreath **Rev:** Value XVI... in 4 lines

Date	Mintage	VG	F	VF	XF	Unc
1655 LW	—	33.00	65.00	135	275	—
1656 LW	—	33.00	65.00	135	275	—
1657 LW	—	33.00	65.00	135	275	—
1658 LW	—	33.00	65.00	135	275	—

KM# 44 1/12 THALER

Silver **Obv:** Crowned imperial eagle with 12 in orb on breast, date in legend, titles of Ferdinand II **Rev:** Crowned lion rampant right

Date	Mintage	VG	F	VF	XF	Unc
1621	—	65.00	135	275	550	—

KM# 45 1/12 THALER

Silver **Obv:** N below lion

Date	Mintage	VG	F	VF	XF	Unc
1621 N Rare	—	—	—	—	—	—

KM# 46 1/12 THALER

Silver **Obv:** Crowned lion rampant left **Obv. Legend:** IN.MANV.DEI.SORTES.MEAE

Date	Mintage	VG	F	VF	XF	Unc
1621	—	65.00	135	275	550	—

KM# 86 1/12 THALER

Silver **Obv:** St. Andrew with cross **Obv. Legend:** RECTE.FACIEN.NEM.IMT

Date	Mintage	VG	F	VF	XF	Unc
1626	—	—	—	—	—	—

KM# 6 1/4 THALER

Silver **Note:** Similar to KM#66.

Date	Mintage	VG	F	VF	XF	Unc
1617	—	80.00	160	275	575	—
1617 (k)	—	80.00	160	275	575	—
1618 (k)	—	80.00	160	275	575	—
1620 (k)	—	80.00	160	275	575	—
1623 HS	—	80.00	160	275	575	—
1624 HS	—	80.00	160	275	575	—

KM# 16 1/4 THALER

Silver **Rev:** Helmeted 8-fold arms

Date	Mintage	VG	F	VF	XF	Unc
1619 (k)	—	—	—	—	—	—

KM# 28 1/4 THALER

Silver **Note:** Struck on octagonal flan.

Date	Mintage	VG	F	VF	XF	Unc
1620 GM Rare	—	—	—	—	—	—

KM# 57 1/4 THALER

Silver **Rev. Legend:** DUX:BR.-ET.LU

Date	Mintage	VG	F	VF	XF	Unc
1622 (w)	—	—	—	—	—	—

KM# 66 1/4 THALER

Silver

Date	Mintage	VG	F	VF	XF	Unc
1623 HP	—	65.00	135	275	550	—
1624 HP	—	65.00	135	275	550	—
1625 HP	—	65.00	135	275	550	—

KM# 79 1/4 THALER

Silver **Rev:** 9-fold arms

Date	Mintage	VG	F	VF	XF	Unc
1625 HS	—	55.00	115	225	450	—
1627 HS	—	55.00	15.00	225	450	—

KM# 89 1/4 THALER

Silver **Rev. Legend:** IN*SPE*ET*-SILENTIO*H.S

Date	Mintage	VG	F	VF	XF	Unc
1629 HS	—	55.00	115	225	450	—
1630 HS	—	55.00	115	225	450	—
1631 HS	—	55.00	115	225	450	—

KM# 97 1/4 THALER

Silver **Obv:** Similar to KM#65 **Rev:** Crowned 9-fold arms

Date	Mintage	VG	F	VF	XF	Unc
1630 HS	—	—	—	—	—	—

KM# 105 1/4 THALER

Silver **Subject:** Death of Christian **Obv:** Ornamented 9-fold arms **Rev:** 10-line inscription with date

Date	Mintage	VG	F	VF	XF	Unc
1633	—	—	—	—	—	—
1633 HS	—	—	—	—	—	—

KM# 119 1/4 THALER

Silver **Obv:** Bust right **Rev:** Crowned 9-fold arms with central shield

Date	Mintage	VG	F	VF	XF	Unc
1635 HS	—	—	—	—	—	—
1636 HS	—	—	—	—	—	—

KM# 126 1/4 THALER

Silver **Obv:** Crowned 11-fold arms with central shield **Rev:** Wildman, tree in right hand, date in legend

Date	Mintage	VG	F	VF	XF	Unc
1636 HS	—	350	650	1,200	2,300	—

KM# 127 1/4 THALER

Silver **Subject:** Death of August I **Rev:** 10-line inscription

Date	Mintage	VG	F	VF	XF	Unc
1636 HS	—	135	275	500	900	—

KM# 128 1/4 THALER

Silver **Obv:** Crowned 7-fold arms with central shield

Date	Mintage	VG	F	VF	XF	Unc
1636 HS	—	200	400	700	1,300	—

KM# 142 1/4 THALER

Silver **Rev:** Crowned 11-fold arms

Date	Mintage	VG	F	VF	XF	Unc
1637 HS	—	150	275	500	875	—
1638 HS	—	150	275	500	875	—
1639 HS	—	150	275	500	875	—
1641 LW	—	150	275	500	875	—
1642 LW	—	150	275	500	875	—
1643 LW	—	150	275	500	875	—
1644 LW	—	150	275	500	875	—

KM# 163 1/4 THALER

Silver **Rev:** 12-fold arms

Date	Mintage	VG	F	VF	XF	Unc
1643 LW	—	85.00	175	325	650	—
1644 LW	—	85.00	175	325	650	—
1645 LW	—	85.00	175	325	650	—
1646 LW	—	85.00	175	325	650	—
1647 LW	—	85.00	175	325	650	—
1648 LW	—	85.00	175	325	650	—

KM# 176 1/4 THALER

Silver **Obv:** Without COADI.D.STIFT.RATZ

Date	Mintage	VG	F	VF	XF	Unc
1647 LW Rare	—	—	—	—	—	—

KM# 190 1/4 THALER

Silver **Subject:** Death of Friedrich V **Rev:** 10-line inscription

Date	Mintage	VG	F	VF	XF	Unc
1648 LW	—	—	—	—	—	—

KM# 205 1/4 THALER

Silver **Rev:** Crowned 12-fold arms, date in legend

Date	Mintage	VG	F	VF	XF	Unc
1649 HS	—	—	—	—	—	—

KM# 206 1/4 THALER

Silver **Obv:** Crowned 12-fold arms **Rev:** Horse leaping left

Date	Mintage	VG	F	VF	XF	Unc
1649 LW	—	150	275	500	875	—
1650 LW	—	150	275	500	875	—
1653 LW	—	150	275	500	875	—

Date	Mintage	VG	F	VF	XF	Unc
1654 LW	—	150	275	500	875	—
1656 LW	—	150	275	500	875	—
1658 LW	—	150	275	500	875	—
1659 LW	—	150	275	500	875	—
1661 LW	—	150	275	500	875	—
1662 LW	—	150	275	500	875	—
1664 LW	—	150	275	500	875	—
1665 LW	—	150	275	500	875	—

KM# 266 1/4 THALER
Silver **Subject:** Death of Christian Ludwig

Date	Mintage	VG	F	VF	XF	Unc
1665 LW	—	100	200	400	800	—

KM# 283 1/4 THALER
Silver **Obv:** Horse leaping left **Rev:** Crowned 12-fold arms

Date	Mintage	VG	F	VF	XF	Unc
1673 RD	—	—	—	—	—	—

KM# 340 1/4 THALER
Silver **Obv:** Crowned 12-fold arms **Rev:** Horse leaping left, 1/4 in oval divides date below

Date	Mintage	VG	F	VF	XF	Unc
1691 III	—	40.00	80.00	150	300	—

KM# 290 1/3 THALER
Silver

Date	Mintage	VG	F	VF	XF	Unc
1674	—	70.00	140	275	550	—

KM# 291 1/3 THALER
Silver **Obv:** Denomination **Rev:** Horse leaping left

Date	Mintage	VG	F	VF	XF	Unc
1674	—	70.00	140	275	550	—
1675	—	70.00	140	275	550	—
1676	—	70.00	140	275	550	—

KM# 344 1/3 THALER
Silver

Date	Mintage	VG	F	VF	XF	Unc
1692 JJJ	—	45.00	90.00	180	360	—
1693 JJJ	—	45.00	90.00	180	360	—

KM# 7 1/2 THALER
Silver

Date	Mintage	VG	F	VF	XF	Unc
1617 (k)	—	90.00	175	325	625	—
1618 (k)	—	90.00	175	325	625	—
1620 (k)	—	90.00	175	325	625	—
1622 HS	—	90.00	175	325	625	—
1623	—	90.00	175	325	625	—
1623 HP	—	90.00	175	325	625	—
1623 HS	—	90.00	175	325	625	—
1624 HS	—	90.00	175	325	625	—
1625 HS	—	90.00	175	325	625	—

KM# 67 1/2 THALER
Silver **Note:** Similar to 1/4 Thaler, KM#66.

Date	Mintage	VG	F	VF	XF	Unc
1623 HP	—	85.00	170	325	625	—
1624 HP	—	85.00	170	325	625	—

KM# 73 1/2 THALER
Silver **Rev:** 9-fold arms

Date	Mintage	VG	F	VF	XF	Unc
1624 HS	—	100	200	400	800	—
1625 HS	—	100	200	400	800	—
1626 HS	—	100	200	400	800	—
1627 HS	—	100	200	400	800	—
1629 HS	—	100	200	400	800	—

KM# 74 1/2 THALER
Silver **Rev:** 10-fold arms

Date	Mintage	VG	F	VF	XF	Unc
1624 HVE	—	140	275	475	950	—

KM# 98 1/2 THALER
Silver

Date	Mintage	VG	F	VF	XF	Unc
1630 HS	—	100	200	400	800	—
1631 HS	—	100	200	400	800	—
1632 HS	—	100	200	400	800	—
1633 HS	—	100	200	400	800	—

KM# 102 1/2 THALER
Silver **Obv:** Similar to 1/4 Thaler, KM#66

Date	Mintage	VG	F	VF	XF	Unc
1632 HS	—	140	225	425	800	—
1633 HS	—	140	225	425	800	—

KM# 106 1/2 THALER
Silver **Subject:** Death of Christian **Obv:** Ornamented 9-fold arms **Rev:** 10-line inscription with date

Date	Mintage	VG	F	VF	XF	Unc
1633 HS	—	—	—	—	—	—

KM# 114 1/2 THALER
Silver **Obv:** Bust right **Rev:** Crowned 9-fold arms with central shield

Date	Mintage	VG	F	VF	XF	Unc
1634 HS	—	140	280	500	1,000	—
1635 HS	—	140	280	500	1,000	—
1636 HS	—	140	280	500	1,000	—

KM# 129 1/2 THALER
Silver **Obv:** Crowned 11-fold arms with central shield **Rev:** Wildman, tree in right hand divides date

Date	Mintage	VG	F	VF	XF	Unc
1636 HS	—	—	—	—	—	—

KM# 130 1/2 THALER
Silver **Subject:** Death of August I **Rev:** 13-line inscription

Date	Mintage	VG	F	VF	XF	Unc
1636 HS	—	180	350	600	1,175	—

KM# 131 1/2 THALER
Silver **Obv:** Crowned 7-fold arms with central shield **Rev:** 10-line inscription

Date	Mintage	VG	F	VF	XF	Unc
1636 HS	—	180	350	600	1,175	—

KM# 143 1/2 THALER
Silver **Rev:** Helmeted 11-fold arms divide date, Gothic letters

Date	Mintage	VG	F	VF	XF	Unc
1637 HS	—	85.00	175	325	650	—
1638 HS	—	85.00	175	325	650	—
1639 HS	—	85.00	175	325	650	—
1640 HS	—	85.00	175	325	650	—
1641 LW	—	85.00	175	325	650	—
1642 LW	—	85.00	175	325	650	—
1643 LW	—	85.00	175	325	650	—

KM# 144 1/2 THALER
Silver **Note:** Latin letters.

Date	Mintage	VG	F	VF	XF	Unc
1637 HS	—	75.00	150	300	600	—

KM# 164 1/2 THALER
Silver **Rev:** Crowned 12-fold arms

Date	Mintage	VG	F	VF	XF	Unc
1643 LW	—	65.00	130	250	500	—
1644 LW	—	65.00	130	250	500	—
1645 LW	—	65.00	130	250	500	—
1646 LW	—	65.00	130	250	500	—
1647 LW	—	65.00	130	250	500	—
1648 LW	—	65.00	130	250	500	—

KM# 165 1/2 THALER
Silver **Subject:** Death of Friedrich's Sister, Margarethe, Wife of Johann Casimir of Saxe-Coburg **Obv:** Helmeted 12-fold arms **Rev:** 10-line inscription with date

Date	Mintage	VG	F	VF	XF	Unc
1643 LW	—	—	—	—	—	—

KM# 191 1/2 THALER

Silver **Subject:** Death of Friedrich V **Obv:** Bust right

Date	Mintage	VG	F	VF	XF	Unc
1648 LW	—	—	—	—	—	—

KM# 207 1/2 THALER

Silver **Obv:** Crowned 12-fold arms **Rev:** Horse leaping left

Date	Mintage	VG	F	VF	XF	Unc
1649 LW	—	165	325	500	975	—
1651 LW	—	165	325	500	975	—
1653 LW	—	165	325	500	975	—
1655 LW	—	165	325	500	975	—
1656 LW	—	165	325	500	975	—
1658 LW	—	165	325	500	975	—
1659 LW	—	165	325	500	975	—
1660 LW	—	165	325	500	975	—
1662 LW	—	165	325	500	975	—
1665 LW	—	165	325	500	975	—

KM# 240 1/2 THALER

Silver **Rev:** Wildman, tree in right hand

Date	Mintage	VG	F	VF	XF	Unc
1657 HS	—	—	—	—	—	—

KM# 258 1/2 THALER

Silver **Note:** Klippe.

Date	Mintage	VG	F	VF	XF	Unc
1664 LW	—	—	—	—	—	—

KM# 267 1/2 THALER

Silver **Subject:** Death of Christian Ludwig **Obv:** 12-fold arms, small crown in legend **Rev:** 11-line inscription with date

Date	Mintage	VG	F	VF	XF	Unc
1665 LW	—	85.00	160	325	650	—
1665 HS	—	85.00	160	325	650	—

KM# 284 1/2 THALER

Silver **Obv:** Horse leaping left **Rev:** Crowned 12-fold arms

Date	Mintage	VG	F	VF	XF	Unc
1673 RD	—	—	—	—	—	—

KM# 341 1/2 THALER

Silver **Obv:** Bust right, date below **Rev:** Halmeted 12-fold arms

Date	Mintage	VG	F	VF	XF	Unc
1691 iii	—	—	—	—	—	—

KM# 328 2/3 THALER

Silver **Obv:** Bust right **Rev:** Horse leaping left in circle, 2/3 in oval divides date below

Date	Mintage	VG	F	VF	XF	Unc
1689 JJJ	—	—	—	—	—	—

KM# 331 2/3 THALER

Silver

Date	Mintage	VG	F	VF	XF	Unc
1690 JJJ	—	40.00	75.00	130	250	350

KM# 345.1 2/3 THALER

Silver **Obv:** Similar to KM#341 but arms break circle at bottom

Date	Mintage	VG	F	VF	XF	Unc
1691 JJJ	—	80.00	140	225	385	—
1692 JJJ	—	80.00	140	225	385	—
1693 JJJ	—	80.00	140	225	385	—
1694 JJJ	—	80.00	140	225	385	—

KM# 346.1 2/3 THALER

Silver

Date	Mintage	VG	F	VF	XF	Unc
1692 JJJ	—	40.00	85.00	160	325	—
1693 JJJ	—	40.00	85.00	160	325	—
1694 JJJ	—	40.00	85.00	160	325	—

KM# 345.2 2/3 THALER

Silver **Ruler:** Georg II Wilhelm **Rev:** FEIN.SILB added above date

Date	Mintage	VG	F	VF	XF	Unc
1694 JJJ	—	80.00	140	220	385	—

KM# 346.2 2/3 THALER

Silver **Rev:** REIN. SILB added above date

Date	Mintage	VG	F	VF	XF	Unc
1697 JJJ	—	40.00	85.00	150	300	—

KM# 9.2 THALER

Silver **Rev:** Helmeted arms divide H-S

Date	Mintage	VG	F	VF	XF	Unc
1617 H-L	—	75.00	150	265	400	—

KM# 9.1 THALER

Silver **Obv. Legend:** CHRISTIANUS. D: G: EL: EP: MIND: DUX. BR: ET: LU* **Rev:** Triple-helmeted 8-fold arms divide H-L **Rev. Legend:** IUSTITIA. - ET. CONCORDIA * ANNO. 1617 **Note:** Dav.#6430.

Date	Mintage	VG	F	VF	XF	Unc
1617 H-L	—	85.00	175	325	525	—

KM# 9.3 THALER

Silver **Obv. Legend:** CHRISTIAN **Rev:** Arms divide half moon- * **Note:** Dav.#6431.

Date	Mintage	VG	F	VF	XF	Unc
1617 (k)	—	75.00	155	290	450	—

KM# 8 THALER

Silver **Note:** Friendship Thaler. Dav. #6429.

Date	Mintage	VG	F	VF	XF	Unc
1617 HL	—	525	900	1,500	2,450	—

KM# 9.4 THALER

Silver **Obv:** Large rosette at top **Rev:** Legend begins at 9 o'clock, divided at top **Note:** Dav. #6432.

Date	Mintage	VG	F	VF	XF	Unc
1618 (k)	—	115	230	500	825	—

KM# 9.6 THALER

Silver **Obv:** Squatter bust, more ornate collar **Note:** Dav. #6435.

Date	Mintage	VG	F	VF	XF	Unc
1619 (k)	—	75.00	150	265	425	—

KM# 17.1 THALER

Silver **Obv:** St. Andrew standing with cross in border of lilies **Rev:** Tri-helmeted arms, date at 8 o'clock **Note:** Dav. #6476.

Date	Mintage	VG	F	VF	XF	Unc
1619	—	140	290	550	975	—
1620	—	140	290	550	975	—
1621	—	140	290	550	975	—
1622	—	140	290	550	975	—

KM# 17.3 THALER

Silver **Rev:** Legend unbroken by shield at bottom **Note:** Dav. #6477.

Date	Mintage	VG	F	VF	XF	Unc
1619 (k)	—	155	325	625	1,100	—
1622 (k)	—	155	325	625	1,100	—

KM# 9.5 THALER

Silver **Obv:** Different bust, large collar **Note:** Dav. #A6433.

Date	Mintage	VG	F	VF	XF	Unc
1619 HGM	—	85.00	175	325	525	—

KM# 9.7 THALER

Silver **Obv:** Changed armor with spiked edge on collar **Note:** Dav. #6436.

Date	Mintage	VG	F	VF	XF	Unc
1620 (k)	—	100	200	400	625	—
1621 (k)	—	100	200	400	625	—

KM# 29.1 THALER

Silver **Obv:** Bust right **Obv. Legend:** CHRISTIANUS ++ D: G: EL. EP. MIND: DUX. B. ET. L **Rev:** 5 helmets above arms, legend ending with orb **Note:** Dav. #6444.

Date	Mintage	VG	F	VF	XF	Unc
1620 H-S	—	75.00	150	265	400	—
1624 H-S	—	75.00	150	265	400	—

KM# 9.8 THALER

Silver **Obv:** Larger bust **Obv. Legend:** BRUN.ET.LU.H/S **Note:** Dav. #6437.

Date	Mintage	VG	F	VF	XF	Unc
1622 H-S	—	85.00	175	325	525	—

KM# 9.9 THALER

Silver **Obv. Legend:** BRU.ET.LU* **Note:** Dav. #6438.

Date	Mintage	VG	F	VF	XF	Unc
1622 (w)	—	85.00	175	325	525	—

KM# 9.10 THALER

Silver **Obv:** Half moon mint mark above bust, drapery with lined sleeves **Rev:** Ornament divides legend **Note:** Dav. #6439.

Date	Mintage	VG	F	VF	XF	Unc
1622 (k)	—	85.00	175	325	525	—

KM# 9.11 THALER
Silver **Obv:** Mint mark S **Obv. Legend:** BRUN ET LUN H **Rev. Legend:** IUSTITIA.-ET.CONCORDIA **Note:** Dav. #6440.

Date	Mintage	VG	F	VF	XF	Unc
16ZZ H-S	—	85.00	175	325	525	—
1623 H-S	—	85.00	175	325	525	—

KM# 17.2 THALER
Silver **Obv:** Without border of lilies **Note:** Dav. #6476A.

Date	Mintage	VG	F	VF	XF	Unc
1622	—	115	230	425	750	—

KM# 9.14 THALER
Silver **Ruler:** Christian **Obv:** Bust right **Rev. Legend:** IUSTITIA ET CO - NCORDIA (or CON - CORDIA) **Note:** Dav. #6441.

Date	Mintage	VG	F	VF	XF	Unc
16ZZ H-S	—	85.00	175	325	525	—
16Z3 H-S	—	85.00	175	325	525	—
16Z4 H-S	—	85.00	175	325	525	—

KM# 9.13 THALER
Silver **Note:** Similar to KM#9.14 but date at left bottom. Dav. #A6440.

Date	Mintage	VG	F	VF	XF	Unc
1622	—	85.00	175	325	525	—

KM# 9.15 THALER
Silver **Rev. Legend:** ET CO-NCORDIA **Note:** Dav. #6441A.

Date	Mintage	VG	F	VF	XF	Unc
1623	—	85.00	175	325	525	—

KM# 9.16 THALER
Silver **Obv:** Bust right in circle of stars **Note:** Dav. #6442.

Date	Mintage	VG	F	VF	XF	Unc
1623	—	85.00	175	325	525	—

KM# 9.12 THALER
Silver **Rev. Legend:** ETCON-CORDIA **Note:** Dav. #6440A.

Date	Mintage	VG	F	VF	XF	Unc
1623 H-S	—	85.00	175	325	525	—

KM# 17.4 THALER
Silver **Obv:** St. Andrew and cross breaking legend at top **Rev:** Arms breaking legend at bottom, date at top left **Note:** Dav. #6478.

Date	Mintage	VG	F	VF	XF	Unc
1623 H-P	—	100	190	350	575	—

KM# 17.5 THALER
Silver **Rev:** Date divided at top, arms divide H-P **Note:** Dav. #6479.

Date	Mintage	VG	F	VF	XF	Unc
1624 H-P	—	115	230	500	875	—

KM# 75.1 THALER
Silver **Obv:** Bust right, legend begins at 10 o'clock **Rev:** 9-fold arms with center shield, 3 helmets above, date divided at top **Note:** Dav. #6443.

Date	Mintage	VG	F	VF	XF	Unc
1624	—	75.00	150	270	425	—

KM# 29.2 THALER
Silver **Obv:** Orb **Obv. Legend:** CHRISTIANVS.D.G.. **Rev:** Arms divide VF-H **Note:** Dav. #6445.

Date	Mintage	VG	F	VF	XF	Unc
1624 VF-H	—	75.00	150	270	425	—

KM# 76.1 THALER
Silver **Obv:** Bust right **Rev:** Helmeted arms supported by 2 lions divide HV16-24E at bottom **Note:** Dav. #6446.

Date	Mintage	VG	F	VF	XF	Unc
1624 HV-E	—	75.00	150	270	425	—

KM# 76.2 THALER
Silver **Rev:** Date divided at top, HV-E below **Note:** Dav. #6447.

Date	Mintage	VG	F	VF	XF	Unc
1624 HV-E	—	75.00	150	270	425	—

KM# 75.2 THALER
Silver **Obv:** Bust right with different drapery, legend begins at top **Rev:** Date at left of plume which divides HV-E **Note:** Dav. #6448.

Date	Mintage	VG	F	VF	XF	Unc
1624 HV-E	—	75.00	150	270	425	—

KM# 75.3 THALER
Silver **Obv:** Different bust, legend begins at 10 o'clock **Rev:** Date left of plume, arms divide HV-E **Note:** Dav. #6449.

Date	Mintage	VG	F	VF	XF	Unc
1624 HV-E	—	75.00	150	270	425	—

KM# 75.4 THALER
Silver **Rev:** Arms divide HU-E **Note:** Dav. #6449A.

Date	Mintage	VG	F	VF	XF	Unc
1624 HU-E	—	75.00	150	270	425	—

KM# 75.5 THALER
Silver **Rev:** Plume above helmeted arms divide date **Note:** Dav. #6450.

Date	Mintage	VG	F	VF	XF	Unc
1624 HV-E	—	75.00	150	265	400	—

KM# 75.6 THALER
Silver **Obv. Legend:** ...DUX.BR.ET.LUN **Rev:** Arms divide L-B **Note:** Dav. #6452.

Date	Mintage	VG	F	VF	XF	Unc
1624 L-B	—	75.00	150	280	450	—

KM# 75.7 THALER
Silver **Obv. Legend:** ...DVX.B.ET.LVNE **Rev:** Arms divide date above and L-B below **Note:** Dav. #6453.

Date	Mintage	VG	F	VF	XF	Unc
1624 L-B	—	75.00	150	280	450	—

KM# 9.17 THALER
Silver **Obv:** Bust right without circle of stars **Rev:** Date divided at top by helmeted arms **Note:** Dav. #6456.

Date	Mintage	VG	F	VF	XF	Unc
1624	—	75.00	150	270	425	—

KM# 9.18 THALER
Silver **Rev:** Date in legend at upper left **Note:** Dav. #6457.

Date	Mintage	VG	F	VF	XF	Unc
1624 LB	—	85.00	165	300	500	—

KM# 29.4 THALER
Silver **Obv:** Small buttons on drapery **Obv. Legend:** MIND.DUX.B.ET.L **Note:** Dav. #6458.

Date	Mintage	VG	F	VF	XF	Unc
1624	—	75.00	150	270	425	—

KM# 76.3 THALER
Silver **Obv. Legend:** CHRISTIANUS **Rev:** Supported arms divide VF-H below **Note:** Dav. #6459.

Date	Mintage	VG	F	VF	XF	Unc
1624 VF-H	—	75.00	150	280	450	—

KM# 29.5 THALER

Silver **Obv. Legend:** ...BR.ET.LU **Rev:** Arms divide HH-O **Note:** Dav. #6460.

Date	Mintage	VG	F	VF	XF	Unc
1624 HH-O	—	75.00	150	280	450	—
1625 HH-O	—	75.00	150	280	450	—

KM# 29.3 THALER

Silver **Obv:** Large buttons on drapery **Obv. Legend:** MIN.DUX.B.E.L **Note:** Dav. #A6458.

Date	Mintage	VG	F	VF	XF	Unc
1624	—	75.00	150	280	450	—

KM# 29.9 THALER

Silver **Obv. Legend:** ...DUX.B.E.L **Rev:** Date above in helmets **Note:** Dav. #A6465.

Date	Mintage	VG	F	VF	XF	Unc
1625	—	75.00	150	280	450	—

KM# 29.6 THALER

Silver **Obv:** Orb, flowers at edge of collar **Obv. Legend:** ...DUX.:B:E:L **Rev:** Date divided below arms **Note:** Dav. #6461.

Date	Mintage	VG	F	VF	XF	Unc
1625	—	75.00	150	280	450	—

KM# 29.7 THALER

Silver **Obv:** H mm S below bust **Obv. Legend:** ...DUX:B.ET.L **Rev:** Date divided by arms within circle **Note:** Dav. #6464.

Date	Mintage	VG	F	VF	XF	Unc
1625 H-S	—	75.00	150	270	425	—

KM# 29.8 THALER

Silver **Obv:** Without mint mark **Note:** Dav. #6464A.

Date	Mintage	VG	F	VF	XF	Unc
1625	—	75.00	150	270	425	—

KM# 29.10 THALER

Silver **Obv. Legend:** ...DUX.B.ET.LU **Rev:** Date below **Note:** Dav. #6465.

Date	Mintage	VG	F	VF	XF	Unc
1625	—	75.00	150	270	425	—

KM# 9.19 THALER

Silver **Obv:** Orb above bust right, legend begins at right **Rev:** Date divided at top by arms **Note:** Dav. #6467.

Date	Mintage	VG	F	VF	XF	Unc
1625	—	75.00	150	280	450	—

KM# 29.11 THALER

Silver **Obv. Legend:** D:G:EL++H mm S++EP **Rev:** Date divided above arms **Note:** Dav. #6468.

Date	Mintage	VG	F	VF	XF	Unc
1626 H-S	—	100	200	425	750	—

KM# 29.12 THALER

Silver **Obv:** Different bust **Rev:** Date divided by curved arms at bottom **Note:** Dav. #6469.

Date	Mintage	VG	F	VF	XF	Unc
1626	—	100	200	425	750	—

KM# 29.13 THALER

Silver **Obv. Legend:** ...LU **Rev:** Arms divide date in straight line **Note:** Dav. #6470.

Date	Mintage	VG	F	VF	XF	Unc
1626	—	100	200	425	750	—

KM# 29.14 THALER

Silver **Obv:** Different bust **Obv. Legend:** CHRISTIANUS. D: G: EL. H mm S EP. MIND. DUX. B. ET .LU **Rev:** Helmeted oval arms, date divided at top **Rev. Legend:** JUSTITIA. ET. - CONCORDIA **Note:** Dav. #6471. Legend varieties exist.

Date	Mintage	VG	F	VF	XF	Unc
1627 H-S	—	85.00	165	300	500	—
1628 H-S	—	85.00	165	300	500	—
1629 H-S	—	85.00	165	300	500	—

KM# 29.15 THALER

Silver **Rev. Legend:** ET.CO.-.NCORDIA **Note:** Dav. #6471A.

Date	Mintage	VG	F	VF	XF	Unc
1627	—	90.00	175	325	525	—

KM# A90 THALER

Silver **Subject:** Death of Wilhelm V's Son, Johann **Obv:** 10-fold arms in ornamented shield **Rev:** 8-line inscription with dates, mintmaster's initials, symbol below **Note:** Dav. #6656.

Date	Mintage	VG	F	VF	XF	Unc
16Z8 HS	—	900	1,800	3,000	—	—

KM# 29.16 THALER

Silver **Obv. Legend:** MIND.DUX.B.ET.L **Rev:** Square topped arms **Note:** Dav. #6473.

Date	Mintage	VG	F	VF	XF	Unc
1629	—	75.00	150	265	400	—

KM# 90 THALER

Silver **Note:** Varieties exist. Dav. #6475.

Date	Mintage	VG	F	VF	XF	Unc
1629 H-S	—	75.00	150	275	450	—
1630 H-S	—	75.00	150	275	450	—
1631 H-S	—	75.00	150	275	450	—
1632 H-S	—	75.00	150	290	550	—
1633 H-S	—	75.00	150	290	550	—

KM# 100 THALER

Silver **Note:** Similar to KM#17, but 5-helmeted 9-fold arms. Dav. #6480.

Date	Mintage	VG	F	VF	XF	Unc
1631 H-S	—	90.00	180	350	625	2,000
1632 H-S	—	90.00	180	350	625	2,000
1633 H-S	—	90.00	180	350	625	2,000

KM# A107 THALER

Silver **Subject:** Death of Wilhelm V's Son, Magnus **Obv:** 10-fold arms in ornamented shield, titles of Magnus **Rev:** Ornament above 6-line inscription with dates, mintmaster's initials, symbol below **Note:** Dav. #6657.

Date	Mintage	VG	F	VF	XF	Unc
1632 HS	—	550	1,100	2,000	4,800	—

KM# 107 THALER

Silver **Subject:** Death of Christian **Note:** Dav. #6482.

Date	Mintage	VG	F	VF	XF	Unc
1633 HS	—	180	300	750	—	—

KM# 115 THALER

Silver **Ruler:** August I **Obv:** Bust of August right in inner circle **Rev:** Helmeted arms **Note:** Prev. Ratzeburg, Dav. #5732. Varieties exist.

Date	Mintage	VG	F	VF	XF	Unc
1634	—	125	255	425	750	—
1635	—	125	255	425	750	—
1636	—	125	255	425	750	—

KM# 116 THALER

Silver **Ruler:** August I **Obv:** Facing bust **Rev:** Date in legend **Note:** Prev. Ratzeburg, Dav. #5733.

Date	Mintage	VG	F	VF	XF	Unc
1634 Rare	—	—	—	—	—	—

Note: Fritz Rudolf Künker Münzenhandlung Auction 95, 9-04, VF-XF realized approximately $9840.

KM# A117 THALER

Silver **Ruler:** August I **Rev:** Legend, date **Rev. Legend:** PATRIIS - UIRTUTIBUS - H/S **Note:** Prev. Ratzeburg, Dav. #5734.

Date	Mintage	VG	F	VF	XF	Unc
1634 Rare	—	—	—	—	—	—

KM# B117 THALER

Silver **Ruler:** August I **Rev:** Legend, date **Rev. Legend:** VIRTUTIBUS - ANNO. DO: **Note:** Prev. Ratzeburg, Dav. #5735.

Date	Mintage	VG	F	VF	XF	Unc
1634 Rare	—	—	—	—	—	—

Note: Fritz Rudolf Künker Münzenhandlung Auction 86, 9-03, XF realized approximately $9180.

KM# A132 THALER

Silver **Ruler:** August I **Obv:** Helmeted arms **Rev:** Wildman **Note:** Prev. Ratzeburg, Dav. #5736.

Date	Mintage	VG	F	VF	XF	Unc
1636	—	130	235	400	650	—

KM# 132 THALER

Silver **Ruler:** August I **Obv:** Legend broken by shield at bottom **Rev:** Wildman holding staff **Note:** Prev. Ratzeburg, Dav. #5736A.

Date	Mintage	VG	F	VF	XF	Unc
1636	—	85.00	155	260	525	—

KM# 133 THALER

Silver **Ruler:** August I **Obv:** Arms **Obv. Legend:** - RATC. DUX ... **Rev:** Wildman **Note:** Prev. Ratzeburg, Dav. #5737A.

Date	Mintage	VG	F	VF	XF	Unc
1636	—	100	165	270	600	—

KM# 135 THALER

Silver **Ruler:** August I **Subject:** Death of August **Obv:** Helmeted arms **Rev:** 9-line inscription **Note:** Prev. Ratzeburg, Dav. #5738. Varieties exist.

Date	Mintage	VG	F	VF	XF	Unc
1636	—	210	425	900	1,800	—

KM# A133 THALER

Silver **Ruler:** August I **Note:** Prev. Ratzeburg Dav. #5737. Similar to KM#132 but legend ...RACE. DUX ...

Date	Mintage	VG	F	VF	XF	Unc
1636	—	100	165	270	600	—

KM# 134.1 THALER

Silver **Subject:** Joint coinage of August I with Friedrich V and Georg of Calenberg **Obv:** Half-length figure of August 3/4 to right **Rev:** Half-length figures of Friedrich and Georg facing each other, date below **Note:** Dav. #6484.

Date	Mintage	VG	F	VF	XF	Unc
1636 HS	—	775	1,300	2,200	3,600	—

KM# 134.2 THALER

Silver **Obv:** Smaller busts **Obv. Legend:** FRIDERIC: ET. GEORG: DUCES. BRUNSVIC. ET. LUN **Note:** Dav. #6485.

Date	Mintage	VG	F	VF	XF	Unc
1636 HS	—	900	1,500	2,400	4,200	—

KM# 145.1 THALER

Silver **Obv:** Bust left breaks circle **Rev:** Helmeted 11-fold arms, date divided below **Note:** Dav. #6491.

Date	Mintage	VG	F	VF	XF	Unc
1637 HS	—	300	650	1,200	2,200	—

KM# 145.2 THALER

Silver **Obv:** Bust left within circle **Note:** Dav. #6491A.

Date	Mintage	VG	F	VF	XF	Unc
1637 HS	—	350	725	1,400	2,400	—

KM# 146.1 THALER

Silver **Obv:** Bust right in ornate circle, script legend **Obv. Legend:** FRIDERICH HERTZOG. ZU. BR. UND. LUNEB. THUMPROBST DES ERTZSTIF BREM. **Rev:** Helmeted arms, H mintmark S, dividing date below **Note:** Dav. #6492.

Date	Mintage	VG	F	VF	XF	Unc
1637 H-S	—	100	200	400	625	—
1638 H-S	—	100	200	400	625	—

KM# 146.2 THALER

Silver **Obv. Legend:** FRIDER(ICH) HERT(Z). ZU. B. U. L. COADI. DS STIF(T)RATZB. THUM(P). D. E(RTZST). B(R) (E) (M) (E). **Note:** Dav. #6494.

Date	Mintage	VG	F	VF	XF	Unc
1637 HS	—	75.00	150	275	450	—
1638 HS	—	75.00	150	275	450	—
1639 HS	—	75.00	150	275	450	—
1640 HS	—	75.00	150	275	450	—
1640 LW	—	75.00	150	275	450	—
1641 LW	—	75.00	150	275	450	—
1642 LW	—	75.00	150	275	450	—
1643 LW	—	75.00	150	275	450	—

KM# 155.1 THALER

Silver **Obv:** Friedrich V **Note:** Dav. #6488.

Date	Mintage	VG	F	VF	XF	Unc
1641 HS	—	115	225	425	800	—
1643 HS	—	115	225	425	800	—
1645 HS	—	115	225	425	800	—
1648 HS	—	115	225	425	800	—
1649 HS Error	—	115	225	425	800	—
ND HS	—	115	225	425	800	—

KM# 155.2 THALER

Silver **Obv:** Baton in right hand **Note:** Dav. #6489.

Date	Mintage	VG	F	VF	XF	Unc
ND(1651)	—	400	775	1,450	2,400	—

KM# 156 THALER

Silver **Obv:** Title:...HERTZOG... **Note:** Dav. #6490.

Date	Mintage	VG	F	VF	XF	Unc
ND(1651) HS	—	140	290	450	975	—

KM# 168 THALER

Silver **Subject:** Death of Friedrich's sister, Margarethe, Wife of Johann Casimir of Saxe-Coburg **Obv:** Helmeted 12-fold arms **Rev:** 12-line inscription with date **Note:** Dav. #6501.

Date	Mintage	VG	F	VF	XF	Unc
1643 LW	—	400	775	1,500	3,600	—

KM# 166 THALER

Silver **Obv:** Similar to KM#169.1 **Rev:** Similar to KM#169.1 but date at lower right **Note:** Dav. #6495.

Date	Mintage	VG	F	VF	XF	Unc
1643 LW	—	115	230	450	875	—

KM# 167 THALER

Silver **Note:** Varieties exist. Dav. #6487.

Date	Mintage	VG	F	VF	XF	Unc
1643 HS	—	145	290	550	925	—
1644 HS	—	145	290	550	925	—
1645 HS	—	145	290	550	925	—
ND HS	—	145	290	550	925	—
ND	—	145	290	550	925	—

KM# 169.1 THALER

Silver **Note:** Dav. #6497.

Date	Mintage	VG	F	VF	XF	Unc
1644 LW	—	85.00	175	400	625	—
1645 LW	—	85.00	175	400	625	—
1646 LW	—	85.00	175	400	625	—
1647 LW	—	85.00	175	400	625	—

KM# 170 THALER

Silver **Note:** Dav. #6486.

Date	Mintage	VG	F	VF	XF	Unc
1644 HS	—	115	230	425	800	—
ND	—	115	230	425	800	—

KM# 169.2 THALER

Silver **Rev:** Date horizontal or slanting right of arms **Note:** Dav. #6498.

Date	Mintage	VG	F	VF	XF	Unc
1647 LW	—	85.00	175	350	575	—
1648 LW	—	85.00	175	350	575	—

KM# 192 THALER

Silver **Subject:** Death of Friedrich V **Note:** Dav. #6500.

Date	Mintage	VG	F	VF	XF	Unc
1648 LW	—	240	475	900	1,500	—

KM# 209 THALER
Silver **Obv:** KM#208 **Rev:** Similar to KM#210, but date divided by wildman **Note:** Mule.

Date	Mintage	VG	F	VF	XF	Unc
1648/49 HS Rare	—	—	—	—	—	—

KM# 211 THALER
Silver **Obv:** Helmeted arms **Obv. Legend:** CHRISTIAN: LUDOVI: CUS D.G. DUX BR: ET LUNEBERG **Rev:** Rearing horse left **Rev. Legend:** SINCERE ET CONSTANTOR ANNO **Note:** Dav. #6521.

Date	Mintage	VG	F	VF	XF	Unc
1649 LW	—	85.00	175	325	500	—
1650 LW	—	85.00	175	325	500	—
1651 LW	—	85.00	175	325	500	—
1652 LW	—	85.00	175	325	500	—
1653 LW	—	85.00	175	325	500	—
1654 LW	—	85.00	175	325	500	—
1655 LW	—	85.00	175	325	500	—
1656 LW	—	85.00	175	325	500	—
1657 LW	—	85.00	175	325	500	—
1658 LW	—	85.00	175	325	500	—
1659 LW	—	85.00	175	325	500	—
1660 LW	—	85.00	175	325	500	—
1661 LW	—	85.00	175	325	500	—
1662 LW	—	85.00	175	325	500	—
1663 LW	—	85.00	175	325	500	—
1664 LW	—	85.00	175	325	500	—
1665 LW	—	85.00	175	325	500	—

KM# 208 THALER
Silver **Obv:** 3/4-length bust right **Rev:** Helmeted 12-fold arms, date in legend **Note:** Dav. #6514.

Date	Mintage	VG	F	VF	XF	Unc
1649 HS	—	190	350	625	1,100	—

KM# 229 THALER
Silver **Subject:** Death of Sybilla, Second Wife of Julius Ernst zu Dannenberg **Obv:** Helmeted 12-fold arms **Rev:** 9-line inscription with date **Note:** Dav. #6523.

Date	Mintage	VG	F	VF	XF	Unc
1652 LW Rare	—	—	—	—	—	—

KM# 237 THALER
Silver **Rev:** Tree in left hand **Note:** Dav. #6518.

Date	Mintage	VG	F	VF	XF	Unc
1654 HS	—	85.00	175	325	550	—
1655 HS	—	85.00	175	325	550	—
1658 HS	—	85.00	175	325	550	—
1659 HS	—	85.00	175	325	550	—
1660 HS	—	85.00	175	325	550	—
1661 HS	—	85.00	175	325	550	—
1662 HS	—	85.00	175	325	550	—
1665 HS	—	85.00	175	325	550	—

KM# 238 THALER
Silver **Rev:** Tree in both hands **Note:** Dav. #6517A.

Date	Mintage	VG	F	VF	XF	Unc
1655 HS	—	85.00	175	325	550	—

KM# 241 THALER
Silver **Obv:** Helmeted 12-fold arms **Rev:** Wildman, PIETATE..., date in legend (die of Georg Wilhelm) **Note:** Mule. Dav. #6522.

Date	Mintage	VG	F	VF	XF	Unc
1657 HS	—	85.00	175	325	550	—
1662 HS	—	85.00	175	325	550	—

KM# 247 THALER
Silver **Subject:** Death of Christian Ludwig's Aunt Clara **Obv:** Horse leaping left in laurel wreath **Rev:** 9-line inscription with date **Note:** Dav. #6524.

Date	Mintage	VG	F	VF	XF	Unc
1658 LW	—	600	1,200	2,400	3,900	—

KM# 210 THALER
Silver **Note:** Dav. #6519.

Date	Mintage	VG	F	VF	XF	Unc
1663 HS	—	75.00	150	290	425	—
1664 HS	—	75.00	150	290	425	—
1665 HS	—	75.00	150	290	425	—

KM# 268 THALER
Silver **Subject:** Death of Christian Ludwig **Note:** Dav. #6525.

Date	Mintage	VG	F	VF	XF	Unc
1665 LW	—	180	425	900	2,000	—
1665 HS	—	180	425	900	2,000	—

KM# 285 THALER
Silver **Obv:** Bust left **Rev:** Horse leaping left, date in legend **Note:** Dav. #6537.

Date	Mintage	VG	F	VF	XF	Unc
1673 RD Rare	—	—	—	—	—	—

KM# 286 THALER
Silver **Obv:** Horse leaping left **Rev:** Helmeted 12-fold arms, date in legend **Note:** Dav. #6538.

Date	Mintage	VG	F	VF	XF	Unc
1673 RD Rare	—	—	—	—	—	—
1674 RD Rare	—	—	—	—	—	—

KM# 287 THALER
Silver **Obv:** Bust left

Date	Mintage	VG	F	VF	XF	Unc
1673 RD Rare	—	—	—	—	—	—

KM# 302 THALER
Silver **Subject:** 100th Anniversary of the University of Helmstedt **Obv:** Samson wrestling lion in cartouche **Note:** Dav. #6543.

Date	Mintage	VG	F	VF	XF	Unc
1676	—	450	900	1,800	3,000	—

KM# 332 THALER
Silver **Obv:** Bust right **Rev:** Horse leaping left in circle broken by ground below which divides date **Note:** Dav. #6539.

Date	Mintage	VG	F	VF	XF	Unc
1690 JJJ Rare	—	—	—	—	—	—

KM# 342 THALER
Silver **Obv:** Helmeted 12-fold arms **Rev:** Horse leaping left, date below **Note:** Dav. #6540.

Date	Mintage	VG	F	VF	XF	Unc
1691	—	500	1,000	2,000	3,400	—
1691 iii	—	500	1,000	2,000	3,400	—

KM# 343 THALER
Silver **Obv:** Bust right **Rev:** Helmeted 12-fold arms, date in legend **Note:** Dav. #6541.

Date	Mintage	VG	F	VF	XF	Unc
1691 iii	—	550	925	1,900	3,400	—

KM# 249 1-1/2 THALER
43.1300 g., Silver, 59 mm. **Obv:** Triple-helmeted 8-fold arms with central shield **Rev:** Rider on rearing horse to right, without value **Note:** Illustration reduced. Dav. #LS125.

Date	Mintage	VG	F	VF	XF	Unc
ND(1622 W)	—	3,600	5,600	8,200	—	—

KM# 250 1-1/2 THALER
42.8000 g., Silver, 62 mm. **Obv:** Crowned CL monogram in laurel wreath surrounded by 14 small shields, date in legend, 1-1/2 punched in **Rev:** Horse leaping left above mining scene, head turned up towards wreath held by arms from clouds **Note:** Illustration reduced. Dav. #LS166.

Date	Mintage	VG	F	VF	XF	Unc
1659 L-W	—	725	1,200	2,050	3,600	—

KM# 251.1 1-1/2 THALER
Silver **Rev:** Horse looking ahead, wreath held in arm from clouds above head **Note:** Dav. #LS164.

Date	Mintage	VG	F	VF	XF	Unc
1659 L-W	—	425	725	1,200	1,900	—

KM# 251.2 1-1/2 THALER
Silver **Note:** Dav. #LS170.

Date	Mintage	VG	F	VF	XF	Unc
1661 L-W	—	425	725	1,200	1,900	—

KM# 251.3 1-1/2 THALER
Silver **Note:** Dav. #LS175. Illustration reduced.

Date	Mintage	VG	F	VF	XF	Unc
1662 L-W	—	425	725	1,200	1,900	—

KM# 251.4 1-1/2 THALER
Silver **Note:** Dav. #LS179.

Date	Mintage	VG	F	VF	XF	Unc
1663 L-W	—	425	725	1,200	1,900	—

KM# 251.5 1-1/2 THALER
Silver, 62 mm. **Note:** Illustration reduced. Dav. #LS190. Varieties exist.

Date	Mintage	VG	F	VF	XF	Unc
1664 L-W	—	425	725	1,200	1,900	—

KM# 303 1-1/2 THALER
Silver **Subject:** 100th Anniversary of the University of Helmstedt **Obv:** Samson wrestling lion in cartouche **Note:** Dav. #6542.

Date	Mintage	VG	F	VF	XF	Unc
1676 Rare	—	—	—	—	—	—

KM# 18 2 THALER
Silver **Note:** Similar to 1 Thaler, KM#9. Dav. #6533. Varieties exist.

Date	Mintage	VG	F	VF	XF	Unc
1619 HGM Rare	—	—	—	—	—	—
1624 H-S Rare	—	—	—	—	—	—
1625 Rare	—	—	—	—	—	—

KM# 77.1 2 THALER
Silver **Obv:** Bust right, H-S below **Obv. Legend:** CHRISTIANUS D: G. EL. EP MIND.-DUX. B. ET. L. **Rev:** Helmeted arms divide date above **Rev. Legend:** IUSTITIA ET CO.-.NCORDIA. ANNO. **Note:** Dav. #6554.

Date	Mintage	VG	F	VF	XF	Unc
1624 H-S Rare	—	—	—	—	—	—

KM# 77.2 2 THALER
Silver **Obv. Legend:** ...+D. G. EL. EP: M + DUX. B. EL. **Note:** Dav. #6555.

Date	Mintage	VG	F	VF	XF	Unc
1624 Rare	—	—	—	—	—	—

KM# 77.3 2 THALER
Silver **Obv. Legend:** ...D: G*H (mm). S*EL. EP. MIND. DUX. B. L. **Rev. Legend:** ...ET-CONCORDIA **Note:** Dav. #6562.

Date	Mintage	VG	F	VF	XF	Unc
1625 H-S Rare	—	—	—	—	—	—

KM# 77.4 2 THALER
Silver **Rev:** Arms divided date below **Note:** Dav. #6563.

Date	Mintage	VG	F	VF	XF	Unc
1625 H-S Rare	—	—	—	—	—	—

KM# 77.5 2 THALER
Silver **Obv. Legend:** Ends: DUX. B. E. L. **Rev:** Date divided at top by plume, shorter and wider shield **Note:** Dav. #6572.

Date	Mintage	VG	F	VF	XF	Unc
1629 H-S Rare	—	—	—	—	—	—

KM# 77.6 2 THALER
Silver **Rev:** Square-topped arms **Note:** Dav. #6573.

Date	Mintage	VG	F	VF	XF	Unc
1629 H-S Rare	—	—	—	—	—	—

KM# 101 2 THALER
Silver **Note:** Dav. #6574. Similar to 1 Thaler, KM#90.

Date	Mintage	VG	F	VF	XF	Unc
1631 HS Rare	—	—	—	—	—	—

KM# 108 2 THALER
Silver **Subject:** Death of Christian **Note:** Dav. #6581. Similar to 1 Thaler, KM#107.

Date	Mintage	VG	F	VF	XF	Unc
1633 HS Rare	—	—	—	—	—	—

KM# 109 2 THALER
65.5000 g., Silver **Obv:** Duke August on horse to right **Rev:** Fortune with sail in hands, battle scene in background without value **Note:** Dav. #LS127.

Date	Mintage	VG	F	VF	XF	Unc
ND +M+ Rare	—	—	—	—	—	—

KM# 137 2 THALER
Silver **Obv:** Half-length figure of August 3/4 right **Rev:** Half-length figures of Friedrich and Georg facing each other, date below **Note:** Joint Coinage of August I with Friedrich V and Georg of Calenberg. Dav. #6483.

Date	Mintage	VG	F	VF	XF	Unc
1636 HS Rare	—	—	—	—	—	—

KM# 138 2 THALER
Silver **Ruler:** August I **Subject:** Death of August **Obv:** Helmeted arms **Rev:** 9-line inscription **Note:** Prev. Ratzeburg, Dav. #A5738.

Date	Mintage	VG	F	VF	XF	Unc
1636 Rare	—	—	—	—	—	—

KM# 157 2 THALER
Silver **Note:** Similar to 1 Thaler, KM#146. Dav. #6493.

Date	Mintage	VG	F	VF	XF	Unc
1641 LW Rare	—	—	—	—	—	—

KM# 174.1 2 THALER
Silver **Obv:** Different bust **Obv. Legend:** ...BR. U. LUN. P. C. D. S. R. E. D. P. D. E. B. **Rev:** Date slanted left of arms **Note:** Dav. #6496.

Date	Mintage	VG	F	VF	XF	Unc
1646 LW	—	1,000	1,750	2,900	4,600	—

KM# 193 2 THALER
Silver **Subject:** Death of Friedrich V **Note:** Similar to 1 Thaler, KM#192. Dav. #6499.

Date	Mintage	VG	F	VF	XF	Unc
1648 LW Rare	—	—	—	—	—	—

KM# 174.2 2 THALER
Silver **Obv. Legend:** ...BR: LUNBURG. **Rev:** Date slanted left of arms **Note:** Dav. #A6498.

Date	Mintage	VG	F	VF	XF	Unc
1648 LW	—	1,000	1,750	2,900	4,600	—

KM# 221 2 THALER
Silver **Note:** Similar to 1 Thaler, KM#211. Dav. #6520.

Date	Mintage	VG	F	VF	XF	Unc
1650 LW Rare	—	—	—	—	—	—

KM# 242.1 2 THALER
Silver **Obv:** Crowned CL monogram in laurel wreath surrounded by 14 small shields, date in legend, 2 punched in **Rev:** Horse leaping left above mining scene, head turned up towards wreath held by arm from clouds **Note:** Dav. #LS162. Illustration reduced.

Date	Mintage	VG	F	VF	XF	Unc
1657 LW	—	600	1,000	1,600	2,600	—

KM# 242.2 2 THALER

Silver **Note:** Dav. #LS165. Illustration reduced.

Date	Mintage	VG	F	VF	XF	Unc
1659 LW	—	600	1,000	1,600	2,600	—

KM# 252.1 2 THALER

Silver **Note:** Similar to 1-1/2 Thaler, KM#251 but 2 punched in. Dav. #LS163. Illustration reduced.

Date	Mintage	VG	F	VF	XF	Unc
1659 LW	—	600	1,000	1,600	2,600	—

KM# 252.2 2 THALER

Silver **Note:** Dav. #LS169.

Date	Mintage	VG	F	VF	XF	Unc
1661 LW	—	600	1,000	1,600	2,600	—

KM# 252.3 2 THALER

Silver **Note:** Dav. #LS174. Illustration reduced.

Date	Mintage	VG	F	VF	XF	Unc
1662 LW	—	600	1,000	1,600	2,600	—

KM# 252.4 2 THALER

Silver **Note:** Dav. #LS178.

Date	Mintage	VG	F	VF	XF	Unc
1663 LW	—	600	1,000	1,600	2,600	—

KM# 252.5 2 THALER

Silver, 64 mm. **Ruler:** Christian Ludwig **Note:** Dav. #LS189. Illustration reduced.

Date	Mintage	VG	F	VF	XF	Unc
1664 LW	—	600	1,000	1,600	2,600	—

KM# 194 2-1/2 THALER

78.0000 g., Silver **Ruler:** Christian Ludwig **Obv:** Duke on rearing horse right **Rev:** Helmeted 12-fold arms, date in legend **Note:** Dav. #LS147A.

Date	Mintage	VG	F	VF	XF	Unc
1648 HS Rare	—	—	—	—	—	—

KM# 80 3 THALER

Silver **Obv:** 3/4-length figure 3/4 to right, helmet on table at right **Rev:** Helmeted and supported 9-fold arms with central shield, Roman numeral date in legend, 3 punched in **Note:** Dav. #LS119.

Date	Mintage	VG	F	VF	XF	Unc
1625 HB Rare	—	—	—	—	—	—

KM# 91 3 THALER

Silver **Rev:** Arabic date divided at top **Note:** Dav. #LS123.

Date	Mintage	VG	F	VF	XF	Unc
1629 HL-HS Rare	—	—	—	—	—	—

KM# 111 3 THALER

87.6500 g., Silver, 65 mm. **Obv:** Duke August on horse to right **Rev:** Fortune with sail in hands, battle scene in background, without value **Note:** Illustration reduced. Dav. #LS126.

Date	Mintage	VG	F	VF	XF	Unc
ND +M+	—	1,600	2,700	4,200	6,000	—

KM# 110 3 THALER

85.0000 g., Silver **Subject:** Death of Christian **Note:** Similar to 1 Thaler, KM#107.

Date	Mintage	VG	F	VF	XF	Unc
1633 HS Rare	—	—	—	—	—	—

KM# 151 3 THALER

86.6000 g., Silver, 81 mm. **Rev:** 3 punched in **Note:** Illustration reduced. Dav. #LS131.

Date	Mintage	VG	F	VF	XF	Unc
1639 HS	—	1,850	3,100	5,100	7,100	—

KM# 177 3 THALER

Silver, 80 mm. **Obv:** Bust right in wreath surrounded by 14 small shields **Rev:** Mining scene, date in legend, 3 punched in **Note:** Illustration reduced. Dav. #LS135.

Date	Mintage	VG	F	VF	XF	Unc
1647 LW	—	1,550	2,900	4,700	6,600	—

KM# 178 3 THALER

Silver **Obv:** Inscription instead of wreath around bust **Note:** Dav. #LS-A135.

Date	Mintage	VG	F	VF	XF	Unc
1647 HR-LW Rare	—	—	—	—	—	—

KM# 195 3 THALER

Silver, 71 mm. **Ruler:** Christian Ludwig **Rev:** 84 g or 3 punched in **Note:** Illustration reduced. Dav. #LS146.

Date	Mintage	VG	F	VF	XF	Unc
1648 HS	—	1,100	2,000	3,550	6,200	—

KM# 222.1 3 THALER

Silver **Obv:** Similar to 1-1/2 Thaler, KM#251 but ca. 85 g or 3 punched in **Note:** Dav. #LS150.

Date	Mintage	VG	F	VF	XF	Unc
1650 LW	—	1,100	2,000	3,550	6,200	—

KM# 230 3 THALER

Silver **Note:** Dav. #LS156.

Date	Mintage	VG	F	VF	XF	Unc
1654 LW	—	775	1,400	2,600	4,300	—

KM# 222.2 3 THALER

Silver **Note:** Dav. #LS159.

Date	Mintage	VG	F	VF	XF	Unc
1657 LW	—	1,100	2,000	3,550	6,200	—

KM# 243 3 THALER

Silver, 72 mm. **Note:** Illustration reduced. Dav. #LS161.

Date	Mintage	VG	F	VF	XF	Unc
1657 LW	—	700	1,300	2,350	3,900	—

KM# 222.3 3 THALER

Silver **Note:** Dav. #LS173.

Date	Mintage	VG	F	VF	XF	Unc
1662 LW	—	1,100	2,000	3,550	6,200	—

KM# 222.4 3 THALER

Silver **Note:** Dav. #LS177.

Date	Mintage	VG	F	VF	XF	Unc
1663 LW	—	1,100	2,000	3,550	6,200	—

KM# 256.1 3 THALER
Silver, 80 mm. **Obv:** 3 punched in at bottom **Note:** Illustration reduced. Dav. #LS181.

Date	Mintage	VG	F	VF	XF	Unc
1663 HS Rare	—	—	—	—	—	—

KM# 222.5 3 THALER
Silver **Note:** Dav. #LS188.

Date	Mintage	VG	F	VF	XF	Unc
1664 LW	—	1,100	2,000	3,550	6,200	—

KM# 256.2 3 THALER
Silver **Note:** Dav. #LS192. Illustration reduced.

Date	Mintage	VG	F	VF	XF	Unc
1665 HS	—	3,100	5,500	8,600	12,000	—

KM# 196 3-1/2 THALER
Silver **Obv:** Duke on rearing horse right **Rev:** Helmeted 12-fold arms, date in legend **Note:** Dav. #LS146b. Approximate weight: 99.00 grams.

Date	Mintage	VG	F	VF	XF	Unc
1648 HS Rare	—	—	—	—	—	—

KM# 81 4 THALER
116.0000 g., Silver **Obv:** 3/4-length figure 3/4 to right, helmet on table at right **Rev:** Helmeted and supproted 9-fold arms with central shield, roman numeral date in legend, without value **Note:** Dav. #LS118.

Date	Mintage	VG	F	VF	XF	Unc
1625 NZ	—	4,700	7,100	10,000	15,000	—

KM# 93 4 THALER
116.0000 g., Silver **Rev:** Arabic date divided at top **Note:** Dav. #LS122.

Date	Mintage	VG	F	VF	XF	Unc
1629 HL-HS Rare	—	—	—	—	—	—

KM# 147 4 THALER
116.0000 g., Silver **Obv:** Facing bust, inscription, date in tablet below, two legends **Rev:** Brunswick helmet surrounded by 14 small shields **Note:** Dav. #LS128.

Date	Mintage	VG	F	VF	XF	Unc
1637 HS	—	—	—	—	—	—

KM# 152 4 THALER
116.0000 g., Silver **Ruler:** Friedrich V **Note:** Similar to 3 Thaler, KM#151 but 4 punched in. Dav. #LS130. Illustration reduced.

Date	Mintage	VG	F	VF	XF	Unc
1639 HS	—	2,750	4,300	6,200	—	—

KM# 179 4 THALER
116.0000 g., Silver, 86 mm. **Note:** Illustration reduced. Dav. #LS134.

Date	Mintage	VG	F	VF	XF	Unc
1647 LW Rare	—	—	—	—	—	—

KM# 180 4 THALER
115.4000 g., Silver, 80 mm. **Obv:** Inscription instead of wreath around bust **Rev:** 4 punched in **Note:** Illustration reduced. Dav. #LS134a.

Date	Mintage	VG	F	VF	XF	Unc
1647 HR-LW	—	—	—	—	—	—

Note: Spink Taisei Zurich Milas sale 4-92 XF realized $12,730

KM# 197 4 THALER
114.9000 g., Silver, 70 mm. **Ruler:** Christian Ludwig **Note:** Similar to 3 Thaler, KM#195. Dav. #LS145. Illustration reduced.

Date	Mintage	VG	F	VF	XF	Unc
1648 HS	—	2,350	3,900	5,900	—	—

KM# 223.1 4 THALER
Silver, 79 mm. **Ruler:** Christian Ludwig **Obv:** Ca. 115 g or 4 punched in **Note:** Similar to 1-1/2 Thaler, KM#251. Dav. #LS149.

Date	Mintage	VG	F	VF	XF	Unc
1650 LW	—	2,300	3,850	5,900	8,500	—

KM# 231 4 THALER
115.3000 g., Silver, 72 mm. **Note:** Illustration reduced. Dav. #LS155.

Date	Mintage	VG	F	VF	XF	Unc
1654 LW	—	1,550	2,650	4,150	—	—

KM# 223.2 4 THALER

Silver **Note:** Dav. #LS158. Illustration reduced.

Date	Mintage	VG	F	VF	XF	Unc
1657 LW	—	2,100	3,550	5,500	7,800	—

KM# 244 4 THALER

115.3000 g., Silver **Rev:** Horse leaping left above mining scene, head turned up towards wreath held by arm from clouds **Note:** Dav. #LS160. Illustration reduced.

Date	Mintage	VG	F	VF	XF	Unc
1657 LW	—	1,850	3,100	5,100	—	—

KM# 223.3 4 THALER

Silver **Note:** Dav. #LS172.

Date	Mintage	VG	F	VF	XF	Unc
1662 LW	—	2,100	3,550	5,500	7,800	—

KM# 223.4 4 THALER

Silver **Note:** Dav. #LS176.

Date	Mintage	VG	F	VF	XF	Unc
1663 LW	—	2,100	3,550	5,500	7,800	—

KM# 257.1 4 THALER

115.1000 g., Silver, 75 mm. **Obv:** 4 punched in at bottom **Rev:** Wildman, tree in right hand, mining scene, in background, date in legend **Note:** Dav. #LS180.

Date	Mintage	VG	F	VF	XF	Unc
1663 HS	—	4,700	7,400	10,500	—	—

KM# 223.5 4 THALER

Silver **Note:** Dav. #LS187. Illustration reduced.

Date	Mintage	VG	F	VF	XF	Unc
1664 LW	—	2,100	3,550	5,500	7,800	—

KM# 257.2 4 THALER

Silver **Rev:** Periods separate legend **Note:** Dav. #LS191.

Date	Mintage	VG	F	VF	XF	Unc
1665 HS	—	4,700	7,400	11,500	—	—

KM# 82 5 THALER

150.0000 g., Silver **Obv:** 3/4-length figure 3/4 to right, helmet on table at right **Rev:** Helmeted and supported 9-fold arms with central shield, Roman numeral date in legend, without value **Note:** Dav. #LS117.

Date	Mintage	VG	F	VF	XF	Unc
1625 NZ Rare	—	—	—	—	—	—

KM# 94 5 THALER

Silver **Rev:** Arabic date divided at top, 5 punched in **Note:** Dav. #LS121.

Date	Mintage	VG	F	VF	XF	Unc
1629 HL-HS Rare	—	—	—	—	—	—

KM# 26.1 5 THALER

Silver **Obv:** Duke **Obv. Legend:** ...GEORG HERTZOG ZU... **Rev:** Helmeted and supported arms **Note:** Dav. #LS141.

Date	Mintage	VG	F	VF	XF	Unc
1638	—	2,800	4,700	7,800	11,500	—

KM# 26.2 5 THALER

Silver **Obv. Legend:** GEORG HIERTZOG ZU... **Note:** Dav. #LS141a. Illustration reduced.

Date	Mintage	VG	F	VF	XF	Unc
1638	—	2,800	4,700	7,800	11,500	—

KM# 153 5 THALER
Silver **Ruler:** Friedrich V **Obv:** Facing bust in baroque frame **Rev:** Helmeted 12-fold arms, date divided at top, 5 punched in **Note:** Dav. #LS129. Illustration reduced.

Date	Mintage	VG	F	VF	XF	Unc
1639 HS	—	5,100	7,800	12,000	15,500	—

KM# 182 5 THALER
Silver **Obv:** Inscription instead of wreath around bust **Note:** Dav. #LS133a.

Date	Mintage	VG	F	VF	XF	Unc
1647 HR-LW Rare	—	—	—	—	—	—

KM# 181 5 THALER
Silver **Rev:** 5 punched in **Note:** Similar to 4 Thaler, KM#179. Dav. #LS133. Illustration reduced.

Date	Mintage	VG	F	VF	XF	Unc
1647 LW	—	4,300	6,600	9,900	13,000	—

KM# 198 5 THALER
144.7000 g., Silver **Obv:** Duke on rearing horse right **Rev:** Helmeted 12-fold arms, date in legend **Note:** Dav. #LS144.

Date	Mintage	VG	F	VF	XF	Unc
1648 HS	—	3,900	650	9,600	—	—

KM# 224.1 5 THALER
Silver **Obv:** 5 punched in **Note:** Similar to 1-1/2 Thaler, KM#251. Dav. #LS148. Illustration reduced.

Date	Mintage	VG	F	VF	XF	Unc
1650 LW	—	3,550	5,900	9,000	12,000	—

KM# 232 5 THALER
Silver **Rev:** Horse above city view of Celle **Note:** Similar to 4 Thaler, KM#231. Dav. #LS186.

Date	Mintage	VG	F	VF	XF	Unc
1654 LW Rare	—	—	—	—	—	—

KM# 245 5 THALER
144.0000 g., Silver **Note:** Similar to 3 Thaler, KM#243. Dav. #LS-A160.

Date	Mintage	VG	F	VF	XF	Unc
1657 LW Rare	—	—	—	—	—	—

KM# 224.2 5 THALER
Silver **Note:** Dav. #LS157.

Date	Mintage	VG	F	VF	XF	Unc
1657 LW	—	3,550	5,900	9,000	12,000	—

KM# 224.3 5 THALER
Silver **Note:** Dav. #LS171.

Date	Mintage	VG	F	VF	XF	Unc
1662 LW	—	3,550	5,900	9,000	12,000	—

KM# 224.4 5 THALER
Silver **Note:** Dav. #LS186.

Date	Mintage	VG	F	VF	XF	Unc
1664 LW	—	3,550	5,900	9,000	12,000	—

KM# 83 6 THALER
174.0000 g., Silver **Obv:** 3/4-length figure 3/4 to right, helmet on table at right **Rev:** Helmeted and supported 9-fold arms with central shield, Roman numeral date in legend, without value **Note:** Dav. #LS116. Illustration reduced.

Date	Mintage	VG	F	VF	XF	Unc
1625 NZ Rare	—	—	—	—	—	—

KM# 183 6 THALER
Silver **Obv:** Bust right in inscription surrounded by 14 small shields **Rev:** Mining scene, date in legend; 6 punched in **Note:** Dav. #LS-A133.

Date	Mintage	VG	F	VF	XF	Unc
1647 HR-LW Rare	—	—	—	—	—	—

KM# 199 6 THALER
Silver **Obv:** Duke on rearing horse right **Rev:** Helmeted 12-fold arms, date in legend **Note:** Dav. #LS143.

Date	Mintage	VG	F	VF	XF	Unc
1648 HS Rare	—	—	—	—	—	—

KM# 233.1 6 THALER
Silver **Obv:** Crowned CL monogram in laurel wreath surrounded by 14 small shields, date in legend, 6 punched in **Rev:** Horse leaping left above city view of Celle, head turned up towards wreath held by arm from clouds **Note:** Dav. #LS153.

Date	Mintage	VG	F	VF	XF	Unc
1654 LW Rare	—	—	—	—	—	—

KM# 233.2 6 THALER
Silver **Note:** Dav. #LS168.

Date	Mintage	VG	F	VF	XF	Unc
1660 LW Rare	—	—	—	—	—	—

KM# 259 6 THALER
Silver **Note:** Similar to 1-1/2 Thaler, KM#251. Dav. #LS185. Illustration reduced.

Date	Mintage	VG	F	VF	XF	Unc
1664 LW	—	5,500	7,800	11,000	15,000	—

KM# 234 8 THALER
Silver **Obv:** Crowned CL monogram in laurel wreath surrounded by 14 small shields, date in legend, 8 punched in **Rev:** Horse leaping left above city view of Celle, head turned up towards wreath held by arms from clouds **Note:** Dav. #LS152. Illustration reduced.

Date	Mintage	VG	F	VF	XF	Unc
1654 LW Rare	—	—	—	—	—	—

Note: Spink Taisei Zurich Milas sale 4-92 XF realized $14,750

KM# 260 8 THALER
Silver **Rev:** Horse looking ahead, wreath held in arm from clouds above head **Note:** Dav. #LS184.

Date	Mintage	VG	F	VF	XF	Unc
1664 LW Rare	—	—	—	—	—	—

KM# 76 10 THALER
289.2000 g., Silver, 75 mm. **Note:** Illustration reduced. Dav. #LS-A116.

Date	Mintage	VG	F	VF	XF	Unc
1625 NZ Rare	—	—	—	—	—	—

Note: Spink Taisei Zurich Milas sale 4-92 VF realized $26,800

KM# 184 10 THALER
Silver **Obv:** Bust right in wreath surrounded by 14 small shields **Rev:** Mining scene, date in legend, 10 punched in **Note:** Dav. #LS132.

Date	Mintage	VG	F	VF	XF	Unc
1647 LW Rare	—	—	—	—	—	—

KM# 225 10 THALER
Silver **Obv:** Crowned CL monogram in laurel wreath surrounded by 14 small shields, date in legend, 10 punched in **Rev:** Horse leaping left above mining scene, head turned up towards wreath held by arm from clouds **Note:** Dav. #LS147.

Date	Mintage	VG	F	VF	XF	Unc
1650 LW Rare	—	—	—	—	—	—

KM# 235.1 10 THALER
Silver **Rev:** Horse above city view of Celle **Note:** Dav. #LS151.

Date	Mintage	VG	F	VF	XF	Unc
1654 LW Rare	—	—	—	—	—	—

KM# 235.2 10 THALER
Silver **Note:** Dav. #LS167.

Date	Mintage	VG	F	VF	XF	Unc
1660 LW Rare	—	—	—	—	—	—

KM# 261 10 THALER
Silver **Note:** Similar to 1-1/2 Thaler, KM#251. Dav. #LS183. Illustration reduced.

Date	Mintage	VG	F	VF	XF	Unc
1664 LW Rare	—	—	—	—	—	—

Note: Spink Taisei Zurich Milas sale 4-92 XF realized $28,810

KM# 262 12 THALER
Silver **Obv:** Crowned CL monogram in laurel wreath surrounded by 14 small shields, date in legend, 12 punched in **Rev:** Horse leaping left above mining scene, head turned up towards wreath held by arm from clouds **Note:** Dav. #LS182.

Date	Mintage	VG	F	VF	XF	Unc
1664 LW Rare	—	—	—	—	—	—

TRADE COINAGE

KM# 48 GOLDGULDEN
3.5000 g., 0.9860 Gold 0.1109 oz. AGW **Obv:** Bust of Christian right in inner circle **Rev:** Crowned arms in inner circle, date at top

Date	Mintage	VG	F	VF	XF	Unc
1621	—	575	1,400	2,750	4,600	—
1624	—	575	1,400	2,750	4,600	—
1628	—	575	1,400	2,750	4,600	—
1630	—	575	1,400	2,750	4,600	—
1631	—	575	1,400	2,750	4,600	—
1633	—	575	1,400	2,750	4,600	—

KM# 78 GOLDGULDEN
3.5000 g., 0.9860 Gold 0.1109 oz. AGW **Subject:** Gold from St. Andreas Mine **Obv:** St. Andrew standing **Rev:** Crowned arms in inner circle

Date	Mintage	VG	F	VF	XF	Unc
1624	—	800	1,750	3,450	6,900	—
1629	—	800	1,750	3,450	6,900	—

KM# 333 1/4 DUCAT
0.8750 g., 0.9860 Gold 0.0277 oz. AGW **Obv:** Georg Wilhelm

Date	Mintage	VG	F	VF	XF	Unc
1690	—	115	230	575	1,400	—

KM# 312 1/2 DUCAT
1.7500 g., 0.9860 Gold 0.0555 oz. AGW **Obv:** Helmeted 12-fold arms, date **Rev:** Horse leaping left, sun above

Date	Mintage	VG	F	VF	XF	Unc
1685 RD	—	260	425	700	1,650	—

KM# 313 1/2 DUCAT
1.7500 g., 0.9860 Gold 0.0555 oz. AGW **Obv:** Bust of George Wilhelm right **Rev:** Rearing horse, date in exergue

Date	Mintage	VG	F	VF	XF	Unc
1685	—	260	425	750	1,750	—
1690	—	260	425	750	1,750	—

KM# 314 1/2 DUCAT
1.7500 g., 0.9860 Gold 0.0555 oz. AGW **Obv:** Crowned arms in order collar

Date	Mintage	VG	F	VF	XF	Unc
1685	—	260	400	650	1,550	—
1688	—	260	400	650	1,550	—
1690	—	260	400	650	1,550	—

KM# 334 1/2 DUCAT
1.7500 g., 0.9860 Gold 0.0555 oz. AGW **Obv:** Bust right

Date	Mintage	VG	F	VF	XF	Unc
1690	—	300	500	775	1,900	—

KM# 49 DUCAT
3.5000 g., 0.9860 Gold 0.1109 oz. AGW **Obv:** Bust right **Rev:** Helmeted 8-fold arms with central shield

Date	Mintage	VG	F	VF	XF	Unc
1621 GM	—	575	1,050	2,050	4,050	—

KM# 50 DUCAT
3.5000 g., 0.9860 Gold 0.1109 oz. AGW **Obv:** Bust right, date in legend **Rev:** Crowned 8-fold arms with central shield

Date	Mintage	VG	F	VF	XF	Unc
(16)21 GM	—	575	1,050	2,050	4,050	—

KM# 87 DUCAT
3.5000 g., 0.9860 Gold 0.1109 oz. AGW **Rev:** 9-fold arms

Date	Mintage	VG	F	VF	XF	Unc
1628 HS	—	600	1,100	2,150	4,200	—
1629 HS	—	600	1,100	2,150	4,200	—

KM# 95 DUCAT
3.5000 g., 0.9860 Gold 0.1109 oz. AGW **Obv:** Crowned 7-fold arms with central shield **Rev:** St. Andrew with cross

Date	Mintage	VG	F	VF	XF	Unc
1629 HP	—	575	1,050	2,050	4,050	—
ND HP	—	575	1,050	2,050	4,050	—

KM# 99 DUCAT
3.5000 g., 0.9860 Gold 0.1109 oz. AGW **Rev:** Date in legend

Date	Mintage	VG	F	VF	XF	Unc
1630 HS	—	575	1,050	2,050	4,050	—
1632 HS	—	575	1,050	2,050	4,050	—
1633 HS	—	575	1,050	2,050	4,050	—

KM# 117 DUCAT
3.5000 g., 0.9860 Gold 0.1109 oz. AGW **Obv:** Bust right **Rev:** Crowned 8-fold arms with central shield of Ratzeburg

Date	Mintage	VG	F	VF	XF	Unc
1634 HS	—	1,000	1,850	3,600	7,000	—

KM# 139 DUCAT
3.5000 g., 0.9860 Gold 0.1109 oz. AGW **Obv:** Standing figure of Friedrich right in inner circle **Rev:** Crowned arms in inner circle

Date	Mintage	VG	F	VF	XF	Unc
1636	—	450	925	1,950	3,800	—
1638	—	450	925	1,950	3,800	—
1639	—	450	925	1,950	3,800	—
1641	—	450	925	1,950	3,800	—
1644	—	450	925	1,950	3,800	—
1647	—	450	925	1,950	3,800	—
1648	—	450	925	1,950	3,800	—
ND	—	450	925	1,950	3,800	—

KM# 150 DUCAT
3.5000 g., 0.9860 Gold 0.1109 oz. AGW **Obv:** Standing figure of duke, head turned right **Rev:** Crowned oval 11-fold arms, date above crown

Date	Mintage	VG	F	VF	XF	Unc
1638 HS	—	575	1,050	2,050	4,050	—
1641 LW	—	575	1,050	2,050	4,050	—

KM# 158 DUCAT
3.5000 g., 0.9860 Gold 0.1109 oz. AGW **Obv:** Duke's head turned to left

Date	Mintage	VG	F	VF	XF	Unc
1642 LW	—	575	1,050	2,050	4,050	—

KM# 159 DUCAT
3.5000 g., 0.9860 Gold 0.1109 oz. AGW **Obv:** Duke turned half right

Date	Mintage	VG	F	VF	XF	Unc
ND LW	—	575	1,050	2,050	4,050	—

KM# 160 DUCAT
3.5000 g., 0.9860 Gold 0.1109 oz. AGW **Rev:** 12-fold arms

Date	Mintage	VG	F	VF	XF	Unc
ND	—	575	1,050	2,050	4,050	—

KM# 185 DUCAT
3.5000 g., 0.9860 Gold 0.1109 oz. AGW **Obv:** Armored bust of Friedrich right in inner circle **Rev:** Crowned arms in inner circle

Date	Mintage	VG	F	VF	XF	Unc
1647	—	450	925	1,950	3,800	—
1648	—	450	925	1,950	3,800	—
ND	—	450	925	1,950	3,800	—

KM# 200 DUCAT
3.5000 g., 0.9860 Gold 0.1109 oz. AGW **Obv:** Bust right **Rev:** Crowned 12-fold arms divide date 1-6/4-8

Date	Mintage	VG	F	VF	XF	Unc
1648 LW	—	450	925	1,950	3,800	—

KM# 226 DUCAT
3.5000 g., 0.9860 Gold 0.1109 oz. AGW

Date	Mintage	VG	F	VF	XF	Unc
1650	—	400	750	1,750	3,550	—
1661	—	400	750	1,750	3,550	—

KM# 227 DUCAT

3.5000 g., 0.9860 Gold 0.1109 oz. AGW **Obv:** Crowned 12-fold arms **Rev:** Horse leaping left in wreath, date in legend

Date	Mintage	VG	F	VF	XF	Unc
1650 LW	—	400	750	1,750	3,550	—
1661 LW	—	400	750	1,750	3,550	—

KM# 263 DUCAT

3.5000 g., 0.9860 Gold 0.1109 oz. AGW **Obv:** Bust of Georg Wilhelm right **Rev:** Crowned arms in inner circle

Date	Mintage	VG	F	VF	XF	Unc
1664	—	800	1,500	2,750	5,100	—
1675	—	800	1,500	2,750	5,100	—

KM# 294 DUCAT

3.5000 g., 0.9860 Gold 0.1109 oz. AGW **Obv:** Bust right **Rev:** Crowned 12-fold arms, date in legend

Date	Mintage	VG	F	VF	XF	Unc
1675 RD	—	800	1,500	2,750	5,100	—

KM# 310 DUCAT

3.5000 g., 0.9860 Gold 0.1109 oz. AGW **Obv:** Helmeted 12-fold arms, date **Rev:** Horse leaping left, sun above

Date	Mintage	VG	F	VF	XF	Unc
1684	—	175	325	750	2,000	—
1685 RD	—	175	325	750	2,000	—
ND III	—	175	325	750	2,000	—

KM# 311 DUCAT

3.5000 g., 0.9860 Gold 0.1109 oz. AGW **Obv:** Crowned arms in garter

Date	Mintage	VG	F	VF	XF	Unc
1684	—	175	325	750	2,000	—
1687	—	175	325	750	2,000	—
1689	—	175	325	750	2,000	—
1691	—	175	325	750	2,000	—
1694	—	175	325	750	2,000	—
1697	—	175	325	750	2,000	—
ND	—	175	325	750	2,000	—

KM# 315 DUCAT

3.5000 g., 0.9860 Gold 0.1109 oz. AGW **Rev:** Rearing horse, date in exergue

Date	Mintage	VG	F	VF	XF	Unc
1685	—	350	575	1,300	2,700	—
1690	—	350	575	1,300	2,700	—

KM# 325 DUCAT

3.5000 g., 0.9860 Gold 0.1109 oz. AGW **Rev:** Date added

Date	Mintage	VG	F	VF	XF	Unc
1688 JJJ	—	350	575	1,300	2,700	—

KM# 335 DUCAT

3.5000 g., 0.9860 Gold 0.1109 oz. AGW **Obv:** Bust right

Date	Mintage	VG	F	VF	XF	Unc
1690 JJJ	—	—	—	—	—	—

Note: Reported, not confirmed

KM# 350 DUCAT

3.5000 g., 0.9860 Gold 0.1109 oz. AGW **Obv:** Helmeted 12-fold arms in Order of the Garter **Rev:** Horse leaping left

Date	Mintage	VG	F	VF	XF	Unc
1693	—	230	375	875	2,150	—
1697	—	230	375	875	2,150	—

KM# 295 2 DUCAT

7.0000 g., 0.9860 Gold 0.2219 oz. AGW **Obv:** Bust right **Rev:** Crowned 12-fold arms, date in legend

Date	Mintage	VG	F	VF	XF	Unc
1675 RD	—	950	2,400	5,000	9,000	—

KM# 296 2 DUCAT

7.0000 g., 0.9860 Gold 0.2219 oz. AGW **Obv:** Horse leaping left **Rev:** Crowned 12-fold arms

Date	Mintage	VG	F	VF	XF	Unc
1675 RD	—	950	2,400	5,000	9,000	—

KM# 297 2 DUCAT

7.0000 g., 0.9860 Gold 0.2219 oz. AGW **Obv:** Bust of Georg Wilhelm right **Rev:** Crowned arms

Date	Mintage	VG	F	VF	XF	Unc
1675	—	950	2,400	5,000	9,000	—
1699	—	950	2,400	5,000	9,000	—

KM# 298 2 DUCAT

7.0000 g., 0.9860 Gold 0.2219 oz. AGW

Date	Mintage	VG	F	VF	XF	Unc
1675	—	950	2,400	5,000	9,000	—
1699	—	950	2,400	5,000	9,000	—
1700	—	950	2,400	5,000	9,000	—

KM# 316 2 DUCAT

7.0000 g., 0.9860 Gold 0.2219 oz. AGW **Obv:** Bust right **Rev:** Horse leaping left, sun above

Date	Mintage	VG	F	VF	XF	Unc
1685 RD	—	1,200	2,700	5,900	9,800	—
1688 RD	—	1,200	2,700	5,900	9,800	—

KM# 317 2 DUCAT

7.0000 g., 0.9860 Gold 0.2219 oz. AGW **Obv:** Bust of George Wilhelm right

Date	Mintage	VG	F	VF	XF	Unc
1685	—	1,200	2,700	5,900	9,800	—
1688	—	1,200	2,700	5,900	9,800	—
1690	—	1,200	2,700	5,900	9,800	—
1699	—	1,200	2,700	5,900	9,800	—

KM# 357 2 DUCAT

7.0000 g., 0.9860 Gold 0.2219 oz. AGW **Rev:** Horse leaping left

Date	Mintage	VG	F	VF	XF	Unc
1699 III	—	1,600	3,800	8,200	11,000	—

KM# 358 2 DUCAT

7.0000 g., 0.9860 Gold 0.2219 oz. AGW **Obv:** Crowned 12-fold arms in Order of the Garter

Date	Mintage	VG	F	VF	XF	Unc
1699 III	—	1,200	2,700	5,900	9,800	—
1700 III	—	1,200	2,700	5,900	9,800	—

KM# 305 4 DUCAT

14.0000 g., 0.9860 Gold 0.4438 oz. AGW **Obv:** Bust right **Rev:** Horse leaping left

Date	Mintage	VG	F	VF	XF	Unc
1681 Rare	—	—	—	—	—	—
1688 JJJ Rare	—	—	—	—	—	—

KM# 306 4 DUCAT

14.0000 g., 0.9860 Gold 0.4438 oz. AGW **Obv:** Crowned arms **Rev:** Rearing horse, date in exergue

Date	Mintage	VG	F	VF	XF	Unc
1681 Rare	—	—	—	—	—	—

KM# 326 4 DUCAT

14.0000 g., 0.9860 Gold 0.4438 oz. AGW **Obv:** Bust of Georg Wilhelm right

Date	Mintage	VG	F	VF	XF	Unc
1688 Rare	—	—	—	—	—	—

PATTERNS

Including off metal strikes

KM#	Date	Mintage	Identification	Mkt Val
Pn1	ND	—	2 Pfennig. Gold. II/GVD/PEN.	—
Pn2	1690	—	1/2 Ducat. Silver. KM#334	400
Pn3	1690 JJ	—	Ducat. Silver. KM#335	475

BRUNSWICK-WOLFENBUTTEL

(Braunschweig-Wolfenbüttel)

Located in north-central Germany. Wolfenbüttel was annexed to Brunswick in 1257. One of the five surviving sons of Albrecht II founded the first line in Wolfenbüttel in 1318. A further division in Wolfenbüttel and Lüneburg was undertaken in 1373. Another division occurred in 1495, but the Wolfenbüttel duchy survived in the younger line. Heinrich IX was forced out of his territory during the religious wars of the mid-sixteenth century by Duke Johann Friedrich I of Saxony and Landgrave Philipp of Hessen in 1542, but was restored to his possessions in 1547. Duke Friedrich Ulrich was forced to cede the Grubenhagen lands, which had been acquired by Wolfenbüttel in 1596, to Lüneburg in 1617. When the succession died out in 1634, the lands and titles fell to the cadet line in Dannenberg. The line became extinct once again and passed to Brunswick-Bevern in 1735 from which a new succession of Wolfenbüttel dukes descended. The ducal family was beset by continual personal and political tragedy during the nineteenth century. Two of the dukes were killed in battles with Napoleon, the territories were occupied by the French and became part of the Kingdom of Westphalia, another duke was forced out by a revolt in 1823. From 1884 until 1913, Brunswick-Wolfenbüttel was governed by Prussia and then turned over to a younger prince of Brunswick who married a daughter of Kaiser Wilhelm II. His reign was short, however, as he was forced to abdicate at the end of World War I.

RULERS

Heinrich VIII der Ältere, 1495-1514
Heinrich IX der Jüngere, 1514-1568
Julius, 1568-1589

...Note: For joint issues of Heinrich IX with Erich II von Calenberg, 1551-1556, see under Brunswick-Calenberg.

Heinrich Julius, 1589-1613
Friedrich Ulrich, 1613-1634
August II, 1634-1666
Rudolf August, 1666-1704
Anton Ulrich, as joint ruler, 1685-1704
alone, 1704-1714

MINT OFFICIALS' INITIALS

Andreasberg Mint

Initial	Date	Name
(d)	1594-1611	Heinrich Depsern, mintmaster
HP	1623-1629	Heinrich Pechstein, mintmaster

Brunswick Mint

Initial	Date	Name
GB/B	1675-1684	Johann Georg Breuer, mintmaster
HCH	1689-1729	Heinrich Christoph Hille, mintmaster

Catlenburg Mint

Initial	Date	Name
VF (ligature), sometimes with H	1623-1624	Urban Felgenhauer

Clausthal Mint

Initial	Date	Name
HS (often with ingot hook	1622-1640	Henning Schreiber
HB	1675-1711	Heinrich Bonhorst

Goslar Mint

Initial	Date	Name
	1543-47	Gregor Ainkhüren, mintmaster
(aa)=	Before 1550	Unknown
(bb)=	1551-55	Unknown
(cc)=	1556-57, 1561	Unknown
(dd)=	1557-58	Unknown
(ee)= ‡	1558-62, 65-70	Hans Küne
(ff)= Stag leaping left	1559	Unknown
	1563	Lazarus Erkel, mintmaster
(gg)=	1563-64	Samuel Salwar
(hh)= ‡	1570-96, 97-99	Andreas Küne
(ii)= or	1596-97	Commission
(d)=	1599-1612	Heinrich Depsern
(o)= or or	1613-1618	Heinrich Oeckeler
(c)	1619-1625	Hans Laffers
HL	1622-1625	Henning Loehr
(k)= S	?-1625	Hermann Schlanbusch
HS (sometimes with crossed keys)	1626-1672	Henning Schlüter
IPE	1672	Julius Philipp Eisendrath
RB	1685-1704	Rudolf Bornemann

Hannover Mint

Initial	Date	Name
RB	1673-1676	Rudolf Bornemann

BRUNSWICK-WOLFENBUTTEL

(Braunschweig-Wolfenbüttel)

Located in north-central Germany. Wolfenbüttel was annexed to Brunswick in 1257. One of the five surviving sons of Albrecht II founded the first line in Wolfenbüttel in 1318. A further division in Wolfenbüttel and Lüneburg was undertaken in 1373. Another division occurred in 1495, but the Wolfenbüttel duchy survived in the younger line. Heinrich IX was forced out of his territory during the religious wars of the mid-sixteenth century by Duke Johann Friedrich I of Saxony and Landgrave Philipp of Hessen in 1542, but was restored to his possessions in 1547. Duke Friedrich Ulrich was forced to cede the Grubenhagen lands, which had been acquired by Wolfenbüttel in 1596, to Lüneburg in 1617. When the succession died out in 1634, the lands and titles fell to the cadet line in Dannenberg. The line became extinct once again and passed to Brunswick-Bevern in 1735 from which a new succession of Wolfenbüttel dukes descended. The ducal family was beset by continual personal and political tragedy during the nineteenth century. Two of the dukes were killed in battles with Napoleon, the territories were occupied by the French and became part of the Kingdom of Westphalia, another duke was forced out by a revolt in 1823. From 1884 until 1913, Brunswick-Wolfenbüttel was governed by Prussia and then turned over to a younger prince of Brunswick who married a daughter of Kaiser Wilhelm II. His reign was short, however, as he was forced to abdicate at the end of World War I.

RULERS

Heinrich VIII der Ältere, 1495-1514
Heinrich IX der Jüngere, 1514-1568
Julius, 1568-1589
...Note: For joint issues of Heinrich IX with Erich II von Calenberg, 1551-1556, see under Brunswick-Calenberg.
Heinrich Julius, 1589-1613
Friedrich Ulrich, 1613-1634
August II, 1634-1666
Rudolf August, 1666-1704
Anton Ulrich, as joint ruler, 1685-1704
alone, 1704-1714

MINT OFFICIALS' INITIALS

Andreasberg Mint

Initial	Date	Name
(d)	1594-1611	Heinrich Depsern, mintmaster
HP	1623-1629	Heinrich Pechstein, mintmaster

Brunswick Mint

Initial	Date	Name
GB/B	1675-1684	Johann Georg Breuer, mintmaster
HCH	1689-1729	Heinrich Christoph Hille, mintmaster

Catlenburg Mint

Initial	Date	Name
VF (ligature), sometimes with H	1623-1624	Urban Felgenhauer

Clausthal Mint

Initial	Date	Name
HS (often with ingot hook	1622-1640	Henning Schreiber
HB	1675-1711	Heinrich Bonhorst

Goslar Mint

Initial	Date	Name
	1543-47	Gregor Ainkhüren, mintmaster
(aa)=	Before 1550	Unknown
(bb)=	1551-55	Unknown
(cc)=	1556-57, 1561	Unknown
(dd)=	1557-58	Unknown
(ee)= ‡	1558-62, 65-70	Hans Küne
(ff)= Stag leaping left	1559	Unknown
	1563	Lazarus Erkel, mintmaster
(gg)=	1563-64	Samuel Salwar
(hh)= ‡	1570-96, 97-99	Andreas Küne
(ii)=	1596-97	Commission

Initial	Date	Name
(d)=	1599-1612	Heinrich Depsern
(o)= or or	1613-1618	Heinrich Oeckeler
(c)	1619-1625	Hans Laffers
HL	1622-1625	Henning Loehr
(k)= HS	?-1625	Hermann Schlanbusch
HS (sometimes with crossed keys)	1626-1672	Henning Schlüter
IPE	1672	Julius Philipp Eisendrath
RB	1685-1704	Rudolf Bornemann

Hannover Mint

Initial	Date	Name
RB	1673-1676	Rudolf Bornemann

Heinrichsstadt Mint

Initial	Date	Name
	1574-85	Heinrich Veeber (Veever), mintmaster

Helmstedt Mint

Initial	Date	Name
	1510-1512	Bartold Lücken, mintmaster

Lauterberg Mint

Initial	Date	Name
HS	1621-1624	Henning Schreiber

Moritzburg Mint

Initial	Date	Name
CH/ch	1622-1625	Lazarus Christian Hopfgarten

Osterode Mint

Initial	Date	Name
	1619-1622	Henning Schreiber
HL	1622-1625	Henning Loehr

Riechenberg Mint

Initial	Date	Name
(jj)=	1531-32	Valentin von Stoghem, mintmaster
(kk)=	1534-35	Beghart Utz, mintmaster
(ll)= or	1535-40	Hans Khöne, mintmaster
(mm)=	1539-40, 42	Vacant
(nn)= stag rampant left holding ingot hook and	1540	Unknown
(oo)=	1540-43	Andreas Blankenhagen, mintmaster
(pp)=	1545	Unknown
(qq)=	1547-48	Johann Dankwerts, mintmaster
(rr)= stag rampant left holding ingot hook	1548-51	Martin Huxter, mintmaster

Wolfenbüttel Mint

Initial	Date	Name
(ss)=	1587-89	Dietrich Ockeler, mintmaster
ICB/ICP	1693-1697	Johann Christoph Bähr
DF	1697	Damian Fritsch

Zellerfeld Mint

Initial	Date	Name
(o)=	1601-1618	Heinrich Oeckeler
(c)=	1619-1625	Hans Laffers
HL	1622-1625	Henniing Loehr
HS (sometimes with crossed keys	1626-1672	Henning Schlüter
RB	1676-1711	Rudolf Bornemann
***	1698-1715	Used in place of mintmasters' initials

MISCELLANEOUS MINT OFFICIALS' INITIALS

Initial	Date	Name
(a) = acorn	ca.1620	Unknown
(b) = or	ca.1620	possibly Henning Schreiber
LB	ca.1620	Lewin Brockmann
WQ	ca.1620	Unknown
HH	1620-1621	Hardeg Hardegen in Weende bei Göttingen
CV	ca.1621	Unknown
HLM	ca.1621	Unknown
IB	ca.1621	Unknown
ID	ca.1621	Unknown
IL	ca.1621	Unknown
CL	ca.1622	Unknown
GL	ca.1622	Unknown
PHM	1650-1718	Philipp Heinrich Müller), goldsmith, die-cutter, medailleur In Nürnberg and Augsburg
GFN	1682-1724	Georg Friedrich Nürnberger, die-cutter and mintmaster In Nürnberg

DUCHY

REGULAR COINAGE

KM# 64 PFENNIG

Copper **Ruler:** Frederich Ulrich **Note:** Similar to KM#130.

Date	Mintage	VG	F	VF	XF	Unc
1617	—	17.00	35.00	75.00	150	—

KM# 130 PFENNIG

Copper **Ruler:** Frederich Ulrich **Obv:** Brunswick helmet with horse **Rev:** Value, date in 4 lines **Note:** Kipper Pfennig.

Date	Mintage	VG	F	VF	XF	Unc
1620	—	12.00	35.00	75.00	150	—
1621	—	16.00	33.00	65.00	140	—

KM# 230 PFENNIG

Copper **Ruler:** Frederich Ulrich **Obv:** Lion rampant left

Date	Mintage	VG	F	VF	XF	Unc
1621	—	15.00	30.00	60.00	120	—

KM# 231 PFENNIG

Copper **Ruler:** Frederich Ulrich **Obv:** Lion in shield **Rev:** 3 helmets

Date	Mintage	VG	F	VF	XF	Unc
ND	—	15.00	30.00	60.00	120	—

KM# 405 PFENNIG

Silver **Ruler:** August II **Note:** Uniface. **Obv.:** Crowned FV monogram divides date.

Date	Mintage	VG	F	VF	XF	Unc
(16)39	—	15.00	30.00	60.00	—	—

KM# 432 PFENNIG

Silver **Ruler:** August II **Note:** Crowned A, date.

Date	Mintage	VG	F	VF	XF	Unc
1647	—	12.00	25.00	50.00	100	—
1657	—	12.00	25.00	50.00	100	—
1661	—	12.00	25.00	50.00	100	—
1664 (s)	—	12.00	25.00	50.00	100	—
1666 (s)	—	12.00	25.00	50.00	100	—
1667 (s) (error)	—	12.00	25.00	50.00	100	—

KM# 466 PFENNIG

Silver **Ruler:** August II **Subject:** 83rd Birthday of August II **Note:** Crowned A, 10 APRIL _ 1661.

Date	Mintage	VG	F	VF	XF	Unc
1661	—	—	—	—	—	—

KM# 496 PFENNIG

Silver **Ruler:** Rudolf August **Note:** Uniface.Guter-Pfennig. Crowned cursive RA monogram, date.

Date	Mintage	VG	F	VF	XF	Unc
1667 (s)	—	12.00	25.00	50.00	100	—
1668 (s)	—	12.00	25.00	50.00	100	—
1669 (s)	—	12.00	25.00	50.00	100	—
1672 IPE	—	12.00	25.00	50.00	100	—
1675 IPE	—	12.00	25.00	50.00	100	—

Date	Mintage	VG	F	VF	XF	Unc
1676 IPE	—	12.00	25.00	50.00	100	—
1677 RB	—	12.00	25.00	50.00	100	—
1679 RB	—	12.00	25.00	50.00	100	—
1680 RB	—	12.00	25.00	50.00	100	—
1681 RB	—	12.00	25.00	50.00	100	—
1682 RB	—	12.00	25.00	50.00	100	—
1684 RB	—	12.00	25.00	50.00	100	—

KM# 556 PFENNIG

Silver **Ruler:** Rudolf August **Note:** Guter-Pfennig. Intertwined cursive RAV monogram, date.

Date	Mintage	VG	F	VF	XF	Unc
1685 RB	—	12.00	25.00	50.00	100	—
1686 RB	—	12.00	25.00	50.00	100	—
1688 RB	—	12.00	25.00	50.00	100	—
1693 RB	—	12.00	25.00	50.00	100	—

KM# 545 1-1/2 PFENNIGE

Silver **Ruler:** Rudolf August **Obv:** Crowned RA monogram **Rev:** Value, date

Date	Mintage	VG	F	VF	XF	Unc
1680	—	15.00	30.00	60.00	125	165

KM# 65 2 PFENNIGE

Copper **Ruler:** Frederich Ulrich **Obv:** Brunswick helmet with horse **Rev:** Value, date in 4 lines

Date	Mintage	VG	F	VF	XF	Unc
1617	—	35.00	75.00	150	300	—

KM# 131 2 PFENNIGE

Copper **Ruler:** Frederich Ulrich **Note:** Similar to KM#65.

Date	Mintage	VG	F	VF	XF	Unc
1620	—	35.00	75.00	150	300	—

KM# 232 2 PFENNIGE

Copper **Ruler:** Frederich Ulrich **Obv:** Lion rampant right **Rev:** Value, date in 4 lines **Note:** Kipper.

Date	Mintage	VG	F	VF	XF	Unc
1621	—	20.00	40.00	85.00	175	—

KM# 133 3 PFENNIG

Copper **Ruler:** Frederich Ulrich **Rev:** Value date in 4 lines

Date	Mintage	VG	F	VF	XF	Unc
1620	—	15.00	35.00	75.00	150	—
1621	—	15.00	35.00	75.00	150	—

KM# 233 3 PFENNIG

Copper **Ruler:** Frederich Ulrich **Obv:** Arms divided horizontally, lion rampant left above, 3 bars below **Rev:** Imperial orb with 3 **Rev. Legend:** MAT D G

Date	Mintage	VG	F	VF	XF	Unc
ND	—	25.00	50.00	100	210	—

KM# 234 3 PFENNIG

Copper **Ruler:** Frederich Ulrich **Rev:** Orb divides date

Date	Mintage	VG	F	VF	XF	Unc
1621	—	25.00	60.00	100	210	—

KM# 235 3 PFENNIG

Copper **Ruler:** Frederich Ulrich **Obv:** Lion walking left **Rev:** Imperial orb with 3

Date	Mintage	VG	F	VF	XF	Unc
ND	—	25.00	50.00	100	210	—

KM# 236 3 PFENNIG

Copper **Ruler:** Frederich Ulrich **Obv:** Lion rampant right **Rev:** Value III. . ., date in 4 lines

Date	Mintage	VG	F	VF	XF	Unc
1621	—	25.00	50.00	100	210	—

KM# 237 3 PFENNIG

Copper **Ruler:** Frederich Ulrich **Obv:** Crowned 'R' between two stars **Rev:** Value 'III' in circle, date in legend **Rev. Legend:** PFENNIGE (date) **Note:** Issued for Regenstein.

Date	Mintage	VG	F	VF	XF	Unc
1621	—	25.00	50.00	100	210	—

KM# 238 3 PFENNIG

Silver **Ruler:** Frederich Ulrich **Obv:** Arms with lion leaping left over 2 sheaves **Rev:** Imperial orb with 3 divides date **Note:** Kipper-3 Pfennig.

Date	Mintage	VG	F	VF	XF	Unc
1621	—	25.00	50.00	100	210	—

KM# 333 3 PFENNIG

Silver **Ruler:** Frederich Ulrich **Note:** Uniface. Crowned FV monogram divides 3 to left, mintmasters initials to right.

Date	Mintage	VG	F	VF	XF	Unc
ND ch	—	—	—	—	—	—

KM# 330 3 PFENNIG

Silver **Ruler:** Frederich Ulrich **Obv:** Lion rampant right **Rev:** Imperial orb with 3 divides date

Date	Mintage	VG	F	VF	XF	Unc
1622	—	25.00	50.00	100	210	—

KM# 331 3 PFENNIG

Silver **Ruler:** Frederich Ulrich **Obv:** Lion rampant right **Rev:** Imperial orbe with 3

Date	Mintage	VG	F	VF	XF	Unc
1622	—	25.00	50.00	100	210	—

KM# 332 3 PFENNIG

Silver **Ruler:** Frederich Ulrich **Obv:** Brunswick helmet with horse

Date	Mintage	VG	F	VF	XF	Unc
1622	—	25.00	50.00	100	210	—
1622 CL	—	25.00	50.00	100	210	—
1622 G	—	25.00	50.00	100	210	—
16ZZ GL	—	25.00	50.00	100	210	—
1623 GL	—	25.00	50.00	100	210	—

KM# 132 3 PFENNIG

Copper **Ruler:** Frederich Ulrich **Obv:** Brunswick helmet with horse **Rev:** Brunswick helmet with horse **Rev. Legend:** PFENNING

Date	Mintage	VG	F	VF	XF	Unc
ND	—	13.00	27.00	50.00	100	—

KM# 458 3 PFENNIG

Silver **Ruler:** August II **Obv:** Crowned A **Rev:** Imperial orb with 3 divides mintmasters initials

Date	Mintage	VG	F	VF	XF	Unc
1659 (s)	—	20.00	40.00	85.00	170	—
1664 (s)	—	20.00	40.00	85.00	170	—

KM# 467 3 PFENNIG

Silver **Ruler:** August II **Subject:** 83rd Birthday of August II **Obv. Legend:** 10 APRIL - 1661

Date	Mintage	VG	F	VF	XF	Unc
1661 (s)	—	—	—	—	—	—

KM# 517 3 PFENNIG

Silver **Ruler:** Rudolf August **Obv:** Crowned RA monogram **Rev:** Imperial orb with 3

Date	Mintage	VG	F	VF	XF	Unc
1675 IPE	—	20.00	40.00	85.00	170	—
1677 RB	—	20.00	40.00	85.00	170	—
1678 RB	—	20.00	40.00	85.00	170	—
1682 RB	—	20.00	40.00	85.00	170	—

KM# 547 3 PFENNIG

Silver **Ruler:** Rudolf August **Obv:** Crowned RA **Obv. Legend:** F. B. LU. L. MUN.

Date	Mintage	VG	F	VF	XF	Unc
1684	—	35.00	75.00	150	300	—

KM# 557 3 PFENNIG

Silver **Ruler:** Rudolf August **Obv:** Crowned intertwined cursive RAV **Rev:** Imperial orb with 3 divides date

Date	Mintage	VG	F	VF	XF	Unc
1685 RB	—	15.00	35.00	75.00	150	—
1692 HCH	—	15.00	35.00	75.00	150	—

KM# 596 3 PFENNIG

Silver **Ruler:** Rudolf August **Obv:** Date

Date	Mintage	VG	F	VF	XF	Unc
1692 HCH	—	15.00	35.00	75.00	150	—

KM# 603 3 PFENNIG

Silver **Ruler:** Rudolf August **Obv:** Horse leaping left **Rev:** Imperial orb with 3 divides date

Date	Mintage	VG	F	VF	XF	Unc
1693	—	15.00	35.00	75.00	150	—

KM# 66 4 PFENNIGE

Copper **Ruler:** Frederich Ulrich **Obv:** Brunswick helmet with horse **Rev:** Value, IIII, date in 4 lines

Date	Mintage	VG	F	VF	XF	Unc
1617	—	20.00	40.00	80.00	160	—

KM# 528 4 PFENNIGE

Silver, 19 mm. **Ruler:** Rudolf August **Obv:** RA monogram divides mintmaster' initials, crown above divides date **Rev:** 3-line inscription **Rev. Inscription:** 4 / GUTE / PF: **Mint:** Zellerfeld **Note:** Ref. W-1869.

Date	Mintage	VG	F	VF	XF	Unc
1677 RB	—	20.00	40.00	85.00	170	—
1679 RB	—	20.00	40.00	85.00	170	—
1681 RB	—	20.00	40.00	85.00	170	—
1684 RB	—	20.00	40.00	85.00	170	—
1685 RB	—	20.00	40.00	85.00	170	—

KM# 548 4 PFENNIGE

Silver **Ruler:** Rudolf August **Obv:** Crowned cursive RA monogram **Rev:** Value IIII. . ., date

Date	Mintage	VG	F	VF	XF	Unc
1684 B	—	20.00	40.00	85.00	170	—

KM# 558 4 PFENNIGE

Silver **Obv:** Crowned intertwined cursive RAV monogram, date in legend **Rev:** Value 4. . . in 3 lines **Note:** Gute.

Date	Mintage	VG	F	VF	XF	Unc
1685	—	20.00	40.00	85.00	170	—
1691	—	20.00	40.00	85.00	170	—
1692	—	20.00	40.00	85.00	170	—

KM# 588 4 PFENNIGE

Silver **Rev:** Value IIII...

Date	Mintage	VG	F	VF	XF	Unc
1691 RB	—	20.00	40.00	85.00	170	—
1694 RB	—	20.00	40.00	85.00	170	—

KM# 589 4-1/2 PFENNIG

Silver **Obv:** Crowned intertwined cursive RAV monogram, date in legend **Rev:** Value 4-1/2. . . in 3 lines **Note:** Gute-4 1/2 Pfennig.

Date	Mintage	VG	F	VF	XF	Unc
1691	—	35.00	75.00	150	300	—

KM# 597 5 PFENNIG

Silver **Obv:** Crowned intertwined cursive RAAV monogram **Rev:** Value V..., date in 4 lines

Date	Mintage	VG	F	VF	XF	Unc
1692 HCH	—	30.00	60.00	120	240	—

KM# 598 5 PFENNIG

Silver **Obv:** Monogram doubled with backwards: RAAVAA

Date	Mintage	VG	F	VF	XF	Unc
1692 HCH	—	30.00	60.00	120	240	—

KM# 599 5 PFENNIG

Silver **Obv:** Simple RAV monogram

Date	Mintage	VG	F	VF	XF	Unc
1692 HCH	—	30.00	60.00	120	240	—

KM# 549 6 PFENNIGE

Silver **Obv:** RA monogram **Rev:** Imperial orb with 6, date

Date	Mintage	VG	F	VF	XF	Unc
1684	—	25.00	50.00	100	200	—

KM# 590 6 PFENNIGE

Silver **Obv:** Crowned intertwined cursive RAV monogram **Rev:** Imperial orb with 6, divides date

Date	Mintage	VG	F	VF	XF	Unc
1691 HCH	—	16.00	35.00	75.00	155	—
1692 HCH	—	16.00	35.00	75.00	155	—

KM# 604 6 PFENNIGE

Silver **Obv:** Horse leaping left

Date	Mintage	VG	F	VF	XF	Unc
1693	—	15.00	30.00	60.00	120	—

KM# 240 FLITTER (2 Pfennig)

Copper **Obv:** Lion rampant left, + below **Rev:** Value in 4 lines

Date	Mintage	VG	F	VF	XF	Unc
ND	—	20.00	35.00	75.00	155	—

KM# 241 FLITTER (2 Pfennig)

Copper **Obv:** Lion walking left, +++ below **Rev:** Value in 3 lines

Date	Mintage	VG	F	VF	XF	Unc
ND	—	20.00	40.00	80.00	160	—

KM# 242 FLITTER (2 Pfennig)

Copper **Obv:** Brunswick helmet with horse **Rev:** Value, date in 4 lines

Date	Mintage	VG	F	VF	XF	Unc
1621	—	20.00	40.00	80.00	160	—
ND	—	20.00	40.00	80.00	160	—

KM# 239 FLITTER (2 Pfennig)

Copper **Obv:** Lion rampant right **Rev:** Value, date in 4 lines **Note:** Kipper-Flitter.

Date	Mintage	VG	F	VF	XF	Unc
1621	—	20.00	40.00	80.00	160	—

KM# 243 FLITTER (2 Pfennig)

Copper **Note:** Uniface. Lion rampant right in cord circle.

Date	Mintage	VG	F	VF	XF	Unc
ND	—	16.00	35.00	75.00	145	—

KM# 245 2 FLITTER

Copper **Obv:** Brunswick helmet with horse

Date	Mintage	VG	F	VF	XF	Unc
1621	—	10.00	20.00	45.00	90.00	—

KM# 244 2 FLITTER

Copper **Obv:** Lion rampant right **Rev:** Value, date in 4 lines **Note:** Kipper-2 Flitter.

Date	Mintage	VG	F	VF	XF	Unc
1621	—	10.00	20.00	45.00	90.00	—

KM# 247 3 FLITTER

Copper **Obv:** Lion rampant left in shield **Rev:** Value, date in 4 lines

Date	Mintage	VG	F	VF	XF	Unc
1621	—	12.00	25.00	55.00	110	—

KM# 248 3 FLITTER

Copper **Rev:** Value only in 3 lines

Date	Mintage	VG	F	VF	XF	Unc
ND	—	12.00	25.00	55.00	110	—

KM# 249 3 FLITTER

Copper **Obv:** Crowned lion rampant left **Rev:** Similar to KM#251

Date	Mintage	VG	F	VF	XF	Unc
1621	—	12.00	25.00	55.00	110	—

KM# 250 3 FLITTER

Copper **Obv:** Lion walking left in shield **Rev:** Value in 3 lines

Date	Mintage	VG	F	VF	XF	Unc
ND	—	12.00	25.00	55.00	110	—

KM# 251 3 FLITTER

Copper **Obv:** Lion rampant right

Date	Mintage	VG	F	VF	XF	Unc
1621	—	12.00	25.00	55.00	110	—

KM# 252 3 FLITTER

Copper **Rev:** Value, date in 5 lines

Date	Mintage	VG	F	VF	XF	Unc
1621	—	10.00	20.00	45.00	90.00	—
1612 (error)	—	13.00	35.00	55.00	110	—

KM# 253 3 FLITTER

Copper **Rev:** Value, date in 4 lines

Date	Mintage	VG	F	VF	XF	Unc
ND	—	10.00	20.00	40.00	85.00	—

KM# 254 3 FLITTER

Copper **Obv:** 2 leopards to left **Rev:** III in imperial orb **Rev. Legend:** FLITTERN

Date	Mintage	VG	F	VF	XF	Unc
ND	—	12.00	25.00	50.00	100	—

KM# 255 3 FLITTER

Copper **Rev:** III in circle **Rev. Legend:** FLITTER 1621

Date	Mintage	VG	F	VF	XF	Unc
1621	—	10.00	20.00	40.00	85.00	—

KM# 256 3 FLITTER

Copper **Rev. Legend:** FLITTER with orb, without date

Date	Mintage	VG	F	VF	XF	Unc
1621	—	10.00	20.00	40.00	85.00	—
ND	—	10.00	20.00	40.00	85.00	—

KM# 257 3 FLITTER

Copper **Obv:** Arms divided horizontally, lion walking left above, * * below **Rev:** Value in 3 lines

Date	Mintage	VG	F	VF	XF	Unc
ND	—	10.00	20.00	40.00	85.00	—

KM# 258 3 FLITTER

Copper **Obv:** Brunswick helmet with horse **Rev:** Ornamented III in circle **Rev. Legend:** FLITTERN. 1621 and ornament

Date	Mintage	VG	F	VF	XF	Unc
1621	—	10.00	20.00	40.00	60.00	90.00
ND	—	10.00	20.00	40.00	60.00	90.00

KM# 259 3 FLITTER

Copper **Rev:** Value, date in 4 lines

Date	Mintage	VG	F	VF	XF	Unc
1621	—	10.00	20.00	40.00	60.00	90.00
1621 HH	—	12.00	25.00	50.00	75.00	110
ND	—	10.00	20.00	40.00	60.00	90.00

KM# 260 3 FLITTER

Copper **Rev:** 3 in imperial orb **Rev. Legend:** FLITTER **

Date	Mintage	VG	F	VF	XF	Unc
ND	—	10.00	20.00	40.00	85.00	—

KM# 246 3 FLITTER

Copper **Obv:** Lion rampant left **Rev:** Value in 3 lines in circle **Note:** Kipper-3 Flitter.

Date	Mintage	VG	F	VF	XF	Unc
ND	—	12.00	25.00	50.00	100	—

KM# 261 3 FLITTER

Copper **Obv:** Lion rampant left in ornamented oval shield, value III above **Note:** Uniface.

Date	Mintage	VG	F	VF	XF	Unc
ND	—	15.00	30.00	60.00	120	—

KM# 262 3 FLITTER

Copper **Obv:** Inscription in 4-part circle **Obv. Inscription:** III/FLIT/TERN/1621 **Note:** Uniface.

Date	Mintage	VG	F	VF	XF	Unc
1621	—	15.00	30.00	60.00	120	—

KM# 334 3 FLITTER

Copper **Obv:** Similar to KM#251 **Rev:** III in imprial orb **Rev. Legend:** 1622 FLITTER

Date	Mintage	VG	F	VF	XF	Unc
1622	—	15.00	30.00	60.00	120	—

KM# 335 3 FLITTER

Copper **Obv:** 2 leopards left **Rev:** 3 in imprial orb **Rev. Legend:** FLITTER

Date	Mintage	VG	F	VF	XF	Unc
1622	—	15.00	30.00	60.00	120	—

KM# 263 6 FLITTER

Copper **Obv:** 2 leopards to left **Rev:** VI in imperial orb **Rev. Legend:** FLITTER 1621 **Note:** Kipper-6 Flitter.

Date	Mintage	VG	F	VF	XF	Unc
1621	—	15.00	30.00	60.00	120	—
ND	—	10.00	20.00	40.00	85.00	—

KM# 343 MATTIER (4 Pfennig)

Silver **Obv:** Crowned FV monogram **Rev:** Value in 4 lines

Date	Mintage	VG	F	VF	XF	Unc
1624	—	16.00	32.00	65.00	130	—
1629	—	16.00	32.00	65.00	130	—

KM# 344 MATTIER (4 Pfennig)

Silver **Note:** Uniface. **Obv:** Crowned FV monogram.

Date	Mintage	VG	F	VF	XF	Unc
1624	—	10.00	25.00	50.00	100	—

KM# 134 MARIENGROSCHEN

Silver **Obv:** Cronwed FV monogram **Rev:** Value I. . . in 3 lines

Date	Mintage	VG	F	VF	XF	Unc
1620	—	11.00	25.00	55.00	110	—
1623	—	11.00	25.00	55.00	110	—
1624	—	11.00	25.00	55.00	110	—
1625	—	11.00	25.00	55.00	110	—
1626	—	11.00	25.00	55.00	110	—
1627	—	11.00	25.00	55.00	110	—
1628	—	11.00	25.00	55.00	110	—
1629	—	11.00	25.00	55.00	110	—
1631	—	11.00	25.00	55.00	110	—
1634	—	11.00	25.00	55.00	110	—
ND	—	11.00	25.00	55.00	110	—

KM# 433 MARIENGROSCHEN

Silver **Obv:** Cronwed A **Rev:** Value, date

Date	Mintage	VG	F	VF	XF	Unc
1647	—	11.00	25.00	55.00	110	—
1652	—	11.00	25.00	55.00	110	—
1656	—	11.00	25.00	55.00	110	—
1657	—	11.00	25.00	55.00	110	—

KM# 434 MARIENGROSCHEN

Silver **Obv:** Brunswick helmet

Date	Mintage	VG	F	VF	XF	Unc
ND (s)	—	—	—	—	—	—

KM# 497 MARIENGROSCHEN

Silver **Obv:** Wildman holding tree with both hands to left

Date	Mintage	VG	F	VF	XF	Unc
1667	—	16.00	32.00	65.00	130	—
1673	—	16.00	32.00	65.00	130	—
1674	—	16.00	32.00	65.00	130	—
1675	—	16.00	32.00	65.00	130	—
1676	—	16.00	32.00	65.00	130	—
1677	—	16.00	32.00	65.00	130	—
1678	—	16.00	32.00	65.00	130	—
1679	—	16.00	32.00	65.00	130	—
1680	—	16.00	32.00	65.00	130	—
1681	—	16.00	32.00	65.00	130	—
1682	—	16.00	32.00	65.00	130	—
1683	—	16.00	32.00	65.00	130	—
1684	—	16.00	32.00	65.00	130	—

KM# 550 MARIENGROSCHEN

Silver **Obv:** Crowned RA monogram **Obv. Legend:** HERZ. ZU. BR. U. LUN

Date	Mintage	VG	F	VF	XF	Unc
1684	—	13.00	27.00	55.00	110	—
1684 B	—	13.00	27.00	55.00	110	—

KM# 567 MARIENGROSCHEN

Silver **Ruler:** Anton Ulrich **Obv:** Wildman holding tree with both hands to left **Rev:** Value I...in 3 lines, date in legend

Date	Mintage	VG	F	VF	XF	Unc
1686	—	16.00	32.00	65.00	130	—
1687	—	16.00	32.00	65.00	130	—
1688	—	16.00	32.00	65.00	130	—
1689	—	16.00	32.00	65.00	130	—

KM# 264 2 MARIENGROSCHEN

Silver

Date	Mintage	VG	F	VF	XF	Unc
1621	—	12.00	25.00	50.00	100	—
1623	—	12.00	25.00	50.00	100	—
1624	—	12.00	25.00	50.00	100	—
1625	—	12.00	25.00	50.00	100	—
1626	—	12.00	25.00	50.00	100	—
1627	—	12.00	25.00	50.00	100	—
1627 (h)	—	12.00	25.00	50.00	100	—
1628	—	12.00	25.00	50.00	100	—
1628 (h)	—	12.00	25.00	50.00	100	—
1629	—	12.00	25.00	50.00	100	—
1629 (h)	—	12.00	25.00	50.00	100	—
1631	—	12.00	25.00	50.00	100	—
1632	—	12.00	25.00	50.00	100	—
1633	—	12.00	25.00	50.00	100	—
1634	—	12.00	25.00	50.00	100	—
1635 (error)	—	12.00	25.00	50.00	100	—

KM# 397 2 MARIENGROSCHEN
Silver

Date	Mintage	VG	F	VF	XF	Unc
1638 (s)	—	12.00	25.00	50.00	100	—
1639 (s)	—	12.00	25.00	50.00	100	—
1640 (s)	—	12.00	25.00	50.00	100	—
1641 (s)	—	12.00	25.00	50.00	100	—
1642 (s)	—	12.00	25.00	50.00	100	—
1643 (s)	—	12.00	25.00	50.00	100	—
1644 (s)	—	12.00	25.00	50.00	100	—
1645 (s)	—	12.00	25.00	50.00	100	—
1646 (s)	—	12.00	25.00	50.00	100	—
1647 (s)	—	12.00	25.00	50.00	100	—
1648 (s)	—	12.00	25.00	50.00	100	—
1649 (s)	—	12.00	25.00	50.00	100	—
1659 (s)	—	12.00	25.00	50.00	100	—
ND (s)	—	12.00	25.00	50.00	100	—

KM# 431 2 MARIENGROSCHEN
Silver

Date	Mintage	VG	F	VF	XF	Unc
1645	—	15.00	35.00	70.00	145	—
1647	—	15.00	35.00	70.00	145	—
1648	—	15.00	35.00	70.00	145	—
1649	—	15.00	35.00	70.00	145	—
1650	—	15.00	35.00	70.00	145	—
1651	—	15.00	35.00	70.00	145	—
1652	—	15.00	35.00	70.00	145	—
1653	—	15.00	35.00	70.00	145	—
1654	—	15.00	35.00	70.00	145	—
1655	—	15.00	35.00	70.00	145	—
1656	—	15.00	35.00	70.00	145	—
1659	—	15.00	35.00	70.00	145	—

KM# 443 2 MARIENGROSCHEN
Silver **Obv:** Crowned AW monogram

Date	Mintage	VG	F	VF	XF	Unc
1654	—	15.00	35.00	70.00	145	—
1655	—	15.00	35.00	70.00	145	—

KM# 498 2 MARIENGROSCHEN
Silver **Note:** Similar to 1 Mariengroschen, KM#497.

Date	Mintage	VG	F	VF	XF	Unc
1667	—	12.00	25.00	50.00	100	—
1673	—	12.00	25.00	50.00	100	—
1674	—	12.00	25.00	50.00	100	—
1675	—	12.00	25.00	50.00	100	—
1676	—	12.00	25.00	50.00	100	—
1677	—	12.00	25.00	50.00	100	—
1679	—	12.00	25.00	50.00	100	—
1680	—	12.00	25.00	50.00	100	—
1681	—	12.00	25.00	50.00	100	—
1682	—	12.00	25.00	50.00	100	—
1683	—	12.00	25.00	50.00	100	—
1684	—	12.00	25.00	50.00	100	—

KM# 568 2 MARIENGROSCHEN
Silver **Ruler:** Anton Ulrich **Obv:** Wildman holding tree with both hands to left **Rev:** Value II. . . in 3 lines, date in legend

Date	Mintage	VG	F	VF	XF	Unc
1686	—	16.00	33.00	70.00	145	—
1687	—	16.00	33.00	70.00	145	—
1688	—	16.00	33.00	70.00	145	—
1689	—	16.00	33.00	70.00	145	—
1690	—	16.00	33.00	70.00	145	—
1691	—	16.00	33.00	70.00	145	—
1692	—	16.00	33.00	70.00	145	—
1693	—	16.00	33.00	70.00	145	—
1697	—	16.00	33.00	70.00	145	—
1698	—	16.00	33.00	70.00	145	—
1699	—	16.00	33.00	70.00	145	—

KM# 551 3 MARIENGROSCHEN
Silver **Obv:** Horse leaping left, date below **Rev:** Value III. . .

Date	Mintage	VG	F	VF	XF	Unc
1684 GFN	—	40.00	90.00	180	—	—

KM# 552 3 MARIENGROSCHEN
Silver **Obv:** Horse leaping right, date below

Date	Mintage	VG	F	VF	XF	Unc
1684 B	—	—	—	—	—	—

KM# 345 4 MARIENGROSCHEN
2.6000 g., Silver, 21.5 mm. **Obv:** Crowned FV monogram **Rev:** Value IIII... in 4 lines

Date	Mintage	VG	F	VF	XF	Unc
1624 date flanking monogram	—	20.00	35.00	75.00	150	—
1624 HS date in legend	—	20.00	35.00	75.00	150	—
1625 (b)	—	20.00	35.00	75.00	150	—

KM# 499 4 MARIENGROSCHEN
Silver **Obv:** Wildman holding tree at right, with both hands, DG after duke's name **Rev:** Value IIII. . . in 3 lines, date in legend

Date	Mintage	VG	F	VF	XF	Unc
1667	—	30.00	60.00	120	—	—

KM# 500 4 MARIENGROSCHEN
Silver **Obv:** D. G. before duke's name

Date	Mintage	VG	F	VF	XF	Unc
1667	—	13.00	27.00	55.00	115	—
1668	—	13.00	27.00	55.00	115	—
1669	—	13.00	27.00	55.00	115	—
1671	—	13.00	27.00	55.00	115	—
1672	—	13.00	27.00	55.00	115	—
1673	—	13.00	27.00	55.00	115	—
1674	—	13.00	27.00	55.00	115	—

KM# 518 4 MARIENGROSCHEN
Silver **Obv:** 4 added next to wildman

Date	Mintage	VG	F	VF	XF	Unc
1675	—	10.00	27.00	55.00	115	—
1676	—	10.00	27.00	55.00	115	—
1677	—	10.00	27.00	55.00	115	—
1678	—	10.00	27.00	55.00	115	—
1679	—	10.00	27.00	55.00	115	—
1681	—	10.00	27.00	55.00	115	—
1683	—	10.00	27.00	55.00	115	—

KM# 574 4 MARIENGROSCHEN
Silver

Date	Mintage	VG	F	VF	XF	Unc
1687	—	10.00	27.00	55.00	115	—
1688	—	10.00	27.00	55.00	115	—
1689	—	10.00	27.00	55.00	115	—
1691	—	10.00	27.00	55.00	115	—
1697	—	10.00	27.00	55.00	115	—

KM# 503 6 MARIENGROSCHEN
Silver **Obv:** Wildman holding tree with both hands to left, 6 added next to wildman, D.G. after duke's name **Rev:** Value VI. . . in 3 lines, date in legend

Date	Mintage	VG	F	VF	XF	Unc
1668	—	25.00	45.00	90.00	185	—
1671	—	25.00	45.00	90.00	185	—
1673	—	25.00	45.00	90.00	185	—
1674	—	25.00	45.00	90.00	185	—
1675	—	25.00	45.00	90.00	185	—
1676	—	25.00	45.00	90.00	185	—
1677	—	25.00	45.00	90.00	185	—
1678	—	25.00	45.00	90.00	185	—

KM# 505 6 MARIENGROSCHEN
Silver **Obv:** Without 6 next go wildman

Date	Mintage	VG	F	VF	XF	Unc
1669	—	20.00	40.00	85.00	175	—
1679	—	20.00	40.00	85.00	175	—
1682	—	20.00	40.00	85.00	175	—

KM# 519 6 MARIENGROSCHEN
Silver **Obv:** Bust right **Rev:** Value VI. . ., date in 4 lines

Date	Mintage	VG	F	VF	XF	Unc
1675	—	35.00	75.00	150	—	—

KM# 569 6 MARIENGROSCHEN
Silver

Date	Mintage	VG	F	VF	XF	Unc
1686	—	25.00	45.00	90.00	185	—
1687	—	25.00	45.00	90.00	185	—
1688	—	25.00	45.00	90.00	185	—
1689	—	25.00	45.00	90.00	185	—
1690	—	25.00	45.00	90.00	185	—
1691	—	25.00	45.00	90.00	185	—
1692	—	25.00	45.00	90.00	185	—
1693	—	25.00	45.00	90.00	185	—
1694	—	25.00	45.00	90.00	185	—
1695	—	25.00	45.00	90.00	185	—
1696	—	25.00	45.00	90.00	185	—
1697	—	25.00	45.00	90.00	185	—
1698	—	25.00	45.00	90.00	185	—
1699	—	25.00	45.00	90.00	185	—
1700	—	25.00	45.00	90.00	185	—

KM# 578 6 MARIENGROSCHEN (1/6 Thaler)
Silver **Obv:** Horse leaping left, value 1/6 in oval below **Rev:** VI...in 3 lines **Rev. Legend:** REMIGIO ALTISSIMI UNI, date

Date	Mintage	VG	F	VF	XF	Unc
1689	—	25.00	45.00	90.00	185	—

KM# 605 6 MARIENGROSCHEN (1/6 Thaler)
Silver **Rev. Legend:** MONETA NOVA BRUNS. & LV:, date

Date	Mintage	VG	F	VF	XF	Unc
1693 HCH	—	25.00	45.00	90.00	185	—

KM# 606 6 MARIENGROSCHEN (1/6 Thaler)
Silver **Rev. Legend:** NACH DEM LEIP. FUSS

Date	Mintage	VG	F	VF	XF	Unc
1693 HCH	—	16.00	35.00	70.00	145	—
1695 HCH	—	16.00	35.00	70.00	145	—
1696 HCH	—	16.00	35.00	70.00	145	—
1697 HCH	—	16.00	35.00	70.00	145	—

KM# 614 6 MARIENGROSCHEN (1/6 Thaler)
Silver **Rev. Legend:** FURSTL. BRUNS. LUNEB. MUNTZ, date

Date	Mintage	VG	F	VF	XF	Unc
1694 HCH	—	16.00	35.00	70.00	145	—

KM# 622 6 MARIENGROSCHEN (1/6 Thaler)
Silver **Obv:** Value VI. . . in 4 lines

Date	Mintage	VG	F	VF	XF	Unc
1696 ICP	—	20.00	40.00	75.00	155	—
1696 ICB	—	20.00	40.00	75.00	155	—
1697 ICP	—	20.00	40.00	75.00	155	—
1697 ICB	—	20.00	40.00	75.00	155	—

Note: Varieties exist

KM# 346 10 MARIENGROSCHEN
Silver **Obv:** Crowned VF monogram, date in legend **Rev:** Value X…in 3 lines

Date	Mintage	VG	F	VF	XF	Unc
1624	—	—	—	—	—	—

KM# 504 12 MARIENGROSCHEN (1/3 Thaler)
Silver

Date	Mintage	VG	F	VF	XF	Unc
1668	—	33.00	65.00	100	210	—
1669	—	33.00	65.00	100	210	—
1670	—	33.00	65.00	100	210	—
1671	—	33.00	65.00	100	210	—
1672	—	33.00	65.00	100	210	—
1673	—	33.00	65.00	100	210	—
1674	—	33.00	65.00	100	210	—
1675	—	33.00	65.00	100	210	—
1676	—	33.00	65.00	100	210	—
1677	—	33.00	65.00	100	210	—
1678	—	33.00	65.00	100	210	—
1679	—	33.00	65.00	100	210	—
1680	—	33.00	65.00	100	210	—
1681	—	33.00	65.00	100	210	—
1682	—	33.00	65.00	100	210	—
1683	—	33.00	65.00	100	210	—
1684	—	33.00	65.00	100	210	—

KM# 570 12 MARIENGROSCHEN (1/3 Thaler)
Silver **Ruler:** Anton Ulrich **Obv:** Wildman holding tree with two hands at left, 12 at left of wildman **Rev:** Value XII…in 3 lines, date in legend

Date	Mintage	VG	F	VF	XF	Unc
1686	—	25.00	45.00	125	200	—
1687	—	25.00	45.00	125	200	—
1688	—	25.00	45.00	125	200	—
1690	—	25.00	45.00	125	200	—
1691	—	25.00	45.00	125	200	—
1692	—	25.00	45.00	125	200	—
1694	—	25.00	45.00	125	200	—
1695	—	25.00	45.00	125	200	—
1696	—	25.00	45.00	125	200	—
1697	—	25.00	45.00	125	200	—
1698	—	25.00	45.00	125	200	—
1699	—	25.00	45.00	125	200	—
1700	—	25.00	45.00	125	200	—

KM# 585 12 MARIENGROSCHEN (1/3 Thaler)
Silver **Obv:** Horse leaping left **Rev:** Value XII. . . in 3 lines, date in legend

Date	Mintage	VG	F	VF	XF	Unc
1690 HCH	—	30.00	60.00	120	240	—
1691 HCH	—	30.00	60.00	120	240	—

KM# 516 24 MARIENGROSCHEN (2/3 Thaler)
Silver

Date	Mintage	VG	F	VF	XF	Unc
1674	—	45.00	85.00	150	300	—
1675	—	45.00	85.00	150	300	—
1676	—	45.00	85.00	150	300	—
1677	—	45.00	85.00	150	300	—
1679	—	45.00	85.00	150	300	—

KM# 521 24 MARIENGROSCHEN (2/3 Thaler)
Silver **Obv:** Bust right **Rev:** Value, date

Date	Mintage	VG	F	VF	XF	Unc
1676 B	—	120	200	325	625	—

KM# 529 24 MARIENGROSCHEN (2/3 Thaler)
Silver **Note:** Similar to KM#516, but V. FEIN. SILB: added below value.

Date	Mintage	VG	F	VF	XF	Unc
1677	—	35.00	75.00	150	300	—
1678	—	35.00	75.00	150	300	—
1679	—	35.00	75.00	150	300	—
1680	—	35.00	75.00	150	300	—
1681	—	35.00	75.00	150	300	—
1682	—	35.00	75.00	150	300	—
1683	—	35.00	75.00	150	300	—
1684	—	35.00	75.00	150	300	—
1685	—	35.00	75.00	150	300	—

KM# 559 24 MARIENGROSCHEN (2/3 Thaler)
Silver **Ruler:** Anton Ulrich **Obv:** Wildman with tree in both hands at right, value at left **Rev:** Value within inner circle, date in legend

Date	Mintage	VG	F	VF	XF	Unc
1685	—	33.00	65.00	125	250	—
1686	—	33.00	65.00	125	250	—
1687	—	33.00	65.00	125	250	—
1688	—	33.00	65.00	125	250	—
1689	—	33.00	65.00	125	250	—
1690	—	33.00	65.00	125	250	—
1691	—	33.00	65.00	125	250	—
1692	—	33.00	65.00	125	250	—
1693	—	33.00	65.00	125	250	—
1694	—	33.00	65.00	125	250	—
1695	—	33.00	65.00	125	250	—
1696	—	33.00	65.00	125	250	—
1697	—	33.00	65.00	125	250	—
1698	—	33.00	65.00	125	250	—
1699	—	33.00	65.00	125	250	—
1700	—	33.00	65.00	125	250	—

KM# 586 24 MARIENGROSCHEN (2/3 Thaler)
Silver

Date	Mintage	VG	F	VF	XF	Unc
1690	—	35.00	75.00	150	300	—
1690 HCH	—	35.00	75.00	150	300	—
1691 HCH	—	35.00	75.00	150	300	—
1692 HCH	—	35.00	75.00	150	300	—
1693 HCH	—	35.00	75.00	150	300	—

KM# 607 24 MARIENGROSCHEN (2/3 Thaler)
Silver **Rev:** Value XXIIII. . .

Date	Mintage	VG	F	VF	XF	Unc
1693 HCH	—	45.00	90.00	185	375	—

KM# 608 24 MARIENGROSCHEN (2/3 Thaler)
Silver **Rev. Legend:** NACH DEN…

Date	Mintage	VG	F	VF	XF	Unc
1693 HCH	—	45.00	90.00	185	375	—
1694 HCH	—	45.00	90.00	185	375	—

KM# 615 24 MARIENGROSCHEN (2/3 Thaler)
Silver **Ruler:** Anton Ulrich **Obv:** Horse leaping left, 2/3 in oval below

Date	Mintage	VG	F	VF	XF	Unc
1694 HCH	—	45.00	90.00	185	375	—
1695 HCH	—	45.00	90.00	185	375	—
1696 HCH	—	45.00	90.00	185	375	—
1697 HCH	—	45.00	90.00	185	375	—
1698 HCH	—	45.00	90.00	185	375	—
1699 HCH	—	45.00	90.00	185	375	—
1700 HCH	—	45.00	90.00	185	375	—

KM# 347 1/2 MARIENGULDEN (1/3 Thaler)
Silver **Obv:** Similar to 1 Mariengulden, KM#342 **Rev:** I/HALBE/MARIE/GULD **Rev. Legend:** BRAUN. MUNTZ…

Date	Mintage	VG	F	VF	XF	Unc
1624	—	150	275	500	925	—

KM# 342 MARIENGULDEN (2/3 Thaler)
Silver

Date	Mintage	VG	F	VF	XF	Unc
1623	—	150	275	450	850	—
1624	—	150	275	450	850	—

KM# 136 3 KREUZER (Groschen)
Silver **Rev. Legend:** IN FOEL. C. N. INVI

Date	Mintage	VG	F	VF	XF	Unc
ND	—	20.00	40.00	75.00	155	—

KM# 137 3 KREUZER (Groschen)
Silver **Rev. Legend:** LABORE. CONSUMIN.

Date	Mintage	VG	F	VF	XF	Unc
ND	—	20.00	40.00	75.00	155	—

KM# 138 3 KREUZER (Groschen)
Silver **Obv:** Shield **Rev:** Double headed eagle, 3 on breast **Rev. Legend:** M. G. V. K. K. V. G. M.

Date	Mintage	VG	F	VF	XF	Unc
16Z0	—	20.00	40.00	75.00	155	—

KM# 140 3 KREUZER (Groschen)
Silver **Rev. Legend:** SI. DE9 PRO. N. Q. C. N.

Date	Mintage	VG	F	VF	XF	Unc
16Z0	—	20.00	40.00	75.00	155	—

KM# 141 3 KREUZER (Groschen)
Silver **Rev. Legend:** SOLI. DEO. GLORIA.

Date	Mintage	VG	F	VF	XF	Unc
ND	—	20.00	40.00	75.00	155	—

KM# 142 3 KREUZER (Groschen)
Silver **Obv. Legend:** Titles of Ferdinand II **Rev. Legend:** SEMPER. PRO. PATRIA.

Date	Mintage	VG	F	VF	XF	Unc
ND (b)	—	20.00	40.00	75.00	155	—

KM# 143 3 KREUZER (Groschen)
Silver **Obv:** Titles of Matthias **Rev:** Arms divided horizontally, lion above, chessboard below **Rev. Legend:** DEUS. EST. UINDEX.

Date	Mintage	VG	F	VF	XF	Unc
1620	—	20.00	40.00	75.00	155	—

KM# 144 3 KREUZER (Groschen)
Silver **Obv:** Imperial eagle, 3 on breast, Z.O.N.H.T.D.G. **Rev:** Crown with horse above **Rev. Legend:** W.G.W.V.F.L.

Date	Mintage	VG	F	VF	XF	Unc
1620	—	20.00	40.00	75.00	155	—

KM# 145 3 KREUZER (Groschen)
Silver **Obv:** Lion left **Obv. Legend:** AGENDO. CONANDO.

Date	Mintage	VG	F	VF	XF	Unc
ND	—	20.00	40.00	75.00	155	—

KM# 146 3 KREUZER (Groschen)
Silver **Obv:** Lion rampant left **Obv. Legend:** FID. B. DESER. DEUS. **Rev:** Titles of Ferdinand II

Date	Mintage	VG	F	VF	XF	Unc
ND	—	20.00	40.00	75.00	155	—

KM# 147 3 KREUZER (Groschen)
Silver **Obv. Legend:** PAR. PR. NO. IR. L.

Date	Mintage	VG	F	VF	XF	Unc
ND	—	20.00	40.00	75.00	155	—

KM# 148 3 KREUZER (Groschen)
Silver **Obv:** Tower to side of lion **Obv. Legend:** TIME. DEVM. ET. DVCE. M.

Date	Mintage	VG	F	VF	XF	Unc
ND	—	20.00	40.00	75.00	155	—

KM# 149 3 KREUZER (Groschen)
Silver **Obv:** Lion rampant left in 3-turretted tower **Obv. Legend:** GOT. D. E. S. N. M. **Rev:** Titles of Matthias

Date	Mintage	VG	F	VF	XF	Unc
ND	—	20.00	40.00	75.00	155	—

KM# 150 3 KREUZER (Groschen)
Silver **Obv:** Deer antlers **Obv. Legend:** ORA. ET. LABORA **Rev:** Titles of Ferdinand II

Date	Mintage	VG	F	VF	XF	Unc
1620	—	20.00	40.00	75.00	155	—

KM# 151 3 KREUZER (Groschen)
Silver **Obv. Legend:** PRO PATRIA, date

Date	Mintage	VG	F	VF	XF	Unc
1620	—	20.00	40.00	75.00	155	—

KM# 152 3 KREUZER (Groschen)
Silver **Obv:** Large rose **Obv. Legend:** SI. DE. PRO. N. Q. C. N. **Rev:** Titles of Matthias

Date	Mintage	VG	F	VF	XF	Unc
1620	—	20.00	40.00	75.00	155	—

KM# 135 3 KREUZER (Groschen)
Silver **Obv:** Imperial eagle, 3 on breast, titles of Matthias **Rev:** 4-fold arms, H below, **Rev. Legend:** GOT. DI. EH. . . **Note:** Kipper-3 Kreuzer.

Date	Mintage	VG	F	VF	XF	Unc
ND	—	20.00	4.00	75.00	155	—
1620	—	20.00	40.00	75.00	155	—

KM# 139 3 KREUZER (Groschen)
Silver **Rev. Legend:** ORA. ET. LABORA. **Note:** Varieties exist.

Date	Mintage	VG	F	VF	XF	Unc
1620	—	20.00	40.00	75.00	155	—

KM# 265 3 KREUZER (Groschen)
Silver **Obv:** Crowned 4-fold arms **Rev:** Crowned imprial eagle, 3 on breast

Date	Mintage	VG	F	VF	XF	Unc
1621	—	20.00	40.00	75.00	155	—

KM# 89 12 KREUZER (1/12 Thaler)
Silver **Obv. Legend:** IS. AL. NO. SIT. QU. SUI. P.

Date	Mintage	VG	F	VF	XF	Unc
1619	—	33.00	65.00	135	275	—

KM# 90 12 KREUZER (1/12 Thaler)
Silver **Obv. Legend:** ORA. ET. LABORA, date **Note:** Varieties exist.

Date	Mintage	VG	F	VF	XF	Unc
(1)619	—	33.00	65.00	135	275	—
(1)619	—	33.00	65.00	135	275	—

Note: Varieties exist

KM# 88 12 KREUZER (1/12 Thaler)
Silver **Obv:** Crowned imperial eagle, 12 in orb on breast, titles of Matthias **Rev:** Crowned 4-fold arms **Rev. Legend:** D. ME. SP. IS. EIN. GRE. V. G., date **Note:** Kipper 12 Kreuzer.

Date	Mintage	VG	F	VF	XF	Unc
1619	—	33.00	65.00	135	275	—
1620	—	33.00	65.00	135	275	—

Note: Varieties exist

KM# 168 12 KREUZER (1/12 Thaler)
Silver **Rev. Legend:** ORA. ET. LABORA. **Note:** Kipper.

Date	Mintage	VG	F	VF	XF	Unc
1620	—	30.00	60.00	120	240	—

KM# 165 12 KREUZER (1/12 Thaler)
Silver **Note:** Klippe-12 Kreuzer.

Date	Mintage	VG	F	VF	XF	Unc
ND	—	30.00	60.00	120	240	—

KM# 154 12 KREUZER (1/12 Thaler)
Silver **Obv:** Brunswick helmet with horse **Rev:** Date in legend **Note:** Varieties exist.

Date	Mintage	VG	F	VF	XF	Unc
1620	—	30.00	60.00	120	240	—
1621	—	30.00	60.00	120	240	—
ND	—	30.00	60.00	120	240	—

KM# 155 12 KREUZER (1/12 Thaler)
Silver **Note:** Varieties exist.

Date	Mintage	VG	F	VF	XF	Unc
1620	—	30.00	60.00	120	240	—
1621	—	30.00	60.00	120	240	—

KM# 157 12 KREUZER (1/12 Thaler)
Silver **Obv:** Oval 4-fold arms **Rev:** Date in legend **Note:** Varieties exist.

Date	Mintage	VG	F	VF	XF	Unc
1620	—	30.00	60.00	120	240	—
1620 (b)	—	30.00	60.00	120	240	—
(1)621 (b)	—	30.00	60.00	120	240	—

KM# 170 12 KREUZER (1/12 Thaler)
Silver **Obv. Legend:** SOLI. DEO. GLORIA. **Note:** Varieties exist.

Date	Mintage	VG	F	VF	XF	Unc
1620	—	30.00	60.00	120	240	—
ND	—	30.00	60.00	120	240	—

KM# 153 12 KREUZER (1/12 Thaler)
Silver **Obv:** Imperial eagle, 12 in orb on breast, titles of Ferdinand II **Rev:** Wildman, tree in right hand **Rev. Legend:** MONE. NO AR. D. B. E. L.

Date	Mintage	VG	F	VF	XF	Unc
1620 CH	—	27.00	55.00	110	225	—
1620 HH	—	27.00	55.00	110	225	—
1620 LB	—	27.00	55.00	110	225	—
1620 WG	—	27.00	55.00	110	225	—
1621	—	27.00	55.00	110	225	—
1621 CV	—	27.00	55.00	110	225	—
1621 IL	—	27.00	55.00	110	225	—
ND	—	27.00	55.00	110	225	—
16ZZ	—	27.00	55.00	110	225	—

KM# 156 12 KREUZER (1/12 Thaler)
Silver **Obv:** Crowned arms with horse in front of column

Date	Mintage	VG	F	VF	XF	Unc
1620	—	30.00	60.00	120	240	—

KM# 158 12 KREUZER (1/12 Thaler)
Silver **Obv:** 9-fold arms divide date

Date	Mintage	VG	F	VF	XF	Unc
1620	—	33.00	65.00	135	275	—
1621	—	33.00	65.00	135	275	—

KM# 159 12 KREUZER (1/12 Thaler)
Silver **Obv:** Crowned imperial eagle, 12 in orb on breast, titles of Matthias **Rev:** Crowned 4-fold arms **Rev. Legend:** ADIVVANTE DEO, date

Date	Mintage	VG	F	VF	XF	Unc
1620	—	33.00	65.00	135	275	—

KM# 160 12 KREUZER (1/12 Thaler)
Silver **Rev. Legend:** LABORE. CONSUMIMUR

Date	Mintage	VG	F	VF	XF	Unc
1620	—	33.00	65.00	135	275	—
ND	—	33.00	65.00	135	275	—

Note: Varieties exist

KM# 161 12 KREUZER (1/12 Thaler)
Silver **Obv. Legend:** SIT NOM: BENEDICTIVM.

Date	Mintage	VG	F	VF	XF	Unc
ND	—	33.00	65.00	135	275	—

Note: Varieties exist

KM# 162 12 KREUZER (1/12 Thaler)
Silver **Obv. Legend:** SOLI. DEO. GLORIA.

Date	Mintage	VG	F	VF	XF	Unc
ND	—	33.00	65.00	135	275	—

Note: Varieties exist.

KM# 163 12 KREUZER (1/12 Thaler)
Silver **Obv:** Central shield with pellet in arms

Date	Mintage	VG	F	VF	XF	Unc
ND	—	33.00	65.00	135	275	—

KM# 164 12 KREUZER (1/12 Thaler)
Silver **Obv:** Titles of Ferdinand II **Rev. Legend:** CONVERTE. ME. DOMINE.

Date	Mintage	VG	F	VF	XF	Unc
ND	—	33.00	60.00	135	275	—

KM# 166 12 KREUZER (1/12 Thaler)
Silver **Rev. Legend:** D. ME. SP. IS. EIN. GRE. V. G.

Date	Mintage	VG	F	VF	XF	Unc
1620	—	33.00	65.00	135	275	—

KM# 167 12 KREUZER (1/12 Thaler)
Silver **Obv:** Titles of Ferdinan II **Rev. Legend:** LABORE. CONSUMIMUR.

Date	Mintage	VG	F	VF	XF	Unc
1620	—	33.00	65.00	135	275	—

KM# 169 12 KREUZER (1/12 Thaler)
Silver **Obv. Legend:** SIT NOM: DOM: BENEDICTUM.

Date	Mintage	VG	F	VF	XF	Unc
ND	—	33.00	65.00	135	275	—

KM# 171 12 KREUZER (1/12 Thaler)
Silver **Obv:** Crowned 3-fold arms **Obv. Legend:** SOLI. DEO. GLORIA. **Rev:** Titles of Matthias

Date	Mintage	VG	F	VF	XF	Unc
ND	—	33.00	65.00	135	275	—

KM# 172 12 KREUZER (1/12 Thaler)
Silver **Obv:** Shield with bars **Obv. Legend:** DURA. PATI-S **Rev:** Titles of Ferdinand II

Date	Mintage	VG	F	VF	XF	Unc
1620	—	35.00	75.00	150	300	—

KM# 266 12 KREUZER (1/12 Thaler)
Silver **Obv:** Crowned imperial eagle, 12 in orb on breast, titles of Ferdinand II **Rev:** Facing bust of St. Jacob

Date	Mintage	VG	F	VF	XF	Unc
1621	—	—	—	—	—	—

KM# 267 12 KREUZER (1/12 Thaler)
Silver **Obv:** Crowned imperial eagle, 12 on breast, titles of Ferdinand II **Rev:** Wildman, tree in right hand

Date	Mintage	VG	F	VF	XF	Unc
1621	—	27.00	50.00	100	210	—
ND	—	27.00	50.00	100	210	—

KM# 268 12 KREUZER (1/12 Thaler)
Silver **Obv:** 12 in orb on breast, date in legend

Date	Mintage	VG	F	VF	XF	Unc
1621	—	27.00	50.00	100	210	—
ND	—	27.00	50.00	100	210	—

KM# 269 12 KREUZER (1/12 Thaler)
Silver **Rev:** Date in legend

Date	Mintage	VG	F	VF	XF	Unc
16Z1	—	27.00	50.00	100	210	—

KM# 270 12 KREUZER (1/12 Thaler)
Silver **Rev:** Date along side wildman

Date	Mintage	VG	F	VF	XF	Unc
1621	—	27.00	50.00	100	210	—

KM# 271 12 KREUZER (1/12 Thaler)
Silver **Obv:** Date in legend

Date	Mintage	VG	F	VF	XF	Unc
1621	—	27.00	50.00	100	210	—

KM# 272 12 KREUZER (1/12 Thaler)
Silver **Obv:** Value in shield on breast of eagle **Rev:** Date along side wildman

Date	Mintage	VG	F	VF	XF	Unc
1621	—	27.00	50.00	100	210	—

KM# 273 12 KREUZER (1/12 Thaler)
Silver **Obv:** Wildman, tree in right hand **Rev:** Crowned imperial eagle, 12 in orb on breast **Rev. Legend:** SAPIENT. ET. CONSTANTE.

Date	Mintage	VG	F	VF	XF	Unc
1621	—	27.00	50.00	100	210	—
ND	—	27.00	50.00	100	210	—

KM# 275 12 KREUZER (1/12 Thaler)
Silver **Obv:** Wildman, tree in right hand, date in legend

Date	Mintage	VG	F	VF	XF	Unc
1621	—	27.00	50.00	100	210	—

KM# 276 12 KREUZER (1/12 Thaler)
Silver **Rev:** 12 on breast

Date	Mintage	VG	F	VF	XF	Unc
1621 ID	—	27.00	50.00	100	210	—
ND	—	27.00	50.00	100	210	—

KM# 277 12 KREUZER (1/12 Thaler)
Silver **Obv:** Brunswick helmet with horse **Obv. Legend:** MO. NO. AR...,date **Rev:** 12 in orb on breast

Date	Mintage	VG	F	VF	XF	Unc
1621	—	27.00	50.00	100	210	—

KM# 278 12 KREUZER (1/12 Thaler)
Silver **Rev:** Date in legend

Date	Mintage	VG	F	VF	XF	Unc
1621	—	27.00	50.00	100	210	—

KM# 279 12 KREUZER (1/12 Thaler)
Silver **Rev:** 12 on breast

Date	Mintage	VG	F	VF	XF	Unc
1621 IB	—	27.00	50.00	100	210	—

KM# 280 12 KREUZER (1/12 Thaler)
Silver **Obv:** Crowned arms with horse in front of column in circle **Rev:** 12 in orb on breast

Date	Mintage	VG	F	VF	XF	Unc
1621	—	27.00	50.00	100	210	—

KM# 281 12 KREUZER (1/12 Thaler)
Silver **Obv:** Crown lion rampant left **Rev:** Date in legend

Date	Mintage	VG	F	VF	XF	Unc
1621	—	27.00	50.00	100	210	—

KM# 282 12 KREUZER (1/12 Thaler)
Silver **Obv:** Lion striding left above ornamented base

Date	Mintage	VG	F	VF	XF	Unc
1621	—	32.00	65.00	135	275	—

KM# 283 12 KREUZER (1/12 Thaler)
Silver **Obv:** Date in legend

Date	Mintage	VG	F	VF	XF	Unc
1621	—	32.00	65.00	135	275	—

KM# 284 12 KREUZER (1/12 Thaler)
Silver **Obv:** Lion rampant left **Rev:** Wildman, tree in right hand **Rev. Legend:** SAPIENTER. . .

Date	Mintage	VG	F	VF	XF	Unc
1621	—	32.00	65.00	135	275	—

KM# 285 12 KREUZER (1/12 Thaler)
Silver **Obv:** Crown imperial eagle, 12 in orb on breast, titles of Ferdinand II **Rev:** Lion rampant right

Date	Mintage	VG	F	VF	XF	Unc
1621	—	32.00	65.00	135	275	—

KM# 286 12 KREUZER (1/12 Thaler)
Silver **Rev. Legend:** SAPIENTER. . .

Date	Mintage	VG	F	VF	XF	Unc
1621	—	32.00	65.00	135	275	—
ND	—	21.00	65.00	135	275	—

KM# 287 12 KREUZER (1/12 Thaler)
Silver **Obv:** Oval 4-fold arms **Obv. Legend:** MON. NOVA. DVCA. . .

Date	Mintage	VG	F	VF	XF	Unc
1621	—	32.00	65.00	135	275	—

KM# 288 12 KREUZER (1/12 Thaler)
Silver **Obv:** St. Andrew with cross **Obv. Legend:** RECTE FACIEN: NEM. TIMEA.

Date	Mintage	VG	F	VF	XF	Unc
1621	—	32.00	65.00	135	275	—
1622	—	32.00	65.00	135	275	—

KM# 289 12 KREUZER (1/12 Thaler)
Silver **Obv:** Wildman, tree in right hand **Obv. Legend:** PRO LEGE ET GREGE, date

Date	Mintage	VG	F	VF	XF	Unc
1621	—	32.00	65.00	135	275	—

KM# 290 12 KREUZER (1/12 Thaler)
Silver **Obv. Legend:** MONE NO B. E. L.

Date	Mintage	VG	F	VF	XF	Unc
ND	—	32.00	65.00	135	275	—

KM# 291 12 KREUZER (1/12 Thaler)
Silver **Obv. Legend:** SAPIENTER. ET: CONSTANTER.

Date	Mintage	VG	F	VF	XF	Unc
1621	—	27.00	55.00	115	230	—

KM# 292 12 KREUZER (1/12 Thaler)
Silver **Obv:** Cowned 2-fold arms, lion rampant left above bars **Obv. Legend:** DEVS ** DO ** MEA. **Rev:** Titles

Date	Mintage	VG	F	VF	XF	Unc
1621	—	32.00	65.00	135	275	—

KM# 293 12 KREUZER (1/12 Thaler)
Silver **Obv:** Lion walking left **Obv. Legend:** CONSILIO. ET. ARMIS.

Date	Mintage	VG	F	VF	XF	Unc
ND	—	32.00	65.00	135	275	—

KM# 294 12 KREUZER (1/12 Thaler)
Silver **Rev. Legend:** IN SPE ET SILENTIO

Date	Mintage	VG	F	VF	XF	Unc
ND	—	32.00	65.00	135	275	—

KM# 295 12 KREUZER (1/12 Thaler)
Silver **Obv:** 2-fold arms divided vertically, lion rampant left on left, 2 leopards on right

Date	Mintage	VG	F	VF	XF	Unc
ND	—	32.00	65.00	135	275	—

KM# 296 12 KREUZER (1/12 Thaler)
Silver **Obv:** Crowned lion rampant left, holding arms **Obv. Legend:** GVDE. GROS.

Date	Mintage	VG	F	VF	XF	Unc
ND	—	32.00	65.00	135	275	—

KM# 297 12 KREUZER (1/12 Thaler)
Silver **Obv:** Lion rampant left **Rev:** SPES. NON. CONFVNDIT, date

Date	Mintage	VG	F	VF	XF	Unc
1621	—	32.00	65.00	135	275	—

KM# 299 12 KREUZER (1/12 Thaler)
Silver **Obv:** Lion rampant right **Obv. Legend:** ALLES STHET BEI GLVC. V. ZEIT.

Date	Mintage	VG	F	VF	XF	Unc
1621	—	32.00	65.00	135	275	—
ND	—	32.00	65.00	135	275	—

KM# 300 12 KREUZER (1/12 Thaler)
Silver **Obv:** Lion passant right

Date	Mintage	VG	F	VF	XF	Unc
1621	—	32.00	65.00	135	275	—

KM# 301 12 KREUZER (1/12 Thaler)
Silver **Obv:** Lion right, tower at side **Obv. Legend:** PRO. LEGE. ET. GREGE, date

Date	Mintage	VG	F	VF	XF	Unc
1621	—	32.00	65.00	135	275	—

KM# 302 12 KREUZER (1/12 Thaler)
Silver **Obv:** 2 leopards **Obv. Legend:** AVDCES OR IVVAT

Date	Mintage	VG	F	VF	XF	Unc
ND	—	32.00	65.00	135	275	—

KM# 303 12 KREUZER (1/12 Thaler)
Silver **Obv. Legend:** NEG. S. -G: MI-date

Date	Mintage	VG	F	VF	XF	Unc
1621	—	32.00	65.00	135	275	—

KM# 304 12 KREUZER (1/12 Thaler)
Silver **Obv:** Old Brunswick helmet with horse **Obv. Legend:** FIDEM. AES: DE. DEI.

Date	Mintage	VG	F	VF	XF	Unc
ND	—	32.00	60.00	120	240	—

KM# 305 12 KREUZER (1/12 Thaler)
Silver **Obv. Legend:** IN. TE. DOMI. SPERA. NON. CON. F.

Date	Mintage	VG	F	VF	XF	Unc
1621	—	30.00	60.00	120	240	—

KM# 306 12 KREUZER (1/12 Thaler)
Silver **Obv:** Helmet with 2 bear paws **Obv. Legend:** IN. DEO. VIRT. FACIEMUS.

Date	Mintage	VG	F	VF	XF	Unc
1621	—	30.00	60.00	120	240	—
ND	—	30.00	60.00	120	240	—

KM# 307 12 KREUZER (1/12 Thaler)
Silver **Obv:** Horse in front of column **Obv. Legend:** PRO. LEGE. ET. GREGE.

Date	Mintage	VG	F	VF	XF	Unc
ND	—	32.00	65.00	135	275	—

KM# 308 12 KREUZER (1/12 Thaler)
Silver **Obv:** 2 bear paws in shield **Obv. Legend:** ARMIS. ET. LEGIBUS.

Date	Mintage	VG	F	VF	XF	Unc
ND	—	30.00	60.00	120	240	—

KM# 298 12 KREUZER (1/12 Thaler)
Silver **Rev:** Lion rampant right in shield **Rev. Legend:** CONSILIO. ET. ARMIS **Note:** Varieties exist.

Date	Mintage	VG	F	VF	XF	Unc
1621	—	32.00	65.00	135	275	—
ND (b)	—	32.00	65.00	135	275	—
ND	—	32.00	65.00	135	275	—

KM# 274 12 KREUZER (1/12 Thaler)
Silver **Obv:** Brunswick helmet with horse **Rev:** Crowned imperial eagle, 12 in orb on breast, date in legend **Note:** Klippe.

Date	Mintage	VG	F	VF	XF	Unc
1621	—	—	—	—	—	—

KM# 310 24 KREUZER (1/6 Thaler)
Silver **Obv:** Crowned imperial eagle, 24 in orb on breast, titles of Ferdinand II, date in legend **Rev:** Brunswick helmet with horse

Date	Mintage	VG	F	VF	XF	Unc
1621	—	75.00	150	300	625	—

KM# 311 24 KREUZER (1/6 Thaler)
Silver **Obv:** 2-fold arms, lion right above bars below **Obv. Legend:** DEV. TI-TVDO ** MEA.

Date	Mintage	VG	F	VF	XF	Unc
1621	—	75.00	150	300	625	—

KM# 309 24 KREUZER (1/6 Thaler)
Silver **Obv:** Crown above Brunswick helmet with horse, 3 arms below **Rev:** Angel standing behind shield with deer left, date in legend **Note:** Kipper-24 Kreuzer.

Date	Mintage	VG	F	VF	XF	Unc
1621	—	75.00	150	300	625	—

KM# 23 1/96 THALER (Körtling)
Silver **Obv:** Brunswick helmet with horse **Rev:** Imperial orb with 96 divides date

Date	Mintage	VG	F	VF	XF	Unc
1605	—	—	—	—	—	—

KM# 35 1/28 THALER
Silver **Obv:** Brunswick helmet with horse **Rev:** Wildman, tree branch in right hand, 28 below

Date	Mintage	VG	F	VF	XF	Unc
1610 (o)	—	—	—	—	—	—

KM# 4 1/24 THALER (Groschen)
Silver **Obv:** Brunswick helmet with horse **Rev:** Imperial orb with 24 **Note:** Ref. W#671.

Date	Mintage	VG	F	VF	XF	Unc
1602	—	25.00	50.00	100	200	—
1603	—	25.00	50.00	100	200	—
1605	—	25.00	50.00	100	200	—

KM# 40 1/24 THALER (Groschen)
Silver **Rev:** Wildman, imperial orb with 24 in right hand, date in legend

Date	Mintage	VG	F	VF	XF	Unc
1613 (o)	—	25.00	55.00	110	225	—
1614 (o)	—	25.00	55.00	110	225	—
1615 (o)	—	25.00	55.00	110	225	—

KM# 67 1/24 THALER (Groschen)
Silver **Obv:** Imperial orb with 24, titles of Matthias, date **Rev:** Rampant lion left **Rev. Legend:** AN. GOT. SE. I. AL. GE.

Date	Mintage	VG	F	VF	XF	Unc
1617	—	16.00	32.00	65.00	130	—
1618	—	16.00	32.00	65.00	130	—

KM# 69 1/24 THALER (Groschen)
Silver **Obv:** Imperial orb with 24, titles of Matthias **Rev:** LIon rampant right **Rev. Legend:** AGENDO CONANDO **Note:** Varieties exist.

Date	Mintage	VG	F	VF	XF	Unc
1617	—	16.00	32.00	65.00	130	—
1619	—	16.00	32.00	65.00	130	—
ND	—	16.00	32.00	65.00	130	—

KM# 68 1/24 THALER (Groschen)
Silver **Note:** Klipper-1/24 Thaler, 5.50 g.

Date	Mintage	VG	F	VF	XF	Unc
1617	—	—	—	—	—	—

KM# 80 1/24 THALER (Groschen)
Silver **Obv:** Imperial orb with 24, titles of Matthias **Rev:** Arms with 2 bear claws (Hoya) **Rev. Legend:** D. MENSCHEN. G. I. V. S. **Note:** Varieties exist.

Date	Mintage	VG	F	VF	XF	Unc
1618	—	16.00	35.00	70.00	145	—
1619	—	16.00	35.00	70.00	145	—

KM# 75 1/24 THALER (Groschen)
Silver **Obv:** 4-fold arms **Obv. Legend:** DOMI. PROVIDEBIT, date

Date	Mintage	VG	F	VF	XF	Unc
1618	—	16.00	35.00	70.00	145	—
1619	—	16.00	35.00	70.00	145	—

KM# 76 1/24 THALER (Groschen)
Silver **Obv:** 2-fold arms divided vertically **Obv. Legend:** BI. GO. IST. RHAT. V. THA. R.

Date	Mintage	VG	F	VF	XF	Unc
1618	—	16.00	35.00	70.00	145	—
1619	—	16.00	35.00	70.00	145	—

KM# 77 1/24 THALER (Groschen)
Silver **Obv:** Rampant lion left **Obv. Legend:** B. GOT. I. RADT. V. DHAD.

Date	Mintage	VG	F	VF	XF	Unc
1618	—	16.00	32.00	65.00	130	—

KM# 78 1/24 THALER (Groschen)
Silver **Obv:** Lion holding key **Obv. Legend:** GOTT. GI: WE. ER. WIL.

Date	Mintage	VG	F	VF	XF	Unc
1618	—	12.00	25.00	55.00	110	—
1619	—	12.00	25.00	55.00	110	—

KM# 79 1/24 THALER (Groschen)
Silver **Obv:** Stag antlers **Obv. Legend:** B. E. GOT. I. RAHT.

Date	Mintage	VG	F	VF	XF	Unc
1618	—	20.00	40.00	85.00	170	—

KM# 92 1/24 THALER (Groschen)
Silver **Obv. Legend:** SOLI. DEO. G.

Date	Mintage	VG	F	VF	XF	Unc
ND	—	16.00	33.00	65.00	130	—

KM# 95 1/24 THALER (Groschen)
Silver **Obv. Legend:** GOTT. BI. WE. ER. WIL.

Date	Mintage	VG	F	VF	XF	Unc
1619	—	13.00	30.00	60.00	120	—

KM# 97 1/24 THALER (Groschen)
Silver **Obv:** Lion rampant left **Obv. Legend:** AGENDO: CONANDO

Date	Mintage	VG	F	VF	XF	Unc
1619	—	13.00	30.00	60.00	120	—
ND	—	13.00	30.00	60.00	120	—

KM# 98 1/24 THALER (Groschen)
Silver **Obv. Legend:** I. A. N. S. Q. S. E. P., date

Date	Mintage	VG	F	VF	XF	Unc
1619	—	13.00	30.00	60.00	120	—

KM# 99 1/24 THALER (Groschen)
Silver **Obv. Legend:** SI. D. P. N. Q. C. N.

Date	Mintage	VG	F	VF	XF	Unc
1619	—	13.00	30.00	60.00	120	—

KM# 100 1/24 THALER (Groschen)
Silver **Obv:** Lion left below crowned band **Obv. Legend:** A DIVVANTE DEO

Date	Mintage	VG	F	VF	XF	Unc
ND	—	12.00	25.00	55.00	110	—

KM# 101 1/24 THALER (Groschen)
Silver **Obv. Legend:** AGENDO: CONANDO

Date	Mintage	VG	F	VF	XF	Unc
1619	—	12.00	25.00	55.00	110	—

KM# 102 1/24 THALER (Groschen)
Silver **Obv:** Lion rampant left in shield **Obv. Legend:** I. A. N. S. Q. S. E. P.

Date	Mintage	VG	F	VF	XF	Unc
1619	—	12.00	25.00	55.00	110	—

KM# 103 1/24 THALER (Groschen)
Silver **Obv:** Crowned lion in gatehouse **Obv. Legend:** FID. N. DE. DEV.

Date	Mintage	VG	F	VF	XF	Unc
ND	—	12.00	25.00	55.00	110	—

KM# 104 1/24 THALER (Groschen)
Silver **Obv:** Lion rampant left in 3-towered gatehouse

Date	Mintage	VG	F	VF	XF	Unc
1619	—	10.00	25.00	50.00	100	—

KM# 105 1/24 THALER (Groschen)
Silver **Obv. Legend:** GOT. DI. EH. S. . M.

Date	Mintage	VG	F	VF	XF	Unc
1619	—	10.00	25.00	50.00	100	—
1620	—	10.00	25.00	50.00	100	—

KM# 106 1/24 THALER (Groschen)
Silver **Obv. Legend:** M. G. C. K.

Date	Mintage	VG	F	VF	XF	Unc
1619	—	10.00	25.00	50.00	100	—

KM# 107 1/24 THALER (Groschen)
Silver **Obv:** Lion walking left **Obv. Legend:** ORA. ET. LABORA.

Date	Mintage	VG	F	VF	XF	Unc
1619	—	10.00	20.00	45.00	90.00	—
1620	—	10.00	20.00	45.00	90.00	—

KM# 108 1/24 THALER (Groschen)
Silver **Obv:** Lion rampant right **Obv. Legend:** DEUS. PROVIDEBIT.

Date	Mintage	VG	F	VF	XF	Unc
1619	—	12.00	25.00	55.00	110	—
ND	—	12.00	25.00	55.00	110	—

KM# A109 1/24 THALER (Groschen)
Silver **Obv. Legend:** DURANT MODERATA

Date	Mintage	VG	F	VF	XF	Unc
ND	—	13.00	30.00	60.00	120	—

KM# 110 1/24 THALER (Groschen)
Silver **Obv. Legend:** IN CRIMEN. COELITS

Date	Mintage	VG	F	VF	XF	Unc
1619	—	12.00	25.00	55.00	110	—
1620	—	12.00	25.00	55.00	110	—

KM# 111 1/24 THALER (Groschen)
Silver **Obv:** Titles of Ferdinand II

Date	Mintage	VG	F	VF	XF	Unc
ND	—	12.00	25.00	55.00	110	—

KM# 112 1/24 THALER (Groschen)
Silver **Rev. Legend:** IUSTIT. ET. CONCOR., date

Date	Mintage	VG	F	VF	XF	Unc
1619	—	12.00	25.00	55.00	110	—

KM# 113 1/24 THALER (Groschen)
Silver **Obv:** Titles of Ferdinand II

Date	Mintage	VG	F	VF	XF	Unc
ND	—	12.00	25.00	55.00	110	—

KM# 116 1/24 THALER (Groschen)
Silver **Obv:** 2 small towers in front of lion, without church

Date	Mintage	VG	F	VF	XF	Unc
1619 (b)	—	12.00	27.00	55.00	115	—

KM# 117 1/24 THALER (Groschen)
Silver **Obv:** Lion rampant right in castle gate with 2 towers **Obv. Legend:** G. V. KR. K. V. G. M.

Date	Mintage	VG	F	VF	XF	Unc
1619 (b)	—	13.00	27.00	55.00	115	—

KM# 118 1/24 THALER (Groschen)
Silver **Obv:** Titles of Ferdinand II **Rev:** Lion waling right **Rev. Legend:** MON: NOV: ARGEN

Date	Mintage	VG	F	VF	XF	Unc
ND	—	13.00	27.00	55.00	115	—

KM# 91 1/24 THALER (Groschen)
Silver **Obv:** 4-fold arms **Obv. Legend:** SI. D. P. N. Q, C. N, date **Note:** Varieties exist.

Date	Mintage	VG	F	VF	XF	Unc
1619	—	16.00	33.00	65.00	130	—

KM# 93 1/24 THALER (Groschen)
Silver **Obv:** 2-fold arms divided horizontally **Obv. Legend:** BI GOTT. IST. RA. V. T. **Note:** Varieties exist.

Date	Mintage	VG	F	VF	XF	Unc
1619	—	13.00	27.00	55.00	115	—
1620	—	13.00	27.00	55.00	115	—

KM# 94 1/24 THALER (Groschen)
Silver **Obv. Legend:** SI. D. P. N. Q. C. N. **Note:** Varieties exist.

Date	Mintage	VG	F	VF	XF	Unc
1619	—	13.00	27.00	55.00	115	—
1620	—	13.00	27.00	55.00	115	—

KM# 96 1/24 THALER (Groschen)
Silver **Obv:** 2 lions on gate with towers **Obv. Legend:** BI. GO. IS. R. V. T. **Note:** Varieties exist.

Date	Mintage	VG	F	VF	XF	Unc
1619	—	13.00	27.00	55.00	115	—

KM# 114 1/24 THALER (Groschen)
Silver **Obv:** Imperial orb with 24, titles of Matthias **Rev:** Lion rampant right, holding up model of church **Rev. Legend:** PRO LEGE. ET. GREGE. **Note:** Varieties exist.

Date	Mintage	VG	F	VF	XF	Unc
1619	—	13.00	27.00	55.00	115	—

KM# 119 1/24 THALER (Groschen)
Silver **Obv:** Titles of Matthias **Rev:** 2 leopards left in circle **Rev. Legend:** GOT: GI: GOT: NIM. **Note:** Varieties exist.

Date	Mintage	VG	F	VF	XF	Unc
1619 (b)	—	13.00	27.00	55.00	115	—
1619	—	13.00	27.00	55.00	115	—
1620	—	13.00	27.00	55.00	115	—

KM# 125 1/24 THALER (Groschen)
Silver **Obv:** Helmeted arms with 2 keys **Obv. Legend:** SOLI. DEO. GLORIA **Note:** Varieties exist.

Date	Mintage	VG	F	VF	XF	Unc
1619	—	12.00	25.00	55.00	110	—
1620	—	12.00	25.00	55.00	110	—
ND	—	12.00	25.00	55.00	110	—
ND	—	12.00	25.00	55.00	110	—

Note: Varieties exist

KM# 115 1/24 THALER (Groschen)
Silver **Note:** Klippe-1/24 Thaler.

Date	Mintage	VG	F	VF	XF	Unc
1619 (b)	—	—	—	—	—	—

KM# 124 1/24 THALER (Groschen)
Silver **Obv:** Arms with 2 bear claws **Obv. Legend:** D. MENSCHEN. G. I. V. S. **Note:** Klippe-1/24 Thaler.

Date	Mintage	VG	F	VF	XF	Unc
1619	—	—	—	—	—	—

KM# 121 1/24 THALER (Groschen)
Silver **Obv:** Stag left **Obv. Legend:** ORA. ET. LABORA.

Date	Mintage	VG	F	VF	XF	Unc
1619	—	20.00	40.00	85.00	155	—

KM# 122 1/24 THALER (Groschen)
Silver **Obv:** Stag antlers **Obv. Legend:** PRO PATRIA, date

Date	Mintage	VG	F	VF	XF	Unc
619 (b)	—	20.00	40.00	85.00	155	—
620 (b)	—	20.00	40.00	85.00	155	—

KM# 123 1/24 THALER (Groschen)
Silver **Obv. Legend:** I. A. N. S. Q. S. E. P. 16-19

Date	Mintage	VG	F	VF	XF	Unc
1619	—	20.00	40.00	85.00	155	—

KM# 126 1/24 THALER (Groschen)
Silver **Obv:** Small tree with 7 branches in circle **Obv. Legend:** ME. G. L. V. KR. K. V. G. M.

Date	Mintage	VG	F	VF	XF	Unc
1619 (b)	—	20.00	40.00	85.00	155	—

KM# 173 1/24 THALER (Groschen)
Silver **Obv:** Imperial orb with 24, titles of Ferdinand II **Rev:** Crowned shield with lion rampant left, value 3 below

Date	Mintage	VG	F	VF	XF	Unc
1620	—	13.00	27.00	55.00	110	—

KM# 174 1/24 THALER (Groschen)
Silver **Rev:** Without 3

Date	Mintage	VG	F	VF	XF	Unc
1620	—	13.00	27.00	55.00	110	—

KM# 175 1/24 THALER (Groschen)
Silver **Rev:** Lion rampant right holding tower

Date	Mintage	VG	F	VF	XF	Unc
1620	—	13.00	27.00	55.00	110	—
1621	—	13.00	27.00	55.00	110	—
ND	—	13.00	27.00	55.00	110	—

KM# 177 1/24 THALER (Groschen)
Silver **Obv:** Arms of Hoya (2 bear claws)

Date	Mintage	VG	F	VF	XF	Unc
1620	—	16.00	33.00	65.00	130	—
ND	—	16.00	33.00	65.00	130	—

KM# 178 1/24 THALER (Groschen)
Silver **Obv:** 2-fold arms, lion left, tower right

Date	Mintage	VG	F	VF	XF	Unc
1620 (a)	—	16.00	33.00	65.00	130	—

KM# 179 1/24 THALER (Groschen)
Silver **Obv:** 4-fold arms

Date	Mintage	VG	F	VF	XF	Unc
1620 (b)	—	16.00	33.00	65.00	130	—

KM# 180 1/24 THALER (Groschen)
Silver **Obv:** Crowned 4-fold arms **Obv. Legend:** ADIVVANTE **Rev:** Imperial orb with 24

Date	Mintage	VG	F	VF	XF	Unc
ND	—	16.00	33.00	65.00	130	—

KM# 181 1/24 THALER (Groschen)
Silver **Obv:** Imperial orb with 24, title of Matthias **Rev. Legend:** GOT. DE. E. S. N. M.

Date	Mintage	VG	F	VF	XF	Unc
ND	—	16.00	33.00	65.00	130	—

KM# 182 1/24 THALER (Groschen)
Silver **Obv:** Titles of Ferdinand II

Date	Mintage	VG	F	VF	XF	Unc
ND	—	16.00	33.00	65.00	130	—

KM# 183 1/24 THALER (Groschen)
Silver **Obv:** Titles of Matthias **Rev:** 4-fold arms **Rev. Legend:** D. M. S. I. E. G. V. G., date

Date	Mintage	VG	F	VF	XF	Unc
1620 (b)	—	16.00	33.00	65.00	130	—

KM# 184 1/24 THALER (Groschen)
Silver **Obv:** Titles of Ferdinand II **Rev. Legend:** IN FOE LC. N. IN. VI.

Date	Mintage	VG	F	VF	XF	Unc
1620	—	16.00	33.00	65.00	130	—
ND	—	16.00	33.00	65.00	130	—

KM# 185 1/24 THALER (Groschen)
Silver **Obv:** Heart-shaped arms **Obv. Legend:** IN. F. O. E. L. C. N. I. N. V.*

Date	Mintage	VG	F	VF	XF	Unc
1620	—	16.00	33.00	65.00	130	—

KM# 188 1/24 THALER (Groschen)
Silver **Obv. Legend:** ORA. ET. LABORA. **Rev:** Without legend

Date	Mintage	VG	F	VF	XF	Unc
ND	—	16.00	33.00	65.00	130	—

KM# 189 1/24 THALER (Groschen)
Silver **Obv. Legend:** SEMPER. PRO. PATRIA.

Date	Mintage	VG	F	VF	XF	Unc
1620 (b)	—	16.00	33.00	65.00	130	—

KM# 190 1/24 THALER (Groschen)
Silver **Obv. Legend:** TIME DEV ET. DVCEM.

Date	Mintage	VG	F	VF	XF	Unc
1620	—	16.00	33.00	65.00	130	—

KM# 191 1/24 THALER (Groschen)
Silver **Obv:** Titles of Ferdinand II **Rev:** 2-fold arms divided horizontally **Rev. Legend:** BI GOTT. IST. RA. V. T.

Date	Mintage	VG	F	VF	XF	Unc
1620	—	16.00	33.00	65.00	130	—

KM# 192 1/24 THALER (Groschen)
Silver **Obv. Legend:** FID. DES. DE., date

Date	Mintage	VG	F	VF	XF	Unc
(16)20	—	16.00	33.00	65.00	135	—

KM# 193 1/24 THALER (Groschen)
Silver **Obv. Legend:** OMNI. CR. DE.

Date	Mintage	VG	F	VF	XF	Unc
1620	—	16.00	33.00	65.00	130	—

KM# 194 1/24 THALER (Groschen)
Silver **Obv. Legend:** ORA. ET. LABORA. *20*

Date	Mintage	VG	F	VF	XF	Unc
(16)20	—	16.00	33.00	65.00	130	—

KM# 195 1/24 THALER (Groschen)
Silver **Obv:** Titles of Ferdinand II **Rev:** 2-fold arms divided vertically **Rev. Legend:** TIME. DEV. ET. DUCEM.

Date	Mintage	VG	F	VF	XF	Unc
ND	—	16.00	33.00	65.00	130	—

KM# 196 1/24 THALER (Groschen)
Silver **Obv:** Imperial orb with 24, titles of Matthias, date **Rev:** Horse leaping left in circle **Rev. Legend:** M. G. V. KR. K. V. G. M.

Date	Mintage	VG	F	VF	XF	Unc
1620 (b)	—	27.00	55.00	115	230	—

KM# 197 1/24 THALER (Groschen)
Silver **Obv:** Imperial orb with 24, titles of Ferdinand II **Rev:** 2 lions holding up 2 towers **Rev. Legend:** PRO LEGE ET GREGE

Date	Mintage	VG	F	VF	XF	Unc
1620 (b)	—	16.00	33.00	65.00	130	—

KM# 199 1/24 THALER (Groschen)
Silver **Obv:** Lion rampant left **Obv. Legend:** SI. DE9. PRO. N. Q. C. N.

Date	Mintage	VG	F	VF	XF	Unc
1620	—	13.00	27.00	55.00	115	—

KM# 200 1/24 THALER (Groschen)
Silver **Obv:** Titles of FerdinandII **Rev. Legend:** AGENDO: CONANDO

Date	Mintage	VG	F	VF	XF	Unc
1620	—	13.00	27.00	55.00	115	—
1621	—	13.00	27.00	55.00	115	—

KM# 201 1/24 THALER (Groschen)
Silver **Obv. Legend:** DEUS. (or DEVS) PROVIDER

Date	Mintage	VG	F	VF	XF	Unc
1620	—	13.00	27.00	55.00	115	—
1621 (b)	—	13.00	27.00	55.00	115	—
ND	—	13.00	27.00	55.00	115	—

KM# 202 1/24 THALER (Groschen)
Silver **Obv. Legend:** FIDE. N. DESER. DEUS.

Date	Mintage	VG	F	VF	XF	Unc
ND	—	13.00	27.00	55.00	115	—

KM# 203 1/24 THALER (Groschen)
Silver **Obv. Legend:** I. A. N. S. Q. S. E. P., date

Date	Mintage	VG	F	VF	XF	Unc
ND	—	13.00	27.00	55.00	115	—

KM# 204 1/24 THALER (Groschen)
Silver **Obv. Legend:** PAR. PRO. S. N. IRA. L. 2. 0.

Date	Mintage	VG	F	VF	XF	Unc
(16)20	—	13.00	27.00	55.00	115	—
ND	—	13.00	27.00	55.00	115	—

KM# 205 1/24 THALER (Groschen)
Silver **Obv:** Crowned lion rampant left **Obv. Legend:** PAR. PRO. S. N. IRA. L.

Date	Mintage	VG	F	VF	XF	Unc
1620	—	13.00	27.00	55.00	115	—
ND	—	13.00	27.00	55.00	115	—

KM# 206 1/24 THALER (Groschen)
Silver **Obv. Legend:** PRO. ARIS. ET. FO.

Date	Mintage	VG	F	VF	XF	Unc
ND	—	13.00	27.00	55.00	115	—

KM# 207 1/24 THALER (Groschen)
Silver **Obv:** Lion left below crowned band **Obv. Legend:** A DIVVANTE DEO

Date	Mintage	VG	F	VF	XF	Unc
1620	—	13.00	27.00	55.00	115	—
1621	—	13.00	27.00	55.00	115	—

KM# 208 1/24 THALER (Groschen)
Silver **Obv:** Imperial orb with 24, titles of Matthias **Rev:** Lion rampant left, tower to side **Rev. Legend:** TIME. DEV. ET. DVCE.

Date	Mintage	VG	F	VF	XF	Unc
1620	—	13.00	27.00	55.00	115	—

KM# 209 1/24 THALER (Groschen)
Silver **Obv:** Titles of Ferdinand II **Rev:** Lion rampant left in 3-towered gatehouse

Date	Mintage	VG	F	VF	XF	Unc
ND	—	13.00	27.00	55.00	115	—
1620	—	13.00	27.00	55.00	115	—

KM# 210 1/24 THALER (Groschen)
Silver **Obv. Legend:** FID. N. DE. DEUS.

Date	Mintage	VG	F	VF	XF	Unc
ND	—	13.00	27.00	55.00	115	—

KM# 212 1/24 THALER (Groschen)
Silver **Obv:** Lion rampant left, gate with 1 tower **Obv. Legend:** M. GL. V. KR. K. V. G. M.

Date	Mintage	VG	F	VF	XF	Unc
1620 (b)	—	13.00	27.00	55.00	115	—

KM# 213 1/24 THALER (Groschen)
Silver **Obv:** Titles of Ferdinand II **Rev:** Gate with 2 towers **Rev. Legend:** NERVI RERVM

Date	Mintage	VG	F	VF	XF	Unc
1620	—	13.00	27.00	55.00	115	—

KM# 214 1/24 THALER (Groschen)
Silver **Obv:** Lion to left below cloverleaf in gate with 2 towers **Obv. Legend:** NERVI. RERUM. **Rev:** Imperial orb with 24

Date	Mintage	VG	F	VF	XF	Unc
1620	—	13.00	27.00	55.00	115	—

KM# 215 1/24 THALER (Groschen)
Silver **Obv:** Lion rampant right **Obv. Legend:** COELITUS. IN GREME

Date	Mintage	VG	F	VF	XF	Unc
1620	—	13.00	27.00	55.00	115	—

KM# 216 1/24 THALER (Groschen)
Silver **Obv. Legend:** NON. PROCRASTIND

Date	Mintage	VG	F	VF	XF	Unc
1620	—	13.00	27.00	55.00	115	—
ND	—	13.00	27.00	55.00	115	—

KM# 217 1/24 THALER (Groschen)
Silver **Obv:** Tower to side of lion **Obv. Legend:** PRO LEGE

Date	Mintage	VG	F	VF	XF	Unc
1620 (b)	—	13.00	27.00	55.00	115	—

KM# 218 1/24 THALER (Groschen)
Silver **Obv. Legend:** TIME. DEV. ET. DVC.

Date	Mintage	VG	F	VF	XF	Unc
1620	—	13.00	27.00	55.00	115	—

KM# 219 1/24 THALER (Groschen)
Silver **Obv:** 2 small towers in front of lion, without church

Date	Mintage	VG	F	VF	XF	Unc
1620 (b)	—	13.00	27.00	55.00	115	—

KM# 220 1/24 THALER (Groschen)
Silver **Obv:** Imperial orb with 24 **Obv. Legend:** M. D. G. R. I. S. A 6-19

Date	Mintage	VG	F	VF	XF	Unc
1620/(1)619	—	—	—	—	—	—

KM# 221 1/24 THALER (Groschen)
Silver **Obv:** Titles of Ferdinand II, date in legend **Rev:** Stag antlers

Date	Mintage	VG	F	VF	XF	Unc
1620	—	20.00	40.00	85.00	170	—
1621	—	20.00	40.00	85.00	170	—

KM# 223 1/24 THALER (Groschen)

Silver **Obv:** Date in legend

Date	Mintage	VG	F	VF	XF	Unc
1620	—	20.00	40.00	85.00	170	—

KM# 224 1/24 THALER (Groschen)

Silver **Obv:** Titles of Ferdinand II **Rev:** Helmeted arms with 2 keys

Date	Mintage	VG	F	VF	XF	Unc
1620	—	16.00	33.00	65.00	130	—

KM# 225 1/24 THALER (Groschen)

Silver **Obv:** Heart-shaped arms with bars **Obv. Legend:** OM. CREAVI. DEVS.

Date	Mintage	VG	F	VF	XF	Unc
1620	—	16.00	33.00	65.00	130	—

KM# 109 1/24 THALER (Groschen)

Silver **Obv. Legend:** DURANT MODERATA **Note:** Klippe, 4.20 G.

Date	Mintage	VG	F	VF	XF	Unc
ND	—	—	60.00	100	—	—

KM# 176 1/24 THALER (Groschen)

Silver **Obv:** Brunswick helmet with horse **Obv. Legend:** F • VL • D • G • DVX • B • E • L **Note:** Varieties exist.

Date	Mintage	VG	F	VF	XF	Unc
1620	—	12.00	25.00	55.00	110	—
1622	—	12.00	25.00	55.00	110	—
1622 CL	—	12.00	25.00	55.00	110	—
1623 GL	—	12.00	25.00	55.00	110	—

KM# 187 1/24 THALER (Groschen)

Silver **Obv:** 4-fold arms **Obv. Legend:** OMNIA. CREAV. DEVS. **Note:** 1/24 Thaler-Klippe.

Date	Mintage	VG	F	VF	XF	Unc
1620	—	16.00	33.00	65.00	130	—

KM# 198 1/24 THALER (Groschen)

Silver **Note:** 1/24 Thaler-Klippe.

Date	Mintage	VG	F	VF	XF	Unc
1620 (b)	—	—	—	—	—	—

KM# 211 1/24 THALER (Groschen)

Silver **Note:** 1/24 Thaler-Klippe.

Date	Mintage	VG	F	VF	XF	Unc
ND	—	—	—	—	—	—

KM# 222 1/24 THALER (Groschen)

Silver **Rev. Legend:** F. E. I. I. D. G. R. I. 6-20 **Note:** 1/24-Klippe.

Date	Mintage	VG	F	VF	XF	Unc
1620	—	—	—	—	—	—

KM# 120 1/24 THALER (Groschen)

Silver **Obv. Legend:** LABOR. CONSUMIMU.

Date	Mintage	VG	F	VF	XF	Unc
ND	—	12.00	25.00	50.00	100	—

KM# 312 1/24 THALER (Groschen)

Silver **Obv:** Imperial orb with 24, titles of Ferdinand II **Rev:** Wildman, tree in right hand **Note:** Kipper coinage.

Date	Mintage	VG	F	VF	XF	Unc
(16)21	—	—	—	—	—	—
ND	—	—	—	—	—	—

KM# 313 1/24 THALER (Groschen)

Silver **Note:** 1/14 Thaler-Klippe.

Date	Mintage	VG	F	VF	XF	Unc
(16)21	—	—	—	—	—	—

KM# 316 1/24 THALER (Groschen)

Silver **Obv:** Brunswick helmet with horse **Note:** 1/24 Thaler/Klippe.

Date	Mintage	VG	F	VF	XF	Unc
1621 ID	—	—	—	—	—	—

KM# 318 1/24 THALER (Groschen)

Silver **Note:** 1/24 Thaler-Klippe.

Date	Mintage	VG	F	VF	XF	Unc
1621	—	—	—	—	—	—

KM# 320 1/24 THALER (Groschen)

Silver **Obv:** Arms of Hoya (2 bear claws) **Note:** 1/24 Thaler-Klippe.

Date	Mintage	VG	F	VF	XF	Unc
1621	—	—	—	—	—	—

KM# 317 1/24 THALER (Groschen)

Silver **Obv:** Horse in front of column, value 3 in legend **Note:** Varieties exist.

Date	Mintage	VG	F	VF	XF	Unc
1621	—	—	—	—	—	—

KM# 314 1/24 THALER (Groschen)

Silver **Obv:** Lion rampant left in ornamented shield

Date	Mintage	VG	F	VF	XF	Unc
1621	—	13.00	27.00	55.00	115	—

KM# 315 1/24 THALER (Groschen)

Silver **Obv:** Lion rampant right holding 2 towers

Date	Mintage	VG	F	VF	XF	Unc
1621	—	13.00	27.00	55.00	115	—

KM# 319 1/24 THALER (Groschen)

Silver **Obv:** Without 3 in legend

Date	Mintage	VG	F	VF	XF	Unc
1621	—	—	—	—	—	—
ND	—	—	—	—	—	—

KM# 321 1/24 THALER (Groschen)

Silver **Obv:** Lion rampant left **Obv. Legend:** SOLI. DEO. GLORIA.

Date	Mintage	VG	F	VF	XF	Unc
1621	—	13.00	27.00	55.00	115	—

KM# 322 1/24 THALER (Groschen)

Silver **Obv. Legend:** MIT. RAT. VNT. THAT.

Date	Mintage	VG	F	VF	XF	Unc
1621	—	13.00	27.00	55.00	115	—

KM# 323 1/24 THALER (Groschen)

Silver **Obv:** Lion rampant right, S at each side **Obv. Legend:** MONE: NOVA, ARGENT

Date	Mintage	VG	F	VF	XF	Unc
1621	—	13.00	27.00	55.00	115	—

KM# 324 1/24 THALER (Groschen)

Silver **Obv. Legend:** CONSILIO. ET. ARM.

Date	Mintage	VG	F	VF	XF	Unc
1621	—	13.00	27.00	55.00	115	—

KM# 325 1/24 THALER (Groschen)

Silver **Obv:** Titles of Matthias **Rev:** Brunswick helmet **Rev. Legend:** ORA. ET. LABORA

Date	Mintage	VG	F	VF	XF	Unc
ND	—	16.00	33.00	65.00	130	—

KM# 326 1/24 THALER (Groschen)

Silver **Obv:** Titles of Ferdinand II **Rev. Legend:** FI. N. DE. DEI.

Date	Mintage	VG	F	VF	XF	Unc
ND	—	16.00	33.00	65.00	130	—
1621	—	16.00	33.00	65.00	130	—

KM# 327 1/24 THALER (Groschen)

Silver **Obv:** Stag antlers **Rev:** Date divided by orb

Date	Mintage	VG	F	VF	XF	Unc
1621	—	20.00	40.00	75.00	155	—

KM# 336 1/24 THALER (Groschen)

Silver **Obv:** Brunwick helmet with horse **Rev:** Imprial orb with 24 divdies date

Date	Mintage	VG	F	VF	XF	Unc
1622 CH	—	13.00	27.00	55.00	115	—

KM# 337 1/24 THALER (Groschen)

Silver **Obv:** Brunswick helmet with horse **Rev:** Imperial orb with 24 divides date

Date	Mintage	VG	F	VF	XF	Unc
1622 HS	—	13.00	27.00	55.00	115	—
1623 HS	—	13.00	27.00	55.00	115	—

KM# 388 1/24 THALER (Groschen)

Silver **Obv:** Brunswick helmet

Date	Mintage	VG	F	VF	XF	Unc
1636 (s)	—	13.00	27.00	55.00	115	—

KM# 553 1/24 THALER (Groschen)

Silver **Obv:** Horse leaping left **Rev:** Imperial orb with 24

Date	Mintage	VG	F	VF	XF	Unc
1684	—	13.00	27.00	55.00	115	—

KM# 591 1/24 THALER (Groschen)

Silver **Obv:** Crowned intertwined cursive RAV monogram, date in legend

Date	Mintage	VG	F	VF	XF	Unc
1691 HCH	—	16.00	33.00	65.00	130	—
1692 HCH	—	16.00	33.00	65.00	130	—
1693 HCH	—	16.00	33.00	65.00	130	—

KM# 609 1/24 THALER (Groschen)

Silver **Rev. Legend:** NACH DEN. . .

Date	Mintage	VG	F	VF	XF	Unc
1693 HCH	—	16.00	33.00	65.00	130	—

KM# 610 1/24 THALER (Groschen)

Silver **Obv:** Horse leaping left **Rev:** Imperial orb with 24

Date	Mintage	VG	F	VF	XF	Unc
1693 HCH	—	16.00	33.00	65.00	130	—

KM# 26 1/16 THALER

Silver **Obv:** Brunswick helmet with horse **Rev:** Wildman, tree branch in right hand, date in legend, 16 at top

Date	Mintage	VG	F	VF	XF	Unc
1605	—	—	—	—	—	—
1606	—	—	—	—	—	—

KM# 329 1/16 THALER

Silver **Obv:** Imperial eagle, 16 in orb on breast, titles of Ferdinand II, date in legend **Rev:** DS in circle

Date	Mintage	VG	F	VF	XF	Unc
(1)621	—	50.00	100	180	360	—
ERR(1)612 (error)	—	50.00	100	180	360	—

KM# 328 1/16 THALER

Silver **Obv:** Lion rampant left **Rev:** DS **Rev. Legend:** PAX. AL. PRO. BELLO. **Note:** Kipper 1/16 Thaler.

Date	Mintage	VG	F	VF	XF	Unc
ND	—	60.00	125	250	500	—

KM# 510 1/16 THALER

Silver **Obv:** Bust right **Rev:** XVI EININ REICHSTHALER…, date in legend

Date	Mintage	VG	F	VF	XF	Unc
1671 GB	—	33.00	65.00	130	260	—
1675 GB	—	33.00	65.00	130	260	—
1676 GB	—	33.00	65.00	130	260	—
1678 GB	—	33.00	65.00	130	260	—

KM# 522 1/16 THALER

Silver **Rev:** Date below value

Date	Mintage	VG	F	VF	XF	Unc
1676 R	—	33.00	65.00	130	260	—
1677 R	—	—	—	—	—	—

KM# 36 1/14 THALER

Silver **Obv:** Brunswick helmet with horse **Rev:** Wildman, tree branch in right hand, 14 in legend

Date	Mintage	VG	F	VF	XF	Unc
1610 (d)	—	27.00	55.00	130	260	—
1610 (o)	—	27.00	55.00	130	260	—

KM# 554 1/12 THALER (2 Groschen)

Silver **Obv:** Horse leaping left, date below **Rev:** 12/EINEN/EEICHS/TAL

Date	Mintage	VG	F	VF	XF	Unc
1684	—	—	—	—	—	—

KM# 600 1/12 THALER (2 Groschen)

Silver **Obv:** Horse leaping left **Rev:** Value 12. . ., LANDMUNTZ in 5 lines **Note:** Varieties exist.

Date	Mintage	VG	F	VF	XF	Unc
1692 HCH	—	13.00	27.00	65.00	130	—
1693 HCH	—	13.00	27.00	65.00	130	—
1695 HCH	—	13.00	27.00	65.00	130	—
1695 ICB	—	13.00	27.00	65.00	130	—
1697 DF	—	13.00	27.00	65.00	130	—

KM# 616 1/12 THALER (2 Groschen)

Silver **Ruler:** Anton Ulrich **Obv. Legend:** NACH DEN…, Horse leaping left, date below horse **Rev:** Value 12. . ., LANDMUNTZ IN 5 lines

Date	Mintage	VG	F	VF	XF	Unc
1694	—	16.00	33.00	75.00	155	—
1695	—	16.00	33.00	75.00	155	—
1697	—	16.00	33.00	75.00	155	—

KM# 626 1/12 THALER (2 Groschen)

Silver **Ruler:** Anton Ulrich **Rev:** Date below value

Date	Mintage	VG	F	VF	XF	Unc
1699 HCH	—	16.00	33.00	75.00	155	—
1700 HCH	—	16.00	33.00	75.00	155	—

KM# 15 1/8 THALER

Silver **Subject:** DEath of Heinrich Juluis' Mother, Hedwig von Brandenburg **Obv:** 11-fold arms **Rev:** 10-line inscription with date

Date	Mintage	VG	F	VF	XF	Unc
1602 (o)	—	—	—	—	—	—

KM# 27 1/8 THALER

Silver **Obv:** 11-fold arms with central shield of Halberstadt arms **Rev:** Wildman, tree branch in right hand

Date	Mintage	VG	F	VF	XF	Unc
1606 (o)	—	—	—	—	—	—

KM# 41 1/8 THALER

Silver **Subject:** Death of Heinrich Julius **Rev:** 9-line inscription with date

Date	Mintage	VG	F	VF	XF	Unc
1613 (o)	—	40.00	80.00	160	325	—

KM# 49 1/8 THALER

Silver **Obv:** 11-fold arms **Obv. Legend:** Without D. G. in titles **Rev:** Wildman, tree in right hand, date in legend

Date	Mintage	VG	F	VF	XF	Unc
1614 (o)	—	40.00	80.00	160	325	—

KM# 127 1/8 THALER

Silver **Obv. Legend:** D. G. in titles

Date	Mintage	VG	F	VF	XF	Unc
1619 (c)	—	40.00	80.00	160	325	—
1620 (c)	—	40.00	80.00	160	325	—
1621 (c)	—	40.00	80.00	160	325	—
1623 HS	—	40.00	80.00	160	325	—
1624 (b)	—	40.00	80.00	160	325	—

KM# 362 1/8 THALER

Silver **Subject:** Death of Friedrich Ulrich's Mother, Elisabeth of Denmark **Obv:** Arms of 2 lions on left facing 3 leopards on right, double legend inscriptions **Rev:** 13-line inscription with date

Date	Mintage	VG	F	VF	XF	Unc
1626 (s)	—	—	—	—	—	—

KM# 367 1/8 THALER

Silver **Obv:** Crowned 11-fold arms **Rev:** Wildman, tree in right hand, date in legend

Date	Mintage	VG	F	VF	XF	Unc
1629 HS	—	40.00	80.00	160	325	—
1634 HS	—	40.00	80.00	160	325	—

KM# 389 1/8 THALER

Silver **Obv:** Crowned 11-fold arms, titles in Latin **Rev:** Wildman, tree in right hand

Date	Mintage	VG	F	VF	XF	Unc
1636 (s)	—	40.00	80.00	160	325	—

KM# 394 1/8 THALER
Silver **Obv:** Titles in German

Date	Mintage	VG	F	VF	XF	Unc
1637 (s)	—	35.00	70.00	160	325	—
1639 (s)	—	35.00	70.00	160	325	—
1641 (s)	—	35.00	70.00	160	325	—
1647 (s)	—	35.00	70.00	160	325	—

KM# 459 1/8 THALER
Silver **Rev:** Wildman holds tree with both hands to his left

Date	Mintage	VG	F	VF	XF	Unc
1659 (s)	—	75.00	150	300	—	—
1664 (s)	—	75.00	150	300	—	—

KM# 460 1/8 THALER
Silver **Rev:** Wildman holds tree across in front of him, date in legend

Date	Mintage	VG	F	VF	XF	Unc
1659 (s)	—	90.00	180	360	—	—

KM# 474 1/8 THALER
3.6000 g., Silver, 29.9 mm. **Subject:** Death of August II **Obv:** 11-line inscription with date **Rev:** Withered tree with skull at base

Date	Mintage	VG	F	VF	XF	Unc
1666	—	75.00	150	225	400	—

KM# 520 1/8 THALER
Silver **Obv:** Crowned 11-fold arms **Rev:** Wildman holding tree with both hands to his left, date in legend

Date	Mintage	VG	F	VF	XF	Unc
1675 IPE	—	—	—	—	—	—

KM# 601 1/8 THALER
Silver **Obv:** Helmeted 11-fold arms divide date **Rev:** Wildman holding tree with both hands to his left

Date	Mintage	VG	F	VF	XF	Unc
1692 RB	—	—	—	—	—	—

KM# 618 1/8 THALER
Silver **Subject:** Death of August Wilhelm's Wife, Christine Sophie **Obv:** Eagle above globe, inscription on ribbon above **Rev:** 13-line inscription

Date	Mintage	VG	F	VF	XF	Unc
MDCVC (1695) ICB	—	40.00	80.00	160	325	—

KM# 611 1/6 THALER
Silver **Obv:** Crowned 12-fold arms **Rev:** Horse leaping left, 1/6 below

Date	Mintage	VG	F	VF	XF	Unc
1693 ICB	—	45.00	90.00	180	360	—
1696 ICB	—	45.00	90.00	180	360	—

KM# 617 1/6 THALER
Silver **Obv:** Horse leaping left **Rev:** Crowned 11-fold arms divide date, 1/6 below

Date	Mintage	VG	F	VF	XF	Unc
1694 ICB	—	50.00	100	200	425	—
1695 ICB	—	50.00	100	200	425	—

KM# 8 1/4 THALER
Silver **Rev:** St. Andrew with cross, date in legend

Date	Mintage	VG	F	VF	XF	Unc
1601 (d)	—	50.00	100	200	425	—
1602 (d)	—	50.00	100	200	425	—
1604 (d)	—	50.00	100	200	425	—
1605 (d)	—	50.00	100	200	425	—
1606 (d)	—	50.00	100	200	425	—
1609 (d)	—	50.00	100	200	425	—
1610 (d)	—	50.00	100	200	425	—
1612 (d)	—	50.00	100	200	425	—

KM# 5 1/4 THALER
Silver **Obv:** 11-fold arms with central shield of Halberstadt arms

Date	Mintage	VG	F	VF	XF	Unc
1601 (d)	—	60.00	120	200	400	—
1601 (o)	—	60.00	120	200	400	—
160Z (d)	—	—	—	—	—	—
160Z (o)	—	—	—	—	—	—
1603 (d)	—	60.00	120	200	400	—
1603 (o)	—	60.00	120	200	400	—
1604 (d)	—	—	—	—	—	—
1604 (o)	—	60.00	120	200	400	—
1605 (o)	—	—	—	—	—	—
1605 (d)	—	60.00	120	200	400	—
1606 (d)	—	—	—	—	—	—
1606 (o)	—	60.00	120	200	400	—
1607 (d)	—	60.00	120	200	400	—
1607 (o)	—	60.00	120	200	400	—
1608 (d)	—	60.00	120	200	400	—
1608 (o)	—	60.00	120	200	400	—
1609 (d)	—	60.00	120	200	400	—
1609 (o)	—	60.00	120	200	400	—
1610 (d)	—	60.00	120	200	400	—
1610 (o)	—	60.00	120	200	400	—
1611 (d)	—	60.00	120	200	400	—
1611 (o)	—	60.00	120	200	400	—
1612 (o)	—	60.00	120	200	400	—
1613 (o)	—	60.00	120	200	400	—

KM# 16 1/4 THALER
Silver **Subject:** Death of Heinrich Julius' Mother, Hedwig von Brandenburg **Note:** Similar to 1 Thaler, KM#18.

Date	Mintage	VG	F	VF	XF	Unc
1602 (o)	—	—	—	—	—	—

KM# 42 1/4 THALER
7.1000 g., Silver, 31.5 mm. **Subject:** Death of Heinrich Julius **Note:** Similar to 1 Thaler, KM#46.

Date	Mintage	VG	F	VF	XF	Unc
1613	—	85.00	165	325	650	—
1613 (o)	—	85.00	165	325	650	—

KM# 43 1/4 THALER
Silver **Note:** Similar to 1 Thaler, KM#47.

Date	Mintage	VG	F	VF	XF	Unc
1613 (o)	—	50.00	100	200	425	—
1614 (o)	—	50.00	100	200	425	—

KM# 50 1/4 THALER
Silver

Date	Mintage	VG	F	VF	XF	Unc
1614 (o)	—	55.00	110	225	440	—
1614/3 (o)	—	—	—	—	—	—
1615 (o)	—	55.00	110	225	440	—
1616 (o)	—	55.00	110	225	440	—
1617 (o)	—	55.00	110	225	440	—
1618	—	55.00	110	225	440	—
1619	—	55.00	110	225	440	—
1619 (c)	—	55.00	110	225	440	—
1620 (c)	—	55.00	110	225	440	—
1621 (c)	—	55.00	110	225	440	—
1622 (c)	—	55.00	110	225	440	—
1624 (c)	—	55.00	110	225	440	—
1624 HL	—	55.00	110	225	440	—
1624 HS	—	55.00	110	225	440	—
1625 (s)	—	55.00	110	225	440	—
1625 HL	—	55.00	110	225	440	—
1626 (s)	—	55.00	110	225	440	—
1627 (s)	—	55.00	110	225	440	—
1628 (s)	—	55.00	110	225	440	—
1629 (s)	—	55.00	110	225	440	—

KM# 59 1/4 THALER
Silver **Obv:** 11-fold arms **Rev:** St. Andrew with cross

Date	Mintage	VG	F	VF	XF	Unc
1616 (o)	—	—	—	—	—	—

KM# 363 1/4 THALER
Silver **Subject:** Death of Friedrich Ulrich's Mother, Elisabeth of Denmark **Note:** Similar to 1 Thaler, KM#365.

Date	Mintage	VG	F	VF	XF	Unc
1626 (s)	—	—	—	—	—	—

KM# 376 1/4 THALER
Silver **Obv:** Crowned 11-fold arms **Rev:** Wildman, tree in right hand, date in legend

Date	Mintage	VG	F	VF	XF	Unc
1631 (s)	—	50.00	100	225	365	—
1632 (s)	—	50.00	100	225	365	—
1634 (s)	—	50.00	100	225	365	—

KM# 377 1/4 THALER
Silver **Obv:** Crowned 11-fold arms **Rev:** St. Jacob, staff in right hand

Date	Mintage	VG	F	VF	XF	Unc
1633 (s)	—	—	—	—	—	—

KM# 390 1/4 THALER
Silver **Note:** Similar to KM#395 but titles in Latin.

Date	Mintage	VG	F	VF	XF	Unc
1636 (s)	—	50.00	100	180	360	—

KM# 395 1/4 THALER
Silver **Obv:** Titles in German

Date	Mintage	VG	F	VF	XF	Unc
1637 (s)	—	33.00	70.00	145	290	—
1638 (s)	—	33.00	70.00	145	290	—
1639 (s)	—	33.00	70.00	145	290	—
1642 (s)	—	33.00	70.00	145	290	—
1654 (s)	—	33.00	70.00	145	290	—
1655 (s)	—	33.00	70.00	145	290	—

KM# 411 1/4 THALER
Silver **Note:** 1/4 2nd Bell Thaler.

Date	Mintage	VG	F	VF	XF	Unc
1643 (s)	—	75.00	150	300	600	—

KM# 435 1/4 THALER
Silver **Obv:** Bust left **Rev:** Crowned 11-fold arms, date in legend

Date	Mintage	VG	F	VF	XF	Unc
1647 (s)	—	—	—	—	—	—

KM# 461 1/4 THALER
Silver **Note:** Similar to KM#395 but wildman holds tree across in front of him.

Date	Mintage	VG	F	VF	XF	Unc
1659 (s)	—	40.00	80.00	160	325	—
1660 (s)	—	40.00	80.00	160	325	—
1665 (s)	—	40.00	80.00	160	325	—

KM# 465 1/4 THALER
Silver

Date	Mintage	VG	F	VF	XF	Unc
1660 (s)	—	75.00	150	300	600	—
1663 (s)	—	75.00	150	300	600	—
1664 (s)	—	75.00	150	300	600	—

KM# 475 1/4 THALER
Silver **Subject:** Death of August II

Date	Mintage	VG	F	VF	XF	Unc
1666	—	160	275	375	650	—

KM# 515 1/4 THALER
Silver **Note:** Similar to KM#395 but wildman holding tree with both hands to his left.

Date	Mintage	VG	F	VF	XF	Unc
1673 IPE	—	40.00	80.00	150	310	—
1684 RD	—	40.00	80.00	150	310	—

KM# 592 1/4 THALER
Silver **Ruler:** Anton Ulrich **Mint:** Zellerfeld

Date	Mintage	VG	F	VF	XF	Unc
1691 RB	—	40.00	80.00	180	360	—

KM# 619 1/4 THALER
Silver **Subject:** Death of August Wilhelm's wife, Christine Sophia **Note:** Similar to 1 Thaler, KM#621.

Date	Mintage	VG	F	VF	XF	Unc
1695 ICB	—	—	—	—	—	—

KM# 612 1/3 THALER
Silver **Obv:** Horse leaping left **Rev:** Crowned 11-fold arms, value 1/3 below

Date	Mintage	VG	F	VF	XF	Unc
1693 ICB	—	—	—	—	—	—
1694 ICB	—	—	—	—	—	—

KM# 6 1/2 THALER
Silver **Obv:** Helmeted 11-fold arms with central shield of Halberstadt arms **Rev:** Wildman, tree branch in right hand

Date	Mintage	VG	F	VF	XF	Unc
1601 (o)	—	85.00	160	250	450	—
1602 (d)	—	85.00	160	250	450	—
1602 (o)	—	85.00	160	250	450	—
1603 (d)	—	85.00	160	250	450	—
1603 (o)	—	85.00	160	250	450	—
1603/Z (o)	—	—	—	—	—	—
1604	—	85.00	160	250	450	—
1604 (o)	—	85.00	160	250	450	—

KM# 9 1/2 THALER
Silver **Rev:** St. Andrew with cross, date in legend

Date	Mintage	VG	F	VF	XF	Unc
1601 (d)	—	250	400	675	1,300	—
1602 (d)	—	250	400	675	1,300	—
1604 (d)	—	250	400	675	1,300	—
1605 (d)	—	250	400	675	1,300	—

KM# 10 1/2 THALER
Silver **Note:** Klippe 1/2 Thaler.

Date	Mintage	VG	F	VF	XF	Unc
1601 (d)	—	—	—	—	—	—

KM# 17 1/2 THALER
Silver **Subject:** Death of Heinrich Julius' Mother, Hedwig von Brandenburg **Note:** Similar to 1 Thaler, KM#18.

Date	Mintage	VG	F	VF	XF	Unc
1602 (o)	—	—	—	—	—	—

KM# 22 1/2 THALER
Silver **Obv:** Without helmets above arms

Date	Mintage	VG	F	VF	XF	Unc
1604 (o)	—	70.00	140	220	425	—
1605 (o)	—	70.00	140	220	425	—
1605 (d)	—	—	—	—	—	—
1606 (o)	—	70.00	140	220	425	—
1607 (o)	—	70.00	140	220	425	—
1608 (o)	—	70.00	140	220	425	—
1609 (o)	—	70.00	140	220	425	—
1610 (o)	—	70.00	140	220	425	—
1611 (o)	—	70.00	140	220	425	—
1611 (d)	—	70.00	140	220	425	—
1612 (o)	—	70.00	140	220	425	—
1613 (o)	—	70.00	140	220	425	—

KM# 28 1/2 THALER
Silver **Rev:** St. Andrew with cross, date in legend

Date	Mintage	VG	F	VF	XF	Unc
1608 (d)	—	—	—	—	—	—
1610 (d)	—	—	—	—	—	—
1612 (d)	—	—	—	—	—	—

KM# 44 1/2 THALER
Silver **Subject:** Death of Heinrich Julius **Note:** Similar to 1 Thaler, KM#46.

Date	Mintage	VG	F	VF	XF	Unc
1613 (o)	—	125	250	375	750	—

KM# 45 1/2 THALER
Silver **Note:** Similar to 1 Thaler, KM#47.

Date	Mintage	VG	F	VF	XF	Unc
1613 (o)	—	60.00	120	200	425	—
1614 (o)	—	60.00	120	200	425	—

KM# 51 1/2 THALER
Silver **Note:** Similar to 1 Thaler, KM#52.

Date	Mintage	VG	F	VF	XF	Unc
1614 (o)	—	55.00	110	175	360	—
1615 (o)	—	55.00	110	175	360	—
1616 (o)	—	55.00	110	175	360	—
1617 (o)	—	55.00	110	175	360	—
1618	—	55.00	110	175	360	—
1619	—	55.00	110	175	360	—
1621 (c)	—	55.00	110	175	360	—
1622 (c)	—	55.00	110	175	360	—
1622 HL	—	55.00	110	175	360	—
1623 (h)	—	55.00	110	175	360	—
1624 (h)	—	55.00	110	175	360	—
1625 (h)	—	55.00	110	175	360	—
1625 HL	—	55.00	110	175	360	—
1626 (s)	—	55.00	110	175	360	—
1627 (s)	—	55.00	110	175	360	—
1628 (s)	—	55.00	110	175	360	—
1629 (h)	—	55.00	110	175	360	—
1632 (s)	—	55.00	110	175	360	—

KM# 70 1/2 THALER
Silver **Obv:** Angel's head and wings above 11-fold arms **Rev:** Wildman, tree in right hand, date in legend

Date	Mintage	VG	F	VF	XF	Unc
1617	—	60.00	120	200	425	—
1618	—	60.00	120	200	425	—
1624	—	60.00	120	200	425	—

KM# 364 1/2 THALER
Silver **Subject:** Death of Friedrich Ulrich's Mother, Elisabeth of Denmark **Note:** Similar to 1 Thaler, KM#365.

Date	Mintage	VG	F	VF	XF	Unc
1626 (h)	—	—	—	—	—	—
1626 (s)	—	—	—	—	—	—

KM# 368 1/2 THALER
Silver **Obv:** Crowned 11-fold arms **Rev:** Wildman, tree in right hand

Date	Mintage	VG	F	VF	XF	Unc
1628 HS	—	60.00	120	200	425	—
1629 HS	—	60.00	120	200	425	—
1631 HS	—	60.00	120	200	425	—
1633 HS	—	60.00	120	200	425	—
1634 HS	—	60.00	120	200	425	—

KM# 378 1/2 THALER
Silver **Obv:** Similar to 1 Thaler, KM#365 **Rev:** St. Jacob with staff in right hand

Date	Mintage	VG	F	VF	XF	Unc
1633 (s)	—	—	—	—	—	—

KM# 382 1/2 THALER
Silver **Obv:** Helmeted 11-fold arms **Rev:** Wildman, tree in right hand, date in legend **Note:** August II.

Date	Mintage	VG	F	VF	XF	Unc
1634 (s)	—	—	—	—	—	—

KM# 391 1/2 THALER
Silver **Note:** Similar to 1/4 Thaler, KM#395.

Date	Mintage	VG	F	VF	XF	Unc
1636 (s)	—	120	200	300	600	—
1637 (s)	—	120	200	300	600	—
1639 (s)	—	120	200	300	600	—
1653 (s)	—	120	200	300	600	—
1655 (s)	—	120	200	300	600	—
1656 (s)	—	120	200	300	600	—

KM# 410 1/2 THALER
Silver

Date	Mintage	VG	F	VF	XF	Unc
1641 (s)	—	—	—	—	—	—
1642 (s)	—	—	—	—	—	—

KM# 412 1/2 THALER
Silver **Note:** 1/2 1st Bell Thaler. Similar to 1 Thaler, KM#418.

Date	Mintage	VG	F	VF	XF	Unc
1643	—	60.00	120	200	400	—

KM# 413 1/2 THALER
Silver **Note:** 1/2 2nd Bell Thaler. Similar to 1 Thaler, KM#419.

Date	Mintage	VG	F	VF	XF	Unc
1643 (s)	—	60.00	120	200	400	—

KM# 414 1/2 THALER
Silver **Note:** 1/2 3rd Bell Thaler.

Date	Mintage	VG	F	VF	XF	Unc
1643	—	80.00	160	325	650	—

KM# 415 1/2 THALER
Silver **Note:** 1/2 4th Bell Thaler.

Date	Mintage	VG	F	VF	XF	Unc
1643	—	70.00	140	250	450	—

KM# 416 1/2 THALER
Silver **Note:** 1/2 5th Bell Thaler.

Date	Mintage	VG	F	VF	XF	Unc
1643 (s)	—	60.00	120	200	375	—

KM# 417 1/2 THALER
Silver **Note:** 1/2 6th Bell Thaler.

Date	Mintage	VG	F	VF	XF	Unc
1643 (s)	—	60.00	120	200	400	—

KM# 454 1/2 THALER
Silver **Note:** Illustration reduced.

Date	Mintage	VG	F	VF	XF	Unc
1656 (s)	—	55.00	110	175	360	—
1663 (s)	—	55.00	110	175	360	—
1664 (s)	—	55.00	110	175	360	—
1665 (s)	—	55.00	110	175	360	—

KM# 468 1/2 THALER
Silver **Rev:** Wildman holds tree across in front of him

Date	Mintage	VG	F	VF	XF	Unc
1661 (s)	—	70.00	140	250	500	—

KM# 476 1/2 THALER
Silver **Subject:** Death of August II **Note:** Similar to 1 Thaler, KM#477.

Date	Mintage	VG	F	VF	XF	Unc
1666	—	135	240	375	650	—

KM# 575 1/2 THALER
Silver **Ruler:** Anton Ulrich **Obv:** Crowned 11-fold arms, date divided below **Rev:** 2 wildman holding 2 interwined trees **Note:** Similar to 1 Thaler, KM#571.

Date	Mintage	VG	F	VF	XF	Unc
1687 RB	—	55.00	110	175	375	—
1691 RB	—	55.00	110	175	375	—
1697 RB	—	55.00	110	175	375	—

KM# A620 1/2 THALER
Silver **Subject:** Death of August Wilhelm's Wife, Christine Sophie **Note:** Similar to 1 Thaler, KM#621.

Date	Mintage	VG	F	VF	XF	Unc
1695 ICB	—	—	—	—	—	—

KM# 620 1/2 THALER
Silver **Obv:** Crowned 11-fold arms **Rev:** Wildman holding tree with both hands to his left, date in legend

Date	Mintage	VG	F	VF	XF	Unc
1695 ICB	—	—	—	—	—	—

KM# 635 1/2 THALER
Silver **Ruler:** Anton Ulrich **Obv:** Crowned 11-fold arms **Rev:** Wildman holding tree to his left with 2 hands, date in legend

Date	Mintage	VG	F	VF	XF	Unc
1700 RB	—	70.00	140	275	575	—

KM# 587 2/3 THALER
Silver **Obv:** Horse leaping left **Rev:** Crowned 11-fold arms divide date, REMIGIO... in legend, value below

Date	Mintage	VG	F	VF	XF	Unc
1690 ICB	—	40.00	85.00	160	325	—
1693 ICB	—	40.00	85.00	160	325	—
1694 ICB	—	40.00	85.00	160	325	—
1695 ICB	—	40.00	85.00	160	325	—

KM# 613 2/3 THALER
Silver **Rev. Legend:** LAND. MUNTZ...

Date	Mintage	VG	F	VF	XF	Unc
1693	—	65.00	135	275	550	—

KM# 623 2/3 THALER
Silver **Obv:** Crowned 12-fold arms **Rev:** Horse leaping left, 2/3 divide date below

Date	Mintage	VG	F	VF	XF	Unc
1696 ICB	—	50.00	100	200	400	—
1697 ICB	—	50.00	100	200	400	—

KM# 624 2/3 THALER
Silver **Obv:** Crowned 11-fold arms, value 2/3 below **Rev:** Horse leaping left, date below **Note:** Varieties exist.

Date	Mintage	VG	F	VF	XF	Unc
1697 DF	—	50.00	100	180	360	—

KM# 627 2/3 THALER
Silver **Ruler:** Anton Ulrich **Obv:** Crowned 14-fold arms divide date **Rev:** Horse leaping left, value 2/3 below

Date	Mintage	VG	F	VF	XF	Unc
1699 HCH	—	75.00	150	300	625	—
1700 HCH	—	75.00	150	300	625	—

KM# 636 2/3 THALER
Silver **Ruler:** Anton Ulrich **Rev:** Date divided by value below horse

Date	Mintage	VG	F	VF	XF	Unc
1700 HCH	—	35.00	75.00	150	310	—

KM# 11 THALER
Silver **Ruler:** Heinrich Julius **Rev:** Cross below right arm **Mint:** Goslar **Note:** Dav. #9087 (6288).

Date	Mintage	VG	F	VF	XF	Unc
1601 (d)	—	100	200	325	525	—

KM# 7 THALER
Silver **Ruler:** Heinrich Julius **Subject:** Heinrich Julius **Obv:** Helmeted 11-fold arms with central shield of Halberstadt arms **Rev:** Wildman, tree trunk in right hand, date in legend **Mint:** Goslar **Note:** Dav.#6285.

Date	Mintage	VG	F	VF	XF	Unc
1601 (d)	—	100	200	325	500	—
1601 (d)	—	100	200	325	500	—
1601 (o)	—	100	200	325	500	—
1602 (d)	—	100	200	325	500	—
1602 (o)	—	100	200	325	500	—
1603 (d)	—	100	200	325	500	—
1603 (o)	—	100	200	325	500	—
1604 (d)	—	100	200	325	500	—
1604 (o)	—	100	200	325	500	—
1605 (d)	—	100	200	325	500	—
1605 (o)	—	100	200	325	500	—
1606 (d)	—	—	—	—	—	—
1606 (o)	—	100	200	325	500	—
1607 (d)	—	—	—	—	—	—
1607 (o)	—	100	200	325	500	—
1608 (d)	—	100	200	325	500	—
1608 (o)	—	100	200	325	500	—
1609 (d)	—	—	—	—	—	—
1609 (o)	—	100	200	325	500	—
1610 (d)	—	100	200	325	500	—
1610 (o)	—	100	200	325	500	—
1611 (d)	—	100	200	325	500	—
1611 (o)	—	100	200	325	500	—
1612 (d)	—	—	—	—	—	—
1612 (o)	—	100	200	325	500	—
1613 (o)	—	100	200	325	500	—

KM# 12.1 THALER
Silver **Rev:** St. Andrew holding cross **Note:** Dav.#6290.

Date	Mintage	VG	F	VF	XF	Unc
1601 (d)	—	100	200	325	525	—
1602 (d)	—	100	200	325	525	—
1603 (d)	—	100	200	325	525	—
1604 (d)	—	100	200	325	525	—
1605 (d)	—	100	200	325	525	—
1606 (d)	—	100	200	325	525	—
1607 (d)	—	100	200	325	525	—
1608 (d)	—	100	200	325	525	—
1609 (d)	—	100	200	325	525	—
1610 (d)	—	100	200	325	525	—
1611 (d)	—	100	200	325	525	—

KM# 12.2 THALER

Silver **Rev:** Left hand over joint of cross **Note:** Dav. #6292.

Date	Mintage	VG	F	VF	XF	Unc
1602 (d)	—	100	200	325	525	—
1603 (d)	—	100	200	325	525	—

KM# 18 THALER

Silver **Subject:** Death of Heinrich Julius' Mother, Hedwig von Brandenburg **Obv:** Central shield of Halberstadt arms. **Rev:** 11-line inscription **Note:** Dav. #6296.

Date	Mintage	VG	F	VF	XF	Unc
1602 (o)	—	180	350	725	1,250	—

KM# 12.3 THALER

Silver **Rev:** St. Andrew within circle of arabesques **Note:** Dav. #6293.

Date	Mintage	VG	F	VF	XF	Unc
1604 (d)	—	100	200	325	525	—
1605 (d)	—	100	200	325	525	—

KM# 24 THALER

Silver **Obv:** Helmeted 11-fold arms with central shield of Halberstadt arms, thick flan **Rev:** St. Andrew with cross, date in legend **Note:** Dav. #6286A.

Date	Mintage	VG	F	VF	XF	Unc
1605 (d)	—	—	—	—	—	—

KM# 47 THALER

Silver **Obv:** Helmeted 11-fold arms, without D. G. in titles **Note:** Dav. #A6303.

Date	Mintage	VG	F	VF	XF	Unc
1613 (o)	—	65.00	145	300	600	—
1614 (o)	—	65.00	145	300	600	—
1615 (o)	—	65.00	145	300	600	—

KM# 52.1 THALER

Silver **Obv:** With D.G. in titles **Note:** Dav.#6303.

Date	Mintage	VG	F	VF	XF	Unc
1613 (o)	—	80.00	175	375	650	—
1614 (o)	—	80.00	175	375	650	—
1615 (o)	—	80.00	175	375	650	—
1616 (o)	—	80.00	175	375	650	1,600
1617 (o)	—	80.00	175	375	650	—
1618 (o)	—	80.00	175	375	650	—
1619 (o)	—	80.00	175	375	650	—
1619 (c)	—	80.00	175	375	650	—
1620 (c)	—	80.00	175	375	650	—
1621 (c)	—	80.00	175	375	650	—
1622 (c)	—	80.00	175	375	650	—
1622 HL-(c)	—	80.00	175	375	650	—
1623 HL-(c)	—	80.00	175	375	650	—
1623 HL	—	80.00	175	375	650	—
1624 HL	—	80.00	175	375	650	—
1625 HL	—	80.00	175	375	650	—
1625	—	80.00	175	375	650	—
1626 (s)	—	80.00	175	375	650	—
1627 (s)	—	80.00	175	375	650	—
1628 (s)	—	80.00	175	375	650	—

KM# 46 THALER

Silver **Subject:** Death of Heinrich Julius **Note:** Dav. #6298.

Date	Mintage	VG	F	VF	XF	Unc
1613 (o)	—	175	325	650	1,400	—

KM# 52.2 THALER

Silver **Rev:** Border of crosses **Note:** Dav. #6303A.

Date	Mintage	VG	F	VF	XF	Unc
1615	—	115	290	525	975	—

KM# 52.3 THALER

Silver **Rev:** Top on tree **Note:** Dav. #6303B.

Date	Mintage	VG	F	VF	XF	Unc
1615	—	115	290	525	975	—

KM# 60 THALER

Silver **Rev:** St. Andrew with cross, date in legend **Note:** Dav. #6305.

Date	Mintage	VG	F	VF	XF	Unc
1616 (o)	—	150	300	525	975	—

KM# 52.4 THALER

Silver **Rev:** With mintmaster initials HS **Note:** Dav. #6306.

Date	Mintage	VG	F	VF	XF	Unc
1622 (h)	—	85.00	190	425	750	—
1623 (h)	—	85.00	190	425	750	—
1624 (h)	—	85.00	190	425	750	—
1625 (h)	—	85.00	190	425	750	—
1626 (h)	—	85.00	190	425	750	—
1627 (h)	—	85.00	190	425	750	—
1628 (h)	—	85.00	190	425	750	—
1629 (h)	—	85.00	190	425	750	—

KM# 365 THALER

Silver **Subject:** Death of Friedrich Ulrich's Mother, Elisabeth of Denmark **Note:** Dav. #6299.

Date	Mintage	VG	F	VF	XF	Unc
1626 (h)	—	215	425	750	1,200	—
1626 (s)	—	215	425	750	1,200	—

KM# 366 THALER

Silver **Rev:** 12-line inscription with month of death as IULI instead of IUNI **Note:** Dav. #6300.

Date	Mintage	VG	F	VF	XF	Unc
1626 (h)	—	240	475	850	1,450	—

KM# 52.5 THALER

Silver **Rev:** Inner pearl border and flowers **Note:** Dav. #6307.

Date	Mintage	VG	F	VF	XF	Unc
1627 (s)	—	85.00	190	375	650	—
1628 (s)	—	85.00	190	375	650	—
1629 (s)	—	85.00	190	375	650	—
1630 (s)	—	85.00	190	375	650	—
1631 (s)	—	85.00	190	375	650	—
1632 (s)	—	85.00	190	375	650	—
1633 (s)	—	85.00	190	375	650	—
1634 (s)	—	85.00	190	375	650	—
1635 (s)	—	85.00	190	375	650	—

Note: Varieties of inner border exists

KM# 380 THALER

Silver **Rev:** St. Jacob divides LAVTEN-TAHL, SI-date **Note:** Dav. #6309.

Date	Mintage	VG	F	VF	XF	Unc
1633 (s)	—	575	1,100	2,750	5,500	—

KM# 381 THALER

Silver **Rev:** St. Jacob divides 16-33 and S-I in 2 lines **Note:** Dav. #6310.

Date	Mintage	VG	F	VF	XF	Unc
1633 (s)	—	575	1,100	2,750	5,500	—

KM# 379 THALER

Silver **Rev:** Date at left of St. Jacob **Note:** Lauthenthal Mining Thalers. Dav. #6308.

Date	Mintage	VG	F	VF	XF	Unc
1633 (s)	—	525	950	1,750	6,500	—
1634 (s)	—	525	950	1,750	6,500	—

KM# 446 THALER

Silver **Note:** Reisse Thaler. Varieties exist. Dav. #6357.

Date	Mintage	VG	F	VF	XF	Unc
ND	—	165	325	775	1,650	—
ND (s)	—	165	325	775	1,650	—

KM# 448 THALER

Silver **Note:** Similar to KM#446 but capped bust and 1 large ship on reverse. Dav. #6360.

Date	Mintage	VG	F	VF	XF	Unc
ND	—	500	1,000	1,850	3,300	—

KM# 449 THALER

Silver **Obv:** Capped bust 3/4 to left **Note:** Dav. #6361.

Date	Mintage	VG	F	VF	XF	Unc
ND	—	500	1,000	1,850	3,300	—

KM# 447.1 THALER

Silver **Obv. Legend:** ...LUNEB:. **Note:** Dav. #6362.

Date	Mintage	VG	F	VF	XF	Unc
ND (s)	—	145	285	575	1,050	—

KM# 447.2 THALER

Silver **Rev:** Mint mark on shore nearer ship **Note:** Dav. #6362A.

Date	Mintage	VG	F	VF	XF	Unc
ND (s)	—	145	285	575	1,050	—

KM# 447.3 THALER

Silver **Obv. Legend:** ...U*LUNE:. **Note:** Dav. #6362B.

Date	Mintage	VG	F	VF	XF	Unc
ND (s)	—	145	285	575	1,050	—

KM# 447.4 THALER

Silver **Rev. Legend:** Larger boat farther from land with mm below, more clouds above **Note:** Dav. #6362C.

Date	Mintage	VG	F	VF	XF	Unc
ND (s)	—	145	285	575	1,050	—

KM# 392.1 THALER

Silver **Obv:** Helmeted 11-fold arms, titles in Latin **Rev:** Wildman, tree in right hand, date in legend **Note:** Dav. #6335.

Date	Mintage	VG	F	VF	XF	Unc
1636 (s)	—	220	450	825	1,500	—

KM# 392.2 THALER

Silver **Obv. Legend:** AUGUST' IUNI. D. -G: -DUX... **Note:** Dav. #6336.

Date	Mintage	VG	F	VF	XF	Unc
1636 (s)	—	220	450	825	1,500	—

KM# 393.1 THALER

Silver **Obv:** Titles in German, AUGUS: HERTZOB--ZU. BR: UND: L. **Note:** Dav. #6337.

Date	Mintage	VG	F	VF	XF	Unc
1636 (s)	—	75.00	165	300	625	—
1637 (s)	—	75.00	165	300	625	—
1638 (s)	—	75.00	165	300	625	—
1639 (s)	—	75.00	165	300	625	—

KM# 396 THALER

Silver **Note:** Similar to KM#444, but wildman holds tree with only his left hand

Date	Mintage	VG	F	VF	XF	Unc
1637	—	—	—	—	—	—

KM# 398.1 THALER

Silver **Obv:** 1/2-length figure left **Obv. Legend:** AUGUSTUS HERTOZOG. ZU. BRAUNS. UND. LUN. **Rev:** Helmeted 11-fold arms, date in legend **Note:** Dav. #6346.

Date	Mintage	VG	F	VF	XF	Unc
1638 (s)	—	85.00	175	350	700	—
1639 (s)	—	85.00	175	350	700	—

KM# 398.2 THALER

Silver **Rev:** Legend unbroken by arms at bottom **Note:** Dav. #6347.

Date	Mintage	VG	F	VF	XF	Unc
1639 (s)	—	85.00	175	350	700	—
1640 (s)	—	85.00	175	350	700	—
1641 (s)	—	85.00	175	350	700	—
1642 (s)	—	85.00	175	350	700	—
1643 (s)	—	85.00	175	350	700	—
1644 (s)	—	85.00	175	350	700	—
1644	—	85.00	175	350	700	—
1645 (s)	—	85.00	175	350	700	—
1646	—	85.00	175	350	700	—

KM# 393.2 THALER

Silver **Obv. Legend:** AUGUS. HERTZ. ZU. BR. U. LUN. **Note:** Dav. #6348.

Date	Mintage	VG	F	VF	XF	Unc
1639	—	75.00	165	325	625	—
1640 (s)	—	75.00	165	325	625	—
1641 (s)	—	75.00	165	325	625	—
1642 (s)	—	75.00	165	325	625	—
1643 (s)	—	75.00	165	325	625	—
1644 (s)	—	75.00	165	325	625	—
1645 (s)	—	75.00	165	325	625	—
1646 (s)	—	75.00	165	325	625	—
1647	—	75.00	165	325	625	—
1647 (s)	—	75.00	165	325	625	—
1648 (s)	—	75.00	165	325	625	—

KM# 418.1 THALER

Silver **Rev. Legend:** ALLES*MIT BEDACHT*ANNO, date **Note:** 1st Bell Thaler. Dav. #6363.

Date	Mintage	VG	F	VF	XF	Unc
1643	—	150	265	500	750	1,150

KM# 419.1 THALER

Silver **Obv:** Small 3/4 length armored figure of August II left. **Obv. Legend:** • AUGUSTUS • HERTZOG • ZU **Rev:** Bell with *UTI * SIC * NISI * below **Rev. Legend:** * ALLES * MIT * BEDACHT * ANNO **Note:** 2nd Bell Thaler. Dav. #6366. Prev. KM#419. Varieties exist.

Date	Mintage	VG	F	VF	XF	Unc
1643	—	150	265	500	775	—
1643 (s)	—	150	265	500	775	—

KM# 422 THALER

Silver **Note:** 3rd Bell Thaler. Dav. #6368.

Date	Mintage	VG	F	VF	XF	Unc
1643	—	220	400	800	2,000	5,000
1643 (s)	—	220	400	800	2,000	5,000

KM# 425 THALER

Silver **Rev:** Clapper style bell with stone block **Note:** 4th Bell Thaler. Dav. #6371.

Date	Mintage	VG	F	VF	XF	Unc
1643	—	200	400	775	1,200	—

KM# 427 THALER

Silver **Note:** 5th Bell Thaler. Dav. #6373.

Date	Mintage	VG	F	VF	XF	Unc
1643 (s)	—	150	275	525	825	—

KM# 428 THALER

Silver **Note:** 6th Bell Thaler. Dav. #6374.

Date	Mintage	VG	F	VF	XF	Unc
1643 (s)	—	150	275	550	875	—

Note: Varieties exist

KM# 429 THALER

Silver **Rev:** Sun above city scene **Note:** 7th Bell Thaler. Dav. #6375. Varieties exist.

Date	Mintage	VG	F	VF	XF	Unc
1643	—	110	250	500	725	—
1643 (s)	—	110	250	500	725	—

KM# 418.2 THALER

Silver **Rev. Legend:** ...BEDACHT. mm.-ANO., date **Note:** Dav. #6364.

Date	Mintage	VG	F	VF	XF	Unc
1643 (s)	—	145	255	475	750	—

KM# 419.2 THALER

Silver **Obv:** Small 3/4 length armored figure of August II left **Note:** Dav. #6366A.

Date	Mintage	VG	F	VF	XF	Unc
1643 HS	—	145	255	475	750	—

KM# 419.3 THALER

Silver **Obv:** Large 3/4 length armored figure of August II left **Note:** Dav. #6366B.

Date	Mintage	VG	F	VF	XF	Unc
1643	—	145	255	475	750	—

Note: 1643 (s) is error.

KM# 420 THALER

Silver **Obv:** Helmeted 11-fold arms **Note:** Dav. #6367.

Date	Mintage	VG	F	VF	XF	Unc
1643 (s)	—	900	1,750	3,500	6,000	—

KM# 423 THALER

Silver **Rev:** UTI SIC NISI below bell **Note:** Dav. #6369.

Date	Mintage	VG	F	VF	XF	Unc
1643	—	180	325	600	1,050	—
1643 (s)	—	180	325	600	1,050	—

KM# 424 THALER

Silver **Obv:** Helmeted 11-fold arms **Note:** Dav. #6370.

Date	Mintage	VG	F	VF	XF	Unc
1643	—	180	325	600	1,050	—

KM# 426 THALER

Silver **Obv:** Helmeted 11-fold arms **Note:** Dav. #6372.

Date	Mintage	VG	F	VF	XF	Unc
1643	—	—	—	—	—	—

KM# 398.3 THALER

Silver **Note:** Dav. #6348.

Date	Mintage	VG	F	VF	XF	Unc
1647 (s)	—	70.00	160	325	550	—
1648 (s)	—	70.00	160	325	550	—
1649 (s)	—	70.00	160	325	550	—
1650 (s)	—	70.00	160	325	550	—

KM# 436 THALER

Silver **Obv:** KM#393 **Rev:** Die of Christian Ludwig von Calenberg, KM#47. **Note:** Mule. Dav. #6339.

Date	Mintage	VG	F	VF	XF	Unc
1648 (s) Rare	—	—	—	—	—	—
1652 (s) Rare	—	—	—	—	—	—

KM# 440.1 THALER

Silver **Obv:** Bust 3/4 to right **Rev:** Similar to KM#441 **Note:** Dav. #6349.

Date	Mintage	VG	F	VF	XF	Unc
1650 (s)	—	110	220	375	600	—
1651 (s)	—	110	220	375	600	—
1651	—	110	220	375	600	—

KM# 393.3 THALER

Silver **Obv. Legend:** AUGUSTUS. HERTZUG... **Note:** Dav. #6340.

Date	Mintage	VG	F	VF	XF	Unc
1650 (s)	—	70.00	160	300	550	—
1651 (s)	—	70.00	160	300	550	—
1652 (s)	—	70.00	160	300	550	—
1653 (s)	—	70.00	160	300	550	—
ND	—	70.00	160	300	550	—

KM# 440.2 THALER

Silver **Rev. Legend:** ANNO, date **Note:** Dav. #6350. Varieties exist.

Date	Mintage	VG	F	VF	XF	Unc
1652 (s)	—	100	200	350	600	—
1653 (s)	—	100	200	350	600	—

KM# 441 THALER

Silver **Note:** Dav. #6351.

Date	Mintage	VG	F	VF	XF	Unc
1652 (s)	—	115	225	425	850	—
1653 (s)	—	115	225	425	850	—
1654 (s)	—	115	225	425	850	—
1655 (s)	—	115	225	425	850	—

KM# 442.1 THALER

Silver **Obv:** Legend reads right to left **Note:** Dav. #6341.

Date	Mintage	VG	F	VF	XF	Unc
1653 (s)	—	80.00	175	325	550	—
1655 (s)	—	80.00	175	325	550	—
1656 (s)	—	80.00	175	325	550	—
1657 (s)	—	80.00	175	325	550	—
1658 (s)	—	80.00	175	325	550	—
1659 (s)	—	80.00	175	325	550	—
1660 (s)	—	80.00	175	325	550	—
1661 (s)	—	80.00	175	325	550	—
1662 (s)	—	80.00	175	325	550	—
1663 (s)	—	80.00	175	325	550	—
1664 (s)	—	80.00	175	325	550	—
1665 (s)	—	80.00	175	325	550	—

KM# 444.1 THALER

Silver **Obv:** Similar to KM#442.1 **Rev:** Similar to KM#444.2 **Note:** Dav. #6343.

Date	Mintage	VG	F	VF	XF	Unc
1655 (s)	—	80.00	175	325	550	—
1657 (s)	—	80.00	175	325	550	—
1658 (s)	—	80.00	175	325	550	—
1659 (s)	—	80.00	175	325	550	—
1660 (s)	—	80.00	175	325	550	—
1661 (s)	—	80.00	175	325	550	—
1662 (s)	—	80.00	175	325	550	—
1663 (s)	—	80.00	175	325	550	—
1664 (s)	—	80.00	175	325	550	—
1665 (s)	—	80.00	175	325	550	—

KM# 455 THALER

Silver **Obv:** Bust left, legend on both sides on ribbons spiraled around laurel wreaths **Note:** Dav. #6352.

Date	Mintage	VG	F	VF	XF	Unc
1656	—	175	300	575	1,000	—

KM# 456 THALER

Silver **Note:** Dav. #6353.

Date	Mintage	VG	F	VF	XF	Unc
1656	—	125	245	500	1,000	—
1657	—	125	245	500	1,000	—
1658	—	125	245	500	1,000	—
1659	—	125	245	500	1,000	—
1661	—	125	245	500	1,000	—
1664	—	125	245	500	1,000	—

KM# 444.2 THALER

Silver **Note:** Dav. #6344.

Date	Mintage	VG	F	VF	XF	Unc
1662	—	100	200	375	650	—
1664	—	100	200	375	650	—
1665	—	100	200	375	650	—
1666 (s)	—	100	200	375	650	—
1667 (s)	—	100	200	375	650	—

KM# 469 THALER

Silver **Obv:** KM#393 **Rev:** Die of George Wilhelm von Calenberg, KM#57 **Note:** Mule. Dav. #6345.

Date	Mintage	VG	F	VF	XF	Unc
1662 (s)	—	150	300	600	1,200	—

KM# 470 THALER

Silver **Note:** Dav. #6354.

Date	Mintage	VG	F	VF	XF	Unc
1664	—	350	700	1,250	2,250	—
1665	—	350	700	1,250	2,250	—
1665 (s)	—	350	700	1,250	2,250	—

KM# 442.2 THALER

Silver **Obv:** Legend reads left to right **Note:** Dav. #6342.

Date	Mintage	VG	F	VF	XF	Unc
1664 (s)	—	100	200	350	600	—
1665 (s)	—	100	200	350	600	—
1666 (s)	—	100	200	350	600	—

KM# 445 THALER

Silver **Note:** Dav. #6355.

Date	Mintage	VG	F	VF	XF	Unc
1665	—	150	300	650	1,100	—
1665 (s)	—	150	300	650	1,100	—
1666	—	150	300	650	1,100	—
1666 (s)	—	150	300	650	1,100	—

KM# 478 THALER

Silver **Obv:** D. G. after duke's name **Note:** Dav. #6378.

Date	Mintage	VG	F	VF	XF	Unc
1666 HS	—	85.00	175	375	675	—
1667 HS	—	85.00	175	375	675	—
1670 HS	—	85.00	175	375	675	—
1673 IPE	—	85.00	175	375	675	—
1674 IPE	—	85.00	175	375	675	—

KM# 477 THALER

Silver **Subject:** Death of August II **Note:** Dav. #6376.

Date	Mintage	VG	F	VF	XF	Unc
1666	—	150	300	650	1,250	2,000

KM# 502 THALER

Silver **Obv:** D. G. before duke's name **Note:** Varieties exist. Dav. #6379.

Date	Mintage	VG	F	VF	XF	Unc
1667 HS	—	65.00	145	285	485	—
1668 HS	—	65.00	145	285	485	—
1669 HS	—	65.00	145	285	485	—
1670 HS	—	65.00	145	285	485	—
1671 HS	—	65.00	145	285	485	—
1672 IPE	—	65.00	145	285	485	—
1673 IPE	—	65.00	145	285	485	—
1674 IPE	—	65.00	145	285	485	—
1675 IPE	—	65.00	145	285	485	—
1676 RB	—	65.00	145	285	485	—
1678 RB	—	65.00	145	285	485	—
1679 RB	—	65.00	145	285	485	—
1680 RB	—	65.00	145	285	485	—
1681 RB	—	65.00	145	285	485	—
1682 RB	—	65.00	145	285	485	—
1683 RB	—	65.00	145	285	485	—

KM# 511 THALER

Silver **Subject:** Capture of the city of Brunswick **Note:** Dav. #6381.

Date	Mintage	VG	F	VF	XF	Unc
1671 RB	—	230	400	750	1,500	—

KM# 512 THALER

Silver **Obv:** Top of bust breaks legend **Note:** Dav. #6382.

Date	Mintage	VG	F	VF	XF	Unc
1671	—	230	400	750	1,500	—
1671 RB	—	230	400	750	1,500	—

KM# 513.1 THALER

Silver **Note:** Dav. #6383.

Date	Mintage	VG	F	VF	XF	Unc
1671	—	175	350	700	1,350	—

Note: Varieties exist

KM# 513.2 THALER

Silver **Note:** Dav. #6384. Varieties exist.

Date	Mintage	VG	F	VF	XF	Unc
1671 RB	—	225	450	950	1,750	—

KM# 514 THALER

Silver **Obv:** Bust enclosed in circle **Note:** Dav. #6385.

Date	Mintage	VG	F	VF	XF	Unc
1671	—	175	375	750	1,500	—

KM# 524 THALER

Silver **Subject:** Death of August II's 3rd Wife, Sophie Elisabeth von Mecklenburg-Gustrow **Obv:** 2 angels holding crowned heart, 2 hands from clouds above **Rev:** 13-line inscription with Roman numeral date **Note:** Dav. #6377.

Date	Mintage	VG	F	VF	XF	Unc
1676	—	250	500	1,000	2,000	—

KM# 523 THALER

Silver **Subject:** Death of August Friedrich, Eldest Son of Anton Ulrich **Note:** Dav. #6398.

Date	Mintage	VG	F	VF	XF	Unc
1676 Rare	—	—	—	—	—	—

Note: Peus Auction 397, 11-08, near unc realized approximately $10,050

KM# 555 THALER

Silver **Note:** Dav. #6380.

Date	Mintage	VG	F	VF	XF	Unc
1684 RB	—	75.00	150	275	500	1,000
1685 RB	—	75.00	150	275	500	1,000

KM# 560 THALER

Silver **Obv:** Bust left enclosed in circle **Rev:** Helmeted 11-fold arms, date in legend **Note:** Dav. #6386.

Date	Mintage	VG	F	VF	XF	Unc
1685	—	1,200	2,500	5,000	8,750	—
1686 RB	—	—	—	—	—	—

KM# 561 THALER

Silver **Obv:** Intertwined cursive mirror-image RAVA monogram **Note:** Dav. #6387.

Date	Mintage	VG	F	VF	XF	Unc
ND	—	1,200	2,000	3,500	5,500	—

KM# 562 THALER

Silver **Obv:** Helmeted 11-fold arms divide date **Rev:** Wildman holding tree with both hands to his left in circle **Note:** Dav. #6388.

Date	Mintage	VG	F	VF	XF	Unc
1685 RB	—	250	500	1,200	2,500	—

KM# 571 THALER

Silver **Note:** Dav. #6392.

Date	Mintage	VG	F	VF	XF	Unc
1686 RB	—	85.00	170	265	480	—
1687 RB	—	85.00	170	265	480	—

KM# 572.1 THALER

Silver **Obv:** Small shield with round base, **Obv. Legend:** with U's **Note:** Dav. #6393.

Date	Mintage	VG	F	VF	XF	Unc
1686 RB	—	85.00	170	265	480	—
1687 RB	—	85.00	170	265	480	—

KM# 572.2 THALER

Silver **Obv:** Large shield with scalloped base **Obv. Legend:** W/V's **Note:** Dav. #6393A.

Date	Mintage	VG	F	VF	XF	Unc
1688 RB	—	85.00	170	265	480	—
1689 RB	—	85.00	170	265	480	—
1690 RB	—	85.00	170	265	480	—
1691 RB	—	85.00	170	265	480	—
1692 RB	—	85.00	170	265	480	—

KM# 576 THALER

Silver **Note:** Dav. #6394.

Date	Mintage	VG	F	VF	XF	Unc
1688 RB	—	375	750	1,400	2,750	—

KM# 577 THALER

Silver **Obv:** Bust of 2 dukes right within inner circle **Note:** Dav. #395.

Date	Mintage	F	VF	XF	Unc	BU
1688 RB	—	150	250	485	875	1,650
1689 RB	—	150	250	485	875	1,650
1690 RB	—	150	250	485	875	1,650
1691 RB	—	150	250	485	875	1,650
1692 RB	—	150	250	485	875	1,650
1693 RB	—	150	250	485	875	1,650
1694 RB	—	150	250	485	875	1,650
1695 RB	—	150	250	485	875	1,650
1696 RB	—	150	250	485	875	1,650
1697 RB	—	150	250	485	875	1,650
1698 RB	—	150	250	485	875	1,650
1699 RB	—	150	250	485	875	1,650
1700 RB	—	150	250	485	875	1,650

KM# 593 THALER

Silver **Note:** Dav. #6389.

Date	Mintage	F	VF	XF	Unc	BU
1691 RB	—	145	230	400	825	1,350
1692 RB	—	145	230	400	825	1,350
1693 RB	—	145	230	400	825	1,350
1694 RB	—	145	230	400	825	1,350
1695 RB	—	145	230	400	825	1,350
1696 RB	—	145	230	400	825	1,350
1697 RB	—	145	230	400	825	1,350
1698 RB	—	145	230	400	825	1,350
1699 RB	—	145	230	400	825	1,350

KM# 602.1 THALER

Silver **Obv:** Bust drapped and armored right **Rev:** Bust drapped right **Note:** Varieties exist. Dav. #6396.

Date	Mintage	F	VF	XF	Unc	BU
1692 RB	—	525	950	1,600	2,750	—
1693 RB	—	525	950	1,600	2,750	—

KM# 602.2 THALER

Silver **Obv:** Bust armored right **Rev:** Bust drapped right **Note:** Varieties exist. Dav. #6397.

Date	Mintage	F	VF	XF	Unc	BU
1694 RB	—	575	1,150	2,000	3,500	—
1695 RB	—	575	1,150	2,000	3,500	—

KM# 621 THALER

Silver **Subject:** Death of August Wilhelm's wife, Christine Sophie **Note:** Dav. #6400.

Date	Mintage	F	VF	XF	Unc	BU
1695	—	500	900	1,750	3,000	—

KM# 628 THALER

Silver **Note:** Similar to KM#637 but small date divided. Dav. #6390.

Date	Mintage	F	VF	XF	Unc	BU
1699 RB	—	175	350	700	1,150	—

KM# 637 THALER
Silver **Ruler:** Anton Ulrich **Obv:** Helmeted 11-fold arms, date in legend **Rev:** Wildman holding tree with both hands to his left **Note:** Dav. #6391.

Date	Mintage	F	VF	XF	Unc	BU
1700 RB	—	145	275	600	1,000	—

KM# 341 1-1/4 THALER
Silver **Note:** Similar to KM#338 but Fortuna divides date on obverse and a different scene upper left on reverse. Dav. #6315.

Date	Mintage	VG	F	VF	XF	Unc
1622	—	1,200	2,100	3,100	5,200	—

KM# 19 1-1/2 THALER
Silver **Subject:** Death of Heinrich JUlius' Mother, Hedwig von Brandenburg **Note:** Similar to 1 Thaler, KM#18. Dav. #6295.

Date	Mintage	VG	F	VF	XF	Unc
1602 (o) Rare	—	—	—	—	—	—

KM# 37 1-1/2 THALER
43.0000 g., Silver, 63 mm. **Ruler:** Heinrich Julius **Note:** Similar to 3 Thaler, KM#29. Varieties with and without denomination. Dav. #LS33.

Date	Mintage	VG	F	VF	XF	Unc
1612 (o)	—	650	1,150	2,100	3,300	—

KM# 81 1-1/2 THALER
43.0000 g., Silver, 71 mm. **Note:** Illustration reduced. Dav. #LS42.

Date	Mintage	VG	F	VF	XF	Unc
1618 (o)	—	900	1,400	2,450	4,150	—

KM# 356 1-1/2 THALER
43.3000 g., Silver **Note:** Similar to 3 Thaler, KM#359 but without denomination shown. Dav. #LS57. Illustration reduced.

Date	Mintage	VG	F	VF	XF	Unc
1625 HS	—	1,250	2,200	4,150	7,100	—

KM# 450.1 1-1/2 THALER
43.0000 g., Silver **Note:** Similar to 2 Thaler, KM#451, but without denomination value punched in. Dav. #LS71. Illustration reduced.

Date	Mintage	VG	F	VF	XF	Unc
1655 (s)	—	425	750	1,400	2,400	—

KM# 464 1-1/2 THALER
43.0000 g., Silver **Subject:** Death of Princess Anna Sophie **Obv:** Crowned arms in wreath **Rev:** 11-line inscription with date **Note:** Dav. #6317.

Date	Mintage	VG	F	VF	XF	Unc
1659 Rare	—	—	—	—	—	—

KM# 450.2 1-1/2 THALER
43.0000 g., Silver **Note:** Similar to 2 Thaler, KM#451.2, with value 1-1/2. Dav. #LS73.

Date	Mintage	VG	F	VF	XF	Unc
1660 (s)	—	425	750	1,400	2,400	—

KM# 450.3 1-1/2 THALER
43.0000 g., Silver, 63 mm. **Ruler:** August II **Note:** Similar to 2 Thaler, KM#451.3. Dav. #LS75. Illustration reduced.

Date	Mintage	VG	F	VF	XF	Unc
1662 (s)	—	425	750	1,400	2,400	—

KM# 450.4 1-1/2 THALER
43.0000 g., Silver, 62 mm. **Ruler:** August II **Obv:** August II mounted right with plumed hat, value stamped below **Rev:** Helmeted arms **Note:** Dav. #LS77. Illustration reduced.

Date	Mintage	VG	F	VF	XF	Unc
1664 (s)	—	425	750	1,400	2,400	—

KM# 479.2 1-1/2 THALER
43.0000 g., Silver **Note:** Dav. #LS88a.

Date	Mintage	VG	F	VF	XF	Unc
1666 IPE	—	350	650	1,250	1,900	—

Note: IPE mintmasters initials indicate later restrike

KM# 479.3 1-1/2 THALER
43.0000 g., Silver **Note:** Dav. #LS88b.

Date	Mintage	VG	F	VF	XF	Unc
1666 RB	—	900	1,400	2,450	4,150	—

KM# 480 1-1/2 THALER
43.0000 g., Silver **Subject:** Death of August II **Note:** Similar to 1 Thaler, KM#477 but denomination 1-1/2 punched in. Dav. #LS94.

Date	Mintage	VG	F	VF	XF	Unc
1666 Rare	—	—	—	—	—	—

KM# 479.1 1-1/2 THALER

43.0000 g., Silver **Subject:** 88th Birthday of August II **Note:** Similar to 2 Thaler, KM#482 with or without value. Dav. #LS88.

Date	Mintage	VG	F	VF	XF	Unc
1666 (s)	—	850	1,150	1,700	2,650	—

KM# 530.1 1-1/2 THALER

43.0000 g., Silver, 64 mm. **Note:** Illustration reduced. Dav. #LS106.

Date	Mintage	VG	F	VF	XF	Unc
1679 RB	—	350	650	1,250	1,900	—

KM# 530.2 1-1/2 THALER

43.0000 g., Silver **Note:** Dav. #LS108.

Date	Mintage	VG	F	VF	XF	Unc
1683 RB	—	350	650	1,250	1,900	—

KM# 530.3 1-1/2 THALER

43.0000 g., Silver **Ruler:** Rudolf August **Note:** Dav. #LS115. Illustration reduced.

Date	Mintage	VG	F	VF	XF	Unc
1686 RB	—	350	650	1,250	1,900	—

KM# 13 2 THALER

Silver **Obv:** Helmeted 11-fold arms with central shield of Halberstadt arms **Rev:** Wildman, tree trunk in right hand, date in legend **Note:** Dav. #6284.

Date	Mintage	VG	F	VF	XF	Unc
1601 (o)	—	1,300	2,100	3,200	—	—
1604 (o)	—	1,300	2,100	3,200	—	—
1605 (o)	—	1,300	2,100	3,200	—	—

KM# 14 2 THALER

Silver **Note:** Similar to 1 Thaler, KM#12 but with cross below right arm. Dav. #6287.

Date	Mintage	VG	F	VF	XF	Unc
1601 (d) Rare	—	—	—	—	—	—

KM# 20 2 THALER

Silver **Subject:** Death of Heinrich Julius' Mother, Hedwig von Brandenburg **Note:** Similar to 1 Thaler, KM#18. Dav. #6294.

Date	Mintage	VG	F	VF	XF	Unc
1602 (o) Rare	—	—	—	—	—	—

KM# 21.1 2 THALER

Silver **Note:** Similar to 1 Thaler, KM#12. Dav. #6291.

Date	Mintage	VG	F	VF	XF	Unc
1603 (d) Rare	—	—	—	—	—	—

KM# 25.1 2 THALER

Silver **Obv:** Helmeted 11-fold arms with central shield of Halberstadt arms **Obv. Legend:** HENRICVS. IVLIVS. . . BRVNSVIC. ET. L. **Rev:** Wildman, tree trunk in right hand, date in legend **Note:** Dav. #6286.

Date	Mintage	VG	F	VF	XF	Unc
1605 (o)	—	425	750	1,250	2,200	—

KM# 25.2 2 THALER

Silver **Obv. Legend:** Ends: ...BRUNSVI. ET. LU. **Note:** Dav. #6286A.

Date	Mintage	VG	F	VF	XF	Unc
1605 (o)	—	425	750	1,250	2,200	—

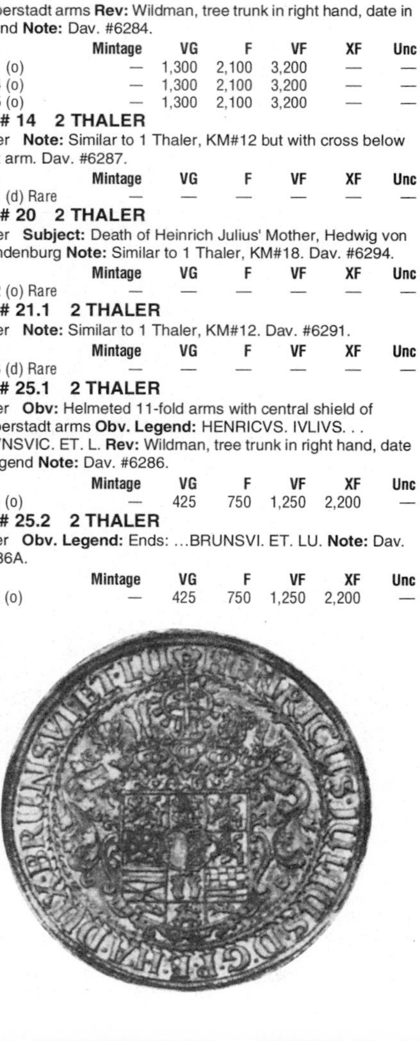

KM# 25.3 2 THALER

Silver **Obv. Legend:** HENRICUS.IULIUS...BRUNSVI.ET.LU. **Note:** Dav. #6286B.

Date	Mintage	VG	F	VF	XF	Unc
1605 (o)	—	425	750	1,250	2,200	—

KM# 21.2 2 THALER

Silver **Note:** Dav. #6289.

Date	Mintage	VG	F	VF	XF	Unc
1607 (d) Rare	—	—	—	—	—	—
1611 (d) Rare	—	—	—	—	—	—

KM# 38 2 THALER

57.2000 g., Silver **Note:** Similar to 3 Thaler, KM#29. Dav. #LS32. Illustration reduced.

Date	Mintage	VG	F	VF	XF	Unc
1612 (o)	—	900	1,550	2,750	4,550	—

Note: Struck with 1-1/2 Thaler dies. Varieties with and without denomination

KM# 48 2 THALER

57.2000 g., Silver **Subject:** Death of Heinrich Julius **Note:** Struck from 1 Thaler dies on thick flan. Similar to 1 Thaler, KM#46. Dav. #6297.

Date	Mintage	VG	F	VF	XF	Unc
1613 (o) Rare	—	—	—	—	—	—

KM# 62 2 THALER

57.2000 g., Silver **Obv:** KM#61 **Rev:** KM#25 **Note:** Mule. Dav. #6301.

Date	Mintage	VG	F	VF	XF	Unc
(1616)/1605 (o)	—	1,300	2,150	3,250	—	—

KM# 61 2 THALER

57.2000 g., Silver **Note:** Dav. #6302.

Date	Mintage	VG	F	VF	XF	Unc
1616 (o)	—	1,550	2,650	4,150	—	—
1621 (c)	—	1,550	2,650	4,150	—	—

KM# 63 2 THALER

57.2000 g., Silver **Obv:** Similar to 1 Thaler, KM#52 **Rev:** St. Andrew with cross, date in legend **Note:** Dav. #6304.

Date	Mintage	VG	F	VF	XF	Unc
1616 (o) Rare	—	—	—	—	—	—

KM# 82 2 THALER

57.0000 g., Silver **Note:** 2 Glucks Thaler. Similar to 1-1/4 Thaler, KM#339, but without value shown. Dav. #6312.

Date	Mintage	VG	F	VF	XF	Unc
ND	—	1,550	2,650	4,150	—	—

KM# 83 2 THALER

57.0000 g., Silver **Note:** Similar to 1-1/2 Thaler, KM#81, but 2 punched in. Dav. #LS41.

Date	Mintage	VG	F	VF	XF	Unc
1618 (o)	—	1,250	2,100	3,300	—	—

Note: Varieties with and without denomination.

KM# 357 2 THALER

57.5300 g., Silver **Note:** Similar to 3 Thaler, KM#359, but 2 punched in. Dav. #LS56.

Date	Mintage	VG	F	VF	XF	Unc
1625 HS	—	1,300	2,300	4,300	7,300	—

KM# 430 2 THALER

57.5300 g., Silver **Note:** 2nd Bell Thaler. Similar to 1 Thaler, KM#419. Dav. #6365.

Date	Mintage	VG	F	VF	XF	Unc
1643 Rare	—	—	—	—	—	—

KM# 451.1 2 THALER

58.0000 g., Silver, 63 mm. **Obv:** Without 2 punched in **Note:** Illustration reduced. Dav. #LS570

Date	Mintage	VG	F	VF	XF	Unc
1655 (s)	—	550	925	1,800	3,300	—

KM# 451.2 2 THALER

58.0000 g., Silver **Obv:** With 2 punched in **Note:** Dav. #LS72. Illustration reduced.

Date	Mintage	VG	F	VF	XF	Unc
1660 (s)	—	375	650	1,250	2,300	—

KM# 451.3 2 THALER

46.9400 g., Silver, 61 mm. **Note:** Illustration reduced. Dav. #LS74.

Date	Mintage	VG	F	VF	XF	Unc
1662 (s)	—	450	775	1,500	2,750	—

KM# 451.4 2 THALER

57.4000 g., Silver, 62 mm. **Rev:** No inner circle **Note:** Illustration reduced. Dav. #LS76.

Date	Mintage	VG	F	VF	XF	Unc
1664 (s)	—	450	775	1,500	2,750	—

KM# 482.2 2 THALER

Silver, 66 mm. **Note:** Illustration reduced. Dav. #LS87A.

Date	Mintage	VG	F	VF	XF	Unc
1666 IPE	—	425	750	1,300	2,350	—

KM# 482.3 2 THALER

Silver **Note:** Dav. #LS87B.

Date	Mintage	VG	F	VF	XF	Unc
1666 RB	—	850	1,700	3,300	5,400	—

Note: The above with mintmaster's initials other than (s) are later restrikes

KM# 483 2 THALER

Silver **Subject:** Death of August II **Note:** Similar to 1 Thaler, KM#477 but 2 punched in. Dav. #LS93.

Date	Mintage	VG	F	VF	XF	Unc
1666 Rare	—	—	—	—	—	—

KM# 481 2 THALER

Silver **Subject:** 88th Birthday of August II **Note:** With 2 punched in. Dav. #LS97C.

Date	Mintage	VG	F	VF	XF	Unc
1666 (s)	—	425	750	1,250	2,200	—

KM# 482.1 2 THALER

Silver **Note:** Similar to KM#482.2. Dav. #LS87. Illustration reduced.

Date	Mintage	VG	F	VF	XF	Unc
1666 (s)	—	450	900	1,750	3,100	—

KM# 531.1 2 THALER

Silver **Note:** Similar to 1-1/2 Thaler, KM#530 but 2 punched in. Dav. #LS105.

Date	Mintage	VG	F	VF	XF	Unc
1679 RB	—	475	900	1,700	3,050	—

KM# 531.2 2 THALER

Silver **Note:** Dav. #LS107.

Date	Mintage	VG	F	VF	XF	Unc
1683 RB	—	475	900	1,700	3,050	—

KM# 563 2 THALER

Silver **Note:** Similar to 3 Thaler, KM#564. Dav. #LS112.

Date	Mintage	VG	F	VF	XF	Unc
1685 RB Rare	—	—	—	—	—	—

KM# 531.3 2 THALER

Silver **Ruler:** Rudolf August **Note:** Dav. #LS114.

Date	Mintage	VG	F	VF	XF	Unc
1686 RB	—	475	900	1,700	3,050	—

KM# 39 2-1/2 THALER

72.0000 g., Silver **Note:** Struck from 1-1/2 Thaler dies. Similar to 3 Thaler, KM#29. Dav. #LS-A32.

Date	Mintage	VG	F	VF	XF	Unc
1612 Rare	—	—	—	—	—	—

KM# 484 2-1/2 THALER

Silver **Note:** Similar to 1-1/2 Thaler, KM#479, 2-1/2 punched in. Dav. #LS86.

Date	Mintage	VG	F	VF	XF	Unc
1666 (s) Rare	—	—	—	—	—	—

KM# 29.1 3 THALER

Silver **Note:** Similar to 5 Thaler, KM#31.1. Dav.#LS26. Illustration reduced.

Date	Mintage	VG	F	VF	XF	Unc
1608 (o)	—	650	1,300	2,400	3,700	—
1609 (o)	—	—	—	—	—	—

KM# 29.2 3 THALER

Silver **Note:** Similar to 5 Thaler, KM#31.1. Dav.#LS29.

Date	Mintage	VG	F	VF	XF	Unc
1610 (o)	—	850	1,700	3,100	5,200	—

KM# 29.3 3 THALER

86.0000 g., Silver, 65 mm. **Note:** Illustration reduced. Varieties exist with differences in background on obverse and ornamentation around arms on reverse. Dav. #LS31.

Date	Mintage	VG	F	VF	XF	Unc
1612 (o)	—	775	1,550	2,800	4,700	—

KM# 72 3 THALER

Silver, 69 mm. **Obv:** Non-marred die **Note:** Illustration reduced. Dav. #LS38.

Date	Mintage	VG	F	VF	XF	Unc
1617 (o)	—	925	1,850	3,700	6,600	—

KM# 71 3 THALER

Silver, 73 mm. **Obv:** Marred die **Rev:** Small horse and shield, 3 stamped in cartouche at bottom **Note:** Illustration reduced. Dav. #LS38a.

Date	Mintage	VG	F	VF	XF	Unc
1617 (o)	—	850	1,700	3,100	5,200	—

KM# 85.1 3 THALER

Silver, 72 mm. **Obv:** KM#71. **Rev:** KM#84. **Note:** Illustration reduced. Dav. #LS38b.

Date	Mintage	VG	F	VF	XF	Unc
1618 (o)	—	850	1,700	3,100	5,200	—

KM# 84 3 THALER

Silver, 69 mm. **Note:** Illustration reduced. Dav. #LS40.

Date	Mintage	VG	F	VF	XF	Unc
1618 (o)	—	775	1,550	2,800	4,700	—

KM# 85.2 3 THALER

Silver **Obv:** KM#712 **Rev:** KM#84. **Note:** Dav. #LS38c.

Date	Mintage	VG	F	VF	XF	Unc
1618 (o)	—	850	1,700	3,100	5,200	—

KM# 348 3 THALER

87.0000 g., Silver, 82 mm. **Rev:** With or without 3 punched in **Note:** Illustration reduced. Dav. #LS51.

Date	Mintage	VG	F	VF	XF	Unc
1624 HS	—	900	1,800	3,550	6,100	—

KM# 349 3 THALER

Silver **Note:** Similar to 1-1/4 Thaler, KM#338, but 3 on globe. Dav. #LS53.

Date	Mintage	VG	F	VF	XF	Unc
1624 Rare	—	—	—	—	—	—

KM# 359 3 THALER

Silver, 68 mm. **Rev:** With or without 3 punched in **Note:** Illustration reduced. Dav. #LS55.

Date	Mintage	VG	F	VF	XF	Unc
1625 HS Rare	—	—	—	—	—	—

KM# A452 3 THALER

Silver **Note:** Similar to 2 Thaler, KM#451.1. Dav. #LS-A70.

Date	Mintage	VG	F	VF	XF	Unc
1655 (s)	—	925	1,700	3,100	5,200	—

KM# 452 3 THALER

Silver **Note:** With or without 3 punched in. Dav. #LS69. Illustration reduced.

Date	Mintage	VG	F	VF	XF	Unc
1655 (s)	—	775	1,550	2,800	4,700	—

KM# 471 3 THALER

Silver **Obv:** Date 1665 in ground below horse **Rev:** With or without 3 punched in **Note:** Similar to 4 Thaler, KM#453. Dav. #LS80.

Date	Mintage	VG	F	VF	XF	Unc
1665/1655 (s)	—	775	1,550	2,800	4,700	—

KM# 485 3 THALER

Silver **Subject:** 88th Birthday of August II **Note:** Similar to 4 Thaler, KM#488 but 3 punched in. Dav. #LS85C.

Date	Mintage	VG	F	VF	XF	Unc
1666 (s) Rare	—	—	—	—	—	—

KM# 486.1 3 THALER

87.0000 g., Silver **Note:** Similar to 2 Thaler, KM#482, but without value shown. Dav. #LS85.

Date	Mintage	VG	F	VF	XF	Unc
1666 (s) Rare	—	—	—	—	—	—

KM# 487 3 THALER

85.0000 g., Silver **Subject:** Death of August II **Note:** Similar to 1 Thaler, KM#477, but without value shown.

Date	Mintage	VG	F	VF	XF	Unc
1666	—	—	—	—	—	—

KM# 486.2 3 THALER

87.0000 g., Silver **Note:** Dav. #LS85A.

Date	Mintage	VG	F	VF	XF	Unc
1666 IPE Rare	—	—	—	—	—	—

KM# 486.3 3 THALER

87.0000 g., Silver **Note:** Dav. #LS85B.

Date	Mintage	VG	F	VF	XF	Unc
1666 RB Rare	—	—	—	—	—	—

Note: Mintmaster's initials other than (s) indicate later restrikes

KM# 525 3 THALER

83.7000 g., Silver, 79 mm. **Subject:** Death of August Friedrich, Eldest Son of Anton Ulrich **Obv:** With or without 3 punched in **Note:** Illustration reduced. Dav. #LS97.

Date	Mintage	VG	F	VF	XF	Unc
1676	—	1,750	3,400	6,000	10,500	—

KM# 533 3 THALER

Silver **Obv:** Altered bust not in circle **Note:** Dav. #LS104.

Date	Mintage	VG	F	VF	XF	Unc
1679 Rare	—	—	—	—	—	—

KM# 532 3 THALER

Silver **Note:** Similar to 5 Thaler, KM#536, but 3 punched in. Dav. #LS101. Illustration reduced.

Date	Mintage	VG	F	VF	XF	Unc
1679	—	2,350	4,300	7,800	12,000	—

KM# 564 3 THALER

78.0000 g., Silver, 76 mm. **Ruler:** Rudolf August **Note:** Illustration reduced. With or without 3 punched in. Dav. #LS111.

Date	Mintage	VG	F	VF	XF	Unc
1685 RB	—	925	1,700	3,100	5,200	—
1685 HH/RB	—	925	1,700	3,100	5,200	—

KM# 30.1 4 THALER

117.0000 g., Silver **Note:** Struck from 1-1/2 Thaler dies in each year. Similar to 3 Thaler, KM#29, but 4 punched in. Dav. #LS25.

Date	Mintage	VG	F	VF	XF	Unc
1608 (o)	—	2,400	4,800	9,700	—	—

KM# 30.2 4 THALER

Silver **Note:** Similar to 3 Thaler, KM#29.3. Dav. #LS30.

Date	Mintage	VG	F	VF	XF	Unc
1612 (o)	—	1,700	3,100	5,600	9,400	—

KM# 74 4 THALER

Silver **Obv:** Marred die **Note:** Dav. #LS37a.

Date	Mintage	VG	F	VF	XF	Unc
1617 (o)	—	1,500	2,800	5,000	8,500	—

KM# 73 4 THALER

Silver **Note:** Similar to 3 Thaler, KM#71, but 4 punched in. Dav. #LS37.

Date	Mintage	VG	F	VF	XF	Unc
1617 (o)	—	1,500	2,800	5,000	8,500	—

KM# 86.2 4 THALER

Silver **Obv. Legend:** Error FRIIDERICUS **Note:** Dav. #LS39a.

Date	Mintage	VG	F	VF	XF	Unc
1618 (o)	—	1,850	3,300	6,100	10,500	—

KM# 87 4 THALER

Silver **Obv:** KM#74 **Rev:** KM#86 **Note:** Mule. Dav. #LS37b.

Date	Mintage	VG	F	VF	XF	Unc
1618 (o)	—	1,700	3,100	5,600	9,400	—

KM# 86.1 4 THALER

Silver **Note:** Similar to 1-1/2 Thaler, KM#81, but 4 punched in. Dav. #LS39.

Date	Mintage	VG	F	VF	XF	Unc
1618 (o)	—	1,700	3,100	5,600	9,400	—

KM# 226 4 THALER

Silver, 81 mm. **Rev:** 4 punched in cartouche at bottom **Note:** Illustration reduced. Dav. #LS46.

Date	Mintage	VG	F	VF	XF	Unc
1620 (c) Rare	—	—	—	—	—	—

KM# 352 4 THALER
117.0000 g., Silver **Rev:** 4 on globe **Note:** Dav. #52a.

Date	Mintage	VG	F	VF	XF	Unc
1624 Rare	—	—	—	—	—	—

KM# 351 4 THALER
117.0000 g., Silver **Note:** Similar to 1-1/4 Thaler, KM#339, but without value shown. Dav. #52.

Date	Mintage	VG	F	VF	XF	Unc
1624 HP Rare	—	—	—	—	—	—

KM# 350 4 THALER
114.9000 g., Silver **Note:** Similar to 3 Thaler, KM#348 but with or without 4 punched in. Dav. #LS50. Illustration reduced.

Date	Mintage	VG	F	VF	XF	Unc
1624 (h)	—	1,700	3,100	5,600	9,400	—

KM# 360 4 THALER
Silver **Note:** Similar to 3 Thaler, KM#359, but 4 punched in. Dav. #LS54.

Date	Mintage	VG	F	VF	XF	Unc
1625 HS Rare	—	—	—	—	—	—

KM# 399 4 THALER
116.0000 g., Silver **Obv:** Similar to 2 Thaler, KM#451 **Rev:** Helmeted 11-fold arms, 2 lions as supporters, Roman numeral date in legend, without value shown **Note:** Dav. #LS65.

Date	Mintage	VG	F	VF	XF	Unc
1638 (s) Rare	—	—	—	—	—	—

KM# 400 4 THALER
114.9000 g., Silver **Obv:** Duke without hat on horse right, TANDEM behind head **Note:** Dav. #LS66.

Date	Mintage	VG	F	VF	XF	Unc
1638 (s) Rare	—	—	—	—	—	—

KM# 453 4 THALER
115.3000 g., Silver, 85 mm. **Ruler:** August II **Note:** Illustration reduced. With or without 4 punched in. Dav. #LS68.

Date	Mintage	VG	F	VF	XF	Unc
1655 HS	—	1,550	2,800	5,200	8,500	—

KM# 472 4 THALER
Silver **Obv:** Date 1665 in ground below horse **Rev:** 4 punched in **Note:** Dav. #LS79.

Date	Mintage	VG	F	VF	XF	Unc
1665/55 (s)	—	1,550	2,800	5,200	8,500	—

KM# 489 4 THALER
Silver, 87 mm. **Subject:** Death of August II **Note:** Illustration reduced. Similar to 1 Thaler, KM#477, but 4 punched in. Dav. #LS92.

Date	Mintage	VG	F	VF	XF	Unc
1666 Rare	—	—	—	—	—	—

Note: Spink Taisei Zurich Milas sale 4-92 XF realized $12,060

KM# 488 4 THALER
114.0500 g., Silver, 87 mm. **Subject:** 88th Birthday of August II **Note:** Illustration reduced. With or without 4 punched in. Dav. #LS84.

Date	Mintage	VG	F	VF	XF	Unc
1666 HS	—	1,700	3,100	5,600	9,400	—

KM# 526 4 THALER
Silver **Subject:** Death of August Friedrich, Eldest Son of Anton Ulrich **Note:** Similar to 3 Thaler, KM#525, but 4 punched in. Dav. #LS96.

Date	Mintage	VG	F	VF	XF	Unc
1676 Rare	—	—	—	—	—	—

KM# 535 4 THALER
Silver **Obv:** Altered bust not in circle **Note:** Dav. #LS103.

Date	Mintage	VG	F	VF	XF	Unc
1679 Rare	—	—	—	—	—	—

KM# 534 4 THALER
Silver **Note:** Similar to 5 Thaler, KM#536, but 4 punched in. Dav. #LS100. Illustration reduced.

Date	Mintage	VG	F	VF	XF	Unc
1679	—	4,300	6,800	10,500	14,500	—

KM# 565 4 THALER
Silver **Note:** Similar to 3 Thaler, KM#564, but 4 punched in. Dav. #LS110.

Date	Mintage	VG	F	VF	XF	Unc
1685 RB	—	1,750	3,050	5,600	9,500	—
1685 HH/RB	—	1,750	3,050	5,600	9,500	—

KM# 31.1 5 THALER
145.6000 g., Silver, 65 mm. **Note:** Illustration reduced. Struck from 3 Thaler dies, 5 punched in. Dav. #LS24.

Date	Mintage	VG	F	VF	XF	Unc
1608 (o)	—	—	—	9,200	13,000	—

KM# 31.4 5 THALER

Silver **Note:** Stamped 5 but having weight of only 3-1/4 Thaler. Dav. #LS28A.

Date	Mintage	VG	F	VF	XF	Unc
1609 (o)	—	—	—	14,500	22,000	—

KM# 31.2 5 THALER

144.2000 g., Silver, 81 mm. **Note:** Illustration reduced. Dav. #LS28.

Date	Mintage	VG	F	VF	XF	Unc
1609 (o)	—	—	—	14,500	21,500	—

KM# 31.3 5 THALER

144.2000 g., Silver **Note:** Dav. #LS-A29. Varieties exist with differences in background on obverse and ornamentation around arms on reverse.

Date	Mintage	VG	F	VF	XF	Unc
1610 (o)	—	—	—	14,500	22,000	—

KM# 53 5 THALER

Silver **Obv:** Helmeted 11-fold arms, 5 punched in **Rev:** Duke fully armored on horse left **Note:** Dav. #LS-A35.

Date	Mintage	VG	F	VF	XF	Unc
MDCXIV (1614) (o) Rare	—	—	—	—	—	—

KM# 54 5 THALER

Silver, 88 mm. **Rev:** 5 punched in cartouche at bottom **Note:** Illustration reduced. Dav. #LS36.

Date	Mintage	VG	F	VF	XF	Unc
1614 (o)	—	—	—	14,500	21,500	—

KM# 227 5 THALER

Silver, 82 mm. **Ruler:** Frederich Ulrich **Note:** Similar to 4 Thaler, KM#226, but 5 punched in. Dav. #LS45. Illustration reduced.

Date	Mintage	VG	F	VF	XF	Unc
1620 (c)	—	—	—	10,500	16,000	—

KM# 353 5 THALER

144.8000 g., Silver, 84 mm. **Note:** Illustration reduced. Similar to 3 Thaler, KM#348, but with or without 5 punched in. Dav. #LS49.

Date	Mintage	VG	F	VF	XF	Unc
1624 (h)	—	—	—	13,500	19,500	—

KM# 401 5 THALER

144.2000 g., Silver **Obv:** Duke without hat on horse right, TANDEM behind head **Rev:** Helmeted 4-fold arms, 2 lions as supporters, without value shown **Note:** Dav. #LS65.

Date	Mintage	VG	F	VF	XF	Unc
MDCXXXVIII (1638) (s) Rare	—	—	—	—	—	—

KM# 402 5 THALER

Silver **Note:** Similar to 4 Thaler, KM#453, but 5 punched in. Dav. #LS67.

Date	Mintage	VG	F	VF	XF	Unc
1655 (s) Rare	—	—	—	—	—	—

KM# 473 5 THALER

Silver **Obv:** Date 1665 in ground below horse **Rev:** 5 punched in **Note:** Dav. #LS78.

Date	Mintage	VG	F	VF	XF	Unc
1665/1655 (s) Rare	—	—	—	—	—	—

KM# 490 5 THALER

Silver **Subject:** 88th Birthday of August II **Note:** Similar to 4 Thaler, KM#488, but with or without 5 punched in. Dav. #LS83.

Date	Mintage	VG	F	VF	XF	Unc
1666 (s)	—	—	—	10,500	16,000	—

KM# 491 5 THALER

Silver **Subject:** Death of August II **Note:** Similar to 1 Thaler, KM#477, but 5 punched in. Dav. #LS91.

Date	Mintage	VG	F	VF	XF	Unc
1666 Rare	—	—	—	—	—	—

KM# 527 5 THALER

Silver **Subject:** Death of August Friedrich, Eldest Son of Anton Ulrich **Note:** Similar to 3 Thaler, KM#525, but 5 punched in. Dav. #LS95.

Date	Mintage	VG	F	VF	XF	Unc
1676 Rare	—	—	—	—	—	—

KM# 537 5 THALER

Silver **Obv:** Altered bust not in circle **Note:** Dav. #LS102.

Date	Mintage	VG	F	VF	XF	Unc
1679 Rare	—	—	—	—	—	—

KM# 536 5 THALER

Silver, 79 mm. **Rev:** 5 punched in **Note:** Illustration reduced. Dav. #LS99.

Date	Mintage	VG	F	VF	XF	Unc
1679 Rare	—	—	—	—	—	—

Note: Spink Taisei Zurich Milas sale 4-92 XF realized $10,050

KM# 566 5 THALER
Silver **Note:** Similar to 3 Thaler, KM#564, but 5 punched in. Dav. #LS109. Illustration reduced.

Date	Mintage	VG	F	VF	XF	Unc
1685 RB Rare	—	—	—	—	—	—

KM# 228 6 THALER
170.9000 g., Silver, 85 mm. **Note:** Illustration reduced. Similar to 4 Thaler, KM#226, but with or without 6 punched in. Dav. #LS44.

Date	Mintage	VG	F	VF	XF	Unc
1620 (c)	—	—	—	17,500	23,500	—

KM# 354 6 THALER
172.6000 g., Silver **Note:** Similar to 3 Thaler, KM#348, but with or without 6 punched in. Dav. #LS48.

Date	Mintage	VG	F	VF	XF	Unc
1624 (h)	—	—	—	13,000	20,000	—

KM# 383 6 THALER
171.0000 g., Silver **Note:** Similar to 10 Thaler, KM#385, but with or without 6 punched in. Dav. #LS61.

Date	Mintage	VG	F	VF	XF	Unc
1634 (s)	—	—	—	14,500	21,500	—

KM# 492 6 THALER
173.1000 g., Silver **Subject:** 88th Birthday of August II **Note:** Similar to 4 Thaler, KM#488, but with or without 6 punched in. Dav. #LS82.

Date	Mintage	VG	F	VF	XF	Unc
1666 (s) Rare	—	—	—	—	—	—

Note: Spink Taisei Zurich Milas sale 4-92 XF realized $11,055

KM# 493 6 THALER
173.1000 g., Silver **Subject:** Death of August II **Note:** Similar to 1 Thaler, KM#477, but 6 punched in. Dav. #LS90.

Date	Mintage	VG	F	VF	XF	Unc
1666 Rare	—	—	—	—	—	—

KM# 538 6 THALER
173.1000 g., Silver **Note:** Similar to 5 Thaler, KM#536, but 6 punched in. Dav. #LS98.

Date	Mintage	VG	F	VF	XF	Unc
1679 Rare	—	—	—	—	—	—

KM# 573 7 THALER
Silver **Note:** Similar to 1-1/2 Thaler, KM#530, but 7 punched in. Dav. #LS113.

Date	Mintage	VG	F	VF	XF	Unc
1686 RB Rare	—	—	—	—	—	—

KM# 384 8 THALER
230.0000 g., Silver **Note:** Similar to 10 Thaler, KM#385, but with or without 8 punched in. Dav. #LS60.

Date	Mintage	VG	F	VF	XF	Unc
1634 (s) Rare	—	—	—	—	—	—

KM# 494 8 THALER
230.0000 g., Silver **Subject:** Death of August II **Note:** Similar to 1 Thaler, KM#477, but 8 punched in. Dav. #LS89.

Date	Mintage	VG	F	VF	XF	Unc
1666 Rare	—	—	—	—	—	—

KM# 32 10 THALER
292.5000 g., Silver **Note:** Struck from 5 Thaler dies. Similar to 3 Thaler, KM#29, but with 10 in cartouche at bottom reverse. Dav. #LS27.

Date	Mintage	VG	F	VF	XF	Unc
1609 (o) Rare	—	—	—	—	—	—

Note: Spink Taisei Zurich Milas sale 4-92 XF realized $18,760

KM# 55 10 THALER
292.5000 g., Silver **Obv:** Helmeted 11-fold arms, value 10 punched in **Rev:** Duke fully armored on horse left, Roman numeral date in legend **Note:** Dav. #LS34.

Date	Mintage	VG	F	VF	XF	Unc
1614 (o) Rare	—	—	—	—	—	—

KM# 56 10 THALER
292.5000 g., Silver **Note:** Dav. #LS35. Similar to 5 Thaler, KM#54, but 10 punched in.

Date	Mintage	VG	F	VF	XF	Unc
1614 (o) Rare	—	—	—	—	—	—

KM# 229 10 THALER
289.9000 g., Silver **Note:** Similar to 4 Thaler, KM#226, but 10 punched in or omitted. Dav. #LS43.

Date	Mintage	VG	F	VF	XF	Unc
1620 (c) Rare	—	—	—	—	—	—

Note: Spink Taisei Zurich Milas sale 4-92 XF realized $15,400

KM# 355 10 THALER
290.0000 g., Silver **Note:** Similar to 3 Thaler, KM#348, but without value shown. Dav. #LS47.

Date	Mintage	VG	F	VF	XF	Unc
1624 (h) Rare	—	—	—	—	—	—

KM# 386 10 THALER
284.8000 g., Silver **Note:** Altered features, especially sun without face. Dav. #LS62.

Date	Mintage	VG	F	VF	XF	Unc
1634 (s) Rare	—	—	—	—	—	—

KM# 385 10 THALER
284.8000 g., Silver, 100 mm. **Note:** Illustration reduced. With or without 10 punched in. Dav. #LS59.

Date	Mintage	VG	F	VF	XF	Unc
1634 (s) Rare	—	—	—	—	—	—

Note: Spink Taisei Zurich Milas sale 4-92 XF realized $37,520

KM# 403 10 THALER
284.0000 g., Silver **Obv:** Duke without hat on horse right, TANDEN behind head **Rev:** Helmeted 11-fold arms, 2 lions as supporters, Roman numeral date in legend, without value shown **Note:** Dav. #LS63.

Date	Mintage	VG	F	VF	XF	Unc
1638 (s) Rare	—	—	—	—	—	—

KM# 495 10 THALER
284.0000 g., Silver **Subject:** 88th Birthday of August II **Note:** Similar to 4 Thaler, KM#488, but 10 punched in. Dav. #LS81.

Date	Mintage	VG	F	VF	XF	Unc
1666 (s) Rare	—	—	—	—	—	—

KM# 387 12 THALER
349.0000 g., Silver **Note:** Similar to 10 Thaler, KM#385, but without value shown. Dav. #LS58.

Date	Mintage	VG	F	VF	XF	Unc
1634 (s) Rare	—	—	—	—	—	—

TRADE COINAGE

KM# A57 DUCAT
3.2500 g., Gold **Ruler:** Heinrich Julius **Rev:** St. Andrew with cross, date in legend **Mint:** Goslar **Note:** Ref. Welter#609A. Struck in gold from same dies as 1/4 Thaler, KM#8.

Date	Mintage	VG	F	VF	XF	Unc
1612 (d)	—	—	—	—	—	—

KM# 57 DUCAT
3.5000 g., 0.9860 Gold 0.1109 oz. AGW **Obv:** Crowned arms in inner circle **Rev:** Wildman holding tree

Date	Mintage	VG	F	VF	XF	Unc
1615 (o)	—	500	1,100	2,400	4,500	—
1617	—	500	1,100	2,400	4,500	—
1618 (o)	—	500	1,100	2,400	4,500	—
1620	—	500	1,100	2,400	4,500	—
1621	—	500	1,100	2,400	4,500	—
1624	—	500	1,100	2,400	4,500	—
1629 (h)	—	500	1,100	2,400	4,500	—
1631 (s)	—	500	1,100	2,400	4,500	—

KM# 361 DUCAT
3.5000 g., 0.9860 Gold 0.1109 oz. AGW **Obv:** Bust of Friedrich Ulrich right in inner circle **Rev:** Crowned arms in inner circle

Date	Mintage	VG	F	VF	XF	Unc
1625 HS	—	600	1,300	3,000	4,800	—
1626 HS	—	600	1,300	3,000	4,800	—

KM# 375 DUCAT
3.5000 g., 0.9860 Gold 0.1109 oz. AGW **Obv:** Friedrich Ulrich standing in inner circle

Date	Mintage	VG	F	VF	XF	Unc
1630 HS	—	425	850	1,850	3,000	—

KM# 404 DUCAT
3.5000 g., 0.9860 Gold 0.1109 oz. AGW **Obv:** Bust of August right in inner circle **Rev:** Crowned arms in inner circle

Date	Mintage	VG	F	VF	XF	Unc
1638 (s)	—	350	725	1,500	2,700	—

KM# 406 DUCAT
3.5000 g., 0.9860 Gold 0.1109 oz. AGW **Obv:** August **Rev:** Date in legend

Date	Mintage	VG	F	VF	XF	Unc
1639 (s)	—	350	725	1,500	2,700	—

KM# 457 DUCAT
3.5000 g., 0.9860 Gold 0.1109 oz. AGW **Obv:** Facing bust of August in hat

Date	Mintage	VG	F	VF	XF	Unc
1658 (s)	—	300	600	1,250	2,500	—

KM# 506 DUCAT
3.5000 g., 0.9860 Gold 0.1109 oz. AGW **Obv:** Crowned arms in inner circle **Rev:** Rearing horse, date in exergue

Date	Mintage	VG	F	VF	XF	Unc
1669	—	450	900	1,900	3,400	—

KM# 546 DUCAT
3.5000 g., 0.9860 Gold 0.1109 oz. AGW **Obv:** Rudolf August **Rev:** War galley at sea, "Jehovah" (in Hebrew) above

Date	Mintage	VG	F	VF	XF	Unc
1680 RB	—	1,000	2,150	4,150	7,150	—

KM# 594 DUCAT
3.5000 g., 0.9860 Gold 0.1109 oz. AGW **Obv:** Bust of 2 dukes right **Rev:** Crowned 11-fold arms, date in legend

Date	Mintage	VG	F	VF	XF	Unc
1691 HCH	—	550	1,100	2,400	4,500	—

KM# 625 DUCAT
3.5000 g., 0.9860 Gold 0.1109 oz. AGW **Ruler:** Anton Ulrich **Obv:** Bust of Rudolf August right **Rev:** Bust of Anton Ulrich right **Note:** Varieties exist.

Date	Mintage	VG	F	VF	XF	Unc
1698 HCH	—	900	2,000	4,600	8,500	—

KM# 595 DUCAT
3.5000 g., 0.9860 Gold 0.1109 oz. AGW **Obv:** Conjoined busts of Rudolf August and Anton Ulrich right **Rev:** Crowned 15-fold arms divide date

Date	Mintage	VG	F	VF	XF	Unc
1699 HCH	—	500	1,000	2,300	4,500	—

KM# A507 2 DUCAT
7.0000 g., Gold **Ruler:** Heinrich Julius **Rev:** St. Andrew with cross, date in legend **Mint:** Goslar **Note:** Ref. Welter#609. Struck in gold from same dies as 1/4 Thaler, KM#8.

Date	Mintage	VG	F	VF	XF	Unc
1608 (d)	—	—	—	—	—	—
1612 (d)	—	—	—	—	—	—

KM# 507 2 DUCAT

7.0000 g., 0.9860 Gold 0.2219 oz. AGW **Obv:** Crowned arms in inner circle **Rev:** Rearing horse, date in exergue

Date	Mintage	VG	F	VF	XF	Unc
1669 (S)	—	975	1,800	3,750	8,500	—

KM# 58 10 DUCAT (Portugalöser)

35.0000 g., 0.9860 Gold 1.1095 oz. AGW **Obv:** 1/2 length figure right **Rev:** Helmeted 11-fold arms, wildman to left, date in legend **Note:** Struck with 1 Thaler dies, KM#7.

Date	Mintage	VG	F	VF	XF	Unc
1615 (o) Rare	—	—	—	—	—	—

PATTERNS

Including off metal strikes

KM#	Date	Mintage	Identification	Mkt Val
PnA2	1625 HS	—	2 Thaler. Gold. KM#357.	—
Pn2	1643 (s)	—	1/4 Thaler. Gold. KM#411.	—
Pn3	1643 (s)	—	Thaler. Gold. 6th bell thaler, KM#428.	—
Pn4	1643 (s)	—	Thaler. Gold. 7th bell thaler, KM#429.	—
Pn5	1687	—	Thaler. Silver. KM#576.	—

BUCHEIM

The Bucheim house were hereditary cupbearers to the archdukes of Austria. Johann Christof III (1619-1657) was the only issuer of coins.

RULERS

Johann Christian, 1619-1657

LORDSHIP

TRADE COINAGE

KM# 1 DUCAT

3.5000 g., 0.9860 Gold 0.1109 oz. AGW **Obv:** Bust of Johann Christian right

Date	Mintage	VG	F	VF	XF	Unc
1650 Rare	—	—	—	—	—	—

BURGMILCHLING

(Wilhermsdorf)

A knight named Heinrich Hartmann Schutzpar, who descended from the late 13th century Hartmann von Schutzpeer (= Schüttle den Speer, same meaning as Shakespeare in English), lived with the nickname Milchling (milkman). Heinrich Hartmann bought the ruined castle of Wilhermsdorf, 15 miles (25km) west of Nüremberg, and its surrounding territory. When he had restored the castle, he renamed it Burgmilchling and was given the title of free baron in 1569. His son succeeded him in 1591 and struck a few coins.

RULERS

Heinrich Hermann, 1591-1649

BARONY

REGULAR COINAGE

KM# 10 THALER

Silver **Obv:** Helmeted four fold arms **Obv. Legend:** + HENR: HERM: L: B: INBVRGMILCHLING ET. WILHERMSDORF **Rev:** 3/4 length laureate bust of Rudolf II with sceptre and orb facing 3/4 right **Rev. Legend:** RVDOLPH • II • ROM: IMP:... **Note:** Dav. #6659.

Date	Mintage	VG	F	VF	XF	Unc
1605	—	1,650	2,875	5,175	8,650	—
1606	434	1,750	2,550	6,500	10,500	—
1608	—	1,650	2,875	5,175	8,650	—
1610	—	1,250	2,500	4,850	7,500	—
1611	—	1,250	2,500	4,850	7,500	—

CAMENZ

(Wilhermsdorf)

A knight named Heinrich Hartmann Schutzpar, who descended from the late 13th century Hartmann von Schutzpeer (= Schüttle den Speer, same meaning as Shakespeare in English), lived with the nickname Milchling (milkman). Heinrich Hartmann bought the ruined castle of Wilhermsdorf, 15 miles (25km) west of Nüremberg, and its surrounding territory. When he had restored the castle, he renamed it Burgmilchling and was given the title of free baron in 1569. His son succeeded him in 1591 and struck a few coins.

RULERS

Heinrich Hermann, 1591-1649

TOWN

REGULAR COINAGE

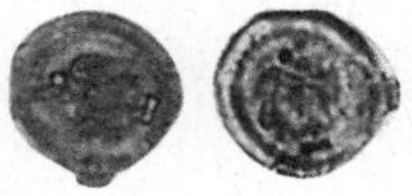

KM# 1 PFENNIG

Copper **Obv:** Arms (angel's wing, three pellets left), value 1 to right. **Note:** Kipper Pfennig. Uniface.

Date	Mintage	VG	F	VF	XF	Unc
ND(1622)	—	10.00	20.00	40.00	85.00	160
1622	—	10.00	20.00	40.00	85.00	160

KM# 2 2 PFENNIG

Copper, 15 mm. **Note:** Kipper 2 Pfennig.

Date	Mintage	VG	F	VF	XF	Unc
16ZZ	—	15.00	30.00	60.00	120	225

KM# 3 3 PFENNIG (Dreier)

Copper, 16 mm. **Obv:** Arms, value 3 PF below **Rev. Inscription:** BONO / PVBL. / CAM. / date **Note:** Kipper 3 Pfennig.

Date	Mintage	VG	F	VF	XF	Unc
1622	—	20.00	40.00	70.00	140	280

PATTERNS

Including off metal strikes

KM#	Date	Mintage	Identification	Mkt Val
Pn1	ND(1622)	—	Pfennig. Silver. KM#1	—

CAMMIN

The town of Cammin in Pomerania (see, near the Baltic coast some 20 miles north-northeast of Stettin), was the seat of a bishopric founded by Adalbert (1139-62). The first Protestant bishop ruled from 1544, but in the next decade, Cammin came under the control of the dukes of Pomerania. From that time until the end of the Thirty Years' War in 1648-50, members of the ducal house were Bishops of Cammin. The part of Pomerania in which Cammin is situated passed with it to Brandenburg-Prussia in 1650. Except for some denars of the 13th century, no coins were struck for the bishopric until the 17th century.

RULERS

Kasimir VII Herzog, of Pomerania, 1574-1602
Franz of Pomerania, 1602-1618
Ulrich of Pomerania, 1618-1622
Bogislaus II (XIV) of Pomerania, 1622-1637
Ernst Bogislaus of Croy, 1637-1650

NOTE: Coinage for Cammin was interchangeable with that of Pomerania, which see for additional pieces that circulated freely in the bishopric.

MINTMASTERS' INITIALS

Initial	Date	Name
GT, sometimes in legature	Ca. 1628-37, 54	Gottfried Tabbert, die-cutter in Stettin
HS	1612-19	Johann (Hans) Schampan in Stettin
(z)= 	1628-30	Unknown
VB	1633-63	Ulrich Butkau in Stettin

ARMS

Bishopric – Cross
Pomerania – Griffen, usually rampant to left

BISHOPRIC

REGULAR COINAGE

KM# 1 DREIER (3 Pfennig)

Silver **Ruler:** Franz **Obv:** Shield of Pomeranian griffin left, ornate helmet above, over all F.I.D.-S.P.O. **Rev:** Imperial orb in baroque shield divides date **Note:** Prev. KM#5. Ref. H#242.

Date	Mintage	VG	F	VF	XF	Unc
(16)15	—	120	275	450	—	—

KM# 2 DREIER (3 Pfennig)

Silver **Ruler:** Franz **Obv:** III / F.H.Z. / S.P. / date **Rev:** Griffin rampant left **Note:** Ref. H#243.

Date	Mintage	VG	F	VF	XF	Unc
1616	—	100	200	385	—	—

KM# 21 DREIER (3 Pfennig)

0.6600 g., Silver **Ruler:** Ulrich **Obv:** Ornate helmet over shield of Pomeranian arms, bishop's cap above divides V.I.D - S. POM **Rev:** Ornate helmet over shield of Pomeranian arms divides date **Note:** Ref. H#253.

Date	Mintage	VG	F	VF	XF	Unc
16Z1	—	35.00	75.00	150	—	—

KM# 25 DREIER (3 Pfennig)

Silver **Ruler:** Ulrich **Obv:** Ornate helmet, feathers at top divide V.H.Z.-S.P. **Rev:** Shield with concave sides, griffin left, date above **Note:** Ref. H#254.

Date	Mintage	VG	F	VF	XF	Unc
16ZZ	—	35.00	75.00	150	—	—

KM# 26 DREIER (3 Pfennig)

Silver **Ruler:** Ulrich **Obv:** Ornate helmet divided date, feathers at top divide V.H.Z.-S.P. **Rev:** Shield with concave sides, griffin left, date above **Note:** Ref. H#254. Varieties exist.

Date	Mintage	VG	F	VF	XF	Unc
(16)ZZ//16ZZ	—	35.00	75.00	150	—	—

KM# 27 1/4 SCHILLING (Dreiling; 1/128 Thaler)

0.7800 g., Silver **Ruler:** Ulrich **Obv:** Crowned griffin to left in circle, titles of Ulrich begin VLRIC9 **Rev:** Large "1Z8" in circle, legend, date **Rev. Legend:** DEVS. PROTECTOR. MEV. **Note:** Ref. H#267.

Date	Mintage	VG	F	VF	XF	Unc
(16)ZZ	—	—	—	—	—	—

KM# 18 WITTEN (4 Pfennig)

0.5400 g., Silver **Ruler:** Ulrich **Obv:** Crowned griffin left in circle, titles of Ulrich begin VLRIC9 **Rev:** Cross, arms divide A-O (Anno)/Z-0 **Rev. Legend:** DEVS. PROTECTOR. MEV. **Note:** Prev. KM#15. Ref. H#262.

Date	Mintage	VG	F	VF	XF	Unc
(16)Z0	—	25.00	50.00	100	225	—

KM# 28 WITTEN (4 Pfennig)

0.5400 g., Silver **Ruler:** Ulrich **Obv:** Crowned griffin to left in circle, titles of Ulrich begin VLRIC9 **Rev:** Short cross in circle, date in angles **Rev. Legend:** DEVS. PROTECTOR. MEV. **Note:** Ref. H#263.

Date	Mintage	VG	F	VF	XF	Unc
16ZZ	—	26.00	50.00	110	240	—

KM# 29 1/2 SCHILLING (1/64 Thaler)

Silver **Ruler:** Ulrich **Obv:** Crowned griffin left in circle **Rev:** Large 6•4 in field, date **Rev. Legend:** DEVS.PROTECTOR.MEV. **Note:** Prev. KM#19. Ref. H#266.

Date	Mintage	VG	F	VF	XF	Unc
(16)22	—	—	—	—	—	—

KM# 30 SCHILLING (1/32 Thaler)

1.5700 g., Silver **Ruler:** Ulrich **Obv:** Crowned griffin left in circle, titles of Ulrich begin VLRIC9 **Rev:** Large 3 • Z in field, date **Rev. Legend:** DEVS. PROTECTOR. MEV. **Note:** Prev. KM#22. Ref. H#265.

Date	Mintage	VG	F	VF	XF	Unc
(16)22	—	—	—	—	—	—

KM# 3 2 SCHILLING (Doppelschilling)

Silver **Ruler:** Franz **Obv:** Crowned griffin to left in circle, titles of Franz **Rev:** Intertwined "DS" in circle, legend, date **Rev. Legend:** ADSIT. AB. ALTO. **Note:** Ref. H#244-45.

Date	Mintage	VG	F	VF	XF	Unc
1616 HS	—	30.00	60.00	120	—	—
1617	—	30.00	60.00	120	—	—

KM# 10 2 SCHILLING (Doppelschilling)
1.3200 g., Silver **Ruler:** Ulrich **Obv:** Crowned griffin to left in circle, titles of Ulrich begin VLRIC9 **Rev:** Intertwined "DS" in circle **Rev. Legend:** DEVS.PROTECTOR.MEV9. **Note:** Ref. H#255.

Date	Mintage	VG	F	VF	XF	Unc
ND(1618-22)	—	50.00	120	300	—	—

KM# 11 2 SCHILLING (Doppelschilling)
1.3200 g., Silver **Ruler:** Ulrich **Obv:** Crowned griffin to left in circle, titles of Ulrich begin VLDARIC9 **Rev:** Intertwined "DS" in circle **Rev. Legend:** DEVS.PROTECTOR.MEV9.

Date	Mintage	VG	F	VF	XF	Unc
ND(1618-22)	—	—	—	—	—	—

Note: Reported, not confirmed

KM# 15 2 SCHILLING (Doppelschilling)
1.3200 g., Silver **Ruler:** Ulrich **Obv:** Crowned griffin to left in circle, titles of Ulrich begin VLDARIC9 **Rev:** Intertwined "DS" in circle divides date **Rev. Legend:** DEVS.PROTECTOR.MEVS. **Note:** Ref. H#256, 258.

Date	Mintage	VG	F	VF	XF	Unc
(16)19	—	30.00	60.00	120	—	—
(16)Z0	—	30.00	60.00	120	—	—

KM# 16 2 SCHILLING (Doppelschilling)
1.3200 g., Silver **Ruler:** Ulrich **Obv:** Crowned griffin to left in circle, titles of Ulrich begin VLDARIC9 **Rev:** Intertwined "DS" in circle, legend, date **Rev. Legend:** DEVS. PROTECTOR. MEVS. **Note:** Ref. H#256.

Date	Mintage	VG	F	VF	XF	Unc
(16)19	—	30.00	60.00	120	—	—

KM# 17 2 SCHILLING (Doppelschilling)
1.3200 g., Silver **Ruler:** Ulrich **Obv:** Crowned griffin to left in circle, titles of Ulrich begin VLRIC9 **Rev:** Intertwined "DS" in circle, date below **Rev. Legend:** DEVS. PROTECTOR. MEVS. **Note:** Ref. H#257, 259-61. Varieties exist.

Date	Mintage	VG	F	VF	XF	Unc
(16)19	—	16.00	40.00	75.00	155	—
(16)Z0	—	16.00	40.00	75.00	155	—
(16)Z1	—	16.00	40.00	75.00	155	—
(16)ZZ	—	16.00	40.00	75.00	155	—

KM# 22 2 SCHILLING (Doppelschilling)
1.3200 g., Silver **Ruler:** Ulrich **Obv:** Crowned griffin to left in circle, titles of Ulrich begin VLRIC9 **Rev:** Intertwined "DS" in circle divides date **Rev. Legend:** DEVS. PROTECTOR. MEVS. **Note:** Ref. H#260-61.

Date	Mintage	VG	F	VF	XF	Unc
(16)Z1	—	16.00	40.00	75.00	155	—
(16)ZZ	—	16.00	40.00	75.00	155	—

KM# 31 2 SCHILLING (Doppelschilling)
1.3200 g., Silver **Ruler:** Ulrich **Obv:** Crowned griffin to left in circle, titles of Ulrich begin VLRIC9 **Rev:** Intertwined "DS" in circle divides date **Rev. Legend:** DEVS. PROTECTOR. MEVS. **Note:** Ref. H#261.

Date	Mintage	VG	F	VF	XF	Unc
16ZZ	—	16.00	40.00	75.00	155	—

KM# 19 DOPPEL-SCHILLING (1/16 Thaler)
Silver **Ruler:** Ulrich **Obv:** Griffin left in oval baroque frame **Rev:** 5-line inscription **Rev. Legend:** DEVS. PROTECTOR. MEVS. **Rev. Inscription:** II / SCHIL / LING / POM / date **Note:** Prev. KM#17. Ref. H#268.

Date	Mintage	VG	F	VF	XF	Unc
(16)Z0	—	30.00	60.00	120	—	—

KM# 32 DOPPEL-SCHILLING (1/16 Thaler)
Silver **Ruler:** Ulrich **Obv:** Crowned griffin left in circle **Rev:** Large Gothic "1 • 6" in field, date **Rev. Legend:** DEVS. PROTECTOR. MEVS. **Note:** Prev. KM#24. Ref. H#264.

Date	Mintage	VG	F	VF	XF	Unc
16ZZ	—	30.00	60.00	120	—	—

KM# 7 1/24 THALER (Groschen)
Silver **Ruler:** Franz **Obv:** Smaller bust right breaks circle at top, titles of Franz **Rev:** Imperial orb with 24 divides date **Rev. Legend:** ADSIT. AB. ALTO. **Note:** Ref. H#237-38.

Date	Mintage	VG	F	VF	XF	Unc
1616	—	15.00	30.00	65.00	130	—
1617	—	15.00	30.00	65.00	130	—

KM# 14 1/24 THALER (Groschen)
1.2800 g., Silver **Ruler:** Ulrich **Obv:** Crowned griffin left, "3" in oval below, titles of Ulrich begin VLDARIC9 **Rev:** Imperial orb with "Z4" divides date **Rev. Legend:** DEVS. PROTECTOR. MEVS. **Note:** Prev. KM#11. Ref. H#246-48. Varieties exist.

Date	Mintage	VG	F	VF	XF	Unc
(16)18	—	20.00	50.00	100	210	—
1618	—	20.00	50.00	100	210	—
(16)19	—	20.00	50.00	100	210	—
(16)Z0	—	20.00	50.00	100	210	—

KM# A2 1/24 THALER (Reichsgroschen)
Silver **Ruler:** Franz **Obv:** Large bust right breaks circle at top, titles of Franz **Rev:** Imperial orb with Z4 in circle, date at end of legend **Rev. Legend:** ADSIT. AB. ALTO. **Note:** Ref. H#235-36.

Date	Mintage	VG	F	VF	XF	Unc
1615 HS	—	60.00	120	275	550	—
1616 HS	—	60.00	120	275	550	—

KM# 5 1/24 THALER (Reichsgroschen)
Silver **Ruler:** Franz **Obv:** Large bust right breaks circle at top, titles of Franz **Rev:** Imperial orb with "24" in circle, date divided by base of cross on orb **Rev. Legend:** ADSIT. AB. ALTO. **Note:** Ref. H#236.

Date	Mintage	VG	F	VF	XF	Unc
1616 HS	—	60.00	120	240	480	—

KM# 4 1/24 THALER (Reichsgroschen)
Silver **Ruler:** Franz **Obv:** Large bust right breaks circle at top, titles of Franz **Rev:** Imperial orb with "Z4" in circle, date at top divided by cross **Rev. Legend:** ADSIT. AB. ALTO. **Note:** Ref. H#236-37.

Date	Mintage	VG	F	VF	XF	Unc
1616 HS	—	65.00	135	275	550	—
1616	—	65.00	135	275	550	—

KM# 8 1/24 THALER (Dreipölker)
Silver **Ruler:** Franz **Obv:** Smaller head right breaks circle at top, value "3" in oval below shoulder, titles of Franz **Rev:** Imperial orb with "Z4" in circle, date divided by cross on top **Rev. Legend:** ADSIT. AB. ALTO. **Note:** Ref. H#237, 340.

Date	Mintage	VG	F	VF	XF	Unc
1616	—	55.00	110	225	450	—
1618	—	55.00	110	225	450	—

KM# 6 1/24 THALER (Dreipölker)
Silver **Ruler:** Franz **Obv:** Smaller head right breaks circle at top, titles of Franz **Rev:** Imperial orb with "Z4" in circle, legend, date **Rev. Legend:** ADSIT. AB. ALTO. **Note:** Ref. H#237.

Date	Mintage	VG	F	VF	XF	Unc
1616	—	55.00	110	225	450	—

KM# 9 1/24 THALER (Dreipölker)
Silver **Ruler:** Franz **Obv:** Crowned griffin left, value "3" in oval below, titles of Franz **Rev:** Imperial orb with "Z4" in circle, date divided by cross on top **Rev. Legend:** ADSIT. AB. ALTO. **Note:** Ref. H#239.

Date	Mintage	VG	F	VF	XF	Unc
1617	—	35.00	75.00	150	—	—

KM# 12 1/24 THALER (Dreipölker)
Silver **Ruler:** Franz **Obv:** Crowned griffin to left, value "3" in oval below, titles of Franz **Rev:** Imperial orb with "Z4" in circle, date divided by cross on top **Rev. Legend:** ADSIT. AB. ALTO. **Note:** Ref. H#241.

Date	Mintage	VG	F	VF	XF	Unc
1618	—	35.00	75.00	150	—	—

KM# 13 1/24 THALER (Dreipölker)
Silver **Ruler:** Franz **Obv:** Crowned griffin left, titles of Franz **Rev:** Imperial orb with "24" in circle, date divided by base of cross on orb **Rev. Legend:** ADSIT. AB. ALTO. **Note:** Ref. H#241.

Date	Mintage	VG	F	VF	XF	Unc
1618	—	35.00	75.00	150	—	—

KM# 20 1/24 THALER (Dreipölker)
1.2800 g., Silver **Ruler:** Ulrich **Obv:** Crowned griffin left, "3" in oval below, titles of Ulrich begin VLRIC9 **Rev:** Imperial orb with "Z4" divides date **Rev. Legend:** DEVS. PROTECTOR. MEVS. **Note:** Ref. H#249.

Date	Mintage	VG	F	VF	XF	Unc
(16)Z0	—	35.00	75.00	150	—	—

KM# 23 1/24 THALER (Dreipölker)
0.9000 g., Silver **Ruler:** Ulrich **Obv:** 4-fold arms with central shield of bishopric (cross), titles of Ulrich begin VLRIC9 **Rev:** Imperial orb with "Z4" divides date **Rev. Legend:** DEVS. PROTECTOR. MEVS. **Note:** Ref. H#250, 252.

Date	Mintage	VG	F	VF	XF	Unc
(16)Z1	—	20.00	45.00	90.00	180	—
(16)ZZ	—	20.00	45.00	90.00	180	—

KM# 24 1/24 THALER (Dreipölker)
0.9000 g., Silver **Ruler:** Ulrich **Obv:** Four-fold arms with central shield of bishopric (cross), crown above, "3" below, titles of Ulrich begin VLRIC9 **Rev:** Imperial orb with "Z4" divides date **Rev. Legend:** DEVS. PROTECTOR. MEVS. **Note:** Ref. H#251.

Date	Mintage	VG	F	VF	XF	Unc
(16)Z1	—	20.00	45.00	90.00	180	—

KM# 33 1/8 THALER (Halber Reichsort)
3.4100 g., Silver **Ruler:** Bogislaw XIV **Subject:** Death of Ulrich **Obv:** Bust left breaks circle at top, titles of Ulrich, date **Rev:** Fierce storm from upper right breaks branch from tree in lower left **Rev. Legend:** + DEO. ASPIRANTE. VIRESCIT. **Note:** Ref. H#276.

Date	Mintage	VG	F	VF	XF	Unc
16ZZ	—	—	—	—	—	—

KM# 90 1/8 THALER (Halber Reichsort)
3.4100 g., Silver **Subject:** Entombment of Hedwig von Braunschweig-Wolfenbüttel, Widow of Ulrich **Obv:** 7-line inscription around titles of Hedwig **Rev:** 10-line inscription with R.N. dates **Note:** Ref. H#391.

Date	Mintage	VG	F	VF	XF	Unc
MIDCLIV (1654)	—	—	—	—	—	—

KM# 34 1/4 THALER (Reichsort)
6.5700 g., Silver **Subject:** Death of Ulrich **Obv:** Bust left, date in legend **Rev:** Rays from sun in upper right through clouds to tree **Rev. Legend:** DEO. ASPIRANTE. VIRESCIT. **Note:** Prev. KM#30. Ref. H#275.

Date	Mintage	VG	F	VF	XF	Unc
1622	—	—	—	—	—	—

KM# 35 1/2 THALER
Silver Weight varies, 13.54-13.67g **Ruler:** Ulrich **Subject:** Death of Ulrich **Obv:** Armored bust to left, date divided in margin at top **Obv. Legend:** VLRICVS. D.G. D: POM. EPISCOP. CAMMIN. **Rev:** Fierce storm from upper right breaks branch from tree in lower left **Rev. Legend:** + DEO. ASPIRANTE. VIRESCIT. **Note:** Ref. H#274.

Date	Mintage	VG	F	VF	XF	Unc
16ZZ	—	900	1,700	3,250	—	—

KM# 75 1/2 THALER

13.6700 g., Silver **Ruler:** Bogislaw XIV **Obv:** Bust right breaks circle at top, titles of Bogislaw **Rev:** Oval ten-fold arms in baroque frame, ducal cap above divides date in legend **Note:** Ref. H#330. Varieties exist.

Date	Mintage	VG	F	VF	XF	Unc
1633	—	600	1,100	2,000	—	—

KM# 76 1/2 THALER

Silver **Ruler:** Bogislaw XIV **Obv:** Bust right breaks circle at top, titles of Bogislaw **Rev:** Squarish ten-fold arms with rounded corners in baroque frame, date divided above, ducal cap at top over all, titles continuous **Note:** Ref. H#331-32. Varieties exist. Prev. KM#90.

Date	Mintage	VG	F	VF	XF	Unc
1633	—	600	1,100	2,000	—	—
1634	—	600	1,100	2,000	—	—

KM# 85 1/2 THALER

13.6700 g., Silver **Ruler:** Bogislaw XIV **Obv:** Bust right breaks circle at top, titles of Bogislaw **Rev:** Oval ten-fold arms in baroque frame, date divided to either side near top of arms, ducal cap above all, titles continuous **Note:** Ref. H#333.

Date	Mintage	VG	F	VF	XF	Unc
1635	—	600	1,100	2,000	—	—

KM# 37 THALER

Silver **Ruler:** Ulrich **Subject:** Death of Ulrich **Obv:** Bust left breaks circle at top, date above head, titles of Ulrich **Rev:** Nine-line inscription with dates **Note:** Dav. #7243. Prev. KM#36.

Date	Mintage	VG	F	VF	XF	Unc
16ZZ	—	1,200	2,250	4,500	8,500	—

KM# 36 THALER

Silver **Ruler:** Ulrich **Obv:** Bust left breaks circle at top, date above head, titles of Ulrich **Rev:** Bust of Philipp II right in ornamented circle, titles of Phillip II of Pomerania-Stettin **Note:** Mule. Dav. #7240. Prev. KM#35.

Date	Mintage	VG	F	VF	XF	Unc
16ZZ Rare	—	—	—	—	—	—

Note: The above coin is a combination of the obverse of KM#37 and the reverse of Pomerania-Stettin KM#6.

KM# 42 THALER

Silver **Ruler:** Bogislaw XIV **Obv:** Bust right **Obv. Legend:** BOGISLAVS. XIV: D: G: DVS. STET. POM. CASSVB. ET. VAN: X **Rev:** Crowned griffin to left holding sword and book in baroque frame, ducal cap above divides date, titles continuous **Mint:** Stettin **Note:** Dav. #7262. Prev. KM#48.1.

Date	Mintage	VG	F	VF	XF	Unc
16Z8 GT(z)	—	300	600	1,200	2,250	—

KM# 43 THALER

Silver **Ruler:** Bogislaw XIV **Obv:** Bust right with bowknot on shoulder, titles of Bogislaw **Obv. Legend:** BOGISLAVS. XIV. D: G: DVS. STE. PO: CAS: E: V: P: RVG **Rev:** Helmeted and supported arms, date **Rev. Legend:** X EP: CAM: CO: GVT ZK: TER: LEOB: E: BV: DO **Mint:** Stettin **Note:** Dav. #7263. Prev. KM#50.1.

Date	Mintage	VG	F	VF	XF	Unc
16Z8 (z)	—	300	600	1,200	2,250	—

KM# 44 THALER

Silver **Ruler:** Bogislaw XIV **Obv:** Bust right in circle, bow on shoulder, titles of Bogislaw **Rev:** Crowned griffin left holding sword and book in baroque frame, ducal cap above divides date, titles continuous **Rev. Legend:** ...ET. BV. DOM. **Mint:** Stettin **Note:** Dav. #7263A.

Date	Mintage	VG	F	VF	XF	Unc
16Z8 (z)	—	300	600	1,200	2,250	—
16Z9 (z)	—	300	600	1,200	2,250	—

KM# 45 THALER

Silver **Ruler:** Bogislaw XIV **Obv:** Without bowknot **Obv. Legend:** ... PR: RV: **Rev:** Ornate helmet over nine-fold arms supported by wildmen with helmets, titles continuous ending with DO:, date **Note:** Dav. #7264. Prev. KM#50.2.

Date	Mintage	VG	F	VF	XF	Unc
16Z8 (z)	—	300	600	1,200	2,250	—

KM# 46 THALER

Silver **Ruler:** Bogislaw XIV **Obv:** Bust right in circle, titles of Bogislaw **Obv. Legend:** ... PR: RV: **Rev:** Ornate helmet over nine-fold arms supported by two wildmen wearing helmets, titles continuous, date **Rev. Legend:** ... DO. **Note:** Dav. #7264A.

Date	Mintage	VG	F	VF	XF	Unc
1628	—	300	600	1,200	2,250	—

KM# 47 THALER

Silver **Ruler:** Bogislaw XIV **Obv:** Bust right in circle, titles of Bogilsaw **Obv. Legend:** ...PR:RV: **Rev:** Ornate helmet over large nine-fold arms supported by two wildmen wearing helmets, date **Rev. Legend:** ...BV:DO **Note:** Dav. #7265. Prev. KM#50.3.

Date	Mintage	VG	F	VF	XF	Unc
16Z8	—	300	600	1,200	2,250	—

KM# 48 THALER

Silver **Ruler:** Bogislaw XIV **Obv:** Bust right in circle, titles of Bogislaw **Obv. Legend:** PR: RVG * **Rev:** Crowned griffin left holding sword and book in baroque frame, ducal cap above divides date, titles contiuous **Rev. Legend:** ... ET. BV. DOM. **Mint:** Stettin **Note:** Dav. #7266. Prev. KM#50.4.

Date	Mintage	VG	F	VF	XF	Unc
16Z8 GT	—	300	600	1,200	2,250	—

KM# 51 THALER

Silver **Ruler:** Bogislaw XIV **Obv:** Bust right in circle, titles of Bogislaw **Obv. Legend:** STE: PO: CAS: E: V: P: RV **Rev:** Crowned griffin left holding sword and book in baroque frame, ducal cap above divides date, titles continuous **Rev. Legend:** ... ET. BV. DOM. **Mint:** Stettin **Note:** Dav. #7267. Prev. KM#48.2.

Date	Mintage	VG	F	VF	XF	Unc
1629 (z)	—	375	675	1,350	2,500	—

KM# 52 THALER

Silver **Ruler:** Bogislaw XIV **Obv:** Bust right in circle, titles of Bogislaw **Obv. Legend:** ...E: V: P: R **Rev:** Crowned griffin left holding sword and book in baroque frame, ducal cap above divides date, titles continuous **Rev. Legend:** ...ET. BV. DOM. **Mint:** Stettin **Note:** Dav. #7267A.

Date	Mintage	VG	F	VF	XF	Unc
16Z9 (z)	—	500	900	1,500	2,850	—

KM# 53 THALER

Silver **Ruler:** Bogislaw XIV **Obv:** Bust right in circle, titles of Bogislaw **Obv. Legend:** ...E: V: P: RVG **Rev:** Crowned griffin left holding sword and book in baroque frame, ducal cap above divides date, titles continuous **Rev. Legend:** ...ET. BV. DOM. **Mint:** Stettin **Note:** Dav. #7267B.

Date	Mintage	VG	F	VF	XF	Unc
16Z9 (z)	—	500	900	1,500	2,850	—

KM# 55 THALER

Silver **Ruler:** Bogislaw XIV **Obv:** Half-length armored figure right with baton, helmet before **Obv. Legend:** ... E. V. P. RV **Rev:** Crowned griffin to left holding sword and book in baroque frame, ducal cap divides date, titles continuous **Rev. Legend:** ... GVTZK. TER. LEOB. ET. BV. DO. **Mint:** Stettin **Note:** Dav. #7268. Prev. KM#64.1.

Date	Mintage	VG	F	VF	XF	Unc
16Z9 (z)	—	875	1,400	2,250	3,850	—

KM# 56 THALER

Silver **Ruler:** Bogislaw XIV **Obv:** Half-length armored figure right holding baton, helmet at right, titles of Bogilsaw **Obv. Legend:** ...E: V: P: RV **Rev:** Crowned griffin to left holding sword and book in baroque frame, ducal cap above divides date, titles continuous **Rev. Legend:** ...GVTZ. TER. LEOB. ET. BV. DOM. **Mint:** Stettin **Note:** Dav. #7268A.

Date	Mintage	VG	F	VF	XF	Unc
16Z9 (z)	—	500	900	1,500	2,850	—

KM# 57 THALER

Silver **Ruler:** Bogislaw XIV **Obv:** Half-length armored figure right holding baton, helmet at right, titles of Bogilsaw **Obv. Legend:** ...E. V. P. RV. **Rev:** Crowned griffin to left holding sword and book in baroque frame, ducal cap above divides date, mintmaster's initials below arms, titles continuous **Rev. Legend:** ...GVTZK. TER. LEOB. ET. BV. DO. **Mint:** Stettin **Note:** Dav. #7268B.

Date	Mintage	VG	F	VF	XF	Unc
16Z9 GT	—	500	900	1,500	2,850	—

KM# 58 THALER

Silver **Ruler:** Bogislaw XIV **Obv:** Half-length armored figure right holding baton, helmet at right, titles of Bogilsaw **Obv. Legend:** ...E. V. P. RV. **Rev:** Crowned griffin left holding sword and book in baroque frame, ducal cap above divides date, mintmaster's initials below arms, titles continuous **Rev. Legend:** ...GVTZK. TER. LEOB. ET. BV. DOM. **Mint:** Stettin **Note:** Dav. #7268C.

Date	Mintage	VG	F	VF	XF	Unc
16Z9 (z)	—	500	900	1,500	2,850	—

KM# 59 THALER

Silver **Ruler:** Bogislaw XIV **Obv. Legend:** E: V: P: R: **Rev:** Ornate helmeted arms supported by two wildmen wearing helmets, titles continuous, legend, date **Rev. Legend:** ... BV: D: **Mint:** Stettin **Note:** Dav. #7269. Prev. KM#64.2.

Date	Mintage	VG	F	VF	XF	Unc
1629 GT(z)	—	875	1,400	2,250	3,850	—

KM# 60 THALER

Silver **Ruler:** Bogislaw XIV **Obv:** Half-length armored figure right holding baton, helmet at right, titles of Bogislaw **Obv. Legend:** ... E: V: P: RV **Rev:** Ornate helmet over nine-fold arms supported by two wildmen wearing helmets, titles continuous, legend, date **Rev. Legend:** ... BV: D: **Mint:** Stettin **Note:** Dav. #7269A.

Date	Mintage	VG	F	VF	XF	Unc
16Z9 (z)	—	500	900	1,500	2,850	—

KM# 61 THALER

Silver **Ruler:** Bogislaw XIV **Obv:** Half-length armored figure right holding baton, helmet at right, titles of Bogislaw **Obv. Legend:** ... E: V: P: R **Rev:** Ornate helmet over nine-fold arms supported by two wildmen wearing helmets, date in legend **Rev. Legend:** ... BV. DO. **Mint:** Stettin **Note:** Dav. #7269B.

Date	Mintage	VG	F	VF	XF	Unc
16Z9 (z)	—	500	900	1,500	2,850	—

KM# 62 THALER

Silver **Ruler:** Bogislaw XIV **Obv:** Half-length armored figure right holding baton, helmet at right, titles of Bogislaw **Obv. Legend:** ... E. V. P. RV. **Rev:** Crowned griffin left holding sword and book in baroque frame, ducal cap above divides date in legend **Rev. Legend:** ... BV. DOM. **Mint:** Stettin **Note:** Dav. #7270.

Date	Mintage	VG	F	VF	XF	Unc
16Z9 (z)	—	500	900	1,500	2,850	—

KM# 54 THALER

Silver **Ruler:** Bogislaw XIV **Obv:** Half-length armored figure right holding baton, helmet at right, titles of Bogilsaw **Obv. Legend:** ...E: V: P: RV **Rev:** Ten-fold arms in baroque frame, ducal cap above divides date, titles continuous **Rev. Legend:** ...BV. DOM. **Mint:** Stettin **Note:** Dav. #A7268.

Date	Mintage	VG	F	VF	XF	Unc
16Z9 GT(z)	—	500	900	1,500	2,850	—

KM# 63 THALER

Silver **Ruler:** Bogislaw XIV **Obv:** Armored bust right in circle, titles of Bogislaw **Obv. Legend:** ... CASE. E. V. P. R **Rev:** Crowned griffin to left holding sword and book in baroque frame, date in legend **Rev. Legend:** ... GVTZK. TER. LEOB. ET. BV. DOM. **Mint:** Stettin **Note:** Dav. #7271. Prev. KM#48.3.

Date	Mintage	VG	F	VF	XF	Unc
1630 (z)	—	400	800	1,350	2,500	—

KM# 65 THALER

Silver **Ruler:** Bogislaw XIV **Obv:** Half-length armored figure right holding baton, helmet at right, titles of Bogislaw **Obv. Legend:** ... E. V. P. RV. **Rev:** Crowned griffin left holding sword and book in baroque frame, ducal cap above divides date, titles continuous **Rev. Legend:** LEOB. E. B. D. **Note:** Dav. #7272. Prev. KM#64.3.

Date	Mintage	VG	F	VF	XF	Unc
1631	—	400	800	1,350	2,500	—

KM# 66 THALER

Silver **Ruler:** Bogislaw XIV **Obv:** Armored bust right in circle, titles of Bogislaw **Obv. Legend:** CAS. EV. PR* **Rev:** Crowned griffin left holding book and sword in baroque frame, ducal cap above divides date, titles continuous **Rev. Legend:** ... LEOB. E. B. D. **Note:** Dav. #7273. Prev. KM#48.4.

Date	Mintage	VG	F	VF	XF	Unc
1631	—	400	800	1,350	2,500	—

KM# 67 THALER

Silver **Ruler:** Bogislaw XIV **Obv:** Bust right **Obv. Legend:** PO: C. E. T. V. P. R **Rev:** Helmeted and supported arms divide date above **Rev. Legend:** EP: CAM: ... **Mint:** Stettin **Note:** Dav. #7274. Prev. KM#71.1. Varieties exist.

Date	Mintage	VG	F	VF	XF	Unc
1631 GT	—	400	800	1,350	2,500	—

KM# 68 THALER

Silver **Ruler:** Bogislaw XIV **Obv:** Bust right in circle, titles of Bogislaw **Obv. Legend:** ... E. V. P. R. **Rev:** Ornate helmet over ten-fold arms supported by two wildmen wearing helmets, titles continuous **Rev. Legend:** EP: CAM: ... **Mint:** Stettin **Note:** Dav. #7275. Prev. KM#71.2.

Date	Mintage	VG	F	VF	XF	Unc
1631 GT	—	500	900	1,500	2,850	—

KM# 69 THALER

Silver **Ruler:** Bogislaw XIV **Obv:** Bust off center to right, hand breaks through legend **Rev:** Ornate helmet over ten-fold arms supported by two wildmen wearing helmets, date in legend **Rev. Legend:** EP: CAM:... **Mint:** Stettin **Note:** Dav. #7276. Prev. KM#71.3.

Date	Mintage	VG	F	VF	XF	Unc
1631 GT	—	750	1,250	2,250	3,850	—

KM# 72 THALER

Silver **Ruler:** Bogislaw XIV **Obv:** Large bust right **Obv. Legend:** ... DVX. STE. P. C. E. V. P. R **Rev:** Large arms, date **Rev. Legend:** EP. CAM. CO. GVTZK. TER. LEOB. ET. BV. DOM **Note:** Dav. #7279. Prev. KM#82.1.

Date	Mintage	VG	F	VF	XF	Unc
163Z	—	400	800	1,350	2,500	—

KM# 73 THALER

Silver **Ruler:** Bogislaw XIV **Obv:** Bust right divides date in legend at top **Rev:** Ornate helmet over ten-fold arms, supported by two wildmen wearing helmets, date in legend **Note:** Dav. #7280. Prev. KM#82.2.

Date	Mintage	VG	F	VF	XF	Unc
1632	—	400	800	1,350	2,500	—

KM# 71 THALER

Silver **Ruler:** Bogislaw XIV **Obv:** Bust right in circle, titles of Bogislaw **Obv. Legend:** ...E. V. P. R. **Rev:** Ornate helmet over nine-fold arms supported by two wildmen wearing helmets, date in legend **Note:** Dav.#7277. Prev. KM#50.5. The '3' and '2' in the date are engraved backwards.

Date	Mintage	VG	F	VF	XF	Unc
163Z	—	400	800	1,350	2,500	—

Note: The "3" and "2" in date are engraved backwards

KM# A77 THALER

Silver **Ruler:** Bogislaw XIV **Obv:** Date in legend above large bust; titles with BOGISLAVS **Obv. Legend:** ... ET. V. P. R. **Rev:** Helmeted and supported ten-fold arms, date in legend **Rev. Legend:** EP: CAM:... **Note:** Dav. #7282. Prev. KM#82.3.

Date	Mintage	VG	F	VF	XF	Unc
1633	—	400	800	1,350	2,500	—
1634	—	400	800	1,350	2,500	—

KM# 78 THALER

Silver **Ruler:** Bogislaw XIV **Obv:** Large bust right breaks circle at top, titles with BOGISLAVS **Obv. Legend:** ... E. V. P. R. **Rev:** Ornate helmet over ten-fold arms supported by two wildmen wearing helmets, date in legend **Rev. Legend:** EP: CAM:... **Note:** Dav. #7282A.

Date	Mintage	VG	F	VF	XF	Unc
1633	—	400	800	1,350	2,500	—

KM# 79 THALER

Silver **Ruler:** Bogislaw XIV **Obv:** Broad bust to right breaks circle at top, titles with BOISLAVS **Obv. Legend:** ... ET. V. P. R. **Rev:** Ornate helmet over ten-fold arms supported by two wildmen wearing helmets, date in legend **Rev. Legend:** EP: CAM:... **Note:** Dav. #7282B.

Date	Mintage	VG	F	VF	XF	Unc
1633	—	400	800	1,350	2,500	—

KM# 82 THALER

Silver **Ruler:** Bogislaw XIV **Obv:** Large bust right breaks circle at top, titles with BOFILAVS **Obv. Legend:** ... ET. V. P. R. **Rev:** Ornate helmet over ten-fold arms supported by two wildmen wearing helmets, date in legend **Rev. Legend:** EP: CAM:... **Note:** Dav. #7282C.

Date	Mintage	VG	F	VF	XF	Unc
1634	—	400	800	1,350	2,500	—

KM# 83 THALER

Silver **Ruler:** Bogislaw XIV **Obv:** Large bust right **Obv. Legend:** DVX: S * P * C * ET * V * P * R * **Rev:** Large arms, date divided by feathers on helmet below legend **Rev. Legend:** TER * LEOB * E * BV **Note:** Dav. #7283. Prev. KM#71.4.

Date	Mintage	VG	F	VF	XF	Unc
1634	—	400	800	1,350	2,500	—

KM# 84 THALER

Silver **Ruler:** Bogislaw XIV **Obv:** Large bust right breaks circle, titles of Bogislaw **Obv. Legend:** DVX. STE. PO. CAS. E. V. P. R **Rev:** Ornate helmet over nine-fold arms supported by two wildmen wearing helmets, date divided by feathers on helmet at top in legend **Rev. Legend:** TER: LEOB: ETBU: DO **Note:** Dav. #7284. Prev. KM#71.5.

Date	Mintage	VG	F	VF	XF	Unc
1634	—	400	800	1,350	2,500	—

KM# 86 THALER

Silver **Ruler:** Bogislaw XIV **Obv:** Large bust right breaks circle, titles of Bogislaw **Obv. Legend:** DVX. S. P. C. E. P. R **Rev:** Ornate helmet over ten-fold arms supported by two wildmen wearing helmets, date divided by featehrs on helmet below legend **Rev. Legend:** EP - * CAM * CO * GVTZK * TER * LEOB * E * BV * - DO **Note:** Dav. #7285. Prev. KM#71.6.

Date	Mintage	VG	F	VF	XF	Unc
1635	—	400	800	1,350	2,500	—

KM# 87 THALER

Silver **Ruler:** Bogislaw XIV **Obv:** Large bust right breaks circle, titles of Bogislaw **Rev:** Ornate helmet over ten-fold arms supported by two wildmen wearing helmets, date divided by feathers on helmet below legend, date in legend **Rev. Legend:** E - * CAM * CO * GV - TZK * TER * L--EOB * E * BV * - D - O * **Note:** Dav. #7286. Prev. KM#71.7.

Date	Mintage	VG	F	VF	XF	Unc
1635	—	400	800	1,350	2,500	—

KM# A88 THALER

Silver **Obv:** Different bust **Obv. Legend:** EOB: ET: BV: **Note:** Dav.#7287. Prev. KM#71.8.

Date	Mintage	VG	F	VF	XF	Unc
1635	—	400	800	1,350	2,500	—

KM# 88 THALER

Silver **Ruler:** Bogislaw XIV **Obv:** Large bust right breaks circle, titles of Bogislaw **Obv. Legend:** S. P. C. E. V. P. R **Rev:** Ornate helmet over ten-fold arms supported by two wildmen wearing helmets, date divided by helmet above arms **Rev. Legend:** EP: CAM:... **Note:** Dav. #7288. Prev. KM#71.9.

Date	Mintage	VG	F	VF	XF	Unc
1636	—	500	900	1,500	2,850	—

KM# 89 THALER

Silver **Ruler:** Bogislaw XIV **Obv:** Large different bust right breaks circle, titles of Bogislaw **Rev:** Ornate helmet over ten-fold arms supported by two wildmen wearing helmets to either side, date divided by helmet above arms **Rev. Legend:** EP - * CAM * CO * G - V - TZK * TER - * LEOB * ET * B - DO * **Note:** Dav. #7289. Prev. KM#71.10.

Date	Mintage	VG	F	VF	XF	Unc
1637	—	500	900	1,500	2,850	—

KM# 91 THALER
Silver **Subject:** Entombment of Hedwig von Braunschweig-Wolfenbüttel, Widow of Ulrich **Obv:** 7-line inscription around titles of Hedwig **Rev:** 10-line inscription with R.N. dates **Note:** Dav. #6316

Date	Mintage	VG	F	VF	XF	Unc
MIDCLIV (1654)	—	—	3,000	5,000	8,500	—

KM# 38 1-1/2 THALER
Silver **Ruler:** Ulrich **Subject:** Death of Ulrich **Obv:** Bust left breaks circle at top, date above head, titles of Ulrich **Rev:** Nine-line inscription with dates **Note:** Dav. #A7243.

Date	Mintage	VG	F	VF	XF	Unc
16ZZ Rare	—	—	—	—	—	—

KM# 39 2 THALER
Silver **Subject:** Death of Ulrich **Obv:** Bust left breaks circle at top, date above head, titles of Ulrich **Rev:** 9-line inscription with dates **Note:** Dav. #7242. Prev. KM#40.

Date	Mintage	VG	F	VF	XF	Unc
16ZZ Rare	—	—	—	—	—	—

KM# 74 2 THALER
Silver **Ruler:** Bogislaw XIV **Obv:** Large bust to right breaks circle at top, titles of Bosislaw end with small date **Rev:** Ornate helmet over ten-fold arms supported by two wildmen wearing helmets to either side, date in legend **Note:** Dav. #7278. Prev. KM#83.

Date	Mintage	VG	F	VF	XF	Unc
163Z Rare	—	—	—	—	—	—

KM# 80 2 THALER
Silver **Ruler:** Bogislaw XIV **Obv:** Large bust right breaks circle at top, titles with BOGISLAVS **Obv. Legend:** E. V. P. R. **Rev:** Ornate helmet over ten-fold arms supported by two wildmen wearing helmets, date in legend **Note:** Dav. #7281. Prev. KM#84.

Date	Mintage	VG	F	VF	XF	Unc
1633 Rare	—	—	—	—	—	—

KM# 40 2-1/2 THALER
Silver **Subject:** Death of Ulrich **Obv:** Bust left breaks circle at top, date above head, titles of Ulrich **Rev:** Nine-line inscription with dates **Note:** Dav. #A7242.

Date	Mintage	VG	F	VF	XF	Unc
16ZZ Rare	—	—	—	—	—	—

KM# 41 3 THALER
Silver **Subject:** Death of Ulrich **Obv:** Bust left breaks circle at top, date above head, titles of Ulrich **Rev:** 9-line inscription with dates **Note:** Dav. #7241. Prev. KM#45.

Date	Mintage	VG	F	VF	XF	Unc
1622	—	5,500	8,500	15,000	—	—

TRADE COINAGE

KM# 49 GOLDGULDEN
3.5000 g., 0.9860 Gold 0.1109 oz. AGW **Ruler:** Bogislaw XIV **Obv:** Bust right in circle, titles of Bogislaw **Rev:** Ornamented shield fo four-folds arms, date above, titles continuous **Rev. Legend:** PL R: EP. CA… **Note:** Fr. #2098.

Date	Mintage	VG	F	VF	XF	Unc
16Z8	—	1,400	2,700	5,100	9,300	—

KM# 50 GOLDGULDEN
3.5000 g., 0.9860 Gold 0.1109 oz. AGW **Ruler:** Bogislaw XIV **Obv:** Large bust right in circle, titles of Bogislaw **Rev:** Narroew four-fold arms divide date at sides and above 1-6Z-8 **Rev. Legend:** EP: CA:… **Note:** Fr. #2098. Prev. KM#60.

Date	Mintage	VG	F	VF	XF	Unc
1628	—	1,400	2,700	5,100	9,300	—

KM# 64 DUCAT
3.5000 g., 0.9860 Gold 0.1109 oz. AGW **Ruler:** Bogislaw XIV **Obv:** Full-length figure facing right, titles of Bogislaw **Rev:** Ten-fold arms in shield within circle, date in legend **Note:** Ref. H#290. Fr. #2100.

Date	Mintage	VG	F	VF	XF	Unc
ND(1630-35)	—	900	1,800	3,200	6,600	—

KM# 70 DUCAT
3.5000 g., 0.9860 Gold 0.1109 oz. AGW **Ruler:** Bogislaw XIV **Obv:** Full-length figure facing right, head divides date, titles of Bogislaw **Rev:** 10-fold arms in shield within circle, date in legend **Note:** Fr. #2100.

Date	Mintage	VG	F	VF	XF	Unc
1631	—	900	1,800	3,200	6,600	—

KM# 81 DUCAT
3.5000 g., 0.9860 Gold 0.1109 oz. AGW **Ruler:** Bogislaw XIV **Obv:** Full-length figure facing right, head divides mintmaster's initials, titles of Bogislaw **Rev:** 10-fold arms in shield within circle, date in legend **Mint:** Stettin **Note:** Fr. #2100. Varieties exist.

Date	Mintage	VG	F	VF	XF	Unc
1633 VB	—	900	1,800	3,200	6,600	—
1634 VB	—	900	1,800	3,200	6,600	—
1635 VB	—	900	1,800	3,200	6,600	—
1636 VB	—	900	1,800	3,200	6,600	—
ND VB	—	900	1,800	3,200	6,600	—

CLEVES

(Cleve, Kleve)

The countship, later duchy, of Cleves, located on both sides of the Rhine at the Dutch border, had its beginnings in the early 11th century. It passed in marriage to the counts of Mark in 1368, who were raised to the rank of duke in Cleves in 1417. In 1511 Jülich, Berg and Ravensberg were obtained by marriage. The last duke died in 1609 without a male heir, causing a great struggle for the various territories between Pfalz-Neuburg, Brandenburg-Prussia and Saxony. (See Jülich-Cleves-Berg for coinage to 1609). Eventually, the first two won out and made a pact to divide the territories between them. Brandenburg-Prussia obtained Cleves, Mark and Ravensberg, while Pfalz-Neuburg received Jülich and Berg. Saxony refused to give up its claims and, though never managing to obtain any territory, the dukes continued to place the arms of Cleves on their coinage throughout the rest of the 17th century. The rulers of Brandenburg-Prussia and Pfalz-Neuburg struck a joint coinage in the disputed territories until the formal division in 1624. The joint coinage struck in Cleves is listed here. That of Jülich-Berg is listed under that name. The special coinage of Brandenburg-Prussia for Mark and Ravensberg are included under those place names.

RULERS
Joint Coinage, 1609-1624
Georg Wilhelm, Markgraf von Brandenburg, 1624-1640
Friedrich Wilhelm, Markgraf von Brandenburg, 1640-1688
Friedrich III, Markgraf von Brandenburg (I of Prussia, as King), 1688-(1701)-1713

MINT MARKS
C - Cleves

MINT OFFICIALS" INITIALS

Initial	Date	Name
(h)	1603-15	Conrad Hoyer in Emmerich
WH	1689-94	Seger Wendel, warden and ? Hoyer, mintmaster in Emmerich
	1615-	Anton Hoyer in Emmerich
	-1618	Arnold Rath, warden in Emmerich
	1618-	Johann Von Wannere, warden in Emmerich

ARMS
Cleves – 8 rods (scepters) with lilies at tip, arranged as spokes in a wheel, small shield in center
Mark – Horizontal band of checkerboard design across center

MONETARY SYSTEM
8 Duit = 1 Stüber
60 Stüber = 1 Reichsthaler
5 Reichsthaler = 1 Friedrich d'Or

REFERENCE:
Sch = Wolfgang Schulten, **Deutsche Münzen aus der Zeit Karls V.**, Frankfurt am Main, 1974

DUCHY

REGULAR COINAGE

KM# 5 3 HELLER
Copper **Obv:** Crowned 6-fold arms **Rev:** III in wreath **Rev. Legend:** NVMMVS. CLIVENSIS **Mint:** Emmerich

Date	Mintage	VG	F	VF	XF	Unc
ND(1609-1615) (h)	—	17.00	37.00	75.00	150	—

KM# 20 3 HELLER
Copper **Rev:** Inscription in wreath, without indication of value **Rev. Inscription:** DV / CLI / VIAE **Note:** Varieties exist.

Date	Mintage	VG	F	VF	XF	Unc
ND(ca.1618)	—	20.00	40.00	80.00	160	—

KM# 25.1 DUIT
Copper, 20 mm. **Ruler:** Friedrich Wilhelm **Obv:** Crowned scepter divides date within wreath **Rev:** Inscription in wreath **Rev. Inscription:** DU / CLI / VIAE

Date	Mintage	VG	F	VF	XF	Unc
1669	—	12.00	30.00	60.00	125	—
1670	—	12.00	30.00	60.00	125	—

KM# 25.2 DUIT
Copper **Ruler:** Friedrich Wilhelm **Obv:** Crowned scepter divides date within wreath **Rev:** Inscription in wreath **Rev. Inscription:** DU / CLIV / IAE

Date	Mintage	VG	F	VF	XF	Unc
1677	—	12.00	30.00	60.00	125	—
1678	—	12.00	30.00	60.00	125	—
1679	—	12.00	30.00	60.00	125	—
1680	—	12.00	30.00	60.00	125	—

KM# 32 DUIT
Copper **Ruler:** Friedrich III **Obv:** Scepter in crowned oval shield with lion supporters **Rev. Inscription:** EEN / DUIT

Date	Mintage	VG	F	VF	XF	Unc
ND(1688-1701)	—	12.00	25.00	50.00	100	—

KM# 37 DUIT
Copper **Ruler:** Friedrich III

Date	Mintage	VG	F	VF	XF	Unc
1692	—	12.00	25.00	50.00	100	—
1693	—	12.00	25.00	50.00	100	—
1694	—	12.00	25.00	50.00	100	—
1695	—	12.00	25.00	50.00	100	—
1696	—	12.00	25.00	50.00	100	—
1697	—	12.00	25.00	50.00	100	—
1698	—	12.00	25.00	50.00	100	—

KM# 6 1/2 STüBER (10 Heller)
Silver **Obv:** Large X in center divides date **Obv. Legend:** NVMMVS. CLIVENSIS **Rev:** XCII in center **Rev. Legend:** CVSVS. EMBRICAE **Note:** Struck at Emmerich Mint.

Date	Mintage	VG	F	VF	XF	Unc
(1)6(0)9 (h)	—	20.00	40.00	80.00	160	—

KM# 7 1/2 STüBER (10 Heller)
Silver **Obv:** Crowned 6-fold arms divide X-O **Rev:** Ornate cross divides X - CII at top and date below **Note:** Varieties exist.

Date	Mintage	VG	F	VF	XF	Unc
(1)609	—	20.00	40.00	80.00	160	—
(1)609 (h)	—	20.00	40.00	80.00	160	—

KM# 8 1/2 STüBER (10-1/2 Heller)
Silver **Rev:** Value XCI

Date	Mintage	VG	F	VF	XF	Unc
(1)609	—	20.00	40.00	80.00	160	—

KM# 15 1/2 STüBER (10-1/2 Heller)
Silver **Rev:** Without indiciation of value

Date	Mintage	VG	F	VF	XF	Unc
ND(ca.1612)	—	20.00	40.00	80.00	160	—

KM# 16 STüBER (21 Heller)
Silver **Obv:** Crowned 6-fold arms divide I-S **Obv. Legend:** NVMMVS. CLIVENSIS **Rev:** Ornate cross **Rev. Legend:** MO. A - RG: CV - SVS: E - MBRI(C) **Mint:** Emmerich **Note:** Varieties exist.

Date	Mintage	VG	F	VF	XF	Unc
ND(ca.1612) (h)	—	20.00	40.00	80.00	160	—

KM# 19 STüBER (21 Heller)
Silver **Rev. Legend:** MON. ARG. CVS. EMB **Note:** Varieties exist.

Date	Mintage	VG	F	VF	XF	Unc
ND(ca.1616-1624)	—	20.00	40.00	80.00	160	—

KM# 30 STüBER (21 Heller)
Silver **Ruler:** Friedrich Wilhelm **Obv:** Square topped shield, crowned **Rev:** Cross florate **Rev. Legend:** MON. ARG. CVS. CLI

Date	Mintage	VG	F	VF	XF	Unc
1668	—	10.00	25.00	55.00	115	—
1669	—	10.00	25.00	55.00	115	—
1670	—	10.00	25.00	55.00	115	—

KM# 21 3 STüBER
Silver **Obv:** Crowned imperial eagle, **Obv. Legend:** III. ST **Rev:** Crowned 6-fold arms **Mint:** Emmerich **Note:** Kipper 3 Stuber. Varieties exist.

Date	Mintage	VG	F	VF	XF	Unc
ND(1619-22)	—	100	200	360	725	—

KM# 9 SCHILLING
Silver **Obv:** Crowned imperial eagle, titles of Rudolf II **Rev:** Crowned 6-fold arms **Note:** Varieties exist.

Date	Mintage	VG	F	VF	XF	Unc
ND(1609-12)	—	20.00	40.00	80.00	160	—
ND(1609-12) (h)	—	20.00	40.00	80.00	160	—

KM# 17 SCHILLING
Silver **Obv:** Titles of Matthias **Note:** Varieties exist.

Date	Mintage	VG	F	VF	XF	Unc
ND(1612-15) (h)	—	20.00	40.00	80.00	160	—

KM# 18 SCHILLING
9.8400 g., Silver **Obv:** Titles of Matthias **Note:** Klippe.

Date	Mintage	VG	F	VF	XF	Unc
ND(1612-15) (h)	—	—	—	—	—	—

KM# 35 1/12 THALER (2 Groschen)

Silver **Ruler:** Friedrich III **Obv:** Crowned ornate 6-fold arms **Rev:** Date **Rev. Inscription:** 12 / EINEN / REICHS / THALER **Mint:** Emmerich

Date	Mintage	VG	F	VF	XF	Unc
1690 WH	—	16.00	30.00	65.00	130	—
1691 WH	—	16.00	30.00	65.00	130	—
1692 WH	—	16.00	30.00	65.00	130	—
1693 WH	—	16.00	30.00	65.00	130	—

KM# 38 1/3 THALER (1/2 Gulden)

Silver **Ruler:** Friedrich III **Obv:** Bust right **Rev:** Crowned 10-fold arms, value (1/3) below, date in legend

Date	Mintage	VG	F	VF	XF	Unc
1693 WH	—	—	—	—	—	—

KM# 36.1 2/3 THALER

Silver **Ruler:** Friedrich III **Obv:** Armored bust to right with undivided legend **Obv. Legend:** FRIDER. III. D.G. M. B. S. R. I. ARC. &. EL. **Rev:** Crowned shield of manifold arms divides mintmaster's initials, value (2/3) below, date at end of legend **Rev. Legend:** MONETA. NOVA. - BRANDENB. **Mint:** Emmerich **Note:** Dav. 281. Varieties exist.

Date	Mintage	VG	F	VF	XF	Unc
1690 WH	—	75.00	150	300	600	—
1691 WH	—	75.00	150	300	600	—
1692 WH	—	75.00	150	300	600	—

KM# 36.2 2/3 THALER

Silver **Ruler:** Friedrich III **Obv:** Armored bust to right divides legend at top **Obv. Legend:** FRIDER. III. D.G. M. - B. S. R. I. ARC. &. EL. **Rev:** Crowned shield of manifold arms divides mintmaster's initials, (2/3) in oval below, date at end of legend **Rev. Legend:** MONETA. NOVA. - BRANDENB. **Mint:** Emmerich **Note:** Dav. 282. Varieties exist.

Date	Mintage	VG	F	VF	XF	Unc
1692 WH	—	75.00	150	300	625	—
1693 WH	—	75.00	150	300	625	—
1694 WH	—	75.00	150	300	625	—
1695 WH	—	75.00	150	300	625	—
1696 WH	—	75.00	150	300	625	—
1696/5 WH	—	75.00	150	300	625	—

KM# 11 THALER

Silver **Rev:** Crowned arms dividing date in inner circle **Note:** Dav. #6665.

Date	Mintage	VG	F	VF	XF	Unc
1604 Rare	—	—	—	—	—	—
1608 Rare	—	—	—	—	—	—
1609 Rare	—	—	—	—	—	—

KM# 10 THALER

Silver **Ruler:** Friedrich III **Obv:** Bust right **Rev:** Helmeted arms **Note:** Dav. #6661.

Date	Mintage	VG	F	VF	XF	Unc
ND Rare	—	—	—	—	—	—

KM# 39 THALER (Albertus)

Silver **Ruler:** Friedrich III **Obv:** Ornate arms, crown above divides date **Rev:** 4 crowned double-F monograms alternating wioth 4 III's, scepter arms in center, inscription between crowns **Note:** Dav. #6221.

Date	Mintage	VG	F	VF	XF	Unc
1695 WH	—	225	400	750	1,500	—

KM# 40 THALER (Albertus)

Silver **Ruler:** Friedrich III **Rev:** Without inscription between crowns **Note:** Dav. #6222.

Date	Mintage	VG	F	VF	XF	Unc
1695 WH Rare	—	—	—	—	—	—

KM# 12 1-1/2 THALER

Silver **Obv:** Bust right **Rev:** Crowned arms dividing date in inner circle **Note:** Klippe. Dav. #6664. Illustration reduced.

Date	Mintage	VG	F	VF	XF	Unc
1608 Rare	—	—	—	—	—	—
1609 Rare	—	—	—	—	—	—

KM# 14 2 THALER

Silver **Rev:** Crowned arms divide date in inner circle **Note:** Dav. #6663.

Date	Mintage	VG	F	VF	XF	Unc
1604 Rare	—	—	—	—	—	—
1608 Rare	—	—	—	—	—	—

KM# 22 2 THALER

Silver **Note:** Klippe. Dav. #6663A.

Date	Mintage	VG	F	VF	XF	Unc
1608 Rare	—	—	—	—	—	—

KM# 13 2 THALER

Silver **Obv:** Bust right **Rev:** Helmeted arms **Note:** Dav. #6660.

Date	Mintage	VG	F	VF	XF	Unc
ND Rare	—	—	—	—	—	—

KM# 23 3 THALER

Silver **Obv:** Bust right **Rev:** Crowned arms divide date in inner circle **Note:** Klippe. Dav. #6662.

Date	Mintage	VG	F	VF	XF	Unc
1609 Rare	—	—	—	—	—	—

COESFELD

The town of Coesfeld in Westphalia is located on the Berkel River some 19 miles (32 kilometers) west of Münster. Although Coesfeld belonged to the bishops of Münster, it was permitted to issue a local minor coinage from the late 16th century until 1763. When the bishopric was secularized in 1802, Coesfeld was acquired by the Rhinegraves of Salm. The latter's territories were soon mediatized in 1806 and became a part of Joachim Murat's grand duchy of Berg. Coesfeld finally passed to Prussia along with the rest of Berg at the conclusion of the Napoleonic Wars.

REFERENCE

H = Wolf Holtmann, "Beschreibung der Coesfelder Kupfermünzen", ***Geschichtsblätter des Kreises Coesfeld***, 1 (1979), pp. 51-71.

PROVINCIAL TOWN

REGULAR COINAGE

KM# 12 HELLER

Copper **Obv:** Facing steer's head in circle, date **Obv. Legend:** STADT. COSVELT **Rev:** I/H within ornamented square

Date	Mintage	VG	F	VF	XF	Unc
1627	—	110	225	450	—	—

KM# 11 PFENNIG

Copper **Obv:** Facing steer's head within circle **Obv. Legend:** STADT. COSVELT **Rev:** Value 'I' within ornamented square **Note:** Varieties exist.

Date	Mintage	VG	F	VF	XF	Unc
1617	—	11.00	22.00	45.00	90.00	—
1627	—	11.00	22.00	45.00	90.00	—
1644	—	11.00	22.00	45.00	90.00	—
1694	—	11.00	22.00	45.00	90.00	—

KM# 5 2 PFENNIG

Copper **Obv:** Facing steer's head in shield, within circle **Obv. Legend:** STADT. COSVEL(D)T. **Rev:** Value 'II' within ornamented square **Note:** Varieties exist.

Date	Mintage	VG	F	VF	XF	Unc
1608	—	12.00	25.00	50.00	100	—
1609	—	12.00	25.00	50.00	100	—
1617	—	12.00	25.00	50.00	100	—
1644	—	12.00	25.00	50.00	100	—
1694	—	12.00	25.00	50.00	100	—

KM# 6 3 PFENNIG

Copper **Obv:** Facing steer's head in circle **Obv. Legend:** STADT. COSVEL(D)T. **Rev:** Value 'III' within ornamented square **Note:** Varieties exist.

Date	Mintage	VG	F	VF	XF	Unc
1609	—	15.00	35.00	70.00	140	—
1617	—	15.00	35.00	70.00	140	—
1644	—	15.00	35.00	70.00	140	—
1650	—	15.00	35.00	70.00	140	—
1699	—	15.00	35.00	70.00	140	—

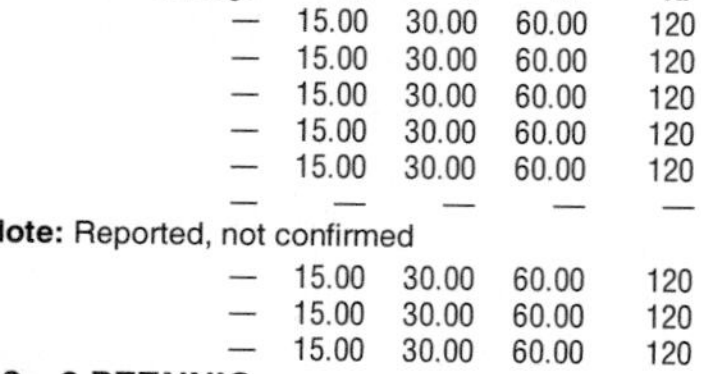

KM# 7 4 PFENNIG

Copper **Obv:** Facing steer's head within shield, circle surrounds **Obv. Legend:** STADT. COSVEL(D)T. **Rev:** Value 'IIII' within ornamented square **Note:** Varieties exist.

Date	Mintage	VG	F	VF	XF	Unc
1609	—	15.00	30.00	60.00	120	—
1617	—	15.00	30.00	60.00	120	—
1634	—	15.00	30.00	60.00	120	—
1644	—	15.00	30.00	60.00	120	—
1650	—	15.00	30.00	60.00	120	—
1673	—	—	—	—	—	—
Note: Reported, not confirmed						
1693	—	15.00	30.00	60.00	120	—
1694	—	15.00	30.00	60.00	120	—
1699	—	15.00	30.00	60.00	120	—

KM# 8 6 PFENNIG

Copper **Obv:** Facing steer's head in shield within circle **Obv. Legend:** STADT. COSVEL(D)T. **Rev:** Value 'VI' within ornamented square **Note:** Varieties exist.

Date	Mintage	VG	F	VF	XF	Unc
1609	—	20.00	40.00	85.00	170	—
1617	—	20.00	40.00	85.00	170	—

KM# 9 8 PFENNIG

Copper **Obv:** Facing steer's head in shield, within circle **Obv. Legend:** STADT. COSVEL(D)T. **Rev:** Value 'VIII' within ornamented square **Note:** Varieties exist.

Date	Mintage	VG	F	VF	XF	Unc
1609	—	15.00	30.00	60.00	125	—
1617	—	15.00	30.00	60.00	125	—
1634	—	15.00	30.00	60.00	125	—
1636 Rare	—	—	—	—	—	—
1691	—	15.00	30.00	60.00	125	—
1694	—	15.00	30.00	60.00	125	—

KM# 10 12 PFENNIG

Copper **Obv:** Facing steer's head in shield, within circle **Obv. Legend:** STADT. COSVELDT. **Rev:** Value 'XII' within ornamented square **Note:** Varieties exist.

Date	Mintage	VG	F	VF	XF	Unc
1616	—	—	—	—	—	—
Note: Reported, not confirmed						
1617	—	45.00	100	225	425	—
1636	—	45.00	100	225	425	—
1663 Rare	—	—	—	—	—	—
Note: Error for 1636						

COLMAR

A city in central Alsace, about 37 miles west of Freiburg in Breisgau, known to exist as early as 823. Colmar became a free imperial city in 1226. It was captured by Swedish forces in 1632, then by the French in 1635 during the Thirty Years' War. It regained its free status in 1649, but was taken back in 1673 and finally annexed by France in 1681.

MONETARY SYSTEM

2 Staber = Rappen (Pfennig)
Plappart = 42 Rappen = 7 Schilling
Dicken = 5 Plappart = 210 Rappen
2 Heller = 1 Pfennig
4 (Vierer) Pfennig = 1 Kreuzer

ARMS

A mace, usually tilted to the left

CITY

REGULAR COINAGE

KM# 6 DOPPELVIERER

Silver **Obv:** Eagle in circle **Obv. Legend:** MONET = N - O + COLMA **Rev:** Long cross **Rev. Legend:** GLOR - IA. IN.E - XCE - L 'DEO.

Date	Mintage	VG	F	VF	XF	Unc
ND(c.1660)	—	—	—	—	—	—

KM# 7 DOPPELVIERER

Silver **Obv:** Eagle in circle **Obv. Legend:** MONET = N - O + COLMA. **Rev:** Long cross **Rev. Legend:** GLOR - IA. IN.E - XCE - L 'DEO. **Note:** Klippe.

Date	Mintage	VG	F	VF	XF	Unc
ND(c.1660) Rare	—	—	—	—	—	—

KM# 4 DOPPELVIERER

Silver, 19.3 mm. **Obv:** Crowned imperial eagle, arms of city (mace)on breast **Obv. Legend:** MON: NO: CIVIT: IM: COLMAR: **Rev:** Long cross dividing legend **Rev. Legend:** S:MA-RTIN-VS. PA-TRON **Note:** Prev. KM#5.

Date	Mintage	VG	F	VF	XF	Unc
ND(c.1660)	—	25.00	50.00	100	200	—

KM# 5 DOPPELVIERER

Silver **Rev. Legend:** GLOR-IA. IN.E-XCE-L'DEO **Note:** Varieties exist. Prev. KM#6.

Date	Mintage	VG	F	VF	XF	Unc
ND(c.1660)	—	—	—	—	—	—
Note: Four pieces known						

KM# 16 4 KREUZER (Batzen)

Silver **Obv:** City arms (mace), date above **Rev:** Imperial eagle in inner circle

Date	Mintage	VG	F	VF	XF	Unc
1666	—	40.00	85.00	150	290	—
1667	—	40.00	85.00	150	290	—
1669	—	40.00	85.00	150	290	—

KM# 15 12 KREUZER (Zwölfer)

Silver **Obv:** Crowned imperial eagle **Rev:** Oval city arms (mace) in baroque frame, value XII.K above

Date	Mintage	VG	F	VF	XF	Unc
ND(c.1660)	—	180	250	475	950	—

KM# 17 12 KREUZER (Zwölfer)

Silver **Obv:** City arms (mace) **Rev:** Crowned imperial eagle

Date	Mintage	VG	F	VF	XF	Unc
1666	—	115	225	425	875	—
1669	—	115	225	425	875	—

KM# 20 30 KREUZER (1/2 Gulden)

Silver **Obv:** City arms in baroque frame divide date, 30 in oval at bottom **Rev:** Crowned imperial eagle

Date	Mintage	VG	F	VF	XF	Unc
1670	—	—	—	—	—	—
Note: Three pieces known						

KM# 22 60 KREUZER (Gulden)

Silver **Rev:** Different shield and incorporating value "60" at bottom, within circle **Note:** Dav. #462.

Date	Mintage	VG	F	VF	XF	Unc
ND	—	275	575	1,150	2,200	—

KM# 21 60 KREUZER (Gulden)

Silver **Obv:** Similar to 12 Kreuzer, KM#17 **Rev:** City arms in baroque frame divides date **Note:** Dav. #461.

Date	Mintage	VG	F	VF	XF	Unc
1670	—	475	900	1,500	2,900	—

KM# 18 THALER

Silver **Obv:** Crowned imperial eagle **Obv. Legend:** LEOPOLD: DG:... **Rev:** City view with COLLMAR on banner above, angel's head above two shields below **Note:** Dav# 5131.

Date	Mintage	VG	F	VF	XF	Unc
1666 Rare	—	—	—	—	—	—

KM# 23 THALER

Silver **Obv:** Small crown and square topped shield **Rev:** COLMAR on banner **Note:** Dav #5133.

Date	Mintage	VG	F	VF	XF	Unc
1670 Rare	—	—	—	—	—	—
Note: Künkler Auction 184, 3-11, VF+ realized approximately $23,750. Moller Auction 10-92 VF/XF realized $15,750						

KM# 24 2 THALER

Silver **Obv:** City view with COLMAR" on banner above, angel's head above two shields below **Obv. Legend:** LEOPOLD: DG:... **Rev:** Crowned double-headed imperial eagle with city arms on breast **Note:** Dav #5132.

Date	Mintage	VG	F	VF	XF	Unc
1670 Rare	—	—	—	—	—	—

COLOGNE

(Köln)

A bishopric was established in the city of Roman foundation in 313 and transformed into an archbishopric by Charlemagne in 785. Joint issues of coinage by the archbishops and the emperors began in the mid-10th century and the first independent ecclesiastic issues appeared in the late 11th century. Upon the breakup of the old duchy of Saxony in 1180, the archbishop obtained the duchy of Westphalia. The archbishops became Electors of the Empire by the Gold Bull of 1356 and continued to gain power and territory during the ensuing centuries. In 1801, Cologne was secularized and its lands west of the Rhine were taken by France. Several principalities divided Cologne's territories east of the Rhine, the largest portions having been taken by Hesse-Darmstadt and Nassau.

RULERS

Hermann IV, Landgraf von Hessen, 1480-1508
Philipp II, Graf von Dhaun-Oberstein, 1508-1515
Hermann V, Graf von Wied, 1515-1546
Adolf III, Graf von Schaumburg-Pinneberg, 1547-1556
Anton, Graf von Schaumburg-Pinneberg, 1556-1558
Johann Gebhard (I), Graf von Mansfeld-Vorderort, 1558-1562
Friedrich IV, Graf von Wied, 1562-1567
Salentin, Graf von Isenburg-Grenzau, 1567-1577
Gebhard (II), Truchsess von Waldburg-Trauchburg, 1577-1583
Ernst, Herzog von Bayern, 1583-1612
Ferdinand, Herzog von Bayern, 1612-1650
Maximilian Heinrich, Herzog von Bayern, 1650-1688
Josef Clemens, Herzog von Bayern, 1688-1723

ARMS

Archbishopric – Cross

EARLY MINT OFFICIALS

Deutz Mint

Date	Name
1547-57	Dietrich Grünwalt, mintmaster
	Jürgen Bornheim, warden
1558-65	Johann Bitter von Raesfeld, mintmaster
1565-72	Peter Bitter von Raesfeld, mintmaster
1565-69	Tilman Wickerath, warden
1569-84	Gabriel Phinoir, warden
1572-79	Reiner Budels, mintmaster
1580	Heinrich Rörichs
1581-1584	Gilles von Siburg, mintmaster
1583-1601	Reiner Budels, mintmaster
1600-	Ulrich von Wernberg, warden
1615-17	Heinrich Lambertz, mintmaster
1617-?	Johann Gerhardt, warden

MINT OFFICIALS' INITIALS

Initials	Date	Name
BS	1641-42	Benedikt Stephani in Bonn

C		Commission, Committee
FE	1638-39	Franz Engels in bonn
FL	Ca.1657	Unknown in Bonn
FW	1693	Friedrich Wendels in Deutz
	1698-1728	In Bonn
IPL/PL	1681-88	Johann Peter Longerich in Bonn
NK	1663-64	Unknown
NL	1693-94	Nikolaus Longerich in Deutz
NR	1672-1725	Norbert Roettiers, die-cutter in Bruxelles
PL	1609-12	Paul Lachentriess in Deutz, die-cutter in Cleves
VFH	1630	Urban Felgenhauer in Marsberg
	1631-50	In Arnsberg
(w)	Ca.1608-12	Werl mint, unknown mintmaster

REFERENCES

N = Alfred Noss, ***Die Münzen und Medaillen von Köln, v. 3, Die Münzen der Erzbischöfe von Köln, 1547-1794***. Cologne, 1926.

Sch = Wolfgang Schulten, ***Deutsche Münzen aus der Zeit Karls V.*** Frankfurt am Main, 1974.

ARCHBISHOPRIC

REGULAR COINAGE

KM# 18 HELLER (1/2 Pfennig)

Silver **Ruler:** Ferdinand **Obv:** C above arms

Date	Mintage	VG	F	VF	XF	Unc
ND(ca.1612-20)	—	7.00	15.00	30.00	60.00	—

KM# 17 HELLER (1/2 Pfennig)

Silver **Ruler:** Ferdinand **Obv:** 4-fold arms of Cologne **Note:** Uniface.

Date	Mintage	VG	F	VF	XF	Unc
ND(ca.1612-20)	—	7.00	15.00	30.00	60.00	—

KM# 65 HELLER (1/2 Pfennig)

Silver **Ruler:** Maximilian Heinrich **Obv:** Arms of Cologne (cross) **Note:** Uniface hohl-type.

Date	Mintage	VG	F	VF	XF	Unc
ND(ca.1680)	—	12.00	25.00	50.00	100	—

KM# 80 2 HELLER (Pfennig)

Silver **Ruler:** Josef Clemens **Obv:** Crowned 4-fold arms of Bavaria-Pfalz divide 2-H

Date	Mintage	VG	F	VF	XF	Unc
1698 FW	—	27.00	55.00	100	200	—

KM# 51 4 HELLER

Silver **Ruler:** Maximilian Heinrich **Obv:** Round arms of Cologne (cross) **Rev:** IIII in center, date in legend

Date	Mintage	VG	F	VF	XF	Unc
1659	—	16.00	33.00	70.00	145	—
1662	—	16.00	33.00	70.00	145	—
1663	—	16.00	33.00	70.00	145	—

KM# 60 4 HELLER

Silver **Ruler:** Maximilian Heinrich **Obv:** Arms of Bavaria **Rev:** IIII in center, date in legend

Date	Mintage	VG	F	VF	XF	Unc
1679	—	—	—	—	—	—

KM# 5 8 HELLER (4 Pfennig)

Silver **Ruler:** Ernst von Bayern **Obv:** 4-fold arms of Bavaria-Pfalz, value 8 in legend **Rev:** 4-fold arms of Cologne, 74 in legend **Note:** Varieties exist.

Date	Mintage	VG	F	VF	XF	Unc
ND(1609-12) PL	—	10.00	25.00	55.00	110	—

KM# 10 8 HELLER (4 Pfennig)

Silver **Ruler:** Ernst von Bayern **Obv:** 2 arms of Pfalz and Bavaria above VIII **Rev:** 4-fold arms of Cologne **Note:** Varieties exist.

Date	Mintage	VG	F	VF	XF	Unc
ND(ca.1610) (w)	—	10.00	25.00	50.00	110	—

KM# 11 8 HELLER (4 Pfennig)

Silver **Ruler:** Ernst von Bayern **Obv:** 4-fold arms of Bavaria-Pfalz **Rev:** VIII above arms of Werl **Rev. Legend:** WERL... **Note:** Varieties exist.

Date	Mintage	VG	F	VF	XF	Unc
ND(ca.1610) (w)	—	15.00	35.00	70.00	145	—

KM# 12 8 HELLER (4 Pfennig)

Silver **Ruler:** Ernst von Bayern **Rev:** Without value

Date	Mintage	VG	F	VF	XF	Unc
ND(ca.1610) (w)	—	15.00	30.00	60.00	120	—

KM# 13 8 HELLER (4 Pfennig)

Silver **Ruler:** Ernst von Bayern **Obv:** 4-fold arms of Cologne **Rev:** VIII above arms of Werl **Rev. Legend:** WERL...

Date	Mintage	VG	F	VF	XF	Unc
ND(ca.1610) (w)	—	15.00	35.00	70.00	145	—

KM# 19 8 HELLER (4 Pfennig)

Silver **Ruler:** Ferdinand **Obv:** 4-fold arms **Obv. Legend:** FERD.D:G... **Rev:** Crowned imperial eagle, 8 HE or HEL in legend at bottom, titles of Matthias

Date	Mintage	VG	F	VF	XF	Unc
ND(1612-19)	—	35.00	70.00	140	285	—

KM# 25 8 HELLER (4 Pfennig)

Silver **Ruler:** Ferdinand **Obv:** Arms of Bavaria, date in legend **Rev:** Arms of Cologne (cross) **Note:** Varieties exist.

Date	Mintage	VG	F	VF	XF	Unc
1630	—	10.00	20.00	40.00	80.00	—
1631	—	10.00	20.00	40.00	80.00	—
1632	—	10.00	20.00	40.00	80.00	—
1633	—	10.00	20.00	40.00	80.00	—
1634	—	10.00	20.00	40.00	80.00	—
1636	—	10.00	20.00	40.00	80.00	—
1637	—	10.00	20.00	40.00	80.00	—
1649	—	10.00	20.00	40.00	80.00	—

KM# 28 8 HELLER (4 Pfennig)

Silver **Obv:** 4-fold arms of Cologne **Rev:** 4-fold arms of Bavaria-Pfalz, date in legend

Date	Mintage	VG	F	VF	XF	Unc
1638 FE	—	10.00	20.00	40.00	80.00	—
1639	—	10.00	20.00	40.00	80.00	—
1640	—	10.00	20.00	40.00	80.00	—
1641 BS	—	10.00	20.00	40.00	80.00	—

KM# 35 8 HELLER (4 Pfennig)

Silver **Ruler:** Ferdinand **Obv:** 4-fold arms of Cologne, date above **Rev:** 4-fold arms of Bavaria-Pfalz between 2 laurel sprigs

Date	Mintage	VG	F	VF	XF	Unc
1642	—	12.00	25.00	50.00	100	—

KM# 40 8 HELLER (4 Pfennig)

Silver **Ruler:** Maximilian Heinrich **Obv:** Arms of Bavaria in small, ornamented shields, date in legend **Rev:** Arms of Cologne (cross) in small, ornamented shields

Date	Mintage	VG	F	VF	XF	Unc
1650	—	10.00	20.00	40.00	85.00	—

KM# 41 8 HELLER (4 Pfennig)

Silver **Ruler:** Maximilian Heinrich **Obv:** Arms of Bavaria in small, ornamented shields, date in legend **Rev:** Arms of Cologne (cross) in small, ornamented shields, posthumous dates in legend **Note:** Mule.

Date	Mintage	VG	F	VF	XF	Unc
1650/51	—	10.00	25.00	50.00	100	—
1650/52	—	10.00	25.00	50.00	100	—

KM# 42 8 HELLER (4 Pfennig)

Silver **Ruler:** Maximilian Heinrich **Obv:** Arms of Bavaria in small, ornamented shields **Rev:** Arms of Cologne, (cross) in small, ornamented shields, date in legend **Note:** Varieties exist.

Date	Mintage	VG	F	VF	XF	Unc
1651	—	10.00	20.00	40.00	80.00	—
1652	—	10.00	20.00	40.00	80.00	—
1653	—	10.00	20.00	40.00	80.00	—
1654	—	10.00	20.00	40.00	80.00	—
1655	—	10.00	20.00	40.00	80.00	—
1656	—	10.00	20.00	40.00	80.00	—
1657	—	10.00	20.00	40.00	80.00	—
1658	—	10.00	20.00	40.00	80.00	—
1659	—	10.00	20.00	40.00	80.00	—
1659	—	10.00	20.00	40.00	80.00	—

KM# 43 8 HELLER (4 Pfennig)

Silver **Ruler:** Maximilian Heinrich **Obv:** Large 8 in shield

Date	Mintage	VG	F	VF	XF	Unc
1654	—	10.00	20.00	40.00	80.00	—
1655	—	10.00	20.00	40.00	80.00	—

KM# 48 8 HELLER (4 Pfennig)

Silver **Ruler:** Maximilian Heinrich **Obv:** Date divided by arms of Bavaria

Date	Mintage	VG	F	VF	XF	Unc
1658	—	—	—	—	—	—

KM# 49 8 HELLER (4 Pfennig)

Silver **Ruler:** Maximilian Heinrich **Obv:** Date divided by arms of Bavaria **Rev:** Arms of Cologne (cross) in small, ornamented shields, date in legend **Note:** Mule.

Date	Mintage	VG	F	VF	XF	Unc
1658	—	—	—	—	—	—

KM# 52 8 HELLER (4 Pfennig)

Silver **Ruler:** Maximilian Heinrich **Obv:** Date divided by arms of Bavaria **Rev:** Arms of Cologne (cross) in small, ornamented shield

Date	Mintage	VG	F	VF	XF	Unc
1659	—	—	—	—	—	—

KM# 61 8 HELLER (4 Pfennig)

Silver **Ruler:** Maximilian Heinrich **Obv:** Arms of Bavaria **Rev:** VIII in center, date in legend

Date	Mintage	VG	F	VF	XF	Unc
1679	—	10.00	20.00	40.00	80.00	—
1680	—	10.00	20.00	40.00	80.00	—

KM# 66 8 HELLER (4 Pfennig)

Silver **Ruler:** Maximilian Heinrich **Obv:** Arms of Cologne **Rev:** Arms of Bavaria, date in legend **Note:** Varieties exist.

Date	Mintage	VG	F	VF	XF	Unc
1681 PL	—	10.00	20.00	40.00	80.00	—
1684 IPL	—	10.00	20.00	40.00	80.00	—
1688 IPL	—	10.00	20.00	40.00	80.00	—

KM# 83 8 HELLER (4 Pfennig)

Silver **Ruler:** Josef Clemens **Obv:** Arms of Bavaria in circle **Rev:** Arms of Cologne (cross) in circle, date at top in legend

Date	Mintage	VG	F	VF	XF	Unc
1699 FW	—	10.00	20.00	40.00	80.00	—
1700 FW	—	10.00	20.00	40.00	80.00	—

KM# 6 PFENNIG

Silver **Ruler:** Ernst von Bayern **Obv:** 4-fold arms with C above **Note:** Uniface schüssel-type.

Date	Mintage	VG	F	VF	XF	Unc
ND(ca.1609)	—	20.00	45.00	90.00	185	—

KM# 7 ALBUS (12 Heller)

Silver **Ruler:** Ernst von Bayern **Obv:** 4-fold arms of Bavaria-Pfalz **Rev:** Arms of Mainz, Trier, Cologne and Bavaria in cruciform

Date	Mintage	VG	F	VF	XF	Unc
ND(1609-12) PL	—	—	—	—	—	—

KM# 55.1 ALBUS (12 Heller)

Silver **Ruler:** Maximilian Heinrich **Obv:** Round arms of Cologne (cross) **Rev. Inscription:** IALBVS / COLS / CH

Date	Mintage	VG	F	VF	XF	Unc
ND(ca.1662/3)	—	16.00	35.00	70.00	145	—

KM# 55.2 ALBUS (12 Heller)

Silver **Ruler:** Maximilian Heinrich **Rev. Inscription:** I / ALBVS / COLSCH

Date	Mintage	VG	F	VF	XF	Unc
ND(ca.1662/3)	—	16.00	35.00	70.00	145	—

KM# 55.3 ALBUS (12 Heller)

Silver **Ruler:** Maximilian Heinrich **Rev. Inscription:** I / ALBVS / COLN / CH

Date	Mintage	VG	F	VF	XF	Unc
ND(ca.1662/3)	—	16.00	35.00	70.00	145	—

KM# 55.4 ALBUS (12 Heller)

Silver **Ruler:** Maximilian Heinrich **Obv:** Shirt cross with shaded arms **Rev. Inscription:** COLN / ISCHER / ALBVS

Date	Mintage	VG	F	VF	XF	Unc
ND(ca.1662/3)	—	16.00	35.00	70.00	145	—

KM# 44 2 ALBUS

1.6000 g., Silver, 20.1 mm. **Ruler:** Maximilian Heinrich **Obv:** Arms of Cologne, 2 AL or ALB below in legend **Rev:** Arms of Bavaria, date in legend **Note:** Varieties exist.

Date	Mintage	VG	F	VF	XF	Unc
1657	—	16.00	32.00	65.00	130	—
1658	—	16.00	32.00	65.00	130	—
1659	—	16.00	32.00	65.00	130	—
1660	—	16.00	32.00	65.00	130	—
1661	—	16.00	32.00	65.00	130	—
1662	—	16.00	32.00	65.00	130	—
1663	—	16.00	32.00	65.00	130	—
1665	—	16.00	32.00	65.00	130	—
1666	—	16.00	32.00	65.00	130	—
1667	—	16.00	32.00	65.00	130	—
1671	—	16.00	32.00	65.00	130	—
1672	—	16.00	32.00	65.00	130	—
1673	—	16.00	32.00	65.00	130	—
1681 PL	—	16.00	32.00	65.00	130	—
1682	—	16.00	32.00	65.00	130	—
1687 IPL	—	16.00	32.00	65.00	130	—
	—	16.00	32.00	65.00	130	—

KM# 45 2 ALBUS

Silver **Ruler:** Maximilian Heinrich **Rev:** Date divided by arms **Note:** Varieties exist.

Date	Mintage	VG	F	VF	XF	Unc
1657	—	16.00	32.00	65.00	130	—
1658	—	16.00	32.00	65.00	130	—
1659	—	16.00	32.00	65.00	130	—

KM# 62 2 ALBUS

Silver **Ruler:** Maximilian Heinrich **Obv:** Date divided by arms

Date	Mintage	VG	F	VF	XF	Unc
1679	—	—	—	—	—	—

KM# 27 4 ALBUS (Blaffert)

Silver **Ruler:** Ferdinand **Obv:** Crowned 4-fold arms of Bavaria-Pfalz **Rev:** Arms of Cologne, date in legend

Date	Mintage	VG	F	VF	XF	Unc
1633	—	33.00	65.00	120	440	—
1635	—	33.00	65.00	120	440	—

KM# 29 4 ALBUS (Blaffert)

Silver **Ruler:** Ferdinand **Obv:** Crowned oval 4-fold arms of Cologne with central shield of Bavaria-Pfalz **Rev:** IIII/ALBVS in square, date in legend

Date	Mintage	VG	F	VF	XF	Unc
1638 FE	—	—	—	—	—	—

KM# 36 4 ALBUS (Blaffert)

Silver **Ruler:** Ferdinand **Obv:** 4-fold arms of Cologne, date in legend **Rev:** Crowned 4-fold arms of Bavaria-Pfalz between 2 laurel sprigs

Date	Mintage	VG	F	VF	XF	Unc
1642 BS	—	27.00	55.00	115	230	—

KM# 70 4 ALBUS (Blaffert)

Silver **Ruler:** Josef Clemens **Obv:** Crowned 4-fold arms of Bavaria-Pfalz **Rev:** Date above arms of Cologne

Date	Mintage	VG	F	VF	XF	Unc
1693 FW	—	25.00	50.00	100	210	—

KM# 14 MARIENGROSCHEN

Silver **Ruler:** Ernst von Bayern **Obv:** Bust of St. Peter above 4-fold arms of Bavaria-Pfalz **Rev:** Madonna and child, date in legend

Date	Mintage	VG	F	VF	XF	Unc
1610	—	25.00	50.00	90.00	180	—
1610	—	15.00	35.00	65.00	130	—

KM# A27 MARIENGROSCHEN

1.3500 g., Silver, 20 mm. **Ruler:** Ferdinand **Obv:** City arms (Cologne cross) above "36" **Obv. Legend:** FERDIN • D • G • ARCH CO • **Rev:** Bavarian arms **Rev. Legend:** S • R • I • P • ELEC • BAV • DVX *

Date	Mintage	VG	F	VF	XF	Unc
1631 VH	—	—	—	—	—	—

KM# A29 MARIENGROSCHEN

1.3500 g., Silver, 20 mm. **Ruler:** Ferdinand **Obv:** Three-line denomination in center *I*/MARI/GRO above "36" **Rev:** Bavarian arms on the Cologne cross above VF **Rev. Legend:** S • R • I • P • ELEC • BAVA • ET • W • DVX • * •

Date	Mintage	VG	F	VF	XF	Unc
1638 VF	—	75.00	150	300	600	—

KM# A33 2 MARIENGROSCHEN

1.1200 g., Silver **Ruler:** Ferdinand **Obv:** Four-part Bavarian arms under elector's hat **Obv. Legend:** FERDI • D • G • AR • LP • COL • **Rev:** Three-line inscription with denomination in center **Rev. Legend:** VON • FEINEM • SILBE • 16*39 • **Rev. Inscription:** • II • / MAR / • GR • **Note:** Legend varieties exist.

Date	Mintage	VG	F	VF	XF	Unc
1639	—	10.00	25.00	50.00	100	—
1640	—	10.00	25.00	50.00	100	—
1641	—	10.00	25.00	50.00	100	—
1642	—	10.00	25.00	50.00	100	—
1643	—	10.00	25.00	50.00	100	—
1644	—	10.00	25.00	50.00	100	—
1645	—	10.00	25.00	50.00	100	—
1649	—	10.00	25.00	50.00	100	—
1650	—	10.00	25.00	50.00	100	—

KM# 50 MARK

Silver **Ruler:** Maximilian Heinrich **Obv:** Crowned arms of Bavaria-Pfalz quartered by cross, arms extending out of shield **Rev:** Date **Rev. Inscription:** I / MARCK / COLSCH

Date	Mintage	VG	F	VF	XF	Unc
1658	—	—	—	—	—	—
1659	—	—	—	—	—	—

KM# 8 1/24 THALER (Groschen)

Silver **Ruler:** Ernst von Bayern **Obv:** Imperial orb with 24, date divided above orb by cross, titles of Rudolf II **Rev:** 4-fold arms of Bavaria-Pfalz **Note:** Varieties exist.

Date	Mintage	VG	F	VF	XF	Unc
1609	—	40.00	85.00	150	300	—
ND(1583-1612)	—	30.00	60.00	150	300	—

KM# 15 1/24 THALER (Groschen)

Silver **Ruler:** Ernst von Bayern **Rev:** Crowned 4-fold arms of Bavaria-Pfalz

Date	Mintage	VG	F	VF	XF	Unc
1610 PL	—	13.00	27.00	50.00	100	—
1611 PL	—	13.00	27.00	50.00	100	—

KM# 16 1/24 THALER (Groschen)

Silver **Ruler:** Ernst von Bayern **Obv:** 1/2 length figure of St. Peter above arms of Cologne **Note:** Klippe.

Date	Mintage	VG	F	VF	XF	Unc
1611 Rare	—	—	—	—	—	—

KM# 71 1/6 THALER (1/4 Gulden)

Silver **Ruler:** Josef Clemens **Obv:** Bust right in circle **Rev:** Crowned 7-fold arms with central shield of 4-fold arms of Bavaria-Pfalz divide date, 1/6 in oval at bottom

Date	Mintage	VG	F	VF	XF	Unc
1693 FW	—	33.00	75.00	155	315	—

KM# 72 1/6 THALER (1/4 Gulden)

Silver **Ruler:** Josef Clemens **Obv:** Bust breaks circle at bottom

Date	Mintage	VG	F	VF	XF	Unc
1693 FW	—	33.00	75.00	155	315	—

KM# 73 1/3 THALER (1/2 Gulden)

Silver **Ruler:** Josef Clemens **Obv:** Bust right in circle **Rev:** Crowned 7-fold arms with central shield of 4-fold arms of Bavaria-Pfalz dividing date, 1/3 in oval at bottom

Date	Mintage	VG	F	VF	XF	Unc
1693 FW	—	—	—	—	—	—

KM# 85 1/3 THALER (1/2 Gulden)

Silver **Ruler:** Josef Clemens **Subject:** Consecration of the Palace Chapel in Bonn **Obv:** Crowned IEC monogram between branches **Rev:** 15-line inscription with date

Date	Mintage	VG	F	VF	XF	Unc
1700	—	500	900	1,700	3,100	—

KM# 74 2/3 THALER (Gulden)

Silver **Ruler:** Josef Clemens **Obv:** Bust right in circle broken at bottom **Rev:** Crowned 7-fold arms with central shield of 4-fold arms of Bavaria-Pfalz divide date, 2/3 in oval at bottom

Date	Mintage	VG	F	VF	XF	Unc
1693 FW	—	—	—	—	—	—

KM# 75 2/3 THALER (Gulden)

Silver **Ruler:** Josef Clemens **Note:** Varieties exist in arrangement of date.

Date	Mintage	VG	F	VF	XF	Unc
1693 NL	—	60.00	120	190	385	—
1694 NL	—	60.00	120	190	385	—

KM# 76 2/3 THALER (Gulden)

Silver **Ruler:** Josef Clemens

Date	Mintage	VG	F	VF	XF	Unc
1694 NL	—	60.00	120	210	425	—

KM# 86 2/3 THALER (Gulden)

Silver **Ruler:** Josef Clemens **Rev:** 12-fold arms

Date	Mintage	VG	F	VF	XF	Unc
1700 FW	—	—	—	—	—	—

KM# 20.1 THALER

Silver **Ruler:** Ferdinand **Obv:** Helmeted 4-fold arms with central shield of Bavaria-Pfalz **Rev:** Figure of St. Peter divides date **Note:** Dav.#5134.

Date	Mintage	VG	F	VF	XF	Unc
1616 Rare	—	—	—	—	—	—

KM# 20.2 THALER

Silver **Ruler:** Ferdinand **Rev:** Circle of laurel around St. Peter **Note:** Dav.#5136. Varieties exist.

Date	Mintage	VG	F	VF	XF	Unc
1617 Rare	—	—	—	—	—	—

KM# 26 THALER

Silver **Ruler:** Ferdinand **Obv:** 1/2 length facing figure of st. Peter **Rev:** Crowned 4-fold arms of Bavaria-Pfalz divide date **Note:** Dav.#5137.

Date	Mintage	VG	F	VF	XF	Unc
1630 Rare	—	—	—	—	—	—

KM# 30 THALER

Silver **Ruler:** Ferdinand **Obv:** Bust right **Rev:** Crowned oval 4-fold arms of Cologne with central shield of Bavaria-Pfalz, date at left of crown in legend **Note:** Dav.#5142.

Date	Mintage	VG	F	VF	XF	Unc
1638 FE Rare	—	500	1,000	1,750	2,700	—

KM# 31 THALER

Silver **Ruler:** Ferdinand **Obv:** Bust 3/4 to right **Rev:** Crown replaced by mitre **Note:** Dav.#5143.

Date	Mintage	VG	F	VF	XF	Unc
1638 FE Rare	—	—	—	—	—	—

KM# 33 THALER

Silver **Ruler:** Ferdinand **Obv:** Bust right, 2 legend inscriptions, inner broken by top of bust **Rev:** Crowned oval 4-fold arms of Bavaria-Pfalz supported by 2 lions, surrounded by circle of 17 small shields, date divided by crown **Note:** Dav.#5144.

Date	Mintage	VG	F	VF	XF	Unc
1639 FE Rare	—	—	—	—	—	—

KM# 46.1 THALER

Silver **Ruler:** Maximilian Heinrich **Obv:** Bust right in circle **Rev:** Crowned oval 4-fold arms of Cologne with central shield of Bavaria-Pfalz **Rev. Legend:** V.- BA. WE. AN. BV. DVX. MA. FR. CO. PIVM. LOS. LO. H-OR **Note:** Dav.#5146.

Date	Mintage	VG	F	VF	XF	Unc
ND(ca.1657) FL Rare	—	—	—	—	—	—

KM# 46.2 THALER

Silver **Ruler:** Maximilian Heinrich **Rev. Legend:** V.-BAV: WE: AN: BVL: DVX: LANDG: LEVCH: MAR: - FRA: **Note:** Dav.#5147.

Date	Mintage	VG	F	VF	XF	Unc
ND(ca.1657)	—	1,250	2,500	5,000	8,500	—

Note: Slight differences in arms and inscription on reverse

KM# 68 THALER
Silver **Ruler:** Sede Vacante **Obv:** St. Peter **Rev:** Nativity **Note:** Dav.#5153.

Date	Mintage	VG	F	VF	XF	Unc
1688	—	400	800	1,500	3,750	6,500

KM# 67 THALER
Silver **Ruler:** Sede Vacante **Obv:** St. Peter holding key up **Rev:** Nativity **Note:** Sede Vacante issue. Dav.#5152.

Date	Mintage	VG	F	VF	XF	Unc
1688	—	1,000	2,000	3,500	6,000	—

KM# 77 THALER
Silver **Ruler:** Josef Clemens **Subject:** Joseph Clemens **Note:** Dav.#5154.

Date	Mintage	F	VF	XF	Unc	BU
1694 NL	—	4,500	7,500	12,500	—	—

KM# 81 THALER
Silver **Ruler:** Josef Clemens **Obv:** Bust right **Rev:** Crowned II's in cruciform, date above crown at top, double C in angles, round Bavarian arms in center **Note:** Dav.#5155.

Date	Mintage	F	VF	XF	Unc	BU
1698 FW	—	7,500	12,500	—	—	—

KM# 21 2 THALER
Silver **Ruler:** Ferdinand **Obv:** Helmeted 4-fold arms with central shield of Bavaria-Pfalz **Rev:** St. Peter divides date **Note:** Dav.#5135.

Date	Mintage	F	VF	XF	Unc	BU
1617 Rare	—	—	—	—	—	—

TRADE COINAGE

KM# 32 DUCAT
3.5000 g., 0.9860 Gold 0.1109 oz. AGW **Ruler:** Ferdinand **Obv:** Radiant Madonna and child in inner circle **Rev:** Crowned arms in inner circle

Date	Mintage	VG	F	VF	XF	Unc
ND(1638)	—	475	900	2,200	4,250	—

KM# 47 DUCAT
3.5000 g., 0.9860 Gold 0.1109 oz. AGW **Ruler:** Maximilian Heinrich **Obv:** Bust right in circle **Rev:** Crowned 4-fold arms of Cologne with central shield of Bavaria-Pfalz, DVCAT at bottom in legend

Date	Mintage	VG	F	VF	XF	Unc
ND(ca.1657)	—	550	1,000	2,550	4,750	—

KM# 56 DUCAT
3.5000 g., 0.9860 Gold 0.1109 oz. AGW **Ruler:** Maximilian Heinrich **Obv:** Bust 3/4 to right, legend broken by top of head **Rev:** Crowned 4-fold arms of Cologne, central shield of Bavaria-Pfalz, date below

Date	Mintage	VG	F	VF	XF	Unc
1664	—	450	850	2,000	4,150	—

KM# 57 DUCAT
3.5000 g., 0.9860 Gold 0.1109 oz. AGW **Ruler:** Maximilian Heinrich **Obv:** Bust right breaks top of circle

Date	Mintage	VG	F	VF	XF	Unc
1665 NK	—	550	950	2,350	4,700	—

KM# 78 DUCAT
3.5000 g., 0.9860 Gold 0.1109 oz. AGW **Ruler:** Josef Clemens **Rev:** Crowned arms in inner circle

Date	Mintage	VG	F	VF	XF	Unc
1694 NL	—	750	1,450	2,850	5,500	—

KM# 82 DUCAT
3.5000 g., 0.9860 Gold 0.1109 oz. AGW **Ruler:** Josef Clemens **Obv:** Bust of Josef Clemens right **Rev:** Seated Madonna and child with crowned arms at right

Date	Mintage	VG	F	VF	XF	Unc
1698 FW	—	1,700	3,350	6,200	12,000	—
1699 FW	—	1,700	3,350	6,200	12,000	—

KM# 79 3 DUCAT
10.5000 g., 0.9860 Gold 0.3328 oz. AGW **Ruler:** Josef Clemens

Date	Mintage	VG	F	VF	XF	Unc
1696 FW	—	4,950	8,300	14,500	22,500	—
1696	—	4,950	8,300	14,500	22,500	—

KM# 69 10 DUCAT (Portugalöser)
35.0000 g., 0.9860 Gold 1.1095 oz. AGW **Ruler:** Sede Vacante **Obv:** St. Peter standing with shield **Note:** Sede Vacante Issue.

Date	Mintage	VG	F	VF	XF	Unc
1688 Rare	—	—	—	—	—	—

FREE CITY

(Köln)
CITY

One of the oldest cities in Europe, Cologne on the Rhine was founded as the Roman colony of Colonia Agrippinensis in 50 A.D. The town grew in importance after becoming the site of a bishopric and later an archbishopric. For two centuries beginning about the mid-10th century, Cologne contained an imperial mint. The archbishops had nominal control of the city until the 12th century. In 1201, Cologne joined the Hanseatic League and gained the right to govern itself in 1288. As the commercial importance of Cologne rose through membership in the League, it finally gained the mint right in 1474 and was soon striking its own coinage. The city remained in the Catholic fold after the Reformation, but its importance as a commercial center waned during the next several centuries. The French occupied Cologne in 1794 and annexed it three years later. At the end of the Napoleonic Wars in 1815, it was acquired by Prussia.

MINT OFFICIALS' INITIALS & MARKS

LETTER	DATE	NAME
	1506-11	Heinrich von Coisfeld, warden
	1511-14	Mintmaster
	1511-14	Arnt von Hamant, warden
	1515-18	Heinrich von Lynnar, mintmaster
	1515-18	Severin von Myle, warden
	1518-?	Johann von Eltmer, mintmaster
	1519-31	Kaspar Rave, warden
	1547-74	Ludwig Gronwalt, mintmaster
	1565-1608	Johann von Worringen, warden
	Ca. 1575	Meister Daniel, die-cutter?
	1567-1602	Jacob Lamberts, die-cutter
	1574-1602	Herbert Gronwalt
	Ca. 1575-79	Heinrich Attendahr, die-cutter
	1602-05	Reiner Gronwalt
	1602-08	Johann Lamberts, die-cutter
	1605-29	Johann Reess
	1608-43	Konrad Duisberg, warden
	1608-25	Peter Schlebusch, die-cutter
	1626-59	Hans Schwertzge, die-cutter
	1629-52	Hermann Cramer
	1642-?	Heinrich Mittweg, die-cutter
	1643-44	Johann Duisberg, warden
	1644-85	Friedrich Rodorff, warden
	1652-80	Kaspar Cramer
	1658-?	Georg Hartmann Plappert, die-cutter
	1659-1700	Jacob Leer, die-cutter
TB	1678-1717	Tobias Bernard, die-cutter in Paris
PN	1680-1698	Peter Newers, mintmaster
P	1685-1702	Johann Post, warden
NL	1699-1700	Nikolaus Longerich, mintmaster

ARMS
Divided horizontally, 3 crowns in upper half, lower half shaded, usually with cross-hatching, but sometimes with other devices.

REFERENCES

N = Alfred Noss, ***Die Münzen und Medaillen von Köln, v. 4, Die Münzen der Städte Köln und Neuss 1474-1794.*** Cologne, 1926

Sch = Wolfgang Schulten, ***Deutsche Münzen aus der Zeit Karls V.*** Frankfurt am Main, 1974.

REGULAR COINAGE

KM# 313 HELLER
Silver **Obv:** City arms (3 crowns above arabesques) in shield, divide date where present **Note:** Uniface hohl-type.

Date	Mintage	VG	F	VF	XF	Unc
ND(1604-11)	10,340,000	5.00	10.00	25.00	55.00	—
1611	2,396,000	5.00	10.00	25.00	55.00	—

KM# 339 HELLER
Silver **Obv:** Intertwined arabesques below crowns **Note:** Uniface.

Date	Mintage	VG	F	VF	XF	Unc
ND(1635-52)	2,761,000	6.00	12.00	30.00	60.00	—

KM# 356 HELLER
Silver **Obv:** Arms not in shield **Note:** Uniface.

Date	Mintage	VG	F	VF	XF	Unc
ND(1653-64)	705,000	5.00	10.00	25.00	55.00	—

KM# 376 HELLER
Silver **Obv:** 2 spirals below crowns, separated by 2 parallel lines **Note:** Uniface.

Date	Mintage	VG	F	VF	XF	Unc
ND(1676-77)	313,000	6.00	12.00	30.00	60.00	—

KM# 395 HELLER
Silver **Obv:** Spirals separated from crowns by single line **Note:** Uniface.

Date	Mintage	VG	F	VF	XF	Unc
ND(1692-94)	—	6.00	12.00	30.00	60.00	—

KM# 330 2 HELLER
Silver **Obv:** City arms (3 crowns above arabesques **Note:** Uniface hohl-type.

Date	Mintage	VG	F	VF	XF	Unc
ND(ca.1625)	—	—	—	—	—	—

KM# 360 4 HELLER
Silver **Obv:** City arms (3 crowns above cross-hatch pattern) **Rev:** IIII in center, HELLER.COLON, date in legend

Date	Mintage	VG	F	VF	XF	Unc
1661	—	16.00	33.00	65.00	170	—
1662	16,000	10.00	20.00	40.00	85.00	—
1663	—	10.00	20.00	40.00	85.00	—
1681	—	10.00	20.00	40.00	85.00	—

KM# 361 4 HELLER
Silver **Rev:** 4 in center

Date	Mintage	VG	F	VF	XF	Unc
1662	—	13.00	27.00	55.00	110	—

KM# 314 8 HELLER (Fettmännchen)
Silver **Obv:** VIII in circle **Obv. Legend:** NVMMVS: COLONIENSIS **Rev:** Value LXX/IIII in circles, date **Rev. Legend:** CVSVS. COLONIAE **Note:** Legend varieties exist.

Date	Mintage	VG	F	VF	XF	Unc
1604	25,000	8.00	16.00	35.00	70.00	—
1605	318,000	8.00	16.00	35.00	70.00	—
1606	250,000	8.00	16.00	35.00	70.00	—
1608	122,000	8.00	16.00	35.00	70.00	—
1609	286,000	8.00	16.00	35.00	70.00	—
1610	213,000	8.00	16.00	35.00	70.00	—
1611	49,000	8.00	16.00	35.00	70.00	—

KM# 315 8 HELLER (Fettmännchen)
Silver **Obv:** VIII in circle **Obv. Legend:** NVMMVS: COLONIENSIS **Rev:** From die of Mulheim mint **Note:** Mule.

Date	Mintage	VG	F	VF	XF	Unc
1605	Inc. above	10.00	25.00	50.00	100	—
1608	Inc. above	10.00	25.00	50.00	100	—
1609	Inc. above	10.00	25.00	50.00	100	—

KM# 317 8 HELLER (Fettmännchen)
Silver **Obv:** From die of Julich **Rev:** KM#314 **Note:** Mule.

Date	Mintage	VG	F	VF	XF	Unc
1609	Inc. above	10.00	25.00	50.00	100	—
1610	Inc. above	10.00	25.00	50.00	100	—

KM# 320 8 HELLER (Fettmännchen)
Silver **Note:** Klippe.

Date	Mintage	VG	F	VF	XF	Unc
1610	—	—	—	—	—	—

KM# 328 8 HELLER (Fettmännchen)
Silver **Rev. Legend:** LXX/VIIII

Date	Mintage	VG	F	VF	XF	Unc
ND	—	6.00	15.00	30.00	65.00	—
1624	23,000	6.00	15.00	30.00	65.00	—
1625	182,000	6.00	15.00	30.00	65.00	—
1626	177,000	6.00	15.00	30.00	65.00	—
1627	104,000	6.00	15.00	30.00	65.00	—
1628	46,000	6.00	15.00	30.00	65.00	—
1629	111,000	6.00	15.00	30.00	65.00	—
1630	40,000	6.00	15.00	30.00	65.00	—
1631	44,000	6.00	15.00	30.00	65.00	—
1633	—	6.00	15.00	30.00	65.00	—
1649	42,000	6.00	15.00	30.00	65.00	—

KM# 375 2 ALBUS

Silver, 20 mm. **Obv:** City arms (3 crowns above 2 intertwined arabesques) in ornate shield, date above 2.ALB in legend below **Rev:** Titles of Leopold I

Date	Mintage	VG	F	VF	XF	Unc
1674	—	10.00	20.00	40.00	80.00	—
1675	—	10.00	20.00	40.00	80.00	—
1676	122,000	10.00	20.00	40.00	80.00	—
1677	77,000	10.00	20.00	40.00	80.00	—
1678	177,000	10.00	20.00	40.00	80.00	—
1681 PN	—	10.00	20.00	40.00	80.00	—
1682 PN	—	10.00	20.00	40.00	80.00	—
1683 PN	—	10.00	20.00	40.00	80.00	—
1684 PN	—	10.00	20.00	40.00	80.00	—
1685 PN	31,000	10.00	20.00	40.00	80.00	—

KM# 332 4 ALBUS (Blaffert)

Silver **Obv:** Oval city arms (3 crowns above 11 flames) in baroque frame, date in legend, 4 below arms **Rev:** Crowned imperial eagle, orb on breast, titles of Ferdinand II

Date	Mintage	VG	F	VF	XF	Unc
1627	20,000	16.00	33.00	70.00	145	—

KM# 334 4 ALBUS (Blaffert)

Silver **Obv:** City arms (3 crowns above 2 intertwined arabesques) in ornate shield, date above, value in legend below

Date	Mintage	VG	F	VF	XF	Unc
1628	97,000	12.00	22.00	40.00	85.00	—
1629	55,000	12.00	22.00	40.00	85.00	—
1630	191,000	12.00	22.00	40.00	85.00	—
1631	56,000	12.00	22.00	40.00	85.00	—
1632	61,000	12.00	22.00	40.00	85.00	—
1633	79,000	12.00	22.00	40.00	85.00	—
1634	67,000	12.00	22.00	40.00	85.00	—
1635	39,000	12.00	22.00	40.00	85.00	—
1636	—	12.00	22.00	40.00	85.00	—

KM# 341 4 ALBUS (Blaffert)

Silver **Rev:** 11 flames in lower 1/2 of arms

Date	Mintage	VG	F	VF	XF	Unc
1636	—	13.00	25.00	50.00	100	—

KM# 346 4 ALBUS (Blaffert)

Silver **Obv:** 2 intertwined arabesques in lower 1/2 of arms **Rev:** Titles of Ferdinand III

Date	Mintage	VG	F	VF	XF	Unc
1638	19,000	13.00	25.00	45.00	100	—
1644	—	13.00	25.00	45.00	100	—
1645	—	13.00	25.00	45.00	100	—
1646	15,000	13.00	25.00	45.00	100	—
1647	12,000	13.00	25.00	45.00	100	—
1648/6	—	13.00	25.00	45.00	100	—
1651	6,000	13.00	25.00	45.00	100	—
1656	12,000	13.00	25.00	45.00	100	—
1657	10,000	13.00	25.00	45.00	100	—
1658	12,000	13.00	25.00	45.00	100	—

KM# 357 4 ALBUS (Blaffert)

Silver **Obv:** Titles of Leopold I

Date	Mintage	VG	F	VF	XF	Unc
1658	Inc. above	16.00	27.00	55.00	115	—
1659	28,000	16.00	27.00	55.00	115	—
1682 PN	—	16.00	27.00	55.00	115	—

KM# 335 8 ALBUS

Silver **Obv:** Crowned imperial eagle, orb on breast, titles of Ferdinand II **Rev:** Large, ornate plumed helmet, 8.ALB in legend below

Date	Mintage	VG	F	VF	XF	Unc
ND(ca.1631)	6,000	40.00	80.00	150	275	—

KM# 336 8 ALBUS

Silver **Obv:** Crowned imperial eagle, 8 in orb on breast, VIII/ALB above **Rev:** City arms (similar to KM#340) divide date, titles of Ferdinand II

Date	Mintage	VG	F	VF	XF	Unc
1633	1,404	33.00	65.00	130	260	—

KM# 340 8 ALBUS

Silver

Date	Mintage	VG	F	VF	XF	Unc
1635	12,000	27.00	45.00	90.00	185	—
1636	15,000	27.00	45.00	90.00	185	—
1637	6,000	27.00	45.00	90.00	185	—

KM# 342 8 ALBUS

Silver **Obv:** Titles of Ferdinand III **Rev:** KM#340 **Note:** Mule.

Date	Mintage	VG	F	VF	XF	Unc
1636	Inc. above	33.00	60.00	115	230	—

KM# 344 8 ALBUS

Silver **Obv:** Titles of Ferdinand III

Date	Mintage	VG	F	VF	XF	Unc
1637	Inc. above	27.00	45.00	90.00	185	—
1639	—	27.00	45.00	90.00	185	—
1641	37,000	27.00	45.00	90.00	185	—
1644	10,000	27.00	45.00	90.00	185	—

KM# 345 8 ALBUS

Silver **Obv:** Inscription in ornamented rhombus **Obv. Inscription:** 8 / ALBUS / COLS

Date	Mintage	VG	F	VF	XF	Unc
1637 Rare	Inc. above	27.00	45.00	90.00	185	—
1641 Rare	Inc. above	27.00	45.00	90.00	185	—
1644 Rare	Inc. above	27.00	45.00	90.00	185	—

KM# 370 1/16 THALER

Silver **Obv:** Similar to KM#371. **Rev:** Crowned imperial eagle, orb on breast, titles of Leopold I

Date	Mintage	VG	F	VF	XF	Unc
1670	—	30.00	55.00	110	225	—

KM# 371 1/16 THALER

1.5000 g., Silver, 21.3 mm. **Note:** Varieties exist.

Date	Mintage	VG	F	VF	XF	Unc
1670	—	27.00	45.00	90.00	185	—
1671	—	27.00	45.00	90.00	185	—

KM# 373 1/8 THALER

Silver

Date	Mintage	VG	F	VF	XF	Unc
1673	—	35.00	75.00	150	300	—
1674	—	50.00	90.00	155	300	—

KM# 374 1/8 THALER

Silver

Date	Mintage	VG	F	VF	XF	Unc
1673	—	45.00	90.00	180	360	—

KM# 386 1/4 THALER

Silver **Obv:** City arms (3 crowns above 2 intertwined arabesques), date above, all in square punched into square flan **Note:** Uniface. Klippe.

Date	Mintage	VG	F	VF	XF	Unc
1683 Rare	—	—	—	—	—	—

KM# 309 1/2 THALER

Silver **Obv:** Helmeted arms (3 crowns above arabesques), supported by lion and griffin, date in legend **Rev:** Crowned imperial eagle, orb on breast, titles of Rudolf II

Date	Mintage	VG	F	VF	XF	Unc
1602	—	1,000	2,000	4,000	—	—

KM# 326 1/2 THALER

Silver **Note:** Similar to 1 Thaler, KM#325.

Date	Mintage	VG	F	VF	XF	Unc
1621	—	—	—	—	—	—
1627	—	—	—	—	—	—

KM# 350 1/2 THALER

Silver **Subject:** Titles of Ferdinand III

Date	Mintage	VG	F	VF	XF	Unc
1641	—	—	—	—	—	—

KM# 387 1/2 THALER

Silver **Obv:** City arms (3 crowns above 2 intertwined arabesques), date above, all in square punched into square flan **Note:** Uniface. Klippe. Coin has weight of 1/2 Thaler.

Date	Mintage	VG	F	VF	XF	Unc
1683 Rare	—	—	—	—	—	—

KM# 397 1/2 THALER

Silver **Obv:** Crowned imperial eagle with orb on breast divide date, **Rev:** Helmeted arms supported by lion and griffin, BVRG 31/36 FVES below arms **Note:** Struck to Burgundian standard of fineness.

Date	Mintage	VG	F	VF	XF	Unc
1699 NL	—	—	—	—	—	—

KM# 396 2/3 THALER (Gulden)

17.1000 g., Silver, 37.6 mm. **Obv:** Supported arms in inner circle **Rev:** Crowned imperial eagle, orb on breast in inner circle **Note:** Varieties exist.

Date	Mintage	VG	F	VF	XF	Unc
1693 PN	—	75.00	150	300	625	—
1694 PN	—	75.00	150	300	625	—
1695 PN	—	75.00	150	300	625	—
1700 IAL	—	75.00	150	300	625	—

KM# 401 2/3 THALER (Gulden)

Silver **Obv:** Arms surrounded by 2 laurel branches **Rev:** Crowned imperial eagle

Date	Mintage	VG	F	VF	XF	Unc
1700 IAL	—	100	185	350	750	—

KM# 400 2/3 THALER (Gulden)

Silver **Rev:** Arms flanked by 2 small palm branches **Note:** Known overstruck on 2/3 Thaler of Anhalt (1677), East Frisia (1694), Hanau (1694) and Saxe-Lauenburg (ca.1680). Some of the under types may show traces of the Franconian Circle countermark of 1693-5.

Date	Mintage	VG	F	VF	XF	Unc
1700 IAL	—	75.00	150	300	625	—

KM# 305.2 THALER

Silver **Note:** Klippe. Dav.#5157A.

Date	Mintage	VG	F	VF	XF	Unc
1601 Rare	5,000	—	—	—	—	—
1602 Rare	—	—	—	—	—	—
1611 Rare	—	—	—	—	—	—

KM# 306.1 THALER

Silver **Obv. Legend:** ROM . IMP . SEMP . AVGVST **Note:** Dav.#5160.

Date	Mintage	VG	F	VF	XF	Unc
1602	Inc. above	300	500	850	1,500	—

KM# 305.1 THALER

Silver **Obv:** Helmeted arms supported by a lion and griffin **Obv. Legend:** MO. NO. ARGEN. CIV. COLONIE **Rev:** Crowned double eagle w/orb on breast **Rev. Legend:** RVDOLP. II. IMP. AVG. P. F. DECRETO **Note:** Varieties exist. Dav.#5157.

Date	Mintage	VG	F	VF	XF	Unc
1602	2,000	400	800	1,500	3,000	—
1611	13,000	400	800	1,500	3,000	—

KM# 306.2 THALER

Silver **Obv. Legend:** ROM. IMP. SEMP. AVGVST **Note:** Dav.#5160A. Klippe.

Date	Mintage	VG	F	VF	XF	Unc
1603 Rare	8,000	—	—	—	—	—
1609 Rare	3,000	—	—	—	—	—
1610 Rare	5,000	—	—	—	—	—
1611 Rare	—	—	—	—	—	—

KM# 306.3 THALER

Silver **Rev. Legend:** ...COLONIAE **Note:** Varieties exist.

Date	Mintage	VG	F	VF	XF	Unc
1611 Rare	—	—	—	—	—	—

KM# 322.2 THALER

Silver **Note:** Dav.#5162.

Date	Mintage	VG	F	VF	XF	Unc
1619	—	1,250	2,100	3,500	—	—

KM# 322.1 THALER

Silver **Obv. Legend:** FERDENANT. II. D.G. EL. RO. IM. SEM. AVG. **Note:** Similar to KM#322.2. Dav.#5161.

Date	Mintage	VG	F	VF	XF	Unc
1619	—	1,150	1,950	3,800	—	—

KM# 325.1 THALER

Silver **Rev:** New shield **Note:** Dav.#5163.

Date	Mintage	VG	F	VF	XF	Unc
1620	—	1,150	1,950	3,350	—	—

KM# 325.2 THALER

Silver **Note:** Dav.#5166.

Date	Mintage	VG	F	VF	XF	Unc
1621	1,040	1,800	3,150	6,100	—	—
1622	6,000	1,650	2,800	5,400	—	—
1623	6,000	1,650	2,800	5,400	—	—
1624	9,000	1,650	2,800	5,400	—	—
1626	7,000	1,650	2,800	5,400	—	—
1627	11,000	1,650	2,800	5,400	—	—

KM# 333 THALER

Silver **Note:** Klippe. Struck on flan of thaler weight from same dies.

Date	Mintage	VG	F	VF	XF	Unc
1627 Rare	Inc. above	—	—	—	—	—

KM# 325.3 THALER

Silver **Obv. Legend:** MO. NO-ARG. CIVI. COL **Rev. Legend:** ...AVGVS **Note:** Dav.#5167.

Date	Mintage	VG	F	VF	XF	Unc
1631	11,000	1,650	2,800	5,400	—	—

KM# 325.4 THALER

Silver **Rev. Legend:** ...AVG **Note:** Dav.#5168.

Date	Mintage	VG	F	VF	XF	Unc
1636/3	5,000	750	1,250	2,500	—	—
1636	Inc. above	750	1,250	2,500	—	—
1637	9,000	750	1,250	2,500	—	—

KM# 343 THALER

Silver **Obv:** KM#325.2 **Rev:** KM#355 **Note:** Mule. Dav.#5169.

Date	Mintage	VG	F	VF	XF	Unc
1636	Inc. above	750	1,250	2,500	—	—

KM# 348 THALER

Silver **Rev:** Titles of Ferdinand III and without inner circles. **Note:** Similar to KM#325.2. Dav.#5171.

Date	Mintage	VG	F	VF	XF	Unc
1638	Inc. above	875	1,450	3,000	—	—
1643	6,000	875	1,450	3,000	—	—
1644	4,000	875	1,450	3,000	—	—
1645	23,000	875	1,450	3,000	—	—

KM# 347 THALER

Silver **Obv:** KM#325.2 **Rev:** KM#348 **Note:** Mule. Dav.#5168.

Date	Mintage	VG	F	VF	XF	Unc
1638	33,000	2,400	4,200	7,800	15,000	—

KM# 355 THALER

Silver **Note:** Similar to KM#325.2, but titles of Ferdinand III. Dav.#5169.

Date	Mintage	VG	F	VF	XF	Unc
1650	3,000	—	—	—	—	—

KM# 362 THALER

Silver **Obv:** 1/2 length crowned figure right holding orb and scepter **Note:** Dav.#5172.

Date	Mintage	VG	F	VF	XF	Unc
1663 Rare	—	—	—	—	—	—

KM# 363 THALER

Silver **Obv:** The Three Kings standing behind oval city arms in baroque frame, date below **Rev:** 3 persons on ship, other figures behind on dock

Date	Mintage	VG	F	VF	XF	Unc
1668 Rare	—	—	—	—	—	—

KM# 398 THALER

Silver **Obv:** Helmeted arms supported by lion and griffin **Rev:** Crowned imperial eagle with orb on breast divide date **Note:** Dav. #5173. Varieties exist.

Date	Mintage	F	VF	XF	Unc	BU
1699 NL	—	400	750	1,300	2,200	—
1700 NL	—	400	750	1,300	2,200	—
1700 IAL	—	400	750	1,300	2,200	—

KM# 310.1 2 THALER

Silver **Obv:** Helmeted arms supported by lion and griffon, Titles of Rudolf II **Rev:** Crowned imperial eagle with orb on breast **Note:** Dav.#A5156.

Date	Mintage	F	VF	XF	Unc	BU
1602 Rare	—	—	—	—	—	—

KM# 311 2 THALER

Silver **Obv. Legend:** ROM.IMP.SEMP.AVGVST **Note:** Klippe. Dav.#5159.

Date	Mintage	F	VF	XF	Unc	BU
1610 Rare	—	—	—	—	—	—

KM# 310.2 2 THALER

Silver **Note:** Klippe.

Date	Mintage	F	VF	XF	Unc	BU
1611 Rare	—	—	—	—	—	—

KM# 327 2 THALER

Silver **Note:** Similar to 1 Thaler, KM#325.2. Dav.#5165.

Date	Mintage	F	VF	XF	Unc	BU
1621 Rare	—	—	—	—	—	—
1622 Rare	—	—	—	—	—	—

KM# 351 2 THALER

Silver **Note:** Similar to 1 Thaler, KM#325.2, but titles of Ferdinand III and without inner circles. Dav.#5170.

Date	Mintage	F	VF	XF	Unc	BU
1643 Rare	—	—	—	—	—	—
1645 Rare	—	—	—	—	—	—

KM# 353 2 THALER

Silver **Note:** Klippe. Dav.#5170A.

Date	Mintage	F	VF	XF	Unc	BU
1645 Rare	—	—	—	—	—	—

KM# 364 2 THALER

Silver **Obv:** The Three King's standing behind oval city arms in baroque frame, date below **Rev:** 3 people in ship, other figures behind on dock

Date	Mintage	F	VF	XF	Unc	BU
1668 Rare	—	—	—	—	—	—
ND Rare	—	—	—	—	—	—

KM# 307.1 3 THALER

Silver **Obv:** Helmeted arms supported by lion and griffon **Rev:** Crowned double eagle w/orb on breast **Note:** Dav.#5156.

Date	Mintage	F	VF	XF	Unc	BU
1601 Rare	—	—	—	—	—	—

KM# 307.2 3 THALER

Silver **Obv:** Helmeted arms supported by lion and griffin **Obv. Legend:** ROM. IMP. SEMP. AVGVST **Rev:** Crowned double eagle w/orb on breast **Note:** Dav#5158. Klippe.

Date	Mintage	F	VF	XF	Unc	BU
1609 Rare	—	—	—	—	—	—
1611 Rare	—	—	—	—	—	—

KM# 331 3 THALER

Silver **Note:** Klippe. Similar to 1 Thaler, KM#325.2. Dav.#5164.

Date	Mintage	F	VF	XF	Unc	BU
1626 Rare	—	—	—	—	—	—

COUNTERMARKED COINAGE

KM# 377 36 ALBUS

Silver **Countermark:** 3 crowns above 36, small P (post) below **Note:** Countermark on Sayn-Wittgenstein 16 Gute Groschen.

CM Date	Host Date	Good	VG	F	VF	XF
ND	ND(ca.1695)	450	850	1,750	3,300	—

KM# 385 36 ALBUS

Silver **Countermark:** 3 crowns above 36, small P (post) below **Note:** Countermark on Sayn-Wittgenstein 2/3 Thaler.

CM Date	Host Date	Good	VG	F	VF	XF
ND	ND(ca.1695)	450	850	1,700	3,300	—

KM# 380 42 ALBUS
Silver **Countermark:** 3 crowns above 42, small P below **Note:** Countermark on Saxe-Gotha 2/3 Thaler.

CM Date	Host Date	Good	VG	F	VF	XF
ND	ND(ca.1695)	500	950	1,850	3,600	—

KM# 378 42 ALBUS
Silver **Countermark:** 3 crowns above 42, small P below **Note:** Countermark on Sayn-Wittgenstein 2/3 Thaler.

CM Date	Host Date	Good	VG	F	VF	XF
ND	ND(ca.1695)	500	950	1,850	3,600	—

KM# 390 44 ALBUS
Silver **Countermark:** 3 crowns above 44, small P below **Note:** Countermark on Saxe-Romhild 2/3 Thaler.

CM Date	Host Date	Good	VG	F	VF	XF
ND	ND(ca.1695)	550	1,100	2,100	3,900	—

KM# 389 46 ALBUS
Silver **Countermark:** 3 crowns above 46, small P below **Note:** Countermark on Mecklenburg-Gustrow 2/3 Thaler, KM#110.

CM Date	Host Date	Good	VG	F	VF	XF
ND	ND(ca.1695)	550	1,100	2,100	3,900	—

KM# 379 50 ALBUS
Silver **Countermark:** 3 crowns above 50, small P below **Note:** Countermark on Lübeck 2/3 Thaler.

CM Date	Host Date	Good	VG	F	VF	XF
ND	ND(ca.1695)	850	1,750	3,200	6,000	—

TRADE COINAGE

KM# 312 GOLDGULDEN
3.5000 g., 0.9860 Gold 0.1109 oz. AGW **Subject:** Titles of Rudolf II **Obv:** City arms with four shields in quatrefoil **Rev:** Crowned imperial eagle, titles of Rudolf II

Date	Mintage	VG	F	VF	XF	Unc
1603	1,069	265	550	1,050	1,850	—
1604	2,605	265	550	1,050	1,850	—
1605 2 known	3,000	—	—	—	—	—
1607	735	265	550	1,050	1,850	—
1608	1,069	265	550	1,050	1,850	—
1609 2 known	3,000	—	—	—	—	—
1610	3,000	265	550	1,050	1,850	—
1611	2,000	265	550	1,050	1,850	—

KM# 316 GOLDGULDEN
6.5300 g., 0.9860 Gold 0.2070 oz. AGW **Obv:** City arms with four shields of quatrefoil **Rev:** Crowned imperial eagle **Note:** Klippe.

Date	Mintage	VG	F	VF	XF	Unc
1605 Rare	—	—	—	—	—	—

KM# 323 GOLDGULDEN
3.5000 g., 0.9860 Gold 0.1109 oz. AGW **Subject:** Titles of Ferdinand II

Date	Mintage	VG	F	VF	XF	Unc
1619	—	350	725	1,450	2,700	—
1621	401	350	725	1,450	2,700	—
1622	8,000	350	725	1,450	2,700	—

KM# 329 GOLDGULDEN
3.5000 g., 0.9860 Gold 0.1109 oz. AGW

Date	Mintage	VG	F	VF	XF	Unc
1624	1,737	425	850	1,700	3,300	—
1625	9,000	425	850	1,700	3,300	—
1628	9,000	425	850	1,700	3,300	—
1631	4,000	425	850	1,700	3,300	—
1633	4,000	425	850	1,700	3,300	—
1634	534	425	850	1,700	3,300	—

KM# 388 1/2 DUCAT
1.7500 g., 0.9860 Gold 0.0555 oz. AGW **Obv:** City arms (3 crowns above 2 intertwined arabesques), date above, all in square punched into square flan **Note:** Uniface. Klippe.

Date	Mintage	VG	F	VF	XF	Unc
1683 Rare	—	—	—	—	—	—

KM# 337 DUCAT
3.5000 g., 0.9860 Gold 0.1109 oz. AGW **Obv:** Arms in inner circle **Rev:** Value in tablet

Date	Mintage	VG	F	VF	XF	Unc
1634	—	1,900	3,800	7,800	14,000	—

KM# 338 DUCAT
3.5000 g., 0.9860 Gold 0.1109 oz. AGW **Subject:** Titles of Ferdinand II

Date	Mintage	VG	F	VF	XF	Unc
1634	—	200	325	725	1,400	—
1635	2,664	200	325	725	1,400	—
1636	12,000	200	325	725	1,400	—

KM# 352 DUCAT
3.5000 g., 0.9860 Gold 0.1109 oz. AGW **Subject:** Titles of Ferdinand III

Date	Mintage	VG	F	VF	XF	Unc
1643	2,806	165	275	600	1,300	—
1644	13,000	165	275	600	1,300	—
Note: Orb in right hand						
1650	5,155	165	275	600	1,300	—
1652	802	—	—	—	—	—
1653	802	—	—	—	—	—
1654	1,670	—	—	—	—	—
1655	4,609	165	275	600	1,300	—
1657	1,202	165	275	600	1,300	—

KM# 358 DUCAT
3.5000 g., 0.9860 Gold 0.1109 oz. AGW **Subject:** Titles of Leopold

Date	Mintage	VG	F	VF	XF	Unc
1659/7	400	1,100	1,950	2,750	4,300	—
1661	—	220	450	825	1,650	—
1662	802	325	650	1,100	2,350	—
1664	2,338	220	450	825	1,650	—
1668	2,271	220	450	825	1,650	—
1672	—	220	450	825	1,650	—

KM# 372 DUCAT
3.5000 g., 0.9860 Gold 0.1109 oz. AGW **Obv:** Laureate bust of Leopold right **Rev:** Similar to KM#352

Date	Mintage	VG	F	VF	XF	Unc
1671	—	300	600	1,300	2,500	—

KM# 365 DUCAT
3.5000 g., 0.9860 Gold 0.1109 oz. AGW **Subject:** Titles of Leopold

Date	Mintage	VG	F	VF	XF	Unc
1681	—	325	650	1,500	2,750	—
1689 PN	—	325	650	1,500	2,750	—
1693 PN	—	325	650	1,500	2,750	—

KM# 321 4 DUCAT
14.0000 g., 0.9860 Gold 0.4438 oz. AGW **Obv:** The Three Wise Men **Rev:** St. Ursula in medieval ship

Date	Mintage	VG	F	VF	XF	Unc
1612 Rare	—	—	—	—	—	—

KM# 308 6 DUCAT
21.0000 g., 0.9860 Gold 0.6657 oz. AGW **Obv:** The Three Wise Men **Rev:** St. Ursula in medieval ship

Date	Mintage	VG	F	VF	XF	Unc
ND(ca.1601) Rare	—	—	—	—	—	—

KM# A309 7 DUCAT
24.5000 g., 0.9860 Gold 0.7766 oz. AGW **Obv:** The Three Wise Men **Rev:** St. Ursula in medieval ship

Date	Mintage	VG	F	VF	XF	Unc
ND(ca.1601) Rare	—	—	—	—	—	—

PATTERNS

Including off metal strikes

KM#	Date	Mintage	Identification	Mkt Val
Pn1	1698 FW	—	Ducat. Silver. KM#82.	—
Pn2	1699 FW	—	8 Heller. Gold. KM#83.	—
Pn3	1700	—	1/3 Thaler. Copper. KM#85.	—
Pn10	ND(1604-11)	—	Heller. Gold. KM#313.	825
Pn11	1610	—	8 Heller. Gold. KM#314.	—
Pn12	1610	—	8 Heller. Gold. KM#317.	—
PnA13	1624	—	8 Heller. Gold. KM#328.	—
Pn13	ND(ca.1625)	—	2 Heller. Gold. KM#330.	—
Pn14	1627	—	8 Heller. Gold. KM#328.	—
Pn15	ND(1635-52)	—	Heller. Gold. KM#339.	—
Pn16	1641	—	8 Albus. Gold. KM#345.	—
Pn17	ND(1653-64)	—	Heller. Gold. KM#356.	—
Pn18	1663	—	4 Heller. Gold. KM#360.	—
Pn19	ND(1676-77)	—	Heller. Gold. KM#376.	—
Pn20	ND(1692-94)	—	Heller. Gold. KM#395.	—
Pn4	1701 FW	—	8 Heller. Gold. KM#83.	—
Pn21	ND(1716)	—	Heller. Gold. KM#410.	700
Pn22	1768	—	4 Heller. Silver. KM#440.	150
Pn23	1789	—	4 Heller. Silver. KM#440.	150
Pn24	ND(1792)	—	Heller. Gold. KM#445.	750
Pn25	1793	—	8 Heller. Silver. KM#446.	—

CONSTANCE

(Konstanz, Kostnitz, Costnitz)

This bishopric, which is centered on the city of the same name, was transferred to that location from Vindinissa in Aargau late in the 6th century. The first episcopal coinage was produced at the end of the 9th century and minting continued intermittently during the next 850 years. By the time of the Protestant Reformation, the bishop had become a Prince of the Empire and ruled over a large expanse of territory encompassing much of what is now southwest Germany and northern Switzerland. In 1527, Bishop Hugo refused to submit to the Reformation and was forced to flee the city. He went to Meersburg, across the lake on the north shore, and it became the bishop's residence until the diocese was secularized in 1802. It was acquired by Baden along with the city at that time.

RULERS

Hugo von Hohenlandenberg, 1st reign, 1496-1529
Balthasar Merklin (Merkler), 1529-1531
Hugo, 2nd reign, 1531-1532
Johann II, Graf von Lupfen, 1532-1537
Johann III von Welza (Weza), 1537-1548
Christoph Metzler von Andelberg, 1548-1561
Marcus Sittich, Graf von Hohenembs, 1561-1589
Andreas, Grossherzog von Österreich, 1589-1600
Johann Georg von Hallwyl, 1601-1604
Jacob, Graf von Fugger-Weissenhorn, 1604-1626
Sixtus Werner von Prassberg, 1626-1627
Johann IV, Truchsess von Waldburg, 1628-1644
Johann Franz I von Prassberg, 1644-1689
Markwart Rudolf von Rodt, 1689-1704

ARMS

Plain cross

MINT MARKS

G = Günzburg Mint

REFERENCES

SCH = Wolfgang Schulten, ***Deutsche Münzen aus der Zeit Karls V.*** Frankfurt am Main, 1974

S = Hugo Frhr. von Saurma-Jeltsch, **Die Saurmasche Münzsammlung deutscher, schweizerischer und polnischer Gepräge von etwa dem Beginn der Groschenzeit bis zur Kipperperiode**, Berlin, 1892.

BISHOPRIC

REGULAR COINAGE

KM# 5 4 HELLER
Copper **Ruler:** Johann Georg **Obv:** Oval arms (cross) in baroque, G. 4. E. above (Georgius Episcopus), all in laurel wreath **Note:** Uniface.

Date	Mintage	VG	F	VF	XF	Unc
ND(1601-1604)	—	16.00	33.00	60.00	125	—

KM# 6 4 HELLER
Copper **Note:** Only 4 above arms.

Date	Mintage	VG	F	VF	XF	Unc
ND(1604-1626)	—	16.00	33.00	60.00	125	—

FREE CITY

Located at the western end of the Bodensee (Lake Constance) and on the German-Swiss border, Constance stands on the site of the late Roman fortress of Constantia. When the bishopric in Aargau was transferred to the place shortly before 600, the town began to grow in importance. An Imperial mint was established in Constance at the beginning of the 11th century and it functioned until about 1250. Constance became an imperial free city in either 1192 or 1255, but the bishop controlled most of its affairs at least until the Protestant Reformation. The city joined the League of Schmalkalden in 1530, but was the lone Protestant holdout in the region after 1547. Karl V took Constance in 1548 and incorporated it into his Austrian realm. The city retained its coinage rights, however, and continued minting until about 1733. Constance became part of Baden in 1803.

MINT OFFICIALS' INITIALS

Initial	Date	Name
	1620	Martin Stoff
	1621-22	Martin Näf and Johann Rudolf Wegerich
	1642	Marx Stütz, warden
	1652-56	Franz Änzinger
	1652-56	Jakob Weingartner, warden
	1676-80	Franz Staiffel
	1676-86	Hans Konrad Betzerin, warden

ARMS

Cross, horizontal bar usually shaded, often a single-headed eagle above

REFERENCE

N = Elisabeth Nau, ***Die Münzen und Medaillen des oberschwäbischen Städte.*** Freiburg im Breisgau, 1964

REGULAR COINAGE

KM# 163 PFENNIG

Billon **Obv:** City arms, 6-pointed star above **Note:** Uniface.

Date	Mintage	VG	F	VF	XF	Unc
ND(1653-55)	—	10.00	20.00	40.00	80.00	—

KM# 175 PFENNIG

Copper **Obv:** City arms, C above **Note:** Uniface.

Date	Mintage	VG	F	VF	XF	Unc
ND(1671-1674)	—	10.00	20.00	40.00	80.00	—

KM# 176 PFENNIG

Copper **Obv:** City arms, date above. **Note:** Varieties exist.

Date	Mintage	VG	F	VF	XF	Unc
1675	—	8.00	16.00	32.00	65.00	—
1676	—	8.00	16.00	32.00	65.00	—
1677	—	8.00	16.00	32.00	65.00	—
1678	—	8.00	16.00	32.00	65.00	—
1679	—	8.00	16.00	32.00	65.00	—
1680	—	8.00	16.00	32.00	65.00	—
1681	—	8.00	16.00	32.00	6.00	—
1684	—	8.00	16.00	32.00	65.00	—
1686	—	8.00	16.00	32.00	65.00	—
1687	—	8.00	16.00	32.00	65.00	—
1688	—	8.00	16.00	32.00	65.00	—
1689	—	8.00	16.00	32.00	65.00	—
1690	—	8.00	16.00	32.00	65.00	—
1691	—	8.00	16.00	32.00	65.00	—

Note: Varieties exist.

KM# 190 PFENNIG

Billon **Obv:** City arms in cartouche, date divided by C above **Note:** Uniface.

Date	Mintage	VG	F	VF	XF	Unc
1700	—	25.00	55.00	110	225	—

KM# 110 2 PFENNIG (Zweier)

Silver **Obv:** City arms in quatrefoil, C above **Note:** Uniface.

Date	Mintage	VG	F	VF	XF	Unc
ND(1622)	—	35.00	75.00	150	—	—

KM# 111 4 PFENNIG (Kreuzer)

Silver **Obv:** Oval city arms, 4 above, all in wreath **Note:** Uniface.

Date	Mintage	VG	F	VF	XF	Unc
ND(ca.1622)	—	45.00	90.00	180	—	—

KM# 134 6 PFENNIG (Sechser)

Silver **Obv:** City arms in quatrefoil **Rev:** Eagle with oval shield on breast divides date and value V-I

Date	Mintage	VG	F	VF	XF	Unc
(16)26	—	60.00	120	240	475	—

KM# 137 6 PFENNIG (Sechser)

Silver **Rev:** Value VI below eagle

Date	Mintage	VG	F	VF	XF	Unc
(16)27	—	60.00	120	240	475	—

KM# 166 KREUZER

Billon **Obv:** City arms with double-cross behind **Rev:** Eagle with arms on breast **Note:** Varieties exist.

Date	Mintage	VG	F	VF	XF	Unc
ND(1657-1705)	—	15.00	30.00	65.00	130	—

KM# 165 KREUZER

Silver **Obv:** City arms with double-cross (*), value 1 below **Rev:** Crowned imperial eagle, titles of Leopold I

Date	Mintage	VG	F	VF	XF	Unc
ND	—	12.00	25.00	55.00	115	—

KM# 130 1/2 BATZEN (2 Kreuzer)

Silver **Obv:** City arms divide date **Rev:** Imperial eagle, 2 in orb on breast, titles of Ferdinand II

Date	Mintage	VG	F	VF	XF	Unc
(16)24	—	30.00	60.00	120	240	—
(16)25	—	30.00	60.00	120	240	—

KM# 131 1/2 BATZEN (2 Kreuzer)

Silver **Obv:** City arms divide date **Rev:** Imperial eagle, 2 in orb on breast, titles of Ferdinand II **Note:** Klippe.

Date	Mintage	VG	F	VF	XF	Unc
(16)24	—	—	—	—	—	—
(16)25	—	—	—	—	—	—

KM# 133 1/2 BATZEN (2 Kreuzer)

Silver **Rev:** Crowned imperial eagle **Note:** Klippe.

Date	Mintage	VG	F	VF	XF	Unc
(16)25	—	—	—	—	—	—

KM# 132 1/2 BATZEN (2 Kreuzer)

Silver **Rev:** Crowned imperial eagle

Date	Mintage	VG	F	VF	XF	Unc
(16)25	—	27.00	55.00	115	230	—
(16)26	—	27.00	55.00	115	230	—

KM# 160 1/2 BATZEN (2 Kreuzer)

Silver **Obv:** Date above arms **Rev:** Value 2 below eagle, titles of Ferdinand III

Date	Mintage	VG	F	VF	XF	Unc
1652	—	25.00	45.00	115	230	—
1653	—	25.00	45.00	115	230	—

KM# 164 1/2 BATZEN (2 Kreuzer)

Silver **Obv:** Date divided by arms

Date	Mintage	VG	F	VF	XF	Unc
1654	—	30.00	60.00	120	240	—

KM# 150 3 KREUZER (Groschen)

Silver **Obv:** Titles of Ferdinand III **Rev:** City arms in ornate shield

Date	Mintage	VG	F	VF	XF	Unc
ND	—	33.00	65.00	120	240	—

KM# 118 3 KREUZER (Groschen)

Silver **Obv:** Crowned imperial eagle, shield on breast, value 3 below, titles of Ferdinand II **Rev:** City arms in quatrefoil **Note:** Varieties exist.

Date	Mintage	VG	F	VF	XF	Unc
ND	—	27.00	55.00	100	210	—

KM# 154 3 KREUZER (Groschen)

Silver **Obv:** Crowned shield divides 1-6 above 2 shields, with 39 below **Rev:** 3 in orb on breast

Date	Mintage	VG	F	VF	XF	Unc
1639	—	25.00	50.00	100	210	—

KM# 180 3 KREUZER (Groschen)

Silver **Obv:** Titles of Leopold I

Date	Mintage	VG	F	VF	XF	Unc
1680	—	25.00	45.00	95.00	195	—

KM# 185 3 KREUZER (Groschen)

Silver **Obv:** City arms in ornate shield, date in legend **Rev:** Titles of Leopold I

Date	Mintage	VG	F	VF	XF	Unc
1694	—	20.00	40.00	75.00	155	—

KM# 151 10 KREUZER

Silver **Obv:** Titles of Ferdinand III **Rev:** Ornate city arms

Date	Mintage	VG	F	VF	XF	Unc
ND	—	45.00	95.00	180	360	—

KM# 119 10 KREUZER

Silver **Obv:** City arms in quatrefoil, date in legend **Rev:** Crowned imperial eagle, value 10 below, titles of Ferdinand II **Note:** Varieties exist.

Date	Mintage	VG	F	VF	XF	Unc
(16)23	—	27.00	55.00	110	225	—
ND	—	22.00	45.00	90.00	180	—

KM# 115 3 BATZEN (Dreibätzener)

Silver **Obv:** City arms, date in legend **Rev:** Imperial eagle, value 3 below, titles of Ferdinand II

Date	Mintage	VG	F	VF	XF	Unc
1622	—	45.00	90.00	180	360	—
ND	—	45.00	90.00	180	360	—

KM# 116 3 BATZEN (Dreibätzener)

Silver **Obv:** Arms divide date

Date	Mintage	VG	F	VF	XF	Unc
1622	—	110	225	450	900	—
1623	—	110	225	450	900	—
1624	—	110	225	450	900	—

KM# 120 3 BATZEN (Dreibätzener)
Silver **Obv:** City arms, date in legend **Rev:** Imperial eagle, value 3 below, titles of Ferdinand II **Note:** Klippe.

Date	Mintage	VG	F	VF	XF	Unc
1623	—	—	—	1,750	3,250	—
1624	—	—	—	1,750	3,250	—

KM# 135 3 BATZEN (12 Kreuzer)
Silver **Rev:** Crowned imperial eagle, value XII below

Date	Mintage	VG	F	VF	XF	Unc
1626	—	40.00	80.00	160	325	—
ND(1626)	—	40.00	80.00	160	325	—

KM# 138 3 BATZEN (12 Kreuzer)
Silver **Obv:** Date above arms **Rev:** Without indication of value

Date	Mintage	VG	F	VF	XF	Unc
1628	—	—	—	—	—	—

KM# 139 3 BATZEN (12 Kreuzer)
Silver **Obv:** City arms in quatrefoil **Rev:** Crowned imperial eagle, value below

Date	Mintage	VG	F	VF	XF	Unc
ND	—	45.00	90.00	180	360	—

KM# 140 3 BATZEN (12 Kreuzer)
Silver **Rev:** 3 arms (1 above 2) between branches

Date	Mintage	VG	F	VF	XF	Unc
ND	—	45.00	90.00	180	360	—

KM# 141 3 BATZEN (12 Kreuzer)
Silver **Obv:** Without branches

Date	Mintage	VG	F	VF	XF	Unc
ND	—	45.00	90.00	180	360	—

KM# 112 15 KREUZER
Silver **Obv:** Saints Pelagius and Conrad behind city arms **Rev:** Crowned imperial eagle, 15 on breast, titles of Ferdinand II

Date	Mintage	VG	F	VF	XF	Unc
ND(1622)	—	150	275	450	850	1,600

KM# 113 15 KREUZER
7.4300 g., Silver **Note:** Klippe.

Date	Mintage	VG	F	VF	XF	Unc
ND	—	—	400	800	1,550	—

KM# 114 15 KREUZER
5.3600 g., Silver **Note:** Octagonal Klippe.

Date	Mintage	VG	F	VF	XF	Unc
ND(1622)	—	—	425	800	1,550	—

KM# 152 15 KREUZER
Silver **Obv:** Oval arms with date below

Date	Mintage	VG	F	VF	XF	Unc
1636	—	45.00	100	190	385	—

KM# 153 15 KREUZER
Silver **Obv:** Titles of Ferdinand III

Date	Mintage	VG	F	VF	XF	Unc
ND	—	—	—	—	—	—

KM# 177 15 KREUZER
Silver **Obv:** Titles of Leopold I

Date	Mintage	VG	F	VF	XF	Unc
1679	—	55.00	115	225	450	—

KM# 136 6 BATZEN (24 Kreuzer)
Silver **Obv:** City arms in quatrefoil **Rev:** Crowned imperial eagle, date below, titles of Ferdinand II

Date	Mintage	VG	F	VF	XF	Unc
1626	—	55.00	115	210	360	—
1627	—	55.00	115	210	360	—
1630	—	55.00	115	210	360	—
1633/0	—	55.00	115	210	360	—
1633	—	55.00	115	210	360	—

KM# 181.1 6 BATZEN (24 Kreuzer)
Silver **Obv:** Large city shield in quadralobe **Obv. Legend:** *MO: NO: CIVI: CONSTANTIEN **Rev:** Crowned imperial eagle, date in exergue **Rev. Legend:** LEOPOLDVS • D • G • R • I • S • A • G • H • B • R

Date	Mintage	VG	F	VF	XF	Unc
1681	—	165	325	600	1,100	2,100

KM# 181.2 6 BATZEN (24 Kreuzer)
Silver **Obv:** Small city shield in more ornate quadralobe **Obv. Legend:** *MONETA: NOVA: CIVITATIS: CONSTANTIENSIS **Rev:** Crowned imperial eagle, date in exergue **Rev. Legend:** LEOPOLDVS . D . G . I . S . A . G . H . ET . B . REX

Date	Mintage	VG	F	VF	XF	Unc
1681	—	200	400	700	1,300	2,400

KM# 121 1/2 THALER
Silver **Obv:** Saints Pelagius and Conrad standing behind city arms **Rev:** Crowned imperial eagle, titles of Ferdinand II

Date	Mintage	VG	F	VF	XF	Unc
ND(1622)	—	600	1,100	2,100	4,000	—

KM# 122 1/2 THALER
Silver **Obv:** St. Pelagius and Conrad standing behind city arms **Rev:** Crowned imperial eagle, titles of Ferdinand II **Note:** Klippe.

Date	Mintage	VG	F	VF	XF	Unc
ND(1622)	—	—	—	—	—	—

KM# 123 1/2 THALER
Silver **Obv:** City arms divide date

Date	Mintage	VG	F	VF	XF	Unc
16Z3	—	275	500	800	1,550	—

KM# 105 THALER
Silver **Obv:** Saints Pelagius and Conrad standing behind city arms **Rev:** Crowned imperial eagle, titles of Ferdinand II **Note:** Struck on thick flan. Dav. #5174.

Date	Mintage	F	VF	XF	Unc	BU
ND(1619-1637) Rare	—	—	—	—	—	—

Note: CNG Triton V, 1-02, gVF realized $29,000

KM# 124 THALER
Silver **Note:** Regiments Thaler. Similar to 2 Thaler, KM#128. Dav. #5176.

Date	Mintage	F	VF	XF	Unc	BU
1623	—	900	1,800	3,200	—	—

KM# 125.1 THALER
Silver **Obv:** Large city shield divides date **Obv. Legend:** MON: NO: CIVITAT: CONSTANTIENSIS **Rev:** Titles of Ferdinand II **Rev. Legend:** FERD: II: D: G: ROM: IMP: ... **Note:** Dav. #5177.

Date	Mintage	F	VF	XF	Unc	BU
16Z3	—	165	300	650	1,250	—
16Z4	—	165	300	650	1,250	—
16Z5	—	165	300	650	1,250	—
16Z6	—	165	300	650	1,250	—

KM# 126 THALER
28.8600 g., Silver **Obv:** City arms divide date **Rev:** Crowned imperial eagle **Note:** Klippe.

Date	Mintage	F	VF	XF	Unc	BU
16Z3	—	2,500	4,500	8,000	—	—

KM# 125.2 THALER
Silver **Obv:** Sprays around shield **Note:** Dav. #5178. Varieties exist.

Date	Mintage	F	VF	XF	Unc	BU
16Z8	—	350	650	1,250	—	—

KM# 142 THALER
Silver **Obv:** City view, CONSTANTIA in exergue **Rev:** Five shields in center surrounded by 22 shields **Note:** Regiments Thaler. Dav. #5179.

Date	Mintage	F	VF	XF	Unc	BU
1629	—	950	1,750	3,500	6,500	8,750

KM# 127 1-1/2 THALER
Silver **Note:** Dav. #5175B. Regiments 1-1/2 Thaler. Klippe.

Date	Mintage	F	VF	XF	Unc	BU
16Z3	—	2,500	4,500	7,500	—	—

KM# A130 2 THALER
56.2900 g., Silver **Obv:** Large city shield divides date **Obv. Legend:** MON: NO: CIVITAT: CONSTANTIENSIS **Rev:** Titles of Ferdinand II **Rev. Legend:** FERD: II: D: G: ROM: IMP: ... **Note:** Dav. #A5177.

Date	Mintage	F	VF	XF	Unc	BU
16Z3	—	6,000	10,500	18,500	—	—

KM# 128 2 THALER
Silver **Note:** Regiments 2 Thaler. Dav. #5171A.

Date	Mintage	F	VF	XF	Unc	BU
16Z3	—	3,500	6,500	10,000	—	—

KM# A126 2 THALER
Silver **Obv:** Large city shield divides date **Obv. Legend:** MON: NO: CIVITAT: CONSTANTIENSIS **Rev:** Crowned imperial eagle **Rev. Legend:** FERD: II: D: G: ROM: IMP: ... **Note:** Dav. #A5177.

Date	Mintage	VG	F	VF	XF	Unc
16Z3 Rare	—	—	—	—	—	—

Note: H.D. Rauch Auction 76, 10-05, VF realized approximately $55,515, WAG Auction 26, 9-04, VF+ realized approximately $16,000

KM# 129 2-1/2 THALER
Silver **Note:** Regiments 2-1/2 Thaler. Klippe. Similar to 2 Thaler, KM#128. Dav. #5175.

Date	Mintage	F	VF	XF	Unc	BU
16Z3 Rare	—	—	—	—	—	—

TRADE COINAGE

KM# 143 GOLDGULDEN
3.5000 g., 0.9860 Gold 0.1109 oz. AGW **Obv:** Arms of Constance **Rev:** Eagle, titles of Ferdinand II, date **Note:** Fr.#843.

Date	Mintage	VG	F	VF	XF	Unc
1629	—	1,150	2,250	5,500	9,500	—

KM# 161 DUCAT
3.5000 g., 0.9860 Gold 0.1109 oz. AGW **Obv:** Oval city arms, date above **Obv. Legend:** DVCATVS • NOVVS • CIVI • CONSTANTENS **Rev:** Crowned imperial eagle, titles of Ferdinand III **Rev. Legend:** FERDINAND: III • D • G • ROM • IMP • S • AVG • **Note:** Fr. #844.

Date	Mintage	VG	F	VF	XF	Unc
1652	—	875	1,750	4,000	7,800	—
1654	—	875	1,750	4,000	7,800	—
ND	—	875	1,750	4,000	7,800	—

KM# 162 DUCAT
3.5000 g., 0.9860 Gold 0.1109 oz. AGW **Ruler:** Johann Franz I **Obv:** Oval city arms, date above **Rev:** Crowned imperial eagle, titles of Ferdinand III **Note:** Klippe.

Date	Mintage	VG	F	VF	XF	Unc
ND	—	—	—	—	—	—

KM# 117 2 DUCAT
7.0000 g., 0.9860 Gold 0.2219 oz. AGW **Obv:** Arms of Constance, date in legend **Rev:** Crowned imperial eagle, titles of Ferdinand II

Date	Mintage	VG	F	VF	XF	Unc
1622 Rare	—	—	—	—	—	—

KM# 155 2 DUCAT
7.0000 g., 0.9860 Gold 0.2219 oz. AGW **Subject:** Titles of Ferdinand III **Note:** Klippe. Fr.#842. (ND1600's).

Date	Mintage	VG	F	VF	XF	Unc
ND(1601) Rare	—	—	—	—	—	—

CORVEY

(Corvei-Corbie-Corbey-Curbei)

Located on the Weser River just east of Höxter in Westphalia, the Benedictine abbey of Corvey was founded in 820 at the instigation of Emperor Ludwig the Pious (814-40) by monks from the monastery of Corbei in Picardy. Not long after it was established, the new abbey received the mint right as stated in the surviving document dated 1 June 833. Over the next several decades, Corvey also received the right to mint coins in several nearby towns including Marsberg and Meppen. Except for a long period between about 1370 and 1500, Corvey produced a long series of coinage. In 1793, the abbey was transformed into a bishopric, but did not long remain an independent entity. Corvey was secularized in 1803 and its territory was acquired by Nassau-Dietz the same year. After having been incorporated into the Kingdom of Westphalia (1807-13) during the Napoleonic Wars, Corvey was absorbed by Prussia in 1813. Corvey struck some joint issues with Höxter and these are included here.

RULERS

Dietrich IV von Beringhausen, 1585-1616
Heinrich V von Aschenbrok, 1616-1624
Johann Christoph von Brambach, 1624-1638
Arnold IV von Waldois, 1638-1661
Christof Bernhard von Galen, 1661-1678
Christof von Bellinghausen, 1678-1696
Florenz von der Velde, 1696-1714

MINT OFFICIALS' INITIALS

HÖXTER MINT

Initials	Date	Name
(b)= HL	1605, 1606-07, 1615-16	Hans Lachentries (Laschentweiss), mintmaster
(c)= HK or or	1612-15	Hans Kayser, mintmaster
	1612-15	Ernst Schrader, warden
	1615-16	Henningh Brauns, warden
(d)=	1619-20, 1631-32	Jakob Pfahler, mintmaster
	1619-24	Jobst Brauns, warden
(e)= or	1620-24, 1638-43	Wolff Albrecht Knorre, mintmaster
(f)=	1646-48	Georg Kruckenberg, mintmaster

(g) = ↘ or ↗	1648-55	Johann Otto, mintmaster
HC	ca.1649	Unknown
	1654-55	Christian Wilckens, warden
VF (usually in ligature or VFH	1655-61	Urban Felgenhauer, mintmaster
	1655-60	Daniel Klögel, warden
GB	1682-85, 1686-89	Gottfried Binnenboss(e) , mintmaster
GIH	1685-86	Georg Jakob Halter, mintmaster
(h)= ✿	1685-89	Johann Odendahl, warden,
	1689-90	and mintmaster
or IO or JO		

Various Mints

Initials	Date	Name
	1606-09	Jakob Pfaler, mintmaster in Marsberg
IO	1694	Johann Odendahl, mintmaster in Münster

ARMS
2-fold divided horizontally, lower half usually shaded by various devices.

REFERENCES
I/S = Peter Ilisch and Arnold Schwede, **Das Münzwesen im Stift Corvey, 1541-1794**, Paderborn, 2007.
W = Joseph Weingärtner, **Die Gold= und Silber=Münzen der Abtei Corvey**, Münster, 1883.

BENEDICTINE ABBEY

REGULAR COINAGE

KM# 24 PFENNIG

Copper, 14.5-16 mm. **Ruler:** Johann Christoph **Obv:** Mitre divides date a 1 - 6 / Z - 1 **Rev:** 3-line inscription **Rev. Inscription:** +I+ / PFEN / NING **Mint:** Höxter **Note:** Ref. I/S-164. Kipper issue.

Date	Mintage	Good	VG	F	VF	XF
16Z1	—	—	900	1,500	2,500	3,750

KM# 33.1 PFENNIG

Copper, 15 mm. **Ruler:** Johann Christoph **Obv:** Arms of Brambach (comb and diagonal bar) **Obv. Legend:** IO. CH. ABB. COR(B). **Rev:** Value I in center, date at top **Rev. Legend:** S. VITVS. **Mint:** Höxter **Note:** Ref. I/S-189; W-719.

Date	Mintage	VG	F	VF	XF	Unc
1638	—	40.00	75.00	150	300	—

KM# 33.2 PFENNIG

Copper, 15 mm. **Ruler:** Johann Christoph **Obv:** Arms of Brambach (comb and diagonal bar) in shield with concave sides **Obv. Legend:** IO. CH. ABB. CORD **Rev:** Value *I* i shield with concave sides, date at end of legend **Rev. Legend:** S. VITVS. AO. **Mint:** Höxter **Note:** Ref. I/S-190.

Date	Mintage	VG	F	VF	XF	Unc
1638	—	40.00	75.00	150	300	—

KM# 40.1 PFENNIG

Copper, 14-16 mm. **Ruler:** Arnold IV **Obv:** Arms of Waldois (ox-head) **Obv. Legend:** ARNOL(D). (D.G.) A(B). COR(B)(E)(I)(N). **Rev:** Value I in circle, date divided above **Rev. Legend:** S(ANCTUS). VIT(V)(U)S **Mint:** Höxter **Note:** Ref. I/S-192, 196, 200, 201; W#725-27. Varieties exist.

Date	Mintage	VG	F	VF	XF	Unc
1641	—	40.00	80.00	150	300	—
1642	—	40.00	80.00	150	300	—
1644	—	40.00	80.00	150	300	—
1646	—	40.00	80.00	150	300	—
(16)46	—	40.00	80.00	150	300	—

KM# 40.2 PFENNIG

Copper, 13.5 mm. **Ruler:** Arnold IV **Obv:** Arms of Waldois (ox-head) in shield with concave sides **Obv. Legend:** ARNOLD. ABB. CORB. **Rev:** Value I between 2 cloverleaves in circle, date divided above **Rev. Legend:** S. VITVS. **Mint:** Höxter **Note:** Ref. I/S-193.

Date	Mintage	VG	F	VF	XF	Unc
1641	—	40.00	80.00	150	300	—

KM# 37 PFENNIG

Silver Weight varies: 0.6-0.35g., 10-14 mm. **Ruler:** Arnold IV **Obv:** "C," with mitre above, divides date **Mint:** Höxter **Note:** Ref. I/S-197, 203, 207, 210, 212, 217, 221, 226, 232, 237, 241-244; W-62, 63. Uniface schüssel-type. Varieties exist.

Date	Mintage	VG	F	VF	XF	Unc
(16)45	—	25.00	50.00	110	200	—
(16)48	—	25.00	50.00	110	200	—
(16)49	—	25.00	50.00	110	200	—
(16)50	—	25.00	50.00	110	200	—
(16)51	—	25.00	50.00	110	200	—
(16)5Z	—	25.00	50.00	110	200	—
(16)53	—	25.00	50.00	110	200	—
(16)54	—	25.00	50.00	110	200	—
(16)55	—	25.00	50.00	110	200	—
(16)56	—	25.00	50.00	110	200	—
(16)57	—	25.00	50.00	110	200	—
(16)58	—	25.00	50.00	110	200	—
(16)59	—	25.00	50.00	110	200	—
(16)60	—	25.00	50.00	110	200	—

KM# 34 PFENNIG

Copper, 16 mm. **Ruler:** Arnold IV **Obv:** Large A in circle, mitre above **Obv. Legend:** D. G. ABBAS. COR. **Rev:** Value I in circle **Rev. Legend:** LANT: MVNT. **Mint:** Höxter **Note:** Ref. I/S-204; W-728.

Date	Mintage	VG	F	VF	XF	Unc
ND(1648)	—	50.00	100	200	400	—

KM# 83 PFENNIG

Silver Weight varies: 0.29-0.56g., 12-15 mm. **Ruler:** Christoph **Obv:** Crowned ornate C divides date **Mint:** Höxter **Note:** Ref. I/S-301; W-169. Uniface schüssel-type.

Date	Mintage	VG	F	VF	XF	Unc
1683	—	135	270	400	775	—

KM# 35 2 PFENNIG

0.6640 g., 0.1883 Silver Weight varies: 0.48-0.68g. 0.0040 oz. ASW, 15 mm. **Ruler:** Arnold IV **Obv:** Spanish shield of 4-fold arms in circle **Obv. Legend:** ARNOLDVS. D. G. EL. ET. CO)N). **Rev:** Imperial orb with 2 **Rev. Legend:** ABBAS. CORBEIEN. **Mint:** Höxter **Note:** Ref. I/S-245; W-134.

Date	Mintage	VG	F	VF	XF	Unc
ND(1660)	—	120	200	425	—	—

KM# 19.1 3 PFENNIG (Dreier)

Silver Weight varies: 0.78-0.89g., 14-18 mm. **Ruler:** Johann Christoph **Obv:** Spanish shield of 4-fold arms divide legend **Obv. Legend:** M(O). N(O). - A(B). C(O). **Rev:** Imperial orb with 3 divides date **Mint:** Höxter **Note:** Ref. I/S-171, 176; W#102-4. Varieties exist.

Date	Mintage	VG	F	VF	XF	Unc
1621	—	—	—	—	—	—
	Note: Reported, not confirmed.					
16ZZ (f)	—	25.00	45.00	90.00	185	—
16Z3 (f)	—	25.00	45.00	90.00	185	—

KM# 19.2 3 PFENNIG (Dreier)

Silver Weight varies: 0.61-1.26g., 18 mm. **Ruler:** Johann Christoph **Obv:** Ornate shield of 4-fold arms in baroque frame divides legend **Obv. Legend:** M(O). N(O). - A(B)(B). C(O). **Rev:** Imperial orb with 3 divides date **Mint:** Höxter **Note:** Ref. I/S-172, 173, 177, 178. Varieties exist.

Date	Mintage	VG	F	VF	XF	Unc
1622 (f)	—	25.00	45.00	90.00	185	—
16ZZ (f)	—	25.00	45.00	90.00	185	—
16Z3 (f)	—	25.00	45.00	90.00	185	—

KM# 36 3 PFENNIG (Dreier)

Copper, 20 mm. **Ruler:** Johann Christoph **Obv:** Arms of Brambach (comb and diagonal bar) in circle **Obv. Legend:** IO. CH. ABB. CORB. **Rev:** Value III in circle, date divided at top **Rev. Legend:** S. VITVS. AO. **Mint:** Höxter **Note:** Ref. I/S-188; W-718.

Date	Mintage	VG	F	VF	XF	Unc
1638	—	40.00	65.00	135	270	—

KM# 41 3 PFENNIG (Dreier)

Copper, 19-20 mm. **Ruler:** Arnold IV **Obv:** Arms of Waldois (ox-head) **Obv. Legend:** ARNOLD ABB. CORB. **Rev:** Value III in circle, date divided at top **Rev. Legend:** S. VITVS. AO. **Mint:** Höxter **Note:** Ref. I/S-191, 195; W#721-23.

Date	Mintage	VG	F	VF	XF	Unc
1641	—	40.00	65.00	135	270	—
164Z	—	40.00	65.00	135	270	—
1642	—	40.00	65.00	135	270	—

KM# 84.1 3 PFENNIG (Dreier)

Silver Weight varies: 0.47-0.79g., 15-16 mm. **Ruler:** Christoph **Obv:** Ornate shield of 4-fold arms in baroque frame, legend curved above **Obv. Legend:** F. C. L. M. **Rev:** Imperial orb with 3 divides date **Mint:** Höxter **Note:** Ref. I/S-298, 299; W-168. Varieties exist.

Date	Mintage	VG	F	VF	XF	Unc
1683	—	30.00	60.00	120	240	—

KM# 84.2 3 PFENNIG (Dreier)

Silver Weight varies: 0.59-0.69g., 15-17 mm. **Ruler:** Christoph **Obv:** Oval shield of 4-fold arms in baroque frame, legend curved above **Obv. Legend:** F. C. L. M. **Rev:** Imperial orb with 3 divides mintmaster's initials **Mint:** Höxter **Note:** Ref. I/S-300.

Date	Mintage	VG	F	VF	XF	Unc
ND(1683) GB	—	20.00	40.00	80.00	160	—

KM# 84.3 3 PFENNIG (Dreier)

Silver Weight varies: 0.67-0.71g., 16 mm. **Ruler:** Christoph **Obv:** Crowned script CA monogram divides F. C. - L. M. **Rev:** Imperial orb with 3 divides date **Mint:** Höxter **Note:** Ref. I/S-296.

Date	Mintage	VG	F	VF	XF	Unc
1683	—	40.00	85.00	170	340	—

KM# 84.4 3 PFENNIG (Dreier)

Silver Weight varies: 0.57-0.71g., 15 mm. **Ruler:** Christoph **Obv:** Crowned C divides date **Rev:** Imperial orb with 3 divides mintmaster's initals **Mint:** Höxter **Note:** Ref. I/S-297.

Date	Mintage	VG	F	VF	XF	Unc
1683 GB	—	20.00	40.00	80.00	160	—

KM# 44 4 PFENNIG

Copper, 20 mm. **Ruler:** Arnold IV **Obv:** Large A in circle, mitre above **Obv. Legend:** D. G. AB(B)AS. COR(VEI). **Rev:** Value IIII in circle, date at end of legend **Rev. Legend:** LANT: MVNT. **Mint:** Höxter **Note:** Ref. I/S-202; W-720. Varieties exist.

Date	Mintage	VG	F	VF	XF	Unc
1648	—	35.00	65.00	135	270	—

KM# 85.1 4 PFENNIG

0.2920 g., 0.2500 Silver Weight varies: 0.36-0.98g. 0.0023 oz. ASW, 16 mm. **Ruler:** Christoph **Obv:** Crowned script CA monogram divides date **Rev:** 3-line inscription **Rev. Inscription:** IIII / GUTE / PF **Mint:** Höxter **Note:** Ref. I/S-293.

Date	Mintage	VG	F	VF	XF	Unc
1683	—	45.00	80.00	160	325	—

KM# 85.2 4 PFENNIG

0.2920 g., 0.2500 Silver Weight varies: 0.55-1.01g. 0.0023 oz. ASW, 16 mm. **Ruler:** Christoph **Obv:** Crowned CA monogram divides mintmaster's initials **Rev:** 3-line inscription, bottom line divides date **Rev. Inscription:** IIII / GUTE / PF **Mint:** Höxter **Note:** Ref. I/S-294.

Date	Mintage	VG	F	VF	XF	Unc
1683 GB	—	50.00	100	210	425	—

KM# 85.3 4 PFENNIG

0.2920 g., 0.2500 Silver Weight varies: 0.79-0.99g. 0.0023 oz. ASW, 16-17 mm. **Ruler:** Christoph **Obv:** Spanish shield of 4-fold arms in baroque frame, legend curved above **Obv. Legend:** F. C. L. M. **Rev:** 3-line inscription, bottom line divides date **Rev. Inscription:** IIII / GUTE / PF **Mint:** Höxter **Note:** Ref. I/S-295; W-167.

Date	Mintage	VG	F	VF	XF	Unc
1683	—	45.00	80.00	160	325	—

KM# B33 2 KREUZER

Silver **Ruler:** Johann Christoph **Obv:** Shield of Corvey arms **Rev:** Imperial orb with 2 **Mint:** Höxter **Note:** Ref. I/S-187.

Date	Mintage	VG	F	VF	XF	Unc
1636	—	—	—	—	—	—

KM# 15.1 12 KREUZER (Schreckenberger)

Silver Weight varies: 1.92-2.93g., 26-27 mm. **Ruler:** Heinrich V **Obv:** Oval shield of 4-fold arms in baroque frame, superimposed on 2 crossed croziers, mitre above divides date, where present **Obv. Legend:** HENRICV(S). D. G. ABBAS. CORBEI. **Rev:** Crowned imperial eagle, 1Z in orb on breast **Rev. Legend:** FERD. II. D. G. ROM. IMP. SEMP. A(V)(G). **Mint:** Höxter **Note:** Ref: I/S-145, 148. Kipper issue. Varieties exist.

Date	Mintage	VG	F	VF	XF	Unc
16Z0	—	40.00	70.00	130	265	—
ND(1620)	—	40.00	70.00	130	265	—

KM# 15.2 12 KREUZER (Schreckenberger)

Silver Weight varies: 2.04-3.00g., 26-28 mm. **Ruler:** Heinrich V **Obv:** Shield of 4-fold arms with concave sides, superimposed on 2 crossed croziers, divides date, where present, mitre above **Obv. Legend:** HENRICVS. D. G. ABBAS. CORBEIE(N). **Rev:** Crowned imperial eagle, 1Z in orb on breast **Rev. Legend:** FERD. II. D. G. ROM. IMP. SEM(P). A(V). **Mint:** Höxter **Note:** Ref. I/S-146, 150. Kipper issue. Varieties exist.

Date	Mintage	VG	F	VF	XF	Unc
16Z0	—	175	325	500	850	—
ND(1620)	—	175	325	500	850	—

KM# 15.2A 12 KREUZER (Schreckenberger)

10.5800 g., Silver, 32x32.5 mm. **Ruler:** Heinrich V **Obv:** Shield of 4-fold arms with concave sides, superimposed on 2 crossed croziers, mitre above **Obv. Legend:** HENRICVS. D. G. ABBAS. CORBEI. **Rev:** Crowned imperial eagle, 1Z in orb on breast **Rev. Legend:** FERD. II. D. G. ROM. IMP. SEMP. AV. **Mint:** Höxter **Note:** Ref. I/S-150.1. Klippe. Kipper issue.

Date	Mintage	VG	F	VF	XF	Unc
ND(1620)	—	—	—	—	—	—

KM# 15.3 12 KREUZER (Schreckenberger)

Silver Weight varies: 2.81-3.64g., 27 mm. **Ruler:** Heinrich V **Obv:** Spanish shield of 4-fold arms, with ornaments at sides, superimposed on 2 crossed croziers, mitre above **Obv. Legend:** HENR. D. G. ABBAS. CORBEIE. **Rev:** Crowned imperial eagle, 1Z in orb on breast **Rev. Legend:** FERD. II. D. G. ROM. IMP. SEMP. A(V)(G). **Mint:** Höxter **Note:** Ref. I/S-149. Kipper issue. Varieties exist.

Date	Mintage	VG	F	VF	XF	Unc
ND(1620)	—	—	—	—	—	—

KM# 16.1 12 KREUZER (Schreckenberger)

Silver Weight varies: 1.84-4.13g., 26-29 mm. **Ruler:** Johann Christoph **Obv:** Oval shield of 4-fold arms in baroque frame, superimposed on 2 crossed croziers, mitre above divides date. **Obv. Legend:** MONETA. NOVA. ABB. CORB(E)(I)(E)(N)(S)(I). **Rev:** Crowned imperial eagle, iZ in orb on breast **Rev. Legend:** FERD. II. D. G(RA). ROM. IMP. SE(M)(P). A(V). **Mint:** Höxter **Note:** Ref. I/S-151. Varieties exist.

Date	Mintage	VG	F	VF	XF	Unc
16Z0	—	40.00	80.00	160	325	—
(16)Z0	—	40.00	80.00	160	325	—

KM# 16.2 12 KREUZER (Schreckenberger)

2.5700 g., Silver, 26-27 mm. **Ruler:** Johann Christoph **Obv:** Oval shield of 4-fold arms in baroque frame, superimposed on 2 crossed croziers, mitre above divides date **Obv. Legend:** MONETA. NOVA. ABB. CORBIEN. **Rev:** Crowned imperial eagle, IZ in orb on breast, date divided by crown at top **Rev. Legend:** FERD. II. D. G. ROM. IMP. SEMP. AV. **Mint:** Höxter **Note:** Ref. I/S-152.

Date	Mintage	VG	F	VF	XF	Unc
1(6)Z0//(16)Z0	—	—	—	—	—	—

KM# 20.2 12 KREUZER (Schreckenberger)

Silver Weight varies: 1.22-2.65g., 24 mm. **Ruler:** Johann Christoph **Obv:** Heart-shaped shield of 4-fold arms in baroque frame, superimposed on 2 crossed croziers, mitre above divides date **Obv. Legend:** MO(N). NO(U)(A). ABB(A)(S). COR(B)(E). **Rev:** Crowned imperial eagle, 1Z in orb on breast **Rev. Legend:** S. M(U)(V)NZ. D. S(T). (Z.) IZ. S(W). P(E). **Mint:** Höxter **Note:** Ref. I/S-158, 166. Kipper issue. Varieties exist.

Date	Mintage	VG	F	VF	XF	Unc
16Z1	—	40.00	80.00	150	300	—
1622	—	40.00	80.00	150	300	—

KM# 20.3 12 KREUZER (Schreckenberger)

Silver Weight varies: 1.53-2.70g., 24 mm. **Ruler:** Johann Christoph **Obv:** Heart-shaped shield of 4-fold arms in baroque frame, superimposed on 2 crossed croziers, mitre aboe, date divided in margin at top **Obv. Legend:** MO. NO. ABBA. COR(P)(B). **Rev:** Crowned imperial eagle, IZ in orb on breast **Rev. Legend:** S. M(U)(V)NZ. D. S. Z. 1Z. S. (P.) **Mint:** Höxter **Note:** Ref. I/S-159, 167. Varieties exist.

Date	Mintage	VG	F	VF	XF	Unc
16Z1	—	27.00	60.00	80.00	150	—
16ZZ	—	27.00	60.00	80.00	150	—

KM# 20.1 12 KREUZER (Schreckenberger)

Silver Weight varies: 1.65-2.82g., 25-27 mm. **Ruler:** Johann Christoph **Obv:** Heart-shaped shield of 4-fold arms in baroque frame, superimposed on 2 crossed croziers, mitre aove divides date **Obv. Legend:** MO. N(O). ABBA. CORBE(I). **Rev:** Crowned imperial eagle, IZ in orb on breast **Rev. Legend:** LANTMVN. DA. ST. 1Z. SW. PE(N). **Mint:** Höxter **Note:** Ref. I/S-157. Varieties exist.

Date	Mintage	VG	F	VF	XF	Unc
16Z1	—	27.00	60.00	80.00	160	—

KM# 20.1A 12 KREUZER (Schreckenberger)

11.0000 g., Silver, 27.5x29 mm. **Ruler:** Johann Christoph **Obv:** Heart-shaped shield of 4-fold arms in baroque frame, superimposed on 2 crossed croziers, mitre above divides date **Obv. Legend:** MO. NO. ABBA. CORBE. **Rev:** Crowned imperial eagle, IZ in orb on breast **Rev. Legend:** LANTMVN. DA. ST. IZ. SW. PE. **Mint:** Höxter **Note:** Ref. I/S-157.1. Klippe. The Z in the reverse legend is retrograde.

Date	Mintage	VG	F	VF	XF	Unc
16Z1	—	—	—	—	—	—

KM# 20.4 12 KREUZER (Schreckenberger)

1.6400 g., Silver, 26 mm. **Ruler:** Johann Christoph **Obv:** Heart-shaped shield of 4-fold arms in baroque frame, superimposed on 2 crossed croziers, mitre above divides date **Obv. Legend:** MO. NO. ABBA. CORBE. **Rev:** Crowned imperial eagle, IZ in orb on breast **Rev. Legend:** STIFTMVN. DA. ST. 1Z. SW. PE. **Mint:** Höxter **Note:** Ref. I/S-160.

Date	Mintage	VG	F	VF	XF	Unc
16Z1	—	30.00	65.00	110	200	—

KM# 20.5 12 KREUZER (Schreckenberger)

1.6200 g., Silver, 23 mm. **Ruler:** Johann Christoph **Obv:** Heart-shaped shield of 4-fold arms in baroque frame, superimposed on 2 crossed croziers, mitre above divides date **Obv. Legend:** MO. NO. ABBA. COR. **Rev:** Crowned imperial eagle, IZ in orb on breast, date divided by crown at top **Rev. Legend:** S. MVNZ. D. S. Z. 1Z. S(W). SP. **Mint:** Höxter **Note:** Ref. I/S-168.

Date	Mintage	VG	F	VF	XF	Unc
16Z1//16ZZ	—	—	—	—	—	—

KM# 20.6 12 KREUZER (Schreckenberger)

Silver Weight varies: 1.68-2.31g., 25 mm. **Ruler:** Johann Christoph **Obv:** Oval shield of 4-fold arms in baroque frame, superimposed on 2 crossed croziers, mitre above, all in circle, date at end of legend **Obv. Legend:** MO(NETA). NO(VA). ABB(AS). CORBE(I). **Rev:** Crowned imperial eagle, IZ in orb on breast **Rev. Legend:** FER(D). II. D. G. RO(M). IM(P). SE(M)(P). A(V). **Mint:** Höxter **Note:** Ref. I/S-154. Varieties exist.

Date	Mintage	VG	F	VF	XF	Unc
16Z1	—	40.00	70.00	125	240	—
(16)Z1	—	40.00	70.00	125	240	—

KM# 20.7 12 KREUZER (Schreckenberger)

Silver Weight varies: 1.48-2.56g., 25-28 mm. **Ruler:** Johann Christoph **Obv:** Oval shield of 4-fold arms in baroque frame, superimposed on 2 crossed croziers, mitre above, all in circle, date at beginning of legend **Obv. Legend:** MO(NETA). NO(VA). ABB. CORBE(I). **Rev:** Crowned imperial eagle, IZ in orb on breast **Rev. Legend:** FER(D). II. D. G. ROM. IM(P). SE(M)(P). A(VG). **Mint:** Höxter **Note:** Ref. I/S-155, 156. Varieties exist.

Date	Mintage	VG	F	VF	XF	Unc
(16)Z1	—	40.00	70.00	125	240	—

KM# 30 MATTIER

Silver Weight varies: 0.74-1.18g., 16-17 mm. **Ruler:** Johann Christoph **Obv:** Oval shield of 4-fold arms, superimposed on 2 crossed croziers, mitre above **Obv. Legend:** I. C(H). D. G. AB(B). COR. **Rev:** 3-line inscription, date divided by mintmaster's symbol below **Rev. Inscription:** I / MATTI / ER **Mint:** Höxter **Note:** Ref. I/S-182, 185; W-110, 111. 1/2 Mariengroschen = 1/72 Thaler.

Date	Mintage	VG	F	VF	XF	Unc
1631 (e)	—	325	550	800	1,300	—
1632 (e)	—	325	550	800	1,300	—

KM# 27 MARIENGROSCHEN

Silver Weight varies: 1.08-1.52g., 20-22 mm. **Ruler:** Johann Christoph **Obv:** Spanish shield of 4-fold arms in circle, date in margin at top **Obv. Legend:** MO(N). NO. ABB(A). CO(R)(B)(E). **Rev:** Seated Madonna with Child, rays around **Rev. Legend:** MARIA.(-) MA(-)T(ER). DO(M)(I). **Mint:** Höxter **Note:** Ref. I/S-170, 175; W-101. Varieties exist. 8 Pfennig = 1/36 Thaler. Prev. KM#23.

Date	Mintage	VG	F	VF	XF	Unc
1622 (f)	—	120	250	375	625	—
1623 (f)	—	120	250	375	625	—

KM# 31 MARIENGROSCHEN

1.7720 g., 0.3750 Silver Weight varies: 1.05-1.80g. 0.0214 oz. ASW, 19-20 mm. **Ruler:** Johann Christoph **Obv:** Oval shield of 4-fold arms, superimposed on 2 crossed croziers, mitre above **Obv. Legend:** IOAN. CH. D. G. A(B)(B). COR(B). **Rev:** 4-line inscription with date **Rev. Legend:** NACH DES CR(E)IS.

ORDNVN(G). **Rev. Inscription:** I / MARI / GROS / (date) **Mint:** Höxter **Note:** Ref. I/S-181, 184; W-101. Varieties exist. 8 Pfennig = 1/36 Thaler.

Date	Mintage	VG	F	VF	XF	Unc
1631 (e)	—	50.00	90.00	165	325	—
163Z (e)	—	600	900	1,300	1,900	—

KM# 45 MARIENGROSCHEN

Silver Weight varies: 0.94-1.37g., 21 mm. **Ruler:** Arnold IV **Obv:** Ornate shield of 4-fold arms, superimposed on crossed sword and crozier, mitre above **Obv. Legend:** ARNOLD. D. G. ABBA. CORB(E). **Rev:** Madonna and Child, rays around, date at end of legend **Rev. Legend:** MARI. MAT. - DEI. **Mint:** Höxter **Note:** Ref. I/S-206; W-132. 1/36 Thaler.

Date	Mintage	VG	F	VF	XF	Unc
1649	—	—	—	—	—	—

KM# 55.1 MARIENGROSCHEN

1.4110 g., 0.3750 Silver Weight varies: 0.70-1.46g. 0.0170 oz. ASW, 20-21 mm. **Ruler:** Arnold IV **Obv:** 3-line inscription i circle **Obv. Legend:** (D.G.) ARNOL. (D.G) EL. ET. CON. AB. COR. **Obv. Inscription:** I / MARI / GRO **Rev:** Madonna with Child divides date in circle **Rev. Legend:** S. MARIA. MATER. DEI. **Mint:** Höxter **Note:** Ref. I/S-219, 225, 236; W-132A, 133. Varieties exist. 1/36 Thaler.

Date	Mintage	VG	F	VF	XF	Unc
1653 (h)	—	40.00	65.00	130	265	—
1654 (h)	—	40.00	65.00	130	265	—
1656	—	—	—	—	—	—

Note: Reported, not confirmed.

KM# 55.2 MARIENGROSCHEN

1.6470 g., 0.3698 Silver Weight varies: 1.45-1.68g. 0.0196 oz. ASW, 20 mm. **Ruler:** Arnold IV **Obv:** 3-line inscription in circle **Obv. Legend:** ARNOL. D. G. EL. ET. CON. AB. COR. **Obv. Inscription:** I / MARI / GRO **Rev:** Madonna with Child in circle, date at end of legend **Rev. Legend:** S. MARIA. MATER. DEI. **Mint:** Höxter **Note:** Ref. I/S-220. 1/36 Thaler.

Date	Mintage	VG	F	VF	XF	Unc
1653 (h)	—	40.00	65.00	120	240	—

KM# A86 MARIENGROSCHEN

Silver Weight varies: 1.03-1.38g., 18 mm. **Ruler:** Christoph **Obv:** Crowned ornately-shaped shield of 4-fold arms in circle **Obv. Legend:** CHRISTO • II • G • AB • COR • **Rev:** 3-line inscription in circle, date at end of legend **Rev. Legend:** SACRI • ROM • IMP • PR. **Rev. Inscription:** I / MARI / GROS **Mint:** Höxter **Note:** Ref. I/S-292. 1/36 Thaler.

Date	Mintage	VG	F	VF	XF	Unc
1683	—	40.00	80.00	160	320	—

KM# 38 2 MARIENGROSCHEN

1.2200 g., Silver, 19 mm. **Ruler:** Arnold IV **Obv:** Oval shield of 4-fold arms in baroque frame, superimposed on 2 crossed croziers, mitre above **Obv. Legend:** ARNOLD D. D. G. AB. COR. **Rev:** 4-line inscription with mintmaster's initials and symbol, value II in first line divides date **Rev. Legend:** VON. FEINEM. SILBER. M. **Rev. Inscription:** II / MARI / (GORS) (GROS) / (initials, symbol) **Mint:** Höxter **Note:** Ref. I/S-198. 16 Pfennig = 1/18 Thaler. Varieties exist.

Date	Mintage	VG	F	VF	XF	Unc
1646 GK(g)	—	—	—	—	—	—

KM# 39 2 MARIENGROSCHEN

Silver, 19 mm. **Ruler:** Arnold IV **Obv:** Oval shield of 4-fold arms in baroque frame, superimposed on 2 crossed croziers, mitre above **Obv. Legend:** ARNOLD. D. G. EL. ET. CO. AB. CO. **Rev:** 4-line inscription with mintmaster's initials, date at end of legend **Rev. Legend:** VON. FEINEM. SILBER. **Rev. Inscription:** II / MARI / GROS / (initials) **Mint:** Höxter **Note:** I/S-199. 16 Pfennig = 1/18 Thaler.

Date	Mintage	VG	F	VF	XF	Unc
1646 GK	—	—	—	—	—	—

KM# 43 2 MARIENGROSCHEN

Silver Weight varies: 0.70-1.36g., 17-19 mm. **Ruler:** Arnold IV **Obv:** Large A in circle divides date, mitre above **Obv. Legend:** D. G. (EL. ET. CON.) (CORBI.) AB(B)(AS). (COR)(B)(E)(I)(N). **Rev:** 4-line inscription with mintmaster's initials or symbol **Rev. Legend:** VON. FEINEM. SILBER. (S. M.) **Rev. Inscription:** II / MAR / GR(O) / (initials-symbol) **Mint:** Höxter **Note:** Ref. I/S-205, 209, 211, 216, 218, 223, 227; W#124-29. Varieties exist.

Date	Mintage	VG	F	VF	XF	Unc
1649 (h)	—	17.00	35.00	70.00	145	—
1649 HC	—	17.00	35.00	70.00	145	—
1650 (h)	—	17.00	35.00	70.00	145	—
1651 (h)	—	17.00	35.00	70.00	145	—
165Z (h)	—	17.00	35.00	70.00	145	—
1653 (h)	—	17.00	35.00	70.00	145	—
1654 (h)	—	17.00	35.00	70.00	145	—
1655 (h)	—	17.00	35.00	70.00	145	—

KM# 56.1 2 MARIENGROSCHEN

1.2910 g., 0.8750 Silver Weight varies: 0.78-1.29g. 0.0363 oz. ASW, 17-18 mm. **Ruler:** Arnold IV **Obv:** Large A in circle, mitre above **Obv. Legend:** D. G. EL. ET. CON. AB. COR(B). **Rev:** 4-line inscription with mintmaster's initials, date at top in margin **Rev. Legend:** VON FEINE(M)(N) SILBE(R). **Rev. Inscription:** II / MAR / GRO(S) / (initials) **Mint:** Höxter **Note:** Ref. I/S-224, 228, 229; W-130. Varieties exist. 16 Pfennig = 1/18 Thaler.

Date	Mintage	VG	F	VF	XF	Unc
1654 VF	—	16.00	33.00	75.00	155	—
1655 VF	—	16.00	33.00	75.00	155	—

KM# 56.2 2 MARIENGROSCHEN

1.2910 g., 0.8750 Silver Weight varies: 0.74-1.56g. 0.0363 oz. ASW, 17-18 mm. **Ruler:** Arnold IV **Obv:** Large A in circle, mitre above **Obv. Legend:** D. G. EL. ET. CON. AB. COR(B). **Rev:** 4-line inscription with mintmaster's initials, date at top in margin **Rev. Legend:** VON. GVTTEM. SILBE(R). **Rev. Inscription:** II / MARI / GRO(S) / (initials) **Mint:** Höxter **Note:** Ref. I/S-230, 235; W-130a, 131. Varieties exist. 16 Pfennig = 1/18 Thaler.

Date	Mintage	VG	F	VF	XF	Unc
1655 VF	—	16.00	33.00	75.00	155	—
1656 VF	—	16.00	33.00	75.00	155	—

KM# 56.3 2 MARIENGROSCHEN

1.2910 g., 0.8750 Silver Weight varies: 0.83-1.26g. 0.0363 oz. ASW, 18 mm. **Ruler:** Arnold IV **Obv:** Large A in circle, mitre above **Obv. Legend:** D. G. EL. ET. CON. AB. CORB. **Rev:** 4-line inscription with mintmaster's initials, date at top of margin **Rev. Legend:** FORTITER. RECTE. PIE. **Rev. Inscription:** II / MARI / GRO / (initials) **Mint:** Höxter **Note:** Ref. I/S-231; W-130. 16 Pfennig = 1/18 Thaler.

Date	Mintage	VG	F	VF	XF	Unc
1655 VF	—	16.00	33.00	75.00	155	—

KM# 86.1 6 MARIENGROSCHEN

Silver Weight varies: 5.47-5.67g., 28 mm. **Ruler:** Christoph **Obv:** 4-line inscription with date **Obv. Legend:** CHRIST(O)P. EL. E. CONF. AB. COR. S. R. I. P. **Rev:** Crowned imperial eagle in circle **Rev. Legend:** LEOPOLD. D. G. ROM. IMP. SEM. AUG. **Rev. Inscription:** VI / MARIEN / GROS / (date) **Mint:** Höxter **Note:** Ref. I/S-286; W-164. 1/6 Thaler.

Date	Mintage	VG	F	VF	XF	Unc
1683	—	80.00	135	240	450	—

KM# 86.2 6 MARIENGROSCHEN

Silver, 28 mm. **Ruler:** Christoph **Obv:** 3-line inscription, date at end of legend **Obv. Legend:** CHRISTP. EL. E. CONF. AB. COR. S. R. I. P. **Rev:** Crowned imperial eagle in circle **Rev. Legend:** LEOPOLD. D. G. ROM. IMPER. SEM. AUG. **Rev. Inscription:** VI / MARIEN / GROS **Mint:** Höxter **Note:** Ref. I/S-287. 1/6 Thaler.

Date	Mintage	VG	F	VF	XF	Unc
1683	—	80.00	135	240	450	—

KM# 88 12 MARIENGROSCHEN

9.4200 g., Silver, 32 mm. **Ruler:** Christoph **Obv:** 4-line inscription with date **Obv. Legend:** CHRISTP. EL. E. CONF. AB. COR. S. R. I. P. **Obv. Inscription:** XII / MARIEN / GROSCH / (date) **Rev:** Crowned imperial eagle in circle **Rev. Legend:** LEOPOLD. D. G. ROM. IMPER. SEM. AVG. **Mint:** Höxter **Note:** Ref. I/S-285. 1/2 Gulden = 1/3 Reichsthaler.

Date	Mintage	VG	F	VF	XF	Unc
1683	—	—	—	—	—	—

KM# 74 24 MARIENGROSCHEN (Gulden)

Silver Weight varies: 15.75-18.90g., 37-40 mm. **Ruler:** Christoph **Obv:** 4-line inscription with date **Obv. Legend:** CHRIST(O)P. EL. E. CONF. AB. COR(B). S. R. I. P. **Rev:** Crowned imperial eagle in circle **Rev. Legend:** LEOPOLD. D. G. ROM. IMP. SEM. A(V)(U)G. **Rev. Inscription:** XXIIII / MARIEN / GROSCH / (date) **Mint:** Höxter **Note:** Ref. I/S-246, 267; W-162A; Dav. 491B. Varieties exist.

Date	Mintage	VG	F	VF	XF	Unc
1682	—	—	—	—	—	—
1683 Rare	—	—	—	—	—	—

Note: An example in VF-XF realized approximately $12,700 in a June 2004 Künker auction.

KM# 69 24 MARIENGROSCHEN (Gulden)

Silver Weight varies: 16.88-17.11g., 40 mm. **Ruler:** Christoph **Obv:** Bust to left in circle **Obv. Legend:** CHRISTOPH. EL. E. CONF. AB. COR. S. R. I. P. **Rev:** 3-line inscription **Rev. Legend:** CANDORE ET AMORE. **Rev. Inscription:** XXIIII / MARIEN / GROSCH **Note:** Ref. I/S-317; W-152; Dav. 488.

Date	Mintage	VG	F	VF	XF	Unc
ND(1682)	—	—	—	—	—	—

KM# 70.1 24 MARIENGROSCHEN (Gulden)

Silver Weight varies: 12.94-17.12g., 39-40 mm. **Ruler:** Christoph **Obv:** Crowned script double ACC monogram **Obv. Legend:** CHRIST. EL. E. CON(F). AB. COR. S. R. I. P. **Rev:** 3-line inscription in circle, date at end of legend, where present **Rev. Legend:** CANDORE ET AMORE. **Rev. Inscription:** XXIIII / MARIEN / GROSCH. **Mint:** Höxter **Note:** Ref. I/S-256, 319; W-156; Dav. 489. Varieties exist.

Date	Mintage	VG	F	VF	XF	Unc
ND(1682)	—	225	375	525	900	—
1682	—	225	375	525	900	—

KM# 70.2 24 MARIENGROSCHEN (Gulden)

Silver, 40 mm. **Ruler:** Christoph **Obv:** Crowned script double ACC monogram, crossed palm branches below **Obv. Legend:** CHRIST. EL. E. CONF. AB. COR. S. R. I. P. **Rev:** 4-line inscription, date at end of legend **Rev. Legend:** CANDORE ET AMORE. **Rev. Inscription:** 24 / MARIEN / GROS(C)(G) / (H)EN. **Mint:** Höxter **Note:** Ref. I/S-257; Dav. 489.

Date	Mintage	VG	F	VF	XF	Unc
1682	—	—	—	—	—	—

KM# 72.1 24 MARIENGROSCHEN (Gulden)

Silver Weight varies: 13.40-16.66g., 36-38 mm. **Ruler:** Christoph **Obv:** Crowned shield of 4-fold arms between 2 palm branches **Obv. Legend:** CHRIST. EL. E. CONF. AB. COR. S. R. I. P. **Rev:** 3-line inscription, date at end of legend **Rev. Legend:** CANDORE. ET. AMORE. **Rev. Inscription:** XXIIII / MARIEN / GROSCH. **Mint:** Höxter **Note:** Ref. I/S-265; W-160; Dav. 490.

Date	Mintage	VG	F	VF	XF	Unc
1682	—	—	—	—	—	—

KM# 73 24 MARIENGROSCHEN (Gulden)

17.0400 g., Silver, 37 mm. **Ruler:** Christoph **Obv:** 4-line inscription with date **Obv. Legend:** CHRISTOP. EL. E. CONF.

AB. COR. S. R. I. P. **Rev:** Crowned imperial eagle in circle **Rev. Legend:** LEOPOLD. D. G. ROM. IMP. SEM. AVG. **Rev. Inscription:** 24 / MARIEN / GROSCH / (date) **Mint:** Höxter **Note:** Ref. I/S-247; W-162; Dav. 491.

Date	Mintage	VG	F	VF	XF	Unc
1682	—	2,800	3,750	4,500	6,500	—

KM# 75 24 MARIENGROSCHEN (Gulden)
16.7500 g., Silver, 40 mm. **Ruler:** Christoph **Obv:** 3-line inscription in circle **Obv. Legend:** CHRISTOPH. EL. E. CONF. AB. COR. S. R. I. P. **Obv. Inscription:** XXIIII / MARIEN / GROSCHEN **Rev:** Large 2/3 in circle **Rev. Legend:** CHRISTOPH. EL. E. CON. A. COR. S. R. I. P. **Mint:** Höxter **Note:** Ref. I/S-320; W-152A. Mule

Date	Mintage	VG	F	VF	XF	Unc
ND(1683)	—	325	575	1,000	1,700	—

KM# 71.1 24 MARIENGROSCHEN (Gulden)
Silver Weight varies: 15.93-16.68g., 37 mm. **Ruler:** Christoph **Obv:** Crowned double script CDGAC monogram **Obv. Legend:** CHRIST. EL. E. CONF. AB. COR. S. R. I. P. **Rev:** 4-line inscription, date at end of legend **Rev. Legend:** CANDORE. ET. AMORE. **Rev. Inscription:** 24 / MARIEN / GROS(C)(G) / (H)EN. **Mint:** Höxter **Note:** Ref. I/S-306, 311; W-157; Dav. 492. Varieties exist.

Date	Mintage	VG	F	VF	XF	Unc
1684 (i)	—	1,500	2,200	2,850	4,200	—

KM# 71.2 24 MARIENGROSCHEN (Gulden)
Silver Weight varies: 15.41-16.79g., 38 mm. **Ruler:** Christoph **Obv:** Crowned double script CDGAC monogram **Obv. Legend:** CHRIST. EL. E. CONF. AB. COR. S. R. I. P. **Rev:** 4-line inscription, date at end of legend **Rev. Legend:** CANDORE. ET. AMORE. **Rev. Inscription:** XXIIII / MARIEN / GROS(C)(G) / (H)EN. **Mint:** Höxter **Note:** Ref. I/S-307, 310. Varieties exist.

Date	Mintage	VG	F	VF	XF	Unc
1684 (i)	—	2,250	3,000	3,750	5,500	—

KM# 72.2 24 MARIENGROSCHEN (Gulden)
Silver Weight varies: 16.05-17.05g., 37 mm. **Ruler:** Christoph **Obv:** Crowned oval shield of 4-fold arms in baroque frame, superimposed on crossed sword and crozier **Obv. Legend:** CHRIST. EL. E. CONF. AB. COR. S. R. I. P. **Rev:** 4-line inscription, date at end of legend **Rev. Legend:** CANDORE ET AMORE. **Rev. Inscription:** XXIIII / MARIEN / GROSG / EN. **Mint:** Höxter **Note:** Ref. I/S-314; W-160.

Date	Mintage	VG	F	VF	XF	Unc
1684 (i)	—	—	—	—	—	—

KM# 7 1/96 THALER
0.7600 g., Silver, 16 mm. **Ruler:** Dietrich IV **Obv:** Spanish shield of 4-fold arms in baroque frame **Rev:** Imperial orb with 96, cross on top flanked by 2 rosettes **Mint:** Höxter **Note:** Ref. I/S-140. Dreier.

Date	Mintage	VG	F	VF	XF	Unc
ND(1612-15)	—	—	—	—	—	—

KM# 5.1 1/24 THALER
Silver Weight varies: 1.27-1.98g., 21 mm. **Ruler:** Dietrich IV **Obv:** Spanish shield of 4-fold arms in baroque frame **Obv. Legend:** DIED. D. G. ABB. CORBIE. **Rev:** Imperial orb with Z4 divides date **Rev. Legend:** RUD. II. RO. IMP. SEM. AU. **Mint:** Höxter **Note:** Ref. I/S-55. Fürstengroschen.

Date	Mintage	VG	F	VF	XF	Unc
1606 HL	—	—	—	—	—	—

KM# 5.4 1/24 THALER
Silver Weight varies: 1.06-1.93g., 20-2 mm. **Ruler:** Dietrich IV **Obv:** Spanish shield of 4-fold arms in baroque frame **Obv. Legend:** THEOD. D. G. ABB. COR(B)(I) **Rev:** Imperial orb with Z4, date divided by cross on top **Rev. Legend:** RVD. II. RO(M). I(M)(P). S. A(V)(G). **Mint:** Höxter **Note:** Ref. I/S#60-62, 67. Fürstengroschen. Varieties exist.

Date	Mintage	VG	F	VF	XF	Unc
1607	—	20.00	35.00	75.00	155	—
1607 HL	—	20.00	35.00	75.00	155	—
1612 HK(c)	—	20.00	35.00	75.00	155	—

KM# 5.2 1/24 THALER
Silver Weight varies: 1.58-1.90g., 21 mm. **Ruler:** Dietrich IV **Obv:** Spanish shield of 4-fold arms in baroque frame **Obv. Legend:** DIED. D. G. ABB. CORBIE. **Rev:** Imperial orb with Z4, date divided by cross on top **Rev. Legend:** RVD. II. RO. I(M). S. A(V). **Mint:** Höxter **Note:** Ref. I/S-57; W-84. Fürstengroschen. Varieties exist.

Date	Mintage	VG	F	VF	XF	Unc
1607 HL	—	20.00	40.00	75.00	155	—

KM# 5.3 1/24 THALER
Silver Weight varies: 1.51-1.93g., 20 mm. **Ruler:** Dietrich IV **Obv:** Ornate shield of 4-fold arms superimposed on 2 crossed croziers, mitre above **Obv. Legend:** DIED. D. G. AB. CORBIE. **Rev:** Imperial orb with Z4 divides date **Rev. Legend:** RVD. II. RO(M). I(M)(P). S. AV(G). **Mint:** Höxter **Note:** Ref. I/S-58, 59. Fürstengroschen. Varieties exist.

Date	Mintage	VG	F	VF	XF	Unc
1607	—	30.00	60.00	120	—	—
1607 HL	—	30.00	60.00	120	—	—

KM# 5.5 1/24 THALER
Silver Weight varies: 1.27-1.94g., 21 mm. **Ruler:** Dietrich IV **Obv:** Ornate shield of 4-fold arms **Obv. Legend:** THEOD. D. G. ABB. COR(BI). **Rev:** Imperial orb with Z4, date divided by cross on top **Rev. Legend:** RVD. II. RO(M). IM(P). S. A(V). **Mint:** Höxter **Note:** Ref. I/S-63. Fürstengroschen. Varieties exist.

Date	Mintage	VG	F	VF	XF	Unc
1607	—	30.00	60.00	120	—	—

KM# 5.6 1/24 THALER
Silver Weight varies: 1.37-1.70g., 21 mm. **Ruler:** Dietrich IV **Obv:** Ornate shield of 4-fold arms superimposed on 2 crossed croziers, mitre above **Obv. Legend:** THEOD. D. G. A(BB). COR(BIE). **Rev:** Imperial orb with Z4, date divided by cross on top **Rev. Legend:** RVD. II. RO(M). IM(P). S. A(V)(G). **Mint:** Höxter **Note:** Ref. I/S-64. Fürstengroschen. Varieties exist.

Date	Mintage	VG	F	VF	XF	Unc
1607	—	30.00	60.00	120	—	—

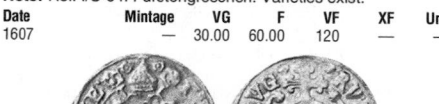

KM# 8.1 1/24 THALER
Silver Weight varies: 1.21-1.75g., 20 mm. **Ruler:** Dietrich IV **Obv:** Spanish shield of 4-fold arms in baroque frame, superimposed on 2 crossed croziers, mitre above **Obv. Legend:** THEOD. D. G. ABB. CORB(I)E. **Rev:** Imperial orb with Z4, date divided by cross on top **Rev. Legend:** RVD(OLP). II. (D.G.) RO(M). IMP. S(EM). A(V)(G). **Mint:** Höxter **Note:** Ref. I/S-71, 80, 83. Fürstengroschen. Varieties exist.

Date	Mintage	VG	F	VF	XF	Unc
161Z	—	60.00	125	200	385	—
ND(1612)	—	60.00	125	200	385	—

KM# 8.2 1/24 THALER
Silver Weight varies: 1.33-1.66g., 21 mm. **Ruler:** Dietrich IV **Obv:** Oval shield of 4-fold arms in baroque frame, superimposed on crossed sword and crozier, mitre above **Obv. Legend:** TEODOR. D. G. ABB. CORB. **Rev:** Imperial orb with Z4, date divided by cross on top **Rev. Legend:** RVD. II. RO(M). IM. S(EM). AV. **Mint:** Höxter **Note:** Ref. I/S-66. Fürstengroschen. Varieties exist.

Date	Mintage	VG	F	VF	XF	Unc
161Z	—	30.00	65.00	100	210	—

KM# 8.3 1/24 THALER
Silver Weight varies: 1.27-1.90g., 20-21 mm. **Ruler:** Dietrich IV **Obv:** Spanish shield of 4-fold arms in baroque frame, superimposed on crossed sword and crozier, mitre above **Obv. Legend:** T(H)E(OD)(O)(R). D. G. ABB. COR(B)(I)(E)(N). **Rev:** Imperial orb with Z4, date divided by cross on top, where present **Rev. Legend:** RVD(OLP). II. (D.G.) R(O)(M). I(M)(P). S. A(V)(G). **Mint:** Höxter **Note:** Ref. I/S-68, 74, 77, 82. Fürstengroschen. Varieties exist.

Date	Mintage	VG	F	VF	XF	Unc
161Z	—	30.00	65.00	100	210	—
ND(1612)	—	30.00	65.00	100	210	—

KM# 8.4 1/24 THALER
Silver Weight varies: 1.24-1.69g., 20 mm. **Ruler:** Dietrich IV **Obv:** Spanish shield of 4-fold arms, superimposed on crossed sword and crozier, mitre above **Obv. Legend:** T(H)EOD(O)(R). D. G. ABB. CORB(I)(E). **Rev:** Imperial orb with Z4, date divided by cross on top **Rev. Legend:** RVD. II. (D.G.) RO(M). I(M)(P). S. A(V)(G). **Mint:** Höxter **Note:** Ref. I/S-69. Fürstengroschen. Varieties exist.

Date	Mintage	VG	F	VF	XF	Unc
161Z HK(c)	—	30.00	60.00	100	200	—

KM# 8.5 1/24 THALER
Silver Weight varies: 1.32-1.74g., 20 mm. **Ruler:** Dietrich IV **Obv:** Spanish shield of 4-fold arms, superimposed on crossed sword and crozier, mitre above **Obv. Legend:** THEOD(O)(R). D. G. ABB. COR(B)(I)(E). **Rev:** Imperial orb with Z4 divides date **Rev. Legend:** RVD(OLP). II. (D.G.) RO(M)(A). I(M)(P). S(EM). A(V). **Mint:** Höxter **Note:** Ref. I/S-70, 79. Fürstengroschen. Varieties exist.

Date	Mintage	VG	F	VF	XF	Unc
161Z	—	30.00	60.00	100	200	—

KM# 8.6 1/24 THALER
Silver Weight varies: 1.07-1.69g., 20-21 mm. **Ruler:** Dietrich IV **Obv:** Ornate shield of 4-fold arms, mitre above **Obv. Legend:** T(H)EOD(OR). D. G. ABB(AS). CORB(IENS). **Rev:** Imperial orb with Z4, date divided by cross on top **Rev. Legend:** RVD. II. (D.G.) RO(M). IM. S(EM). A(V)(G). **Mint:** Höxter **Note:** Ref. I/S-72. Fürstengroschen. Varieties exist.

Date	Mintage	VG	F	VF	XF	Unc
161Z HK(c)	—	30.00	60.00	100	200	—

KM# 8.7 1/24 THALER
Silver Weight varies: 1.43-1.60g., 20 mm. **Ruler:** Dietrich IV **Obv:** Ornate shield of 4-fold arms, mitre above **Obv. Legend:** THEOD. D. G. ABB. CORBIENS. **Rev:** Imperial orb with Z4 divides date **Rev. Legend:** RVD. II. D. G. ROM. IM. S. AVG. **Mint:** Höxter **Note:** Ref. I/S-73. Fürstengroschen.

Date	Mintage	VG	F	VF	XF	Unc
161Z	—	30.00	60.00	100	200	—

KM# 8.8 1/24 THALER
Silver Weight varies: 1.27-1.68g., 20 mm. **Ruler:** Dietrich IV **Obv:** Ornate shield of 4-fold arms,superimposed on crossed sword and crozier, mitre above **Obv. Legend:** T(H)EOD(OR). D. G. ABB. COR(B)(IE)(N). **Rev:** Imperial orb with Z4, date divided by cross on top **Rev. Legend:** RVD(OLP). II. (D.G.) RO(M). IM(P). S(EM)(P). A(V)(G). **Mint:** Höxter **Note:** Ref. I/S-75 76, 84. Fürstengroschen. Varieties exist.

Date	Mintage	VG	F	VF	XF	Unc
161Z HK(c)	—	20.00	45.00	90.00	180	—
ND(1612)	—	20.00	45.00	90.00	180	—

KM# 8.9 1/24 THALER
Silver Weight varies: 1.38-1.53g., 20 mm. **Ruler:** Dietrich IV **Obv:** Ornate shield of 4-fold arms, superimposed on crossed sword and crozier, mitre above **Obv. Legend:** T(H)EOD(OR). D. G. ABB. CO(RBIE). **Rev:** Imperial orb with Z4 divides date **Rev. Legend:** RVD(OL). II. D. G. RO(M). IM. S(EM). AV(G). **Mint:** Höxter **Note:** Ref. I/S-78. Fürstengroschen. Varieties exist.

Date	Mintage	VG	F	VF	XF	Unc
161Z	—	30.00	60.00	100	200	—

KM# 8.10 1/24 THALER
Silver Weight varies: 1.22-1.86g., 20 mm. **Ruler:** Dietrich IV **Obv:** Ornate shield of 4-fold arms, superimposed on 2 crossed croziers, mitre above **Obv. Legend:** THEOD(D). D. G. ABB. CORB(I)(E). **Rev:** Imperial orb with Z4 divides date **Rev. Legend:** RVD(OLP). II. RO(M)(A). IM(P). S(EM). A(V)(G)(V)(ST). **Mint:** Höxter **Note:** Ref. I/S-81, 85. Fürstengroschen. Varieties exist.

Date	Mintage	VG	F	VF	XF	Unc
161Z	—	20.00	45.00	90.00	180	—
ND(1612)	—	20.00	45.00	90.00	180	—

KM# 12.1 1/24 THALER
Silver Weight varies: 1.17-1.65g., 20-21 mm. **Ruler:** Dietrich IV **Obv:** Oval shield of 4-fold arms in baroque frame, superimposed on crossed sword and crozier, mitre above **Obv. Legend:** T(H)EOD(O)(R). D(E). G(R). AB(B). COR(B)(I). **Rev:** Imperial orb with Z4, date divided by cross on top **Rev. Legend:** MATI(AS). (D.G.) R(O). I(M). S. A(V). **Mint:** Höxter **Note:** Ref. I/S-86, 102, 118, 119, 131, 132, 133. Fürstengroschen. Varieties exist.

Date	Mintage	VG	F	VF	XF	Unc
1613 HK(c)	—	20.00	45.00	90.00	180	—
1614 (c)	—	20.00	45.00	90.00	180	—
1615	—	20.00	45.00	90.00	180	—
1615 (c)	—	20.00	45.00	90.00	180	—
1616	—	20.00	45.00	90.00	180	—
1616 (d)	—	20.00	45.00	90.00	180	—

KM# 12.4 1/24 THALER
Silver Weight varies: 1.34-1.68g., 20 mm. **Ruler:** Dietrich IV **Obv:** Spanish shield of 4-fold arms in baroque frame, superimposed on crossed sword and crozier, mitre above **Obv. Legend:** T(H)EOD(OR). D. G. ABB(AS). COR(B)(I). **Rev:** Imperial orb with Z4 divides date **Rev. Legend:** MAT(TH)I(A). (I.) (D.G.) RO. I(M). S(E). A(V)(G). **Mint:** Höxter **Note:** Ref. I/S-92, 93, 111, 112. Fürstengroschen. Varieties exist.

Date	Mintage	VG	F	VF	XF	Unc
1613	—	20.00	45.00	90.00	180	—
1613 HK(c)	—	20.00	45.00	90.00	180	—
1614 (c)	—	20.00	45.00	90.00	180	—

KM# 12.3 1/24 THALER
Silver Weight varies: 1.06-1.96g., 20-21 mm. **Ruler:** Dietrich IV **Obv:** Spanish shield of 4-fold arms in baroque frame, superimposed on crossed sword and crozier, mitre above **Obv. Legend:** T(H)E(O)(D)(D)(OR)(VS). D(E). G(R). AB(B)(AS). C(OR)(B)(I)(E). **Rev:** Imperial orb with Z4, date divided by cross on top **Rev. Legend:** MAT(T)(H)(I)(AS). (D.G.) R(O). I(M)(P). S(EM). A(V)(G). **Mint:** Höxter **Note:** Ref. I/S#89-91, 103-110, 116, 121-125, 137-139. Fürstengroschen. Varieties exist.

Date	Mintage	VG	F	VF	XF	Unc
1613	—	20.00	35.00	75.00	155	—
1613 HK(c)	—	20.00	35.00	75.00	155	—
1613 (c)	—	20.00	35.00	75.00	155	—
1614	—	20.00	35.00	75.00	155	—
1614 (c)	—	20.00	35.00	75.00	155	—
ND(1614) (c)	—	20.00	35.00	75.00	155	—
1615	—	20.00	35.00	75.00	155	—
1615 (c)	—	20.00	35.00	75.00	155	—
1616	—	20.00	35.00	75.00	155	—
1616 (d)	—	20.00	35.00	75.00	155	—

KM# 12.7 1/24 THALER
Silver Weight varies: 1.18-1.76g., 19-21 mm. **Ruler:** Dietrich IV **Obv:** Ornate shield of 4-fold arms, superimposed on crossed sword and crozier, mitre above **Obv. Legend:** T(H)EOD(O)(R). D. G. AB(B). C(O)(R)(B)(I). **Rev:** Imperial orb with Z4, date divided by cross on top **Rev. Legend:** MAT(T)(H)I(AS). D. G. R(O)(M). I(M)(P). S(E). A(V)(G). **Mint:** Höxter **Note:** Ref. I/S#97-99, 113-115, 127-129. Fürstengroschen. Varieties exist.

Date	Mintage	VG	F	VF	XF	Unc
1613	—	20.00	45.00	90.00	180	—
1613 HK(c)	—	20.00	45.00	90.00	180	—
1613 (c)	—	20.00	45.00	90.00	180	—
1614	—	20.00	45.00	90.00	180	—
1614 (c)	—	20.00	45.00	90.00	180	—
1641 (c) error for 1614	—	20.00	45.00	90.00	180	—
1615	—	20.00	45.00	90.00	180	—
1615 (c)	—	20.00	45.00	90.00	180	—

KM# 12.2 1/24 THALER
Silver Weight varies: 1.14-1.55g., 20-21 mm. **Ruler:** Dietrich IV **Obv:** Oval shield of 4-fold arms in baroque frame, superimposed on crossed sword and crozier, mitre above **Obv. Legend:** TEODOR. D. G. ABB. CORB. **Rev:** Imperial orb with Z4 divides date **Rev. Legend:** MATIAS. II. RO. IM. S. A. **Mint:** Höxter **Note:** Ref. I/S-87, 88. Fürstengroschen.

Date	Mintage	VG	F	VF	XF	Unc
1613	—	20.00	45.00	90.00	180	—
1613 HK(c)	—	20.00	45.00	90.00	180	—

KM# 12.5 1/24 THALER
Silver Weight varies: 1.06-1.75g., 20 mm. **Ruler:** Dietrich IV **Obv:** Ornate shield of 4-fold arms, mitre above **Obv. Legend:** TEO(D)(U)OR. D. G. ABBAS. CORB. **Rev:** Imperial orb with Z4, date divided by cross on top **Rev. Legend:** MATI. D. G. RO. I(M). S. A(V). **Mint:** Höxter **Note:** Ref. I/S-94; W-86. Fürstengroschen.

Date	Mintage	VG	F	VF	XF	Unc
1613 HK(c)	—	25.00	50.00	100	200	—

KM# 12.6 1/24 THALER
Silver Weight varies: 1.50-1.77g., 20 mm. **Ruler:** Dietrich IV **Obv:** Ornate shield of 4-fold arms, mitre above **Obv. Legend:** THEOD. D. G. ABBAS. CORB. **Rev:** Imperial orb with Z4 divides date **Rev. Legend:** MATIAS. II. RO. IM. S. A(V). **Mint:** Höxter **Note:** Ref. I/S-95, 96. Fürstengroschen.

Date	Mintage	VG	F	VF	XF	Unc
1613	—	25.00	50.00	100	200	—
1613 HK(c)	—	25.00	50.00	100	200	—

KM# 12.8 1/24 THALER
1.4100 g., Silver, 20 mm. **Ruler:** Dietrich IV **Obv:** Ornate shield of 4-fold arms, superimposed on crossed sword and crozier, mitre above **Obv. Legend:** T(H)EOD(OR). D. G. ABB. COR(B)(I). **Rev:** Imperial orb with Z4 divides date **Rev. Legend:** MATIA(S). (I.) D. G. RO. I(M). S. A(V). **Mint:** Höxter **Note:** Ref. I/S-100, 101. Fürstengroschen. Varieties exist.

Date	Mintage	VG	F	VF	XF	Unc
1613	—	25.00	50.00	100	200	—
1613 HK(c)	—	25.00	45.00	85.00	165	—

KM# 14.1 1/24 THALER
Silver Weight varies: 1.05-1.72g., 19-22 mm. **Ruler:** Dietrich IV **Obv:** Spanish shield of 4-fold arms in baroque frame **Obv. Legend:** T(H)EOD(OR). D. G. ABB(AS). COR(B). **Rev:** Imperial orb with Z4, date divided by cross on top **Rev. Legend:** MAT(H)I. D. G. RO. I(M). S. A(V). **Mint:** Höxter **Note:** Ref. I/S-120, 134-136. Fürstengroschen. Varieties exist.

Date	Mintage	VG	F	VF	XF	Unc
1615	—	20.00	45.00	90.00	180	—
1616	—	20.00	45.00	90.00	180	—
1616 (d)	—	20.00	45.00	90.00	180	—

KM# 14.2 1/24 THALER
1.5400 g., Silver, 21 mm. **Ruler:** Dietrich IV **Obv:** Spanish shield of 4-fold arms in baroque frame, superimposed on 2 crossed croziers, mitre above **Obv. Legend:** THEOD. D. G. ABB. CORBIE. **Rev:** Imperial orb with Z4, date divided by cross on top **Rev. Legend:** MATI. D. G. RO. IMP. S. AV. **Mint:** Höxter **Note:** Ref. I/S-126. Fürstengroschen.

Date	Mintage	VG	F	VF	XF	Unc
1615	—	30.00	50.00	100	210	—

KM# 13.1 1/24 THALER
Silver Weight varies: 0.83-1.28g., 16-19 mm. **Ruler:** Heinrich V **Obv:** Two ornately-shaped shield of arms, superimposed on 2 crossed croziers, mitre above **Obv. Legend:** HENR. D. G. ABB. C(O)(R)(B). **Rev:** Imperial orb with Z4, date divided by cross on top **Rev. Legend:** MAT(I). D. G. R. I(M). S. A(V). **Mint:** Höxter **Note:** Ref. I/S#141-143; W-95, 96. 12 Pfennig. Kipper issue. Varieties exist.

Date	Mintage	VG	F	VF	XF	Unc
1619	—	20.00	40.00	80.00	160	—
1619 (e)	—	20.00	40.00	80.00	160	—

KM# 13.1A 1/24 THALER
3.7900 g., Silver, 19.5x19.5 mm. **Ruler:** Heinrich V **Obv:** Two ornately-shaped shields of arms, superimposed on 2 crossed croziers, mitre above **Obv. Legend:** HENR. D. G. ABB. C. **Rev:** Imperial orb with Z4, date divided by cross on top **Rev. Legend:** MATI. D. G. R. I. S. A. **Mint:** Höxter **Note:** Ref. I/S-141.1. 12 Pfennig. Kipper issue. Klippe.

Date	Mintage	VG	F	VF	XF	Unc
1619	—	—	—	—	—	—

KM# 13.2 1/24 THALER
Silver Weight varies: 0.62-0.91g., 16-17 mm. **Ruler:** Heinrich V **Obv:** Two ornately-shaped shield of arms, superimposed on 2 crossed croziers, mitre above **Obv. Legend:** HENR. D. G. ABB. C. **Rev:** Imperial orb with Z4, date divided by cross on top **Rev. Legend:** FERD. II. D. G. R. I. (S.) (A.) **Mint:** Höxter **Note:** Ref. I/S-147. 12 Pfennig. Kipper issue. Varieties exist.

Date	Mintage	VG	F	VF	XF	Unc
16Z0	—	30.00	65.00	115	225	—
(1)6Z0	—	30.00	65.00	115	225	—
(16)Z0	—	30.00	65.00	115	225	—

KM# 17 1/24 THALER
1.1200 g., Silver, 20 mm. **Ruler:** Johann Christoph **Obv:** Ornate shield of Corvey arms in baroque frame, superimposed on 2 crossed croziers, mitre above **Obv. Legend:** MONE. NO. A. B. C. **Rev:** imperial orb with Z4, date at beginning of legend. **Rev. Legend:** FERD. II. D. G. R. I. **Mint:** Höxter **Note:** Ref. I/S-153. Fürstengroschen. Kipper issue.

Date	Mintage	VG	F	VF	XF	Unc
(16)Z0	—	30.00	65.00	115	225	—

KM# 28 1/24 THALER
1.8000 g., Silver, 23.5 mm. **Ruler:** Johann Christoph **Obv:** Spanish shield of 4-fold arms in baroque frame within circle **Obv. Legend:** MONET. NO. ABBA. CORBE. **Rev:** Imperial orb with 24 divides date **Rev. Legend:** FERD. II. D. G. RO. IM. SE. A. **Mint:** Höxter **Note:** Ref. I/S-169, 174. Fürstengroschen.

Date	Mintage	VG	F	VF	XF	Unc
1622 (f)	—	20.00	40.00	80.00	160	—
1623 (f)	—	20.00	40.00	80.00	160	—

KM# A33 1/24 THALER
Silver **Ruler:** Johann Christoph **Obv:** Oval shield of 4-fold arms, mitre above **Rev:** Imperial orb with 24 divides date **Mint:** Höxter **Note:** Ref. I/S-186. Fürstengroschen.

Date	Mintage	VG	F	VF	XF	Unc
1633 (e)	—	25.00	50.00	100	200	—

KM# 87.1 1/24 THALER
Silver Weight varies: 1.16-1.91g., 21 mm. **Ruler:** Christoph **Obv:** Crowned Spanish shield of 4-fold arms **Obv. Legend:** CHRISTO. D. G. AB. COR(B). **Rev:** Imperial orb with 24, date at end of legend **Rev. Legend:** SACRI. ROM. IMP. PR. **Mint:** Höxter **Note:** Ref. I/S-288; W-165. Groschen.

Date	Mintage	VG	F	VF	XF	Unc
1683	—	20.00	40.00	80.00	160	—

KM# 87.2 1/24 THALER
1.8400 g., Silver, 21 mm. **Ruler:** Christoph **Obv:** Crowned ornate Spanish shield of 4-fold arms in baroque frame **Obv. Legend:** CHRISTOPH. D. G. AB. CORB. **Rev:** Imperial orb with 24, date at end of legend **Rev. Legend:** DES. HEILIGEN. R. R. F. ANNO. **Mint:** Höxter **Note:** Ref. I/S-289; W-166. Groschen.

Date	Mintage	VG	F	VF	XF	Unc
1683	—	20.00	40.00	75.00	150	—

KM# 87.3 1/24 THALER
Silver Weight varies: 1.30-1.66g., 21 mm. **Ruler:** Christoph **Obv:** Crowned ornately-shaped shield of 4-fold arms superimposed on crossed sword and crozier **Obv. Legend:** CHRISTO. D. G. AB. COR. **Rev:** Imperial orb with 24, date at end of legend **Rev. Legend:** SACRI. ROM. IMP. PR. **Mint:** Höxter **Note:** Ref. I/S-290. Groschen.

Date	Mintage	VG	F	VF	XF	Unc
1683	—	20.00	40.00	75.00	150	—

KM# 87.4 1/24 THALER
Silver Weight varies: 1.05-1.72g., 21 mm. **Ruler:** Christoph **Obv:** Crowned ornately-shaped shield of 4-fold arms, superimposed on crossed sword and crozier, palm frond at left and right **Obv. Legend:** CHRISTO. D. G. AB. COR(B). **Rev:** Imperial orb with 24, date at end of legend **Rev. Legend:** SACRI. ROM. IMP. PR. **Mint:** Höxter **Note:** Ref. I/S-291. Groschen.

Date	Mintage	VG	F	VF	XF	Unc
1683	—	35.00	75.00	135	240	—

KM# 21.1 1/21 THALER (Schilling)
Silver Weight varies: 1.64-2.46g., 25 mm. **Ruler:** Johann Christoph **Obv:** Heart-shaped shield of 4-fold arms in baroque frame, superimposed on 2 crossed croziers, mitre above divides date **Obv. Legend:** MO. NO. ABB(A). CORBE(I)(I). **Rev:** Crowned imperial eagle, orb on breast **Rev. Legend:** LANTMVNZ. (Z1) (XXI). ZVM. R. D(A). **Mint:** Höxter **Note:** Ref. I/S-162; W-100. Kipper issue. Varieties exist.

Date	Mintage	VG	F	VF	XF	Unc
16Z1	—	25.00	45.00	90.00	185	—
1621	—	25.00	45.00	90.00	185	—

KM# 21.2 1/21 THALER (Schilling)
Silver Weight varies: 1.56-2.68g., 24-26 mm. **Ruler:** Johann Christoph **Obv:** Heart-shaped shield of 4-fold arms in baroque frame, superimposed on 2 crossed croziers, mitre above divides date **Obv. Legend:** MO. NO. ABB(A)(S). CORBEI(I). **Rev:** Crowned imperial eagle, Z1 in orb on breast **Rev. Legend:** LANTMVN(T)Z. (Z1) (XXI). ZVM. R. D(A)(L). **Mint:** Höxter **Note:** Ref. I/S-163; W-100. Kipper issue. Varieties exist.

Date	Mintage	VG	F	VF	XF	Unc
16Z1	—	25.00	45.00	90.00	185	—
(16)Z1	—	25.00	45.00	90.00	185	—

KM# 22 1/21 THALER (Schilling)
2.2200 g., Silver, 27 mm. **Ruler:** Johann Christoph **Obv:** Oval shield of 4-fold arms in baroque frame, superimposed on 2 crossed croziers, date at end of legend **Obv. Legend:** MO. NO. ABB. CORBEI. **Rev:** Crowned imperial eagle, Z1 in orb on breast **Rev. Legend:** LANT. MVNTZ. Z1. ZVM R(I). D(AL). **Mint:** Höxter **Note:** Ref. I/S-161. Kipper issue. Varieties exist.

Date	Mintage	VG	F	VF	XF	Unc
(16)Z1	—	25.00	45.00	90.00	185	—

KM# A15 1/16 THALER (Doppelschilling)
2.4400 g., Silver, 24 mm. **Ruler:** Dietrich IV **Obv:** Oval shield of 4-fold arms in baroque frame, superimposed on crossed sword and crozier, mitre above **Obv. Legend:** TEODOR. D. G. ABB. CORBI. **Rev:** Crowned imperial eagle, 16 in orb on breast, date divided by crown on top **Rev. Legend:** MATI. D. G. - RO I S A. **Mint:** Höxter **Note:** Ref. I/S-117.

Date	Mintage	VG	F	VF	XF	Unc
1615	—	—	—	—	—	—

KM# 59 1/4 THALER
Silver Weight varies: 7.03-7.36., 30 mm. **Ruler:** Arnold IV **Obv:** Spanish shield of 4-fold arms, superimposed on crossed sword and crozier, divides date and mintmaster's initials, mitre above, value 4 in semi-oval at top **Obv. Legend:** ARNOLDVS. D. G. EL. E. CONF. AB. CORBEIENS. **Rev:** Full-length standing figure of St. Vitus holding book and palm branch **Rev. Legend:** SANCTVS. VITVS. PATRONVS. CORBEIENSI. **Mint:** Höxter **Note:** Ref. I/S-240; W-121.

Date	Mintage	VG	F	VF	XF	Unc
1657 VFH	—	—	—	—	—	—

KM# 51 1/2 THALER
Silver Weight varies: 14.36-14.38g., 35 mm. **Ruler:** Arnold IV **Obv:** Full-length standing figure of St. Vitus divides date **Obv. Legend:** SANCTVS. VITVS. PATRON. CORB. **Rev:** Crucifix divides MRA - IOES **Rev. Legend:** IN. ÆTER. VERBV. - DOMINI. MANET. **Mint:** Höxter **Note:** Ref. I/S-215; W-119. Known struck on thick flan, weighing 21.50-22.50g.

Date	Mintage	VG	F	VF	XF	Unc
165Z	—	—	—	—	—	—

KM# A56 1/2 THALER
14.3000 g., Silver, 36 mm. **Ruler:** Arnold IV **Obv:** Oval shield of 4-fold arms in baroque frame, mitre above, top of crozier in margin, 2 ornate helmets to upper left and right **Obv. Legend:** D. G. ARNOLD. EL. ET. COM. ABBA. **Rev:** Full-length facing figure of St. Vitus, holding book and palm branch, date divided at lower left and right **Rev. Legend:** SANCTVS. VITVS. PATRON. CORB. **Mint:** Höxter **Note:** Ref. I/S-222.

Date	Mintage	VG	F	VF	XF	Unc
1654	—	—	—	—	—	—

KM# 60 1/2 THALER
Silver Weight varies: 14.16-14.33g., 37 mm. **Ruler:** Arnold IV **Obv:** Oval shield of 4-fold arms, superimposed on 2 crossed croziers, divides date and mintmaster's initials, mitre above, ornate helmet at left and right **Obv. Legend:** ARNOLDVS. D. G. EL. E. CONF. AB. CORBE. **Rev:** Full-length standing figure of St. Vitus **Rev. Legend:** SANCTVS. VITVS. PATRONVS. CORBEIE. **Mint:** Höxter **Note:** Ref. I/S-239; W-120.

Date	Mintage	VG	F	VF	XF	Unc
1657 VFH	—	—	—	—	—	—

KM# 65.1 16 GUTE GROSCHEN (Gulden)
Silver Weight varies: 16.66-16.74g., 38 mm. **Ruler:** Christoph **Obv:** Crowned shield of 4-fold arms, superimposed on crossed sword and crozier, between 2 palm branches **Obv. Legend:** CHRIST. EL. E. CONF. AB. COR. S. R. I. P. **Rev:** 3 or 4-line inscription in circle, date at end of legend **Rev. Legend:** CANDORE. ET. AMORE. **Rev. Inscription:** 16 / GUTE (/) GR (/) OS(G)(CH) (/) EN. **Mint:** Höxter **Note:** Ref. I/S-261; W-159a; Dav. 493.

Date	Mintage	VG	F	VF	XF	Unc
1682	—	200	400	575	1,100	—

KM# 65.2 16 GUTE GROSCHEN (Gulden)
16.6500 g., Silver, 38 mm. **Ruler:** Christoph **Obv:** Crowned oval shield of 4-fold arms in baroque frame, superimposed on crossed sword and crozier **Obv. Legend:** CHRIST. EL. E. CONF. AB. COR. S. R. I. P. **Rev:** 4-line inscription in circle, date at end of legend **Rev. Legend:** CANDORE. ET. AMORE. **Rev. Inscription:** 16 / GUTE / GROSG / EN. **Mint:** Höxter **Note:** Ref. I/S-260; Dav. 493.

Date	Mintage	VG	F	VF	XF	Unc
1682	—	200	400	575	1,100	—

KM# 65.3 16 GUTE GROSCHEN (Gulden)
16.0600 g., Silver, 37 mm. **Ruler:** Christoph **Obv:** Crowned Spanish shield of 4-fold arms with oramented sides, superimposed on crossed sword and crozier **Obv. Legend:** CHRIST. EL. E. CONF. AB. COR. S. R. I. P. **Rev:** 3-line inscription in circle, date at end of legend **Rev. Legend:** CANDORE. ET. AMORE. **Rev. Inscription:** 16 / GUTE GR / OSGEN. **Mint:** Höxter **Note:** Ref. I/S-262.

Date	Mintage	VG	F	VF	XF	Unc
1682	—	200	400	575	1,100	—

KM# 66.1 16 GUTE GROSCHEN (Gulden)
Silver Weight varies: 15.44-16.80g., 37 mm. **Ruler:** Christoph **Obv:** Crowned shield of 4-fold arms, superimposed on crossed sword and crozier, between 2 palm branches **Obv. Legend:** CHRIST. EL. E. CONF. AB. COR. S. R. I. P. **Rev:** 4-line inscription, date at end of legend **Rev. Legend:** IN DOMINO CONFIDO. **Rev. Inscription:** 16 / GUTE / GROSCH / EN. **Mint:** Höxter **Note:** Ref. I/S-263; W-159b; Dav. 495.

Date	Mintage	VG	F	VF	XF	Unc
1682	—	200	400	575	1,100	—

KM# 66.2 16 GUTE GROSCHEN (Gulden)
16.8400 g., Silver, 37 mm. **Ruler:** Christoph **Obv:** Crowned Spanish shield of 4-fold arms with ornamented sides, superimposed on crossed sword and crozier **Obv. Legend:** CHRIST. EL. E. CONF. AB. COR. S. R. I. P. **Rev:** 4-line inscription in circle, date at end of legend **Rev. Legend:** IN DOMINO. CONFIDO. **Rev. Inscription:** 16 / GUTE / GROSCH / EN. **Mint:** Höxter **Note:** Ref. I/S-264.

Date	Mintage	VG	F	VF	XF	Unc
1682	—	200	400	575	1,100	—

KM# 67 16 GUTE GROSCHEN (Gulden)
Silver Weight varies: 16.59-16.78g., 38 mm. **Ruler:** Christoph **Obv:** Crowned script double ACC monogram, palm fronds crossed below **Obv. Legend:** CHRIST. EL. E. CONF. AB. COR. S. R. I. P. **Rev:** 4-line inscription in circle, date at end of legend **Rev. Legend:** CANDORE ET AMORE. **Rev. Inscription:** 16 / GUTE (/) GR (/) OS(G)(CH) (/) EN. **Mint:** Höxter **Note:** Ref. I/S-254; W-155b; Dav. 494.

Date	Mintage	VG	F	VF	XF	Unc
1682	—	2,750	3,500	4,200	6,500	—

KM# 68 16 GUTE GROSCHEN (Gulden)
Silver Weight varies: 14.56-16.64g., 37 mm. **Ruler:** Christoph **Obv:** Crowned script double AC monogram **Obv. Legend:** CHRIST. EL. E. CONF. AB. COR. S. R. I. P. **Rev:** 4-line inscription in circle, date at end of legend **Rev. Legend:** IN DOMINO CONFIDO. **Rev. Inscription:** 16 / GUTE / GROSCH / EN. **Mint:** Höxter **Note:** Ref. I/S-255; W-155a.

Date	Mintage	VG	F	VF	XF	Unc
1682	—	—	—	—	—	—

KM# 94 16 GUTE GROSCHEN (Gulden)
Silver Weight varies: 14.49-16.80g., 37-38 mm. **Ruler:** Christoph **Obv:** Crowned script double CDGAC monogram **Obv. Legend:** CHRIST. EL. E. CONF. AB. COR. S. R. I. P. **Rev:** 4-line inscription, date at end of legend **Rev. Legend:** CANDORE ET AMORE. **Rev. Inscription:** 16 / GUTE / GROSG / EN. **Mint:** Höxter **Note:** Ref. I/S-305, 309; Dav. 496. Varieties exist.

Date	Mintage	VG	F	VF	XF	Unc
1684 (i)	—	—	—	—	—	—

KM# 95 16 GUTE GROSCHEN (Gulden)
16.7500 g., Silver, 37 mm. **Ruler:** Christoph **Obv:** Bust to right in circle **Obv. Legend:** CHRISTOP. D. G. EL. E. CONF. AB. COR. S. R. I. P. **Rev:** 4-line inscription, date at end of legend **Rev. Legend:** CANDORE ET AMORE. **Rev. Inscription:** 16 / GUTE / GROSG / EN. **Mint:** Höxter **Note:** Ref. I/S-303; W-151; Dav. 497.

Date	Mintage	VG	F	VF	XF	Unc
1684 (i)	—	275	450	800	1,400	—

KM# 96 16 GUTE GROSCHEN (Gulden)
Silver Weight varies: 16.55-16.77g., 37 mm. **Ruler:** Christoph **Obv:** Crowned oval shield of 4-fold arms in baroque frame, superimposed on crossed sword and crozier **Obv. Legend:** CHRIST. EL. E. CONF. AB. COR. S. R. I. P. **Rev:** 4-line inscription, date at end of legend **Rev. Legend:** CANDORE. ET. AMORE. **Rev. Inscription:** 16 / GUTE / GROSG / EN. **Mint:** Höxter **Note:** Ref. I/S-313; W-158B; Dav. 498.

Date	Mintage	VG	F	VF	XF	Unc
1684 (i)	—	—	—	—	—	—

KM# 79.1 2/3 THALER (Gulden)
Silver Weight varies: 13.13-18.80g., 38-40 mm. **Ruler:** Christoph **Obv:** Bust to right in circle **Obv. Legend:** CHRIST(O)P(H). EL. E. CON(E)F. AB. COR. S. R. I. P(R). **Rev:** Crowned ornate shield of 4-fold arms, superimposed on crossed sword and crozier, palm fronds at left and right, 2/3 in oval below, date at end of legend **Rev. Legend:** CANDORE ET - AMORE. **Mint:** Höxter **Note:** Ref. I/S-248, 268, 269; W-144, 146, 147; Dav. 479, 481, 483. Varieties exist.

Date	Mintage	VG	F	VF	XF	Unc
1682	—	200	400	850	1,750	3,500
1683	—	165	325	750	1,500	3,000

KM# 76 2/3 THALER (Gulden)
Silver Weight varies: 16.28-16.97g., 39-40 mm. **Ruler:** Christoph **Obv:** Bust to right in circle **Obv. Legend:** CHRISTOPH. EL. E. CONF. AB. COR. S. R. I. P. **Rev:** Large 2/3 in wreath, date at top in margin **Rev. Legend:** CANDORE ET AMORE. **Mint:** Höxter **Note:** Ref. I/S-249, 272; W-145a, 149; Dav. 477.

Date	Mintage	VG	F	VF	XF	Unc
1682	—	1,000	1,800	2,600	3,800	—
1683	—	1,000	1,800	2,600	3,800	—

KM# 80.3 2/3 THALER (Gulden)
Silver Weight varies: 15.49-16.76g., 37 mm. **Ruler:** Christoph **Obv:** Crowned script double CAC monogram **Obv. Legend:** CHRIST. EL. E. CONF. AB. COR. S. R. I. P. **Rev:** Large 2/3 in circle, date at end of legend **Rev. Legend:** CANDORE ET AMORE. **Mint:** Höxter **Note:** Ref. I/S-252, 308; W-153A; Dav. 484. Varieties exist.

Date	Mintage	VG	F	VF	XF	Unc
1682	—	375	600	850	1,450	—
1684 (i)	—	1,500	2,200	2,800	4,750	—

KM# 77 2/3 THALER (Gulden)
Silver Weight varies: 16.31-16.95g., 38-40 mm. **Ruler:** Christoph **Obv:** Bust to right in circle **Obv. Legend:** CHRISTOPH. EL. E. CONF. AB. COR. S. R. I. P. **Rev:** Large 2/3 in circle, date at top in margin **Rev. Legend:** CANDORE ET AMORE. **Mint:** Höxter **Note:** Ref. I/S-250, 273, 274; W-145b; Dav. 477.

Date	Mintage	VG	F	VF	XF	Unc
1682	—	190	375	600	1,100	—

KM# 78 2/3 THALER (Gulden)
Silver Weight varies: 16.79-16.93g., 41 mm. **Ruler:** Christoph **Obv:** Bust to right in circle **Obv. Legend:** CHRISTOPH. EL. E. CONF. AB. COR. S. R. I. P. **Rev:** Large 2/3 in circle **Rev. Legend:** CANDORE ET AMORE. **Mint:** Höxter **Note:** Ref. I/S-315; W-150A/B; Dav. 478.

Date	Mintage	VG	F	VF	XF	Unc
ND(1682)	—	500	875	1,400	2,400	—

KM# 80.1 2/3 THALER (Gulden)
Silver Weight varies: 15.12-16.68g., 40 mm. **Ruler:** Christoph **Obv:** Crowned script double CAC monogram, palm fronds crossed below **Obv. Legend:** CHRIST. EL. E. CONF. AB. COR. S. R. I. P. **Rev:** Large 2/3 in circle, date at end of legend **Rev. Legend:** CANDORE ET AMORE. **Mint:** Höxter **Note:** Ref. I/S-251; W-153.

Date	Mintage	VG	F	VF	XF	Unc
1682	—	—	—	—	—	—

KM# 80.2 2/3 THALER (Gulden)
16.8500 g., Silver, 37 mm. **Ruler:** Christoph **Obv:** Crowned script double AC monogram **Obv. Legend:** CHRIST. EL. E. CONF. AB. COR. S. R. I. P. **Rev:** Large 2/3, 4 small ornamental diamonds around, all in circle, date at end of legend **Rev. Legend:** IN DOMINO CONFIDO. **Mint:** Höxter **Note:** Ref. I/S-253.

Date	Mintage	VG	F	VF	XF	Unc
1682	—	—	—	—	—	—

KM# 82 2/3 THALER (Gulden)
17.0100 g., Silver, 38-40 mm. **Ruler:** Christoph **Obv:** Crowned shield of 4-fold arms, superimposed on crossed sword and crozier, between 2 crossed palm branches **Obv. Legend:** CHRIST. EL. E. CONF. AB. COR. S. R. I. P. **Rev:** Large 2/3 with 4 small diamonds around, in circle, date at end of legend **Rev. Legend:** IN DOMINO CONFIDO. **Mint:** Höxter **Note:** Ref. I/S-258, 259; W-158.

Date	Mintage	VG	F	VF	XF	Unc
1682	—	—	—	—	—	—

KM# 81 2/3 THALER (Gulden)
Silver Weight varies: 16.41-16.86g., 38-39 mm. **Ruler:** Christoph **Obv:** Crowned script double ChAC monogram **Obv. Legend:** CHRIST. EL. E. CON. AB. COR. S. R. I. P. **Rev:** Large 2/3 in circle, date at end of legend, where present **Rev. Legend:** CANDORE ET AMORE **Mint:** Höxter **Note:** Ref. I/S-276, 277, 318; Dav. 485. Varieties exist.

Date	Mintage	VG	F	VF	XF	Unc
1683	—	—	—	—	—	—
ND(1684)	—	1,600	3,000	5,500	—	—

KM# 79.2 2/3 THALER (Gulden)
17.2200 g., Silver, 38 mm. **Ruler:** Christoph **Obv:** Bust to right in circle **Obv. Legend:** CHRISTOPH. EL. E. CONF. AB. COR. S. R. I. P. **Rev:** Large 2/3 in circle, date at end of legend **Rev. Legend:** CANDORE. ET. AMORE. **Mint:** Höxter **Note:** Ref. I/S-275.

Date	Mintage	VG	F	VF	XF	Unc
1683	—	—	—	—	—	—

KM# 79.3 2/3 THALER (Gulden)
16.5600 g., Silver, 39 mm. **Ruler:** Christoph **Obv:** Bust to right in circle **Obv. Legend:** CHRISTOPH. EL. E. CONF. AB. COR. S. R. I. P. **Rev:** Large 2/3, 4 small diamonds around, all in circle **Rev. Legend:** CHRISTOPH. EL. E. CONF. AB. COR. S. R. I. P. **Mint:** Höxter **Note:** Ref. I/S-316.

Date	Mintage	VG	F	VF	XF	Unc
ND(1683)	—	—	—	—	—	—

KM# 89 2/3 THALER (Gulden)
Silver Weight varies: 14.29-17.28g., 39 mm. **Ruler:** Christoph **Obv:** Bust to right in circle **Obv. Legend:** CHRIST(OPH). EL. E. CON. A(B). COR. S. R. I. P. **Rev:** Large 2/3 divides date 1 - 6 / 8 - 3 in circle **Rev. Legend:** CANDORE. ET AMORE. **Mint:** Höxter **Note:** Ref. I/S-278; W-150a; Dav. 480.

Date	Mintage	VG	F	VF	XF	Unc
1683	—	190	375	600	1,100	—

KM# 90 2/3 THALER (Gulden)
16.9800 g., Silver, 40 mm. **Ruler:** Christoph **Obv:** Bust to right in circle, date at end of legend **Obv. Legend:** CHRIST. EL. E. CON. A(B). COR. S. R. I. P. **Rev:** Large 2/3 in circle **Rev. Legend:** CANDORE ET AMORE. **Mint:** Höxter **Note:** Ref. I/S-279; W-150b; Dav. 480A.

Date	Mintage	VG	F	VF	XF	Unc
1683	—	—	—	—	—	—

KM# 91.1 2/3 THALER (Gulden)
17.1100 g., Silver, 39 mm. **Ruler:** Christoph **Obv:** Large 2/3, 4 small ornamental diamonds around, all in circle **Obv. Legend:** CHRISTO(PH). EL. E. CON(F). A(B). COR. S. R. I. P. **Rev:** Crowned ornately-shaped shield of 4-fold arms, superimposed on crossed sword and crozier, date at end of legend **Rev. Legend:** CANDORE. ET. AMORE. **Mint:** Höxter **Note:** Ref. I/S-281; W-161; Dav. 482.

Date	Mintage	VG	F	VF	XF	Unc
1683	—	—	—	—	—	—

KM# 91.2 2/3 THALER (Gulden)
16.0200 g., Silver, 39 mm. **Ruler:** Christoph **Obv:** Large 2/3, 4 small ornamental diamonds around, all in circle **Obv. Legend:** CHRISTOPH. EL. E. CON. A. COR. S. R. I. P. **Rev:** Crowned ornately-shaped shield of 4-fold arms, superimposed on crossed sword and crozier, value (2/3) in oval below, date at end of legend **Rev. Legend:** CANDORE. ET - AMORE. **Mint:** Höxter **Note:** Ref. I/S-282.

Date	Mintage	VG	F	VF	XF	Unc
1683	—	—	—	—	—	—

KM# 91.3 2/3 THALER (Gulden)
Silver, 38-40 mm. **Ruler:** Christoph **Obv:** Large 2/3 in circle **Obv. Legend:** CHRISTO. EL. E. CONF. AB. COR. S. R. I. P. **Rev:** Crowned ornate shield of 4-fold arms, superimposed on crossed sword and crozier, palm fronds at sides, value (2/3) in oval below, date at end of legend **Rev. Legend:** CANDORE ET - AMORE. **Mint:** Höxter **Note:** Ref. I/S-283.

Date	Mintage	VG	F	VF	XF	Unc
1683	—	—	—	—	—	—

KM# 91.4 2/3 THALER (Gulden)
Silver Weight varies: 16.81-17.02g., 40 mm. **Ruler:** Christoph **Obv:** Large 2/3 divides date as 1 - 6 / 8 - 3 in circle **Obv. Legend:** CHRIST(OPH). EL. E. CON. AB. COR. S. R. I. P. **Rev:** Crowned ornate shield of 4-fold arms, superimposed on crossed sword and crozier, palm fronds at sides, value (2/3) in oval blow, date at end of legend **Rev. Legend:** CANDORE. ET - AMORE. **Mint:** Höxter **Note:** Ref. I/S-280. Mule.

Date	Mintage	VG	F	VF	XF	Unc
1683//1683	—	—	—	—	—	—

KM# 91.5 2/3 THALER (Gulden)
16.8200 g., Silver, 39 mm. **Ruler:** Christoph **Obv:** Large 2/3 divides date as 1 - 6 / 8 - 3 in circle **Obv. Legend:** CHRIST. EL. E. CON. AB. COR. S. R. I. P. **Rev:** Crowned script double ChAC monogram **Rev. Legend:** CANDORE. ET. AMORE. **Mint:** Höxter **Note:** Ref. I/S-284.

Date	Mintage	VG	F	VF	XF	Unc
1683	—	—	—	—	—	—

KM# 97 2/3 THALER (Gulden)
Silver Weight varies: 16.38-17.98g., 40 mm. **Ruler:** Christoph **Obv:** Bust to left in circle **Obv. Legend:** CHRISTOPH. EL. E. CONF. AB. COR. S. R. I. P. **Rev:** Crowned ornate shield of 4-fold arms, superimposed on crossed sword and crozier, palm fronds at sides, value (2/3) in oval below, date at end of legend **Rev. Legend:** CANDORE. ET - AMORE. **Mint:** Höxter **Note:** Ref. I/S-271; W-148.

Date	Mintage	VG	F	VF	XF	Unc
1683	—	200	400	700	1,250	—

KM# 98 2/3 THALER (Gulden)
16.5600 g., Silver, 37 mm. **Ruler:** Christoph **Obv:** Crowned script double CChAC monogram **Obv. Legend:** CHRIST. EL. E. CONF. AB. COR. S. R. I. P. **Rev:** Large 2/3 in circle, date at end of legend **Rev. Legend:** CANDORE. ET. AMORE. **Mint:** Höxter **Note:** Ref. I/S-304.

Date	Mintage	VG	F	VF	XF	Unc
1684 (i)	—	1,200	2,200	3,800	—	—

KM# 99.1 2/3 THALER (Gulden)
16.5600 g., Silver, 37 mm. **Ruler:** Christoph **Obv:** Crowned oval shield of 4-fold arms in baroque frame, superimposed on crossed sword and crozier **Obv. Legend:** CHRIST. EL. E. CONF. AB. COR. S. R. I. P. **Rev:** Large 2/3 in circle, date at end of legend **Rev. Legend:** CANDORE ET AMORE. **Mint:** Höxter **Note:** Ref. I/S-312; W-158A; Dav. 486.

Date	Mintage	VG	F	VF	XF	Unc
1684 (i)	—	—	—	—	—	—

KM# 99.2 2/3 THALER (Gulden)
16.9000 g., Silver, 39 mm. **Ruler:** Christoph **Obv:** Bust to right in circle **Obv. Legend:** CHRISTOPH. EL. E. CONF. AB. COR. S. R. I. P. **Rev:** Crowned ornately-shaped shield of 4-fold arms, superimposed on crossed sword and crozier, date at end of legend **Rev. Legend:** CANDORE. ET. AMORE. **Mint:** Höxter **Note:** Ref. I/S-270.

Date	Mintage	VG	F	VF	XF	Unc
1684	—	—	—	—	—	—

KM# 105 2/3 THALER (Gulden)
Silver Weight varies: 14.21-15.78g., 36-40 mm. **Ruler:** Christoph **Obv:** Crowned script double CAC monogram **Obv. Legend:** CHRIST. EL. E. CONF. AB. COR. S. R. I. P. **Rev:** Large 2/3 with 4 small diamonds around, in circle, date at end of legend **Rev. Legend:** IN DOMINO CONFIDO. **Mint:** Höxter **Note:** Ref. I/S-328; W-154; Dav. 487.

Date	Mintage	VG	F	VF	XF	Unc
1690	—	1,750	2,500	3,500	5,500	—

KM# 6 THALER
28.7100 g., Silver, 45 mm. **Ruler:** Dietrich IV **Obv:** Full-length standing figure of St. Vitus divides S - V and 2 small shields of arms, date divided at top **Obv. Legend:** THEODORVS. D. G. - A - BBAS. CORBIEN. **Rev:** Crowned imperial eagle, Z4 in orb on breast **Rev. Legend:** RVDOLP. II. D. G. ROMANOR. IIMP. SEMP. AVG. **Mint:** Höxter **Note:** Ref. I/S-56; W-82; Dav. 5182. 24 Groschen.

Date	Mintage	VG	F	VF	XF	Unc
1607 HL Rare	—	—	—	—	—	—

KM# 10 THALER
Silver Weight varies: 28.87-29.09g., 43 mm. **Ruler:** Dietrich IV **Obv:** Full-length standing figure of St. Vitus, 2 small shields of arms at left and right **Obv. Legend:** TEODORVS. D. G. ABBAS. CORBE. **Rev:** Crowned imperial eagle, orb on breast, crown divides date at top **Rev. Legend:** MATIAS. II. D. G. ROMA. IMP. SEM. AVG. **Mint:** Höxter **Note:** Ref. I/S-65, 130; W-83. Dav. 5184.

Date	Mintage	VG	F	VF	XF	Unc
161Z Rare	—	—	—	—	—	—

Note: A VF example realized approximately $11,250 in a September 2003 USB auction.

Date	Mintage	VG	F	VF	XF	Unc
1616 Rare	—	—	—	—	—	—

KM# 18 THALER
28.7900 g., Silver, 42 mm. **Ruler:** Heinrich V **Obv:** Oval shield of 4-fold arms in baroque frame, superimposed on 2 crossed croziers, mitre above **Obv. Legend:** HENRICVS. D. G. ABBAS. CORBEIENSIS. **Rev:** Crowned imperial eagle, orb on breast, date divided by crown at top **Rev. Legend:** FERDINAND. II. D. G. ROM. IMP. SEMP. AV. **Mint:** Höxter **Note:** Ref. I/S-144; W-91; Dav. 5185.

Date	Mintage	VG	F	VF	XF	Unc
16Z0 Rare	—	—	—	—	—	—

KM# 29 THALER
Silver Weight varies: 28.73-28.99g., 42 mm. **Ruler:** Johann Christoph **Obv:** Ornate shield of 4-fold arms, superimposed on 2 crossed croziers, mitre above **Obv. Legend:** D. G. IOAN(N). CHRISTOP. EL. ET. CONF. ABB. CORB. **Rev:** Crowned imperial eagle, orb on breast, date divided by crown at top **Rev. Legend:** FERDINAN. II. D. G. RO. IM. SEM. AUG. **Mint:** Höxter **Note:** Ref. I/S-179; W-106; Dav. 5186. Prev. KM#24.

Date	Mintage	VG	F	VF	XF	Unc
1624 Rare	—	—	—	—	—	—

KM# 32 THALER

Silver Weight varies: 28.36-29.03g., 43-45 mm. **Ruler:** Johann Christoph **Obv:** Oval shield of 4-fold arms in baroque frame, superimposed on 2 crossed croziers, mitre above divides date **Obv. Legend:** IOAN. CHRISTOP(H). D. G. ABB(AS). CORBEIE(N)(S)(IS). **Rev:** Full-length figure of St. Vitus **Rev. Legend:** SANCTVS. VITVS. PATRONVS. CORBEI(E)N(S). **Mint:** Höxter **Note:** Ref. I/S-180, 183; W-107, 108; Dav. 5187, 5188. Varieties exist.

Date	Mintage	VG	F	VF	XF	Unc
1631 (e)	—	1,750	3,500	6,000	—	—
1632 (e)	—	1,750	3,500	6,000	—	—

KM# 50 THALER

Silver Weight varies: 28.17-29.25g., 44 mm. **Ruler:** Arnold IV **Obv:** Oval shield of 4-fold arms in baroque frame, mitre above between 2 ornate helmets **Obv. Legend:** D. G. ARNOLD. EL. ET. CONF. ABBA. CORBE. **Rev:** Full-length figure of St. Vitus, date at end of legend **Rev. Legend:** SANCTVS. VITVS. PATRONVS. **Mint:** Höxter **Note:** Ref. I/S-208; W-115; Dav. 5190.

Date	Mintage	VG	F	VF	XF	Unc
1650 Rare	—	—	—	—	—	—

KM# 52 THALER

28.0800 g., Silver, 44 mm. **Ruler:** Arnold IV **Obv:** Oval shield of 4-fold arms in baroque frame, mitre above, ornate helmet to right, sword hilt to left **Obv. Legend:** D. G. ARNOLD. EL. ET. CONF. ABBA. CORBE. **Rev:** Full-length figure of St. Vitus, date at end of legend **Rev. Legend:** SANCTVS. VITVS. PATRONVS. **Mint:** Höxter **Note:** Ref. I/S-214; W-115a; Dav. 5192.

Date	Mintage	VG	F	VF	XF	Unc
165Z	—	2,000	4,000	6,500	9,500	—

KM# 57.1 THALER

Silver Weight varies: 28.83-29.33g., 42 mm. **Ruler:** Arnold IV **Obv:** Oval shield, with top and bottom curled inward, of 4-fold arms, superimposed on 2 crossed croziers, mitre above, sword hilt at upper left, ornate helmet at upper right, date and mintmaster's initials divided at lower left and right **Obv. Legend:** ARNOLDVS. DEI. GRATIA. EL. E. CONFIR. AB. CORB. **Rev:** Full-length facing figure of St. Vitus holding book and palm branch **Rev. Legend:** SANCTVS. VITVS. PATRONVS. CORBEIENSIS. **Mint:** Höxter **Note:** Ref. I/S-234; W-116; Dav. 5194.

Date	Mintage	VG	F	VF	XF	Unc
1656 VFH	—	750	1,450	2,750	4,750	—

KM# 57.2 THALER

Silver Weight varies: 28.53-29.22g., 41 mm. **Ruler:** Arnold IV **Obv:** Oval shield of 4-fold arms, superimposed on 2 crossed croziers, divides date and mintmaster's initials, mitre above, ornate helmet at left and right **Obv. Legend:** ARNOLDVS. DEI. GRATIA. EL. E. CON. AB. CORB. **Rev:** Full-length standing figure of St. Vitus holding book and palm branch **Rev. Legend:** SANCTVS. VITVS. PATRONVS. CORBEIENSIS. **Mint:** Höxter **Note:** Ref. I/S-238; W-117; Dav. 5195.

Date	Mintage	VG	F	VF	XF	Unc
1657 VFH	—	1,250	2,500	4,500	7,500	—

KM# 92.1 THALER

Silver Weight varies: 27.75-29.21g., 49 mm. **Ruler:** Christoph **Obv:** Oval shield of 4-fold arms in baroque frame, 3 ornate helmets and mitre above **Obv. Legend:** CHRISTOPHORVS. D. G. ELECT. ET. CONF. ABBAS. CORBEI. S. R. I. P. **Rev:** 3/4-length figure of St. Vitus holdig palm branch and book on which a bird is standing, date at end of legend **Rev. Legend:** SACTVS. VITVS. PATRONVS. CORBEIENSIS. **Mint:** Höxter **Note:** Ref. I/S-266; W-136; Dav. 5197.

Date	Mintage	VG	F	VF	XF	Unc
1683 GB	—	450	850	1,650	2,850	—

KM# 92.2 THALER

Silver Weight varies: 28.00-29.59g., 50 mm. **Ruler:** Christoph **Obv:** Oval shield of 4-fold arms in baroque frame, 3 ornate helmets and mitre above **Obv. Legend:** CHRISTOPHORVS. D. G. ELECT. ET. COF. ABBAS. CORBEI. S. R. I. P. **Rev:** 3/4-length figure of St. Vitus holding palm branch and book on which a bird is standing, lion's head at lower right, date at end of legend **Rev. Legend:** SANCTVS. VITVS. PATRONVS. CORBEIENSIS. **Mint:** Höxter **Note:** Ref. I/S-322; W-137; Dav. 5198.

Date	Mintage	VG	F	VF	XF	Unc
1686	—	850	1,600	2,250	3,200	—

KM# 92.3 THALER

Silver Weight varies: 28.73-33.51g., 50 mm. **Ruler:** Christoph **Obv:** Oval shield of 4-fold arms in baroque frame, 3 ornate helmets and mitre above, mintmaster's initials divided by bottom of arms **Obv. Legend:** CHRISTOPHORVS. D. G. ELECT. ET. CONF. ABBAS. CORBEI. S. R. I. P. **Rev:** 3/4-length figure of St. Vitus holding palm branch and book on which a bird is standing, date at end of legend **Rev. Legend:** SANCTVS. VITVS. PATRONVS. CORBEIENSIS. **Mint:** Höxter **Note:** Ref. I/S-321; W-137; Dav. 5198A.

Date	Mintage	VG	F	VF	XF	Unc
1686 GIH	—	850	1,600	2,250	3,200	—

KM# 100.1 THALER

28.4000 g., Silver, 48 mm. **Ruler:** Christoph **Obv:** Bust to right, double legend **Obv. Legend:** Inner: CHRISTOPHORVS. D. G. EL. E. CONF. AB. CORB. S. R. I. P. Outer: LEOPOLDVS. I. ET. MAGNVS. ROM. IMPER. S. A. TVRCARVM. DOMITOR. **Rev:** Spanish shield of 4-fold arms, 3 ornate helmets and 1/2-length figure of St. Vitus above, date at end of legend **Rev. Legend:** SANCTVS. VITVS. PATRONVS. CORBEIENSIS. **Mint:** Höxter **Note:** Ref. I/S-323; W-138; Dav. 5199.

Date	Mintage	VG	F	VF	XF	Unc
1688 GB Rare	—	—	—	—	—	—

KM# 101.1 THALER

Silver Weight varies: 28.91-29.35g., 48 mm. **Ruler:** Christoph **Obv:** Spanish shield of 4-fold arms, superimposed on crossed sword and crozier, 3 ornate helmets and 3/4-length figure of St. Vitus above, date divided by bottom of arms **Obv. Legend:** ST. VITVS. PATR - CORBEIENSIS. **Rev:** Laureate bust to right in circle **Rev. Legend:** LEOPOLD. I. &. MAGNVS. D. G. ROM. IMP. SEMP. AVG. TVRCAR. DOMITOR. **Mint:** Höxter **Note:** Ref. I/S-324; W-139; Dav. 5200.

Date	Mintage	VG	F	VF	XF	Unc
1688 GB	—	3,250	5,500	9,000	—	—

KM# 101.2 THALER
Silver Weight varies: 28.30-28.60g., 49 mm. **Ruler:** Christoph **Obv:** Spanish shield of 4-fold arms, superimposed on crossed sword and crozier, 3 ornate helmets and 3/4-length figure of St. Vitus above, date divided by bottom of arms **Obv. Legend:** ST. VITVS. PATR - CORBEIENSIS. **Rev:** 3/4-length figure of St. Vitus holding palm branch and book on which a bird is standing, lion's head at lower right, date at end of legend **Rev. Legend:** SANCTVS. VITVS. PARTONVS. CORBEIENSIS. **Mint:** Höxter **Note:** Ref. I/S-325. Mule of obverse of KM#101.1 and reverse of KM#92.2.

Date	Mintage	VG	F	VF	XF	Unc
1688//1686 GB	—	—	—	—	—	—

Note: An example in VF realized approximately $11,120 in a Gorny & Mosch auction in October 2009.

KM# 100.2 THALER
28.2000 g., Silver, 49 mm. **Ruler:** Christoph **Obv:** Bust to right, double legend **Obv. Legend:** Inner: CHRISTOPHORVS. D. G. EL. E. CONF. AB. CORB. S. R. I. P. Outer: LEOPOLDVS. I. ET. MAGNVS. ROM. IMPER. S. A. TVRCARVM. DOMITOR. **Rev:** Spanish shield of 4-fold arms, superimposed on crossed sword and crozier, 3 ornate helmets and 3/4-length figure of St. Vitus above, head divides mintmaster's initials, date at end of legend **Rev. Legend:** SANCTVS. VITVS. PATRONVS. CORBEIENSIS. **Mint:** Höxter **Note:** Ref. I/S-326; Dav. 5202.

Date	Mintage	VG	F	VF	XF	Unc
1690 IO Rare	—	—	—	—	—	—

KM# 101.3 THALER
Silver Weight varies: 28.23-29.19g., 48 mm. **Ruler:** Christoph **Obv:** Spanish shield of 4-fold arms, superimposed on crossed sword and crozier, 3 ornate helmets above, head divides mintmaster's initials, date at end of legend **Obv. Legend:** SANCTVS. VITVS. PATRONVS. CORBEIENSIS. **Rev:** Laureate bust to right in circle **Rev. Legend:** LEOPOLD. I. &. MAGNVS. D. G. ROM. IMP. SEMP. AVG. TVRCAR. DOMITOR. **Mint:** Höxter **Note:** Ref. I/S-327; W-140; Dav. 5201.

Date	Mintage	VG	F	VF	XF	Unc
1690 IO Rare	—	—	—	—	—	—

KM# 106 THALER
Silver Weight varies: 28.90-29.07g., 40 mm. **Ruler:** Christoph **Obv:** Spanish shield of 4-fold arms, superimposed on crossed sword and crozier, 3 ornate helmets and 1/2-length figure of St. Vitus above, date at end of legend **Obv. Legend:** CHRISTOPH. D. G. ELECT. ET. CONF. ABBAS. CORBEI. S. R. I. P. **Rev:** Laureate armored bust to right **Rev. Legend:** +LEOPOLD. I. &. MAGNVS. D. G. ROM. IMP. SEMP. AVG. TVRCAR. DOMITOR. **Mint:** Münster **Note:** Ref. I/S-330; W-142; Dav. 5204.

Date	Mintage	VG	F	VF	XF	Unc
1694 JO Rare	—	—	—	—	—	—

KM# 107 THALER
28.9700 g., Silver, 40 mm. **Ruler:** Christoph **Obv:** Spanish shield of 4-fold arms, superimposed on crossed sword and crozier, divides date, 3 ornate helmets and mitre above **Obv. Legend:** +CHRISTOPHORVS. D. G. ELECT. ET. CONF. ABBAS. CORBEI. S. R. I. P. **Rev:** Laureate armored bust to right **Rev. Legend:** +LEOPOLD. I. &. MAGNVS. D. G. ROM. IMP. SEMP. AVG. TVRCAR. DOMITOR. **Mint:** Münster **Note:** Ref. I/S-329; W-141; Dav. 5203.

Date	Mintage	VG	F	VF	XF	Unc
1694 JO Rare	—	—	—	—	—	—

KM# 108 THALER
Silver Weight varies: 28.75-29.54g., 42 mm. **Ruler:** Florenz **Obv:** Oval shield of 4-fold arms in baroque frame, superimposed on crossed sword and crozier, 3 ornate helmets and mitre divide mintmaster's initials above **Obv. Legend:** FLORENTIUS. D. G. ABBAS. CORBEIENSIS. S. R. I. PRIN. **Rev:** Full-length figure of St. Vitus with palm branch, book and bird, lion passant behind, date at end of legend **Rev. Legend:** SANCTVS. VITVS. PATRONVS. CORBEIENSIS. **Mint:** Osnabrück **Note:** Ref. I/S-331; W-170; Dav. 5205.

Date	Mintage	VG	F	VF	XF	Unc
1698 HLO	—	400	750	1,350	2,550	—

KM# 16 1-1/2 THALER
43.8000 g., Silver, 43 mm. **Ruler:** Dietrich IV **Obv:** Full-length standing figure of St. Vitus, two small shield of arms at left and right **Obv. Legend:** TEODORVS. D. G. ABBAS. CORBE. **Rev:** Crowned imperial eagle, orb on breast, crown divided date on top **Rev. Legend:** MATIAS. II. D. G. ROMA. IMP. SEM. AVG. **Mint:** Höxter **Note:** Ref. I/S-130.1

Date	Mintage	VG	F	VF	XF	Unc
1616 Rare	—	—	—	—	—	—

KM# 11 2 THALER
Silver Weight varies: 57.23-58.44g., 44 mm. **Ruler:** Dietrich IV **Obv:** Full-length standing figure of St. Vitus divides 2 small shields of arms **Obv. Legend:** TEODORVS. D. G. ABBAS. CORBE. **Rev:** Crowned imperial eagle, date divided by crown at top **Rev. Legend:** MATIAS. II. D. G. ROMA. IMP. SEM. AVG. **Mint:** Höxter **Note:** Ref. I/S-65.1, 130.2; W-80, 81; Dav. 5183.

Date	Mintage	VG	F	VF	XF	Unc
161Z Rare	—	—	—	—	—	—
1616 Rare	—	—	—	—	—	—

KM# 58 2 THALER
Silver **Ruler:** Arnold IV **Obv:** Oval shield, with top and bottom curled inward, of 4-fold arms, superimposed on 2 crossed crozier, mitre above, sword hilt at upper left, ornate helmet at upper right, date and mintmaster's initials divided at lower left and right **Obv. Legend:** ARNOLDVS. DEI. GRATIA. EL. E. CONFIR. AB. CORB. **Rev:** Full-length facing figure of St. Vits holding book and palm branch **Rev. Legend:** SANCTVS. VITVS. PATRONVS. CORBEIENSIS. **Mint:** Höxter **Note:** Ref. I/S-234.1; W-114; Dav. 5193.

Date	Mintage	VG	F	VF	XF	Unc
1656 VFH Rare	—	—	—	—	—	—

KM# 93 2 THALER
Silver Weight varies: 56.04-58.18g., 49 mm. **Ruler:** Christoph **Obv:** Oval shield of 4-fold arms in baroque frame, 3 ornate helmets and mitre above **Obv. Legend:** CHRISTOPHORVS. D. G. ELECT. ET. CONF. ABBAS. CORBEI. S. R. I. P. **Rev:** 3/4-length figure of St. Vitus holding palm branch and book on which a bird is standing, date at end of legend **Rev. Legend:** SANCTVS. VITVS. PATRONVS. CORBEIENSIS. **Mint:** Höxter **Note:** Ref. I/S-266.1; W-135; Dav. 5196.

Date	Mintage	VG	F	VF	XF	Unc
1683 GB Rare	—	—	—	—	—	—

Note: An example in VF realized approximately $20,325 in a UBS auction in September 2003.

TRADE COINAGE

KM# 42 DUCAT
3.5000 g., 0.9860 Gold 0.1109 oz. AGW **Ruler:** Arnold IV **Obv:** 4-fold arms, date in legend **Obv. Legend:** D. G. ARNOLDUS. CORBIENSIS. **Rev:** Full-length figure of St. Vitus **Rev. Legend:** SANCTVS. VITVS. PATRONVS. **Mint:** Höxter **Note:** Ref. I/S-194; W-112.

Date	Mintage	VG	F	VF	XF	Unc
1642	—	1,200	2,400	4,800	9,000	—

KM# 54 DUCAT
3.5000 g., 0.9860 Gold Weight varies: 3.46-3.49g. 0.1109 oz. AGW, 21.5 mm. **Ruler:** Arnold IV **Obv:** Oval shield of 4-fold arms in baroque frame, mitre above, sword hilt to left, ornate helmet to right, date at end of legend **Obv. Legend:** D. G. ARNOLD. EL. ET. CON. AB. **Rev:** Full-length figure of St. Vitus, DVCA downward to right of saint **Rev. Legend:** SANC. VITVS. PAT - RONVS. CORB. **Mint:** Höxter **Note:** Ref. I/S-213; W-112A.

Date	Mintage	VG	F	VF	XF	Unc
165Z	—	1,200	2,400	4,800	9,000	—

KM# 61 DUCAT
Gold **Ruler:** Arnold IV **Mint:** Höxter **Note:** Ref. I/S-233. No description available.

Date	Mintage	VG	F	VF	XF	Unc
1656 VFH	—	—	—	—	—	—

Note: Reported, not confirmed.

PATTERNS

Including off metal strikes

KM#	Date	Mintage	Identification	Mkt Val
Pn1	1632	—	Thaler. Tin. KM#32.1.	125
Pn2	1683	—	Thaler. Tin. KM#92.1.	125

COTTBUS

A provincial town about 70 miles southeast of Berlin. There was a mint for Brandenburg located in it during the 13th century. Cottbus and the surrounding territory belonged to Brandenburg from 1462 except 1807-13 when it was controlled by Saxony. Coins were issued during the Kipper Period.

TOWN

REGULAR COINAGE

KM# 1 PFENNIG
Copper **Note:** Uniface. Kipper Pfennig. Crayfish, head at top.

Date	Mintage	VG	F	VF	XF	Unc
ND(1622)	—	16.00	30.00	65.00	135	—

KM# 2 PFENNIG
Copper, 14 mm. **Note:** S-C at lower left and right (Stadt Cottbus). Varieties exist.

Date	Mintage	VG	F	VF	XF	Unc
ND(1622)	—	13.00	27.00	65.00	135	—

DORTMUND

(Tremoniensis)

Dortmund is located in Westphalia, 50 miles east of Düsseldorf. It was the site of an imperial mint from the 10th to early 16th century and later had its own city coinage, dated pieces being known from 1553 to 1760. In 1803 Dortmund was annexed to Nassau-Dillenburg and passed to Prussia in 1815.

MINT OFFICIALS' INITIALS

Initials	Date	Name
NL	1688-95	Nikolaus Longerich
(t) 	1631-50	Simon Textor
	1650-88	Ernst Textor

ARMS
Eagle with wings spread, head usually turned to left.

CITY

REGULAR COINAGE

KM# 5 1/8 SCHILLING (1-1/2 Pfennig)

Silver **Note:** Uniface. Eagle, head left, in circle.

Date	Mintage	VG	F	VF	XF	Unc
ND(ca.1625/30)	—	—	—	—	—	—

KM# 6 1/8 SCHILLING (1-1/2 Pfennig)

Silver **Note:** Eagle not in circle and D below.

Date	Mintage	VG	F	VF	XF	Unc
ND(ca.1630/35)	—	—	—	—	—	—

KM# 71 1/8 SCHILLING (1-1/2 Pfennig)

Silver **Note:** Eagle, head right, in circle of pellets, NL below.

Date	Mintage	VG	F	VF	XF	Unc
ND(1688-95) NL	—	—	—	—	—	—

KM# 70 3 PFENNIG

Silver **Obv:** Eagle, head right, divides TRE-MON **Rev. Inscription:** III / PFEN / NING

Date	Mintage	VG	F	VF	XF	Unc
ND(ca.1680) (t)	—	40.00	85.00	175	—	—

KM# 67 8 HELLER

Billon **Obv:** Eagle, head right **Obv. Legend:** TREMONIENSIS **Rev:** VIII in center, date in legend

Date	Mintage	VG	F	VF	XF	Unc
1676 (t)	—	—	—	—	—	—

KM# 7 6 PFENNING (1/2 Schilling)

Silver **Obv:** Eagle, head left, in circle **Obv. Legend:** TREMONIENSIS **Rev:** Inscription, date in circle **Rev. Inscription:** VI / PFENN / ING

Date	Mintage	VG	F	VF	XF	Unc
1631 (t)	—	35.00	75.00	150	—	—

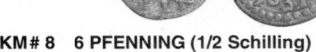

KM# 8 6 PFENNING (1/2 Schilling)

Silver **Obv:** Eagle, not in circle

Date	Mintage	VG	F	VF	XF	Unc
1631	—	35.00	75.00	150	300	—

KM# 45 6 PFENNING (1/2 Schilling)

Silver **Obv:** Date in legend **Rev. Inscription:** VI / PFEN / NING

Date	Mintage	VG	F	VF	XF	Unc
1651	—	33.00	65.00	120	225	—

KM# 46 6 PFENNING (1/2 Schilling)

Silver **Rev:** Inscription, date **Rev. Inscription:** VI / PFEN / NING

Date	Mintage	VG	F	VF	XF	Unc
1651	—	33.00	65.00	120	225	—

KM# 49 6 PFENNING (1/2 Schilling)

Silver **Rev. Inscription:** VI / PFEN / NING **Note:** Varieties exist.

Date	Mintage	VG	F	VF	XF	Unc
ND(1658-88)	—	13.00	27.00	55.00	110	—
ND(1658-88) (t)	—	13.00	27.00	55.00	110	—

KM# 9 SCHILLING

Silver **Obv:** Eagle, head left, in circle, titles of Ferdinand II **Rev:** 1 / SCHIL / LING / date **Note:** These are also known with countermarks of arms of the county of Mark (checkerboard).

Date	Mintage	VG	F	VF	XF	Unc
1631 (t)	—	20.00	40.00	80.00	160	—
1632 (t)	—	20.00	40.00	80.00	160	—
1633 (t)	—	20.00	40.00	80.00	160	—
1635 (t)	—	20.00	40.00	80.00	160	—
1640 (t)	—	20.00	40.00	80.00	160	—

KM# 36 SCHILLING

Silver **Obv:** Eagle's head to right

Date	Mintage	VG	F	VF	XF	Unc
1641 (t)	—	20.00	40.00	80.00	160	—

KM# 35 SCHILLING

Silver **Obv:** Titles of Ferdinand III **Note:** Often found with countermark of Mark arms.

Date	Mintage	VG	F	VF	XF	Unc
1641 (t)	—	20.00	40.00	80.00	160	—
1643 (t)	—	20.00	40.00	80.00	160	—
1644 (t)	—	20.00	40.00	80.00	160	—
1646 (t)	—	20.00	40.00	80.00	160	—
1647 (t)	—	20.00	40.00	80.00	160	—
1653 (t)	—	20.00	40.00	80.00	160	—
1655 (t)	—	20.00	40.00	80.00	160	—
1656 (t)	—	20.00	40.00	80.00	160	—

KM# 10 1/52 THALER (Schilling)

1.5800 g., Silver, 21 mm. **Obv:** Imperial orb with 52 divides date **Obv. Legend:** MON. NO. CIV. IMP. TREMONI. **Rev:** Eagle, head left, in circle **Rev. Legend:** FERDI. II. D. G. RO. IM(P). SEMP. AV. **Note:** Ref. B-172.

Date	Mintage	VG	F	VF	XF	Unc
1631 (t)	—	35.00	80.00	135	250	—

KM# 14 1/16 THALER (Halber Blamüser)

Silver **Obv:** Titles of Ferdinand II, value 16 in legend at bottom **Rev:** Eagle, head left, in circle, date in legend

Date	Mintage	VG	F	VF	XF	Unc
1632 (t)	—	85.00	170	300	625	—
1633 (t)	—	85.00	170	300	625	—
1637 (t)	—	85.00	170	300	625	—

KM# 25 1/16 THALER (Halber Blamüser)

Silver **Rev:** Eagle's head right

Date	Mintage	VG	F	VF	XF	Unc
1637 (t)	—	85.00	170	300	625	—

KM# 29 1/16 THALER (Halber Blamüser)

Silver **Rev:** Titles of Ferdinand III, value 16 bottom

Date	Mintage	VG	F	VF	XF	Unc
1639 (t)	—	150	250	350	725	—
1640 (t)	—	150	250	350	725	—
1642 (t)	—	150	250	350	725	—
1645 (t)	—	150	250	350	725	—
1646 (t)	—	150	250	350	725	—
1647 (t)	—	150	250	350	725	—
1648 (t)	—	150	250	350	725	—
1650 (t)	—	150	250	350	725	—

KM# 47 1/16 THALER (Halber Blamüser)

2.3000 g., Silver, 24 mm. **Obv:** Value 16 in legend above bust

Date	Mintage	VG	F	VF	XF	Unc
1656 (t)	—	75.00	150	300	600	—
1658 (t)	—	75.00	150	300	600	—

KM# 65 1/16 THALER (Dütchen)

1.6000 g., Silver, 22.4 mm. **Obv:** Titles of Leopold I

Date	Mintage	VG	F	VF	XF	Unc
1670 (t)	—	16.00	33.00	65.00	130	—
1671 (t)	—	16.00	33.00	65.00	130	—
1672 (t)	—	16.00	33.00	65.00	130	—

KM# 50 1/13 THALER (4 Stüber)

Silver **Obv:** Titles of Leopold I, value 13 above in legend

Date	Mintage	VG	F	VF	XF	Unc
1659 (t)	—	300	600	1,200	2,300	4,250
1660 (t)	—	75.00	150	275	550	—

KM# 17 1/4 THALER

Silver **Obv:** Crowned 1/2-length bust of emperor right, titles of Ferdinand II **Rev:** Eagle, head left, in circle, date in legend

Date	Mintage	VG	F	VF	XF	Unc
1634 (t)	—	—	—	—	—	—
1637 (t)	—	—	—	—	—	—

KM# 38 1/4 THALER

Silver **Obv:** Bust of emperor right, titles of Ferdinand III **Rev:** Eagle, head left, in circle, double legend, date in outer legend

Date	Mintage	VG	F	VF	XF	Unc
1646 (t)	—	—	—	—	—	—

KM# 72 2/3 THALER (Gulden)

Silver **Obv:** Laureate bust right, titles of Leopold I **Rev:** Eagle, head left, value 2/3 in oval below, date in legend

Date	Mintage	VG	F	VF	XF	Unc
1688 NL	—	—	—	—	—	—

Note: The few known specimens have countermark on obverse of leaping horse left, IP on flank, for monetary warden-general of the Lower Rhine-Westphalian imperial circle, Johann Post (1682-1702)

KM# 11.1 THALER

Silver **Obv:** Eagle in circle **Rev:** 1/2-length crowned and armored figure of emperor right holding scepter over right shoulder, titles of Karl V, date in legend

Date	Mintage	VG	F	VF	XF	Unc
16Z1 Rare	—	—	—	—	—	—

KM# 11.3 THALER

Silver **Note:** Klippe. Dav. #5207A.

Date	Mintage	VG	F	VF	XF	Unc
1631 (t) Rare	—	—	—	—	—	—

KM# 11.2 THALER

Silver **Obv:** Crowned half figure with scepter right **Obv. Legend:** FERDINANDVS. II. DG. RO. IMP. SEM. AVGB.--S. **Rev:** Legend, eagle, date **Rev. Legend:** MON. NO. CIVIT. IMP. TREMONIENSIS **Note:** Dav. #5207.

Date	Mintage	VG	F	VF	XF	Unc
1631 (t) Rare	—	—	—	—	—	—

KM# 11.4 THALER

Silver **Obv. Legend:** MONE. NOV... **Note:** Dav. #5209.

Date	Mintage	VG	F	VF	XF	Unc
163Z (t) Rare	—	—	—	—	—	—

Note: WAG Auction 43, 9-07, XF realized approximately $47,925, Künker Auction 113 6-06, XF realized approximately, $23,260

KM# 11.5 THALER
Silver **Note:** Klippe. Dav. #5209A.

Date	Mintage	VG	F	VF	XF	Unc
163Z (t) Rare	—	—	—	—	—	—

KM# 18.1 THALER
Silver **Obv:** Date in field before bust **Obv. Legend:** FERDI. , II. DG: ROM: IMPERIA: SEMP. AVG-X. **Rev. Legend:** MONETA: NOV: CIVIT: IMPERIA: TREMONIENS. **Note:** Dav. #5210.

Date	Mintage	VG	F	VF	XF	Unc
1634 (t) Rare	—	—	—	—	—	—

KM# 18.2 THALER
Silver **Note:** Dav. #5212.

Date	Mintage	VG	F	VF	XF	Unc
1635 (t)	—	650	1,250	2,500	4,750	—

KM# 18.3 THALER
Silver **Note:** Dav. #5213.

Date	Mintage	VG	F	VF	XF	Unc
1636 (t) Rare	—	—	—	—	—	—

KM# 27.1 THALER
Silver **Obv:** Eagle, head left, in circle, double legend, date divided by eagle's legs **Rev:** Bust of emperor right, titles of Ferdinand III **Note:** Dav. #5215.

Date	Mintage	VG	F	VF	XF	Unc
ND(1637-48) Rare	—	—	—	—	—	—

Note: Fritz Rudolf Künker Münzenhandlung Auction 98, 3-05, VF realized approximately $46,000.

KM# 27.2 THALER
Silver **Obv. Legend:** ...ROM. IMP. SEMP. AVGVSTVS. **Note:** Dav. #5216.

Date	Mintage	VG	F	VF	XF	Unc
ND(1637-48) Rare	—	—	—	—	—	—

KM# 27.3 THALER
Silver **Note:** Klippe. Dav. #5216A.

Date	Mintage	VG	F	VF	XF	Unc
ND(1637-48) Rare	—	—	—	—	—	—

KM# 27.4 THALER
Silver **Rev:** Date divided by eagle **Note:** Dav. #5217.

Date	Mintage	VG	F	VF	XF	Unc
1638 Rare	—	—	—	—	—	—
1640 Rare	—	—	—	—	—	—

KM# 27.5 THALER
Silver **Obv:** Harnessed bust right **Note:** Dav. #5218.

Date	Mintage	VG	F	VF	XF	Unc
1646 Rare	—	—	—	—	—	—

KM# 27.6 THALER
Silver **Obv:** Different bust **Note:** Dav. #5220.

Date	Mintage	VG	F	VF	XF	Unc
1647 Rare	—	—	—	—	—	—

KM# 27.7 THALER
Silver

Date	Mintage	VG	F	VF	XF	Unc
1650 Rare	—	—	—	—	—	—

KM# 48 THALER
Silver **Rev:** Date in outer legend **Note:** Dav. #5221.

Date	Mintage	VG	F	VF	XF	Unc
1657 (t) Rare	—	—	—	—	—	—

Note: Bank Leu Auction 46 5-88 VF realized $14,000

KM# 55.1 THALER
Silver **Note:** Dav. #5223.

Date	Mintage	VG	F	VF	XF	Unc
1660 (t)	—	1,450	3,250	6,250	—	—
1668 (t)	—	1,440	3,250	6,250	—	—

KM# 55.2 THALER
Silver **Note:** Klippe. Dav. #5223A.

Date	Mintage	VG	F	VF	XF	Unc
1668 (t) Rare	—	—	—	—	—	—

KM# 55.4 THALER
Silver **Note:** Klippe. Dav. #5224A.

Date	Mintage	VG	F	VF	XF	Unc
1683 Rare	—	—	—	—	—	—

Note: Künker Auction 163, 1-10, VF+ realized approximately $11,935, Bank Leu Auction 46 5-88 VF realized $18,000

KM# 55.3 THALER
Silver **Obv:** Different bust with longer hair and softer looking drapings **Note:** Dav. #5224.

Date	Mintage	VG	F	VF	XF	Unc
1683 Rare	—	—	—	—	—	—

Note: Künker Auction 163, 1-10, VF+ realized approximately $11,935, Swiss Bank sale 19 1-88 VF/XF realized $23,400

KM# 55.5 THALER
Silver **Obv:** Larger letters in wider legend **Note:** Dav. #5225.

Date	Mintage	VG	F	VF	XF	Unc
1688 NL Rare	—	—	—	—	—	—

KM# 75 THALER
Silver **Obv:** Large bust not in circle **Rev:** Double legend broken at top by eagle, head of which divides mintmaster's initials from date **Note:** Dav. #5226.

Date	Mintage	VG	F	VF	XF	Unc
1695 NL Rare	—	—	—	—	—	—

Note: Bank Leu Auction 46 5-88 VF realized $26,000

KM# 77 THALER
Silver **Note:** Dav. #5227.

Date	Mintage	VG	F	VF	XF	Unc
1698 Rare	—	—	—	—	—	—

Note: Bank Leu Auction 46 5-88 VF-XF realized $35,000

KM# 39 1-1/2 THALER
Silver **Obv:** Bust of emperor right, titles of Ferdinand III **Rev:** Eagle, head left, in circle, double legend, date divided by legs

Date	Mintage	VG	F	VF	XF	Unc
1647 Rare	—	—	—	—	—	—

Note: May be a 2 Thaler. Similar to KM#40.3, listed as a 2 Thaler

KM# 12.1 2 THALER
Silver **Obv:** Eagle in circle **Obv. Legend:** + MO + NO + CIVI + IMP + TREMONIENSIS **Rev:** 1/2-length crowned and armored figure of emperor right holding scepter over right shoulder, titles of Karl V, date in reverse legend **Note:** Similar to 1 Thaler, KM#18 but date in reverse legend. Dav. #5206.

Date	Mintage	VG	F	VF	XF	Unc
1631 (t) Rare	—	—	—	—	—	—

KM# 12.2 2 THALER
Silver **Obv. Legend:** MONE. NOV... **Note:** Dav. #5208.

Date	Mintage	VG	F	VF	XF	Unc
163Z (t) Rare	—	—	—	—	—	—

KM# 13 2 THALER
Silver **Note:** Klippe. Dav. #5208A.

Date	Mintage	VG	F	VF	XF	Unc
163Z (t) Rare	—	—	—	—	—	—

KM# 20 2 THALER
Silver **Note:** Klippe. Dav. #5211A.

Date	Mintage	VG	F	VF	XF	Unc
1635 (t) Rare	—	—	—	—	—	—

KM# 19 2 THALER
Silver **Obv:** Eagle in circle **Obv. Legend:** + MO + NO + CIVI + IMP + TREMONIENSIS **Rev:** 1/2-length crowned and armored figure of emperor right holding scepter over right shoulder, titles of Karl V **Note:** Similar to 1 Thaler, KM#18. Dav. #5211.

Date	Mintage	VG	F	VF	XF	Unc
1635 (t) Rare	—	—	—	—	—	—

KM# 40.1 2 THALER
Silver **Obv:** Bust of emperor right, titles of Ferdinand III **Rev:** Eagle, head left, in circle, double legend **Note:** Dav. #5214.

Date	Mintage	VG	F	VF	XF	Unc
ND(1637-48) Rare	—	—	—	—	—	—

KM# 40.2 2 THALER
Silver **Note:** Dav. #5214A.

Date	Mintage	VG	F	VF	XF	Unc
ND(1637-48) Rare	—	—	—	—	—	—

KM# 40.3 2 THALER
Silver **Rev:** Date divided by eagle's legs **Note:** Dav. #5219.

Date	Mintage	VG	F	VF	XF	Unc
1647 Rare	—	—	—	—	—	—

Note: 1647 may actually be 1-1/2 Thaler as KM#39

KM# 40.4 2 THALER
Silver **Note:** Klippe. Dav. #5219A.

Date	Mintage	VG	F	VF	XF	Unc
1647 Rare	—	—	—	—	—	—

KM# 56.2 2 THALER
Silver **Note:** Klippe. Dav. #5222A.

Date	Mintage	VG	F	VF	XF	Unc
1660 (t) Rare	—	—	—	—	—	—

KM# 56.1 2 THALER
Silver **Note:** Dav. #5222.

Date	Mintage	VG	F	VF	XF	Unc
1660 (t) Rare	—	—	—	—	—	—

Note: Bank Leu Auction 46 5-88 XF realized $22,000

Date	Mintage	VG	F	VF	XF	Unc
1668 (t) Rare	—	—	—	—	—	—

KM# 56.3 2 THALER
Silver **Obv:** Large letters in wide legend **Note:** Dav. #A5225.

Date	Mintage	VG	F	VF	XF	Unc
1688 NL Rare	—	—	—	—	—	—

KM# 56.4 2 THALER
Silver **Note:** Klippe. Dav. #A5225A.

Date	Mintage	VG	F	VF	XF	Unc
1688 NL Rare	—	—	—	—	—	—

KM# 76 2 THALER
Silver **Obv:** Large bust not in circle **Rev:** Double legend broken at top by eagle, head of which divides mintmasters initials from date **Note:** Dav. #A5226.

Date	Mintage	VG	F	VF	XF	Unc
1695 NL Rare	—	—	—	—	—	—

TRADE COINAGE

KM# 15 GOLDGULDEN
3.5000 g., 0.9860 Gold 0.1109 oz. AGW **Obv:** Ferdinand II standing in inner circle **Rev:** Large orb in center circle

Date	Mintage	VG	F	VF	XF	Unc
1632 Rare	—	—	—	—	—	—

KM# 16 GOLDGULDEN
3.5000 g., 0.9860 Gold 0.1109 oz. AGW **Rev:** Imperial orb in hexalobe

Date	Mintage	VG	F	VF	XF	Unc
1633	—	850	1,750	3,500	6,500	—
1635/3	—	850	1,750	3,500	6,500	—

KM# 22 DUCAT
3.5000 g., 0.9860 Gold 0.1109 oz. AGW **Obv:** Full-length facing standing figure of emperor, titles of Ferdinand II in legend **Rev:** Eagle, head left, divides date above four-line inscription

Date	Mintage	VG	F	VF	XF	Unc
1635	—	1,750	3,750	7,500	13,500	—

KM# 24 DUCAT
3.5000 g., 0.9860 Gold 0.1109 oz. AGW **Rev:** Eagle, head right, date in legend

Date	Mintage	VG	F	VF	XF	Unc
1636	—	750	1,800	3,750	7,000	—

KM# 26 DUCAT
3.5000 g., 0.9860 Gold 0.1109 oz. AGW **Rev:** Eagle's head to left

Date	Mintage	VG	F	VF	XF	Unc
1637	—	750	1,800	3,750	7,000	—

KM# 30 DUCAT
3.5000 g., 0.9860 Gold 0.1109 oz. AGW **Rev:** Three-line inscription with posthumous date, titles of Ferdinand II

Date	Mintage	VG	F	VF	XF	Unc
1639	—	1,000	2,400	5,000	9,500	—

KM# 37 DUCAT
3.5000 g., 0.9860 Gold 0.1109 oz. AGW **Obv:** Figure of emperor divides date, titles of Ferdinand III **Rev:** Eagle, head left

Date	Mintage	VG	F	VF	XF	Unc
1644 (t)	—	750	1,800	3,750	7,000	—
1655 (t)	—	750	1,800	3,750	7,000	—

KM# 58 DUCAT
3.5000 g., 0.9860 Gold 0.1109 oz. AGW **Obv:** Leopold standing in inner circle **Rev:** Displayed eagle in inner circle **Note:** Fr #860

Date	Mintage	VG	F	VF	XF	Unc
1660	—	2,000	4,000	8,500	15,000	—

KM# 59 DUCAT
3.5000 g., 0.9860 Gold 0.1109 oz. AGW **Rev:** Date divided by eagle's head

Date	Mintage	VG	F	VF	XF	Unc
1663 (t)	—	2,500	4,500	9,000	16,000	—

KM# 66 DUCAT
3.5000 g., 0.9860 Gold 0.1109 oz. AGW **Obv:** Laureate bust of emperor right, titles of Leopold I **Rev:** Eagle, head left, date in legend

Date	Mintage	VG	F	VF	XF	Unc
1670 (t) Rare	—	—	—	—	—	—

DROSSEN

A town in Brandenburg and mint site in the 13th century. Drossen received the right to coin Pfennigs in 1369. Local coinage was also struck during the Kipper Period.

TOWN

REGULAR COINAGE

KM# 1 PFENNIG
Copper **Obv:** Eagle in shield divides sideways date, D below. **Note:** Kipper Pfennig. Uniface.

Date	Mintage	VG	F	VF	XF	Unc
16ZZ	—	32.00	65.00	135	275	—

KM# 2 PFENNIG
Copper **Obv:** Eagle in shield, date above divided by D. **Note:** Uniface.

Date	Mintage	VG	F	VF	XF	Unc
16ZZ	—	25.00	55.00	110	220	—

KM# 3 PFENNIG
0.6000 g., Copper, 14 mm. **Obv:** Eagle, head left, D below.

Date	Mintage	VG	F	VF	XF	Unc
ND(1622)	—	15.00	30.00	60.00	125	—

DULMEN

A town in Westphalia some 18 miles southwest of Munster. Between 1590 and 1625 a series of copper coins were struck for local use.

REFERENCE

W = Joseph Weingärtner, ***Beschreibung der Kupfermünzen Westfalens nebst historischen Nachrichten,*** 2 vols. Paderborn, 1872-81.

TOWN

REGULAR COINAGE

KM# 1 PFENNIG
Copper **Obv:** Arms, (cross in shield), legend, date around **Obv. Legend:** STADT DVLMEN **Rev:** Value I in circle with ornaments around **Note:** Ref. W#197. Varieties exist.

Date	Mintage	Good	VG	F	VF	XF
ND(c.1609)	—	65.00	120	200	350	—
1625	—	65.00	120	200	350	—

KM# 2 2 PFENNIG
Copper **Obv:** Arms, legend, date around **Obv. Legend:** STADT DVLMEN **Rev:** Value II in circle with ornaments around **Note:** Ref. W#195. Varieties exist.

Date	Mintage	Good	VG	F	VF	XF
1609	—	65.00	125	250	500	—
1625	—	100	200	400	825	—

KM# 3 3 PFENNIG
Copper **Obv:** Arms, legend, date around **Obv. Legend:** STADT DVLMEN **Rev:** Value III in circle with ornaments around **Note:** Ref. W#192. Varieties exist.

Date	Mintage	Good	VG	F	VF	XF
1609	—	90.00	175	350	700	—
1625	—	100	200	425	875	—

KM# 4 4 PFENNIG
Copper **Obv:** Arms, legend, date around **Obv. Legend:** STADT DVLMEN **Rev:** Value IIII in square with circle ornaments around **Note:** Ref. W#190. Varieties exist.

Date	Mintage	Good	VG	F	VF	XF
1609	—	160	325	650	—	—

KM# 5 6 PFENNIG
Copper, 22 mm. **Obv:** Arms, legend, date around **Obv. Legend:** STADT DVLMEN **Rev:** Value VI in circle with ornaments around **Note:** Ref. W#187. Varieties exist.

Date	Mintage	Good	VG	F	VF	XF
1609	—	40.00	85.00	175	350	—
1622	—	40.00	85.00	175	350	—

EAST FRIESLAND

The countship, and later principality, of East Friesland was located along the North Sea coast between the Rivers Ems and Weser. By the late 14th and early 15th centuries, several powerful families controlled various areas of what was to become the countship. The Cirksena family of Greetsyl managed to emerge during this period as a leading force in the region through astute marriages and sometimes by armed might. Ulrich I Cirksena was created the first count of East Friesland in 1454. This confirmed his line as the ruling dynasty with the capital at Aurich. In 1654, the count was raised to the rank of prince. In 1744, the Cirksenas became extinct and East Friesland passed to Prussia, which maintained the mint at Aurich for the new province. East Friesland became part of Hannover at the end of the Napoleonic Wars in 1815, but returned to Prussian control when Hannover itself was absorbed by Prussia in 1866.

RULERS

Enno III, 1599-1625
Rudolph Christian, 1625-1628
Ulrich II, 1628-1648
Enno IV Ludwig, 1648-1660
Georg Christian, 1660-1665
Christine Charlotte, regent, 1665-1690
Christian Eberhard, 1665-1708

MINT MARKS

A - Berlin
B - Breslau
D - Aurich
F - Magdeburg
Star - Dresden

MINT OFFICIALS' INITIALS

Initial	Date	Name
	1519-26	Uko Hessena, warden in Emden
(a)=	ca. 1528	Johann?, mintmaster
(b)=	ca. 1529-32	Hinrich, mintmaster
(c)=	1532-39	Martin Nycamer, mintmaster
	1533-40	Hinrich Scrapper, warden
(d)=	1558-63	Heinrich Meinerts, mintmaster
(e)=	1563-74?	Dirk Iden Kruitkremer, mintmaster
(f)=	1574-82	Johann Iden, mintmaster
	1577-99	Franz Munting, die-cutter
(g)=	1582-1602	Joest Janssen van Strijp, mintmaster
(h)=	1602-11	Franz Munting in Emden
(i)=	1611-13	Meinhard Caspars in Emden
(j)=	1614-17	Jacob Stalpert in Emden
(k)=	1617-24	Johann von Romunde in Emden
HS	1626-72	Henning Schlüter in Zellerfeld
(l)=	1629-32	Unknown
(m)= or or with or without BH	1660-65	Unknown
(n)=	Ca.1690	Unknown at Esens
FBP	Ca.1693-1700	Unknown

MONETARY SYSTEM

Witte = 4 Hohlpfennig = 1/3 Schilling = 1/20 Schaf = 1/10 Stuber
Ciffert = 6 Witten
Stuber = 10 Witten = 1/30 Reichstaler
Schaf = 20 Witten = 2 Stuber
Flindrich = 3 Stuber
Schilling = 6 Stuber
288 Pfennige = 54 Stuber = 36 Mariengroschen = 1 Reichsthaler

COUNTSHIP

REGULAR COINAGE

KM# 10 WITTE (1/10 Stüber)

Silver **Obv:** Harpy facing (arms of Cirksena family) **Rev:** Date across center, imperial orb above, 1/Z0 below

Date	Mintage	VG	F	VF	XF	Unc
1603 (h)	—	60.00	125	250	—	—
1604 (h)	—	60.00	125	250	—	—

KM# 46 WITTE (1/10 Stüber)

Silver **Note:** Uniface. Schussel type. Shield with harpy divides date, mintmaster's symbol above.

Date	Mintage	VG	F	VF	XF	Unc
1621 (k)	—	60.00	125	250	—	—

KM# 34 3 WITTEN

Silver **Obv:** Harpy, titles of Enno III **Rev:** Value 3 in imperial orb **Rev. Legend:** DA. PAC...

Date	Mintage	VG	F	VF	XF	Unc
ND(ca.1617-20)	—	—	—	—	—	—

KM# 15 CIFFERT (1/2 Stüber)

Silver **Ruler:** Enno III **Obv:** Crowned harpy arms divid H-S (Halb Stuber), date above crown **Rev:** Ornate cross, O-F/H-S in angles **Rev. Legend:** DA. PA... **Mint:** Emden

Date	Mintage	VG	F	VF	XF	Unc
1612 (i)	76,956	25.00	50.00	100	210	—
ND	—	25.00	50.00	100	210	—

KM# 18 CIFFERT (1/2 Stüber)

Silver **Rev:** Date in angles of cross instead of letters

Date	Mintage	VG	F	VF	XF	Unc
1612 (i)	Inc. above	27.00	55.00	110	225	—

KM# 16 CIFFERT (1/2 Stüber)

Silver **Note:** Klippe.

Date	Mintage	VG	F	VF	XF	Unc
ND (i)	—	—	—	—	—	—

KM# 17 CIFFERT (1/2 Stüber)

Silver **Obv:** Arms divide date, without H-S **Note:** Klippe.

Date	Mintage	VG	F	VF	XF	Unc
(16)12 (i)	Inc. above	16.00	35.00	75.00	155	—

KM# 35 1/4 STüBER (2-1/2 Witten)

Silver **Obv:** Harpy, titles of Enno III **Rev:** Imperial orb **Rev. Legend:** DA. PAC...

Date	Mintage	VG	F	VF	XF	Unc
ND(ca.1617-20)	—	13.00	27.00	55.00	110	—

KM# 19 STüBER

Silver **Ruler:** Enno III **Obv:** Crowned harpy arms divide I-S (1 Stuber), date above crown **Rev:** Ornate cross in quatrefoil, DA. PA... around **Mint:** Emden

Date	Mintage	VG	F	VF	XF	Unc
1612 (i)	122,769	17.00	35.00	75.00	155	—
ND	230,868	17.00	35.00	75.00	155	—

KM# 21 STüBER

Silver **Obv:** S-I divided by date

Date	Mintage	VG	F	VF	XF	Unc
ND	Inc. above	17.00	35.00	75.00	155	—

KM# 20 STüBER

Silver **Note:** Klippe.

Date	Mintage	VG	F	VF	XF	Unc
ND (i)	—	—	—	—	—	—

KM# 47 STüBER

Silver **Obv:** Crowned harpy arms divide I-S **Rev:** Ornate cross

Date	Mintage	VG	F	VF	XF	Unc
ND(1628-48)	—	32.00	65.00	435	275	—

KM# 23 SCHAF (2 Stüber)

Silver **Ruler:** Enno III **Obv:** Crowned harpy arms divide 2-S, date above crown **Rev:** Ornate cross **Rev. Legend:** DA. PACEM... **Mint:** Emden

Date	Mintage	VG	F	VF	XF	Unc
1612 (i)	72,240	15.00	30.00	65.00	130	—
ND (j)	179,865	15.00	30.00	65.00	130	—
ND (k)	46,332	15.00	30.00	65.00	130	—

KM# 24 SCHAF (2 Stüber)

Silver **Note:** Klippe.

Date	Mintage	VG	F	VF	XF	Unc
ND	—	—	—	—	—	—

KM# 55 SCHAF (2 Stüber)

Silver **Obv:** Crowned harpy arms divide 2-S, date above crowne **Rev:** Ornate cross

Date	Mintage	VG	F	VF	XF	Unc
1632	—	40.00	80.00	160	325	—
1633	—	40.00	80.00	160	325	—
ND	—	40.00	80.00	160	325	—

KM# 66 SCHAF (2 Stüber)

Silver **Obv:** Crowned harpy arms, titles of Enno Ludwig **Rev:** Ornate cross **Rev. Legend:** DA. PACEM...

Date	Mintage	VG	F	VF	XF	Unc
ND	—	15.00	30.00	60.00	120	—

KM# 67 FLINDRICH (3 Stüber)

Silver **Obv:** Crowned harpy arms, ENNO... **Rev:** Crowned imperial eagle, orb on breast, titles of Ferdinand II

Date	Mintage	VG	F	VF	XF	Unc
ND	—	40.00	80.00	125	250	—
ND (k)	—	40.00	80.00	125	250	—

KM# 22 5 STüBER

Silver **Ruler:** Enno III **Obv:** Small harpy arms divide date, crowned helmet above **Rev:** Crowned imperial eagle, 1/10 in orb on breast **Rev. Legend:** DA. PACEM... **Mint:** Emden

Date	Mintage	VG	F	VF	XF	Unc
1612 (i)	129,690	40.00	85.00	150	300	—
ND (k)	139,975	40.00	85.00	150	300	—
ND	176,055	40.00	85.00	150	300	—

KM# 69 SCHILLING (6 Stüber)

Silver **Ruler:** Enno III **Obv:** Crowned imperial eagle, titles of Rudolf II **Rev:** Crowned six-fold arms, MO-NO. ENN... **Mint:** Emden

Date	Mintage	VG	F	VF	XF	Unc
ND(1612) (i)	236,054	33.00	65.00	120	240	—

KM# 70 SCHILLING (6 Stüber)

Silver **Ruler:** Enno III **Obv:** Crowned shield of 6-fold arms **Rev:** Crowned imperial eagle **Mint:** Emden

Date	Mintage	VG	F	VF	XF	Unc
ND(1614) (j)	1,815,495	33.00	65.00	120	240	—
ND(1617) (k)	72,618	33.00	65.00	120	240	—

KM# 45 SCHILLING (6 Stüber)

Silver **Obv:** Crowned imperial eagle, orb on breast, titles of Ferdinand II **Rev:** Crowned harpy arms **Note:** Kipper Schilling.

Date	Mintage	VG	F	VF	XF	Unc
ND(1620/1)	—	40.00	80.00	150	300	—

KM# 57 SCHILLING (6 Stüber)

Silver **Obv:** Crowned six-fold arms

Date	Mintage	VG	F	VF	XF	Unc
1633 (l)	—	—	—	—	—	—

KM# 72 SCHILLING (6 Stüber)

Silver **Obv:** Titles of Leopold I **Rev:** Titles of Enno Ludwig

Date	Mintage	VG	F	VF	XF	Unc
ND	—	—	—	—	—	—

KM# 71 SCHILLING (6 Stüber)

Silver **Note:** Klippe.

Date	Mintage	VG	F	VF	XF	Unc
ND (j)	—	—	—	—	—	—
ND (k)	—	—	—	—	—	—

KM# 65 28 STüBER (Gulden)

Silver **Obv:** Crowned imperial eagle, orb with 28 on breast, titles of Leopold I **Rev:** Crowned four-fold arms, titles of Enno Ludwig

Date	Mintage	VG	F	VF	XF	Unc
ND	—	675	975	1,350	2,200	—

KM# 26 1/2 THALER

Silver **Note:** Klippe.

Date	Mintage	VG	F	VF	XF	Unc
1614 (j)	—	—	—	—	—	—

KM# 32 1/2 THALER

Silver **Note:** Similar to 1 thaler, KM#27.

Date	Mintage	VG	F	VF	XF	Unc
1616 (j)	—	—	—	—	—	—

KM# 27.1 THALER

Silver **Ruler:** Enno III **Obv:** Armored bust to right in circle, date at end of legend **Obv. Legend:** ENNO + COM + ET + DO - FRI(S) + ORIE(N)(T) + **Rev:** Crowned imperial eagle, imperial orb on breast **Rev. Legend:** DA + PACEM + DOMINE + IN + DIEBVS + NOS(T)(R) **Mint:** Emden **Note:** Varieties exist. Dav. #7122.

Date	Mintage	VG	F	VF	XF	Unc
1614 (j)	26,032	325	525	1,000	1,600	—
1615 (j)	11,976	325	525	1,000	1,600	—
1616 (j)	Inc. above	500	800	1,550	2,400	—
1617 (k)	4,464	500	800	1,550	2,400	—
1619 (k)	Inc. above	500	800	1,550	2,400	—
16ZZ (k)	—	325	525	1,000	1,600	—

KM# 27.2 THALER

Silver **Ruler:** Enno III **Obv:** Armored bust to right in circle **Rev:** Crowned imperial eagle, imperial orb on breast **Mint:** Emden **Note:** Dav. #7123.

Date	Mintage	VG	F	VF	XF	Unc
ND(1614) (j)	Inc. above	500	800	1,500	2,500	—

KM# 28 THALER
Silver **Ruler:** Enno III **Obv:** Armored bust to right in circle, date at end of legend **Rev:** Crowned imperial eagle, imperial orb on breast **Mint:** Emden **Note:** Klippe. Dav. #7122A.

Date	Mintage	VG	F	VF	XF	Unc
1615 (j) Rare	—	—	—	—	—	—
1616 (j) Rare	—	—	—	—	—	—
1617 (k) Rare	—	—	—	—	—	—

KM# 48 THALER
Silver **Obv:** Facing bust, harpy arms below **Rev:** Crowned imperial eagle, orb on breast, date in legend **Note:** Dav. #7125.

Date	Mintage	VG	F	VF	XF	Unc
1629 (l) Rare	—	—	—	—	—	—

KM# 56 THALER
Silver **Rev:** Date divided to lower left and right of eagle **Note:** Dav. #7126.

Date	Mintage	VG	F	VF	XF	Unc
1632 (l) Rare	—	—	—	—	—	—

KM# 36 1-1/2 THALER
Silver **Subject:** Enno III **Note:** Klippe. Similar to 1 Thaler, KM#27. Dav. #7121.

Date	Mintage	VG	F	VF	XF	Unc
1617 (k) Rare	—	—	—	—	—	—
1619 (k) Rare	—	—	—	—	—	—
1622 (k) Rare	—	—	—	—	—	—

KM# 37 1-1/2 THALER
Silver **Obv:** Count on horse leaping right over landscape with town, ship, etc., legend quartered by four small shields **Obv. Legend:** DEO. CONFID… **Rev:** Female figure of Peace sitting, background of town, harbor with ship, etc. **Rev. Legend:** DA. PACEM… **Note:** Dav. #LS366.

Date	Mintage	VG	F	VF	XF	Unc
ND Rare	—	—	—	—	—	—

KM# 30 2 THALER
Silver **Ruler:** Enno III **Obv:** Armored bust to right in circle, date at end of legend **Obv. Legend:** ENNO + COM + ET + DO • FRI(S) + ORIE(N)(T) + **Rev:** Crowned imperial eagle, imperial orb on breast **Rev. Legend:** DA + PACEM + DOMINE + IN + DIEBVS + NOS(T) (R) **Mint:** Emden **Note:** Klippe. Dav. #A7120.

Date	Mintage	VG	F	VF	XF	Unc
1614 (j)	—	2,000	3,250	6,000	—	—
1615 (j) Rare	—	—	—	—	—	—
1617 (k) Rare	—	—	—	—	—	—
1619 (k) Rare	—	—	—	—	—	—

KM# 29 2 THALER
Silver **Ruler:** Enno III **Subject:** Enno III **Obv:** Armored bust to right in circle, date at end of legend **Rev:** Crowned imperial eagle, imperial orb on breast **Mint:** Emden **Note:** Dav. #A7120.

Date	Mintage	VG	F	VF	XF	Unc
1614 (j) Rare	—	—	—	—	—	—

KM# 38 2 THALER
Silver **Obv:** Count on horse leaping right over landscape with town, etc., legend quartered by four small shields **Obv. Legend:** DEO. CONFID… **Rev:** Female figure of Peace sitting, background of town, harbor with ship, etc. **Rev. Legend:** DA. PACEM… **Note:** Dav. #LS365.

Date	Mintage	VG	F	VF	XF	Unc
ND Rare	—	—	—	—	—	—

KM# 49 2 THALER
Silver **Obv:** Crowned imperial eagle, orb on breast, date in legend **Rev:** Facing bust of Ulrich II, harpy arms below **Note:** Dav. #7124.

Date	Mintage	VG	F	VF	XF	Unc
1629 (l) Rare	—	—	—	—	—	—
1632 (l) Rare	—	—	—	—	—	—

TRADE COINAGE

KM# 73 GOLDGULDEN
3.5000 g., 0.9860 Gold 0.1109 oz. AGW **Ruler:** Enno III **Rev:** Crowned imperial eagle, orb on breast **Rev. Legend:** DA. PACEM...

Date	Mintage	VG	F	VF	XF	Unc
ND(1614)	324	750	1,650	4,000	7,700	—

KM# 31 GOLDGULDEN
3.5000 g., 0.9860 Gold 0.1109 oz. AGW **Obv:** Bust of Enno right, date in legend **Rev:** Four shields in cruciform separated by arms of cross

Date	Mintage	VG	F	VF	XF	Unc
1615	576	625	1,350	3,600	6,900	—

KM# 33 GOLDGULDEN
3.5000 g., 0.9860 Gold 0.1109 oz. AGW **Note:** Klippe.

Date	Mintage	VG	F	VF	XF	Unc
1616	—	1,450	2,800	5,600	8,800	—

KM# 74 GOLDGULDEN
3.5000 g., 0.9860 Gold 0.1109 oz. AGW **Obv:** Christ standing **Rev:** Crowned arms

Date	Mintage	VG	F	VF	XF	Unc
ND	—	550	1,200	3,250	6,000	—

KM# 75 1/2 DUCAT
1.7500 g., 0.9860 Gold 0.0555 oz. AGW **Obv:** Crowned arms **Rev:** Cross in circle

Date	Mintage	VG	F	VF	XF	Unc
ND	—	325	625	1,250	2,150	—

KM# 25 DUCAT
3.5000 g., 0.9860 Gold 0.1109 oz. AGW **Obv:** Five-line inscription in ornamented square MON. AVE/ENN… **Rev:** Full-length figure of knight standing to right with sword and shield divides date

Date	Mintage	VG	F	VF	XF	Unc
1612	2,035	950	1,900	4,600	8,200	—

PRINCIPALITY

REGULAR COINAGE

KM# 95 CIFFERT (1/2 Stüber)
Silver **Obv:** Arms divide H-S, date above crown **Rev:** O-F/H-S in angles of cross

Date	Mintage	VG	F	VF	XF	Unc
1660	—	16.00	35.00	75.00	155	—

KM# 106 CIFFERT (1/2 Stüber)
Silver **Obv:** Crowned harpy arms, titles of Christian Eberhard

Date	Mintage	VG	F	VF	XF	Unc
ND (n)	—	16.00	35.00	75.00	155	—

KM# 107 1/4 STüBER (2-1/2 Witten)
Billon **Obv:** Titles of Christian Eberhard **Rev. Legend:** IN. DEO…

Date	Mintage	VG	F	VF	XF	Unc
ND(ca.1665-1708)	—	13.00	27.00	55.00	110	—

KM# 96 STüBER
Silver

Date	Mintage	VG	F	VF	XF	Unc
1660	—	27.00	60.00	115	230	—
ND	—	27.00	60.00	115	230	—

KM# 130 STüBER
Silver

Date	Mintage	VG	F	VF	XF	Unc
ND(1690-1708)	—	27.00	60.00	115	230	—

KM# 99 SCHAF (2 Stüber)
Silver **Obv:** Titles of Georg Christian

Date	Mintage	VG	F	VF	XF	Unc
ND	—	16.00	35.00	75.00	155	—

KM# 109 SCHAF (2 Stüber)
Silver **Obv:** Titles of Christian Eberhard **Rev. Legend:** LAND. MUNTZ.

Date	Mintage	VG	F	VF	XF	Unc
ND	—	15.00	30.00	65.00	130	—

KM# 132 FLINDRICH (3 Stüber)
Silver **Obv:** Crowned harpy arms **Rev:** Value, date

Date	Mintage	VG	F	VF	XF	Unc
1697	—	15.00	30.00	65.00	130	—
1698	—	15.00	30.00	65.00	130	—

KM# 97 4 STüBER
Silver **Obv:** Bust of Enno Ludwig right **Rev:** Crowned harpy shield, date in legend

Date	Mintage	VG	F	VF	XF	Unc
1660	—	—	—	—	—	—

KM# 100 SCHILLING (6 Stüber)
Silver **Obv:** Titles of Georg Christian

Date	Mintage	VG	F	VF	XF	Unc
ND (m)	—	85.00	160	325	650	—

KM# 110 SCHILLING (6 Stüber)
Silver **Ruler:** Christian Eberhard

Date	Mintage	VG	F	VF	XF	Unc
ND	—	30.00	70.00	145	290	—
1693 FBP	—	30.00	70.00	145	290	—
1694 FBP	—	30.00	70.00	145	290	—
1696 FBP	—	30.00	70.00	145	290	—
1697 FBP	—	30.00	70.00	145	290	—
1700 FBP	—	30.00	70.00	145	290	—

KM# 98 28 STüBER (Gulden)
Silver **Obv:** Titles of Georg Christian

Date	Mintage	VG	F	VF	XF	Unc
ND	—	175	325	675	—	—

KM# 108 30 STüBER (Gulden)
Silver **Obv:** 30 in orb on breast of eagle **Rev:** Crowned six-fold arms divide 30-ST, titles of Christian Eberhard

Date	Mintage	VG	F	VF	XF	Unc
ND (m)	—	160	300	600	1,175	—

KM# 104 1/24 THALER
Silver **Obv:** Bust right **Rev:** Crowned imperial eagle, 24 in orb on breast, titles of Leopold I

Date	Mintage	VG	F	VF	XF	Unc
ND (z) Rare	—	—	—	—	—	—

KM# 85 1/16 THALER (2 Schilling)
Silver **Subject:** Death of Juliane of Hesse-Darmstadt, Wife of Ulrich II

Date	Mintage	VG	F	VF	XF	Unc
1659 HS	—	55.00	110	185	360	—

KM# 105 1/12 THALER (2 Groschen)
Silver **Obv:** Bust right **Rev:** Crowned harpy arms, date in legend

Date	Mintage	VG	F	VF	XF	Unc
1661	—	—	—	—	—	—

KM# 86 1/8 THALER
Silver **Subject:** Death of Juliane of Hesse-Darmstadt, Wife of Ulrich II **Note:** Similar to 1 Thaler, KM#89.

Date	Mintage	VG	F	VF	XF	Unc
1659 HS	—	115	200	375	750	—

KM# 87 1/4 THALER
Silver **Subject:** Death of Juliane of Hesse-Darmstadt, Wife of Ulrich II **Note:** Similar to 1 Thaler, KM#89.

Date	Mintage	VG	F	VF	XF	Unc
1659 HS	—	300	500	750	1,400	—

KM# 134 1/4 THALER
Silver **Subject:** Death of Christine Charlotte of Wurttemberg, Wife of Georg Christian **Obv:** Crowned momogram **Rev:** Inscription with date, loveknot below

Date	Mintage	VG	F	VF	XF	Unc
1699	—	165	375	600	1,100	—

KM# 135 1/4 THALER
Silver **Obv:** Arms of East Friesland and Wurttemberg

Date	Mintage	VG	F	VF	XF	Unc
1699	—	—	—	—	—	—

KM# 145 1/4 THALER
Silver **Subject:** Death of Eberhardine Sophie of Ottingen, Wife of Christian Eberhard

Date	Mintage	VG	F	VF	XF	Unc
1700	—	275	475	900	1,800	—

KM# 101 1/3 THALER
Silver **Obv:** Crowned imperial eagle, titles of Leopold I **Rev:** Crowned six-fold arms, value 3.EIN.RT, below, titles of Georg Christian **Note:** Varieties exist.

Date	Mintage	VG	F	VF	XF	Unc
ND (m)	—	80.00	140	275	550	—

KM# 111 1/3 THALER
Silver **Obv:** Crowned four-fold arms of Wurttemberg, central shield of harpy arms, titles of Christine Charlotte **Rev:** Crowned six-fold arms, value 3.EIN.RT, below, titles of Christian Eberhard

Date	Mintage	VG	F	VF	XF	Unc
ND	—	—	—	—	—	—

KM# 112 1/3 THALER
Silver **Obv:** Crowned imperial eagle, titles of Leopold I **Rev:** Crowned six-fold arms, value 3.EIN.RT. below, titles of Christian Eberhard

Date	Mintage	VG	F	VF	XF	Unc
ND (m)	—	50.00	100	200	425	—

KM# 88 1/2 THALER
Silver **Subject:** Death of Juliane of Hesse-Darmstadt, Wife of Ulrich II **Note:** Similar to 1 Thaler, KM#89.

Date	Mintage	VG	F	VF	XF	Unc
1659 HS	—	260	375	700	1,350	—

KM# 131 2/3 THALER (Gulden)
Silver **Obv:** Bust right **Rev:** Crowned six-fold arms, value 2/3 in oval below divides date **Note:** Varieties exist.

Date	Mintage	VG	F	VF	XF	Unc
1694	—	750	1,500	3,000	6,000	11,000
1694 FBP	—	300	700	1,500	—	—

KM# 89 THALER
Silver **Subject:** Death of Juliane of Hesse-Darmstadt, Wife of Ulrich II **Obv:** 12-line inscription **Rev:** Crowned shield **Note:** Dav. #7127.

Date	Mintage	VG	F	VF	XF	Unc
1659 HS	—	600	1,000	1,850	2,750	—

KM# 102.1 THALER
Silver **Note:** Dav. #7128.

Date	Mintage	VG	F	VF	XF	Unc
ND (m) Rare	—	—	—	—	—	—

KM# 102.2 THALER
28.7700 g., Silver **Obv:** Different bust with longer hair **Obv. Legend:** ... ET. W. **Note:** Dav. #7129.

Date	Mintage	VG	F	VF	XF	Unc
ND (m) Rare	—	—	—	—	—	—

Note: Fritz Rudolf Künker Münzenhandlung Auction 127, 6-07, VF realized approximately $21,470.

KM# 103 THALER
Silver **Obv:** Facing bust **Note:** Dav. #7130.

Date	Mintage	VG	F	VF	XF	Unc
ND (m) Rare	—	—	—	—	—	—

KM# 120 THALER
28.8300 g., Silver **Subject:** 20th Anniversary of Regency of Christine Charlotte of Wurttemburg **Obv:** Facing bust **Rev:** Crowned joined oval arms of East Freisland and Wurttemberg, date in inner of two legends **Note:** Dav. #7132.

Date	Mintage	VG	F	VF	XF	Unc
1685 BH (m) Rare	—	—	—	—	—	—

Note: Fritz Rudolf Künker Münzenhandlung Auction 90, 3-03, near XF realized approximately $23,215.

KM# 121.1 THALER
Silver **Obv:** Bust of Christian Eberhard right **Rev:** Crowned six-fold arms divide date, two legends **Rev. Legend:** Outer: DA PAC...; inner: CHARITATE & CANDORE ERIGIMUR **Note:** Dav. #7133.

Date	Mintage	VG	F	VF	XF	Unc
1685 BH (m) Rare	—	—	—	—	—	—

KM# 121.2 THALER
Silver **Note:** Dav. #7134.

Date	Mintage	VG	F	VF	XF	Unc
1686	—	—	—	—	—	—

Note: Reported, not confirmed

KM# A134 THALER
Silver **Obv:** Bust right **Rev:** Ornate helmeted six-fold arms, date below **Note:** Dav. #7135.

Date	Mintage	VG	F	VF	XF	Unc
1698 FBP Rare	—	—	—	—	—	—

KM# A102 1-1/2 THALER
43.4700 g., Silver **Ruler:** Georg Christian **Obv:** Bust with long hair, right **Rev:** Three crowned helmets above six fold arms **Note:** As Dav. #7129

Date	Mintage	VG	F	VF	XF	Unc
ND (m) Rare	—	—	—	—	—	—

Note: Fritz Rudolf Künker Münzenhandlung Auction 93, 6-04, VF-XF realized approximately $67,700.

KM# 122 2 THALER
Silver **Subject:** 20th Anniversary of Regency of Christine Charlotte of Wurttemberg **Obv:** Facing bust **Rev:** Crowned joined oval arms of East Friesland and Wurttemberg, date in inner of two legends **Note:** Dav. #7131.

Date	Mintage	VG	F	VF	XF	Unc
1685 BH (m) Rare	—	—	—	—	—	—

PATTERNS

Including off metal strikes

KM#	Date	Mintage	Identification	Mkt Val
Pn1	ND (i)	—	Ciffert. Gold And Silver. Klippe. KM#16.	—
Pn2	ND (k)	—	Flindrich. Gold. KM#67.	—
Pn3	1659 HS	—	Thaler. Lead. KM#89.	—

EICHSTATT

(Eichstadt)

A bishopric in central Bavaria, which was founded in 745. The imperial mint was established about 908 and episcopal coinage began in the 11th century. Eichstätt was secularized in 1802 and given to Salzburg. It passed to Bavaria in 1805.

RULERS

Johann Conrad von Gemmingen, 1595-1612
Johann Christoph von Westerstetten, 1612-1636
Marquard II, Schenk von Castell, 1636-1685
Johann Eucharius, Schenk von Castell, 1685-1697
Johann Martin von Eyb, 1697-1704

MINT OFFICIALS' INITIALS

Initial	Date	Name
(c), GFN	1682-1724	Georg Friedrich Nürnberger, mintmaster and die-cutter in Nürnberg
(d)	ca.1606	Paulus Bietherr in Nürnberg
(h) 2 horseshoes	1626-28	Bartholomaus Holeisen in Augsburg
IB	ca.1634-37	Unknown
VM	ca. 1569-1603	Valentin Maler, die-cutter in Nürnberg

ARMS

A bishop's crozier

BISHOPRIC

REGULAR COINAGE

KM# 16 PFENNIG

Copper, 13 mm. **Obv:** Oval Eichstatt arms divide date, I above **Note:** Kipper Pfennig. Uniface.

Date	Mintage	VG	F	VF	XF	Unc
1621	—	33.00	65.00	125	250	—

KM# 17 PFENNIG

Copper **Note:** Shield is flat on top, pointed bottom.

Date	Mintage	VG	F	VF	XF	Unc
1621	—	75.00	150	300	600	—

KM# 18 1/2 KREUZER

Copper **Obv:** Bishop's staff between two crosses **Note:** Kipper 1/2 Kreuzer. Uniface.

Date	Mintage	VG	F	VF	XF	Unc
ND(1621/2)	—	25.00	40.00	80.00	160	—

KM# 26 1/2 KREUZER

Silver **Obv:** Two shields of Eichstatt and Westerstetten arms, date above **Rev:** Imperial orb with 1/2

Date	Mintage	VG	F	VF	XF	Unc
1623	—	65.00	130	220	385	—
1624	—	65.00	130	220	385	—

KM# 19 KREUZER

Copper **Obv:** Bishop's staff **Rev:** I/KREI/ZER **Note:** Kipper Kreuzer. Varieties exist.

Date	Mintage	VG	F	VF	XF	Unc
ND(1621/2)	—	20.00	40.00	80.00	160	—

KM# 20 KREUZER

Copper **Rev:** KREIZER/I **Note:** Varieties exist.

Date	Mintage	VG	F	VF	XF	Unc
ND(1621/2)	—	20.00	40.00	80.00	160	—

KM# 31 KREUZER

Silver **Obv:** Bishop's mitre above two shilds of Eichstatt and Westerstetten arms, date below **Rev:** Horseshoes above legend, pine cone of Augsburg below **Rev. Inscription:** CONFIRMET / ET / CONSERVET / DEVS

Date	Mintage	VG	F	VF	XF	Unc
1628 (h)	—	32.00	65.00	135	230	—

KM# 40 KREUZER

Silver **Obv:** Two shields of Eichstsattt and Castell arms, angel's head above divides I.E.-E.E. **Rev:** Double cross forming star, value I in central circle, date in legend

Date	Mintage	VG	F	VF	XF	Unc
1694 (c)	—	16.00	35.00	75.00	155	—

KM# 28 2 KREUZER (1/2 Batzen)

Silver **Obv:** Crowned imperial eagle, two in orb on breast, titles of Ferdinand II **Rev:** Four-fold arms of Eichstatt and Westerstetten in circle, date above in legend

Date	Mintage	VG	F	VF	XF	Unc
1623	—	27.00	45.00	90.00	180	—

KM# 27 2 KREUZER (1/2 Batzen)

Silver **Obv:** Imperial orb with Z, titles of Ferdinand II **Rev:** Two shields of Eichstatt and Westerstetten arms in circle **Note:** Varieties exist.

Date	Mintage	VG	F	VF	XF	Unc
ND(1623)	—	27.00	50.00	100	200	—

KM# 29 2 KREUZER (1/2 Batzen)

Silver **Obv:** Two in orb **Rev:** Date above shields **Note:** Varieties exist.

Date	Mintage	VG	F	VF	XF	Unc
1623	—	20.00	40.00	80.00	160	—
1624	—	20.00	40.00	80.00	160	—
1634	—	20.00	40.00	80.00	160	—
1634 IB	—	20.00	40.00	80.00	160	—

KM# 38 2 KREUZER (1/2 Batzen)

Silver **Rev:** Two oval arms, date in legend

Date	Mintage	VG	F	VF	XF	Unc
1636 IB	—	16.00	35.00	75.00	155	—

KM# 39 2 KREUZER (1/2 Batzen)

Silver **Obv:** Titles of Ferdinand III

Date	Mintage	VG	F	VF	XF	Unc
1637 IB	—	16.00	35.00	75.00	155	—

KM# 41 2 KREUZER (1/2 Batzen)

Silver **Obv:** Crowned imperial eagle, value 2 in shield on breast, date and titles of Leopold I in legend **Rev:** Four-fold arms of cathedral chapter and Castell arms, with central shield of Eichstatt arms

Date	Mintage	VG	F	VF	XF	Unc
1694 (c)	282,000	16.00	35.00	75.00	150	—

KM# 23 3 KREUZER (Groschen)

Silver **Obv:** Crowned imperial eagle, 3 in orb on breast, titles of Ferdinand II **Rev:** Four-fold arms of Eichstatt and Westerstetten, date in legend at top **Note:** Varieties exist.

Date	Mintage	VG	F	VF	XF	Unc
1622	—	50.00	100	250	500	1,300
1623	—	50.00	100	250	500	1,300

KM# 42 4 KREUZER (Batzen)

Silver **Obv:** Four-fold arms of cathedral chapter and Castell between palm branches, angel's head with mitre above **Rev:** St. Willibald standing, value (4) below

Date	Mintage	VG	F	VF	XF	Unc
1694 GFN	135,000	40.00	75.00	140	265	550

KM# 35 10 KREUZER

Silver **Obv:** Crowned imperial eagle, X.K. in shield on breast, titles of Ferdinand II **Rev:** Two oval arms of Eichstatt and Westerstetten in baroque frame, date in legend

Date	Mintage	VG	F	VF	XF	Unc
1634 IB	—	275	425	575	1,050	—

KM# 36 10 KREUZER

Silver **Rev:** Value 10 in shield on eagle's breast **Note:** Varieties exist.

Date	Mintage	VG	F	VF	XF	Unc
1635 IB	—	200	300	500	1,000	—
1636 IB	—	200	300	500	1,000	—
1637 IB	—	200	300	500	1,000	—

KM# 21 24 KREUZER

Silver **Obv:** Westerstetten arms in baroque frame **Obv. Legend:** MONETA. NOVA... **Rev:** Eichstatt arms in baroque frame, (24) in legend at top **Note:** Kipper 24 Kreuzer.

Date	Mintage	VG	F	VF	XF	Unc
ND(1621)	—	175	350	700	1,400	—

KM# 22 24 KREUZER

Silver **Rev:** Value in field above arms **Note:** Varieties exist.

Date	Mintage	VG	F	VF	XF	Unc
ND(1621)	—	175	350	700	1,400	—

KM# 15 1/4 THALER (24 Kreuzer)

Silver **Obv:** Three leopards left (cathedral chapter arms) **Obv. Legend:** MONETA. NOVA... **Rev:** Eichstatt arms in baroque frame divide date

Date	Mintage	VG	F	VF	XF	Unc
1620 Rare	—	—	—	—	—	—

KM# 5 1/2 THALER

Silver **Rev:** Madonna and child

Date	Mintage	VG	F	VF	XF	Unc
1606 (d)	500	600	1,000	2,000	3,500	—

KM# 6 1/2 THALER

Silver **Rev:** St. Wilibaldus seated

Date	Mintage	VG	F	VF	XF	Unc
1606 (d)	500	1,000	1,900	3,750	7,200	—

KM# 7 1/2 THALER

Silver **Obv:** Crowned imperial eagle, titles of Rudolf II **Rev:** Four-fold arms of Eichstatt and Gemmingen, angel's head and wings above, date divided below

Date	Mintage	VG	F	VF	XF	Unc
1606 (d)	500	—	—	—	—	—

KM# 43 1/2 THALER

Silver **Obv:** Johann Eucharius

Date	Mintage	VG	F	VF	XF	Unc
1694 GFN Rare	192	—	—	—	—	—

KM# 44 1/2 THALER

Silver **Rev:** St. Wilibaldus standing

Date	Mintage	VG	F	VF	XF	Unc
1694 GFN	3,392	300	600	1,000	1,800	—

KM# 8 THALER

Silver **Rev:** Madonna and child **Note:** Dav. #5228.

Date	Mintage	VG	F	VF	XF	Unc
1606 (d) Rare	1,000	—	—	—	—	—

Note: Dr. Busso Peus Nachfolger Auction 390, 5-07, XF-VF realized approximately $27,200.

KM# 9 THALER

Silver **Rev:** St. Wilibaldus seated **Note:** Dav. #5229.

Date	Mintage	VG	F	VF	XF	Unc
1606 (d) Rare	999	—	—	—	—	—

Note: Dr. Busso Peus Nachfolger Auction 390, 5-07, XF-VF realized approximately $11,550.

KM# 10 THALER

Silver **Obv:** Crowned imperial eagle, titles of Rudolf II **Rev:** Four-fold arms of Eichstatt and Gemmingen, angel's head and wings above, date divided below **Note:** Dav. #5230.

Date	Mintage	VG	F	VF	XF	Unc
1606 (d) Rare	1,002	—	—	—	—	—

KM# 24.1 THALER

Silver **Obv:** Crowned imperial eagle, orb on breast, titles of Ferdinand II **Rev:** Two oval arms of Eichstatt and Westerstetten in baroque frame, angel's head above, date below **Note:** Dav. #5231.

Date	Mintage	VG	F	VF	XF	Unc
1622 Rare	—	—	—	—	—	—

KM# 25 THALER

Silver **Obv:** Floral spray instead of angel's head **Note:** Dav. #5233.

Date	Mintage	VG	F	VF	XF	Unc
1622 Rare	—	—	—	—	—	—

KM# 24.2 THALER

Silver **Obv:** Two pointed arms and cherub face in cartouche, date in frame below **Note:** Varieties exist. Dav. #5232.

Date	Mintage	VG	F	VF	XF	Unc
1622 Rare	—	—	—	—	—	—

KM# 30 THALER
Silver **Subject:** Johann Christoph **Obv:** Four-fold arms of Eichstatt and Westerstetten, two helmets and mitre above, date in legend at top **Note:** Dav. #5234.

Date	Mintage	VG	F	VF	XF	Unc
1626 Rare	—	—	—	—	—	—

Note: Künker Auction 134, 1-08, Unc realized approx. $50,300

KM# 45 THALER
Silver **Subject:** Johann Eucharius **Note:** Dav. #5235.

Date	Mintage	VG	F	VF	XF	Unc
1694 GFN	2,208	375	750	1,250	3,000	7,500

KM# 46 THALER
Silver **Rev:** St. Wilibaldus standing **Note:** Dav. #5236.

Date	Mintage	VG	F	VF	XF	Unc
1694 GFN	24,000	125	250	400	900	1,850

KM# 47 2 THALER
Silver **Rev:** St. Wilibaldus standing **Note:** Dav. #5236A.

Date	Mintage	VG	F	VF	XF	Unc
1694 GFN Rare	—	—	—	—	—	—

TRADE COINAGE

KM# 32 GOLDGULDEN
3.2300 g., 0.9860 Gold 0.1024 oz. AGW **Ruler:** Johann Christoph **Obv:** Two coats of arms in inner circle **Rev:** St. Walburga standing behind arms divides date

Date	Mintage	VG	F	VF	XF	Unc
1633	—	775	1,650	3,850	6,750	—

KM# 33 GOLDGULDEN
3.1800 g., Gold, 23 mm. **Ruler:** Johann Christoph **Obv:** Two adjacent oval shields of arms in baroque frame **Obv. Legend:** IOAN. CHRIST. D. G. EPS. EYSTETENS. **Rev:** St. Willibald standing behind shield of arms which divides date **Rev. Legend:** SANCTVS. - WILLIBALD9 **Note:** Fr. 903.

Date	Mintage	VG	F	VF	XF	Unc
1633	—	775	1,650	3,850	6,750	—
1634	—	775	1,650	3,850	6,750	—
1635 IB	—	775	1,650	3,850	6,750	—

KM# 34 GOLDGULDEN
3.2000 g., Gold, 23 mm. **Ruler:** Johann Christoph **Obv:** Two adjacent oval shields of arms in baroque frame **Obv. Legend:** IOAN. CHRIST. D. G. EPS. EYSTETENS. **Rev:** St. Walburga standing behind shield of arms which divides date **Rev. Legend:** SANCTA. WALP - VRGIS. VIRGO. **Note:** Fr. 904.

Date	Mintage	VG	F	VF	XF	Unc
1633	—	775	1,650	3,850	6,750	—

KM# 37 DUCAT
3.4700 g., 0.9860 Gold 0.1100 oz. AGW **Ruler:** Johann Christoph **Obv:** St. Willibald behind shield of arms **Obv. Legend:** IOHAN CHRISTO ... **Rev:** Imperial eagle in inner circle, date in legend **Rev. Legend:** FERDINAND ...

Date	Mintage	VG	F	VF	XF	Unc
1635 IB	—	1,000	2,100	4,800	8,500	—

KM# A45 5 DUCAT (1/2 Portugalöser)
17.5000 g., 0.9860 Gold 0.5547 oz. AGW **Note:** Struck with 1/2 Thaler dies, KM#44.

Date	Mintage	VG	F	VF	XF	Unc
1694 GFN Rare	—	—	—	—	—	—

KM# A46 10 DUCAT (Portugalöser)
0.9860 Gold **Note:** Struck with 1 Thaler dies, KM#45.

Date	Mintage	VG	F	VF	XF	Unc
1694 GFN Rare	—	—	—	—	—	—

EINBECK

(Eimbeck)

The town of Einbeck, near the confluence of the Leine and Ilme Rivers, 38 miles (65 kilometers) south of Hannover, was associated early on with the nearby monastery of St. Alexander which was founded about 1080. Its first mention as a town came in 1274 and soon thereafter it was the location of a mint for the dukes of Brunswick-Grubenhagen. At some point during the 15th century, Einbeck obtained the mint right and began striking its own local coinage in 1498. By an edict of Johann Friedrich, Duke of Brunswick-Lüneburg-Calenberg (1665-79) in 1674, the minting of silver coinage was halted, but the town continued striking undated copper pfennigs until 1717.

MINT OFFICIALS' INITIALS

Initial	Date	Name
(a)shield with half of seal ring in top, bottom shaded	1616-18	Heinrich von der Ecke
AS	1668-71	Andreas Schele
(b)same as (a)	1623-25	Hans von der Ecke der Jüngere
(c) crossed halberds	1628	Georg Krukenberg
HE (combined in oval)	1604-05	Hans von der Ecke der Ältere
HE (combined in oval)	1606-18	Heinrich von der Ecke
HH (sometimes in ligature)	1672-74	Hans Hallensen
IK or (d) halberd	1629	Unknown
VF (sometimes in ligature)	1659	Urban Felgenhauer

ARMS

Large Gothic 'E', later in 17th century, a Latin 'E'

REFERENCE

B = Heinrich Buck, ***Die Münzen der Stadt Einbeck.*** Hildeshiem and Leipzig, 1939.

PROVINCIAL TOWN

REGULAR COINAGE

KM# 15 FLITTER (1/2 Pfennig)
Copper **Obv:** Crowned Gothic E **Rev:** Date **Rev. Legend:** I/FLIT/TER **Note:** Klipper Flitter.

Date	Mintage	VG	F	VF	XF	Unc
(1)620	—	20.00	40.00	85.00	175	—

KM# 16 FLITTER (1/2 Pfennig)
Copper, 15 mm. **Obv:** Crowned ornate gothic E **Rev:** Value I in circle, date in legend **Rev. Legend:** EINBEK **Note:** Varieties exist.

Date	Mintage	VG	F	VF	XF	Unc
1620	—	20.00	40.00	85.00	175	—
1621	—	20.00	40.00	85.00	175	—
1612 Error	—	20.00	40.00	85.00	175	—
1622	—	20.00	40.00	85.00	175	—

KM# 19 3 FLITTER
Copper **Obv:** Crowned Gothie C **Rev:** III in circle, date **Rev. Legend:** FLITTER **Note:** Klipper 3 Flitter. Varieties exist.

Date	Mintage	VG	F	VF	XF	Unc
16Z1	—	20.00	40.00	85.00	175	—
1Z61 Error	—	20.00	40.00	85.00	175	—
1621	—	20.00	40.00	85.00	175	—

KM# 22 PFENNIG
Silver **Obv:** Gothic E, date above, in shield surrounded by circle of pellets **Note:** Uniface. Schüssel type. Varieties exist.

Date	Mintage	VG	F	VF	XF	Unc
16Z3	—	16.00	35.00	70.00	145	—
16Z4	—	16.00	35.00	70.00	145	—
ND(1623/4)	—	16.00	35.00	70.00	145	—

KM# 32 PFENNIG
Silver **Note:** Crowned Gothic E divides date in circle of pellets. Varieties exist.

Date	Mintage	VG	F	VF	XF	Unc
16Z9	—	16.00	35.00	70.00	145	—
1660	—	16.00	35.00	70.00	145	—

KM# 35 PFENNIG
Silver **Note:** Crowned Roman E divides date in circle of pellets. Varieties exist.

Date	Mintage	VG	F	VF	XF	Unc
1631	—	16.00	35.00	70.00	145	—
1632	—	16.00	35.00	70.00	145	—
1634	—	16.00	35.00	70.00	145	—
1635	—	16.00	35.00	70.00	145	—
1638	—	16.00	35.00	70.00	145	—
1641	—	16.00	35.00	70.00	145	—

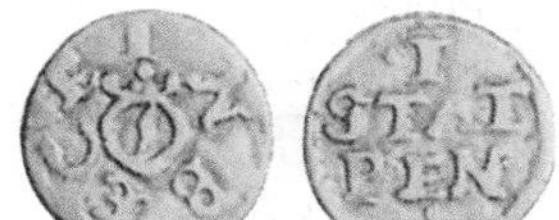

KM# 40 PFENNIG
Copper **Obv:** EINBECK around **Rev:** Value **Note:** Varieties exist.

Date	Mintage	VG	F	VF	XF	Unc
ND(1647-1717)	—	15.00	30.00	55.00	110	—

KM# 41 PFENNIG
Copper **Obv:** With rosette **Note:** Varieties exist.

Date	Mintage	VG	F	VF	XF	Unc
ND(1647-1717)	—	15.00	30.00	55.00	110	—

KM# 51 PFENNIG
Silver **Note:** Uniface. Crowned Gothic E divides date.

Date	Mintage	VG	F	VF	XF	Unc
1668	—	13.00	33.00	65.00	135	—
1668 AS	—	13.00	33.00	65.00	135	—

KM# 67 PFENNIG
Silver **Note:** Schussel type. Crowned Roman E divides date and mintmasters initials.

Date	Mintage	VG	F	VF	XF	Unc
1673 HH	—	13.00	33.00	65.00	135	—

KM# 20 3 PFENNIG (1/96 Thaler)
Silver **Obv:** Crowned Gothic E **Rev:** Imperial orb with 3 divides date

Date	Mintage	VG	F	VF	XF	Unc
1622	—	20.00	40.00	80.00	165	—
1635	—	20.00	40.00	80.00	165	—

KM# 21 3 PFENNIG (1/96 Thaler)
Silver **Obv:** Smaller E **Rev:** Smaller imperial orb on ornamented rhombus

Date	Mintage	VG	F	VF	XF	Unc
1622	—	20.00	40.00	80.00	165	—

KM# 52 3 PFENNIG (1/96 Thaler)
Silver **Obv:** Crowned Gothic E, EINBECK, date **Rev:** Imperial orb with 3

Date	Mintage	VG	F	VF	XF	Unc
1668 AS	—	13.00	27.00	55.00	110	—
1669 AS	—	13.00	27.00	55.00	110	—
1670 AS	—	13.00	27.00	55.00	110	—

KM# 53 3 PFENNIG (1/96 Thaler)
Silver **Obv. Legend:** EIMBEC

Date	Mintage	VG	F	VF	XF	Unc
1668 AS	—	15.00	30.00	60.00	125	—

KM# 60 3 PFENNIG (1/96 Thaler)
Silver **Obv. Legend:** EINBEC

Date	Mintage	VG	F	VF	XF	Unc
1670 AS	—	15.00	30.00	60.00	125	—
1672 HH	—	15.00	30.00	60.00	125	—
1673 HH	—	15.00	30.00	60.00	125	—

KM# 5 1/96 THALER (3 Pfennig)
Silver **Obv:** Crowned Gothic E **Rev:** Imperial orb with 96 divides date

Date	Mintage	VG	F	VF	XF	Unc
1604	—	55.00	120	200	450	—
1604 HE	—	55.00	120	200	450	—
1605 HE	—	55.00	120	200	450	—
ND	—	55.00	120	200	450	—

KM# 54 4 PFENNIG (Gute)
Silver **Obv:** Crowned Gothic E, MO. NO. EINBECIC, date around **Rev. Legend:** IIII/GUTE/PF

Date	Mintage	VG	F	VF	XF	Unc
1668 AS	—	20.00	40.00	85.00	170	—
1669 AS	—	20.00	40.00	85.00	170	—

KM# 68 4 PFENNIG (Gute)
Silver **Obv. Legend:** EINBEC

Date	Mintage	VG	F	VF	XF	Unc
1673 HH	—	20.00	40.00	85.00	170	—

KM# 23 MARIENGROSCHEN
Silver **Obv:** Crowned Gothic E, date in legend **Rev:** Madonna and child **Note:** Varieties exist.

Date	Mintage	VG	F	VF	XF	Unc
16Z3	—	20.00	45.00	90.00	185	—
16Z4	—	20.00	45.00	90.00	185	—
1659 VF	—	20.00	45.00	90.00	185	—
1668 AS	—	20.00	45.00	90.00	185	—
1669 AS	—	20.00	45.00	90.00	185	—
1670 AS	—	20.00	45.00	90.00	185	—
1673 HH	—	20.00	45.00	90.00	185	—
1674 HH	—	20.00	45.00	90.00	185	—

KM# 61 2 MARIENGROSCHEN
Silver **Obv:** Crowned Large E, date in legend **Rev. Legend:** II/MARI/GR

Date	Mintage	VG	F	VF	XF	Unc
1671 AS	—	300	600	1,200	2,400	—

KM# 62 4 MARIENGROSCHEN
Silver **Obv:** Crowned Large E, date in legend **Rev. Legend:** IIII/MARIEN/GROS

Date	Mintage	VG	F	VF	XF	Unc
1671 AS	—	135	275	550	1,100	—

KM# 55 6 MARIENGROSCHEN
Silver **Obv:** Crowned Gothic E **Rev:** Date in legend **Rev. Legend:** VI/MARIEN/GROS

Date	Mintage	VG	F	VF	XF	Unc
1669 AS	—	40.00	85.00	160	325	—
1671 AS	—	40.00	85.00	160	325	—
1673 HH	—	40.00	85.00	160	325	—
1674 HH	—	40.00	85.00	160	325	—

KM# 63 6 MARIENGROSCHEN
Silver **Obv:** Crowned Large E date in legend **Rev:** Date **Rev. Inscription:** VI / MARIEN / GROSCH

Date	Mintage	VG	F	VF	XF	Unc
1671 AS	—	275	500	1,000	1,800	—

KM# 64 12 MARIENGROSCHEN
Silver **Obv:** Crowned Large E **Rev:** Date **Rev. Legend:** XII/MARIEN/GROSCH

Date	Mintage	VG	F	VF	XF	Unc
1671 AS	—	450	850	1,650	3,000	—

KM# 65 24 MARIENGROSCHEN (2/3 Thaler)
Silver **Obv:** Crowned Gothic E, date in legend **Rev. Inscription:** XXIIII / MARIEN / GROS **Note:** Dav. #502.

Date	Mintage	VG	F	VF	XF	Unc
1671	—	—	—	—	—	—

Note: Reported, not confirmed

KM# 66 24 MARIENGROSCHEN (2/3 Thaler)
Silver **Obv:** Crowned Large E **Rev:** Value, date **Rev. Legend:** XXIIII **Note:** Dav. #503.

Date	Mintage	VG	F	VF	XF	Unc
1671 AS	—	—	—	—	—	—

Note: Reported, not confirmed

KM# 17 12 KREUZER (Schreckenberger)
Silver **Obv:** Crowned imperial eagle, 12 in orb on breast, titles of Ferdinand II **Rev:** Crowned Gothic E in shield **Note:** Kipper 12 Kreuzer.

Date	Mintage	VG	F	VF	XF	Unc
ND(1620-21)	—	150	300	600	—	—

KM# 7 1/24 THALER (Groschen)
Silver **Obv:** Imperial orb with 24, cross divides date, titles of Rudolf II **Rev:** Crowned Gothic E **Note:** Klippe.

Date	Mintage	VG	F	VF	XF	Unc
1604 HE Rare	—	—	—	—	—	—

KM# 6 1/24 THALER (Groschen)
Silver **Obv:** Imperial orb with 24, cross divides date, titles of Rudolf II **Rev:** Crowned Gothic E **Note:** Varieties exist.

Date	Mintage	VG	F	VF	XF	Unc
1604 HE	—	20.00	40.00	85.00	175	—
1605 HE	—	20.00	40.00	85.00	175	—
1606 HE	—	20.00	40.00	85.00	175	—
1607 HE	—	20.00	40.00	85.00	175	—

KM# 10 1/24 THALER (Groschen)
Silver **Obv:** Titles of Matthias **Note:** Varieties exist.

Date	Mintage	VG	F	VF	XF	Unc
1614	—	20.00	40.00	80.00	165	—
1615	—	20.00	40.00	80.00	165	—
1616	—	20.00	40.00	80.00	165	—
1616 (a)	—	20.00	40.00	80.00	165	—
1617	—	20.00	40.00	80.00	165	—
1617 (a)	—	20.00	40.00	80.00	165	—

KM# 11 1/24 THALER (Groschen)
Silver **Rev:** Date divided at top **Note:** Kipper 1/24 Thaler. Varieties exist.

Date	Mintage	VG	F	VF	XF	Unc
1618	—	20.00	40.00	85.00	175	—
1619	—	20.00	40.00	85.00	175	—
1602 Error	—	20.00	40.00	85.00	175	—

KM# 18 1/24 THALER (Groschen)
Silver **Obv:** Titles of Ferdinand II

Date	Mintage	VG	F	VF	XF	Unc
1620	—	30.00	60.00	120	240	—

KM# 56 1/24 THALER (Groschen)
Silver **Obv:** Imperial orb with 24, titles of Leopold I **Rev:** Crowned Gothic E, date in legend

Date	Mintage	VG	F	VF	XF	Unc
1669 AS	—	20.00	40.00	85.00	175	—
1670 AS	—	20.00	40.00	85.00	175	—
1671 AS	—	20.00	40.00	85.00	175	—

KM# 29 1/2 REICHSORT (1/8 Thaler)
Silver **Obv:** Cross on imperial orb above divides date in legend, titles of Ferdinand II **Obv. Inscription:** EIN / HALB / REICHS / ORT **Rev:** Crowned Gothic E

Date	Mintage	VG	F	VF	XF	Unc
1628	—	—	—	—	—	—

KM# 24 1/4 THALER
Silver **Obv:** Crowned imperial eagle, orb on breast, titles of Ferdinand II **Rev:** Crowned Gothic E, date in legend **Note:** Varieties exist.

Date	Mintage	VG	F	VF	XF	Unc
1624 (b)	—	600	1,000	1,600	2,900	—
1625 (b)	—	600	1,000	1,600	2,900	—
1628 (c)	—	600	1,000	1,600	2,900	—

KM# 25 1/2 THALER
Silver **Obv:** Crowned imperial eagle, orb on breast, titles of Ferdinand II **Rev:** Crowned Gothic E in ornamented shield, date in legend **Note:** Varieties exist.

Date	Mintage	VG	F	VF	XF	Unc
1624 (b)	—	750	1,400	2,300	3,500	—
1625 (b)	—	750	1,400	2,300	3,500	—
1627	—	750	1,400	2,300	3,500	—

KM# 12 THALER
Silver **Obv:** Crowned imperial eagle, orb on breast, titles of Matthias **Rev:** Crowned Gothic E in ornamented shield, date in legend **Note:** Dav. #5237.

Date	Mintage	VG	F	VF	XF	Unc
1618 (a) Rare	—	—	—	—	—	—

KM# 26 THALER
Silver **Obv:** Titles of Ferdinand II **Rev:** Angel's head above Gothic E **Note:** Dav. #5238.

Date	Mintage	VG	F	VF	XF	Unc
1624 Rare	—	—	—	—	—	—

KM# 27 THALER

Silver **Rev:** Titles of Ferdinand II **Note:** Dav. #5239.

Date	Mintage	VG	F	VF	XF	Unc
1624 (b)	—	1,500	3,000	5,100	8,400	—

KM# 28 THALER

Silver **Note:** Dav. #5241.

Date	Mintage	VG	F	VF	XF	Unc
1624 (b)	—	750	1,500	3,000	5,000	—
1625 (b)	—	750	1,500	3,000	6,000	—
1627	—	900	1,750	3,300	7,200	—
1628 (c)	—	750	1,500	3,300	6,000	—
1631	—	900	1,750	3,900	7,200	—

KM# 45 THALER

Silver **Note:** Dav. #5242.

Date	Mintage	VG	F	VF	XF	Unc
1659 VF Rare	—	—	—	—	—	—

KM# 30 2 THALER

Silver **Obv:** Crowned ornate Gothic E superimposed on cross in circle, date at end of legend **Obv. Legend:** MONETA NOVA EIMBECENSIS **Rev:** Crowned imperial eagle, Z4 in orb on breast, titles of Maximilian II **Note:** Dav. #5240. Struck from KM#28 dies.

Date	Mintage	VG	F	VF	XF	Unc
1628 (c) Rare	—	—	—	—	—	—

KM# 50 2 THALER

Silver **Note:** Struck from KM#36 dies. Dav. #5243.

Date	Mintage	VG	F	VF	XF	Unc
1660 VF Rare	—	—	—	—	—	—

TRADE COINAGE

KM# 13 GOLDGULDEN

3.5000 g., 0.9860 Gold 0.1109 oz. AGW **Obv:** Imperial eagle, orb on breast, titles of Ferdinand II **Rev:** Crowned Gothic E, date in legend

Date	Mintage	VG	F	VF	XF	Unc
1619 Reported not confirmed	—	—	—	—	—	—

KM# 31 GOLDGULDEN

3.5000 g., 0.9860 Gold 0.1109 oz. AGW **Obv:** Crowned imperial eagle, orb on breast, titles of Ferdinand II **Rev:** Crowned Gothic E in city gate with 2 towers which divides date, lion left above gate

Date	Mintage	VG	F	VF	XF	Unc
1628 Rare	—	—	—	—	—	—

KM# 33 GOLDGULDEN

3.5000 g., 0.9860 Gold 0.1109 oz. AGW **Rev:** Gothic E in city gate with 2 towers

Date	Mintage	VG	F	VF	XF	Unc
1629 IK Rare	—	—	—	—	—	—
1629 (d) Rare	—	—	—	—	—	—

PATTERNS

Including off metal strikes

KM#	Date	Mintage	Identification	Mkt Val
Pn1	1633	—	Thaler. Copper. KM#28.	—

TRIAL STRIKES

KM#	Date	Mintage	Identification	Mkt Val
TS1	1636	—	Thaler. Silver. Klippe, obverse, KM#36.	—

ELLWANGEN

Founded as a Benedictine Abbey about 764 but not recognized as a town until about 1229, Ellwangen is located in northern Württemberg about 18 miles northwest of Nordlingen. The Abbey was reorganized as a college in 1460. The mint right was obtained in 1555. The town was mediatized and the properties given to Württemberg in 1803.

RULERS

Wolfgang von Hausen, 1584-1603
Johann Christoph I von Westerstetten, 1603-1613
Johann Christoph II von Freyberg-Eisenberg, 1613-1620
Johann Jakob Blarer von Wartensee, 1621-1654
Johann Rudolf von Rechberg, 1654-1660
Johann Christoph III von Freyberg-Eisenberg, 1660-1674
Johann Christoph IV Adelmann von Adelmannsfelden, 1674-1687
Heinrich Christoph von Wolfframsdorf, 1687-1689
Ludwig Anton, Pfalzgraf bei Rhein und zu Neuburg, 1689-1694
Franz Ludwig von der Pfalz, 1694-1732

MINT OFFICIALS' INITIALS

Initials	Date	Name
(a) horseshoe	Ca.1620-68	Johann Bartholomaus Holesen der Altere in Augsburg
(b) horseshoe	1668-97	Johann Christoph Holeisen in Augsburg
CIL	1683-1707	Christoph Jakob Leherr, die-cutter in Augsburg
GFN	1682-1704	George Friedrich Nurnberger in Nüremberg

PROVOSTSHIP

Abbey

REGULAR COINAGE

KM# 5 PFENNIG

Copper **Ruler:** Johann Jakob Blarer **Obv:** Mitre with cross above divides date 1 - 6/Z - 1 **Rev. Legend:** I/PFEN/NING/++

Date	Mintage	VG	F	VF	XF	Unc
16Z1	—	—	—	—	—	—

KM# 6 2 KREUZER (1/2 Batzen)

Silver **Ruler:** Johann Jakob Blarer **Obv:** Crowned imperial eagle, Z in orb on breast, titles of Ferdinand II **Rev:** 2 oval arms, angel's head above, date below **Note:** Varieties exist.

Date	Mintage	VG	F	VF	XF	Unc
(16)24 (a)	—	20.00	40.00	85.00	175	350
(16)25 (a)	—	20.00	40.00	85.00	175	350
(16)26 (a)	—	20.00	40.00	85.00	175	350

KM# 15 3 KREUZER (Groschen)

Silver **Ruler:** Ludwig Anton **Subject:** Death of Ludwig Anton **Obv:** Crowned oval 4-fold arms in baroque frame **Rev:** 7-line inscription with date, value 3 in imperial orb below

Date	Mintage	VG	F	VF	XF	Unc
1694 Rare	—	—	—	—	—	—

KM# 16 1/4 THALER

Silver **Ruler:** Ludwig Anton **Subject:** Death of Ludwig Anton **Obv:** Crowned oval 4-fold arms in baroque frame **Rev:** 6-line inscription with date, value in imperial orb below

Date	Mintage	VG	F	VF	XF	Unc
1694 GFN Rare	—	—	—	—	—	—

KM# 7 THALER

Silver **Ruler:** Johann Jakob Blarer **Obv:** Oval 4-fold arms, angel's head and wings above, date in cartouche below **Rev:** Crowned imperial eagle, orb on breast, arms (pinecone) of Augsburg below, titles of Ferdinand II **Note:** Dav. #5244.

Date	Mintage	VG	F	VF	XF	Unc
1624 (a)	—	2,500	4,500	6,500	10,000	—

KM# 10 THALER

Silver **Ruler:** Heinrich Christoph **Obv:** Bust right **Rev:** Helmeted and mitred oval 4-fold arms, date below divided by small Augsburg arms **Note:** Dav. #5245.

Date	Mintage	VG	F	VF	XF	Unc
1689 CIL-(b) Rare	—	—	—	—	—	—

KM# 11 THALER

Silver **Ruler:** Heinrich Christoph **Obv:** Bust right **Rev:** Romulus and Remus with wolf in landscape, ornate 4-fold arms above divide date **Note:** Dav. #5246.

Date	Mintage	VG	F	VF	XF	Unc
1689 CIL Rare	—	—	—	—	—	—

EMDEN

A seaport on the Ems River adjoining the North Sea was founded in the 9th century and became a pirate lair in the 14th century. It was taken by Hamburg and East Friesland in 1431. Hamburg sold its local holdings to East Friesland in 1453. Emden became a Free City of the Empire in 1595, was transferred to Prussia in 1744, and then became a Free Port in 1751. It was passed to Holland in 1806, Hannover in 1815 and Prussia in 1866.

MINT OFFICIALS' INITIALS

Initial	Date	Name
IG, G	Pre-1603	Jonas Georgens
CP	Ca.1619	Unknown
CP	1673-74	Christian Pfahler
IS	1648-50	Jacob Schweiger
JR	Ca.1681	Unknown

ARMS

Upper half of crowned harpy (because of the association with East Friesland) above a stone wall, waves below.

REFERENCE

K = ***Nachtrag zum Münz- und Medaillen – Kabinet des Grafen Karl zu Inn- und Knyphausen.*** Hannover, 1877.

FREE CITY

REGULAR COINAGE

KM# 3 2 STUBER

Silver, 24 mm. **Obv:** Shield of city arms **Obv. Legend:** CIVITAT. EMBDENSIS. **Rev:** Floriated cross in circle **Rev. Legend:** BENEDICTVS. DOMINVS. DEVS. **Note:** Ref. K#9656.

Date	Mintage	VG	F	VF	XF	Unc
ND(17th c)	—	45.00	90.00	180	—	—

KM# 26.1 2 STUBER

Silver, 25 mm. **Obv:** Crowned shield of city arms divides 2 - S **Obv. Legend:** DA. PACEM. DOMINE. **Rev:** Ornate floriated cross, with quatrefoil in center, in circle **Rev. Legend:** LEOPOLD: I. D: G: ROM: IMP: S: A: **Note:** Ref. K-6300.

Date	Mintage	VG	F	VF	XF	Unc
ND(1675-80)	—	45.00	100	180	360	—

KM# 26.2 2 STUBER

Silver, 25 mm. **Obv:** Crowned shield of city arms divides 2 - S **Obv. Legend:** MONE. NOV. CIVI. EMBDEN. **Rev:** Ornate floriated cross, with quatrefoil in center, in circle **Rev. Legend:** BENEDICTVS. DOMINVS. DEVS. **Note:** Ref. K-6301.

Date	Mintage	VG	F	VF	XF	Unc
ND(1680-90)	—	40.00	85.00	150	300	—

KM# 4.1 6 STUBER

Silver **Obv:** Shield of city arms **Obv. Legend:** CIVIT. EMBDEN. **Rev:** Crowned imperial eagle, orb on breast **Rev. Legend:** FERD. II. D. G. ? **Note:** Ref. K#9653. 29-30mm.

Date	Mintage	VG	F	VF	XF	Unc
ND(1619-37)	—	25.00	50.00	100	—	—

KM# 4.3 6 STUBER

Silver, 29-30 mm. **Obv:** Shield of city arms **Obv. Legend:** MONNO - CIV + - EMBD. **Rev:** Crowned imperial eagle, orb on breast **Rev. Legend:** FERD. II D G ROM IMP. SEM. AVG. **Note:** Ref. K#9655.

Date	Mintage	VG	F	VF	XF	Unc
ND(1619-37)	—	20.00	45.00	90.00	—	—

KM# 27 6 STUBER

Silver, 29-30 mm. **Obv:** Crowned shield of city arms, date at end of legend, where present **Obv. Legend:** DA PACEM DOMINE **Rev:** Crowned imperial eagle divides mintmaster's initials, where present **Rev. Legend:** LEOP: I. D: G: RO(M): - IMP: SEM: AUG: **Note:** Ref. K-6292, 9652. Varieties exist.

Date	Mintage	VG	F	VF	XF	Unc
1674 CP	—	40.00	80.00	160	325	—
ND(1680-90)	—	40.00	80.00	160	325	—

KM# 11 28 STUBER (2/3 Thaler - Gulden)

Silver **Note:** Klippe.

Date	Mintage	VG	F	VF	XF	Unc
ND(1624-37) Rare	—	—	—	—	—	—

KM# 10.1 28 STUBER (2/3 Thaler - Gulden)

Silver

Date	Mintage	VG	F	VF	XF	Unc
ND(1624-37)	—	45.00	95.00	190	385	—

KM# 10.2 28 STUBER (2/3 Thaler - Gulden)

Silver **Obv:** Crowned arms with modified ornamentation **Note:** Dav. #508.

Date	Mintage	VG	F	VF	XF	Unc
ND(1624-37)	—	45.00	95.00	190	385	—

KM# 16 28 STUBER (2/3 Thaler - Gulden)

Silver **Obv:** Titles of Ferdinand III

Date	Mintage	VG	F	VF	XF	Unc
ND(1624-57)	—	55.00	100	190	385	—

KM# 28 1/3 THALER

Silver **Obv:** Crowned shield of city arms, palm fronds at each side **Obv. Legend:** DA. PACEM. - DOMINE. **Rev:** Crowned imperial eagle **Rev. Legend:** LEOP. I. D. G. ROM. IMP. SEM. AVG. **Note:** 30-31mm.

Date	Mintage	VG	F	VF	XF	Unc
ND(1680-1700)	—	825	1,500	2,700	—	—

KM# 29 1/3 THALER

Silver, 30 mm. **Obv:** Crowned shield of city arms divides date, value (1/3) in oval below **Obv. Legend:** MONETA NOVA - CIVIT: EMBD: **Rev:** Crowned imperial eagle, orb on breast **Rev. Legend:** LEOPOLD: I. D: G: ROM: IMP: SEM: AUG: **Note:** Ref. K-6291.

Date	Mintage	VG	F	VF	XF	Unc
1687	—	650	1,100	1,600	2,600	—

KM# 30 2/3 THALER (Gulden)

Silver **Obv:** Value 2/3 below crossing of branches **Note:** Varieties exist.

Date	Mintage	VG	F	VF	XF	Unc
1684	—	35.00	100	180	360	—
1688	—	35.00	100	180	360	—
1689	—	35.00	100	180	360	—
1690	—	35.00	100	180	360	—
1691	—	35.00	100	180	360	—

KM# 31 2/3 THALER (Gulden)

Silver **Rev:** Crowned arms of Emden (harpy on wall above waves) divide date, value 2/3 in oval below

Date	Mintage	VG	F	VF	XF	Unc
1687	—	80.00	160	300	600	—

KM# 32 2/3 THALER (Gulden)

Silver **Rev:** Smaller arms within palm branches

Date	Mintage	VG	F	VF	XF	Unc
1687	—	65.00	130	240	475	—

KM# 33 2/3 THALER (Gulden)

Silver **Obv:** Date divided above crown, value divided by crossing of branches

Date	Mintage	VG	F	VF	XF	Unc
1688	—	65.00	130	240	475	—

KM# 5.1 THALER

Silver **Obv:** Crowned double eagle with orb on breast, titles of Ferdinand Ii **Rev:** Crowned arms with CP between crown and arms. **Note:** Dav. #5247.

Date	Mintage	VG	F	VF	XF	Unc
ND(1619-37) CP	—	450	900	1,750	5,500	—

KM# 5.2 THALER

Silver **Obv:** Crowned imperial eagle, orb on breast **Rev:** Crowned city arms in ornate frame **Note:** Varieties exist. Dav. #5248.

Date	Mintage	VG	F	VF	XF	Unc
ND(1624-37)	—	275	500	1,000	2,000	—

KM# 20 THALER

Silver **Obv:** Arms above city divide date **Note:** Dav. #5249.

Date	Mintage	VG	F	VF	XF	Unc
ND(1673-74) CP Rare	—	—	—	—	—	—

KM# 21.1 THALER

27.9700 g., Silver, 46 mm. **Obv:** Arms above city view divide date **Obv. Legend:** MO: NO: CI: - EMBDENS. **Rev:** Crowned imperial eagle, orb on breast **Rev. Legend:** LEOPOLD: I: D:G: ROM: IMP: SEMP: AUGUSTUS. **Note:** Dav. 5251.

Date	Mintage	VG	F	VF	XF	Unc
1674 Rare	—	—	—	—	—	—

Note: Fritz Rudolf Künker Münzenhandlung Auction 127, 6-07, nearly XF realized approximately $28,180.

KM# 21.2 THALER

28.0000 g., Silver, 46 mm. **Obv:** Crowned shield of city arms, flanked by angels from clouds at left and right, divides legend, all above city view **Obv. Legend:** MO: NO: - CI: EMB. **Rev:** Crowned imperial eagle, orb on breast, date at end of legend **Rev. Legend:** LEOPOLDUS I. DEI GR: ROMA: IMP: SEM: AUGUS: **Note:** Ref. Dav. 5251 variant.

Date	Mintage	VG	F	VF	XF	Unc
1674 Rare	—	—	—	—	—	—

KM# 22 THALER

Silver **Obv:** Crowned imperial eagle with orb on breast **Note:** Dav. #5250.

Date	Mintage	VG	F	VF	XF	Unc
1674 CP	—	2,750	5,500	9,500	—	—

KM# 23.1 THALER

Silver **Note:** Dav. #5252.

Date	Mintage	VG	F	VF	XF	Unc
1674 CP	—	950	1,500	2,750	4,500	—

KM# 24 THALER

Silver **Obv:** Rampant lion left, 40 S and date in legend **Rev:** Knight standing behind shield of arms, imperial eagle above harpy **Note:** Dav. #5253.

Date	Mintage	VG	F	VF	XF	Unc
1675	—	1,200	2,200	3,500	5,750	—

KM# 25 THALER

Silver **Obv:** Rampant lion left holding city arms, 40 in legend below **Rev:** Shield of imperial eagle only **Note:** Dav. #5254.

Date	Mintage	VG	F	VF	XF	Unc
ND(ca.1675)	—	300	700	1,350	2,500	—

KM# 23.2 THALER

Silver **Obv:** Narrow legend **Rev:** Without inner circle **Note:** Varieties exist. Dav. #5255.

Date	Mintage	VG	F	VF	XF	Unc
1689 JR	—	1,500	3,000	5,500	—	—

KM# A21 2 THALER

57.9800 g., Silver, 57 mm. **Obv:** City view, crowned shield of city arms above, supported by 2 angels in clouds, divides curved legend **Obv. Legend:** MO: NO: - CI: EMB: **Rev:** Crowned imperial eagle, orb on breast, date at end of legend **Rev. Legend:** LEOPOLDUS I. DEI GR: ROMA: IMP: SEM: AUGUS: **Note:** Dav. #A5251

Date	Mintage	VG	F	VF	XF	Unc
1674CP Rare	—	—	—	—	—	—

TRADE COINAGE

Formerly listed 18th Century 2, 2-1/4, 3-1/4, and 4 Ducat issues are considered medals by leading authorities. Currently unlisted in the Standard Catalog series.

KM# 15 DUCAT

3.5000 g., 0.9860 Gold 0.1109 oz. AGW **Note:** Many varieties exist.

Date	Mintage	VG	F	VF	XF	Unc
1635	—	550	1,200	2,750	5,500	—
1644	—	550	1,200	2,750	5,500	—
1651	—	550	1,200	2,750	5,500	—
1663	—	550	1,200	2,750	5,500	—
1668	—	550	1,200	2,750	5,500	—
1674 Rare	—	—	—	—	—	—
Note: Künker Auction 139, 3-08, VF-XF realized approximately $19,370						
1676	—	550	1,200	2,750	5,500	—
1681	—	550	1,200	2,750	5,500	—
1687	—	550	1,200	2,750	5,500	—
1689	—	700	1,500	3,250	6,500	—
1694 Rare	—	—	—	—	—	—
Note: Künker Auction 125, 6-07, XF-Unc realized approximately $26,795						
1698	—	550	1,200	2,750	6,500	—
ND	—	550	1,200	2,750	6,500	—

KM# 35 2 DUCAT

7.0000 g., 0.9860 Gold 0.2219 oz. AGW **Obv:** Knight standing in inner circle **Rev:** Four line inscription in ornamental tablet

Date	Mintage	VG	F	VF	XF	Unc
1694	—	3,500	5,500	9,500	16,500	—

ERBACH

The lords of Erbach, located in the Odenwalde about 20 miles to the southeast of Darmstadt, are known from the early 12th century. Beginning in the early 13th century and lasting until 1806, the rulers of Erbach held the office of hereditary cupbearer to the elector-counts palatine of the Rhine. The rank of count was obtained from the emperor in 1532. The countship was divided by the four sons of Georg IV in 1605, although they struck a joint coinage. The family patrimony was further divided during the later 17th and early 18th centuries. Only some rulers of the several branches struck coins. Erbach was mediatized and its lands went to Hesse-Darmstadt in 1806.

RULERS

George IV, 1564-1605
Friedrich Magnus von Erbach-Reichenberg--Fürstenau, 1605-1618
Ludwig II von Erbach, 1605-1643
Johann Kasimir von Erbach-Wildenstein--Breuberg, 1605-1627
Georg Albrecht I von Erbach, 1605-1647
Georg Ludwig I, 1647-1693
Philipp Ludwig, 1693-1720

MINT OFFICIALS' INITIALS

Initial	Date	Name
ID	1691-92	Johann Ditmar in Darmstadt
ILI	1675-78	Jurgen Lippoldt Jaster in Breuberg
PPP	1675	Peter Paul Peckstein in Breuberg

COUNTSHIP

REGULAR COINAGE

KM# 7 PFENNIG

Silver **Obv:** E above 4-fold arms, all in circle of pellets **Note:** Uniface.

Date	Mintage	VG	F	VF	XF	Unc
ND(1623)	—	70.00	140	275	550	—

KM# 9 2 KREUZER (1/2 Batzen)

Silver **Rev:** Date Z - 3 divided by orb

Date	Mintage	VG	F	VF	XF	Unc
(16)Z3	Inc. above	75.00	165	350	600	—

KM# 8 2 KREUZER (1/2 Batzen)

Silver **Obv:** Imperial orb with Z, titles of Ferdinand II **Rev:** 4-fold arms divide Z - 3 **Rev. Legend:** MON: COM: IN: ERPACH **Note:** Varieties exist.

Date	Mintage	VG	F	VF	XF	Unc
(16)Z3	109,000	85.00	175	375	775	—

KM# 5 3 KREUZER (Groschen)

Silver **Obv:** Crowned imperial eagle, 3 in orb on breast, titles of Ferdinand II **Rev:** 4-fold arms **Note:** Varieties exist.

Date	Mintage	VG	F	VF	XF	Unc
ND(1622)	—	75.00	150	300	625	—

KM# 10 4 KREUZER (Batzen)

Silver **Obv:** Crowned imperial eagle, 4 in orb on breast, titles of Ferdinand II **Rev:** 4-fold arms

Date	Mintage	VG	F	VF	XF	Unc
1623 Reported, not confirmed	—	—	—	—	—	—

KM# 6 12 KREUZER (6 Albus)

Silver **Obv:** Crowned imperial eagle, 12 in orb on breast, titles of Ferdinand II and date in legend **Rev:** Crowned 4-fold arms **Rev. Legend:** IO CAS. E. GEORG. ALB. C. I. ERB. D. I. BRE

Date	Mintage	VG	F	VF	XF	Unc
1622	—	80.00	165	325	675	—

KM# 15 60 KREUZER (2/3 Thaler)

Silver **Note:** Varieties exist.

Date	Mintage	VG	F	VF	XF	Unc
1675 PPP	38,000	1,000	2,000	4,000	6,000	—
1675 ILI	—	1,250	2,500	5,000	9,000	—
1675 ILP	—	—	—	—	—	—
1675	—	—	—	—	—	—

KM# 11 THALER

Silver **Obv:** Titles of Ferdinand II **Note:** Dav. #6666. Varieties exist.

Date	Mintage	VG	F	VF	XF	Unc
1623	157,000	100	200	375	750	—
1624	—	100	200	375	750	—

KM# 12 THALER

Silver **Rev:** Date in legend **Note:** Dav. #6667.

Date	Mintage	VG	F	VF	XF	Unc
1624	Inc. above	150	300	500	900	—

KM# 16 THALER

Silver **Obv:** 4-fold arms **Obv. Legend:** MONETA NOVA ARGENTEA **Rev:** Similar to 60 Kreuzer, KM#15

Date	Mintage	VG	F	VF	XF	Unc
1675	—	—	—	—	—	—
Note: Reported, not confirmed						

KM# 13 GOLDGULDEN

3.5000 g., 0.9860 Gold 0.1109 oz. AGW **Obv:** Crowned imperial eagle, titles of Ferdinand II **Rev:** 4-fold arms, date above

Date	Mintage	VG	F	VF	XF	Unc
1624	—	—	—	—	—	—
Note: Reported, not confirmed						

ERBACH-BREUBERG

RULER

George VI, 1647-1678

COUNTSHIP

REGULAR COINAGE

KM# 5 GULDEN (2/3 Thaler)

Silver **Ruler:** George VI **Obv:** Bust left, titles of George VI **Rev:** Crowned 4-fold arms, legend, date **Rev. Legend:** PRO DEO ET PATRIA **Note:** Dav 510

Date	Mintage	VG	F	VF	XF	Unc
1675	—	1,000	2,000	4,000	7,700	—

ERBACH-FURSTENAU

RULER

Georg Albrecht II, 1647-1717

COUNTSHIP

REGULAR COINAGE

KM# 15 2 ALBUS (4 Kreuzer)

Silver

Date	Mintage	VG	F	VF	XF	Unc
1691 ID	—	40.00	85.00	160	325	—

KM# 17 1/12 THALER (2 Groschen)

Silver **Obv:** Similar to 2 Albus, KM#15 **Rev:** Inscription in wreath **Rev. Inscription:** 12 / EINEN / REICHS / THALER / date

Date	Mintage	VG	F	VF	XF	Unc
1691 ID Rare	—	—	—	—	—	—

KM# 16 15 KREUZER (1/4 Gulden - 1/6 Thaler)
Silver

Date	Mintage	VG	F	VF	XF	Unc
1691 ID	—	75.00	150	300	600	1,200

KM# 5 30 KREUZER (1/2 Gulden - 1/3 Thaler)
Silver **Note:** Similar to 60 Kreuzer, KM#9 but 30 in bottom legend.

Date	Mintage	VG	F	VF	XF	Unc
1675 PPP	—	—	—	—	—	—
1676 ILI	—	—	—	—	—	—

Note: Reported, not confirmed

KM# 7 30 KREUZER (1/2 Gulden - 1/3 Thaler)
38.5000 g., Silver **Note:** Klippe. Struck on square flan.

Date	Mintage	VG	F	VF	XF	Unc
1676 ILI Rare	—	—	—	—	—	—

KM# 6 60 KREUZER (2/3 Thaler - 1 Gulden)
Silver **Obv:** Facing bust with long wig, 60 below in oval **Rev:** Similar to 60 Kreuzer, KM#9 **Note:** Varieties exist. Dav 511 and 513

Date	Mintage	VG	F	VF	XF	Unc
1675	—	1,000	2,000	4,000	7,700	—
1676	—	1,000	2,000	4,000	7,700	—

KM# 8 60 KREUZER (2/3 Thaler - 1 Gulden)
Silver **Rev:** Date in legend **Note:** Dav 512 Klippe

Date	Mintage	VG	F	VF	XF	Unc
1676 ILI Rare	—	—	—	—	—	—

KM# 9 60 KREUZER (2/3 Thaler - 1 Gulden)
Silver **Note:** Dav 513

Date	Mintage	VG	F	VF	XF	Unc
1676 ILI	—	1,000	2,000	4,000	7,700	—

KM# 10 60 KREUZER (2/3 Thaler - 1 Gulden)
Silver **Obv:** Bust left **Note:** Dav 515

Date	Mintage	VG	F	VF	XF	Unc
1676 ILI	—	1,000	2,000	4,000	7,700	—

ERFURT

The city of Erfurt is located in northern Thuringia (Thüringen), about 12.5 miles (21 kilometers) west of Weimar. It was a place of some importance as early as 741 when it became a branch bishopric of Mainz. The archbishops of the latter city remained very much involved in the affairs of Erfurt throughout the High Middle Ages and even located one of their mints there from the 11th through the 13th centuries. An imperial mint also produced coinage in Erfurt during the 12th century. By the mid-13th century, however, the town gained enough power to force the archbishop to grant it self-governing rights. Erfurt was given the right to mint its own coins in 1341 and 1354, and a long series of coins began which lasted until the beginning of the 19th century. Having joined the Hanseatic League during the early 15th century, Erfurt was at the height of its power and prestige, but events began to cause the decline of the city. Saxony managed to wrest control of Erfurt away from Mainz in 1483. During the Thirty Years' War, the city was seized and occupied by Swedish forces in 1631. The treaties which ended the war in 1648 gave control of Erfurt back to Mainz, but the good citizens refused to submit. The city held out until 1664 when it was captured by the archbishop's forces. It remained under Mainz until 1803, when the archbishopric was secularized, and then passed to Prussia.
Free City, 1601-1631
Swedish Occupation, 1631-1648

MINT OFFICIALS' INITIALS

Initial	Date	Name
(a)=	ca. 1548	Unknown
(b)=	ca. 1562	Unknown
FG	ca. 1561-62	Unknown
HL (in ligature)	1592-99	Hans Liphard, mintmaster
	1597-?	Hans Weber, warden
FG/G	1599-1607	Florian Gruber
(c)= or HG/G	1607-09	Hieronymus Kronberger (Gronberger)
AW	1617-24	Asmus Wagner
IS	1624-35	Johann Schneider (known as Weissmantel)
	1625	Jakob Zeuner of Freiburg
EW	Ca.1632	Unknown
CZ	1650-59	Christof Ziegler
ICD	1673-76	Johann Christoph Dürr
	Ca.1675	Johann Georg Philipp Reipp, warden
MW	Ca.1676-81	Marcus Weissmantel
D	Ca.1683	Unknown
GFS	1689	Georg Friedrich Staude
ICS	1690-91	Johann Christoph Staude

ARMS
6-spoked wheel of Mainz, sometimes in 2-fold shield, half of which is 3 vertical bars (Capellendorf).

CITY

REGULAR COINAGE

KM# 2 PFENNIG
Silver **Obv:** Two arms side-by-side, wheel left, six pales right, date divided by E above, mintmaster's initial below **Note:** Uniface. Prev. KM#5.

Date	Mintage	VG	F	VF	XF	Unc
1602 G	—	15.00	35.00	75.00	150	—
1603 G	—	15.00	35.00	75.00	150	—
1603	—	15.00	35.00	75.00	150	—
1605 G	—	15.00	35.00	75.00	150	—
1607 HG	—	15.00	35.00	75.00	150	—
1609 HG	—	15.00	35.00	75.00	150	—
1609 (c)	—	15.00	35.00	75.00	150	—

KM# 25 PFENNIG
Silver **Obv:** Wheel arms in cartouche, date divided by E above **Note:** Kipper Pfennig.

Date	Mintage	VG	F	VF	XF	Unc
1620	—	13.00	27.00	55.00	110	—
1622	—	13.00	27.00	55.00	110	—

KM# 33 PFENNIG
Silver **Obv:** Wheel arms divide date, + E + above

Date	Mintage	VG	F	VF	XF	Unc
1622	—	13.00	27.00	55.00	110	—

KM# 27 2 SCHERF (Pfennig)
Copper **Obv:** 2-fold arms, wheel left, pales right, BPE above **Rev:** II/S/date **Note:** Kipper 2 Scherf.

Date	Mintage	VG	F	VF	XF	Unc
16Z1	—	10.00	20.00	40.00	80.00	—

KM# 28 3 SCHERF (1-1/2 Pfennig)
Copper **Obv:** 2-fold arms, wheel left, pales right, BPE above **Rev. Inscription:** III / S **Note:** Kipper 3 Scherf. Varieties exist.

Date	Mintage	VG	F	VF	XF	Unc
16Z1	—	10.00	20.00	40.00	80.00	—

KM# 38 3 SCHERF (1-1/2 Pfennig)
Copper **Rev:** Date **Rev. Inscription:** III / SCHERF

Date	Mintage	VG	F	VF	XF	Unc
1622	—	10.00	20.00	40.00	80.00	—

KM# 29 6 SCHERF (3 Pfennig)
1.1000 g., Copper, 15.6 mm. **Obv:** Wheel arms **Obv. Legend:** +ERFVRTENSIVM **Rev. Legend:** BONO PVBLICO **Rev. Inscription:** VI / S / date **Note:** Kipper 6 Scherf. Varieties exist.

Date	Mintage	VG	F	VF	XF	Unc
16Z1	—	13.00	27.00	50.00	100	—

KM# 39 6 SCHERF (3 Pfennig)
Copper **Obv. Inscription:** VI / SCHERF **Rev:** Date

Date	Mintage	VG	F	VF	XF	Unc
1622	—	13.00	27.00	50.00	100	—

KM# 8 3 PFENNIG (Dreier)
Silver **Obv:** Helmeted shield with wheel arms **Rev:** Helmeted shield with pales, date above, FG below

Date	Mintage	VG	F	VF	XF	Unc
1601 FG	—	30.00	60.00	120	240	—
1604 FG	—	13.00	27.00	55.00	110	—

KM# 13 3 PFENNIG (Dreier)
Silver **Obv:** Wheel arms in cartouche **Rev:** Helmeted wheel arms divide date **Note:** Prev. KM#15.

Date	Mintage	VG	F	VF	XF	Unc
1613	—	13.00	27.00	55.00	110	—

KM# 34 3 PFENNIG (Dreier)
Silver **Obv:** Ornamented wheel **Note:** Kipper 3 Pfennig.

Date	Mintage	VG	F	VF	XF	Unc
1622	—	8.00	16.00	35.00	75.00	—

KM# 35 3 PFENNIG (Dreier)
Copper **Obv:** Ornamented wheel **Note:** Kipper 3 Pfennig. Varieties exist.

Date	Mintage	VG	F	VF	XF	Unc
1622	—	10.00	20.00	40.00	80.00	—

KM# 36 3 PFENNIG (Dreier)
Billon **Rev:** Date divided near bottom **Note:** Kipper 3 Pfennig. Varieties exist.

Date	Mintage	VG	F	VF	XF	Unc
16ZZ	—	10.00	20.00	40.00	80.00	—

KM# 44 3 PFENNIG (Dreier)
Silver **Obv:** Wheel arms in cartouche **Rev:** Helmeted wheel arms, date divided above **Note:** Varieties exist.

Date	Mintage	VG	F	VF	XF	Unc
1623	—	10.00	20.00	40.00	80.00	—
1623 AW	—	10.00	20.00	40.00	80.00	—
1624	—	10.00	20.00	40.00	80.00	—
1625	—	10.00	20.00	40.00	80.00	—
1650	—	10.00	20.00	40.00	80.00	—
1655	—	10.00	20.00	40.00	80.00	—
1656	—	10.00	20.00	40.00	80.00	—

KM# 30 12 SCHERF (6 Pfennig)
Copper, 18 mm. **Obv:** Wheels arms, date **Obv. Legend:** ERFVRTENSIVM **Rev. Inscription:** XII / SCHERF **Note:** Kipper 12 Scherf. Varieties exist.

Date	Mintage	VG	F	VF	XF	Unc
16Z1	—	27.00	55.00	80.00	165	—
16ZZ	—	27.00	55.00	80.00	165	—

KM# 37 12 PFENNIG
Copper **Obv:** Wheel arms in ornamented shield **Rev:** Date **Rev. Inscription:** 12 / PFENNI / GE **Note:** Kipper 3 Kreuzer or 1/24 Thaler. Varieties exist. Prev. Mainz, KM #31.

Date	Mintage	VG	F	VF	XF	Unc
16ZZ	—	15.00	32.00	65.00	130	—

KM# 41 1/24 THALER (Groschen)
Copper **Obv:** Helmeted wheel arms, another wheel above helmet, date in legend **Rev:** Wheel arms in ornamented shield, Z4 above **Note:** Kipper Groschen. Varieties exist.

Date	Mintage	VG	F	VF	XF	Unc
(16)ZZ	—	26.00	40.00	85.00	170	—
1623	—	26.00	40.00	85.00	170	—
11623 Error	—	26.00	40.00	85.00	170	—

KM# 40 1/24 THALER (Groschen)
Silver **Obv:** Helmeted wheel arms, another wheel above helmet, date in legend **Rev:** Wheel arms in ornamented shield, Z4 above **Note:** Varieties exist.

Date	Mintage	VG	F	VF	XF	Unc
16ZZ	—	16.00	33.00	75.00	155	—
1622	—	16.00	33.00	75.00	155	—
1623 AW	—	16.00	33.00	75.00	155	—
1623 IS	—	16.00	33.00	75.00	155	—
1623	—	16.00	33.00	75.00	155	—

KM# 97 1/24 THALER (Groschen)
Silver **Subject:** Peace of Westphalia **Obv. Inscription:** ...GRATIAR / MONIMENT. F. F. / ANNO 1650 / 8 SEPT **Rev:** Jehovah in Hebrew above, rays streaming down, hand from clouds below holding palm and laurel branches with wheel, in band above legend **Rev. Legend:** SUPER HIS SERVATA QVIESCO

Date	Mintage	VG	F	VF	XF	Unc
1650	—	160	325	650	1,350	—

KM# 14 1/4 THALER

7.1400 g., Silver, 29 mm. **Obv:** Shield of city arms supported by 2 wildmen, ornate helmet surmounted by wheel of Mainz above **Obv. Legend:** MON: ARGENTEA CIVITATIS EREFVRDI. **Rev:** Ornate shield of 4-fold arms with central shield of Erfurt in baroque frame, angel's head above, date divided below **Rev. Legend:** DATE CÆSARIS CÆSARI QVÆ. DEI - DEO. **Note:** Ref. L-490.

Date	Mintage	VG	F	VF	XF	Unc
1617 Rare	—	—	—	—	—	—

Note: A VF example realized approximately $7,420 in a UBS auction September 2007.

KM# 17 1/3 THALER (1/2 Gulden)

Silver **Obv:** Supported arms **Rev:** Arms with angel head above, date divided below

Date	Mintage	VG	F	VF	XF	Unc
1617	—	—	—	—	—	—
1618	—	—	—	—	—	—

KM# 31 1/3 THALER (1/2 Gulden)

Silver **Rev:** 5-fold arms, date in legend

Date	Mintage	VG	F	VF	XF	Unc
1621	—	325	625	1,000	2,000	—

KM# 98 30 KREUZER (1/2 Gulden)

Silver **Subject:** Peace of Westphalia **Obv. Inscription:** … GRATIARUM / MONIMENT / FIERIFECIT / Ao 1650. 8. SEPT. **Rev:** Jehovah in Hebrew above, rays streaming down, hand from clouds below holding palm and laurel branches with wheel

Date	Mintage	VG	F	VF	XF	Unc
1650 Rare	—	—	—	—	—	—

KM# 15 1/2 THALER

Silver, 35 mm. **Obv:** Shield of city arms supported by 2 wildmen, ornate helmet surmounted by wheel of Mainz above **Obv. Legend:** MO: NO: ARGENTEA: CIVITATIS: EREFORD. **Rev:** Ornate shield of 4-fold arms, with central shield of Erfurt, in baroque frame, angel's head above, date divided to lower left and right **Rev. Legend:** DATE CÆSARIS CÆSARI. ET QVÆ - DEI . DEO.

Date	Mintage	VG	F	VF	XF	Unc
1617 Rare	—	—	—	—	—	—

Note: An example in VF-XF realized approximately $4,650 in a Gorny & Mosch auction of March 2003.

KM# 42 1/2 THALER

Silver **Obv:** Oval wheel arms in baroque frame, date in legend **Rev:** Ornamented 5-fold arms, value 21 gl (groschen) below

Date	Mintage	VG	F	VF	XF	Unc
1622	—	—	—	—	—	—

KM# 18 2/3 THALER (Gulden)

Silver **Obv:** Supported arms, date divided above **Rev:** Arms with angel head above

Date	Mintage	VG	F	VF	XF	Unc
1617	—	—	—	—	—	—

KM# 5 60 KREUZER (Gulden)

Silver **Obv:** Helmeted city arms, wildman and wildwoman as supporters, wheel of Mainz above **Obv. Legend:** MON. REIPVBLIC CIVITATIS - ERFFORDI **Rev:** Two angels suspended holding wreath in center in which date, small shield below with "60", legend divided by four small shields of arms **Rev. Inscription:** AVF. IEDES. SCHIS. / EN. MEIN. R. DIS IAR / ZV. VORN. 100. 60. 40. / GEBEN. WAR. 29. AVG. & 5. SEPT. **Note:** Dav. #5256

Date	Mintage	VG	F	VF	XF	Unc
1603 FG	—	450	900	1,750	3,250	—

KM# 99 60 KREUZER (Gulden)

Silver **Subject:** Peace of Westphalia **Obv. Inscription:** … GRATIARUM / MONIMENT / FIERIFECIT / Ao 1650. 8. SEPT.

Date	Mintage	VG	F	VF	XF	Unc
1650 Rare	—	—	—	—	—	—

KM# 16.1 THALER

Silver **Obv:** Supported arms **Rev:** Arms with angel head above, date divided below, 16-13 **Note:** Dav. #5257.

Date	Mintage	VG	F	VF	XF	Unc
1613	—	325	650	1,200	2,000	—

KM# 16.3 THALER

Silver **Rev:** Squares with dots at sides of arms, symbols before and after date **Note:** Dav. #5259.

Date	Mintage	VG	F	VF	XF	Unc
1617	—	100	225	475	950	—

KM# 16.4 THALER

Silver **Obv. Legend:** MO:…EFFFORD **Rev:** Alchemy symbols at sides **Note:** Dav. #5260.

Date	Mintage	VG	F	VF	XF	Unc
1617	—	125	250	500	1,000	—

KM# 19.1 THALER

Silver **Rev:** Date above arms instead on angel's head **Note:** Dav. #5262.

Date	Mintage	VG	F	VF	XF	Unc
1617 AW	—	150	300	550	1,100	—
1618 AW	—	150	300	550	1,100	—

KM# 19.2 THALER

Silver **Rev:** AW. IS below shield **Note:** Dav. #5262A.

Date	Mintage	VG	F	VF	XF	Unc
1617 AW-IS	—	200	400	750	1,250	—

KM# 16.6 THALER

Silver **Obv. Legend:** MON…ERFFORDENSIS **Rev:** Alchemy symbols at sides **Note:** Dav. #A5259.

Date	Mintage	VG	F	VF	XF	Unc
1617	—	350	700	1,150	—	—

KM# 16.2 THALER

Silver, 41 mm. **Obv:** Helmeted shield of city arms, with wildman and wildwoman as supporters, wheel of Mainz above **Obv. Legend:** MON: ARGENTEA CIVITATIS EREFORDENSIS. **Rev:** Shield of 4-fold arms, with central shield of Erfurt, in baroque frame, date divided below, 1.6 - 1.7 **Rev. Legend:** DATE. CÆSARIS. CÆSARI. ET QVÆ. DEI. DEO. **Note:** Dav. 5258.

Date	Mintage	VG	F	VF	XF	Unc
1617	—	175	325	650	1,250	—

KM# 32 THALER

Silver **Obv:** Ornamented oval wheel arms, date in legend **Rev:** 4-fold arms with central shield, 24 below **Note:** Kipper Thaler. Varieties exist.

Date	Mintage	VG	F	VF	XF	Unc
16Z1	—	900	1,750	3,250	5,750	—
16ZZ	—	900	1,750	3,250	5,750	—

KM# 19.3 THALER

Silver **Obv:** Helmeted and supported oval shield **Rev:** AW below shield **Note:** Dav. #5263.

Date	Mintage	VG	F	VF	XF	Unc
1621 AW	—	600	1,200	2,250	4,000	—

KM# 19.4 THALER

Silver **Rev:** Date above shield, I-S at sides and E-W below

Date	Mintage	VG	F	VF	XF	Unc
1632 IS-EW Reported not confirmed	—	—	—	—	—	—

KM# 16.5 THALER

Silver **Obv. Legend:** MON:...ERFFORDENSIS **Rev:** Alchemy symbols at sides **Note:** Dav. #5274.

Date	Mintage	VG	F	VF	XF	Unc
1637	—	250	500	1,000	2,000	—

KM# 101 THALER

Silver **Obv:** Angel putting sword in sheath, treading on dead bodies, nearby a tablet surmounted by skull **Obv. Legend:** MORS IVGLANS CEDIT VITA SAL VSQ. REDIT. **Obv. Inscription:** A. 1683. SVMMA MORTV / ORVM / 9437 **Rev:** Inscription at top **Rev. Inscription:** HOC REDEVNTE PERIT CONTAGIOSA LVES; ERPHORDIA A PESTE LIBERA ANNO 1683. EXEVNTE in exergue **Note:** Leitzmann #811.

Date	Mintage	VG	F	VF	XF	Unc
1683 D Rare	—	—	—	—	—	—

KM# 102 THALER

Silver **Obv:** Angel putting sword in sheath, treading on dead bodies, without skull on tablet **Obv. Inscription:** SUM. D.A. 1683. ZV. ERFF. ERSTORB. PERSON. 9437. **Note:** Plague Double Thaler. Leitzmann #812.

Date	Mintage	VG	F	VF	XF	Unc
1683 D Rare	—	—	—	—	—	—

KM# 7 2 THALER

Silver **Obv:** Helmeted city arms divide date, wildman and wildwoman as supporters, wheel of Mainz above **Rev:** 2 angels suspended holding wreath in center **Note:** Dav. #A5256.

Date	Mintage	VG	F	VF	XF	Unc
1603 Rare	—	—	—	—	—	—

KM# 20 2 THALER

Silver **Obv:** Date aabove arms instead of on angel's head **Note:** Dav. #5261.

Date	Mintage	VG	F	VF	XF	Unc
1617 AW Rare	—	—	—	—	—	—

KM# 43 2 THALER

Silver **Obv:** Ornamented oval wheel arms, date in legend **Rev:** 4-fold arms with central shield, 48 below **Note:** Kipper 2 Thaler.

Date	Mintage	VG	F	VF	XF	Unc
16ZZ Rare	—	—	—	—	—	—

TRADE COINAGE

KM# 26 GOLDGULDEN

3.5000 g., 0.9860 Gold 0.1109 oz. AGW **Obv:** Helmeted arms divide date in inner circle **Rev:** Arms in inner circle **Note:** Fr.#916.

Date	Mintage	VG	F	VF	XF	Unc
1620	—	2,500	4,500	7,500	12,500	—
1622	—	2,500	4,500	7,500	12,500	—
ND1670	—	2,500	4,500	7,500	12,500	—

KM# 100 DUCAT

3.5000 g., 0.9860 Gold 0.1109 oz. AGW **Obv:** Wheel arms divide date **Rev:** 5-fold arms

Date	Mintage	VG	F	VF	XF	Unc
1670 Rare	—	—	—	—	—	—

OCCUPATION COINAGE

Issued by Swedish forces 1631-48

KM# 69 1/4 THALER

Silver **Subject:** Death of Gustavus Adolphus **Obv:** Crowned 4-fold arms with central shield, 2 inscriptions around, date divided by crown **Rev:** Grapevine growing out of skull resting on ground, 2 inscriptions around with date

Date	Mintage	VG	F	VF	XF	Unc
1633	—	65.00	125	275	500	—

KM# 50 1/2 THALER

Silver **Obv:** "Jehovah" in Hebrew in rayed oval above, inscription below fronds on E **Obv. Inscription:** A. DOMINO / FACTVM. EST / ISTVD **Rev:** 11-line inscription with R.N. date

Date	Mintage	VG	F	VF	XF	Unc
1631 Rare	—	—	—	—	—	—

KM# 58 1/2 THALER

Silver **Obv:** Bust of Gustavus II Adolphus 3/4 to right **Rev:** Crowned oval 4-fold arms with central shield in baroque frame, wheel below divides date

Date	Mintage	VG	F	VF	XF	Unc
1632 Rare	—	—	—	—	—	—

KM# 57 1/2 THALER

Silver **Note:** Similar to 1 Thaler, KM#59.

Date	Mintage	VG	F	VF	XF	Unc
1632 Rare	—	—	—	—	—	—

KM# A70 1/2 THALER

Silver **Obv:** King laying in state, battle in background **Obv. Legend:** GUSTAVUS ADOLPHUS MAGNUS... **Rev:** King in triumphant chariot, crowned by Religion and Justice, crushing his enemies below **Rev. Legend:** DUX GLORIOS: PRINC: PIUS: HEROS...

Date	Mintage	VG	F	VF	XF	Unc
1633	—	—	—	—	—	—

KM# 86 1/2 THALER

Silver **Note:** Similar to 1 Thaler, KM#87.

Date	Mintage	VG	F	VF	XF	Unc
1645	—	600	1,100	1,900	—	—
1648 Rare	—	—	—	—	—	—

KM# 49 THALER

Silver **Obv:** 2 branches below inscription

Date	Mintage	VG	F	VF	XF	Unc
1631 Unique	—	—	—	—	—	—

KM# 51 THALER

Silver **Obv:** 11-line inscription with R.N. date **Rev:** "Jehovah" in Hebrew in rayed oval above, below fronds on E **Rev. Inscription:** A. DOMINO. / FACTVM. EST / ISTVD **Note:** Dav. #4544.

Date	Mintage	VG	F	VF	XF	Unc
1631	—	300	600	1,250	2,500	—

KM# 53 THALER

Silver **Obv:** Arabic numeral date below 12-line inscription **Note:** Dav. #4545.

Date	Mintage	VG	F	VF	XF	Unc
1631	—	350	700	1,450	2,750	—

KM# 52 THALER

Silver **Note:** Klippe. Dav. #4545A.

Date	Mintage	VG	F	VF	XF	Unc
1631 Rare	—	—	—	—	—	—

KM# 61 THALER

Silver **Rev:** Without small wheel below arms **Note:** Swedish issue. Dav. #4547.

Date	Mintage	VG	F	VF	XF	Unc
1632 Rare	—	—	—	—	—	—

KM# 59 THALER

Silver **Subject:** 1st Anniversary of Victory at Leipzig **Note:** Dav. #4546.

Date	Mintage	VG	F	VF	XF	Unc
1632	—	200	500	1,150	2,250	—

KM# 60 THALER

Silver **Obv:** Bust of Gustavus II Adolphus 3/4 to right **Rev:** Crowned oval 4-fold arms with central shield in baroque frame, wheel below divides date **Note:** Dav. #4548.

Date	Mintage	VG	F	VF	XF	Unc
1632 Rare	—	—	—	—	—	—

KM# 62 THALER

Silver **Subject:** Death of Gustavus Adolphus **Obv:** Grapevine growing out of skull resting on ground, 2 inscriptions around with date **Rev:** Crowned 4-fold arms with central shield, 2 inscriptions around, date divided by crown

Date	Mintage	VG	F	VF	XF	Unc
1632 Rare	—	—	—	—	—	—

KM# 77 THALER

Silver **Obv:** King lying in state, battle in background **Obv. Legend:** GUSTAVUS ADOLPHUS MAGNUS... **Rev:** King in triumphant chariot, crowned by Religion and Justice, crushing his enemies below **Rev. Legend:** DUX FLORIOS : PRINC : PIUS:... **Note:** Dav. #5272.

Date	Mintage	Good	VG	F	VF	XF
1633	—	200	450	1,000	2,250	4,000

KM# 70 THALER

Silver **Obv:** Helmeted and supported arms, wheel above divides date **Obv. Legend:** + MON x REIPVBLICAE x CIVITATIS x ERFFORDI x **Rev:** Angels holding "Jehovah" in Hebrew in oval above city view, all in wreath divided by 4 small arms **Note:** Ref. L-563; Dav. 5270.

Date	Mintage	VG	F	VF	XF	Unc
1633	—	1,200	2,250	4,750	7,500	—

KM# 71 THALER

Silver **Obv:** Gustavus Adolphus lying in state with battle in background **Rev:** King in chariot crushing enemies below **Note:** Dav. #5272.

Date	Mintage	VG	F	VF	XF	Unc
1634	—	550	1,150	2,250	4,000	—

KM# 87 THALER

Silver **Subject:** Christina **Note:** Dav. #4570.

Date	Mintage	F	VF	XF	Unc	BU
1645	—	700	1,500	3,000	5,000	—
1648	—	1,650	2,850	5,500	9,500	—

KM# 72 1-1/2 THALER

Silver **Obv:** Helmeted and supported arms, wheel above divides date **Rev:** Angels holding "Jehovah" in Hebrew in oval above city view, all in wreath divided by 4 small arms **Note:** Dav. #5269A.

Date	Mintage	VG	F	VF	XF	Unc
1603 Rare	—	—	—	—	—	—
1633 Rare	—	—	—	—	—	—

KM# A78 1-1/2 THALER

Silver **Obv:** King lying in state, battle in background **Obv. Legend:** GUSTAVUS ADOLPHUS MAGNUS... **Rev:** King in triumphant chariot, crowned by Religion and Justice, crushing his enemies below **Rev. Legend:** DUX FLORIOS : PRINC : PIUS:... **Note:** Dav. #5271, 275.

Date	Mintage	Good	VG	F	VF	XF
1633	—	—	—	—	—	—

KM# 73 2 THALER

Silver **Obv:** Helmeted and supported arms, wheel above divides date **Rev:** Angels holding "Jehovah" in Hebrew in oval above city view, all in wreath divided by 4 small arms **Note:** Dav. #5269.

Date	Mintage	VG	F	VF	XF	Unc
1633 Rare	—	—	—	—	—	—

KM# 78 2 THALER

59.7000 g., Silver **Obv:** King lying in state, battle in background **Obv. Legend:** GUSTAVUS ADOLPHUS MAGNUS... **Rev:** King in triumphant chariot, crowned by Religion and Justice, crushing his enemies below **Rev. Legend:** DUX FLORIOS : PRINC : PIUS:... **Note:** Dav. #5271A, 274.

Date	Mintage	VG	F	VF	XF	Unc
1633	—	750	1,250	2,500	4,250	—

KM# 76 2 THALER

Silver **Obv:** Gustavus Adolphus seated in chariot left, raising sword to clouds in heaven, date divided by small ornate oval arms below **Rev:** King lying in state, angels with Jehovah above, 8 inscribed ovals around, 7 of which have baldachini above them in legend **Note:** Dav. #5273.

Date	Mintage	VG	F	VF	XF	Unc
1634 Rare	—	—	—	—	—	—

KM# 79 3 THALER

83.7000 g., Silver **Obv:** King lying in state, battle in background **Obv. Legend:** GUSTAVUS ADOLPHUS MAGNUS... **Rev:** King in triumphant chariot, crowned by Religion and Justice, crushing his enemies below **Rev. Legend:** DUX GLORIOS : PRINC : PIUS:... **Note:** Dav. #5271B, 273.

Date	Mintage	VG	F	VF	XF	Unc
1633	—	950	1,650	2,750	4,500	—

KM# 80 4 THALER

116.0000 g., Silver **Obv:** King lying in state, battle in background **Obv. Legend:** GUSTAVUS ADOLPHUS MAGNUS... **Rev:** King in triumphant chariot, crowned by Religion and Justice, crushing his enemies below **Rev. Legend:** DUX FLORIOS : PRINC : PIUS:... **Note:** Dav. #5271C, 272.

Date	Mintage	VG	F	VF	XF	Unc
1633	—	1,350	2,750	4,250	7,500	—

KM# A81 5 THALER

Silver **Obv:** King lying in state, battle in background **Obv. Legend:** GUSTAVUS ADOLPHUS MAGNUS... **Rev:** King in triumphant chariot, crowned by Religion and Justice, crushing his enemies below **Rev. Legend:** DUX FLORIOS : PRINC : PIUS:... **Note:** Dav. #275A. Weight varies: 139.00-152.00 grams.

Date	Mintage	Good	VG	F	VF	XF
1634	—	—	—	—	—	—

KM# 64 DUCAT

3.5000 g., 0.9860 Gold 0.1109 oz. AGW **Rev:** Date in outer legend

Date	Mintage	VG	F	VF	XF	Unc
1631 Rare	—	—	—	—	—	—
1632 Rare	—	—	—	—	—	—

KM# 54 DUCAT

3.5000 g., 0.9860 Gold 0.1109 oz. AGW **Obv:** Gustavus Adolphus **Note:** Fr.#923.

Date	Mintage	VG	F	VF	XF	Unc
1631 Unique	—	—	—	—	—	—
1632 Rare	—	—	—	—	—	—
1634	—	275	550	1,100	2,250	—

KM# 63 DUCAT

3.5000 g., 0.9860 Gold 0.1109 oz. AGW **Rev:** Crown above inscription in inner circle **Note:** Fr.#919.

Date	Mintage	VG	F	VF	XF	Unc
1632	—	150	325	650	1,200	—
1633	—	150	325	650	1,200	—
1634	—	150	325	650	1,200	—

KM# 74 DUCAT

3.5000 g., 0.9860 Gold 0.1109 oz. AGW **Rev:** Date below shield

Date	Mintage	VG	F	VF	XF	Unc
1633 Rare	—	—	—	—	—	—
1634	—	275	550	1,100	2,250	—

KM# 81 DUCAT

3.5000 g., 0.9860 Gold 0.1109 oz. AGW **Rev:** Shield divides date **Note:** Prev. KM#77.

Date	Mintage	VG	F	VF	XF	Unc
1634	—	500	1,000	2,000	4,000	—

KM# 82 DUCAT

3.5000 g., 0.9860 Gold 0.1109 oz. AGW **Rev:** Date above crown **Note:** Prev. KM#78.

Date	Mintage	VG	F	VF	XF	Unc
1634	—	500	1,000	2,000	4,000	—

KM# 85 DUCAT

3.5000 g., 0.9860 Gold 0.1109 oz. AGW **Obv:** Bust of Christina facing 1/2 left in inner circle **Rev:** Crowned arms in inner circle

Date	Mintage	VG	F	VF	XF	Unc
1644 Rare	—	—	—	—	—	—
1645	—	300	750	1,850	3,750	—

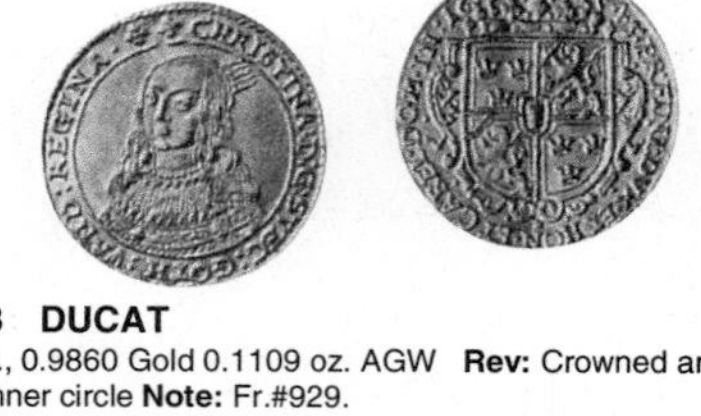

KM# 88 DUCAT

3.5000 g., 0.9860 Gold 0.1109 oz. AGW **Rev:** Crowned arms without inner circle **Note:** Fr.#929.

Date	Mintage	VG	F	VF	XF	Unc
1645	—	300	725	1,850	3,750	—
1646 Rare	—	—	—	—	—	—
1647	—	300	725	1,850	3,750	—
1648	—	300	725	1,850	3,750	—

KM# 91 DUCAT

3.5000 g., 0.9860 Gold 0.1109 oz. AGW **Obv:** Bust of Christina right in inner circle **Rev:** Crowned arms with ornamentation **Note:** Fr.#930.

Date	Mintage	VG	F	VF	XF	Unc
1646 Rare	—	—	—	—	—	—
1647 Rare	—	—	—	—	—	—
1648	—	1,000	2,150	4,250	7,500	—

KM# 93 DUCAT

3.5000 g., 0.9860 Gold 0.1109 oz. AGW **Rev:** Small crown above arms

Date	Mintage	VG	F	VF	XF	Unc
1648	—	300	725	1,850	3,750	—

KM# 94 DUCAT

3.5000 g., 0.9860 Gold 0.1109 oz. AGW **Obv:** Bust of Christina right without inner circle **Rev:** Crowned arms without ornamentation

Date	Mintage	VG	F	VF	XF	Unc
1648 Unique	—	—	—	—	—	—

KM# 75 2 DUCAT

7.0000 g., 0.9860 Gold 0.2219 oz. AGW **Obv:** Skull below grape vine in inner circle **Rev:** Crowned arms in inner circle **Note:** Fr.#923a.

Date	Mintage	VG	F	VF	XF	Unc
1633 Rare	—	—	—	—	—	—

KM# 92 2 DUCAT

7.0000 g., 0.9860 Gold 0.2219 oz. AGW **Obv:** Christina with radiant "Jehovah" in Hebrew **Rev:** Crowned ornate arms **Note:** Fr.#928.

Date	Mintage	VG	F	VF	XF	Unc
1646	—	1,000	2,000	3,750	7,500	11,500

KM# A55 3 DUCAT

10.5000 g., 0.9860 Gold 0.3328 oz. AGW **Subject:** Victory **Obv:** Radiant "Jehovah" in Hebrew above legend and ornamentation **Rev:** 11 line inscription with date below **Note:** Fr.#918.

Date	Mintage	VG	F	VF	XF	Unc
1631 Rare	—	—	—	—	—	—

KM# 55 4 DUCAT

14.0000 g., 0.9860 Gold 0.4438 oz. AGW **Obv:** Radiant "Jehovah" in Hebrew above legend and ornamentation **Rev:** 11 line inscription with date below

Date	Mintage	VG	F	VF	XF	Unc
1631 Rare	—	—	—	—	—	—

KM# 84 4 DUCAT

14.0000 g., 0.9860 Gold 0.4438 oz. AGW **Obv:** Crowned king lying in state, battlefield in background **Obv. Legend:** GUSTAVUS ADOLPHUS MAGNUS... **Rev:** King in chariot between two angels running over his enemies **Rev. Legend:** DUX GLORIOS • PRINC : PIUS • HEROS... **Note:** Prev. KM#80. Fr.#923. Struck with 1/2 Thaler dies, KM #A70.

Date	Mintage	VG	F	VF	XF	Unc
1634 Rare	—	—	—	—	—	—

KM# 65 5 DUCAT (1/2 Portugalöser)

17.5000 g., 0.9860 Gold 0.5547 oz. AGW **Obv:** Laureate bust of Gustavus Adolphus in inner circle **Rev:** Crowned arms in inner circle, date in legend **Note:** Fr.#922.

Date	Mintage	VG	F	VF	XF	Unc
1632 Rare	—	—	—	—	—	—

KM# 89 5 DUCAT (1/2 Portugalöser)

17.5000 g., 0.9860 Gold 0.5547 oz. AGW **Obv:** Bust of Christina in inner circle **Rev:** Crowned arms in inner circle, crown divides date **Note:** Fr.#927.

Date	Mintage	VG	F	VF	XF	Unc
1645 Rare	—	—	—	—	—	—
1648 Rare	—	—	—	—	—	—

KM# 66 8 DUCAT

28.0000 g., 0.9860 Gold 0.8876 oz. AGW **Obv:** Laureate bust of Gustavus Adolphus in inner circle **Rev:** Crowned arms in inner circle, date in legend **Note:** Fr.#921.

Date	Mintage	VG	F	VF	XF	Unc
1632 Rare	—	—	—	—	—	—

KM# 56 10 DUCAT (Portugalöser)

35.0000 g., 0.9860 Gold 1.1095 oz. AGW **Subject:** Victory **Obv:** Radiant "Jehovah" in Hebrew above legend and ornamentation **Rev:** 10-line legend with R.N. date below **Note:** Fr.#917.

Date	Mintage	VG	F	VF	XF	Unc
1631 Rare	—	—	—	—	—	—

KM# 67 10 DUCAT (Portugalöser)

35.0000 g., 0.9860 Gold 1.1095 oz. AGW **Obv:** Within inner circle **Rev:** Within inner circle **Note:** Fr.#920.

Date	Mintage	VG	F	VF	XF	Unc
1632 Rare	—	—	—	—	—	—

KM# 68 10 DUCAT (Portugalöser)

35.0000 g., 0.9860 Gold 1.1095 oz. AGW **Obv:** Laureate bust of Gustavus Adolphus in inner circle **Rev:** Crowned arms in inner circle, date in legend

Date	Mintage	VG	F	VF	XF	Unc
1632 Rare	—	—	—	—	—	—

KM# 83 10 DUCAT (Portugalöser)

35.0000 g., 0.9860 Gold 1.1095 oz. AGW **Obv:** Gustavus Adolphus lying in state **Rev:** King riding triumphantly in chariot **Note:** Prev. KM#79. Fr.#924.

Date	Mintage	VG	F	VF	XF	Unc
1634 Rare	—	—	—	—	—	—

KM# 90 10 DUCAT (Portugalöser)

35.0000 g., 0.9860 Gold 1.1095 oz. AGW **Note:** Fr.#926.

Date	Mintage	VG	F	VF	XF	Unc
1645 Rare	—	—	—	—	—	—

Note: Stack's Kroisos Sale, 1-08, XF realized $75,000

Date	Mintage	VG	F	VF	XF	Unc
1648 Rare, 2 known	—	—	—	—	—	—

PATTERNS

Including off metal strikes

KM#	Date	Mintage	Identification	Mkt Val
Pn1	1631	—	2 Thaler. Silver. A Domino.	—
Pn2	1631	—	2 Thaler. Silver. A Domino, Klippe.	—
Pn3	1631	—	3 Thaler. Silver. A Domino, Klippe.	—
Pn4	1632	—	Ducat. Silver. KM#63.	—
Pn5	1632	—	10 Ducat. Silver. KM#68, weight of 1/2 Thaler.	—
Pn6	1646	—	2 Ducat. Silver. KM#92, weight of 1/2 Thaler.	—

TRIAL STRIKES

KM#	Date	Mintage	Identification	Mkt Val
TS1	1618	—	2/3 Thaler. Lead. 4-fold arms with central shield, date in legend.	—

ESSEN

The city of Essen lies in the Ruhr Valley, about 18 miles (30 kilometers) northeast of Düsseldorf and about the same distance west of Dortmund. A Benedictine abbey for women was founded in the place during the first half of the 9th century and the town of Essen grew up around the religious institution. The earliest coinage was of the imperial type pfennigs dating from the first half of the 11th century. The abbess attained the distinction as a princess of the Empire in 1275 and it is from that time that coinage of the abbesses themselves first dates. In the general secularization of the Empire in 1802-03, Essen was given to Prussia, but passed to Berg in 1806. Prussia regained possession of the monastery and city at the end of the Napoleonic Wars in 1815. There was no coinage during the 16th century.

RULERS

Margaretha Elisabeth, Grafin von Manderscheid-Geroldstein, 1598-1604
Elisabeth IX von Berg, 1604-1614
Maria Clara, Grafin von Spaur, 1614-1644
Anna Eleonora, Grafin von Stauffen, 1645-1646
Anna Salome I, Grafin von Salm-Reifferscheidt, 1646-1688
Anna Salome II, Grafin von Manderscheid-Blankenheim, 1689-1691
Bernhardine Sophie, Grafin von Ostfriesland-Ritberg, 1691-1726

MINT OFFICIALS' INITIALS

Initial	Date	Name
CBH	1660-72	Christian Bornhorst
N(crossed swords)L	1686-99	Nikolaus Longerich, mintmaster in Bonn

REFERENCE

K = Heinz Josef Kramer, ***Das Stift Essen Münzen und Medaillen***. Münster, 1993.

ABBEY

REGULAR COINAGE

KM# 5 8 HELLER (1/120 Thaler)

Silver **Ruler:** Anne Salome I **Obv:** Arms of Salm (2 fish), date **Obv. Legend:** MONETA. NOVA **Rev:** VIII in center **Rev. Legend:** NVMMVS. ESSENSIS **Note:** Varieties exist.

Date	Mintage	VG	F	VF	XF	Unc
1656	—	20.00	40.00	95.00	180	—
1657	—	20.00	40.00	95.00	180	—
(1)657	—	20.00	40.00	95.00	180	—

KM# 30 8 HELLER (1/120 Thaler)

Silver **Ruler:** Anna Salome II **Obv:** 4-fold arms, date above **Rev:** VIII **Rev. Legend:** MONE. NOVA. ESSENDIS

Date	Mintage	VG	F	VF	XF	Unc
1691 NL	—	25.00	45.00	100	210	—

KM# 15 1/120 THALER

Silver **Ruler:** Anne Salome I **Obv:** Arms of Salm **Obv. Legend:** SINGULA. COLL: IUVAT **Rev:** Inscription, date **Rev. Legend:** NUMMUS. ESSEND **Rev. Inscription:** 120 / I.REIC / HSTHA / LER **Note:** Varieties exist. Ref. K#54.

Date	Mintage	VG	F	VF	XF	Unc
1671	79,000	20.00	40.00	85.00	170	—
1672 Rare	—	—	—	—	—	—

KM# 11 ALBUS (1/104 Thaler)

Silver **Ruler:** Anne Salome I **Obv:** Crowned 4-fold arms **Rev. Legend:** (104) EINNER REICHSTAHLER **Rev. Inscription:** I / ALBVS / ESSEN / date

Date	Mintage	VG	F	VF	XF	Unc
1662	30,000	27.00	55.00	100	200	—

KM# 19 1/40 THALER (2 Albus)

Silver **Ruler:** Anne Salome I **Obv:** Crowned Salm arms, date in legend **Rev:** Value **Rev. Inscription:** 40 / I. REIC / HSTHA / LER **Note:** Varieties exist.

Date	Mintage	VG	F	VF	XF	Unc
1674	15,000	33.00	75.00	125	240	—
1675	Inc. above	33.00	75.00	125	240	—

KM# 12 MARK (1/26 Thaler)

Silver **Ruler:** Anne Salome I **Obv:** 4-fold arms with central shield divide date **Rev. Legend:** (26) EINEN REICHS THALER **Rev. Inscription:** I / MARCK / ESSEN / DISCH

Date	Mintage	VG	F	VF	XF	Unc
1662	6,000	135	240	375	675	—

KM# 16 1/16 THALER (5 Albus)

Silver **Ruler:** Anne Salome I **Obv:** 4-fold arms with central shield **Rev:** Date in legend **Rev. Inscription:** XVI / I. REICH / HSTHA / LER

Date	Mintage	VG	F	VF	XF	Unc
1671	—	45.00	110	165	335	—

KM# 31 1/6 THALER

Silver **Ruler:** Anna Salome II **Obv:** Crowned 4-fold arms, (1/6) below in legend **Rev:** Madonna and child surrounded by flames, date in legend

Date	Mintage	VG	F	VF	XF	Unc
1691 NL	—	165	290	425	850	—

KM# 9 1/2 THALER

Silver **Ruler:** Anne Salome I **Obv:** Crowned 5-fold arms divides ANNO - date **Rev:** Madonna holding child standing on crescent surrounded by flames **Note:** Ref. K#44.

Date	Mintage	VG	F	VF	XF	Unc
1672 CBH Rare	—	—	—	—	—	—

Note: Only one example of this coin is known, in Vienna; Described as a gulden but same diameter as thaler, most likely struck with thaler dies

KM# 10 THALER

Silver **Ruler:** Anne Salome I **Obv:** Bust of Anna Salome I facing 3/4 left **Obv. Legend:** ANN: SLAO: V. G.: G. FVRSTIN. ZV. ESS. GEBORN: GRAFIN. Z. S: * **Rev:** Crowned five-fold arms divides date **Rev. Legend:** OVI-LITEM. AVFFERT... **Note:** Dav. #5276.

Date	Mintage	VG	F	VF	XF	Unc
1660 Rare	—	—	—	—	—	—

KM# 17 THALER
Silver **Ruler:** Anne Salome I **Obv:** Crowned 5-fold arms divides ANNO - date **Obv. Legend:** ANNA SALOME. D:G:PRIN: ESEND:COMITISSA SALMEN: **Rev:** Madonna holding child standing on crescent surrounded by flames **Rev. Legend:** SUBTUUM PRAESIDIUM CONFUGIMUS **Note:** Dav. #5277.

Date	Mintage	VG	F	VF	XF	Unc
1672 CBH Rare	—	—	—	—	—	—

KM# 25 THALER
Silver **Ruler:** Anne Salome I **Obv:** Crowned five-fold arms divides date **Rev:** City view in lower 1/2, battle scene in upper half with saint in clouds above, date in chronogram in legend **Note:** Dav. #5278.

Date	Mintage	VG	F	VF	XF	Unc
1680 Rare	—	—	—	—	—	—

Note: Künker Auction 170, 6-10 VF realized approximately $27,235

KM# 26 THALER
Silver **Ruler:** Anne Salome I **Obv:** Bust left, titles of Leopold I **Note:** Dav. #5279.

Date	Mintage	VG	F	VF	XF	Unc
1680 Rare	—	—	—	—	—	—

TRADE COINAGE

KM# 18 DUCAT
3.5000 g., 0.9860 Gold 0.1109 oz. AGW **Ruler:** Anne Salome I **Obv:** Crowned 4-fold arms, dividing date **Rev:** Madonna standing holding child **Note:** Fr. 932.

Date	Mintage	VG	F	VF	XF	Unc
1672 CBH Rare	—	—	—	—	—	—

PATTERNS

Including off metal strikes

KM#	Date	Mintage	Identification	Mkt Val
Pn1	1660	—	Thaler. Tin. KM#10.	350

FINSTINGEN

(Fenestrange, Fenetrange)

A city located 28 miles south of Saarbrucken in France, Moselle Department. To Lorraine in 1665.

RULER
Diana

FREE CITY

REGULAR COINAGE

KM# 10 1/4 ECU
Silver **Obv:** Crowned arms **Obv. Legend:** DIANA. PRINC: : S: IMP: MARCH LE HAVRE. **Rev:** St. Maurice on horseback **Rev. Legend:** SANCTVS MAVRITIVS. PATRONVS. VINSTIN.

Date	Mintage	VG	F	VF	XF	Unc
ND(CA.1613) Rare	—	—	—	—	—	—

FRANCONIA

(Franken)

Franconia became a territorial part of the empire established by Charlemagne and remained a division of Germany until early modern times. It was situated north of Bavaria between the Palatinate and the Upper Palatinate and formed the basis for the Franconian Circle (see) of the Empire from the 16th century. During the Thirty Years' War, Bernhard of Saxe-Weimar took control of the area and proclaimed himself Duke of Franconia, having coins struck with his name and titles thus stylized, a circumstance which did not outlive him.

RULER
Bernhard of Saxe-Weimar, 1633-1639

MINT OFFICIALS' INITIALS

Initial	Date	Name
CS	1622-54	Conrad Stutz, Franconian Circle, die-cutter in Fürth

DUCHY

REGULAR COINAGE

KM# 5 1/2 BATZEN (2 Kreuzer)
Silver **Ruler:** Bernhard **Obv:** Crowned oval shield of ducal Saxony arms in baroque frame, value 28 R in oval above **Obv. Legend:** BERNHARD. D. G. D. - SAX. IVL. CL. E. MON. **Rev:** Full-length facing figure of Christ, holding orb in left hand, divides date **Rev. Legend:** SALVATOR MVN - DI AD IVLIANOS. **Mint:** Würzburg **Note:** 1/28 Reichsthaler or Schilling.

Date	Mintage	VG	F	VF	XF	Unc
1633	—	33.00	65.00	130	260	—
1634	—	110	250	375	600	—

KM# 6.1 BATZEN (4 Kreuzer)
Silver **Ruler:** Bernhard **Obv:** Crowned squarish shield of ducal Saxony arms in baroque frame, value IIII K in oval above **Obv. Legend:** BERNHARD. D.G. DVX. SAXONI. IVL. C. E. M. **Rev:** Full-lentgh standing figure of Christ facing divides date **Rev. Legend:** SALVATOR. MV - NDI. ADIUVANOS

Date	Mintage	VG	F	VF	XF	Unc
1633	—	25.00	50.00	100	210	—

KM# 6.2 BATZEN (4 Kreuzer)
Silver **Ruler:** Bernhard **Obv:** Crowned oval shield of ducal Saxony arms in baroque frame, value IIII K above in oval **Obv. Legend:** BERNHARD. D.G. DVX. SAX. IVL. CL. E. MO. **Rev:** Full-length facing figure of Christ, holding orb in left hand, divides date **Rev. Legend:** SALVATOR MV - NDI ADIVUANOS. **Mint:** Würzburg

Date	Mintage	VG	F	VF	XF	Unc
1633	—	25.00	50.00	100	210	—
1634	—	45.00	100	180	325	—

KM# 10 1/28 THALER (1 Schilling)
Silver **Ruler:** Bernhard **Obv:** Crowned oval arms, 28 in oval above **Rev:** Full-length standing figure of Christ facing divides date

Date	Mintage	VG	F	VF	XF	Unc
1633	—	—	—	—	—	—

KM# 7 THALER
Silver **Obv:** Facing bust of Gustav Adolf, arms below **Rev:** Christ standing facing with orb **Note:** Dav. #A6670.

Date	Mintage	VG	F	VF	XF	Unc
1632 Rare	—	—	—	—	—	—

KM# 8 THALER
Silver **Obv:** Facing bust of Axel Oxensteirna, arms below **Rev:** Lion left with sword and crown **Note:** Dav. #B6670.

Date	Mintage	VG	F	VF	XF	Unc
ND Rare	—	—	—	—	—	—

Note: Dr. Busso Peus Nachfolger Auction 390, 5-07, XF-Unc realized approximately $16,995.

KM# 9 THALER
Silver, 42 mm. **Ruler:** Bernhard **Obv:** Facing 1/2-length armored bust, small crowned shield of arms of ducal Saxony below **Obv. Legend:** BERNHARD: D. G DVX. SAXO - NIÆ IVLIÆ. CLIVIÆ. ET MON. **Rev:** Shield of arms with ornate helmet above dividing date **Rev. Legend:** NACH DEM. ALTEN - SCHROT. V: KORN. **Note:** Dav.#7539.

Date	Mintage	VG	F	VF	XF	Unc
1633 Rare	—	—	—	—	—	—

KM# 11 THALER
Silver, 42 mm. **Ruler:** Bernhard **Obv:** Facing 1/2-length armored bust, small crowned shield of arms of ducal Saxony below **Obv. Legend:** BERNHARD' D:G: DVX. - SAXO. IVL. CL. ET. MON. **Rev:** "Jehovah" in Hebrew in oval with rays, hand extending from heaven with wreath, small oval arms in baroque frame divide date **Rev. Legend:** QVOD. DEVS. VULT. HOC. SEMP. FIT. **Mint:** Fürth **Note:** Dav. #7539. (C6670). Prev. KM #9.

Date	Mintage	VG	F	VF	XF	Unc
1634 CS Rare	—	—	—	—	—	—

TRADE COINAGE

KM# 12 GOLDGULDEN
Gold **Ruler:** Bernhard **Obv:** Shield of ducal Saxony arms **Rev:** Figure of Christ standing **Note:** Fr. 3016.

Date	Mintage	VG	F	VF	XF	Unc
1634 Rare	—	—	—	—	—	—

FRANCONIAN CIRCLE

(Franken)

Franconia became a territorial part of the empire established by Charlemagne and remained a division of Germany until early modern times. It was situated north of Bavaria between the Palatinate and the Upper Palatinate and formed the basis for the Franconian Circle (see) of the Empire from the 16th century. During the Thirty Years' War Bernhard of Saxe-Weimar took control of the area and proclaimed himself Duke of Franconia, having coins struck with his name and titles thus stylized, a circumstance which did not outlive him.

RULER
Bernhard of Saxe-Weimar, 1633-1639

MINT MARKS
F – Furth Mint
N – Nuremberg Mint
S – Schwabach Mint

MINT OFFICIALS' INITIALS

Initial	Date	Name
CS	1622-54	Conrad Stutz, Franconian Circle, die-cutter in Furth
GFN	1682-1710	Georg Friedrich Nurnberger

NOTE: The usual design of most coins of the Franconian Circle incorporates the four arms of Bamberg, Brandenburg-Ansbach, Brandenburg-Bayreuth and Nuremberg.

IMPERIAL CIRCLE

REGULAR COINAGE

KM# 5 3 HELLER
Silver **Obv:** Four arms, date divided to left and right, F below **Rev:** III/HELL/ER **Mint:** Fürth

Date	Mintage	VG	F	VF	XF	Unc
1624F	—	—	—	—	—	—

KM# 15 KREUZER
Silver **Obv:** Four arms divided date, star below **Rev:** Cross and St. Andrew's cross above and below 8-spoked wheel

Date	Mintage	VG	F	VF	XF	Unc
1637	—	—	—	—	—	—

KM# 6 2 KREUZER (1/2 Batzen)
Silver **Obv:** Imperial orb with 2 divides date, titles of Ferdinand II **Rev:** Four arms, F below **Rev. Legend:** AD LEG: IM... **Mint:** Fürth

Date	Mintage	VG	F	VF	XF	Unc
1624F	—	25.00	55.00	110	220	—

KM# 7 2 KREUZER (1/2 Batzen)
Silver, 18 mm. **Obv:** Cross at top divides date **Rev:** Four arms in cruciform, F between 2 at lower right **Rev. Legend:** AD LEG: IM... **Mint:** Fürth

Date	Mintage	VG	F	VF	XF	Unc
1624F	—	30.00	60.00	120	240	—

KM# 16 2 KREUZER (1/2 Batzen)
Silver **Obv:** Imperial orb with 2 divides date **Rev:** Similar to 4 Kreuzer, KM#10

Date	Mintage	VG	F	VF	XF	Unc
1637	—	33.00	60.00	120	230	—

KM# 17 2 KREUZER (1/2 Batzen)
Silver **Obv:** Imperial eagle, 2 in orb on breast, titles of Ferdinand III

Date	Mintage	VG	F	VF	XF	Unc
1637	—	55.00	110	175	335	—

KM# 8 4 KREUZER (1 Batzen)
Silver **Obv:** Similar to KM#10 but date in legend **Rev:** Four arms in cruciform, F between 2 at lower right **Rev. Legend:** AD LEG: IMP...

Date	Mintage	VG	F	VF	XF	Unc
1624	—	—	—	—	—	—

KM# 10 4 KREUZER (1 Batzen)
Silver **Mint:** Fürth

Date	Mintage	VG	F	VF	XF	Unc
1625F	—	40.00	85.00	150	300	—

KM# 12 1/28 THALER (1 Schilling)
Silver **Obv:** Crowned imperial eagle, Z8 in orb on breast, titles of Ferdinand II **Rev:** Four arms **Mint:** Fürth

Date	Mintage	VG	F	VF	XF	Unc
16Z4F	—	—	—	—	—	—

KM# 20 1/3 THALER (1/2 Gulden)
Silver **Note:** Similar to 2/3 Thaler, KM#21.

Date	Mintage	VG	F	VF	XF	Unc
1693 GFN	—	—	—	—	—	—

KM# 21 2/3 THALER (Gulden)
Silver, 37.4 mm.

Date	Mintage	VG	F	VF	XF	Unc
1693 GFN	—	65.00	120	200	360	—

KM# 9 THALER
Silver **Obv:** Crowned imperial eagle, orb on breast, titles of Ferdinand II **Rev:** Four oval arms in baroque frames in form of X, palm sprays around, date in legend **Note:** Dav. #6668.

Date	Mintage	VG	F	VF	XF	Unc
1624 CS	—	1,250	2,500	4,500	7,500	—

KM# 13 THALER
36.0000 g., Silver **Note:** Klippe. Dav. #6668A.

Date	Mintage	VG	F	VF	XF	Unc
1624 CS Rare	—	—	—	—	—	—

KM# 11 THALER
Silver **Obv:** Facing heads of four rulers in oval frames in cruciform, smaller arms in cruciform in center **Rev:** Female allegorical figures of Justice and Peace seated on bench, two angels above, "JEHOVAH" in Hebrew with rays at top, Roman numeral date in legend **Note:** Dav. #6669.

Date	Mintage	VG	F	VF	XF	Unc
1625 CS Rare	—	—	—	—	—	—

Note: Leu Numismatik AG Auction 85, 10-02, good XF realized approximately $11,975.

COUNTERMARKED COINAGE

1693-1695

KM# 31.15 60 KREUZER (Gulden)
Silver **Countermark:** 60 K/FC monogram **Note:** Countermarked on Sayn-Wittgenstein-Hohnstein 2/3 Thaler, KM#52.

CM Date	Host Date	Good	VG	F	VF	XF
ND(1693-5)	1674 IZW	—	—	—	—	—

KM# 30.1 60 KREUZER (Gulden)
Silver **Countermark:** 60K/FC monogram **Note:** Countermark on Montfort 2/3 Thaler, KM#45.

CM Date	Host Date	Good	VG	F	VF	XF
ND(1693-5)	1675	—	120	200	400	675

KM# 30.2 60 KREUZER (Gulden)
Silver **Countermark:** 60K/FC monogram **Note:** Countermark on Montfort 60 Kreuzer, KM#61.

CM Date	Host Date	Good	VG	F	VF	XF
ND(1693-5)	1679	—	120	200	400	675

KM# 30.3 60 KREUZER (Gulden)
Silver **Countermark:** 60K/FC monogram **Note:** Countermark on Montfort 60 Kreuzer, KM#76.

CM Date	Host Date	Good	VG	F	VF	XF
ND(1693-5)	1690 FIG	—	120	200	400	650

KM# 30.4 60 KREUZER (Gulden)
Silver **Countermark:** 60K/FC monogram **Note:** Countermark on Montfort 60 Kreuzer, KM#78.

CM Date	Host Date	Good	VG	F	VF	XF
ND(1693-5)	1690 FIG	—	120	200	400	675

KM# 30.5 60 KREUZER (Gulden)
Silver **Countermark:** 60K/FC monogram **Note:** Countermark on Montfort 60 Kreuzer, KM#78.

CM Date	Host Date	Good	VG	F	VF	XF
ND(1693-95)	1690	—	85.00	150	300	550

KM# 31.1 60 KREUZER (Gulden)
Silver **Countermark:** 60K/FC monogram **Note:** Countermark on Anhalt-Desau 2/3 Thaler, KM#6.2.

CM Date	Host Date	Good	VG	F	VF	XF
ND(1693-5)	1693 IEG	—	55.00	100	220	350

KM# 31.2 60 KREUZER (Gulden)
Silver **Countermark:** 60K/FC monogram **Note:** Countermark on Anhalt-Harzegerode 2/3 Thaler, KM#1.1.

CM Date	Host Date	Good	VG	F	VF	XF
ND(1693-5)	ND1675-79	—	55.00	100	220	350

KM# 31.3 60 KREUZER (Gulden)
Silver **Countermark:** 60K/FC monogram **Note:** Countermark on Anhalt-Harzegerode 2/3 Thaler, KM#1.4.

CM Date	Host Date	Good	VG	F	VF	XF
ND(1693-5)	1679 SD	—	55.00	100	220	350

KM# 31.4 60 KREUZER (Gulden)
Silver **Countermark:** 60K/FC monogram **Note:** Countermark on Anhalt-Harzegerode 2.3 Thaler, KM#1.4.

CM Date	Host Date	Good	VG	F	VF	XF
ND(1693-5)	1676 CP	—	55.00	100	220	350

KM# 31.5 60 KREUZER (Gulden)
Silver **Countermark:** 60K/FC monogram **Note:** Countermark on Anhalt-Zerbst 2/3 Thaler, KM#19.6.

CM Date	Host Date	Good	VG	F	VF	XF
ND(1693-5)	1679 CP	—	55.00	100	220	350

KM# 31.6 60 KREUZER (Gulden)
Silver **Countermark:** 60K/FC monogram **Note:** Countermark on Emden 2/3 Thaler, KM#30.

CM Date	Host Date	Good	VG	F	VF	XF
ND(1693-5)	1688	—	55.00	100	220	350

KM# 31.7 60 KREUZER (Gulden)
Silver **Countermark:** 60K/FC m onogram **Note:** Countermark on Henneberg-Ilmenau 2/3 Thaler, KM#10.

CM Date	Host Date	Good	VG	F	VF	XF
ND(1693-5)	1692-93 BA	—	55.00	100	220	350

KM# 31.8 60 KREUZER (Gulden)
Silver **Countermark:** 60K/FC monogram **Note:** Countermark on Lauenberg 2/3 Thaler.

CM Date	Host Date	Good	VG	F	VF	XF
ND(1693-5)	1678	—	55.00	100	220	350

KM# 31.9 60 KREUZER (Gulden)
Silver **Countermark:** 60K/FC monogram **Note:** Countermark on Lubeck 2/3 Thaler, KM#62.

CM Date	Host Date	Good	VG	F	VF	XF
ND(1693-5)	1678	—	55.00	100	220	350

KM# 31.10 60 KREUZER (Gulden)
Silver **Countermark:** 60K/FC monogram **Note:** Countermark on Münster 24 Mariengroschen, KM#101.

CM Date	Host Date	Good	VG	F	VF	XF
ND(1693-5)	1693 JO	—	55.00	100	220	350

KM# 31.11 60 KREUZER (Gulden)
Silver **Countermark:** 60K/FC monogram **Note:** Countermark on Pfalz-Sulzbach Gulden.

CM Date	Host Date	Good	VG	F	VF	XF
ND(1693-5)	1690-91	—	55.00	100	220	350

KM# 31.12 60 KREUZER (Gulden)
Silver **Countermark:** 60K/FC monogram **Note:** Countermark on Saxe-Weimar Gulden.

CM Date	Host Date	Good	VG	F	VF	XF
ND(1693-5)	1677-78	—	55.00	100	220	350

KM# 31.13 60 KREUZER (Gulden)
Silver **Countermark:** 60K/FC monogram **Note:** Countermark on Sayn-Wittgenstein-Wittgenstein 2/3 Thaler, KM#79.

CM Date	Host Date	Good	VG	F	VF	XF
ND(1693-5)	1676	—	55.00	100	220	350

KM# 31.14 60 KREUZER (Gulden)
Silver **Countermark:** 60K/FC monogram **Note:** Countermark on Henneberg-Ilmenau 2/3 Thaler, KM#9. Prev. KM#31.

CM Date	Host Date	Good	VG	F	VF	XF
ND(1693-5)	1692 BA	—	120	200	400	650

TRADE COINAGE

KM# A13 4 DUCAT
14.0000 g., 0.9860 Gold 0.4438 oz. AGW

Date	Mintage	VG	F	VF	XF	Unc
1625 CS Rare	—	—	—	—	—	—

Note: Similar to 1 Thaler, KM#11, struck from same dies.

FRANKENTHAL

Located about 6 miles northwest of Mannheim, Frankenthal was besieged by the Spaniards during the Thirty Years' War and forced to strike obsidional coinage.

NOTE: The horizontal line below VII represents 1/2.

TOWN

SIEGE COINAGE

Frankenthal was besieged by the Spaniards during the Thirty Years War and forced to strike obsidional coinage.

KM# 1 7-1/2 BATZEN
4.5000 g., Silver **Obv:** City arms above value, the horizontal line below VII represents 1/2. **Obv. Legend:** FRANCKENTHALER: NOTH • M • 16 • 23. **Obv. Inscription:** BATZ / VII. **Note:** Uniface. Klippe.

Date	Mintage	VG	F	VF	XF	Unc
1623	—	1,150	1,650	3,000	5,700	—

KM# 3.1 15 BATZEN
8.7000 g., Silver **Obv:** Town arms above value **Obv. Legend:** FRANCKENTHALER • NOTH • M • 16 • 23. **Obv. Inscription:** BATZ / XV. **Note:** Uniface. Klippe.

Date	Mintage	VG	F	VF	XF	Unc
1623	—	400	700	1,400	2,700	—

KM# 3.2 15 BATZEN
8.7000 g., Silver **Obv. Legend:** FRANCKEN • NOTHM • 1623

Date	Mintage	VG	F	VF	XF	Unc
1623	—	—	—	—	—	—

Note: Reported, not confirmed

KM# 4.2 GULDEN
7.1000 g., Silver **Obv:** Town arms with F below divide date without value punch **Obv. Legend:** GOTT • IST • VNSER • ECKSTEIN

Date	Mintage	VG	F	VF	XF	Unc
1623	—	700	1,350	2,700	5,000	—

KM# 4.1 GULDEN
7.1000 g., Silver **Obv:** Town arms with F below divide date, value 1 punched in below outside legend. **Obv. Legend:** GOTT • IST • VNSER • ECKSTEIN **Note:** Uniface. Klippe.

Date	Mintage	VG	F	VF	XF	Unc
1623	—	750	1,500	2,800	5,500	—

KM# 6.1 2 GULDEN
Silver **Obv:** Without value punch **Obv. Legend:** GOTT • IST • VNSER • ECKSTEIN.

Date	Mintage	VG	F	VF	XF	Unc
1623	—	450	825	1,600	3,000	—

KM# 9.1 2 GULDEN
Silver **Obv:** F between two stars, value 2 in round indent **Obv. Legend:** GOTT • IST • VNSER • ECKSTEIN

Date	Mintage	VG	F	VF	XF	Unc
1623	—	550	825	1,600	3,000	—

KM# 9.2 2 GULDEN
Silver **Obv:** F between 2 stars, value 2 punched in all four corners **Obv. Legend:** GOTT • IST • VNSER • ECKSTEIN

Date	Mintage	VG	F	VF	XF	Unc
1623	—	500	925	1,700	3,300	—

KM# 9.3 2 GULDEN
Silver **Obv:** F between 2 stars, without value punch **Obv. Legend:** GOTT • IST • VNSER • ECKSTEIN

Date	Mintage	VG	F	VF	XF	Unc
1623	—	850	1,650	2,900	4,200	—

KM# 9.4 2 GULDEN
Silver **Obv:** City arms surrounded by six arcs, forming one circle **Obv. Legend:** DEVS • PETRA • NOSTRA • ANGVLARIS • 1623.

Date	Mintage	VG	F	VF	XF	Unc
1623 Rare	—	—	—	—	—	—

KM# 5 2 GULDEN
Silver **Obv:** Town arms with F below divide date, value 2 punched in below outside legend **Obv. Legend:** DEVS • PETRA • NOSTRA • ANGVLARIS **Note:** Weight varies 14.0-14.3 grams. Uniface. Klippe.

Date	Mintage	VG	F	VF	XF	Unc
1623	—	900	1,735	2,700	5,000	—

KM# 6.2 2 GULDEN
Silver **Obv. Legend:** GOTT • IST • VNSER • ECKSTEIN.

Date	Mintage	VG	F	VF	XF	Unc
1623	—	400	825	1,600	3,000	—

KM# 7.1 4 GULDEN
Silver **Obv:** Town arms with F below divide date, value 4 punched in below outside legend. **Obv. Legend:** DEVS • PETRA • NOSTRA • ANGVLARIS **Note:** Weight varies 28.0-28.5 g. Uniface. Klippe.

Date	Mintage	VG	F	VF	XF	Unc
1623	—	950	1,650	2,500	3,250	6,500

KM# 7.2 4 GULDEN
Silver **Obv:** Value 4 punched in below outside legend, without F below town arms **Obv. Legend:** DEVS • PETRA • NOSTRA • ANGVLARIS

Date	Mintage	VG	F	VF	XF	Unc
1623	—	650	1,200	2,500	4,500	—

KM# 8 4 GULDEN
Silver **Obv:** value 4 punched in below outside legend. **Obv. Legend:** GOTT • IST • VNSER • ECKSTEIN

Date	Mintage	VG	F	VF	XF	Unc
1623	—	950	1,650	2,500	3,500	—

TRADE COINAGE

KM# 11 DUCAT
3.5000 g., 0.9860 Gold 0.1109 oz. AGW **Obv:** Town arms with F below divide date, legend, no value shown **Obv. Legend:** GOTT • IST • VNSER • ECKSTEIN **Note:** Klippe, uniface.

Date	Mintage	VG	F	VF	XF	Unc
1623 Rare	—	—	—	—	—	—

KM# 12 2 DUCAT
6.6800 g., Gold **Obv:** Town arms with F below divide date, legend, no value shown. **Obv. Legend:** GOTT • IST • VNSER • ECKSTEIN **Note:** Uniface.

Date	Mintage	VG	F	VF	XF	Unc
1623 Rare	—	—	—	—	—	—

Note: Peus Auction 390, 5-07, XF realized approximately $35,350

KM# 13 2 DUCAT
6.6800 g., Gold **Obv:** Town arms encircled by three storm clouds, legend **Obv. Legend:** DEVS • PETRA • NOSTRA • ANGVLARIS • 1623 F

Date	Mintage	VG	F	VF	XF	Unc
1623 Rare	—	—	—	—	—	—

FRANKFURT AM MAIN

One of the largest cities of modern Germany, Frankfurt is located on the north bank of the Main River about 25 miles (42 kilometers) upstream from where it joins the Rhine at Mainz. It was the site of a Roman camp in the first century. Frankfurt was a commercial center from the early Middle Ages and became a favored location for imperial councils during the Carolingian period because of its central location. An imperial mint operated from early times and had a large production during the 12th to 14th centuries. Local issues were produced from at least the mid-14th century, but it was not until 1428 that the city was officially granted the right to coin its own money. In establishing the seven permanent electors of the Empire in 1356, the Golden Bull also made Frankfurt the site of those elections and increased the prestige of the city even further. Frankfurt remained a free city until 1806 and then was the capital of the Grand Duchy of Frankfurt from 1810 until 1814, only to regain its free status in 1815. The city chose the wrong side in the Austro-Prussian War of 1866 and thus was absorbed by victorious Prussia in the latter year.

MINT MARKS
F = Frankfurt

MINT OFFICIALS' INITIALS

Initial	Date	Name
PM	1567-1603	Philipp Mussler, warden
LS	1611-30	Lorenz Schilling, diecutter
(a) or or or AE or C AE	1618-25, 27-36	Caspar Ayrer
HE, HS	1625-27	Hans Schmidt
GN	1644-45	George Nurnberger der Jungere
AM	1637-44	Johann Anselm Munch
(h) (3 acorns)	1646-66	Johann Ludwig Hallaicher
(f) and/or MR	1666-89	Michael Faber
IF, IIF	1690-1737	Johann Jeremias Freytag

NOTE: In some instances old dies were used with initials beyond the date range of the man that held the position.

FREE CITY

REGULAR COINAGE

KM# 16 PFENNIG
Silver **Obv:** Crowned eagle left in circle **Note:** Uniface, schüssel-type.

Date	Mintage	VG	F	VF	XF	Unc
ND(1606) Rare	—	—	—	—	—	—

KM# 24 PFENNIG
Silver **Obv:** Crowned eagle, head left in circle, around FRANCFVRTI, date. **Note:** Uniface, schüssel-type. Varieties exist.

Date	Mintage	VG	F	VF	XF	Unc
1609	—	20.00	50.00	100	200	—
1610	—	20.00	50.00	100	200	—

KM# 68 PFENNIG
Silver **Obv:** Shield with crowned eagle, head left, divides date, F above.

Date	Mintage	VG	F	VF	XF	Unc
16Z1	—	20.00	50.00	100	200	—

KM# 73 PFENNIG
Silver **Note:** Shield with crowned eagle, head left, date above divided by F.

Date	Mintage	VG	F	VF	XF	Unc
16ZZ	—	15.00	33.00	65.00	130	—

KM# 69 DREIER (3 Pfennig)
Silver **Obv:** Crowned eagle, head left, in shield, divides date, F above **Rev:** Imperial orb with 3 **Note:** Kipper Dreier.

Date	Mintage	VG	F	VF	XF	Unc
1621	—	—	—	—	—	—

Note: Reported, not confirmed

KM# A20 ENGLISH (7 Heller)
Silver **Obv:** 4-fold shield, Frankfurt crowned eagle in each quadrant **Obv. Legend:** MON ETA NOV **Rev:** Ornate floriated cross in circle **Rev. Legend:** ANGLIE • FRANCF • 1601 **Note:** Ref. J/F#261.

Date	Mintage	VG	F	VF	XF	Unc
1601	—	275	525	1,000	1,800	—

Note: Orignally issued in the late Middle Ages to facilitate exchange with English sterling or pennies which circulated widely in continental Europe.

KM# 99 1/4 KREUZER
Silver **Obv:** Crowned eagle, head left divides date in circle of pellets, 1/4 below **Note:** Uniface, schüssel-type.

Date	Mintage	VG	F	VF	XF	Unc
1647 Rare	—	—	—	—	—	—

Note: Reported, not confirmed

KM# 60 KREUZER
Silver **Obv:** Crowned eagle, head left, in shield, F above, all within wreath **Rev:** Date **Rev. Inscription:** I / KREVTZ / ER **Note:** Kipper Kreuzer. Varieties exist.

Date	Mintage	VG	F	VF	XF	Unc
1620	—	85.00	175	675	750	—
16Z0	—	40.00	80.00	160	320	—
1622	—	40.00	80.00	160	320	—
16ZZ	—	40.00	80.00	160	320	—

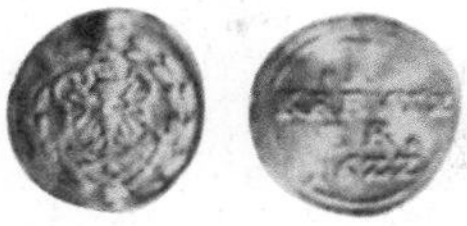

KM# 74 KREUZER
Silver **Obv:** Eagle, head left, in shield, F above, all in laurel wreath **Note:** Kipper Kreuzer. Varieties exist.

Date	Mintage	VG	F	VF	XF	Unc
16ZZ	—	25.00	55.00	115	230	—
16Z3	—	30.00	65.00	180	260	—

KM# 77 KREUZER
Silver **Obv:** Eagle's head to right

Date	Mintage	VG	F	VF	XF	Unc
16Z3	—	25.00	55.00	120	250	—

KM# 135 KREUZER
Silver **Obv:** Crowned displayed eagle, head to right, in circle **Rev:** Date divided by F above 3-line inscription with mintmaster's initials, all in laurel wreath **Rev. Inscription:** KREU / TZER / (initials) **Mint:** Frankfurt

Date	Mintage	VG	F	VF	XF	Unc
1666 MF	—	40.00	80.00	160	320	—

KM# 139 KREUZER
Silver, 16 mm. **Obv:** Crowned displayed eagle, head to left, in circle **Rev:** Date divided by F above 3-line inscription with mintmaster's initials, all in laurel wreath **Rev. Inscription:** KREU / TZER / (initals) **Mint:** Frankfurt

Date	Mintage	VG	F	VF	XF	Unc
1668 MF	—	40.00	80.00	160	320	—
1669 MF	—	40.00	80.00	160	320	—
1676 MF	—	30.00	70.00	150	300	—

KM# 151 KREUZER
Silver **Rev:** Inscription divides date in circle **Rev. Legend:** NACH • DEM • SCHLUS • DER • V • STAND **Rev. Inscription:** F / KREV / TZER

Date	Mintage	VG	F	VF	XF	Unc
1693 IIF	—	30.00	65.00	130	260	—
1695 IIF	—	30.00	65.00	130	260	—

KM# 158 KREUZER
Silver **Obv:** Floral design above inscription **Obv. Inscription:** FRANC / FURT **Rev. Inscription:** I / KREU / ZER

Date	Mintage	VG	F	VF	XF	Unc
ND(ca.1695) 1 known; Rare	—	—	—	—	—	—

KM# 61 2 KREUZER (Halbbatzen)
Silver **Obv:** Crowned eagle, head left, in shield **Rev:** Date **Rev. Inscription:** II / KREVTZ / ER **Note:** Varieties exist.

Date	Mintage	VG	F	VF	XF	Unc
16Z0	—	150	300	500	—	—

KM# 87.1 ALBUS
Silver **Obv:** Crowned eagle, in inner circle, head left **Obv. Legend:** REIP • FRANCOFVRT **Rev:** Inscription in laurel wreath and inner circle **Rev. Inscription:** ALBVS / + / date

Date	Mintage	VG	F	VF	XF	Unc
1637	—	16.00	30.00	65.00	130	—
1637 AM	—	16.00	30.00	65.00	130	—
1638 AM	—	16.00	30.00	65.00	130	—
1639 AM	—	16.00	30.00	65.00	130	—
1640 AM	—	16.00	30.00	65.00	130	—
1642 (h)	—	—	—	—	—	—
Note: Reported, not confirmed						
1647 (a)	—	16.00	30.00	65.00	130	—
1647 (h)	—	16.00	30.00	65.00	130	—
1654 (h)	—	16.00	30.00	65.00	130	—
1655 (h)	—	16.00	30.00	65.00	130	—

KM# 87.2 ALBUS
Silver **Obv:** Without inner circles **Obv. Legend:** ...REIPVB **Rev:** Without inner circles **Rev. Legend:** ALBVS / + / date

Date	Mintage	VG	F	VF	XF	Unc
1647 (h)	—	16.00	30.00	65.00	130	—
1648 (h)	—	16.00	30.00	65.00	130	—

KM# 87.3 ALBUS
Silver **Obv. Legend:** REIP...

Date	Mintage	VG	F	VF	XF	Unc
1648 (h)	—	16.00	30.00	60.00	120	—

KM# 105 ALBUS
Silver **Rev:** Date / ++ / ALBVS

Date	Mintage	VG	F	VF	XF	Unc
1648 (h)	—	30.00	60.00	120	240	—

KM# 108.1 ALBUS
Silver **Obv. Legend:** REIPUB: FRANCOFURT **Rev:** Inscription divided by cross below, in laurel wreath **Rev. Inscription:** ALBVS / date

Date	Mintage	VG	F	VF	XF	Unc
1649 (h)	—	27.00	55.00	100	200	—
1651 (h)	—	27.00	55.00	100	200	—
1652 (h)	—	27.00	55.00	100	200	—

KM# 107.1 ALBUS
Silver **Obv:** Eagle head left **Rev:** Inscription divided by cross below, in laurel wreath **Rev. Inscription:** I / ALBVS / date **Note:** Varieties exist.

Date	Mintage	VG	F	VF	XF	Unc
1649 (h)	—	15.00	35.00	70.00	145	—
1650 (h)	—	15.00	35.00	70.00	145	—
1651 (h)	—	15.00	35.00	70.00	145	—
1652 (h)	—	15.00	35.00	70.00	145	—
1653	—	15.00	35.00	70.00	145	—
1657	—	15.00	35.00	70.00	145	—

KM# 107.2 ALBUS
Silver **Obv:** Eagle head right **Rev:** Inscription divided by cross below, in laurel wreath **Rev. Inscription:** I / ALBVS / date

Date	Mintage	VG	F	VF	XF	Unc
1651 (h)	—	20.00	40.00	80.00	160	—
1652 (h)	—	20.00	40.00	80.00	160	—
1653 (h)	—	20.00	40.00	80.00	160	—
1653	—	20.00	40.00	80.00	160	—
1654	—	20.00	40.00	80.00	160	—

KM# A108 ALBUS
Silver **Obv:** Smaller eagle, head left **Rev:** ALBVS around, date intact

Date	Mintage	VG	F	VF	XF	Unc
1655 Rare	—	—	—	—	—	—

KM# 108.2 ALBUS
Silver **Obv:** Eagle left in inner circle **Rev:** ALBUS above cross, date flanking, within inner circle **Rev. Legend:** REIPVB FRANCOFURT **Note:** Varieties exist.

Date	Mintage	VG	F	VF	XF	Unc
1655 (h)	—	27.00	40.00	80.00	160	—
1655	—	27.00	40.00	80.00	160	—
1656 (h)	—	27.00	40.00	80.00	160	—
1656	—	27.00	40.00	80.00	160	—
1657 (h)	—	27.00	40.00	80.00	160	—
1657	—	27.00	40.00	80.00	160	—
1666 (f)	—	27.00	40.00	80.00	160	—
1667 (f)	—	27.00	40.00	80.00	160	—
1668 (f)	—	27.00	40.00	80.00	160	—
1669 (f)	—	27.00	40.00	80.00	160	—
1670 (f)	—	27.00	40.00	80.00	160	—
1671 (f)	—	27.00	40.00	80.00	160	—
1680 (f)	—	27.00	40.00	80.00	160	—
1681 (f)	—	27.00	40.00	80.00	160	—

KM# 152.1 ALBUS
Silver **Rev:** I/ ALBUS/ date and mintmasters initials divided by cross **Rev. Legend:** NACH • DEM • SCHLUS • DER • V • STäND

Date	Mintage	VG	F	VF	XF	Unc
1693 IIF	—	27.00	55.00	75.00	125	240
1695 IIF	—	27.00	55.00	75.00	125	240

KM# 152.2 ALBUS
Silver **Rev. Legend:** ...V • STAEND

Date	Mintage	VG	F	VF	XF	Unc
1693 IIF	—	27.00	55.00	75.00	125	240
1695 IIF	—	27.00	55.00	75.00	125	240

KM# 152.3 ALBUS
Silver **Rev. Legend:** ...V • STEND

Date	Mintage	VG	F	VF	XF	Unc
1693 IIF	—	27.00	55.00	75.00	125	240
1695 IIF	—	27.00	55.00	75.00	125	240

KM# 25 ALBUS (8 Heller)
Silver **Obv:** Crowned eagle, head left, date in legend **Rev:** Cross divides 8 **Rev. Legend:** NOVVS • ALBVS

Date	Mintage	VG	F	VF	XF	Unc
1609	—	65.00	140	300	600	—

KM# 31.3 ALBUS (8 Heller)
Silver **Obv. Legend:** NO • ALB • FRANCOFVRTENS[IS] **Rev:** Inscription within laurel wreath **Rev. Inscription:** VIII / * / date

Date	Mintage	VG	F	VF	XF	Unc
1610	—	33.00	65.00	130	230	—
1611	—	33.00	65.00	130	230	—

KM# 31.1 ALBUS (8 Heller)
Silver **Obv:** Crowned eagle, head left **Obv. Legend:** NO • ALBVS • FRANCOFVRTENSIS **Rev:** Inscription in laurel wreath **Rev. Inscription:** VIII / ++ / date **Note:** Varieties exist.

Date	Mintage	VG	F	VF	XF	Unc
1610	—	33.00	65.00	120	230	—
1612	—	33.00	65.00	120	230	—

KM# 31.2 ALBUS (8 Heller)
Silver **Obv. Legend:** ... FRANCOFVRTENS **Rev:** Inscription within laurel wreath **Rev. Inscription:** ALB / + / 1610

Date	Mintage	VG	F	VF	XF	Unc
1610	—	33.00	65.00	125	250	—

KM# 32 ALBUS (8 Heller)
Silver **Note:** Klippe.

Date	Mintage	VG	F	VF	XF	Unc
1610	—	—	—	—	—	—

KM# 136 ALBUS (8 Heller)
Silver **Obv:** Eagle head right, without inner circle

Date	Mintage	VG	F	VF	XF	Unc
1651 (h)	—	35.00	70.00	140	285	—

KM# 153 2 ALBUS
Silver **Obv:** Similar to 1 Albus, KM#108 **Rev:** Inscription and mintmasters' initials divided by cross **Rev. Inscription:** II / ALBUS / date **Note:** Varities exist.

Date	Mintage	VG	F	VF	XF	Unc
1693 IIF	—	25.00	50.00	100	200	—
1694 IIF	—	30.00	60.00	120	240	—

KM# 62 6 KREUZER
Silver **Obv:** Crowned eagle, head left, F on breast **Rev:** Date in laurel wreath **Rev. Inscription:** VI / KREVTZ / ER **Note:** Varieties exist.

Date	Mintage	VG	F	VF	XF	Unc
16Z0 (a)	—	135	275	525	1,050	—
16Z0 AE	—	135	275	525	1,050	—

KM# 30 12 KREUZER (Zwölfer)
Silver **Obv:** Crowned eagle, head left, F in heart-shaped shield on breast **Rev:** Crowned imperial eagle, (12) in orb on breast, titles of Rudolf II, date in legend **Note:** Varieties exist.

Date	Mintage	VG	F	VF	XF	Unc
1610 With 12 in orb	—	65.00	130	300	625	—
1611	—	75.00	180	400	900	—
161Z	—	75.00	180	400	900	—
1612	—	75.00	180	400	900	—

KM# 37 12 KREUZER (Zwölfer)
Silver **Obv:** Titles of Matthias

Date	Mintage	VG	F	VF	XF	Unc
1612 Rare	—	—	—	—	—	—

KM# 63 12 KREUZER (Zwölfer)
Silver **Obv:** Crowned imperial eagle, 1Z in orb on breast, titles of Ferdinand II **Rev:** Crowned eagle, head left, in shield divides date **Note:** Varieties exist.

Date	Mintage	VG	F	VF	XF	Unc
16Z0 (a)	—	175	350	700	1,400	—
16Z1	—	175	350	700	1,400	—

KM# 70 12 KREUZER (Zwölfer)
Silver **Obv:** Eagle with F on breast

Date	Mintage	VG	F	VF	XF	Unc
ND(1621/2) 2 known; Rare	—	—	—	—	—	—

KM# 154 6 ALBUS (12 Kreuzer)
Silver **Obv:** Similar to 1 Albus, KM#108 **Rev:** VI/ ALBUS/ date and mintmasters initials divided by cross

Date	Mintage	VG	F	VF	XF	Unc
1693 IIF	—	50.00	100	200	400	—

MB# 44 TURNOSGROSCHEN
Silver **Obv:** Crowned eagle in circle, date at end of legend **Obv. Legend:** +TVRONVS. FRANCKEFORT. **Rev:** Cross in circle surrounded by band of lilies in arches **Rev. Legend:** Outer: SIT NOMEN ... **Note:** Ref. J/F#239, 253, 255b, 258h, 260 Klippe. Weight varies: 2.51-2.75 g.

Date	Mintage	VG	F	VF	XF	Unc
1601 rare	—	—	—	—	—	—

KM# 15.3 TURNOSGROSCHEN
Silver **Obv. Legend:** FRANCOFVRDI

Date	Mintage	VG	F	VF	XF	Unc
1606	—	45.00	95.00	190	385	—

KM# 13.2 TURNOSGROSCHEN
Silver **Obv:** Crowned eagle, head left, date **Obv. Legend:** TVRONVS • FRANCOFVRDI **Rev:** Small cross in circle, surrounded by circle of none fleur-de-lis in arches **Rev. Legend:** SIT • NOMEN • DOMINI • BENEDICTVM

Date	Mintage	VG	F	VF	XF	Unc
1606	—	55.00	110	225	450	—

KM# 13.3 TURNOSGROSCHEN
Silver **Obv. Legend:** TVRONVS CIVIT • FRANCOFVRDI:

Date	Mintage	VG	F	VF	XF	Unc
1606	—	55.00	110	225	450	—

KM# 15.1 TURNOSGROSCHEN
Silver **Obv. Legend:** TVRONVS: CIVIT • FRANCOFVRTENSIS **Rev:** Cross in quatrilobe

Date	Mintage	VG	F	VF	XF	Unc
1606	—	45.00	95.00	190	385	—

KM# 15.2 TURNOSGROSCHEN
Silver **Obv. Legend:** FRANCOFVRTENS

Date	Mintage	VG	F	VF	XF	Unc
1606	—	45.00	95.00	190	385	—

KM# 17.1 TURNOSGROSCHEN
Silver **Obv. Legend:** TVRONVS • CIVIT • FRANCFVRTEN[S] **Rev:** Large cross with flourishes in angles

Date	Mintage	VG	F	VF	XF	Unc
1606	—	45.00	95.00	180	360	—
ND	—	125	250	560	1,050	—

KM# 17.2 TURNOSGROSCHEN
Silver **Obv. Legend:** FRANCFVRTENSIS

Date	Mintage	VG	F	VF	XF	Unc
1606	—	60.00	160	400	675	—

KM# 17.3 TURNOSGROSCHEN
Silver **Obv:** Eagle's head divides date **Obv. Legend:** FRANCOFVRTENS **Rev:** Flourishes around cross

Date	Mintage	VG	F	VF	XF	Unc
1606	—	90.00	185	375	775	—

KM# 18.1 TURNOSGROSCHEN
Silver **Obv:** Crowned eagle, date **Obv. Legend:** CIVIT FRANCOFVRT[EN] **Rev:** Short ornamented cross without flourishes in angles

Date	Mintage	F	VF	XF	Unc	BU
1606	—	55.00	110	200	385	—

KM# 18.2 TURNOSGROSCHEN
Silver **Obv. Legend:** TVRONVS • CIVIT • FRANCFVRTEN **Rev:** Short cross without flourishes and ornaments

Date	Mintage	F	VF	XF	Unc	BU
1606	—	55.00	110	200	385	—

KM# 19 TURNOSGROSCHEN
Silver **Obv:** With CIVIT **Rev:** Cross with ornaments in three angles **Note:** Klippe.

Date	Mintage	VG	F	VF	XF	Unc
1606	—	—	—	—	—	—

KM# 137.1 TURNOSGROSCHEN
Silver **Rev:** Large cross without flourishes

Date	Mintage	VG	F	VF	XF	Unc
1666 (f)	—	55.00	110	225	450	—

KM# 137.2 TURNOSGROSCHEN
Silver **Rev:** Large cross with flourishes

Date	Mintage	VG	F	VF	XF	Unc
1680 MF	—	65.00	135	275	575	—
1689 MF-IF	—	65.00	135	275	575	—

KM# 146 60 KREUZER (2/3 Thaler)
Silver **Obv. Legend:** MONETA • NOVA... **Note:** Varieties exist.

Date	Mintage	VG	F	VF	XF	Unc
1672 MF	—	45.00	100	200	385	—
1673 MF	—	45.00	100	200	385	—
1674 MF	—	45.00	100	200	385	—
1675 MF	—	45.00	100	200	385	—

KM# 150 60 KREUZER (2/3 Thaler)
Silver **Obv. Legend:** FRANCFVRTER • STADT • MUNTZ **Note:** Varieties exist.

Date	Mintage	VG	F	VF	XF	Unc
1690 IIF	—	45.00	100	200	425	—
1691 IIF	—	45.00	100	200	425	—
1693 IIF	—	45.00	100	200	425	—
1695 IIF	—	45.00	100	200	425	—

KM# 155 60 KREUZER (2/3 Thaler)
Silver **Obv:** Eagle not in circle

Date	Mintage	VG	F	VF	XF	Unc
1694 IIF	—	75.00	150	300	600	—

KM# 75 1/8 THALER
Silver **Note:** Similar to 1 Thaler, KM#72 but 1/8 in orb on breast.

Date	Mintage	VG	F	VF	XF	Unc
16Z2 AE Rare	—	—	—	—	—	—

KM# 45 1/6 THALER (1/4 Gulden)
Silver, 25 mm. **Subject:** Centenary of Reformation **Note:** Weight varies 4.25-4.40 grams. Same dies as a goldgulden.

Date	Mintage	VG	F	VF	XF	Unc
1617	—	100	250	500	1,000	—

KM# 20 1/4 THALER
Silver **Note:** Similar to 1 Thaler, KM#22.

Date	Mintage	VG	F	VF	XF	Unc
1606	—	—	—	—	—	—

KM# 29 1/4 THALER
7.0000 g., Silver, 29 mm. **Subject:** Centenary of Reformation

Date	Mintage	VG	F	VF	XF	Unc
1617	—	—	—	—	—	—

KM# 53 1/4 THALER
7.0000 g., Silver **Obv:** Large cross with eagle in a small center shield

Date	Mintage	VG	F	VF	XF	Unc
1619 AE	—	600	950	1,500	2,750	—
Note: Strikes dated 1619 have a mint mark on either the obverse or reverse side						
1620 AE	—	600	950	1,500	2,750	—

KM# 71 1/4 THALER
7.0000 g., Silver **Rev:** 1/4 in orb, date in legend

Date	Mintage	VG	F	VF	XF	Unc
16Z1 (a)	—	—	—	—	—	—
16ZZ (a) AE	—	—	—	—	—	—

KM# 156 1/4 THALER
7.0000 g., Silver **Note:** Similar to 1/2 Thaler, KM#157.

Date	Mintage	VG	F	VF	XF	Unc
1694 IIF	—	250	600	1,200	2,500	—

KM# 159 1/4 THALER
7.0000 g., Silver **Obv:** Without angels **Rev:** Without circle around eagle

Date	Mintage	VG	F	VF	XF	Unc
1695 IIF	—	1,050	1,650	3,000	6,000	—

KM# 117 1/3 THALER (1/2 Gulden)
Silver **Subject:** Coronation of Leopold I **Obv:** Laureate bust of Leopold right, date in legend **Rev:** Crowned imperial eagle, F in heart-shaped shield on breast

Date	Mintage	VG	F	VF	XF	Unc
1658	—	600	950	1,700	3,300	—

KM# 21 1/2 THALER
Silver **Note:** Similar to 1 Thaler KM#45, titles of Rudolf II.

Date	Mintage	VG	F	VF	XF	Unc
1606 Rare	—	—	—	—	—	—
1610 Rare	—	—	—	—	—	—
1611 Rare	—	—	—	—	—	—

KM# 50 1/2 THALER
Silver **Obv:** Titles of Matthias **Note:** Klippe.

Date	Mintage	VG	F	VF	XF	Unc
1618 AE	—	—	—	—	—	—
Note: Reported, not confirmed						

KM# 64 1/2 THALER
Silver **Note:** Similar to Thaler KM#65, titles of Ferdinand II.

Date	Mintage	VG	F	VF	XF	Unc
1619 (a) AE on obv. AE (a) on rev.	—	—	—	—	—	—
1620 AE Rare	—	—	—	—	—	—

KM# 76 1/2 THALER
Silver **Note:** Similar to 1 Thaler, KM#72.

Date	Mintage	VG	F	VF	XF	Unc
16ZZ AE Rare	—	—	—	—	—	—

KM# 106 1/2 THALER
Silver **Subject:** End of Thirty Years War **Obv:** City view, FRANCOFVRT in cartouche below **Rev:** Crowned eagle, head left, date above **Rev. Legend:** NOMEN • DOMINI • TVRRIS • FORTISSIMA

Date	Mintage	VG	F	VF	XF	Unc
1648 (h)	—	1,750	3,400	5,000	8,500	—

KM# 145 1/2 THALER
Silver **Obv:** Cross **Rev:** Eagle **Note:** Varieties exist.

Date	Mintage	VG	F	VF	XF	Unc
1670 MF	—	1,200	2,000	3,750	7,750	—
1671 MF	—	1,200	2,000	3,750	7,750	—

KM# 157 1/2 THALER
Silver **Obv:** City view **Rev:** Eagle

Date	Mintage	VG	F	VF	XF	Unc
1694 IIF	—	1,350	2,500	5,000	10,000	—

KM# 160 1/2 THALER
Silver **Obv:** Alternate city view **Rev:** Revised imperial eagle

Date	Mintage	VG	F	VF	XF	Unc
1695 IIF Rare	—	—	—	—	—	—
1696 IIF Rare	—	—	—	—	—	—

KM# 162 1/2 THALER
Silver **Note:** Similar to 1/2 Thaler, KM#145 but value 1/2 added below eagle on reverse.

Date	Mintage	VG	F	VF	XF	Unc
1696 IIF Rare	—	—	—	—	—	—

KM# 22 THALER
Silver **Obv:** Cross **Rev:** Titles of Rudolph II, eagle **Note:** Dav.#5281. Varieties exist.

Date	Mintage	VG	F	VF	XF	Unc
1606 rare	—	—	—	—	—	—
Note: Dr. Busso Peus auction #395, 5-08, VF realized $14,300						

KM# 34 THALER
Silver **Obv:** Eagle in baroque ornament on plain cross **Rev:** Titles of Rudolf II **Note:** Dav.#5283. Varieties exist.

Date	Mintage	VG	F	VF	XF	Unc
1610 rare	—	—	—	—	—	—
Note: Dr. Busso Peus auction #394, 10-07, VF realized approximately $12,450						
1611 rare	—	—	—	—	—	—

KM# 46 THALER
Silver **Rev:** Titles of Matthias **Note:** Dav.#5285.

Date	Mintage	VG	F	VF	XF	Unc
1617	—	900	2,000	4,000	—	—
1618 AE (a)	—	900	2,000	4,000	—	—

KM# 61.1 THALER
Silver **Obv:** Eagle in oval shield on cross **Rev:** Titles of Ferdinand II, crowned imperial eagle **Note:** Dav.#5287. Prev. KM#65.1.

Date	Mintage	VG	F	VF	XF	Unc
16Z0 AE	—	80.00	200	400	800	—
ND AE	—	100	250	500	1,000	—

KM# 72.1 THALER
Silver **Obv:** Eagle on shield at center of cross date, legends in small letters **Rev:** Crowned imperial eagle, legends in small letters **Note:** Both dates exist with the year on the reverse side, 1620 exists with the year on the obverse as well. 16Z1 AE strikes have inverted N's in their legends. Dav.#5289.

Date	Mintage	VG	F	VF	XF	Unc
16Z0 AE	—	70.00	150	300	600	—
16Z1 AE	—	70.00	150	300	600	—

KM# 72.2 THALER
Silver **Obv:** Eagle in shield at center of cross, legend in small letters **Rev:** Crowned imperial eagle, date, legend in small letters

Date	Mintage	VG	F	VF	XF	Unc
16Z0 AE	—	65.00	140	280	600	—

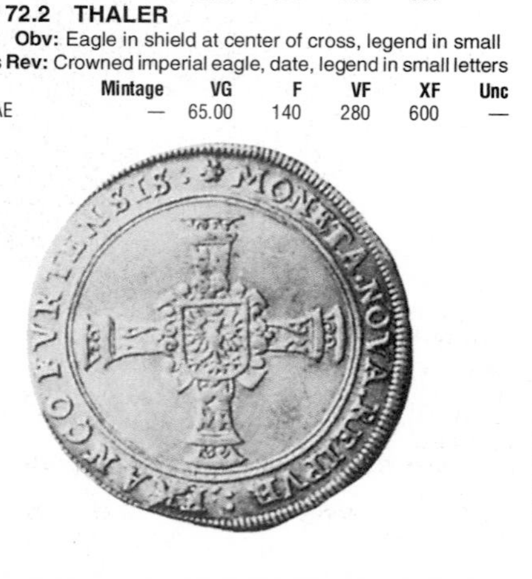

KM# 61.2 THALER
Silver **Obv:** Eagle in shield on cross within double circle **Rev:** Crowned imperial eagle **Note:** Dav.#5287C. Prev. KM#65.2.

Date	Mintage	VG	F	VF	XF	Unc
16Z0 AE	—	120	300	600	900	—

KM# 72.3 THALER
Silver **Obv:** Eagle in shield at center of cross, date, legends in large letters **Rev:** Crowned imperial eagle, legends in large letters **Note:** Dav.#5289.

Date	Mintage	VG	F	VF	XF	Unc
16Z1 AE	—	70.00	150	300	600	—
16ZZ AE	—	70.00	150	300	600	—
1622 AE	—	80.00	170	350	700	—

KM# 72.4 THALER
Silver **Obv:** Eagle on shield at center of cross, large letters **Rev:** Crowned imperial eagle, date, large letters

Date	Mintage	VG	F	VF	XF	Unc
16Z1 AE	—	70.00	150	300	600	—
16ZZ AE	—	70.00	150	300	600	—

KM# 65.3 THALER
Silver **Obv:** Eagle in oval shield on cross,large letters **Rev:** Crowned imperial eagle, large letters **Note:** Prev. KM#65.4. Year on either side.

Date	Mintage	VG	F	VF	XF	Unc
16Z3 AE	—	100	250	500	1,000	—

KM# 65.1 THALER
Silver **Obv:** Eagle in oval shield at center of cross, angel heads at ends, small letters **Rev:** Crowned double-headed imperial eagle, small letters **Note:** Dav.#5290. Prev. KM65.3. Both dates exist with the date on either side

Date	Mintage	VG	F	VF	XF	Unc
16Z3 AE	—	75.00	160	320	650	—
16Z4 AE	—	85.00	200	400	800	—

KM# 88.1 THALER
Silver **Rev:** Eagle faces right on cross **Note:** Dav.#5291. Prev. KM#65.6.

Date	Mintage	VG	F	VF	XF	Unc
16Z4 AE	—	80.00	180	375	730	—
16Z5 HS	—	80.00	180	375	730	—
16Z6 HS	—	80.00	180	375	730	—

Note: 16Z6 dates exist with the year on either obverse and reverse 1626 on reverse exists

Date	Mintage	VG	F	VF	XF	Unc
16Z6	—	100	220	850	900	—

KM# 88.2 THALER

Silver **Obv:** Eagle faces left on roundeded shield in center of cross within circle **Rev:** Crowned double-headed imperial eagle within circle **Note:** Dav.#5293. Prev. KM#65.5.

Date	Mintage	VG	F	VF	XF	Unc
16Z5 AE	—	100	250	500	1,000	—
16Z5 HS	—	80.00	180	375	750	—
16Z6 HS	—	80.00	180	375	750	—
1627 HS	—	80.00	180	375	750	—
1627 AE	—	100	250	500	1,000	—
163Z AE	—	100	250	500	1,000	—
1634 AE	—	80.00	180	375	750	—
1635 AE	—	80.00	180	375	750	—
1636 AM	—	100	250	500	1,000	—
1637 AM	—	100	250	500	1,000	—

KM# 78 THALER

Silver **Obv:** Crowned eagle, head left, in laurel wreath, date divided below tail **Rev:** City view, FRANCOFORDIA above, FROTECTORE DEO in band at top

Date	Mintage	VG	F	VF	XF	Unc
16Z5 LS	—	—	5,000	8,000	11,000	—

KM# 88.3 THALER

Silver **Obv:** Crowned eagle on shield in center of cross within circle **Rev:** Titles of Ferdinand III **Note:** Dav.#5294. Prev. KM#88. Varieties exist. Legends in small letters in both obverse and reverse.

Date	Mintage	VG	F	VF	XF	Unc
1638 AM	—	100	250	500	1,000	—
1639 AM	—	100	250	500	1,000	—
1641 AM	—	120	300	600	1,200	—
1642 AM	—	120	300	600	1,200	—
1643 AM	—	140	350	750	1,500	—
1644 GN Unique	—	—	—	—	—	—

KM# 95 THALER

Silver **Obv:** Crowned eagle on small shield in center of designed cross within circle **Rev:** Date divided by crown at top **Note:** Dav.#5295 and 5296.

Date	Mintage	VG	F	VF	XF	Unc
1644 GN	—	—	200	5,000	9,000	—
1645 GN	—	—	2,500	6,000	10,000	—
1646 (h)	—	—	750	1,500	3,000	—
1647 (h)	—	—	750	1,500	3,000	—

KM# 101 THALER

Silver **Obv:** Crowned eagle on shield in center of cross within circle **Rev:** Date in legend. Imperial eagle, titles of Ferdinandus II. **Note:** Dav.#5297. Legends in small letters in both obverse and reverse.

Date	Mintage	VG	F	VF	XF	Unc
1647 (h)	—	—	750	1,500	3,000	—
1650 (h)	—	—	1,000	2,000	4,000	—
1651 (h)	—	—	1,200	2,500	5,500	—
1652 (h)	—	—	1,200	2,500	5,500	—
1655 (h)	—	—	1,200	2,500	5,500	—

KM# 115 THALER

Silver **Obv:** KM#101 **Rev:** KM#78

Date	Mintage	VG	F	VF	XF	Unc
1650 (h) Unique	—	—	—	—	—	—

KM# 123 THALER

Silver **Note:** Similar to KM#101 but titles of Leopold I. Dav.#5298.

Date	Mintage	VG	F	VF	XF	Unc
1658 (h) Rare	—	—	—	—	—	—

KM# 138 THALER

Silver **Obv:** Crowned eagle on larger shield in center of designed cross within circle **Rev:** Titles of Leopold I **Note:** Dav.#5299. Varieties exist.

Date	Mintage	VG	F	VF	XF	Unc
1667 MF	—	—	1,200	2,500	5,000	—
1669 MF	—	—	1,500	3,500	7,000	—
1671 MF	—	—	1,200	2,500	5,000	—
1674 MF	—	—	1,500	3,500	7,000	—
1694 IIF	—	—	2,000	6,000	12,500	—

KM# 161 THALER

Silver **Obv:** Heraldic angel above city view, within circle **Rev:** Crowned double-headed imperial eagle **Note:** Dav.#5300. Legends in small letters on both sides.

Date	Mintage	VG	F	VF	XF	Unc
1695 IIF	—	1,750	3,500	6,000	12,500	—
1696 IIF	—	1,750	3,500	6,000	12,500	—

KM# 23 2 THALER

Silver **Obv:** Crowned eagle on shield in center of cross within designed circle **Rev:** Titles of Rudolph II **Note:** Dav.#5280. Varieties exist.

Date	Mintage	VG	F	VF	XF	Unc
1606 Rare	—	—	—	—	15,000	—

KM# 35 2 THALER

Silver **Note:** Struck with 1 Thaler dies, thick flan. Titles of Rudolf II. Varieties exist. Dav.#5282.

Date	Mintage	VG	F	VF	XF	Unc
1610 Rare	—	—	—	—	11,000	—

KM# 51 2 THALER

Silver **Note:** Similar to 1 Thaler, KM#46. Dav.#5284.

Date	Mintage	VG	F	VF	XF	Unc
1618 AE	—	—	—	—	—	—

Note: Reported, not confirmed

KM# 66.1 2 THALER

Silver **Note:** Similar to 1 Thaler, KM#65.1. Dav.#5286.

Date	Mintage	VG	F	VF	XF	Unc
16Z0 AE Rare	—	—	—	—	—	—

KM# 66.2 2 THALER

Silver **Note:** Similar to 1 Thaler, KM#88. Varieties exist. Dav.#5292.

Date	Mintage	VG	F	VF	XF	Unc
1637 AM Unique	—	—	—	—	—	—

KM# 102 2 THALER
Silver **Note:** Similar to 1 Thaler, KM#100. Dav.#A5296.

Date	Mintage	VG	F	VF	XF	Unc
1647 (h) Rare	—	—	—	—	—	—

KM# 103 2 THALER
Silver **Note:** Similar to 1 Thaler, KM#101. Dav.#A5297.

Date	Mintage	VG	F	VF	XF	Unc
1647 (h) Rare	—	—	—	—	—	—

TRADE COINAGE

KM# 36 GOLDGULDEN
3.5000 g., 0.9860 Gold 0.1109 oz. AGW **Obv:** St. John standing in inner circle, arms at bottom **Rev:** Crowned imperial eagle in inner circle, date in legend, titles of Rudolf II

Date	Mintage	VG	F	VF	XF	Unc
1611	—	300	900	1,800	3,500	—

KM# 38 GOLDGULDEN
3.5000 g., 0.9860 Gold 0.1109 oz. AGW **Obv:** Enthroned king in center panel flanked by angels **Rev:** Angel blowing trumpet, eagle preparing to place wreath on angel's head

Date	Mintage	VG	F	VF	XF	Unc
1612	—	1,600	3,500	6,000	11,000	—

KM# 39.1 GOLDGULDEN
3.5000 g., 0.9860 Gold 0.1109 oz. AGW **Subject:** Coronation of Matthias

Date	Mintage	VG	F	VF	XF	Unc
1612	—	350	800	1,500	2,800	—

KM# 39.2 GOLDGULDEN
3.5000 g., 0.9860 Gold 0.1109 oz. AGW **Rev:** Without inner circle

Date	Mintage	VG	F	VF	XF	Unc
1612	—	350	850	1,700	3,500	—

KM# 47 GOLDGULDEN
3.8000 g., 0.9860 Gold 0.1205 oz. AGW **Subject:** Centennial of the Reformation **Rev:** Angel inside double circle of legend

Date	Mintage	VG	F	VF	XF	Unc
1617	—	—	3,500	8,000	12,000	—

KM# 48 GOLDGULDEN
3.5000 g., 0.9860 Gold 0.1109 oz. AGW **Note:** Klippe.

Date	Mintage	VG	F	VF	XF	Unc
1617 Rare	—	—	—	—	—	—

KM# 49.1 GOLDGULDEN
3.5000 g., 0.9860 Gold 0.1109 oz. AGW **Obv:** St. John standing **Rev:** Titles of Matthias

Date	Mintage	VG	F	VF	XF	Unc
1617	—	200	400	900	2,000	—

KM# 49.2 GOLDGULDEN
3.5000 g., 0.9860 Gold 0.1109 oz. AGW **Obv:** St. John standing with small shield **Rev:** Titles of Matthias

Date	Mintage	VG	F	VF	XF	Unc
1618 AE	—	200	350	600	1,200	—

KM# 54 GOLDGULDEN
3.5000 g., 0.9860 Gold 0.1109 oz. AGW **Obv:** St. John standing right with oval shield **Rev:** Titles of Matthias

Date	Mintage	VG	F	VF	XF	Unc
1619 AE	—	200	380	750	1,500	—

KM# 55 GOLDGULDEN
3.5000 g., 0.9860 Gold 0.1109 oz. AGW **Obv:** St. John standing right **Rev:** Crowned imperial eagle, titles of Ferdinand II

Date	Mintage	VG	F	VF	XF	Unc
1619 AE	—	250	500	1,000	1,750	—

KM# 56 GOLDGULDEN
3.5000 g., 0.9860 Gold 0.1109 oz. AGW **Subject:** Coronation of Ferdinand II **Obv:** Crown, small eagle divides circle below **Rev:** Seated figure facing within circle, titles of Ferdinand II

Date	Mintage	VG	F	VF	XF	Unc
1619	—	250	500	1,200	2,400	—

KM# 67 GOLDGULDEN
3.5000 g., 0.9860 Gold 0.1109 oz. AGW **Obv:** St. John standing right **Rev:** Orb in trefoil within inner circle

Date	Mintage	VG	F	VF	XF	Unc
16Z0	—	200	350	700	1,000	—
16-20	—	300	600	1,000	2,000	—
16Z1	—	200	350	700	1,000	—
16Z1 (a)	—	200	350	700	1,000	—
16ZZ (a)	—	200	350	700	1,000	—
16Z4 (a)	—	—	—	—	—	—

Note: Reported but not confirmed.

Date	Mintage	VG	F	VF	XF	Unc
16Z5	—	200	350	700	1,500	—

KM# 40.1 2 GOLDGULDEN
7.0000 g., 0.9860 Gold 0.2219 oz. AGW **Subject:** Coronation of Matthias II **Obv:** Laureate bust of Matthias right in inner circle **Rev:** Large crown in inner circle between sun and moon **Note:** Prev. KM#40.

Date	Mintage	VG	F	VF	XF	Unc
1612	—	800	2,000	4,000	7,000	—

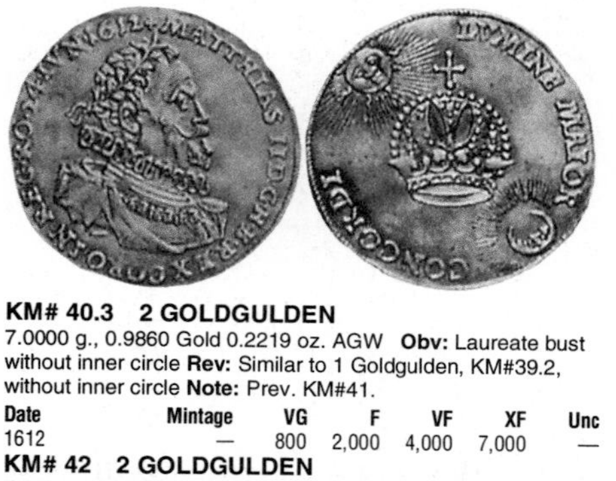

KM# 40.3 2 GOLDGULDEN
7.0000 g., 0.9860 Gold 0.2219 oz. AGW **Obv:** Laureate bust without inner circle **Rev:** Similar to 1 Goldgulden, KM#39.2, without inner circle **Note:** Prev. KM#41.

Date	Mintage	VG	F	VF	XF	Unc
1612	—	800	2,000	4,000	7,000	—

KM# 42 2 GOLDGULDEN
7.0000 g., 0.9860 Gold 0.2219 oz. AGW **Obv:** Enthroned king in center panel flanked by angels **Rev:** Angel blowing trumpet, eagle preparing to pace wreath on angel's head

Date	Mintage	VG	F	VF	XF	Unc
1612 Rare	—	—	—	—	—	—

KM# 40.2 2 GOLDGULDEN
7.0000 g., 0.9860 Gold 0.2219 oz. AGW **Rev:** Similar to 1 Goldgulden, KM#39.1, with inner circle

Date	Mintage	VG	F	VF	XF	Unc
1612 Rare	—	—	—	—	—	—

KM# 58 1/2 DUCAT
1.7500 g., 0.9860 Gold 0.0555 oz. AGW **Subject:** Coronation of Ferdinand II **Obv:** Crowned F above II, crossed palm and laurel branches, behind crown **Rev:** Crown with crossed palm and laurel branches behind, all above 5-line inscription with date

Date	Mintage	VG	F	VF	XF	Unc
1619 Rare	—	—	—	—	—	—

KM# 59 1/2 DUCAT
1.7500 g., 0.9860 Gold 0.0555 oz. AGW **Note:** Klippe.

Date	Mintage	VG	F	VF	XF	Unc
1619 Rare	—	—	—	—	—	—

KM# 124 1/2 DUCAT
1.7500 g., 0.9860 Gold 0.0555 oz. AGW **Subject:** Coronation of Leopold I **Obv:** Crown above 5-line inscription and date **Rev:** Crowned globe with hand holding scepter at left, arm holding sword at right

Date	Mintage	VG	F	VF	XF	Unc
1658	—	200	380	750	1,500	—

KM# 125 1/2 DUCAT
1.7500 g., 0.9860 Gold 0.0555 oz. AGW **Obv:** Leopold I

Date	Mintage	VG	F	VF	XF	Unc
ND(1658) Rare	—	—	—	—	—	—

KM# 52 DUCAT
3.5000 g., 0.9860 Gold 0.1109 oz. AGW **Subject:** Sighting of a Comet **Obv:** Comet passing from right to left in laurel wreath **Rev:** Hands in prayer at center, flaming altar at right, stalks at left **Note:** Klippe.

Date	Mintage	VG	F	VF	XF	Unc
1618 Rare	—	—	—	—	—	—

KM# A70 DUCAT
3.5000 g., 0.9860 Gold 0.1109 oz. AGW **Subject:** Coronation of Ferdinand II **Obv:** Hand from clouds extended right, holding crown, inscription on ribbon winding in-and-out, all in laurel wreath **Rev:** Arabesque above 6-line inscription, date in Roman numerals

Date	Mintage	VG	F	VF	XF	Unc
MCCXIX (1619)	—	—	600	1,300	2,500	4,800

KM# 79 DUCAT
3.5000 g., 0.9860 Gold 0.1109 oz. AGW **Obv:** Bust in circle, titles of Ferdinand II **Rev:** Imperial crown above crossed sword and sceptre, crossed palm and laurel branches behind **Note:** Klippe.

Date	Mintage	VG	F	VF	XF	Unc
ND(1619) Rare	—	—	—	—	—	—

Note: Peus Auction #390 5-07, XF realized approximately $8500.

KM# 80 DUCAT
3.5000 g., 0.9860 Gold 0.1109 oz. AGW **Note:** Similar to KM#79 except reverse has hands from clouds holding royal crown above imperial crown.

Date	Mintage	VG	F	VF	XF	Unc
ND(1619) Rare	—	—	—	—	—	—

KM# 85 DUCAT
3.5000 g., 0.9860 Gold 0.1109 oz. AGW **Obv:** Eagle in oval shield **Rev:** Inscription within square

Date	Mintage	VG	F	VF	XF	Unc
1633 AE (a)	—	250	400	750	1,400	—
1634 AE (a)	—	200	350	650	1,200	—
1635 AE (a)	—	200	350	650	1,200	—
1636 AE (a)	—	200	350	650	1,200	—
1637 AM (a)	—	200	350	650	1,200	—
1638 AM (a)	—	200	350	650	1,200	—
1639 AM (a)	—	200	350	650	1,200	—
1640 AM (a)	—	200	350	650	1,200	—
1641 AM (a)	—	200	350	650	1,200	—
1642 AM (a)	—	200	350	650	1,200	—
1643 AM (a)	—	200	350	650	1,200	—

Date	Mintage	VG	F	VF	XF	Unc
1644 AM (a)	—	200	350	650	1,200	—
ND AM (a)	—	300	500	900	1,800	—

KM# 96.1 DUCAT

3.5000 g., 0.9860 Gold 0.1109 oz. AGW **Obv:** Angel holding shield of arms **Obv. Legend:** ...NOMEN **Rev:** 4-line legend in cartouche, angel head above, date flanking

Date	Mintage	VG	F	VF	XF	Unc
16-44 GN (a)	—	250	600	1,000	2,000	—
1645 GN	—	250	600	1,000	2,000	—

Note: N of mint mark is inverted

KM# 97.1 DUCAT

3.5000 g., 0.9860 Gold 0.1109 oz. AGW **Obv:** Crowned eagle with head to left, date divided below tail as 1-6-4-6 in inner circle **Rev:** 5-line legend in ornamental cartouche

Date	Mintage	VG	F	VF	XF	Unc
1646 (h)	—	180	300	520	900	—

KM# 104.1 DUCAT

3.5000 g., 0.9860 Gold 0.1109 oz. AGW **Obv:** Crowned eagle with head to left **Rev:** Mintmark

Date	Mintage	VG	F	VF	XF	Unc
1646	—	200	350	650	1,250	—
1646 (h)	—	200	350	650	1,250	—
1647 (h)	—	200	350	650	1,250	—
1648 (h)	—	200	350	650	1,250	—
1649 (h)	—	200	350	650	1,250	—
1652 (h)	—	180	320	550	1,000	—
1654 (h)	—	180	320	550	1,000	—

KM# 97.2 DUCAT

3.5000 g., 0.9860 Gold 0.1109 oz. AGW **Obv:** Legend ends with date

Date	Mintage	VG	F	VF	XF	Unc
1646 (h)	—	200	350	750	1,250	—

KM# 104.2 DUCAT

3.5000 g., 0.9860 Gold 0.1109 oz. AGW **Obv:** With eagle's head to right

Date	Mintage	VG	F	VF	XF	Unc
ND	—	250	450	800	1,500	—
1649 (h)	—	200	360	700	1,200	—
1650 (h)	—	200	360	700	1,200	—
1651 (h)	—	200	360	700	1,200	—
1652 (h)	—	200	360	700	1,200	—
1653 (h)	—	200	360	700	1,200	—
1654 (h)	—	200	360	700	1,200	—
1655 (h)	—	200	360	700	1,200	—
1656 (h)	—	200	360	700	1,200	—
1657 (h)	—	200	360	700	1,200	—
1658 (h)	—	200	360	700	1,200	—
1660 (h)	—	200	360	700	1,200	—
1666 (h)	—	200	360	700	1,200	—

KM# 126 DUCAT

3.5000 g., 0.9860 Gold 0.1109 oz. AGW **Subject:** Coronation of Leopold I **Obv:** Crown above 5-line inscription and Roman numeral date **Rev:** Crowned glove with hand holding scepter at left, arm holding sword at right

Date	Mintage	VG	F	VF	XF	Unc
MDCLVIII (1658)	—	250	550	1,000	2,000	—

KM# 57 2 DUCAT

7.0000 g., 0.9860 Gold 0.2219 oz. AGW **Subject:** Coronation of Ferdinand II **Obv:** Laureate bust of Ferdinand II right in inner circle **Rev:** Crown above crossed sword and scepter, laurel wreath above in inner circle **Note:** Klippe.

Date	Mintage	VG	F	VF	XF	Unc
MDCXIX (1619) Unique	—	—	—	—	—	—

KM# 81 2 DUCAT

7.0000 g., 0.9860 Gold 0.2219 oz. AGW **Subject:** Coronation of Ferdinand II **Obv:** Head from clouds extended right, holding crown, inscription on ribbon winding in-and-out, all in laurel wreath **Rev:** Arabesque above 6-line inscription, date in Roman numerals **Note:** Similar to 1 Ducat, KM#70.

Date	Mintage	VG	F	VF	XF	Unc
MDCXIX (1619)	—	950	2,200	4,400	8,000	—

KM# 86 2 DUCAT

7.0000 g., 0.9860 Gold 0.2219 oz. AGW

Date	Mintage	VG	F	VF	XF	Unc
1633 AE (a)	—	400	900	1,800	3,000	6,000
1634 AE (a)	—	400	900	1,800	3,000	6,000
1635 AE (a)	—	400	900	1,800	3,000	6,000
1637 AM (a)	—	400	900	1,800	3,000	6,000

KM# 127 2 DUCAT

7.0000 g., 0.9860 Gold 0.2219 oz. AGW **Subject:** Coronation of Leopold I **Obv:** Crown above 5-line inscription, Roman numeral date **Rev:** Crowned globe with hand holding scepter at left and arm holding sword at right

Date	Mintage	VG	F	VF	XF	Unc
1658	—	500	1,500	3,000	6,000	7,500

KM# 43 3 DUCAT

10.5000 g., 0.9860 Gold 0.3328 oz. AGW **Subject:** Coronation of Matthias **Obv:** Matthias on rearing horse right, city in background **Rev:** Crowned imperial eagle surrounded by 7 shields of arms

Date	Mintage	VG	F	VF	XF	Unc
ND(1612) Rare	—	—	—	—	500	—

KM# A128 3 DUCAT

Gold **Subject:** Coronation of Leopold I **Obv:** Crown above 5-line inscription and Roman numeral date **Rev:** Crowned globe w/hand holding scepter at left, arms holding sword at right

Date	Mintage	VG	F	VF	XF	Unc
1658 Rare	—	—	—	—	—	—

Note: Auction Peus 390 2007 XF/Unc realized approximately $8600.

KM# 128 4 DUCAT

14.0000 g., 0.9860 Gold 0.4438 oz. AGW **Subject:** Coronation of Leopold I **Obv:** Crown above 5-line inscription, Roman numeral date **Rev:** Crowned globe with hand holding scepter at left, arm holding sword at right

Date	Mintage	VG	F	VF	XF	Unc
MDCLVIII (1658) Rare	—	—	—	—	—	—

KM# A23 5 DUCAT

17.5000 g., 0.9860 Gold 0.5547 oz. AGW **Note:** Struck with 1/2 Thaler dies, KM#21.

Date	Mintage	VG	F	VF	XF	Unc
1606 Rare	—	—	—	—	—	—

KM# 44 5 DUCAT

17.5000 g., 0.9860 Gold 0.5547 oz. AGW **Subject:** Coronation of Matthias **Obv:** Matthias on rearing horse right, city in background **Rev:** Crowned imperial eagle surrounded by 7 shields of arms

Date	Mintage	VG	F	VF	XF	Unc
ND(1612) Rare	—	—	—	—	—	—

KM# B108 5 DUCAT

17.5000 g., 0.9860 Gold 0.5547 oz. AGW **Note:** Struck with 1/2 Thaler dies, KM#106.

Date	Mintage	VG	F	VF	XF	Unc
1648 (h) Rare	—	—	—	—	—	—

KM# 82 5 DUCAT

17.5000 g., 0.9860 Gold 0.5547 oz. AGW **Subject:** Coronation of Leopold I **Obv:** Imperial crown with 2 angel supporters above 6-line inscription, Roman numeral date **Rev:** Similar to 4 Ducat, KM#128

Date	Mintage	VG	F	VF	XF	Unc
NDMDCLVIII (1658) Rare	—	—	—	—	—	—

KM# B23 10 DUCAT (Portugalöser)

35.0000 g., 0.9860 Gold 1.1095 oz. AGW

Date	Mintage	VG	F	VF	XF	Unc
1606 Rare	—	—	—	—	—	—

Note: Struck with 1 Thaler dies, KM#22

PATTERNS

Including off metal strikes

KM#	Date	Mintage	Identification	Mkt Val
Pn5	1601	—	English. Gold. KM#A20.	—
Pn7	1606	—	Turnosgroschen. Gold. Klippe, KM#19.	—
Pn8	1606	—	1/4 Thaler. Gold. KM#20.	—
Pn9	1612	—	2 Goldgulden. Silver. KM#40.	375
Pn10	ND(1612)	—	3 Ducat. Silver. Matthias, KM#43.	450
Pn11	ND(1612)	—	5 Ducat. Silver. Matthias, KM#44.	800
Pn12	1617	—	1/6 Thaler. Silver. 12.0000 g. Klippe, KM#45.	—
Pn13	1617	—	Goldgulden. Silver. KM#47.	—
Pn14	1617	—	Goldgulden. Silver. Klippe, KM#48.	—
Pn15	1618	—	Ducat. Silver. Klippe, KM#52.	350
Pn16	1618	—	Ducat. Silver. Comet, KM#52.	275
Pn17	1619	—	1/2 Ducat. Silver. Ferdinand II, KM#58.	300
Pn18	1619	—	1/2 Ducat. Silver. Klippe, Ferdinand II, KM#59.	400
Pn19	1619	—	Ducat. Silver. KM#70.	350
Pn20	ND(1619)	—	Ducat. Copper. Klippe, KM#79.	300
Pn21	ND(1619)	—	Ducat. Silver. Klippe, Ferdinand II, KM#79.	450
Pn22	ND(1619)	—	Ducat. Silver. Klippe, KM#80.	450
Pn23	ND(1619)	—	2 Ducat. Silver. Ferdinand II, KM#57.	525
Pn24	ND(1619)	—	2 Ducat. Bronze. KM#57.	175
Pn25	1619	—	2 Ducat. Silver. Ferdinand II, KM#81.	450
Pn26	1651 (h)	—	Albus. Gold. KM#108.	—
Pn27	1658	—	1/2 Ducat. Silver. Crown above inscription, KM#125.	130
Pn28	ND(1658)	—	1/2 Ducat. Silver. Leopold I, KM#125.	225
Pn29	ND(1658)	—	Ducat. Silver. Leopold I, KM#126.	270
Pn30	ND(1658)	—	2 Ducat. Silver. Leopold I, KM#127.	300
Pn31	ND(1658)	—	4 Ducat. Silver. Leopold I, KM#128.	450
Pn32	1658	—	5 Ducat. Silver. KM#82.	475
Pn33	1667 (f)	—	Albus. Gold. KM#136.	—
Pn34	1695 IIF	—	1/4 Thaler. Gold. KM#159.	—

FRANKFURT AM ODER

A provincial city in Brandenburg, established on the Oder River about 50 miles east of Berlin in the 13th century. Local copper coins were struck during the Kipper Period. Today, the river Oder creates a natural boundary line between Germany and Poland.

CITY

REGULAR COINAGE

KM# 1 PFENNIG

0.3000 g., Copper, 13.2 mm. **Obv:** Two joined arms, helmet left, hen facing left on right, F below, ornamentation above. Varieties exist. **Note:** Kipper Pfennig. Uniface.

Date	Mintage	VG	F	VF	XF	Unc
ND(1621)	—	20.00	40.00	70.00	130	—

KM# 2 PFENNIG
Copper, 15 mm. **Obv:** Two joined arms, helmet left, hen facing left on right, date above **Note:** Varieties exist.

Date	Mintage	VG	F	VF	XF	Unc
1622	—	27.00	45.00	80.00	165	—
16ZZ	—	27.00	45.00	80.00	165	—

FREIBURG IM BREISGAU

CITY

Located in Baden about 35 miles north of Basel and east of the Rhine, Freiburg was a free city in the early 12th century. A century later the city lost its free status when it fell to the counts of Urach. In 1368, Freiburg became a Hapsburg possession and it remained so until 1803. In 1805 the city was united to Baden. Freiburg struck coins from the 14th century until 1739. As a member of the Rappenmünzbund from 1387 until 1584, Freiburg struck coins in accordance with the provisions of that monetary union of South German and Swiss entities.

ARMS

Raven's head, usually turned to the left.

REFERENCES

B = Udo Becker, **Freiburger Münzen**, Freiburg im Breisgau, 1970.
Sch = Wolfgang Schulten, ***Deutsche Münzen aus der Zeit Karls V.***, Frankfurt am Main, 1974

S = Hugo Frhr. Von Saurma-Jeltsch, **Die Saurmasche Münzsammlung deutscher, schweizerischer und polnischer Gepräge von etwa dem Beginn der Groschenzeit bis zur Kipperperiode**, Berlin, 1892.

REGULAR COINAGE

KM# 40 KREUZER
Silver **Obv:** Raven's head left in shield, date in legend **Rev:** Cross in shield **Rev. Legend:** SALVE...

Date	Mintage	VG	F	VF	XF	Unc
1624	—	27.00	55.00	115	230	—

KM# 45 3 KREUZER (Groschen)
Silver **Obv:** Raven's head left in shield, date in legend **Rev:** Cross in shield, 3 above **Rev. Legend:** SALVE...

Date	Mintage	VG	F	VF	XF	Unc
ND(ca. 1625)	—	—	—	—	—	—

KM# 5 10 KREUZER
Silver **Obv:** Raven's head left divides date, 10 in legend below **Rev:** Madonna seated on throne

Date	Mintage	VG	F	VF	XF	Unc
16Z0	—	700	1,400	2,750	5,000	—

KM# 10 12 KREUZER
Silver **Obv:** Raven's head left divides date, 1Z in legend at bottom **Rev:** Cross in ornamented shield **Rev. Legend:** DOMINE...

Date	Mintage	VG	F	VF	XF	Unc
16Z0	—	—	—	—	—	—

KM# 15 1/4 THALER
Silver **Obv:** Similar to 1 Thaler, KM#25 **Rev:** Eagle, head left **Rev. Legend:** SI.DEVS...

Date	Mintage	VG	F	VF	XF	Unc
16Z0 Rare	—	—	—	—	—	—

KM# 20 1/2 THALER
Silver **Obv:** Similar to 1 Thaler, KM#25 **Rev:** Eagle with head left **Rev. Legend:** SI.DEVS...

Date	Mintage	VG	F	VF	XF	Unc
16Z0 Rare	—	—	—	—	—	—

KM# 25 THALER
Silver **Rev. Legend:** DOMINE... **Note:** Dav. #5302.

Date	Mintage	VG	F	VF	XF	Unc
16Z0	—	1,200	2,200	3,900	6,600	—

KM# 27 THALER
Silver **Obv:** Different head and smaller letters **Rev:** Smaller eagle and letters **Note:** Dav. #5302A.

Date	Mintage	VG	F	VF	XF	Unc
16Z0 Rare	—	—	—	—	—	—

KM# 26 THALER
Silver **Obv:** Raven's head left in ornamented shield, date above **Note:** Dav. #5303.

Date	Mintage	VG	F	VF	XF	Unc
16Z0 Rare	—	—	—	—	—	—

KM# 50 THALER
Silver **Note:** Dav. #5304.

Date	Mintage	VG	F	VF	XF	Unc
1626	—	1,150	2,250	3,750	7,000	—
1627	—	1,150	2,250	3,750	7,000	—
1628	—	1,150	2,250	3,750	7,000	—
1629	—	1,150	2,250	3,750	7,000	—

KM# 51 THALER
Silver **Note:** Klippe. Dav. #5304A.

Date	Mintage	VG	F	VF	XF	Unc
1627 Rare	—	—	—	—	—	—
1628 Rare	—	—	—	—	—	—

KM# 30 2 THALER
Silver **Note:** Similar to 1 Thaler, KM#25. Dav. #5201.

Date	Mintage	VG	F	VF	XF	Unc
16Z0 Rare	—	—	—	—	—	—

TRADE COINAGE

KM# 35 GOLDGULDEN
3.5000 g., 0.9860 Gold 0.1109 oz. AGW **Obv:** Madonna and child facing **Rev:** 4-fold arms of Freiburg, date in legend **Note:** Fr. 1028.

Date	Mintage	VG	F	VF	XF	Unc
1622 Rare	—	—	—	—	—	—

FREISING

A Bishopric located in central Bavaria, was founded in 724. It became the site of an imperial mint in the 11th century. Bracteates of the bishops appeared c. 1150. The bishops were made princes of the empire in the 17th century. It became secularized in 1802 with part of the territories going to Bavaria and the rest to Salzburg.

RULERS

Ernst, Herzog von Bayern, 1566-1612
Stephan von Sieboldsdorf, 1612-1618
Veit Adam von Gebeck, 1618-1651
Albert Sigismund, Herzog von Bayern, 1652-1685
Joseph Clemens, Herzog von Bayern, 1685-1694
Johann Franz Eckher Freiherr von Kapfing, 1695-1727

MINT OFFICIALS' INITIALS

Initial	Date	Name
*, PHM	Ca.1685-1719	Philipp Heinrich Muller, medailleur in Augsburg

BISHOPRIC

REGULAR COINAGE

KM# 5 HELLER
Silver **Obv:** Freising and Gebeck family arms in adjoining shield, date above, F below. **Note:** Kipper Heller. Uniface. Hohl type.

Date	Mintage	VG	F	VF	XF	Unc
1622	—	—	—	—	—	—

KM# 6 HELLER
Silver **Obv:** Band connecting both arms at top replaces date. **Note:** Uniface.

Date	Mintage	VG	F	VF	XF	Unc
ND(ca.1622)	—	—	—	—	—	—

KM# 7 2 HELLER (Pfennig)
Copper **Obv:** Joined VA monogram in wreath **Rev:** Crowned head left in circle

Date	Mintage	VG	F	VF	XF	Unc
ND(ca.1622)	—	40.00	85.00	175	350	—

KM# 8 2 HELLER (Pfennig)
Copper **Obv:** Feather crown on head left in circle **Rev:** Large Z (2 Heller) in wreath

Date	Mintage	VG	F	VF	XF	Unc
ND(ca.1622)	—	22.00	45.00	85.00	190	—

KM# 9 4 HELLER (1/2 Kreuzer)
Copper, 15 mm. **Obv:** Crowned head left in wreath **Rev:** Value 4 in wreath **Note:** Kipper 4 Heller.

Date	Mintage	VG	F	VF	XF	Unc
ND(ca.1622)	—	30.00	60.00	125	250	—

KM# 10 KREUZER
Copper **Obv:** Feather crown on head left in wreath **Rev:** Script K in wreath **Note:** Kipper Kreuzer

Date	Mintage	VG	F	VF	XF	Unc
ND(ca.1622)	—	—	—	—	—	—

KM# 11 24 KREUZER (Sechsbätzner)
Billon **Obv:** Crowned imperial eagle, 24 in orb on breast, titles of Ferdinand II **Rev:** Crowned head left in oval cartouche, date in legend **Note:** Kipper 24 Kreuzer

Date	Mintage	VG	F	VF	XF	Unc
1622	—	70.00	130	260	—	—

FRIEDBERG

(Burg Friedberg in der Wetterau)

The fortified town of Friedberg, located in Hesse about 15 miles (25 kilometers) north of Frankfurt am Main, dates from Roman times. It attained free status in 1211 and was the site of an imperial mint until the mid-13th century. In 1349 Friedberg passed to the countship of Schwarzburg, losing its free status shortly thereafter. Local nobles began electing one among themselves to the office of burgrave-for-life. The burgraves obtained the mint right in 1541 and recognized only the emperor as overlord. In 1802 Friedberg passed in fief to Hesse-Darmstadt and was mediatized in 1818.

RULERS

Johann Eberhard von Cronberg, 1577-1617
Konrad Low von Steinfurt, 1617-1632
Wolf Adolf von Karben, 1632-1671
Johann Eitel I von Diede zu Fürstenstein, 1671-1685
Phillipp Adolf Rau von Holzhausen, 1685-1692
Johann IV Schiltz von Görtz, 1692-1699
Adolf Johann Karl von Bettendorf, 1700-1705

MINT OFFICIALS' INITIALS

Initials	Date	Name
AL	1674-76	Adam Longerich
CB	1688-90	Conrad Bethmann
HS	1625-72	Henning Schlüter in Zellerfeld
(r) and/or R, HR	1618-22	Hans Rück

RA	1679-88	Johann Reinhard Arnold
VBW	1684-88, 1702-14	Ulrich Burkhard Willerding in Mainz

ARMS

Wall with 3 towers, often with imperial eagle which has shield of Austrian arms on breast

REFERENCES

L = Ernst Lejeune, "Die Münzen der reichsunmittelbaren Burg Friedberg i.d. Wetterau," **Berliner Münzblätter**, N.F., v. 24 (1903), pp. 336ff.

Sch = Wolfgang Schulten, ***Deutsche Münzen aus der Zeit Karls V.***, Frankfurt am Main, 1974.

S = Hugo Frhr. Von Saurma-Jeltsch, ***Die Saurmasche Münzsammlung deutscher, schweizerischer und polnischer Gepräge von etwa dem Beginn der Groschenzeit bis zur Kipperperiode***, Berlin, 1892.

IMPERIAL CITY

REGULAR COINAGE

KM# 32 PFENNIG

Silver **Ruler:** Konrad Löw **Note:** 4-fold arms divide date in circle of pellets.

Date	Mintage	VG	F	VF	XF	Unc
16Z3	—	20.00	45.00	90.00	—	—

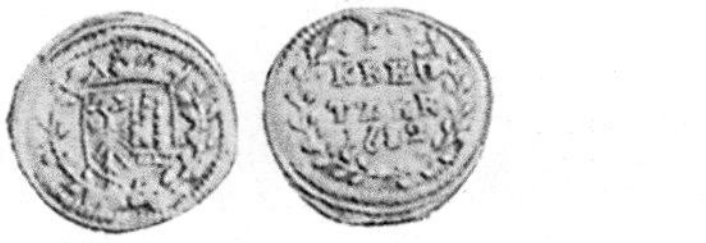

KM# 47 KREUZER

Silver **Ruler:** Johann Eitel I **Obv:** Crowned 2-fold arms in laurel wreath **Rev:** I/ KREV/ TZER/ date/ mintmasters initials in laureal wreath **Note:** Varieties exist.

Date	Mintage	VG	F	VF	XF	Unc
1679 RA	—	15.00	35.00	75.00	155	—
1680 RA	—	15.00	35.00	75.00	155	—
1680	—	15.00	35.00	75.00	155	—
1682	—	15.00	35.00	75.00	155	—
1683	—	15.00	35.00	75.00	155	—
1684	—	15.00	35.00	75.00	155	—

KM# 56 KREUZER

Silver **Ruler:** Philipp Adolf Rau

Date	Mintage	VG	F	VF	XF	Unc
1685	—	10.00	25.00	55.00	115	—
1686	—	10.00	25.00	55.00	115	—

KM# 41 2 KREUZER (Halbbatzen)

Silver **Ruler:** Wolf Adolf **Rev:** Without Z in orb

Date	Mintage	VG	F	VF	XF	Unc
1657 HS	—	27.00	60.00	110	215	—

KM# 40 2 KREUZER (Halbbatzen)

Silver **Ruler:** Wolf Adolf **Obv:** Crowned rampant lion left with bend superimposed (Kraichen arms) in laurel wreath **Note:** Varieties exist.

Date	Mintage	VG	F	VF	XF	Unc
1657 HS	—	27.00	60.00	110	215	—
1658 HS	—	27.00	60.00	110	215	—

KM# 55 ALBUS

Silver **Ruler:** Johann Eitel I **Obv:** Ornamented 4-fold arms divide mintmasters initials **Rev:** Date in laurel wreath **Rev. Legend:** I/ ALBVS

Date	Mintage	VG	F	VF	XF	Unc
1683 RA	—	80.00	160	280	550	—

KM# 10 3 KREUZER (Groschen)

Silver **Ruler:** Konrad Löw **Obv:** Crowned imperial eagle, 3 in orb on breast, titles of Matthias and date in legend **Rev:** 4-fold arms **Rev. Legend:** CASTR • IMP **Note:** Varieties exist.

Date	Mintage	VG	F	VF	XF	Unc
ND(1618) (r)	96,000	30.00	65.00	135	275	—
1618 (R)	Inc. above	30.00	65.00	135	275	—
1619 (r)	43,000	30.00	65.00	135	275	—

KM# 20 3 KREUZER (Groschen)

Silver **Ruler:** Konrad Löw **Obv:** Titles of Ferdinand II

Date	Mintage	VG	F	VF	XF	Unc
16Z0 (r)	28,000	27.00	60.00	110	225	—
1623	—	27.00	60.00	110	225	—

KM# 27 3 KREUZER (Groschen)

Silver **Ruler:** Konrad Löw **Obv:** Date in legend

Date	Mintage	VG	F	VF	XF	Unc
16Z1	—	25.00	50.00	100	200	—

KM# 26 3 KREUZER (Groschen)

Silver **Ruler:** Konrad Löw **Obv:** Arms divide date **Rev:** Crowned imperial eagle with orb on breast **Note:** Kipper 3 Kreuzer.

Date	Mintage	VG	F	VF	XF	Unc
16Z1 (r)	—	25.00	50.00	100	200	—
16ZZ (r)	—	25.00	50.00	100	200	—
16ZZ (r)	—	25.00	50.00	100	200	—

KM# 48 3 KREUZER (Groschen)

Silver **Ruler:** Johann Eitel I **Note:** Similar to KM#49 but date in legend.

Date	Mintage	VG	F	VF	XF	Unc
1679	—	27.00	60.00	110	225	—

KM# 49 3 KREUZER (Groschen)

Silver **Ruler:** Johann Eitel I **Obv:** Crowned double-headed imperial eagle **Rev:** Date divided by crown

Date	Mintage	VG	F	VF	XF	Unc
1679	—	27.00	60.00	110	225	—

KM# 57 6 KREUZER

Silver **Ruler:** Johann Eitel I **Obv:** Phillipp Adolf Rau **Rev:** Crown divides circle and date above **Note:** Varieties exist.

Date	Mintage	VG	F	VF	XF	Unc
1688 RA	—	45.00	90.00	180	360	—
1688	—	45.00	90.00	180	360	—
1688 VBW	—	45.00	90.00	180	360	—

KM# 21 12 KREUZER (Zwölfer)

Silver **Ruler:** Konrad Löw **Obv:** Shield of 4-fold arms **Obv. Legend:** CASTR.IMP... **Rev:** Crowned imperial eagle, 1Z in orb on breast, titles of Ferdinand II and date in legend **Note:** Kipper coinage.

Date	Mintage	VG	F	VF	XF	Unc
16Z0	—	—	—	—	—	—

KM# 28 12 KREUZER (Zwölfer)

Silver **Ruler:** Konrad Löw **Obv:** Date in legend

Date	Mintage	VG	F	VF	XF	Unc
16Z1	—	—	—	—	—	—

KM# 50 15 KREUZER (1/4 Gulden)

Silver **Ruler:** Johann Eitel I **Obv:** Church façade within circle, legend around border **Rev:** Date in legend **Note:** Varieties exist.

Date	Mintage	VG	F	VF	XF	Unc
1679 RA	—	40.00	80.00	160	325	—

KM# 45 30 KREUZER (1/3 Thaler)

Silver **Ruler:** Johann Eitel I

Date	Mintage	VG	F	VF	XF	Unc
1674 AL	—	95.00	190	380	725	—

KM# 46 60 KREUZER (2/3 Thaler)

Silver **Ruler:** Johann Eitel I **Note:** Varieties exist.

Date	Mintage	VG	F	VF	XF	Unc
1674 AL	—	72.00	125	240	475	—
1675 AL	—	72.00	125	240	475	—
1676 AL	—	72.00	125	240	475	—

KM# 11 1/4 THALER (Teston)

Silver **Ruler:** Konrad Löw **Obv:** Oval 4-fold arms in baroque frame **Rev:** Crowned imperial eagle, arms of Austria on breast date separated by eagle's neck, titles of Matthias

Date	Mintage	VG	F	VF	XF	Unc
1618 (r) Reported, not confirmed	3,201	—	—	—	—	—
1619 (r)	19,000	—	—	—	—	—

KM# 22 1/4 THALER (Teston)

Silver **Ruler:** Konrad Löw **Rev:** Titles of Ferdinand II

Date	Mintage	VG	F	VF	XF	Unc
1620 (r)	2,852	—	—	—	—	—

Note: Reported, not confirmed

KM# 29 1/4 THALER (Teston)

Silver **Ruler:** Konrad Löw **Note:** Similar to 1/2 Thaler, KM#30 but orb on breast of eagle.

Date	Mintage	VG	F	VF	XF	Unc
ND(1622) HB	—	—	—	—	—	—

KM# 30 1/2 THALER

Silver **Ruler:** Konrad Löw **Obv:** Standing armored figure **Rev:** Austrian arms on eagle's breast

Date	Mintage	VG	F	VF	XF	Unc
ND(1622) R	—	350	625	1,200	—	—

KM# 33 1/2 THALER

Silver **Ruler:** Konrad Löw **Obv:** Standing armored figure **Rev:** Date in legend

Date	Mintage	VG	F	VF	XF	Unc
1623 R	—	450	900	1,700	—	—

KM# 12 THALER

Silver **Ruler:** Konrad Löw **Obv:** St. George and dragon with shields in legend **Rev:** Crowned double eagle with Austrian arms on breast, date divided by neck, 2 arms below, titles of Rudolph II **Note:** Dav. #5308.

Date	Mintage	VG	F	VF	XF	Unc
1618 Reported, not confirmed	198	—	—	—	—	—
1619 (r) Rare	505	—	—	—	—	—

KM# 23 THALER

Silver **Ruler:** Konrad Löw **Rev:** Date divided above claws of eagle. **Note:** Similar to KM#34. Dav. #5309.

Date	Mintage	VG	F	VF	XF	Unc
1620 Reported, not confirmed	630	—	—	—	—	—
16ZZ R	—	650	1,250	2,250	4,500	—

KM# 34 THALER

Silver **Ruler:** Konrad Löw **Obv:** Standing armored figure **Rev:** Titles of Ferdinand II **Note:** Dav. #5310.

Date	Mintage	VG	F	VF	XF	Unc
16Z3	—	500	1,000	2,000	4,000	—

KM# 58 THALER

Silver **Ruler:** Philipp Adolf Rau **Obv:** Armored equestrian, left, above date, flanked by shields **Rev:** Titles of Leopold I **Note:** Dav. #5311.

Date	Mintage	VG	F	VF	XF	Unc
1688 CB	—	2,250	4,500	8,300	13,500	—

KM# 60 THALER

Silver **Ruler:** Philipp Adolf Rau **Obv:** Armored equestrian, right, flanked by shields **Rev:** Titles of Leopold I **Note:** Dav. #5312.

Date	Mintage	VG	F	VF	XF	Unc
1690 CB	—	2,050	4,150	7,500	13,000	—

KM# 14 2 THALER

Silver **Ruler:** Konrad Löw **Obv:** St. George and dragon with shields in legend **Rev:** Crowned double eagle with Austrian arms on breast, date divided by neck, 2 arms below, titles of Rudolph II **Note:** Dav. #5307.

Date	Mintage	VG	F	VF	XF	Unc
1619 (r) Rare	110	—	—	—	—	—

TRADE COINAGE

KM# 7 GOLDGULDEN

3.5000 g., 0.9860 Gold 0.1109 oz. AGW **Ruler:** Konrad Löw **Obv:** 4-fold arms **Rev:** Crowned imperial eagle, titles of Rudolf II

Date	Mintage	VG	F	VF	XF	Unc
ND Rare	5,101	—	—	—	—	—

KM# 13 GOLDGULDEN

3.5000 g., 0.9860 Gold 0.1109 oz. AGW **Ruler:** Konrad Löw **Obv:** Crowned imperial eagle, Austrian arms on breast, titles of Matthias and date in legend **Rev:** 4-fold arms, family arms to left and right in legend

Date	Mintage	VG	F	VF	XF	Unc
1618 (r) Rare	1,359	—	—	—	—	—

KM# 15 GOLDGULDEN

3.5000 g., 0.9860 Gold 0.1109 oz. AGW **Ruler:** Konrad Löw **Obv:** Date divided by eagle's neck

Date	Mintage	VG	F	VF	XF	Unc
1619 (r) Rare	2,529	—	—	—	—	—

KM# 24 GOLDGULDEN

3.5000 g., 0.9860 Gold 0.1109 oz. AGW **Ruler:** Konrad Löw **Obv:** Titles of Ferdinand II and date in legend

Date	Mintage	VG	F	VF	XF	Unc
16Z0 (r) Rare	2,673	—	—	—	—	—

KM# 25 GOLDGULDEN

3.5000 g., 0.9860 Gold 0.1109 oz. AGW **Ruler:** Konrad Löw **Note:** Klippe.

Date	Mintage	VG	F	VF	XF	Unc
16Z0 (r) Unique	—	—	—	—	—	—

KM# 31 GOLDGULDEN

3.5000 g., 0.9860 Gold 0.1109 oz. AGW **Ruler:** Konrad Löw **Obv:** Date in legend **Rev:** Crowned double-headed imperial eagle

Date	Mintage	VG	F	VF	XF	Unc
16ZZ R	—	3,500	6,000	10,000	18,000	—

PATTERNS

Including off metal strikes

KM#	Date	Mintage	Identification	Mkt Val
Pn1	16ZZ RA	—	Thaler. Gold. KM#23.	—

FUGGER

A wealthy banking and commercial family of Augsburg, which first came into prominence about 1370 and became the bankers of the Hapsburgs by 1475. In 1500 they were given the county of Kirchberg and the lordship of Weissenborn (in Swabia) as security for a loan. The emperor made them hereditary counts of these areas and gave them the mint right in 1534. There was a complicated succession with many lines and few coin issuers. The land was mediatized to Bavaria and Württemberg in 1806.

FAMILY ARMS

2 lilies on adjacent fields

REFERENCE

K = Johann Veit Kull, ***"Die Münzen des gräflichen und fürstlichen Hauses Fugger,"*** *Mitteilungen der Bayerischen Numismatischen Gesellschaft 8 (1889)*, pp. 1-96.

Sch = Wolfgang Schulten, ***Deutsche Münzen aus der Zeit Karls V.*** Frankfurt am Main, 1974.

FUGGER-BABENHAUSEN

RULERS

(Issuers of Coinage Only)

Maximilian II zu Babenhausen, 1598-1629
Johann III zu Babenhausen, 1598-1633
Sebastian zu Kirchheim-Worth, guardian of Sigmund Joseph and Johann Rudolf zu Babenhausen, 1668-1677
Sigmund Joseph zu Babenhausen, 1685-1696
Johann Rudolf zu Babenhausen, 1685-1693

COUNTSHIP

REGULAR COINAGE

KM# 11 HELLER (1/420 Gulden)

Copper **Obv:** Arms in wreath **Rev:** MAX divides date in frame, C CC C above, X X below **Note:** Kipper Heller.

Date	Mintage	VG	F	VF	XF	Unc
1621	—	—	—	—	—	—

KM# 12 PFENNIG (1/210 Gulden)

Copper **Obv:** MAX divides date in frame, C C above, X below **Rev:** Arms in wreath **Note:** Kipper Pfennig.

Date	Mintage	VG	F	VF	XF	Unc
1621	—	45.00	85.00	145	275	—
1622	—	45.00	85.00	145	275	—

KM# 13 1/2 KREUZER (1/20 Gulden)

Copper **Obv:** Arms in wreath **Rev:** MAX divides date in frame, 120 below **Note:** Kipper 1/2 Kreuzer.

Date	Mintage	VG	F	VF	XF	Unc
1621	—	25.00	50.00	100	200	—

KM# 20 1/2 KREUZER (1/20 Gulden)

Copper **Rev:** IF monogram in frame, date above, 120 below

Date	Mintage	VG	F	VF	XF	Unc
1622	—	27.00	55.00	110	225	—

KM# 21 KREUZER (1/60 Gulden)

Copper, 17 mm. **Obv:** Arms in wreath **Rev:** K in ornamented round shield divides date, MAX. F above, 60 below **Note:** Kipper Kreuzer.

Date	Mintage	VG	F	VF	XF	Unc
1622	—	22.00	40.00	80.00	165	—

KM# 22 KREUZER (1/60 Gulden)
Copper **Obv:** Arms in wreath divides date, MAX above, K below. **Note:** Uniface.

Date	Mintage	VG	F	VF	XF	Unc
1622	—	22.00	40.00	80.00	165	—

KM# 23 KREUZER (1/60 Gulden)
Copper **Obv:** MAX • F, date above, 60 below.

Date	Mintage	VG	F	VF	XF	Unc
1622	—	22.00	40.00	80.00	165	—

KM# 24 KREUZER (1/60 Gulden)
Copper **Note:** Similar to KM#23 but MAX.

Date	Mintage	VG	F	VF	XF	Unc
1622	—	15.00	25.00	50.00	100	—

KM# 25 KREUZER (1/60 Gulden)
Silver **Obv:** Arms in heart-shaped shield **Obv. Legend:** MAX • F • L... **Rev:** Eight-armed cross, I in center, K-R-E-I-Z-E-R-++ in angles of cross

Date	Mintage	VG	F	VF	XF	Unc
ND	—	25.00	40.00	75.00	155	—

KM# 5 2 KREUZER (1/2 Batzen)
Silver **Obv:** Arms **Obv. Legend:** MAX • FVG... **Rev:** Imperial orb with 2 **Rev. Legend:** GLO • ET • HO...

Date	Mintage	VG	F	VF	XF	Unc
ND(ca.1620)	—	40.00	70.00	125	240	—

KM# 6 2 KREUZER (1/2 Batzen)
Silver **Rev. Legend:** PAX • ET • VERIT...

Date	Mintage	VG	F	VF	XF	Unc
ND(ca.1620)	—	40.00	70.00	125	240	—

KM# 7 2 KREUZER (1/2 Batzen)
Silver **Rev. Legend:** NON EST PAX...

Date	Mintage	VG	F	VF	XF	Unc
ND(ca.1620)	—	40.00	70.00	125	240	—

KM# 8 2 KREUZER (1/2 Batzen)
Silver **Rev. Legend:** PAX ET HONOS...

Date	Mintage	VG	F	VF	XF	Unc
ND(ca.1620)	—	40.00	70.00	125	240	—

KM# 9 2 KREUZER (1/2 Batzen)
Silver **Obv:** Crowned imperial eagle, 2 in orb on breast, titles of Ferdinand II

Date	Mintage	VG	F	VF	XF	Unc
ND(ca.1620)	—	40.00	70.00	125	240	—

KM# 30 6 KREUZER
Silver **Obv:** Crowned four-fold arms, F-S above, date divided in points of crown **Rev:** Crowned intertwined cipher, two palm branches below, 6 in frame

Date	Mintage	VG	F	VF	XF	Unc
1676	2,470	—	—	—	—	—

KM# 35 6 KREUZER
Silver **Obv:** Bust right, VI below **Rev:** Crowned four-fold arms, date in legend

Date	Mintage	VG	F	VF	XF	Unc
1684	—	—	—	—	—	—

KM# 14 12 KREUZER (Zwölfer)
Silver **Obv:** Crowned imperial eagle, 12 in orb on breast, titles of Ferdinand II **Rev:** Oval four-fold arms, date divided below **Note:** Kipper 12 Kreuzer.

Date	Mintage	VG	F	VF	XF	Unc
1621	—	—	—	—	—	—

KM# 31 15 KREUZER (1/4 Gulden)
Silver

Date	Mintage	VG	F	VF	XF	Unc
1676	941,000	90.00	185	375	775	—
1677	Inc. above	90.00	185	375	775	—

KM# 36 15 KREUZER (1/4 Gulden)
Silver **Obv:** Bust right, XV below **Rev:** Crowned four-fold arms, date in legend divided by crown

Date	Mintage	VG	F	VF	XF	Unc
1684	—	120	225	450	900	—

KM# 32 60 KREUZER (2/3 Thaler - Gulden)
Silver **Obv:** Crowned four-fold arms divide F-S, date above **Rev:** Intertwined cipher, 60 in frame below with palm branches

Date	Mintage	VG	F	VF	XF	Unc
1676	858	—	—	—	—	—

KM# 10 1/24 THALER (Groschen)
Silver **Obv:** Arms **Obv. Legend:** MAX: FVGGER... **Rev:** 24/ AVF • EIN/ REICHS/ TALER in frame

Date	Mintage	VG	F	VF	XF	Unc
ND(ca.1620)	—	—	—	—	—	—

KM# 37 2/3 THALER (60 Kreuzer - Gulden)
Silver **Obv:** Bust right **Rev:** 2/3 in wreath, date below

Date	Mintage	VG	F	VF	XF	Unc
1684	—	—	—	—	—	—

KM# 15 THALER (120 Kreuzer)
Silver **Obv:** Crowned imperial eagle, 120 in frame below, titles of Ferdinand II **Rev:** Four-fold arms divide date

Date	Mintage	VG	F	VF	XF	Unc
1621	—	500	1,000	1,800	3,000	—

KM# 16 THALER (120 Kreuzer)
Silver **Obv:** Ornate shield within circle **Rev:** Crown above double-headed imperial eagle within circle **Note:** Dav. #6672. Varieties exist.

Date	Mintage	VG	F	VF	XF	Unc
1621	—	275	500	775	1,800	3,000

KM# 17 THALER (120 Kreuzer)
Silver **Obv:** Ornate shield divides date within circle **Rev:** Crown above double-headed imperial eagle **Note:** Dav. #6673.

Date	Mintage	VG	F	VF	XF	Unc
1621	—	195	350	650	1,500	2,700
1623	—	195	350	650	1,500	2,700

KM# 27 THALER (120 Kreuzer)
Silver **Rev:** Titles of Ferdinand II **Note:** Dav. #6674.

Date	Mintage	VG	F	VF	XF	Unc
1624	—	425	775	1,300	2,150	—

TRADE COINAGE

KM# 18 GOLDGULDEN
3.5000 g., 0.9860 Gold 0.1109 oz. AGW **Note:** Fr. 1037.

Date	Mintage	VG	F	VF	XF	Unc
ND	—	1,000	2,000	3,650	5,600	—

KM# 26 DUCAT
3.5000 g., 0.9860 Gold 0.1109 oz. AGW **Obv:** 3 oval shields within circle **Rev:** Crowned imperial eagle within circle **Note:** Fr. 1038.

Date	Mintage	VG	F	VF	XF	Unc
1622	—	—	2,000	4,500	9,000	15,000

KM# 19 4 DUCAT
14.0000 g., 0.9860 Gold 0.4438 oz. AGW **Obv:** Crowned imperial eagle, titles of Ferdinand II **Rev:** Four-fold arms, date divided below

Date	Mintage	VG	F	VF	XF	Unc
1621 Rare	—	—	—	—	—	—

KM# A28 6 DUCAT
21.0000 g., 0.9860 Gold 0.6657 oz. AGW **Obv:** Ornate shield divides date within circle **Rev:** Crown above double-headed imperial eagle **Note:** Struck with 1 Thaler dies, KM#17.

Date	Mintage	VG	F	VF	XF	Unc
1621 Rare	—	—	—	—	—	—

KM# B28 8 DUCAT
27.0000 g., 0.9860 Gold 0.8559 oz. AGW **Obv:** Ornate shield divides date within circle **Rev:** Crown above double-headed imperial eagle **Note:** Struck with 1 Thaler dies, KM#17.

Date	Mintage	VG	F	VF	XF	Unc
1621 Rare	—	—	—	—	—	—

KM# C28 10 DUCAT (Portugalöser)
35.0000 g., 0.9860 Gold 1.1095 oz. AGW **Obv:** Ornate shield divides date within circle **Rev:** Crown above double-headed imperial eagle **Note:** Struck with 1 Thaler dies, KM#17.

Date	Mintage	VG	F	VF	XF	Unc
1621 Rare	—	—	—	—	—	—

KM# 28 11 DUCAT
38.5000 g., 0.9860 Gold 1.2204 oz. AGW **Obv:** Ornate shield divides date within circle **Rev:** Crown above double-headed imperial eagle **Note:** Struck with 1 Thaler dies, KM#17.

Date	Mintage	VG	F	VF	XF	Unc
1621 Rare	—	—	—	—	—	—

KM# A29 12 DUCAT
42.0000 g., 0.9860 Gold 1.3314 oz. AGW **Obv:** Ornate shield divides date within circle **Rev:** Crown above double-headed imperial eagle **Note:** Struck with 1 Thaler dies, KM#17.

Date	Mintage	VG	F	VF	XF	Unc
1621 Rare	—	—	—	—	—	—

KM# B29 13 DUCAT
45.0000 g., 0.9860 Gold 1.4265 oz. AGW **Obv:** Ornate shield divides date within circle **Rev:** Crown above double-headed imperial eagle **Note:** Struck with 1 Thaler dies, KM#17.

Date	Mintage	VG	F	VF	XF	Unc
1621 Rare	—	—	—	—	—	—

KM# 29 15 DUCAT
52.5000 g., 0.9860 Gold 1.6642 oz. AGW **Obv:** Ornate shield divides date within circle **Rev:** Crown above double-headed imperial eagle **Note:** Struck with 1 Thaler dies, KM#17.

Date	Mintage	VG	F	VF	XF	Unc
1621 Rare	—	—	—	—	—	—

FUGGER-BABENHAUSEN-WELLENBURG

RULERS

(Issuers of Coinage Only)

Georg IV zu Babenhausen-Wellenburg, 1598-1643

COUNTSHIP

REGULAR COINAGE

KM# 7 KREUZER
Copper **Obv:** Similar to KM#5, but G-F above and L-F below arms.

Date	Mintage	VG	F	VF	XF	Unc
1622	—	33.00	55.00	110	220	—

KM# 5 KREUZER
Copper, 15x18 mm. **Note:** Kipper Kreuzer. Varieties exist.

Date	Mintage	VG	F	VF	XF	Unc
1622	—	33.00	55.00	110	220	—

KM# 6 KREUZER
Copper **Obv:** Square arms **Rev:** Date below value **Note:** Varieties exist.

Date	Mintage	VG	F	VF	XF	Unc
1622	—	33.00	55.00	110	220	—

KM# 11 2 KREUZER (1/2 Batzen)
Silver **Obv:** Ornate shield within circle **Rev:** Crown above double-headed imperial eagle within circle **Note:** Varieties exist.

Date	Mintage	VG	F	VF	XF	Unc
1624	—	27.00	45.00	75.00	155	—

KM# 9 12 KREUZER (Zwölfer)
Silver **Obv:** Half-length bust right divides date

Date	Mintage	VG	F	VF	XF	Unc
1622	—	125	250	450	900	—

KM# 8 12 KREUZER (Zwölfer)
Silver **Ruler:** Georg IV **Obv:** Crowned bust holding orb and scepter **Rev:** Crowned imperial eagle, 12 on breast, titles of Ferdinand II **Mint:** Wasserburg **Note:** Kipper 12 Kreuzer.

Date	Mintage	VG	F	VF	XF	Unc
ND	—	90.00	135	250	425	—

KM# 10 THALER
Silver **Ruler:** Georg IV **Obv:** Armored equestrian, left, 4-fold arms below divides circle **Rev:** Titles of Ferdinand II **Mint:** Wasserburg **Note:** Kipper Thaler. Dav. #6671.

Date	Mintage	VG	F	VF	XF	Unc
1622	—	250	450	1,150	2,250	—

FUGGER-GLOTT

RULERS

(Issuers of Coinage Only)

Franz Ernst zu Glott, 1673-1711

COUNTSHIP

REGULAR COINAGE

KM# 5 THALER
Silver **Obv:** Crowned ornate shield **Rev:** Titles of Leopold I **Note:** Dav. #6675.

Date	Mintage	F	VF	XF	Unc	BU
1694	—	450	850	1,500	2,750	—

FUGGER-NORDENDORF

RULERS

(Issuers of Coinage Only)

Marquard zu Nordendorf, 1601-1624
Nikolaus zu Nordendorf, 1611-1676

COUNTSHIP

REGULAR COINAGE

KM# 5 PFENNIG (1/210 Gulden)
Copper **Obv:** Arms in wreath **Rev:** NF monogram in frame, CXC below **Note:** Kipper Pfennig. Klippe.

Date	Mintage	VG	F	VF	XF	Unc
ND(c.1622)	—	—	—	—	—	—

KM# 7 1/2 KREUZER (1/120 Gulden)
Copper **Obv:** Arms in wreath, NF monogram above **Rev. Inscription:** HALB / KREIC / ER / date **Note:** Kipper 1/2 Kreuzer.

Date	Mintage	VG	F	VF	XF	Unc
1622	—	25.00	40.00	80.00	165	—

KM# 6 1/120 GULDEN (1/2 Kreuzer)
Copper **Obv:** Oval ornamented arms in wreath **Rev:** NF monogram, date above, 120 below **Note:** Varieties exist.

Date	Mintage	VG	F	VF	XF	Unc
1622	—	22.00	40.00	80.00	160	—

KM# 8 1/60 GULDEN (Kreuzer)
Copper **Obv:** Ornamented oval arms in wreath **Rev:** MQF monogram, date divided above, 60 below **Note:** Kipper 1/60 Gulden. Varieties exist.

Date	Mintage	VG	F	VF	XF	Unc
1622	—	25.00	40.00	80.00	160	—

KM# 9 1/60 GULDEN (Kreuzer)
Copper **Obv:** Arms in wreath **Rev:** MQF monogram, date divided above and 60 below, cloverleaf to left

Date	Mintage	VG	F	VF	XF	Unc
1622	—	25.00	40.00	80.00	160	—

KM# 10 1/60 GULDEN (Kreuzer)
Copper **Obv:** MQF monogram, date divided above and 60 below, cloverleaf at left. **Note:** Uniface.

Date	Mintage	VG	F	VF	XF	Unc
1622	—	20.00	40.00	80.00	160	—

KM# 11 1/60 GULDEN (Kreuzer)
Copper, 17 mm. **Obv:** Ornamental oval arms in wreath **Rev:** NF monogram between two rosettes, date above, 60 below **Note:** Varieties exist.

Date	Mintage	VG	F	VF	XF	Unc
1622	—	20.00	40.00	80.00	160	—

KM# 12 THALER
Silver **Obv:** Ornate oval arms within circle **Obv. Legend:** * MARQUARDT • FVGGE(R) • F:H:V... **Rev:** Crowned imperial eagle, titles of Ferdinand II **Note:** Dav. #6670.

Date	Mintage	VG	F	VF	XF	Unc
1623	—	1,250	2,500	4,750	7,500	—

FUGGER-PFIRT

RULERS

(Issuers of Coinage Only)

Wilhelm zu Pfirt, 1601-1659

COUNTSHIP

REGULAR COINAGE

KM# 5 4 PFENNIG
Copper, 17 mm. **Obv:** Lily arms in wreath, 4 above, W below. **Note:** Uniface. Kipper 4 Pfennig.

Date	Mintage	VG	F	VF	XF	Unc
ND(c.1621/22)	—	35.00	75.00	150	300	—

FULDA

Located in central Germany, the abbey was founded in 744. The abbot became prince of the empire in the late 10th century. The first coins were struck in the 11th century. It became a bishopric in 1752 and in 1803, Fulda was secularized and passed successively to Orange-Nassau, Westphalia, Hesse-Cassel and Prussia.

RULERS

Balthasar von Dernbach, 1570-1606
under control of the Teutonic Order, 1576-1602
Johann Friedrich von Schwalbach, 1606-1622
Johann Bernhard, Schenk von Schweinsberg, 1623-1632
Johann Adolf von Hoheneck, 1633-1635
Hermann Georg von Neuhof, 1635-1644
Joachim von Graveneck, 1644-1671
Bernhard Gustav Adolf, Markgraf von Baden, 1671-1677
Placidus von Droste zu Erwite, 1678-1700
Adalbert I von Schleifras, 1700-1714

MINT OFFICIALS' INITIALS

Initial	Date	Name
OS	Ca.1600	Unknown
PHM	Ca.1688	P.H. Müller

ARMS

Plain cross, sometimes in shield divided vertically with 3 long-stemmed flowers of cathedral chapter.

REFERENCES

SCH = Wolfgang Schulten, ***Deutsche Münzen aus der Zeit Karls V.*** Frankfurt am Main, 1974

S = Hugo Frhr. von Saurma-Jeltsch, **Die Saurmasche Münzsammlung deutscher, schweizerischer und polnischer Gepräge von etwa dem Beginn der Groschenzeit bis zur Kipperperiode**, Berlin, 1892.

ABBEY

REGULAR COINAGE

KM# 5 PFENNIG

Silver **Ruler:** Balthasar **Obv:** 4-fold arms of Fulda and Dernbach, B above. **Note:** Uniface. Schussel-type.

Date	Mintage	VG	F	VF	XF	Unc
ND(ca.1602-06)	—	33.00	65.00	130	265	—

KM# 22 ALBUS

Silver **Ruler:** Placidus

Date	Mintage	VG	F	VF	XF	Unc
1679	—	65.00	150	250	425	—

KM# 6 3 KREUZER (Groschen)

Silver **Ruler:** Balthasar **Obv:** 4-fold arms in Fulda and Dernbach in oval baroque frame **Rev:** Crowned imperial eagle, 3 in orb on breast, titles of Rudolf II

Date	Mintage	VG	F	VF	XF	Unc
ND(ca.1602-06) OS	—	55.00	120	225	425	—

KM# 7 3 KREUZER (Groschen)

Silver **Ruler:** Balthasar **Rev:** Square 4-fold arms

Date	Mintage	VG	F	VF	XF	Unc
ND(ca.1602-06)	—	55.00	120	225	425	—

KM# 15 1/8 THALER

Silver **Ruler:** Bernhard Gustav Adolf **Obv:** Legend with Roman numeral date **Rev:** Arms

Date	Mintage	VG	F	VF	XF	Unc
MDCLXXII (1672)	—	95.00	200	325	600	—

KM# 16 THALER

Silver **Ruler:** Bernhard Gustav Adolf **Note:** Dav. #5315.

Date	Mintage	VG	F	VF	XF	Unc
1672	—	500	1,000	2,200	4,500	7,500

KM# 17 THALER

Silver **Ruler:** Bernhard Gustav Adolf **Note:** Dav. #5316.

Date	Mintage	VG	F	VF	XF	Unc
1672	—	500	1,000	2,000	3,250	6,500

KM# 25 THALER

Silver **Ruler:** Placidus **Obv:** Bust of Placidus right **Rev:** Mitered and helmeted 4-fold arms with cross above, date in legend **Note:** Dav. #5318.

Date	Mintage	VG	F	VF	XF	Unc
1687	—	600	1,200	2,250	3,750	7,000

KM# 26 THALER

Silver **Ruler:** Placidus **Note:** Klippe. Dav. #5318A.

Date	Mintage	VG	F	VF	XF	Unc
1687	—	—	—	—	—	—

Note: Reported, not confirmed

KM# 29 THALER

Silver **Ruler:** Placidus **Note:** Dav. #5996.

Date	Mintage	VG	F	VF	XF	Unc
1688	—	400	900	2,250	4,750	8,000

KM# 30 1-1/4 THALER

Silver **Ruler:** Placidus **Note:** Similar to 1 Thaler, KM#29. Dav. #--.

Date	Mintage	VG	F	VF	XF	Unc
1688	—	1,200	2,500	5,000	9,000	—

KM# 8 2 THALER

Silver **Ruler:** Balthasar **Obv:** Crowned imperial eagle, titles of Rudolf II and date in legend **Rev:** Helmeted 4-fold arms **Note:** Klippe. Dav. #5313.

Date	Mintage	VG	F	VF	XF	Unc
1605 Rare	—	—	—	—	—	—

KM# 10 2 THALER

Silver **Ruler:** Balthasar **Note:** Klippe. Dav. #5314A.

Date	Mintage	VG	F	VF	XF	Unc
1606 Rare	—	—	—	—	—	—

KM# 9 2 THALER

Silver **Ruler:** Balthasar **Rev:** Orb on breast of eagle **Note:** Dav. #5314.

Date	Mintage	VG	F	VF	XF	Unc
1606 Rare	—	—	—	—	—	—

KM# 27 2 THALER

Silver **Ruler:** Placidus **Obv:** Bust right **Rev:** Mitered and helmeted 4-fold arms with cross above, date in legend **Note:** Dav. #5317.

Date	Mintage	VG	F	VF	XF	Unc
1687 Rare	—	—	—	—	—	—

KM# 28 2 THALER

Silver **Ruler:** Placidus **Note:** Klippe. Dav. #5317A.

Date	Mintage	VG	F	VF	XF	Unc
1687 Rare	—	—	—	—	—	—

TRADE COINAGE

KM# 18 1/4 DUCAT

0.8750 g., 0.9860 Gold 0.0277 oz. AGW **Ruler:** Bernhard Gustav Adolf **Obv:** St. Boniface **Rev:** AFBG monogram

Date	Mintage	VG	F	VF	XF	Unc
1672	—	325	700	1,700	3,700	—

KM# 19 1/2 DUCAT

1.7500 g., 0.9860 Gold 0.0555 oz. AGW **Ruler:** Bernhard Gustav Adolf **Obv:** St. Boniface **Rev:** AFBG monogram

Date	Mintage	VG	F	VF	XF	Unc
1672	—	550	1,200	2,800	6,000	—

KM# 20 DUCAT

3.5000 g., 0.9860 Gold 0.1109 oz. AGW **Ruler:** Bernhard Gustav Adolf **Obv:** St. Boniface above shield of arms **Rev:** AFBG monogram

Date	Mintage	VG	F	VF	XF	Unc
1672	—	725	1,750	4,200	9,100	—

KM# 35 DUCAT

3.5000 g., 0.9860 Gold 0.1109 oz. AGW **Ruler:** Placidus **Obv:** Bust of Placidus right **Rev:** Helmeted arms

Date	Mintage	VG	F	VF	XF	Unc
1692	—	1,800	3,600	9,100	17,500	—

KM# 21 2 DUCAT

7.0000 g., 0.9860 Gold 0.2219 oz. AGW **Ruler:** Bernhard Gustav Adolf **Obv:** St. Boniface above shield of arms **Rev:** AFBG monogram

Date	Mintage	VG	F	VF	XF	Unc
1672 Rare	—	—	—	—	—	—

KM# 36 2 DUCAT

7.0000 g., 0.9860 Gold 0.2219 oz. AGW **Ruler:** Placidus **Obv:** Bust of Placidus right **Rev:** Helmeted arms

Date	Mintage	VG	F	VF	XF	Unc
1692 Rare	—	—	—	—	—	—

KM# A30 7 DUCAT

24.5000 g., 0.9860 Gold 0.7766 oz. AGW **Ruler:** Placidus

Date	Mintage	VG	F	VF	XF	Unc
1688 Rare	—	—	—	—	—	—

Note: Struck with 1 Thaler dies, KM#29

KM# A31 7 DUCAT

24.5000 g., 0.9860 Gold 0.7766 oz. AGW **Ruler:** Placidus **Note:** Struck with 1 Thaler dies, KM#29.

Date	Mintage	VG	F	VF	XF	Unc
1688 Rare	—	—	—	—	—	—

KM# 31 8 DUCAT

28.0000 g., 0.9860 Gold 0.8876 oz. AGW **Ruler:** Placidus **Note:** Struck with 1 Thaler dies, KM#29.

Date	Mintage	VG	F	VF	XF	Unc
1688 Rare	—	—	—	—	—	—

KM# 32 10 DUCAT (Portugalöser)

35.0000 g., 0.9860 Gold 1.1095 oz. AGW **Ruler:** Placidus **Note:** Struck with 1 Thaler dies, KM#29.

Date	Mintage	VG	F	VF	XF	Unc
1688 Rare	—	—	—	—	—	—

FURSTENBERG

A noble family with holdings in Baden and Württemberg. The lord of Fürstenberg assumed the title of Count in the 13th century, which was raised to the rank of Prince in 1664. The Fürstenberg possessions were mediatized in 1806.

FURSTENBERG-HEILIGENBERG

RULERS

Friedrich IV, 1598-1617
Wilhelm II, 1617-1618
Egon VIII, 1618-1635
Hermann Egon, 1635-1674
Anton Egon, 1674-1716

COUNTSHIP

REGULAR COINAGE

KM# 5 KREUZER

Copper **Ruler:** Egon VIII **Obv:** 4-fold arms of Heiligenberg and Werdenberg, HB above in wreath **Rev:** Inscription in wreath **Rev. Inscription:** I / CREI / ZER **Note:** Kipper Kreuzer. Varieties exist.

Date	Mintage	VG	F	VF	XF	Unc
ND(c.1621/2)	—	375	750	1,500	—	—

KM# 6 3 KREUZER (Groschen)

Silver **Ruler:** Egon VIII **Obv:** Bust right **Rev:** Crowned imperial eagle, 3 in orb on breast, titles of Ferdinand II and date in legend

Date	Mintage	VG	F	VF	XF	Unc
1623	—	—	—	—	—	—

KM# 7 6 KREUZER

Silver **Ruler:** Egon VIII **Obv:** Ornamented helmet **Rev:** Crowned imperial eagle, 6 in orb on breast, titles of Ferdinand II

Date	Mintage	VG	F	VF	XF	Unc
ND(1623)	—	—	—	—	—	—

KM# 8 12 KREUZER (Dreibätzner)

Silver **Ruler:** Egon VIII **Obv:** Crowned shield of arms in ornamented frame **Rev:** Crowned imperial eagle, 1Z in orb on breast, titles of Ferdinand II

Date	Mintage	VG	F	VF	XF	Unc
ND(1623)	—	—	—	—	—	—

KM# 9 THALER

Silver **Ruler:** Egon VIII **Obv:** Crowned oval shield of arms in ornamented frame **Obv. Legend:** EGON: CO: IN: FVRSTENB. H. ET. W. LA. IN. BARE. **Rev:** Crowned imperial eagle in circle **Rev. Legend:** FERDINAND: II: ROM: IMPER: SEMPER: AVG: **Note:** Dav. #6677.

Date	Mintage	F	VF	XF	Unc	BU
ND(1623) Rare	—	—	—	—	—	—

KM# 10 2 THALER

Silver **Ruler:** Egon VIII **Obv:** Crowned shield of oval arms in ornamented frame **Obv. Legend:** EGON. CO. IN. FVRSTENB. H. ET. W. LA. IN. BARE. **Rev:** Crowned imperial eagle in circle **Rev. Legend:** FERDINAND. II. ROM. IMPER. SEMPER. AVG. **Note:** Dav. #6676.

Date	Mintage	F	VF	XF	Unc	BU
ND(1623) Rare	—	—	—	—	—	—

PRINCIPALITY

REGULAR COINAGE

KM# 16 THALER

Silver **Ruler:** Hermann Egon **Obv:** Armored bust to right **Obv. Legend:** HERMAN. EGON. D.G. LANDGRAVE IN FVRSTENBERG. **Rev:** Crowned shield of Fürstenberg arms, with small shield of 4-fold arm on eagle's breast **Rev. Legend:** COMES. IN. HEILIGENB. WERD. S. R. I. P. **Note:** Dav. #6678. Varieties exist.

Date	Mintage	F	VF	XF	Unc	BU
1670 Rare	—	—	—	—	—	—

FURSTENWALDE

The provincial town of Furstenwalde in Prussia is located on the River Spree some 30 miles east-southeast of central Berlin. A local kipper coinage was struck during the Thirty Years' War.

PROVINCIAL TOWN

REGULAR COINAGE

KM# 3 PFENNIG

Copper, 13 mm. **Obv:** Tree in oval shield, date above, F • W below. **Note:** Uniface.

Date	Mintage	VG	F	VF	XF	Unc
16Z1	—	40.00	85.00	175	—	—
1621	—	40.00	85.00	175	—	—
16ZZ	—	40.00	85.00	175	—	—

KM# 1 PFENNIG

Copper **Obv:** Two adjoining oval arms, eagle in left, tree in right, date above, FW below. **Note:** Kipper Pfennig. Uniface. Varieties exist.

Date	Mintage	VG	F	VF	XF	Unc
1621	—	40.00	85.00	190	375	—

Date	Mintage	VG	F	VF	XF	Unc
16Z1	—	40.00	85.00	190	375	—
16ZZ	—	40.00	85.00	190	375	—

KM# 4 PFENNIG

Copper **Obv:** Tree in ornately-shaped shield divides FW, date above. Varieties exist. **Note:** Uniface.

Date	Mintage	VG	F	VF	XF	Unc
1621	—	75.00	150	300	—	—
16Z1	—	75.00	150	300	—	—

KM# 5 PFENNIG

Copper **Obv:** Tree dividing FW in ornately-shaped shield, date above. **Note:** Uniface.

Date	Mintage	VG	F	VF	XF	Unc
1621	—	75.00	150	300	—	—
16Z1	—	75.00	150	300	—	—

KM# 6 PFENNIG

Copper **Obv:** Tree in ornamented oval arms divide FW near bottom, date above. **Note:** Uniface.

Date	Mintage	VG	F	VF	XF	Unc
1621	—	75.00	150	300	—	—
16Z1	—	75.00	150	300	—	—

KM# 7 PFENNIG

Copper **Obv:** Oval tree arms in baroque frame, date divided above, F-W divided below. **Note:** Uniface.

Date	Mintage	VG	F	VF	XF	Unc
1621	—	60.00	125	250	—	—

KM# 8 PFENNIG

Copper **Obv:** F-W divided above and date divided below arms. **Note:** Uniface.

Date	Mintage	VG	F	VF	XF	Unc
1621	—	55.00	110	225	—	—

KM# 9 PFENNIG

Copper **Obv:** Tree between two eagles, date divided above, F-W divided below. **Note:** Uniface.

Date	Mintage	VG	F	VF	XF	Unc
1621	—	75.00	150	300	—	—

KM# 10 PFENNIG

Copper **Note:** Tree divides F-W in oval baroque frame, date divided above.

Date	Mintage	VG	F	VF	XF	Unc
1622	—	75.00	150	300	—	—

KM# 2 PFENNIG

Copper **Note:** FW above, date below arms.

Date	Mintage	VG	F	VF	XF	Unc
16ZZ	—	80.00	160	225	—	—

FURTH

City 5 miles northwest of Nürnberg. Originally a Franconian settlement dating from the 8th century. Mentioned in 1007 when village was given to Bishopric of Bamberg. Claimed by Ansbach and Nürnberg in late medieval period. Captured briefly by Gustavus II Adolphus in 1632 during the 30 Years War. Town passed to Bavaria in 1806 and was chartered in 1808.

RULERS

Swedish

MONEYERS' INITIALS

Initial	Date	Name
CS	1632	Conrad Stutz

SWEDISH ADMINISTRATION

REGULAR COINAGE

KM# 3 PFENNIG

Silver **Obv:** "JEHOVAH" in Hebrew, rays streaming down on GA monogram dividing date, value I below. **Note:** Uniface.

Date	Mintage	VG	F	VF	XF	Unc
1632	—	45.00	100	180	360	—

KM# 4 1/28 GULDEN

Silver **Obv:** Crowned 4-fold arms with central shield, (28) above **Rev:** Figure of Christ holding orb divides date

Date	Mintage	VG	F	VF	XF	Unc
1632 CS Unique	—	—	—	—	—	—

KM# 5 4 KREUZER (Batzen)

Silver **Obv:** Half-length bust of Gustavus Adolphus 3/4 right holding sword over shoulder **Rev:** Crown above 4-fold arms with central shield divides date, value at top (IIII.K.)

Date	Mintage	VG	F	VF	XF	Unc
1632 CS	—	250	650	1,500	3,000	—

KM# 6 4 KREUZER (Batzen)

Silver **Obv:** Crown above 4-fold arms supported by two lions, value at top (IIII. K.) **Rev:** Figure of Christ holding orb divides date **Note:** Varieties exist.

Date	Mintage	VG	F	VF	XF	Unc
1632	—	75.00	150	300	600	—

KM# 7 4 KREUZER (Batzen)

Silver **Obv:** Arms and lions within inner circle

Date	Mintage	VG	F	VF	XF	Unc
1632	—	80.00	170	350	725	—

KM# 8 4 KREUZER (Batzen)

Silver **Obv:** Crowned shield

Date	Mintage	VG	F	VF	XF	Unc
1632	—	80.00	170	350	725	—

KM# 9 THALER

Silver **Obv:** Gustabus Adolphus **Rev:** Christ wtih orb, "JEHOVAH" in Hebrew above **Note:** Dav. #4549.

Date	Mintage	F	VF	XF	Unc	BU
1632 CS Rare	—	—	—	—	—	—

Note: Künker Auction 185, 3-11, XF realized approximately $55,690. Dr. Busso Peus Nachfolger Auction 390, 5-07, XF realized approximately $19,035.

TRADE COINAGE

KM# 10 DUCAT

3.5000 g., 0.9860 Gold 0.1109 oz. AGW **Obv:** Gustabus Adolphus standing right, divides date **Rev:** Crowned arms

Date	Mintage	VG	F	VF	XF	Unc
1632 CS Rare	—	—	—	—	—	—

PATTERNS

Including off metal strikes

KM#	Date	Mintage	Identification	Mkt Val
Pn1	1632 CS	—	Ducat. Silver. KM#10	—

GLOGAU

A city on the Oder River in Silesia (present-day Poland), about 105 miles northeast of Dresden, Glogau was the seat of a duchy, which passed successively to Poland in 1476, to Austria in 1526 and to Prussia in 1740. A rather scarce city coinage was struck during the early part of the Thirty Years' War.

MINT OFFICIALS' INITIALS

Initials	Date	Name
PN1	1621	Mathes Jachtmann
IC	1622	Johann Curtz aus Haynau
IH	1623	Johann Jacob Huser
	1624	Balthasar Zwirner
	1624	Peter Geldner, coinage leaseholder
	1624	Peter John
	1624	Jeremias Reinwaldt
	1625	Jacob Jamniter, coinage leaseholder

CITY

REGULAR COINAGE

KM# 1 KREUZER

Silver **Obv:** Silesian eagle, titles of Ferdinand II **Rev:** 4-fold arms divide date **Note:** Kipper Kreuzer.

Date	Mintage	VG	F	VF	XF	Unc
(16)ZZ	—	25.00	50.00	100	200	—

KM# 2 3 KREUZER (Groschen)

Silver **Note:** Kipper 3 Kreuzer. Varieties exist.

Date	Mintage	VG	F	VF	XF	Unc
1622 IC	—	40.00	80.00	160	325	650

KM# 3 3 KREUZER (Groschen)

Silver **Obv:** Laureate bust right, titles of Ferdinand II, date in legend **Rev:** Silesian eagle, value 3 below

Date	Mintage	VG	F	VF	XF	Unc
1622 IC	—	50.00	100	200	425	—

KM# 4 3 KREUZER (Groschen)

Silver **Obv:** Silesian eagle, titles of Ferdinand II **Rev:** Two shields above value 3 in oval

Date	Mintage	VG	F	VF	XF	Unc
1622 IC	—	30.00	65.00	135	275	—

KM# 5 3 KREUZER (Groschen)

Silver **Obv:** Silesian eagle, value 3 below, titles of Ferdinand II, date in legend **Rev:** Madonna and child **Note:** Klippe.

Date	Mintage	VG	F	VF	XF	Unc
1622	—	—	—	—	—	—

KM# 6 3 KREUZER (Groschen)

Silver **Obv:** Silesian eagle, value 3 below, titles of Ferdinand II **Rev:** Ornate gothic G, date in legend

Date	Mintage	VG	F	VF	XF	Unc
16ZZ IH	—	—	—	—	—	—

KM# 7 24 KREUZER

Silver **Obv:** Similar to KM#8, titles of Ferdinand II **Rev:** Silesian eagle **Note:** Kipper 24 Kreuzer

Date	Mintage	VG	F	VF	XF	Unc
1622 IC	—	90.00	170	300	625	—

KM# 8 24 KREUZER

Silver

Date	Mintage	VG	F	VF	XF	Unc
1622 IC	—	90.00	170	300	625	—
1622 IH	—	90.00	170	300	625	—

KM# 9 1/4 THALER

Silver **Note:** Similar to 24 Kreuzer KM#8, but 1/4 below bust and without date.

Date	Mintage	VG	F	VF	XF	Unc
ND(1622) IC	—	—	—	—	—	—

GOLDBERG

A provincial town in Silesia founded in 1211 at the site of a gold mine. A local coinage was struck during the Kipper period of the Thirty Years' War.

MINT OFFICIALS' INITIALS

Initials	Date	Name
GH	1612-23	Georg Heinecke
HB	Ca.1623	Unknown
MH	1604-20	Uncertain, perhaps Melchior Hoffmann in Kolln an der Spree

PROVINCIAL TOWN

REGULAR COINAGE

KM# 1 HELLER

Copper **Obv:** Silesian eagle above three mounds, value I below. **Note:** Uniface.

Date	Mintage	VG	F	VF	XF	Unc
ND(1621-22)	—	—	—	—	—	—

KM# 2 HELLER

Copper **Obv:** Silesian eagle above straight line, value I below divides mintmaster's initials. **Note:** Uniface.

Date	Mintage	VG	F	VF	XF	Unc
ND(1621-22) GH	—	—	—	—	—	—

KM# 3 HELLER

Copper **Obv:** Three circles with an eagle, GB and date. **Note:** Uniface.

Date	Mintage	VG	F	VF	XF	Unc
(16)23	—	—	—	—	—	—

KM# 4 2 HELLER

Copper **Obv:** Silesian eagle above three mounds, vlaue II below. **Note:** Uniface. Kipper 2 Heller.

Date	Mintage	VG	F	VF	XF	Unc
ND(1621-22)	—	—	—	—	—	—

KM# 5 3 HELLER

Copper **Obv:** Silesian eagle above three mounds, value III below. **Note:** Uniface. Kipper 3 Heller.

Date	Mintage	VG	F	VF	XF	Unc
ND(1621/2)	—	35.00	70.00	145	—	—

KM# 6 3 HELLER

Copper **Obv:** Smaller eagle dividing G-B. **Note:** Uniface.

Date	Mintage	VG	F	VF	XF	Unc
ND(1621-22)	—	35.00	70.00	145	—	—

KM# 7 3 HELLER

Copper **Obv:** H before III below eagle. **Note:** Uniface.

Date	Mintage	VG	F	VF	XF	Unc
ND(1621-22)	—	35.00	70.00	145	—	—

KM# 11 3 HELLER

Copper **Obv:** Silesian eagle above three mounds divides date 1-6/2-2 and G-B, ++III++ below **Note:** Uniface.

Date	Mintage	VG	F	VF	XF	Unc
16ZZ	—	45.00	90.00	180	365	—
16Z3	—	45.00	90.00	180	365	—

KM# 8 3 HELLER

Copper **Obv:** Silesian eagle above three mounds in circle, around +16. G. III. B. 22+ **Note:** Uniface.

Date	Mintage	VG	F	VF	XF	Unc
1622	—	45.00	90.00	180	365	—

KM# 9 3 HELLER

Copper **Obv:** Silesian eagle above three mounds divides date and G-B, value III below. **Note:** Uniface.

Date	Mintage	VG	F	VF	XF	Unc
16ZZ	—	45.00	90.00	180	365	—
ZZ61 MH Error date	—	45.00	90.00	180	365	—

KM# 10 3 HELLER

Copper **Obv:** H before III below **Note:** Uniface.

Date	Mintage	VG	F	VF	XF	Unc
16ZZ	—	45.00	90.00	180	365	—

KM# 12 3 HELLER

Copper **Obv:** Three circles, eagle in top circle divides 1-6, bottom two circles have GB and III, 22 below. **Note:** Uniface.

Date	Mintage	VG	F	VF	XF	Unc
1622	—	50.00	100	200	425	—

KM# 14 3 HELLER

Copper **Obv:** Silesian eagle above three mounds divides date 1-6/2-3, G III B below **Note:** Uniface.

Date	Mintage	VG	F	VF	XF	Unc
1623	—	37.00	75.00	150	300	—

KM# 15 3 HELLER

Copper **Obv:** G-B separated by mounds, G III H below **Note:** Uniface.

Date	Mintage	VG	F	VF	XF	Unc
1623 GH	—	45.00	90.00	180	360	—

KM# 16 3 HELLER

Copper **Obv:** Silesian eagle above three mounds, GB and III, date divided near top in trefoil. **Note:** Uniface.

Date	Mintage	VG	F	VF	XF	Unc
(16)23	—	33.00	65.00	135	270	—
(16)23 HB	—	33.00	65.00	135	270	—

KM# 17 3 HELLER

Copper **Obv:** Three mounds, GB and III, date in center trefoil **Note:** Uniface.

Date	Mintage	VG	F	VF	XF	Unc
(16)23	—	45.00	90.00	180	360	—

KM# 18 3 HELLER

Copper **Obv:** Date 16/23 above, GB and III below, three mounds in center in trefoil. **Note:** Uniface.

Date	Mintage	VG	F	VF	XF	Unc
1623	—	45.00	90.00	180	360	—

KM# 19 3 HELLER

Copper **Obv:** Three mounds above, 16-23 below, GB III in center in trefoil **Note:** Uniface.

Date	Mintage	VG	F	VF	XF	Unc
1623	—	45.00	90.00	180	360	—

KM# 20 3 HELLER

Copper **Obv:** GB above, III and 23 below, three mounds in center in trefoil **Note:** Uniface.

Date	Mintage	VG	F	VF	XF	Unc
(16)23	—	45.00	90.00	180	360	—

KM# 21 3 HELLER

Copper **Obv:** III above, GB and 23 below in trefoil **Note:** Uniface.

Date	Mintage	VG	F	VF	XF	Unc
(16)23	—	45.00	90.00	180	360	—

KM# 22 3 HELLER

Copper **Obv:** Three circles, eagle in top circle divides date, GB and III in lower circles **Note:** Uniface.

Date	Mintage	VG	F	VF	XF	Unc
(16)23	—	45.00	90.00	180	360	—

KM# 23 3 HELLER

Copper **Obv:** Three circles, 23 in top, GB and III in lower circles **Note:** Uniface.

Date	Mintage	VG	F	VF	XF	Unc
(16)23	—	45.00	90.00	180	360	—

KM# 24 3 HELLER

Copper **Obv:** Three mounds replace 23 in top circle which divides date **Note:** Uniface.

Date	Mintage	VG	F	VF	XF	Unc
(16)23	—	45.00	90.00	180	360	—
(16)23 GH	—	45.00	90.00	180	360	—

KM# 25 3 HELLER

Copper **Obv:** Circle divided into four segments, Silesian eagle top left, GB top right, three mounds above 2 bottom left, III above 3 bottom right. **Note:** Uniface.

Date	Mintage	VG	F	VF	XF	Unc
(16)23	—	50.00	100	200	425	—

GORLITZ

A provincial city located about 60 miles east of Dresden on the Neisse River in Upper Lusatia (Oberlausitz). Görlitz received the mint right in 1330. Kipper coins were issued there during the early part of the Thirty Years' War. The city passed to Prussia in 1815.

REFERENCES

Sch = Wolfgang Schulten, ***Deutsche Münzen aus der Zeit Karls V.***, Frankfurt am Main, 1976.

S = Hugo Frhr. Von Saurma-Jeltsch, **Die Saurmasche Münzsammlung deutscher, schweizerischer und polnischer Gepräge von etwa dem Beginn der Groschenzeit bis zur Kipperperiode**, Berlin, 1892.

PROVINCIAL CITY

REGULAR COINAGE

KM# 1 PFENNIG

Copper **Obv:** Large crown above G divides date. **Note:** Kipper Pfennig. Uniface.

Date	Mintage	VG	F	VF	XF	Unc
ND(1621-22)	—	13.00	25.00	45.00	90.00	—
16Z1	—	13.00	25.00	45.00	90.00	—

KM# 2 PFENNIG

Copper **Obv:** GOR, crown above, date below. **Note:** Uniface.

Date	Mintage	VG	F	VF	XF	Unc
1622	—	—	—	—	—	—

KM# 3 DREIER (3 Pfennig)

Copper **Obv:** Three arms (crown, lion, eagle) arranged in clover leaf, value 3 in center, G-O-R between shields around **Note:** Uniface.

Date	Mintage	VG	F	VF	XF	Unc
ND(1621-22)	—	—	—	—	—	—
1622	—	—	—	—	—	—

KM# 4 3 KREUZER (Groschen)

0.5000 g., Billon, 16.8 mm. **Obv:** Lion rampant left, date in legend **Rev:** Crowned imperial eagle, 3 in orb on breast, titles of Ferdinand II **Note:** Kipper 3 Kreuzer. Varieties exist.

Date	Mintage	VG	F	VF	XF	Unc
ND(1621-22)	—	55.00	110	225	450	—
16ZZ	—	55.00	110	225	450	—
1622	—	55.00	110	225	450	—
1623	—	55.00	110	225	450	—

GORZE

A monastery located within the city of Gorze southeast of Metz in Lorraine, was founded in 745 by Bishop Chrodegang. In 1543 it and the city were captured from the duke of Guise and taken possession of by the French. It was secularized in 1580 but remained a cloister until 1752.

RULERS

Charles de Guise, 1572-1603
Karl von Remoncourt, 1603-1648

ABBEY

REGULAR COINAGE

KM# 10 TESTON

Silver **Ruler:** Karl **Obv:** Head to right **Obv. Legend:** CAR • A LOTH • D • A • ET S • S • A • G • SVP • DNS • GORZ • AB **Rev:** Shield of Lothringen arms **Rev. Legend:** MONETA NOVA GORZIAE CVSA

Date	Mintage	VG	F	VF	XF	Unc
ND(1603-30)	—	—	—	—	—	—

KM# 20 THALER

Silver **Ruler:** Karl **Obv:** Bust to right **Obv. Legend:** CAROL. A. LOTH. D. ET. S. S. A. G. SVPRE. DNS. GORZ. AB. **Rev:** Crowned shield of manifold arms in ornamented frame **Rev. Legend:** MONETA. ARGENTEA. GORZIÆ. CVSA. **Note:** Dav. #5319

Date	Mintage	VG	F	VF	XF	Unc
ND(1603-30) Rare	—	—	—	—	—	—

KM# 21 THALER

Silver **Ruler:** Karl **Obv:** Bust to right in circle **Obv. Legend:** CAROL. A LOTH. D. ET. S. S. A. G. SVP. DNS. GORZIENS. AB. **Rev:** Crowned shield of manifold arms in ornamented frame **Rev. Legend:** MONETA. ARGENTEA. GORZIENSIS. CVSSA. **Note:** Dav. #5320.

Date	Mintage	VG	F	VF	XF	Unc
ND(1603-30) Rare	—	—	—	—	—	—

KM# 22 THALER

Silver **Ruler:** Karl **Obv:** Bust to right divides date, in circle **Obv. Legend:** CAROLVS. A LOTH. D. ET. S. S. A. G. SVP. DNS. GORZ. A. **Rev:** Crowned shield of manifold arms in ornamented frame **Rev. Legend:** MONETA. ARGENTEA GORZIÆ. CVSA. **Note:** Dav. #5321.

Date	Mintage	VG	F	VF	XF	Unc
1630 Rare	—	—	—	—	—	—

KM# 35 THALER

Silver **Ruler:** Karl **Obv:** Partial date end of legend above bust **Note:** Dav. #5321A.

Date	Mintage	VG	F	VF	XF	Unc
(1640) Rare	—	—	—	—	—	—

TRADE COINAGE

KM# 30 2 DUCAT

7.0000 g., 0.9860 Gold 0.2219 oz. AGW **Ruler:** Karl **Obv:** Bust to right in circle **Obv. Legend:** CAR • A • LOTH • D • S • S • A • G • SVP • DNS • GO • AB • **Rev:** Crowned shield of manifold arms in ornamented frame **Rev. Legend:** MONETA • AVREA • GORZ • CVSA •

Date	Mintage	VG	F	VF	XF	Unc
ND(1603-30) Rare	—	—	—	—	—	—

GOSLAR

The small city of Goslar is located on the northern flank of the Harz Mountains, about 26 miles (44 kilometers) west of Halberstadt. It was founded as a free city by Emperor Heinrich I (918-936) about the year 920 and was later a royal residence, as well as the site of an imperial mint. Goslar was ideally situated close to mines in the Harz Mountains which produced an abundance of metals including copper and silver among others. The growing town became a member of the Hanseatic League in the mid-14th century and was soon producing its own coinage. The free imperial status of Goslar came to an end in 1802 when it passed to the rule of Prussia. It became a part of the Kingdom of Westphalia from 1807 until 1813, after which it was returned to Prussia for a short time. It was then assigned to Hannover in the peace which ended the Napoleonic Wars in 1815. When Hannover was annexed by Prussia in 1866, Goslar was once again in the Prussian fold.

MINT OFFICIALS' INITIALS

Initials	Date	Name
CHS	1674-75	Christoph Heinrich Schluter
GK	Ca.1619-28	Georg Kruckenberg
ICB	1663-68	Johann Christoph Bahr
IW	Ca.1671	Unknown, possibly Julius Wefer

ARMS

Crowned eagle

REFERENCES

C = Heinrich Philipp Cappe, **Beschreibung der Münzen von Goslar**, Dresden, 1860.

Sch = Wolfgang Schulten, ***Deutsche Münzen aus der Zeit Karls V.***, Frankfurt am Main, 1976.

S = Hugo Frhr. Von Saurma-Jeltsch, **Die Saurmasche Münzsammlung deutscher, schweizerischer und polnischer Gepräge von etwa dem Beginn der Groschenzeit bis zur Kipperperiode,** Berlin, 1892.

FREE CITY

REGULAR COINAGE

KM# 20 FLITTER

Copper **Obv:** Eagle with G on breast **Rev. Inscription:** I / FLIT / TER / date **Note:** Kipper Flitter.

Date	Mintage	VG	F	VF	XF	Unc
(1)6Z0	—	10.00	25.00	45.00	90.00	—

KM# 21 FLITTER

Copper **Rev. Inscription:** I / FLITTER / date

Date	Mintage	VG	F	VF	XF	Unc
(1)6Z0	—	10.00	25.00	45.00	90.00	—

KM# 42 PFENNIG

Billon **Obv. Inscription:** GOS / date **Note:** Uniface, hohl-type.

Date	Mintage	VG	F	VF	XF	Unc
16Z8	—	33.00	55.00	110	225	—
1633	—	33.00	55.00	110	225	—
1638	—	33.00	55.00	110	225	—
164Z	—	33.00	55.00	110	225	—

KM# 41 PFENNIG

Billon **Obv:** Eagle in ornately-shaped shield, GOS (or GOSL) above divides date **Note:** Uniface, hohl-type. Varieties exist.

Date	Mintage	VG	F	VF	XF	Unc
1628	—	33.00	55.00	110	225	—
1629	—	33.00	55.00	110	225	—
1630	—	33.00	55.00	110	225	—
1676	—	33.00	55.00	110	225	—
1677	—	33.00	55.00	110	225	—
1693	—	33.00	55.00	110	225	—

KM# 50 PFENNIG

Billon **Obv:** Crowned G divides date.

Date	Mintage	VG	F	VF	XF	Unc
1634	—	33.00	65.00	120	240	—

KM# 61 PFENNIG

Billon **Obv:** GOS/ date **Note:** Uniface. Varieties exist.

Date	Mintage	VG	F	VF	XF	Unc
1664	—	33.00	60.00	110	225	—
1668	—	33.00	60.00	110	225	—

KM# 12 3 PFENNIG (Dreier)

Silver **Obv:** Eagle in ornamented shield **Rev:** Imperial orb with 3 divides date above

Date	Mintage	VG	F	VF	XF	Unc
1615	—	—	—	—	—	—

KM# 13 3 PFENNIG (Dreier)

Silver **Obv:** Eagle

Date	Mintage	VG	F	VF	XF	Unc
1616	—	—	—	—	—	—

KM# 32 3 PFENNIG (Dreier)

Silver **Obv:** Eagle in ornately-shaped shield, GOSLAR above **Note:** Kipper 3 Pfennig.

Date	Mintage	VG	F	VF	XF	Unc
1622	—	33.00	65.00	130	265	—

KM# 33 3 PFENNIG (Dreier)

Silver **Obv:** Eagle arms in baroque frame

Date	Mintage	VG	F	VF	XF	Unc
1622	—	33.00	65.00	130	265	—

KM# 34 3 PFENNIG (Dreier)

Silver, 18 mm. **Obv:** Eagle, head left, G on breast **Rev:** Imperial orb with 3 divides date, all in rhombus

Date	Mintage	Good	VG	F	VF	XF
1622	—	—	40.00	85.00	175	220

KM# 65 3 PFENNIG (Dreier)

Silver **Rev:** Without rhombus

Date	Mintage	VG	F	VF	XF	Unc
1671 IW	—	20.00	40.00	80.00	160	—

KM# 70 3 PFENNIG (Dreier)

Silver **Obv:** GOS/ LAR/ date **Rev:** Imperial orb with 3

Date	Mintage	VG	F	VF	XF	Unc
1676	—	20.00	40.00	80.00	160	—

KM# 71 3 PFENNIG (Dreier)

Silver **Obv:** GOS/ date

Date	Mintage	VG	F	VF	XF	Unc
1676	—	20.00	40.00	80.00	160	—

KM# 60 4 PFENNIG (Gute)

Silver **Obv:** Eagle **Rev. Inscription:** IIII / GUTE / 16PF63 / mintmaster's initials (if present)

Date	Mintage	VG	F	VF	XF	Unc
1663 ICB	—	16.00	40.00	80.00	160	—
1668 ICB	—	16.00	40.00	80.00	160	—
1676	—	16.00	40.00	80.00	160	—

KM# 39 6 PFENNIG

Silver **Obv:** Crowned imperial eagle, 6 in orb on breast, titles of Ferdinand II **Rev:** Madonna and child, date in legend

Date	Mintage	VG	F	VF	XF	Unc
1623	—	—	—	—	—	—

KM# 29 MARIENGROSCHEN

Silver **Obv:** Madonna and child surrounded by flames **Rev:** Eagle, date in legend

Date	Mintage	VG	F	VF	XF	Unc
16Z1	—	—	—	—	—	—

KM# 62 MARIENGROSCHEN

Silver **Note:** Similar to KM#29

Date	Mintage	VG	F	VF	XF	Unc
1668 ICB	—	40.00	80.00	130	265	—
1671 ICB	—	30.00	60.00	100	200	—

KM# 43 1/36 THALER

Silver **Obv:** Madonna and child surrounded by flames **Rev:** Eagle, date divided below, 36 in imperial orb above

Date	Mintage	VG	F	VF	XF	Unc
1628 GK	—	—	—	—	—	—

KM# 5 1/24 THALER (Groschen)

Silver **Obv:** Eagle head left **Rev:** Imperial orb with 24 divides date, titles of Rudolf II

Date	Mintage	VG	F	VF	XF	Unc
1605	—	—	—	—	—	—

KM# 14 1/24 THALER (Groschen)
Silver **Rev:** Titles of Matthias

Date	Mintage	VG	F	VF	XF	Unc
1615	—	20.00	35.00	75.00	155	—
1618	—	20.00	35.00	75.00	155	—
1619	—	20.00	35.00	75.00	155	—
1620	—	20.00	35.00	75.00	155	—

KM# 24 1/24 THALER (Groschen)
Silver **Obv:** Titles of Ferdinand II **Note:** Kipper 1/24 Thaler.

Date	Mintage	VG	F	VF	XF	Unc
ND	—	27.00	45.00	80.00	160	—

KM# 30 1/24 THALER (Groschen)
Silver **Obv:** Imperial orb with 24, titles of Ferdinand II, date in legend **Rev:** Eagle

Date	Mintage	VG	F	VF	XF	Unc
(16)21	—	27.00	45.00	80.00	160	—

KM# 35 1/24 THALER (Groschen)
Silver **Obv:** Crowned imperial eagle, 24 in orb on breast, titles of Ferdinand II **Rev:** Helmeted eagle arms

Date	Mintage	VG	F	VF	XF	Unc
1622	—	27.00	45.00	80.00	160	—

KM# 40 1/24 THALER (Groschen)
Silver **Obv:** Imperial orb with 24 divides date above, titles of Ferdinand II

Date	Mintage	VG	F	VF	XF	Unc
16Z3 GK	—	27.00	45.00	80.00	160	—

KM# A12 12 KREUZER
Silver **Obv:** Crowned imperial eagle, 12 in orb on breast, titles of Ferdinand II and date (where present) in legend **Rev:** Eagle in circle

Date	Mintage	VG	F	VF	XF	Unc
1620	—	33.00	75.00	125	250	—
ND(1620/1)	—	33.00	75.00	125	250	—

KM# 28 12 KREUZER
Silver **Rev:** Date in legend **Note:** Varieties exist.

Date	Mintage	VG	F	VF	XF	Unc
1621	—	33.00	75.00	125	250	—

KM# 23 24 KREUZER
Silver **Obv:** Crowned imperial eagle, 24 in orb on breast, titles of Ferdinand II **Rev:** Eagle in circle

Date	Mintage	VG	F	VF	XF	Unc
ND(1620/21)	—	45.00	100	180	360	—

KM# 31 1/6 THALER (4 Groschen)
Silver **Obv:** Madonna and child, date in legend **Rev:** Crowned imperial eagle, 4 in orb on breast, titles of Ferdinand II **Note:** Kipper 1/6 Thaler.

Date	Mintage	VG	F	VF	XF	Unc
(16)21	—	70.00	140	230	475	—

KM# 68 1/6 THALER (4 Groschen)
Silver **Obv:** Eagle, value 1/6 below **Rev. Inscription:** IIII / GVTE / GROSCH / EN / date **Note:** 4 Gute Groschen 1/6 Thaler.

Date	Mintage	VG	F	VF	XF	Unc
1674 CHS	—	—	—	—	—	—

KM# 56 1/4 THALER (6 Groschen)
Silver **Obv:** Madonna and child surrounded by flames, eagle in shield below **Rev:** Crowned imperial eagle, 6 in orb on breast, date divides above claws, titles of Leopold I

Date	Mintage	VG	F	VF	XF	Unc
1659	—	—	—	—	—	—

KM# 10.1 1/2 THALER (12 Groschen)
Silver **Obv:** Madonna and child surrounded by flames, eagle in shield below **Rev:** Titles of Rudolf II **Note:** Dav. #5322.

Date	Mintage	VG	F	VF	XF	Unc
1610	—	450	1,100	1,800	3,200	—

KM# 10.2 1/2 THALER (12 Groschen)
Silver **Rev. Legend:** RUDOL * II * ROM * IMPER * SEMP * AU **Note:** Dav. #5323.

Date	Mintage	F	VF	XF	Unc	BU
1611	—	600	1,050	1,800	3,200	—

KM# 11 1/2 THALER (12 Groschen)
Silver **Rev:** 24 in orb on eagle's breast

Date	Mintage	VG	F	VF	XF	Unc
1610	—	—	—	—	—	—

KM# 36 1/2 THALER (12 Groschen)
Silver **Obv:** Crowned imperial eagle, 1Z in orb on breast, titles of Ferdinand II **Rev:** Madonna and child surrounded by flames, eagle in shield below, date in legend

Date	Mintage	VG	F	VF	XF	Unc
16ZZ GK	—	—	—	—	—	—

KM# 37 1/2 THALER (12 Groschen)
Silver **Obv:** Titles of Ferdinand II **Note:** Dav. #5324.

Date	Mintage	VG	F	VF	XF	Unc
16ZZ	—	750	1,300	1,950	3,300	—
16ZZ GK	—	750	1,300	1,950	3,300	—
16Z3	—	750	1,300	1,950	3,300	—
16Z8	—	750	1,300	1,950	3,300	—

KM# 38 1/2 THALER (12 Groschen)
Silver **Obv:** Z4 in orb on eagle's breast

Date	Mintage	VG	F	VF	XF	Unc
16ZZ	—	800	1,400	2,400	4,300	—

KM# 44.1 1/2 THALER (12 Groschen)
Silver **Obv:** Date at bottom **Note:** Dav. #5325.

Date	Mintage	VG	F	VF	XF	Unc
16Z8	—	750	1,300	1,950	3,300	—
16Z8 GK	—	750	1,300	1,950	3,300	—

KM# 44.2 1/2 THALER (12 Groschen)
Silver **Obv. Legend:** ...D: G: ROM: IMP: SEMP • AU • **Note:** Dav. #5326.

Date	Mintage	VG	F	VF	XF	Unc
16Z9 GK	—	750	1,300	1,950	3,300	—

KM# 51 1/2 THALER (12 Groschen)
Silver **Rev:** Date divided by eagle's claws, titles of Ferdinand III **Note:** Dav. #5327.

Date	Mintage	VG	F	VF	XF	Unc
1637	—	750	1,300	1,950	3,300	—

Note: Dates 1638 and 1642 probably do not exist; listing in Davenport due to misreading of Cappe

KM# 57 1/2 THALER (12 Groschen)
Silver **Obv:** Radiant Madonna above arms **Rev:** Titles of Leopold I

Date	Mintage	VG	F	VF	XF	Unc
1659	—	—	—	—	—	—

KM# 55.1 1/2 THALER (12 Groschen)
Silver **Note:** Similar to KM# 63. Dav. #5328.

Date	Mintage	VG	F	VF	XF	Unc
1650 Error of 1659	—	750	1,300	1,950	3,300	—

KM# 55.2 1/2 THALER (12 Groschen)
Silver **Obv:** Date divided above eagle's claws, titles of Leopold I **Note:** Dav. #5329.

Date	Mintage	VG	F	VF	XF	Unc
1659	—	750	1,300	1,950	3,300	—

KM# 69 24 MARIENGROSCHEN (2/3 Thaler)
Silver **Obv:** Helmeted arms with plumes **Rev:** Value and date within inner circle **Note:** Similar to KM#99.

Date	Mintage	VG	F	VF	XF	Unc
1675 CHS	—	80.00	135	275	550	—
1676 CHS	—	80.00	135	275	550	—

KM# 67 16 GUTE GROSCHEN (2/3 Thaler)
Silver **Obv:** 2/3 added below eagle **Rev:** Value XVI...

Date	Mintage	VG	F	VF	XF	Unc
1674 CHS	—	150	275	450	900	—
1675 CHS	—	125	250	450	900	—

KM# A67 16 GUTE GROSCHEN (2/3 Thaler)
Silver **Obv:** 2/3 below eagle **Rev. Inscription:** 16 / GUTE / GROSCH / EN / date **Note:** Mule of KM67 and KM66

Date	Mintage	VG	F	VF	XF	Unc
1674	—	100	200	375	775	—

KM# 66 16 GUTE GROSCHEN (2/3 Thaler)
Silver **Obv:** Eagle **Rev. Inscription:** 16 / GUTE / GROSCH / EN / date

Date	Mintage	VG	F	VF	XF	Unc
1674 CHS	—	100	200	375	775	—

TRADE COINAGE

KM# 45 GOLDGULDEN
3.5000 g., 0.9860 Gold 0.1109 oz. AGW **Obv:** Helmeted arms in inner circle **Rev:** Crowned imperial eagle in inner circle

Date	Mintage	VG	F	VF	XF	Unc
1628	—	1,450	3,000	6,000	10,000	—
ND	—	1,450	3,000	6,000	10,000	—

KM# 6 DUCAT
3.5000 g., 0.9860 Gold 0.1109 oz. AGW **Obv:** Imperial orb in trefoil, titles of Rudolf II and date in legend **Rev:** Eagle, head left **Note:** Fr.#1072.

Date	Mintage	VG	F	VF	XF	Unc
1605	—	1,600	3,300	7,800	12,000	—

KM# 25 DUCAT
3.5000 g., 0.9860 Gold 0.1109 oz. AGW **Obv:** Crowned imperial eagle, orb on breast, titles of Ferdinand II **Rev:** Helmeted city arms

Date	Mintage	VG	F	VF	XF	Unc
ND GK	—	1,500	2,800	5,800	10,000	—

KM# 26 DUCAT
3.5000 g., 0.9860 Gold 0.1109 oz. AGW **Obv:** Bust of Ferdinand II right **Rev:** Shield of arms **Note:** Fr.#1070.

Date	Mintage	VG	F	VF	XF	Unc
ND	—	1,400	2,650	5,600	8,900	—

KM# 27 DUCAT
3.5000 g., 0.9860 Gold 0.1109 oz. AGW **Obv:** Ferdinand II in inner circle **Note:** Fr.#1071.

Date	Mintage	VG	F	VF	XF	Unc
ND	—	1,100	2,150	4,500	7,200	—

GOTTINGEN

The provincial city of Göttingen is located in present-day Niedersachsen, 12 miles (20 km) south of Northeim and about 60 miles (100 km) south of Hannover. Göttingen is first mentioned in a document of 953 and received some limited self-governing rights in 1210. It was a seat of the Brunswick dukes from 1286 until 1442. By the 14th century, Göttingen was one of the foremost members of the Hanseatic League and obtained the mint right from the duke of Brunswick in 1351 and again in 1368. The earliest coinage of Göttingen consists of bracteates from the beginning of the 13th century, but dated coins begin in 1410 and continue intermittently until 1664. Coins of the Göttingen type with dates after 1664 are spurious issues of Count Gustav von Sayn-Wittgenstein. The town passed along with the rest of Brunswick-Hannover to Prussia in 1866.

MINT OFFICIALS' INITIALS

Initial	Date	Name
H, HL	1601-06	Hans Liphart
(e)= 	1601-07	Hans Lachentries, mintmaster
	1601-20, 1622	Hardege Hardege, warden
	1613	Andreas Laffert, mintmaster
(h)=  or 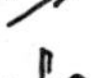	1614, 1624-25	Valentin Block, mintmaster
or (i)=		

(f)= 	1614-17	Hans Schlessewigk, mintmaster
	1618-19	Heinrich von der Ecke, mintmaster
(g)= 	1619-20, 1622	Steffen Ulmer, mintmaster
	1620-22	Hans Rukop, mintmaster
	1623-24	Levin Brockmann, mintmaster
	1624-26?	Franz Helfte, mintmaster
WN	1625-64	Wilhelm Nordmeier, warden
VB	1624-25	Valentin Block, warden
(j)=  or (k)=  +IE/IEV	1626-29	Jacob Eisenvalet, mintmaster
	1634-35, 1637-38, 1641	Heinrich Eichenberg, mintmaster
PL	1655-64	Peter (Heinrich) Lohr, mintmaster

REFERENCE

K = Anton Kapelhoff, ***Die Münzen Ostrieslands.*** Aurich, 1982.

S = Ulrich E. G. Schrock, ***Münzen der Stadt Göttingen,*** Brement, 1987.

PROVINCIAL CITY

REGULAR COINAGE

KM# 15 3 FLITTER

Copper **Obv:** Gothic G between rosettes **Rev:** III/ FLITTER/ date **Note:** Kipper 3 Flitter.

Date	Mintage	VG	F	VF	XF	Unc
1620	—	27.00	45.00	80.00	165	—
1621	—	27.00	45.00	80.00	165	—

KM# 16 PFENNIG

Copper **Obv:** Crowned gothic G **Rev:** I, date above **Note:** Kipper Pfennig.

Date	Mintage	VG	F	VF	XF	Unc
1621	—	27.00	45.00	80.00	165	—

KM# 26 PFENNIG

Copper **Obv:** Crowned gothic G divides date, where present. **Note:** Uniface schüssel type.

Date	Mintage	VG	F	VF	XF	Unc
ND(ca.1623-64)	—	20.00	40.00	80.00	165	—
(16)33 IE	—	20.00	40.00	80.00	165	—
1634	—	20.00	40.00	80.00	165	—
1635	—	20.00	40.00	80.00	165	—
1637	—	20.00	40.00	80.00	165	—
1638	—	20.00	40.00	80.00	165	—
1641	—	20.00	40.00	80.00	165	—
1656	—	20.00	40.00	80.00	165	—
1656 WN	—	20.00	40.00	80.00	165	—
1658	—	20.00	40.00	80.00	165	—
1659	—	20.00	40.00	80.00	165	—
1660	—	20.00	40.00	80.00	165	—
1661	—	20.00	40.00	80.00	165	—
1664	—	20.00	40.00	80.00	165	—

KM# 17 2 PFENNIG

Copper **Obv:** Crowned Gothic G **Rev:** II, date above **Note:** Kipper 2 Pfennig.

Date	Mintage	VG	F	VF	XF	Unc
1621	—	30.00	60.00	120	240	—

KM# 18 2 PFENNIG

Copper **Rev:** Date divided above and below II in quatrefoil

Date	Mintage	VG	F	VF	XF	Unc
1621	—	27.00	50.00	100	210	—

KM# 6 3 PFENNIG (Dreier)

Silver **Obv:** Crowned Gothic G **Rev:** Imperial orb with 3 divides date

Date	Mintage	VG	F	VF	XF	Unc
1601	—	27.00	55.00	110	225	—
1602	—	27.00	55.00	110	225	—

KM# 7 3 PFENNIG (Dreier)

Silver **Obv:** Crowned Gothic G in shield **Rev:** Imperial orb with 3 divides date in quatrefoil

Date	Mintage	VG	F	VF	XF	Unc
1602	—	33.00	65.00	130	265	—
1603	—	33.00	65.00	130	265	—

KM# A8 3 PFENNIG (Dreier)

Silver **Obv:** Crowned "G" in ornate shield **Rev:** Imperial orb with 3 in oval, cross on orb divides date, arabesque ornaments around oval

Date	Mintage	VG	F	VF	XF	Unc
160Z	—	35.00	75.00	150	300	—

KM# 19 3 PFENNIG (Dreier)

Silver **Obv:** Crowned Gothic G **Rev:** III, date above

Date	Mintage	VG	F	VF	XF	Unc
16Z1	—	25.00	40.00	75.00	155	—

KM# 20 3 PFENNIG (Dreier)

Silver **Note:** Varieties exist.

Date	Mintage	VG	F	VF	XF	Unc
16Z1	—	16.00	30.00	75.00	155	—

KM# 25 3 PFENNIG (Dreier)

Silver **Obv:** Crowned Gothic G **Rev:** Imperial orb with 3 divides date **Note:** Kipper 3 Pfennig.

Date	Mintage	VG	F	VF	XF	Unc
16ZZ	—	30.00	60.00	120	240	—
1623	—	30.00	60.00	120	240	—

KM# A30 3 PFENNIG (Dreier)

Silver **Obv:** Crowned ornate "G" **Rev:** Imperial orb with 3 divides date

Date	Mintage	VG	F	VF	XF	Unc
1635	—	33.00	65.00	130	265	—

KM# 35 3 PFENNIG (Dreier)

Silver **Obv:** Crowned Gothic G between two stars **Note:** Varieties exist.

Date	Mintage	VG	F	VF	XF	Unc
1657	—	27.00	55.00	115	230	—
1658	—	27.00	55.00	115	230	—
1659	—	27.00	55.00	115	230	—
1674	—	27.00	55.00	115	230	—
1675	—	27.00	55.00	115	230	—
1684 ILA	—	27.00	55.00	115	230	—

KM# 36 3 PFENNIG (Dreier)

Silver **Obv:** Crowned Gothic G, GOTTINGEN above

Date	Mintage	VG	F	VF	XF	Unc
1658	—	—	—	—	—	—

KM# 55 3 PFENNIG (Dreier)

Silver **Obv:** Crowned Gothic G divides date **Rev:** Imperial orb with 3 between two stars

Date	Mintage	VG	F	VF	XF	Unc
1672	—	—	—	—	—	—

KM# 21 4 PFENNIG

Copper **Obv:** Crowned Gothic G **Rev:** IIII, date above **Note:** Kipper 4 Pfennig.

Date	Mintage	VG	F	VF	XF	Unc
16Z1	—	20.00	40.00	80.00	160	—

KM# 22 4 PFENNIG

Copper **Note:** Similar to 3 Pfennig, KM#20 but IIII.

Date	Mintage	VG	F	VF	XF	Unc
16Z1	—	16.00	35.00	70.00	140	—

KM# 23 4 PFENNIG

Copper, 16.7 mm. **Rev:** IIII, date above

Date	Mintage	VG	F	VF	XF	Unc
16Z1	—	20.00	40.00	80.00	160	—

KM# 24 4 PFENNIG

Copper **Rev:** Value 4

Date	Mintage	VG	F	VF	XF	Unc
16Z1	—	—	—	—	—	—

KM# 45 4 PFENNIG

Silver **Obv:** Crowned Gothic G divides date **Rev:** IIII/G.PEN. (or PENI)

Date	Mintage	VG	F	VF	XF	Unc
1660	—	—	—	—	—	—
1664	—	—	—	—	—	—

KM# 39 MARIENGROSCHEN

Silver **Obv:** Crowned Gothic 'G', date **Obv. Legend:** MO • NO • GOTTIN • **Rev:** Madonna and child with rays around

Date	Mintage	VG	F	VF	XF	Unc
16ZZ	—	45.00	95.00	190	290	—

KM# 37 MARIENGROSCHEN

Silver **Obv:** Crowned Gothic G, date in legend **Rev:** Madonna and child

Date	Mintage	VG	F	VF	XF	Unc
1658	—	33.00	65.00	130	265	—
1659	—	33.00	65.00	130	265	—
1660	—	33.00	65.00	130	265	—

KM# 5 1/24 THALER (Groschen)

Silver **Obv:** Crowned Gothic G **Obv. Legend:** MO. NO. GOTTINGE. **Rev:** Imperial orb with Z4 divides date **Rev. Legend:** RU. II. RO. IM. SEM. AUG.

Date	Mintage	VG	F	VF	XF	Unc
1601 (e)	—	20.00	40.00	75.00	155	—
1602 (e)	—	20.00	40.00	75.00	155	—
1603 (e)	—	20.00	40.00	75.00	155	—
1605 (e)	—	20.00	40.00	75.00	155	—
1606 (e)	—	20.00	40.00	75.00	155	—
1606	—	20.00	40.00	75.00	155	—

KM# 8 1/24 THALER (Groschen)

Silver **Obv:** Crowned Gothic G **Obv. Legend:** MO. NO. GOTTINGE. **Rev:** Imperial orb with Z4 divides date **Rev. Legend:** RU. II. RO. IM. SEM. AUG. **Note:** Klippe.

Date	Mintage	VG	F	VF	XF	Unc
1603 (e) Rare	—	—	—	—	—	—
1605 (e) Rare	—	—	—	—	—	—
1606 Rare	—	—	—	—	—	—

KM# A9 1/24 THALER (Groschen)

Silver **Rev:** Without value Z4 in imperial orb **Note:** The dies for this coin may have been intended to strike goldgulden, but only known in silver.

Date	Mintage	VG	F	VF	XF	Unc
1606	—	20.00	40.00	85.00	170	—

KM# 11 1/24 THALER (Groschen)

Silver **Obv:** Imperial orb with 24 divides date, titles of Rudolf II **Rev:** Crowned Gothic G, but without value Z4 in imperial orb **Note:** Dies for this coin may have been intended to strike goldgulden, but only known in silver.

Date	Mintage	VG	F	VF	XF	Unc
1606	—	20.00	40.00	75.00	155	—

KM# 10 1/24 THALER (Groschen)

Silver **Obv:** Crowned Gothic G **Obv. Legend:** MO. NO. GOTTINGENSIS. **Rev:** Imperial orb with 24 divides date **Rev. Legend:** MATTHIAS. ROM. IM. S. **Note:** Varieties exist.

Date	Mintage	VG	F	VF	XF	Unc
1610	—	25.00	50.00	80.00	160	—
1614 (f)	553,000	25.00	50.00	80.00	160	—
1615 (f)	1,307,000	25.00	50.00	80.00	160	—
1615	Inc. above	25.00	50.00	80.00	160	—
1616	2,094,000	25.00	50.00	80.00	160	—
1617	1,676,000	25.00	50.00	80.00	160	—
1618	1,751,000	25.00	50.00	80.00	160	—
1619	1,368,000	25.00	50.00	80.00	160	—
1619 (g)	Inc. above	25.00	50.00	80.00	160	—
1620 (g)	1,912,000	25.00	50.00	80.00	160	—
ND (g)	—	25.00	50.00	80.00	160	—

KM# 12 1/24 THALER (Groschen)

Silver **Note:** Klippe.

Date	Mintage	VG	F	VF	XF	Unc
1614 Rare	—	—	—	—	—	—
1617 Rare	—	—	—	—	—	—

KM# A11 1/24 THALER (Groschen)

Silver **Note:** Ref. S#112, 119. Klippe.

Date	Mintage	VG	F	VF	XF	Unc
1614 (f) Rare	—	—	—	—	—	—
1617 Rare	—	—	—	—	—	—

KM# 14 1/8 THALER (1/2 Reichsort)

Silver **Obv:** Crowned ornate 'G' superimposed on cross in circle **Obv. Legend:** MONETA • NOVA GOTTINGENSIS • **Rev:** Date, titles of Ferdinand II

Date	Mintage	VG	F	VF	XF	Unc
16Z4	—	—	—	—	—	—

KM# 13 1/8 THALER (1/2 Reichsort)
Silver **Obv:** Crowned ornate "G" superimposed on cross in circle **Obv. Legend:** MONETA.NOVA - GOTTINGENSIS **Rev:** Titles of Ferdinand II **Rev. Inscription:** EIN / HALBE / REICHS / OERT / date **Note:** Ref. S#150.

Date	Mintage	VG	F	VF	XF	Unc
16Z4	—	—	—	—	—	—

KM# 29 1/4 THALER
Silver **Obv:** Small crowned Gothic G in ornamented frame divides date 1-6/Z-6 **Rev:** Crowned imperial eagle, orb on breast, titles of Ferdinand II

Date	Mintage	VG	F	VF	XF	Unc
1626 IEV(j)	—	—	—	—	—	—

KM# 30 1/4 THALER
Silver **Obv:** Crowned Gothic G, date in legend

Date	Mintage	VG	F	VF	XF	Unc
1627 IE(j)	—	—	—	—	—	—

KM# 43 1/2 THALER
Silver **Obv:** City arms in ornamented shield within circle, mintmaster's symbol and date **Obv. Legend:** MONETA • NOVA • GOTTINGENSIS **Rev:** Crowned imperial eagle, orb on breast, titles of Ferdinand II

Date	Mintage	VG	F	VF	XF	Unc
16Z4 (i)	—	—	—	—	—	—

KM# 44 1/2 THALER
Silver **Obv:** Large crowned 'G' superimposed on cross in circle, date **Obv. Legend:** MONET • NOVA GOTT **Rev:** Crowned imperial eagle, orb on breast, titles of Ferdinand II

Date	Mintage	VG	F	VF	XF	Unc
16Z8 IE(k)	—	—	—	—	—	—

KM# 46 1/2 THALER
Silver **Obv:** Crowned imperial eagle, orb on breast, titles of Leopold I **Rev:** Helmeted arms, crowned Gothic G above divides date

Date	Mintage	VG	F	VF	XF	Unc
1660 PL Rare	—	—	—	—	—	—

KM# 47 2/3 THALER (Gulden)
Silver **Obv:** Crowned imperial eagle, orb on breast, titles of Leopold I **Rev:** Helmeted arms, Gothic G above divides date

Date	Mintage	VG	F	VF	XF	Unc
1660 PL Rare	—	—	—	—	—	—

KM# 27 THALER
Silver **Obv:** Shield of city arms, ornate helmet above, all in circle, date at end of legend **Obv. Legend:** MONETA. NOVA. GOTTINGENSIS. **Rev:** Crowned imperial eagle, orb on breast **Rev. Legend:** FERDI. II. D.G. RO. IMP. SEMP. AVG. **Note:** Dav. #5330.

Date	Mintage	F	VF	XF	Unc	BU
1624 VB(h) Rare	—	—	—	—	—	—

KM# 28 THALER
Silver **Obv:** Crowned Gothic G in ornate frame, date at end of legend **Obv. Legend:** MONETA. NOVA. GOTTINGENSIS. **Rev:** Crowned imperial eagle, orb on breast **Rev. Legend:** FERDI. II. D.G. RO. IMP. SEMP. AVG. **Note:** Dav. #5331.

Date	Mintage	F	VF	XF	Unc	BU
1625 VB(h) Rare	—	—	—	—	—	—

KM# 38 THALER
Silver **Obv:** Shield of city arms surmounted with ornate helmet, Gothic G above divides date **Obv. Legend:** MONETA NOVA - GOTTINGENSIS. **Rev:** Crowned imperial eagle, 24 in orb on breast **Rev. Legend:** LEOPOLDVS. I. D.G. ROM. IMP. SEM. AVGVST. **Note:** Dav. #5332.

Date	Mintage	F	VF	XF	Unc	BU
1659 PL Rare	—	—	—	—	—	—

KM# A38 2 THALER
Silver **Note:** As thaler, struck from same dies.

Date	Mintage	VG	F	VF	XF	Unc
1659 PL Rare	—	—	—	—	—	—

KM# 40 2 THALER
Silver **Obv:** Crowned Imperial Eagle, 24 in orb on breast, titles of Leopold I **Rev:** Helmeted arms, Gothis 'G' above divides date **Note:** Struck from same dies as KM#38.

Date	Mintage	VG	F	VF	XF	Unc
1659 PL Rare	—	—	—	—	—	—

TRADE COINAGE

KM# A48 3 DUCAT
10.1900 g., 0.9860 Gold 0.3230 oz. AGW **Obv:** Shield of arms in inner circle **Rev:** Crowned Imperial Eagle in inner circle

Date	Mintage	VG	F	VF	XF	Unc
1660 PL Rare	—	—	—	—	—	—

KM# 48 4 DUCAT
14.0000 g., 0.9860 Gold 0.4438 oz. AGW **Obv:** Shield of arms in inner circle **Rev:** Crowned imperial eagle in inner circle **Note:** Fr.#1073.

Date	Mintage	VG	F	VF	XF	Unc
1660 Rare	—	—	—	—	—	—

PATTERNS

Including off metal strikes

KM#	Date	Mintage	Identification	Mkt Val
Pn1	1660 PL	—	2/3 Thaler. Lead. KM#47.	—

GREIFSWALD

Located near the Baltic coast about 18 miles (30 kilometers) southeast of Stralsund, Greifswald was an important trading center in Pomerania. Originally founded by merchants and traders from Holland about 1240, the town obtained civic rights from the duke of Pomerania some ten years later. In 1270, Greifswald allied itself with the Hanseatic League and obtained the mint right in 1398. Issues of silver small denominations continued into the 16th century. The city was besieged by the Swedes in 1631 and the Imperial Colonel Franz Ludwig Perusi, who commanded the defending garrison, had emergency coinage struck. After the capitulation of the imperial forces, Sweden held the city for most of the time between 1631 and 1715, then Denmark obtained it for a short while until 1721. After the Danish interlude, Greifswald returned to Swedish control until 1815, when all of Pomerania still held by Sweden was taken by Prussia.

ARMS

Field of cross-hatching divided by horizontal bar with a pellet in center.

REFERENCES

Sch = *Wolfgang Schulten,* ***Deutsche Münzen aus der Zeit Karls V.****, Frankfurt am Main, 1976.*

S = *Hugo Frhr.* ***Von Saurma-Jeltsch, Die Saurmasche Münzsammlung deutscher, schweizerischer und polnischer Gepräge von etwa dem Beginn der Groschenzeit bis zur Kipperperiode****, Berlin, 1892.*

Friedrich Wiegand, ***"Das Notgeld der Stadt Greifswald vom Jahre 1631," Berlineer Münzblätter 33 (1912), pp. 275-80.***

NOTE: All siege coinage of Greifswald is rare.

NOTE: Silver strikes were produced of KM#1, 3-5 in 1812. They are valued between $125. and $350 in VF.

CITY

OBSIDIONAL COINAGE

KM# 1 SCHILLING
29.0700 g., Lead Or Tin, 36-37 mm. **Obv:** Griffin left, front foot on tree stump, divides date, value 'I' above, all in pointillate circle **Obv. Legend:** NECESSITAS. GRYPSWALDENSIS. **Rev:** Crowned imperial eagle, shield of city arms on breast, in pointillate circle **Rev. Legend:** FERD. II. ROM. IMPF. SEMP. AVGVST &c.

Date	Mintage	VG	F	VF	XF	Unc
1631	—	—	—	5,000	6,000	—

KM# 2 SCHILLING
Lead Or Pewter **Obv:** Griffin rampant left on tree stump with new branches divides date, value 1 above, smaller module. **Obv. Legend:** GRYPSWALDENSIS ... **Note:** Uniface.

Date	Mintage	VG	F	VF	XF	Unc
1631 Rare	—	—	—	—	—	—

KM# 3 2 SCHILLING
Lead Or Tin, 33 mm. **Obv:** Griffin left, front foot on tree stump, divides date, value 'II' above, all in pointillate circle **Obv. Legend:** NECESSITAS. GRYPSWALDENSIS. **Rev:** Crowned imperial eagle, shield of city arms on breast, in pointillate circle **Rev. Legend:** FERD. II. ROM. IMPF. SEMP. AVGVST &c.

Date	Mintage	VG	F	VF	XF	Unc
1631	—	—	—	3,500	4,500	—

KM# 4 3 SCHILLING
Lead Or Tin, 40 mm. **Obv:** Griffin left, front foot on tree stump, divides date, value 'III' above, in pointillate circle **Obv. Legend:** NECESSITAS. GRYPESWALDIÆ. **Rev:** Crowned imperial eagle, shield of city arms on breast, in pointillate circle. **Rev. Legend:** FERD. II. ROM. IMPF. SEMP. AVGVST &c.

Date	Mintage	VG	F	VF	XF	Unc
1631	—	—	—	3,500	4,650	—

KM# 5 4 SCHILLING
Lead Or Tin, 37 mm. **Obv:** Griffin left, front foot on tree stump, divides date, value 'IIII' above, all in pointillate circle **Obv. Legend:** NECESSITAS. GRYPSWALDIÆ. **Rev:** Crowned imperial eagle, shield of city arms on breast, in pointillate circle **Rev. Legend:** FERD. II. ROM. IMPF. SEMP. AVGVST &c.

Date	Mintage	VG	F	VF	XF	Unc
1631	—	—	—	4,500	5,750	—

GRONSFELD

(Gronsveld, Gronsvelt)

The free barony of Gronsfeld was located southeast of Maastricht, near the Netherlands – German border. It was acquired by the countship of Bronkhorst-Batenburg by marriage in 1432. The lordship of Alpen was added by marriage in 1450. The rank of count was granted by the emperor in either 1585 or 1588. The ruling line became extinct in 1719 and Gronsfeld was divided among several heirs. A portion went to Diepenbroich, centered on Empel, near the Rhine in Westphalia. The other part was inherited by the countship of Töring, which was vassal to Limburg-Styrum.

RULERS

Johann II, 1588-1617
Jobst Maximilian, 1617-1662
Johann Franz, 1662-1719

MINT OFFICIALS' INITIALS

Initials	Date	Name
PN	1680-98	Peter Newers, mintmaster in Cologne

ARMS

Batenburg – crowned rampant lion left
Gronsfeld – 3 globes or spheres, usually arranged in triangular shape

REFERENCE

D = P.J.A.M. van Daalen, ***De Munten van het Graafschap Gronsveld***. Gronsveld, 1964.

COUNTSHIP

STANDARD COINAGE

KM# 13 4 MYTE
Copper **Ruler:** Jobst Maximilian **Obv:** Eagle, date **Rev:** Value: IIII

Date	Mintage	Good	VG	F	VF	XF
(16)38	—	27.00	55.00	115	200	—

KM# 8 DUIT
Copper **Ruler:** Jobst Maximilian **Obv:** Crowned shield of Batenburg lion in wreath **Rev:** Inscription in wreath, small shield of Gronsfeld arms at top **Rev. Inscription:** CO/ METAT/ GRON

Date	Mintage	Good	VG	F	VF	XF
ND(1617-62)	—	30.00	60.00	120	240	—

KM# 11 DUIT
Copper **Ruler:** Jobst Maximilian **Obv:** Crowned shield of Batenburg arms divides date in wreath **Rev:** Inscription in wreath, small Gronsfeld arms at bottom **Rev. Inscription:** IN/ GRON/ CVS

Date	Mintage	Good	VG	F	VF	XF
1636	—	30.00	60.00	120	240	—

KM# 9 OORD (1/4 Stuiver = 2 Duit)
Copper **Ruler:** Jobst Maximilian **Obv:** Crowned B-E over G in circle **Obv. Legend:** Titles of Jobst Maximilian **Rev:** Crowned four-fold arms with central shield in circle, titles continuous

Date	Mintage	Good	VG	F	VF	XF
ND(1617-62)	—	27.00	55.00	110	225	—

KM# 10 OORD (1/4 Stuiver = 2 Duit)
Copper **Ruler:** Jobst Maximilian **Obv:** Crowned four-fold arms with central shield **Obv. Legend:** Titles of Jobst Maximilian **Rev:** Four small shields of arms below large crown

Date	Mintage	Good	VG	F	VF	XF
ND(1617-62)	—	27.00	55.00	110	225	—

KM# 12 OORD (1/4 Stuiver = 2 Duit)
Copper **Ruler:** Jobst Maximilian **Obv:** Crowned bust to left **Obv. Legend:** Titles of Jobst Maximilian **Rev:** Crowned four-fold arms with central shield **Rev. Legend:** Titles of Ferdinand III

Date	Mintage	Good	VG	F	VF	XF
ND(1637-62)	—	25.00	50.00	100	210	—

KM# 18 1/3 THALER (1/2 Gulden)
Silver **Ruler:** Johann Franz **Obv:** Crowned arms **Obv. Legend:** Titles of Johann Franz **Rev:** Value 1/3 divides date **Rev. Legend:** Titles continuous

Date	Mintage	Good	VG	F	VF	XF
1688 PN	—	185	375	775	—	—
1692 PN	—	185	375	775	—	—
1693 PN	—	185	375	775	—	—

KM# 19 2/3 THALER (Gulden)
Silver **Ruler:** Johann Franz **Obv:** Crowned arms **Obv. Legend:** IOAN FRAN COMES AN BRONCKHORST IN GRONSFELDT (ET) **Rev:** Value 2/3 divides date **Rev. Legend:** (ET) EBERST L. B. IN BATTENB. ET RIMB. D. IN ALPEN ET HO(NNEPP). **Note:** D-67a; Dav. 529.

Date	Mintage	Good	VG	F	VF	XF
1688 PN	—	300	575	1,150	—	—
1692 PN	—	300	575	1,150	—	—
1693 PN	—	300	575	1,150	—	—

KM# 20 2/3 THALER (Gulden)
Silver **Ruler:** Johann Franz **Obv:** Crowned eight-fold arms, left four have central shield of Gronsfeld, date at end of legend **Obv. Legend:** IOAN: FRAN: COMES. A. BRONCKHORST. IN. GRONSFELT. **Rev:** Crowned script CBE monogram with palm fronds on either side, value 2/3 in oval below **Rev. Legend:** EBERST. L. B. I(N) BATT. & (ET) - RIMB. D. I(N). ALP. E (ET) HONN. **Note:** D-70, 70a; Dav. 530.

Date	Mintage	Good	VG	F	VF	XF
1692 PN	—	300	575	1,150	—	—
1693 PN	—	300	575	1,150	—	—
ND PN	—	300	575	1,150	—	—

KM# 21 2/3 THALER (Gulden)
Silver **Ruler:** Johann Franz **Obv:** Bust to left **Obv. Legend:** IOAN. FRANC: EX. ANTIQUA. BRONCKHORSTIO(R). **Rev:** Crowned manifold arms divide date and mintmaster's initials **Rev. Legend:** GRONSFELDIANORVM - COMITUM. FAMILIA. **Note:** D-71, 71a; Dav. 531.

Date	Mintage	Good	VG	F	VF	XF
1693 PN	—	300	575	1,150	—	—
1694 PN	—	300	575	1,150	—	—

KM# 16 THALER
Silver **Ruler:** Jobst Maximilian **Obv:** 4-line inscription, "Jehovah" in Hebrew above, ornament below **Rev:** Crowned arms in double legend **Note:** Dav. #4502. Prev. KM#10.

Date	Mintage	VG	F	VF	XF	Unc
ND(1658)	—	1,100	2,250	4,500	8,500	—

KM# 17 THALER
Silver **Ruler:** Jobst Maximilian **Obv:** Date below inscription **Rev:** Large crowned arms within single legend **Note:** Dav. #4503. Prev. KM#11.

Date	Mintage	VG	F	VF	XF	Unc
1658	—	2,000	4,000	7,500	13,500	—

KM# 15 2 THALER
57.9000 g., Silver, 56 mm. **Ruler:** Jobst Maximilian **Obv:** 4-line inscription, "Jehovah" in Hebrew above dividing date, ornament below **Rev:** Crowned arms in double legend **Note:** Klippe. Dav. #4501. Prev. KM#5.

Date	Mintage	VG	F	VF	XF	Unc
1642 Rare	—	—	—	—	—	—

Note: Hess-Divo AG Auction 300, 10-04, VF realized approximately $65,840.

TRADE COINAGE

KM# 14 DUCAT
3.4140 g., 0.9860 Gold 0.1082 oz. AGW **Ruler:** Jobst Maximilian **Obv:** Crowned four-fold arms with central shield **Obv. Legend:** MO • NO • AV • IVST • MAX • C • A • BR • IN • GR • **Rev:** Inscription in circle **Rev. Legend:** Titles continuous **Rev. Inscription:** date / IVSTVS / VI PALMA / FLORE / BIT **Note:** Prev. Fr. #86h.

Date	Mintage	VG	F	VF	XF	Unc
ND	—	1,000	2,000	4,000	7,500	—
1641	—	1,000	2,000	4,000	7,500	—
1642	—	1,000	2,000	4,000	7,500	—
1657	—	1,000	2,000	4,000	7,500	—
1664	—	1,000	2,000	4,000	7,500	—

GUBEN

A provincial town located about 25 miles south-southwest of Frankfurt am Oder. Guben passed to Brandenburg in about 1311 and then to Bohemia in 1368. Local coins were struck there during the Kipper Period of the Thirty Years' War. The town belonged to Saxony from 1635 until 1815 when it reverted to Prussia.

MINTMASTER"S INITIALS

Initials	Date	Name
ZL	Ca.1622	Unknown

PROVINCIAL TOWN

REGULAR COINAGE

KM# 3 PFENNIG
Copper **Obv:** Pfennig symbol in G **Note:** Uniface. Varieties exist.

Date	Mintage	VG	F	VF	XF	Unc
16Z1	—	25.00	45.00	85.00	190	—
1621	—	25.00	45.00	85.00	190	—
16ZZ	—	25.00	45.00	85.00	190	—
1622	—	25.00	45.00	85.00	190	—

KM# 1 PFENNIG
Copper **Obv:** Large crown above G divides date **Note:** Kipper Pfennig. Uniface. Varieties exist.

Date	Mintage	VG	F	VF	XF	Unc
16Z1	—	25.00	45.00	85.00	190	—
1621	—	25.00	45.00	85.00	190	—

Note: Above are possibly issues of Gorlitz

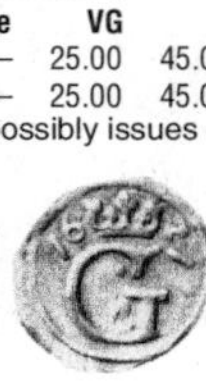

KM# 2 PFENNIG
Copper **Obv:** Small crown above large G divides date, dot in center **Note:** Uniface.

Date	Mintage	VG	F	VF	XF	Unc
16Z1	—	25.00	45.00	85.00	190	—
1621	—	25.00	45.00	85.00	190	—

KM# 4 3 KREUZER (Groschen)
Silver **Obv:** Crowned imperial eagle, 3 in orb on breast, titles of Ferdinand II **Rev:** Crown above triple-turreated gate, date in legend **Note:** Kipper 3 Kreuzer.

Date	Mintage	VG	F	VF	XF	Unc
1621	—	—	—	—	—	—
1622	—	—	—	—	—	—

KM# 5 3 KREUZER (Groschen)
Silver **Obv:** Bust right, titles of Ferdinand II **Rev:** Crowned triple-turreted gate, wtih G, 3 in oval below

Date	Mintage	VG	F	VF	XF	Unc
(1)622 ZL Rare	—	—	—	—	—	—

KM# 6 1/24 THALER (Groschen)
Silver **Obv:** Imperial orb with 24, titles of Ferdinand II **Rev:** Gothic G in circle, crown above divides date **Note:** Kipper 1/24 Thaler. Varieties exist.

Date	Mintage	VG	F	VF	XF	Unc
1622	—	33.00	65.00	130	265	—

GUTENBURG

ABBEY

REGULAR COINAGE

KM# 1 KREUZER
Copper, 20 mm. **Ruler:** Roman **Obv:** 4-iine inscription **Obv. Inscription:** BERG / WERKS. ZV / GVTEN / BVRG **Rev:** 3-line inscription with date **Rev. Inscription:** I / CREVZER / (date) **Mint:** Sankt Blasien

Date	Mintage	VG	F	VF	XF	Unc
1694	—	1,000	2,000	4,000	—	—

KM# 2 3 KREUZER
1.5400 g., Copper **Ruler:** Roman **Obv:** 4-line inscription **Obv. Inscription:** BERG / WERKS. ZV / GVTEN / BVRG **Rev:** 3-line inscription with date **Rev. Inscription:** III / CREVZER / (date) **Mint:** Sankt Blasien

Date	Mintage	VG	F	VF	XF	Unc
1694	—	125	250	500	1,000	—

KM# 3 15 KREUZER
4.2200 g., Copper **Ruler:** Roman **Obv:** Flaming iron furnace in circle **Obv. Legend:** EX. DVRO. LIQVIDVM. REDDITVR. QVIS. RE. **Rev:** 3-line inscription with date **Rev. Legend:** BVRGWERKS. ZV. GVTENBVRG. **Rev. Inscription:** XV / CREVZER / (date) **Mint:** Sankt Blasien

Date	Mintage	VG	F	VF	XF	Unc
1694	—	150	300	600	1,150	—

KM# 4 GULDEN
11.4100 g., Copper **Ruler:** Roman **Obv:** Flaming iron furnace in circle **Obv. Legend:** DVROS. INFERRVM. LAPIDES. CONVERTO. LIQVESCES. **Rev:** 3-line inscription with date **Rev. Legend:** BVRGWERKS. ZV. GVTENBVRG. **Rev. Inscription:** 1 / GVLDEN / (date) **Mint:** Sankt Blasien

Date	Mintage	VG	F	VF	XF	Unc
1694	—	250	650	1,350	2,750	—

HAGENAU

A city located in Alsace north of Strasburg, emerged in the 12th century. In 1257 Hagenau became a free imperial city but did not obtain the mint right until the 16th century. Although it passed, with other parts of Alsace, to France in 1648, coins continued to be minted in the emperor's name. In 1679 it was completely absorbed into France.

MINT OFFICIALS' INITIALS

Initial	Date	Name
	1600-1624	Philipp Wulvesheim, Mint Superintendant
	1600-1603 (d.1604)	Jakob Dietrich
	1600-1622	Hans Zaberer, Warden
	1603-1606	Ernst Knorr
	1606-1625	Hans Caspar Mock, Mintmaster
	1625-1634 (d.1636)	Mint Superintendant
	1622-ca.1630	Jakob Zeck, Warden
	1625-1630	Andreas Welland
	1630-1634	Johann Modersdorfer
	1634-1636	Johann Christian Herrmann, Mint Superintendant
(p) or GHP	1664-1673	Georg Hartmann Plappert

ARMS

Open rose with five petals

REFERENCE

E/L = Arthur Engel and Ernest Lehr, **Numismatique de l'Alsace**, Paris, 1887.

FREE IMPERIAL CITY

REGULAR COINAGE

KM# 5 HELLER
Silver **Obv:** Rose **Rev:** Rose

Date	Mintage	VG	F	VF	XF	Unc
ND Rare	—	—	—	—	—	—

KM# 14 PFENNIG
Silver **Obv:** City arms, H above **Note:** Uniface. Schussel type.

Date	Mintage	VG	F	VF	XF	Unc
ND(ca.1603/5)	754,000	20.00	35.00	75.00	155	—

KM# 15 PFENNIG
Silver **Obv:** Rose with H in center **Note:** Unifaace, schussel type.

Date	Mintage	VG	F	VF	XF	Unc
ND(ca.1603/5)	Inc. above	16.00	33.00	65.00	130	—

KM# 18 PFENNIG
Silver **Obv:** Rose **Rev:** Rose

Date	Mintage	VG	F	VF	XF	Unc
ND(ca.1608/14)	523,000	16.00	33.00	65.00	130	—

KM# 40 PFENNIG
Silver **Note:** Uniface.

Date	Mintage	VG	F	VF	XF	Unc
ND(ca.1625/6)	226,000	13.00	27.00	40.00	85.00	—

KM# 17 KREUZER
Silver **Obv:** City arms, date above **Rev:** Crowned imperial eagle, 1 in orb on breast, titles of Rudolf II

Date	Mintage	VG	F	VF	XF	Unc
1604 3 known	—	—	—	—	—	—

KM# 50 KREUZER
Silver **Rev:** Titles of Leopold I

Date	Mintage	VG	F	VF	XF	Unc
1664	—	15.00	30.00	60.00	120	—
1668	—	15.00	30.00	60.00	120	—
1669	—	15.00	30.00	60.00	120	—
1670	—	15.00	30.00	60.00	120	—
1671	—	15.00	30.00	60.00	120	—

KM# 41 2 KREUZER (1/2 Batzen)
Silver **Obv:** Shield of city arms, date above, where present, all in circle **Obv. Legend:** MONETA. HAGENO(I)ENSIS. **Rev:** Titles of Ferdinand II **Rev. Inscription:** II / KREUTZ / ER **Note:** E/L-65 (ND). Varieties exist.

Date	Mintage	VG	F	VF	XF	Unc
1625	—	15.00	30.00	60.00	120	—
ND	—	15.00	30.00	60.00	120	—

KM# 51 2 KREUZER (1/2 Batzen)
Silver **Obv:** Shield of city arms, date above, all in circle **Obv. Legend:** MONETA. NOV. CIV. HAGENOIEN(SIS). **Rev:** Crowned imperial eagle, value 2 in orb on breast, titles of Leopold I **Note:** E/L-

Date	Mintage	VG	F	VF	XF	Unc
1664 (p)	—	15.00	30.00	60.00	120	—
1665 (p)	—	15.00	30.00	60.00	120	—
1666 (p)	—	15.00	30.00	60.00	120	—
1667 (p)	524,000	15.00	30.00	60.00	120	—
1668 (p)	—	15.00	30.00	60.00	120	—

KM# 6 3 KREUZER (Groschen)
Silver **Obv:** Shield of city arms, date above, all in circle **Obv. Legend:** MONETA. HAGENOIENSIS. **Rev:** Crowned imperial eagle, value 3 in orb on breast **Rev. Legend:** RVDOL. II. RO. IMP. AVG. P. F. DEC. **Note:** E/L-17,20,23.

Date	Mintage	VG	F	VF	XF	Unc
1601	172,000	16.00	33.00	65.00	130	—
1602	144,000	16.00	33.00	65.00	130	—
1603	67,000	16.00	33.00	65.00	130	—
1604	115,000	16.00	33.00	65.00	130	—
1607	84,000	16.00	33.00	65.00	130	—
1608	44,000	16.00	33.00	65.00	130	—
1610	—	16.00	33.00	65.00	130	—
ND	—	16.00	33.00	65.00	130	—

KM# 16 3 KREUZER (Groschen)
Silver **Note:** Klippe.

Date	Mintage	VG	F	VF	XF	Unc
1603 Rare	—	—	—	—	—	—
1604 Rare	—	—	—	—	—	—

KM# 25 3 KREUZER (Groschen)
Silver **Rev:** Titles of Matthias

Date	Mintage	VG	F	VF	XF	Unc
ND(1612-19) Rare	—	—	—	—	—	—

KM# 11 4 KREUZER (Batzen)
Silver **Obv:** City arms, date above **Obv. Legend:** MONETA. ARGEN. CIVIT. HAGEN. **Rev:** Crowned imperial eagle, 4 in orb on breast, titles of Rudolf II

Date	Mintage	VG	F	VF	XF	Unc
1601	—	40.00	85.00	145	290	—
1602	—	40.00	85.00	145	290	—
1603	—	40.00	85.00	145	290	—
1604	—	40.00	85.00	145	290	—
1607	—	40.00	85.00	145	290	—
1608	—	40.00	85.00	145	290	—
1609	—	40.00	85.00	145	290	—

KM# 12 4 KREUZER (Batzen)
Silver **Obv:** Shield ornately-shaped, no date

Date	Mintage	VG	F	VF	XF	Unc
ND 3 known	—	—	—	—	—	—

KM# 36 4 KREUZER (Batzen)
Silver **Obv:** City arms **Rev:** Titles of Ferdinand II in legend **Rev. Inscription:** RAHTS / GELT

Date	Mintage	VG	F	VF	XF	Unc
ND	7,000	100	175	350	625	—

KM# 55 4 KREUZER (Batzen)
Silver **Obv:** City arms, date above **Rev:** Titles of Leopold I **Rev. Inscription:** RAHTS / GELT / date

Date	Mintage	VG	F	VF	XF	Unc
1666	—	100	175	350	625	—
1667	—	100	175	350	625	—

KM# 37 12 KREUZER (Zwölfer = Dreibätzner)
4.2200 g., Silver **Obv:** City arms in circle, date above, where present **Obv. Legend:** MONETA. ARGENT. CIVIT. HAGEN. **Rev:** Crowned imperial eagle, orb with value "IZ" on breast **Rev. Legend:** FERDINAND. II. ROM. IMP. SEM. AVG. **Note:** Kipper coinage.

Date	Mintage	VG	F	VF	XF	Unc
1621	—	120	260	425	800	—
ND(1621/2)	—	85.00	170	350	650	—

KM# 39 12 KREUZER (Zwölfer = Dreibätzner)
4.2200 g., Silver **Rev. Legend:** IVSTITIA MAMET IN AETER

Date	Mintage	VG	F	VF	XF	Unc
1623 Rare	—	—	—	—	—	—

KM# 42 12 KREUZER (Zwölfer = Dreibätzner)
4.2200 g., Silver

Date	Mintage	VG	F	VF	XF	Unc
1625	71,000	55.00	115	220	425	—
1626	Inc. above	55.00	115	220	425	—

KM# 53 12 KREUZER (Zwölfer = Dreibätzner)
4.5600 g., Silver **Obv:** Shield of city arms in baroque frame, date at end of legend **Obv. Legend:** MONE. ARGEN. CIVIT. HAGENOIENSIS. **Rev:** Imperial eagle with orb on breast **Rev. Legend:** LEOPOLD. I. D.G. ROMAN. IMP. SEMP. AVG. **Note:** E/L-70.

Date	Mintage	VG	F	VF	XF	Unc
1665	—	45.00	90.00	175	325	—

KM# 52.1 12 KREUZER (Zwölfer = Dreibätzner)
Silver Weight varies: 4.10-4.22g. **Obv:** Squarish shield of city arms with concave sides, date above, all in circle **Obv. Legend:** MON. ARGENT. CIVI(T). HAGENOEINSIS. **Rev:** Crowned imperial eagle, orb on breast, value 'XII' in oval at top **Rev. Legend:** LEOPOLD. I. D.G. ROM. IMP. SE. AVG. **Note:** E/L-88. Varieties exist.

Date	Mintage	VG	F	VF	XF	Unc
1665	—	45.00	100	175	325	—
1666	—	45.00	100	175	325	—
1667	10,000	45.00	100	175	325	—
1668	10,000	45.00	100	175	325	—
1669	—	45.00	100	175	325	—

KM# 58 12 KREUZER (Zwölfer = Dreibätzner)
4.9200 g., Silver **Obv:** Plain shield of city arms in circle **Obv. Legend:** MONET. ARGE. CIV. HAGENOENSIS. **Rev:** Crowned imperial eagle, orb with three pellets on breast, all in circle, value (XII) in cartouche at top **Rev. Legend:** LEOPOLD. I. D.G. ROM. IMP. S. AVG. **Note:** E/L-90.

Date	Mintage	VG	F	VF	XF	Unc
ND(ca1665)	—	60.00	115	235	475	—

KM# 52.2 12 KREUZER (Zwölfer = Dreibätzner)
4.9500 g., Silver **Obv:** Shield of city arms in ornate frame, date above, all in circle **Obv. Legend:** MONE. ARGEN. CIVIT. HAGENOIENSIS. **Rev:** Imperial eagle, orb on breast with single pellet, value (XII) at top **Rev. Legend:** LEOPOLD. I. D.G. ROM. IMP. SE. AVG. **Note:** E/L-83.

Date	Mintage	VG	F	VF	XF	Unc
1668	—	70.00	125	200	425	—

KM# 28.1 18 KREUZER (1/4 Thaler = Dicken)
Silver **Obv:** Shield of city arms with small ornaments at left, top and right, all in circle **Obv. Legend:** HAGENOIA * IMPERII * CANERA. **Rev:** Crowned imperial eagle, orb on breast **Rev. Legend:** IVSTITIA. MANET. IN. AETER.

Date	Mintage	VG	F	VF	XF	Unc
ND(c.1614)	38,000	55.00	120	225	450	—

KM# 29 18 KREUZER (1/4 Thaler = Dicken)
Silver **Note:** Klippe.

Date	Mintage	VG	F	VF	XF	Unc
ND Rare	—	—	—	—	—	—

KM# 28.2 18 KREUZER (1/4 Thaler = Dicken)
Silver **Obv:** Plain city arms **Obv. Legend:** IVSTITIA. MANET... **Rev:** Crowned imperial eagle, orb on breast **Note:** Prev. KM#28.

Date	Mintage	VG	F	VF	XF	Unc
1614	501,000	40.00	85.00	145	325	—

KM# 38 18 KREUZER (1/4 Thaler = Dicken)
Silver **Note:** Kipper 18 Kreuzer.

Date	Mintage	VG	F	VF	XF	Unc
1621	—	115	200	300	575	—

KM# 56 30 KREUZER (1/2 Gulden; 1/3 Thaler)
Silver

Date	Mintage	VG	F	VF	XF	Unc
1668	4,000	200	300	425	775	—
1669	—	200	300	425	775	—
1671	4,000	200	300	425	775	—

KM# 65 30 KREUZER (1/2 Gulden; 1/3 Thaler)
Silver **Obv:** Not enclosed in circles **Rev:** Not enclosed in circles

Date	Mintage	VG	F	VF	XF	Unc
1673 2 known	—	—	—	—	—	—

KM# 35 60 KREUZER (Guldentaler)
Silver **Obv:** City arms in ornate shield **Rev:** Date divided by eagle's tail, titles of Ferdinand II

Date	Mintage	F	VF	XF	Unc	BU
1620 2 known	—	—	—	—	—	—

KM# 66 60 KREUZER (Guldentaler)
19.2100 g., Silver, 36 mm. **Obv:** Shield of city arms in ornate frame divides date, value LX.K. above **Obv. Legend:** MONETA. ARG. CAM. AC. CIVIT. HAGENOENSIS. **Rev:** Crowned imperial eagle, orb on breast **Rev. Legend:** LEOPOLD. I. D.G. ROMANOR. IMP. SEMPER AUGUS. **Note:** E/L-93; Dav. 533.

Date	Mintage	VG	F	VF	XF	Unc
1673	—	550	1,000	1,700	3,150	—

KM# 57 60 KREUZER (Gulden = 2/3 Thaler)
Silver **Obv:** Shield of city arms in ornate frame divides sideways date, value LX - K above **Obv. Legend:** NVM. ARG. IMP. CAME. AC. CIVIT. HAGENO. **Rev:** Crowned imperial eagle, orb on breast **Rev. Legend:** LEOPOLD. I. D.G. ROMAN. IMP(E). SEM(P). AVG. **Note:** E/L-81, 86; Dav. 532.

Date	Mintage	VG	F	VF	XF	Unc
1668	2,000	600	1,100	1,800	3,250	—
1669	—	600	1,100	1,800	3,250	—

KM# 46 THALER

Silver **Obv:** City arms in ornate frame **Obv. Legend:** FERDINANDVS.II.D:G:... **Rev:** Crowned imperial eagle **Note:** Dav. #5333.

Date	Mintage	VG	F	VF	XF	Unc
1635 Rare	—	—	—	—	—	—

KM# 54 THALER

Silver **Obv:** City arms on shield **Obv. Legend:** LEOPOLDVS:I:D:G:... **Rev:** Crowned imperial eagle **Note:** Dav. #5334.

Date	Mintage	VG	F	VF	XF	Unc
1665 GH-P Rare	—	—	—	—	—	—

KM# 59 THALER

Silver **Obv:** City arms **Obv. Legend:** LEOPOLDVS:I:D:G:... **Rev:** Crowned imperial eagle **Rev. Legend:** ... HGEN **Note:** Dav. #5335.

Date	Mintage	VG	F	VF	XF	Unc
1668 GH-P Rare	—	—	—	—	—	—

TRADE COINAGE

KM# 13 GOLDGULDEN

3.5000 g., 0.9860 Gold 0.1109 oz. AGW **Obv:** Arms of Hagenau with date above in inner circle **Rev:** Crowned imperial eagle in inner circle, titles of Rudolf II

Date	Mintage	VG	F	VF	XF	Unc
1601	2,613	2,300	5,400	9,200	15,000	—
1604	1,474	2,300	5,400	9,200	15,000	—
1608	1,407	2,300	5,400	9,200	15,000	—
1609	670	2,300	5,400	9,200	15,000	—
1610	2,077	2,300	5,400	9,200	15,000	—
1611	1,608	2,300	5,400	9,200	15,000	—

KM# 26 GOLDGULDEN

3.5000 g., 0.9860 Gold 0.1109 oz. AGW **Obv:** St. John standing **Rev:** Imperial eagle, titles of Rudolf II

Date	Mintage	VG	F	VF	XF	Unc
ND	8,308	1,450	3,050	5,400	9,900	—

KM# 27 GOLDGULDEN

3.5000 g., 0.9860 Gold 0.1109 oz. AGW **Rev:** Titles of Matthias

Date	Mintage	VG	F	VF	XF	Unc
ND	5,025	1,650	3,300	6,100	11,000	—

KM# 45 GOLDGULDEN

3.5000 g., 0.9860 Gold 0.1109 oz. AGW **Rev:** Titles of Ferdinand II

Date	Mintage	VG	F	VF	XF	Unc
1634 Rare	1,340	—	—	—	—	—

HALBERSTADT

Bishopric transferred to Halberstadt, about 30 miles southwest of Magdeburg, in 820. Bishops were given the coin right in 989. The town received its charter in 998, and its coin right in 1363. The bishopric was assigned to Brandenburg as a secular principality in 1648. Dated city coinage was struck from 1519-1691.

RULERS

Heinrich Julius, Herzog von Braunschweig-Wolfenbüttel, 1566-1613
Heinrich Karl, Herzog von Braunschweig-Wolfenbüttel, 1613-1615
Rudolf III, Herzog von Braunschweig-Wolfenbüttel, 1615-1616
Christian, Herzog von Braunschweig-Wolfenbüttel, 1616-1624
Christian Wilhelm. Markgraf von Brandenburg-Preussen, 1625-1627
Leopold Wilhelm von Österreich, 1627-1648

MINT OFFICIALS' INITIALS

Initial	Date	Name
CZ	1628-31	Christoph Ziegenhorn
HS	1626-72	Henning Schluter in Zellerfeld
HS	1614-26	Henning Schreiber
IA	1653-65	Johann Arendsburg
ICS	1690-95	Johann Christoph Seehte in Magdeburg
(b)	1633-34	Unknown
(c)	1663	Unknown

ARMS

2-fold divided vertically, right half usually shaded.

REFERENCES

T = Otto Tornau, **Die Halberstädter Münzen der neueren Zeit**, Halberstadt, n.d.

Sch = Wolfgang Schulten, ***Deutsche Münzen aus der Zeit Karls V.***, Frankfurt am Main, 1976.

S = Hugo Frhr. Von Saurma-Jeltsch, **Die Saurmasche Münzsammlung deutscher, schweizerischer und polnischer Gepräge von etwa dem Beginn der Groschenzeit bis zur Kipperperiode**, Berlin, 1892.

BISHOPRIC

REGULAR COINAGE

KM# 7 1/24 THALER (Groschen)

Silver **Obv:** Value 24 **Note:** Varieties exist.

Date	Mintage	VG	F	VF	XF	Unc
1614	—	16.00	30.00	50.00	100	—
1615	—	16.00	30.00	50.00	100	—

KM# 10 1/24 THALER (Groschen)

Silver **Obv:** Value 24

Date	Mintage	VG	F	VF	XF	Unc
1616	—	16.00	30.00	50.00	100	—
1619	—	16.00	30.00	50.00	100	—

KM# 13 1/24 THALER (Groschen)

Silver **Obv:** Date divided by cross below legend

Date	Mintage	VG	F	VF	XF	Unc
1618	—	16.00	30.00	50.00	100	—

KM# 22 1/24 THALER (Groschen)

Silver **Obv:** Titles of Ferdinand II

Date	Mintage	VG	F	VF	XF	Unc
16ZZ	—	16.00	33.00	55.00	110	—
16Z3	—	16.00	33.00	55.00	110	—

KM# 55 1/24 THALER (Groschen)

Silver **Obv:** Helmeted oval arms **Rev:** Imperial orb with 4Z (error), date divided in legend at top

Date	Mintage	VG	F	VF	XF	Unc
1628 CZ	—	16.00	33.00	55.00	110	—

KM# 51 1/8 THALER

Silver **Subject:** Death of Christian **Obv:** Crowned 11-fold arms, double legends around **Rev:** 10-line inscription with Roman numeral date

Date	Mintage	VG	F	VF	XF	Unc
MDCXXVII (1627) HS Error	—	—	—	—	—	—

KM# 41 1/2 REICHSORT (1/8 Thaler)

Silver **Obv:** Oval arms in baroque frame below divide date **Obv. Inscription:** EIN. / HALB.REIC. / ORT **Rev:** St. Stephen standing

Date	Mintage	VG	F	VF	XF	Unc
16Z5	—	—	—	—	—	—

KM# 46 1/4 THALER

Silver **Subject:** Death of Christian **Obv:** Crowned 11-fold arms, double legends around **Rev:** 8-line inscription with Roman numeral date

Date	Mintage	VG	F	VF	XF	Unc
1626 HS	—	—	—	—	—	—

KM# 59 1/4 THALER

Silver **Obv:** Oval arms in baroque frame **Rev:** St. Stephen standing divides date **Note:** Varieties exist.

Date	Mintage	VG	F	VF	XF	Unc
1629 CZ	—	300	600	1,200	2,400	—
1631 CZ	—	300	600	1,200	2,400	—

KM# 69 1/4 THALER

Silver **Obv:** Helmeted oval arms

Date	Mintage	VG	F	VF	XF	Unc
1631 CZ	—	300	600	1,200	2,400	—

KM# 52 REICHSORT (1/4 Thaler)

Silver **Obv:** Oval arms in baroque frame **Rev:** Date **Rev. Inscription:** EIN. / REICHS. / ORTH.

Date	Mintage	VG	F	VF	XF	Unc
16Z8 CZ	—	250	500	950	1,750	—

KM# 47 1/2 THALER

Silver **Subject:** Death of Christian **Obv:** Crowned 11-fold arms, double legends around **Rev:** 9-line inscription around

Date	Mintage	VG	F	VF	XF	Unc
1626 HS	—	—	—	—	—	—

KM# 45 GULDEN (1/2 Reichsthaler)

Silver **Obv:** Oval arms in baroque frame **Rev:** St. Stephen standing divides date

Date	Mintage	VG	F	VF	XF	Unc
16Z5 HS	—	90.00	180	360	725	—

KM# 53 GULDEN (1/2 Reichsthaler)

Silver **Obv:** Ornately-helmeted oval arms **Note:** Varieties exist.

Date	Mintage	VG	F	VF	XF	Unc
16Z8 CZ	—	65.00	135	275	550	—
1628 CZ	—	65.00	135	275	550	—
16Z9 CZ	—	65.00	135	275	550	—
1629 CZ	—	65.00	135	275	550	—
ND CZ	—	65.00	135	275	550	—

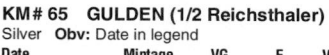

KM# 65 GULDEN (1/2 Reichsthaler)

Silver **Obv:** Date in legend

Date	Mintage	VG	F	VF	XF	Unc
1630 CZ	—	85.00	175	360	725	—
1631 CZ	—	85.00	175	360	725	—

KM# 26 THALER

Silver **Obv:** Titles of Christian around legend **Obv. Inscription:** GOTTES / FREVNDT / DER PFAFFEN / FEINDT **Rev:** Arm from cloud on right holding sword upright, date **Rev. Legend:** TOVT. AVEC. DIEV **Note:** Dav.#6320.

Date	Mintage	VG	F	VF	XF	Unc
1622	—	350	750	1,550	2,600	—
16ZZ	—	400	800	1,750	2,900	—

KM# 27 THALER

Silver **Obv. Legend:** FREINDT (error) **Note:** Dav.#6320A.

Date	Mintage	VG	F	VF	XF	Unc
1622	—	450	925	1,900	3,150	—

KM# 28 THALER

Silver **Rev:** Jesuit cap on point of sword **Note:** Dav.#6322.

Date	Mintage	VG	F	VF	XF	Unc
1622	—	575	1,050	2,000	4,050	—

KM# 29 THALER

Silver **Rev:** Crown on point of sword **Note:** Dav.#6323.

Date	Mintage	VG	F	VF	XF	Unc
1622	—	700	1,400	2,300	4,600	—

KM# 38 THALER

Silver **Obv:** 5 helmets above 11-fold arms, titles of Christian **Rev:** Wildman, tree trunk in right hand **Rev. Legend:** HONESTUM. PRO. PATRIA. ANNO. date HS **Note:** Dav.#6324.

Date	Mintage	VG	F	VF	XF	Unc
1623 HS	—	900	1,800	3,300	6,000	—

KM# 39 THALER

Silver **Rev. Legend:** DEO.ET.PATRIAE.ANNO. date HS **Note:** Dav.#6325.

Date	Mintage	VG	F	VF	XF	Unc
1623 HS	—	750	1,450	3,300	5,500	—

KM# 40 THALER

Silver **Obv:** Ornately-helmeted oval arms **Rev:** St. Stephen standing divides date **Note:** Dav.#5339.

Date	Mintage	VG	F	VF	XF	Unc
16Z3	—	150	300	600	1,200	—

KM# 43 THALER

Silver **Obv:** Helmeted shield **Note:** Dav.#5343.

Date	Mintage	VG	F	VF	XF	Unc
16Z5	—	250	500	800	1,500	—

KM# 48 THALER

Silver **Rev:** Symbol of Mercury below left 1/2 of date **Note:** Dav.#5345.

Date	Mintage	VG	F	VF	XF	Unc
1626 HS	—	300	600	1,250	2,000	—

KM# 49.1 THALER

Silver **Subject:** Death of Christian **Obv:** Crowned 11-fold arms, double legends broken by crown **Rev:** 10-line inscription with Roman numeral date **Note:** Dav.#6327.

Date	Mintage	VG	F	VF	XF	Unc
1626 HS	—	300	500	1,000	1,850	—

KM# 49.2 THALER

Silver **Obv:** Crown breaks outer legend only **Note:** Dav.#6328. Varieties exist.

Date	Mintage	VG	F	VF	XF	Unc
1626	—	300	600	1,200	2,000	—

KM# 56.1 THALER

Silver **Note:** Similar to KM#56.2. Dav.#5346.

Date	Mintage	VG	F	VF	XF	Unc
16Z8 CZ	—	225	450	750	1,350	—

KM# 60 THALER

Silver **Obv:** Date divided by helmet **Note:** Dav.#5347.

Date	Mintage	VG	F	VF	XF	Unc
16Z9 CZ	—	125	250	400	800	—

KM# 56.2 THALER

Silver **Note:** Dav.#5348. Varieties exist.

Date	Mintage	VG	F	VF	XF	Unc
16Z9 CZ	—	95.00	185	325	750	—

KM# 61 THALER

Silver **Note:** Klippe. Dav.#5347A.

Date	Mintage	VG	F	VF	XF	Unc
16Z9 CZ Rare	—	—	—	—	—	—

KM# 66.1 THALER

Silver **Obv:** Date in legend **Note:** Dav.#5349.

Date	Mintage	VG	F	VF	XF	Unc
1630 CZ	—	175	350	750	1,250	—

KM# 66.2 THALER
Silver **Obv:** Dots between date in outer legend **Note:** Dav.#5351. Varieties exist.

Date	Mintage	VG	F	VF	XF	Unc
1631 CZ	—	175	350	750	1,250	—

KM# 30 1-1/4 THALER
36.0000 g., Silver **Note:** Similar to 1 Thaler, KM#26 with value punched in. Dav.#6322A.

Date	Mintage	VG	F	VF	XF	Unc
16ZZ Rare	—	—	—	—	—	—

KM# 31 1-1/2 THALER
44.0000 g., Silver **Note:** Similar to 1 Thaler, KM#26 with value punched in. Dav.#6322A.

Date	Mintage	VG	F	VF	XF	Unc
16ZZ Rare	—	—	—	—	—	—

KM# 12 2 THALER
Silver **Obv:** Ornately-helmeted pointed oval arms, date divided in legend at top **Rev:** St. Stephen standing **Note:** Dav.#5337.

Date	Mintage	VG	F	VF	XF	Unc
1617 HS Rare	—	—	—	—	—	—

KM# 14 2 THALER
Silver **Obv:** Ornately-helmeted oval arms, date divided by plumes near top **Rev:** St. Stephen standing **Note:** Dav.#5338.

Date	Mintage	VG	F	VF	XF	Unc
1618 Rare	—	—	—	—	—	—
16Z8 CZ Rare	—	—	—	—	—	—

KM# 50 2 THALER
Silver **Subject:** Death of Christian **Obv:** Similar to reverse of 1 Thaler, KM#39 but with date 1620 **Rev:** 8-line inscription with Roman Numeral date **Note:** Mule. Dav.#6326.

Date	Mintage	VG	F	VF	XF	Unc
1620/1626 HS Rare	—	—	—	—	—	—

KM# 33 2 THALER
Silver **Note:** Similar to 1 Thaler, KM#26, but Jesuit cap on point of sword. Dav.#6321.

Date	Mintage	VG	F	VF	XF	Unc
1622 Rare	—	—	—	—	—	—

KM# 32 2 THALER
Silver **Note:** Similar to 1 Thaler, KM#26. Dav.#6319.

Date	Mintage	VG	F	VF	XF	Unc
1622 Rare	—	—	—	—	—	—

KM# 44.1 2 THALER
Silver **Note:** Similar to 1 Thaler, KM#56.

Date	Mintage	VG	F	VF	XF	Unc
16Z5 Rare	—	—	—	—	—	—

KM# 44.2 2 THALER
Silver **Note:** Similar to 1 Thaler, KM#56.2.

Date	Mintage	VG	F	VF	XF	Unc
1626 HS Rare	—	—	—	—	—	—

KM# 70 2 THALER
Silver **Note:** Dav.#5350.

Date	Mintage	VG	F	VF	XF	Unc
1631 CZ Rare	—	—	—	—	—	—

KM# 11 3 THALER
Silver **Obv:** Ornately-helmeted pointed oval arms, date divided in legend at top **Rev:** St. Stephen standing **Note:** Dav.#5336.

Date	Mintage	VG	F	VF	XF	Unc
1617 HS Rare	—	—	—	—	—	—

TRADE COINAGE

KM# 8 GOLDGULDEN
3.5000 g., 0.9860 Gold 0.1109 oz. AGW **Obv:** Arms divide date in inner circle **Rev:** St. Stephen standing in inner circle

Date	Mintage	VG	F	VF	XF	Unc
1615 1 known	1,165	—	—	—	—	—
1616 Rare	1,353	—	—	—	—	—
1617 Rare	594	—	—	—	—	—

KM# 34 DUCAT
3.5000 g., 0.9860 Gold 0.1109 oz. AGW **Obv. Inscription:** GOTTES / FREINT / VND / DER PAFFE / FEINT **Note:** Similar to 1 Thaler, KM#26.

Date	Mintage	VG	F	VF	XF	Unc
1622 Rare	—	—	—	—	—	—

KM# 35 2 DUCAT
7.0000 g., 0.9860 Gold 0.2219 oz. AGW **Note:** Similar to 1 Thaler, KM#26.

Date	Mintage	VG	F	VF	XF	Unc
1622 Rare	—	—	—	—	—	—

KM# 36 2 DUCAT
7.0000 g., 0.9860 Gold 0.2219 oz. AGW **Rev:** Jesuit cap on point of sword

Date	Mintage	VG	F	VF	XF	Unc
1622 Rare	—	—	—	—	—	—

KM# 37 10 DUCAT (Portugalöser)
35.0000 g., 0.9860 Gold 1.1095 oz. AGW **Note:** Similar to 1 Thaler, KM#26.

Date	Mintage	VG	F	VF	XF	Unc
1622 Rare	—	—	—	—	—	—

CATHEDRAL CHAPTER

REGULAR COINAGE

KM# 6 1/24 THALER (Groschen)
Silver **Rev:** Date divided by cross below legend

Date	Mintage	VG	F	VF	XF	Unc
1614	—	16.00	30.00	50.00	100	—
1615 (c)	—	16.00	30.00	50.00	100	—

KM# 5 1/24 THALER (Groschen)
Silver **Obv:** Ornate helmet above arms **Rev:** Imperial orb with Z4, date divided in legend above, titles of Matthias **Note:** Varieties exist.

Date	Mintage	VG	F	VF	XF	Unc
1614	—	16.00	30.00	50.00	100	—
1614 (c)	—	16.00	30.00	50.00	100	—
1615 (c)	—	16.00	30.00	50.00	100	—
1615	—	16.00	30.00	50.00	100	—

KM# 9 1/24 THALER (Groschen)
Silver **Obv:** Ornate helmet above arms **Rev:** Imperial orb with Z4 within circle, date divided at top **Note:** Varieties exist.

Date	Mintage	VG	F	VF	XF	Unc
1616	—	13.00	27.00	50.00	100	—
1617	—	13.00	27.00	50.00	100	—
1617 (c)	—	13.00	27.00	50.00	100	—
1618 (c)	—	13.00	27.00	50.00	100	—
1618 HS	—	13.00	27.00	50.00	100	—
1618	—	13.00	27.00	50.00	100	—
1619	—	13.00	27.00	50.00	100	—

KM# 42 REICHSORT (1/4 Thaler)
Silver **Obv:** Oval arms in baroque frame below divide date **Obv. Legend:** EIN.ORTS.THA/LER **Rev:** St. Stephen standing

Date	Mintage	VG	F	VF	XF	Unc
16Z5 (c)	—	—	—	—	—	—

TRADE COINAGE

KM# 54 GOLDGULDEN
Gold **Obv:** Helmeted arms in inner circle **Rev:** St. Stephen standing divides date and moneyers initials **Note:** Fr. 1074.

Date	Mintage	VG	F	VF	XF	Unc
1628 CZ	—	1,250	2,500	4,500	8,500	—
ND(1628) CZ	—	1,250	2,500	4,500	8,500	—

KM# 58 GOLDGULDEN
Gold **Rev:** Date divided by St. Stephen standing **Note:** Fr. 1074.

Date	Mintage	VG	F	VF	XF	Unc
1629	—	1,250	2,500	4,500	8,500	—
ND(1631)	—	1,250	2,500	4,500	8,500	—

CITY

REGULAR COINAGE

KM# 75 PFENNIG
Silver **Note:** Uniface. Schussel-type. City arms, date.

Date	Mintage	VG	F	VF	XF	Unc
1633	—	—	—	—	—	—

KM# 76 3 PFENNIG (Dreier)
Silver **Obv:** City arms **Rev:** Imperial orb with 3

Date	Mintage	VG	F	VF	XF	Unc
1633	—	30.00	60.00	120	240	—

KM# 77 1/24 THALER (Groschen)
Silver **Obv:** Helmeted city arms **Obv. Legend:** NACH. REICHS. SCHR: V: KOR **Rev:** Imperial orb with Z4 **Rev. Legend:** MON.NOVA...

Date	Mintage	VG	F	VF	XF	Unc
1633 (d)	—	20.00	40.00	75.00	150	—
1634 (d)	—	20.00	40.00	75.00	150	—

KM# 78.1 THALER
Silver **Obv:** Capped and helmeted small oval arms **Obv. Legend:** MON: NOU: CIU: ... **Rev:** St. Stephan standing **Note:** Dav.#5352.

Date	Mintage	VG	F	VF	XF	Unc
1633 (d) Rare	—	—	—	—	—	—

KM# 80 THALER
Silver **Rev:** Date in legend **Note:** Dav.#5354.

Date	Mintage	VG	F	VF	XF	Unc
1663	—	650	1,250	2,850	5,000	—

KM# 78.2 THALER
Silver **Obv. Legend:** MONETA. NOVA. ARG: ... **Rev:** St. Stephen standing divides date **Note:** Dav.#5355.

Date	Mintage	VG	F	VF	XF	Unc
1663 (e) Rare	—	—	—	—	—	—

KM# 81 1-1/2 THALER
Silver **Note:** Similar to 1 Thaler, KM#80, with value punched in on reverse. Dav.#5353A.

Date	Mintage	VG	F	VF	XF	Unc
1663 Rare	—	—	—	—	—	—

KM# 82 2 THALER
Silver **Note:** Similar to 1 Thaler, KM#80, with value punched in on reverse. Dav.#5353.

Date	Mintage	VG	F	VF	XF	Unc
1663 Rare	—	—	—	—	—	—

TRADE COINAGE

FR# 79 GOLDGULDEN

3.5000 g., 0.9860 Gold 0.1109 oz. AGW **Obv:** Crowned and helmeted arms in inner circle **Rev:** St. Stephen standing divides date

Date	Mintage	VG	F	VF	XF	Unc
1633 Rare	—	—	—	—	—	—

JOINT COINAGE

Cathedral Chapter and City

KM# 20 3 PFENNIG (Dreier)

Billon **Obv:** Helmeted episcopal arms divide date **Rev:** City arms, 3 in circle above

Date	Mintage	VG	F	VF	XF	Unc
16ZZ	—	20.00	40.00	85.00	175	—
ND	—	20.00	40.00	85.00	175	—

KM# 21 3 PFENNIG (Dreier)

Billon **Obv:** St. Stephen standing above episcopal arms **Rev:** City arms, 3 in circle below

Date	Mintage	VG	F	VF	XF	Unc
ND	—	30.00	60.00	120	240	—

KM# 24 1/24 THALER (Groschen)

Silver **Obv:** Oval episcopal arms, date divided above helmet **Rev. Legend:** MONETA NO...

Date	Mintage	VG	F	VF	XF	Unc
16ZZ	—	22.00	45.00	90.00	180	—

KM# 23 1/24 THALER (Groschen)

Silver **Obv:** Imperial orb with 24 above city arms, titles of Ferdinand II **Rev:** Helmeted episcopal arms, date divided in legend at top **Note:** Kipper 1/24 Thaler.

Date	Mintage	VG	F	VF	XF	Unc
16ZZ	—	16.00	33.00	70.00	150	—

KM# 25 1/24 THALER (Groschen)

Silver **Note:** Klippe.

Date	Mintage	VG	F	VF	XF	Unc
16ZZ Rare	—	—	—	—	—	—

KM# 85 THALER

Silver **Obv:** Helmeted city arms **Rev:** St. Stephan **Note:** Dav.#5356.

Date	Mintage	VG	F	VF	XF	Unc
1691 IC-S	—	125	250	550	1,200	4,500

PATTERNS

Including off metal strikes

KM#	Date	Mintage	Identification	Mkt Val
Pn1	1622	—	Ducat. Silver. KM#34.	—
Pn2	1628 CZ	—	Gulden. Gold. KM#53.	—
Pn3	ND CZ	—	Gulden. Gold. KM#53.	—
Pn4	1630 CZ	—	Thaler. Gold. KM#66.	—
Pn5	1631 CZ	—	1/4 Thaler. Gold. Arms in frame. KM#59.	6,500
Pn6	1631 CZ	—	1/4 Thaler. Gold. Helmeted arms. KM#69.	6,500

HALL

(Schwäbisch Hall)
(Hall am Kocher)

This city in Swabia, situated on the River Kocher 34 miles (56 kilometers) northeast of Stüttgart, was founded at an early date, probably because of the presence of natural salt in the area. Small silver coins struck beginning in the second half of the 12th century and called *haller* were the origin of both the denomination and its name which has come down over the centuries as *heller.* Hall was made a free imperial city in 1276 and was given the right to strike its own coins in 1396. The city soon began to mint hellers with an open hand on the obverse and a cross on the reverse. These coins became known as *handelshellers* and the hand became the symbol of the city. Hall produced some coins during each of the following centuries, but total mintages were never very high. Most coins issued during the 18th century were commemorative in nature and usually only struck in a single year. The last city coins were produced in 1798. Württemberg annexed the city in 1803 as part of Napoleon's consolidation plans for Germany.

MINT OFFICIAL'S INITIALS

Initials	Date	Name
MB	1659-1725	Martin Brunner

ARMS

Usually 2-fold, but also found in separate shields, Open-palmed hand with fingers pointed upwards or a cross.

REFERENCE

R = Albert Raff, ***Die Münzen und Medaillen der Stadt Schwäbisch Hall***, Freiburg im Breisgau, 1986.

FREE CITY

REGULAR COINAGE

KM# 5 PFENNIG

Silver, 12-13 mm. **Obv:** Two adjacent shields of arms, cross in left, open hand in right, rising eagle above, date below. **Note:** Uniface.

Date	Mintage	VG	F	VF	XF	Unc
1664	—	10.00	20.00	40.00	85.00	—
1675	—	10.00	20.00	40.00	85.00	—
1681	—	10.00	20.00	40.00	85.00	—
1697	—	10.00	20.00	40.00	85.00	—

KM# 7 PFENNIG

Silver, 13 mm. **Obv:** Two adjacent shields of arms, cross in left, hand in right, date below, imperial eagle rising up from behind above **Note:** Uniface. R-59.1.

Date	Mintage	VG	F	VF	XF	Unc
1696	—	10.00	20.00	40.00	85.00	—

KM# 6 1/2 KREUZER

Silver, 14 mm. **Obv:** Two adjacent shields of arms, cross in left, open hand in right, eagle rising from behind divides data above, value 1/2 in cartouche below **Note:** Uniface. R-54.

Date	Mintage	VG	F	VF	XF	Unc
1664	—	10.00	25.00	50.00	100	—

PATTERNS

Including off metal strikes

KM#	Date	Mintage	Identification	Mkt Val
Pn1	1681	—	Pfennig. Gold. KM#5.	—

HALTERN

A provincial town located about 25 miles southwest of Münster in Westphalia. Two series of copper coins were struck for local use in 1595 and 1624.

ARMS

A halter, as for a horse.

REFERENCE

W = Joseph Weingärtner, **Beschreibung der Kupfermünzen Westfalens nebst historischen Nachrichten**, 2 vols., Paderborn, 1872-81.

PROVINCIAL TOWN

REGULAR COINAGE

KM# 1 3 PFENNIG

Copper **Obv:** Arms in ornamented shield, STADT. HALTEREN, date around **Rev:** Value III in ornamented rectangle

Date	Mintage	VG	F	VF	XF	Unc
1624	—	150	300	625	1,250	—

KM# 2 6 PFENNIG

Copper **Obv:** Arms in ornamented shield, STADT. HALTEREN, date around **Rev:** Value VI in ornamented rectangle

Date	Mintage	VG	F	VF	XF	Unc
1624	—	175	375	750	1,400	—

KM# 3 9 PFENNIG

Copper **Obv:** Arms in ornamented shield, STADT. HALTEREN, date around **Rev:** Value VIIII in ornamented rectangle

Date	Mintage	VG	F	VF	XF	Unc
1624	—	225	450	900	1,800	—

HAMBURG

The city of Hamburg is located on the Elbe River about 75 miles from the North Sea. It was founded by Charlemagne in the 9th century. In 1241 it joined Lubeck to form the Hanseatic League. The mint right was leased to the citizens in 1292. However, the first local halfpennies had been struck almost 50 years earlier. In 1510 Hamburg was formally made a Free City, though, in fact, it had been free for about 250 years. It was occupied by the French during the Napoleonic period. In 1866 it joined the North German Confederation and became a part of the German Empire in 1871. The Hamburg coinage is almost continuous up to the time of World War I.

MINT OFFICIALS' INITIALS

Initial	Date	Name
	1592-1606	Matthias Mörsch, warden
(f)=	1599-1605	Claus Flegel
(g)=monk's head left	1606-1619	Matthias Mörsch, (Moors)
	1618-19	Jacob Stoer, warden
(h)= or	1619-20	Henning Hanses
(i)= or	1620-34	Christoff Fuessel (Feustal)
(j)= or with or without MF	1635-68	Matthias Freude der Altere
	1635-?	Jacob Stoer, warden (2nd)
(k)= with or without MF	1668-73	Matthias Freude der Jungere
HL	1673-92	Hermann Luders
	1691-1718	Jacob Schroeder, warden
IR	1692-1724	Jochim Rustmeyer

FREE CITY

REGULAR COINAGE

KM# 5.1 SCHERF (1/2 Pfennig)

Copper **Obv:** City arms **Rev:** I.S, blank field or rosette above, ornaments below **Note:** Prev. KM#7.1. Varieties exist.

Date	Mintage	VG	F	VF	XF	Unc
ND(1572-1605)	—	15.00	35.00	75.00	150	—

KM# 8 PFENNIG

Copper **Obv:** City arms **Rev:** Inscription, date **Rev. Inscription:** I / PEN / NING / **Note:** Prev. KM#52.

Date	Mintage	VG	F	VF	XF	Unc
1621	—	—	—	—	—	—

KM# 180 3 PFENNIG

Silver **Obv:** Date, inscription in octagonal frame **Obv. Inscription:** HAMB: / STADT / GELD **Rev:** 3P. in octagonal frame **Note:** Prev. KM#65.

Date	Mintage	VG	F	VF	XF	Unc
1632	—	—	—	—	—	—

KM# 157 SECHSLING (6 Pfennig)

Silver **Obv:** City arms in circle **Rev:** Inscription, date **Rev. Inscription:** I / SOES / LIN(G) **Note:** Prev. KM#53. Varieties exist.

Date	Mintage	VG	F	VF	XF	Unc
(1)621 (i)	—	16.00	33.00	65.00	130	—
1624 (i)	—	16.00	33.00	65.00	130	—
1635 (i)	—	16.00	33.00	65.00	130	—
1636 (j)	—	16.00	33.00	65.00	130	—
1641 (j)	—	16.00	33.00	65.00	130	—
1646 (j)	—	16.00	33.00	65.00	130	—
1648 (j)	—	16.00	33.00	65.00	130	—
1659 (j)	—	16.00	33.00	65.00	130	—
1660 (j)	—	16.00	33.00	65.00	130	—
1669 (k)	—	16.00	33.00	65.00	130	—
1670 (k)	—	16.00	33.00	65.00	130	—

KM# 107 1/2 SCHILLING (6 Pfennig)
Silver **Obv:** Crowned imperial eagle, 1/2 on breast, titles of Ferdinand II **Rev:** City arms in circle **Note:** Prev. KM#40. Kipper coinage.

Date	Mintage	VG	F	VF	XF	Unc
ND(1620/21) (i)	—	33.00	75.00	150	315	—

KM# 108 SCHILLING (12 Pfennig)
Silver **Obv:** City arms within circle **Rev:** Crowned imperial eagle, I on breast, titles of Ferdinand II **Note:** Prev. KM#41. Kipper coinage. Varieties exist.

Date	Mintage	VG	F	VF	XF	Unc
ND(1620/21) (i)	—	33.00	75.00	150	315	—

KM# 239 SCHILLING (12 Pfennig)
Silver **Rev:** Inscription, date **Rev. Inscription:** I / SCHIL / LING **Note:** Prev. KM#88.

Date	Mintage	VG	F	VF	XF	Unc
1669 (k)	—	12.00	25.00	55.00	110	—
1670 (k)	—	12.00	25.00	55.00	110	—

KM# 110 2 SCHILLING (1/16 Thaler)
Silver **Obv:** City arms in circle **Rev:** Crowned imperial eagle, Z in orb on breast, titles of Ferdinand II **Note:** Prev. KM#42. Kipper coinage.

Date	Mintage	VG	F	VF	XF	Unc
ND(1620/21) (i)	—	20.00	40.00	75.00	150	—

KM# 170 2 SCHILLING (1/16 Thaler)
Silver **Rev:** Inscription, date **Rev. Inscription:** II / SCHIL / LING / **Note:** Prev. KM#58.

Date	Mintage	VG	F	VF	XF	Unc
(1)623 (i)	—	16.00	33.00	75.00	155	—
(1)624 (i)	—	16.00	33.00	75.00	155	—

KM# 171 2 SCHILLING (1/16 Thaler)
Silver **Rev:** Inscription, date **Rev. Inscription:** II / SCHIL / LING **Note:** Prev. KM#59. Varieties exist.

Date	Mintage	VG	F	VF	XF	Unc
1624 (i)	—	15.00	30.00	65.00	130	—
1627 (i)	—	15.00	30.00	65.00	130	—
1628 (i)	—	15.00	30.00	65.00	130	—
ND(1631) (i)	—	15.00	30.00	65.00	130	—
1636 (j)	—	15.00	30.00	65.00	130	—
1637 (j)	—	15.00	30.00	65.00	130	—
1639 (j)	—	15.00	30.00	65.00	130	—
1641 (j)	—	15.00	30.00	65.00	130	—
1646 (j)	—	15.00	30.00	65.00	130	—
1647 (j)	—	15.00	30.00	65.00	130	—
1659 (j)	—	15.00	30.00	65.00	130	—
1660 (j)	—	15.00	30.00	65.00	130	—
1669 (k)	—	15.00	30.00	65.00	130	—
1670 (k)	—	15.00	30.00	65.00	130	—
(1)672	—	15.00	30.00	65.00	130	—

KM# 258 2 SCHILLING (1/16 Thaler)
Silver **Obv:** Crowned imperial eagle, 2/S on breast, date in legend **Rev:** Madonna and child, small oval city arms below resting on crescent **Note:** Prev. KM#98.

Date	Mintage	VG	F	VF	XF	Unc
1673 MF	—	20.00	40.00	80.00	160	—

KM# 265 2 SCHILLING (1/16 Thaler)
Silver **Obv:** Madonna with scepter and child **Rev:** 2 on eagle's breast **Note:** Prev. KM#102. Varieties exist.

Date	Mintage	VG	F	VF	XF	Unc
1674 HL	—	20.00	45.00	90.00	185	—
1675 HL	—	20.00	45.00	90.00	185	—
1677 HL	—	20.00	45.00	90.00	185	—
1678 HL	—	20.00	45.00	90.00	185	—
1687 HL	—	20.00	45.00	90.00	185	—
1688 HL	—	20.00	45.00	90.00	185	—
1689 HL	—	20.00	45.00	90.00	185	—

KM# 299 2 SCHILLING (1/16 Thaler)
Silver **Obv:** City arms between palm branches **Rev:** Value on breast of double-headed imperial eagle **Note:** Prev. KM#125.

Date	Mintage	VG	F	VF	XF	Unc
1692 IR	—	15.00	30.00	60.00	120	—
1693 IR	—	15.00	30.00	60.00	120	—
1695 IR	—	15.00	30.00	60.00	120	—

KM# 113 4 SCHILLING (1/4 Mark)
Silver **Obv:** City arms, date divided among towers **Rev:** Crowned imperial eagle, IIII in rhombus on breast, titles of Ferdinand II **Note:** Prev. KM#43.

Date	Mintage	VG	F	VF	XF	Unc
1620 (g)	—	85.00	160	300	625	—

KM# 241 4 SCHILLING (1/4 Mark)
Silver **Obv:** City arms within circle **Rev:** Inscription, date, titles of Leopold I **Rev. Inscription:** IIII / SCHIL / LING **Note:** Prev. KM#89.

Date	Mintage	VG	F	VF	XF	Unc
1669 (k)	—	40.00	80.00	150	315	—

KM# 159 4 SCHILLING (1/8 Thaler)
Silver **Obv:** City arms in circle, date divided by towers **Rev:** Crowned imperial eagle, 4 in orb on breast, titles of Ferdinand II and date inlegend **Note:** Prev. KM#54.

Date	Mintage	VG	F	VF	XF	Unc
1621 (i)	—	65.00	125	275	550	—

KM# 167 4 SCHILLING (1/8 Thaler)
Silver **Obv:** Towered building facade within beaded circle **Rev:** Date only in legend **Note:** Prev. KM#57.

Date	Mintage	VG	F	VF	XF	Unc
(1)6ZZ (i)	—	60.00	120	240	475	—
(1)623 (i)	—	60.00	120	240	475	—

KM# 224 4 SCHILLING (1/8 Thaler)
Silver **Rev:** Titles of Ferdinand III **Note:** Prev. KM#75.

Date	Mintage	VG	F	VF	XF	Unc
1642 (j)	—	60.00	120	240	475	—

KM# 22 8 SCHILLING (1/4 Thaler)
Silver **Obv:** Crowned imperial eagle, 8 in orb on breast, titles f Rudolf II and date in legend **Rev:** City arms in circle **Note:** Prev. KM#12. Varieties exist.

Date	Mintage	VG	F	VF	XF	Unc
(1)602 (f)	—	55.00	120	225	450	—
(1)606 (g)	—	55.00	120	225	450	—
1607 (g)	—	55.00	120	225	450	—
(1)608 (g)	—	55.00	120	225	450	—
1608 (g)	—	55.00	120	225	450	—
ND (g)	—	55.00	120	225	450	—

KM# 116 8 SCHILLING (1/4 Thaler)
Silver **Obv:** Towered building facade within beaded circle **Rev:** Titles of Ferdinand II **Note:** Prev. KM#44. Varieties exist.

Date	Mintage	VG	F	VF	XF	Unc
(1)620 (i)	—	45.00	110	200	425	—
(1)621 (i)	—	45.00	110	200	425	—
(1)622 (i)	—	45.00	110	200	425	—
1622 (i)	—	45.00	110	200	425	—

KM# 117 8 SCHILLING (1/4 Thaler)
Silver **Obv:** Date divided by towers within beaded circle **Rev:** Value on breast of double-headed eagle within beaded circle **Note:** Prev. KM#45.

Date	Mintage	VG	F	VF	XF	Unc
1620 (i)	—	45.00	110	200	425	—
1622 (i)	—	45.00	110	200	425	—

KM# 161 8 SCHILLING (1/2 Mark)
Silver **Obv:** City arms, date divided among towers **Rev:** Crowned imperial eagle, value VIII in rhombus on breast, titles of Ferdinand II **Note:** Prev. KM#55.

Date	Mintage	VG	F	VF	XF	Unc
16Z1 (i)	—	—	—	—	—	—
1631 (i)	—	—	—	—	—	—

KM# 230 8 SCHILLING (1/2 Mark)
Silver **Obv:** City arms in circle, date in legend **Rev:** 8 in orb on breast, titles of Ferdinand III **Note:** Prev. KM#80.

Date	Mintage	VG	F	VF	XF	Unc
1653 (j)	—	—	—	—	—	—

KM# 231 8 SCHILLING (1/2 Mark)
Silver **Obv:** Titles of Leopold I **Note:** Prev. KM#81.

Date	Mintage	VG	F	VF	XF	Unc
1659 (j)	—	—	—	—	—	—
1667 (j)	—	—	—	—	—	—

KM# 232 8 SCHILLING (1/2 Mark)

Silver, 60 mm. **Obv:** Date in legend **Note:** Prev. KM#85. Illustration reduced.

Date	Mintage	VG	F	VF	XF	Unc
1668 (k)	—	135	350	650	1,175	—

KM# 243 8 SCHILLING (1/2 Mark)

Silver **Obv:** City arms in circle **Rev:** Value inscription, date at end, titles of Leopold I **Rev. Inscription:** VIII / SCHIL / LING **Note:** Prev. KM#90.

Date	Mintage	VG	F	VF	XF	Unc
1669 (k)	—	—	—	—	—	—

KM# 250 8 SCHILLING (1/2 Mark)

Silver **Obv:** Towered building facade within beaded circle **Rev:** Value on breast of double-headed imperial eagle within beaded circle **Note:** Prev. KM#95.

Date	Mintage	VG	F	VF	XF	Unc
1672 (k)	—	65.00	135	240	650	—

KM# 309 1/2 MARK (8 Schilling)

Silver **Obv:** City arms in baroque shield, date below **Rev:** Crowned imperial eagle, 1/2 in orb on breast, titles of Leopold I **Note:** Prev. KM#127.

Date	Mintage	VG	F	VF	XF	Unc
1694 IR	—	80.00	175	350	650	—

KM# 24 16 SCHILLING (1/2 Thaler)

Silver **Obv:** Date in legend **Note:** Prev. KM#13. Similar to KM#32.

Date	Mintage	VG	F	VF	XF	Unc
1602 (f)	—	—	—	—	—	—

KM# 32 16 SCHILLING (1/2 Thaler)

Silver **Obv:** Towered building facade within beaded circle **Rev:** Value on breast of double-headed imperial eagle within beaded circle **Note:** Prev. KM#15. Varieties exist.

Date	Mintage	VG	F	VF	XF	Unc
1605 (f)	—	55.00	110	235	475	—
(1)607 (g)	—	55.00	110	235	475	—
(1)608 (g)	—	55.00	110	235	475	—
1610 (g)	—	55.00	110	235	475	—
ND (f)	—	55.00	110	235	475	—

KM# 86 16 SCHILLING (1/2 Thaler)

Silver **Rev:** Date divided among towers **Note:** Prev. KM#26.

Date	Mintage	VG	F	VF	XF	Unc
1611 (g)	—	—	—	—	—	—

KM# 98 16 SCHILLING (1/2 Thaler)

Silver **Obv:** Titles of Matthias **Note:** Prev. KM#33.

Date	Mintage	VG	F	VF	XF	Unc
1619 (h)	—	—	—	—	—	—

KM# 120 16 SCHILLING (1/2 Thaler)

Silver **Obv:** Date divided by towers within beaded circle **Rev:** Titles of Ferdinand II **Note:** Prev. KM#46. Varieties exist.

Date	Mintage	VG	F	VF	XF	Unc
1620 (g)	—	80.00	175	300	600	—
16Z1 (i)	—	80.00	175	300	600	—
1629 (i)	—	80.00	175	300	600	—

KM# 164 16 SCHILLING (1/2 Thaler)

Silver **Obv:** Towered building facade within beaded circle **Rev:** Value on breast of double-headed imperial eagle within beaded circle **Note:** Prev. KM#56. Varieties exist.

Date	Mintage	VG	F	VF	XF	Unc
(1)6Z1 (i)	—	55.00	115	250	475	—
(1)6ZZ (i)	—	55.00	115	250	475	—
(1)6Z3 (i)	—	55.00	115	250	475	—
1624 (i)	—	55.00	115	250	475	—
(1)625 (i)	—	55.00	115	250	475	—
1629 (i)	—	55.00	115	250	475	—
1632 (i)	—	55.00	115	250	475	—
1634 (j)	—	55.00	115	250	475	—
1636 (j)	—	55.00	115	250	475	—

KM# 217 16 SCHILLING (1/2 Thaler)

Silver **Obv:** Titles of Ferdinand III **Note:** Prev. KM#70. Varieties exist.

Date	Mintage	VG	F	VF	XF	Unc
1638 (j)	—	55.00	115	250	475	—
1640 (j)	—	55.00	115	250	475	—
1641 (j)	—	55.00	115	250	475	—
1642 (j)	—	55.00	115	250	475	—
1644 (j)	—	55.00	115	250	475	—
1645 (j)	—	55.00	115	250	475	—

KM# 259 16 SCHILLING (1/2 Thaler)

Silver **Obv:** Titles of Leopold I **Note:** Prev. KM#99.

Date	Mintage	VG	F	VF	XF	Unc
1673 MF (k)	—	120	275	500	1,025	—

KM# 245 16 SCHILLING (Mark)

Silver **Rev:** Value inscription, titles of Leopold I and date in legend **Rev. Inscription:** XVI / SCHIL / LING **Note:** Prev. KM#92.

Date	Mintage	VG	F	VF	XF	Unc
1669 (k)	—	—	—	—	—	—

KM# 252 16 SCHILLING (Mark)

Silver **Obv:** City arms within inner circle **Rev:** Double-headed eagle with 16 S in orb on breast **Note:** Prev. KM#96.

Date	Mintage	VG	F	VF	XF	Unc
1672 (k)	—	125	250	500	1,025	—

KM# 311 MARK

Silver **Obv:** City arms in baroque shield, date below **Obv. Legend:** HAMBURGER-STADT GELDT **Rev:** Crowned imperial eagle, 1 in orb on breast, titles of Leopold I **Rev. Legend:** LEOPOLDUS DG: ROMA: IMP: SEM: AU **Note:** Prev. KM#128.

Date	Mintage	VG	F	VF	XF	Unc
1694 IR	—	110	200	375	775	—

KM# 254 32 SCHILLING (2 Mark)

Silver **Obv:** City arms within inner circle **Rev:** Double-headed eagle in inner circle, date at end of legend **Note:** Prev. KM#97.

Date	Mintage	VG	F	VF	XF	Unc
1672 (k)	—	200	425	725	1,350	—

KM# 262 32 SCHILLING (2 Mark)

Silver **Note:** Prev. KM#100. Similar to KM#101 but 39 mm.

Date	Mintage	VG	F	VF	XF	Unc
1673 MF (k)	—	95.00	185	350	775	—

KM# 30 32 SCHILLING (Thaler)

Silver **Rev:** Titles of Rudolf II and date in reverse legend. **Note:** Dav. #5357. Prev. KM#14. Varieties exist. Similar to KM#35.

Date	Mintage	VG	F	VF	XF	Unc
1603 (f)	—	165	325	550	1,100	—
1604 (f)	—	165	325	550	1,100	—
1605 (f)	—	165	325	550	1,100	—
(1)607 (g)	—	80.00	160	475	1,100	—
1608 (g)	—	165	325	550	1,100	—
(1)608 (g)	—	80.00	160	475	1,100	—

KM# 75.1 32 SCHILLING (Thaler)

Silver **Note:** Dav. #5358. Prev. KM#16.1. Similar to KM#16.2 but with straight wall.

Date	Mintage	VG	F	VF	XF	Unc
(1)606 (g)	—	165	325	550	1,100	—
1606 (g)	—	165	325	550	1,100	—
1607 (g)	—	165	325	550	1,100	—

KM# 35 32 SCHILLING (Thaler)

Silver **Obv:** City arms within inner circle, date in legend **Rev:** Crowned double-headed imperial eagle, date in legend **Note:** Dav. #5359. Prev. KM#17. Varieties exist.

Date	Mintage	VG	F	VF	XF	Unc
1606/1607 (g)	—	160	325	600	1,300	—
1606/(1)607 (g)	—	160	325	600	1,300	—
(1)606/(1)606 (g)	—	160	325	600	1,300	—
(1)607/(1)606 (g)	—	160	325	600	1,300	—
(1)607/(1)607 (g)	—	160	325	600	1,300	—
(1)608/1608 (g)	—	160	325	600	1,300	—
(1)608/(1)608 (g)	—	160	325	600	1,300	—

KM# 75.2 32 SCHILLING (Thaler)

Silver **Obv:** City arms within inner circle **Rev:** Crowned imperial eagle with 3Z in orb on breast **Note:** Dav. #5361. Prev. KM#16.2. Varieties exist.

Date	Mintage	VG	F	VF	XF	Unc
(1)607 (g)	—	150	300	575	1,200	—
(1)608 (g)	—	150	300	575	1,200	—
1608 (g)	—	150	300	575	1,200	—
1610 (g)	—	150	300	575	1,200	—
ND (g)	—	150	300	575	1,200	—

KM# 77 32 SCHILLING (Thaler)

Silver **Obv:** City arms' towers divide date 1 (tower) 6 (tower) 1 (tower) 0 **Rev:** Crowned double-headed imperial eagle with 3Z in orb on breast **Note:** Dav. #5360. Prev. KM#20. Varieties exist.

Date	Mintage	VG	F	VF	XF	Unc
1608 (g)	—	150	300	575	1,200	—
1610 (g)	—	150	300	575	1,200	—
1611 (g)	—	150	300	575	1,200	—
161Z (g)	—	150	300	575	1,200	—

KM# 88.1 32 SCHILLING (Thaler)

Silver **Rev:** Titles of Matthias **Note:** Dav. #5362. Prev. KM#27.1.

Date	Mintage	VG	F	VF	XF	Unc
1613 (g)	—	900	1,600	3,000	6,000	—
1616 (g)	—	900	1,600	3,000	6,000	—

KM# 88.2 32 SCHILLING (Thaler)

Silver **Obv:** City arms' towers divide date numerals **Obv. Legend:** MONETA ? NOVA CIVITATIS HAMBURGENSIS **Rev:** Crowned imperial eagle with 3Z in orb on breast, titles of Matthias **Rev. Legend:** MATTHIAS ? D:G:ROMA IMPE: SEM: AUGU: **Note:** Dav. #5363. Prev. KM#27.2. Varieties exist.

Date	Mintage	VG	F	VF	XF	Unc
1619 (h)	—	300	600	1,200	—	—

KM# 100 32 SCHILLING (Thaler)

Silver **Obv:** City arms' towers divide date numerals **Rev:** Crowned imperial eagle with 3Z in orb on breast, titles of Ferdinand II **Note:** Dav. #5364. Prev. KM#34. Varieties exist.

Date	Mintage	VG	F	VF	XF	Unc
1619 (h)	—	75.00	150	300	600	—
1620 (g)	—	—	—	—	—	—
1620 (i)	—	75.00	150	300	600	—
1621 (i)	—	75.00	150	300	600	—
1622 (i)	—	75.00	150	300	600	—
1625 (i)	—	75.00	150	300	600	—

KM# 123 32 SCHILLING (Thaler)

Silver **Note:** Dav. #5365. Prev. KM#47. Varieties exist.

Date	Mintage	VG	F	VF	XF	Unc
1620 (i)	—	90.00	175	325	675	—
1621 (i)	—	90.00	175	325	675	—
(1)621 (i)	—	90.00	175	325	675	—
(16)21 (i)	—	90.00	175	325	675	—
(1)622 (i)	—	90.00	175	325	675	—
1623 (i)	—	90.00	175	325	675	—
(1)623 (i)	—	90.00	175	325	675	—
(16)23 (i)	—	90.00	175	325	675	—
1624 (i)	—	90.00	175	325	675	—
(1)624 (i)	—	90.00	175	325	675	—
(1)625 (i)	—	90.00	175	325	675	—
1626 (i)	—	90.00	175	325	675	—
1628 (i)	—	90.00	175	325	675	—
1629 (i)	—	90.00	175	325	675	—
1630 (i)	—	90.00	175	325	675	—
1631 (i)	—	90.00	175	325	675	—
1632 (i)	—	90.00	175	325	675	—
1634 (i)	—	90.00	175	325	675	—
1635 (j)	—	90.00	175	325	675	—
1636 (j)	—	90.00	175	325	675	—
1636 MF (j)	—	90.00	175	325	675	—
1637 (j)	—	90.00	175	325	675	—
ND (j)	—	90.00	175	325	675	—

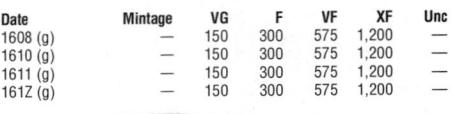

KM# 210.1 32 SCHILLING (Thaler)

Silver **Rev:** Titles of Ferdinand III **Note:** Dav. #5366. Prev. KM#67.1.

Date	Mintage	VG	F	VF	XF	Unc
1637 (j)	—	135	275	450	850	—
1638 (j)	—	135	275	450	850	—
1640 (j)	—	135	275	450	850	—
1641 (j)	—	135	275	450	850	—
1642 (j)	—	135	275	450	850	—
1644 (j)	—	135	275	450	850	—
1645 (j)	—	135	275	450	850	—
1646 (j)	—	135	275	450	850	—

KM# 210.2 32 SCHILLING (Thaler)

Silver **Obv:** City arms in inner circle, date divided at top **Rev:** Double-headed imperial eagle, titles of Ferdinand II **Note:** Dav. #5367. Prev. KM#67.2. Varieties exist.

Date	Mintage	VG	F	VF	XF	Unc
1643 (j)	—	165	340	575	1,150	—
1645 (j)	—	165	340	575	1,150	—
1647 (j)	—	165	340	575	1,150	—
1648 (j)	—	165	340	575	1,150	—
1649 (j)	—	165	340	575	1,150	—
1650 (j)	—	165	340	575	1,150	—
1651 (j)	—	165	340	575	1,150	—
1652 (j)	—	165	340	575	1,150	—
1653 (j)	—	165	340	575	1,150	—

KM# 263 32 SCHILLING (Thaler)

Silver **Rev:** Double-headed imperial eagle, titles of Leopold. **Note:** Dav. #5368. Prev. KM#101.

Date	Mintage	VG	F	VF	XF	Unc
1673 MF (k)	—	275	425	850	1,650	—

KM# 279 48 SCHILLING (Thaler)

Silver **Subject:** Peace of Nymwegan **Note:** Dav. #5370. Prev. KM#115.

Date	Mintage	VG	F	VF	XF	Unc
1680 HL	—	850	1,650	3,000	5,500	—

KM# 285 48 SCHILLING (Thaler)

Silver **Obv:** Crowned imperial eagle, orb on breast, titles of Leopold I **Rev:** City arms, date divided to left and right of towers, all in palm wreath **Note:** Dav. #5372. Prev. KM#119.

Date	Mintage	VG	F	VF	XF	Unc
1687 HL	—	1,350	2,500	4,250	7,500	—

KM# 313 2 MARK

Silver **Obv:** City arms in baroque shield, date below **Rev:** Crowned imperial eagle, 2 in orb on breast, titles of Leopold I **Note:** Prev. KM#129.

Date	Mintage	VG	F	VF	XF	Unc
1694 IR	—	220	450	825	1,650	—

KM# 20 1/128 THALER (3 Pfennig)

Silver **Obv:** City arms in circle **Rev:** Imperial orb with 128, titles of Rudolf II **Note:** Prev. KM#10. Varieties exist.

Date	Mintage	VG	F	VF	XF	Unc
1601	—	27.00	55.00	115	230	—

KM# 26 1/128 THALER (3 Pfennig)

Silver **Obv:** City arms **Obv. Legend:** MO. NOV. CIVI. HAMBVRG **Rev:** Imperial orb with 1Z8 , titles of Rudolf II in legend **Note:** Prev. KM#1.

Date	Mintage	VG	F	VF	XF	Unc
ND(1602-05)	—	25.00	50.00	100	200	—

KM# 126 1/96 THALER

Silver **Obv:** City arms in circle, date in legend **Rev:** Imperial orb with titles of Ferdinand II and date in legend **Note:** Prev. KM#48.

Date	Mintage	VG	F	VF	XF	Unc
(1)6Z0 (g)	—	25.00	45.00	90.00	185	—

KM# 267 1/96 THALER

Silver **Obv:** City arms between palm branches **Rev:** 96 between palm branches, date in legend **Note:** Prev. KM#103.

Date	Mintage	VG	F	VF	XF	Unc
1675 HL	—	20.00	40.00	70.00	145	—

KM# 13 1/64 THALER (6 Pfennig)

Silver **Obv:** City arms in inner circle **Rev:** Imperial eagle, orb with 64, date in legend **Note:** Prev. KM#8.

Date	Mintage	VG	F	VF	XF	Unc
(1)601 (f)	—	20.00	45.00	90.00	185	—
(1)602 (f)	—	20.00	45.00	90.00	185	—
(1)603 (f)	—	20.00	45.00	90.00	185	—
(1)605 (f)	—	20.00	45.00	90.00	185	—

KM# 219 1/48 THALER (Schilling)

Silver **Obv:** City arms in circle **Rev:** 48 in shield, date in legned **Note:** Prev. KM#71. Varieties exist.

Date	Mintage	VG	F	VF	XF	Unc
1639 (j)	—	33.00	65.00	130	265	—
1641 (j)	—	33.00	65.00	130	265	—
1646 (j)	—	33.00	65.00	130	265	—
1659 (j)	—	33.00	65.00	130	265	—
1660 (j)	—	33.00	65.00	130	265	—

KM# 269 1/48 THALER (Schilling)

Silver **Obv:** City arms between palm branches **Rev:** 48 between palm branches, date in legend **Note:** Prev. KM#104. Varieties exist.

Date	Mintage	VG	F	VF	XF	Unc
1675 HL	—	30.00	65.00	130	265	—
1676 HL	—	30.00	65.00	130	265	—
1680 HL	—	30.00	65.00	130	265	—
1687 HL	—	30.00	65.00	130	265	—

KM# 305 1/48 THALER (Schilling)

Silver **Rev:** 48/REICHS/DALER, date in legend **Note:** Prev. KM#126.

Date	Mintage	VG	F	VF	XF	Unc
1693 IR	—	25.00	55.00	110	225	—

KM# 102 1/20 THALER (24 Pfennig)

Silver **Obv:** Two interlocking shields of Lübeck and Hamburg arms above DALER-A-20.STVC and below 24, all in a circle, date at end of legend **Obv. Legend:** MONETA. HAMBVRGENSIS **Rev:** Crowned imperial eagle, titles of Matthias **Note:** Ref. G#851. Prev. KM#32.

Date	Mintage	VG	F	VF	XF	Unc
1619	—	—	—	—	—	—

Note: Companion issue of Lübeck (city), KM#43

KM# 15 1/16 THALER (2 Schilling)

Silver **Obv:** City arms in circle, date above **Obv. Legend:** MON - NOV - HAMB - VRG. **Rev:** Shield with crowned imperial eagle, 16 in orb on breast, small imperial crown above **Rev. Legend:** RVDO. - II.D.G. - RO.I.S. - A.P.F.D. **Note:** Prev. KM#11. Varieties exist.

Date	Mintage	VG	F	VF	XF	Unc
(1)601 (f)	—	20.00	40.00	80.00	160	—
(1)602 (f)	—	20.00	40.00	80.00	160	—
(1)603 (f)	—	20.00	40.00	80.00	160	—
(1)604 (f)	—	20.00	40.00	80.00	160	—
(1)605 (f)	—	20.00	40.00	80.00	160	—
(1)607 (g)	—	20.00	40.00	80.00	160	—
(1)608 (g)	—	20.00	40.00	80.00	160	—

KM# 90 1/16 THALER (2 Schilling)

Silver **Rev:** Titles of Matthias **Note:** Prev. KM#28.

Date	Mintage	VG	F	VF	XF	Unc
1614 (g)	—	25.00	45.00	90.00	180	—

KM# 92 1/16 THALER (2 Schilling)

Silver **Obv:** Date in legend **Rev:** Imperial eagle with 16 in orb on breast **Note:** Prev. KM#29. Varieties exist.

Date	Mintage	VG	F	VF	XF	Unc
1614 (g)	—	20.00	40.00	85.00	175	—
1615 (g)	—	20.00	40.00	85.00	175	—
1616 (g)	—	20.00	40.00	85.00	175	—
1617 (g)	—	20.00	40.00	85.00	175	—

KM# 94 1/16 THALER (2 Schilling)

Silver **Rev. Legend:** NON. MIHI. D. SED. NOM. TVO **Note:** Prev. KM#30.

Date	Mintage	VG	F	VF	XF	Unc
1617	—	33.00	60.00	120	240	—

KM# 38 1/4 THALER (Schau)

Silver **Obv:** City arms in baroque frame, ornate helmet above **Obv. Legend:** DA.PACEM.DOMIN:—IN.DIE:NOSTRIS **Rev:** Nativity scene **Rev. Legend:** IESUS. E: KINT: GEBOREN. V: EIN. IUNCKFRA: AUSERKORN. **Note:** Prev. KM#21.

Date	Mintage	VG	F	VF	XF	Unc
ND(1606-19)	—	—	—	—	—	—

KM# 39 1/4 THALER (Schau)

Silver **Obv:** City arms in baroque frame, ornate helmet above **Obv. Legend:** DA.PACEM.DOMIN:—IN.DIE:NOSTRIS **Rev:** Nativity scene **Rev. Legend:** PVER. NATVS. EST. NOVIS. E. FILIVS. DATVS. ETS. NOBIS. **Note:** Prev. KM#22. Varieties exist.

Date	Mintage	VG	F	VF	XF	Unc
ND(1606-19)	—	75.00	150	325	650	—

KM# 129 1/4 THALER (Schau)

Silver **Obv:** City arms in baroque frame, ornate helmet **Obv. Legend:** DA.PACEM.DOMIN:—IN.DIE:NOSTRIS **Rev:** Nativity scene **Rev. Legend:** PVER. NATVS. EST. NOBI. E. FILIVS. DATVS. ETS. **Note:** Prev. KM#35.

Date	Mintage	VG	F	VF	XF	Unc
ND(1620-34)	—	75.00	150	325	650	—

KM# 184 1/4 THALER (Schau)

Silver **Obv:** The Annunciation **Obv. Legend:** AVE MARIA GRATIA. PLENA. DOMINVS TECUM **Rev:** The Nativity **Rev. Legend:** IESUS. E. KINT. GEBORN. V: EIN. IUNCKFRA: AVSERKORN **Note:** Prev. KM#72.

Date	Mintage	VG	F	VF	XF	Unc
ND(1635-68)	—	60.00	150	300	625	—

KM# 185 1/4 THALER (Schau)

Silver **Obv:** The Annunciation **Obv. Legend:** AVE MARIA GRATIA. PLENA. DOMINVS TECUM **Rev:** The Nativity **Rev. Legend:** PVER NATUS. EST. NOBI E FILIVS. DATVS. EST. NOBIS **Note:** Prev. KM#73.

Date	Mintage	VG	F	VF	XF	Unc
ND(1635-68)	—	60.00	150	300	625	—

KM# 186 1/4 THALER (Schau)

Silver **Obv:** City arms in shield, ornate helmet above **Obv. Legend:** DA PACEM DOMINE **Rev:** The Nativity **Rev. Legend:** IESUS. E. KINT. GEBORN. V: EIN. IUNCKFRA: AVSERKORN **Note:** Prev. KM#74.

Date	Mintage	VG	F	VF	XF	Unc
ND(1635-68)	—	80.00	160	325	650	—

KM# 187 1/4 THALER (Schau)

Silver **Obv:** City arms in shield, ornate helmet **Obv. Legend:** DA PACEM DOMINE **Rev:** The Nativity **Rev. Legend:** PVER NATUS. EST. NOBI E FILIVS. DATVS. EST. **Note:** Prev. KM#77.

Date	Mintage	VG	F	VF	XF	Unc
ND(1635-68)	—	80.00	160	325	650	—

KM# 288 1/4 THALER (Schau)

Silver **Obv:** City arms in sprays **Obv. Legend:** * MONETA NOVA CIVITATIS HAMBURGEN: **Rev:** Crowned imperial eagle **Rev. Legend:** LEOPOLDUS • D: G: ROMA: IMP: SEM: AUG • **Note:** Prev. KM#118.

Date	Mintage	Good	VG	F	VF	XF
ND(1687)	—	55.00	130	275	550	1,100

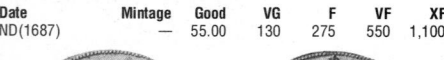

KM# 290 1/4 THALER (Schau)

Silver **Obv:** City arms inside 2 palm branches **Obv. Legend:** MONETA NOVA CIVITATIS HAMBURGEN:. **Rev:** Crowned Imperial Eagle, 4 in orb on breast, titles of Leopold I **Note:** Prev. KM#124.

Date	Mintage	VG	F	VF	XF	Unc
ND(1687)	—	120	300	450	850	—

KM# 271 1/3 THALER

Silver **Obv:** Arms divide date, value in orb below **Rev:** Crowned imperial eagle **Note:** Prev. KM#105.

Date	Mintage	VG	F	VF	XF	Unc
ND(1675) HL	—	120	275	400	825	—
1679 HL	—	120	275	400	825	—

KM# 43 1/2 THALER (Schau)

14.4000 g., Silver, 35 mm. **Obv:** City arms in baroque frame, ornate helmet **Obv. Legend:** DA.PACEM.DOMIN:--IN.DIE:NOSTRIS **Rev:** Nativity scene **Rev. Legend:** PVER. NATVS. EST. NOVIS. E. FILIVS. DATVS. ETS. **Note:** Prev. KM#A23.

Date	Mintage	F	VF	XF	Unc	BU
ND(1606-19)	—	130	270	550	1,100	—

KM# 42 1/2 THALER (Schau)

14.4000 g., Silver **Obv:** City arms in baroque frame, ornate helmet **Obv. Legend:** DA. PACEM. DOMIN: — IN. DIE: NOSTRIS **Rev:** Nativity scene **Rev. Legend:** PVER. NATVS. EST. NOVIS. E. FILIVS. DATVS. ETS. **Note:** Prev. KM#23. Klippe; struck on square flan of 1/2 Thaler weight.

Date	Mintage	VG	F	VF	XF	Unc
ND(1606-19)	—	150	300	600	1,200	—

KM# 190 1/2 THALER (Schau)

Silver **Obv:** Nativity scene **Obv. Legend:** PVER NATVS. EST. NOBI E: FILIVS. DATVS EST. NOBIS. ESA: IX **Rev:** Baptism of Christ **Rev. Legend:** CHRIST. D: HEIL: TAUF. NI: AN. V: SEI: VORLAUF: IM. IORD **Note:** Prev. KM#78.

Date	Mintage	VG	F	VF	XF	Unc
ND(1635-68)	—	110	215	450	925	—

KM# 191 1/2 THALER (Schau)

Silver **Obv:** The Annunciation **Obv. Legend:** AVE MARIA GRATIA. PLENA. DOMINVS **Rev:** The Nativity **Rev. Legend:** PVER NATUS. EST. NOBI E FILIVS. DATVS. EST. **Note:** Prev. KM#79.

Date	Mintage	VG	F	VF	XF	Unc
ND(1635-68)	—	110	215	450	925	—

KM# 273 2/3 THALER

Silver **Obv:** Arms divide date, value below in orb **Rev:** Crowned imperial eagle **Note:** Prev. KM#106. Similar to 1/3 Thaler, KM#105, but value 2/3.

Date	Mintage	VG	F	VF	XF	Unc
ND(1675) HL	—	120	275	500	1,000	—
ND(1675)	—	120	275	500	1,000	—
1679 HL	—	120	275	500	1,000	—

KM# 315 THALER

Silver **Obv:** City arms in baroque frame **Rev:** Crowned imperial eagle **Note:** Dav. #5374. Prev. KM#130.

Date	Mintage	F	VF	XF	Unc	BU
1694 IR	—	190	375	600	1,350	—

KM# 46 THALER (Schau)

Silver **Obv:** City arms in ornamented oval shield, ornate helmet above **Obv. Legend:** DA. PACEM. DOMI. — IN. DIE: NOSTRÍS **Rev:** Nativity scene **Rev. Legend:** GLORIA. IN. EXC — ELSIS. DEO **Note:** Ref. G#1528. Prev. KM#24.

Date	Mintage	VG	F	VF	XF	Unc
ND(1606-19)	—	90.00	180	350	775	—

KM# 132 THALER (Schau)

Silver **Obv:** City arms in rectangular shield with rounded bottom, ornate helmet above **Obv. Legend:** DA. PACEM... **Rev:** Madonna with rays around **Rev. Legend:** SI. DEVS. PRO. NOBIS. — QVIS. CONTRA. NOS **Note:** Ref. G#1547. Prev. KM#36.

Date	Mintage	VG	F	VF	XF	Unc
ND(1620-34)	—	90.00	180	350	775	—

KM# 194 THALER (Schau)

Silver **Obv:** Nativity scene **Obv. Legend:** PVER NATVS. EST. NOBI E: FILIVS. DATVS EST. NOBIS. **Rev:** Baptism of Christ **Rev. Legend:** CHRIST. D: HEIL: TAUF. NI: AN. V: SEI: VORLAUF: IM. **Note:** Ref. G#1585. Prev. KM#82.

Date	Mintage	VG	F	VF	XF	Unc
ND(1635-68)	—	80.00	160	325	600	—

KM# 197 THALER (Schau)

Silver **Obv:** The Annunciation **Obv. Legend:** AVE MARIA GRATIA. PLENA. DOMINVS **Rev:** The Nativity **Rev. Legend:** PVER NATUS. EST. NOBI E FILIVS. DATVS. EST. **Note:** Ref. G#1587. Prev. KM#83.

Date	Mintage	VG	F	VF	XF	Unc
ND(1635-68)	—	80.00	160	325	600	—

KM# 198 THALER (Schau)
Silver **Obv:** Engaged couple, Jehovah in Hebrew and dove above center **Obv. Legend:** QUOS DEUS CONIUNXIT **Rev:** Wedding at Cana **Rev. Legend:** IESUS CHRIST: MACHET **Note:** Ref. G#1600. Prev. KM#84.

Date	Mintage	VG	F	VF	XF	Unc
ND(1635-68)	—	80.00	160	325	600	—

KM# 48 1-1/4 THALER (Schau)
Silver **Obv:** City arms in ornamented shield, ornate helmet above **Obv. Legend:** DA. PACEM. DOMI. — IN. DIEBVS. NOSTRIS **Rev:** Madonna with sceptre standing on crescent **Rev. Legend:** VERBVM. DOMINI. — MANET. IN ÆTERNVM **Note:** Ref. G#1524. Prev. KM#A25.

Date	Mintage	VG	F	VF	XF	Unc
ND(1606-19)	—	220	375	575	1,000	—

KM# 50 1-1/2 THALER (Schau)
Silver **Obv:** City arms in ornate shield, ornate helmet above **Obv. Legend:** DA. PACEM. DOMINE'. IN — DIEBVS. NOSTRIS **Rev:** Madonna with sword and sceptre, child with orb **Rev. Legend:** SI. DEVS. PRO. NOBIS. — QVIS. CONTRA. NOS. **Note:** Dav. #LS-301. Ref. G#1521. Prev. KM#B25.

Date	Mintage	VG	F	VF	XF	Unc
ND(1606-19)	—	550	1,000	1,950	3,250	—

KM# 51 1-1/2 THALER (Schau)
Silver **Obv:** City arms in ornamented oval shield, ornate helmet above **Obv. Legend:** DA. PACEM. DOMI. — IN. DIE: NOSTRIS **Rev:** Nativity scene **Rev. Legend:** GLORIA. IN. EXC — ELSIS. DEO **Note:** Ref. G#1528. Prev. KM#C25.

Date	Mintage	VG	F	VF	XF	Unc
ND(1606-19)	—	255	425	650	1,100	—

KM# 134 1-1/2 THALER (Schau)
Silver, 60 mm. **Obv:** Christ joining a couple in marriage **Obv. Legend:** QUOS DEUS CONIUNXIT — HOMO NON SEPARET **Rev:** Wedding at Cana **Rev. Legend:** IESUS CHRISTUS MACHET WASSER ZU WEIN. IN. CANA. GAL: IOH. II **Note:** Ref. G#1541. Prev. KM#37. Illustration reduced.

Date	Mintage	VG	F	VF	XF	Unc
ND(1620-34)	—	290	550	875	1,450	—

KM# 135 1-1/2 THALER (Schau)
Silver, 60 mm. **Obv:** Marriage scene **Obv. Legend:** WAS GOTT ZUSAMMEN FVGET — DAS SOL KEIN MENSCH SCHEIDEN **Rev:** Similar to KM#37, but variant scene and legend **Rev. Legend:** ...Z. WEIN. IN. CANA. GALI. IOHA. II **Note:** Ref. G#1544. Prev. KM#38. Illustration reduced.

Date	Mintage	VG	F	VF	XF	Unc
ND(1620-34)	—	290	550	875	1,450	—

KM# 136 1-1/2 THALER (Schau)
Silver, 59 mm. **Obv:** Crucifixion scene **Obv. Legend:** CHRISTUS IST UMB UNSER SUNDE WILLEN. GESTORBEN. UND **Rev:** Ascension, Christ with cross and banner **Rev. Legend:** UMB. UNSER. GERECHTIGKEIT. WILLEN. WIDER. AUFFERSTANDE **Note:** Ref. G#1551. Prev. KM#39. Illustration reduced.

Date	Mintage	VG	F	VF	XF	Unc
ND(1620-34)	—	325	575	950	1,650	—

KM# 200 1-1/2 THALER (Schau)
Silver **Obv:** The Nativity **Obv. Legend:** IESUS EIN KINDT GEBORN. V. EINER IUNCKFRAUW: AUSERKORN **Rev:** Baptism of Christ **Rev. Legend:** CHRIST: D. HEILIG: TAUF: NIM. AN. V. SEIM: VORLAUFFER IM. IOR:. **Note:** Ref. G#1582, 1584. Prev. KM#A85. Varieties exist.

Date	Mintage	VG	F	VF	XF	Unc
ND(1635-68)	—	255	425	650	1,100	—

KM# 201 1-1/2 THALER (Schau)
Silver **Obv:** Angel with band: HEIL SEI GOTT IN DER HÖH' **Obv. Legend:** IESUS EIN KINDT GEBORN. V. EINER IUNCKFRAUW: AUSERKORN **Rev:** Baptism of Christ **Rev. Legend:** CHRIST: D. HEILIG: TAUF: NIM. AN. V. SEIM: VORLAUFFER IM. IOR:. **Note:** Ref. G#1583a. Prev. KM#B85.

Date	Mintage	VG	F	VF	XF	Unc
ND(1635-68)	—	255	425	650	1,100	—

KM# 202 1-1/2 THALER (Schau)
Silver **Obv:** Engaged couple, Jehovah in Hebrew and dove at top center **Obv. Legend:** QUOS DEIUS CONIUNXIT **Rev:** Wedding at Cana **Rev. Legend:** IESUS CHRISTUS MACHET **Note:** Prev. KM#C85.

Date	Mintage	VG	F	VF	XF	Unc
ND(1635-68)	—	255	425	650	1,100	—

KM# 203 1-1/2 THALER (Schau)
Silver, 60 mm. **Obv:** Christ performing marriage with a couple **Obv. Legend:** WAS GOT ZUSAMMEN **Rev:** Cana wedding scene, but with couple under canopy, Christ and Mary at left, cellar master at right **Rev. Legend:** IESUS CHRISTUS MACHET **Note:** Prev. KM#D85. Illustration reduced.

Date	Mintage	VG	F	VF	XF	Unc
ND(1635-68)	—	220	375	500	950	—

KM# 54 2 THALER
Silver **Note:** Dav. #A5358. Prev. KM#18. Similar to 32 Schilling, KM#35, but date in obverse legend.

Date	Mintage	F	VF	XF	Unc	BU
(1)606	—	825	1,650	3,000	4,900	—
1607	—	825	1,650	3,000	4,900	—

KM# 55 2 THALER
Silver **Note:** Dav. #A5359. Prev. KM#19. Similar to 32 Schilling, KM#35.

Date	Mintage	F	VF	XF	Unc	BU
(1)606/(1)606 Rare	—	—	—	—	—	—

KM# 79 2 THALER
Silver **Note:** Dav. #A5360. Prev. KM#25. Similar to 32 Schilling, KM#77.

Date	Mintage	VG	F	VF	XF	Unc
1610	—	825	1,650	3,000	4,900	—

KM# 182 2 THALER
Silver **Note:** Dav. #A5365. Prev. KM#66. Similar to 32 Schilling, KM#123.

Date	Mintage	VG	F	VF	XF	Unc
1632 Rare	—	—	—	—	—	—
1636 Rare	—	—	—	—	—	—

KM# 282 2 THALER
Silver **Subject:** Peace of Nymwegen **Note:** Dav. #5369. Prev. KM#116. Similar to 48 Schilling, KM#115.

Date	Mintage	VG	F	VF	XF	Unc
1680 HL	—	2,800	4,900	8,300	13,000	—

KM# 293 2 THALER

Silver **Obv:** Crowned imperial eagle, orb on breast, titles of Leopold I **Rev:** City arms, date divided left and right of towes, all in palm wreath **Note:** Dav. #5371. Prev. KM#120.

Date	Mintage	VG	F	VF	XF	Unc
1687 HL	—	1,500	3,000	5,300	8,300	—

KM# 317 2 THALER

Silver **Note:** Dav. #5373. Prev. KM#131. Similar to 1 Thaler, KM#130.

Date	Mintage	VG	F	VF	XF	Unc
1694 IR	—	2,250	3,750	6,400	9,800	—

KM# 56 2 THALER (Schau)

Silver, 56 mm. **Obv:** City arms in oval shield, ornate helmet above, 2 young females as supporters **Obv. Legend:** DA. PACEM. DOMINE. IN. — DIEBVS. NOSTRIS **Rev:** Madonna with sceptre and standing on crescent with child who holds orb **Rev. Legend:** SI. DEVS. PRO. NOBIS. — QVIS. CONTRA. NOS **Note:** Ref. G#1522. Prev. KM#D25.

Date	Mintage	VG	F	VF	XF	Unc
ND(1606-19)	—	525	900	1,500	2,650	—

KM# 57 2 THALER (Schau)

Silver **Obv:** City arms in ornate shield, ornamented helmet above **Obv. Legend:** DA. PACEM **Rev:** Madonna with sceptre and standing on crescent with child who holds orb **Rev. Legend:** SI. DEVS. PRO. NOBIS. — QVIS. CONTRA. NOV **Note:** Dav. #LS-306. Ref. G#1522a. Prev. KM#E25.

Date	Mintage	VG	F	VF	XF	Unc
ND(1606-19)	—	375	675	1,300	2,250	—

KM# 58 2 THALER (Schau)

Silver, 53 mm. **Obv:** City arms in rectangular shield, ornate helmet above **Obv. Legend:** DA. PACEM. DOMINE. IN. — DIEBVS. NOSTRIS **Rev:** Madonna with sceptre and standing on crescent with child who holds orb **Rev. Legend:** SI. DEVS. PRO. NOBIS. — QVIS. CONTRA. NOV **Note:** Dav. #LS-309. Ref. G#1523. Prev. KM#F25. Illustration reduced.

Date	Mintage	VG	F	VF	XF	Unc
ND(1606-19)	—	750	1,350	2,650	4,500	—

KM# 59 2 THALER (Schau)

Silver **Obv:** City arms in ornamented oval shield, ornate helmet above **Obv. Legend:** DA. PACEM. DOMI. — IN. DIEBVS. NOSTRIS **Rev:** Madonna with sceptre standing on crescent **Rev. Legend:** VERBVM. DOMINI. — MANET. IN ÆTERNVM **Note:** Ref. G#1524. Prev. KM#G25. Struck from the same dies as 1-1/4 Thaler, KM#48

Date	Mintage	VG	F	VF	XF	Unc
ND(1606-19)	—	900	1,500	2,800	4,500	—

KM# 60 2 THALER (Schau)

Silver **Obv:** City arms in oval shield, ornate helmet above, 2 young females as supporters **Obv. Legend:** DA. PACEM. DOMINE. IN. — DIEBVS. NOSTRIS **Rev:** Fortuna on the sea being attacked by Envy **Rev. Legend:** FORTUNÆ COMES IN VIDIA FR **Note:** Ref. G#1525. Prev. KM#H25.

Date	Mintage	VG	F	VF	XF	Unc
ND(1606-19)	—	500	1,000	2,250	—	—

KM# 62 2 THALER (Schau)

Silver, 60 mm. **Obv:** City arms in ornamented oval shield, ornate helmet above **Obv. Legend:** DA. PACEM. DOMI. — IN. DIEBVS. NOSTRIS **Rev:** Christ performing marriage of a couple **Rev. Legend:** QUOS. DEVS. CINIVNXIT. HOMO. NON. SEPARET **Note:** Ref. G#1526-27. Prev. KM#I25. Illustration reduced.

Date	Mintage	VG	F	VF	XF	Unc
ND(1606-19)	—	900	1,500	2,800	4,500	—

KM# 81 2 THALER (Schau)

Silver **Obv:** Madonna with sword and sceptre, child with orb **Obv. Legend:** SI. DEVS. PRO. NOBIS. — QVIS. CONTRA. NOS **Rev:** The Resurrection scene **Rev. Legend:** +ICK BIN DE VPERSTANDING VND DAT LEYENT **Note:** Ref. G#1534. Prev. KM#J25.

Date	Mintage	VG	F	VF	XF	Unc
ND(ca.1610-15)	—	375	675	1,050	1,900	—

KM# 63 2 THALER (Schau)

Silver **Obv:** Nativity scene **Obv. Legend:** PVER. NATVS. EST. NOBIS: ET. FILIVS. DATVS. EST. NOBIS. ESAIA: IX: CA: **Rev:** Scene of 3 wise king's visit to Holy Family **Rev. Legend:** GLORIA. IN. EXCELSIS. DEO. ET. IN. TERRA. PAX. LVCÆ. II. CAPITTEL **Note:** Ref. G#1535a. Prev. KM#K25.

Date	Mintage	VG	F	VF	XF	Unc
ND(1606-19)	—	375	675	1,050	1,900	—

KM# 105 2 THALER (Schau)

Silver **Obv:** Marriage ceremony scene **Obv. Legend:** QUOS DEUS CONIUNXIT HOMO NON SEPARET **Rev:** Wedding at Cana **Rev. Legend:** IESUS CHRISTUS MACHET WASSER ZU GUDEM WEINN. IOHA **Note:** Ref. G#1536. Prev. KM#A35.

Date	Mintage	VG	F	VF	XF	Unc
ND(1619-20)	—	375	675	1,050	1,900	—

KM# 139 2 THALER (Schau)

Silver, 60 mm. **Obv:** The Annunciation **Obv. Legend:** ZACHARIA: WIRD EIN SOHN GLOBT + MARIA MIT GOTTS. SOHN BEGABT **Rev:** Baptism scene **Rev. Legend:** CHRIST: DE: EHILG: TAUF: NIMPT. AN. V: SEIM. VORLAUFFER. IM. IORDAN **Note:** Ref. G#1539. Prev. KM#A52. Illustration reduced.

Date	Mintage	VG	F	VF	XF	Unc
ND(1620-34)	—	375	675	1,050	1,900	—

KM# 140 2 THALER (Schau)

Silver **Obv:** The Annunciation **Obv. Legend:** ZACHARIA: WIRD EIN SOHN GLOBT + MARIA MIT GOTTS. SOHN BEGABT **Rev:** Armored rider on horseback **Rev. Legend:** IUSTITIA — ET — CONCORDIA **Note:** Ref. G#1540. Prev. KM#B52.

Date	Mintage	VG	F	VF	XF	Unc
ND(ca.1620)	—	375	675	1,050	1,900	—

KM# 142 2 THALER (Schau)

Silver, 58 mm. **Obv:** Christ joining a couple in marriage **Obv. Legend:** QUOS DEUS CONIUNXIT — HOMO NON SEPARET **Rev:** Wedding at Cana **Rev. Legend:** IESUS CHRISTUS MACHET WASSER ZU WEIN. IN. CANA. GAL: IOH. II **Note:** Ref. G#1542-43. Prev. KM#C52. Varieties exist.

Date	Mintage	VG	F	VF	XF	Unc
ND(1620-34)	—	350	600	975	1,750	—

KM# 143 2 THALER (Schau)

Silver **Obv:** Marriage scene **Obv. Legend:** WAS GOTT ZUSAMMEN FVGET — DAS SOL KEIN MENSCH SCHEIDEN **Rev:** Similar to KM#134, but variant scene and legend **Rev. Legend:** ...Z. WEIN. IN. CANA. GALI. IOHA. II **Note:** Ref. G#1545-46. Prev. KM#D52. Varieties exist.

Date	Mintage	VG	F	VF	XF	Unc
ND(1620-34)	—	270	500	725	1,350	—

KM# 145 2 THALER (Schau)

Silver, 57 mm. **Obv:** Nativity scene with 3 shepherds **Obv. Legend:** PUER NATUS EST NOBIS **Rev:** Visit of 3 wise Kings **Rev. Legend:** GLORIA. IN. EXCELSIS. DEO **Note:** Ref. G#1549. Prev. KM#E52. Illustration reduced.

Date	Mintage	VG	F	VF	XF	Unc
ND(1620-34)	—	425	725	1,150	2,050	—

KM# 146 2 THALER (Schau)

Silver **Obv:** Flight of the Holy Family to Egypt **Obv. Legend:** CHRISTUS. FLEUCH. IN. EGYPTE. LAND. DAS. IH. HEROD. NICH. MEHR: FAND **Rev:** Ascension, Christ with cross and banner **Rev. Legend:** UMB. UNSER. GERECHTIGKEIT. WILLEN. WIDER. AUFFERSTANDE **Note:** Ref. G#1552. Prev. KM#F52. Illustration reduced.

Date	Mintage	VG	F	VF	XF	Unc
ND(1620-34)	—	425	725	1,150	2,050	—

KM# 205 2 THALER (Schau)

Silver **Obv:** The Nativity **Obv. Legend:** IESUS EIN KINDT GEBORN **Rev:** Baptism of Christ **Rev. Legend:** CHRIST: D. HEILIG: TAUF: NIM **Note:** Ref. G#1580-81, 1581a, 1583. Prev. KM#E85. Illustration reduced. Varieties exist.

Date	Mintage	VG	F	VF	XF	Unc
ND(1635-68)	—	375	650	975	1,650	—

KM# 206 2 THALER (Schau)

Silver **Obv:** The Annunciation **Obv. Legend:** AVE MARIA GRATIA. PLENA. DOMINVS **Rev:** The Nativity **Rev. Legend:** PVER NATUS. EST. NOBI E FILIVS. DATVS. EST. **Note:** Ref. G#1586. Prev. KM#F85.

Date	Mintage	VG	F	VF	XF	Unc
ND(1635-68)	—	425	675	1,150	2,050	—

KM# 207 2 THALER (Schau)

Silver **Obv:** Engaged couple, Jehovah in Hebrew and dove at top center **Obv. Legend:** QUOS DEIUS CONIUNXIT **Rev:** Wedding at Cana **Rev. Legend:** IESUS CHRISTUS MACHET **Note:** Ref. G#1594, 1598. Prev. KM#G85. Varieties exist.

Date	Mintage	VG	F	VF	XF	Unc
ND(1635-68)	—	425	675	1,150	2,050	—

KM# 208 2 THALER (Schau)

Obv: Engaged couple, Jehovah in Hebrew and dove at top center **Obv. Legend:** WAS GOTT ZUSAMN FVGT **Rev:** Wedding at Cana **Rev. Legend:** IESUS CHRISTUS MACHET **Note:** Ref. G#1599. Prev. KM#H85.

Date	Mintage	VG	F	VF	XF	Unc
ND(1635-68)	—	425	675	1,150	2,050	—

KM# 64 2-1/2 THALER (Schau)

Silver **Obv:** City arms in baroque shield, ornate helmet above **Obv. Legend:** DA. PACEM. DOMIN: IN — DIEBVS. NOSTRIS **Rev:** Madonna with sceptre and standing on crescent with child who holds orb **Rev. Legend:** SI. DEVS. PRO. NOBIS. — QVIS. CONTRA. NOV **Note:** Ref. G#1522b. Prev. KM#L25.

Date	Mintage	VG	F	VF	XF	Unc
ND(1606-19)	—	425	725	1,350	2,500	—

KM# 66 3 THALER (Schau)

Silver **Obv:** City arms in baroque shield, ornate helmet above **Obv. Legend:** DA. PACEM. DOMIN: IN — DIEBVS. NOSTRIS **Rev:** Madonna with sceptre and standing on crescent with child who holds orb **Rev. Legend:** SI. DEVS. PRO. NOBIS. — QVIS. CONTRA. NOV **Note:** Ref. G#1522b. Prev. KM#M25. Struck with same dies as 2-1/2 Thaler, KM#64.

Date	Mintage	VG	F	VF	XF	Unc
ND(1606-19)	—	450	750	1,450	2,550	—

KM# 83 3 THALER (Schau)

Silver **Obv:** Madonna with sword and sceptre, child with orb **Obv. Legend:** SI. DEVS. PRO. NOBIS. — QVIS. CONTRA. NOS **Rev:** The Resurrection scene **Rev. Legend:** +ICK BIN DE VPERSTANDING VND DAT LEYENT **Note:** Ref. G#1533. Prev. KM#A26.

Date	Mintage	VG	F	VF	XF	Unc
ND(ca.1610-15)	—	450	750	1,450	2,550	—

KM# 147 3 THALER (Schau)
Silver, 60 mm. **Obv:** Marriage scene **Obv. Legend:** WAS GOTT ZUSAMMEN FVGET — DAS SOL KEIN MENSCH SCHEIDEN **Rev:** Similar to KM#134, but variant scene and legend **Rev. Legend:** ...Z. WEIN. IN. CANA. GALI. IOHA. II **Note:** Ref. G#1544. Prev. KM#H52. Illustration reduced.

Date	Mintage	VG	F	VF	XF	Unc
ND(1620-34)	—	400	675	1,050	1,650	—

KM# 209 3 THALER (Schau)
Silver **Obv:** Engaged couple, Jehovah in Hebrew and dove at top center **Obv. Legend:** QUOS DEIUS CONIUNXIT **Rev:** Wedding at Cana **Rev. Legend:** IESUS CHRISTUS MACHET **Note:** Ref. G#1597. Prev. KM#I85. Illustration reduced.

Date	Mintage	VG	F	VF	XF	Unc
ND(1635-68)	—	350	650	950	1,450	—

KM# 67 3-1/2 THALER (Schau)
Silver **Obv:** City arms in oval shield, ornate helmet above, 2 young females as supporters **Obv. Legend:** DA. PACEM. DOMINE. IN. — DIEBVS. NOSTRIS **Rev:** Madonna with sceptre standing on crescent with child who holds orb **Rev. Legend:** SI. DEVS. PRO. NOBIS. — QVIS. CONTRA. NOV **Note:** Ref. G#1522. Prev. KM#N25.

Date	Mintage	VG	F	VF	XF	Unc
ND(1606-19)	—	525	825	1,500	2,700	—

TRADE COINAGE

KM# 18 GOLDGULDEN
3.5000 g., 0.9860 Gold 0.1109 oz. AGW **Obv:** St. Peter **Note:** Prev. KM#9.

Date	Mintage	VG	F	VF	XF	Unc
ND(1606-12) (g)	—	425	850	2,450	5,300	—
1608 (g)	—	425	850	2,450	5,300	—

KM# 96 GOLDGULDEN
3.5000 g., 0.9860 Gold 0.1109 oz. AGW **Rev:** Titles of Matthias **Note:** Prev. KM#31.

Date	Mintage	VG	F	VF	XF	Unc
1617 (g)	—	600	1,100	3,200	6,800	—
1619 (g)	—	600	1,100	3,200	6,800	—

KM# 178 GOLDGULDEN
3.5000 g., 0.9860 Gold 0.1109 oz. AGW **Rev:** Titles of Ferdinand II **Note:** Prev. KM#61.

Date	Mintage	VG	F	VF	XF	Unc
1628 (i)	—	425	850	2,450	5,300	—

KM# 215 GOLDGULDEN
3.5000 g., 0.9860 Gold 0.1109 oz. AGW **Rev:** Titles of Ferdinand III **Note:** Prev. KM#68.

Date	Mintage	VG	F	VF	XF	Unc
1637 (j) Rare	—	—	—	—	—	—

KM# 275 GOLDGULDEN
3.5000 g., 0.9860 Gold 0.1109 oz. AGW **Obv:** Helmeted oval arms **Rev:** Crowned imperial eagle, titles of Leopold I **Note:** Prev. KM#108.

Date	Mintage	VG	F	VF	XF	Unc
1675 HL	—	425	725	2,100	3,900	—

KM# 283 1/4 DUCAT
0.8750 g., 0.9860 Gold 0.0277 oz. AGW **Note:** Prev. KM#117.

Date	Mintage	VG	F	VF	XF	Unc
1680 HL	—	195	350	750	1,250	—
ND1692 IR	—	195	350	750	1,250	—

KM# 327 1/4 DUCAT
0.8750 g., 0.9860 Gold 0.0277 oz. AGW **Obv:** Madonna and child **Rev:** Annunciation scene **Note:** Prev. KM#140.

Date	Mintage	VG	F	VF	XF	Unc
ND(1700)	—	220	400	900	1,500	—

KM# 277 1/2 DUCAT
1.7500 g., 0.9860 Gold 0.0555 oz. AGW **Note:** Prev. KM#107.

Date	Mintage	VG	F	VF	XF	Unc
1675 HL	—	150	275	650	1,250	—

KM# 301 1/2 DUCAT
1.7500 g., 0.9860 Gold 0.0555 oz. AGW **Obv:** Crowned imperial eagle, titles of Leopold I **Note:** Prev. KM#134.

Date	Mintage	VG	F	VF	XF	Unc
ND(1692-1704) IR	—	225	450	850	1,450	—

KM# 221 DUCAT
3.5000 g., 0.9860 Gold 0.1109 oz. AGW **Note:** Prev. KM#69.

Date	Mintage	VG	F	VF	XF	Unc
1641 (j)	—	200	350	600	1,000	—
1642 (j)	—	200	350	600	1,000	—
1643 (j)	—	200	350	600	1,000	—
1644 (j)	—	200	350	600	1,000	—
1645 (j)	—	200	350	600	1,000	—
1646 (j)	—	200	350	600	1,000	—
1647 (j)	—	200	350	600	1,000	—
1649 (j)	—	200	350	600	1,000	—
1650 (j)	—	200	350	600	1,000	—
1651 (j)	—	200	350	600	1,000	—
1652 (j)	—	200	350	600	1,000	—
1653 (j)	—	200	350	600	1,000	—
1654 (j)	—	200	350	600	1,000	—
1655 (j)	—	200	350	600	1,000	—
1656 (j)	—	200	350	600	1,000	—
1657 (j)	—	200	350	600	1,000	—
1658 (j)	—	200	350	600	1,000	—
1659 (j)	—	200	350	600	1,000	—
1660 (j)	—	200	350	600	1,000	—
1661 (j)	—	200	350	600	1,000	—
1662 (j)	—	200	350	600	1,000	—
1663 (j)	—	200	350	600	1,000	—
1664 (j)	—	200	350	600	1,000	—
1665 (j)	—	200	350	600	1,000	—
1666 (j)	—	200	350	600	1,000	—
1667 (j)	—	200	350	600	1,000	—

KM# 235 DUCAT
3.5000 g., 0.9860 Gold 0.1109 oz. AGW **Rev:** Madonna and child **Note:** Prev. KM#86.

Date	Mintage	VG	F	VF	XF	Unc
1668 (k)	—	225	450	950	1,750	—
1669 MF (k)	—	225	450	950	1,750	—
1671	—	225	450	950	1,750	—
1674 HL	—	225	450	950	1,750	—
1675 HL	—	225	450	950	1,750	—
1692	—	225	450	950	1,750	—

KM# 295 DUCAT
3.5000 g., 0.9860 Gold 0.1109 oz. AGW **Obv:** Arms in branches **Rev:** Crowned imperial eagle **Note:** Prev. KM#121.

Date	Mintage	VG	F	VF	XF	Unc
1689 HL	—	475	800	2,000	3,700	—
1692 IR	—	475	800	2,000	3,700	—
1695	—	475	800	2,000	3,700	—
1698	—	475	800	2,000	3,700	—

KM# 320 DUCAT
3.5000 g., 0.9860 Gold 0.1109 oz. AGW **Rev:** Madonna with shield of arms **Note:** Prev. KM#132.

Date	Mintage	VG	F	VF	XF	Unc
1694 IR	—	350	750	1,600	3,000	—

KM# 228 2 DUCAT
7.0000 g., 0.9860 Gold 0.2219 oz. AGW **Obv:** Madonna and child in inner circle **Rev:** Madonna and child in inner circle, date in legend **Note:** Prev. KM#76.

Date	Mintage	VG	F	VF	XF	Unc
1649 MF (j)	—	650	1,250	3,250	5,750	—
1660 MF (j)	—	650	1,250	3,250	5,750	—
1666 MF	—	650	1,250	3,250	5,750	—

KM# 247 2 DUCAT
7.0000 g., 0.9860 Gold 0.2219 oz. AGW **Obv:** Arms with lion supporters **Rev:** Madonna and child, date in legend **Note:** Prev. KM#91.

Date	Mintage	VG	F	VF	XF	Unc
1669 MF (k)	—	475	875	1,950	3,600	—
1672	—	475	875	1,950	3,600	—
1674 HL	—	475	875	1,950	3,600	—
1679	—	475	875	1,950	3,600	—
1681	—	475	875	1,950	3,600	—
1685	—	475	875	1,950	3,600	—
1690	—	475	875	1,950	3,600	—

Date	Mintage	VG	F	VF	XF	Unc
1692	—	475	875	1,950	3,600	—
1694	—	475	875	1,950	3,600	—

KM# 256 2 DUCAT

7.0000 g., 0.9860 Gold 0.2219 oz. AGW **Obv:** Crowned imperial eagle, titles of Leopold I **Rev:** City arms between two palm branches **Note:** Prev. KM#109.

Date	Mintage	VG	F	VF	XF	Unc
ND(1672-92) HL	—	—	—	—	—	—
ND(1692-1705) IR	—	—	—	—	—	—

KM# 297 2 DUCAT

7.0000 g., 0.9860 Gold 0.2219 oz. AGW **Obv:** Crowned imperial eagle, titles of Leopold I **Rev:** Arms in cartouche **Note:** Prev. KM#122.

Date	Mintage	VG	F	VF	XF	Unc
1689 HL	—	800	1,800	4,000	7,000	—
1692	—	800	1,800	4,000	7,000	—
1696	—	800	1,800	4,000	7,000	—
1698	—	800	1,800	4,000	7,000	—

KM# 150 2-1/2 DUCAT (1/4 Portugalöser)

8.7500 g., 0.9860 Gold 0.2774 oz. AGW **Note:** Prev. KM#49. Similar to 5 Ducat, KM#153.

Date	Mintage	VG	F	VF	XF	Unc
ND(c.1620) Rare	—	—	—	—	—	—

KM# 303 2-1/2 DUCAT (1/4 Portugalöser)

8.7500 g., 0.9860 Gold 0.2774 oz. AGW **Obv:** Crowned imperial eagle, titles of Leopold I **Rev:** Madonna and child **Note:** Prev. KM#135.

Date	Mintage	VG	F	VF	XF	Unc
ND(1692-1705) IR Rare	—	—	—	—	—	—

KM# 69 5 DUCAT (1/2 Portugalöser)

17.9400 g., Gold **Obv:** City arms in ornamented oval shield, ornate helmet above **Obv. Legend:** DA. PACEM. DOMI. — IN. DIEBVS. NOSTRIS **Rev:** Madonna with sceptre standing on crescent **Rev. Legend:** VERBVM. DOMINI. — MANET. IN ÆTERNVM **Note:** Ref. G#1524. Prev. KM#O25. Struck from the same dies as 1 1/4 Thaler, KM#48.

Date	Mintage	VG	F	VF	XF	Unc
ND(1606-19) Rare	—	—	—	—	—	—

KM# 153 5 DUCAT (1/2 Portugalöser)

17.5000 g., 0.9860 Gold 0.5547 oz. AGW **Note:** Prev. KM#50.

Date	Mintage	F	VF	XF	Unc	BU
ND(c.1620) Rare	—	—	—	—	—	—

KM# 175 5 DUCAT (1/2 Portugalöser)

17.5000 g., 0.9860 Gold 0.5547 oz. AGW **Rev:** Titles of Ferdinand II **Note:** Prev. KM#60. Struck with 1 Thaler dies.

Date	Mintage	F	VF	XF	Unc	BU
1624 Rare	—	—	—	—	—	—

Note: Stack's International sale, 3/88 XF realized $16,500

KM# 323 5 DUCAT (1/2 Portugalöser)

17.5000 g., 0.9860 Gold 0.5547 oz. AGW **Obv:** Arms in cartouche **Rev:** Crowned imperial eagle, titles of Leopold I **Note:** Prev. KM#133.

Date	Mintage	F	VF	XF	Unc	BU
1695 IR Rare	—	—	—	—	—	—

KM# 72 10 DUCAT (Portugalöser)

Gold **Obv:** City arms in ornate shield, ornate helmet above **Obv. Legend:** DA. PACEM. DOMINE'. IN — DIEBVS. NOSTRIS **Rev:** Madonna with sword and sceptre, child with orb **Rev. Legend:** SI. DEVS. PRO. NOBIS. — QVIS. CONTRA. NOS **Note:** Ref. G#1521. Prev. KM#P25. Struck from the same dies as 1 1/2 Thaler, KM#50.

Date	Mintage	VG	F	VF	XF	Unc
ND(1606-19) Rare	—	—	—	—	—	—

KM# 155 10 DUCAT (Portugalöser)

35.0000 g., 0.9860 Gold 1.1095 oz. AGW **Rev:** Similar to 5 Ducat, KM#153. **Note:** Prev. KM#51. Illustration reduced.

Date	Mintage	F	VF	XF	Unc	BU
ND(c.1620) Rare	—	—	—	—	—	—

KM# 238 10 DUCAT (Portugalöser)

35.0000 g., 0.9860 Gold 1.1095 oz. AGW **Note:** Prev. KM#87. Similar to KM#155.

Date	Mintage	F	VF	XF	Unc	BU
ND(1668-73) Rare	—	—	—	—	—	—

KM# 325 10 DUCAT (Portugalöser)

35.0000 g., 0.9860 Gold 1.1095 oz. AGW **Subject:** Peace of Ryswick **Obv:** Winged victory standing on prone human figure between palm and pine trees, sailing ships in background **Obv. Legend:** PAX MARE PAX TERRAM PAX VRBES PAX BEATAGROS **Rev:** City view, sailing ships in foreground, Hamburg below, Jehovah in Hebrew in clouds above, legend curves above and below **Rev. Legend:** HÆC VRDS TUTA DEI CLIPEO - PRO TECTA MANEBIT **Note:** Prev. KM#138. (Ref: Gaedechens III: 1681)

Date	Mintage	F	VF	XF	Unc	BU
ND(1697) Rare	—	—	—	—	—	—

HAMELN

Hamlin, Hamelin, Quernhameln

City on the Weser River 26 miles southwest of Hannover grew around the abbey of St. Boniface beginning in the 8th century. In 1259 it passed from the abbey of Fulda to the bishopric of Minden, then to the dukes of Brunswick. Became a member of the Hanseatic league and obtained the mint right in the late 15th century and struck coins until 1695. This is the town of the legend of the Pied Piper.

MINTOFFICIALS' INITIALS

Initials	Date	Name
CF or (e)	1615-18	Christof Feustel (Feistel)
DK	1624-25	Unknown
IB or (n)	1671-73	Jonas Bose (Bosen)
(a)	1606-08	Christof Dies (Diess, Dyss)
(b)	1609	Sebastian Schoras
(c)	1611-12	Gert Koler
(d)	1612-15	Jakob Pfahler (Pfaler)
(f)	1619-?	Nicolaus (Claws) Oppermann
(g)	1622-24	Georg Arendes (Arndt, Arndts)
(h)	1626-32	Unknown, perhaps Simon timke
(i)	1633	Unknown
(j)	1635-41	Caspar Hoffmann
(k)	1655-56	Johann Otte (Otto)
(m)	1668-70, 1673	(Peter) Paul Pechstein

ARMS

2 mill rinds, often in front of twin-towered church.

CITY

REGULAR COINAGE

KM# 36 PFENNIG

Silver **Obv:** Arms in shield divide Q-H, date above. **Note:** Uniface schussel type.

Date	Mintage	VG	F	VF	XF	Unc
(1)6ZZ	—	27.00	55.00	115	230	—
(1)6Z3	—	27.00	55.00	115	230	—
16Z3	—	27.00	55.00	115	230	—
(1)6Z5	—	27.00	55.00	115	230	—

KM# 40 PFENNIG

Silver **Obv:** Shield divides date, QH above **Note:** Uniface.

Date	Mintage	VG	F	VF	XF	Unc
(16)24	—	27.00	55.00	115	230	—

KM# 51 PFENNIG

Copper **Rev:** Date added **Rev. Inscription:** 33 / STAT / PEN

Date	Mintage	VG	F	VF	XF	Unc
(16)3Z/(16)33	—	13.00	33.00	60.00	125	—
1633/(16)33	—	13.00	33.00	60.00	125	—

KM# 70 PFENNIG

Silver **Obv:** Arms divide date **Note:** Uniface, schussel type.

Date	Mintage	VG	F	VF	XF	Unc
1668	—	35.00	75.00	150	—	—
1669	—	35.00	75.00	150	—	—
1672	—	35.00	75.00	150	—	—

KM# 50 PFENNIG (Stadtpfennig)
Copper **Obv:** Arms, date in legend **Rev. Inscription:** I / STAT / PEN **Note:** Varieties exist.

Date	Mintage	VG	F	VF	XF	Unc
(16)3Z	—	35.00	75.00	160	325	—
ND	—	35.00	75.00	160	325	—
(16)33	—	35.00	75.00	160	325	—
(1)634	—	35.00	75.00	160	325	—
(1)635	—	—	—	—	—	—
Note: Reported, not confirmed						
1636	—	50.00	100	200	425	—
1637	—	—	—	—	—	—
Note: Reported, not confirmed						
1639	—	—	—	—	—	—
Note: Reported, not confirmed						
1641	—	—	—	—	—	—
Note: Reported, not confirmed						
1643	—	—	—	—	—	—
Note: Reported, not confirmed						
1644	—	—	—	—	—	—
Note: Reported, not confirmed						
1645	—	—	—	—	—	—
Note: Reported, not confirmed						
1650	—	—	—	—	—	—
Note: Reported, not confirmed						
1653	—	—	—	—	—	—
Note: Reported, not confirmed						
1655	—	—	—	—	—	—
Note: Reported, not confirmed						

KM# 82 2 PFENNIG
Silver **Obv:** Arms divide date **Rev. Inscription:** II / GUTE / PF **Note:** Gute 2 Pfennig.

Date	Mintage	VG	F	VF	XF	Unc
1672	—	20.00	45.00	90.00	—	—

KM# 16 3 PFENNIG (Dreier)
Silver **Obv:** Arms in shield **Rev:** Imperial orb with 3, date divided above

Date	Mintage	VG	F	VF	XF	Unc
1619	—	30.00	60.00	120	—	—
16ZZ (g)	—	30.00	60.00	120	—	—
16Z3 (g)	—	30.00	60.00	120	—	—

KM# 37 3 PFENNIG (Dreier)
Silver **Obv:** Arms in front of church divide Q-H

Date	Mintage	VG	F	VF	XF	Unc
1622 (g)	—	30.00	60.00	120	—	—

KM# 65 3 PFENNIG (Dreier)
Silver **Obv:** Arms in shield **Rev:** Imperial orb with 3 divides date

Date	Mintage	VG	F	VF	XF	Unc
1655 (k)	4,000	45.00	90.00	175	—	—
1656 (k)	—	45.00	90.00	175	—	—

KM# 71 3 PFENNIG (Dreier)
Silver **Obv:** Arms, date in legend **Rev:** Imperial orb with 3

Date	Mintage	VG	F	VF	XF	Unc
1668 (m)	—	18.00	35.00	75.00	150	—

KM# 83 3 PFENNIG (Dreier)
Silver **Obv:** Arms **Rev:** Imperial orb with 3, date divided above

Date	Mintage	VG	F	VF	XF	Unc
1672 (n)	—	10.00	20.00	40.00	80.00	—

KM# 90 3 PFENNIG (Dreier)
Silver **Obv:** Arms, 3 above, date divided below **Note:** Uniface.

Date	Mintage	VG	F	VF	XF	Unc
1695	—	—	—	—	—	—

KM# A90 3 PFENNIG (Dreier)
Silver **Obv:** Arms, 4 small stars around **Note:** Uniface.

Date	Mintage	VG	F	VF	XF	Unc
ND(ca. late 17th c.)	—	—	—	—	—	—

KM# 54 4 PFENNIG (4 Stadtpfennig; Mattier)
Copper **Obv:** Arms **Rev:** IIII in cartouche divides date, STAT above, PEN below

Date	Mintage	VG	F	VF	XF	Unc
1633	—	37.00	75.00	150	300	—
1635 (j)	—	37.00	75.00	150	300	—
1636 (j)	—	37.00	75.00	150	300	—
1639	—	—	—	—	—	—
Note: Reported, not confirmed						
1648	—	37.00	75.00	150	300	—
1650	—	—	—	—	—	—
Note: Reported, not confirmed						

KM# 72 4 PFENNIG (4 Stadtpfennig; Mattier)
1.0000 g., Silver, 16.7 mm. **Obv:** Arms divide date **Rev. Inscription:** IIII / GUTE / PF

Date	Mintage	VG	F	VF	XF	Unc
1668 (m)	—	13.00	33.00	55.00	110	—
1669 (m)	—	13.00	33.00	55.00	110	—
1672 (n)	—	13.00	33.00	55.00	110	—
1627 (n) Error; Rare	—	—	—	—	—	—

KM# 91 6 PFENNIG
Silver **Obv:** 6 above arms, date divided below **Note:** Uniface.

Date	Mintage	VG	F	VF	XF	Unc
1695	—	—	—	—	—	—

KM# 25 FLITTER
Copper **Obv:** Church with 2 towers **Rev. Inscription:** I / FLIT / TER / date **Note:** Kipper Flitter.

Date	Mintage	VG	F	VF	XF	Unc
16Z0	—	13.00	33.00	65.00	130	—
1645	—	—	—	—	—	—
Note: Reported, not confirmed						
1653	—	—	—	—	—	—
Note: Reported, not confirmed						

KM# 26 2 FLITTER
Copper **Obv:** Arms in front of church divide date as 1-6/Z-0 **Rev. Inscription:** II / FLIT / TRN

Date	Mintage	VG	F	VF	XF	Unc
16Z0	—	20.00	40.00	80.00	160	—
16Z1	—	20.00	40.00	80.00	160	—

KM# 27 3 FLITTER
Copper **Note:** Kipper 3 Flitter.

Date	Mintage	VG	F	VF	XF	Unc
16Z0	—	17.00	35.00	75.00	150	—
16Z1	—	17.00	35.00	75.00	150	—

KM# 34 3 FLITTER
Copper, 17 mm. **Obv:** City arms **Rev:** 4-line inscription with date **Rev. Inscription:** III / FLITT / REN / (date)

Date	Mintage	VG	F	VF	XF	Unc
16Z1	—	40.00	80.00	160	325	—

KM# A28 GOSLAR (1/12 Schilling)
Silver **Obv:** Oval city arms, 4 small rosettes around **Rev. Inscription:** I / GOS / LAR

Date	Mintage	VG	F	VF	XF	Unc
ND(ca.1620)	—	—	—	—	—	—

KM# 28.1 GOSKEN
Copper **Obv:** City arms, IZ below **Rev:** 'I' in center, ANNO, date around

Date	Mintage	VG	F	VF	XF	Unc
16Z0	—	35.00	75.00	155	310	—

KM# 28.2 GOSKEN
Copper **Obv:** City gate, arms in entrance, date above **Rev:** I/GOS/KEN

Date	Mintage	VG	F	VF	XF	Unc
1620	—	35.00	75.00	155	310	—

KM# 29 1-1/2 GOSKEN
Copper **Obv:** Arms, .8. above **Rev:** 1-1/2 in center, ANNO / 16Z0 around

Date	Mintage	VG	F	VF	XF	Unc
16Z0	—	40.00	80.00	160	325	—

KM# 30 2 GOSKEN
Copper **Obv:** Arms in front of church divide date as 1-6/Z-0 **Rev:** II center, GOSKEN around

Date	Mintage	VG	F	VF	XF	Unc
16Z0	—	35.00	75.00	150	300	—

KM# 31 2 GOSKEN
Copper **Rev:** Date also in legend

Date	Mintage	VG	F	VF	XF	Unc
16Z0	—	35.00	75.00	150	300	—
16Z1	—	35.00	75.00	150	300	—

KM# 35 2 GOSKEN
Copper **Rev:** Date only in legend

Date	Mintage	VG	F	VF	XF	Unc
16Z1	—	35.00	75.00	150	300	—

KM# 33 3 GOSKEN
Copper **Rev:** Date also in legend

Date	Mintage	VG	F	VF	XF	Unc
16Z0	—	25.00	45.00	75.00	155	—

KM# 32 3 GOSKEN
Copper **Obv:** Arms in front of church divide date as 1-6/Z-0 **Rev:** III in center, GOSKEN around **Note:** Kipper 3 Gosken.

Date	Mintage	VG	F	VF	XF	Unc
16Z0	—	25.00	45.00	75.00	155	—

KM# 38 MARIENGROSCHEN
Silver **Obv:** Arms divide date **Rev:** Madonna and child **Note:** Varieties exist.

Date	Mintage	VG	F	VF	XF	Unc
(1)622 (g)	—	27.00	55.00	115	235	—
(1)6Z3 (g)	—	27.00	55.00	115	235	—
1623 (g)	—	27.00	55.00	115	235	—
1624 (g)	—	27.00	55.00	115	235	—
1655 (k)	82,000	27.00	55.00	115	235	—
1668 (m)	—	27.00	55.00	115	235	—
1669 (m)	—	27.00	55.00	115	235	—

KM# 80 4 MARIENGROSCHEN
Silver **Obv:** Church with 2 towers, arms between **Rev. Inscription:** IIII / MARIE / GROS

Date	Mintage	VG	F	VF	XF	Unc
1671 IB	—	85.00	175	325	650	—

KM# 73 6 MARIENGROSCHEN
Silver **Obv:** Church with 2 towers, arms between within inner circle **Rev. Legend:** MONETA NOVA 1669 **Rev. Inscription:** VI / MARIEN / GROS **Note:** Varieties exist.

Date	Mintage	VG	F	VF	XF	Unc
1668 (m)	—	45.00	95.00	190	385	—
1669 (m)	—	45.00	95.00	190	385	—
1672 IB	68,000	45.00	95.00	190	385	—

KM# 81 12 MARIENGROSCHEN
Silver **Obv:** Church with 2 towers **Rev:** Inscription within inner circle, legend around **Rev. Inscription:** XII / MARIEN / GROS

Date	Mintage	VG	F	VF	XF	Unc
1671 IB	65,000	60.00	120	240	480	—
1672 IB	55,000	60.00	120	240	480	—
1672	—	60.00	120	240	480	—

KM# 5 1/96 THALER
Silver **Obv:** Arms in front of church **Rev:** Imperial orb with 96 divides date in ornamented rhombus

Date	Mintage	VG	F	VF	XF	Unc
1606	—	150	300	600	1,100	—
1608	—	—	—	—	—	—

KM# 6.2 1/24 THALER (Groschen)

Silver **Rev:** Date divided by cross in outer circle

Date	Mintage	VG	F	VF	XF	Unc
1606	—	20.00	40.00	85.00	175	—
1607	—	20.00	40.00	85.00	175	—
1609	—	20.00	40.00	85.00	175	—

KM# 6.1 1/24 THALER (Groschen)

Silver **Obv:** Arms in front of church **Rev:** Imperial orb with Z4, date divided by cross within inner circle, titles of Rudolf II **Note:** Varieties exist.

Date	Mintage	VG	F	VF	XF	Unc
ND (a)	—	20.00	40.00	80.00	165	—
1606 (a)	—	20.00	40.00	80.00	165	—
1607 (a)	—	20.00	40.00	80.00	165	—
1608 (a)	—	20.00	40.00	80.00	165	—
1609 (a)	—	20.00	40.00	80.00	165	—
1609	—	20.00	40.00	80.00	165	—
1609 (b)	—	20.00	40.00	80.00	165	—
1611 (c)	—	20.00	40.00	80.00	165	—

KM# 10 1/24 THALER (Groschen)

Silver **Rev:** Titles of Matthias **Note:** Varieties exist.

Date	Mintage	VG	F	VF	XF	Unc
1612 (c)	—	20.00	40.00	80.00	165	—
1612 (d)	—	20.00	40.00	80.00	165	—
1613 (d)	—	20.00	40.00	80.00	165	—
1614 (d)	—	20.00	40.00	80.00	165	—
1614 (e)	—	20.00	40.00	80.00	165	—
1615/3	—	20.00	40.00	80.00	165	—
1615 (d)	—	20.00	40.00	80.00	165	—
1615 (e)	—	20.00	40.00	80.00	165	—
1616 (e)	60,000	20.00	40.00	80.00	165	—
1617 (e)	—	20.00	40.00	80.00	165	—
1618 (e)	—	20.00	40.00	80.00	165	—

KM# 15 1/24 THALER (Groschen)

Silver **Note:** Klippe.

Date	Mintage	VG	F	VF	XF	Unc
(16)18 (e)	—	—	—	—	—	—

KM# 18 1/24 THALER (Groschen)

Silver **Note:** Klippe.

Date	Mintage	VG	F	VF	XF	Unc
(16)19 (f)	—	—	—	—	—	—

KM# 17 1/24 THALER (Groschen)

Silver **Note:** Kipper 1/24 Thaler. Varieties exist.

Date	Mintage	VG	F	VF	XF	Unc
1619 (f)	—	20.00	40.00	80.00	165	—
(1)619 (f)	—	20.00	40.00	80.00	165	—
(16)19 (f)	—	20.00	40.00	80.00	165	—
(16)Z0 (f)	—	20.00	40.00	80.00	165	—

KM# 19 1/24 THALER (Groschen)

Silver **Note:** Kipper 1/24 Thaler. Varieties exist.

Date	Mintage	VG	F	VF	XF	Unc
(16)19 (f)	—	20.00	40.00	80.00	160	—
(16)20 (f)	—	20.00	40.00	80.00	160	—
(1)620 (f)	—	20.00	40.00	80.00	160	—
ND (f)	—	20.00	40.00	80.00	160	—
(1)6ZZ (g)	—	20.00	40.00	80.00	160	—
1622	—	20.00	40.00	80.00	160	—
1623 (g)	—	20.00	40.00	80.00	160	—

KM# 56 1/24 THALER (Groschen)

Silver **Rev:** Date between church towers

Date	Mintage	VG	F	VF	XF	Unc
1633 (i)	—	—	—	—	—	—

KM# 57 1/24 THALER (Groschen)

Silver **Rev:** Titles of Ferdinand III **Note:** Varieties exist.

Date	Mintage	VG	F	VF	XF	Unc
(16)36 (j)	—	25.00	40.00	80.00	165	—
(16)37 (j)	—	25.00	40.00	80.00	165	—
(16)39 (j)	—	25.00	40.00	80.00	165	—
1641 (j)	21,000	25.00	40.00	80.00	165	—
(1)641 (j)	Inc. above	25.00	40.00	80.00	165	—
1655 (k)	—	25.00	40.00	80.00	165	—

KM# 58 1/24 THALER (Groschen)

Silver **Obv:** Titles of Ferdinand III

Date	Mintage	VG	F	VF	XF	Unc
(1)638 (j)	—	—	—	—	—	—

KM# 7 1/16 THALER (Doppel-Schilling)

Silver **Obv:** Arms in front of church **Rev:** Crowned imperial eagle, 16 in orb on breast, titles of Rudolf II, date divided by crown at top

Date	Mintage	VG	F	VF	XF	Unc
ND	—	200	400	750	1,500	—
1607 (a)	—	200	400	750	1,500	—
1608 (a)	—	200	400	750	1,500	—

KM# 42.1 1/8 THALER (1/2 Reichsort)

Silver **Obv:** Titles of Ferdinand II **Obv. Inscription:** I / HALBR. / R.ORT / date **Rev:** Arms in front of church

Date	Mintage	VG	F	VF	XF	Unc
1624	—	—	—	—	—	—

KM# 42.2 1/8 THALER (1/2 Reichsort)

Silver **Obv:** Titles of Ferdinand II **Obv. Inscription:** I / HALBR. / R.ORT / date **Rev:** Arms in front of church, date divided above value

Date	Mintage	VG	F	VF	XF	Unc
16Z4 (h)	—	—	—	—	—	—

KM# 44 1/8 THALER (1/2 Reichsort)

Silver **Rev:** Date in legend **Rev. Inscription:** EIN / HALB. / RIKES / ORT

Date	Mintage	VG	F	VF	XF	Unc
1625 (h)	—	—	—	—	—	—

KM# 39.1 1/4 THALER (6 Groschen)

Silver **Obv:** Arms in front of Church, date in legend **Rev:** Crowned imperial eagle, 6 on breast, titles of Ferdinand II

Date	Mintage	VG	F	VF	XF	Unc
1623	—	—	—	—	—	—

KM# 39.2 1/4 THALER (6 Groschen)

Silver **Obv:** Arms in front of church, date between towers **Rev:** Crowned imperial eagle, 6 on breast, titles of Ferdinand II

Date	Mintage	VG	F	VF	XF	Unc
16Z3 (g)	—	—	—	—	—	—

KM# 66 1/4 THALER (6 Groschen)

Silver **Obv:** Arms in front of church **Rev:** Crowned imperial eagle, orb without value on breast, titles of Ferdinand III and date in legend

Date	Mintage	VG	F	VF	XF	Unc
1656	—	—	—	—	—	—

KM# 41 1/2 THALER (12 Groschen)

Silver **Obv:** Crowned imperial eagle, 1Z in orb on breast, titles of Ferdinand II **Rev:** Arms in front of church, date between two towers

Date	Mintage	VG	F	VF	XF	Unc
16Z4 (h)	—	—	—	—	—	—
16Z5 (h)	—	—	—	—	—	—
1627 (h)	—	—	—	—	—	—
1629 (h)	—	—	—	—	—	—

KM# 43 1/2 THALER (12 Groschen)

Silver **Rev:** Date in legend

Date	Mintage	VG	F	VF	XF	Unc
(1)625 DK	—	—	—	—	—	—

KM# 52 1/2 THALER (12 Groschen)

Silver **Obv:** Without value in orb on eagle's breast **Rev:** Date divided left and right of church

Date	Mintage	VG	F	VF	XF	Unc
163Z (h)	—	—	—	—	—	—

KM# 55 1/2 THALER (12 Groschen)

Silver **Rev:** Date between church towers

Date	Mintage	VG	F	VF	XF	Unc
1633 (h)	—	—	—	—	—	—

KM# 8 THALER (24 Groschen)

Silver **Obv:** Church with arms in entrance way, date above in inner circle **Obv. Legend:** MONETA. NOVA: CIVITATIS. Q. HAMEL. x **Rev:** Crowned imperial eagle with orb on breast **Rev. Legend:** • RVDOL. II. D. G. ROM. IMP. SE. AVGVST. **Note:** Dav. #5375.

Date	Mintage	VG	F	VF	XF	Unc
1608 (a)	—	2,050	3,350	5,600	9,000	—

KM# 11 THALER (24 Groschen)

Silver **Obv:** Church with arms in entrance way **Obv. Legend:** • MONE • NOVA • CIVI • QVE • HAMELEN • **Rev:** Crowned imperial eagle with orb on breast **Rev. Legend:** MATTH • I • ROMA IMPE • SEMP • AV • **Note:** Dav.#A5377.

Date	Mintage	VG	F	VF	XF	Unc
1614 (d)	—	—	—	—	—	—
1617 GF	1,540	—	—	—	—	—

KM# 12 THALER (24 Groschen)

Silver **Obv:** Church wtih arms in entrance way in inner circle **Obv. Legend:** • MONETA. NOVA. CIVITATIS Q. HAMELE. **Rev:** Crowned imperial eagle with orb on breast, date above **Rev. Legend:** MATH. I. D. G. ROM. IM. SEM. AVGVS. **Note:** Klippe. Dav.#5376. Illustration reduced.

Date	Mintage	VG	F	VF	XF	Unc
1614 (d) Rare	—	—	—	—	—	—

KM# 13 THALER (24 Groschen)

Silver **Obv:** 24 in orb on breast of eagle, titles of Matthias **Rev:** Arms in front of church, date divided by central tower of church **Note:** Klippe. Dav. #5376.

Date	Mintage	VG	F	VF	XF	Unc
1615 (d)	—	—	—	—	—	—
1616 (d)	1,000	—	—	—	—	—

Note: Reported, not confirmed

KM# A13 THALER (24 Groschen)

Silver **Obv:** Church with arms in entrance way, date above in inner circle **Obv. Legend:** MONETA • NOVA • CIVITA • Q • HAMELEN **Rev:** Crowned imperial eagle with orb on breast **Rev. Legend:** MATHI • I • D • G • RO IMP • SEM • AVGVS • **Note:** Dav.#5376.

Date	Mintage	VG	F	VF	XF	Unc
1615	—	—	—	—	—	—

KM# A14 THALER (24 Groschen)

Silver **Obv:** Church with arms in entrance way, date above **Obv. Legend:** • MONETA • NOVA • CIVITATIS • QVERN • HAME LEN • **Rev:** Crowned imperial eagle with orb on breast **Rev. Legend:** MATTH • I • ROMA • IMPE • SEMP • AV • **Note:** Dav.#5376B.

Date	Mintage	VG	F	VF	XF	Unc
1616//1617	—	—	—	—	—	—

KM# 45 THALER (24 Groschen)
Silver **Note:** Dav. #5377.

Date	Mintage	VG	F	VF	XF	Unc
1625 DK	—	2,050	3,350	5,600	9,000	—

KM# 45.1 THALER (24 Groschen)
Silver **Obv:** Church with arms in entrance way **Obv. Legend:** MO•NO•REIP. QUERN HAMELN **Rev:** Crowned imperial eagle with orb on breast **Rev. Legend:** D: G. FERDI. Z. ROM. IMP. S. A.

Date	Mintage	VG	F	VF	XF	Unc
1625 D+K	—	—	—	—	—	—

KM# 45.2 THALER (24 Groschen)
Silver **Obv:** Church with arms in entrance way **Obv. Legend:** MO. NO. REIP. QUERN. HAMELN. **Rev:** Crowned imperial eagle with orb on breast **Rev. Legend:** D: G. FERD. Z. ROM .. IMP. SEM. AVG. **Note:** Dav. #5377A.

Date	Mintage	VG	F	VF	XF	Unc
1625 D+K	—	2,050	3,350	5,600	9,000	—

KM# 45.3 THALER (24 Groschen)
Silver **Obv:** Church with arms in entrance way **Obv. Legend:** MO • NO •• REIP • QUERN • HAMELN • ANNO • **Rev:** Crowned imperial eagle with orb on breast **Rev. Legend:** D • G • FERDI • Z • ROM • IMP • SEM • A • **Note:** Dav.#5377B.

Date	Mintage	VG	F	VF	XF	Unc
(1)1625 D+K	—	2,050	3,350	5,600	9,000	—

KM# 46.1 THALER (24 Groschen)
Silver **Obv. Legend:** D: G. FERDI. Z. ROM. - IMP * S * AUGU * **Rev:** Date between towers **Rev. Legend:** NOM - * NOUA * REIP ... * **Note:** Dav. #5378.

Date	Mintage	VG	F	VF	XF	Unc
(1)625 (h)	—	2,050	3,350	5,600	9,000	—

KM# 46.2 THALER (24 Groschen)
Silver **Obv. Legend:** ... Z.- ROM. IMP. S. A. **Note:** Dav. #5379.

Date	Mintage	VG	F	VF	XF	Unc
1625 (h)	—	2,050	3,350	5,600	9,000	—

KM# 46.3 THALER (24 Groschen)
Silver **Rev:** Three mint mark 1 above church **Rev. Legend:** MONE. NOVA. REIP. QVER. HAMLEN. **Note:** Dav. #5380.

Date	Mintage	VG	F	VF	XF	Unc
(16) (h) Rare	—	—	—	—	—	—

KM# 53.1 THALER (24 Groschen)
Silver **Obv. Legend:** FERDI. Z. DG. ROM ... **Note:** Dav. #5382.

Date	Mintage	VG	F	VF	XF	Unc
1632 (h)	—	2,050	3,350	5,600	9,000	—

KM# 53.2 THALER (24 Groschen)
Silver **Obv. Legend:** FERDI. Z. ROM. - ... **Note:** Dav. #5383.

Date	Mintage	F	VF	XF	Unc	BU
1632 (h)	—	2,050	3,350	5,600	9,000	—

KM# 60.1 THALER (24 Groschen)
Silver **Obv. Legend:** FERDI: III: D: G: - ROM: ... **Rev:** Church in decorative border, arms below **Note:** Dav. #5384.

Date	Mintage	VG	F	VF	XF	Unc
1639 (j)	—	2,050	3,350	5,600	9,000	—

KM# 60.2 THALER (24 Groschen)
Silver **Rev:** Heart above church **Note:** Varieties exist. Dav. #5385.

Date	Mintage	VG	F	VF	XF	Unc
1656 (k) Rare	—	—	—	—	—	—

KM# 76 THALER (24 Groschen)
Silver **Obv:** Crowned imperial eagle, titles of Leopold I **Rev:** Arms in front of church, date between towers **Note:** Dav. #5386.

Date	Mintage	VG	F	VF	XF	Unc
1669 (m) Rare	—	—	—	—	—	—

KM# 9 2 THALER
Silver **Obv:** Arms in front of church **Rev:** Crowned imperial eagle, 16 in orb on breast, titles of Rudolf II, date divided by crown at top

Date	Mintage	VG	F	VF	XF	Unc
1608 (a)	—	—	—	—	—	—

KM# 14 2 THALER
Silver **Obv:** Crowned imperial eagle, date divided by crown, titles of Matthias **Rev:** Arms in front of church, date in legend **Note:** Mule.

Date	Mintage	VG	F	VF	XF	Unc
1616//1617 Rare	—	—	—	—	—	—

KM# 61 2 THALER
Silver **Obv:** Crowned imperial eagle, orb on breast, date in legend below, titles of Ferdinand III

Date	Mintage	VG	F	VF	XF	Unc
1639 (j) Rare	—	—	—	—	—	—

TRADE COINAGE

KM# 59 GOLDGULDEN
3.5000 g., 0.9860 Gold 0.1109 oz. AGW **Obv:** Crowned imperial eagle, titles of Ferdinand III **Rev:** Arms in front of church, date in legend at top

Date	Mintage	VG	F	VF	XF	Unc
1638 (j) Rare	—	—	—	—	—	—

KM# 62 GOLDGULDEN
3.5000 g., 0.9860 Gold 0.1109 oz. AGW **Rev:** Date in legend at bottom

Date	Mintage	VG	F	VF	XF	Unc
(16)39 (j) Rare	—	—	—	—	—	—

KM# 74 GOLDGULDEN
3.5000 g., 0.9860 Gold 0.1109 oz. AGW **Obv:** Arms in front of church **Rev:** Bare-headed soldier standing 3/4 to left with sword and baton, legend **Rev. Legend:** DER.GER - HT.WI.N - V.

Date	Mintage	VG	F	VF	XF	Unc
ND(1668) Rare	—	—	—	—	—	—

KM# 75 GOLDGULDEN
3.5000 g., 0.9860 Gold 0.1109 oz. AGW **Obv:** Crowned imperial eagle, titles of Leopold I **Rev:** City arms in front of church, date above

Date	Mintage	VG	F	VF	XF	Unc
1668 Rare	—	—	—	—	—	—

KM# 85 GOLDGULDEN
3.5000 g., 0.9860 Gold 0.1109 oz. AGW **Rev:** Orb on eagle's breast, date divided by crown

Date	Mintage	VG	F	VF	XF	Unc
1672 Rare	—	—	—	—	—	—

KM# 67 DUCAT
3.5000 g., 0.9860 Gold 0.1109 oz. AGW **Obv:** City arms in front of church **Rev:** Full-length figure of Ferdinand III divides date

Date	Mintage	VG	F	VF	XF	Unc
1656 Rare	—	—	—	—	—	—

KM# 47 4 DUCAT
14.0000 g., 0.9860 Gold 0.4438 oz. AGW **Obv:** Arms in front of church, date between towers **Obv. Legend:** Inner: AMOR - VINZIT - OMNIA; Outer: DES. MENSCHEN. RVM. IST. WIE IN. WEISE. BLOM **Rev:** Bouquet of six flowers, heart pierced by two arrows below, double lily above

Date	Mintage	VG	F	VF	XF	Unc
1625 (h) Rare	—	—	—	—	—	—

KM# 48 10 DUCAT (Portugalöser)
35.0000 g., 0.9860 Gold 1.1095 oz. AGW **Note:** Struck with 1 Thaler dies, KM#46.

Date	Mintage	VG	F	VF	XF	Unc
(1)1625 (h) Rare	—	—	—	—	—	—

PATTERNS

Including off metal strikes

KM#	Date	Mintage	Identification	Mkt Val
Pn2	1672	—	12 Groschen. Gold. KM#81. Crowned imperial eagle, orb on breast, titles of Leopold I, crown divides date at top. Mule.	—

HAMM

A provincial city located in Westphalia, some 20 miles northeast of Dortmund, in the county of Mark. When the ruling house of Mark (see Cleves and Julich-Berg) became extinct in 1609, its territories, including Hamm, went to Brandenburg-Prussia in 1624 after a dispute with Pfalz-Neuburg. Hamm struck a local copper coinage from 1609 to 1749.

ARMS
Fesse of checkerboard

CITY

REGULAR COINAGE

KM# 6 HELLER
Copper **Obv:** H above arms in ornamented shield **Note:** Uniface.

Date	Mintage	VG	F	VF	XF	Unc
ND(ca.1609)	—	13.00	27.00	50.00	100	—

KM# 7 PFENNIG
Copper **Obv:** H above arms in ornamented shield **Rev:** Large I **Note:** Varieties exist.

Date	Mintage	VG	F	VF	XF	Unc
ND(ca. 1609)	—	13.00	27.00	50.00	100	—

KM# 8 2 PFENNIG
Copper **Obv:** H above arms in ornamented shield **Rev:** Large II **Note:** Varieties exist.

Date	Mintage	VG	F	VF	XF	Unc
ND(ca. 1609)	—	13.00	27.00	50.00	100	—

KM# 46 2 PFENNIG
Copper **Obv:** HAM above arms **Rev:** II above date

Date	Mintage	VG	F	VF	XF	Unc
1637	—	13.00	27.00	50.00	100	—

KM# 9 3 PFENNIG
Copper **Obv:** Arms in ornamented shield, H - A - M around in legend **Rev:** Value III in circle

Date	Mintage	VG	F	VF	XF	Unc
ND(ca.1609)	—	12.00	27.00	50.00	100	—

KM# 10 3 PFENNIG
Copper **Obv:** H above arms

Date	Mintage	VG	F	VF	XF	Unc
ND(ca.1609)	—	12.00	27.00	50.00	100	—

KM# 12 3 PFENNIG
Copper **Obv:** .S.H. above arms

Date	Mintage	VG	F	VF	XF	Unc
ND(ca.1609)	—	12.00	27.00	50.00	100	—

KM# 11 3 PFENNIG
Copper **Obv:** H above arms in ornamented shield **Rev:** Large III **Note:** Varieties exist.

Date	Mintage	VG	F	VF	XF	Unc
ND(ca.1609)	—	11.00	20.00	40.00	80.00	—
1618	—	11.00	20.00	40.00	80.00	—

KM# 28 3 PFENNIG
Copper **Obv:** Arms in ornamented shield, STADT. HAM. AN. D., date around **Rev:** Value III in ornamented circle

Date	Mintage	VG	F	VF	XF	Unc
1619	—	12.00	27.00	50.00	100	—
1630	—	12.00	27.00	50.00	100	—

KM# 41 3 PFENNIG
Copper **Obv:** HAM above arms **Rev:** Value III, date below

Date	Mintage	VG	F	VF	XF	Unc
1635	—	12.00	27.00	50.00	100	—

KM# 43 3 PFENNIG
Copper **Obv:** Arms, STADT - date - HAM around **Rev:** Value III in circle

Date	Mintage	VG	F	VF	XF	Unc
1635	—	12.00	27.00	50.00	100	—

KM# 42 3 PFENNIG
Copper **Obv:** Arms, STADT. HAM around **Rev:** Value III above date **Note:** Varieties exist.

Date	Mintage	VG	F	VF	XF	Unc
1635	—	12.00	27.00	50.00	100	—
1637	—	12.00	27.00	50.00	100	—

KM# 50 3 PFENNIG
Copper **Obv:** Arms, STADT. HAMM, date around **Rev. Legend:** III/PFEN

Date	Mintage	VG	F	VF	XF	Unc
1648	—	12.00	27.00	50.00	100	—

KM# 55 3 PFENNIG
Copper **Rev:** III only

Date	Mintage	VG	F	VF	XF	Unc
1652	—	11.00	20.00	50.00	100	—

KM# 56 3 PFENNIG
Copper **Obv:** H above ornamented arms, H-A-M around in legend **Rev:** III in ornamented square divides date

Date	Mintage	VG	F	VF	XF	Unc
(16)58	—	11.00	27.00	50.00	100	—

KM# 57 3 PFENNIG
Copper **Obv:** H above ornamented arms **Rev:** III above date

Date	Mintage	VG	F	VF	XF	Unc
1658	—	11.00	27.00	50.00	100	—
1661	—	11.00	27.00	50.00	100	—

KM# 58 3 PFENNIG
Copper **Obv:** Arms, HAMM. date around **Rev:** Value III

Date	Mintage	VG	F	VF	XF	Unc
1659	—	10.00	20.00	35.00	75.00	—

KM# 59 3 PFENNIG
Copper **Obv:** Legend S. HAMM. date

Date	Mintage	VG	F	VF	XF	Unc
1659	—	10.00	20.00	35.00	75.00	—

KM# 60 3 PFENNIG
Copper **Obv:** Arms, STADT. HAMM. date around **Rev:** III in palm wreath

Date	Mintage	VG	F	VF	XF	Unc
1669	—	8.00	20.00	35.00	75.00	—
1676	—	8.00	20.00	35.00	75.00	—
1679	—	8.00	20.00	35.00	75.00	—

KM# 65 3 PFENNIG
Copper **Obv:** Arms, STADT. HAMM, date around **Rev:** III PFEN. in palm wreath

Date	Mintage	VG	F	VF	XF	Unc
(16)74	—	7.00	20.00	35.00	75.00	—
1680	—	7.00	20.00	35.00	75.00	—
1682	—	7.00	20.00	35.00	75.00	—
1686	—	7.00	20.00	35.00	75.00	—

KM# 66 3 PFENNIG
Copper **Rev:** III in ornamented circle

Date	Mintage	VG	F	VF	XF	Unc
1676	—	7.00	20.00	35.00	75.00	—

KM# 70 3 PFENNIG
Copper **Obv:** HVS below arms

Date	Mintage	VG	F	VF	XF	Unc
1684	—	7.00	20.00	35.00	75.00	—

KM# 71 3 PFENNIG
Copper **Obv:** Arms **Rev:** Value within wreath

Date	Mintage	VG	F	VF	XF	Unc
1687	—	7.00	20.00	35.00	75.00	—
1699	—	7.00	20.00	35.00	75.00	—
1700	—	7.00	20.00	35.00	75.00	—

KM# 72 3 PFENNIG
Copper, 19-21 mm. **Obv:** Shield of town arms, date above **Obv. Legend:** STADT - HAMM **Rev:** 2-line inscription within wreath **Rev. Inscription:** III / PFEN

Date	Mintage	VG	F	VF	XF	Unc
1687	—	7.00	20.00	35.00	75.00	—
1692	—	7.00	20.00	35.00	75.00	—
1693	—	7.00	20.00	35.00	75.00	—
1696	—	7.00	20.00	35.00	75.00	—

KM# 75 3 PFENNIG
Copper, 20 mm. **Obv:** Shield of town arms, date below **Obv. Legend:** STADT - HAMM **Rev:** 2-line inscription within wreath **Rev. Inscription:** III / PFEN **Note:** Varieties exist.

Date	Mintage	VG	F	VF	XF	Unc
1690	47,000	7.00	20.00	35.00	75.00	—
1699	—	7.00	20.00	35.00	75.00	—

KM# 76 3 PFENNIG
Copper **Obv. Inscription:** STADT / date / HAMM

Date	Mintage	VG	F	VF	XF	Unc
1696	—	7.00	20.00	35.00	75.00	—

KM# 14 4 PFENNIG
Copper **Obv:** H-A-M around in legend

Date	Mintage	VG	F	VF	XF	Unc
ND(ca.1609)	—	13.00	30.00	55.00	110	—

KM# 13 4 PFENNIG
Copper **Obv:** H above arms in ornamented shield **Rev:** Large IIII **Note:** Varieties exist.

Date	Mintage	VG	F	VF	XF	Unc
ND(ca.1609)	—	13.00	30.00	55.00	110	—

KM# 35 4 PFENNIG
Copper **Obv:** Arms, around STADT. HAM. ANNO. date **Rev:** IIII in ornamented oval

Date	Mintage	VG	F	VF	XF	Unc
1620	—	11.00	20.00	40.00	80.00	—

KM# 40 4 PFENNIG
Copper **Obv:** Date **Obv. Legend:** STADT. AHM. AN. D **Note:** Varieties exist.

Date	Mintage	VG	F	VF	XF	Unc
1630	—	11.00	20.00	40.00	80.00	—
1650	—	11.00	20.00	40.00	80.00	—

KM# 47 4 PFENNIG
Copper **Obv:** Arms, around STADT. HAM **Rev:** IIII above date

Date	Mintage	VG	F	VF	XF	Unc
1637	—	11.00	20.00	40.00	80.00	—

KM# 16 6 PFENNIG
Copper **Rev:** Date above VI, H-A-M around legend

Date	Mintage	VG	F	VF	XF	Unc
1609	—	13.00	27.00	50.00	100	—

KM# 15 6 PFENNIG
Copper **Obv:** H above arms in ornamented shield **Rev:** Large VI **Note:** Varieties exist.

Date	Mintage	VG	F	VF	XF	Unc
ND(ca.1609)	—	16.00	33.00	65.00	130	—

KM# 26 6 PFENNIG
Copper **Obv:** H-A-M around legend **Rev:** Date below value **Note:** Varieties exist.

Date	Mintage	VG	F	VF	XF	Unc
(1)614	—	27.00	55.00	110	225	—
(1)618	—	13.00	27.00	45.00	90.00	—
1620	—	13.00	27.00	45.00	90.00	—

KM# 36 6 PFENNIG
Copper **Obv:** H above arms, without H-A-M

Date	Mintage	VG	F	VF	XF	Unc
1620	—	16.00	33.00	65.00	130	—

KM# 44 6 PFENNIG
Copper **Rev:** ANNO above value

Date	Mintage	VG	F	VF	XF	Unc
1635	—	13.00	27.00	50.00	100	—

KM# 45 6 PFENNIG
Copper **Obv:** HAM above arms **Note:** Varieties exist.

Date	Mintage	VG	F	VF	XF	Unc
1635	—	11.00	20.00	35.00	75.00	—

KM# 5 12 PFENNIG
Copper **Obv:** H above arms

Date	Mintage	VG	F	VF	XF	Unc
(16)05	—	15.00	30.00	60.00	120	—

KM# 19 12 PFENNIG
Copper **Rev:** Date below value **Note:** Varieties exist.

Date	Mintage	VG	F	VF	XF	Unc
1609	—	15.00	30.00	60.00	120	—
1610	—	15.00	30.00	60.00	120	—
1618	—	15.00	30.00	60.00	120	—

KM# 17 12 PFENNIG
Copper **Obv:** H above arms in ornamented shield **Rev:** Large XII

Date	Mintage	VG	F	VF	XF	Unc
ND(ca.1609)	—	13.00	27.00	55.00	115	—

KM# 18 12 PFENNIG
Copper **Obv:** H-A-M around legend

Date	Mintage	VG	F	VF	XF	Unc
ND(ca.1609)	—	15.00	30.00	60.00	125	—

KM# 27 12 PFENNIG
Copper **Obv:** Without H above arms **Note:** Varieties exist.

Date	Mintage	VG	F	VF	XF	Unc
(1)614	—	20.00	40.00	80.00	160	—
1618	—	20.00	40.00	80.00	160	—
1620	—	20.00	40.00	80.00	160	—

HANAU

Located 14 miles east of Frankfurt am Main, Hanau is the site of a Roman frontier settlement. The line of counts can be traced back to the mid-11th century. The county was divided into the lines of Hanau-Lichtenberg and Hanau-Münzenberg in 1451.

HANAU-LICHTENBERG

The younger line of the counts of Hanau. Lands in Alsace, acquired through marriage, the counts taking up residence in Buchsweiler, some 14 miles west of Hagenau. The elder Münzenberg line became extinct in 1642 and all lands passed to Lichtenberg. Raised to the rank of prince in 1696. Became extinct in 1736 and passed to Hesse-Darmstadt in 1785.

RULERS
Johann Reinhard I, 1599-1625
Philipp Wolfgang, 1625-1641
Friedrich Casimir, 1641-1685
Philipp Reinhard, 1685-1712

MINT OFFICIALS' INITIALS

Buchsweiler Mint

Initial	Date	Name
BM, IBM	1663-72	Johann Brettmacher
GHP, HP	1672-73	Georg Hartmann Plappert
IFL	1661-62	Johann Friedrich Lauer
IMG, MG	1659-60	Johann Martin Ganser

Darmstadt Mint

Initial	Date	Name
R	1696-1727	Johann C. Roth, die-cutter

Hanau Mint

Initial	Date	Name
	1603-1607	Peter Arenburch
	1607-1612	Simon Tympe (Timpf)
	1609-1613/14	Gerhard Bodenback, warden
	1613-?	Jakob Thomann
	1613-	Peter Binder, warden
	1614-1616	Melchior Küttner
	1619-1620	Hans Baldwin
IMG, MG	1658-74	Johann Martin Ganser
SM	1674-95	Sebastian Müller

Heidelberg Mint

Initial	Date	Name
IL, JL	1659-1711	Johann Link, die-cutter

Willstett Mint

Initial	Date	Name
	1622-1623	Martin Thomann

Wörth Mint

Initial	Date	Name
(b)= 	1596-1601	Jakob Dietrich
V	1601-02	Konrad Vogel

ARMS
Hanau only = 3 chevrons, but often 4-fold arms with central chevron shield.
Hanau-Lichtenberg = 3 chevrons on left, rampant lion on right.
Ochsenstein = 2 horizontal bars

REFERENCE:
S = Reinhard Suchier, **Die Münzen der Grafen von Hanau**, Hanau, 1897.

COUNTSHIP

REGULAR COINAGE

KM# 11 PFENNIG
Silver **Ruler:** Johann Reinhard I **Obv:** Hohl-type. 4-fold arms with central chevron shield, IR above **Note:** Uniface.

Date	Mintage	VG	F	VF	XF	Unc
ND(1605)	75,000	11.00	25.00	50.00	100	—

KM# 13 PFENNIG
Silver **Ruler:** Johann Reinhard I **Obv:** 3 conjoined shields, IR above. **Note:** Uniface, hohl-type.

Date	Mintage	VG	F	VF	XF	Unc
ND(1609)	63,000	13.00	27.00	55.00	110	—

KM# 77 PFENNIG
Silver **Obv:** Crowned Hanau arms divide H - M, date divided below **Note:** Uniface, hohl-type.

Date	Mintage	VG	F	VF	XF	Unc
1676	—	16.00	30.00	65.00	130	—

KM# 87 PFENNIG
Silver **Note:** Date below divided by SM.

Date	Mintage	VG	F	VF	XF	Unc
1681 SM	—	16.00	33.00	65.00	130	—

KM# 88 PFENNIG
Silver **Note:** Arms divide H-M/S-M.

Date	Mintage	VG	F	VF	XF	Unc
ND(1683-85) SM	—	16.00	33.00	65.00	130	—

KM# 14 2 PFENNIG (1/2 Kreuzer)
Silver **Ruler:** Johann Reinhard I **Obv:** Hanau arms in shield divide I-R, swan to left above. **Note:** Uniface.

Date	Mintage	VG	F	VF	XF	Unc
ND(1609-12)	1,073,000	12.00	25.00	55.00	110	—

KM# 33 2 PFENNIG (1/2 Kreuzer)
Silver **Obv:** Hanau arms divide I - R, date above **Note:** Uniface, hohl-type.

Date	Mintage	VG	F	VF	XF	Unc
1624	—	15.00	35.00	70.00	—	—

KM# 26 4 PFENNIG (Kreuzer)
Silver **Obv:** Crowned arms of Hanau, titles of Ferdinand II **Rev:** Chevron arms, titles of Johann Reinhard I

Date	Mintage	VG	F	VF	XF	Unc
ND(1619-25) Unique	—	—	—	—	—	—

KM# 20 8 PFENNIG (Albus)
Silver **Ruler:** Johann Reinhard I **Obv:** Four-fold arms with central chevron shield **Rev:** I. LIECHT etc. around **Rev. Inscription:** VIII / PFENNIG / date, DO.

Date	Mintage	VG	F	VF	XF	Unc
1610	81,000	33.00	65.00	130	265	—
1611	—	33.00	65.00	130	265	—

KM# 97 ALBUS (8 Pfennig)
Silver **Obv:** Crowned arms **Rev. Inscription:** I / ALBUS / date

Date	Mintage	VG	F	VF	XF	Unc
1693 SM	—	33.00	65.00	130	265	—

Date	Mintage	VG	F	VF	XF	Unc
1694 SM	—	33.00	65.00	130	265	—
1695 SM	—	33.00	65.00	130	265	—

KM# 32 KREUZER

Silver **Obv:** Titles of Ferdinand II **Obv. Inscription:** I / KREI / ZER **Rev:** 5-fold arms with central chevron shield, date above **Note:** Varieties exist.

Date	Mintage	VG	F	VF	XF	Unc
1623	—	20.00	40.00	75.00	155	—
1624	—	20.00	40.00	75.00	155	—

KM# 63 KREUZER

Silver **Obv:** Crowned six-fold arms in laurel wreath **Rev:** Inscription in laurel wreath **Rev. Inscription:** I / KREVTZ / date / ER

Date	Mintage	VG	F	VF	XF	Unc
1663 Unique	—	—	—	—	—	—

KM# 68 KREUZER

Silver **Rev. Inscription:** I / KREV / TZER

Date	Mintage	VG	F	VF	XF	Unc
ND(1667-68)	—	15.00	35.00	70.00	145	—

KM# 69 KREUZER

Silver **Rev. Inscription:** I / KREVTZ / ER

Date	Mintage	VG	F	VF	XF	Unc
ND(1667-68)	—	15.00	35.00	70.00	145	—

KM# 78 KREUZER

Silver **Obv:** Crowned Hannau-Lichtenberg arms in laurel wreath **Rev:** Inscription in laurel wreath **Rev. Inscription:** 16 I 76 / KREU / TZER / S.M.

Date	Mintage	VG	F	VF	XF	Unc
1676 SM	—	12.00	25.00	55.00	110	—

KM# 79 KREUZER

0.4000 g., Silver, 15.4 mm. **Rev. Inscription:** I / KREV / TZER / date / SM **Note:** Varieties exist.

Date	Mintage	VG	F	VF	XF	Unc
1676 SM	—	10.00	20.00	45.00	90.00	—
1677 SM	—	10.00	20.00	45.00	90.00	—
1678 SM	—	10.00	20.00	45.00	90.00	—
1679 SM	487,000	10.00	20.00	45.00	90.00	—
1679 MS Error	Inc. above	10.00	20.00	45.00	90.00	—
1680 SM	—	10.00	20.00	45.00	90.00	—
1681 SM	—	10.00	20.00	45.00	90.00	—
1682 SM	—	10.00	20.00	45.00	90.00	—
1683 SM	—	10.00	20.00	45.00	90.00	—

KM# 85 KREUZER

Silver **Obv:** Crowned heart-shaped three-fold arms without laurel wreath

Date	Mintage	VG	F	VF	XF	Unc
1680 SM	—	15.00	30.00	60.00	120	—
1681 SM	—	15.00	30.00	60.00	120	—

KM# 102 KREUZER

Silver **Ruler:** Philipp Reinhard **Obv:** Crowned oval Hanau-Lichtenberg arms **Rev. Inscription:** I / KREV / TZER / date

Date	Mintage	VG	F	VF	XF	Unc
1695	—	—	—	—	—	—

KM# 45 2 KREUZER (1/2 Batzen)

Silver **Obv:** II/KREUTZ/ER, titles of Ferdinand II **Rev:** Four-fold arms with central chevron shield, date above

Date	Mintage	VG	F	VF	XF	Unc
1631	—	12.00	25.00	50.00	100	—
1632	—	12.00	25.00	50.00	100	—

KM# 50 2 KREUZER (1/2 Batzen)

Silver **Obv:** Round seven-fold arms **Rev:** Imperial orb with two in curve-sided rhombus divides date

Date	Mintage	VG	F	VF	XF	Unc
1647	—	—	—	—	—	—

KM# 51 2 KREUZER (1/2 Batzen)

Silver **Obv:** Crowned seven-fold arms **Rev:** Imperial orb with Z (or 2), date divided by cross above, all in wreath **Note:** Varieties exist.

Date	Mintage	VG	F	VF	XF	Unc
1647	—	10.00	20.00	45.00	90.00	—
1647 MG	—	10.00	20.00	45.00	90.00	—
1648 MG	—	10.00	20.00	45.00	90.00	—
1651 MG	—	10.00	20.00	45.00	90.00	—
1653 MG	—	10.00	20.00	45.00	90.00	—
1654 MG	—	10.00	20.00	45.00	90.00	—
1655 MG	—	10.00	20.00	45.00	90.00	—
1656 MG	—	10.00	20.00	45.00	90.00	—
1657 MG	—	10.00	20.00	45.00	90.00	—
1658	—	10.00	20.00	45.00	90.00	—
1666	—	10.00	20.00	45.00	90.00	—
1667	—	10.00	20.00	45.00	90.00	—
1667 MG	—	10.00	20.00	45.00	90.00	—
1668 MG	—	10.00	20.00	45.00	90.00	—
1669 MG	—	10.00	20.00	45.00	90.00	—
1670 MG	—	10.00	20.00	45.00	90.00	—
1671 MG	—	10.00	20.00	45.00	90.00	—
1672 MG	—	10.00	20.00	45.00	90.00	—
1680 SM	—	10.00	20.00	45.00	90.00	—
1681 SM	—	10.00	20.00	45.00	90.00	—
1682 SM	—	10.00	20.00	45.00	90.00	—
1684 SM	—	10.00	20.00	45.00	90.00	—

KM# 60 2 KREUZER (1/2 Batzen)

Silver **Obv:** Crowned seven-fold arms with date below in laurel wreath **Rev:** Inscription in laurel wreath **Rev. Inscription:** HANAW (or U) / LICHTEN / BERGI / SCHE / 2K

Date	Mintage	VG	F	VF	XF	Unc
1660 MG	—	—	—	—	—	—

KM# 62 2 KREUZER (1/2 Batzen)

Silver **Obv:** Date above crown

Date	Mintage	VG	F	VF	XF	Unc
1661 IFL	—	11.00	25.00	50.00	100	—
1662 IFL	—	11.00	25.00	50.00	100	—
1663 IBM	—	11.00	25.00	50.00	100	—

KM# 64 2 KREUZER (1/2 Batzen)

Silver **Obv:** Date divided by arms

Date	Mintage	VG	F	VF	XF	Unc
1663 IBM	—	11.00	25.00	50.00	100	—
1664/3	—	11.00	25.00	50.00	100	—
1664	—	11.00	25.00	50.00	100	—
1665	—	11.00	25.00	50.00	100	—

KM# 80 2 KREUZER (1/2 Batzen)

Silver **Obv:** Crowned 7-fold arms, date in legend **Rev:** Imperial orb with Z (for 2), cross above, all in wreath

Date	Mintage	VG	F	VF	XF	Unc
1678 SM	—	—	—	—	—	—

KM# 90 2 KREUZER (1/2 Batzen)

Silver **Obv:** Crowned 7-fold arms **Rev:** Imperial orb with 2, date divided by cross above, all in wreath

Date	Mintage	VG	F	VF	XF	Unc
1687	—	—	—	—	—	—

KM# 4 3 KREUZER (Groschen)

Silver **Ruler:** Johann Reinhard I **Obv:** 4-fold arms with central chevron arms, date above **Obv. Legend:** IOAN. REINH. COM. IN. HANAW. **Rev:** Crowned imperial eagle, 3 in orb on breast **Rev. Legend:** RVDOL. II. RO. IMP. AVG. P. F. DEC. **Note:** Varieties exist.

Date	Mintage	VG	F	VF	XF	Unc
1601	—	12.00	25.00	40.00	85.00	—
1601 V	—	12.00	25.00	40.00	85.00	—
1602	—	12.00	25.00	40.00	85.00	—
1603	—	12.00	25.00	40.00	85.00	—
1604	—	12.00	25.00	40.00	85.00	—
1605	43,000	12.00	25.00	40.00	85.00	—
1606	79,000	12.00	25.00	40.00	85.00	—
1607	93,000	12.00	25.00	40.00	85.00	—
1608	—	12.00	25.00	40.00	85.00	—
1609	—	12.00	25.00	40.00	85.00	—
ND(1610/11)	62,000	12.00	25.00	40.00	85.00	—
1614 Posthumous	—	12.00	25.00	40.00	85.00	—

KM# 5 3 KREUZER (Groschen)

Silver **Obv:** 4-fold arms with central chevron arms, date above **Rev:** Crowned imperial eagle, 3 in orb on breast **Note:** Klippe.

Date	Mintage	VG	F	VF	XF	Unc
1602 Rare	—	—	—	—	—	—

KM# 7 3 KREUZER (Groschen)

Silver **Obv:** 4-fold arms with central chevron arms without date **Rev:** Inscription in laurel wreath **Rev. Inscription:** Date / FORTVNAM / VINCE / FERENDO **Note:** Klippe.

Date	Mintage	VG	F	VF	XF	Unc
1602	—	—	—	—	—	—

KM# 21 3 KREUZER (Groschen)

1.3000 g., Silver, 20.9 mm. **Ruler:** Johann Reinhard I **Obv:** Shield **Rev:** Double headed eagle **Rev. Legend:** Titles of Matthias **Note:** Varieties exist.

Date	Mintage	VG	F	VF	XF	Unc
161Z	28,000	20.00	40.00	65.00	120	—
ND	12,000	20.00	40.00	65.00	120	—

KM# 34 3 KREUZER (Groschen)

Silver **Obv:** Titles of Ferdinand II

Date	Mintage	VG	F	VF	XF	Unc
1624	—	—	—	—	—	—

KM# 98 2 ALBUS (Batzen)

Silver, 22-23 mm. **Ruler:** Philipp Reinhard **Obv:** Crowned oval shield of 6-fold arms with central shield in baroque frame **Obv. Legend:** PHILIP. REINHAR. D. G. Z. HANAU. **Rev:** 4-line inscription with date **Rev. Legend:** NACH. DEM SCHLUS. DER. V. STÆND. **Rev. Inscription:** II / ALBUS / (date) / SM

Date	Mintage	VG	F	VF	XF	Unc
1693 SM	—	30.00	55.00	115	230	—
1694 SM	—	30.00	55.00	115	230	—

KM# 99.2 6 ALBUS (12 Kreuzer)

Silver **Ruler:** Philipp Reinhard **Obv:** Crowned arms **Obv. Legend:** PHILIP. REINHARD: G: Z: HANAU **Rev. Legend:** NACH • DEM. SCHLUS • DER • STAEND

Date	Mintage	VG	F	VF	XF	Unc
1693	—	30.00	65.00	135	270	—

KM# 99.1 6 ALBUS (12 Kreuzer)

Silver **Ruler:** Philipp Reinhard **Obv:** Crowned arms **Note:** Varieties exist.

Date	Mintage	VG	F	VF	XF	Unc
1693 SM	—	27.00	55.00	115	230	—
1694 SM	—	27.00	55.00	115	230	—

KM# 27 12 KREUZER (Dreibätzner/3 Batzen)

Silver **Obv:** Crowned imperial eagle, 12 in orb on breast, SVB. VMB... **Obv. Legend:** Four-fold arms with central chevron shield, date above **Note:** Varieties exist.

Date	Mintage	VG	F	VF	XF	Unc
1619	—	45.00	100	190	325	650
1620	—	45.00	100	190	325	650
1621	—	45.00	100	190	325	650
ND	—	45.00	100	190	325	650

KM# 35 12 KREUZER (Dreibätzner/3 Batzen)

Silver **Obv:** Shield below date within circle **Rev:** Without 12 in orb, (XII) at top, titles of Ferdinand II

Date	Mintage	VG	F	VF	XF	Unc
1624	—	55.00	110	235	475	—
1625	—	55.00	110	235	475	—

KM# 38 12 KREUZER (Dreibätzner/3 Batzen)

Silver **Obv:** Shield below date within beaded circle, Philipp Wolfgang in legend **Rev:** Double-headed imperial eagle within beaded circle **Note:** Varieties exist.

Date	Mintage	VG	F	VF	XF	Unc
1626	—	60.00	120	235	475	—
1629	—	60.00	120	235	475	—
1630	—	60.00	120	235	475	—
1631	—	60.00	120	235	475	—

KM# 61 12 KREUZER (Dreibätzner/3 Batzen)

Silver **Obv:** Crowned imperial eagle, orb on breast, value (XII) above, titles of Leopold I **Rev:** Crowned six-fold arms, date above crown

Date	Mintage	VG	F	VF	XF	Unc
1660 MG	—	80.00	160	300	600	—
1661/0 IFL	—	80.00	160	300	600	—
1662 IFL	—	80.00	160	300	600	—
ND(1662) IFL	—	80.00	160	300	600	—
ND(1663) FM Error for BM	—	80.00	160	300	600	—

KM# 65 12 KREUZER (Dreibätzner/3 Batzen)

Silver **Obv:** Date divided by crowned arms **Rev:** Double-headed imperial eagle within beaded circle

Date	Mintage	VG	F	VF	XF	Unc
1664	—	80.00	160	300	600	—
1665	—	80.00	160	300	600	—

KM# 70 30 KREUZER (1/3 Thaler)

Silver **Obv:** Bust right **Rev:** Crowned seven-fold arms divide date, value 30 in cartouche at bottom

Date	Mintage	VG	F	VF	XF	Unc
1668 BM	—	—	—	—	—	—
ND(1669)	—	—	—	—	—	—
1672 MG	651	—	—	—	—	—
1673 MG	—	—	—	—	—	—

KM# 75 30 KREUZER (1/3 Thaler)

Silver **Rev:** Date in legend

Date	Mintage	VG	F	VF	XF	Unc
1675 SM Unique	—	—	—	—	—	—

KM# 6 TESTONE (24 Kreuzer)

Silver **Obv:** Four-fold arms with central chevron shield, date above

Date	Mintage	VG	F	VF	XF	Unc
1601	—	80.00	160	220	375	650
1608	—	80.00	160	220	375	650
1609	—	80.00	160	220	375	650
1610	49,000	80.00	160	220	375	650
1611	—	80.00	160	220	375	650
161Z	42,000	80.00	160	220	375	650
1613	16,000	80.00	160	220	375	650
ND(1614-18)	77,000	80.00	160	220	375	650
1621	—	80.00	160	220	375	650
ND(1621)	—	80.00	160	220	375	650

KM# 12 TESTONE (24 Kreuzer)

Silver **Ruler:** Johann Reinhard I **Note:** Klippe.

Date	Mintage	VG	F	VF	XF	Unc
1608 Rare	—	—	—	—	—	—

KM# 30 TESTONE (24 Kreuzer)

Silver **Obv:** Bust right in inner circle **Rev:** 4-fold arms with central chevron shield, date above **Note:** Kipper Testone. Lightweight - 3.6-3.7 grams.

Date	Mintage	VG	F	VF	XF	Unc
ND(1622)	—	45.00	85.00	150	270	—

KM# 8 1/2 THALER

Silver **Obv:** Bust of Johann Reinhard right in inner circle, legend around **Rev:** 4-fold arms on shield

Date	Mintage	VG	F	VF	XF	Unc
ND Rare	—	—	—	—	—	—

KM# 71.1 60 KREUZER (2/3 Thaler)

Silver **Rev:** 60 in cartouche below arms

Date	Mintage	VG	F	VF	XF	Unc
1668 BM	—	85.00	150	220	425	—
ND(1668) BM	—	85.00	150	220	425	—

KM# 71.2 60 KREUZER (2/3 Thaler)

Silver **Rev:** Crowned arms divide GH-P at sides

Date	Mintage	VG	F	VF	XF	Unc
ND(1669-72) GHP	—	90.00	150	225	475	—

KM# 71.3 60 KREUZER (2/3 Thaler)

Silver **Rev:** GH-P divided at bottom of crowned arms

Date	Mintage	VG	F	VF	XF	Unc
ND(1669-72) HP	—	100	180	250	500	—

KM# 71.4 60 KREUZER (2/3 Thaler)

Silver

Date	Mintage	VG	F	VF	XF	Unc
1672 MG	18,000	85.00	150	210	385	—
1673 MG	—	85.00	150	210	385	—
1674 MG	—	85.00	150	210	385	—

KM# 71.5 60 KREUZER (2/3 Thaler)

Silver **Note:** Simple and ornate bust varieties exist.

Date	Mintage	VG	F	VF	XF	Unc
1675 SM	—	100	160	240	475	—
1676 SM	—	100	160	240	475	—
1680/76 SM	—	100	160	240	475	—
1680 SM	—	100	160	240	475	—

KM# 95 60 KREUZER (2/3 Thaler)

Silver

Date	Mintage	VG	F	VF	XF	Unc
1691 SM	—	—	—	—	—	—

KM# 96 60 KREUZER (2/3 Thaler)

Silver **Rev:** Oval arms and date divided by crown above **Note:** Varieties exist.

Date	Mintage	VG	F	VF	XF	Unc
1693 SM	—	85.00	150	220	450	—
1693 IL-SM	—	85.00	150	220	450	—
1694 SM	—	85.00	150	220	450	—
1695 SM	—	85.00	150	220	450	—

KM# 9 THALER

Silver **Obv:** Johann Reinhard **Note:** Dav. #6693.

Date	Mintage	VG	F	VF	XF	Unc
ND	2,570	1,000	2,000	4,000	7,000	—

KM# 15 THALER

Silver **Ruler:** Johann Reinhard I **Obv:** Large bust breaking circle at top and bottom **Rev:** Shield dividing date **Note:** Dav. #6694.

Date	Mintage	VG	F	VF	XF	Unc
1609	—	1,250	2,750	4,500	7,500	—

KM# 36 THALER

Silver **Obv:** Smaller full bust within circle **Rev:** Date above shield **Note:** Dav. #6696.

Date	Mintage	VG	F	VF	XF	Unc
1624	—	825	1,650	2,850	5,000	—

KM# 39 THALER

Silver **Obv:** Crowned imperial eagle, orb on breast, titles of Ferdinand II **Rev:** Oval arms in baroque frame, date divided above **Note:** Dav. #6697.

Date	Mintage	VG	F	VF	XF	Unc
1626 Rare	—	—	—	—	—	—

KM# 40 THALER

Silver **Obv:** Bust of Philipp Wolfgang right **Rev:** Four-fold arms with central chevron shield, date divided around **Note:** Dav. #6698.

Date	Mintage	VG	F	VF	XF	Unc
1629 Rare	—	—	—	—	—	—

KM# 52.1 THALER

Silver **Obv:** Crowned imperial eagle, orb on breast, titles of Ferdinand III **Rev:** Crowned ornate seven-fold arms divide date **Note:** Dav. #6699.

Date	Mintage	VG	F	VF	XF	Unc
1647 MG Rare	—	—	—	—	—	—

Note: Dr. Busso Peus Nachfolger Auction 383, 4-05, VF realized approximately $10,695.

Date	Mintage	VG	F	VF	XF	Unc
1648 MG Rare	—	—	—	—	—	—
1655 MG Rare	—	—	—	—	—	—

KM# 52.2 THALER

Silver **Obv:** Titles of Leopold I **Rev. Legend:** FRIDERICVS. CASIMIRVS... **Note:** Dav. #6700.

Date	Mintage	VG	F	VF	XF	Unc
1658 MG Rare	—	—	—	—	—	—

KM# 53 THALER

Silver **Obv:** Bust right **Note:** Dav. #A6701.

Date	Mintage	VG	F	VF	XF	Unc
ND MG Rare	—	—	—	—	—	—

KM# 66 THALER

Silver **Obv:** Bust right in circle **Rev:** Helmeted seven-fold arms divide date **Note:** Dav. #6702.

Date	Mintage	VG	F	VF	XF	Unc
1664 BM Rare	—	—	—	—	—	—

Note: Künker Auction 163, 1-10, XF realized approximately $15,445. Hess-Divo AG Auction 297, 10-03, VF/XF realized approximately $21,250.

Date	Mintage	VG	F	VF	XF	Unc
1673 HP Rare	—	—	—	—	—	—

KM# 86 THALER

Silver **Obv:** Large bust without circle **Rev:** Date in legend **Note:** Dav. #6703.

Date	Mintage	VG	F	VF	XF	Unc
1680 SM Rare	—	—	—	—	—	—

KM# 100 THALER
Silver **Ruler:** Philipp Reinhard **Obv:** Philipp Reinhard **Rev:** Helmeted seven-fold arms, date in legend **Note:** Dav. #6704.

Date	Mintage	VG	F	VF	XF	Unc
1694 SM Rare	—	—	—	—	—	—

KM# 101 THALER
Silver **Ruler:** Philipp Reinhard **Rev:** Crowned oval seven-fold arms, date divided at bottom **Note:** Dav. #6705.

Date	Mintage	VG	F	VF	XF	Unc
1694 JL-SM Rare	—	—	—	—	—	—

Note: Rauch Auction 85, 11-09 XF realized approx. $27,100

KM# 103.1 THALER
Silver **Ruler:** Philipp Reinhard **Obv:** Bust right **Rev:** City view, angel above, crowned and supported oval seven-fold arms below divide date **Note:** Dav. #6706.

Date	Mintage	VG	F	VF	XF	Unc
1695	—	1,750	3,000	5,500	9,500	—

KM# 103.2 THALER
Silver **Ruler:** Philipp Reinhard **Obv:** Bust with different armor, R below **Note:** Dav. #6707.

Date	Mintage	VG	F	VF	XF	Unc
1695 R Rare	—	—	—	—	—	—

KM# 10.1 2 THALER
Silver **Ruler:** Johann Reinhard I **Obv:** Bust of Johann Reinhard right **Rev:** Similar to 1 Thaler, KM#9 **Note:** Dav. #6691.

Date	Mintage	VG	F	VF	XF	Unc
ND Rare	—	—	—	—	—	—

KM# 10.2 2 THALER
Silver **Ruler:** Johann Reinhard I **Rev. Legend:** IN-LIECH: ET-OCHSE... **Note:** Dav. #6692.

Date	Mintage	VG	F	VF	XF	Unc
ND Rare	—	—	—	—	—	—

KM# 23 2 THALER
Silver **Obv:** Crowned imperial eagle, titles of Matthias and date in legend **Rev:** Helmeted four-fold arms with central chevron shield **Note:** Dav. #6695.

Date	Mintage	VG	F	VF	XF	Unc
1613 Rare	—	—	—	—	—	—

KM# 67 2 THALER
Silver **Obv:** Bust right in circle **Rev:** Helmeted seven-fold arms divide date **Note:** Dav. #6701.

Date	Mintage	VG	F	VF	XF	Unc
1664 BM Rare	—	—	—	—	—	—

KM# 104 2 THALER
Silver **Ruler:** Philipp Reinhard **Note:** Similar to 1 Thaler, KM#103.

Date	Mintage	VG	F	VF	XF	Unc
1695 Rare	—	—	—	—	—	—

TRADE COINAGE

KM# 22 GOLDGULDEN
3.5000 g., 0.9860 Gold 0.1109 oz. AGW **Ruler:** Johann Reinhard I **Obv:** Bust right **Rev:** Four-fold arms, legend, date **Rev. Legend:** MONE[TA] NO[VA] AUREA BABENHU [SAE] CU [SA] **Mint:** Babenhausen

Date	Mintage	VG	F	VF	XF	Unc
(1)612 Unique	—	—	—	—	—	—

KM# 24 GOLDGULDEN
3.5000 g., 0.9860 Gold 0.1109 oz. AGW **Obv:** Arms in inner circle **Rev:** Crowned imperial eagle in inner circle

Date	Mintage	VG	F	VF	XF	Unc
ND(1612)	—	1,500	3,000	5,500	9,500	—
1613	252	1,500	3,000	5,500	9,500	—

KM# 25 GOLDGULDEN
3.5000 g., 0.9860 Gold 0.1109 oz. AGW **Obv:** Date above arms

Date	Mintage	VG	F	VF	XF	Unc
1613	Inc. above	1,250	2,750	5,000	9,000	—
1614	828	1,250	2,750	5,000	9,000	—
1615	540	—	—	—	—	—
Note: Reported, not confirmed						
1617	360	1,250	2,750	5,000	9,000	—
1618	1,350	1,250	2,750	5,000	9,000	—
1619	1,224	—	—	—	—	—
Note: Reported, not confirmed						

KM# 37 GOLDGULDEN
3.5000 g., 0.9860 Gold 0.1109 oz. AGW **Obv:** Titles of Ferdinand II

Date	Mintage	VG	F	VF	XF	Unc
1624	—	2,500	4,500	9,000	17,500	—

KM# 54 DUCAT
3.5000 g., 0.9860 Gold 0.1109 oz. AGW **Obv:** Ornamental arms **Rev:** Four-line inscription and date in branches, "Jehovah" (in Hebrew) at top

Date	Mintage	VG	F	VF	XF	Unc
1647 Rare	—	—	—	—	—	—

Note: Swiss Bank Auction 25, 9-90 VF realized $13,845

KM# 55 DUCAT
3.5000 g., 0.9860 Gold 0.1109 oz. AGW **Obv:** Bust of Philipp Casimir right in inner circle **Rev:** Helmeted arms in inner circle

Date	Mintage	VG	F	VF	XF	Unc
ND(1660) Rare	—	—	—	—	—	—

KM# 76 DUCAT
3.5000 g., 0.9860 Gold 0.1109 oz. AGW **Obv:** Bust right **Rev:** Crown above seven-fold arms divides date

Date	Mintage	VG	F	VF	XF	Unc
1675 SM Rare	—	—	—	—	—	—

KM# 89 DUCAT
3.5000 g., 0.9860 Gold 0.1109 oz. AGW **Obv:** Bust of Philipp Reinhard right **Rev:** Crowned ornate seven-fold arms divide S-M

Date	Mintage	VG	F	VF	XF	Unc
ND(1685/6) SM Rare	—	—	—	—	—	—

KM# 31 2 DUCAT
7.0000 g., 0.9860 Gold 0.2219 oz. AGW **Obv:** Bust right **Rev:** Helmeted four-fold arms with central shield, 2 DVCAT in cartouche at bottom, date in legend

Date	Mintage	VG	F	VF	XF	Unc
16ZZ Rare	—	—	—	—	—	—

KM# 91 6 DUCAT
21.0000 g., 0.9860 Gold 0.6657 oz. AGW **Obv:** Bust right **Rev:** Helmeted seven-fold arms, date in legend

Date	Mintage	VG	F	VF	XF	Unc
1688 Rare	—	—	—	—	—	—

KM# 92 10 DUCAT (Portugalöser)
35.0000 g., 0.9860 Gold 1.1095 oz. AGW **Obv:** Bust right **Rev:** Helmeted seven-fold arms, date in legend **Note:** Struck with 1 Thaler dies, but only known in gold.

Date	Mintage	VG	F	VF	XF	Unc
1688 Rare	—	—	—	—	—	—

KM# 105 10 DUCAT (Portugalöser)
35.0000 g., 0.9860 Gold 1.1095 oz. AGW **Ruler:** Philipp Reinhard **Obv:** Bust Philipp Reinhard right **Rev:** City view, angel above, crowned and supported seven-fold arms below divide date **Note:** Struck with Thaler dies, KM#103.1.

Date	Mintage	VG	F	VF	XF	Unc
1695 Rare	—	—	—	—	—	—

PATTERNS

Including off metal strikes

KM#	Date	Mintage	Identification	Mkt Val
Pn1	1694 JL-SM	—	Thaler. Gold. KM#101	—

HANAU-MUNZENBERG

Elder line of Hanau founded in division of 1451, but became extinct in 1642 and fell to the line Lichtenberg, line. Hanau-Münzenberg passed to Hesse-Cassel in 1736 upon extinction of Hanau-Lichtenberg.

RULERS

Philipp Ludwig II, 1580-1612
Philipp Moritz, 1612-1638
  Katharina Belgia of Nassau-Orange, regent, 1612-1626
Philipp Ludwig III, 1638-1641
  Sibylle Christine, regent, 1638-1641
Johann Ernst, 1641-1642

MINT OFFICIALS' INITIALS

Initial	Date	Name
IA, IAL, (a)	1638-39	J(ohann?) Adelmann

ARMS

Hanau only = 3 chevrons, but often 4-fold arms with central chevron shield.

Hanau-Lichtenberg = 3 chevrons on left, 2 horizontal bars of Ochsenstein on right.

REFERENCE

S = Reinhard Suchier, **Die Münzen der Grafen von Hanau**, Hanau, 1897.

COUNTSHIP

REGULAR COINAGE

KM# 5 PFENNIG
Silver **Obv:** Shield of Hanau chevron arms in circle of pellets **Note:** Uniface. Hohl type.

Date	Mintage	VG	F	VF	XF	Unc
ND(1603)	663,000	75.00	150	300	—	—

KM# 6 PFENNIG
Silver **Note:** PL above arms.

Date	Mintage	VG	F	VF	XF	Unc
ND(1604)	1,361,000	75.00	150	300	—	—

KM# 9 PFENNIG
Silver **Obv:** PL above three shields of arms arranged two above one **Note:** Uniface, Hohl-type.

Date	Mintage	VG	F	VF	XF	Unc
ND(1605)	457,000	45.00	100	190	385	—

KM# 13 PFENNIG
Silver **Obv:** Crown above three arms **Note:** Uniface.

Date	Mintage	VG	F	VF	XF	Unc
ND(1606/7)	—	45.00	100	190	385	—

KM# 14 PFENNIG
Silver **Obv:** Crown divides P - L, lower shield divides date **Note:** Uniface.

Date	Mintage	VG	F	VF	XF	Unc
1609	—	45.00	90.00	180	360	—

KM# 15 PFENNIG
Silver **Obv:** P. L. C. H. E. R. D. I. M., date around three shields **Note:** Uniface.

Date	Mintage	VG	F	VF	XF	Unc
1609	—	45.00	90.00	180	360	—
1610	—	45.00	90.00	180	360	—

KM# 25 PFENNIG
Silver **Obv:** Legend P. L. C. I. H., date **Note:** Uniface.

Date	Mintage	VG	F	VF	XF	Unc
1610	—	45.00	90.00	180	360	—

KM# 50 KREUZER
Silver **Rev. Inscription:** I / KREVT / ZER / date

Date	Mintage	VG	F	VF	XF	Unc
16ZZ	—	—	—	—	—	—

KM# 51 KREUZER
Silver **Rev. Inscription:** I / KREVTZ / ER / date

Date	Mintage	VG	F	VF	XF	Unc
16ZZ	—	—	—	—	—	—

KM# 49 KREUZER
Silver **Obv:** Crown above three shields, two above one **Rev. Inscription:** I / KRVTZE / R / date **Note:** Kipper Kreuzer.

Date	Mintage	VG	F	VF	XF	Unc
16ZZ	—	—	—	—	—	—

KM# 60 KREUZER
Silver **Obv:** Crown above three shields, two above one, date in legend **Rev:** Imperial orb with 2 in wreath **Note:** Varieties exist.

Date	Mintage	VG	F	VF	XF	Unc
1638	—	—	—	—	—	—
1638 IAL	—	—	—	—	—	—

KM# 16 ALBUS (2 Kreuzer)
Silver **Obv:** Crown above three shields, two above one **Rev:** 2:CR/VIII/date

Date	Mintage	VG	F	VF	XF	Unc
1609	—	55.00	110	220	440	—

KM# 17 ALBUS (2 Kreuzer)
Silver **Rev. Inscription:** ALB / VIII / date

Date	Mintage	VG	F	VF	XF	Unc
1609	—	65.00	125	275	575	—
1610	—	65.00	125	275	575	—

KM# 29 ALBUS (2 Kreuzer)
Silver **Rev. Inscription:** ALB / NOVVS / date

Date	Mintage	VG	F	VF	XF	Unc
1611	12,000	75.00	150	300	600	—

KM# 10 3 KREUZER (Groschen)
Silver **Ruler:** Philipp Ludwig II **Obv:** Crowned imperial eagle, 3 in orb on breast, titles of Rudolf II **Rev:** Three shields of arms, two above one

Date	Mintage	VG	F	VF	XF	Unc
ND(1605)	898,000	12.00	25.00	55.00	110	—

KM# 11 3 KREUZER (Groschen)
Silver **Ruler:** Philipp Ludwig II **Obv:** Four-fold arms

Date	Mintage	VG	F	VF	XF	Unc
ND(1605-09)	Inc. above	12.00	25.00	50.00	100	—

KM# 12 3 KREUZER (Groschen)
Silver **Ruler:** Philipp Ludwig II **Note:** Klippe.

Date	Mintage	VG	F	VF	XF	Unc
ND(1605-09)	—	—	—	—	—	—

KM# 32 3 KREUZER (Groschen)
Silver, 21 mm. **Ruler:** Philipp Moritz **Obv:** Crowned Spanish shield of 4-fold arms, with central shield, in circle **Obv. Legend:** MON. ... HAN(AV). RI(M). E. MVNT. **Rev:** Crowned imperial eagle, 3 in circle on breast, date at end of legend **Rev. Legend:** MATTH(IAS.)I. D: G. IM. RO. SE(M). A(V). **Note:** Varieties exist.

Date	Mintage	VG	F	VF	XF	Unc
161Z	Inc. above	13.00	27.00	55.00	115	—
1613	84,000	13.00	27.00	55.00	115	—
1614	111,000	13.00	27.00	55.00	115	—
1615	—	13.00	27.00	55.00	115	—
1618	47,000	13.00	27.00	55.00	115	—
1619	53,000	13.00	27.00	55.00	115	—

KM# 30 3 KREUZER (Groschen)
Silver **Ruler:** Philipp Ludwig II **Obv:** Crowned oval four-fold arms, titles of Philipp Ludwig II **Rev:** Titles of Matthias and date in legend

Date	Mintage	VG	F	VF	XF	Unc
1612	—	16.00	36.00	75.00	150	—

KM# 31 3 KREUZER (Groschen)
Silver **Ruler:** Philipp Ludwig II **Obv. Legend:** MON. TVT. HAN... **Rev:** Crowned oval four-fold arms in baroque frame

Date	Mintage	VG	F	VF	XF	Unc
161Z	68,000	16.00	33.00	75.00	150	—

KM# 38 3 KREUZER (Groschen)
Silver **Ruler:** Philipp Moritz **Rev:** Titles of Ferdinand II

Date	Mintage	VG	F	VF	XF	Unc
(16)19	72,000	13.00	27.00	55.00	115	—

KM# 46 3 KREUZER (Groschen)
Silver **Ruler:** Philipp Moritz **Obv:** Arms divide date, titles of Philipp Moritz **Rev:** Crowned imperial eagle within beaded circle **Note:** Kipper issue. Varieties exist.

Date	Mintage	VG	F	VF	XF	Unc
16Z1	—	16.00	33.00	65.00	130	—
16ZZ	—	16.00	33.00	65.00	130	—

KM# 26 12 KREUZER (6 Albus)
Silver **Obv:** Crown above 3 shields of arms, 2 above 1 **Rev:** Crowned imperial eagle, 12 in orb on breast, titles of Rudolf II and date in legend

Date	Mintage	VG	F	VF	XF	Unc
1610	8,000	110	225	460	925	—
ND(1610)	Inc. above	110	225	460	925	—

KM# 39 12 KREUZER (6 Albus)
Silver **Obv:** Crowned four-fold arms divide date **Rev:** Crowned imperial eagle, 1Z in orb on breast, titles of Ferdinand II **Note:** Varieties exist.

Date	Mintage	VG	F	VF	XF	Unc
1619	—	110	225	475	975	—
16Z0	—	110	225	475	975	—

KM# 40 24 KREUZER (12 Albus)
Silver **Obv:** Crowned 4-fold arms divide date **Rev:** Crowned imperial eagle, titles of Ferdinand II **Note:** Varieties exist.

Date	Mintage	VG	F	VF	XF	Unc
1619	—	55.00	110	225	450	—
16Z0	—	55.00	110	225	450	—

KM# 36 TESTONE (6 Batzen)
Silver **Obv:** Bust right, two legends around **Rev:** Crowned four-fold arms, date in legend **Note:** Varities exist.

Date	Mintage	VG	F	VF	XF	Unc
1614	12,000	110	250	500	1,000	1,800
1615	3,000	—	—	—	—	—

Note: Reported, not confirmed

Date	Mintage	VG	F	VF	XF	Unc
1618/4	16,000	110	250	500	1,000	1,800
1618	Inc. above	110	250	500	1,000	1,800
1619/8/4	34,000	110	250	500	1,000	1,800
16Z0	10,000	—	—	—	—	—

Note: Reported, not confirmed

KM# 48 TESTONE (6 Batzen)
Silver **Obv:** Bust right **Rev:** Crowned four-fold arms divide date **Note:** Varieties exist.

Date	Mintage	VG	F	VF	XF	Unc
16Z1	—	150	300	600	1,200	—
16ZZ	—	150	300	600	1,200	—

KM# 18 27 ALBUS (Guldenthaler)
Silver **Obv:** Bust right **Rev. Inscription:** ALBVS / XXVII / Ao. / date

Date	Mintage	F	VF	XF	Unc	BU
1609	—	—	—	—	—	—

KM# 27 27 ALBUS (Guldenthaler)
Silver **Rev. Inscription:** ALB / XX / VII / date

Date	Mintage	F	VF	XF	Unc	BU
1610	646	—	—	—	—	—
ND	—	—	—	—	—	—

KM# 28 27 ALBUS (Guldenthaler)
Silver **Rev:** Crown above three shields of arms, two above one; date between two top shields, lower one divides 27/ALB

Date	Mintage	F	VF	XF	Unc	BU
1610	Inc. above	—	—	—	—	—
1611	525	—	—	—	—	—

Note: Reported, not confirmed

Date	Mintage	F	VF	XF	Unc	BU
ND	—	—	—	—	—	—

KM# 47 SCHILLING (1/28 Thaler)
Silver **Obv:** Crown above three shields, two above one; lower shield divides date **Rev. Legend:** HANAVIS+LANDMVNTZ **Rev. Inscription:** I / SCHILL

Date	Mintage	VG	F	VF	XF	Unc
1621 Rare	—	—	—	—	—	—
1622 Rare	—	—	—	—	—	—

KM# 53 1/4 THALER
Silver **Obv:** Crowned imperial eagle, orb on breast, titles of Ferdinand II and date in legend **Rev:** Crowned arms of Hanau-Munzenberg and Nassau-Orange in ornamented shield, titles of Katharina Belgia

Date	Mintage	VG	F	VF	XF	Unc
16Z3	—	—	—	—	—	—

KM# 54 1/4 THALER
Silver **Rev:** Without ornamentation on shield

Date	Mintage	VG	F	VF	XF	Unc
16Z3	—	—	—	—	—	—

KM# 55 1/2 THALER
Silver **Obv:** Crowned imperial eagle, orb on breast, titles of Ferdinand II and date in legend **Rev:** Crowned arms of Hanau-Munzenberg and Nassau-Orange in ornamented shield, titles of Katharina Belgia

Date	Mintage	VG	F	VF	XF	Unc
16Z3	—	—	—	—	—	—
16Z4	—	—	—	—	—	—

KM# 19 THALER
Silver **Obv:** Bust right **Rev:** Crowned imperial eagle, orb on breast, titles of Rudolf II and date in legend **Note:** Dav. #6681.

Date	Mintage	VG	F	VF	XF	Unc
1609 Rare	—	—	—	—	—	—

KM# 20 THALER
Silver **Obv:** Bust right **Rev:** Crowned four-fold arms with central shield **Note:** Struck on oval flan. Dav. #6682.

Date	Mintage	VG	F	VF	XF	Unc
ND Rare	—	—	—	—	—	—

KM# 33 THALER
Silver **Subject:** Death of Philipp Ludwig II **Obv:** Bust right **Rev:** Seven-line inscription with date **Note:** Dav. #6683.

Date	Mintage	VG	F	VF	XF	Unc
1612 Rare	—	—	—	—	—	—

KM# 34 THALER
Silver **Obv:** Crowned imperial eagle, orb on breast, titles of Matthias **Rev:** Crowned arms of Hanau-Munzenberg and Nassau-Orange divide date, titles of Katharina Belgia **Note:** Dav. #6685.

Date	Mintage	VG	F	VF	XF	Unc
1613	685	—	—	—	—	—
Note: Reported, not confirmed						
1614 Rare	1,431	—	—	—	—	—
1615	539	—	—	—	—	—
Note: Reported, not confirmed						
1618	659	—	—	—	—	—
Note: Reported, not confirmed						
1619	546	—	—	—	—	—
Note: Reported, not confirmed						

KM# 45 THALER
Silver **Obv:** Titles of Ferdinand II

Date	Mintage	VG	F	VF	XF	Unc
16Z0	2,584	—	—	—	—	—
Note: Reported, not confirmed						

KM# 52.2 THALER
Silver **Obv:** Crowned ornate shield within circle **Obv. Legend:** MONETA: NOVA:... **Rev:** Crown above double-headed imperial eagle within circle **Note:** Varieties exist. Dav. #6688.

Date	Mintage	VG	F	VF	XF	Unc
1622	—	150	300	550	1,250	—
1623	—	150	300	550	1,250	—
16Z4	—	150	300	550	1,250	—
16Z5	—	150	300	550	1,250	—
16Z6	—	150	300	550	1,250	—
16Z7	—	150	300	550	1,250	—

KM# 52.1 THALER
Silver **Obv:** Crowned ornate shield within circle **Rev:** Crown above double-headed eagle within circle **Note:** Dav. #6686.

Date	Mintage	VG	F	VF	XF	Unc
16ZZ	—	150	300	550	1,250	—
16Z3	—	150	300	550	1,250	—

KM# 56 THALER
Silver **Obv:** Partial date in legend **Rev:** Crowned oval four-fold arms with central shield in baroque frame divide date **Note:** Accession Thaler. Dav. #6689.

Date	Mintage	VG	F	VF	XF	Unc
16Z6/16Z- Rare	—	—	—	—	—	—

KM# 61 THALER
Silver **Obv:** Diamond design divides date within circle **Rev:** Titles of Ferdinand III **Note:** Dav. #6690.

Date	Mintage	VG	F	VF	XF	Unc
1638 IA	—	2,000	4,000	6,500	10,000	—

KM# 21 2 THALER
Silver **Obv:** Bust right **Rev:** Crowned imperial eagle, orb on breast, titles of Rudolf II and date in legend **Note:** Dav. #6680.

Date	Mintage	VG	F	VF	XF	Unc
1609 Rare	—	—	—	—	—	—

KM# 57 2 THALER
Silver **Obv:** Crowned ornate shield within circle **Rev:** Crown above double-headed eagle within circle **Note:** Dav. #6687.

Date	Mintage	VG	F	VF	XF	Unc
16Z6	—	900	1,450	2,250	3,250	—

TRADE COINAGE

KM# 7 GOLDGULDEN
3.5000 g., 0.9860 Gold 0.1109 oz. AGW **Obv:** Full-length standing figure of Rudolf II, titles in legend **Rev:** crowned four-fold arms divide date

Date	Mintage	VG	F	VF	XF	Unc
1604	585	—	—	—	—	—
Note: Reported, not confirmed						

KM# 8 GOLDGULDEN
3.5000 g., 0.9860 Gold 0.1109 oz. AGW **Obv:** Crowned imperial eagle, titles of Rudolf II **Rev:** Crown above three shields, two above one; date divided below

Date	Mintage	VG	F	VF	XF	Unc
1604	Inc. above	—	—	—	—	—
Note: Reported, not confirmed						

Date	Mintage	VG	F	VF	XF	Unc
1605	450	—	—	—	—	—
Note: Reported, not confirmed						
1606	378	—	—	—	—	—
Note: Reported, not confirmed						
1607	486	—	—	—	—	—
Note: Reported, not confirmed						
1608	990	—	—	—	—	—
Note: Reported, not confirmed						

KM# 35 GOLDGULDEN
3.5000 g., 0.9860 Gold 0.1109 oz. AGW **Obv:** Crowned imperial eagle, orb on breast, titles of Matthias **Rev:** Crowned arms of Hanau-Munzenberg and Nassau-Orange, titles of Katharina Belgia, date

Date	Mintage	VG	F	VF	XF	Unc
1613	2,194	—	—	—	—	—
Note: Reported, not confirmed						
1614	2,007	—	—	—	—	—
Note: Reported, not confirmed						

KM# 37 GOLDGULDEN
3.5000 g., 0.9860 Gold 0.1109 oz. AGW **Obv:** Date in legend **Rev:** Crown above three shields of arms, two above one

Date	Mintage	VG	F	VF	XF	Unc
1615	756	—	—	—	—	—
1619	1,332	—	—	—	—	—
Note: Reported, not confirmed						

KM# 41 GOLDGULDEN
3.5000 g., 0.9860 Gold 0.1109 oz. AGW **Obv:** Titles of Ferdinand II

Date	Mintage	VG	F	VF	XF	Unc
1619	8,000	—	—	—	—	—
Note: Reported, not confirmed						

KM# 62 DUCAT
3.5000 g., 0.9860 Gold 0.1109 oz. AGW **Obv:** Crowned four-fold arms in rhombus within palm branches **Rev:** Inscription in rhombus, date divided along four sides as 1-6/3-8 **Rev. Inscription:** DV / CATVS / COMITATVS / HANO / M

Date	Mintage	VG	F	VF	XF	Unc
1638 (a) Rare	—	—	—	—	—	—

KM# 63 DUCAT
3.5000 g., 0.9860 Gold 0.1109 oz. AGW **Obv:** Standing full-length figure, crowned oval four-fold arms at left **Rev:** Date, inscription **Rev. Inscription:** /DVCATVS / NOVVS / CVRATE / LAE. HANO / VIENSIS

Date	Mintage	VG	F	VF	XF	Unc
1638 IAL Rare	—	—	—	—	—	—

KM# 64 DUCAT
3.5000 g., 0.9860 Gold 0.1109 oz. AGW **Obv:** Standing full-length figure of soldier at left looking right, crowned four-fold arms at right **Rev:** Inscription in ornamented square, date divided below **Rev. Inscription:** DVCATVS / NOVVS / CVRATE / LAE. HANO / VIENSIS

Date	Mintage	VG	F	VF	XF	Unc
1639 IA Rare	—	—	—	—	—	—

HANNOVER

Located in North Central Germany, Hannover had its beginnings as early as the 12th century. The city obtained the mint right in 1331, but fell under the control of the dukes of Brunswick who later made it their residence. Hannover eventually became the capitol of the Kingdom of the same name. The city coinage lasted until 1674.

MINT OFFICIALS' INITIALS

Initial	Date	Name
(g)= or MK	1616	Melchior Kohl
(h)= or	1616-18	Valentin Block
	1618-19	Andreas Fricke
(i)= or TB	1619-20, 22-28	Tönnies Bremer
MB (sometimes in ligature	1628-66	Moritz Bergmann
AS	1666-74	Andreas Schele

ARMS

3-petaled cloverleaf or complex arms consisting of twin-towered city gate, 3-petaled cloverleaf in portal and rampant lion left between towers.

PROVINCIAL CITY

REGULAR COINAGE

KM# 10 PFENNIG
Silver **Note:** Uniface. Arms, date above. Varieties exist

Date	Mintage	VG	F	VF	XF	Unc
1618	—	32.00	65.00	135	270	—
16Z8	54,000	32.00	65.00	135	270	—
1635 MB	—	32.00	65.00	135	270	—
1636 MB	58,000	32.00	65.00	135	270	—
1639 MB	26,000	32.00	65.00	135	270	—

Date	Mintage	VG	F	VF	XF	Unc
1640 MB	8,000	32.00	65.00	135	270	—
1641 MB	30,000	32.00	65.00	135	270	—
164Z MB	4,000	32.00	65.00	135	270	—
1644 MB	27,000	32.00	65.00	135	270	—
1645 MB	12,000	32.00	65.00	135	270	—
1646 MB	30,000	32.00	65.00	135	270	—
1647 MB	—	32.00	65.00	135	270	—
1648 MB	—	32.00	65.00	135	270	—
1650 MB	11,000	32.00	65.00	135	270	—
1653 MB	—	32.00	65.00	135	270	—
1656 MB	—	32.00	65.00	135	270	—
1657 MB	—	32.00	65.00	135	270	—
1658 MB	21,000	32.00	65.00	135	270	—
1659 MB	14,000	32.00	65.00	135	270	—
1660 MB	—	32.00	65.00	135	270	—
1661 MB	—	32.00	65.00	135	270	—
1663	—	32.00	65.00	135	270	—
1664 MB	—	32.00	65.00	135	270	—
1665 MB	—	32.00	65.00	135	270	—
1666 AS	—	32.00	65.00	135	270	—
1667 AS	—	32.00	65.00	135	270	—
1668 AS	—	32.00	65.00	135	270	—
1670 AS	51,000	32.00	65.00	135	270	—

KM# 50 PFENNIG

Copper **Obv:** Arms, HANO around **Note:** Uniface.

Date	Mintage	VG	F	VF	XF	Unc
ND(c.1650)	—	—	—	—	—	—

KM# 64 2 PFENNIG

Silver **Obv:** Arms, date above **Rev. Inscription:** II / GUTE / PEN **Note:** Gute 2 Pfennig.

Date	Mintage	VG	F	VF	XF	Unc
1666 AS	—	—	—	—	—	—

Note: Although the dies exist for this coin, no struck specimens are known

KM# 17 3 PFENNIG (Dreier)

Silver **Obv:** Complete arms **Rev:** Imperial orb with 3 divides date

Date	Mintage	VG	F	VF	XF	Unc
16ZZ	—	27.00	60.00	120	240	—
16ZZ (i)	—	27.00	60.00	120	240	—
16Z3 (i)	—	27.00	60.00	120	240	—

KM# 46 3 PFENNIG (Dreier)

Silver **Obv:** Arms, HANNOVER above **Rev:** Imperial orb with 3 divides date **Note:** Varieties exist.

Date	Mintage	VG	F	VF	XF	Unc
1646 MB	—	22.00	45.00	90.00	180	—
1648 MB	10,000	22.00	45.00	90.00	180	—
1649 MB	20,000	22.00	45.00	90.00	180	—
1650 MB	—	22.00	45.00	90.00	180	—
ND(1650) MB	—	22.00	45.00	90.00	180	—
1651 MB	14,000	22.00	45.00	90.00	180	—
1652 MB	9,000	22.00	45.00	90.00	180	—
1653 MB	—	22.00	45.00	90.00	180	—
1654 MB	8,000	22.00	45.00	90.00	180	—
1655 MB	9,000	22.00	45.00	90.00	180	—
1656 MB	8,000	22.00	45.00	90.00	180	—
1657 MB	3,000	22.00	45.00	90.00	180	—
1658 MB	12,000	22.00	45.00	90.00	180	—
1659 MB	—	22.00	45.00	90.00	180	—
1660 MB	—	22.00	45.00	90.00	180	—
1661 MB	—	22.00	45.00	90.00	180	—
1663 MB	—	22.00	45.00	90.00	180	—
1664 MB	—	22.00	45.00	90.00	180	—

KM# 76 3 PFENNIG (Dreier)

Silver **Obv:** Arms divide date, HANNOVER above **Rev:** Imperial orb with 3

Date	Mintage	VG	F	VF	XF	Unc
1667 AS	—	25.00	50.00	100	210	—
1668 AS	—	25.00	50.00	100	210	—

KM# 85 3 PFENNIG (Dreier)

Silver **Obv:** Arms, HANNOVER above **Rev:** Imperial orb with 3 divides date

Date	Mintage	VG	F	VF	XF	Unc
1670 AS	67,000	25.00	50.00	100	210	—
1673 AS	33,000	25.00	50.00	100	210	—
1674/3 AS	32,000	25.00	50.00	100	210	—

KM# 65 4 PFENNIG

Silver **Obv:** Arms, legend, date **Obv. Legend:** HANNOVER **Rev. Inscription:** IIII / GUTE (or GVTE) / PEN **Note:** Gute 4 Pfennig.

Date	Mintage	VG	F	VF	XF	Unc
1666 AS	—	—	—	—	—	—
1667 AS	—	—	—	—	—	—

KM# 18 MARIENGROSCHEN

Silver **Obv:** Arms in shield, date in legend **Rev:** Madonna and child **Note:** Kipper Mariengroschen. Varieties exist.

Date	Mintage	VG	F	VF	XF	Unc
16ZZ	—	32.00	65.00	135	275	—
(1)6ZZ	—	32.00	65.00	135	275	—
(1)6ZZ (i)	—	32.00	65.00	135	275	—
16Z3	—	32.00	65.00	135	275	—
16Z3 (i)	—	32.00	65.00	135	275	—
(1)6Z3 (i)	—	32.00	65.00	135	275	—
(1)6Z3	—	32.00	65.00	135	275	—

KM# 19 MARIENGROSCHEN

Silver **Note:** Klippe.

Date	Mintage	VG	F	VF	XF	Unc
(1)6Z3 (i)	—	—	—	—	—	—

KM# 52 MARIENGROSCHEN

Silver **Obv:** Arms in shield, date in legend **Rev:** Madonna and child **Note:** Varieties exist.

Date	Mintage	VG	F	VF	XF	Unc
1652 MB	11,000	32.00	65.00	130	265	—
1653 MB	7,000	32.00	65.00	130	265	—
1654 MB	3,000	32.00	65.00	130	265	—
1655 MB	8,000	32.00	65.00	130	265	—
1656 MB	5,000	32.00	65.00	130	265	—
1657 MB	10,000	32.00	65.00	130	265	—
1658 MB	10,000	32.00	65.00	130	265	—
1659 MB	2,000	32.00	65.00	130	265	—
1660 MB	—	32.00	65.00	130	265	—

KM# 61 MARIENGROSCHEN

Silver **Rev:** Date at top

Date	Mintage	VG	F	VF	XF	Unc
1661 MB	—	—	—	—	—	—

KM# 62 MARIENGROSCHEN

Silver **Rev:** Date above arms **Note:** Varieties exist.

Date	Mintage	VG	F	VF	XF	Unc
1664 MB	—	32.00	65.00	130	265	—
1665 MB	—	32.00	65.00	130	265	—
1666 MB	—	32.00	65.00	130	265	—

KM# 66 MARIENGROSCHEN

Silver **Obv:** Arms in ornamented shield, date above **Rev:** Madonna and child

Date	Mintage	VG	F	VF	XF	Unc
1666 AS	—	25.00	50.00	100	200	—
1667 AS	—	25.00	50.00	100	200	—
1668 AS	—	25.00	50.00	100	200	—
1670 AS	80,000	25.00	50.00	100	200	—

KM# 67 MARIENGROSCHEN

Silver **Obv:** Date in legend

Date	Mintage	VG	F	VF	XF	Unc
1666 AS	—	—	—	—	—	—

KM# 77 MARIENGROSCHEN

Silver **Obv:** Arms not in shield

Date	Mintage	VG	F	VF	XF	Unc
1668 AS	—	—	—	—	—	—

KM# 6 1/24 THALER (Groschen)

Silver **Note:** Klippe.

Date	Mintage	VG	F	VF	XF	Unc
1616	—	—	—	—	—	—

KM# 5 1/24 THALER (Groschen)

Silver **Obv:** Arms in ornamented shield **Rev:** Imperial orb with Z4, date divided at top in legend by cross, titles of Matthias **Note:** Varieties exist.

Date	Mintage	VG	F	VF	XF	Unc
1616	—	35.00	75.00	150	315	—
1616 (g)	—	35.00	75.00	150	315	—
1616 MK	—	35.00	75.00	150	315	—
1616 (h)	—	35.00	75.00	150	315	—
1617 (h)	58,000	35.00	75.00	150	315	—
1716 (h) Error	—	35.00	75.00	150	315	—

KM# 7 1/24 THALER (Groschen)

Silver **Rev:** Complex arms **Note:** Varieties exist.

Date	Mintage	VG	F	VF	XF	Unc
1616	—	35.00	65.00	130	265	—
1616 (g)	—	35.00	65.00	130	265	—
1616 MK	—	35.00	65.00	130	265	—
1617	Inc. above	35.00	65.00	130	265	—
1617 (h)	Inc. above	35.00	65.00	130	265	—
1618	—	35.00	65.00	130	265	—
1619 (h)	—	35.00	65.00	130	265	—
16Z0	—	35.00	65.00	130	265	—

KM# 15 1/24 THALER (Groschen)

Silver **Note:** Klippe.

Date	Mintage	VG	F	VF	XF	Unc
16Z0	—	—	—	—	—	—

KM# 16 1/24 THALER (Groschen)

Silver **Obv:** Titles of Ferdinand II **Note:** Kipper 1/24 Thaler. Small flan.

Date	Mintage	VG	F	VF	XF	Unc
(1)6Z0	—	—	—	—	—	—

KM# 20 1/24 THALER (Groschen)

Silver **Obv:** Date divided by cross just above orb, titles of Ferdinand II **Note:** Varieties exist.

Date	Mintage	VG	F	VF	XF	Unc
16Z3 (i)	—	35.00	75.00	150	315	—
1626 (i)	—	35.00	75.00	150	315	—
1632 MB	—	35.00	75.00	150	315	—
1633 MB	3,000	35.00	75.00	150	315	—
1636 MB	—	35.00	75.00	150	315	—

KM# 38 1/24 THALER (Groschen)

Silver **Note:** Varieties exist.

Date	Mintage	VG	F	VF	XF	Unc
1639 MB	6,000	35.00	75.00	150	315	—
1640 MB	13,000	35.00	75.00	150	315	—
1640	Inc. above	35.00	75.00	150	315	—
1641 MB	10,000	35.00	75.00	150	315	—
1642 MB	—	35.00	75.00	150	315	—
1644 MB	9,000	35.00	75.00	150	315	—
1645 MB	4,000	35.00	75.00	150	315	—
1646 MB	11,000	35.00	75.00	150	315	—
1647 MB	2,000	35.00	75.00	150	315	—

KM# 54 1/24 THALER (Groschen)

Silver **Obv:** Date divided by imperial orb with Z4 as 16/M - 58/B and titles of Leopold I

Date	Mintage	VG	F	VF	XF	Unc
1658 MB	1,744	—	—	—	—	—
1659 MB	—	—	—	—	—	—

KM# 71 1/24 THALER (Groschen)

Silver **Obv:** 24 in orb

Date	Mintage	VG	F	VF	XF	Unc
1666 AS	—	—	—	—	—	—

KM# 68 2 MARIENGROSCHEN

Silver **Note:** Varieties exist.

Date	Mintage	VG	F	VF	XF	Unc
1666 AS	—	50.00	100	200	400	—
1667 AS	—	50.00	100	200	400	—
1668 AS	—	50.00	100	200	400	—
1669 AS	—	50.00	100	200	400	—

KM# 69 4 MARIENGROSCHEN

Silver **Note:** Varieties exist.

Date	Mintage	VG	F	VF	XF	Unc
1666 AS	—	20.00	40.00	80.00	155	—
1667 AS	—	20.00	40.00	80.00	155	—
1667	—	20.00	40.00	80.00	155	—
1669 AS	—	20.00	40.00	80.00	155	—
1670 AS	—	20.00	40.00	80.00	155	—
1671	—	20.00	40.00	80.00	155	—
1674/0 AS	—	20.00	40.00	80.00	155	—
1674/1 AS	—	20.00	40.00	80.00	155	—

KM# 22 1/2 REICHSORT (1/8 Thaler)

Silver **Obv:** Titles of Ferdinand II and date **Obv. Inscription:** EIM / HALB / REICHS / ORT **Rev:** Complex arms

Date	Mintage	VG	F	VF	XF	Unc
16Z4 (i)	—	—	—	—	—	—

KM# 26 1/2 REICHSORT (1/8 Thaler)
Silver **Obv:** Date in legend **Note:** Varieties exist.

Date	Mintage	VG	F	VF	XF	Unc
16Z5 (i)	1,334	300	600	1,100	2,100	—
16Z8 MB	1,118	300	600	1,100	2,100	—
16Z9 MB	2,033	300	600	1,100	2,100	—

KM# 70 1/2 REICHSORT (1/8 Thaler)
Silver **Obv:** Lion flanked by towers below date **Rev:** Inscription within circle **Rev. Legend:** LEOPOLD • I • D • G • ROMINUS • SEMP • AUG **Rev. Inscription:** I / HALBER / REICHS / ORT

Date	Mintage	VG	F	VF	XF	Unc
1666 AS	—	275	600	1,300	2,750	—

KM# 78 6 MARIENGROSCHEN
Silver **Note:** Varieties exist.

Date	Mintage	VG	F	VF	XF	Unc
1668 AS	—	32.00	65.00	130	265	—
1668	—	32.00	65.00	130	265	—
1669 AS	—	32.00	65.00	130	265	—
1671	42,000	32.00	65.00	130	265	—
1673 AS	134,000	32.00	65.00	130	265	—
1674 AS	58,000	32.00	65.00	130	265	—

KM# 88 6 MARIENGROSCHEN
Silver **Obv:** Date in legend

Date	Mintage	VG	F	VF	XF	Unc
1674	—	35.00	75.00	150	300	—
1674 AS	—	35.00	75.00	150	300	—

KM# 79 12 MARIENGROSCHEN
Silver **Note:** Varieties exist.

Date	Mintage	VG	F	VF	XF	Unc
1669 AS	—	35.00	75.00	150	290	—
1670 AS	—	35.00	75.00	150	290	—
1671	—	35.00	75.00	150	290	—
1672	107,000	35.00	75.00	150	290	—
1674	—	35.00	75.00	150	290	—
1674 AS	—	35.00	75.00	150	290	—

KM# 86 12 MARIENGROSCHEN
Silver **Rev. Inscription:** XII / MARIEN / GROSCH / date

Date	Mintage	VG	F	VF	XF	Unc
1672 AS	Inc. above	45.00	90.00	180	360	—
1673 AS	12,000	45.00	90.00	180	360	—

KM# 23 1/4 THALER (Reichsort)
Silver **Obv:** Twin towered building with larger clover on door than KM#25.2. **Rev:** Crowned imperial eagle, orb on breast

Date	Mintage	VG	F	VF	XF	Unc
16Z4 (i)	—	—	—	—	—	—
16Z9 MB	988	—	—	—	—	—

KM# 53 1/4 THALER (Reichsort)
Silver **Obv:** Crowned imperial eagle, orb on breast with value 4 (altered from 6), date divided by tail, titles of Ferdinand III **Rev:** Complex arms

Date	Mintage	VG	F	VF	XF	Unc
1654 MB	—	—	—	—	—	—

KM# 72 1/4 THALER (Reichsort)
Silver **Obv:** Titles of Leopold I

Date	Mintage	VG	F	VF	XF	Unc
1666 AS	—	—	—	—	—	—

KM# 24 1/2 THALER
Silver **Obv:** Twin towered building with larger clover on door than KM#25.2. **Rev:** Crowned imperial eagle, orb on breast

Date	Mintage	VG	F	VF	XF	Unc
16Z4 (i)	—	—	—	—	—	—
16Z9 MB	1,966	—	—	—	—	—

KM# 27 1/2 THALER
Silver **Obv:** W/1Z (groschen) in imperial orb

Date	Mintage	VG	F	VF	XF	Unc
16Z5 (i)	—	1,250	2,500	4,000	6,800	—
16Z6 (i)	1,150	1,000	2,200	4,000	6,800	—

KM# 30 1/2 THALER
Silver **Note:** Klippe.

Date	Mintage	VG	F	VF	XF	Unc
16Z9 MB Rare	—	—	—	—	—	—

KM# 73 1/2 THALER
Silver **Obv:** Titles of Leopold I

Date	Mintage	VG	F	VF	XF	Unc
1666 AS	—	—	—	—	—	—

KM# 87 24 MARIENGROSCHEN (2/3 Thaler - Gulden)
Silver **Note:** Similar to 12 Mariengroschen, KM#79, but value XXIIII.

Date	Mintage	VG	F	VF	XF	Unc
1672 AS	—	—	—	—	—	—

KM# 89 24 MARIENGROSCHEN (2/3 Thaler - Gulden)
Silver **Obv:** Lion rampant left above three-petaled cloverleaf **Rev. Inscription:** 24 / MARIEN / GROSCH / date

Date	Mintage	VG	F	VF	XF	Unc
1674 AS	3,608	750	1,600	3,100	—	—

KM# 25.1 THALER
Silver **Obv:** Twin towered building with larger clover on door than KM#25.2. **Rev:** Crowned imperial eagle, orb on breast **Note:** Dav. #5388.

Date	Mintage	VG	F	VF	XF	Unc
16Z4 (i)	—	550	1,000	1,650	—	—

KM# 28.1 THALER
Silver **Rev:** Z4 (groschen) in imperial orb **Note:** Dav. #5389.

Date	Mintage	VG	F	VF	XF	Unc
16Z5 (i)	5,748	550	1,000	1,650	—	—

KM# 28.2 THALER
Silver **Rev:** Without 24 in imperial orb **Note:** Dav. #5389A.

Date	Mintage	VG	F	VF	XF	Unc
16Z5 (i)	Inc. above	650	1,200	2,050	4,150	—

KM# 25.2 THALER
Silver **Obv:** Twin towered building, lion rampant left between towers, small cloverleaf on door **Rev:** Crowned imperial eagle with orb on breast in inner circle **Note:** Dav. #5390.

Date	Mintage	VG	F	VF	XF	Unc
16Z9 MB	3,344	650	1,200	2,050	4,250	—

KM# 35 THALER
Silver **Obv:** Shield of complex arms, horned helmet above **Rev:** Crowned imperial eagle, Z4 in orb on breast, date divided by crown at top, titles of Ferdinand II **Note:** Dav. #5392.

Date	Mintage	VG	F	VF	XF	Unc
1630 MB	2,130	725	1,250	2,150	4,400	—

KM# 37 THALER
Silver **Obv:** Lion flanked by towers within beaded circle, without date **Rev:** Z-4 on breast of double-headed imperial eagle within beaded circle **Note:** Dav. #5393.

Date	Mintage	VG	F	VF	XF	Unc
1631 MB	1,780	600	1,100	1,800	3,850	—
1635 MB	—	650	1,200	2,050	4,150	—
1636 MB	—	650	1,200	2,050	4,150	—
1637 MB	311	725	1,250	2,150	4,400	—

KM# 39 THALER
Silver **Rev:** Tail divides date, titles of Ferdinand III **Note:** Dav. #5394.

Date	Mintage	VG	F	VF	XF	Unc
1639 MB Rare	464	—	—	—	—	—

KM# 47 THALER
Silver **Rev:** Date divided at top by crown **Note:** Dav. #5395.

Date	Mintage	VG	F	VF	XF	Unc
1646 MB	128	850	1,500	3,000	—	—

KM# 48 THALER
Silver **Rev:** 24 in orb on breast **Note:** Dav. #5396.

Date	Mintage	VG	F	VF	XF	Unc
1649 MB Unique	—	—	—	—	—	—

KM# 60.1 THALER
Silver **Obv:** Similar to KM#25.2 but without date **Rev:** Titles of Leopold I **Note:** Dav. #5397.

Date	Mintage	VG	F	VF	XF	Unc
1660 MB	—	850	1,500	3,000	—	—

KM# 60.2 THALER
Silver **Rev:** Date not divided **Rev. Legend:** LEOPOLDVS... **Note:** Dav. #5398.

Date	Mintage	VG	F	VF	XF	Unc
1665 Rare	—	—	—	—	—	—

KM# 74 THALER
Silver **Obv:** Lion flanked by towers below date **Rev:** Double-headed imperial eagle **Note:** Dav. #5399.

Date	Mintage	VG	F	VF	XF	Unc
1666 AS	—	650	1,200	2,250	4,500	7,500
1670 AS	—	650	1,200	2,250	4,500	—

KM# 8 2 THALER
Silver **Obv:** Complex arms, date in legend at top **Rev:** Crowned imperial eagle, orb on breast, titles of Matthias **Note:** Dav. #5387.

Date	Mintage	VG	F	VF	XF	Unc
1616 Rare	—	—	—	—	—	—

KM# 36 2 THALER
Silver **Obv:** Shield of complex arms, horned helmet above **Rev:** Crowned imperial eagle, Z4 in orb on breast, date divided by crown at top, titles of Ferdinand II **Note:** Dav. #5391.

Date	Mintage	VG	F	VF	XF	Unc
1630 MB Rare	—	—	—	—	—	—

TRADE COINAGE

KM# 9 GOLDGULDEN
3.5000 g., 0.9860 Gold 0.1109 oz. AGW **Obv:** Crowned imperial eagle, orb on breast, titles of Matthias **Rev:** Complex arms, date above **Note:** Fr. #1156.

Date	Mintage	VG	F	VF	XF	Unc
1616	—	1,250	2,800	5,500	9,500	—

KM# 29 GOLDGULDEN
3.5000 g., 0.9860 Gold 0.1109 oz. AGW **Obv:** Titles of Ferdinand II **Note:** Fr. #1156.

Date	Mintage	VG	F	VF	XF	Unc
16Z5 TB	488	1,000	2,150	4,300	7,200	—
16Z8 TB	2,960	875	1,800	3,600	6,000	—
16Z9 MB	2,061	875	1,800	3,600	6,000	—
1630 MB	627	1,000	2,150	4,300	7,200	—
1633 MB	323	1,000	2,150	4,300	7,200	—
1635 MB	527	1,000	2,150	4,300	7,200	—

KM# 51 GOLDGULDEN
3.5000 g., 0.9860 Gold 0.1109 oz. AGW **Obv:** Titles of Ferdinand III

Date	Mintage	VG	F	VF	XF	Unc
1650 MB	—	1,150	2,400	4,700	8,000	—

KM# 45 DUCAT
3.5000 g., 0.9860 Gold 0.1109 oz. AGW **Obv:** Crowned imperial eagle, orb on breast, titles of Matthias **Rev:** Complex arms, date above, legend **Rev. Legend:** DUCAT: NOV... **Note:** Fr. #1157.

Date	Mintage	VG	F	VF	XF	Unc
1640 MB	1,057	1,800	3,300	6,000	10,000	—

KM# A75 DUCAT
3.5000 g., 0.9860 Gold 0.1109 oz. AGW **Obv:** Titles of Leopold I

Date	Mintage	VG	F	VF	XF	Unc
1666	—	1,200	2,400	4,800	8,400	—
1667 AS	—	1,200	2,400	4,800	8,400	—

KM# A54 3 DUCAT
10.5000 g., 0.9860 Gold 0.3328 oz. AGW **Obv:** Crowned imperial eagle, orb on breast with value 4 (altered from 6), date divided by tail, titles of Ferdinand III **Rev:** Complex arms **Note:** Struck with 1/4 Thaler dies, KM#53.

Date	Mintage	VG	F	VF	XF	Unc
1654 MB Rare	—	—	—	—	—	—

KM# 75 3 DUCAT
10.5000 g., 0.9860 Gold 0.3328 oz. AGW **Obv:** Titles of Leopold I **Note:** Fr. #1157. Struck with 1/4 Thaler dies, KM#72.

Date	Mintage	VG	F	VF	XF	Unc
1666 AS Rare	—	—	—	—	—	—

HATZFELD

The origins of this old noble family in Hesse were in the territory around the now ruined castle of Hatzfeld on the Eder River, about 16 miles (26km) north-northwest of Marburg. The earliest known lord of Hatzfeld is Kraft I (1265-1301), whose sons Gottfried I and Kraft II divided their patrimony upon his death. The elder line died out in 1575, but several branches of the younger line continued to thrive into the modern era and undergoing numerous divisions over the next three centuries. The first such division occurred in about 1420, creating the lines of Hatzfeld-Weisweiler and Hatzfeld-Wildenburg. Hatzfeld-Weisweiler was further divided in 1508 into Hatzfeld-Weisweiler-Merten, Hatzfeld-Weisweiler-Werther and Hatzfeld-Weisweiler-Weisweiler. Hatzfeld-Weisweiler-Werther established a cadet line in Schönstein in 1539 and the lord was raised to the rank of count in 1671. A further division of Hatzfeld-Weisweiler-Werther in 1766 created a new branch of Hatzfeld-Weisweiler-Trachenberg, whose count was made a prince in 1803. Meanwhile, the ruler of Hatzfeld-Weisweiler-Weisweiler was raised to a count in 1635 and his son was reconfirmed in the title in 1698. A later count of this line was made a Prussian prince in 1870 and a new line of Hatzfeld-Wildenburg was established from it in 1874.

The original Hatzfeld-Wildenburg line was the only branch of the dynasty which issued coins. Cadet lines were established from it at Heckenbeuhel in 1490 and at Krottendorf in 1569. The latter received part of the countship of Gleichen in 1639, then Trachenberg in 1641, the same year the lord was raised to the rank of count. A further division was effected in 1677 and resulted in the lines of Hatzfeld-Wildenburg-Rosenberg (extinct in 1722) and Hatzfeld-Wildenburg-Krottendorf-Gleichen. The count of Hatzfeld-Wildenburg-Gleichen became a Prussian prince in 1741 and a Prince of the Empire in 1748, but the line died out in 1794 and most of the family's territories were divided between the Archbishopric of Mainz and the Bishopric of Würzburg.

MINT OFFICIALS
Christian Moller, die-cutter at Nürnberg, ca. 1666
H.N. Kolb, mintmaster at Niederstetten, ca. 1684-1685

ARMS
A house anchor (used to strengthen walls of buildings)

REFERENCE
V = Franz-Eugen Volz, "Die Münzen und Medaillen des gräflichen Hauses Hatzfeldt," in Wolf-Dieter Müller-Jahneke and Franz-Eugen Volz, ***Die Münzen und Medaillen der gräflicher Häuser Sayn***, Frankfurt am Main, 1975.

HATZFELD-GLEICHEN-TRACHENBERG

Established from the addition of territories to Hatzfeld-Wildenburg-Krottendorf in 1639 and further divided in 1677 into Hatzfeld-Wildenburg-Rosenberg and Hatzfeld-Wildenburg-Krottendorf.

RULERS
Melchior I, 1630-1658, Count 1641
Hermann, 1658-77
Heinrich, 1677-83 and
Sebastian II, 1677-96
Franz, 1683-1738

COUNTSHIP

REGULAR COINAGE

KM# 5 3 GUTE KREUZER (Groschen)
Silver **Ruler:** Franz **Obv:** 3 in small circle of points above GVTE/KREUTZ, year, titles of Franz II **Rev:** Crowned 6-fold arms in ornamented frame **Mint:** Niederstetten **Note:** Varieties exist.

Date	Mintage	VG	F	VF	XF	Unc
1684	—	45.00	90.00	180	360	—

KM# 6 3 GUTE KREUZER (Groschen)
Silver **Ruler:** Franz **Obv:** 3 in small circle of points above inscription **Obv. Inscription:** BVTHE / KREVT / ZER, MONETA: HAZFELDIACA **Mint:** Niederstetten

Date	Mintage	VG	F	VF	XF	Unc
ND(ca.1685)	—	45.00	90.00	180	360	—

KM# 7 3 GUTE KREUZER (Groschen)
Silver **Ruler:** Franz **Rev:** GVTE/KRVT/ZER **Mint:** Niederstetten

Date	Mintage	VG	F	VF	XF	Unc
ND(ca.1685)	—	45.00	90.00	180	360	—

KM# 1 THALER
Silver **Ruler:** Melchior I **Obv:** Armored bust of Melchior right **Rev:** Seated Madonna and child, Hatzfeld arms below **Mint:** Nürnberg **Note:** Dav. #6709.

Date	Mintage	F	VF	XF	Unc	BU
ND(1666)	—	2,000	3,750	7,000	—	—

KM# 2 THALER
Silver **Ruler:** Hermann **Obv:** Armored and draped bust to right **Obv. Legend:** HERMAN. HATZFELDT. CO: GLEICH: D: CROTTORF. / + FERD: III. DG: ROM: I:S:A: **Rev:** Madonna seated with Child in clouds, rays around, small shield of Hatzfeld arms below **Rev. Legend:** PROTECTRIX. NE. DESERAS: AFF: FAM: HATZFELDTICAM. AVGE. FODINAS. **Note:** Dav. 6710.

Date	Mintage	F	VF	XF	Unc	BU
ND(1666)	—	1,750	3,000	6,500	—	—

TRADE COINAGE

KM# 3 DUCAT
3.5000 g., 0.9860 Gold 0.1109 oz. AGW **Ruler:** Melchior I **Obv:** Mantled bust to right **Mint:** Nürnberg **Note:** Fr.#1186.

Date	Mintage	VG	F	VF	XF	Unc
ND(1666)	—	2,950	5,600	9,900	16,000	—

KM# 4 DUCAT
Gold **Ruler:** Hermann **Obv:** Bust of Hermann right, titles of Hermann and Ferdinand III in legend **Rev:** Madonna and Child on cloud with shield of Hatzfield arms **Rev. Legend:** PROTECTRIX. NE: DESERAS ... **Note:** Fr. #1187.

Date	Mintage	VG	F	VF	XF	Unc
ND(1666) Rare	—	—	—	—	—	—

HATZFELD-WILDENBURG-KROTTENDORF

Created from the division of Hatzfeld-Wildenburg in 1569, but reformed in the next generation into Hatzfeld-Gleichen-Trachenberg with the addition of territory.

RULER
Sebastian I, 1569-1630

LORDSHIP

REGULAR COINAGE

KM# 1 THALER

Silver **Obv:** Facing bust of Sebastian I **Rev:** Standing figures of Honor and Virtue, date below **Rev. Legend:** HONOS ET VIRTVS **Note:** Dav. #9249.

Date	Mintage	F	VF	XF	Unc	BU
1597(1666)	—	—	—	12,000	20,000	—

Note: Although dated 1597, the above coin was actually struck in Nuremberg in 1666

TRADE COINAGE

KM# 2 DUCAT

3.5000 g., 0.9860 Gold 0.1109 oz. AGW **Obv:** Facing bust of Sebastian I **Rev:** Standing figures of Honor and Virtue, date below **Rev. Legend:** HONOS ET VIRTVS **Mint:** Nurnberg **Note:** Fr. #1185.

Date	Mintage	VG	F	VF	XF	Unc
1597(1666)	—	—	—	13,500	22,500	—

Note: Although dated 1597, the coin was actually struck in Nüremberg in 1666

HELFENSTEIN

A line of rulers, eventually counts, with lands near Ulm in Swabia, who traced their origins back to the early 12th century. The family had several divisions of the patrimony, the last occurring in 1548 when the two lines of Helfenstein-Gundelfingen and Helfenstein-Wiesensteig were established. Both became extinct in 1627 and titles passed to Furstenberg and Bavaria, the latter obtaining all of Helfenstein by 1752.

ARMS

Helfenstein – elephant to right

Gundelfingen – long leaf

REFERENCE

B/E = Christian Binder, Julius Ebner, **Württembergische Münz- und Medaillen-Kunde**, 2 vols., Stuttgart, 1910-12.

HELFENSTEIN-GUNDELFINGEN

RULERS

Froben, 1573-1622

Georg Wilhelm, 1622-1627

COUNTSHIP

TRADE COINAGE

KM# 1 GOLDGULDEN

3.5000 g., 0.9860 Gold 0.1109 oz. AGW **Ruler:** Froben **Obv:** Oval 4-fold arms in baroque frame, date above **Rev:** Crowned imperial eagle, arms of Austria and Burgundy on breast, titles of Rudolf II

Date	Mintage	VG	F	VF	XF	Unc
1611 Rare	—	—	—	—	—	—

Note: Stack's Kroisos sale, 1-08, Strong VF realized $40,000

HELFENSTEIN-WIESENSTEIG

RULERS

Rudolf V, 1570-1601

Rudolf VI, 1601-1627

COUNTSHIP

REGULAR COINAGE

KM# 1 1/24 THALER (Groschen)

Silver **Ruler:** Rudolf VI **Note:** Counterstamp of elephant and branches, 4-fold arms on Groschen of Magdeburg City KM#240.

Date	Mintage	VG	F	VF	XF	Unc
16ZZ Rare	—	—	—	—	—	—

KM# 2 24 KREUTZER (Dreibätzner)

Silver **Ruler:** Rudolf VI **Obv:** Crowned 4-fold arms, titles of Rudolf VI **Rev:** Crowned imperial eagle, 24 in orb on breast, titles of Ferdinand II **Note:** Kipper 24 Kreutzer. Varieties exist.

Date	Mintage	VG	F	VF	XF	Unc
ND(1621/2)	—	375	750	1,600	3,000	—

KM# 3 24 KREUTZER (Dreibätzner)

Silver **Ruler:** Rudolf VI **Obv:** Bust of Rudolf VI right **Rev:** Crowned imperial eagle, 24 in orb on breast, titles of Ferdinand II **Note:** Varieties exist.

Date	Mintage	VG	F	VF	XF	Unc
ND(1621/2)	—	—	—	—	—	—

KM# 4 24 KREUTZER (Dreibätzner)

Silver **Ruler:** Rudolf VI **Obv:** Elephant right in crowned and ornamented oval, titles of Rudolf VI **Rev:** Crowned imperial eagle, value (24) in legend below, titles of Ferdinand II

Date	Mintage	VG	F	VF	XF	Unc
ND(1621/2)	—	750	1,250	—	—	—

HENNEBERG

The line of counts of Henneberg in southern Thüringia, who traced their ancestors back to the late eighth century became extinct in 1583. The territories went mostly to Saxony with smaller parts to Hesse-Cassel and Brandenburg. Several Saxon duchies issued coins at Ilmenau. In 1660 Henneberg was divided again and redistributed among the duchies of both Albertine Saxony (Electoral Saxony and Saxe-Zeitz) and Ernestine Saxony (Saxe-Gotha and Saxe-Weimar). Each struck coins for its portion.

Joint Sovereignty of Electoral Saxony, Saxe-Gotha, Saxe-Altenburg and Saxe-Weimar

RULERS

Friedrich Wilhelm I of Saxe-Altenburg, 1583-1602, Regent 1591-1601 for Christian II of Electoral Saxony

Johann III of Saxe-Weimar, 1583-1605

Johann Philipp I of Saxe-Altenburg, 1602-39

Friedrich VIII of Saxe-Altenburg, 1602-25

Johann Wilhelm IV of Saxe-Altenburg, 1602-32

Friedrich Wilhelm IV of Saxe-Altenburg, 1603-60

Johann Ernst IV of Saxe-Weimar, 1605-26

Friedrich VII of Saxe-Weimar, 1605-22

Wilhelm IV of Saxe-Weimar, 1605-60

Albrecht II of Saxe-Weimar, 1605-44

Johann Friedrich VI of Saxe-Weimar, 1605-28

Friedrich Wilhelm of Saxe-Weimar, 1605-19

Bernhard of ISaxe-Weimar, 1605-39

Ernst I of Saxe-Gotha (III of Saxe-Weimar), 1605-60

Johann Georg I of Electoral Saxony, 1611-56

MINT MARK

S – Schleusingen Mint

ARMS

Hen standing or walking left

M = Otto Merseburger, **Sammlung Otto Merseburger umfassend Münzen und Medaillen von Sachsen**, Leipzig, 1894.

Sch = Wolfgang Schulten, ***Deutsche Münzen aus der Zeit Karls V.***, Frankfurt am Main, 1976.

S = Hugo Frhr. Von Saurma-Jeltsch, **Die Saurmasche Münzsammlung deutscher, schweizerischer und polnischer Gepräge von etwa dem Beginn der Groschenzeit bis zur Kipperperiode**, Berlin, 1892.

L. Deahna, "Zur hennebergischen Münzkunde," **Frankfurter Münzzeitung** 11 (1911), pp. 194-5, 203-6.

COUNTSHIP

REGULAR COINAGE

KM# 2 3 KREUZER (Groschen)

Silver **Obv:** Date divided at top and bottom **Rev:** Hen in heart-shaped ornamented shield

Date	Mintage	VG	F	VF	XF	Unc
16Z1	—	20.00	45.00	90.00	185	—

KM# 3 3 KREUZER (Groschen)

Silver **Obv:** Date divided near lower shield and 3 in legend at bottom

Date	Mintage	VG	F	VF	XF	Unc
16Z1	—	20.00	45.00	90.00	185	—

KM# 1 3 KREUZER (Groschen)

Silver **Obv:** 3 shields of arms, imperial orb with 3 above, titles of Joahnn Georg I **Rev:** Hen left in ornamental oval **Note:** Kipper 3 Kreuzer.

Date	Mintage	VG	F	VF	XF	Unc
ND(1621)	—	—	—	—	—	—

KM# 7 3 KREUZER (Groschen)

Silver **Obv:** Date in legend, with or without S below orb **Note:** Varieties exist.

Date	Mintage	VG	F	VF	XF	Unc
16ZZ	—	20.00	45.00	90.00	185	—
16ZZ S	—	20.00	45.00	90.00	185	—
1622	—	20.00	45.00	90.00	185	—

KM# 5 24 KREUZER (Doppelschreckenberger)

Silver **Obv:** Date divided by lower shield

Date	Mintage	VG	F	VF	XF	Unc
16Z1	—	27.00	60.00	110	225	—
16Z1 S	—	27.00	60.00	110	225	—
16ZZ S	—	27.00	60.00	110	225	—

KM# 4 24 KREUZER (Doppelschreckenberger)

Silver **Obv:** 3 shields of arms, imperial orb with 24 above, date divided at top and bottom **Rev:** Hen in heart-shaped ornamented shield **Note:** Kipper 24 Kreuzer.

Date	Mintage	VG	F	VF	XF	Unc
16Z1	—	27.00	60.00	110	225	—

KM# 6 24 KREUZER (Doppelschreckenberger)

Silver **Obv:** Date divided by orb at top, with or without S below orb **Note:** Varieties exist.

Date	Mintage	VG	F	VF	XF	Unc
1621 S	—	27.00	60.00	110	225	—
16Z1 S	—	27.00	60.00	110	225	—
16Z1	—	27.00	60.00	110	225	—
16ZZ S	—	27.00	60.00	110	225	—
16ZZ	—	27.00	60.00	110	225	—
1622 S	—	27.00	60.00	110	225	—

KM# 8 24 KREUZER (Doppelschreckenberger)

Silver **Obv:** 24 in orb

Date	Mintage	VG	F	VF	XF	Unc
16ZZ	—	27.00	60.00	110	225	—
16ZZ S	—	27.00	60.00	110	225	—

KM# 9 24 KREUZER (Doppelschreckenberger)

Silver **Rev:** Hen left in oval within baroque frame

Date	Mintage	VG	F	VF	XF	Unc
16ZZ	—	33.00	65.00	120	130	265

KM# 10 24 KREUZER (Doppelschreckenberger)

Silver **Obv:** Value in orb 24

Date	Mintage	VG	F	VF	XF	Unc
1622 S	—	33.00	65.00	130	265	—

KM# 12 1/2 THALER

Silver **Obv:** 3 shields of arms, imperial orb above, date divided at top **Rev:** Hen left in heart-shaped ornamented shield

Date	Mintage	VG	F	VF	XF	Unc
16ZZ S Rare	—	—	—	—	—	—

KM# 11 40 GROSCHEN (2 Guldentaler)

Silver, 38 mm. **Ruler:** Johann Georg I **Obv:** 3 shields of arms, 2 over 1, imperial orb above, date divided at top, 40 in cartouche at bottom **Rev:** Hen left in heart-shaped ornamented shield **Note:** Kipper issue.

Date	Mintage	VG	F	VF	XF	Unc
1622S	—	7,000	11,500	20,000	—	—

Note: Hess-Divo Auction 295, 5-03, VF realized approximately $15,735

KM# 13 40 GROSCHEN (2 Guldentaler)

Silver, 38 mm. **Ruler:** Johann Georg I **Obv:** 3 shields of arms, 2 over 1, imperial orb above, date divided at top **Rev:** Hen left in heart-shaped ornamented shield **Mint:** Schleusingen **Note:** Kipper issue.

Date	Mintage	VG	F	VF	XF	Unc
16ZZ S Rare	—	—	—	—	—	—

KM# 14 40 GROSCHEN (2 Guldentaler)
19.8500 g., Silver, 38 mm. **Ruler:** Johann Georg I **Obv:** 3 shields of arms, 2 over 1, imperial orb above, date divided by lower shield, value (40) in cartouche at bottom **Obv. Legend:** IOHAN: GEORG: D: - G: EL: ET: REL. DVC. **Rev. Legend:** SAXONIAE. MONETA: HENNEBERGICA. **Mint:** Schleusingen **Note:** Kipper issue.

Date	Mintage	VG	F	VF	XF	Unc
1622 S Rare	—	—	—	—	—	—

Note: An example in XF realized approximately $15,750 in a May 2003 Hess-Divo auction.

KM# 15 3 THALER
Silver **Ruler:** Johann Georg I **Obv:** 3 shields of arms, 2 over 1, imperial orb above, date divided by lower arms **Rev:** Hen left in heart-shaped ornamented shield **Mint:** Schleusingen **Note:** Kipper issue.

Date	Mintage	VG	F	VF	XF	Unc
1622 S Rare	—	—	—	—	—	—

SUCCESSION TO SAXE-GOTHA
Ernestine LIne

RULER
Ernst I, 1660-1675

REGULAR COINAGE

KM# 21 GROSCHEN
Silver **Subject:** Partition of Henneberg and Homage to Ernst **Obv:** Crowned 2-fold arms of Saxony and Henneberg **Rev:** 8-line inscription with date

Date	Mintage	VG	F	VF	XF	Unc
1661	—	15.00	30.00	60.00	120	—

KM# 22 1/4 THALER
Silver **Subject:** Partition of Henneberg and Homage to Ernst **Obv:** Crowned 5-fold arms **Rev:** 8-line inscription with Roman numeral date

Date	Mintage	VG	F	VF	XF	Unc
1661	—	—	—	—	—	—

KM# 23 THALER
Silver **Subject:** Partition of Henneberg and Homage to Ernst **Obv:** Crowned 5-fold arms **Rev:** 11-line inscription with Roman numeral date **Note:** Dav. #7446.

Date	Mintage	VG	F	VF	XF	Unc
1661	—	450	900	1,850	3,000	—

SUCCESSION TO SAXE-WEIMAR

RULERS
Wilhelm IV, 1660-62
Johann Ernst II, 1662-83
Wilhelm Ernst, 1683-1728
Johann Ernst, 1683-1707

REGULAR COINAGE

KM# 31 DREIER (3 Pfennig)
Silver **Subject:** Partition of Henneberg and Homage to Wilhelm IV **Obv:** Adjacent ornate arms of Saxony and Henneberg divide date, below Heneb. Hul=/digungs=/muntz **Rev:** 6-line inscription

Date	Mintage	VG	F	VF	XF	Unc
1661	—	16.00	33.00	65.00	135	—

KM# 32 GROSCHEN
Silver **Subject:** Partition of Henneberg and Homage to Wilhelm IV **Obv:** Crowned 5-fold arms **Rev:** 7-line inscription with date

Date	Mintage	VG	F	VF	XF	Unc
1661	—	16.00	33.00	65.00	130	—

KM# 33 1/4 THALER
Silver **Subject:** Partition of Henneberg and Homage to Wilhelm IV **Obv:** Bust right **Rev:** Crown above 2 small arms of Saxony and Hennenberg divides date, 5-line inscription below

Date	Mintage	VG	F	VF	XF	Unc
1661	—	—	—	—	—	—

KM# 34 1/2 THALER
Silver **Subject:** Partition of Henneberg and Homage to Wilhelm IV **Obv:** Bust right **Rev:** Crown above 2 small arms of Saxony and Henneberg divides date, 5-line inscription below surrounded by flames and rays

Date	Mintage	VG	F	VF	XF	Unc
1661	—	170	325	550	1,100	—

KM# 35 THALER
Silver **Subject:** Partition of Henneberg and Homage to Wilhelm IV **Obv:** Bust right **Rev:** Crown above 2 small arms of Saxony and Henneberg divides date, 5-line inscription below surrounded by flames and rays **Note:** Dav. #7548.

Date	Mintage	VG	F	VF	XF	Unc
1661	—	350	750	1,600	2,750	—

HENNEBERG-ILMENAU
SUCCESSION TO SAXE-GOTHA AND WEIMAR

RULERS
Friedrich I of Saxe-Gotha, 1680-91
Friedrich II of Saxe-Gotha, 1691-1732
Wilhelm Ernst of Saxe-Weimar, 1683-1728
Johann Ernst of Saxe-Weimar, 1683-1707

Initials	Date	Name
BA	1691-1702	Bastian Altmann at Ilmenau

REGULAR COINAGE

KM# 11 HELLER
Copper, 21 mm. **Obv:** Crowned rooster right

Date	Mintage	VG	F	VF	XF	Unc
1693	—	10.00	27.00	55.00	110	—
1694	—	10.00	27.00	55.00	110	—

KM# 7 DREIER (3 Pfennig)
Silver **Obv:** Crowned arms, date **Rev:** Hen right

Date	Mintage	VG	F	VF	XF	Unc
1692	—	20.00	40.00	80.00	160	—

KM# 12 DREIER (3 Pfennig)
Silver **Obv:** Hen right **Rev:** Inscription with date

Date	Mintage	VG	F	VF	XF	Unc
1693	—	20.00	40.00	80.00	160	—

KM# 8.1 2 GROSCHEN
Silver **Rev:** Large crown, small arms

Date	Mintage	VG	F	VF	XF	Unc
1692 BA	—	33.00	65.00	130	265	—

KM# 8.2 2 GROSCHEN
Silver **Rev:** Small crown, large arms

Date	Mintage	VG	F	VF	XF	Unc
1692 BA	—	45.00	90.00	180	360	—

KM# 13 1/3 THALER (1/2 Gulden)
Silver **Obv:** Crowned arms, date **Rev:** Hen right, value 1/3 below

Date	Mintage	VG	F	VF	XF	Unc
1693 BA	—	27.00	65.00	120	240	—

KM# 5 2/3 THALER (Gulden)
Silver **Note:** Mining 2/3 Thaler. Similar to KM#10 but larger arms.

Date	Mintage	VG	F	VF	XF	Unc
1691 BA	—	—	—	—	—	—

KM# 9 2/3 THALER (Gulden)
Silver **Obv:** Crown divides date **Note:** Varieties exist.

Date	Mintage	VG	F	VF	XF	Unc
1692 BA	—	45.00	90.00	180	360	—

KM# 10 2/3 THALER (Gulden)
Silver **Obv:** Smaller arms **Note:** Varieties exist.

Date	Mintage	VG	F	VF	XF	Unc
1692 BA	—	45.00	90.00	180	360	—
1693 BA	—	45.00	90.00	180	360	—
1694 BA	—	45.00	90.00	180	360	—

KM# 14 THALER

Silver **Rev:** "JEVOVAH" in Hebrew letters above hen **Note:** Dav. #7481.

Date	Mintage	VG	F	VF	XF	Unc
1693 BA	—	325	750	1,550	3,750	6,000

KM# 15 THALER

Silver **Rev:** Small hen left in wreath, legend in 3 circles **Note:** Dav. #7482.

Date	Mintage	VG	F	VF	XF	Unc
1693 BA	—	825	1,500	2,650	4,950	—

KM# 16 THALER

Silver **Rev:** Crowned hen walking right **Rev. Legend:** PINGVESCIT DUM ERUIT **Note:** Dav. #7484.

Date	Mintage	VG	F	VF	XF	Unc
1694 BA	—	375	700	1,200	2,800	—

KM# 25 THALER

Silver **Rev. Legend:** IN RUTILO.. **Note:** Dav. #7485.

Date	Mintage	VG	F	VF	XF	Unc
1695 BA	—	400	775	1,500	3,000	—

KM# 26 THALER

Silver **Rev. Legend:** CRESCIT ET HOC... **Note:** Dav. #7486.

Date	Mintage	VG	F	VF	XF	Unc
1696 BA	—	270	550	1,050	2,350	—

KM# 28 THALER

Silver **Rev:** Date below hen in ribbon bow **Rev. Legend:** WEIL GOTTES... **Note:** Dav. #7487.

Date	Mintage	VG	F	VF	XF	Unc
1697 BA	—	250	525	1,050	2,500	—

KM# 30 THALER

Silver **Note:** Dav. #7488.

Date	Mintage	VG	F	VF	XF	Unc
1698 BA	—	375	750	1,500	3,400	—

KM# 31 THALER

Silver **Note:** Dav. #7489.

Date	Mintage	VG	F	VF	XF	Unc
1699 BA	—	375	725	1,450	3,250	—

KM# 32 THALER

Silver **Obv:** 2 helmets with plumes and supporters **Rev:** Ribbons instead of palm branches around shields **Note:** Dav. #7490.

Date	Mintage	VG	F	VF	XF	Unc
1699 BA	—	280	525	1,150	3,000	—

KM# 35 THALER
Silver **Ruler:** Bernard III **Obv:** 2 ornate helmets, figures at right and left **Rev:** Crown above two shields of arms **Note:** Dav. #7491.

Date	Mintage	F	VF	XF	Unc	BU
1700 BA	—	325	575	1,150	2,800	—

SUCCESSION TO SAXE-MEININGEN

RULER
Bernhard III, 1680-1706

REGULAR COINAGE

KM# 6 HELLER
Copper **Obv:** Crowned Saxon arms **Rev:** Date **Rev. Inscription:** I / HELLER / H.MEIN **Note:** Varieties exist.

Date	Mintage	VG	F	VF	XF	Unc
1691	—	7.00	16.00	30.00	60.00	—
1694	—	7.00	16.00	30.00	60.00	—
1696	—	7.00	16.00	30.00	60.00	—
1697	—	7.00	16.00	30.00	60.00	—
1699	—	7.00	16.00	30.00	60.00	—
1700	—	7.00	16.00	30.00	60.00	—

KM# 17 HELLER
Copper **Obv:** Arms between palm branches **Note:** Varieties exist.

Date	Mintage	VG	F	VF	XF	Unc
1694	—	7.00	16.00	30.00	60.00	—
1695	—	7.00	16.00	30.00	60.00	—
1696	—	7.00	16.00	30.00	60.00	—
1699	—	7.00	16.00	30.00	60.00	—

KM# 18 HELLER
Copper **Obv:** Crowned Saxon arms **Rev:** Date **Rev. Legend:** I/HELLER/HEN: MEI

Date	Mintage	VG	F	VF	XF	Unc
1694	—	7.00	16.00	30.00	60.00	—

KM# 19 HELLER
Copper **Rev:** Date **Rev. Inscription:** I / HELLER / HEN: MEIN

Date	Mintage	VG	F	VF	XF	Unc
1694	—	7.00	16.00	30.00	60.00	—

KM# 20 HELLER
Copper **Rev:** Date **Rev. Inscription:** I / HELLER / HEN: MEIN

Date	Mintage	VG	F	VF	XF	Unc
1694	—	7.00	16.00	30.00	60.00	—

KM# 21 HELLER
Copper **Obv:** Arms between palm branches

Date	Mintage	VG	F	VF	XF	Unc
1694	—	7.00	16.00	30.00	60.00	—

KM# 27 HELLER
Copper **Obv:** Crowned Saxon arms between palm branches **Rev:** Hen right, date below

Date	Mintage	VG	F	VF	XF	Unc
1696	—	6.00	13.00	27.00	55.00	—

KM# 29 HELLER
Copper **Obv:** Without palm branches

Date	Mintage	VG	F	VF	XF	Unc
1697	—	6.00	13.00	27.00	55.00	—
1699	—	6.00	13.00	27.00	55.00	—

KM# 38 HELLER
Copper **Obv:** Crowned hen right on 3 mounds **Rev:** Hen right, date below

Date	Mintage	VG	F	VF	XF	Unc
1700	—	7.00	20.00	37.00	75.00	—

KM# 39 HELLER
Copper **Obv:** Crowned Saxon arms **Rev. Inscription:** H / MEIN / HELLER

Date	Mintage	VG	F	VF	XF	Unc
1700	—	7.00	20.00	35.00	70.00	—

KM# 36 HELLER
Copper **Obv:** Crowned hen right on 3 mounds **Rev:** Date **Rev. Inscription:** H / MEIN / HELLER **Note:** Varieties exist.

Date	Mintage	VG	F	VF	XF	Unc
1700	—	7.00	20.00	37.00	75.00	—

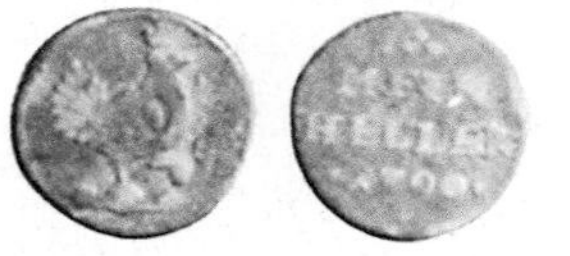

KM# 37 HELLER
Copper **Rev:** Date **Rev. Inscription:** MEIN. / HELLER **Note:** Varieties exist.

Date	Mintage	VG	F	VF	XF	Unc
1700	—	7.00	20.00	37.00	75.00	—

KM# 24 2 KREUZER (1/2 Batzen)
Silver **Obv:** Crowned arms in palm branches, 2 above **Rev:** Date **Rev. Inscription:** NACH / DEM / FRANCKI / SCHEN KREIS / SCHLVS

Date	Mintage	VG	F	VF	XF	Unc
1694	—	—	—	—	—	—

KM# 22 1/36 THALER (8 Pfennig)
Silver **Obv:** 2 oval arms of Saxony and Henneberg in cartouche, crown above **Rev:** Date **Rev. Inscription:** 36 / EININ. R. / THALER

Date	Mintage	VG	F	VF	XF	Unc
1694	—	—	—	—	—	—
1695	—	—	—	—	—	—

KM# 23 1/18 THALER (16 Pfennig)
Silver **Obv:** 2 oval arms of Saxony and Henneberg in cartouche, crown above **Rev:** Date **Rev. Inscription:** 1 8 / EIN. R. / THALER

Date	Mintage	VG	F	VF	XF	Unc
1694	—	—	—	—	—	—

HERFORD

Herford town grew up around the Benedictine abbey of the same name, located about 9 miles northeast of Bielefeld in Westphalia. Herford became a free imperial city in 1631 but had this status removed in 1647. In 1803 it became a possession of Prussia. A series of local coins were struck in Herford from about 1580 until 1670.

TOWN

REGULAR COINAGE

KM# 1 PFENNIG
Copper **Obv:** City arms **Obv. Legend:** CIVITAS HERVORIA **Rev:** I in center of legend **Rev. Legend:** ANNO 1636

Date	Mintage	VG	F	VF	XF	Unc
1636	—	200	500	900	1,750	—

KM# 2 PFENNIG
Copper **Obv. Legend:** CIVITAS HERVORD...

Date	Mintage	VG	F	VF	XF	Unc
1636	—	55.00	120	175	350	—

KM# 3 2 PFENNIG
Copper **Obv:** City arms **Obv. Legend:** CIVITAS HERVORIA **Rev:** II in center of legend **Rev. Legend:** ANNO 1636

Date	Mintage	VG	F	VF	XF	Unc
1636	—	200	400	700	1,400	—

KM# 4 2 PFENNIG
Copper **Obv. Legend:** CIVITAS HERVORD...

Date	Mintage	VG	F	VF	XF	Unc
1636	—	40.00	85.00	150	300	—

KM# 5 3 PFENNIG
Copper **Obv:** City arms **Obv. Legend:** CIVITAS HERVORIA **Rev:** III in center of legend **Rev. Legend:** ANNO 1636

Date	Mintage	VG	F	VF	XF	Unc
1636	—	200	400	700	1,400	—

KM# 6 6 PFENNIG
Copper **Obv:** City arms, legend, date **Obv. Legend:** CIVITAS HERVORIA **Rev:** VI in ornamented circle

Date	Mintage	VG	F	VF	XF	Unc
1636	—	200	400	700	1,400	—

KM# 7 6 PFENNIG
Copper **Obv. Legend:** CIVITAS HERVORD

Date	Mintage	VG	F	VF	XF	Unc
1636	—	20.00	40.00	70.00	140	—

KM# 17 6 PFENNIG
Copper **Obv:** City arms, legend, VI at bottom **Obv. Legend:** STADT HERVORD **Rev:** Crowned scepter divides date in ornamented circle

Date	Mintage	VG	F	VF	XF	Unc
1670	—	18.00	32.00	65.00	135	—

KM# 8 12 PFENNIG
Copper **Obv:** City arms, legend, date **Obv. Legend:** CIVITAS. HERVORDIA **Rev:** XII in ornamented circle

Date	Mintage	VG	F	VF	XF	Unc
1636	—	75.00	150	300	600	—

KM# 9 12 PFENNIG
Copper **Obv:** ANO before date

Date	Mintage	VG	F	VF	XF	Unc
1636	—	37.00	75.00	150	300	—

KM# 18 12 PFENNIG
Copper

Date	Mintage	VG	F	VF	XF	Unc
1670	—	20.00	40.00	80.00	160	—

KM# 10 MARIENGROSCHEN (1/36 Thaler)
Silver **Obv:** City arms, imperial orb with 36 above, legend, date **Obv. Legend:** STAD. HERBORD ANO **Rev:** Madonna and child **Rev. Legend:** MARIEN - GROSCH **Note:** Varieties exist.

Date	Mintage	VG	F	VF	XF	Unc
1638	—	25.00	50.00	100	200	—
1640	—	25.00	50.00	100	200	—
1646	—	25.00	50.00	100	200	—

KM# 15 1/72 THALER (Matthier)
Silver **Obv:** Oval city arms in ornamented circle **Rev. Inscription:** 72 / EHT / HERV / MTIER / date

Date	Mintage	VG	F	VF	XF	Unc
1646	—	450	800	1,400	2,600	—

KM# 11 1/24 THALER (Groschen)
Silver **Obv:** City arms **Rev:** Imperial orb with 24, date above, titles of Ferdinand III **Rev. Legend:** IMPERIALIS. HERVOLDIA.

Date	Mintage	VG	F	VF	XF	Unc
1638	—	—	—	—	—	—

KM# 16 1/24 THALER (Groschen)
Silver **Obv. Legend:** MON. NOVA. REIP. HERVORD.

Date	Mintage	VG	F	VF	XF	Unc
1646	—	90.00	180	360	—	—

KM# 13 1/2 THALER
Silver **Obv:** City arms divide date **Obv. Legend:** MONETA.NOVA.REIP.HERVORD. **Rev:** Crowned imperial eagle, orb on breast, titles of Ferdinand III

Date	Mintage	VG	F	VF	XF	Unc
1640	—	—	—	—	—	—

KM# 12 THALER
Silver **Obv:** City arms divide date as 1-6/3-8 **Rev:** Crowned imperial eagle, orb on breast, titles of Ferdinand III **Note:** Dav. #5400.

Date	Mintage	VG	F	VF	XF	Unc
1638 Rare	—	—	—	—	—	—
1640 Rare	—	—	—	—	—	—

COUNTERMARKED COINAGE

In 1647, the Elector of Brandenburg, Friedrich Wilhelm (1640-88), took possession of his newly acquired countship of Ravensberg. Herford was located within that territory and the 1636 copper coinage of the town was countermarked to reflect the change in regime. The countermarks used were either a shield of the Herford arms (horizontal bar) or the electoral scepter of Brandenburg. In some cases, both countermarks were used. Another countermark consisting of a horizontal bar in a shield with suspended hunting horn above and sphere below, reportedly representing the Rhenish Imperial Knighthood, was used during this period.

KM# 21 2 PFENNIG
Copper **Note:** Countermark of Herford arms on 2 Pfennig, KM#3 or 4.

CM Date	Host Date	Good	VG	F	VF	XF
ND(1647)	1636	85.00	165	325	550	—

KM# 24 3 PFENNIG
Copper **Note:** Countermark of Rhemish Imperial Knights on 3 Pfennig, KM#5.

CM Date	Host Date	Good	VG	F	VF	XF
ND(1647-50)	1636	75.00	150	300	500	—

KM# 28 6 PFENNIG
Copper **Note:** Countermark of Herford and Sceptor arms on 6 Pfennig, KM#6 or 7.

CM Date	Host Date	Good	VG	F	VF	XF
ND(1647)	1636	50.00	100	200	—	—

KM# 27 6 PFENNIG
Copper **Note:** Countermark of Sceptor arms on 6 Pfennig, KM#6 or 7.

CM Date	Host Date	Good	VG	F	VF	XF
ND(1647)	1636	50.00	100	200	—	—

KM# 31 12 PFENNIG
Copper **Note:** Countermark of Herford and Sceptor arms on 12 Pfennig, KM#8 or 9.

CM Date	Host Date	Good	VG	F	VF	XF
ND(1647)	1636	60.00	180	250	—	—

TRADE COINAGE

KM# 14 DUCAT
3.5000 g., 0.9860 Gold 0.1109 oz. AGW **Obv:** 5-line inscription with date in ornamental square **Rev:** Crowned imperial eagle, orb on breast, titles of Ferdinand III

Date	Mintage	F	VF	XF	Unc	BU
1641 Rare	—	—	—	—	—	—

HERSFELD

Benedictine abbey founded in 769 about 24 miles north-northeast of Fulda. In 1606 the landgraves of Hesse-Cassel replaced the abbots as administrators of Hersfeld. The abbey was secularized and became a part of Hesse-Cassel in 1648.

RULERS
Joachim Ruhl, 1591-1606
Otto of Hesse-Cassel, 1606-1617
Wilhelm II of Hesse-Cassel, 1617-1627
Imperial Occupation, 1627-1631
Wilhelm II of Hesse Cassel, 1631-1637
Hermann III of Hesse-Cassel, 1637-1648

SECULARIZED ABBEY

REGULAR COINAGE

KM# 1 1/2 THALER
14.5800 g., Silver **Ruler:** Wilhelm II **Obv:** Crowned and mantled 2-fold arms, double-barred cross of Hersfeld left, crowned Hessian lion right **Obv. Legend:** GUILIELMUS D: G: P: A: D: H: A: H: **Rev:** Facing open hand raised from clouds below, all-seeing eye in palm, fore and middle fingers raised vertically, date at end of legend **Rev. Legend:** FIDE • SED • CUI • VIDE • **Note:** Hoffmeister 804.

Date	Mintage	VG	F	VF	XF	Unc
16Z1	—	1,750	2,500	4,500	7,000	—

KM# 2 THALER
Silver **Ruler:** Wilhelm II **Obv:** Crowned and mantled 2-fold arms with mitre above, double-barred cross of Hersfeld left, crowned Hessian lion right **Obv. Legend:** GUILIELMUS D:G:P:A:D:H:A:H: **Rev:** Facing open hand raised from clouds below, all-seeing eye in palm, fore and middle fingers raised vertically, date at end of legend **Rev. Legend:** FIDE. SED. CUI. VIDE.

Date	Mintage	VG	F	VF	XF	Unc
16Z1 Rare	—	—	—	—	—	—

HESSE-CASSEL

KM# 315 HELLER
Silver **Ruler:** Karl **Obv:** Crowned CL Monogram divides date as 1-6/8-5. **Note:** Schussel-type. Prev. KM#316.

Date	Mintage	VG	F	VF	XF	Unc
1683	—	55.00	115	235	475	—
1685	—	55.00	115	235	475	—
1686	—	55.00	115	235	475	—
1688	—	55.00	115	235	475	—
1690	—	55.00	115	235	475	—
1697	—	55.00	115	235	475	—

KM# 307 HELLER
Silver **Ruler:** Karl **Obv:** Crowned C, date divided as 16-83 **Note:** Schussel-type. Uniface.

Date	Mintage	VG	F	VF	XF	Unc
1683	—	65.00	135	275	550	—

KM# 60 2 HELLER
0.3600 g., Silver, 14.5 mm. **Ruler:** Moritz **Obv:** Crowned Hessian lion in Spanish shield, ML above, Z-H divided left and right, date divided below **Note:** S#686. Kipper issue, uniface.

Date	Mintage	VG	F	VF	XF	Unc
(1)6Z3	—	60.00	125	250	500	—
16Z3	—	60.00	125	250	500	—

KM# 316 2 HELLER
0.2800 g., Silver, 15 mm. **Ruler:** Karl **Obv:** Crowned CL monogram divides date as 1 - 6/8 - 5. **Mint:** Cassel **Note:** S#1293. Uniface.

Date	Mintage	VG	F	VF	XF	Unc
1685	—	55.00	100	160	280	—

KM# 241.1 3 HELLER
Silver **Ruler:** Wilhelm VI **Obv:** Crowned W in palm wreath **Rev:** III, date divided above and to sides

Date	Mintage	VG	F	VF	XF	Unc
1655 AG	—	55.00	115	235	475	—
1656 AG	—	55.00	115	235	475	—
1657 AG	—	55.00	115	235	475	—

KM# 241.2 3 HELLER
Silver **Ruler:** Wilhelm VI **Rev:** III/date

Date	Mintage	VG	F	VF	XF	Unc
1658	—	—	—	—	—	—

Note: Reported, not confirmed

KM# 267 3 HELLER
Silver **Ruler:** Wilhelm VII **Obv:** Crowned W between palm branches **Rev:** Shield with 3, roses besides, date above

Date	Mintage	VG	F	VF	XF	Unc
1665 IGB	—	55.00	115	235	475	—

KM# 280 3 HELLER
Silver **Ruler:** Wilhelm VII **Obv:** Crowned W between palm branches **Rev:** Value 3 in oval baroque frame divides date as 1-6/7-0

Date	Mintage	VG	F	VF	XF	Unc
1668	—	55.00	115	235	475	—
1670	—	55.00	115	235	475	—

KM# 291 3 HELLER
Silver, 13-14 mm. **Ruler:** Karl **Obv:** Crowned script C between palm branches **Rev:** Value '3' in oval baroque frame divides date as 1-6/7-3 **Mint:** Cassel

Date	Mintage	VG	F	VF	XF	Unc
1673	—	55.00	115	235	475	—
1674	—	55.00	115	235	475	—
1677	—	55.00	115	235	475	—
1679	—	55.00	115	235	475	—
1681	—	55.00	115	235	475	—
1684	—	55.00	115	235	475	—
1686	—	55.00	115	235	475	—
1694	—	55.00	115	235	475	—
1699	—	55.00	115	235	475	—

KM# 5 4 HELLER
Silver Weight varies: 0.66-1.06g., 15-17 mm. **Ruler:** Moritz **Obv:** Crowned Hessian lion to left in Spanish shield divides date, MLZH above **Rev:** Ornate Hessian helmet, 4-H above **Note:** S-579,584,589,591,592,593,595,595.2,596,598,598.1,600,602,604,612,618, 622-3,624a; Saurma 2268. Varieties exist, mainly with the helmet on the reverse.

Date	Mintage	VG	F	VF	XF	Unc
1601	—	10.00	25.00	50.00	100	—
1602	—	10.00	25.00	50.00	100	—
160Z	—	10.00	25.00	50.00	100	—
(1)603	—	10.00	25.00	50.00	100	—
(1)604	—	10.00	25.00	50.00	100	—
1604	—	10.00	25.00	50.00	100	—
1605	—	10.00	25.00	50.00	100	—
1606	—	10.00	25.00	50.00	100	—
1609	—	10.00	25.00	50.00	100	—
1610	—	10.00	25.00	50.00	100	—
1611	—	10.00	25.00	50.00	100	—
(16)14	—	—	—	—	—	—

Note: Reported, not confirmed.

KM# 30.1 4 HELLER
0.5800 g., Silver, 15-16 mm. **Ruler:** Moritz **Obv:** Hessian lion in German shield divides date, MLZH above. **Rev:** Hessian helmet, horns divide 4-H **Rev. Legend:** LANDT. MUNTZ. **Note:** S-642. Kipper issue.

Date	Mintage	VG	F	VF	XF	Unc
(1)6Z1	—	20.00	45.00	90.00	180	—

KM# 30.2 4 HELLER
0.6000 g., Silver, 15-16 mm. **Ruler:** Moritz **Obv:** Hessian lion in Spanish shield divides date as 1-6/Z-1, MLZH above **Rev:** Hessian helmet, horns divide 4 - H **Rev. Legend:** LANDT. MUNTZ. **Note:** S-643. Kipper issue.

Date	Mintage	VG	F	VF	XF	Unc
16Z1	—	40.00	80.00	160	325	—

MB# 31 4 HELLER (Gute Dreier)
0.8100 g., Silver, 16.5 mm. **Ruler:** Moritz **Obv:** Hessian lion left in Spanish shield, which divides date, MLZH above **Rev:** Hessian helmet divides 4 - H **Note:** Ref. S#644.

Date	Mintage	VG	F	VF	XF	Unc
(1)6Z1	—	25.00	50.00	100	200	—

KM# 32 4 HELLER (Gute Dreier)

Silver, 16 mm. **Ruler:** Moritz **Obv:** Crowned Hessian lion to left in Spanish shield divides date, MLZH above **Rev:** Ornate Hessian helmet, 4 H above **Note:** S-675, 675.1, 685, 685.1. Varieties exist.

Date	Mintage	VG	F	VF	XF	Unc
(1)6ZZ	—	20.00	45.00	75.00	150	—
16ZZ	—	20.00	45.00	75.00	150	—
(1)6Z3	—	20.00	45.00	75.00	150	—
16Z3	—	20.00	45.00	75.00	150	—

KM# 245 4 HELLER (1/3 Albus)

Silver, 16 mm. **Ruler:** Wilhelm VI **Obv:** Crowned W in palm wreath **Rev:** IIII, date divided above and at sides, mintmaster's initials below **Note:** Varieties exist with value as IIII or II.II.

Date	Mintage	VG	F	VF	XF	Unc
1656 AG	—	10.00	20.00	40.00	80.00	—
1657 AG	—	10.00	20.00	40.00	80.00	—
1657 IGB	—	10.00	20.00	40.00	80.00	—
1657 IGB	—	10.00	20.00	40.00	80.00	—
1658 IGB	—	10.00	20.00	40.00	80.00	—

KM# 251 4 HELLER (1/3 Albus)

Silver **Ruler:** Wilhelm VI **Obv:** Crowned ornamented W between palm branches **Rev:** Date / IIII / mintmaster initials

Date	Mintage	VG	F	VF	XF	Unc
1661 IGB	—	30.00	65.00	135	270	—
1663 IGB	—	30.00	65.00	135	270	—

KM# 256 4 HELLER (1/3 Albus)

Silver, 14-15 mm. **Ruler:** Wilhelm VII **Obv:** Hessian lion in crowned Spanish shield between palm branches **Rev:** Date/ IIII/ mintmaster initials **Mint:** Cassel

Date	Mintage	VG	F	VF	XF	Unc
1663 IGB	—	45.00	90.00	180	360	—
1665 IGB	—	45.00	90.00	180	360	—
1668 IGB	—	45.00	90.00	180	360	—
1670 IGB	—	45.00	90.00	180	360	—

KM# 290 4 HELLER (1/3 Albus)

Silver **Ruler:** Karl **Obv:** Crowned shield with Hessian lion left, palm branches flank **Rev:** Value, date **Note:** Varieties exist.

Date	Mintage	VG	F	VF	XF	Unc
1671 IGB	—	10.00	20.00	40.00	85.00	—
1673 IGB	—	10.00	20.00	40.00	85.00	—
1674 IGB	—	10.00	20.00	40.00	85.00	—
1675 IGB	—	10.00	20.00	40.00	85.00	—
1676 IGB	—	10.00	20.00	40.00	85.00	—
1677 IGB	—	10.00	20.00	40.00	85.00	—
1678 IGB	—	10.00	20.00	40.00	85.00	—
1679 IGB	—	10.00	20.00	40.00	85.00	—
1680 IGB	—	10.00	20.00	40.00	85.00	—
1681 IH	—	10.00	20.00	40.00	85.00	—
1682 IH	—	10.00	20.00	40.00	85.00	—
1682 IVF	—	10.00	20.00	40.00	85.00	—
1685 IVF	—	10.00	20.00	40.00	85.00	—
1687 IVF	—	10.00	20.00	40.00	85.00	—
1690 IVF	—	10.00	20.00	40.00	85.00	—
1691 IVF	—	10.00	20.00	40.00	85.00	—
1692 IVF	—	10.00	20.00	40.00	85.00	—
1694 IVF	—	10.00	20.00	40.00	85.00	—
1697 IVF	—	10.00	20.00	40.00	85.00	—
1699	—	10.00	20.00	40.00	85.00	—

KM# 215 6 HELLER (1/2 Albus)

Silver **Ruler:** Wilhelm VI **Obv:** Hessian lion **Obv. Legend:** WILHELMVS • HASS • LAND • PRINC • HERSF • **Rev:** Helmet divides date, value 6 between horns

Date	Mintage	VG	F	VF	XF	Unc
1651	—	90.00	185	275	575	—

KM# 242 6 HELLER (1/2 Albus)

Silver **Ruler:** Wilhelm VI **Obv:** Crowned W in wreath, date divided at sides, 1-6 above, 5-6 below **Rev:** Hessian lion, value VI below **Note:** Varieties exist.

Date	Mintage	VG	F	VF	XF	Unc
1655 AG	—	65.00	135	275	550	—
1656 AG	—	40.00	80.00	160	325	—
1657 AG	—	40.00	80.00	160	325	—
1657 IGB	—	40.00	80.00	160	325	—
1658 IGB	—	40.00	80.00	160	325	—

KM# 257 6 HELLER (1/2 Albus)

Silver **Ruler:** Wilhelm VI **Obv:** Crowned and ornamented W date below, between 2 palm branches

Date	Mintage	VG	F	VF	XF	Unc
1663 IGB	—	45.00	90.00	180	360	—

KM# 269 6 HELLER (1/2 Albus)

Silver **Ruler:** Wilhelm VII **Obv:** Crowned W between palm branches, date below in one line

Date	Mintage	VG	F	VF	XF	Unc
1668	—	40.00	80.00	160	325	—

KM# 281 6 HELLER (1/2 Albus)

Silver, 16 mm. **Ruler:** Wilhelm VII **Obv:** Crowned W between palm branches, date divided at sides, 1-6 above, 7-0 below **Note:** S#1204.

Date	Mintage	VG	F	VF	XF	Unc
1670	—	40.00	80.00	160	325	—

KM# 292 6 HELLER (1/2 Albus)

Silver **Ruler:** Karl **Obv:** Crowned script C, date divided at sides, 1-6 above, 7-3 below, palm branches at sides

Date	Mintage	VG	F	VF	XF	Unc
1673	—	45.00	90.00	180	360	—

KM# 298 6 HELLER (1/2 Albus)

Silver, 16-17 mm. **Ruler:** Karl **Obv:** Crowned script C, date below, palm branches at sides **Rev:** Crowned Hessian lion to left, value VI below **Note:** Varieties exist in date numeral placement.

Date	Mintage	VG	F	VF	XF	Unc
1675	—	15.00	30.00	60.00	120	—
1679	—	15.00	30.00	60.00	120	—
1686	—	15.00	30.00	60.00	120	—
1688	—	15.00	30.00	60.00	120	—
1695	—	15.00	30.00	60.00	120	—

KM# 246 8 HELLER (1/48 Thaler)

Silver, 17 mm. **Ruler:** Wilhelm VI **Obv:** Value 'VIII' in circle, W.L.Z.H. and date in legend **Rev:** Crowned Hessian lion, mintmaster's monogram below, all in circle **Note:** Varieties exist.

Date	Mintage	VG	F	VF	XF	Unc
1657 IGB	—	45.00	90.00	180	360	—
1658 IGB	—	45.00	90.00	180	360	—
1659 IGB	—	45.00	90.00	180	360	—

KM# 293 8 HELLER (1/48 Thaler)

Silver **Ruler:** Karl **Obv:** Crowned script C, date divided 1-6 above, 7-3 below, palm branches at sides **Rev:** VIII in heart-shaped cartouche

Date	Mintage	VG	F	VF	XF	Unc
1673	—	40.00	80.00	160	325	—

KM# 49 3 KREUZER

Silver **Subject:** Lordship of Epstein **Obv:** Crowned arms of Eppstein **Rev:** Imperial eagle, 3 in circle on breast, titles of MAVR etc. and of Ferdinand II, date in legend **Note:** Kipper 3 Kreuzer.

Date	Mintage	VG	F	VF	XF	Unc
(1)622 TS	—	—	—	—	—	—
(1)623	—	—	—	—	—	—

Note: Reported, not confirmed

KM# 48 3 KREUZER

Silver **Ruler:** Moritz **Obv:** Crowned Hessian lion to right above C in oval baroque shield, date divided above **Rev:** Imperial orb with 3 **Note:** Kipper 3 Kreuzer.

Date	Mintage	VG	F	VF	XF	Unc
1622 C	—	65.00	135	275	550	—

KM# A49 3 KREUZER

Silver **Ruler:** Moritz **Obv:** Crowned arms of Eppstein **Obv. Legend:** CONSILIO ET VIRTUTE... **Rev:** Imperial eagle, 3 in circle on breast **Rev. Legend:** F • E • II • D • G • R • I • S • A •6ZZ

Date	Mintage	VG	F	VF	XF	Unc
(1)6ZZ TS Rare	—	—	—	—	—	—
(1)6ZZ shamrock Rare	—	—	—	—	—	—
(1)622 cross Rare	—	—	—	—	—	—

KM# 50 3 KREUZER

Silver **Ruler:** Moritz **Subject:** Lordship of Plesse **Obv:** Arms of Plesse (pothooks) **Note:** Kipper 3 Kreuzer

Date	Mintage	VG	F	VF	XF	Unc
(1)622 TS	—	—	—	—	—	—
(1)6ZZ shamrock	—	—	—	—	—	—
(1)622 shamrock	—	—	—	—	—	—

KM# 58.2 12 KREUZER (Schreckenberger)

Silver **Ruler:** Moritz **Obv:** Crowned arms of Eppstein, flanked by crosses, titles of Maurice in legend, date

Date	Mintage	VG	F	VF	XF	Unc
1621 V, pothook within	—	75.00	150	300	600	—
1622 V, pothook within	—	75.00	150	300	600	—

KM# 37 12 KREUZER (Schreckenberger)

Silver **Ruler:** Moritz **Obv:** Angel above arms, date in legend, titles of Moritz **Rev:** Imperial eagle, 12 in circle on breast **Note:** Varieties exist.

Date	Mintage	VG	F	VF	XF	Unc
16Z1 3 crossed pothooks	—	55.00	110	225	450	—
(1)6Z1 3 crossed pothooks	—	65.00	135	275	550	—
16ZZ 3 crossed pothooks	—	55.00	110	225	450	—
16ZZC 3 crossed pothooks	—	75.00	150	300	600	—
1622 3 crossed pothooks	—	65.00	135	275	550	—
(1)622 3 crossed pothooks	—	65.00	135	275	550	—

KM# 33 12 KREUZER (Schreckenberger)

Silver **Ruler:** Moritz **Obv:** Hessian helmet in circle, horms with three or more branches **Obv. Legend:** MAUR • D • G • LAND • HASS • date **Rev:** Crowned imperial eagle, 12 in circle on breast **Rev. Legend:** FERD • II • D • G • ROM • IMP • SEM • AUGU **Note:** Kipper 12 Kreuzer. Prev. KM #33.1.

Date	Mintage	VG	F	VF	XF	Unc
ND	—	75.00	150	300	600	—
1621 1 pothook (or rose)	—	45.00	90.00	180	360	—
16Z1 1 pothook	—	45.00	90.00	180	360	—
(1)621 1 pothook	—	45.00	90.00	180	360	—
16Z1 C 3 crossed pothooks	—	45.00	90.00	180	360	—
1621 3 crossed pothooks	—	45.00	90.00	180	360	—
16Z1 3 crossed pothooks	—	40.00	80.00	160	325	—
(1)621 3 crossed pothooks	—	40.00	80.00	160	325	—
(1)6Z1 3 crossed pothooks	—	40.00	80.00	160	325	—
16Z(1) rose	—	60.00	125	250	500	—
(1)622 small ring	—	60.00	125	250	500	—
(1)622	—	60.00	125	250	500	—

KM# 58.1 12 KREUZER (Schreckenberger)

Silver **Ruler:** Moritz **Obv:** Hessian lion in pearl circle **Obv. Legend:** ...SPES NON CONFVNDIT

Date	Mintage	VG	F	VF	XF	Unc
1621 O Rare	—	—	—	—	—	—

KM# 54 12 KREUZER (Schreckenberger)

Silver **Ruler:** Moritz **Obv:** Hessian lion in double circle, ornaments between the circles, date in legend **Rev:** Crowned imperial eagle, 12 on breast, titles of Ferdinand II

Date	Mintage	VG	F	VF	XF	Unc
(1)621 3 crossed pothooks	—	65.00	135	275	550	—
(1)621. V, pothook within and rose	—	45.00	90.00	180	360	—
1621 V, pothook within and rose	—	45.00	90.00	180	360	—
16Z1 V, pothook within	—	45.00	90.00	180	360	—
1621 V, pothook within	—	45.00	90.00	180	360	—
(1)621//16Z1	—	80.00	165	335	675	—
(1)6Z1//16Z1	—	80.00	165	335	675	—
(1)622	—	60.00	140	280	575	—
(1)622 TS	—	65.00	135	275	550	—
(16)Z2 rose	—	65.00	135	275	550	—

Note: Date on reverse

Date	Mintage	VG	F	VF	XF	Unc
(16)22 L	—	65.00	135	275	550	—

Note: Date on reverse

KM# 36 12 KREUZER (Schreckenberger)

Silver **Ruler:** Moritz **Obv:** Hessian lion in circle without shield **Obv. Legend:** MAUR • D • G • LAND • HASS **Rev:** Crowned imperial eagle, 12 in shield on breast **Rev. Legend:** FERD • II • D • G • ROM • IMP • SEM • AUGU

Date	Mintage	VG	F	VF	XF	Unc
ND rose	—	75.00	150	300	600	—
16Z1 rose	—	45.00	90.00	180	360	—
(1)6Z1 rose	—	45.00	90.00	180	360	—
1621 TS	—	45.00	90.00	180	360	—
(1)621 TS	—	40.00	80.00	160	325	—
(1)621 cross	—	45.00	90.00	180	360	—
1621 3 crossed pothooks	—	45.00	90.00	180	360	—
1622 3 crossed pothooks	—	45.00	90.00	180	360	—
(1)622 1 pothook	—	45.00	90.00	180	360	—
(1)622 TS	—	45.00	90.00	180	360	—
(1)622 3 crossed pothooks	—	55.00	110	225	450	—
(1)6ZZ 3 crossed pothooks	—	55.00	110	220	435	—
16ZZ rose	—	55.00	110	220	435	—
1622 rose	—	55.00	110	220	435	—
(1)622 rose	—	55.00	110	220	435	—
1622 cross	—	55.00	110	220	435	—
16ZZ small ring	—	55.00	110	220	435	—
1622	—	55.00	110	220	435	—
16ZZ	—	55.00	110	220	435	—
(1)6ZZ/16ZZ	—	—	—	—	—	—

Note: Reported, not confirmed

KM# 34 12 KREUZER (Schreckenberger)

Silver **Ruler:** Moritz **Obv:** Hessian helmet in circle **Obv. Legend:** MAUR... **Note:** Klippe.

Date	Mintage	VG	F	VF	XF	Unc
(1)6Z1 Rare	—	—	—	—	—	—

Note: Date on obverse

Date	Mintage	VG	F	VF	XF	Unc
1621 Rare	—	—	—	—	—	—

Note: Date on reverse

KM# 39 12 KREUZER (Schreckenberger)

Silver **Ruler:** Moritz **Obv:** Hessian lion in oval or round shield, date **Obv. Legend:** CONSILIO ET VIRTUTE

Date	Mintage	VG	F	VF	XF	Unc
(1)621 3 crossed pothooks	—	65.00	135	275	550	—
(1)621/(1)621 3 crossed pothooks	—	65.00	135	275	550	—
(1)621	—	65.00	135	275	550	—
(1)621/621	—	65.00	135	275	550	—

KM# A39 12 KREUZER (Schreckenberger)

Silver **Ruler:** Moritz **Obv:** Hessian lion in crowned shield **Rev:** Imperial eagle, 12 in circle on breast, date

Date	Mintage	VG	F	VF	XF	Unc
(1)6ZZ star	—	80.00	165	335	675	—
(16)ZZ star	—	80.00	165	335	675	—
(16)22 star	—	80.00	165	335	675	—
(16)22 2 stars	—	80.00	165	335	675	—

KM# 52 12 KREUZER (Schreckenberger)

Silver **Ruler:** Moritz **Note:** Klippe. Similar to KM#36.1, but date on reverse.

Date	Mintage	VG	F	VF	XF	Unc
(1)6ZZ	—	—	—	—	—	—

Note: Reported, not confirmed

KM# 56 24 KREUZER (2 Schreckenberger)

Silver **Subject:** Lordship of Eppstein **Obv:** Crowned arms of Eppstein (3 chevrons), date in legend **Obv. Legend:** CONSILIO ET VIRTUTE **Rev:** Crowned imperial eagle, 24 in shield on breast, titles of Ferdinand II **Note:** Kipper 24 Kreuzer.

Date	Mintage	VG	F	VF	XF	Unc
(1)622 Rare	—	—	—	—	—	—
(1)6ZZ Rare	—	—	—	—	—	—

KM# 4 ALBUS (12 Heller)

Silver **Ruler:** Moritz **Obv:** Crowned Hessian lion to left, date below, legend divided by four small shields of arms **Obv. Legend:** MAUR • D • G • L - ANDGR • HASSIÆ. **Rev:** Ornate Hessian helmet **Rev. Legend:** VALET • I • ALBVM • VEL • 1Z OBVL(OS) • HASS(ICOS) • **Note:** Ref. S#597. Varieties exist.

Date	Mintage	VG	F	VF	XF	Unc
160Z	—	50.00	100	200	400	—
1604	—	45.00	90.00	180	360	—
1607	—	45.00	90.00	180	360	—

KM# 8 ALBUS (12 Heller)

Silver **Obv:** Hessian lion in circle, legend divided by 4 small shields **Rev:** Helmet in circle, date above **Rev. Legend:** VALET I ALBVM • VEL • 12 • OBVLOS HASSIACOS

Date	Mintage	VG	F	VF	XF	Unc
(16)05	—	35.00	75.00	150	290	—
(16)06	—	35.00	75.00	150	290	—
(16)07	—	35.00	75.00	150	290	—

KM# 9 ALBUS (12 Heller)

Silver **Obv:** Date divided below lion **Rev:** Date above helmet, between the horns.

Date	Mintage	VG	F	VF	XF	Unc
1607/(16)07	—	50.00	100	210	425	—

KM# 10 ALBUS (12 Heller)

Silver, 19-21 mm. **Ruler:** Moritz **Obv:** Date only below lion

Date	Mintage	VG	F	VF	XF	Unc
1607	—	20.00	45.00	80.00	160	—

KM# 16 ALBUS (12 Heller)

Silver **Ruler:** Moritz **Obv:** Without small shields in legend, date divided below lion **Rev. Legend:** ALB • HASSIAC • VALET 1Z • OBVLOS

Date	Mintage	VG	F	VF	XF	Unc
1610	—	65.00	135	275	550	—

KM# 21 ALBUS (12 Heller)

Silver **Ruler:** Moritz **Obv:** Date in legend

Date	Mintage	VG	F	VF	XF	Unc
1610	—	65.00	130	260	525	—
1611	—	65.00	130	260	525	—

KM# 40 ALBUS (12 Heller)

Silver **Ruler:** Moritz **Obv:** Hessian lion in circle **Obv. Legend:** MAUR • D • G • LAND • HAS • **Rev:** Helmet divides date **Rev. Legend:** 1 • ALB • LANDT MUNTZ **Note:** Kipper Albus.

Date	Mintage	VG	F	VF	XF	Unc
16Z1	—	40.00	85.00	175	350	—

KM# 57 ALBUS (12 Heller)

Silver **Ruler:** Moritz **Obv:** Hessian lion, date in legend **Rev:** Helmet **Rev. Legend:** ALB9 • HASSIAC9 • VALET • 1Z • OBUL **Note:** Varieties exist.

Date	Mintage	VG	F	VF	XF	Unc
16ZZ TS	—	35.00	75.00	155	315	—
(1)6ZZ TS	—	35.00	75.00	155	315	—
(1)6Z3 TS	—	35.00	75.00	155	315	—
16Z3 TS	—	35.00	75.00	155	315	—
1624 TS	—	35.00	75.00	155	315	—

KM# 216 ALBUS (12 Heller)

Silver **Ruler:** Wilhelm VI **Obv:** Hessian lion in circle **Obv. Legend:** WILHELMVS HASS: LAND PRINC • HERSF • **Rev:** Helmet, I between, horns, date divided

Date	Mintage	VG	F	VF	XF	Unc
1651 AG	—	30.00	65.00	135	275	—

KM# 224 ALBUS (12 Heller)

Silver **Ruler:** Wilhelm VI **Obv:** Crowned W in palm wreath **Rev:** Crowned Hessian lion, date divided as 16-5Z

Date	Mintage	VG	F	VF	XF	Unc
165Z	—	25.00	55.00	110	220	—

KM# 225 ALBUS (12 Heller)

Silver **Ruler:** Wilhelm VI **Obv:** Crowned W in laurel wreath, date divided as 1-6/5-Z **Rev:** Crowned Hessian lion

Date	Mintage	VG	F	VF	XF	Unc
165Z	—	25.00	55.00	110	220	—

KM# A225 ALBUS (12 Heller)

Silver **Ruler:** Wilhelm VI **Obv:** Crowned W in palm wreath, date divided 1-6 / 5Z. **Rev:** Crowned Hessian lion

Date	Mintage	VG	F	VF	XF	Unc
165Z	—	25.00	55.00	110	220	—

KM# 235 ALBUS (12 Heller)

Silver **Ruler:** Wilhelm VI **Obv:** Crowned W in palm wreath divides date 1-6/5-3 **Rev:** Crowned Hessian lion, mintmaster initials below **Note:** Varieties exist.

Date	Mintage	VG	F	VF	XF	Unc
1653 AG	—	25.00	55.00	110	215	—
1654 AG	—	25.00	55.00	110	215	—
1655 AG	—	25.00	55.00	110	215	—
1656 AG	—	25.00	55.00	110	215	—
1657 AG	—	25.00	45.00	90.00	185	—
1657 .o.	—	40.00	75.00	150	300	—
1657	—	40.00	75.00	150	300	—
1657 GB	—	40.00	75.00	150	300	—
1657 IGB	—	40.00	75.00	150	300	—
1658 IGB	—	40.00	75.00	150	300	—
1659 IGB	—	55.00	90.00	125	265	—

KM# 252 ALBUS (12 Heller)

Silver **Ruler:** Wilhelm VI **Obv:** Crowned W with ribbons between palm branches, date in one line **Rev:** Crowned Hessian lion, mint master initials below **Note:** Varieties exist.

Date	Mintage	VG	F	VF	XF	Unc
1661 IGB	—	25.00	50.00	100	200	—
166Z IGB	—	25.00	50.00	100	200	—
1662 IGB	—	25.00	50.00	100	200	—
1663 IGB	—	25.00	50.00	100	200	—

KM# A252 ALBUS (12 Heller)

Silver **Ruler:** Wilhelm VI **Obv:** Crowned W between palm branches, date below in one line or as 1-6/6-1

Date	Mintage	VG	F	VF	XF	Unc
1661 IGB	—	50.00	100	200	400	—

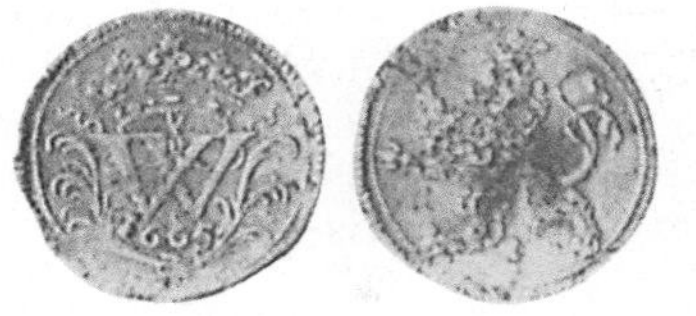

KM# 268 ALBUS (12 Heller)

Silver **Ruler:** Wilhelm VII **Obv:** Crowned W with ribbons, similar to KM #252 but more ornamented **Rev:** Hessian lion, similar to KM #235

Date	Mintage	VG	F	VF	XF	Unc
1665 IGB	—	30.00	65.00	135	275	—
1667 IGB	—	30.00	65.00	135	275	—
1668 IGB	—	30.00	65.00	135	275	—

KM# A282 ALBUS (12 Heller)

Silver **Ruler:** Wilhelm VII **Obv:** Crowned W without ribbons, within palm branches, date below **Rev:** Hessian lion

Date	Mintage	VG	F	VF	XF	Unc
1668 IGB	—	50.00	100	200	400	—

KM# 282 ALBUS (12 Heller)

Silver **Ruler:** Wilhelm VII **Obv:** W within palm branches, date as 1-6/7-0

Date	Mintage	VG	F	VF	XF	Unc
1670 IGB	—	40.00	80.00	160	325	—

KM# 294 ALBUS (12 Heller)

Silver **Ruler:** Karl **Obv:** Crowned double, mirror-image script CL monogram divides date between palm branches **Rev:** Crowned Hessian lion, mintmasters monogram below

Date	Mintage	VG	F	VF	XF	Unc
1673 IGB	—	45.00	90.00	185	335	—

KM# 296 ALBUS (12 Heller)

Silver **Ruler:** Karl **Obv:** Date below C **Note:** Varieties exist especially in design and date placement.

Date	Mintage	VG	F	VF	XF	Unc
1673 IGB	—	15.00	30.00	60.00	120	—
1674 IGB	—	15.00	30.00	60.00	120	—
1675 IGB	—	15.00	30.00	60.00	120	—
1676 IGB	—	15.00	30.00	60.00	120	—
1677 IGB	—	15.00	30.00	60.00	120	—
1678 IGB	—	15.00	30.00	60.00	120	—
1679 IGB	—	15.00	30.00	60.00	120	—
1680 IGB	—	15.00	30.00	60.00	120	—
1680 IH	—	15.00	30.00	60.00	120	—
1681 IH	—	15.00	30.00	60.00	120	—
1681 IVF	—	15.00	30.00	60.00	120	—
1682 IVF	—	15.00	30.00	60.00	120	—
1683 IVF	—	15.00	30.00	60.00	120	—
1684 IVF	—	15.00	30.00	60.00	120	—
1685 IVF	—	15.00	30.00	60.00	120	—
1686 IVF	—	15.00	30.00	60.00	120	—
1687 IVF	—	15.00	30.00	60.00	120	—
1688 IVF	—	15.00	30.00	60.00	120	—
1689 IVF	—	15.00	30.00	60.00	120	—
1690 IVF	—	15.00	30.00	60.00	120	—

KM# 295 ALBUS (12 Heller)

Silver **Ruler:** Karl **Obv:** Crowned C divides date 1-6 / 7-3, between palm branches

Date	Mintage	VG	F	VF	XF	Unc
1673 IGB	—	25.00	45.00	90.00	185	—
1673 GIB error	—	—	—	—	—	—

KM# 330 ALBUS (12 Heller)

Silver **Ruler:** Karl **Obv:** Crowned CL monogram divides date as 1-6 / 9-1 **Rev:** Lion left without shield **Note:** Variety of crown designs exist.

Date	Mintage	VG	F	VF	XF	Unc
1690	—	—	—	—	—	—
Note: Reported, not confirmed						
1691 IVF	—	20.00	40.00	75.00	155	—
1692 IVF	—	20.00	40.00	75.00	155	—

KM# 331 ALBUS (12 Heller)

Silver **Ruler:** Karl **Obv:** Crowned CL, date flanking as 1-6 / 9-1 **Rev:** Crowned shield with lion **Note:** Many shield and crown varieties exist.

Date	Mintage	VG	F	VF	XF	Unc
1691 IVF	—	20.00	40.00	75.00	155	—
1692 IVF	—	20.00	40.00	75.00	155	—
1693 IVF	—	20.00	40.00	75.00	155	—

KM# 333 ALBUS (12 Heller)

Silver **Ruler:** Karl **Obv:** Bust right **Rev:** Scirpt C, crown above divides date

Date	Mintage	VG	F	VF	XF	Unc
1693 IVF	—	65.00	135	275	550	—

KM# 342 ALBUS (12 Heller)

Silver **Ruler:** Karl **Obv:** Crowned double-script C monogram, L-Z-H between **Rev:** Hessian lion divides date **Note:** Varieties exist in date placement.

Date	Mintage	VG	F	VF	XF	Unc
1694 IVF	—	15.00	30.00	65.00	130	—
1695 IVF	—	15.00	30.00	65.00	130	—
1696 IVF	—	15.00	30.00	65.00	130	—
1697 IVF	—	15.00	30.00	65.00	130	—
1698	—	15.00	30.00	65.00	130	—
1699	—	15.00	30.00	65.00	130	—
1700	—	15.00	30.00	65.00	130	—

KM# A72 2 ALBUS (4 Kreuzer)

Silver **Ruler:** Moritz **Obv:** Hessian lion, date below; all in circle **Obv. Legend:** MAU • D: G • LAND • HASS • C • C • D • Z • E • N • **Rev:** Helmet with two horns **Rev. Legend:** ALB 9 HASS • DVPLIC • VALET 24 • OBUL:

Date	Mintage	VG	F	VF	XF	Unc
16ZZ TS Rare	—	—	—	—	—	—

KM# 72 2 ALBUS (4 Kreuzer)

Silver **Ruler:** Moritz **Obv:** Hessian arms in baroque shield **Obv. Legend:** MAUR: D: G: LAND: HASS: CO: C • D: 2 • E • N • **Rev:** • II •/ ALBUS/ date **Rev. Legend:** VON • REICHS • THALER • SILBER

Date	Mintage	VG	F	VF	XF	Unc
16Z4 TS Rare	—	—	—	—	—	—
16Z5 Rare	—	—	—	—	—	—

KM# 151 2 ALBUS (4 Kreuzer)

Silver **Ruler:** Wilhelm V **Obv:** Hessian lion in circle, date divided around lion **Rev:** Value, Z between horns, helmet **Rev. Legend:** VON REICHS TAHLER SILBER

Date	Mintage	VG	F	VF	XF	Unc
1635	—	—	—	—	—	—

KM# 334 2 ALBUS (4 Kreuzer)

Silver **Ruler:** Karl **Obv:** Bust right **Rev:** 2 crowned script C's between palm branches, date in legend

Date	Mintage	VG	F	VF	XF	Unc
1693 IVF	—	140	250	475	950	—

KM# 305 4 ALBUS (1/8 Thaler)

Silver **Ruler:** Karl **Obv:** Crowned Hessian lion **Rev:** IIII/ ALBUS, date in legend

Date	Mintage	VG	F	VF	XF	Unc
1681 IH	—	55.00	110	225	450	—

KM# 306 4 ALBUS (1/8 Thaler)

Silver **Ruler:** Karl **Obv:** Hessian lion in empty field, without legend **Rev:** IIII/ ALBUS, date **Note:** KM#306 is a possible pattern.

Date	Mintage	VG	F	VF	XF	Unc
1681 IH Rare	—	—	—	—	—	—

KM# 85 1/96 THALER (4 Heller)

Silver, 14 mm. **Ruler:** Wilhelm V **Obv:** Ornate helmet divides date, WLZH above **Rev:** 5-line inscription **Rev. Inscription:** 96 / EIN • R • / TAHLER / WERT / TS **Mint:** Cassel

Date	Mintage	VG	F	VF	XF	Unc
(16)Z7 TS	—	—	—	—	—	—
(16)Z8 TS	—	65.00	110	210	425	—

KM# 103 1/96 THALER (4 Heller)

Silver **Ruler:** Wilhelm V **Obv:** WLH above ornate helmet **Rev. Inscription:** 96 / EIN • R • / TAHLER / WERT / TS

Date	Mintage	VG	F	VF	XF	Unc
(16)Z8 TS	—	65.00	110	210	425	—

KM# 104 1/96 THALER (4 Heller)

Silver **Ruler:** Wilhelm V **Obv:** WLZH above helmet **Rev. Inscription:** 96 • ST • EIN / R • TAHL / WERT / TS

Date	Mintage	VG	F	VF	XF	Unc
(16)Z8 TS	—	65.00	110	210	425	—

KM# 112.1 1/96 THALER (4 Heller)

Silver, 14 mm. **Ruler:** Wilhelm V **Obv:** Ornate helmet divides date at bottom, W.L.Z.H. above **Rev:** 5-line inscription **Rev. Inscription:** 96 / EINN • R / TAHLER / WERTH / TS **Mint:** Cassel

Date	Mintage	VG	F	VF	XF	Unc
(16)Z8 TS	—	55.00	95.00	190	385	—
(16)Z9 TS	—	55.00	95.00	190	385	—
(16)29 TS	—	55.00	95.00	190	385	—
(16)30 TS	—	55.00	95.00	190	385	—
(16)31 TS	—	55.00	95.00	190	385	—
(16)33 TS	—	55.00	95.00	190	385	—

Date	Mintage	VG	F	VF	XF	Unc
(16)35 shamrock	—	55.00	95.00	190	385	—
(16)35 TS	—	55.00	95.00	190	385	—

KM# 112.2 1/96 THALER (4 Heller)

Silver **Ruler:** Wilhelm V **Obv:** Helmet, WLZH above **Rev. Inscription:** • 96 • / EINN • R / TALL • / WERT **Note:** Varieties exist.

Date	Mintage	VG	F	VF	XF	Unc
ND GK, crossed pothooks	—	55.00	95.00	190	385	—
ND shamrock	—	55.00	95.00	190	385	—
1637 shamrock	—	55.00	95.00	190	385	—

KM# 158 1/96 THALER (4 Heller)

Silver **Ruler:** Wilhelm V **Obv:** Ornate helmet, WLZH above **Rev. Inscription:** • 96 • / EINN • R / THALL / date

Date	Mintage	VG	F	VF	XF	Unc
1636 shamrock	—	55.00	95.00	190	385	—

KM# 168 1/96 THALER (4 Heller)

Silver **Ruler:** Wilhelm V **Obv:** Helmet, WL above, date between horns **Rev. Inscription:** 96 / EINN • R / THALL / WERT

Date	Mintage	VG	F	VF	XF	Unc
(16)37 shamrock	—	55.00	95.00	190	385	—

KM# 169 1/96 THALER (4 Heller)

Silver **Ruler:** Wilhelm VI **Obv:** Helmet, WLZ above, H between horns, date divided **Rev. Inscription:** 96 / EINN • R / TAHLL / WERT

Date	Mintage	VG	F	VF	XF	Unc
(16)37 AG	—	55.00	95.00	190	385	—
(16)40 AG	—	55.00	95.00	190	385	—
ND AG	—	55.00	95.00	190	385	—

KM# 199 1/96 THALER (4 Heller)

Silver **Ruler:** Wilhelm VI **Obv:** Helmet, WLZH above, divides date as 3-9 **Rev. Inscription:** 96 / EINN • R / TAHLL / VVERT

Date	Mintage	VG	F	VF	XF	Unc
(16)39 GK	—	45.00	95.00	190	385	—

KM# 200 1/96 THALER (4 Heller)

Silver **Ruler:** Wilhelm VI **Obv:** Helmet, date between horns **Rev. Inscription:** 96 / EINNR • / TAHLL / WERT

Date	Mintage	VG	F	VF	XF	Unc
(16)39 GK	—	45.00	95.00	190	385	—

KM# 211 1/96 THALER (4 Heller)

Silver **Ruler:** Wilhelm VI **Obv:** Helmet, WLZ above, H between horns, date divided **Rev. Inscription:** 96 / EINN • R / TAHLL / WERT

Date	Mintage	VG	F	VF	XF	Unc
(16)40 AG	—	—	—	—	—	—
(16)46 AG	—	—	—	—	—	—

KM# 207 1/96 THALER (4 Heller)

Silver **Ruler:** Wilhelm VI **Obv:** Helmet, WLH above, date divided **Rev. Inscription:** 96 / S • EIN R / TAHLER / WERT

Date	Mintage	VG	F	VF	XF	Unc
(16)45 AG	—	—	—	—	—	—

KM# A212 1/96 THALER (4 Heller)

Silver, 16 mm. **Ruler:** Wilhelm VI **Obv:** Helmet, WLZH above, date divided **Rev. Inscription:** 96 / EINN • R / THALL • / WERT **Mint:** Cassel **Note:** Varieties exist.

Date	Mintage	VG	F	VF	XF	Unc
(16)49 AG	—	70.00	120	185	300	—
(16)50 AG	—	70.00	120	185	300	—

KM# 239 1/96 THALER (4 Heller)

Silver **Ruler:** Wilhelm VI **Obv:** Crowned W divides date as 1-6/5-3 in palm wreath **Rev:** Hessian lion divides 9-6

Date	Mintage	VG	F	VF	XF	Unc
1653 AG	—	75.00	150	300	625	—
1654 AG	—	75.00	150	300	625	—

KM# 212 1/64 THALER (6 Heller)

Silver **Ruler:** Wilhelm VI **Obv:** Hessian lion in shield within circle **Obv. Legend:** WILHEL: LANDQ • ZV • HESSEN **Rev. Inscription:** 64 / ST • EINN / R • TAHLER / WERTH

Date	Mintage	VG	F	VF	XF	Unc
1646 AG	—	30.00	60.00	120	240	—
1647 AG	—	30.00	60.00	120	240	—
1649 AG	—	30.00	60.00	120	240	—

KM# 236 1/64 THALER (6 Heller)
Silver **Ruler:** Wilhelm VI **Obv:** Crowned W in palm wreath, date divided above 1-6, below 5-3 **Rev:** Hessian lion divides 6-4

Date	Mintage	VG	F	VF	XF	Unc
1653 AG	—	—	—	—	—	—
1653	—	—	—	—	—	—

KM# 105.1 1/48 THALER (8 Heller)
Silver **Ruler:** Wilhelm V **Obv:** Hessian arms **Obv. Legend:** WIL • LAN • HAS **Rev. Legend:** 48 • ST • EIN THAL WERT

Date	Mintage	VG	F	VF	XF	Unc
16Z8 Rare	—	—	—	—	—	—

KM# 105.2 1/48 THALER (8 Heller)
Silver **Ruler:** Wilhelm V **Obv:** Crowned arms **Obv. Legend:** WILHE: -LAN • HAS **Rev:** Date divided below **Rev. Legend:** 48 ST • EIN • RE TAHLER WERT **Note:** Prev. KM #145. Legend varieties WILHE, WILHL, WILHEL; HA, HAS.

Date	Mintage	VG	F	VF	XF	Unc
1634 3 crossed pothooks, Rare	—	—	—	—	—	—

KM# 106 1/32 THALER (Albus)
Silver **Ruler:** Wilhelm V **Obv:** Helmet, I between horns, title of Wilhelm in legend **Rev:** Value, date **Rev. Inscription:** 3Z / STUCK • / EIN • • RICHS / THALER • / WEHRT **Note:** Nearly 80 varieties exist in obverse legend and reverse value writing combinations.

Date	Mintage	VG	F	VF	XF	Unc
16Z8 TS	—	25.00	50.00	100	200	—
16Z9 TS	—	25.00	50.00	100	200	—
1630 TS	—	25.00	50.00	100	200	—
1631 TS	—	25.00	50.00	100	200	—
163Z TS	—	25.00	50.00	100	200	—
1633 TS	—	25.00	50.00	100	200	—
1634 TS	—	25.00	50.00	100	200	—
1635	—	25.00	50.00	100	200	—
1635 o	—	25.00	50.00	100	200	—
1635 shamrock	—	25.00	50.00	100	200	—
1636 shamrock	—	25.00	50.00	100	200	—
1637 shamrock	—	25.00	50.00	100	200	—

KM# 205 1/32 THALER (Albus)
Silver **Ruler:** Wilhelm VI **Note:** Similar to KM#106. Varieties exist.

Date	Mintage	VG	F	VF	XF	Unc
1640 GK	—	27.00	55.00	110	220	—
1641 GK Rare	—	—	—	—	—	—
1645 AG	—	27.00	55.00	110	220	—
1648 .o.	—	27.00	55.00	110	220	—
1650 AG	—	27.00	55.00	110	220	—

KM# 84 1/2 REICHSORT (1/8 Thaler)
Silver **Ruler:** Wilhelm V **Obv:** Hessian helmet, 8-pointed star between horns **Obv. Legend:** WILHELM • D • G... **Rev:** value and date **Rev. Inscription:** EIN / HALBER / REICHS= / ORT **Note:** Legend varieties.

Date	Mintage	VG	F	VF	XF	Unc
16Z7 TS	—	180	375	750	1,500	—
16Z8 TS	—	150	300	625	1,250	—

KM# 152 1/2 REICHSORT (1/8 Thaler)
Silver **Ruler:** Wilhelm V **Obv:** Hessian lion in Spanish shield within circle **Obv. Legend:** WIHEL: D: G: LAND: HASS: C • C • Z • E • N **Rev:** Value and date **Rev. Inscription:** EINN / HALBER / REICHS / ORTH

Date	Mintage	VG	F	VF	XF	Unc
1635 shamrock Rare	—	—	—	—	—	—

KM# 166.1 1/2 REICHSORT (1/8 Thaler)
Silver **Ruler:** Wilhelm V **Obv:** Tree in storm **Obv. Legend:** VNO VOLENTE HUMILIS LEVABOR **Rev:** Valus and date **Rev. Inscription:** 1 / HALLBER / REICHS • / ORTH • / 16-37

Date	Mintage	VG	F	VF	XF	Unc
1637 GK crossed pothooks	—	175	375	750	1,500	—

KM# 166.2 1/2 REICHSORT (1/8 Thaler)
Silver **Ruler:** Wilhelm V **Rev. Inscription:** EINN / HALBER / ...

Date	Mintage	VG	F	VF	XF	Unc
1637 GK	—	—	—	—	—	—

Note: Reported, not confirmed

KM# 17 1/8 THALER (1/2 Reichsort)
Silver **Ruler:** Moritz **Obv:** Crowned Hessian lion in ornamented German shield, helmet above, 4 small arms divide legend **Obv. Legend:** MAURI: - D: GLAN - :HASS: C • - • D • Z • E • N • **Rev:** Two crossed lances with pennants divide date, branches above, bell and hour glass below, 4 small arms divide legend **Rev. Legend:** CONSILio - et • VIRTU - TE: MO: - NO: IMP **Note:** S#615.

Date	Mintage	VG	F	VF	XF	Unc
1610 Rare	—	—	—	—	—	—

KM# 73 1/8 THALER (1/2 Reichsort)
Silver **Ruler:** Moritz **Obv:** Crowned Hessian lion in circle, four small shields divide legned **Obv. Legend:** MAU: D: - G • LAND - HASS: C. - C • D • Z • E • N **Rev:** Two crossed lances with pennants divide date, branches above, bell and hourglass below **Rev. Legend:** CONSILI(O) - ET • VIR: - TUTE • M(O) - NO: IM: **Mint:** Cassel **Note:** S#691, 696, 703. Varieties exist.

Date	Mintage	VG	F	VF	XF	Unc
16Z4 TS	—	150	300	600	1,200	—
16Z5 TS	—	150	300	600	1,200	—
16Z6 TS	—	150	300	600	1,200	—
1627 TS	—	—	—	—	—	—

Note: Reported, not confirmed

KM# 113 1/8 THALER (1/2 Reichsort)
Silver **Ruler:** Wilhelm V **Obv:** Hessian lion, date above, four small shields divide legend **Obv. Legend:** WILHEL • -D • G • LA • -HASS • C • - C • D • Z • N • **Rev:** Tree in storm, four small shields divide legend **Rev. Legend:** DEO • VOL -ENTE • - HUMILIS -LEVABOR

Date	Mintage	VG	F	VF	XF	Unc
16Z9 TS	—	185	375	775	1,550	—

KM# 123 1/8 THALER (1/2 Reichsort)
Silver **Ruler:** Wilhelm V **Obv:** Lion divides date as 1-6/3-0; legend divided by four small sheilds **Obv. Legend:** WILHEL... **Rev:** Tree in storm, four houses beside; four small shield divide legend **Rev. Legend:** DEO VOLENTE HUMILIS LEVABOR **Note:** Reverse legend shield position changes.

Date	Mintage	VG	F	VF	XF	Unc
1630	—	185	375	775	1,550	—
1631	—	185	375	775	1,550	—

KM# 124 1/8 THALER (1/2 Reichsort)
Silver **Ruler:** Wilhelm V **Subject:** Death of Moritz **Obv:** 7-line inscription, date **Rev:** Two crossed flags, branches above, hourglass below **Rev. Legend:** MAURITI • MEMENTO MORI • CONSIL • E • VIRTUTE

Date	Mintage	VG	F	VF	XF	Unc
163Z TS	—	150	300	600	1,200	—

KM# 134.1 1/8 THALER (1/2 Reichsort)
Silver **Ruler:** Wilhelm V **Obv:** Hessian lion without small arms in legend, date between hind claws **Obv. Legend:** WILH: D: G: L: HASS: C: C: D: Z: E: N: TS **Rev:** Tree in storm **Rev. Legend:** IEHOVA • VOLENTE • HUMILIS • LEVABOR

Date	Mintage	VG	F	VF	XF	Unc
1633 TS without houses	—	150	300	625	1,250	—
1633 TS two houses	—	150	300	625	1,250	—

KM# 134.2 1/8 THALER (1/2 Reichsort)
Silver **Ruler:** Wilhelm V **Obv:** Lion divides date as 1-6/3-3 **Obv. Legend:** WILHELM • D • G • LAND • HASS • COM • C • D • ZEN **Rev:** Tree in storm **Rev. Legend:** IEHOVA • VOLENTE • HUMILIS • LEVABOR

Date	Mintage	VG	F	VF	XF	Unc
1633 TS//clover two houses	—	150	300	625	1,250	—
1635 .o.//clover without houses	—	150	300	625	1,250	—
1637 //clover without houses	—	150	300	625	1,250	—

KM# 134.3 1/8 THALER (1/2 Reichsort)
Silver **Ruler:** Wilhelm V **Obv:** Date in band below lion

Date	Mintage	VG	F	VF	XF	Unc
1633 TS	—	150	300	625	1,250	—

KM# 134.4 1/8 THALER (1/2 Reichsort)
Silver **Ruler:** Wilhelm V **Obv:** Lion, date in legend **Obv. Legend:** WILH • D • G • LAND • HAS • AO • 1636 **Rev:** Tree in storm **Rev. Legend:** IEHOVA • VOLENTE • HUMILIS • LEVABOR **Note:** Varieties exist.

Date	Mintage	VG	F	VF	XF	Unc
1636 clover without houses	—	175	375	775	1,550	—

KM# 170 1/8 THALER (1/2 Reichsort)
Silver **Ruler:** Wilhelm V **Obv:** Lion, date divided around lion as 1-6/3-7 or 1-3/6-7 or 16-37, without small shields breaking legend **Rev:** Tree in storm, 4 or 5 houses **Rev. Legend:** VNO • VOLENTE • HUMILIS • LEVABOR **Note:** Varieties exist.

Date	Mintage	VG	F	VF	XF	Unc
1637	—	175	350	700	1,400	—
Note: Date reads vertically						
1637	—	175	350	700	1,400	—
Note: Date reads horizontally						
1637	—	175	350	700	1,400	—
Note: Date split as 16-37						

KM# 317 1/8 THALER (1/2 Reichsort)
Silver **Ruler:** Karl **Obv:** Hession lion **Obv. Legend:** C • L • Z • H • F • Z • H • C • D • Z • N • U • S • **Rev:** Value within legend **Rev. Legend:** HESS LAND MUNTZ

Date	Mintage	VG	F	VF	XF	Unc
1685 IVF	—	45.00	90.00	180	360	—
1.6.89 IVF	—	45.00	90.00	180	360	—
1689 IVF	—	45.00	90.00	180	360	—

KM# 319 1/8 THALER (1/2 Reichsort)
Silver **Ruler:** Karl **Obv:** Arms, titles of Karl **Rev:** Swan, date in legend **Note:** Similar to 1 Thaler, KM#322. Some sources consider this a medal.

Date	Mintage	VG	F	VF	XF	Unc
1686	—	—	—	—	—	—

KM# 335 1/8 THALER (1/2 Reichsort)
Silver **Ruler:** Karl **Obv:** Bust right **Obv. Legend:** CAROL • DG • HASS • LANDG **Rev:** Four crowned CC monograms forming a cross, date in legend

Date	Mintage	VG	F	VF	XF	Unc
1693 IVF	—	—	800	1,600	3,250	—

KM# 171 1/8 THALER
Silver, 25 mm. **Ruler:** Wilhelm V **Subject:** Death of Wilhelm V **Obv:** 7-line inscription with Arabic numeral dates **Obv. Legend:** WILHEL. V. DICT,. CONSTANS. HASS: LANDGRAVI: **Obv. Inscription:** NAT,. / 14. FEBR. Ao. / 160Z. MORT: / 21. SEP: A: 1637. / REG: A(o): 10.M.7. / D: 4. VIX(IT): A: (35) / (35.) M. 7. D. 7. / .GK. **Rev:** Palm tree in storm, four houses **Rev. Legend:** VNO VOLENTE HUMILIS LEVABOR. **Mint:** Cassel **Note:** S#996.

Date	Mintage	VG	F	VF	XF	Unc
1637 GK	—	165	230	460	925	—

KM# 217 1/8 THALER
Silver **Ruler:** Wilhelm VI **Subject:** Death of Amalie Elisabth von Hanau, Wife of Wilhelm V, mother of Wilhelm VI **Obv:** 9-line inscription with Arabic numeral dates **Obv. Legend:** AMELIA ELISABETHA HASS: LANDGR: HANOVIÆ COMES: **Rev:** Mountain with miner in mine, winged heart and sun above, clouds and storm at left and right **Rev. Legend:** WIEDER MACHT UND LIST. MEIN FELS GOTT IST. **Rev. Inscription:** NATA / Z9 IAN: 160Z / PR: PIETATE FIDE / AC CONSTANT INCL / POST 13 AN: TUTEL / AC REGI: GLORIOS / PLACIDA MORTE / OBYT. 8. AUG. / A 1651 G **Mint:** Cassel **Note:** S#1161.

Date	Mintage	VG	F	VF	XF	Unc
1651 AG	—	160	325	650	1,300	—

KM# 226 1/8 THALER
Silver **Ruler:** Wilhelm VI **Obv:** Crowned shield of manifold arms,

with central shield of Hessian lion, all in baroque frame, date flanking as 1-6/5-2 **Obv. Legend:** WILH(ELM,)(.) DG. LAND(G). HASS. PRIN. HERSF. C(O). C(A). D(I). Z(I). N: t SCHA. **Rev:** Sailing ship to left in circle **Rev. Legend:** VELA (• LEVANTUR) • HIS • VENTIS (• LEVANTUR) **Mint:** Cassel **Note:** S#1069, 1075, 1082, 1089. Varieties exist.

Date	Mintage	VG	F	VF	XF	Unc
165Z	—	800	1,600	3,250	6,500	—
1653	—	800	1,600	3,250	6,500	—
1654 AG	—	—	—	—	—	—
1655 AG	—	800	1,600	3,250	6,500	—

KM# 258 1/8 THALER

Silver **Ruler:** Wilhelm VI **Subject:** Death of Wilhelm VI **Obv:** Armored bust 3/4 to right **Obv. Legend:** WILHELM • VI • D • G • LANDG • HASS • PR • HERSE • CO • CA • DE • ZI • NI • ET • SCHAW • **Rev:** 10-line inscription with Roman numeral dates, legend divided by 7 small shields of arms **Rev. Legend:** PIE - TATE. - FIDE - ET - IVS - TI - TIA. **Rev. Inscription:** NASCITVR / AN. M.DC.XXIX / .XXIII. MAII. VIXIT. / ANN. XXXIV. MENS. / I.D. XXI. REGNA. / AN. XII. M. IX. DIE / XXI. OBIT. XVI. JVL. / A.-M.DC.-LX / III / .IGB. **Mint:** Cassel **Note:** S#1155.

Date	Mintage	VG	F	VF	XF	Unc
MDCLXIII (1663) IGB	—	185	375	775	1,550	—

KM# 270 1/8 THALER

Silver **Ruler:** Wilhelm VII **Subject:** Hedwig Sophie of Brandenburg, Wife of Wilhelm VII **Obv:** Large shield of manifold arms incorporating Hesse on left and Brandenburg on right, large crown above, knotted cord around **Obv. Legend:** HEDWIG • SOPHIA • V: G: G: L: Z: H: G: A: C: S: D: M: Z: B: W: V: V: REGENT: **Rev:** Terrestrial globe hanging on a heart, sword cutting connecting rope **Rev. Legend:** DISSOLVER - ANNO (date) **Mint:** Cassel **Note:** S#1218.

Date	Mintage	VG	F	VF	XF	Unc
1669	—	675	1,350	2,750	5,500	—

KM# 283 1/8 THALER

Silver, 24 mm. **Ruler:** Wilhelm VII **Subject:** Death of Wilhelm VII **Obv:** Shield of manifold arms with central shield of Hessian lion, 5 ornate helmets above **Obv. Legend:** WILHELM • VII • D • G • LANDG • HASS • PR • HERSE • COM • C • D • Z • N • ET • SHAW * **Rev:** 9-line inscription with Arabic numeral dates in wreath **Rev. Inscription:** NATVS / CASSELLIS. 21. / IVN. 1651. OBIIT IN / IPSO REGIM. PROPY / LÆO PARISIIS. 21. NOV. / 1670. VIXIT DIV. / QVIA BENE VIXIT / ANNOS. 19. / MENS. 5. **Mint:** Cassel **Note:** S#1211.

Date	Mintage	VG	F	VF	XF	Unc
1670 IGB	—	150	300	600	1,200	—

KM# 336 1/8 THALER

Silver **Ruler:** Karl **Obv:** Crowned shield **Obv. Legend:** C • L • Z • H • F • Z • H • G • Z • C • D • Z • N • U • S • **Rev:** Value within legend **Rev. Inscription:** VIII / EINEN / THALER **Note:** Varieties exist.

Date	Mintage	VG	F	VF	XF	Unc
1693 IVF	—	60.00	120	240	475	—
1693 IVF star	—	60.00	120	240	475	—

KM# 12 1/4 THALER (Ortstaler)

Silver **Ruler:** Moritz **Obv:** Crowned Hessian lion, date below, four small shields divide legend **Obv. Legend:** MAVRI • S -E • D • G • LA - ND • HASS - C • C • D • Z • E • N **Rev:** Helmet, shamrock between horns **Rev. Legend:** BENEDICTIO DEI E NOVIS • FODI • FRANCOBER

Date	Mintage	VG	F	VF	XF	Unc
1607 Rare	—	—	—	—	—	—

KM# 18 1/4 THALER (Ortstaler)

Silver **Ruler:** Moritz **Obv:** Hessian lion, helmet above; four small shields divide legend **Obv. Legend:** MAURI • -D • G • LAN • - HASS • C • -C • D • Z • ET N • **Rev:** Two crossed flags, branches above, hourglass below **Rev. Legend:** MON • NOV • IMP • CONSILIO ET VIRTVTE

Date	Mintage	VG	F	VF	XF	Unc
1610 Rare	—	—	—	—	—	—

KM# 64 1/4 THALER (Ortstaler)

Silver **Ruler:** Moritz **Obv:** Hessian lion, legend divided by 4 small shields **Rev:** 2 crossed flags divide date, hourglass and bell below, branches above, legend divided by 4 small shields **Rev. Legend:** CONSIL -IO • E • VIR • -TVTEMO • -NO • IMP:

Date	Mintage	VG	F	VF	XF	Unc
1623 TS	—	225	450	900	1,850	—
16Z4 TS	—	225	450	900	1,850	—
16Z5 TS Rare	—	—	—	—	—	—
16Z6 TS	—	225	450	900	1,850	—

KM# 86 1/4 THALER (Ortstaler)

Silver **Ruler:** Wilhelm V **Obv:** Bust of Wilhelm right divides date as 1-6/Z-7, titles of Wilhelm in legend **Rev:** 5-fold arms **Rev. Legend:** UNO

Date	Mintage	VG	F	VF	XF	Unc
1627 Rare	—	—	—	—	—	—

KM# 107 1/4 THALER (Ortstaler)

Silver **Ruler:** Wilhelm V **Obv:** Hessian arms in Spanish shield **Obv. Legend:** WILHELM • D • G • LAND • H • A • H • C • C • D • Z • E • N **Rev:** Tree in storm, date in legend **Rev. Legend:** DEO... **Note:** Varieties exist.

Date	Mintage	VG	F	VF	XF	Unc
(1)6Z8	—	275	550	1,100	2,200	—
(16)Z8	—	275	550	1,100	2,200	—
(1)6Z9	—	275	550	1,100	2,200	—
1630 TS	—	275	550	1,100	2,200	—
1631 two houses	—	275	550	1,100	2,200	—

KM# 125 1/4 THALER (Ortstaler)

Silver **Ruler:** Wilhelm V **Subject:** Death of Moritz **Obv:** 7-line inscription **Rev:** Two crossed flags, branches above, hourglass below **Rev. Legend:** MAURITI • MEMENTO MORI CONSI: E: VIRTU

Date	Mintage	VG	F	VF	XF	Unc
163z TS	—	550	1,100	2,250	4,500	—

KM# 138 1/4 THALER (Ortstaler)

Silver **Ruler:** Wilhelm V **Obv:** Oval arms in oval baroque frame, titles of Wilhelm in legend **Obv. Legend:** WILHELM • D • G • LANDGRAV • HASS • COM • C • DIZ • Z • E • N **Rev:** Tree in storm, four houses, date **Rev. Legend:** IEHOVA...

Date	Mintage	VG	F	VF	XF	Unc
(1)633 TS	—	250	500	1,000	2,000	—

KM# A170 1/4 THALER (Ortstaler)

Silver **Ruler:** Wilhelm V **Obv:** Lion in Spanish shield, 1-6 / 3-5 **Obv. Legend:** WILHELM D G LAND HASS... **Rev:** Tree in storm, houses beside **Rev. Legend:** IEHOVA VOLENTE HUMILIS...

Date	Mintage	VG	F	VF	XF	Unc
1635 clover Rare	—	—	—	—	—	—

KM# 172.1 1/4 THALER (Ortstaler)

Silver **Ruler:** Wilhelm V **Obv:** Hessian lion divides date **Rev:** Tree in storm, 4, 5, or 6 houses **Rev. Legend:** VNO VOLENTE HUMILIS LEVABOR **Note:** Many varieties exist.

Date	Mintage	VG	F	VF	XF	Unc
1637 AG two crossed pothooks	—	300	600	1,200	2,400	—
1637 GK	—	300	600	1,200	2,400	—

KM# 172.2 1/4 THALER (Ortstaler)

Silver **Ruler:** Wilhelm V **Obv:** Hessian lion divides date **Rev:** Tree in storm, 3, 4 or 5 houses **Rev. Legend:** IEHOVA VOLENTE HUMILIS LEVABOR

Date	Mintage	VG	F	VF	XF	Unc
(16)37 clover	—	300	600	1,200	2,400	—

KM# 172.3 1/4 THALER (Ortstaler)

Silver **Ruler:** Wilhelm V **Obv:** Hessian lion, date flanking **Rev:** Tree in storm, 3, 4 or 5 houses **Rev. Legend:** IEHOVA VOLENTE HUMILIS LEVABOR

Date	Mintage	VG	F	VF	XF	Unc
1637	—	300	600	1,200	2,400	—

KM# 172.4 1/4 THALER (Ortstaler)

Silver **Ruler:** Wilhelm V **Obv:** Hessian lion, date flanking as 3-7 **Rev:** Tree in storm, 3, 4 or 5 houses **Rev. Inscription:** IEHOVA...

Date	Mintage	VG	F	VF	XF	Unc
(16)37 GK	—	300	600	1,200	2,400	—

KM# 173 1/4 THALER (Ortstaler)

Silver **Ruler:** Wilhelm V **Subject:** Death of Wilhelm V **Obv:** 9-line inscription, Arabic numeral date **Rev:** Tree in storm, 4 houses **Rev. Legend:** VNO VOLENTE HUMILIS LEVABOR

Date	Mintage	VG	F	VF	XF	Unc
1637 GK crossed pothooks	—	185	375	750	1,500	—

Note: Due to engraving style, GK often reads as GR

KM# 196 1/4 THALER (Ortstaler)

Silver **Ruler:** Wilhelm VI **Obv:** Hessian lion, date divided among paws as 1-63-8, star in front denotes Wilhelm VI **Rev:** Tree in storm, 3 houses **Rev. Legend:** IEHOVA VOLENTE HUMILIS LEVABOR

Date	Mintage	VG	F	VF	XF	Unc
1638 LH Rare	—	—	—	—	—	—

KM# 218 1/4 THALER (Ortstaler)

Silver **Ruler:** Wilhelm VI **Subject:** Death of Amalie Elisabeth von Hanau, Wife of Wilhelm V **Obv:** 9-line inscription **Rev:** Mountain with miner in mine, heart and sun above, clouds and storm besides **Rev. Legend:** WIDER MACHT UND LIST MEIN FELS GOTT IST

Date	Mintage	VG	F	VF	XF	Unc
1651 AG	—	225	450	925	1,850	—

KM# 228 1/4 THALER (Ortstaler)

Silver **Ruler:** Wilhelm VI **Obv:** Crowned manifold arms in baroque frame divide date at 1-6/5-Z **Obv. Legend:** WIL: DG: LAND: HASS: PRIN: HERS: CO: CA: DI: ZI: N:& SCH • **Rev:** Sailing ship left **Note:** Varieties exist.

Date	Mintage	VG	F	VF	XF	Unc
165Z	—	800	1,600	3,250	6,500	—
1653	—	—	—	—	—	—

Note: Reported, not confirmed

Date	Mintage	VG	F	VF	XF	Unc
1654 AG	—	800	1,600	3,250	6,500	—
1655 AG	—	800	1,600	3,250	6,500	—

Note: Peus Auction 4-03, XF/VF example realized $3775.

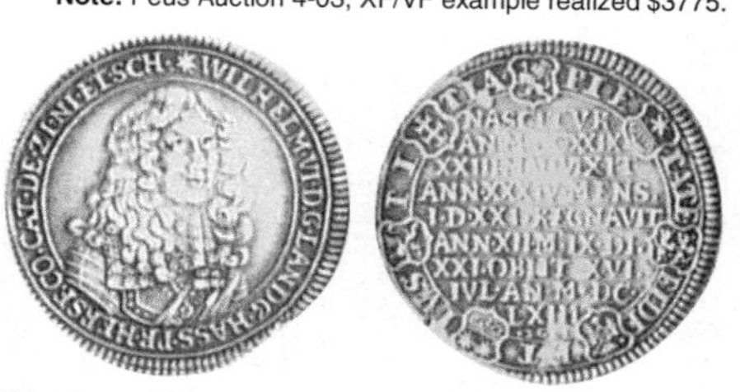

KM# 259 1/4 THALER (Ortstaler)

Silver **Ruler:** Wilhelm VI **Subject:** Death of Wilhelm VI **Obv:** Bust half left **Obv. Legend:** WILHELM • VI • G • G • LANDG • HASS • PR • HERSF • CO • CAT • DE • ZI • NI • ET • SCH **Rev:** 10-line inscription, R.N. date **Rev. Legend:** PIE -TATA • -FIDE - ET -IVS - TI -TIA -

Date	Mintage	VG	F	VF	XF	Unc
MDCLXIII (1663) IGB	—	375	775	1,575	3,150	—

KM# 271 1/4 THALER (Ortstaler)

Silver **Ruler:** Wilhelm VII **Obv:** Hessian and Brandenburg arms in crowned divided shield **Obv. Legend:** HEDWIG • SOPHIA.... **Rev:** Terrestrial globe hanging on a heart, sword cuts the rope **Rev. Legend:** DISSOLVER **Note:** Similar to 1 Thaler, KM#273.

Date	Mintage	VG	F	VF	XF	Unc
1669	—	800	1,600	3,250	6,500	—

Note: Peus Auction 4-03, XF/VF realized $5100.

KM# 284 1/4 THALER (Ortstaler)
Silver **Ruler:** Wilhelm VII **Subject:** Death of Wilhelm VII **Obv:** 7-fold Hessian arms with 5 helmets **Obv. Legend:** WILHELM • VII • D • G • LANDG • HASS • PR • HERSF • COM • C • D • Z • N • ET • SCHAV * **Rev:** 10-line inscription, R.N. date

Date	Mintage	VG	F	VF	XF	Unc
MDCLXX (1670) Rare	—	—	—	—	—	—

KM# 308 1/4 THALER (Ortstaler)
7.3000 g., Silver, 27.4 mm. **Ruler:** Karl **Subject:** Death of Hedwig Sophie von Brandenburg, Wife of Wilhelm VI **Obv:** Hessian and Brandenburg arms in divided crowned shield **Obv. Legend:** HEDWIGIS: SOPHIA • HASS: PR • H • NAT • PR • ELECT: BRANDENB: **Rev:** 9-line inscription with date

Date	Mintage	VG	F	VF	XF	Unc
1.6.83	—	900	1,800	3,600	7,200	—

Note: Peus Auction 4-03, VF realized $2830.

KM# 321 1/4 THALER (Ortstaler)
Silver **Ruler:** Karl **Obv:** Crowned arms between palm branches, date below **Rev:** Swan with crown around its neck on pedestal, double C monogram and lion above **Note:** Similar to 1 Thaler, KM#322. Some sources consider this a medal.

Date	Mintage	VG	F	VF	XF	Unc
1686 IVF	—	—	—	—	—	—

KM# 337 1/4 THALER (Ortstaler)
Silver **Ruler:** Karl **Obv:** Bust right **Obv. Legend:** CAROL • DG •-•-• HASS • LANDG **Rev:** Double CL monogram in cross angles, crowned

Date	Mintage	VG	F	VF	XF	Unc
1693 IVF	—	450	900	1,850	3,700	—

KM# 22 1/2 THALER
Silver **Ruler:** Moritz **Obv:** Hessian lion in ornamented shield, helmet above, titles of Moritz in legend **Rev:** Crossed flags divide date, branches above, bell and hourglass below **Rev. Legend:** CONSILIO...

Date	Mintage	VG	F	VF	XF	Unc
1611 Rare	—	—	—	—	—	—

KM# 43 1/2 THALER
23.9000 g., Silver **Ruler:** Moritz **Obv:** Helmet above shield with lion, legend between four small shields **Rev:** Crossed lances dividing date at center, legend between four small shields **Note:** Klippe.

Date	Mintage	VG	F	VF	XF	Unc
1621 Unique	—	—	—	—	—	—

KM# 65 1/2 THALER
Silver **Ruler:** Moritz **Obv:** Crowned Hessian lion, 4 small shields divide legend; titles of Maurice **Rev:** Crossed flags divide date, branches above, bell and hourglass below, four small shields divide legend

Date	Mintage	VG	F	VF	XF	Unc
1623 TS	—	450	900	1,800	3,600	—
16Z4 TS	—	400	800	1,600	3,250	—
16Z5 TS	—	400	800	1,600	3,250	—
1626 TS	—	400	800	1,600	3,250	—
1627	—	—	—	—	—	—

Note: Reported, not confirmed

KM# 87 1/2 THALER
Silver **Ruler:** Wilhelm V **Obv:** Facing bust divides date, titles of Wilhelm V in legend **Rev:** Hessian arms in Spanish shield, 3 helmets **Rev. Legend:** UNO • VOLENTE • HUMILIS • LEVABOR •

Date	Mintage	VG	F	VF	XF	Unc
16Z7 TS Rare	—	—	—	—	—	—

KM# 88 1/2 THALER
Silver **Ruler:** Wilhelm V **Obv:** Bust right divides date 1-6/Z-7 or as 16-Z7, titles of Wilhelm V **Obv. Legend:** WILHELM • D • G • LAND • HASS • ADMI • HIR • C • C • D • Z • E • N **Rev:** Hessian arms in German shield, 3 helmets **Rev. Legend:** UNO VOLENTE • HUMILIS • LEVABOR •

Date	Mintage	VG	F	VF	XF	Unc
16Z7 TS Rare	—	—	—	—	—	—
1627	—	—	—	—	—	—

Note: Reported, not confirmed

KM# 108.1 1/2 THALER
Silver **Ruler:** Wilhelm V **Obv:** 5-fold arms in baroque French shield **Obv. Legend:** WILHELM • D • G • LAND • HASS • AD • H • COM • C • D • Z • E • N **Rev:** Tree in storm, without houses, date **Rev. Legend:** DEO • VOLENTE • HUMILIS • LEVABOR •

Date	Mintage	VG	F	VF	XF	Unc
16Z8 TS Rare	—	—	—	—	—	—

KM# 108.2 1/2 THALER
Silver **Ruler:** Wilhelm V **Obv:** Crowned arms in baroque shield **Rev:** Tree in storm, with houses only in 1631 and 1632 **Note:** Reverse background varieties exist.

Date	Mintage	VG	F	VF	XF	Unc
1629 TS	—	600	1,200	2,400	4,800	—
1630 TS	—	600	1,200	2,400	4,800	—
1631	—	500	1,000	2,000	4,000	—
163Z	—	500	1,000	2,000	4,000	—

KM# 126 1/2 THALER
Silver **Ruler:** Wilhelm V **Subject:** Death of Moritz **Obv:** 9-line inscription, Arabic date **Rev:** Two crossed flags, branches above **Rev. Legend:** MAURITI • MEMENTO MORI • CONSILIO ET VIRTUTE •

Date	Mintage	VG	F	VF	XF	Unc
1632 TS	—	500	1,000	2,000	4,000	—

KM# 126a 1/2 THALER
Tin **Ruler:** Wilhelm V **Subject:** Death of Moritz **Obv:** 9-line inscription **Rev:** Two crossed flags, branches above **Note:** Off-metal strike of KM#126.

Date	Mintage	VG	F	VF	XF	Unc
1632 TS	—	—	180	360	725	—

KM# 139 1/2 THALER
Silver **Ruler:** Wilhelm V **Obv:** Hessian arms in ornamented oval, crowned, date 1-6-3-3 divided around crown, titles of Wilhelm **Rev:** Tree in storm, 4 houses, date as 633 **Rev. Legend:** IEHOVA...

Date	Mintage	VG	F	VF	XF	Unc
1633//(1)633 clover	—	550	1,100	2,250	4,500	—

KM# 140 1/2 THALER
Silver **Ruler:** Wilhelm V **Obv:** Bust right divides date **Rev:** Hessian arms in ornamented oval, crowned **Rev. Legend:** FATA • CONSILITS • POTIORA

Date	Mintage	VG	F	VF	XF	Unc
1633	—	—	—	—	—	—

Note: Reported, not confirmed

KM# 146 1/2 THALER
Silver **Ruler:** Wilhelm V **Obv:** Bust right, no legend **Rev:** Ornamented oval arms, no legend **Note:** Some sources consider this a medal.

Date	Mintage	VG	F	VF	XF	Unc
1634	—	—	—	—	—	—

KM# 153 1/2 THALER
Silver **Ruler:** Wilhelm V **Obv:** Crowned Hessian lion divides date as 1-6/3-5 around, titles of Wilhelm in legend **Rev:** Tree in storm **Rev. Legend:** IEHOVA...

Date	Mintage	VG	F	VF	XF	Unc
1635 LH clover	—	340	685	1,375	2,750	—

KM# 160.1 1/2 THALER
Silver **Ruler:** Wilhelm V **Obv:** Crowned Hessian lion divides date as 16-36 **Rev:** Tree in storm, 4 houses **Rev. Legend:** IEHOVA...

Date	Mintage	VG	F	VF	XF	Unc
1636 2 crosses	—	275	575	1,150	1,550	—
1637 clover	—	335	675	1,350	2,750	—

KM# 175.1 1/2 THALER
Silver **Ruler:** Wilhelm VI **Obv:** Hessian lion, star in front (denotes Wilhelm VI) **Obv. Legend:** WILHEL[M] • D: G: LAND[GRA] • HASS • C[OM] • C • D • Z • E • N • **Rev:** Tree in storm, houses **Rev. Legend:** IEHOVA VOLENTE HUMILIS LEVABOR **Note:** Date placement varies.

Date	Mintage	VG	F	VF	XF	Unc
1637 clover	—	190	385	775	1,550	—
1637 GK crossed pothooks	—	190	385	775	1,550	—
1638 LH	—	190	385	775	1,550	—
1639 GK crossed pothooks	—	190	385	775	1,550	—

KM# 160.2 1/2 THALER
Silver **Ruler:** Wilhelm V **Obv:** Crowned Hessian lion **Rev:** Tree in storm, houses **Rev. Legend:** VNO... **Note:** Varieties exist.

Date	Mintage	VG	F	VF	XF	Unc
1637 AG	—	375	750	1,500	3,000	—
1637 LH	—	325	650	1,350	1,700	—
1637 O	—	375	750	1,500	3,000	—

KM# 160.3 1/2 THALER
Silver **Ruler:** Wilhelm V **Obv:** Crowned Hessian lion **Rev:** Tree in storm, houses **Rev. Legend:** VNO...

Date	Mintage	VG	F	VF	XF	Unc
1637 GK two pothooks	—	400	800	1,600	3,250	—

KM# 174 1/2 THALER
Silver **Ruler:** Wilhelm V **Subject:** Death of Wilhelm V **Obv:** 10-line inscription, Arabic date **Obv. Legend:** WILHELM9 • V • DICT9 • CONSTANS • HASS: LANDGR: **Rev:** Tree in storm **Rev. Legend:** VNO VOLENTE HUMILIS LEVABOR

Date	Mintage	VG	F	VF	XF	Unc
1637 GK two pothooks	—	680	1,375	2,750	5,500	—

KM# 175.2 1/2 THALER
Silver **Ruler:** Wilhelm VI **Obv:** Hessian lion, star. **Rev:** Tree in storm, houses **Rev. Legend:** VNO...

Date	Mintage	VG	F	VF	XF	Unc
1637 GH crossed pothooks	—	190	385	775	1,550	—

KM# 219 1/2 THALER
Silver **Ruler:** Wilhelm VI **Subject:** Death of Amalie Elisabeth von Hanau, Wife of Wilhelm V, mother of William VI **Obv:** 9-line inscription with Arabic numeral date **Rev:** Mountain with miner in mine, heart and sun above, clouds and storm besides **Note:** Similar to 1/4 Thaler, KM#218.

Date	Mintage	VG	F	VF	XF	Unc
1651 AG	—	500	1,050	2,100	4,200	—

KM# 231 1/2 THALER
Silver **Ruler:** Wilhelm VI **Obv:** Crowned Hessian arms in baroque frame divide date, titles of Wilhelm in legend **Rev:** Sailing ship left **Rev. Legend:** VELA VENTIS HIS LEVANTVR **Note:** Varieties exist.

Date	Mintage	VG	F	VF	XF	Unc
1652	—	900	1,800	3,600	7,200	—
1653	—	900	1,800	3,600	7,200	—
1654 AG	—	—	—	—	—	—
1655 AG	—	900	1,800	3,600	7,200	—

Note: Reported, not confirmed (1654 AG)

KM# 261 1/2 THALER
Silver **Ruler:** Wilhelm VI **Subject:** Death of Wilhelm VI **Obv:** Bust right **Obv. Legend:** WILHELM • VI • D • G • LANDG • HASS • PR • HERS • CO • C • D • Z • N • ET • SCHAW **Rev:** 10-line inscription, date in R.N.

Date	Mintage	VG	F	VF	XF	Unc
MDCLXIII (1663) IGB	—	425	850	1,700	3,400	—

KM# 272 1/2 THALER

Silver **Ruler:** Wilhelm VII **Obv:** Hessian and brandburg arms in divided crowned shield **Obv. Legend:** HEDWIG • SOPHIA • V: G: G: L: Z: H: G: A: C: S: D: M: Z: B: W: V: V: REGENT: **Rev:** Terrestrial globe hanging on a heart, sword cuts the rope **Rev. Legend:** DISSOLVER **Note:** Similar to 1 Thaler, KM#273.

Date	Mintage	VG	F	VF	XF	Unc
1669	—	685	1,350	2,750	5,500	—

KM# 286 1/2 THALER

Silver **Ruler:** Wilhelm VII **Rev:** Inscription with Arabic numerals date in wreath **Note:** Struck with a 1/4 Thaler die

Date	Mintage	VG	F	VF	XF	Unc
1670	—	—	—	—	—	—

Note: Reported, not confirmed

KM# 285 1/2 THALER

Silver **Ruler:** Wilhelm VII **Subject:** Death of Wilhelm VII **Obv:** Helmeted arms **Obv. Legend:** WILHELM • VII • D • G • LANDG • HASS • PR • HERSF • COM C • D • Z • N • ET SCHAVENB **Rev:** 11-line inscription with R.N. date

Date	Mintage	VG	F	VF	XF	Unc
MDCLXX (1670) Rare	—	—	—	—	—	—

KM# 309 1/2 THALER

Silver **Ruler:** Karl **Subject:** Death of Hedwig Sophie von Brandenburg, Wife of Wilhelm VI **Obv:** Hessian and Brandenburg arms in crowned divided shield **Obv. Legend:** HEDWIGIS: SOPHIA • HASS: PR • H • NAT • PR • ELECT: BRANDENB: **Rev:** 9-line inscription with date

Date	Mintage	VG	F	VF	XF	Unc
1683	—	685	1,350	2,750	5,500	—

KM# 318 1/2 THALER

10.7000 g., Silver, 23 mm. **Ruler:** Karl **Obv:** Star **Rev:** Star **Note:** Believed by many now to be a medal

Date	Mintage	VG	F	VF	XF	Unc
1685	—	—	—	—	—	—

KM# 338 1/2 THALER

Silver **Ruler:** Karl **Obv:** Bust right **Obv. Legend:** CAROL • DG • -- HASS: LANDG • **Rev:** Hessian arms in Spanish shield, 5 helmets

Date	Mintage	VG	F	VF	XF	Unc
1693 IVF	—	750	1,500	3,000	6,000	—

KM# 19 THALER

Silver **Ruler:** Moritz **Obv:** Hessian lion in oval cartouche, helmet above, legend divided by 4 small shields **Obv. Legend:** MAURITIUS • D.G • LAND. HASS. CO • IN • C•D•Z•E•N• **Rev:** Branches above crossed flags, divided date in the side angles, hourglass and bell below, four small shields divide legend **Rev. Legend:** CONSILIO ET VIRTVTE. MON. NOV. IMP. **Note:** Dav.#6711; S#613.1.

Date	Mintage	VG	F	VF	XF	Unc
1610 Rare	—	—	—	—	—	—

KM# 20 THALER

Silver **Ruler:** Moritz **Obv:** Crowned Hessian lion in oval baroque frame, ornate helmet above, legend divided by 4 small shields of arms **Obv. Legend:** MAVRITI(V'). - D:G. LAND: - HASS. CO. - I(N). C.D.Z.E.N. **Rev:** Crossed flags divide date, bell and hourglass below, legend divided by 4 small shields of arms **Rev. Legend:** CONSILI(-)O. (-) ET. VIR(-)TU(= -)TE. MO(N) - NOV. IMP: **Note:** Dav.#6712; S#613, 620.1. Varieties exist.

Date	Mintage	VG	F	VF	XF	Unc
1610	—	700	1,200	2,400	4,800	—
1611	—	700	1,200	2,400	4,800	—

KM# 23 THALER

Silver **Ruler:** Moritz **Obv:** Hessian lion in oval shield, ornate helmet above **Obv. Legend:** MAVRITI - D.G. LAND - HASSIÆ - CO. IN. CAT. **Rev:** Two crossed lances, branches above, bell and hourglass below, date divided at left and right **Rev. Legend:** CONSILI - O. ET. VIR - TVTE. MO. - NOV. IMP. **Note:** Dav.#6713; S#620.

Date	Mintage	VG	F	VF	XF	Unc
1611	—	700	1,200	2,400	5,000	—

KM# 44 THALER

Silver, 40 mm. **Ruler:** Moritz **Obv:** Crowned Hessian lion in oval baroque frame, ornate helmet above, four small shields divide legend **Obv. Legend:** MAURIT: - D:G. LAND - HASS: CO. - C.D.Z.E.N: **Rev:** Two crossed lances with pennants divide date, branches above, bell and hourglass below **Rev. Legend:** CONSILIO - ET. VIRTUTE - MONETA - NOV: IMP: **Note:** Dav.#6716; S#625.

Date	Mintage	VG	F	VF	XF	Unc
1621 3 crossed ingot hooks	—	600	1,100	2,200	4,500	—

KM# 45 THALER

Silver **Ruler:** Moritz **Obv:** Crowned Hessian lion in oval baroque frame, ornate helmet above, four small shields divide legend **Obv. Legend:** MAURIT: - D:G. LAND. - HASS: CO. - C.D.Z.E.N. **Rev:** Two crossed lances with pennants, branches above, bell and hourglass below, date at end of legend **Rev. Legend:** MONETA. NOV. IMP. CONSILIO ET VIRTUTE. **Note:** Dav.#6717.

Date	Mintage	VG	F	VF	XF	Unc
1621	—	600	1,100	2,200	4,500	—

Note: Reported, not confirmed

KM# 69.2 THALER

Silver **Ruler:** Moritz **Obv:** Crowned Hessian lion in circle, four small shields of arms divide legend **Obv. Legend:** MA(U)(V)R(I)(T): D: - G: LAN(D): - HASS(IÆ): C(O): - C: D: Z: E: N: **Rev:** Two crossed lances with pennants divide date, branches above, bell and hourglass below, legend divided by 4 small shields of arms **Rev. Legend:** CONSILI(O) - ET. VIR - TU(T)(E). MO(N) - NOV(A). IM(P). **Mint:** Cassel **Note:** Dav.#6723; S#680, 688, 694, 698, 707. Varieties exist.

Date	Mintage	VG	F	VF	XF	Unc
16Z3 TS	—	100	220	460	1,200	—
16Z3	—	120	250	500	1,450	—
16Z4 TS	—	100	200	430	1,100	—
16Z5 TS	—	100	200	430	1,100	—
16Z6 TS	—	100	200	430	1,100	—
16Z7 TS	—	100	220	460	1,200	—

KM# 66 THALER

Silver **Ruler:** Moritz **Obv:** Crowned Hessian lion in oval baroque frame, ornate helmet above, four small shields divide legend **Obv. Legend:** MAVRIT(I)' - D.G. LAND. - HASS. CO. - (I.)C.D.Z.E.N. **Rev:** Two crossed lances with pennants, branches above, bell and hourglass divide date below, legend divided by 4 small shields of arms **Rev. Legend:** CONSILIO - ET VIRTVTE. - MON. NOV. IMP. **Note:** Dav.#6718.

Date	Mintage	VG	F	VF	XF	Unc
1623	—	700	1,200	2,400	5,000	—

KM# 67 THALER

Silver **Ruler:** Moritz **Obv:** Crowned Hessian lion in oval baroque frame, ornate helmet above, four small shields divide legend **Obv. Legend:** MAUR(ITI'). - D.G. LAND. - HASS. CO. - I.C.D.Z.E.N. **Rev:** Two crossed lances with pennants divide date, branches above, bell and hourglass below, legend divided by 4 small shields of arms **Rev. Legend:** CONSILIO - ET VIRTUTE. - MON. NOVA. IMP. **Note:** Dav.#6719.

Date	Mintage	VG	F	VF	XF	Unc
1623	—	700	1,200	2,400	5,000	—

KM# 68 THALER

Silver **Ruler:** Moritz **Obv:** Crowned Hessian lion in oval baroque frame, ornate helmet above, four small shields divide legend **Obv. Legend:** MAURIT(I'). - D.G. LAND. - HASS. CO. - I.C.D.Z.E.N. **Rev:** Two crossed lances with pennants, branches above, bell and hourglass below divide date, legend divided by 4 small shields of arms **Rev. Legend:** CONSILIO ET VIRTUTE. MONETA NOV. IMP. **Note:** Dav.#6720; S#678.

Date	Mintage	VG	F	VF	XF	Unc
1623	—	700	1,200	2,400	5,000	—

KM# 69.1 THALER

Silver **Ruler:** Moritz **Obv:** Crowned Hessian lion in circle, legend divided by 4 small shields of arms **Obv. Legend:** MAURIT: D.G. LAN(D). - HASS. CO. - C.D.Z.E.N. **Rev:** Two crossed lances with pennants divide date, branches above, bell and hourglass below, legend divided by 4 small shields of arms **Rev. Legend:** CONSILIO E(T): - VIRTUTE MONETA - NOV(A). IM(P): **Mint:** Cassel **Note:** Dav.#6721.

Date	Mintage	VG	F	VF	XF	Unc
16Z3 TS	—	100	220	460	1,200	—

KM# 71 THALER

Silver **Ruler:** Moritz **Obv:** Crowned Hessian lion in circle, legend divided by 4 small shields of arms **Obv. Legend:** MAU: - G. LAND. - HASSIÆ - C.C.D.E.N. **Rev:** Two crossed lances with pennants divide date, branches above, bell and hourglass below, legend divided by 4 small shields of arms **Rev. Legend:** CONSIL - IO. E. VIR - TUTE. M. - NO: IMP **Mint:** Cassel **Note:** S#681.1. Struck on Thaler flan with 1/2 Thaler dies.

Date	Mintage	VG	F	VF	XF	Unc
1623 TS Rare	—	—	—	—	—	—

KM# 76 THALER

Silver **Ruler:** Moritz **Obv:** Crowned Hessian lion in circle, four small shields of arms divide legend **Obv. Legend:** MAUR: D: - G: LAND: - HASS: C: - C:D:Z:E:N. **Rev:** Two crossed lances with pennants divide date, branches above, bell and hourglass below, legend divided by 4 small shields of arms **Rev. Legend:** CONSILI - ET VIRTU - MON: NO: AURE: IM. **Mint:** Cassel **Note:** Dav. #6724; S#700. The reverse die was intended for a gold issue, as indicated by the word AURE in the legend.

Date	Mintage	VG	F	VF	XF	Unc
16Z6 TS Rare	—	—	—	—	—	—

KM# 89 THALER
Silver **Ruler:** Wilhelm V **Obv:** Facing armored bust in partial circle, inner legend with date curved above head **Obv. Legend:** WILHELM. D.G. LAND. HASS. ADMI. HIRS. C.C.D.Z.E.. **Rev:** 4-fold arms with central shield of Hesse, 3 ornate helmets above **Rev. Legend:** Outer: UNO: VOLENTE. HUMILIS. LEVABOR. MO: NO: IM: Inner: ANNO. DOMINE. (date). **Mint:** Cassel **Note:** Dav.#6728; S#721.

Date	Mintage	VG	F	VF	XF	Unc
16Z7 TS	—	650	1,200	2,800	6,000	—

KM# 91 THALER
Silver **Ruler:** Wilhelm V **Obv:** Facing bust, *ANNO* *1627* without band around head **Rev:** Helmeted arms IN 5-fold Spanish shield **Note:** Dav.#6729.

Date	Mintage	VG	F	VF	XF	Unc
16Z7 TS	—	600	1,100	2,500	5,500	—

KM# 92 THALER
Silver **Ruler:** Wilhelm V **Obv:** Facing bust of Wilhelm V without date **Rev:** Helmeted arms in 5-fold German shield, date in legend which starts at the bottom **Rev. Legend:** VNO COLENTE HVMILIS LEVABOR **Note:** Dav.#6731. Varieties exist.

Date	Mintage	VG	F	VF	XF	Unc
1627 TS	—	550	1,000	2,400	5,000	—

KM# 93 THALER
Silver **Ruler:** Wilhelm V **Obv:** Facing bust which divides date **Rev:** Helmeted arms, date in legend starting at the bottom **Rev. Legend:** VNO VOLENTE HVMILIS LEVABOR **Note:** Dav.#6732. Date on both sides.

Date	Mintage	VG	F	VF	XF	Unc
16Z7 TS	—	550	1,000	2,400	5,000	—

KM# 95 THALER
Silver **Ruler:** Wilhelm V **Obv:** Facing bust, bust divides date **Rev:** Helmeted arms in 5-fold Spanish shield **Rev. Legend:** UNO VOLENTE HUMILIS LEVABOR MO NO IM **Note:** Dav.#6733. Varieties exist.

Date	Mintage	VG	F	VF	XF	Unc
16Z7 TS	—	500	950	2,200	4,800	—

KM# 96 THALER
Silver **Ruler:** Wilhelm V **Obv:** Bust right **Rev:** Helmeted arms in 5-fold Spanish shield **Rev. Legend:** UNO VOLENTE NUMILIS LEVABOR MO NO IM **Note:** Dav.#6734. Varieties exist, star or rose at end of date.

Date	Mintage	VG	F	VF	XF	Unc
16Z7 TS	—	400	850	2,000	4,500	—

KM# 98.1 THALER
Silver **Ruler:** Wilhelm V **Obv:** Ornate shield of 4-fold arms with central shield of Hesse, 3 ornate helmets above **Obv. Legend:** WILHELM. D.G. LAND. HASS. ADM. HIRS. C.C.D.Z.E.N. **Rev:** Palm tree in storm with lightning, with or without clouds, sun above with Hebrew "JEHOVAH" and date at end of legend **Rev. Legend:** DEO. VOLENTE. HUMILIS. LEVA(b)(B)OR. ANNO. **Mint:** Cassel **Note:** Dav.#6735; S#732-3. Varieties exist.

Date	Mintage	VG	F	VF	XF	Unc
16Z7 TS	—	180	350	750	1,500	—
(1)6Z7 TS	—	170	350	680	1,350	—

KM# 98.2 THALER
Silver **Ruler:** Wilhelm V **Obv:** 3 helmets above 5-fold Spanish arms in square shield w/round bottom **Obv. Legend:** WILHELM • D • G • LAND... **Rev:** Palm tree in storm **Note:** Dav.#6736.

Date	Mintage	VG	F	VF	XF	Unc
16Z8 TS	—	170	330	680	1,350	—
16Z9 TS	—	170	330	680	1,350	—

KM# 115.1 THALER
Silver **Ruler:** Wilhelm V **Obv:** 5-fold arms in crowned oval, crown divides date **Obv. Legend:** WILHELMUS • D: G: LANDTGRAVIVS • HASSIAE • COM: IN: C: D: Z: E: NID **Rev:** Tree in storm, sun above w/Hebrew "JEHOVAH" without houses in the background beside the tree **Rev. Legend:** DEO • VOLETE • HUMILIS • LEVABOR **Note:** Dav.#6737.

Date	Mintage	VG	F	VF	XF	Unc
16Z9 TS	—	110	230	480	950	—
1630 TS	—	110	230	480	950	—

KM# 117 THALER
Silver **Ruler:** Wilhelm V **Obv:** Hessian arms in 5-fold oval, without crown **Obv. Legend:** WILHELMUS • D: G: LANDTGRAV: HASS: CO: C: D: Z: E: N **Rev:** Palm tree in storm **Rev. Legend:** DEO • VILETE • HUMILIS • LEVABOR • ANNO •(date)

Date	Mintage	VG	F	VF	XF	Unc
16Z9 TS	—	110	230	520	1,200	—

KM# 115.2 THALER
Silver **Ruler:** Wilhelm V **Obv. Legend:** LANDTGRAVIUS...C • D • Z • N **Rev:** Tree in storm, town in background **Note:** Dav.#6741.

Date	Mintage	VG	F	VF	XF	Unc
1630 TS	—	150	320	660	1,300	—
1631 TS	—	140	300	630	1,250	—

KM# 120 THALER
Silver **Ruler:** Wilhelm V **Obv:** Bust of Wilhelm V right, date M-D-C-XXX in corners **Rev:** Tree in storm, town in background **Rev. Legend:** DEO VOLENTE HUMILIS LEVABOR **Note:** Klippe. Dav.#6743.

Date	Mintage	VG	F	VF	XF	Unc
MDCXXX (1630)	—	—	2,000	3,500	6,000	—

KM# 115.3 THALER
Silver **Ruler:** Wilhelm V **Obv:** Hessian arms in 5-fold Spanish shield **Obv. Legend:** WILHELM9 • D: G: LANDGRAVI9 **Note:** Dav.#6745.

Date	Mintage	VG	F	VF	XF	Unc
1631 TS	—	140	300	630	1,250	—
1632 TS	—	140	300	630	1,250	—

KM# 115.4 THALER

Silver **Ruler:** Wilhelm V **Obv:** Crown breaks through upper inner circle **Note:** Dav.#6745A.

Date	Mintage	VG	F	VF	XF	Unc
1631	—	85.00	165	300	550	—

KM# 115.6 THALER

Silver **Ruler:** Wilhelm V **Obv:** Hessian arms in 5-fold oval **Obv. Legend:** WILHELM9: D: G: LANDGRAVI9: **Rev:** Palmtree in storm, town in background **Rev. Legend:** IEHOVA **Note:** Dav.#6749.

Date	Mintage	VG	F	VF	XF	Unc
163Z clover//TS	—	150	340	700	1,400	—
1633 clover//TS	—	150	340	700	1,400	—
1634 TS//rose	—	140	300	630	1,250	—
1634 clover//TS	—	—	—	—	—	—
1634 TS//clover	—	140	300	630	1,250	—
1634 clover//rose	—	—	—	—	—	—

KM# 115.5 THALER

Silver **Ruler:** Wilhelm V **Rev. Legend:** V[U]NO.VOLENTE **Note:** Dav.#6746.

Date	Mintage	VG	F	VF	XF	Unc
1632	—	85.00	165	300	550	—

KM# 128 THALER

Silver, 43 mm. **Ruler:** Wilhelm V **Subject:** Death of Moritz **Obv:** 10-line inscription with dates **Obv. Legend:** MAURITI,. LANDGRAVI,. HASSIÆ. DEO.ET.IMPERIO. FIDUS: **Obv. Inscription:** NATUS. / Z5. MAI. AN(N)O. / 157Z. MORTUUS. / 15. MARTII. ANNO. / 163Z. REGNAVIT. / ANNOS. 34. MENSES. / 6. DIES. ZZ. / VIXIT. ANNOS. 59. / MENSES. 10. / DIES. 10. **Rev:** Two crossed lances with pennants, branches above, bell and hourglass below **Rev. Legend:** MAURITI. MEMENTO. MORI. CONSILIO. ET. VIRTUTE. **Mint:** Cassel **Note:** Dav.#6726; S#811. Varieties exist.

Date	Mintage	VG	F	VF	XF	Unc
1632 TS	—	100	22.00	450	950	—

KM# 141 THALER

Silver **Ruler:** Wilhelm V **Obv:** Bust right **Obv. Legend:** WILHELM9 • D: G: LANDGRAVI9 HASSIAE • C: C: D: Z: ET: N: **Rev:** Hessian arms in 5-fold oval Spanish shield **Rev. Legend:** FATA CONSILIIS POTIORA **Note:** Dav.#6748.

Date	Mintage	VG	F	VF	XF	Unc
1633 clover	—	900	1,700	2,800	5,400	10,000
1633 crossed pothooks	—	900	1,700	2,800	5,400	10,000
1633 mercury stick	—	900	1,700	2,800	5,400	10,000
1633	—	—	—	—	—	—
Note: Reported, not confirmed						
1634 crossed pothooks	—	900	1,700	2,800	5,400	10,000

KM# 143 THALER

Silver **Ruler:** Wilhelm V **Obv:** Hessian lion left, date scattered in field **Rev:** Tree in storm, town in background **Rev. Legend:** IEHOVA VOLENTE HUMILIS LEVABOR **Note:** Dav.#6752; 6753. Number of houses varies, 4 or 5.

Date	Mintage	VG	F	VF	XF	Unc
1635 LH clover//star	—	150	300	650	1,250	—
1635 LH star//star	—	150	300	650	1,250	—
1636 LH star//star	—	150	300	650	1,250	—
1636 LH star//clover	—	150	300	650	1,250	—

KM# 115.7 THALER

Silver **Ruler:** Wilhelm V **Rev. Legend:** IEHOV **Note:** Dav.#6751.

Date	Mintage	VG	F	VF	XF	Unc
1635	—	85.00	165	300	550	—

KM# 162.1 THALER

Silver **Ruler:** Wilhelm V **Obv:** Hessian lion divides date in inner circle **Rev:** Tree in storm, village in background **Note:** Dav.#6755.

Date	Mintage	VG	F	VF	XF	Unc
1636 LH clover//star	—	150	300	650	1,250	—
1636 LH star//clover	—	150	300	650	1,250	—
1637 LH clover star//star	—	150	300	650	1,250	—

KM# 179.2 THALER

Silver **Ruler:** Wilhelm VI **Obv:** Crowned lion dividing date, star in front **Rev:** Tree in storm **Note:** Dav.#6775.

Date	Mintage	VG	F	VF	XF	Unc
1637 LH	—	150	320	620	1,200	—
1638 LH	—	150	320	620	1,200	—

KM# 179.3 THALER

Silver **Ruler:** Wilhelm VI **Obv:** Crowned lion left, star in front **Rev:** Tree in storm, no houses **Note:** Dav.#6775A.

Date	Mintage	VG	F	VF	XF	Unc
1637 LH	—	150	320	620	1,200	—
1638 LH	—	150	320	620	1,200	—

KM# 162.2 THALER

Silver **Ruler:** Wilhelm V **Obv:** Hessian lion left **Rev:** Tree in storm **Note:** Dav.#6757.

Date	Mintage	VG	F	VF	XF	Unc
1637 .o.//star	—	150	300	650	1,250	—

KM# 162.3 THALER
Silver **Ruler:** Wilhelm V **Obv:** Hessian lion left, 16-37 flanking **Rev. Legend:** IEHOVA **Note:** Dav.#6760.

Date	Mintage	VG	F	VF	XF	Unc
1637 G crossed pothooks k	—	150	300	650	1,250	—
1637 GK / crossed pothooks	—	150	300	650	1,250	—

KM# 162.4 THALER
Silver **Ruler:** Wilhelm V **Obv:** 16-37 flanking lion **Rev. Legend:** IEHOVA... **Note:** Dav.#6761.

Date	Mintage	VG	F	VF	XF	Unc
1637 GK crossed pothooks	—	85.00	165	300	550	—

KM# 162.5 THALER
Silver **Ruler:** Wilhelm V **Obv:** Lion rampant left, date divided by lion above **Note:** Dav.#6762.

Date	Mintage	VG	F	VF	XF	Unc
1637 LH clover	—	85.00	165	300	550	—

KM# 162.6 THALER
Silver **Ruler:** Wilhelm V **Obv:** Hessian lion left, 16-37 flanking **Rev. Legend:** VNO VOLETE HUMILIS LEVABOR **Note:** Dav.#6763; A6764.

Date	Mintage	VG	F	VF	XF	Unc
1637 AG	—	150	300	650	1,250	—
1637 G crossed pothooks K	—	150	300	650	1,250	—

KM# 162.7 THALER
Silver **Ruler:** Wilhelm V **Obv:** Lion's legs divide G-H, mint mark between legs **Note:** Dav.#A6764.

Date	Mintage	VG	F	VF	XF	Unc
1637 GH	—	85.00	165	300	550	—

KM# 176 THALER
Silver **Ruler:** Wilhelm V **Obv:** Date between hind feed **Note:** Dav.#6759. Varieties exist.

Date	Mintage	VG	F	VF	XF	Unc
1637 LH	—	85.00	165	300	550	—

KM# 177 THALER
Silver **Ruler:** Wilhelm V **Subject:** Death of Wilhelm V **Obv:** 10-line inscription with Roman numeral date **Obv. Legend:** WILHELM9 • V • DICT9 • CONSTANS • HASS: LANDGRAVIVS **Rev:** Tree in storm, (4, 5, 6, or 7 houses) **Note:** Dav.#6765.

Date	Mintage	VG	F	VF	XF	Unc
MDCXXXVII (1637) G crossed pothooks K	—	250	500	1,000	2,000	—

KM# 178 THALER
Silver **Ruler:** Wilhelm V **Subject:** Death of Wilhelm V **Obv:** 10-line inscription with arabic numeral date **Obv. Legend:** WILHELM9 • V • DICT9 • CONSTANS • HASS • LANDGRAVIVS **Rev. Legend:** VNO VOLENTE HUMILIS LEBABOR **Note:** Dav.#6766.

Date	Mintage	VG	F	VF	XF	Unc
1637 G crossed pothooks K	—	275	600	1,200	2,400	—

KM# 179.1 THALER
Silver **Ruler:** Wilhelm VI **Obv:** Crowned lion left with star in front, date below **Note:** Dav.#6771.

Date	Mintage	VG	F	VF	XF	Unc
1637 LH	—	150	320	620	1,200	—
1637 GK	—	150	320	620	1,200	—

KM# 180.1 THALER
Silver **Ruler:** Wilhelm VI **Obv:** Crowned lion left with star in front, date below, L mint mark H behind **Obv. Legend:** ...C: D: Z: E: N: **Rev:** Tree in storm **Note:** Dav.#6770.

Date	Mintage	VG	F	VF	XF	Unc
1637 LH	—	150	320	620	1,200	—

KM# 180.2 THALER
Silver **Ruler:** Wilhelm VI **Obv:** Crowned lion left with star in front, date below **Obv. Legend:** ...C: D: Z: ETN: **Rev:** Tree in storm **Rev. Legend:** VNO VOLENTE HUMILIS LEVABOR **Note:** Dav.#6773.

Date	Mintage	VG	F	VF	XF	Unc
1637 LH	—	150	320	620	1,200	—

KM# 181 THALER
Silver **Ruler:** Wilhelm VI **Obv:** Crowned lion left with star in front, date curved at right behind lion **Note:** Dav.#6772.

Date	Mintage	VG	F	VF	XF	Unc
1637 GK	—	85.00	165	300	550	—

KM# 180.3 THALER
Silver **Ruler:** Wilhelm VI **Obv:** Lion left, star at left **Obv. Legend:** WILHEL • D • G • LANDGRA **Rev:** Tree in storm **Note:** Dav.#6776.

Date	Mintage	VG	F	VF	XF	Unc
1638 LH	—	150	320	620	1,200	—

KM# 180.4 THALER
Silver **Ruler:** Wilhelm VI **Obv:** Crowned lion left with star in front, date curved below, LH above **Rev:** Tree in storm **Note:** Dav.#180.4.

Date	Mintage	VG	F	VF	XF	Unc
1638 LH	—	150	320	620	1,200	—

KM# 179.4 THALER
Silver **Ruler:** Wilhelm VI **Obv:** Crowned lion dividing date, G (mint mark) K above **Obv. Legend:** WILHELM • D • G • LAND • HASS • C: C • D • Z • ET • N **Rev:** Tree in storm **Note:** Dav.#6778.

Date	Mintage	VG	F	VF	XF	Unc
1639 GK	—	150	320	620	1,200	—

Note: Sometimes the poor die engraving reads GK as GR

KM# 220 THALER
Silver **Ruler:** Wilhelm VI **Subject:** Death of Amalie Elisabeth von Hanau, Wife of Wilhelm V **Obv:** 10-line inscription, date in Arabic numerals **Obv. Legend:** AMALIA ELISABETHA • HASSIAE LANDGRAVIA • HANOVIAE COMES: **Rev:** Mountain with miner in mine, hear and sun above, clouds and storm beside **Note:** Similar to 1/4 Thaler, KM#218. Dav.#6768.

Date	Mintage	VG	F	VF	XF	Unc
1651 AG	—	500	1,000	2,100	4,200	—

KM# 232.1 THALER
Silver **Ruler:** Wilhelm VI **Obv:** Crowned 7-fold arms in baroque frame divide date as 1-6/5-Z **Obv. Legend:** WILHELM9: DG • LANDG • HASS: PRINC: HERSF: COM: CATZ • DIETZ • ZIGEN • NID • ET • SCHA • **Rev:** Sailing ship left **Rev. Legend:** HIS VENTIS VELA LEVANTUR **Note:** Dav.#6779.

Date	Mintage	VG	F	VF	XF	Unc
165Z Rare	—	—	—	—	—	—

KM# 232.4 THALER
Silver **Ruler:** Wilhelm VI **Obv. Legend:** ...& SCH[A] **Rev:** Sailing ship left **Note:** Dav.#6783.

Date	Mintage	VG	F	VF	XF	Unc
1653 Rare	—	—	—	—	—	—
1654 AG Rare	—	—	—	—	—	—
1655 AG	—	—	3,000	6,000	10,000	—

KM# 232.2 THALER
Silver **Ruler:** Wilhelm VI **Rev. Legend:** VELA VENTIS HIS LEVANTUR **Note:** Dav.#6781.

Date	Mintage	VG	F	VF	XF	Unc
1653 Rare	—	—	—	—	—	—

KM# 232.3 THALER
Silver **Ruler:** Wilhelm VI **Obv. Legend:** CO • CA • DI • ZI • NI • U • SCHAW **Rev:** Sailing ship left **Note:** Dav.#6781A.

Date	Mintage	VG	F	VF	XF	Unc
1653 Rare	—	—	—	—	—	—

KM# 250 THALER

Silver **Ruler:** Wilhelm VI **Obv:** Bust right **Obv. Legend:** WILHELM • D • G • LANDG • HASS: PR • HERSF • CO • C • D • Z • N • ET • SCHAU **Rev:** Crowned 7-fold arms in French shield within palm branches **Rev. Legend:** FIDE ET IUSTITIA **Note:** Dav.#6784.

Date	Mintage	VG	F	VF	XF	Unc
1660 IGB	—	600	1,200	2,500	5,000	—

KM# 254 THALER

Silver **Ruler:** Wilhelm VI **Obv:** Bust right in wreath **Rev:** Crowned oval arms between palm branches, date in legend **Note:** Dav.#6784A.

Date	Mintage	VG	F	VF	XF	Unc
1661 IGB	—	750	1,500	3,000	7,000	—

KM# 263 THALER

Silver **Ruler:** Wilhelm VI **Obv:** Bust right **Obv. Legend:** WILHELM • D • G • LANDG • HAS • PR • HERSE • CO • C • D • Z • N • ET • SC **Rev:** Crowned 7-fold arms in Franch shield within palm branches **Rev. Legend:** FIDE ET IVSTITIA **Note:** Dav.#6784B.

Date	Mintage	VG	F	VF	XF	Unc
1663 IGB Rare	—	—	—	—	—	—

KM# 264 THALER

Silver **Ruler:** Wilhelm VI **Subject:** Death of Wilhelm VI **Obv:** Bust half-right **Obv. Legend:** WILHELM • VI • D • G • LANDG • HASS • PR • HERSF • COM • CAT • DEC • ZIEG • NID • ET • SCHAWEN • **Rev:** 10-Line inscription with Roman numeral date **Note:** Dav.#6785.

Date	Mintage	VG	F	VF	XF	Unc
MDCLXIII (1663) IGB	—	320	750	1,450	2,850	—

KM# 273 THALER

Silver **Ruler:** Wilhelm VII **Subject:** Hedwig Sophie's death **Obv:** Hessian and Brandenberg arms in crowned divised shield **Rev:** Terrestrial globe hanging on a heart, sword cuts the rope **Note:** Dav.#6786.

Date	Mintage	VG	F	VF	XF	Unc
1669	—	600	1,200	2,700	6,200	—
1671	—	600	1,200	2,700	6,200	—

KM# 274 THALER

Silver **Ruler:** Wilhelm VII **Subject:** Hedwig Sophie's death **Obv:** Hessian and Brandenberg arms in crowned divided shield, date as 1-6/6-9 flanking **Obv. Legend:** HEDWIG • SOPHIA • V: G: G: L: Z: H: G: A: C: S: D: M: Z: B: WIT: V: V: REGENTIN **Rev:** Terrestrial globe hanging on a heart, sword cuts the rope **Rev. Legend:** DISSOLVER **Note:** Dav.#6786A.

Date	Mintage	VG	F	VF	XF	Unc
1669	—	600	1,200	2,700	5,200	—

KM# 287 THALER

Silver **Ruler:** Wilhelm VII **Subject:** Death of Wilhelm VII **Obv:** Hessian arms in shield, 5 helmets above **Obv. Legend:** WILHELM • VII • D • G • LANG • HASS • PR • HERSF • COM • CAT • DEC • ZIEG • NIED ET SCHAV **Rev:** 11-line inscription in wreath with Roman numeral date **Note:** Dav.#6788.

Date	Mintage	VG	F	VF	XF	Unc
MDCLXX (1670) IGB	—	950	1,800	3,500	6,500	—

KM# 288 THALER

Silver **Ruler:** Wilhelm VII **Subject:** Death of Wilhelm VII **Rev:** 6-line inscription **Note:** Dav.#6788A.

Date	Mintage	VG	F	VF	XF	Unc
1670 IGB	—	500	1,000	2,000	3,750	—

KM# 310 THALER

Silver **Ruler:** Karl **Subject:** Death of Hedwig Sophie von Brandenburg, Wife of Wilhelm VI **Obv:** Crowned arms of Hesse and Brandenburg, date 16-49 below **Rev:** 16-line inscription with Roman numeral date **Note:** Dav.#6787.

Date	Mintage	VG	F	VF	XF	Unc
1683	—	500	1,000	2,000	3,750	—

KM# 311 THALER

Silver **Ruler:** Karl **Subject:** Death of Hedwig Sophie **Rev:** 16-line inscription, Roman numeral date **Rev. Legend:** HEDWIGIS SOPHIA NATA PRINC: ELECT: BRANDENBVRGICA **Note:** Dav.#6787A.

Date	Mintage	VG	F	VF	XF	Unc
MDCLXXXIII (1683)	—	500	1,200	2,300	4,500	—

KM# 322 THALER

Silver **Ruler:** Karl **Obv:** Bust right **Rev:** Swan with crown around its neck on pedestal, double-C monogram and lion above **Note:** Dav.#--. Most authorities now consider this a medal.

Date	Mintage	VG	F	VF	XF	Unc
1686 IVF	—	—	—	—	—	—

KM# 325.1 THALER

Silver, 36 mm. **Ruler:** Karl **Obv:** Head right **Obv. Legend:** CAROL: D • G • -HASS: LANDG **Rev:** 7-fold arms in oval, branches flanking **Note:** Dav.#6789.

Date	Mintage	VG	F	VF	XF	Unc
1687 IVF	—	700	1,400	2,800	5,600	—

KM# 325.2 THALER

Silver, 40 mm. **Ruler:** Karl **Obv:** Bust right **Obv. Legend:** CAROLUS... **Rev:** 7-fold arms in oval, plam branches flanking **Note:** Dav.#6790.

Date	Mintage	VG	F	VF	XF	Unc
1692 IVF	—	600	1,200	2,500	5,000	—

KM# 325.3 THALER

Silver **Ruler:** Karl **Obv:** Bust right **Rev:** Crowned oval arms with 16-I-V-F-92 below **Note:** Dav.#6791.

Date	Mintage	VG	F	VF	XF	Unc
1692 IVF	—	600	1,200	2,500	5,000	—

KM# 325.4 THALER

Silver **Ruler:** Karl **Obv:** Larger bust **Rev:** Crowned oval arms **Note:** Dav.#6792.

Date	Mintage	VG	F	VF	XF	Unc
1693 IVF	—	700	1,400	2,800	5,600	—

KM# 340 THALER

Silver **Ruler:** Karl **Obv:** Bust right **Rev:** Helmeted arms divide date **Note:** Dav.#6793.

Date	Mintage	VG	F	VF	XF	Unc
1693	—	450	850	1,600	2,750	—

KM# 46 1-1/2 THALER

Silver **Ruler:** Moritz **Obv:** Crowned Hessian lion in oval baroque frame, ornate helmet above, four small shields divide legend **Obv. Legend:** MAURIT: - D:G. LAND - HASS: CO. - C.D.Z.E.N: **Rev:** Two crossed lances with pennants divide date, branches above, bell and hourglass below, 4 small shields divide legend **Rev. Legend:** CONSILIO - ET. VIRTUTE - MONETA - NOV: IMP: **Note:** Klippe. Dav.#6715. Struck from Thaler dies, KM#44.

Date	Mintage	VG	F	VF	XF	Unc
16Z1 3 crossed ingot hooks Rare	—	—	—	—	—	—

Note: Reported, not confirmed

KM# 47 2 THALER

Silver **Ruler:** Moritz **Obv:** Crowned Hessian lion in oval baroque frame, ornate helmet above, four small shields divide legend **Obv. Legend:** MAURIT: - D:G. LAND - HASS: CO. - C.D.Z.E.N: **Rev:** Two crossed lances with pennants, branches above, bell and hourglass below, 4 small shields divide legend **Rev. Legend:** CONSILIO - ET. VIRTTE - MNETA - NOV: IMP: **Note:** Klippe. Dav.#6714. Struck from Thaler dies, KM#44.

Date	Mintage	VG	F	VF	XF	Unc
16Z1 3 crossed ingot hooks Rare	—	—	—	—	—	—

Note: Reported, not confirmed

KM# 80 2 THALER

Silver **Ruler:** Moritz **Obv:** Hessian lion **Obv. Legend:** MAUR: D: G: LAND: HASS: C: C: Z: E: N: **Rev:** Two crossed flags **Rev. Legend:** CONSILIO ET • VIRTUTE • MON NOVA IM **Note:** Similar to 1 Thaler, KM#69, but struck on a thick flan. Dav.#6722.

Date	Mintage	VG	F	VF	XF	Unc
16Z5 TS Rare	—	—	—	—	—	—

Note: Reported, not confirmed

KM# 119 2 THALER

Silver, 54 mm. **Ruler:** Moritz **Obv:** Hessian lions **Obv. Legend:** MAURIT: D: G: LAND: HASSIAE • C: C: D: Z: E: N: **Rev:** Two crossed flags **Rev. Legend:** CONSILI: ET • VIRTU: MONETA • NOVA • IMP: **Note:** Dav.#LS311. Wide 2 Thaler similar to Thaler KM #19, but obverse and reverse the four shields dividing the legends are much bigger and go into the central design area.

Date	Mintage	VG	F	VF	XF	Unc
16Z7 TS	—	—	2,000	3,900	7,800	—

Note: Moller Auction 10, 10-92 VF-XF realized $20,800

KM# 109 2 THALER

Silver **Ruler:** Wilhelm V **Obv:** Hessian arms in 5-fold Spanish shield, three helmets above **Obv. Legend:** WILHELMUS • D • G • LAND... **Rev:** Palm tree in storm, without houses **Rev. Legend:** DEO • VOLENTE • HUMILIS • LEVABOR • ANNO... **Note:** Dav.#LS312.

Date	Mintage	VG	F	VF	XF	Unc
16Z8 TS	—	—	2,000	3,900	7,800	—
16Z9 TS	—	—	2,000	3,900	7,800	—

KM# 121 2 THALER

Silver **Ruler:** Wilhelm V **Obv:** Hessian arms in 5-fold Spanish shield, 3 helmets above **Obv. Legend:** WILHELMUS D • G • LANDGRAVIUS HASSIAE • COMES C • D • Z • ET NIDDA **Rev:** Palm tree in storm, six houses flanking **Rev. Legend:** DEO • VOLENTE HUMILIS LEVABOR **Note:** Dav.#LS315.

Date	Mintage	VG	F	VF	XF	Unc
MDCXXX (1630) TS Rare	—	—	—	—	—	—

Note: Auction Peus #371, 2002 EF realized $7900.

KM# 122 2 THALER

Silver **Ruler:** Wilhelm V **Obv:** Bust of Wilhelm V right, date M-D-C-XXX in corners **Rev:** Tree in storm, town in background **Rev. Legend:** DEO VOLENTE HUMILIS LEVABOR **Note:** Klippe. Dav.#6742.

Date	Mintage	VG	F	VF	XF	Unc
MDCXXX (1630) Rare	—	—	—	—	—	—

KM# 129 2 THALER

Silver **Ruler:** Wilhelm V **Subject:** Death of Moritz **Obv:** 10-line inscription with dates **Obv. Legend:** MAURITI,. LANDGRAVI,. HASSIÆ. DEO.ET.IMPERIO.FIDUS: **Rev:** Two crossed lances with pennants, branches above, bell and hourglass below **Rev. Legend:** MAURITI. MEMENTO. MORI. CONSILIO. ET. VIRTUTE. **Rev. Inscription:** NATUS. / Z5. MAI. ANO. / 157Z. MORTUUS. / 15. MARTII. ANNO. / 163Z. REGNAVIT. / ANNOS. 34. MENSES. / 6. DIES. ZZ. / VIXIT. ANNOS. 59. / MENSES. 10. / DIES. 10. **Mint:** Cassel **Note:** Dav.#6725. Struck from Thaler dies, KM#128.

Date	Mintage	VG	F	VF	XF	Unc
1632 TS	—	—	—	—	—	—

Note: Reported, not confirmed

KM# 149 2 THALER

Silver **Ruler:** Wilhelm V **Obv:** Bust left **Note:** Similar to Thaler, KM#142 but struck on a thick flan.

Date	Mintage	VG	F	VF	XF	Unc
1634	—	—	—	—	—	—

KM# 147 2 THALER

Silver **Ruler:** Wilhelm V **Obv:** Hessian arms in 5-fold oval shield, 3 helmets above, Roman numeral date in legend **Obv. Legend:** WILHELMUS9 D: G: LANDGRAVI9 • HASSIAE • COM: C: D: Z: E: N: **Rev:** Palm tree in storm, village in background **Rev. Legend:** IEHOVA • VOLENTE • HUMILIS • LEVABOR • **Note:** Similar to KM#121. Dav.#LS316.

Date	Mintage	VG	F	VF	XF	Unc
MDCXXXIIII (1634) TS Rare	—	—	—	—	—	—

Note: Auction Peus 371, 2002, XF realized $7800. Formerly listed Dav. #6747, KM #148 has been deleted as an error listing.

KM# 154 2 THALER

Silver **Ruler:** Wilhelm V **Obv:** crowned Hessian lion to left, legend FATA CONSILIIS POTIORA in inner circle **Obv. Legend:** WILHELM9 D: G: LANDGRAVI9 HASSIAE • COM: C: D: Z: ET • N: ANNO... **Rev:** Tree in storm, 6 houses flanking **Rev. Legend:** IEHOVA VOLENTE HUMILIS LEVABOR **Note:** Dav.#LS318 and LS319 have been combined into one listing.

Date	Mintage	VG	F	VF	XF	Unc
MDCXXXV (1635) L clover H	—	—	—	—	—	—

Note: Auction Peus 383, 2005, VF realized $7500.

KM# 182.1 2 THALER

Silver **Ruler:** Wilhelm V **Obv:** Crowned lion left, dividing date, mintmark below **Obv. Legend:** WILHELM9 • D: G • LANDGRAVI9 • HASSIAE • C: C: D: Z: ET • N: **Rev:** Palm tree in storm, 6 or 8 houses **Rev. Legend:** U[V]NO VOLENTE HUMILIS LEVABOR **Note:** Dav.#6756.

Date	Mintage	VG	F	VF	XF	Unc
1637 .o. Rare	—	—	—	—	—	—
1637 AG Rare	—	—	—	—	—	—

KM# 182.2 2 THALER
Silver **Ruler:** Wilhelm V **Obv:** Lion, date between hind legs **Obv. Legend:** WILHELM9 • D: G: LANDGRAVI9 • HASS: COM: C • D: Z • E • N **Rev. Legend:** IEHOVA VOLENTE HUMILIS LEVABOR **Note:** Dav.#6758.

Date	Mintage	VG	F	VF	XF	Unc
1637 GK crossed pothooks Rare	—	—	—	—	—	—

KM# 183 2 THALER
Silver **Ruler:** Wilhelm V **Subject:** Death of Wilhelm V **Obv:** 10-line inscription, Roman numeral date **Obv. Legend:** WILHELM9 • V • DICT9 • CONSTANS • HASS: LANDGRAVIS **Rev:** Tree in storm, 5 houses **Rev. Legend:** VNO • VOLENTE • HUMILIS • LEVABOR **Note:** Dav.#6764. Legend varieties.

Date	Mintage	VG	F	VF	XF	Unc
1637 G two pothooks K Rare	—	—	—	—	—	—

KM# 184 2 THALER
Silver **Ruler:** Wilhelm VI **Obv:** Lion, date below, star in front **Obv. Legend:** WILHELM9 • D: G: LANDGRAVI9 • HASSIAE • COM: C: D: Z: E: N: **Rev:** Palm tree in storm, 5 houses **Rev. Legend:** IEHOVA VOLENTE HUMILIS LEVABOR **Note:** Similar to 1 Thaler, KM#162. Dav.#6769.

Date	Mintage	VG	F	VF	XF	Unc
1637 L clover H Rare	—	—	—	—	—	—

Note: Auction Moeller 47, 2007, VF+ realized $19,000.

KM# 198 2 THALER
Silver **Ruler:** Wilhelm VI **Obv:** Star in front of lion denoting Wilhelm VI **Note:** Dav.#6774.

Date	Mintage	VG	F	VF	XF	Unc
1638 LH	—	—	—	—	—	—

Note: Reported, not confirmed

KM# 237.1 2 THALER
Silver **Ruler:** Wilhelm VI **Obv:** Crowned manifold arms in baroque frame divide date as 1-6/5-3 **Rev:** Sailing ship left **Note:** Dav.#6780.

Date	Mintage	VG	F	VF	XF	Unc
1653 Rare	—	—	—	—	—	—

KM# 222 2 THALER
Silver **Ruler:** Wilhelm VI **Subject:** Death of Amalie Elisabeth von Hanau, Wife of Wilhelm V **Obv:** Crowned 7-fold arms in baroque frame, date divided as 1-6/5-3 **Obv. Legend:** WILHELM9: DG: LANDG: HASS: PRINC: HERSF: COM: CATz • DIETz • ZIGEN: NID: t SCHA: **Rev:** Sailing ship left **Rev. Legend:** VELA VENTIS HIS LEVANTUR **Note:** Same dies as KM#221. Dav.#6767.

Date	Mintage	VG	F	VF	XF	Unc
1651 AG Rare	—	—	—	—	—	—
1653 Rare	—	—	—	—	—	—

KM# 237.2 2 THALER
Silver **Ruler:** Wilhelm VI **Obv. Legend:** ...et SCHA **Note:** Dav.#6782.

Date	Mintage	VG	F	VF	XF	Unc
1655 Rare	—	—	—	—	—	—

KM# 99 3 THALER
Silver, 54 mm. **Ruler:** Moritz **Note:** Dav.#LS310; S#705. Similar to 2 Thaler, KM#119. Struck on a thick flan.

Date	Mintage	VG	F	VF	XF	Unc
16Z7 TS Very very rare	—	—	—	—	—	—

KM# 118 3 THALER
Silver **Ruler:** Wilhelm V **Obv:** Hessian arms in Spanish shield, 3 helmets above **Obv. Legend:** WILHELMUS • D • G • LAND • HASSIAE • ADMIN • HIRS • COM • C • D • Z • E • N **Rev:** Palm tree in storm, no houses **Rev. Legend:** DEO • VOLENTE • HUMILIS • LEVABOR **Note:** Dav.#LS313. Similar to 2 Thaler, KM#109.

Date	Mintage	VG	F	VF	XF	Unc
16Z9 TS Rare	—	—	—	—	—	—

KM# 155 3 THALER
Silver **Ruler:** Wilhelm V **Obv:** Crowned Hessian lion left, inner legend: FATA CONSILIIS POTIORA **Obv. Legend:** WILHEMUS9 • D:G: LANDGRAVI9 • HASSIAE • COM: C: D: Z: ET • N: **Rev:** Palm tree in storm, 6 houses **Rev. Legend:** IEHOVA VOLENTE HUMILIS LEVABOR **Note:** Similar to 2 Thaler, KM#154. Struck on a thick flan.

Date	Mintage	VG	F	VF	XF	Unc
1635 LH Rare	—	—	—	—	—	—

TRADE COINAGE

KM# 77 GOLDGULDEN
3.5000 g., 0.9860 Gold 0.1109 oz. AGW **Ruler:** Moritz **Obv:** Hessian arms in shield **Obv. Legend:** MAUR: D: G: LAND: HASS: C • C • D: Z: E • N **Rev:** Cruciform arms in inner circle, date in legend **Rev. Legend:** MONETA • NOVA • AUREA • HASS:

Date	Mintage	VG	F	VF	XF	Unc
16Z4 TS Rare	—	—	—	—	—	—
16Z6 TS Rare	—	—	—	—	—	—

Note: Peus Auction #379 4-2005 1626 XF realized $18,100.

KM# 100 GOLDGULDEN
3.5000 g., 0.9860 Gold 0.1109 oz. AGW **Ruler:** Wilhelm V **Obv:** Bust of Wilhelm V right in inner circle **Obv. Legend:** WILHELM • D • G• LAND • HASS • A • H • C • C • D • Z • **Rev:** Hessian arms in Spanish shield, date in legend **Rev. Legend:** VNO NOLENTE HUMILIS LEVABOR

Date	Mintage	VG	F	VF	XF	Unc
1627 Rare	—	—	—	—	—	—

KM# 101 GOLDGULDEN
3.5000 g., 0.9860 Gold 0.1109 oz. AGW **Ruler:** Wilhelm V **Obv:** Head right, date as 1-6/2-7 **Obv. Legend:** WILHELM9 • D: G: LAND: HASS: ADM: HIR **Rev:** Hessian arms in Spanish shield

Date	Mintage	VG	F	VF	XF	Unc
1627 Rare	—	—	—	—	—	—

Note: Auction Peus #379, 2004 VF realized $14,500.

KM# 110 GOLDGULDEN
3.5000 g., 0.9860 Gold 0.1109 oz. AGW **Ruler:** Wilhelm V **Obv:** Hessian arms in Spanish shield **Obv. Legend:** WILHELM • D • G • L[AND] • HASS • [A • H •] C • C • D • Z • E • N **Rev:** Tree in storm, no houses **Rev. Legend:** DEO • VOLENTE • HUMILIS • LEVABOR • **Note:** Varieties exist.

Date	Mintage	VG	F	VF	XF	Unc
(16)Z8 TS	—	400	800	1,600	2,800	—
1629 TS	—	400	800	1,600	2,800	—
1630 TS	—	400	800	1,600	2,800	—
1631 TS	—	400	800	1,600	2,800	—
163Z TS	—	400	800	1,600	2,800	—
1633 TS	—	400	800	1,600	2,800	—
1634	—	400	800	1,600	2,800	—

KM# 130 GOLDGULDEN
3.5000 g., 0.9860 Gold 0.1109 oz. AGW **Ruler:** Wilhelm V **Obv:** Hessian arms in Spanish shield **Obv. Legend:** WILHELM • D • G • LAND • HASS • C • C • D • Z • E • N **Rev:** Tree in storm, 2 houses **Note:** Date placement varieties exist.

Date	Mintage	VG	F	VF	XF	Unc
1631	—	400	800	1,600	2,800	—
163Z	—	400	800	1,600	2,800	—

KM# 144 GOLDGULDEN
3.5000 g., 0.9860 Gold 0.1109 oz. AGW **Ruler:** Wilhelm V **Obv:** Hessian arms in Spanish shield, date above **Obv. Legend:** WILHELM • D • G • LAND • HASS • C • C • D • Z • E • N **Rev:** Tree in storm, no houses **Rev. Legend:** IEHOVA • VOLENTE • HUMILIS • LEVABOR

Date	Mintage	VG	F	VF	XF	Unc
1633	—	400	800	1,600	2,800	—
1633 TS	—	400	800	1,600	2,800	—
1634	—	400	800	1,600	2,800	—
1634 TS	—	400	800	1,600	2,800	—

KM# 156 GOLDGULDEN
3.5000 g., 0.9860 Gold 0.1109 oz. AGW **Ruler:** Wilhelm V **Obv:** Hessian lion in Spanish shield, roses flanking **Obv. Legend:** WILHEL[M]: D • G • LAND • HASS • C • C • D • Z • E • N **Rev:** Willow tree in storm, no houses **Rev. Legend:** IEHOVA VOLENTE HUMILIS LEVABOR

Date	Mintage	VG	F	VF	XF	Unc
(1)635 clover	—	550	1,000	2,200	4,400	—
(16)35 clover	—	550	1,000	2,200	4,400	—
(1)63 clover	—	550	1,000	2,200	4,400	—
1636 clover	—	550	1,000	2,200	4,400	—
(1)637	—	550	1,000	2,200	4,400	—
1637 clover	—	550	1,000	2,200	4,400	—

KM# 157 GOLDGULDEN
3.5000 g., 0.9860 Gold 0.1109 oz. AGW **Ruler:** Wilhelm V **Obv:** Hessian lion in Spanish shield, roses flanking, date above **Obv. Legend:** WILHEL[M]: D • G • LAND • HASS • C • C • D • Z • E • N **Rev:** Tree in storm, 2 houses **Rev. Legend:** IEHOVA VOLENTE HUMILIS LEVABOR

Date	Mintage	VG	F	VF	XF	Unc
1637 below lion	—	550	1,000	2,200	4,400	—
1637 behind lion	—	550	1,000	2,200	4,400	—

KM# 185 GOLDGULDEN
3.5000 g., 0.9860 Gold 0.1109 oz. AGW **Ruler:** Wilhelm V **Obv:** Hessian lion in Spanish shield, date as 1-6/3-7 **Obv. Legend:** WILHEL: D: G: LAND: HASS: COM: C: D: Z: E: N: **Rev:** Tree in storm, 4 houses **Rev. Legend:** IEHOVA VOLENTE HUMILIS LEVABOR

Date	Mintage	VG	F	VF	XF	Unc
1637 G two crosshooks K	—	550	1,000	2,200	4,400	—

KM# 186.1 GOLDGULDEN
3.5000 g., 0.9860 Gold 0.1109 oz. AGW **Ruler:** Wilhelm VI **Obv:** Crowned Hessian lion left, star before **Obv. Legend:** WILHE[LM] • D • G • LAND • HASS • C • C • D • Z • E • N **Rev:** Tree in storm, 3 or 4 houses **Rev. Legend:** IEHOVA VOLENTE HUMILIS LEVABOR

Date	Mintage	VG	F	VF	XF	Unc
1637 clover	—	650	1,250	2,500	4,800	—
1637 G crossed pothooks K	—	650	1,250	2,500	4,800	—
1638	—	650	1,250	2,500	4,800	—
1638 LH	—	—	—	—	—	—
1638 GK	—	—	—	—	—	—
1639 GK	—	—	—	—	—	—

KM# 186.2 GOLDGULDEN
3.5000 g., 0.9860 Gold 0.1109 oz. AGW **Ruler:** Wilhelm VI **Obv:** Hessian lion, star in front **Rev:** Tree in storm, 3 houses **Rev. Legend:** VNO VOLENTE HUMILIS LEVABOR

Date	Mintage	VG	F	VF	XF	Unc
1637 GXK	—	650	1,250	2,500	4,800	—

KM# 131 DUCAT
3.5000 g., 0.9860 Gold 0.1109 oz. AGW **Ruler:** Wilhelm V **Subject:** Death of Moritz **Obv:** 7-line inscription, Arabic numeral date **Obv. Legend:** MAURITI9 • HASS: LAND • DEO • ET • IMPERIO • FIDUS • **Rev:** Crossed flags, branches above, bell and hourglass below **Rev. Legend:** MAURITI • MEMENTO MORI • CONSIL • E • VIRTUTE

Date	Mintage	VG	F	VF	XF	Unc
1632 TS Rare	—	—	—	—	—	—

KM# 189 DUCAT
3.5000 g., 0.9860 Gold 0.1109 oz. AGW **Ruler:** Wilhelm V **Subject:** Death of Wilhelm V **Obv:** 10-line inscription, Arabic numeral date **Rev:** Tree in storm, 4, 5, or 6 houses

Date	Mintage	VG	F	VF	XF	Unc
1637	—	300	650	1,250	2,400	—
1637 G crossed pothooks K	—	300	650	1,250	2,400	—
1637 GK	—	—	—	—	—	—

Note: Reported, not confirmed

Date	Mintage	VG	F	VF	XF	Unc
1637 crossed pothooks	—	300	650	1,250	2,400	—
1637 AG	—	300	650	1,250	2,400	—
1637 TS	—	—	—	—	—	—

Note: Reported, not confirmed

KM# 190 DUCAT
3.5000 g., 0.9860 Gold 0.1109 oz. AGW **Ruler:** Wilhelm VI **Subject:** Death of Amalie Elizabeth von Hanau, Wife of Wilhelm V **Obv:** Crowned Hessian diamond arms in laurel wreath **Obv. Legend:** AMELIA ELIZABET • LANDGR • ZU HES voRM • U • REGENTIN **Rev:** Mountain with miner in mine, heart and sun above, clouds and storm flanking **Rev. Legend:** WIEDER MACHT UNDT LIST • MEIN FELS GOTT IST •

Date	Mintage	VG	F	VF	XF	Unc
ND(1651) AG Rare	—	—	—	—	—	—

Note: Only 3 pieces known. Auction Peus 383, 2005, VF realized $11,600.

KM# 233 DUCAT
3.5000 g., 0.9860 Gold 0.1109 oz. AGW **Ruler:** Wilhelm VI **Obv:** Crowned 7-fold Hessian arms in ornamented shield date as 1-6/5-2 **Obv. Legend:** WILHELM9: D • G • LAND: HAS: PRIN: HERSF: C • C • D • Z • N • ET SCHAW **Rev:** Sailing ship **Rev. Legend:** VELA VENTIS HIS LEVANTUR

Date	Mintage	VG	F	VF	XF	Unc
1652	—	650	1,250	2,500	4,800	—
1653	—	—	—	—	—	—

Note: Reported, not confirmed

KM# 255 DUCAT
3.5000 g., 0.9860 Gold 0.1109 oz. AGW **Ruler:** Wilhelm VI **Obv:** Bust of Wilhelm VI right in inner circle **Obv. Legend:** WILHELM • D • G • LAND • HASS • PR• H • C • C • Z • N • ET • SCH **Rev:** Crowned arms, date in legend **Rev. Legend:** FIDE ET IUSTITIA

Date	Mintage	VG	F	VF	XF	Unc
1661 Rare	—	—	—	—	—	—
1663 Rare	—	—	—	—	—	—

Note: Auction UBS 69, 2007, VF relazied $12,250

KM# 265 DUCAT
3.5000 g., 0.9860 Gold 0.1109 oz. AGW **Ruler:** Wilhelm VI **Subject:** Death of Wilhelm VI **Obv:** Facing bust **Rev:** 9-line inscription, Arabic numeral date **Rev. Legend:** PIETATE • FIDE • ET • IUSTITIA

Date	Mintage	VG	F	VF	XF	Unc
1663	—	—	—	—	—	—

Note: Reported, not confirmed

KM# 276 DUCAT
3.5000 g., 0.9860 Gold 0.1109 oz. AGW **Ruler:** Wilhelm VII **Obv:** Bust of Hedwig Sophie right in inner circle **Obv. Legend:** HEDWIG • SOPHIA • V: G: G: L: Z: H: G: A: C: S: D: M: Z: B: W: V: V: REGENTIN **Rev:** Terrestrial globe hanging on a heart, sword cuts the rope **Rev. Legend:** DISSOLVER

Date	Mintage	VG	F	VF	XF	Unc
1669 Rare	—	—	—	—	—	—

Note: Two pieces known. Auction Peus 383, 2005, XF realzed $29,000

KM# 289 DUCAT
3.5000 g., 0.9860 Gold 0.1109 oz. AGW **Ruler:** Wilhelm VII **Subject:** Death of Wilhelm VII **Obv:** Helmeted Hessian arms in inner circle **Rev:** 8-line inscription

Date	Mintage	VG	F	VF	XF	Unc
1670 Rare	—	—	—	—	—	—

KM# 299 DUCAT
3.5000 g., 0.9860 Gold 0.1109 oz. AGW **Ruler:** Karl **Obv:** 10-line inscription, Arabic numeral date **Rev:** View of Edder river and surrounding landscape **Rev. Legend:** AN • GOTTES • SEGEN • IST • ALLES • GELEGEN

Date	Mintage	VG	F	VF	XF	Unc
1677 Rare	—	—	—	—	—	—

KM# 323 DUCAT
3.5000 g., 0.9860 Gold 0.1109 oz. AGW **Ruler:** Karl **Obv:** Crowned Hessian arms in oval, date below **Obv. Legend:** CAROLUS • D • G • H • L • PR • H • C • C • D • Z • N • ET • S **Rev:** Swan on pedestal **Rev. Legend:** CANDIDE ET CONSTANTER **Note:** Similar to medal (former 1 Thaler), KM#322.

Date	Mintage	VG	F	VF	XF	Unc
1686 IVF Rare	—	—	—	—	—	—

KM# 341 DUCAT
3.5000 g., 0.9860 Gold 0.1109 oz. AGW **Ruler:** Karl **Obv:** Bust right **Obv. Legend:** CAROL • D • G • HASS • LANDG • **Rev:** Crowned double, mirror-image C monogram, date above

Date	Mintage	VG	F	VF	XF	Unc
1693	—	—	—	—	—	—

Note: Reported, not confirmed

KM# 240 1-1/4 DUCAT
4.3750 g., 0.9860 Gold 0.1387 oz. AGW **Ruler:** Wilhelm VI **Obv:** Crowned 7-fold Hessian arms in ornamented shield **Obv. Legend:** WILHELM9: D G LANDG: HASS PRIN • HERSF • C • C • D • Z • N • T: SCHA **Rev:** Sailing ship **Rev. Legend:** VELA VENTIS HIS LEVANTUR

Date	Mintage	VG	F	VF	XF	Unc
1654 AG Rare	—	—	—	—	—	—

KM# 132 2 DUCAT
7.0000 g., 0.9860 Gold 0.2219 oz. AGW **Ruler:** Wilhelm V **Subject:** Death of Mortiz **Obv:** 7-line inscription Arabic numeral date **Rev:** Crossed flags, branches above, bell and hourglass below **Rev. Legend:** MAURITI MEMENTO MORI • CONSI: E: VIRTU

Date	Mintage	VG	F	VF	XF	Unc
1632 TS Rare	—	—	—	—	—	—

KM# 133 2 DUCAT
7.0000 g., 0.9860 Gold 0.2219 oz. AGW **Ruler:** Wilhelm V **Obv:** Arms divide date in inner circle **Rev:** Willow tree bending in storm in inner circle

Date	Mintage	VG	F	VF	XF	Unc
1632	—	—	—	—	—	—

Note: Reported, not confirmed

KM# 191 2 DUCAT
7.0000 g., 0.9860 Gold 0.2219 oz. AGW **Ruler:** Wilhelm V **Obv:** Crowned Hessian lion in Spanish shield, date as 1-6/3-7 **Obv. Legend:** WILHEL: D: G: LAND: HASS: COM: C: D: Z: E: N: **Rev:** Willow tree bending in storm **Rev. Legend:** IEHOVA VOLENTE HUMILIS LEVABOR

Date	Mintage	VG	F	VF	XF	Unc
1637 GK Rare	—	—	—	—	—	—

KM# 192 2 DUCAT
7.0000 g., 0.9860 Gold 0.2219 oz. AGW **Ruler:** Wilhelm V **Subject:** Death of Wilhelm V **Obv:** 10-line inscription Arabic numeral date **Rev:** Tree in storm, 4 houses **Rev. Legend:** VNO VOLENTE HUMILIS LEVABOR

Date	Mintage	VG	F	VF	XF	Unc
1637 GK crossed pothooks Rare	—	—	—	—	—	—

Note: Some read GK as GR due to poor die engraving

KM# 223 2 DUCAT
7.0000 g., 0.9860 Gold 0.2219 oz. AGW **Ruler:** Wilhelm VI **Subject:** Death of Amalie Elisabeth von Hanau, Wife of Wilhelm V **Obv:** Arms in laurel wreath **Rev:** Mountain with miner in mine, heart and sun above, slouds and storm flanking **Rev. Legend:** WIDER MACHT UND LIST MEIN FELS GOTT IST

Date	Mintage	VG	F	VF	XF	Unc
ND(1651)	—	—	—	—	—	—

Note: Reported, not confirmed

KM# 234 2 DUCAT
7.0000 g., 0.9860 Gold 0.2219 oz. AGW **Ruler:** Wilhelm VI **Obv:** Hessian arms **Rev:** Sailing ship **Note:** Similar to 1 Goldgulden, KM#233.

Date	Mintage	VG	F	VF	XF	Unc
1652 Rare	—	—	—	—	—	—

KM# 312 2 DUCAT
7.0000 g., 0.9860 Gold 0.2219 oz. AGW **Ruler:** Karl **Subject:** Death of Hedwig Sophia, Regend for Wilhelm VII **Obv:** Hessian and Brandenburg arms in divided crowned shield **Obv. Legend:** HEDWIGIS SOPHIA HASS • L • PR • H • HAT • PR • ELECT • BRANDENB • **Rev:** 7-line inscription and date

Date	Mintage	VG	F	VF	XF	Unc
1683	—	—	—	—	—	—

Note: Reported, not confirmed

KM# 313 2 DUCAT
7.0000 g., 0.9860 Gold 0.2219 oz. AGW **Ruler:** Karl **Subject:** Death of Elizabeth Henrietta, Wife of Karl **Obv:** Bust of Elizabeth Henrietta right **Obv. Legend:** HENRIETTA ELISABETA... **Rev:** Crown on pedestal

Date	Mintage	VG	F	VF	XF	Unc
1683 Rare	—	—	—	—	—	—

KM# 243 3 DUCAT
10.5000 g., 0.9860 Gold 0.3328 oz. AGW **Ruler:** Wilhelm VI **Obv:** Crowned manifold arms in baroque frame divide date at 1-6/5-5 **Obv. Legend:** WILHELM9 • DG • LANDG: HASS • PRIN • HERSF • CO: CA • DI • ZI • ET • SCHAW **Rev:** Sailing ship left **Rev. Legend:** VELA VENTIS HIS LEVANTUR

Date	Mintage	VG	F	VF	XF	Unc
1655 AG Rare	—	—	—	—	—	—

Note: Reported, not confirmed

KM# 102 4 DUCAT
14.0000 g., 0.9860 Gold 0.4438 oz. AGW **Ruler:** Moritz **Obv:** Crowned Hessian lion left **Obv. Legend:** MAUR • D • G • LANDG • HASS • C • C • D • Z • E • N **Rev:** Crossed flags, branches above, bell and hourglass below **Rev. Legend:** CONSILIO ET VIRTUTE MON • NOVA IM

Date	Mintage	VG	F	VF	XF	Unc
1627 Rare	—	—	—	—	—	—

KM# 194 4 DUCAT
14.0000 g., 0.9860 Gold 0.4438 oz. AGW **Ruler:** Wilhelm V **Subject:** Death of Wilhelm V **Obv:** 9-line inscription, Arabic numeral date **Obv. Legend:** WILHELM: V • DICT9 • CONSTANS • HASS • LANDGRVIVS **Rev:** Palm tree in storm, 4 houses **Rev. Legend:** VNO VOLENTE HUMILIS LEVABOR

Date	Mintage	VG	F	VF	XF	Unc
1637 GK crossed pothooks Rare	—	—	—	—	—	—

KM# 278 4 DUCAT
14.0000 g., 0.9860 Gold 0.4438 oz. AGW **Ruler:** Wilhelm VII **Subject:** Death of Hedwig Sophie **Obv:** Hessian and Brandenburg arms in divided crowned shield **Obv. Legend:** HEDWIG • SOPHIA • V • G • G... **Rev:** Terrestrial globe hanging on a heat, sword cuts the rope **Rev. Legend:** DISSOLVER **Note:** Similar to 1 Thaler, KM#273.

Date	Mintage	VG	F	VF	XF	Unc
1669 Rare	—	—	—	—	—	—

Note: Reported, not confirmed

KM# 244 5 DUCAT (1/2 Portugalöser)
17.5000 g., 0.9860 Gold 0.5547 oz. AGW **Ruler:** Wilhelm VI **Obv:** Crowned Hessian arms, date as 1-6/5-5 **Rev:** Sailing ship **Rev. Legend:** VELA VENTIS HIS LAVABOR

Date	Mintage	VG	F	VF	XF	Unc
1655	—	—	—	—	—	—

Note: Reported, not confirmed

KM# 111 6 DUCAT
21.0000 g., 0.9860 Gold 0.6657 oz. AGW **Ruler:** Wilhelm V **Obv:** Hessian arms in Spanish shield, 3 helmets above **Rev:** Palm tree in storm, date in legend

Date	Mintage	VG	F	VF	XF	Unc
1628	—	—	—	—	—	—

Note: Reported, not confirmed

KM# 150 6 DUCAT
21.0000 g., 0.9860 Gold 0.6657 oz. AGW **Ruler:** Wilhelm V **Obv:** Bust of Wilhelm V right, date in field **Rev:** Palm tree in storm **Rev. Legend:** IEHOVA...

Date	Mintage	VG	F	VF	XF	Unc
1634	—	—	—	—	—	—

Note: Reported, not confirmed

PATTERNS

Including off metal strikes

KM#	Date	Mintage	Identification	Mkt Val
Pn4	1610	—	4 Heller. Gold. KM#5.	—
Pn5	1610	—	Thaler. Gold. KM#19.	—
Pn6	1628 TS	—	Thaler. Tin. KM#98.	—
Pn7	1634 TS	—	Thaler. Tin. KM#115.	—
Pn8	1638 LH	—	1/2 Thaler. Gold. KM#197.	—
Pn9	1651 AG	—	1/2 Thaler. Gold. KM#219.	—
Pn10	1669	—	Thaler. Gold. KM#274.	—
Pn11	1681	—	3 Heller. Gold. KM#291.	—
Pn12	1686	—	Ducat. Copper. KM#323.	—
Pn13	1686	—	Ducat. Gold. KM#323.	—

HESSE-DARMSTADT

Founded by the youngest of Philipp I's four sons upon the death of their father in 1567, Hesse-Darmstadt was one of the two main branches of the family which survived past the beginning of the 17th century. The Countship of Hanau-Lichtenberg was acquired through marriage when the male line of that principality failed in 1736. Ludwig X was forced to cede that territory to France in 1801. In 1803, Darmstadt acquired part of the Palatinate, the city of Friedberg, part of the city of Mainz, and the Duchy of Westphalia in a general settlement with France. The Landgrave was elevated to the status of Grand Duke in 1806 and reacquired Hesse-Homburg. In 1815 the Congress of Vienna awarded Hesse-Darmstadt the city of Worms and all of Mainz. These were relinquished, along with Hesse-Homburg, to Prussia in 1866 and Hesse-Darmstadt was called just Hesse from 1867 onwards. Hesse became part of the German Empire in 1871, but ceased to exist as a semi-sovereign state at the end of World War I.

RULERS
Ludwig V, 1596-1626
Georg II, 1626-1661
Ludwig VI, 1661-1678
Ludwig VII, 1678
Ernst Ludwig, 1678-1739

MINT MARKS
N Nidda, 1622

MINT OFFICIALS' INITIALS

Initial	Date	Name
GLC	1695-1708	Gabriel Le Clerc, die-cutter and medailleur in Cassel
HIS	1619 1623	Johann Schenckh, warden Mintmaster
IAR, AR	1693-1705	Johann Adam Rephun
ICF	1681	Johann Carl Falkner
ICR, R	1696-1707	J.C. Roth, medailleur
ID	1691-93	Johann Dittmar
IS	1654-87	Johann Sartorius
IW	1625-28	Jacob Wiesener (Wiesemann) in Nidda

REFERENCES

PA = Prinz Alexander von Hessen, **Hessisches Münzcabinet**, Darmstadt, 1877-85.

S = Hugo Frhr. von Saurma-Jeltsch, **Die Saurmasche Münzsammlung deutscher, schweizerischer und polnischer Gepräge von etwa dem Beginn der Groschenzeit bis zur Kipperperiode**, Berlin, 1892.

LANDGRAVIATE

REGULAR COINAGE

MB# 5 PFENNIG
Silver **Ruler:** Ludwig V **Obv:** Shield of Hessian lion, 'LL' above **Note:** Ref. S#2271. Uniface schüssel-type.

Date	Mintage	VG	F	VF	XF	Unc
ND(1607-1626)	—	—	—	—	—	—

KM# 13 PFENNIG
Silver **Ruler:** Ludwig V **Obv:** Cross with M-H / N-F in angles **Note:** Uniface, schüssel-type.

Date	Mintage	VG	F	VF	XF	Unc
ND(1623-36)	—	30.00	60.00	120	240	—

Note: Minted for coin union of 1623-1626 between Mainz, Hesse-Darmstadt, Nassau and Frankfurt. See Frankfurt, 2 Kreuzer for additional coinage mandated by the union

KM# 21.1 PFENNIG
Billon **Ruler:** Ludwig V **Obv:** Hessian lion on shield, Z-H flanking, L-L above, date below **Note:** Uniface, schüssel-type. (LLZH = Ludwig Landgraf zu Hessen).

Date	Mintage	VG	F	VF	XF	Unc
1623	—	30.00	60.00	120	240	—
ND	—	—	—	—	—	—

Note: Reported, not confirmed

KM# 14 PFENNIG
Silver **Ruler:** Georg II **Obv:** Shield with wheel of Mainz left of Hessian lion. **Note:** Uniface, schüssel-type.

Date	Mintage	VG	F	VF	XF	Unc
ND(1637-39)	—	55.00	110	225	450	—

Note: In 1636 Frankfurt and Nassau finished the cooperation with the union of 1623 because of bad quality of product from the mint at Mainz. Mainz and Hesse-Darmstadt continued with the cooperation until 1639. So it is likely that this Pfennig was minted for the same reason after 1636.

KM# 21.2 PFENNIG
Silver **Ruler:** Georg II **Obv:** Lion in spanish shield **Note:** Uniface, schüssel-type.

Date	Mintage	VG	F	VF	XF	Unc
ND(1654-61) IS Rare	—	—	—	—	—	—

KM# 45 PFENNIG
Silver **Ruler:** Georg II **Obv:** Hessian lion in Spanish shield divides date upwards on left and downwards on right, mintmasters initials above. **Note:** Uniface.

Date	Mintage	VG	F	VF	XF	Unc
1656 IS	—	35.00	75.00	150	300	—
1658 IS Rare	—	—	—	—	—	—
ND(1654-61) IS Rare	—	—	—	—	—	—
1659	—	—	—	—	—	—

Note: Reported, not confirmed

KM# A72 PFENNIG
Billon **Ruler:** Ernst Ludwig **Obv:** Hessian lion in crowned shield, H-D above, date in diameter as 1-6 / 8-Z **Note:** Uniface, schüssel-type.

Date	Mintage	VG	F	VF	XF	Unc
168Z IS Rare	—	—	—	—	—	—

KM# 72 PFENNIG
Silver **Ruler:** Ernst Ludwig **Obv:** Hessian lion in crowned shield divides date and mintmasters initials at 1-6 / 8-5 / I-S. **Note:** Uniface, schüssel-type.

Date	Mintage	VG	F	VF	XF	Unc
1685 IS	—	45.00	90.00	185	375	—
1692	—	45.00	90.00	185	375	—
1693	—	45.00	90.00	185	375	—
1698	—	45.00	90.00	185	375	—

KM# 84 PFENNIG
Silver **Ruler:** Ernst Ludwig **Obv:** Hessian lion in shield, H-D above, date below.

Date	Mintage	VG	F	VF	XF	Unc
1692	—	45.00	90.00	180	360	—
1693	—	45.00	90.00	180	360	—
1696	—	45.00	90.00	180	360	—
1699	—	45.00	90.00	180	360	—

KM# 83 PFENNIG
Silver **Ruler:** Ernst Ludwig **Obv:** Hessian lion in shield, rose above, date beside as 1-6 / 9-3 **Note:** Uniface.

Date	Mintage	VG	F	VF	XF	Unc
1693	—	50.00	100	210	425	—

KM# 88 PFENNIG
Silver **Ruler:** Ernst Ludwig **Obv:** Hessian lion in Spanish shield, date below. **Note:** Uniface, schüssel-type.

Date	Mintage	VG	F	VF	XF	Unc
1699	—	30.00	60.00	125	250	—

KM# 15 2 PFENNIG

Silver **Ruler:** Ludwig V **Obv:** Hessian lion divides L-L / Z-H **Rev. Inscription:** II / PFENIG / date

Date	Mintage	VG	F	VF	XF	Unc
1621	—	100	210	425	—	—
1622	—	100	210	425	—	—

KM# 41.1 ALBUS

Silver **Ruler:** Georg II **Obv:** Hessian lion in laurel wreath **Rev:** Value and date within legend **Rev. Legend:** GEORG LANDGRAF ZV HESS around *I*/ ALBVS

Date	Mintage	VG	F	VF	XF	Unc
1654 IS	—	25.00	55.00	110	220	—
1655 IS	—	25.00	55.00	110	220	—
1655	—	—	—	—	—	—
1656 IS	—	—	—	—	—	—

Note: Requires confirmation.

Date	Mintage	VG	F	VF	XF	Unc
1657 IS	—	—	—	—	—	—

Note: Requires confirmation.

KM# 41.2 ALBUS

Silver **Ruler:** Georg II **Obv:** Hessian lion in inner circle, laurel wreath around **Rev:** Value and date within legend **Rev. Legend:** GEORG LANDGRAF ZV HESS around *I*/ ALBVS **Note:** Varieties exist: with or without berries in the laurel wreath, or Small crown on lion within or breaking circle.

Date	Mintage	VG	F	VF	XF	Unc
1656 IS	—	25.00	55.00	110	220	—
1656 SI Rare	—	—	—	—	—	—
1657 IS	—	15.00	35.00	70.00	145	—
1658 IS	—	15.00	35.00	70.00	145	—

KM# 71.1 ALBUS

Silver **Ruler:** Ernst Ludwig **Obv:** Hessian lion in shield divides I-S, HESS DARM above, all within laurel wreath **Rev:** Inscription within laurel wreath **Rev. Inscription:** I / ALBVS / date **Note:** Varieties exist.

Date	Mintage	VG	F	VF	XF	Unc
1680 IS	—	25.00	50.00	100	200	—
1681 IS	—	25.00	50.00	100	200	—
1682 IS	—	20.00	40.00	80.00	160	—
1683 IS	—	20.00	40.00	80.00	160	—
1684 IS	—	20.00	40.00	80.00	160	—
1687 IS	—	20.00	40.00	80.00	160	—

KM# 71.2 ALBUS

Silver **Ruler:** Ernst Ludwig **Obv:** Hessian lion in shield within laurel wreath, rose above **Rev:** Inscription within laurel wreath **Rev. Inscription:** *I*/ ALBVS/ date

Date	Mintage	VG	F	VF	XF	Unc
1686	—	25.00	50.00	100	200	—

KM# 71.3 ALBUS

Silver **Ruler:** Ernst Ludwig **Obv:** Hessian lion in shield, HES DAR above, all within laurel wreath **Rev:** *I*/ ALBVS/ date within laurel wreath **Note:** Legend varieties exist.

Date	Mintage	VG	F	VF	XF	Unc
1692 ID	—	25.00	50.00	100	200	—
1692	—	25.00	50.00	100	200	—
1693 IA-R	—	20.00	40.00	80.00	160	—
1694 I.A.R.	—	20.00	40.00	80.00	160	—
1695 I.A.R.	—	20.00	40.00	80.00	160	—

KM# 71.4 ALBUS

Silver **Ruler:** Ernst Ludwig **Obv:** Hessian lion in shield, H.D. above, all within laurel wreath **Rev:** I/ ALBUS/ date/ mint mark, all within laurel wreath **Note:** Varieties exist with Spanish or French shield.

Date	Mintage	VG	F	VF	XF	Unc
1697 IAR	—	15.00	30.00	65.00	130	—
1699 IAR	—	15.00	30.00	65.00	130	—

KM# 82 2 ALBUS

Silver **Ruler:** Ernst Ludwig **Obv:** Manifold Hessian arms in Spanish shield, HD above, all within laurel wreath **Rev:** II/ ALBUS/ date/ mint mark, all within laurel wreath **Note:** Varieties exit.

Date	Mintage	VG	F	VF	XF	Unc
1692 ID	—	15.00	30.00	65.00	130	—
1693 IAR	—	11.00	25.00	55.00	110	—
1694 IAR	—	11.00	25.00	55.00	110	—
1695 IAR	—	11.00	25.00	55.00	110	—
1697 IAR	—	11.00	25.00	55.00	110	—

KM# 19.1 KREUZER

Silver **Ruler:** Ludwig V **Obv:** Hessian lion divides H-LZ, L above, N below

Date	Mintage	VG	F	VF	XF	Unc
1622 N	—	20.00	40.00	80.00	160	—

KM# 19.2 KREUZER

Silver **Ruler:** Ludwig V **Rev. Inscription:** KREVT / ZER

Date	Mintage	VG	F	VF	XF	Unc
1622 N	—	20.00	40.00	80.00	160	—

KM# 17.1 KREUZER

Silver **Ruler:** Ludwig V **Obv:** Hessian lion divides L-L / Z-H **Rev. Inscription:** *I* / KREVTZ / ER / date **Mint:** Darmstadt

Date	Mintage	VG	F	VF	XF	Unc
16ZZ	—	75.00	150	300	600	—
1622 D	—	75.00	150	300	600	—
1622	—	75.00	150	300	600	—

KM# 17.2 KREUZER

Silver **Ruler:** Ludwig V **Rev. Inscription:** I / KREVT / ZER **Mint:** Darmstadt

Date	Mintage	VG	F	VF	XF	Unc
1622	—	75.00	150	300	600	—
16ZZ	—	75.00	150	300	600	—

KM# 17.3 KREUZER

Silver **Ruler:** Ludwig V **Rev. Inscription:** I / KREV / TZER **Mint:** Darmstadt

Date	Mintage	VG	F	VF	XF	Unc
1622	—	75.00	150	300	600	—
16ZZ	—	75.00	150	300	600	—

KM# 18.1 KREUZER

Silver **Ruler:** Ludwig V **Obv:** Hessian lion divides H-L, L above, N below **Rev. Inscription:** .I. / KREVTZ / ER / date **Mint:** Nidda **Note:** Varieties exist

Date	Mintage	VG	F	VF	XF	Unc
1622N	—	55.00	115	235	475	—
16ZZN	—	55.00	115	235	475	—
1622 Rare	—	—	—	—	—	—

KM# 18.2 KREUZER

Silver **Ruler:** Ludwig V **Obv:** Hessian lion divides Z-H, LL above, N below **Rev. Inscription:** KREV / TZER **Mint:** Nidda

Date	Mintage	VG	F	VF	XF	Unc
16ZZN Rare	—	—	—	—	—	—

KM# 18.3 KREUZER

Silver **Ruler:** Ludwig V **Rev. Inscription:** KREVTZ / ER **Mint:** Nidda

Date	Mintage	VG	F	VF	XF	Unc
16ZZN	—	55.00	115	235	475	—

KM# 70.1 KREUZER

Silver **Ruler:** Ernst Ludwig **Obv:** Hessian lion in French shield between laurel branches, H.D above (1699 has Spanish shield) **Rev:** Value and date between laurel branches **Rev. Inscription:** *I* / KREU / TZER

Date	Mintage	VG	F	VF	XF	Unc
1680 IS	—	15.00	30.00	65.00	130	—
1681 IS	—	15.00	30.00	65.00	130	—
1682 IS	—	15.00	30.00	65.00	130	—
1683 IS	—	15.00	30.00	65.00	130	—
1684	—	—	—	—	—	—

Note: Reported, not confirmed

Date	Mintage	VG	F	VF	XF	Unc
1689 IS	—	15.00	30.00	65.00	130	—
1699 IAR	—	15.00	30.00	65.00	130	—

KM# 73 KREUZER

Silver **Ruler:** Ernst Ludwig **Obv:** Hessian lion (with crown) in Spanish shield, L-E beside, laurel wreath around **Rev. Inscription:** I / KREV / TZER / 1685

Date	Mintage	VG	F	VF	XF	Unc
1685 Rare	—	—	—	—	—	—

Note: Reported, not confirmed

KM# 74 KREUZER

Silver **Ruler:** Ernst Ludwig **Obv:** Hessian lion (uncrowned) in Spanish shield, S-P besides, laurel wreath around **Rev. Inscription:** I / KREU / TZER / 1686 / LBM

Date	Mintage	VG	F	VF	XF	Unc
1686 LBM	—	20.00	35.00	75.00	155	—

Note: Reported, not confirmed

KM# 70.2 KREUZER

Silver **Ruler:** Ernst Ludwig **Obv:** Lion in shield, H.D. above, laurel branches around **Rev:** Inscription in laurel branches around **Rev. Inscription:** I / KREV / TZER / date

Date	Mintage	VG	F	VF	XF	Unc
1699 IAR	—	7.00	15.00	30.00	60.00	—

KM# 8 3 KREUZER (Groschen)

Silver **Ruler:** Ludwig V **Obv:** Hessian arms in Spanish shield, value (3) above **Obv. Legend:** LVDOVICVS • D • G • LANDGRA: HASS* **Rev:** Hssian helmet, date **Rev. Legend:** IN TE DOMINE CONFIDO

Date	Mintage	VG	F	VF	XF	Unc
1619	—	80.00	160	375	775	—

KM# 10 12 KREUZER (Schreckenberger)

Silver **Ruler:** Ludwig V **Obv:** Hessian arms in Spanish sheild, 12 above **Obv. Legend:** LVDOVICVS • D • G • LANDGRA: HASS •*• **Rev:** Helmet, date in legend

Date	Mintage	VG	F	VF	XF	Unc
1619	—	85.00	175	375	775	—

KM# 65.1 60 KREUZER (Gulden)

Silver **Ruler:** Ludwig VI **Obv:** Bust with long hair right **Obv. Legend:** LVDOVIC • VI • D • G • HASSLANDGRAV • PRINC • HERSF * **Rev:** Crowned arms divides mintmaster initials, date above **Rev. Legend:** FVRSTLICHE HESSIS che landmvntz * **Note:** Tall letters.

Date	Mintage	VG	F	VF	XF	Unc
1674 IS	—	150	300	600	1,200	—

KM# 65.2 60 KREUZER (Gulden)

Silver **Ruler:** Ludwig VI **Obv:** Bust with long hair right **Obv. Legend:** LVDOVIC • VI • D • G • HASS • LANDGRAV • PRINC • HERSF * **Rev:** Crowned arms divides I-S, date above **Rev. Legend:** FVRSTLICHE • HESSISC HE LAND MVNTZ* **Note:** Short letters.

Date	Mintage	VG	F	VF	XF	Unc
1674	—	150	300	600	1,200	—
1674 IS	—	—	—	—	—	—

Note: Reported, not confirmed

KM# A5 1/8 THALER

3.6500 g., Silver, 30 mm. **Ruler:** Ludwig V **Subject:** Death of Georg I's second wife, Eleonore von Württemberg **Obv:** 6-line inscription within square ornamented with foliage, R.N. date above **Obv. Inscription:** F • ELEONORA / L • Z • H • G • H • Z • / W • STARB • XII / IAN • IHRES / ALTERS • LXVI / IHAR **Rev:** 2 shields of arms, Hesse on left, Württemberg on right, H ★ W above **Note:** Ref. PA#1541.

Date	Mintage	VG	F	VF	XF	Unc
MDCXVIII (1618) Rare	—	—	—	—	—	—

KM# 55 1/8 THALER

Silver **Ruler:** Georg II **Obv:** 6-line inscription with Arabic numeral date **Obv. Legend:** DNI DNI GEORGII II L HPH C C DZ H S Y ET B **Rev:** Oak tree with band reading: AETERNI SACRVM **Rev. Legend:** NVM EXEQ PRIN OPT PH PRVD BENEFI

Date	Mintage	VG	F	VF	XF	Unc
1661	—	550	1,100	2,250	4,500	—

Note: The former 55.1 with Roman numeral date does not exist.

KM# 7 1/4 THALER

Silver **Ruler:** Ludwig V **Obv:** 5 shields of arms in cruciform, Hesse in center, Ziegenhain, Katzenelbogen, Diez. **Obv. Legend:** LVDOVICVS • D • G • LANDGRA: HASSIAE **Rev:** Helmet, date in legend **Rev. Legend:** IN • TE • DOMINO • CONFIDO •

Date	Mintage	VG	F	VF	XF	Unc
1618	—	—	1,900	3,850	7,750	—

KM# 12 1/4 THALER

Silver **Ruler:** Ludwig V **Obv:** 5-fold Hessian arms in Spanish shield, ornaments around **Obv. Legend:** LVDOVICVS: D: G: LANDGRA: HASSI * **Rev:** Hessian helmet, date in legend **Rev. Legend:** IN • TE • DOMINO • CONFIDO •

Date	Mintage	VG	F	VF	XF	Unc
1618	—	—	1,800	3,600	7,200	—
1619	—	—	1,800	3,600	7,200	—
16Z1 Rare	—	—	—	—	—	—

KM# 11 1/4 THALER

Silver **Ruler:** Ludwig V **Obv:** 5-fold Hessian arms **Obv. Legend:** LVDOVICVS • D • G • LANDGRA • HASS **Rev:** Hessian helmet, date in legend **Rev. Legend:** IN • DOMINO • CONFIDO • **Note:** Klippe.

Date	Mintage	VG	F	VF	XF	Unc
1619	—	—	—	—	—	—

Note: Reported, not confirmed

KM# 56 1/4 THALER

Silver **Ruler:** Georg II **Subject:** Death of Georg II **Obv:** 8-line inscription with R.N. date **Obv. Legend:** DNI • DNI • GEORGII II • LANDHAS • PR • HERSF • COM CDZHS • Y & B **Obv. Inscription:** NASCITUR / XVII • MART MDCV / OBIT • XI • JVNII / MDC • LXI • VIXIT • AN / NOS LVI • MENSES / III • REGNAVIT • / • ANNOS XXXIV / MENX • X • **Rev:** Oak tree, with band reading AETERNITATI SACRVM **Rev. Legend:** NVM EXEQVIAL • PRINCIPIS • OPTIMI • PII • PRVDENTIS • BENEF:

Date	Mintage	VG	F	VF	XF	Unc
MDCLXI (1661)	—	—	825	1,675	3,350	7,700

KM# 26 1/2 THALER

Silver **Ruler:** Ludwig V **Obv:** Bust of Ludwig V right **Obv. Legend:** LUDOUIUS: D: G: LANDGR • HASSIÆ • COM • IN • CA • **Rev:** Hessian arms in Spanish shield, date in legend **Rev. Legend:** IN TE * DOMINE * CONFIDO: **Note:** Legend varieties.

Date	Mintage	VG	F	VF	XF	Unc
1625 IW pothook Rare	—	—	—	—	—	—
1626 IW Rare	—	—	—	—	—	—

KM# 31 1/2 THALER

Silver **Ruler:** Georg II **Obv:** Bust of Georg II right **Obv. Legend:** D • G • GEORGIVS • HASSIÆ • LANDGRAVIVS • **Rev:** Hessian arms in ornaments, date in legend **Rev. Legend:** SECVNDVM • VOLVNTATEM • TVAM • DOMINE • **Note:** 1/4 Thaler Octagonal Klippe.

Date	Mintage	VG	F	VF	XF	Unc
1627 Rare	—	—	—	—	—	—

KM# 57 1/2 THALER

Silver **Ruler:** Georg II **Subject:** Death of Georg II **Obv:** 8-line inscription with R.N. date **Obv. Legend:** DNI • DNI • GEORGII • II • LAND • HAS • PR: HERSF: COM CDZ • N • S • Y • ET B + **Obv. Inscription:** NASCITUR / XVII • MAR M • DC • V / OBIT • XI • JVNII • / MDCLXI • VVIXIT • AN / NOS • LVI • MENSES / III • REGNAVIT • ANNOS • XXXIV / MENS • X • **Rev:** Oak tree, with band reading AETERNITATI SACRVM **Rev. Legend:** MVM • EXEQVIAL • PRINCIPIS • OPTIMI • PII • PRVDENTIS • BENEF: +

Date	Mintage	VG	F	VF	XF	Unc
MDCLXI (1661) Rare	—	—	—	—	—	—

KM# 80 1/2 THALER

Silver **Ruler:** Ernst Ludwig **Obv:** Bust right **Obv. Legend:** ERNESTVS • LVDOVICVS • I • D • G • HASS • LANDGRAV • PRINC • HERSF * **Rev:** Hessian arms in oval shield with crown, crown above divides date **Rev. Legend:** MONETA • NOVA • ARGENTEA • DARMSTADINA * **Note:** Legend varieties.

Date	Mintage	VG	F	VF	XF	Unc
1691 Rare	—	—	—	—	—	—
1693 IA-R	—	—	—	—	—	—

Note: Reported, not confirmed

KM# 90 1/2 THALER

Silver **Ruler:** Ernst Ludwig **Obv:** Bust right **Obv. Legend:** ERNEST • LUD • I • D • G • HASS • LANDG • PRINC • HERSF * **Rev:** Hessian arms in German shield with 5 helmets **Rev. Legend:** • MONETA • NOVA • ARGENTEA • DARMSTADINA

Date	Mintage	VG	F	VF	XF	Unc
1696 IA-R Rare	—	—	2,500	5,000	10,000	—

Note: Dates of 1697, 1700 and ND formerly listed with this type have been confirmed as not existing or errors in previous catalog appearances

KM# 91 1/2 THALER

Silver **Ruler:** Ernst Ludwig **Obv:** 7-fold Hessian arms in baroque cartouche supported by 2 miners, sun and clouds above, R.N. date below **Obv. Legend:** GOTT • BAUE • DAS • HAUS • HESSEN • DARMSTATT **Rev:** Mining scene, man turning windlass in foreground, sun and 3 fires in background **Rev. Legend:** SO • BLICKEN • DIE ERSTLING • DES • SEGENS • HERFUR * **Note:** Mining 1/2 Thaler.

Date	Mintage	VG	F	VF	XF	Unc
MDCXCVI (1696) GLC	—	—	2,100	4,200	8,400	—
MDCXCVI (1696) IAR-R	—	—	—	—	—	—

Note: Reported, not confirmed

Date	Mintage	VG	F	VF	XF	Unc
MDCXCVI (1696)	—	—	—	—	—	—

Note: Reported, but the small mint mark has probably been missed

KM# 22 THALER

Silver **Ruler:** Ludwig V **Obv:** Bust of Ludwig V right **Obv. Legend:** LVDOUICUS • D: G • LANDG: HASSIÆ: CO • I • CA * **Rev:** Hessian manifold arms in German shield with helmet above, ornaments besides, date in legend **Rev. Legend:** INTE: DOMINE: * : CONFIDO: ANNO **Note:** Dav. #6795.

Date	Mintage	VG	F	VF	XF	Unc
1623	—	300	600	1,000	1,600	—
16Z3	—	300	600	1,000	1,600	—

KM# 23.1 THALER

Silver **Ruler:** Ludwig V **Obv:** Bust right, IHS below shoulder **Obv. Legend:** LVDOVICVS: D: G: LANDG: HASSIÆ • COM: I: CA * **Rev:** Hessian manifold arms in German shield, ornaments beside, 3 helmets above **Rev. Legend:** IN TE: DOMINE: CONFIDO: ANN **Note:** Dav. #6796.

Date	Mintage	VG	F	VF	XF	Unc
1623 IHS	—	250	500	1,000	2,000	—
1623 Rare	—	—	—	—	—	—
16Z3 IHS	—	250	500	1,000	2,000	—
16Z3 Rare	—	—	—	—	—	—

KM# 23.2 THALER

Silver **Ruler:** Ludwig V **Obv:** Bust right, I.W. below shoulder **Note:** Dav. #6797.

Date	Mintage	VG	F	VF	XF	Unc
1625 IW	—	250	500	1,000	2,000	—

KM# 23.3 THALER

Silver **Ruler:** Ludwig V **Obv:** Bust right **Obv. Legend:** LVDOVICVS • D: G • LANDGR • HASSIÆ: COM • IN: CA **Rev:** I-W divided by arms **Rev. Legend:** INTE • DOMINE • CONFIDO ANN **Note:** Dav. #6798.

Date	Mintage	VG	F	VF	XF	Unc
1626 IW pothook	—	400	1,000	2,000	4,000	—
(1)626 IW pothook	—	400	1,000	2,000	4,000	—
(1)6Z6 IW pothook	—	400	1,000	2,000	4,000	—

KM# 29 THALER

Silver **Ruler:** Ludwig V **Subject:** Death of Ludwig V **Obv:** 8-line inscription, R.N. date **Obv. Legend:** LUDOVICUS • DICTUS • FIDELIS • HASSIÆ • LANDGRAVIUS • **Obv. Inscription:** NATUS • / XXVI • SEPTEMB • / ANNI • M • D • LXXVII • / MORTUUS • XXVII • / JVLII • ANNI M • D • C • XXVI • REGNAVIT • / ANNOS • XXX • MENS • / V • DIES • XIX • **Rev. Legend:** PATRI • PATRIÆ • IMMORTALITATE • DONATO • around, in center: VIVIT •/ POST • FVNERA •/ VIRTUS **Note:** Dav. #6800.

Date	Mintage	VG	F	VF	XF	Unc
MDCXXVI (1626) Rare	—	—	—	—	—	—

KM# 33 THALER

Silver **Ruler:** Georg II **Obv:** Youthful bust of Georg II right divides date **Rev:** 3 helmets above arms **Note:** Dav. #6801.

Date	Mintage	VG	F	VF	XF	Unc
1627 IW	—	—	—	—	—	—

Note: Reported, not confirmed

KM# 36 THALER

Silver, 35 mm. **Ruler:** Georg II **Subject:** 200th Anniversary, Marburg University **Obv:** Bust right **Rev:** 13-line inscription **Note:** Dav. #6802.

Date	Mintage	VG	F	VF	XF	Unc
1627 Rare	—	—	—	—	—	—

Note: This is currently considered a medal.

KM# 34 THALER

Silver **Ruler:** Georg II **Rev:** Date above helmets **Note:** Dav. #--.

Date	Mintage	VG	F	VF	XF	Unc
1627 IW	—	—	—	—	—	—

Note: Now thought to be an incorrect listing

KM# 37 THALER

Silver **Ruler:** Georg II **Subject:** Death of Anna Margarethe von Diepholz, 1st Wife of Philipp zu Butzbach **Obv:** 8-line inscription, R.N. date **Obv. Inscription:** NATUS / XXIV • SEPTEMB • / ANNI • M • D • LXXVII • / MORTUUS • XXVII • **Rev:** 2 kneeling females, hand from clouds with crown, to one side figures of Satan and Death

Date	Mintage	VG	F	VF	XF	Unc
1629 Rare	—	—	—	—	—	—

Note: Currently thought to be an issue of Hesse-Butzbach, founded by Philip III (Son of Georg II of Hesse-Darmstadt) in 1609, and returned to Hesse-Darmstadt in 1643 at his death.

KM# 48 THALER

Silver **Ruler:** Georg II **Obv:** Mature bust right **Obv. Legend:** :D: G: GEORGIVS • HASSIÆ • LAND • GRAVIVS • COM: IN • C: **Rev:** 5-fold Hessian arms in Spanish sheild, 3 helmets, date in legend **Rev. Legend:** IS SECVNDVM • VOLVNTATEM • TVAM • DOMINE • **Note:** Dav. #6803.

Date	Mintage	VG	F	VF	XF	Unc
1657 IS Rare	—	—	—	—	—	—
1658	—	—	—	—	—	—

Note: Reported, not confirmed

Date	Mintage	VG	F	VF	XF	Unc
1658 IS Rare	—	—	—	—	—	—

KM# 58 THALER

Silver **Ruler:** Georg II **Subject:** Death of Georg II **Obv:** 8-line inscrption, R.N. date **Obv. Legend:** DNI • DNI • GEORGII • II • LAND • HAS • PR: HERSF • COM • C • D • Z • N • S • Y • & • B • + **Obv. Inscription:** NASCITVR / XVII • MART MDC / V • ORBIIT • XI • JVNII / MDC • LXI • VIXIT • AN / NOS LVI MENSES / III REGNAVIT • / ANNOS • XXXIV / MENS • X **Rev:** Oak tree, with band reading AETERNITATI SACRVM **Rev. Legend:** NVM • EXEQVIAL: PRINCIPIS • OPTIMI • PII • PRVDENTIS • BENEFICI + **Note:** Dav. #6805.

Date	Mintage	VG	F	VF	XF	Unc
MDCLXI (1661) Rare	—	—	—	—	—	—

KM# 81 THALER

Silver **Ruler:** Ernst Ludwig **Obv:** Bust of Ernst Ludwig right **Obv. Legend:** ERNESTVS • LVDOVICVS • I • D • G • HASS • LANDGRAV • PRINC • HERSF * **Rev:** 7-fold Hessian arms in oval cartouche, crown divides date **Rev. Legend:** MONETA • NOVA • ARGENTEA • DARMSTADINA * **Note:** Dav. #6806.

Date	Mintage	VG	F	VF	XF	Unc
1691 Rare	—	—	—	—	—	—

KM# 87 THALER

Silver **Ruler:** Ernst Ludwig **Obv:** Bust right **Obv. Legend:** ERNEST • LVD • I • D • G • HASS • LANDGR • PR • HERSF * **Rev:** 7-fold Hessian arms in oval cartouche, crown divides date **Rev. Legend:** MONETA • NOVA • ARGENTEA • DARMSTADINA * **Note:** Dav. #6807.

Date	Mintage	VG	F	VF	XF	Unc
1693 IAR	—	—	—	—	—	—

Note: Reported, not confirmed

KM# 93 THALER

Silver **Ruler:** Ernst Ludwig **Obv:** Bust right **Obv. Legend:** ERNEST • LVD • I • D • G • HASS • LANDGRAV • PRINC • HERSF **Rev:** 7-fold Hessian arms in German shield, 5 helmets above, date divided below **Rev. Legend:** MONETA • NOVA • ARGENTEA • DARMSTADINA **Note:** Dav. #6808.

Date	Mintage	VG	F	VF	XF	Unc
1696 ICR-IAR Rare	—	—	—	—	—	—

KM# 95.1 THALER

Silver **Ruler:** Ernst Ludwig **Obv:** Bust right in armor, rosette, R below **Obv. Legend:** ERNEST • LVD • I • D • G • HASS • LANDGR • PRINC • HERSF **Rev:** Hessian arms in baroque oval frame supported by 2 lions, crown divides date, Elephant order and IAR below **Rev. Legend:** MONETA • NOVA • ARGENTEA • DARMSTADINA **Note:** Dav. #6809 and Dav. #6811.

Date	Mintage	VG	F	VF	XF	Unc
1696 ICR-IAR	—	—	1,200	2,500	5,000	—
1697 R-IAR	—	—	1,200	2,500	5,000	—

KM# 94 THALER

Silver **Ruler:** Ernst Ludwig **Obv:** Two miners supporting 7-fold Hessian arms in baroque cartouche, sun and clouds above, Roman numeral date below **Obv. Legend:** GOTT • BAUE • DAS • HAUS • HESSEN • DARMSTATT • **Rev:** Mining scene, man turning windlass in foregorund, suna dn 3 fires in background **Rev. Legend:** SO • BLICKEN • DIE ERSTLING • DES • SEGENS • HERFUR **Note:** Dav. #6810. Mining Thaler.

Date	Mintage	VG	F	VF	XF	Unc
1696	—	1,250	2,500	4,500	7,500	—
1696 IAR	—	1,250	2,500	4,500	7,500	—
1696 GLC Rare	—	—	—	—	—	—
1696 IAR GLC F Rare	—	—	—	—	—	—
1696 IAR R	—	1,250	2,500	4,500	7,500	—

KM# 95.2 THALER

Silver **Ruler:** Ernst Ludwig **Obv:** Bust right in armor **Obv. Legend:** ERNEST • LVD • I • D • G • HASS • LANDGR • PR • HERSF * **Rev:** 7-fold Hessian arms in baroque oval supported by 2 lions, crown divides date, Elephant order and IAR below **Rev. Legend:** MONETA NOVA ARGENTEA DARMSTADINA **Note:** Dav. #6811A.

Date	Mintage	VG	F	VF	XF	Unc
1697 IAR	—	450	900	2,000	4,000	—

KM# 95.3 THALER

Silver **Ruler:** Ernst Ludwig **Obv:** bust right in armor, with rosette, R below **Obv. Legend:** ERNEST • LVD • I • D • G • HASS • LANDGR • PRINC • HERSF **Rev:** Hessian arms in baroque oval supported by 2 lions, crown divides date, Elephant order below **Rev. Legend:** MONETA • NOVA • ARGENTEA • DARMSTADINA **Note:** Dav. #6812. Varieties exist.

Date	Mintage	VG	F	VF	XF	Unc
1700 R-IAR Rare	—	—	—	—	—	—

KM# 24 2 THALER

Silver **Ruler:** Ludwig V **Note:** Similar to 1 Thaler, KM#22. Dav. #6794.

Date	Mintage	VG	F	VF	XF	Unc
16Z3 Rare	—	—	—	—	—	—

KM# 30 2 THALER

Silver **Ruler:** Ludwig V **Subject:** Death of Ludwig V **Obv:** 8-line inscription with R.N. date **Obv. Legend:** LUDOVICUS • DICTUS • FIDELIS • HASSIÆ • LANDGRAVIUS • **Obv. Inscription:** NATUS • / XXIV • SEPTEMB • / ANNOS • XXX • MENS • / V • DIES • XIX • **Rev. Legend:** PATRI • PATRIÆ • IMMORTALITATE • DONATO around, in center VIVIT • / POST • FVNERA • / VIRTUS **Note:** Dav. #6799. Thick planchet, dies of KM#29.

Date	Mintage	VG	F	VF	XF	Unc
MDCXXVI (1626) Rare	—	—	—	—	—	—

TRADE COINAGE

KM# 59 1/2 DUCAT

1.7500 g., 0.9860 Gold 0.0555 oz. AGW **Ruler:** Georg II **Subject:** Death of Georg II **Obv:** 7-line inscription with Arabic numeral date **Rev:** Oak tree at center

Date	Mintage	VG	F	VF	XF	Unc
1661	—	200	650	1,400	2,800	—

KM# 25 DUCAT

3.5000 g., 0.9860 Gold 0.1109 oz. AGW **Ruler:** Ludwig V **Obv:** Crowned arms in inner circle **Rev:** 3 helmets in inner circle, date in legend

Date	Mintage	VG	F	VF	XF	Unc
1621 Rare	—	—	—	—	—	—
1623	—	—	1,200	2,500	5,000	—

KM# 40 DUCAT

3.5000 g., 0.9860 Gold 0.1109 oz. AGW **Ruler:** Georg II **Obv:** Bust of Georg II left with long hair, in inner circle **Rev:** Arms in inner circle, date in legend

Date	Mintage	VG	F	VF	XF	Unc
1651	—	—	—	—	—	—

Note: Reported, not confirmed

KM# 43 DUCAT

3.5000 g., 0.9860 Gold 0.1109 oz. AGW **Ruler:** Georg II **Obv:** Bearded bust

Date	Mintage	VG	F	VF	XF	Unc
1655	—	650	1,500	3,500	7,000	—
1656	—	600	1,400	3,000	6,000	—
1658	—	650	1,500	3,500	7,000	—

KM# 61 DUCAT

3.5000 g., 0.9860 Gold 0.1109 oz. AGW **Ruler:** Georg II **Subject:** Death of Georg II **Obv:** 7-line inscription, with Roman numeral date **Rev:** Oak tree at center

Date	Mintage	VG	F	VF	XF	Unc
MDCLXI (1661)	—	450	1,000	2,500	5,000	—

KM# 68 DUCAT

3.5000 g., 0.9860 Gold 0.1109 oz. AGW **Ruler:** Ludwig VI **Obv:** Bust of Ludwig VI right **Rev:** Crowned arms, date in legend **Rev. Legend:** INTE DOMINE SPERAVI 1675 clover

Date	Mintage	VG	F	VF	XF	Unc
1675 IS	—	450	1,000	2,800	4,600	—

KM# B139 DUCAT

3.5000 g., Gold **Ruler:** Ernst Ludwig **Obv:** Bust right **Rev:** Lion in a square, crowned EL monogram four times around

Date	Mintage	VG	F	VF	XF	Unc
ND(1696-1707)	—	—	—	—	—	—

KM# A139 25 DUCAT

Gold **Ruler:** Ernst Ludwig **Obv:** Bust right, titles of Ernst Ludwig **Rev:** Ornate oval 6-fold arms with central shield, 5 helmets above

Date	Mintage	Good	VG	F	VF	XF
ND(1696-1707) R Rare	—	—	—	—	—	—

PATTERNS

Including off metal strikes

KM#	Date	Mintage	Identification	Mkt Val
PnA1	1626	—	Thaler. Tin. KM#29.	200
Pn1	1657 IS	—	Albus. Gold. KM#41.	—
PnA2	1674 IS	—	60 Kreuzer. Silver. Thaler size planchet, KM#66.	—
Pn2	1696 GLC-R	—	1/2 Thaler. Lead. KM#91.	—

HESSE-HOMBURG

Located in west central Germany, Hesse-Homburg was created from part of Hesse-Darmstadt in 1622. The landgraviate had six villages, along with Homburg (today Bad Homburg), and is mostly known for its famous landgrave, Friedrich II. Commander of the Brandenburg cavalry, Friedrich II (with the silver leg) won the Battle of Fehrbellin in 1675. Hesse-Homburg was mediatized to Hesse-Darmstadt during 1801-15, after which it acquired full sovereignty once again, along with the lordship of Meisenheim. The Homburg line became extinct in 1866, and along with Hesse-Darmstadt, was annexed by Prussia.

RULERS

Friedrich I, 1622-1638
Margaretha Elisabeth von Leiningen-Westerburg-Schaumburg, regent, 1638-1650
Ludwig Philipp, 1638-1643
Wilhelm Christof, 1643-1669
Friedrich II, 1681-1708

MINT OFFICIALS' INITIALS

Initial	Date	Name
RA	ca.1692	Johann Reinhard Arnold

LANDGRAVIATE

REGULAR COINAGE

KM# 6 2 ALBUS

Silver **Ruler:** Friedrich II **Obv:** Arms, HH above, in palm branches **Rev:** II/ ALBUS/ date in laurel wreath **Note:** Varieties exist in thickness of arms.

Date	Mintage	VG	F	VF	XF	Unc
1692	—	175	350	700	1,400	—

KM# 7 2/3 THALER (Gulden)

Silver **Ruler:** Friedrich II **Obv:** Bust right **Rev:** Crowned arms, (2/3) below, date in legend

Date	Mintage	VG	F	VF	XF	Unc
1692 RA	—	—	1,800	3,600	7,500	—

Note: Friedrich without Elephant order

Date	Mintage	VG	F	VF	XF	Unc
1692 Restrike	—	—	—	1,500	2,800	—

Note: Friedrich with Elephant order

KM# 8 2/3 THALER (Gulden)

Silver **Ruler:** Friedrich II **Obv:** Crowned arms, 2/3 below, date in legend **Rev:** Large 2/3 in laurel wreath

Date	Mintage	VG	F	VF	XF	Unc
1692 RA	—	—	—	1,100	2,200	—

Note: See note below KM#9

KM# 9 2/3 THALER (Gulden)

Silver **Ruler:** Friedrich II **Obv:** Crowned arms, (2/3) below, date in legend **Rev:** Large 2/3 in laurel wreath

Date	Mintage	VG	F	VF	XF	Unc
ND	—	—	—	1,300	2,600	—

Note: KM#8-9 are restrikes and die-couplings of KM#7 with Hohenlohe-Schillingsfurst 2/3 Thaler, KM#28. Struck in 1860, the original, although rusty, dies were used

TRADE COINAGE

KM# 5 DUCAT

3.5000 g., 0.9860 Gold 0.1109 oz. AGW **Ruler:** Friedrich II **Obv:** Bust of Friedrich right **Rev:** 2 men right and left of mountain, trying to climb

Date	Mintage	VG	F	VF	XF	Unc
1690 Rare	—	—	—	—	—	—

Note: Three known

Date	Mintage	VG	F	VF	XF	Unc
ND Rare	—	—	—	—	—	—

Note: One known

HESSE-MARBURG

When Hesse was divided among four brothers in 1567, one line of landgraves became centered on Marburg, 45 miles southwest of Cassel. Failing to provide any offspring to continue the line after one ruler, Hesse-Marburg reverted to Hesse-Cassel in 1604.

RULER

Ludwig (III) IV, 1567-1604

Initial	Date	Name
(c)=	1594-ca.1603	Peter Arnsburg (Arnsburgk) in Marburg

LANDGRAVIATE

REGULAR COINAGE

KM# 1 HELLER

Silver **Obv:** Hessian lion in shield divides Z-H, LL above. **Note:** Uniface, schüssel-type.

Date	Mintage	VG	F	VF	XF	Unc
ND	—	55.00	115	235	475	—

KM# 2 HELLER

Silver **Obv:** Hessian lion in shield, LL above **Note:** Uniface, schüssel-type.

Date	Mintage	VG	F	VF	XF	Unc
ND	—	150	300	600	1,200	—

KM# 3 ALBUS

Silver **Obv:** Three helmets above 5-fold arms **Rev:** Helmet **Rev. Legend:** ALBVS * NOVVS - HASSIAE

Date	Mintage	VG	F	VF	XF	Unc
ND Rare	—	—	—	—	—	—

KM# 10 1/4 THALER

Silver **Ruler:** Ludwig (III) IV **Subject:** Death of Ludwig IV **Obv:** Three ornate helmets in circle **Obv. Legend:** LVDOVICVS. D.G. LANDGR. HASSIÆ. CO. I. CA. **Rev:** 6-line inscription with Roman numeral date **Rev. Inscription:** OBIIT / A.D. MDCIIII / M. OCTOB. D. IX. / H.VII. VIXIT. / A. LXVII. M. IIII / D.XII. H.VI. **Note:** Ref. S#530, PA#228.

Date	Mintage	VG	F	VF	XF	Unc
MDCIIII (1604)	—	300	600	1,200	2,400	—

KM# 11 1/2 THALER

Silver **Obv:** Half-length figure to left, holding helmet, head divides, four small shields divide legend **Rev:** Three helmets

Date	Mintage	VG	F	VF	XF	Unc
1604	—	—	1,500	3,000	6,000	—

KM# 12 1/2 THALER

Silver **Subject:** Death of Ludwig IV **Obv:** Eight-line inscription **Rev:** Three crowned helmets

Date	Mintage	VG	F	VF	XF	Unc
MDCIIII (1604) Rare	—	—	—	—	—	—

KM# 9 THALER

Silver **Obv:** 1/2-Half-length figure 3/4 left holding helmet and sword1/2- **Rev:** Crowned Hessian lion, four small shields divide legend **Note:** Dav. #6814.

Date	Mintage	VG	F	VF	XF	Unc
1603 Rare	—	—	—	—	—	—

Note: Peus Auction 375, 4-03, VF realized approximately $6,570.

Date	Mintage	VG	F	VF	XF	Unc
1604 Rare	—	—	—	—	—	—

KM# 14 THALER

Silver **Obv:** Half-length figure 3/4 left, holding helmet and sword **Rev:** Three helmets above oval 5-fold arms **Note:** Dav. #6816.

Date	Mintage	VG	F	VF	XF	Unc
1604	—	—	2,500	5,000	10,000	—

KM# 15 THALER

Silver **Subject:** Death of Ludwig IV **Obv:** 8-line inscription with Roman numeral date **Rev:** Crowned Hessian lion, four small shields divide legend **Note:** Dav. #6817.

Date	Mintage	VG	F	VF	XF	Unc
MDCIIII (1604) Rare	—	—	—	—	—	—

KM# 17 2 THALER

Silver **Obv:** Similar to 1 thaler, KM#9 **Rev:** Crowned Hessian lion, four small shields divide legend **Note:** Dav. #6813.

Date	Mintage	VG	F	VF	XF	Unc
1604 Rare	—	—	—	—	—	—

KM# 16 2 THALER

Silver **Note:** Similar to 1 Thaler, KM#14. Dav. #6815.

Date	Mintage	VG	F	VF	XF	Unc
1604 Rare	—	—	—	—	—	—

Note: Künker Auction 98, 3-05, VF realized approximately $22,425.

HILDESHEIM

A bishopric located in Westphalia, about 18 miles southeast of Hannover, was established in 822. The first mint was installed in the Mundburg Castle c. 977. Hildesheim coins were minted there although the bishopric didn't legally receive the mint right until 1054. There was no episcopal coinage during most of the 16th century, the first being produced only during the reign of Ernst of Bavaria. In 1803 it was secularized and assigned to Prussia. From 1807-1813 it formed part of the Kingdom of Westphalia and in 1813 was given to Hannover.

RULERS

Ernst of Bavaria, 1573-1612
Ferdinand of Bavaria, 1612-50
Maximilian Heinrich of Bavaria, 1650-88
Jobst Edmund von Brabeck, 1688-1702

MINT OFFICIALS' INITIALS

Hildesheim Mint

Initials	Date	Name
GB	1689-90	Georg Binnebohs
GH	Ca.1621-24	?
HB	1674-1711	Heinrich Bonhorst in Clausthal
HS, HIS	1692, 1694-1702	Heinrich Justus Sebastiani
IH	Ca.1611	?, die-cutter
LZ	1678-90	Levin Zernemann, die-cutter in Clausthal and Brunswick
PL	1663-65	Peter Lohr
SC	1660-92, 1693	Simon Conrad

Moritzberg Mint

(Closed 1634)

Initial	Date	Name
CG	1628-33	Caspar Gieseler
(a)= or	1598-1608	Christoph Diess
(b)= (HL)	1608-12	Hans Lachentress
(e)=	1612-18	Andreas Fricke
(f)=	1622-23	Christian Hopfgarten

Peine Mint

1608-1627

Initial	Date	Name
(c)=	1608-09	Paul Lachentress
(d)=	1609-11	Caspar Kohl
(a)= or	1611-12	Christoph Diess
(g)=	1620-22	Carl Solter

ARMS

Hildesheim (bishopric): Parted per pale gold and red.
Peine: Wolf leaping left above two corn sheaves.

BISHOPRIC

REGULAR COINAGE

KM# 31 FLITTER

Copper **Ruler:** Ferdinand **Obv:** Crowned 4-fold arms of Bavaria-Pfalz, with central shield of Hildesheim **Rev. Inscription:** I / FLIT / TER **Note:** Kipper Flitter.

Date	Mintage	VG	F	VF	XF	Unc
ND(1621/22)	—	13.00	33.00	60.00	120	—

KM# 45 PFENNIG

Silver **Ruler:** Maximilian Heinrich **Obv:** Crowned MH monogram divides date as 1-6/6-3.

Date	Mintage	VG	F	VF	XF	Unc
1663	170,000	20.00	33.00	65.00	130	—

KM# 55 PFENNIG

Silver **Ruler:** Jobst Edmund **Obv:** Crowned script JE monogram divides date where present **Note:** Uniface.

Date	Mintage	VG	F	VF	XF	Unc
ND(1688-1702)	—	15.00	30.00	60.00	120	240
1691	—	15.00	30.00	60.00	120	240
1692	—	15.00	30.00	60.00	120	240

KM# 73 PFENNIG

Copper **Ruler:** Jobst Edmund **Obv:** Crowned script JE monogram **Rev. Inscription:** I / PFENNIG / SCHEIDE / MUNTZ / date

Date	Mintage	VG	F	VF	XF	Unc
1693	—	9.00	20.00	40.00	80.00	—
1695	—	9.00	20.00	40.00	80.00	—
1696	—	9.00	20.00	40.00	80.00	—
1700	—	9.00	20.00	40.00	80.00	—

KM# 80 2 PFENNIG

Silver **Ruler:** Jobst Edmund **Obv:** Crowned script JE monogram **Rev. Inscription:** II / PFEN / date

Date	Mintage	VG	F	VF	XF	Unc
1696	—	15.00	30.00	60.00	120	—

KM# 33 3 PFENNIG (1/96 Thaler; Dreier)

Silver **Ruler:** Ferdinand **Obv:** Crowned 4-fold arms of Bavaria-Pfalz, with central shield of Hildesheim arms **Rev:** Imperial orb with 3 divides date **Mint:** Moritzberg

Date	Mintage	VG	F	VF	XF	Unc
16ZZ (f)	—	45.00	90.00	180	360	—

KM# 34 3 PFENNIG (1/96 Thaler; Dreier)

Silver **Ruler:** Ferdinand **Obv:** Arms of Peine in ornate shield

Date	Mintage	VG	F	VF	XF	Unc
16ZZ	—	60.00	115	225	450	—

KM# 46 3 PFENNIG (1/96 Thaler; Dreier)

Silver **Ruler:** Maximilian Heinrich **Obv:** Crowned 4-fold arms of Bavaria-Pfalz, with central shield of Hildesheim arms **Note:** Varieties exist.

Date	Mintage	VG	F	VF	XF	Unc
1663	178,000	11.00	25.00	55.00	110	—
1664	221,000	8.00	18.00	35.00	70.00	—

KM# 60 3 PFENNIG (1/96 Thaler; Dreier)

Silver **Ruler:** Jobst Edmund **Obv:** 4-fold arms of Hildesheim and Brabeck, F. B. H. L. M. above

Date	Mintage	VG	F	VF	XF	Unc
1690	—	—	—	—	—	—
1691	—	—	—	—	—	—

KM# 65 4 PFENNIG

Silver **Ruler:** Jobst Edmund **Obv:** Crowned script JE monogram divides date **Rev. Inscription:** IIII / PFEN(N) / F. B. H. L. M.

Date	Mintage	VG	F	VF	XF	Unc
1691	—	11.00	20.00	45.00	90.00	—
1692	—	11.00	20.00	45.00	90.00	—

KM# 47 MARIENGROSCHEN

Silver **Ruler:** Maximilian Heinrich **Obv:** Crowned 4-fold arms of Bavaria-Pfalz, with central shield of Hildesheim arms **Rev:** Madonna and child, date in legend

Date	Mintage	VG	F	VF	XF	Unc
1663	191,000	33.00	55.00	115	230	—

KM# 68 MARIENGROSCHEN

Silver **Ruler:** Jobst Edmund **Obv:** Madonna and child **Rev. Inscription:** I / MARIEN / GROS / date

Date	Mintage	VG	F	VF	XF	Unc
1692	—	33.00	55.00	115	230	—

KM# 61 6 MARIENGROSCHEN

Silver **Ruler:** Jobst Edmund **Obv:** 4-fold arms of Hildesheim and Brabeck, bishop's cap above, crozier and sword crossed behind in form of St. Andrew's cross **Rev. Inscription:** VI / MARIEN / GROSCH / date **Mint:** Hildesheim

Date	Mintage	VG	F	VF	XF	Unc
1689 GB	—	40.00	85.00	150	300	—
1690	—	40.00	85.00	150	300	—

KM# 74 6 MARIENGROSCHEN

Silver **Ruler:** Jobst Edmund **Obv:** Bust right **Rev. Legend:** NACH DEM... **Rev. Inscription:** VI / MARIEN / GROSCH / date **Mint:** Hildesheim

Date	Mintage	VG	F	VF	XF	Unc
1693 HIS	—	40.00	80.00	140	265	—
1694 HIS	—	40.00	80.00	140	265	—

KM# 75 12 MARIENGROSCHEN (1/3 Thaler)

Silver **Ruler:** Jobst Edmund **Obv:** Bust left **Rev. Legend:** NACH DEM... **Rev. Inscription:** XII / MARIEN / GROSCH / date

Date	Mintage	VG	F	VF	XF	Unc
1693	—	—	—	—	—	—

KM# 62 24 MARIENGROSCHEN (2/3 Thaler)

Silver **Ruler:** Jobst Edmund **Obv:** Bust right in circle **Rev. Legend:** IN PACE ET AEGUITATE... **Rev. Inscription:** 24 / MARIEN / GROSH / date

Date	Mintage	VG	F	VF	XF	Unc
1690	—	—	—	—	—	—
1691	—	1,450	2,750	5,500	—	—
1692	—	—	—	—	—	—

KM# 69 24 MARIENGROSCHEN (2/3 Thaler)

Silver **Ruler:** Jobst Edmund **Obv:** Crowned oval 4-fold arms of Hildesheim and Brabeck

Date	Mintage	VG	F	VF	XF	Unc
1692	—	—	—	—	—	—

KM# 70 24 MARIENGROSCHEN (2/3 Thaler)

Silver **Ruler:** Jobst Edmund **Rev. Legend:** NACH DEM LEIPZIGE FUES. **Rev. Inscription:** XXIIII / MARIEN... **Mint:** Hildesheim

Date	Mintage	VG	F	VF	XF	Unc
1692	—	135	300	475	975	—
1693 HS	—	135	300	475	975	—
1694 HS	—	135	300	475	975	—
1697 HS	—	135	300	475	975	—

KM# 76 24 MARIENGROSCHEN (2/3 Thaler)

Silver **Ruler:** Jobst Edmund **Obv:** Bust right in circle **Rev. Legend:** IN PACE ET AEGUITATE... **Rev. Inscription:** XXIIII / MARIEN / GROSCH, date **Mint:** Hildesheim

Date	Mintage	VG	F	VF	XF	Unc
1693 SC	—	—	—	—	—	—

KM# 77 24 MARIENGROSCHEN (2/3 Thaler)

Silver **Ruler:** Jobst Edmund **Obv:** Crowned oval 4-fold arms of Hildesheim and Brabeck **Mint:** Hildesheim

Date	Mintage	VG	F	VF	XF	Unc
1693 HS	—	—	—	—	—	—
1693 SC	—	—	—	—	—	—

KM# 78 24 MARIENGROSCHEN (2/3 Thaler)

Silver **Ruler:** Jobst Edmund **Obv:** Bust right not in circle **Rev. Legend:** NACH DEM LEIPZIGER FUES **Mint:** Hildesheim

Date	Mintage	VG	F	VF	XF	Unc
1693 HIS	—	375	650	1,100	2,150	—
1694 HIS	—	375	650	1,100	2,150	—
1697 HIS	—	375	650	1,100	2,150	—

KM# 85 24 MARIENGROSCHEN (2/3 Thaler)

Silver **Ruler:** Jobst Edmund **Obv:** Bust left **Rev:** Date in legend **Rev. Inscription:** XXIIII / MARIEN / GROSCH / V:FEINEM SILVER / HIS **Mint:** Hildesheim

Date	Mintage	VG	F	VF	XF	Unc
1698 HIS	—	—	—	—	—	—

KM# 90 24 MARIENGROSCHEN (2/3 Thaler)

Silver **Ruler:** Jobst Edmund **Obv:** Bust right **Rev:** Date in legend **Rev. Inscription:** XXIIII / MARIEN / GROSCH / VIFEINEM SILVER / HIS **Mint:** Hildesheim

Date	Mintage	VG	F	VF	XF	Unc
1700 HIS	—	250	500	1,000	2,000	—

KM# 11 1/96 THALER (3 Pfennig; Dreier)

Silver **Ruler:** Ernst **Rev:** Imperial orb in rhombus divides date **Mint:** Moritzberg **Note:** Varieties exist.

Date	Mintage	VG	F	VF	XF	Unc
1601 (a)	—	35.00	70.00	140	285	—
160Z (a)	—	35.00	70.00	140	285	—
1604 (a)	—	35.00	70.00	140	285	—
1605 (a)	—	35.00	70.00	140	285	—
ND(ca.1608)	—	35.00	70.00	140	285	—
ND (b)	—	35.00	70.00	140	285	—

KM# 13 1/96 THALER (3 Pfennig; Dreier)

Silver **Ruler:** Ernst **Obv:** Small shield of Peine arms below 4-fold arms

Date	Mintage	VG	F	VF	XF	Unc
ND(ca.1609)	—	20.00	35.00	75.00	155	—

KM# 14 1/96 THALER (3 Pfennig; Dreier)

Silver **Ruler:** Ernst **Rev:** Imperial orb with 96 in ornamented oval

Date	Mintage	VG	F	VF	XF	Unc
1609	—	20.00	45.00	90.00	185	—

KM# 12 1/96 THALER (3 Pfennig; Dreier)

Silver **Ruler:** Ernst **Obv:** Small shield of Peine arms below arms **Mint:** Moritzberg

Date	Mintage	VG	F	VF	XF	Unc
ND(ca.1609)	—	20.00	35.00	75.00	155	—
ND (d)	—	20.00	35.00	75.00	155	—

KM# 9.1 1/24 THALER (Groschen)

Silver **Ruler:** Ernst **Obv:** Crowned shield of 4-fold arms of Bavaria-Pfalz, central shield of Hildesheim **Obv. Legend:** ERN. D.G. COL. AR. EL. A. H. **Rev:** Imperial orb with Z4, cross divides date **Rev. Legend:** RVDOL. II. ROM. IMP. SEM. A. **Mint:** Moritzberg **Note:** Cappe 132-43. Previous KM #9. Varieties exist.

Date	Mintage	VG	F	VF	XF	Unc
1601	—	16.00	32.00	65.00	130	—
1601 (a)	—	16.00	32.00	65.00	130	—
1602 (a)	—	16.00	32.00	65.00	130	—
1603 (a)	—	16.00	32.00	65.00	130	—
1604 (a)	—	16.00	32.00	65.00	130	—
1605 (a)	—	16.00	32.00	65.00	130	—
1606 (a)	—	16.00	32.00	65.00	130	—
1607 (a)	—	13.00	32.00	65.00	130	—
1607	—	13.00	32.00	65.00	130	—
1608 (b)	—	13.00	32.00	65.00	130	—
1609 (b)	—	13.00	32.00	65.00	130	—

KM# 9.2 1/24 THALER (Groschen)

Silver **Ruler:** Ernst **Obv:** Shield of 4-fold arms of Bavaria-Pfalz, central shield of Hildesheim, electoral hat above **Obv. Legend:** ERN. D.G. COL. AR. EL. A. H. **Rev:** Crowned imperial eagle, Z4 in orb on breast **Rev. Legend:** RVDOL. II. ROM. IMP. SEM. A. **Mint:** Moritzberg **Note:** Cappe 112-14.

Date	Mintage	VG	F	VF	XF	Unc
ND(1608-12) (b)	—	16.00	35.00	70.00	145	—

KM# 15 1/24 THALER (Groschen)

Silver **Ruler:** Ernst **Obv:** Small shield of Peine arms below arms **Rev:** Date divided by top of cross in legend **Mint:** Peine

Date	Mintage	VG	F	VF	XF	Unc
1609	—	16.00	35.00	75.00	155	—
1609 (c)	—	16.00	35.00	75.00	155	—
1609 (d)	—	16.00	35.00	75.00	155	—

KM# 20 1/24 THALER (Groschen)

Silver **Ruler:** Ernst **Obv:** Shield of 4-fold arms of Bavaria-Pfalz with central shield of Hildesheim, superimposed on 2 crossed croziers, electoral hat above, small shield of Peine arms below **Rev:** Imperial orb with Z4 divides date, 4-line inscription with date below **Rev. Inscription:** NUIE TOPL. / SILBR GROS. / STIFT HILDESH. / (date) **Note:** Cappe 182. Prev. listed as 1/12 Thaler.

Date	Mintage	VG	F	VF	XF	Unc
1611	—	27.00	45.00	75.00	150	—

KM# 24 1/24 THALER (Groschen)
Silver **Ruler:** Ferdinand **Rev:** Titles of Matthias **Mint:** Moritzberg

Date	Mintage	VG	F	VF	XF	Unc
1613 (e)	—	15.00	30.00	65.00	130	—
1614 (e)	—	15.00	30.00	65.00	130	—
1615 (e)	—	15.00	30.00	65.00	130	—
1616 (e)	—	15.00	30.00	65.00	130	—
1617 (e)	—	15.00	30.00	65.00	130	—
1618 (e)	—	15.00	30.00	65.00	130	—

KM# 25 1/24 THALER (Groschen)
Silver **Ruler:** Ferdinand **Rev:** Imperial orb with Z4, date divided in legend at top, titles of Matthias **Note:** Kipper 1/24 Thaler.

Date	Mintage	VG	F	VF	XF	Unc
1619	—	—	—	—	—	—

KM# 26 1/24 THALER (Groschen)
Silver **Ruler:** Ferdinand **Note:** Similar to KM#24, but titles of Ferdinand II.

Date	Mintage	VG	F	VF	XF	Unc
1619	—	15.00	30.00	65.00	130	—
1620	—	15.00	30.00	65.00	130	—
1621	—	15.00	30.00	65.00	130	—

KM# 30 1/24 THALER (Groschen)
Silver **Ruler:** Ferdinand **Obv:** Ornate shield of Peine arms **Rev:** Imperial orb with Z4, date divided in legend at top, titles of Ferdinand II **Mint:** Peine

Date	Mintage	VG	F	VF	XF	Unc
1620 (g)	—	20.00	35.00	75.00	155	—
1622	—	20.00	35.00	75.00	155	—

KM# 32 1/24 THALER (Groschen)
Silver **Ruler:** Ferdinand **Mint:** Hildesheim **Note:** Similar to KM#24 but date divided in obverse legend at top.

Date	Mintage	VG	F	VF	XF	Unc
16Z1	—	15.00	30.00	65.00	130	—
16Z1 GH	—	15.00	30.00	65.00	130	—
16Z3 GH	—	15.00	30.00	65.00	130	—
16Z4 GH	—	15.00	30.00	65.00	130	—

KM# 48 1/24 THALER (Groschen)
Silver **Ruler:** Maximilian Heinrich **Obv:** Crowned 4-fold arms of Bavaria-Pfalz with central shield of Hildesheim arms **Rev:** Imperial orb with Z4 divides date

Date	Mintage	VG	F	VF	XF	Unc
1663	980	—	—	—	—	—

KM# 66 1/24 THALER (Groschen)
Silver **Ruler:** Jobst Edmund **Obv:** 4-fold arms of Hildesheim and Brabeck **Rev:** Imperial orb with Z4 divides date

Date	Mintage	VG	F	VF	XF	Unc
1691	—	15.00	30.00	65.00	130	—

KM# 10 1/16 THALER (2 Schilling)
Silver **Ruler:** Ernst **Obv:** Shield of 4-fold arms of Bavaria-Pfalz, central shield of Hildesheim, superimposed on floriated cross, electoral hat above **Obv. Legend:** ERN.(-)D.G. AR(H).(-)CO. E(L).(-)(AD.)H(IL). **Rev:** Crowned imperial eagle, 16 in orb on breast, titles of Rudolf II and date divided by crown in legend at top, where present **Rev. Legend:** RVD. II. D.G. RO. I(MP). S(EM). A. **Mint:** Moritzberg **Note:** Cappe 115-16, 144. Varieties exist.

Date	Mintage	VG	F	VF	XF	Unc
1602	—	27.00	60.00	110	220	—
1603	—	27.00	60.00	110	220	—
1604	—	27.00	60.00	110	220	—
1605	—	27.00	60.00	110	220	—
1606	—	27.00	60.00	110	220	—
1607	—	27.00	60.00	110	220	—
1608 (b)	—	27.00	60.00	110	220	—
ND(1608-12) (b)	—	27.00	60.00	110	220	—
(16)09 (b)	—	27.00	60.00	110	220	—
1609 (b)	—	27.00	60.00	110	220	—
1609 (d)	—	27.00	60.00	110	220	—

KM# 16 1/16 THALER (2 Schilling)
Silver **Ruler:** Ernst **Rev:** Small shield of Peine arms below 4-fold arms

Date	Mintage	VG	F	VF	XF	Unc
ND(ca.1609)	—	45.00	90.00	180	360	—

KM# 57 1/16 THALER (2 Schilling)
Silver **Ruler:** Jobst Edmund **Obv:** Bust right **Rev. Inscription:** XVI / EINEN / REICHS / THAL., date in legend

Date	Mintage	VG	F	VF	XF	Unc
1689	—	85.00	175	350	725	—
1691	—	85.00	175	350	725	—
1692	—	85.00	175	350	725	—

KM# 67 1/12 THALER (2 Groschen)
Silver **Ruler:** Jobst Edmund **Obv:** Crowned 4-fold arms of Hildesheim and Brabeck **Rev. Inscription:** 12 / EINEN / REICHS / THAL / date

Date	Mintage	VG	F	VF	XF	Unc
1691	—	33.00	55.00	110	220	—
1692	—	100	200	425	—	—

KM# 71 1/12 THALER (2 Groschen)
Silver **Ruler:** Jobst Edmund **Obv:** Bust right **Rev:** Date in legend **Rev. Inscription:** 12 / EINEN / REICHS / THAL / HIS **Mint:** Hildesheim

Date	Mintage	VG	F	VF	XF	Unc
1692 HIS	—	40.00	70.00	130	265	—
1693 HIS	—	40.00	70.00	130	265	—
1694 HIS	—	40.00	70.00	130	265	—
1696 HIS	—	40.00	70.00	130	265	—
1700 HIS	—	40.00	70.00	130	265	—

KM# 79 1/12 THALER (2 Groschen)
Silver **Ruler:** Jobst Edmund **Rev. Inscription:** 12 / EINEN / REICHS / THAL / date

Date	Mintage	VG	F	VF	XF	Unc
1693	—	40.00	70.00	130	265	—

KM# 82 1/12 THALER (2 Groschen)
Silver **Ruler:** Jobst Edmund **Obv:** Crowned script JE monogram **Rev:** Date in legend **Rev. Inscription:** 12 / EINEN / REICHS / THAL / HIS **Mint:** Hildesheim

Date	Mintage	VG	F	VF	XF	Unc
1697 HIS	—	40.00	70.00	130	265	—
1700 HIS	—	40.00	70.00	130	265	—

KM# 40 1/2 ORT (1/8 Thaler)
Silver **Ruler:** Ferdinand **Obv:** Bust right **Rev:** Imperial orb divides G-H above **Rev. Inscription:** EIN / HALB / REICHS / ORTH / date, **Mint:** Hildesheim

Date	Mintage	VG	F	VF	XF	Unc
16Z4 GH	—	1,500	2,900	5,700	—	—

KM# 35 1/4 THALER
Silver **Ruler:** Ferdinand **Obv:** Bust right **Rev:** Crowned 4-fold arms of Bavaria-Pfalz with central shield of Hildesheim arms in ornate frame, date divides mintmaster's initials below **Mint:** Hildesheim **Note:** Varieties exist.

Date	Mintage	VG	F	VF	XF	Unc
16Z3 GH Rare	—	—	—	—	—	—
16Z4 GH Rare	—	—	—	—	—	—

KM# 42 1/4 THALER
Silver **Ruler:** Ferdinand **Rev:** Date at top of legend **Mint:** Moritzberg **Note:** Varieties exist.

Date	Mintage	VG	F	VF	XF	Unc
16Z5 (f) Rare	—	—	—	—	—	—

KM# 36 1/2 THALER
Silver **Ruler:** Ferdinand **Obv:** Bust right **Rev:** Crowned 4-fold arms of Bavaria-Pfalz with central shield of Hildesheim arms in ornate frame, date divides mintmaster's initials below **Mint:** Hildesheim

Date	Mintage	VG	F	VF	XF	Unc
16Z3 GH	—	—	—	—	—	—

KM# 41 1/2 THALER
Silver **Ruler:** Ferdinand **Rev:** Date at top of legend

Date	Mintage	VG	F	VF	XF	Unc
16Z3 GH	—	460	925	1,850	—	—
16Z4 (f)	—	460	925	1,850	—	—
1630 CG	—	460	925	1,850	—	—

KM# 49 2/3 THALER (Gulden)
Silver **Ruler:** Maximilian Heinrich **Obv:** Crowned 4-fold arms of Bavaria-Pfalz with central shield of Hildesheim arms **Rev:** Madonna and child, date in legend **Mint:** Hildesheim

Date	Mintage	VG	F	VF	XF	Unc
1663 PL	88	—	—	—	—	—

KM# 21 THALER
Silver **Ruler:** Ernst **Obv:** Bust right in circle, date divided by top of head **Rev:** Crowned, ornate 4-fold arms of Bavaria-Pfalz with central shield Hildesheim arms, small shield of Peine arms below, IH on edge **Mint:** Hildesheim **Note:** Dav. #5402.

Date	Mintage	VG	F	VF	XF	Unc
1611 IH Rare	—	—	—	—	—	—

KM# 23 THALER
Silver **Ruler:** Ferdinand **Obv:** Bust right in circle **Rev:** Crowned 4-fold arms of Bavaria-Pfalz with central shield of Hildesheim arms in ornate frame **Note:** Dav. #5403.

Date	Mintage	VG	F	VF	XF	Unc
ND(ca.1612) Rare	—	—	—	—	—	—

KM# 27 THALER

Silver **Ruler:** Ferdinand **Obv:** Similar to KM#37 but date 1 - 6 divided by crown and 1 - 9 divided by arms at sides **Note:** Dav. #5404.

Date	Mintage	VG	F	VF	XF	Unc
1619 Rare	—	—	—	—	—	—

KM# 37.1 THALER

Silver **Ruler:** Ferdinand **Mint:** Hildesheim **Note:** Dav. #5405.

Date	Mintage	VG	F	VF	XF	Unc
1623 GH	—	300	600	1,150	2,000	—

KM# 39 THALER

Silver **Ruler:** Ferdinand **Rev:** Similar to KM#37 but date below arms **Mint:** Hildesheim **Note:** Dav. #5405B.

Date	Mintage	VG	F	VF	XF	Unc
1623 GH	—	300	600	1,200	2,100	—

KM# 38 THALER

Silver **Ruler:** Ferdinand **Mint:** Hildesheim **Note:** Klippe. Dav. #5405A.

Date	Mintage	VG	F	VF	XF	Unc
1623 GH Rare	—	—	—	—	—	—

KM# 37.2 THALER

Silver **Ruler:** Ferdinand **Obv:** Larger bust **Mint:** Hildesheim **Note:** Varieties exist. Dav. #5406.

Date	Mintage	VG	F	VF	XF	Unc
1623 GH	—	240	475	800	1,800	—
16Z4 GH	—	240	475	800	1,800	—
1625 GH	—	240	475	800	1,800	—
1630	—	240	475	800	1,800	—
1630 CG	—	240	475	800	1,800	—
1631 CG	—	240	475	800	1,800	—

KM# 50 THALER

Silver **Ruler:** Maximilian Heinrich **Obv:** Crowned 4-fold arms of Bavaria-Pfalz with central shield of Hildesheim arms **Rev:** Madonna and child, date in legend **Mint:** Hildesheim

Date	Mintage	VG	F	VF	XF	Unc
1663 PL Rare	—	—	—	—	—	—

KM# 56 THALER

Silver **Ruler:** Jobst Edmund **Obv:** Leopold I **Rev:** Ornate helmeted arms of Hildesheim, Madonna and child above, date in legend **Mint:** Hildesheim **Note:** Sede vacante. Dav. #5407.

Date	Mintage	VG	F	VF	XF	Unc
1688 HB/LZ	800	300	500	950	1,700	3,000

KM# 63 THALER

Silver **Ruler:** Jobst Edmund **Rev:** Helmeted 4-fold arms of Hildesheim and Brabeck in oval supported by two female figures, all dividing date **Mint:** Hildesheim **Note:** Dav. #5408.

Date	Mintage	VG	F	VF	XF	Unc
1690	—	2,000	4,000	7,000	12,000	—
1690 GB	—	2,000	4,000	7,000	12,000	—

KM# 72 THALER

Silver **Ruler:** Jobst Edmund **Rev:** Ornately-helmeted 4-fold arms of Hildesheim and Brabeck divide date **Mint:** Hildesheim **Note:** Dav. #5409.

Date	Mintage	VG	F	VF	XF	Unc
1692 SC Rare	—	—	—	—	—	—

KM# 81 THALER

Silver **Ruler:** Jobst Edmund **Obv:** Bust right **Mint:** Hildesheim **Note:** Dav. #5410.

Date	Mintage	VG	F	VF	XF	Unc
1696 HS Rare	—	—	—	—	—	—

KM# 83 THALER

Silver **Ruler:** Jobst Edmund **Obv:** Helmeted arms **Rev:** Full-length facing standing figure of St. Anthony **Rev. Legend:** SANCTUS ANTHONIUS... **Mint:** Hildesheim **Note:** Mining Thaler. Dav. #5411.

Date	Mintage	VG	F	VF	XF	Unc
1697 HIS	—	500	1,000	2,000	4,250	—

KM# 84.1 THALER

Silver **Ruler:** Jobst Edmund **Rev. Legend:** HÆC... **Mint:** Hildesheim **Note:** Mining Thaler. Dav. #5412.

Date	Mintage	VG	F	VF	XF	Unc
1697 HIS	—	350	700	1,500	3,250	—
1698 HIS	—	350	700	1,500	3,250	—
1699 HIS	—	350	700	1,500	3,250	—

KM# 84.2 THALER

Silver **Ruler:** Jobst Edmund **Rev. Legend:** ...SANCTI ANTONII EREMITAE **Note:** Dav. #5413.

Date	Mintage	F	VF	XF	Unc	BU
1698	—	350	700	1,500	3,250	—

KM# 91 THALER

Silver **Ruler:** Jobst Edmund **Obv:** Arms in circle and date in legend **Mint:** Hildesheim **Note:** Mining Thaler. Dav. #5414.

Date	Mintage	VG	F	VF	XF	Unc
1700 HIS Rare	—	—	—	—	—	—

KM# 92 THALER

Silver **Ruler:** Jobst Edmund **Obv:** Ornately-helmeted 4-fold arms **Rev:** St. Anthony in circle **Mint:** Hildesheim **Note:** Mining Thaler. Dav. #5415.

Date	Mintage	VG	F	VF	XF	Unc
1700 HIS Rare	—	—	—	—	—	—

KM# 22 2 THALER

Silver **Ruler:** Ernst **Mint:** Hildesheim **Note:** Similar to 1 Thaler, KM#21. Dav. #5401.

Date	Mintage	VG	F	VF	XF	Unc
1611 IH Rare	—	—	—	—	—	—

TRADE COINAGE

KM# 64 DUCAT

3.5000 g., 0.9860 Gold 0.1109 oz. AGW **Ruler:** Jobst Edmund **Obv:** Bust of Jobst Edmund right **Rev:** Helmeted arms, date below **Mint:** Hildesheim

Date	Mintage	VG	F	VF	XF	Unc
1690	—	1,000	2,300	5,500	9,500	—
1694 HS	—	1,000	2,300	5,500	9,500	—
1695 HS	—	1,000	2,300	5,500	9,500	—

KM# 51 2 DUCAT

7.0000 g., 0.9860 Gold 0.2219 oz. AGW **Ruler:** Maximilian Heinrich **Obv:** Crowned oval 4-fold arms of Bavaria-Pfalz in ornate frame, date divided below **Rev:** Madonna seated facing with child

Date	Mintage	VG	F	VF	XF	Unc
1664 Rare	—	—	—	—	—	—

FREE CITY

The town of Hildesheim grew up around the seat of the bishopric and was made a free imperial city in the mid-13th century. The first civic coinage was struck in 1428 and continued more or less continually until the second half of the 18th century. The last silver coins were struck for the city in 1764 and copper coinage was last produced in 1772. Hildesheim came under the control of Prussia in 1803 and like the bishopric, became part of the Kingdom of Westphalia 1807-13. It was awarded to the Kingdom of Hannover in 1813 and reverted to Prussia when the latter absorbed Hannover in 1866.

MINTMASTERS' INITIALS

Initials	Date	Name
(a)=	1573-74, 1589-90,1592-94, 1600-01	Christoph Dyss der Altere
(b)=	1601-03	Henning Hans (Johannis)
(c)=	1603-06	Christoph Diess der Jungere
(d)=	1614-22	Matthais Weber
(e)=	1622-30	Andreas Fricke
	1631-32	Caspar Gieseler
(f)=	1645-48	Caspar Kohl
(g)=	1666-72	Jonas Bose
	1673-74	Peter Paul Peckstein
(h)= I B	1674-95	Jonas Bose
HL	1696-1710	Hans Luders

SUPERVISORS

Date	Name
1666-72	Jonas Bose
1696	Joachim Heinrich Bose and Kurd Eberling

MINT WARDENS

Date	Name
1693-96	Hans Luders
1601	Adrian Reimers
1601-19	Jobst Brauns
1615-47	Heinrich Ruden

DIE-CUTTERS

Date	Name
1618-19	Isaac Henniges
1619-28	Lazarus Arens
1630	Isaac Henniges
1637-39	Barthold Kretzer
1666	Henning Benneken
1666-74	Tobias Reuss in Clausthal
1666-68	Paul Franzel
1675-90	Jurgen Lippold Jaster
1691	Heinrich Andreas Fricke

ARMS

Old style are quartered red and gold, new style have upper half of crowned eagle above quarterly.

REGULAR COINAGE

KM# 176 FLITTER (Heller)

Copper **Obv:** Arms in shield with flat top and rounded botttom

Date	Mintage	VG	F	VF	XF	Unc
16Z0	—	12.00	25.00	50.00	100	—

KM# 177 FLITTER (Heller)

Copper **Obv:** Oval arms **Rev. Inscription:** I / FLIT / TER / date

Date	Mintage	VG	F	VF	XF	Unc
(1)6Z0	—	12.00	25.00	50.00	100	—

KM# 178 FLITTER (Heller)

Copper **Obv:** Ornamented arms

Date	Mintage	VG	F	VF	XF	Unc
(16)Z0	—	12.00	25.00	50.00	100	—

KM# 179 FLITTER (Heller)

Copper **Rev. Inscription:** 116 / FLIT / TER / ZO

Date	Mintage	VG	F	VF	XF	Unc
16Z0	—	12.00	25.00	50.00	100	—

KM# 180 FLITTER (Heller)

Copper **Obv:** Ornately-shaped arms **Rev. Inscription:** I / FLIT / TER / date

Date	Mintage	VG	F	VF	XF	Unc
(1)6Z0	—	12.00	25.00	50.00	100	—

KM# 181 FLITTER (Heller)

Copper **Obv:** Oval arms **Rev. Inscription:** I / FLIT / TER

Date	Mintage	VG	F	VF	XF	Unc
ND(1620/21)	—	12.00	25.00	50.00	100	—

KM# 182 FLITTER (Heller)

Copper **Obv:** Ornately-shaped arms

Date	Mintage	VG	F	VF	XF	Unc
ND(1620/21)	—	12.00	25.00	50.00	100	—

KM# 175 FLITTER (Heller)

Copper **Obv:** Oval arms, date above **Rev. Inscription:** I / FLIT / TER **Note:** Kipper Flitter.

Date	Mintage	VG	F	VF	XF	Unc
16Z0	—	12.00	25.00	50.00	100	—

KM# 135 PFENNIG

Silver **Obv:** Arms divide date, H above **Note:** Uniface. Varieties exist.

Date	Mintage	VG	F	VF	XF	Unc
16Z8	—	27.00	55.00	110	225	—
1628	—	27.00	55.00	110	225	—
1630	—	27.00	55.00	110	225	—
1631	—	27.00	55.00	110	225	—
163Z	—	27.00	55.00	110	225	—
1637	—	27.00	55.00	110	225	—
1639	—	27.00	55.00	110	225	—
1645	—	27.00	55.00	110	225	—
1648	—	50.00	100	200	400	—
1659	—	27.00	55.00	110	225	—
1660	—	27.00	55.00	110	225	—
1661	—	27.00	55.00	110	225	—
1663	—	27.00	55.00	110	225	—
1666	—	27.00	55.00	110	225	—
1667	—	27.00	55.00	110	225	—
1676	—	27.00	55.00	110	225	—
1686	—	27.00	55.00	110	225	—
1691	—	27.00	55.00	110	225	—
1695	—	27.00	55.00	110	225	—

KM# 227 2 PFENNIG (Stadt)

Billon **Obv:** Arms in oval shield with pointed bottom, HILDES, date around **Rev. Inscription:** II / STAT / PENN

Date	Mintage	VG	F	VF	XF	Unc
1666	—	13.00	27.00	55.00	110	—

KM# 245 2 PFENNIG (Stadt)

Billon **Obv:** 16 HILDES 86 around arms

Date	Mintage	VG	F	VF	XF	Unc
1686	—	13.00	27.00	55.00	110	—

KM# 252 2 PFENNIG (Stadt)

Billon, 13.8 mm. **Obv:** City arms **Rev:** Value, date **Note:** Varieties exist.

Date	Mintage	VG	F	VF	XF	Unc
1695	—	10.00	20.00	55.00	110	—
1696	—	10.00	20.00	55.00	110	—

KM# 183 3 PFENNIG (1/96 Thaler; Dreier)

Billon **Obv:** Arms in oval **Rev:** Imperial orb with 3 **Note:** Kipper 3 Pfennig.

Date	Mintage	VG	F	VF	XF	Unc
ND(1620/21)	—	20.00	40.00	75.00	155	—

KM# 187 3 PFENNIG (1/96 Thaler; Dreier)

Billon **Obv:** Oval arms **Rev:** Imperial orb with 3 divides date **Note:** Varieties exist.

Date	Mintage	VG	F	VF	XF	Unc
16ZZ (e)	—	10.00	27.00	55.00	110	—
16ZZ	—	10.00	27.00	55.00	110	—
1638 (e)	—	10.00	27.00	55.00	110	—

KM# 188 3 PFENNIG (1/96 Thaler; Dreier)

Billon **Obv:** Similar to KM#220 but HILDESHEIM above plain arms **Note:** Varieties exist.

Date	Mintage	VG	F	VF	XF	Unc
16ZZ (e)	—	8.00	20.00	40.00	75.00	—
16Z3	—	8.00	20.00	40.00	75.00	—
1648	—	8.00	20.00	40.00	75.00	—

KM# 221 3 PFENNIG (1/96 Thaler; Dreier)

Billon **Note:** Klippe.

Date	Mintage	VG	F	VF	XF	Unc
1659 Rare	—	—	—	—	—	—

KM# 220 3 PFENNIG (1/96 Thaler; Dreier)

Billon **Obv:** HILDES above ornately-shaped arms **Rev:** Imperial orb with value divides date **Note:** Varieties exist.

Date	Mintage	VG	F	VF	XF	Unc
1659	—	10.00	20.00	40.00	85.00	—
1660	—	10.00	20.00	40.00	85.00	—
1661	—	10.00	20.00	40.00	85.00	—
1672	—	10.00	20.00	40.00	85.00	—
1676	—	10.00	20.00	40.00	85.00	—
1679	—	10.00	20.00	40.00	85.00	—
1680	—	10.00	20.00	40.00	85.00	—
1683	—	10.00	20.00	40.00	85.00	—
1685	—	10.00	20.00	40.00	85.00	—
1686	—	10.00	20.00	40.00	85.00	—
1687	—	10.00	20.00	40.00	85.00	—
1690	—	10.00	20.00	40.00	85.00	—
1691	—	10.00	20.00	40.00	85.00	—
1692	—	10.00	20.00	40.00	85.00	—
1694	—	10.00	20.00	40.00	85.00	—
1700	—	10.00	20.00	40.00	85.00	—

KM# 251 4 PFENNIG

Billon **Obv:** Arms within square **Rev:** Value with PF dividing date below **Rev. Inscription:** IIII / STADT / 17PF16 **Note:** Varieties exist.

Date	Mintage	VG	F	VF	XF	Unc
1691	—	15.00	30.00	60.00	120	—
1692	—	15.00	30.00	60.00	120	—

KM# 226 4 PFENNIG (Matthier)

Billon **Obv:** Arms **Obv. Legend:** MO. NO. CIVIT. HILDES. **Rev. Inscription:** IIII / STAT / PENNI / date **Note:** Stadt 4 Pfennig.

Date	Mintage	VG	F	VF	XF	Unc
1663	—	15.00	30.00	60.00	125	—
1666	—	15.00	30.00	60.00	125	—

KM# 238 4 PFENNIG (Matthier)

Billon **Rev. Inscription:** IIII / GUTE / 16PF75 **Note:** Gute 4 Pfennig. Varieties exist.

Date	Mintage	VG	F	VF	XF	Unc
ND(ca.1675)	—	15.00	30.00	60.00	125	—
1675	—	15.00	30.00	60.00	125	—
1676	—	15.00	30.00	60.00	125	—
(1)676	—	15.00	30.00	60.00	125	—
1679	—	15.00	30.00	60.00	125	—
1680	—	15.00	30.00	60.00	125	—

KM# 239 4 PFENNIG (Matthier)

Billon **Rev. Inscription:** 1IIII6 /GUTE / 7PF6

Date	Mintage	VG	F	VF	XF	Unc
1676	—	—	—	—	—	—

KM# A12 1/2 KORTLING (2 Gosler; 2 Pfennig)

Silver **Obv:** Shield of old city arms divide Z - G, date divided by H above **Note:** Ref. B/B#100. Uniface.

Date	Mintage	VG	F	VF	XF	Unc
1601	—	—	—	—	—	—

KM# 190 MARIENGROSCHEN

Silver **Note:** Klippe.

Date	Mintage	VG	F	VF	XF	Unc
(1)6ZZ	—	—	—	—	—	—
(1)6ZZ (e)	—	—	—	—	—	—
(1)6Z3 (e)	—	—	—	—	—	—

KM# 189 MARIENGROSCHEN

1.2200 g., Silver **Obv:** 4-fold arms, date above **Rev:** Madonna and child **Note:** Varieties exist.

Date	Mintage	VG	F	VF	XF	Unc
(1)6ZZ (e)	—	15.00	35.00	75.00	150	—
(1)6ZZ (e)	—	15.00	35.00	75.00	150	—
(1)6Z3 (e)	—	15.00	35.00	75.00	150	—
(1)6Z4	—	15.00	35.00	75.00	150	—
(1)660	—	15.00	35.00	75.00	150	—
1661	—	15.00	35.00	75.00	150	—
(1)663	—	15.00	35.00	75.00	150	—
(1)666	—	15.00	35.00	75.00	150	—
1666	—	15.00	35.00	75.00	150	—
1667	—	15.00	35.00	75.00	150	—
1668	—	15.00	35.00	75.00	150	—
1685	—	15.00	35.00	75.00	150	—
1687	—	15.00	35.00	75.00	150	—

KM# 228 6 MARIENGROSCHEN (1/6 Thaler)

Silver **Obv:** Large arms in oval shield, pointed at bottom **Rev:** Inscription in laurel wreath **Rev. Inscription:** VI / MARIEN / GROSCH / date

Date	Mintage	VG	F	VF	XF	Unc
1666 (g)	—	65.00	135	275	575	—

KM# 229 6 MARIENGROSCHEN (1/6 Thaler)

Silver **Note:** Klippe.

Date	Mintage	VG	F	VF	XF	Unc
1666 (g)	—	—	—	—	—	—

KM# 230 6 MARIENGROSCHEN (1/6 Thaler)

Silver **Note:** Varieties exist.

Date	Mintage	VG	F	VF	XF	Unc
1667	—	35.00	70.00	140	285	—
1668	—	35.00	70.00	140	285	—
1669	—	35.00	70.00	140	285	—
1673	—	35.00	70.00	140	285	—
1674	—	35.00	70.00	140	285	—
1689	—	35.00	70.00	140	285	—
1690	—	35.00	70.00	140	285	—
1693	—	35.00	70.00	140	285	—
1694	—	35.00	70.00	140	285	—
1694 (h)	—	35.00	70.00	140	285	—
1696 HL	—	35.00	70.00	140	285	—

KM# 236 12 MARIENGROSCHEN (1/3 Thaler)
Silver

Date	Mintage	VG	F	VF	XF	Unc
1674	—	65.00	165	325	650	—
1675	—	65.00	165	325	650	—
1676	—	65.00	165	325	650	—
1677	—	65.00	165	325	650	—
1680	—	65.00	165	325	650	—
1681	—	65.00	165	325	650	—
1693	—	65.00	165	325	650	—
1695 HL	—	100	200	550	1,150	—
1696 HL	—	135	275	550	1,150	—
1697 HL	—	135	275	550	1,150	—
1700 HL	—	135	275	550	1,150	—

KM# 237 24 MARIENGROSCHEN (2/3 Thaler)
Silver **Obv:** Small arms in ovoid shield, pointed at bottom, ornate helmet above, 3/4 length figure of maiden above helmet **Rev:** Value, date below **Rev. Inscription:** 24 / MARIEN / GROSCH **Note:** Varieties exist.

Date	Mintage	VG	F	VF	XF	Unc
1674	—	85.00	175	375	675	—
1680	—	85.00	175	375	675	—
1681	—	85.00	175	375	675	—
1683	—	85.00	175	375	675	—
1684	—	85.00	175	375	675	—
1685	—	85.00	175	375	675	—
1686	—	85.00	175	375	675	—
1687	—	85.00	175	375	675	—
1688	—	85.00	175	375	675	—
1689	—	85.00	175	375	675	—
1690	—	85.00	175	375	675	—
1691	—	85.00	175	375	675	—
1692	—	85.00	175	375	675	—
1693	—	85.00	175	375	675	—
1694 (h)	—	80.00	160	300	575	—
1694 HL	—	80.00	160	300	575	—
1694	—	85.00	175	375	675	—
1695 HL	—	80.00	160	300	575	—
1696 HL	—	80.00	160	300	575	—
1697 HL	—	80.00	160	300	575	—
1698 HL	—	80.00	160	300	575	—
1699 HL	—	80.00	160	300	575	—
1700 HL	—	80.00	160	300	575	—

KM# 143 1/96 THALER (3 Pfennig; Dreier)
Billon **Obv:** Arms divde date, mintmaster's mark above **Rev:** Imperial orb with 96 in ornamented frame

Date	Mintage	VG	F	VF	XF	Unc
1601 (b)	—	40.00	80.00	160	325	—

KM# 144 1/96 THALER (3 Pfennig; Dreier)
Billon **Obv:** Arms, mintmaster's mark above **Rev:** Large imperial orb with 96 divides date

Date	Mintage	VG	F	VF	XF	Unc
1601 (b)	—	35.00	70.00	145	290	—
160Z (b)	—	35.00	70.00	145	290	—
160Z	—	35.00	70.00	145	290	—
1603 (b)	—	35.00	70.00	145	290	—
1606	—	35.00	70.00	145	290	—

KM# 153 1/96 THALER (3 Pfennig; Dreier)
Billon **Obv:** Oval arms **Rev:** Imperial orb with 96, mintmaster's mark above

Date	Mintage	VG	F	VF	XF	Unc
ND(1601-3) (b)	—	20.00	35.00	70.00	140	—
ND(1605-6) (c)	—	20.00	35.00	70.00	140	—

KM# 154 1/96 THALER (3 Pfennig; Dreier)
Billon **Obv:** Arms, mintmaster's mark above **Rev:** Imperial orb with 96 in oval baroque frame

Date	Mintage	VG	F	VF	XF	Unc
ND(1601-3) (b)	—	20.00	35.00	70.00	140	—

KM# 155 1/96 THALER (3 Pfennig; Dreier)
Billon **Obv:** Arms in ornate shield, without mintmaster's mark **Rev:** Imperial orb without value in three-lobed triangular frame

Date	Mintage	VG	F	VF	XF	Unc
ND(1601-3)	—	20.00	35.00	70.00	140	—

KM# 156 1/96 THALER (3 Pfennig; Dreier)
Billon **Rev:** Imperial orb without value in ornamented rhombus

Date	Mintage	VG	F	VF	XF	Unc
ND(1601-3)	—	20.00	35.00	75.00	150	—

KM# 157 1/96 THALER (3 Pfennig; Dreier)
Billon **Rev:** Large imperial orb without value, but symbol

Date	Mintage	VG	F	VF	XF	Unc
ND(1601-3)	—	20.00	35.00	75.00	150	—

KM# 148 1/96 THALER (3 Pfennig; Dreier)
Billon **Rev:** Smaller imperial orb with 96 in ornamented rhombus

Date	Mintage	VG	F	VF	XF	Unc
160Z (b)	—	27.00	55.00	110	225	—
1603 (b)	—	27.00	55.00	110	225	—
1606	—	27.00	55.00	110	225	—

KM# 150 1/96 THALER (3 Pfennig; Dreier)
Billon **Obv:** Arms, mintmaster's mark above **Rev:** Imperial orb with 96 in oval baroque frame, date above

Date	Mintage	VG	F	VF	XF	Unc
160Z (b)	—	27.00	55.00	110	225	—
ND (b)	—	27.00	55.00	110	225	—

KM# 151 1/96 THALER (3 Pfennig; Dreier)
Billon **Obv:** Helmet, mintmaster's mark above, divides date **Rev:** Imperial orb with 96 in oval cartouche, date above

Date	Mintage	VG	F	VF	XF	Unc
160Z (b)	—	27.00	55.00	110	225	—

KM# 152 1/96 THALER (3 Pfennig; Dreier)
Billon **Obv:** Mintmaster's mark below helmet **Rev:** Without date

Date	Mintage	VG	F	VF	XF	Unc
160Z (b)	—	27.00	55.00	110	225	—

KM# 149 1/96 THALER (3 Pfennig; Dreier)
Billon **Obv:** Mintmaster's mark left of arms

Date	Mintage	VG	F	VF	XF	Unc
1603 (c)	—	27.00	55.00	110	225	—

KM# 160 1/96 THALER (3 Pfennig; Dreier)
Billon **Obv:** Arms **Rev:** Large imperial orb with 96, mintmaster's mark at upper left

Date	Mintage	VG	F	VF	XF	Unc
ND(1605-6) (c)	—	20.00	35.00	75.00	150	—

KM# 161 1/96 THALER (3 Pfennig; Dreier)
Billon **Obv:** Oval arms **Rev:** Imperial orb with 96 divides date in ornamented rhombus, mintmaster's mark in one quadrant

Date	Mintage	VG	F	VF	XF	Unc
ND(1605-6) (c)	—	20.00	33.00	55.00	120	—

KM# 146 1/24 THALER (Reichsgroschen)
Silver **Note:** Klippe.

Date	Mintage	VG	F	VF	XF	Unc
1601 (b)	—	—	—	—	—	—
160Z (b)	—	—	—	—	—	—
1603 (b)	—	—	—	—	—	—

KM# 145 1/24 THALER (Reichsgroschen)
Silver **Obv:** Ornate shield of new city arms, ornate helmet above, crest of helmet is female figure **Obv. Legend:** MONO. RE - IP. HILD. **Rev:** Imperial orb with Z4 divides date, legend in Latin letters **Rev. Legend:** RVDOL. II. ROM. IMP. SEM. A. **Note:** Varieties exist.

Date	Mintage	VG	F	VF	XF	Unc
1601	—	20.00	33.00	55.00	115	—
1601 (b)	—	20.00	33.00	55.00	115	—
160Z (b)	—	20.00	33.00	55.00	115	—
1603 (b)	—	20.00	33.00	55.00	115	—

Date	Mintage	VG	F	VF	XF	Unc
1605	—	20.00	33.00	55.00	115	—
1605 (c)	—	20.00	33.00	55.00	115	—

KM# 137 1/24 THALER (Reichsgroschen)
Silver **Obv:** Ornately-shaped shield of new city arms in circle **Obv. Legend:** MO(N)(E): NO(VA): REIP(VB): HILDE(S)(EN). **Rev:** Imperial orb with Z4 divides date **Rev. Legend:** RVDOL. II. ROM. IMP. SEM. AV. **Note:** B/B-69, 74, 75, 81, 85. Varieties exist.

Date	Mintage	VG	F	VF	XF	Unc
1601 (a)	—	20.00	33.00	55.00	100	—
1601	—	20.00	33.00	55.00	100	—
1601 (b)	—	20.00	33.00	55.00	100	—
160Z (b)	—	20.00	33.00	55.00	100	—

KM# 139 1/24 THALER (Reichsgroschen)
Silver **Obv:** Arms, ornate helmet above **Rev:** Imperial orb with Z4 divides date, titles of Rudolf II, partly in Gothic letters **Note:** B/B-86. Varieties exist.

Date	Mintage	VG	F	VF	XF	Unc
1602 (b)	—	20.00	35.00	70.00	145	—
1603 (b)	—	20.00	35.00	70.00	145	—
1603 (c)	—	20.00	35.00	70.00	145	—
1604 (c)	—	20.00	35.00	70.00	145	—
1605 (c)	—	20.00	35.00	70.00	145	—
1605	—	20.00	35.00	70.00	115	—
1606	—	20.00	35.00	70.00	115	—
1606 (c)	—	20.00	35.00	70.00	115	—

KM# 162 1/24 THALER (Reichsgroschen)
Silver **Note:** Klippe.

Date	Mintage	VG	F	VF	XF	Unc
1602 (b)	—	—	—	—	—	—
1606 (c)	—	—	—	—	—	—

KM# 165 1/24 THALER (Reichsgroschen)
Silver **Obv:** Titles of Matthias **Note:** Varieties exist.

Date	Mintage	VG	F	VF	XF	Unc
(1)614 (d)	—	20.00	33.00	55.00	115	—
1614 (d)	—	20.00	33.00	55.00	115	—
1615 (d)	—	20.00	33.00	55.00	115	—

KM# 166 1/24 THALER (Reichsgroschen)
Silver **Obv:** Date in legend **Note:** Varieties exist.

Date	Mintage	VG	F	VF	XF	Unc
(1)614 (d)	—	20.00	33.00	55.00	115	—
(1)614	—	20.00	33.00	55.00	115	—
1615 (d)	—	20.00	33.00	55.00	115	—
1616 (d)	—	20.00	33.00	55.00	115	—
1618	—	20.00	33.00	55.00	115	—
1619	—	20.00	33.00	55.00	115	—

KM# 167 1/24 THALER (Reichsgroschen)
Silver **Obv:** Arms **Rev:** Titles of Mathias **Note:** Varieties exist.

Date	Mintage	VG	F	VF	XF	Unc
1614 (d)	—	20.00	33.00	55.00	115	—
1615 (d)	—	20.00	33.00	55.00	115	—
1616 (d)	—	20.00	33.00	55.00	115	—

KM# 168 1/24 THALER (Reichsgroschen)
Silver **Obv:** Date in legend **Note:** Varieties exist.

Date	Mintage	VG	F	VF	XF	Unc
(1)614 (d)	—	20.00	33.00	55.00	115	—
1614 (d)	—	20.00	33.00	55.00	115	—
1615 (d)	—	20.00	33.00	55.00	115	—
1616 (d)	—	20.00	33.00	55.00	115	—
1617 (d)	—	20.00	33.00	55.00	115	—
1618 (d)	—	20.00	33.00	55.00	115	—
1619 (d)	—	20.00	33.00	55.00	115	—
1619	—	20.00	33.00	55.00	115	—

KM# 169 1/24 THALER (Reichsgroschen)
Silver **Note:** Klippe.

Date	Mintage	VG	F	VF	XF	Unc
1616 (d)	—	—	—	—	—	—

KM# 170 1/24 THALER (Reichsgroschen)
Silver **Note:** Klippe.

Date	Mintage	VG	F	VF	XF	Unc
1619 (d)	—	—	—	—	—	—

KM# 185 1/24 THALER (Reichsgroschen)
Silver **Note:** Klippe.

Date	Mintage	VG	F	VF	XF	Unc
(1)6Z0 (d)	—	—	—	—	—	—
(1)6Z1	—	—	—	—	—	—

KM# 184 1/24 THALER (Reichsgroschen)
Silver **Obv:** Titles of Ferdinand II **Note:** Kipper 1/24 Thaler. Varieties exist.

Date	Mintage	VG	F	VF	XF	Unc
(1)6Z0	—	20.00	33.00	55.00	115	—
16Z0	—	20.00	33.00	55.00	115	—

Date	Mintage	VG	F	VF	XF	Unc
16Z0 (d)	—	20.00	33.00	55.00	115	—
(1)6Z0 (d)	—	20.00	33.00	55.00	115	—
ND(1620/21)	—	20.00	33.00	55.00	115	—
(1)6Z1	—	20.00	33.00	55.00	115	—
(1)6Z1 (d)	—	20.00	33.00	55.00	115	—

KM# 192 1/24 THALER (Reichsgroschen)

Silver **Obv:** Arms, ornate helmet and figure of maiden above

Date	Mintage	VG	F	VF	XF	Unc
16ZZ	—	20.00	33.00	55.00	115	—
16ZZ (e)	—	20.00	33.00	55.00	115	—

KM# 194 1/24 THALER (Reichsgroschen)

Silver **Obv:** Large ornamented arms **Rev:** Imperial orb with 24 or Z4 divides date

Date	Mintage	VG	F	VF	XF	Unc
16ZZ	—	20.00	33.00	55.00	115	—

KM# 191 1/24 THALER (Reichsgroschen)

Silver **Obv:** Imperial orb with 24 or Z4 divides date **Rev:** Arms, ornate helmet above **Note:** Varieties exist.

Date	Mintage	VG	F	VF	XF	Unc
1622 (e)	—	20.00	33.00	55.00	115	—
16ZZ (e)	—	20.00	33.00	55.00	115	—
16ZZ	—	20.00	33.00	55.00	115	—
16Z3 (e)	—	20.00	33.00	55.00	115	—
16Z3	—	20.00	33.00	55.00	115	—

KM# 193 1/24 THALER (Reichsgroschen)

Silver **Obv:** Oval arms **Rev:** Date in legend **Note:** Varieties exist.

Date	Mintage	VG	F	VF	XF	Unc
16ZZ	—	20.00	33.00	55.00	115	—
16Z3 (e)	—	20.00	33.00	55.00	115	—
16Z4 (e)	—	20.00	33.00	55.00	115	—

KM# 216 1/24 THALER (Reichsgroschen)

Silver **Obv:** Arms, ornate helmet and figure of maiden above **Note:** Varieties exist.

Date	Mintage	VG	F	VF	XF	Unc
1645 (f)	—	20.00	33.00	65.00	130	—
1646 (f)	—	20.00	33.00	65.00	130	—
1647 (f)	—	20.00	33.00	65.00	130	—

KM# 215 1/24 THALER (Reichsgroschen)

Silver **Obv:** Imperial orb with Z4 divides date, titles of Ferdinand III **Rev:** Arms

Date	Mintage	VG	F	VF	XF	Unc
1645 (f)	—	20.00	33.00	65.00	130	—

KM# 225 1/24 THALER (Reichsgroschen)

Silver **Obv:** Titles of Leopold I

Date	Mintage	VG	F	VF	XF	Unc
1661 (g)	—	—	—	—	—	—

KM# 246 1/24 THALER (Reichsgroschen)

Silver **Obv:** Oval arms with pointed bottom, ornate helmet and figure of maiden above **Obv. Legend:** DA PACEM... **Rev:** Imperial orb with 24 or Z4 divides date **Rev. Legend:** HILDESHEI STADT GELDT **Note:** Varieties exist.

Date	Mintage	VG	F	VF	XF	Unc
1688	—	16.00	30.00	60.00	120	—
1689	—	16.00	30.00	60.00	120	—
1691	—	16.00	30.00	60.00	120	—
1692	—	16.00	30.00	60.00	120	—
1693	—	16.00	30.00	60.00	120	—
1695	—	16.00	30.00	60.00	120	—
1695 HL	—	16.00	30.00	60.00	120	—
1696 HL	—	16.00	30.00	60.00	120	—
1697 HL	—	16.00	30.00	60.00	120	—
1698 HL	—	16.00	30.00	60.00	120	—
1699 HL	—	16.00	30.00	60.00	120	—
1700 HL	—	16.00	30.00	60.00	120	—

KM# 147 1/16 THALER (2 Schilling)

Silver **Obv:** Date divided by arms

Date	Mintage	VG	F	VF	XF	Unc
1601 (b)	—	—	—	—	—	—

KM# 140.1 1/16 THALER (2 Schilling)

Silver **Obv:** New city arms in ornamented shield with concave sides superimposed on floriated cross, date divided above shield **Obv. Legend:** MO. NO - REIP - HILDE - NSHE(IM). **Rev:** Crowned imperial eagle, 16 in orb on breast **Note:** B/B-84. Varieties exist. Previous KM #140.

Date	Mintage	VG	F	VF	XF	Unc
1601	—	33.00	80.00	160	325	—
1601 (b)	—	33.00	80.00	160	325	—
1601 (b)	—	—	—	—	—	—
160Z (c) Rare	—	—	—	—	—	—
1605	—	33.00	80.00	160	325	—
1606	—	33.00	80.00	160	325	—

KM# 140.2 1/16 THALER (2 Schilling)

Silver **Obv:** New city arms in ornamented shield with concave sides superimposed on floriated cross divide date **Obv. Legend:** MO. NO - REIP - HILDE - NSHE(IM). **Rev:** Crowned imperial eagle, 16 in orb on breast **Note:** B/B-95.

Date	Mintage	VG	F	VF	XF	Unc
1601 (b)	—	33.00	80.00	140	220	—

KM# 186 1/16 THALER (Doppelschilling)

Silver **Obv:** Oval arms, ornate helmet and figure of maiden above **Rev:** Crowned imperial eagle, 16 in orb on breast, titles of Ferdinand II **Note:** Kipper issue.

Date	Mintage	VG	F	VF	XF	Unc
16Z0	—	—	—	—	—	—

KM# 196 1/2 REICHSORT (1/8 Thaler)

Silver **Ruler:** Ferdinand **Obv:** EIN / HALB / RICHS (or REICHS) / ORT, titles of Ferdinand II and date **Rev:** Oval arms, ornate helmet and figure of maiden above **Mint:** Moritzberg **Note:** Varieties exist.

Date	Mintage	VG	F	VF	XF	Unc
16Z3 (e)	—	—	—	—	—	—
16Z4 (e)	—	—	—	—	—	—
16Z5 (e)	—	—	—	—	—	—
16Z6 (e)	—	—	—	—	—	—
16Z7/6 (e)	—	—	—	—	—	—

KM# 204 1/2 REICHSORT (1/8 Thaler)

Silver **Obv. Inscription:** Date / EIN / HALB / REICHS / ORT

Date	Mintage	VG	F	VF	XF	Unc
16Z4 (E)	—	—	—	—	—	—

KM# 203 1/2 REICHSORT (1/8 Thaler)

Silver **Note:** Klippe.

Date	Mintage	VG	F	VF	XF	Unc
16Z4 (e)	—	—	—	—	—	—

KM# 197 1/4 THALER (Reichsort)

Silver **Obv:** Crowned imperial eagle, orb on breast, titles of Ferdinand II around, date divided in legend at top **Rev:** Ornate arms, ornate helmet and figure of maiden above **Note:** Varieties exist.

Date	Mintage	VG	F	VF	XF	Unc
16Z3 (e) Rare	—	—	—	—	—	—
16Z4 (e) Rare	—	—	—	—	—	—
16Z5 (e) Rare	—	—	—	—	—	—
16Z6 (e) Rare	—	—	—	—	—	—

Note: Künker Auction 90, 3-03, XF realized approximately $12,700

KM# 159 1/2 THALER

Silver **Obv:** Crowned imperial eagle, orb on breast, titles of Rudolf II **Rev:** Oval arms in baroque frame, figure of maiden above divides date

Date	Mintage	VG	F	VF	XF	Unc
1603 (b)	—	—	—	—	—	—

KM# 198 1/2 THALER

Silver **Obv:** Crowned imperial eagle, orb on breast, titles of Ferdinand II around, date divided in legend at top **Rev:** Ornately-shaped arms, ornate helmet and figure of maiden above

Date	Mintage	VG	F	VF	XF	Unc
16Z3 (e)	—	—	—	—	—	—
16Z4/3 (e)	—	—	—	—	—	—

KM# 206 1/2 THALER

Silver **Obv:** Arms in shield with rounded bottom, flat top

Date	Mintage	VG	F	VF	XF	Unc
16Z4 (e)	—	—	—	—	—	—

KM# 205 1/2 THALER

Silver **Obv:** Oval arms **Note:** Varieties exist.

Date	Mintage	VG	F	VF	XF	Unc
16Z4 (e) Rare	—	—	—	—	—	—
16Z5 (e) Rare	—	—	—	—	—	—
16Z6 (e) Rare	—	—	—	—	—	—
16Z7 (e) Rare	—	—	—	—	—	—
16Z8 (e) Rare	—	—	—	—	—	—

KM# 208 1/2 THALER

Silver **Note:** Klippe.

Date	Mintage	VG	F	VF	XF	Unc
16Z6 (e) Rare	—	—	—	—	—	—

KM# 164 THALER

28.0000 g., Silver **Note:** Similar to 2 Thaler, KM#172. Dav. #LS325.

Date	Mintage	VG	F	VF	XF	Unc
ND(1618)	—	3,000	5,000	8,000	13,500	—

Note: Exists with Hildesheim orb or plain orb

KM# 195.1 THALER

Silver **Obv. Legend:** MONETA * NOVE * - * REIPUB * HILDES **Note:** Similar to KM#195.1. Dav. #5417.

Date	Mintage	VG	F	VF	XF	Unc
16ZZ MW	—	450	900	1,500	2,800	—

KM# 199 THALER

Silver **Obv:** Date divided in legend at bottom **Note:** Dav. #5418.

Date	Mintage	VG	F	VF	XF	Unc
16Z3 (e)	—	375	750	1,450	2,500	—

KM# 200 THALER

Silver **Obv:** Date left of crown at top **Note:** Dav. #5418.

Date	Mintage	VG	F	VF	XF	Unc
16Z3 (e)	—	375	750	1,450	2,500	—
16Z4 (e)	—	375	750	1,450	2,500	—

KM# 195.2 THALER

Silver **Obv:** Crowned imperial eagle, orb on breast, titles of Ferdinand II around, date divided in legend at top **Rev:** Oval arms in baroque frame, ornate helmet and figure of maiden above **Note:** Dav. #5419.

Date	Mintage	VG	F	VF	XF	Unc
16Z4 (e)	—	250	500	950	1,650	—

KM# 195.3 THALER

Silver **Obv:** Crowned eagle within inner circle **Rev:** Crown above double-headed imperial eagle within beaded circle **Note:** Dav. #5420.

Date	Mintage	VG	F	VF	XF	Unc
16Z4 (e)	—	250	500	950	1,650	—
16Z5 (e)	—	250	500	950	1,650	—
16Z6 (e)	—	250	500	950	1,650	—
16Z7 (e)	—	250	500	950	1,650	—
16Z8 (e)	—	250	500	950	1,650	3,500
1631	—	250	500	950	1,650	—

KM# 250 THALER

Silver **Note:** Similar to KM#72 but titles of Leopold I around, date divided in legend at top. Dav. #5421.

Date	Mintage	VG	F	VF	XF	Unc
1690	—	800	1,600	2,800	4,500	—

KM# 141 THALER (24 Groschen)

Silver **Obv:** Shield of new city arms at bottom, ornate helmet above with figure of young female as crest **Obv. Legend:** MONETA. NOVA. ARG. - REIP. HILDENSHEIM. **Rev:** Crowned imperial eagle, Z4 in orb on breast, date divided by tail below **Rev. Legend:** RVDOL. II. D.G. ROMA. IMPER. SEMPER. AVGVS. **Note:** Dav. #9302, 5416.

Date	Mintage	VG	F	VF	XF	Unc
160Z (b) Rare	—	—	—	—	—	—

KM# A170 1-1/4 THALER

Silver **Note:** Dav. #LS324. Weight varies: 34.00-36.00 grams. Similar to 2 Thaler, KM#172.

Date	Mintage	VG	F	VF	XF	Unc
ND1618) Rare	—	—	—	—	—	—

KM# 171 1-1/2 THALER

Silver **Note:** Dav. #LS323. Weight varies: 43.00-44.00 grams. Similar to 2 Thaler, KM#172.

Date	Mintage	VG	F	VF	XF	Unc
ND(1618)	—	3,000	4,800	7,800	11,500	—

KM# 172 2 THALER

Silver **Note:** Dav. #LS322. Weight varies: 57.00-58.00 grams.

Date	Mintage	VG	F	VF	XF	Unc
ND(1618)	—	3,000	5,000	8,000	13,500	—

Note: Exists with Hildesheim orb or plain orb

KM# 173 2-1/2 THALER

74.0000 g., Silver **Note:** Cross-reference number Dav. #LS321. Similar to 2 Thaler, KM#172.

Date	Mintage	VG	F	VF	XF	Unc
ND(1618) Rare	—	—	—	—	—	—

KM# 174 3 THALER

87.0000 g., Silver **Note:** Dav. #LS320. Similar to 2 Thaler, KM#172.

Date	Mintage	VG	F	VF	XF	Unc
ND(1618) Rare	—	—	—	—	—	—

TRADE COINAGE

KM# 201 1/2 GOLDGULDEN

1.7500 g., 0.9860 Gold 0.0555 oz. AGW **Obv:** Arms in baroque frame **Rev:** Crowned imperial eagle, titles of Ferdinand II and date in legend

Date	Mintage	VG	F	VF	XF	Unc
1623 (e)	—	800	1,600	3,500	7,000	—

KM# 209 1/2 GOLDGULDEN

1.7500 g., 0.9860 Gold 0.0555 oz. AGW **Obv:** Oval arms with pointed bottom, ornate helmet and figure of maiden above **Rev:** Crowned imperial eagle, orb on breast, titles of Ferdinand II around, date in legend at top

Date	Mintage	VG	F	VF	XF	Unc
1627 (e)	—	800	1,600	3,500	7,000	—

KM# 158 GOLDGULDEN

3.5000 g., 0.9860 Gold 0.1109 oz. AGW **Obv:** Arms, ornate helmet and figure of maiden above divide date **Rev:** Crowned imperial eagle, orb on breast, titles of Rudolf II

Date	Mintage	VG	F	VF	XF	Unc
1602 (b)	—	1,000	1,950	4,600	8,500	—
1603 (b)	—	1,000	1,950	4,600	8,500	—
1606/3 (b)	—	1,000	1,950	4,600	8,500	—

KM# 202 GOLDGULDEN

3.5000 g., 0.9860 Gold 0.1109 oz. AGW **Rev:** Titles of Ferdinand II, date divided in legend at top

Date	Mintage	VG	F	VF	XF	Unc
1623 (e)	—	800	1,800	3,750	7,500	—
1627 (e)	—	800	1,800	3,750	7,500	—
1628 (e)	—	800	1,800	3,750	7,500	—

KM# 235 GOLDGULDEN

3.5000 g., 0.9860 Gold 0.1109 oz. AGW **Rev:** Titles of Leopold I

Date	Mintage	VG	F	VF	XF	Unc
1672	—	3,000	6,000	10,000	18,500	—

KM# A196 4 GOLDGULDEN

14.4800 g., 0.9860 Gold 0.4590 oz. AGW **Rev:** Titles of Ferdinand II **Note:** Struck with 1 Thaler dies, KM#195.3.

Date	Mintage	VG	F	VF	XF	Unc
16Z6 (e) Rare	—	—	—	—	—	—

PATTERNS

Including off metal strikes

KM#	Date	Mintage	Identification	Mkt Val
Pn1	16Z4	—	Mariengroschen. Gold.	—
Pn2	16Z6 (e)	—	1/2 Thaler. Gold.	—
Pn4	1700	—	3 Pfennig. Copper.	—

HOHENGEROLDSECK

The line of these lords, who had lands in Baden, began in the late 12th century. Upon the extinction of the dynasty in 1634, the territory passed to Cronberg and finally to Leyen in 1692.

RULER

Jakob, 1569-1634

LORDSHIP

REGULAR COINAGE

KM# 1 12 KREUZER (Schreckenberger)

Silver **Obv:** Crowned imperial eagle, 12 in orb on breast, titles of Ferdinand II **Rev:** Arms **Note:** Kipper 12 Kreuzer.

Date	Mintage	VG	F	VF	XF	Unc
ND(1621/2)	—	—	—	—	—	—

Note: Many forgeries known to exist

HOHENLOHE

A countship located in the vicinity of Uffenheim in Franconia and originally centered on the village and castle of present-day Hohlach. The ruling family derived its name from the place name and has been traced back as far as the 10th century. The counts gradually acquired various territories between Offenheim to Bad Mergentheim and beyond that became the basis for the many branches of the dynasty. The first of these was Weikersheim with its castle overlooking the confluence of the Vorbach with the Tauber River. In 1472, the surviving elder branch of counts was divided into Hohenlohe-Weikersheim and Hohenlohe Neuenstein. The former became extinct in 1545 and its lands reverted to Hohenlohe-Neuenstein, which itself was divided once again into Hohenlohe-Neuenstein-Neuenstein (Protestant) and Hohenlohe-Neuenstein-Waldenburg (Catholic) in 1551. Hohenlohe-Neuenstein-Neuenstein was further divided in 1610 (see) and Hohenlohe-Neuenstein-Waldenburg underwent the same process in 1600 with the establishment of Hohenlohe-Waldenburg-Pfedelbach, Hohenlohe-Waldenburg-Schillingsfürst and Hohenlohe-Waldenburg-Waldenburg. See the sections under each of these branches for the subsequent history of each. The lands of all branches of Hohenlohe were mediatized in 1806, thereafter passing to Bavaria and Württemberg.

JOINT COINAGE

From 1594 to 1622 a joint coinage was issued for all the counts of the various branches of Hohenlohe. See under each branch for names and dates of individual rulers.

MINT MARKS

N = Neuenstein (Kipper period)
S = Schwabach

MINT OFFICIALS' INITIALS

Initial	Date	Name
	1594-?	Paul Diether
	1615-21	Herr Müller

ARMS

Hohenlohe – 2 leopards passant left
Langenburg – crowned lion passant left or right above Lozengy field.

REFERENCE

A = Joseph Albrecht, **Münzgeschichte des Hauses Hohenlohe**, Öhringen, 1865.

COUNTSHIP

From 1594 to 1622 a joint coinage was issued for all the counts of the various branches of Hohenlohe. See under each branch for names and dates of individual rulers.

MINT MARKS

N – Neuenstein (Kipper period)

MINT OFFICIALS' INITIALS

Initials	Date	Name
	1594-?	Paul Diether
I	1615-21	Herr Müller

JOINT COINAGE

KM# 9 PFENNIG

Silver **Obv:** Shields of Hohenlohe and Langenburg arms **Note:** A-20, 25, 31ff. Uniface. Varieties exist.

Date	Mintage	VG	F	VF	XF	Unc
1603	—	27.00	45.00	85.00	170	—
1604	—	27.00	45.00	85.00	170	—
1605	—	27.00	45.00	85.00	170	—
1606	—	27.00	45.00	85.00	170	—
1609	—	27.00	45.00	85.00	170	—
1610	—	27.00	45.00	85.00	170	—
1615	—	27.00	45.00	85.00	170	—
1616	—	27.00	45.00	85.00	170	—

KM# 24 PFENNIG

Silver **Obv:** Langenburg arms with lion striding right, 1 above **Note:** Kipper Pfennig.

Date	Mintage	VG	F	VF	XF	Unc
ND1621/2)	—	—	—	—	—	—

KM# 25 PFENNIG

Silver **Obv:** Lion striding left

Date	Mintage	VG	F	VF	XF	Unc
ND(1621/2)	—	—	—	—	—	—

KM# 26 2 PFENNIG (1/2 Kreuzer)

Silver **Obv:** Shields of Hohenlohe and Langenburg arms with 2 above **Note:** Uniface.

Date	Mintage	VG	F	VF	XF	Unc
ND1621/2	—	—	—	—	—	—

KM# 8 1/84 THALER (3 Pfennig)

Silver **Obv:** Four-fold arms in ornamented shield **Rev:** Imperial orb with 84 divides date in rhombus **Note:** A-24, 26b, 27, 30, 32b. Varieties exist.

Date	Mintage	VG	F	VF	XF	Unc
1602	—	27.00	55.00	100	200	—
1603	—	27.00	55.00	100	200	—
1604	—	27.00	55.00	100	200	—
1605	—	27.00	55.00	100	200	—
1606	—	27.00	55.00	100	200	—
1609	—	27.00	55.00	100	200	—
1615	—	27.00	55.00	100	200	—

KM# 33 3 KREUZER (Groschen)

Silver **Rev:** Four-fold arms

Date	Mintage	VG	F	VF	XF	Unc
1622	—	33.00	60.00	120	240	—

KM# 34 3 KREUZER (Groschen)

Silver **Obv:** Imperial orb with 3 **Rev:** Hohenlohe arms, date above

Date	Mintage	VG	F	VF	XF	Unc
1622	—	33.00	60.00	120	240	—

KM# 32 3 KREUZER (Groschen)

Silver **Obv:** Crowned imperial eagle, 3 in orb on breast **Rev:** Hohenlohe arms, date in legend **Note:** Kipper 3 Groschen.

Date	Mintage	VG	F	VF	XF	Unc
1622	—	33.00	60.00	120	240	—

KM# 28 12 KREUZER (Schreckenberger)
Silver **Rev:** Four-fold arms divide date

Date	Mintage	VG	F	VF	XF	Unc
1621	—	27.00	70.00	130	265	—

KM# 29 12 KREUZER (Schreckenberger)
Silver **Rev:** Arms, date above

Date	Mintage	VG	F	VF	XF	Unc
1621	—	27.00	65.00	130	265	—

KM# 30 12 KREUZER (Schreckenberger)
Silver **Rev:** Crowned four-fold arms

Date	Mintage	VG	F	VF	XF	Unc
ND(1621)	—	27.00	65.00	130	265	—

KM# 27 12 KREUZER (Schreckenberger)
Silver **Obv:** Crowned imperial eagle, 12 in orb on breast, titles of Ferdinand II **Rev:** Crowned four-fold arms divide date **Note:** Klippe. Kipper 12 Kreuzer.

Date	Mintage	VG	F	VF	XF	Unc
1621	—	27.00	65.00	130	265	—

KM# 31 24 KREUZER (Doppelschreckenberger)
Silver **Obv:** Crowned shield of 4-fold arms divides date **Obv. Legend:** MO. NO. CO. DE HOE(N). E(T). DO. IN. LA(N)(G). **Rev:** Crowned imperial eagle, 24 in orb on breast **Rev. Legend:** FERDIN. II. D. G. RO(M). IM. SE(M). AV(G)(V). **Mint:** Neuenstein **Note:** A#78-82. Varieties exist.

Date	Mintage	VG	F	VF	XF	Unc
1621	—	45.00	90.00	180	360	—
1621 N	—	45.00	90.00	180	360	—
ND(1621)	—	45.00	90.00	180	360	—

KM# 35 24 KREUZER (Doppelschreckenberger)
Silver **Obv:** Crowned imperial eagle, 24 in orb on breast, MON: NOV:... **Rev:** Crowned four-fold arms, date in legend

Date	Mintage	VG	F	VF	XF	Unc
1622	—	45.00	90.00	180	360	—
1622 N	—	45.00	90.00	180	360	—

KM# 36 24 KREUZER (Doppelschreckenberger)
Silver **Obv:** Crowned four-fold arms divide date **Rev:** Crowned imperial eagle, 24 in circle on breast, titles of Ferdinand II

Date	Mintage	VG	F	VF	XF	Unc
(16)22	—	45.00	90.00	180	360	—

KM# 37 24 KREUZER (Doppelschreckenberger)
Silver **Obv:** Count's crown above 4-fold arms **Rev:** Crowned imperial eagle, 24 in orb on breast **Rev. Legend:** PIETATE...

Date	Mintage	VG	F	VF	XF	Unc
1622	—	45.00	90.00	180	360	—

KM# 10 1/4 THALER
Silver **Note:** Similar to KM#16.

Date	Mintage	VG	F	VF	XF	Unc
1607 Rare	—	—	—	—	—	—
1609 Rare	—	—	—	—	—	—
1610 Rare	—	—	—	—	—	—

KM# 16 1/4 THALER
Silver **Obv:** Count on horse with shield to left, titles of Matthias

Date	Mintage	VG	F	VF	XF	Unc
1615 Rare	—	—	—	—	—	—

KM# 12 1/3 THALER (1/2 Gulden)
Silver **Obv:** Count on horse in armor with shield to left, titles of Matthias

Date	Mintage	VG	F	VF	XF	Unc
1608 Rare	—	—	—	—	—	—

KM# 11 1/2 THALER
Silver **Obv:** Count on horse with shield to left, titles of Matthias

Date	Mintage	VG	F	VF	XF	Unc
1607 Rare	—	—	—	—	—	—
1609 Rare	—	—	—	—	—	—
1610 Rare	—	—	—	—	—	—

KM# 17 1/2 THALER
Silver **Obv:** Titles of Matthias

Date	Mintage	VG	F	VF	XF	Unc
1615 Rare	—	—	—	—	—	—

KM# 5 THALER
Silver **Obv:** 4-fold arms in ornamented shield, date above **Rev:** Crowned imperial eagle, orb on breast, titles of Rudolf II **Note:** Dav# 6818.

Date	Mintage	VG	F	VF	XF	Unc
1601	—	150	350	750	1,650	—

KM# 6 THALER
Silver **Obv:** Count on horse with shield to left, titles of Matthias **Note:** Varieties exist. Dav. #6819.

Date	Mintage	VG	F	VF	XF	Unc
1603	—	125	300	650	1,500	—
1605	—	125	300	650	1,500	—
1607	—	125	300	650	1,500	—
1608	—	125	300	650	1,500	—
1609	—	125	300	650	1,500	—
1610	—	125	300	650	1,500	—

KM# 18 THALER
Silver **Obv:** Count on horse with shield to left, titles of Matthias **Note:** Dav. #6820.

Date	Mintage	VG	F	VF	XF	Unc
1615	—	150	350	750	1,650	—

KM# 19 GOLDGULDEN
3.5000 g., 0.9860 Gold 0.1109 oz. AGW **Obv:** 4-fold arms divide date **Rev:** Crowned imperial eagle, orb on breast, titles of Matthias

Date	Mintage	VG	F	VF	XF	Unc
1615	—	1,500	3,000	6,000	10,500	—

TRADE COINAGE

KM# 7 DUCAT
3.5000 g., 0.9860 Gold 0.1109 oz. AGW **Obv:** 4-fold arms of Hohenlohe and Waldenburg in ornamented frame divide date, legend begins with small imperial orb **Obv. Legend:** MO.NO.COM... **Rev:** Armored and laureate figure of knight with large sword at side, helmet at feet, titles of Rudolf II

Date	Mintage	VG	F	VF	XF	Unc
1608	—	—	—	—	—	—
1610	—	—	—	—	—	—

KM# 13 DUCAT
3.5000 g., 0.9860 Gold 0.1109 oz. AGW **Obv:** 4-fold arms of Hohenlohe and Waldenburg divide date as 1-6/0-8 **Obv. Legend:** M: NO; COM:... **Rev:** Crowned imperial eagle, orb on breast, titles of Rudolf II

Date	Mintage	VG	F	VF	XF	Unc
1608	—	—	—	—	—	—

KM# 20 DUCAT
3.5000 g., 0.9860 Gold 0.1109 oz. AGW **Obv:** Four-fold arms in ornamented shield divide date **Rev:** Knight standing 3/4 right, titles of Matthias

Date	Mintage	VG	F	VF	XF	Unc
1615 Rare	—	—	—	—	—	—

KM# 15 2 DUCAT
7.0000 g., 0.9860 Gold 0.2219 oz. AGW **Obv:** Four-fold arms in ornamented shield divide date **Rev:** Knight standing 3/4 right, titles of Rudolf II

Date	Mintage	VG	F	VF	XF	Unc
1610 Rare	—	—	—	—	—	—

KM# 21 2 DUCAT
7.0000 g., 0.9860 Gold 0.2219 oz. AGW **Rev:** Titles of Matthias

Date	Mintage	VG	F	VF	XF	Unc
1615 Rare	—	—	—	—	—	—

KM# 22 3 DUCAT
10.5000 g., 0.9860 Gold 0.3328 oz. AGW **Obv:** Knight on horseback **Rev:** Ornate helmets, date above **Note:** Similar to 1 Thaler, KM#18.

Date	Mintage	VG	F	VF	XF	Unc
1615 Rare	—	—	—	—	—	—

KM# 23 4 DUCAT
14.0000 g., 0.9860 Gold 0.4438 oz. AGW **Obv:** Knight on horseback **Rev:** Ornate helmets, date above **Note:** Similar to 1 Thaler, KM#18.

Date	Mintage	VG	F	VF	XF	Unc
1615 Rare	—	—	—	—	—	—

HOHENLOHE-LANGENBURG

A branch of Hohenlohe-Neuenstein founded in 1610 and was the Protestant line of the family. It was divided again in 1701, Langenburg being one of the cointinuing entities. The count gained princely rank in 1764, but lost his territory as a result of the mediatization of 1806.

RULERS
Philipp Ernst, 1610-1629
Ludwig Krato, 1629-1632
Joachim Albrecht, 1632-1675
Heinrich Friedrich, 1675-1699
Albrecht Wolfgang, 1699-1715

MINT MARKS
K - Kirchberg
L - Langenburg

MINTMASTERS' INITIALS

Date	Name
1621-23	Egidius Poller at Kirchberg
1621-22	Gerhard Dreyer von Hanau at Langenburg
1622	Jeremias Delssner at Langenburg
1622-23	Jacob de Lannon at Langenburg

COUNTSHIP

REGULAR COINAGE

KM# 16 1/84 THALER (3 Pfennig)
Silver **Obv:** Adjacent shields of Hohenlohe and Langenburg arms crown above **Rev:** Imperial orb with 84 divides date in rhombus

Date	Mintage	VG	F	VF	XF	Unc
1623	—	—	—	—	—	—

KM# 14 3 KREUZER (Groschen)
Silver

Date	Mintage	VG	F	VF	XF	Unc
16Z3	—	—	—	—	—	—

KM# 15 3 KREUZER (Groschen)
Silver **Obv:** 4-fold arms without crown divide date

Date	Mintage	VG	F	VF	XF	Unc
(16)23	—	—	—	—	—	—

KM# 5 12 KREUZER (Schreckenberger)
Silver **Obv:** Crowned 4-fold arms divide date **Rev:** Crowned imperial eagle, 1Z in orb on breast, titles of Ferdianand II **Note:** Kipper 12 Kreuzer

Date	Mintage	VG	F	VF	XF	Unc
16Z1	—	27.00	55.00	110	220	—

KM# 9 12 KREUZER (Schreckenberger)
Silver **Rev:** Date in legend

Date	Mintage	VG	F	VF	XF	Unc
16ZZ	—	27.00	55.00	110	220	—

KM# 7 24 KREUZER (Doppelschreckenberg)
Silver **Obv:** Bust right **Rev:** Crowned four-fold arms

Date	Mintage	VG	F	VF	XF	Unc
16Z1	—	80.00	160	300	600	—
16ZZ	—	80.00	160	300	600	—

KM# 8 24 KREUZER (Doppelschreckenberg)
Silver **Rev:** Z4 in legend at bottom

Date	Mintage	VG	F	VF	XF	Unc
1621	—	80.00	160	300	600	—

KM# 13 24 KREUZER (Doppelschreckenberg)
Silver **Obv:** Titles of Ferdinand II

Date	Mintage	VG	F	VF	XF	Unc
ND(1621/22)	—	80.00	160	300	600	—

KM# 6 24 KREUZER (Doppelschreckenberg)
Silver **Obv:** Facing bust, 24 in legend **Rev:** Four-fold arms divide date **Note:** Kipper 24 Kreuzer

Date	Mintage	VG	F	VF	XF	Unc
16Z1	—	90.00	170	300	600	—

KM# 12 24 KREUZER (Doppelschreckenberg)
Silver **Obv:** Crowned four-fold arms **Note:** Varieties exist.

Date	Mintage	VG	F	VF	XF	Unc
16ZZ	—	33.00	75.00	140	285	—
16ZZ K	—	33.00	75.00	140	285	—
16ZZ L	—	33.00	75.00	140	285	—

KM# 10 24 KREUZER (Doppelschreckenberg)
Silver **Obv:** Bust right, date below **Rev:** Crowned imperial eagle, Z4 in orb on breast

Date	Mintage	VG	F	VF	XF	Unc
16ZZ K	—	80.00	160	325	650	—

KM# 11 24 KREUZER (Doppelschreckenberg)
Silver **Obv:** Bust right **Rev:** Date in legend

Date	Mintage	VG	F	VF	XF	Unc
16ZZ	—	90.00	180	360	725	—

KM# 17 THALER
Silver **Subject:** 50th Anniversary of Territorial Division **Obv:** 4-fold arms in inner circle, legend around **Rev:** Crowned imperial eagle **Note:** Dav. #6832.

Date	Mintage	VG	F	VF	XF	Unc
16Z3	—	850	1,500	2,500	3,750	—

KM# 18 THALER
Silver **Obv:** Oval arms in baroque frame divide date **Note:** Dav. #6833.

Date	Mintage	VG	F	VF	XF	Unc
1623	—	900	1,650	2,750	4,500	—

HOHENLOHE-NEUENSTEIN-NEUENSTEIN

The division of 1551 established the Protestant line of counts at Neuenstein and the Catholic line at Waldenburg.

RULERS
Wolfgang, 1575-1610
Kraft, 1610-1641
Wolfgang Julius, 1641-1698

MINT MARKS
A - Augsburg

MINT OFFICIALS' INITIALS

Initials	Date	Name
IIR	1623-24	Johann Jacob Rephun at Neuenstein
GFN	1682-1724	Georg Friedrich Nürnberger at Nüremberg

COUNTSHIP

REGULAR COINAGE

KM# 10 HELLER
Silver **Obv:** Adjacent arms of Hohenlohe and Langenburg in two shields, CGVH above, date below. **Note:** Uniface.

Date	Mintage	VG	F	VF	XF	Unc
(16)23	—	33.00	70.00	130	265	—

KM# 15 1/84 THALER (3 Pfennig - 1 Dreier)
Silver **Obv:** Solitary Hohenlohe arms in crowned rhombus, CG-VH divided near top **Rev:** Imperial orb with 84 divides date in rhombus

Date	Mintage	VG	F	VF	XF	Unc
1623 A	—	45.00	90.00	180	360	—

KM# 21 1/84 THALER (3 Pfennig - 1 Dreier)
Silver **Obv:** Two leopards right in Hohenlohe arms

Date	Mintage	VG	F	VF	XF	Unc
16Z4 IIR	—	45.00	90.00	180	360	—

KM# 11 KREUZER
Silver

Date	Mintage	VG	F	VF	XF	Unc
16Z3	—	40.00	80.00	160	325	—

KM# 12 2 KREUZER (1/2 Batzen)
Silver **Obv:** Imperial orb with 2, titles of Ferdinand II **Rev:** Crowned 3-fold arms, date in legend

Date	Mintage	VG	F	VF	XF	Unc
1623	—	45.00	90.00	180	360	—
1624	—	45.00	90.00	180	360	—

KM# 13 2 KREUZER (1/2 Batzen)
Silver **Obv:** Date divided by orb

Date	Mintage	VG	F	VF	XF	Unc
1623	—	45.00	90.00	180	360	—

KM# 20 2 KREUZER (1/2 Batzen)
Silver **Obv:** Imperial orb with 2 **Rev:** Crowned adjacent arms of Hohenlohe and Langenburg, date above

Date	Mintage	VG	F	VF	XF	Unc
16Z4	—	45.00	90.00	180	360	—

KM# 23 2 KREUZER (1/2 Batzen)
Silver **Obv:** Z in orb on breast

Date	Mintage	VG	F	VF	XF	Unc
1628	—	45.00	90.00	180	360	—

KM# 14 3 KREUZER (Groschen)
Silver **Obv:** Crowned imperial eagle, 3 in shield on breast, titles of Ferdinand II **Rev:** 4-fold arms, date above

Date	Mintage	VG	F	VF	XF	Unc
1623	—	55.00	100	200	400	—
1623 A	—	55.00	100	200	400	—

KM# 30 4 KREUZER (Batzen)
Silver

Date	Mintage	VG	F	VF	XF	Unc
1697 GFN	—	25.00	55.00	110	220	—

KM# 5 12 KREUZER (Schreckenberger)
Silver **Obv:** Crowned imperial eagle, 12 in orb on breast, titles of Ferdinand II **Rev:** Crowned 4-fold arms divide date

Date	Mintage	VG	F	VF	XF	Unc
1621	—	—	—	—	—	—

KM# 6 24 KREUZER (Doppelschreckenberger)
Silver **Ruler:** Kraft **Obv:** Crowned shield of 4-fold arms divides date **Obv. Legend:** CRAFT COM. DE. HOEN. ET. DO. I. LANG. **Rev:** Crowned imperial eagle, 24 in orb on breast **Rev. Legend:** FERDIN. II. D. G. ROM. IM. SEM. AVGV. **Mint:** Neuenstein **Note:** A-103. Kipper issue.

Date	Mintage	VG	F	VF	XF	Unc
1621	—	45.00	95.00	190	385	—

KM# 8 24 KREUZER (Doppelschreckenberger)
Silver **Obv:** Crowned 4-fold arms, date in legend **Rev:** Crowned imperial eagle, 24 in orb on breast **Rev. Legend:** PIETATE... **Mint:** Weickersheim **Note:** Joint issues with Philipp Ernst of Hohenlohe-Neuenstein-Langenburg.

Date	Mintage	VG	F	VF	XF	Unc
1622	—	115	235	475	—	—

KM# 7 24 KREUZER (Doppelschreckenberger)
Silver **Obv:** Bust right **Rev:** Crowned 4-fold arms, date above

Date	Mintage	VG	F	VF	XF	Unc
1622	—	225	450	800	1,350	—

KM# 9 24 KREUZER (Doppelschreckenberger)
Silver **Obv:** Crowned 4-fold arms divide date, titles of Kraft and Philipp Ernst

Date	Mintage	VG	F	VF	XF	Unc
1622	—	250	500	975	—	—

KM# 16 THALER
Silver **Obv:** Crowned imperial eagle, titles of Ferdinand II **Rev:** Crowned 4-fold arms divide date **Note:** Dav. #6823.

Date	Mintage	VG	F	VF	XF	Unc
1623	—	1,400	2,700	5,400	9,000	—

KM# 18 THALER

Silver **Note:** Dav. #6824.

Date	Mintage	VG	F	VF	XF	Unc
1623	—	300	550	1,100	2,200	—
1624	—	350	650	1,200	2,400	—

KM# 17 THALER

Silver **Note:** Klippe. Dav. #6823A.

Date	Mintage	VG	F	VF	XF	Unc
1623 Rare	—	—	—	—	—	—

KM# 19.1 THALER

Silver **Note:** Sole issue of Hohenlohe-Neuenstein-Neuenstein. Varieties exist. Dav. #6825.

Date	Mintage	VG	F	VF	XF	Unc
1623	—	180	350	775	1,500	—
1624	—	240	475	1,000	2,100	—
1625	—	240	475	1,000	2,100	—

KM# 19.2 THALER

Silver **Note:** Dav. #6826.

Date	Mintage	VG	F	VF	XF	Unc
16Z4	—	210	350	775	1,600	3,000

KM# 22 THALER

Silver **Note:** Klippe. Dav. #6825A

Date	Mintage	VG	F	VF	XF	Unc
1625 Rare	—	—	—	—	—	—

KM# 25 THALER

Silver **Obv:** Ornate 4-fold arms with central shield, three helmets above **Rev:** Knight on horseback springing left, globe below divides date **Note:** Dav. #6827.

Date	Mintage	VG	F	VF	XF	Unc
163Z	—	350	650	1,150	2,100	—

KM# 31 THALER

Silver **Note:** Dav. #6831.

Date	Mintage	VG	F	VF	XF	Unc
1697 GFN	—	180	350	700	1,500	2,400

TRADE COINAGE

KM# 26 DUCAT

3.5000 g., 0.9860 Gold 0.1109 oz. AGW **Obv:** Ornate 4-fold arms with central shield, three helmets above **Rev:** Knight on horseback springing left, globe below divides date

Date	Mintage	VG	F	VF	XF	Unc
1632 Rare	—	—	—	—	—	—

KM# 32 DUCAT

3.5000 g., 0.9860 Gold 0.1109 oz. AGW

Date	Mintage	VG	F	VF	XF	Unc
1697 GFN	—	—	850	1,800	3,600	6,600

KM# 33 8 DUCAT

28.0000 g., 0.9860 Gold 0.8876 oz. AGW **Note:** Similar to 1 Thaler, KM#31.

Date	Mintage	VG	F	VF	XF	Unc
1697 GFN Rare	—	—	—	—	—	—

HOHENLOHE-NEUENSTEIN-OEHRINGEN

This principality was located in southern Germany. The Neuenstein-Öhringen line was founded in 1610 and the first prince of the empire from this line was proclaimed in 1764. The line became extinct in 1805 and the lands passed to Ingelfingen.

RULERS

Johann Friedrich I, 1641-1702
Wolfgang Julius von Neuenstein, 1641-1698
Siegfried von Weikersheim, 1645-1684
Johann Ludwig von Künzelsau, 1641-1689

MINT OFFICIALS' INITIALS

Initial	Date	Name
(a) = 2 horseshoes	1668-97	Johann Christoph Holeisen at Augsburg

COUNTSHIP

REGULAR COINAGE

KM# 17 1/8 THALER

Silver **Ruler:** Johann Friedrich I **Mint:** Augsburg **Note:** Similar to 1/4 Thaler, KM#18. Struck from ducat dies, KM# 22.

Date	Mintage	VG	F	VF	XF	Unc
1699 (a)	—	135	275	500	1,025	—

KM# 18 1/4 THALER

7.2000 g., Silver **Ruler:** Johann Friedrich I **Mint:** Augsburg **Note:** Struck from ducat dies, KM# 22.

Date	Mintage	VG	F	VF	XF	Unc
1699 (a)	—	135	275	525	1,025	—

KM# 19 1/2 THALER (60 Kreuzer)

Silver **Ruler:** Johann Friedrich I **Obv:** Knight on horse leaping left over globe below, which divides date, DEO - DUCE before and after knight, titles of Johann Friedrich I around and value "1/2 Thr. 60 Kr" in margin at bottom **Rev:** Ornately shaped shield of 4-fold arms with central shield, 3 ornate helmets above, titles continued **Mint:** Augsburg **Note:** Albrecht 131.

Date	Mintage	VG	F	VF	XF	Unc
1699 (a)	—	135	275	525	1,025	—

KM# 15 THALER

Silver **Ruler:** Johann Friedrich I **Rev:** Age of count is 79 in legend **Mint:** Augsburg **Note:** Dav. #6828.

Date	Mintage	VG	F	VF	XF	Unc
1696 (a)	—	325	600	1,200	2,000	4,000

KM# 20 THALER

Silver **Ruler:** Johann Friedrich I **Obv:** Knight on horse leaping left over globe below, which divides date, DEO - DUCE before and after knight, value "1/2 Thr. 60 kr" in margin at bottom **Obv. Legend:** IOHAN. FRIDERIC. COMES. DE. - HOHENLOHE. ET. GLEICHEN **Rev:** Ornately-shaped shield of 4-fold arms with central shield, 3 ornate helmets above **Rev. Legend:** DOM. IN LANGENB. & CRANICHF. SEN & FEVD. ADMIN. ÆT. S. 83. **Mint:** Augsburg **Note:** Struck from 1/2 Thaler dies, KM#19, on thick flan, retaining statement of value as "1/2 Thr. 60 kr." Dav. #6830.

Date	Mintage	VG	F	VF	XF	Unc
1699 (a)	—	325	600	1,250	2,100	4,150

KM# 21 2 THALER

Silver **Ruler:** Johann Friedrich I **Obv:** Knight on horse leaping left over globe below, which divides date, DEO - DUCE before and after knight, value "1/2 Thr. 60 kr" in margin at bottom **Obv. Legend:** IOHAN. FRIDERIC. COMES. DE. - HOHENLOHE. ET. GLEICHEN. **Rev:** Ornately-shaped shield of 4-fold arms with central shield, 3 ornate helmets above **Rev. Legend:** DOM. IN LANGENB. & CRANICHF. SEN & FEVD. ADMIN. ÆT. S. 83. **Mint:** Augsburg **Note:** Struck from 1/2 Thaler dies, KM#19, on thick flan, retaining statement of value as "1/2 Thr. 60 kr." Dav# 6829.

Date	Mintage	VG	F	VF	XF	Unc
1699 (a) Rare	—	—	—	—	—	—

TRADE COINAGE

KM# 22 DUCAT

3.5000 g., 0.9860 Gold 0.1109 oz. AGW **Ruler:** Johann Friedrich I **Obv:** Equestrian figure of knight riding left above globe dividing date in inner circle **Rev:** Arms topped by 3 helms **Mint:** Augsburg

Date	Mintage	VG	F	VF	XF	Unc
1699 (a)	—	725	1,400	2,700	4,500	—

KM# 23 2 DUCAT

7.0000 g., 0.9860 Gold 0.2219 oz. AGW **Ruler:** Johann Friedrich I **Mint:** Augsburg

Date	Mintage	VG	F	VF	XF	Unc
1699 (a) Rare	—	—	—	—	—	—

KM# 25 7 DUCAT

24.5000 g., 0.9860 Gold 0.7766 oz. AGW **Ruler:** Johann Friedrich I **Obv:** Knight on horse leaping left, globe below divides date **Rev:** Ornate 4-fold arms with central shield, 3 ornate helmets above **Mint:** Augsburg

Date	Mintage	VG	F	VF	XF	Unc
1700 (a) Rare	—	—	—	—	—	—

HOHENLOHE-NEUENSTEIN-WEIKERSHEIM

Established as a branch of Hohenlohe-Neuenstein in the division of 1610, it became extinct in one generation and passed to Hohenlohe-Neuenstein-Neuenstein from which line the younger brothers ruled Weikersheim until 1756.

RULERS

Georg Friedrich, 1610-1645
Siegfried, 1645-1684

MINT MARK

N – Nuremberg

COUNTSHIP

REGULAR COINAGE

KM# 5.1 THALER

Silver **Obv:** Horseman left, shield below divides date within circle **Obv. Legend:** GEORGE: FRID: COM: -DE: **Rev:** Crowned double eagle with orb on breast **Note:** Dav. #6821.

Date	Mintage	VG	F	VF	XF	Unc
1623	—	450	825	1,300	2,500	—

KM# 5.2 THALER

Silver **Obv:** Shield below horse divides date and breaks through inner circle **Note:** Dav. #6822.

Date	Mintage	VG	F	VF	XF	Unc
16Z4	—	525	900	1,450	2,650	—

HOHENLOHE-PFEDELBACH

Established as one of three lines of the Waldenburg (Catholic) branch of Hohenlohe in 1600. It became extinct in 1728, passed to Hohenlohe-Bartenstein. A new line was established as Hohenlohe-Bartenstein-Pfedelbach (which see).

RULER

Ludwig Gottfried, 1685-1728

COUNTSHIP

REGULAR COINAGE

KM# 5 PFENNIG

Silver **Note:** Uniface. Adjacent shields of Hohenlohe and Langenburg arms, LE above.

Date	Mintage	VG	F	VF	XF	Unc
ND(ca.1610)	—	27.00	55.00	110	225	—

KM# 14 2 KREUZER (1/2 Batzen)

Silver **Obv:** Crowned arms within circle, date above **Rev:** Value within orb

Date	Mintage	VG	F	VF	XF	Unc
1623	—	55.00	110	190	385	—

KM# 10 3 KREUZER (Groschen)

Silver **Obv:** Crowned four-fold arms divide date **Rev:** Crowned imperial eagle, 3 in orb on breast, titles of Ferdinand II

Date	Mintage	VG	F	VF	XF	Unc
(16)21	—	25.00	50.00	100	200	—
(16)ZZ	—	25.00	50.00	100	200	—

KM# 11 24 KREUZER (Doppelschreckenberger)

Silver **Obv:** 4-fold arms, date divided by crown above **Rev:** Crowned imperial eagle, 24 in orb on breast, titles of Ferdinand II

Date	Mintage	VG	F	VF	XF	Unc
1621	—	35.00	75.00	150	300	—

KM# 12 24 KREUZER (Doppelschreckenberger)

Silver **Rev:** Date divided by arms

Date	Mintage	VG	F	VF	XF	Unc
1622	—	35.00	75.00	150	300	—

KM# 13 THALER

Silver **Note:** Similar to KM#15 but titles of Ludwig Eberhard on reverse. Dav. #6834.

Date	Mintage	VG	F	VF	XF	Unc
1622	—	850	1,350	2,450	4,500	—

KM# 15 THALER

Silver **Subject:** Joint Coinage with Philipp Heinrich of Hohenlohe-Waldenburg-Waldenburg **Obv:** Titles of both counts **Rev:** Crown above double-headed imperial eagle within circle **Note:** Dav. #6835.

Date	Mintage	VG	F	VF	XF	Unc
1623	—	625	1,200	2,300	3,850	—

PATTERNS

Including off metal strikes

KM#	Date	Mintage	Identification	Mkt Val
Pn1	1622	—	Thaler. Gold. KM#13	—

HOHENLOHE-WALDENBURG-SCHILLINGSFURST

In 1600 the Pfedelbach, Waldenburg and Schillingsfürst lines of Hohenlohe were established from Waldenburg, the Catholic branch of the family. Waldenburg became extinct in 1679 with all lands passing to Schillingsfurst. The count gained the rank of prince in 1744, but the line only lasted until mediatization in 1806.

RULERS

Georg Friedrich II, 1600-1635
Moritz Friedrich, 1635-1646
Georg Adolf, 1646-1656
Ludwig Gustav, 1656-1697
Philipp Ernst, 1697-1753

MINT MARKS

F - Friedberg

MINTMASTERS' INITIALS

Initial	Date	Name
AD	1689-90	Andreas Dittmar
GFN	1682-1724	Georg Friedrich Nürnberger in Nuremberg
IR	ca.1690	

NOTE: Mints functioned at Bartenstein and Schillingsfürst during the Kipper Period.

COUNTSHIP

REGULAR COINAGE

KM# 19 1/84 THALER (3 Pfennig)
Silver **Ruler:** Ludwig Gustav **Obv:** Crowned arms of Hohenlohe and Langenburg in ornamented shield **Rev:** Imperial orb with 84 divides date

Date	Mintage	VG	F	VF	XF	Unc
1685	—	33.00	65.00	130	265	—

KM# 20 1/84 THALER (3 Pfennig)
Silver **Ruler:** Ludwig Gustav **Obv:** 3 shields of arms, 2 larger above, 1 smaller below divides date, F in middle, crown above **Rev:** Imperial orb with 84 in ornamented rhombus, alchemical symbols to left and right of orb **Note:** Varieties exist.

Date	Mintage	VG	F	VF	XF	Unc
1685 F	—	25.00	55.00	110	220	—
1689 AD	—	25.00	55.00	110	220	—
1690 AD	—	25.00	55.00	110	220	—
1690 IR	—	25.00	55.00	110	220	—
1690	—	25.00	55.00	110	220	—
1691	—	25.00	55.00	110	220	—

KM# 5 3 KREUZER (Groschen)
Silver **Ruler:** Georg Friedrich II **Obv:** Imperial orb with 3 divides date, titles of Ferdinand II **Rev:** Crowned round 4-fold arms **Note:** Kipper 3 Kreuzer.

Date	Mintage	VG	F	VF	XF	Unc
1622	—	35.00	75.00	150	300	—

KM# 15 3 KREUZER (Groschen)
Silver **Ruler:** Ludwig Gustav

Date	Mintage	VG	F	VF	XF	Unc
1684	—	35.00	75.00	150	300	—
ND	—	35.00	75.00	150	300	—

KM# 21 1/24 THALER (3-3/4 Kreuzer)
Silver **Ruler:** Ludwig Gustav **Obv:** Imperial orb with 24, titles of Ludwig Gustav **Rev:** Crowned oval 4-fold arms

Date	Mintage	VG	F	VF	XF	Unc
ND	—	—	—	—	—	—

KM# 29 4 KREUZER (Batzen)
Silver **Ruler:** Ludwig Gustav

Date	Mintage	VG	F	VF	XF	Unc
1696	—	20.00	45.00	90.00	185	—

KM# 18 6 KREUZER
Silver **Ruler:** Ludwig Gustav **Obv:** Similar to 4 Kreuzer, KM#29 **Rev:** Phoenix in flames, F. VI K. above, date in legend

Date	Mintage	VG	F	VF	XF	Unc
1685	—	45.00	90.00	180	360	—

KM# 25 6 KREUZER
Silver **Ruler:** Ludwig Gustav

Date	Mintage	VG	F	VF	XF	Unc
1691	—	45.00	90.00	180	360	—

KM# 30 1/15 THALER (2 Groschen)
Silver **Ruler:** Ludwig Gustav **Obv:** Crowned 4-fold arms between palm branches **Rev:** Date in legend **Rev. Legend:** +XV / + / EINEN / REICHS / THALR / GFN

Date	Mintage	VG	F	VF	XF	Unc
1696 GFN	—	—	—	—	—	—

KM# 22 1/12 THALER (2 Groschen)
2.5900 g., Silver **Ruler:** Ludwig Gustav **Obv. Legend:** LVDGVST.COMAB.HOHENLO.DI.LANG **Rev. Legend:** 12 EINEN REICHS THALER /date **Note:** Varieties exist.

Date	Mintage	VG	F	VF	XF	Unc
1685	—	27.00	65.00	120	240	—
1686	—	27.00	65.00	120	240	—
1689	—	27.00	65.00	120	240	—
1690	—	27.00	65.00	120	240	—
1691	—	27.00	65.00	120	240	—
1692	—	27.00	65.00	120	240	—

KM# 26 15 KREUZER
Silver **Ruler:** Ludwig Gustav **Obv:** Bust right **Rev:** Hohenlohe arms, crown above divides date, value XV below

Date	Mintage	VG	F	VF	XF	Unc
1692	—	165	375	575	1,150	—

KM# 27 15 KREUZER
Silver **Ruler:** Ludwig Gustav **Rev:** Date undivided in legend

Date	Mintage	VG	F	VF	XF	Unc
1692	—	165	375	575	1,150	—

KM# 10 24 KREUZER (Doppelschreckenberger)
Silver **Ruler:** Georg Friedrich II **Obv:** Bust right, date in legend above, value in legend below **Rev:** 4-fold arms, titles of Georg Friedrich in legend

Date	Mintage	VG	F	VF	XF	Unc
1621	—	350	700	1,350	2,650	—

KM# 6 24 KREUZER (Doppelschreckenberger)
Silver **Ruler:** Georg Friedrich II **Obv:** Bust right **Rev:** Crowned imperial eagle, 24 on breast **Note:** Kipper 24 Kreuzer.

Date	Mintage	VG	F	VF	XF	Unc
ND(1621/2)	—	—	—	—	—	—

KM# 7 24 KREUZER (Doppelschreckenberger)
Silver **Ruler:** Georg Friedrich II **Obv:** Bust right divides date **Rev:** Crowned 4-fold arms, value (24) in legend

Date	Mintage	VG	F	VF	XF	Unc
1622	—	—	—	—	—	—

KM# 8 24 KREUZER (Doppelschreckenberger)
Silver **Ruler:** Georg Friedrich II **Obv:** Bust right **Rev:** Date in legend

Date	Mintage	VG	F	VF	XF	Unc
16ZZ	—	—	—	—	—	—

KM# 9 24 KREUZER (Doppelschreckenberger)
Silver **Ruler:** Georg Friedrich II **Obv:** Bust right **Rev:** 4-fold arms in ornamented square, value (24) below, date in legend

Date	Mintage	VG	F	VF	XF	Unc
1622	—	—	—	—	—	—

KM# 28 2/3 THALER (Gulden)
Silver **Ruler:** Ludwig Gustav

Date	Mintage	VG	F	VF	XF	Unc
1693	—	—	—	—	—	—

Note: Reportedly struck in Frankfurt about 1861-62

KM# 16 THALER
Silver **Ruler:** Ludwig Gustav **Note:** Dav. #6836.

Date	Mintage	VG	F	VF	XF	Unc
1684 Rare	—	—	—	—	—	—

KM# 31 THALER
Silver **Ruler:** Ludwig Gustav **Note:** Dav. #6837.

Date	Mintage	VG	F	VF	XF	Unc
MDCXCVI (1696) GFN	—	550	1,000	2,000	3,500	—

KM# 35 THALER
Silver **Ruler:** Philipp Ernst **Obv:** Titles of Philipp Ernst **Note:** Dav. #6838.

Date	Mintage	VG	F	VF	XF	Unc
MDCC (1700 GFN)	—	650	1,200	2,500	4,000	—

TRADE COINAGE

KM# 17 DUCAT
3.5000 g., 0.9860 Gold 0.1109 oz. AGW **Ruler:** Ludwig Gustav

Date	Mintage	VG	F	VF	XF	Unc
1684 Rare	—	—	—	—	—	—

KM# 32 DUCAT

3.5000 g., 0.9860 Gold 0.1109 oz. AGW **Ruler:** Ludwig Gustav **Obv:** Bust left **Obv. Legend:** L. G. S. R. I. C. A-H. E. D. I. L **Rev:** Crowned and mantled arms

Date	Mintage	VG	F	VF	XF	Unc
1696 Rare	—	—	—	—	—	—

KM# 36 8 DUCAT

28.0000 g., 0.9860 Gold 0.8876 oz. AGW **Ruler:** Philipp Ernst **Note:** Struck with 1 Thaler dies, KM#35. Actual weight = 8-1/4 ducat.

Date	Mintage	VG	F	VF	XF	Unc
MDCC (1700 GFN) Rare	—	—	—	—	—	—

HOHENLOHE-WALDENBURG-WALDENBURG

Founded in the division of Waldenburg in 1600 and extinct in 1679. Possessions passed to Hohenlohe-Waldenburg-Schillingsfürst.

RULERS

Philipp Heinrich, 1600-1644
Wolfgang Friedrich, 1644-1658
Philipp Gottfried, 1658-1679

Mints functioned at Waldenburg and Untersteinbach.

COUNTSHIP

REGULAR COINAGE

KM# 1 3 KREUZER (Groschen)

Silver **Obv:** Crowned imperial eagle, 3 in orb on breast, titles of Ferdinand II **Rev:** Four-fold arms **Note:** Kipper 3 Kreuzer. Varieties exist.

Date	Mintage	VG	F	VF	XF	Unc
ND(1621/2)	—	—	—	—	—	—

HOHENZOLLERN-HECHINGEN

Located in southern Germany, the Hechingen line was founded in 1576. The family received the mint right in 1471 and the counts were raised to the rank of prince of the empire in 1623. As a result of the 1848 revolutions the prince abdicated in favor of Prussia in 1849.

RULERS

Eitel Friedrich IV, 1576-1605
Johann Georg, 1605-1623
Eitel Fridrich V, 1623-1662
Philipp Christoph Friedrich, 1662-1671
Friedrich Wilhelm, 1671-1735

ARMS

Hohenzollern: Quartered square, upper left and lower right dark, upper right and lower left light (black and silver).

Hereditary Imperial Chamberlain: Two crossed sceptres.

REFERENCE:

B = Emil Bahrfeldt, **Das Münz- und Geldwesen der Fürstenthümer Hohenzollern**, Berlin, 1900.

PRINCIPALITY

REGULAR COINAGE

KM# 5 3 KREUZER (Groschen)

Silver **Obv:** Crowned imperial eagle, 3 in orb on breast, titles of Rudolf II **Rev:** Two conjoined shields of Hohenzollern and hereditary chamberlain's arms, date above

Date	Mintage	VG	F	VF	XF	Unc
1606	—	—	—	—	—	—

KM# 13 3 KREUZER (Groschen)

Silver **Obv:** Value (3) in legend below eagle

Date	Mintage	VG	F	VF	XF	Unc
1622	Inc. above	95.00	150	275	550	—

KM# 12 3 KREUZER (Groschen)

Silver **Obv:** Date in legend, titles of Ferdinand II **Rev:** Bust right **Note:** Kipper 3 Kreuzer.

Date	Mintage	VG	F	VF	XF	Unc
1622	691,000	50.00	100	200	385	—

KM# 14 3 KREUZER (Groschen)

Silver **Obv:** Bust right, value (3) in legend below **Rev:** Crowned four-fold arms, CAM. HAER..., date in legend **Note:** Varieties exist.

Date	Mintage	VG	F	VF	XF	Unc
1622	Inc. above	100	200	375	725	—

KM# 15 12 KREUZER (Dreibätzner)

Silver **Ruler:** Johann George **Obv:** Bust right **Rev:** Crowned imperial eagle, 12 in orb on breast, titles of Ferdinand II, date divided in legend at top **Note:** Kipper 12 Kreuzer.

Date	Mintage	VG	F	VF	XF	Unc
1622	39,000	—	—	—	—	—

KM# 10 24 KREUZER (1/4 Thaler = Sechsbätzner)

Silver **Obv:** Crowned 4-fold arms **Rev:** Crowned imperial eagle, 24 in orb on breast, titles of Ferdinand II, date divided at top **Note:** Kipper 24 Kreuzer or Sechsbätzner.

Date	Mintage	VG	F	VF	XF	Unc
1621	19,000	75.00	135	250	—	—

KM# 17 24 KREUZER (1/4 Thaler = Sechsbätzner)

Silver **Note:** Klippe.

Date	Mintage	VG	F	VF	XF	Unc
16ZZ	Inc. above	—	—	—	—	—

KM# 19 24 KREUZER (1/4 Thaler = Sechsbätzner)

Silver **Note:** Klippe.

Date	Mintage	VG	F	VF	XF	Unc
16ZZ	Inc. above	—	—	—	—	—

KM# 16 24 KREUZER (1/4 Thaler = Sechsbätzner)

Silver **Obv:** Bust right **Rev:** Crowned four-fold arms, CAM: HAER..., date in legend **Note:** Varieties exist.

Date	Mintage	VG	F	VF	XF	Unc
16ZZ	223,000	65.00	130	265	—	—

KM# 18 24 KREUZER (1/4 Thaler = Sechsbätzner)

Silver **Obv:** Value (24) below bust

Date	Mintage	VG	F	VF	XF	Unc
16ZZ	Inc. above	65.00	130	285	—	—

KM# 11 48 KREUZER (1/2 Thaler)

Silver **Obv:** Crowned 4-fold arms **Rev:** Crowned mperial eagle, 48 in orb on breast, titles of Ferdinand II, date divided in legend at top **Note:** Kipper 48 Kreuzer.

Date	Mintage	VG	F	VF	XF	Unc
1621	31,000	—	—	—	—	—

KM# 20 THALER

Silver **Obv:** St. George on horse right, dragon below **Rev:** Two adjacent helmeted arms of Hohenzollern and hereditary chamberlain **Note:** Dav. #6839.

Date	Mintage	VG	F	VF	XF	Unc
ND(1622) Rare	—	—	—	—	—	—

KM# 21 THALER

Silver **Obv:** Crowned imperial eagle, titles of Ferdinand II, date in legend **Rev:** Bust right **Note:** Dav. #6840.

Date	Mintage	VG	F	VF	XF	Unc
1623 Rare	140	—	—	—	—	—

HOHENZOLLERN-SIGMARINGEN

Located in southern Germany, the Sigmaringen line was founded in 1576. The counts obtained the mint right in 1471 and were raised to the rank of Prince of the Empire in 1623. As a result of the 1848 revolutions the prince abdicated in favor of Prussia in 1849.

RULERS

Karl II, 1576-1606
Johann, 1606-1638
Meinrad I, 1638-1681
Maximilian, 1681-1689
Meinrad II, 1689-1715

ARMS

Hohenzollern: Quartered square, upper left and lower right dark, upper right and lower left light (black and silver).

Sigmaringen – stag left

REFERENCE

B = Emil Bahrfeldt, **Das Münz- und Geldwesen der Fürstenthümer Hohenzollern**, Berlin, 1900.

PRINCIPALITY

REGULAR COINAGE

KM# 5 4 PFENNIG

Copper **Obv:** Hohenzollern arms in baroque frame **Rev:** IIII in wreath **Note:** Kipper 4 Pfennig.

Date	Mintage	VG	F	VF	XF	Unc
ND(1621/22)	—	45.00	95.00	190	275	—

KM# 6 3 KREUZER (Groschen)

Silver **Obv:** Crowned oval Hohenzollern arms in baroque frame **Rev:** Crowned imperial eagle, 3 in orb on breast, titles of Ferdinand II, date in legend

Date	Mintage	VG	F	VF	XF	Unc
1622	428,000	—	—	—	—	—

KM# 7 3 KREUZER (Groschen)

Silver **Rev:** Arms in shield with rounded bottom and flat top

Date	Mintage	VG	F	VF	XF	Unc
1622	Inc. above	—	—	—	—	—

KM# 8 3 KREUZER (Groschen)

Silver **Obv:** Bust of Ferdinand II right, titles around **Rev:** Crowned imperial eagle, shield on breast, value 3 in legend at bottom, date **Rev. Legend:** MON. NOVA. ARG. ZOLL.

Date	Mintage	VG	F	VF	XF	Unc
1622	Inc. above	—	—	—	—	—

KM# 9 24 KREUZER (1/4 Thaler - Sechsbätzner)

Silver **Obv:** Ornately-shaped 4-fold arms with central shield dividing date **Rev:** Crowned imperial eagle, Z4 in orb n breast, titles of Ferdinand II

Date	Mintage	VG	F	VF	XF	Unc
16ZZ	56,000	450	900	1,800	—	—

KM# 10 24 KREUZER (1/4 Thaler - Sechsbätzner)

Silver **Obv:** 4-fold arms **Rev:** 24 in orb

Date	Mintage	VG	F	VF	XF	Unc
ND(1622)	Inc. above	475	850	1,600	—	—

KM# 11 THALER

Silver **Ruler:** Johann **Subject:** In the name Johann's younger brother, Ernst Georg (d.1625). **Obv:** Oval 4-fold arms of Hohenzollern and Sigmaringen with central shield in baroque frame, titles of Ernst Georg **Rev:** Crowned imperial eagle, orb on breast, titles of Ferdinand II and date in legend

Date	Mintage	VG	F	VF	XF	Unc
16ZZ Rare	—	—	—	—	—	—

HOHNSTEIN

(Hohenstein)

The counts of Hohnstein, based in the Harz Mountains of central Germany, about 15 miles northeast of Nordhausen, descended from a line dating to the mid-12th century. With the death of Ernst VII in 1593, the dynasty became extinct and the lands were divided among several ecclesiastical and secular principalities. Eventually, most of the territories of Hohnstein went to Brandenburg-Prussia and Brunswick-Wolfenbüttel. Some of these princes struck coinage for Hohnstein.

RULERS

Friedrich Ulrich, Herzog von Braunschweig-Wolfenbüttel, 1613-1634
Johann VIII, Graf von Sayn-Wittgenstein, 1634-1657
Gustav, Graf von Sayn-Wittgenstein, 1657-1701

NOTE: For coinage after 1634, see Sayn-Wittgenstein-Hohnstein.

MINT MARKS

EL - Ellrich

MINT OFFICIALS' INITIALS

Initial	Date	Name
(f)= thistle	1620-21	
CO	1613-23	Claus Oppermann at Bayreuth
DF	1684	Daniel Friese at Klettenberg
HCH	1686	Heinrich Christoph Hille at Klettenberg
HM	1675-76	Henning Müller at Ellrich and Klettenberg
HS	1621-24	Henning Schreiber at Lauterberg
IZW	1673-76	Julius Zacharias Wefer at Ellrich
JA, JLA	1684	Johann Leonard Ahrensburg at Klettenberg
JCB	1687-88	Johann Christoph Bar at Klettenberg
PL	1675-76	Peter Lohr at Ellrich and maybe Klettenberg
TLK	1684-90	Thomas Ludolf Koch in Klettenberg

ARMS

Usually 4-fold arms, checkerboard in upper left and lower right, lion passant left above five bars in upper right and lower left, central shield with stag left.

Hohnstein only - checkerboard
Klettenberg only - stag left
Lutterberg only - lion rampant left

REFERENCE

S = Peter N. Schulten, **Die Münzen der Grafen von Hohnstein von den ersten Anfängen im Mittelalter bis zum Aussterben des gräfliches Hauses 1593**, Osnabrück, 1997.

COUNTSHIP

REGULAR COINAGE

KM# 34 6 FLITTER (3 Pfennig)

Copper **Obv:** Hohnstein arms, E-L above **Rev:** VI in center, FLITTER, date around **Mint:** Elrich

Date	Mintage	VG	F	VF	XF	Unc
16Z1	—	80.00	145	275	575	—

KM# 35 6 FLITTER (3 Pfennig)

Copper **Rev:** Imperial orb with VI, cross on orb divides date

Date	Mintage	VG	F	VF	XF	Unc
16Z1	—	85.00	145	275	575	—

KM# 12 3 PFENNIG (Dreier)

Copper **Obv:** Klettingberg arms **Rev:** III/PFEN/NING

Date	Mintage	VG	F	VF	XF	Unc
ND(1620/21)	—	60.00	120	235	475	—

KM# 10 3 PFENNIG (Dreier)

Billon **Obv:** Vertically divided two-fold arms, date above **Rev:** Imperial orb with 3 **Note:** Kipper 3 Pfennig.

Date	Mintage	VG	F	VF	XF	Unc
16Z0	—	65.00	120	235	475	—

KM# 11 3 PFENNIG (Dreier)

Copper **Obv:** Hohnstein arms, E-L above **Mint:** Elrich **Note:** Struck at Ellrich Mint.

Date	Mintage	VG	F	VF	XF	Unc
ND(1620/21)	—	60.00	120	235	475	—

KM# 33 3 PFENNIG (Dreier)
Copper **Obv:** Lutterberg arms **Rev:** Imperial orb with 3 divides date

Date	Mintage	VG	F	VF	XF	Unc
16Z1	—	60.00	120	235	475	—

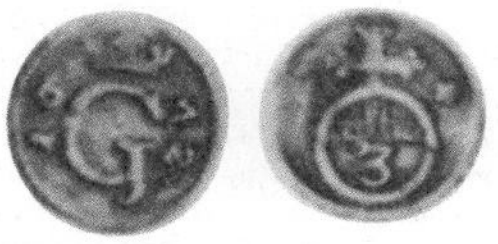

KM# 50 3 PFENNIG (Dreier)
Copper **Obv:** Crowned uncial G divides date **Rev:** Imperial orb with 3

Date	Mintage	VG	F	VF	XF	Unc
167Z	—	45.00	85.00	175	350	—

KM# 51 3 PFENNIG (Dreier)
Copper **Obv:** Ornamented shield, date above

Date	Mintage	VG	F	VF	XF	Unc
167Z	—	45.00	85.00	175	350	—

KM# 13 8 PFENNIG
Copper **Obv:** Crowned Klettenberg arms **Rev:** VIII in center, PFENNING around **Note:** Kipper 8 Pfennig.

Date	Mintage	VG	F	VF	XF	Unc
ND(1620/21)	—	60.00	115	225	450	—

KM# 5 3 KREUZER (Groschen)
Silver **Obv. Inscription:** IN GOTS GEWALT HAB ICH GESTALT. SO DER HERR GIEBT, DAS MIR GENOGT. **Rev:** Imperial orb with 3, date **Note:** Kipper 3 Kreuzer.

Date	Mintage	VG	F	VF	XF	Unc
1619	—	—	—	—	—	—

KM# 14 3 KREUZER (Groschen)
Silver **Obv:** Crowned Hohnstein arms **Rev:** Crowned imperial eagle, value (3) in legend below, date

Date	Mintage	VG	F	VF	XF	Unc
1620	—	65.00	120	235	475	—

KM# 15 3 KREUZER (Groschen)
Silver **Rev:** 3 in orb on breast

Date	Mintage	VG	F	VF	XF	Unc
1620	—	65.00	120	235	475	—

KM# 6 12 KREUZER (Schreckenberger)
Silver **Obv:** Crowned imperial eagle, 1Z in orb on breast, titles of Matthias **Rev:** Three shields, one above two, SIT NOM...

Date	Mintage	VG	F	VF	XF	Unc
ND(1619)	—	—	—	—	—	—

KM# 17 12 KREUZER (Schreckenberger)
Silver **Obv:** Four-fold arms with central shield **Rev:** Wildman holding tree in right hand, 12 in right field, date **Rev. Legend:** PRO: LEGE: ET: GREGE:

Date	Mintage	VG	F	VF	XF	Unc
1620 (f)	—	33.00	90.00	140	265	—

KM# 18 12 KREUZER (Schreckenberger)
Silver **Rev:** Value (12) below wildman

Date	Mintage	VG	F	VF	XF	Unc
1620	—	33.00	60.00	115	220	—

KM# 19 12 KREUZER (Schreckenberger)
Silver **Rev:** Wildman divides 1-2

Date	Mintage	VG	F	VF	XF	Unc
1620	—	40.00	100	165	300	—

KM# 20 12 KREUZER (Schreckenberger)
Silver **Obv:** Three shields of arms, one above two **Rev:** Wildman holding tree in right hand, 12 in right field

Date	Mintage	VG	F	VF	XF	Unc
1620	—	27.00	60.00	115	225	—
1621	—	27.00	60.00	115	225	—

KM# 22 12 KREUZER (Schreckenberger)
Silver **Obv:** Upper shield of arms divides L-W

Date	Mintage	VG	F	VF	XF	Unc
1620	—	27.00	60.00	115	225	—

KM# 23 12 KREUZER (Schreckenberger)
Silver **Obv:** Three shields of arms, one above two **Rev:** Wildman, 1Z at right, date **Rev. Legend:** PRO LEGE...

Date	Mintage	VG	F	VF	XF	Unc
1620	—	27.00	65.00	125	230	—

KM# 24 12 KREUZER (Schreckenberger)
Silver **Obv:** Crowned Hohnstein arms **Obv. Legend:** PAPS - SN - IL4G - GROS **Rev:** Crowned imperial eagle, 1Z in orb on breast, titles of Ferdinand II

Date	Mintage	VG	F	VF	XF	Unc
ND(1620/21)	—	27.00	80.00	145	250	—

KM# 25 12 KREUZER (Schreckenberger)
Silver **Rev:** Lion left above arms

Date	Mintage	VG	F	VF	XF	Unc
ND(1620/21)	—	27.00	80.00	145	250	—

KM# 26 12 KREUZER (Schreckenberger)
Silver **Obv:** Three shields of arms, one above two, 12 between lower two, date **Obv. Legend:** PRO LEGE... **Rev:** Wildman, tree branch in right hand

Date	Mintage	VG	F	VF	XF	Unc
16Z0	—	27.00	60.00	120	225	—

KM# 27 12 KREUZER (Schreckenberger)
Silver **Obv:** Crowned Hohnstein arms divide date near top **Rev:** Crowned imperial eagle, 12 in orb on breast, SUB: UMBRA **Mint:** Bayreuth

Date	Mintage	VG	F	VF	XF	Unc
1620 CO	—	—	—	—	—	—

KM# 28 12 KREUZER (Schreckenberger)
Silver **Rev:** Without value in orb on eagle's breast **Mint:** Bayreuth

Date	Mintage	VG	F	VF	XF	Unc
1620 CO	—	—	—	—	—	—

KM# 29 12 KREUZER (Schreckenberger)
Silver, 28.5 mm. **Obv:** 5-fold arms with central shield of Klettenberg arms, date in legend **Rev:** 12 in orb on eagle's breast

Date	Mintage	VG	F	VF	XF	Unc
1620	—	33.00	80.00	140	240	—

KM# 39 12 KREUZER (Schreckenberger)
Silver **Obv:** Similar to KM#23 but upper shield divides L-W

Date	Mintage	VG	F	VF	XF	Unc
1620	—	33.00	65.00	120	230	—
1621	—	33.00	65.00	120	230	—

KM# 16 12 KREUZER (Schreckenberger)
Silver **Obv:** Two-fold arms divided horizontally in ornamented shield divides C-O, date divided above **Rev:** Crowned imperial eagle, 12 in orb on breast **Rev. Legend:** SUB: UMBRA: ALARUM: TUAR **Mint:** Bayreuth **Note:** Kipper 12 Kreuzer. Varieties exist.

Date	Mintage	VG	F	VF	XF	Unc
1620 CO	—	—	—	—	—	—

KM# 21 12 KREUZER (Schreckenberger)
Silver **Rev:** Value 1Z below wildman **Note:** Varieties exist.

Date	Mintage	VG	F	VF	XF	Unc
1620	—	27.00	60.00	120	230	—
16Z1	—	27.00	60.00	120	230	—

KM# 36 12 KREUZER (Schreckenberger)
Silver **Obv:** Three shields of arms, value 12 in middle **Rev:** Wildman holding tree in right hand **Note:** Varieties exist.

Date	Mintage	VG	F	VF	XF	Unc
1621	—	27.00	60.00	120	230	—
1621 (f)	—	27.00	60.00	120	230	—

KM# 37 12 KREUZER (Schreckenberger)
2.1300 g., Silver **Obv:** 1Z between two lower shields **Note:** Varieties exist.

Date	Mintage	VG	F	VF	XF	Unc
16Z1	—	33.00	65.00	120	240	—

KM# 40 12 KREUZER (Schreckenberger)
Silver **Obv:** Three shields of arms, two above one **Rev:** Wildman, town at left, date **Rev. Legend:** DEO: ET: PATRIAE **Note:** Varieties exist.

Date	Mintage	VG	F	VF	XF	Unc
1621 (f)	—	27.00	80.00	140	240	—

KM# 41.1 12 KREUZER (Schreckenberger)
Silver **Obv:** Crowned three-fold arms **Rev:** Wildman, branch in his right, 12 on left, DEO...

Date	Mintage	VG	F	VF	XF	Unc
1621	—	27.00	80.00	140	240	—

KM# 41.2 12 KREUZER (Schreckenberger)
Silver **Rev:** Similar to reverse legend of KM#38.

Date	Mintage	VG	F	VF	XF	Unc
1621	—	27.00	80.00	140	240	—

KM# 42 12 KREUZER (Schreckenberger)
Silver **Obv:** Crowned imperial eagle, 1Z in orb on breast **Rev:** Wildman, date **Rev. Legend:** PRO LEGE...

Date	Mintage	VG	F	VF	XF	Unc
1621	—	33.00	80.00	140	240	—

KM# 43 12 KREUZER (Schreckenberger)
Silver **Obv:** Crowned imperial eagle, 12 in orb on breast, titles of Ferdinand II **Rev:** Three shields, one above two, 1Z at bottom

Date	Mintage	VG	F	VF	XF	Unc
1621	—	—	—	—	—	—

KM# 38 12 KREUZER (Schreckenberger)
Silver **Rev:** Date **Rev. Legend:** PRO: LEGE:...

Date	Mintage	VG	F	VF	XF	Unc
1621	—	33.00	70.00	125	230	—

KM# 30 24 KREUZER (Doppelschreckenberger)
Silver **Obv:** Crowned imperial eagle, Z4 in orb on breast, titles of Ferdinand II **Rev:** Crowned Hohnstein arms

Date	Mintage	VG	F	VF	XF	Unc
ND(1620/21)	—	50.00	100	200	400	—

KM# 44 24 KREUZER (Doppelschreckenberger)
Silver **Rev:** Date in legend

Date	Mintage	VG	F	VF	XF	Unc
1621	—	50.00	100	200	400	—

KM# 45 24 KREUZER (Doppelschreckenberger)
Silver **Obv:** Crowned arms of two leopards left, value (24) below **Rev:** Wildman, tree branch in right hand, town in right background, date **Rev. Legend:** DEO. ET...

Date	Mintage	VG	F	VF	XF	Unc
1621	—	50.00	100	200	400	—

KM# 46 24 KREUZER (Doppelschreckenberger)
Silver **Rev:** Date **Rev. Legend:** PRO. LEGE...

Date	Mintage	VG	F	VF	XF	Unc
1621	—	50.00	100	200	400	—

KM# 47 24 KREUZER (Doppelschreckenberger)
Silver **Ruler:** Friedrich Ulrich **Obv:** Crowned Klettenberg arms **Rev:** Z4 on left of wildman **Mint:** Bayreuth

Date	Mintage	VG	F	VF	XF	Unc
1621 CO	—	—	—	—	—	—

KM# 48 24 KREUZER (Doppelschreckenberger)
Silver **Obv:** Crowned imperial eagle, Z4 in orb on breast, titles of Ferdinand II and date in legend **Rev:** Crowned Lutterberg arms

Date	Mintage	VG	F	VF	XF	Unc
1621	—	—	—	—	—	—

KM# 31 6 BATZEN (Sechsbätzner - 24 Kreuzer)
Silver **Obv:** Crowned Hohnstein arms, date divided in legend by crown **Rev:** Crowned imperial eagle, 6 in orb on breast **Rev. Legend:** SUB: ULTRA... **Mint:** Bayreuth

Date	Mintage	VG	F	VF	XF	Unc
1620 CO	—	—	—	—	—	—

KM# 52 MARIENGROSCHEN
Silver **Ruler:** Gustav **Obv:** Crowned G divides date **Rev:** Madonna and child **Mint:** Elrich

Date	Mintage	VG	F	VF	XF	Unc
1672	—	25.00	40.00	75.00	150	—
1673	—	25.00	40.00	75.00	150	—

KM# 53 MARIENGROSCHEN
Silver **Ruler:** Gustav **Obv:** Crowned vertically divided 2-fold arms divide date **Mint:** Elrich

Date	Mintage	VG	F	VF	XF	Unc
1672	—	30.00	50.00	90.00	180	—

KM# 54 12 MARIENGROSCHEN (1/3 Thaler - 1/2 Gulden)
Silver **Ruler:** Gustav **Obv:** Klettenberg arms **Rev:** Date at end of legend **Rev. Legend:** PIE... **Rev. Inscription:** XII / MARIA / GROS **Mint:** Elrich

Date	Mintage	VG	F	VF	XF	Unc
1672	—	150	275	550	—	—

KM# 55 12 MARIENGROSCHEN (1/3 Thaler - 1/2 Gulden)
Silver **Ruler:** Gustav **Obv:** Klettenberg arms **Rev. Inscription:** XII / MARIEN / GROSCH **Mint:** Elrich

Date	Mintage	VG	F	VF	XF	Unc
1672	—	150	275	550	—	—
1673 IZW	—	150	275	550	—	—

KM# 58 12 MARIENGROSCHEN (1/3 Thaler - 1/2 Gulden)
Silver **Ruler:** Gustav **Obv:** Bust right **Mint:** Elrich

Date	Mintage	VG	F	VF	XF	Unc
1673	—	175	325	650	—	—
1673 IZW	—	175	325	650	—	—
1674 IZW	—	175	325	650	—	—

KM# 59 24 MARIENGROSCHEN (2/3 Thaler - Gulden)
Silver **Ruler:** Gustav **Obv:** Klettenberg arms **Rev. Inscription:** XXIIII / MARIEN / GROSCH **Mint:** Elrich **Note:** Dav#927.

Date	Mintage	VG	F	VF	XF	Unc
1673 IZW	—	80.00	160	325	650	—
1675	—	80.00	160	325	650	—

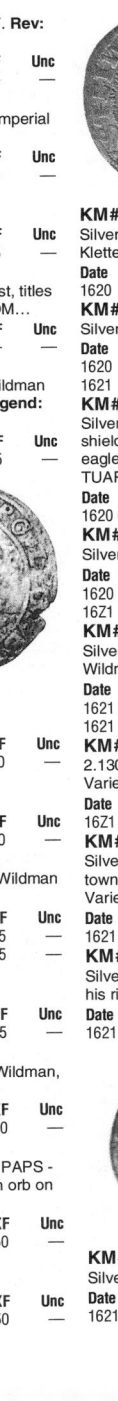

KM# 60 24 MARIENGROSCHEN (2/3 Thaler - Gulden)

Silver **Ruler:** Gustav **Obv:** Bust right **Mint:** Elrich **Note:** Dav#928.

Date	Mintage	VG	F	VF	XF	Unc
1673 IZW	—	150	275	550	—	—
1674 IZW	—	150	275	550	—	—

KM# 32 1/24 THALER (Groschen)

Silver **Obv:** Imperial orb with Z4, titles of Ferdinand II and date **Rev:** Crowned Hohnstien arms, (3) below **Note:** Kipper 1/24 Thaler.

Date	Mintage	VG	F	VF	XF	Unc
1620	—	—	—	—	—	—
ND	—	—	—	—	—	—

KM# 56 1/24 THALER (Groschen)

Silver **Ruler:** Gustav **Obv:** Klettenberg arms **Rev:** Imperial orb with Z4 titles of Gustav **Mint:** Elrich **Note:** Kipper coinage.

Date	Mintage	VG	F	VF	XF	Unc
ND(1672)	—	—	—	—	—	—

KM# 57 1/24 THALER (Groschen)

Silver **Ruler:** Gustav **Rev:** Date at end of legend **Rev. Legend:** PIE.ET.CAUTE **Mint:** Elrich **Note:** Kipper coinage.

Date	Mintage	VG	F	VF	XF	Unc
1672	—	—	—	—	—	—

KM# 75 1/24 THALER (Groschen)

Silver **Ruler:** Gustav **Obv:** Hohnstein arms divide mitmasters initials **Rev:** Imperial orb with 24 divides date at 1-6/8-4 **Mint:** Klettenberg **Note:** Kipper coinage.

Date	Mintage	VG	F	VF	XF	Unc
1684 DF	—	—	—	—	—	—

KM# 76 1/12 THALER

Silver **Ruler:** Gustav **Obv:** Crowned 6-fold arms with central shield divide date as 1-6/8-4 **Rev. Inscription:** 12 / EINEN / REICHS / THAL / ER **Mint:** Klettenberg

Date	Mintage	VG	F	VF	XF	Unc
1684 DF	—	—	—	—	—	—

KM# 62 1/3 THALER

Silver **Ruler:** Gustav **Obv:** Bust right **Rev:** Crowned 6-fold arms with central shield, value 1/3 in oval below, date at end of legend **Rev. Legend:** UT PRESSA PALM **Mint:** Elrich

Date	Mintage	VG	F	VF	XF	Unc
1674 IZW	—	75.00	150	275	550	—
1676 PL	—	75.00	150	275	550	—

KM# 63 1/3 THALER

Silver **Ruler:** Gustav **Rev:** Date at end of legend **Rev. Legend:** PIE ET CAUTE-ANNO **Mint:** Elrich

Date	Mintage	VG	F	VF	XF	Unc
1674 IZW	—	75.00	150	275	550	—

KM# 66 1/3 THALER

Silver **Ruler:** Gustav **Rev:** Date at end of legend **Rev. Legend:** TANDEN FORTUNA-OBSTETRILE **Mint:** Elrich

Date	Mintage	VG	F	VF	XF	Unc
1676 PL	—	75.00	150	275	550	—

KM# 67 1/3 THALER

Silver **Ruler:** Gustav **Rev:** Date divided by arms **Mint:** Elrich

Date	Mintage	VG	F	VF	XF	Unc
1676	—	65.00	135	250	500	—
1676 PL	—	65.00	135	250	500	—
1677	—	65.00	135	250	500	—

KM# 61 2/3 THALER

Silver **Ruler:** Gustav **Obv:** Bust right **Rev:** Arms, 2/3 below, date at end of inscription **Rev. Inscription:** PIET * CAVTE * **Mint:** Elrich

Date	Mintage	VG	F	VF	XF	Unc
1673	—	75.00	150	300	600	—

KM# 64 2/3 THALER

Silver **Ruler:** Gustav **Rev:** Crowned 6-fold arms with central shield, value 2/3 in oval at bottom of shield, date at end of legend **Rev. Legend:** PIE ET CAUTE. ANNO **Mint:** Elrich **Note:** Dav#907. Varieties exist.

Date	Mintage	VG	F	VF	XF	Unc
1674 IZW	—	55.00	115	235	475	—

KM# 65 2/3 THALER

Silver **Ruler:** Gustav **Rev:** Date at end of legend **Rev. Legend:** UT PRESSA PALM **Mint:** Elrich **Note:** Dav#908-09. Varieties exist.

Date	Mintage	VG	F	VF	XF	Unc
1674 IZW	—	55.00	115	235	475	—
1675 IZW	—	55.00	115	235	475	—
1675 PL	—	55.00	115	235	475	—
1676 PL	—	55.00	115	235	475	—

KM# 68 2/3 THALER

Silver **Ruler:** Gustav **Rev:** Large crowned 6-fold arms with central shield divides date, 2/3 in oval at bottom **Rev. Legend:** AD. PALMUM. PRESSA. LAETIUE. SURGIT **Mint:** Elrich **Note:** Dav#911.

Date	Mintage	VG	F	VF	XF	Unc
1676 PL	—	80.00	160	325	650	—

KM# 69 2/3 THALER

Silver **Ruler:** Gustav **Rev:** Crowned 6-fold arms with central shield, value 2/3 in oval below, date at end of legend **Rev. Legend:** TANDEM FORTUNA-OBSTETRICE **Mint:** Elrich **Note:** Dav#915.

Date	Mintage	VG	F	VF	XF	Unc
1676 PL	—	75.00	150	300	600	—

INGOLSTADT

A city in Upper Bavaria (Oberbayern) on the Danube at the junction with the Schutter, some 45 miles (75km) north of Munich. When Bavaria was divided in 1375 by the sons of Stephan I, Ingolstadt became the capital of one of the three duchies, but lost that status when the line died out in 1334 and the territory went to the Munich line (see Bavaria). A university was founded in the city in 1472, but was transferred to Landshut in 1800 and then to Munich in 1826. The city was besieged by Gustavus Adolphus in 1632-33 and obsidional coinage was produced to meet the emergency.

REFERENCE

B = Joseph P. Beierlein, **Medaillen und Münzen des Gesammthauses Wittelsbach**, 2 vols., Munich, 1897-1901.

CITY

OBSIDIONAL COINAGE

KM# 1 1/4 GULDEN

4.3500 g., Silver **Ruler:** (no Ruler Information) **Obv:** Crowned Madonna holding child in right arm, palm branch in left, standing on dragon, divides date 16-33 **Obv. Legend:** SANCTA. MARIA. DE. VICTORIA. INGOLSTA **Rev:** View of the city, date 1632 in ribbon and band above **Rev. Legend:** VRBIS. TVTELA. CIVIVM. PATRONA. **Note:** Klippe. Beierlein 806.

Date	Mintage	VG	F	VF	XF	Unc
1633//1632 Rare	—	—	—	—	—	—

ISENBURG

The lands of the counts of Isenburg lay on both sides of the Main River to the east of Frankfurt. The dynasty traces its lineage back to the 10th century and began issuing coins in the mid-13th century. The county underwent many divisions in the Middle Ages, but by the early 17th century only one dominant branch was producing coins. This was Isenburg-Birstein, divided once again into Isenburg-Offenbach-Birstein and Isenburg-Büdingen in 1635. The latter was further divided into four branches in 1673/1687 and two of the substrata became extinct in 1725 and 1780 respectively. Isenburg-Offenbach-Birstein was raised to the rank of prince in 1744 and all other branches had to relinquish their sovereignty to his descendant in 1806. The latter lost his sole leadership in 1813 because he sided with Napoleon and the lands of Isenburg-Offenbach-Birstein were mediatized to Hesse-Darmstadt in 1815. The subdivisions of Isenburg-Büdigen did not issue a regular coinage, but struck the series of the quasi-official snipe hellers during the 19th century.

RULERS

Wolfgang Ernst von Birstein, 1596-1633
Wolfgang Heinrich von Offenbach-Birstein, 1633-1635
Johann Ludwig von Offenbach-Birstein, 1635-1685
Johann Philipp (in Offenbach), 1685-1718

Isenburg-Büdingen

Johann Ernst, 1633-1685
Johann Kasimir, 1685-1693
Ernst Kasimir I, 1693-1749

MINT OFFICIALS' INITIALS

Initial	Date	Name
	1618-1619	Melchior (Michael) Kuttner, in Offenbach
A	CA.1681	
HB, IHB	ca. 1693	
IRA, RA	ca. 1670-1679	

COUNTSHIP

REGULAR COINAGE

KM# 27 KREUZER

Silver **Obv:** Crowned arms **Obv. Legend:** MONETA... **Rev:** I/KREVTZ/ER/date **Rev. Legend:** YSENBVRG. BVDINGEN. **Note:** Kipper Kreuzer.

Date	Mintage	VG	F	VF	XF	Unc
16ZZ	39,000	—	—	—	—	—

KM# 28 KREUZER

Silver **Obv:** I/KREVTZ/ER/date **Obv. Legend:** MONETA... **Rev:** Crowned arms, 5-pointed star on both sides **Rev. Legend:** YSENBVRG. BVDINGEN.

Date	Mintage	VG	F	VF	XF	Unc
16Z3	—	—	—	—	—	—

KM# 35 KREUZER

Silver **Obv:** Crowned arms in laurel wreath **Rev:** I/KREU/TZER/date/A in laurel wreath

Date	Mintage	VG	F	VF	XF	Unc
1681 A	—	135	265	500	1,025	—

KM# 36 ALBUS

Silver **Obv:** Crowned arms between laurel branches **Rev:** *I*/ALBVS/date/R.A., between laurel branches

Date	Mintage	VG	F	VF	XF	Unc
1681 RA	—	160	275	500	1,025	—

KM# 5 3 KREUZER (Groschen)

Silver **Obv:** Crowned arms divide date **Rev:** Crowned imperial eagle, 3 in orb on breast, titles of Matthias **Mint:** Budingen

Date	Mintage	VG	F	VF	XF	Unc
1618	—	475	950	1,900	—	—

KM# 22 3 KREUZER (Groschen)

Silver **Rev:** Titles of Ferdinand II and date repeated at end... S. AV. 19.

Date	Mintage	VG	F	VF	XF	Unc
1619	—	300	600	—	—	—

KM# 42 2 ALBUS (Doppelalbus)

Silver **Obv:** Crowned arms between palm branches, titles of Johann Philipp and Wilhelm Moritz **Rev:** *II*/ALBUS/date/H*B **Rev. Legend:** NACH DEM...

Date	Mintage	VG	F	VF	XF	Unc
1693 HB	—	135	225	400	725	—

KM# 6 6 KREUZER

Silver **Obv:** Crowned arms divide date **Rev:** Crowned imperial eagle, 6 in orb on breast, titles of Matthias **Mint:** Budingen **Note:** Varieties exist.

Date	Mintage	VG	F	VF	XF	Unc
1618	—	200	350	600	1,100	—

KM# 40 12 KREUZER

Silver **Obv:** Crowned arms between palm branches, titles of Johann philipp and Wilhelm Moritz **Rev. Legend:** NACH. DEM. SCHLUS... **Rev. Inscription:** XII / KREU / TZER / date / HB

Date	Mintage	VG	F	VF	XF	Unc
1693 HB	—	—	—	—	—	—

KM# 26 4 GROSCHEN

Silver **Obv:** Arms, date in legend **Obv. Legend:** DURA, PATI, VIRTUS **Rev:** Imperial eagle with 4G on breast, titles of Ferdinand II **Note:** Kipper 4 Groschen.

Date	Mintage	VG	F	VF	XF	Unc
1621	—	—	—	—	—	—

KM# 7 1/8 THALER

Silver **Obv:** Crowned arms divide date **Rev:** Imperial eagle, titles of Matthias **Mint:** Budingen

Date	Mintage	VG	F	VF	XF	Unc
1618	—	—	—	—	—	—

KM# 18 1/4 THALER

Silver, 29.5 mm. **Obv:** Crowned arms divide date, titles of Wolfgang Ernst **Rev:** Crowned imperial eagle, orb on breast, titles of Matthias **Note:** Varieties exist.

Date	Mintage	VG	F	VF	XF	Unc
1618	—	135	300	425	800	1,500
1619	—	135	300	425	800	1,500

KM# 30 60 KREUZER (1 Gulden = 2/3 Thaler)
Silver **Obv:** Ornate arms between two laurel branches, date in legend **Rev:** Crowned imperial eagle, 60 in orb on breast, titles of Leopold I **Note:** Varieties exist.

Date	Mintage	VG	F	VF	XF	Unc
1670 IRA	—	500	825	1,600	3,200	—
1676 IRA	—	500	825	1,600	3,200	—
1678 IRA	—	500	825	1,600	3,200	—
1679 IRA	—	500	825	1,600	3,200	—

KM# 41 60 KREUZER (1 Gulden = 2/3 Thaler)
Silver **Rev:** Crowned arms between palm branches divide date, titles of Johann Philipp and Wilhelm Moritz

Date	Mintage	VG	F	VF	XF	Unc
1693 IHB	—	525	975	1,850	3,600	—

KM# 19 THALER
Silver **Obv:** Ornate baroque arms, double legend, titles of Wolfgang Ernst **Rev:** Crowned imperial eagle, orb on breast, titles of Matthias, date in legend **Note:** Mining Thaler. Dav. #6841.

Date	Mintage	VG	F	VF	XF	Unc
1618 Rare	—	—	—	—	—	—

KM# 25 THALER
Silver **Obv:** Crowned arms, titles of Wolfgang Ernst **Rev:** Titles of Ferdinand II **Note:** Dav. #6842.

Date	Mintage	VG	F	VF	XF	Unc
1620 Rare	—	—	—	—	—	—

KM# 43 2 THALER
Silver **Obv:** Crowned ornate oval arms, titles of Johann Philipp and Wilhelm Moritz, date in legend **Rev:** Crowned imperial eagle, titles of Leopold I **Note:** Dav. #6843.

Date	Mintage	VG	F	VF	XF	Unc
1694 Rare	—	—	—	—	—	—

TRADE COINAGE

KM# 20 DUCAT
3.5000 g., 0.9860 Gold 0.1109 oz. AGW **Obv:** Ornate baroque arms divide date, titles of Wolfgang Ernst in legend **Rev:** Crowned imperial eagle, orb on breast, titles of Matthias **Note:** Varieties exist.

Date	Mintage	VG	F	VF	XF	Unc
1618 Rare	—	—	—	—	—	—

KM# 21 2 DUCAT
7.0000 g., 0.9860 Gold 0.2219 oz. AGW **Obv:** Arms of Isenburg **Rev:** Crowned imperial eagle

Date	Mintage	VG	F	VF	XF	Unc
1619 Rare	—	—	—	—	—	—

ISNY

This south German city, some 17 miles NE of Lindau and the shore of the Bodensee (Lake Constance), is first mentioned in the 11th century. It acquired its imperial city status from Emperor Karl IV in 1365 and the mint right in 1507 from Maximilian I. A regular coinage began the following year and continued, on-and-off, until the early 18th century. The city was acquired by Württemberg in 1803 and lost its position as a free city.

MINT OFFICIALS' INITIALS

Initials	Date	Name
PI	1695-1702	Hans Jakob Hau

ARMS

Early arms – horseshoe in shield

Later arms - crowned eagle with horseshoe in shield on breast

Also, sometimes a large, six-pointed star

REFERENCE

N = Elisabeth Nau, ***Die Münzen und Medaillen des oberschwäbischen Städte***, Freiburg im Breisgau, 1964.

FREE CITY

REGULAR COINAGE

KM# 5 PFENNIG
Copper **Obv:** Crowned eagle arms divide date (when present) **Note:** Uniface. Varieties exist.

Date	Mintage	VG	F	VF	XF	Unc
ND(ca.1623)	—	16.00	27.00	45.00	90.00	—
1695	—	16.00	27.00	45.00	90.00	—

KM# 10 PFENNIG
Copper **Obv:** Eagle without crown above

Date	Mintage	VG	F	VF	XF	Unc
1695	—	16.00	27.00	45.00	90.00	—
1696	—	16.00	27.00	45.00	90.00	—

KM# 11 PFENNIG
Copper **Obv:** Small crowned eagle on arms divide date

Date	Mintage	VG	F	VF	XF	Unc
1698	—	16.00	27.00	45.00	90.00	—

KM# 12 PFENNIG
Copper **Obv:** Small crowned eagle divides date

Date	Mintage	VG	F	VF	XF	Unc
1699	—	16.00	27.00	45.00	90.00	—
1700	—	16.00	27.00	45.00	90.00	—

KM# 6 2 KREUZER (Halbbatzen)
Silver **Obv:** Eagle, legend, date **Obv. Legend:** MON: NO: CIVI: ISSEN: **Rev:** Crowned imperial eagle, value Z in orb on breast, titles of Ferdinand II

Date	Mintage	VG	F	VF	XF	Unc
16Z3	—	—	—	—	—	—

KM# 7 12 KREUZER (Dreibätzner)
Silver **Obv:** Eagle with city arms on breast in ornamented shield divides date, .XII.K. above **Rev:** STAT/MYNZ in round cartouche **Note:** Varieties exist.

Date	Mintage	VG	F	VF	XF	Unc
16Z3	—	—	—	—	—	—

JAGERNDORF

A duchy in Silesia, centered on the town of the same name, which is located on the Oppa (Opava) River, some 14 miles (23km) northwest of Troppau. From earliest recorded times, Jägerndorf had been part of Silesia, but passed to the Duchy of Troppau in 1340. When Troppau was divided by sons of a duke who had died in 1366, Jägerndorf together with Ratibor formed one of the subdivisions. Jägerndorf was occupied by Hungary 1483-93, then by Bohemia through the agency of Johann von Schellenberg in 1493. Johann's son, George, who ruled Jägerndorf on behalf of Bohemia from 1506 to 1523, sold the duchy to Georg the Pious, Margrave of Brandenburg-Ansbach in the latter year. Jägerndorf was briefly in the hands of the Elector of Brandenburg and also for a short period was obtained by the Habsburgs. It shortly thereafter passed to the princes of Liechtenstein who ruled it until the end of World War I in 1918.

RULERS

Georg Friedrich von Brandenburg-Ansbach 1543-1603
Joachim Friedrich von Brandenburg, 1603-1606
Johann Georg von Brandenburg-Ansbach, 1607-1623

MINT OFFICIALS' INITIALS

Initial	Date	Name
Cp	1613-20	Caspar Hennemann
FVC, VCF	1610-12	Franz Carl Uhle
	1610-12	Valentin Janus
	1564-1606	Leonhard Emich, superintendent

DUCHY

REGULAR COINAGE

KM# 30 3 PFENNIG (Dreier - Gröschel)
Silver **Obv:** Ornate helmet divides date **Rev:** Crowned Silesian eagle **Note:** Varieties exist.

Date	Mintage	VG	F	VF	XF	Unc
1610	—	27.00	55.00	110	225	450
1611	—	27.00	55.00	110	225	450
1612	—	27.00	55.00	110	225	450

KM# 53 KREUZER
Silver **Ruler:** Johann Georg **Obv:** Five shields of arms arranged around central pellet **Rev:** 6-line inscription with date **Note:** Varieties exist.

Date	Mintage	VG	F	VF	XF	Unc
1618	—	65.00	125	225	450	—
ND	—	65.00	125	225	450	—

KM# 31 3 KREUZER (Groschen)
Silver **Ruler:** Johann Georg **Obv:** Bust to right, value (3) below **Obv. Legend:** IOA. GEO. D. - G. MA(R). BR(A). **Rev:** Crowned shield of 4-fold armscentral shield of Silesia, date at end of legend **Rev. Legend:** GRO. ARG. III. CRV. **Note:** Varieties exist.

Date	Mintage	VG	F	VF	XF	Unc
(1)610 (d)	—	25.00	45.00	90.00	180	—
(1)611 (d)	—	25.00	45.00	90.00	180	—
1612 (d)	—	25.00	45.00	90.00	180	—
1613 CP	—	25.00	45.00	90.00	180	—
1614 CP	—	25.00	45.00	90.00	180	—
1615 CP	—	25.00	45.00	90.00	180	—
1616 CP	—	25.00	45.00	90.00	180	—
1617 CP	—	25.00	45.00	90.00	180	—
1618 CP	—	25.00	45.00	90.00	180	—
1619 CP	—	25.00	45.00	90.00	180	—
1620 CP	—	25.00	45.00	90.00	180	—
1621	—	25.00	45.00	90.00	180	—

KM# 39 3 KREUZER (Groschen)
Silver **Note:** Klippe. Varieties exist.

Date	Mintage	VG	F	VF	XF	Unc
1611	—	—	—	—	—	—
1614 CP	—	—	—	—	—	—
1616 CP	—	—	—	—	—	—
1619 CP	—	—	—	—	—	—

KM# 46 3 GROSCHEN
Silver **Obv:** Bust right **Rev:** Two co-joined shields of arms, crowne above, 4-line inscription with date

Date	Mintage	VG	F	VF	XF	Unc
1612	—	—	—	—	—	—

KM# 32 1/4 THALER
Silver **Ruler:** Johann Georg **Obv:** Armored bust to right divides date in circle **Obv. Legend:** IOHAN. GEOR. DG. MARCHIO. BRA. **Rev:** Crowned shield of 4-fold arms, central shield of Silesia in baroque frame **Rev. Legend:** DVX. CARNOVIENSIS.

Date	Mintage	VG	F	VF	XF	Unc
1610 FVC/(d)	—	—	—	—	—	—

KM# 6 1/2 THALER
Silver **Ruler:** Georg Friedrich **Obv:** Half-length armored bust right **Rev:** Ornate cross with shields of arms in angle, shield in center, date in legend at top **Note:** Schrötter 1198.

Date	Mintage	VG	F	VF	XF	Unc
1602 (b)	—	1,200	2,150	3,300	5,750	—

KM# 13 1/2 THALER
Silver **Ruler:** Joachim Friedrich **Obv:** Half-length armored bust right divides date **Obv. Legend:** IOACHIM. FRID. D.G. MARCHIO. BRANDE. SAC. **Rev:** Ornate 6-fold arms with central shield **Rev. Legend:** ROMA. IMPE. ARCHICAMER. ET. ELECTOR.

Date	Mintage	VG	F	VF	XF	Unc
1606 (b)	—	1,700	2,900	4,500	8,500	—

KM# 14 1/2 THALER

Silver **Obv:** Half-length armored bust right, titles of Johann Georg **Rev:** Oval 12-folds arms, three helmets above

Date	Mintage	VG	F	VF	XF	Unc
ND	—	1,050	1,800	3,600	—	—

KM# 33 1/2 THALER

Silver **Ruler:** Johann Georg **Obv:** Half-length bust right divides date **Rev:** 12-fold arms, three helmets above

Date	Mintage	VG	F	VF	XF	Unc
1610 FVC/(d)	—	1,050	1,800	3,600	—	—

KM# 40 1/2 THALER

Silver **Ruler:** Johann Georg **Obv:** Half-length armored bust right, date below

Date	Mintage	VG	F	VF	XF	Unc
1611 FVC/(d)	—	1,050	1,800	3,600	—	—

KM# 62 1/2 THALER (36 Kreuzer)

Silver **Obv:** Half-length bust right **Rev:** Crowned 4-fold arms with central shield, date in legend

Date	Mintage	VG	F	VF	XF	Unc
1621	—	350	700	1,400	—	—

KM# 8 THALER

Silver **Ruler:** Georg Friedrich **Obv:** Half-length armored figure to right **Obv. Legend:** MO. NO. ARG. GEOR. F. MAR. BRAN. Z. SL. DVC. **Rev:** Large floriated cross, small shield of Silesia arms in center, shield of arms in each angle, date at end of legend **Rev. Legend:** SI. DEVS. PRONOB. QVIS. CONTRA. NOS. **Note:** Dav. #6844.

Date	Mintage	VG	F	VF	XF	Unc
1601 (b)	—	550	1,150	2,100	3,600	—
1602 (b)	—	550	1,150	2,100	3,600	—

KM# 15 THALER

Silver **Ruler:** Joachim Friedrich **Obv:** Half-length armored figure to right divides date **Obv. Legend:** IOACHIM. FRIDERIC. D.G. MARCHIO. BRANDE. SAC. **Rev:** Shield of manifold arms, 3 ornate helmets above **Rev. Legend:** ROM. IMP. ARC - CAM. ET. ELEC. **Note:** Dav. #6846.

Date	Mintage	VG	F	VF	XF	Unc
1606 (b) Rare	—	—	—	—	—	—

KM# 16 THALER

Silver **Rev:** Oval shield with V-C-F above **Note:** Similar to KM#17. Dav. #6848.

Date	Mintage	VG	F	VF	XF	Unc
ND VCF	—	425	900	1,800	3,000	—

KM# 17 THALER

Silver **Rev:** Spanish arms **Note:** Dav. #6851.

Date	Mintage	VG	F	VF	XF	Unc
ND	—	375	800	1,600	2,750	—

KM# 18 THALER

Silver **Obv:** Half-figure right breaks upper legend **Rev:** Helmeted oval arms with F-V-C above **Note:** Dav. #6853.

Date	Mintage	VG	F	VF	XF	Unc
ND FVC	—	350	850	1,750	2,950	—

KM# 34 THALER

Silver **Ruler:** Johann Georg **Obv:** Half-length armored figure to right with helmet, date in margin at top **Obv. Legend:** IOHAN. GEORG. D.G. MARCHIO. BRANDENB. **Rev:** Shield of manifold arms, 3 ornate helmets above **Rev. Legend:** DVX. CARN - OVIENSIS. **Note:** Dav. #6855.

Date	Mintage	VG	F	VF	XF	Unc
1610 FVC/(d)	—	450	950	1,900	3,300	—

KM# 35 THALER

Silver **Ruler:** Johann Georg **Obv:** Half-length armored figure to right, helmet before at right, date at top in margin **Obv. Legend:** IOHAN. GEORG. D.G. MARCHIO. BRANDENB. **Rev:** Small shield of manifold arms, 3 ornate helmets above , crests of which divide mintmaster's initials **Rev. Legend:** DVX. CARNO - VIENSIS. **Note:** Dav. #6855A.

Date	Mintage	VG	F	VF	XF	Unc
1610 FVC/(d)	—	475	1,000	2,100	3,600	—

KM# 41 THALER

Silver **Ruler:** Johann Georg **Obv:** Half-length armored figure, turned 3/4 to right, date in exergue **Obv. Legend:** IOHAN. GEORG. D.G. MARCHI. BRAND. **Rev:** Shield of manifold arms, 3 ornate helmets above **Rev. Legend:** DVX. CAR. - NOVIEN. **Note:** Dav. #6856.

Date	Mintage	VG	F	VF	XF	Unc
1611 (d)	—	775	1,500	3,050	4,950	—

KM# 42 THALER
Silver **Rev. Legend:** DVX. CARN-O. VIENSIS **Note:** Dav. #6856A.

Date	Mintage	VG	F	VF	XF	Unc
1611 FVC	—	775	1,500	3,050	4,950	—

KM# 47 THALER
Silver **Ruler:** Johann Georg **Obv:** Half-length armored figure to right, date in exergue **Obv. Legend:** IOHAN. GEORG. D.G. MARCHI. BRAN(D). **Rev:** Shield of manifold arms, 3 ornate helmets above **Rev. Legend:** DVX. CAR(-)(N)(-)(O) - (N)(O.)VIENSIS. **Note:** Varieties exist. Dav. #6858.

Date	Mintage	VG	F	VF	XF	Unc
1612 FVC/(d)	—	775	1,500	3,050	4,950	—

KM# 19 2 THALER
Silver **Ruler:** Joachim Friedrich **Obv:** Half-length armored figure to right divides date **Obv. Legend:** IOACHIM. FRIDERIC. D.G. MARCHIO. BRANDE. SAC. **Rev:** Shield of manifold arms, 3 ornate helmets above **Rev. Legend:** ROM. IMP. ARC - CAM. ET. ELEC. **Note:** Dav. #6845.

Date	Mintage	VG	F	VF	XF	Unc
1606 (b) Rare	—	—	—	—	—	—

Note: Fritz Rudolf Künker Münzenhandlung Auction 131, 10-07, VF realized approximately $9,915.

KM# 20 2 THALER
Silver **Obv:** Half-figure right **Rev:** Helmeted oval arms **Note:** Dav. #6847.

Date	Mintage	VG	F	VF	XF	Unc
ND VCF Rare	—	—	—	—	—	—

Note: Künker Auction 113, 6-06, VF realized approximately $10,115. Künker Auction 147, 2-09, XF realized approximately $10,950.

KM# 21 2 THALER
Silver **Note:** Similar to 1 Thaler, KM#17. Dav. #6850.

Date	Mintage	VG	F	VF	XF	Unc
ND Rare	—	—	—	—	—	—

KM# 22 2 THALER
Silver **Obv:** Half-figure right breaks upper legend **Rev:** Helmeted oval arms with F-V-C above **Note:** Dav. #6852.

Date	Mintage	VG	F	VF	XF	Unc
ND FVC Rare	—	—	—	—	—	—

KM# 36 2 THALER
Silver **Ruler:** Johann Georg **Obv:** Half-length armored figure right to with helmet, date in margin at top **Obv. Legend:** IOHAN. GEORG. D.G. MARCHIO. BRANDENB. **Rev:** Shield of manifold arms, 3 ornate helmets above **Rev. Legend:** DVX. CARN - OVIENSIS. **Note:** Dav. #6854.

Date	Mintage	VG	F	VF	XF	Unc
1610 FVC/(d) Rare	—	—	—	—	—	—

Note: Rauch Auction 85, 11-09, XF realized approximately $9,785. Fritz Rudolf Künker Münzenhandlung Auction 135, 01-08, VF realized approximately $9,970

KM# 48 2 THALER
Silver **Ruler:** Johann Georg **Obv:** Half-length armored figure to right, date in exergue **Obv. Legend:** IOHAN. GEORG. D.G. MARCHIO. BRAND. **Rev:** Shield of manifold arms, 3 ornate helmets above **Rev. Legend:** DVX. CARNO - VIENSIS. **Note:** Dav. #6857.

Date	Mintage	VG	F	VF	XF	Unc
1612 FVC/(d) Rare	—	—	—	—	—	—

Note: Fritz Rudolf Künker Münzenhandlung Auction 98, 3-05, VF realized approximately $20,685

KM# 12 3 THALER
Silver **Note:** Similar to 1 Thaler, KM#17. Dav. #6849.

Date	Mintage	VG	F	VF	XF	Unc
ND Rare	—	—	—	—	—	—

TRADE COINAGE

KM# 51 1/2 DUCAT
1.7500 g., 0.9860 Gold 0.0555 oz. AGW **Obv:** Crowned arms divide date **Rev:** Six-line inscription

Date	Mintage	VG	F	VF	XF	Unc
1615	—	375	750	1,350	2,350	—
1617	—	375	750	1,350	2,350	—
1620	—	375	750	1,350	2,350	—
1621	—	375	750	1,350	2,350	—
1622	—	375	750	1,350	2,350	—

KM# 60 1/2 DUCAT
1.7500 g., 0.9860 Gold 0.0555 oz. AGW **Note:** Klippe.

Date	Mintage	VG	F	VF	XF	Unc
1620	—	—	—	—	—	—

KM# 37 DUCAT
3.5000 g., 0.9860 Gold 0.1109 oz. AGW **Obv:** Johann Georg standing right divides date **Rev:** 12-fold arms, three helmets above

Date	Mintage	VG	F	VF	XF	Unc
1610	—	1,000	2,250	4,250	7,500	—

KM# 43 DUCAT
3.5000 g., 0.9860 Gold 0.1109 oz. AGW **Rev:** Crowned 12-fold arms, date in legend

Date	Mintage	VG	F	VF	XF	Unc
1611	—	1,000	2,250	4,250	7,500	—

KM# 49 DUCAT
3.5000 g., 0.9860 Gold 0.1109 oz. AGW **Obv:** Half-length bust of Johann Georg right **Rev:** Crowned 12-fold arms, date in legend

Date	Mintage	VG	F	VF	XF	Unc
1612	—	600	1,200	2,400	4,500	—
1620	—	600	1,200	2,400	4,500	—

KM# 50 DUCAT
3.5000 g., 0.9860 Gold 0.1109 oz. AGW **Rev:** Crowned oval arms

Date	Mintage	VG	F	VF	XF	Unc
1614	—	600	1,200	2,400	4,500	—
1616	—	600	1,200	2,400	4,500	—
1617	—	600	1,200	2,400	4,500	—

KM# 61 DUCAT
3.5000 g., 0.9860 Gold 0.1109 oz. AGW **Obv:** Crowned arms divide date **Rev:** Six-line inscription **Note:** Thick planchet.

Date	Mintage	VG	F	VF	XF	Unc
1620	—	750	1,500	3,600	6,000	—
1621	—	—	—	—	—	—

KM# 52 2 DUCAT
7.0000 g., 0.9860 Gold 0.2219 oz. AGW **Obv:** Crowned arms divide date **Rev:** Six-line inscription **Note:** Thick planchet.

Date	Mintage	VG	F	VF	XF	Unc
1617	—	1,950	4,000	8,000	14,000	—

KM# 54 2 DUCAT
7.0000 g., 0.9860 Gold 0.2219 oz. AGW **Obv:** Johann Georg standing right **Rev:** Crowned oval arms, date in legend

Date	Mintage	VG	F	VF	XF	Unc
1618	—	1,150	2,400	4,500	8,000	13,500
1620	—	1,150	2,400	4,500	8,000	13,500
1621	—	1,150	2,400	4,500	8,000	13,500
ND	—	1,150	2,400	4,500	8,000	13,500

KM# 55 3 DUCAT

10.5000 g., 0.9860 Gold 0.3328 oz. AGW **Obv:** Johann Georg standing right **Rev:** Crowned oval arms, date in legend

Date	Mintage	VG	F	VF	XF	Unc
ND FVC Rare	—	—	—	—	—	—

KM# A56 3 DUCAT

10.5000 g., 0.9860 Gold 0.3328 oz. AGW **Obv:** Half-length bust Johann Georg right divides date, titles of Johann Georg **Rev:** Crowned 4-fold arms with central shield in baroque frame **Note:** Struck with 1/4 Thaler dies, KM#32.

Date	Mintage	VG	F	VF	XF	Unc
1610 FVC Rare	—	—	—	—	—	—

KM# 23 4 DUCAT

14.0000 g., 0.9860 Gold 0.4438 oz. AGW **Obv:** Half-length armored bust Johann Georg right with titles **Rev:** Oval 12-fold arms, three helmets above **Note:** Struck with 1/2 Thaler dies, KM#14.

Date	Mintage	VG	F	VF	XF	Unc
ND FVC	—	—	—	—	—	—

KM# 38 4 DUCAT

14.0000 g., 0.9860 Gold 0.4438 oz. AGW **Ruler:** Johann Georg **Obv:** Half-length armored bust to right divides date **Rev:** Shield of 12-fold arms, three helmets above **Note:** Struck with 1/2 Thaler dies, KM#33.

Date	Mintage	VG	F	VF	XF	Unc
1610 FVC/(d) Rare	—	—	—	—	—	—

KM# 25 5 DUCAT (1/2 Portugalöser)

17.5000 g., 0.9860 Gold 0.5547 oz. AGW **Note:** Struck with 1/2 Thaler dies, KM#14.

Date	Mintage	VG	F	VF	XF	Unc
ND VCF	—	—	—	—	—	—

KM# 44 5 DUCAT (1/2 Portugalöser)

17.5000 g., 0.9860 Gold 0.5547 oz. AGW **Ruler:** Johann Georg **Obv:** Half-length armored figure to right, date in exergue **Obv. Legend:** IOHAN. GEORG. D.G. MARCH. BRA. **Rev:** Shield of manifold arms, 3 ornate helmets above **Rev. Legend:** DVX. CAR - NOVIEN. **Note:** Struck with 1/2 Thaler dies, KM#40.

Date	Mintage	VG	F	VF	XF	Unc
1611 FVC/(d) Rare	—	—	—	—	—	—

KM# A45 7 DUCAT

24.5000 g., 0.9860 Gold 0.7766 oz. AGW **Note:** Struck with 1 Thaler dies.

Date	Mintage	VG	F	VF	XF	Unc
1611 Rare	—	—	—	—	—	—

KM# B45 8 DUCAT

28.0000 g., 0.9860 Gold 0.8876 oz. AGW **Note:** Struck with 1 Thaler dies.

Date	Mintage	VG	F	VF	XF	Unc
1611 Rare	—	—	—	—	—	—

KM# 28 10 DUCAT (Portugalöser)

35.0000 g., 0.9860 Gold 1.1095 oz. AGW **Note:** Struck with 1 Thaler dies.

Date	Mintage	VG	F	VF	XF	Unc
ND Rare	—	—	—	—	—	—

KM# 45 10 DUCAT (Portugalöser)

35.0000 g., 0.9860 Gold 1.1095 oz. AGW **Ruler:** Johann Georg **Obv:** Half-length armored figure to right, date in exergue **Obv. Legend:** IOHAN. GEORG. D.G. MARCHI. BRAND. **Rev:** Shield of manifold arms, 3 ornate helmets above **Rev. Legend:** DVX. CARN - O. VIENSIS. **Note:** Struck with Thaler dies, KM#42.

Date	Mintage	VG	F	VF	XF	Unc
1611 FVC/(d) Rare	—	—	—	—	—	—

KM# 26 12 DUCAT

42.0000 g., 0.9860 Gold 1.3314 oz. AGW **Note:** Struck with 2 Thaler dies, KM#22.

Date	Mintage	VG	F	VF	XF	Unc
ND FVC Rare	—	—	—	—	—	—

PATTERNS

Including off metal strikes

KM#	Date	Mintage	Identification	Mkt Val
Pn2	1611	—	Thaler. Lead. KM#41	—
Pn3	1612 FVC	—	Thaler. Lead. KM#47	—

JEVER

A lordship lying on the North Sea coast, Jever's earliest coinage dates from the late 10th and early 11th centuries. For several centuries Jever experienced political disintegration until one powerful lord united the district in the early 15th century. The noble line fell extinct in 1575 and Jever passed by marriage to Oldenburg, then successively to Anhalt-Zerbst in 1667, Russia in 1793, Holland in 1807, Russia again in 1813, and finally to Oldenburg again in 1818.

The coinage struck for Jever under Oldenburg can be distinguished by prominence given to the Jever arms - a lion rampant to the left usually in a central shield imposed over the four-fold arms of Oldenburg and Delmenhorst.

RULERS

Johann XVI von Oldenburg, 1575-1603
Anton Günther von Oldenburg, 1603-1667
Johann Rudolph von Anhalt-Zerbst, 1667 only
Karl Wilhelm von Anhalt-Zerbst, 1667-1718

MINT OFFICIALS' INITIALS

Initial	Date	Name
CDZ, GDZ, Z	1663-71	Georg David Ziegenhorn
CP	1674-91	Christian Pfahler
GW	(ca.1698)	?
IA, IAQ	1666-76	Johann Arendsburg
	1614-22	Nikolaus Wintgens
	1637-49	Gerhard Dreyer
	1649-51	Jürgen Detleffs
	1658-62	Jürgen Hartmann

REFERENCE

M = Johann Friedrich L. Th. Merzdorf, **Die Münzen und Medaillen Jeverlands**, Oldenburg, 1862.

LORDSHIP

REGULAR COINAGE

KM# 5 SCHWAREN

Billon **Ruler:** Anton Günther **Obv:** Cross, titles of Anton Günther **Rev:** Jever lion, titles

Date	Mintage	VG	F	VF	XF	Unc
ND	7,549	75.00	150	300	—	—

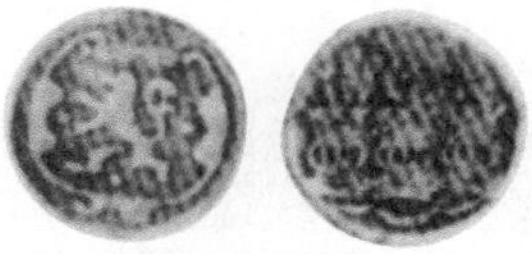

KM# 15 1/4 STUBER (Örtgen)

Billon **Ruler:** Anton Günther **Obv:** Jever lion left **Rev:** 3 ornate helmets

Date	Mintage	VG	F	VF	XF	Unc
ND(c. 1614-1622)	—	20.00	45.00	90.00	180	—

KM# 16 1/4 STUBER (Örtgen)

Billon **Ruler:** Anton Günther **Obv:** Cross, titles of Anton Gunther **Rev:** Crowned 4-fold arms with central shield of Jever lion, titles

Date	Mintage	VG	F	VF	XF	Unc
ND	—	70.00	120	225	450	—

KM# 17 1/4 STUBER (Örtgen)

Billon **Ruler:** Anton Günther **Rev:** Jever lion, titles **Note:** Varieties exist.

Date	Mintage	VG	F	VF	XF	Unc
ND	—	20.00	40.00	80.00	165	—

KM# 86 1/4 STUBER (Örtgen)

Billon **Ruler:** Karl Wilhelm **Obv:** Jever lion arms **Obv. Legend:** MON. PRINC. ANH. D. I. &. K. **Rev. Inscription:** IN / DOMINO / FIDUCIA / NOST. **Note:** Varieties exist.

Date	Mintage	VG	F	VF	XF	Unc
ND(1667-1718)	—	13.00	27.00	55.00	115	—

KM# 85 1/4 STUBER (Örtgen)

Billon **Ruler:** Karl Wilhelm **Obv:** Crowned Jever lion left **Obv. Legend:** MON:NOVA JEVEREN **Rev:** Legend, date **Rev. Inscription:** IN / DEO / FACIEM / VIRT **Note:** Varieties exist.

Date	Mintage	VG	F	VF	XF	Unc
1690	—	20.00	40.00	80.00	165	—
1699	—	20.00	40.00	80.00	165	—

KM# 6 1/2 STUBER

Billon **Ruler:** Anton Günther **Obv:** Crowned 4-fold arms with central shield of Jever lion, titles of Anton Gunther **Rev:** Ornate cross, 1-EV/H-S in 4 angles **Rev. Legend:** IN. M-DOM-SOR-MEA. **Note:** Varieties exist.

Date	Mintage	VG	F	VF	XF	Unc
ND	—	16.00	33.00	65.00	130	—

KM# 7 1/2 STUBER

Billon **Ruler:** Anton Günther **Rev:** I-E/H-S in angles of cross **Rev. Legend:** AUX-IL. M-EA-D. **Note:** Varieties exist.

Date	Mintage	VG	F	VF	XF	Unc
ND	—	18.00	35.00	75.00	150	—

KM# 87 1/2 STUBER

Billon **Ruler:** Karl Wilhelm **Obv:** Ornate burgundian cross **Obv. Legend:** MON-NOV--IEVE-REN **Rev:** Denomination, date

Date	Mintage	VG	F	VF	XF	Unc
1690	—	75.00	150	300	600	—

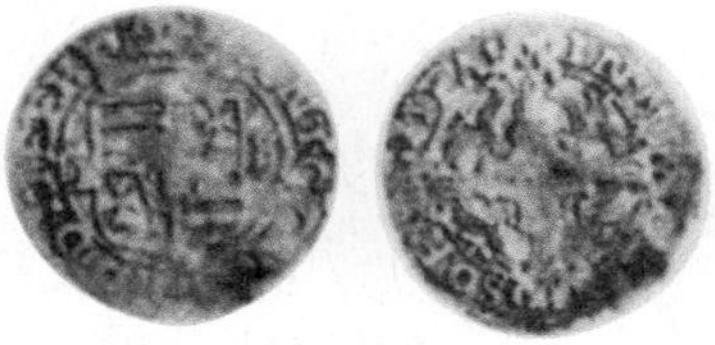

KM# 24 STUBER (10 Witten)

Billon **Ruler:** Anton Günther **Obv:** Crowned 4-fold arms with central shield of Jever lion divides I-S, titles of Anton Gunther **Rev:** Ornate cross **Rev. Legend:** IN. M-DOM-SOR-MEA

Date	Mintage	VG	F	VF	XF	Unc
ND(c. 1618-1620)	—	20.00	45.00	90.00	185	—

KM# 55 STUBER (10 Witten)

Billon **Ruler:** Anton Günther **Rev. Legend:** AUX-IL. M-EA-DOM **Note:** Varieties exist.

Date	Mintage	VG	F	VF	XF	Unc
ND(c. 1660)	—	20.00	45.00	90.00	185	—

KM# 56 STUBER (10 Witten)

Billon **Ruler:** Anton Günther **Obv:** Ornate burgundian cross **Obv. Legend:** MON-NOV--IEVE-REN **Rev. Inscription:** I / IEVER / STU:VER **Note:** Varieties exist.

Date	Mintage	VG	F	VF	XF	Unc
ND	—	95.00	195	325	650	—

KM# 57 STUBER (10 Witten)

Billon **Ruler:** Anton Günther **Obv. Legend:** MON-PRIN. ANHA-D. IE. **Note:** Varieties exist.

Date	Mintage	VG	F	VF	XF	Unc
ND	—	35.00	75.00	150	300	—

KM# 88 STUBER (10 Witten)

Billon **Ruler:** Karl Wilhelm **Rev. Inscription:** .I. / STUVER. / .1690

Date	Mintage	VG	F	VF	XF	Unc
1690	—	16.00	35.00	70.00	140	—

KM# 9.1 2 STUBER (Schaf)
Billon **Ruler:** Anton Günther **Obv:** Crowned 4-fold arms with central shield of Jever lion divides II-S, titles of Anton Gunther **Rev:** Ornate cross **Rev. Legend:** IN MANIBVS DOMINI SOR. MEAE*

Date	Mintage	VG	F	VF	XF	Unc
ND	—	27.00	55.00	90.00	180	—

KM# 9.2 2 STUBER (Schaf)
Billon **Ruler:** Anton Günther **Obv:** Value 2-S

Date	Mintage	VG	F	VF	XF	Unc
ND	—	27.00	55.00	90.00	180	—

KM# 9.3 2 STUBER (Schaf)
Billon **Ruler:** Anton Günther **Note:** Klippe.

Date	Mintage	VG	F	VF	XF	Unc
ND	—	—	—	—	—	—

KM# 13 2 STUBER (Schaf)
Billon **Ruler:** Anton Günther **Obv:** Imperial orb inside 2. GROOT. 18 WIT. **Obv. Legend:** Titles of Matthias **Rev:** 4-fold arms with central concave shield of Jever lion, helmet above

Date	Mintage	VG	F	VF	XF	Unc
ND	—	27.00	55.00	90.00	180	—

KM# 18.1 2 STUBER (Schaf)
Billon **Ruler:** Anton Günther **Obv:** Titles of Matthias

Date	Mintage	VG	F	VF	XF	Unc
ND(1614-1619)	—	27.00	55.00	90.00	180	—

KM# 18.2 2 STUBER (Schaf)
Billon **Ruler:** Anton Günther **Obv:** 2 GROOT 18 WIT around small imperial orb within ornamented oval **Obv. Legend:** IN MANIB...

Date	Mintage	VG	F	VF	XF	Unc
ND(1614-1622)	—	27.00	55.00	90.00	180	—

KM# 18.3 2 STUBER (Schaf)
Billon **Ruler:** Anton Günther **Note:** Klippe.

Date	Mintage	VG	F	VF	XF	Unc
ND(1614-1622)	—	—	—	—	—	—

KM# 19 2 STUBER (Schaf)
Billon **Ruler:** Anton Günther **Rev. Legend:** DA. PACEM. DOMINE. IN. DIEBVS. NOSTRIS.

Date	Mintage	VG	F	VF	XF	Unc
ND	—	27.00	55.00	90.00	180	—

KM# 20 2 STUBER (Schaf)
Billon **Ruler:** Anton Günther **Rev. Legend:** AUXILIUM. MEUM.

Date	Mintage	VG	F	VF	XF	Unc
ND	—	27.00	55.00	90.00	180	—

KM# 64 2 STUBER (Schaf)
Billon **Ruler:** Karl Wilhelm **Obv:** Crowned Anhalt arms divide 2-S, titles of Karl Wilhelm **Rev:** Ornate burgundian cross **Rev. Legend:** MONETA NOVA IEVERNSIS

Date	Mintage	VG	F	VF	XF	Unc
ND	—	27.00	55.00	90.00	180	—

KM# 65 2 STUBER (Schaf)
Billon **Ruler:** Karl Wilhelm **Obv:** Crowned 4-fold arms with central shield of Jever lion divides 2-S, titles of Karl Wilhelm **Rev:** Ornate burgundian cross **Rev. Legend:** IN. DOMINO. FIDUCIA. NOSTRA.

Date	Mintage	VG	F	VF	XF	Unc
ND	—	27.00	55.00	90.00	180	—

KM# 10.1 GROTEN (4 Pfennig)
Billon **Ruler:** Anton Günther **Obv:** Crowned 4-fold arms with central shield of Jever lion, titles of Anton Gunther **Rev:** I/OLDEN/BVRGER/GROT/* **Rev. Legend:** AVXILIVM...

Date	Mintage	VG	F	VF	XF	Unc
ND	—	55.00	110	225	450	—

KM# 10.2 GROTEN (4 Pfennig)
Billon **Ruler:** Anton Günther **Rev. Inscription:** 1 / OLDE / GROT / date

Date	Mintage	VG	F	VF	XF	Unc
1658	—	55.00	110	225	450	—
1659	—	55.00	110	225	450	—

KM# 11 GROTEN (4 Pfennig)
Billon **Ruler:** Anton Günther **Obv:** Arms divide I-G

Date	Mintage	VG	F	VF	XF	Unc
ND	—	55.00	110	225	450	—

KM# 12 2 GROTE (Krumster)
Silver **Ruler:** Anton Günther **Obv:** Crowned 4-fold arms with central shield of Jever lion, titles of Anton Gunther **Rev:** Imperial orb **Rev. Legend:** Inner: 2 GROOT 18 WIT; outer: IN. MANIB. DOMI. SORTE, ME.

Date	Mintage	VG	F	VF	XF	Unc
ND	—	70.00	140	275	550	—

KM# 21 2 GROTE (Krumster)
Silver **Ruler:** Anton Günther **Obv. Legend:** Outer: Titles of Matthias **Rev:** Helmeted, ornate 4-fold arms with central shield Jever lion **Note:** Varieties exist.

Date	Mintage	VG	F	VF	XF	Unc
ND(1614-1619)	—	70.00	140	275	550	—

KM# 90 MALL SCHILLING (6 Stüber)
Silver **Ruler:** Karl Wilhelm **Rev:** Crowned imperial eagle, titles of Leopold I, date in legend

Date	Mintage	VG	F	VF	XF	Unc
1698 GW	—	80.00	140	225	385	—
1699 GW	—	150	300	600	—	—

KM# 75 1/192 THALER (Bläffert)
Billon **Ruler:** Karl Wilhelm **Obv:** Jever lion left **Obv. Legend:** CAROL. WILH:. **Rev:** PRIN. ANHALT. 77. around 19Z.

Date	Mintage	VG	F	VF	XF	Unc
(16)77	—	—	—	—	—	—

KM# 30 1/36 THALER (Mariengroschen)
Silver **Ruler:** Anton Günther **Obv:** Crowned ornate 4-fold arms with central shield of Jever lion divides 7-G **Rev:** Imperial eagle with 36 in oval above, titles of Ferdinand III

Date	Mintage	VG	F	VF	XF	Unc
ND(1637-1657)	—	55.00	120	200	425	—

KM# 43 1/36 THALER (Mariengroschen)
Silver **Ruler:** Anton Günther **Obv:** Crowned 4-fold arms with central shield of Jever lion **Rev:** XXXVI./.EIN/RTAL. **Rev. Legend:** AUXILIUM MEUM A DOMINO, date

Date	Mintage	VG	F	VF	XF	Unc
1658	—	55.00	120	200	425	—
1659	—	55.00	120	200	425	—

KM# 44 1/36 THALER (Mariengroschen)
Silver **Ruler:** Anton Günther **Rev. Legend:** AUXILIUM... **Rev. Inscription:** 36 / EIN / R. TAL. / date **Note:** Varieties exist.

Date	Mintage	VG	F	VF	XF	Unc
1659	—	40.00	90.00	180	360	—
1660	—	40.00	90.00	180	360	—
1664	—	40.00	90.00	180	360	—
1665	—	40.00	90.00	180	360	—
1666	—	40.00	90.00	180	360	—

KM# 45 1/36 THALER (Mariengroschen)
Silver **Ruler:** Anton Günther **Obv:** Crowned Jever lion left **Obv. Legend:** MON. PRIN. ANHAL... **Rev. Legend:** IN. DOMINO. FIDVCIA. NOSTRA. **Rev. Inscription:** 36 / EIN / RTAL / * **Note:** Varieties exist.

Date	Mintage	VG	F	VF	XF	Unc
ND	—	55.00	120	200	385	—
ND IAQ	—	55.00	120	200	385	—

KM# 58 1/18 THALER (4 Grote)
Silver **Ruler:** Anton Günther **Obv:** Crowned 4-fold arms with central shield of Jever lion, titles of Anton Gunther **Rev. Legend:** AUXILIUM...date **Rev. Inscription:** 18 / EIN / R. TAL. / Z **Note:** Varieties exist.

Date	Mintage	VG	F	VF	XF	Unc
1658 (d)	—	115	225	450	900	—
1659 (d)	—	115	225	450	900	—
1660 (d)	—	115	225	450	900	—
1663 Z	—	115	225	450	900	—
1664 Z	—	115	225	450	900	—
1665 Z	—	115	225	450	900	—
1666 Z	—	115	225	450	900	—

KM# 70 1/18 THALER (4 Grote)
Silver **Ruler:** Karl Wilhelm **Obv:** Crowned Jever lion arms **Rev. Legend:** IN DOMINO...date **Rev. Inscription:** 18 / EINEN / REICHS / THALER

Date	Mintage	VG	F	VF	XF	Unc
1671	—	—	—	—	—	—

KM# 71 1/18 THALER (4 Grote)
Silver **Ruler:** Karl Wilhelm **Obv:** Anhalt arms **Obv. Legend:** MON. PRINC. ANH... **Rev. Legend:** IN DOMINO **Rev. Inscription:** 18 / EINEN / RIAL **Note:** Varieties exist.

Date	Mintage	VG	F	VF	XF	Unc
ND	—	—	—	—	—	—

KM# 50 2 SCHILLING (1/16 Thaler)
Silver **Ruler:** Anton Günther **Obv:** Crowned 4-fold arms with central shield of Jever **Rev:** Titles continued **Rev. Inscription:** II / SCHIL / LNIG / date

Date	Mintage	VG	F	VF	XF	Unc
1654	—	—	—	—	—	—

KM# 73 1/16 THALER (3 Schilling)
Silver **Ruler:** Karl Wilhelm **Obv:** Bust right, titles of Karl Wilhelm **Rev. Legend:** IN. DOMIN:... **Rev. Inscription:** XVI / REICHS / THAL. / CP

Date	Mintage	VG	F	VF	XF	Unc
ND(1674-1691)	—	45.00	100	190	385	—

KM# 22 12 GROTE (1/6 Thaler)
Silver **Ruler:** Anton Günther **Obv:** Crowned imperial eagle, orb on breast, titles of Matthias **Rev:** Crowned 4-fold arms with central shield of Jever lion, titles of Anton Gunther

Date	Mintage	VG	F	VF	XF	Unc
ND(1614-1619)	—	—	—	—	—	—

KM# 25 12 GROTE (1/6 Thaler)
Silver **Ruler:** Anton Günther **Obv:** Titles of Ferdinand II **Note:** Klippe.

Date	Mintage	VG	F	VF	XF	Unc
ND(1619-1637)	—	—	—	—	—	—

KM# 41 12 GROTE (1/6 Thaler)
Silver **Ruler:** Anton Günther **Obv:** Bust turned 1/4 to right **Rev:** Crowned 4-fold arms with central shield of Jever lion, XII.GROT below **Rev. Legend:** AVXILIVM and date

Date	Mintage	VG	F	VF	XF	Unc
1658	—	1,650	3,100	—	—	—
1659	—	—	—	—	—	—

KM# 80 1/6 THALER
Silver **Ruler:** Karl Wilhelm **Obv:** Crowned ornate helmet with 3 tall feathers **Rev:** Crowned ornate CWFZA monogram, value (1/6) below, date in legend

Date	Mintage	VG	F	VF	XF	Unc
1689 CP	—	—	—	—	—	—
1690 CP	—	200	400	750	1,500	—

KM# 23 1/4 THALER
Silver **Ruler:** Anton Günther **Obv:** Crowned 4-fold arms with central shield of Jever lion **Rev:** Crowned imperial eagle, orb on breast, titles of Matthias **Note:** Varieties exist.

Date	Mintage	VG	F	VF	XF	Unc
ND(1614-1619)	—	—	—	—	—	—

KM# 42 24 GROTE (1/3 Thaler)
Silver **Ruler:** Anton Günther **Obv:** Bust turned 1/4 right **Rev:** Crowned 4-fold arms with central shield of Jever lion, XXIIII GROT below **Rev. Legend:** AUXILIUM MEUM A DOMINO, date **Note:** Varieties exist.

Date	Mintage	VG	F	VF	XF	Unc
1658	207,000	225	400	750	1,500	—
1659	Inc. above	225	400	750	1,500	—
1660	Inc. above	225	400	750	1,500	—

KM# 69 1/3 THALER (1/2 Gulden)
Silver **Ruler:** Karl Wilhelm **Obv:** Crowned Jever lion in laurel wreath **Rev:** Mintmaster's initials, date in legend **Rev. Inscription:** III / EINEN / REICHS / THALER /

Date	Mintage	VG	F	VF	XF	Unc
1671 GDZ	—	140	225	350	725	—

KM# 72 1/3 THALER (1/2 Gulden)
Silver **Ruler:** Karl Wilhelm **Obv:** Crowned ornate helmet with 3 tall feathers **Rev:** Date in legend **Rev. Inscription:** III / EINEN / REICHS / THALER **Note:** Varieties exist.

Date	Mintage	VG	F	VF	XF	Unc
1671 CDZ	—	85.00	160	300	625	—
167Z IAG	—	65.00	140	275	550	—
1675 CP	—	75.00	150	240	575	—
1676 IA	—	75.00	150	240	575	—

KM# 26 1/2 THALER
Silver **Ruler:** Anton Günther **Obv:** Crowned 4-fold arms with central shield of Jever lion **Rev:** Crowned imperial eagle, orb on breast, titles of Matthias **Note:** Klippe.

Date	Mintage	VG	F	VF	XF	Unc
ND(1614-1619)	—	—	—	—	—	—

KM# 66 1/2 THALER
Silver **Ruler:** Karl Wilhelm **Subject:** Death of Johann Rudolph **Obv:** Bust right **Rev:** Crowned arms of Anhalt, birth and death dates in legend

Date	Mintage	VG	F	VF	XF	Unc
1667	—	—	—	—	—	—

KM# 35 28 STUBER (Gulden)
Silver, 42 mm. **Ruler:** Anton Günther **Obv:** Crowned 4-fold arms with central shield of Jever lion, value (28) below **Obv. Legend:** FLOR • ANT • GV • C(28) • ED • D •LI • E • K - **Rev:** Crowned imperial eagle, 28 in orb on breast **Rev. Legend:** FERD • III • D • G • ROM • IMP • SEMP • AVG • **Note:** Varieties exist. Dav.#713.

Date	Mintage	VG	F	VF	XF	Unc
ND(c. 1640)	—	45.00	90.00	180	360	—

KM# 40 28 STUBER (Gulden)
Silver **Ruler:** Anton Günther **Obv:** Crowned shield within circle **Obv. Legend:** FLOR • AN • GV. C • O (28) E • D • D • I • IE • E • K **Rev:** Value in circle on breast of crowned imperial eagle, 28 in orb on breast within circle **Rev. Legend:** FERD • II • D • G • ROM • IMP • SEMP • AV • **Note:** Varieties exist. Dav. #714.

Date	Mintage	VG	F	VF	XF	Unc
ND(1649-51)	—	33.00	65.00	150	315	—

KM# 59 28 STUBER (Gulden)
Silver **Ruler:** Anton Günther **Obv:** Crowned shield within circle, without value in legend **Obv. Legend:** FLOR • AN • GU • C • O • E • E • DI • IE • E • K • **Rev:** Crowned imperial eagle **Rev. Legend:** • LEOPOLD • D • G • ROM • IMPER • SEMP • AUG * **Note:** Varieties exist. Dav.#715.

Date	Mintage	VG	F	VF	XF	Unc
ND(c. 1660)	—	700	1,300	2,200	3,400	—

KM# 46 48 GROTE (2/3 Thaler)
Silver **Ruler:** Anton Günther **Obv:** Bust turned 1/4 right **Rev:** Crowned 4-fold arms with central shield of Jever lion, 16.48. GROT. 59 above **Rev. Legend:** AUXILIUM MEUM A DOMINO **Note:** Dav.#716.

Date	Mintage	VG	F	VF	XF	Unc
1659	—	575	1,100	2,000	3,350	—
ND(1660)	—	575	1,100	2,000	3,350	—

KM# 47 48 GROTE (2/3 Thaler)
Silver **Ruler:** Anton Günther **Rev:** Date in legend **Note:** Varieties exist. Dav.#717.

Date	Mintage	VG	F	VF	XF	Unc
1659	—	575	1,100	2,000	3,350	—
1660	—	575	1,100	2,000	3,350	—

KM# 48 48 GROTE (2/3 Thaler)
Silver **Ruler:** Anton Günther **Rev:** Value XXXXVIII GROT. below arms **Note:** Dav.#718.

Date	Mintage	VG	F	VF	XF	Unc
1659 Rare	—	—	—	—	—	—

KM# 89 2/3 THALER (Gulden)
Silver **Ruler:** Karl Wilhelm **Obv:** Crowned ornate helmet with 3 tall feathers **Rev:** Crowned ornate CWFZA monogram, 2/3 below, date in legend **Note:** Dav.#581.

Date	Mintage	VG	F	VF	XF	Unc
1690 CP	—	—	—	—	—	—

KM# 74 40 STUBER (Thaler)
Silver **Ruler:** Karl Wilhelm **Obv:** Knight behind shield **Rev:** Rampant lion left **Note:** Varieties exist.

Date	Mintage	VG	F	VF	XF	Unc
1676	—	550	1,000	1,850	3,600	—
1677	—	550	1,000	1,850	3,600	—
1678	—	550	1,000	1,850	3,600	—

KM# 60 48 GROTE (Thaler weight)
Silver **Ruler:** Anton Günther **Obv. Legend:** Ends with ...IE. ET. KN. **Note:** Approximately 29 grams.

Date	Mintage	VG	F	VF	XF	Unc
1660	—	500	950	1,700	3,400	—

KM# 62 THALER
Silver **Ruler:** Anton Günther **Obv:** Bust left **Obv. Legend:** ANT. GVNT. C. OL. **Rev:** Crowned arms **Note:** Dav. #7114.

Date	Mintage	VG	F	VF	XF	Unc
1664	—	500	1,000	2,250	3,750	—

KM# A61 48 GROTE (2 Thaler weight)
Silver **Ruler:** Anton Günther **Obv:** Bust turned 1/4 right **Rev:** Crowned 4-fold arms with central shield of Jever lion, 16.48. GROT. 59 above **Rev. Legend:** AUXILIUM MEUM A DOMINO **Note:** Varieties exist. Dav.#7111.

Date	Mintage	VG	F	VF	XF	Unc
1659	—	750	1,250	—	—	—
ND(1660)	—	750	1,250	—	—	—

KM# 61 48 GROTE (2 Thaler weight)
Silver **Ruler:** Anton Günther **Obv. Legend:** Ends with ...IE. ET. KN. **Rev:** Date in legend **Note:** Approximately 58 grams. Dav.#7118.

Date	Mintage	VG	F	VF	XF	Unc
1660	—	1,000	2,000	3,500	—	—

TRADE COINAGE

KM# 63 DUCAT
3.5000 g., 0.9860 Gold 0.1109 oz. AGW **Ruler:** Anton Günther **Obv:** Bust right **Rev:** Crowned 4-fold arms with central shield of Jever lion in palm wreath **Rev. Legend:** AUXILIUM ..., date

Date	Mintage	VG	F	VF	XF	Unc
1664	—	1,450	2,650	4,650	7,000	—

JULICH

The capital city of the duchy of Jülich is located on the Roer River 16 miles northeast of Aachen near the border with the Netherlands. The Roman town of Juliacum became the seat of the counts of Jülich by the mid-9th century and that of the dukes beginning in 1356. Three major sieges took place against the city and the first occurred in 1543. In the early 17th century Jülich was besieged twice, in 1610 by Prince Moritz of Nassau-Orange (1618-1625) and in 1621-22 by Count Henry of 's-Heerenberg (d.1638).

REFERENCE

N = Hartwig Neumann, **Die Jülicher Notklippen von 1543, 1610, 1721/22**, Jülich, 1974.

CITY

SIEGE COINAGE

1610

Obsidional coinage issued by Baron Johann von Rauschenberg, governor of Jülich on behalf of the Hapsburg Archduke Leopold, imperial administrator for the disputed lands of Jülich, Cleve, Berg, Mark, and Ravensberg. Most, if not all, of the following items were fashioned or cut from silver or gold dinnerware, some hammered flat and countermarked with identifying stamps and value stamps. There are two types of identifying stamps:

A - in oval, a crowned R (Rauschenberg) above 16L10 (L = Leopold).

B - in oval, V/I. R/1610 (Johann von Rauschenberg).

KM# 1 THALER
Silver **Note:** Weight varies: 1.54-3.50 grams. Uniface, oblong and irregular. Stamp B and I in oblong stamp. Varieties exist.

Date	Mintage	VG	F	VF	XF	Unc
1610	—	1,100	1,800	2,800	4,000	—

KM# 2 THALER
Silver **Note:** On square piece.

Date	Mintage	VG	F	VF	XF	Unc
1610	—	1,100	1,800	2,800	4,000	—

KM# 3 THALER
Silver **Note:** On octagonal piece.

Date	Mintage	VG	F	VF	XF	Unc
1610	—	1,100	1,800	2,800	4,000	—

KM# 4 2 THALER
Silver **Note:** Weight varies: 5.77-6.20 grams. Uniface. Square. Stamp A and II in square stamp.

Date	Mintage	VG	F	VF	XF	Unc
1610	—	800	1,300	2,000	5,600	—

KM# 5 2 THALER
Silver **Note:** Weight varies: 5.98-6.20 grams. Varieties exist.

Date	Mintage	VG	F	VF	XF	Unc
1610	—	1,600	2,600	4,000	5,600	—

KM# 6 2 THALER
Silver **Note:** Weight varies: 2.70-9.30 grams. Small irregular, four sided. Varieties exist.

Date	Mintage	VG	F	VF	XF	Unc
1610	—	1,400	2,300	3,500	5,000	—

KM# 7 3 THALER
Silver **Note:** Weight varies: 7.94-10.00 grams. Uniface, irregular half circle.

Date	Mintage	VG	F	VF	XF	Unc
1610	—	1,300	2,200	3,300	4,800	—

KM# 8 3 THALER
Silver **Note:** Square with rounded corners.

Date	Mintage	VG	F	VF	XF	Unc
1610	—	1,300	2,200	3,300	4,800	—

KM# 9 3 THALER
Silver **Note:** Weight varies: 8.60-9.40 grams. Octagonal flan. Varieties exist.

Date	Mintage	VG	F	VF	XF	Unc
1610	—	1,200	2,000	3,100	4,500	—

KM# 10 3 THALER
9.0100 g., Silver **Note:** Square with rounded ends. Stamp B and II in oblong stamp.

Date	Mintage	VG	F	VF	XF	Unc
1610	—	1,450	2,400	3,700	5,300	—

KM# 11 3 THALER
9.0100 g., Silver **Note:** Stamp B and III in rectangular stamp.

Date	Mintage	VG	F	VF	XF	Unc
1610	—	1,400	2,300	3,500	5,100	—

KM# 15 4 THALER
Silver **Note:** Similar to KM#13, but with stamp B.

Date	Mintage	VG	F	VF	XF	Unc
1610	—	1,800	2,900	4,400	6,000	—

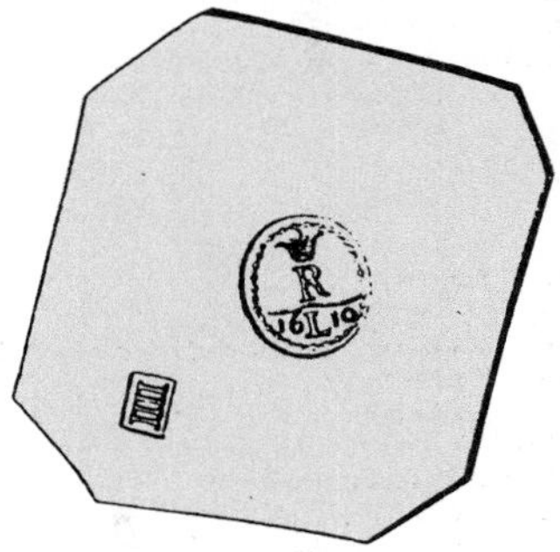

KM# 12 4 THALER
Silver **Note:** Weight varies: 11.80-17.42 grams. Uniface irregular octagon. Stamp A and IIII in rectangle.

Date	Mintage	VG	F	VF	XF	Unc
1610	—	1,800	2,900	4,400	6,000	—

KM# 13 4 THALER
Silver **Note:** Weight varies: 11.76-15.78 grams. Irregular rectangle. Stamp A and IIII in oblong stamp. Varieties exist.

Date	Mintage	VG	F	VF	XF	Unc
1610	—	900	1,450	2,200	6,000	—

KM# 14 4 THALER
26.2000 g., Silver **Note:** Unevenly round. Stamp A and IIII in rectangle.

Date	Mintage	VG	F	VF	XF	Unc
1610	—	1,800	2,900	4,400	6,000	—

KM# 16 5 THALER
Silver **Note:** Weight varies: 17.00-18.00 grams. Uniface square with rounded corners. Stamp A and IIIII in rectangle.

Date	Mintage	VG	F	VF	XF	Unc
1610	—	1,900	3,000	4,500	6,500	—

KM# 17 5 THALER
24.7100 g., Silver **Note:** Irregular flan.

Date	Mintage	VG	F	VF	XF	Unc
1610 Rare	—	—	—	—	—	—

Note: Fritz Rudolf Künker Münzenhandlung Auction 122, 3-07, nearly XF realized approximately $14,550

KM# 18 6 THALER

11.8000 g., Silver **Note:** Uniface triangle with rounded angles. Stamp B, V in square at left, I in rectangle at right.

Date	Mintage	VG	F	VF	XF	Unc
1610	—	2,000	3,300	5,000	7,000	—

KM# 19 6 THALER

28.0700 g., Silver **Note:** Piece from bowl rim, square with rounded angles at bottom.

Date	Mintage	VG	F	VF	XF	Unc
1610	—	2,000	3,300	5,000	7,000	—

KM# 20 7 THALER

24.8700 g., Silver, 67 mm. **Note:** Illustration reduced. Uniface triangle with rounded angles. Stamp A in each angle, VII in rectangle at center.

Date	Mintage	VG	F	VF	XF	Unc
1610	—	2,000	3,300	5,000	7,000	—

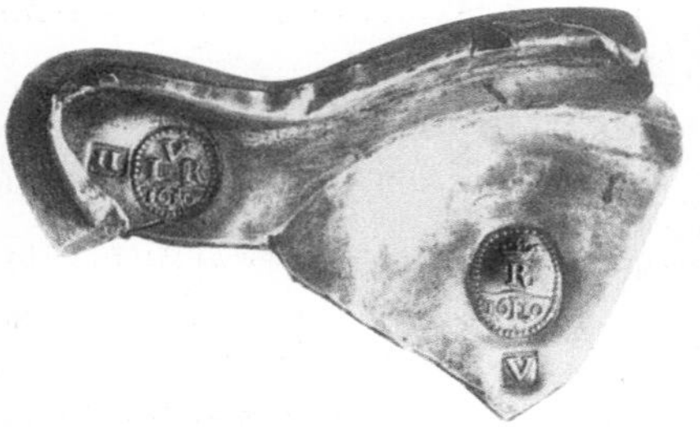

KM# 21 7 THALER

28.7900 g., Silver **Obv:** Stamp B top left with II in rectangle nearby, stamp A with V in square nearby. **Note:** Illustration reduced. Actual size: 81mm wide. Piece from rim of plate. Varieties exist.

Date	Mintage	VG	F	VF	XF	Unc
1610	—	2,000	3,400	5,300	7,500	—

KM# 22 8 THALER

25.6400 g., Silver **Note:** Uniface square. Stamp A in center, eagle in shield-shaped stamp at left and right, II in square stamp twice each above and below.

Date	Mintage	VG	F	VF	XF	Unc
1610	—	2,000	3,400	5,300	7,500	—

KM# 23 8 THALER

37.5000 g., Silver, 85 mm. **Note:** Illustration reduced. Baroque ornamented handle of tableware. Stamp B, V square at left, III in rectangle at right, stamp A on other side.

Date	Mintage	VG	F	VF	XF	Unc
1610	—	2,000	3,500	5,500	8,000	—

KM# 24 8 THALER

37.5000 g., Silver **Note:** Trapezoid. Stamp B in center, V in square left and III in rectangle at right.

Date	Mintage	VG	F	VF	XF	Unc
1610	—	2,000	3,300	5,000	7,000	—

KM# 25 9 THALER

42.0000 g., Silver **Note:** Rim of baroque ornamented cup in uneven square with rounded corners. Stamp B, V in square at left, IIII in rectangle at right, on other side, arms of Rauschenberg (lion upper right, arrow lower left), winged helmet above, IvR below.

Date	Mintage	VG	F	VF	XF	Unc
1610	—	2,400	4,000	6,000	9,000	—

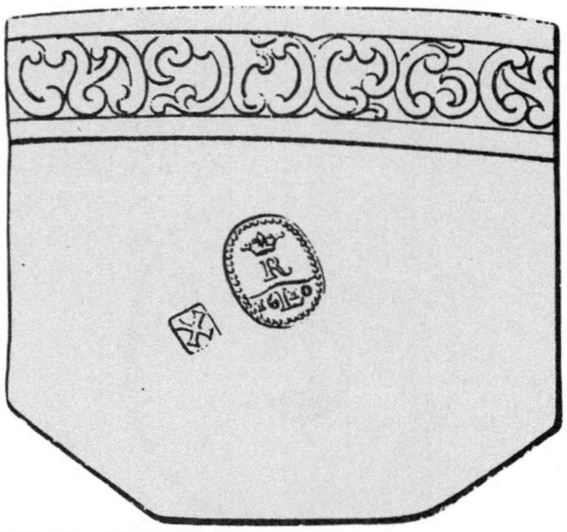

KM# 26 10 THALER

Silver **Note:** Rim of plate, rounded at one end, inner cut end has rounded corners. Large ornate version of stamp A and VIGILANTE/DEO in two lines below. Other side: Stamp A and X in rectangle. Illustration reduced.

Date	Mintage	VG	F	VF	XF	Unc
1610	—	2,700	7,000	10,000	18,000	—

KM# 27 10 THALER

30.5000 g., Silver **Note:** Uniface irregular square from edge of large bowl. Stamp A and X in square. Varieties exist.

Date	Mintage	VG	F	VF	XF	Unc
1610	—	2,700	4,500	7,000	10,000	—

KM# 28 10 THALER

Silver **Note:** Weight varies: 48.90-53.45 grams. Large piece from rim of plate. Stamp A and X in square.

Date	Mintage	VG	F	VF	XF	Unc
1610 Rare	—	—	—	—	—	—

Note: Fritz Rudolf Künker Münzenhandlung Auction 122, 3-07, nearly XF realized approximately $39,675

KM# 29 10 THALER

Silver **Note:** Similar to KM#27, but stamp B.

Date	Mintage	VG	F	VF	XF	Unc
1610	—	3,000	5,000	7,500	11,000	—

KM# 30 15 THALER

69.8000 g., Silver **Note:** Irregular square with rounded corners. Stamp A and X in rectangle at left, V in square at right, large engraved version of A on other side.

Date	Mintage	VG	F	VF	XF	Unc
1610 Rare	—	—	—	—	—	—

KM# 31 15 THALER

65.1900 g., Silver **Note:** Stamp A in center, X in rectangular at left, a second A at lower right with IIIII in long rectangle at left.

Date	Mintage	VG	F	VF	XF	Unc
1610 Rare	—	—	—	—	—	—

KM# 32 20 THALER

90.8000 g., Silver **Note:** Irregular square with rounded corners. Two A stamps at upper left and right, each with X in square nearby. Smaller Thaler denominations exist.

Date	Mintage	VG	F	VF	XF	Unc
1610 Rare	—	—	—	—	—	—

KM# 33 40 THALER

Gold **Note:** Weight varies: 6.66-6.72 grams. Uniface square with rounded corners. Stamp A in center and at each corner, X in squarish stamp in between along each side. Varieties exist.

Date	Mintage	VG	F	VF	XF	Unc
1610 Rare	—	—	—	—	—	—

SIEGE COINAGE

1621-22

Obsidional coinage issued by Friedrich Pithan, governor of the city. There are 3 main types of stamps:

A - Small shield, F above P monogram divides 16 - Z1/Z - S (2 Stüber).

B - Slightly larger shield, F above P monogram divides 16 - Z1/4 - S (4 Stüber).

C - Large shield with extended corners in upper left and right, F above P monogram divides 16 - Z1/IN - GVL/BE - LE and G below, (beseiged in Jülich).

KM# 34 2 STUBER

Silver **Note:** Weight varies: 1.30-1.60 grams. Uniface round. Stamp A. Varieties exist.

Date	Mintage	VG	F	VF	XF	Unc
16Z1	—	550	850	1,150	1,900	—

KM# 35 2 STUBER

Silver **Note:** Weight varies: 0.66-0.81 grams. Triangle with rounded angles. Stamp A. Varieties exist.

Date	Mintage	VG	F	VF	XF	Unc
16Z1	—	550	850	1,150	1,900	—

KM# 36 2 STUBER

Silver **Note:** Weight varies: 0.57-0.71 grams. Octagon. Stamp A.

Date	Mintage	VG	F	VF	XF	Unc
16Z1	—	1,100	1,800	2,900	5,200	—

KM# 37 4 STUBER

Silver **Note:** Weight varies: 0.94-1.62 grams. Uniface irregular round. Stamp B in center. Varieties exist.

Date	Mintage	VG	F	VF	XF	Unc
16Z1	—	1,200	2,000	3,400	6,300	—

KM# 38 4 STUBER

1.2400 g., Silver **Note:** Irregular triangle. Stamp B on one side, GVLICH engraved on other.

Date	Mintage	VG	F	VF	XF	Unc
16Z1	—	1,200	2,000	3,400	6,300	—

KM# 39 4 STUBER

Silver **Note:** Weight varies: 1.92-2.00 grams. Triangular piece from contemporary coin. Stamp B.

Date	Mintage	VG	F	VF	XF	Unc
16Z1	—	2,500	4,300	7,500	12,500	—

KM# 40 8 STUBER

Silver **Note:** Weight varies: 6.05-6.50 grams. Uniface rhombus with rounded corners. Stamp C in center, stamp A in each corner with top inward.

Date	Mintage	VG	F	VF	XF	Unc
16Z1	—	1,350	2,500	4,200	8,000	—

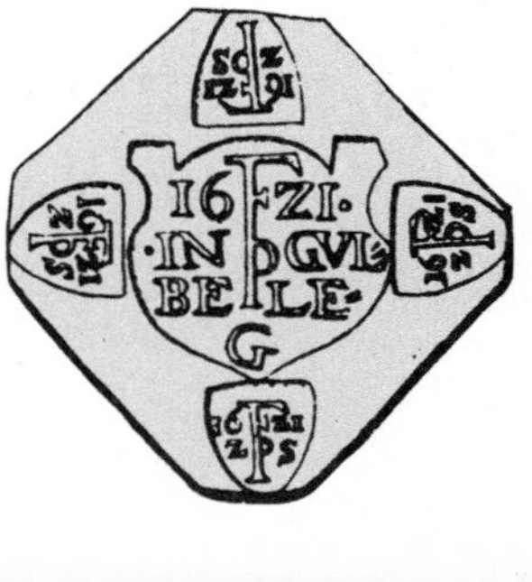

KM# 41 8 STUBER

Silver **Note:** Octagonal flan. Varieties exist.

Date	Mintage	VG	F	VF	XF	Unc
16Z1	—	1,350	2,500	4,200	8,000	—

KM# 42 10 STUBER

7.5800 g., Silver **Note:** Uniface pentagon. Stamp C in center, stamp A five times, tops inward.

Date	Mintage	VG	F	VF	XF	Unc
16Z1	—	1,600	2,700	4,200	8,000	—

KM# 43 12 STUBER

Silver **Note:** Weight varies: 7.17-7.20 grams. Uniface round. Stamp C in center, stamp A six times, tops inward.

Date	Mintage	VG	F	VF	XF	Unc
16Z1	—	1,350	2,500	4,200	8,000	—

KM# 44 12 STUBER

6.3300 g., Silver **Note:** Hexagonal flan.

Date	Mintage	VG	F	VF	XF	Unc
16Z1	—	1,350	2,500	4,200	8,000	—

KM# 45 14 STUBER

Silver **Note:** Weight varies: 4.85-7.70 grams. Uniface seven-sided. Stamp C in center, stamp A seven times at angles, tops inward. Varieties exist.

Date	Mintage	VG	F	VF	XF	Unc
16Z1	—	1,350	2,500	4,200	8,000	—

KM# 46 14 STUBER

Silver **Note:** Round flan.

Date	Mintage	VG	F	VF	XF	Unc
16Z1	—	1,350	2,500	4,200	8,000	—

KM# 47 16 STUBER

Silver **Note:** Weight varies: 6.76-6.80 grams. Uniface square with rounded corners. Stamp C in center, stamp B in each of four corners.

Date	Mintage	VG	F	VF	XF	Unc
16Z1	—	1,600	2,700	4,200	8,000	—

KM# 48 16 STUBER

7.0000 g., Silver **Note:** Octagon. Stamp C in cetner, stamp A in each angle, tops inward.

Date	Mintage	VG	F	VF	XF	Unc
16Z1	—	1,850	3,100	5,000	9,250	—

KM# 49 16 STUBER

7.0200 g., Silver **Note:** Round. Stamp C in center, stamp A eight times, tops inward.

Date	Mintage	VG	F	VF	XF	Unc
16Z1	—	1,850	3,100	5,000	9,250	—

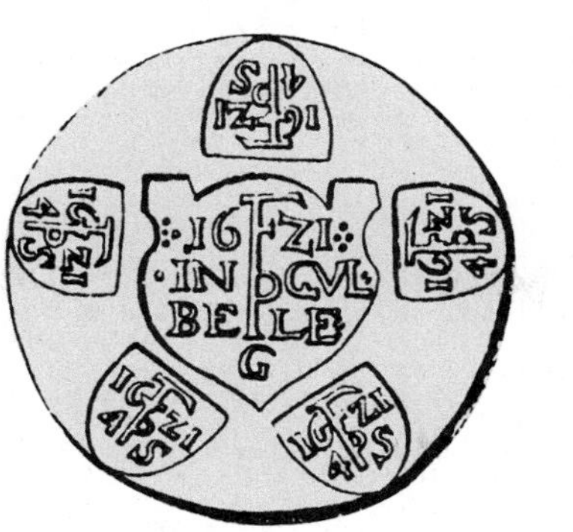

KM# 50 20 STUBER

Silver **Note:** Weight varies: 6.99-15.50 grams. Uniface round. Stamp C in center, stamp B five times, tops inward.

Date	Mintage	VG	F	VF	XF	Unc
16Z1	—	1,700	3,200	4,400	8,500	—

KM# 51 20 STUBER

Silver **Note:** Weight varies: 6.60-7.11 grams. Pentagon flan.

Date	Mintage	VG	F	VF	XF	Unc
16Z1	—	1,700	3,200	4,400	8,500	—

KM# 52 24 STUBER

7.6700 g., Silver **Note:** Uniface round. Stamp C in cetner, four A and B stamps alternating, tops inward.

Date	Mintage	VG	F	VF	XF	Unc
16Z1	—	1,350	3,200	4,400	8,500	—

KM# 53 32 STUBER

Silver **Note:** Uniface round. Stamp C in center, stamp B eight times, tops inward.

Date	Mintage	VG	F	VF	XF	Unc
16Z1	—	1,900	3,300	5,000	9,250	—

KM# 54 THALER

Silver **Note:** Weight varies: 27.19-28.08 grams. Uniface. Stmap C on one side of round flan, usually a contemporary thaler or Spanish 8 Reales, hammered flat. Varieties exist.

Date	Mintage	VG	F	VF	XF	Unc
16Z1	—	1,100	3,000	4,000	8,000	—

Note: Note also that many other pieces of this type, on varying size flans with various weights below 10 grams, were probably meant to be passed as thalers, even though no value is stated on coin

JULICH-BERG

The earliest counts of Jülich, located between Aachen and the Rhine (see Jülich, City), are known from the mid-9th century. Successive counts added territories to the nucleus of their domains and obtained the mint right in 1237. Count Wilhelm V (1328-62) attained the rank of Margrave in 1336 and was raised to that of Duke as Wilhelm I in 1356. His son, Wilhelm II, married Maria of Geldern, thus enlarging the duchy greatly. His younger brother married the heiress of Berg (along the east bank of the Rhine) and Ravensberg (in Westphalia). Geldern passed to the Egmont family in 1423 for lack of legitimate heirs in the Jülich line. Jülich itself fell to the younger branch of the family in Berg-Ravensberg in the same year. From this time on, the duchy was known as Jülich-Berg. Wilhelm IV died in 1511 without a male heir and his daughter, Maria, had married Duke Johann III of Cleve the year before. In 1521, the three duchies were united as Jülich-Cleve Berg (see). Following the great controversy after the death of Duke Johann Wilhelm in 1609, Jülich and Berg were occupied jointly by Brandenburg and Pfalz-Neuburg. The latter acquired Jülich-Berg outright in 1624, while Cleve, Mark and Ravensberg went to Brandenburg-Prussia. The dual duchy remained with the Wittelsbachs of the Palatinate until 1801, in which year France occupied it. In the peace settlement at the end of the Napoleonic Wars in 1815, Jülich-Berg was given to Prussia.

RULERS

Disputed, 1609-1624
Wolfgang Wilhelm von Pfalz-Neuburg, 1624-1653
Philipp Wilhelm von Pfalz-Neuburg, 1653-1679
Johann Wilhelm von Pfalz-Neuburg, 1679-1716

MINT MARKS

D - Düsseldorf

MINTOFFICIALS' INITIALS

Initial	Date	Name
IL	1659-1700	Jakob Leer, die-cutter
IL	1689-90	Johann Linck, die-cutter in Heidelberg
ST	1628-35	Simon Timpff
(h) (linden leaf)	1636-65	Simon Huber
(j) (crossed ingot hooks) or IL	1670-81	Johann Longerich in Mülheim
(n) (crossed ingot hooks) or NL	1681-91	Nikolaus Longerich in Mülheim

ARMS

Berg: Lion with double tail rampant to left.
Cleve: Eight rods (scepters) with lilies at tips arranged as spokes in a wheel, small shield in center.
Jülich: Lion with single tail rampant to left.
Mark: Checkerboard in horizontal band across center.
Pfalz: Lion rampant to left.
Ravensberg: Three chevrons.

REFERENCES

N = Alfred Noss, ***Die Münzen von Berg und Jülich-Berg I***, Munich, 1929.

Sch = Wolfgang Schulten, ***Deutsche Münzen aus der Zeit Karls V.***, Frankfurt am Main, 1976.

DUCHY

REGULAR COINAGE

KM# 11 HELLER

Silver **Ruler:** Wolfgang Wilhelm **Obv:** Rampant lion right **Note:** Uniface.

Date	Mintage	VG	F	VF	XF	Unc
ND(ca.1631)	—	15.00	30.00	65.00	130	—

KM# 78 HELLER

Billon **Obv:** Rampant lion left, NL between hind legs **Note:** Uniface.

Date	Mintage	VG	F	VF	XF	Unc
ND(ca.1685)	—	15.00	32.00	65.00	130	—

KM# 79 HELLER

Billon **Note:** Without mintmaster's initials.

Date	Mintage	VG	F	VF	XF	Unc
ND(ca.1685)	—	15.00	32.00	65.00	130	—

KM# 5 2 HELLER

Silver **Obv:** Lion rampant left **Obv. Legend:** 2 HELLER LEICHT **Note:** Uniface.

Date	Mintage	VG	F	VF	XF	Unc
ND(ca.1628)	—	13.00	27.00	55.00	115	—

KM# 13 2 HELLER (4 Pfennig)

Silver **Note:** Lion rampant left divides date, value 4 between hind legs.

Date	Mintage	VG	F	VF	XF	Unc
(16)36	—	13.00	27.00	55.00	115	—

KM# 50 4 HELLER (Cologne)

Silver **Obv:** Lion rampant right **Obv. Legend:** NVMMVS. IVLIAC. ET. MON **Rev:** Value: IIII in center, legend, date **Rev. Legend:** HELLER. SCHWAR.

Date	Mintage	VG	F	VF	XF	Unc
1662	—	—	—	—	—	—

KM# 25 5 HELLER (Light)

Silver **Obv:** Lion rampant left **Obv. Legend:** MON. IVLIACENSIS **Rev:** Large V in center, date **Rev. Legend:** HELLER LICHT **Note:** Varieties exist.

Date	Mintage	VG	F	VF	XF	Unc
1640 (h)	—	12.00	24.00	50.00	100	—
1641 (h)	—	12.00	24.00	50.00	100	—
(1)641 (h)	—	12.00	24.00	50.00	100	—
(16)42 (h)	—	12.00	24.00	50.00	100	—
1643 (h)	—	12.00	24.00	50.00	100	—
(1)643 (h)	—	12.00	24.00	50.00	100	—
(16)43 (h)	—	12.00	24.00	50.00	100	—

Date	Mintage	VG	F	VF	XF	Unc
(16)44 (h)	—	12.00	24.00	50.00	100	—
ND (h)	—	12.00	24.00	50.00	100	—

KM# 39 5 HELLER (Light)

Silver **Obv:** Lion rampant left **Obv. Legend:** MON. IVLIACENSIS **Rev:** Large V in center, date **Rev. Legend:** HELLER LICHT **Note:** Varieties exist.

Date	Mintage	VG	F	VF	XF	Unc
(1)655	—	12.00	24.00	50.00	100	—

KM# 44 6 HELLER (Light)

Silver **Obv:** Lion rampant left **Obv. Legend:** NVM. IVLIACENSIS. ET **Rev:** Imperial orb with 6, HEL. LE below in legend, MONT - date above

Date	Mintage	VG	F	VF	XF	Unc
(1)659	—	10.00	20.00	35.00	75.00	—
1659	—	10.00	20.00	35.00	75.00	—

KM# 6 8 HELLER (1/74 Thaler)

Silver **Obv:** Legend, VIII in center **Obv. Legend:** NVMMVS IVLIACEN **Rev:** Legend, Lxx/VIII in center

Date	Mintage	VG	F	VF	XF	Unc
ND	—	10.00	20.00	40.00	85.00	—

KM# 7 8 HELLER (1/74 Thaler)

Silver **Rev:** Legend, date **Rev. Legend:** CVSVS DVSSELDORP **Note:** Varieties exist.

Date	Mintage	VG	F	VF	XF	Unc
(16)28	—	10.00	20.00	40.00	80.00	—
(1)628	—	10.00	20.00	40.00	80.00	—
(16)29	—	10.00	20.00	40.00	80.00	—
(1)629	—	10.00	20.00	40.00	80.00	—
(1)630	—	10.00	20.00	40.00	80.00	—
(1)631	—	10.00	20.00	40.00	80.00	—
(1)631 ST	—	10.00	20.00	40.00	80.00	—
(1)648 (h)	—	10.00	20.00	40.00	80.00	—
1649	—	10.00	20.00	40.00	80.00	—
(1)649	—	10.00	20.00	40.00	80.00	—
(1)649 (h)	—	10.00	20.00	40.00	80.00	—

KM# 33 8 HELLER (1/74 Thaler)

Silver **Rev:** Rampant lion left in shield **Note:** Varieties exist.

Date	Mintage	VG	F	VF	XF	Unc
(1)649	—	10.00	20.00	40.00	80.00	—
1650	—	10.00	20.00	40.00	80.00	—
(1)650	—	10.00	20.00	40.00	80.00	—
1651	—	10.00	20.00	40.00	80.00	—
(1)651	—	10.00	20.00	40.00	80.00	—
1652	—	10.00	20.00	40.00	80.00	—
(1)652	—	10.00	20.00	40.00	80.00	—
(1)653	—	10.00	20.00	40.00	80.00	—

KM# 54 8 HELLER (1/74 Thaler)

Silver **Obv:** Legend, date **Obv. Legend:** MONE. IVLIA. ET. MONT **Note:** Varieties exist.

Date	Mintage	VG	F	VF	XF	Unc
1663	—	10.00	20.00	40.00	80.00	—
1663	—	10.00	20.00	40.00	80.00	—
(1)664	—	10.00	20.00	40.00	80.00	—
(16)64	—	10.00	20.00	40.00	80.00	—

KM# 51 8 HELLER (1/74 Thaler)

Silver **Obv:** Lion rampant left, date **Obv. Legend:** MONE. IVLIA. ET. MONT. **Rev:** VIII in center **Rev. Legend:** CVSVS. DVSSELDORP.

Date	Mintage	VG	F	VF	XF	Unc
1663	—	10.00	25.00	50.00	100	—

KM# 53 8 HELLER (1/74 Thaler)

Silver **Obv:** VIII in ceneter **Obv. Legend:** NVMMVS. IVLIACEN **Rev:** Rampant lion left in shield **Rev. Legend:** CVSVS. DVSSELDORP.

Date	Mintage	VG	F	VF	XF	Unc
1663	—	10.00	25.00	50.00	100	—

KM# 52 8 HELLER (1/74 Thaler)

Silver **Obv:** Lion rampant left in shield, date **Obv. Legend:** CVSVS. DVSSELDORP. **Rev:** KM#51 **Note:** Mule.

Date	Mintage	VG	F	VF	XF	Unc
1663	—	10.00	20.00	40.00	85.00	—

KM# 57 8 HELLER (1/74 Thaler)

Silver **Rev:** Date in legend

Date	Mintage	VG	F	VF	XF	Unc
1664	—	10.00	20.00	40.00	80.00	—

KM# 63 8 HELLER (1/74 Thaler)

Silver **Obv:** Titles of Philipp Wilhelm, date **Rev:** VIII in center **Rev. Legend:** MON. IVL. ET. MONT. **Note:** Varieties exist.

Date	Mintage	VG	F	VF	XF	Unc
1676 (j)	—	10.00	20.00	45.00	90.00	—
1676 I(j)L	—	10.00	20.00	45.00	90.00	—
1677 I(j)L	—	10.00	20.00	45.00	90.00	—
1678 I(j)L	—	10.00	20.00	45.00	90.00	—
1679 I(j)L	—	10.00	20.00	45.00	90.00	—

KM# 64 8 HELLER (1/74 Thaler)

Silver **Obv:** Value: VIII in center **Obv. Legend:** MONE. IVLIA. ET. MONT. **Rev:** Arms of Salm (two salmon) in shield **Rev. Legend:** SINGVLA. COLL. IVV. **Note:** Mule.

Date	Mintage	VG	F	VF	XF	Unc
ND	—	—	—	—	—	—

Note: This coin is a mule of reverse type KM#63 and obverse of a fettmannchen of the abbey of Essen date 1671, KM#78

KM# 72 8 HELLER (1/74 Thaler)

Silver **Obv:** Titles of Johann Wilhelm II **Note:** Varieties exist.

Date	Mintage	VG	F	VF	XF	Unc
1682 N(n)L	—	15.00	30.00	60.00	120	—
1683 N(n)L	—	15.00	30.00	60.00	120	—

KM# 14 ALBUS

Silver **Obv:** Crowned lion rampant left **Obv. Legend:** NVMMVS. IVLIACEN. **Rev:** Value **Rev. Inscription:** I / ALBg / LEIC / HT **Note:** Light Albus.

Date	Mintage	VG	F	VF	XF	Unc
ND(ca.1636) (h)	—	—	—	—	—	—

KM# 15 ALBUS

Silver **Rev:** Legend, date **Rev. Legend:** CVSVS. DVSSELDOR **Note:** Varieties exist.

Date	Mintage	VG	F	VF	XF	Unc
(1)636	—	16.00	35.00	75.00	155	—
(1)636 (h)	—	16.00	35.00	75.00	155	—
(1)637 (h)	—	16.00	35.00	75.00	155	—

KM# 32 ALBUS

Silver **Obv:** Lion rampant left **Obv. Legend:** MONETA. IVLIACENSIS **Rev:** Value, legend, date **Rev. Legend:** CVSVS. DVSSELDOR **Rev. Inscription:** I / ALBVS / LEICH / T

Date	Mintage	VG	F	VF	XF	Unc
1648 (h)	—	—	—	—	—	—

KM# 37 ALBUS

Silver **Rev. Inscription:** I / ALB / LEIC / HT **Note:** Varieties exist.

Date	Mintage	VG	F	VF	XF	Unc
1654	—	15.00	35.00	70.00	145	—
1655	—	15.00	35.00	70.00	145	—
1658	—	15.00	35.00	70.00	145	—

KM# 62 2 ALBUS (1/2 Bläffert)

Silver **Obv:** Lion rampant left, titles of Philipp Wilhelm **Rev:** Date at end of inscription **Rev. Legend:** MONET. NOV. IVLIACENSIS **Rev. Inscription:** 2 / ALBVS / COLSCH **Note:** Varieties exist.

Date	Mintage	VG	F	VF	XF	Unc
1674 (j)	—	10.00	20.00	40.00	85.00	—
1675 (j)	—	10.00	20.00	40.00	85.00	—
1676 (j)	—	10.00	20.00	40.00	85.00	—
1676 I(j)L	—	10.00	20.00	40.00	85.00	—
1677 I(j)L	—	10.00	20.00	40.00	85.00	—
1678 I(j)L	—	10.00	20.00	40.00	85.00	—
1679 I(j)L	—	10.00	20.00	40.00	85.00	—

KM# 68 2 ALBUS (1/2 Bläffert)

Silver **Obv. Legend:** SOLI. DEO. GLORIA. D. S **Rev. Legend:** MONETA. NOVA. ARGENTEA.

Date	Mintage	VG	F	VF	XF	Unc
1677	—	—	—	—	—	—

KM# 71 2 ALBUS (1/2 Bläffert)

Silver **Obv:** Titles of Johann Wilhelm II **Note:** Varieties exist.

Date	Mintage	VG	F	VF	XF	Unc
1681 I(j)L	—	10.00	20.00	40.00	85.00	—
1682 N(n)L	—	10.00	20.00	40.00	85.00	—
1683 N(n)L	—	10.00	20.00	40.00	85.00	—
1684 N(n)L	—	10.00	20.00	40.00	85.00	—
1685 N(n)L	—	10.00	20.00	40.00	85.00	—
1688/5 N(n)L	—	10.00	20.00	40.00	85.00	—
1690 N(n)L	—	10.00	20.00	40.00	85.00	—

KM# 16 4 ALBUS (Bläffert)

Silver **Obv:** Crowned 8-fold arms with central shield of Pfalz **Obv. Legend:** IN. DEO... **Rev:** Date at end of inscription **Rev. Legend:** MONE. NOVA. IVLIACEN. ET. MONT. **Rev. Inscription:** IIII / ALBVS / COLSCH **Note:** Varieties exist.

Date	Mintage	VG	F	VF	XF	Unc
(1)636 (h)	—	15.00	35.00	70.00	145	—
1636 (h)	—	15.00	35.00	70.00	145	—
ND(1638) (h)	—	15.00	35.00	70.00	145	—
1639 (h)	—	15.00	35.00	70.00	145	—
(1)641	—	15.00	35.00	70.00	145	—
1643 (h)	—	15.00	35.00	70.00	145	—
1644 (h)	—	15.00	35.00	70.00	145	—
(1)644 (h)	—	15.00	35.00	70.00	145	—
1645 (h)	—	15.00	35.00	70.00	145	—
1646 (h)	—	15.00	35.00	70.00	145	—

KM# 18 4 ALBUS (Bläffert)

Silver **Obv:** Date in legend

Date	Mintage	VG	F	VF	XF	Unc
1638 (h)	—	16.00	35.00	75.00	155	—

KM# 19 4 ALBUS (Bläffert)

Silver **Rev. Legend:** NVMMVS. IVLIACEN...

Date	Mintage	VG	F	VF	XF	Unc
1639 (h)	—	16.00	35.00	75.00	155	—

KM# 30 4 ALBUS (Bläffert)

Silver **Obv:** Date divided below arms

Date	Mintage	VG	F	VF	XF	Unc
164Z	—	16.00	35.00	75.00	155	—

KM# 31 4 ALBUS (Bläffert)

Silver **Obv:** Date in Roman numerals between MEA and CONSOL

Date	Mintage	VG	F	VF	XF	Unc
(16)42	—	16.00	35.00	75.00	155	—

KM# 77 4 ALBUS (Bläffert)

Silver **Obv:** Titles of Johann Wilhelm II **Rev:** Lion rampant left on line above inscription, date at end of inscription **Rev. Legend:** MONE. NOV... **Rev. Inscription:** 4. ALB. COL

Date	Mintage	VG	F	VF	XF	Unc
1684 N(n)L	—	—	—	—	—	—

KM# 8 5 ALBUS

Silver **Obv:** Crowned 8-fold arms with central shield of Pfalz divides date **Obv. Legend:** IN. DEO. MEA. CONSOLATIO. **Rev:** Ornate cross with lion left **Rev. Legend:** MON. NOVA. IVLIACENSIS. V. ALB.

Date	Mintage	VG	F	VF	XF	Unc
1629	—	30.00	65.00	130	265	—

KM# 10 5 ALBUS

Silver **Note:** Varieties exist.

Date	Mintage	VG	F	VF	XF	Unc
(1)630	—	25.00	50.00	100	210	—
(1)631	—	25.00	50.00	100	210	—
(1)63Z	—	25.00	50.00	100	210	—
(1)633	—	25.00	50.00	100	210	—

KM# 26 10 ALBUS (Light)

Silver **Obv:** 8-fold arms with central shield of Pfalz **Obv. Legend:** IN. DEO... **Rev:** Ornamented square tablet with inscription, date divided above and below **Rev. Legend:** MO. NOVA... **Rev. Inscription:** X / ALBVS / LICHT

Date	Mintage	VG	F	VF	XF	Unc
1640 (h)	—	150	300	625	—	—

KM# 29 10 ALBUS (Light)

Silver **Rev:** Date in tablet

Date	Mintage	VG	F	VF	XF	Unc
1641 (h)	—	—	—	—	—	—

KM# 60 1/16 THALER (1/2 Schilling)
Silver **Obv:** Crowned 8-fold arms with central shield of Pfalz, titles of Philipp Wilhelm **Rev:** Date at end of inscription **Rev. Legend:** (j) MON. ARGE. IVLIACENSI **Rev. Inscription:** XVI / I. REICHS / THALER **Note:** Varieties exist.

Date	Mintage	VG	F	VF	XF	Unc
1671 (j)	—	80.00	140	225	450	—
1672 (j)	—	80.00	140	225	450	—

KM# 100 1/12 THALER (1/8 Gulden)
Silver **Obv:** Crowned oval 9-fold arms with central shield **Rev:** Date at end of inscription **Rev. Inscription:** 12 / EINEN / REICHS / THAL

Date	Mintage	VG	F	VF	XF	Unc
1700 HLO	—	55.00	115	235	475	—

KM# 101 1/12 THALER (1/8 Gulden)
Silver **Obv:** Round arms **Rev:** THALER

Date	Mintage	VG	F	VF	XF	Unc
1700 HLO	—	50.00	100	200	425	—

KM# 102 1/12 THALER (1/8 Gulden)
Silver **Obv:** Arms flat on top, rounded at bottom **Note:** Varieties exist.

Date	Mintage	VG	F	VF	XF	Unc
1700 HLO	—	50.00	100	200	425	—

KM# 61 1/8 THALER (Schilling)
Silver **Obv:** Crowned 8-fold arms with central shield of Pfalz, titles of Philipp Wilhelm **Rev:** Date at end of inscription **Rev. Inscription:** VIII / I. REICHS / THALER **Note:** Varieties exist.

Date	Mintage	VG	F	VF	XF	Unc
1673 (j)	—	80.00	160	325	650	—
1675 (j)	—	80.00	160	325	650	—

KM# 70 1/8 THALER (Schilling)
Silver **Obv:** Crowned 8-fold arms with central shield of Pfalz divides date, titles of Johann Wilhelm II **Rev:** Rampant lion left holding large oval with 8/I.R **Rev. Legend:** MONET. NOV. IVLIACENS. ET. MONT. **Note:** Permisser Schilling.

Date	Mintage	VG	F	VF	XF	Unc
1680 I(j)L	—	—	—	—	—	—

Note: This coin circulated on par with similar pieces of Liege and Brabant

KM# 35 1/6 THALER (1/4 Gulden)
Silver **Subject:** Death of Wolfgang Wilhelm **Obv:** 11-line inscription with date **Rev:** 5-line inscription with date in chronogram between palm leaves

Date	Mintage	VG	F	VF	XF	Unc
1653	—	250	500	1,000	2,000	—

KM# 81 1/6 THALER (1/4 Gulden)
Silver **Obv:** Bust right **Rev:** Crowned 8-fold arms with central shield of Pfalz, value (1/6) below, date

Date	Mintage	VG	F	VF	XF	Unc
1689 N(n)L	—	115	225	425	850	—

KM# 93 1/6 THALER (1/4 Gulden)
Silver **Rev:** 9-fold arms with central shield

Date	Mintage	VG	F	VF	XF	Unc
1691 N(n)L	—	—	—	—	—	—

KM# 94 1/6 THALER (1/4 Gulden)
Silver **Obv:** Large 1/6 in laurel wreath

Date	Mintage	VG	F	VF	XF	Unc
1691 N(n)L	—	—	—	—	—	—

KM# 36 1/4 THALER
Silver **Subject:** Death of Wolfgang Wilhelm **Obv:** 11-line inscription with date **Rev:** 5-line inscription with date in chronogram between palm leaves

Date	Mintage	VG	F	VF	XF	Unc
1653	—	325	650	1,360	2,560	—

KM# 98 1/4 THALER
Silver **Obv:** Bust right, date below **Rev:** Four small crowned shields in cruciform, shield in center, a crowned ornate IW monogram between each shield

Date	Mintage	VG	F	VF	XF	Unc
1696 HHK	—	—	—	—	—	—

KM# 65 2/3 THALER (Gulden)
Silver **Obv:** Bust of Philipp Wilhelm right **Rev:** 8-fold arms with central shield of Pfalz, crown above divides date, value (2/3) below

Date	Mintage	VG	F	VF	XF	Unc
1676 I(j)L	—	375	750	1,500	2,750	—

KM# 66 2/3 THALER (Gulden)
Silver **Rev:** Date above crown

Date	Mintage	VG	F	VF	XF	Unc
1676 I(j)L	—	375	750	1,500	2,750	—

KM# 82 2/3 THALER (Gulden)
Silver **Obv:** Bust right **Rev:** Date divided by value (2/3) at bottom

Date	Mintage	VG	F	VF	XF	Unc
1689	—	275	550	1,100	2,200	—
1689 NL/(n)	—	275	550	1,100	2,200	—

KM# 83 2/3 THALER (Gulden)
Silver **Rev:** Crowned 8-fold arms with central shield of Pfalz, value (2/3) below, date in legend **Note:** Varieties exist.

Date	Mintage	VG	F	VF	XF	Unc
1689 (n)NL	—	275	550	1,100	2,200	—
1690 N(n)L	—	275	550	1,100	2,200	—
1690 (n)NL	—	275	550	1,100	2,200	—
1690 NL/(n)	—	275	550	1,100	2,200	—
1690 (n)	—	275	550	1,100	2,200	—
1691 N(n)L	—	275	550	1,100	2,200	—

KM# 90 2/3 THALER (Gulden)
Silver **Obv:** Reverse of KM#83 **Rev:** KM#82 without countermark **Note:** Mule.

Date	Mintage	VG	F	VF	XF	Unc
1690 N(n)L	—	—	—	—	—	—

KM# 95 2/3 THALER (Gulden)
Silver **Rev:** Similar to KM#83, but 9-fold arms in shield

Date	Mintage	VG	F	VF	XF	Unc
1691 N(n)L	—	300	650	1,200	2,400	—

KM# 96 2/3 THALER (Gulden)
Silver

Date	Mintage	VG	F	VF	XF	Unc
1691 IL/N(n)L	—	300	650	1,200	2,400	—
1691 NL/N(n)L	—	300	650	1,200	2,400	—

KM# 103 2/3 THALER (Gulden)
Silver **Rev:** Crowned oval 9-fold arms with central shield

Date	Mintage	VG	F	VF	XF	Unc
1700 HLO	—	800	1,300	1,800	3,150	—

KM# 104 2/3 THALER (Gulden)
Silver **Obv:** Different bust **Rev:** Small oval arms

Date	Mintage	VG	F	VF	XF	Unc
1700 HLO	—	800	1,300	1,800	3,150	—

KM# 105 2/3 THALER (Gulden)
Silver **Rev:** Date divided near bottom by oval arms

Date	Mintage	VG	F	VF	XF	Unc
1700 HLO	—	800	1,300	1,800	3,150	—

KM# 106 2/3 THALER (Gulden)
Silver **Obv:** High collar on neck of bust **Rev:** Larger oval arms

Date	Mintage	VG	F	VF	XF	Unc
1700 HLO	—	800	1,300	1,800	3,150	—

KM# 27 THALER
Silver **Obv:** Bust right, double legend **Rev:** Crowned arms in cartouche **Note:** Dav. #6861.

Date	Mintage	VG	F	VF	XF	Unc
1640	—	1,600	3,300	5,400	—	—

KM# 40 THALER
Silver **Obv:** Bust right with hair neatly tied back with bow **Rev:** Crowned arms in order chain **Note:** Dav. #6865.

Date	Mintage	VG	F	VF	XF	Unc
1655 Rare	—	—	—	—	—	—

KM# 55 THALER
Silver **Obv:** Bust right with loose flying hair **Note:** Dav. #6867.

Date	Mintage	VG	F	VF	XF	Unc
1663 Rare	—	—	—	—	—	—

Note: USB Auction 65, 9-06, VF realized approximately $14,645

KM# 58 THALER
Silver **Obv:** Half-facing bust without inner circle **Note:** Dav. #6868.

Date	Mintage	VG	F	VF	XF	Unc
1667 Rare	—	—	—	—	—	—

KM# 73 THALER
Silver **Note:** Dav. #6870.

Date	Mintage	VG	F	VF	XF	Unc
1682 N(n)L Rare	—	—	—	—	—	—

Note: Fritz Rudolf Künker Münzenhandlung Auction 134, 1-08, nearly XF realized approximately $8,860; Auktionshaus Meister & Sonntag Auction 5, 9-07, XF realized approximately $23,035

KM# 84 THALER
Silver **Obv:** Longer bust showing shoulder **Rev:** Crowned round arms in order collar **Note:** Dav. #6871.

Date	Mintage	VG	F	VF	XF	Unc
1689 IL Rare	—	—	—	—	—	—

KM# 91 THALER
Silver **Subject:** Death of Philipp Wilhelm **Note:** Dav. #6872.

Date	Mintage	VG	F	VF	XF	Unc
1690 NL Rare	—	—	—	—	—	—

KM# 92 THALER
Silver **Obv:** Smaller bust within legend **Obv. Legend:** I. W. D. G. C. P. R. S. R. I. ARCHIT. & EL. **Rev:** Crowned round arms in Order collar **Note:** Dav. #6873.

Date	Mintage	VG	F	VF	XF	Unc
1690 IL Rare	—	—	—	—	—	—

KM# 41 1-1/2 THALER
Silver **Obv:** Bust right **Rev:** Crowned arms divide date **Note:** Dav. #6864.

Date	Mintage	VG	F	VF	XF	Unc
1655 Rare	—	—	—	—	—	—

KM# 12 2 THALER
Silver **Obv:** Bust right within double legend **Rev:** Crowned arms in Order chain **Note:** Dav. #6860.

Date	Mintage	VG	F	VF	XF	Unc
1631 Rare	—	—	—	—	—	—

KM# 42 2 THALER
Silver **Obv:** Bust right with hair neatly tied back with bow **Rev:** Crowned arms in Order chain **Note:** Dav. #6863.

Date	Mintage	VG	F	VF	XF	Unc
1655 Rare	—	—	—	—	—	—

KM# 56 2 THALER
Silver **Obv:** Bust right with loose flying hair **Note:** Dav. #6866.

Date	Mintage	VG	F	VF	XF	Unc
1663 Rare	—	—	—	—	—	—

KM# 74 2 THALER
Silver **Note:** Similar to 1 Thaler, KM#73. Dav. #6869.

Date	Mintage	VG	F	VF	XF	Unc
1682 N(n)L Rare	—	—	—	—	—	—

Note: Auktionshaus H.D. Rauch GmbH Auction 76, 10-05, VF realized approximately $44,510; Westfälische Auktionsgesellschaft Auction 29, 2-05, VF-XF realized approximately $40,840

KM# 43 4 THALER
Silver **Obv:** Bust right with hair neatly tied back with bow **Rev:** Crowned arms in Order chain **Note:** Dav. #6862.

Date	Mintage	VG	F	VF	XF	Unc
1655 Rare	—	—	—	—	—	—

TRADE COINAGE

KM# 17 DUCAT
3.5000 g., 0.9860 Gold 0.1109 oz. AGW **Obv:** Wolfgang Wilhelm **Rev:** Date in legend

Date	Mintage	VG	F	VF	XF	Unc
1636	—	500	1,200	2,500	4,250	—
1643	—	500	1,200	2,500	4,250	—
1650	—	500	1,200	2,500	4,250	—

KM# 38 DUCAT
3.5000 g., 0.9860 Gold 0.1109 oz. AGW **Obv:** Philip Wilhelm **Rev:** Crown divides date

Date	Mintage	VG	F	VF	XF	Unc
1654	—	650	1,350	2,750	4,750	—
1659	—	650	1,350	2,750	4,750	—
1660	—	650	1,350	2,750	4,750	—
1663	—	650	1,350	2,750	4,750	—
1665	—	650	1,350	2,750	4,750	—
1668	—	650	1,350	2,750	4,750	—
1670	—	650	1,350	2,750	4,750	—
1672	—	650	1,350	2,750	4,750	—
1674	—	650	1,350	2,750	4,750	—
1677	—	650	1,350	2,750	4,750	—

KM# 67 DUCAT
3.5000 g., 0.9860 Gold 0.1109 oz. AGW **Obv:** Philip Wilhelm

Date	Mintage	VG	F	VF	XF	Unc
1676	—	500	1,150	2,250	4,000	—

KM# 75 DUCAT
3.5000 g., 0.9860 Gold 0.1109 oz. AGW **Obv:** Bust of Johan Wilhelm II right **Rev:** Crowned 8-fold arms with central shield of Pfalz, date divided above crown

Date	Mintage	VG	F	VF	XF	Unc
1682 N(n)L	—	950	2,250	4,500	7,500	—
1683 N(n)L	—	950	2,250	4,500	7,500	—

KM# 76 DUCAT
3.5000 g., 0.9860 Gold 0.1109 oz. AGW **Obv:** Larger bust of Johann Wilhelm **Note:** Varieties exist.

Date	Mintage	VG	F	VF	XF	Unc
1683	—	950	2,250	4,500	7,500	—
1686 N(n)L	—	950	2,250	4,500	7,500	—

KM# 97 DUCAT
3.5000 g., 0.9860 Gold 0.1109 oz. AGW **Rev:** Crowned round 9-fold arms with central shield, date in legend

Date	Mintage	VG	F	VF	XF	Unc
1691 IL//NL	—	950	2,250	4,500	7,500	—

KM# 28 2 DUCAT
7.0000 g., 0.9860 Gold 0.2219 oz. AGW **Obv:** Bust of Wolfgang Wilhelm right, titles in legend **Rev:** Bust of second wife, Katharina Charlotte right, titles in legend

Date	Mintage	VG	F	VF	XF	Unc
ND(1640) Rare	—	—	—	—	—	—

KM# 34 2 DUCAT
7.0000 g., 0.9860 Gold 0.2219 oz. AGW **Obv:** Bust of Johann Wilhelm II right **Rev:** Bust of Marie Anne left

Date	Mintage	VG	F	VF	XF	Unc
ND(1679) Rare	—	—	—	—	—	—

KM# A91 10 DUCAT
35.0000 g., 0.9860 Gold 1.1095 oz. AGW **Obv:** Johann Wilhelm longer bust showing shoulder **Rev:** Crowned round arms in Order collar **Note:** Struck with 1 Thaler dies, KM#84.

Date	Mintage	VG	F	VF	XF	Unc
1689 IL Rare	—	—	—	—	—	—

COUNTERMARKED COINAGE

KM# 80 2/3 THALER (Gulden)
Silver **Countermark:** Leaping horse of Brunswick **Obv:** 8-fold arms with central shield of Pfalz, titles of Johann Wilhelm II, date above crown **Rev:** Ship sailing away right, value (2/3) in oval below, oval countermark at right of ship

CM Date	Host Date	Good	VG	F	VF	XF
ND	1688 N(n)L	—	—	—	—	—

PATTERNS

Including off metal strikes

KM#	Date	Mintage	Identification	Mkt Val
Pn2	1700 HLO	—	1/12 Thaler. Copper. KM#101	—

JULICH-CLEVE-BERG

United by marriage in 1510 and formally constituted as a single entity in 1521, the Duchies of Jülick, Cleve and Berg followed a single path during most of the 16th century. Following the death of the last ruler in 1609, the various territories were divided among rival claimants to the inheritance. See Jülich-Berg for a more complete overview of the history.

RULER
Johann Wilhelm I, 1592-1609

MINTMASTERS' PRIVY MARKS

Mark	Date	Name
(h)	1613-15	Heinrich Wintgens in Mülheim
(i)	1602-08	Johann Lambers, die-cutter
(r)	1604-05	Johann Rees in Mülheim
(w)	1611-13	Heinrich Wintgens in Huissen and Emmerich

MINTS
Emmerich in Cleve
Huissen in Cleve
Mülheim in Berg

REFERENCES
N = Alfred Noss, **Die Münzen von Berg und Jülich-Berg I**, Munich, 1929.
Sch = Wolfgang Schulten, **Deutsche Münzen aus der Zeit Karls V.**, Frankfurt am Main, 1976.
S = Hugo Frhr. Von Saurma-Jeltsch, **Die Saurmasche Münzsammlung deutscher, schweizerischer und polnischer Gepräge von etwa dem Beginn der Groschenzeit bis zur Kipperperiode**, Berlin, 1892.

DUCHY

REGULAR COINAGE

KM# 5 1/8 STUBER (Deut)
Copper **Obv:** Crowned arms vertically divided into three parts **Obv. Legend:** MO. POSS. PRIN. CVS. **Rev:** Inscription in wreath **Rev. Inscription:** IN / HVES / SEN **Mint:** Huissen **Note:** Varieties exist.

Date	Mintage	VG	F	VF	XF	Unc
ND	1,286,000	15.00	30.00	60.00	—	—

KM# 6 1/8 STUBER (Deut)
Copper **Rev:** CVSA/HVIS/SIAE in wreath **Note:** Varieties exist.

Date	Mintage	VG	F	VF	XF	Unc
ND	Inc. above	15.00	25.00	50.00	—	—

KM# 10 HELLER
Silver **Note:** Uniface, 5-fold arms, date above.

Date	Mintage	VG	F	VF	XF	Unc
(1)604	206,000	8.00	25.00	35.00	70.00	—

KM# 11 HELLER
Silver **Note:** Mintmaster's symbol above arms instead of date.

Date	Mintage	VG	F	VF	XF	Unc
ND (r)	130,000	8.00	25.00	35.00	70.00	—

KM# 23 1/4 STUBER (Örtchen/Örtgen)
Copper **Obv:** Crowned arms of Julich and Berg divide date **Obv. Legend:** MO-POSSI-PRINC-IVL. ET-MON **Rev:** Crowned 6-fold arms **Rev. Legend:** IVSTITIA. THRONVM. FIRMAT. **Note:** Varieties exist.

Date	Mintage	VG	F	VF	XF	Unc
1609	—	30.00	65.00	130	265	—
1611	45,000	30.00	65.00	130	265	—

KM# 21 8 HELLER (1/74 Thaler)
Silver **Note:** Mule. Two reverses dies of KM#12.

Date	Mintage	VG	F	VF	XF	Unc
(1)604/(1)608	—	—	—	—	—	—

KM# 12 8 HELLER (1/74 Thaler)
Silver **Obv:** VIII in circle **Obv. Legend:** NVMMVS. IVLIACENSI **Rev:** LXX/IIII in circle, legend, date **Rev. Legend:** CVSVS. MOLHEMI **Note:** Varieties exist.

Date	Mintage	VG	F	VF	XF	Unc
(1)604 (r)	23,000	13.00	27.00	55.00	110	—
(1)605 (r)	326,000	13.00	27.00	55.00	110	—
(1)606 (r)	445,000	13.00	27.00	55.00	110	—
(1)607 (r)	228,000	13.00	27.00	55.00	110	—
(1)608 (r)	110,000	13.00	27.00	55.00	110	—
(1)609 (r)	84,000	13.00	27.00	55.00	110	—

KM# 20 8 HELLER (1/74 Thaler)
Silver **Obv:** KM#12 with legend NVMMVS. COLONIEN **Rev:** Obverse of Cologne, KM#11 **Note:** Mule. Varieties exist.

Date	Mintage	VG	F	VF	XF	Unc
(1)605 (r)	—	13.00	27.00	55.00	110	—
(1)608 (r)	—	13.00	27.00	55.00	110	—
(1)609 (r)	—	13.00	27.00	55.00	110	—

KM# 19 8 HELLER (1/74 Thaler)
Silver **Obv:** Date in legend

Date	Mintage	VG	F	VF	XF	Unc
(1)605 (r)	Inc. above	13.00	27.00	55.00	110	—

KM# 24 8 HELLER (1/74 Thaler)
Silver **Obv:** KM#12 **Rev:** Reverse of Cologne, KM#11, legend, date **Rev. Legend:** CVSVS. COLONIAE **Note:** Mule.

Date	Mintage	VG	F	VF	XF	Unc
(1)609 (r)	—	—	—	—	—	—

KM# 34 STUBER (21 Heller = 1/56 Thaler)
Silver **Obv:** Crowned 6-fold arms divide I-S **Obv. Legend:** MO: NO: AR: POSS: PRI: 21. h. **Rev:** Ornate cross with lily in center, rampant lion left in upper right and lower left angles of cross, 21 in upper left and H in lower right **Rev. Legend:** 56. DVC-: IVLIE - CLI: E - MONT: **Mint:** Huissen **Note:** Varieties exist.

Date	Mintage	VG	F	VF	XF	Unc
ND(1611-13)	404,000	33.00	65.00	130	265	—

KM# 35 STUBER (21 Heller = 1/56 Thaler)
Silver **Rev:** Upper right and lower left angles of cross have a lily and upper left and lower right a rampant lion **Note:** Varieties exist. Illustration reduced.

Date	Mintage	VG	F	VF	XF	Unc
ND(1611-13)	Inc. above	33.00	65.00	130	265	—

KM# 36 STUBER (16 Heller = 1/3 Albus)
Silver **Obv:** Crowned imperial eagle, 16 in orb on breast, titles of Matthias **Rev:** 6-fold arms **Rev. Legend:** MO:POSS:PRIN... **Mint:** Mülheim

Date	Mintage	VG	F	VF	XF	Unc
ND	—	33.00	65.00	130	265	—

KM# 37 STUBER (16 Heller = 1/3 Albus)
Silver **Rev:** Crowned 6-fold arms **Rev. Legend:** MO. NO. AR. POSS. PRI.

Date	Mintage	VG	F	VF	XF	Unc
ND	—	33.00	65.00	130	265	—

KM# 26 SCHILLING
Silver **Obv:** Crowned 6-fold arms, (two each of Julich, Mark, Berg) **Rev:** Crowned imperial eagle, titles of Rudolf **Rev. Legend:** MO. NO. POS ... IV. ET. MONT. **Note:** Varieties exist.

Date	Mintage	VG	F	VF	XF	Unc
ND(1609-12)	—	45.00	90.00	180	360	—
ND(1609-12) (w)	—	45.00	90.00	180	360	—

KM# 27 SCHILLING
Silver **Obv:** 6-fold arms of Julich, Cleve, Berg, Mark, Ravensberg, and Mors **Obv. Legend:** IVL. CLE. MONT. **Rev:** Crown above double-headed imperial eagle within rope wreath **Mint:** Emmerich **Note:** Varieties exist.

Date	Mintage	VG	F	VF	XF	Unc
ND(1609-12) (w)	323,000	33.00	65.00	130	265	—

KM# 25 SCHILLING
Silver **Obv:** Ornate 5-fold arms **Obv. Legend:** MONETA. NO. ARGEN. POSS. PRINCIP. **Rev:** Inscription in wreath **Rev. Inscription:** IVSTITIA / THRONVM / FIRMAT. Ao/date **Mint:** Huissen

Date	Mintage	VG	F	VF	XF	Unc
1609	—	200	375	750	1,500	—

KM# 40 SCHILLING
Silver **Obv:** Small crown above arms **Rev:** Crown above double-headed imperial eagle within circle **Mint:** Mülheim

Date	Mintage	VG	F	VF	XF	Unc
ND(1612-13) (h)	54,000	45.00	90.00	180	360	—

KM# 39 SCHILLING

Silver **Obv:** Crowned shield within circle **Rev:** Titles of Matthias **Note:** Varieties exist.

Date	Mintage	VG	F	VF	XF	Unc
ND(1612-13) (w)	Inc. above	33.00	65.00	130	265	—

KM# 41 SCHILLING

Silver **Rev:** Imperial orb on eagle's breast **Note:** Varieties exist.

Date	Mintage	VG	F	VF	XF	Unc
ND(1612-13) (h)	Inc. above	45.00	90.00	180	360	—

KM# 38 STUBER (3 Kreuzer)

Silver **Obv:** (3) in legend at bottom, MO: POS... **Rev. Legend:** ... 16.H(eller)

Date	Mintage	VG	F	VF	XF	Unc
ND	—	—	—	—	—	—

KM# 14 THALER

Silver **Note:** Klippe. Dav. #6108A.

Date	Mintage	VG	F	VF	XF	Unc
1604 (j) Rare	Inc. above	—	—	—	—	—

KM# 13 THALER

Silver **Note:** Similar to KM#14, but not a klippe. Varieties exist. Dav. #6108.

Date	Mintage	VG	F	VF	XF	Unc
1604 (j) Rare	3,145	—	—	—	—	—
1605 (r/j) Rare	4,403	—	—	—	—	—

KM# 30 THALER

Silver **Rev:** Crowned arms divide date **Note:** Dav. #6108B.

Date	Mintage	VG	F	VF	XF	Unc
1609 (r/j) Rare	2,580	—	—	—	—	—

KM# 28 THALER

Silver **Subject:** Death of Johann Wilhelm **Obv:** 6-line inscription **Rev:** Arms **Mint:** Huissen **Note:** Dav. #6109.

Date	Mintage	VG	F	VF	XF	Unc
1609 (w) Rare	—	—	—	—	—	—

KM# 16 2 THALER

Silver **Note:** Klippe.

Date	Mintage	VG	F	VF	XF	Unc
1604 (j) Rare	—	—	—	—	—	—

KM# 15 2 THALER

Silver **Note:** Similar to KM#16 but not a klippe. Dav. #6107.

Date	Mintage	VG	F	VF	XF	Unc
1604 (j) Rare	—	—	—	—	—	—

KM# 42 2 THALER

50.8000 g., Silver **Obv:** Crowned shield divides date within circle **Rev:** Crown above double-headed imperial eagle within circle **Mint:** Mülheim **Note:** Klippe. Dav. #6110.

Date	Mintage	VG	F	VF	XF	Unc
1613 (h) Unique	—	—	—	—	—	—

Note: Fritz Rudolf Künker Münzenhandlung Auction 90, 3-03, XF realized approximately $54,175

KM# 17 3 THALER

Silver **Note:** Similar to 2 Thaler, KM#16. Klippe. Dav. #6106.

Date	Mintage	VG	F	VF	XF	Unc
1604 (j) Rare	—	—	—	—	—	—

TRADE COINAGE

KM# 18 GOLDGULDEN

3.5000 g., 0.9860 Gold 0.1109 oz. AGW **Obv:** Four small shields of arms in points of quatrefoil, 6-fold arms, in center date in legend **Rev:** Crowned imperial eagle, orb on breast **Note:** Varieties exist.

Date	Mintage	VG	F	VF	XF	Unc
1604	271	525	1,050	2,200	5,500	—
1605	3,930	450	950	2,000	4,800	—
1608	68	525	1,050	2,200	5,500	—
1609	3,320	450	950	2,000	4,800	—

KM# 43 GOLDGULDEN

3.5000 g., 0.9860 Gold 0.1109 oz. AGW **Obv:** Titles of Matthias **Rev:** Crowned 6-fold arms, legend, date **Mint:** Mülheim

Date	Mintage	VG	F	VF	XF	Unc
1613 (h)	1,220	450	850	1,750	4,500	—

KM# 29 DUCAT

3.5000 g., 0.9860 Gold 0.1109 oz. AGW **Obv:** Full-length figure of emperor (Rudolf II) wearing crown, carrying orb and scepter, striding right, divides date **Obv. Legend:** MO: NO: AVRE-POSS: PRIN. **Rev:** Crowned 6-fold arms, legend, **Rev. Legend:** DVCAT : IVL: CLI ET: MONT.

Date	Mintage	VG	F	VF	XF	Unc
1609 Rare	85	—	—	—	—	—

KAUFBEUREN

As a free city in Bavaria 55 miles southwest of Munich, Kaufbeuren was established c. 842. It enjoyed the status of an imperial city from 1286 until 1803, at which time it passed to Bavaria. A local coinage was struck in the city from about 1540 until 1748.

MINT OFFICIALS' SYMBOLS

Initials	Date	Name
(f) = pinecone divides two horseshoes	1714-41	Christian Ernst Müller, die-cutter in Augsburg

ARMS

Divided vertically, half of imperial eagle on left, right side divided diagonally from upper left to lower right by band, a 6-pointed star above and below.

REFERENCE

N = Elisabeth Nau, **Die Münzen und Medaillen des oberschwäbischen Städte**, Freiburg im Breisgau, 1964.

FREE CITY

REGULAR COINAGE

KM# 5 PFENNIG

Copper, 11 mm. **Obv:** City arms in variety of shield shapes **Note:** Ref. N-113. Uniface Schüssel-type. Kipper coinage. Varieties exist.

Date	Mintage	Good	VG	F	VF	XF
ND(1622)	—	24.00	45.00	75.00	155	—

KM# 6 KREUZER

Copper, 15 mm. **Obv:** City arms **Rev:** Imperial eagle, 1 in orb on breast **Note:** Ref. N-112, 117. Kipper coinage. Varieties exist.

Date	Mintage	Good	VG	F	VF	XF
ND(1622)	—	16.00	40.00	70.00	145	—

KM# 7 KREUZER

Copper Weight varies: 0.81-1.40g., 16-17 mm. **Obv:** City arms, date above **Rev:** Imperial eagle, I in orb on breast **Note:** Ref. N-115, 116. Kipper coinage. Varieties exist.

Date	Mintage	Good	VG	F	VF	XF
1622	—	16.00	40.00	70.00	145	—
16ZZ	—	16.00	40.00	70.00	145	—

KM# 8 KREUZER

0.5300 g., Copper, 16-17 mm. **Obv:** Shield of city arms, date above **Rev:** Crowned imperial eagle, value 1 in orb on breast **Note:** Ref. N-114. Kipper coinage. Varieties exist.

Date	Mintage	Good	VG	F	VF	XF
1622	—	16.00	40.00	70.00	145	—
16ZZ	—	16.00	40.00	70.00	145	—

KEMPTEN

The site of Kempten, 81 miles southwest of Munich, predates the Roman town known as Cambodunum. A monastery was founded there as early as 752 from St. Gall (in present-day Switzerland), but the famous abbey was refounded in 773/4 by Hildegard, wife of Charlemagne. A town grew up around the abbey and was the site of an imperial mint from the early 13th century. In 1289 Kempten became a free imperial city and in 1348 the abbot became a prince of the empire. The city obtained the right to mint coins in 1510 and struck a series from 1511 until 1730. The abbots struck coins in the 12th and 13th centuries, then again from 1572 infrequently until 1748. In 1803 the abbey was secularized and, together with the city, was joined to Bavaria.

RULERS

Johann Adam Renner von Almendingen, 1594-1607
Heinrich VIII von Ulm-Langenrhein, 1607-1616
Johann Eucharius von Wolffurth, 1616-1631
Johann Willibald Schenk von Kastel, 1631-1639
Romanus Bernhard Giel von Gielsperg, 1639-1678
Bernhard Gustav von Baden, 1678
Ruprecht von Bodnau (Bodman), 1678-1728

MINT OFFICIALS' INITIALS

Initial	Date	Name
MW	?	?
(h)= 2 horseshoes		Mintmasters at Augsburg

ARMS

Facing bust of St. Hildegard, usually in shield.

REFERENCE

H = Clemens Maria Haertle, **Die Münzen und Medaillen des Stiftes und der Stadt Kempten, Kempten**, 1993.

ABBEY

REGULAR COINAGE

KM# 5 PFENNIG

Silver Weight varies: 0.27-0.32g., 12 mm. **Ruler:** Johann Eucharius **Obv:** Arms in shield divide M - C (Monasterium Campidonensis), above .I.E.A. (Ioannes Eucharius Abbas) **Note:** Ref. H#171-3; G-30, 31. Uniface Schüssel-type. Varieties exist.

Date	Mintage	VG	F	VF	XF	Unc
ND(1616-31)	—	—	—	—	—	—

KM# 6 PFENNIG

Silver, 13x13 mm. **Ruler:** Johann Eucharius **Obv:** Arms in shield divide M - C (Monasterium Campidonensis), above .I.E.A. (Ioannes Eucharius Abbas) **Note:** Ref. H-174. Klippe.

Date	Mintage	VG	F	VF	XF	Unc
ND(1616-31) Rare	—	—	—	—	—	—

KM# 7 PFENNIG

Copper Weight varies: 0.36-0.43g., 12-13 mm. **Ruler:** Johann Eucharius **Obv:** Facing bust of St. Hildegard **Rev:** Value in 2 lines of inscription **Rev. Inscription:** CC / XXXX / (blossom) **Note:** Ref. H-189, 192; G-34.

Date	Mintage	VG	F	VF	XF	Unc
ND(1616-31)	—	—	—	—	—	—

KM# 11 KREUZER

Silver **Ruler:** Johann Eucharius **Obv:** Facing bust of St. Hildegard, date at end of legend **Obv. Legend:** B' HILDENV. MO. CAM. **Rev:** Eight-armed cross with four short and four long arms, 1 in small oval shield in center **Rev. Legend:** FERDI. II. ROM. IMP. SEMP. A. **Note:** Varieties exist.

Date	Mintage	VG	F	VF	XF	Unc
1623	—	10.00	27.00	55.00	115	—
1624	—	10.00	27.00	55.00	115	—

KM# 12 KREUZER

Copper Weight varies: 0.92-1.04g., 19 mm. **Ruler:** Johann Eucharius **Obv:** Facing bust of St. Hildegard divides date **Rev:** Crowned Imperial Eagle **Note:** Ref. H-175, 176; G-32.

Date	Mintage	VG	F	VF	XF	Unc
1623	—	—	—	—	—	—

KM# 13 KREUZER

Copper Weight varies: 0.80-1.20g., 16 mm. **Ruler:** Johann Eucharius **Obv:** Two-fold arms divided vertically, facing bust of St. Hildegard on left, wolf rampant left above diagonal bands from upper right to lower left in right half **Rev:** Crowned imperial eagle, I in orb on breast **Note:** Ref. H#177-188; G-33. Kipper coinage.

Date	Mintage	VG	F	VF	XF	Unc
ND(1622-23)	—	33.00	75.00	150	300	—

KM# 14 2 KREUZER (Halbbatzen)

Silver Weight varies: 0.76-1.20g., 19 mm. **Ruler:** Johann Eucharius **Obv:** Facing bust of St. Hildegard, date at end of legend **Obv. Legend:** B. HILDE. FVN. M(O). CAM(PID)(O). **Rev:** Imperial orb with 2 **Rev. Legend:** FERDINA(N)D. II. RO(M). I(M)(P). S(E)(MP). A. **Note:** Ref. H#122-41, 143-52; G-23, 24, 26, 27. Varieties exist.

Date	Mintage	VG	F	VF	XF	Unc
1623	—	16.00	35.00	70.00	145	—
1624	—	16.00	35.00	70.00	145	—
1625	—	16.00	35.00	70.00	145	—
1626	—	16.00	35.00	70.00	145	—

KM# 18 2 KREUZER (Halbbatzen)

1.4000 g., Silver, 17x17 mm. **Ruler:** Johann Eucharius **Obv:** Facing bust of St. Hildegard, date at end of legend **Obv. Legend:** B. HILDE. FVN. M. CAMPID. **Rev:** Imperial orb with 2 **Rev. Legend:** FERDINAND. II. ROM. IM. S. A. **Note:** Ref. H-142; G-25. Klippe.

Date	Mintage	VG	F	VF	XF	Unc
1624 Rare	—	—	—	—	—	—

KM# 10 12 KREUZER (Zwölfer; Dreibätzner)

1.9400 g., Silver, 25 mm. **Obv:** Half-length figure of St. Lucius right, arms of Kempten below, date at end of legend **Obv. Legend:** IO. EVCARIVS - D. G. AB. CAM. **Rev:** Crowned imperial eagle, 1Z in orb on breast **Rev. Legend:** FERDI. II. ROM. IMP. SEMPER. AVG. **Note:** Ref. H-121; G-22. 12 Kreuzer. Kipper coinage.

Date	Mintage	VG	F	VF	XF	Unc
(16)22	—	—	—	—	—	—

KM# 15 1/6 THALER

11.0100 g., Silver, 26 mm. **Ruler:** Johann Eucharius **Obv:** Half-length figure of St. Lucius right, arms of Kempten below, abbot's mitre above **Obv. Legend:** IO. IVCHARIVS. D. G. ABBAS. CAMPIDO. **Rev:** 5-line inscription with date in baroque frame **Rev. Inscription:** VI / AVF. EIN / REICHS / TALER / (date) **Note:** Ref. H-120; G-21. Varieties exist.

Date	Mintage	VG	F	VF	XF	Unc
1623	—	—	—	—	—	—

KM# 16 THALER

Silver Weight varies: 27.56-29.23g., 41-44 mm. **Ruler:** Johann Eucharius **Obv:** Facing figure of St. Hildegard holding church model to left, shield of 2-fold arms in baroque frame below in front, date in margin between church model towers **Obv. Legend:** B. HILDEGARDIS. FVND. MO. CAMPIDON. **Rev:** Crowned imperial eagle, orb on breast, in circle **Rev. Legend:** FERDINANDVS. II. ROM. IMP. SEMP. AVGVSTVS. **Note:** Ref. H#106-16; G-18; Dav. 5422. Varieties exist.

Date	Mintage	VG	F	VF	XF	Unc
16Z3	—	900	1,600	2,750	4,000	—

KM# 17 THALER

Silver, 41x44 mm. **Ruler:** Johann Eucharius **Obv:** Facing figure of St. Hildegard holding church model to left, shield of 2-fold arms in baroque frame below in front, date in margin between church model towers **Obv. Legend:** B. HILDEGARDIS. FVND. MO. CAMPIDON/ **Rev:** Crowned imperial eagle, orb on breast, in circle **Rev. Legend:** FERDINANDVS. II. ROM. IMP. SEMP. AVGVSTVS.2 **Note:** Ref. H-117; G-19. Klippe.

Date	Mintage	VG	F	VF	XF	Unc
16Z3 Rare	—	—	—	—	—	—

KM# 19 THALER

Silver, 41 mm. **Ruler:** Johann Eucharius **Obv:** Facing figure of St. Hildegard holding church model to left, small oval shield of arms in baroque frame below in front, date at end of legend **Obv. Legend:** B. HILDEGARDIS. FVN. M. CAMPIDONENSIS. **Rev:** Crowned imperial eagle in circle **Rev. Legend:** FERDINANDVS. II. ROM. IMP. SEMP. AVGVSTVS. **Note:** Ref. H-118; G-20; Dav. 5423.

Date	Mintage	VG	F	VF	XF	Unc
16Z5	—	900	1,600	2,750	4,000	—

KM# 32 THALER

Silver Weight varies: 28.82-29.12g., 44 mm. **Ruler:** Ruprecht **Obv:** Oval shield of 4-fold arms with central shield, in baroque frame, superimposed on crossed sword, crozier and scepter, mitre above **Obv. Legend:** RVPERT. D. G. S. R. I. PRINC. & A. CAMPID. AVG. ROM. IMP. ARCHIMARS. **Rev:** Crowned facing bust of St. Hildegard in circle, date divided in margin above **Rev. Legend:** S. HILDEGARD. IIMP. EX - SVEV. DVCIB. FVNDATR. **Note:** Ref. H-215; G-41; Dav. 5424.

Date	Mintage	VG	F	VF	XF	Unc
1694 (h)	—	240	475	850	2,500	4,900

TRADE COINAGE

KM# 25 DUCAT

3.5000 g., 0.9860 Gold Weight varies: 3.20-3.50g. 0.1109 oz. AGW, 22 mm. **Ruler:** Johann Willibald **Obv:** Shield of 4-fold arms, four helmets above, date at end of legend **Obv. Legend:** D: G: IO: WILLIB: AB: CAM - A: R: IM: A: M: S: R: I: P:. **Rev:** Crowned imperial eagle in circle **Rev. Legend:** FERD: II. D:G. ROM: IMP: SEM: AVG:. **Note:** Ref. H-193; G-35.

Date	Mintage	VG	F	VF	XF	Unc
1631 (h) Rare	—	—	—	—	—	—

KM# 30 DUCAT

3.5000 g., 0.9860 Gold Weight varies: 3.44-3.49g. 0.1109 oz. AGW, 22 mm. **Ruler:** Ruprecht **Obv:** Shield of 4-fold arms with central shield, 4 ornate helmets above **Obv. Legend:** +RVPERT. (D.G.) S. R. I. P. & A. CAMP. AVG. ROM. IMP. ARCHIMARS(C). **Rev:** Oval shield with facing bust of St. Hildegard, ornate helmet above with crest of Genius holding sword and scepter, date at end of legend **Rev. Legend:** S. HILDEGARDIS (IMP - ERATRIX) (-) FVNDATRIX. **Mint:** Augsburg **Note:** Ref. H-209, 211, 212; G#37-39; Fr. 1423. Varieties exist.

Date	Mintage	VG	F	VF	XF	Unc
1692 (h)	—	625	1,350	3,350	6,750	—
1693 (h)	—	625	1,350	3,350	6,750	—
1695 (h)	—	625	1,350	3,350	6,750	—

KM# 31.1 2 DUCAT

7.0000 g., 0.9860 Gold Weight varies: 6.90-6.97g. 0.2219 oz. AGW, 28 mm. **Ruler:** Ruprecht **Obv:** Ornate shield of 4-fold arms with central shield, 4 ornate helmets above **Obv. Legend:** RVPERT. D. G. S. R. I. PRINC. & A. CAMPID. AVG. ROM. IMP. ARCHIMARS. **Rev:** Facing bust of St. Hildegard in ornately shaped shield, ornate helmet above topped with figure of Genius holding sword and scepter, date at end of legend **Rev. Legend:** +ST HILDEGARDIS IMP - ERATRIX FVNDATRIX. **Note:** Ref. H-205; G-36a; Fr. 1422.

Date	Mintage	VG	F	VF	XF	Unc
1693 (h)	—	1,300	2,650	5,300	9,500	—

Note: An example in XF+ realized approximately $14,725 in a Westfälische AG auction of September 2008.

KM# 31.2 2 DUCAT

7.0000 g., 0.9860 Gold Weight varies: 6.92-6.97g. 0.2219 oz. AGW, 28 mm. **Ruler:** Ruprecht **Obv:** Ornate shield of 4-fold arms with central shield, 4 ornate helmets above **Obv. Legend:** RVPERT. D. G. S. R. I. PRINC. & A. CAMPID. AVG. ROM. IMP. ARCHIMARS. **Rev:** Facing bust of St. Hildegard in oval shield, ornate helmet above topped with figure of Genius holding sword and scepter, date at end of legend **Rev. Legend:** +ST HILDEGARDIS IMP - ERATRIX FVNDATRIX. **Note:** Ref. H-206; G-30b; Fr. 1422.

Date	Mintage	VG	F	VF	XF	Unc
1693 (h)	—	1,500	2,800	5,500	10,000	—

FREE CITY

REGULAR COINAGE

KM# 52 PFENNIG
0.2600 g., Silver, 7 mm. **Obv:** K in wreath **Note:** Ref. H-1414; Nau 205a. Uniface.

Date	Mintage	VG	F	VF	XF	Unc
ND	—	10.00	25.00	55.00	115	—

KM# 51 PFENNIG
Copper Weight varies: 0.36-0.98g., 7 mm. **Obv:** Crowned imperial eagle, K in Spanish shield below **Rev:** Value in 2-line inscription **Rev. Inscription:** CC / XXXX **Note:** Ref. H-1457, 1458; Nau 179. Kipper coinage.

Date	Mintage	VG	F	VF	XF	Unc
ND(1622-23)	—	45.00	90.00	150	300	—

KM# 63 1/2 KREUZER
Silver Weight varies: 0.31-0.55g., 15 mm. **Obv:** 3 small shields of arms arranged with tops towards rim, upper shield divides date, K between two at bottom **Note:** Ref. H#1384-87; Nau 199. Uniface.

Date	Mintage	VG	F	VF	XF	Unc
1623	—	18.00	40.00	65.00	120	—

KM# 53 KREUZER
Copper Weight varies: 0.37-1.42g., 16 mm. **Obv:** Crowned imperial eagle, K in shield on breast **Rev:** 4-line inscription with date **Rev. Inscription:** I / KREI / ZER / (date) **Note:** Ref. H#1422-40, 1444-56; Nau 190. Kipper coinage. Varieties exist.

Date	Mintage	VG	F	VF	XF	Unc
1622	—	25.00	45.00	90.00	—	—

KM# 54 KREUZER
Copper Weight varies: 091-1.29g., 15-16 mm. **Obv:** Crowned imperial eagle, K in shield on breast **Rev:** 4-line inscription with date **Rev. Inscription:** I / KREI / TZER / (date) **Note:** Ref. H#1441-3. Kipper coinage. Varieties exist.

Date	Mintage	VG	F	VF	XF	Unc
1622	—	75.00	150	325	—	—

KM# 72 KREUZER
Silver Weight varies: 0.62-0.87g., 17 mm. **Obv:** Eagle in oval shield superimposed on double cross, date at end of legend **Obv. Legend:** MON. NO(VA). CI(VIT). CAMPID(O). **Rev:** Crowned imperial eagle, I in orb on breast **Rev. Legend:** FERD(INAND). II. RO(M). I(M)(P). S. A(V). **Note:** Ref. H#1371-83; G-204, 205. Varieties exist.

Date	Mintage	VG	F	VF	XF	Unc
1623	—	33.00	65.00	130	265	—
1625	—	33.00	65.00	130	265	—

KM# 64 KREUZER
0.7800 g., Silver, 17 mm. **Obv:** Eagle in Spanish shield superimposed on double cross, legend, date at end of legend **Obv. Legend:** MON. NO. CIVIT. CAMPID. **Rev:** Crowned imperial eagle, I in orb on breast **Rev. Legend:** FERDINAND. II. ROM. IM. S. A. **Note:** Ref. H-1370; Nau 198.

Date	Mintage	VG	F	VF	XF	Unc
1623	—	35.00	70.00	130	265	—

KM# 65 2 KREUZER (Halbbatzen)
Silver Weight varies: 1.05-1.31g., 19 mm. **Obv:** Three-fold arms in quatrefoil **Obv. Legend:** MON. NO. CI. CAMPIDO. **Rev:** Crowned imperial eagle, 2 in orb on breast, date at end of legend **Rev. Legend:** FERDINANDVS. II. ROM. IMP. S. A(VG). **Note:** Ref. H#1042-48; Nau 196, 197. Varieties exist.

Date	Mintage	VG	F	VF	XF	Unc
1623	—	13.00	30.00	55.00	115	—

KM# 71 2 KREUZER (Halbbatzen)
Silver Weight varies: 0.74-1.21g., 18 mm. **Obv:** Crowned imperial eagle, 2 in orb on breast, date at end of legend **Obv. Legend:** MON. NO. CI. CAMPIDO. **Rev:** Three small ornately-shaped shield of arms, bottoms to center, in circle **Rev. Legend:** FERDINANDVS. II. ROM. IMP. S(EM). A(V). **Note:** Ref. H#1049-63; Nau 200-3. Varieties exist.

Date	Mintage	VG	F	VF	XF	Unc
1624	—	10.00	25.00	55.00	110	—
1625	—	10.00	25.00	55.00	110	—

KM# 66 3 KREUZER (Groschen)
Silver Weight varies: 1.55-1.86g., 22 mm. **Obv:** Three small shields of arms, bottoms to center in circle, date at end of legend **Obv. Legend:** MON. NOVA. CIVIT. CAMPIDO(N). **Rev:** Crowned imperial eagle, 3 in orb on breast **Rev. Legend:** FERDINANDVS. - II. ROM. IM. S. A(V). **Note:** Ref. H#1344-49; Nau 194, 195. Varieties exist.

Date	Mintage	VG	F	VF	XF	Unc
1623	—	25.00	50.00	100	200	—

KM# 55 1/24 THALER (5 Kreuzer)
1.9000 g., Silver, 24 mm. **Obv:** Crowned imperial eagle, K in shield on breast **Obv. Legend:** MONETA. NO(VA). CI(VIT). CAMPIDONENSIS. **Obv. Inscription:** XXIIII / AVF. EIN / REICHS / TALER. **Rev:** 4-line inscription **Note:** Ref. H#1350-52; Nau 178. Kipper coinage.

Date	Mintage	VG	F	VF	XF	Unc
ND(1622/23)	—	550	800	1,100	1,500	—

KM# 56 12 KREUZER (Zwölfer; Dreibätzner)
Silver, 23-25 mm. **Obv:** Crowned imperial eagle in shield divides date, +XII+ above **Obv. Legend:** MON. NO. CIVIT. CAMPIDONENSIS. **Rev:** STAT / MVNTZ above cross branches, in ornate oval baroque frame **Note:** Ref. H-399, 400; Nau 186, 187. Kipper coinage. Varieties exist.

Date	Mintage	VG	F	VF	XF	Unc
1622	—	—	—	—	—	—

KM# 57 12 KREUZER (Zwölfer; Dreibätzner)
0.9900 g., Silver, 23-25 mm. **Obv:** Crowned imperial eagle in ornamented Spanish shield, .XII. above **Obv. Legend:** MON. NOVA. CIVIT. CAMPIDONENSIS. **Rev:** 3-line inscription with date in baroque frame **Rev. Inscription:** STAT: / MVNTZ / (date) **Note:** Ref. H-401; Nau 188. Kipper coinage.

Date	Mintage	VG	F	VF	XF	Unc
1622	—	—	—	—	—	—

KM# 58 12 KREUZER (Zwölfer; Dreibätzner)
2.7000 g., Silver, 26-28 mm. **Obv:** Imperial eagle in ornamented shield, XII.K above **Obv. Legend:** MONETA. NOVA. CIVITATIS. CAMPIDONENSIS. **Rev:** 3-line inscription with date in baroque frame **Rev. Inscription:** STAT. / MVNTZ / (date) **Note:** Ref. H-402; Nau 189. Kipper coinage.

Date	Mintage	VG	F	VF	XF	Unc
1622	—	—	—	—	—	—

KM# 67 12 KREUZER (Zwölfer; Dreibätzner)
Silver Weight varies: 1.71-2.12g., 24-25 mm. **Obv:** Crowned imperial eagle in ornamented shield, .XII. above **Obv. Legend:** MONETA. NOVA. CIVIT. CAMPIDONENSIS. **Rev:** 3-line inscription with date **Rev. Inscription:** STAT. / MINTZ / (date) **Note:** Ref. H#403-5; Nau 193. Kipper coinage. Varieties exist.

Date	Mintage	VG	F	VF	XF	Unc
1623	—	600	900	1,200	2,000	—

KM# A59 1/8 THALER
Silver Weight varies: 3.19-3.38g., 28-29 mm. **Obv:** Three small shields of Austria, Burgundy and Tyrol, 2 above 1, date at top **Obv. Legend:** MONETA. NOVA. CIVITAT. CAMPIDONENSIS. **Rev:** Half-length laureate and armored figure 3/4 to right, scepter over right shoulder, small shield with imperial eagle below **Rev. Legend:** +FERDINANDVS. II. D.G. - ROM. IMP. SEMP. AVGVS. **Note:** Ref. H-380, 381; N-185.

Date	Mintage	VG	F	VF	XF	Unc
1622	—	675	1,000	1,550	2,550	—

KM# 59 1/4 THALER
Silver Weight varies: 6.88-7.40g., 28-32 mm. **Obv:** 3 small shields, 2 above 1, date centered above upper 2 shields **Obv. Legend:** MONETA. NOVA. CIVIT. CAMPIDONENSIS. **Rev:** Half-length laureate and armored figure, turned 3/4 right, holding sword hilt and scepter, small shield of crowned imperial eagle below **Rev. Legend:** FERDINANDVS. II D. G. - ROM. IMP. SEMP. AVG. **Note:** Ref. H#370-79; Nau 182-84. Varieties exist.

Date	Mintage	VG	F	VF	XF	Unc
1622	—	225	525	800	1,550	—

KM# 61 1/2 THALER
Silver Weight varies: 14.02-14.89g., 33 mm. **Obv:** Imperial eagle in Spanish shield in center, large crown above, small shield at left, right and below, date at end of legend **Obv. Legend:** MONETA. NOVA. CIVIT. CAMPIDONENSIS. **Rev:** Half-length laureate and armored figure, turned 3/4 right, holding sword hilt and scepter, small shield of crowned imperial eagle below **Rev. Legend:** FERDINANDVS. II. D. G. ROM. IMP. SEMP. AVGVST. **Note:** Ref. H-322; Nau 181.

Date	Mintage	VG	F	VF	XF	Unc
1622	—	1,350	2,150	3,250	6,000	—

KM# 73 1/2 THALER
Silver **Note:** Struck from dies of 1 Thaler, KM#69.

Date	Mintage	VG	F	VF	XF	Unc
1623	—	1,150	2,000	3,000	5,600	—

KM# 68A 1/2 THALER
14.6700 g., Silver, 40 mm. **Obv:** Spanish shield with imperial eagle in center, large crown above, 3 small oval shields of arms in baroque frames at left, bottom and right, date at end of legend **Obv. Legend:** MONETA. NOVA. CIVITA. CAMPIDONENSIS. **Rev:** Large high-collared laureate bust to right in circle **Rev. Legend:** FERDINANDVS. II. D. G. ROMA. IMP. SEMP. AVGVSTVS. **Note:** Ref. H-321; Nau 191. Struck on thin flan from Thaler dies, KM#69.

Date	Mintage	VG	F	VF	XF	Unc
1623 Rare	—	—	—	—	—	—

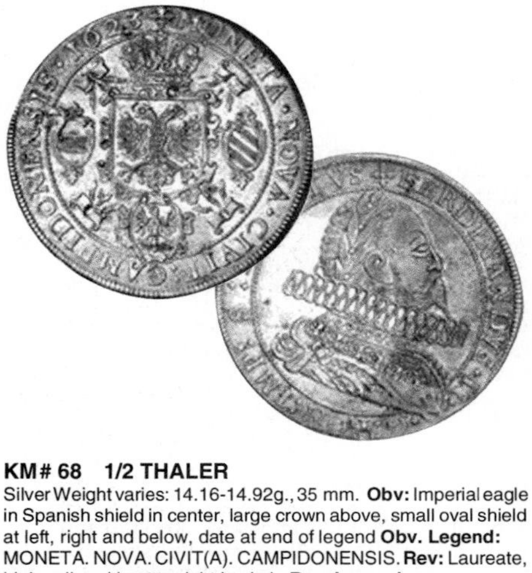

KM# 68 1/2 THALER
Silver Weight varies: 14.16-14.92g., 35 mm. **Obv:** Imperial eagle in Spanish shield in center, large crown above, small oval shield at left, right and below, date at end of legend **Obv. Legend:** MONETA. NOVA. CIVIT(A). CAMPIDONENSIS. **Rev:** Laureate, high-collared bust to right in circle **Rev. Legend:** FERDINANDVS. II. D. G. ROM. IMP. SEMP. AVGVST(VS). **Note:** Ref. H#323-7; Nau 192. Varieties exist.

Date	Mintage	VG	F	VF	XF	Unc
1623	—	1,350	2,150	3,250	5,000	—

KM# 62 THALER

Silver Weight varies: 28.48-28.95g., 42 mm. **Obv:** Modified Spanish shield with imperial eagle in center, large crown above, 3 small shields of arms at left, bottom and right, date at end of legend **Obv. Legend:** MONETA. NOVA. CIVIT. CAMPIDONENSIS. **Rev:** Armored and laureate high-collared half-length figure, turned 3/4 to right, holding orb and scepter **Rev. Legend:** FERDINANDVS. II. D. G. ROM. IMP. SEMPE(R). AVG. **Note:** Ref. H-269, 270; Nau 180; Dav. 5425. Varieties exist.

Date	Mintage	VG	F	VF	XF	Unc
1622	—	1,300	2,250	3,700	6,000	—

KM# 69 THALER

Silver Weight varies: 28.38-29.29g., 40-41 mm. **Obv:** Spanish shield with imperial eagle in center, large crown above, 3 small oval shields of arms in baroque frames at left, bottom and right, date at end of legend **Obv. Legend:** MONETA. NOVA. CIVITA. CAMPIDONENESIS. **Rev:** Large high-collared laureate bust to right in circle **Rev. Legend:** FERDINANDVS. II. D. G. ROM(A). IMP. SEM(P). AVGVSTVS. **Note:** Ref. H#279-84; Nau 191; Dav. 5427. Varieties exist.

Date	Mintage	VG	F	VF	XF	Unc
1623	—	650	1,250	2,500	4,500	—

KM# A70 THALER (Regimentsthaler)

Silver Weight varies: 20.23-22.69g., 39-41 mm. **Obv:** City view, ribbon band above with CAMPIDONVM, 4-line inscription in exergue within cartouche, divides date below, small oval shields left and right, imperial eagle to left, vertical band on empty field to right, die-cutter's name GVLIELMVS HOLENAWER **Obv. Inscription:** PRÆSIDIVM / IOVÆ CONSTANS / ET CERTA / COLVMNA **Rev:** 8 small oval shields of arms of town council members in baroque frames, seven around one in center, 3 angels' heads with wings at top and upper left and right, various other floral ornaments distributed around in field **Note:** Haertle 290, 292.

Date	Mintage	VG	F	VF	XF	Unc
16Z5 DS	—	875	1,250	1,700	2,500	—

KM# 70 2 THALER

57.9300 g., Silver, 40 mm. **Obv:** Spanish shield with imperial eagle in center, large crown above, 3 small oval shields of arms in baroque frames at left, bottom and right, date at end of legend **Obv. Legend:** MONETA. NOVA. CIVITA. CAMPIDONENSIS. **Rev:** Large high-collared laureate bust to right in circle **Rev. Legend:** FERDINANDVS. II. D. G. ROM(A). IMP. SEMP. AVGVSTVS. **Note:** Ref. H-28, Nau 191. Dav. 5426.

Date	Mintage	VG	F	VF	XF	Unc
1623 Rare	—	—	—	—	—	—

TRADE COINAGE

KM# B70 9 DUCAT

31.2500 g., Gold, 40-41 mm. **Obv:** City view, ribbon band above with CAMPIDONVM, 4-line inscription in exergue within cartouche, divides date below, small oval shields left and right, imperial eagle to left, vertical band on empty field to right, die-cutter's name GVLIELMVS HOLENAWER **Obv. Inscription:** PRÆSIDIVM / IOVÆ CONSTANS / ET CERTA / COLVMNA **Rev:** 8 small oval shields of arms of town council members in baroque frames, seven around one in center, 3 angels' heads with wings at top and upper left and right, various other floral ornaments distributed around in field **Note:** Haertle 291. Struck from Thaler dies, KM #A70.

Date	Mintage	VG	F	VF	XF	Unc
16Z5 DS Rare	—	—	—	—	—	—

PATTERNS

Including off metal strikes

KM#	Date	Mintage	Identification	Mkt Val
Pn7	1622	—	Thaler. Tin. KM#62.	—
Pn9	1623	—	Thaler. Lead. KM#69.	—
Pn8	16Z3	—	Thaler. Lead. KM #16.	—
Pn9A	1624	—	2 Kreuzer. Gold. 1.5700 g. 18 mm. KM#71.	12,000
Pn10	1694 (h)	—	Thaler. Lead. KM #32.	—

KOLLN

(Cöln)

Originally a separate settlement on the River Spree just southeast of medieval Berlin when first mentioned in 1238, Kölln has been over the centuries absorbed by the great capital city. It was early on the site of a chief mint for the Brandenburg margraves, but also had a short-lived copper coinage during the opening era of the Thirty Years' War.

CITY

REGULAR COINAGE

KM# 1 SCHERF (1/2 Pfennig)

Copper **Ruler:** (no Ruler Information) **Note:** Uniface; Eagle in shield, start to either side of tail, date above.

Date	Mintage	VG	F	VF	XF	Unc
16Z0	—	20.00	45.00	85.00	190	—
16Z1	—	20.00	45.00	85.00	190	—
1621	—	20.00	45.00	85.00	190	—

KM# 2 SCHERF (1/2 Pfennig)

Copper **Ruler:** (no Ruler Information) **Note:** Uniface; Eagle in shield, start to either side of tail, date above; varities exist.

Date	Mintage	VG	F	VF	XF	Unc
1621	—	20.00	45.00	85.00	190	—
16Z1	—	20.00	45.00	85.00	190	—

KROSSEN

(Crossen)

A town situated on the Oder River, about 30 miles southeast of Frankfurt am Oder, founded in 1005. At first the center of a Silesian duchy, Krossen passed to Brandenburg in 1509 by marriage. During much of the 17th century, Krossen was a mint site for the electors of Brandenburg-Prussia, but during the Kipper Period a local coinage was struck.

PROVINCIAL TOWN

REGULAR COINAGE

KM# 5 PFENNIG

Billon **Obv:** Arms with two shields, C below **Note:** Kipper. Uniface.

Date	Mintage	Good	VG	F	VF	XF
ND(1621-22)	—	40.00	70.00	125	250	—

KUSTRIN

(Custrin)

A town on the Oder River, almost due east of Berlin about 50 miles. It came under the control of the Teutonic Order in 1259, later passing to Brandenburg. Local coinage was issued by the town during the Kipper Period.

TOWN

REGULAR COINAGE

KM# 5 PFENNING

Bronze, 14 mm. **Obv:** Shield of two-fold arms, date divided by C above **Note:** Uniface. Kipper Pfennig.

Date	Mintage	VG	F	VF	XF	Unc
(1)621	—	33.00	55.00	100	200	—
1621	—	33.00	55.00	100	200	—
(1)622	—	33.00	55.00	100	200	—
1622	—	33.00	55.00	100	200	—

KYRITZ

This provincial town is located about 50 miles northwest of Berlin. A few small copper coins were issued during the 16th and 17th centuries.

TOWN

REGULAR COINAGE

KM# 5 PFENNIG

Copper **Note:** Uniface. Two adjacent shields of arms, eagle (Brandenburg) on left, double fleur-de-lis on right, "C" below.

Date	Mintage	Good	VG	F	VF	XF
ND(1619-22)	—	40.00	70.00	125	250	—

Note: This issue is distinguished from similar coins of Crossen by lack of a crossbar on the double fleur-de-lis

LAUINGEN

Lauingen, a town on the Danube in Bavaria, about halfway between Ulm and Donauworth, issued a few copper coins during the emergency Kipper Period of the Thirty Years' War.

TOWN

REGULAR COINAGE

KM# 5 1/4 KREUZER (2 Heller)

Copper 0 **Obv:** Monk's head left in wreath **Rev:** Value Z (2) in wreath **Note:** Kipper 1/4 Kreuzer.

Date	Mintage	VG	F	VF	XF	Unc
ND(1620-22)	—	30.00	65.00	135	275	—

KM# 6 1/2 KREUZER (4 Heller)

Copper 0 **Obv:** Crowned monk's head left in wreath **Rev:** Value 4 in wreath **Note:** Kipper 1/2 Kreuzer.

Date	Mintage	VG	F	VF	XF	Unc
ND(1620-22)	—	27.00	55.00	110	220	—

KM# 7 KREUZER (4 Pfennig)
Copper 0 **Note:** Kipper Kreuzer. Similar to 1/2 Kreuzer, KM#6, but ornate script K in wreath on reverse.

Date	Mintage	VG	F	VF	XF	Unc
ND(1620-22)	—	—	—	—	—	—

LEININGEN

The counts, landgraves and princes of Leiningen trace their origin back to early 12th century Alsace. Over the ensuing centuries, through marriage and division, Leiningen became a house of numerous lines with far-flung possessions situated from southwest Germany, throughout the Rhineland, Hesse and Bavaria. Only several of the Leiningen branches struck coins in the 17th and 19th centuries.

LEININGEN-DAGSBURG-FALKENBURG

This line of counts was founded upon the division of Leiningen-Dagsburg-Hartenburg in 1541. The lands of Leiningen-Dagsburg-Falkenburg were located west of Koblenz near the present-day border with Belgium. Its possessions were annexed by France in 1801.

RULERS
Johann Ludwig, 1593-1625
Ludwig of Westerburg, 1597-1622
Emich XII, 1625-1658

MINT OFFICIAL
David Niderlander, warden in Dagsburg, 1620-1621

COUNTSHIP

REGULAR COINAGE

KM# 13 ALBUS (2 Kreuzer)
Silver **Ruler:** Johann Ludwig **Obv:** Crowned oval 4-fold arms with central shield (cross), date in legend **Rev:** Crowned imperial eagle, 2 in orb on breast, titles of Ferdinand **Mint:** Heidesheim **Note:** Varieties exist.

Date	Mintage	VG	F	VF	XF	Unc
1624	—	60.00	110	165	300	—

KM# 5 12 KREUZER (Dreibatzner)
Silver **Obv:** Crowned 4-fold arms w/central shield, (cross) divides date **Rev:** Crowned imperial eagle with 12 in orb on breast, titles of Ferdinand II **Note:** Varieties exist.

Date	Mintage	VG	F	VF	XF	Unc
ND	—	165	275	420	725	—
1620	5,088	200	300	475	825	—

KM# 6 1/4 THALER
Silver **Ruler:** Johann Ludwig **Obv:** Crowned 4-fold arms with central shield (cross) divides date **Rev:** Crowned imperial eagle, titles of Ferdinand II **Mint:** Heidesheim

Date	Mintage	VG	F	VF	XF	Unc
ND	1,044	325	525	700	1,300	—
1620	4,340	325	525	700	1,300	—

KM# 7 THALER
Silver **Obv:** Crowned ornate oval arms divide date **Rev:** Crowned double eagle with orb on breast **Note:** Dav. #6878.

Date	Mintage	VG	F	VF	XF	Unc
1623	—	1,000	1,800	3,250	—	—

KM# 8 THALER
Silver **Rev:** Crowned shield-shaped arms divide date **Note:** Dav. #6879.

Date	Mintage	VG	F	VF	XF	Unc
1623	—	1,150	2,000	3,500	—	—

KM# 9 THALER
Silver **Rev:** Crowned ornate shield-shaped arms, date in legend **Note:** Dav. #6880.

Date	Mintage	VG	F	VF	XF	Unc
1623	—	1,150	2,000	3,500	—	—

KM# 10 THALER
Silver **Obv:** Date divided below crowned double eagle **Rev:** Crowned ornate oval arms **Note:** Dav. #6881.

Date	Mintage	VG	F	VF	XF	Unc
1623	—	1,150	2,000	3,500	—	—

KM# 11 THALER
Silver **Obv:** Crowned ornate oval arms divide slanting date near bottom **Rev:** Crown above double-headed imperial eagle within circle **Note:** Dav. #6882.

Date	Mintage	VG	F	VF	XF	Unc
1623	—	750	1,350	2,750	—	—
1624	—	750	1,350	2,750	—	—

KM# 14 THALER
Silver **Rev:** Date in straight line divided near bottom **Note:** Dav. #6883.

Date	Mintage	VG	F	VF	XF	Unc
1624	—	800	1,500	3,000	5,000	—

KM# 12 2 THALER
Silver **Obv:** Crowned ornate arms **Rev:** Crowned double eagle **Note:** Dav. #6877.

Date	Mintage	VG	F	VF	XF	Unc
1623 Rare	—	—	—	—	—	—

Note: Giessener Munzhandlung Auction 9 3-76 XF realized $13,420

LEININGEN-LEININGEN

Established by the division of Leiningen-Westerburg in 1547, Leiningen-Leiningen was located some 12 miles southwest of Worms in the Rhineland. When the line fell extinct in 1705, its possessions passed to Leiningen-Schaumburg.

RULERS
Ludwig, 1597-1622
Johann Casimir, 1622-1635
Philipp zu Rikingen, 1635-1668
Ludwig Eberhard, 1668-1688
Philipp Ludwig, 1688-1705

COUNTSHIP

REGULAR COINAGE

KM# 5 PFENNIG
Silver **Obv:** Shield of arms divided into three sections: 1) eagle, 2) two fish, 3) cross **Note:** Uniface.

Date	Mintage	Good	VG	F	VF	XF
ND	444,000	85.00	160	225	400	—

KM# 7 PFENNIG
Silver **Obv:** Small crown above LG **Note:** Varieties exist.

Date	Mintage	Good	VG	F	VF	XF
ND	Inc. above	100	165	250	450	—

KM# 6 PFENNIG
Silver **Ruler:** Ludwig **Obv:** 3 small shields with rounded bottoms towards rims, two above one, LG between top two, Z - L divided by shield on bottom **Mint:** Grünstadt

Date	Mintage	Good	VG	F	VF	XF
ND	Inc. above	85.00	160	225	400	—

KM# 9 8 PFENNIG (2 Kreuzer = 1/2 Batzen)
1.4000 g., Silver, 19.7 mm. **Note:** Klippe.

Date	Mintage	Good	VG	F	VF	XF
1610	Inc. above	—	—	—	—	—

KM# 8 8 PFENNIG (2 Kreuzer = 1/2 Batzen)
Silver **Ruler:** Ludwig **Obv:** Crown above three small shields with rounded bottoms toward rim, two above one, LG between top two, Z-L divided by shield on bottom, titles of Ludwig in legend **Rev:** Titles continued from obverse in legend **Rev. Inscription:** VIII/PFENIG/date, **Mint:** Grünstadt **Note:** Varieties exist.

Date	Mintage	Good	VG	F	VF	XF
1610	99,000	45.00	100	160	300	—
1611	32,000	60.00	110	180	325	—

KM# 12 3 KREUZER (Groschen)
Silver **Ruler:** Ludwig **Obv:** Crowned 4-fold arms with central shield (cross), titles fo Ludwig in legend **Rev:** Crowned imperial eagle, 3 in orb on breast, titles of Rudolf II **Mint:** Grünstadt **Note:** Varieties exist.

Date	Mintage	Good	VG	F	VF	XF
1611	36,000	33.00	75.00	150	300	—
ND	Inc. above	33.00	75.00	150	300	—

KM# 13 3 KREUZER (Groschen)
Silver **Ruler:** Ludwig **Obv:** Crowned shield within circle **Rev:** Titles of Matthias **Mint:** Grünstadt **Note:** Varieties exist.

Date	Mintage	Good	VG	F	VF	XF
ND	163,000	33.00	75.00	150	300	—

KM# 20 3 KREUZER (Groschen)
Silver **Obv:** Titles of Ferdinand II **Rev:** Date divided by arms **Note:** Varieties exist.

Date	Mintage	Good	VG	F	VF	XF
1620	—	33.00	75.00	150	300	—
ND	—	33.00	75.00	150	300	—

KM# 21 3 KREUZER (Groschen)
Silver **Ruler:** Ludwig **Obv:** Date in legend **Mint:** Grünstadt **Note:** Varieties exist.

Date	Mintage	Good	VG	F	VF	XF
(16)22	—	33.00	75.00	150	300	—
(1)622	—	33.00	75.00	150	300	—

KM# 22 3 KREUZER (Groschen)
Silver **Note:** Klippe.

Date	Mintage	Good	VG	F	VF	XF
1622	—	—	—	—	—	—

KM# 14 1/4 THALER
Silver **Ruler:** Ludwig **Obv:** Bust of Ludwig right **Rev:** Crowned 4-fold arms with central shield (cross) divides date **Rev. Legend:** DER. RECHT. GLAUBT… **Mint:** Grünstadt **Note:** Varieties exist.

Date	Mintage	VG	F	VF	XF	Unc
ND	6,939	350	700	1,400	2,750	—
1614	17,000	375	750	1,500	2,900	—

KM# 18 1/2 THALER
Silver **Obv:** Bust right, date below **Rev:** Crowned 4-fold arms iwth central shield **Rev. Legend:** DER. RECHT. GLAUBT…

Date	Mintage	VG	F	VF	XF	Unc
1614	—	—	—	—	—	—

KM# 16 THALER
Silver **Ruler:** Ludwig **Obv:** Bust right in circle **Obv. Legend:** LVD • COM • IN • LEI • ET • RI • DOM • IN • WES • ET • SC • S • R • I • S • L • **Rev:** Crowned ornate 4-fold arms divide date **Rev. Legend:** DER RECHT GLAV: - LAEWIG LEBT **Mint:** Grünstadt **Note:** Dav. #6875.

Date	Mintage	VG	F	VF	XF	Unc
1612 2 known	—	—	—	—	—	—

Note: Gorny & Mosch Giessener Münzhandlung Auction 148, 3-06, good VF realized approximately $21,460.

KM# 17 THALER
Silver **Obv:** Large bust **Rev:** Arms with less ornamentation **Note:** Dav. #6876.

Date	Mintage	VG	F	VF	XF	Unc
1613	1,274	2,250	4,000	6,500	—	—

KM# 10 2 THALER
Silver **Obv:** Bust right, date in front **Rev:** Crowned arms **Note:** Dav. #6874.

Date	Mintage	VG	F	VF	XF	Unc
1610 Rare	—	—	—	—	—	—

KM# 11 2 THALER
Silver **Obv:** Different bust **Rev:** Different shield of arms divides date **Rev. Legend:** GOT. DVT. RETEN. SO DVN. GLAVBEN. **Note:** Klippe.

Date	Mintage	VG	F	VF	XF	Unc
1610 Rare	—	—	—	—	—	—

TRADE COINAGE

KM# 15 GOLDGULDEN
3.5000 g., 0.9860 Gold 0.1109 oz. AGW **Ruler:** Ludwig **Obv:** Bust right in circle, date below. **Obv. Legend:** LV.C.I.L.E.R.D.I. W.S.E.F.S.R.I.S.L(IB). **Rev:** Four-fold arms with central shield, crown above in margin **Rev. Legend:** DER.RECHT.GLAVBT. IA.EWIG.LEB(T). **Mint:** Grünstadt **Note:** Varieties exist.

Date	Mintage	VG	F	VF	XF	Unc
161Z	1,593	500	775	1,750	3,900	—
(1)614	3,488	425	775	1,650	3,250	—
1617	—	425	775	1,650	3,250	—
1618	—	425	775	1,650	3,250	—
1619	—	425	775	1,650	3,250	—
1620	—	500	775	1,750	3,900	—

LEININGEN-SCHAUMBURG-KLEEBERG

This subdivision of Leiningen-Westerburg was established in 1547 and centered in Nassau to the southwest of Limburg. It was further divided in 1695 but none of those branches issued coins.

RULERS
Christof, 1585-1632 and
Philipp Jacob, 1585-1612 and
Reinhart VII, 1585-1655
Georg Wilhelm, 1632-1695

MINT OFFICIALS' INITIALS

Initials	Date	Name
CS	Ca.1663	?
DZ	1670-91	Dietrich Zimmermann at Leiningen
IAB	Ca.1685-89	Johann Adam Bottcher (Bottiger)
	1625-26	Henning Kiessel at Cramberg
	1626-28	Christian Gobel, die-cutter at Cramberg
	1628	Georg Wied at Cramberg

COUNTSHIP

REGULAR COINAGE

KM# 5 PFENNIG
Silver **Obv:** Four-fold arms, LW above. **Mint:** Cramberg **Note:** Kipper Pfennig. Uniface. Varieties exist.

Date	Mintage	Good	VG	F	VF	XF
ND(1621/2)	—	80.00	165	300	600	—

KM# 6 PFENNIG
Silver **Mint:** Cramberg **Note:** Four-fold arms. Varieties exist.

Date	Mintage	Good	VG	F	VF	XF
ND(1621/2)	—	35.00	80.00	150	300	—

KM# 7 PFENNIG
Silver **Note:** LS above arms.

Date	Mintage	Good	VG	F	VF	XF
ND(1621/2)	—	35.00	80.00	150	300	—

KM# 4 PFENNIG
Silver **Ruler:** Reinhart VII **Obv:** Shield of eagle arms, 'L' above, all in circle of pellets **Mint:** Cramberg **Note:** Uniface.

Date	Mintage	VG	F	VF	XF	Unc
ND (1632-55)	—	100	160	225	425	—

KM# 26 8 HELLER
Silver **Ruler:** Georg Wilhelm **Obv:** Cross in shield (Schaumburg), titles of Georg Wilhelm **Rev:** VIII/mintmaster's initials, legend: titles and date **Mint:** Leiningen **Note:** Varieties exist.

Date	Mintage	VG	F	VF	XF	Unc
1676 DZ	—	85.00	165	350	675	—
(1)676	—	85.00	165	350	675	—

KM# 20 KREUZER
Silver **Obv:** Crowned four-fold arms **Rev:** Inscription, mintmaster's initials in wreath **Rev. Inscription:** I/KREVTZ/date/

Date	Mintage	VG	F	VF	XF	Unc
1663 CS	—	—	—	—	—	—

KM# 21 KREUZER
Silver **Rev. Inscription:** I/KREVT/ZER/16CS63

Date	Mintage	VG	F	VF	XF	Unc
1663 CS	—	—	—	—	—	—

KM# 40 KREUZER
Silver **Obv:** Crowned eagle aarms in wreath **Rev:** Inscription in wreath **Rev. Inscription:** I/KREV/TZER/date/mintmaster's initials **Note:** Varieties exist.

Date	Mintage	VG	F	VF	XF	Unc
1685 IAB	—	120	275	425	800	—
1686 IAB	—	120	275	425	800	—

KM# 11 2 KREUZER
Silver **Obv:** Imperial orb with Z, titles of Ferdinand II **Rev:** Ornate cross, small arms in each angle **Note:** Varieties exist.

Date	Mintage	VG	F	VF	XF	Unc
ND(1626)	—	120	275	425	800	—

KM# 9 2 KREUZER
Silver **Obv:** Imperial orb with Z divides date, titles of Reinhart VII **Rev:** Ornate cross, small arms in each angle **Note:** Varieties exist.

Date	Mintage	VG	F	VF	XF	Unc
(16)Z9	—	—	—	—	—	—
ND	—	—	—	—	—	—

KM# 10 2 KREUZER
Silver **Obv:** Titles of Christof **Note:** Varieties exist.

Date	Mintage	VG	F	VF	XF	Unc
ND	—	—	—	—	—	—

KM# 8 3 KREUZER (Groschen)
Silver **Obv:** Crowned imperial eagle, 3 in orb on breast, titles of Ferdinand II and date in legend **Rev:** Four-fold arms, titles of Christof **Note:** Varieties exist.

Date	Mintage	VG	F	VF	XF	Unc
1622	—	60.00	120	240	—	—
ND	—	60.00	120	240	—	—

KM# 42 6 KREUZER
Silver **Obv:** Bust right, value (VI) below in legend **Rev:** Eagle in circle, legend, date divided by mintmaster's initials **Rev. Legend:** SOLI DEO GLORIA **Note:** Varieties exist.

Date	Mintage	VG	F	VF	XF	Unc
1689 IAB	—	165	325	525	1,000	—

KM# 41 15 KREUZER
Silver **Obv:** Bust right **Rev:** Eagle in circle, legend, date **Rev. Legend:** MONETA NOVA ARGENTEA

Date	Mintage	VG	F	VF	XF	Unc
1687	—	65.00	135	275	550	—

KM# 43 15 KREUZER
Silver **Obv:** Value XV below bust in legend **Rev:** Legend, date **Rev. Legend:** SOLI DEO GLORIA **Note:** Varieties exist.

Date	Mintage	VG	F	VF	XF	Unc
1689	—	50.00	115	220	425	—

KM# 45 15 KREUZER
Silver **Rev:** Crowned four-fold arms with central shield (cross) **Note:** Varieties exist.

Date	Mintage	VG	F	VF	XF	Unc
1690	—	40.00	85.00	135	265	—

Date	Mintage	VG	F	VF	XF	Unc
1691	—	40.00	85.00	135	265	—
1692	—	40.00	85.00	135	265	—

KM# 46 15 KREUZER
Silver **Note:** Similar to KM#45, but value (XV) below arms on reverse.

Date	Mintage	VG	F	VF	XF	Unc
1691	—	65.00	135	250	600	—

KM# 48 15 KREUZER
Silver **Note:** Without indication of value.

Date	Mintage	VG	F	VF	XF	Unc
1692	—	65.00	135	250	600	—

KM# 25 60 KREUZER (Gulden = 2/3 Thaler)
Silver **Ruler:** Georg Wilhelm **Obv:** Bust right, value 60 below **Rev:** Crowned four-fold arms with central shield (cross) in palm branches, date in legend **Mint:** Westerburg **Note:** Varieties exist.

Date	Mintage	VG	F	VF	XF	Unc
1675 DZ	—	650	1,325	2,650	—	—
1676 DZ	—	850	1,700	3,250	—	—
1677 DZ Dav# 608B	—	900	1,800	3,300	—	—

KM# 28 60 KREUZER/16 GUTE GROSCHEN (Gulden = 2/3 Thaler)
Silver **Rev. Inscription:** XVI/GUTE/GROSCH

Date	Mintage	VG	F	VF	XF	Unc
1676	—	—	—	—	—	—

KM# 27 60 KREUZER/16 GUTE GROSCHEN (Gulden = 2/3 Thaler)
Silver **Obv:** Bust right, value below **Rev:** Legend, date **Rev. Legend:** SOLI DEO GLORIA **Rev. Inscription:** 16 / GUTE / GROSCH / EN, **Note:** Varieties exist.

Date	Mintage	VG	F	VF	XF	Unc
1676	—	1,125	2,250	4,500	—	—

KM# 15 ALBUS
Silver **Obv:** Crowned four-fold arms with central shield (cross), titles of Georg Wilhelm **Rev:** ALBVS/date in laurel wreath

Date	Mintage	VG	F	VF	XF	Unc
1657	—	—	—	—	—	—

KM# 49 2 ALBUS (4 Kreuzer = Batzen)
Silver **Obv:** Crowned four-fold arms with central shield (cross), L.W above, in laurel wreath **Rev:** II/ALBUS/date, legend **Rev. Legend:** NACH.DEM.SCHLUS.DER.V.STAEND.

Date	Mintage	VG	F	VF	XF	Unc
1693	—	—	—	—	—	—

KM# 29 16 GUTE GROSCHEN (Gulden = 2/3 Thaler)
Silver **Ruler:** Georg Wilhelm **Obv:** Bust right **Rev:** 16/GUTE/GROSCH/EN, legend, date **Rev. Legend:** SOLI DEO GLORIA **Mint:** Westerburg

Date	Mintage	VG	F	VF	XF	Unc
1676	—	1,100	2,200	4,200	—	—

KM# 30 16 GUTE GROSCHEN (Gulden = 2/3 Thaler)
Silver **Obv:** Eagle, legend **Obv. Legend:** MONETA NOVA ARGENTEA

Date	Mintage	VG	F	VF	XF	Unc
1676	—	—	—	—	—	—

KM# 31 24 MARIENGROSCHEN (Gulden = 2/3 Thaler)
Silver **Obv:** Bust right **Rev:** 24/MARIE/GROS, legend, date **Rev. Legend:** SOL DEO GLORIA

Date	Mintage	VG	F	VF	XF	Unc
1676	—	—	—	—	—	—

KM# 36 24 MARIENGROSCHEN (Gulden = 2/3 Thaler)
Silver **Obv. Legend:** XXIIII/MARIE*/GROSCH/date, legend **Rev:** GKIRUA. IN* ECCELSIS*DEO

Date	Mintage	VG	F	VF	XF	Unc
1677	—	—	—	—	—	—

KM# 47 1/12 THALER (2 Groschen)
Silver **Obv:** Crowned oval four-fold arms with central shield (cross) **Rev:** 12/EINEN/REICHS/THALER/1691 in palm wreath **Note:** Varieties exist.

Date	Mintage	VG	F	VF	XF	Unc
1691	—	—	—	—	—	—

KM# 32 1/3 THALER (1/2 Gulden)
Silver **Obv:** Bust right **Rev:** Crowned four-fold arms with central shield (cross) in palm wreath, legend, mintmaster's initials, date **Rev. Legend:** NACH DEM (1/3) LEIBZIGER EVS

Date	Mintage	VG	F	VF	XF	Unc
1676 DZ	—	165	335	675	1,150	—

KM# 33 1/3 THALER (1/2 Gulden)
Silver **Obv:** Bust right, value (1/3) below **Rev:** Legend, date **Rev. Legend:** SOLI DEO GLORIA

Date	Mintage	VG	F	VF	XF	Unc
1676 DZ	—	200	375	750	1,500	—

KM# 34 2/3 THALER (Gulden)
Silver **Obv:** Bust right, value (2/3) below **Rev:** Crowned four-fold arms with central shield in palm wreath, legend, date **Rev. Legend:** SOLI DEO GLORIA **Note:** Varieties exist.

Date	Mintage	VG	F	VF	XF	Unc
1675	—	375	675	1,250	2,400	—
1676 DZ	—	375	675	1,250	2,400	—

Note: Known struck to weight of 1/2 Thaler, 14.72g.

KM# 35 2/3 THALER (Gulden)
Silver **Obv:** Older bust **Rev:** Larger crown **Note:** Varieties exist.

Date	Mintage	VG	F	VF	XF	Unc
1676 DZ	—	375	675	1,250	2,400	—
1676	—	375	675	1,250	2,400	—

KM# 37 2/3 THALER (Gulden)
Silver **Obv:** Two flowers below bust **Rev:** Value (2/3) at bottom

Date	Mintage	VG	F	VF	XF	Unc
1677	—	400	750	1,350	2,400	—

LIEGNITZ

Liegnitz is located in Silesia, 40 miles (67 kilometers) west-northwest of Breslau, and was one of the two seats for the dukes of Silesia-Liegnitz-Brieg (see). The town was given the mint right by Duke Ludwig III (1420-41) in 1425 and a series of small denominations ensued. Liegnitz passed to the Habsburgs, along with the rest of the duchy, in 1675.

MINT OFFICIAL'S INITIAL

Initials	Date	Name
GH	1622-23	Georg Heinecke, mintmaster

ARMS

2 crossed keys, often with Bohemian lion rampant left

REFERENCE

F/S = Ferdinand Friedensburg and Hans Seger, ***Schlesiens Münzen und Medaillen der neuren Zeit,*** Breslau, 1901 (reprint Frankfurt/Main, 1976).

S = Hugo Frhr. Von Saurma-Jeltsch, ***Die Saurmasche Münzsammlung deutscher, schweizerischer und polnischer Gepräge von etwa dem Beginn der Groschenzeit bis zur Kipperperiode,*** Berlin, 1892.

S/Sch = Hugo Frhr. Von Saurma-Jelsch, ***Schlesische Münzen und Medaillen, Breslau, 1883.***

TOWN

STANDARD COINAGE

KM# 3 2 HELLER
0.2900 g., Copper **Obv:** Crossed keys divide mintmaster's initials, 'L' above, 'II' below **Note:** Ref. F/S#3596. Kipper coinage. Uniface.

Date	Mintage	VG	F	VF	XF	Unc
ND(1622-23) GH	—	28.00	50.00	90.00	160	—

KM# 5 3 HELLER
0.4800 g., Copper **Obv:** 3 small round shields, 1 above 2, upper has 'L' and divides mintmaster's initials, lower left crossed keys, lower right Bohemian lion, value 'III' at bottom **Note:** Ref. F/S-3594; S/Sch-78. Kipper coinage. Uniface.

Date	Mintage	VG	F	VF	XF	Unc
ND(1622-23) GH	—	18.00	35.00	60.00	110	—

KM# 6 3 HELLER
Copper **Obv:** Crossed keys at left, Bohemian lion at right, 'L' above, G III H in exergue **Note:** Ref. F/S#3595. Kipper coinage. Uniface.

Date	Mintage	VG	F	VF	XF	Unc
ND(1622-23) GH	—	18.00	35.00	50.00	85.00	—

KM# 7 3 HELLER
0.2800 g., Copper **Obv:** Trefoil with 'L' in upper lobe which divides mintmaster's initials, crossed keys in lower left, Bohemian lion in lower right, value 'III' at bottom **Note:** Ref. F/S#3593. Kipper coinage. Uniface.

Date	Mintage	VG	F	VF	XF	Unc
ND(1622-23) GH	—	16.00	35.00	65.00	120	—

KM# 8 3 HELLER
Copper **Obv:** Trefoil with crossed keys, 'L' in upper lobe which divides date, mintmaster's initials in lower lobes **Note:** Ref. S/Sch#3591. Kipper coinage. Uniface.

Date	Mintage	VG	F	VF	XF	Unc
16ZZ GH	—	—	—	—	—	—

KM# 9 3 HELLER
Copper **Obv:** Trefoil with 'L' in upper lobe which divides date, Bohemian lion in lower left, crossed keys in lower right, mintmaster's initials in lower lobes **Note:** Ref. F/S#3592. Kipper coinage. Uniface.

Date	Mintage	VG	F	VF	XF	Unc
16ZZ GH	—	—	—	—	—	—

LINDAU

A town located on the northeast shore of Lake Constance, Lindau dates from the early 9th century. After acquiring the status of free imperial city in 1274, a local coinage was produced for Lindau on and off during the next 5 centuries. During the Kipper Period of the Thirty Years' War, a variety of coins from South German issuing authorities were counterstamped with the linden tree symbol of Lindau. These are not listed here. In 1732 a joint coinage with the towns of Isny, Wangen, and Leutkirch was struck. After the Napoleonic Wars, in 1805, Lindau was made a part of Bavaria.

MINT

Langenargen, of the Swabian imperial circle located in Montfort

MINT OFFICIALS' INITIALS

Initial	Date	Name
	1682-1712	Hans Jakob Kickh
	1685, 1712-19	Johann Albrecht Riedlin von Ulm, die-cutter

IMPERIAL CITY

REGULAR COINAGE

KM# 5 PFENNIG

Billon **Obv:** 5-leaved linden tree divides date **Note:** Uniface. Varieties exist.

Date	Mintage	Good	VG	F	VF	XF
1661	—	5.00	16.00	30.00	60.00	—
1663	—	5.00	16.00	30.00	60.00	—
1665	—	5.00	16.00	30.00	60.00	—
1675	—	5.00	16.00	30.00	60.00	—
1679	—	5.00	16.00	30.00	60.00	—
1681	—	5.00	16.00	30.00	60.00	—
1682	—	5.00	16.00	30.00	60.00	—
1683	—	5.00	16.00	30.00	60.00	—
1684	—	5.00	16.00	30.00	60.00	—
1686	—	5.00	16.00	30.00	60.00	—
1687	—	5.00	16.00	30.00	60.00	—
1689	—	5.00	16.00	30.00	60.00	—
1691	—	5.00	16.00	30.00	60.00	—
1692	—	5.00	16.00	30.00	60.00	—
1693	—	5.00	16.00	30.00	60.00	—
1694	—	5.00	16.00	30.00	60.00	—
1695	—	5.00	16.00	30.00	60.00	—
1696	—	5.00	16.00	30.00	60.00	—
1697	—	5.00	16.00	30.00	60.00	—
ND	—	5.00	16.00	30.00	60.00	—

LIPPE

The lords of Lippe first established their territory in Westphalia to the west of the Weser River in the early 12th century. The dynasty acquired the rank of count in the early 16th century. In 1613 Lippe was divided into four branches: Lippe-Detmold, Lippe-Sternberg (extinct in 1620 and reverted to Detmold), Lippe-Bracke, and Lippe-Alverdissen. The latter inherited half of the county of Schauenburg (Schaumburg) and founded the line of Schaumburg-Lippe in 1640 (q.v.). Lippe-Brucke became extinct in 1790 and its possessions fell back to the senior branch of Lippe-Detmold, which lasted into the 20th century.

RULERS

Simon VI, 1563-1613
Simon VII, 1613-1627
Hermann Adolf, 1652-1666
Simon Heinrich, 1666-1697

MINT OFFICIALS' INITIALS

Initial	Date	Name
(a)=	1599-1601	Peter Busch von Bielefeld
	1601-04	Alexander Wacherwald, warden
(b)=	1601-02	Caspar Hover
(c)=	1602-06	Henning Hansen
(d)=	1604-06	Ernst Schroder, warden
(e)=	1606-10	Engelbert (Engelhard) Hausmann
	1606-?	Borchard Lachtorp, warden
(f)=	1610-18	Caspar Kholl (Kohl, Khol) in Blomberg

ARMS

5-petaled rose

COUNTSHIP

REGULAR COINAGE

KM# 5 GOSLER (1/2 Pfennig)

Silver **Ruler:** Simon VI **Obv:** Rose in circle **Note:** Uniface.

Date	Mintage	VG	F	VF	XF	Unc
ND(1601)	—	65.00	135	275	550	—

KM# 13 3 PFENNIG (Dreier = 1/96 Thaler)

Silver Weight varies: 0.70-0.88g, 17-18 mm. **Ruler:** Simon VI **Obv:** Lippe rose **Obv. Legend:** S. C. E. N. D. D. E. L. **Rev:** Imperial orb with 06 divides date, small annulet to each side **Mint:** Detmold **Note:** Ref. W#213-14.

Date	Mintage	VG	F	VF	XF	Unc
1610 Rare	—	—	—	—	—	—
161Z Rare	—	—	—	—	—	—

KM# 6 1/96 THALER (Dreier = 3 Pfennig)

Silver Weight varies: 0.70-0.88g **Ruler:** Simon VI **Obv:** Rose **Obv. Legend:** S G V E H Z L **Rev:** Imperial orb with 96 divides date **Note:** Ref. W#169.

Date	Mintage	VG	F	VF	XF	Unc
1601	—	100	185	300	625	—
1602 (c)	—	75.00	135	225	450	—
160Z	—	—	—	—	—	—
1605(1602)	—	100	185	300	625	—

KM# 9 1/96 THALER (Dreier = 3 Pfennig)

Silver **Ruler:** Simon VI **Obv:** Rose **Obv. Legend:** S. C. E. N. D. D. L. **Rev:** Imperial orb with 96 in rhombus divides date

Date	Mintage	VG	F	VF	XF	Unc
1608	—	85.00	165	275	550	—

KM# 14 1/96 THALER (Dreier = 3 Pfennig)

Silver **Ruler:** Simon VI **Obv:** Rose **Rev:** Imperial orb with 96 divides date

Date	Mintage	VG	F	VF	XF	Unc
1610	—	—	—	—	—	—

KM# 7 MARIENGROSCHEN (1/36 Thaler)

Silver **Ruler:** Simon VI **Obv:** 4-fold arms in ornate shield **Rev:** Madonna and child, date in legend **Note:** Ref. G/H#88; W#171-72. Varieties exist.

Date	Mintage	VG	F	VF	XF	Unc
1601 (c)	—	33.00	70.00	120	230	—
1605 (d)	—	33.00	70.00	120	230	—
1605 (e)	—	33.00	70.00	120	230	—
(1)605 (e)	—	33.00	70.00	120	230	—
(1)606 (e)	—	33.00	70.00	120	230	—
1607 (e)	—	33.00	70.00	120	230	—
(1)607 (e)	—	33.00	70.00	120	230	—
1608 (e)	—	33.00	70.00	120	230	—

KM# 8 1/24 THALER (Fürstengroschen)

Silver **Ruler:** Simon VI **Obv:** Ornate helmet above 4-fold arms **Obv. Legend:** SIM. C. E. - N. D. I. L. **Rev:** Imperial orb with Z4, date divided upper left and right **Rev. Legend:** RUD. II. RO. IM. S. A. **Note:** Ref. G/H-78, 84, 86; W-193, 194, 200, 212. Varieties exist.

Date	Mintage	VG	F	VF	XF	Unc
1607 (e)	—	27.00	45.00	90.00	185	—
1608 (e)	—	27.00	45.00	90.00	185	—
1608 (f)	—	27.00	45.00	90.00	185	—
1609 (f)	—	27.00	45.00	90.00	185	—
1610 (f)	—	27.00	45.00	90.00	185	—
1610 (g)	—	27.00	45.00	90.00	185	—
1610 (h)	—	27.00	45.00	90.00	185	—
1611 (h)	—	27.00	45.00	90.00	185	—
1612 (h)	—	27.00	45.00	90.00	185	—
161Z (h)	—	27.00	45.00	90.00	185	—
1613 (h)	—	27.00	45.00	90.00	185	—
ND Rare	—	—	—	—	—	—

KM# 17 1/24 THALER (Fürstengroschen)

Silver **Ruler:** Simon VI **Obv:** Crowned shield **Rev:** Titles of Matthias **Note:** Varieties exist.

Date	Mintage	VG	F	VF	XF	Unc
1613 (h)	—	27.00	45.00	100	200	—
1613	—	27.00	45.00	100	200	—

KM# 10 THALER

Silver **Ruler:** Simon VI **Note:** Dav. #6884.

Date	Mintage	VG	F	VF	XF	Unc
1601 Rare	—	—	—	—	—	—

KM# 15 THALER

Silver **Ruler:** Simon VI **Obv:** Helmeted arms **Rev:** Crowned imperial eagle with date divided below **Note:** Dav. #6886.

Date	Mintage	VG	F	VF	XF	Unc
1612 (h) Rare	—	—	—	—	—	—

KM# 16 2 THALER

Silver **Ruler:** Simon VI **Obv:** Helmeted arms **Obv. Legend:** RVDOL. II. D. **Rev:** Crowned imperial eagle with date divided below **Note:** Dav. #6885.

Date	Mintage	VG	F	VF	XF	Unc
1612 (h) Rare	—	—	—	—	—	—

LIPPE-DETMOLD

The Counts of Lippe ruled over a small state in northwestern Germany. In 1528/9 they became counts; in 1720 they were raised to the rank of princes, but did not use the title until 1789. Another branch of the family ruled the even smaller Schaumburg-Lippe. Lippe joined North German Confederation in 1866, and became part of the German Empire in 1871. When the insane Prince Alexander succeeded to the throne in 1895, the main branch reached an end, and a ten-year testamentary dispute between the Biesterfeld and the Schaumburg-Lippe lines followed - a Wilhelmine cause celebre. The Biesterfeld line gained the principality in 1905, but abdicated in 1918. In 1947 Lippe was absorbed by the German Land of North Rhine-Westphalia.

RULERS

Simon VI, 1563-1613
Simon VII, 1613-1627
Simon Ludwig, 1627-1636
Simon Philip, 1636-1650
Johann Bernhard, 1650-1652
Hermann Adolf, 1652-1666
Simon Heinrich, 1666-1697
Friedrich Adolf, 1697-1718

MINT OFFICIALS' INITIALS

Initial	Date	Name
B/TB	1678-1716	Thomas (or Tobias) Bernard, die-cutter in Paris
IH/(e)	1671-95	Johann Hoffmann in Detmold
(a)=	1610-18	Caspar Kholl (Kohl, Khol) at Blomberg
(b)=	1619-20	Jacob Pfahler of Marsberg
(c)=	1618	Valentin Riemer
(d)=	1620-21	Ippo Rizema (Ritzema)
	c.1636-55	Michael Kuttner
	1655-58	Johann Kuttneer, superintendant
	1658-60	Christoph Henning Schluter
	1661-69	Hans Georg Moser

COUNTSHIP

REGULAR COINAGE

KM# 11 1/2 PFENNIG (Groschen)

Copper **Ruler:** Simon VII **Obv:** Rose in circle **Rev:** Value 1/2 in ornate rectangle **Note:** Kipper 1/2 Pfennig. Varieties exist.

Date	Mintage	VG	F	VF	XF	Unc
ND(1619)	100,000	10.00	25.00	55.00	115	—

KM# 35 1/2 PFENNIG (Groschen)

0.3200 g., Silver **Ruler:** Simon VII **Obv:** Rose in shield divides date as 2 - 1, crown above. **Note:** Uniface.

Date	Mintage	VG	F	VF	XF	Unc
(16)21	—	12.00	25.00	55.00	110	—

KM# 43 1/2 PFENNIG (Groschen)

1.0000 g., Copper, 16 mm. **Ruler:** Simon VII **Obv:** Rose in ring of 5 small stars alternating with 5 pellets, in circle of pellets **Rev:** Value 1/2 in ornate rectangle, 4 small stars flank upper and lower ornaments, a lily flanks 1/2, in circle of pellets

Date	Mintage	VG	F	VF	XF	Unc
ND(1623)	—	15.00	32.00	65.00	135	—

KM# 50 1/2 PFENNIG (Groschen)

Copper **Ruler:** Simon Philip **Obv:** Linear circle **Rev:** Lily-like ornamentation on sides of rectangle, without outer circle

Date	Mintage	VG	F	VF	XF	Unc
ND(1636-38)	98,000	10.00	25.00	55.00	110	—

KM# 60 1/2 PFENNIG (Groschen)

Copper **Ruler:** Simon Philip **Rev:** 1/2 within 4 floral ornaments **Note:** Varieties exist.

Date	Mintage	VG	F	VF	XF	Unc
ND(1644-69)	623,000	10.00	25.00	55.00	110	—

KM# 92 1/2 PFENNIG (Groschen)

Billon **Ruler:** Simon Heinrich **Obv:** Rose in center, variety of small stars, rosettes, pellets and/or crosses around **Rev:** 1/2 in center, variety of ornaments around **Note:** Varieties exist.

Date	Mintage	VG	F	VF	XF	Unc
ND(1675-92)	86,000	15.00	32.00	65.00	135	—

KM# 12 PFENNIG

Copper **Ruler:** Simon VII **Obv:** Rose in circle **Rev:** Value 1 in ornate rectangle

Date	Mintage	VG	F	VF	XF	Unc
ND(1619)	90,000	32.00	65.00	130	265	—

KM# 25 PFENNIG

Copper **Ruler:** Simon VII **Obv:** DITMAL around rose **Rev:** ANNO, date around value 1 **Note:** Varieties exist.

Date	Mintage	VG	F	VF	XF	Unc
1620	—	25.00	50.00	100	210	—

KM# 44 PFENNIG

Copper **Ruler:** Simon VII **Obv:** Rose in ring of 5 small stars alternating with 5 pellets in circle of pellets **Rev:** Value 1 in ornate rectangle, 4 small stars flank upper and lower ornaments, a lily at either side of 1/2, in circle of pellets

Date	Mintage	VG	F	VF	XF	Unc
ND(1623)	—	25.00	50.00	100	210	—

KM# 51 PFENNIG

Copper **Ruler:** Simon Philip **Obv:** Legend is around rose **Obv. Legend:** LIPP.LANT.MVN(T)Z **Rev:** Value 1 in rectangle, lily-like decorations on sides

Date	Mintage	VG	F	VF	XF	Unc
ND(1636-38)	142,000	20.00	40.00	85.00	175	—

KM# 61 PFENNIG

Copper **Ruler:** Simon Philip **Obv:** Rose, 5 large rosettes and 5 small stars around **Rev:** 1 within 4 floral ornaments, flanked by 4 rosettes **Note:** Varieties exist.

Date	Mintage	VG	F	VF	XF	Unc
ND(1644-69)	422,000	20.00	40.00	85.00	175	—

KM# 94 PFENNIG

Billon **Ruler:** Simon Heinrich **Obv:** Rose in circle **Rev:** 1 in circle

Date	Mintage	VG	F	VF	XF	Unc
ND(1675-92)	72,000	—	—	—	—	—

KM# 62 1-1/2 PFENNIG (1/192 Thaler)

Copper **Ruler:** Simon Philip **Obv:** Leged is around rose **Obv. Legend:** LIPP.LANT.MVNTZ **Rev:** Value 1-1/2 surrounded by circle of small stars and rosettes **Note:** Varieties exist.

Date	Mintage	VG	F	VF	XF	Unc
ND(1644-69)	192,000	12.00	25.00	50.00	100	—

KM# 96 1-1/2 PFENNIG (1/192 Thaler)

Copper **Ruler:** Simon Heinrich **Obv:** Rose **Rev. Legend:** 1-1/2/LIPP/PFEN/NINGE

Date	Mintage	VG	F	VF	XF	Unc
ND(1675-92)	288,000	12.00	25.00	50.00	100	—

KM# 13 2 PFENNIG

Copper **Ruler:** Simon VII **Obv:** Rose in circle **Rev:** Value II in ornate rectangle **Note:** Kipper 2 Pfennig.

Date	Mintage	VG	F	VF	XF	Unc
ND(1619)	66,000	9.00	20.00	45.00	90.00	—

KM# 26 2 PFENNIG

Copper **Ruler:** Simon VII **Obv:** DITMAL around rose **Rev:** ANNO, date around II **Note:** Varieties exist.

Date	Mintage	VG	F	VF	XF	Unc
1620	—	16.00	33.00	65.00	170	—

KM# 45 2 PFENNIG

Copper **Ruler:** Simon VII **Obv:** Rose in ring of 5 small stars alternating with 5 pellets in circle of pellets **Rev:** Value II in ornate rectangle, 4 small stars flank upper and lower ornaments, a lily on sides of 1/2 in circle of pellets **Note:** Varieties exist.

Date	Mintage	VG	F	VF	XF	Unc
ND(1623)	—	16.00	33.00	65.00	130	—

KM# 52 2 PFENNIG

Copper **Ruler:** Simon Philip **Obv:** Legend around rose **Obv. Legend:** LIPP.LANT.MVN(T)Z **Rev:** Value II in rectangle, lily-like decorations at sides

Date	Mintage	VG	F	VF	XF	Unc
ND(1636-38)	287,000	16.00	33.00	65.00	130	—

KM# 63 2 PFENNIG

Copper **Ruler:** Simon Philip **Obv:** Legend around rose **Obv. Legend:** LIPP.LANT.MVNTZ **Rev:** II within 8 floral ornaments **Note:** Varieties exist.

Date	Mintage	VG	F	VF	XF	Unc
ND(1644-69)	186,000	16.00	33.00	65.00	130	—

KM# 21 3 PFENNIG

Silver **Ruler:** Simon VII **Obv:** Rose, around DITMAL **Rev:** Imperial eagle, 3 in orb on breast

Date	Mintage	VG	F	VF	XF	Unc
ND(1619-20)	—	27.00	55.00	110	225	—

KM# 14 3 PFENNIG

Copper **Ruler:** Simon VII **Obv:** Rose in circle **Rev:** Value III in ornate rectangle **Note:** Kipper 3 Pfennig. Varieties exist.

Date	Mintage	VG	F	VF	XF	Unc
ND(1619)	15,000	20.00	45.00	95.00	190	—

KM# 15 3 PFENNIG

Copper **Ruler:** Simon VII **Obv:** DITMAL around rose **Rev:** ANNO, date around **Note:** Varieties exist.

Date	Mintage	VG	F	VF	XF	Unc
1619	Inc. above	27.00	50.00	100	210	—

KM# 27 3 PFENNIG

Silver **Ruler:** Simon VII **Obv:** Rose, titles of Simon VII **Rev:** Crowned imperial eagle, 3 in orb on breast, titles of Matthias (sic) and date

Date	Mintage	VG	F	VF	XF	Unc
1620	—	20.00	40.00	80.00	160	—
16Z0	—	20.00	40.00	80.00	160	—

KM# 41 3 PFENNIG

Silver **Ruler:** Simon VII **Obv:** 4-fold arms **Rev:** Imperial eagle, 3 in orb on breast, date divided above

Date	Mintage	VG	F	VF	XF	Unc
1622	—	16.00	32.00	65.00	130	—

KM# 46 3 PFENNIG

Silver **Ruler:** Simon VII **Obv:** Rose in ring of 5 small stars alternating with 5 pellets in circle of pellets **Rev:** Value III in ornate rectangle, 4 small stars flank upper and lower ornaments, a lily on sides of 1/2 in circle of pellets **Note:** Varieties exist.

Date	Mintage	VG	F	VF	XF	Unc
ND(1623)	—	20.00	40.00	80.00	160	—

KM# 53 3 PFENNIG

Silver **Ruler:** Simon Philip **Obv:** Legend around rose **Obv. Legend:** LIPP.LANT.MVN(T)Z **Rev:** Value III in rectangle, lily-like decorations at sides

Date	Mintage	VG	F	VF	XF	Unc
ND(1636-38)	435,000	9.00	27.00	55.00	110	—

KM# 64 3 PFENNIG

Silver **Ruler:** Simon Philip **Obv:** Rose in circle **Obv. Legend:** LIPPE. LANTMVNTZ. **Rev:** Value 'III' in ornamented border **Note:** Varieties exist.

Date	Mintage	VG	F	VF	XF	Unc
ND(1644-69)	320,000	9.00	27.00	55.00	110	—

KM# 65 6 PFENNIG

Copper **Ruler:** Simon Philip **Obv:** Legend around rose **Obv. Legend:** LIPP.LANT.MVNTZ **Rev:** VI in square, 8 lily-like floral ornaments around **Note:** Varieties exist.

Date	Mintage	VG	F	VF	XF	Unc
ND(1644-69)	167,000	10.00	25.00	45.00	90.00	—

Note: This 6 Pfennig was later countermarked, in 1671, by a small rose with thick petals and again, in 1685, by a double rose

KM# 75 6 PFENNIG

Copper **Ruler:** Simon Heinrich **Countermark:** Small rose with thick petals

Date	Mintage	VG	F	VF	XF	Unc
ND(1671)	—	10.00	25.00	40.00	70.00	—

KM# 102 6 PFENNIG

Copper **Ruler:** Simon Heinrich **Countermark:** Second countermark a double rose

Date	Mintage	VG	F	VF	XF	Unc
ND(1685)	—	14.00	27.00	55.00	110	—

KM# 36 3 FLITTER (1-1/2 Pfennig)

Copper **Ruler:** Simon VII **Obv:** Rose in shield **Rev:** III/FLITTERN/date **Note:** Kipper 3 Flitter.

Date	Mintage	VG	F	VF	XF	Unc
(1)6Z1	—	10.00	27.00	50.00	100	—

KM# 77 MATTIER (4 Pfennig)

Silver **Ruler:** Simon Heinrich **Obv:** Rose in laurel wreath **Rev. Legend:** 16172/MATTIER/GR.LIPP.L./M(UNTZ) **Note:** Varieties exist.

Date	Mintage	VG	F	VF	XF	Unc
1672	35,000	16.00	35.00	75.00	155	—

KM# 78 MATTIER (4 Pfennig)

Silver **Ruler:** Simon Heinrich **Obv:** Rose with alternating rosettes, stars or pellets **Note:** Varieties exist.

Date	Mintage	VG	F	VF	XF	Unc
1672	Inc. above	16.00	35.00	75.00	155	—
1673	32,000	16.00	35.00	75.00	155	—
1683	22,000	16.00	35.00	75.00	155	—

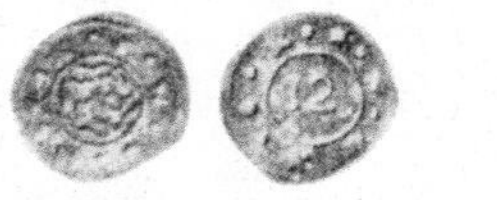

KM# 93 1/12 MARIENGROSCHEN

Copper **Ruler:** Simon Heinrich **Rev:** Value 12

Date	Mintage	VG	F	VF	XF	Unc
ND(1675-92)	Inc. above	33.00	65.00	130	260	—

KM# 95 1/6 MARIENGROSCHEN

Copper **Ruler:** Simon Heinrich **Obv:** Rose **Obv. Legend:** GREFLIGE.LIPP **Rev:** Imperial orb with 6 **Rev. Legend:** LANDT. MUNTZ(E) **Note:** Varieties exist.

Date	Mintage	VG	F	VF	XF	Unc
ND(1675-92)	Inc. above	20.00	40.00	85.00	170	—

KM# 42 MARIENGROSCHEN (1/36 Thaler)

Silver **Ruler:** Simon VII **Obv:** 4-fold arms, titles of Simon VII **Rev:** Madonna and child, date in legend **Note:** Varieties exist.

Date	Mintage	VG	F	VF	XF	Unc
(1)622	42,000	120	200	325	675	—

KM# 76 MARIENGROSCHEN (1/36 Thaler)

Silver **Ruler:** Simon Heinrich **Obv:** Rose in laurel wreath, 36 below **Rev:** I/MARI/GROS, date **Rev. Legend:** GRE.PIPP.LANDT.MUNTZ **Note:** Varieties exist.

Date	Mintage	VG	F	VF	XF	Unc
1671	5,400	33.00	60.00	120	240	—
1672	18,000	33.00	60.00	120	240	—

KM# 79 MARIENGROSCHEN (1/36 Thaler)

Silver **Ruler:** Simon Heinrich **Rev. Inscription:** I / MARI / GROZ, date **Note:** Varieties exist.

Date	Mintage	VG	F	VF	XF	Unc
1672	30,000	40.00	65.00	130	260	—

KM# 90 MARIENGROSCHEN (1/36 Thaler)

Silver **Ruler:** Simon Heinrich **Rev:** Date **Rev. Legend:** G.LIP.LANT.MUNZ

Date	Mintage	VG	F	VF	XF	Unc
1673	—	60.00	115	200	425	—

KM# 54 2 MARIENGROSCHEN (1/18 Thaler)

Silver **Ruler:** Simon Philip **Obv:** Crowned 4-fold arms, date **Obv. Legend:** DEO.FAVENTE **Rev. Legend:** GRAF: LIPP. LANDT. MV(N) **Rev. Inscription:** II / MAR / GR **Note:** Varieties exist.

Date	Mintage	VG	F	VF	XF	Unc
1638	25,000	30.00	65.00	130	265	—

KM# 70 2 MARIENGROSCHEN (1/18 Thaler)

Silver **Ruler:** Hermann Adolf **Obv:** Crowned HA monogram, date above **Rev. Inscription:** II / MARI / GR **Note:** Varieties exist.

Date	Mintage	VG	F	VF	XF	Unc
1658	—	80.00	165	335	675	—

KM# 80 2 MARIENGROSCHEN (1/18 Thaler)
Silver **Ruler:** Simon Heinrich **Obv:** Crowned SH monogram **Obv. Legend:** GR. LIPP. SILB. MUNZ **Rev. Legend:** 18. EINEN. R. THAL. WERT **Rev. Inscription:** 16 II 72 / MARI / GR **Note:** Varieties exist.

Date	Mintage	VG	F	VF	XF	Unc
1672	8,550	16.00	33.00	65.00	130	—

KM# 81 2 MARIENGROSCHEN (1/18 Thaler)
Silver **Ruler:** Simon Heinrich **Rev:** Date in legend **Note:** Varieties exist.

Date	Mintage	VG	F	VF	XF	Unc
1672	6,300	16.00	33.00	65.00	130	—

KM# 71 4 MARIENGROSCHEN (1/9 Thaler)
Silver **Ruler:** Hermann Adolf **Obv:** Crowned HA monogram, date above **Obv. Legend:** GR. LIPP. SILBER. MVNTZ **Rev. Legend:** 9. EINEN. THALER. WEHRT **Rev. Inscription:** IIII / MARI / GR **Note:** Varieties exist.

Date	Mintage	VG	F	VF	XF	Unc
1658	—	135	275	550	1,050	—

KM# 82 4 MARIENGROSCHEN (1/9 Thaler)
Silver **Ruler:** Simon Heinrich **Obv:** Crowned SH monogram, date **Obv. Legend:** G(R). LIPP. SILBER. MVN(T)Z **Note:** Varieties exist.

Date	Mintage	VG	F	VF	XF	Unc
1672 IH/(e)	14,000	20.00	45.00	80.00	155	—

KM# 83 4 MARIENGROSCHEN (1/9 Thaler)
Silver **Ruler:** Simon Heinrich **Rev:** Date in legend **Note:** Varieties exist.

Date	Mintage	VG	F	VF	XF	Unc
1672 IH	12,000	20.00	45.00	80.00	155	—
1672 IH/(e)	Inc. above	20.00	45.00	80.00	155	—

KM# 84 4 MARIENGROSCHEN (1/9 Thaler)
Silver **Ruler:** Simon Heinrich **Rev:** Date **Rev. Inscription:** IIII / MARIEN / GROS **Note:** Varieties exist.

Date	Mintage	VG	F	VF	XF	Unc
1672 IH	59,000	33.00	65.00	130	265	—

KM# A85 6 MARIENGROSCHEN (1/6 Thaler)
Silver **Ruler:** Simon Heinrich **Obv:** Crowned 4-fold arms **Rev. Legend:** G. KIPP. SILBER. MUNTZ. ANNO **Rev. Inscription:** VI / MARIEN / GROS / date

Date	Mintage	VG	F	VF	XF	Unc
1671	—	160	325	650	1,300	—

KM# 85 6 MARIENGROSCHEN (1/6 Thaler)
Silver **Ruler:** Simon Heinrich **Obv:** Crowned 4-fold arms **Rev. Legend:** GR. LIPP. SILBER. MUNTZ **Rev. Inscription:** VI / MARIEN / GROSS / date **Note:** Varieties exist.

Date	Mintage	VG	F	VF	XF	Unc
1672 IH	23,000	115	200	375	775	—

KM# 101 24 MARIENGROSCHEN (2/3 Thaler)
Silver **Ruler:** Simon Heinrich **Obv:** Crowned 4-fold arms in baroque frame, value (2/3) below **Rev:** Date **Rev. Inscription:** XXIIII / MARIEN / GROSCH

Date	Mintage	VG	F	VF	XF	Unc
1683 IH	1,815	1,000	1,800	3,000	6,000	—

KM# 16 12 KREUZER (Driebatzner)
Silver **Ruler:** Simon VII **Obv:** Large, ornate helmet above 4-fold arms **Rev:** Crowned imperial eagle, 12 in orb on breast, titles of Matthias, date **Note:** Varieties exist.

Date	Mintage	VG	F	VF	XF	Unc
1619	8,012	160	325	650	1,300	—

KM# 17 12 KREUZER (Driebatzner)
Silver **Ruler:** Simon VII **Obv:** Titles of Ferdinand II **Note:** Varieties exist.

Date	Mintage	VG	F	VF	XF	Unc
1619	224,000	150	300	575	1,150	—
16Z0 (b)	—	150	300	575	1,150	—

KM# 28 12 KREUZER (Driebatzner)
Silver **Ruler:** Simon VII **Rev:** Crowned 4-fold arms

Date	Mintage	VG	F	VF	XF	Unc
16Z0	—	150	300	575	1,150	—

KM# 29 12 KREUZER (Driebatzner)
Silver **Ruler:** Simon VII **Rev:** Single large rose in shield, large crown above

Date	Mintage	VG	F	VF	XF	Unc
16Z0	—	150	300	575	1,150	—

KM# 37 12 KREUZER (Driebatzner)
Silver **Ruler:** Simon VII **Obv. Legend:** LANDTMVNZ - ZV - **Rev:** Date in legend **Note:** Varieties exist.

Date	Mintage	VG	F	VF	XF	Unc
1621	—	150	300	575	1,150	—

KM# 38 12 KREUZER (Driebatzner)
Silver **Ruler:** Simon VII **Obv:** Legend ends GS **Note:** Varieties exist.

Date	Mintage	VG	F	VF	XF	Unc
1621	—	150	300	575	1,150	—

KM# 97 15 KREUZER (1/6 Thaler)
Silver **Ruler:** Simon Heinrich **Obv:** Crowned imperial eagle, XV in orb on breast, titles of Leopold I **Rev:** Helmeted arms, titles of Simon Heinrich **Note:** Varieties exist.

Date	Mintage	VG	F	VF	XF	Unc
ND(ca. 1675)	4,800	—	—	—	—	—

KM# 5 1/24 THALER (Fürstengroschen)
Silver **Ruler:** Simon VII **Obv:** Ornate helmet above 4-fold arms **Rev:** Imperial orb with Z4, cross above divides date,titles of Matthias **Note:** Varieties exist.

Date	Mintage	VG	F	VF	XF	Unc
1614 (a)	—	27.00	55.00	110	220	—
1614 (b)	—	27.00	55.00	110	220	—
1615 (a)	—	27.00	55.00	110	220	—
1615 (b)	—	27.00	55.00	110	220	—
1615	—	27.00	55.00	110	2,202	—
1616 (a)	—	27.00	55.00	110	220	—
1616 (b)	—	27.00	55.00	110	220	—
1616	—	27.00	55.00	110	220	—
1617 (b)	452,000	27.00	55.00	110	220	—
1618 (b)	—	27.00	55.00	110	220	—
1618 (c)	—	27.00	55.00	110	220	—

KM# 18 1/24 THALER (Fürstengroschen)
Silver **Ruler:** Simon VII **Obv:** Helmeted shield within circle **Rev:** Date in legend **Note:** Varieties exist.

Date	Mintage	VG	F	VF	XF	Unc
1619 (b)	165,000	20.00	45.00	90.00	185	—

KM# 19 1/24 THALER (Fürstengroschen)
Silver **Ruler:** Simon VII **Rev:** Titles of Ferdinand II **Note:** Varieties exist.

Date	Mintage	VG	F	VF	XF	Unc
1619 (b)	289,000	20.00	45.00	90.00	185	—
1620 (b)	—	20.00	45.00	90.00	185	—
(1)6Z0	—	20.00	45.00	90.00	185	—

KM# 55 1/24 THALER (Fürstengroschen)
Silver **Ruler:** Simon Philip **Obv:** Helmeted 4-fold arms **Rev:** Titles of Ferdinand III **Rev. Legend:** MONET: NOV. COMIT. LIPP **Note:** Varieties exist.

Date	Mintage	VG	F	VF	XF	Unc
1638	14,000	60.00	115	225	475	—
1639	Inc. above	80.00	160	325	650	—

KM# 103 1/24 THALER (Fürstengroschen)

Silver **Ruler:** Simon Heinrich **Obv:** Helmeted 4-fold arms, titles of Simon Heinrich **Rev:** Imperial orb with 24, cross above divides date **Rev. Legend:** GREFLIGE. LIPP. LANDT. MUNTZ **Note:** Groschen 1/24 Thaler. Varieties exist.

Date	Mintage	VG	F	VF	XF	Unc
1685 IH	432,000	45.00	90.00	180	360	—
1689 IH	502,000	60.00	115	210	425	—

KM# 31 1/21 THALER (1-1/2 Schilling)

Silver **Ruler:** Simon VII **Obv:** Date, 4-fold arms **Obv. Legend:** LANT MVNZ. XII. ZT TH **Rev:** Value in circle on breast of double-headed imperial eagle

Date	Mintage	VG	F	VF	XF	Unc
1620	—	110	200	375	775	—

KM# 30 1/21 THALER (1-1/2 Schilling)

Silver **Ruler:** Simon VII **Obv:** Crowned imperial eagle, 21 in orb on breast **Obv. Legend:** LANT MVNZ 21. ZUM. R. DALER **Rev:** Crowned 4-fold arms, date in legend **Note:** Kipper 1/21 Thaler. Varieties exist.

Date	Mintage	VG	F	VF	XF	Unc
1620 (b)	—	110	200	375	775	—

KM# 32 1/21 THALER (1-1/2 Schilling)

Silver **Ruler:** Simon VII **Obv:** Helmeted arms **Rev:** Value in legend XXI **Note:** Varieties exist.

Date	Mintage	VG	F	VF	XF	Unc
1620	—	100	175	325	675	—
1621	—	100	175	325	675	—

KM# 39 1/21 THALER (1-1/2 Schilling)

Silver **Ruler:** Simon VII **Obv:** Helmeted 4-fold arms, titles of Simon VII, date **Obv. Legend:** LANT MVNZ 21. ZUM. R. DALER

Date	Mintage	VG	F	VF	XF	Unc
1621	—	100	175	325	675	—

KM# 40 1/21 THALER (1-1/2 Schilling)

Silver **Ruler:** Simon VII **Obv:** Helmeted 4-fold arms **Rev:** Without value in orb on eagle's breast

Date	Mintage	VG	F	VF	XF	Unc
1621	—	80.00	165	325	650	—

KM# A72 1/4 THALER

Silver **Ruler:** Hermann Adolf **Obv:** Facing bust, turned slightly right, date in legend **Rev:** Crowned 4-fold arms in ornamented frame **Rev. Legend:** SPES. CONFISA...

Date	Mintage	VG	F	VF	XF	Unc
1658	—	2,500	4,250	7,500	14,500	—

KM# 86 1/3 THALER (1/2 Gulden)

Silver **Ruler:** Simon Heinrich **Rev:** Date in legend **Rev. Inscription:** III / EINEN / REICHS / THAL / I(e)H **Note:** Varieties exist.

Date	Mintage	VG	F	VF	XF	Unc
1672 I(e)H	41,000	55.00	100	200	425	—

KM# 72 1/2 THALER

Silver **Ruler:** Hermann Adolf **Obv:** Facing bust, turned slightly right, date in legend **Rev:** Crowned 4-fold arms in ornamented frame **Rev. Legend:** SPES.CONFISA **Note:** Varieties exist.

Date	Mintage	VG	F	VF	XF	Unc
1658	—	1,650	3,250	6,500	13,000	—

KM# 6 THALER

Silver **Ruler:** Simon VII **Obv:** Crowned imperial eagle with orb on breast, date **Obv. Legend:** MATIAS. I.D.G **Note:** Dav. #6888.

Date	Mintage	VG	F	VF	XF	Unc
1614 (a) Rare	—	—	—	—	—	—

KM# 9 THALER

Silver **Ruler:** Simon VII **Obv:** Helmeted arms within circle **Rev:** Crown above double-headed imperial eagle within circle **Rev. Legend:** MATHI * D * G ** **Note:** Dav. #6890.

Date	Mintage	VG	F	VF	XF	Unc
1617	—	6,500	12,000	20,000	—	—
1618 (d) Rare	—	—	—	—	—	—

KM# 33 THALER

Silver **Ruler:** Simon VII **Rev. Legend:** FERDINAND.II.D.G... **Note:** Dav. #6892.

Date	Mintage	VG	F	VF	XF	Unc
1620 Rare	—	—	—	—	—	—

KM# 47 THALER

Silver **Ruler:** Simon VII **Obv:** Helmeted arms within beaded circle **Rev:** Crown above double-headed eagle within beaded circle **Rev. Legend:** FERDINANDVS: II: D: G: ... **Note:** Dav. #6893.

Date	Mintage	VG	F	VF	XF	Unc
16Z3	3,754	1,200	2,500	4,500	8,000	—

KM# 73 THALER

Silver **Ruler:** Hermann Adolf **Note:** Dav. #6894.

Date	Mintage	VG	F	VF	XF	Unc
1658	—	400	800	1,850	4,500	—

KM# 87 THALER

Silver **Ruler:** Simon Heinrich **Note:** Dav. #6895.

Date	Mintage	VG	F	VF	XF	Unc
1672 IH	610	600	1,200	2,500	4,850	—

KM# 88 THALER

Silver **Ruler:** Simon Heinrich **Rev:** Date above helmeted arms **Note:** Dav. #6895A.

Date	Mintage	VG	F	VF	XF	Unc
1672 IH	—	650	1,250	2,650	5,000	—

KM# 89 THALER

Silver **Ruler:** Simon Heinrich **Obv:** Larger head on bust **Note:** Dav. #6896.

Date	Mintage	VG	F	VF	XF	Unc
1672 IH	910	650	1,250	2,650	5,000	—

KM# 100 THALER

Silver **Ruler:** Simon Heinrich **Obv:** Bust left **Rev:** Crowned mantled arms **Note:** Dav. #6897.

Date	Mintage	VG	F	VF	XF	Unc
1681	223	1,000	2,000	3,750	6,500	—

KM# 104 THALER

Silver **Ruler:** Simon Heinrich **Obv:** Bust right **Rev:** Crowned and supported arms above palm sprays **Note:** Dav. #6899.

Date	Mintage	VG	F	VF	XF	Unc
1685 IH	194	800	1,600	3,200	5,500	—

KM# 110 THALER

Silver **Ruler:** Simon Heinrich **Rev:** Crowned arms **Note:** Dav. #6900.

Date	Mintage	VG	F	VF	XF	Unc
1692 IH Rare	140	—	—	—	—	—

KM# 7 2 THALER

Silver **Ruler:** Simon VII **Obv:** Helmeted arms **Obv. Legend:** I.D.G... **Rev:** Crowned imperial eagle with orb on breast, date below **Note:** Dav. #6887.

Date	Mintage	VG	F	VF	XF	Unc
1614 (a) Rare	—	—	—	—	—	—

KM# 10 2 THALER

Silver **Ruler:** Simon VII **Rev:** Date in legend divided by crown **Rev. Legend:** MATHI*... **Note:** Dav. #6889.

Date	Mintage	VG	F	VF	XF	Unc
1617 Rare	—	—	—	—	—	—
1618 (d) Rare	—	—	—	—	—	—

KM# 34 2 THALER

Silver **Ruler:** Simon VII **Rev. Legend:** FERDINAND. II... **Note:** Dav. #6891.

Date	Mintage	VG	F	VF	XF	Unc
1620 Rare	—	—	—	—	—	—

KM# 105 2 THALER

Silver **Ruler:** Simon Heinrich **Obv:** Bust right **Rev:** Crowned and supported arms above palm sprays **Note:** Dav. #6898.

Date	Mintage	VG	F	VF	XF	Unc
1685 Rare	—	—	—	—	—	—

TRADE COINAGE

KM# 8 GOLDGULDEN

3.5000 g., 0.9860 Gold 0.1109 oz. AGW **Ruler:** Simon VII **Obv:** Ornate helmet above 4-fold arms **Rev:** Crowned imperial eagle, orb on breast, date divided by legs of eagle, titles of Matthias

Date	Mintage	VG	F	VF	XF	Unc
1615 Rare	—	—	—	—	—	—

KM# 20 GOLDGULDEN

3.5000 g., 0.9860 Gold 0.1109 oz. AGW **Ruler:** Simon VII **Obv:** Arms topped by helm in inner circle **Rev:** Crowned imperial eagle, date in legend, titles of Matthias

Date	Mintage	VG	F	VF	XF	Unc
1619 Rare	—	—	—	—	—	—

KM# 91 DUCAT

3.5000 g., 0.9860 Gold 0.1109 oz. AGW **Ruler:** Simon Heinrich **Obv:** Bust of Simon Heinrich right **Rev:** Arms **Rev. Legend:** CLEMENTE DEO...

Date	Mintage	VG	F	VF	XF	Unc
1673 IH	186	1,800	3,750	7,000	12,000	—
1685	—	1,800	3,750	7,000	12,000	—

KM# 106 DUCAT

3.5000 g., 0.9860 Gold 0.1109 oz. AGW **Ruler:** Simon Heinrich **Obv:** Bust right **Rev:** Crowned oval 4-fold arms, supported by 2 lions, palm fronds and date below **Rev. Legend:** NEC TEMERE NEC TIMIDE

Date	Mintage	VG	F	VF	XF	Unc
1685 IH	276	2,700	5,600	10,000	17,500	—

KM# 107 1-1/2 DUCAT

5.2500 g., 0.9860 Gold 0.1664 oz. AGW **Ruler:** Simon Heinrich **Obv:** Bust of Simon Heinrich right **Rev:** Crowned arms

Date	Mintage	VG	F	VF	XF	Unc
1685	—	3,600	5,400	9,000	16,000	—
1692 IH	—	3,600	5,400	9,000	16,000	—

KM# 108 3 DUCAT

10.5000 g., 0.9860 Gold 0.3328 oz. AGW **Ruler:** Simon Heinrich **Obv:** Bust of Simon Heinrich right **Rev:** Crowned arms

Date	Mintage	VG	F	VF	XF	Unc
1685 Rare	—	—	—	—	—	—
1692 Rare	—	—	—	—	—	—

KM# 109 4 DUCAT

14.0000 g., 0.9860 Gold 0.4438 oz. AGW **Ruler:** Simon Heinrich **Obv:** Bust of Simon Heinrich right **Rev:** Crowned arms

Date	Mintage	VG	F	VF	XF	Unc
1685 Rare	—	—	—	—	—	—

KM# A74 5 DUCAT

17.5000 g., 0.9860 Gold 0.5547 oz. AGW **Ruler:** Hermann Adolf

Date	Mintage	VG	F	VF	XF	Unc
1658 Rare	—	—	—	—	—	—

Note: Struck with 1/2 Thaler dies, KM#72

KM# 111 6 DUCAT

21.0000 g., 0.9860 Gold 0.6657 oz. AGW **Ruler:** Simon Heinrich **Note:** Struck with 1 Thaler dies, KM#110.

Date	Mintage	VG	F	VF	XF	Unc
1692 IH Rare	—	—	—	—	—	—

PATTERNS

Including off metal strikes

KM#	Date	Mintage	Identification	Mkt Val
Pn2	1672 IH	—	Thaler. Gold. KM#87.	—
Pn3	1673 IH	—	Ducat. Silver. Weight of 1/4 Thaler, KM#91.	—
Pn4	1673 IH	—	Ducat. Silver. Bust right. Crowned ornate arms. Klippe, weight of 1/4 Thaler, KM#91.	—
Pn5	1685 IH	—	Thaler. Gold. KM#104.	—
Pn6	1685 IH	—	Ducat. Silver. Weight of 1/4 Thaler, KM#106.	850

LORRAINE

(Lothringen)

Lorraine was established as a kingdom for Lothaire in the mid-9th century and was a part of the Carolingian Empire. It emerged as a duchy in the early 10th century and eventually became a buffer state between Germany and France. By 955, following several revolts which had their roots in Lorraine, Emperor Otto I (936-73) divided the territory in Lower Lorraine, which later became Brabant, and Upper Lorraine, the region which stretched along the Meuse and Mosel Rivers southwards to Burgundy. It is the latter entity, often associated with Alsace (see), which has come down to modern Europe as Lorraine.

The duchy was often a source of contention between the emperors and the kings of France, especially in the 17th century. France occupied it several times, from 1634-41, 1643-44, 1654-61, and 1673-75, and then again 1690-97. In 1736, Duke Franz III married Maria Theresa, daughter of Emperor Karl VI and reigned as Emperor Franz I (1745-65). He exchanged Lorraine with France at the end of 1736 and received the Grand Duchy of Tuscany as compensation in the following year. The former King of Poland, Stanislaw Leszczinski, succeeded Franz III (I) in Lorraine, but the duchy was finally incorporated into France upon his death in 1766. Along with Alsace, Lorraine was acquired by the German Empire after the defeat of France by Prussia in the Franco-Prussian War of 1870-71. The Treaty of Versailles returned Alsace and Lorraine to France in 1919.

RULERS

Renatus II, 1473-1508
Anton, 1508-1544
Franz I, 1544-1545
Nikolaus von Vaudemont, administrator 1545-1552
Karl II, 1545-1608
Heinrich, 1608-1624
Nikolaus, 1624-1625
Franz II, 1625, coins issued in his name 1625-32 by the Badenweiler Mint
Karl III, 1625-34, 1661-73 (died 1675)
Karl IV, 1675-1690
French Occupation, 1690-97
Leopold, (1690) 1697-1729
Franz III, 1729-1736

MINTS

Badenweiler
Florence
Nancy
Romarti (Remiremont)
Stenay

MINT MARKS

G – Unknown mint official at Nancy, late 16th-early 17th c.
A – Paris

ARMS

Lorraine – band from upper left to lower right on which 3 small eagles
Bar – two fish standing on tails, four small crosses around

MONETARY SYSTEM

3 Deniers = 1 Liard
4 Liards = 1 Sol
25 Sols = 1 Livre
6 Livres = 1 Ecu
4 Ecus = 1 Louis D'or

DUCHY

STANDARD COINAGE

KM# 25 OBOL

Copper **Ruler:** Karl III and Nikolaus **Obv:** Crowned double cross **Rev:** Ornamental cross **Mint:** Nancy

Date	Mintage	VG	F	VF	XF	Unc
ND(1624-25)	—	20.00	40.00	80.00	160	—

KM# 26 OBOL

Copper **Ruler:** Karl III and Nikolaus **Obv:** Jerusalem cross **Rev:** Crowned double cross

Date	Mintage	VG	F	VF	XF	Unc
ND(1624-25)	—	20.00	40.00	80.00	160	—

KM# 27 OBOL
Copper **Ruler:** Karl III **Obv:** Two-part arms **Rev:** Crowned bird

Date	Mintage	VG	F	VF	XF	Unc
ND(1625-34)	—	18.00	35.00	75.00	150	—

KM# 50 OBOL
Copper **Ruler:** French Occupation **Obv:** Sword through crowned double cross **Rev:** Jerusalem cross

Date	Mintage	VG	F	VF	XF	Unc
ND(1634-41)	—	130	260	—	—	—

KM# 10 DENIER
Silver **Ruler:** Heinrich **Obv:** Crowned cross of Lorraine in cartouche **Rev:** Crowned eagle

Date	Mintage	VG	F	VF	XF	Unc
ND(1608-24)	—	20.00	45.00	85.00	175	—

KM# 11 DENIER
Silver **Ruler:** Heinrich **Obv:** Two-sectioned coat of arms **Rev:** Crowned cross of Lorraine between crowned eagles **Mint:** Nancy

Date	Mintage	VG	F	VF	XF	Unc
ND(1608-24)	—	20.00	45.00	85.00	175	—

KM# 12 DENIER
Silver **Ruler:** Heinrich **Obv:** Crowned "H" monogram **Rev:** Arms of Lorraine

Date	Mintage	VG	F	VF	XF	Unc
ND(1608-24)	—	20.00	45.00	85.00	175	—

KM# 28 DENIER
Silver **Ruler:** Karl III and Nikolaus **Obv:** Crowned eagles **Rev:** Crowned arms of Lorraine

Date	Mintage	VG	F	VF	XF	Unc
ND	—	20.00	45.00	85.00	175	—
1625	—	20.00	45.00	85.00	175	—

KM# 40 DENIER
Silver **Ruler:** Karl III **Obv:** Two crowned arms **Rev:** Crowned eagle

Date	Mintage	VG	F	VF	XF	Unc
ND(1626-34)	—	20.00	45.00	85.00	175	—

KM# 41 DENIER
Silver **Ruler:** Karl III **Obv:** Crowned cartouche with arms of Lorraine

Date	Mintage	VG	F	VF	XF	Unc
ND(1626-34)	—	20.00	45.00	85.00	175	—

KM# 51 DENIER
Silver **Ruler:** French Occupation **Obv:** Two-part arms **Rev:** Crowned eagle

Date	Mintage	VG	F	VF	XF	Unc
ND(1634-61)	—	—	—	—	—	—

KM# 52 DENIER
Silver **Ruler:** French Occupation **Obv:** Round arms of Lorraine

Date	Mintage	VG	F	VF	XF	Unc
ND(1634-61)	—	20.00	45.00	85.00	175	—

KM# 70 DENIER
Copper **Ruler:** Leopold Joseph as Leopold I **Obv:** Crowned arms **Rev:** Monogram within four crosses

Date	Mintage	VG	F	VF	XF	Unc
ND(1697-1729)	—	20.00	40.00	80.00	160	—

KM# 71 DENIER
Copper **Ruler:** Leopold Joseph as Leopold I **Rev:** Monogram with cross above and eagles at sides and bottom

Date	Mintage	VG	F	VF	XF	Unc
ND(1697-1729)	—	20.00	40.00	80.00	160	—

KM# 14 2 DENIER
Silver **Ruler:** Heinrich **Obv:** Crowned arms **Rev:** Crowned "H"

Date	Mintage	VG	F	VF	XF	Unc
ND(1608-24)	—	20.00	45.00	85.00	175	—

KM# 15 2 DENIER
Silver **Ruler:** Heinrich **Obv:** Crowned cross of Lorraine **Rev:** Jerusalem cross

Date	Mintage	VG	F	VF	XF	Unc
ND(1608-24)	—	20.00	45.00	85.00	175	—

KM# 13 2 DENIER
Silver **Ruler:** Heinrich **Obv:** Crown above 2 adjacent arms **Rev:** Crowned eagle **Mint:** Nancy **Note:** Legend varieties exist.

Date	Mintage	VG	F	VF	XF	Unc
ND G	—	25.00	50.00	100	210	—
1623	—	25.00	50.00	100	210	—
1624	—	25.00	50.00	100	210	—

KM# 29 2 DENIER
Silver **Ruler:** Karl III and Nikolaus **Obv:** Crowned eagle **Rev:** Crowned two-part arms between crosses of Lorraine

Date	Mintage	VG	F	VF	XF	Unc
1624	—	25.00	50.00	100	210	—
1625	—	25.00	50.00	100	210	—

KM# 42 2 DENIER
Silver **Ruler:** Karl III **Obv:** Large crown above two adjacent shields of arms **Rev:** Crowned eagle

Date	Mintage	VG	F	VF	XF	Unc
ND(1625-34)	—	15.00	30.00	65.00	130	—

KM# 43 2 DENIER
Silver **Ruler:** Karl III **Obv:** Two crowned arms **Rev:** Crowned cross of Lorraine

Date	Mintage	VG	F	VF	XF	Unc
ND(1625-34)	—	15.00	35.00	70.00	145	—

KM# 53 2 DENIER
Silver **Ruler:** French Occupation **Obv:** Crowned two-part arms **Rev:** Crowned eagle

Date	Mintage	VG	F	VF	XF	Unc
ND(1634-61)	—	—	—	—	—	—

KM# 74 15 DENIERS
Silver **Ruler:** Leopold Joseph as Leopold I **Obv:** Crowned double L monogram, three small eagles in field **Obv. Legend:** LEOP • I • D • G • D • LOT • BA • REX • IER • **Rev:** Cross of Lorraine with eagles in angles

Date	Mintage	VG	F	VF	XF	Unc
ND(1697-1729)	—	30.00	65.00	135	265	—

KM# 76 30 DENIERS
Silver **Ruler:** Leopold Joseph as Leopold I **Obv:** Crowned double L monogram, three small eagles in field **Rev:** Cross of Lorraine with eagles in angles **Note:** Similar to 15 Deniers, KM#74.

Date	Mintage	VG	F	VF	XF	Unc
ND(1697-1729)	—	30.00	65.00	135	275	—

KM# 77 30 DENIERS
Silver **Ruler:** Leopold Joseph as Leopold I **Obv:** Monogram in block letters **Rev:** Cross of Lorraine with eagles in angles **Note:** Similar to 15 Deniers, KM#74.

Date	Mintage	VG	F	VF	XF	Unc
ND(1697-1729)	—	30.00	65.00	135	275	—

KM# 82 SOL
Silver **Ruler:** Leopold Joseph as Leopold I **Obv:** Crown above two oval arms **Rev:** Crowned eagle **Mint:** Nancy

Date	Mintage	VG	F	VF	XF	Unc
ND(1697-1729)	—	15.00	35.00	70.00	145	—

KM# 83 SOL
Silver **Ruler:** Leopold Joseph as Leopold I **Obv:** Crowned two-part arms **Rev:** Eagle

Date	Mintage	VG	F	VF	XF	Unc
ND(1697-1729)	—	15.00	35.00	70.00	145	—

KM# 16 1/4 TESTON
Silver **Ruler:** Heinrich **Obv:** Bust right **Rev:** Cross of Lorraine

Date	Mintage	VG	F	VF	XF	Unc
ND(1608-24)	—	110	220	425	875	—

KM# 44 1/4 TESTON
Silver **Ruler:** Karl III **Obv:** Bust right **Rev:** Crowned arms **Mint:** Nancy

Date	Mintage	VG	F	VF	XF	Unc
1629	—	110	220	425	875	—

KM# 60 1/4 TESTON
Silver **Ruler:** Karl III **Obv:** Armored bust **Rev:** Crowned shield of arms

Date	Mintage	VG	F	VF	XF	Unc
1663	—	75.00	150	275	550	—
1664	—	75.00	150	275	550	—
1665	—	75.00	150	275	550	—
1666	—	75.00	150	275	550	—
1668	—	75.00	150	275	550	—

KM# 61 1/2 TESTON
Silver **Ruler:** Karl III **Obv:** Armored bust **Mint:** Nancy

Date	Mintage	VG	F	VF	XF	Unc
1663	—	80.00	165	325	650	—
1664	—	80.00	165	325	650	—
1665	—	80.00	165	325	650	—
1666	—	80.00	165	325	650	—
1668	—	—	—	—	—	—

KM# 84 1/2 TESTON
Silver **Ruler:** Leopold Joseph as Leopold I **Obv:** Bust right **Rev:** Crowned arms

Date	Mintage	VG	F	VF	XF	Unc
1700	—	65.00	135	275	575	—

KM# 17.1 TESTON
9.0000 g., Silver **Ruler:** Heinrich **Obv:** Bust of Heinrich **Obv. Legend:** HENRI. DG. DVX. LOTH. MARCH. DC. BG **Mint:** Nancy

Date	Mintage	VG	F	VF	XF	Unc
ND(1608-24)	—	65.00	135	275	575	—

KM# 17.2 TESTON
9.0000 g., Silver **Ruler:** Heinrich **Obv. Legend:** ...MARC. DC. BG.

Date	Mintage	VG	F	VF	XF	Unc
ND(1608-24)	—	65.00	135	275	575	—

KM# 18 TESTON
9.0000 g., Silver **Ruler:** Heinrich

Date	Mintage	VG	F	VF	XF	Unc
1614	—	65.00	135	275	575	—
1615	—	65.00	135	275	575	—

KM# 30 TESTON
9.0000 g., Silver **Ruler:** Karl III and Nikolaus **Mint:** Nancy

Date	Mintage	VG	F	VF	XF	Unc
1624	—	160	325	675	1,300	—
1625	—	160	325	675	1,300	—
1627	—	160	325	675	1,300	—

KM# 35 TESTON
9.0000 g., Silver **Ruler:** Franz II **Mint:** Badenweiler

Date	Mintage	VG	F	VF	XF	Unc
1626	—	80.00	160	325	600	—
1627	—	80.00	160	325	600	—
1628	—	80.00	160	325	600	—
1629	—	80.00	160	325	600	—
1630	—	80.00	160	325	600	—
1631	—	80.00	160	325	600	—

KM# 45 TESTON
9.0000 g., Silver **Ruler:** Karl III

Date	Mintage	VG	F	VF	XF	Unc
1626	—	110	200	425	850	—
1627	—	110	200	425	850	—
1628	—	110	200	425	850	—
1629	—	110	200	425	850	—

Date	Mintage	VG	F	VF	XF	Unc
1630	—	110	200	425	850	—
1632	—	110	200	425	850	—

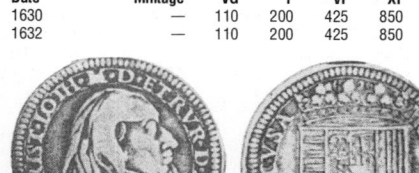

KM# 47 TESTON

9.0000 g., Silver **Ruler:** Karl III **Obv:** Cloaked bust of Christine **Obv. Legend:** CHRIST • LOTH. M. D... **Rev:** Crowned arms **Rev. Legend:** ... FLORENT. CVSA. **Mint:** Florence

Date	Mintage	VG	F	VF	XF	Unc
1630	—	25,000	50,000	80,000	—	—

KM# 55 TESTON

9.0000 g., Silver **Obv:** Bust right **Rev:** Crowned arms

Date	Mintage	VG	F	VF	XF	Unc
1634	—	120	240	450	900	—
1635	—	120	240	450	900	—

KM# 56 TESTON

9.0000 g., Silver **Ruler:** Karl III **Mint:** Romarti

Date	Mintage	VG	F	VF	XF	Unc
1638	—	300	600	950	1,850	—
1639	—	300	600	950	1,850	—

KM# 62 TESTON

9.0000 g., Silver **Mint:** Nancy **Note:** Varieties exist.

Date	Mintage	VG	F	VF	XF	Unc
1663	—	80.00	160	325	650	—
1665	—	80.00	160	325	650	—
1666	—	80.00	160	325	650	—
1667	—	80.00	160	325	650	—
1668	—	80.00	160	325	650	—
1669	—	80.00	160	325	650	—

KM# 90 TESTON

Silver **Ruler:** Leopold Joseph as Leopold I **Obv:** Bust right **Rev:** Crowned plain oval arms **Mint:** Nancy

Date	Mintage	VG	F	VF	XF	Unc
1700	—	175	375	775	1,550	—

KM# 91 TESTON

Silver **Ruler:** Leopold Joseph as Leopold I **Rev:** Cross of Lorraine on crowned ornate oval arms

Date	Mintage	VG	F	VF	XF	Unc
1700	—	175	375	775	1,550	—

KM# 92 TESTON

Silver **Ruler:** Leopold Joseph as Leopold I **Obv:** Bust right **Obv. Legend:** LEOP • I • D • G • D • LOT • BA • REX • IE • **Rev:** Crowned oval shield within cartouche **Rev. Legend:** IN • TE • DOMINE • SPERAVI •

Date	Mintage	VG	F	VF	XF	Unc
1700	—	175	375	775	1,550	—

KM# 5 THALER

Silver **Ruler:** Karl II **Obv:** Bust of Karl II left, date on shoulder **Rev:** Eagle above crowned, mantled and supported arms **Note:** Dav. #6901.

Date	Mintage	VG	F	VF	XF	Unc
1601	—	900	1,800	3,500	6,500	—
1603	—	900	1,800	3,500	6,500	—

KM# 6 THALER

Silver **Ruler:** Karl II **Obv:** Bust breaking circle at bottom, date below **Rev:** Eagle above crowned, helmeted and mantled arms, seven shields around and two monograms in field **Note:** Dav. #6902.

Date	Mintage	VG	F	VF	XF	Unc
1603 Rare	—	—	—	—	—	—

KM# 36 THALER

Silver **Ruler:** Franz II **Obv:** Bust of Franz II right **Rev:** Date above crowned arms **Note:** Dav. #6903.

Date	Mintage	VG	F	VF	XF	Unc
1630 Rare	—	—	—	—	—	—
1632 Rare	—	—	—	—	—	—

KM# 37 THALER

Silver **Ruler:** Franz II **Obv:** Crowned arms divide date at sides **Rev:** Madonna standing in oval of flames **Note:** Dav. #6904.

Date	Mintage	VG	F	VF	XF	Unc
1632 Rare	—	—	—	—	—	—

KM# 63 THALER

Silver **Ruler:** Karl III, 2nd reign **Note:** Thick flan.

Date	Mintage	VG	F	VF	XF	Unc
1665 Rare	—	—	—	—	—	—
1668 Rare	—	—	—	—	—	—

KM# 104 THALER

Silver **Ruler:** Leopold Joseph as Leopold I **Obv:** Bust of Leopold I right **Rev:** Crowned oval arms **Note:** Dav. #6905.

Date	Mintage	VG	F	VF	XF	Unc
1700	—	1,000	2,000	3,750	7,000	—

KM# 48 CHARLES D'OR

3.3600 g., 0.9520 Gold 0.1028 oz. AGW **Obv:** Bust of Karl III right **Rev:** Cross of crowned C monograms **Mint:** Paris

Date	Mintage	VG	F	VF	XF	Unc
1612A	—	1,900	3,750	6,300	10,500	—

KM# 64 CHARLES D'OR
3.3600 g., 0.9520 Gold 0.1028 oz. AGW **Obv:** Karl III **Mint:** Nancy **Note:** Fr. #157.

Date	Mintage	VG	F	VF	XF	Unc
1661	—	1,250	2,750	5,320	9,500	—
1662	—	1,250	2,750	5,320	9,500	—
1665	—	1,250	2,750	5,320	9,500	—
1668	—	1,250	2,750	5,320	9,500	—
1669	—	1,250	2,750	5,320	9,500	—

KM# 115 LEOPOLD D'OR
6.6900 g., 0.9170 Gold 0.1972 oz. AGW **Ruler:** Leopold Joseph as Leopold I **Obv:** Laureate head right **Obv. Legend:** LEOP • I • D • G • D • LOT • BAR • REX • IE • **Rev:** Crowned L's in cruciform, double crosses at angles **Rev. Legend:** TV • DOMINE • SPES • MEA **Mint:** Nancy **Note:** Fr. #158.

Date	Mintage	VG	F	VF	XF	Unc
1700	—	1,600	3,500	5,750	10,000	—

TRADE COINAGE

KM# 19 1/2 GOLDGULDEN
1.7500 g., 0.9860 Gold 0.0555 oz. AGW **Ruler:** Heinrich **Obv:** Arms **Obv. Legend:** HENRI. D: G. LOTH **Rev:** St. Nicholas standing **Mint:** Nancy **Note:** Fr. #153.

Date	Mintage	VG	F	VF	XF	Unc
ND(1608-24)	—	900	1,800	3,000	5,500	—

KM# 20 GOLDGULDEN
3.5000 g., 0.9860 Gold 0.1109 oz. AGW **Ruler:** Heinrich **Mint:** Nancy **Note:** Fr. #152.

Date	Mintage	VG	F	VF	XF	Unc
ND(1608-24)	—	295	650	1,100	1,850	—

KM# 21.1 GOLDGULDEN
3.5000 g., 0.9860 Gold 0.1109 oz. AGW **Ruler:** Heinrich **Obv:** Bust of Henri **Obv. Legend:** ... MARC. DC. BG. **Note:** Fr. #154.

Date	Mintage	VG	F	VF	XF	Unc
ND(1608-24)	—	700	1,650	3,250	6,000	—

KM# 21.2 GOLDGULDEN
3.5000 g., 0.9860 Gold 0.1109 oz. AGW **Ruler:** Heinrich **Obv. Legend:** ... MARCH. DC. BG. **Note:** Fr. #154.

Date	Mintage	VG	F	VF	XF	Unc
ND(1608-24)	—	700	1,650	3,250	6,000	—

KM# 22 GOLDGULDEN
3.5000 g., 0.9860 Gold 0.1109 oz. AGW **Ruler:** Heinrich **Obv:** Head right **Note:** Fr. #154.

Date	Mintage	VG	F	VF	XF	Unc
1617	—	700	1,650	3,250	6,000	—

KM# 57 PISTOLE
6.6500 g., 0.9000 Gold 0.1924 oz. AGW **Obv:** Crowned arms **Obv. Legend:** CAROLVS. D: G... **Rev:** Cross of Jerusalem **Mint:** Romarti **Note:** Fr. #156.

Date	Mintage	VG	F	VF	XF	Unc
1639	—	850	1,750	3,200	5,800	—
ND	—	850	1,750	3,200	5,800	—

KM# A57 2 PISTOLES
13.3000 g., 0.9000 Gold 0.3848 oz. AGW **Ruler:** Karl III **Obv:** Date over large crown above manifold arms with central shield of Lorraine, small cross of Lorraine to either side, titles of Karl III **Obv. Legend:** CAROLUS. D: G... **Rev:** Cross of Jerusalem within octolobe **Rev. Legend:** DA. MIHI. VIRTV. CONTRA. HOSTES. TVOS. **Mint:** Romarti

Date	Mintage	VG	F	VF	XF	Unc
1631	—	1,200	2,600	4,500	7,750	—

LOWENBERG

(Lwowek, Lvuvek)

The city of Löwenberg is located in northwestern Silesia twenty miles southwest of Liegnitz. The Emperor Matthias as king of Bohemia granted the city permission to coin a commemorative thaler on the occasion of a shooting match festival held there in 1615.

MINT OFFICIAL

HR = Hans Rieger der Ältere, die-cutter in Breslau, ca. 1610-1653.

REFERENCES

L/S = Ferdinand Friedensburg and Hans Seger, **Schlesiens Münzen und Medaillen der neueren Zeit**, Breslau, 1901.
J/M = Norbert Jaschke and Fritz P. Maercker, **Schlesische Münzen und Medaillen**, Ihringen, 1985.

PROVINCIAL TOWN

REGULAR COINAGE

KM# 2 HELLER
Silver **Obv:** Lion striding to left **Note:** Ref. L/S-3599. Uniface. Kipper issue.

Date	Mintage	VG	F	VF	XF	Unc
ND(1621)	—	35.00	75.00	155	—	—

KM# 3 3 HELLER
Copper **Obv:** Lion to left in trefoil, date below **Note:** Ref. J/M-932. Uniface. Kipper issue.

Date	Mintage	VG	F	VF	XF	Unc
1622	—	—	—	—	—	—

KM# 6 THALER
Silver **Rev:** Without buds around border **Note:** Dav. #5429A.

Date	Mintage	VG	F	VF	XF	Unc
1615 HR	—	200	450	1,000	2,000	—

KM# 5 THALER
Silver **Subject:** Shooting festival of 1615 **Obv:** 5-line inscription above ornate shield of 2-fold arms, which divides date below **Obv. Inscription:** KLEINOT / DES GROSEN / SCHISSEN. ZV / LEWENBERG / 23. AVGVSTI. **Rev:** Crowned imperial eagle, large ornate shield of manifold arms on breast, crown divides 2-line inscription **Rev. Inscription:** MAT - THI: / ROM. - IMP: **Note:** Dav. 5429.

Date	Mintage	VG	F	VF	XF	Unc
1615 HR	—	200	450	1,000	2,000	4,000

KM# 7 THALER
Silver **Subject:** Shooting festival of 1615 **Obv:** 5-line inscription above ornate shield of 2-fold arms, which divides date below **Obv. Inscription:** KLEINOT / DES GROSSEN / SCHISSEN. ZV / LEWENBERG / 23. AVGVSTI. **Rev:** Crowned imperial eagle, large ornate shield of manifold arms on breast, crown divides 2-line inscription **Rev. Inscription:** MAT - THI: / ROM. - IMP: **Note:** Dav. 5430.

Date	Mintage	VG	F	VF	XF	Unc
1615 HR	—	275	600	1,350	2,800	—

KM# 8 2 THALER
Silver **Subject:** Shooting festival of 1615 **Obv:** 5-line inscription above ornate shield of 2-fold arms, which divides date below **Obv. Inscription:** KLEINOT / DES GROSEN / SCHISSEN. ZV / LEWENBERG / 23. AVGVSTI. **Rev:** Crowned imperial eagle, large ornate shield of manifold arms on breast, crown divides 2-line inscription **Rev. Inscription:** MAT - THI: / ROM. - IMP: **Note:** Dav. 5428.

Date	Mintage	VG	F	VF	XF	Unc
1615 HR Rare	—	—	—	—	—	—

LOWENSTEIN-WERTHEIM

The countship of Löwenstein was established by a division of the lineage of Calw in northern Württemberg, in 1152. Löwenstein was sold to the Habsburgs in 1281 from which it eventually passed to the Palatinate (Pfalz) in 1441. A new line of counts was established in 1476 from the electoral Palatinate. Wertheim was obtained by marriage in 1600. The division of 1635 resulted in the separation of Löwenstein-Wertheim into 2 branches, Protestant and Catholic.

RULERS

Ludwig II, 1541-1611
Christoph Ludwig, 1611-1618 and
Ludwig III, 1611-1635 and
Wolfgang Ernst, 1611-1636 and
Johann Dietrich, 1611-1644
Friedrich Ludwig, 1618-1635

MINT OFFICIALS

Date	Name
1622 (February)	Heinrich Westermann in Wertheim
1622 (July)	Ernst Knorr the Elder in Wertheim

REFERENCES

K = Ulrich Klein, "Die Münzen der Grafen und Fürsten von Löwenstein-Wertheim," **700 Jahre Stadt Löwenstein**, Löwenstein (Württemberg), 1987.
W = Ferdinand Wibel, **Zur Münzgeschichte der Grafen von Wertheim und des Gesamthauses Löwenstein-Wertheim**, Hamburg, 1880.

COUNTSHIP

REGULAR COINAGE

KM# 14 HELLER
Copper, 25 mm. **Ruler:** Johann Dietrich **Obv:** Bust to right **Obv. Legend:** I. THEO. COM. LE. RO. SVP. CHASP. **Rev:** Crowned shield of 9-fold arms, date at end of legend **Rev. Legend:** IN. CVGNON. CVSVS. **Mint:** Cugnon **Note:** W#177. Prev. Löwenstein-Wertheim-Rochefort KM#12.

Date	Mintage	VG	F	VF	XF	Unc
1623	—	—	—	—	—	—

KM# 3 3 KREUZER (Groschen)
Silver **Ruler:** Wolfgang Ernst and Johann Dietrich **Obv:** Shield of 4-fold arms divides date **Obv. Legend:** MONETA. NOVA. ARG. ROK. **Rev:** Crowned imperial eagle, 3 in orb on breast **Rev. Legend:** SVB. VMB. ALARVM. TVARVM. **Mint:** Wertheim **Note:** Prev. Löwenstein-Wertheim-Rochefort KM#5.

Date	Mintage	VG	F	VF	XF	Unc
(16)16	—	—	—	—	—	—
1616	—	—	—	—	—	—

KM# 4 3 KREUZER (Groschen)
Silver **Ruler:** Wolfgang Ernst and Johann Dietrich **Obv:** Three small shields of arms, 2 above 1 **Obv. Legend:** MONETA. NOVA. ARG. ROK. **Rev:** Crowned imperial eagle, 3 in orb on breast **Rev. Legend:** SVB. VMB. ALARVM. TVARVM. **Mint:** Wertheim **Note:** Prev. Löwenstein-Wertheim-Rochefort KM#6. Varieties exist.

Date	Mintage	VG	F	VF	XF	Unc
ND(1616)	—	—	—	—	—	—

KM# 1 SCHILLING
Silver **Ruler:** Johann Dietrich **Obv:** Crowned shield of 4-fold arms **Obv. Legend:** MO. NOVA - ARG - ORDINE - CLER. **Rev:** Crowned imperial eagle in circle **Rev. Legend:** NISI TV DOMINE NOBISCVM EPVS. **Note:** Imitation of issue of Schaumburg-Pinneberg KM#75. CLER in obv. legend = Comitis Löwenstein Et Rochefort.

Date	Mintage	VG	F	VF	XF	Unc
ND(1611-35)	—	450	625	850	1,550	—

KM# 26 SCHILLING
Silver **Ruler:** Johann Dietrich **Obv:** Bust to right **Rev:** Date in legend **Mint:** Cugnon **Note:** W#176.

Date	Mintage	VG	F	VF	XF	Unc
1626	—	—	—	—	—	—

KM# 5 12 KREUZER (4 Stüber=Dreibätzner)
Silver **Ruler:** Johann Dietrich **Obv:** Bust to right **Obv. Legend:** SIT. NOMEN. DOMINI. BENEDICTVM. **Rev:** Shield of 4-fold arms, date above, where present **Rev. Legend:** MONETA. NOVA. ARGENTIA. CHA. R. **Mint:** Cugnon **Note:** Prev. Löwenstein-Wertheim-Rochefort KM#7. Varieties exist.

Date	Mintage	VG	F	VF	XF	Unc
1617	—	—	—	—	—	—
ND(ca1618)	—	—	—	—	—	—

KM# 9 12 KREUZER (4 Stüber=Dreibätzner)
Silver **Ruler:** Johann Dietrich **Obv:** Bust to right **Obv. Legend:** + SI. DEVS. PRO. NOBIS. QVI. CONT. NOS. **Rev:** Crowned imperial eagle **Rev. Legend:** SVB. VMBRA. ALARVM. TVARVM **Mint:** Wertheim **Note:** Kipper. Prev. Löwenstein-Wertheim-Rochefort KM#11.

Date	Mintage	VG	F	VF	XF	Unc
ND(1621-2)	—	—	—	—	—	—

KM# 10 12 KREUZER (4 Stüber=Dreibätzner)
3.6800 g., Silver **Ruler:** Wolfgang Ernst and Johann Dietrich **Obv:** Crowned shield of 4-fold arms **Obv. Legend:** MONETA - NOVA - ARG * ROK. **Rev:** Crowned imperial eagle **Rev. Legend:** SVB. VMBRA. ALARVM. TUARVM. **Mint:** Rochefort **Note:** Kipper. Prev. Löwenstein-Wertheim-Rochefort KM#10.

Date	Mintage	VG	F	VF	XF	Unc
ND(1622-23)	—	450	625	850	1,550	—

KM# 2 THALER
Silver **Ruler:** Christoph Ludwig **Obv:** Bust to right **Rev:** Helmeted arms **Note:** W#99. Prev. KM#5.

Date	Mintage	VG	F	VF	XF	Unc
ND(1611-18) Rare	—	—	—	—	—	—

KM# 16 THALER
Silver Weight varies: 27.50-28.00g. **Ruler:** Johann Dietrich **Obv:** Armored bust to right in circle, date at top in margin. **Obv. Legend:** IO. THEOD. COM. IN LEWENSTEIN. WERTH. ROCHEF. **Rev:** Shield of 4-fold arms with central shield, 2 ornate helmets flank crest above **Rev. Legend:** ET. MONTAGV. SV. P. IN CHASPIERRE ET CVGNON - ETZ. **Mint:** Cugnon **Note:** Dav. #6909; W#171, 175. Prev. Löwenstein-Wertheim-Rochefort KM#13. Varieties exist.

Date	Mintage	VG	F	VF	XF	Unc
1623	—	1,000	2,000	4,000	6,500	—
ND(1624)	—	—	—	—	—	—

KM# 17 THALER
Silver Weight varies: 27.50-28.00g. **Ruler:** Johann Dietrich **Obv:** Armored bust to right in circle, date at top in margin **Obv. Legend:** IO. THEOD. COM. IN LEWENSTEIN. WERGI. ROCHEF. **Rev:** Ornate shield of 4-fold arms with central shield, 2 ornate helmets flank crest above **Rev. Legend:** ET. MONTACV. SV. P. IN CHASFIERRE. **Mint:** Cugnon **Note:** Dav. #6910; W#172. Prev. Löwenstein-Wertheim-Rochefort KM#14.

Date	Mintage	VG	F	VF	XF	Unc
1623	—	1,000	2,000	4,000	6,500	—

KM# 18 THALER
Silver Weight varies: 27.50-28.00g., 42-43 mm. **Ruler:** Johann Dietrich **Obv:** Crowned shield of 4-fold arms with central shield in ornamented frame **Obv. Legend:** IO. THEOD. COM. IN. LEWENSTEIN. WERTH. ROCHEF + **Rev:** Crowned imperial eagle, orb on breast, date at end of legend **Rev. Legend:** FERDINAND. II. D.G. ROM. IMP. SEMP. AVGVST. **Mint:** Wertheim **Note:** Dav. #6911; W#169-70. Prev. Löwenstein-Wertheim-Rochefort KM#15.

Date	Mintage	VG	F	VF	XF	Unc
1623	—	450	900	1,650	2,750	—
1624	—	450	900	1,650	2,750	—

KM# 22 THALER
Silver, 42-43 mm. **Ruler:** Johann Dietrich **Obv:** Draped and armored bust to right, date in margin at top **Obv. Legend:** IO. THEOD. COM. IN LEWENSTEIN. WERTH. ROCHEF. **Rev:** Crowned shield of 9-fold arms in ornamented frame **Rev. Legend:** ET. MONTAGV. SV. P. IN CHASPIERRE ET CVGNON - ETZ. **Mint:** Cugnon **Note:** Dav. #6912; W#173. Prev. Löwenstein-Wertheim-Rochefort KM#16.

Date	Mintage	VG	F	VF	XF	Unc
1624 Rare	—	—	—	—	—	—

KM# 24 THALER
Silver Weight varies: 27.50-28.00g., 44 mm. **Ruler:** Johann Dietrich **Obv:** Large armored bust to right in circle, date in margin at top **Obv. Legend:** IO. THEOD. COM IN LEWENSTEIN. WERTH. ROCHEF. **Rev:** Crowned 4-fold arms with central shield, in ornamented frame **Rev. Legend:** ET. MONTAGV. SV. P. IN CHASPIERRE ET CVGNON - ETZ. **Mint:** Cugnon **Note:** Dav. #6913; W#174. Prev. Löwenstein-Wertheim-Rochefort KM#17.

Date	Mintage	VG	F	VF	XF	Unc
1625 Rare	—	—	—	—	—	—

JOINT COINAGE

KM# 20 HELLER
Silver **Ruler:** Christoph Ludwig, Friedrich Ludwig, and Ludwig III **Obv:** Shield of 4-fold arms, date **Note:** Uniface. W#95. Prev. KM#13.

Date	Mintage	VG	F	VF	XF	Unc
1624	—	—	—	—	—	—

KM# 6 2 KREUZER (1/2 Batzen)
Silver **Ruler:** Wolfgang Ernst and Johann Dietrich **Obv:** 2-fold arms divided horizontally, lozenges above, lion walking to right below **Obv. Legend:** ZV: GOTT: MEIN: HOFFNVNG **Rev:** Imperial orb with Z **Rev. Legend:** SOLI: DEO: GLORIA. **Note:** Kipper. K#1b.

Date	Mintage	VG	F	VF	XF	Unc
ND(1619-22)	—	—	—	—	—	—

KM# 7 3 KREUZER (Groschen)
Silver **Ruler:** Wolfgang Ernst and Johann Dietrich **Obv:** Shield of 4-fold arms **Rev:** Crowned imperial eagle, 3 in orb on breast, titles of Ferdinand II **Mint:** Wertheim **Note:** Kipper. W#98.

Date	Mintage	VG	F	VF	XF	Unc
ND(1619-24)	—	—	—	—	—	—

KM# 8 3 KREUZER (Groschen)
Silver **Ruler:** Wolfgang Ernst and Johann Dietrich **Obv:** 2-fold arms divided horizontally **Rev:** Crowned imperial eagle, 3 in orb on breast, titles of Ferdinand II **Mint:** Wertheim **Note:** Kipper. K#1a. Prev. KM#10.

Date	Mintage	VG	F	VF	XF	Unc
1621	—	600	1,200	—	—	—

KM# 11 24 KREUZER (Sechsbätzner)
Silver **Ruler:** Wolfgang Ernst and Johann Dietrich **Obv:** Crowned rampant lion to right **Rev:** Crowned imperial eagle, 24 in orb on breast, titles of Ferdinand II **Mint:** Wertheim **Note:** Kipper. W#97.

Date	Mintage	VG	F	VF	XF	Unc
ND(ca.1622)	—	—	—	—	—	—

KM# 12 THALER
Silver, 43 mm. **Ruler:** Wolfgang Ernst and Johann Dietrich **Obv:** Two half-length figures facing each other, date in exergue **Obv. Legend:** WOLF. ERN. ET. IOH. THEO. COM. I. LEW. WERTH. R.M. DN. I.S.C.B. H.N. **Rev:** Crowned imperial eagle, orb on breast **Rev. Legend:** FERDINAND. II. D.G. RO. IMP. SEMP. AU. H. B. **Mint:** Wertheim **Note:** Dav. #6906; W#96. Varieties exist.

Date	Mintage	VG	F	VF	XF	Unc
1622 Rare	—	—	—	—	—	—

LOWENSTEIN-WERTHEIM-ROCHEFORT

Rochefort was the Catholic branch of Löwenstein-Wertheim, established in 1635. From 1622 until about 1650, coinage for Löwenstein-Wertheim-Rochefort was struck at the mint of Cugnon in Luxembourg. The ruler was made Prince of the Empire in 1711. All lands in his possession were mediatized in 1806.

RULERS
Wolfgang Ernst, (1611)-1635-1636 and
Johann Dietrich, (1611)-1635-1644
Ferdinand Karl, 1644-1672
Maximilian Karl, 1672-1718

MINT
Cugnon in Luxembourg

MINT OFFICIALS' INITIALS

Initial	Date	Name
(a) = 6-pointed star or PHM	1677-1718	Philipp Heinrich Müller, die-cutter in Augsburg
FS	ca.1691-7	Friedrich Schattauer

REFERENCES
K = Ulrich Klein, "Die Münzen der Grafen und Fürsten von Löwenstein-Wertheim," **700 Jahre Stadt Löwenstein**, Löwenstein (Württemberg), 1987.

W = Ferdinand Wibel, **Zur Münzgeschichte der Grafen von Wertheim und des Gesamthauses Löwenstein-Wertheim**, Hamburg, 1880.

COUNTSHIP
Catholic Branch
REGULAR COINAGE

KM# 28 DENIER (Pfennig)
Copper Weight varies: 0.88-1.32g. **Ruler:** Ferdinand Karl **Obv:** Bust to right in circle **Obv. Legend:** FERDINAN. CHARLE. **Rev:** Four fleurs-de-lis in field **Rev. Legend:** DEN. DE. LA. SOV. DE. CVGN. **Mint:** Cugnon **Note:** W#206.

Date	Mintage	VG	F	VF	XF	Unc
ND(1644-50)	—	—	—	—	—	—

KM# 30 DENIER (Pfennig)
Copper Weight varies: 0.88-1.32g. **Ruler:** Ferdinand Karl **Obv:** Bust to right **Obv. Legend:** FERDINAN.CHARLE **Rev:** Three large rosettes **Rev. Legend:** DEN. DE. LA. SOV. DE. CVGN. **Mint:** Cugnon **Note:** W#202-5. Varieties exist.

Date	Mintage	VG	F	VF	XF	Unc
ND(1644-50)	—	16.00	32.00	65.00	130	—

KM# 29.2 DENIER (Pfennig)
Copper Weight varies: 0.88-1.32g. **Ruler:** Ferdinand Karl **Obv:** Bust to right **Obv. Legend:** F.C.C.D.L.RO.S.S.D.CH.CVG. **Rev:** 3 rosettes in circle **Rev. Legend:** DENIER + DE + CVGNON **Mint:** Cugnon

Date	Mintage	VG	F	VF	XF	Unc
ND(1644-50)	—	16.00	32.00	65.00	130	—

KM# 31 DENIER (Pfennig)
Billon **Ruler:** Ferdinand Karl **Obv:** Bust to right **Obv. Legend:** FERDINAN.CHARLE **Rev:** Four fleurs-de-lis in field **Rev. Legend:** DEN.DE.LA.SOV.DE.CVG. **Mint:** Cugnon **Note:** W#187.

Date	Mintage	VG	F	VF	XF	Unc
ND(1644-50)	—	16.00	32.00	65.00	135	—

KM# 32 DENIER (Pfennig)
Billon **Ruler:** Ferdinand Karl **Rev:** Three rosettes **Rev. Legend:** DEN.DE.LA.SOV.DE.CVGN. **Mint:** Cugnon

Date	Mintage	VG	F	VF	XF	Unc
ND(1644-50)	—	13.00	30.00	65.00	130	—

KM# 25 DENIER (Pfennig)
Copper Weight varies: 0.88-1.32g. **Ruler:** Ferdinand Karl **Obv:** Bust to right **Obv. Legend:** F.C.C.D.L.R(o).S.S... **Rev:** Two fleurs-de-lis above rosette, date at end of legend **Rev. Legend:** DENIER. DE. CVGNON **Mint:** Cugnon **Note:** W#188-9. Varieties exist.

Date	Mintage	Good	VG	F	VF	XF
1645	—	—	16.00	35.00	75.00	150
1649	—	—	13.00	27.00	55.00	110

KM# 26 DENIER (Pfennig)
Copper Weight varies: 0.88-1.32g. **Ruler:** Ferdinand Karl **Obv:** Bust to right **Obv. Legend:** F.C.C.D.L.RO.S.S... **Rev:** Two fleurs-de-lis above rosette, date at end of legend **Rev. Legend:** DENIER. TOVRNOIS. **Mint:** Cugnon **Note:** W#190, 192-4. Varieties exist.

Date	Mintage	VG	F	VF	XF	Unc
1645	—	13.00	30.00	65.00	130	—
1649	—	13.00	30.00	65.00	130	—

KM# 27 DENIER (Pfennig)
Copper Weight varies: 0.88-1.32g. **Ruler:** Ferdinand Karl **Obv:** Bust to right **Rev:** Date around field of four rosettes **Rev. Legend:** PRINCE DE CUGNON **Mint:** Cugnon **Note:** W#191.

Date	Mintage	VG	F	VF	XF	Unc
1645	—	13.00	30.00	65.00	130	—

KM# 33 DENIER (Pfennig)
Copper Weight varies: 0.88-1.32g. **Ruler:** Ferdinand Karl **Obv:** Bust to right **Obv. Legend:** F.C.C.D.L.RO.S.S... **Rev:** Four fleurs-de-lis in field, date at end of legend **Rev. Legend:** DENIER DE CVGNON **Mint:** Cugnon **Note:** W#195-7, 207. Varieties exist.

Date	Mintage	VG	F	VF	XF	Unc
1649	—	13.00	30.00	65.00	130	—
ND(1644-50)	—	13.00	30.00	65.00	130	—

KM# 29.1 DENIER (Pfennig)
Copper Weight varies: 0.88-1.32g. **Ruler:** Ferdinand Karl **Obv:** Bust to right **Obv. Legend:** F.C.C.D.L.RO.S.S.D.CH.CVG. **Rev:** Three large rosettes, date at end of legend **Rev. Legend:** DENIER DE CVGNON **Mint:** Cugnon **Note:** W#198-201. Varieties exist.

Date	Mintage	VG	F	VF	XF	Unc
1649	—	15.00	35.00	75.00	150	—
ND(1644-50)	—	15.00	35.00	75.00	150	—

KM# 20 DOUBLE TOURNOIS (2 Deniers)
Copper Weight varies: 2.40-2.45g. **Ruler:** Johann Dietrich **Obv:** Bust to right in circle. **Obv. Legend:** I. T. H. C. D. LE. RO. S. S. D. CH. CVGN. **Rev:** 4 fleurs-de-lis with rosette in center, date at end of legend **Rev. Legend:** DOVBLE.TOVRNOIS. **Mint:** Cugnon **Note:** W#178-86. Varieties exist.

Date	Mintage	VG	F	VF	XF	Unc
1633	—	20.00	33.00	55.00	110	—
1634	—	20.00	33.00	55.00	110	—
1635	—	30.00	50.00	75.00	155	—
1643	—	30.00	50.00	75.00	155	—

KM# 35 KREUZER
Billon **Ruler:** Maximilian Karl **Obv:** Crowned 3-fold arms **Obv. Legend:** M. C. COM. IN - LOW. WERTH. **Rev:** 4-line inscription with date **Rev. Inscription:** 1/KREU/TZER/(date). **Mint:** Wertheim **Note:** W#213, 215. Varieties exist.

Date	Mintage	VG	F	VF	XF	Unc
1697 FS	—	25.00	50.00	100	210	—

KM# 37 3 KREUZER (Groschen)
Silver **Ruler:** Maximilian Karl **Rev:** Four-fold arms **Mint:** Wertheim

Date	Mintage	VG	F	VF	XF	Unc
1697 FS	—	40.00	100	185	325	—

KM# 36.1 4 KREUZER (Batzen)
Silver, 25 mm. **Ruler:** Maximilian Karl **Obv:** Crowned oval 8-fold arms, date divided by crown in margin **Obv. Legend:** MAX. KARO(L). COM. IN LOW. WERTHEIM. **Rev:** Crowned imperial eagle, 4 in orb on breast **Rev. Legend:** LEOPOLDVS. D.G. ROM. IMP. S. AVG. **Mint:** Wertheim **Note:** W#211, 213. Varieties exist. Prev. KM#36.

Date	Mintage	VG	F	VF	XF	Unc
1697 FS	—	55.00	90.00	180	275	—

KM# 36.2 4 KREUZER (Batzen)
Silver, 25 mm. **Ruler:** Maximilian Karl **Obv:** Crowned shield of 8-fold arms, date divided by crown in margin **Obv. Legend:** MAX. KAROL. COM. IN LOW. WERTHEIM. L **Rev:** Shield of 9-fold arms in circle **Rev. Legend:** LEOPOLDVS. D.G. ROM. IMP. S. AVG. **Mint:** Wertheim **Note:** W#212.

Date	Mintage	VG	F	VF	XF	Unc
1697 FS	—	60.00	100	190	360	—

KM# A38 1/2 THALER
14.6800 g., Silver, 34 mm. **Ruler:** Maximilian Karl **Obv:** Armored bust to right **Obv. Legend:** MAX. CAROL. COMES IN LÖWENSTEIN WERTHEIM. **Rev:** Ornate shield of 8-fold arms divides date and die-cutter's initials near bottom, 3 ornate helmets above **Rev. Legend:** ROCHEF. ET MONT. SV. PR. IN CHAS. D. IN SCHARPF. BR. HERB. ET NEUFF. **Mint:** Wertheim

Date	Mintage	Good	VG	F	VF	XF
1697 FS	—	—	—	—	—	—

KM# 38 THALER
Silver, 40-41 mm. **Ruler:** Maximilian Karl **Obv:** Armored bust to right, die-cutter's initials below **Obv. Legend:** MAX • CAROL • COMES IN LOWENSTEIN WERTHEIM • **Rev:** Ornate shield of 8-fold arms divides date and die-cutter's initials near bottom, 3

ornate helmets above **Rev. Legend:** *ROCH • ET MON • S • PR • IN CHAS • D • IN SCHAR • BR • KER • CAS • HERB • ET NEUF **Mint:** Wertheim **Note:** Ref. W-210; Dav. 6914.

Date	Mintage	VG	F	VF	XF	Unc
1697 PHM//FS	—	750	1,500	3,000	6,500	—

Note: Künker Auction 163, 1-10, nearly Unc realized approximately $12,640.

TRADE COINAGE

KM# 34 DUCAT
3.3900 g., Gold **Ruler:** Maximilian Karl **Obv:** Armored bust turned slightly to right in circle **Obv. Legend:** MAX. CAR. COM. IN LEWENST. WERTH. ROCH. ET MONS. SVPR. **Rev:** Crowned ornately-shaped shield of 8-fold arms, crossed palm fronds divide date below **Rev. Legend:** IN CHASSEP. DOM. IN SCHARH. EREVB. HERB. ET NEVSCH. **Mint:** Cugnon **Note:** FR#1459; W#209.

Date	Mintage	VG	F	VF	XF	Unc
1692 Rare	—	—	—	—	—	—

PRINCIPALITY
Catholic Branch
REGULAR COINAGE

KM# 24 DENIER (Pfennig)
1.0900 g., Copper **Obv:** Bust of Ferdinand Charles right **Obv. Legend:** GERDIN. CHARLE **Rev:** Three rosettes, dot in center **Rev. Legend:** DEN. D.L. SOV. D. CVGN. **Mint:** Cugnon

Date	Mintage	VG	F	VF	XF	Unc
ND(1623-24)	—	25.00	55.00	110	225	—

KM# 18 SCHILLING
Silver **Obv:** Bust right, titles in legend **Rev:** Titles, date in legend **Mint:** Cugnon

Date	Mintage	VG	F	VF	XF	Unc
1626	—	—	—	—	—	—

KM# 22 ESCALIN
Silver **Obv:** Rampant lion left with sword and shield **Obv. Legend:** IO.THEOD COM.D.LEW. **Rev:** Crowned eight-fold arms

Date	Mintage	F	VF	XF	Unc	BU
1626	—	—	—	—	—	—

PATTERNS
Including off metal strikes

KM#	Date	Mintage	Identification	Mkt Val
Pn1	1692	—	Ducat. Silver. KM#34.	450

LOWENSTEIN-WERTHEIM-VIRNEBURG

The Protestant branch of the family dates from the division of 1635. There was a further division in 1721 into 3 branches, 2 of which survived more than one generation, only to be mediatized in 1806.

RULERS
Friedrich Ludwig, 1635-1658
Ludwig Ernst, 1658-1681 and
Friedrich Eberhard, 1658-1683
Eucharius Kasimir, 1681-1698
Heinrich Friedrich, 1683-1721

MINT OFFICIALS' INITIALS

Initial	Date	Name
FS	ca.1691-7	Friedrich Schattauer

REFERENCES
K = Ulrich Klein, "Die Münzen der Grafen und Fürsten von Löwenstein-Wertheim," **700 Jahre Stadt Löwenstein**, Löwenstein (Württemberg), 1987.
W = Ferdinand Wibel, **Zur Münzgeschichte der Grafen von Wertheim und des Gesamthauses Löwenstein-Wertheim**, Hamburg, 1880.

COUNTSHIP
Protestant Branch
REGULAR COINAGE

KM# 10 KREUZER
Silver, 15-18 mm. **Ruler:** Eucharius Kasimir Heinrich Friedrich **Obv:** Crowned three-fold arms **Obv. Legend:** E. C. COM. IN. (-) LO(-)W. WERTHEI(M). **Rev:** 4-line inscription with date in wreath **Rev. Inscription:** I / KREU / TZER / (date). **Mint:** Wertheim **Note:** Varieties exist. W#101-2, 110, 112.

Date	Mintage	VG	F	VF	XF	Unc
1691	—	35.00	70.00	110	225	—
1697 FS	—	35.00	70.00	110	225	—

KM# 11 KREUZER
Silver **Ruler:** Eucharius Kasimir Heinrich Friedrich **Obv:** Crowned shield of 3-fold arms, no legend **Rev:** 4-line inscription with date **Rev. Inscription:** I / KREU / TZER / (date). **Mint:** Wertheim **Note:** W#103, 113.

Date	Mintage	VG	F	VF	XF	Unc
1691	—	15.00	30.00	65.00	135	—
1697	—	15.00	30.00	65.00	135	—

KM# 13 KREUZER
Silver **Ruler:** Eucharius Kasimir Heinrich Friedrich **Obv:** Crowned shield of 3-fold arms in wreath, no legend **Rev:** 4-line inscription with date **Rev. Inscription:** I / KREU / TZER / (date). **Mint:** Wertheim **Note:** W#104.

Date	Mintage	VG	F	VF	XF	Unc
1692	—	30.00	60.00	100	200	—

KM# 5 3 KREUZER (Groschen)
Silver **Ruler:** Ludwig Ernst and Friedrich Eberhard **Obv:** Shield of 4-fold arms **Rev:** Crowned imperial eagle, 3 in orb on breast, titles of Ferdinand II **Mint:** Wertheim **Note:** W#100.

Date	Mintage	VG	F	VF	XF	Unc
ND(1635-37)	—	—	—	—	—	—

KM# 12 4 KREUZER (Batzen)
Silver **Ruler:** Eucharius Kasimir Heinrich Friedrich **Obv:** Crowned shield of 9-fold arms, date in legend **Rev:** Imperial orb with 4 **Mint:** Wertheim **Note:** W#101.

Date	Mintage	VG	F	VF	XF	Unc
1691 FS	—	—	—	—	—	—

KM# 14 4 KREUZER (Batzen)
Silver **Ruler:** Eucharius Kasimir Heinrich Friedrich **Obv:** Shield of 9-fold arms, crown above divides date in margin **Obv. Legend:** EUCH. CASIM. COM IN LOW. WERTHEIM. **Rev:** Imperial orb with 4 **Rev. Legend:** ROCHEF. VIRNENBURG. GEILDORF. **Mint:** Wertheim **Note:** W#109.

Date	Mintage	VG	F	VF	XF	Unc
1697 FS	—	85.00	150	235	475	—

KM# 15 1/2 THALER
14.6600 g., Silver **Ruler:** Eucharius Kasimir Heinrich Friedrich **Obv:** In half of design, 2 arms holding onto tree branches, band over DUM SCINDITUR FRANGOR, in other half, 2 men working beneath fruit tree, band above ME CONIUNCTIO SERVAT. **Obv. Legend:** EUCH. CASIM. CO. IN LEWENST. WERTH. ROCHEF. VIRNEB. **Rev:** Ornate shield of 9-fold arms divides date near bottom, 4 ornate helmets above **Rev. Legend:** GEILDORF & MONT. S. PR. IN CHASS. D. IN SCHAR. BR. HERB & NEUCH. **Mint:** Wertheim **Note:** W#108.

Date	Mintage	VG	F	VF	XF	Unc
1697 FS	—	2,650	3,650	4,900	7,000	—

KM# 16 THALER
Silver Dav. #6908; W#107. **Ruler:** Heinrich Friedrich **Obv:** In half of design, 2 arms holding onto tree branches, band over DUM SCINDITUR FRANGOR, in other half, 2 men working beneath fruit tree, band above ME CONIUNCTIO SERVAT. **Obv. Legend:** EUCH. CASIM. CO. IN LEWENST. WERTH. ROCHEF. VIRNEB. **Rev:** Ornate shield of 9-fold arms divides date near bottom, 4 ornate helmets above **Rev. Legend:** GEILDORF & MONT. S. PR. IN CHASS. D. IN SCHAR. BR. HERB & NEUCH. **Mint:** Wertheim **Note:** Struck at Wertheim. Varieties exist. Dav. #6908.

Date	Mintage	VG	F	VF	XF	Unc
1697 FS	—	500	900	1,750	3,250	6,000

KM# 17 2 THALER
Silver **Ruler:** Eucharius Kasimir Heinrich Friedrich **Obv:** In half of design, 2 arms holding onto tree branches, band over DUM SCINDITUR FRANGOR, in other half, 2 men working beneath fruit tree, band above ME CONIUNCTIO SERVAT. **Obv. Legend:** EUCH. CASIM. CO. IN LEWENST. WERTH. ROCHEF. VIRNEB. **Rev:** Ornate shield of 9-fold arms divides date near bottom, 4 ornate helmets above **Rev. Legend:** GEILDORF & MONT. S. PR. IN CHASS. D. IN SCHAR. BR. HERB & NEUCH. **Mint:** Wertheim **Note:** Dav. #6907; W#105.

Date	Mintage	Good	VG	F	VF	XF
1697 FS Rare	—	—	—	—	—	—

LUBECK

The bishopric was established at Lubeck ca. 1160. The first coins were struck ca. 1190. The bishops became Protestant during the Reformation. Territories were absorbed into Oldenburg during the reign of the last bishop. All the bishops of Lubeck from 1586 until 1802 were dukes of Schleswig-Holstein-Gottorp.

RULERS
Johann Adolf, 1586-1607
Johann Friedrich, 1607-1634
Johann X, 1634-1655
Johann Georg, 1655 (Feb.-Dec.)
Christian Albrecht, 1655-1666
August Friedrich, 1666-1705

MINT OFFICIALS' INITIALS

Initial	Date	Name
AGAH, GAH	Ca.1690	Georg Albrecht Hille?
HR	Ca.1615	Hans Rucke?
HR	1673-1715	Hans Ridder
IG, JG	1603-08	Jonas Georgen in Steinbeck bei Hamburg
MM	1661-66	Michael Moller in gottorp
MP, P	1596-1611	Matthias Puls
PS	Ca.1618	Peter Schrader?

ARMS

Lubeck: A cross.
Schleswig: 2 lions walking left.
Holstein: Nettleleaf.

MONETARY SYSTEM

(1/192 Thaler = 3 Pfennig)

BISHOPRIC

REGULAR COINAGE

KM# 57 1/192 THALER (3 Pfennig)

Silver **Ruler:** Christian Albrecht **Obv:** Shield of Schleswig arms **Obv. Legend:** CRRIST. ALB. D. G. E. L. H. N. **Rev:** Value 192 between ornaments in center, date at end of legend **Rev. Legend:** DVX. SCHLES. ET. HOLS. **Mint:** Gottorp **Note:** Ref. B-749, 750. Dreiling.

Date	Mintage	VG	F	VF	XF	Unc
166Z MM	—	10.00	20.00	45.00	90.00	—
1663 MM	—	10.00	20.00	45.00	90.00	—

KM# 55 1/96 THALER (6 Pfennig)

Silver **Ruler:** Christian Albrecht **Obv:** Holstein arms in center **Obv. Legend:** CHRISTIA. ALBR. D. G. E. L. H. N. **Rev:** 96 in ornamented shield, date at end of legend **Rev. Legend:** DVX. SCHLESW. ET. HOLS. **Mint:** Gottorp **Note:** Ref. B-753. Sechsling.

Date	Mintage	VG	F	VF	XF	Unc
1661 MM	—	20.00	40.00	85.00	—	—

KM# 5 2 SCHILLING

Silver **Ruler:** Johann Friedrich **Obv:** Armored horseman riding to right, Z SL below **Rev:** 5-line inscription **Rev. Inscription:** V. G. G. / IOH. FRI /. E B. Z. B. V. / L. E. Z. N. H / Z. S. H. **Note:** Ref. B-793. This issue struck for use in both Bremen and Lübeck.

Date	Mintage	VG	F	VF	XF	Unc
ND	—	150	300	600	—	—

KM# 6 2 SCHILLING

Silver **Ruler:** Johann Friedrich **Obv:** Armored horseman riding to left, Z SL below **Rev:** 5-line inscription **Rev. Inscription:** V. G. G. / IOH. FRI / .E B. Z. B. V. / L. E. Z. N. H / Z. S. H. **Note:** Ref. B-794. This issue struck for use in both Bremen and Lübeck.

Date	Mintage	VG	F	VF	XF	Unc
ND	—	150	300	600	—	—

KM# 8.1 4 SCHILLING

1.8500 g., Silver **Ruler:** Johann Friedrich **Obv:** Armored horseman riding to right, 4 : S.L. below **Rev:** 5-line inscription **Rev. Inscription:** V. G. G. / JOH. FRID / E. B. Z. B. V. / L. E. Z. N. H. / Z. S. H. **Note:** Ref. B-791. This issue was struck for use in both Bremen and Lübeck. Varieties exist.

Date	Mintage	VG	F	VF	XF	Unc
ND	—	100	200	400	775	—

KM# 8.2 4 SCHILLING

Silver **Ruler:** Johann Friedrich **Obv:** Armored horseman riding to left, 4.SL below **Rev:** 5-line inscription **Rev. Inscription:** V. G. G. / IOH. FRID / E. B. Z. B. V. / L. E. Z. N. H. / Z. S. H. **Note:** Ref. B-792. This issue was struck for use in both Bremen and Lübeck. Varieties exist.

Date	Mintage	VG	F	VF	XF	Unc
ND	—	100	200	400	775	—

KM# 40 1/36 THALER (Doppelgroten)

Silver **Ruler:** Johann Friedrich **Obv:** Shield of 8-fold arms with central shield of Lübeck cross, three helmets above **Obv. Legend:** IOHAN. FRIDERICH. ARCHIEP. BREM. **Rev:** Shield with 2 crossed keys, date at end of legend **Rev. Legend:** MONETA. NOVA. BREMER. GROTTE. **Note:** Ref. B-756. This coin was struck for use in both Bremen and Lubeck.

Date	Mintage	VG	F	VF	XF	Unc
1611 Rare	—	—	—	—	—	—

KM# 46 1/24 THALER (Groschen)

Silver **Ruler:** Johann Friedrich **Obv:** Shield of 8-fold arms with central shield of Lübeck cross **Obv. Legend:** IOH. FRI. D. G. A. ET. E. EP. B. E. L. **Rev:** Imperial orb with Z4 divides date **Rev. Legend:** MATTI. D. G. R. IM. S. A. **Note:** Ref. B-759a. Kipper issue.

Date	Mintage	VG	F	VF	XF	Unc
(16)19	—	35.00	75.00	150	—	—

KM# 47 1/24 THALER (Groschen)

Silver, 22x22 mm. **Ruler:** Johann Friedrich **Obv:** Shield of 8-fold arms with central shield of Lübeck cross **Obv. Legend:** IOH. FRI. D. G. A. ET. E. EP. B. E. L. **Rev:** Imperial orb with Z4 divides date **Rev. Legend:** MATTI. D.. G. R. IM. S. A. **Note:** Ref. B-759a. Klippe.

Date	Mintage	VG	F	VF	XF	Unc
(16)19	—	35.00	75.00	150	—	—

KM# 48 1/24 THALER (Groschen)

Silver **Ruler:** Johann Friedrich **Obv:** Shield of 8-fold arms with central shield of Lübeck cross **Obv. Legend:** I. FRI. D. G. A. E. EP. B. E. L(V). **Rev:** Imperial orb with Z4, date divided in margin at top **Rev. Legend:** MAT. D. G. R. IM. S. A. **Note:** Ref. B-759b,c. Varieties exist.

Date	Mintage	VG	F	VF	XF	Unc
(1)619	—	35.00	75.00	150	—	—

KM# 51 1/24 THALER (Groschen)

Silver **Ruler:** Johann Friedrich **Obv:** Shield of 3-fold arms, Bremen and Lübeck above Holstein **Obv. Legend:** IOHAN. FRI. D. G. A. E. E(P). B(R). **Rev:** Imperial orb with Z4, date at end of legend **Rev. Legend:** FER(DI). (II.) D. G. R. I. S. A(V). **Note:** Ref. B-760. Varieties exist. Kipper issue.

Date	Mintage	VG	F	VF	XF	Unc
(1)6Z1	—	50.00	100	210	—	—
(16)Z1	—	50.00	100	210	—	—

KM# 15 1/16 THALER

Silver **Ruler:** Johann Adolf **Obv:** Shield of 6-fold arms with central shield of Lübeck cross, 3 helmets above **Obv. Legend:** I. A. D. G. D. S. H. S. D. C. O. **Rev:** Imperial orb with 16 divides date **Rev. Legend:** RVDOL. II. D. G. RO. IM. SE. AV. **Note:** Ref. B-764.

Date	Mintage	VG	F	VF	XF	Unc
1601	—	40.00	80.00	160	325	—

KM# 17 1/16 THALER

Silver **Ruler:** Johann Adolf **Obv:** Shield of 6-fold arms with central shield of Lübeck cross, 3 helmets above **Obv. Legend:** I. A. D. G. - D. S. H. S. (D)(I). **Rev:** Imperial orb with 16, date at end of legend **Rev. Legend:** RVDOL. II. D. G. RO. I. S. A(V). **Note:** Ref. B#765-69. Varieties exist.

Date	Mintage	VG	F	VF	XF	Unc
(1)60Z	—	25.00	50.00	100	210	—
1603	—	25.00	50.00	100	210	—
(1)604	—	25.00	50.00	100	210	—
1604	—	25.00	50.00	100	210	—
(1)606	—	25.00	50.00	100	210	—
(1)607	—	25.00	50.00	100	210	—

KM# 41 1/16 THALER

Silver **Ruler:** Johann Friedrich **Obv:** Shield of 8-fold arms with central shield of Bremen key and Lübeck cross, 3 helmets above **Obv. Legend:** IOHA. FRID. - ARCH(I). P. BR. **Rev:** Crowned imperial eagle, crossed keys in orb on breast, value 1-6 divided by eagle's necks, date at end of legend **Rev. Legend:** RVDOL. II. D. G. ROM. IMP. SEM. AVG(V). **Note:** Ref. B-770. Varieties exist.

Date	Mintage	VG	F	VF	XF	Unc
1611	—	27.00	55.00	115	230	—

KM# 44 1/16 THALER

Silver **Ruler:** Johann Friedrich **Obv:** Shield of 8-fold arms with central shield of Bremen key and Lübeck cross, 3 helmets above **Obv. Legend:** IOH(A)(N). FR(I)(D). (-) (D.G.) A(RCH). E(T). E(P). B(R). **Rev:** Crowned imperial eagle, crossed keys in orb on breast, value 1 - 6 divided by eagle's necks, date at end of legend **Rev. Legend:** MATT(HIA)(S). D.(-)G. R(O)(M). I(M)(P). S(E)(M). A(V)(U)(G). **Note:** Ref. B-772, 774, 776, 778. Varieties exist.

Date	Mintage	VG	F	VF	XF	Unc
1613	—	25.00	50.00	100	200	—
1614	—	25.00	50.00	100	200	—
(1)615 HR	—	25.00	50.00	100	200	—
(1)616	—	25.00	50.00	100	200	—
(1)616 HR	—	25.00	50.00	100	200	—
(1)617	—	25.00	50.00	100	200	—

KM# 42 1/16 THALER (Düttchen)

Silver **Ruler:** Johann Friedrich **Obv:** Shield of 8-fold arms with central shield of Lübeck cross and Bremen key **Obv. Legend:** IOHAN. FRI(E)D(R)(I). (D.G.) AR(C)(H)(I). (E)(T). EP. B(R)(E). E(T). L(V)(B)(I). **Rev:** Three helmets, value 16 below, date at end of legend **Rev. Legend:** HER. NO(R)(W). D(V)(U)X. SL(E)(S). E(T). H(O)(L)(S). **Note:** Ref. B-771, 773, 775, 777, 779, 781. Varieties exist.

Date	Mintage	VG	F	VF	XF	Unc
161Z	—	25.00	50.00	100	200	—
1613	—	25.00	50.00	100	200	—
1614	—	25.00	50.00	100	200	—
1615	—	25.00	50.00	100	200	—
1616	—	25.00	50.00	100	200	—
(1)617	—	25.00	50.00	100	200	—

KM# 56 1/16 THALER (Düttchen)

Silver **Ruler:** Christian Albrecht **Obv:** Bust to right **Obv. Legend:** CRIST. ALB. D. G. E. L. H. N. D. S. ET. H. **Rev:** 4-line inscription with mintmaster's initials, date at end of legend **Rev. Legend:** PER. ASPERA. AD. ASTRA. **Rev. Inscription:** XVI / 1 REIC(HS) / (HS)(/)THA / (initials) **Mint:** Gottorp **Note:** Ref. B#785-89. Varieties exist.

Date	Mintage	VG	F	VF	XF	Unc
1661 MM	—	30.00	65.00	130	265	—
166Z MM	—	30.00	65.00	130	265	—
1663 MM	—	30.00	65.00	130	265	—
1664 MM	—	30.00	65.00	130	265	—
1665 MM	—	30.00	65.00	130	265	—

KM# 60 1/16 THALER (Düttchen)

Silver **Ruler:** August Friedrich **Obv:** Bust to right **Obv. Legend:** A. F. D. G. E. E. L. H. N. D. S. E. H. **Rev:** 4-line inscription with date **Rev. Legend:** DEO SORSQ. SALVSQ. ME(A). **Rev. Inscription:** XVI / REICHS / THAL(E) / (date) **Note:** Ref. B-790. Varieties exist.

Date	Mintage	VG	F	VF	XF	Unc
1678 (f)	—	35.00	75.00	150	315	—

KM# 45 1/16 THALER (Doppelschilling)

Silver **Ruler:** Johann Friedrich **Obv:** Shield of 8-fold arms with central shield of Bremen key and Lübeck cross, 3 helmets above **Obv. Legend:** I(O)(H). F(RI) (-) D. G. (-) A. E. E(P). B. (L.) **Rev:** Crowned imperial eagle, shield of Bremen key on breast, no value indicated, date at end of legend **Rev. Legend:** MATT(HIA)(S). D. G. R(O). I(M). S. A(V). **Note:** Ref. B-780, 782-3. Varieties exist.

Date	Mintage	VG	F	VF	XF	Unc
(1)617	—	25.00	50.00	100	200	—
(1)618	—	25.00	50.00	100	200	—
(1)618 PS	—	25.00	50.00	100	200	—
(1)619	—	25.00	50.00	100	200	—

KM# 50 1/16 THALER (Doppelschilling)

Silver **Ruler:** Johann Friedrich **Obv:** Shield of 8-fold arms with central shield of Bremen key and Lübeck cross, 3 helmets above **Obv. Legend:** I. F. D. G. - A. E. E. B. **Rev:** Crowned imperial eagle, shield of Bremen key on breast, no value indicated, date at end of legend **Rev. Legend:** FERDIN(AN). D. G. R. I(M). S. A. **Note:** Ref. B-784.

Date	Mintage	VG	F	VF	XF	Unc
(1)6Z0	—	35.00	75.00	150	290	—

KM# 9 4 GROSCHEN (1/6 Thaler)

Silver **Ruler:** Johann Friedrich **Obv:** Bust to right **Obv. Legend:** IOHAN. FRIDR. D. G. ARC. E. EP. BR. E. L(V). **Rev:** Shield of 8-fold arms with central shield of Lübeck cross, value 4 GROS. above **Rev. Legend:** HERRES. NOR. DVX. SLES. E(T). HOLS. **Note:** Ref. B-798b-d. Issued for use in both Bremen and Lübeck.

Date	Mintage	VG	F	VF	XF	Unc
ND	—	475	950	1,800	3,600	—

KM# 10 4 GROSCHEN (1/6 Thaler)

Silver **Ruler:** Johann Friedrich **Obv:** Bust to right **Obv. Legend:** IOHAN. FRIDR. D. G. ARC. E. EP. BR. E. L. **Rev:** Shield of 8-fold arms with central shield of Lübeck cross, no value indicated **Rev. Legend:** HERRES. NOR. DVX. SLES. ET. HOLS. **Note:** Ref. B-798a. Issued for use in both Bremen and Lübeck.

Date	Mintage	VG	F	VF	XF	Unc
ND	—	475	950	1,800	3,600	—

KM# 25 1/2 THALER

Silver **Ruler:** Johann Adolf **Obv:** Armored bust to right **Obv. Legend:** IOH. ADOL. D. G. EPIS. LVBE. HER. NORW. **Rev:** Shield of 6-fold arms, with central shield of Lübeck cross, divides date, 3 helmets above divide mintmaster's initials **Rev. Legend:** DVX. SLES. - E(T). HOLS(A). **Mint:** Steinbeck bei Hamburg **Note:** Ref. B-806, 807.

Date	Mintage	VG	F	VF	XF	Unc
1606 JG	—	—	—	—	—	—
1607 JG	—	2,000	4,000	7,700	—	—

KM# 34 1/2 THALER

Silver **Ruler:** Johann Adolf **Obv:** Armored bust to right **Obv. Legend:** IOH. ADOL. - D. G. EPIS. LVBE. HER. NORW. **Rev:** Shield of 6-fold arms, with central shield of Oldenburg arms, date and mintmaster's initials divided among 3 helmets above **Rev. Legend:** DVX. SL. HO. S. E. D. CO. O. E. D. **Note:** Ref. B-808.

Date	Mintage	VG	F	VF	XF	Unc
1608 MP	—	—	—	—	—	—

KM# 62 2/3 THALER (Gulden)

Silver **Ruler:** August Friedrich **Obv:** Armored bust to right, value (2/3) below shoulder **Obv. Legend:** AVGVST. DRID. D. G. EL. E(P). L(U)(V)(B). H. N. D. S. (E.) H. **Rev:** Crowned Spanish shield of 7-fold arms, with central shield of Lübeck cross, superimposed on crossed sword and crozier, between 2 palm branches, date at end of legend **Rev. Legend:** DEO SORSQ. SALVSQ. MEA. **Note:** Ref. B-801, 802; Dav. 621. Varieties exist.

Date	Mintage	VG	F	VF	XF	Unc
1678 (f)	—	60.00	115	235	475	—
1678	—	60.00	115	235	475	—
1688	—	60.00	115	235	475	—

KM# 61 2/3 THALER (Gulden)

Silver **Ruler:** August Friedrich **Obv:** Large AF monogram between palm branches, bishop's mitre above **Obv. Legend:** AVGVST. FRIDER. D. G. E. EP. L(V)(U)B. H. N. D. S. E. H. **Rev:** Crowned Spanish shield of 7-fold arms, with central shield of Lübeck cross, superimposed on crossed sword and crozier, between palm branches, value (2/3) in oval cartouche below, date at end of legend **Rev. Legend:** DEO SORSQ. SA - L(V)(U)SQ. MEA. **Note:** Ref. B-800; Dav. 620.

Date	Mintage	VG	F	VF	XF	Unc
1678 (f)	—	650	1,300	2,400	4,800	—
1678	—	650	1,300	2,400	4,800	—

KM# 68 2/3 THALER (Gulden)

Silver **Ruler:** August Friedrich **Obv:** Small armored bust to right **Obv. Legend:** AUGUST. FRID. D. G. EL. EP. LUB. H. N. D. S. H. **Rev:** Small shield of 7-fold arms, with central shield of Lübeck cross, superimposed on crossed sword and crozier, between 2 palm branches, date at end of legend **Rev. Legend:** A. DEO. SORSQ. SALVSQ. MEA. **Note:** Ref. B-803, 804; Dav. 622.

Date	Mintage	VG	F	VF	XF	Unc
1689	—	60.00	115	235	475	—
1690 GAH	—	60.00	115	235	475	—
1690 AG/AH	—	60.00	115	235	475	—

KM# 16 THALER

Silver **Ruler:** Johann Adolf **Obv:** Armored bust to left with scepter in right hand **Obv. Legend:** +IOH. ADOL. D. G. - EPISCO. LVB. HÆ. NOR. **Rev:** Squarish shield of 6-fold arms, with central shield of Lübeck divides date, 3 helmets above, mintmaster's initials above center helmet **Rev. Legend:** DVX. SL. HO. S. E. DI. CO. O. E. D. **Note:** Ref. B-811; Dav. 5431.

Date	Mintage	VG	F	VF	XF	Unc
(1)601 MP Rare	—	—	—	—	—	—

KM# 18 THALER

Silver, 41-42 mm. **Ruler:** Johann Adolf **Obv:** Half-length armored figure to left holding baton **Obv. Legend:** IOH. ADOL. DG. - EPIS. LVB. - HE. NOR. **Rev:** Small Spanish shield of Lübeck cross in center, 6 small Spanish shields of arms around, date divided by shield at bottom **Rev. Legend:** +DVX. SLES. HOLSA. STOR. E. DITM. COM. OL. E. DE. **Note:** Ref. B-812; Dav. 5432.

Date	Mintage	VG	F	VF	XF	Unc
(1)602 MP Rare	—	—	—	—	—	—

KM# 19 THALER

Silver, 40 mm. **Ruler:** Johann Adolf **Obv:** Armored bust to right holding baton **Obv. Legend:** IOH. ADOL. D. G. EPISCOP. LVBECE. HERRES. NOR. **Rev:** Ornate Spanish shield of 6-fold arms with central shield of Lübeck cross divides date, 3 helmets above **Rev. Legend:** DVX. SL. HO. S. - E. DI. CO. O. E. D. **Note:** Ref. B-814; Dav. 5433.

Date	Mintage	VG	F	VF	XF	Unc
1603 MP Rare	—	—	—	—	—	—

KM# 20 THALER

Silver, 39-40 mm. **Ruler:** Johann Adolf **Subject:** Mutual Oath of Allegiance with King Christian IV of Denmark **Obv:** Half-length armored figure to left holding baton, 30 OCTO below arm **Obv. Legend:** IOH. ADOL. D. - G. EPISCOP. LVBE. HER. NORW. **Rev:** Ornate Spanish shield of 6-fold arms with central shield of Lübeck cross divides date, 3 helmets above **Rev. Legend:** DVX. SL. HO. S. - E. DI. CO. O. E. D. **Note:** Ref. B-813; Dav. 5434.

Date	Mintage	VG	F	VF	XF	Unc
1603 MP Rare	—	—	—	—	—	—

KM# 21 THALER

Silver, 40 mm. **Ruler:** Johann Adolf **Obv:** Half-length armored figure to left holding baton **Obv. Legend:** IOH. ADOL. D. G. EPISCOP. LVBE. HER. NORW. **Rev:** Ornate Spanish shield of 6-fold arms with central shield of Lübeck cross divides date, mintmaster's initials divided by 3 helmets above **Rev. Legend:** DVX. SL. HO. S. - E. DI. CO. O. E. D. **Note:** Ref. B-815; Dav. 5435.

Date	Mintage	VG	F	VF	XF	Unc
1604 IG Rare	—	—	—	—	—	—

KM# 22 THALER

Silver, 38 mm. **Ruler:** Johann Adolf **Obv:** Armored bust to right holding baton **Obv. Legend:** IOH. ADOL. D. G. EPISCOP. LVBECE. HERES. NOR. **Rev:** Squarish shield of 6-fold arms, with central shield of Lübeck cross, divides mintmaster's initials, 3 helmets above divide date **Rev. Legend:** DVX. SL. H. S. - E. DI. CO: O. E D. **Note:** Ref. Dav. 5436.

Date	Mintage	VG	F	VF	XF	Unc
(1)604 MP	—	1,000	2,000	3,750	7,000	—

KM# 23 THALER

Silver, 41 mm. **Ruler:** Johann Adolf **Obv:** Armored bust to right holding baton **Obv. Legend:** IOH. ADOL. D. G. EPISCOP. LVBECE. HERES. NOR. **Rev:** Squarish shield of 6-fold arms, with central shield of Lübeck cross, divides date, 3 helmets above **Rev. Legend:** DVX. SL. H. S. - E. DI. CO. O. E. D. **Note:** Ref. Dav. A5437.

Date	Mintage	VG	F	VF	XF	Unc
(1)605	—	1,000	2,000	3,750	7,000	—

KM# 24 THALER

Silver, 41-42 mm. **Ruler:** Johann Adolf **Obv:** Armored bust to right holding baton **Obv. Legend:** IOH. ADOL. D. G. EPISCOP. LVBECE. HERES. NOR. **Rev:** Squarish shield of 6-fold arms, with central shield of Lübeck cross, 3 helmets above, date divided among helmets and mintmaster's initials divided by center helmet **Rev. Legend:** DVX. SL. HO. S. E. DI. CO: E. D. **Note:** Ref. B-816; Dav. 5437.

Date	Mintage	VG	F	VF	XF	Unc
1605 MP	—	1,000	2,000	3,750	7,000	—

KM# 29 THALER

Silver, 40 mm. **Ruler:** Johann Adolf **Obv:** Armored bust to right **Obv. Legend:** IOH. ADOL. D. G. EPISCOP. LVBE. HER. NORWE. **Rev:** Ornate Spanish shield of 6-fold arms, with central shield of Lübeck cross, divides date, 3 helmets above, center helmet divides mintmaster's initials **Rev. Legend:** DVX. SL: HO: (-) S:(-) E. DI. CO. O. E. D. **Mint:** Steinbeck bei Hamburg **Note:** Ref. B-817, 823; Dav. 5439.

Date	Mintage	VG	F	VF	XF	Unc
1606 IG	—	1,000	2,000	3,750	7,000	—
1607 IG	—	1,000	2,000	3,750	7,000	—

KM# 26.1 THALER

Silver **Ruler:** Johann Adolf **Obv:** Armored bust to right holding baton **Obv. Legend:** IOH. ADOL. D. G. EPISCOP. LVBECE. HERES. NOR. **Rev:** Squarish shield of 6-fold arms, with central shield of Lübeck cross, date divided among 3 helmets above, mintmaster's initials divided by center helmet **Rev. Legend:** D: S. H. S. E. D(I). - CO. E. D. M. N. S. **Note:** Ref. B-818, 820; Dav. 5438.

Date	Mintage	VG	F	VF	XF	Unc
1606 MP	—	1,250	2,250	4,500	8,000	—
1607 MP	—	1,250	2,250	4,500	8,000	—
1610 MP	—	1,250	2,250	4,500	8,000	—

KM# 26.2 THALER

Silver **Ruler:** Johann Adolf **Obv:** Armored bust to right **Obv. Legend:** IOH. ADOL. D. G. EPISCOP. LVBECE. HERES. NOR. **Rev:** Squarish shield of 6-fold arms, with central shield of Lübeck cross, date divided among 3 helmets above, mintmaster's initials divided by center helmet **Rev. Legend:** D. S. H. S. E. D. - C. O. E. D. **Note:** Ref. B-819; Dav. 5438A.

Date	Mintage	VG	F	VF	XF	Unc
1606	—	1,250	2,250	4,500	8,000	—

KM# 28 THALER

Silver, 38x39 mm. **Ruler:** Johann Adolf **Obv:** Armored bust to right holding baton **Obv. Legend:** IOH. ADOL. D. G. EPISCOP. LVBE. HER. NORWE. **Rev:** Ornate Spanish shield of 6-fold arms, with central shield of Lübeck cross, divides date, 3 helmets above, center helmet divides mintmaster's initials **Rev. Legend:** DV. SL. HO. S. - E. DI. CO. O. E. D. **Mint:** Steinbeck bei Hamburg **Note:** Ref. Dav. A5439. Klippe.

Date	Mintage	VG	F	VF	XF	Unc
1606 IG Rare	—	—	—	—	—	—

KM# 35 THALER

Silver, 40 mm. **Ruler:** Johann Adolf **Obv:** Armored bust to right holding baton **Obv. Legend:** IOH. ADOL. D. G. EPISCOP. LVBEC. HERES. NOR. **Rev:** Squarish shield of 6-fold arms, with central shield of Lübeck cross, date divided among 3 helmets above, center helmet divides minmaster's initials **Rev. Legend:** D. S. H. S. E. D. - C. O. E. D. M. N. S. **Note:** Ref. B-824; Dav. 5440. Struck after resignation of bishop.

Date	Mintage	VG	F	VF	XF	Unc
1608 MP Rare	—	—	—	—	—	—

KM# 36 THALER

Silver, 42 mm. **Ruler:** Johann Adolf **Obv:** Armored bust to right **Obv. Legend:** IOH. ADOL. D. G. EPISCOP. LVBE. HER. NORWE. **Rev:** Ornately-shaped shield of 5-fold arms with central shield of Oldenburg, date divided among 3 helmets above, mintmaster's initials divided by crest of middle helmet **Rev. Legend:** DVX: SL. HO: S: E: DI. CO. O. E. DE. **Mint:** Steinbeck bei Hamburg **Note:** Ref. B-825; Dav. 5441. Struck after the resignation of the bishop.

Date	Mintage	VG	F	VF	XF	Unc
1608 IG Rare	—	—	—	—	—	—

KM# 63 THALER

Silver, 40 mm. **Ruler:** August Friedrich **Obv:** Small, thin armored bust to right **Obv. Legend:** AUGUST. FRID. D. G. EL. EP. LUB. H. N. DUX. S. E. H. **Rev:** Large crowned Spanish shield of 7-fold arms, with central shield of Lübeck cross, superimposed on crossed sword and crozier, between 2 palm branches, date at end of legend **Rev. Legend:** STORM. & DIT. COM. IN OLD. & DELM. **Note:** Ref. B-831, 832; Dav. 5442.

Date	Mintage	VG	F	VF	XF	Unc
1678 HR Rare	—	—	—	—	—	—
1683 HR Rare	—	—	—	—	—	—

KM# 65 THALER

Silver, 42 mm. **Ruler:** August Friedrich **Obv:** Large, full armored bust to right **Obv. Legend:** AUGUST. FRID. D. G. EL. EP. LUB. H. N. DUX. S. E. H. **Rev:** Small crowned shield of 7-fold arms, with central shield of Lübeck cross, superimposed on crossed sword and crozier, between 2 palm branches, date at end of legend **Rev. Legend:** STORM. & DIT. COM. IN OLD. & DELM. **Note:** Ref. Dav. A5443.

Date	Mintage	VG	F	VF	XF	Unc
1683 HR Rare	—	—	—	—	—	—

KM# 66 THALER

Silver, 45 mm. **Ruler:** August Friedrich **Obv:** Large armored bust to right **Obv. Legend:** AVGVST. FRIDERIC. D. G. ELECT. EPISCOP. LUBECENS. **Rev:** Spanish shield of 7-fold arms, 3 helmets above, date divided below **Rev. Legend:** HÆR. NORW. DVX. SCHLÆS. HOL. STORM. &. DIT. COM. OLD. & DEL. **Note:** Ref. B-833; Dav. 5443.

Date	Mintage	VG	F	VF	XF	Unc
1687 BM Rare	—	—	—	—	—	—

KM# 30 1-1/2 THALER

Silver **Ruler:** Johann Adolf **Obv:** Shield of 6-fold arms, with central shield of Lübeck cross, 3 helmets above, date below **Obv. Legend:** IOH. ADO. D. G. EPIS. LVB. HER. NOR. DVX. SCHL. E. HOL. **Rev:** Armored bust to right holding baton **Rev. Legend:** STOR. E. DIT. COM. OL. E. DEL. &. VIVIT. POST. FVNERA. VIRTVS. **Note:** Ref. B-822; Dav. LS442.

Date	Mintage	VG	F	VF	XF	Unc
1607 Rare	—	—	—	—	—	—

KM# 31 2 THALER
Silver **Ruler:** Johann Adolf **Obv:** Shield of 6-fold arms, with central shield of Lübeck cross, divides date, 3 helmets above **Obv. Legend:** IOH. ADO. D. G. EPIS. LVB. HER. NOR. DVX. SCHL. E. HOL. **Rev:** Half-length figures of bishop and his wife **Rev. Legend:** STOR. E. DIT. COM. OL. E. DEL. & VIVAT. POST. FVNERA. VIRTVS. **Mint:** Steinbeck bei Hamburg **Note:** Ref. B-821a; Dav. LS439.

Date	Mintage	VG	F	VF	XF	Unc
1607 IG Rare	—	—	—	—	—	—

KM# 32 2 THALER
Silver **Ruler:** Johann Adolf **Obv:** Shield of 6-fold arms, with central shield of Lübeck cross, divides date, 3 helmets above **Obv. Legend:** IOH ADO D G EPIS LVB HER NOR DVX SCHL E HOL **Rev:** Figures of bishop and his wife, who offers crown to husband **Rev. Legend:** STOR E DIT COM OL E DEL & VIVAT POST FVNERA VITRVS. **Note:** Ref. B-821b; Dav. LS440.

Date	Mintage	VG	F	VF	XF	Unc
1607 P Rare	—	—	—	—	—	—

KM# 33 3 THALER
Silver **Ruler:** Johann Adolf **Obv:** Shield of 6-fold arms, with central shield of Lübeck cross, divides date, 3 helmets above **Obv. Legend:** IOH. ADO. D. G. EPIS. LVB. HER. NOR. DVX. SCHL. E. HOL. **Rev:** Half-length figures of bishop and his wife **Rev. Legend:** STOR. E. DIT. COM. OL. E. DEL. & VIVAT. POST. FVNERA. VIRTVS. **Mint:** Steinbeck bei Hamburg **Note:** Ref. B-821c; Dav. LS438. Struck from same dies as 2 Thaler, KM#31.

Date	Mintage	VG	F	VF	XF	Unc
1607 IG Rare	—	—	—	—	—	—

TRADE COINAGE

KM# 43 GOLDGULDEN
Gold **Ruler:** Johann Friedrich **Obv:** Shield of manifold arms, 2-fold central shield of Bremen and Lübeck, 3 helmets above **Obv. Legend:** IO • FR • D • G • A • E • EP • B • ET • L • D • S • H • **Rev:** Full-length standing figure of St. Peter, date nearby **Rev. Legend:** VIVIT POST FVNERA VIRTVS. **Note:** Ref. B-839; Fr. 1504.

Date	Mintage	VG	F	VF	XF	Unc
1612 Rare	—	—	—	—	—	—

KM# A45 GOLDGULDEN
Gold **Ruler:** Johann Friedrich **Obv:** Shield of manifold arms, 2-fold central shield of Bremen and Lübeck, 3 helmets above **Obv. Legend:** I • F • D • G • A • E • EP • B • E • L • D • S • H • **Rev:** Full-length standing figure of St. Peter, date nearby **Rev. Legend:** VIVIT POST FVNERA VIRTVS • **Note:** Ref. B-840.

Date	Mintage	VG	F	VF	XF	Unc
1618 Rare	—	—	—	—	—	—

KM# 67 DUCAT
3.5000 g., 0.9860 Gold 0.1109 oz. AGW **Ruler:** August Friedrich **Obv:** Armored bust to right **Obv. Legend:** AVGVST. FRID. D. G. EL. EP. LVB. H. N. D. S. E. H. **Rev:** Crowned shield of 7-fold arms with central shield of Lübeck cross between 2 palm branches, date at end of legend **Rev. Legend:** A DEO SORSQ SALVSQ MEA. **Note:** Ref. B-841.

Date	Mintage	VG	F	VF	XF	Unc
1688	—	2,700	5,400	9,800	16,500	—
1689	—	2,700	5,400	9,800	16,500	—

KM# 69 DUCAT
3.5000 g., 0.9860 Gold 0.1109 oz. AGW **Ruler:** Christian Albrecht **Obv:** Armored bust to right **Obv. Legend:** +CHRIST. ALB. D. G. H. N. DVX. SLES & HOL. **Rev:** Crowned shield of 7-fold arms, with central shield of Lübeck cross, between 2 palm branches, mintmaster's initials and date below in cartouche **Rev. Legend:** PER ASPERA AD ASTRA. **Note:** Ref. B-842. Struck after the bishop's assignment as co-adjutor of Lübeck.

Date	Mintage	VG	F	VF	XF	Unc
1689 HIL	—	3,000	6,000	10,500	18,500	—

KM# A17 10 DUCAT (Portugalöser)
35.0000 g., 0.9860 Gold 1.1095 oz. AGW **Ruler:** Johann Adolf **Obv:** Armored bust to left **Obv. Legend:** +IOH. ADOL D. G. - EPISCO. LVB. HÆ. NOR. **Rev:** Squarish shield of 6-fold arms, with central shield of Lübeck cross, divides date, 3 helmets above **Rev. Legend:** DVX. SL. HO. S. E. DI. CO. O. E. D. **Note:** Struck with Thaler dies, KM#16.

Date	Mintage	VG	F	VF	XF	Unc
(1)601 MP Rare	—	—	—	—	—	—

KM# A33 10 DUCAT (Portugalöser)
Gold **Ruler:** Johann Friedrich **Obv:** Armored figure to right, 8 small oval shields of arms around **Rev:** Cross in circle, 3 marginal legends **Rev. Legend:** Outer: IOHAN: FRIEDRICH: D:G: ARCH: ET. EP: BRE: ET. LVB.; Middle: HERRES • NORW • DVX • SLES • ET • HOLSACIÆ •; Inner: NOCH • PORTOGALISC: SCHROT: V: KO: **Note:** Ref. B-854; Fr. 1505.

Date	Mintage	VG	F	VF	XF	Unc
ND(1607-34) Rare	—	—	—	—	—	—

FREE CITY

Lübeck became a free city of the empire in 1188 and from c. 1190 into the 13th century an imperial mint existed in the town. It was granted the mint right in 1188, 1226 and 1340, but actually began its first civic coinage c.1350. Occupied by the French during the Napoleonic Wars, it was restored as a free city in 1813 and became part of the German Empire in 1871.

MINT OFFICIALS' INITIALS

Initials	Date	Name
(aa)=	1583-1603?	Claes Roethusen
(a)=	1603-14	Statius Wessel II
(bb)=	1617-18	Claus Jaeger
(b)=	1609-44	Heinrich von der Klähren
(c)=	1645-60	Hans Wilms
(d)=	1662-66	Matthias Freude
IF	Ca.1665-67	Dietrich Philipp Zachau
(e)=	1667-72	Lorenz Wagener
(f)=	1673-1715	Hans Ridder

REGULAR COINAGE

KM# 27 1/192 THALER (3 Pfennig)
Silver **Obv:** Imperial orb with 192, date at end of legend **Obv. Legend:** MON(E). NO(VA). L(V)(U)(B)(E)(C). **Rev:** Crowned imperial eagle **Rev. Legend:** CIVITA(T). IMPER(I)(A)(L). **Note:** Ref. B#473-98. Varieties exist.

Date	Mintage	VG	F	VF	XF	Unc
(160)9 (b)	—	10.00	20.00	40.00	80.00	—
(16)12 (b)	—	10.00	20.00	40.00	80.00	—
(16)20 (b)	—	10.00	20.00	40.00	80.00	—
(16)21 (b)	—	10.00	20.00	40.00	80.00	—
(16)22 (b)	—	10.00	20.00	40.00	80.00	—
(16)24 (b)	—	10.00	20.00	40.00	80.00	—
(16)25 (b)	—	10.00	20.00	40.00	80.00	—
(16)26 (b)	—	10.00	20.00	40.00	80.00	—
(16)27 (b)	—	10.00	20.00	40.00	80.00	—
(16)28 (b)	—	10.00	20.00	40.00	80.00	—
(16)29 (b)	—	10.00	20.00	40.00	80.00	—
(16)92 (b) Error for 1629	—	10.00	20.00	40.00	80.00	—
(16)30 (b)	—	10.00	20.00	40.00	80.00	—
(16)30	—	10.00	20.00	40.00	80.00	—
(16)31 (b)	—	10.00	20.00	40.00	80.00	—
(16)32 (b)	—	10.00	20.00	40.00	80.00	—
(16)33 (b)	—	10.00	20.00	40.00	80.00	—
(1)633 (b)	—	10.00	20.00	40.00	80.00	—
(16)34	—	10.00	20.00	40.00	80.00	—
(16)35 (b)	—	10.00	20.00	40.00	80.00	—
(16)36 (b)	—	10.00	20.00	40.00	80.00	—
(16)37 (b)	—	10.00	20.00	40.00	80.00	—
(16)38 (b)	—	10.00	20.00	40.00	80.00	—
(16)39 (b)	—	10.00	20.00	40.00	80.00	—
(16)41 (b)	—	10.00	20.00	40.00	80.00	—
(16)42 (b)	—	10.00	20.00	40.00	80.00	—
(16)43 (b)	—	10.00	20.00	40.00	80.00	—
(16)44 (b)	—	10.00	20.00	40.00	80.00	—
(16)45 (b)	—	10.00	20.00	40.00	80.00	—
(16)45 (c)	—	10.00	20.00	40.00	80.00	—
(16)46 (c)	—	10.00	20.00	40.00	80.00	—
(16)47 (c)	—	10.00	20.00	40.00	80.00	—
(16)48 (c)	—	10.00	20.00	40.00	80.00	—
(16)49 (c)	—	10.00	20.00	40.00	80.00	—
(16)50 (c)	—	10.00	20.00	40.00	80.00	—
(16)50	—	10.00	20.00	40.00	80.00	—
(16)51 (c)	—	10.00	20.00	40.00	80.00	—
(16)52 (c)	—	10.00	20.00	40.00	80.00	—
(16)54 (c)	—	10.00	20.00	40.00	80.00	—
1655	—	10.00	20.00	40.00	80.00	—
ND (c)	—	10.00	20.00	40.00	80.00	—
(16)65 (d)	—	10.00	20.00	40.00	80.00	—
(16)66 (d)	—	10.00	20.00	40.00	80.00	—
(16)67 (e)	—	10.00	20.00	40.00	80.00	—
(16)71 (e)	—	10.00	20.00	40.00	80.00	—
(16)72 (e)	—	10.00	20.00	40.00	80.00	—
(16)75 (f)	—	10.00	20.00	40.00	80.00	—
ND (f)	—	10.00	20.00	40.00	80.00	—
(16)90	—	10.00	20.00	40.00	80.00	—
(16)92	—	10.00	20.00	40.00	80.00	—
(16)97 (f)	—	10.00	20.00	40.00	80.00	—
(16)98 (f)	—	10.00	20.00	40.00	80.00	—

KM# A58 1/192 THALER (3 Pfennig)
Silver **Obv:** Imperial orb with 192, date at end of legend **Obv. Legend:** MONE. NO. - (crown) CE. **Rev:** Crowned imperial eagle **Rev. Legend:** CIVITAT. IMPE. NOL. **Note:** Ref. B-479b.

Date	Mintage	VG	F	VF	XF	Unc
(16)25	—	—	—	—	—	—

KM# 88 1/192 THALER (3 Pfennig)
Silver **Obv:** Imperial orb with 192 **Obv. Legend:** MONE. NO. L(U)(V)B(E). **Rev:** Crowned imperial eagle, date at end of legend **Rev. Legend:** CIVITA(T). IMP. **Note:** Ref. B#509b-514, 518. Varieties exist.

Date	Mintage	VG	F	VF	XF	Unc
(16)55	—	10.00	20.00	40.00	80.00	—
(16)56	—	10.00	20.00	40.00	80.00	—
(16)57	—	10.00	20.00	40.00	80.00	—
(16)58	—	10.00	20.00	40.00	80.00	—
(16)59	—	10.00	20.00	40.00	80.00	—
(16)60 (c)	—	10.00	20.00	40.00	80.00	—
(16)68	—	10.00	20.00	40.00	80.00	—

KM# A9 1/128 THALER (3 Pfennig)
Silver **Obv:** Imperial orb wtih 128, date at end of legend **Obv. Legend:** MONE. NO. LVBEC. **Rev:** Crowned imperial eagle **Rev. Legend:** CIVITA(TI)S. IMPERIAL. **Note:** Ref. B-471, 472. Varieties exist. Previous KM#9. Dreiling.

Date	Mintage	VG	F	VF	XF	Unc
(1)603 (a)	—	13.00	27.00	55.00	115	—
(1)604 (a)	—	13.00	27.00	55.00	115	—

KM# 117 4 PFENNIG
Silver **Obv:** 4-line inscription with date **Obv. Legend:** LVB: STAD(T): GELDT. **Rev:** Crowned imperial eagle, city arms on breast **Rev. Legend:** LEOP. D. G. RO. IM. SEM. AVG. **Rev. Inscription:** IIII / PFEN / NIG / (date) **Note:** Ref. B-465.

Date	Mintage	VG	F	VF	XF	Unc
1687	—	15.00	30.00	60.00	—	—

KM# A5 1/64 THALER (6 Pfennig)
Silver **Obv:** Imperial orb with 64, date at end of legend **Obv. Legend:** MONE. NO(VA). LVBEC(K). **Rev:** Crowned imperial eagle **Rev. Legend:** CIVITATIS IMPERIAL. **Note:** Ref. B#436-8. Sechsling. Varieties exist. Prev. KM#5.

Date	Mintage	VG	F	VF	XF	Unc
(1)601 (aa)	—	16.00	35.00	70.00	145	—
(1)603 (a)	—	16.00	35.00	70.00	145	—
(1)604 (a)	—	16.00	35.00	70.00	145	—

KM# A50 1/96 THALER (6 Pfennig)
Silver **Obv:** Cross with city arms in center, value 96 in margin at bottom, date at end of legend **Obv. Legend:** MO(N)(E). NO(VA). - LVB(E)(C)(E). **Rev:** Crowned imperial eagle in circle **Rev. Legend:** CIVITA(T)(IS). IMPER(I)(AL). **Note:** Ref. B#439-63. Sechsling. Varieties exist. Prev. KM#50.

Date	Mintage	VG	F	VF	XF	Unc
(1)620 (b)	—	10.00	20.00	40.00	80.00	—
(16)20 (b)	—	10.00	20.00	40.00	80.00	—
(16)21 (b)	—	10.00	20.00	40.00	80.00	—
(16)22 (b)	—	10.00	20.00	40.00	80.00	—
(16)23 (b)	—	10.00	20.00	40.00	80.00	—
(16)24 (b)	—	10.00	20.00	40.00	80.00	—
LVBE (b)	—	10.00	20.00	40.00	80.00	—
(16)29 (b)	—	10.00	20.00	40.00	80.00	—
(16)43 (b)	—	10.00	20.00	40.00	80.00	—
(16)44 (b)	—	10.00	20.00	40.00	80.00	—
(16)45 (b)	—	10.00	20.00	40.00	80.00	—
(16)45 (c)	—	10.00	20.00	40.00	80.00	—
(16)46 (c)	—	10.00	20.00	40.00	80.00	—
(16)47 (c)	—	10.00	20.00	40.00	80.00	—
(16)48 (c)	—	10.00	20.00	40.00	80.00	—
(16)49 (c)	—	10.00	20.00	40.00	80.00	—
(16)50 (c)	—	10.00	20.00	40.00	80.00	—
(16)54 (c)	—	10.00	20.00	40.00	80.00	—
(16)59 (c)	—	10.00	20.00	40.00	80.00	—
1661 (d)	—	10.00	20.00	40.00	80.00	—
1662 (d)	—	10.00	20.00	40.00	80.00	—
1664 (d)	—	10.00	20.00	40.00	80.00	—
1665 (d)	—	10.00	20.00	40.00	80.00	—
(16)66 (d)	—	10.00	20.00	40.00	80.00	—
(16)69 (e)	—	10.00	20.00	40.00	80.00	—
1669 (e)	—	1.00	20.00	40.00	80.00	—
1670 (e)	—	10.00	20.00	40.00	80.00	—
(16)75 (f)	—	10.00	20.00	40.00	80.00	—
1675 (f)	—	10.00	20.00	40.00	80.00	—
(16)76 (f)	—	10.00	20.00	40.00	80.00	—
1676 (f)	—	10.00	20.00	40.00	80.00	—

KM# A80 1/96 THALER (6 Pfennig)
Silver **Obv:** Cross with city arms in center, value 96 in margin at bottom, date at end of legend **Obv. Legend:** MONE. NO - LVBECE. **Rev:** Crowned imperial eagle in circle **Rev. Legend:** CIVITAT. IMPERIAL. **Note:** B-448c. Klippe. Previous KM#80.

Date	Mintage	VG	F	VF	XF	Unc
(16)46 (c)	—	—	—	—	—	—

KM# A86 1/96 THALER (6 Pfennig)
Silver **Obv:** Cross with city arms in center, value 96 in margin at bottom, date at end of legend **Obv. Legend:** MONE. NO - LVBE. **Rev:** Crowned imperial eagle, date at end of legend **Rev. Legend:** CIVITAT. IMP. **Note:** Ref. B-453a. Sechsling. Previous KM#86.

Date	Mintage	VG	F	VF	XF	Unc
(16)54//(16)54 (c)	—	—	—	—	—	—

KM# 53 SCHILLING (1/48 Thaler)
Silver **Obv:** City arms in quatrefoil superimposed on cross, value 48 in margin at bottom, date at end of legend **Obv. Legend:** MONE. NO(V)(U)(A). - L(V)(U)BE(C)(E)(N). **Rev:** Crowned imperial eagle **Rev. Legend:** CI(V)(U)ITAT(IS). IMPERIA(L)(I)(S). **Note:** Ref. B#404-12. Varieties exist.

Date	Mintage	VG	F	VF	XF	Unc
(1)6Z0 (b)	—	10.00	20.00	40.00	80.00	—
(1)620 (b)	—	10.00	20.00	40.00	80.00	—
(16)20 (b)	—	10.00	20.00	40.00	80.00	—
(1)65Z (c)	—	10.00	20.00	40.00	80.00	—
(16)5Z (c)	—	10.00	20.00	40.00	80.00	—
ND(1652) (c)	—	10.00	20.00	40.00	80.00	—
1662 (d)	—	10.00	20.00	40.00	80.00	—
1667 (e)	—	10.00	20.00	40.00	80.00	—
1668 (e)	—	10.00	20.00	40.00	80.00	—
1669 (e)	—	10.00	20.00	40.00	80.00	—
1670 (e)	—	10.00	20.00	40.00	80.00	—
1671 (e)	—	10.00	20.00	40.00	80.00	—

KM# A43 2 SCHILLING (1/20 Thaler)
Silver **Obv:** St. John with lamb above city arms of Lübeck, symbol of mayor Alexander Lüneburg (castle tower) in legend between date **Obv. Legend:** MONETA - LVBECEN. **Rev:** Arms of Lübeck and Hamburg, 3-line inscription above, 24 (symbol for Pfennig) below **Rev. Legend:** DOMINE. SERVA. NOS. **Rev. Inscription:**

DALER / A. / 20. STVC. **Note:** Ref. B-364. Joint issue with Hamburg.

Date	Mintage	VG	F	VF	XF	Unc
1619 (b)	—	—	—	—	—	—

KM# A56 4 SCHILLING (1/8 Thaler)

Silver **Obv:** St. John holding lamb, shield of city arms below in margin divides date **Obv. Legend:** MON(E). NO(VA). - LVBEC(E)(N). **Rev:** Crowned imperial eagle, value 4 in orb on breast **Rev. Legend:** FERDINAND. II. D. G. RO. IM(P). S(E)(M). A(V). **Note:** Ref. B#279-88. 1/2 Ortsthaler. Varieties exist. Previous KM#56.

Date	Mintage	VG	F	VF	XF	Unc
1622 (b)	—	40.00	80.00	160	325	—
1623 (b)	—	40.00	80.00	160	325	—
1629 (b)	—	40.00	80.00	160	325	—
1630 (b)	—	40.00	80.00	160	325	—
1634 (b)	—	40.00	80.00	160	325	—
1635 (b)	—	40.00	80.00	160	325	—
1636 (b)	—	40.00	80.00	160	325	—
1637 (b)	—	40.00	80.00	160	325	—

KM# 71 4 SCHILLING (1/8 Thaler)

Silver **Obv:** St. John with lamb, shield of city arms below in margin divides date **Obv. Legend:** MONE. NO. - LVBECE(N). **Rev:** Crowned imperial eagle, value 4 in orb on breast **Rev. Legend:** FERDINAND. III. D. G. RO. IMP. SE(M). A. **Note:** Ref. B-287, 288. 1/2 Ortsthaler. Varieties exist.

Date	Mintage	VG	F	VF	XF	Unc
1639 (b)	—	33.00	65.00	130	265	—
1646 (c)	—	33.00	65.00	130	265	—

KM# A6 8 SCHILLING (1/4 Thaler)

Silver **Obv:** St. John holding lamb, shield of city arms below, date at end of legend **Obv. Legend:** MONE. NO(VA). - LVBECE(NS). **Rev:** Crowned imperial eagle, value 8 in orb on breast **Rev. Legend:** RVDOL. II. D. G. IMP. SE. AVGVS. **Note:** Ref. B#252-257. Ortsthaler. Varieties exist. Previous KM#6.

Date	Mintage	VG	F	VF	XF	Unc
1601 (aa)	—	60.00	180	300	600	—
(1)603 (a)	—	60.00	180	300	600	—
(1)606 (a)	—	60.00	180	300	600	—
(1)609 (a)	—	60.00	180	300	600	—
1610 (a)	—	60.00	180	300	600	—
(1)612 (a)	—	60.00	180	300	600	—

KM# 39 8 SCHILLING (1/4 Thaler)

Silver **Obv:** St. John holding lamb, shield of city arms below divides date **Obv. Legend:** MONE. NOVA. - LVBECNS. **Rev:** Crowned imperial eagle, value 8 in orb on breast **Rev. Legend:** MATTHAIS. I. D. G. IMP. SE. AVGVS. **Note:** Ref. B-258. Ortsthaler.

Date	Mintage	VG	F	VF	XF	Unc
1617 (bb)	—	—	—	—	—	—

KM# A41 8 SCHILLING (1/4 Thaler)

Silver **Obv:** St. John holding lamb, shield of city arms below, date at end of legend **Obv. Legend:** MONE. NOVA. - LVBEC(E)NS. **Rev:** Crowned imperial eagle, value 8 in orb on breast **Rev. Legend:** MATTHIAS. I. D. G. IMP. SE. AVGVS. **Note:** Ref. B-259. Ortsthaler. Varieties exist. Previous KM#41.

Date	Mintage	VG	F	VF	XF	Unc
(1)619 (b)	—	55.00	115	235	475	—
(16)19 (b)	—	55.00	115	235	475	—

KM# A51 8 SCHILLING (1/4 Thaler)

Silver **Obv:** St. John holding lamb, shield of city arms below, date at end of legend **Obv. Legend:** MONE. NO(VA). (CIV.) - LVBECEN(S). **Rev:** Crowned imperial eagle, value 8 in orb on breast **Rev. Legend:** FERDINAND. II. D. G. RO. IM(P). S(E). AV(G)(VS). **Note:** Ref. B-260, 261. Ortsthaler. Varieties exist. Previous KM#51.

Date	Mintage	VG	F	VF	XF	Unc
(16)20 (b)	—	90.00	180	360	—	—
(16)Z0 (b)	—	90.00	180	360	—	—
(16)21 (b)	—	90.00	180	360	—	—

KM# A55 8 SCHILLING (1/4 Thaler)

Silver **Obv:** St. John holding lamb, shield of city arms below, date divided at bottom **Obv. Legend:** MO(N)(E). N(O)(V)(A). - LVBE(C)(E)(N)(S). **Rev:** Crowned imperial eagle, value 8 in orb on breast **Rev. Legend:** FERDINAN(D). II. D. G. R(O). I(M)(P). S(E)(M)(P). A(V)(G). **Note:** Ref. B#261a, 262-74b. Ortsthaler. Varieties exist. Previous KM#55.

Date	Mintage	VG	F	VF	XF	Unc
1621 (b)	—	75.00	150	300	600	—
1622 (b)	—	75.00	150	300	600	—
1623 (b)	—	75.00	150	300	600	—
1625 (b)	—	75.00	150	300	600	—
1626 (b)	—	75.00	150	300	600	—
1627 (b)	—	75.00	150	300	600	—
1628 (b)	—	75.00	150	300	600	—
1629 (b)	—	75.00	150	300	600	—
1631 (b)	—	75.00	150	300	600	—
1632 (b)	—	75.00	150	300	600	—
1633 (b)	—	75.00	150	300	600	—
1634 (b)	—	75.00	150	300	600	—
1635 (b)	—	75.00	150	300	600	—
1637 (b)	—	75.00	150	300	600	—

KM# A67 8 SCHILLING (1/4 Thaler)

Silver **Obv:** St. John holding lamb, shield of city arms below, date divided at bottom **Obv. Legend:** MONE. NO. - LVBECEN. **Rev:** Crowned imperial eagle, value 8 in orb on breast **Rev. Legend:** FERDINAND. III. D. G. RO. IIMP. SEM. A. **Note:** Ref. B#274c, d. Ortsthaler. Varieties exist. Prev. KM#67.

Date	Mintage	VG	F	VF	XF	Unc
1637 (b)	—	75.00	150	300	600	—

KM# A78 8 SCHILLING (1/4 Thaler)

Silver **Obv:** St. John holding lamb, shield of city arms below, date at end of legend **Obv. Legend:** MONE. NO. - LVBECEN. **Rev:** Crowned imperial eagle, value 8 in orb on breast **Rev. Legend:** FERDINAND. III. D. G. RO. IMP. SEM. A(V). **Note:** Ref. B-275, 276. Ortsthaler. Varieties exist. Previous KM#78.

Date	Mintage	VG	F	VF	XF	Unc
1645 (c)	—	—	—	—	—	—
1646 (c)	—	—	—	—	—	—

KM# A7 16 SCHILLING (1/2 Thaler)

Silver **Obv:** St. John holding lamb, shield of city arms below, date at end of legend **Obv. Legend:** MONE. NOVA. - LVBECENS. **Rev:** Crowned imperial eagle, value 16 in orb on breast **Rev. Legend:** RVDOL(PHVS). II. D. G. IMP. SE. AVGVS. **Note:** Ref. B-217, 218. Varieties exist. Previous KM#7.

Date	Mintage	VG	F	VF	XF	Unc
1601 (aa)	—	—	—	—	—	—
(1)603 (a)	—	—	—	—	—	—

KM# A26 16 SCHILLING (1/2 Thaler)

Silver **Obv:** St. John holding lamb, shield of city arms below divides date **Obv. Legend:** MONE(TA). NOVA. - LVBECENS. **Rev:** Crowned imperial eagle, value 16 in orb on breast **Rev. Legend:** RVDOL. II. D. G. IMP. SE. AVGVS. **Note:** Ref. B#219-22. Varieties exist. Previous KM#26.

Date	Mintage	VG	F	VF	XF	Unc
(1)608 (a)	—	110	220	450	925	—
(1)609 (a)	—	110	220	450	925	—
1610 (a)	—	110	220	450	925	—
(1)61Z (a)	—	110	220	450	925	—

KM# A42 16 SCHILLING (1/2 Thaler)

Silver **Obv:** St. John holding lamb, shield of city arms below divides date **Obv. Legend:** MONE. NOVA. - LVBECENS. **Rev:** Crowned imperial eagle, value 16 in orb on breast **Rev. Legend:** MATTHIAS. I. D. G. IMP. SE. AVGVS. **Note:** Ref. B-223. Previous KM#42.

Date	Mintage	VG	F	VF	XF	Unc
1619 (b)	—	—	—	—	—	—

KM# 52 16 SCHILLING (1/2 Thaler)

Silver **Obv:** St. John holding lamb, shield of city arms below divides date **Obv. Legend:** MON(E). NO(VA). - LVBEC(E)(N)(S)(I). **Rev:** Crowned imperial eagle, value 16 in orb on breast **Rev. Legend:** FERDINAND. II. D. G. RO(M). I(M)(P). S(E)(M)(P). A(V)(GVS). **Note:** Ref. B#224-236. Varieties exist.

Date	Mintage	VG	F	VF	XF	Unc
16Z0 (b)	—	275	425	875	1,550	—
1621 (b)	—	275	425	875	1,550	—
1622 (b)	—	275	425	875	1,550	—
1623 (b)	—	275	425	875	1,550	—
1625 (b)	—	275	425	875	1,550	—
1626 (b)	—	275	425	875	1,550	—
1627 (b)	—	275	425	875	1,550	—
1628 (b)	—	275	425	875	1,550	—
1629/8 (b)	—	575	1,300	2,300	3,500	—
1629 (b)	—	275	425	875	1,550	—
1631 (b)	—	275	425	875	1,550	—
1632 (b)	—	275	425	875	1,550	—
1633 (b)	—	275	425	875	1,550	—
1635 (b)	—	275	425	875	1,550	—

KM# A75 16 SCHILLING (1/2 Thaler)

Silver **Obv:** St. John holding lamb, shield of city arms below divides date **Obv. Legend:** MONE. NOVA. - LVBECENS. **Rev:** Crowned imperial eagle, value 16 in orb on breast **Rev. Legend:** FERDINAND. III. D. G. ROM. IMP. SEM. A. **Note:** Ref. B-237. Prev. KM#75.

Date	Mintage	VG	F	VF	XF	Unc
1640 (b)	—	165	350	700	1,400	—

KM# A81 16 SCHILLING (1/2 Thaler)

Silver **Obv:** Standing St. John with paschel lamb facing, arms below, undivided date at top **Obv. Legend:** * MONE. NOVA - LVBECEN. **Rev:** Crowned imperial eagle, value 16 in orb on breast **Rev. Legend:** FERDINAND: III: D: G: ROM • IMP • SEM(P): A. **Note:** Ref. B-238. Prev. KM#81.

Date	Mintage	VG	F	VF	XF	Unc
1646 (c)	—	165	350	700	1,400	—

KM# A87 16 SCHILLING (1/2 Thaler)

Silver **Obv:** St. John holding lamb, shield of city arms below **Obv. Legend:** MONE NO. - LUBECENS. **Rev:** Crowned imperial eagle, value 16 in orb on breast, date divided by crown at top **Rev. Legend:** FERDINAND. III. D. G. RO. IMP. SEM. A. **Note:** Ref. B-239. Prev. KM#87.

Date	Mintage	VG	F	VF	XF	Unc
1654 (c)	—	165	350	700	1,400	—

KM# 97 16 SCHILLING (1/2 Thaler)

Silver **Obv:** St. John holding lamb, shield of city arms below **Obv. Legend:** MONETA. NOVA - LVBECENSIS. **Rev:** Crowned imperial eagle, value 16 in orb on breast, dated divided between tail and claws **Rev. Legend:** LEOPOLDUS. D. G. ROM. IMP. SEMP. AV. **Note:** Ref. B-240.

Date	Mintage	VG	F	VF	XF	Unc
1662 (d)	—	1,250	2,500	4,500	7,000	12,000

KM# 116 16 SCHILLING (1/2 Thaler)

Silver **Obv:** St. John holding lamb, shield of city arms below **Obv. Legend:** MONETA. NOVA - LUBECENSIS. **Rev:** Crowned imperial eagle, value 16 in orb on breast, date divided below tail **Rev. Legend:** LEOPOLDUS. - D. G. ROMA. I. S. A. **Note:** Ref. B-241, 242. Varieties exist.

Date	Mintage	VG	F	VF	XF	Unc
1681 (f)	—	—	—	—	—	—
Note: Reported, not confirmed.						
1683	—	—	—	—	—	—

KM# 106 32 SCHILLING (Gulden)

18.3200 g., 0.7500 Silver 0.4417 oz. ASW **Obv:** Crowned imperial eagle in wreath **Obv. Legend:** CIVITATIS - IMPERIAL. **Rev:** Crowned shield of city arms in wreath divides date **Rev. Legend:** 32. SCHILLING. LVBE. STADT. GELT. **Note:** Ref. B-289; Dav. 624.

Date	Mintage	VG	F	VF	XF	Unc
1671 (e)	—	110	225	450	900	—

KM# 107 32 SCHILLING (Gulden)

18.3200 g., 0.7500 Silver 0.4417 oz. ASW **Obv:** Crowned imperial eagle, small shield of mayor's arms below **Obv. Legend:** MONET(A). NOVA - CIVIT. IMP. LVB(E). **Rev:** Crowned shield of city arms in baroque frame, date at end of legend **Rev. Legend:** 32. SCHIL(L)ING. STADT. GELD(T). **Note:** Ref. B-290; Dav. 625. Varieties exist.

Date	Mintage	VG	F	VF	XF	Unc
1672 (e)	—	90.00	180	360	725	—

KM# A77 1/24 THALER (2 Schilling)

Silver **Obv:** Imperial eagle, with city arms on breast, superimposed on cross **Obv. Legend:** CIVI - TATIS - IMPER - IALIS. **Rev:** 4-line inscription with date **Rev. Legend:** LVBECHS STADT GELDT. **Rev. Inscription:** 24 / REICHS / DALER / (date) **Note:** Ref. B-365. Prev. KM#77.

Date	Mintage	VG	F	VF	XF	Unc
1644 (b)	—	—	—	—	—	—

KM# A79 1/24 THALER (2 Schilling)

Silver **Obv:** Crowned imperial eagle, shield of mayor's arms below **Obv. Legend:** CI(V)(U)ITAT(IS) - IMPERIA(L)(I)(S). **Rev:** 4-line inscription with date **Rev. Legend:** L(V)(U)BEC(K)(H)S. STAD(T). GELD(T). **Rev. Inscription:** 24 (or Z4) / REICHS / DALER / (date) **Note:** Ref. B#366-85. Varieties exist. Prev. KM#79.

Date	Mintage	VG	F	VF	XF	Unc
1645 (c)	—	20.00	45.00	95.00	190	—
1646 (c)	—	20.00	45.00	95.00	190	—
1647 (c)	—	20.00	45.00	95.00	190	—
1648 (c)	—	20.00	45.00	95.00	190	—
1649 (c)	—	20.00	45.00	95.00	190	—
1650 (c)	—	20.00	45.00	95.00	190	—
1651 (c)	—	20.00	45.00	95.00	190	—
1652 (c)	—	20.00	45.00	95.00	190	—
1653 (c)	—	20.00	45.00	95.00	190	—
1654 (c)	—	20.00	45.00	95.00	190	—
1655 (c)	—	20.00	45.00	95.00	190	—
1656 (c)	—	20.00	45.00	95.00	190	—
1657 (c)	—	20.00	45.00	95.00	190	—
1658 (c)	—	20.00	45.00	95.00	190	—
1659 (c)	—	20.00	45.00	95.00	190	—
1660 (c)	—	20.00	45.00	95.00	190	—
1665 IF/(d)	—	20.00	45.00	95.00	190	—
1666 IF/(d)	—	20.00	45.00	95.00	190	—
1667 IF	—	20.00	45.00	95.00	190	—
1692 (f)	—	20.00	45.00	95.00	190	—
1693 (f)	—	20.00	45.00	95.00	190	—
1696 (f)	—	20.00	45.00	95.00	190	—
1700 (f)	—	20.00	45.00	95.00	190	—

KM# A57 1/16 THALER (3 Schilling)

Silver **Obv:** Crowned imperial eagle, city arms on breast, superimposed on cross **Obv. Legend:** CIVI - TATIS - IMPER - IALIS. **Rev:** 4-line inscription with date **Rev. Legend:** L(V)(U)BEC(H)(K)S. STADT. GELDT. **Rev. Inscription:** 16 / REICHS / DALER / (date) **Note:** Ref. B#334-55. Düttchen. Previous KM#57. Varieties exist.

Date	Mintage	VG	F	VF	XF	Unc
1623 (b)	—	33.00	65.00	130	265	—
1624 (b)	—	33.00	65.00	130	265	—
1629 (b)	—	33.00	65.00	130	265	—
1642 (b)	—	33.00	65.00	130	265	—
1643 (b)	—	33.00	65.00	130	265	—
1644 (b)	—	33.00	65.00	130	265	—
1645 (c)	—	33.00	65.00	130	265	—
1646 (c)	—	33.00	65.00	130	265	—
1647 (c)	—	33.00	65.00	130	265	—
1648 (c)	—	33.00	65.00	130	265	—
1649 (c)	—	33.00	65.00	130	265	—
1651 (c)	—	33.00	65.00	130	265	—
1659 (c)	—	33.00	65.00	130	265	—
1660 (c)	—	33.00	65.00	130	265	—
1662 (d)	—	33.00	65.00	130	265	—
1667 (e)	—	33.00	65.00	130	265	—
1669 (e)	—	33.00	65.00	130	265	—
1670 (d) Error/mule	—	33.00	65.00	130	265	—
1670 (e)	—	33.00	65.00	130	265	—
1671 (e)	—	33.00	65.00	130	265	—
1672 (e)	—	33.00	65.00	130	265	—
1673 (e)	—	33.00	65.00	130	265	—
1683 (f)	—	33.00	65.00	130	265	—

KM# 7 16 SCHILLING (1/2 Thaler)

Silver **Obv:** Figure of St. John holding Lamb, city arms below, date in legend **Obv. Legend:** MONETA. NOVA. - LVBECENS. **Rev:** Crowned imperial eagle, 16 in orb on breast **Rev. Legend:** RVDOL(PHVS). II. D. G. IMP. SE. AVGVS. **Note:** Varieties exist.

Date	Mintage	VG	F	VF	XF	Unc
ND	—	—	—	—	—	—

KM# A8 THALER (32 Schilling)

Silver, 42 mm. **Obv:** Facing figure of St. John holding lamb, shield of city arms below, small shield of mayor's arms at left, date at end of legend **Obv. Legend:** MONETA. NOVA. - LVBECENS. **Rev:** Crowned imperial eagle, 3Z in orb on breast **Rev. Legend:** RVDOLPHVS. II. D. G. IMP. SE. AVGVS. **Note:** Ref. B#128-31; Dav. 5444. Varieties exist. Arms of Mayor Gotthard v. Höveln (1600-09).

Date	Mintage	VG	F	VF	XF	Unc
1601 (aa)	—	125	300	700	1,250	—
(1)601 (aa)	—	125	300	700	1,250	—
(1)602 (aa)	—	125	300	700	1,250	—
(1)603 (a)	—	125	300	700	1,250	—
(1)604 (a)	—	125	300	700	1,250	—

KM# A23 THALER (32 Schilling)

Silver, 41 mm. **Obv:** Facing figure of St. John holding lamb, shield of city arms divides date below, small shield of mayor's arms at left **Obv. Legend:** MONETA. NOVA. - LVBECENS. **Rev:** Crowned imperial eagle, 3Z in orb on breast **Rev. Legend:** RVDOLPHVS. II. D. G. IMP. SE. AVGVS. **Note:** Ref. B#132-35; Dav. #5445. Prev. KM#23. Varieties exist. Arms of Mayor Gotthard v. Höveln (1600-09).

Date	Mintage	VG	F	VF	XF	Unc
(1)605 (a)	—	100	250	500	1,250	—
(1)607 (a)	—	100	250	500	1,250	—
(1)608 (a)	—	100	250	500	1,250	—
(1)609 (a)	—	100	250	500	1,250	—

KM# A35 THALER (32 Schilling)

Silver, 41 mm. **Obv:** Facing figure of St. John holding lamb, shield of city arms divides date below, small shield of mayor's arms at left and right **Obv. Legend:** MONE(TA). NO(VA). - LVBECENS. **Rev:** Crowned imperial eagle, 32 in orb on breast **Rev. Legend:** RVDOLPHVS. II. D. G. IMP. SE. AVGVS. **Note:** Ref. B-140, 141a, 142a; Dav. 5446. Prev. KM#35. Varieties exist. Arms of Mayor Alexander Lüneburg (1609-27).

Date	Mintage	VG	F	VF	XF	Unc
1610 (a)	—	65.00	125	275	650	—
1611 (a)	—	65.00	125	275	650	—
1612 (a)	—	65.00	125	275	650	—

KM# 38 THALER (32 Schilling)

Silver, 40-41 mm. **Obv:** Facing figure of St. John holding lamb, shield of city arms divides date below, small shield of mayor's arms at left and right **Obv. Legend:** MONE(TA). NO(VA). - LVB(E)(I)CEN(S). **Rev:** Crowned imperial eagle, 32 in orb on breast **Rev. Legend:** MATTHIAS. I. D. G. IMP. SE. AVGVS. **Note:** Ref. B-142b, 143-49; Dav. 5447. Varieties exist. Arms of Mayor Alexander Lüneburg (1609-27).

Date	Mintage	VG	F	VF	XF	Unc
1612 (a)	—	65.00	125	275	650	—
1613 (a)	—	65.00	125	275	650	—
1614 (a)	—	65.00	125	275	650	—
1615 (a)	—	65.00	125	275	650	—
1616 (a)	—	65.00	125	275	650	—
1617 (bb)	—	65.00	125	275	650	—
1618 (bb)	—	—	—	—	—	—
Note: Reported, not confirmed						
1619 (b)	—	60.00	120	245	550	—

KM# 54 THALER (32 Schilling)
Silver **Obv:** Facing figure of St. John holding lamb, shield of city arms divides date below, small shield of mayor's arms at left (and right) **Obv. Legend:** MONE. NOV(A). - LVBECEN(S)(I)(S). **Rev:** Crowned imperial eagle, 32 in orb on breast **Rev. Legend:** FERDINAND. II. D. G. RO(M)(A). IM(P). S(E)(M)(P). A(V)(G)(VS). **Note:** Ref. B#150-168b; Dav. 5449. Varieties exist. Arms of Mayor Alexander Lüneburg (1609-27), followed by Lorenz Möller (1627-34), then Heinrich Köhler (1634-41).

Date	Mintage	VG	F	VF	XF	Unc
1620 (b)	—	70.00	150	350	1,000	—
1621 (b)	—	70.00	150	350	1,000	—
1622 (b)	—	70.00	150	350	1,000	—
1623 (b)	—	70.00	150	350	1,000	—
1624 (b)	—	70.00	150	350	1,000	—
1625 (b)	—	70.00	150	350	1,000	—
1626 (b)	—	70.00	150	350	1,000	—
1627 (b)	—	70.00	150	350	1,000	—

KM# A60 THALER (32 Schilling)
Silver **Obv:** Facing half-length figure of St. John holding lamb, shield of city arms in baroque frame below in front divides date, small shield of mayor's arms below at left **Obv. Legend:** MONE. NOVA. - LVBECENSI. **Rev:** Crowned imperial eagle, 32 in orb on breast **Rev. Legend:** FERDINAND. II. D. G. RO. IMP. SEMP. AV. **Note:** Ref. B-157b; Dav. 5449B. Prev. KM#60. Arms of Mayor Lorenz Möller (1627-34).

Date	Mintage	VG	F	VF	XF	Unc
1627 (b)	—	75.00	150	250	400	—

KM# A61 THALER (32 Schilling)
Silver **Obv:** Half-length facing figure of St. John with lamb, shield of city arms below in front divides two mayors' arms and date **Obv. Legend:** MONE. NOV(A) - LVBECENS. **Rev:** Crowned imperial imperial eagle, 32 in orb on breast **Rev. Legend:** FERDINAND. II. D. G. RO(M)(A). I(M)(P). SEM(P). A(V). **Note:** Ref. Dav. 5449C. Prev. KM#61. Varieties exist. Arms of Mayors Lorenz Möller (1627-34) and Heinrich Köhler (1634-41).

Date	Mintage	VG	F	VF	XF	Unc
1627 (b)	—	65.00	130	285	750	—
1628 (b)	—	65.00	130	285	750	—
1629 (b)	—	65.00	130	285	750	—
1630 (b)	—	65.00	130	285	750	—
1631 (b)	—	65.00	130	285	750	—
1632 (b)	—	65.00	130	285	750	—
1633 (b)	—	65.00	130	285	750	—
1634 (b)	—	65.00	130	285	750	—
1635 (b)	—	65.00	130	285	750	—

KM# A65 THALER (32 Schilling)
Silver **Obv:** Facing half-length figure of St. John with lamb, shield of city arms below in front divides date and mayor's arms **Obv. Legend:** MONE. NOVA - LVBECENS. **Rev:** Crowned imperial eagle, 32 in orb on breast **Rev. Legend:** FERDINAND. II. D. G. RO(M). IM(P). SEM(P). A(V) **Note:** Ref. B#164b, 165-68; Dav. 5449D. Prev. KM#65. Arms of Mayor Heinrich Köhler (1634-41).

Date	Mintage	VG	F	VF	XF	Unc
1634 (b)	—	70.00	150	350	1,000	—
1635 (b)	—	70.00	150	350	1,000	—
1636 (b)	—	70.00	150	350	1,000	—
1637 (b)	—	70.00	150	350	1,000	—
1638 (b)	—	70.00	150	350	1,000	—

KM# A69 THALER (32 Schilling)
Silver, 41-42 mm. **Obv:** Facing figure of St. John holding lamb, shield of city arms divides date below, small shield of mayor's arms at left **Obv. Legend:** MONE. NOVA. - LVBEC(E)NS. **Rev:** Crowned imperial eagle, 32 in orb on breast **Rev. Legend:** FERDINAND. III. D. G. RO. IMP. SEMP. AV. **Note:** Ref. B#168c-170; Dav. 5450. Prev. KM#69. Varieties exist. Arms of Mayor Heinrich Köhler (1634-41).

Date	Mintage	VG	F	VF	XF	Unc
1638 (b)	—	175	375	850	1,450	—
1639 (b)	—	175	375	850	1,450	—
1640 (b)	—	175	375	850	1,450	—

KM# A76 THALER (32 Schilling)
Silver, 42-43 mm. **Obv:** Facing figure of St. John holding lamb, shield of city arms below, small shield of mayor's arms at left, date at end of legend **Obv. Legend:** MONE. NOVA. - LVBECE(N)(S). **Rev:** Crowned imperial eagle, 32 in orb on breast **Rev. Legend:** FERDINAND. III. D. G. RO. IMP. SEMP. AV(G). **Note:** Ref. B#171-78; Dav. 5451. Prev. KM#76. Varieties exist. Arms of Mayor Heinrich Köhler (1634-41) to 1642, then Christoph Gerdes (1641-61).

Date	Mintage	VG	F	VF	XF	Unc
1641 (b)	—	150	350	800	1,350	—
1642 (b)	—	150	350	800	1,350	—
1645 (c)	—	150	350	800	1,350	—
1646 (c)	—	150	350	800	1,350	—
1647 (c)	—	150	350	800	1,350	—
1648 (c)	—	150	350	800	1,350	—
1649 (c)	—	150	350	800	1,350	—
1650 (c)	—	150	350	800	1,350	—

KM# 95 THALER (32 Schilling)
Silver, 43 mm. **Obv:** Small facing figure of St. John holding lamb, large shield of city arms below, small shield of mayor's arms at left, date at end of legend **Obv. Legend:** MONE. NOVA. - LVBECE. **Rev:** Crowned imperial eagle, 32 in orb on breast **Rev. Legend:** LEOPOLDVS. D. G. RO. IMP. SEMP. AVG. **Note:** Ref. B-179; Dav. 5452. Arms of Mayor Christoph Gerdes (1641-61).

Date	Mintage	VG	F	VF	XF	Unc
1660 (c)	—	425	900	1,650	2,850	—

KM# 96 THALER (32 Schilling)
Silver, 44 mm. **Obv:** Large facing figure of St. John holding lamb, shield of city arms below, small shield of mayor's arms at left, date at end of legend **Obv. Legend:** MONETA. NOVA. - LUBEC. **Rev:** Crowned imperial eagle, 32 in orb on breast **Rev. Legend:** LEOPOLDUS. D: G. ROM: IMP: SEMP: AU: **Note:** Ref. B-180; Dav. 5453. Arms of Mayor Christoph Gerdes (1641-61).

Date	Mintage	VG	F	VF	XF	Unc
1661 (c)	—	425	900	1,650	2,850	—

KM# 98 THALER (32 Schilling)
Silver **Obv:** Facing figure of St. John holding lamb, shield of city arms below, small shield of mayor's arms at left **Obv. Legend:** MONETA. NOVA. - LUBECENSIS. **Rev:** Crowned imperial eagle, 32 in orb on breast, date divided by tail **Rev. Legend:** LEOPOLDUS. D. G. ROM. IMP. SEMP. AU. **Note:** Ref. B-181a; Dav. 5454. Arms of Mayor Hermann v. Dorne (1661-65).

Date	Mintage	VG	F	VF	XF	Unc
1662 (d) Rare	—	—	—	—	—	—

KM# 99 THALER (32 Schilling)
Silver, 42 mm. **Obv:** Facing figure of St. John holding lamb, shield of city arms below, small shield of mayor's arms at left **Obv. Legend:** MONETA. NOVA. - LUBECENSIS. **Rev:** Crowned imperial eagle, 3Z in orb on breast, date at end of legend **Rev. Legend:** LEOPOLDUS. D. G. ROM(A). I(M). S(E). A. **Note:** Ref. B-181b, 182; Dav. 5455. Varieties exist. Arms of Mayor Hermann v. Dorne (1661-65).

Date	Mintage	VG	F	VF	XF	Unc
1662 (d)	—	350	350	1,250	2,250	—
1663 (d)	—	350	650	1,250	2,250	—

KM# 105 THALER (32 Schilling)

Silver **Obv:** Facing figure of St. John holding lamb, shield of city arms below, small shield of mayor's arms at left **Obv. Legend:** MONETA. NOVA. - LUBECENSIS **Rev:** Crowned imperial eagle, 32 in orb on breast, date at end of legend **Rev. Legend:** LEOPOLD: D. G. RO: IM. SE. AV. **Note:** Ref. B-183; Dav. 5456. Arms of Mayor David Gloxin (1669-71).

Date	Mintage	VG	F	VF	XF	Unc
1670 (e)	—	300	650	1,200	2,000	—

KM# 108 THALER (32 Schilling)

Silver, 41-42 mm. **Obv:** Facing figure of St. John holding lamb, shield of city arms below, small shield of mayor's arms at left **Obv. Legend:** MONETA. NOVA. - L(V)(U)BECENSIS. **Rev:** Crowned imperial eagle, 32 in orb on breast, date at end of legend **Rev. Legend:** LEOPOLDUS. D. G. ROMA. I. S. A. **Rev. Inscription:** LEOPOLDUS. D: G: ROMA: I: S: A: **Note:** Ref. B-184; Dav. 5457. Arms of Mayor Matthäus Rodde (1671-77).

Date	Mintage	VG	F	VF	XF	Unc
1673 (e)	—	375	875	1,500	2,500	—

KM# 109 THALER (32 Schilling)

Silver, 38 mm. **Obv:** Small full-length facing figure of St. John holding lamb, ornate shield of city arms below in front **Obv. Legend:** MONETA. NOVA. - LUBECENSIS. **Rev:** Crowned imperial eagle, 32 in orb on breast, small shield of mayor's arms below, date at end of legend **Rev. Legend:** LEOPOLDUS. D. G. - ROM. I. S. A. **Edge Lettering:** PRISCA VIRTVTE FIDEQUE **Note:** Ref. B-185; Dav. 5458. Arms of Mayor Matthäus Rodde (1671-77).

Date	Mintage	VG	F	VF	XF	Unc
1676 (f)	—	600	1,250	2,500	5,000	—

KM# 115 THALER (32 Schilling)

Silver, 39 mm. **Obv:** Small full-length facing figure of St. John holding lamb, shield of city arms in baroque frame below in front **Obv. Legend:** MONETA. NOVA. - LUBECENSIS. **Rev:** Crowned imperial eagle, 3Z in orb on breast, small shield of mayor's arms divides date below **Rev. Legend:** LEOPOLDUS. - D. G. ROMA. I. S. A. **Note:** Ref. B-186. 187; Dav. 5459. Arms of Johann Ritter (1677-1700).

Date	Mintage	VG	F	VF	XF	Unc
1680 (f)	—	400	800	1,500	2,500	—
1683 (f)	—	400	800	1,500	2,500	—

KM# A68 THALER (32 Schilling)

Silver **Obv:** Facing half-length figure of St. John holding lamb, shield of city arms in baroque frame below in front divides date and mayor's arms **Obv. Legend:** MONE. NOVA - LVBECENS. **Rev:** Crowned imperial eagle, 32 in orb on breast **Rev. Legend:** FERDINAND II. D. G. RO. IMP. SEMP AV. **Note:** Ref. B-168b; Dav. 5449A. Prev. KM#68.

Date	Mintage	VG	F	VF	XF	Unc
1683 (b) error for 1638	—	75.00	150	350	1,100	—

KM# 120 THALER (32 Schilling)

Silver, 39 mm. **Obv:** Small full-length facing figure of St. John holding lamb, shield of city arms in baroque frame below in front **Obv. Legend:** MONETA. NOVA. - LUBECENSIS. **Rev:** Crowned imperial eagle, 3Z in orb on breast, small shield of mayor's arms divides date below **Rev. Legend:** LEOPOLDUS. D. G. - ROMA. IMP. SE. AUG. **Edge Lettering:** PRISCA . VIRTVTE . FIDEQVE **Note:** Ref. B-188, 189; Dav. 5460. Arms of Mayor Johann Ritter (1677-1700).

Date	Mintage	VG	F	VF	XF	Unc
1690 (f)	—	600	1,250	2,250	4,000	—
1696 (f)	—	600	1,250	2,250	4,000	—

KM# A10 THALER

Silver **Obv:** Crowned imperial eagle, city arms on breast, arms of mayor in legend **Obv. Legend:** ADVERSVS. HOSTES. NVLLA - PRÆTEREVNDA. EST. OCCASIO. **Rev:** Full-length figure of St. John **Rev. Legend:** MEDIOCRITAS. IN. OMNI - RE. EST. OTIMA. **Note:** Ref. B-136a,b; Dav. #LS331. Varieties exist. Previous KM#10. Broad flan. Arms of Mayor Gotthard v. Höveln (1600-09).

Date	Mintage	VG	F	VF	XF	Unc
ND(1603-09) (a) Rare	—	—	—	—	—	—

KM# A28 THALER

Silver **Obv:** Crowned imperial eagle, city arms on breast, arms of mayor in legend **Obv. Legend:** ADVERSVS. HOSTES. NVLLA - PRÆTEREVNDA. EST. OCCASIO. **Rev:** Full-length figure of St. John **Rev. Legend:** MEDIOCRITAS. IN. OMNI - RE. EST. OPTIMA. **Note:** Ref. B-137a; Dav. LS336. Prev. KM#28. Broad flan. Arms of Mayor Alexander Lüneburg (1609-27).

Date	Mintage	VG	F	VF	XF	Unc
ND(1609-16) (a) Rare	—	—	—	—	—	—

KM# A40 THALER

Silver **Obv:** Crowned imperial eagle, shield of city arms on breast, arms of mayor in legend **Obv. Legend:** ADVERSVS. HOSTES. NVLLA - PRÆTEEREVNDA. EST. OCCASIO. **Rev:** Full-length figure of St. John **Rev. Legend:** MEDIOCRITAS. IN. OMNI - RE. EST. OPTIMA. **Note:** Ref. B-138; Dav. LS337. Prev. KM#40. Broad flan. Arms of Mayor Alexander Lüneburg (1609-27).

Date	Mintage	VG	F	VF	XF	Unc
ND(1617-18) (bb) Rare	—	—	—	—	—	—

KM# A44 THALER

Silver **Obv:** Crowned imperial eagle, shield of city arms on breast, arms of mayor in legend **Obv. Legend:** ADVERSVS. HOSTES. NVLLA - PRÆTEREVNDA. EST. OCCASIO. **Rev:** Full-length figure of St. John **Rev. Legend:** MEDIOCRITAS. IN. OMNI - RE. EST. OPTIMA. **Note:** Ref. B-139a,b; Dav. LS341. Prev. KM#44. Broad flan. Arms of Mayor Alexander Lüneburg (1609-27).

Date	Mintage	VG	F	VF	XF	Unc
ND(1619-27) (b) Rare	—	—	—	—	—	—

KM# A11 THALER

Silver **Obv. Legend:** Ends: ....OCCASIO **Note:** Dav. #LS331a. Prev. KM#11.

Date	Mintage	VG	F	VF	XF	Unc
ND(1603-09) (a)	—	450	850	1,500	2,500	4,000

KM# A12 1-1/2 THALER

Silver **Obv:** Crowned imperial eagle, shield of city arms on breast, arms of mayor in margin below **Obv. Legend:** ADVERSVS. HOSTES. NVLLA - PRÆTEREVNDA. EST. OCCASIO. **Rev:** Full-length figure of St. John **Rev. Legend:** MEDIOCRITAS. IN. OMNI - RE. EST. OPTIMA. **Note:** Ref. B-136c; Dav. LS330. Prev. KM#12. Broad flan. Arms of Mayor Gotthard v. Höveln (1600-09).

Date	Mintage	VG	F	VF	XF	Unc
ND(1603-09) (a) Rare	—	—	—	—	—	—

KM# A29 1-1/2 THALER

Silver **Obv:** Crowned imperial eagle, shield of city arms on breast, arms of mayor in margin below **Obv. Legend:** ADVERSVS. HOSTES. NVLLA - PRÆTEREVNDA. EST. OCCASIO. **Rev:** Full-length figure of St. John **Rev. Legend:** MEDIOCRITAS. IN. OMNI - RE. EST. OPTIMA. **Note:** Ref. B-137b,c; Dav. LS333. Prev. KM#29. Broad flan. Arms of Mayor Alexander Lüneburg (1609-27).

Date	Mintage	VG	F	VF	XF	Unc
ND(1609-1616) (a) Rare	—	—	—	—	—	—

KM# A30 1-1/2 THALER

Silver **Note:** Similar to 1 thaler, KM#28. Dav. #LS335. Prev. KM#30.

Date	Mintage	VG	F	VF	XF	Unc
ND(1609-16) (a) Rare	—	—	—	—	—	—

KM# A46 1-1/2 THALER

Silver **Obv:** Crowned imperial eagle, shield of city arms on breast, arms of mayor in margin below **Obv. Legend:** ADVERSVS. HOSTES. NVLLA - PRÆTEREVNDA. EST. OCCASIO. **Rev:** Full-length figure of St. John **Rev. Legend:** MEDIOCRITAS. IN. OMNI - RE. EST. OPTIMA. **Note:** Ref. B-139c; Dav. LS340. Prev. KM#46. Broad flan. Arms of Mayor Alexander Lüneburg (1609-27).

Date	Mintage	VG	F	VF	XF	Unc
ND(1619-27) (b) Rare	—	—	—	—	—	—

KM# 14 2 THALER

Silver **Obv. Legend:** ACCASIO **Note:** Dav. #LS329a.

Date	Mintage	VG	F	VF	XF	Unc
ND(1603-09) (a) Rare	—	—	—	—	—	—

KM# A15 2 THALER

Silver **Obv:** Crowned imperial eagle, shield of city arms on breast, arms of mayor in margin at bottom **Obv. Legend:** ADVERSVS. HOSTES. NVLLA - PRÆTEREVNDA. EST. OCCASIO. **Rev:** Full-length figure of St. John **Rev. Legend:** MEDIOCRITAS. IN. OMNI - RE. EST. OPTIMA. **Note:** Ref. B-136d; Dav. LS329b. Prev. KM#15. Broad flan. Arms of Mayor Gotthard v. Höveln (1600-09).

Date	Mintage	VG	F	VF	XF	Unc
ND(1603-09) (a)	—	1,600	2,650	4,400	7,200	—

KM# A13 2 THALER

Silver **Note:** Similar to 4 Thaler, KM#19. Varieties exist. Dav. #LS329. Prev. KM#13.

Date	Mintage	VG	F	VF	XF	Unc
ND(1603-09) (a) Rare	—	—	—	—	—	—

KM# A24 2 THALER

Silver, 41 mm. **Obv:** Facing figure of St. John holding lamb, shield of city arms below divides date **Obv. Legend:** MONETA. NOVA. - LVBECENS. **Rev:** Crowned imperial eagle, 3Z in orb on breast **Rev. Legend:** RVDOLPHVS. II. D. G. IMP. SE. AVGVS. **Note:** Ref. B-132c; Dav. A5445. Prev. KM#24.

Date	Mintage	VG	F	VF	XF	Unc
(1)605 (a) Rare	—	—	—	—	—	—

KM# A31 2 THALER

Silver **Obv:** Crowned imperial eagle, shield of city arms on breast, arms of mayor in margin at bottom **Obv. Legend:** ADVERSVS. HOSTES. NVLLA - PRÆTEREVNDA. EST. OCCASIO. **Rev:** Full-length figure of St. John **Rev. Legend:** MEDIOCRITAS. IN. OMNI - RE. EST. OPTIMA. **Note:** Ref. B-137d,e; Dav. LS332. Prev. KM#31. Broad flan. Arms of Mayor Alexander Lüneburg (1609-27).

Date	Mintage	VG	F	VF	XF	Unc
ND(1609-16) (a) Rare	—	—	—	—	—	—

KM# A32 2 THALER

Silver **Note:** Similar to 1 Thaler, KM#28 but obverse legend: NVLLA*-PRAE... Dav. #LS334. Prev. KM#32.

Date	Mintage	VG	F	VF	XF	Unc
ND(1609-16) (a)	—	1,600	2,650	4,400	7,200	—

KM# 37 2 THALER

Silver, 41 mm. **Obv:** Facing half-length figure of St. John with lamb, shield of city arms below in front divides date and mayor's arms **Obv. Legend:** MONE. NOVA. - LVBECENS. **Rev:** Crowned imperial eagle, 32 in orb on breast **Rev. Legend:** RVDOLPHVS. II. D. G. IMP. SE. AVGVS. **Note:** Ref. B-141b; Dav. A5446. Thick flan.

Date	Mintage	VG	F	VF	XF	Unc
1611 (a) Rare	—	—	—	—	—	—

KM# A47 2 THALER

Silver **Obv:** Crowned imperial eagle, shield of city arms on breast, arms of mayor in margin at bottom **Obv. Legend:** ADVERSVS. HOSTES. NVLLA - PRÆTEREVNDA. EST. OCCASIO. **Rev:** Full-length figure of St. John **Rev. Legend:** MEDIOCRITAS. IN. OMNI - RE. EST. OPTIMA. **Note:** Ref. B-139d; Dav. #LS339. Prev. KM#47. Broad flan. Arms of Mayor Alexander Lüneburg (1609-27).

Date	Mintage	VG	F	VF	XF	Unc
ND(1619-27) (b) Rare	—	—	—	—	—	—

KM# 58 2 THALER

Silver **Obv:** Facing half-length figure of St. John with lamb, shield of city arms in baroque frame below divides date and mayor's arms **Obv. Legend:** MONE. NOVA: - LVBECENS: **Rev:** Crowned imperial eagle, 32 in orb on breast **Rev. Legend:** FERDINAND. II. D: G: (RO.) IMP: SEM(P) AV: **Note:** Ref. B-154a, 157e, 158e; Dav. 5448. Varieties exist. Thick flan.

Date	Mintage	VG	F	VF	XF	Unc
1624 (b) Rare	—	—	—	—	—	—
1627 (b) Rare	—	—	—	—	—	—
1628 (b) Rare	—	—	—	—	—	—

KM# A16 2-1/2 THALER

Silver **Obv:** Crowned imperial eagle, shield of city arms on breast, arms of mayor in margin below **Obv. Legend:** ADVERSVS. HOSTES. NVLLA - PRÆTEREVNDA. EST. OCCASIO. **Rev:** Full-length figure of St. John **Rev. Legend:** MEDIOCRITAS. IN. OMNI - RE. EST. OPTIMA. **Note:** Ref. B-136e; Dav. LS328. Prev. KM#16. Broad flan. Arms of Mayor Gotthard v. Höveln (1600-09).

Date	Mintage	VG	F	VF	XF	Unc
ND(1603-09) (a) Rare	—	—	—	—	—	—

KM# B17 3 THALER

Silver **Obv:** Crowned imperial eagle, shield of city arms on breast, arms of mayor in margin at bottom **Obv. Legend:** ADVERSVS. HOSTES. NVLLA - PRÆTEREVNDA. EST. OCCASIO. **Rev:** Full-length figure of St. John **Rev. Legend:** MEDIOCRITAS. IN. OMI - RE. EST. OPTIMA. **Note:** Ref. B-136f,g; Dav. LS327. Prev. KM#17. Varieties exist. Broad flan. Arms of Mayor Gotthard v. Höveln (1600-09).

Date	Mintage	VG	F	VF	XF	Unc
ND(1603-09) (a)	—	2,400	3,850	6,700	9,600	—

KM# A19 4 THALER

Silver **Obv:** Crowned imperial eagle, shield of city arms on breast, arms of mayor in margin at bottom **Obv. Legend:** ADVERSVS. HOSTES. NVLLA - PRÆTEREVNDA. EST. OCCASIO. **Rev:** Full-length figure of St. John **Rev. Legend:** MEDIOCRITAS. IN. OMNI - RE. EST. OPTIMA. **Note:** Ref. B-136h; Dav. Varieties exist. Dav. #LS326. Prev. KM#19. Broad flan. Arms of Mayor Gotthard v. Höveln (1600-09).

Date	Mintage	VG	F	VF	XF	Unc
ND(1603-09) (a) Rare	—	—	—	—	—	—

KM# A48 4 THALER

Silver **Obv:** Crowned imperial eagle, shield of city arms on breast, arms of mayor in margin at bottom **Obv. Legend:** ADVERSVS. HOSTES. NVLLA - PRÆTEREVNDA. EST. OCCASIO. **Rev:** Full-length figure of St. John **Rev. Legend:** MEDIOCRITAS. IN. OMNI - RE. EST. OPTIMA. **Note:** Ref. B-139e; Dav. LS338. Prev. KM#48. Broad flan. Arms of Mayor Alexander Lüneburg (1609-27).

Date	Mintage	VG	F	VF	XF	Unc
ND(1619-27) (b)	—	3,200	5,600	8,000	13,000	—

KM# 59 4 THALER

Silver, 41 mm. **Obv:** Facing figure of St. John holding lamb, shield of city arms in baroque frame below divides date **Obv. Legend:** MONE. NOV. - LVBECENS. **Rev:** Crowned imperial eagle, 32 in orb on breast **Rev. Legend:** FERDINAND. II. D. G. RO. IMP. SEMP. AV. **Note:** Ref. B-156k; Dav. #A5448. Thick flan.

Date	Mintage	VG	F	VF	XF	Unc
1626 (b) Rare	—	—	—	—	—	—

TRADE COINAGE

KM# A21 GOLDGULDEN

3.5000 g., 0.9860 Gold 0.1109 oz. AGW **Obv:** Orb in shield in inner circle, shield divides date **Rev:** Crowned imperial eagle in inner circle **Note:** Prev. KM#21.

Date	Mintage	VG	F	VF	XF	Unc
(1)603 (a)	—	1,050	2,250	4,500	7,500	—
(1)603 (aa)	—	1,050	2,250	4,500	7,500	—
(1)608 (a)	—	1,050	2,250	4,500	7,500	—
1617 (bb)	—	1,050	2,250	4,500	7,500	—
1619 (b)	—	1,050	2,250	4,500	7,500	—
1622 (b)	—	1,050	2,250	4,500	7,500	—
1623 (b)	—	1,050	2,250	4,500	7,500	—
1624 (b)	—	1,050	2,250	4,500	7,500	—
1627 (b)	—	1,050	2,250	4,500	7,500	—
1629	—	1,050	2,250	4,500	7,500	—
1637 (b)	—	1,050	2,250	4,500	7,500	—
1651	—	1,050	2,250	4,500	7,500	—
1657	—	1,050	2,250	4,500	7,500	—
1663	—	1,050	2,250	4,500	7,500	—
1670	—	1,050	2,250	4,500	7,500	—
1675 (f)	—	1,050	2,250	4,500	7,500	—

KM# A25 GOLDGULDEN
3.5000 g., 0.9860 Gold 0.1109 oz. AGW **Obv:** Shield of arms in inner circle **Note:** Prev. KM#25.

Date	Mintage	VG	F	VF	XF	Unc
1605	—	650	1,350	2,700	4,500	—
1611	—	650	1,350	2,700	4,500	—
1613	—	650	1,350	2,700	4,500	—
1619	—	650	1,350	2,700	4,500	—
1625	—	650	1,350	2,700	4,500	—
1631	—	650	1,350	2,700	4,500	—
1636	—	650	1,350	2,700	4,500	—
1637	—	650	1,350	2,700	4,500	—

KM# A85 1/4 DUCAT
0.8750 g., 0.9860 Gold 0.0277 oz. AGW **Obv:** Orb in shield **Rev:** Crowned imperial eagle **Note:** Prev. KM#85.

Date	Mintage	VG	F	VF	XF	Unc
ND(1650)	—	240	475	900	1,650	—

KM# 110 1/4 DUCAT
0.8750 g., 0.9860 Gold 0.0277 oz. AGW **Obv:** Emperor standing **Rev:** Crowned imperial eagle

Date	Mintage	VG	F	VF	XF	Unc
1679 (f)	—	210	425	675	1,250	—
1683 (f)	—	210	425	675	1,250	—
1690 (f)	—	210	425	675	1,250	—
1692 (f)	—	210	425	675	1,250	—
1693 (f)	—	210	425	675	1,250	—
1694 (f)	—	210	425	675	1,250	—
1697 (f)	—	210	425	675	1,250	—

KM# 111 1/2 DUCAT
1.7500 g., 0.9860 Gold 0.0555 oz. AGW **Obv:** Emperor standing **Rev:** Crowned imperial eagle

Date	Mintage	VG	F	VF	XF	Unc
1679 (f)	—	250	500	1,000	1,700	—
1682	—	250	500	1,000	1,700	—
1683 (f)	—	250	500	1,000	1,700	—
1688	—	250	500	1,000	1,700	—
1690 (f)	—	250	500	1,000	1,700	—
1692 (f)	—	250	500	1,000	1,700	—
1693 (f)	—	250	500	1,000	1,700	—
1697 (f)	—	250	500	1,000	1,700	—
1698	—	250	500	1,000	1,700	—

KM# A22 DUCAT
3.5000 g., 0.9860 Gold 0.1109 oz. AGW **Obv:** Full-length facing armored figure of emperor, date at end of legend **Obv. Legend:** MONE(TA). NO(VA). (-) A(-)V(-)R(-)EA. LVBEC. **Rev:** Crowned imperial eagle, shield of city arms on breast **Rev. Legend:** CIVITATIS. - IMPERIALIS. **Note:** Ref. B#596-601. Varieties exist. Prev. KM#22.

Date	Mintage	VG	F	VF	XF	Unc
(1)603 (a)	—	600	1,100	2,200	3,600	—
(1)604 (a)	—	600	1,100	2,200	3,600	—
(1)606 (a)	—	600	1,100	2,200	3,600	—
(1)607 (a)	—	600	1,100	2,200	3,600	—
(1)608 (a)	—	600	1,100	2,200	3,600	—
(1)609 (a)	—	600	1,100	2,200	3,600	—

KM# A36 DUCAT
3.5000 g., 0.9860 Gold 0.1109 oz. AGW **Obv:** Full-length facing armored figure of emperor **Obv. Legend:** MON(E)(T)(A). NO(-)(V)(-)(A) - A(-)(V)(U)R(-)E(A). L(V)(U)B(E)(C). **Rev:** Crowned imperial eagle, shield of city arms on breast, shield of mayor's arms divides date below **Rev. Legend:** CI(V)(U)ITAT(I)(S) - IMPERI(A)(L)(IS). **Note:** Ref. B#602, 602A, 602B, 603-34, 636. Varieties exist. Prev. KM#36.

Date	Mintage	VG	F	VF	XF	Unc
1610 (a)	—	240	475	900	1,500	—
161Z (a)	—	240	475	900	1,500	—
1613 (a)	—	240	475	900	1,500	—
1614 (a)	—	240	475	900	1,500	—
1615 (a)	—	240	475	900	1,500	—
1627 (b)	—	240	475	900	1,500	—
1629 (b)	—	240	475	900	1,500	—
1630 (b)	—	240	475	900	1,500	—
1631 (b)	—	240	475	900	1,500	—
1632 (b)	—	—	—	—	—	—
1634 (b)	—	—	—	—	—	—
1636	—	240	475	900	1,500	—
1643 (b)	—	—	—	—	—	—
1645 (c)	—	—	—	—	—	—
1647	—	240	475	900	1,500	—
1648/7 (c)	—	—	—	—	—	—
1649	—	240	475	900	1,500	—
1652	—	240	475	900	1,500	—
1656	—	240	475	900	1,500	—
1657	—	240	475	900	1,500	—
1659	—	240	475	900	1,500	—
1660	—	240	475	900	1,500	—
1663	—	240	475	900	1,500	—
1664	—	240	475	900	1,500	—
1667	—	240	475	900	1,500	—
1672	—	240	475	900	1,500	—
1674	—	240	475	900	1,500	—
1677	—	240	475	900	1,500	—
1683	—	240	475	900	1,500	—
1684	—	240	475	900	1,500	—
1689	—	240	475	900	1,500	—
1690	—	240	475	900	1,500	—
1691	—	240	475	900	1,500	—
1695	—	240	475	900	1,500	—
1697	—	240	475	900	1,500	—
1700	—	240	475	900	1,500	—

KM# 89 2 DUCAT
7.0000 g., 0.9860 Gold 0.2219 oz. AGW **Obv:** Knight with imperial orb and sceptre **Rev:** Crowned double-headed eagle with city arms on breast

Date	Mintage	VG	F	VF	XF	Unc
1656 (c)	—	950	1,700	4,000	6,700	—
1658 (c)	—	950	1,700	4,000	6,700	—
1660 (c)	—	950	1,700	4,000	6,700	—
1666 (d)	—	950	1,700	4,000	6,700	—
1667	—	950	1,700	4,000	6,700	—
1672 (e)	—	950	1,700	4,000	6,700	—
1674 (f)	—	950	1,700	4,000	6,700	—
1675 (f)	—	950	1,700	4,000	6,700	—
1676 (f)	—	950	1,700	4,000	6,700	—
1678 (f)	—	950	1,700	4,000	6,700	—
1681	—	950	1,700	4,000	6,700	—
1682 (f)	—	950	1,700	4,000	6,700	—
1686	—	950	1,700	4,000	6,700	—
1690	—	950	1,700	4,000	6,700	—
1691 (f)	—	950	1,700	4,000	6,700	—
1694	—	950	1,700	4,000	6,700	—
1699	—	950	1,700	4,000	6,700	—

KM# 70 4 DUCAT
14.0000 g., 0.9860 Gold 0.4438 oz. AGW **Obv:** Full-length facing armored figure of emperor **Obv. Legend:** MONE. NO - VA - AVREA . LVB. **Rev:** Crowned imperial eagle, shield of city arms on breast, shield of mayor's arms divides date at bottom **Rev. Legend:** CIVITATIS - IMPERIAL. **Note:** Ref. B-611b. Struck on thick flan from Ducat dies, KM#A36.

Date	Mintage	VG	F	VF	XF	Unc
1638 (b) Rare	—	—	—	—	—	—

KM# A62 5 DUCAT (1/2 Portugalöser)
17.5000 g., 0.9860 Gold 0.5547 oz. AGW **Obv:** Crowned impeerial eagle, shield of city arms on breast, date at end of legend **Obv. Legend:** EX AVRO. SOLIDO - LIB. IMPER. CIVITAS. LVB. FF **Rev:** Emperor enthroned, 1627 - ANO below **Rev. Legend:** SERVA. NOS. DOMINE. NE. PEREAMVS. **Note:** Ref. B-664. Prev. KM#62.

Date	Mintage	VG	F	VF	XF	Unc
1628 (b) Rare	—	—	—	—	—	—

KM# A66 5 DUCAT (1/2 Portugalöser)
17.5000 g., 0.9860 Gold 0.5547 oz. AGW **Obv:** City arms in center of large ornate cross, date at end of legend **Obv. Legend:** EX. AVRO. SOLIDO - LIB. IMPER. CIVITAS. LVB. FF. **Rev:** Figure of St. John **Rev. Legend:** SERVA. NOS. DOMINE. NE. PEREAMVS. **Note:** Ref. B-665. Prev. KM#66.

Date	Mintage	VG	F	VF	XF	Unc
1636 (b) Rare	—	—	—	—	—	—

KM# A109 10 DUCAT (Portugalöser)
35.0000 g., 0.9860 Gold 1.1095 oz. AGW **Note:** Struck with 1 Thaler dies, KM#108.

Date	Mintage	VG	F	VF	XF	Unc
1673 (e) Rare	—	—	—	—	—	—

PATTERNS

Including off metal strikes

KM#	Date	Mintage	Identification	Mkt Val
Pn1	1665 (d)	—	1/96 Thaler. Gold. KM#50.	—
PnA2	(16)67 (e)	—	Dreiling. Gold. KM#27.	750
PnA3	1669 (e)	—	1/96 Thaler. Gold. KM#50.	—
PnA4	(16)71 (e)	—	Dreiling. Gold. KM#27.	—
Pn6	1681 (f)	—	16 Schilling. Gold. Weight of 2-1/2 Ducat, KM#116.	—
Pn7	1683	—	16 Schilling. Gold. Weight of 2-1/2 Ducat, KM#116.	—
Pn8	1683 (f)	—	1/16 Thaler. Gold. Weight of 2 Ducat, KM#A57.	—
Pn9	1687	—	4 Pfennig. Gold. Weight of 1/2 Ducat, KM#117.	—
Pn10	1692 (f)	—	1/24 Thaler. Gold. Weight of 1 Ducat, KM#79.	—
Pn11	(16)98 (f)	—	Dreiling. Gold. KM#27.	375

LUCKAU

Situated about 45 miles (75 km) south-southeast of Berlin, Luckau was the centrally most important town in Lower Lusatia on the way to Dresden. A mint functioned in the town during the 13th and 14th centuries and a mintmaster is mentioned there in the early 15th century. Luckau produced a series of coins for local use during the early period of the Thirty Years' War.

PROVINCIAL TOWN

REGULAR COINAGE

KM# 1 PFENNIG (Kipper)
Copper **Ruler:** (no Ruler Information) **Obv:** Lion leaping left in oval baroque frame, date above **Note:** Uniface.

Date	Mintage	VG	F	VF	XF	Unc
16ZZ Rare	—	—	—	—	—	—

KM# 2 PFENNIG (Kipper)
Copper **Ruler:** (no Ruler Information) **Obv:** Lion leaping left in ornately-shaped shield, date above **Note:** Uniface; varieties exist.

Date	Mintage	VG	F	VF	XF	Unc
16ZZ	—	75.00	150	300	—	—
1622	—	75.00	150	300	—	—
16Z2	—	75.00	150	300	—	—

KM# 3 PFENNIG
Billon **Ruler:** (no Ruler Information) **Obv:** Lion leaping left in ornately-shaped shield, date above **Note:** Uniface; varieties exist.

Date	Mintage	VG	F	VF	XF	Unc
16ZZ Rare	—	—	—	—	—	—

KM# 4 3 KREUZER (Kipper - Groschen)
Silver **Ruler:** (no Ruler Information) **Obv:** Steer walking left **Obv. Legend:** MONETA. NOVA. LUCCANA. **Rev:** Crowned imperial eagle, 3 in orb on breast, titles of Ferdinand II **Note:** Varieties exist.

Date	Mintage	VG	F	VF	XF	Unc
ND(1621/2) Rare	—	—	—	—	—	—

KM# 5 1/24 THALER (Kipper - Groschen)
Silver **Ruler:** (no Ruler Information) **Obv:** Steer walking left, date in margin **Obv. Legend:** MONETA. NOVA. LUCCANA. **Rev:** Crowned imperial eagle, Z4 in orb on breast, titles of Ferdinand II **Note:** Varieties exist.

Date	Mintage	VG	F	VF	XF	Unc
1622 Rare	—	—	—	—	—	—

LUNEBURG

This city 50 miles southeast of Hamburg, chartered in 1247, became a powerful member of The Hanseatic League and received the mint right in 1293. It passed to Hannover in 1705 and to Prussia in 1866. Using a pun on the city name "luna", they showed a half moon on larger coins. Lüneburg had a local coinage, which was produced intermittently from 1293 until 1777.

MINT OFFICIALS' INITIALS

Initials	Date	Name
(a)= 	1599-1605	Claus Flegel
(c)= ,AT	1643-49	Andreas Tympfe
(d)= and/or CHS	Ca.1660-	Christoph Hennig Schluter
(e)= 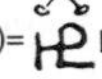 HL	1676-89	Hermann Luders
(b)= 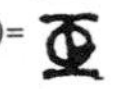	1612-45, 49	Jonas Georgens
Knight on horseback rearing left and/or IG (monogram)		
JJJ	1687-1705	Jobst Jacob Janisch in Celle

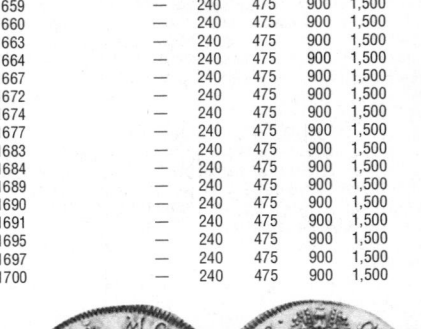

ARMS

City gate, usually with 3 towers, lion rampant or leopard left in portal. Often depicted with St. John (patron saint) above towers.

REFERENCES

Sch = Wolfgang Schulten, ***Deutsche Münzen aus der Zeit Karls V.***, Frankfurt am Main, 1976.

S = Hugo Frhr. Von Saurma-Jeltsch, ***Die Saurmasche Münzsammlung deutscher, schweizerischer und polnischer Gepräge von etwa dem Beginn der Groschenzeit bis zur Kipperperiode***, Berlin, 1892.

K = Wilhelm Knigge, ***Münz-u. Medaillen-Kabinet***, Hannover, 1901.

Kn = Karl Graf zu Inn- und Knyphausen, ***Erster Nachtrag zum Münz- und Medaillen-Kabinet***, Hannover, 1877.

CITY

REGULAR COINAGE

KM# 40 FLITTER (1/2 Pfennig)

Silver **Obv:** Lion rampant left **Rev. Inscription:** I/FLIT/TER/date **Note:** Kipper Flitter.

Date	Mintage	VG	F	VF	XF	Unc
(1)6Z0	—	33.00	60.00	110	220	—
(1)6Z1	—	33.00	60.00	110	220	—
ND	—	33.00	60.00	110	220	—

KM# 70 FLITTER (1/2 Pfennig)

Silver **Obv:** Lion rampant left **Rev. Inscription:** 1S/date/LUN

Date	Mintage	Good	VG	F	VF	XF
1641	—	12.00	25.00	50.00	100	—

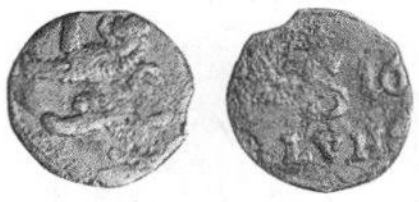

KM# 90 SCHERF (1/2 Pfennig)

Copper **Obv:** Lion rampant left **Rev:** Large S divides date, value 1 above, LVN below **Note:** Varieties exist.

Date	Mintage	VG	F	VF	XF	Unc
1675	—	10.00	22.00	45.00	90.00	—
1683	—	10.00	22.00	45.00	90.00	—
1684	—	10.00	22.00	45.00	90.00	—
1691	—	10.00	22.00	45.00	90.00	—
1694	—	10.00	22.00	45.00	90.00	—

KM# 45 PFENNIG

Copper **Obv:** City arms **Rev. Inscription:** I / PEN / NIG / date

Date	Mintage	VG	F	VF	XF	Unc
16Z1	—	10.00	20.00	40.00	80.00	—
16ZZ	—	10.00	20.00	40.00	80.00	—

KM# 46 PFENNIG

Copper **Obv. Legend:** MONET. CI. LVNEBVRG

Date	Mintage	VG	F	VF	XF	Unc
16Z1	—	10.00	20.00	40.00	85.00	—

KM# 48 PFENNIG

Copper **Rev. Inscription:** I / PEN / NING / date

Date	Mintage	VG	F	VF	XF	Unc
(1)6ZZ	—	10.00	20.00	40.00	85.00	—

KM# 49 PFENNIG

Silver **Obv:** Rampant lion left **Note:** Uniface.

Date	Mintage	VG	F	VF	XF	Unc
ND	—	10.00	20.00	40.00	80.00	—

KM# 47 3 PFENNIG

Copper **Obv:** City arms **Rev. Inscription:** III / PEN / NIG / date **Note:** Kipper 3 Pfennig.

Date	Mintage	VG	F	VF	XF	Unc
16Z1	—	15.00	30.00	60.00	120	—

KM# 50 3 PFENNIG

Copper **Obv. Legend:** ...LUNEBURG

Date	Mintage	VG	F	VF	XF	Unc
(1)6ZZ	—	15.00	30.00	60.00	120	—

KM# 44 SECHSLING (6 Pfennig)

Silver **Obv:** City arms **Obv. Legend:** MONET. CI. LUNEBURG **Rev. Legend:** STADT GELT. ANO **Rev. Inscription:** I / SECS / LING, date

Date	Mintage	VG	F	VF	XF	Unc
(1)6Z1	—	40.00	65.00	130	265	—

KM# 51 1/64 THALER (1/2 Schilling)

Silver **Obv:** Imperial orb with 64, titles of Ferdinand II and date in legend **Rev:** City arms **Rev. Legend:** MO NO CP. LUNEBURG

Date	Mintage	VG	F	VF	XF	Unc
16ZZ IG	—	33.00	60.00	120	240	—

KM# 62 1/64 THALER (1/2 Schilling)

Silver **Rev. Legend:** MO: NO: CIV: LUNEBURGENSIS

Date	Mintage	VG	F	VF	XF	Unc
1627 (b)	—	33.00	60.00	120	240	—

KM# 71 1/64 THALER (1/2 Schilling)

Silver **Rev:** Legend, date **Rev. Legend:** STADT: GELDT **Note:** Varieties exist.

Date	Mintage	VG	F	VF	XF	Unc
1643	—	27.00	55.00	110	220	—
1647	—	27.00	55.00	110	220	—

KM# 56 1/32 THALER (Schilling)

Silver **Obv:** City arms, date in legend **Rev:** Ornamented quatrefoil with 32 in center **Rev. Legend:** DA. PAC...

Date	Mintage	VG	F	VF	XF	Unc
(1)6Z3 (b)	—	25.00	45.00	90.00	180	—

KM# 58 1/32 THALER (Schilling)

Silver **Rev:** Date in legend **Note:** Varieties exist.

Date	Mintage	VG	F	VF	XF	Unc
16Z6 IG	—	20.00	33.00	75.00	150	—
1627 (b)	—	20.00	33.00	75.00	150	—
1629 (b)	—	20.00	33.00	75.00	150	—

KM# 73 1/32 THALER (Schilling)

Silver, 20.9 mm. **Rev:** Date in legend **Note:** Similar to KM#58. Varieties exist.

Date	Mintage	VG	F	VF	XF	Unc
1647	—	20.00	33.00	75.00	150	—
1648	—	20.00	33.00	75.00	150	—

KM# 10 1/16 THALER (2 Schilling)

Silver **Obv:** St. John above city arms **Obv. Legend:** MO: NO. C. - LVNEBVR **Rev:** Crowned imperial eagle, 16 in orb on breast, titles of Rudolf II and date in legend

Date	Mintage	VG	F	VF	XF	Unc
(1)601 (A)	—	—	—	—	—	—

KM# 32 1/16 THALER (2 Schilling)

Silver **Obv:** Titles of Matthias **Note:** Varieties exist.

Date	Mintage	VG	F	VF	XF	Unc
1614 (b)	—	45.00	80.00	120	240	—
1615 (b)	—	45.00	80.00	120	240	—
1616 (b)	—	45.00	80.00	120	240	—

KM# 41 1/16 THALER (2 Schilling)

Silver **Obv:** City arms divide date **Obv. Legend:** MO. NO. CI. LVNAEBVRGE. **Rev:** St. John, value (16) below **Rev. Legend:** DA. PAC. D: I.-DIEB. NOS. **Note:** Kipper 1/16 Thaler.

Date	Mintage	VG	F	VF	XF	Unc
1620 (b)	—	—	—	—	—	—

KM# 52 1/16 THALER (2 Schilling)

Silver **Obv:** City arms in shield imposed on cross, which divides legend **Obv. Legend:** MONE-LUNE-BURG-date **Rev:** St. John, value 16 between feet **Rev. Legend:** DA. PA... **Note:** Varieties exist.

Date	Mintage	VG	F	VF	XF	Unc
(1)6ZZ (b)	—	55.00	85.00	140	260	—
(1)6Z4 (b)	—	55.00	85.00	140	260	—

KM# 59 1/16 THALER (2 Schilling)

Silver **Obv:** Date above arms **Note:** Varieties exist.

Date	Mintage	VG	F	VF	XF	Unc
16Z6 (b)	—	27.00	55.00	100	200	—
1627 (b)	—	27.00	55.00	100	200	—
16Z8 (b)	—	27.00	55.00	100	200	—
16Z9 (b)	—	27.00	55.00	100	200	—
1632 (b)	—	27.00	55.00	100	200	—
1633 (b)	—	27.00	55.00	100	200	—
1637 (b)	—	27.00	55.00	100	200	—
1643 (c)	—	27.00	55.00	100	200	—
1644	—	27.00	55.00	100	200	—
1646 AT	—	27.00	55.00	100	200	—
1647 (c)	—	27.00	55.00	100	200	—
1647 AT	—	27.00	55.00	100	200	—

KM# 85 1/16 THALER (2 Schilling)

Silver **Obv:** Date divided by mintmaster's initials or symbol in legend

Date	Mintage	VG	F	VF	XF	Unc
1660 (d)	—	27.00	55.00	100	200	—
1677 (e)	—	27.00	55.00	100	200	—

KM# 57 1/4 THALER

Silver **Obv:** Crowned imperial eagle, orb on breast, titles of Ferdinand II and date **Rev:** City arms, date in legend

Date	Mintage	VG	F	VF	XF	Unc
(1)6Z5/1625 (b)	—	100	185	360	725	—

KM# A53 8 SCHILLING

Silver **Obv:** City arms, date in margin **Obv. Legend:** MON • NOV • CIV • LUNEBERGEN • **Rev:** Crowned imperial eagle, 8 in orb on breast **Rev. Legend:** FERDINANDUS • II • DG • RO • I • S • A •

Date	Mintage	VG	F	VF	XF	Unc
16ZZ (b)	—	—	—	—	—	—

KM# 63 8 SCHILLING

Silver **Rev:** 8 in orb on imperial eagle's breast and date **Note:** Varieties exist.

Date	Mintage	VG	F	VF	XF	Unc
(1)6ZZ (b)	—	—	—	—	—	—
1629 (b)	—	120	225	425	850	—
1632 (b)	—	120	225	425	850	—

KM# 86 8 SCHILLING

Silver **Obv:** Titles of Leopold I

Date	Mintage	VG	F	VF	XF	Unc
1660 CHS (d)	—	—	—	—	—	—

KM# 53 16 SCHILLING (1/2 Thaler)

Silver **Obv:** Towered building facade within beaded circle **Rev:** Value in circle on breast of double-headed imperial eagle within beaded circle **Note:** Varieties exist.

Date	Mintage	VG	F	VF	XF	Unc
16ZZ (b)	—	275	500	725	1,450	—
16Z9 (b)	—	275	500	725	1,450	—
1632 (b)	—	275	500	725	1,450	—

KM# 11 THALER OF 32 SCHILLING

Silver **Obv:** Gate and towers **Obv. Legend:** MONETA. NOVA: CIVI: LVNEBVGENS **Rev:** Crowned imperial eagle with orb and 32 on breast **Rev. Legend:** RVDOLP: II. G. RO. I. SE. AVG. P. F. D. **Note:** Dav. #5461.

Date	Mintage	VG	F	VF	XF	Unc
1601 Rare	—	—	—	—	—	—

KM# 12 THALER OF 32 SCHILLING

Silver **Obv. Legend:** ...IM. SEM. AUGU. P. F. D. **Rev. Legend:** ...CIUITATTS. LUNEBURGENSIS **Note:** Dav. #5462.

Date	Mintage	VG	F	VF	XF	Unc
1602 Rare	—	—	—	—	—	—

KM# 14 THALER OF 32 SCHILLING

Silver **Obv:** Tilted small shield below towered building facade, within beaded circle **Rev:** Value in circle on breast of double-headed imperial eagle, crown above **Note:** Dav. #5464.

Date	Mintage	VG	F	VF	XF	Unc
1609	—	250	500	1,000	1,750	—
1610	—	250	500	1,000	1,750	—
1611	—	250	500	1,000	1,750	—
1612	—	250	500	1,000	1,750	—

KM# 20 THALER OF 32 SCHILLING

Silver **Obv:** KM#12 **Rev:** KM#31 **Note:** Mule. Dav. #A5465.

Date	Mintage	VG	F	VF	XF	Unc
1610 Rare	—	—	—	—	—	—

KM# 21 THALER OF 32 SCHILLING

Silver **Obv:** Crowned helmeted arms **Rev:** Standing figure facing, profile right within crescent at left **Note:** Similar to 2 Thaler, KM#22. Dav. #LS342A.

Date	Mintage	VG	F	VF	XF	Unc
ND(1611-12) Rare	—	—	—	—	—	—

KM# 25 THALER OF 32 SCHILLING

Silver **Obv:** Lion on shield between feet **Note:** Similar to 2 Thaler, KM#30 but with fuller cape. Dav. #LS346.

Date	Mintage	VG	F	VF	XF	Unc
ND(1612) Rare	—	—	—	—	—	—

KM# 26 THALER OF 32 SCHILLING

Silver **Obv:** Similar to 2 Thaler, KM#29, inner legend **Note:** Dav. #LS348.

Date	Mintage	VG	F	VF	XF	Unc
ND(1612) Rare	—	—	—	—	—	—

KM# 24 THALER OF 32 SCHILLING

Silver **Obv:** T between feet **Note:** Similar to 2 Thaler, KM#15. Dav. #LS-B342.

Date	Mintage	VG	F	VF	XF	Unc
ND(1612) Rare	—	—	—	—	—	—

KM# 31 THALER OF 32 SCHILLING

Silver **Obv:** Towers divide date **Rev:** Titles of Matthias **Note:** Dav. #5465.

Date	Mintage	VG	F	VF	XF	Unc
1613	—	400	950	2,000	3,500	—
1615	—	400	950	2,000	3,500	—
1617 (b)	—	400	950	2,000	3,500	—
1619	—	400	950	2,000	3,500	—

KM# 33 THALER OF 32 SCHILLING

Silver **Obv:** Date divided 1-6-1-7 by towers **Rev:** Crowned double-headed imperial eagle **Note:** Dav. #5465A.

Date	Mintage	VG	F	VF	XF	Unc
1617	—	450	1,000	2,200	3,750	—

KM# 34 THALER OF 32 SCHILLING

Silver **Obv:** Lion on shield between feet **Note:** Similar to 2 Thaler, KM#30. Dav. #LS344A.

Date	Mintage	VG	F	VF	XF	Unc
ND(1617) Rare	—	1,100	2,000	3,900	6,600	—

KM# 54 THALER OF 32 SCHILLING

Silver **Obv:** Without date in legend **Note:** Dav. #5468.

Date	Mintage	VG	F	VF	XF	Unc
ND(1619-37) (b)	—	650	1,250	2,500	4,500	—

KM# 55 THALER OF 32 SCHILLING

Silver **Rev:** Titles of Ferdinand II **Note:** Dav. #5466.

Date	Mintage	VG	F	VF	XF	Unc
16ZZ (b)	—	125	250	550	1,250	4,000
1623	—	125	250	550	1,250	4,000
16Z4 (b)	—	125	250	550	1,250	4,000
16Z5	—	125	250	550	1,250	4,000
1626 (b)	—	125	250	500	1,250	4,000

KM# 60 THALER OF 32 SCHILLING

Silver **Obv:** Towered building facade within circle **Rev:** Value in circle of breast of double-headed imperial eagle, crown above, date in legend **Note:** Dav. #5467.

Date	Mintage	VG	F	VF	XF	Unc
1626 (b)	—	135	275	675	1,750	—
1627	—	135	275	675	1,750	—
1628	—	135	275	675	1,750	—
1629	—	135	275	675	1,750	—
1630	—	135	275	675	1,750	—
163Z	—	135	275	675	1,750	—
1636	—	135	275	675	1,750	—

KM# 87 THALER OF 32 SCHILLING

Silver **Obv:** Large towers **Rev:** Titles of Leopold I **Note:** Dav. #5469.

Date	Mintage	VG	F	VF	XF	Unc
1660 CHS Rare	—	—	—	—	—	—

KM# 27 1-1/2 THALER

Silver **Note:** Similar to 2 Thaler, KM#30 but with fuller cape. Dav. #LS-A346.

Date	Mintage	VG	F	VF	XF	Unc
ND(1612) Rare	—	—	—	—	—	—

KM# 35 1-1/2 THALER

Silver **Note:** Similar to 2 Thaler, KM#30. Dav. #LS344.

Date	Mintage	VG	F	VF	XF	Unc
ND(1617) Rare	—	—	—	—	—	—

KM# 13 2 THALER

Silver **Obv:** Gate and towers **Rev:** Crowned imperial eagle with orb and 32, titles of Rudolph **Note:** Dav. #5463.

Date	Mintage	VG	F	VF	XF	Unc
1606	—	1,150	1,900	3,150	4,700	—

KM# 15 2 THALER

Silver **Rev:** T between feet **Note:** Dav. #LS-A342.

Date	Mintage	VG	F	VF	XF	Unc
ND(1609)	—	1,800	3,000	4,800	7,200	—

KM# 22 2 THALER

Silver **Obv:** Crowned helmeted arms **Rev:** Standing figure facing, profile right within crescent at left **Note:** Dav. #LS342.

Date	Mintage	VG	F	VF	XF	Unc
ND(1611-12)	—	1,000	1,800	3,600	6,000	—

KM# 23 2 THALER

Silver **Obv:** Crowned helmeted arms **Obv. Legend:** QVISCONTRA NOS… **Rev:** Standing figure facing, profile right within crescent at left **Note:** Dav. #LS342a.

Date	Mintage	VG	F	VF	XF	Unc
ND(1611-12)	—	900	1,600	3,400	5,800	—

KM# 30 2 THALER

Silver **Rev:** Lion between shield between feet **Note:** Dav. #LS343.

Date	Mintage	VG	F	VF	XF	Unc
ND(1612)	—	1,800	3,000	4,800	7,200	—

KM# 29 2 THALER

Silver **Obv:** Inner legend **Obv. Legend:** QUIS - CONTRA NOS **Note:** Dav. #LS347.

Date	Mintage	VG	F	VF	XF	Unc
ND(1612) Rare	—	—	—	—	—	—

KM# 28 2 THALER

Silver **Note:** Similar to KM#30 but with fuller cape. Dav. #LS345.

Date	Mintage	VG	F	VF	XF	Unc
ND(1612) Rare	—	—	—	—	—	—

TRADE COINAGE

KM# 6 GOLDGULDEN

3.5000 g., 0.9860 Gold 0.1109 oz. AGW **Obv:** Imperial eagle in inner circle **Rev:** St. John standing in inner circle

Date	Mintage	VG	F	VF	XF	Unc
1601	1,233	450	900	1,800	3,000	—
1602	343	450	900	1,800	3,000	—
1603	—	450	900	1,800	3,000	—
1604	—	450	900	1,800	3,000	—
1606	155	450	900	1,800	3,000	—
1607	—	450	900	1,800	3,000	—
1609	733	450	900	1,800	3,000	—
1610	784	450	900	1,800	3,000	—
1612	900	450	900	1,800	3,000	—
1613	220	450	900	1,800	3,000	—
1614	396	450	900	1,800	3,000	—
1615	432	450	900	1,800	3,000	—
1616	288	450	900	1,800	3,000	—
1617 (b)	828	450	900	1,800	3,000	—
1623	—	450	900	1,800	3,000	—
1629	—	450	900	1,800	3,000	—
1635	—	450	900	1,800	3,000	—

KM# 39 GOLDGULDEN

3.5000 g., 0.9860 Gold 0.1109 oz. AGW **Obv:** St. John standing

Date	Mintage	VG	F	VF	XF	Unc
ND(1613-37)	—	700	1,450	2,700	4,500	—

KM# 61 GOLDGULDEN

3.5000 g., 0.9860 Gold 0.1109 oz. AGW **Obv:** Bust of St. John in inner circle **Rev:** Orb in trilobe

Date	Mintage	VG	F	VF	XF	Unc
1626	—	600	1,150	2,450	4,100	—
1629	—	600	1,150	2,450	4,100	—

KM# 42 2-1/2 GOLDGULDEN

8.7500 g., 0.9860 Gold 0.2774 oz. AGW **Obv:** St. John standing in inner circle **Rev:** Arms superimposed on cross in inner circle

Date	Mintage	VG	F	VF	XF	Unc
ND(ca.1620) Rare	—	—	—	—	—	—

KM# 43 3 GOLDGULDEN

10.5000 g., 0.9860 Gold 0.3328 oz. AGW **Obv:** St. John standing in inner circle **Rev:** Arms superimposed on cross in inner circle

Date	Mintage	VG	F	VF	XF	Unc
ND(ca.1612) Rare	—	—	—	—	—	—

KM# 72 DUCAT

3.5000 g., 0.9860 Gold 0.1109 oz. AGW **Obv:** St. John standing in oval, arms at bottom **Rev:** Crescent moon with face right in inner circle

Date	Mintage	VG	F	VF	XF	Unc
1645	—	750	1,500	2,950	4,950	—
1647	—	750	1,500	2,950	4,950	—

KM# A31 6 DUCAT

21.0000 g., 0.9860 Gold 0.6657 oz. AGW **Rev:** St. John standing facing at center, crescent moon with face right in inner circle **Note:** Struck with 2 Thaler dies, KM#29. Actual weight 19.90 grams.

Date	Mintage	VG	F	VF	XF	Unc
ND(1612) Rare	—	—	—	—	—	—

KM# 98 6 DUCAT

21.0000 g., 0.9860 Gold 0.6657 oz. AGW **Obv:** St. John standing holding lamb beside two palm trees, harbor scene in background **Rev:** Face in crescent, huntsman above, fisherman below

Date	Mintage	VG	F	VF	XF	Unc
ND(1650) Rare	—	—	—	—	—	—

KM# 99 10 DUCAT

35.0000 g., 0.9860 Gold 1.1095 oz. AGW **Obv:** St. John standing holding lamb beside two palm trees, harbor scene in background **Rev:** Face in crescent, huntsman above, fisherman above

Date	Mintage	VG	F	VF	XF	Unc
ND(1650) Rare	—	—	—	—	—	—

MAGDEBURG

The small 9th century settlement on the Elbe River, about 85 miles (140 km) west-southwest of Berlin, grew into an important religious and trading center. A convent was established in Magdeburg by Otto the Great (962-73) in 937, while he was still King of the Germans and not yet Emperor. Otto followed this pious act by placing an imperial mint in the town in 942 and facilitated the establishment of an archbishopric there in 968. It was not long before the archbishops were striking coins, in the name of the emperor at first, then in their own names beginning in the late 11th-early 12th century. Archiepiscopal coinage was struck more or less continuously from the late 14th century until 1679. Long under the influence of Brandenburg-Prussia, the Archbishopric of Magdeburg passed, along with the city, into the possession of that powerful state in 1680.

RULERS

Ernst, Herzog von Sachsen, 1476-1513
Albrecht IV, Markgraf von Brandenburg, Administrator, 1513-1545
Johann Albrecht, Markgraf von Brandenburg, 1545-1551
Friedrich IV, Markgraf von Brandenburg, 1551-1552
Sigmund, Markgraf von Brandenburg, 1552-1566
Joachim Friedrich, Markgraf von Brandenburg, 1566-1598
Regents of the Chapter, 1598-1607
Christian Wilhelm von Brandenburg, 1608-1631
Leopold Wilhelm of Austria, 1631-1638
Regents of the Chapter, 1635-1638
August von Sachsen-Weissenfels, 1638-1680

MINT OFFICIALS' INITIALS

Initial	Date	Name
(a)= and/or GM	1595-1613	Georg Meinhard in Halle
(b)=	1613-17	Jonas Wedemeyer in Halle
IH/H	1614	Isaak Henniges, die-cutter
	1617-?	Heinrich Mayer
W	Ca.1619-22	
FD	1622	Franz Thimo
H	Ca.1622	
	1622	Anton Koburger the Elder
AK	1623-25	Anton Koburger the Younger
MK	1638	
ML	1638	
(c)= and/or PS	1638-41	Peter Schrader
ABK	1668	Anton Bernhard Koburger
HHF	1668-77	Hans Heinrich Friese in Halle
(d)=	1675-85	Johann Georg Breyer (Breuer), die-cutter and mintmaster in Brunswick City
SM	Ca.1677	
AF	Ca.1679	

ARMS

Archbishopric and cathedral chapter - 2-fold arms, divided horizontally in half, usually upper, foliated or floral ornament or otherwise shaded to denote red, lower half blank to denote silver, sometimes with patron Saint Moritz.

REFERENCES

S = Friedrich Freiherrn von Schrötter, ***Beschreibung der Neuzeitlichen Münzen des Erzstifts und der Stadt Magdeburg 1400-1682***. Magdeburg, 1909.

B = Emil Bahrfeldt, Magdeburger Münzen. Nachträge und Berichtigungen zu Friedrich Freiherrn v. Schrötters Buche über die neuzeitlichen Münzen von Magdeburg, ***Berliner Münzblätter*** 43 (1922), pp. 290-91, 345-46, 390-93, 410ff.

Saur = Hugo Frhr. Von Saurma-Jeltsch, ***Die Saurmasche Münzsammlung deutscher, schweizerischer und polnischer Gepräge von etwa dem Beginn der Groschenzeit bis zur Kipperperiode***. Berlin, 1892,

Sch = Wolfgang Schulten, ***Deutsche Münzen aus der Zeit Karls V***. Frankfurt am Main, 1974.

ARCHBISHOPRIC

REGULAR COINAGE

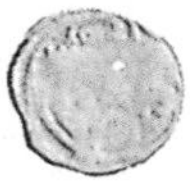

KM# 70 PFENNIG

Silver **Obv:** 4-fold arms with central shield of Madgeburg, date above. **Note:** Uniface. Schussel type.

Date	Mintage	VG	F	VF	XF	Unc
(16)ZZ	—	10.00	20.00	40.00	80.00	—

KM# 75 PFENNIG

Silver **Obv:** Arms divide mintmaster's initials **Note:** Varieties exist.

Date	Mintage	VG	F	VF	XF	Unc
(16)Z3	—	10.00	20.00	40.00	80.00	—
(16)Z4	—	10.00	20.00	40.00	80.00	—

KM# 76 PFENNIG

Silver **Obv:** Adjacent arms of Brandenburg and Zollern, date above **Rev:** Imperial orb in shield divides mintmaster's initials

Date	Mintage	VG	F	VF	XF	Unc
(16)Z3	—	10.00	20.00	40.00	80.00	—

KM# 25 3 PFENNIG (Dreier)

Silver **Obv:** Helmeted eagle arms of Brandenburg, date divided at top **Rev:** Imperial orb with 3 in ornamented oval frame

Date	Mintage	VG	F	VF	XF	Unc
1613	—	20.00	40.00	75.00	155	—
1615	—	—	—	—	—	—

KM# 41 3 PFENNIG (Dreier)

Silver **Obv:** Three shields of arms, Brandenburg, Zollern, and Magdeburg **Rev:** Imperial orb with 3

Date	Mintage	VG	F	VF	XF	Unc
1615	—	20.00	40.00	75.00	155	—

KM# 49 3 PFENNIG (Dreier)

Silver **Obv:** Four-fold arms with central shield of Magdeburg in cartouche **Rev:** Imperial orb with 3 divides date near top

Date	Mintage	VG	F	VF	XF	Unc
1617	—	20.00	40.00	75.00	155	—

KM# 50 3 PFENNIG (Dreier)

Silver **Obv:** Adjacent shields of Brandenburg and Zollern

Date	Mintage	VG	F	VF	XF	Unc
1617 (b)	—	25.00	45.00	90.00	185	—

KM# 67 3 PFENNIG (Dreier)

Silver **Obv:** Four-fold arms with central shield of Magdeburg, small annulet at either side and above **Rev:** Imperial orb with 3 divides date **Note:** Kipper 3 Pfennig. Varieties exist.

Date	Mintage	VG	F	VF	XF	Unc
16Z1	—	20.00	40.00	75.00	155	—

KM# 72 3 PFENNIG (Dreier)

Silver **Obv:** 5-line inscription with date, Brandenburg eagle in oval shield divides lower three lines **Obv. Inscription:** CHRIS / WIL: D: G: / P: A:-M: C / H.-D: P: / date **Rev:** Imperial orb with 3 divides mintmaster's initials in ornamented rhombus **Note:** Varieties exist.

Date	Mintage	VG	F	VF	XF	Unc
(16)ZZ FD	—	33.00	60.00	110	225	—
(16)ZZ FD-H	—	33.00	60.00	110	225	—

KM# 71 3 PFENNIG (Dreier)

Silver **Obv:** Four-fold arms with central shield of Magdeburg, date above **Rev:** Imperial orb with 3 in ornamented rhombus

Date	Mintage	VG	F	VF	XF	Unc
16ZZ	—	20.00	40.00	75.00	155	—
16ZZ FD	—	20.00	40.00	75.00	155	—

KM# 77 3 PFENNIG (Dreier)

Silver **Obv:** Adjacent arms of Brandenburg and Magdeburg, date above **Rev:** Imperial orb with 3 divides mintmaster's initials **Note:** Varieties exist.

Date	Mintage	VG	F	VF	XF	Unc
16Z3 AK	—	33.00	60.00	110	225	—
16Z4 AK	—	33.00	60.00	110	225	—

KM# 53 4 GROSCHEN (3 Kreuzer - Schreckenberger)

Silver **Obv:** Crowned imperial eagle with orb on breast **Rev:** Four-fold arms with central shield of Magdeburg superimposed on ornamented cross **Note:** Kipper 4 Groschen. Varieties exist.

Date	Mintage	VG	F	VF	XF	Unc
ND(1619-22)	—	40.00	80.00	150	290	—

KM# 54 4 GROSCHEN (3 Kreuzer - Schreckenberger)

Silver **Obv:** Crowned ornate shield **Rev:** Value 4 in imperial orb **Note:** Varieties exist.

Date	Mintage	VG	F	VF	XF	Unc
ND(1619-22)	—	40.00	80.00	150	290	—

KM# 55 4 GROSCHEN (3 Kreuzer - Schreckenberger)

Silver **Obv:** Smaller cross **Note:** Varieties exist.

Date	Mintage	VG	F	VF	XF	Unc
ND(1619-22) W	—	40.00	80.00	150	290	—

KM# 7 1/24 THALER (Groschen)

Silver **Obv:** Imperial orb with Z4 divides date, titles of Rudolf II **Rev:** St. Moritz standing full-length holding flag and chapter arms in shield **Note:** Cathedral Chapter issue. Varieties exist.

Date	Mintage	VG	F	VF	XF	Unc
1607 (a)	—	33.00	55.00	110	220	—

KM# 26 1/24 THALER (Groschen)

Silver **Obv:** Helmeted Magdeburg arms **Rev:** Small imperial orb with Z4 divides date, below adjacent arms of Brandenburg and Zollern

Date	Mintage	VG	F	VF	XF	Unc
1613 (b)	—	13.00	27.00	35.00	115	—

KM# 27 1/24 THALER (Groschen)

Silver **Ruler:** Christian Wilhelm **Obv:** Oval Magdeburg arms, ornate helmet above **Obv. Legend:** CRIS. WIL. D.G. PA. A. G. P. G MB **Rev:** Imperial orb with 'Z4' divides date **Rev. Legend:** MATI. D.G. RO. IM. SEM. AV **Note:** Varieties exist.

Date	Mintage	VG	F	VF	XF	Unc
1613 (b)	—	13.00	27.00	55.00	115	—
1614 (b)	—	13.00	27.00	55.00	115	—
1614	—	13.00	27.00	55.00	115	—

KM# 34 1/24 THALER (Groschen)

Silver **Ruler:** Christian Wilhelm **Obv:** Magdeburg arms above two adjacent arms, Brandenburg and Zollern **Note:** Varieties exist.

Date	Mintage	VG	F	VF	XF	Unc
1614 (b)	—	13.00	27.00	55.00	115	—

KM# 37 1/24 THALER (Groschen)

Silver **Obv:** Shields with pointed bottoms and scalloped tops **Note:** Varieties exist.

Date	Mintage	VG	F	VF	XF	Unc
1614 (b)	—	13.00	27.00	55.00	115	—
1615 (b)	—	13.00	27.00	55.00	115	—

KM# 33 1/24 THALER (Groschen)

Silver **Obv:** Four-fold arms with central shield of Magdeburg

Date	Mintage	VG	F	VF	XF	Unc
1614	—	13.00	27.00	55.00	115	—

KM# 36 1/24 THALER (Groschen)

Silver **Obv:** Arms in oval shields

Date	Mintage	VG	F	VF	XF	Unc
1614 (b)	—	13.00	27.00	55.00	115	—

KM# 35 1/24 THALER (Groschen)

Silver **Note:** Klippe

Date	Mintage	VG	F	VF	XF	Unc
1614 (b)	—	—	—	—	—	—

KM# 42 1/24 THALER (Groschen)

Silver **Rev. Legend:** MARCH. BR. D. PRVS. **Note:** Varieties exist.

Date	Mintage	VG	F	VF	XF	Unc
1615 (b)	—	16.00	30.00	65.00	130	—

KM# 43 1/24 THALER (Groschen)
Silver **Ruler:** Christian Wilhelm **Obv:** Four-fold arms in various shapes, with central shield of Magdeburg **Note:** Varieties exist.

Date	Mintage	VG	F	VF	XF	Unc
1615 (b)	—	16.00	30.00	65.00	130	—
1616 (b)	—	16.00	30.00	65.00	130	—
1617 (b)	—	16.00	30.00	65.00	130	—

KM# 44 1/24 THALER (Groschen)
Silver **Obv:** Titles of Matthias **Note:** Varieties exist.

Date	Mintage	VG	F	VF	XF	Unc
1615 (b)	—	16.00	30.00	65.00	130	—

KM# 51 1/24 THALER (Groschen)
Silver **Rev. Legend:** COAD. HALB. M. B. D. P. **Note:** Varieties exist.

Date	Mintage	VG	F	VF	XF	Unc
1617 (b)	—	16.00	30.00	65.00	130	—

KM# 52 1/24 THALER (Groschen)
Silver **Obv:** 16-fold arms with central shield of Magdeburg arms **Rev:**

Imperial orb with Z4 divides date, titles of Christian Wilhelm **Rev. Legend:** PRO: LE-GE. ET.-GREGE **Note:** Klippe. Reverse of this coin struck with same dies as goldgulden, KM#47.

Date	Mintage	VG	F	VF	XF	Unc
1617 (b)	—	20.00	40.00	80.00	—	—

KM# 58 1/24 THALER (Groschen)
Silver **Ruler:** Christian Wilhelm **Obv:** Four-fold arms with central shield of Magdeburg, titles of Christian Wilhelm **Rev:** Imperial orb with Z4, date divided above **Note:** Kipper Coinage. Varieties exist.

Date	Mintage	VG	F	VF	XF	Unc
1619	—	16.00	30.00	65.00	130	—
16Z0	—	16.00	30.00	65.00	130	—
(16)Z0	—	16.00	30.00	65.00	130	—
16Z1	—	16.00	30.00	65.00	130	—
(16)Z1	—	16.00	30.00	65.00	130	—
(16)1Z Error	—	16.00	30.00	65.00	130	—

KM# 65 1/24 THALER (Groschen)
Silver **Note:** Klippe.

Date	Mintage	VG	F	VF	XF	Unc
(16)Z0	—	—	—	—	—	—

KM# 73 1/24 THALER (Groschen)
Silver **Rev:** Arms divide mintmaster's initials

Date	Mintage	VG	F	VF	XF	Unc
16ZZ FD	—	16.00	30.00	65.00	130	—

KM# 74 1/24 THALER (Groschen)
Silver **Rev:** Date above arms

Date	Mintage	VG	F	VF	XF	Unc
16ZZ	—	16.00	30.00	65.00	130	—

KM# 78 1/24 THALER (Groschen)
Silver **Obv:** Imperial orb with Z4 divides mintmaster's initials, date divided at top **Rev:** Three oval shields of arms, Magdeburg above Brandenburg and Zollern

Date	Mintage	VG	F	VF	XF	Unc
16Z3 AK	—	20.00	35.00	75.00	155	—
16Z4 AK	—	20.00	35.00	75.00	155	—

KM# 145 1/24 THALER (Groschen)
Silver **Ruler:** August **Obv:** Oval 2-fold arms of Magdeburg and Saxony in baroque frame **Obv. Legend:** AUGUSTUS. DEI. GRAT. P. A. **Rev:** Imperial orb with '24' divides mintmaster's initials, date at end of legend **Rev. Legend:** A - M. DUX. SAX.- I. C. E. M. **Note:** Varieties exist.

Date	Mintage	VG	F	VF	XF	Unc
1668 ABK	—	13.00	27.00	55.00	115	—
1669 HHF	—	13.00	27.00	55.00	115	—
1670 HHF	—	13.00	27.00	55.00	115	—

KM# 38 1/16 THALER (Doppelschilling)
Silver **Obv:** Crowned imperial eagle, 16 in orb on breast, crown at top divides date, titles in legend **Rev:** Four-fold arms with central shield of Magdeburg superimposed on ornate cross **Rev. Legend:** MO. N. NO-CRISTI.-WIL. AR-EP. MAG. **Note:** Klippe.

Date	Mintage	VG	F	VF	XF	Unc
1614	—	—	—	—	—	—

KM# 45 1/16 THALER (Doppelschilling)
Silver **Note:** Similar to KM#38 but round.

Date	Mintage	VG	F	VF	XF	Unc
1615	—	—	—	—	—	—

KM# 59 1/16 THALER (Doppelschilling)
Silver **Note:** Kipper 1/16 Thaler. Varieties exist.

Date	Mintage	VG	F	VF	XF	Unc
1619	—	85.00	175	350	—	—

KM# 66 1/16 THALER (Doppelschilling)
Silver **Obv. Legend:** CRI-SIA-WIL-HEL **Rev:** Intertwined DS (Doppelschilling), titles in legend with date

Date	Mintage	VG	F	VF	XF	Unc
(16)Z0	—	—	—	—	—	—

KM# 15 1/14 THALER (Doppelgroschen)
Silver **Obv:** Facing bust turned slightly right **Rev:** Small imperial orb with 14 divides date above **Rev. Inscription:** NEWE. TOP / PEL. SILBER / GROSCHEN / G(a)M

Date	Mintage	VG	F	VF	XF	Unc
1610 G(a)M	—	—	—	—	—	—

KM# 18 1/14 THALER (Doppelgroschen)
Silver **Obv:** Bust right **Obv. Inscription:** NE-WE / TOPPEL. SIL / BER. GROS: / G(a)M **Rev:** Small imperial orb with 14 divides date and first line of inscription **Note:** Varieties exist.

Date	Mintage	VG	F	VF	XF	Unc
161Z G(a)M	—	—	—	—	—	—

KM# 56 1/12 THALER
Silver **Obv:** Value 1Z in imperial orb **Note:** Varieties exist.

Date	Mintage	VG	F	VF	XF	Unc
ND(1619/22)	—	33.00	65.00	120	240	—

KM# 57 1/12 THALER
Silver **Obv:** Smaller cross **Note:** Varieties exist.

Date	Mintage	VG	F	VF	XF	Unc
ND(1619/22)	—	33.00	65.00	120	240	—

KM# 91 1/12 THALER
Silver **Obv:** Half-length bust right **Rev. Inscription:** EIN / HALBER / REICHS / ORT / date

Date	Mintage	VG	F	VF	XF	Unc
16Z4 AK	—	—	—	—	—	—

KM# 146 1/6 THALER
Silver **Ruler:** August **Obv:** Half-length bust right, value (1/6) below **Rev:** Crowned four-fold arms with central shield of Magdeburg divides date and mintmaster's initials

Date	Mintage	VG	F	VF	XF	Unc
1668 ABK	—	55.00	110	225	450	—

KM# 147 1/6 THALER
Silver **Rev:** Date in legend **Note:** Varieties exist.

Date	Mintage	VG	F	VF	XF	Unc
1668 HHF	—	45.00	75.00	150	290	—
1669 HHF	—	45.00	75.00	150	290	—

KM# 165 1/6 THALER
Silver **Rev:** Value (1/6) at bottom **Note:** Varieties exist.

Date	Mintage	VG	F	VF	XF	Unc
1670 HHF	—	33.00	60.00	110	220	—

KM# 166 1/6 THALER
Silver **Rev:** Large bust **Note:** Varieties exist.

Date	Mintage	VG	F	VF	XF	Unc
1670 HHF	—	33.00	60.00	110	220	—

KM# 79 1/4 THALER
Silver **Obv:** 3/4-length bust right **Obv. Inscription:** PRO.LEGE.-ET.GREGE **Rev:** Small helmeted arms of Magdeburg in center, oval arms of Brandenburg above and Zollern below divided inscription, margin of 14 small oval arms **Note:** Varieties exist.

Date	Mintage	VG	F	VF	XF	Unc
ND (b)	—	—	—	—	—	—
(16)Z3 AK	—	—	—	—	—	—

KM# 81 1/4 THALER
Silver **Obv:** Half-length bust right

Date	Mintage	VG	F	VF	XF	Unc
(16)Z3 AK	—	—	—	—	—	—

KM# 92 1/4 THALER
Silver **Rev:** 15-fold arms with central shields of Magdeburg and Brandenburg above that of Zollern, date in legend

Date	Mintage	VG	F	VF	XF	Unc
(16)Z4 AK	—	—	—	—	—	—

KM# 80 1/4 THALER
Silver **Note:** Klippe.

Date	Mintage	VG	F	VF	XF	Unc
ND (b)	—	—	—	10,000	11,500	—

KM# 105 1/4 THALER
Silver **Obv:** Helmeted arms of Magdeburg divide date and mintmaster's initials **Rev:** Full-length figure of St. Moritz holding Magdeburg banner in right hand, shield with imperial eagle in left hand **Note:** Cathedral Chapter issue.

Date	Mintage	VG	F	VF	XF	Unc
1638 MK	—	135	275	375	650	—

KM# 106 1/4 THALER
Silver **Obv:** Date divided above

Date	Mintage	VG	F	VF	XF	Unc
1638 PS (c)	—	135	275	375	650	—

KM# 130 1/4 THALER
Silver **Obv:** Facing bust of August **Rev:** Four-fold arms with central shield of Magdeburg, bishop's mitre above, date divided in legend at top

Date	Mintage	VG	F	VF	XF	Unc
1640 PS	—	—	—	—	—	—

KM# 148 1/3 THALER (1/2 Gulden)
Silver **Ruler:** August **Obv:** Value (1/3) below bust **Rev:** 4-fold arms with central shield of Magdeburg divide date and mintmaster's initials **Note:** Varieties exist.

Date	Mintage	VG	F	VF	XF	Unc
1668 ABK	—	55.00	100	210	425	—

KM# 149 1/3 THALER (1/2 Gulden)
Silver **Rev:** Date in legend **Note:** Varieties exist.

Date	Mintage	VG	F	VF	XF	Unc
1668 HHF	—	35.00	65.00	125	250	—
1669 HHF	—	35.00	65.00	125	250	—

KM# 152 1/3 THALER (1/2 Gulden)
Silver **Rev:** Date divided by crown

Date	Mintage	VG	F	VF	XF	Unc
1669 HHF	—	35.00	65.00	125	250	—

KM# 153 1/3 THALER (1/2 Gulden)
Silver **Obv:** Larger bust without circle

Date	Mintage	VG	F	VF	XF	Unc
1669 HHF	—	35.00	65.00	125	250	—
1670 HHF	—	35.00	65.00	125	250	—

KM# 167 1/3 THALER (1/2 Gulden)
Silver **Rev:** Value (1/3) at bottom

Date	Mintage	VG	F	VF	XF	Unc
1670 HHF	—	45.00	80.00	150	300	—

KM# 168 1/3 THALER (1/2 Gulden)
Silver **Obv:** Larger head **Note:** Varieties exist.

Date	Mintage	VG	F	VF	XF	Unc
1670 HHH	—	40.00	80.00	150	290	—
1671 HHH	—	40.00	80.00	150	290	—
1672 HHH	—	40.00	80.00	150	290	—
1674 HHH	—	40.00	80.00	150	290	—
1675 HHH	—	40.00	80.00	150	290	—

KM# 19 1/2 THALER
Silver **Obv:** Half-length bust right, imperial orb at lower right **Rev:** Three helmets above 13-fold arms with central shield of Magdeburg

Date	Mintage	VG	F	VF	XF	Unc
(1)61Z GM	—	—	—	—	—	—

KM# 85 1/2 THALER (20 Groschen)
Silver **Obv:** 3/4-length bust right **Obv. Inscription:** PRO. LEG.--ET. GREGE **Rev:** Small helmeted arms of Magdeburg in center, oval arms above, Zollern below divided inscription, margin of 14 small oval arms

Date	Mintage	VG	F	VF	XF	Unc
ND	—	—	—	—	—	—

KM# 68 1/2 THALER (20 Groschen)
Silver **Obv:** Oval four-fold arms with central shield of Brandenburg in cartouche **Rev:** Angel above heart-shaped shield of Magdeburg, date above, 20 G. in cartouche in margin at bottom **Note:** Kipper 1/2 Thaler. Varieties exist.

Date	Mintage	VG	F	VF	XF	Unc
16Z1	—	—	—	—	—	—

KM# 82 1/2 THALER (20 Groschen)
Silver **Note:** Varieties exist. Photo reduced.

Date	Mintage	VG	F	VF	XF	Unc
ND	—	135	325	450	850	—
(16)Z3	—	135	325	450	850	—
(16)Z4 AK	—	135	325	450	850	—
16Z4 AK	—	135	325	450	850	—

KM# 86 1/2 THALER (20 Groschen)
Silver **Obv:** Half-length bust right **Rev:** 15-fold arms with central shield of Magdeburg

Date	Mintage	VG	F	VF	XF	Unc
(16)Z3 AK	—	—	—	—	—	—

KM# 93 1/2 THALER (20 Groschen)
Silver **Rev:** 16-fold arms with central shields of Magdeburg and Brandenburg above that of Zollern, date in legend **Note:** Varieties exist.

Date	Mintage	VG	F	VF	XF	Unc
16Z4 AK	—	300	575	1,100	2,200	—
(16)Z4 AK	—	300	575	1,100	2,200	—
(16)Z5 AK	—	300	575	1,100	2,200	—

KM# 83 1/2 THALER (20 Groschen)
Silver **Obv:** Half-length bust right **Rev:** 16-fold arms with central shield of Magdeburg

Date	Mintage	VG	F	VF	XF	Unc
ND	—	—	—	—	—	—

KM# 84 1/2 THALER (20 Groschen)
Silver **Obv. Legend:** CRIST. D. G. P. ADM...WILHJ

Date	Mintage	VG	F	VF	XF	Unc
ND	—	—	—	—	—	—

KM# 107 1/2 THALER (20 Groschen)
Silver **Obv:** Helmeted arms of Magdeburg divide date and mintmaster's initials **Rev:** Full-length figure of St. Moritz holding Magdeburg banner in right hand, shield with imperial eagle in left hand

Date	Mintage	VG	F	VF	XF	Unc
1638 (c)	—	165	300	650	1,150	—

KM# 108 1/2 THALER (20 Groschen)
Silver **Obv:** Date divided above arms **Note:** Varieties exist.

Date	Mintage	VG	F	VF	XF	Unc
1638 PS (c)	—	260	450	675	1,225	—

KM# 131 1/2 THALER (20 Groschen)
Silver **Obv:** Facing bust of August **Rev:** 4-fold arms with central shield of Magdeburg, bishop's mitre above, date divided in legend at top **Note:** Varieties exist.

Date	Mintage	VG	F	VF	XF	Unc
1640 PS Rare	—	—	—	—	—	—

KM# 155 2/3 THALER (Gulden)
Silver **Note:** Varieties exist.

Date	Mintage	VG	F	VF	XF	Unc
1669 HHF	—	80.00	125	200	385	—

KM# 156 2/3 THALER (Gulden)
Silver **Obv:** Without circle around bust **Note:** Varieties exist.

Date	Mintage	VG	F	VF	XF	Unc
1669 HHF	—	80.00	125	200	385	—
1670 HHF	—	80.00	125	200	385	—

KM# 169 2/3 THALER (Gulden)
Silver **Obv:** Larger bust **Note:** Varieties exist.

Date	Mintage	VG	F	VF	XF	Unc
1670 HHF	—	45.00	80.00	150	300	—
1671 HHF	—	45.00	80.00	150	300	—
1672 HHF	—	45.00	80.00	150	300	—
1673 HHF	—	45.00	80.00	150	300	—
1674 HHF	—	45.00	80.00	150	300	—

KM# 171 2/3 THALER (Gulden)
Silver **Ruler:** August **Rev:** Arms divide 2/3-T, date divided below arms **Note:** Varieties exist.

Date	Mintage	VG	F	VF	XF	Unc
1674	—	45.00	80.00	150	300	—
1675	—	45.00	80.00	150	300	—

KM# 173 2/3 THALER (Gulden)
Silver **Rev:** Swan swimming right, value 2/3 in oval below, legend, date **Rev. Legend:** SILENDO. ET. SPERANDO. **Note:** Varieties exist.

Date	Mintage	VG	F	VF	XF	Unc
1675 (d)	—	45.00	80.00	150	300	—
ND (d)	—	45.00	80.00	150	300	—

KM# 172 2/3 THALER (Gulden)
Silver **Rev:** 21-fold arms divide three stars - 2/3

Date	Mintage	VG	F	VF	XF	Unc
1675 (d)	—	45.00	80.00	150	300	—

KM# 174 2/3 THALER (Gulden)
Silver **Obv:** Bust right wtih lion's head on shoulder **Rev:** Date divided by arms

Date	Mintage	VG	F	VF	XF	Unc
1675 HHF	—	45.00	80.00	150	300	—

KM# 175.1 2/3 THALER (Gulden)
Silver **Ruler:** August **Rev:** Shield with indented sides

Date	Mintage	VG	F	VF	XF	Unc
1675 HHF	—	45.00	80.00	150	300	—

KM# 175.2 2/3 THALER (Gulden)
Silver **Ruler:** August **Obv:** Date below bust

Date	Mintage	VG	F	VF	XF	Unc
1675 HHF	—	45.00	80.00	150	300	—
1676 HHF	—	45.00	80.00	150	300	—

KM# 176 2/3 THALER (Gulden)

Silver **Rev:** Mintmaster's initials divided by value below arm **Note:** Varieties exist.

Date	Mintage	VG	F	VF	XF	Unc
1676 HHF	—	45.00	80.00	150	300	—

KM# 179 2/3 THALER (Gulden)

Silver **Obv:** Bust right with lion's head on shoulder, mintmaster's initials below **Note:** Varieties exist.

Date	Mintage	VG	F	VF	XF	Unc
1679 AF	—	55.00	100	200	385	—

KM# 5 THALER

Silver **Obv:** Helmeted arms with divided date above and G-M below **Rev:** Saint standing with standard and shield **Note:** Cathedral Chapter issue. Varieties exist. Dav.#5471.

Date	Mintage	VG	F	VF	XF	Unc
1602 GM	1,000	125	285	600	1,250	2,500
1603 GM	1,525	125	285	600	1,250	2,500
1604 GM	3,432	125	285	600	1,250	2,500
1605 GM	6,371	125	285	600	1,250	2,500
1606 GM	7,080	125	285	600	1,250	2,500
1607 GM	4,401	125	285	600	1,250	2,500

KM# 8 THALER

Silver **Ruler:** Christian Wilhelm **Obv:** Bust of Christian Wilhelm right **Obv. Legend:** CHRIST: WILH: D: G: P: ARCHIEP: MAGD: P: G: M: B: **Rev:** Helmeted arms with divided date above, G-M below **Note:** Dav.#5473.

Date	Mintage	VG	F	VF	XF	Unc
1608 GM	—	650	1,250	2,500	4,250	—
1609 GM	—	650	1,250	2,500	4,250	—

KM# 9 THALER

Silver **Ruler:** Christian Wilhelm **Obv:** Narrower bust **Obv. Legend:** CHRISTI:... **Note:** Dav.#5474. Varieties exist.

Date	Mintage	VG	F	VF	XF	Unc
1608 GM	—	200	550	1,200	2,500	—
1609 GM	—	200	550	1,200	2,500	—
1610 GM	—	200	550	1,200	2,500	—
1611 GM	—	200	550	1,200	2,500	—
1612 GM	—	200	550	1,200	2,500	—

KM# 16 THALER

Silver **Rev:** G-M in legend **Note:** Dav.#5474A.

Date	Mintage	VG	F	VF	XF	Unc
1611 GM	—	250	600	1,300	2,750	—

KM# 17 THALER

Silver **Obv. Legend:** CHRISTI: VILH:... **Rev:** G16-11M below arms **Note:** Dav.#5474B.

Date	Mintage	VG	F	VF	XF	Unc
1611 GM	—	250	600	1,300	2,750	—

KM# 20 THALER

Silver **Rev:** Legend starting on the right **Note:** Dav.#5474C.

Date	Mintage	VG	F	VF	XF	Unc
1612 GM	—	250	600	1,300	2,750	—

KM# 21 THALER

Silver **Rev:** G-M divided by arms **Note:** Dav.#5474D.

Date	Mintage	VG	F	VF	XF	Unc
1612 GM	—	250	600	1,300	2,750	—

KM# 22 THALER

Silver **Obv. Legend:** ...ARCHIEP: IAGD:... **Note:** Dav.#5474E.

Date	Mintage	VG	F	VF	XF	Unc
1612 GM	—	250	600	1,300	2,750	—

KM# 23 THALER

Silver **Obv:** Longer bust right **Rev:** Date divided in legend at top **Note:** Dav.#5475.

Date	Mintage	VG	F	VF	XF	Unc
1612 GM	—	350	750	1,450	2,850	—

KM# 24 THALER

Silver **Obv. Legend:** CHRISTIAN... **Note:** Dav.#5475A.

Date	Mintage	VG	F	VF	XF	Unc
1612 GM	—	350	750	1,450	2,850	—

KM# 28 THALER

Silver **Obv:** Different bust with wing collar **Rev:** Date divided by helmets above arms **Note:** Dav.#5476.

Date	Mintage	VG	F	VF	XF	Unc
1613 GM	—	300	650	1,350	2,800	—

KM# 29 THALER

Silver **Obv:** Half-bust facing **Obv. Legend:** CHRIS. WILH D. G. -P. ADM. MAG. D. PR. **Note:** Dav.#5477.

Date	Mintage	VG	F	VF	XF	Unc
1613 GM Rare	—	—	—	—	—	—

KM# 31 THALER

Silver **Rev:** Fourteen shields surround legend which surrounds Bishop's shield with small shields above and below **Rev. Legend:** PRO: LEGE.-ET. GREGE **Note:** Dav.#5479.

Date	Mintage	VG	F	VF	XF	Unc
ND	—	350	750	1,500	3,000	—

KM# 32 THALER

Silver **Ruler:** Christian Wilhelm **Obv:** Large facing figure **Rev:** Different frames and shapes of center shield **Note:** Dav.#5480.

Date	Mintage	VG	F	VF	XF	Unc
ND IH-(b)	—	700	1,350	2,750	4,750	—

KM# 30 THALER

Silver **Obv:** Small half-bust right **Obv. Legend:** CHRIST. WILH. AR. EP. MAGDEB. MAR. BRAND. D. PRVS. **Note:** Dav.#5478.

Date	Mintage	VG	F	VF	XF	Unc
1613 IH/(b) Rare	—	—	—	—	—	—
1613 (b) Rare	—	—	—	—	—	—

KM# 39 THALER

Silver **Obv:** Date above figure **Obv. Legend:** CRISTI. WILH. D: G. AR... **Rev:** St. Mortitz standing with standard and shield, Cathedral at left **Note:** Dav.#5482.

Date	Mintage	VG	F	VF	XF	Unc
1614 IH-(b) Rare	—	—	—	—	—	—

KM# 69 THALER

Silver **Obv:** Oval four-fold arms with central shield of Brandenburg in cartouche **Rev:** Angel above heart-shaped shield of Magdeburg, date above

Date	Mintage	VG	F	VF	XF	Unc
16Z1 Rare	—	—	—	—	—	—
1621 Rare	—	—	—	—	—	—

KM# 87 THALER

Silver **Ruler:** Christian Wilhelm **Obv:** Bust right, date below **Rev:** Similar to Dav. #5480 but center arms helmeted with staffs **Note:** Dav. #5483.

Date	Mintage	VG	F	VF	XF	Unc
1623 AK	—	300	600	1,200	2,500	—

KM# 88 THALER

Silver **Obv:** Without date below bust **Note:** Dav. #5484.

Date	Mintage	VG	F	VF	XF	Unc
ND	—	300	600	1,200	2,500	—

KM# 89 THALER

Silver **Obv. Legend:** CHRIS. WILH. D: G: P. ADM. MAG. MARCH. BR. DVX. P: COAD. HALB: **Note:** Dav. #5485.

Date	Mintage	VG	F	VF	XF	Unc
ND	—	300	600	1,200	2,500	—

KM# 90 THALER

Silver **Obv. Legend:** CRIS. WILH... **Note:** Dav. #5485A.

Date	Mintage	VG	F	VF	XF	Unc
ND	—	300	600	1,200	2,500	—

KM# 94 THALER

Silver **Obv:** Legend, date **Obv. Legend:** CRIS. WIL: D: G: P: AD: M: COA: HAL: MAR: BR: DVX: PRV **Note:** Dav. #5486.

Date	Mintage	VG	F	VF	XF	Unc
1624 AK	—	200	400	750	1,500	—

KM# 95 THALER

Silver **Obv. Legend:** CHRIS: WILH: D: G: POST: AD: MAG: E: HALB: M: B: D: P **Note:** Dav. #5487.

Date	Mintage	VG	F	VF	XF	Unc
(16)24 AK	—	145	270	650	1,300	—

KM# 97 THALER

Silver **Ruler:** Christian Wilhelm **Obv. Legend:** CHRIS*WILH*... **Rev:** Shield separating A-K, date in legend **Note:** Dav. #5490.

Date	Mintage	VG	F	VF	XF	Unc
(16)24 AK	—	145	270	650	1,300	—
(16)25 AK	—	145	270	650	1,300	—

KM# 96 THALER

Silver **Rev:** Shield separating Z-4 and A-K **Note:** Dav. #5488. Varieties exist.

Date	Mintage	VG	F	VF	XF	Unc
(16)Z4 AK	—	—	—	—	—	—
1624 AK	—	180	350	775	1,500	—

KM# 98 THALER

Silver **Ruler:** Christian Wilhelm **Obv. Legend:** CRIS: WIL: D: G: POSTVL:... **Note:** Dav. #5491.

Date	Mintage	VG	F	VF	XF	Unc
(16)25 AK	—	180	350	775	1,500	—

KM# 99 THALER

Silver **Obv. Legend:** CRIS. WILH. D: G. P... **Note:** Dav. #5492. Varieties exist.

Date	Mintage	VG	F	VF	XF	Unc
ND	—	180	350	775	1,500	—

KM# 100 THALER

Silver **Note:** Similar to KM#99 but without helmet above arms.

Date	Mintage	VG	F	VF	XF	Unc
ND	—	210	450	850	1,600	—

KM# 109 THALER

Silver **Note:** Cathedral Chapter issue. Similar to KM#110 but PS-X below arms. Dav. #5495.

Date	Mintage	VG	F	VF	XF	Unc
1638 PS(c)	—	240	475	1,150	2,100	—

KM# 110 THALER

Silver **Obv:** M-K divided above helmeted arms **Note:** Dav. #5495A.

Date	Mintage	VG	F	VF	XF	Unc
1638 MK	—	270	550	1,200	2,200	—

KM# 111 THALER

Silver **Obv:** M-K divided below helmeted arms **Note:** Dav. #5495B.

Date	Mintage	VG	F	VF	XF	Unc
1638 MK	—	270	550	1,200	2,200	—

KM# 112 THALER

Silver **Obv:** PS-X divided below helmeted arms **Note:** Dav. #5495C.

Date	Mintage	VG	F	VF	XF	Unc
1638 PS(c)	—	240	475	1,150	2,100	—

KM# 113 THALER

Silver **Obv:** PS dividing date below helmeted arms **Note:** Dav. #5495D.

Date	Mintage	VG	F	VF	XF	Unc
1638 PS	—	240	475	1,150	2,100	—

KM# 114 THALER

Silver **Obv:** PSX dividing date below helmeted arms **Note:** Dav. #5495E.

Date	Mintage	VG	F	VF	XF	Unc
1638 PS(c)	—	240	475	1,150	2,100	—

KM# 115 THALER

Silver **Obv:** PS left of arms, date divided by arms **Note:** Dav. #5496.

Date	Mintage	VG	F	VF	XF	Unc
1638 PS(c)	—	270	550	1,200	2,200	—

KM# 116 THALER

Silver **Obv:** PS-X and 16-38 below arms **Note:** Dav. #5496A.

Date	Mintage	VG	F	VF	XF	Unc
1638 PS(c)	—	270	550	1,200	2,200	—

KM# 117 THALER

Silver **Obv:** P S X below arms **Note:** Dav. #5496B.

Date	Mintage	VG	F	VF	XF	Unc
1638 PS(c)	—	270	550	1,200	2,200	—

KM# 118 THALER

Silver **Obv:** P S X right and 16-38 below arms **Note:** Dav. #5496C. Varieties exist.

Date	Mintage	VG	F	VF	XF	Unc
1638 PS(c)	—	270	550	1,200	2,200	—

KM# 119 THALER

Silver **Obv:** 11-line inscription **Note:** Dav. #5497. Varieties exist.

Date	Mintage	VG	F	VF	XF	Unc
1638 PS(c)	—	425	850	1,750	3,850	—

KM# 120 THALER

Silver **Rev:** City view at left **Note:** Dav. #5498. Varieties exist.

Date	Mintage	VG	F	VF	XF	Unc
1638 PS(c)S/ML	—	350	775	1,550	3,150	—

KM# 132 THALER

Silver **Obv:** Facing bust **Obv. Legend:** AUGUSTUS. D: G. POSTULATUS. ARCHIEPISCOPUS. MAGDEBURGEN **Rev:** Helmeted arms, PS-X at sides, date divided at top **Rev. Legend:** PRIMAS. GERMA: DUX-SAX. IUL. CL. E. MONT. **Note:** Dav. #5502.

Date	Mintage	VG	F	VF	XF	Unc
1640 PS(c)	—	375	650	1,300	3,050	—

KM# 133 THALER

Silver **Ruler:** August **Obv. Legend:** ...POSTUL: ARCHIEP:... **Note:** Dav. #5502A.

Date	Mintage	VG	F	VF	XF	Unc
1640 PS(c)	—	375	650	1,300	3,050	—

KM# 136 THALER

Silver **Rev:** Arms divide PS-X **Rev. Legend:** ...DU-X. SAX... **Note:** Dav. #5503.

Date	Mintage	VG	F	VF	XF	Unc
1641 PS(c)	—	525	1,100	2,300	3,900	—

KM# 137 THALER

Silver **Obv. Legend:** ...POSTULATUS. ARCHIEPISCOPUS... **Note:** Dav. #5503A.

Date	Mintage	VG	F	VF	XF	Unc
1641 PS(c)	—	525	1,100	2,300	3,900	—

KM# 138 THALER

Silver **Obv. Legend:** ...MAGDEBURGE **Note:** Dav. #5503B.

Date	Mintage	VG	F	VF	XF	Unc
1641 PS(c)	—	525	1,100	2,300	3,900	—

KM# 157 THALER

Silver **Obv:** Facing bust with longer, curlier hair **Obv. Legend:** ... POST: ADMI: ARCHI = EP: MADGEB. **Rev:** Date in legend **Note:** Dav. #5504.

Date	Mintage	VG	F	VF	XF	Unc
1669 HHF	—	1,150	2,300	4,300	7,800	—

KM# 158 THALER

Silver **Obv:** Bust right **Obv. Legend:** ARCHI-EP **Note:** Dav. #5505.

Date	Mintage	VG	F	VF	XF	Unc
1669 HHF	—	1,750	3,450	6,300	9,800	—

KM# 159 THALER

Silver **Rev. Legend:** ...I.C.E.M. **Note:** Dav. #5505A.

Date	Mintage	VG	F	VF	XF	Unc
1669 HHF	—	1,750	3,450	6,300	9,800	—

KM# 177 THALER

Silver **Obv:** Larger bust right **Obv. Legend:** D. G. AUGUSTUS... **Note:** Dav. #5506.

Date	Mintage	VG	F	VF	XF	Unc
1677 HHF-SM	—	1,750	3,450	6,300	9,800	—

KM# 178 THALER

Silver **Obv:** Different harnessed bust **Note:** Dav. #5507.

Date	Mintage	VG	F	VF	XF	Unc
1677 HHF-SM	—	1,750	3,450	6,300	9,800	—

KM# 6 2 THALER

Silver **Note:** Cathedral Chapter issue. Similar to 1 Thaler, KM#5. Dav. #5470.

Date	Mintage	VG	F	VF	XF	Unc
1603 GM Rare	—	—	—	—	—	—
1606 GM Rare	—	—	—	—	—	—

KM# 10 2 THALER

Silver **Obv:** Bust right **Rev:** Helmeted arms with divided date above and G M below **Note:** Archepiscopal issue. Dav. #5472.

Date	Mintage	VG	F	VF	XF	Unc
1609 GM Rare	—	—	—	—	—	—

KM# 40 2 THALER

Silver **Obv:** Half-figure facing with head right, date above **Rev:** St. Moritz standing with standard and shield, Cathedral at left **Note:** Dav. #5481.

Date	Mintage	VG	F	VF	XF	Unc
1614 (b)-IH Rare	—	—	—	—	—	—

KM# 101 2 THALER

Silver **Ruler:** Christian Wilhelm **Obv. Legend:** CHRIS * WILH * ... **Rev:** Shield separating A-K, dte in legend **Note:** Similar to 1 Thaler, KM#97. Dav. #5489.

Date	Mintage	VG	F	VF	XF	Unc
1625 AK Rare	—	—	—	—	—	—

KM# 124 2 THALER

Silver **Obv:** Eleven-line inscription **Rev:** Saint standing with banner, sword, and shield **Note:** Dav. #A5497.

Date	Mintage	VG	F	VF	XF	Unc
1638 PS(c) Rare	—	—	—	—	—	—

KM# 122 2 THALER

Silver **Note:** Similar to 1 Thaler, KM#110 but date divided 16-38-PXS. Dav. #5494B.

Date	Mintage	VG	F	VF	XF	Unc
1638 PS(c) Rare	—	—	—	—	—	—

KM# 123 2 THALER
Silver **Subject:** Enthronement of August von Sachsen-Weissenfels **Note:** Similar to 1 Thaler, KM#115. Dav. #A5496.

Date	Mintage	VG	F	VF	XF	Unc
1638 PS(c) Rare	—	—	—	—	—	—

KM# 121 2 THALER
Silver **Note:** Cathedral Chapter issue. Similar to 1 Thaler, KM#110 but with date divided 16-P X S-38. Dav. #5494A.

Date	Mintage	VG	F	VF	XF	Unc
1638 PS(c) Rare	—	—	—	—	—	—

KM# 134 2 THALER
Silver **Obv:** Facing bust **Rev:** Helmeted arms **Note:** Dav. #5501.

Date	Mintage	VG	F	VF	XF	Unc
1640 PS(c) Rare	—	—	—	—	—	—

TRADE COINAGE

KM# 46 1/2 GOLDGULDEN
1.7500 g., 0.9860 Gold 0.0555 oz. AGW **Obv:** Bust of Christian Wilhelm right in inner circle **Rev:** Arms in inner circle

Date	Mintage	VG	F	VF	XF	Unc
ND(1613)	—	575	1,350	3,500	6,500	—

KM# 47 GOLDGULDEN
3.5000 g., 0.9860 Gold 0.1109 oz. AGW **Obv:** Bust of Christian Wilhelm right in inner circle **Rev:** Arms in inner circle

Date	Mintage	VG	F	VF	XF	Unc
ND(1613) (b)	—	—	—	—	—	—
1615	—	800	1,950	4,600	9,500	—
(16)23	—	800	1,950	4,600	9,500	—
ND	282	800	1,950	4,600	9,500	—

KM# 61 GOLDGULDEN
3.5000 g., 0.9860 Gold 0.1109 oz. AGW **Note:** Hexagonal klippe.

Date	Mintage	VG	F	VF	XF	Unc
ND(1613) (b) Rare	—	—	—	—	—	—

KM# 48 2 GOLDGULDEN
7.0000 g., 0.9860 Gold 0.2219 oz. AGW **Obv:** Bust of Christian Wilhelm right in inner circle **Rev:** Three vertical shields in circle of fourteen shields

Date	Mintage	VG	F	VF	XF	Unc
ND (b) Rare	—	—	—	—	—	—

KM# 125 DUCAT
3.5000 g., 0.9860 Gold 0.1109 oz. AGW **Obv:** Oval arms topped by helmet dividing date, in inner circle **Rev:** St. Maurice standing with banner, sword, and shield in inner circle **Note:** Cathedral Chapter issue.

Date	Mintage	VG	F	VF	XF	Unc
1638 PS(c)	—	350	775	1,550	2,750	—

KM# 126 DUCAT
3.5000 g., 0.9860 Gold 0.1109 oz. AGW **Subject:** Enthronement of Archbishop August **Obv:** Nine-line inscription with date **Rev:** St. Moritz

Date	Mintage	VG	F	VF	XF	Unc
1638	—	400	875	1,750	3,500	—

KM# 135 DUCAT
3.5000 g., 0.9860 Gold 0.1109 oz. AGW **Ruler:** August **Obv:** August

Date	Mintage	VG	F	VF	XF	Unc
1640 PS	—	475	1,000	2,150	4,000	—
1641 PS	—	475	1,000	2,150	4,000	—

CITY

The city of Magdeburg encompassed the seat of the archbishopric. The town received the mint right in 1479 but had already been striking local coinage in the previous century. Magdeburg was besieged in 1550-1551 and again in 1629, during the Thirty Years' War, leading to interesting obsidional coinages. In 1631 the imperial forces under Tilly burned Magdeburg to the ground causing the deaths of 30,000 inhabitants, an act which shocked all of Europe. The city was rebuilt in 1638 and was absorbed by Brandenburg in 1680. The last city coinage is dated 1682. Magdeburg became a mint for Brandenburg-Prussia (q.v.) beginning in 1683. The city was taken by the French in 1806 and reverted to Prussia in 1814.

MINT OFFICIALS' INITIALS

Initial	Date	Name
(a)= [mark] or [mark]	1571-1606	Konrad Hundt
HS	1614-26	Henning Schreiber in Halberstadt
(b)= [mark] or [mark] and/or HM	1616-18	Heinrich Meyer
PS	1622-39	Peter Schrader
IL	1664-75	Johann Liebmann, warden in Berlin
HPK	1661-63	Hans Philipp Koburger
EFS	1669-70	Ernst Friedrich Schneider
CP	1672-78, 82-83	Christoph Pflug
IE	1673, 78-80	Johann Elers

ARMS

City gate, usually with two towers, maiden holding wreath above gate; sometimes just maiden with wreath.

REFERENCES

S = Friedrich Freiherrn von Schrötter, ***Beschreibung der Neuzeitlichen Münzen des Erzstifts und der Stadt Magdeburg 1400-1682***. Magdeburg, 1909.

Saur = Hugo Frhr. Von Saurma-Jelsch, ***Die Saurmasche Münzsammlung deutscher, schweizerischer und polnischer Gepräge von etwa dem Beginn der Groschenzeit bis zur Kipperperiode***. Berlin, 1892.

REGULAR COINAGE

KM# 230 PFENNIG
Copper **Obv:** City arms, date below **Note:** Kipper Pfennig. Uniface. Varieties exist.

Date	Mintage	VG	F	VF	XF	Unc
16Z1	—	7.00	13.00	27.00	55.00	—

KM# 265 PFENNIG
Silver **Obv:** City arms, date divided above **Note:** Uniface.

Date	Mintage	VG	F	VF	XF	Unc
1630	—	7.00	15.00	30.00	60.00	—

KM# 266 PFENNIG
Silver **Obv:** City arms divide date **Note:** Uniface.

Date	Mintage	VG	F	VF	XF	Unc
(16)30	—	7.00	15.00	30.00	60.00	—

KM# 318 PFENNIG
Silver **Obv:** City arms **Rev. Inscription:** 1 / PFENG / date / mintmaster's initials

Date	Mintage	VG	F	VF	XF	Unc
1675 CP	—	6.00	12.00	25.00	55.00	—

KM# 212 3 PFENNIG (Dreier)
Silver **Obv:** City arms **Rev:** Imperial orb with 3 divides date **Note:** Varieties exist.

Date	Mintage	VG	F	VF	XF	Unc
1617 (b)	—	16.00	33.00	65.00	130	—

KM# 236 3 PFENNIG (Dreier)
Silver **Obv:** City arms in oval baroque frame **Rev:** Imperial orb with 3 divides date within ornamented rhombus **Note:** Varieties exist.

Date	Mintage	VG	F	VF	XF	Unc
16ZZ	—	16.00	30.00	55.00	110	—

KM# 239 3 PFENNIG (Dreier)
Silver **Obv:** Without M below arms **Note:** Varieties exist.

Date	Mintage	VG	F	VF	XF	Unc
16ZZ	—	13.00	27.00	55.00	110	—
16Z3	—	13.00	27.00	55.00	110	—
16Z3 PS	—	13.00	27.00	55.00	110	—
1670	—	13.00	27.00	55.00	110	—
1670 EFS	—	13.00	27.00	55.00	110	—
1673 CP	—	13.00	27.00	55.00	110	—
1674 CP	—	13.00	27.00	55.00	110	—
1675 CP	—	13.00	27.00	55.00	110	—
1676 CP	—	13.00	27.00	55.00	110	—
1677	—	13.00	27.00	55.00	110	—
1679 IE	—	13.00	27.00	55.00	110	—
1680 IE	—	13.00	27.00	55.00	110	—

KM# 237 3 PFENNIG (Dreier)
Silver **Rev:** Larger orb without rhombus divides date

Date	Mintage	VG	F	VF	XF	Unc
16ZZ	—	16.00	30.00	55.00	110	—

KM# 238 3 PFENNIG (Dreier)
Silver **Obv:** City arms, M below, all in circle **Rev:** Imperial orb with 3 divides date

Date	Mintage	VG	F	VF	XF	Unc
16ZZ	—	16.00	30.00	50.00	100	—

KM# 232 4 GROSCHEN
(12 Kreuzer - Schreckenberger)
Silver **Obv:** City arms, date above **Rev:** Crowned imperial eagle, 4 in orb on breast, titles of Ferdinand II **Note:** Kipper 4 Groschen. Varieties exist.

Date	Mintage	VG	F	VF	XF	Unc
16Z1	—	55.00	90.00	180	360	—

KM# 331 4 GROSCHEN
(12 Kreuzer - Schreckenberger)
Silver **Obv:** City arms **Rev. Legend:** VERBUM DOMINI... **Rev. Inscription:** IIII / GUTE / GROSCHEN / date / mintmaster's initials **Note:** Gute 4 Groschen.

Date	Mintage	VG	F	VF	XF	Unc
1682 CP	—	—	—	—	—	—

KM# 206 1/24 THALER (Groschen)
Silver **Obv:** City arms **Obv. Legend:** MO. NO. CI. MAGDEBVR. **Rev:** Imperial orb with Z4 divides date, titles of Rudolf II **Note:** Varieties exist. Weight varies: 2.2-2.4 grams.

Date	Mintage	VG	F	VF	XF	Unc
1601 (a)	—	16.00	35.00	75.00	155	—
1606 (a)	—	16.00	35.00	75.00	155	—

KM# 210 1/24 THALER (Groschen)
Silver **Obv:** Crowned city arms, titles of Matthias, date divided in legend at top **Note:** Weight varies: 2.2-2.4 grams.

Date	Mintage	VG	F	VF	XF	Unc
1616 (b)	—	13.00	30.00	65.00	130	—

KM# 211 1/24 THALER (Groschen)
Silver **Obv:** Without crown above arms **Note:** Varieites exist. Weight varies: 2.2-2.4 grams.

Date	Mintage	VG	F	VF	XF	Unc
1616 (b)	—	13.00	30.00	65.00	130	—
1617 (b)	—	13.00	30.00	65.00	130	—
1617	—	13.00	30.00	65.00	130	—
1618	—	13.00	30.00	65.00	130	—

KM# 225 1/24 THALER (Groschen)
Silver **Note:** Kipper 1/24 Thaler. Struck on smaller flan. Weight varies: 0.45-1.24 grams.

Date	Mintage	VG	F	VF	XF	Unc
1619	—	25.00	35.00	65.00	130	—

KM# 226 1/24 THALER (Groschen)
4.8100 g., Silver **Note:** Klippe.

Date	Mintage	VG	F	VF	XF	Unc
1619	—	33.00	60.00	120	240	—

KM# 233 1/24 THALER (Groschen)
Silver **Obv:** Titles of Ferdinand II **Note:** Varieties exist.

Date	Mintage	VG	F	VF	XF	Unc
16Z1	—	25.00	40.00	65.00	130	—

KM# 234 1/24 THALER (Groschen)
Silver **Obv:** Date above arms **Note:** Varieties exist.

Date	Mintage	VG	F	VF	XF	Unc
16Z1	—	25.00	40.00	65.00	130	—

KM# 240 1/24 THALER (Groschen)
Silver **Obv:** Date divided by cross on orb **Note:** Varieties exist. Weight varies: 1.90-2.30 grams.

Date	Mintage	VG	F	VF	XF	Unc
16ZZ	—	20.00	33.00	65.00	130	—

KM# 253 1/24 THALER (Groschen)
Silver **Obv:** City arms **Rev:** Date divided in legend at top **Note:** Varieties exist.

Date	Mintage	VG	F	VF	XF	Unc
16Z3 PS	—	20.00	33.00	65.00	130	—
16Z4 PS	—	20.00	33.00	65.00	130	—
16Z6 PS	—	20.00	33.00	65.00	130	—
1630 PS	—	20.00	33.00	65.00	130	—
1631 PS	—	20.00	33.00	65.00	130	—

KM# 254 1/24 THALER (Groschen)
Silver **Obv:** Date divided above arms **Note:** Varieties exist.

Date	Mintage	VG	F	VF	XF	Unc
16Z3 PS	—	20.00	33.00	65.00	130	—

KM# 261 1/24 THALER (Groschen)
Billon **Obv:** City arms **Rev:** Rose in circle, date **Rev. Legend:** NECESSI(TAS): CARET. LEGE **Note:** Weight varies: 0.75-1.20 grams.

Date	Mintage	VG	F	VF	XF	Unc
16Z9	—	20.00	33.00	65.00	130	—

Note: These siege coins are often found with a rose countermark

KM# 280 1/24 THALER (Groschen)
Silver **Obv:** City arms **Rev:** Imperial orb with 24, titles of Leopold I and date in legend **Rev. Legend:** MO. NO...

Date	Mintage	VG	F	VF	XF	Unc
1661 HPK	—	20.00	33.00	65.00	130	—

KM# 286 1/24 THALER (Groschen)
Silver **Obv:** City arms **Obv. Legend:** MAG DE BURGER **Rev. Legend:** STAD-GELD **Rev. Inscription:** 23 / 1 R: / THALER / date

Date	Mintage	VG	F	VF	XF	Unc
1668 IL	—	20.00	33.00	65.00	130	—

KM# 287 1/24 THALER (Groschen)
Silver **Obv:** City arms **Rev. Inscription:** 24 / EINEN / REICHS / THALER / date

Date	Mintage	VG	F	VF	XF	Unc
1669	—	20.00	33.00	65.00	130	—

KM# 288 1/24 THALER (Groschen)
Silver **Rev:** Border of flowers and arches

Date	Mintage	VG	F	VF	XF	Unc
1669	—	15.00	33.00	65.00	130	—

KM# 289 1/24 THALER (Groschen)
Silver **Rev:** Imperial orb wtih 24 divides date, border of flowers and arches **Note:** Varieties exist.

Date	Mintage	VG	F	VF	XF	Unc
1669	—	20.00	33.00	65.00	130	—
1670 EFS	—	20.00	33.00	65.00	130	—

KM# 296 1/24 THALER (Groschen)
Silver **Rev:** Imperial orb with 24 divides date in circle, border of laurel leaves **Note:** Varieties exist.

Date	Mintage	VG	F	VF	XF	Unc
1670 EFS	—	20.00	33.00	65.00	130	—

KM# 298 1/24 THALER (Groschen)
Silver **Rev:** Imperial orb with 24 divides mintmaster's initials left and date right **Rev. Legend:** VERB. DOM. MANET. IN. AETERN. **Note:** Varieties exist.

Date	Mintage	VG	F	VF	XF	Unc
1670 EFS	—	20.00	33.00	65.00	130	—

KM# 299 1/24 THALER (Groschen)
Silver **Rev:** Date and mintmaster's initials divided by orb **Note:** Varieties exist.

Date	Mintage	VG	F	VF	XF	Unc
1670 EFS	—	20.00	33.00	65.00	130	—
1672 CP	—	20.00	33.00	65.00	130	—
1673 CP	—	20.00	33.00	65.00	130	—
1674 CP	—	20.00	33.00	65.00	130	—
1675 CP	—	20.00	33.00	65.00	130	—
1676 CP	—	20.00	33.00	65.00	130	—
1679 IE	—	20.00	33.00	65.00	130	—
1680 IE	—	20.00	33.00	65.00	130	—

KM# 295 1/24 THALER (Groschen)
Silver **Rev:** Orb divides mintmaster's initials left and date right

Date	Mintage	VG	F	VF	XF	Unc
1670 EFS	—	20.00	33.00	65.00	130	—

KM# 297 1/24 THALER (Groschen)
Silver **Rev:** Date and mintmaster's initials divided ".E.F. 16-70. S." in circle around orb

Date	Mintage	VG	F	VF	XF	Unc
1670 EFS	—	20.00	33.00	65.00	130	—

KM# 323 1/24 THALER (Groschen)
Silver **Obv:** City arms in oval baroque frame

Date	Mintage	VG	F	VF	XF	Unc
1677 CP	—	20.00	33.00	65.00	130	—

KM# 334 1/24 THALER (Groschen)
Silver **Obv:** City arms, MO. NO... in half circle above **Rev. Legend:** VERB. DOM... **Rev. Inscription:** 24 / EINEN / REICHS / THAL / date

Date	Mintage	VG	F	VF	XF	Unc
1682 CP	—	20.00	33.00	65.00	130	—

KM# 235 1/16 THALER (Doppelschilling)
Silver **Obv:** Intertwined DS, date above **Obv. Legend:** MO. NO... **Rev:** Crowned imperial eagle, blank orb on breast, titles of Ferdinand II **Note:** Kipper 1/16 Thaler.

Date	Mintage	VG	F	VF	XF	Unc
16Z1	—	—	—	—	—	—

KM# 256 1/2 ORT (1/8 Thaler)
Silver **Obv:** City arms **Obv. Legend:** MO. NO. CI... **Rev:** Date divided by small orb at top, titles of Ferdinand II **Rev. Inscription:** EIN / HALB / REICHS / ORT **Note:** Varieties exist.

Date	Mintage	VG	F	VF	XF	Unc
16Z4 PS	—	—	—	—	—	—

KM# 302 1/6 THALER
Silver **Obv:** City arms **Rev:** Inscription between laurel and palm branches, date divided by orb at top **Rev. Legend:** VERBUM. DOMINI... **Rev. Inscription:** VI / EINEN / REICHS / THALER / mintmaster's initials

Date	Mintage	VG	F	VF	XF	Unc
1672 CP	—	—	—	—	—	—

KM# 231 12 KREUZER
(4 Groschen - Schreckenberger)
Silver **Obv:** City arms, date above **Rev:** Crowned imperial eagle, 1Z in orb on breast, titles of Ferdinand II **Note:** Kipper 12 Kreuzer. Varieties exist.

Date	Mintage	VG	F	VF	XF	Unc
16Z1	—	40.00	65.00	100	210	—

KM# 249 6 GROSCHEN (Ort - 1/4 Thaler)
Silver **Obv:** Helmeted city arms in shield **Rev:** Crowned imperial eagle, 6 in orb on breast, titles of Ferdinand II, date divided at top **Rev. Legend:** MO. NO. CIVI...

Date	Mintage	VG	F	VF	XF	Unc
16Z3 PS	—	115	220	400	800	—

KM# 250 6 GROSCHEN (Ort - 1/4 Thaler)
Silver **Obv:** City arms **Rev:** Value in circle on breast of double-headed imperial eagle, crown above **Note:** Varieties exist.

Date	Mintage	VG	F	VF	XF	Unc
16Z3 PS	—	90.00	185	375	750	—
16Z4 PS	—	90.00	185	375	750	—

KM# 259 6 GROSCHEN (Ort - 1/4 Thaler)
Silver **Obv:** City arms **Rev. Legend:** NECESSITAS. LEGEM. NON. HABET. **Rev. Inscription:** VI / GROSCHEN / MAGDEBVR: / STATGELT / date

Date	Mintage	VG	F	VF	XF	Unc
16Z9	—	100	200	375	775	—

Note: The above are often found with a rose countermark

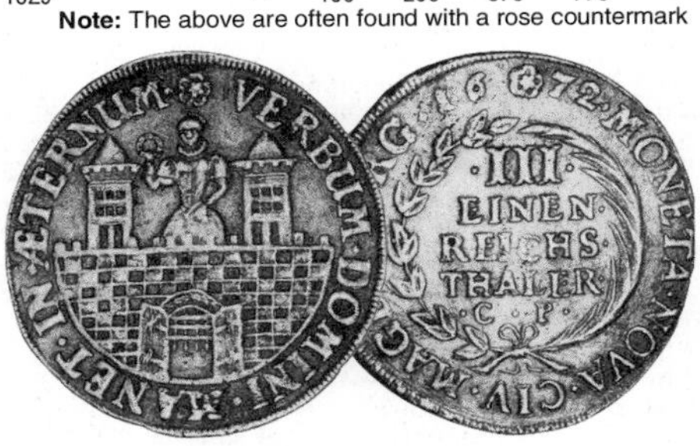

KM# 300 1/3 THALER (1/2 Gulden)
Silver **Note:** Varieties exist.

Date	Mintage	VG	F	VF	XF	Unc
1670 EFS	—	80.00	140	210	425	—
1671	—	80.00	140	210	425	—
1672 CP	—	80.00	140	210	425	—
1673 CP	—	80.00	140	210	425	—
1674 CP	—	80.00	140	210	425	—

KM# 314 1/3 THALER (1/2 Gulden)
Silver **Obv:** Value 1/3 in oval baroque frame within oak and palm branches, date at top **Rev:** City arms

Date	Mintage	VG	F	VF	XF	Unc
1674 CP	—	85.00	160	260	525	—

KM# 319 1/3 THALER (1/2 Gulden)
Silver **Obv:** City view from river, "Jehovah" in rayed oval above **Rev:** Helmeted four-fold arms, date in legend

Date	Mintage	VG	F	VF	XF	Unc
1675 CP	—	—	—	—	—	—

KM# 332 8 GUTE GROSCHEN
Silver **Obv:** City arms **Rev. Legend:** VERBUM DOMINI... **Rev. Inscription:** VIII / GUTE / GROSCHEN / date, mintmaster's initials

Date	Mintage	VG	F	VF	XF	Unc
1682 CP	—	—	—	—	—	—

KM# 213 12 GROSCHEN (1/2 Thaler)
Silver **Obv:** City arms, date above **Rev:** Crowned imperial eagle, 1Z in orb on breast, titles of Matthias

Date	Mintage	VG	F	VF	XF	Unc
1617 HM	—	—	—	—	—	—

KM# 251 12 GROSCHEN (1/2 Thaler)
Silver **Obv:** Helmeted city arms in shield **Rev:** Date divided by crown at top, titles of Ferdinand II

Date	Mintage	VG	F	VF	XF	Unc
16Z3 PS	—	300	500	950	1,800	—

KM# 252 12 GROSCHEN (1/2 Thaler)
Silver **Obv:** Plain city arms **Rev:** Value in circle on breast of double-headed imperial eagle, crown above **Note:** Varieties exist.

Date	Mintage	VG	F	VF	XF	Unc
16Z3 PS	—	225	400	775	1,550	—
16Z4 PS	—	225	400	775	1,550	—
16Z5 PS	—	225	400	775	1,550	—
16Z7 PS	—	225	400	775	1,550	—
1630 PS	—	225	400	775	1,550	—

KM# 260 12 GROSCHEN (1/2 Thaler)
Silver **Obv:** City arms **Rev. Legend:** NECESSITAS. LEGEM. NON. HABET. **Rev. Inscription:** XII / GROSCHEN / MAGDEBVR: / STATGELT / date **Note:** Varieties exist.

Date	Mintage	VG	F	VF	XF	Unc
16Z9	—	135	275	550	1,150	—

KM# 214 1/2 THALER (12 Groschen)
Silver **Subject:** Centennial of the Protestant Reformation **Note:** Similar to 1 Thaler, KM#215.

Date	Mintage	VG	F	VF	XF	Unc
1617	—	135	225	400	675	—

KM# 273 1/2 THALER (12 Groschen)
Silver **Obv:** City arms, date in legend **Rev:** Crowned imperial eagle, bust of emperor in oval on breast, titles of Ferdinand III

Date	Mintage	VG	F	VF	XF	Unc
1639	—	—	—	—	—	—

KM# 324 1/2 THALER (12 Groschen)
Silver **Obv:** City view from river, "Jehovah" in rayed oval above **Rev:** Helmeted four-fold arms, date in legend

Date	Mintage	VG	F	VF	XF	Unc
1678 IE	—	—	—	—	—	—

KM# 301 16 GUTE GROSCHEN
Silver **Obv:** City arms in oval baroque frame **Rev:** Inscription in laurel and palm wreath **Rev. Inscription:** XVI / GUTE / GROSCHEN / date

Date	Mintage	VG	F	VF	XF	Unc
1672 CP	—	400	675	1,200	2,100	—
1673 CP	—	400	675	1,200	2,100	—

KM# 306 16 GUTE GROSCHEN
Silver **Rev:** GROSCH:... **Note:** Varieties exist.

Date	Mintage	VG	F	VF	XF	Unc
1673 CP	—	400	675	1,200	2,100	—
1674 CP	—	400	675	1,200	2,100	—

KM# 313 16 GUTE GROSCHEN
Silver **Obv:** Round arms in floral ring **Obv. Legend:** MONETA. NOVA...

Date	Mintage	VG	F	VF	XF	Unc
1674 CP	—	400	675	1,200	2,100	—

KM# 333 16 GUTE GROSCHEN
Silver **Obv:** City arms **Rev. Legend:** VERBUM DOMINI... **Rev. Inscription:** XVI / GUTE / GROSCHEN / date / mintmaster's initials **Note:** Varieties exist.

Date	Mintage	VG	F	VF	XF	Unc
1682 CP	—	135	275	525	1,050	—

KM# 303 2/3 THALER (Gulden)
Silver **Obv:** Helmeted four-fold arms **Obv. Legend:** MONETA. NOVA... **Rev:** Inscription divided by 2/3, all in laurel and palm wreath **Rev. Inscription:** VERBUM / DOMINI / MANET.IN. / AETERNUM / date **Note:** Varieties exist.

Date	Mintage	VG	F	VF	XF	Unc
1672 CP	—	—	—	—	—	—

KM# 304 2/3 THALER (Gulden)
Silver **Obv:** City arms in oval baroque frame **Note:** Varieties exist.

Date	Mintage	VG	F	VF	XF	Unc
1672 CP	—	—	—	—	—	—

KM# 305 2/3 THALER (Gulden)
Silver **Obv:** City arms **Rev:** Inscription divided by 2/3, in laurel and palm wreath **Rev. Inscription:** VERBUM / DOMINI / MANET.IN. / AETERNUM / date

Date	Mintage	VG	F	VF	XF	Unc
1672 CP	—	—	—	—	—	—

KM# 316 2/3 THALER (Gulden)
Silver **Obv:** City arms in oval baroque frame **Rev:** Inscription divided by 2/3, in laurel and palm wreath **Rev. Inscription:** VERBUM / DOMINI / MANET.IN. / AETERNUM / date

Date	Mintage	VG	F	VF	XF	Unc
1674 CP	—	65.00	125	235	475	—

KM# 317.2 2/3 THALER (Gulden)
Silver, 34 mm. **Obv:** City arms with lower part in half circle, date divided by rosette above. **Obv. Legend:** MONETA. NOV. CIV. MAGDEBURG **Rev:** 4-line inscription, value '2/3' in oval below, laurel and palm branches in margin **Rev. Inscription:** VERV / DOMINI / MAET. IN /ÆTERN

Date	Mintage	VG	F	VF	XF	Unc
1674 cp	—	45.00	90.00	180	360	—

KM# 315 2/3 THALER (Gulden)
Silver **Note:** Varieties exist.

Date	Mintage	VG	F	VF	XF	Unc
1674 CP	—	65.00	125	200	425	—
1675 CP	—	65.00	125	200	425	—

KM# 317.1 2/3 THALER (Gulden)
Silver **Obv:** City arms in circle, date divided by rosette at top **Obv. Legend:** MONETA. NOV: CIV. MAGDEBURG **Rev:** 4-line inscription, value '2/3' in oval below, border of laurel and palm branches **Rev. Inscription:** VERB. / DOMINI / MANET. IN / ÆTERN **Note:** Varieties exist.

Date	Mintage	VG	F	VF	XF	Unc
1674 CP	—	45.00	90.00	180	360	—

KM# 320 2/3 THALER (Gulden)
Silver **Note:** Varieties exist.

Date	Mintage	VG	F	VF	XF	Unc
1675 CP	—	45.00	90.00	180	360	—

KM# 321 2/3 THALER (Gulden)
Silver **Obv:** Date complete in obverse legend **Note:** Varieties exist.

Date	Mintage	VG	F	VF	XF	Unc
1675 CP	—	55.00	100	190	385	—
1676 CP	—	55.00	100	190	385	—

KM# 325 2/3 THALER (Gulden)
Silver **Obv:** City arms, date divided at top **Rev:** Similar to KM#320

Date	Mintage	VG	F	VF	XF	Unc
1678 CP	—	55.00	100	190	385	—

KM# 208 THALER (24 Groschen)
Silver **Obv:** Young lady above city gate **Rev:** Crowned imperial ealge with 24 in orb on breast, date above **Note:** Dav. #5508.

Date	Mintage	VG	F	VF	XF	Unc
1603 (a) Rare	—	—	—	—	—	—

KM# 216 THALER (24 Groschen)
Silver **Note:** Dav. #5509A. Klippe.

Date	Mintage	VG	F	VF	XF	Unc
1617 HM Rare	—	—	—	—	—	—

KM# 217 THALER (24 Groschen)
Silver **Obv:** Young lady above city gate, date above **Obv. Legend:** MATTHIAS: II: D: G: ROM: IMP: SEM: AV: **Rev:** Crowned imperial eagle, H-M below **Rev. Legend:** MONETA: NO: CI: MAGDEBVRGK **Note:** Dav. #5510.

Date	Mintage	VG	F	VF	XF	Unc
1617 HM	—	600	1,400	3,050	6,000	—

KM# 218 THALER (24 Groschen)
Silver **Obv. Legend:** MATTHI-II-D-G-RO-IMP-SEM-A **Rev. Legend:** MO NO. AVR. CI. MAGDEBVR **Note:** Dav. #5511.

Date	Mintage	VG	F	VF	XF	Unc
1617	—	600	1,400	3,050	6,000	—

KM# 215 THALER (24 Groschen)
Silver **Subject:** 100th Anniversary of the Reformation **Obv:** Crowned imperial eagle with arms on breast **Rev:** Half busts of Huss and Luther within double legend **Note:** Dav. #5509. Varieties exist.

Date	Mintage	VG	F	VF	XF	Unc
1617	—	650	1,300	2,400	5,200	—
1617 HM	—	—	—	—	—	—

KM# 221 THALER (24 Groschen)
Silver **Obv. Legend:** MATHI. D. G. ROM. -IMP. SEMP. AVGVS. **Rev:** Legend, date **Rev. Legend:** MON * NOVA * CIVITAT * MAGDEBVRCK **Note:** Dav. #5512.

Date	Mintage	VG	F	VF	XF	Unc
1618	—	600	1,400	3,050	6,000	—

KM# 222 THALER (24 Groschen)
28.5300 g., Silver **Subject:** Founding of the City **Obv:** Emperor Otto I (936-73) on horseback to right, date in exergue **Rev:** Crowned imperial eagle, 4-fold arms on breast **Note:** Dav. #5514.

Date	Mintage	VG	F	VF	XF	Unc
1618 Rare	—	—	—	—	—	—

KM# 241 THALER (24 Groschen)
Silver **Obv:** Emperor riding galloping horse right, date divided below **Rev:** Wagon pulled left towards city by two doves and two swans with standing Venus and the Three Graces, four-line inscription in tablet below divides date

Date	Mintage	VG	F	VF	XF	Unc
16ZZ HS	—	1,700	3,050	4,500	10,000	—

KM# 242 THALER (24 Groschen)
Silver **Obv:** Emperor Otto I and Empress Edith enthroned, imperial eagle in shield centered above, four-line inscription with foundation date 938 below **Rev:** City view, arms above in band MAGDA-BVRG, divide Roman numeral date, three-line inscription in cartouche below

Date	Mintage	VG	F	VF	XF	Unc
16ZZ PS Rare	—	—	—	—	—	—

KM# 255 THALER (24 Groschen)
Silver **Obv:** Large city arms, towers break circle at upper left and right **Rev:** Crowned imperial eagle, 'Z4' in orb on breast, date divided by crown at top, mintmaster's initials divided to left and right of eagle's claws **Rev. Legend:** FERDINAND II - D:G: RO: IM. S.A **Note:** Dav. #5516. Varieties exist.

Date	Mintage	VG	F	VF	XF	Unc
16Z3 PS	—	125	250	750	1,650	—
16Z4 PS	—	125	250	750	1,650	—
16Z5 PS	—	125	250	750	1,650	—
16Z6 PS	—	125	250	750	1,650	—
16Z7 PS	—	125	250	750	1,650	—
16Z8 PS	—	125	250	750	1,650	—
16Z9 PS	—	125	250	750	1,650	—
1630 PS	—	125	250	750	1,650	—

KM# A255 THALER (24 Groschen)

Silver, 41.5 mm. **Rev:** Mintmaster's initials divided by eagles' necks to left and right.

Date	Mintage	VG	F	VF	XF	Unc
1630 PS	—	125	250	750	1,650	—

KM# 267 THALER (24 Groschen)

Silver **Subject:** Rebuilding the City **Obv:** Maiden above helmeted arms **Rev:** Crowned imperial eagle with Emperor's bust, legend in straight lines around **Note:** Dav. #5518.

Date	Mintage	VG	F	VF	XF	Unc
1638 PS	—	350	650	1,350	2,250	—

KM# 268 THALER (24 Groschen)

Silver **Subject:** Reconstruction of the City, 1638-1642 **Obv:** Maiden facing, flanked by towers **Rev:** Oval shield on breast of double-headed imperial eagle **Note:** Dav. #5520.

Date	Mintage	VG	F	VF	XF	Unc
1638 PS	—	250	550	1,200	2,250	—

KM# 282 THALER (24 Groschen)

Silver **Rev:** Helmeted arms with girl above dividing date **Note:** Dav. #5521.

Date	Mintage	VG	F	VF	XF	Unc
1661 HPK	—	1,750	3,250	6,000	10,000	—

KM# 283 THALER (24 Groschen)

Silver **Rev:** Girl above city gate dividing date **Note:** Dav. #5523.

Date	Mintage	VG	F	VF	XF	Unc
1661 HPK	—	1,750	3,250	6,000	10,000	—

KM# 285 THALER (24 Groschen)

Silver **Rev. Legend:** MONETA: ARGENTEA: CIVITATIS. MAGDEBVRG **Note:** Dav. #5524.

Date	Mintage	VG	F	VF	XF	Unc
1662 HPK	—	1,750	3,250	6,000	10,000	—

KM# 307 THALER (24 Groschen)

Silver **Obv:** "Jehovah" in Hebrew above city view **Note:** Dav. #5526.

Date	Mintage	VG	F	VF	XF	Unc
1673 CP	—	1,500	3,000	5,000	9,000	—

KM# 308 THALER (24 Groschen)

Silver **Obv. Legend:** MON. NO. CIV. MAGDEB. **Note:** Dav. #5527.

Date	Mintage	VG	F	VF	XF	Unc
1673 CP	—	1,200	2,200	4,000	6,500	—

KM# 326 THALER (24 Groschen)

Silver **Rev:** Girl breaks legend at top and divides date **Note:** Dav. #5528.

Date	Mintage	VG	F	VF	XF	Unc
1678 IE	—	1,250	2,250	4,000	6,500	—
1680 IE	—	1,250	2,250	4,000	6,500	—

KM# 330 THALER (24 Groschen)

Silver **Rev:** Inner circle ends with legend **Note:** Dav. #5529.

Date	Mintage	VG	F	VF	XF	Unc
1680 IE	—	1,400	2,400	4,250	7,000	—

KM# 335 THALER (24 Groschen)

Silver **Subject:** Deliverance from the Plague **Obv:** City view, sun shining from clouds, inscription in band above **Rev:** Two maidens in landscape, Eye of God with rays in clouds above, inscription in band above, three-line inscription with date below

Date	Mintage	VG	F	VF	XF	Unc
168Z CP Rare	—	—	—	—	—	—

KM# 309 1-1/4 THALER

Silver **Note:** Dav. #A5525.

Date	Mintage	VG	F	VF	XF	Unc
1673 CP Rare	—	—	—	—	—	—

KM# 243 1-1/2 THALER

Silver **Subject:** Founding of the City by Emperor Otto I the Great **Obv:** Emperor riding galloping horse right, date divided below **Rev:** Wagon pulled left towards city by two doves and two swar with standing Venus and the Three Graces, four-line inscrir in tablet below divides date

Date	Mintage	VG	F	VF	XF	Unc
16ZZ HS Rare	—	—	—	—		

KM# 310 1-1/2 THALER

Silver **Note:** Similar to 1-1/4 Thaler, KM#309. ...525.

Date	Mintage	VG	F	VF	XF	Unc
1673 CP Rare	—	—	—		—	—

KM# 227 2 THALER

Silver **Subject:** Founding of the City **Obv:** Emperor Otto on horseback right **Rev:** Crowned double eagle with shield on breast **Note:** Dav. #5513.

Date	Mintage	VG	F	VF	XF	Unc
1618 Rare	—	—	—	—	—	—

KM# 245 2 THALER

Silver **Note:** Hexagonal klippe.

Date	Mintage	VG	F	VF	XF	Unc
16ZZ HS Rare	—	—	—	—	—	—

KM# 244 2 THALER

Silver **Obv:** Emperor riding galloping horse right, date divided below **Rev:** Wagon pulled left by two doves and two swans with standing Venus and the Three Graces, four-line inscription in tablet below divides date

Date	Mintage	VG	F	VF	XF	Unc
16ZZ HS Rare	—	—	—	—	—	—

KM# 257 2 THALER

Silver **Note:** Similar to 1 Thaler, KM#255. Dav. #5515.

Date	Mintage	VG	F	VF	XF	Unc
1624 PS Rare	—	—	—	—	—	—
1625 PS Rare	—	—	—	—	—	—

KM# 269 2 THALER

Silver **Subject:** Rebuilding of the City **Obv:** Crowned double eagle with Emperor's bust, legend in straight lines around **Rev:** Maiden above helmeted arms **Note:** Dav. #5517.

Date	Mintage	VG	F	VF	XF	Unc
1638 PS Rare	—	—	—	—	—	—

KM# 270 2 THALER

Silver **Subject:** Reconstruction of the City, 1638-1642 **Obv:** Maiden facing, flanked by towers **Rev:** Oval shield on breast of double-headed imperial eagle **Note:** Dav. #5519. Similar to 1 Thaler, KM#268.

Date	Mintage	VG	F	VF	XF	Unc
1638 PS Rare	—	—	—	—	—	—

KM# 284 2 THALER

Silver **Rev:** Girl above city gate dividing date **Note:** Dav. #5522.

Date	Mintage	VG	F	VF	XF	Unc
1661 HPK Rare	—	—	—	—	—	—

KM# 311 2 THALER

Silver **Note:** Dav. #5525. Similar to 1-1/4 Thaler, KM#309.

Date	Mintage	VG	F	VF	XF	Unc
1673 CP Rare	—	—	—	—	—	—

Note: Giessener Munzhandlung Auction 6 11-73 VF realized approximately $6,300

KM# 246 3 THALER

Silver **Subject:** Founding of the City by Emperor Otto I the Great **Obv:** Emperor riding galloping horse right, date divided below **Rev:** Wagon pulled left towards city by two doves and two swans with standing Venus and the Three Graces, four-line inscription in tablet divides date

Date	Mintage	VG	F	VF	XF	Unc
16ZZ HS Rare	—	—	—	—	—	—

TRADE COINAGE

KM# 207 GOLDGULDEN

3.5000 g., 0.9860 Gold 0.1109 oz. AGW **Obv:** Crowned imperial eagle in inner circle, titles of Rudolf II **Rev:** Young women above two-towered city gate in inner circle

Date	Mintage	VG	F	VF	XF	Unc
1605 (a)	—	650	1,200	2,650	4,750	—
1606 (a)	—	650	1,200	2,650	4,750	—

KM# 219 GOLDGULDEN

3.5000 g., 0.9860 Gold 0.1109 oz. AGW **Obv:** Titles of Matthias

Date	Mintage	VG	F	VF	XF	Unc
1617 (b)	—	1,050	2,250	4,750	8,900	—

KM# 220 GOLDGULDEN

3.5000 g., 0.9860 Gold 0.1109 oz. AGW **Obv:** Crowned imperial eagle in inner circle, titles of Matthias **Rev:** Arms topped by helmet in inner circle

Date	Mintage	VG	F	VF	XF	Unc
ND	—	800	1,700	3,600	6,600	—

KM# 247 GOLDGULDEN

3.5000 g., 0.9860 Gold 0.1109 oz. AGW **Obv:** Titles of Ferdinand II

Date	Mintage	VG	F	VF	XF	Unc
1622 PS	—	290	600	975	2,600	—
1624 PS	—	350	800	1,650	3,350	—

…258 GOLDGULDEN

…, 0.9860 Gold 0.1109 oz. AGW **Rev:** Titles of Ferdinand …arieties exist.

Date	Mintage	VG	F	VF	XF	Unc
16…	—	290	600	975	2,600	—
1627 …	—	290	600	975	2,600	—
1628 PS	—	290	600	975	2,600	—
1629 PS	—	290	600	975	2,600	—
1630 PS	—	290	600	975	2,600	—

KM# 271 DUCAT

3.5000 g., 0.9860 Gold 0.1109 oz. AGW **Subject:** Rebuilding of the City **Obv:** Crowned imperial eagle in inner circle **Rev:** Value and date in tablet

Date	Mintage	VG	F	VF	XF	Unc
1638 PS	—	425	875	1,700	3,500	—
1641 PS	—	425	875	1,700	3,500	—
1642 PS	—	425	875	1,700	3,500	—

KM# 312 DUCAT

3.5000 g., 0.9860 Gold 0.1109 oz. AGW **Rev:** Arms topped by helmet in inner circle

Date	Mintage	VG	F	VF	XF	Unc
1673 CP	—	850	2,000	4,250	8,500	—

KM# 274 2 DUCAT

7.0000 g., 0.9860 Gold 0.2219 oz. AGW **Obv:** Crowned imperial eagle in inner circle **Rev:** Young woman above two-towered city gate

Date	Mintage	VG	F	VF	XF	Unc
1639 Rare	—	—	—	—	—	—

KM# 322 2 DUCAT

7.0000 g., 0.9860 Gold 0.2219 oz. AGW **Obv:** View of Magdeburg **Rev:** Arms topped by helmet in inner circle

Date	Mintage	VG	F	VF	XF	Unc
1675 CP Rare	—	—	—	—	—	—

KM# A323 4 DUCAT

14.0000 g., 0.9860 Gold 0.4438 oz. AGW **Obv:** View of Magdeburg **Rev:** Arms topped by helmet

Date	Mintage	VG	F	VF	XF	Unc
1675 CP Rare	—	—	—	—	—	—

KM# 272 5 DUCAT (1/2 Portugaloser)

17.5000 g., 0.9860 Gold 0.5547 oz. AGW **Subject:** Rebuilding of the City **Obv:** Crowned imperial eagle with Emperor's bust, legend in straight lines around **Rev:** Maiden above helmeted arms

Date	Mintage	VG	F	VF	XF	Unc
1638 PS Rare	—	—	—	—	—	—

KM# 224 10 DUCAT (Portugaloser)

35.0000 g., 0.9860 Gold 1.1095 oz. AGW **Obv:** Crowned imperial eagle with shield on breast **Rev:** Emperor Otto on horseback right **Note:** Varieties exist.

Date	Mintage	VG	F	VF	XF	Unc
1618 (b)	—	—	—	14,500	20,000	—

KM# 248 10 DUCAT (Portugaloser)

35.0000 g., 0.9860 Gold 1.1095 oz. AGW **Subject:** Founding of the City by Emperor Otto I the Great **Obv:** Emperor riding galloping horse right, date divided below **Rev:** Wagon pulled left towards city by two doves and two swans with standing Venus and the Three Graces, four-line inscription in tablet below divides date

Date	Mintage	VG	F	VF	XF	Unc
16ZZ HS	—	—	—	12,000	17,500	—

PATTERNS

Including off metal strikes

KM#	Date	Mintage	Identification	Mkt Val
Pn1	ND(1623)	—	1/4 Thaler. Copper. Klippe.	—

TRIAL STRIKES

KM#	Date	Mintage	Identification	Mkt Val
TS1	1617	—	1/30 Thaler. Silver. Klippe. Imperial orb wtih 30, cross divides date.	—

MAINZ

Mainz, located on the Rhine 25 miles west of Frankfurt, became an archbishopric in 747. It was a residence and mint of Charlemagne, and the Imperial Mint established then functioned into the 11th century. The archbishops were recognized as presidents of the electoral college and arch-chancellors of the Empire by the Golden Bull of 1356. In 1797, Mainz was ceded to France and in 1801 the French annexed all of the territories on the left bank of the Rhine. The remaining lands were secularized in 1803 and portions were divided between Hesse-Darmstadt, Nassau and Prussia.

Mainz became a Free City of the Empire in 1118 but lost the title in 1163 through an unsuccessful revolt against ecclesiastical authority. The city obtained the mint right in 1420 but rarely availed itself of the privilege. It was occupied by Sweden from 1631 to 1635 during the 30 Years' War. Siege coins were struck in 1793 when the French garrison was besieged by the Prussians.

RULERS

Wolfgang von Dalberg, 1582-1601
Johann Adam von Bicken, 1601-1604
Johann Schweickhard von Kronberg, 1604-1626
Georg Friedrich von Greiffenklau zu Wollrath, 1626-1629
Anselm Casimir Wamboldt von Umstaedt, 1629-1647
Swedish, 1631-1635
Johann Philipp, Graf von Schönborn, 1647-1673
Lothar Friedrich, Freiherr von Metternich-Burscheid, 1673-1675
Damian Hartard, Freiherr von der Leyen, 1675-1678
Karl Heinrich von Metternich-Winneburg, Jan.-Sept. 1679
Anselm Franz, Freiherr von Ingelheim, 1679-1695
Lothar Franz, Graf von Schönborn, 1695-1729

MINT OFFICIALS' INITIALS

Initial	Date	Name
AD	1690	Andreas Dittmar in Erfurt
	1690-92	In Mainz
AE	1618-36	Kaspar Ayrer in Frankfurt am Main
AK	Ca.1693	
AL	1678-83	Adam Longerich in Coblenz
	1683-84	In Mainz
BR	Ca.1641	
BS	1629-33	Benedict Stephani
CB	1692-96	Conrad Bethmann in Aschaffenburg
DA	1627-29, 33-36	Daniel Ayrer in Mainz
Et	1643-44	Ernst Textor
ET	1644-51	Etherius Hettinger
F, MF	1652-83	Matthias Fischer
GB	1692	Johann Gerhard Bender in Mainz
GFN	1682-1724	Georg Friedrich Nurnberger in Nürnberg
GFS	1689	Georg Friedrich Staude in Erfurt
HC	Ca.1641	
ICD	1673-76	Johann Christoph Durr in Erfurt
ICS	1690-91	Johann Christoph Staude in Erfurt
IGL	1691-92	Johann (Hans) Georg Langbehn (Langbein) in Aschaffenburg
IH	1675-76	Johann Horcher, mint treasurer in Erfurt
IS	Ca.1602	
KD	Ca.1676	
LS	1611-30	Lorenz Schilling, die-cutter in Frankfurt am Main
MG	1642	Johann Martin Ganser in Hanau
PE	Ca.1642	
VBW	1684-88, 1702-14	Ulrich Burkhard Willerding
	1586-1607	Andreas Wachsmuth the Elder
	1609-19	Hennig Kissels in Aschaffenburg
	1621-23	Andreas Wachsmuth the Younger
	1622-?	Johann Wolf Palm, warden
	Ca.1628	Philipp Schad (Scheid), warden
	1629-?	Michael Kapp (Capp), warden
	1636-40	Adolf Koch, warden
	1636-42	Philipp Schad, warden 2nd time
	1640-42	Hans Georg Dumwald von Geinhausen, warden
	1690-?	Johann Jacob Birkenholz, warden
	1691-?	Johann Georg Bickel, die-cutter

ARMS

A wheel with six spokes

REFERENCES

PA = Alexander, Prinz von Hessen, ***Mainzisches Münzcabinet***, Darmstadt, 1882. (rpt. Münster-Angelmodde, 1968)

K = Fritz Rudolf Künker, ***Erzbistum Mainz – Eine bedeutende Sammlung aus rheinischen Adelsbesitz.*** (auction catalog) Osnabrück, 1992.

S = Hugo Frhr. Von Saurma-Jeltsch, ***Die Saurmasche Münzsammlung deutscher, schweizerischer und polnischer Gepräge von etwa dem Beginn der Groschenzeit bis zur Kipperperiode.*** Berlin, 1892.

Sch = Wolfgang Schulten, ***Deutsche Münzen aus der Zeit Karls V.*** Frankfurt am Main, 1974.

St = Theodor Stenzel, "Die churfürstlich mainzischen Münzen und Medaillen neuerer Zeit," ***Numismatische Zeitung*** 31 (1864), cols. 73ff; 32 (1865), cols. 27ff.

H = Tassilo Hoffmann, "Mainzer inedita und Rarissima im Gothaer Münzkabinett," ***Deutsche Münzblätter*** 54 (1934), pp. 167-70.

ARCHBISHOPRIC - ELECTORATE

REGULAR COINAGE

KM# 54 8 HELLER

Silver **Obv. Inscription:** G / ARS / 8. **Note:** Uniface.

Date	Mintage	VG	F	VF	XF	Unc
ND	—	100	200	425	850	—

KM# 5 PFENNIG

Silver **Obv:** 4-fold arms of Mainz and Bicken, IA above **Note:** Uniface. Schussel type. Varieties exist.

Date	Mintage	VG	F	VF	XF	Unc
ND(1601-04)	—	8.00	15.00	35.00	70.00	—

KM# 30 PFENNIG

Silver **Obv:** Arms of Mianz (wheel), ML (Mainzer Landmunze) above **Note:** Uniface. Hohl type.

Date	Mintage	VG	F	VF	XF	Unc
ND(1622)	—	8.00	15.00	35.00	70.00	—

KM# 39 PFENNIG

Silver **Obv:** Crowned 4-fold arms of Mainz and Umstadt **Note:** Uniface.

Date	Mintage	VG	F	VF	XF	Unc
ND(1629-47)	—	8.00	15.00	35.00	70.00	—

KM# 91 PFENNIG
Silver **Obv:** 2-fold arms divided vertically, Mainz on left, Unstadt right, mintmaster's initials above **Note:** Uniface.

Date	Mintage	VG	F	VF	XF	Unc
ND(1643-46) ET	—	8.00	15.00	35.00	70.00	—

KM# 97 PFENNIG
Silver **Obv:** 2-fold arms of Mainz and Schonborn divided vertically, 6-petalled rose above **Note:** Uniface.

Date	Mintage	VG	F	VF	XF	Unc
ND(1647-73)	—	8.00	15.00	35.00	70.00	—

KM# 99 PFENNIG
Silver **Obv:** MF above arms **Note:** Uniface.

Date	Mintage	VG	F	VF	XF	Unc
ND(1647-73?)	—	8.00	15.00	35.00	70.00	—

KM# 98 PFENNIG
Silver **Obv:** W. W. above arms **Note:** Uniface, schussel type.

Date	Mintage	VG	F	VF	XF	Unc
ND(1647-73?)	—	8.00	15.00	35.00	70.00	—

KM# 132 PFENNIG
Silver **Obv:** Arms of Mainz and Leyen divided vertically **Note:** Uniface.

Date	Mintage	VG	F	VF	XF	Unc
ND(1675-78)	—	8.00	15.00	30.00	60.00	—

KM# 156 PFENNIG
Silver **Obv:** Crowned arms of Mainz, date divided near top **Rev:** Imperial orb with 1 in cartouche

Date	Mintage	VG	F	VF	XF	Unc
1677	—	8.00	15.00	30.00	60.00	—

KM# 175 PFENNIG
Silver **Obv:** Arms of Mainz and Ingelheim divided vertically, mintmaster's initials above **Note:** Uniface. Varieties exist.

Date	Mintage	VG	F	VF	XF	Unc
ND(ca.1680/1) MF	—	8.00	15.00	30.00	60.00	—
ND(ca.1692/6) CB	—	8.00	15.00	30.00	60.00	—

KM# 157 2 PFENNIG
Silver **Obv:** Three shields of arms around cetner, lower one divides date **Rev. Inscription:** II / PFEN

Date	Mintage	VG	F	VF	XF	Unc
1677	—	—	—	—	—	—

KM# 133 3 PFENNIG
Silver **Obv:** Three separate arms of Mainz, Leyen, and Worms, crown above central shield, two crossed palm branches below **Rev:** Imperial orb with 3 in cartouche divides date **Note:** Varieties exist.

Date	Mintage	VG	F	VF	XF	Unc
1675 ICD	—	11.00	20.00	40.00	80.00	—
1676 ICD	—	12.00	20.00	40.00	85.00	—

KM# 144 3 PFENNIG
Silver **Obv:** Three arms of Mainz, Leyen, and Worms in triangular cartouche, crown above, D. H. E. M. at top **Rev:** Imperial orb with 3 divides date **Note:** Varieties exist.

Date	Mintage	VG	F	VF	XF	Unc
1676 IH	—	11.00	20.00	40.00	85.00	—
1676 ICD	—	11.00	20.00	40.00	85.00	—
1677 ICD	—	11.00	20.00	40.00	85.00	—
1677	—	11.00	20.00	40.00	85.00	—

KM# 176 3 PFENNIG
Silver **Obv:** 4-fold arms of Mainz and Ingelheim in palm leaves, AF-EM above **Rev:** Imperial orb with 3 divides date in laurel wreath **Note:** Varieties exist.

Date	Mintage	VG	F	VF	XF	Unc
1680	—	11.00	20.00	40.00	85.00	—
1681	—	11.00	20.00	40.00	85.00	—
1682	—	11.00	20.00	40.00	85.00	—
1685	—	11.00	20.00	40.00	85.00	—
1686	—	11.00	20.00	40.00	85.00	—
1688	—	11.00	20.00	40.00	85.00	—
1689	—	11.00	20.00	40.00	85.00	—
1690 ICS	—	11.00	20.00	40.00	85.00	—

KM# 146 6 PFENNIG (Sechser)
Silver **Obv:** Date in legend **Rev:** Orb divides mintmaster's initials

Date	Mintage	VG	F	VF	XF	Unc
1676 ICD	—	27.00	45.00	80.00	160	—

KM# 145 6 PFENNIG (Sechser)
Silver **Obv:** Crowned 3-fold arms **Rev:** Imperial orb with 6, date in legend **Note:** Struck at Erfurt.

Date	Mintage	VG	F	VF	XF	Unc
1676	—	33.00	55.00	95.00	190	—

KM# 147 6 PFENNIG (Sechser)
Silver **Obv:** Crowned 3-fold arms of Mainz, Leyen, and Worms, date in legend **Rev:** Imperial orb with 6 divides mintmaster's initials, within palm branches **Note:** Varieties exist.

Date	Mintage	VG	F	VF	XF	Unc
1676 KD	—	25.00	40.00	75.00	155	—
1676 ICD	—	25.00	40.00	75.00	155	—

KM# 158 6 PFENNIG (Sechser)
Silver **Rev:** Facing bust of St. Martin, value 6 in round frame below

Date	Mintage	VG	F	VF	XF	Unc
1677	—	27.00	40.00	75.00	155	—

KM# 115 KREUZER
Silver **Obv:** 2-fold arms divided vertically, Mainz (wheel) on left and Schonborn on right, in laurel wreath **Rev:** Value, inscription in laurel wreath **Rev. Inscription:** I / KREVTZ / date / initials,

Date	Mintage	VG	F	VF	XF	Unc
1661 MF	—	15.00	35.00	70.00	145	—

KM# 203 KREUZER
Silver **Obv:** 4-fold arms of Mainz and Ingelheim in laurel wreath **Rev:** Value in laurel wreath **Rev. Inscription:** I / KREU / TZER / date /initials **Note:** Varieties exist.

Date	Mintage	VG	F	VF	XF	Unc
1691 AD	—	15.00	30.00	60.00	125	—
1693 CB	—	15.00	30.00	60.00	125	—

KM# 81 2 KREUZER (1 Albus)
Silver **Obv:** 4-fold arms of Mainz and Umstadt in laurel wreath **Rev:** Imperial orb with 2, date above, legend, mintmaster's initials **Rev. Legend:** MAINTZER. ALBVS.

Date	Mintage	VG	F	VF	XF	Unc
1641 BS	—	40.00	80.00	140	265	—

KM# 215 3 KREUZER (Groschen)
Silver **Subject:** Death of Anselm Franz **Obv:** Crowned oval ornate 4-fold arms of Mainz and Ingelheim **Rev:** 6-line inscription with dates, small imperial orb with 3 at bottom

Date	Mintage	VG	F	VF	XF	Unc
1695	—	55.00	115	235	475	—

KM# 204 12 KREUZER
Silver **Obv:** Crowned 4-fold arms of Mainz and Ingelheim in palm branches **Rev. Legend:** CHURFURSTL... **Rev. Inscription:** XII / KREU / TZER / date / initials **Note:** Varieties exist.

Date	Mintage	VG	F	VF	XF	Unc
1691 IGL	—	33.00	65.00	135	265	—
1692 IGL	—	33.00	65.00	135	265	—
1692 CB	—	33.00	65.00	135	265	—

KM# 208 12 KREUZER
Silver **Rev. Legend:** NACH. DE. SCHLUS...

Date	Mintage	VG	F	VF	XF	Unc
1693 CB	—	30.00	60.00	120	240	—
1694 CB	—	30.00	60.00	120	240	—

KM# 177 15 KREUZER (1/4 Gulden)
Silver **Obv:** Bust right **Obv. Legend:** Crowned 4-fold arms of Mainz and Ingelheim, palm branches at each side, value (15) in legend below, date in legend at top

Date	Mintage	VG	F	VF	XF	Unc
1680 MF	—	—	—	—	—	—

KM# 195 15 KREUZER (1/4 Gulden)
Silver **Obv:** Value XV below shoulder of bust **Rev:** Date divided in legend by mintmaster's initials **Note:** Varieties exist.

Date	Mintage	VG	F	VF	XF	Unc
1689 GFS	—	27.00	55.00	90.00	185	—
1690 ICS	—	27.00	55.00	90.00	185	—
1691 ICS	—	27.00	55.00	90.00	185	—

KM# 200 15 KREUZER (1/4 Gulden)
Silver **Rev:** Value XV at bottom **Note:** Varieties exist.

Date	Mintage	VG	F	VF	XF	Unc
1690 AD	—	60.00	100	210	425	—

KM# 120 30 KREUZER (1/3 Thaler)
Silver **Obv:** Bust right **Rev:** 6-fold arms with central shield of Schonborn, value 30 in legend at bottom, date in legend **Note:** Varieties exist.

Date	Mintage	VG	F	VF	XF	Unc
1671 MF	—	65.00	135	275	550	—
1672 MF	—	65.00	135	275	550	—

KM# 135 30 KREUZER (1/3 Thaler)
Silver **Rev:** Crowned 4-fold arms of Mainz and Worms with central shield of Leyen, palm branches at either side, value (30) below, date in legend **Note:** Varieties exist.

Date	Mintage	VG	F	VF	XF	Unc
1675 MF	—	65.00	135	275	525	—
1676 MF	—	65.00	135	275	525	—

KM# 134 30 KREUZER (1/3 Thaler)
Silver **Rev:** Crowned 6-fold arms with central shield of Metternich, value 30 and date in legend

Date	Mintage	VG	F	VF	XF	Unc
1675 MF	—	120	235	475	950	—

KM# 148 30 KREUZER (1/3 Thaler)
Silver **Rev:** Very small arms, date divided in legend at top

Date	Mintage	VG	F	VF	XF	Unc
1676	—	—	—	—	—	—

KM# 162 30 KREUZER (1/3 Thaler)
Silver **Rev:** 4-fold arms of Mainz and Worms, with inner shield of 4-fold arms of Winneburg and Beilstein, with central shield of Metternich, in laurel wreath, crown above

Date	Mintage	VG	F	VF	XF	Unc
1679 MF	—	—	—	—	—	—

KM# 178 30 KREUZER (1/3 Thaler)
Silver **Rev:** Crowned 4-fold arms of Mainz and Ingelheim, palm branch at each side, value 30 in legend below, legend, date **Rev. Legend:** DEXTERA DOMINI - EXALTAVIT ME

Date	Mintage	VG	F	VF	XF	Unc
1680 MF	—	—	—	—	—	—

KM# 121 60 KREUZER (2/3 Thaler)
Silver **Obv:** Date in legend **Rev:** Value 60 at bottom **Note:** Varieties exist.

Date	Mintage	VG	F	VF	XF	Unc
1671 MF	—	75.00	150	300	600	—
1672 MF	—	75.00	150	300	600	—

KM# 123 60 KREUZER (2/3 Thaler)

Silver, 37 mm. **Rev:** Crowned 6-fold arms with central shield of Metternich, value (60) in legend at bottom, date in legend **Note:** Varieties exist.

Date	Mintage	VG	F	VF	XF	Unc
1673 MF	—	75.00	150	300	600	—
1674 MF	—	75.00	150	300	600	—
1675 MF	—	75.00	150	300	600	—

KM# 136 60 KREUZER (2/3 Thaler)

Silver **Rev:** Crowned 4-fold arms of Mainz and Worms with central shield of Leyen divide date and mintmaster's initials, ERFFURT in small band below, value in legend at bottom **Note:** Varieties exist.

Date	Mintage	VG	F	VF	XF	Unc
1675 ICD	—	65.00	135	275	550	—

KM# 141 60 KREUZER (2/3 Thaler)

Silver **Obv:** Different bust **Note:** Varieties exist.

Date	Mintage	VG	F	VF	XF	Unc
1675 MF	—	90.00	180	325	650	—
1676 MF	—	90.00	180	325	650	—

KM# 137 60 KREUZER (2/3 Thaler)

Silver **Rev:** Without ERFFURT, palm branches at sides of arms, date in legend

Date	Mintage	VG	F	VF	XF	Unc
1675 MF	—	600	1,000	2,000	3,600	—

KM# 138 60 KREUZER (2/3 Thaler)

Silver **Rev:** Large crown above arms, without palm branches, arms divide date and mintmaster's initials

Date	Mintage	VG	F	VF	XF	Unc
1675 ICD	—	600	1,000	2,000	3,600	—

KM# 139 60 KREUZER (2/3 Thaler)

Silver **Rev:** Palm branches crossed below arms

Date	Mintage	VG	F	VF	XF	Unc
1675 ICD	—	600	1,000	2,000	3,600	—

KM# 140 60 KREUZER (2/3 Thaler)

Silver **Rev:** Squarish arms with date divided in legend at top

Date	Mintage	VG	F	VF	XF	Unc
1675 ICD	—	160	325	650	1,300	—

KM# 163 60 KREUZER (2/3 Thaler)

Silver **Obv:** Bust right **Rev:** 4-fold arms of Mainz and Worms, inner shield of 4-fold arms of Winneburg and Beilstein, central shield of Metternich, in laurel wreath, crown above value 60 in legend below

Date	Mintage	VG	F	VF	XF	Unc
1679 MF	—	160	325	750	1,500	—

KM# 179 60 KREUZER (2/3 Thaler)

Silver **Rev:** Youthful bust and value 60. **Note:** Similar to KM#201.

Date	Mintage	VG	F	VF	XF	Unc
1680 MF	—	60.00	115	200	425	—

KM# 201 60 KREUZER (2/3 Thaler)

Silver **Obv:** Older bust **Note:** Varieties exist.

Date	Mintage	VG	F	VF	XF	Unc
1690 AD	—	80.00	165	275	575	—
1693 CB	—	80.00	165	275	575	—
1695 CB	—	80.00	165	275	575	—

KM# 32 ALBUS (2 Kreuzer)

Silver **Obv:** Ornamented shield of Mainz arms in circle with laurel wreath around, M*L (Mainzer Landmunze) in legend at top **Rev:** I/ALBVS in laurel wreath **Note:** Kipper Albus.

Date	Mintage	VG	F	VF	XF	Unc
ND(1622)	—	—	—	—	—	—

KM# 93 ALBUS (2 Kreuzer)

4.2200 g., Silver **Note:** Klippe.

Date	Mintage	VG	F	VF	XF	Unc
1644 ET Rare	—	—	—	—	—	—

KM# 92 ALBUS (2 Kreuzer)

Silver **Obv:** 4-fold arms of Mainz and Ulmstadt in laurel wreath **Rev:** Inscription in laurel wreath **Rev. Inscription:** I / ALBVS / date / initials **Note:** Varieties exist.

Date	Mintage	VG	F	VF	XF	Unc
1644 ET	—	13.00	27.00	55.00	115	—
1645 ET	—	13.00	27.00	55.00	115	—
1646 ET	—	13.00	27.00	55.00	115	—

KM# 100 ALBUS (2 Kreuzer)

Silver **Note:** Varieties exist.

Date	Mintage	VG	F	VF	XF	Unc
1648 ET	—	8.00	16.00	35.00	70.00	—
1650 ET	—	8.00	16.00	35.00	70.00	—
1651 ET	—	8.00	16.00	35.00	70.00	—
1652 MF	—	8.00	16.00	35.00	70.00	—
1653 MF	—	8.00	16.00	35.00	70.00	—
1654 MF	—	8.00	16.00	35.00	70.00	—
1655 MF	—	8.00	16.00	35.00	70.00	—
1656 MF	—	8.00	16.00	35.00	70.00	—
1657 MF	—	8.00	16.00	35.00	70.00	—
1658 MF	—	8.00	16.00	35.00	70.00	—

KM# 117 ALBUS (2 Kreuzer)

Silver **Obv:** 6-fold arms with central shield of Schonborn **Note:** Varieties exist.

Date	Mintage	VG	F	VF	XF	Unc
1664 MF	—	8.00	16.00	35.00	70.00	—
1666 MF	—	8.00	16.00	35.00	70.00	—
1667 MF	—	8.00	16.00	35.00	70.00	—
1668 MF	—	8.00	16.00	35.00	70.00	—
1669 MF	—	8.00	16.00	35.00	70.00	—
1670 MF	—	8.00	16.00	35.00	70.00	—
1671 MF	—	8.00	16.00	35.00	70.00	—

KM# 129 ALBUS (2 Kreuzer)

Silver **Obv:** Central shield of Metternich arms

Date	Mintage	VG	F	VF	XF	Unc
1674 MF	—	13.00	27.00	55.00	115	—

KM# 159 ALBUS (2 Kreuzer)

Silver **Obv:** 4-fold arms of Mainz and Worms with central shield of Leyen, in laurel wreath

Date	Mintage	VG	F	VF	XF	Unc
1678 MF	—	13.00	27.00	55.00	115	—

KM# 164 ALBUS (2 Kreuzer)

Silver Weight varies: 0.82-0.91g., 17-18 mm. **Ruler:** Karl Heinrich **Obv:** Three small adjacent shields of arms, Mainz upper left, Worms upper right, 4-fold arms of Winneburg and Beilstein, with central shield of Metternich, in lower shield, electoral hat above, crossed palm branches below **Rev:** 4-line inscription with date and mintmaster's initials in laurel wreath **Rev. Inscription:** I / ALBVS / (date) / initials

Date	Mintage	VG	F	VF	XF	Unc
1679 MF	—	30.00	60.00	100	200	—

KM# 165 ALBUS (2 Kreuzer)

Silver Weight varies: 0.82-0.91g., 17-18 mm. **Ruler:** Karl Heinrich **Obv:** Three small adjacent shields of arms, Mainz upper left, Worms upper right, 4-fold arms of Winneburg and Beilstein, with central shield of Metternich, in lower shield, electoral hat above **Rev:** 4-line inscription with date and mintmaster's initials in laurel wreath **Rev. Inscription:** I / ALBVS / (date) / (initials)

Date	Mintage	VG	F	VF	XF	Unc
1679 MF	—	30.00	60.00	100	200	—

KM# 166 ALBUS (2 Kreuzer)

Silver **Obv:** 4-fold arms of Mainz and Worms, with inner shield of 4-fold arms of Winneburg and Beilstein, with central shield of Metternich, in laurel wreath

Date	Mintage	VG	F	VF	XF	Unc
1679 MF	—	16.00	35.00	75.00	150	—

KM# 167 ALBUS (2 Kreuzer)

0.9100 g., Silver, 18 mm. **Obv:** 4-fold arms of Mainz and Ingelheim in laurel wreath **Rev:** Value in laurel wreath **Rev. Inscription:** I / ALBVS / date / initials **Note:** Varieties exist.

Date	Mintage	VG	F	VF	XF	Unc
1679 MF	—	13.00	27.00	55.00	115	—
1680 MF	—	13.00	27.00	55.00	115	—
1681 MF	—	13.00	27.00	55.00	115	—
1692 CB	—	13.00	27.00	55.00	115	—
1692 GB	—	13.00	27.00	55.00	115	—

KM# 216 ALBUS (2 Kreuzer)

4.2200 g., Silver **Rev. Legend:** NACHDEMSCHL. D. V. STAND.

Date	Mintage	VG	F	VF	XF	Unc
1695 CB	—	13.00	27.00	55.00	115	—

KM# 184 2 ALBUS (4 Kreuzer)

Silver Weight varies: 1.79-1.91g., 21 mm. **Obv:** 4-fold arms of Mainz and Ingelheim in laurel wreath **Rev:** Value in laurel wreath **Rev. Inscription:** II / ALBVS / date / initials **Note:** Varieties exist.

Date	Mintage	VG	F	VF	XF	Unc
1681 MF	—	20.00	45.00	90.00	185	—
1690 AD	—	20.00	45.00	90.00	185	—
1691 AD	—	20.00	45.00	90.00	185	—
1693 CB	—	20.00	45.00	90.00	185	—

KM# 202 2 ALBUS (4 Kreuzer)

Silver **Mint:** Erfurt

Date	Mintage	VG	F	VF	XF	Unc
1690 ICS	—	20.00	45.00	90.00	185	—

KM# 209 2 ALBUS (4 Kreuzer)

Silver **Rev. Legend:** NACH. DEM. SCHLUS. DER. V. STAND.

Date	Mintage	VG	F	VF	XF	Unc
1693 CB	—	16.00	35.00	75.00	150	—
1694 CB	—	16.00	35.00	75.00	150	—
1695 CB	—	16.00	35.00	75.00	150	—

KM# 124 GROSCHEN (3 Kreuzer)

Silver **Subject:** Death of Johann Philipp and Accession of Lothar Friedrich **Obv:** Crowned 6-fold arms with central shield of Schonborn in palm branches **Rev:** Crowned 6-fold arms with central shield of Metternich in palm branches, date in legend

Date	Mintage	VG	F	VF	XF	Unc
1673	—	50.00	100	210	425	—

KM# 142 GROSCHEN (3 Kreuzer)

Silver **Subject:** Death of Lothar Friedrich **Obv:** Crowned 6-fold arms with central shield of Metternich, palm branches at sides **Rev:** 12-line inscription with dates

Date	Mintage	VG	F	VF	XF	Unc
1675	—	50.00	100	210	425	—

KM# 160 GROSCHEN (3 Kreuzer)

Silver **Subject:** Death of Damian Hartard **Obv:** Crowned 4-fold arms with central shield of Leyen in palm branches **Rev:** 9-line inscription with date

Date	Mintage	VG	F	VF	XF	Unc
1678	—	50.00	100	210	425	—

KM# 168 GROSCHEN (3 Kreuzer)

Silver **Subject:** Death of Karl Heinrich **Obv:** Crowned 4-fold arms with central shield of Metternich **Rev:** 10-line inscription with dates

Date	Mintage	VG	F	VF	XF	Unc
1679	—	50.00	100	210	425	—

KM# 217 GROSCHEN (3 Kreuzer)

Silver **Subject:** Death of Anselm Franz and Accessin of Lothar Franz **Obv:** Crowned 6-fold arms with central shield of Schonborn, date in legend **Rev:** Crowned 4-fold arms of Mainz and Ingelheim, titles of Anselm Franz

Date	Mintage	VG	F	VF	XF	Unc
1695	—	80.00	140	210	425	—

KM# 149 4 GROSCHEN

Silver **Obv:** Bust right **Rev:** 3-fold arms of Mainz, Worms and Leyen divide date, crown above **Rev. Legend:** C. F. M. SILBER M above, IIII. GUT. GROSCH below

Date	Mintage	VG	F	VF	XF	Unc
1676	—	50.00	100	210	425	—

KM# 150 4 GROSCHEN

Silver **Rev. Legend:** C. F. M. L. M. V. FEIN. SIL, IIII. GUT. GROSCH. **Note:** Varieties exist.

Date	Mintage	VG	F	VF	XF	Unc
1676	—	50.00	100	210	425	—

KM# 186 SOL

Silver **Subject:** French Occupation **Obv:** Crowned ornamented oval, within four intertwined cursive L's (for Louis XIV) **Rev:** Value 1 in center

Date	Mintage	VG	F	VF	XF	Unc
ND(1689)	—	60.00	120	210	425	—

KM# 187 SOL

Silver **Rev:** 1/SOL/date

Date	Mintage	VG	F	VF	XF	Unc
1689	—	50.00	100	210	425	—

KM# 188 2 SOLS

Silver **Subject:** French Occupation **Obv:** Crowned ornamented oval, within four intertwined L's (for Louis XIV), value (3) in legend below **Obv. Legend:** MONE. NOV-ARGENTEA **Rev. Legend:** GLOR. IN. EXCELS. DEO. **Rev. Inscription:** II / SOLS / date

Date	Mintage	VG	F	VF	XF	Unc
1689	—	85.00	165	275	575	—

KM# 189 1/24 THALER (Groschen)

Silver **Obv:** Crowned 4-fold arms of Mainz and Ingelheim in baroque frame **Rev:** Imperial orb with value: 24 divides date near top **Rev. Legend:** CHURFURST... **Mint:** Erfurt

Date	Mintage	VG	F	VF	XF	Unc
1689 GFS	—	45.00	100	165	300	—

KM# 210 1/24 THALER (Groschen)

Silver **Obv:** Ornate round arms **Rev:** Legend, date **Rev. Legend:** NACH DEM LEIPZIGER FUSS

Date	Mintage	VG	F	VF	XF	Unc
1693 ICS	—	45.00	100	165	300	—

KM# 125 1/12 THALER (Doppelgroschen)

Silver **Subject:** Death of Johann Philipp and Accession of Lothar Friedrich **Obv:** Crowned 6-fold arms of Mainz, Worms, and Wurzburg with central shield of Schonborn, palm branches at sides **Rev:** Crowned 6-fold arms of Mainz with central shield of Metternich, palm branches at sides, date in legend

Date	Mintage	VG	F	VF	XF	Unc
1673	—	90.00	180	360	725	—

KM# 143 1/12 THALER (Doppelgroschen)

Silver **Subject:** Death of Lothar Friedrich **Obv:** Crowned 6-fold arms with central shield of Metternich, palm branches at sides **Rev:** 12-line inscription/date

Date	Mintage	VG	F	VF	XF	Unc
1675	—	80.00	150	300	—	—

KM# 190 1/12 THALER (Doppelgroschen)

Silver **Rev. Inscription:** 12 / EINEN / REICHS / THALER / date **Mint:** Erfurt **Note:** Varieties exist.

Date	Mintage	VG	F	VF	XF	Unc
1689 GFS	—	20.00	35.00	65.00	130	—
1690 ICS	—	20.00	35.00	65.00	130	—
1691 AD	—	33.00	70.00	120	180	—
1692 AD	—	20.00	35.00	65.00	130	—
1692 CB	—	20.00	35.00	65.00	130	—

KM# 205 1/12 THALER (Doppelgroschen)

Silver **Rev. Inscription:** 12 / EINEN / THALER / date

Date	Mintage	VG	F	VF	XF	Unc
1691 ICS	—	—	—	—	—	—

KM# 161 1/8 THALER

Silver **Subject:** Death of Damian Hartard **Obv:** Crowned 4-fold arms of Mainz and Worms between palm branches **Rev:** 9-line inscription with dates

Date	Mintage	VG	F	VF	XF	Unc
1678	—	100	210	425	—	—

KM# 169 1/8 THALER

Silver **Subject:** Death of Karl Heinrich **Obv:** Crowned 4-fold arms of Mainz and Worms with 4-fold central shield of Metternich arms with central shield of Mainz alone, palm branches at sides **Rev:** 10-line inscription with dates

Date	Mintage	VG	F	VF	XF	Unc
1679	—	65.00	135	210	425	—

KM# 191 1/6 THALER

Silver **Subject:** French Occupation **Obv:** Crowned ornamented oval, within four intertwined cursive L's (for Louis XIV) **Obv. Legend:** MONETA. NOVA. ARGENTEA **Rev:** Large 1/6 in center, GLORIA..., date in legend

Date	Mintage	VG	F	VF	XF	Unc
1689	—	115	235	475	950	—

KM# 6 1/4 THALER

Silver **Obv:** Oval 4-fold arms of Mainz and Bicken, mitre above **Rev:** St. Martin riding left on horse, kneeling beggar underneath, wheel of Mainz in cartouche below, date in legend

Date	Mintage	VG	F	VF	XF	Unc
160Z	—	65.00	135	210	425	—

KM# 15 1/4 THALER

Silver **Subject:** Laying of Cornerstone for New Archepiscopal Residence at Aschaffenburg **Obv:** Ornate 4-fold arms of Mainz and Kronberg, three helmets above **Rev:** View of castle, Roman numeral date in legend **Note:** Varieties exist.

Date	Mintage	VG	F	VF	XF	Unc
1614 LS	—	675	1,000	1,350	2,150	—

KM# 63 1/4 THALER

Silver **Obv:** Bust of Anselm Casimir right **Rev:** Helmeted 4-fold arms of Mainz and Umstadt

Date	Mintage	VG	F	VF	XF	Unc
ND	—	375	650	1,000	2,150	—

KM# 61 1/4 THALER

Silver **Obv:** Bust right **Rev:** 4-fold arms of Mainz and Umstadt, three helmets above, date in legend

Date	Mintage	VG	F	VF	XF	Unc
1636	—	375	650	1,000	1,800	—

KM# 62 1/4 THALER

Silver **Obv:** Smaller bust and value 1/4 below

Date	Mintage	VG	F	VF	XF	Unc
1636	—	375	650	1,000	1,800	—

KM# 127 1/3 THALER (30 Kreuzer)

Silver **Obv:** Bust right, date in legend **Rev:** Triangle with streaming rays above Metternich arms (three mussel shells) **Rev. Legend:** IN TRIBVS PACITVM EST MEO. ECCL. 25

Date	Mintage	VG	F	VF	XF	Unc
1673 Rare	—	—	—	—	—	—

KM# 126 1/3 THALER (30 Kreuzer)

Silver **Obv:** Bust right **Rev:** Crowned 6-fold arms with central shield of Metternich, date in legend **Note:** Varieties exist.

Date	Mintage	VG	F	VF	XF	Unc
1673 MF	—	110	200	400	825	—

KM# 192 1/3 THALER (30 Kreuzer)

Silver **Subject:** French Occupation **Obv:** Crowned ornamented oval, within four intertwined cursive L's (for Louis XIV) **Obv. Legend:** MONETA. NOVA. ARGENTEA. **Rev:** Large 1/3 in center, GLORIA..., date in legend

Date	Mintage	VG	F	VF	XF	Unc
1689	—	275	450	750	1,500	—

KM# 11 1/2 THALER

Silver **Obv:** Oval 4-fold arms of Mainz and Bicken, three helmets above **Rev:** St. Martin riding horse left, beggar below ar right, round arms of Mainz in ornamented frame in margin at lower left, date in legend at top

Date	Mintage	VG	F	VF	XF	Unc
1603	—	800	1,350	2,000	3,300	—

KM# 16 1/2 THALER

Silver **Subject:** Laying the Cornerstone of the New Archepiscopal Residence at Aschaffenburg **Obv:** Ornate 4-fold arms of Mainz and Kronberg, three helmets above **Rev:** View of castle, Roman numeral date in legend

Date	Mintage	VG	F	VF	XF	Unc
1614 LS	—	800	1,350	2,000	3,300	—

KM# 17 1/2 THALER

Silver **Note:** Klippe.

Date	Mintage	VG	F	VF	XF	Unc
1614 LS	—	700	1,500	2,400	4,200	—

KM# 50 1/2 THALER

Silver **Obv:** Bust turned 1/4 to right **Rev:** Ornate 4-fold arms of Mainz and Umstadt, three helmets above, date in legend

Date	Mintage	VG	F	VF	XF	Unc
1630 LS/AD	—	2,000	3,500	6,000	—	—

KM# 69 1/2 THALER

Silver **Obv:** Bust right

Date	Mintage	VG	F	VF	XF	Unc
1637 BS	—	2,000	3,500	6,000	—	—

KM# 80 1/2 THALER

Silver **Obv:** Crowned 4-fold arms of Mainz and Umstadt **Rev:** Inscription in laurel wreath **Rev. Legend:** S: ROM: IMP **Rev. Inscription:** Date / MONETA NOVA / ARGENTEA / MOGVNITINA **Note:** Varieties exist.

Date	Mintage	VG	F	VF	XF	Unc
1640	—	525	900	1,500	2,600	—
1641	—	525	900	1,500	2,600	—
1642	—	525	900	1,500	2,600	—

KM# 82 1/2 THALER

Silver **Subject:** Meeting of Imperial Diet in Regensburg **Obv:** Wreath in outer margin enclosing crowned arms of the seven electors in cartouches, above the standing imperial eagle, inscription in center within laurel wreath **Obv. Inscription:** REICHS / TAG / ZV REGEN / SPVRG / date **Rev:** Laureate bust of emperor right, shield of Regensburg arms below, angel's head under crown above, titles of Ferdinand III **Note:** Show 1/2 Thaler.

Date	Mintage	VG	F	VF	XF	Unc
1641 HC/BR	—	1,300	2,350	4,200	—	—

KM# 84 1/2 THALER

Silver **Obv:** 4-fold arms of Mainz and Umstadt in baroque frame, half eagle and flowers on each side **Rev:** Inscription in laurel wreath, titles of Anselm Casimir **Rev. Inscription:** Date / MONETA: NOVA / ARGENTEA / MOGVN / TINAE **Note:** Varieties exist.

Date	Mintage	VG	F	VF	XF	Unc
1642 MG	—	525	900	1,500	2,600	—
1645 MG	—	525	900	1,500	2,600	—

KM# 193 2/3 THALER (60 Kreuzer)

Silver **Subject:** French Occupation **Obv:** Crowned ornamented oval, four intertwined cursive L's (for Louis XIV) **Obv. Legend:** MONETA NOVA ARGENTEA **Rev:** Large 2/3 in center, GLORIA..., date in legend

Date	Mintage	VG	F	VF	XF	Unc
1689	—	1,600	2,800	5,200	—	—

KM# 194 2/3 THALER (60 Kreuzer)

Silver **Obv:** Smaller oval with crown dividing date, without legend

Date	Mintage	VG	F	VF	XF	Unc
1689	—	1,600	2,800	5,200	—	—

KM# 4 THALER

Silver **Note:** Dav. #9468.

Date	Mintage	VG	F	VF	XF	Unc
1601	—	1,750	2,750	5,500	9,500	—

KM# 7 THALER

Silver **Obv:** Capped and helmeted arms **Rev:** St. Martin facing on horseback, beggar under horse **Note:** Dav. #5531. Varieties exist.

Date	Mintage	VG	F	VF	XF	Unc
1602	—	550	1,150	2,200	4,200	—

KM# 8 THALER

Silver **Rev:** Beggar at rear of horse **Note:** Dav. #5533. Varieties exist.

Date	Mintage	VG	F	VF	XF	Unc
1602	—	550	1,150	2,200	4,200	—
1603	—	550	1,150	2,200	4,200	—

KM# 19 THALER

Silver, 46 mm. **Note:** Dav. #5536A.

Date	Mintage	VG	F	VF	XF	Unc
1614	—	1,250	2,300	3,600	7,200	—

KM# 20 THALER

Silver **Note:** Klippe. Dav. #5536B.

Date	Mintage	VG	F	VF	XF	Unc
1614 LS	—	2,700	4,500	7,200	—	—

KM# 18 THALER

Silver **Subject:** Laying of Cornerstone for New Archepiscopal Residence at Aschaffenburg **Obv:** Crowned and helmeted shield **Rev:** Aschaffenburg Castle **Note:** Thick Thaler. Dav. #5536.

Date	Mintage	VG	F	VF	XF	Unc
1614 LS	—	1,250	2,300	3,600	7,200	—

KM# 22 THALER

Silver **Note:** Similar to KM#23 but sterner portrait of Johann on obverse and ANNO added in reverse legend. Dav. #5537.

Date	Mintage	VG	F	VF	XF	Unc
1618	—	1,250	2,300	3,600	6,400	—

KM# 23 THALER

Silver **Note:** Dav. #5539.

Date	Mintage	VG	F	VF	XF	Unc
1619	—	1,300	2,500	4,600	7,400	—

KM# 35 THALER

Silver **Obv:** Bust of Georg Friedrich right, LS on arm **Rev:** Helmeted arms **Note:** Dav. #5541.

Date	Mintage	VG	F	VF	XF	Unc
1627 AE	—	600	1,300	3,000	4,800	—

KM# 34 THALER

Silver **Note:** Similar to KM#35 but smaller bust with date and LS on arm and smaller shield on reverse. Dav. #5540.

Date	Mintage	VG	F	VF	XF	Unc
1627 AE	—	450	1,000	2,200	3,750	—

KM# 40 THALER

Silver **Obv:** Closer bust with date and LS on arm **Rev:** Helmeted arms with AD left, mint mark right **Note:** Dav. #5543.

Date	Mintage	VG	F	VF	XF	Unc
1629 LS/DA	—	500	1,100	2,500	4,000	—
ND AD Rare	—	—	—	—	—	—

KM# 51 THALER

Silver **Obv:** Facing bust of Anselm **Rev:** Helmeted arms **Note:** Dav. #5544.

Date	Mintage	VG	F	VF	XF	Unc
1629 LS/DA	—	1,550	3,000	5,400	9,000	—

KM# 53 THALER

Silver **Obv:** Bust of Anselm right **Note:** Dav. #5546.

Date	Mintage	VG	F	VF	XF	Unc
1630 BS	—	400	800	1,500	2,550	—

KM# 52 THALER

Silver **Note:** Octagonal klippe. Dav. #5545.

Date	Mintage	VG	F	VF	XF	Unc
1630 BS	—	3,600	6,400	9,000	—	—

KM# 64 THALER

Silver **Obv:** Different cloak on bust **Obv. Legend:** ANSELMI. **Rev. Legend:** MONET-A: NOVA: ARGENTEA: MOG-V-NTINA. **Note:** Dav. #5547.

Date	Mintage	VG	F	VF	XF	Unc
1636	—	425	875	1,750	2,900	—

KM# 65 THALER

Silver **Obv. Legend:** ANSELMUS... **Note:** Dav. #5548.

Date	Mintage	VG	F	VF	XF	Unc
1636	—	190	375	675	1,150	—
1637 BS	—	190	375	675	1,150	—
1641 BS	—	190	375	675	1,150	—
ND BS	—	190	375	675	1,150	—
ND	—	190	375	675	1,150	—

KM# 70 THALER

Silver **Rev:** Date below shield **Note:** Dav. #5549.

Date	Mintage	VG	F	VF	XF	Unc
1637 BS	—	250	500	1,000	2,700	—
1638 BS	—	250	500	1,000	2,700	—
1639 BS	—	250	500	1,000	2,700	—

KM# 72 THALER

Silver **Obv:** Similar to 3 Thaler, KM#73 **Rev:** Similar to KM#65 **Note:** Dav. #5551.

Date	Mintage	VG	F	VF	XF	Unc
1639 BS	—	275	600	1,250	2,800	—

KM# 83 THALER

Silver **Subject:** Meeting of Imperial Diet in Regensburg **Obv:** Laureate bust of emperor right, shield of Regensburg arms below, angel's head under crown above, titles of Ferdinand III **Rev:** Wreath in outer margin enclosing crowned arms of the seven electors in cartouches, above the standing imperial eagle, inscription in center within laurel wreath **Rev. Inscription:** REICHS / TAG / ZV REGEN / SPVRG / date **Note:** Show Thaler.

Date	Mintage	VG	F	VF	XF	Unc
1641 HC/BR Rare	—	—	—	—	—	—

KM# 85 THALER

Silver **Obv:** Facing bust of Anselm **Rev:** Helmeted arms with mitre divide date **Note:** Dav. #5552. Varieties exist.

Date	Mintage	VG	F	VF	XF	Unc
1642 MG	—	600	1,200	2,400	4,200	—

KM# 86 THALER

Silver **Obv:** Without MOG on legend **Note:** Dav. #5553. Varieties exist.

Date	Mintage	VG	F	VF	XF	Unc
1642 MG	—	600	1,200	2,400	4,200	—

KM# 94 THALER

Silver **Obv:** Bust right **Rev:** Helmeted arms, date above **Note:** Dav. #5554.

Date	Mintage	VG	F	VF	XF	Unc
1644	—	350	725	1,550	3,000	—

KM# 109 THALER

Silver **Obv:** Facing bust of Johann Philipp left **Rev:** Capped and helmeted arms **Note:** Dav. #5556.

Date	Mintage	VG	F	VF	XF	Unc
ND ET	—	1,200	2,000	3,750	7,000	—

KM# 110 THALER

Silver **Obv:** Bust of Johann Philipp right **Note:** Dav. #5558.

Date	Mintage	VG	F	VF	XF	Unc
1658 MF	—	900	1,750	3,500	6,500	—

KM# 130 THALER

Silver **Note:** Similar to 2 Thaler, KM#131. Dav. #5560.

Date	Mintage	VG	F	VF	XF	Unc
1674 MF	—	3,000	6,000	9,000	—	—

KM# 151 THALER

Silver **Obv:** Bust of Damian Hartard right **Rev:** Helmeted arms **Note:** Dav. #5562.

Date	Mintage	VG	F	VF	XF	Unc
1676 MF	—	1,350	2,750	5,000	9,000	—

KM# 152 THALER

Silver **Obv. Legend:** ... D. G. S. S. M. A. E. **Rev. Legend:** S. R. I. P. G. AR. CAN. PR. EL. EP. WORM. **Note:** Dav. #5563.

Date	Mintage	VG	F	VF	XF	Unc
1676	—	1,500	3,000	5,500	9,500	—

KM# 153 THALER

Silver **Obv. Legend:** ... HARTARDT. D. G. S. S. MOG. ARCH. E. **Note:** Dav. #5564.

Date	Mintage	VG	F	VF	XF	Unc
1676 ICD	—	1,500	3,000	5,500	9,500	—

KM# 170 THALER

Silver **Obv:** Bust of Karl Heinrich right **Rev:** Helmeted arms **Note:** Dav. #5566.

Date	Mintage	VG	F	VF	XF	Unc
1679 MF	—	2,500	4,500	7,500	12,000	—

KM# 180 THALER

Silver **Subject:** Peace of Nymegen **Obv:** Bust of Anselm Franz right **Rev:** Hand holding scale weighing sword and olive branch **Note:** Dav. #5567.

Date	Mintage	VG	F	VF	XF	Unc
ND	—	700	1,600	3,250	5,750	—

KM# 181 THALER

Silver **Rev:** Helmeted arms **Note:** Dav. #5569. Varieties exist.

Date	Mintage	VG	F	VF	XF	Unc
1680 MF	—	250	600	1,250	2,750	—
1682 MF	—	250	600	1,250	2,750	—
1682 AL	—	250	600	1,250	2,750	—
1682 VBW	—	250	600	1,250	2,750	—

KM# 206 THALER

Silver **Rev:** Different shaped arms **Note:** Dav. #5570.

Date	Mintage	VG	F	VF	XF	Unc
1691 AD	—	450	900	1,750	3,500	—
1691 CB	—	675	1,200	2,250	4,500	—

KM# 211 THALER

Silver **Rev:** Without inner circle **Note:** Dav. #5571. Varieties exist.

Date	Mintage	VG	F	VF	XF	Unc
1692 CB	—	450	900	1,750	3,500	—
1693 CB	—	450	900	1,750	3,500	—

KM# 212 THALER

Silver **Obv:** Bust right **Rev:** Helmeted round 4-fold arms of Mainz and Ingelheim, date in legend

Date	Mintage	VG	F	VF	XF	Unc
1693 AK	—	2,000	3,750	6,500	—	—

KM# 214 THALER

Silver **Obv:** Different bust **Rev:** Smaller, altered arms **Note:** Dav. #5572.

Date	Mintage	VG	F	VF	XF	Unc
1694 CB	—	450	900	1,750	3,500	—
1695 CB	—	450	900	1,750	3,500	—

KM# 219 THALER

Silver **Obv:** Bust of Lothar Franz right **Rev:** Capped round arms with crozier and sword, cross above cap, date divided below **Note:** Dav. #5574.

Date	Mintage	VG	F	VF	XF	Unc
1696	—	500	950	1,800	3,750	—

KM# 10 2 THALER

Silver **Obv:** Capped and helmeted arms **Rev:** St. Martin on horseback facing out, beggar at rear of horse **Note:** Dav. #5532.

Date	Mintage	VG	F	VF	XF	Unc
1602 Rare	—	—	—	—	—	—

KM# 9 2 THALER

Silver **Obv:** Capped and helmeted arms **Rev:** St. Martin facing on horseback, beggar under horse **Note:** Similar to 1 Thaler, KM#7. Dav. #5530. Varieties exist.

Date	Mintage	VG	F	VF	XF	Unc
1602 Rare	—	—	—	—	—	—

KM# 29 2 THALER

Silver **Subject:** Laying of the Cornerstone for the New Archepiscopal Residence at Schaffenburg **Note:** Similar to 1 Thaler, KM#18. Thick flan.

Date	Mintage	VG	F	VF	XF	Unc
1614 LS	—	3,000	5,500	8,500	—	—

KM# 24 2 THALER

Silver **Obv:** Bust facing in inner circle, arms below divides legend **Rev:** Castle in inner circle **Note:** Similar to 1 Thaler, KM#23. Dav. #5538.

Date	Mintage	VG	F	VF	XF	Unc
1619 Rare	—	—	—	—	—	—

KM# 41 2 THALER

Silver **Obv:** Bust of Georg Friedrich right **Rev:** Helmeted arms **Note:** Dav. #5542.

Date	Mintage	VG	F	VF	XF	Unc
1629 LS/AD Rare	—	—	—	—	—	—

KM# 95 2 THALER

Silver **Obv:** Bust of Anselm right **Rev:** Helmeted arms **Note:** Dav. #A5554.

Date	Mintage	VG	F	VF	XF	Unc
1644	—	2,000	3,500	5,500	9,500	—

KM# 111 2 THALER

Silver **Obv:** Facing bust of Johann Philipp left **Rev:** Capped and helmeted arms **Note:** Dav. #5555.

Date	Mintage	VG	F	VF	XF	Unc
ND ET Rare	—	—	—	—	—	—

KM# 112 2 THALER

Silver **Obv:** Bust of Johann Philipp right in inner circle **Note:** Similar to 1 Thaler, KM#110. Dav. #5557.

Date	Mintage	VG	F	VF	XF	Unc
1658 MF	—	3,500	6,500	10,000	17,000	—

KM# 131 2 THALER

Silver **Obv:** Bust of Lothar Friedrich **Note:** Dav. #5559.

Date	Mintage	VG	F	VF	XF	Unc
1674 MF	—	2,800	4,200	7,500	12,000	—

KM# 154 2 THALER

Silver **Note:** Dav. #5561.

Date	Mintage	VG	F	VF	XF	Unc
1676 MF	—	1,500	3,000	5,250	9,000	—

KM# 171 2 THALER

Silver **Obv:** Bust of Karl Heinrich right **Rev:** Helmeted arms **Note:** Similar to 1 Thaler, KM#170. Dav. #5565.

Date	Mintage	VG	F	VF	XF	Unc
1679 MF	—	3,750	7,500	12,500	—	—

KM# 182 2 THALER

Silver **Obv:** Bust of Anselm Franz right **Note:** Dav. #5568. Varieties exist.

Date	Mintage	VG	F	VF	XF	Unc
1680 MF	—	3,000	5,000	8,500	14,500	—
1685 VBW	—	3,000	5,000	8,500	14,500	—

KM# 207 2 THALER

Silver **Obv:** Bust of Anselm Franz right **Rev:** Helmeted arms **Note:** Similar to 1 Thaler, KM#181 but different arms. Varieties exist.

Date	Mintage	VG	F	VF	XF	Unc
1691 AD	—	3,600	6,500	10,000	—	—
1691 CB	—	3,600	6,500	10,000	—	—

KM# 213 2 THALER

Silver **Obv:** Bust of Anselm Franz right **Rev:** Helmeted arms without inner circle **Note:** Similar to 1 Thaler, KM#211.

Date	Mintage	VG	F	VF	XF	Unc
1693 AK	—	5,900	9,500	16,000	—	—

KM# 218 2 THALER

Silver **Obv:** Bust of Lothar Franz right **Rev:** Capped round arms with crozier and sword, cross above cap, date divided below **Note:** Similar to 1 Thaler, KM#219.

Date	Mintage	VG	F	VF	XF	Unc
1695 AK	—	5,900	9,500	16,000	—	—

KM# 73 3 THALER

Silver **Obv:** Bust of Anselm Casimir right **Rev:** Helmeted arms in wreath **Note:** Dav. #5550.

Date	Mintage	VG	F	VF	XF	Unc
1639	—	8,500	16,000	22,000	—	—

TRADE COINAGE

KM# 33 GOLDGULDEN

3.5000 g., 0.9860 Gold 0.1109 oz. AGW **Obv:** Arms in inner circle **Rev:** Four batons cruciform with shields of arms in angles in inner circle

Date	Mintage	VG	F	VF	XF	Unc
16Z6	40,000	450	1,000	1,750	3,300	—
16Z7 AE	Inc. above	450	1,000	1,750	3,300	—
1627 DA	—	—	—	—	—	—

KM# 36 GOLDGULDEN

3.5000 g., 0.9860 Gold 0.1109 oz. AGW **Rev:** St. Martin and beggar in inner circle

Date	Mintage	VG	F	VF	XF	Unc
16Z8	—	2,250	4,500	7,000	9,900	—

KM# 37 DUCAT

3.5000 g., 0.9860 Gold 0.1109 oz. AGW

Date	Mintage	VG	F	VF	XF	Unc
16Z8	—	295	575	1,200	2,000	—
16Z9	—	295	575	1,200	2,000	—

KM# 38 DUCAT

3.5000 g., 0.9860 Gold 0.1109 oz. AGW **Note:** Klippe.

Date	Mintage	VG	F	VF	XF	Unc
1628	—	1,300	2,650	5,100	11,000	—

KM# 42 DUCAT

3.5000 g., 0.9860 Gold 0.1109 oz. AGW **Obv:** Facing bust of Anselm Casimir in inner circle **Rev:** Arms in inner circle

Date	Mintage	VG	F	VF	XF	Unc
1629	—	1,000	2,150	4,150	9,100	—

KM# 60 DUCAT

3.5000 g., 0.9860 Gold 0.1109 oz. AGW **Obv:** Anselm Casimir **Rev:** Crowned arms in inner circle

Date	Mintage	VG	F	VF	XF	Unc
1633 BS	—	265	525	925	2,000	—
1638 BS	—	265	525	925	2,000	—
1644	—	265	525	925	2,000	—
ND BS	—	265	525	925	2,000	—

KM# 66 DUCAT

3.5000 g., 0.9860 Gold 0.1109 oz. AGW **Obv:** Bust of Anselm Casimir right **Rev:** Arms in inner circle

Date	Mintage	VG	F	VF	XF	Unc
1636	—	290	575	1,150	2,500	—
1638	—	290	575	1,150	2,500	—

KM# 67 DUCAT

3.5000 g., 0.9860 Gold 0.1109 oz. AGW **Obv:** Arms divide date in inner circle **Rev:** Value in tablet

Date	Mintage	VG	F	VF	XF	Unc
1636	—	200	375	825	1,600	—
1641 BS	—	200	375	825	1,600	—

KM# 87 DUCAT

3.5000 g., 0.9860 Gold 0.1109 oz. AGW

Date	Mintage	VG	F	VF	XF	Unc
1642 MG	—	265	525	1,050	2,200	—
1646	—	265	525	1,050	2,200	—

KM# 96 DUCAT

3.5000 g., 0.9860 Gold 0.1109 oz. AGW **Obv:** Crowned arms in wreath

Date	Mintage	VG	F	VF	XF	Unc
1645	—	200	375	825	1,600	—
1646 ET	—	200	375	825	1,600	—

KM# 101 DUCAT

3.5000 g., 0.9860 Gold 0.1109 oz. AGW **Obv:** Bust of Johann Philip facing

Date	Mintage	VG	F	VF	XF	Unc
1648 ET	—	425	825	1,400	2,750	—
1649 ET	—	425	825	1,400	2,750	—
1650	—	425	825	1,400	2,750	—

KM# 105 DUCAT

3.5000 g., 0.9860 Gold 0.1109 oz. AGW **Obv:** Bust of Johann Philip left

Date	Mintage	VG	F	VF	XF	Unc
1650 ET	—	325	625	1,050	2,100	—
1651	—	325	625	1,050	2,100	—
1651/0	—	325	625	1,050	2,100	—

KM# 106 DUCAT

3.5000 g., 0.9860 Gold 0.1109 oz. AGW **Obv:** Large bust of Johann Philip left

Date	Mintage	VG	F	VF	XF	Unc
1652 MF	—	325	625	1,050	2,100	—
1653 MF	—	325	625	1,050	2,100	—

KM# 107 DUCAT

3.5000 g., 0.9860 Gold 0.1109 oz. AGW **Obv:** Small bust of Johann Philip left

Date	Mintage	VG	F	VF	XF	Unc
1652 MF	—	215	425	700	1,400	—
1653 MF	—	215	425	700	1,400	—
1654 MF	—	215	425	700	1,400	—
1655 MF	—	215	425	700	1,400	—
1657 MF	—	215	425	700	1,400	—
1658 MF	—	350	700	1,650	2,750	—
1659 MF	—	350	700	1,650	2,750	—
1660 MF	—	215	425	700	1,400	—
1661 MF	—	215	425	700	1,400	—

KM# 108 DUCAT

3.5000 g., 0.9860 Gold 0.1109 oz. AGW **Obv. Legend:** (I) OANN...

Date	Mintage	VG	F	VF	XF	Unc
1655 MF	—	215	425	700	1,400	—

KM# 116 DUCAT

3.5000 g., 0.9860 Gold 0.1109 oz. AGW **Obv:** Large bust of Johann Philip left

Date	Mintage	VG	F	VF	XF	Unc
1663 MF	—	240	500	900	1,650	—
1664 MF	—	240	500	900	1,650	—

KM# 118 DUCAT

3.5000 g., 0.9860 Gold 0.1109 oz. AGW **Obv:** Small bust of Johann Philip right

Date	Mintage	VG	F	VF	XF	Unc
1667	—	215	375	700	1,200	—
1668 MF	—	215	375	700	1,200	—
1670	—	215	375	700	1,200	—

KM# 122 DUCAT

3.5000 g., 0.9860 Gold 0.1109 oz. AGW **Obv:** Large bust of Johann Philip right

Date	Mintage	VG	F	VF	XF	Unc
1671 MF	—	230	425	750	1,300	—

KM# 128 DUCAT

3.5000 g., 0.9860 Gold 0.1109 oz. AGW **Obv:** Bust of Lothar Friedrich right in inner circle

Date	Mintage	VG	F	VF	XF	Unc
1673 MF	—	1,550	3,100	6,500	11,000	—

KM# 155 DUCAT

3.5000 g., 0.9860 Gold 0.1109 oz. AGW **Obv:** Bust of Damian Hartard right in inner circle

Date	Mintage	VG	F	VF	XF	Unc
1676 MF	—	825	1,950	4,550	8,300	—

KM# 172 DUCAT

3.5000 g., 0.9860 Gold 0.1109 oz. AGW **Obv:** Bust of Karl Heinrich right **Rev:** Crowned 4-fold arms with central shield of Metternich in palm branches, date in legend

Date	Mintage	VG	F	VF	XF	Unc
1679 MF	—	—	—	—	—	—

KM# 185 DUCAT
3.5000 g., 0.9860 Gold 0.1109 oz. AGW **Obv:** Bust of Anselm Franz right in inner circle

Date	Mintage	VG	F	VF	XF	Unc
1684 AL	—	550	1,050	2,500	4,150	—

KM# 220 DUCAT
3.5000 g., 0.9860 Gold 0.1109 oz. AGW **Subject:** Treaty of Ryswick

Date	Mintage	VG	F	VF	XF	Unc
ND(1696) GFN	—	475	825	1,250	2,050	—

KM# 221 DUCAT
3.5000 g., 0.9860 Gold 0.1109 oz. AGW **Subject:** Treaty of Ryswick **Rev:** Altar wtih burning weapons on top

Date	Mintage	VG	F	VF	XF	Unc
1696	—	295	525	925	1,650	—

KM# 222 DUCAT
3.5000 g., 0.9860 Gold 0.1109 oz. AGW **Subject:** Treaty of Ryswick **Rev:** Minerva standing

Date	Mintage	VG	F	VF	XF	Unc
1696	—	275	550	1,100	2,300	—

KM# 43 2 DUCAT
7.0000 g., 0.9860 Gold 0.2219 oz. AGW **Obv:** Facing bust of Anselm Casimir in inner circle **Rev:** Arms in inner circle **Note:** Struck with 1 Ducat dies.

Date	Mintage	VG	F	VF	XF	Unc
1629	—	1,200	2,700	7,000	12,000	—

KM# 68 2 DUCAT
7.0000 g., 0.9860 Gold 0.2219 oz. AGW **Obv:** Bust of Anselm Casimir right **Rev:** Arms in inner circle **Note:** Struck with 1 Ducat dies.

Date	Mintage	VG	F	VF	XF	Unc
1636	—	1,250	2,500	5,400	9,900	—

KM# 71 2 DUCAT
7.0000 g., 0.9860 Gold 0.2219 oz. AGW **Obv:** Small crowned arms

Date	Mintage	VG	F	VF	XF	Unc
ND	—	275	450	825	1,750	—
1638 BS	—	275	450	825	1,750	—

KM# 74 2 DUCAT
7.0000 g., 0.9860 Gold 0.2219 oz. AGW **Obv:** Large crowned arms

Date	Mintage	VG	F	VF	XF	Unc
1639 BS	—	300	500	900	1,950	—

KM# 88 2 DUCAT
7.0000 g., 0.9860 Gold 0.2219 oz. AGW **Obv:** Facing bust of Anselm Casimir in inner circle **Rev:** Crowned arms in inner circle

Date	Mintage	VG	F	VF	XF	Unc
1642	—	925	1,850	3,200	5,900	—

KM# 89 2 DUCAT
7.0000 g., 0.9860 Gold 0.2219 oz. AGW **Obv:** Bust of Anselm Casimir right in inner circle

Date	Mintage	VG	F	VF	XF	Unc
1642 MG	—	475	925	1,600	3,050	—
1644 ET	—	475	925	1,600	3,050	—
1646 ET	—	475	925	1,600	3,050	—
1647 ET	—	475	925	1,600	3,050	—

KM# 90 2 DUCAT
7.0000 g., 0.9860 Gold 0.2219 oz. AGW **Obv:** Bust of Anselm Casimir right in inner circle **Rev:** Arms topped by three helmets in inner circle

Date	Mintage	VG	F	VF	XF	Unc
1642 MG	—	650	1,300	2,950	4,550	—

KM# 183 2 DUCAT
7.0000 g., 0.9860 Gold 0.2219 oz. AGW **Subject:** Anselm Franz

Date	Mintage	VG	F	VF	XF	Unc
1680 MF	—	800	2,100	5,600	7,900	—

KM# 223 2 DUCAT
7.0000 g., 0.9860 Gold 0.2219 oz. AGW **Subject:** Treaty of Ryswick **Obv:** Crowned and mantled arms **Rev:** Concordia seated left with wreath and cornucopia

Date	Mintage	VG	F	VF	XF	Unc
ND(1696)	—	625	1,250	2,350	3,950	—

KM# 224 2 DUCAT
7.0000 g., 0.9860 Gold 0.2219 oz. AGW **Subject:** Treaty of Ryswick **Rev:** Altar with burning weapons on top

Date	Mintage	VG	F	VF	XF	Unc
1696	—	450	875	1,650	3,300	—

KM# 225 2 DUCAT
7.0000 g., 0.9860 Gold 0.2219 oz. AGW **Subject:** Treaty of Ryswick **Rev:** Minerva standing

Date	Mintage	VG	F	VF	XF	Unc
1696	—	450	875	1,650	3,300	—

KM# 21 3 DUCAT
10.5000 g., 0.9860 Gold 0.3328 oz. AGW **Subject:** Laying the Cornerstone for the New Archepiscopal Residence at Aschaffenburg **Note:** Similar to 1 Thaler, KM#18.

Date	Mintage	VG	F	VF	XF	Unc
1614 LS	—	7,300	11,000	16,000	—	—

KM# A132 5 DUCAT (1/2 Portugaloser)
17.5000 g., 0.9860 Gold 0.5547 oz. AGW **Note:** Struck with 1 Thaler dies, KM#130.

Date	Mintage	VG	F	VF	XF	Unc
1674 MF Rare	—	—	—	—	—	—

KM# A156 5 DUCAT (1/2 Portugaloser)
17.5000 g., 0.9860 Gold 0.5547 oz. AGW **Obv:** Hartard bust right within inner circle **Obv. Legend:** DAMIAN HARTARD: DG: ARCHIEPVS: MOGVNTINVS: **Rev. Legend:** S•R•I•P•GERM •ARCHICAN & PRIN: EL: EPS: WOR: **Note:** Struck with 1 Thaler dies, KM#154. Fr. #1659a.

Date	Mintage	VG	F	VF	XF	Unc
1676 MF Rare	—	—	—	—	—	—

KM# A184 5 DUCAT (1/2 Portugaloser)
17.5000 g., 0.9860 Gold 0.5547 oz. AGW

Date	Mintage	VG	F	VF	XF	Unc
1680 MF	—	—	—	15,000	24,000	—
1682 MF	—	—	—	15,000	24,000	—

KM# B156 7 DUCAT
24.5000 g., 0.9860 Gold 0.7766 oz. AGW **Obv:** Bust of Damian Hortard right **Rev:** Helmeted arms **Note:** Struck with 1 Thaler dies, KM#151.

Date	Mintage	VG	F	VF	XF	Unc
1676 MF Rare	—	—	—	—	—	—

KM# B184 10 DUCAT (Portugaloser)
35.0000 g., 0.9860 Gold 1.1095 oz. AGW **Obv:** Bust right **Rev:** Helmeted arms **Note:** Struck with 1 Thaler dies, KM#181.

Date	Mintage	VG	F	VF	XF	Unc
1680 MF	—	—	—	17,000	25,000	—
1682 MF	—	—	—	17,000	25,000	—
1684 AL	—	—	—	17,000	25,000	—

TRADE COINAGE

Swedish Issues - 1631-1635

KM# 500 DUCAT
3.5000 g., 0.9860 Gold 0.1109 oz. AGW **Obv:** Gustav II Adolf facing

Date	Mintage	VG	F	VF	XF	Unc
1631 Rare	—	—	—	—	—	—

KM# 502 DUCAT
3.5000 g., 0.9860 Gold 0.1109 oz. AGW **Obv:** Bust right

Date	Mintage	VG	F	VF	XF	Unc
1632 HA	—	260	525	1,150	2,300	—
1632 HE	—	260	525	1,150	2,300	—

KM# 503 DUCAT
3.5000 g., 0.9860 Gold 0.1109 oz. AGW **Obv. Inscription:** IN PVGNIS...

Date	Mintage	VG	F	VF	XF	Unc
1632	—	1,100	1,800	2,750	—	—

KM# 504 DUCAT
3.5000 g., 0.9860 Gold 0.1109 oz. AGW **Obv:** Bust right **Rev. Inscription:** IN PVGNIS...

Date	Mintage	VG	F	VF	XF	Unc
1632	—	300	600	1,200	2,500	—

KM# 505 DUCAT
3.5000 g., 0.9860 Gold 0.1109 oz. AGW **Rev. Inscription:** HEROS MAGNANIMBS...

Date	Mintage	VG	F	VF	XF	Unc
1632	—	1,500	2,500	4,500	—	—

KM# 506 DUCAT
3.5000 g., 0.9860 Gold 0.1109 oz. AGW **Obv:** Ruler standing **Rev. Inscription:** IN PVGNIS / FVERATLEO, REX...

Date	Mintage	VG	F	VF	XF	Unc
1632	—	1,500	2,500	4,500	—	—

KM# 507 DUCAT
3.5000 g., 0.9860 Gold 0.1109 oz. AGW **Rev:** Crowned shield

Date	Mintage	VG	F	VF	XF	Unc
1632	—	1,500	2,500	4,500	—	—

KM# 508 DUCAT
3.5000 g., 0.9860 Gold 0.1109 oz. AGW **Rev. Legend:** DVCATVS NOVVU

Date	Mintage	VG	F	VF	XF	Unc
1632	—	1,500	2,500	4,500	—	—

KM# 511 DUCAT
3.5000 g., 0.9860 Gold 0.1109 oz. AGW **Obv:** Facing bust of Kristina **Rev:** Crowned shield

Date	Mintage	VG	F	VF	XF	Unc
ND(1635) Rare	—	—	—	—	—	—

KM# 501 2 DUCAT
7.0000 g., 0.9860 Gold 0.2219 oz. AGW **Obv:** Gustav II Adolf **Rev:** Arms in inner circle

Date	Mintage	VG	F	VF	XF	Unc
1631	—	3,000	5,500	9,500	—	—

KM# 509 2 DUCAT
7.0000 g., 0.9860 Gold 0.2219 oz. AGW **Obv:** Gustav II Adolf profile **Rev:** Value and date on tablet

Date	Mintage	VG	F	VF	XF	Unc
1632	—	3,000	5,500	9,500	—	—

KM# 510 2 DUCAT
7.0000 g., 0.9860 Gold 0.2219 oz. AGW **Obv:** Gustav II Adolf standing

Date	Mintage	VG	F	VF	XF	Unc
1632	—	4,250	7,000	12,500	—	—

KM# 512 2 DUCAT
7.0000 g., 0.9860 Gold 0.2219 oz. AGW **Obv:** Facing bust of Kristina **Rev:** Crowned shield

Date	Mintage	VG	F	VF	XF	Unc
ND(1635) Rare	—	—	—	—	—	—

MAINZ AND HESSE-DARMSTADT

JOINT COINAGE

Mainz and Hesse-Darmstadt

KM# 1 HELLER
Silver **Obv:** Hesse lion and Mainz wheel in shield, L above **Note:** Uniface.

Date	Mintage	VG	F	VF	XF	Unc
ND(1623-26)	—	15.00	35.00	80.00	165	—

KM# 651 HELLER
Silver **Obv:** Hesse lion and Mainz wheel in shield, L above **Note:** Uniface. Previous KM #1.

Date	Mintage	VG	F	VF	XF	Unc
ND(1623-26)	—	25.00	60.00	120	240	—

KM# 684.1 2 KREUZER (Albus)
0.6000 g., Silver, 17 mm. **Obv:** Adjacent oval arms of Mainz and Hesse, M-H above, date below, in laurel wreath **Rev:** Imperial orb with 'Z' **Rev. Legend:** MEINTZ. VND. HES. DARMS. **Note:** Varieties exist.

Date	Mintage	VG	F	VF	XF	Unc
16Z9	—	18.00	40.00	80.00	165	—
1630	—	18.00	40.00	80.00	165	—
1638	—	18.00	40.00	80.00	165	—

KM# 684.2 2 KREUZER (Albus)
Silver **Obv:** Adjacent oval arms of Mainz and Hesse, M-H above, date below, all in laurel wreath **Rev:** Imperial orb with 'Z' **Rev. Legend:** MEINTZ. VND. HES. DARMST.

Date	Mintage	VG	F	VF	XF	Unc
163Z	—	16.00	40.00	80.00	165	—
1635	—	16.00	40.00	80.00	165	—
1637	—	16.00	40.00	80.00	165	—
1638	—	16.00	40.00	80.00	165	—
1639	—	16.00	40.00	80.00	165	—

KM# 684.3 2 KREUZER (Albus)
Silver **Obv:** Adjacent oval arms of Mainz and Hesse, M-H above, date below, no laurel wreath **Rev:** Imperial orb with 'Z' **Rev. Legend:** MEINTZ. VND. HAS. DARMST. BS (Bundes Scheidemünze)

Date	Mintage	VG	F	VF	XF	Unc
1637	—	13.00	40.00	80.00	165	—
1638	—	13.00	40.00	80.00	165	—
1639	—	13.00	40.00	80.00	165	—

HESSE-DARMSTADT, MAINZ, NASSAU-SAARBRÜCKEN, & FRAN

Mainz joined a union with Hesse-Darmstadt, Nassau-Saarbrucken and Frankfurt to strike some minor coins during the Thirty Years' War. Official coinage was to be minted at Frankfurt. Unofficial issues struck by Mainz foiled the union, ending the four-state corroboration in 1636. A two-state union for Hesse-Darmstadt and Mainz continued to mint amended Halbbatzen in Mainz from 1637-1639.

JOINT COINAGE

Mainz, Hesse-Darmstadt, Nassau-Saarbrücken and Frankfurt am Main

KM# 652 PFENNIG
Silver **Obv:** Cross with M-H/N-F in angles **Note:** Uniface. Schussel type.

Date	Mintage	VG	F	VF	XF	Unc
ND(1623-30)	—	35.00	70.00	120	225	—

KM# 653.1 2 KREUZER (Albus)
Silver **Obv:** Imperial orb with Z divides date **Obv. Legend:** MEINTZ. HAS. NAS. FRANC **Rev:** Ornate cross, arms of each of four members of monetary union in angles

Date	Mintage	VG	F	VF	XF	Unc
16Z5	—	13.00	30.00	55.00	115	—
16Z8 Æ	—	13.00	30.00	55.00	115	—
16Z8 HE	—	13.00	30.00	55.00	115	—
1629 Æ	—	13.00	30.00	55.00	115	—
16Z9 HE	—	13.00	30.00	55.00	115	—
16Z9 HS	—	13.00	30.00	55.00	115	—
(16)Z9	—	13.00	30.00	55.00	115	—
1630 Æ	—	13.00	30.00	55.00	115	—
163Z	—	13.00	30.00	55.00	115	—
1635	—	13.00	30.00	55.00	115	—
1635 HE	—	13.00	30.00	55.00	115	—
1636	—	13.00	30.00	55.00	115	—
1636 BS	—	13.00	30.00	55.00	115	—
ND	—	13.00	30.00	55.00	115	—

KM# 653.2 2 KREUZER (Albus)
Silver **Obv:** Imperial orb with Z divides date **Obv. Legend:** MEINTZ. HAS. NAS. FRANC. **Rev:** Ornate cross, arms of each of 4 members of the monetary union in angles

Date	Mintage	VG	F	VF	XF	Unc
16Z9	—	—	—	—	—	—

FRENCH OCCUPATION

REGULAR COINAGE

KM# 550 UNKNOWN DENOMINATION
12.6000 g., Silver **Note:** Klippe. Crowned arms of Mainz in ornate baroque shield, griffin rampant at right, legend: KURF MAINZ - NOTH MVN, date in cartouche above.

Date	Mintage	VG	F	VF	XF	Unc
1688 Rare	—	—	—	—	—	—

KM# 551 UNKNOWN DENOMINATION
Pewter, 34 mm. **Note:** Octagonal klippe. Date struck separately below round impression of arms.

Date	Mintage	VG	F	VF	XF	Unc
1688	—	—	—	—	—	—

PATTERNS

Including off metal strikes

KM#	Date	Mintage	Identification	Mkt Val
Pn6	16Z7 Æ	—	2 Kreuzer. Gold. KM#653.1.	—
Pn1	1629 BS	—	Thaler. Pewter. KM#51.	—
Pn7	1636	—	2 Kreuzer. Gold. KM#653.1.	—
Pn2	ND(1647) VBW	—	Pfennig. Gold. VBW above arms. KM#98.	—
Pn3	1652 MF	—	Albus. Gold. KM#100.	—
Pn4	1658 MF	—	Albus. Gold. KM#100.	—
Pn5	1674 MF	—	Albus. Gold. KM#129.	—
Pn8	1679 MF	—	Albus. Gold. KM#164.	—
Pn9	1680	—	3 Pfennig. Gold. KM#176.	—
Pn10	1682 MF	—	Thaler. Gold. KM#181.	22,500
Pn11	1684 AL	—	Thaler. Gold. KM#181.	22,500
Pn12	1690 AD	—	2 Albus. Gold. KM#184.	—
Pn13	1695 AK	—	2 Thaler. Pewter. KM#218.	—

MANSFELD

A small, silver mining state, located between Anhalt and Thuringia. Bracteats were struck c. 1200. The ruling family of Mansfeld was much divided during the 15th and 16th centuries and they were prolific coin issuers during this period. The county of Mansfeld was annexed to Electoral Saxony in 1780 and then passed to Prussia in 1815.

RULERS

Vorderort Line

BORNSTEDT
- Bruno II, 1546-1615
- Wolfgang III, 1615-1638
- Bruno III, 1615-1644
- Joachim Friedrich, 1615-1623
- Philip V, 1615-1657
- Karl Adam, 1638-1662
- Georg Albrecht, 1657-1696
- Maximilian Philip, 1657-1664
- Franz Maximilian, 1644-1692
- Heinrich Franz, 1644-1715

EISLEBEN
- Jobst II, 1579-1619
- Ernst IV, 1579-1609
- Hoyer Christof, 1579-1587
- Johann Georg II, 1619-1647

FRIEDEBURG
- Peter Ernst I, 1532-1604

ARNSTEIN
- Wilhelm I, 1601-1615

ARTERN
- Johann Georg IV, 1585-1615
- Volrat VI, 1585-1627

Hinterort Line
- Ernst VI, 1567-1609
- Friedrich Christof, 1579-1631
- David, 1592-1628
- Ernst Ludwig, 1631-1632
- Christian Friedrich, 1632-1666

MINT MARKS
- A, AR - Artern
- B - Blumrode
- F - Friedeburg
- K - Katharinenrieth
- L, LS - Leimbach
- M -- Mansfeld
- MF - Thal Mansfeld
- NA - New-Asseburg
- OWS - Oberwiederstedt bei Hettstedt
- V - Voigtstedt
- W - Welbsleben

MINT OFFICIALS' INITIALS

Initial	Date	Name
ABK	1667-80	Anton Bernhard Koburger in Eisleben
AK	1615-32	Anton Koburger (the Elder) in Eisleben
CW	1688-1739	Christian Wermuth, die-cutter in Gotha

DM		Daniel Mebes in Gerbstadt
GB		Unknown
GM	1595-1615	Georg Meinhart in Eisleben
HB		Hardenberg in Wiederstadt
HB		Hans Bergkmann in Artern
HI	1619-23	Hans (Johann/Heinrich)Jacob in Saalfeld
HPK	1632-65	Hans (Johann) Philipp Koburger in Eisleben
HS		Hans Simons
IS	1621-?	Johann Sommer in Artern
PH		Philipp von Hausen in Arnstein castle Johann/Jacob Elias

ARMS

Mansfeld (lordship) – two rows of three lozenges (diamond shapes)

Old Mansfeld (until about 1550) – 4-fold with Querfurt in upper left and lower right, Mansfeld in upper right and lower left

New Mansfeld (from about 1550 onwards) – 4-fold of old Mansfeld in upper left and lower right, Arnstein in upper right, Heldrungen in lower left

Querfurt – six horizontal bars, every other one shaded

Arnstein – eagle

Heldrungen – rampant lion striding upwards to left on checkered diagonal bar

REFERENCE

T = Otto Tornau, ***Münzwesen und Münzen der Grafschaft Mansfeld***, Prague, 1937.

JOINT COINAGE

I – Günther IV, Ernst II, Hoyer VI, Gebhard VII, Albrecht VII
II – Ernst II, Hoyer VI, Gebhard VII, Albrecht VII
III – Hoyer VI, Gebhard VII, Albrecht VII, Philipp II
IV – Hoyer VI, Gebhard VII, Albrecht VII, Johann Georg I

COUNTSHIP

ANONYMOUS COINAGE

1619-1625

KM# 6 3 FLITTER (1-1/2 Pfennig)

Copper **Obv:** Rampant lion left (Heldrungen) divides date in ornamented shield **Rev. Inscription:** III / FLIT / TER

Date	Mintage	VG	F	VF	XF	Unc
(16)Z1	—	25.00	55.00	115	—	—

KM# 7 3 FLITTER (1-1/2 Pfennig)

Copper **Obv:** Oval Querfurt arms (four horizontal bars), value III above

Date	Mintage	VG	F	VF	XF	Unc
ND(1621/22)	—	25.00	50.00	105	—	—

KM# 19 PFENNIG

Silver **Obv:** 4-fold arms divide mintmaster's initials, date above **Note:** Uniface, Schussel type. Varieties exist.

Date	Mintage	VG	F	VF	XF	Unc
(16)24 HI	—	15.00	30.00	65.00	130	—
(16)25 AK	—	15.00	30.00	65.00	130	—
1625 AK	—	15.00	30.00	65.00	130	—

KM# 5 3 PFENNIG (Dreier)

Silver **Obv:** 4-fold arms divide date, mintmaster's initials above **Rev:** Small imperial orb with 3 in ornamented rhombus

Date	Mintage	VG	F	VF	XF	Unc
(16)19	—	—	—	—	—	—

KM# 9 3 PFENNIG (Dreier)

Copper **Obv:** 4-fold arms, date above **Rev:** Rampant lion left in shield (Heldrungen), value 3 above

Date	Mintage	VG	F	VF	XF	Unc
16Z1	—	12.00	25.00	40.00	65.00	—

KM# 10 3 PFENNIG (Dreier)

Copper **Obv:** Rampant lion left in shield **Rev:** Imperial orb with 3 divides date

Date	Mintage	VG	F	VF	XF	Unc
(16)Z1	—	12.00	24.00	45.00	90.00	—

KM# 11 3 PFENNIG (Dreier)

Copper **Obv:** Rampant lion left in circle **Rev:** Ornamented heart-shaped shield with 3

Date	Mintage	VG	F	VF	XF	Unc
ND(1621/22)	—	12.00	24.00	45.00	90.00	—

KM# 12 3 PFENNIG (Dreier)

Copper **Obv:** Value III above lion

Date	Mintage	VG	F	VF	XF	Unc
ND(1621/22)	—	12.00	24.00	45.00	90.00	—

KM# 8 3 PFENNIG (Dreier)

Copper **Obv:** 3-fold arms **Rev:** Imperial orb with 3 **Note:** Kipper 3 Pfennig.

Date	Mintage	VG	F	VF	XF	Unc
ND(1621/22)	—	12.00	24.00	45.00	90.00	—

KM# 13 3 PFENNIG (Dreier)

Silver **Obv:** 4-fold arms, crown above divides mintmaster's initials **Rev:** Imperial orb with 3, cross divides date **Mint:** Saalfeld **Note:** Varieties exist.

Date	Mintage	VG	F	VF	XF	Unc
16ZZ HI	—	10.00	20.00	40.00	80.00	—
16Z3 HI	—	10.00	20.00	40.00	80.00	—

KM# 14 3 PFENNIG (Dreier)

Silver **Obv:** Mintmaster's initials divided by arms **Mint:** Saalfeld **Note:** Varieties exist.

Date	Mintage	VG	F	VF	XF	Unc
16ZZ HI	—	10.00	20.00	40.00	80.00	—
16Z3 HI	—	10.00	20.00	40.00	80.00	—

KM# 15 3 PFENNIG (Dreier)

Silver **Obv:** 4-fold arms, crown above divides mintmaster's initials **Rev:** Orb divides date within ornamented rhombus **Mint:** Saalfeld

Date	Mintage	VG	F	VF	XF	Unc
16ZZ HI	—	13.00	27.00	55.00	110	—

KM# 16 3 PFENNIG (Dreier)

Silver **Obv:** 3-fold arms, crown above divides mintmaster's initials **Rev:** Imperial orb with 3, cross divides date **Mint:** Saalfeld

Date	Mintage	VG	F	VF	XF	Unc
16ZZ HI	—	13.00	27.00	55.00	110	—

KM# 17 3 PFENNIG (Dreier)

Silver **Obv:** Mintmaster's initials divided by arms **Mint:** Saalfeld

Date	Mintage	VG	F	VF	XF	Unc
16ZZ HI	—	13.00	27.00	55.00	110	—

KM# 18 3 PFENNIG (Dreier)

Silver **Obv:** Without crown above arms **Mint:** Saalfeld

Date	Mintage	VG	F	VF	XF	Unc
16ZZ HI	—	13.00	27.00	55.00	110	—

MANSFELD-ARTERN

Founded in the division of 1530/32, Artern became extinct in 1631 and its lands and titles reverted to Bornstedt.

RULERS

Johann Georg IV, 1585-1615
Philipp Ernst, 1585-1631

JOINT COINAGE

I - Volrat VI, Jobst II, and Wolfgang III
II - Volrat VI, Jobst II, Wolfgang III and Bruno III
III - Volrat VI and Jobst II
IIIa - Volrat VI, Wolfgang III and Albrecht Wolff
IIIb - Volrat VI, Philipp Ernst and Albrecht Wolff
IV - Volrat VI, Wolfang III and Johann Georg II
V - Philipp Ernst, Wolfgang III and Johann Georg II

COUNTSHIP

JOINT COINAGE

KM# 60 FLITTER (1/2 Pfennig)

Copper **Ruler:** Volrat VI, Philipp Ernst, Albrecht Wolff **Obv:** Rampant lion left (Heldrungen) in ornamented shield **Rev:** Querfurt arms (four horizontal bars) in shield **Note:** Kipper Flitter. Struck at Thal Mansfeld Mint.

Date	Mintage	VG	F	VF	XF	Unc
ND(1621/22)	—	—	—	—	—	—

KM# 65 3 FLITTER (1-1/2 Pfennig)

Copper **Ruler:** Volrat VI, Philipp Ernst, Albrecht Wolff **Mint:** Katharinenrieth

Date	Mintage	VG	F	VF	XF	Unc
(16)Z1	—	—	—	—	—	—

KM# 61 3 FLITTER (1-1/2 Pfennig)

Copper **Ruler:** Volrat VI, Philipp Ernst, Albrecht Wolff **Obv:** Rampant lion left (Heldrungen) in ornate shield **Rev:** Querfurt arms (four horizontal bars) below **Rev. Inscription:** III / FLITT / ER **Mint:** Thal Mansfeld **Note:** Kipper 3 Flitter. Varieties exist.

Date	Mintage	VG	F	VF	XF	Unc
ND(1621/22)	—	65.00	130	265	—	—

KM# 62 3 FLITTER (1-1/2 Pfennig)

Copper **Ruler:** Volrat VI, Philipp Ernst, Albrecht Wolff **Rev:** Date divided by arms **Note:** Varieties exist.

Date	Mintage	VG	F	VF	XF	Unc
1621	—	25.00	55.00	115	—	—

KM# 63 3 FLITTER (1-1/2 Pfennig)

Copper **Ruler:** Volrat VI, Philipp Ernst, Albrecht Wolff **Rev:** III above Querfurt arms **Note:** Varieties exist.

Date	Mintage	VG	F	VF	XF	Unc
ND(1621/22)	—	25.00	55.00	115	—	—

KM# 64 3 FLITTER (1-1/2 Pfennig)

Copper **Ruler:** Volrat VI, Philipp Ernst, Albrecht Wolff **Obv:** Two-fold arms divided vertically in ornate shield **Rev:** III in circle, date **Rev. Legend:** FLITTER **Note:** Varieties exist.

Date	Mintage	VG	F	VF	XF	Unc
16Z1	—	25.00	55.00	115	—	—

KM# 31 3 PFENNIG (Dreier)

Copper **Ruler:** Volrat VI, Philipp Ernst, Albrecht Wolff **Obv:** Four-fold arms, small heart above **Rev:** Imperial orb with 3 divides date **Mint:** Thal Mansfeld

Date	Mintage	VG	F	VF	XF	Unc
1618	—	20.00	40.00	80.00	160	—
161Z Error for 16Z1	—	20.00	40.00	80.00	160	—

KM# 66 3 PFENNIG (Dreier)

Copper **Ruler:** Volrat VI, Philipp Ernst, Albrecht Wolff **Obv:** Arnstein eagle in circle **Rev:** Imperial orb with 3 **Mint:** Thal Mansfeld

Date	Mintage	VG	F	VF	XF	Unc
ND(1621/22)	—	27.00	55.00	110	225	—
ND(1621/22) MF	—	27.00	55.00	110	225	—

KM# 67 3 PFENNIG (Dreier)

Copper **Ruler:** Volrat VI, Philipp Ernst, Albrecht Wolff **Obv:** Two-fold arms divided vertically in ornate shield **Rev:** Imperial orb with 3 divides date, in rhombus

Date	Mintage	VG	F	VF	XF	Unc
16Z1	—	16.00	33.00	65.00	130	—

KM# 68 3 PFENNIG (Dreier)

Copper **Ruler:** Volrat VI, Philipp Ernst, Albrecht Wolff **Obv:** 4-fold arms, K above **Rev:** Imperial orb with 3 divides date **Mint:** Katharinenrieth

Date	Mintage	VG	F	VF	XF	Unc
(16)Z1 K	—	12.00	25.00	55.00	110	—
16Z1 K	—	12.00	25.00	55.00	110	—
1621 K	—	12.00	25.00	55.00	110	—

KM# 69 3 PFENNIG (Dreier)

Copper **Ruler:** Volrat VI, Philipp Ernst, Albrecht Wolff **Obv:** Date divided by arms **Mint:** Katharinenrieth

Date	Mintage	VG	F	VF	XF	Unc
(16)21/16Z1 K	—	30.00	60.00	120	—	—

KM# 70 3 PFENNIG (Dreier)

Copper **Ruler:** Volrat VI, Philipp Ernst, Albrecht Wolff **Obv:** Four-fold arms divide date, A above **Rev:** Imperial orb with 3 divides A-R **Mint:** Artern **Note:** Varieties exist.

Date	Mintage	VG	F	VF	XF	Unc
(16)1Z A/AR Error for Z1	—	—	—	—	—	—

KM# 114 GROSCHEN

Silver **Ruler:** Volrat VI, Philipp Ernst, Albrecht Wolff **Subject:** Death of Volrat VI **Obv:** Crowned four-fold arms **Rev:** 7-line inscription with dates **Note:** Varieties exist.

Date	Mintage	VG	F	VF	XF	Unc
16Z7	—	15.00	30.00	65.00	130	—

KM# 72 12 KREUZER (Schreckenberger)

Silver **Ruler:** Volrat VI, Philipp Ernst, Albrecht Wolff **Obv:** Crowned four-fold arms divide mintmaster's initials **Mint:** Artern

Date	Mintage	VG	F	VF	XF	Unc
ND(1621/22) HB	—	65.00	135	225	385	—

KM# 73 12 KREUZER (Schreckenberger)

Silver **Ruler:** Volrat VI, Philipp Ernst, Albrecht Wolff **Obv:** Three small shields of arms, above two, upper one divides date **Rev:** St. George slaying dragon at right

Date	Mintage	VG	F	VF	XF	Unc
16Z1	—	65.00	135	225	425	—

KM# 74 12 KREUZER (Schreckenberger)

Silver **Ruler:** Volrat VI, Philipp Ernst, Albrecht Wolff **Obv:** Single arms at bottom divides date

Date	Mintage	VG	F	VF	XF	Unc
(16)Z1	—	65.00	135	225	425	—

KM# 76 12 KREUZER (Schreckenberger)

Silver **Ruler:** Volrat VI, Philipp Ernst, Albrecht Wolff **Rev:** Helmet with eight small banners from top, date in legend

Date	Mintage	VG	F	VF	XF	Unc
1621	—	85.00	140	275	550	—

KM# 78 12 KREUZER (Schreckenberger)

Silver **Ruler:** Volrat VI, Philipp Ernst, Albrecht Wolff **Obv:** Three small shields of arms, one above two, upper one divides date

Date	Mintage	VG	F	VF	XF	Unc
1621	—	65.00	135	225	425	—

KM# 79 12 KREUZER (Schreckenberger)

Silver **Ruler:** Volrat VI, Philipp Ernst, Albrecht Wolff **Obv:** Two adjacent ornate shields of arms, date above **Mint:** Hettstedt

Date	Mintage	VG	F	VF	XF	Unc
16Z1 HS	—	115	195	275	450	—

KM# 71 12 KREUZER (Schreckenberger)

Silver **Ruler:** Volrat VI, Philipp Ernst, Albrecht Wolff **Obv:** Four-fold arms **Rev:** Crowned imperial eagle, 1Z in orb on breast **Note:** Kipper 12 Kreuzer.

Date	Mintage	VG	F	VF	XF	Unc
ND(1621/22)	—	65.00	135	225	425	—

KM# 75 12 KREUZER (Schreckenberger)

Silver **Ruler:** Volrat VI, Philipp Ernst, Albrecht Wolff **Obv:** Three small shields of arms, one above two, upper one divides date **Rev:** Crowned imperial eagle, 1Z in orb on breast, titles of Ferdinand II **Note:** Varieties exist.

Date	Mintage	VG	F	VF	XF	Unc
16Z1	—	65.00	135	225	450	—

KM# 77 12 KREUZER (Schreckenberger)

Silver **Ruler:** Volrat VI, Philipp Ernst, Albrecht Wolff **Obv:** Two adjacent ornate shields of arms, date above **Rev:** Crowned imperial eagle 1Z in orb on breast, titles of Ferdinand II **Note:** Varieties exist.

Date	Mintage	VG	F	VF	XF	Unc
16Z1	—	85.00	160	275	550	—

KM# 81 24 KREUZER (Doppelschreckenburger)

Silver **Ruler:** Volrat VI, Philipp Ernst, Albrecht Wolff **Rev:** Crowned imperial eagle, Z4 in orb on breast

Date	Mintage	VG	F	VF	XF	Unc
ND(1621/22)	—	35.00	75.00	150	300	—

KM# 82 24 KREUZER (Doppelschreckenburger)

Silver **Ruler:** Volrat VI, Philipp Ernst, Albrecht Wolff **Obv:** Ornamented four-fold arms **Rev:** Crowned imperial eagle, Z4 in orb on breast, titles of Ferdinand II

Date	Mintage	VG	F	VF	XF	Unc
ND(1621/22)	—	35.00	75.00	150	300	—

KM# 80 24 KREUZER (Doppelschreckenburger)
Silver **Ruler:** Volrat VI, Philipp Ernst, Albrecht Wolff **Obv:** Angel above heart-shaped two-fold arms **Rev:** Two adjacent ornate shields of arms, value Z4 above **Note:** Kipper 24 Kreuzer.

Date	Mintage	VG	F	VF	XF	Unc
ND(1621/22)	—	35.00	75.00	150	300	—

KM# 83 30 KREUZER
Silver **Ruler:** Volrat VI, Philipp Ernst, Albrecht Wolff **Obv:** Angel above three-fold arms **Rev:** Crowned imperial eagle, 30 in orb on breast **Note:** Kipper 30 Kreuzer.

Date	Mintage	VG	F	VF	XF	Unc
ND(1621/22)	—	75.00	150	300	600	1,100

KM# 88 1/24 THALER
Silver **Ruler:** Volrat VI, Wolfgang III, Johann Georg II **Rev:** Date and mintmaster's initials divided by orb **Mint:** Saalfeld

Date	Mintage	VG	F	VF	XF	Unc
16ZZ HI	—	27.00	55.00	90.00	185	—

KM# 87 1/24 THALER
Silver **Ruler:** Volrat VI, Wolfgang III, Johann Georg II **Obv:** Two helmets above four-fold arms **Rev:** Imperial orb with 24 divides mintmaster's initials, cross above divides date **Mint:** Saalfeld **Note:** Varieties exist.

Date	Mintage	VG	F	VF	XF	Unc
16ZZ HI	—	27.00	55.00	90.00	185	—
16Z3 HI	—	27.00	55.00	90.00	185	—
(16)Z3 HI	—	27.00	55.00	90.00	185	—
16Z4 HI	—	27.00	55.00	90.00	185	—

KM# 89 1/24 THALER
Silver, 22.7 mm. **Ruler:** Philipp Ernst, Wolfgang III, Johann Georg II **Obv:** Four-fold arms divide mintmaster's initials, date above **Rev:** Imperial orb with Z4 **Note:** Varieties exist.

Date	Mintage	VG	F	VF	XF	Unc
16ZZ AK	—	20.00	45.00	80.00	160	—
16Z3 AK	—	20.00	45.00	80.00	160	—
16Z4 AK	—	20.00	45.00	80.00	160	—
16Z4 HI	—	20.00	45.00	80.00	160	—
1624 HI	—	20.00	45.00	80.00	160	—
16Z5 AK	—	20.00	45.00	80.00	160	—
1625 AK	—	20.00	45.00	80.00	160	—
1626 AK	—	20.00	45.00	80.00	160	—
16Z7 AK	—	20.00	45.00	80.00	160	—
16Z8 AK	—	20.00	45.00	80.00	160	—

KM# 103 1/24 THALER
Silver **Ruler:** Volrat VI, Wolfgang III, Johann Georg II **Obv:** Two helmets above oval arms **Rev:** Imperial orb with 24 divides mintmaster's initials, cross above divides date

Date	Mintage	VG	F	VF	XF	Unc
16Z4	—	27.00	55.00	100	200	—

KM# 104 1/24 THALER
Silver **Ruler:** Philipp Ernst, Wolfgang III, Johann Georg II **Mint:** Saalfeld

Date	Mintage	VG	F	VF	XF	Unc
16Z4 HI	—	27.00	55.00	100	200	—

KM# 105 1/24 THALER
Silver **Ruler:** Volrat VI, Wolfgang III, Johann Georg II **Obv:** Four-fold arms divide mintmaster's initials, date above **Mint:** Saalfeld

Date	Mintage	VG	F	VF	XF	Unc
1624 HI	—	27.00	55.00	100	200	—

KM# 115 1/24 THALER
Silver **Ruler:** Volrat VI, Wolfgang III, Johann Georg II **Rev:** Imperial orb with 24 or Z4, date divided in legend at top **Mint:** Eisleben

Date	Mintage	VG	F	VF	XF	Unc
16Z7 AK	—	27.00	55.00	100	200	—

KM# 120 1/24 THALER
Silver **Ruler:** Volrat VI, Wolfgang III, Johann Georg II **Rev:** Date divided at top in legend **Mint:** Eisleben

Date	Mintage	VG	F	VF	XF	Unc
1629 AK	—	33.00	60.00	110	220	—

KM# 119 1/24 THALER
Silver **Ruler:** Philipp Ernst, Wolfgang III, Johann Georg II **Rev:** Imperial orb with 24 or Z4 **Mint:** Eisleben **Note:** Varieties exist.

Date	Mintage	VG	F	VF	XF	Unc
1629 AK	—	33.00	60.00	110	220	—

KM# 121 1/24 THALER
Silver **Ruler:** Volrat VI, Wolfgang III, Johann Georg II **Rev:** Date divided by orb **Mint:** Eisleben **Note:** Varieties exist.

Date	Mintage	VG	F	VF	XF	Unc
16Z9/1630 AK	—	33.00	60.00	110	220	—
1629/1630 AK	—	33.00	60.00	110	220	—

KM# 122 1/24 THALER
Silver **Ruler:** Volrat VI, Wolfgang III, Johann Georg II **Mint:** Eisleben **Note:** Name of an unknown Wilhelm Georg replaces that of Wolfgang III; probably a die-cutter's error.

Date	Mintage	VG	F	VF	XF	Unc
1629/1630 AK	—	—	—	—	—	—

KM# 130 1/24 THALER
Silver **Ruler:** Volrat VI, Wolfgang III, Johann Georg II **Rev:** Date divided by orb **Mint:** Eisleben **Note:** Varieties exist.

Date	Mintage	VG	F	VF	XF	Unc
1630 AK	—	33.00	60.00	110	220	—

KM# 131 1/24 THALER
Silver **Ruler:** Volrat VI, Wolfgang III, Johann Georg II **Obv:** Mintmaster's initials above arms **Mint:** Eisleben

Date	Mintage	VG	F	VF	XF	Unc
1630 AK	—	33.00	60.00	110	220	—

KM# 10 1/21 THALER
Silver **Ruler:** Volrat VI, Jobst II, Wolfgang III **Obv:** Two helmets above four-fold arms **Rev:** Imperial orb with Z1 divides mintmaster's initials, cross above divides date **Mint:** Eisleben **Note:** Varieties exist.

Date	Mintage	VG	F	VF	XF	Unc
1616 AK	—	—	—	—	—	—

KM# 19 1/21 THALER
Silver **Ruler:** Volrat VI, Jobst II, Wolfgang III, Bruno III **Mint:** Eisleben

Date	Mintage	VG	F	VF	XF	Unc
1617 AK	—	—	—	—	—	—
Note: Reported, not confirmed						
1618 AK	—	—	—	—	—	—
Note: Reported, not confirmed						

KM# 5 1/4 THALER
Silver **Ruler:** Volrat VI, Jobst II, Wolfgang III, Bruno III **Subject:** Death of Johann Georg IV **Obv:** Four-fold arms divide mintmaster's initials, two helmets above divide date **Rev:** Seven-line inscription with dates, legend divided by orb and three small shields **Rev. Inscription:** TRAV / IST / MIS / LISH **Mint:** Eisleben

Date	Mintage	VG	F	VF	XF	Unc
1615 GM	—	—	—	—	—	—

KM# 11 1/4 THALER
Silver **Ruler:** Volrat VI, Jobst II, Wolfgang III **Obv:** Four-fold arms, date and mintmaster's initials between and around two helmets above **Rev:** St. George slaying dragon at right **Mint:** Eisleben **Note:** Varieties exist.

Date	Mintage	VG	F	VF	XF	Unc
1616 AK	—	80.00	140	220	425	—

KM# 20 1/4 THALER
Silver **Ruler:** Volrat VI, Jobst II, Wolfgang III, Bruno III **Obv:** Date and mintmaster's initials divided **Mint:** Eisleben

Date	Mintage	VG	F	VF	XF	Unc
1617 AK	—	80.00	140	220	425	—

KM# 35 1/4 THALER
Silver **Ruler:** Volrat VI, Jobst II, Wolfgang III, Bruno III **Obv:** Mintmaster's initials between helmets **Mint:** Eisleben

Date	Mintage	VG	F	VF	XF	Unc
1619 AK	—	80.00	140	220	425	—

KM# 36 1/4 THALER
Silver **Ruler:** Volrat VI, Jobst II **Obv:** St. George slaying dragon at right **Rev:** Ornate four-fold arms, two helmets above divide date and mintmaster' initials **Mint:** Saalfeld

Date	Mintage	VG	F	VF	XF	Unc
1619 HI	—	45.00	90.00	180	360	—

KM# 50 1/4 THALER
Silver **Ruler:** Volrat VI, Wolfgang III, Johann Georg II **Obv:** St. George slaying dragon, titles of Philipp Ernst **Rev:** Four-fold arms, two helmets above divided by date and mintmaster's initials **Mint:** Saalfeld **Note:** Spruch 1/4 Thaler. Varieties exist.

Date	Mintage	VG	F	VF	XF	Unc
16Z0 HI	—	45.00	90.00	180	360	—
16Z3 HI	—	45.00	90.00	180	360	—

KM# 90 1/4 THALER
Silver **Ruler:** Volrat VI, Wolfgang III, Johann Georg II **Obv:** Date left of St. George **Rev:** Mintmaster's initials divided by arms **Mint:** Saalfeld

Date	Mintage	VG	F	VF	XF	Unc
16ZZ HI	—	45.00	90.00	180	360	—

KM# 94 1/4 THALER
Silver **Ruler:** Volrat VI, Wolfgang III, Johann Georg II **Rev:** Date in legend, mintmaster's initials divided by arms **Mint:** Saalfeld

Date	Mintage	VG	F	VF	XF	Unc
1623 HI	—	45.00	90.00	180	360	—

KM# 95 1/4 THALER
Silver **Ruler:** Volrat VI, Wolfgang III, Johann Georg II **Rev:** Date divided at top **Mint:** Saalfeld

Date	Mintage	VG	F	VF	XF	Unc
1623 HI	—	45.00	90.00	180	360	—

KM# 96 1/4 THALER
Silver **Ruler:** Volrat VI, Wolfgang III, Johann Georg II **Rev:** Date between two helmets **Mint:** Saalfeld

Date	Mintage	VG	F	VF	XF	Unc
16Z3 HI	—	45.00	90.00	180	360	—

KM# 97 1/4 THALER
Silver **Ruler:** Volrat VI, Wolfgang III, Johann Georg II **Rev:** Date in legend at top, mintmaster's initials divided by arms **Mint:** Saalfeld

Date	Mintage	VG	F	VF	XF	Unc
1623 HI	—	—	—	—	—	—

KM# 107 1/4 THALER
Silver **Ruler:** Volrat VI, Wolfgang III, Johann Georg II **Rev:** Date between helmets **Mint:** Saalfeld

Date	Mintage	VG	F	VF	XF	Unc
1624 HI	—	45.00	90.00	180	360	—

KM# 106 1/4 THALER
Silver **Ruler:** Volrat VI, Wolfgang III, Johann Georg II **Rev:** Date divided by arms **Mint:** Eisleben **Note:** Varieties exist.

Date	Mintage	VG	F	VF	XF	Unc
16Z4 AK	—	45.00	80.00	160	325	—
16Z6 AK	—	45.00	80.00	160	325	—

KM# 108 1/4 THALER
Silver **Ruler:** Volrat VI, Wolfgang III, Johann Georg II **Rev:** Date divided by arms **Mint:** Saalfeld **Note:** Varieties exist.

Date	Mintage	VG	F	VF	XF	Unc
1624 HI	—	45.00	90.00	180	360	—

KM# 116 1/4 THALER
Silver **Ruler:** Volrat VI, Wolfgang III, Johann Georg II **Subject:** Death of Volrat VI **Obv:** St. George slaying dragon at right **Rev:** Seven-line inscription with dates, imperial orb above

Date	Mintage	VG	F	VF	XF	Unc
16Z7	—	—	—	—	—	—
Note: Reported, not confirmed						

KM# 123 1/4 THALER
Silver **Ruler:** Philipp Ernst, Wolfgang III, Johann Georg II **Rev:** Mintmaster's initials between helmets **Mint:** Eisleben

Date	Mintage	VG	F	VF	XF	Unc
16Z9 AK	—	45.00	90.00	180	360	—
1630 AK	—	—	—	—	—	—
Note: Reported, not confirmed						

KM# 6 1/2 THALER
Silver **Ruler:** Philipp Ernst, Wolfgang III, Johann Georg II **Subject:** Death of Johann Georg IV **Obv:** Four-fold arms divide mintmaster's initials, two helmets above divide date **Rev:** Seven-line inscription with dates, legend divided by orb and three small shields **Rev. Legend:** TRAV-UST-MIS-LICH **Mint:** Eisleben **Note:** Varieties exist.

Date	Mintage	VG	F	VF	XF	Unc
1615 GM	—	—	—	—	—	—

KM# 7 1/2 THALER
Silver **Ruler:** Philipp Ernst, Wolfgang III, Johann Georg II **Obv:** Date in legend **Mint:** Eisleben **Note:** Varieties exist.

Date	Mintage	VG	F	VF	XF	Unc
1615 GM	—	—	—	—	—	—

KM# 12 1/2 THALER
Silver **Ruler:** Volrat VI, Jobst II, Wolfgang III **Obv:** Four-fold arms, date and mintmaster's initials between and around two helmets above **Rev:** St. George slaying dragon at right **Mint:** Eisleben **Note:** Varieties exist.

Date	Mintage	VG	F	VF	XF	Unc
1616 AK	—	165	325	550	1,100	—
1617 AK	—	165	325	550	1,100	—

KM# 21 1/2 THALER
Silver **Ruler:** Volrat VI, Jobst II, Wolfgang III, Bruno III **Obv:** Date and mintmaster's initials divided by arms **Mint:** Eisleben

Date	Mintage	VG	F	VF	XF	Unc
1617 AK	—	165	325	450	875	—

KM# 22 1/2 THALER
Silver **Ruler:** Volrat VI, Wolfgang III, Johann Georg II **Obv. Legend:** VOLRATH • IOBST • E • WOLFGANG... **Mint:** Eisleben **Note:** Spruch 1/2 Thaler. Broad flan. Varieties exist.

Date	Mintage	VG	F	VF	XF	Unc
1617 AK	—	165	325	550	1,100	—
1618 AK	—	165	325	550	1,100	—
1619 AK	—	165	325	550	1,100	—

KM# 32 1/2 THALER
Silver **Ruler:** Volrat VI, Jobst II, Wolfgang III, Bruno III **Obv:** Mintmaster's initials between helmets **Mint:** Eisleben **Note:** Varieties exist.

Date	Mintage	VG	F	VF	XF	Unc
1618 AK	—	165	325	550	1,100	—
1619 AK	—	165	325	550	1,100	—

KM# 33 1/2 THALER
Silver **Ruler:** Volrat VI, Jobst II, Wolfgang III, Bruno III **Obv:** Date between helmets **Mint:** Eisleben

Date	Mintage	VG	F	VF	XF	Unc
(16)18 AK	—	165	325	550	1,100	—

KM# 38 1/2 THALER
Silver **Rev:** Date divided by arms **Note:** Varieties exist.

Date	Mintage	VG	F	VF	XF	Unc
1619 AK	—	165	325	550	1,100	—
16Z3 HI	—	165	325	550	1,100	—
16Z4 HI	—	165	325	550	1,100	—

KM# 37 1/2 THALER
Silver **Ruler:** Volrat VI, Jobst II **Obv:** St. George slaying dragon at right **Rev:** Ornate four-fold arms, two helmets above divide date and mintmaster's initials **Mint:** Saalfeld

Date	Mintage	VG	F	VF	XF	Unc
1619 HI	—	165	325	550	1,100	—

KM# 51 1/2 THALER
Silver **Ruler:** Volrat VI, Wolfgang III, Johann Georg II **Rev:** Date and mintmaster's initials between helmets **Mint:** Saalfeld

Date	Mintage	VG	F	VF	XF	Unc
16Z0 HI	—	165	325	550	1,100	—

KM# 52 1/2 THALER
Silver **Ruler:** Volrat VI, Wolfgang III, Johann Georg II **Obv. Legend:** VOLRAT • IOBST • WOLFGANG • E • BRUNO... **Mint:** Saalfeld **Note:** Varieties exist.

Date	Mintage	VG	F	VF	XF	Unc
16Z0 HI	—	165	325	550	1,100	—
16Z4 HI	—	165	325	550	1,100	—

KM# 91 1/2 THALER
Silver **Ruler:** Volrat VI, Wolfgang III, Johann Georg II **Rev:** Date divided by arms **Note:** Varieties exist.

Date	Mintage	VG	F	VF	XF	Unc
16ZZ HI	—	45.00	90.00	180	360	—
16Z3 HI	—	45.00	90.00	180	360	—
16Z4 HI	—	45.00	90.00	180	360	—
16Z4 AK	—	45.00	90.00	180	360	—
16Z5 AK	—	45.00	90.00	180	360	—
16Z6 AK	—	45.00	90.00	180	360	—

KM# 92 1/2 THALER
Silver **Ruler:** Philipp Ernst, Wolfgang III, Johann Georg II **Obv:** Date left of St. George **Rev:** Mintmaster's initials divided by arms **Mint:** Saalfeld **Note:** Varieties exist.

Date	Mintage	VG	F	VF	XF	Unc
16ZZ HI	—	55.00	100	180	360	—

KM# 100 1/2 THALER
Silver **Ruler:** Volrat VI, Wolfgang III, Johann Georg II **Rev:** Date in legend at top, mintmaster's initials divided by arms **Mint:** Saalfeld **Note:** Varieties exist.

Date	Mintage	VG	F	VF	XF	Unc
16Z3 HI	—	55.00	100	180	360	—
16Z4 HI	—	55.00	100	180	360	—
16Z5 HI	—	55.00	100	180	360	—

KM# 99 1/2 THALER
Silver **Ruler:** Volrat VI, Wolfgang III, Johann Georg II **Mint:** Saalfeld **Note:** Broad flan.

Date	Mintage	VG	F	VF	XF	Unc
16Z3 HI	—	55.00	100	180	360	—

KM# 98 1/2 THALER
Silver **Ruler:** Philipp Ernst, Wolfgang III, Johann Georg II **Obv:** Date at top in legend **Mint:** Saalfeld

Date	Mintage	VG	F	VF	XF	Unc
16Z3 HI	—	55.00	100	180	360	—

KM# 101 1/2 THALER
Silver **Ruler:** Volrat VI, Wolfgang III, Johann Georg II **Rev:** Date divided in legend at top **Mint:** Saalfeld

Date	Mintage	VG	F	VF	XF	Unc
16Z3 HI	—	55.00	100	180	360	—

KM# 109 1/2 THALER
Silver **Ruler:** Volrat VI, Wolfgang III, Johann Georg II **Rev:** Date divided by arms **Mint:** Saalfeld

Date	Mintage	VG	F	VF	XF	Unc
16Z4 HI	—	55.00	100	180	360	—

KM# 110 1/2 THALER
Silver **Ruler:** Volrat VI, Wolfgang III, Johann Georg II **Rev:** Date between two helmets **Mint:** Saalfeld

Date	Mintage	VG	F	VF	XF	Unc
16Z4 HI	—	55.00	100	180	360	—

KM# 117 1/2 THALER
Silver **Ruler:** Volrat VI, Wolfgang III, Johann Georg II **Subject:** Death of Volrat VI **Obv:** St. George slaying dragon at right **Rev:** Seven-line inscription with dates, imperial orb above

Date	Mintage	VG	F	VF	XF	Unc
16Z7	—	—	—	—	—	—

KM# 124 1/2 THALER
Silver **Ruler:** Volrat VI, Wolfgang III, Johann Georg II **Rev:** Mintmaster's initials between helmets **Mint:** Eisleben

Date	Mintage	VG	F	VF	XF	Unc
16Z9 AK	—	175	350	675	—	—

KM# 132 1/2 THALER
Silver **Ruler:** Volrat VI, Wolfgang III, Johann Georg II **Rev:** Mintmaster's initials also divided by arms **Mint:** Eisleben

Date	Mintage	VG	F	VF	XF	Unc
1630 AK	—	—	—	—	—	—

KM# 133 1/2 THALER
Silver **Ruler:** Volrat VI, Wolfgang III, Johann Georg II **Rev:** Date between helmets **Mint:** Eisleben

Date	Mintage	VG	F	VF	XF	Unc
1630 AK	—	—	—	—	—	—

KM# 8 THALER
Silver **Ruler:** Volrat VI, Wolfgang III, Johann Georg II **Subject:** Death of Johann Georg IV **Obv:** Helmeted arms divide date above, G-M below **Rev:** Seven-line inscription **Mint:** Eisleben **Note:** Varieties exist. Dav. #6949.

Date	Mintage	VG	F	VF	XF	Unc
1615 GM	—	1,250	2,500	4,500	7,500	—

KM# 13 THALER
Silver **Ruler:** Volrat VI, Jobst II, Wolfgang III **Obv. Legend:** BOLRA. IOBST. E. WOLFG. P. **Mint:** Eisleben **Note:** Varieties exist. Dav. #6950.

Date	Mintage	VG	F	VF	XF	Unc
1616 AK	—	75.00	190	265	400	—
1617 AK	—	75.00	190	265	400	—

KM# 16 THALER
Silver **Ruler:** Volrat VI, Jobst II, Wolfgang III **Obv:** Date divided by shield **Mint:** Eisleben **Note:** Varieties exist. Dav. #6952.

Date	Mintage	VG	F	VF	XF	Unc
1616 AK	—	75.00	190	265	400	—
1617 AK	—	75.00	190	265	400	—

KM# 15 THALER
Silver **Ruler:** Volrat VI, Jobst II, Wolfgang III **Obv:** A-K divided in helmets **Mint:** Eisleben **Note:** Dav. #6951A.

Date	Mintage	VG	F	VF	XF	Unc
1616 AK	—	—	—	—	—	—

KM# 17 THALER
Silver **Ruler:** Volrat VI, Jobst II, Wolfgang III, Bruno III **Obv:** Date divided in helmets, A-K below **Obv. Legend:** VOLRAT. IOBST. WOLF. E. BRV. **Mint:** Eisleben **Note:** Varieties exist.

Date	Mintage	VG	F	VF	XF	Unc
1616 AK	—	75.00	190	275	425	—
1617 AK	—	75.00	190	275	425	—
1618 AK	—	75.00	190	275	425	—
1619 AK	—	75.00	190	275	425	—

KM# 14 THALER
Silver **Ruler:** Volrat VI, Jobst II, Wolfgang III **Obv:** Solid or divided date in helmets **Mint:** Eisleben **Note:** Varieties exist. Dav. #6991.

Date	Mintage	VG	F	VF	XF	Unc
1616 AK	—	75.00	190	275	425	—
1617 AK	—	75.00	190	275	425	—

KM# 23 THALER
Silver **Ruler:** Volrat VI, Jobst II, Wolfgang III, Bruno III **Obv:** Clover and A-K between helmets, date divided by shield below **Mint:** Eisleben **Note:** Varieties exist.

Date	Mintage	VG	F	VF	XF	Unc
1617 AK	—	75.00	190	275	425	—
1618 AK	—	75.00	190	275	425	—
1619 AK	—	75.00	190	275	425	—

KM# 27 THALER
Silver **Ruler:** Volrat VI, Jobst II, Wolfgang III, Bruno III **Rev:** Helmeted arms divide date and initials below **Note:** Varieties exist. Dav. #6967.

Date	Mintage	VG	F	VF	XF	Unc
1617 AK	—	75.00	190	265	400	—
1618 AK	—	75.00	190	265	400	—
1619 AK	—	115	225	375	600	—
16Z1 HI	—	75.00	190	265	400	—
16ZZ HI	—	—	—	—	—	—

Date	Mintage	VG	F	VF	XF	Unc
1624 HI	—	75.00	190	265	400	—
1625 HI	—	75.00	190	265	400	—
1626 HI	—	75.00	190	265	400	—
1627 HI	—	75.00	190	265	400	—

KM# 24 THALER

Silver **Ruler:** Volrat VI, Jobst II, Wolfgang III, Bruno III **Obv:** A-K below **Mint:** Eisleben **Note:** Dav. #6955A.

Date	Mintage	VG	F	VF	XF	Unc
1617 AK	—	75.00	190	275	425	—
1618 AK	—	75.00	190	275	425	—
1619 AK	—	75.00	190	275	425	—

KM# 25 THALER

Silver **Ruler:** Volrat VI, Jobst II, Wolfgang III, Bruno III **Obv:** A-K above date **Mint:** Eisleben **Note:** Dav. #6955B.

Date	Mintage	VG	F	VF	XF	Unc
1617 AK	—	75.00	190	275	425	—
1618 AK	—	75.00	190	275	425	—
1619 AK	—	75.00	190	275	425	—

KM# 26 THALER

Silver **Ruler:** Volrat VI, Jobst II, Wolfgang III, Bruno III **Obv:** Without A-K **Note:** Dav. #6955C.

Date	Mintage	VG	F	VF	XF	Unc
1617	—	75.00	190	275	425	—
1618	—	75.00	190	275	425	—
1619	—	75.00	190	275	425	—

KM# 39 THALER

Silver **Ruler:** Volrat VI, Jobst II **Obv:** Helmeted arms, X/H. I/date between helmets **Obv. Legend:** VOLRATH. ET. IOBST. PATR. COM. ET. COM. **Mint:** Saalfeld **Note:** Varieties exist. Dav. #6956.

Date	Mintage	VG	F	VF	XF	Unc
1619 HI	—	75.00	190	265	400	—
1620 HI	—	75.00	190	265	400	—

KM# 40 THALER

Silver **Ruler:** Volrat VI, Jobst II **Obv:** St. George and dragon **Obv. Legend:** VOLRATH ET. JOBST. PATRVELES **Rev:** Wreaths horizontal **Mint:** Saalfeld **Note:** Varieties exist. Dav. #6957.

Date	Mintage	VG	F	VF	XF	Unc
1619 HI	—	100	200	375	700	—

KM# 41 THALER

Silver **Ruler:** Volrat VI, Jobst II **Rev:** Wreaths vertical **Note:** Varieties exist. Dav. #6957A.

Date	Mintage	VG	F	VF	XF	Unc
1619 HI	—	100	200	375	700	—

KM# 42 THALER

Silver **Ruler:** Volrat VI, Jobst II **Rev:** X/HI/date between helmets **Mint:** Saalfeld **Note:** Varieties exist. Dav. #6969.

Date	Mintage	VG	F	VF	XF	Unc
1619 HI	—	75.00	190	285	450	—
1620 HI	—	75.00	190	285	450	—
1621 HI	—	75.00	190	285	450	—
1622 HI	—	75.00	190	285	450	—

KM# 54 THALER

Silver **Ruler:** Volrat VI, Wolfgang III, Johann Georg II **Obv. Legend:** VOLRAT. WOLF: IOH: GEOR: PATR: CO: E: DO: **Mint:** Saalfeld **Note:** Varieties exist. Dav. #6960.

Date	Mintage	VG	F	VF	XF	Unc
1620 HI	—	75.00	190	265	400	—
1621 HI	—	75.00	190	265	400	—
1622 HI	—	75.00	190	265	400	—

KM# 55 THALER

Silver, 43 mm. **Ruler:** Volrat VI, Wolfgang III, Johann Georg II **Obv. Legend:** VOLR: WOLF: IOH: GEOR: PATR. **Rev:** Spanish or German shields **Note:** Varieties exist. Dav. #6962.

Date	Mintage	VG	F	VF	XF	Unc
16Z0 HI	—	75.00	190	285	450	—
16Z1 HI	—	75.00	190	285	450	—
16ZZ HI	—	75.00	190	285	450	—
16Z3 HI	—	80.00	195	300	500	—
16Z4 HI	—	75.00	190	285	450	—
16Z4 AK	—	100	200	325	675	—
16Z5 AK	—	100	200	325	675	—
16Z6 AK	—	100	200	325	675	—
16Z7 AK	—	100	200	325	675	—

KM# 53 THALER

Silver **Ruler:** Volrat VI, Jobst II **Rev:** X/O/H-I between helmets, date divided below **Mint:** Saalfeld **Note:** Dav. #6958.

Date	Mintage	VG	F	VF	XF	Unc
1620 HI	—	75.00	190	265	400	—

KM# 85 THALER

Silver **Ruler:** Volrat VI, Wolfgang III, Johann Georg II **Rev:** H-I divided by shield **Mint:** Saalfeld **Note:** Dav. #6963A.

Date	Mintage	VG	F	VF	XF	Unc
1621 HI	—	75.00	190	265	400	—
1622 HI	—	75.00	190	265	400	—
1623 HI	—	75.00	190	265	400	—

KM# 84 THALER

Silver **Ruler:** Volrat VI, Wolfgang III, Johann Georg II **Mint:** Saalfeld **Note:** Similar to KM#85 but HI between helmets. Dav. #6963.

Date	Mintage	VG	F	VF	XF	Unc
1621 HI	—	75.00	190	265	400	—
1622 HI	—	75.00	190	265	400	—
1623 HI	—	75.00	190	265	400	—

KM# 102 THALER

Silver **Ruler:** Volrat VI, Wolfgang III, Johann Georg II **Obv. Legend:** VOLRAT. WOLFGANG. E. IOHAN. GEORG. PATRVELIS. **Mint:** Saalfeld **Note:** Dav. #6964.

Date	Mintage	VG	F	VF	XF	Unc
1623 HI	—	120	225	450	900	—
1624 HI	—	120	225	450	900	—

KM# 118 THALER

Silver **Ruler:** Volrat VI, Wolfgang III, Johann Georg II **Subject:** Death of Volrat VI **Obv:** St. George and dragon **Rev:** Seven-line inscription **Note:** Dav. #6965.

Date	Mintage	VG	F	VF	XF	Unc
1627	—	1,215	250	475	950	—

KM# 125 THALER

Silver **Ruler:** Volrat VI, Wolfgang III, Johann Georg II **Obv. Legend:** PHILIP: ERN: SEN: WOL: ET: IO-HA. GEOR. PA: **Rev:** Helmeted arms divide date and A-K **Note:** Dav. #6970. Varieties exist.

Date	Mintage	VG	F	VF	XF	Unc
1629	—	75.00	190	265	400	—
1630	—	75.00	190	265	400	—

KM# 126 THALER

Silver **Ruler:** Volrat VI, Wolfgang III, Johann Georg II **Rev:** A-K between helmets **Note:** Dav. #6970A. Varieties exist.

Date	Mintage	VG	F	VF	XF	Unc
1629	—	115	225	350	550	—

KM# 9 2 THALER

Silver **Ruler:** Volrat VI, Wolfgang III, Johann Georg II **Subject:** Death of Johann Georg IV **Obv:** Helmeted arms divide date above, G-M below **Rev:** Seven-line inscription **Mint:** Eisleben **Note:** Dav. #6948. Varieties exist.

Date	Mintage	VG	F	VF	XF	Unc
1615 GM Rare	—	—	—	—	—	—

KM# 28 2 THALER

Silver **Ruler:** Volrat VI, Jobst II, Wolfgang III, Bruno III **Rev:** Helmeted arms divide date and initials below **Note:** Spruch 2 Thaler. Varieties exist. Dav. #6966.

Date	Mintage	VG	F	VF	XF	Unc
1617 AK	—	2,250	4,500	8,000	—	—
1618 AK	—	2,250	4,500	8,000	—	—
1619 AK	—	2,250	4,500	8,000	—	—
1621 HI	—	2,250	4,500	8,000	—	—
16Z5 AK	—	2,250	4,500	8,000	—	—

KM# 34 2 THALER

Silver **Ruler:** Volrat VI, Jobst II, Wolfgang III, Bruno III **Obv:** Helmeted arms with divided date and A-K between helmets **Obv. Legend:** VOLRAT. IOBST. WOLF. E. BRV. **Mint:** Eisleben **Note:** Dav. #6954.

Date	Mintage	VG	F	VF	XF	Unc
1618 AK	—	2,250	4,500	8,000	—	—

KM# 56 2 THALER

Silver **Ruler:** Volrat VI, Wolfgang III, Johann Georg II **Obv. Legend:** VOLRAT. WOLF: IOH: GEOR: PATR: CO: E: DO: **Mint:** Saalfeld **Note:** Dav. #6959.

Date	Mintage	VG	F	VF	XF	Unc
1620 HI	—	2,250	4,500	8,000	—	—

KM# 86 2 THALER

Silver **Ruler:** Volrat VI, Wolfgang III, Johann Georg II **Rev:** X/HI/date between helmets **Note:** Dav. #6968.

Date	Mintage	VG	F	VF	XF	Unc
16Z1 HI	—	2,250	4,500	8,000	—	—

KM# 112 2 THALER

Silver **Ruler:** Volrat VI, Wolfgang III, Johann Georg II **Obv. Legend:** VOLR: WOLF: IOH: GEOR: PATR. **Rev:** Spanish or German shields **Note:** Varieties exist. Dav. #6961.

Date	Mintage	VG	F	VF	XF	Unc
1626	—	1,850	3,750	7,000	—	—

TRADE COINAGE

KM# 57 1/2 GOLDGULDEN

1.7500 g., 0.9860 Gold 0.0555 oz. AGW **Ruler:** Volrat VI, Wolfgang III, Johann Georg II **Obv:** St. George and dragon in inner circle **Rev:** Three shields as trilobe, date divided at bottom

Date	Mintage	VG	F	VF	XF	Unc
1620	—	750	1,150	2,600	5,500	—

KM# 18 GOLDGULDEN

3.5000 g., 0.9860 Gold 0.1109 oz. AGW **Ruler:** Volrat VI, Jobst II, Wolfgang III, Bruno III **Obv. Legend:** VOLRATH • IOBST • E • WOLFGANG...

Date	Mintage	VG	F	VF	XF	Unc
1616	—	400	650	1,350	3,000	—
1617	—	400	650	1,350	3,000	—

KM# 29 GOLDGULDEN

3.5000 g., 0.9860 Gold 0.1109 oz. AGW **Ruler:** Volrat VI, Wolfgang III, Johann Georg II **Obv. Legend:** VOLRAT • IOBST • WOLFGANG • E • BRUNO...

Date	Mintage	VG	F	VF	XF	Unc
1617	—	400	650	1,350	3,000	—
1618	—	400	650	1,350	3,000	—

KM# 43 GOLDGULDEN

3.5000 g., 0.9860 Gold 0.1109 oz. AGW **Ruler:** Volrat VI, Jobst II **Obv. Legend:** VOLRAT • ET • JOBST ...

Date	Mintage	VG	F	VF	XF	Unc
1619	—	400	650	1,350	3,000	—

KM# 58 GOLDGULDEN

3.5000 g., 0.9860 Gold 0.1109 oz. AGW **Ruler:** Volrat VI, Wolfgang III, Johann Georg II **Obv. Legend:** VOLRAT • ET • IOBST...

Date	Mintage	VG	F	VF	XF	Unc
16Z0 HI	—	350	525	1,150	2,750	—
16Z1 HI	—	350	525	1,150	2,750	—
16Z6 AK	—	350	525	1,150	2,750	—

KM# 134 GOLDGULDEN

3.5000 g., 0.9860 Gold 0.1109 oz. AGW **Ruler:** Volrat VI, Wolfgang III, Johann Georg II **Rev:** Three shields as trilobe, date divided at bottom

Date	Mintage	VG	F	VF	XF	Unc
1630	—	475	875	1,850	3,750	—

KM# 93 2 GOLDGULDEN

7.0000 g., 0.9860 Gold 0.2219 oz. AGW **Ruler:** Volrat VI, Wolfgang III, Johann Georg II **Obv:** St. George slaying dragon at right, date at left **Rev:** Ornate four-fold arms, two helmets above, Mintmaster's initials divided by arms **Mint:** Saalfeld

Date	Mintage	VG	F	VF	XF	Unc
16ZZ HI Rare	—	—	—	—	—	—

KM# 113 2 GOLDGULDEN

7.0000 g., 0.9860 Gold 0.2219 oz. AGW **Ruler:** Volrat VI, Wolfgang III, Johann Georg II **Rev:** Date divided by arms **Mint:** Eisleben

Date	Mintage	VG	F	VF	XF	Unc
16Z6 AK Rare	—	—	—	—	—	—

KM# 127 2 GOLDGULDEN

7.0000 g., 0.9860 Gold 0.2219 oz. AGW **Ruler:** Philipp Ernst, Wolfgang III, Johann Georg II **Rev:** Two helmets above divided by date and mintmaster's initials **Mint:** Eisleben **Note:** Varieties exist.

Date	Mintage	VG	F	VF	XF	Unc
16Z9 AK Rare	—	—	—	—	—	—

KM# 59 2 DUCAT

7.0000 g., 0.9860 Gold 0.2219 oz. AGW **Ruler:** Philipp Ernst **Obv:** St. George slaying dragon, titles of Philipp Ernst **Rev:** Four-fold arms, two helmets above divided by date and mintmaster's initials **Mint:** Saalfeld

Date	Mintage	VG	F	VF	XF	Unc
16Z0 HI Rare	—	—	—	—	—	—

KM# 111 2 DUCAT

7.0000 g., 0.9860 Gold 0.2219 oz. AGW **Rev:** Date between helmets **Mint:** Saalfeld

Date	Mintage	VG	F	VF	XF	Unc
16Z4 HI Rare	—	—	—	—	—	—

KM# 30 3 DUCAT

10.5000 g., 0.9860 Gold 0.3328 oz. AGW **Ruler:** Volrat VI, Jobst II, Wolfgang III, Bruno III **Obv:** Four-fold arms, date and mintmaster's initials between two helmets above **Rev:** St. George slaying dragon at right **Mint:** Eisleben

Date	Mintage	VG	F	VF	XF	Unc
1617 AK Rare	—	—	—	—	—	—
1619 AK Rare	—	—	—	—	—	—

KM# 135 4 DUCAT

14.0000 g., 0.9860 Gold 0.4438 oz. AGW **Ruler:** Philipp Ernst, Wolfgang III, Johann Georg II **Mint:** Eisleben **Note:** Struck with 1 Thaler dies, KM#27.

Date	Mintage	VG	F	VF	XF	Unc
1630 AK Rare	—	—	—	—	—	—

KM# 136 4 DUCAT

14.0000 g., 0.9860 Gold 0.4438 oz. AGW **Ruler:** Philipp Ernst, Wolfgang III, Johann Georg II **Mint:** Eisleben **Note:** Struck with 1 Thaler dies, KM#42.

Date	Mintage	VG	F	VF	XF	Unc
1630 AK Rare	—	—	—	—	—	—

MANSFELD-BORNSTEDT

Founded upon the division of Mansfeld in 1530/32. Raised to the rank of Prince of the Empire in 1709. The line became extinct in 1780 and its titles fell to Colloredo.

RULERS

Bruno II, 1546-1615
Wolfgang III, 1615-1638
Karl Adam, 1638-1662
Franz Maximilian, 1644-1692
Heinrich Franz, 1644-1715
Georg Albrecht, 1657-1696
Maximilian Philipp, 1657-1664
Karl Franz, 1692-1717

JOINT COINAGE

V - Wolfgang III, Bruno III, Joachim Friedrich and Philipp V

REFERENCE

T = Otto Tornau, **Münzwesen und Münzen der Grafschaft Mansfeld**, Prague, 1937.

COUNTSHIP

STANDARD COINAGE

KM# 55 2 PFENNIG

Copper **Ruler:** Bruno II, Wilhelm I, Johann Georg IV, Volrat VI and Jobst II **Obv:** 3-fold arms, .I.I. above **Mint:** Schraplau **Note:** Kipper 2 Pfennig. Uniface.

Date	Mintage	VG	F	VF	XF	Unc
ND(1621/22)	—	—	—	—	—	—

KM# 31 3 PFENNIG (Dreier)

Silver **Ruler:** Bruno II, Wilhelm I, Johann Georg IV, Volrat VI and Jobst II **Obv:** Ornate 4-fold arms with mintmaster's initials above **Rev:** Imperial orb with 3 divides date, within ornamented rhombus **Mint:** Eisleben **Note:** Varieties exist.

Date	Mintage	VG	F	VF	XF	Unc
161Z GM	—	—	—	—	—	—
1613 GM	—	—	—	—	—	—

KM# 56 3 PFENNIG (Dreier)

Copper **Obv:** Round 4-fold arms **Rev:** Imperial orb with 3 divides date **Note:** Kipper 3 Pfennig. Varieties exist.

Date	Mintage	Good	VG	F	VF	XF
(16)Z1	—	11.00	22.00	45.00	90.00	—

KM# 57 3 PFENNIG (Dreier)

Copper **Ruler:** Bruno II, Wilhelm I, Johann Georg IV, Volrat VI and Jobst II **Obv:** Rampant lion to left (Heldrungen), OWS below **Rev:** Imperial orb with 3 **Mint:** Oberwiederstedt bei Hettstedt

Date	Mintage	Good	VG	F	VF	XF
ND(1621/22) OWS	—	20.00	33.00	65.00	130	—

KM# 58 3 PFENNIG (Dreier)

Copper **Ruler:** Bruno II, Wilhelm I, Johann Georg IV, Volrat VI and Jobst II **Obv:** 4-fold arms, W above **Rev:** Imperial orb with 3 divides date **Mint:** Welbsleben

Date	Mintage	Good	VG	F	VF	XF
(16)Z1 W	—	20.00	33.00	65.00	130	—

KM# 59 3 PFENNIG (Dreier)

Copper **Ruler:** Wolfgang III and David **Obv:** 3-fold arms in ornate shield **Rev:** Imperial orb with 3 **Mint:** Schraplau **Note:** Varieties exist.

Date	Mintage	Good	VG	F	VF	XF
ND(1621/22)	—	20.00	33.00	65.00	130	—

KM# 60 3 PFENNIG (Dreier)

Copper **Ruler:** Wolfgang III and David **Obv:** 3-fold arms in ornate shield **Note:** Uniface.

Date	Mintage	Good	VG	F	VF	XF
ND(1621/22)	—	20.00	33.00	65.00	130	—

KM# 61 3 PFENNIG (Dreier)

Copper **Ruler:** Wolfgang III and David **Obv:** 4-fold arms, date above **Rev:** Rampant lion to left (Heldrungen) in circle, 3 below **Note:** Varieties exist.

Date	Mintage	Good	VG	F	VF	XF
16Z1	—	11.00	20.00	40.00	85.00	—

KM# 62 3 PFENNIG (Dreier)

Copper **Ruler:** Wolfgang III and David **Rev:** Lion in squarish shield, value 3 above

Date	Mintage	Good	VG	F	VF	XF
16Z1	—	11.00	20.00	40.00	85.00	—

KM# 63 3 PFENNIG (Dreier)

Copper **Ruler:** Wolfgang III and David **Rev:** Ornately-shaped shield

Date	Mintage	Good	VG	F	VF	XF
16Z1	—	11.00	20.00	40.00	85.00	—

KM# 64 3 PFENNIG (Dreier)

Copper **Ruler:** Wolfgang III and David **Rev:** Value: I.I.I. above lion arms

Date	Mintage	Good	VG	F	VF	XF
16Z1	—	11.00	20.00	40.00	85.00	—

KM# 65 3 PFENNIG (Dreier)

Copper **Ruler:** Wolfgang III and Joachim Friedrich **Obv:** Shield of Arnstein eagle divides date, F above **Rev:** Imperial orb with 3 **Mint:** Friedeburg

Date	Mintage	Good	VG	F	VF	XF
(16)Z1	—	20.00	33.00	65.00	130	—

KM# 40 GROSCHEN

Silver **Ruler:** Bruno II, Wilhelm I, Volrat VI and Jobst II **Subject:** Death of Bruno II **Obv:** 4-fold arms divide mintmaster's initials **Rev:** 8-line inscription with dates **Mint:** Eisleben **Note:** Varieties exist.

Date	Mintage	VG	F	VF	XF	Unc
1615 GM	—	—	—	—	—	—

KM# 32 3-1/2 GROSCHEN

Silver **Ruler:** Bruno II, Wilhelm I, Johann Georg I, Volrat VI and Jobst II **Obv:** 4-fold arms divide 3 1/Z - gl, two helmets above, date in legend

Date	Mintage	VG	F	VF	XF	Unc
161Z	—	—	—	—	—	—

KM# 66 12 KREUZER (Schreckenburger)

Silver **Ruler:** Wolfgang III, Bruno III and Joachim Friedrich **Obv:** Crowned imperial eagle, 1Z in orb on breast, titles of Ferdinand II **Rev:** Crowned 4-fold arms divide date, angel above **Note:** Kipper 12 Kreuzer.

Date	Mintage	VG	F	VF	XF	Unc
(16)21	—	55.00	115	235	475	—

KM# 67 12 KREUZER (Schreckenburger)

Silver **Ruler:** Wolfgang III, Bruno III, Joachim Friedrich and Philipp V **Obv:** Crowned 4-fold arms **Rev:** St. George slaying dragon at right, date divided by imperial orb in legend at top

Date	Mintage	VG	F	VF	XF	Unc
16Z1	—	55.00	115	235	475	—

KM# 68 12 KREUZER (Schreckenburger)

Silver **Ruler:** Wolfgang III, Bruno III, Joachim Friedrich and Philipp V **Obv:** Value (1Z) at bottom

Date	Mintage	VG	F	VF	XF	Unc
16Z1	—	55.00	115	235	475	—

KM# 69 12 KREUZER (Schreckenburger)

Silver **Ruler:** Wolfgang III, Bruno III, Joachim Friedrich and Philipp V **Obv:** 3 small shields of arms around central point, titles of Wolfgang III **Rev:** Three small shields of arms around central point, titles of Wolfgang III **Rev. Legend:** FATA. VIAM. INVENIENT

Date	Mintage	VG	F	VF	XF	Unc
1621	—	55.00	115	235	475	—

KM# 70 12 KREUZER (Schreckenburger)

Silver **Ruler:** Wolfgang III, Bruno III, Joachim Friedrich and Philipp V **Rev:** St. George slaying dragon at right

Date	Mintage	VG	F	VF	XF	Unc
1621	—	55.00	115	235	475	—

KM# 71 12 KREUZER (Schreckenburger)

Silver **Ruler:** Wolfgang III, Bruno III, Joachim Friedrich and Philipp V **Obv:** 4-fold arms **Rev:** Crowned imperial eagle, 1Z in orb on breast, legend, date **Rev. Legend:** FATA. VIAM. INVENIENT

Date	Mintage	VG	F	VF	XF	Unc
16Z1	—	55.00	115	235	475	—
1621	—	55.00	115	235	475	—

KM# 72 12 KREUZER (Schreckenburger)

Silver **Ruler:** Wolfgang III and Joachim Friedrich **Obv:** Crowned 4-fold arms divide date, angel above **Rev:** Crowned imperial eagle, 1Z in orb on breast

Date	Mintage	VG	F	VF	XF	Unc
16Z1	—	55.00	115	235	475	—

KM# 73 12 KREUZER (Schreckenburger)

Silver **Ruler:** Wolfgang III and Joachim Friedrich **Obv:** 4-fold arms surmounted on cross with lilies at ends, titles of Joachim Friedrich

Date	Mintage	VG	F	VF	XF	Unc
ND(1621/22)	—	55.00	115	235	475	—

KM# 75 24 KREUZER (Doppelschreckenberger)

Silver **Ruler:** Wolfgang III **Obv:** Ornate 4-fold arms of Mansfeld, angel's head and wings above **Obv. Legend:** WOL: COM: E: E: I. MANS. ND: I. H. **Rev:** Three small ornate shields of arms, 1 above 2, upper shield divides 2 - 4, date at end of legend **Rev. Legend:** RATA. VIAM. INVENIENT. **Mint:** Schraplau **Note:** Kipper 24 Kreuzer.

Date	Mintage	Good	VG	F	VF	XF
16Z1 Rare	—	—	—	—	—	—

KM# 95 1/2 ORT (1/8 Thaler)

Silver **Ruler:** Wolfgang III and Joachim Friedrich **Obv:** Two helmets above 4-fold arms, titles of Karl Adam **Rev. Inscription:** EIN. / HALB. / REICHS. / ORT. / date

Date	Mintage	VG	F	VF	XF	Unc
1655	—	—	—	—	—	—

KM# 20 1/28 THALER

Silver **Ruler:** Bruno II, Wilhelm I, Johann Georg IV, Volrat VI and Jobst II **Obv:** Two hlemets above 4-fold arms **Rev:** Imperial orb with Z8 divides date **Note:** Varieties exist.

Date	Mintage	VG	F	VF	XF	Unc
1610	—	45.00	90.00	180	—	—
1610 GM	—	45.00	90.00	180	—	—
1611 GM	—	45.00	90.00	180	—	—

KM# 22 1/28 THALER

Silver **Ruler:** Bruno II, Wilhelm I, Johann Georg IV, Volrat VI and Jobst II **Rev:** Date in legend **Mint:** Eisleben **Note:** Varieties exist.

Date	Mintage	VG	F	VF	XF	Unc
1611 GM	—	65.00	135	275	—	—

KM# 23 1/28 THALER

Silver **Ruler:** Bruno II, Wilhelm I, Johann Georg IV, Volrat VI and Jobst II **Mint:** Eisleben **Note:** Mule. Reverse of issue of Friedrich Christoph of Eigentliche-Hinterort.

Date	Mintage	VG	F	VF	XF	Unc
1611 GM	—	—	—	—	—	—

KM# 77 1/24 THALER

Silver **Ruler:** Wolfgang III, Bruno III, Joachim Friedrich and Philipp V **Obv:** Crowned 4-fold arms **Rev:** Imperial orb with 24, date divided in legend at top **Note:** Kipper 1/24 Thaler. Prev. KM #74.

Date	Mintage	VG	F	VF	XF	Unc
16Z1	—	—	—	—	—	—

KM# 102 1/24 THALER

Silver **Ruler:** Wolfgang III, Bruno III, Joachim Friedrich and Philipp V **Obv:** Ornamented oval 4-folds arms, titles of Karl Adam **Rev:** Imperial orb with 24 divides date **Mint:** Eisleben

Date	Mintage	VG	F	VF	XF	Unc
1657 HPK	—	—	—	—	—	—

KM# 116 1/24 THALER

Silver **Ruler:** Franz Maximilian and Heinrich Franz **Obv:** Date divided by cross on top of orb **Mint:** Eisleben

Date	Mintage	VG	F	VF	XF	Unc
1668 ABK	—	30.00	60.00	120	—	—

KM# 115 1/24 THALER

Silver **Ruler:** Franz Maximilian and Heinrich Franz **Obv:** Imperial orb with 24 divides date and mintmaster's initials **Rev:** Crowned 4-fold arms **Mint:** Eisleben **Note:** Varieties exist.

Date	Mintage	VG	F	VF	XF	Unc
1668 ABK	—	30.00	60.00	120	—	—
1670 ABK	—	30.00	65.00	135	—	—
1673 ABK	—	50.00	100	210	—	—

KM# 117 1/24 THALER

Silver **Ruler:** Franz Maximilian and Heinrich Franz **Rev:** Without crown above arms **Mint:** Eisleben **Note:** Varieties exist.

Date	Mintage	VG	F	VF	XF	Unc
1668 ABK	—	30.00	60.00	120	—	—

KM# 27 1/21 THALER

Silver **Ruler:** Franz Maximilian and Heinrich Franz **Rev:** Without value shown in orb **Mint:** Eisleben

Date	Mintage	VG	F	VF	XF	Unc
1611 GM	—	16.00	33.00	65.00	130	—

KM# 24 1/21 THALER

Silver **Ruler:** Franz Maximilian and Heinrich Franz **Mint:** Eisleben **Note:** Varieties exist.

Date	Mintage	VG	F	VF	XF	Unc
1611 GM	—	16.00	33.00	65.00	130	—
161Z GM	—	16.00	33.00	65.00	130	—
161Z	—	16.00	33.00	65.00	130	—
1613 GM	—	16.00	33.00	65.00	130	—
1614 GM	—	16.00	33.00	65.00	130	—
1615 GM	—	16.00	33.00	65.00	130	—

KM# 26 1/21 THALER

Silver **Ruler:** Franz Maximilian and Heinrich Franz **Rev:** Date divided by orb **Mint:** Eisleben **Note:** Varieties exist.

Date	Mintage	VG	F	VF	XF	Unc
1611	—	16.00	33.00	65.00	130	—
1611 GM	—	16.00	33.00	65.00	130	—
161Z GM	—	16.00	33.00	65.00	130	—

KM# 33 1/21 THALER

Silver **Ruler:** Bruno II, Wilhelm I, Volrat VI and Jobst II **Obv:** Ornamented 4-fold arms **Rev:** Imperial orb with Z1 divides mintmaster's initials, date in legend **Mint:** Eisleben

Date	Mintage	VG	F	VF	XF	Unc
161Z GM	—	16.00	33.00	60.00	120	240

KM# 25 1/21 THALER

Silver **Ruler:** Franz Maximilian and Heinrich Franz **Mint:** Eisleben **Note:** Klippe.

Date	Mintage	VG	F	VF	XF	Unc
1613 GM	—	15.00	30.00	55.00	110	—

KM# 28 1/8 THALER

Silver **Ruler:** Bruno II, Wilhelm I, Johann Georg IV, Volrat VI and Jobst II **Obv:** 4-fold arms divide date and mintmaster's initials, angel above **Rev:** St. George slaying dragon **Mint:** Eisleben

Date	Mintage	VG	F	VF	XF	Unc
1611 GM	—	185	375	775	—	—

KM# 29 1/8 THALER

Silver **Mint:** Eisleben **Note:** Varieties exist.

Date	Mintage	VG	F	VF	XF	Unc
1611 GM	—	185	375	775	—	—
161Z GM	—	185	375	775	—	—

KM# 41 1/8 THALER

Silver **Ruler:** Bruno II, Wilhelm I, Johann Georg IV, Volrat VI and Jobst II **Subject:** Death of Bruno II **Obv:** 4-fold arms, mintmaster's initials above **Rev:** 8-line inscription with dates **Mint:** Eisleben

Date	Mintage	VG	F	VF	XF	Unc
1615 GM	—	—	—	—	—	—

KM# 5 1/4 THALER

Silver **Ruler:** Bruno II, Wilhelm I (V) and Johann Georg IV **Obv:** Two helmets divided by date above 4-fold arms **Rev:** St. George slaying dragon, imperial orb above horse's head **Mint:** Eisleben **Note:** Varieties exist.

Date	Mintage	VG	F	VF	XF	Unc
(1)604 GM	—	65.00	120	200	425	—
1605 GM	—	65.00	120	200	425	—
1606 GM	—	65.00	120	200	425	—

KM# 13 1/4 THALER

Silver **Ruler:** Bruno II, Wilhelm I, Johann Georg IV and Volrat VI **Mint:** Eisleben **Note:** Varieties exist.

Date	Mintage	VG	F	VF	XF	Unc
1607 GM	—	65.00	120	200	425	—
1608 GM	—	65.00	120	200	425	—
1609 GM	—	65.00	120	200	425	—
1610 GM	—	65.00	120	200	425	—
161Z GM	—	65.00	120	200	425	—
1613 GM	—	65.00	120	200	425	—
1614 GM	—	65.00	120	200	425	—
1615 GM	—	65.00	120	200	425	—
ND GM	—	65.00	120	200	425	—

KM# 42 1/4 THALER

Silver **Ruler:** Bruno II, Wilhelm I, Johann Georg IV and Volrat VI **Subject:** Death of Bruno II **Obv:** St. George slaying dragon at left, sword raised above head **Rev:** 8-line inscription with dates **Mint:** Eisleben **Note:** Varieties exist.

Date	Mintage	VG	F	VF	XF	Unc
1615 GM	—	135	225	450	875	—

KM# 83 1/4 THALER

Silver **Ruler:** Wolfgang III and Johann Georg II **Obv:** St. George slaying dragon, imperial orb above horse's head **Rev:** Two helmets above 4-fold arms divide date **Mint:** Eisleben **Note:** Varieties exist.

Date	Mintage	VG	F	VF	XF	Unc
1635 HPK	—	115	175	300	600	—

KM# 96 1/4 THALER

Silver **Ruler:** Wolfgang III and Johann Georg II **Obv:** Two helmets above 4-fold arms, date divided by arms, titles of Karl Adam **Rev:** St. George slaying dragon, imperial orb above horse's head **Mint:** Eisleben

Date	Mintage	VG	F	VF	XF	Unc
1655 HPK	—	115	165	275	550	—
1660 HPK	—	—	—	—	—	—

Note: Reported, not confirmed

KM# 105 1/4 THALER

Silver **Ruler:** Wolfgang III and Johann Georg II **Rev:** Obverse of issue of Christoph Friedrich of Eigentliche-Hinterort **Mint:** Eisleben **Note:** Mule.

Date	Mintage	VG	F	VF	XF	Unc
1660 HPK	—	—	—	—	—	—

KM# 108 1/4 THALER

Silver **Ruler:** Franz Maximilian and Heinrich Franz **Obv:** St. George slaying dragon below **Rev:** 4-fold arms, two helmets above divided by date, mintmaster's initials outside helmets **Mint:** Eisleben

Date	Mintage	VG	F	VF	XF	Unc
1667 ABK	—	135	200	325	650	—

KM# 119 1/3 THALER (1/2 Gulden)

Silver **Ruler:** Franz Maximilian and Heinrich Franz **Rev:** Palm branches at sides of arms, mintmaster's initials below **Mint:** Stolberg

Date	Mintage	VG	F	VF	XF	Unc
1669 ABK	—	55.00	80.00	220	385	—

KM# 120 1/3 THALER (1/2 Gulden)

Silver **Ruler:** Franz Maximilian and Heinrich Franz **Rev:** Without palm branches **Mint:** Stolberg

Date	Mintage	VG	F	VF	XF	Unc
1669 ABK	—	55.00	80.00	220	385	—

KM# 118 1/3 THALER (1/2 Gulden)

Silver **Obv:** St. George slaying dragon. value 1/3 in oval at bottom **Rev:** 4-fold arms divide mintmaster's initials, crown above divides date **Mint:** Stolberg **Note:** Varieties exist.

Date	Mintage	VG	F	VF	XF	Unc
1669 ABK	—	33.00	55.00	100	210	—
1670 ABK	—	33.00	55.00	100	210	—

KM# 125 1/3 THALER (1/2 Gulden)

Silver **Ruler:** Franz Maximilian and Heinrich Franz **Rev:** Arms divide date and mintmaster's initials **Mint:** Stolberg **Note:** Varieties exist.

Date	Mintage	VG	F	VF	XF	Unc
1670 ABK	—	27.00	50.00	110	220	—
1671 ABK	—	27.00	50.00	110	220	—
1672 ABK	—	27.00	50.00	110	220	—
1673 ABK	—	27.00	50.00	110	220	—

KM# 127 1/3 THALER (1/2 Gulden)

Silver **Ruler:** Franz Maximilian and Heinrich Franz **Rev:** 4-fold oval arms divide mintmaster's initials, crown above divides date **Mint:** Stolberg

Date	Mintage	VG	F	VF	XF	Unc
1673 ABK	—	30.00	55.00	110	220	—

KM# 6 1/2 THALER

Silver **Ruler:** Bruno II, Wilhelm I (V) and Johann Georg IV **Mint:** Eisleben **Note:** Varieties exist.

Date	Mintage	VG	F	VF	XF	Unc
(1)604 GM	—	65.00	135	275	550	—
1605 GM	—	65.00	135	275	550	—
1606 GM	—	65.00	135	275	550	—

KM# 10 1/2 THALER

Silver **Ruler:** Bruno II, Wilhelm I, Johann Georg IV and Volrat VI **Mint:** Eisleben

Date	Mintage	VG	F	VF	XF	Unc
1606 GM	—	60.00	110	225	450	—
1607 GM	—	60.00	110	225	450	—
1608 GM	—	60.00	110	225	450	—
1609 GM	—	60.00	110	225	450	—
1610 GM	—	60.00	110	225	450	—
1611 GM	—	60.00	110	225	450	—
161Z GM	—	60.00	110	225	450	—
1613 GM	—	60.00	110	225	450	—
1614 GM	—	60.00	110	225	450	—
1615 GM	—	60.00	110	225	450	—
ND GM	—	60.00	110	225	450	—

KM# 14 1/2 THALER

Silver **Ruler:** Bruno II, Wilhelm I, Johann Georg IV and Volrat VI **Mint:** Eisleben **Note:** Broad flan.

Date	Mintage	VG	F	VF	XF	Unc
1608 GM	—	—	—	—	—	—

KM# 34 1/2 THALER

Silver **Ruler:** Bruno II, Wilhelm I, Johann Georg IV, Volrat VI and Jobst II **Obv:** Date in legend **Mint:** Eisleben **Note:** Varieties exist.

Date	Mintage	VG	F	VF	XF	Unc
161Z GM	—	—	—	—	—	—

KM# 43 1/2 THALER

Silver **Ruler:** Bruno II, Wilhelm I, Johann Georg IV, Volrat VI and Jobst II **Subject:** Death of Bruno II **Obv:** St. George slaying dragon at left, sword raised above head **Rev:** 8-line inscription with dates **Mint:** Eisleben **Note:** Varieties exist.

Date	Mintage	VG	F	VF	XF	Unc
1615 GM	—	—	—	—	—	—

KM# 84 1/2 THALER

Silver **Ruler:** Wolfgang III and Johann Georg II **Obv:** St. George slaying dragon, imperial orb above horse's head **Rev:** Two helmets above 4-fold arms divide date **Mint:** Eisleben **Note:** Varieties exist.

Date	Mintage	VG	F	VF	XF	Unc
1635 HPK	—	115	220	375	775	—
1638 HPK	—	115	220	375	775	—

KM# 97 1/2 THALER

Silver **Ruler:** Wolfgang III and Johann Georg II **Obv:** Two helmets above 4-fold arms, date divided by arms, titles of Karl Adam **Rev:** St. George slaying dragon, imperial orb above horse's head **Mint:** Eisleben **Note:** Varieties exist.

Date	Mintage	VG	F	VF	XF	Unc
1655 HPK	—	75.00	150	300	600	—
1657 HPK	—	75.00	150	300	600	—
1658 HPK	—	75.00	150	300	600	—
1659 HPK	—	75.00	150	300	600	—
1660 HPK	—	75.00	150	300	600	—

KM# 109 1/2 THALER

Silver **Ruler:** Wolfgang III and Johann Georg II **Obv:** St. George slaying dragon below **Rev:** 4-fold arms divide date, two helmets above, mintmaster's initials outside helmets **Mint:** Eisleben **Note:** Varieties exist.

Date	Mintage	VG	F	VF	XF	Unc
1667 HPK	—	65.00	135	275	550	—

KM# 107 2/3 THALER (Gulden)

Silver **Ruler:** Franz Maximilian and Heinrich Franz **Obv:** St. George slaying dragon, value: 2/3 in oval at bottom **Rev:** 4-fold arms divide mintmaster's initials crown above divides date **Mint:** Eisleben **Note:** Varieties exist.

Date	Mintage	VG	F	VF	XF	Unc
1665 ABK	—	55.00	85.00	190	290	—
1675 ABK	—	55.00	85.00	190	290	—
1676 ABK	—	55.00	85.00	190	290	—

KM# 128 2/3 THALER (Gulden)

Silver **Ruler:** Franz Maximilian and Heinrich Franz **Rev:** Two helmets above arms instead of crowne, date outside left helmet **Mint:** Eisleben **Note:** Varieties exist.

Date	Mintage	VG	F	VF	XF	Unc
1675 ABK	—	40.00	65.00	120	240	—

KM# 129 2/3 THALER (Gulden)

Silver **Ruler:** Franz Maximilian and Heinrich Franz **Rev:** Date divided by helmets **Mint:** Eisleben **Note:** Varieties exist.

Date	Mintage	VG	F	VF	XF	Unc
1675 ABK	—	45.00	80.00	130	250	—

KM# 130 2/3 THALER (Gulden)

Silver **Ruler:** Franz Maximilian and Heinrich Franz **Rev:** Date and mintmaster's initials divided by arms **Mint:** Eisleben **Note:** Varieties exist.

Date	Mintage	VG	F	VF	XF	Unc
1675 ABK	—	45.00	80.00	125	250	—
1676 ABK	—	45.00	80.00	125	250	—

KM# 131 2/3 THALER (Gulden)

Silver **Ruler:** Franz Maximilian and Heinrich Franz **Obv:** Date divided in legend near top **Mint:** Eisleben **Note:** Varieties exist.

Date	Mintage	VG	F	VF	XF	Unc
1676 ABK	—	45.00	80.00	125	250	—
ND ABK	—	45.00	80.00	125	250	—

KM# 7 THALER

Silver **Ruler:** Bruno II, Wilhelm I (V) and Johann Georg IV **Obv:** Helmeted arms, G-M and date above **Obv. Legend:** BRVNO. SENIOR. WILH: H: GE: P: **Rev:** St. George and dragon, orb at upper right **Rev. Legend:** COM: E: DOMI: I: MAN-SFE: NO: D: I: H: **Mint:** Eisleben **Note:** Dav. #6916.

Date	Mintage	VG	F	VF	XF	Unc
1604 GM	—	75.00	190	275	750	1,500
1605 GM	—	75.00	190	275	750	1,500
1606 GM	—	75.00	190	275	750	1,500
1607 GM	—	75.00	190	275	750	1,500

KM# 8 THALER

Silver **Ruler:** Bruno II, Wilhelm I (V) and Johann Georg IV **Obv:** St. George and dragon **Obv. Legend:** COMI: E: DOMI: IN: MANSFE: NOB: DO: I. h: **Rev:** St. George and dragon, legend similar to KM#7 but with single dots **Note:** Mule. Dav. #6917.

Date	Mintage	VG	F	VF	XF	Unc
ND(1604)	—	125	250	400	900	—

KM# 9 THALER

Silver **Ruler:** Bruno II, Wilhelm I, Johann Georg IV and Volrat VI **Obv. Legend:** BRVNO. SENI: WILH: HA: GE: VOLR: P. **Mint:** Eisleben **Note:** Dav. #6919.

Date	Mintage	VG	F	VF	XF	Unc
1605	—	75.00	195	300	775	—
1607	—	75.00	195	300	775	—
1608	—	75.00	195	300	775	—
(1)609	—	75.00	195	300	775	—
1609	—	75.00	195	300	775	—
1610	—	75.00	195	300	775	—
1611	—	75.00	195	300	775	—
1612	—	75.00	195	300	775	—
1613 GM	—	75.00	195	300	775	—
1614 GM	—	75.00	195	300	775	—
1615 GM	—	75.00	195	300	775	—

KM# 36 THALER

Silver **Ruler:** Bruno II, Wilhelm I, Johann Georg IV and Volrat VI **Obv. Legend:** BRVNO. S: WILH. HANS. GEOR. VOLRAT. P. **Mint:** Eisleben **Note:** Dav. #6921.

Date	Mintage	VG	F	VF	XF	Unc
1612 GM	—	85.00	200	325	850	—
1613 GM	—	85.00	200	325	850	—
1614 GM	—	85.00	200	325	850	—
1615 GM	—	85.00	225	325	850	—
ND	—	85.00	225	325	850	—

KM# 37 THALER

Silver **Ruler:** Bruno II, Wilhelm I, Johann Georg IV, Volrat VI and Jobst II **Obv. Legend:** BRVNO: S: WILH. HANS: G. VOL: IOB: P: **Mint:** Eisleben **Note:** Dav. #6922.

Date	Mintage	VG	F	VF	XF	Unc
1612 GM	—	120	300	650	—	—

KM# 44 THALER

Silver **Ruler:** Bruno II, Wilhelm I, Johann Georg IV, Volrat VI and Jobst II **Subject:** Death of Bruno **Obv:** Large GM, hooves within circle **Mint:** Eisleben **Note:** Dav. #6923.

Date	Mintage	VG	F	VF	XF	Unc
1615 GM	—	120	225	350	875	—

KM# 45 THALER

Silver **Ruler:** Bruno II, Wilhelm I, Johann Georg IV, Volrat VI a nd Jobst II **Obv:** Small GM, hooves break circle **Mint:** Eisleben **Note:** Dav. #6923A.

Date	Mintage	VG	F	VF	XF	Unc
1615 GM	—	130	230	375	900	—

KM# 35 THALER

Silver **Ruler:** Bruno II, Wilhelm I, Johann Georg IV and Volrat VI **Note:** Klippe. Dav. #6919D.

Date	Mintage	VG	F	VF	XF	Unc
1615 Rare	—	—	—	—	—	—

KM# 48 THALER

Silver **Ruler:** Wolfgang III, Bruno III, Joachim Friedrich and Philipp V **Obv. Legend:** WOLFGAN: BRVNO: IOACHIM: FRIDERIC. ET. PHILIP: F. **Rev:** Date and HI between helmets **Note:** Dav. #6924.

Date	Mintage	VG	F	VF	XF	Unc
1619	—	90.00	225	350	875	—

KM# 49 THALER

Silver **Ruler:** Wolfgang III, Bruno III, Joachim Friedrich and Philipp V **Rev:** H-I divided by helmets **Note:** Dav. #6924A.

Date	Mintage	VG	F	VF	XF	Unc
1619	—	90.00	225	350	875	—

KM# 50 THALER

Silver **Ruler:** Wolfgang III and Bruno III **Obv. Legend:** WOLFGAN: ET. BRVNO: FRAT: COM: ET: DOMI: **Note:** Dav. #6925.

Date	Mintage	VG	F	VF	XF	Unc
1619 XHI	—	90.00	225	350	875	—
1620 XHI	—	90.00	225	350	875	—
1622 XHI	—	90.00	225	350	875	—

KM# 80 THALER

Silver **Ruler:** Wolfgang III and Johann Georg II **Obv. Legend:** WOLFG: ET. IOHA: GEOR: PAT: COMI: ET. **Mint:** Eisleben **Note:** Dav. #6927.

Date	Mintage	VG	F	VF	XF	Unc
1631 HPK	—	75.00	195	300	775	—
1632 HPK	—	75.00	195	300	775	—
1635 HPK	—	75.00	195	300	775	—
1637 HPK	—	75.00	195	300	775	—
1638 HPK	—	75.00	195	300	775	—
ND HPK	—	75.00	195	300	775	—

KM# 81 THALER

Silver **Ruler:** Wolfgang III and Johann Georg II **Obv. Legend:** ...IOHAN. GEORG... **Rev:** Double-helmeted arms **Mint:** Eisleben **Note:** Dav. #6928.

Date	Mintage	VG	F	VF	XF	Unc
ND HPK	—	145	285	550	1,250	—

KM# 98 THALER

Silver **Ruler:** Wolfgang III and Johann Georg II **Obv:** Helmeted arms, date divided below **Rev:** St. George and the dragon **Mint:** Eisleben **Note:** Dav. #6930.

Date	Mintage	VG	F	VF	XF	Unc
1655 HPK	—	75.00	195	350	875	—
1656 HPK	—	75.00	195	350	875	—
1657 HPK	—	75.00	195	350	875	—
1658 HPK	—	75.00	195	350	875	—
1659 HPK	—	75.00	195	350	875	—
1660 HPK	—	75.00	195	350	875	—

KM# 110 THALER

Silver **Ruler:** Franz Maximilian and Heinrich Franz **Obv:** Large winged dragon **Obv. Legend:** FRANZ MAX. HEINR. FRANZ. COMIT. I. MANSFELT. **Mint:** Eisleben **Note:** Dav. #6931.

Date	Mintage	VG	F	VF	XF	Unc
1667 ABK	—	100	250	450	1,000	—

KM# 111 THALER
Silver **Ruler:** Franz Maximilian and Heinrich Franz **Obv:** Small winged dragon **Mint:** Eisleben **Note:** Dav. #6931A.

Date	Mintage	VG	F	VF	XF	Unc
1667 ABK	—	100	250	450	1,000	—

KM# 15 2 THALER
Silver **Ruler:** Bruno II, Wilhelm I, Johann Georg IV and Volrat VI **Obv. Legend:** BRVNO. SENI: WILLH: HA: GE: VOLR: P. **Mint:** Eisleben **Note:** Dav. #6918. Similar to 1 Thaler, KM#9.

Date	Mintage	VG	F	VF	XF	Unc
1609 GM	—	850	1,650	3,200	5,500	—
1615 GM	—	850	1,650	3,200	5,500	—

KM# 38 2 THALER
Silver **Ruler:** Bruno II, Wilhelm I, Johann Georg IV and Volrat VI **Obv. Legend:** BRVNO. S. WILH. HANS. GEOR. VOLRAT. P. **Mint:** Eisleben **Note:** Dav. #6920.

Date	Mintage	VG	F	VF	XF	Unc
1612 GM	—	850	1,650	3,200	5,500	—

KM# 85 2 THALER
Silver **Ruler:** Wolfgang III and Johann Georg II **Obv:** St. George right and dragon **Obv. Legend:** WOLFG: ET. IOHA: GEOR: PAT: COMI: ET. **Mint:** Eisleben **Note:** Dav. #6926.

Date	Mintage	VG	F	VF	XF	Unc
1635 HPK	—	850	1,650	3,200	5,500	—

KM# 99 2 THALER
Silver **Ruler:** Wolfgang III and Johann Georg II **Obv:** St. George slaying dragon **Rev:** Helmeted arms, date divided below **Mint:** Eisleben **Note:** Similar to 1 Thaler, KM#98. Dav. #6929.

Date	Mintage	VG	F	VF	XF	Unc
1655 HPK Rare	—	—	—	—	—	—
1656 HPK Rare	—	—	—	—	—	—
Note: Künker Auction 122, 3-07, XF realized approximately $24,420.						
1657 HPK Rare	—	—	—	—	—	—

KM# 11 3 THALER
Silver **Ruler:** Bruno II, Wilhelm I (V) and Johann Georg IV **Obv:** Helmeted arms **Obv. Legend:** BRVNO. SENIOR. WILH: H: GE: P: **Rev:** St. George and dragon **Mint:** Eisleben **Note:** Dav. #6915.

Date	Mintage	VG	F	VF	XF	Unc
1606 GM Rare	—	—	—	—	—	—

TRADE COINAGE

KM# 12 GOLDGULDEN
3.5000 g., 0.9860 Gold 0.1109 oz. AGW **Ruler:** Bruno II, Wilhelm I (V) and Johann Georg IV

Date	Mintage	VG	F	VF	XF	Unc
1606	—	500	1,000	2,000	4,000	—

KM# 30 GOLDGULDEN
3.5000 g., 0.9860 Gold 0.1109 oz. AGW **Ruler:** Bruno II, Wilhelm I (V) and Johann Georg IV **Rev:** Three shields as trilobe, date divided at bottom

Date	Mintage	VG	F	VF	XF	Unc
1611	—	550	1,100	2,200	4,500	—

KM# 39 GOLDGULDEN
3.5000 g., 0.9860 Gold 0.1109 oz. AGW **Ruler:** Bruno II, Wilhelm I, Johann Georg IV, Volrat VI and Jobst II **Obv:** Three shields of arms in trefoil form, bottom arms divide date **Rev:** St. George slaying dragon **Note:** Varieties exist.

Date	Mintage	VG	F	VF	XF	Unc
1614 Rare	—	—	—	—	—	—

KM# 47 GOLDGULDEN
3.5000 g., 0.9860 Gold 0.1109 oz. AGW **Ruler:** Bruno II, Wilhelm I, Johann Georg IV, Volrat VI and Jobst II **Subject:** Death of Bruno II **Obv:** 4-fold arms divide mintmaster's initials **Rev:** 8-line inscription with dates **Mint:** Eisleben **Note:** Varieties exist.

Date	Mintage	VG	F	VF	XF	Unc
1615 GM	—	—	—	—	—	—

KM# 46 GOLDGULDEN
3.5000 g., 0.9860 Gold 0.1109 oz. AGW **Ruler:** Bruno II, Wilhelm I, Johann Georg IV, Volrat VI and Jobst II

Date	Mintage	VG	F	VF	XF	Unc
1615	—	500	1,000	1,950	4,000	—
ND	—	500	1,000	1,950	4,000	—

KM# 126 1/4 DUCAT
0.8750 g., 0.9860 Gold 0.0277 oz. AGW **Ruler:** Franz Maximilian and Heinrich Franz **Obv:** St. George and dragon **Rev:** Arms, value and date

Date	Mintage	VG	F	VF	XF	Unc
1670	—	220	325	575	1,150	—
1671	—	220	325	575	1,150	—

KM# 82 DUCAT
3.5000 g., 0.9860 Gold 0.1109 oz. AGW **Ruler:** Wolfgang III and Johann Georg II **Rev:** Value and date on tablet

Date	Mintage	VG	F	VF	XF	Unc
1631	—	425	825	1,800	3,500	—
1632	—	425	825	1,800	3,500	—
1635	—	425	825	1,800	3,500	—
1638	—	425	825	1,800	3,500	—

KM# 101 DUCAT
3.5000 g., 0.9860 Gold 0.1109 oz. AGW **Ruler:** Wolfgang III and Johann Georg II

Date	Mintage	VG	F	VF	XF	Unc
1656	—	475	975	2,100	4,000	—

KM# 112 DUCAT
3.5000 g., 0.9860 Gold 0.1109 oz. AGW **Ruler:** Franz Maximilian and Heinrich Franz **Obv:** St. George slaying dragon **Obv. Legend:** FRANZ MAX

Date	Mintage	VG	F	VF	XF	Unc
1667	—	—	—	—	—	—

KM# 135 DUCAT
3.5000 g., 0.9860 Gold 0.1109 oz. AGW **Ruler:** Franz Maximilian and Heinrich Franz **Obv:** St. George horseback right slaying dragon **Obv. Legend:** FRANZ • MAX • HEINR • FRANZ • COMIT • IN MANSFELT **Rev:** Ornate crowned arms in order chain **Rev. Legend:** • NOB • DOM • INHELD • UNGENSEB • E • SER • **Note:** Fr#1573.

Date	Mintage	VG	F	VF	XF	Unc
1687	—	285	575	1,150	1,950	—

KM# 86 2 DUCAT
7.0000 g., 0.9860 Gold 0.2219 oz. AGW **Ruler:** Wolfgang III and Johann Georg II **Obv:** St. George slaying dragon, imperial orb above horse's head **Rev:** Two helmets above 4-fold arms, date divided by arms **Mint:** Eisleben **Note:** Varieties exist.

Date	Mintage	VG	F	VF	XF	Unc
1635 HPK	—	975	1,750	3,250	5,750	—

KM# 100 2 DUCAT
7.0000 g., 0.9860 Gold 0.2219 oz. AGW **Ruler:** Wolfgang III and Johann Georg II **Obv:** Two helmets above 4-fold arms, date divided by arms, titles of Karl Adam **Rev:** St. George slaying dragon, imperial orb above horse's head **Mint:** Eisleben

Date	Mintage	VG	F	VF	XF	Unc
1655 HPK	—	1,450	2,450	4,800	8,500	—

KM# 113 2 DUCAT
7.0000 g., 0.9860 Gold 0.2219 oz. AGW **Ruler:** Franz Maximilian and Heinrich Franz **Obv:** St. George slaying dragon **Obv. Legend:** FRANZ MAX...

Date	Mintage	VG	F	VF	XF	Unc
1667	—	1,250	2,100	4,200	7,500	—

KM# 21 3 DUCAT
10.5000 g., 0.9860 Gold 0.3328 oz. AGW **Ruler:** Bruno II, Wilhelm I, Johann Georg IV and Volrat VI **Mint:** Eisleben **Note:** Similar to 1/2 Thaler, KM#6.

Date	Mintage	VG	F	VF	XF	Unc
1610 GM Rare	387	—	—	—	—	—
1615 GM Rare	—	—	—	—	—	—

KM# 106 3 DUCAT
10.5000 g., 0.9860 Gold 0.3328 oz. AGW **Ruler:** Karl Adam **Obv:** Two helmets above 4-fold arms, date divided by arms, titles of Karl Adam **Rev:** St. George slaying dragon, imperial orb above horse's head **Mint:** Eisleben

Date	Mintage	VG	F	VF	XF	Unc
1660 HPK	—	1,600	3,100	5,800	10,500	—

KM# 114 3 DUCAT
10.5000 g., 0.9860 Gold 0.3328 oz. AGW **Ruler:** Franz Maximilian and Heinrich Franz **Obv:** St. George slaying dragon **Obv. Legend:** FRANZ MAX • HEINR • FRANZ... **Mint:** Eisleben

Date	Mintage	VG	F	VF	XF	Unc
1667 AB-K	—	1,600	3,000	6,000	10,000	—

KM# 87 5 DUCAT (1/2 Portugaloser)
17.5000 g., 0.9860 Gold 0.5547 oz. AGW **Ruler:** Wolfgang III and Johann Georg II **Obv:** St. George slaying dragon, imperial orb above horse's head **Rev:** Two helmets above 4-fold arms divide date **Mint:** Eisleben **Note:** Varieties exist.

Date	Mintage	VG	F	VF	XF	Unc
1635 HPK	—	3,000	4,500	7,500	13,500	—
1637 HPK	—	3,000	4,500	7,500	13,500	—

KM# 88 10 DUCAT (Portugaloser)
35.0000 g., 0.9860 Gold 1.1095 oz. AGW **Ruler:** Wolfgang III and Johann Georg II **Obv. Legend:** WOLFG: ET. IOHA: GEOR: PAT: COMI: ET. **Note:** Similar to 1 Thaler, KM#80. Varieties exist.

Date	Mintage	VG	F	VF	XF	Unc
1635 HPK Rare	—	—	—	—	—	—
1637 HPK Rare	—	—	—	—	—	—

MANSFELD-EIGENTLICHE-HINTERORT

Founded in 1486 when the Hinterort line of Mansfeld was divided into this and the Schraplau branches. Upon the extinction of Eigentliche-Hinterort in 1666, the lands and titles reverted to Mansfeld-Vorderort-Bornstedt.

RULERS
Albrecht VII, 1486-1560
Volrat V, 1560-1578
Johann I, 1560-1567
Karl I, 1560-1594
Friedrich Christoph zu Hedersleben, 1567-1631
Ernst VI, 1567-1609
Kaspar, 1578-1586
Friedrich III, 1586-1593
David, 1592-1628
Friedrich Christoph, 1609-1631
Ernst Ludwig, 1631-1632
Christian Friedrich, 1632-1666

JOINT COINAGE
I – Albrecht VII, Philipp II, Johann Georg I
II – Albrecht VII, Johann Georg I, Peter Ernst I, Christoph II
III – Volrat V, Johann I, Karl I
IV – Volrat V, Johann I
V – Volrat V, Karl I
VI - Ernst VI and Friedrich Christoph
VII - Ernst VI, Friedrich Christoph and David
VIII - Friedrich Christoph and David

REFERENCE
T = Otto Tornau, ***Münzwesen und Münzen der Grafschaft Mansfeld***, Prague, 1937.

COUNTSHIP

JOINT COINAGE

KM# 87 3 FLITTER (1-1/2 Pfennig)
Copper **Rev:** Value: FLITTER **Mint:** Eisleben

Date	Mintage	VG	F	VF	XF	Unc
16Z1 M	—	35.00	75.00	150	—	—

KM# 86 3 FLITTER (1-1/2 Pfennig)
Copper **Obv:** Four-fold arms, M above **Rev:** III in center, FLITTER, date around **Mint:** Mansfeld **Note:** Kipper 3 Flitter.

Date	Mintage	VG	F	VF	XF	Unc
16Z1 M	—	35.00	75.00	150	—	—

KM# 88 PFENNIG
Copper **Obv:** 4-fold arms divide mintmaster's initials, date above **Mint:** Gerbstadt **Note:** Uniface.

Date	Mintage	VG	F	VF	XF	Unc
16Z1 DM	—	30.00	60.00	125	—	—

KM# 142 PFENNIG
Silver **Obv:** Oval four-fold arms, date above divides mintmaster's initials **Mint:** Eisleben **Note:** Anonymous Kipper. Uniface. Schussel type.

Date	Mintage	VG	F	VF	XF	Unc
16Z3 AK	—	—	—	—	—	—

KM# 35 3 PFENNIG (Dreier)
Silver **Obv:** Helmeted four-fold arms **Rev:** Small imperial orb with 3 divides date, in ornamented rhombus

Date	Mintage	VG	F	VF	XF	Unc
1611	—	33.00	60.00	110	220	—

KM# 55 3 PFENNIG (Dreier)
Silver **Obv:** Four-fold arms, mintmaster's initials above **Rev:** Imperial orb with 3 divides date **Mint:** Eisleben

Date	Mintage	VG	F	VF	XF	Unc
161Z GM	—	33.00	60.00	110	220	—

KM# 56 3 PFENNIG (Dreier)
Silver **Rev:** Value in orb III **Mint:** Eisleben

Date	Mintage	VG	F	VF	XF	Unc
161Z GM	—	33.00	60.00	110	220	—

KM# 89 3 PFENNIG (Dreier)
Silver **Obv:** Crowned four-fold arms divide date and mintmaster's initials **Rev:** Imperial orb with 3 in rhombus **Mint:** Eisleben **Note:** Anonymous Kipper. Varieties exist.

Date	Mintage	VG	F	VF	XF	Unc
16Z1 AK	—	16.00	35.00	70.00	145	—
16ZZ AK	—	16.00	35.00	70.00	145	—

KM# 97 3 PFENNIG (Dreier)
Copper **Rev:** Arms in oval shield **Note:** Varieties exist.

Date	Mintage	Good	VG	F	VF	XF
ND(1621/22)	—	18.00	37.00	75.00	150	—

KM# 90 3 PFENNIG (Dreier)
Copper **Obv:** Rampant lion (Heldrungen) left, value III above **Rev:** Large "B" between annulets and stars **Mint:** Blumrode

Date	Mintage	Good	VG	F	VF	XF
ND(1621/22) B	—	18.00	37.00	75.00	150	—

KM# 91 3 PFENNIG (Dreier)

Copper **Obv:** Large "B" between floral ornaments **Rev:** Value 3 in ornamented heart-shaped shield **Mint:** Blumrode

Date	Mintage	Good	VG	F	VF	XF
ND(1621/22) B	—	18.00	37.00	75.00	150	—

KM# 92 3 PFENNIG (Dreier)

Copper **Obv:** Four-fold arms with M above **Rev:** Imperial orb with 3 in double rhombus **Mint:** Mansfeld

Date	Mintage	Good	VG	F	VF	XF
ND(1621/22) M	—	18.00	37.00	75.00	150	—

KM# 93 3 PFENNIG (Dreier)

Copper **Obv:** Oval four-fold arms, M above **Rev:** Imperial orb with 3 divides date **Mint:** Mansfeld

Date	Mintage	Good	VG	F	VF	XF
(16)21 M	—	18.00	37.00	75.00	150	—

KM# 94 3 PFENNIG (Dreier)

Copper **Obv:** Arms in squarish shield **Mint:** Mansfeld

Date	Mintage	Good	VG	F	VF	XF
(16)Z1 M	—	18.00	37.00	75.00	150	—

KM# 95 3 PFENNIG (Dreier)

Copper **Obv:** Four-fold arms in heart-shaped shield, III above **Rev:** Heart-shaped shield with 3

Date	Mintage	Good	VG	F	VF	XF
ND(1621/22)	—	18.00	37.00	75.00	150	—

KM# 96 3 PFENNIG (Dreier)

Copper **Obv:** Without value **Rev. Legend:** *3 PFENNIG...

Date	Mintage	Good	VG	F	VF	XF
ND(1621/22)	—	18.00	37.00	75.00	150	—

KM# 98 3 PFENNIG (Dreier)

Copper **Obv:** Date above four-fold arms **Rev:** Imperial orb with 3

Date	Mintage	Good	VG	F	VF	XF
16Z1	—	20.00	40.00	85.00	175	—

KM# 99 3 PFENNIG (Dreier)

Copper **Obv:** Ornamented four-fold arms **Rev:** Imperial orb with 3, date divided above

Date	Mintage	Good	VG	F	VF	XF
16Z1	—	20.00	40.00	85.00	175	—

KM# 100 3 PFENNIG (Dreier)

Copper **Obv:** Oval arms

Date	Mintage	Good	VG	F	VF	XF
(16)Z1	—	20.00	40.00	85.00	175	—
(16)22	—	20.00	40.00	85.00	175	—

KM# 101 3 PFENNIG (Dreier)

Copper **Obv:** Four-fold arms, date above **Rev:** Ornamented oval frame with 3, date above

Date	Mintage	Good	VG	F	VF	XF
16Z1/16Z1	—	20.00	40.00	85.00	175	—

KM# 102 3 PFENNIG (Dreier)

Copper **Obv:** Heart-shaped four-fold arms **Rev:** 3 in large ornamented frame divides date

Date	Mintage	Good	VG	F	VF	XF
(16)21	—	20.00	40.00	85.00	175	—

KM# 124 3 PFENNIG (Dreier)

Copper **Obv:** St. George slaying dragon at right **Rev:** Imperial orb with 3 divides date

Date	Mintage	Good	VG	F	VF	XF
(16)ZZ	—	—	—	—	—	—

KM# 122 3 PFENNIG (Dreier)

Silver **Rev:** Without rhombus **Mint:** Eisleben **Note:** Varieties exist.

Date	Mintage	VG	F	VF	XF	Unc
16ZZ AK	—	27.00	55.00	110	220	—

KM# 123 3 PFENNIG (Dreier)

Silver **Obv:** Crowned four-fold arms divide mintmaster's initials **Rev:** Imperial orb with 3 divides date **Mint:** Eisleben **Note:** Varieties exist.

Date	Mintage	VG	F	VF	XF	Unc
16ZZ AK	—	27.00	55.00	110	220	—
16Z3 AK	—	27.00	55.00	110	220	—

KM# 120 3 PFENNIG (Dreier)

Silver **Obv:** Crown above four-fold arms divide date **Rev:** Imperial orb with 3 in rhombus

Date	Mintage	VG	F	VF	XF	Unc
16ZZ	—	27.00	55.00	110	220	—

KM# 121 3 PFENNIG (Dreier)

Silver **Obv:** Four-fold arms, crown above divides mintmaster's initials **Rev:** Imperial orb with 3 divides date, within rhombus **Mint:** Eisleben

Date	Mintage	VG	F	VF	XF	Unc
16ZZ AK	—	27.00	55.00	110	220	—

KM# 104 6 PFENNIG

Copper **Obv:** Date above arms

Date	Mintage	VG	F	VF	XF	Unc
16Z1	—	16.00	27.00	55.00	115	—

KM# 105 6 PFENNIG

Copper **Obv:** Imperial orb with 6

Date	Mintage	VG	F	VF	XF	Unc
16Z1	—	16.00	27.00	55.00	115	—

KM# 103 6 PFENNIG

Copper **Obv:** Ornate four-fold arms, eight-pointed star above **Rev:** VI/PFENNIG above imperial orb **Note:** Kipper 6 Pfennig.

Date	Mintage	VG	F	VF	XF	Unc
ND(1621/22)	—	9.00	20.00	40.00	80.00	—

KM# 168 GROSCHEN (1/28 Thaler)

Silver **Subject:** Death of David **Obv:** Crown divides date above ornaented oval four-fold arms **Rev:** Eight-line inscription with dates **Note:** Varieties exist.

Date	Mintage	VG	F	VF	XF	Unc
(16)Z8	—	—	—	—	—	—

KM# 186 GROSCHEN (1/28 Thaler)

Silver **Subject:** Death of Friedrich Christoph **Obv:** Five-line inscription with dates, titles of Friedrich Christoph **Rev:** Crowned oval four-fold arms **Rev. Legend:** GEDVLDT IN . VNSHVLDT. **Note:** Varieties exist.

Date	Mintage	VG	F	VF	XF	Unc
(16)31	—	135	225	450	—	—

KM# 190 GROSCHEN (1/28 Thaler)

Silver **Subject:** Death of Ernest Ludwig **Obv:** Crowned oval four-fold arms **Rev:** Seven-line inscription with date **Note:** Varieties exist.

Date	Mintage	VG	F	VF	XF	Unc
(1)632	—	—	—	—	—	—

KM# 107 12 KREUZER (Schreckenburger)

Silver **Rev:** Angel above four-fold arms

Date	Mintage	VG	F	VF	XF	Unc
ND(1621/22)	—	65.00	120	200	385	—

KM# 108 12 KREUZER (Schreckenburger)

Silver **Rev:** Ornamented oval arms

Date	Mintage	VG	F	VF	XF	Unc
ND(1621/22)	—	65.00	120	200	385	—

KM# 109 12 KREUZER (Schreckenburger)

Silver **Obv:** Crowned imperial eagle, 1Z in orb on breast, titles of Ferdinand II **Rev:** Crowned four-fold arms, titles of Friedrich Christoph

Date	Mintage	VG	F	VF	XF	Unc
ND(1621/22)	—	65.00	120	200	385	—

KM# 110 12 KREUZER (Schreckenburger)

Silver **Obv:** Arms divide mintmaster's initials **Rev:** Date **Rev. Legend:** IUST. NVN.-VS

Date	Mintage	VG	F	VF	XF	Unc
16Z1 GB	—	65.00	120	200	385	—
161Z GB	—	65.00	120	200	385	—

Note: Error with retrograde B

KM# 112 12 KREUZER (Schreckenburger)

Silver **Rev:** Titles of David in legend

Date	Mintage	VG	F	VF	XF	Unc
ND(1621/22)	—	—	—	—	—	—

KM# 111 12 KREUZER (Schreckenburger)

Silver **Obv:** Crowned imperial eagle, 1Z in orb on breast, titles of Ferdinand II **Rev:** Crowned four-fold arms, titles of Friedrich Christoph **Mint:** Hedersleben **Note:** Struck at Hedersleben Mint.

Date	Mintage	VG	F	VF	XF	Unc
1621	—	65.00	120	200	385	—

KM# 113 12 KREUZER (Schreckenburger)

Silver **Rev:** Date added **Mint:** Schraplau **Note:** Struck at Schraplau Mint.

Date	Mintage	VG	F	VF	XF	Unc
16Z1	—	85.00	155	235	475	—

KM# 106 12 KREUZER (Schreckenburger)

Silver **Obv:** St. George slaying dragon at left **Rev:** Crowned four-fold arms **Note:** Varieties exist.

Date	Mintage	VG	F	VF	XF	Unc
ND(1621/22)	—	65.00	120	200	385	—

KM# 16 1/28 THALER

Silver **Obv:** Imperial orb with Z8, date in legend at top **Rev:** Inscription above four-fold arms dividing mintmaster's initials **Rev. Inscription:** BEI GOT / IST RAHT / VND THAT **Mint:** Eisleben **Note:** Spruch 1/28 Thaler.

Date	Mintage	VG	F	VF	XF	Unc
1606 GM	—	75.00	150	300	—	—

KM# 17 1/28 THALER

Silver **Rev. Inscription:** BEI / GOTT IST / RAHT VND / TH-AT **Mint:** Eisleben

Date	Mintage	VG	F	VF	XF	Unc
ND GM	—	50.00	100	210	—	—

KM# 30 1/28 THALER

Silver **Obv:** Date divided by cross on orb **Rev:** Date divided by arms **Mint:** Eisleben

Date	Mintage	VG	F	VF	XF	Unc
1610/1610 GM	—	40.00	80.00	150	300	—

KM# 31 1/28 THALER

Silver **Rev:** Date divided by arms

Date	Mintage	VG	F	VF	XF	Unc
1610	—	35.00	75.00	150	—	—

KM# 32 1/28 THALER

Silver **Obv:** Imperial orb with Z8 divides mintmaster's initials, titles of Friedrich Christoph and date in legend **Rev:** Helmeted four-fold arms **Mint:** Eisleben **Note:** Varieties exist.

Date	Mintage	VG	F	VF	XF	Unc
1610 GM	—	65.00	135	275	—	—

KM# 39 1/28 THALER

Silver **Rev:** Date divided by orb, mintmaster's initials in legend at top **Mint:** Eisleben **Note:** Varieties exist.

Date	Mintage	VG	F	VF	XF	Unc
1611 GM	—	35.00	75.00	150	—	—

KM# 36 1/28 THALER

Silver **Obv:** Imperial orb with 28, Date divided by cross on orb **Rev:** Inscription above four-fold arms dividing mintmaster's initials **Rev. Inscription:** BEI / GOTT IST / RAHT VND / TH-AT **Mint:** Eisleben

Date	Mintage	VG	F	VF	XF	Unc
1611 GM	—	60.00	120	240	—	—

KM# 37 1/28 THALER

Silver **Obv:** Mintmaster's initials divided by cross **Mint:** Eisleben

Date	Mintage	VG	F	VF	XF	Unc
1611 GM	—	35.00	75.00	150	—	—

KM# 38 1/28 THALER

Silver **Obv:** Titles of Friedrich Christoph **Rev:** Imperial orb with Z8 divides mintmaster's initials, date in legend **Mint:** Eisleben

Date	Mintage	VG	F	VF	XF	Unc
1611 GM	—	35.00	75.00	150	—	—

KM# 40 1/28 THALER

Silver **Rev:** Mintmaster's initials divided by arms **Mint:** Eisleben

Date	Mintage	VG	F	VF	XF	Unc
1611 GM	—	35.00	75.00	150	—	—

KM# 84 1/24 THALER

Silver, 23 mm. **Obv:** Crowned four-fold arms divide mintmaster's initials, titles of Freidrich Christoph **Rev:** Imperial orb with 24 divides date **Mint:** Eisleben **Note:** Varieties exist. Kipper 1/24 Thaler.

Date	Mintage	VG	F	VF	XF	Unc
16Z0 AK	—	20.00	45.00	80.00	155	—
16Z8 AK	—	20.00	45.00	80.00	155	—
16Z9 AK	—	20.00	45.00	80.00	155	—
1630 AK	—	20.00	45.00	80.00	155	—
1631 AK	—	20.00	45.00	80.00	155	—

KM# 115 1/24 THALER

Silver **Obv:** Lion rampant left (Heldrungen) **Rev:** Imperial orb with 24, titles of Ferdinand II and date in legend **Note:** Varieties exist.

Date	Mintage	VG	F	VF	XF	Unc
(16)Z1	—	27.00	55.00	100	210	—
ND(1621/22)	—	27.00	55.00	100	210	—

KM# 117 1/24 THALER

Silver **Rev:** Date divided at top in legend **Note:** Varieties exist.

Date	Mintage	VG	F	VF	XF	Unc
(16)Z1	—	15.00	30.00	65.00	130	—

KM# 118 1/24 THALER

Silver **Obv:** Crowned four-fold arms divide mintmaster's initials **Rev:** Imperial orb with Z4, cross above divides date **Mint:** Eisleben **Note:** Varieties exist.

Date	Mintage	VG	F	VF	XF	Unc
16Z1 AK	—	11.00	25.00	55.00	110	—
16Z4 AK	—	11.00	25.00	55.00	110	—
16Z5 AK	—	11.00	25.00	55.00	110	—
16Z6 AK	—	11.00	25.00	55.00	110	—

KM# 114 1/24 THALER

Silver **Obv:** Imperial orb with 24, titles of David in legend **Rev:** Lion rampant left (Heldrungen) **Rev. Legend:** FATA. VIAM. INVENIE.

Date	Mintage	VG	F	VF	XF	Unc
ND(1621/22)	—	27.00	55.00	110	210	—

KM# 116 1/24 THALER

Silver **Obv:** Crowned four-fold arms **Rev:** Imperial orb with Z4

Date	Mintage	VG	F	VF	XF	Unc
ND(1621/22)	—	15.00	30.00	65.00	130	—

KM# 125 1/24 THALER

Silver **Obv:** Imperial orb with 24, cross divides mintmaster's initials, date divided at top **Rev:** Helmet with six small pennants above four-fold arms **Mint:** Eisleben

Date	Mintage	VG	F	VF	XF	Unc
16ZZ AK	—	15.00	30.00	65.00	130	—

KM# 127 1/24 THALER
Silver **Rev:** Change in legend from D. I. MANSF... **Rev. Legend:** MANSF... **Mint:** Eisleben

Date	Mintage	VG	F	VF	XF	Unc
16ZZ AK	—	15.00	30.00	65.00	130	—

KM# 128 1/24 THALER
Silver **Rev:** Mintmaster's initials divided by arms **Mint:** Eisleben

Date	Mintage	VG	F	VF	XF	Unc
16ZZ AK	—	15.00	30.00	65.00	130	—

KM# 126 1/24 THALER
Silver **Obv:** Imperial orb with 24 or Z4 divides mintmaster's initials, date divided in legend at top **Rev:** Helmeted four-fold arms **Mint:** Eisleben **Note:** Varieties exist.

Date	Mintage	VG	F	VF	XF	Unc
16ZZ AK	—	15.00	30.00	65.00	130	—

KM# 147 1/24 THALER
Silver **Rev:** Mintmaster's initials divided by orb **Mint:** Eisleben

Date	Mintage	VG	F	VF	XF	Unc
16Z4 AK	—	13.00	27.00	55.00	115	—

KM# 161 1/24 THALER
Silver **Obv:** Imperial orb with date divided at top **Rev:** Crowned four-fold arms divide mintmaster's initials, titles of Friedrich Christoph **Mint:** Eisleben **Note:** Varieties exist.

Date	Mintage	VG	F	VF	XF	Unc
16Z7 AK	—	11.00	25.00	50.00	100	—
16Z8 AK	—	11.00	25.00	50.00	100	—
16Z9 AK	—	11.00	25.00	50.00	100	—
1630 AK	—	11.00	25.00	50.00	100	—

KM# 162 1/24 THALER
Silver **Obv:** Four-fold arms, crown above divides mintmaster's initials **Rev:** Imperial orb with 24 or Z4, date divided in legend at top **Mint:** Eisleben **Note:** Varieties exist.

Date	Mintage	VG	F	VF	XF	Unc
16Z7 AK	—	11.00	25.00	55.00	115	—
16Z8 AK	—	11.00	25.00	55.00	115	—

KM# 173 1/24 THALER
Silver **Rev:** Imperial orb with 24 divides date **Mint:** Eisleben

Date	Mintage	VG	F	VF	XF	Unc
16Z9 AK	—	15.00	30.00	65.00	130	—

KM# 174 1/24 THALER
Silver **Obv:** Crowned round arms, mintmaster's initials divided by crown above arms **Mint:** Eisleben

Date	Mintage	VG	F	VF	XF	Unc
16Z9 AK	—	15.00	30.00	65.00	130	—

KM# 185 1/24 THALER
Silver **Rev:** Orb divides both date and mintmaster's initials **Mint:** Eisleben

Date	Mintage	VG	F	VF	XF	Unc
1630/Z4 AK	—	15.00	30.00	65.00	130	—

Note: Reverse die of KM#147 with date altered from 16Z4 to 1630

KM# 208 1/24 THALER
Silver **Obv:** Crowned four-fold arms divide mintmaster's initials, date divided in legend at top **Rev:** Imperial orb with 24, date divided in legend at top **Mint:** Eisleben **Note:** Varieties exist.

Date	Mintage	VG	F	VF	XF	Unc
(16)45/1646 HPK	—	15.00	30.00	65.00	130	—
(16)45/1647 HPK	—	15.00	30.00	65.00	130	—

KM# 209 1/24 THALER
Silver **Mint:** Eisleben **Note:** Date only on reverse. Varieties exist.

Date	Mintage	VG	F	VF	XF	Unc
1646 HPK	—	15.00	30.00	65.00	130	—
1647 HPK	—	15.00	30.00	65.00	130	—

KM# 41 1/21 THALER
Silver **Obv:** Imperial orb with Z1, mintmaster's initials divided by cross on orb **Rev. Inscription:** BEI / GOTT IST / RAHT VND / TH-AT **Mint:** Eisleben

Date	Mintage	VG	F	VF	XF	Unc
1611 GM	—	25.00	50.00	100	210	—
161Z GM	—	25.00	50.00	100	210	—

KM# 43 1/21 THALER
Silver **Obv:** Mintmaster's initials divided by cross on orb **Rev:** Mintmaster's initials divided by arms **Mint:** Eisleben

Date	Mintage	VG	F	VF	XF	Unc
1611 GM	—	25.00	50.00	100	210	—
1613 GM	—	25.00	50.00	100	210	—

KM# 42 1/21 THALER
Silver **Obv:** Mintmaster's initials divided in legend at top, date divided by orb **Mint:** Eisleben **Note:** Varieties exist.

Date	Mintage	VG	F	VF	XF	Unc
1611 GM	—	25.00	50.00	100	210	—
161Z	—	25.00	50.00	100	210	—
1613 GM	—	25.00	50.00	100	210	—
1615 GM	—	25.00	50.00	100	210	—

KM# 44 1/21 THALER
Silver **Obv:** Imperial orb with Z1 divides date and mintmaster's initials **Rev:** Helmeted four-fold arms **Mint:** Eisleben **Note:** Varieties exist.

Date	Mintage	VG	F	VF	XF	Unc
1611 GM	—	30.00	60.00	120	240	—

KM# 45 1/21 THALER
Silver **Obv:** Date divided in legend at top **Mint:** Eisleben **Note:** Varieties exist.

Date	Mintage	VG	F	VF	XF	Unc
1611 GM	—	30.00	60.00	120	240	—
161Z GM	—	30.00	60.00	120	240	—

KM# 58 1/21 THALER
Silver **Obv:** Mintmaster's initials divided at top of legend **Mint:** Eisleben **Note:** Varieties exist.

Date	Mintage	VG	F	VF	XF	Unc
161Z GM	—	30.00	65.00	130	265	—
1615 GM	—	30.00	65.00	130	265	—

KM# 57 1/21 THALER
Silver **Obv:** Reverse of Mansfeld-Vorderort-Borstedt KM#24 **Mint:** Eisleben

Date	Mintage	VG	F	VF	XF	Unc
161Z GM	—	30.00	65.00	130	265	—

KM# 61 1/21 THALER
Silver **Obv:** Mintmaster's initials divided by arms **Mint:** Eisleben

Date	Mintage	VG	F	VF	XF	Unc
1616 AK	—	35.00	75.00	150	300	—

KM# 46 1/8 THALER
Silver **Obv:** St. George slaying dragon at left **Rev:** Inscription above four-fold arms which divide date and mintmaster's initials **Rev. Inscription:** BEI GOT / IST RATH / VND THAT **Mint:** Eisleben **Note:** Spruch 1/8 Thaler.

Date	Mintage	VG	F	VF	XF	Unc
1611 GM	—	—	—	—	—	—

KM# 47 1/4 THALER
Silver **Obv:** St. George slaying dragon at left **Rev:** Inscription above four-fold arms which divide date and mintmaster's initials **Rev. Inscription:** BEI GOT / IST RATH / VND THAT **Mint:** Eisleben **Note:** Spruch 1/4 Thaler. Varieties exist.

Date	Mintage	VG	F	VF	XF	Unc
1611 GM	—	65.00	135	275	550	—
1613 GM	—	65.00	135	275	550	—
1614 GM	—	65.00	135	275	550	—
1615 GM	—	65.00	135	275	550	—

KM# 48 1/4 THALER
Silver **Obv:** Four-fold arms divide mintmaster's initials, helmet above divides date, titles of Friedrich Christoph **Rev:** St. George slaying dragon at left **Mint:** Eisleben **Note:** Varieties exist.

Date	Mintage	VG	F	VF	XF	Unc
1611 GM	—	75.00	150	300	600	—
161Z GM	—	75.00	150	300	600	—

KM# 62 1/4 THALER
Silver **Obv:** St. George slaying dragon at left **Rev:** Ornamented 4-fold arms divide mintmaster's initials, crown above divides date **Rev. Legend:** BEY. GOTT. IST. RATH. VND. THAT **Mint:** Eisleben **Note:** Varieties exist.

Date	Mintage	VG	F	VF	XF	Unc
1616 AK	—	75.00	150	300	600	—
1618 AK	—	75.00	150	300	600	—

KM# 65 1/4 THALER
Silver **Rev:** Date divided by arms and mintmaster's initials divided by crown **Mint:** Eisleben

Date	Mintage	VG	F	VF	XF	Unc
1617 AK	—	75.00	150	300	600	—

KM# 66 1/4 THALER
Silver **Rev:** Date and mintmaster's initials divided **Mint:** Eisleben

Date	Mintage	VG	F	VF	XF	Unc
1617 AK	—	75.00	150	300	600	—

KM# 72 1/4 THALER
Silver **Obv:** St. George slaying dragon at left, titles of Friedrich Christoph **Rev:** Four-fold arms divide mintmaster's initials near top, helmet above divides date **Rev. Legend:** PATIENTA - VINCIT - OMNIA **Mint:** Saalfeld **Note:** Spruch 1/4 Thaler.

Date	Mintage	VG	F	VF	XF	Unc
1619 HI	—	75.00	150	300	600	—

KM# 80 1/4 THALER
Silver **Rev:** Date and mintmaster's initials divided, legend differs from KM#66. **Rev. Legend:** EST. DEVS. AYXUKUI. CIBSUKUI. QVE. POTIS. **Mint:** Saalfeld

Date	Mintage	VG	F	VF	XF	Unc
16Z0 HI	—	75.00	150	300	600	—

KM# 129 1/4 THALER
Silver **Obv:** St. George slaying dragon at left, titles of Friedrich Christoph **Rev:** Helmeted four-fold arms divide date and mintmaster's initials **Mint:** Eisleben **Note:** Varieties exist.

Date	Mintage	VG	F	VF	XF	Unc
16ZZ AK	—	80.00	160	325	650	—
16ZZ	—	80.00	160	325	650	—
16Z3 AK	—	80.00	160	325	650	—
16Z4 AK	—	80.00	160	325	650	—

KM# 163 1/4 THALER
Silver **Subject:** Death of David **Obv:** Six-line inscription with dates **Rev:** Crowned four-fold arms divide date and mintmaster's initials **Mint:** Eisleben

Date	Mintage	VG	F	VF	XF	Unc
Z8 AK	—	—	—	—	—	—

KM# 164 1/4 THALER
Silver **Obv:** Seven-line inscription **Mint:** Eisleben

Date	Mintage	VG	F	VF	XF	Unc
(16)Z8 AK	—	—	—	—	—	—

KM# 165 1/4 THALER
Silver **Obv:** Eight-line inscription **Mint:** Eisleben

Date	Mintage	VG	F	VF	XF	Unc
(16)Z8 AK	—	—	—	—	—	—

KM# 175 1/4 THALER
Silver **Obv:** St. George slaying dragon at left, titles of Friedrich Christoph **Rev:** Helmeted four-fold arms with date divided by helmet above arms **Mint:** Eisleben **Note:** Varieties exist.

Date	Mintage	VG	F	VF	XF	Unc
16Z9	—	75.00	150	300	600	—
ND AK	—	75.00	150	300	600	—

KM# 187 1/4 THALER
Silver **Subject:** Death of Friedrich Christoph **Obv:** St. George slaying dragon at left **Rev:** Eight-line inscription with dates **Note:** Varieties exist.

Date	Mintage	VG	F	VF	XF	Unc
1631	—	—	—	—	—	—

KM# 191 1/4 THALER
Silver **Subject:** Death of Ernst Ludwig **Obv:** St. George slaying dragon at left **Rev:** Seven-line inscription with dates **Note:** Varieties exist.

Date	Mintage	VG	F	VF	XF	Unc
(1)63Z	—	—	—	—	—	—

KM# 200 1/4 THALER
Silver **Mint:** Eisleben **Note:** Similar to 1/2 Thaler, KM#201. Varieties exist.

Date	Mintage	VG	F	VF	XF	Unc
1641 HPK	—	40.00	80.00	160	325	—
1642 HPK	—	40.00	80.00	160	325	—
1649 HPK	—	40.00	80.00	160	325	—
1649	—	40.00	80.00	160	325	—
1653 HPK	—	40.00	80.00	160	325	—
1661 HPK	—	40.00	80.00	160	325	—

KM# 227 1/4 THALER
Silver **Rev:** Mintmaster's initials and date divided by helmet **Mint:** Eisleben **Note:** Varieties exist.

Date	Mintage	VG	F	VF	XF	Unc
1663 HPK	—	85.00	165	335	675	—

KM# 228 1/4 THALER
Silver **Rev:** Date divided by arms **Mint:** Eisleben **Note:** Varieties exist.

Date	Mintage	VG	F	VF	XF	Unc
1663 HPK	—	—	—	—	—	—
1665 HPK	—	—	—	—	—	—

KM# 15 1/2 THALER
Silver **Obv:** St. George slaying dragon to left **Rev:** Helmeted arms with helmets dividing date **Mint:** Eisleben **Note:** Spruch 1/2 Thaler. Similar to 1 Thaler, KM#7.

Date	Mintage	VG	F	VF	XF	Unc
1605 GM	—	—	—	—	—	—

KM# 23 1/2 THALER
Silver **Obv:** St. George slaying dragon to left **Rev:** Shield dividing date and G - M, three-line inscription above **Mint:** Eisleben **Note:** Similar to 1 Thaler, KM#18. Varieties exist.

Date	Mintage	VG	F	VF	XF	Unc
1609 GM	—	55.00	95.00	150	300	—
1611 GM	—	55.00	95.00	150	300	—

KM# 49 1/2 THALER

Silver **Obv:** St. George slaying dragon at left **Rev:** Inscription above four-fold arms which divide date and mintmaster's initials **Rev. Inscription:** BEI GOT / IST RATH / VND THAT **Mint:** Eisleben **Note:** Varieties exist.

Date	Mintage	VG	F	VF	XF	Unc
1611 GM	—	80.00	165	325	650	—
1613 GM	—	80.00	165	325	650	—
1614 GM	—	80.00	165	325	650	—
1615 GM	—	80.00	165	325	650	—

KM# 50 1/2 THALER

Silver **Obv:** Four-fold divide mintmaster's initials, helmet above divides date, titles of Friedrich Christoph **Rev:** St. George slaying dragon at left **Mint:** Eisleben **Note:** Varieties exist.

Date	Mintage	VG	F	VF	XF	Unc
1611 GM	—	80.00	165	325	650	—
161Z GM	—	80.00	165	325	650	—
1613 GM	—	80.00	165	325	650	—
1617 AK	—	80.00	165	325	650	—

KM# 63 1/2 THALER

Silver **Obv:** St. George slaying dragon at left **Rev:** Ornamented four-fold arms divide mintmaster's initials, crown above divides date **Rev. Legend:** BEY. GOTT. IST. RATH. VND. THAT **Mint:** Eisleben **Note:** Spruch 1/2 Thaler.

Date	Mintage	VG	F	VF	XF	Unc
1616 AK	—	—	—	—	—	—

KM# 67 1/2 THALER

Silver **Obv:** St. George slaying dragon to left **Rev:** Crowned shield divides date and A - K **Mint:** Eisleben **Note:** Broad flan. Similar to 1 Thaler, KM#64.

Date	Mintage	VG	F	VF	XF	Unc
1617 AK	—	—	—	—	—	—

KM# 68 1/2 THALER

Silver **Obv:** St. George slaying dragon to left **Rev:** Crowned shield divides date and A - K **Mint:** Eisleben **Note:** Normal flan. Similar to 1 Thaler, KM#64. Varieties exist.

Date	Mintage	VG	F	VF	XF	Unc
1617 AK	—	175	235	290	475	—
1618 AK	—	175	235	290	475	—

KM# 73 1/2 THALER

Silver **Obv:** St. George slaying dragon at left, titles of Friedrich Christoph **Rev:** Four-fold arms divide mintmaster's initials near top, helmet above divides date **Rev. Legend:** PATIENTA - VINCIT - OMNIA **Mint:** Saalfeld **Note:** Varieties exist.

Date	Mintage	VG	F	VF	XF	Unc
1619 HI	—	—	—	—	—	—

KM# 82 1/2 THALER

Silver **Note:** Similar to 1 Thaler, KM#75 but mintmaster's initials above date. Varieties exist.

Date	Mintage	VG	F	VF	XF	Unc
16Z0 HI	—	135	220	275	475	—
16Z1 AK	—	135	220	275	475	—
1624 AK	—	135	220	275	475	—

KM# 81 1/2 THALER

Silver **Rev:** Ornamented four-fold arms divide mintmaster's initials, crown above divides date **Rev. Legend:** EST DEVS. AUXILIO. CONSILIO. QVE. POTIS. **Mint:** Saalfeld

Date	Mintage	VG	F	VF	XF	Unc
16Z0 HI	—	—	—	—	—	—

KM# 130 1/2 THALER

Silver **Obv:** St. George slaying dragon at left, titles of Friedrich Christoph **Rev:** Helmeted four-fold arms divide date and mintmaster's initials **Mint:** Eisleben **Note:** Varieties exist.

Date	Mintage	VG	F	VF	XF	Unc
16ZZ AK	—	45.00	85.00	150	300	—
16Z3 AK	—	45.00	85.00	150	300	—
16Z4 AK	—	45.00	85.00	150	300	—
16Z9 AK	—	45.00	85.00	150	300	—

KM# 131 1/2 THALER

Silver **Rev:** Date divided by helmet above arms **Mint:** Eisleben **Note:** Varieties exist.

Date	Mintage	VG	F	VF	XF	Unc
(16)ZZ AK	—	60.00	120	225	450	—
16Z9 AK	—	60.00	120	225	450	—

KM# 151 1/2 THALER

Silver **Obv:** St. George slaying dragon at left **Rev:** Helmeted four-fold arms divide date and mintmaster's initials near bottom **Mint:** Eisleben

Date	Mintage	VG	F	VF	XF	Unc
16Z6 AK	—	100	200	350	725	—

KM# 152 1/2 THALER

Silver **Rev:** Mansfeld-Artern, KM#91 **Mint:** Eisleben

Date	Mintage	VG	F	VF	XF	Unc
16Z6 AK	—	100	200	350	725	—

KM# 166 1/2 THALER

Silver **Subject:** Death of David **Obv:** Seven-line inscription **Rev:** Crowned four-fold arms divid date and mintmaster's initials. **Mint:** Eisleben **Note:** Varieties exist.

Date	Mintage	VG	F	VF	XF	Unc
16Z8 AK	—	—	—	—	—	—

KM# 188 1/2 THALER

Silver **Subject:** Death of Friedrich Christoph **Obv:** Eight-line inscription with dates **Rev:** St. George slaying dragon at left **Rev. Legend:** GEDVLDT. IN. VNSCHVLDT. TREW IST WILPRET. **Note:** Varieties exist.

Date	Mintage	VG	F	VF	XF	Unc
1631	—	—	450	750	1,350	—

KM# 192 1/2 THALER

Silver **Subject:** Death of Ernst Ludwig **Obv:** St. George slaying dragon at left **Rev:** Seven-line inscription with dates

Date	Mintage	VG	F	VF	XF	Unc
1632	—	—	—	—	—	—

KM# 201 1/2 THALER

Silver **Mint:** Eisleben **Note:** Varieties exist.

Date	Mintage	VG	F	VF	XF	Unc
1642 HPK	—	60.00	120	190	325	—
1646	—	60.00	120	190	325	—
1649 HPK	—	60.00	120	190	325	—
1649	—	60.00	120	190	325	—
1651 HPK	—	60.00	120	190	325	—
1653 HPK	—	60.00	120	190	325	—

KM# 220 1/2 THALER

Silver **Rev:** Mintmaster's initials also divided by helmet **Mint:** Eisleben **Note:** Varieties exist.

Date	Mintage	VG	F	VF	XF	Unc
1651 HPK	—	—	—	—	—	—

KM# 225 1/2 THALER

Silver **Obv:** Date in legend **Mint:** Eisleben

Date	Mintage	VG	F	VF	XF	Unc
1661 HPK	—	55.00	110	225	450	—

KM# 229 1/2 THALER

Silver **Rev:** Date divided by legend **Mint:** Eisleben **Note:** Varieties exist.

Date	Mintage	VG	F	VF	XF	Unc
1663 HPK	—	45.00	85.00	110	155	—
1664 HPK	—	45.00	85.00	110	155	—
1665 HPK	—	45.00	85.00	110	155	—

KM# 24 2/3 THALER (Gulden)

Silver **Obv:** St. George slaying dragon to left **Rev:** Shield dividing date and G-M, 3-line inscription above **Mint:** Eisleben **Note:** Spruch 2/3 Thaler. Broad flan. Similar to 1 Thaler, KM#18.

Date	Mintage	VG	F	VF	XF	Unc
1609 GM	—	—	—	—	—	—

KM# 148 2/3 THALER (Gulden)

Silver **Obv:** St. George slaying dragon to left **Rev:** Shield of arms divide mintmaster's initials **Mint:** Eisleben **Note:** Similar to 1 Thaler, KM#145.

Date	Mintage	VG	F	VF	XF	Unc
1624 AK	—	—	—	—	—	—

KM# 5 THALER

Silver **Obv:** Crowned imperial eagle above crowned arms divide date and G-M, titles of Rudolf II **Rev. Legend:** ERNESTVS. FRI: CHRIST: E. DAVID. CO. MANSF: **Mint:** Eisleben **Note:** Dav. #6996.

Date	Mintage	VG	F	VF	XF	Unc
1602 GM	—	165	325	550	—	—
1603 GM	—	165	325	550	—	—

KM# 9 THALER

Silver **Rev. Legend:** ERNESTVS. E: FRID: CHRIST: CO: E: DO: I: MANSFEL **Mint:** Eisleben **Note:** Dav. #6998.

Date	Mintage	VG	F	VF	XF	Unc
1603 GM	—	175	375	650	—	—

KM# 7 THALER

Silver **Obv:** Helmeted arms with helmets dividing G-M **Rev:** St. George left and dragon **Mint:** Eisleben **Note:** Dav. #6974.

Date	Mintage	VG	F	VF	XF	Unc
1603 GM	—	75.00	190	285	450	—
1605 GM	—	75.00	190	285	450	—

KM# 8 THALER

Silver **Obv:** Arms divide G-M **Mint:** Eisleben **Note:** Varieties exist. Dav. #6974A.

Date	Mintage	VG	F	VF	XF	Unc
1603 GM	—	75.00	190	285	450	—
1605 GM	—	75.00	190	285	450	—
1615 GM Error for 1605	—	75.00	190	285	450	—

KM# 13 THALER

Silver **Obv:** Helmeted arms with divided date above and G-M below **Rev. Legend:** ...D: I: MAN **Mint:** Eisleben **Note:** Varieties exist. Dav. #7000.

Date	Mintage	VG	F	VF	XF	Unc
1604 GM	—	75.00	195	300	500	—
1605 GM	—	75.00	195	300	500	—
1606 GM	—	75.00	195	300	500	—
1607 GM	—	75.00	195	300	500	—
1608 GM	—	75.00	195	300	500	—
1609 GM	—	75.00	195	300	500	—
1611 GM	—	75.00	195	300	500	—

KM# 18 THALER

Silver **Obv:** St. George left and dragon **Rev:** Shield dividing date and G-M, three-line inscription above **Note:** Dav. #6977.

Date	Mintage	VG	F	VF	XF	Unc
1606	—	85.00	200	350	600	—
1607	—	85.00	200	350	600	—
1608	—	85.00	200	350	600	—
1609	—	85.00	200	350	600	—
1610	—	85.00	200	350	600	—
1611	—	85.00	200	350	600	—
1612	—	85.00	200	350	600	—
1613	—	85.00	200	350	600	—
1614	—	85.00	200	350	600	—
1615	—	85.00	200	350	600	—

KM# 33 THALER

Silver **Obv:** Helmeted arms, divided date above and initials below **Rev:** St. George and dragon **Mint:** Eisleben **Note:** Dav. #7002.

Date	Mintage	VG	F	VF	XF	Unc
1610 GM	—	75.00	195	300	500	—
1611 GM	—	75.00	195	300	500	—
1612 GM	—	75.00	195	300	500	—
1613 GM	—	75.00	195	300	500	—
1614 GM	—	75.00	195	300	500	—
1615 GM	—	75.00	195	300	500	—
1616 AK	—	75.00	195	300	500	—
1617 AK	—	75.00	195	300	500	—
1618 AK	—	75.00	195	300	500	—
1619 AK	—	75.00	195	300	500	—
1621 AK	—	75.00	195	300	500	—

KM# 52 THALER

Silver **Obv:** G-M above arms, date below **Mint:** Eisleben **Note:** Dav. #7003.

Date	Mintage	VG	F	VF	XF	Unc
1611 GM	—	75.00	190	265	400	—

KM# 53 THALER

Silver **Obv:** Without initials above arms **Note:** Dav. #7003A.

Date	Mintage	VG	F	VF	XF	Unc
1611	—	75.00	190	265	400	—

KM# 51 THALER

Silver **Rev:** Four-line inscription above shield **Mint:** Eisleben **Note:** Dav. #6977A.

Date	Mintage	VG	F	VF	XF	Unc
1611 GM	—	85.00	200	350	600	—
1614 GM	—	85.00	200	350	600	—
1615 GM	—	85.00	200	350	600	—

KM# 64 THALER

Silver **Rev:** Crowned shield divide date and A-K **Mint:** Eisleben **Note:** Dav. #6979.

Date	Mintage	VG	F	VF	XF	Unc
1616	—	75.00	190	285	450	—
1618	—	75.00	190	285	450	—
1620	—	75.00	190	285	450	—

KM# 69 THALER

Silver **Rev:** A-K above date **Mint:** Eisleben **Note:** Dav. #6979A.

Date	Mintage	VG	F	VF	XF	Unc
1617	—	75.00	190	285	450	—
1618	—	75.00	190	285	450	—
1619	—	75.00	190	285	450	—

KM# 74 THALER

Silver **Rev:** A-K above crown **Mint:** Eisleben **Note:** Dav. #6979B.

Date	Mintage	VG	F	VF	XF	Unc
1619	—	75.00	190	275	450	—

KM# 75 THALER

Silver **Mint:** Saalfeld **Note:** Dav. #6980.

Date	Mintage	VG	F	VF	XF	Unc
1619 H-I	—	75.00	195	325	550	—
1620 H-I	—	75.00	195	325	550	—

KM# 76 THALER

Silver **Obv:** St. George and dragon **Rev:** Helmeted arms, date divided above, A-K divided at center **Mint:** Eisleben **Note:** Dav. #7005.

Date	Mintage	VG	F	VF	XF	Unc
1619 AK	—	75.00	195	325	550	—
1620 AK	—	75.00	195	325	550	—

KM# 83 THALER

Silver **Rev:** H-I above date **Note:** Dav. #6980A.

Date	Mintage	VG	F	VF	XF	Unc
1620	—	75.00	195	300	550	—

KM# 119 THALER

Silver **Obv:** St. George and dragon smaller **Rev:** Crowned arms dividing date and H-I **Mint:** Saalfeld **Note:** Dav. #6981.

Date	Mintage	VG	F	VF	XF	Unc
1621	—	100	220	400	750	—

KM# 132 THALER

Silver **Obv. Legend:** DAVID: C. E. DO: I. MANSF. NO: DO: I. HEL SE. E. SC. **Rev:** Spanish shield divides A-K **Rev. Legend:** BEI: GOTT: IST: RAHT. VNND THATT **Mint:** Eisleben **Note:** Dav. #6982.

Date	Mintage	VG	F	VF	XF	Unc
1622	—	100	220	400	750	—

KM# 133 THALER

Silver **Rev:** A-K above date **Mint:** Eisleben **Note:** Dav. #6982A.

Date	Mintage	VG	F	VF	XF	Unc
1622	—	100	220	400	750	—

KM# 134 THALER

Silver **Rev:** Heart-shaped shield, A-K above date **Mint:** Eisleben **Note:** Dav. #6982B.

Date	Mintage	VG	F	VF	XF	Unc
1622	—	100	220	400	750	—

KM# 135 THALER

Silver **Rev:** Date above A-K **Mint:** Eisleben **Note:** Dav. #7006.

Date	Mintage	VG	F	VF	XF	Unc
1622	—	85.00	200	400	850	1,850
1623	—	85.00	200	400	850	1,850
1624	—	85.00	200	400	850	1,850
1625	—	85.00	200	400	850	1,850

KM# 136 THALER

Silver **Obv:** Small rider within circle above dragon on back **Mint:** Eisleben **Note:** Dav. #7006A.

Date	Mintage	VG	F	VF	XF	Unc
1622 AK	—	85.00	200	400	850	—

KM# 137 THALER

Silver **Rev:** A-K above date **Mint:** Eisleben **Note:** Dav. #7006B.

Date	Mintage	VG	F	VF	XF	Unc
1622	—	85.00	200	400	850	—
1623	—	85.00	200	400	850	—
1624	—	85.00	200	400	850	—
1625	—	85.00	200	400	850	—

KM# 138 THALER

Silver **Rev. Legend:** MANSF. NOBILES. DOM… **Mint:** Eisleben **Note:** Dav. #7007.

Date	Mintage	VG	F	VF	XF	Unc
1622 AK	—	85.00	200	400	850	—

KM# 139 THALER

Silver **Obv:** St. George left and dragon **Obv. Legend:** FRIDERI: CHRIS: ET. DAVID. CO: E: D: IN **Rev:** Helmeted arms dividing date and A-K below **Mint:** Eisleben **Note:** Dav. #7013. Varieties exist for legend and shield.

Date	Mintage	VG	F	VF	XF	Unc
1622	—	85.00	200	350	650	—
1623	—	85.00	200	350	650	—
1624	—	85.00	200	350	650	—
1625	—	85.00	200	350	650	—
1626	—	85.00	200	350	650	—

KM# 143 THALER

Silver **Obv. Legend:** DAVID: C. E. DO: I. MANSF. NO: DO: I. HEL. SE. E. SC. **Rev. Legend:** IN. MANSF. NOBI. DOM. IN. HEL. SEB. ET. SC. **Mint:** Eisleben **Note:** Mule. Dav. #6986.

Date	Mintage	VG	F	VF	XF	Unc
1623 AK	—	100	250	475	1,000	—

KM# 144 THALER

Silver **Obv. Legend:** ...DOM. I. MANS. N: D. I. H: S: E. S: **Rev. Legend:** BEI. GOTT. IST. RAHT. VNND. THADT **Mint:** Eisleben **Note:** Mule. Dav. #6987.

Date	Mintage	VG	F	VF	XF	Unc
1623 AK	—	100	250	475	1,000	—

KM# 146 THALER

Silver **Rev. Legend:** IN. MANSF. NOBI. DOM... **Mint:** Eisleben **Note:** Dav. #7008.

Date	Mintage	VG	F	VF	XF	Unc
1623 AK	—	100	250	475	1,000	—

KM# 145 THALER

Silver **Mint:** Eisleben **Note:** Dav. #6989.

Date	Mintage	VG	F	VF	XF	Unc
1623 A-K	—	85.00	200	350	650	—
1624 A-K	—	85.00	200	350	650	—
1625 A-K	—	85.00	200	350	650	—
1626 A-K	—	85.00	200	350	650	—
1627 A-K	—	85.00	200	350	650	—
1628 A-K	—	85.00	200	350	650	—

KM# 156 THALER

Silver **Obv:** Date below St. George **Rev:** Date above crowned arms in legend **Mint:** Eisleben **Note:** Dav. #6990.

Date	Mintage	VG	F	VF	XF	Unc
1624	—	85.00	200	350	650	—
1626//624 AK	—	85.00	200	350	650	—

KM# 150 THALER

Silver **Rev:** Date divided above arms **Mint:** Eisleben **Note:** Dav. #7014.

Date	Mintage	VG	F	VF	XF	Unc
1625 AK	—	100	250	475	1,000	—
1626 AK	—	85.00	200	400	850	—

KM# 153 THALER

Silver **Obv. Legend:** DAVID: CO: ET. DO: IN. MANSF. N. :D: I. H. S. E. **Rev. Legend:** MANST. NO. DO. IN. HEL. SEB. ET. SC. **Mint:** Eisleben **Note:** Mule. Dav. #6983.

Date	Mintage	VG	F	VF	XF	Unc
1626//1622 AK	—	85.00	200	400	850	—

KM# 154 THALER

Silver **Rev. Legend:** COM. ET. DOM. IN. MANSF. NO. DOM. IN. HEL: **Mint:** Eisleben **Note:** Mule. Dav. #6984.

Date	Mintage	VG	F	VF	XF	Unc
1626//1622 AK	—	75.00	190	275	450	—

KM# 155 THALER

Silver **Rev:** Double helmets and complex arms **Mint:** Eisleben **Note:** Mule. Dav. #6985.

Date	Mintage	VG	F	VF	XF	Unc
1626//1622 AK	—	85.00	200	385	750	—

KM# 157 THALER

Silver **Rev:** Elaborate shield **Mint:** Eisleben **Note:** Dav. #6990A.

Date	Mintage	VG	F	VF	XF	Unc
1626//1626 AK	—	85.00	200	350	650	—

KM# 158 THALER

Silver **Obv:** Date below St. George **Rev:** Shield of arms divides A - K **Mint:** Eisleben **Note:** Dav. #6991.

Date	Mintage	VG	F	VF	XF	Unc
1626//1625 AK	—	85.00	200	385	750	—

KM# 159 THALER

Silver **Rev:** Crowned arms divide date and A-K **Mint:** Eisleben **Note:** Dav. #6993.

Date	Mintage	VG	F	VF	XF	Unc
1626 AK	—	85.00	200	350	650	—

KM# 167 THALER

Silver **Subject:** Death of David **Obv:** Seven-line inscription **Rev:** Crowned arms **Mint:** Eisleben **Note:** Dav. #6994.

Date	Mintage	VG	F	VF	XF	Unc
1628 AK	—	130	265	450	900	—

KM# 176 THALER

Silver **Obv. Legend:** FRIDERI: CHRI:... **Rev. Legend:** MANSF: NOBI. DOM. IN. HEL... **Mint:** Eisleben **Note:** Dav. #7010.

Date	Mintage	VG	F	VF	XF	Unc
1629 AK	—	85.00	200	375	700	—
1630 AK	—	85.00	200	375	700	—

KM# 177 THALER

Silver **Rev:** Initials divided by helmets, date below **Mint:** Eisleben **Note:** Dav. #7011.

Date	Mintage	VG	F	VF	XF	Unc
1629 AK	—	85.00	200	350	650	—

KM# 189 THALER

Silver **Subject:** Death of Friedrich Christoph **Note:** Dav. #7012.

Date	Mintage	VG	F	VF	XF	Unc
1631	—	150	300	650	1,500	—

KM# 193 THALER

Silver **Subject:** Death of Ernst Ludwig **Obv:** St. George and dragon **Rev:** Seven-line inscription **Note:** Dav. #7016.

Date	Mintage	VG	F	VF	XF	Unc
1632 Rare	—	—	—	—	—	—

KM# 202 THALER

Silver **Rev:** Helmeted arms dividing date above and HP-K below **Mint:** Eisleben **Note:** Dav. #7019.

Date	Mintage	VG	F	VF	XF	Unc
1642 HPK	—	75.00	190	285	600	—
1643 HPK	—	75.00	190	285	600	—
1644 HPK	—	75.00	190	285	600	—
1645 HPK	—	75.00	190	285	600	—
1646 HPK	—	75.00	190	285	600	—
1647 HPK	—	75.00	190	285	600	—
1648 HPK	—	75.00	190	285	600	—
1649 HPK	—	75.00	190	285	600	—
1651 HPK	—	75.00	190	285	600	—
1652 HPK	—	75.00	190	285	600	—
1653 HPK	—	75.00	190	285	600	—
1663 HPK	—	75.00	190	285	600	—
1665 HPK	—	75.00	190	285	600	—

KM# 211 THALER

Silver **Rev:** Without initials **Note:** Dav. #7019A.

Date	Mintage	VG	F	VF	XF	Unc
1648	—	75.00	190	285	600	—
1649	—	75.00	190	285	600	—
1651	—	75.00	190	285	600	—

KM# 221 THALER

Silver **Rev:** HP-K above date **Mint:** Eisleben **Note:** Dav. #7019B.

Date	Mintage	VG	F	VF	XF	Unc
1651	—	75.00	190	285	600	—

KM# 222 THALER

Silver **Obv:** St. George slaying dragon to left **Rev:** Helmeted arms divide date and mintmaster's initials **Mint:** Eisleben **Note:** Dav. #7021.

Date	Mintage	VG	F	VF	XF	Unc
1653 HPK	—	85.00	200	350	750	2,250
1661 HPK	—	85.00	200	350	750	2,250
1662 HPK	—	85.00	200	350	750	2,250
1663 HPK	—	85.00	200	350	750	2,250
1664 HPK	—	85.00	200	350	750	2,250
1665 HPK	—	85.00	200	350	750	2,250
ND HP-K	—	85.00	200	350	750	2,250

KM# 6 2 THALER

Silver **Obv:** Crowned double eagle above crowned arms **Rev:** St. George left and dragon **Mint:** Eisleben **Note:** Dav. #6995.

Date	Mintage	VG	F	VF	XF	Unc
1602 GM	—	1,850	3,250	5,750	—	—

KM# 11 2 THALER

Silver **Rev. Legend:** ERNESTVS. E: FRID: CHRIST: CO: E: DO: I: MANSFEL **Mint:** Eisleben **Note:** Dav. #6997.

Date	Mintage	VG	F	VF	XF	Unc
1603 GM	—	1,850	3,250	5,750	—	—

KM# 10 2 THALER

Silver **Obv:** Helmeted arms with helmets dividing G-M **Rev:** St. George left and dragon **Mint:** Eisleben **Note:** Dav. #6973.

Date	Mintage	VG	F	VF	XF	Unc
1603 GM	—	1,850	3,250	5,750	—	—

KM# 14 2 THALER

Silver **Obv:** Helmeted arms with divided date above and G-M below **Rev:** St. George and dragon **Rev. Legend:** NOBILES. DOMINI… **Mint:** Eisleben **Note:** Dav. #6999.

Date	Mintage	VG	F	VF	XF	Unc
1604 GM	—	1,850	3,250	5,750	—	—
1606 GM	—	1,850	3,250	5,750	—	—

KM# 20 2 THALER

Silver **Obv:** St. George slaying dragon to left **Rev:** Shield of arms divides date and G-M **Mint:** Eisleben **Note:** Similar to 1 Thaler, KM#18. Dav. #6976.

Date	Mintage	VG	F	VF	XF	Unc
1607 GM	—	1,850	3,250	5,750	—	—
1610 GM	—	1,850	3,250	5,750	—	—
1611 GM	—	1,850	3,250	5,750	—	—
1615 GM	—	1,850	3,250	5,750	—	—

KM# 25 2 THALER

Silver **Rev. Legend:** NOBILIS. DOMINVS… **Mint:** Eisleben **Note:** Dav. #6999A.

Date	Mintage	VG	F	VF	XF	Unc
1609 GM	—	1,850	3,250	5,750	—	—

KM# 34 2 THALER

Silver **Obv:** Shield of arms, bullets divide date • 1 • 6 … **Rev:** St. George slaying dragon, horse left **Mint:** Eisleben **Note:** Similar to 1 Thaler, KM#33. Dav. #7001.

Date	Mintage	VG	F	VF	XF	Unc
1610 GM	—	1,850	3,250	5,750	—	—
1612 GM	—	1,850	3,250	5,750	—	—

KM# 70 2 THALER

Silver **Rev:** Crowned shield divides date and A-K **Mint:** Eisleben **Note:** Dav. #6978.

Date	Mintage	VG	F	VF	XF	Unc
1617 AK	—	1,850	3,250	5,750	—	—

KM# 85 2 THALER

Silver **Obv:** St. George and dragon **Rev:** Helmeted arms with date divided above and H-I divided at center **Mint:** Saalfeld **Note:** Dav. #7004.

Date	Mintage	VG	F	VF	XF	Unc
1620 HI	—	1,850	3,250	5,750	—	—

KM# 149 2 THALER

Silver **Note:** Similar to 1 Thaler, KM#145. Dav. #6988.

Date	Mintage	VG	F	VF	XF	Unc
1624 AK	—	1,850	3,250	5,750	—	—

KM# 178 2 THALER

Silver **Obv:** St. George and dragon **Rev:** Helmeted arms divide date and mintmaster's initials **Mint:** Eisleben **Note:** Dav. #3250.

Date	Mintage	VG	F	VF	XF	Unc
16Z9 AK	—	—	—	—	—	—

KM# 194 2 THALER

Silver **Subject:** Death of Ernst Ludwig **Obv:** St. George and dragon **Rev:** Seven-line inscription **Note:** Dav. #7015.

Date	Mintage	VG	F	VF	XF	Unc
1632 Rare	—	—	—	—	—	—

KM# 206 2 THALER

Silver **Rev:** Helmeted arms dividing date above and HP-K below **Mint:** Eisleben **Note:** Similar to 1 Thaler, KM#202. Dav. #7018.

Date	Mintage	VG	F	VF	XF	Unc
1644 HPK	—	1,850	3,250	5,500	—	—
1646 HPK	—	1,850	3,250	5,500	—	—
1651 HPK	—	1,850	3,250	5,500	—	—
1665 HPK	—	1,850	3,250	5,500	—	—

KM# 223 2 THALER

Silver **Obv:** St. George slaying dragon, horse left **Rev:** Helmeted arms divide mintmaster's initials **Mint:** Eisleben **Note:** Similar to 1 Thaler, KM#222. Dav. #7020.

Date	Mintage	VG	F	VF	XF	Unc
1653 HPK	—	1,850	3,250	5,500	—	—
1662 HPK	—	1,850	3,250	5,500	—	—

KM# 26 3 THALER

Silver **Obv:** St. George slaying dragon to left **Rev:** Shield of arms divide date above, mintmaster's initials below **Mint:** Eisleben **Note:** Similar to 1 Thaler, KM#18. Dav. #6975.

Date	Mintage	VG	F	VF	XF	Unc
1609 GM Rare	—	—	—	—	—	—

KM# 160 4 THALER
Silver **Obv:** St. George and dragon **Rev:** Crowned arms **Mint:** Eisleben **Note:** Dav. #6992.

Date	Mintage	VG	F	VF	XF	Unc
1626 AK Rare	—	—	—	—	—	—

KM# 210 4 THALER
Silver **Note:** Similar to 1 Thaler, KM#202. Dav. #7017.

Date	Mintage	VG	F	VF	XF	Unc
1646 Rare	—	—	—	—	—	—

TRADE COINAGE

KM# 19 GOLDGULDEN
3.5000 g., 0.9860 Gold 0.1109 oz. AGW **Obv:** St. George slaying dragon **Rev:** Two-line inscription above arms **Mint:** Eisleben

Date	Mintage	VG	F	VF	XF	Unc
1606	—	400	825	1,650	3,300	—
1607 GM	—	—	—	—	—	—
1608 GM	—	—	—	—	—	—
1609 GM	—	—	—	—	—	—
1610 GM	—	—	—	—	—	—
1611 GM	—	—	—	—	—	—
1612 GM	—	—	—	—	—	—
1613 GM	—	—	—	—	—	—
1614 GM	—	—	—	—	—	—
1618	—	400	825	1,650	3,300	—

KM# 21 GOLDGULDEN
3.5000 g., 0.9860 Gold 0.1109 oz. AGW **Rev:** Arms topped by helmet in inner circle

Date	Mintage	VG	F	VF	XF	Unc
1607	—	400	825	1,650	3,300	—

KM# 140 GOLDGULDEN
3.5000 g., 0.9860 Gold 0.1109 oz. AGW **Rev:** Arms topped by helmet in inner circle

Date	Mintage	VG	F	VF	XF	Unc
1622	—	550	1,100	2,150	4,500	—

KM# 59 2 GOLDGULDEN
7.0000 g., 0.9860 Gold 0.2219 oz. AGW **Obv:** St. George slaying dragon at left **Rev:** Inscription above four-fold arms which divide date and mintmaster's initials **Rev. Inscription:** BEI GOT/IST RATH/VND THAT **Mint:** Eisleben **Note:** Varieties exist.

Date	Mintage	VG	F	VF	XF	Unc
1614 GM Rare	—	—	—	—	—	—
1615 GM Rare	—	—	—	—	—	—

KM# 77 DUCAT
3.5000 g., 0.9860 Gold 0.1109 oz. AGW **Obv:** St. George and dragon in inner circle **Rev:** Crowned arms in inner circle

Date	Mintage	VG	F	VF	XF	Unc
1619	—	400	750	1,500	3,500	—

KM# 141 DUCAT
3.5000 g., 0.9860 Gold 0.1109 oz. AGW **Obv:** St. George slaying dragon at left **Rev:** Arms topped by helmet in inner circle

Date	Mintage	VG	F	VF	XF	Unc
1622	—	275	550	1,150	2,750	—

KM# 207 DUCAT
3.5000 g., 0.9860 Gold 0.1109 oz. AGW

Date	Mintage	VG	F	VF	XF	Unc
1644	—	225	450	1,150	2,200	—
1647	—	225	450	1,150	2,200	—
1652	—	225	450	1,150	2,200	—

KM# 169 1-3/4 DUCAT
6.1250 g., 0.9860 Gold 0.1942 oz. AGW **Subject:** Death of David **Obv:** Seven-line inscription with dates **Rev:** Crowned four-fold arms divide date and mintmaster's initials **Mint:** Eisleben

Date	Mintage	VG	F	VF	XF	Unc
(16)Z8 AK Rare	—	—	—	—	—	—

KM# 54 2 DUCAT
7.0000 g., 0.9860 Gold 0.2219 oz. AGW **Obv:** St. George slaying dragon left **Rev:** Inscription above four-fold arms which divide date and mintmaster's initials **Rev. Inscription:** BEI GOT / IST RATH / VND THAT

Date	Mintage	VG	F	VF	XF	Unc
1611 Rare	—	—	—	—	—	—

KM# 170 2 DUCAT
7.0000 g., 0.9860 Gold 0.2219 oz. AGW **Subject:** Death of David **Obv:** Six-line inscription with dates **Rev:** Crowned four-fold arms divide date and mintmaster's initials

Date	Mintage	VG	F	VF	XF	Unc
(16)Z8 AK Rare	—	—	—	—	—	—

KM# 171 2 DUCAT
7.0000 g., 0.9860 Gold 0.2219 oz. AGW **Obv:** Eight-line inscription with dates **Mint:** Eisleben

Date	Mintage	VG	F	VF	XF	Unc
(16)Z8 AK Rare	—	—	—	—	—	—

KM# 195 2 DUCAT
7.0000 g., 0.9860 Gold 0.2219 oz. AGW **Subject:** Death of Ernst Ludwig **Obv:** St. George slaying dragon at left **Rev:** Seven-line inscription with dates

Date	Mintage	VG	F	VF	XF	Unc
(1)63Z Rare	—	—	—	—	—	—

KM# 203 2 DUCAT
7.0000 g., 0.9860 Gold 0.2219 oz. AGW **Rev:** Four-fold arms divide mintmaster's initials, helmet above divides date **Note:** Varieties exist.

Date	Mintage	VG	F	VF	XF	Unc
1642 HPK	—	1,000	2,000	4,000	6,500	—
1649 HPK	—	1,000	2,000	4,000	6,500	—

KM# 172 2-3/4 DUCAT
9.6200 g., 0.9860 Gold 0.3049 oz. AGW **Subject:** Death of David **Obv:** Seven-line inscription with dates **Rev:** Crowned four-fold arms divide date and mintmaster's initials **Mint:** Eisleben **Note:** Varieties exist.

Date	Mintage	VG	F	VF	XF	Unc
16Z8 AK Rare	—	—	—	—	—	—

KM# 60 3 DUCAT
10.5000 g., 0.9860 Gold 0.3328 oz. AGW **Obv:** St. George slaying dragon at left **Rev:** Inscription above four-fold arms which divide date and mintmaster's initials **Rev. Inscription:** BEI GOT / IST RATH / VND THAT **Note:** Spruch 3 Ducat.

Date	Mintage	VG	F	VF	XF	Unc
1614 GM	—	2,050	3,900	7,000	12,500	—
1615 GM Rare	—	—	—	—	—	—

KM# 212 3 DUCAT
10.5000 g., 0.9860 Gold 0.3328 oz. AGW **Rev:** Helmeted four-fold arms divide date and mintmaster's initials **Mint:** Eisleben

Date	Mintage	VG	F	VF	XF	Unc
1649 Rare	—	—	—	—	—	—
1649 HPK Rare	—	—	—	—	—	—

KM# 204 4 DUCAT
14.0000 g., 0.9860 Gold 0.4438 oz. AGW **Obv:** St. George slaying dragon to left **Rev:** Date divided by helmet, four-fold arms divide mintmaster's initials **Mint:** Eisleben

Date	Mintage	VG	F	VF	XF	Unc
1642 HPK Rare	—	—	—	—	—	—

KM# 213 4 DUCAT
14.0000 g., 0.9860 Gold 0.4438 oz. AGW **Rev:** Helmeted four-fold arms divide date and mintmaster's initials **Mint:** Eisleben

Date	Mintage	VG	F	VF	XF	Unc
1649 HPK Rare	—	—	—	—	—	—

KM# 22 5 DUCAT (1/2 Portugaloser)
14.0000 g., 0.9860 Gold 0.4438 oz. AGW **Obv:** St. George slaying dragon to left **Rev:** Shield dividing date and G-M, 3 line inscription above **Mint:** Eisleben **Note:** Spruch 5 Ducat. Similar to 1 Thaler, KM#18.

Date	Mintage	VG	F	VF	XF	Unc
1608 GM Rare	—	—	—	—	—	—
1609 GM Rare	—	—	—	—	—	—

KM# 71 5 DUCAT (1/2 Portugaloser)
14.0000 g., 0.9860 Gold 0.4438 oz. AGW **Obv:** St. George slaying dragon to left **Rev:** Crowned shield divides date and A-K **Mint:** Eisleben **Note:** Similar to 1 Thaler, KM#64.

Date	Mintage	VG	F	VF	XF	Unc
1617 AK Rare	—	—	—	—	—	—

KM# 226 5 DUCAT (1/2 Portugaloser)
14.0000 g., 0.9860 Gold 0.4438 oz. AGW **Obv:** St. George slaying dragon to left **Rev:** Shield of arms divides H-PK at top, date below **Mint:** Eisleben **Note:** Similar to 1 Thaler, KM#222.

Date	Mintage	VG	F	VF	XF	Unc
1661 HPK Rare	—	—	—	—	—	—

KM# 12 10 DUCAT (Portugaloser)
35.0000 g., 0.9860 Gold 1.1095 oz. AGW **Obv:** St. George slaying dragon left **Obv. Legend:** ERNESTVS. FRI: CHRIST: E. DAVID. CO. MANSF: **Rev:** Crowned double eagle above crowned arms divide date and G-M **Mint:** Eisleben

Date	Mintage	VG	F	VF	XF	Unc
1603 GM Rare	—	—	—	—	—	—

KM# 205 10 DUCAT (Portugaloser)
35.0000 g., 0.9860 Gold 1.1095 oz. AGW **Obv:** St. George slaying dragon on horse to left **Rev:** Seven flags above arms divide date **Mint:** Eisleben **Note:** Struck with 1 Thaler dies, KM#202.

Date	Mintage	VG	F	VF	XF	Unc
1642 HPK Rare	—	—	—	—	—	—

MANSFELD-EISLEBEN

This line resulted from the division of 1530/32. Upon the extinction of Eisleben in 1710, all lands and titles reverted to the Bornstedt line.

RULERS
Jobst II, 1579-1619
Johann Georg II, 1619-1647
Hoyer Christof II, 1647-1663
Johann Georg III, 1663-1710

REFERENCE
T = Otto Tornau, **Münzwesen und Münzen der Grafschaft Mansfeld**, Prague, 1937.

COUNTSHIP

REGULAR COINAGE

KM# 21 3 FLITTER (1-1/2 Pfennig)
Copper **Obv:** Four-fold arms, L above **Rev:** III in center, FLITTER, date in legend **Mint:** Leimbach **Note:** Kipper 3 Flitter.

Date	Mintage	VG	F	VF	XF	Unc
16Z1 L	—	—	—	—	—	—

KM# 22 3 PFENNIG
Copper **Obv:** St. George right slaying dragon **Rev:** Imperial orb with 3 divides L-S **Mint:** Leimbach **Note:** Kipper 3 Pfennig.

Date	Mintage	VG	F	VF	XF	Unc
ND(1621/22) LS	—	32.00	65.00	130	265	—

KM# 24 3 PFENNIG
Copper **Obv:** Four-fold arms **Rev:** Imperial orb with 3 divides L-S **Mint:** Leimbach **Note:** Varieties exist.

Date	Mintage	VG	F	VF	XF	Unc
ND(1621/22) LS	—	32.00	65.00	130	265	—

KM# 25 3 PFENNIG
Copper **Obv:** L above arms **Rev:** Date divided by orb **Mint:** Leimbach **Note:** Varieties exist.

Date	Mintage	VG	F	VF	XF	Unc
16Z1 L/LS	—	32.00	65.00	130	265	—
(16)Z1 L/LS	—	32.00	65.00	130	265	—

KM# 23 3 PFENNIG
Copper **Obv:** St. George right slaying dragon divides date **Rev:** L-S divided above imperial orb with 3 **Mint:** Leimbach

Date	Mintage	VG	F	VF	XF	Unc
(16)Z1 LS	—	32.00	65.00	130	265	—
(16)ZZ LS	—	32.00	65.00	130	265	—

KM# 30 3 PFENNIG
Copper **Obv:** Date above arms **Mint:** Leimbach

Date	Mintage	VG	F	VF	XF	Unc
(16)ZZ LS	—	32.00	65.00	130	265	—

KM# 32 3 PFENNIG
Copper **Obv:** Four-fold arms divide date, L above **Rev:** Imperial orb with 3 divides L-S **Mint:** Leimbach

Date	Mintage	VG	F	VF	XF	Unc
(16)ZZ L/LS	—	32.00	65.00	130	265	—

KM# 31 3 PFENNIG
Copper **Rev:** Orb divides date and mint initials **Mint:** Leimbach **Note:** Varieties exist.

Date	Mintage	VG	F	VF	XF	Unc
(16)ZZ LS	—	32.00	65.00	130	265	—

KM# 45 3 PFENNIG (Dreier)
Silver **Obv:** Ornamented oval four-fold arms divide date **Rev:** Small imperial orb with 3 divides mintmaster's initials in ornamented rhombus **Mint:** Eisleben

Date	Mintage	VG	F	VF	XF	Unc
1634 HPK	—	20.00	45.00	90.00	180	—

KM# 75 3 PFENNIG (Dreier)
Silver **Obv:** Crowned four-fold arms, mintmaster's initials above **Rev:** Imperial orb with 3, date above **Mint:** Eisleben

Date	Mintage	VG	F	VF	XF	Unc
1671 ABK	—	—	—	—	—	—

KM# 76 6 PFENNIG (Sechser)
Silver **Obv:** Imperial orb with 6 divides mintmaster's initials **Rev:** Crowned four-fold arms divide date **Mint:** Eisleben **Note:** Varieties exist.

Date	Mintage	VG	F	VF	XF	Unc
1671 ABK	—	—	—	—	—	—

KM# 20 12 KREUZER (Schreckenburger)
Silver **Obv:** Crowned imperial eagle, 12 in orb on breast, titles of Ferdinand II **Rev:** Four-fold arms divide date, angel above **Note:** Kipper 12 Kreuzer.

Date	Mintage	VG	F	VF	XF	Unc
(16)20	—	40.00	70.00	135	275	—

KM# 26 12 KREUZER (Schreckenburger)
Silver **Obv:** Ornamented 4-fold arms, date in legend **Rev:** Crowned imperial eagle, 12 in orb on breast, (NA) at bottom in legend **Mint:** Neu-Asseburg **Note:** Varieties exist.

Date	Mintage	VG	F	VF	XF	Unc
16Z1 NA	—	40.00	70.00	134	275	—

KM# 27 12 KREUZER (Schreckenburger)
Silver **Obv:** 2 ornate helmets above oval with L, date in legend **Rev:** Crowned imperial eagle, 1Z in orb on breast, titles of Johann Georg II **Mint:** Leimbach

Date	Mintage	VG	F	VF	XF	Unc
16Z1 L	—	40.00	70.00	135	275	—

KM# 28 1/24 THALER (Groschen)
Silver **Obv:** St. George right slaying dragon **Rev:** Four-fold arms, value Z4 below, date in legend

Date	Mintage	VG	F	VF	XF	Unc
1621	—	—	—	—	—	—

KM# 29 1/24 THALER (Groschen)
Silver **Obv:** Crowned four-fold arms **Rev:** Imperial orb with 24

Date	Mintage	VG	F	VF	XF	Unc
ND(1621/22)	—	16.00	35.00	70.00	145	—

KM# 39 1/24 THALER (Groschen)
Silver **Obv:** Four-fold arms divide mintmaster's initials, date above **Rev:** Imperial orb with 24 **Mint:** Eisleben **Note:** Varieties exist.

Date	Mintage	VG	F	VF	XF	Unc
1630	—	20.00	40.00	80.00	160	—
163Z AK	—	20.00	40.00	80.00	160	—
1633 HPK	—	20.00	40.00	80.00	160	—
1634 HPK	—	20.00	40.00	80.00	160	—
1635 HPK	—	20.00	40.00	80.00	160	—
1636 HPK	—	20.00	40.00	80.00	160	—
1644 HPK	—	20.00	40.00	80.00	160	—

KM# 40 1/24 THALER (Groschen)
Silver **Obv:** Mintmaster's initials above arms **Rev:** Date divided at top **Mint:** Eisleben **Note:** Varieties exist.

Date	Mintage	VG	F	VF	XF	Unc
1623 HPK Error for 1632	—	—	—	—	—	—
163Z HPK	—	20.00	40.00	80.00	160	—
1636 HPK	—	20.00	40.00	80.00	160	—
1637 HPK	—	20.00	40.00	80.00	160	—
1638 HPK	—	20.00	40.00	80.00	160	—
1639 HPK	—	20.00	40.00	80.00	160	—
1640 HPK	—	20.00	40.00	80.00	160	—
1640	—	20.00	40.00	80.00	160	—
1641 HPK	—	20.00	40.00	80.00	160	—
1642 HPK	—	20.00	40.00	80.00	160	—
ND HPK	—	20.00	40.00	80.00	160	—

KM# 44 1/24 THALER (Groschen)
Silver **Rev:** Date divided by imperial orb **Mint:** Eisleben **Note:** Varieties exist.

Date	Mintage	VG	F	VF	XF	Unc
1636 HPK	—	20.00	40.00	80.00	160	—
1637 HPK	—	20.00	40.00	80.00	160	—
1640 HPK	—	20.00	40.00	80.00	160	—
1645 HPK	—	20.00	40.00	80.00	160	—

KM# 50 1/24 THALER (Groschen)
Silver **Obv:** Mintmaster's initials divided by arms **Mint:** Eisleben **Note:** Varieties exist.

Date	Mintage	VG	F	VF	XF	Unc
1641 HPK	—	20.00	40.00	80.00	160	—
1645 HPK	—	20.00	40.00	80.00	160	—
1646 HPK	—	20.00	40.00	80.00	160	—
1647 HPK	—	20.00	40.00	80.00	160	—

KM# 51 1/24 THALER (Groschen)
Silver **Subject:** Death of Johann Georg II **Obv:** Eight-line inscription with dates **Rev:** Imperial orb with 24 **Rev. Legend:** DENNOCH **Note:** Varieties exist.

Date	Mintage	VG	F	VF	XF	Unc
1647	—	—	—	—	—	—

KM# 55 1/24 THALER (Groschen)
Silver **Obv:** Four-fold arms divide mintmaster's initials **Rev:** Imperial orb with 24 divides date **Mint:** Eisleben **Note:** Varieties exist.

Date	Mintage	VG	F	VF	XF	Unc
1648 HPK	—	16.00	35.00	70.00	145	—
1652 HPK	—	16.00	35.00	70.00	145	—
1657 HPK	—	16.00	35.00	70.00	145	—
ND HPK	—	16.00	35.00	70.00	145	—

KM# 65 1/24 THALER (Groschen)
Silver **Obv:** Imperial orb with 24 divides date and mintmaster's initials **Rev:** Crowned four-fold arms **Mint:** Eisleben **Note:** Varieties exist.

Date	Mintage	VG	F	VF	XF	Unc
1668 ABK	—	16.00	35.00	70.00	145	—
1669 ABK	—	16.00	35.00	70.00	145	—
1670 ABK	—	16.00	35.00	70.00	145	—

KM# 66 1/6 THALER
Silver **Obv:** Value 1/6 below St. George on horse to right slaying dragon **Mint:** Eisleben **Note:** Varieties exist.

Date	Mintage	VG	F	VF	XF	Unc
1668 ABK	—	50.00	100	210	425	—
1669 ABK	—	50.00	100	210	425	—

KM# 68 1/6 THALER
Silver **Rev:** Mintmaster's initials below arms **Mint:** Eisleben

Date	Mintage	VG	F	VF	XF	Unc
1669 ABK	—	50.00	100	210	425	—

KM# 11 1/4 THALER
Silver **Mint:** Saalfeld **Note:** Klippe.

Date	Mintage	VG	F	VF	XF	Unc
1619 HI	—	—	—	—	—	—

KM# 10 1/4 THALER
Silver **Subject:** Death of Jobst II **Obv:** Crowned four-fold arms divide date and mintmaster's initials **Rev:** Eight-line inscription with dates **Mint:** Saalfeld **Note:** Varieties exist.

Date	Mintage	VG	F	VF	XF	Unc
1619 HI	—	—	—	—	—	—

KM# 41 1/4 THALER
Silver **Obv:** St. George right slaying dragon **Rev:** Ornate four-fold arms divide date, mintmaster's initials between two helmets above **Mint:** Eisleben **Note:** Varieties exist.

Date	Mintage	VG	F	VF	XF	Unc
1632 HPK	—	—	—	—	—	—
1634 HPK	—	—	—	—	—	—

KM# 52 1/4 THALER
Silver **Subject:** Death of Johann Georg II **Obv:** Eight-line inscription with dates **Rev:** St. George right slaying dragon **Note:** Varieties exist.

Date	Mintage	VG	F	VF	XF	Unc
1647	—	200	400	750	1,500	—

KM# 60 1/4 THALER
Silver **Obv:** St. George right slaying dragon **Rev:** Ornate four-fold arms, date and mintmaster's initials in legend **Mint:** Eisleben **Note:** Spruch 1/4 Thaler.

Date	Mintage	VG	F	VF	XF	Unc
1667 ABK	—	80.00	140	235	475	—

KM# 67 1/3 THALER (1/2 Gulden)
Silver **Obv:** St. George on horse right slaying dragon, value 1/3 below **Rev:** Shield of arms divides date above, ABK below **Mint:** Eisleben **Note:** Varieties exist.

Date	Mintage	VG	F	VF	XF	Unc
1668 ABK	—	45.00	80.00	150	300	—
1669 ABK	—	45.00	80.00	150	300	—
1670 ABK	—	45.00	80.00	150	300	—
1671 ABK	—	45.00	80.00	150	300	—
1672 ABK	—	45.00	80.00	150	300	—
1673 ABK	—	45.00	80.00	150	300	—

KM# 69 1/3 THALER (1/2 Gulden)
Silver **Rev:** Mintmaster's initials divided below arms **Mint:** Eisleben

Date	Mintage	VG	F	VF	XF	Unc
1669 ABK	—	45.00	80.00	150	300	—

KM# 12 1/2 THALER
Silver **Subject:** Death of Jobst II **Obv:** St. George left slaying dragon **Rev:** Eight-line inscription with dates **Mint:** Saalfeld

Date	Mintage	VG	F	VF	XF	Unc
1619 HI	—	85.00	140	200	385	—

KM# 13 1/2 THALER
Silver **Obv:** Crowned four-fold arms divide date and mintmaster's initials **Mint:** Saalfeld

Date	Mintage	VG	F	VF	XF	Unc
1619 HI	—	85.00	140	200	385	—

KM# 42 1/2 THALER
Silver **Obv:** St. George right slaying dragon **Rev:** Ornate four-fold arms with date between helmets, mintmaster's initials divided by arms **Mint:** Eisleben **Note:** Varieties exist.

Date	Mintage	VG	F	VF	XF	Unc
1634 HPK	—	—	—	—	—	—

KM# 53 1/2 THALER
Silver **Subject:** Death of Johann George II **Obv:** Eight-line inscription with dates **Rev:** St. George right slaying dragon **Note:** Varieties exist.

Date	Mintage	VG	F	VF	XF	Unc
1647	—	—	—	—	—	—

KM# 5 THALER
Silver **Obv:** St. George slaying the dragon **Rev:** Helmeted arms **Mint:** Eisleben **Note:** Dav. #6932.

Date	Mintage	VG	F	VF	XF	Unc
1603 GM	—	85.00	200	325	550	—
1604 GM	—	85.00	200	325	550	—
1605 GM	—	85.00	200	325	550	—
1606 GM	—	85.00	200	325	550	—
1607 GM	—	85.00	200	325	550	—
1608 GM	—	85.00	200	325	550	—
1609 GM	—	85.00	200	325	550	—
1610 GM	—	85.00	200	325	550	—
1611 GM	—	85.00	200	325	550	—

KM# 6 THALER
Silver **Rev. Legend:** COM: E: DOMI: IN: MANSFE: NOB: **Mint:** Eisleben **Note:** Dav. #6933.

Date	Mintage	VG	F	VF	XF	Unc
1608 GM	—	90.00	220	300	550	—

KM# 14 THALER
Silver **Subject:** Death of Jobst II **Obv:** St. George left with dragon **Rev:** Eight-line inscription **Mint:** Saalfeld **Note:** Dav. #6935.

Date	Mintage	VG	F	VF	XF	Unc
1619 HI	—	175	400	850	1,750	—

KM# 15 THALER
Silver **Mint:** Saalfeld **Note:** Klippe. Dav. #6935A.

Date	Mintage	VG	F	VF	XF	Unc
1619 HI Rare	—	—	—	—	—	—

KM# 34 THALER
Silver **Ruler:** Johann Georg II **Obv:** St. George right with dragon **Rev:** Helmeted arms with date and A-K between helmets **Mint:** Eisleben **Note:** Dav. #6936.

Date	Mintage	VG	F	VF	XF	Unc
16Z9 AK	—	95.00	215	475	750	—

KM# 43 THALER
Silver **Obv. Legend:** HP-K below arms **Rev. Legend:** MANSF: NO. DOM: IN. HELDRVNG: SE: ET. SC: **Mint:** Eisleben **Note:** Dav. #6937.

Date	Mintage	VG	F	VF	XF	Unc
1634 HPK	—	95.00	215	475	750	—

KM# 54 THALER
Silver **Subject:** Death of Johann George II **Note:** Dav. #6938.

Date	Mintage	VG	F	VF	XF	Unc
1647	—	300	750	1,500	3,250	—

KM# 61 THALER
Silver **Obv:** St. George and dragon right **Obv. Legend:** IOAN. GEOR. COMES. I. MANSF. NOB. DYNASTA... **Rev:** Helmeted arms, legend, date, ABK **Rev. Legend:** FORTITER. ET CONSTANTER. **Mint:** Eisleben **Note:** Dav. #6940.

Date	Mintage	VG	F	VF	XF	Unc
1667 ABK	—	100	225	485	850	—

KM# 62 THALER
Silver **Rev:** AB-K by helmets, date divided below **Mint:** Eisleben **Note:** Dav. #6941.

Date	Mintage	VG	F	VF	XF	Unc
1667 ABK	—	100	225	485	850	—

KM# 63 THALER
Silver **Rev. Legend:** NOB: DOM: IN: HELDRUNGEN. SEB. E. SR: **Mint:** Eisleben **Note:** Dav. #6942.

Date	Mintage	VG	F	VF	XF	Unc
1667 ABK	—	95.00	215	475	750	—

KM# 70 THALER
Silver **Obv. Legend:** ...GEORG... **Rev:** Date between helnets, AB-K below arms **Mint:** Eisleben **Note:** Dav. #6944.

Date	Mintage	VG	F	VF	XF	Unc
1669 ABK	—	75.00	190	375	650	—
1671 ABK	—	75.00	190	375	650	—

KM# 35 2 THALER
Silver **Subject:** Death of Jobst II **Obv:** St. George on horse to left slaying dragon below **Rev:** 8-line inscription with crossed flags dividing H-I **Mint:** Saalfeld **Note:** Dav. #6934.

Date	Mintage	VG	F	VF	XF	Unc
1619 HI Rare	—	—	—	—	—	—

KM# 64 2 THALER
Silver **Obv:** St. George right and dragon **Obv. Legend:** IOAN. GEOR. COMES. I MANSF. NOB. DYNASTA... **Rev:** Helmeted arms, legend, date, ABK **Rev. Legend:** FORTITER. ET. CONSTANTER. **Mint:** Eisleben **Note:** Dav. #6939.

Date	Mintage	VG	F	VF	XF	Unc
1667 ABK Rare	—	—	—	—	—	—

KM# 77 2 THALER
Silver **Obv. Legend:** ...GEORG... **Rev:** Date between helmets, AB-K below arms **Mint:** Eisleben **Note:** Dav. #6943.

Date	Mintage	VG	F	VF	XF	Unc
1671 ABK Rare	—	—	—	—	—	—

TRADE COINAGE

KM# 46 GOLDGULDEN
3.5000 g., 0.9860 Gold 0.1109 oz. AGW

Date	Mintage	VG	F	VF	XF	Unc
1632	—	375	675	1,350	2,850	—
1635	—	375	675	1,350	2,850	—
1636	—	375	675	1,350	2,850	—
1637	—	375	675	1,350	2,850	—

MANSFELD-FRIEDEBURG

Founded in the division of 1530/32 and became extinct in 1604. Titles passed to Bornstedt.

RULERS
Peter Ernst I, 1532-1604
Peter Ernst IV, 1580-1626
Gebhard VIII von Arnstein, 1586-1601

JOINT COINAGE
I – Peter Ernst I, Christoph II, Johann Hoyer III
II – Peter Ernst I, Johann Albrecht, Johann Hoyer III, Bruno II, Hoyer Christoph
III – Peter Ernst I, Johann Albrecht, Bruno II, Hoyer Christoph, Johann Georg IV
IV – Peter Ernst I, Bruno II, Hoyer Christoph, Gebhard VIII, Johann Georg IV
V – Peter Ernst I, Bruno II, Christoph II, Gebhard VIII, Johann Georg IV
VI - Peter Ernst I, Bruno II, Gebhard VIII and Johann Georg IV
VII - Peter Ernst I, Bruno II, Wilhelm I and Johann Georg IV

REFERENCE
T = Otto Tornau, **Münzwesen und Münzen der Grafschaft Mansfeld**, Prague, 1937.

COUNTSHIP

JOINT COINAGE
- VI

KM# 12 1/2 THALER
Silver **Obv:** Shield of arms, date above **Obv. Legend:** PETER. ERN: BRVNO: WILH: HA: GE: P: **Rev:** St. George on horse to right slaying dragon below **Mint:** Eisleben **Note:** Broad flan. Varieties exist.

Date	Mintage	VG	F	VF	XF	Unc
160Z GM	—	65.00	120	225	375	—

KM# 11 1/2 THALER
Silver **Obv:** 4-fold arms, two helmets above divided by date and mintmaster's initials **Rev:** St. George right slaying dragon **Mint:** Eisleben **Note:** Varieties exist.

Date	Mintage	VG	F	VF	XF	Unc
160Z GM	—	65.00	120	225	375	—
(1)603 GM	—	65.00	120	225	375	—
(1)604 GM	—	65.00	120	225	375	—
1604 GM	—	65.00	120	225	375	—

KM# 7 THALER
Silver **Obv:** Helmeted arms **Obv. Legend:** PETER. ERN: BRVNO: GE: HA: GE: P: **Rev:** St. George right with dragon **Mint:** Eisleben **Note:** Dav. #6945.

Date	Mintage	VG	F	VF	XF	Unc
1601 GM	—	95.00	230	325	675	—

KM# 9 THALER
Silver **Obv. Legend:** PETER. ERN: BRVNO: WILH: HA: GE: P: **Mint:** Eisleben **Note:** Dav. #6947.

Date	Mintage	VG	F	VF	XF	Unc
1601 GM	—	75.00	190	275	475	900
160Z GM	—	75.00	190	275	475	900
1603 GM	—	75.00	190	275	475	900
1604 GM	—	75.00	190	275	475	900

JOINT COINAGE
- VII

KM# 10 1/4 THALER
Silver **Obv:** 4-fold arms, two helmets above divided by date and mintmaster's initials **Rev:** St. George right slaying dragon **Note:** Varieties exist.

Date	Mintage	VG	F	VF	XF	Unc
160Z GM	—	80.00	140	250	400	—
(1)603 GM	—	80.00	140	250	400	—

KM# 13 4 THALER
Silver **Obv:** GM at top in legend, date below, shield of arms below date **Rev:** St. George on horse to right slaying dragon below **Mint:** Eisleben **Note:** Dav. #6946.

Date	Mintage	VG	F	VF	XF	Unc
160Z GM Rare	—	—	—	—	—	—

TRADE COINAGE

KM# 14 GOLDGULDEN
3.5000 g., 0.9860 Gold 0.1109 oz. AGW **Obv:** Three shields as trilobe, date divided at bottom **Rev:** St. George and dragon in inner circle **Note:** Joint Coinage VII.

Date	Mintage	VG	F	VF	XF	Unc
1603	—	350	725	1,500	3,000	—

MANSFELD-SCHRAPLAU

This branch was founded on the division of 1486. It became extinct in 1602 and its lands passed to Eigentliche-Hinterort.

RULER
Heinrich II, 1591-1602

REFERENCE
T = Otto Tornau, **Münzwesen und Münzen der Grafschaft Mansfeld**, Prague, 1937.

COUNTSHIP

REGULAR COINAGE

KM# 8 1/4 THALER
Silver **Obv:** Helmeted four-fold arms divide date **Rev:** St. George left slaying dragon **Mint:** Eisleben

Date	Mintage	VG	F	VF	XF	Unc
160Z GM	—	—	—	—	—	—

Note: Reported, not confirmed

KM# 5 1/2 THALER

Silver **Obv:** Helmeted four-fold arms divide date **Rev:** St. George left slaying dragon **Note:** Broad flan. Spruch 1/2 Thaler.

Date	Mintage	VG	F	VF	XF	Unc
1601 GM	—	60.00	130	210	425	—

KM# 9 1/2 THALER

Silver **Mint:** Eisleben **Note:** Normal flan.

Date	Mintage	VG	F	VF	XF	Unc
160Z GM	—	60.00	130	210	425	—

KM# 6 THALER

Silver **Obv:** Helmeted arms **Rev:** St. George and dragon **Mint:** Eisleben **Note:** Dav. #6972.

Date	Mintage	VG	F	VF	XF	Unc
1601 GM	—	125	325	475	900	—
1602 GM	—	125	325	475	900	—

KM# 7 2 THALER

Silver **Obv:** Helmeted arms **Rev:** St. George and dragon **Note:** Dav. #6971.

Date	Mintage	VG	F	VF	XF	Unc
1601 GM	—	1,000	2,000	3,500	6,500	—

MARK

The countship of Mark was established in the early 13th century in Westphalia, with the capital located in the town of Hamm. Through marriages during the 14th century, Mark inherited the countships of Berg and Cleve. By the late 15th century, those three countships were united with those of Jülich and Ravensberg and all five figured in the succession controversy stemming from the extinction of the ruling line in 1609. Mark, along with Cleve and Ravensberg, went to Brandenburg-Prussia in 1624. Several decades later, the electors/margraves of Brandenburg struck a special local coinage for Mark.

RULERS

Johann Wilhelm, 1592-1609
Georg Wilhelm, Markgraf von Brandenburg, 1619-1640
Friedrich Wilhelm, Markgraf von Brandenburg, 1640-1688

ARMS

Horizontal bar of checkerboard design

REFERENCES

L = Busso Peus, **Grafschaft Mark (Sammlung Ernst Lejeune)**, auction Catalog 262, Frankfurt am Main, 19 June 1961.
N = Erich Neumann, **Brandenburg-preussische Münzprägungen**, vol. 1, **1415-1701**, Cologne, 1998.
Sch = Wolfgang Schulten, **Deutsche Münzen aus der Zeit Karls V.**, Frankfurt am Main, 1974.

COUNTSHIP

REGULAR COINAGE

KM# 9 6 PFENNIG (1/104 Thaler)

Billon **Ruler:** Friedrich Wilhelm **Obv:** Crowned 4-fold arms of Mark and Cleves **Obv. Legend:** MONET MARCANA **Rev:** 4-line inscription with date **Rev. Inscription:** VI / PFEN / NING / (date) **Mint:** Lünen **Note:** Varieties exist.

Date	Mintage	VG	F	VF	XF	Unc
1660	15,000	80.00	160	325	650	—
1663	—	80.00	160	325	650	—

KM# 6 SCHILLING (1/52 Thaler)

Silver **Ruler:** Friedrich Wilhelm **Obv:** Crowned 4-fold arms of Mark and Cleves **Obv. Legend:** MONET MARCANA **Rev:** Inscription, legend, date **Rev. Legend:** MON NOV CIV LUNENSIS **Rev. Inscription:** I / SCHIL / LING / MM (Moneta Marcena), **Mint:** Lünen **Note:** Varieties exist.

Date	Mintage	VG	F	VF	XF	Unc
1659	7,600	45.00	90.00	190	385	—

KM# 7 SCHILLING (1/52 Thaler)

Silver **Ruler:** Friedrich Wilhelm **Obv:** Crowned shield of 4-fold arms **Obv. Legend:** FRID. WILH. V. G. G. MAR. **Rev:** 4-line inscription with value, date at end of legend **Rev. Legend:** MON. NOV. MARCANA. **Rev. Inscription:** I / SCHIL / LING / 52 **Mint:** Lünen **Note:** Varieties exist.

Date	Mintage	VG	F	VF	XF	Unc
1659	Inc. above	30.00	65.00	135	275	—
1660	44,000	30.00	65.00	135	275	—

KM# 8 2 SCHILLING (1/16 Thaler; 1/2 Blämuser)

Silver Weight varies: 2.32-2.54g., 25-26 mm. **Ruler:** Friedrich Wilhelm **Obv:** Bust to right, value (16) above in margin **Obv. Legend:** FRID. WILH. V. G. G. MARGG. Z. BRAN. **Rev:** Brandenburg eagle, scepter arms on breast, arms of Cleves and Mark on wings, date at end of legend **Rev. Legend:** MONETA. NOVA. MARCANA. **Mint:** Lünen **Note:** Lejeune 1359; Schrötter 2092, 2099. Varieties exist.

Date	Mintage	VG	F	VF	XF	Unc
1659	4,700	275	550	1,100	2,200	—
1660	10,000	275	50.00	1,100	2,200	—

KM# 3 20 SCHILLING

Silver **Ruler:** Georg Wilhelm **Obv:** Crowned 9-fold arms in baroque frame **Obv. Legend:** IN DEO SPES ET SALUS MEA **Rev:** Crowned imperial eagle, orb on breast **Rev. Legend:** NVMMVS ARG CO MAR VIG SOLID **Mint:** Huissen **Note:** Prev. Brandenburg-Prussia KM #5.

Date	Mintage	VG	F	VF	XF	Unc
ND(ca.1620's)	—	2,400	4,750	8,500	—	—

KM# 5 THALER

Silver **Ruler:** Friedrich Wilhelm **Obv:** 3/4 facing bust **Rev:** Eagle with three shields on breast and wings, crown above divided date **Mint:** Lünen **Note:** Dav. #6189. Prev. Brandenburg-Prussia KM #291.

Date	Mintage	VG	F	VF	XF	Unc
1657 Rare	—	—	—	—	—	—

KM# 10 THALER

Silver **Ruler:** Friedrich Wilhelm **Obv:** Bust right in circle **Rev:** Eagle with three arms on breast and wings, date divided by legend **Mint:** Lünen **Note:** Dav. #6190. Prev. Brandenburg-Prussia KM #316.

Date	Mintage	VG	F	VF	XF	Unc
1660 MM Rare	—	—	—	—	—	—

TRADE COINAGE

KM# 8A DUCAT

3.5000 g., 0.9860 Gold 0.1109 oz. AGW **Ruler:** Friedrich Wilhelm **Obv:** Facing bust of Friedrich Wilhelm in inner circle **Rev:** Capped four-fold arms **Mint:** Lünen **Note:** Prev. Brandenburg-Prussia KM #306. Fr. #2271.

Date	Mintage	VG	F	VF	XF	Unc
1659 MM Rare	—	—	—	—	—	—

KM# 11 DUCAT

3.5000 g., 0.9860 Gold 0.1109 oz. AGW **Ruler:** Friedrich Wilhelm **Obv:** Bust of Friedrich Wilhelm right in inner circle **Rev:** Capped arms divide date in inner circle **Mint:** Lünen **Note:** Prev. Brandenburg-Prussia KM #317. Fr. #2272.

Date	Mintage	VG	F	VF	XF	Unc
1660 Rare	—	—	—	—	—	—
1662 Rare	—	—	—	—	—	—

KM# 12 DUCAT

3.5000 g., 0.9860 Gold 0.1109 oz. AGW **Ruler:** Friedrich Wilhelm **Obv:** Facing bust of Friedrich Wilhelm in inner circle **Rev:** Capped arms in inner circle, date in legend **Mint:** Lünen **Note:** Prev. Brandenburg-Prussia KM #334. Fr. #2273.

Date	Mintage	VG	F	VF	XF	Unc
1664 Rare	—	—	—	—	—	—

MARSBERG

A town in Westphalia, which is located on the Diemel River west of Warburg. Its origins are obscure, but Marsberg had a mint in the 13th century. During the first half of the 17th century, Marsberg had a local coinage, some issues being struck in the name of the archbishop/elector of Cologne. The town was included in the Kingdom of Westphalia from 1807 to 1813 and passed to Prussia in 1815.

RULERS

Ernst von Bayern, 1583-1612
Ferdinand von Bayern, 1612-1650

MINT OFFICIALS' INITIALS

Initial	Date	Name
VFH	1630	Urban Felgenhauer
(a)= [mark]	1601-18	Jacob Pfahler

TOWN

REGULAR COINAGE

KM# 21 PFENNIG

0.8000 g., Copper **Obv:** I in circle **Obv. Legend:** FERDINAN ELECT **Rev:** A and upright key in center, small shield above with cross of Cologne divides date **Rev. Legend:** MARSPERG

Date	Mintage	VG	F	VF	XF	Unc
1638	—	80.00	175	350	725	—

KM# 22 PFENNIG

0.8000 g., Copper **Rev:** Date undivided in legend

Date	Mintage	VG	F	VF	XF	Unc
1638	—	80.00	175	650	725	—

KM# 23 PFENNIG

0.2400 g., Silver **Obv:** Upright key, two-towered city gate behind **Rev:** Large A, four rosettes around

Date	Mintage	VG	F	VF	XF	Unc
ND	—	—	—	—	—	—

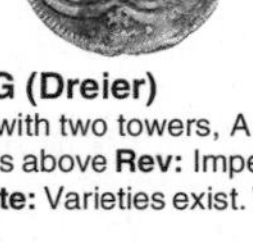

KM# 7 3 PFENNIG (Dreier)

Silver **Obv:** City gate with two towers, A and upright key in entrance, Cologne cross above **Rev:** Imperial orb with 3 divides date, all within trefoil **Note:** Varieties exist. Weight varies: 0.7-0.8 grams.

Date	Mintage	VG	F	VF	XF	Unc
1606 (a)	—	180	360	725	—	—

KM# 11 3 PFENNIG (Dreier)

Silver **Obv:** Three shields of arms, one above two, date divided by one above **Rev:** Without date **Note:** Varieties exist.

Date	Mintage	VG	F	VF	XF	Unc
1609 (a)	—	275	550	1,000	1,950	—

KM# 15 3 PFENNIG (Dreier)
Silver **Rev:** Date divided by orb

Date	Mintage	VG	F	VF	XF	Unc
1614	—	—	—	—	—	—

KM# 20 SCHILLING (1/28 Thaler)
2.5200 g., Silver **Obv:** Large A and upright key in front of two-towered city gate, date scattered about design, mintmaster's monogram **Obv. Legend:** MONETA NOV CI MONT MARTIS **Rev:** Crowned imperial eagle, Z8 in orb on breast, titles of Ferdinand II

Date	Mintage	VG	F	VF	XF	Unc
1630 VFH	—	325	650	1,350	—	—

KM# 12 1/28 THALER (Groschen)
1.4000 g., Silver **Ruler:** Ernst **Obv:** Three shields of arms, one above two **Rev:** Imperial orb with Z8, titles of Rudolf II, date divided by cross at top **Mint:** Marsberg

Date	Mintage	VG	F	VF	XF	Unc
1609 (a)	—	225	375	775	—	—

KM# 5 1/24 THALER (Groschen)
Silver, 20.2 mm. **Ruler:** Ernst **Obv:** 3 shields of arms, one above two **Rev:** Imperial orb with Z4, titles of Rudolf II, date divided by cross at top **Mint:** Marsberg **Note:** Varieties exist. Weight varies: 1.5-1.7 grams.

Date	Mintage	VG	F	VF	XF	Unc
1601 (a)	—	33.00	60.00	120	240	—
1606 (a)	—	33.00	60.00	120	240	—
1606	—	33.00	60.00	120	240	—
1607	—	33.00	60.00	120	240	—
1608 (a)	—	33.00	60.00	120	240	—
1609 (a)	—	33.00	60.00	120	240	—
1610 (a)	—	33.00	60.00	120	240	—
1611 (a)	—	33.00	60.00	120	240	—

KM# 6 1/24 THALER (Groschen)
Silver **Obv:** A and upright key in two-towered city gate, small shield above with cross of Cologne **Rev:** Date divided by upper part of orb **Note:** Varieties exist.

Date	Mintage	VG	F	VF	XF	Unc
1605	—	55.00	110	225	450	—
1606	—	55.00	110	225	450	—
1607	—	55.00	110	225	450	—

KM# 8 1/24 THALER (Groschen)
Silver **Rev:** Value in orb 24, date divided by cross at top

Date	Mintage	VG	F	VF	XF	Unc
1606	—	55.00	100	180	360	—

KM# 9 1/24 THALER (Groschen)
Silver **Ruler:** Ernst **Rev:** Date undivided in legend **Mint:** Marsberg

Date	Mintage	VG	F	VF	XF	Unc
1608 (a)	—	55.00	100	180	360	—

KM# 10 1/24 THALER (Groschen)
Silver **Ruler:** Ernst **Rev:** Value erroneously 4Z in orb **Mint:** Marsberg

Date	Mintage	VG	F	VF	XF	Unc
1608 (a)	—	55.00	100	180	360	—

KM# 16 1/24 THALER (Groschen)
Silver **Obv:** Shield with A and upright key superimposed on cross **Rev:** 4Z in orb, titles of Matthias **Note:** Varieties exist.

Date	Mintage	VG	F	VF	XF	Unc
1614	—	60.00	120	200	385	—
1615	—	60.00	120	200	385	—

KM# 17 1/24 THALER (Groschen)
Silver **Obv:** A and upright key in two-towered city gate, small shield above, date divided by cross at top **Rev:** Titles of Matthias **Note:** Varieties exist.

Date	Mintage	VG	F	VF	XF	Unc
1616	—	125	250	500	1,050	—
1617	—	125	250	500	1,050	—

MECKLENBURG

The dukes of Mecklenburg trace their origins from one Niklot, prince of the pagan Slavonic tribe of the Obotrites in the Baltic region, who was killed in battle in 1160 by Duke Heinrich the Lion of Saxony. Niklot's eldest son, Przibislaw II (1160-81), converted to Christianity in 1170 and was made Prince of Meckelnburg, the region in northern Germany lying along the Baltic between Holstein and Pomerania. Mecklenburg was divided in 1227 into the four lines of Mecklenburg, Werle, Rostock and Parchim. The two sons of Heinrich II the Lion (1287-1329), Albrecht II (1329-79) and Johann I (1329-1393), were raised to the rank of duke in 1348 and ruled jointly until 1352, when they divided their land into the Mecklenburg and Stargard branches. The dukes of Mecklenburg had their main seat of power in ruling their domains at the castle in Schwerin, but younger brothers sometimes were granted Güstrow, which they controlled independently of the main line. A completely independent line of Mecklenburg-Güstrow was established in 1610 and became extinct in 1695. The two main lines of Mecklenburg-Schwerin and Mecklenburg-Strelitz were founded in 1658.

RULERS
Karl I, 1603-1610

MINT OFFICIALS' PRIVY MARKS

Marienehe Mint

Mark	Date	Name
(j)=acorn	1601-05	Nicolaus Isebein

ARMS
Mecklenburg – crowned steer's head facing, usually with ring in nose
Schwerin – 2-fold arms divided horizontally, upper half shaded by cross-hatching
Stargard – arm with ribbon tied around, emerging from clouds at right, holding ring in hand
Werle – facing steer's head with open crown

REFERENCES
K = Michael Kunzel, ***Das Münzwesen Mecklenburgs von 1492 bis 1892***, Berlin, 1994.
E = Carl Friedrich Evers, ***Mecklenburgische Münz-Verfassung***, 2 vols., Schwerin, 1798-99.

DUCHY

STANDARD COINAGE

KM# 2 2 SCHILLING (Doppelschilling)
Silver **Ruler:** Ulrich III **Obv:** 4-fold arms with central shield of Schwerin, at left, above and right V - HZ - M, date at end of legend **Obv. Legend:** AETERNVM. NON. PECCABIS. **Rev:** Large intertwined 'DS,' small imperial orb in the 'D' **Rev. Legend:** MEMORARE. NOVISSIM(A). TVA. E. I(N). **Mint:** Marienehe **Note:** Ref. K#127-28. Known struck on thick flan with weight of 6.75 g. Varieties exist.

Date	Mintage	VG	F	VF	XF	Unc
(1)601 (n)	—	—	—	—	—	—
(1)60Z (n)	—	—	—	—	—	—

MECKLENBURG-GUSTROW

The shortest in duration of the Mecklenburg divisions was founded in 1610 by Johann Albrecht II, son of Johann VII of Mechlenburg-Schwerin. His son, Gustav Adolf was the last of the line when he died in 1695. Mecklenburg-Strelitz was the claimant thereafter.

RULERS
Ulrich III, regent, 1555-1603
Karl I, 1603-1610
Johann Albrecht II, 1611-1636
Gustav Adolph, 1636-1695

MINT OFFICIALS' PRIVY MARKS

Boizenburg Mint

Mark	Date	Name
(a)=	1608-09	Simon Ludermann
(b)=	1615-18	Joachim Konecke
(c)=crowned heart	1618	Samuel Nebeltau

Gadebusch Mint

Mark	Date	Name
(d)=acorn	1605-08	Nicolaus Isebein

Gluckstadt Mint

Mark	Date	Name
	1692-93	Christoph Woldtrecht

Groien Mint

Mark	Date	Name
	1615-18	Lorentz Leiser
(e)=crowned heart	1618	Samuel Nebeltau
(f) front half of unicorn left	1621-22	Nicolaus Netzebrandt
(g)= hand to right	1622-24	Heinrich Hantschen
(h)=	1632-35	Hans Puls

Gustrow Mint

Mark	Date	Name
	1668	Daniel Syvertz
(l)= lion left	1670-73	Hans Memmies der Altere
(ii)= lion left and/or IM	1673-83	Johann (Hans) Memmies der Jüngere

Marienehe Mint

Mark	Date	Name
(j)=acorn	1601-05	Nicolaus Isebein

Rostock Mint

Mark	Date	Name
(k)= lion left and/or IM	1686-95	Johann (Hans) Memmies der Jüngere

Schwaan Mint

Mark	Date	Name
HIH or	1692-93	Heinrich Johann Hille

Wismar Mint

Mark	Date	Name
	1666, 1668	Henning Stor

DUCHY

REGULAR COINAGE

KM# 35 PFENNIG
Copper **Obv:** Facing steer's head, titles of Johann Albrecht II **Rev. Inscription:** 1 / PFEN / NING / date **Mint:** Groien

Date	Mintage	Good	VG	F	VF	XF
16Z1	—	75.00	150	300	600	—

KM# 36 2 PFENNIG
Copper **Rev:** Similar to 3 Pfennig, KM#37 but value II on reverse. **Mint:** Groien **Note:** Varieties exist.

Date	Mintage	Good	VG	F	VF	XF
1621	—	27.00	55.00	110	220	—
16Z1	—	27.00	55.00	110	220	—

KM# 37 3 PFENNIG
Copper **Rev:** Value III **Mint:** Groien

Date	Mintage	Good	VG	F	VF	XF
16Z1	—	35.00	75.00	150	300	—
16ZZ	—	35.00	75.00	150	300	—

KM# 94 3 PFENNIG
Copper **Obv:** GA monogram in laurel wreath **Rev:** III/date **Rev. Legend:** LANDWITT **Mint:** Gustrow **Note:** Varieties exist.

Date	Mintage	Good	VG	F	VF	XF
1674	—	8.00	15.00	30.00	60.00	—
1675	—	8.00	15.00	30.00	60.00	—
1676	—	8.00	15.00	30.00	60.00	—
1677	—	8.00	15.00	30.00	60.00	—
1678	—	8.00	15.00	30.00	60.00	—
1679	—	8.00	15.00	30.00	60.00	—
ND	—	8.00	15.00	30.00	60.00	—

KM# 109 3 PFENNIG
Copper **Mint:** Rostock **Note:** Varieties exist.

Date	Mintage	Good	VG	F	VF	XF
1688	29,000	8.00	15.00	30.00	60.00	—
1690	27,000	8.00	15.00	30.00	60.00	—
1692	211,000	8.00	15.00	30.00	60.00	—
1692 (k)	149,000	8.00	15.00	30.00	60.00	—

KM# 45 SECHSLING (6 Pfennig)
Silver **Ruler:** Johann Albrecht II **Obv:** Similar to 3 Pfennig, KM#37 **Rev:** Inscription divided by mint symbol **Rev. Inscription:** I / SOSLI / MECHE / LNVB / date **Mint:** Groien

Date	Mintage	VG	F	VF	XF	Unc
16ZZ (g)	—	13.00	35.00	65.00	130	—
16Z4 (g)	—	13.00	35.00	65.00	130	—

KM# 46 SECHSLING (6 Pfennig)
Silver **Ruler:** Johann Albrecht II **Rev:** Date divided by mint symbol **Rev. Inscription:** 1 / SOSLI / NG MEC / HELN / date **Mint:** Groien

Date	Mintage	VG	F	VF	XF	Unc
16ZZ (g)	—	13.00	35.00	65.00	130	—

KM# 120 SECHSLING (6 Pfennig)
Billon **Obv:** Crowned GA monogram, legend, and date **Obv. Legend:** ANNO **Rev:** Imperial orb with 6 **Mint:** Rostock

Date	Mintage	VG	F	VF	XF	Unc
1692	124,000	11.00	22.00	55.00	110	—

KM# 38 SCHILLING
Silver **Obv:** Similar to 3 Pfennig, KM#37 **Rev. Inscription:** 1 SCHIL / LING / date **Mint:** Groien **Note:** Varieties exist.

Date	Mintage	VG	F	VF	XF	Unc
1621	—	16.00	40.00	75.00	155	—
16Z1	—	16.00	40.00	75.00	155	—

KM# 47 SCHILLING
Silver **Ruler:** Johann Albrecht II **Obv:** 5-fold arms, titles of

Johann Albrecht **Rev:** Inscription, date divided by mint symbol. **Rev. Inscription:** I / SCHIL / LING ME / CHELN / BVRG / (date). **Mint:** Groien **Note:** Varieties exist.

Date	Mintage	VG	F	VF	XF	Unc
16ZZ (g)	—	13.00	33.00	65.00	130	—
16Z3/Z (g)	—	13.00	33.00	65.00	130	—
16Z3 (g)	—	13.00	33.00	65.00	130	—
16Z4/3 (g)	—	13.00	33.00	65.00	130	—
16Z4 (g)	—	13.00	33.00	65.00	130	—

KM# 5 2 SCHILLING (Doppelschilling)

Silver **Obv:** Ornate four-fold arms with central shield, legend, mintmaster's symbol **Obv. Legend:** Z - CH - M **Rev:** Intertwined DS in shield, imperial orb above, date. below

Date	Mintage	VG	F	VF	XF	Unc
(1)603 (j)	17,000	40.00	85.00	150	300	—
(1)604 (j)	24,000	40.00	85.00	150	300	—

KM# 6 2 SCHILLING (Doppelschilling)

Silver **Rev:** Date around shield **Note:** Varieties exist.

Date	Mintage	VG	F	VF	XF	Unc
1604 (j)	Inc. above	27.00	65.00	135	275	—
1605 (j)	3,109	27.00	65.00	135	275	—
1606 (d)	8,280	27.00	65.00	135	275	—
1607 (d)	5,909	27.00	65.00	135	275	—
1608 (d)	9,348	27.00	65.00	135	275	—
1608 (a)	13,000	27.00	65.00	135	275	—
1609 (a)	58,000	27.00	65.00	135	275	—

KM# 20 2 SCHILLING (Doppelschilling)

Silver **Obv:** Similar to KM#5 but date in place of four letters in legend **Note:** Varieties exist.

Date	Mintage	VG	F	VF	XF	Unc
1614	—	24.00	45.00	80.00	160	—
1615 (b)	131,000	24.00	45.00	80.00	160	—
1615	139,000	24.00	45.00	80.00	160	—
1616 (b)	—	24.00	45.00	80.00	160	—
1616	120,000	24.00	45.00	80.00	160	—
1617 (b)	218,000	24.00	45.00	80.00	160	—
1617	273,000	24.00	45.00	80.00	160	—
1618	—	24.00	45.00	80.00	160	—
ND (b)	—	24.00	45.00	80.00	160	—

KM# 27 2 SCHILLING (Doppelschilling)

Silver **Rev:** Date in legend **Note:** Varieties exist.

Date	Mintage	VG	F	VF	XF	Unc
1617	—	24.00	45.00	80.00	150	—
1618	—	24.00	45.00	80.00	150	—
ND	—	24.00	45.00	80.00	150	—

KM# 29 2 SCHILLING (Doppelschilling)

Silver **Obv:** KM#13 **Rev:** KM#15 **Note:** Mule.

Date	Mintage	VG	F	VF	XF	Unc
1617/1618	—	—	—	—	—	—

KM# 28 2 SCHILLING (Doppelschilling)

Silver **Ruler:** Johann Albrecht II **Rev:** Date only in legend **Mint:** Boizenburg **Note:** Varieties exist.

Date	Mintage	VG	F	VF	XF	Unc
1618	—	24.00	45.00	80.00	160	—
1618 (c)	—	24.00	45.00	80.00	160	—

KM# 22 4 SCHILLING

Silver **Ruler:** Johann Albrecht II **Obv:** Crowned four-fold arms with central shield divide date, titles of Johann Albrecht II **Rev:** Crowned imperial eagle, titles of Matthias **Mint:** Boizenburg **Note:** Kipper 4 Schilling. Varieties exist.

Date	Mintage	VG	F	VF	XF	Unc
1616 (b)	26,000	35.00	65.00	135	275	—
ND (b)	—	35.00	65.00	135	275	—
ND	—	35.00	65.00	135	275	—

KM# 23 4 SCHILLING

Silver **Ruler:** Johann Albrecht II **Rev:** Imperial orb on eagle's breast **Mint:** Boizenburg **Note:** Varieties exist.

Date	Mintage	VG	F	VF	XF	Unc
1616 (b)	—	35.00	65.00	135	275	—
ND	—	35.00	65.00	135	275	—

KM# 24 4 SCHILLING

Silver **Ruler:** Johann Albrecht II **Rev:** Value 4 in imperial orb **Mint:** Boizenburg **Note:** Varieties exist.

Date	Mintage	VG	F	VF	XF	Unc
1616 (b)	—	35.00	65.00	135	275	—
ND	—	35.00	65.00	135	275	—

KM# 39 1/2 ORT (1/8 Thaler)

Silver **Ruler:** Johann Albrecht II **Obv:** Four-fold arms with central shield, three helmets above **Rev:** HALB/REICHS/ORTH/date **Mint:** Groien **Note:** Varieties exist.

Date	Mintage	VG	F	VF	XF	Unc
16Z1 (f)	—	90.00	165	325	—	—
16Z1	—	90.00	165	325	—	—

KM# 40 1/2 ORT (1/8 Thaler)

Silver **Ruler:** Johann Albrecht II **Obv:** Bust right **Mint:** Groien **Note:** Varieties exist.

Date	Mintage	VG	F	VF	XF	Unc
16Z1 (f)	—	120	200	425	—	—

KM# 50 1/2 ORT (1/8 Thaler)

Silver **Ruler:** Johann Albrecht II **Obv:** Date divided by bust **Mint:** Groien **Note:** Varieties exist.

Date	Mintage	VG	F	VF	XF	Unc
(1)6ZZ/16ZZ (f)	—	120	200	425	—	—

KM# 51 1/2 ORT (1/8 Thaler)

Silver **Ruler:** Johann Albrecht II **Obv:** Bust facing, slightly to right **Rev:** Four-fold arms with central shield, date in legend **Mint:** Groien **Note:** Varieties exist.

Date	Mintage	VG	F	VF	XF	Unc
16ZZ (g)	—	80.00	140	200	385	—

KM# 72 1/2 ORT (1/8 Thaler)

Silver **Ruler:** Johann Albrecht II **Obv:** Bust half right in inner circle **Rev:** 4-fold arms **Mint:** Groien **Note:** Similar to 1/4 Thaler, KM#52. Varieties exist.

Date	Mintage	VG	F	VF	XF	Unc
1634 (h)	—	—	—	—	—	—

KM# 100 GULDEN (1/2 Thaler)

Silver **Obv:** Crowned 7-fold arms **Rev. Inscription:** EIN / GVLDEN / MECKLEN / BVRGS / date **Mint:** Gustrow **Note:** Varieties exist. Dav. #671.

Date	Mintage	VG	F	VF	XF	Unc
1679	—	225	400	700	1,425	—
1680	—	225	400	700	1,425	—

KM# 111 24 MARIENGROSCHEN (Gulden = 2/3 Thaler)

Silver **Obv:** Bust right **Rev:** Inscription, legend, date **Rev. Legend:** MONETA NOVA ARGENTEA **Rev. Inscription:** XXIIII / MARIEN / GROSS **Mint:** Glückstadt **Note:** Dav. #676.

Date	Mintage	VG	F	VF	XF	Unc
1689	—	85.00	180	300	600	—

Note: Struck in 1692

KM# 48 1/96 THALER (Sechsling = 6 Pfennig)

Silver **Ruler:** Johann Albrecht II **Obv:** Similar to 3 Pfennig, KM#37 **Rev:** Imperial orb with 96, mint mark, date **Rev. Legend:** HERTZ MECH **Mint:** Groien

Date	Mintage	VG	F	VF	XF	Unc
16ZZ (g)	—	—	—	—	—	—

KM# 90 1/96 THALER (Sechsling = 6 Pfennig)

Billon **Ruler:** Gustav Adolph **Obv:** GA monogram in laurel wreath **Rev:** Value 96 in shield, date in legend **Mint:** Gustrow **Note:** Varieties exist.

Date	Mintage	VG	F	VF	XF	Unc
1671 (i)	—	20.00	35.00	75.00	155	—
1675 (ii)	—	20.00	35.00	75.00	155	—
1676 (ii)	—	20.00	35.00	75.00	155	—
1677 (ii)	—	20.00	35.00	75.00	155	—
1679 (ii)	—	20.00	35.00	75.00	155	—
1688 (k)	206,000	20.00	35.00	75.00	155	—
1689 (k)	96,000	20.00	35.00	75.00	155	—
1689	—	20.00	35.00	75.00	155	—
1692 (k)	—	75.00	150	300	—	—
ND	—	20.00	35.00	75.00	155	—

Note: Mintage icluded in KM#120.

KM# 49 1/48 THALER (Schilling)

Silver **Ruler:** Johann Albrecht II **Obv:** Five-fold arms, titles of Johann Albrecht **Rev:** Imperial orb with 48 divides date **Mint:** Groien

Date	Mintage	VG	F	VF	XF	Unc
16ZZ (f)	—	—	—	—	—	—

KM# 80 1/48 THALER (Schilling)

Silver **Obv:** 7-fold arms **Rev:** Inscription, date in legend **Rev. Inscription:** 48 / EINEN / REICH / DALE **Mint:** Wismar **Note:** Varieties exist.

Date	Mintage	VG	F	VF	XF	Unc
1666	14,000	—	—	—	—	—

KM# 91 1/48 THALER (Schilling)

Silver **Ruler:** Gustav Adolph **Rev. Inscription:** 48 / REICHS / DALER / date **Mint:** Gustrow **Note:** Varieties exist.

Date	Mintage	VG	F	VF	XF	Unc
1671 (i)	—	16.00	30.00	65.00	130	—
1675 (ii)	—	16.00	30.00	65.00	130	—
1676 (ii)	—	16.00	30.00	65.00	130	—
1677 (ii)	—	16.00	30.00	65.00	130	—
1679 (ii)	—	16.00	30.00	65.00	130	—
1680 (ii)	—	16.00	30.00	65.00	130	—
1694 (k)	—	16.00	30.00	65.00	130	—

KM# 112 1/48 THALER (Schilling)

Silver **Obv:** Crowned GA monogram, legend, date **Obv. Legend:** ANNO **Rev:** Value 48 in wreath **Note:** Varieties exist.

Date	Mintage	VG	F	VF	XF	Unc
1689	—	16.00	30.00	65.00	130	—
1691	—	16.00	30.00	65.00	130	—
1692	504,000	13.00	27.00	65.00	130	—

KM# 113 1/24 THALER (Doppelschilling)

Silver **Obv:** Crowned GA monogram, legend, date **Obv. Legend:** Imperial orb with 24 divides mintmaster's initials **Note:** Varieties exist.

Date	Mintage	VG	F	VF	XF	Unc
1689 IM	1,440,000	25.00	50.00	100	—	—
1692 HIH	36,000	35.00	70.00	140	—	—
1692	—	60.00	120	240	—	—

KM# 121 1/24 THALER (Doppelschilling)

Silver **Ruler:** Gustav Adolph **Obv:** Crowned 7-fold arms **Rev:** Date in legend **Rev. Inscription:** 24 / EINEN / REICHS / THAL **Mint:** Schwaan **Note:** Varieties exist.

Date	Mintage	VG	F	VF	XF	Unc
1692 HIH	Inc. above	40.00	80.00	165	325	—

KM# 122 1/24 THALER (Doppelschilling)

Silver **Rev:** Imperial orb with 24 divides mintmaster's initials, date in legend

Date	Mintage	VG	F	VF	XF	Unc
1692	—	60.00	120	240	—	—

KM# 92 1/16 THALER (Dutchen)

Silver **Ruler:** Gustav Adolph **Obv:** 7-fold arms **Rev. Inscription:** 16 / REICHS / DALER / date **Mint:** Gustrow **Note:** Varieties exist.

Date	Mintage	VG	F	VF	XF	Unc
1671 (i)	—	40.00	80.00	160	325	—
1672 (i)	—	40.00	80.00	160	325	—
1673 (i)	—	45.00	90.00	180	360	—

KM# 95 1/16 THALER (Dutchen)
Silver **Ruler:** Gustav Adolph **Obv:** Bust right **Rev:** Date in legend **Rev. Inscription:** XVI / REICHS / THALER / mintmaster's initials **Mint:** Rostock **Note:** Varieties exist.

Date	Mintage	VG	F	VF	XF	Unc
1677 (k) IM	—	45.00	90.00	190	385	—
1678 (k)	—	45.00	90.00	190	385	—

KM# 99 1/16 THALER (Dutchen)
Silver **Ruler:** Gustav Adolph **Rev. Inscription:** XVI / REICH / THAL **Mint:** Gustrow **Note:** Varieties exist.

Date	Mintage	VG	F	VF	XF	Unc
1678	—	55.00	110	225	450	—

KM# 124 1/12 THALER
Silver **Obv:** Crowned ornate GA monogram

Date	Mintage	VG	F	VF	XF	Unc
1692	—	—	—	—	—	—

KM# 125 1/12 THALER
Silver **Ruler:** Gustav Adolph **Obv:** Crowned 7-fold arms divide date **Rev. Inscription:** 12 / EINEN / REICHS / THAL / mintmaster's initials **Mint:** Schwaan

Date	Mintage	VG	F	VF	XF	Unc
1692 HIH	Inc. above	60.00	120	—	—	—

KM# 123 1/12 THALER
Silver **Ruler:** Gustav Adolph **Obv:** Crowned 7-fold arms **Rev. Inscription:** 12 / EINEN / REICHS / THAL / date **Mint:** Glückstadt **Note:** Varieties exist.

Date	Mintage	VG	F	VF	XF	Unc
1692 HIH	—	—	—	—	—	—
1692	36,000	—	—	—	—	—

KM# 114 1/6 THALER
Silver **Ruler:** Gustav Adolph **Obv:** Bust right **Rev. Legend:** MONETA... **Rev. Inscription:** VI / EINEN / REICHS / THAL / date **Mint:** Glückstadt

Date	Mintage	VG	F	VF	XF	Unc
1689	—	85.00	165	275	550	—

Note: Struck in 1692

KM# 126 1/6 THALER
Silver **Ruler:** Gustav Adolph **Rev. Legend:** NACH DEM... **Mint:** Schwaan

Date	Mintage	VG	F	VF	XF	Unc
1692 HIH	—	—	—	—	—	—

KM# 127 1/6 THALER
Silver **Ruler:** Gustav Adolph **Obv:** Crowned seven-fold arms divide mintmaster's initials **Mint:** Schwaan

Date	Mintage	VG	F	VF	XF	Unc
1692 HIH	—	—	—	—	—	—

KM# 41 1/4 THALER (Ort)
Silver **Ruler:** Johann Albrecht II **Obv:** Bust right divides date **Rev:** 4-fold arms with central shield, three helmets above **Mint:** Groien **Note:** Varieties exist.

Date	Mintage	VG	F	VF	XF	Unc
16Z1 (f)	—	200	375	600	1,200	—
16ZZ (f)	—	200	375	600	1,200	—

KM# 52 1/4 THALER (Ort)
Silver **Ruler:** Johann Albrecht II **Obv:** Bust half right in inner circle **Rev:** 4-fold arms, helmets above **Mint:** Groien **Note:** Varieties exist.

Date	Mintage	VG	F	VF	XF	Unc
16ZZ (g)	—	225	400	750	1,500	—

KM# 7 1/2 THALER
Silver **Ruler:** Ulrich III **Obv:** Half-length armored bust right holding scepter, head divides date, titles of Karl **Rev:** 5-fold arms supported by steer and griffin, three helmets above **Mint:** Gadebusch

Date	Mintage	VG	F	VF	XF	Unc
1607 (d)	—	—	—	—	—	—

KM# 10 1/2 THALER
Silver **Ruler:** Karl I **Obv:** Half-length armored bust right holding imperial orb **Rev:** 5-fold arms, three helmets above **Mint:** Boizenburg

Date	Mintage	VG	F	VF	XF	Unc
1608 (a)	—	—	—	—	—	—

KM# 15 1/2 THALER
Silver **Ruler:** Karl I **Obv:** Date in legend above duke's head **Mint:** Boizenburg

Date	Mintage	VG	F	VF	XF	Unc
1609 (a)	—	—	—	—	—	—

KM# 42 1/2 THALER
Silver **Ruler:** Johann Albrecht II **Obv:** 4-fold arms with central shield, three helmets above **Mint:** Groien **Note:** Varieties exist.

Date	Mintage	VG	F	VF	XF	Unc
16Z1 (f)	—	275	550	1,100	2,200	—
16Z1	—	275	550	1,100	2,200	—
16ZZ (f)	—	275	550	1,100	2,200	—
16ZZ (g)	—	275	550	1,100	2,200	—

KM# 53 1/2 THALER
Silver **Ruler:** Johann Albrecht II **Obv:** Bust half right in inner circle **Rev:** 4-fold arms, helmets above **Mint:** Groien **Note:** Similar to 1/4 Thaler, KM#52. Varieties exist.

Date	Mintage	VG	F	VF	XF	Unc
16ZZ (g)	—	400	725	1,400	2,600	—
16Z3 (g)	—	400	725	1,400	2,600	—
(1)634 (h)	—	400	725	1,400	2,600	—

KM# 60 1/2 THALER
Silver **Ruler:** Johann Albrecht II **Obv:** Small bust right **Rev:** 4-fold arms, helmets above **Mint:** Groien **Note:** Similar to 1/4 Thaler, KM#52.

Date	Mintage	VG	F	VF	XF	Unc
16Z4 (g)	—	—	—	—	—	—

KM# 108 2/3 THALER (Gulden)
Silver **Ruler:** Gustav Adolph **Obv:** Bust right, date below **Rev:** Crowned 7-fold arms divide mintmaster's initials, value (2/3) in oval at bottom **Mint:** Rostock

Date	Mintage	VG	F	VF	XF	Unc
1687 IM	—	—	—	—	—	—

KM# 110 2/3 THALER (Gulden)
Silver **Mint:** Rostock **Note:** Varieties exist. Dav. #672.

Date	Mintage	VG	F	VF	XF	Unc
1688	—	100	200	335	675	—

KM# 115 2/3 THALER (Gulden)
Silver **Mint:** Glückstadt **Note:** Dav. #675.

Date	Mintage	VG	F	VF	XF	Unc
1689	—	85.00	170	300	600	—

Note: Struck in 1692

KM# 8 THALER
Silver **Ruler:** Karl I **Obv:** Bust right dividing date **Obv. Legend:** CAROLUS. DEI. GRACIA. DUX. MEGAPOLENSI. **Rev:** Helmeted arms **Rev. Legend:** PRIN. VA. COM. -SU. ROS. - - TOC. E. STAR. D. **Mint:** Gadebusch **Note:** Dav. #7044.

Date	Mintage	VG	F	VF	XF	Unc
1607 (d)	—	1,200	2,500	4,500	—	—

KM# 9 THALER
Silver **Ruler:** Karl I **Obv:** Bust half facing right **Obv. Legend:** ...MEGAPOLENS **Mint:** Gadebusch **Note:** Dav. #7045.

Date	Mintage	VG	F	VF	XF	Unc
1607 (d) Rare	—	—	—	—	—	—

KM# 11 THALER
Silver **Ruler:** Karl I **Obv:** Bust half facing right with scepter dividing date **Obv. Legend:** ... MEGAPOLENSI **Rev:** Helmeted and supported arms **Mint:** Gadebusch **Note:** Dav. #7047.

Date	Mintage	VG	F	VF	XF	Unc
1608 (d)	—	2,150	4,200	7,200	—	—

KM# 12 THALER
Silver **Ruler:** Karl I **Obv:** Bust right with orb in hand **Mint:** Boizenburg **Note:** Dav. #7050.

Date	Mintage	VG	F	VF	XF	Unc
1608 (a)	—	2,150	2,700	5,400	9,000	—
1609	—	2,150	2,700	5,400	9,000	—

KM# 16 THALER
Silver **Obv:** Without orb **Note:** Dav. #7050A.

Date	Mintage	VG	F	VF	XF	Unc
1609 (a)	—	2,150	2,700	5,400	9,000	—

KM# 21 THALER
Silver **Obv:** Bust right **Obv. Legend:** IOHANNES. ALBERTVS. D: G: DVX. MEGAPOLE **Rev:** Helmeted arms, date **Rev. Legend:** NON. EST. MORTALE. QVOD. OPTO. AN: DO: **Note:** Dav. #7051.

Date	Mintage	VG	F	VF	XF	Unc
1615	—	1,450	3,000	4,800	—	—

KM# 25 THALER
Silver **Subject:** Death of Margaret Elisabeth, Wife of Johann Albrecht **Obv:** Helmeted arms **Rev:** Eight-line inscription **Note:** Dav. #7052.

Date	Mintage	VG	F	VF	XF	Unc
1616 Rare	—	—	—	—	—	—

KM# 30 THALER
Silver **Ruler:** Johann Albrecht II **Obv:** Bust right **Obv. Legend:** IOANNES. ALBERTVS. D: G: COAD. EPISC. RATZEBURG **Rev:** Helmeted arms dividing date **Rev. Legend:** DVX. MEGAPOLENSIS. NON. EST MORTALE. QUOD: OPTO. X. **Mint:** Boizenburg **Note:** Dav. #7053.

Date	Mintage	VG	F	VF	XF	Unc
1618 (b)	—	1,450	3,000	4,800	—	—

KM# 43 THALER
Silver **Ruler:** Johann Albrecht II **Obv:** Bust right dividing date **Obv. Legend:** HANS. ALBRECHT: V: G: G: HER: ZV. MECHLEN: **Rev:** Helmeted arms, unicorn **Rev. Legend:** FVRST. ZV. WEN: GRA: ZV: SWE: D: L: R: V: S: HER **Mint:** Groien **Note:** Dav. #7054.

Date	Mintage	VG	F	VF	XF	Unc
16Z1 (f)	—	1,050	2,100	4,200	—	—

KM# 44 THALER
Silver **Rev:** Without unicorn in legend **Note:** Dav. #7054A.

Date	Mintage	VG	F	VF	XF	Unc
16Z1	—	1,050	2,100	4,200	—	—

KM# 54 THALER
Silver **Ruler:** Johann Albrecht II **Obv. Legend:** ... MECHLN **Rev:** Unicorn in legend **Rev. Legend:** ... GRA ... ZV ... **Mint:** Groien **Note:** Dav. #7055.

Date	Mintage	VG	F	VF	XF	Unc
16ZZ (f)	—	550	1,150	2,200	3,600	—

KM# 55 THALER
Silver **Ruler:** Johann Albrecht II **Obv:** Thinner bust **Rev:** Unicorn in legend **Rev. Legend:** FVRST. ZVWEN: GRA...Z:... **Mint:** Groien **Note:** Dav. #7055A.

Date	Mintage	VG	F	VF	XF	Unc
16ZZ (f)	—	550	1,150	2,200	3,600	—

KM# 56 THALER
Silver **Ruler:** Johann Albrecht II **Obv:** Facing bust **Rev:** Helmeted arms, hand, date **Rev. Legend:** NON. EST. MORTALE. QVOD: OPTO: **Mint:** Groien **Note:** Dav. #7057.

Date	Mintage	VG	F	VF	XF	Unc
16ZZ (g)	—	900	1,800	3,000	4,800	—
16Z3	—	900	1,800	3,000	4,800	—

KM# 57 THALER
Silver **Ruler:** Johann Albrecht II **Obv:** Bust right, scalloped lace collar **Rev:** Helmeted arms **Mint:** Groien **Note:** Dav. #7058.

Date	Mintage	VG	F	VF	XF	Unc
16ZZ (g)	—	425	950	2,150	3,600	—
16Z3 (g)	—	425	950	2,150	3,600	—

KM# 59 THALER
Silver **Rev. Legend:** QVOD: hand OPTO: **Note:** Dav. #7058A.

Date	Mintage	VG	F	VF	XF	Unc
16Z3	—	425	950	2,150	3,600	—

KM# 61 THALER
Silver **Ruler:** Johann Albrecht II **Obv:** Full lace collar without dots, shoulder circles, dashes **Mint:** Groien **Note:** Dav. #7058B.

Date	Mintage	VG	F	VF	XF	Unc
16Z4 (g)	—	400	775	1,600	2,700	—

KM# 62 THALER
Silver **Ruler:** Johann Albrecht II **Obv:** Full lace collar with dots, shoulder circles, dots **Mint:** Groien **Note:** Dav. #7058C.

Date	Mintage	VG	F	VF	XF	Unc
16Z4 (g)	—	400	775	1,600	2,700	—

KM# 65 THALER

Silver **Obv:** Facing bust **Obv. Legend:** V. G. G. HANS. ALBRECHT. HERT. Z. MECHELN. **Rev. Legend:** MONETA. NOVA. MEGELENB. **Note:** Dav. #7059.

Date	Mintage	VG	F	VF	XF	Unc
1633	—	1,600	3,300	5,400	—	—

KM# 66 THALER

Silver **Ruler:** Johann Albrecht II **Obv. Legend:** NON EST MORTALE-QUOD OPTO **Mint:** Groien **Note:** Dav. #7060.

Date	Mintage	VG	F	VF	XF	Unc
1633 (h)	—	1,000	1,500	4,200	6,600	—
1634 (h)	—	1,000	1,500	4,200	6,600	—
1635 (h)	—	1,000	1,500	4,200	6,600	—

KM# 67 THALER

Silver **Ruler:** Johann Albrecht II **Obv:** Small bust, dots lower breast plate **Mint:** Groien **Note:** Dav. #7060A.

Date	Mintage	VG	F	VF	XF	Unc
1633 (h)	—	1,000	2,100	4,200	6,600	—

KM# 73 THALER

Silver **Ruler:** Johann Albrecht II **Obv:** Large bust, stars lower breast plate **Rev. Legend:** NON EST MORTAL:-QUAD OPTO **Mint:** Groien **Note:** Varieties exist. Dav. #7060B.

Date	Mintage	VG	F	VF	XF	Unc
1634 (h)	—	1,000	2,100	4,200	6,600	—

KM# 82 THALER

Silver **Obv:** Bust right, date below **Obv. Legend:** DEI GRATIA. GUSTAV. ADOLPHUS. DUX. MECKLENBURG **Rev:** Helmeted and supported arms **Rev. Legend:** QVID. RETRIBUAM. DOMINO **Note:** Dav. #7062.

Date	Mintage	VG	F	VF	XF	Unc
1668 Rare	—	—	—	—	—	—

KM# 96 THALER

Silver **Obv:** Without inner circle **Obv. Legend:** D. G. GVST. ADOLP: DVX. MECKLENB: **Rev:** Helmeted arms in palm sprays in inner circle **Note:** Dav. #7064.

Date	Mintage	VG	F	VF	XF	Unc
1677 Rare	—	—	—	—	—	—

KM# 97 THALER

Silver **Obv. Legend:** ...ADOLP.- DVX... **Note:** Dav. #7065.

Date	Mintage	VG	F	VF	XF	Unc
1677 Rare	—	—	—	—	—	—

Note: Fritz Rudolf Künker Münzenhandlung Auction 92, 6-04, VF realized approximately $8,225

KM# 105 THALER

Silver **Ruler:** Gustav Adolph **Obv:** Bust right dividing date, continuous legend **Rev:** Helmeted arms supported by 2 griffins **Note:** Dav. #7067.

Date	Mintage	VG	F	VF	XF	Unc
1680	—	850	1,800	3,300	5,700	—

KM# 106 THALER

Silver **Rev:** Helmeted arms supported by a buffalo and griffin **Note:** Dav. #7068.

Date	Mintage	VG	F	VF	XF	Unc
1680 Rare	—	—	—	—	—	—

KM# 116 THALER

Silver **Note:** Dav. #7069.

Date	Mintage	VG	F	VF	XF	Unc
1689 Rare	—	—	—	—	—	—

KM# 128 THALER

Silver **Ruler:** Gustav Adolph **Obv. Legend:** D. G. GUSTAVUS ADOLPHUS DUX... **Rev:** Helmeted, hatted and supported arms **Mint:** Gustrow **Note:** Dav. #7070.

Date	Mintage	VG	F	VF	XF	Unc
1692 IM Rare	—	—	—	—	—	—

KM# 129 THALER

Silver **Ruler:** Gustav Adolph **Obv:** Without IM below **Rev:** HI-H below arms **Mint:** Schwaan **Note:** Dav. #7071.

Date	Mintage	VG	F	VF	XF	Unc
1693 HIH Rare	—	—	—	—	—	—

KM# 130 THALER

Silver **Subject:** Death of Gustav Adolf **Note:** Dav. #7072.

Date	Mintage	VG	F	VF	XF	Unc
1696 Rare	—	—	—	—	—	—

KM# 13 1-1/2 THALER

Silver **Ruler:** Karl I **Obv:** Bust right with orb in hand **Mint:** Gadebusch **Note:** Similar to 1 Thaler, KM#12. Dav. #7049.

Date	Mintage	VG	F	VF	XF	Unc
1608 (d) Rare	—	—	—	—	—	—

KM# 14 2 THALER

Silver **Ruler:** Karl I **Obv:** Bust right with scepter dividing date **Rev:** Helmeted and supported arms **Mint:** Gadebusch **Note:** Dav. #7046.

Date	Mintage	VG	F	VF	XF	Unc
1608 (d) Rare	—	—	—	—	—	—

KM# 17 2 THALER

Silver **Ruler:** Karl I **Obv:** Bust right with orb in hand **Mint:** Boizenburg **Note:** Similar to 1 Thaler, KM#12. Dav. #7048.

Date	Mintage	VG	F	VF	XF	Unc
1609 (a) Rare	—	—	—	—	—	—

KM# 26 2 THALER

Silver **Ruler:** Johann Albrecht II **Subject:** Death of Margaret Elisabeth, Wife of Johann Albrecht **Obv:** Helmeted arms **Rev:** 8-line inscription **Note:** Dav. #7052A.

Date	Mintage	VG	F	VF	XF	Unc
1616 Rare	—	—	—	—	—	—

KM# 31 2 THALER

Silver **Ruler:** Johann Albrecht II **Obv:** Bust right **Obv. Legend:** IOANNES. ALBERTVS. D: G: COAD. EPISC. RATZEBURG **Rev:** Helmeted arms dividing date **Rev. Legend:** DVX. MEGAPOLENSIS. NON. EST MOTALE. QUOD: OPTO. X. **Mint:** Boizenburg **Note:** Similar to 1 Thaler, KM#30. Dav. #7053A.

Date	Mintage	VG	F	VF	XF	Unc
1618 (b) Rare	—	—	—	—	—	—

KM# 58 2 THALER

Silver **Ruler:** Johann Albrecht II **Obv:** Facing bust **Rev:** Helmeted arms, hand, date **Rev. Legend:** NON. EST. MORTALE. QVOD: OPTO: **Mint:** Groien **Note:** Similar to 1 Thaler, KM#56. Dav. #7056.

Date	Mintage	VG	F	VF	XF	Unc
16ZZ (f) Rare	—	—	—	—	—	—

KM# 83 2 THALER

Silver **Obv:** Bust of Gustav Adolf right, date below **Rev:** Helmeted and supported arms **Note:** Dav. #7061.

Date	Mintage	VG	F	VF	XF	Unc
1668 Rare	—	—	—	—	—	—

KM# 98 2 THALER

Silver **Obv:** Bust right without inner circle **Rev:** Hatted arms in palm sparys **Note:** Dav. #7063.

Date	Mintage	VG	F	VF	XF	Unc
1677 Rare	—	—	—	—	—	—

KM# 107 2 THALER

Silver **Obv:** Bust right dividing date without inner circle **Rev:** Helmeted and supported arms **Note:** Dav. #7066.

Date	Mintage	VG	F	VF	XF	Unc
1680 Rare	—	—	—	—	—	—

TRADE COINAGE

KM# 68 DUCAT

3.5000 g., 0.9860 Gold 0.1109 oz. AGW **Ruler:** Johann Albrecht II **Obv:** Standing figure of Johann Albrecht, head turned half right **Mint:** Groien

Date	Mintage	VG	F	VF	XF	Unc
1633 (h)	—	1,000	2,150	5,500	10,000	—

KM# 69 DUCAT

3.5000 g., 0.9860 Gold 0.1109 oz. AGW **Ruler:** Johann Albrecht II **Obv:** Bust half right in inner circle **Rev:** 4-fold arms, helmets above **Mint:** Groien **Note:** Similar to 1/2 Ort, KM#72.

Date	Mintage	VG	F	VF	XF	Unc
1633 (h) Rare	—	—	—	—	—	—

KM# 81 DUCAT

3.5000 g., 0.9860 Gold 0.1109 oz. AGW **Ruler:** Gustav Adolph **Obv:** Bust of Gustav Adolph right in inner circle **Rev:** Arms in inner circle, date in legend **Mint:** Wismar

Date	Mintage	VG	F	VF	XF	Unc
1666 (h)	1,000	950	2,050	4,750	7,750	—
1668	—	950	2,050	4,750	7,750	—

KM# 93 DUCAT
3.5000 g., 0.9860 Gold 0.1109 oz. AGW **Mint:** Gustrow

Date	Mintage	VG	F	VF	XF	Unc
1671	—	900	1,900	4,750	7,750	—
1672	—	900	1,900	4,750	7,750	—
1674	—	900	1,900	4,750	7,750	—
1680 IM	—	900	1,900	4,750	7,750	—
1686	—	900	1,900	4,750	7,750	—
1687	—	900	1,900	4,750	7,750	—
1688 PP	—	900	1,900	4,750	7,750	—
1689 PP	—	900	1,900	4,750	7,750	—

KM# 70 2 DUCAT
7.0000 g., 0.9860 Gold 0.2219 oz. AGW **Obv:** Johann Albrecht standing in inner circle **Rev:** Arms in inner circle

Date	Mintage	VG	F	VF	XF	Unc
1633	—	4,000	7,500	11,500	18,500	—

KM# 71 3 DUCAT
10.5000 g., 0.9860 Gold 0.3328 oz. AGW **Obv:** Johann Albrecht standing in inner circle **Rev:** Arms in inner circle

Date	Mintage	VG	F	VF	XF	Unc
1633 Rare	—	—	—	—	—	—

PATTERNS

Including off metal strikes

KM#	Date	Mintage	Identification	Mkt Val
Pn1	1689	—	1/6 Thaler. Copper. KM#114	—

MECKLENBURG-SCHWERIN

The duchy of Mecklenburg was located along the Baltic coast between Holstein and Pomerania. Schwerin was annexed to Mecklenburg in 1357. During the Thirty Years' War, the dukes of Mecklenburg sided with the Protestant forces against the emperor. Albrecht von Wallenstein, the imperialist general, ousted the Mecklenburg dukes from their territories in 1628. They were restored to their lands in 1632. In 1658 the Mecklenburg dynasty was divided into two lines. No coinage was produced for Mecklenburg-Schwerin from 1708 until 1750. The 1815 Congress of Vienna elevated the duchy to the status of grand duchy and it became a part of the German Empire in 1871 until 1918 when the last grand duke abdicated.

RULERS
Adolf Friedrich I, 1592-1628, 1632-1658
Christian Ludwig I, 1658-1692
Friedrich Wilhelm, 1692-1713

MINT MARKS
A - Berlin
B - Hannover

MINT OFFICIALS' INITIALS & PRIVY MARKS

DOMITZ MINT

Initial or Mark	Date	Name
(a)=	1669-73	Henning Kemper
WE	1675-79	Werner Eberhardt

GADEBUSCH MINT

Initial or Mark	Date	Name
(b)=	1611-19	Simon Ludemann
(c)= mermaid or CE	1621-24	Christian Emerich

RATZEBURG MINT

Initial or Mark	Date	Name
(d)= and AH	1678(Jan.–May)	Andreas Hille
(e)= and/or PBH	1678-79	Peter Brasshaver
DB monogram	1679-81	Dietrich Bauer
(f)=	1682-85	Michael Wagner
(g) none	1686-89	Gabriel Christian Rodatz

SCHWERIN MINT

Initial or Mark	Date	Name
(h)=	1651-52	Berthold Krause
	1658-63	Peter Lohe
ZDK	1695-1708	Zacharias Daniel Kelpe

WISMAR MINT

Initial or Mark	Date	Name
(l)= or ID	1625, 1632-47	Johann Dase

DUCHY

REGULAR COINAGE

KM# 40 PFENNIG
Copper **Ruler:** Adolf Friedrich I **Obv:** Facing steer head; titles of Adolph Friedrich **Rev:** Date **Rev. Inscription:** I / PFEN / NING **Mint:** Gadebusch **Note:** Varieties exist.

Date	Mintage	Good	VG	F	VF	XF
1621	—	15.00	35.00	70.00	145	—
16Z1	—	15.00	35.00	70.00	145	—
(1)622	—	15.00	35.00	70.00	145	—

KM# 41 2 PFENNIG (Zweier)
Copper **Ruler:** Adolf Friedrich I **Obv:** Facing steer head, titles of Adolph Friedrich **Rev. Inscription:** Z / PFEN / NING / date **Mint:** Gadebusch **Note:** Varieties exist.

Date	Mintage	Good	VG	F	VF	XF
1621	—	27.00	55.00	110	225	—

KM# 42 2 PFENNIG (Zweier)
Copper **Ruler:** Adolf Friedrich I **Rev. Inscription:** II / PFEN / NING / date **Note:** Varieties exist.

Date	Mintage	Good	VG	F	VF	XF
1621	—	27.00	55.00	110	225	—

KM# 43 3 PFENNIG (Dreier)
Copper **Ruler:** Adolf Friedrich I **Obv:** Facing steer head, titles of Adolph Friedrich **Mint:** Gadebusch **Note:** Varieties exist.

Date	Mintage	Good	VG	F	VF	XF
1621	—	10.00	20.00	40.00	80.00	—
1622	—	10.00	20.00	40.00	80.00	—

KM# 95 3 PFENNIG (Dreiling)
Silver **Ruler:** Christian Ludwig I **Obv:** Crowned CL monogram **Rev:** Imperial orb with 3 divides date **Mint:** Domitz **Note:** Varieties exist.

Date	Mintage	VG	F	VF	XF	Unc
1676	—	15.00	30.00	60.00	125	—
1677	—	15.00	30.00	60.00	125	—

KM# 85 SECHSLING (6 Pfennig)
Silver **Ruler:** Christian Ludwig I **Obv:** Facing steer head, titles of Christian Ludwig **Rev:** Date **Rev. Inscription:** I / SOSLING / MECHLE / NBVRG **Mint:** Schwerin **Note:** Varieties exist.

Date	Mintage	VG	F	VF	XF	Unc
1661	—	—	—	—	—	—

KM# 96 SECHSLING (6 Pfennig)
Silver **Ruler:** Christian Ludwig I **Obv:** Crowned CL monogram, **Obv. Legend:** LANDMVNZ **Rev:** Date **Rev. Inscription:** I/SECHS/LING **Mint:** Domitz

Date	Mintage	VG	F	VF	XF	Unc
1676	—	—	—	—	—	—

KM# 44 SCHILLING
Silver **Ruler:** Adolf Friedrich I **Obv:** Facing steer head, titles of Adolph Friedrich **Rev:** Value and date **Rev. Inscription:** 1 / SCHIL / LING **Mint:** Gadebusch

Date	Mintage	VG	F	VF	XF	Unc
1621 (c)	—	—	—	—	—	—

KM# 86 SCHILLING
Silver **Ruler:** Christian Ludwig I **Obv:** Crowned 7-fold arms **Rev:** Value and date **Rev. Inscription:** 1 / SCHILLI / NG MECH / LENBVRG **Mint:** Schwerin **Note:** Varieties exist.

Date	Mintage	VG	F	VF	XF	Unc
1661	—	—	—	—	—	—

KM# 97 SCHILLING
Silver **Ruler:** Christian Ludwig I **Obv:** Crowned CL monogram, date **Obv. Legend:** LANDMVNTZ **Rev:** Value and mintmasters symbol **Rev. Inscription:** I / SCHIL / LING ME / CKELN / BVRG **Mint:** Domitz **Note:** Varieties exist.

Date	Mintage	VG	F	VF	XF	Unc
1670 (a)	—	20.00	45.00	90.00	185	—
1671 (a)	—	20.00	45.00	90.00	185	—
1672 (a)	—	20.00	45.00	90.00	185	—

KM# 10 2 SCHILLING (Doppelschilling)
Silver **Ruler:** Adolf Friedrich I **Obv:** 4-fold arms with central shield, titles of Adolph Friedrich **Rev:** Large intertwined DS divides date **Mint:** Gadebusch

Date	Mintage	VG	F	VF	XF	Unc
1611 (b)	—	27.00	65.00	135	265	—

KM# 21 2 SCHILLING (Doppelschilling)
Silver **Ruler:** Adolf Friedrich I **Mint:** Gadebusch **Note:** Klippe 2 Schilling.

Date	Mintage	VG	F	VF	XF	Unc
1613 (b)	—	—	—	—	—	—

KM# 19 2 SCHILLING (Doppelschilling)
Silver **Ruler:** Adolf Friedrich I **Rev:** DS in shield **Note:** Varieties exist.

Date	Mintage	VG	F	VF	XF	Unc
1613 (b)	—	33.00	65.00	135	265	—
(16)15 (b)	—	33.00	65.00	135	265	—

KM# 20 2 SCHILLING (Doppelschilling)
Silver **Ruler:** Adolf Friedrich I **Rev:** Date in legend **Mint:** Gadebusch **Note:** Varieties exist.

Date	Mintage	VG	F	VF	XF	Unc
1613 (b)	—	27.00	55.00	115	220	—
(1)613 (b)	—	27.00	55.00	115	220	—
1614 (b)	—	27.00	55.00	115	220	—
(1)614 (b)	—	27.00	55.00	115	220	—
(16)14 (b)	—	27.00	55.00	115	220	—
(16)15 (b)	—	27.00	55.00	115	220	—

KM# 22 2 SCHILLING (Doppelschilling)
Silver **Ruler:** Adolf Friedrich I **Mint:** Gadebusch **Note:** Similar to KM#20 but part of date divided by shield, rest below shield. Varieties exist.

Date	Mintage	VG	F	VF	XF	Unc
1614 (b)	—	27.00	55.00	115	220	—
1615 (b)	—	27.00	55.00	115	220	—
(16)15 (b)	—	27.00	55.00	115	220	—
1616 (b)	—	27.00	55.00	115	220	—

KM# 33 2 SCHILLING (Doppelschilling)
Silver **Ruler:** Adolf Friedrich I **Rev:** DS not in shield **Mint:** Gadebusch **Note:** Varieties exist.

Date	Mintage	VG	F	VF	XF	Unc
(16)16 (b)	—	25.00	50.00	100	210	—
1616 (b)	—	25.00	50.00	100	210	—
(1)6(1)7 (b)	—	25.00	50.00	100	210	—
1617 (b)	—	25.00	50.00	100	210	—
ND(1618) (b)	—	25.00	50.00	100	210	—

KM# 130 2 SCHILLING (Doppelschilling)
Silver **Ruler:** Friedrich Wilhelm **Obv:** Crowned 7-fold arms **Rev:** Date, mintmaster's initials **Rev. Inscription:** II / SCHIL / LING **Mint:** Schwerin **Note:** Varieties exist.

Date	Mintage	VG	F	VF	XF	Unc
1696 ZDK	—	16.00	35.00	75.00	155	—
1699 ZDK	10,000	16.00	35.00	75.00	155	—

KM# 135 4 GUTE GROSCHEN (1/6 Thaler)
Silver **Ruler:** Friedrich Wilhelm **Obv:** Bust right **Rev:** Legend is 4 crowned ornate FW monograms in cruciform around date in circle in center, VIER GVTE GROS CEN **Mint:** Schwerin

Date	Mintage	VG	F	VF	XF	Unc
1698	—	—	—	—	—	—

KM# 136 16 GUTE GROSCHEN (2/3 Thaler)
Silver **Ruler:** Friedrich Wilhelm **Obv:** Bust right **Rev:** Date **Rev. Inscription:** XVI / GVTE / GROSCH / EN **Mint:** Schwerin

Date	Mintage	VG	F	VF	XF	Unc
1698	60	—	—	—	—	—

KM# 75 1/192 THALER (Dreiling)
Silver **Ruler:** Adolf Friedrich I **Obv:** Date in legend **Mint:** Wismar **Note:** Varieties exist.

Date	Mintage	VG	F	VF	XF	Unc
(16)43	—	25.00	55.00	110	220	—
(16)45	—	25.00	55.00	110	220	—

KM# 87 1/192 THALER (Dreiling)
Silver **Ruler:** Christian Ludwig I **Obv:** Titles of Christian Ludwig **Rev:** Imperial orb divides date **Mint:** Schwerin

Date	Mintage	VG	F	VF	XF	Unc
1661	—	—	—	—	—	—

KM# 5 1/192 THALER (Dreiling)
Silver **Ruler:** Friedrich Wilhelm **Obv:** Facing steer head, titles of Adolph Friedrich **Rev:** Imperial orb with 192 **Mint:** Gadebusch

Date	Mintage	VG	F	VF	XF	Unc
ND	—	—	—	—	—	—

KM# 47 1/96 THALER (Sechsling)
Silver **Ruler:** Adolf Friedrich I **Obv:** Facing steer head, titles of Adolph Friedrich, date in legend **Rev:** Imperial orb with 96 **Mint:** Gadebusch **Note:** Varieties exist.

Date	Mintage	VG	F	VF	XF	Unc
(1)622 CE	—	25.00	50.00	100	210	—
(16)22 CE	—	25.00	50.00	100	210	—
(16)23 CE	—	25.00	50.00	100	210	—

KM# 48 1/96 THALER (Sechsling)
Silver **Ruler:** Adolf Friedrich I **Obv:** Date divided by steer's head **Mint:** Gadebusch **Note:** Varieties exist.

Date	Mintage	VG	F	VF	XF	Unc
(1)622 CE	—	25.00	50.00	100	210	—
(16)22 CE	—	25.00	50.00	100	210	—
(16)22	—	25.00	50.00	100	210	—
(16)23 CE	—	25.00	50.00	100	210	—
(16)23	—	25.00	50.00	100	210	—

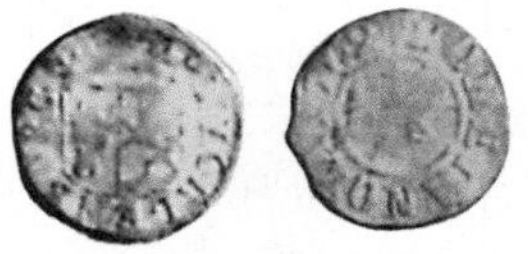

KM# 137 1/96 THALER (Sechsling)
Silver **Ruler:** Friedrich Wilhelm **Obv:** Date in legend **Rev:** Value: 96 on imperial orb **Mint:** Schwerin **Note:** Varieties exist.

Date	Mintage	VG	F	VF	XF	Unc
1698	125,000	15.00	30.00	65.00	130	—
1699	115,000	15.00	30.00	65.00	130	—

KM# 11 1/64 THALER
Silver **Ruler:** Adolf Friedrich I **Obv:** Facing steer head in shield, titles of Adolph Friedrich **Rev:** Imperial orb with 64, date in legend **Mint:** Gadebusch

Date	Mintage	VG	F	VF	XF	Unc
161Z (b)	—	—	—	—	—	—
1613 (b)	—	—	—	—	—	—

KM# 12 1/64 THALER
Silver **Ruler:** Adolf Friedrich I **Rev:** Date divided by imperial orb **Mint:** Gadebusch

Date	Mintage	VG	F	VF	XF	Unc
161Z (b)	—	—	—	—	—	—

KM# 49 1/48 THALER (Schilling)

Silver **Ruler:** Adolf Friedrich I **Obv:** Facing steer head in shield, titles of Adolph Friedrich **Rev:** Imperial orb with 48 **Mint:** Gadebusch **Note:** Varieties exist.

Date	Mintage	VG	F	VF	XF	Unc
1622 CE	—	15.00	35.00	70.00	145	—
(16)22 CE	—	15.00	35.00	70.00	145	—

KM# 115 1/48 THALER (Schilling)

Silver **Ruler:** Christian Ludwig I **Obv:** Crowned CL monogram **Rev:** Date **Rev. Inscription:** 48 / EINEN / REICHS / THALER **Mint:** Ratzeburg

Date	Mintage	VG	F	VF	XF	Unc
1678	—	—	—	—	—	—

KM# 138 1/48 THALER (Schilling)

Silver **Ruler:** Friedrich Wilhelm **Obv:** Crowned ornate FW monogram **Rev:** Crowned 2-fold arms divided vertically, date **Rev. Legend:** MONETA (48) NOVA **Mint:** Schwerin

Date	Mintage	VG	F	VF	XF	Unc
1698	—	—	—	—	—	—

KM# 60 1/24 THALER (Groschen)

Silver **Ruler:** Adolf Friedrich I **Obv:** 4-fold arms with central shield, titles of Adolph Friedrich **Rev:** Date, small imperial orb at top **Rev. Inscription:** 24 / REICHS / DALER **Mint:** Wismar **Note:** Varieties exist.

Date	Mintage	VG	F	VF	XF	Unc
1632 (i)	—	40.00	75.00	160	325	—
1633 (i)	—	40.00	75.00	160	325	—
1646 (i)	—	40.00	75.00	160	325	—
1647 (i)	—	40.00	75.00	160	325	—
1650 (i)	—	40.00	75.00	160	325	—
1651 (h)	—	40.00	75.00	160	325	—
1652 (h)	—	40.00	75.00	160	325	—

KM# 80 1/24 THALER (Doppelschilling)

Silver **Ruler:** Christian Ludwig I **Obv:** Bust right **Mint:** Schwerin **Note:** Varieites exist.

Date	Mintage	VG	F	VF	XF	Unc
1659	—	—	—	—	—	—

KM# 88 1/24 THALER (Doppelschilling)

Silver **Ruler:** Christian Ludwig I **Obv:** 7-fold arms

Date	Mintage	VG	F	VF	XF	Unc
1661	—	—	—	—	—	—

KM# 98 1/24 THALER (Doppelschilling)

Silver **Ruler:** Christian Ludwig I **Obv:** Crowned CL monogram within Order chain **Mint:** Domitz **Note:** Varieties exist.

Date	Mintage	VG	F	VF	XF	Unc
1670 (a)	—	33.00	60.00	125	250	—
1671 (a)	—	33.00	60.00	125	250	—
1672 (a)	—	33.00	60.00	125	250	—
1673 (a)	—	33.00	60.00	125	250	—

KM# 123 1/24 THALER (Doppelschilling)

Silver **Ruler:** Christian Ludwig I **Obv:** Bust right

Date	Mintage	VG	F	VF	XF	Unc
1682	—	—	—	—	—	—

Note: Reported, not confirmed

KM# 131 1/24 THALER (Doppelschilling)

Silver **Ruler:** Friedrich Wilhelm **Obv:** Crowned 7-fold arms **Rev:** Date, mintmasters initials **Rev. Inscription:** 24 / EINEN / REICHS / THALER **Mint:** Schwerin **Note:** Varieties exist.

Date	Mintage	VG	F	VF	XF	Unc
1696 ZDK	203,000	—	—	—	—	—

KM# 53 1/16 THALER (Dutchen)

Silver **Ruler:** Adolf Friedrich I **Obv:** 4-fold arms with central shield, titles of Adolph Friedrich **Rev:** Date, small imperial orb above **Rev. Inscription:** 16 / REICHS / DALER **Mint:** Wismar **Note:** Varieties exist.

Date	Mintage	VG	F	VF	XF	Unc
1632 (i)	—	45.00	80.00	180	360	—
1633 (i)	—	45.00	80.00	180	360	—
1646 (i)	—	45.00	80.00	180	360	—

KM# 110 1/16 THALER (Dutchen)

Silver **Ruler:** Christian Ludwig I **Obv:** Bust right **Rev:** Mintmasters initials, date in legend **Rev. Inscription:** XVI / REICHS / DALER **Mint:** Domitz **Note:** Varieties exist.

Date	Mintage	VG	F	VF	XF	Unc
1676 WE	—	40.00	75.00	150	300	—
1677 WE	—	40.00	75.00	150	300	—

KM# 111 1/16 THALER (Dutchen)

Silver **Ruler:** Christian Ludwig I **Rev:** Mintmasters initials **Rev. Inscription:** XVI / REICHS / THAL(E)R **Mint:** Ratzeburg **Note:** Varieties exist.

Date	Mintage	VG	F	VF	XF	Unc
1676	—	40.00	75.00	150	300	—
1678 PBH	—	40.00	75.00	150	300	—
1678 (f)	—	40.00	75.00	150	300	—

Note: 1678 with star mint mark struck ca.1682-1685

KM# 46 1/8 THALER (1/2 Reichsort)

Silver **Ruler:** Adolf Friedrich I **Rev:** Date **Rev. Inscription:** HALB / REICH / S ORTH **Mint:** Gadebusch **Note:** Klippe 1/8 Thaler.

Date	Mintage	VG	F	VF	XF	Unc
1621 (c)	—	—	—	—	—	—

KM# 45 1/8 THALER (1/2 Reichsort)

Silver **Ruler:** Adolf Friedrich I **Obv:** 1/2-length bust right, titles of Adolph Friedrich **Rev:** Date **Rev. Inscription:** HALB / REICHS / ORTH **Mint:** Gadebusch **Note:** Varieties exist.

Date	Mintage	VG	F	VF	XF	Unc
1621 (c)	—	60.00	120	200	425	—
1622 CE	—	60.00	120	200	425	—

KM# 50 1/8 THALER (1/2 Reichsort)

Silver **Ruler:** Adolf Friedrich I **Rev:** 4-fold arms with central shield, 3 helmets above, date divided above **Mint:** Gadebusch

Date	Mintage	VG	F	VF	XF	Unc
(1)622 CE	—	—	—	—	—	—

KM# 56 1/8 THALER (1/2 Reichsort)

Silver **Ruler:** Adolf Friedrich I **Note:** Similar to KM#46, but not Klippe.

Date	Mintage	VG	F	VF	XF	Unc
1625	—	—	—	—	—	—

Note: Reported, not confirmed

KM# 54 1/4 THALER (Reichsort)

Silver **Ruler:** Adolf Friedrich I **Obv:** 1/2 length bust right, titles of Adolph Friedrich **Rev:** 4-fold arms with central shield dividing date, 3 helmets above **Mint:** Gadebusch

Date	Mintage	VG	F	VF	XF	Unc
(1)623 CE	—	—	—	—	—	—

KM# 62 1/4 THALER (Reichsort)

Silver **Ruler:** Adolf Friedrich I **Subject:** Death of Anna Marie, Wife of Adolph Friedrich I **Obv:** 10-line inscription with date **Rev:** 4-line inscription

Date	Mintage	VG	F	VF	XF	Unc
1634	—	—	—	—	—	—

KM# 103 1/3 THALER (1/2 Gulden)

Silver **Ruler:** Christian Ludwig I **Obv:** Crowned CL monogram, 1/3 in oval below **Rev:** Crowned 7-fold arms, in order chain, date in legend **Mint:** Domitz

Date	Mintage	VG	F	VF	XF	Unc
1671 (a)	—	—	—	—	—	—

KM# 116 1/3 THALER (1/2 Gulden)

Silver **Ruler:** Christian Ludwig I **Obv:** Bust right, 1/3 in oval below **Rev:** Crowned 7-fold arms, supporters at sides, Order chain at bottom, date in legend **Mint:** Domitz **Note:** Varieties exist.

Date	Mintage	VG	F	VF	XF	Unc
1678 WE	—	—	—	—	—	—

KM# 31 1/2 THALER

Silver **Ruler:** Adolf Friedrich I **Obv:** 1/2 length bust right, titles of Adolph Friedrich **Rev:** 4-fold arms with central shield supported, 3 helmets above, date in upper left legend **Note:** Varieties exist.

Date	Mintage	VG	F	VF	XF	Unc
1615 (b)	—	—	—	—	—	—
1618 (b)	—	—	—	—	—	—
(1)622	—	—	—	—	—	—
(1)623 CE	—	—	—	—	—	—

KM# 63 1/2 THALER

Silver **Ruler:** Adolf Friedrich I **Subject:** Death of Anna Maria, Wife of Adolph Friedrich I **Obv:** 11-line inscription with date **Rev:** 6-line inscription

Date	Mintage	VG	F	VF	XF	Unc
1634	—	—	—	—	—	—

KM# 90 1/2 THALER

Silver **Ruler:** Christian Ludwig I **Obv:** Bust right **Rev:** Crowned and mantled 7-fold arms, Order chain around, date divided at bottom of crown **Mint:** Domitz

Date	Mintage	VG	F	VF	XF	Unc
1669	—	—	—	—	—	—

KM# 89 2/3 THALER (Gulden)

Silver **Ruler:** Christian Ludwig I **Obv:** Crowned CL monogram, 2/3 in oval below **Rev:** Crowned and mantled 7-fold arms, Order chain around, date divided at bottom of crown **Mint:** Domitz **Note:** Dav. #665. Varieties exist.

Date	Mintage	VG	F	VF	XF	Unc
1670 (a)	—	650	1,400	2,750	5,200	—
1671 (a)	—	650	1,400	2,750	5,200	—

KM# 104 2/3 THALER (Gulden)

Silver **Ruler:** Christian Ludwig I **Obv:** Without mantle, angels hold up crown **Mint:** Domitz **Note:** Dav. #666. Varieties exist.

Date	Mintage	VG	F	VF	XF	Unc
1671 (a)	—	600	1,200	2,400	4,500	—
1672 (a)	—	600	1,200	2,400	4,500	—
1673 (a)	—	600	1,200	2,400	4,500	—

KM# A106 2/3 THALER (Gulden)

Silver **Ruler:** Christian Ludwig I **Obv:** Bust of Christian right with value in oval below **Rev:** Angels support crowned arms, Order chain below **Note:** Dav. #667-669. Varieties exist.

Date	Mintage	VG	F	VF	XF	Unc
1675 WE	—	65.00	135	275	575	—
1676 WE	—	65.00	135	275	575	—
1677 WE	—	65.00	135	275	575	—
1678 (d)	—	65.00	135	275	575	—
1678 (f) Star	—	65.00	135	275	575	—
1688 (g)	—	65.00	135	275	575	—

KM# 106 2/3 THALER (Gulden)

Silver **Ruler:** Christian Ludwig I **Obv:** Armored bust **Rev:** Different crown, small order chain under shield

Date	Mintage	VG	F	VF	XF	Unc
1676 (d)	—	50.00	100	210	425	—
1678 (d) AH	—	50.00	100	210	425	—
1678 (e) PBH	—	50.00	100	210	425	—
1680 DB	—	50.00	100	210	425	—

KM# 13 THALER

Silver **Ruler:** Adolf Friedrich I **Obv:** Bust of Adolf right **Rev:** Fortuna **Mint:** Gadebusch **Note:** Dav. #7023.

Date	Mintage	VG	F	VF	XF	Unc
1612 (b)	—	450	950	2,050	4,050	—

KM# 14 THALER

Silver **Ruler:** Adolf Friedrich I **Obv:** Longer bust right **Rev:** Helmeted arms **Mint:** Gadebusch **Note:** Dav. #7025.

Date	Mintage	VG	F	VF	XF	Unc
1612 (b)	—	450	875	1,500	2,500	—

KM# 23 THALER

Silver **Ruler:** Adolf Friedrich I **Rev:** Helmeted and supported arms, divided date **Mint:** Gadebusch **Note:** Dav. #7026.

Date	Mintage	VG	F	VF	XF	Unc
1613 (b)	—	250	750	1,500	4,050	—
1614 (b)	—	250	750	1,500	4,050	—
1615 (b)	—	270	575	1,100	2,050	—
1616 (b)	—	270	575	1,100	2,050	—
1617 (b)	—	280	575	1,250	2,800	—
1618 (b)	—	280	575	1,250	2,800	—

KM# 24 THALER

Silver **Ruler:** Adolf Friedrich I **Rev:** Date not divided in legend **Mint:** Gadebusch **Note:** Dav. #7026A.

Date	Mintage	VG	F	VF	XF	Unc
1613 (b)	—	325	750	1,500	3,750	—
1614 (b)	—	325	750	1,500	3,750	—
1615 (b)	—	325	750	1,500	3,750	—
1616 (b)	—	325	750	1,500	3,750	—
1617 (b)	—	325	750	1,500	3,750	—
1618 (b)	—	280	625	1,450	3,450	—

KM# 25 THALER

Silver **Ruler:** Adolf Friedrich I **Mint:** Gadebusch **Note:** Similar to 2 Thaler, KM#27. Dav. #LS359.

Date	Mintage	VG	F	VF	XF	Unc
1613 (b) Rare	—	—	—	—	—	—

KM# 51 THALER

Silver **Ruler:** Adolf Friedrich I **Obv:** Bust right **Obv. Legend:** ADOLPH.FRIDR.V G.G. HERTZ. Z. MECKLENBVR **Rev:** Helmeted arms, date **Rev. Legend:** F. Z. -W. -G. Z. S. D. L. R. V.S. HER **Mint:** Gadebusch **Note:** Dav. #7027.

Date	Mintage	VG	F	VF	XF	Unc
1622 CE	—	280	625	1,450	3,450	—

KM# 52 THALER

Silver **Ruler:** Adolf Friedrich I **Obv:** Bust right **Obv. Legend:** ...HERT. Z. **Rev:** Date dividied **Rev. Legend:** ...G. Z. S. D. L. R. -V. S. HER. H **Mint:** Gadebusch **Note:** Dav. #7028.

Date	Mintage	VG	F	VF	XF	Unc
1622 CE Rare	—	—	—	—	—	—

KM# 55 THALER

Silver **Ruler:** Adolf Friedrich I **Obv:** Different bust right **Rev:** Helmeted and supported arms **Mint:** Gadebusch **Note:** Dav. #7029.

Date	Mintage	VG	F	VF	XF	Unc
1623 CE	—	280	625	1,450	3,450	—
16Z3 CE	—	280	625	1,450	3,450	—

KM# 61 THALER

Silver **Ruler:** Adolf Friedrich I **Obv:** Facing bust **Rev:** Helmeted arms **Mint:** Wismar **Note:** Dav. #7030.

Date	Mintage	VG	F	VF	XF	Unc
1633 (i)	—	625	1,200	2,250	3,800	—
1634 (i)	—	650	1,300	2,450	4,050	—

KM# 64 THALER

Silver **Ruler:** Adolf Friedrich I **Subject:** Death of Anna Maria, Wife of Adolf Friedrich **Obv:** 12-line inscription **Rev:** Sun **Rev. Inscription:** VIVIT.POST / FUNERA / VIRTUS **Note:** Dav. #7031.

Date	Mintage	VG	F	VF	XF	Unc
1634 Rare	—	—	—	—	—	—

Note: Fritz Rudolf Künker Münzenhandlung Auction 92, 6-04, XF realized approximately $10,880

KM# 66 THALER

Silver **Ruler:** Adolf Friedrich I **Obv:** Facing bust **Rev:** Helmeted arms **Mint:** Wismar **Note:** Dav. #7033.

Date	Mintage	VG	F	VF	XF	Unc
1637 (i)	—	375	825	1,550	2,800	—
1639 (i)	—	375	825	1,550	2,800	—
1642 (i)	—	375	825	1,550	2,800	—
1647 (i)	—	375	825	1,550	2,800	—

KM# 91 THALER

Silver **Ruler:** Christian Ludwig I **Obv:** Head of Christian Ludwig right **Rev:** Similar to KM#99 **Mint:** Domitz **Note:** Dav. #7034.

Date	Mintage	VG	F	VF	XF	Unc
1669 (a)	—	750	1,450	2,500	4,050	—
1670 (a)	—	750	1,450	2,500	4,050	—

KM# 99 THALER

Silver **Ruler:** Christian Ludwig I **Obv:** Bust right **Note:** Dav. #7036.

Date	Mintage	VG	F	VF	XF	Unc
1670	—	1,900	3,750	6,300	9,400	—

KM# 100 THALER

Silver **Ruler:** Christian Ludwig I **Obv:** Smaller bust right **Obv. Legend:** CHRISTIAN: LVDOVI:D: G: DVX MEGAPOLITAN **Note:** Dav. #7037.

Date	Mintage	VG	F	VF	XF	Unc
1670	—	1,900	3,750	8,100	14,000	—

KM# 105 THALER

Silver **Ruler:** Christian Ludwig I **Rev:** Crowned arms **Rev. Legend:** NON EST MORT-ALE... **Note:** Dav. #7038.

Date	Mintage	VG	F	VF	XF	Unc
1671	—	950	1,900	3,750	8,100	—

KM# 107 THALER

Silver **Ruler:** Christian Ludwig I **Subject:** Death of Duke Johann Georg of Mirow **Note:** Dav. #LS363.

Date	Mintage	VG	F	VF	XF	Unc
1675	—	1,500	3,150	5,600	9,400	—

KM# 112 THALER

Silver **Ruler:** Christian Ludwig I **Obv. Legend:** ...LUDOV: D: G: DUX... **Rev. Legend:** NON EST MOR-TALE.. **Mint:** Domitz **Note:** Dav. #7041.

Date	Mintage	VG	F	VF	XF	Unc
1677 WE Rare	—	—	—	—	—	—

KM# 120 THALER

Silver **Ruler:** Christian Ludwig I **Obv:** Different bust right **Obv. Legend:** CHRIST. LVD. D. G... **Rev:** Crowned arms in Order band, date below **Note:** Dav. #7043.

Date	Mintage	VG	F	VF	XF	Unc
1681 Rare	—	—	—	—	—	—

KM# 15 1-1/2 THALER

Silver **Ruler:** Adolf Friedrich I **Obv:** Bust of Adolf Friedrich right **Rev:** Fortuna with sail, tree and cavalry riding right in background **Mint:** Gadebusch **Note:** Similar to 3 Thaler, KM#18. Dav. #LS353.

Date	Mintage	VG	F	VF	XF	Unc
1612 (b) Rare	—	—	—	—	—	—

KM# 26 1-1/2 THALER

Silver **Ruler:** Adolf Friedrich I **Obv:** Half-length figure of Adolf Friedrich right **Rev:** Fortuna with sail, tree at right, cavalry riding left **Mint:** Gadebusch **Note:** Similar to 2 Thaler, KM#27. Dav. #LS358.

Date	Mintage	VG	F	VF	XF	Unc
1613 (b) Rare	—	—	—	—	—	—

KM# 108 1-1/2 THALER

Silver **Ruler:** Christian Ludwig I **Subject:** Death of Duke Johann Georg of Mirow **Obv:** Bust half right **Rev:** Multi-line inscription **Note:** Similar to 1 Thaler, KM#107. Dav. #LS362.

Date	Mintage	VG	F	VF	XF	Unc
1675 Rare	—	—	—	—	—	—

Note: Rauch New York Auction 1-09, VF realized approximately $19,245.

KM# 113 1-1/2 THALER

Silver **Ruler:** Christian Ludwig I **Obv:** Facing bust of Adolf Friedrich **Rev:** Helmeted arms **Mint:** Domitz **Note:** Similar to 2 Thaler, KM#114. Dav. #7040.

Date	Mintage	VG	F	VF	XF	Unc
1677 WE Rare	—	—	—	—	—	—

KM# 16 2 THALER

Silver **Ruler:** Adolf Friedrich I **Obv:** Bust right **Rev:** Fortuna standing with sail, tree and cavalry riding right in background **Note:** Dav. #7022.

Date	Mintage	VG	F	VF	XF	Unc
1612 (b) Rare	—	—	—	—	—	—

Note: Fritz Rudolf Künker Münzenhandlung Auction 96, 9-04, VF-XF realized approximately $9,225

KM# 17 2 THALER

Silver **Ruler:** Adolf Friedrich I **Rev:** Helmeted arms, date divided at left in legend **Mint:** Gadebusch **Note:** Dav. #7024.

Date	Mintage	VG	F	VF	XF	Unc
1612 (b)	—	3,900	6,400	11,500	—	—

KM# 27 2 THALER

Silver **Ruler:** Adolf Friedrich I **Obv:** Bust right in inner circle **Rev:** Fortuna with sail, tree at right, cavalry riding left **Mint:** Gadebusch **Note:** Dav. #LS357.

Date	Mintage	VG	F	VF	XF	Unc
1613 (b)	—	2,300	3,900	6,500	10,500	—

KM# 34 2 THALER

Silver **Ruler:** Adolf Friedrich I **Subject:** Death of Margaret Elizabeth, Wife of Johann Albrecht **Obv:** Helmeted arms **Rev:** 10-line inscription **Note:** Dav. #LS360.

Date	Mintage	VG	F	VF	XF	Unc
1616 Rare	—	—	—	—	—	—

KM# 67 2 THALER

Silver **Ruler:** Adolf Friedrich I **Obv:** Facing bust **Rev:** Helmeted arms **Mint:** Wismar **Note:** Similar to 1 Thaler, KM#66. Dav. #7032.

Date	Mintage	VG	F	VF	XF	Unc
1639 (i) Rare	—	—	—	—	—	—

KM# 101 2 THALER

Silver **Ruler:** Christian Ludwig I **Obv:** Bust right **Rev:** Crowned arms **Note:** Similar to 1 Thaler, KM#99.

Date	Mintage	VG	F	VF	XF	Unc
1670 Rare	—	—	—	—	—	—

KM# 109 2 THALER

Silver **Ruler:** Christian Ludwig I **Subject:** Death of Duke Johann Georg of Nirow **Obv:** Bust facing **Rev:** Multi-line inscription **Note:** Similar to 1 Thaler, KM#107. Dav. #LS361.

Date	Mintage	VG	F	VF	XF	Unc
1675 Rare	—	—	—	—	—	—

KM# 114 2 THALER

Silver **Ruler:** Christian Ludwig I **Obv:** Bust of Christian Ludwig right in inner circle **Rev:** Crowned and mantled arms in bands, date and initials above **Mint:** Domitz **Note:** Dav. #7040.

Date	Mintage	F	VF	XF	Unc	BU
1677 WE Rare	—	—	—	—	—	—

KM# 121 2 THALER

Silver **Ruler:** Christian Ludwig I **Obv:** Different bust right without inner circle **Rev:** Crowned arms in order band, date below **Note:** Dav. #7042.

Date	Mintage	F	VF	XF	Unc	BU
1681 Rare	—	—	—	—	—	—

KM# 18 3 THALER
Silver **Ruler:** Adolf Friedrich I **Obv:** Bust of Adolf Friedrich right **Rev:** Fortuna with sail, tree and cavalry riding right in background **Mint:** Gadebusch **Note:** Dav. #LS351.

Date	Mintage	VG	F	VF	XF	Unc
1612 (b) Rare	—	—	—	—	—	—

KM# 28 3 THALER
Silver **Ruler:** Adolf Friedrich I **Obv:** Bust of Adolf Friedrich right **Rev:** Fortuna with sail, tree at right, cavalry riding left in background **Mint:** Gadebusch **Note:** Similar to 2 Thaler, KM#27. Dav. #LS356.

Date	Mintage	VG	F	VF	XF	Unc
1613 (b) Rare	—	—	—	—	—	—

KM# 29 4 THALER
Silver **Ruler:** Adolf Friedrich I **Obv:** Bust of Adolf Friedrich right **Rev:** Fortuna with sail, tree at right, cavalry riding left in background at left **Mint:** Gadebusch **Note:** Similar to 2 Thaler, KM#27. Dav. #LS355.

Date	Mintage	VG	F	VF	XF	Unc
1613 (b) Rare	—	—	—	—	—	—

KM# 30 5 THALER
Silver **Ruler:** Adolf Friedrich I **Obv:** Bust of Adolf Friedrich right **Rev:** Fortuna with sail, tree at right, cavalry riding left in background at left **Note:** Similar to 2 Thaler, KM#27. Dav. #LS354.

Date	Mintage	VG	F	VF	XF	Unc
1613 Rare	—	—	—	—	—	—

TRADE COINAGE

KM# 32 GOLDGULDEN
3.5000 g., 0.9860 Gold 0.1109 oz. AGW **Ruler:** Adolf Friedrich I **Obv:** Bust of Adolf Friedrich right in inner circle **Rev:** Helmeted arms in inner circle **Mint:** Gadebusch

Date	Mintage	VG	F	VF	XF	Unc
1615 (b)	—	1,500	2,950	6,200	9,900	—
1616 (b)	—	1,500	2,950	6,200	9,900	—
ND (b)	—	—	—	—	—	—

KM# 57 GOLDGULDEN
3.5000 g., 0.9860 Gold 0.1109 oz. AGW **Ruler:** Adolf Friedrich I **Obv:** Different bust of Adolf Friedrich right in inner circle **Mint:** Wismar

Date	Mintage	VG	F	VF	XF	Unc
1625 ID	—	975	1,950	3,900	6,500	—

KM# 65 GOLDGULDEN
3.5000 g., 0.9860 Gold 0.1109 oz. AGW **Ruler:** Adolf Friedrich I **Obv:** Facing bust, slightly right **Rev:** 4-fold arms with central shield, date in legend **Mint:** Wismar

Date	Mintage	VG	F	VF	XF	Unc
1634 (i)	—	1,150	2,500	4,950	8,300	—

KM# A19 3 GOLDGULDEN
10.5000 g., 0.9860 Gold 0.3328 oz. AGW **Ruler:** Adolf Friedrich I **Obv:** Bust of Adolf right **Rev:** Fortuna **Mint:** Gadebusch **Note:** Struck with 1 Thaler dies, KM#13.

Date	Mintage	VG	F	VF	XF	Unc
1612 (b) Rare	—	—	—	—	—	—

KM# A68 4 GOLDGULDEN
14.0000 g., 0.9860 Gold 0.4438 oz. AGW **Ruler:** Adolf Friedrich I **Obv:** Bust of Adolf right **Rev:** Helmeted arms **Mint:** Wismar **Note:** Struck with 1 Thaler dies, KM#66

Date	Mintage	VG	F	VF	XF	Unc
1637 (i) Rare	—	—	—	—	—	—

KM# B19 5 GOLDGULDEN
17.5000 g., 0.9860 Gold 0.5547 oz. AGW **Ruler:** Adolf Friedrich I **Obv:** Bust right **Rev:** Fortuna **Mint:** Gadebusch **Note:** Struck with 1 Thaler dies, KM#13.

Date	Mintage	VG	F	VF	XF	Unc
1612 (b) Rare	—	—	—	—	—	—

KM# C19 6 GOLDGULDEN
21.0000 g., 0.9860 Gold 0.6657 oz. AGW **Ruler:** Adolf Friedrich I **Obv:** Bust right **Rev:** Fortuna **Mint:** Gadebusch **Note:** Struck with 1 Thaler dies, KM#13.

Date	Mintage	VG	F	VF	XF	Unc
1612 (b) Rare	—	—	—	—	—	—

KM# A40 6 GOLDGULDEN
21.0000 g., 0.9860 Gold 0.6657 oz. AGW **Ruler:** Adolf Friedrich I **Obv:** Bust of Adolf right **Rev:** Helmeted arms **Mint:** Wismar **Note:** Struck with 1 Thaler dies, KM#66.

Date	Mintage	VG	F	VF	XF	Unc
1639 (i) Rare	—	—	—	—	—	—
1642 (i) Rare	—	—	—	—	—	—

KM# B68 8 GOLDGULDEN
28.0000 g., 0.9860 Gold 0.8876 oz. AGW **Ruler:** Adolf Friedrich I **Obv:** Bust of Adolf right **Rev:** Helmeted arms **Mint:** Wismar **Note:** Struck with 1 Thaler dies, KM#66.

Date	Mintage	VG	F	VF	XF	Unc
1637 (i) Rare	—	—	—	—	—	—

KM# D19 10 GOLDGULDEN
35.0000 g., 0.9860 Gold 1.1095 oz. AGW **Ruler:** Adolf Friedrich I **Obv:** Bust of Adolf right **Rev:** Fortuna **Mint:** Gadebusch **Note:** Struck with 1 Thaler dies, KM#13.

Date	Mintage	VG	F	VF	XF	Unc
1612 (b) Rare	—	—	—	—	—	—

KM# 68 DUCAT
3.5000 g., 0.9860 Gold 0.1109 oz. AGW **Ruler:** Adolf Friedrich I **Obv:** Bust of Adolf Friedrich in inner circle **Rev:** Arms topped with 3 helmets in inner circle, date in legend **Mint:** Wismar

Date	Mintage	VG	F	VF	XF	Unc
1639 (i)	—	800	1,750	3,550	6,700	—

KM# 102 DUCAT
3.5000 g., 0.9860 Gold 0.1109 oz. AGW **Ruler:** Christian Ludwig I **Obv:** Bust of Christian Ludwig right in inner circle **Rev:** Arms in inner circle

Date	Mintage	VG	F	VF	XF	Unc
1670	—	1,100	2,200	5,400	10,500	—
1671	—	1,100	2,200	5,400	10,500	—
1681	—	1,100	2,200	5,400	10,500	—

KM# 132 DUCAT
3.5000 g., 0.9860 Gold 0.1109 oz. AGW **Ruler:** Friedrich Wilhelm **Obv:** Crowned FW monogram

Date	Mintage	VG	F	VF	XF	Unc
1696	850	1,450	3,050	7,100	11,500	—

KM# 134 DUCAT
3.5000 g., 0.9860 Gold 0.1109 oz. AGW **Ruler:** Friedrich Wilhelm **Rev:** Crowned FW monogram

Date	Mintage	VG	F	VF	XF	Unc
1696	Inc. above	1,450	3,050	7,100	11,500	—

KM# 133 DUCAT
3.5000 g., 0.9860 Gold 0.1109 oz. AGW **Ruler:** Friedrich Wilhelm **Obv:** Bust of Friedrich Wilhelm right **Rev. Legend:** NON EST MORTALE...

Date	Mintage	VG	F	VF	XF	Unc
1696	Inc. above	1,450	3,050	7,100	11,500	—

KM# 69 2 DUCAT
7.0000 g., 0.9860 Gold 0.2219 oz. AGW **Ruler:** Adolf Friedrich I **Obv:** Bust of Adolf Friedrich in inner circle **Rev:** Arms topped with 3 helmets in inner circle, date in legend **Mint:** Wismar **Note:** Klippe. Similar to 1 Ducat, KM#68.

Date	Mintage	VG	F	VF	XF	Unc
1639 (i) Rare	—	—	—	—	—	—

KM# 122 2 DUCAT
7.0000 g., 0.9860 Gold 0.2219 oz. AGW **Ruler:** Christian Ludwig I **Obv:** Christian Ludwig

Date	Mintage	VG	F	VF	XF	Unc
1681 Rare	—	—	—	—	—	—

KM# A45 10 DUCAT
35.0000 g., 0.9860 Gold 1.1095 oz. AGW **Ruler:** Adolf Friedrich I **Obv:** Bust of Adolf Friedrich right in inner circle **Rev:** Helmeted arms **Mint:** Wismar **Note:** Struck with 1 Thaler dies, KM#66.

Date	Mintage	VG	F	VF	XF	Unc
1647 (i) Rare	—	—	—	—	—	—

Note: Struck with 1 Thaler dies, KM#66

PIEFORTS

KM#	Date	Mintage	Identification	Mkt Val
P1	1678 (e) PBH	—	2/3 Thaler. Silver. 36.5000 g. Dav.#668, KM#106.	—
P2	1680 DB	—	2/3 Thaler. Silver. Dav.#668, KM#106.	—

MECKLENBURG-STRELITZ

The duchy of Mecklenburg was located along the Baltic Coast between Holstein and Pomerania. The Strelitz line was founded in 1658 when the Mecklenburg line was divided into two lines. The 1815 Congress of Vienna elevated the duchy to the status of grand duchy. It became a part of the German Empire in 1871 until 1918 when the last grand duke died.

RULER
Adolf Friedrich II, 1658-1708

DUCHY

REGULAR COINAGE

KM# 4 THALER
Silver **Ruler:** Adolph Friedrich II **Obv:** Bust to right dividing date **Rev:** Helmeted, crowned and supported arms **Mint:** Strelitz **Note:** Dav. #7073.

Date	Mintage	VG	F	VF	XF	Unc
1694 Rare	—	—	—	—	—	—

MEMMINGEN

This former free imperial city is located in southern Bavaria, about 35 miles southwest of Augsburg. It is the site of an early church foundation of the mid-8th century, but the town itself is mentioned only from the first part of the 11th century. In 1286, free city status and mint rights were granted.

The town struck bracteates into the 14th century. A local town coinage was also issued in the 17th and early 18th centuries. The city was annexed to Bavaria in 1802.

MINTMASTERS
Johannes Vogel, 1622-1623 and 1635-1636

ARMS
Normally 2-fold, divided vertically, half of imperial eagle on left, cross on right.

FREE CITY

REGULAR COINAGE

KM# 10 2 KREUZER (1/2 Batzen)
Silver **Obv:** City arms, legend and date **Obv. Legend:** MEMINGEN **Rev:** 2 in baroque frame **Rev. Legend:** STATT MU(V)NZ **Note:** Varieties exist.

Date	Mintage	Good	VG	F	VF	XF
1635	—	—	75.00	150	300	625
1636	—	—	75.00	150	300	625

KM# 6 3 KREUZER (Groschen)
Silver **Obv:** City arms in oval baroque frame divide date **Rev:** Inscription in oval baroque frame **Rev. Inscription:** ST: /MEM: /.3. **Note:** Varieties exist.

Date	Mintage	Good	VG	F	VF	XF
1623	—	—	85.00	175	350	725

KM# 5 12 KREUZER (Dreibatzner)
Silver **Obv:** City arms in oval baroque frame divide date, XII above **Rev:** Inscription in oval baroque frame **Rev. Inscription:** STAT / MEMIN / GEN **Note:** Varieties exist.

Date	Mintage	Good	VG	F	VF	XF
16ZZ	—	—	65.00	135	275	550
1622	—	—	65.00	135	275	550
1623	—	—	65.00	135	275	550

MEDALLIC COINAGE

KM# M1 THALER
Silver **Note:** Regiments Thaller.

Date	Mintage	Good	VG	F	VF	XF
1623	—	—	75.00	150	300	525

KM# M2 10 DUCAT
35.0000 g., 0.9860 Gold 1.1095 oz. AGW **Note:** Regiments 10 Ducat; Struck with 1 Thaler dies, KM#M1.

Date	Mintage	Good	VG	F	VF	XF
1623 Rare	—	—	—	—	—	—

Note: Bowers and Merena Guia Sale, 3-88 AU realized $29,700

METZ

The capital of Lorraine (Lothringen), Metz is located 36 miles (60 km) west of Saarbrücken and 80 mi. (132 km) west-northwest of Strasburg in present-day France. It has existed as a place prior to the Roman conquest of Gaul and was named by the Romans Divodurum. It was the site of a bishopric at least from the 4th century which grew in importance in the High Middle Ages. Metz functioned as the location of an imperial mint from the 9th through early 12th centuries and the first coins of the bishops were struck in the mid-10th century. The city was attacked and occupied Metz during 1552 and 1553, at which time the coinage of the bishops began to assume the French model upon forfeiting their rights to the conquerors. The Peace of Westphalia ending the Thirty Years' War in 1648 gave formal recognition to the seizure of the city and the last local coinage was issued around 1660.

RULERS

Heinrich II, Herzog von Lothringen, 1484-1505
Johann IV, Herzog von Lothringen, 1505-1550
Under Guardianship of the Cathedral Chapter, 1505-1519
Nikolaus, Herzog von Lothringen-Mercoeur, administrator 1529-1548
Karl I, Herzog von Lothringen-Guise, 1550-51, Administrator 1551-1574
Robert von Lenoncourt, 1551-1553, cardinal 1538
Franz von Beauquerre de Peguillon, 1555-1568 (d.1591)
Ludwig II, Herzog von Lothringen-Guise, 1568-1578
Karl II, Herzog von Lothringen-Guise, 1578-1607
Annas von Peruffe d'Escars von Givry, 1608-1612
Heinrich III, Marquis von Verneuil, 1612-1652 (d.1682)
Under Guardianship of the Cathedral Chapter, 1612-1621

ARMS

Cross

REFERENCES

Sch = Wolfgang Schulten, ***Deutsche Münzen aus der Zeit Karls V***, Frankfurt am Main, 1974.

S = Hugo Frhr. Von Saurma-Jeltsch, ***Die Saurmasche Münzsammlung deutscher, schweizerischer und polnischer Gepräge von etwa dem Beginn der Groschenzeit bis zur Kipperperiode,*** Berlin, 1892.

BISHOPRIC

REGULAR COINAGE

KM# 7 DENIER
Silver **Ruler:** Heinrich III **Obv:** Crown on cross, mitre **Obv. Legend:** VIC. HENRI. D. G. EPVS. METENSIS. **Rev:** Crowned H **Rev. Legend:** MONETA. NOVA. VICENSIS.

Date	Mintage	VG	F	VF	XF	Unc
ND(1612-52)	—	65.00	135	275	550	—

KM# 10 2 DENIER
Silver **Ruler:** Heinrich III **Obv:** Crown on cross, mitre **Rev:** Crowned "Alerion"

Date	Mintage	VG	F	VF	XF	Unc
ND(1612-52)	—	65.00	135	275	575	—

MB# 2 1/4 ECU
8.5000 g., Silver, 30 mm. **Ruler:** Karl II **Obv:** Bust to left in circle, date below shoulder, where present **Obv. Legend:** CAROL. D. G. CARD. LOTH. EP. ARGENT. ET. MET **Rev:** Spanish shield of 4-fold complex arms, with central shield of Lothringen, cardinals hat and cross above **Rev. Legend:** ALSAS. LANGRA. **Note:** Prev. KM#4.

Date	Mintage	VG	F	VF	XF	Unc
1601	—	100	225	350	625	—

CITY

The pre-Roman settlement of Metz was the seat of a bishopric from the 4th century (see) and became a free imperial city in the 13th century. The city was accorded the right to mint its own coins in 1383, which production came to an end after the conclusion of the Peace of Westphalia, the treaty ending the Thirty Years' War in 1648-50. The city and surrounding territory then formally passed to France. The last city coinage was struck in 1650.

CITY ARMS

Shield divided vertically into two sections, right half usually shaded

REFERENCES

Sch = Wolfgang Schulten, ***Deutsche Münzen aus der Zeit Karls V.***, Frankfurt am Main, 1976.

S = Hugo Frhr. Von Saurma-Jeltsch, ***Die Saurmasche Münzsammlung deutscher, schweizerischer und polnischer Gepräge von etwa dem Beginn der Groschenzeit bis zur Kipperperiode,*** Berlin, 1892.

REGULAR COINAGE

KM# 41 1/2 GROSCHEN
Silver **Obv:** Small cross in circle, star in each angle, 2 marginal legends **Obv. Legend:** Outer: SIT. NOM. DNINRI. IHV. XPI. BNDICT. Inner: SEMIGROSS. METEN. **Rev:** St. Stephen kneeling between 2 small shields of arms, date in exergue **Rev. Legend:** S. STEPHA - PROTO. ME. **Note:** Boudeau 1661.

Date	Mintage	VG	F	VF	XF	Unc
1652	—	—	—	—	—	—

KM# 4 6 GROSCHEN (1/2 Franc)
Silver **Obv:** Oval city arms in baroque frame, value "VI.G." in exergue **Obv. Legend:** MONETA. CIVITA. METENSIS. **Rev:** Bust of St. Stephen left, date in exergue **Rev. Legend:** S • STEPHAN • PROTHOM **Note:** Prev. KM#1. Varieties exist.

Date	Mintage	VG	F	VF	XF	Unc
1611	—	40.00	80.00	140	275	—
1612	—	40.00	80.00	140	275	—
1613	—	40.00	80.00	140	275	—
1614	—	40.00	80.00	140	275	—
1616	—	40.00	80.00	140	275	—
1617	—	40.00	80.00	140	275	—
16Z3	—	40.00	80.00	140	275	—
1641	—	40.00	80.00	140	275	450

KM# 6 12 GROSCHEN (Franc)
Silver **Obv:** Oval city arms in baroque frame, value "XII.G." in exergue **Obv. Legend:** MONETA. NOVA. METENSIS **Rev:** Bust of St. Stephen left, date in exergue **Note:** Prev. KM#2. Varieties exist.

Date	Mintage	VG	F	VF	XF	Unc
1611	—	45.00	100	180	360	—
1613	—	45.00	100	180	360	—
1614	—	45.00	100	180	360	—
1616	—	45.00	100	180	360	—
1617	—	45.00	100	180	360	—
1649	—	45.00	100	180	360	—
1657	—	45.00	100	180	360	—

KM# 15 1/4 THALER (Teston)
Silver **Note:** Prev. KM#6.

Date	Mintage	VG	F	VF	XF	Unc
1628	—	27.00	55.00	100	210	—

KM# 35 1/4 THALER (Teston)
Silver **Obv:** Ornate arms **Obv. Legend:** MONETA CIVITA METENSIS **Rev:** Bust of St. Stephan left, value 1/4 below **Rev. Legend:** ❊ S. STEPANVS PROTOMARTYR **Note:** Prev. KM#20.

Date	Mintage	VG	F	VF	XF	Unc
1640	—	1,100	2,200	4,400	—	—

KM# 23 1/2 THALER
Silver **Obv:** Arms in scalloped frame **Obv. Legend:** MONETA CIVITA METENSIS **Rev:** Bust of St. Stephan left, value 1/2 below **Rev. Legend:** S.STEPHANVS PROTOMARTIR **Note:** Prev. KM#23.

Date	Mintage	VG	F	VF	XF	Unc
1638	—	—	1,800	3,500	6,800	—

KM# 17 THALER
Silver **Obv:** Imperial eagle, city arms on breast, date **Obv. Legend:** MONETA. NOVA. METENSIS **Rev:** Full-length standing figure of St. Stephan holding palm branch in elongated oval **Note:** Dav. #5580. Prev. KM#8. Varieties exist.

Date	Mintage	VG	F	VF	XF	Unc
1628	—	120	240	500	825	—
1629	—	120	240	500	825	—
1630	—	120	240	500	825	—

Date	Mintage	VG	F	VF	XF	Unc
1631	—	120	240	500	825	—
1632	—	120	240	500	825	—
1633	—	120	240	500	825	—
1634	—	120	240	500	825	—

KM# 25 THALER

Silver **Obv:** City arms in hexalobe, date **Obv. Legend:** MONETA CIVITATISMETEN **Rev:** Full-length standing figure of St. Stephan holding palm branch in elongated oval **Note:** Dav. #5581. Prev. KM#13.

Date	Mintage	VG	F	VF	XF	Unc
1638	—	165	325	650	1,250	—

KM# 26 THALER

Silver **Obv:** Oval city arms in baroque frame, date **Obv. Legend:** MONETA CIVITATIS METEN **Rev:** Full-length standing figure of St. Stephan holding palm branch in elongated oval **Rev. Legend:** S • STE[JAMVS • • PROTHOMART **Note:** Dav. #5582. Prev. KM#14.

Date	Mintage	VG	F	VF	XF	Unc
1638	—	220	450	750	1,450	—

KM# 27 THALER

Silver **Obv:** City arms with scalloped sides in ornamented frame, date **Obv. Legend:** MONETA CIVITAMETENSIS **Rev:** Bust of St. Stephan left in circle **Rev. Legend:** S. STEPHANVS PROTOMARTIR. **Note:** Dav. #5583. Prev. KM#15. Varieties exist.

Date	Mintage	VG	F	VF	XF	Unc
1638	—	100	200	350	725	—
1639	—	100	200	350	725	—
1640	—	100	200	350	725	—
1641	—	100	200	350	725	—
1643	—	100	200	350	725	—
1645	—	100	200	350	725	—

KM# 28 THALER

Silver **Obv:** City arms with scalloped sides in ornamented frame, date **Obv. Legend:** MONETA CIVITA METENSIS **Rev:** Bust of St. Stephan left in circle **Rev. Legend:** S. STEPHANVS PROTHOMART **Note:** Dav. #5583A. Prev. KM#16.

Date	Mintage	VG	F	VF	XF	Unc
1638	—	100	200	350	725	—

KM# 38 THALER

Silver **Obv:** City arms with scalloped sides in ornamented frame, date **Obv. Legend:** MONETA CIVITA METENSIS **Rev:** Bust of St. Stephan left in circle **Rev. Legend:** S STEPHANVS • PROTO • MARTIR **Note:** Dav. #5583B. Prev. KM#22. Varieties exist.

Date	Mintage	VG	F	VF	XF	Unc
1646	—	100	200	350	725	—
1647	—	100	200	350	725	—
1650	—	100	200	350	725	—

KM# 18 2 THALER

Silver **Note:** Dav. A5580.

Date	Mintage	VG	F	VF	XF	Unc
1630 Rare	—	—	—	—	—	—

KM# 20 2 THALER

Silver **Obv:** Imperial eagle, city arms on breast, date **Obv. Legend:** MONETA. NOVA. METENSIS **Rev:** Full-length standing figure of St. Stephan in elongated oval **Note:** Prev. KM#A10.

Date	Mintage	VG	F	VF	XF	Unc
1630 Rare	—	—	—	—	—	—

TRADE COINAGE

KM# 12 GOLDGULDEN

3.5000 g., 0.9860 Gold 0.1109 oz. AGW **Obv:** City arms in hexalobe **Obv. Legend:** FLORENVS. CIVITAT. METENS. **Rev:** Full-length figure of St. Stephan standing, holding stone and palm branch, divides date, all in elongated oval **Note:** Fr. #164. Prev. KM#A4. Varieties exist.

Date	Mintage	VG	F	VF	XF	Unc
1620	—	290	500	825	1,650	—
1623	—	290	500	825	1,650	—
1624	—	290	500	825	1,650	—
1631	—	290	500	825	1,650	—
ND	—	290	500	825	1,650	—

KM# 33 GOLDGULDEN

3.5000 g., 0.9860 Gold 0.1109 oz. AGW **Obv:** City arms in hexalobe **Obv. Legend:** FLORENVS. CIVITAT. METENS. **Rev:** Bust of St. Stephan to left **Note:** Fr. #165. Prev. KM#18.

Date	Mintage	VG	F	VF	XF	Unc
1639	—	575	1,050	2,250	3,950	—

MINDEN

The town of Minden in Westphalia, some 60 miles east of Osnabruck, was made the seat of a bishopric by Charlemagne in 803. The bishop gained the mint right in 997 and obtained the right to maintain a mint at Eisleben in 1045. Only a small variety of coin types were struck during the first half of the 17th century, most notably the city seige issues of 1634. For the coinage of Bishop Christian, see listings for him under Brunswick-Luneburg-Celle. As part of the Peace of Westphalia ending the Thirty Years' War in 1648, Minden was secularized and handed over to Brandenburg-Prussia. The latter established a mint for the territory in Minden with coins first struck in 1652. From 1807 until 1814, Minden was part of the Kingdom of Westphalia and was returned to Prussia thereafter.

RULERS

Christian von Braunschweig-Luneburg, 1599-1633
Franz Wilhelm von Wartenberg, 1633-1648

ARMS

2 crossed keys

REFERENCE

S = Ewald Stange, **Geld- und Münzgeschichte des Bistums Minden**, Berlin, 1915.

BISHOPRIC

TRADE COINAGE

KM# 13 DUCAT

3.5000 g., 0.9860 Gold 0.1109 oz. AGW **Ruler:** Franz Wilhelm **Obv:** Christ handing key to St. Peter, titles of Franz Wilhelm **Rev:** 4-fold arms with central shield of Wartenberg, crossed sword and crozier behind, titles continued around

Date	Mintage	VG	F	VF	XF	Unc
ND(ca.1643) Rare	500	—	—	—	—	—

TOWN

STANDARD COINAGE

KM# 5 3 PFENNIG (Dreier; Körtling)

Silver **Obv:** Crossed keys divide 1 - 6, 34 below **Rev. Inscription:** III / PENNI

Date	Mintage	VG	F	VF	XF	Unc
1634	—	600	1,000	1,850	3,300	—

SIEGE COINAGE

KM# 6 MATTHIER (1/2 Mariengroschen; 4 Pfennig)

Silver **Obv:** MIN / OBSES, crossed keys below divide date **Rev. Inscription:** EIN / MATTI / ER

Date	Mintage	VG	F	VF	XF	Unc
1634	6,156	225	450	900	1,800	—

KM# 7 MARIENGROSCHEN

Silver **Obv:** Inscription, crossed keys below divide date **Obv. Inscription:** MIN / OBSES **Rev. Inscription:** I / GROS

Date	Mintage	VG	F	VF	XF	Unc
1634	24,000	155	310	625	—	—

KM# 8 2 MARIENGROSCHEN

Silver **Obv:** Crossed keys, legend, date **Obv. Legend:** MINDA OBSESSA Ao **Rev. Legend:** DVRVM TELVM NECESSITAS **Rev. Inscription:** II / GROS

Date	Mintage	VG	F	VF	XF	Unc
1634	4,549	275	525	1,050	—	—

KM# 9 4 MARIENGROSCHEN (1/2 Kopstucke)
Silver **Obv:** Crossed keys, legend, date **Obv. Legend:** MINDA OBSESSA Ao **Rev. Legend:** DVRVM TELVM NECESSITAS **Rev. Inscription:** IIII / GROS

Date	Mintage	VG	F	VF	XF	Unc
1634	70,000	—	—	—	—	—

KM# 10 4 MARIENGROSCHEN (1/2 Kopstucke)
Copper **Obv:** Two stamps: Crossed keys and IIIIG. **Note:** Uniface, square, approximately 13.4 grams.

Date	Mintage	VG	F	VF	XF	Unc
ND(1634)	—	200	400	700	1,250	—

KM# 10a 4 MARIENGROSCHEN (1/2 Kopstucke)
7.6000 g., Tin

Date	Mintage	VG	F	VF	XF	Unc
ND(1634)	—	—	—	—	—	—

KM# 12 8 MARIENGROSCHEN (Kopstucke)
Copper **Obv:** Crossed keys, legend, date **Obv. Legend:** MINDA OBSESSA Ao **Rev. Legend:** DVRVM TELVM NECESSITAS **Rev. Inscription:** VIII/GROS

Date	Mintage	VG	F	VF	XF	Unc
1634	2,099	—	—	—	—	—

KM# 11 8 MARIENGROSCHEN (Kopstucke)
Silver **Obv:** Inscription in circle **Obv. Inscription:** MINDA / OBSESSA / date **Rev:** Inscription in circle, countermarked with two crossed keys **Rev. Inscription:** 8 / GROS / CHEN **Shape:** Square **Note:** Approximately 3.6 grams.

Date	Mintage	VG	F	VF	XF	Unc
1634	—	90.00	170	325	650	—

MITTWEIDA

The town of Mittweida in Saxony is located 11 miles (18km) north of Chemnitz. During the Kipper Period of the Thirty Years' War, a local coinage was struck there.

REFERENCE
M = Otto Merseburger, **Sammlung Otto Merseburger umfassend Münzen und Medaillen von Sachsen**, Leipzig, 1894.

PROVINCIAL TOWN

KIPPER COINAGE

KM# 1 3 PFENNIG (Dreier)
Lead **Ruler:** (no Ruler Information) **Obv:** Town arms (two lions), MZ (Mittweidischer Zeichen) above **Rev:** Value '3' and date **Note:** M-2650.

Date	Mintage	VG	F	VF	XF	Unc
16Z1 Rare	—	—	—	—	—	—

MOMPELGART

(Mömpelgard, Mümpelgard, Montbéliard)

The Countship of Mömpelgart was located southwest of the Rhine, between the County of Burgundy and the Landgraviate of Upper Alsace. Its capital was the town of the same name situated near the confluence of the Allaine and Lisaine Rivers, 36 miles (60 kilometers) northeast of Besançon. When the last count of the old line died without a male heir, the territory and titles passed by way of his daughter Henriette through her marriage in 1408 to Count Eberhard IV of Württemberg (ruled 1417-19). Eberhard's son, Ludwig I (1419-50), inherited Mömpelgart outright when his mother died in 1444. The Countship was ruled from this point by either the Counts (dukes from 1495) of Württemberg themselves or their brothers and cousins until a separate line was established in 1608. When that line became extinct in 1723, the titles and lands reverted to Württemberg. France annexed Mömpelgart in 1796 and all association with Württemberg ended.

RULERS
Friedrich I, 1558-1608
Under guardianship of his uncle, Ludwig III (Duke 1568-93)
Ludwig Friedrich, 1608-1631
Leopold Friedrich, 1631-1662
Georg II, 1662-1699
French Occupation, 1684-1697
Leopold Eberhard, 1699-1723

MINT MARKS
M – Mömpelgart Mint
R – Reichenweier (Riquewihr Mint

MINT OFFICIALS' INITIALS

Initial	Date	Name
	1579-1616	Franz Briot
	1613-19	Franz Guichart
	1622	André Hubner
	1623-24	Jacob Kolb
	1624-25	3 brothers Wittenauer
S	1692	Johann Friedrich Schattauer, die-cutter and mintmaster in Brenz

ARMS
Mömpelgart – 2 fish standing on tails
Württemberg – 3 stag horns
Flag with eagle (Hereditary flag-bearer of the Empire)
Teck – field of lozenges (diamond shapes)
Urach – hunting horn

REFERENCE
B&E = Christian Binder and Julius Ebner, **Württembergische Münz- und Medaillen-Kunde**, 2 vols., Stuttgart, 1910-12.

COUNTSHIP

REGULAR COINAGE

KM# 4 KREUZER
Silver **Ruler:** Ludwig Friedrich **Obv:** Mömpelgart arms, titles of Ludwig Friedrich **Rev:** 'LF' monogram, 4 fleur-de-lis in cruciform, date **Rev. Legend:** M—N—M—

Date	Mintage	VG	F	VF	XF	Unc
(1)622	—	45.00	95.00	190	385	—

KM# 5 KREUZER
Silver **Ruler:** Ludwig Friedrich **Obv:** Mömpelgart arms, 'I' left and right, titles of Ludwig Friedrich **Rev:** 'LF' monogram, 4 fleur-de-lis in cruciform, 'I' left and right, date

Date	Mintage	VG	F	VF	XF	Unc
1622	—	45.00	95.00	190	385	—

KM# 7 2 KREUZER (1/2 Batzen = Halbbatzen)
0.8800 g., Silver **Ruler:** Ludwig Friedrich **Obv:** Württemberg arms, titles of Ludwig Friedrich **Rev:** Mömpelgart arms, date **Rev. Legend:** MON: NOVA: MONT:

Date	Mintage	VG	F	VF	XF	Unc
1622	—	75.00	150	300	600	—

Note: Known also struck on thick flan of 2.82 grams

KM# 8 2 KREUZER (1/2 Batzen = Halbbatzen)
0.8800 g., Silver **Ruler:** Ludwig Friedrich **Obv:** 3 small shields of arms, 2 above 1, which divides date below, value '2' at top, titles of Ludwig Friedrich **Rev:** Flag with eagle, 'M' below, titles continued

Date	Mintage	VG	F	VF	XF	Unc
1624 M	22,000	80.00	165	335	675	—

KM# 9 3 KREUZER (Groschen)
Silver **Ruler:** Ludwig Friedrich **Obv:** Württemberg arms, '3' above, titles of Ludwig Friedrich **Rev:** Mömpelgart arms, '3' above, date **Rev. Legend:** MON:NOVA:MOMP: **Note:** Weight varies 1.03-1.24 grams.

Date	Mintage	VG	F	VF	XF	Unc
16Z3	143,000	75.00	150	310	625	—
16Z4	124,000	75.00	150	310	625	—

KM# 9a 3 KREUZER (Groschen)
3.8000 g., Silver **Ruler:** Ludwig Friedrich **Obv:** Württemberg arms, '3' above, titles of Ludwig **Rev:** Mömpelgart arms, '3' above, date **Rev. Legend:** MON:NOVA:MOMP: **Note:** Klippe.

Date	Mintage	VG	F	VF	XF	Unc
16Z4	—	—	—	—	—	—

KM# 15 12 KREUZER (Dreibätzner)
Silver **Ruler:** Ludwig Friedrich **Obv:** Bust right, value '12' below, titles of Ludwig Friedrich **Rev:** Crowned 4-fold arms divide date **Rev. Legend:** SECVNDM.VOLVNTATEM.DEI.

Date	Mintage	VG	F	VF	XF	Unc
1622	—	650	1,300	2,300	4,400	—

KM# 16 12 KREUZER (Dreibätzner)
Silver **Ruler:** Ludwig Friedrich **Obv:** 3 small shields of arms, 2 above 1, value '12' above, titles of Ludwig Friedrich **Rev:** Shield with eagle flag, date **Rev. Legend:** COMES.MOMPELGART

Date	Mintage	VG	F	VF	XF	Unc
1623	—	650	1,300	2,300	4,400	—

KM# 17 12 KREUZER (Dreibätzner)
Silver **Ruler:** Ludwig Friedrich **Obv:** 3 small shields of arms, 2 above 1, value '12' above, titles of Ludwig Friedrich **Rev:** Shield with eagle flag, date **Rev. Legend:** MONTPELIGAR or MONTBELIGAR

Date	Mintage	VG	F	VF	XF	Unc
1624	—	650	1,300	2,300	4,400	—

KM# 18 2 SCHILLING
Silver **Ruler:** Ludwig Friedrich **Obv:** 3 small shields of arms, 2 above 1, value '2' above, titles of Ludwig Friedrich **Rev:** Shield with eagle flag, date **Rev. Legend:** MONTPELIGAR or MONTBELIGAR

Date	Mintage	VG	F	VF	XF	Unc
1624	31,000	450	900	1,750	3,300	—
1625	41,000	450	900	1,750	3,300	—

KM# 19 1/4 THALER
Silver **Ruler:** Ludwig Friedrich **Obv:** Bust right in circle, titles of Ludwig Friedrich **Rev:** Crowned 4-fold arms divide II—II (=1/4 Taler), date **Rev. Legend:** SECVNDVM. VOLVNTATEM. DEI

Date	Mintage	VG	F	VF	XF	Unc
1622	—	—	—	—	—	—

KM# 20 1/2 THALER (Shooting)
Silver **Ruler:** Ludwig Friedrich **Obv:** Large 'LF' monogram in circle, wreath border **Rev:** Crossbow vertical divides date in circle, wreath border

Date	Mintage	VG	F	VF	XF	Unc
1612	—	—	—	—	—	—

Note: The '2' in the date is retrograde

KM# 2 1/2 THALER (Shooting)
Silver **Ruler:** Ludwig Friedrich **Obv:** Large 'LF' monogram in circle, wreath border **Rev:** Crossbow vertical divides date in circle, wreath border **Note:** Ref. B/E#41. The '2' in the date is retrograde.

Date	Mintage	VG	F	VF	XF	Unc
1612	—	—	—	—	—	—

KM# 21 2/3 THALER (Gulden)
Silver **Ruler:** Georg II **Obv:** Bust right, titles of Georg II **Rev:** Crowned oval 4-fold arms within palm branches, date **Rev. Legend:** CONCORDIA.RES.PARVÆ.CRESCVNT

Date	Mintage	VG	F	VF	XF	Unc
1692 S	—	—	—	—	—	—

KM# A24 2/3 THALER (Gulden)
Silver **Ruler:** Georg II **Obv:** Bust right, titles of Georg II **Rev:** Crowned oval 4-fold arms within pal branches, date at end of legend **Rev. Legend:** CONCORDIA. RES. PARVÆ. CRESCVNT **Note:** Ref. B/E#69.

Date	Mintage	VG	F	VF	XF	Unc
1692 S	—	—	—	—	—	—

KM# 22 THALER (Shooting)
Silver **Ruler:** Ludwig Friedrich **Obv:** Large 'LF' monogram in circle, wreath border **Rev:** Crowned 4-fold arms in rhombus divide date, all within circle, wreath border

Date	Mintage	VG	F	VF	XF	Unc
1614 Rare	—	—	—	—	—	—

KM# 23 THALER (Shooting)
Silver **Ruler:** Ludwig Friedrich **Obv:** Ruffed collared bust in circle, titles of Ludwig Friedrich **Rev:** Crowned ornate 4-fold arms, date **Rev. Legend:** SECVNDVM . VOLVNTATEM . DEI **Note:** Dav. 7075, Varieties Exist.

Date	Mintage	VG	F	VF	XF	Unc
1622	11,000	3,000	5,500	9,000	—	—

Note: Fritz Rudolf Künker Münzenhandlung Auction 134, 1-08, VF realized approximately $7,680; Hess-Divo AG Auction 304, 5-06, VF realized approximately $15,640; Fritz Rudolf Künker Münzenhandlung Auction 98, 3-05, VF realized approximately $5,070

Date	Mintage	VG	F	VF	XF	Unc
16Z3 Rare	—	—	—	—	—	—

KM# 24 2 THALER
Silver **Ruler:** Ludwig Friedrich **Obv:** Bust in circle, titles of Ludwig Friedrich **Rev:** Crowned ornate 4-fold arms, date **Rev. Legend:** SECVNDVM. VOLVNTATEM. DEI

Date	Mintage	VG	F	VF	XF	Unc
1624 Rare	—	—	—	—	—	—

TRADE COINAGE

KM# 11 1/4 DUCAT
Gold **Ruler:** Ludwig Friedrich **Obv:** Mömpelgart arms, titles of Ludwig **Rev:** 'LF' monogram, 4 fleur-de-lis in cruciform, date **Rev. Legend:** M—N—M— **Note:** Ref. B&E#44. Struck from the same dies as Kreuzer KM#4.

Date	Mintage	VG	F	VF	XF	Unc
(1)622	—	1,450	2,900	4,300	7,800	—

KM# 12 1/2 DUCAT
Gold **Ruler:** Ludwig Friedrich **Obv:** Württemberg arms, titles of Ludwig Friedrich **Rev:** Mömpelgart arms, date **Rev. Legend:** MON: NOVA: MONT: **Note:** Ref. B&E#43. Struck from the same dies as 2 Kreuzer, KM#7.

Date	Mintage	VG	F	VF	XF	Unc
1622	—	1,800	3,250	5,000	8,700	—

MONTFORT

The countship of Montfort was located in the extreme southern part of Württemberg along the northern shore of the Bodensee (Lake Constance) and the area extending southeast of the lake known as the Vorarlberg. The castle of Montfort is situated next to the mint town of Langenargen on the Bodensee between Lindau and Friedrichshafen. The House of Montfort oriinated from the marriage of Hugo I, Count Palatine of Tübingen (1162-82) and Elizabeth, Countess and heir of Bregenz, Montfort and Sigmaringen. Their elder son, Rudolf I (1182-1230), took part of Bregenz and Montfort, thus establishing that line of counts. The sons of Hugo II divided their patrimony, founding separate lines of Montfort and Werdenberg. It was during the 13th century that the counts of Montfort began striking their first coins in the form of bracteats. The next generation again divided the lands into the branches of Montfort-Feldkirch, Montfort-Bregenz and Montfort-Tettnang. Feldkirch fell extinct in 1390 and passed to Austria. The Bregenz line only lasted until 1338 and was reunited to that of Tettnang. In 1353, the two sons of Wilhelm II founded the lines of Montfort-Neu-Bregenz and Montfort-Tettnang. Both branches struck coins, but the latter became extinct in 1574 and the lands and titles reverted to Bregenz, which then took the name of Montfort-Tettnang. Half of the territory of Montfort was sold to Austria in 1523. The last count sold the remainder to Austria in 1780.

RULERS

Montfort-Neu-Breganz (Tettnang from 1574)
Johann VI, 1573-1619
Hugo and Johann VII, 1619-1625
Hugo XIV, 1619-1662
Johann VIII, 1662-1686
Anton II, regent, 1686-1693
Anton III, 1693-1733
Ernst Max Josef, 1733-1758
Franz Xavier, 1758-1780

MINTMASTERS' INITIALS

Initial	Date	Name
L		Langenargen Mint
(a) = pomegranate	Ca.1636-37	Hans Apfelfelder (Appenfelder), mintmaster
	Ca. 1621	Gottfried Gannsser, warden
	1622	Jakob Wegerich, mintmaster
	1623	Hans Heinrich Schmidt, mintmaster and warden
	Ca. 1625	Leonard Hau, die-cutter
	Ca. 1625	Daniel Sailer, die-cutter in Augsburg
	Ca. 1626-27	Christoph Molventer, die-cutter
	Ca. 1627	Heinrich Kolb, die-cutter in Ulm
(c)= anchor	Ca. 1675-79	Jakob Haltmeyer, mintmaster
	Ca. 1675-79	Andreas Kees, warden
	Ca. 1681	Bartholomäus Kessler, warden
	Ca. 1691	Hans Jakob Kick, mintmaster
FG, FIG	1690-94	Franz Joseph Gülly of Lucerne, mintmaster
	1695	Hans Georg Gülly, mintmaster
IK	1696-1724	Johann Künle (Kühnlein), warden and mintmaster

ARMS

Hanging banner with three pendenticles, the center one longer than those on left and right, three small rings equidistant along top of banner

REFERENCES

B/E = Christian Binder & Julius Ebner, ***Württembergische Münz- und Medaillen-Kunde,*** v. 2, Stuttgart, 1912.

Sch = Wolfgang Schulten, ***Deutsche Münzen aus der Zeit Karls V. Frankfurt am Main, 1974.***

COUNTSHIP

STANDARD COINAGE

KM# 13 4 HELLER (2 Pfennig)
Copper, 17 mm. **Obv:** Monogram HGZM in pearl circle, IIII at top, date at bottom **Rev:** Montfort arms between flowers

Date	Mintage	VG	F	VF	XF	Unc
1622	—	200	325	675	1,300	—

KM# 22 PFENNIG
Copper **Obv:** Flag in cartouche divides date, "H" above **Note:** Uniface.

Date	Mintage	VG	F	VF	XF	Unc
1624	—	200	325	675	1,300	—

KM# 22a PFENNIG
Silver **Obv:** Flag in cartouche divides date, "H" above **Note:** Uniface.

Date	Mintage	VG	F	VF	XF	Unc
1624	—	—	—	—	—	—

KM# 30 PFENNIG
Copper, 22 mm. **Obv:** Flag in cartouche divides date, "H" above **Note:** Uniface

Date	Mintage	VG	F	VF	XF	Unc
(16)27	—	200	325	675	1,300	—

KM# 32 PFENNIG
Copper, 12 mm. **Obv:** Montfort arms divide date, "H" above **Note:** Uniface.

Date	Mintage	VG	F	VF	XF	Unc
(16)29	—	200	325	675	1,300	—

KM# 35 PFENNIG
Copper, 11 mm. **Obv:** Flag on plain shield **Note:** Uniface.

Date	Mintage	VG	F	VF	XF	Unc
ND(1662-86)	—	160	325	650	1,300	—

KM# 48 PFENNIG
Copper, 13 mm. **Obv:** Crowned arms in elongated shield divides date **Note:** Uniface.

Date	Mintage	VG	F	VF	XF	Unc
1676	—	165	325	650	1,300	—

KM# A14 2 PFENNIG
Silver **Ruler:** Anton III **Obv:** Crowned shield of Montfort arms divides date and mintmaster's initials, value (2) below **Mint:** Langenargen **Note:** Ref. B/E#155a. Uniface.

Date	Mintage	VG	F	VF	XF	Unc
1696 IK	—	—	—	—	—	—

KM# 14 1/2 KREUZER
Copper, 16 mm. **Obv:** Arms with "H" between flowers above, "K" below divides date **Note:** Uniface.

Date	Mintage	VG	F	VF	XF	Unc
1622	—	200	325	675	1,300	—

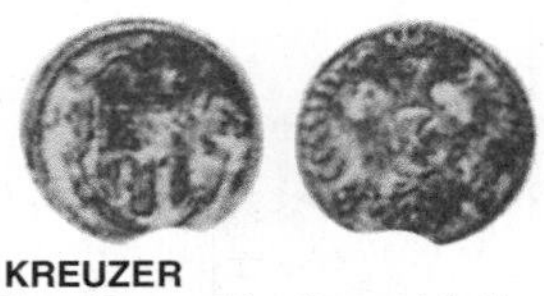

KM# 17 KREUZER
0.6600 g., Silver, 16 mm. **Obv:** Crowned double eagle, "K" in orb on breast **Rev:** Montfort arms divide date

Date	Mintage	VG	F	VF	XF	Unc
1623	—	200	375	700	1,300	—

KM# 25 KREUZER
Silver **Obv:** Double eagle, "1" in orb on breast **Obv. Legend:** FER II... **Rev:** Montfort arms on double cross

Date	Mintage	VG	F	VF	XF	Unc
1625	—	200	375	700	1,300	—

KM# 28 KREUZER
Silver **Obv. Legend:** FERD II...

Date	Mintage	VG	F	VF	XF	Unc
1626	—	200	375	700	1,300	—

KM# 36 KREUZER
Silver **Obv:** Crowned double eagle, "I" on breast **Rev:** Montfort arms in cartouche

Date	Mintage	VG	F	VF	XF	Unc
ND(1662-86)	—	165	300	600	1,175	—

KM# 70 KREUZER
Silver **Obv:** Crowned double eagle with "I" on breast dividing date **Rev:** Crowned arms **Rev. Legend:** ...MON.

Date	Mintage	VG	F	VF	XF	Unc
1680	—	135	300	600	1,175	—

KM# 71 KREUZER
Silver **Rev. Legend:** ...MONTF.

Date	Mintage	VG	F	VF	XF	Unc
1680	—	135	275	525	1,025	—

KM# 90 KREUZER
Silver, 15 mm. **Obv:** Armored bust right **Rev:** Crowned arms between palm fronds

Date	Mintage	VG	F	VF	XF	Unc
1696	—	80.00	165	335	675	—

KM# 91 KREUZER
Silver **Ruler:** Anton III **Obv:** Crowned shield **Obv. Legend:** ... MON. **Rev:** Crowned double eagle, "I" in orb on breast **Mint:** Langenargen

Date	Mintage	VG	F	VF	XF	Unc
(16)96	—	65.00	135	275	550	—
(16)96 IK	—	65.00	135	275	550	—
(16)97 IK	—	—	—	—	—	—

KM# 92 KREUZER
Silver **Rev. Legend:** ...MONTF.

Date	Mintage	VG	F	VF	XF	Unc
1696 IK	—	80.00	165	335	675	—

KM# 93 KREUZER
Silver **Rev. Legend:** ...MON:F.

Date	Mintage	VG	F	VF	XF	Unc
1696	—	80.00	165	335	675	—

KM# 18 2 KREUZER
1.2500 g., Silver, 18 mm. **Obv:** Orb with denomination **Obv. Legend:** FERD.II... **Rev:** Church flag in ornamented shield

Date	Mintage	VG	F	VF	XF	Unc
ND	—	45.00	95.00	190	385	—

KM# 19 2 KREUZER
Silver, 19 mm. **Rev:** Montfort arms in ornamentation and legend

Date	Mintage	VG	F	VF	XF	Unc
1623	—	35.00	75.00	150	300	—
1624	—	35.00	75.00	150	300	—

KM# 27 2 KREUZER

Silver **Note:** Double dot legend dividers; (16)26 date also exists with a Lindau countermark.

Date	Mintage	VG	F	VF	XF	Unc
1625	—	30.00	65.00	135	275	—
1626	—	30.00	65.00	135	275	—
(16)26	—	30.00	65.00	135	275	—
(16)27	—	30.00	65.00	135	275	—
(16)28	—	30.00	65.00	135	275	—
1629	—	30.00	65.00	135	275	—
(16)29	—	30.00	65.00	135	275	—
(16)29(29) Error date	—	30.00	65.00	135	275	—

KM# 26 2 KREUZER

Silver **Note:** Single dot legend dividers.

Date	Mintage	VG	F	VF	XF	Unc
1625	—	35.00	75.00	150	300	—

KM# 83 4 KREUZER

4.0000 g., Silver, 23 mm. **Obv:** Manteled arms with helmet and flag **Obv. Legend:** ...COMES.IN... **Rev:** Crowned imperial eagle, 4 in orb on breast **Rev. Legend:** ...COMES.IN...

Date	Mintage	VG	F	VF	XF	Unc
1694	—	35.00	75.00	150	300	—
(16)94	—	35.00	75.00	150	300	—

KM# 85 4 KREUZER

4.0000 g., Silver **Ruler:** Anton III **Obv. Legend:** "COM:" **Mint:** Langenargen **Note:** Many varieties exist.

Date	Mintage	VG	F	VF	XF	Unc
(16)94	—	35.00	75.00	150	300	—
1695	—	35.00	75.00	150	300	—
1697	—	35.00	75.00	150	300	—

KM# 84 4 KREUZER

Silver **Ruler:** Anton III **Obv:** Manteled arms with helmet and mitre above **Obv. Legend:** ANTONIVS. COMES.IN. MONTFOR. **Rev:** Crowned imperial eagle, 4 in orb on breast **Rev. Legend:** LEOPOLDVS. D.G. ROM. IMP. S. AVG.

Date	Mintage	VG	F	VF	XF	Unc
1694	—	35.00	75.00	150	300	—

KM# 8 12 KREUZER

Silver

Date	Mintage	VG	F	VF	XF	Unc
1621	—	1,000	1,950	—	—	—

KM# 9 12 KREUZER

2.0000 g., Silver, 26 mm. **Obv:** Armored bust left with sword on right shoulder and sceptre in left hand **Rev:** Crowned imperial eagle, 12 in orb on breast **Note:** Kipper.

Date	Mintage	VG	F	VF	XF	Unc
ND	—	1,000	2,000	—	—	—

KM# 11 12 KREUZER

Silver **Obv:** Montfort shield in field next to bust

Date	Mintage	VG	F	VF	XF	Unc
ND	—	1,000	2,000	—	—	—

KM# 40 15 KREUZER

Silver, 31 mm. **Obv:** Crowned Montfort arms between palm branches **Rev:** Crowned imperial eagle above XV **Rev. Legend:** IN. MONTFORT.

Date	Mintage	VG	F	VF	XF	Unc
1674	—	220	435	875	—	—

KM# 41 15 KREUZER

Silver **Obv:** Crowned Montfort arms between palm branches **Obv. Legend:** MONTFOR. **Rev:** Crowned imperial eagle above XV

Date	Mintage	VG	F	VF	XF	Unc
1674	—	220	435	875	—	—

KM# 42 15 KREUZER

Silver, 31 mm. **Obv:** Crowned Montfort arms between palm branches **Obv. Legend:** I.MONTFORT: **Rev:** Crowned imperial eagle above XV

Date	Mintage	VG	F	VF	XF	Unc
1674	—	220	435	875	—	—

KM# 43 15 KREUZER

5.6500 g., Silver, 29 mm. **Ruler:** Johann VIII **Obv:** Armored bust right **Obv. Legend:** IOANN... **Rev:** Crowned arms between 2 branches **Mint:** Langenargen

Date	Mintage	VG	F	VF	XF	Unc
1675 (c)	—	150	300	600	—	—

KM# 44 15 KREUZER

5.6500 g., Silver, 29 mm. **Ruler:** Johann VIII **Obv:** Armored bust right **Obv. Legend:** IOANNES... **Rev:** Crowned arms between 2 branches **Mint:** Langenargen

Date	Mintage	VG	F	VF	XF	Unc
1675 (c)	—	150	300	600	—	—

KM# 49 15 KREUZER

Silver **Ruler:** Johann VIII **Obv:** Armored bust right, dots at beginning and end of legend **Rev:** Crowned arms between 2 branches **Mint:** Langenargen

Date	Mintage	VG	F	VF	XF	Unc
1676 (c)	—	60.00	120	235	475	—

KM# 50 15 KREUZER

Silver **Ruler:** Johann VIII **Obv:** Armored bust right, without dots at beginning and end of legend **Rev:** Crowned arms between 2 branches **Mint:** Langenargen

Date	Mintage	VG	F	VF	XF	Unc
1676 (c)	—	60.00	120	235	475	—

KM# 51 15 KREUZER

Silver **Ruler:** Johann VIII **Obv:** Armored bust right, tight curls **Mint:** Langenargen

Date	Mintage	VG	F	VF	XF	Unc
1676 (c)	—	60.00	120	235	475	—

KM# 52 15 KREUZER

Silver **Ruler:** Johann VIII **Obv:** Armored bust right, continuous legend below **Rev:** Crowned arms between 2 branches **Mint:** Langenargen

Date	Mintage	VG	F	VF	XF	Unc
1678 (c)	—	50.00	100	210	425	—

KM# 53 15 KREUZER

Silver **Ruler:** Johann VIII **Obv:** Armored bust right, divides legend at bottom **Rev:** Crowned arms between 2 branches **Mint:** Langenargen

Date	Mintage	VG	F	VF	XF	Unc
1678 (c)	—	50.00	100	210	425	—

KM# 54 15 KREUZER

Silver **Ruler:** Johann VIII **Obv:** Armored bust right, divides legend **Obv. Legend:** ...COM + - + MES... **Rev:** Crowned arms between 2 branches **Mint:** Langenargen

Date	Mintage	VG	F	VF	XF	Unc
1678 (c)	—	50.00	100	210	425	—

KM# 58 15 KREUZER

Silver **Ruler:** Johann VIII **Obv:** Armored bust right, continuous legend **Rev:** Crowned arms between 2 branches **Mint:** Langenargen

Date	Mintage	VG	F	VF	XF	Unc
1679 (c)	—	50.00	100	210	425	—

KM# 59 15 KREUZER

Silver **Ruler:** Johann VIII **Obv:** Armored bust right, divides legend **Obv. Legend:** "COMES * - * DE" **Rev:** Crowned arms between 2 branches **Mint:** Langenargen

Date	Mintage	VG	F	VF	XF	Unc
1679 (c)	—	50.00	100	210	425	—

KM# 82 15 KREUZER

Silver, 30 mm. **Ruler:** Anton II **Obv:** Armored bust right **Rev:** Crowned arms between 2 branches

Date	Mintage	VG	F	VF	XF	Unc
1692	—	50.00	100	210	425	—

KM# 55 30 KREUZER (1/2 Gulden)

Silver **Ruler:** Johann VIII **Obv:** Armored bust **Rev:** Crowned arms between branches

Date	Mintage	VG	F	VF	XF	Unc
1678 (c)	—	225	450	900	1,800	—

KM# 60 30 KREUZER (1/2 Gulden)
Silver **Obv:** Armored bust **Rev:** Heart-shaped shield

Date	Mintage	VG	F	VF	XF	Unc
1679	—	225	450	900	1,800	—

KM# 75 30 KREUZER (1/2 Gulden)
Silver, 33 mm. **Ruler:** Anton II **Obv:** Armored bust **Rev:** Crowned arms between branches **Mint:** Langenargen

Date	Mintage	VG	F	VF	XF	Unc
1690	—	200	350	700	1,400	—
1690 FG	—	200	350	700	1,400	—
1691/10 FIG	—	—	—	—	—	—

KM# 79 30 KREUZER (1/2 Gulden)
Silver **Ruler:** Anton II **Obv:** Armored bust right **Rev:** Crowned arms between branches **Mint:** Langenargen

Date	Mintage	VG	F	VF	XF	Unc
1691 FIG	—	200	350	700	1,400	—

KM# 56 60 KREUZER (Gulden)
18.5000 g., Silver, 37 mm. **Ruler:** Johann VIII **Obv:** Bust right **Rev:** Crowned arms between branches **Mint:** Langenargen

Date	Mintage	VG	F	VF	XF	Unc
1678 (c)	—	120	235	475	950	—

KM# 57 60 KREUZER (Gulden)
Silver **Obv:** Bust right **Rev:** Crowned arms between branches, heart-shaped shield

Date	Mintage	VG	F	VF	XF	Unc
1678	—	150	300	600	1,150	—

KM# 61 60 KREUZER (Gulden)
Silver **Ruler:** Johann VIII **Obv:** Bust right **Rev:** Crowned arms between branches **Mint:** Langenargen **Note:** This coin also exists with Franconian Circle and Salzburg countermarks.

Date	Mintage	VG	F	VF	XF	Unc
1679 (c)	—	120	235	475	950	—

KM# 62 60 KREUZER (Gulden)
Silver **Ruler:** Johann VIII **Obv:** Bust right **Rev:** Crowned arms between branches, legend in rope borders **Mint:** Langenargen

Date	Mintage	VG	F	VF	XF	Unc
1679 (c)	—	115	225	450	950	—

KM# 63 60 KREUZER (Gulden)
Silver **Ruler:** Johann VIII **Obv:** Bust right, legend divided at bottom **Rev:** Crowned arms between branches **Mint:** Langenargen

Date	Mintage	VG	F	VF	XF	Unc
1679 (c)	—	100	210	425	850	—

KM# 64 60 KREUZER (Gulden)
Silver **Ruler:** Johann VIII **Obv:** Portrait with modified nose **Rev:** Crowned arms between branches **Mint:** Langenargen

Date	Mintage	VG	F	VF	XF	Unc
1679 (c)	—	135	275	525	1,050	—

KM# 76 60 KREUZER (Gulden)
16.2500 g., Silver, 38 mm. **Ruler:** Anton II **Obv:** Portrait with loose curls **Rev:** Crowned arms between 2 branches **Mint:** Langenargen **Note:** This coin also exists with Franconian Circle countermark.

Date	Mintage	VG	F	VF	XF	Unc
1690 FG	—	100	210	425	850	—

KM# 77 60 KREUZER (Gulden)
Silver **Ruler:** Anton II **Obv:** Portrait with tight curls **Rev:** Crowned arms between 2 branches **Mint:** Langenargen **Note:** This coin also exists with Franconian Circle countermark.

Date	Mintage	VG	F	VF	XF	Unc
1690 FIG	—	100	210	425	850	—

KM# 78 60 KREUZER (Gulden)
Silver **Ruler:** Anton II **Obv:** Portrait with tight scale-like curls **Rev:** Large crown **Mint:** Langenargen **Note:** This coin also exists with Franconian Circle countermark.

Date	Mintage	VG	F	VF	XF	Unc
1690	—	100	210	425	850	—

KM# 80 60 KREUZER (Gulden)
Silver **Ruler:** Anton II **Obv. Legend:** ...ADMINI. **Mint:** Langenargen

Date	Mintage	VG	F	VF	XF	Unc
1691 FIG	—	100	210	425	850	—

KM# 81 60 KREUZER (Gulden)

Silver **Ruler:** Anton II **Obv. Legend:** ...ADMINIST. **Mint:** Langenargen

Date	Mintage	VG	F	VF	XF	Unc
1691/0 FIG	—	100	210	425	850	—
1691 FIG	—	100	210	425	850	—
1691	—	100	210	425	850	—
1691 E	—	100	210	425	850	—

KM# 24 1/4 THALER

Silver **Ruler:** Hugo and Johann VII **Obv:** Shield of Montfort arms. **Rev:** Bust of Ferdinand II.

Date	Mintage	VG	F	VF	XF	Unc
1624	—	450	900	1,800	3,500	—

KM# 86 1/4 THALER

Silver **Ruler:** Anton III **Obv:** Bust right **Rev:** Manteled arms with helmet and flag

Date	Mintage	VG	F	VF	XF	Unc
1694	—	450	900	1,800	3,500	—

KM# A87 1/2 THALER

Silver **Ruler:** Anton III **Obv:** Armored bust right

Date	Mintage	VG	F	VF	XF	Unc
1694	—	400	800	1,600	3,200	—

KM# 87 1/2 THALER

14.6500 g., Silver, 36 mm. **Ruler:** Anton III **Obv:** Draped armored bust right **Rev:** Arms **Mint:** Augsburg

Date	Mintage	VG	F	VF	XF	Unc
1695	—	400	800	1,600	3,200	—

Note: Contemporary counterfeit of 1695 coin is struck from smaller oval shaped dies in lower grade silver

KM# 45 2/3 THALER (Gulden)

18.3000 g., Silver **Ruler:** Johann VIII **Obv:** Portrait with loose curls **Note:** This coin also exists with Franconian Circle countermark.

Date	Mintage	VG	F	VF	XF	Unc
1675	—	135	300	600	1,225	—

KM# 46 2/3 THALER (Gulden)

Silver **Ruler:** Johann VIII **Obv:** Portrait with tight curls

Date	Mintage	VG	F	VF	XF	Unc
1675	—	165	335	675	1,375	—

KM# 47 2/3 THALER (Gulden)

Silver **Ruler:** Johann VIII **Rev:** Arms ornamented with 2 griffin heads

Date	Mintage	VG	F	VF	XF	Unc
1675	—	200	375	700	1,425	—

KM# 65 2/3 THALER (Gulden)

Silver **Ruler:** Johann VIII **Obv:** Armored bust **Rev:** Montfort arms, denomination "2/3"

Date	Mintage	VG	F	VF	XF	Unc
1679	—	200	375	700	1,425	—

KM# 5 THALER

Silver **Ruler:** Hugo and Johann VII **Obv:** Helmeted arms within beaded circle **Rev:** Double-headed imperial eagle, value in orb on breast **Note:** Dav.#7077.

Date	Mintage	VG	F	VF	XF	Unc
16Z0	—	195	375	725	1,250	—

KM# 6 THALER

Silver **Ruler:** Hugo and Johann VII **Obv:** Arabesque begins legend **Rev:** Arabesque before date **Note:** Dav.#7077A.

Date	Mintage	VG	F	VF	XF	Unc
16Z0	—	275	550	925	1,500	—

KM# 7 THALER

Silver **Ruler:** Hugo and Johann VII **Obv:** Arms with pointed shield **Rev:** Double-headed imperial eagle, value in orb on breast **Note:** Dav.#7078.

Date	Mintage	VG	F	VF	XF	Unc
16Z0	—	220	450	825	1,400	—

KM# 12 THALER

Silver **Ruler:** Hugo and Johann VII **Obv:** Arms with rounded shield **Rev:** Double-headed imperial eagle, value in orb on breast **Note:** Dav.#7079.

Date	Mintage	VG	F	VF	XF	Unc
16Z1	—	270	550	1,000	1,700	—

KM# 15 THALER

Silver **Ruler:** Hugo and Johann VII **Obv:** 1/2 Length bust right, small shield below **Rev:** Double-headed imperial eagle within beaded circle, crown above **Rev. Legend:** FERDINAN:II:... **Note:** Dav.#7080.

Date	Mintage	VG	F	VF	XF	Unc
16ZZ	—	625	1,150	1,900	—	—

KM# 16 THALER

Silver **Ruler:** Hugo and Johann VII **Rev. Legend:** FERDINANDVS II...

Date	Mintage	VG	F	VF	XF	Unc
16ZZ	—	750	1,250	2,150	—	—

KM# 20 THALER
Silver **Ruler:** Hugo and Johann VII **Obv:** Bust 1/4 right divides date, small shield below **Rev:** Double-headed imperial eagle within beaded circle, crown above **Note:** Single dot legend dividers; Dav.#7081.

Date	Mintage	VG	F	VF	XF	Unc
1623	—	600	1,100	1,800	—	—

KM# 21 THALER
Silver **Ruler:** Hugo and Johann VII **Obv:** Bust right divides date, small shield below **Obv. Legend:** MONETA NOVA HVGONIS... **Rev:** Double-headed imperial eagle within circle, crown above **Note:** Double-dot legend dividers; Dav.#7082.

Date	Mintage	VG	F	VF	XF	Unc
16Z3	—	575	1,050	1,750	—	—

KM# 31 THALER
Silver **Ruler:** Hugo XIV **Obv:** St. John of Montfort standing with shield at left, date below, double legend **Rev:** Crowned double eagle with orb on breast **Note:** Dav.#7084.

Date	Mintage	VG	F	VF	XF	Unc
1627 Rare	—	—	—	—	—	—

KM# 33 THALER
Silver **Ruler:** Johann VIII **Obv:** Bust of Johann VIII with arms **Rev:** Crowned double eagle **Note:** Dav.#7085.

Date	Mintage	VG	F	VF	XF	Unc
ND Rare	—	—	—	—	—	—

KM# 72 THALER
Silver **Ruler:** Johann VIII **Obv:** Helmeted, mitred and draped arms with banner behind **Note:** Dav.#7086.

Date	Mintage	VG	F	VF	XF	Unc
1680	—	575	1,150	2,300	3,950	—

KM# 88 THALER
29.3000 g., Silver, 40 mm. **Ruler:** Anton III **Obv:** Rounded shield, helmeted, mantled arms within beaded cirrcle **Obv. Legend:** ANTONIVS... **Rev:** Double-headed imperial eagle, value in orb on breast within beaded circle, crown above **Rev. Legend:** LEOPOLDVS... **Note:** Dav.#7087.

Date	Mintage	VG	F	VF	XF	Unc
1694	—	450	900	1,750	3,300	—
1695/4	—	450	900	1,750	3,300	—
1695	—	450	900	1,750	3,300	—
1696 IK	—	450	900	1,750	3,300	—

KM# 89 THALER
Silver **Ruler:** Anton III **Obv:** Bust of Anton right **Rev:** Helmeted, mitred and draped arms with banner behind **Note:** Dav.#7088.

Date	Mintage	VG	F	VF	XF	Unc
1694	—	950	1,750	3,350	6,200	—

KM# 29 2 THALER
Silver **Ruler:** Hugo XIV **Obv:** Helmeted, mitred and draped arms **Rev:** Crowned double eagle **Note:** Dav.#7083.

Date	Mintage	VG	F	VF	XF	Unc
1626 Rare	—	—	—	—	—	—

PATTERNS

Including off metal strikes

KM#	Date	Mintage	Identification	Mkt Val
Pn1	ND(1520-40)	—	1/2 Thaler. Copper. MB#3.	—
Pn2	1627	—	Thaler. Gold. KM#31	—
Pn3	1720	—	Thaler. Copper. KM#120.	2,000
Pn4	1732	—	Pfennig. Copper. KM#102	—
Pn5	1736	—	1/2 Kreuzer. Copper. KM#150	—

MUHLHAUSEN IN ALSACE

(Mühlhausen, Mulhouse)

Not to be confused with the Mühlhausen in Thüringen, this town is located in southern Alsace, 58 miles (96 km) south of Strassburg. Mühlhausen was made a free imperial city during the 14th century. The town did not exercise its right to strike coins until the early phase of the Thirty Years' War. At the conclusion of hostilities in 1648, Mühlhausen joined the Swiss Confederation, but was annexed to France in 1798.

ARMS

A millwheel, sometimes just half a millwheel and half an eagle.

FREE CITY

REGULAR COINAGE

KM# 1 RAPPEN (Pfennig)
Silver **Obv:** Half eagle and half a mill-wheel in circle within circle of pellets **Note:** Uniface hohl-type.

Date	Mintage	VG	F	VF	XF	Unc
ND(ca.1623)	—	65.00	135	275	550	—

KM# 2 RAPPEN (Pfennig)
Silver **Obv:** Half eagle and half a mill-wheel in circle within shield **Note:** Uniface. Hohl-type.

Date	Mintage	VG	F	VF	XF	Unc
(ca.1623)	—	65.00	135	275	550	—

KM# 3.1 1/2 KREUZER
Silver **Obv:** Arms as Rappen, KM#1, date **Obv. Legend:** MO. NO. MILHVSINA **Rev:** Ornate cross **Rev. Legend:** EX. VNO. OMN: NOST. SAL(VS).

Date	Mintage	VG	F	VF	XF	Unc
1622	—	65.00	135	275	575	—
1623	—	65.00	135	275	575	—

KM# 3.2 1/2 KREUZER
Silver **Obv:** Arms as Rappen, date **Obv. Legend:** MO. NO. MILHVSINA **Rev:** Ornate cross **Rev. Legend:** EX. VNO. OMN: NOST. SAL(VS). **Note:** Klippe.

Date	Mintage	VG	F	VF	XF	Unc
1623	—	—	—	—	—	—

KM# 4 KREUZER
Silver **Obv:** City arms, date divided at top **Obv. Legend:** MO. NO: MILHVSINA **Rev:** Ornate cross **Rev. Legend:** EX. VNO. OMN: NOST. SAL(VS).

Date	Mintage	VG	F	VF	XF	Unc
1623	—	200	375	700	1,350	—

KM# 5 KREUZER
Silver **Obv:** City arms **Obv. Legend:** MO. NO: MILHVSINA **Rev:** Ornate cross **Rev. Legend:** EX. VNO. OMN: NOST. SAL(VS).

Date	Mintage	VG	F	VF	XF	Unc
1623	—	200	375	700	1,350	—

KM# 6 BATZEN (4 Kreuzer)
Silver **Obv:** Shield of city arms superimposed on long cross, MONETA, etc. **Rev:** Imperial eagle, 1 in orb on breast, date below, EX VNO, etc.

Date	Mintage	VG	F	VF	XF	Unc
1623	—	400	725	1,425	2,850	—

KM# 7 DREIBATZNER (12 Kreuzer)
Silver **Obv:** Shield of city arms superimposed on long cross, MONETA, etc. **Obv. Legend:** MON—OVAMI—NA. **Rev:** Crowned Imperial Eagle with 12 in orb on breast, EX VNO, etc.

Date	Mintage	VG	F	VF	XF	Unc
1623	—	—	—	—	—	—

KM# 8 DREIBATZNER (12 Kreuzer)
Silver **Obv:** Ornate city arms, date **Obv. Legend:** MONETA ★ NOVA ★ MILHVSINIA ★ **Rev:** Crowned Imperial Eagle with value '12' below eagle, EX VNO, etc.

Date	Mintage	VG	F	VF	XF	Unc
1623	—	—	—	—	—	—

KM# 9.1 THALER
Silver **Obv:** Rappant Lion left holding city arms, MONETA, etc. **Rev:** Crowned imperial eagle **Rev. Legend:** EX VNO OMNIS NOSTRA SALVS **Note:** Dav. #5586.

Date	Mintage	VG	F	VF	XF	Unc
1623 Rare	—	—	—	—	—	—

KM# 9.2 THALER
Silver **Obv:** Rappant Lion left holding city arms, MONETA, etc. **Rev:** Crowned Imperial Eagle **Rev. Legend:** EX VNO OMNIS NOSTRA SALVS **Note:** Klippe. Dav. #5586A.

Date	Mintage	VG	F	VF	XF	Unc
1623 Rare	—	—	—	—	—	—

KM# 10.1 THALER
Silver **Obv:** Rappant Lion left holding city arms, MONETA, etc.

Rev: Crowned imperial eagle **Rev. Legend:** EX VNO OMNIS NOSTRA SAL **Note:** Dav. #5587.

Date	Mintage	VG	F	VF	XF	Unc
1623	—	750	1,250	2,250	4,000	—

KM# 10.2 THALER
Silver **Obv:** Rappant Lion left holding city arms, MONETA, etc. **Rev:** Crowned Imperial Eagle **Rev. Legend:** EX VNO OMNIS NOSTRA SAL **Note:** Klippe. Dav. #5587A.

Date	Mintage	VG	F	VF	XF	Unc
1623 Rare	—	—	—	—	—	—

KM# 11 THALER
Silver **Obv:** Ornate city arms, date in margin above, MONETA, etc. **Rev:** Crowned imperial eagle **Rev. Legend:** EX VNO OMNIS NOSTRA SALVS **Note:** Dav. #5588.

Date	Mintage	VG	F	VF	XF	Unc
1623	—	400	750	1,250	2,500	—

MUHLHAUSEN THURINGEN

The city of Mühlhausen is located 20 miles (34km) north-northwest of Gotha and is one of the oldest towns in Thuringia (Thüringen). Walls and fortifications were built during the reign of Emperor Heinrich I (918-36), who gave Mühlhausen a number of special privileges. An imperial mint was located there in the 12th and 13th centuries. After obtaining the right to mint its own coinage, Mühlhausen issued a long series dated from 1496-1767. Mühlhausen came under Prussian rule in 1802, then was dominated by Westphalia from 1807. It was returned to Prussia in 1815, by the terms of the peace which ended the Napoleonic Wars.

MINT OFFICIALS' INITIALS

Initial	Date	Name
	1616	Lubert Hausmann of Cassel
	1618-20	Andreas Weber
	1618-19	Zacharias Wolf, warden
	1621	Jacob Wossner of Munden
	1621-22	Heinrich Schwellenburg
	1626-72	Henning Schluter of Zellerfeld
	1665	Hieronymus Hollenbach, die-cutter
IZW and/or X	1676	Julius Zacharias Wefer (Weber)
	1676	Henning Christoph Meyer, warden

NOTE: Coinage of 1665 minted in Zellerfeld, Brunswick.

ARMS

Archaic type: Upper half of eagle above mill-rind.

Newer type: Eagle with two mill-rinds on wings.

NOTE: there are some variations on the above types found on some coins.

REFERENCES

B = Gerd Behr, "Übersicht über die Münzen der Stadt Mühlhausen von 1523 bis 1767," **IV. Bezirksmünzausstellung**, Erfurt, 1975, p. 24-31.

Sch = Wolfgang Schulten, **Deutsche Münzen aus der Zeit Karls V**, Frankfurt am Main, 1974.

S = Hugo Frhr. Von Saurma-Jeltsch, **Die Saurmasche Münzsammlung deutscher, schweizerischer und polnischer Gepräge von etwa dem Beginn der Groschenzeit bis zur Kipperperiode,** Berlin, 1892.

FREE CITY

REGULAR COINAGE

KM# 15 PFENNINGE
Copper **Obv:** Muhlhausen eagle, date divided by tail **Note:** Uniface. Kipper Pfennige.

Date	Mintage	VG	F	VF	XF	Unc
(16)Z1	—	50.00	100	200	400	—

KM# 16 3 PFENNINGE (Dreier)
Copper **Obv:** Muhlhausen eagle, head divides 3 - , tail divides date **Note:** Kipper 3 Pfenninge. Uniface. Varieties exist.

Date	Mintage	VG	F	VF	XF	Unc
(16)21	—	85.00	175	350	600	1,000
(16)22	19,000	30.00	65.00	125	250	500

KM# 5 1/24 THALER (Groschen)
Silver **Obv:** Muhlhausen eagle **Obv. Legend:** MON. NO. IM. CI. MULHUS **Rev:** Imperial orb with Z4, titles of Matthias, date divided at top

Date	Mintage	VG	F	VF	XF	Unc
1619	—	—	—	—	—	—

KM# 26 2/3 THALER (Gulden)
Silver **Obv:** Helmeted shield **Rev. Legend:** CIVIT... **Note:** Dav. #688.

Date	Mintage	VG	F	VF	XF	Unc
1676 IZW	—	450	925	1,650	—	—

KM# 6 THALER
Silver **Obv:** Shield with crowned eagle arms, 2 mill-rinds on wings, ornate helmet above **Obv. Legend:** MON: NOV: CIV: — IMP: MULHUS. **Rev:** Crowned imperial eagle, orb on breast, titles of Matthias, date divided by crown at top **Note:** Dav. #5584.

Date	Mintage	VG	F	VF	XF	Unc
1619 Rare	—	—	—	—	—	—

Note: Fritz Rudolf Künker Münzenhandlung Auction 113, 6-06, VF realized approximately $10,115

KM# 25 THALER
Silver **Rev:** Crowned imperial eagle, orb with Z4, titles of Leopold **Note:** Dav. #5585.

Date	Mintage	VG	F	VF	XF	Unc
1665	500	700	1,350	2,850	5,500	—

SIEGE COINAGE

KM# 7 DUCAT
3.5000 g., 0.9860 Gold 0.1109 oz. AGW **Obv:** Legend, Muhlhausen eagle **Obv. Legend:** MON: NOV: CIVI - IMP : MULHUS **Rev:** Crowned imperial eagle, orb on breast, date divided at top, titles of Matthias

Date	Mintage	VG	F	VF	XF	Unc
1619 Rare	—	—	—	—	—	—

MUNSTER

St. Ludger founded the bishopric near the end of the 8th or the beginning of the 9th century in Westphalia. The town of Münster, which means "monastery," grew up around the ecclesiastical establishment (which see). The earliest anonymous coins of the bishopric date from the late 11th century and a long series of issues in the name of the bishops followed over the centuries. In 1802, Münster was secularized and divided among several principalities. Those were soon mediatized and part of the territory went to Hannover. Münster belonged to the Duchy of Berg from 1806 until 1810, then to France until 1814, when it was acquired by Prussia.

During the 16th and 17th centuries treasury tokens, mostly counterstamped with the arms or initials of the current treasurer were issued. These were replaced in the middle of the 17th century by Cathedral coins, showing St. Paul with a sword. They last appeared at the end of the 18th century.

RULERS

Ernst, Herzog von Bayern, 1585-1612
Ferdinand, Herzog von Bayern, 1612-1650
Christof Bernhard von Galen, 1650-1678
Ferdinand von Fürstenberg, 1678-1683
Maximilian Heinrich von Bayern, 1683-1688
Friedrich Christian von Plettenberg, 1688-1706

MINT OFFICIALS' INITIALS & PRIVY MARKS

Initials or Privy Mark	Date	Name
EK	1638-56	Englebert Kettler
GS	Ca.1683-88	Gottfried Storp
HLO, HO	1696-1700, 1704, 1706	Heinrich Lorenz Odendahl
IL	1664-80	Johann Longerich
IO/JO	1692-96	Johann Odendahl
(a) – bird	1638-1656	Engelbert Kettler
(b) – flower		?
(c) - rosette		?

ARMS

Horizontal bar, usually shaded by cross-hatching

REFERENCES

G = Hermann Grote, "Die Münsterschen Münzen des Mittelalters", **Münzstudien** 1 (1855), pp. 177-330, 346-54; 2 (1861), pp. 984-91.

Sch = Wolfgang Schulten, **Deutsche Münzen aus der Zeit Karls V**, Frankfurt am Main, 1974.

S = Hugo Frhr. Von Saurma-Jeltsch, **Die Saurmasche Münzsammlung deutscher, schweizerischer und polnischer Gepräge von etwa dem Beginn der Groschenzeit bis zur Kipperperiode,** Berlin, 1892.

BISHOPRIC

REGULAR COINAGE

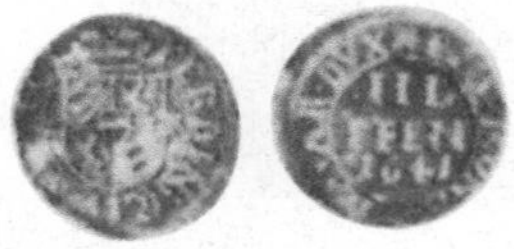

KM# 36 3 PFENNIG (1/112 Thaler)
Silver **Obv:** Crowned 4-fold arms with central shield of Munster, titles of Ferdinand, (112) in legend at bottom **Rev:** Titles in legend **Rev. Inscription:** III / PFEN / date **Note:** Varieties exist.

Date	Mintage	VG	F	VF	XF	Unc
1641 EK	—	20.00	40.00	75.00	155	—
1645 EK	—	20.00	40.00	75.00	155	—
1646 EK	—	20.00	40.00	75.00	155	—

KM# 40 3 PFENNIG (1/112 Thaler)
Silver **Obv:** Crowned 4-fold arms, titles of Ferdinand, (112) in legend at bottom **Rev:** Bust of St. Paul, date also in legend **Rev. Inscription:** III / PFEN / date

Date	Mintage	VG	F	VF	XF	Unc
1643 EK	—	25.00	50.00	100	210	—

KM# 44 3 PFENNIG (1/112 Thaler)
Silver **Rev:** Inscription, titles in legend **Rev. Inscription:** III / PFEN / date

Date	Mintage	VG	F	VF	XF	Unc
1647	—	20.00	40.00	75.00	155	—
1648	—	20.00	40.00	75.00	155	—

KM# 58 3 PFENNIG (1/112 Thaler)
Silver **Obv:** 4-fold arms with central shield of Galen (3 wolf traps), titles of Christoph Bernhard, (112) in legend at bottom **Rev:** Inscription, titles in legend **Rev. Inscription:** III / PFEN / date **Note:** Varieties exist.

Date	Mintage	VG	F	VF	XF	Unc
1652	—	20.00	40.00	75.00	155	—
1653	—	20.00	40.00	75.00	155	—
1655	—	20.00	40.00	75.00	155	—

KM# 37 4 PFENNIG (1/84 Thaler)
Silver **Obv:** Crowned 4-fold arms, titles of Ferdinand, (80) in legend at bottom **Rev:** Inscription, titles in legend **Rev. Inscription:** IIII / PFEN / date

Date	Mintage	VG	F	VF	XF	Unc
1641 EK	—	20.00	45.00	90.00	180	—

KM# 41 4 PFENNIG (1/84 Thaler)
Silver **Rev:** Value: 4

Date	Mintage	VG	F	VF	XF	Unc
1643 EK	—	20.00	45.00	90.00	180	—

KM# 25 6 PFENNIG (1/56 Thaler)
Silver **Obv:** Crowned 4-fold arms in rhombus-form, titles of Ferdinand in legend, (56) in legend at bottom **Rev:** Inscription, titles in legend **Rev. Inscription:** VI / PFEN / date **Note:** Varieties exist.

Date	Mintage	VG	F	VF	XF	Unc
1639 EK	—	20.00	35.00	75.00	155	—
1641 EK	—	20.00	35.00	75.00	155	—
1642 EK	—	20.00	35.00	75.00	155	—
1643 EK	—	20.00	35.00	75.00	155	—
1645 EK	—	20.00	35.00	75.00	155	—
1646 EK	—	20.00	35.00	75.00	155	—
1648 EK	—	20.00	35.00	75.00	155	—

KM# 59 6 PFENNIG (1/56 Thaler)
Silver **Obv:** 4-fold arms with central shield of Galen (3 wolf traps), titles of Christoph Bernhard, (56) in legend at bottom **Rev. Inscription:** VI / PFEN(N) / date **Note:** Varieties exist.

Date	Mintage	VG	F	VF	XF	Unc
1652	—	20.00	40.00	75.00	155	—
1654	—	20.00	40.00	75.00	155	—
1655	—	20.00	40.00	75.00	155	—

KM# 117 6 PFENNIG (1/56 Thaler)
Silver **Obv:** Crowned 6-fold arms with central shield of Plettenberg (line down center of shield), titles of Friedrich Christian in legend **Rev:** Inscription, legend, (56) at bottom **Rev. Legend:** EPISCOPVS. MONASTERIENS **Rev. Inscription:** VI / PFEN / date **Note:** Varieties exist.

Date	Mintage	VG	F	VF	XF	Unc
1695 JO	—	15.00	30.00	60.00	120	—
1696 HO	—	15.00	30.00	60.00	120	—

KM# 30 SCHILLING (1/28 Thaler)
Silver **Obv:** Crowned 4-fold arms iwth central shield of Munster, titles of Ferdinand, (28) in legend at bottom **Rev:** 1/2-length bust of St. Paul, below 1.SCHIL / date **Note:** Varieties exist.

Date	Mintage	VG	F	VF	XF	Unc
1640 (a)	—	25.00	50.00	100	200	—
1641 (a)	—	25.00	50.00	100	200	—
1647 (a)	—	25.00	50.00	100	200	—

KM# 31 SCHILLING (1/28 Thaler)
Silver **Ruler:** Ferdinand **Rev:** Date in legend **Note:** Varieties exist.

Date	Mintage	VG	F	VF	XF	Unc
1640 EK	—	25.00	50.00	100	200	—
1642 EK	—	25.00	50.00	100	200	—
1643 EK	—	25.00	50.00	100	200	—
1645 EK	—	25.00	50.00	100	200	—
1646 EK	—	25.00	50.00	100	200	—
1647 EK	—	25.00	50.00	100	200	—
1648 EK	—	25.00	50.00	100	200	—

KM# 55 SCHILLING (1/28 Thaler)
Silver **Obv:** Cathedral arms with 1/2-length bust of St. Paul divides date **Rev:** Crowned imperial eagle, orb on breast, titles of Ferdinand III, (28) in legend at bottom **Note:** Sede vacante issue.

Date	Mintage	VG	F	VF	XF	Unc
1650	—	60.00	115	210	425	—

KM# 60 SCHILLING (1/28 Thaler)
Silver **Obv:** Crowned 4-fold arms with central shield of Galen arms, titles of Christoph Bernhard, (28) in legend at bottom **Rev:** Similar to KM#30 **Note:** Varieties exist.

Date	Mintage	VG	F	VF	XF	Unc
1652 EK	—	20.00	40.00	75.00	155	—
1653 EK	—	20.00	40.00	75.00	155	—
1654 EK	—	20.00	40.00	75.00	155	—

KM# 66 SCHILLING (1/28 Thaler)
Silver **Rev:** Date divided by head of St. Paul

Date	Mintage	VG	F	VF	XF	Unc
1655 EK	—	20.00	40.00	75.00	155	—

KM# 118 SCHILLING (1/28 Thaler)
Silver **Obv:** Crowned 6-fold arms with central shield of Plettenberg, titles of Friedrich Christian, (28) in legend at bottom

Date	Mintage	VG	F	VF	XF	Unc
1695 JO	—	16.00	35.00	70.00	145	—
1696 HO	—	16.00	35.00	70.00	145	—
1697 HO	—	16.00	35.00	70.00	145	—

KM# 32 2 SCHILLING (1/14 Thaler)
Silver **Obv:** Crowned 4-fold arms with central shield of Munster, titles of Ferdinand, (14) in legend at bottom **Rev:** Full-length figure of St. Paul with sword, date in legend

Date	Mintage	VG	F	VF	XF	Unc
1640 (a)	—	35.00	75.00	150	300	—

KM# 38 2 SCHILLING (1/14 Thaler)
Silver **Ruler:** Ferdinand **Rev:** Date divided by figure of saint **Note:** Varieties exist.

Date	Mintage	VG	F	VF	XF	Unc
1640 (a)	—	35.00	75.00	150	300	—
1641 (a)	—	35.00	75.00	150	300	—
1643 (a)	—	35.00	75.00	150	300	—
1645 (a)	—	35.00	75.00	150	300	—
1646 (a)	—	35.00	75.00	150	300	—
1647 (a)	—	35.00	75.00	150	300	—
1648	—	35.00	75.00	150	300	—

KM# 46 2 SCHILLING (1/14 Thaler)
Silver **Rev:** Date divided at top

Date	Mintage	VG	F	VF	XF	Unc
1648	—	35.00	75.00	150	300	—

KM# 61 2 SCHILLING (1/14 Thaler)
Silver **Obv:** Central shield of Galen arms, titles of Christoph Bernhard **Note:** Varieties exist.

Date	Mintage	VG	F	VF	XF	Unc
1652 (a)	—	35.00	75.00	150	300	—
1654 (a)	—	35.00	75.00	150	300	—
1655 (a)	—	35.00	75.00	150	300	—
1678 IL	—	35.00	75.00	150	300	—

KM# 120 2 SCHILLING (1/14 Thaler)
Silver **Obv:** Crowned 6-fold arms with central shield of Plettenberg, titles of Friedrich Christian

Date	Mintage	VG	F	VF	XF	Unc
1696 HLO	—	—	—	—	—	—

KM# 100 12 MARIENGROSCHEN (1/2 Gulden)
Silver **Obv:** Crowned oval 6-fold arms with central shield of Plettenberg, titles of Friedrich Christian **Rev:** Inscription, titles in legend **Rev. Inscription:** XII / MARIEN / GROS / date. **Note:** Similar to 24 Mariengroschen, KM#101. Varieties exist.

Date	Mintage	VG	F	VF	XF	Unc
1692 JO	—	35.00	75.00	150	300	—
1693 JO	—	35.00	75.00	150	300	—
1694 JO	—	35.00	75.00	150	300	—

KM# 102 24 MARIENGROSCHEN (Gulden)
Silver **Rev:** ...GROSCH

Date	Mintage	VG	F	VF	XF	Unc
1692 IO	—	50.00	100	210	425	—

KM# 101 24 MARIENGROSCHEN (Gulden)
Silver **Obv:** Crowned oval 6-fold arms with central shield of Plettenberg, titles of Friedrich Christian **Rev:** Inscription, titles in legend **Rev. Inscription:** XXIIII / MARIEN / GROS / date **Note:** Varieties exist.

Date	Mintage	VG	F	VF	XF	Unc
1692 JO	—	50.00	100	210	425	—
1693 JO	—	50.00	100	210	425	—
1694 JO	—	50.00	100	210	425	—

KM# 111 24 MARIENGROSCHEN (Gulden)
Silver **Rev:** ...GROSCH **Note:** Varieties exist.

Date	Mintage	VG	F	VF	XF	Unc
1694 JO	—	45.00	90.00	180	360	—
1695 JO	—	45.00	90.00	180	360	—

KM# 110 24 MARIENGROSCHEN (Gulden)
Silver **Obv:** Shield of arms squared at top, round at bottom (Spanish type)

Date	Mintage	VG	F	VF	XF	Unc
1694 JO	—	45.00	90.00	180	360	—

KM# 85 1/4 GULDEN (4 Schilling)
Silver **Obv:** Crowned 8-fold arms with central shield of Galen arms, titles of Christoph Bernhard, date **Rev:** Inscription, 6/EIN R. TR. below in laurel wreath **Rev. Inscription:** 1/4 / REICHS / GVLDEN / IIII SCHIL / VIII PFENN / MVNST / date

Date	Mintage	VG	F	VF	XF	Unc
1678 IL	—	—	—	—	—	—

KM# 86 1/4 GULDEN (4 Schilling)
Silver **Obv:** Crowned 8-fold arms with central shield of Galen arms, titles of Christoph Bernhard, date **Rev:** Inscription, 3/EIN R. TR. below in laurel wreath **Rev. Inscription:** 1/2 / REICHS / GVLDEN / VIIII SCHIL / IIII PFENNI

Date	Mintage	VG	F	VF	XF	Unc
1678 IL	—	—	—	—	—	—

KM# 87 GULDEN (18 Schilling)
Silver **Obv:** Crowned 8-fold arms with central shield of Galen arms, titles of Christoph Bernhard, date **Rev:** Inscription, 1-1/2/EIN-RTLR below **Rev. Inscription:** I / REICHS / GVLDEN / XVIII SCHIL / VIII PFENNI / MVNST / date

Date	Mintage	VG	F	VF	XF	Unc
1678	—	—	—	—	—	—

KM# 103 1/48 THALER (Halbgroschen)
Silver **Obv:** Crowned FC monogram **Rev:** Inscription, legend, date **Rev. Legend:** F.M.L. MVNTZ **Rev. Inscription:** 48 / I / REICHS / TH **Note:** Varieties exist.

Date	Mintage	VG	F	VF	XF	Unc
1692 JO	—	13.00	27.00	50.00	100	—

KM# 88 1/24 THALER (Groschen)
Silver **Obv:** Crowned 8-fold arms with central shield of Galen arms, titles of Christoph Bernhard **Rev:** Inscription, date in legend **Rev. Inscription:** 24 / I / REICHS / THAL., FVRST?, **Note:** Varieties exist.

Date	Mintage	VG	F	VF	XF	Unc
1678 IL	—	20.00	45.00	90.00	185	—

KM# 104 1/24 THALER (Groschen)
Silver **Obv:** Crowned oval 6-fold arms with central shield of Plettenberg, titles of Friedrich Christian **Rev:** FVRST..., date in legend **Rev. Inscription:** 24 / I / REICHS / THAL. **Note:** Varieties exist.

Date	Mintage	VG	F	VF	XF	Unc
1692 IO	—	16.00	35.00	75.00	155	—
1693 IO	—	16.00	35.00	75.00	155	—

KM# 89 1/16 THALER
Silver **Obv:** Crowned 8-fold arms with central shield of Galen arms divide date **Rev:** 1/2-length bust of St. Paul with sword and book, below XVI/R. tr.

Date	Mintage	VG	F	VF	XF	Unc
1678 IL	—	33.00	65.00	135	275	—

KM# 105 1/12 THALER (Doppelgroschen)
Silver **Obv:** Crowned 6-fold arms with central shield of Plettenberg arms, titles of Friedrich Christian **Rev:** Legend, date, value **Rev. Legend:** FVRSTL? **Rev. Inscription:** 12 / EINEN / REICHS / THAL **Note:** Varieties exist.

Date	Mintage	VG	F	VF	XF	Unc
1692 IO	—	27.00	55.00	110	220	—
1692 JO	—	27.00	55.00	110	220	—
1693 IO	—	27.00	55.00	110	220	—
1693 JO	—	27.00	55.00	110	220	—
1695 IO	—	27.00	55.00	110	220	—
1695 JO	—	27.00	55.00	110	220	—
1696 JO	—	27.00	55.00	110	220	—

KM# 90 1/8 THALER (Blamuser)
Silver **Obv:** Crowned 8-fold arms with central shield of Galen arms divides date **Rev:** 1/2-length bust of St. Paul with sword and book, VIII/R. tr. below **Note:** Varieties exist.

Date	Mintage	VG	F	VF	XF	Unc
1678 IL	—	65.00	120	210	425	—

KM# 5 1/4 THALER
Silver **Obv:** Crowned 4-fold arms with central shield of Munster, titles of Ferdinand **Rev:** Full-length figure of St. Paul divides date **Note:** Varieties exist.

Date	Mintage	VG	F	VF	XF	Unc
1633	—	—	—	—	—	—
1637	—	—	—	—	—	—

KM# 6 1/2 THALER
Silver **Obv:** Crowned 4-fold arms with central shiedl of Munster, titles of Ferdinand **Rev:** Full-length figure of St. Paul divides date

Date	Mintage	VG	F	VF	XF	Unc
1633	—	—	—	—	—	—
1635 (b)	—	—	—	—	—	—

KM# 56 1/2 THALER
Silver **Obv:** Cathedral arms with 1/2-length bust of St. Paul divides date **Rev:** Full-length figure of Ferdinand III with sword and orb

Date	Mintage	VG	F	VF	XF	Unc
1650	—	—	—	—	—	—

KM# 106 2/3 THALER (Gulden)
Silver **Obv:** 1/2-length bust of St. Paul with sword and book, value 2/3 below **Rev:** Crowned 6-fold arms with central shield of Plettenberg divide date, titles of Friedrich Christian

Date	Mintage	VG	F	VF	XF	Unc
1692 IO	—	—	—	—	—	—

KM# 7 THALER
Silver **Obv:** Mitered arms, legend **Obv. Legend:** FERDINANDVS... **Rev:** St. Paul standing dividing date, mint mark between feet **Note:** Dav. #5589.

Date	Mintage	VG	F	VF	XF	Unc
1633 (c) Rare	—	—	—	—	—	—

KM# 8 THALER
Silver **Obv:** Crowned arms **Rev:** St. Paul **Note:** Dav. #5591.

Date	Mintage	VG	F	VF	XF	Unc
1633	—	275	550	950	1,900	—
1633 (b)	—	275	550	950	1,900	—
1634 (b)	—	275	550	950	1,900	—
1635 (b)	—	275	550	950	1,900	—
1635	—	275	550	950	1,900	—
1635 (a)	—	275	550	950	1,900	—
1636 (a)	—	275	550	950	1,900	—
1637 (a)	—	275	550	950	1,900	—
1638 (a)	—	275	550	950	1,900	—
1639 (a)	—	275	550	950	1,900	—
1640 (a)	—	275	550	950	1,900	—
1643 (a)	—	275	550	950	1,900	—
1645 (a)	—	275	550	950	1,900	—
1646 (a)	—	275	550	950	1,900	—

KM# 11 THALER
Silver **Note:** Klippe. Dav. #5591A.

Date	Mintage	VG	F	VF	XF	Unc
1634 (b) Rare	—	—	—	—	—	—

KM# 12 THALER
Silver **Rev:** St. Paul above city view, date below **Note:** Dav. #5593.

Date	Mintage	VG	F	VF	XF	Unc
1638 EK	—	1,750	3,500	6,500	10,500	—
1647 EK	—	—	—	—	—	—

KM# 13 THALER

Silver **Obv:** St. Paul in cloud above city view, date below **Rev:** Adoration of the Magi **Note:** Dav. #5595.

Date	Mintage	VG	F	VF	XF	Unc
1638 EK	—	—	—	—	—	—
1647 EK	—	800	1,600	3,250	6,000	—

KM# 14 THALER

Silver **Obv:** Adoration of the Magi **Rev:** Circumcision of Jesus **Note:** Dav. #5596.

Date	Mintage	VG	F	VF	XF	Unc
ND(1647) EK	—	200	350	650	1,750	3,000

KM# 47 THALER

Silver **Subject:** Peace of Westphalia **Obv:** 1/2-length figure of St. Paul with sword and book, titles of Emperor Ferdinand III and Bishop Ferdinand I **Obv. Inscription:** BONVM CERTAMEN / CERTABE. FIDEM / SERVAVI **Rev:** Two arms from clouds at left and right, shaking hands and clasping caduceus and olive branches, 5-line inscription with date **Note:** Broad flan.

Date	Mintage	VG	F	VF	XF	Unc
1648	—	190	375	700	1,250	—

KM# 57 THALER

Silver **Note:** Sede vacante. Dav. #5597.

Date	Mintage	VG	F	VF	XF	Unc
1650 EK	—	425	1,200	2,400	6,000	—
1651 EK	—	—	—	—	—	—

KM# 62 THALER

Silver **Rev:** St. Paul **Note:** Dav. #5599.

Date	Mintage	VG	F	VF	XF	Unc
1652 (a)	—	200	450	1,000	2,000	—
1653 (a)	—	250	550	1,150	2,250	—
1654 (a)	—	250	550	1,150	2,250	—

KM# 67 THALER

Silver **Obv:** Helmeted arms **Rev:** St. Paul standing, date divided above in legend **Note:** Dav. #5600.

Date	Mintage	VG	F	VF	XF	Unc
1659	—	725	1,450	3,250	6,500	—

KM# 68 THALER

Silver **Rev:** Crucifix dividing date, inner legend **Note:** Dav. #5601.

Date	Mintage	VG	F	VF	XF	Unc
1659	—	300	650	1,350	2,800	—

KM# 76 THALER

Silver **Rev:** Oval arms **Note:** Dav. #5603A.

Date	Mintage	VG	F	VF	XF	Unc
1661	—	300	600	1,300	2,250	—

KM# 77 THALER

Silver **Obv:** Different city view **Rev:** Elaborate frame for arms **Note:** Size varies: 39-40mm. Dav. #5604.

Date	Mintage	VG	F	VF	XF	Unc
1661	—	325	650	130	2,600	5,500

KM# 75 THALER

Silver **Rev:** Bust of St. Paul above city view **Note:** Broad flan. Varieties exist. Dav. #5603.

Date	Mintage	VG	F	VF	XF	Unc
MDCLXI (1661)	—	120	240	600	1,150	—

KM# 91 THALER

Silver **Subject:** Death of the Bishop **Rev:** 11-line inscription **Note:** Broad flan. Dav. #5605.

Date	Mintage	VG	F	VF	XF	Unc
MDCLXXVIII (1678)	—	325	650	1,300	2,650	—

KM# 95 THALER

Silver **Obv:** Leopold **Note:** Sede vacante. Dav. #5607.

Date	Mintage	VG	F	VF	XF	Unc
1683 GS	—	600	1,200	2,600	4,250	—

KM# 97 THALER

Silver **Obv:** Different bust of Leopold right **Rev:** Saint with sword and book dividing date **Note:** Dav. #5608. Sede vacante. Varieties exist.

Date	Mintage	VG	F	VF	XF	Unc
1688 GS	—	300	600	1,250	3,250	6,000

KM# 107 THALER

Silver **Obv:** Bust of Friedrich Christian right **Rev:** Crowned oval arms dividing I-O, date in legend above **Note:** Dav. #5609.

Date	Mintage	VG	F	VF	XF	Unc
1693 IO Rare	—	—	—	—	—	—

Note: Künker Auction 180, 1-11, XF/Unc realized approximately $19,855.

KM# 108 THALER

Silver **Rev:** Helmeted arms, I-O at sides, date in legend **Note:** Dav. #5610.

Date	Mintage	VG	F	VF	XF	Unc
1693 JO	—	1,250	3,600	7,200	12,500	—
1695 JO	—	1,250	3,600	7,200	12,500	—

KM# 112 THALER

Silver **Rev:** Helmeted square arms, J-O at sides **Note:** Dav. #5611.

Date	Mintage	VG	F	VF	XF	Unc
1694 JO	—	1,250	3,600	7,200	12,500	—

KM# 113 THALER

Silver **Rev:** Crowned arms in palm branches, J-O at sides **Note:** Dav. #5612.

Date	Mintage	VG	F	VF	XF	Unc
1694 JO	—	1,250	3,600	7,200	12,500	—

KM# 114 THALER

Silver **Rev:** Date divided at top **Note:** Dav. #5613.

Date	Mintage	VG	F	VF	XF	Unc
1694	—	1,250	3,600	7,200	12,500	—

KM# 121 THALER

Silver **Obv. Legend:** FRIDERICVS. CHRISTIANVS... **Rev:** Crowned oval arms in palm branches, date above, J-O at sides **Note:** Dav. #5614.

Date	Mintage	VG	F	VF	XF	Unc
1696 JO	—	—	2,600	4,300	7,600	12,000

KM# 122 THALER

Silver **Obv. Legend:** FRIDER: CHRISTI:... **Note:** Dav. #5615.

Date	Mintage	VG	F	VF	XF	Unc
1696	—	—	1,550	3,250	6,500	11,000
1696 HLO	—	—	1,550	3,250	6,500	11,000

KM# 123 THALER

Silver **Note:** Dav. #5616.

Date	Mintage	VG	F	VF	XF	Unc
1697 HLO	—	—	1,550	3,250	6,500	11,000
1698 HLO	—	—	1,550	3,250	6,500	11,000

KM# 124 THALER

Silver **Rev:** Date below arms diviided by mintmaster's initials

Date	Mintage	VG	F	VF	XF	Unc
1699 IO	—	—	1,550	3,250	6,500	11,000

KM# 49 1-1/4 THALER (Shau)

35.8800 g., Silver, 51 mm. **Ruler:** Ferdinand **Subject:** Peace of Westphalia **Obv:** Two angels above city view **Obv. Legend:** HINC • TOTI • PAX • INSONAT • ORBI **Obv. Inscription:** MONASTERIVM / WESTPHA / 1648 **Rev:** Clasped hands in front of two crossed cornucopiae, date in chronogram **Rev. Legend:** C • SARIS ET. REGVM. IVNXIT. PAX. AVREA. DEXTER. AS. 24. 8bris. **Note:** Prev. X#M11.

Date	Mintage	F	VF	XF	Unc	BU
1648 EK	—	—	1,050	1,500	—	—

KM# 15 1-1/4 THALER

Silver **Obv:** Crowned arms **Rev:** St. Paul above city view **Note:** Klippe. Dav. #A5592.

Date	Mintage	VG	F	VF	XF	Unc
1638 EK Rare	—	—	—	—	—	—
1647 EK Rare	—	—	—	—	—	—

KM# 48 1-1/4 THALER

Silver **Ruler:** Ferdinand **Subject:** Peace of Westphalia **Obv:** 1/2-length figure of St. Paul with sword and book, titles of Emperor Ferdinand III and Bishop Ferdinand I **Obv. Inscription:** BONVM CERTAMEN / CERTAVI. FIDEN / SERVAVI **Rev:** Two arms from clouds at left and right, clasped hands and holding caduceus and olive branches, 5-line inscription with date

Date	Mintage	VG	F	VF	XF	Unc
1648 Rare	—	—	—	—	—	—

KM# 17 1-1/2 THALER

Silver **Obv:** Crowned oval shield arms **Rev:** St. Paul above city view, date below **Note:** Klippe. Similar to 1 Thaler, KM#12.

Date	Mintage	VG	F	VF	XF	Unc
1638 EK Rare	—	—	—	—	—	—

KM# 16 1-1/2 THALER

Silver **Obv:** St. Paul in cloud above city view, date below **Rev:** Adoration of the Magi **Note:** Klippe. Similar to 1 Thaler, KM#13. Dav. #A5594.

Date	Mintage	VG	F	VF	XF	Unc
1638 EK Rare	—	—	—	—	—	—

KM# 9 2 THALER

Silver **Obv:** Crowned oval arms **Rev:** St. Paul above city view, date below **Note:** Similar to 1 Thaler, KM#12. Dav. #5590.

Date	Mintage	VG	F	VF	XF	Unc
1633 Rare	—	—	—	—	—	—
1633 (b) Rare	—	—	—	—	—	—
1634 (b) Rare	—	—	—	—	—	—
1636 (a) Rare	—	—	—	—	—	—
1637 (a) Rare	—	—	—	—	—	—
1639 (a) Rare	—	—	—	—	—	—

KM# 20 2 THALER

Silver **Obv:** St. Paul in cloud above city view, date below **Rev:** Adoration of the Magi **Note:** Similar to 1 Thaler, KM#13. Dav. #5594.

Date	Mintage	VG	F	VF	XF	Unc
1638 EK Rare	—	—	—	—	—	—
1647 EK	—	—	—	—	—	—

Note: Reported, not confirmed

KM# 18 2 THALER

Silver **Obv:** Crowned arms **Rev:** St. Paul above city view **Note:** Dav. #B5592.

Date	Mintage	VG	F	VF	XF	Unc
1638 EK Rare	—	—	—	—	—	—
1647 EK Rare	—	—	—	—	—	—

KM# 19 2 THALER

Silver **Note:** Klippe. Dav. #C5592.

Date	Mintage	VG	F	VF	XF	Unc
1638 EK Rare	—	—	—	—	—	—
1647 EK Rare	—	—	—	—	—	—

KM# 63 2 THALER

Silver **Obv:** Standing St. Paul facing divides date **Rev:** Arms **Note:** Similar to 1 Thaler, KM#62. Dav. #5598.

Date	Mintage	VG	F	VF	XF	Unc
1652 (a) Rare	—	—	—	—	—	—
1653 Rare	—	—	—	—	—	—
1654 Rare	—	—	—	—	—	—

KM# 69 2 THALER

Silver **Obv:** Helmeted arms **Rev:** Crucifix dividing date, inner legend **Note:** Similar to 1 Thaler, KM#68. Dav. #A5601.

Date	Mintage	VG	F	VF	XF	Unc
1659 Rare	—	—	—	—	—	—

KM# 79 2 THALER

Silver **Rev:** Oval arms

Date	Mintage	VG	F	VF	XF	Unc
1661	—	650	1,150	2,100	3,350	—

KM# 78 2 THALER

Silver **Note:** Broad flan. Dav. #5602.

Date	Mintage	VG	F	VF	XF	Unc
MDCLXI (1661)	—	1,000	2,000	3,950	6,600	—

KM# 96 2 THALER

Silver **Note:** Sede vacante. Similar to 1 Thaler, KM#95. Dav. #5606.

Date	Mintage	VG	F	VF	XF	Unc
1683 GS Rare	—	—	—	—	—	—

KM# 115 2 THALER

Silver **Obv:** Bust right **Rev:** Crowned arms in palm branches **Note:** Dav. #A5612.

Date	Mintage	VG	F	VF	XF	Unc
1694 JO Rare	—	—	—	—	—	—

KM# 29 2-1/2 THALER

72.8600 g., Silver **Ruler:** Ferdinand **Obv:** Crowned arms **Rev:** St. Paul above city view **Note:** Klippe. Same as Dav. 5592. Illustration reduced.

Date	Mintage	VG	F	VF	XF	Unc
1638 EK Rare	—	—	—	—	—	—

Note: Fritz Rudolf Künker Münzenhandlung Auction 140, 6-08, VF realized approximately $28,685; Fritz Rudolf Künker Münzenhandlung Auction 84, 6-03, VF realized approximately $14,615

KM# 21 3 THALER

Silver **Obv:** Crowned arms **Rev:** St. Paul above city view **Note:** Dav. #D5592.

Date	Mintage	VG	F	VF	XF	Unc
1638 EK Rare	—	—	—	—	—	—

KM# 22 3 THALER

Silver **Note:** Klippe. Dav. #5592.

Date	Mintage	VG	F	VF	XF	Unc
1638 EK Rare	—	—	—	—	—	—

KM# 116 3 THALER

Silver **Note:** Dav. #LS364. Illustration reduced.

Date	Mintage	VG	F	VF	XF	Unc
1694 JO Rare	—	—	—	—	—	—

Note: Spink Taisei Zurich Milas sale 4-92 XF realized $12,230

TRADE COINAGE

KM# 10 DUCAT

3.5000 g., 0.9860 Gold 0.1109 oz. AGW **Obv:** Crowned arms **Rev:** St. Paul standing

Date	Mintage	VG	F	VF	XF	Unc
1633	—	1,350	2,700	5,250	9,500	—
1634	—	1,350	2,700	5,250	9,500	—
1635	—	1,350	2,700	5,250	9,500	—
1636	—	1,350	2,700	5,250	9,500	—
1637	—	1,350	2,700	5,250	9,500	—

KM# 23 DUCAT

3.5000 g., 0.9860 Gold 0.1109 oz. AGW

Date	Mintage	VG	F	VF	XF	Unc
1638	—	900	1,600	3,900	6,500	—
1640	—	900	1,600	3,900	6,500	—
1641	—	900	1,600	3,900	6,500	—

KM# 24 DUCAT

3.5000 g., 0.9860 Gold 0.1109 oz. AGW **Obv:** Crowned oval 4-fold arms with central shield of Munster **Rev:** 5-line inscription with date divided in first line, in wreath

Date	Mintage	VG	F	VF	XF	Unc
1638	—	975	1,750	4,200	6,750	—
1639	—	975	1,750	4,200	6,750	—

KM# 26 DUCAT

3.5000 g., 0.9860 Gold 0.1109 oz. AGW **Note:** Klippe.

Date	Mintage	VG	F	VF	XF	Unc
1639 Rare	—	—	—	—	—	—

KM# 33 DUCAT

3.5000 g., 0.9860 Gold 0.1109 oz. AGW **Rev:** Date in last of four lines

Date	Mintage	VG	F	VF	XF	Unc
1640	—	900	1,600	3,900	6,500	—
1641	—	900	1,600	3,900	6,500	—
1647	—	900	1,600	3,900	6,500	—

KM# 64 DUCAT

3.5000 g., 0.9860 Gold 0.1109 oz. AGW **Obv:** Crowned arms **Rev:** Value in branches

Date	Mintage	VG	F	VF	XF	Unc
1652	—	1,050	2,300	4,400	8,000	—
1665	—	1,050	2,300	4,400	8,000	—

KM# 65 DUCAT

3.5000 g., 0.9860 Gold 0.1109 oz. AGW **Note:** Klippe.

Date	Mintage	VG	F	VF	XF	Unc
1652 Rare	—	—	—	—	—	—

KM# 43 DUCAT

3.5000 g., 0.9860 Gold 0.1109 oz. AGW **Obv:** Madonna and child **Rev:** Crowned arms

Date	Mintage	VG	F	VF	XF	Unc
ND(1661-78)	—	3,350	6,700	11,000	17,000	—

KM# 92 DUCAT

3.5000 g., 0.9860 Gold 0.1109 oz. AGW **Subject:** Death of Christoph Bernhard

Date	Mintage	VG	F	VF	XF	Unc
1678	—	1,050	2,300	4,300	8,000	—

KM# 109 DUCAT

3.5000 g., 0.9860 Gold 0.1109 oz. AGW **Obv:** Bust of Friedrich Christian right **Rev:** Crowned oval arms, date in legend

Date	Mintage	VG	F	VF	XF	Unc
1693 IO	—	2,250	4,500	7,000	12,500	—

KM# 119 DUCAT

3.5000 g., 0.9860 Gold 0.1109 oz. AGW **Obv:** Bust of Friedrich Christian right **Rev:** Crowned arms

Date	Mintage	VG	F	VF	XF	Unc
1695 JO	—	1,500	3,250	6,000	10,000	—

KM# 34 2 DUCAT

7.0000 g., 0.9860 Gold 0.2219 oz. AGW **Obv:** Crowned arms **Rev:** 3-line inscription and date in branches **Note:** Klippe.

Date	Mintage	VG	F	VF	XF	Unc
1640 Rare	—	—	—	—	—	—

KM# 45 2 DUCAT

7.0000 g., 0.9860 Gold 0.2219 oz. AGW **Obv:** Crowned oval 4-fold arms with central shield of Munster **Rev:** 4-line inscription with date in last line, in wreath **Note:** Klippe.

Date	Mintage	VG	F	VF	XF	Unc
1647 Rare	—	—	—	—	—	—

KM# 35 2 DUCAT

7.0000 g., 0.9860 Gold 0.2219 oz. AGW **Obv:** Madonna and child **Rev:** Crowned arms

Date	Mintage	VG	F	VF	XF	Unc
ND(1661-78)	—	2,750	5,500	9,000	16,500	—

KM# 39 3 DUCAT

10.5000 g., 0.9860 Gold 0.3328 oz. AGW **Obv:** Crowned oval 4-fold arms with central shield of Munster **Rev:** 4-line inscription with date in last line, in wreath

Date	Mintage	VG	F	VF	XF	Unc
1641 Rare	—	—	—	—	—	—

KM# 80 3 DUCAT

10.5000 g., 0.9860 Gold 0.3328 oz. AGW **Obv:** Helmeted arms **Rev:** St. Paul above city view **Note:** Similar to 1 Thaler, KM#75.

Date	Mintage	VG	F	VF	XF	Unc
1661 Rare	—	—	—	—	—	—

KM# 81 3 DUCAT

10.5000 g., 0.9860 Gold 0.3328 oz. AGW, 34.5 mm. **Obv:** Ornate helmeted 9-fold arms **Obv. Legend:** CHRIST: BERN: D. G: EPIS. PRINCEPS • MONA **Rev:** 1/2-length figure of Charlemagne right holding orb and sceptre **Rev. Legend:** CAROLVS • MAGNVS • FVNDATOR

Date	Mintage	VG	F	VF	XF	Unc
ND(1661-78)	—	2,500	4,500	7,500	12,500	—

KM# 70 4 DUCAT
14.0000 g., 0.9860 Gold 0.4438 oz. AGW **Obv:** Arms **Rev:** Crucifix dividing date, inner legend **Note:** Similar to 1 Thaler, KM#68.

Date	Mintage	VG	F	VF	XF	Unc
1659 Rare	—	—	—	—	—	—

KM# 82 6 DUCAT
21.0000 g., 0.9860 Gold 0.6657 oz. AGW **Obv:** Helmeted arms **Rev:** Bust of St. Paul, city view of Munster below

Date	Mintage	VG	F	VF	XF	Unc
1661	—	1,550	3,150	5,900	9,400	—

KM# 93 6 DUCAT
21.0000 g., 0.9860 Gold 0.6657 oz. AGW **Subject:** Death of Christian Bernhard **Rev:** 11-line inscription **Note:** Similar to 1 Thaler, KM#91.

Date	Mintage	VG	F	VF	XF	Unc
MDCLXXVIII (1678)	—	3,150	5,600	9,400	15,500	—

CITY

The town of Münster in Westphalia grew up around the cathedral church after the founding of the bishopric there in the late 8th or early 9th century. As Münster grew in importance, it received a charter near the end of the 12th century. The townspeople continually struggled with the ecclesiastical authorities to regain or maintain their rights. Münster became a leading member of the Hanseatic League during the 13th and 14th centuries, but their control began to ebb in the early years of the Protestant Reformation. During 1534-35, the Anabaptists, lead by Johann of Leyden, established a short-lived "kingdom" in Münster and were ruthlessly suppressed by the Church and Imperial forces. The bishops had lived for many years at Ahaus, 35 miles northwest of Münster because of the frequent strife with the citizens of the city. In 1660, Bishop Christof Bernhard von Galen besieged Münster and after taking away all the city's privileges, made it his principal seat of governance. However, the city continued to strike its own coinage, a series of copper issues begun the 16th century and continued intermittently through the last years of the 18th century.

MINT OFFICIALS' INITIALS

Initials	Date	Name
IP	1601-04	Johann Potthof der Altere
	1604-35	Hermann Potthof
	1635-ca.1644	Johann Potthof der Jüngere
	ca.1640	Englebert Kettler
	1645-77	Johann Scharlaken
	1678-79	Engelbert Johann Scharlaken
	1680-1723	Johann Tomhulse

NOTE: Numbers on some 3 Schilling and 12 Pfennig coins ranging from 1 to 11 are die numbers.

ARMS
As Bishopric, a horizontal bar

REFERENCES
P = Busso Peus, "Das Geld- und Münzwesen der Stadt Münster i. W.," **Quellen und Forschungen zur Geschichte der Stadt Münster** 4 (1931). Pp. 1-90.
Sch = Wolfgang Schulten, **Deutsche Münzen aus der Zeit Karls V**, Frankfurt am Main, 1974.

REGULAR COINAGE

KM# 330 HELLER
Copper **Obv:** Small, plain city arms with point in center **Obv. Legend:** STADT. MVNSTER **Rev:** Value, I/H in ornamented circle

Date	Mintage	Good	VG	F	VF	XF
ND(1700-1740)	—	9.00	18.00	37.00	75.00	—

KM# 315 PFENNIG
Copper **Obv:** Narrow shield of arms, legend continuous, stops are +'s

Date	Mintage	Good	VG	F	VF	XF
ND(ca.1650)	—	8.00	15.00	30.00	60.00	—

KM# 320 PFENNIG
Copper **Obv:** Stops are 6-pointed stars

Date	Mintage	Good	VG	F	VF	XF
ND(ca.1700)	—	8.00	15.00	30.00	60.00	—

KM# 331 PFENNIG
Copper **Obv:** Shield shaped more ornately, with bottom ending in sharp point **Rev:** Value smaller

Date	Mintage	Good	VG	F	VF	XF
ND(ca.1700)	—	8.00	15.00	30.00	60.00	—

KM# 301 2 PFENNING
Copper **Obv:** Lion rampant left holding shield of Munster arms **Obv. Legend:** STAD-T. MV-NSTER **Rev:** Value II in ornamented square **Note:** Struck 1603 to 1697 in varieties.

Date	Mintage	Good	VG	F	VF	XF
ND(1603-97)	—	11.00	20.00	40.00	80.00	—

KM# 302 3 PFENNING
Copper **Obv:** City arms in ornate frame, legend, date **Obv. Legend:** STADT. MVNSTER. ANo. **Rev:** III in circle, ornamented border **Note:** Struck in varieties during 17th century.

Date	Mintage	Good	VG	F	VF	XF
1602	—	8.00	15.00	30.00	60.00	—

KM# 327 3 PFENNING
Copper **Rev:** Small module

Date	Mintage	Good	VG	F	VF	XF
1662	—	—	—	—	—	—

KM# 303 4 PFENNIG
Copper **Obv:** Small city arms in ornate frame, legend, date **Obv. Legend:** STADT. MVNSTER. ANo **Rev:** Value IIII in ornate rectangle

Date	Mintage	Good	VG	F	VF	XF
1602	—	13.00	27.00	50.00	100	—

Note: Struck until end of 17th century

KM# 304 4 PFENNIG
Copper **Note:** Similar to 2 Pfennig, KM#301, but value IIII.

Date	Mintage	Good	VG	F	VF	XF
ND	—	8.00	15.00	30.00	60.00	—

Note: Struck 1689 to 1694 in varieties

KM# 305 6 PFENNIG
Copper **Obv:** City arms in ornate frame, legend, date **Obv. Legend:** STADT. MV-NSTER. A-No **Rev:** Value VI in ornamented rectangle

Date	Mintage	Good	VG	F	VF	XF
1602	—	25.00	55.00	80.00	155	—

Note: Varieties exist. Struck until about 1637. Some pieces are known countermarked 1660 (during siege).

KM# 306 12 PFENNIG
Copper **Obv:** City arms in ornate frame, legend, jewel countermark **Obv. Legend:** STADT. MVNSTER **Rev:** Value XII with date divided among ciphers, all in ornately framed rectangle, a number from 1 to 11 at top

Date	Mintage	Good	VG	F	VF	XF
1602	—	30.00	65.00	100	200	—

Note: Struck until about 1635

KM# 307 3 SCHILLING
Copper **Obv:** City arms in ornate frame, lion supporters on each side, STADT above, MVNSTER below near bottom, a small countermark - a jewel. **Rev:** Value III in central rectangle, date divided between three I's of value, in ornamented frame, small M in oval above, small S in oval below **Rev. Legend:** 1 (OR OTHER NUMBER UP TO 10)-QVI DAT-PAVPERI-NON INDIGEBIT **Note:** Struck until about 1639.

Date	Mintage	Good	VG	F	VF	XF
1602 IP	—	30.00	65.00	100	200	—

KM# 310 3 SCHILLING
Copper **Obv:** Additional countermark, small city arms with date 1639 in center, near top

Date	Mintage	Good	VG	F	VF	XF
1639	—	—	—	—	—	—

COUNTERMARKED SIEGE COINAGE

1660

KM# 71 6 PFENNIG
Copper **Countermark:** 1660 **Note:** Countermark on KM#305.

Date	Mintage	Good	VG	F	VF	XF
ND	—	—	—	—	—	—

SIEGE COINAGE

KM# 321 1/2 THALER

Silver **Obv. Legend:** MONAST: WESTPH: OBSESSVM **Note:** Uniface. Klippe. City arms in baroque frame, date divided by jewel at top

Date	Mintage	Good	VG	F	VF	XF
1660	—	115	225	500	825	950

KM# 322 1/2 THALER

Silver **Obv:** City arms in baroque frame, large jewel above **Rev. Inscription:** MONAST: / OBSES= / SVM / date **Note:** Klippe.

Date	Mintage	VG	F	VF	XF	Unc
1660	—	—	—	—	—	—

KM# 323 THALER

Silver **Obv:** Legend, date **Obv. Legend:** MONAST: WESTPH: OBSESSVM **Note:** Uniface.

Date	Mintage	VG	F	VF	XF	Unc
1660	—	135	275	600	900	—

KM# 324 2 DUCAT

7.0000 g., 0.9860 Gold 0.2219 oz. AGW **Note:** Klippe. Struck with 1/2 Thaler dies, KM#321.

Date	Mintage	VG	F	VF	XF	Unc
1660 Rare	—	—	—	—	—	—

KM# 325 3 DUCAT

10.5000 g., 0.9860 Gold 0.3328 oz. AGW **Note:** Klippe. Struck with 1/2 Thaler dies, KM#321.

Date	Mintage	VG	F	VF	XF	Unc
1660 Rare	—	—	—	—	—	—

KM# 326 5 DUCAT

17.5000 g., 0.9860 Gold 0.5547 oz. AGW **Note:** Klippe. Struck with 1 Thaler dies, KM#19.

Date	Mintage	VG	F	VF	XF	Unc
1660 Rare	—	—	—	—	—	—

CATHEDRAL CHAPTER

REGULAR COINAGE

KM# 405 HELLER

Copper **Obv:** Legend, St. Paul seated on chair **Obv. Legend:** SANCTVS. PAVLVS. APOST. **Rev:** Legend, date, small I above H **Rev. Legend:** BVRSA DOMINORVM

Date	Mintage	Good	VG	F	VF	XF
1608	—	18.00	37.00	75.00	155	—
1608 with countermark	—	18.00	37.00	75.00	155	—

Note: The 1608 with countermark issues are found with countermark of Galen arms (3 wolftraps) at bottom of reverse

KM# 406 HELLER

Copper **Obv:** Legend, facing bust of St. Paul **Obv. Legend:** SANCTVS. PAVLVS. APOST. **Rev:** Legend, date, value: I **Rev. Legend:** BVRSA DOMINORVM

Date	Mintage	Good	VG	F	VF	XF
1608	—	15.00	32.00	65.00	130	—
1608 with countermark	—	15.00	32.00	65.00	130	—

Note: The 1608 with countermark issues are found with countermark of Galen arms (3 wolftraps) at bottom of reverse

KM# 410 HELLER

Copper **Obv:** Inscription in circle **Obv. Inscription:** ELE / I **Note:** Uniface.

Date	Mintage	Good	VG	F	VF	XF
ND	—	50.00	100	210	425	—

Note: Struck during the first half of the 17th century

KM# 415 HELLER

Copper **Obv:** 1/2-length figure of St. Paul holding sword and book divides S-P **Obv. Legend:** MO. CATH. ECCL. MONAS. **Rev:** Wreath of palm leaves, legend: date in center as 16/61 **Note:** Varieties exist.

Date	Mintage	Good	VG	F	VF	XF
1661	—	9.00	18.00	37.00	75.00	—

KM# 416 PFENNIG

Copper **Obv:** Full-length facing figure of St. Paul divides S-P near bottom. **Obv. Legend:** M: CATHED: ECCL: MONASTA **Rev:** Large 'I' divides date in wreath

Date	Mintage	Good	VG	F	VF	XF
1661	—	9.00	18.00	37.00	75.00	—
1699	—	9.00	18.00	37.00	75.00	—

KM# 407 2 PFENNING

Copper **Obv:** Legend, St. Paul seated **Obv. Legend:** SANCTVS. PAVLVS. APOST **Rev:** Legend, date, value: II **Rev. Legend:** BVRSA DOMINORVM

Date	Mintage	Good	VG	F	VF	XF
1608	—	11.00	20.00	40.00	85.00	—
1608 with countermark	—	—	20.00	40.00	85.00	—

Note: The 1608 with countermark issues are found with countermark of Galen arms (3 wolftraps) at bottom of reverse

KM# 411 2 PFENNING

Copper **Note:** Uniface. ELE/II in circle.

Date	Mintage	Good	VG	F	VF	XF
ND	—	60.00	115	225	475	—

Note: Struck during the first half of the 17th century

KM# 417 2 PFENNING

Copper **Obv:** 3/4-length figure of St. Paul with sword and book, S.P. below **Obv. Legend:** MO. CATH. ECCL. MONAS **Rev:** Value, II in center divides date, wreath of palm leaves **Note:** Varieties exist.

Date	Mintage	VG	F	VF	XF	Unc
1661	—	12.00	25.00	50.00	100	—
1699	—	12.00	25.00	50.00	100	—

KM# 400 3 PFENNING

Copper **Note:** Varieties exist.

Date	Mintage	Good	VG	F	VF	XF
1603	—	10.00	20.00	40.00	85.00	—
1608	—	10.00	20.00	40.00	85.00	—
1608 with countermark	—	10.00	20.00	40.00	85.00	—

Note: The 1608 with countermark issues are found with countermark of Galen arms (3 wolftraps) at bottom of reverse

KM# 412 3 PFENNING

Copper **Obv:** Inscription in circle **Obv. Inscription:** ELE / III **Note:** Uniface.

Date	Mintage	Good	VG	F	VF	XF
ND	—	65.00	135	275	575	—

Note: Struck during the first half of the 17th century

KM# 418 3 PFENNING

Copper **Note:** Varieties exist.

Date	Mintage	Good	VG	F	VF	XF
1661	—	8.00	13.00	33.00	75.00	—
1669	—	8.00	13.00	33.00	75.00	—
1692	—	8.00	13.00	33.00	75.00	—
1696	—	8.00	13.00	33.00	75.00	—
1699	—	8.00	13.00	33.00	75.00	—

KM# 401 4 PFENNIG

Copper **Note:** Similar to 3 Pfenning KM#400. Varieties exist.

Date	Mintage	Good	VG	F	VF	XF
1603	—	15.00	30.00	60.00	125	—
1608	—	15.00	30.00	60.00	125	—
1608 with countermark	—	15.00	30.00	60.00	125	—

Note: The 1608 with countermark issues are found with countermark of Galen arms (3 wolftraps) at bottom of reverse

KM# 413 4 PFENNIG

Copper **Obv:** Inscription in circle **Obv. Inscription:** ELE / IIII **Note:** Uniface. Varieties exist.

Date	Mintage	Good	VG	F	VF	XF
ND	—	85.00	175	350	700	—

Note: Struck during the first half of the 17th century

KM# 419 4 PFENNIG

Copper **Rev:** Baroque frame around IIII/date instead of wreath **Note:** Varieties exist.

Date	Mintage	Good	VG	F	VF	XF
1661	—	9.00	16.00	35.00	75.00	—
1692	—	9.00	16.00	35.00	75.00	—
1696	—	9.00	16.00	35.00	75.00	—
1699	—	9.00	16.00	35.00	75.00	—

KM# 402 6 PFENNIG

Copper **Note:** Varieties exist.

Date	Mintage	Good	VG	F	VF	XF
1603	—	13.00	27.00	55.00	110	—
1608	—	13.00	27.00	55.00	110	—

Note: Some 1608 issues have countermark of Galen arms (3 wolftraps) at bottom of reverse

Date	Mintage	Good	VG	F	VF	XF
1633	—	13.00	27.00	55.00	110	—

KM# 403 12 PFENNIG

Copper **Note:** Similar to 6 Pfennig, KM#402, but value on reverse XII. Varieties exist.

Date	Mintage	Good	VG	F	VF	XF
1603	—	27.00	55.00	110	225	—
1608	—	27.00	55.00	110	225	—
1608 with countermark	—	27.00	55.00	110	225	—

Note: The 1608 with countermark issues are found with countermark of Galen arms (3 wolftraps) at bottom of reverse

Date	Mintage	Good	VG	F	VF	XF
1633	—	27.00	55.00	110	225	—

KM# 404 3 SCHILLING

Copper **Obv:** St. Paul on horse galloping left **Obv. Legend:** SAVLE. SAVLE QUID. ME. PERSEQVE. **Rev:** Inscription, date above, countermark below in shield form with EVB/von Brabeck arms, all in ornamented circle **Rev. Inscription:** ++ S ++ I ++ I ++ I ++, **Note:** Varieties exist.

Date	Mintage	Good	VG	F	VF	XF
1603	—	13.00	27.00	55.00	115	—
1608	—	13.00	27.00	55.00	115	—
1608 with countermark	—	13.00	27.00	55.00	115	—

Note: The 1608 with countermark issues are found with countermark of Galen arms (3 wolftraps) at bottom of reverse

Date	Mintage	Good	VG	F	VF	XF
1633	—	20.00	40.00	80.00	160	—

MUNSTERBERG

The duchy of Münsterberg was located in Silesia south of the city of Breslau. It was united with the duchy of Öls from 1495 until 1569, when Karl II sold Münsterberg to Bohemia from which it eventually was acquired by Austria in 1647. The line of dukes continued to rule in Öls, however. Austria granted the duchy to Count Johann Weikhard of Auersperg in 1653 and made him duke of Münsterberg the next year. Auersperg sold Münsterberg to Prussia in 1793.

MUNSTERBERG-ÖLS

The duchies of Munsterberg and Oels were located in Silesia, south and north of Breslau respectively. Munsterberg passed to Bohemia in 1462 and was created a separate duchy. Oels was acquired in 1495 and the two became a single entity under a long dynastic succession. The last duke died in 1647 and Munsterberg passed to Austria, while Oels was acquired through marriage by Wurttemberg (see Wurttemberg-Oels). In 1653, the count of Auersperg received Munsterberg and was made duke there in 1654 (see Munsterberg).

RULERS

Karl II, 1587-1617
Heinrich Wenzel, 1617-1639
Karl Friedrich, 1617-1647

MINT OFFICIALS' INITIALS

Initial	Date	Name
(a)= *‿* or ***	1611-12	Christoph Hedwiger in Oels
(b)= [symbol]	1612-14	Basilius von Sonn in Oels
(c)= HT monogram	1614-16	Hans Tuchmann in Oels
BH	1619-21	Burkhart Hase in Oels
HT	1620-22	Hans Tuchmann, mintmaster and warden in Oels
BZ	1622-23	Balthasar Zwirner, mint-lessee

ARMS

Horizontal bar across upper half of shield.

DUCHY

REGULAR COINAGE

KM# 67 3 HELLER

Silver **Ruler:** Heinrich Wenzel & Karl Friedrich **Obv:** Three small shields of arms in trefoil form, III above two upper shields, lower shield divides date and mintmaster's initials **Mint:** Öls **Note:** Uniface.

Date	Mintage	VG	F	VF	XF	Unc
1622 BZ	—	15.00	30.00	65.00	130	—
1623 BZ	—	15.00	30.00	65.00	130	—

KM# 68 3 HELLER

Silver **Ruler:** Heinrich Wenzel & Karl Friedrich **Obv:** Crowned shield of Münsterberg arms divides date, value 'III. H' below **Mint:** Öls **Note:** Uniface.

Date	Mintage	VG	F	VF	XF	Unc
1622	—	15.00	30.00	60.00	120	—
1622 BZ	—	15.00	30.00	60.00	120	—
1623 BZ	—	15.00	30.00	60.00	120	—

KM# 72 6 HELLER

Silver **Ruler:** Heinrich Wenzel & Karl Friedrich **Obv:** Two adjacent shields of arms, Öls in left, Glatz in right, crown above, date divided at sides, value 'VI' below **Rev:** Silesian eagle **Mint:** Öls

Date	Mintage	VG	F	VF	XF	Unc
1623	—	20.00	45.00	90.00	185	—

KM# 9 3 PFENNIG (Dreier)

Silver **Ruler:** Karl II **Obv:** Silesian eagle, shield of Münsterberg arms on breast, date divided to lower left and right **Rev:** Four small shields of arms in cruciform **Mint:** Öls

Date	Mintage	VG	F	VF	XF	Unc
1612	—	—	—	—	—	—

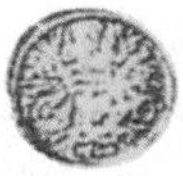

KM# 58 1/4 KREUZER (Pfennig)

Silver **Ruler:** Heinrich Wenzel & Karl Friedrich **Obv:** Silesian eagle, Münsterberg arms on breast **Mint:** Öls **Note:** Uniface. Prev. KM#61.

Date	Mintage	VG	F	VF	XF	Unc
ND(ca.1621) Rare	—	—	—	—	—	—

KM# 5 3 KREUZER (Groschen)

Silver **Ruler:** Karl II **Obv:** Bust to right, with wide ruffed collar, 3 in oval below **Obv. Legend:** CAROL. D. G. D. - MVNS. ET. OLS. **Rev:** Shield of 4-fold arms, with central shield of Münsterberg, small imperial orb above, date at end of legend **Rev. Legend:** CO. GLA. SVP. - CAP. V. SL. **Mint:** Öls **Note:** Varieties exist.

Date	Mintage	VG	F	VF	XF	Unc
(1)611 (a)	—	16.00	35.00	70.00	145	—
(1)61Z (a)	—	16.00	35.00	70.00	145	—
(1)61Z (b)	—	16.00	35.00	70.00	145	—
(1)613 (b)	—	16.00	35.00	70.00	145	—
(1)614 (b)	—	16.00	35.00	70.00	145	—
(1)614 (c)	—	16.00	35.00	70.00	145	—
(1)615 (c)	—	16.00	35.00	70.00	145	—
(1)616 (c)	—	16.00	35.00	70.00	145	—

KM# 39 3 KREUZER (Groschen)

Silver, 20 mm. **Ruler:** Heinrich Wenzel & Karl Friedrich **Obv:** Ornately-shaped shield of 4-fold arms, with central shield of Münsterberg, small imperial orb above **Obv. Legend:** D: G. HEIN. WEN. &. CAR. FRID. FR. **Rev:** Silesian eagle, (3) in oval below, date at end of legend **Rev. Legend:** D(V)(U). S. I. MONS. & - OLS. CO. GL. **Mint:** Öls **Note:** Kipper issue. Varieties exist.

Date	Mintage	VG	F	VF	XF	Unc
(1)619 BH	—	16.00	35.00	70.00	145	—
(1)619	—	16.00	35.00	70.00	145	—
(1)620 BH	—	16.00	35.00	70.00	145	—
(1)620 HT	—	16.00	35.00	70.00	145	—
(1)621 BH	—	16.00	35.00	70.00	145	—
(1)621 HT	—	16.00	35.00	70.00	145	—
(1)622 HT	—	16.00	35.00	70.00	145	—

KM# 69 3 KREUZER (Groschen)

0.8400 g., Silver **Ruler:** Heinrich Wenzel & Karl Friedrich **Obv:** Two adjacent shields of arms, Öls in left, Liegnitz in right, crown above, value '3' below **Obv. Legend:** D. G. HEN. WEN. U. CA. FR. F. D. S. **Rev:** Silesian eagle in circle, date at end of legend **Rev. Legend:** MON. NO. ARGENT. OL. **Mint:** Öls **Note:** Varieties exist.

Date	Mintage	VG	F	VF	XF	Unc
16ZZ BZ	—	20.00	40.00	80.00	160	—
16Z3 BZ	—	20.00	40.00	80.00	160	—

KM# 70 3 KREUZER (Groschen)

Silver **Ruler:** Heinrich Wenzel & Karl Friedrich **Obv:** Two adjacent shields of arms, Öls in left, Glatz in right, crown above, value '3' in oval below **Obv. Legend:** D. G. HEN. WEN. U. CAR. FRI. FR. **Rev:** Silesian eagle in circle, date at end of legend **Rev. Legend:** DVC. SI. MV. ET. OLS.... CO. GLA. **Mint:** Öls

Date	Mintage	VG	F	VF	XF	Unc
1622 BZ	—	20.00	45.00	90.00	185	—

KM# 59 24 KREUZER (Doppelschreckenberger)

Silver **Ruler:** Heinrich Wenzel & Karl Friedrich **Obv:** Crowned shield of 4-fold arms, with central shield of Münsterberg, in baroque frame **Obv. Legend:** D. G. HEIN. WEN. ET. CAR. FRID. FRA. **Rev:** Silesian eagle in circle, date in margin at top, value (24) in margin at bottom **Rev. Legend:** DVC. SIL. MONS. - ET. OLS. CO. GLA. **Mint:** Öls **Note:** Kipper coinage. Varieties exist. Prev. KM#62.

Date	Mintage	VG	F	VF	XF	Unc
1621 BH	—	60.00	100	210	425	—
1621 HT	—	60.00	100	210	425	—
1621	—	60.00	100	210	425	—

KM# 60 24 KREUZER (Doppelschreckenberger)

Silver **Ruler:** Heinrich Wenzel & Karl Friedrich **Obv:** Two armored busts facing each other, date in exergue **Obv. Legend:** D. G. HEIN. WENC. ET. CAROL. FRID. FRATR. **Rev:** Crowned shield of 4-fold arms, with central shield of Münsterberg, value (24) below in margin **Rev. Legend:** DVC. SIL. MONS. - ET. OLS. CO. GLAC. **Mint:** Öls **Note:** Kipper coinage. Varieties exist. Prev. KM#63.

Date	Mintage	VG	F	VF	XF	Unc
1621 HT	—	45.00	85.00	135	275	—
1622 HT	—	45.00	85.00	135	275	—
1622	—	45.00	85.00	135	275	—
1622 BZ	—	45.00	85.00	135	275	—
1623 BZ	—	45.00	85.00	135	275	—
1623	—	45.00	85.00	135	275	—

KM# 71 24 KREUZER (Doppelschreckenberger)

Silver **Ruler:** Heinrich Wenzel & Karl Friedrich **Rev:** Date at end of legend **Mint:** Öls **Note:** Kipper coinage.

Date	Mintage	VG	F	VF	XF	Unc
1622 HT	—	—	—	—	—	—

KM# 61 48 KREUZER (4 Schreckenberger)

Silver **Ruler:** Heinrich Wenzel & Karl Friedrich **Obv:** Crowned shield of 4-fold arms, with central shield of Münzenberg, in baroque frame **Obv. Legend:** D. G. HEIN. WEN. ET. CAR. FRID. FRA. **Rev:** Silesian eagle in circle, date in margin at top, value (48) in margin at bottom **Rev. Legend:** DVC. SIL. MONS. - ET. OLS. CO. GLA. **Mint:** Öls **Note:** Kipper coinage. Varieties exist. Prev. KM#64.

Date	Mintage	VG	F	VF	XF	Unc
1621 BH	—	85.00	160	300	600	—
1621 HT	—	85.00	160	300	600	—
1621	—	85.00	160	300	600	—

KM# 62 48 KREUZER (4 Schreckenberger)

Silver **Ruler:** Heinrich Wenzel & Karl Friedrich **Obv:** Crowned shield of 4-fold arms, with central shield of Münsterberg, in baroque frame **Obv. Legend:** D. G. HEIN. WEN. ET. CAR. FRID. FRA. **Rev:** Silesian eagle in circle, date in margin at top, no value indicated in margin at bottom **Rev. Legend:** DVC. SIL. MONS. ET. OLS. CO. GLA. **Mint:** Öls **Note:** Kipper coinage. Prev. KM#65.

Date	Mintage	VG	F	VF	XF	Unc
1621	—	—	—	—	—	—

KM# 33 1/8 THALER

Silver **Ruler:** Karl II **Subject:** Death of Karl II **Obv:** Armored bust, with wide ruffed collar, to right in circle **Obv. Legend:** +MEM. CAR. II. DV. SI. MONS. OLS. SVP. CAP. SIL. **Rev:** 5-line inscription in circle with Roman numeral date **Rev. Legend:** +INT. IVGLV. ET. SVSP. IEL. DO. ET. TO. PATR. **Rev. Inscription:** OBIIT. / A. MDCXVII / M. IAN. XXVIII / NO. MED / MAT. **Mint:** Öls

Date	Mintage	VG	F	VF	XF	Unc
MDCXVII (1617)	—	100	175	375	775	—

KM# 18 1/4 THALER

Silver **Ruler:** Karl II **Obv:** High-collared armored bust to right in circle, legend begins with small imperial orb at top **Obv. Legend:** CAROLVS. D. G. DVX. MVNSTER. ET. OLS. CO. GLA. **Rev:** Crowned shield of 4-fold arms, with central shield of Münsterberg, date at end of legend **Rev. Legend:** SVPREM. PER VT. - SIL. CAPIT. **Mint:** Öls

Date	Mintage	VG	F	VF	XF	Unc
(1)613 (b)	—	90.00	180	360	725	—
(1)614 (b)	—	90.00	180	360	725	—

KM# 10 1/2 THALER

Silver **Ruler:** Karl II **Obv:** High-collared armored bust to right in circle, legend begins with small imperial orb at top **Obv. Legend:** CAROL. D. G. DVX. MVNSTER. ET. OLS. CO. GLA. **Rev:** Small shield of arms in center divides date, 4 small shields of arms around, all in circle **Rev. Legend:** SVPREMVS. PER VT - SIL. CAPITANEVS. **Mint:** Öls

Date	Mintage	VG	F	VF	XF	Unc
161Z (a)	—	600	1,200	2,200	4,200	—

KM# 19 1/2 THALER

Silver **Ruler:** Karl II **Obv:** High-collared armored bust to right in circle, legend begins with small imperial orb at top **Obv. Legend:** CAROL. D. G. DVX. MVNSTER. ET. OLS. CO. GLA. **Rev:** Ornate shield of 4-fold arms, with central shield, 3 ornate helmets above, date at end of legend **Rev. Legend:** SVPREMVS. PER VT. - SIL. CAPIT. **Mint:** Öls

Date	Mintage	VG	F	VF	XF	Unc
(1)613 (b)	—	700	1,500	2,850	5,500	—

KM# 26 1/2 THALER

Silver **Ruler:** Karl II **Obv:** Armored bust, with ruffed collar, to right in circle **Rev:** Ornate shield of 4-fold arms, with central shield, 3 ornate helmets above, date at end of legend **Mint:** Öls

Date	Mintage	VG	F	VF	XF	Unc
(1)614 (b)	—	—	—	—	—	—

KM# 34 1/2 THALER

Silver **Ruler:** Karl II **Subject:** Death of Karl II **Obv:** Armored bust, with wide ruffed collar, to right in circle **Obv. Legend:** +MEM. CAROL. II. DVX. SIL. MONS. OLS. SVP. CAP. SIL. **Rev:** 7-line inscription with Roman numeral dates **Rev. Legend:** PAT. PA. AD. BHAT. IMMORT. TRANSL. OBIIT. SVM. **Rev. Inscription:** SVOR. ET. / PAT. DESID. AN. / MDCXVII. M. IAN. / XXVIII. / HO. MAT. / DIMI. X. AET. / LXXII. MIN. / XII. HEBD. **Mint:** Öls

Date	Mintage	VG	F	VF	XF	Unc
MDCXVII (1617)	—	235	475	850	1,500	—

KM# 40 1/2 THALER

Silver **Ruler:** Heinrich Wenzel & Karl Friedrich **Obv:** Busts of two dukes facing each other **Rev:** Shield of 4-fold arms, with central shield of Münsterberg, three small helmets above, date at end of legend **Mint:** Öls **Note:** Varieties exist.

Date	Mintage	VG	F	VF	XF	Unc
(1)619 BH	—	100	200	400	800	—
(1)620 BH	—	100	200	400	800	—
(1)621 BH	—	100	200	400	800	—

KM# 49 1/2 THALER

Silver **Ruler:** Heinrich Wenzel & Karl Friedrich **Obv:** Two half-length armored figures facing each other, date in exergue, small imperial orb at top in margin **Obv. Legend:** D.G. HEINRI• WENC• ET• CAROL • FRID (E) • FRAT• **Rev:** Shield of 4-fold arms, with central shield of Münsterberg, 5 ornate helmets above **Rev. Legend:** DVC • SIL • MONS - • ET • OLS • CO • GLA • **Mint:** Öls **Note:** Prev. KM#A55.

Date	Mintage	F	VF	XF	Unc	BU
1620 BH	—	100	200	400	800	—
1621 BH	—	100	200	400	800	—

KM# 50 1/2 THALER

Silver **Ruler:** Heinrich Wenzel & Karl Friedrich **Obv:** Half-length armored figure to right, legend divided by small shields of arms at left, top, right, and 2 shields below **Obv. Legend:** D. G. HEIN - RICVS - WENCES - LAVS. ET. **Rev:** Half-length armored figure to left divides date near top, legend divided by small shields of arms at left, top, right, and 2 shields below **Rev. Legend:** CAR. FRID - ER. DV. SI. - MONS. ET. O - LS. CO. GLA. **Mint:** Öls **Note:** Prev. KM#55.

Date	Mintage	VG	F	VF	XF	Unc
1620 BH	—	100	200	400	800	—

KM# 6 THALER

Silver **Ruler:** Karl II **Obv:** Armored bust, with large ruffed collar, to right in circle, legend begins with small imperial orb at top **Obv. Legend:** CAROLVS. D. G. DVX. MVNST. ET. OLS. CO. GLA. **Rev:** Ornate shield of 4-fold arms, with central shield, 3 ornate helmets above, date at end of legend **Rev. Legend:** SVPREM. PER VT. - SIL. CAPIT. **Mint:** Öls **Note:** Ref. Dav. 7089.

Date	Mintage	VG	F	VF	XF	Unc
(1)611	—	650	1,300	2,750	5,500	9,400
(1)61Z (a)	—	275	550	1,100	2,200	3,850

KM# 20 THALER

Silver **Ruler:** Karl II **Obv:** Armored bust, with large ruffed collar, to right in circle **Obv. Legend:** CAROLVS. D. G. DVX. MVNST. ET. OLS. CO. GLA. **Rev:** Ornate shield of 4-fold arms, with central shield, 3 ornate helmets above, date at end of legend **Rev. Legend:** SVPREM. PER VT. - SIL. CAPIT. **Mint:** Öls **Note:** Dav. 7091.

Date	Mintage	VG	F	VF	XF	Unc
(1)613 (b)	—	875	1,750	3,700	6,900	11,500
(1)616 (c)	—	875	1,750	3,700	6,900	11,500

KM# 27 THALER

Silver **Ruler:** Karl II **Obv:** Armored bust, with wide ruffed collar, to right in circle **Obv. Legend:** CAROLVS. D. G. DVX. MVNST. ET. OLS. CO. GLA. **Rev:** Ornate shield of 4-fold arms, with central shield, 3 ornate helmets above, date at end of legend **Rev. Legend:** SVPREM. PER VT. - SIL. CAPIT. **Mint:** Öls **Note:** Ref. Dav. 7092.

Date	Mintage	VG	F	VF	XF	Unc
(1)614 (b)	—	750	1,500	3,200	6,000	—
(1)615 (c)	—	750	1,500	3,200	6,000	—

KM# 35 THALER

28.8200 g., Silver **Ruler:** Karl II **Subject:** Death of Karl II **Obv:** Armored bust, with wide ruffed collar, to right in circle, small shield of 4-fold arms, with central shield below, 2 margin legends with Roman numeral dates **Obv. Legend:** Outer: MEM. FVN. CAR. II. S. IMP. PR. DVX. - SIL. MVNS. OLS. CO. GLA. OP. MER.

Inner: +NAT. M.DXLV. APR. XV. MOR. - XXVIII. IANV. D.C.XVII. **Rev:** 8-line inscription, arabesque below **Rev. Inscription:** FIDES. / DEO. ET. REGI. / PATRIÆ. GRAT. / SVIS. DESIDER. / - VIXIT - / SPE. I. MORT. GLOR. / NON. TERR. SED. / CŒL. COGIT. **Mint:** Öls **Note:** Ref. F&S 2211; Dav. 7093.

Date	Mintage	VG	F	VF	XF	Unc
MDCXVII (1617)	—	500	1,050	2,350	5,400	9,000

KM# 41 THALER

Silver **Ruler:** Heinrich Wenzel & Karl Friedrich **Obv:** Facing busts with ornament below **Rev:** Helmeted arms **Mint:** Öls **Note:** Ref. Dav. 7094.

Date	Mintage	VG	F	VF	XF	Unc
1619 BH	—	725	1,500	3,050	5,200	—

KM# 42 THALER

Silver **Ruler:** Heinrich Wenzel & Karl Friedrich **Obv:** Half-length armored figure to right, legend divided by small shield of arms at left, top, right, and 2 shields below **Obv. Legend:** D. G. HEIN - RICUS - WENCES - LAUS. ET. **Rev:** Half-length armored figure to left divides date, legend divided by small shield of arms at left, top, right, and 2 shields below **Rev. Legend:** CAR. FRID - ER. DU. SI. - MONS. ET. O - LS. CO. GLA. **Mint:** Öls **Note:** Ref. Dav. 7096.

Date	Mintage	VG	F	VF	XF	Unc
1619 BH	—	500	1,050	2,350	4,950	—
1620 BH	—	500	1,050	2,350	4,950	—

KM# 43 THALER

Silver **Ruler:** Heinrich Wenzel & Karl Friedrich **Obv:** Two half-length armored figures facing each other, date in exergue **Obv. Legend:** D. G. HEINRI. WENCES. ET. CAROL. FRIDE. FRAT. **Rev:** Shield of 4-fold arms, with central shield, 3 ornate helmets above **Rev. Legend:** DUC. SIL. MONS. - ET. OLS. CO. GLA. **Mint:** Öls **Note:** Ref. Dav. 7097. Varieties exist.

Date	Mintage	VG	F	VF	XF	Unc
1619 BH	—	—	—	—	—	—
1620 BH	—	325	775	1,650	2,750	—

KM# 51 2 THALER

Silver **Ruler:** Heinrich Wenzel & Karl Friedrich **Obv:** Half-length armored figure to right, legend divided by small shield of arms at left, top, right, and 2 shields below **Obv. Legend:** D. G. HEIN - RICUS - WENCES - LAUS. ET. **Rev:** Half-length armored figure to left divides date, legend divided by small shield of arms at left, top, right, and 2 shields below **Rev. Legend:** CAR. FRID - ER. DU. SI. - MONS. ET. O - LS. CO. GLA. **Mint:** Öls **Note:** Ref. Dav. 7095. Prev. KM#56.

Date	Mintage	VG	F	VF	XF	Unc
1620 BH Rare	—	—	—	—	—	—

KM# 21 3 THALER

Silver **Ruler:** Karl II **Obv:** Armored bust, with large ruffed collar, to right in circle, legend begins with small imperial orb at top **Obv. Legend:** CAROLVS. D. G. DVX. MVNST. ET. OLS. CO. GLA. **Rev:** Ornate shield of 4-fold arms, with central shield, 3 ornate helmets above, date at end of legend **Rev. Legend:** SVPREM. PER VT. - SIL. CAPIT. **Mint:** Öls **Note:** Ref. Dav. 7090.

Date	Mintage	VG	F	VF	XF	Unc
(1)61Z (a) Rare	—	—	—	—	—	—

TRADE COINAGE

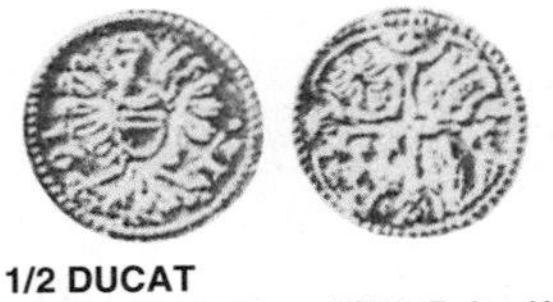

KM# 11 1/2 DUCAT

1.7500 g., 0.9860 Gold 0.0555 oz. AGW **Ruler:** Karl II **Obv:** Silesian eagle with shield of Öls arms on breast, date divided to lower left and right **Rev:** Long cross with small shield in each angle **Mint:** Öls **Note:** Fr. 3250.

Date	Mintage	VG	F	VF	XF	Unc
1612	—	575	850	1,750	3,100	—

KM# 32 1/2 DUCAT

1.7500 g., 0.9860 Gold 0.0555 oz. AGW **Ruler:** Karl II **Obv:** Crowned shield of 4-fold arms, with central shield, in baroque frame, C.H. - Z.M. divided above **Rev:** Silesian eagle, with shield on breast, divides date and mintmaster's initials **Mint:** Öls **Note:** Ref. Fr. 3251.

Date	Mintage	VG	F	VF	XF	Unc
1616 (c)	—	425	725	1,400	2,500	—

KM# 7 DUCAT

3.5000 g., 0.9860 Gold 0.1109 oz. AGW **Ruler:** Karl II **Obv:** Bust to right in circle **Rev:** Crowned shield of arms **Mint:** Öls **Note:** Ref. Fr. 3249. Varieties exist.

Date	Mintage	VG	F	VF	XF	Unc
1611	—	800	1,700	3,300	6,000	—
1612	—	800	1,700	3,300	6,000	—
1613	—	800	1,700	3,300	6,000	—
1614	—	800	1,700	3,300	6,000	—
1615 (c)	—	800	1,700	3,300	6,000	—
1616 (c)	—	800	1,700	3,300	6,000	—

KM# 22 DUCAT

3.5000 g., 0.9860 Gold 0.1109 oz. AGW **Ruler:** Karl II **Obv:** Armored bust, with wide ruffed collar, breaks circle at top **Obv. Legend:** CAROL. D. G. DVX. MVNST. ET. OLS. **Rev:** Crowned shield of 4-fold arms, with central shield, date at end of legend **Rev. Legend:** CO. GLA. SVP. PER - VT. SIL. CAP. **Mint:** Öls **Note:** Ref. Fr. 3249.

Date	Mintage	VG	F	VF	XF	Unc
(1)613	—	800	1,700	3,300	6,000	—

KM# 44 DUCAT

3.5000 g., 0.9860 Gold 0.1109 oz. AGW **Ruler:** Heinrich Wenzel & Karl Friedrich **Obv:** Armored bust of Heinrich Wenzel to right in circle **Rev:** Armored bust of Karl Friedrich to left in circle **Mint:** Öls **Note:** Fr. 3264. Varieties exist.

Date	Mintage	VG	F	VF	XF	Unc
1619 BH	—	900	1,800	3,600	7,200	—
1620 BH	—	900	1,800	3,600	7,200	—
1621 BH	—	900	1,800	3,600	7,200	—

KM# 45 DUCAT

3.5000 g., 0.9860 Gold 0.1109 oz. AGW **Ruler:** Heinrich Wenzel & Karl Friedrich **Obv:** Armored bust to right breaks circle at top **Rev:** Armored bust to left, dividing date, breaks circle at top **Mint:** Öls **Note:** Fr. 3264.

Date	Mintage	VG	F	VF	XF	Unc
1619	—	900	1,800	3,600	7,200	—

KM# 12 2 DUCAT

7.0000 g., 0.9860 Gold 0.2219 oz. AGW **Ruler:** Karl II **Obv:** High-collared armored bust to right in circle, legend begins with small imperial orb at top **Obv. Legend:** CAROLVS. D. G. DVX. MVNSTER. ET. OLS. CO. GLA. **Rev:** Crowned shield of 4-fold arms, with central shield of Münsterberg, date at end of legend **Rev. Legend:** SVPREM. PER VT. - SIL. CAPIT. **Mint:** Öls **Note:** Fr. 3248.

Date	Mintage	VG	F	VF	XF	Unc
(1)61Z (a)	—	1,800	3,600	8,200	14,000	—

KM# 28 2 DUCAT

7.0000 g., 0.9860 Gold 0.2219 oz. AGW **Ruler:** Karl II **Obv:** Armored bust, with ruffed collar, to right in circle **Rev:** Ornate shield of 4-fold arms, with central shield, 3 ornate helmets above, date at end of legend **Mint:** Öls **Note:** Ref. Fr. 3245.

Date	Mintage	VG	F	VF	XF	Unc
1614	—	1,100	2,300	4,800	9,400	—
1615 (c)	—	1,100	2,300	4,800	9,400	—

KM# 36 2 DUCAT

7.0000 g., 0.9860 Gold 0.2219 oz. AGW **Ruler:** Karl II **Subject:** Death of Karl II **Rev:** Five-line inscription **Mint:** Öls **Note:** Ref. Fr. 3255.

Date	Mintage	VG	F	VF	XF	Unc
1617	—	2,450	5,300	11,500	16,000	—

KM# 63 2 DUCAT

7.0000 g., 0.9860 Gold 0.2219 oz. AGW **Ruler:** Heinrich Wenzel & Karl Friedrich **Obv:** Half-length armored figure to right, legend divided by small shield of arms at left, top, right, and 2 shields below **Rev:** Half-length armored figure to left divides date, legend divided by small shield of arms at left, top, right, and 2 shields below **Mint:** Öls **Note:** Ref. Fr. 3263. Prev. KM#66.

Date	Mintage	VG	F	VF	XF	Unc
1621 BH	—	1,100	2,150	5,200	8,600	—

KM# 13 3 DUCAT

10.5000 g., 0.9860 Gold 0.3328 oz. AGW **Ruler:** Karl II **Obv:** High-collared armored bust to right in circle, legend begins with small imperial orb at top **Obv. Legend:** CAROL. D. G. DVX. MVNSTER. ET. OLS. CO. GLA. **Rev:** Small shield of arms in center divides date, 4 small shields of arms around, all in circle **Rev. Legend:** SVPREMVS. PER VT. - SIL. CAPITANEVS. **Mint:** Öls **Note:** Fr. 3247.

Date	Mintage	VG	F	VF	XF	Unc
161Z (a)	—	1,450	2,900	6,500	13,000	—

KM# 23 3 DUCAT

10.5000 g., 0.9860 Gold 0.3328 oz. AGW **Ruler:** Karl II **Obv:** Armored bust, with large collar, to right in circle, legend begins with small imperial orb at top **Obv. Legend:** CAROL. D. G. DVX. MVNSTER. ET. OLS. CO. GLA. **Rev:** Ornate shield of 4-fold arms, with central shield, 3 ornate helmets above, date at end of legend **Rev. Legend:** SVPREMVS. PER VT. - SIL. CAPIT. **Mint:** Öls **Note:** Ref. Fr. 3244.

Date	Mintage	VG	F	VF	XF	Unc
1613 (b)	—	1,700	3,500	7,800	12,500	—
1614	—	1,700	3,500	7,800	12,500	—

KM# 46 3 DUCAT

10.5000 g., 0.9860 Gold 0.3328 oz. AGW **Ruler:** Heinrich Wenzel & Karl Friedrich **Obv:** Two half-length armored figures facing each other, date in exergue **Obv. Legend:** D. G. HEINRI. WENC. ET. CAROL. FRIDE. FRAT. **Rev:** Oval shield of 4-fold arms, with central shield, 3 ornate helmets above **Rev. Legend:** DUC. SI. MONS. - ET. OLS. CO. GLA. **Mint:** Öls **Note:** Varieties exist.

Date	Mintage	VG	F	VF	XF	Unc
1619 BH	—	1,300	2,750	6,200	10,000	—
1621 BH	—	1,300	2,750	6,200	10,000	—
1621 HT	—	1,300	2,750	6,200	10,000	—
1622 HT	—	1,300	2,750	6,200	10,000	—

KM# 52 3 DUCAT

10.5000 g., 0.9860 Gold 0.3328 oz. AGW **Ruler:** Heinrich Wenzel & Karl Friedrich **Obv:** Half-length armored figure to right, legend divided by small shield of arms at left, top, right, and 2 shields below **Rev:** Half-length armored figure to left divides date, legend divided by small shield of arms at left, top, right, and 2 shields below **Mint:** Öls **Note:** Ref. Fr. 3362. Prev. KM#57.

Date	Mintage	VG	F	VF	XF	Unc
1620 BH	—	1,300	2,500	5,400	11,000	—
1621 BH	—	1,300	2,500	5,400	11,000	—

KM# 14 4 DUCAT

14.0000 g., 0.9860 Gold 0.4438 oz. AGW **Ruler:** Karl II **Obv:** High-collared armored bust to right in circle, legend begins with small imperial orb at top **Obv. Legend:** CAROL. D. G. DVX. MVNSTER. ET. OLS. CO. GLA. **Rev:** Small shield of arms in center divides date, 4 small shields of arms around, all in circle **Rev. Legend:** SVPREMVS. PER VT. - SIL. CAPITANEVS. **Mint:** Öls **Note:** Fr. 3246.

Date	Mintage	VG	F	VF	XF	Unc
161Z (a)	—	2,350	4,600	9,200	16,000	—

KM# 24 4 DUCAT

14.0000 g., 0.9860 Gold 0.4438 oz. AGW **Ruler:** Karl II **Obv:** Armored bust, with large collar, to right in circle, legend begins with small imperial orb at top **Obv. Legend:** CAROL. D. G. DVX. MVNSTER. ET. OLS. CO. GLA. **Rev:** Ornate shield of 4-fold arms, with central shield, 3 ornate helmets above, date at end of legend **Rev. Legend:** SVPREMVS. PER VT. - SIL. CAPIT. **Mint:** Öls **Note:** Ref. Fr. 3243.

Date	Mintage	VG	F	VF	XF	Unc
1613 (b)	—	2,750	5,400	11,000	19,000	—
1615 (c)	—	2,750	5,400	11,000	19,000	—

KM# 47 4 DUCAT

14.0000 g., 0.9860 Gold 0.4438 oz. AGW **Ruler:** Heinrich Wenzel & Karl Friedrich **Obv:** Two half-length armored figures facing each other **Obv. Legend:** D. G. HEINRI. WENC. ET. CAROL. FRID. FRAT. **Rev:** Spanish shield of 4-fold arms, with central shield, 3 ornate helmets above, date at end of legend **Rev. Legend:** DVC. SIL. MONS. ET. - OLS. CO. GLA. **Mint:** Öls **Note:** Prev. KM#47.1.

Date	Mintage	VG	F	VF	XF	Unc
1619 BH	—	1,850	3,850	8,600	15,500	—
1621 BH	—	1,850	3,850	8,600	15,500	—

KM# 54 4 DUCAT

14.0000 g., 0.9860 Gold 0.4438 oz. AGW **Ruler:** Heinrich Wenzel & Karl Friedrich **Obv:** Half-length armored figure to right, legend divided by small shield of arms at left, top, right, and 2 shields below **Obv. Legend:** D. G. HEIN - RICUS - WENCES - LAUS. ET. **Rev:** Half-length armored figure to left divides date, legend divided by small shield of arms at left, top, right, and 2 shields below **Rev. Legend:** CAR. FRID - ER. DV. SI. - MONS. ET. O - LS. CO. GLA. **Mint:** Öls **Note:** Ref. Fr. 3261. Prev. KM#58.

Date	Mintage	VG	F	VF	XF	Unc
1620 BH	—	1,850	3,850	8,600	14,500	—

KM# 53 4 DUCAT

Gold **Ruler:** Heinrich Wenzel & Karl Friedrich **Obv:** Two half-length armored figures facing each other, date in exergue, small imperial orb at top in margin **Obv. Legend:** D.G. HEINRI • WENC • ET • CAROL • FRID • FRAT • **Rev:** Shield of 4-fold arms, with central shield of Münsterberg, 5 ornate helmets above **Rev. Legend:** DVC • SIL • MONS • - •ET • OLS • CO • GLA • **Mint:** Öls **Note:** Struck from 1/2 Thaler dies, KM#49. Prev. KM#47.3.

Date	Mintage	VG	F	VF	XF	Unc
1620 BH Rare	—	—	—	—	—	—

Date	Mintage	VG	F	VF	XF	Unc
1621 BH Rare	—	—	—	—	—	—

Note: UBS Gold & Numismatics Auction 69, 1-07, VF-XF realized approximately $8,875

KM# 64 4 DUCAT

14.0000 g., 0.9860 Gold 0.4438 oz. AGW **Ruler:** Heinrich Wenzel & Karl Friedrich **Obv:** Two half-length armored figures facing each other, date in exergue **Obv. Legend:** D. G. HEINRI. WENC. ET. CAROL. FRIDE. FRAT. **Rev:** Oval shield of 4-fold arms, with central shield, three ornate helmets above **Rev. Legend:** DUC. SI. MONS. - ET. OLS. CO. GLA. **Mint:** Öls **Note:** Prev. KM#47.2.

Date	Mintage	VG	F	VF	XF	Unc
1621 HT Rare	—	—	—	—	—	—
1622 HT Rare	—	—	—	—	—	—

Note: Fritz Rudolf Künker Münzenhandlung Auction 135, 1-08, XF realized approximately $16,985

KM# 8 5 DUCAT

17.5000 g., 0.9860 Gold 0.5547 oz. AGW **Ruler:** Karl II **Obv:** Armored bust to right in circle **Rev:** Shield of 4-fold arms, with central shield, 3 ornate helmets above **Mint:** Öls **Note:** Ref. Fr. 3242.

Date	Mintage	VG	F	VF	XF	Unc
(1)611	—	1,800	3,600	7,200	12,000	—
(1)61Z (a)	—	1,800	3,600	7,200	12,000	—

KM# 15 5 DUCAT

17.5000 g., 0.9860 Gold 0.5547 oz. AGW **Ruler:** Karl II **Obv:** Armored bust, with large ruffed collar, to right in circle **Obv. Legend:** CAROLVS. D. G. DVX. MNVST. ET. OLS. CO. GLA. **Rev:** Ornate shield of 4-fold arms, with central shield, 3 ornate helmets above, date at end of legend **Rev. Legend:** SVPREM. PER VT. - SIL. CAPIT. **Mint:** Öls **Note:** Fr. 3242. Varieties exist.

Date	Mintage	VG	F	VF	XF	Unc
(1)61Z (a)	—	1,800	3,600	7,200	12,000	—
(1)613 (b)	—	1,800	3,600	7,200	12,000	—
(1)616 (c)	—	1,800	3,600	7,200	12,000	—

KM# 29 5 DUCAT

17.5000 g., 0.9860 Gold 0.5547 oz. AGW **Ruler:** Karl II **Mint:** Öls **Note:** Ref. Fr. 3242.

Date	Mintage	VG	F	VF	XF	Unc
(1)615	—	1,800	3,600	7,200	12,000	—

KM# 55 5 DUCAT

17.5000 g., 0.9860 Gold 0.5547 oz. AGW **Ruler:** Heinrich Wenzel & Karl Friedrich **Obv:** Two half-length armored figures facing each other, date in exergue **Rev:** Shield of 4-fold arms, with central shield of Münzenberg, 3 ornate helmets above **Mint:** Öls **Note:** Ref. Fr. 3257. Varieties exist. Prev. KM#59.

Date	Mintage	VG	F	VF	XF	Unc
(1)6Z0 BH	—	1,800	3,600	7,200	12,000	22,000
(1)6Z1 BH	—	1,800	3,600	7,200	12,000	22,000

KM# A9 6 DUCAT

21.0000 g., 0.9860 Gold 0.6657 oz. AGW **Ruler:** Karl II **Obv:** Bust of Karl II right **Rev:** Helmeted ornate arms **Note:** Fr.#3241.

Date	Mintage	VG	F	VF	XF	Unc
1611	—	3,950	7,800	19,000	35,000	—

KM# 30 6 DUCAT

21.0000 g., 0.9860 Gold 0.6657 oz. AGW **Ruler:** Karl II **Obv:** Date below bust **Mint:** Öls **Note:** Ref. Fr. 3241.

Date	Mintage	VG	F	VF	XF	Unc
(1)615 (c)	—	6,100	12,000	21,500	35,000	—
(1)616 (c)	—	6,100	12,000	21,500	35,000	—

KM# 31 6 DUCAT

21.0000 g., 0.9860 Gold 0.6657 oz. AGW **Ruler:** Karl II **Obv:** Armored bust, with wide collar, to right in circle, legend begins with small imperial orb at top **Obv. Legend:** CAROLVS. D. G. DVX. MVNST. ET. OLS. CO. GLA. **Rev:** Ornate shield of 4-fold arms, with central shield, 3 ornate helmets above, date at end of legend **Rev. Legend:** SVPREM. PER VT. - SIL. CAPIT. **Mint:** Öls **Note:** Ref. Fr. 3241.

Date	Mintage	VG	F	VF	XF	Unc
(1)615 (c)	—	6,100	12,000	21,500	35,000	—
(1)616 (c)	—	6,100	12,000	21,500	35,000	—

KM# 37 6 DUCAT

21.0000 g., 0.9860 Gold 0.6657 oz. AGW **Ruler:** Karl II **Subject:** Death of Karl II **Obv:** Armored bust, with wide ruffed collar, to right in circle **Obv. Legend:** +MEM. CAROL. II. DVX. SIL. MONS. OLS. SVP. CAP. SIL. **Rev:** 7-line inscription with Roman numeral dates in circle **Rev. Legend:** PAT. PA. AD. BHAT. IMMORT. TRANSL. OBIIT. SVM. **Rev. Inscription:** SVOR. ET. / PAT. DESID. AN. / MDCXVII. M. IAN. / XXVIII. / HO. MAT. / DIMI. X. AET. / LXXII. MIN. / XII. HEBD. **Mint:** Öls **Note:** Ref. Fr. 3254.

Date	Mintage	VG	F	VF	XF	Unc
MDCXVII (1617) Rare	—	—	—	—	—	—

KM# 48 6 DUCAT

21.0000 g., 0.9860 Gold 0.6657 oz. AGW **Ruler:** Heinrich Wenzel & Karl Friedrich **Obv:** Half-length armored figure to right, legend divided by small shield of arms at left, top, right, and 2 shields below **Obv. Legend:** D. G. HEIN - RICVS - WENCES - LAVS. ET. **Rev:** Half-length armored figure to left divides date near top, legend divided by small shield of arms at left, top, right, and 2 shields below **Rev. Legend:** CAR. FRID - ER. DV. SI. - MONS. ET. O - LS. CO. GLA. **Mint:** Öls

Date	Mintage	VG	F	VF	XF	Unc
1619 BH Rare	—	—	—	—	—	—

KM# 56 6 DUCAT

21.0000 g., 0.9860 Gold 0.6657 oz. AGW **Ruler:** Heinrich Wenzel & Karl Friedrich **Obv:** Two half-length armored figures facing each other, date in exergue **Rev:** Ornate shield of 4-fold arms, with central shield of Münzenberg, 3 ornate helmets above **Mint:** Öls **Note:** Ref. Fr. 3256. Prev. KM#A60

Date	Mintage	VG	F	VF	XF	Unc
16Z0 Rare	—	—	—	—	—	—

KM# 57 8 DUCAT

28.0000 g., 0.9860 Gold 0.8876 oz. AGW **Ruler:** Heinrich Wenzel & Karl Friedrich **Obv:** Two half-length armored figures facing each other, date in exergue **Obv. Legend:** D. G. HEINRI. WENCES. ET. CAROL. FRIDE. FRAT. **Rev:** Shield of 4-fold arms, with central shield of Münsterberg, 3 ornate helmets above **Rev. Legend:** DUC. SIL. MONS. - ET. OLS. CO. GLA. **Mint:** Öls **Note:** Prev. KM#60.

Date	Mintage	VG	F	VF	XF	Unc
1620 BH Rare	—	—	—	—	—	—

KM# 16 9 DUCAT

31.5000 g., 0.9860 Gold 0.9985 oz. AGW **Ruler:** Karl II **Obv:** Armored bust, with large ruffed collar, to right in circle **Obv. Legend:** CAROLVS. D. G. DVX. MVNST. ET. OLS. CO. GLA. **Rev:** Ornate shield of 4-fold arms, with central shield, 3 ornate helmets above, date at end of legend **Rev. Legend:** SVPREM. PER VT. - SIL. CAPIT. **Mint:** Öls **Note:** Fr. 3240. Struck from Thaler dies, KM#20.

Date	Mintage	VG	F	VF	XF	Unc
(1)61Z (a) Rare	—	—	—	—	—	—

KM# 17 10 DUCAT

35.0000 g., 0.9860 Gold 1.1095 oz. AGW **Ruler:** Karl II **Obv:** Armored bust, with large ruffed collar, to right in circle **Obv. Legend:** CAROLVS. D. G. DVX. MVNST. ET. OLS. CO. GLA. **Rev:** Ornate shield of 4-fold arms, with central shield, 3 ornate helmets above, date at end of legend **Rev. Legend:** SVPREM. PER VT. - SIL. CAPIT. **Mint:** Öls **Note:** Fr. 3239. Struck from Thaler dies, KM#20.

Date	Mintage	VG	F	VF	XF	Unc
(1)61Z (a) Rare	—	—	—	—	—	—

KM# 25 10 DUCAT

35.0000 g., 0.9860 Gold 1.1095 oz. AGW **Ruler:** Karl II **Obv:** Armored bust, with ruffed collar, to right in circle **Obv. Legend:** CAROLVS. D. G. DVX. MVNST. ET. OLS. CO. GLA. **Rev:** Ornate shield of 4-fold arms, with central shield, 3 ornate helmets above, date at end of legend **Rev. Legend:** SVPREM. PER VT. - SIL. CAPIT. **Mint:** Öls **Note:** Ref. Fr. 3239.

Date	Mintage	VG	F	VF	XF	Unc
(1)613 (b) Rare	—	—	—	—	—	—

KM# A38 10 DUCAT

35.0000 g., 0.9860 Gold 1.1095 oz. AGW **Ruler:** Karl II **Obv:** Armored bust to right, with ruffed collar, in circle **Obv. Legend:** CAROLVS. D. G. DVX. MUNST. ET. OLS. CO. GLA. **Rev:** Ornate shield of 4-fold arms, with central shield, 3 ornate helmets above, date at end of legend **Rev. Legend:** SVPREM. PER VT. - SIL. CAPIT. **Mint:** Öls

Date	Mintage	VG	F	VF	XF	Unc
(1)616 (c) Rare	—	—	—	—	—	—

KM# 38 10 DUCAT

35.0000 g., 0.9860 Gold 1.1095 oz. AGW **Ruler:** Karl II **Subject:** Death of Karl II **Obv:** Armored bust, with wide ruffed collar, to right in circle, small shield of 4-fold arms with central shield below, 2 margin legends **Obv. Legend:** Outer: MEM. FVN. CAR. II. S. IMP. PR. DVX. - SIL. MVNS. OLS. CO. GLA. OP. MER. Inner: +NAT. M.DXLV. APR. XV. MOR. - XXVIII. IANV. D. C. XVII. **Rev:** 8-line inscription, arabesque below **Rev. Inscription:** FIDVS. / DEO. ET. REGI. / PATRIÆ. GRAT. / SVIS. DESIDER. / - VIXIT - / SPE. I. MORT. GLOR. / NON. TERR. SED. / CĐL. COGIT. **Mint:** Öls **Note:** Ref. Fr. 3253.

Date	Mintage	VG	F	VF	XF	Unc
MDCXVII (1617) Rare	—	—	—	—	—	—

KM# A39 12-1/2 DUCAT

43.7500 g., 0.9860 Gold 1.3868 oz. AGW **Ruler:** Karl II **Subject:** Death of Karl II **Obv:** Armored bust, with wide ruffed collar, to right in circle, small shield of 4-fold arms below, 2 margin legends **Obv. Legend:** Outer: MEM. FVN. CAR. II. S. IMP. PR. DVX. - SIL. MVNS. OLS. CO. GLA. OP. MER. Inner: +NAT. M.DXLV. APR. XV. MOR. - XXVIII. IANV. D.C.XVII. **Rev:** 8-line inscription with Roman numeral dates, arabesque below **Rev. Inscription:** FIDVS. / DEO. ET. REGI. / PATRIÆ. GRAT. / SVIS. DESIDER. / - VIXIT - / SPE. I. MORT. GLOR. / NON. TERR. SED. / CĐL. COGIT. **Mint:** Öls **Note:** Struck with Thaler dies, KM#35.

Date	Mintage	VG	F	VF	XF	Unc
1617 Rare	—	—	—	—	—	—

MURBACH & LUDERS

Murbach and Lüders were neighboring abbeys in Upper Alsace founded in the 8th century. Almost from their inception they had a common ruling abbot. A local 12th and 13th century coinage preceded the official granting in 1544 of the right to mint coins. Their territories were absorbed into France in 1680, and secularization followed in 1764.

ABBOTS

Andreas, Erzherzog von Österreich, 1587-1600
Leopold V, Erzherzog von Österreich, 1601-1625, abdicated
Johann Wilhelm, Erzherzog von Österreich, (1625) 1632-1662
Colomban von Andlau, 1663-1665
Franz Egon, Fürst von Fürstenberg-Heiligenberg, 1665-1682

MINTS

Ensisheim
Gebweiler (French Guebwiller)

ARMS

Murbach – hand raised vertically with first two fingers extended in sign of Episcopal benediction
Lüders – dog rampant left

REFERENCES

D = Jean-Paul Divo, **Numismatique de Murbach**, Zurich, 1998.

De = Jean DeMay, **Les Monnaies d'Alsace**, Bruxelles/Paris, 1976.

ABBEY

REGULAR COINAGE

KM# 1 RAPPEN (Pfennig)

Ruler: Leopold V **Obv:** 4-fold arms of abbeys in circle of pellets **Mint:** St. Amarin **Note:** Ref. De#27. Uniface.

Date	Mintage	VG	F	VF	XF	Unc
(1614-25)	—	75.00	150	300	—	—

KM# 32 RAPPEN (Pfennig)

Silver **Ruler:** Leopold-Wilhelm **Obv:** 3-fold arms of Murbach, Lüders and Austria within circle inside circle of pellets **Mint:** Gebweiler **Note:** Ref. D#117. Uniface hohl-type.

Date	Mintage	VG	F	VF	XF	Unc
ND(1659-62)	—	60.00	120	240	—	—

KM# 33 RAPPEN (Pfennig)

Silver **Ruler:** Johann Rudolf Stör **Obv:** 2-fold arms of Murbach and Lüders in circle, within circle of pellets **Mint:** Gebweiler **Note:** Ref. D#118. Uniface.

Date	Mintage	VG	F	VF	XF	Unc
ND(1659-62)	—	75.00	150	300	—	—

KM# 44 RAPPEN (Pfennig)

Silver **Ruler:** Columban **Obv:** 3-fold arms of Andlau, Murbach and Lüders in circle within circle of pellets **Mint:** Gebweiler **Note:** Ref. D#127. Uniface hohl-type.

Date	Mintage	VG	F	VF	XF	Unc
ND(1663-65)	—	90.00	180	360	725	—

KM# 60 RAPPEN (Pfennig)

Billon **Ruler:** Franz Egon **Obv:** Arms of Furstenberg with those of Murbach and Luders **Mint:** Gebweiler **Note:** Uniface. Ref. D#132. Prev. KM#1.

Date	Mintage	VG	F	VF	XF	Unc
ND(1665-82)	—	65.00	135	275	—	—

KM# 13 BATZEN

Silver **Ruler:** Leopold V **Obv:** Adjacent shields of 2 abbeys, date above, value 'I' in circle below **Obv. Legend:** MONETA NOVA ... **Rev:** Full-length standing figure of St. Leodegar facing **Mint:** Ensisheim **Note:** Ref. D#97. Varieties exist.

Date	Mintage	VG	F	VF	XF	Unc
1624	—	55.00	115	235	475	—

KM# 34 BATZEN

Silver **Ruler:** Leopold-Wilhelm **Obv:** Bust of Leopold Wilhelm to right **Rev:** Crowned and mitered 4-fold arms **Mint:** Gebweiler **Note:** Ref. D#112-114. Varieties exist.

Date	Mintage	VG	F	VF	XF	Unc
ND(1659-62)	—	40.00	80.00	165	335	—

KM# 35 BATZEN

Silver **Ruler:** Leopold-Wilhelm **Obv:** Bust of Leopold Wilhelm to right **Rev:** 2 adjacent shields of arms, Austria on left, crown above, Murbach and Lüders on right, miter above **Rev. Legend:** S. LEODEGARI ... **Mint:** Gebweiler **Note:** Ref. D#115.

Date	Mintage	VG	F	VF	XF	Unc
ND(1659-62)	—	50.00	100	210	425	—

KM# 47 BATZEN

Silver **Ruler:** Columban **Obv:** Ornately-shaped 4-fold arms, titles of Columban **Rev:** Facing figure of St. Leodegar divides date **Mint:** Gebweiler **Note:** Ref. D#120.

Date	Mintage	VG	F	VF	XF	Unc
1663	—	55.00	110	225	450	—

KM# 48 BATZEN

Silver **Ruler:** Columban **Obv:** Ornately-shaped 4-fold arms in Spanish shield, date above, titles of Columban **Rev:** Facing figure of St. Leodegar **Mint:** Gebweiler **Note:** Ref. D#121.

Date	Mintage	VG	F	VF	XF	Unc
1663	—	55.00	110	225	450	—

KM# 49 BATZEN

Silver **Ruler:** Columban **Obv:** 4-fold arms, titles of Columban **Rev:** Figure of St. Leodegar, date at end of legend **Mint:** Gebweiler **Note:** Ref. D#122.

Date	Mintage	VG	F	VF	XF	Unc
1663	—	55.00	110	225	450	—

KM# 2 2 BATZEN (Doppelbätzner)

Silver **Ruler:** Leopold V **Obv:** Adjacent shields of 2 abbeys, value 2 in circle below **Obv. Legend:** MONETA NOVA ... **Rev:** Full-length standing figure of St. Leodegar facing **Mint:** Gebweiler **Note:** Ref. D#96.

Date	Mintage	VG	F	VF	XF	Unc
ND(1614-25)	—	65.00	135	275	550	—

KM# 15 2 BATZEN (Doppelbätzner)

Billon **Ruler:** Leopold V **Obv:** Adjacent shields of 2 abbeys, date above, value 2 in circle below **Obv. Legend:** MONETA • NOVA • MVR • ETLVDR **Rev:** Full length standing figure of St. Leodegar facing **Mint:** Gebweiler **Note:** Ref. D#92. Prev. KM#30.

Date	Mintage	VG	F	VF	XF	Unc
1624//1624	—	65.00	135	275	550	—

KM# 16 2 BATZEN (Doppelbätzner)

Silver **Ruler:** Leopold V **Obv:** Adjacent shields of 2 abbeys, date above, value 2 in circle below **Obv. Legend:** MONETA NOVA ... **Rev:** Full-length standing figure of St. Leodegar facing **Mint:** Gebweiler **Note:** Ref. D#93-95. Varieties exist.

Date	Mintage	VG	F	VF	XF	Unc
1624	—	60.00	125	275	575	—
1625	—	60.00	125	275	575	—

KM# 28 2 BATZEN (Doppelbätzner)

Silver **Obv:** Adjacent shields of 2 abbeys, date above, value 2 in circle below **Obv. Legend:** MONETA NOVA ... **Rev:** Full-length standing figure of St. Leodegar facing **Mint:** Gebweiler **Note:** Ref. D#108-110. Varieties exist.

Date	Mintage	VG	F	VF	XF	Unc
1631	—	60.00	125	275	575	—
1632	—	60.00	125	275	575	—

KM# 38 2 BATZEN (Doppelbätzner)

Silver **Ruler:** Leopold-Wilhelm **Obv:** Bust of Leopold Wilhelm right in circle **Rev:** Crowned and mitered 4-fold arms, value 2 in oval at top **Mint:** Gebweiler **Note:** Ref. D#111.

Date	Mintage	VG	F	VF	XF	Unc
ND(1659-62)	—	60.00	125	275	575	—

KM# 51 2 BATZEN (Doppelbätzner)

Silver **Ruler:** Columban **Obv:** 4-fold arms in Spanish shield divide date, value 2 in cartouche at top, titles of Columban **Rev:** Enthroned figure of St. Leodegar **Mint:** Gebweiler **Note:** Ref. D#119.

Date	Mintage	VG	F	VF	XF	Unc
1663	—	—	—	—	—	—

KM# 40 KREUZER

Silver **Ruler:** Leopold-Wilhelm **Obv:** Bust right, titles of Leopold Wilhelm **Rev:** 2 adjacent shields of arms, austria on left, crown above, Murbach and Lüders on right, miter above **Rev. Legend:** S. LEODEGARI ... **Note:** Ref. D#116.

Date	Mintage	VG	F	VF	XF	Unc
ND(1659-62)	—	35.00	75.00	150	300	—

KM# 53 KREUZER

Silver **Ruler:** Columban **Obv:** 4-fold arms, titles of Columban **Rev:** 1/2-length bust of St. Leodegar to right, date in margin **Mint:** Gebweiler **Note:** Ref. D#126.

Date	Mintage	VG	F	VF	XF	Unc
1663	—	—	—	—	—	—

KM# 3 2 KREUZER (Halbbatzen)

Silver **Ruler:** Leopold V **Obv:** 4-fold arms, titles of Leopold V **Rev:** 1/2-length facing bust of St. Leodegar **Mint:** Ensisheim **Note:** Ref. D#98-99.

Date	Mintage	VG	F	VF	XF	Unc
ND(1614-25)	—	50.00	100	175	360	—

KM# 42 2 KREUZER (Halbbatzen)

Silver **Ruler:** Leopold-Wilhelm **Obv:** Bust right in circle, titles of Leopold Wilhelm **Rev:** 2 adjacent shields of arms, austria on left, crown above, Murbach and Lüders on right, miter above **Rev. Legend:** S. LEODEGARI ... **Mint:** Ensisheim **Note:** Ref. De#36.

Date	Mintage	VG	F	VF	XF	Unc
ND(1659-62)	—	50.00	100	175	360	—

KM# 55 2 KREUZER (Halbbatzen)

Silver **Ruler:** Columban **Obv:** 4-fold arms, titles of Columban **Rev:** St. Leodegar divides date **Mint:** Ensisheim **Note:** Ref. D#123.

Date	Mintage	VG	F	VF	XF	Unc
1663	—	—	—	—	—	—

KM# 56 2 KREUZER (Halbbatzen)

Silver **Ruler:** Columban **Obv:** 4-fold arms, titles of Columban **Rev:** Bust of St. Leodegar divides date **Mint:** Ensisheim **Note:** Ref. D#124.

Date	Mintage	VG	F	VF	XF	Unc
1663	—	—	—	—	—	—

KM# 58 2 KREUZER (Halbbatzen)

Billon **Ruler:** Columban **Obv:** 4-fold arms, titles of Columban **Obv. Legend:** COLVMBAN. E. AP... **Rev:** Facing bust of St. Leodegar, date at end of legend **Mint:** Ensisheim **Note:** Ref. D#125. Prev. KM#5.

Date	Mintage	VG	F	VF	XF	Unc
1664	—	20.00	45.00	90.00	180	—

KM# 64 10 KREUZER (Zehner)

Silver **Ruler:** Franz Egon **Obv:** Bust right in circle, titles of Franz Egon **Rev:** Crowned and mitered 4-fold arms, titles continued, date in exergue, value 'X' in oval at top **Mint:** Gebweiler **Note:** Ref. D#130-31. Prev. KM#50.

Date	Mintage	VG	F	VF	XF	Unc
1666	—	50.00	100	200	400	—
1667	—	50.00	100	200	400	—

KM# 4 12 KREUZER (Zwölfer = Dreibätzner)

Silver **Ruler:** Leopold V **Obv:** Bust right, titles of Leopold V **Rev:** Crowned 4-fold arms, value (12) at bottom **Mint:** Ensisheim **Note:** Ref. D#86.

Date	Mintage	VG	F	VF	XF	Unc
ND(1614-25)	—	150	275	500	—	—

KM# 5 12 KREUZER (Zwölfer = Dreibätzner)

Silver **Ruler:** Leopold V **Obv:** Bust right, titles of Leopold V **Rev:** Crowned 4-fold arms, no indication of value **Mint:** Ensisheim **Note:** Ref. D#87.

Date	Mintage	VG	F	VF	XF	Unc
ND(1614-25)	—	150	300	600	—	—

KM# 6 12 KREUZER (Zwölfer = Dreibätzner)

Silver **Ruler:** Leopold V **Obv:** 2 adjacent ornately-shaped shields of Murbach and Lüders arms, value 12 in oval cartouche below **Obv. Legend:** MONETA NOVA ... **Rev:** 1/2-length bust of St. Leodegar to right **Mint:** Gebweiler **Note:** Ref. D#88-91. Varieties exist.

Date	Mintage	VG	F	VF	XF	Unc
ND(1614-25)	—	135	275	550	—	—

KM# 62 12 KREUZER (Zwölfer = Dreibätzner)

Silver **Ruler:** Franz Egon **Obv:** Bust right in circle, titles of Franz Egon **Rev:** Crowned and mitered 4-fold arms, titles continued, date in exergue, no indication of value **Mint:** Gebweiler **Note:** Ref. D#128.

Date	Mintage	VG	F	VF	XF	Unc
1665	—	—	—	—	—	—

KM# 66 12 KREUZER (Zwölfer = Dreibätzner)

Silver **Ruler:** Franz Egon **Obv:** Bust right in circle, titles of Franz Egon **Rev:** Crowned and mitered 4-fold arms, titles continued, date in exergue, value 'XII' at top **Mint:** Gebweiler **Note:** Ref. D#129.

Date	Mintage	VG	F	VF	XF	Unc
1666	—	—	—	—	—	—

KM# 8 1/4 THALER

7.4900 g., Silver **Ruler:** Leopold V **Obv:** Bust right, titles of Leopold V, date to lower left of shoulder (where present) **Rev:** Crowned 3-fold arms, titles continued **Mint:** Ensisheim **Note:** Ref. D#77-85. Prev. KM#23. Varieties exist.

Date	Mintage	VG	F	VF	XF	Unc
(1)621	—	175	350	700	1,500	—
ND	—	175	350	700	1,500	—

KM# 24 THALER

Silver **Obv:** St. Leodegarius with shield **Obv. Legend:** LEODEGARIVS... **Rev:** Crowned imperial eagle **Rev. Legend:** FERDINANDVS • II • D:G:• **Mint:** Ensisheim **Note:** Dav. #5617. Prev. KM#12.

Date	Mintage	VG	F	VF	XF	Unc
ND(ca. 1630)	—	290	525	1,000	1,850	—

KM# 10 THALER

Silver **Ruler:** Leopold V **Obv:** Bust of Leopold right, date below at left **Rev:** Crowned imperial shield, arms of the abbeys at left and right **Note:** Dav. #5620. Prev. KM#28.

Date	Mintage	VG	F	VF	XF	Unc
1624 Requires confirmation	—	775	1,500	2,750	4,400	—
1623	—	775	1,500	2,750	4,400	—
1625	—	775	1,500	2,750	4,400	—

KM# 20 THALER

Silver **Ruler:** Leopold V **Obv:** Date in front of bust **Note:** Dav. #5620A. Prev. KM#35.

Date	Mintage	VG	F	VF	XF	Unc
1625	—	775	1,500	2,750	4,400	—

KM# 22 THALER

Silver **Ruler:** Leopold-Wilhelm **Obv:** Seated St. Lodegarius with right arm raised, small shield between feet **Rev:** Crowned double-headed imperial eagle **Note:** Dav. #5618. Prev. KM#15. Varieties exist.

Date	Mintage	VG	F	VF	XF	Unc
ND(1626-32)	—	400	800	1,500	2,500	—

KM# 25 THALER

Silver **Obv. Legend:** LEODEGARIvS **Note:** Dav. #5617A. Prev. KM#13.

Date	Mintage	VG	F	VF	XF	Unc
ND(ca. 1630)	—	275	500	975	1,750	—

KM# 26 THALER

Silver **Obv:** St. Leodegarius with shield **Obv. Legend:** LEODEGARIVs... **Rev:** Crowned double-headed imperial eagle **Note:** Dav. #5617B. Prev. KM#14.

Date	Mintage	VG	F	VF	XF	Unc
ND(ca 1630)	—	275	500	975	1,750	—

NASSAU

The Countship of Nassau had its origins in the area of the Lahn of the central Rhineland, with territory on both sides of that river. The first count who attained the title with recognition from the emperor was Walram in 1158. His grandsons, Walram I (1255-88) and Otto I (1255-90), divided their patrimony. Walram claimed the left bank of the Lahn and made Weisbaden his principal seat, whereas Otto took the right bank and ruled from Siegen. Thus, the division of 1255 established the two main lines over the ensuing centuries.

Several times, various branches of the family issued joint coinage, notably in the late 17th and again in the early 19th centuries. Eventually, through extinction of the various lines and the elevation of one ruler to the throne of the Netherlands, all Nassau was reunited under the house of Nassau-Weilburg.

RULERS

Johann Franz Desideratus of Siegen, 1638-1699
Heinrich of Dillenburg, 1662-1701
Wilhelm Moritz of Siegen, 1664-1691
Heinrich Casimir of Dietz, 1664-1696
Franz Alexander of Hademar, 1679-1711

MINT OFFICIALS' INITIALS

Initials	Date	Name
GOH	1681-1682	Gottfried Oto Hoyer, mintmaster in Herborn
HCM	1682-1682	Heinrich (Henning) Christian Müller, mintmaster in Herborn
IA	1684-1691	Jürgen Ahrens (Jörg or Georg Arens) Mintmaster in Herborn
IDS	1681	Johann Dietrich Schlüter, die-cutter

ARMS

Nassau – lion rampant left on field of billets (small vertical rectangles)
Holzappel – griffin rampant left holding apple

REFERENCE

I = Julius Isenbeck, ***Das nassauische Münzwesen***, Wiesbaden, 1879.

PRINCIPALITY

Joint Rulers

RULERS

Johann Franz of Siegen
Heinrich of Dillenburg
Wilhelm Moritz of Siegen
Heinrich Casimir of Dietz
Franz Alexander of Hademar

JOINT COINAGE

KM# 1 ALBUS

Silver Weight varies: 0.75-0.87g., 17-19 mm. **Obv:** Nassau lion to left incircle **Obv. Legend:** MON. NOV. PRINCIP. NASSOVI(Æ)(AE). **Rev:** 4-line inscription in laurel wreath **Rev. Inscription:** 1 / ALBVS/(date) / (mintmaster's initials) **Mint:** Herborn **Note:** Isenbeck 155-59.

Date	Mintage	VG	F	VF	XF	Unc
1681 GOH	—	35.00	75.00	150	300	—

KM# 2 ALBUS

Silver Weight varies: 0.58-0.95g., 17-19 mm. **Obv:** Shield of Nassau arms, FVRST(L). NASSA above in straight line, all in laurel wreath **Rev:** 4-line inscription in laurel wreath **Rev. Inscription:** I / ALBVS / (date) / (mintmaster's initials) **Mint:** Herborn **Note:** Isenbeck 160-63, 165-68, 172-73, 183-84. Varieties exist.

Date	Mintage	VG	F	VF	XF	Unc
1681 GOH	—	18.00	40.00	65.00	130	—
1682 GOH	—	18.00	40.00	65.00	130	—
1682 HCM	—	18.00	40.00	65.00	130	—
1683 HCM	—	18.00	40.00	65.00	130	—
1684 HCM	—	18.00	40.00	65.00	130	—
1684 IA	—	18.00	40.00	65.00	130	—

KM# 3 2 ALBUS

Silver Weight varies: 1.46-1.90g., 20-23 mm. **Obv:** Crowned shield of 4-fold arms **Obv. Legend:** MON. NOV. PRINCIP. NASSOVI(Æ)(E). **Rev:** 4-line inscription with date **Rev. Inscription:** II / ALBVS / (date) / (mintmaster's initials) **Mint:** Herborn **Note:** Isenbeck 154, 164, 169, 174-75. Varieties exist.

Date	Mintage	VG	F	VF	XF	Unc
1681 GOH	—	50.00	115	190	360	—
1682 GOH	—	50.00	115	190	360	—
1683 HCM	—	50.00	115	190	360	—
1684 HCM	—	50.00	115	190	360	—

KM# 5 2 ALBUS

Silver Weight varies: 1.46-1.85g., 20-23 mm. **Obv:** Crowned shield of 4-fold arms **Obv. Legend:** MONETA. NO(V)(U)(A). NASSO(V)(U)IÆ. **Rev:** 4-line inscription with date **Rev. Inscription:** II / ALB(V)(U)S / (date) / (mintmaster's initials) **Mint:** Herborn **Note:** Isenbeck 170-71, 176-82, 185-86. Varieties exist.

Date	Mintage	VG	F	VF	XF	Unc
1683 HCM	—	50.00	100	225	425	—
1684 HCM	—	85.00	200	325	575	—
1684 IA	—	30.00	65.00	135	275	—
Note: Some examples of this date have AI initials in error.						
1685 IA	—	30.00	65.00	135	275	—

KM# 4 THALER

Silver Weight varies: 28.86-29.98g., 44 mm. **Obv:** Half-length armored figures of five princes standing in row, large date in exergue **Obv. Legend:** IOHAN: FRANC. HENRIC. GUIL: MAUR. HENR: CASIM. FRANC: ALEXAND. **Rev:** Crowned shield of 4-fold arms supported by 2 lions **Rev. Legend:** D. G. NASSOVIÆ. PRINCIP. COM. CATTIMELIB. VIAND. ET. DEC. DOM. IN. BEILST. **Mint:** Herborn **Note:** Isenbeck 153; Dav. 7098.

Date	Mintage	VG	F	VF	XF	Unc
1681 GOH-IDS	—	900	1,800	3,600	6,000	—

NASSAU-DIETZ

A branch of the Ottonian line established at the division of Nassau-Dillenburg in 1606. The count attained the rank of prince in 1652. Through marriage Nassau-Dietz became related to the House of Orange in the Netherlands and to the royal line in England. When King William III of England died in 1702, the Prince of Nassau-Dietz became Prince of Orange and all Nassau possessions in the Netherlands passed to him. Orange was lost to France in 1713, but the prince became hereditary *stadtholder* of the Netherlands in 1748. The Prince of Nassau-Dietz gained Fulda in 1803, but had to cede Dietz over to Nassau-Weilburg in 1814, upon becoming the first of the royal house of the Netherlands.

RULERS

Ernst Casimir, 1606-1632
Heinrich Casimir I, 1632-1640
Wilhelm Friedrich Casimir, 1640-1664, Prince from 1652
Heinrich Casimir II, 1664-1696
Johann Wilhelm Friso, 1696-1711
Wilhelm IV, 1711-1751
Wilhelm V, 1751-1806, under regency 1751-1766
Wilhelm Friedrich, 1806-1814 (King Willem I of the Netherlands, 1815-40)

MINT OFFICIALS' INITIALS

Initials	Date	Name
ECD	1683	Ernst Caspar Dürr, mintmaster
	Sept 1691	Johann Jakob Hoffman, mintmaster in Beilstein
	Sept-Dec 1691	Dietrich Zimmermann, mintmaster in Beilstein
FA	1691-1696	Ludwig Christian Friedrich Arnold, mintmaster in Beilstein
IIE	1740-70	Johann Jacob Encke, mintmaster in Hanau
IGH	?-1760	Johann Georg Holtzhey, die-cutter in Amsterdam

PRINCIPALITY

REGULAR COINAGE

KM# 2 2 ALBUS

Silver **Ruler:** Heinrich Casimir II **Obv:** Crowned shield of 6-fold arms with central shield in laurel wreath **Rev:** 4-line inscription with date and mintmaster's initials between two laurel branches **Rev. Inscription:** II / ALBUS / (date) / F.A **Mint:** Beilstein **Note:** Isenbeck 296.

Date	Mintage	VG	F	VF	XF	Unc
1692 FA	—	—	—	—	—	—

KM# 3 15 KREUZER (1/4 Gulden; 1/6 Thaler)

Silver **Ruler:** Heinrich Casimir II **Obv:** Armored bust to right **Obv. Legend:** HEINR. CASIM. FVRST. ZV. NASSAV. **Rev:** Crowned shield of 6-fold arms with central shield, supported by 2 lions, date at top, value (XV) at bottom **Rev. Legend:** ERBSTATHAL - IN. FRISLAND. **Mint:** Beilstein **Note:** Isenbeck 295.

Date	Mintage	VG	F	VF	XF	Unc
1692 FA	—	—	—	—	—	—

KM# 4 60 KREUZER (Gulden; 2/3 Thaler)

Silver **Ruler:** Heinrich Casimir II **Obv:** Armored bust to right **Obv. Legend:** H.D. FVRST. Z. NASS. ERBSTATHALTER IN FRISLAND. **Rev:** Crowned shield of manifold arms supported by 2 lions, date divided below shield, value '60' in cartouche at bottom **Rev. Legend:** VNTER. REGIRVNG. DER. D - VRCHL. F. V. N. P. V. ORANIEN. **Mint:** Beilstein **Note:** Isenbeck 292.

Date	Mintage	VG	F	VF	XF	Unc
1692 FA	—	—	—	—	—	—

KM# 1 2/3 THALER (Gulden)
15.1000 g., Silver, 38 mm. **Ruler:** Heinrich Casimir II **Obv:** Draped bust to right **Obv. Legend:** H. C. FVRST. Z. NASS. ERBSTATHALTER. IN FRISLAND. **Rev:** Crowned shield of 6-fold arms, with central shield, divides date, value (2/3) in oval at bottom **Rev. Legend:** VNTER. REGIRVNG. DER D (-) VRCHL. (F)(E). V. N. P. V. ORANIEN. **Mint:** Beilstein **Note:** Isenbeck 290-91; Dav. 701.

Date	Mintage	VG	F	VF	XF	Unc
1691	—	900	1,650	2,750	—	—

KM# 5 2/3 THALER (Gulden)
15.3000 g., Silver, 38 mm. **Ruler:** Heinrich Casimir II **Obv:** Draped and armored bust to right **Obv. Legend:** H. C. FVRST. Z. NASS. ERBSTATHALTER. IN. FRISLAND. **Rev:** Crowned shield of manifold arms, supported by 2 lions, divides date near bottom, value (2/3) in oval below **Rev. Legend:** VNTER. REGIRVNG. DER. D - VRCHL. F. V. N. P. V. ORANIEN. **Mint:** Beilstein **Note:** Isenbeck 293; Dav. 702.

Date	Mintage	VG	F	VF	XF	Unc
1692	—	425	750	1,500	3,000	6,000

KM# 6 2/3 THALER (Gulden)
15.3000 g., Silver, 38 mm. **Ruler:** Heinrich Casimir II **Obv:** Armored and draped bust to right **Obv. Legend:** H. C. FVRST. Z. NASS. ERBSTATHALTER. IN. FRISLAND. **Rev:** Crowned shield of manifold arms, supported by 2 lions, date divided below, value (2/3) in oval at bottom. **Rev. Legend:** VNTER. REGIRVNG. DER. DV - RCHL. F. V. N. P. V. ORANIEN. **Mint:** Beilstein **Note:** Isenbeck 294; Dav. 703.

Date	Mintage	VG	F	VF	XF	Unc
1692	—	—	—	—	—	—

TRADE COINAGE

KM# 7 6-1/2 DUCAT
Gold **Ruler:** Heinrich Casimir II **Subject:** Death of Heinrich Casimir II **Obv:** Shield of arms **Rev:** Inscription **Mint:** Beilstein

Date	Mintage	VG	F	VF	XF	Unc
ND(1696)	—	1,400	2,000	3,000	4,500	—

NASSAU-DILLENBURG

One of the divisions of the Ottonian line of the house of Nassau which was founded in 1290 by Heinrich I, son of Otto I (1255-1290). Through the years this branch developed strong ties with the Netherlands. The last duke of Nassau-Dillenburg, Christian, died in 1739 and the lands passed to Nassau-Dietz.

RULER
Heinrich, 1662-1701

PRINCIPALITY

REGULAR COINAGE

KM# 4 15 KREUZER (1/4 Gulden; 1/6 Thaler)
Silver Weight varies: 5.00-5.90g., 29-31 mm. **Ruler:** Heinrich **Obv:** Draped bust to right in circle, value (XV) below shoulder **Obv. Legend:** HENRICVS. D.G. NASSOV. PRINC. **Rev:** Crowned shield of 4-fold arms divides date in circle **Rev. Legend:** COM. CATTIMEL. VIAND & DEC. DOM. IN. BEI(L)(S)(T). **Mint:** Herborn **Note:** Isenbeck 189-201, 207-10, 220-3, 225, 233. Varieties exist.

Date	Mintage	VG	F	VF	XF	Unc
1685 IA	—	80.00	165	250	450	—
1686 IA	—	80.00	165	250	450	—
1688 IA	—	80.00	165	250	450	—
1689 IA	—	80.00	165	250	450	—

KM# 5 15 KREUZER (1/4 Gulden; 1/6 Thaler)
Silver Weight varies: 5.18-5.70g., 29-31 mm. **Ruler:** Heinrich **Obv:** Draped bust to right, value (XV) below shoulder, in circle **Obv. Legend:** HENRICVS. D G. NASSOV. PRINC. **Rev:** Crowned shield of oval 4-fold arms between 2 palm fronds, date divided by crown **Rev. Legend:** COM. CATTIMEL. VIAN(.)(D) & dEC. DOM. IN. BEIL(.)(ST). **Mint:** Herborn **Note:** Isenbeck 202-204.

Date	Mintage	VG	F	VF	XF	Unc
1686 IA	—	75.00	120	175	325	—

KM# 6 15 KREUZER (1/4 Gulden; 1/6 Thaler)
Silver Weight varies: 5.18-5.70g., 29-31 mm. **Ruler:** Heinrich **Obv:** Drapted bust to right, value (XV) below shoulder **Obv. Legend:** HENRICVS. D G. NASSOV. PRINC. **Rev:** Crowned shield of 4-fold arms divide date **Rev. Legend:** COM. CATTIMEL. VIAND & DEC. DOM. IN. BEIL. **Mint:** Herborn **Note:** Isenbeck 206.

Date	Mintage	VG	F	VF	XF	Unc
1686 IA	—	75.00	120	175	325	—

KM# 8 15 KREUZER (1/4 Gulden; 1/6 Thaler)
Silver Weight varies: 5.18-5.70g., 29-31 mm. **Ruler:** Heinrich **Obv:** Draped bust to right, value (XV) below shoulder **Obv. Legend:** HENRICVS. D(.)G. NASSOV. PRINC. **Rev:** Crowned shield of oval 4-fold arms, palm fronds at left and right, date divided by crown, all in circle **Rev. Legend:** COM(.) CATTIMEL. VIAND & DEC. DOM. IN. BEIL. **Mint:** Herborn **Note:** Isenbeck 211, 218.

Date	Mintage	VG	F	VF	XF	Unc
1686 IA	—	75.00	125	200	425	—
1687 IA	—	75.00	125	200	425	—

KM# 9 15 KREUZER (1/4 Gulden; 1/6 Thaler)
Silver Weight varies: 5.18-5.90g., 29-31 mm. **Ruler:** Heinrich **Obv:** Draped bust to right, value (XV) below shoulder **Obv. Legend:** HENRICVS. D(.)G. NASSOV. PRINC. **Rev:** Shield of 4-fold arms, crown above divides date **Rev. Legend:** COM. CATTIMEL. VIAND & DEC. DOM. IN. BEIL. **Mint:** Herborn **Note:** Isenbeck 212, 224, 239.

Date	Mintage	VG	F	VF	XF	Unc
1686 IA	—	80.00	165	250	450	—
1688 IA	—	80.00	165	250	450	—
1689 IA	—	80.00	165	250	450	—

KM# 7 15 KREUZER (1/4 Gulden; 1/6 Thaler)
Silver Weight varies: 5.00-5.90g., 29-31 mm. **Ruler:** Heinrich **Obv:** Draped bust to right, value (XV) below shoulder **Obv. Legend:** HENRIC(V)(U)S. D.G. NASSOV. PRINC. **Rev:** Crowned shield of 4-fold arms divide date in circle **Rev. Legend:** COM. CATTIMEL. VIAND & DEC. DOM. IN. BEI(L)(S). **Mint:** Herborn **Note:** Isenbeck 213-17, 226-32, 243-45.

Date	Mintage	VG	F	VF	XF	Unc
1686 IA	—	60.00	100	180	360	—
1687 IA	—	60.00	100	180	360	—
1688 IA	—	60.00	100	180	360	—
1689 IA	—	60.00	100	180	360	—
1690 IA	—	60.00	100	180	360	—

KM# 11 15 KREUZER (1/4 Gulden; 1/6 Thaler)
5.7200 g., Silver, 31 mm. **Ruler:** Heinrich **Obv:** Draped bust to right, value (XV) below shoulder **Obv. Legend:** HENRICVS. D:G. NASSOV. PRINC. **Rev:** Crowned shield of 4-fold arms in baroque frame, date above **Rev. Legend:** COM. CATTIMEL. VIAND & DEC. DOM. IN. BEIL. **Mint:** Herborn **Note:** Isenbeck 246.

Date	Mintage	VG	F	VF	XF	Unc
1691 IA	—	85.00	175	285	550	—

KM# 12 15 KREUZER (1/4 Gulden; 1/6 Thaler)
5.5000 g., Silver, 31 mm. **Ruler:** Heinrich **Obv:** Draped bust to right **Obv. Legend:** HENRICVS. D.G. NASSOV. PRINC. **Rev:** Shield of 4-fold arms in baroque frame, date divided by crown above, value (XV) in cartouche at bottom **Rev. Legend:** COM. CATTIMEL. VIAN - D & DEC. DOM. IN BEIL. **Note:** Isenbeck 247.

Date	Mintage	VG	F	VF	XF	Unc
1692	—	85.00	175	285	550	—

KM# 3 2/3 THALER (Gulden)
19.3800 g., Silver, 38 mm. **Ruler:** Heinrich **Obv:** Draped bust to right **Obv. Legend:** HENRICUS. D:G. NASSOV. PRINC. **Rev:** Crowned shield of 4-fold arms supported by 2 lions, date divided to lower left and right, value (2/3) in oval at bottom **Rev. Legend:** COM. CATTIMEL. VIAND - & DEC. DOM. IN. BEILSTEI. **Mint:** Herborn **Note:** Isenbeck 188; Dav. 697.

Date	Mintage	VG	F	VF	XF	Unc
1684 HCM	—	—	—	—	—	—

KM# 2 THALER
29.2700 g., Silver, 41 mm. **Ruler:** Heinrich **Obv:** Draped bust to right **Obv. Legend:** HENRICUS: D:G: NASSOV: PRINC: **Rev:** Crowned shield of 4-fold arms supported by 2 lions, date divided to lower left and right **Rev. Legend:** COM. CATTIMEL. VIAND & DEC. DOM. IN BEILSTEIN. **Mint:** Herborn **Note:** Isenbeck 187; Dav. 7099.

Date	Mintage	VG	F	VF	XF	Unc
1683	—	—	7,500	9,000	12,000	—

TRADE COINAGE

KM# 10 DUCAT
3.5000 g., Gold, 23 mm. **Ruler:** Heinrich **Obv:** Draped and armored bust to right **Obv. Legend:** HENRICUS. D:G. NASSOV. PRINC. **Rev:** Crowned shield of 4-fold arms, ornaments on left and right, date divided to lower left and right **Rev. Legend:** CO: CATTI: VIAN & DEC. D: IN. BEIL. **Mint:** Herborn **Note:** Isenbeck 219; Fr. 1785.

Date	Mintage	VG	F	VF	XF	Unc
1688	—	5,000	9,000	14,500	22,500	—

NASSAU-HOLZAPPEL-SCHAUMBURG

This minor branch of Nassau-Dillenburg came into being when the younger brother of the Count of Nassau-Dillenburg married the heiress of the Lordships of Holzappel and Schaumburg in 1653. The couple died without a male heir and Holzappel-Schaumburg passed through the marriage of their daughter to Anhalt-Bernburg-Hoym in 1707.

RULERS
Adolf, 1653-1676
Elisabeth Charlotte, 1676-1707

MINT OFFICIALS' INITIALS

Initials	Date	Name
IS	1676	Jakob Schmitzen (Schmitzger), mintmaster
CB	1683-1694	Conrad Bethmann, mintmaster in Cramberg
IHB	1694-1696	Joseph Heinrich Bockelmann, mintmaster
DZ	1696-1698	Dietrich Zimmermann, mintmaster in Cramberg

PRINCIPALITY

REGULAR COINAGE

KM# 1 PFENNIG
1.0000 g., Silver, 12 mm. **Ruler:** Adolf **Obv:** Crown above holzappel (crab-apple) branch in circle **Mint:** Cramberg **Note:** Isenbeck 258-259. Uniface schüssel type.

Date	Mintage	VG	F	VF	XF	Unc
ND(1653-76)	—	35.00	60.00	110	225	—

KM# 17 PFENNIG
0.1400 g., Silver, 11 mm. **Ruler:** Elisabeth Charlotte **Obv:** Crowned shield of griffin arms divide date, where present, or mintmaster's initials **Mint:** Cramberg **Note:** Isenbeck 286-88. Uniface. Varieties exist.

Date	Mintage	VG	F	VF	XF	Unc
1693	—	—	—	—	—	—
ND CB	—	225	450	900	—	—
ND DZ	—	—	—	—	—	—

KM# 13 8 HELLER
Silver Weight varies: 0.50-0.58g., 15-16 mm. **Ruler:** Elisabeth Charlotte **Obv:** Griffin arms in circle **Obv. Legend:** ELISABETH CH. F. Z. N. G. Z. H. **Rev:** Value 'VIII,' date and mintmaster's initials in 3 lines within circle **Rev. Legend:** MONE. NOVA. HOLTZAPPEL. **Mint:** Cramberg **Note:** Isenbeck 282-84.

Date	Mintage	VG	F	VF	XF	Unc
1685 CB	—	450	675	850	1,300	—

KM# 11 KREUZER
Silver Weight varies: 0.36-0.59g., 14-16 mm. **Ruler:** Elisabeth Charlotte **Obv:** Crowned shield of Holzappel arms (griffin) **Obv. Legend:** MON(E). NASS(A). HOLTZA(P)(P). **Rev:** 5-line inscription with date and mintmaster's initials in laurel wreath **Rev. Inscription:** I / KREU / TZER / (date) / CB. **Mint:** Cramberg **Note:** Isenbeck 265-69, 275-77, 281.

Date	Mintage	VG	F	VF	XF	Unc
1683 CB	—	65.00	135	275	550	—
1684 CB	—	55.00	110	225	450	—
1685 CB	—	55.00	110	225	450	—
1686/5 CB	—	425	600	850	1,700	—

KM# 9 ALBUS
Silver Weight varies: 0.60-0.93g., 16-18 mm. **Ruler:** Elisabeth Charlotte **Obv:** Crowned 4-fold arms with central shield within larger 4-fold arms **Obv. Legend:** MONE. NASS(A). (-) HOLTZAPP. **Rev:** 4-line inscription with date and mintmaster's initials in laurel wreath **Rev. Inscription:** I / ALBUS / (date) / CB. **Mint:** Cramberg **Note:** Isenbeck 263-64, 272-74. Varieties exist.

Date	Mintage	VG	F	VF	XF	Unc
1683 CB	—	125	250	500	1,025	—
1684 CB	—	—	—	—	—	—

KM# 12 ALBUS
3.0000 g., Silver, 19 mm. **Ruler:** Elisabeth Charlotte **Obv:** Crowned heart-shaped 2-fold arms of Nassau and Holzappel **Obv. Legend:** ADOLPH. F. Z. N. G. Z. H. **Rev:** 4-line inscription with date and mintmaster's initials in laurel wreath **Rev. Inscription:** I / ALBVS / (date) / CB **Mint:** Cramberg **Note:** Isenbeck 260. Mule of obverse of Adolf (never issued) with reverse of Elisabeth Charlotte.

Date	Mintage	VG	F	VF	XF	Unc
1684 CB	—	—	—	950	1,650	3,300

KM# 10 2 ALBUS
Silver Weight varies: 1.25-1.87g., 21-22 mm. **Ruler:** Elisabeth Charlotte **Obv:** Crowned 4-fold arms with central shield within larger 4-fold arms **Obv. Legend:** MONE(TA). (-) NASS. (-) HOLTZAP(P)(E). **Rev:** 4-line inscription with date and mintmaster's initials **Rev. Inscription:** II / ALB(V)(U)S / (date) / CB. **Mint:** Cramberg **Note:** Isenbeck 261-62, 270-71. Varieties exist.

Date	Mintage	VG	F	VF	XF	Unc
1683 CB	—	700	950	1,300	2,300	—
1684 CB	—	875	1,250	2,000	3,300	—

KM# 14 2 ALBUS
1.3500 g., Silver, 20 mm. **Ruler:** Elisabeth Charlotte **Obv:** Griffin arms to left in circle **Obv. Legend:** ELISABETH. CH F. Z. N. G. Z. H. **Rev:** 5-line inscription with date and mintmaster's initials **Rev. Legend:** MONE. NOVA - HOLTZAPPEL. **Rev. Inscription:** 2 / ALBUS / COLSCH / (date) / CB. **Mint:** Cramberg **Note:** Isenbeck 280.

Date	Mintage	VG	F	VF	XF	Unc
1685 CB	—	—	—	—	—	—

KM# 15 15 KREUZER (1/4 Gulden; 1/6 Thaler)
Silver Weight varies: 5.63-8.66g., 31 mm. **Ruler:** Elisabeth Charlotte **Obv:** Crowned 4-fold arms, with central shield within larger 4-fold arms, divide date at 1 - 6/8 - 5, value (XV) at bottom **Obv. Legend:** ELISAB: CHARL. - F. Z. N. G. Z. HOLT. **Rev:** Hand from clouds at upper left sending rays to sailboat at right on sea, anchor below, all in circle **Rev. Legend:** SPES - NESCIA - FALLI. **Mint:** Cramberg **Note:** Isenbeck 278-279.

Date	Mintage	VG	F	VF	XF	Unc
1685 CB Rare	—	—	—	—	—	—

Note: Example in Meister & Sonntag auction, Sept 2007, in VF realized $16,750.

KM# 4 30 KREUZER (1/2 Gulden; 1/3 Thaler)
9.2100 g., Silver, 32 mm. **Ruler:** Adolf **Obv:** Armored bust to right, value (30) in cartouche below **Obv. Legend:** ADOLPH. FVRST. - ZV. NASSAW. **Rev:** Crowned 4-fold arms with central shield within larger 4-fold arms between 2 palm fronds, date at end of legend **Rev. Legend:** MONETA. NASS: HOLTZAPEL. **Note:** Isenbeck 255.

Date	Mintage	VG	F	VF	XF	Unc
1676 Rare	—	—	—	—	—	—

KM# 3 30 KREUZER (1/2 Gulden; 1/3 Thaler)
9.2100 g., Silver, 32 mm. **Ruler:** Adolf **Obv:** Armored bust to right, value (30) in cartouche below **Obv. Legend:** ADOLPH. FURST. - ZU. NASSAW. **Rev:** Crowned 4-fold arms, with central shield within larger 4-fold arms, divide date **Rev. Legend:** MONETA. NASS: HOLTZAPEL. **Mint:** Cramberg **Note:** Isenbeck 256.

Date	Mintage	VG	F	VF	XF	Unc
1676 IS Rare	—	—	—	—	—	—

KM# 6 1/3 THALER (1/2 Gulden)
9.9000 g., Silver, 31 mm. **Ruler:** Adolf **Obv:** Armored bust to right, value (1/3) below shoulder **Obv. Legend:** ADOLPH. FVRST. - ZV. NASSAW. **Rev:** Crowned 4-fold arms with central shield in larger 4-fold arms, date at end of legend **Rev. Legend:** MONETA. NASS: HOLTZAPEL. **Mint:** Cramberg **Note:** Isenbeck 257.

Date	Mintage	VG	F	VF	XF	Unc
1676 Rare	—	—	—	—	—	—

KM# 5 60 KREUZER (Gulden; 2/3 Thaler)
Silver Weight varies: 18.30-18.66g., 38 mm. **Ruler:** Adolf **Obv:** Armored bust to right, value (60) in cartouche below **Obv. Legend:** ADOLPH - F(V)(U)RST. - Z(V)(U) NASSAW. **Rev:** Crowned 4-fold arms, with central shield within larger 4-fold arms, divide date **Rev. Legend:** MONETA. NASS: HOLTZAPEL. **Mint:** Cramberg **Note:** Isenbeck 248-54; Dav. 699. Varieties exist.

Date	Mintage	VG	F	VF	XF	Unc
1676	—	3,000	4,000	5,200	9,500	—
1676 IS	—	3,000	4,000	5,200	9,500	—

KM# 7 2/3 THALER (Gulden)
Silver **Ruler:** Adolf **Obv:** Armored bust to right, value (2/3) below shoulder **Obv. Legend:** ADOLPH FVRST. - ZV. NASSAW. **Rev:** Crowned 4-fold arms with central shield within larger 4-fold arms divide date **Rev. Legend:** MONETA NASS: HOLTZAPEL. **Mint:** Cramberg **Note:** Dav. 698.

Date	Mintage	VG	F	VF	XF	Unc
1676 Rare	—	—	—	—	—	—

KM# 18 2/3 THALER (Gulden)
16.9700 g., Silver, 35 mm. **Ruler:** Elisabeth Charlotte **Obv:** Crowned 4-fold arms with central shield in larger 4-fold arms, palm fronds at left and right, value (2/3) in oval below **Obv. Legend:** ELIS: CHARL: F. Z. N. GEB - G. Z. HOLTZAPELL. **Rev:** Hand from clouds at upper left sending rays to sailboat at right on sea, anchor below, all in circle, date at end of legend **Rev. Legend:** NACH DEM LEIPZIGER FUS. **Mint:** Cramberg **Note:** Isenbeck 285; Dav. 700.

Date	Mintage	VG	F	VF	XF	Unc
1694 IHB Rare	—	—	—	—	—	—

NASSAU-IDSTEIN

A short-lived branch of the Walramian line, Nassau-Idstein was established when Nassau-Weilburg-Saarbrücken underwent division in 1625. The second and last Count of Idstein was raised to the rank of Prince in 1688, but died childless in 1721. At first, the properties reverted to Saarbrücken, but soon passed to Ottweiler in 1723 and eventually reverted to Weilburg in 1728.

RULERS
Johann, 1625-1677
Georg August Samuel, 1677-1721, Prince in 1688

MINT OFFICIALS' INITIALS

Initials	Date	Name
	1692-?	Georg Hartmann Plappert, mintmaster
HH	1692	Hans Heinrich Hanskammer, mintmaster
ML	1692	Matthias Longerich von Mainz, mintmaster

PRINCIPALITY

REGULAR COINAGE

KM# 2 15 KREUZER (1/4 Gulden; 1/6 Thaler)
Silver Weight varies: 4.80-5.06g., 28-31 mm. **Ruler:** Georg August Samuel **Obv:** Armored bust to right, value 'XV' lower left of shoulder **Obv. Legend:** GEORG. A(V)(U)G(V)(U)ST. (-) V. (-) G. G. - FURST. Z(V)(U). NAS(S). **Rev:** Shield of 8-fold arms, crown above divides date **Rev. Legend:** HONESTE. ET. DECENTER. **Note:** Isenbeck 95-98. Varieties exist.

Date	Mintage	VG	F	VF	XF	Unc
1692 HH	—	175	250	475	1,150	—
1692 ML	—	175	250	475	1,150	—

KM# 1 1/6 THALER
Silver Weight varies: 5.00-5.26g., 29-30 mm. **Ruler:** Georg August Samuel **Obv:** Crowned shield of 8-fold arms **Obv. Legend:** G. A. D. G. P. N. C. S. E. S. D. I. L. W. E. I. **Rev:** Large '1/6' in center, date at top **Rev. Legend:** HONESTE. ET. DECENTER. **Note:** Isenbeck 92, 94.

Date	Mintage	VG	F	VF	XF	Unc
1691	—	350	725	—	—	—
1692	—	—	—	—	—	—

KM# 3 60 KREUZER (Gulden; 2/3 Thaler)
Silver, 37-38 mm. **Ruler:** Georg August Samuel **Obv:** Armored bust to right, '60' in oval cartouche below **Obv. Legend:** GEORG. AVGVST - V. G. G. FURST. ZV. NASS. **Rev:** Shield of 8-fold

arms, crown above divides date **Rev. Legend:** HONESTE. ET. DECENTER. **Note:** Isenbeck 93; Dav. 695.

Date	Mintage	VG	F	VF	XF	Unc
1692 ML Rare	—	—	—	—	—	—

NASSAU-SIEGEN

Nassau-Siegen was a branch of the Ottonian line established when four brothers divided Nassau-Dillenburg in 1606. At first, they ruled jointly and all were raised to the rank of Prince between 1652 and 1664. However, as a result of the religious divisions engendered by the Reformation and exacerbated by the Thirty Years' War, two of their sons founded Catholic and Protestant sub-branches. The Protestant line became extinct in 1734 and the Catholic line in 1743, the titles and territories of both thereafter passing to Nassau-Dietz.

RULERS

Johann I, 1606-1623
Johann II, 1623-1638
Wilhelm, 1623-1638
Johann Moritz, 1623-1679, Prince in 1664
Georg Friedrich, 1623-1674, Prince in 1664
Heinrich, 1623-1652
Catholic Branch
Johann Franz Desideratus, 1638-1699, Prince in 1652
Wilhelm Hyacinth, 1699-1743
Protestant Branch
Wilhelm Moritz, 1652-1691, Prince in 1664
Friedrich Wilhelm I Adolf, 1691-1722
Friedrich Wilhelm II, 1722-1734

PRINCIPALITY

REGULAR COINAGE

KM# 1 1/16 THALER (2 Schilling)
Silver Weight varies: 1.65-1.68g., 22-23 mm. **Ruler:** Johann Moritz **Obv:** Crowned shield of 4-fold arms in circle **Obv. Legend:** IOH. MAVR. NASSA. PRINS. **Rev:** Maltese cross in circle, date at end of legend **Rev. Legend:** XVI. AVF. I. REICHST. **Note:** Isenbeck 151-52.

Date	Mintage	VG	F	VF	XF	Unc
1671	—	225	325	650	1,300	—
1672	—	225	325	650	1,300	—

NASSAU-WEILBURG

As a branch of the Walramian line, Nassau-Weilburg was established upon the division of Nassau-Weilburg-Saarbrücken in 1625. The Count was raised to the rank of Prince in 1737. Following the conclusion of the Napoleonic Wars, the ruler became Duke of all Nassau in 1816. Nassau was absorbed by Prussia in 1866 and became the province of Hesse-Nassau when it was joined to Hesse-Cassel.

RULERS

Ernst Casimir, 1625-1655
Friedrich, 1655-1675
Friedrich Wilhelm I, 1675-1684
Johann Ernst, 1675-1719
Karl August, 1719-1753, Prince in 1737
Karl, 1753-1788
Friedrich Wilhelm II, 1788-1816

MINT OFFICIALS' INITIALS

Initials	Date	Name
	1691-92	Justus Adam Böttger
	1692-1700	Johann Dietrich Schlütere

COUNTSHIP

REGULAR COINAGE

KM# 2 15 KREUZER (1/4 Gulden; 1/6 Thaler)
Silver **Ruler:** Johann Ernst **Obv:** Bust to right, value (XV) below **Obv. Legend:** IOH. ERN. COM. NASS. WEILB. **Rev:** Crowned shield of 8-fold arms with ornaments to left and right, date at end of legend **Rev. Legend:** SINCERE. ET. CONSTANTER. **Mint:** Wiesbaden **Note:** Isenbeck 100.

Date	Mintage	VG	F	VF	XF	Unc
1690	—	—	—	—	—	—

KM# 1 15 KREUZER (1/4 Gulden; 1/6 Thaler)
Silver **Ruler:** Johann Ernst **Obv:** Bust to right, value (XV) below **Obv. Legend:** IOH. ERN. COM. NASS. WEILB. **Rev:** Crowned shield of 8-fold arms between 2 palm branches, date at end of legend **Rev. Legend:** SINCERE. ET. CONSTANTER. **Mint:** Wiesbaden **Note:** Isenbeck 99.

Date	Mintage	VG	F	VF	XF	Unc
1690	—	—	—	—	—	—

KM# 3 THALER
28.3500 g., Silver, 42 mm. **Ruler:** Johann Ernst **Obv:** Armored bust to right **Obv. Legend:** IOHANN. ERNEST. G. Z. N. S. **Rev:** Ornate shield of 8-fold arms, 7 ornate helmets above, divides ANNO - (date) below **Rev. Legend:** V. Z. S. W. H. Z. L. W. V. I. **Mint:** Wiesbaden **Note:** Isenbeck 101; Dav. 7100.

Date	Mintage	VG	F	VF	XF	Unc
1691 Rare	—	—	—	—	—	—

NASSAU-WEILBURG-SAARBRUCKEN

As a branch of the Walramian line, Nassau-Weilburg was divided several times, first in 1429 when separate countships were established in Saarbrücken and Weilburg. The Nassau-Saarbrücken family came to an end in 1574 and the land and titles were returned to Nassau-Weilburg. New branches of Idstein, Saarbrücken and Weilburg came into existence in 1625. Nassau-Weilburg-Saarbrücken, together with Mainz, Hesse-Darmstadt and Frankfurt am Main, issued some joint coinages during the early part of the 17th century. See Mainz for those issues.

RULERS

Ludwig II, 1593-1625

COUNTSHIP

REGULAR COINAGE

KM# 5 2 KREUZER (Halbbatzen)
2.1000 g., Silver, 20x20 mm. **Ruler:** Ludwig II **Subject:** Centennial of the Reformation **Obv:** Ornate shield of 4-fold arms with central shield **Obv. Legend:** L + G + Z + N + S + V + S + H + Z + L + W + V + ITZ + **Rev:** 6-line inscription with date **Rev. Inscription:** IVBI / LEVS. EV / ANGELII / REPVRGA / TI. NVM' / (date) **Mint:** Kirchheim **Note:** Isenbeck 88. Klippe.

Date	Mintage	VG	F	VF	XF	Unc
1617	—	—	—	—	—	—

NEURUPPIN

A provincial town located 35 miles (60km) northwest of Berlin, Neuruppin became a mint site for the margraves of Brandenburg in the early 16th century. A local coinage was produced during the first part of the Thirty Years' War.

PROVINCIAL TOWN

REGULAR COINAGE

KM# 1 PFENNIG
Copper **Obv:** Brandenburg eagle in circle, head divides N ? R. **Note:** Uniface. Kipper Pfennig.

Date	Mintage	VG	F	VF	XF	Unc
ND(1621-22)	—	17.00	35.00	70.00	140	—

KM# 2 PFENNIG
Copper, 13 mm. **Obv:** Brandenburg eagle in circle divides date, head divides N ? R **Note:** Uniface. Kipper Pfennig. Varieties exist.

Date	Mintage	VG	F	VF	XF	Unc
(16)Z1	—	18.00	37.00	75.00	150	—
(16)21	—	18.00	37.00	75.00	150	—
(16)ZZ	—	18.00	37.00	75.00	150	—

NORDHAUSEN

Located north of Thuringia (Thüringen) and 25 miles (40km) northeast of Mühlhausen in Thuringia, the town of Nordhausen is found mentioned in records from as early as 874. It was the site of an imperial mint in the 12th and 13th centuries and was designated a free imperial city in 1253. Coinage was struck locally from about this time until nearly the end of the 17th century, but issues were not continuous throughout this period. Nordhausen was annexed at first to Prussia in 1803 and this was made a permanent arrangement in 1813.

MINT OFFICIALS' INITIALS

Initials	Date	Name
HG	1618-24	Hans Gruber
CM	1624	Conrad Marquard
IK	1660	Johann König
AD	1685-86	Andreas Detmar

ARMS

Eagle, head left, sometimes crowned

FREE IMPERIAL CITY

REGULAR COINAGE

KM# 3 3 PFENNIG
Silver **Obv:** Eagle, head left in circle **Rev:** Imperial orb in ornamented rhombus

Date	Mintage	VG	F	VF	XF	Unc
ND(ca.1610)	—	30.00	65.00	130	265	—

KM# 5 3 PFENNIG
Silver **Obv:** City arms in ornamented oval **Rev:** Imperial orb in ornamented rhombus

Date	Mintage	VG	F	VF	XF	Unc
ND(ca.1615)	—	35.00	75.00	150	300	—

KM# 6 3 PFENNIG
Silver **Obv:** City arms in ornamented oval **Rev:** Imperial orb with 3 divides date

Date	Mintage	VG	F	VF	XF	Unc
1615	—	35.00	75.00	150	300	—

KM# 22 3 PFENNIG
Copper **Obv:** City arms **Rev:** Imperial orb with 3 divides date **Note:** Kipper 3 Pfennig.

Date	Mintage	VG	F	VF	XF	Unc
1622	—	45.00	90.00	180	360	—

KM# 25 12 KREUZER (Schreckenberger)
Silver **Obv:** Crowned city arms in ornate frame **Obv. Legend:** MO. NO. CI. IM. NORTHAVSN **Rev:** Crowned imperial eagle, 12 in orb on breast **Rev. Legend:** FERD. II. ROM. IMP. SEMP. A

Date	Mintage	VG	F	VF	XF	Unc
ND(ca.1622)	—	45.00	85.00	160	325	—

KM# 23 12 KREUZER (Schreckenberger)
Silver **Obv:** Ornate helmet above small city arms, MO. NO. C - IM. NORT **Rev:** Crowned imperial eagle, 12 in orb on breast, titles of Ferdinand II and date **Note:** Kipper 12 Kreuzer.

Date	Mintage	VG	F	VF	XF	Unc
16ZZ	—	40.00	75.00	155	300	—

KM# 24 12 KREUZER (Schreckenberger)
Silver **Note:** Similar to KM#23 but MO. OCI - IM. NORT on obverse and 12 in orb and no date on reverse.

Date	Mintage	VG	F	VF	XF	Unc
ND(ca.1622)	—	45.00	85.00	160	325	—

KM# 37 16 GUTE GROSCHEN (2/3 Thaler = Gulden)
Silver **Obv:** Pointed oval shield of city arms, ornate helmet above **Obv. Legend:** CIVITATIS - NORTHUSÆ. **Rev:** 4-line inscription with date in circle **Rev. Legend:** MONEAT NOVA ARGENTEA **Rev. Inscription:** 16 / GUTE / GROSCHEN / (date) **Note:** Dav. #708.

Date	Mintage	VG	F	VF	XF	Unc
1685	—	450	900	1,800	—	—

KM# 35 24 MARIENGROSCHEN (2/3 Thaler)
Silver **Obv:** Shield of pointed oval city arms, ornate helmet above **Obv. Legend:** CIVITATIS - NORTHUSÆ. **Rev:** 4-line inscription with date in circle **Rev. Legend:** MONETA : NOVA : ARGENTEA* **Rev. Inscription:** XXIIII / MARIEN / GROSCH: / date **Note:** Dav. #706.

Date	Mintage	VG	F	VF	XF	Unc
1685	—	325	650	1,300	2,600	—
1686	—	325	650	1,300	2,600	—

KM# 36 24 MARIENGROSCHEN (2/3 Thaler)
Silver **Obv:** Shield of squarish city arms with rounded top and bottom, ornate helmet above **Obv. Legend:** CIVITATIS + NORTHUSÆ. **Rev:** 5-line inscription with date in broken circle **Rev. Legend:** MONETA. NOVA. ARGENTEA. **Rev. Inscription:** XXIII / MARIEN / GROSC / HEN. / (date) **Note:** Dav. #707.

Date	Mintage	VG	F	VF	XF	Unc
1685 AD	—	450	900	1,800	3,600	—

KM# 7 1/24 THALER (Groschen)
Silver **Obv:** Ornate helmet over small city arms, MO. NO. CI. NORTHA. **Rev:** Imperial orb with Z4, date divided at top, titles of Matthias

Date	Mintage	VG	F	VF	XF	Unc
1616	—	45.00	95.00	190	385	—

KM# 8 1/24 THALER (Groschen)
Silver **Obv:** Oval city arms, MON. IMPE.NORTHAVS **Rev:** Similar to KM#7 **Note:** Varieties exist.

Date	Mintage	VG	F	VF	XF	Unc
1616	—	35.00	75.00	150	360	—
1617	—	35.00	75.00	150	360	—
1618	—	35.00	75.00	150	360	—

KM# 16 1/24 THALER (Groschen)
Silver **Obv:** Small oval city arms, MO : NO :... **Rev:** Imperial orb with 4 **Note:** Kipper 1/24 Thaler.

Date	Mintage	VG	F	VF	XF	Unc
1620	—	90.00	180	360	—	—

KM# 40 2/3 THALER (Gulden)
Silver **Obv:** Ornate helmet divides date above shield of city arms **Obv. Legend:** MO:N. LIB. IMPER CIVITATIS. NORTHUSÆ. **Rev:** Column, sun left, personification of wind right, value (2/3) in oval below **Rev. Legend:** *INCLINATA RURSUS - IN DEO ERIGAR: **Note:** Dav. #704.

Date	Mintage	VG	F	VF	XF	Unc
1685 AD	—	675	1,350	2,750	5,000	—

KM# 41 2/3 THALER (Gulden)
Silver **Obv:** Shield of squarish city arms with rounded top and bottom, ornate helmet divides date above **Obv. Legend:** MO: NO: LI: IMPER: CIVITATIS NORTHUS. **Rev:** Column with sun shining at left, personification of wind at right, value (2/3) in oval below **Rev. Legend:** INCLINATA. RURSU - S. IN DEO ERIGAR. **Note:** Dav. #705.

Date	Mintage	VG	F	VF	XF	Unc
1685 AD	—	800	1,600	3,200	6,300	—

KM# 11 THALER
Silver **Obv:** Helmeted arms, date above **Obv. Legend:** MO. NO. **Rev:** Crowned imperial eagle with orb **Rev. Legend:** MATTHI. I. D: G. ROMA... **Note:** Dav. #5621.

Date	Mintage	VG	F	VF	XF	Unc
1616 Rare	—	—	—	—	—	—

KM# 18.1 THALER
Silver **Obv. Legend:** MON: MOV: CIV.-IMP: NORTHUS. **Rev. Legend:** FERDI. II ... **Note:** Dav.#5623.

Date	Mintage	VG	F	VF	XF	Unc
1620	—	1,450	2,900	6,000	10,000	—

KM# 19 THALER
Silver **Obv:** Crowned eagle separating H-G above in shield at bottom **Obv. Legend:** * MON. NOV. CIVI * IMP • NORTHUS... **Rev:** Crowned imperial eagle, date divided above **Note:** Dav.#5626.

Date	Mintage	VG	F	VF	XF	Unc
1620 HG	—	1,450	2,900	5,800	10,000	—
1623 HG	—	1,450	2,900	5,800	10,000	—

KM# 18.2 THALER
Silver **Obv. Legend:** * MON • NOV • CIV* * IMP • NORTHUS **Rev:** Crowned imperial eagle **Note:** Dav.#5626A

Date	Mintage	VG	F	VF	XF	Unc
1620 HG	—	1,450	2,900	6,000	10,000	—

KM# 27 THALER
Silver **Obv:** Helmeted arms in fancy decoration **Obv. Legend:** MO: NOV: CIV: - IMP: NORTHVS: **Rev:** Crowned imperial eagle **Note:** Dav.#5627.

Date	Mintage	VG	F	VF	XF	Unc
1623	—	1,450	2,900	5,800	10,000	—

KM# 30 THALER
Silver **Obv:** Without initials in arms **Rev:** Initials C-M above crowned imperial eagle, date not divided in legend **Rev. Legend:** MON. NO. CIV.-IM. **Note:** Dav.#5629.

Date	Mintage	VG	F	VF	XF	Unc
1624 CM	—	1,500	3,000	5,500	9,600	—

KM# 29 THALER
Silver **Obv:** H-G in arms **Obv. Legend:** MON. MO. CIVI... **Note:** Varieties exist. Dav.#5628.

Date	Mintage	VG	F	VF	XF	Unc
1624 HG	—	1,200	2,400	4,800	8,300	—

KM# 32 THALER
Silver **Obv:** Date divided above helmeted arms **Rev:** Crowned imperial eagle **Rev. Legend:** LEOPOLDVS. D. G... **Note:** Dav.#5631.

Date	Mintage	VG	F	VF	XF	Unc
1660 IK	—	1,400	2,700	5,700	9,600	—

KM# 20 2 THALER
Silver **Obv:** Helmeted arms with fancy decoration **Rev:** Crowned imperial eagle, date divided above **Note:** Dav.#5622.

Date	Mintage	VG	F	VF	XF	Unc
1620 Rare	—	—	—	—	—	—

KM# 28 2 THALER
Silver **Rev:** Crowned eagle dividing H-G above **Note:** Dav.#5625.

Date	Mintage	VG	F	VF	XF	Unc
1623 HG Rare	—	—	—	—	—	—

KM# 33 2 THALER
Silver **Obv:** Date divided above helmeted arms **Rev:** Crowned imperial eagle **Note:** Dav.#5630.

Date	Mintage	VG	F	VF	XF	Unc
1660 IK Rare	—	—	—	—	—	—

TRADE COINAGE

KM# 13 DUCAT
3.5000 g., 0.9860 Gold 0.1109 oz. AGW **Obv:** Theodosis seated facing **Rev:** Shield of arms in inner circle **Note:** Fr. #1792.

Date	Mintage	VG	F	VF	XF	Unc
1619 Rare	—	—	—	—	—	—

KM# 14 4 DUCAT
Gold **Obv:** City arms **Rev:** Crowned imperial eagle, titles of Ferdinand II **Note:** Fr.#1791.

Date	Mintage	VG	F	VF	XF	Unc
1619 Rare	—	—	—	—	—	—

NORTHEIM

(Nordheim)

The city of Northeim, lying 15 miles north of Gottingen in Brunswick-Luneburg, is known from records dating to the early 11th century. Never gaining status as a Free City of the Empire, Northeim was under the control of the dukes of Brunswick-Luneburg who allowed a local coinage to be struck from the 16th century until 1676.

MINT OFFICIALS' INITIALS

Initial	Date	Name
(a)=	1609-14	Jakob Pfahler
	1614-16	Dietrich Schmidt, warden
	1617	Andreas Einbeck, warden
(b)= or or	1615-18	Valentin Block
	1618-21	Heinrich von Eck
	Ca. 1619-20	Henning Westermann
	Ca. 1620-21	Wilhelm Nordmeier, warden
	1621	Philipp Kahle
	1622	Levin Brockmann
	1622-23	Hans von Eck
PL or (pl)	1662-70	Peter Lohr
WN	1655-59	Wilhelm Nordmeier
(c)= and/or	1671-76	Johann Heinrich Hoffman

CITY

REGULAR COINAGE

KM# 12 FLITTER (1/2 Pfennig)
Copper **Obv:** N flanked by 3-petalled leaf, 8-pointed star above and below **Rev. Inscription:** *1* / FLIT / TER **Note:** Kipper Flitter.

Date	Mintage	Good	VG	F	VF	XF
ND(1621/22)	—	15.00	30.00	60.00	125	—

KM# 13 PFENNIG
Copper **Obv:** N flanked by various ornaments, star above and below **Rev. Inscription:** I / PFEN / NING **Note:** Kipper Pfennig. Varieties exist.

Date	Mintage	Good	VG	F	VF	XF
ND(1621/22)	—	15.00	30.00	60.00	125	—

KM# 19 PFENNIG
Silver **Obv:** Crowned gothic N superimposed on cross **Note:** Uniface. Schussel type. Varieties exist.

Date	Mintage	VG	F	VF	XF	Unc
ND(ca.1623)	—	20.00	40.00	80.00	165	—

KM# 25 PFENNIG
Copper **Obv:** Crowned gothic N divides date **Rev. Inscription:** I / STAT / PEN **Note:** Stadt Pfennig. Varieties exist.

Date	Mintage	Good	VG	F	VF	XF
1655	—	18.00	37.00	75.00	150	—
1656	—	18.00	37.00	75.00	150	—
1657	—	18.00	37.00	75.00	150	—

KM# 36 PFENNIG
Silver **Obv:** Crowned gothic N divides date **Note:** Uniface. Schussel type. Varieties exist.

Date	Mintage	VG	F	VF	XF	Unc
1664	—	16.00	35.00	75.00	155	—
1667	—	16.00	35.00	75.00	155	—
1669	—	16.00	35.00	75.00	155	—
1673 (c)	—	16.00	35.00	75.00	155	—
1674 (c)	—	16.00	35.00	75.00	155	—
1675 (c)	—	16.00	35.00	75.00	155	—
1676 (c)	—	16.00	35.00	75.00	155	—

KM# 15 3 PFENNIG

Copper **Obv:** Crowned gothic N divides date **Rev:** III in circle, around PFENN. NIGE

Date	Mintage	Good	VG	F	VF	XF
16Z1	—	12.00	25.00	50.00	100	—

KM# 14 3 PFENNIG

Copper **Obv:** Crowned gothic N between two rosettes **Rev:** III in circle, legend, date **Rev. Legend:** PFENN. NIG **Note:** Kipper Pfennig.

Date	Mintage	Good	VG	F	VF	XF
16Z1	—	12.00	25.00	50.00	100	—

KM# 17 3 PFENNIG (Dreier)

Silver **Obv:** Gothic N superimposed on cross **Rev:** Imperial orb with 3, cross on orb divides date

Date	Mintage	F	VF	XF	Unc
16ZZ	—	33.00	65.00	135	275	—

KM# 20 3 PFENNIG (Dreier)

Silver **Obv:** Gothic N superimposed on cross

Date	Mintage	F	VF	XF	Unc
16Z3	—	33.00	65.00	135	275	—

KM# 26 3 PFENNIG (Dreier)

Copper **Obv:** Mintmasters' initials divided at bottom

Date	Mintage	Good	VG	F	VF	XF
1655 WN	—	10.00	20.00	40.00	80.00	—

KM# 27 3 PFENNIG (Dreier)

Copper **Obv:** Crowned gothic N superimposed on cross, date divided in legend **Rev. Inscription:** III / STAT / PEN / NI

Date	Mintage	Good	VG	F	VF	XF
1655	—	12.00	25.00	50.00	100	—

KM# 35 3 PFENNIG (Dreier)

Silver, 19.4 mm. **Obv:** Crowned gothic N divides date **Rev:** Imperial orb with 3 **Note:** Varieties exist.

Date	Mintage	VG	F	VF	XF	Unc
166Z	—	20.00	40.00	75.00	155	—
1664	—	20.00	40.00	75.00	155	—
1665	—	20.00	40.00	75.00	155	—
1666	—	20.00	40.00	75.00	155	—
1669	—	20.00	40.00	75.00	155	—
1670 (c)	—	20.00	40.00	75.00	155	—
1671 (c)	—	20.00	40.00	75.00	155	—
1672 (c)	—	20.00	40.00	75.00	155	—
1673 (c)	—	20.00	40.00	75.00	155	—
1674 (c)	—	20.00	40.00	75.00	155	—
1675 (c)	—	20.00	40.00	75.00	155	—
1676 (c)	—	20.00	40.00	75.00	155	—

KM# 16 4 PFENNIG

Copper **Obv:** Crowned gothic N between two rosettes **Rev:** IIII in circle, around PFENNINGE, date **Note:** Kipper Pfennig. Varieties exist.

Date	Mintage	Good	VG	F	VF	XF
16Z1	—	30.00	60.00	120	240	—

KM# 40 4 PFENNIG

Silver **Obv:** Crowned gothic N divides date **Rev. Inscription:** IIII / GUTE / PF **Note:** Gute 4 Pfennig. Varieties exist.

Date	Mintage	VG	F	VF	XF	Unc
1670 (pl)	—	27.00	45.00	80.00	160	—
1670 (c)	—	27.00	45.00	80.00	160	—
1671 (c)	—	27.00	45.00	80.00	160	—
1672 (c)	—	27.00	45.00	80.00	160	—
1673 (c)	—	27.00	45.00	80.00	160	—

KM# 21 MARIENGROSCHEN

Silver **Obv:** Crowned ornate gothic N superimposed on cross, legend, date **Obv. Legend:** MO. NO. NORTHE. **Rev:** Madonna and child in circle **Rev. Legend:** MARIA. M-AT. DOM.

Date	Mintage	VG	F	VF	XF	Unc
16Z3	—	27.00	55.00	110	220	—

KM# 28 MARIENGROSCHEN

Silver **Obv:** Crowned gothic N, legend, date **Obv. Legend:** MO. NO. NORTHE **Rev:** Madonna and child **Rev. Legend:** MAR. MATER. DO. **Note:** Varieties exist.

Date	Mintage	VG	F	VF	XF	Unc
1655 WN	—	20.00	35.00	75.00	155	—
166Z	—	20.00	35.00	75.00	155	—
1664	—	20.00	35.00	75.00	155	—
1665	—	20.00	35.00	75.00	155	—
1666	—	20.00	35.00	75.00	155	—
1669	—	20.00	35.00	75.00	155	—

Date	Mintage	VG	F	VF	XF	Unc
1670	—	20.00	35.00	75.00	155	—
1671	—	20.00	35.00	75.00	155	—

KM# 41 4 MARIENGROSCHEN (1/9 Thaler)

Silver **Obv:** Similar to 6 Mariengroschen KM#38 but legend variation, date **Obv. Legend:** STAD. NORTHEIM. **Rev. Legend:** VON FEINEM SILBER **Rev. Inscription:** IIII / MARIEN / GROS **Note:** Varieties exist.

Date	Mintage	VG	F	VF	XF	Unc
1671 (c)	—	—	—	—	—	—

KM# 38 6 MARIENGROSCHEN (1/6 Thaler)

Silver **Obv:** Castle of five towers, lion below **Obv. Legend:** NORTHEIMISCH STADTGELD **Rev:** Value in center; legend and date around **Rev. Legend:** ANNO DOMINI **Note:** Varieties exist.

Date	Mintage	VG	F	VF	XF	Unc
1669 PL	—	40.00	80.00	155	315	—
1669 (pl)	—	40.00	80.00	155	315	—
1670 (pl)	—	40.00	80.00	155	315	—
1671 (c)	—	40.00	80.00	155	315	—
1672 (c)	—	40.00	80.00	155	315	—

KM# 44 24 MARIENGROSCHEN (2/3 Thaler)

Silver **Obv:** Similar to 6 Mariengroschen KM#38 but legend variation, date **Obv. Legend:** ANNO CHRISTI **Rev. Legend:** MON: NOVA CIVIT: NORTHEIMENSIS **Rev. Inscription:** XXIIII / MARIEN / GROSCH / mintmaster's initials **Note:** Varieties exist.

Date	Mintage	VG	F	VF	XF	Unc
1674 (c)	—	—	—	—	—	—

KM# 5 1/24 THALER (Reichsgroschen)

Silver **Obv:** Imperial orb with Z4, date divided by cross on orb, titles of Matthias **Rev:** Crowned gothic N superimposed on long-armed cross **Rev. Legend:** MON: CIVIT: NORTHEIM

Date	Mintage	VG	F	VF	XF	Unc
1614 (a)	—	27.00	55.00	110	220	—

KM# 6 1/24 THALER (Reichsgroschen)

Silver **Rev:** Without cross in background **Rev. Legend:** MO. NO: CIVI. NORTHEIM **Note:** Varieties exist.

Date	Mintage	VG	F	VF	XF	Unc
1615 (b)	—	24.00	45.00	90.00	170	—
1616	—	24.00	45.00	90.00	170	—

KM# 7 1/24 THALER (Reichsgroschen)

Silver, 19.4 mm. **Obv:** Date divided in legend at top **Note:** Varieties exist.

Date	Mintage	VG	F	VF	XF	Unc
1616	—	24.00	45.00	85.00	170	—
1616 (b)	—	24.00	45.00	85.00	170	—
1618	—	24.00	45.00	85.00	170	—
1619	—	24.00	45.00	85.00	170	—
(1)6Z0	—	24.00	45.00	85.00	170	—
16Z0	—	24.00	45.00	85.00	170	—

KM# 11 1/24 THALER (Reichsgroschen)

Silver **Note:** Klippe.

Date	Mintage	VG	F	VF	XF	Unc
16Z0	—	—	—	—	—	—

KM# 10 1/24 THALER (Reichsgroschen)

Silver **Obv:** Titles of Ferdinand II

Date	Mintage	VG	F	VF	XF	Unc
16Z0	—	27.00	55.00	100	200	—

KM# 18 1/24 THALER (Reichsgroschen)

Silver **Obv:** Imperial orb with Z4, cross on orb divides date, titles of Ferdinand II **Rev:** Crowned gothic N with cross in background **Rev. Legend:** MONE. NOVA. NORTHEIM.

Date	Mintage	VG	F	VF	XF	Unc
16ZZ	—	27.00	55.00	100	210	—

KM# 39 1/24 THALER (Reichsgroschen)

Silver **Rev:** Date left of crown

Date	Mintage	VG	F	VF	XF	Unc
1670	—	27.00	55.00	100	190	—

KM# 42 1/24 THALER (Reichsgroschen)

Silver **Obv:** Imperial orb with Z4, titles of Leopold I **Rev:** Date **Rev. Legend:** MO. NO. NORTHEI

Date	Mintage	VG	F	VF	XF	Unc
1671 (c)	—	27.00	55.00	100	210	—

KM# 37 THALER

Silver **Obv:** Lion dividing P-L city arms of 5-towered gateway **Rev:** Crowned imperial eagle with arms on breast, date below, titles of Leopold **Note:** Dav. #5632.

Date	Mintage	VG	F	VF	XF	Unc
1665 PL Rare	—	—	—	—	—	—

KM# 43 THALER

Silver **Obv:** Arms and 24 on breast of eagle **Rev:** Details added into arms **Rev. Legend:** MON: NOVA. CICIT:... **Note:** Dav. #5633.

Date	Mintage	VG	F	VF	XF	Unc
1671 (c) Rare	—	—	—	—	—	—

NURNBERG

(Nuremberg)

The Franconian town of Nürnberg, located some 120 miles (200 kilometers) north-northwest of Munich, is known from documents at least as early as 1050. It was already mentioned as the site of an imperial mint in 1062 and its early massive fortifications probably date from this period. The first identifiable coins struck in the imperial mint are from the reign of Emperor Konrad III von Hohenstaufen (1138-52). In 1219, Emperor Friedrich II (1215-50) granted free status to Nürnberg and the mint continued to strike imperial coinage from that date. In 1422, the city received the right to strike its own coins and the first issues in silver appeared two years later. The first gold coins of Nürnberg date from about 1429. From then onwards, an almost unbroken succession of coinage was produced by the Nürnberg mint. On 15 September 1806, Nürnberg formally became part of Bavaria, although the last city coins were struck in 1807.

MINT OFFICIALS' INITIALS

Initial or Mark	Desc.	Date	Name
DSD		End of 17th century	Daniel Sigmund Dockler, die-cutter
H/GH		1679-1712	George Hautsch (1745), die-cutter
I.L.OE., OEXELEIN			Johann Leonhard Oexelein
K.R.			George Knoll and Riedner
(a)=	3 wheat ears	1616-18, 20-ca.31	Hans Putzere
(b)=	Star	1619-39	Hans Christoph Lauer
(c)=	Cross	1622-57	Georg Nurnberger (elder)
(d)=	Star	1639-45	Hans David Lauer
(e)=	Cross	1655-77	Georg Nurnberger (younger)
(f)= and/or GFN	Cross	1677-1716	Georg Friedrich Nurnberger

CITY ARMS

Divided vertically, eagle (or half eagle) on left, six diagonal bars downward to right on right side.

Paschal Lamb

The paschal lamb, Lamb of God or Agnes Dei was used in the gold Ducat series. It appears standing on a globe holding a banner with the word "PAX" (peace).

REFERENCES

K = Hans-Jörg Kellner, **Die Münzen der Freien Reichsstadt Nürnberg**, Grünwald bei München, 1957.

Sch = Wolfgang Schulten, **Deutsche Münzen aus der Zeit Karls V.**, Frankfurt am Main, 1976.

S = Hugo Frhr. Von Saurma-Jeltsch, **Die Saurmasche Münzsammlung deutscher, schweizerischer und polnischer Gepräge von etwa dem Beginn der Groschenzeit bis zur Kipperperiode**, Berlin, 1892.

FREE IMPERIAL CITY

TOKEN COINAGE

REGULAR COINAGE

KM# 54 3 HELLER

Copper **Obv:** Nurnberg arms divide date, 3 H above **Note:** Uniface. Kipper 3 Heller.

Date	Mintage	VG	F	VF	XF	Unc
1622	—	—	—	—	—	—

KM# 5 PFENNIG

Billon **Obv:** Two adjacent shields of arms, date above, N below **Note:** Varieties exist. Known struck on thick flan using two dies of 1598, so not uniface. Kellner 267.

Date	Mintage	VG	F	VF	XF	Unc
1601	—	10.00	20.00	40.00	85.00	—
1602	—	10.00	20.00	40.00	85.00	—
1603	—	10.00	20.00	40.00	85.00	—
1604	—	10.00	20.00	40.00	85.00	—
1605	—	10.00	20.00	40.00	85.00	—
1606	—	10.00	20.00	40.00	85.00	—
1607	—	10.00	20.00	40.00	85.00	—
1609	—	10.00	20.00	40.00	85.00	—
1610	—	10.00	20.00	40.00	85.00	—
1611	—	10.00	20.00	40.00	85.00	—
1612	—	10.00	20.00	40.00	85.00	—
1613	—	10.00	20.00	40.00	85.00	—

KM# 9 PFENNIG

Billon **Note:** Klippe. Uniface.

Date	Mintage	VG	F	VF	XF	Unc
1602	—	—	—	—	—	—
1604	—	—	—	—	—	—

KM# 21 PFENNIG

Billon **Obv:** Two adjacent oval arms, date above, N below **Note:** Uniface. Varieties exist.

Date	Mintage	VG	F	VF	XF	Unc
1614	—	10.00	25.00	50.00	100	—
1615	—	10.00	25.00	50.00	100	—
1616	—	10.00	25.00	50.00	100	—
1617	—	10.00	25.00	50.00	100	—
1618	—	10.00	25.00	50.00	100	—
1619	—	10.00	25.00	50.00	100	—
1620	—	10.00	25.00	50.00	100	—

KM# 35 PFENNIG

Billon **Obv:** Nurnberg arms divide date, value I above **Note:** Kipper Pfennig.

Date	Mintage	VG	F	VF	XF	Unc
1620	—	15.00	30.00	60.00	125	—
1621	—	16.00	32.00	65.00	130	—

KM# 45 PFENNIG

Silver **Obv:** Nurnberg arms divide date, N above **Note:** Uniface.

Date	Mintage	VG	F	VF	XF	Unc
1621	—	100	200	350	600	—

KM# 55 PFENNIG

Copper **Obv:** City arms in rhomboid shaped shield **Note:** Uniface. Kellner 272.

Date	Mintage	VG	F	VF	XF	Unc
ND(1622)	—	13.00	27.00	55.00	110	—

KM# 35a PFENNIG

Copper

Date	Mintage	VG	F	VF	XF	Unc
1622	—	11.00	20.00	40.00	80.00	—

KM# 64 PFENNIG

Billon **Note:** Uniface. Varieties exist.

Date	Mintage	VG	F	VF	XF	Unc
1623	—	11.00	22.00	45.00	90.00	—
1624	—	11.00	22.00	45.00	90.00	—
1625	—	11.00	22.00	45.00	90.00	—
1627	—	11.00	22.00	45.00	90.00	—
1628	—	11.00	22.00	45.00	90.00	—
1629	—	11.00	22.00	45.00	90.00	—
1630	—	11.00	22.00	45.00	90.00	—
1631	—	11.00	22.00	45.00	90.00	—
1632	—	11.00	22.00	45.00	90.00	—
1633	—	11.00	22.00	45.00	90.00	—
1634	—	11.00	22.00	45.00	90.00	—
1635	—	11.00	22.00	45.00	90.00	—
1636	—	11.00	22.00	45.00	90.00	—
1637	—	11.00	22.00	45.00	90.00	—
1638	—	11.00	22.00	45.00	90.00	—
1639	—	11.00	22.00	45.00	90.00	—
1640	—	11.00	22.00	45.00	90.00	—
1641	—	11.00	22.00	45.00	90.00	—
1642	—	11.00	22.00	45.00	90.00	—
1643	—	11.00	22.00	45.00	90.00	—
1644	—	11.00	22.00	30.00	90.00	—
1646	—	11.00	22.00	45.00	90.00	—
1647	—	11.00	22.00	45.00	90.00	—
1649	—	11.00	22.00	45.00	90.00	—
1650	—	11.00	22.00	45.00	90.00	—
1652	—	11.00	22.00	45.00	90.00	—
1654	—	11.00	22.00	45.00	90.00	—
1655	—	11.00	22.00	45.00	90.00	—
1656	—	11.00	22.00	45.00	90.00	—
1657	—	11.00	22.00	45.00	90.00	—
1658	—	11.00	22.00	45.00	90.00	—
1659	—	11.00	22.00	45.00	90.00	—
1660	—	11.00	22.00	45.00	90.00	—
1661	—	11.00	22.00	45.00	90.00	—
1662	—	11.00	22.00	45.00	90.00	—
1663	—	11.00	22.00	45.00	90.00	—
1664	—	11.00	22.00	45.00	90.00	—
1665	—	11.00	22.00	45.00	90.00	—
1666	—	11.00	22.00	45.00	90.00	—
1667	—	11.00	22.00	45.00	90.00	—
1668	—	11.00	22.00	45.00	90.00	—
1669	—	11.00	22.00	45.00	90.00	—
1670	—	11.00	22.00	45.00	90.00	—
1671	—	11.00	22.00	45.00	90.00	—
1672	—	11.00	22.00	45.00	90.00	—
1673	—	11.00	22.00	45.00	90.00	—
1674	—	11.00	22.00	45.00	90.00	—

KM# 86 PFENNIG

Billon **Obv:** Two adjacent oval arms, surmounted by angel's head, date above, N below **Note:** Varieties exist.

Date	Mintage	VG	F	VF	XF	Unc
1628	—	13.00	27.00	55.00	110	—
1629	—	13.00	27.00	55.00	110	—
1630	—	13.00	27.00	55.00	110	—
1631	—	13.00	27.00	55.00	110	—

KM# 193 PFENNIG

Billon, 13.9 mm. **Obv:** Nurnberg arms divide date, S.I. above, + to lower right **Note:** Uniface. Varieties exist.

Date	Mintage	VG	F	VF	XF	Unc
1675 (e)	—	10.00	20.00	40.00	80.00	—
1676 (e)	—	10.00	20.00	40.00	80.00	—
1677 (e)	—	10.00	20.00	40.00	80.00	—
1678 (f)	—	10.00	20.00	40.00	80.00	—
1679 (f)	—	10.00	20.00	40.00	80.00	—
1680 (f)	—	10.00	20.00	40.00	80.00	—
1681 (f)	—	10.00	20.00	40.00	80.00	—
1682 (f)	—	10.00	20.00	40.00	80.00	—
1683 (f)	—	10.00	20.00	40.00	80.00	—
1684 (f)	—	10.00	20.00	40.00	80.00	—
1685 (f)	—	10.00	20.00	40.00	80.00	—
1686 (f)	—	10.00	20.00	40.00	80.00	—
1687 (f)	—	10.00	20.00	40.00	80.00	—
1688 (f)	—	10.00	20.00	40.00	80.00	—
1689 (f)	—	10.00	20.00	40.00	80.00	—
1690 (f)	—	10.00	20.00	40.00	80.00	—
1692 (f)	—	10.00	20.00	40.00	80.00	—
1693 (f)	—	10.00	20.00	40.00	80.00	—
1695 (f)	—	10.00	20.00	40.00	80.00	—
1696 (f)	—	10.00	20.00	40.00	80.00	—
1698 (f)	—	10.00	20.00	40.00	80.00	—
1699 (f)	—	10.00	20.00	40.00	80.00	—
1700 (f)	—	10.00	20.00	40.00	80.00	—

KM# 174 1-1/2 PFENNIG

Silver **Obv:** Nurnberg arms divide date, value 1 1/2 (pfg) above **Rev:** N, 1 1/2 (pfg) below

Date	Mintage	VG	F	VF	XF	Unc
1659 (e)	—	—	—	—	—	—

KM# 36 2 PFENNIG (Zweier)

Silver **Obv:** Nurnberg arms divide date, value II above **Note:** Uniface.

Date	Mintage	VG	F	VF	XF	Unc
1620	—	11.00	20.00	33.00	70.00	—

KM# 36a 2 PFENNIG (Zweier)

Copper **Obv:** Nurnberg arms divide date, value II above **Note:** Uniface

Date	Mintage	VG	F	VF	XF	Unc
1621	—	9.00	18.00	37.00	75.00	—
1622	—	9.00	18.00	37.00	75.00	—

KM# 65 2 PFENNIG (Zweier)

Silver **Obv:** Two adjacent shields or arms, II divides date above, N below **Note:** Varieties exist.

Date	Mintage	VG	F	VF	XF	Unc
1623	—	8.00	16.00	30.00	60.00	—
1624	—	8.00	16.00	30.00	60.00	—
1628	—	8.00	16.00	30.00	60.00	—
1630	—	8.00	16.00	30.00	60.00	—
1631	—	8.00	16.00	30.00	60.00	—
1633	—	8.00	16.00	30.00	60.00	—

KM# 28 3 PFENNIG (Dreier)

Silver **Subject:** Enlargement of the City Hall **Obv:** Nurnberg arms in baroque frame, date above **Rev:** 4-line inscription **Note:** Similar to 3 Pfennig, KM#22

Date	Mintage	VG	F	VF	XF	Unc
1616	—	16.00	33.00	60.00	120	—

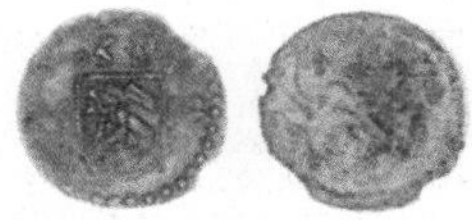

KM# 56 3 PFENNIG (Dreier)

Copper **Obv:** Shield of arms, date at sides, 3 and a pfennigmark above **Note:** Uniface.

Date	Mintage	VG	F	VF	XF	Unc
1622	—	—	—	—	—	—

KM# 66 3 PFENNIG (Dreier)

Silver **Obv:** Two adjacent shields of arms, date above, N below **Rev:** Imperial orb with 3 in baroque frame

Date	Mintage	VG	F	VF	XF	Unc
1623	—	11.00	20.00	35.00	70.00	—
1624	—	11.00	20.00	35.00	70.00	—
1625	—	11.00	20.00	35.00	70.00	—

KM# 107 3 PFENNIG (Dreier)

Silver **Obv:** Nurnberg arms in baroque frame, date divided near top

Date	Mintage	VG	F	VF	XF	Unc
1631	—	13.00	27.00	45.00	90.00	—

KM# 108 3 PFENNIG (Dreier)

Silver **Obv:** Nurnberg arms in ornamented rhombus **Rev:** Imperial orb with 3 divides date, all in ornamented rhombus

Date	Mintage	VG	F	VF	XF	Unc
1631	—	11.00	20.00	35.00	70.00	—
1632	—	11.00	20.00	35.00	70.00	—
1659	—	11.00	20.00	35.00	70.00	—
1662	—	—	—	—	—	—

KM# 6 3 PFENNIG (1/84 Gulden)

Silver **Obv:** Ornamented oval shield of city arms divide date **Rev:** Imperial orb with 84 in ornamented rhombus **Note:** Varieties exist. Kellner 250.

Date	Mintage	VG	F	VF	XF	Unc
1601	—	11.00	20.00	35.00	70.00	—
1602	—	11.00	20.00	35.00	70.00	—
1603	—	11.00	20.00	35.00	70.00	—
1604	—	11.00	20.00	35.00	70.00	—
1605	—	11.00	20.00	35.00	70.00	—
1606	—	11.00	20.00	35.00	70.00	—
1607	—	11.00	20.00	35.00	70.00	—
1608	—	11.00	20.00	35.00	70.00	—
1609	—	11.00	20.00	35.00	70.00	—
1610	—	11.00	20.00	35.00	70.00	—
1611	—	11.00	20.00	35.00	70.00	—
1612	—	11.00	20.00	35.00	70.00	—
1613	—	11.00	20.00	35.00	70.00	—

KM# 22 3 PFENNIG (1/84 Gulden)

Silver **Obv:** Nurnberg arms in baroque frame, date above **Rev:** Imperial orb with 84 in laurel wreath

Date	Mintage	VG	F	VF	XF	Unc
1614	—	11.00	20.00	35.00	70.00	—
1615	—	11.00	20.00	35.00	70.00	—
1616	—	11.00	20.00	35.00	70.00	—

KM# 29 3 PFENNIG (1/84 Gulden)

Silver **Obv:** Oval arms

Date	Mintage	VG	F	VF	XF	Unc
1617	—	11.00	20.00	35.00	70.00	—
1618	—	11.00	20.00	35.00	70.00	—
1619	—	11.00	20.00	35.00	70.00	—
1620	—	11.00	20.00	35.00	70.00	—

KM# 46 1/84 GULDEN (3 Pfennig)

Copper **Obv:** Heart-shaped Nurnberg arms in baroque frame, date divided at top **Rev:** 84 in wreath **Note:** Varieties exist.

Date	Mintage	VG	F	VF	XF	Unc
1621 (a)	—	11.00	20.00	35.00	70.00	—
1622 (a)	—	11.00	20.00	35.00	70.00	—
1622 (b)	—	11.00	20.00	35.00	70.00	—
1622 (c)	—	11.00	20.00	35.00	70.00	—

KM# 40 1/2 KREUZER (2 Pfennig)

Silver **Obv:** Nurnberg arms divide date, 1/2 K above **Note:** Uniface.

Date	Mintage	VG	F	VF	XF	Unc
1620	—	11.00	20.00	35.00	70.00	—

KM# 37 KREUZER (4 Pfennig)

Copper **Obv:** Nurnberg arms, N above **Rev. Inscription:** I / KREUTZ / ER / date **Note:** Kipper Kreuzer. Varieties exist.

Date	Mintage	VG	F	VF	XF	Unc
1620	—	11.00	20.00	37.00	75.00	—
1621	—	11.00	20.00	37.00	75.00	—
1622	—	11.00	20.00	37.00	75.00	—

KM# 68 KREUZER (4 Pfennig)

Silver **Obv:** Double cross (x on ++) **Rev:** Two adjacent arms, date above, I below

Date	Mintage	VG	F	VF	XF	Unc
1623 (c)	—	11.00	20.00	35.00	70.00	—
1624 (a)	—	11.00	20.00	35.00	70.00	—
1630 (a)	—	11.00	20.00	35.00	70.00	—

KM# 67 KREUZER (4 Pfennig)

Silver **Obv:** Imperial eagle, orb on breast with I **Rev:** Two adjacent shields of arms, date above, N below **Note:** Varieties exist.

Date	Mintage	VG	F	VF	XF	Unc
1623	—	13.00	27.00	45.00	90.00	—

KM# 90 KREUZER (4 Pfennig)

Silver **Obv:** Double cross **Rev:** Nurnberg arms in ornamented shield divide date

Date	Mintage	VG	F	VF	XF	Unc
1629 (b)	—	11.00	24.00	40.00	85.00	—

KM# 100 KREUZER (4 Pfennig)

Silver **Obv:** Two coats of arms below date with N at bottom **Rev:** Double cross. Legend begins with star **Note:** Similar to 1 Thaler, KM#51. Varieties exist.

Date	Mintage	VG	F	VF	XF	Unc
1630 (b)	—	11.00	20.00	35.00	70.00	—
	—	—	—	—	—	—
1631 (b)	—	11.00	20.00	35.00	70.00	—
1632 (b)	—	11.00	20.00	35.00	70.00	—
1633 (b)	—	11.00	20.00	35.00	70.00	—
1634 (b)	—	11.00	20.00	35.00	70.00	—
1635 (b)	—	11.00	20.00	35.00	70.00	—
1636 (b)	—	11.00	20.00	35.00	70.00	—
1637 (b)	—	11.00	20.00	35.00	70.00	—
1638 (b)	—	11.00	20.00	35.00	70.00	—
1639 (b)	—	11.00	20.00	35.00	70.00	—
1640 (b)	—	11.00	20.00	35.00	70.00	—
1641 (b)	—	11.00	20.00	35.00	70.00	—

KM# 109 KREUZER (4 Pfennig)

Silver **Obv:** Double cross **Rev:** Two adjacent shields of arms with date above

Date	Mintage	VG	F	VF	XF	Unc
1631 (a)	—	11.00	20.00	35.00	70.00	—
1631 (b)	—	11.00	20.00	35.00	70.00	—

KM# 151 KREUZER (4 Pfennig)

Silver **Note:** Legend begins with cross. Varieties exist.

Date	Mintage	VG	F	VF	XF	Unc
1639 (c)	—	11.00	20.00	35.00	70.00	—
1641 (c)	—	11.00	20.00	35.00	70.00	—
1642 (c)	—	11.00	20.00	35.00	70.00	—
1643 (c)	—	11.00	20.00	35.00	70.00	—

Date	Mintage	VG	F	VF	XF	Unc
1645 (c)	—	11.00	20.00	35.00	70.00	—
1646 (c)	—	11.00	20.00	35.00	70.00	—
1647 (c)	—	11.00	20.00	35.00	70.00	—
1654 (c)	—	11.00	20.00	35.00	70.00	—
1656 (c)	—	11.00	20.00	35.00	70.00	—
1659 (e)	—	11.00	20.00	35.00	70.00	—
1661 (e)	—	11.00	20.00	35.00	70.00	—
1662 (3)	—	11.00	20.00	35.00	70.00	—
1664 (e)	—	11.00	20.00	35.00	70.00	—
1667 (e)	—	11.00	20.00	35.00	70.00	—
1670 (e)	—	11.00	20.00	35.00	70.00	—
1673 (e)	—	11.00	20.00	35.00	70.00	—

KM# 194 KREUZER (4 Pfennig)

Silver **Obv:** Double cross, mint mark (++) divides date at top **Rev:** Oval Nurnberg arms in baroque frame **Note:** Varieties exist.

Date	Mintage	VG	F	VF	XF	Unc
1676 (e)	—	11.00	20.00	35.00	70.00	—
1678 (f)	—	11.00	20.00	35.00	70.00	—
1679 (f)	—	11.00	20.00	35.00	70.00	—
1680 (f)	—	11.00	20.00	35.00	70.00	—
1681 (f)	—	11.00	20.00	35.00	70.00	—

KM# 215 KREUZER (4 Pfennig)

Silver, 16.5 mm. **Obv:** Double cross, date in margin, mint mark (++) at top **Rev:** Two adjacent arms, angel's head above, N below **Note:** Varieties exist.

Date	Mintage	VG	F	VF	XF	Unc
1691 (f)	—	10.00	20.00	35.00	70.00	—
1692 (f)	—	10.00	20.00	35.00	70.00	—
1693 (f)	—	10.00	20.00	35.00	70.00	—
1694 (f)	—	10.00	20.00	35.00	70.00	—
1700 (f)	—	10.00	20.00	35.00	70.00	—

KM# 38 2 KREUZER (1/2 Batzen)

Silver **Obv:** Ornately-shaped Nurnberg arms **Rev. Inscription:** II / KREUTZ / ER / date

Date	Mintage	VG	F	VF	XF	Unc
1620	—	13.00	22.00	40.00	80.00	—
1620 (a)	—	13.00	22.00	40.00	80.00	—

KM# 57 2 KREUZER (1/2 Batzen)

Silver **Obv:** Nurnberg arms, N above **Note:** Kipper Kreuzer. Varieties exist.

Date	Mintage	VG	F	VF	XF	Unc
1620	—	13.00	27.00	45.00	90.00	—
1621	—	13.00	27.00	45.00	90.00	—
1622	—	13.00	27.00	45.00	90.00	—

KM# 157 2 KREUZER (1/2 Batzen)

Silver **Obv:** Eagle, head right **Rev:** Nurnberg arms, 2.K. above

Date	Mintage	VG	F	VF	XF	Unc
ND(1643) (c)	—	11.00	20.00	40.00	85.00	—

KM# 184 2 KREUZER (1/2 Batzen)

Silver **Obv:** Nurnberg arms divide date, 2 above **Rev:** Crowned imperial eagle, Nurnberg arms on breast, titles of Leopold I

Date	Mintage	VG	F	VF	XF	Unc
1665 (e)	—	13.00	24.00	45.00	90.00	—

KM# 200 2 KREUZER (1/2 Batzen)

Silver **Rev:** II K. above arms

Date	Mintage	VG	F	VF	XF	Unc
1680 (f)	—	16.00	27.00	55.00	110	—

KM# 221 2 KREUZER (1/2 Batzen)

Silver **Rev:** 2 on eagle's breast

Date	Mintage	VG	F	VF	XF	Unc
1694 (f)	—	13.00	24.00	45.00	90.00	—
1695 (f)	—	13.00	24.00	45.00	90.00	—

KM# 222 4 KREUZER (Batzen)

Silver **Obv:** Oval Nurnberg arms in baroque frame, date divided below **Rev:** Crowned imperial eagle, 4 in oval on breast, titles of Leopold I

Date	Mintage	VG	F	VF	XF	Unc
1694 (F)	—	16.00	35.00	75.00	155	—

KM# 58 5 KREUZER

Silver **Obv:** Nürnberg arms divide date, V.K. above **Rev:** Crowned imperial eagle, Nurnberg arms on breast, titles of Leopold I **Note:** Kipper 5 Kreuzer. Varieties exist.

Date	Mintage	VG	F	VF	XF	Unc
1622 (a)	—	20.00	35.00	75.00	155	—
1622 (b)	—	20.00	35.00	75.00	155	—
1622 (c)	—	20.00	35.00	75.00	155	—

KM# 39 6 KREUZER

Silver **Obv:** Nurnberg arms in baroque frame **Rev. Inscription:** VI / KREUTZ / ER / date

Date	Mintage	VG	F	VF	XF	Unc
1620	—	16.00	35.00	75.00	155	—

KM# 201 6 KREUZER

Silver **Obv:** Shield of city arms divides date, value K/VI in two lines above **Obv. Legend:** + MON: NOV: ARGENT: REIP: NORIMBERG **Rev:** Crowned imperial eagle with small shield of Nürnberg arms on breast **Rev. Legend:** LEOPOLDVS: D: G: ROM: IMPER: S: A. **Note:** Varieties exist.

Date	Mintage	VG	F	VF	XF	Unc
1680 (f)	—	20.00	40.00	80.00	160	—

KM# 59 10 KREUZER (1/12 Thaler)

Silver **Obv:** Nurnberg arms divide date, value X.K above **Rev:** Crowned imperial eagle, Nurnberg arms on breast, titles of Ferdinand II **Note:** Kipper 10 Kreuzer. Varieties exist.

Date	Mintage	VG	F	VF	XF	Unc
1622 (a)	—	20.00	35.00	75.00	155	—
1622 (b)	—	20.00	35.00	75.00	155	—
1622 (c)	—	20.00	35.00	75.00	155	—

KM# 60 15 KREUZER (1/8 Thaler)

Silver **Note:** Kipper 15 Kreuzer. Varieties exist.

Date	Mintage	VG	F	VF	XF	Unc
1622 (a)	—	11.00	25.00	55.00	110	—
1622 (b)	—	11.00	25.00	55.00	110	—
1622 (c)	—	11.00	25.00	55.00	110	—

KM# 61 20 KREUZER

Silver **Obv:** Nurnberg arms divide date, value K. / XX above **Rev:** Crowned imperial eagle, Nurnberg arms on breast, titles of Ferdinand II **Note:** Kipper 20 Kreuzer. Varieties exist.

Date	Mintage	VG	F	VF	XF	Unc
1622 (a)	—	25.00	50.00	100	200	—
1622 (c)	—	25.00	50.00	100	200	—

KM# 7 30 KREUZER (1/2 Reichsgulden)
Silver **Obv:** Two shields of arms **Obv. Inscription:** RE SPVB / NVRENBERG / F•F **Rev:** Crowned imperial eagle, 30 in orb on breast **Note:** Varieties exist. Kellner 142.

Date	Mintage	VG	F	VF	XF	Unc
MDCI (1601)	—	100	200	400	800	—
MDCII (1602)	—	100	200	400	800	—
MDCIII (1603)	—	100	200	400	800	—
MDCIV (1604)	—	100	200	400	800	—
MDCV (1605)	—	100	200	400	800	—
MDCVI (1606)	—	100	200	400	800	—
MDCVII (1607)	—	100	200	400	800	—
MDCVIII (1608)	—	100	200	400	800	—
MDCIX (1609)	—	100	200	400	800	—
MDCX (1610)	—	100	200	400	800	—
MDCXI (1611)	—	100	200	400	800	—

KM# 18 30 KREUZER (1/2 Reichsgulden)
Silver **Obv:** 2 shields of arms, angel heads above, date below. **Rev:** Crowned imperial eagle, 30 in orb on breast, titles of Matthias **Note:** Varieties exist.

Date	Mintage	VG	F	VF	XF	Unc
1613	—	100	200	400	800	—
1614	—	100	200	400	800	—
1615	—	100	200	400	800	—
1616	—	100	200	400	800	—
1617	—	100	200	400	800	—
1618	—	100	200	400	800	—
1619	—	100	200	400	800	—

KM# 41 30 KREUZER (1/2 Reichsgulden)
Silver **Obv:** Titles of Ferdinand II **Note:** Varieties exist.

Date	Mintage	VG	F	VF	XF	Unc
1620	—	100	200	400	800	—
1621	—	100	200	400	800	—
1622 (b)	—	100	200	400	800	—
1623 (b)	—	100	200	400	800	—
1624 (b)	—	100	200	400	800	—
1625 (b)	—	100	200	400	800	—
1626 (b)	—	100	200	400	800	—
1627 (b)	—	100	200	400	800	—
1628 (b)	—	100	200	400	800	—
1629 (b)	—	100	200	400	800	—
1630 (b)	—	100	200	400	800	—
1631 (b)	—	100	200	400	800	—
1632 (b)	—	100	200	400	800	—
1633 (b)	—	100	200	400	800	—
1635 (b)	—	100	200	400	800	—
1636 (b)	—	100	200	400	800	—
1637 (b)	—	100	200	400	800	—

KM# 62 30 KREUZER (1/4 Thaler)
Silver **Obv:** Nurnberg arms divide date, value K. /XXX above **Rev:** Crowned imperial eagle, Nurnberg arms on breast, titles of Leopold I **Note:** Kipper 30 Kreuzer. Varieties exist.

Date	Mintage	VG	F	VF	XF	Unc
1622 (a)	—	—	—	—	—	—
1622 (b)	—	—	—	—	—	—
1622 (c)	—	—	—	—	—	—

KM# 75 30 KREUZER (1/2 Gulden)
Silver **Obv:** Winged Genius, shield of arms at both sides of legs, date below **Rev:** Crowned double-headed imperial eagle, orb on breast **Note:** Varieties exist.

Date	Mintage	VG	F	VF	XF	Unc
1625 (c)	—	120	235	475	950	—
1626 (c)	—	120	235	475	950	—
1627 (c)	—	120	235	475	950	—
1628 (c)	—	120	235	475	950	—
1629 (c)	—	120	235	475	950	—
1631 (c)	—	120	235	475	950	—

KM# 101 30 KREUZER (1/2 Gulden)
Silver **Rev:** St. Sebald holding model of church, two small arms at both sides of legs, Roman numeral date at bottom **Note:** Varieties exist.

Date	Mintage	VG	F	VF	XF	Unc
1630 (c)	—	100	200	400	800	—
1631 (c)	—	100	200	400	800	—
1632 (c)	—	100	200	400	800	—
1633 (c)	—	100	200	400	800	—
1634 (c)	—	100	200	400	800	—
1635 (c)	—	100	200	400	800	—
1636 (c)	—	100	200	400	800	—
1637 (c)	—	100	200	400	800	—

KM# 140 30 KREUZER (1/2 Gulden)
Silver **Obv:** Two shields of arms, angel heads above, date below **Rev:** Crowned imperial eagle, 30 in orb on breast, titles of Ferdinand II **Note:** Varieties exist.

Date	Mintage	VG	F	VF	XF	Unc
1638 (b)	—	75.00	150	300	600	—
1639 (b)	—	75.00	150	300	600	—
1640 (d)	—	75.00	150	300	600	—
1642 (d)	—	75.00	150	300	600	—

KM# 141 30 KREUZER (1/2 Gulden)
Silver **Obv:** St. Sebald holding model of Church, two small arms at both sides of legs, Roman numeral date at bottom **Note:** Varieties exist.

Date	Mintage	VG	F	VF	XF	Unc
1638 (c)	—	100	200	400	800	—
1639 (c)	—	100	200	400	800	—
1640 (c)	—	100	200	400	800	—
1641 (c)	—	100	200	400	800	—
1642 (c)	—	100	200	400	800	—
1643 (c)	—	100	200	400	800	—
1645 (c)	—	100	200	400	800	—
1646 (c)	—	100	200	400	800	—

KM# 165 30 KREUZER (1/2 Gulden)
Silver **Obv:** Figure of St. Sebald divides date at middle **Note:** Varieties exist.

Date	Mintage	VG	F	VF	XF	Unc
1650 (c)	—	100	200	400	800	—
1657 (c)	—	100	200	400	800	—
1658 (e)	—	100	200	400	800	—

KM# 8 60 KREUZER
Silver **Obv:** Two shields of arms **Obv. Inscription:** RESPVB / NVRENBERG / F • F **Rev:** Crowned imperial eagle, 60 in orb on eagle's breast **Rev. Legend:** +RVDOLPH: II: ROM: - IMP: AVG: P: F: DEC: **Note:** Reichsgulden 60 Kreuzer. Varieties exist. Dav. #89; Kellner 127.

Date	Mintage	VG	F	VF	XF	Unc
MDCI (1601)	—	120	165	300	600	—
MDCII (1602)	—	120	165	300	600	—
MDCIII (1603)	—	120	165	300	600	—
MDCIV (1604)	—	120	165	300	600	—
MDCV (1605)	—	120	165	300	600	—
MDCVI (1606)	—	120	165	300	600	—
MDCVII (1607)	—	120	165	300	600	—
MDCVIII (1608)	—	120	165	300	600	—
MDCIX (1609)	—	120	165	300	600	—
MDCX (1610)	—	120	165	300	600	—
MDCXI (1611)	—	120	165	300	600	—
MDCXII (1612)	—	120	165	300	600	—

KM# 19 60 KREUZER
Silver **Obv:** 2 Adjacent angels with rounded shields on chest, inscription above, date below **Rev:** Crowned double-headed imperial eagle, value in orb on breast **Note:** Titles of Matthias. Varieties exist. Dav. #90.

Date	Mintage	VG	F	VF	XF	Unc
1613	—	120	165	300	600	—
1614	—	120	165	300	600	—
1615	—	120	165	300	600	—
1616	—	120	165	300	600	—
1617	—	120	165	300	600	—
1618	—	120	165	300	600	—
1619	—	120	165	300	600	—

KM# 42 60 KREUZER
Silver **Note:** Similar to 30 Kreuzer, KM#41 but 60 in orb on eagle's breast, titles of Ferdinand II. Varieties exist. Dav. #91.

Date	Mintage	VG	F	VF	XF	Unc
1620	—	120	165	300	600	—
1621	—	120	165	300	600	—
1622 (b)	—	120	165	300	600	—
1623 (b)	—	120	165	300	600	—
1624 (b)	—	120	165	300	600	—
1625 (b)	—	120	165	300	600	—
1626 (b)	—	120	165	300	600	—
1627 (b)	—	120	165	300	600	—
1628 (b)	—	120	165	300	600	—
1629 (b)	—	120	165	300	600	—
1631 (b)	—	120	165	300	600	—
1632 (b)	—	120	165	300	600	—
1633 (b)	—	120	165	300	600	—
1634 (b)	—	120	165	300	600	—
1635 (b)	—	120	165	300	600	—

KM# 63 60 KREUZER (1/2 Thaler)
Silver **Obv:** Value: K./LX above **Rev:** Crowned double-headed imperial eagle, small shield on breast **Note:** Kipper 60 Kreuzer.

Date	Mintage	VG	F	VF	XF	Unc
1622 (b)	—	120	200	335	675	—
1622 (c)	—	120	200	335	675	—

KM# 74 60 KREUZER (1/2 Thaler)
Silver **Obv:** Two oval arms in baroque frame, angel's head above, date in legend **Rev:** Crowned double-headed imperial eagle, 60 in orb on eagle breast **Note:** Reichsgulden 60 Kreuzer. Dav. #92.

Date	Mintage	VG	F	VF	XF	Unc
1624 (a)	—	100	165	300	600	—

KM# 76 60 KREUZER (1/2 Thaler)
Silver **Rev:** Winged Genius, shield of arms at both sides of legs, date below **Note:** Varieties exist. Dav. #93.

Date	Mintage	VG	F	VF	XF	Unc
1625 (c)	—	120	200	375	750	—
1626 (c)	—	120	200	375	750	—
1627 (c)	—	120	200	375	750	—
1628 (c)	—	120	200	375	750	—
1629 (c)	—	120	200	375	750	—

KM# 102 60 KREUZER (1/2 Thaler)
Silver **Obv:** St. Sebald holding model of church, 2 small arms

at both sides of legs, Roman numeral date at bottom **Rev:** Crowned imperial eagle, 60 in orb on breast **Note:** Varieties exist.

Date	Mintage	VG	F	VF	XF	Unc
1630 (c)	—	100	180	300	600	—
1631 (c)	—	100	180	300	600	—
1632 (c)	—	100	180	300	600	—
1633 (c)	—	100	180	300	600	—
1634 (c)	—	100	180	300	600	—
1635 (c)	—	100	180	300	600	—
1636 (c)	—	100	180	300	600	—
1637 (c)	—	100	180	300	600	—

KM# 102.1 60 KREUZER (1/2 Thaler)

Silver **Obv. Legend:** FERDINAND: II: D: G: ROM. IMP SEM... **Rev:** St. Sebald holding model of church, two small arms at both sides of legs, Roman numeral date at bottom **Note:** Dav. #94.

Date	Mintage	VG	F	VF	XF	Unc
1630 (c)	—	100	180	300	600	—
1631 (c)	—	100	180	300	600	—
1632 (c)	—	100	180	300	600	—
1633 (c)	—	100	180	300	600	—
1634 (c)	—	100	180	300	600	—

KM# 102.2 60 KREUZER (1/2 Thaler)

Silver **Obv. Legend:** FERDINAND: II: DG: ROM. SE: AU:... **Note:** Varieties exist. Dav. #95.

Date	Mintage	VG	F	VF	XF	Unc
1635 (c)	—	100	180	300	600	—
1636 (c)	—	100	180	300	600	—
1637 (c)	—	100	180	300	600	—

KM# 142 60 KREUZER (1/2 Thaler)

Silver **Obv:** Titles of Ferdinand III **Rev:** Angel head above two shields, date between **Note:** Varieties exist. Dav. #96.

Date	Mintage	VG	F	VF	XF	Unc
1638 (b)	—	100	190	300	625	—
1639 (d)	—	100	190	300	625	—
1640 (b)	—	100	190	300	625	—

KM# 143 60 KREUZER (1/2 Thaler)

Silver **Rev:** Roman numeral date below saint **Note:** Varieties exist. Dav. #97.

Date	Mintage	VG	F	VF	XF	Unc
1638 (c)	—	100	180	300	600	—
1639 (c)	—	100	180	300	600	—
1640 (c)	—	100	180	300	600	—
1641 (c)	—	100	180	300	600	—
1642 (c)	—	100	180	300	600	—
1643 (c)	—	100	180	300	600	—
1645 (c)	—	100	180	300	600	—
1646 (c)	—	100	180	300	600	—

KM# 166 60 KREUZER (1/2 Thaler)

Silver **Rev:** St. Sebald divides date **Note:** Varieties exist. Dav. #98.

Date	Mintage	VG	F	VF	XF	Unc
1650 (c)	—	100	180	300	600	—
1657 (c)	—	100	180	300	600	—
1658 (e)	—	100	180	300	600	—

KM# 180 60 KREUZER (1/2 Thaler)

Silver **Obv:** Titles of Leopold I **Note:** Varieties exist. Dav. #99.

Date	Mintage	VG	F	VF	XF	Unc
1660 (e)	—	110	200	300	625	—

KM# A29 1/21 THALER (Reichsgroschen)

Silver **Subject:** Centennial of the Reformation **Obv:** Basket held by robed hand from right, inverted over lit candle **Obv. Legend:** ECCLESIA NORI - CA IUBILANS. **Rev:** 4-line inscription containing date in chronogram in ornamented square tablet, angel's head and wings above **Note:** Saurma 1149.

Date	Mintage	VG	F	VF	XF	Unc
MDLLVVVII (1617)	—	—	—	—	—	—

KM# 69 1/9 THALER

Silver **Obv:** 3 small oval shields of arms, 1 above 2 divides date **Rev:** Crowned imperial eagle, 9 in shield on breast, titles of Ferdinand II

Date	Mintage	VG	F	VF	XF	Unc
1623 (b)	—	25.00	55.00	110	220	—
1624 (b)	—	25.00	55.00	110	220	—

KM# 144 1/9 THALER

Silver **Obv:** Titles of Ferdinand III

Date	Mintage	VG	F	VF	XF	Unc
1638 (b)	—	27.00	55.00	115	230	—
1644 (d)	—	27.00	55.00	115	230	—

KM# 47 1/8 THALER

Silver **Note:** Without indication of value.

Date	Mintage	VG	F	VF	XF	Unc
1621 (b)	—	27.00	55.00	115	230	—
1623 (b)	—	27.00	55.00	115	230	—

KM# 77 1/8 THALER

Silver **Rev:** 1/8 in oval on eagle's breast **Note:** Varieties exist.

Date	Mintage	VG	F	VF	XF	Unc
1625 (b)	—	25.00	55.00	110	220	—
1626 (b)	—	25.00	55.00	110	220	—
1628 (b)	—	25.00	55.00	110	220	—
1629 (b)	—	25.00	55.00	110	220	—
1630 (b)	—	25.00	55.00	110	220	—
1631 (b)	—	25.00	55.00	110	220	—
1632 (b)	—	25.00	55.00	110	220	—
1634 (b)	—	25.00	55.00	110	220	—

KM# 132 1/8 THALER

Silver **Rev:** Oval Nurnberg arms in baroque frame divide date **Note:** Varieties exist.

Date	Mintage	VG	F	VF	XF	Unc
1635 (b)	—	25.00	55.00	110	220	—
1636 (b)	—	25.00	55.00	110	220	—
1637 (b)	—	25.00	55.00	110	220	—

KM# 145 1/8 THALER

3.6900 g., Silver, 26 mm. **Obv:** Heart shaped Nurnberg arms in frame divide date **Rev:** Crowned double headed eagle, denomination in oval on breast

Date	Mintage	VG	F	VF	XF	Unc
1638 (b)	—	25.00	55.00	110	220	—
1640 (d)	—	25.00	55.00	110	220	—
1641 (d)	—	25.00	55.00	110	220	—
1643 (d) Unique	—	—	—	—	—	—

KM# 217 1/8 THALER

Silver **Obv:** Laureate bust of Leopold I to right **Rev:** Eagle holding two shields of arms in talons, date between shields, 1/8 in cartouche at bottom

Date	Mintage	VG	F	VF	XF	Unc
1693 GFN	—	30.00	65.00	135	275	—

KM# 70 1/6 THALER

Silver **Obv:** 6 in shield on eagle's breast

Date	Mintage	VG	F	VF	XF	Unc
1623 (b)	—	30.00	65.00	135	275	—
1624 (b)	—	30.00	65.00	135	275	—

KM# 146 1/6 THALER

Silver **Obv:** Titles of Ferdinand III **Note:** Varieties exist.

Date	Mintage	VG	F	VF	XF	Unc
1638 (b)	—	30.00	65.00	135	275	—
1639 (b)	—	30.00	65.00	135	275	—
1641 (d)	—	30.00	65.00	135	275	—
1642 (d)	—	30.00	65.00	135	275	—
1643 (d)	—	30.00	65.00	135	275	—

KM# 48 1/4 THALER

Silver **Note:** Similar to 1/8 Thaler, KM#47. Varieties exist.

Date	Mintage	VG	F	VF	XF	Unc
1621	—	45.00	85.00	160	325	—
1622	—	45.00	85.00	160	325	—
1623 (a)	—	45.00	85.00	160	325	—
1623 (b)	—	45.00	85.00	160	325	—
1624 (a)	—	45.00	85.00	160	325	—
1624 (b)	—	45.00	85.00	160	325	—
1624 (c)	—	45.00	85.00	160	325	—
1625 (a)	—	45.00	85.00	160	325	—

KM# 80 1/4 THALER

Silver **Obv:** 3 shields of arms **Rev:** 1/4 in orb on breast of eagle **Note:** Similar to 1/8 Thaler, KM#47. Varieties exist.

Date	Mintage	VG	F	VF	XF	Unc
1626 (a)	—	45.00	85.00	160	325	—
1627 (a)	—	45.00	85.00	160	325	—
1628 (a)	—	45.00	85.00	160	325	—
1629 (a)	—	45.00	85.00	160	325	—
1631 (a)	—	45.00	85.00	160	325	—
1632 (a)	—	45.00	85.00	160	325	—
1633 (a)	—	45.00	85.00	160	325	—
1634 (a)	—	45.00	85.00	160	325	—
1635 (a)	—	45.00	85.00	160	325	—
1636 (a)	—	45.00	85.00	160	325	—
1637 (a)	—	45.00	85.00	160	325	—

KM# 147 1/4 THALER

Silver **Obv:** Titles of Ferdinand III

Date	Mintage	VG	F	VF	XF	Unc
1638 (a)	—	45.00	95.00	190	385	—
1640 (a)	—	45.00	95.00	190	385	—
1645 (a)	—	45.00	95.00	190	385	—

KM# 218 1/4 THALER

Silver

Date	Mintage	VG	F	VF	XF	Unc
1693 GFN	—	75.00	150	300	600	—

KM# 148 1/3 THALER (1/2 Gulden)

Silver **Obv:** Large oval Nurnberg arms in baroque frame, date divided below, 1/3 in cartouche at bottom **Rev:** Crowned imperial eagle, Nurnberg arms on breast, titles of Ferdinand III **Note:** Varieties exist.

Date	Mintage	VG	F	VF	XF	Unc
1638 (c)	—	45.00	95.00	190	385	—
1639 (c)	—	45.00	95.00	190	385	—
1640 (c)	—	45.00	95.00	190	385	—
1641 (c)	—	45.00	95.00	190	385	—
1642 (c)	—	45.00	95.00	190	385	—
1645 (c)	—	45.00	95.00	190	385	—
1646 (c)	—	45.00	95.00	190	385	—
1657 (c)	—	45.00	95.00	190	385	—
1658 (e)	—	45.00	95.00	190	385	—

KM# 23 1/2 THALER

Silver **Obv:** Three small oval arms in baroque frames, one above two, date below **Rev:** Crowned imperial eagle, titles of Matthias **Note:** Varieties exist.

Date	Mintage	VG	F	VF	XF	Unc
1614	—	55.00	110	225	450	—
1615	—	55.00	110	225	450	—
1616	—	55.00	110	225	450	—

KM# 30 1/2 THALER

Silver **Subject:** Centennial of the Reformation **Obv:** Basket held by robed hand from right, inverted over lit candle, cherub's head and wings in each corner **Obv. Legend:** ECCLESIA NORI - CA IUBILANS. **Rev:** 4-line inscription containing date in chronogram in ornamented square tablet, angel's head and wings above, floral ornaments in each corner **Rev. Inscription:** MARTINVS / LVTHERVS / THEOLOGIE / D:. **Note:** Klippe.

Date	Mintage	VG	F	VF	XF	Unc
MDLLVVVII (1617) Rare	—	—	—	—	—	—

KM# 49 1/2 THALER

Silver **Obv:** Titles of Ferdinand II **Rev:** Upper arms (eagle) divide date **Note:** Varieties exist.

Date	Mintage	VG	F	VF	XF	Unc
1621 (a)	—	50.00	100	210	425	—
1623 (a)	—	50.00	100	210	425	—
1624 (a)	—	50.00	100	210	425	—

KM# 50 1/2 THALER

Silver **Rev:** Upper arms are imperial eagle **Note:** Varieties exist.

Date	Mintage	VG	F	VF	XF	Unc
1621 (b)	—	50.00	100	210	425	—
1623 (b)	—	50.00	100	210	425	—
1624 (b)	—	50.00	100	210	425	—
1625 (b)	—	50.00	100	210	425	—
1625 (c)	—	50.00	100	210	425	—

KM# 78 1/2 THALER

Silver **Obv:** 3 shields of arms **Rev:** 1/2 in orb on eagle's breast **Note:** Similar to 1/8 Thaler, KM#47. Varieties exist.

Date	Mintage	VG	F	VF	XF	Unc
1625 (b)	—	50.00	100	210	425	—
1626 (b)	—	50.00	100	210	425	—
1628 (b)	—	50.00	100	210	425	—

KM# 103 1/2 THALER

Silver **Obv:** Similar to KM#129 but inscription in chronogram **Obv. Inscription:** PAX BONA NVNC REDEAT MARS PEREATQVE FEROX, date **Rev:** Crowned imperial eagle, sword and scepter in claws, imperial bust in shield on breast

Date	Mintage	VG	F	VF	XF	Unc
ND(1630) (b)	—	65.00	135	275	550	—

KM# 110 1/2 THALER

Silver **Obv:** Date in chronogram **Obv. Inscription:** VIVIDA PAX CHRISTI SERVERT NOS TEMPORE TRISTI

Date	Mintage	VG	F	VF	XF	Unc
ND(1631) (b)	—	65.00	135	275	550	—

KM# 129 1/2 THALER

Silver **Obv:** 3 Shields above city view, date in chronogram **Obv. Inscription:** SVBVENIAT FINIS IVDICIVMVE PIIS **Rev:** Crowned double-headed imperial eagle, without sword, scepter or imperial bust

Date	Mintage	VG	F	VF	XF	Unc
ND(1633) (b)	—	65.00	135	275	550	—

KM# 182 1/2 THALER

Silver **Obv:** City view with "Jehovah" in Hebrew above, Roman numeral date in cartouche below **Rev:** Three ornate shields of amrs, one above two **Note:** Varieties exist.

Date	Mintage	VG	F	VF	XF	Unc
1661 (e)	—	65.00	135	275	550	—
1662 (e)	—	65.00	135	275	550	—
1680 (f)	—	65.00	135	275	550	—

KM# 219 1/2 THALER

Silver **Obv:** Three oval shields of arms in baroque frame, one above two, date in margin at upper left **Rev:** Crowned imperial eagle, Nurnberg arms on breast, titles of Leopold I around

Date	Mintage	VG	F	VF	XF	Unc
1693 GFN	—	65.00	135	275	550	—

KM# 149 2/3 THALER (Gulden)

Silver **Obv:** Large oval Nurnberg arms in baroque frame, value and date divided near top of arms **Rev:** Crowned imperial eagle, Nurnberg arms on breast, titles of Ferdinand III **Note:** Varieties exist.

Date	Mintage	VG	F	VF	XF	Unc
1638 (c)	—	90.00	180	360	725	—
1639 (c)	—	90.00	180	360	725	—
1640 (c)	—	90.00	180	360	725	—
1641 (c)	—	90.00	180	360	725	—
1642 (c)	—	90.00	180	360	725	—
1645 (c)	—	90.00	180	360	725	—
1646 (c)	—	90.00	180	360	725	—
1657 (c)	—	90.00	180	360	725	—
1658 (e)	—	90.00	180	360	725	—

KM# 24 THALER

Silver **Obv:** Three shields with date below **Obv. Legend:** MATTHIAS... **Rev:** Crowned double eagle **Note:** Dav. #5634.

Date	Mintage	VG	F	VF	XF	Unc
1614	—	300	650	1,250	2,150	—
1615	—	300	650	1,250	2,150	—
1616	—	300	650	1,250	2,150	—
1617	—	200	500	1,000	1,750	—
1618	—	250	600	1,200	2,000	—
1619	—	250	600	1,200	2,000	—

KM# 51 THALER

Silver **Obv:** Three shields with date above **Rev. Legend:** FERDINANDVS. II: **Note:** Dav. #5635.

Date	Mintage	VG	F	VF	XF	Unc
1621 (a) Rare	—	—	—	—	—	—

Note: Hess-Divo AG Auction 301, 5-05, nice XF realized approximately $20,725

KM# 52 THALER

Silver **Obv:** Upper shield with imperial eagle **Rev:** Crowned double-headed imperial eagle, without sword, scepter or imperial bust **Rev. Legend:** FERDINANDI. II... **Note:** Dav. #5636.

Date	Mintage	VG	F	VF	XF	Unc
1621 (b)	—	60.00	120	210	450	850
1622 (b)	—	60.00	120	210	450	—
1622 (c)	—	60.00	120	210	450	—
1623 (b)	—	60.00	120	210	450	775
1623 (c)	—	60.00	120	210	450	775
1624 (b)	—	60.00	120	210	450	775
1624 (c)	—	60.00	120	210	450	—
1625 (b)	—	60.00	120	210	450	—
1625 (c)	—	60.00	120	210	450	—
1626 (b)	—	60.00	120	210	450	—
1626 (c)	—	60.00	120	210	450	—
1627 (b)	—	60.00	120	210	450	775
1627 (c)	—	60.00	120	210	450	775
1628 (b)	—	60.00	120	210	450	—

KM# 71 THALER

Silver **Obv:** 3 Ornate rounded shields, upper shield is imperial eagle, divided date above **Rev:** Crowned double-headed imperial eagle, without sword, scepter and imperial breast **Rev. Legend:** FERDINANDVS. II:... **Note:** Dav. #5637.

Date	Mintage	VG	F	VF	XF	Unc
1623 (a)	—	60.00	120	220	475	800
1624 (a)	—	60.00	120	220	475	800
1624 (c)	—	60.00	120	220	475	—
1625 (a)	—	60.00	120	220	475	—
1628 (a)	—	60.00	120	220	475	—

KM# 81 THALER

Silver **Rev. Legend:** ...NVRENBERGENSIS. **Note:** Dav. #5639.

Date	Mintage	VG	F	VF	XF	Unc
1626	—	1,750	3,500	6,000	—	—

KM# 83 THALER

Silver **Obv:** Equestrian figure **Rev:** Winged cherub, date in roman numerals **Rev. Legend:** ...NVRENBERGENSIS. **Note:** Dav. #5640.

Date	Mintage	VG	F	VF	XF	Unc
1627	—	—	—	7,500	11,500	—
1628 Rare	—	—	—	—	—	—

Note: Fritz Rudolf Künker Münzenhandlung Auction 134, 1-08, XF realized approximately $12,550; Hess-Divo AG Auction 301, 5-05, XF realized approximately $20,725

Date	Mintage	VG	F	VF	XF	Unc
1630 Rare	—	—	—	—	—	—

KM# 89 THALER

Silver **Rev:** Three shields above city view, date in chronogram in exergue **Rev. Inscription:** CANDIDIA PAX REDEAT / PAX REGNET IN OR. / BE. ET. IN VRBE. / **Note:** Dav. #5643.

Date	Mintage	VG	F	VF	XF	Unc
ND(1628) (b) Rare	—	—	—	—	—	—

Note: Fritz Rudolf Künker Münzenhandlung Auction 134, 1-08, VF realized approximately $10,705; Hess-Divo AG Auction 301, 5-05, VF+ realized approximately $17,410

KM# 93 THALER

Silver **Obv:** Arms in frame with face above and below **Rev:** Crowned imperial eagle with shield on breast **Note:** Dav. #5646.

Date	Mintage	VG	F	VF	XF	Unc
1629 (a)	—	500	1,000	2,150	5,750	—
1630 (a)	—	500	1,000	2,150	5,750	—
1631 (a)	—	500	1,000	2,150	5,750	—

KM# 87 THALER

Silver **Obv:** 3 shields supported by 2 mermaids **Rev:** Crowned imperial eagle with shield on breast **Note:** Dav. #5641.

Date	Mintage	VG	F	VF	XF	Unc
16Z8 (a)	—	700	1,350	2,750	4,850	—

KM# 91 THALER

Silver **Obv:** Date in chronogram in exergue **Obv. Inscription:** VENI AVT SVBVENITV / IS O CHRISTE RED / EMPTOR **Rev:** Bust on breast of crowned double-headed eagle, larger crown above **Note:** Dav. #5644.

Date	Mintage	VG	F	VF	XF	Unc
ND(1629) (B)	—	100	210	425	775	—

KM# 94 THALER

Silver **Obv:** Three shields dividing date above **Rev:** Crowned imperial eagle **Note:** Dav. #5647.

Date	Mintage	VG	F	VF	XF	Unc
1629 (b)	—	70.00	145	300	600	—
1630 (b)	—	70.00	145	300	600	—
1631 (b)	—	70.00	145	300	600	—
1632 (b)	—	70.00	145	300	600	—
1633 (b)	—	70.00	145	300	600	—
1634 (b)	—	70.00	145	300	600	—
1635 (b)	—	70.00	145	300	600	—
1636 (b)	—	70.00	145	300	600	—
1637 (b)	—	70.00	145	300	600	—

KM# 88 THALER

Silver **Obv:** Cherub surrounded by three shields, date in exergue **Rev:** Crowned imperial eagle with arms on breast **Note:** Dav. #5642.

Date	Mintage	VG	F	VF	XF	Unc
1628 (c)	—	80.00	150	325	650	—

KM# 92 THALER

Silver **Obv:** Arms in cartouche **Rev:** Crowned imperial eagle with arms on breast **Note:** Dav. #5645.

Date	Mintage	VG	F	VF	XF	Unc
1629 (c)	—	275	550	950	1,650	—

KM# 104 THALER

Silver **Obv:** Cherub in center of 3 shields, date in exergue, legend, breast **Obv. Legend:** MONETA. NOVA. ARGENTEA... **Rev:** Crowned imperial eagle with arms on breast **Note:** Dav. #5648.

Date	Mintage	VG	F	VF	XF	Unc
1630 (c)	—	90.00	180	350	600	1,400

KM# 105 THALER

Silver **Obv:** Three shields above city view, legend in exergue **Obv. Legend:** NVRINBERGA DIV CHRISTI SIT TVTA SVB VMBRA **Rev:** Crowned imperial eagle with bust on breast **Note:** Dav. #5649.

Date	Mintage	VG	F	VF	XF	Unc
1630 (b)	—	195	400	900	2,300	—

KM# 111 THALER

Silver **Obv:** Inscription in exergue, date in chronogram **Obv. Inscription:** VIVIDA PAX CHRISTI SERVETNOS TEMPORE TRISTI **Note:** Dav. #5650.

Date	Mintage	VG	F	VF	XF	Unc
ND(1631) (b)	—	230	450	1,050	2,000	—

KM# 119 THALER

Silver **Obv:** Cherub surrounded by three shields, date in exergue **Rev:** Crowned imperial eagle with arms on breast, titles of Ferdinand II **Note:** Dav. #5651.

Date	Mintage	VG	F	VF	XF	Unc
1632 (c)	—	90.00	180	400	900	—
1634 (c)	—	100	200	425	950	—
ND (c)	—	90.00	180	400	900	—

KM# 118 THALER

Silver **Obv:** Bust of Gustav II Adolphus right **Rev:** Crowned arms **Note:** Swedish issue. Dav. #4550.

Date	Mintage	VG	F	VF	XF	Unc
1632 (b)	—	230	425	900	2,150	5,900

KM# 130 THALER

Silver **Obv:** Shields above city view, date in chronogram in exergue **Obv. Inscription:** PAX ADSIT BELLVM FVGIAT PESTISQVE SEVERA **Rev:** Crowned double-headed imperial eagle without sword and scepter **Note:** Dav. #5652.

Date	Mintage	VG	F	VF	XF	Unc
ND(1633) (b)	—	230	500	975	1,650	—

KM# 133 THALER

Silver **Obv:** Arms in frame **Rev:** Cherub flying above city view, date in chronogram **Note:** Dav. #5653.

Date	Mintage	VG	F	VF	XF	Unc
ND(1635) (b)	—	700	1,500	3,000	6,000	15,000

KM# 134 THALER

Silver **Obv:** Cherub surrounded by three shields with date above **Rev:** Crowned double-headed imperial eagle with shield on breast **Note:** Dav. #5654.

Date	Mintage	VG	F	VF	XF	Unc
1635 (c)	—	120	240	575	900	—
1636 (c)	—	120	240	575	900	—
1637 (c)	—	120	240	575	900	—

KM# 138 THALER

Silver **Rev. Legend:** FERDINAND: II:... **Note:** Dav. #5655.

Date	Mintage	VG	F	VF	XF	Unc
1637 (c)	—	120	240	575	900	—
1638 (c)	—	120	240	575	900	—

KM# 139 THALER

Silver **Obv:** Three shields in cartouche with date in frame below **Rev:** Crowned imperial eagle **Note:** Dav. #5656.

Date	Mintage	VG	F	VF	XF	Unc
1637 (b)	—	180	325	650	1,100	—
1638 (b)	—	180	325	650	1,100	—
1639 (b)	—	180	325	650	1,100	—
1641 (d)	—	180	325	650	1,100	—

KM# 150 THALER

Silver **Obv:** Arms in frame **Rev:** Crowned imperial eagle with shield **Note:** Dav. #5657.

Date	Mintage	VG	F	VF	XF	Unc
1638 (c)	—	325	650	1,150	1,950	—

KM# 156 THALER

Silver **Obv:** Angel between two shields, Roman numeral date below **Rev:** Crowned imperial eagle with arms on breast **Note:** Dav. #5658.

Date	Mintage	VG	F	VF	XF	Unc
1642 (c)	—	425	900	2,450	4,900	12,000
1645 (c)	—	425	900	2,450	4,900	12,000
1646 (c)	—	425	900	2,450	4,900	12,000
1648 (c)	—	425	900	2,450	4,900	12,000
1649 (c)	—	425	900	2,450	4,900	12,000
MDCLVII (1657) (c)	—	425	900	2,450	4,900	12,000

KM# 172 THALER

Silver **Obv:** 3 Shields **Rev:** "Jehovah" above city view, Roman numeral date in ornate frame below **Note:** Dav. #5659.

Date	Mintage	VG	F	VF	XF	Unc
MDCLVIII (1658) (c)	—	225	450	1,000	2,500	5,750
1661 (c)	—	225	450	1,000	2,500	5,750
1662 (c)	—	225	450	1,000	2,500	5,750
1663 (c)	—	225	450	1,000	2,500	5,750
1677 (c)	—	225	450	1,000	2,500	5,750

KM# 202 THALER

Silver **Obv:** 3 Shields **Rev:** Different city view and ornate frame **Note:** Dav. #5661.

Date	Mintage	VG	F	VF	XF	Unc
MDCLXXX (1680) (f)	—	180	350	600	950	1,500

KM# 203 THALER

Silver **Rev:** Crowned eagle above City Hall, seated figure of Nuremburg in foreground **Note:** Dav. #5663.

Date	Mintage	VG	F	VF	XF	Unc
ND(1688) PHM-F	—	—	—	3,000	5,500	8,500

KM# 204 THALER

Silver **Obv:** Different city view **Rev:** D. S. D. below figure, without cross **Note:** Dav. #5664.

Date	Mintage	VG	F	VF	XF	Unc
ND(1688) DSD	—	—	—	3,500	6,000	9,500

KM# 220 THALER

Silver **Obv:** Bust of Leopold right **Rev:** Eagle above two shields, date between, GFN below **Note:** Dav. #5665.

Date	Mintage	VG	F	VF	XF	Unc
1693 GFN	—	145	300	650	1,200	2,400

KM# 223 THALER

Silver **Obv:** Three shields with decorations, GFN below **Rev:** "Jehovah" above city view, Roman numeral date in ornate frame below **Note:** Dav. #5666.

Date	Mintage	VG	F	VF	XF	Unc
MDCXCIV (1694) GFN	—	145	300	650	1,100	2,200

KM# 224 THALER

Silver **Rev:** Crowned imperial eagle wtih arms on breast **Note:** Dav. #5667.

Date	Mintage	VG	F	VF	XF	Unc
1694 GFN	—	1,000	2,000	4,250	8,750	15,000

KM# 228 THALER

Silver **Obv:** Eye of God above city view, Roman numeral date in cartouche below **Rev:** Angel with two shields of arm **Note:** Dav. #5668.

Date	Mintage	VG	F	VF	XF	Unc
MDCXCVI (1696) GFN	—	90.00	180	450	1,100	2,100

KM# 230 THALER

Silver **Subject:** Peace of Ryswick **Obv:** "Jehovah" above city view, inscription and date below **Rev:** Peace standing above two genii holding shields of arms **Note:** Dav. #5669.

Date	Mintage	VG	F	VF	XF	Unc
1698 GFN	—	180	450	950	1,800	3,000

KM# 82 2 THALER

Silver **Obv:** 3 shields dividing date above **Rev:** Crowned imperial eagle, titles of Ferdinand II **Note:** Dav. #5638.

Date	Mintage	VG	F	VF	XF	Unc
1626 Rare	—	—	—	—	—	—

Note: Hess-Divo AG Auction 301, 5-05, VF-XF realized approximately $26,525

KM# 84 2 THALER

Silver **Obv:** Equestrian figure of Ferdinand II right **Rev:** Winged cherub with two shields of arms, date in exergue **Note:** Dav. #A5640.

Date	Mintage	VG	F	VF	XF	Unc
MDCXXVII (1627)	—	—	—	8,300	15,000	—
MDCXXVIII (1628)	—	—	—	8,300	15,000	—
MDCXXX (1630)	—	—	—	8,300	15,000	—

KM# 205 2 THALER

Silver **Note:** Similar to 1 Thaler, KM#203. Dav. #5662.

Date	Mintage	VG	F	VF	XF	Unc
ND(1688) PHM (F) Rare	—	—	—	—	—	—

KM# 206 3 THALER

Silver **Obv:** 3 shields of arms **Rev:** City view and ornate frame, date within **Note:** Similar to 1 Thaler, KM#202. Dav. #5660.

Date	Mintage	VG	F	VF	XF	Unc
1680 (f) Rare	—	—	—	—	—	—

TRADE COINAGE

MB# 100 GOLDGULDEN

3.5000 g., 0.9860 Gold 0.1109 oz. AGW **Obv:** Eagle in circle **Obv. Legend:** MONE. REIPVB. - NVRENBERG. **Rev:** Full-length facing figure of St. Lawrence divides date **Rev. Legend:** SANCTVS - LAVRENTIVS. **Note:** Fr#1807. Ref. K#17.

Date	Mintage	VG	F	VF	XF	Unc
1604	—	275	500	925	1,800	—

KM# 10 GOLDGULDEN

3.5000 g., 0.9860 Gold 0.1109 oz. AGW **Obv:** Eagle with N on breast **Obv. Legend:** + NVREMBERG + MONE + REIPVB **Rev:** St. Lawerence **Rev. Legend:** SANCTVS - LAVRENTIVS

Date	Mintage	VG	F	VF	XF	Unc
1611	—	240	500	850	1,550	—
1612	—	240	500	850	1,550	—
1613	—	240	500	850	1,550	—

KM# 15 GOLDGULDEN

3.5000 g., 0.9860 Gold 0.1109 oz. AGW **Obv:** Matthias and Anna **Rev:** Three shields of arms

Date	Mintage	VG	F	VF	XF	Unc
1612	—	725	1,650	2,750	4,700	—

KM# 25.1 GOLDGULDEN

3.5000 g., 0.9860 Gold 0.1109 oz. AGW **Obv:** Oval arms in ornate frame **Rev:** St. Lawrence standing holding gridiron facing right

Date	Mintage	VG	F	VF	XF	Unc
1614	—	325	550	775	1,600	—
1615	—	325	550	775	1,600	—

KM# 25.2 GOLDGULDEN

3.5000 g., 0.9860 Gold 0.1109 oz. AGW **Rev:** St. Lawrence standing holding gridiron facing left

Date	Mintage	VG	F	VF	XF	Unc
1617	—	325	550	825	1,650	—

KM# 31 GOLDGULDEN

3.5000 g., 0.9860 Gold 0.1109 oz. AGW **Obv:** Angel above arms **Rev:** St. Lawrence standing holding gridiron

Date	Mintage	VG	F	VF	XF	Unc
1618	—	350	600	1,050	2,100	—

KM# 32 GOLDGULDEN

3.5000 g., 0.9860 Gold 0.1109 oz. AGW **Obv:** Oval arms

Date	Mintage	VG	F	VF	XF	Unc
1619	—	350	600	1,050	2,100	—

KM# 43 GOLDGULDEN

3.5000 g., 0.9860 Gold 0.1109 oz. AGW **Obv:** Oval arms **Rev:** St. Lawrence standing

Date	Mintage	VG	F	VF	XF	Unc
1620	—	240	500	850	1,550	—
1621	—	240	500	850	1,550	—
1622	—	240	500	850	1,550	—

KM# 44 GOLDGULDEN

3.5000 g., 0.9860 Gold 0.1109 oz. AGW **Obv:** Eagle with N on shield **Note:** Varieties exist.

Date	Mintage	VG	F	VF	XF	Unc
1620	—	325	550	925	1,950	—
1621	—	325	550	925	1,950	—
1623	—	325	550	925	1,950	—

KM# 73 GOLDGULDEN

3.5000 g., 0.9860 Gold 0.1109 oz. AGW **Obv:** Displayed eagle with N on breast **Rev:** St. Sebaldus **Note:** Varieties exist.

Date	Mintage	VG	F	VF	XF	Unc
1623	—	1,600	3,200	7,500	12,500	—
1624	—	1,600	3,200	7,500	12,500	—
1625	—	1,600	3,200	7,500	12,500	—
1626	—	1,600	3,200	7,500	12,500	—
1633	—	1,600	3,200	7,500	12,500	—
1634	—	1,600	3,200	7,500	12,500	—
1636	—	1,600	3,200	7,500	12,500	—
1637	—	1,600	3,200	7,500	12,500	—
1642	—	1,600	3,200	7,500	12,500	—
1643	—	1,600	3,200	7,500	12,500	—
1646	—	1,600	3,200	7,500	12,500	—
1686	—	1,600	3,200	7,500	12,500	—

KM# 72 GOLDGULDEN

3.5000 g., 0.9860 Gold 0.1109 oz. AGW **Obv:** Eagle with N on shield **Note:** Varieties exist.

Date	Mintage	VG	F	VF	XF	Unc
1623	—	350	725	1,250	2,000	—
1626	—	350	725	1,250	2,000	—
1629	—	350	725	1,250	2,000	—
1632	—	350	725	1,250	2,000	—
1634	—	350	725	1,250	2,000	—
1635	—	350	725	1,250	2,000	—
1636	—	350	725	1,250	2,000	—
1639	—	350	725	1,250	2,000	—
1640	—	350	725	1,250	2,000	—
1686	—	350	725	1,250	2,000	—

KM# 95 GOLDGULDEN

3.5000 g., 0.9860 Gold 0.1109 oz. AGW **Obv:** Oval arms in cartouche in inner circle

Date	Mintage	VG	F	VF	XF	Unc
1629	—	2,400	4,800	9,000	14,400	—
1630	—	2,400	4,800	9,000	14,400	—

KM# 16 2 GOLDGULDEN

7.0000 g., 0.9860 Gold 0.2219 oz. AGW **Obv:** Jugate busts of Matthias and Anna right **Rev:** Three shields in inner circle, date at bottom

Date	Mintage	VG	F	VF	XF	Unc
1612 Rare	—	—	—	—	—	—

KM# 26 2 GOLDGULDEN

7.0000 g., 0.9860 Gold 0.2219 oz. AGW **Obv:** Oval arms in cartuoche in inner circle **Rev:** St. Lawrence standing holding gridiron and book

Date	Mintage	VG	F	VF	XF	Unc
1614 Rare	—	—	—	—	—	—

KM# 27 2 GOLDGULDEN

7.0000 g., 0.9860 Gold 0.2219 oz. AGW **Obv:** Imperial eagle **Note:** Varieties exist.

Date	Mintage	VG	F	VF	XF	Unc
1615 Rare	—	—	—	—	—	—
1617 Rare	—	—	—	—	—	—
1618 Rare	—	—	—	—	—	—
1619 Rare	—	—	—	—	—	—

KM# 53 2 GOLDGULDEN

7.0000 g., 0.9860 Gold 0.2219 oz. AGW **Obv:** Titles of Ferdinand II

Date	Mintage	VG	F	VF	XF	Unc
1621	—	—	—	—	—	—

KM# 17 3 GOLDGULDEN

10.5000 g., 0.9860 Gold 0.3328 oz. AGW **Obv:** Displayed eagle wtih N on breast in inner circle **Rev:** St. Lawrence standing holding gridiron and book

Date	Mintage	VG	F	VF	XF	Unc
1612 Rare	—	—	—	—	—	—

KM# 20 3 GOLDGULDEN

10.5000 g., 0.9860 Gold 0.3328 oz. AGW **Obv:** Imperial eagle

Date	Mintage	VG	F	VF	XF	Unc
1613 Rare	—	—	—	—	—	—

KM# 79 6 GOLDGULDEN

21.0000 g., 0.9860 Gold 0.6657 oz. AGW **Obv:** Imperial eagle

Date	Mintage	VG	F	VF	XF	Unc
1625 (c) Rare	—	—	—	—	—	—

KM# 245 1/32 DUCAT

0.1094 g., 0.9860 Gold 0.0035 oz. AGW **Obv:** Shield of arms **Rev:** Paschal lamb

Date	Mintage	VG	F	VF	XF	Unc
ND(1700)	—	50.00	100	200	325	650

KM# 246 1/16 DUCAT

0.2188 g., 0.9860 Gold 0.0069 oz. AGW **Obv:** Crowned arms in branches **Rev:** Paschal lamb

Date	Mintage	VG	F	VF	XF	Unc
ND(1700)	—	100	135	190	300	600

KM# 247 1/16 DUCAT

0.2188 g., 0.9860 Gold 0.0069 oz. AGW **Note:** Klippe.

Date	Mintage	VG	F	VF	XF	Unc
ND(1700)	—	65.00	95.00	130	210	425

KM# 248 1/8 DUCAT

0.4375 g., 0.9860 Gold 0.0139 oz. AGW **Obv:** Crowned arms in branches **Rev:** Paschal lamb

Date	Mintage	VG	F	VF	XF	Unc
ND(1700) GFN	—	95.00	125	190	250	500

KM# 249 1/8 DUCAT

0.4375 g., 0.9860 Gold 0.0139 oz. AGW **Note:** Klippe.

Date	Mintage	VG	F	VF	XF	Unc
ND(1700) GFN	—	95.00	125	190	250	500

KM# 250 1/4 DUCAT

0.8750 g., 0.9860 Gold 0.0277 oz. AGW **Obv:** Crowned arms in branches **Rev:** Paschal lamb

Date	Mintage	VG	F	VF	XF	Unc
1700 GFN	—	130	175	235	325	650

KM# 251 1/4 DUCAT

0.8750 g., 0.9860 Gold 0.0277 oz. AGW **Note:** Klippe.

Date	Mintage	VG	F	VF	XF	Unc
1700	—	130	175	235	325	650

KM# 252 1/4 DUCAT

0.8750 g., 0.9860 Gold 0.0277 oz. AGW

Date	Mintage	VG	F	VF	XF	Unc
ND(1700) GFN	—	85.00	115	160	220	425

KM# 253 1/4 DUCAT

0.8750 g., 0.9860 Gold 0.0277 oz. AGW **Obv:** Crowned arms in branches **Rev:** Paschal lamb **Note:** Klippe.

Date	Mintage	VG	F	VF	XF	Unc
ND(1700)	—	85.00	115	160	220	425

KM# 216 1/2 DUCAT

1.7500 g., 0.9860 Gold 0.0555 oz. AGW **Obv:** Three shields of arms **Rev:** Paschal lamb, date in exergue

Date	Mintage	VG	F	VF	XF	Unc
1692	—	225	450	725	975	—

KM# 254 1/2 DUCAT

1.7500 g., 0.9860 Gold 0.0555 oz. AGW **Obv:** Three shields of arms **Rev:** Paschal lamb, date in legend

Date	Mintage	VG	F	VF	XF	Unc
1700 GFN	—	175	265	350	525	1,000
1700 CGL	—	175	265	350	525	1,000
Note: Restruck 1746-55)						
1700 IMF	—	175	265	350	525	1,000
Note: Restruck 1755-64						

KM# 255 1/2 DUCAT

1.7500 g., 0.9860 Gold 0.0555 oz. AGW

Date	Mintage	VG	F	VF	XF	Unc
1700	—	175	265	350	525	1,000

KM# 256 1/2 DUCAT

1.7500 g., 0.9860 Gold 0.0555 oz. AGW **Note:** Klippe.

Date	Mintage	VG	F	VF	XF	Unc
1700	—	175	265	400	600	1,150

KM# 112 DUCAT

3.5000 g., 0.9860 Gold 0.1109 oz. AGW **Obv:** Bust of Gustav II Adolphus facing **Rev:** Crowned arms **Note:** Swedish issue.

Date	Mintage	VG	F	VF	XF	Unc
1631	—	550	1,150	2,250	4,250	—

KM# 120 DUCAT

3.5000 g., 0.9860 Gold 0.1109 oz. AGW **Obv:** Bust of Gustav II Adolphus facing **Rev:** Crowned arms **Note:** Swedish issue.

Date	Mintage	VG	F	VF	XF	Unc
1632 (b)	—	250	500	800	1,750	—

KM# 121 DUCAT

3.5000 g., 0.9860 Gold 0.1109 oz. AGW **Obv:** Gustav II Adolphus standing **Rev:** Crowned arms **Note:** Swedish issue.

Date	Mintage	VG	F	VF	XF	Unc
1632	—	350	700	1,350	2,750	—

KM# 122 DUCAT

3.5000 g., 0.9860 Gold 0.1109 oz. AGW **Obv:** Bust of Gustav II Adolphus right **Rev:** 7-line inscription in wreath **Note:** Swedish issue.

Date	Mintage	VG	F	VF	XF	Unc
1632	—	500	1,000	2,000	3,750	—

KM# 123 DUCAT

3.5000 g., 0.9860 Gold 0.1109 oz. AGW **Obv:** Arms **Rev:** Paschal lamb holding palm frond atop globe **Note:** City coinage resumed.

Date	Mintage	VG	F	VF	XF	Unc
1632	—	195	275	425	725	—

KM# 131 DUCAT

3.5000 g., 0.9860 Gold 0.1109 oz. AGW **Obv:** Ornate arms **Rev:** Cross from cloud above lying lamb

Date	Mintage	VG	F	VF	XF	Unc
1633	—	250	400	650	1,150	—

KM# 135 DUCAT

3.5000 g., 0.9860 Gold 0.1109 oz. AGW **Obv:** Displayed eagle **Rev:** Two shields of arms hanging from knotted ribbon, date in chronogram

Date	Mintage	VG	F	VF	XF	Unc
ND(1635)	—	600	1,400	2,400	4,000	—

KM# 136 DUCAT

3.5000 g., 0.9860 Gold 0.1109 oz. AGW **Obv:** Ornate arms **Rev:** 4-line inscription in ornate square frame

Date	Mintage	VG	F	VF	XF	Unc
1635 (b)	—	200	350	550	1,000	2,000
1636 (b)	—	200	350	550	1,000	2,000
1637 (b)	—	200	350	550	1,000	2,000
1638 (b)	—	200	350	550	1,000	2,000
1639 (b)	—	200	350	550	1,000	2,000
1640 (d)	—	200	350	550	1,000	2,000
1641 (d)	—	200	350	550	1,000	2,000
1642 (d)	—	200	350	550	1,000	2,000
1643 (d)	—	200	350	550	1,000	2,000
1644 (d)	—	200	350	550	1,000	2,000
1645 (d)	—	200	350	550	1,000	2,000

KM# 137 DUCAT

3.5000 g., 0.9860 Gold 0.1109 oz. AGW **Subject:** Peace ducat **Obv:** Displayed eagle **Rev:** Genius standing with two shields, date in chronogram **Note:** Varieties exist

Date	Mintage	VG	F	VF	XF	Unc
ND(1635) (c)	—	250	500	775	1,450	—
ND(1637) (c)	—	200	350	525	1,000	2,000
ND(1640) (c)	—	250	425	650	1,150	2,250
ND(1648) (c)	—	200	350	525	1,000	2,000
ND(1686) (f)	—	200	350	525	1,000	2,000

KM# 155 DUCAT

3.5000 g., 0.9860 Gold 0.1109 oz. AGW **Obv:** Eagle with head to left **Rev:** Two adjacent arms, angel's head above, date in chronogram

Date	Mintage	VG	F	VF	XF	Unc
1640 (c)	—	250	500	775	1,450	—

KM# 158 DUCAT

3.5000 g., 0.9860 Gold 0.1109 oz. AGW **Obv:** Displayed eagle **Rev:** Winged figure staning with two shields

Date	Mintage	VG	F	VF	XF	Unc
1646 (c)	—	450	650	1,250	2,000	—
1647 (c)	—	450	650	1,250	2,000	—

KM# 159 DUCAT

3.5000 g., 0.9860 Gold 0.1109 oz. AGW **Obv:** Three shields of arms **Rev:** Paschal lamb

Date	Mintage	VG	F	VF	XF	Unc
1649 (c)	—	350	500	850	1,500	—

KM# 167 DUCAT

3.5000 g., 0.9860 Gold 0.1109 oz. AGW **Obv:** 6-line inscription, arms divide date at bottom **Rev:** Hand reaching down from heaven with laurel wreath above globe

Date	Mintage	VG	F	VF	XF	Unc
1650 (c)	—	600	900	1,600	2,750	—

KM# 168 DUCAT

3.5000 g., 0.9860 Gold 0.1109 oz. AGW **Subject:** Treaty of Westphalia **Obv:** Hand holds laurel wreath above displayed eagle **Rev:** 6-line inscription, above arms divide Roman numeral date at bottom

Date	Mintage	VG	F	VF	XF	Unc
ND(1650) (c)	—	600	900	1,750	2,850	—

KM# 173 DUCAT

3.5000 g., 0.9860 Gold 0.1109 oz. AGW **Obv:** Laureate bust of Leopold I right **Rev:** Three shields above date

Date	Mintage	VG	F	VF	XF	Unc
1658	—	1,700	3,300	6,000	10,000	—

KM# 181 DUCAT

3.5000 g., 0.9860 Gold 0.1109 oz. AGW **Obv:** Shield of arms **Rev:** 4-line inscription and date in tablet

Date	Mintage	VG	F	VF	XF	Unc
1660	—	675	1,350	2,850	4,200	—

KM# 257 DUCAT

3.5000 g., 0.9860 Gold 0.1109 oz. AGW **Obv:** Three shields of arms **Rev:** Paschal lamb, date in chronogram

Date	Mintage	VG	F	VF	XF	Unc
MDCC (1700) GFN	—	265	425	575	800	1,500
MDCC (1700)	—	265	425	575	800	1,500

KM# 258 DUCAT

3.5000 g., 0.9860 Gold 0.1109 oz. AGW **Obv:** 3 shields of arms **Rev:** Paschal lamb, date in chronogram **Note:** Klippe.

Date	Mintage	VG	F	VF	XF	Unc
MDCC (1700) GFN	—	225	350	525	750	1,450
MDCC (1700) CGL	—	225	350	525	750	1,450
Note: Restruck 1746-55						
MDCC (1700) IMF	—	225	350	525	750	1,450
Note: Restruck 1755-64						

KM# 113 2 DUCAT

7.0000 g., 0.9860 Gold 0.2219 oz. AGW **Note:** Swedish occupation. Similar to 1 Ducat, KM#112.

Date	Mintage	VG	F	VF	XF	Unc
1631	—	900	1,800	3,750	7,500	—

KM# 124 2 DUCAT

7.0000 g., 0.9860 Gold 0.2219 oz. AGW **Note:** Similar to 1 Ducat, KM#120.

Date	Mintage	VG	F	VF	XF	Unc
1632	—	750	1,500	3,250	6,500	—

KM# 125 2 DUCAT

7.0000 g., 0.9860 Gold 0.2219 oz. AGW **Subject:** Death of Gustav II Adolfus

Date	Mintage	VG	F	VF	XF	Unc
1632	—	850	1,750	3,500	7,500	—

KM# 126 2 DUCAT

7.0000 g., 0.9860 Gold 0.2219 oz. AGW **Obv:** Shield of arms **Rev:** Paschal lamb holding palm fron on globe

Date	Mintage	VG	F	VF	XF	Unc
1632	—	475	900	1,700	2,800	—

KM# 160 2 DUCAT

7.0000 g., 0.9860 Gold 0.2219 oz. AGW **Obv:** Three shields of arms **Rev:** Paschal lamb

Date	Mintage	VG	F	VF	XF	Unc
1649 (c)	—	475	900	1,750	3,000	—

KM# 169 2 DUCAT

7.0000 g., 0.9860 Gold 0.2219 oz. AGW **Obv:** 7-line inscription inside outer legend, arms above **Rev:** Hand reaching down from heaven with laurel wreath for hands reaching from globe, all in inner circle

Date	Mintage	VG	F	VF	XF	Unc
1650 (c)	—	600	1,200	2,400	3,550	—

KM# 259 2 DUCAT

7.0000 g., 0.9860 Gold 0.2219 oz. AGW **Obv:** Three shields of arms **Rev:** Paschal lamb, date in chronogram

Date	Mintage	VG	F	VF	XF	Unc
MDCC (1700) GFN	—	425	575	825	1,250	—

KM# 260 2 DUCAT

7.0000 g., 0.9860 Gold 0.2219 oz. AGW **Obv:** Three shields of arms **Rev:** Paschal lamb, date in chronogram **Note:** Klippe.

Date	Mintage	VG	F	VF	XF	Unc
MDCC (1700) GFN	—	1,000	2,000	3,700	6,500	—

KM# A105 3 DUCAT

10.5000 g., 0.9860 Gold 0.3328 oz. AGW **Obv:** 3 shields of arms above city view, inscription in exergue, date in chronogram **Obv. Inscription:** PAX BONA... **Rev:** Crowned imperial eagle with bust on breast **Note:** Struck with 1/2 Thaler dies, KM#103.

Date	Mintage	VG	F	VF	XF	Unc
ND(1630) (b) Rare	—	—	—	—	—	—

KM# 161 3 DUCAT
10.5000 g., 0.9860 Gold 0.3328 oz. AGW **Obv:** 5-line inscription over shield of arms **Rev:** Paschal lamb, date in chronogram **Note:** Klippe.

Date	Mintage	VG	F	VF	XF	Unc
1648 Rare	—	—	—	—	—	—

KM# 170 3 DUCAT
10.5000 g., 0.9860 Gold 0.3328 oz. AGW **Obv:** 7-line inscription inside outer legend, arms above **Rev:** Hand reaching down from heaven with laurel wreath for hands reaching from globe, all in inner circle **Shape:** Square **Note:** Klippe. Date in chronogram.

Date	Mintage	VG	F	VF	XF	Unc
MDCL (1650) (c)	—	2,300	4,500	8,000	13,000	—

KM# 261 3 DUCAT
10.5000 g., 0.9860 Gold 0.3328 oz. AGW **Obv:** Three shields with dove flying above **Rev:** Lamb holding banner on globe in inner circle **Note:** Klippe. Date in chronogram.

Date	Mintage	VG	F	VF	XF	Unc
MDCC (1700)	—	1,750	3,200	6,200	8,500	—

KM# 114 4 DUCAT
14.0000 g., 0.9860 Gold 0.4438 oz. AGW **Obv:** 3 shields of arms above city view, inscription in exergue, date in chronogram **Obv. Inscription:** VIVIDIA PAX..., **Rev:** Crowned imperial eagle with bust on breast **Note:** Struck with 1/2 Thaler dies, KM#110. Date as chronogram.

Date	Mintage	VG	F	VF	XF	Unc
VIVIDXCIIVMII (1631) (b) Rare	—	—	—	—	—	—

KM# A131 4 DUCAT
14.0000 g., 0.9860 Gold 0.4438 oz. AGW **Obv:** 3 shields of arms above city view, inscription in exergue, date in chronogram **Obv. Inscription:** SVBVENIAT FINIS... **Rev:** Crowned imperial eagle, titles of Ferdinand II **Note:** Struck with 1/2 Thaler dies, KM#129.

Date	Mintage	VG	F	VF	XF	Unc
ND(1633) (b) Rare	—	—	—	—	—	—

KM# 171 4 DUCAT
14.0000 g., 0.9860 Gold 0.4438 oz. AGW **Obv:** 7-line inscription inside outer legend, arms above **Rev:** Hand reaching down from heaven with laurel wreath for hands reaching from globe, all in inner circle

Date	Mintage	VG	F	VF	XF	Unc
1650 (c) Rare	—	—	—	—	—	—

KM# 183 4 DUCAT
14.0000 g., 0.9860 Gold 0.4438 oz. AGW **Obv:** City view with "Jehovah" in Hebrew above, Roman numeral date in cartouche below **Rev:** Three ornate shields of arms, one above two **Note:** Struck with 1/2 Thaler dies, KM#182.

Date	Mintage	VG	F	VF	XF	Unc
1662 (e) Rare	—	—	—	—	—	—

KM# 190 4 DUCAT
14.0000 g., 0.9860 Gold 0.4438 oz. AGW **Obv:** Laureate bust of Leopold I right **Rev:** Cherub left holding two shields of arms

Date	Mintage	VG	F	VF	XF	Unc
ND(1670) Rare	—	—	—	—	—	—

KM# A203 4 DUCAT
14.0000 g., 0.9860 Gold 0.4438 oz. AGW **Obv:** Three shields of arms **Rev:** City view with "Jehovah" in Hebrew above, Roman numeral date in cartouche below **Note:** Struck with 1/2 Thaler dies, KM#182.

Date	Mintage	VG	F	VF	XF	Unc
MDCLXXX (1680) Rare	—	—	—	—	—	—

KM# 231 4 DUCAT
14.0000 g., 0.9860 Gold 0.4438 oz. AGW **Subject:** Peace of Ryswick **Obv:** City view with "Jehovah" in Hebrew above, inscription and date below **Rev:** Peace standing above two cherubs holding shields of amrs

Date	Mintage	VG	F	VF	XF	Unc
1698 GFN Rare	—	—	—	—	—	—

KM# 127 5 DUCAT
17.5000 g., 0.9860 Gold 0.5547 oz. AGW **Obv:** Bust of Gustav II Adolphus right **Rev:** Crowned arms **Note:** Swedish issue.

Date	Mintage	VG	F	VF	XF	Unc
1632 (b) Rare	—	—	—	—	—	—

KM# 191 5 DUCAT
17.5000 g., 0.9860 Gold 0.5547 oz. AGW **Obv:** Bust of Leopold right **Rev:** Cherub walking left iwth two shields of arms **Note:** City coinage resumed.

Date	Mintage	VG	F	VF	XF	Unc
ND(1670) Rare	—	—	—	—	—	—

KM# 195 5 DUCAT
17.5000 g., 0.9860 Gold 0.5547 oz. AGW **Obv:** Cherub walking left iwth two shields of arms **Rev:** City view with "Jehovah" in Hebrew above, date in exergue

Date	Mintage	VG	F	VF	XF	Unc
1677 (c) Rare	—	—	—	—	—	—

KM# 225 5 DUCAT
17.5000 g., 0.9860 Gold 0.5547 oz. AGW **Obv:** Three shields with decorations, angel head above **Rev:** City view with "Jehovah" in Hebrew above date below

Date	Mintage	VG	F	VF	XF	Unc
MDCXCIV (1694) Rare	—	—	—	—	—	—

KM# 229 5 DUCAT
17.5000 g., 0.9860 Gold 0.5547 oz. AGW **Obv:** Eye of God above city view, Roman numeral date in exergue below **Rev:** Angel with two shields of arms **Note:** Struck with 1 Thaler dies, KM#228.

Date	Mintage	VG	F	VF	XF	Unc
MDCXCVI (1696) GFN Rare	—	—	—	—	—	—

KM# 232 5 DUCAT
17.5000 g., 0.9860 Gold 0.5547 oz. AGW **Obv:** City view with "Jehovah" in Hebrew above, inscription and date below **Rev:** Peace standing above two genii holding shields of arms **Note:** Struck with 1 Thaler dies, KM#230.

Date	Mintage	VG	F	VF	XF	Unc
1698 GFN	—	—	—	6,600	10,000	—

KM# 115 6 DUCAT
21.0000 g., 0.9860 Gold 0.6657 oz. AGW **Obv:** 3 shields of arms above city view, inscription in exergue, date in chronogram **Rev:** Crowned imperial eagle with bust on breast **Note:** Swedish issue. Similar to 4 Ducat, KM#114.

Date	Mintage	VG	F	VF	XF	Unc
1631 (b) Rare	—	—	—	—	—	—

KM# 128 6 DUCAT
21.0000 g., 0.9860 Gold 0.6657 oz. AGW **Obv:** Bust of Gustav II Adolphus right **Rev:** Crowned arms **Note:** City coinage resumed. Similar to 5 Ducat, KM#127.

Date	Mintage	VG	F	VF	XF	Unc
1632 Rare	—	—	—	—	—	—

KM# 192 6 DUCAT
21.0000 g., 0.9860 Gold 0.6657 oz. AGW **Obv:** Laureate bust of Leopold I right **Rev:** Cherub left holding two shields of arms

Date	Mintage	VG	F	VF	XF	Unc
ND(1670) Rare	—	—	—	—	—	—

KM# 234 6 DUCAT
21.0000 g., 0.9860 Gold 0.6657 oz. AGW **Obv:** City view with "Jehovah" in Hebrew above, inscription and date below **Rev:** Peace standing above two genii holding shields of arms **Note:** Similar to 5 Ducat, KM#232.

Date	Mintage	VG	F	VF	XF	Unc
1698 GFN	—	—	—	7,200	11,500	—

KM# 235 6 DUCAT
21.0000 g., 0.9860 Gold 0.6657 oz. AGW **Note:** Klippe.

Date	Mintage	VG	F	VF	XF	Unc
1698 GFN Rare	—	—	—	—	—	—

KM# 116 8 DUCAT
28.0000 g., 0.9860 Gold 0.8876 oz. AGW **Note:** Swedish issue. Similar to 4 Ducat, KM#114.

Date	Mintage	VG	F	VF	XF	Unc
1631 (b) Rare	—	—	—	—	—	—

KM# 226 8 DUCAT
28.0000 g., 0.9860 Gold 0.8876 oz. AGW **Obv:** Crowned imperial eagle with arms on breast **Rev:** City view with "Jehovah" in Hebrew above, date below **Note:** City coinage resumed.

Date	Mintage	VG	F	VF	XF	Unc
1694 GFN Rare	—	—	—	—	—	—

KM# 240 8 DUCAT
28.0000 g., 0.9860 Gold 0.8876 oz. AGW **Note:** Klippe. Similar to 5 ducat, KM#232.

Date	Mintage	VG	F	VF	XF	Unc
1698 GFN Rare	—	—	—	—	—	—

KM# 241 9 DUCAT
31.5000 g., 0.9860 Gold 0.9985 oz. AGW **Note:** Similar to 5 ducat, KM#232.

Date	Mintage	VG	F	VF	XF	Unc
1698 GFN Rare	—	—	—	—	—	—

KM# 85 10 DUCAT
35.0000 g., 0.9860 Gold 1.1095 oz. AGW **Obv:** Equestrian figure of Ferdinand II right **Rev:** Cherub standing holding two shields of arms, Roman numeral date in exergue **Note:** Struck with 2 Thaler dies, KM#84.

Date	Mintage	VG	F	VF	XF	Unc
ND(1627) Rare	—	—	—	—	—	—
ND(1630) Rare	—	—	—	—	—	—

KM# 117 10 DUCAT
35.0000 g., 0.9860 Gold 1.1095 oz. AGW **Note:** Swedish issue. Similar to 4 Ducat, KM#114.

Date	Mintage	VG	F	VF	XF	Unc
1631 (b) Rare	—	—	—	—	—	—

KM# 189 10 DUCAT
35.0000 g., 0.9860 Gold 1.1095 oz. AGW **Obv:** Laureate bust of Leopold I right **Rev:** Cherub holding two shields of arms **Note:** City coinage resumed.

Date	Mintage	VG	F	VF	XF	Unc
ND(1670) Rare	—	—	—	—	—	—

KM# 208 10 DUCAT
35.0000 g., 0.9860 Gold 1.1095 oz. AGW **Obv:** Eye of God above city view, 4-line inscription in exergue **Rev:** Crowned eagle above City Hall, seated figure of Nurnberg in foreground **Note:** Struck with 1 Thaler dies, KM#203.

Date	Mintage	VG	F	VF	XF	Unc
ND(1688) PHM/(f) Rare	—	—	—	—	—	—

KM# 227 10 DUCAT
35.0000 g., 0.9860 Gold 1.1095 oz. AGW **Note:** Similar to 8 Ducat, KM#226.

Date	Mintage	VG	F	VF	XF	Unc
1694 GFN Rare	—	—	—	—	—	—

KM# 209 12 DUCAT
42.0000 g., 0.9860 Gold 1.3314 oz. AGW **Obv:** Eye of God above city view, 4-line inscription in exergue **Rev:** Crowned eagle above City Hall, seated figure of Nurnberg in foreground **Note:** Struck with 1 Thaler dies, KM#203.

Date	Mintage	VG	F	VF	XF	Unc
ND(1688) PHM/(f) Rare	—	—	—	—	—	—

KM# 210 14 DUCAT
49.0000 g., 0.9860 Gold 1.5533 oz. AGW **Obv:** Eye of God above city view, 4-line inscription in exergue **Rev:** Crowned eagle above City Hall, seated figure of Nurnberg in foreground **Note:** Struck with 1 Thaler dies, KM#203.

Date	Mintage	VG	F	VF	XF	Unc
ND(1688) PHM/(f) Rare	—	—	—	—	—	—

MEDALLIC COINAGE

PATTERNS

Including off metal strikes

KM#	Date	Mintage	Identification	Mkt Val
Pn3	1610	—	Pfennig. Gold. Two-side strike	—
Pn4	1612	—	Goldgulden. Silver. KM#15	500
Pn5	ND(1617)	—	Goldgulden. Silver. KM#30; date in chronogram.	125
Pn6	1650	—	3 Ducat. Silver. KM#170. Klippe.	350
Pn7	ND(1700) GFN	—	2 Ducat. Silver. KM#259. Date in chronogram.	250
Pn8	1711	—	Ducat. Silver. KM#276	150
Pn9	ND(1712)	—	Ducat. Silver. KM#277. Date in chronogram, Karl VI.	150
Pn10	1739 (g)	—	Pfennig. Gold.	700
Pn11	1740 (g)	—	Pfennig. Gold.	700
Pn12	1756 L/MF	—	20 Kreuzer. Gold. Weight of 3 Ducat.	5,000
Pn13	1756 L/MF	—	20 Kreuzer. Gold. Weight of 6 Ducat.	7,500
Pn14	1758 F	—	Kreuzer. Gold. Weight of 1/2 Ducat.	—
Pn15	1759 MF	—	10 Kreuzer. Gold. Weight of 2 Ducat.	4,000

OLDENBURG

The county of Oldenburg was situated on the North Sea-coast, to the east of the principality of East Friesland. It was originally part of the old duchy of Saxony and the first recorded lord ruled from the beginning of the 11th century. The first count was named in 1091and had already acquired the county of Delmenhorst prior to that time. The first identifiable Oldenburg coinage was struck in the first half of the 13thcentury. Oldenburg was divided into Oldenburg and Delmenhorst in 1270, but the two lines were reunited by marriage five generations later. Through another marriage to the heiress of the duchy of Schleswig and county of Holstein, the royal house of Denmark descended through the Oldenburg line beginning in 1448, while a junior branch continued as counts of Oldenburg. The lordship of Jever was added to the county's domains in 1575. In 1667, the last count died without a direct heir and Oldenburg reverted to Denmark until 1773. In the following year, Oldenburg was given to the bishop of Lübeck, of the Holstein-Gottorp line, and raised to the status of a duchy. Oldenburg was occupied several times during the Napoleonic Wars and became a grand duchy in 1829. In 1817, Oldenburg acquired the principality of Birkenfeld from Prussia and struck coins in denominations used there. World War I spelled the end of temporal power for the grand duke in 1918, but the title has continued up to the present time. Grand Duke Anton Gunther was born in 1923.

RULERS
Anton Gunther, 1603-1667
Friedrich III of Denmark, 1667-1670
Christian V of Denmark, 1670-1699
Friedrich IV of Denmark, 1699-1730

MINT OFFICIALS' INITIALS

Initial	Date	Name
(a)= .:. or [symbol] or [symbol]	1614-22	Nicolaus Wintgens
	1616-44	Anton Paris, warden
Z	1622-37	
(b)= [crescent] or [symbol]	1637-49	Gerhard Dreyer
(c)= [symbol]	1649-51	Jurgen Detleffs
	1653-	Konrad Delbruck
(d)= [symbol] or [symbol] or [symbol]	1658-67	Jurgen Hartmann in Munden
	1660-62	Hermann Vogelsang, warden and die-cutter
Z	1663-71	Georg David Ziegenhorn, mintmaster
IGP	Ca. 1665	Unknown die-cutter
CW	1680-1702	Christopher Woltereck in Gluckstadt

ARMS
Oldenburg: Two bars on field.
Delmenhorst: Cross with pointed bottom bar.
Jever: Lion rampant to left.
NOTE: Coins struck for lordship of Jever are listed under the latter.

COUNTSHIP

REGULAR COINAGE

KM# 5 SCHWAREN (3 Light Pfennig)
Silver **Ruler:** Friedrich V **Obv:** Delmenhorst arms in circle, titles of Anton Gunther **Rev. Inscription:** I / OLD.B / VR.SW / ARN

Date	Mintage	VG	F	VF	XF	Unc
ND	—	—	—	—	—	—

KM# 21 GROTEN (1/144 Thaler)
Silver **Ruler:** Anton Günther **Obv:** Crown above 3 small arms, Oldenburg and Jever above Delmenhorst, titles of Anton Gunther **Rev:** Titles continued **Rev. Inscription:** I / OLDEN / BORG / GROT **Note:** Varieties exist.

Date	Mintage	VG	F	VF	XF	Unc
ND(1614-22)	—	30.00	60.00	120	240	—

KM# 22 GROTEN (1/144 Thaler)
Silver **Ruler:** Anton Günther **Rev. Inscription:** I / OLDEN / BVRG / GROT **Note:** Varieties exist.

Date	Mintage	VG	F	VF	XF	Unc
ND(1614-22)	—	30.00	60.00	120	240	—

KM# 31 GROTEN (1/144 Thaler)
Silver **Ruler:** Anton Günther **Obv:** 3 Shields **Obv. Legend:** EN.OLDEN.BVRG.GROT **Rev:** Crowned imperial eagle, orb on breast, titles of Ferdinand II **Note:** Varieties exist.

Date	Mintage	VG	F	VF	XF	Unc
ND(1619-22)	—	16.00	35.00	75.00	155	—

KM# 32 GROTEN (1/144 Thaler)
Silver **Ruler:** Anton Günther **Obv:** Arms of Oldenburg and Delmenhorst above Jever arms **Rev. Legend:** EIN or EEN OLDEN... **Note:** Varieties exist.

Date	Mintage	VG	F	VF	XF	Unc
ND(1619-22)	—	20.00	45.00	90.00	185	—
ND(1619-22) (a)	—	20.00	45.00	90.00	185	—

KM# 75 GROTEN (1/144 Thaler)

Silver **Ruler:** Anton Günther **Obv:** Jever arms divide date, legend **Obv. Legend:** I GROT.OLD.BOR.LANT.G **Rev:** Titles of Ferdinand III **Note:** Varieties exist.

Date	Mintage	VG	F	VF	XF	Unc
(16)51	—	25.00	50.00	100	200	—
1651	—	25.00	50.00	100	200	—

KM# 77 2 GROTE (1/36 Thaler)

Silver **Ruler:** Anton Günther **Obv:** Crown at top, 2 small arms above 1 **Rev:** Date **Rev. Inscription:** XXXVI / EIN / R.TALAVXILIVM...

Date	Mintage	VG	F	VF	XF	Unc
1658	—	70.00	140	275	550	—
1659 (d)	—	70.00	140	275	550	—

KM# 20 1/2 SCHILLING (Flindrich)

Silver **Ruler:** Anton Günther **Obv:** Crowned 4-fold arms, titles of Anton Gunther **Rev:** Crowned imperial eagle, orb on breast, titles of Matthias **Note:** Varieties exist.

Date	Mintage	VG	F	VF	XF	Unc
ND(1612-19)	—	60.00	120	235	475	—

KM# 23 1/2 SCHILLING (Flindrich)

Silver **Ruler:** Anton Günther **Obv:** Ornate floriated cross, Jever lion in center **Obv. Legend:** SORS. MEA... **Rev:** Arms in six-foil

Date	Mintage	VG	F	VF	XF	Unc
ND(1614-1622)	—	60.00	120	235	475	—

KM# A32 1/2 SCHILLING (Flindrich)

Silver **Ruler:** Anton Günther **Obv:** Titles of Ferdinand II **Note:** Previous KM#32.

Date	Mintage	VG	F	VF	XF	Unc
ND(1619-37)	—	—	—	—	—	—

KM# 60 1/2 SCHILLING (Flindrich)

Silver **Ruler:** Anton Günther **Obv:** Titles of Ferdinand III **Rev:** Ornaments around arms **Note:** Varieties exist.

Date	Mintage	VG	F	VF	XF	Unc
ND(1637-57)	—	—	—	—	—	—

KM# 28 SCHILLING (6 Stuber)

Silver **Ruler:** Anton Günther **Note:** Klippe Schilling.

Date	Mintage	VG	F	VF	XF	Unc
ND(1614-19)	—	—	—	—	—	—

KM# 24 SCHILLING (6 Stuber)

Silver **Ruler:** Anton Günther **Obv:** Crowned imperial eagle **Obv. Legend:** IN.MANIBVS... **Rev:** Crowned 4-fold arms, titles of Anton Gunther **Note:** Varieties exist.

Date	Mintage	VG	F	VF	XF	Unc
ND(1614)	—	20.00	45.00	90.00	185	—

KM# 25 SCHILLING (6 Stuber)

Silver **Ruler:** Anton Günther **Obv:** Crowned shield **Rev:** Imperial orb on eagle's breast **Note:** Varieties exist.

Date	Mintage	VG	F	VF	XF	Unc
ND(1614)	—	20.00	45.00	90.00	185	—

KM# 26 SCHILLING (6 Stuber)

Silver **Ruler:** Anton Günther **Obv:** Crowned shield **Rev:** Titles of Matthias **Note:** Varieties exist.

Date	Mintage	VG	F	VF	XF	Unc
ND(1614-19)	—	20.00	45.00	90.00	185	—

KM# 27 SCHILLING (6 Stuber)

Silver **Ruler:** Anton Günther **Obv:** Crowned shield **Rev:** Imperial orb on eagle's breast **Note:** Varieties exist.

Date	Mintage	VG	F	VF	XF	Unc
ND(1614-19)	—	20.00	45.00	90.00	185	—

KM# 33 SCHILLING (6 Stuber)

Silver **Ruler:** Anton Günther **Obv:** Crowned shield **Rev:** Titles of Ferdinand II **Note:** Varieties exist.

Date	Mintage	VG	F	VF	XF	Unc
ND(1619-37)	—	33.00	70.00	175	350	—

KM# 100 SCHILLING (6 Stuber)

Silver **Ruler:** Anton Günther **Obv:** Titles of Ferdinand III **Note:** Varieties exist.

Date	Mintage	VG	F	VF	XF	Unc
ND(1637-57)	—	—	—	—	—	—

KM# 76 SCHILLING (6 Stuber)

Silver **Ruler:** Anton Günther **Obv:** Crowned shield **Rev:** Titles of Leopold I

Date	Mintage	VG	F	VF	XF	Unc
ND(1657-67)	—	75.00	150	300	625	—

KM# 80 SCHILLING (6 Stuber)

Silver **Ruler:** Anton Günther **Obv:** Crowned AG monogram, titles of Anton Gunther **Rev:** 2-fold arms, Jever above Delmenhorst **Rev. Legend:** IN.MA.DOMI.SORS.MEA

Date	Mintage	VG	F	VF	XF	Unc
ND	—	—	—	—	—	—

KM# 81 SCHILLING (6 Stuber)

Silver **Ruler:** Anton Günther **Obv:** VG monogram in error

Date	Mintage	VG	F	VF	XF	Unc
ND	—	—	—	—	—	—

KM# 55 15 SCHAF (Gulden)

Silver **Ruler:** Anton Günther **Obv:** Crowned 4-fold arms, titles of Anton Gunther **Rev:** Crowned imperial eagle, 15 in orb on breast **Rev. Legend:** IN.MANIBVS **Note:** Varieties exist.

Date	Mintage	VG	F	VF	XF	Unc
ND(1620)	—	275	550	1,100	2,200	—

KM# 56 15 SCHAF (30 Stuber)

Silver **Ruler:** Anton Günther **Obv:** 30 in orb on eagle's breast

Date	Mintage	VG	F	VF	XF	Unc
ND	—	—	—	—	—	—

KM# 35 1/4 MARK (8 Grote)

Silver **Ruler:** Anton Günther **Note:** Klippe 1/4 Mark.

Date	Mintage	VG	F	VF	XF	Unc
ND	—	—	—	—	—	—

KM# 34 1/4 MARK (8 Grote)

Silver **Ruler:** Anton Günther **Obv:** Crown above 3 small shields of arms, 2 above 1, titles of Anton Gunther **Rev:** value inscription in center **Rev. Inscription:** 1/4 / OLDENB / MARCK.ZU / 8. GROT. OD / IEV. 6 / STV **Note:** Varieties exist.

Date	Mintage	VG	F	VF	XF	Unc
ND (a)	—	80.00	160	325	650	—

KM# 36 1/4 MARK (8 Grote)

Silver **Ruler:** Anton Günther **Rev:** Legend is 5 lines **Rev. Legend:** /IEV. 5 3/4 **Note:** Varieties exist.

Date	Mintage	VG	F	VF	XF	Unc
ND (a)	—	115	230	450	900	—

KM# 37 1/2 MARK (16 Grote)

Silver **Ruler:** Anton Günther **Rev. Inscription:** 1/2 / OLDENBV / MARCK. ZU / XVI. GROT / OD. IEVER / 11 1/2. STV **Note:** Varieties exist.

Date	Mintage	VG	F	VF	XF	Unc
ND (a)	—	450	900	1,800	3,500	—

KM# 38 1/2 MARK (16 Grote)

Silver **Ruler:** Anton Günther **Rev. Inscription:** 1/2 / OLDEN / BVRGER / MARCK.ZU / XVI / GROOT **Note:** Varieties exist.

Date	Mintage	VG	F	VF	XF	Unc
ND	—	550	1,200	3,000	7,000	—

KM# 41 MARK (32 Grote)

Silver **Ruler:** Anton Günther **Obv:** Legend is continuation, in error, of titles

Date	Mintage	VG	F	VF	XF	Unc
ND (a)	—	—	—	—	—	—

KM# 40 MARK (32 Grote)

Silver **Ruler:** Anton Günther **Rev. Inscription:** OLDENB / MARCK / ZU / XXXII / GROOT. OD / IEV. 23 / STV **Note:** Similar to 1/4 Mark, KM#34. Varieties exist.

Date	Mintage	VG	F	VF	XF	Unc
ND (a)	—	625	1,250	2,300	4,400	—

KM# 44 MARK (32 Grote)

Silver **Ruler:** Anton Günther **Obv:** Crown above 3 small shields of arms, 2 above 1, titles of Anton Gunther **Rev. Inscription:** ...IEV.24 / STV **Note:** Varieties exist.

Date	Mintage	VG	F	VF	XF	Unc
ND (a)	—	—	—	—	—	—

KM# 45 MARK (32 Grote)

Silver **Ruler:** Anton Günther **Rev. Inscription:** I / OLDEN / BVRGER / MARCK. ZV / XXXII / GROOT **Note:** Varieties exist.

Date	Mintage	VG	F	VF	XF	Unc
ND (a)	—	725	1,500	2,500	4,200	—

KM# 39 MARK (32 Grote)

Silver **Ruler:** Anton Günther **Obv:** Crown above 3 small shields, 2 above 1 **Rev:** Crowned imperial eagle, imperial orb on breast, titles of Ferdinand II **Rev. Legend:** OLDENB. MARCK. ZU. 32. GROT. OD. IEV. 23 STV

Date	Mintage	VG	F	VF	XF	Unc
ND(1619-22) (a) Rare	—	—	—	—	—	—

KM# 42 MARK (32 Grote)
Silver **Ruler:** Anton Günther **Rev:** Crowned imperial eagle, imperial orb on breast, titles of Ferdinand II **Rev. Legend:** OLDENB • MARCK • ZU • 32 GROT • OD • IEV • 24 ST **Note:** Varieties exist.

Date	Mintage	VG	F	VF	XF	Unc
ND(1619-22) (a) Rare	—	—	—	—	—	—

KM# 43 MARK (32 Grote)
Silver **Ruler:** Anton Günther **Note:** Klippe Mark.

Date	Mintage	VG	F	VF	XF	Unc
ND(1619-22) (a) Rare	—	—	—	—	—	—

KM# 90 1/8 THALER
Silver **Ruler:** Anton Günther **Subject:** Death of Anton Gunther **Obv:** 9-line inscription with dates **Rev:** Crowned 4-fold arms **Rev. Legend:** AUXILIUM MEUM A DOMINO **Note:** Varieties exist.

Date	Mintage	VG	F	VF	XF	Unc
1667	—	85.00	165	300	550	—

KM# 46 1/4 THALER
Silver **Ruler:** Anton Günther **Obv:** Bust of Anton Gunther right, titles in legend **Rev:** 4-fold arms, 3 helmets above, titles continued in legend

Date	Mintage	VG	F	VF	XF	Unc
ND(1619) (a)	—	—	—	—	—	—

KM# 47 1/4 THALER
Silver **Ruler:** Anton Günther **Obv:** Crowned imperial eagle, imperial orb on breast, titles of Ferdinand II **Rev:** Crowned 4-fold arms, titles of Anton Gunther **Note:** Varieties exist.

Date	Mintage	VG	F	VF	XF	Unc
ND(1619-22)	—	—	—	—	—	—

KM# 91 1/4 THALER
Silver **Ruler:** Anton Günther **Subject:** Death of Anton Gunther **Obv:** 9-line inscription with date **Rev:** Crowned 4-fold arms **Rev. Legend:** AUXILIUM MEUM A DOMINO

Date	Mintage	VG	F	VF	XF	Unc
1667	—	—	—	—	—	—

KM# 29 1/2 THALER
Silver **Ruler:** Anton Günther **Obv:** Crowned imperial eagle, imperial orb on breast, titles of Matthias **Rev:** 4-fold arms, 2 helmets above, titles of Anton Gunther

Date	Mintage	VG	F	VF	XF	Unc
ND(1614-19) (a)	—	—	—	—	—	—

KM# 48 1/2 THALER
Silver **Ruler:** Anton Günther **Obv:** Bust of Anton Gunther, right, titles in legend **Rev:** 4-fold arms, 3 helmets above, titles continued in legend **Note:** Klippe 1/2 Thaler.

Date	Mintage	VG	F	VF	XF	Unc
ND(1619) (a)	—	—	—	—	—	—

KM# 62 1/2 THALER
Silver **Ruler:** Anton Günther **Subject:** Death of Anton Gunther's Sister **Obv:** Helmeted arms **Obv. Legend:** ANNA \ SOPHIA.. **Rev:** 8-line inscription **Note:** Varieties exist.

Date	Mintage	VG	F	VF	XF	Unc
1639 (b)	—	—	—	—	—	—

KM# 61 1/2 THALER
Silver **Ruler:** Anton Günther **Subject:** Death of Anton Gunther's Sister **Obv:** 7-line inscription **Rev:** 8-line inscription with Roman numeral dates

Date	Mintage	VG	F	VF	XF	Unc
1639	—	—	—	—	—	—

KM# 92 1/2 THALER
Silver **Ruler:** Anton Günther **Subject:** Death of Anton Gunther **Obv:** Crowned 4-fold arms **Rev:** 9-line inscription with dates **Rev. Legend:** AUXILIUM MEUM A DOMINO

Date	Mintage	VG	F	VF	XF	Unc
1667	—	125	265	500	975	—

KM# 97 2/3 THALER (Gulden)
17.3230 g., 0.7500 Silver 0.4177 oz. ASW **Ruler:** Christian V **Obv:** Large Shield with open crown on top supported by two wildmen **Obv. Legend:** COMITAT : OLDENB : ET DELM : * **Rev:** Large 2/3 in center, date in legend **Rev. Legend:** MONETA NOVA ARGENTEA . 1690.C*W. or .C.W.* **Mint:** Glückstadt

Date	Mintage	VG	F	VF	XF	Unc
1690 CW	—	5,000	10,000	17,500	30,000	—

KM# 98 2/3 THALER (Gulden)
Silver **Ruler:** Christian V **Obv:** Wildmen supporting crowned shield **Rev:** Large 2/3 within legend

Date	Mintage	VG	F	VF	XF	Unc
1690	—	4,000	6,000	9,250	—	—

Note: Some of these gulden are known with the countermark of the Franconian Circle, valued at 60 Kreuzer

KM# 63 3/4 THALER
21.2000 g., Silver **Ruler:** Anton Günther **Subject:** Death of Anton Gunther's Sister **Obv:** Helmeted arms **Obv. Legend:** ANNA.SOPHIA.. **Rev:** 8-line inscription

Date	Mintage	VG	F	VF	XF	Unc
1639 (b)	—	—	—	—	—	—

Note: Thalers Dav. #7113, Dav. #7113A and Dav. #7114 formerly listed in Oldenburg are now located in Jever

KM# 6 THALER
Silver **Ruler:** Anton Günther **Obv. Legend:** ... RO + IMPER • SEMP + AVGV • **Note:** Dav. #7102.

Date	Mintage	VG	F	VF	XF	Unc
ND (a) Rare	—	—	—	—	—	—

KM# 7 THALER
Silver **Ruler:** Anton Günther **Obv. Legend:** ROM + IMPERA + SEMP + AVG **Note:** Klippe Thaler. Dav. #7103.

Date	Mintage	VG	F	VF	XF	Unc
ND (a)	—	4,500	7,500	12,500	—	—

KM# 8 THALER
Silver **Ruler:** Anton Günther **Obv:** Helmeted 4-fold shield **Rev:** Crowned double-headed imperial eagle **Rev. Legend:** ROM • IMPERAT • SEMP • AVGV **Note:** Dav. #7104.

Date	Mintage	VG	F	VF	XF	Unc
ND (a)	—	3,500	7,000	12,000	—	—

KM# 9 THALER
Silver **Ruler:** Anton Günther **Obv. Legend:** COMES: IN: OLDENB **Rev. Legend:** ET • DELMENH • DOM... **Note:** Dav. #7107.

Date	Mintage	VG	F	VF	XF	Unc
ND (a)	—	1,200	2,000	3,250	—	—

KM# 10 THALER
Silver **Ruler:** Anton Günther **Obv. Legend:** COM • OLDENBVRG • **Rev. Legend:** ET • DEL • DO • IN • **Note:** Dav. #7107A.

Date	Mintage	VG	F	VF	XF	Unc
ND (a)	—	1,200	2,000	3,250	—	—

KM# 11 THALER
Silver **Ruler:** Anton Günther **Note:** Klippe Thaler. Dav. #7107B.

Date	Mintage	VG	F	VF	XF	Unc
ND (a)	—	2,400	4,000	7,500	—	—

KM# 12 THALER
Silver **Ruler:** Anton Günther **Obv:** Helmeted arms **Rev:** Crowned imperial eagle with orb on breast, titles of Ferdinand II **Note:** Dav, #7109.

Date	Mintage	VG	F	VF	XF	Unc
ND (a)	—	1,000	2,100	4,200	6,900	—

KM# 64 THALER
Silver **Ruler:** Anton Günther **Subject:** Death of Anton Gunther's Sister **Obv:** Helmeted arms **Obv. Legend:** ANNA • SOPHIA... **Rev:** 8-line inscription **Note:** Dav. #7110.

Date	Mintage	VG	F	VF	XF	Unc
1639 (b)	—	1,400	2,700	5,400	9,000	—

KM# 84 THALER
Silver **Ruler:** Anton Günther **Subject:** 82nd Birthday of Count

Anton Gunther **Obv:** Bust right, AETAT: 82 at left, REGIMI at right **Rev:** Helmeted arms separating IG-P, date in legend **Note:** Dav. #7115.

Date	Mintage	VG	F	VF	XF	Unc
1665 IGP	—	1,000	2,100	4,200	8,400	—

KM# 86 THALER

Silver **Ruler:** Anton Günther **Subject:** 83rd Birthday of Count Anton Gunther **Obv:** Bust right, within inner circle - AETATIS. 83 at left, REGIMINIS. 63 at right **Rev:** Helmeted arms, date in legend **Note:** Dav. #7116.

Date	Mintage	VG	F	VF	XF	Unc
1666	—	1,150	2,350	4,800	8,300	—

KM# 93 THALER

Silver **Ruler:** Anton Günther **Subject:** Death of Count Anton Gunther **Obv:** Crowned arms **Rev:** 9-line inscription **Note:** Dav. #7118.

Date	Mintage	VG	F	VF	XF	Unc
1667	—	1,600	3,300	6,000	10,000	20,000

KM# 65 1-1/4 THALER

35.0000 g., Silver **Ruler:** Anton Günther **Note:** Klippe 1-1/4 Thaler; Similar to 1 Thaler, KM#9. Dav. #--.

Date	Mintage	VG	F	VF	XF	Unc
ND (a) Rare	—	—	—	—	—	—

KM# 66 1-1/2 THALER

Silver **Ruler:** Anton Günther **Obv:** Bust of Anton Gunther right **Rev:** Helmeted arms **Note:** Klippe. Dav. #7106.

Date	Mintage	VG	F	VF	XF	Unc
ND (a) Rare	—	—	—	—	—	—

Note: Fritz Rudolf Künker Münzenhandlung Auction 69, 10-01, XF realized approximately $13,895

KM# 13 2 THALER

58.0000 g., Silver **Ruler:** Anton Günther **Note:** Octagonal Klippe 2 Thaler; Similar to 1 Thaler, KM#9. Dav. #--.

Date	Mintage	VG	F	VF	XF	Unc
ND (a) Rare	—	—	—	—	—	—

Note: Thalers Dav. #7111 and Dav. #7112 formerly listed in Oldenberg are now located under Jever

KM# 14 2 THALER

58.0000 g., Silver **Ruler:** Anton Günther **Rev. Legend:** RO ++ IMPER • SEMP ++ AVGV • **Note:** Klippe. Similar to 1 Thaler, KM#8. Dav. #7101.

Date	Mintage	VG	F	VF	XF	Unc
ND (a) Rare	—	—	—	—	—	—

Note: Dr. Busso Peus Nachfolger Auction 373, 10-02, XF realized approximately $24,760

KM# 15 2 THALER

58.0000 g., Silver **Ruler:** Anton Günther **Note:** Similar to KM#16 but reverse legend ends ...RN. Dav. #7105.

Date	Mintage	VG	F	VF	XF	Unc
ND (a) Rare	—	—	—	—	—	—

KM# 16 2 THALER

58.0000 g., Silver **Ruler:** Anton Günther **Rev. Legend:** ...KNIP **Note:** Dav. #7105A. Illustration reduced.

Date	Mintage	VG	F	VF	XF	Unc
ND (a) Rare	—	—	—	—	—	—

KM# 17 2 THALER

58.0000 g., Silver **Ruler:** Anton Günther **Obv:** Helmeted arms **Rev:** Crowned imperial eagle with orb on breast **Note:** Dav. #7108.

Date	Mintage	VG	F	VF	XF	Unc
ND Rare	—	—	—	—	—	—

KM# 94 2 THALER

58.0000 g., Silver **Ruler:** Anton Günther **Subject:** Death of Anton Gunther **Obv:** Crowned arms **Rev:** 9-line inscription **Note:** Dav. #7117.

Date	Mintage	VG	F	VF	XF	Unc
1667 Rare	—	—	—	—	—	—

TRADE COINAGE

KM# 82 3 DUCAT

10.5000 g., 0.9860 Gold 0.3328 oz. AGW **Ruler:** Anton Günther **Obv:** Bust of Anton Gunther facing 1/3 right **Rev:** Crowned arms

Date	Mintage	VG	F	VF	XF	Unc
1660	—	4,800	7,800	14,000	21,000	—

KM# 95 4 DUCAT

14.0000 g., 0.9860 Gold 0.4438 oz. AGW **Ruler:** Anton Günther **Subject:** Death of Anton Gunther **Obv:** 9-line inscription with dates **Rev:** Crowned 4-fold arms **Rev. Legend:** AUXILIUM MEUM A DOMINO **Note:** Struck with 1/2 Thaler dies, KM#92

Date	Mintage	VG	F	VF	XF	Unc
1667 Rare	—	—	—	—	—	—

KM# 87 5 DUCAT

17.5000 g., 0.9860 Gold 0.5547 oz. AGW **Ruler:** Anton Günther **Subject:** 83rd Birthday of Anton Gunther **Obv:** Bust right **Rev:** Helmeted arms **Note:** Struck with 1 Thaler dies, KM#86.

Date	Mintage	VG	F	VF	XF	Unc
1666 Rare	—	—	—	—	—	—

KM# 85 10 DUCAT

35.0000 g., 0.9860 Gold 1.1095 oz. AGW **Ruler:** Anton Günther **Subject:** 82nd Birthday of Anton Gunther **Obv:** Bust right **Rev:** Helmeted arms **Note:** Struck with 1 Thaler dies, KM#84.

Date	Mintage	VG	F	VF	XF	Unc
1665 IGP Rare	—	—	—	—	—	—

KM# 88 10 DUCAT

35.0000 g., 0.9860 Gold 1.1095 oz. AGW **Ruler:** Anton Günther **Subject:** 83rd Birthday of Anton Gunther **Note:** Similar to 5 Ducat, KM#87. Struck with 1 Thaler dies, KM#86.

Date	Mintage	VG	F	VF	XF	Unc
1666 Rare	—	—	—	—	—	—

KM# 89 10 DUCAT

35.0000 g., 0.9860 Gold 1.1095 oz. AGW **Ruler:** Anton Günther **Obv:** Bust left

Date	Mintage	VG	F	VF	XF	Unc
1666 Rare	—	—	—	—	—	—

KM# 96 10 DUCAT

35.0000 g., 0.9860 Gold 1.1095 oz. AGW **Ruler:** Anton Günther **Subject:** Death of Anton Gunther **Note:** Similar to 4 Ducat, KM#95. Struck with 1 Thaler dies, KM#93

Date	Mintage	VG	F	VF	XF	Unc
1667 Reported, not confirmed	—	—	—	—	—	—

OPPELN AND RATIBOR

The two duchies of Oppeln and Ratibor in Silesia came into existence in the 12th-13th centuries and produced parallel lines of rulers down to the 16th century. The Ratibor ducal line became extinct in 1522 and the titles passed to Oppeln. The latter died out as well in 1532 and both duchies passed first to Brandenburg, then to a succession of rulers of the Habsburg house, Transylvania and the royal line of Poland. The Habsburgs finally gained sole possession in 1664, but Oppeln-Ratibor went to Prussia in 1740, along with most of the rest of Silesia.

RULERS

Gabriel Bethlen, Prince of Transylvania 1622-1625
Wladislaus IV, King of Poland 1647-1648
Karl Ferdinand, Prince of Poland 1648-1655
Johann Kasimir, King of Poland 1655-1664

MINT OFFICIALS' INITIALS

Initial	Date	Name
BZ	1620-24	Balthasar Zwirner, mintmaster in Oppeln
GG	1647	Gabriel Görloff, mintmaster in Oppeln
AT	1650-60	Andreas Tympf, mintmaster in Posen
TT	1660-68	Thomas Tympf, mintmaster in Bromberg

ARMS

Bethlen family – two geese facing each other, arrow piercing both necks, all encircled by snake with tail in its mouth

REFERENCES

F/S = Ferdinand Friedensburg and Hans Seger, **Schlesiens Münzen und Medaillen der Neueren Zeit**, Breslau, 1901 (reprint Frankfurt/Main)

J/M = Norbert Jaschke and Fritz P. Maercker, **Schlesische Münzen und Medaillen**, Ihringen, 1985.

S/Sch = Hugo Frhr. Von Saurma-Jeltsch, **Schlesische Münzen und Medaillen**, Breslau, 1883.

DUCHY

REGULAR COINAGE

KM# 15 DENAR (Pfennig)

0.5000 g., Silver **Ruler:** Gabriel Bethlen **Obv:** 2-fold arms of Hungary divide mintmaster's initials **Obv. Legend:** GAB. D. G. SA. RO. IM. TRA. PR. PA. R. **Rev:** Madonna and Child in circle, date at end of legend **Rev. Legend:** PATRONA. HVN. **Mint:** Oppeln **Note:** Ref. F/S#2918. Prev. Transylvania, KM#120.

Date	Mintage	VG	F	VF	XF	Unc
16Z3 BZ	—	—	—	—	—	—

KM# 50 3 PFENNIG (Dreier, Gröschel)

Silver **Ruler:** Karl Ferdinand **Obv:** Polish falcon with 2-fold arms on breast **Rev:** Imperial orb with '3' divides date in ornamented rhombus **Mint:** Oppeln **Note:** Ref. F/S#2941.

Date	Mintage	VG	F	VF	XF	Unc
1654	—	45.00	95.00	175	325	—

KM# 5 3 GROSCHER (Dreigröscher)

1.7000 g., Silver, 20-21 mm. **Ruler:** Gabriel Bethlen **Obv:** Armored bust to right **Obv. Legend:** GAB(R). D. G. SAC. R. IM. TRA. P(R). **Rev:** Value 'III' above small crowned shield, Silesian eagle to left, flying eagle to right, date **Rev. Inscription:** GROS. ARG. / TRIP. OPO. / ET. RAT. / BZ. **Mint:** Oppeln **Note:** Ref. F/S#2907, 2914. Prev. Transylvania, KM#156.

Date	Mintage	VG	F	VF	XF	Unc
16ZZ BZ	—	105	195	300	625	—
1623 BZ	—	105	195	300	625	—

KM# 17 3 GROSCHER (Dreigröscher)

Silver **Ruler:** Gabriel Bethlen **Obv:** Armored bust to right **Obv. Legend:** GAB(R). D. G. SAC. R. IM. TRA. P(R). **Rev:** Value 'III' above small crowned shield, Silesian eagle to left, flying eagle to right, date divided among devices, 4-line inscription below **Mint:** Oppeln **Note:** Ref. F/S#2915. Prev. Transylvania, KM#155. Klippe.

Date	Mintage	VG	F	VF	XF	Unc
1623 BZ Rare	—	—	—	—	—	—

KM# 18 3 GROSCHER (Dreigröscher)

Silver **Ruler:** Gabriel Bethlen **Obv:** Crowned bust to right **Obv. Legend:** GABR. D. G. SA. RO. IM. TRA. PR. **Rev:** Value 'III' above small crowned shield, Silesian eagle to left, flying eagle to right, date divided among devices, 4-line inscription below **Rev. Inscription:** GROS. ARG. / TRIP. OPO. / ET. RAT. / BZ. **Mint:** Oppeln **Note:** Ref. F/S#2916. Prev. Transylvania, KM#157.

Date	Mintage	VG	F	VF	XF	Unc
1623 BZ	—	—	—	—	—	—

KM# 7 2 KREUZER

Silver **Ruler:** Gabriel Bethlen **Obv:** Bethlen family arms **Obv. Legend:** GABR. D. G. SAC. RO. IM. TRA. PR. **Rev:** Silesian eagle, value '2' in oval below, date at end of legend **Rev. Legend:** B. TRE. HV. DN. SI. CO. OP. R. A. **Mint:** Oppeln **Note:** Ref. F/S#2910.

Date	Mintage	VG	F	VF	XF	Unc
16ZZ BZ	—	—	—	—	—	—

KM# 9 3 KREUZER (Groschen)

Silver, 17 mm. **Ruler:** Gabriel Bethlen **Obv:** Bust to right, value '3' in oval below **Obv. Legend:** GAB. D. G. SA. - R. IM. TR. PR. P. **Rev:** Bethlen family arms, small shield with mintmaster's initials at top, date at end of legend **Rev. Legend:** REG. HV. DN. SI. CO. OP. RAT. **Mint:** Oppeln **Note:** Ref. F/S#2909, 2917. Kipper Coinage. Weight varies: .80-1.10 g. Varieties exist.

Date	Mintage	VG	F	VF	XF	Unc
16ZZ	—	125	250	465	925	—
16ZZ BZ	—	125	250	465	925	—
16Z3 BZ	—	125	250	465	925	—

KM# 27 3 KREUZER (Groschen)

Silver **Ruler:** Wladislaus IV **Obv:** Crowned bust to right, value (3) below **Obv. Legend:** VL. IV. D. G. R. - POL. ET. S. **Rev:** Crowned shield of Polish arms (falcon), date downward along right side, mintmaster's initials along left side **Rev. Legend:** MO. AR. DV. OPO. E. RAT. **Mint:** Oppeln **Note:** Ref. F/S#2919.

Date	Mintage	VG	F	VF	XF	Unc
1647 GG	—	—	—	—	—	—

KM# 52 3 KREUZER (Groschen)

Silver **Ruler:** Karl Ferdinand **Obv:** Bust to right in circle **Obv. Legend:** CAROLUS. FERDIN. D:G. PRINCEP. & S. **Rev:** Crowned ornate 4-fold arms with central shield, value '3' in oval below, date at end of legend **Rev. Legend:** EPIS. WRA. & PLO - DVX. OP & R. **Mint:** Oppeln **Note:** Ref. F/S#2940.

Date	Mintage	VG	F	VF	XF	Unc
1654	—	—	—	—	—	—

KM# 71 3 KREUZER (Groschen)

Silver **Ruler:** Johann Kasimir **Obv:** Laureate bust to right, value '3' in oval below **Obv. Legend:** IOAN. CAS. D G. R - EX. P. &. SV. M. D. L. **Rev:** Crowned Polish falcon in circle, date at end of legend **Rev. Legend:** MONETA. NOVA. REG. POLON. **Mint:** Oppeln **Note:** Ref. F/S#2942-44. Varieties exist.

Date	Mintage	VG	F	VF	XF	Unc
1657 AT	—	—	—	—	—	—
1658	—	—	—	—	—	—
1660 TT	—	—	—	—	—	—

KM# 73 3 KREUZER (Groschen)

Silver **Ruler:** Johann Kasimir **Obv:** Laureate bust to right, value '3' in oval below **Obv. Legend:** IO. CAS. D G. REX. - P. &. S. M. DL. R. P. **Rev:** Crowned Polish falcon in circle, date at end of legend **Rev. Legend:** MON. ARGENT. - REG. POL. **Mint:** Oppeln **Note:** Ref. F/S#2945.

Date	Mintage	VG	F	VF	XF	Unc
1661 TT	—	—	—	—	—	—

KM# 11 6 KREUZER

Silver **Ruler:** Gabriel Bethlen **Obv:** 2-fold arms of Hungary divide mintmaster's initials **Obv. Legend:** GABRIEL. D.G. SAC. RO. IM. TRAN. PR. PA. **Rev:** Madonna and Child on crescent, in circle, date at end of legend **Rev. Legend:** PATRONA. HVNGARIAR. **Mint:** Oppeln **Note:** Ref. F/S#2908. Kipper Coinage.

Date	Mintage	VG	F	VF	XF	Unc
1622 BZ	—	—	—	—	—	—

KM# 20 24 KREUZER (Vierundzwanziger)

2.7000 g., Silver **Ruler:** Gabriel Bethlen **Obv:** Armored bust to right in circle, value (24) below **Obv. Legend:** GABRIEL. D G. SAC. - RO. IM. ET TRA. PRI. P. **Rev:** Crowned 4-fold arms with central shield of Bethlen family arms, date at end of legend **Rev. Legend:** REG. HV. DN. SI. CO. AC. OP. RA. DVX. **Mint:** Oppeln **Note:** Ref. F/S#2913. Kipper Coinage.

Date	Mintage	VG	F	VF	XF	Unc
1.263 (error) BZ	—	125	250	450	900	—
1623 BZ	—	125	250	450	900	—

KM# 22 GROSCHEN

Silver **Ruler:** Gabriel Bethlen **Obv:** Large crown divides date above 4-line inscription **Obv. Inscription:** GABRIEL / D. G. S. R. I. ET / TRA. PRI / BZ. **Rev:** Silesian eagle in circle **Rev. Legend:** GROSS. DVX. OPPAL. ET. RATIBOR. **Mint:** Oppeln **Note:** Kipper Coinage. Klippe.

Date	Mintage	VG	F	VF	XF	Unc
1623 BZ Rare	—	—	—	—	—	—

KM# 24 1/2 THALER

Silver **Ruler:** Gabriel Bethlen **Obv:** Bust right in circle **Obv. Legend:** GABRIEL. D:G. SAC. ROM. IMP. ET. TRA. PRI. P. **Rev:** Crowned ornamented shield of 4-fold arms with central shield of Bethlen, date divided at upper left and right as 1 - 6 / Z - 3, mintmaster's initials divided at lower left and right **Rev. Legend:** REG. HV. DN. SI. CO. AC. OPO. RAT. DVX. SIL. **Mint:** Oppeln **Note:** Ref. F/S#2911. Klippe.

Date	Mintage	VG	F	VF	XF	Unc
16Z3 BZ Rare	—	—	—	—	—	—

KM# 25 1/2 THALER

Silver **Ruler:** Gabriel Bethlen **Obv:** Bust right in circle **Obv. Legend:** GABRIEL. D:G. SAC. RO. IM. ET. TRAN. PRI. P. **Rev:** Crowned ornamented shield of 4-fold arms with central shield of Bethlen, date at end of legend **Rev. Legend:** REG. HV. DN. SI. CO. AC. OP. RA. DVX. **Mint:** Oppeln **Note:** Ref. F/S#2912. Klippe.

Date	Mintage	VG	F	VF	XF	Unc
1623 Rare	—	—	—	—	—	—

KM# 29 1/2 THALER

Silver **Ruler:** Karl Ferdinand **Obv:** Bust left **Obv. Legend:** CAROLVS. FERDINAN. D.G. PRIN. P. ET. SV. **Rev:** Crowned 4-fold arms with central shield divide date **Rev. Legend:** EPIS. WRATIS. & PLO. DVX. OPPO. & RAT. **Mint:** Oppeln **Note:** Ref. F/S#2931. Octagonal Klippe.

Date	Mintage	VG	F	VF	XF	Unc
1653 Rare	—	—	—	—	—	—

KM# 54 1/2 THALER

Silver **Ruler:** Karl Ferdinand **Obv:** Bust right in circle **Obv. Legend:** CAROLUS. FERDINAND. D.G. PRINC. POL. &. S. **Rev:** Crowned 4-fold arms with central shield in oval baroque frame, date at end of legend **Rev. Legend:** EPIS. WRAT. & PLO. DUX. OPP. & RAT. **Mint:** Oppeln **Note:** Ref. F/S#2938. Klippe.

Date	Mintage	VG	F	VF	XF	Unc
1654 Rare	—	—	—	—	—	—

KM# 55 1/2 THALER

Silver **Ruler:** Karl Ferdinand **Obv:** Bust right in circle **Obv. Legend:** CAROLUS. FERDINAND. D.G. PRINC. POL. &. S. **Rev:** Crowned 4-fold arms with central shield in oval baroque frame, date at end of legend **Rev. Legend:** EPIS. WRAT. & PLO. DUX. OPP. & RAT. **Mint:** Oppeln **Note:** Ref. F/S#2939. Octagonal klippe.

Date	Mintage	VG	F	VF	XF	Unc
1654 Rare	—	—	—	—	—	—

KM# 31 THALER

Silver **Ruler:** Karl Ferdinand **Obv:** Bust left **Obv. Legend:** CAROLVS. FERDINANDVS. D.G. PRINCEP. POL. ET. SVECI. **Rev:** Crowned 4-fold ams with central shield in ornamented Spanish shield divide date **Rev. Legend:** EPIS. WRATIS. ET. PLO. DVX. OPPOLI. ET. RATI. **Note:** Dav#5118. Ref. F/S#2929. Prev. Breslau KM#113.

Date	Mintage	VG	F	VF	XF	Unc
1653 Rare	—	—	—	—	—	—

KM# 32 THALER

Silver **Ruler:** Karl Ferdinand **Obv:** Bust left **Obv. Legend:** CAROLVS. FERDINANDVS. D.G. PRINCEP. POL. ET. SVECI. **Rev:** Crowned 4-fold arms with central shield in ornamented Spanish shield divide date **Rev. Legend:** EPIS. WRATIS. ET. PLO. DVX. OPPOLI. ET. RATI. **Note:** Dav#5118a. Ref. F/S#2930. Octagonal Klippe. Prev. Breslau KM#114.

Date	Mintage	VG	F	VF	XF	Unc
1653 Rare	—	—	—	—	—	—

KM# 57 THALER

Silver **Ruler:** Karl Ferdinand **Obv:** Bust right in circle **Obv. Legend:** CAROLUS. FERDINANDUS. D.G. PRINCEPS. POL. &. SUEC. **Rev:** Crowned 4-fold arms with central shield in oval baroque frame, date at end of legend **Rev. Legend:** EPIS. WRAT. & PLO. DUX. OPPOL. & RATI. **Note:** Dav#5119. Ref. F/S#2935. Prev. Breslau KM#127.

Date	Mintage	VG	F	VF	XF	Unc
1654 Rare	—	—	—	—	—	—

KM# 58 THALER

Silver **Ruler:** Karl Ferdinand **Obv:** Bust right in circle **Obv. Legend:** CAROLUS. FERDINANDUS. D.G. PRINCEPS. POL. &. SUEC. **Rev:** Crowned 4-fold arms with central shield in oval baroque frame, date at end of legend **Rev. Legend:** EPIS. WRAT. & PLO. DUX. OPPOL. & RATI. **Note:** Dav#5119A. Ref. F/S#2936. Klippe. Prev. Breslau KM#128.

Date	Mintage	VG	F	VF	XF	Unc
1654 Rare	—	—	—	—	—	—

KM# 59 THALER

Silver **Ruler:** Karl Ferdinand **Obv:** Bust right in circle **Obv. Legend:** CAROLUS. FERDINANDUS. D.G. PRINCEPS. POL. &. SUEC. **Rev:** Crowned 4-fold arms with central shield in oval baroque frame, date at end of legend **Rev. Legend:** EPIS. WRAT. & PLO. DUX. OPPOL. & RATI. **Note:** Dav#5119B. Ref. F/S#2937. Octagonal Klippe. Prev. Breslau KM#129.

Date	Mintage	VG	F	VF	XF	Unc
1654 Rare	—	—	—	—	—	—

KM# 13 2 THALER

Silver **Ruler:** Gabriel Bethlen **Obv:** Armored bust right in circle, date behind shoulder **Obv. Legend:** GABRIEL. D G. SA. RO. IM. ET. TRANSSYL. PRINCEP. **Rev:** Crowned 4-fold arms with central shield of Bethlen family arms in ornamented frame **Rev. Legend:** PAR. RE. HVN. DO. SIC. CO. AC. OPOL. RA. DVX. **Note:** Dav#7119. Ref. F/S#2906. Klippe.

Date	Mintage	VG	F	VF	XF	Unc
16ZZ Rare	—	—	—	—	—	—

KM# 34 2 THALER

Silver **Ruler:** Karl Ferdinand **Obv:** Bust left **Obv. Legend:** CAROLVS. FERDINANDVS. D.G. PRINCEP. POL. ET. SVECI. **Rev:** Crowned 4-fold arms with central shield in ornamented Spanish shield divide date **Rev. Legend:** EPIS. WRATIS. ET. PLO. DVX. OPPOLI. ET. RATI. **Note:** Dav#5117. Ref. F/S#2928. Octagonal Klippe. Prev. Breslau KM#115.

Date	Mintage	VG	F	VF	XF	Unc
1653 Rare	—	—	—	—	—	—

TRADE COINAGE

KM# 61 1/2 DUCAT

1.7500 g., 0.9860 Gold 0.0555 oz. AGW, 17.3 mm. **Ruler:** Karl Ferdinand **Obv:** Bust right **Obv. Legend:** CAROL. FERD. D.G. PRINC. P. & S. **Rev:** Crowned 4-fold arms with central shield, date at end of legend **Rev. Legend:** EPI - WRA & PL - D. OP. & R. **Note:** Ref. J/M#227.

Date	Mintage	VG	F	VF	XF	Unc
1654 Rare	—	—	—	—	—	—

KM# 36 DUCAT

3.5000 g., 0.9860 Gold 0.1109 oz. AGW **Ruler:** Karl Ferdinand **Obv:** Bust left **Obv. Legend:** CAROLVS. FERDINAN. D.G. PRIN. P. ET. SV. **Rev:** Crowned 4-fold arms with central shield divide date **Rev. Legend:** EPIS. WRATIS. & PLO. DVX. OPPO. & RAT. **Note:** Fr#512b. Prev. Breslau KM#116.

Date	Mintage	VG	F	VF	XF	Unc
1653 Rare	—	—	—	—	—	—

KM# 63 DUCAT

3.5000 g., 0.9860 Gold 0.1109 oz. AGW **Ruler:** Karl Ferdinand **Obv:** Bust right **Obv. Legend:** CAROLUS FERDINAND. D.G. PRINC. P. & S. **Rev:** Crowned 4-fold arms with central shield, date at end of legend **Rev. Legend:** EPIS. WRAT. & PLO. DUX OPP. & R. **Note:** Ref. J/M#226.

Date	Mintage	VG	F	VF	XF	Unc
1654 Rare	—	—	—	—	—	—

KM# 38 2 DUCAT

7.0000 g., 0.9860 Gold 0.2219 oz. AGW **Ruler:** Karl Ferdinand **Obv:** Bust left **Obv. Legend:** CAROLVS. FERDINAN. D.G. PRIN. P. ET. SV. **Rev:** Crowned 4-fold arms with central shield divide date **Rev. Legend:** EPIS. WRATIS. & PLO. DVX. OPPO. & RAT. **Note:** Fr#511a. Ref. F/S#2926. Prev. Breslau KM#117.

Date	Mintage	VG	F	VF	XF	Unc
1653	—	2,300	4,600	7,500	11,500	—

KM# 39 2 DUCAT

Gold **Ruler:** Karl Ferdinand **Obv:** Bust left **Obv. Legend:** CAROLVS. FERDINAN. D.G. PRIN. P. ET. SV. **Rev:** Crowned 4-fold arms with central shield divide date **Rev. Legend:** EPIS. WRATIS. & PLO. DVX. OPPO. & RAT. **Note:** Fr#512a. Octagonal Klippe. Prev. Breslau KM#118.

Date	Mintage	VG	F	VF	XF	Unc
1653 Rare	—	—	—	—	—	—

KM# 65 2 DUCAT

7.0000 g., 0.9860 Gold 0.2219 oz. AGW **Ruler:** Karl Ferdinand **Obv:** Bust right in circle **Obv. Legend:** CAROLUS. FERDINAND. D.G. PRINC. POL. &. S. **Rev:** Crowned 4-fold arms with central shield in oval baroque frame, date at end of legend **Rev. Legend:** EPIS. WRAT. & PLO. DUX. OPP. & RAT. **Note:** Ref. F/S#2934.

Date	Mintage	VG	F	VF	XF	Unc
1654 Rare	—	—	—	—	—	—

KM# 41 3 DUCAT

10.5000 g., 0.9860 Gold 0.3328 oz. AGW **Ruler:** Karl Ferdinand **Obv:** Bust left **Obv. Legend:** CAROLVS. FERDINAN. D.G. PRIN. P. ET. SV. **Rev:** Crowned 4-fold arms with central shield divide date **Rev. Legend:** EPIS. WRATIS. & PLO. DVX. OPPO. & RAT. **Note:** Fr#509a. Ref. F/S#2922. Prev. Breslau KM#119. Struck on thick flan from Ducat dies, KM#36.

Date	Mintage	VG	F	VF	XF	Unc
1653	—	2,900	5,800	9,200	17,500	—

KM# 44 3 DUCAT

10.5000 g., 0.9860 Gold 0.3328 oz. AGW **Ruler:** Karl Ferdinand **Obv:** Bust left **Obv. Legend:** CAROLVS. FERDINAN. D.G. PRIN. P. ET. SV. **Rev:** Crowned 4-fold arms with central shield divide date **Rev. Legend:** EPIS. WRATIS. & PLO. DVX. OPPO. & RAT. **Note:** Fr#510a. Ref. F/S#2925. Octagonal Klippe. Prev. Breslau KM#120.

Date	Mintage	VG	F	VF	XF	Unc
1653 Rare	—	—	—	—	—	—

KM# 42 3 DUCAT

10.5000 g., 0.9860 Gold 0.3328 oz. AGW **Ruler:** Karl Ferdinand **Obv:** Bust left **Obv. Legend:** CAROLVS. FERDINAN. D.G. PRIN. P. ET. SV. **Rev:** Crowned 4-fold arms with central shield divide date **Rev. Legend:** EPIS. WRATIS. & PLO. DVX. OPPO. & RAT. **Note:** Ref. F/S#2923. Klippe.

Date	Mintage	VG	F	VF	XF	Unc
1653 Rare	—	—	—	—	—	—

KM# 43 3 DUCAT

10.5000 g., 0.9860 Gold 0.3328 oz. AGW **Ruler:** Karl Ferdinand **Obv:** Bust left **Obv. Legend:** CAROLVS. FERDINAN. D.G. PRIN. P. ET. SV. **Rev:** Crowned 4-fold arms with central shield divide date **Rev. Legend:** EPIS. WRATIS. & PLO. DVX. OPPO. & RAT. **Note:** Ref. F/S#2924. Hexagonal Klippe.

Date	Mintage	VG	F	VF	XF	Unc
1653 Rare	—	—	—	—	—	—

KM# 67 3 DUCAT

10.5000 g., 0.9860 Gold 0.3328 oz. AGW **Ruler:** Karl Ferdinand **Obv:** Bust right in circle **Obv. Legend:** CAROLUS. FERDINAND. D.G. PRINC. POL. &. S. **Rev:** Crowned 4-fold arms with central shield in oval baroque frame, date at end of legend **Rev. Legend:** EPIS. WRAT. & PLO. DUX. OPP. & RAT. **Note:** Ref. F/S#2933.

Date	Mintage	VG	F	VF	XF	Unc
1654 Rare	—	—	—	—	—	—

KM# 46 4 DUCAT

14.0000 g., 0.9860 Gold 0.4438 oz. AGW **Ruler:** Karl Ferdinand **Obv:** Bust left **Obv. Legend:** CAROLVS. FERDINAN. D.G. PRIN. P. ET. SV. **Rev:** Crowned 4-fold arms with central shield divide date **Rev. Legend:** EPIS. WRATIS. & PLO. DVX. OPPO. & RAT. **Note:** Ref. F/S#2921. Struck from 1/2 Thaler dies, KM#29.

Date	Mintage	VG	F	VF	XF	Unc
1653 Rare	—	—	—	—	—	—

KM# 69 4 DUCAT

14.0000 g., 0.9860 Gold 0.4438 oz. AGW **Ruler:** Karl Ferdinand **Obv:** Bust right in circle **Obv. Legend:** CAROLUS. FERDINAND. D.G. PRINC. POL. &. S. **Rev:** Crowned 4-fold arms with central shield in oval baroque frame, date at end of legend **Rev. Legend:** EPIS. WRAT. & PLO. DUX. OPP. & RAT. **Note:** Ref. F/S#2932. Octagonal Klippe. Struck from 1/2 Thaler dies, KM#54.

Date	Mintage	VG	F	VF	XF	Unc
1654	—	—	—	—	—	—

KM# 48 10 DUCAT

35.0000 g., 0.9860 Gold 1.1095 oz. AGW **Ruler:** Karl Ferdinand **Obv:** Bust left **Obv. Legend:** CAROLVS. FERDINANDVS. D.G. PRINCEP. POL. ET. SVECI. **Rev:** Crowned 4-fold arms with central shield in ornamented Spanish shield divide date **Rev. Legend:** EPIS. WRATIS. ET. PLO. DVX. OPPOLI. ET. RATI. **Note:** Ref. F/S#2920. Struck from Thaler dies, KM#31.

Date	Mintage	VG	F	VF	XF	Unc
1653 Rare	—	—	—	—	—	—

Note: Künker Auction 147, 2-09, F/VF realized approximately $11,920.

OSNABRUCK

RULERS

Konrad IV, Graf von Rietberg, 1482-1508
Erich II, Herzog von Braunschweig-Grubenhagen, 1508-1532
Franz, Graf von Waldeck, 1532-1553
Johann IV, Graf von Hoya, 1553-1574
Heinrich II, Herzog von Sachsen-Lauenburg, 1574-1585
Wilhelm von Schenking, 1585
Bernhard, Graf von Waldeck, 1585-1591
Philip Sigismund, Herzog von Braunschweig, 1591-1623
Eitel Friedrich von Hohenzollern, 1623-1625
Franz Wilhelm, Graf von Wartenberg, 1625-1634
Gustav Gustavson, Graf von Wasaborg, 1634-1648
Franz Wilhelm, Graf von Wartenberg, 1648-1661
Ernst August, Herzog von Braunschweig, 1662-1698
Sede Vacante, 1698
Karl Joseph von Lothringen, 1698-1715

ARMS

Wheel w/6 spokes (usually) and also on city+
Braunschweig (Brunswick): 2 leopards
Hoya: 2 bear paws
Minden: 2 crossed keys
Münster: Broad horizontal bar
Paderborn: Cross
Rietburg: Eagle
Waldeck: 8-pointed star
Wartenberg: Crowned lion rampant left

MINT OFFICIALS' INITIALS

Initial	Date	Name
EK	1605-06	Elias Kempfzer, mintmaster in Annaberg, Saxony for cathedral chapter
IL	Ca. 1633	Johann Loidtmann
EK	1637	Engelbert Kettler
	1641-?	Johann and Heinrich Pothoff
	1655-71	Hermann von der Hardt at Melle
HS	1625-72	Henning Schlüter in Zellerfeld
AS	1666-74	Andreas Scheele in Hannover City

REFERENCE

K = Karl Kennepohl, **Die Münzen von Osnabrück**, München, 1938.

Sch = Wolfgang Schulten, ***Deutsche Münzen aus der Zeit Karls V.*** Frankfurt am Main, 1974

BISHOPRIC

REGULAR COINAGE

KM# 62 1-1/2 PFENNIG (1/8 Schilling)

Silver Weight varies: 0.38-0.45g., 12-13 mm. **Ruler:** Franz Wilhelm **Obv:** Osnabrück arms in hexalobe **Rev:** 3-line inscription with date **Rev. Inscription:** 16 I 57 / I–I / F.O.P. **Mint:** Melle **Note:** K-254.

Date	Mintage	VG	F	VF	XF	Unc
1657	38,640	30.00	65.00	100	210	—

KM# 64 1-1/2 PFENNIG (1/8 Schilling)

0.3000 g., Silver, 13 mm. **Ruler:** Franz Wilhelm **Obv:** Osnabrück arms in plain circle **Rev:** 3-line inscription with date **Rev. Inscription:** 16(tall I divides)57 / I–I / F.O.P. **Mint:** Melle **Note:** K-255.

Date	Mintage	VG	F	VF	XF	Unc
1657	Inc. above	30.00	65.00	100	210	—

KM# 66 2 PFENNIG (1/6 Schilling)

Silver Weight varies: 0.43-0.65g., 13-15 mm. **Ruler:** Franz Wilhelm **Obv:** Osnabrück arms **Rev:** Large Roman numeral II divides date / F.O.P. **Mint:** Melle **Note:** K-253. Varieties exist.

Date	Mintage	VG	F	VF	XF	Unc
1657	27,468	25.00	55.00	95.00	210	—

KM# 67 2 PFENNIG (1/6 Schilling)

0.5300 g., Silver, 13 mm. **Ruler:** Franz Wilhelm **Obv:** Osnabrück arms **Rev:** 3-line inscription with date **Rev. Inscription:** II / 1657 / F.O.P. **Mint:** Melle **Note:** K-253d.

Date	Mintage	VG	F	VF	XF	Unc
1657	Inc. above	25.00	55.00	95.00	210	—

KM# 68 3 PFENNIG (1/4 Schilling)

Silver Weight varies: 0.41-0.78g., 15-16 mm. **Ruler:** Franz Wilhelm **Obv:** Osnabrück arms in baroque frame **Rev:** 3-line inscription with date **Rev. Inscription:** 1657 / III / F.O.P. **Mint:** Melle **Note:** K-252. Varieties exist.

Date	Mintage	VG	F	VF	XF	Unc
1657	18,648	40.00	80.00	140	275	—

KM# 70 4 PFENNIG (1/3 Schilling)

Silver Weight varies: 0.83-0.92g., 18 mm. **Ruler:** Franz Wilhelm **Obv:** Osnabrück arms in baroque frame **Rev:** 3-line inscription with date **Rev. Inscription:** 1657 / IIII / F.O.P. **Mint:** Melle **Note:** K-251. Varieties exist.

Date	Mintage	VG	F	VF	XF	Unc
1657	13,041	30.00	60.00	120	230	—

KM# 72 5 PFENNIG (1/50 Thaler)

1.3000 g., Silver, 18 mm. **Ruler:** Franz Wilhelm **Obv:** Osnabrück arms **Rev:** 3-line inscription with date **Rev. Inscription:** 1657 / V / F.O.P. **Mint:** Melle **Note:** K-250.

Date	Mintage	VG	F	VF	XF	Unc
1657	5,900	35.00	75.00	150	300	—

KM# 74 6 PFENNIG (1/2 Schilling)

Silver Weight varies: 1.00-1.30g., 17-18.5 mm. **Ruler:** Franz Wilhelm **Obv:** Osnabrück arms in baroque frame **Rev:** 3-line inscription with mintmaster's initials **Rev. Inscription:** 1657/ VI / F.O.P. **Mint:** Melle **Note:** K-249. Varieties exist.

Date	Mintage	VG	F	VF	XF	Unc
1657	9,780	35.00	75.00	155	—	—

KM# 111 6 PFENNIG (1/2 Schilling)

Silver Weight varies: 0.77-1.46g., 17-19 mm. **Ruler:** Ernst August I **Obv:** Crowned EA monogram in palm branches **Rev:** 5-line inscription with date **Rev. Inscription:** (date) / VI / PFENN(I) / OSNAB / (4Z) **Mint:** Melle **Note:** K-274, 277, 281. Varieties exist

Date	Mintage	VG	F	VF	XF	Unc
1664	—	35.00	70.00	125	240	—
1665	—	35.00	70.00	125	240	—
1666	—	35.00	70.00	125	240	—

KM# 25 SCHILLING

Silver Weight varies: 1.58-1.98g., 11x12-13x14 mm. **Ruler:** Franz Wilhelm **Obv:** W above Osnabrück arms **Mint:** Osnabrück **Note:** K-218. Uniface. Klippe. Siege issue.

Date	Mintage	VG	F	VF	XF	Unc
ND(1633)	—	—	—	—	—	—

KM# 53 1/28 THALER (Fürstengroschen)

Silver Weight varies: 1.25-1.66g., 20-21 mm. **Ruler:** Franz Wilhelm **Obv:** Crowned shield of Wartenberg arms divide date **Obv. Legend:** FRAN. GVIL. EP. O. R. M. V. S. R. I. P. **Rev:** 1/2-length figure of St. Peter holding key and book, value 28 in exergue **Rev. Legend:** S. PETRVS. PATRON. OSNAB(R). **Mint:** Melle **Note:** K-239. Varieties exist.

Date	Mintage	VG	F	VF	XF	Unc
1656	—	50.00	110	220	—	—

KM# 80 1/28 THALER (Fürstengroschen)

Silver Weight varies: 1.60-1.78g., 22 mm. **Ruler:** Franz Wilhelm **Obv:** Cardinal's hat above 4-fold arms with central shield of Wartenberg **Obv. Legend:** F. G. S. R. E. C. P. E. O. R. M. V. S. R. I. P. **Rev:** 1/2-length figure of St. Peter holding key and book, value 28 below, date divided at top **Rev. Legend:** S. PETR: PATR: OSNAB: **Mint:** Melle **Note:** K-257.

Date	Mintage	VG	F	VF	XF	Unc
1661	—	50.00	110	220	—	—

KM# 24 SCHILLING (12 Pfennig)

Copper, 30-31 mm. **Ruler:** Franz Wilhelm **Obv:** Crown above large FWE monogram in ornamented border **Rev:** Osnabrück arms divide date above .X.I.I. in ornamented border **Mint:** Osnabrück **Note:** K-214.

Date	Mintage	Good	VG	F	VF	XF
1633 IL	—	175	325	500	700	1,400

KM# 50 SCHILLING (1/21 Thaler)

Silver Weight varies: 1.70-2.03g., 23.5-24 mm. **Ruler:** Franz Wilhelm **Obv:** 3 shields of arms, 2 above 1, lower shield divides value 2 - 1 **Obv. Legend:** F - G. E. O. M. V. C. R. S. R. I. - P. **Rev:** 3 shields of arms, 2 above 1 **Rev. Legend:** C. D. W. E. S. D. R. W. E. H. **Mint:** Osnabrück **Note:** K-228.

Date	Mintage	VG	F	VF	XF	Unc
ND(1642-49)	—	45.00	90.00	180	—	—

KM# 99 SCHILLING (1/21 Thaler)

Silver Weight varies: 1.92-2.21g., 23 mm. **Ruler:** Ernst August I **Obv:** Crowned EA monogram, date divided above, value (Z1) at bottom **Obv. Legend:** F. OSNABRUG - LANDT. MVN. **Rev:** Crowned shield of 12-fold arms **Rev. Legend:** SOLA. BONA - QVÆ. HONESTA. **Mint:** Melle **Note:** K-266.

Date	Mintage	VG	F	VF	XF	Unc
1663	—	65.00	150	300	475	—

KM# 27 2 SCHILLING

3.5000 g., Silver, 17x16 mm. **Ruler:** Franz Wilhelm **Obv:** Wheel arms of Osnabrück **Mint:** Osnabrück **Note:** K-217. Uniface. Klippe. Siege issue.

Date	Mintage	VG	F	VF	XF	Unc
ND(1633)	—	—	—	—	—	—

KM# 29 3 SCHILLING (Schreckenberger)

Copper, 32-33 mm. **Ruler:** Franz Wilhelm **Obv:** Crown above FWE monogram in ornamented border **Rev:** Shield of Osnabrück arms divide date above value I.I.I. S., all in ornamented border **Mint:** Osnabrück **Note:** K-213.

Date	Mintage	Good	VG	F	VF	XF
1633 IL	—	100	200	325	500	700

KM# 83 GROSCHEN (1/24 Thaler)

Silver Weight varies: 1.80-2.16g., 22-23 mm. **Ruler:** Ernst August I **Obv:** Crowned EA monogram **Obv. Legend:** SOLA. BONA QVÆ. HONESTA. **Rev:** Crowned shield of Osnabrück arms, date divided above **Rev. Legend:** F - OSNABRUG. LANDTMUN. **Mint:** Zellerfeld **Note:** K-264.

Date	Mintage	VG	F	VF	XF	Unc
1662 HS	—	45.00	90.00	180	—	—

KM# 100 GROSCHEN (1/24 Thaler)

Silver Weight varies: 1.75-2.37g., 20-22 mm. **Ruler:** Ernst August I **Obv:** Crowned EA monogram **Obv. Legend:** SOLA. BONA. QV(Æ)(AE). HONES(T)(A). **Rev:** Crowned shield of Osnabrück arms, date divided above, value (Z4) at bottom **Rev. Legend:** F. OSNABR(U)(V)(G). - LAN(D)(T). MVN(D)(T). **Mint:** Melle **Note:** K-267, 272, 273. Varieties exist.

Date	Mintage	VG	F	VF	XF	Unc
1663	—	40.00	85.00	140	240	—
1664	—	40.00	85.00	140	240	—

KM# 101 GROSCHEN (1/24 Thaler)

1.2300 g., Silver, 20 mm. **Ruler:** Ernst August I **Obv:** Crowned EA monogram **Obv. Legend:** SOLA. BONA. QVÆ. HONESTA. **Rev:** Crowned shield of Osnabrück arms divides value Z - 4, date divided above **Rev. Legend:** F. OSNABRVG. LANDT. MVN. **Mint:** Melle **Note:** K-268.

Date	Mintage	VG	F	VF	XF	Unc
1663	—	45.00	90.00	180	—	—

KM# 102 GROSCHEN (1/24 Thaler)

1.8400 g., Silver, 20 mm. **Ruler:** Ernst August I **Obv:** Crowned EA monogram, date divided above **Obv. Legend:** SOLA BONA. QVÆ. HONESTA. **Rev:** Crowned shield of Osnabrück arms, value (Z4) at bottom **Rev. Legend:** F. OSNABRV. - LANT. MV. **Mint:** Melle **Note:** K-269. Mule mule of obverse die of Mariengroschen, KM#107 with reverse of KM#100.

Date	Mintage	VG	F	VF	XF	Unc
1663	—	45.00	90.00	180	—	—

KM# 105 MATIER

(1/2 Mariengroschen = 1/72 Thaler)

Silver Weight varies: 0.70-0.87g., 16 mm. **Ruler:** Ernst August I **Obv:** Crowned EA monogram **Obv. Legend:** SOLA. BONA. QVÆ. HONESTA. **Rev:** 3-line inscription with date **Rev. Inscription:** EIN / MATIER / (date) **Mint:** Melle **Note:** K-271.

Date	Mintage	VG	F	VF	XF	Unc
1663	—	40.00	85.00	140	275	—

KM# 107 MARIENGROSCHEN (1/36 Thaler)

Silver Weight varies: 1.24-1.35g., 21 mm. **Ruler:** Ernst August I **Obv:** Crowned EA monogram, date divided above **Obv. Legend:** SOLA. BONA. QVÆ. HONESTA. **Rev:** Madonna and child, rays around **Rev. Legend:** MARIEN - GROSCHE. **Mint:** Melle **Note:** K-270.

Date	Mintage	VG	F	VF	XF	Unc
1663	—	45.00	90.00	180	—	—

KM# 57 2 MARIENGROSCHEN
(1/18 Thaler=14 Pfennig)
Silver Weight varies: 1.24-1.44g., 18-19 mm. **Ruler:** Franz Wilhelm **Obv:** Crowned FWE monogram **Obv. Legend:** FRAN. GVIL. E. O. R. M. V. **Rev:** 3-line inscription, date at end of legend **Rev. Legend:** MONE - NO - ARGENT. **Rev. Inscription:** II / MARI / GRO **Mint:** Melle **Note:** K-241.

Date	Mintage	VG	F	VF	XF	Unc
1656	7,416	70.00	150	300	—	—

KM# 115 2 MARIENGROSCHEN
(1/18 Thaler=14 Pfennig)
Silver Weight varies: 1.18-1.47g., 17-19 mm. **Ruler:** Ernst August I **Obv:** Crowned EA monogram **Obv. Legend:** SOLA. BONA. QUÆ. HONESTA. **Rev:** 4-line inscription with date **Rev. Legend:** 18. A(U)(V)F. EIN. REICHS. THALER. **Rev. Inscription:** II / MARIE / GROS / (date) **Mint:** Melle **Note:** K-276, 280, 283, 286. Varieties exist.

Date	Mintage	VG	F	VF	XF	Unc
1665	—	40.00	80.00	160	—	—
1666	—	40.00	80.00	160	—	—
1667	—	40.00	80.00	160	—	—
1668	—	40.00	80.00	160	—	—

KM# 125.1 2 MARIENGROSCHEN
(1/18 Thaler=14 Pfennig)
1.6000 g., Silver, 19 mm. **Ruler:** Ernst August I **Obv:** Braunschweig helmet with horse crest **Obv. Legend:** ERN. AUG. B. Z. O. H. Z. B. U. L. **Rev:** 4-line inscription with date **Rev. Legend:** VON. FEINEM. SILBER. **Rev. Inscription:** 11 / MARI / GR / (date) **Mint:** Melle **Note:** K-292.

Date	Mintage	VG	F	VF	XF	Unc
1669	—	65.00	135	275	—	—

KM# 125.2 2 MARIENGROSCHEN
(1/18 Thaler=14 Pfennig)
0.9200 g., Silver, 19.5 mm. **Ruler:** Ernst August I **Obv:** Braunschweig helmet with horse crest **Obv. Legend:** ERNEST. AUGUST. B. Z. O. H. Z. B. V. L. **Rev:** 4-line inscription with date **Rev. Legend:** VON FEINEM SILBER. **Rev. Inscription:** II / MARIE / GROS / (date) **Mint:** Melle **Note:** K-293.

Date	Mintage	VG	F	VF	XF	Unc
1669	—	65.00	135	275	—	—

KM# 59 4 MARIENGROSCHEN
(1/9 Thaler = 1/2 Kopfstuck)
Silver Weight varies: 2.44-2.45g., 22-23 mm. **Ruler:** Franz Wilhelm **Obv:** Crowned shield of Wartenberg arms divide date **Obv. Legend:** FRAN. GVIL. EP. O. R. M. V. S. R. I. (P.) **Rev:** 3-line inscription **Rev. Legend:** MONETT - NOVA - ARGENTEA. **Rev. Inscription:** IIII / MARI(E) / GRO(S) **Mint:** Melle **Note:** K-240, 248. Varieties exist.

Date	Mintage	VG	F	VF	XF	Unc
1656	25,515	50.00	110	225	—	—
1657	—	50.00	110	225	—	—

KM# 127 4 MARIENGROSCHEN (1/9 Thaler)
Silver Weight varies: 2.20-2.46g., 22-23 mm. **Ruler:** Ernst August I **Obv:** Braunschweig helmet with horse crest **Obv. Legend:** ERNEST. AUGUST. B. Z. O. H. Z. B. U. L. **Rev:** 3-line inscription, date at end of legend **Rev. Legend:** VON FEINEM SILBER. **Rev. Inscription:** IIII / MARIE / GROS **Mint:** Melle **Note:** K-291. Varieties exist.

Date	Mintage	VG	F	VF	XF	Unc
1669	—	65.00	145	200	360	—

KM# 129 6 MARIENGROSCHEN (1/6 Thaler)
3.6000 g., Silver, 26 mm. **Ruler:** Ernst August I **Obv:** Braunschweig helmet with horse crest **Obv. Legend:** ERNEST. AUGUST. B. Z. O. H. Z. B. U. L. **Rev:** 3-line inscription, date at end of legend **Rev. Legend:** VON FEINEM SILBER. **Rev. Inscription:** VI / MARIE / GROS **Mint:** Melle **Note:** K-290.

Date	Mintage	VG	F	VF	XF	Unc
1669	—	550	900	1,500	2,800	—

KM# 130 12 MARIENGROSCHEN
(1/3 Thaler = 1/2 Gulden)
Silver Weight varies: 6.52-7.50g., 30-31 mm. **Ruler:** Ernst August I **Obv:** Braunschweig helmet with horse crest **Obv. Legend:** ERNEST. A(V)(U)GUST. B. Z. O. H. Z. B. U. L. **Rev:** 3-line inscription with mintmaster's initials, where present, date at end of legend **Rev. Legend:** VON FEINEM SILBER. **Rev. Inscription:** XII / MARIEN / GROS **Mint:** Hannover **Note:** K-287, 288, 294, 295. Varieties exist.

Date	Mintage	VG	F	VF	XF	Unc
1669 AS	—	70.00	150	225	450	—
1669	—	70.00	150	225	450	—
1670	—	70.00	150	225	450	—
1670 AS	—	70.00	150	225	450	—

KM# 131 12 MARIENGROSCHEN
(1/3 Thaler = 1/2 Gulden)
Silver Weight varies: 5.75-7.40g., 29-33 mm. **Ruler:** Ernst August I **Obv:** Braunschweig helmet with horse crest enclosed in circle **Obv. Legend:** ERNEST. AUGUST. B. Z. . H. Z. B. V. L. **Rev:** 3-line inscription, date at end of legend **Rev. Legend:** VON FEINEM SILBER. **Rev. Inscription:** XII / MARIEN / GROS **Mint:** Hannover **Note:** K-289, 296. Varieties exist.

Date	Mintage	VG	F	VF	XF	Unc
1669	—	70.00	150	225	450	—
1670	—	70.00	150	225	450	—

KM# 132 12 MARIENGROSCHEN
(1/3 Thaler = 1/2 Gulden)
Silver Weight varies: 7.04-7.50g., 29-32 mm. **Ruler:** Ernst August I **Obv:** Braunschweig helmet with horse crest **Obv. Legend:** ERNEST. A(U)(V)GUST. B. Z. O. H. Z. B. U. L. **Rev:** 3-line inscription, date at end of legend **Rev. Legend:** VON FEINEM SILBER **Rev. Inscription:** XII / MARIEN / GROS **Mint:** Melle **Note:** K-297-299, 302, 306. Varieties exist.

Date	Mintage	VG	F	VF	XF	Unc
1671	—	70.00	150	225	450	—
1672	—	70.00	150	225	450	—
1674	—	70.00	150	225	450	—
1675	—	70.00	150	225	450	—
1676	—	70.00	150	225	450	—

KM# 150 12 MARIENGROSCHEN
(1/3 Thaler = 1/2 Gulden)
8.0800 g., Silver, 31.5 mm. **Ruler:** Ernst August I **Obv:** Braunschweig helmet with horse crest **Obv. Legend:** ERNEST AVGUST. B. Z. O. H. Z. B. U. L. **Rev:** 3-line inscription, date at end of legend **Rev. Legend:** SOLA BONA QVÆ HONESTA. **Rev. Inscription:** XII / MARIEN / GROS. **Mint:** Melle **Note:** K-305.

Date	Mintage	VG	F	VF	XF	Unc
1676	—	75.00	165	360	—	—

KM# 137 24 MARIENGROSCHEN
(2/3 Thaler = Gulden)
Silver Weight varies: 15.91-16.68g., 33-36 mm. **Ruler:** Ernst August I **Obv:** Braunschweig helmet with horse crest **Obv. Legend:** ERNEST AVG(U)(V)ST. B. Z. O. H. Z. B. U. L. **Rev:** 3-line inscription, date at end of legend **Rev. Legend:** SOLA BONA QVÆ HONESTA. **Rev. Inscription:** XXIIII / MARIEN / GROS. **Mint:** Melle **Note:** K-300, 303; Dav. 411. Varieties exist.

Date	Mintage	VG	F	VF	XF	Unc
1675	—	60.00	120	250	400	—
1676	—	75.00	150	275	425	—

KM# 136 24 MARIENGROSCHEN
(2/3 Thaler = Gulden)
Silver Weight varies: 12.31-14.60g., 33-36 mm. **Ruler:** Ernst August I **Obv:** Braunschweig helmet with horse crest **Obv. Legend:** ERNEST AVGUST. B. Z. O. H. Z. B. U. L. **Rev:** 3-line inscription, date at end of legend **Rev. Legend:** VON FEINEM SILBER **Rev. Inscription:** XXIIII / MARIEN / GROS. **Mint:** Melle **Note:** K-301, 304; Dav. 412. Varieties exist.

Date	Mintage	VG	F	VF	XF	Unc
1675	—	70.00	150	225	450	—
1676	—	70.00	150	225	450	—

KM# 118 1/16 THALER (1/2 Blamüser)
Silver Weight varies: 1.43-1.72g., 19-20 mm. **Ruler:** Ernst August I **Obv:** Braunschweig helmet with horse crest **Obv. Legend:** ERNES(T). AUG. B. Z. O. H. Z. B. U. LU(NE). **Rev:** 4-line inscription with date **Rev. Legend:** SOLA. BONA. Q(U)(V)Æ. HONESTA. **Rev. Inscription:** XVI / I. REI(C)(G)(H)S / THALE(R) / (date) **Mint:** Melle **Note:** K-275, 279, 285. Varieties exist.

Date	Mintage	VG	F	VF	XF	Unc
1665	—	25.00	50.00	100	210	425
1666	—	25.00	50.00	100	210	425
1668	—	25.00	50.00	100	210	425

KM# 55 1/14 THALER
(2 Fürstengroschen = 1-1/2 Schilling)
Silver Weight varies: 2.00-2.67g., 24-25 mm. **Ruler:** Franz Wilhelm **Obv:** Crowned shield of Wartenberg arms, value (14) below **Obv. Legend:** FRAN. GV(I)L. EP - O. R. M. V. S. R. I. P. **Rev:** St. Peter standing, holding key and book, divides date **Rev. Legend:** S. PETRVS. PAT - RO: OSNABRV: **Mint:** Melle **Note:** K-237, 238, 247. Varieties exist.

Date	Mintage	VG	F	VF	XF	Unc
1656	—	50.00	100	200	—	—
1657	—	50.00	100	200	—	—

KM# 76 1/14 THALER
(2 Fürstengroschen = 1-1/2 Schilling)
Silver Weight varies: 2.30-3.70g., 24-25 mm. **Ruler:** Franz Wilhelm **Obv:** Crowned shield of Wartenberg arms divides date, value (14) below **Obv. Legend:** FRAN. GVIL. E(P). - (P.) O. R. M. V. S. R. I. (P.) **Rev:** St. Peter standing holding key and book **Rev. Legend:** S. PETRVS. PAT(R) - (R)O: OSNABRV(G). **Mint:** Melle **Note:** K-244-246. Varieties exist.

Date	Mintage	VG	F	VF	XF	Unc
1657	—	125	300	600	1,200	—

KM# 122 1/14 THALER
(2 Fürstengroschen = 1-1/2 Schilling)
Silver Weight varies: 2.62-3.10g., 24 mm. **Ruler:** Ernst August I **Obv:** Crowned EA monogram, value (14) at bottom **Obv. Legend:** F. OSNABR(V)(U)G - LANDT. MVNT. **Rev:** Crowned shield of 12-fold arms with central shield of Osnabrück, date at end of leged **Rev. Legend:** SOLA. BONA. Q(V)(U)Æ. HONESTA. **Mint:** Melle **Note:** K-282, 284. Varieties exist.

Date	Mintage	VG	F	VF	XF	Unc
1667	—	55.00	125	180	360	—
1668	—	55.00	125	180	360	—

KM# 60 1/8 THALER (Blamüser)
Silver Weight varies: 4.25-4.95g., 28-30 mm. **Ruler:** Franz Wilhelm **Obv:** Crowned shield of Wartenberg arms divides date, value (8) below **Obv. Legend:** FRAN.-GVIL - EP - O. R. M. V. S. R. I. P. **Rev:** St. Peter standing, holding key and book **Rev.**

Legend: S. PETRVS-PATR - O. OSNABRVG. **Mint:** Melle **Note:** K-236.

Date	Mintage	VG	F	VF	XF	Unc
1656	1,136	550	800	1,500	3,000	—

KM# 84 1/8 THALER

Silver 3.27-3.63g., 26 mm. **Ruler:** Ernst August I **Obv:** Armored and mantled youthful bust to right **Obv. Legend:** ERNESTVS AVGVSTVS D. G. EPIS. OSNABRVG. DVX. BRVN. ET. LVN. **Rev:** Crowned shield of manifold arms, with central shield of Osnabrück, divides mintmaster's initials, date at end of legend **Rev. Legend:** SOLA BONA. QVÆ HONESTA. ANNO. **Mint:** Zellerfeld **Note:** K-263. Prev. KM-85.

Date	Mintage	VG	F	VF	XF	Unc
1662 HS	—	—	—	—	—	—

KM# 85 1/4 THALER

Silver Weight varies: 7.02-7.30g., 34 mm. **Ruler:** Ernst August I **Obv:** Armored and mantled youthful bust to right **Obv. Legend:** ERNESTVS AVGVSTVS. D. G. EPIS. OSNABRVG. DVX BRVN. ET LVNE. **Rev:** Crowned shield of manifold arms, with central shield of Osnabrück divides mintmaster's initials, date at end of legend **Rev. Legend:** SOLA BONA. QVÆ HONESTA. ANNO. **Mint:** Zellerfeld **Note:** K-262. Prev. KM-86.

Date	Mintage	VG	F	VF	XF	Unc
1662 HS	—	—	—	—	—	—

KM# 30 1/2 THALER

Silver Weight varies: 14.50-14.52g., 22x22-24x24 mm. **Ruler:** Franz Wilhelm **Obv:** St. Peter standing behind shield of 4-fold arms, holding key and book, divides date **Mint:** Osnabrück **Note:** K-216. Uniface Klippe. Siege issue.

Date	Mintage	VG	F	VF	XF	Unc
1633	—	—	—	—	—	—

KM# 86 1/2 THALER

Silver Weight varies: 13.67-14.50g., 37-39 mm. **Ruler:** Ernst August I **Obv:** Armored and mantled youthful bust to right **Obv. Legend:** ERNESTVS. AVGVSTVS. D. G. EPIS. OSNABRVG. DVX. BRVN. ET. LVNE. **Rev:** Crowned shield of manifold arms, with central shield of Osnabrück, divides mintmaster's initials, date at end of legend **Rev. Legend:** SOLA. BONA. QVÆ. HONESTA. ANNO. **Mint:** Zellerfeld **Note:** K-261. Prev. KM-88.

Date	Mintage	VG	F	VF	XF	Unc
1662 HS	—	—	—	—	—	—

KM# 22 THALER

Silver Weight varies: 28.50-29.40g., 41 mm. **Ruler:** Franz Wilhelm **Obv:** Bust to right in circle **Obv. Legend:** FRANCISCVS. GVILIEMVS. D: G. SAC. ROM. IMP. PRINC. **Rev:** Shield of 4-fold arms with 4-fold central shield in baroque frame, date above **Rev. Legend:** EPS. OSNABVRG. MINDEN. VERD: COM. D. WARTTENBERG. **Mint:** Köln **Note:** K-212; Dav. 5670.

Date	Mintage	VG	F	VF	XF	Unc
1631	—	2,200	4,400	8,300	14,000	—

KM# 33 THALER

Silver Weight varies: 28.60-29.30g., 27x28-27x30 mm. **Ruler:** Franz Wilhelm **Obv:** St. Peter standing behind shield of 4-fold arms, holding key and book, divides date **Mint:** Osnabrück **Note:** K-215. Klippe. Uniface. Siege issue.

Date	Mintage	VG	F	VF	XF	Unc
1633	—	1,100	2,400	3,500	4,950	—

KM# 46 THALER

Silver Weight varies: 27.45-29.00g., 41-42 mm. **Ruler:** Franz Wilhelm **Obv:** Bust to right breaks circle at bottom **Obv. Legend:** FRANC: GVIL: D. G. S. R. I. PRINC: **Rev:** Oval 4-fold arms, with oval 4-fold central shield, divide date near top **Rev. Legend:** EPS. OSNAB. MINDE - VERD. COM. DE. WART. **Mint:** Münster **Note:** K-224, 225; Dav. 5672. Date and mintmaster's initials effaced from reverse die on dateless examples.

Date	Mintage	VG	F	VF	XF	Unc
1637 EK Rare	—	—	—	—	—	—
ND(ca.1637) EK	—	1,400	2,750	6,100	—	—

KM# 78 THALER

Silver Weight varies: 28.60-28.80g., 40 mm. **Ruler:** Franz Wilhelm **Obv:** Mantled bust to right **Obv. Legend:** FRANC. GVIL. D. G. S. R. I. PRINC. **Rev:** Round shield of 4-fold arms with central shield of Wartenberg, date divided above left and right, where present **Rev. Legend:** EPS. RATIS. OSNAB. MIND - VERD. COM. DE. WARTEN. **Mint:** Melle **Note:** K-242, 243; Dav. 5672.

Date	Mintage	VG	F	VF	XF	Unc
1657 Rare	—	—	—	—	—	—
ND(1657) Rare	—	—	—	—	—	—

KM# 82 THALER

28.7000 g., Silver, 43 mm. **Ruler:** Franz Wilhelm **Obv:** Elderly bust to right in cardinal's cap and robe, date at end of legend **Obv. Legend:** FRAN. GVIL. D. G. S. R. E. CARDIN. PRESB. **Rev:** Cardinal's hat above oval shield of 4-fold arms with central shield of Wartenberg **Rev. Legend:** EPS. RATISB. OSNAB. MIND - VERD. COM. DE. WART. S. R. I. P. **Mint:** Melle **Note:** K-256.

Date	Mintage	VG	F	VF	XF	Unc
1661 Rare	—	—	—	—	—	—

KM# 87 THALER

Silver Weight varies: 28.65-29.00g., 44-45 mm. **Ruler:** Ernst August I **Obv:** Armored and mantled youthful bust to right **Obv. Legend:** ERNESTVS. AVGVSTVS. D: G. EPIS: OSNABRVG: DVX. BRVN: ET. LVNE: **Rev:** Shield of 12-fold arms with central shield of Osnabrück, 5 ornate helmets above, date at end of legend **Rev. Legend:** SOLA. BONA. QVÆ. HONESTA. ANNO. **Mint:** Zellerfeld **Note:** K-260, 265. Dav. 5673. The Thaler dated 1663 was struck at the Melle mint. Prev. KM-90.

Date	Mintage	VG	F	VF	XF	Unc
1662 HS	—	875	1,750	3,450	6,900	—
1663	—	1,050	2,150	4,300	—	—

KM# A230 1-1/2 THALER

43.1000 g., Silver, 41x42 mm. **Ruler:** Franz Wilhelm **Obv:** Bust to right breaks legend at bottom **Obv. Legend:** FRANC: GVIL: D. G. S. R. I. PRINC: **Rev:** Oval 4-fold arms with oval 4-fold central shield in baroque frame **Rev. Legend:** EPS. OSNAB. MINDE - VERD. COM. DE. WART. **Mint:** Münster **Note:** K-225ex. Klippe.

Date	Mintage	VG	F	VF	XF	Unc
ND(1637) EK Rare	—	—	—	—	—	—

KM# B230 2 THALER

54.8000 g., Silver, 42 mm. **Ruler:** Franz Wilhelm **Obv:** Bust to right breaks legend at bottom **Obv. Legend:** FRANC: GVIL: D. G. S. R. I. PRINC: **Rev:** Shield of oval 4-fold arms with oval 4-fold central shield in baroque frame **Rev. Legend:** EPS. OSNAB. MINDE - VERD. COM. DE. WART. **Mint:** Münster **Note:** K-225ex; Dav. B5671.

Date	Mintage	VG	F	VF	XF	Unc
ND(1637) Rare	—	—	—	—	—	—

KM# C230 2 THALER

57.8500 g., Silver, 41x42 mm. **Ruler:** Franz Wilhelm **Obv:** Bust to right breaks legend at bottom **Obv. Legend:** FRANC: GVIL: D. G. S. R. I. PRINC: **Rev:** Oval 4-fold arms with oval 4-fold central shield in baroque frame **Rev. Legend:** EPS. OSNAB. MINDE - VERD. COM. DE. WART. **Mint:** Münster **Note:** K-225ex; Dav. C5671. Klippe.

Date	Mintage	VG	F	VF	XF	Unc
ND(1637) Rare	—	—	—	—	—	—

KM# 230 3 THALER

86.0000 g., Silver, 42 mm. **Ruler:** Franz Wilhelm **Obv:** Bust to right breaks legend at bottom **Obv. Legend:** FRANC: GVIL: D. G. S. R. I. PRINC: **Rev:** Oval 4-fold arms with oval 4-fold central shield in baroque frame **Rev. Legend:** EPS. OSNAB. MINDE - VERD. COM. DE. WART. **Mint:** Münster **Note:** K-225ex; Dav. 5671.

Date	Mintage	VG	F	VF	XF	Unc
ND(1637) Rare	—	—	—	—	—	—

KM# 90 3 THALER

84.7200 g., Silver, 85-86 mm. **Ruler:** Ernst August I **Obv:** Large shield of 12-fold arms with central shield of Osnabrück, 5 ornate helmets above, outer margin of laurel wreath **Obv. Legend:** ERNESTVS AVGVSTVS. D: G EPIS: OSNABRVG: DVX BRVN: ET LVNE: **Rev:** Crossed sword and crozier above city view, value 3 stamped at bottom, outer margin of laurel wreath **Rev. Legend:** IVNGVNTVR. FELICITER. **Mint:** Zellerfeld **Note:** K-259c; Dav. 229. Prev. KM-93.

Date	Mintage	VG	F	VF	XF	Unc
ND(1662) HS Rare	—	—	—	—	—	—

KM# 92 4 THALER

115.4000 g., Silver, 88 mm. **Ruler:** Ernst August I **Obv:** Large shield of 12-fold arms with central shield of Osnabrück, 5 ornate helmets above, outer margin of laurel wreath **Obv. Legend:** ERNESTVS AVGVSTVS. D: G EPIS: OSNABRVG: DVX BRVN: ET LVNE: **Rev:** Arm from clouds holds wheel of Osnabrück by ribbon, city view in background, value 4 stamped at bottom, outer margin of laurel wreath **Rev. Legend:** HOC AXE. FELICIVS CVRRET. **Mint:** Zellerfeld **Note:** K-258; Dav. 230. Struck from same obverse die as KM-94. Prev. KM-95.

Date	Mintage	VG	F	VF	XF	Unc
ND(1662) HS Rare	—	—	—	—	—	—

KM# 91 4 THALER

115.9700 g., Silver, 85 mm. **Ruler:** Ernst August I **Obv:** Large shield of 12-fold arms with central shield of Osnabrück, 5 ornate helmets above, outer margin of laurel wreath **Obv. Legend:** ERNESTVS AVGVSTVS. D: G EPIS OSNABRVG: DVX BRVN: ET LVNE: **Rev:** Crossed sword and crozier above city view, value 4 stamped at bottom, outer margin of laurel wreath **Rev. Legend:** IVNGVNTVR. FELICITER. **Mint:** Zellerfeld **Note:** K-259b; Dav. 228. Struck with same obverse die as KM-95. Prev. KM-94.

Date	Mintage	VG	F	VF	XF	Unc
ND(1662) HS Rare	—	—	—	—	—	—

KM# 94 5 THALER

139.3000 g., Silver, 85-86 mm. **Ruler:** Ernst August I **Obv:** Large shield of 12-fold arms with central shield of Osnabrück, 5 ornate helmets above, outer margin of laurel wreath **Obv. Legend:** ERNESTVS AVGVSTVS. D: G EPIS: OSNABRVG: DVX BRVN: ET LVNE: **Rev:** Crossed sword and crozier above city view, value 5 stamped at bottom, outer margin of laurel wreath **Rev. Legend:** IVNGVNTVR. FELICITER. **Mint:** Zellerfeld **Note:** K-259a; Dav. 227. Illustration reduced. Prev. KM-97.

Date	Mintage	VG	F	VF	XF	Unc
ND(1662) HS Rare	—	—	—	—	—	—

TRADE COINAGE

KM# 48 DUCAT

3.5000 g., 0.9860 Gold 0.1109 oz. AGW, 22 mm. **Ruler:** Franz Wilhelm **Obv:** Full-length facing figure of St. Peter, holding key and book, in circle **Obv. Legend:** FRAN. GVIL. EP - O. M. V. P. R. S. R. I. P **Rev:** Oval 4-fold arms in baroque frame, superimposed on crossed sword and crozier, date divided near bottom **Rev. Legend:** CO - DE. WART. ET - S. D. I. W. E. - H. **Mint:** Münster **Note:** K-223; Fr. 1938.

Date	Mintage	VG	F	VF	XF	Unc
1637 EK	—	1,000	2,000	4,150	7,700	—

KM# 52 DUCAT

3.5000 g., 0.9860 Gold 0.1109 oz. AGW, 22 mm. **Ruler:** Franz Wilhelm **Obv:** Three small shield of arms in circle, 2 above 1. **Obv. Legend:** F - G. E. O. M. V. P. R. S. R. I - P. **Rev:** Three small shields of arms in circle, 2 above 1 **Rev. Legend:** C. D. W. E. S. D. I. W. E. H. **Mint:** Münster **Note:** K-227; Fr. 1939.

Date	Mintage	VG	F	VF	XF	Unc
ND(1642)	—	1,100	2,550	4,950	9,100	—

KM# 120 DUCAT

3.5000 g., 0.9860 Gold 0.1109 oz. AGW, 21 mm. **Ruler:** Ernst August I **Obv:** Bust to right in circle **Obv. Legend:** ERNEST. AVG. D G. EP: OSNAB: DVX. BRVN: ET LV: **Rev:** Crowned shield of 12-fold arms with central shield of Osnabrück, superimposed on crossed sword and crozier, date at end of legend **Rev. Legend:** SOLA. BONA. QUÆ. HONESTA **Mint:** Melle **Note:** K-278; Fr. 1940.

Date	Mintage	VG	F	VF	XF	Unc
1666	—	1,500	3,300	6,600	11,500	—

KM# 95 2 DUCAT

Gold Weight varies: 6.85-6.86g., 26 mm. **Ruler:** Ernst August I **Obv:** Armored and mantled youthful bust to right **Obv. Legend:** ERNESTVS AVGVSTVS D. G. EPIS. OSNABRVG. DVX. BRUN. ET. LVN. **Rev:** Crowned shield of manifold arms, with central shield of Osnabrück, divides mintmaster's initials, date at end of legend **Rev. Legend:** SOLA BONA. QVÆ HONESTA. ANNO. **Mint:** Zellerfeld **Note:** K-263a. Struck from 1/8 Thaler dies, KM-84.

Date	Mintage	VG	F	VF	XF	Unc
1662 HS Rare	—	—	—	—	—	—

KM# 97 5 DUCAT

16.7700 g., Gold, 34 mm. **Ruler:** Ernst August I **Obv:** Armored and mantled youthful bust to right. **Obv. Legend:** ERNESTVS AVGVSTVS D. G. EPIS. OSNABRVG. DVX BRVN. ET LVNE. **Rev:** Crowned shield of manifold arms, with central shield of Osnabrück, divides mintmaster's initials, date at end of legend **Rev. Legend:** SOLA BONA. QVÆ HONESTA. ANNO. **Mint:** Zellerfeld **Note:** K-262ex. Struck from 1/4 Thaler dies, KM-85.

Date	Mintage	VG	F	VF	XF	Unc
1662 HS Rare	—	—	—	—	—	—

KM# 109 15 DUCAT

51.0900 g., Gold, 44 mm. **Ruler:** Ernst August I **Obv:** Armored and mantled youthful bust to right **Obv. Legend:** ERNESTVS. AVGVSTVS. D: G. EPIS: OSNABRVG: DVX. BRVN: ET. LVNE: **Rev:** Shield of 12-fold arms with central shield of Osnabrück, 5 ornate helmets above, date at end of legend **Rev. Legend:** SOLA BONA. QVÆ HONESTA. ANNO **Mint:** Melle **Note:** K-265ex. Struck with Thaler dies, KM#90. Prev. KM#2.

Date	Mintage	VG	F	VF	XF	Unc
1663 1 known	—	—	—	—	—	—

CATHEDRAL CHAPTER

MINT
Eversburg

REGULAR COINAGE

KM# 10 PFENNIG

Copper, 14.5 mm. **Obv:** St. Peter on throne holding key and book, arms of Osnabrück below in front **Obv. Legend:** DOM CAPITEL OSNABRVK. **Rev:** Value I divides date in ornameted circle **Mint:** Eversburg **Note:** K-207

Date	Mintage	Good	VG	F	VF	XF
1606	—	25.00	42.00	85.00	150	—

KM# 13 2 PFENNIG

Copper, 16-17 mm. **Obv:** St. Peter on throne holding key and book, arms of Osnabrück below in front **Obv. Legend:** DOM CAPITEL. ZV . OSNABRVK. **Rev:** Value divides date as 1 I 60 I 6 **Mint:** Eversburg **Note:** K-206.

Date	Mintage	Good	VG	F	VF	XF
1606 EK	—	150	300	600	950	—

KM# 15 3 PFENNIG

Copper, 19-20 mm. **Obv:** St. Peter on throne holding key and book, arms of Osnabrück below in front **Obv. Legend:** DOM CAPITEL. ZV. OSNABRVGK. **Rev:** Value with date divided as 1 I 6 I 0 I 6 in ornamented rectangle **Mint:** Eversburg **Note:** K-205.

Date	Mintage	Good	VG	F	VF	XF
1606 EK	—	25.00	42.00	85.00	—	—

KM# 3 6 PFENNIG

Copper, 25 mm. **Obv:** St. Peter on throne holding key and book, arms of Osnabrück below in front **Obv. Legend:** DOM CAPITEL. ZV. OSNABRVGK. **Rev:** Large VI in circle, ornamented border with date at top **Mint:** Eversburg **Note:** K-201.

Date	Mintage	Good	VG	F	VF	XF
1605	—	27.00	55.00	115	—	—

KM# 17 6 PFENNIG

Copper, 22-23 mm. **Obv:** St. Peter on throne holding key and book, arms of Osnabrück below in front **Obv. Legend:** DOM CAPITEL. ZV. OSNABRVGK. **Rev:** Value divides date as 1 V 60 I 6 in ornamented rectangle **Mint:** Eversburg **Note:** K-204.

Date	Mintage	Good	VG	F	VF	XF
1606 EK	—	27.00	55.00	115	—	—

KM# 6 9 PFENNIG

Copper, 29-30 mm. **Obv:** St. Peter on throne holding key and book, arms of Osnabrück below in front **Obv. Legend:** DOM CAPITEL. ZV. OSNABRVGK. **Rev:** Value IX in Gothic letters in circle, ornamented border with date at top **Mint:** Eversburg **Note:** K-200.

Date	Mintage	Good	VG	F	VF	XF
1605	—	25.00	50.00	100	160	—

KM# 19 9 PFENNIG

Copper, 25-26 mm. **Obv:** St. Peter on throne holding key and book, arms of Osnabrück below in front **Obv. Legend:** DOM CAPITEL. ZV. OSNABRVGK. **Rev:** Value divides date as 1 V 6 I 0 II 6 I **Mint:** Eversburg **Note:** K-203.

Date	Mintage	Good	VG	F	VF	XF
1606 EK	—	175	300	450	725	—

KM# 8 12 PFENNIG (Schilling)

Copper, 32 mm. **Obv:** St. Peter on throne under Gothic canopy, holding key and book, arms of Osnabrück below in front **Obv. Legend:** DOM CAPITEL ZV OSNABRVGK **Rev:** Value XII in Gothic letters in circle, ornamented border with date at top **Mint:** Eversburg **Note:** K-199.

Date	Mintage	Good	VG	F	VF	XF
1605	—	40.00	80.00	160	—	—

KM# 20 12 PFENNIG (Schilling)

Copper, 28-29 mm. **Obv:** St. Peter on throne holding key and book, arms of Osnabrück below in front **Obv. Legend:** DOM CAPITEL - ZV - OSNABRVGK. **Rev:** Value divides date as 1 X 60 I 6 I **Mint:** Eversburg **Note:** K-202.

Date	Mintage	Good	VG	F	VF	XF
1606 EK	—	65.00	125	225	425	—

KM# 154 THALER

Silver Weight varies: 29.05-29.12g., 41 mm. **Ruler:** Sede Vacante **Obv:** Full-length facing figure of St. Peter, holding book and keys, small shield of Osnabrück arms below in front, all in circle **Obv. Legend:** CAPITULUM CATHEDRALE OSNABRUGENSE SEDE VACANTE **Rev:** Church with short crosses, stars and long trail banner above, legend contains date in chronogram **Rev. Legend:** orlet Vr Intenebrls LVX tVa et tenebræ tVæ erVnt sICVt MerIDIes Isa læ. 58. **Mint:** Hannover **Note:** K-307; Dav. 5674.

Date	Mintage	VG	F	VF	XF	Unc
1698	1,381	300	600	1,200	2,000	—

KM# A154 THALER

Silver Weight varies: 29.05-29.12g., 41 mm. **Ruler:** Sede Vacante **Obv:** Full-length facing figure of St. Peter, holding book and keys, small shield of Osnabrück arms below in front **Obv. Legend:** CAPITULUM CATHEDRALE OSNABRUGENSE SEDE VACANTA **Rev:** Church with tall crosses, stars and short trail banner above, legend contains date in chronogram **Rev. Legend:** orlet Vr Intenebrls LVX tVa et tenebræ tVæ erVnt sICVt MerIDIes Isa læ. 58. **Mint:** Hannover **Note:** K-307; Dav. 5674A.

Date	Mintage	VG	F	VF	XF	Unc
1698	Inc. above	325	675	1,350	2,250	—

SWEDISH OCCUPATION

REGULAR COINAGE

KM# 35 THALER
Silver **Ruler:** Gustav Gustavson **Obv:** Bust of Gustavus Adolphus left **Rev:** Crown above inscription **Rev. Inscription:** IOHAN • 10/ EIN • GVTER • HIRT/ LESSET • SEIN • LE:/ BEN • FVR • DIE •/ SCHAAFFE •/ OSNABRVGK/ +1663+ **Note:** Dav. #4551.

Date	Mintage	VG	F	VF	XF	Unc
1633 Rare	—	—	—	—	—	—

KM# 36 THALER
Silver **Ruler:** Gustav Gustavson **Obv:** Bust of Gustavus Adolphus left **Rev:** Crown above inscription **Rev. Inscription:** ...HRT / LESST • SEIN • LE/ BEN • F • DI • SCH/ AFFE/ 16 0SNABR 33 **Note:** Dav. #4553.

Date	Mintage	VG	F	VF	XF	Unc
1633	—	550	1,150	2,250	4,250	—

KM# 37 THALER
Silver **Ruler:** Gustav Gustavson **Rev:** Date divided below inscription **Rev. Inscription:** ...SCHAFFE/ OSNABRVG **Note:** Dav. #4554.

Date	Mintage	VG	F	VF	XF	Unc
1633	—	240	475	1,200	2,100	—

KM# 38 THALER
Silver **Ruler:** Gustav Gustavson **Rev:** Date above inscription in legend **Rev. Inscription:** ...SCHAFFE/ OSNABRV **Note:** Dav. #4555.

Date	Mintage	VG	F	VF	XF	Unc
1633	—	350	850	1,850	3,050	—

KM# 39 THALER
Silver **Ruler:** Gustav Gustavson **Rev. Inscription:** ...LESSET • SEIN/ LEBEN • F • DIE •/... **Note:** Dav. #4556.

Date	Mintage	VG	F	VF	XF	Unc
1633	—	450	975	1,950	3,150	—

KM# 42 2 THALER
Silver **Ruler:** Gustav Gustavson **Obv:** Bust of Gustavus Adolphus left **Rev:** Crown above 6-line inscription **Rev. Inscription:** ... HRT / LESST • SEIN • LE / BEN • F • DI • SCH / AFFE / 16 OSNABR 33. **Note:** Dav. #4552.

Date	Mintage	VG	F	VF	XF	Unc
1633 Unique	—	—	—	—	—	—

TRADE COINAGE

KM# 43 DUCAT
3.5000 g., 0.9860 Gold 0.1109 oz. AGW **Ruler:** Gustav Gustavson **Obv:** Laureate bust of Gustav II Adolphus left **Rev:** Crown above 5-line legend **Note:** Fr. #1943.

Date	Mintage	VG	F	VF	XF	Unc
1633	—	550	1,100	2,150	3,800	—

KM# 44 10 DUCAT
35.0000 g., 0.9860 Gold 1.1095 oz. AGW **Ruler:** Gustav Gustavson **Obv:** Laureate bust of Gustav II Adolphus left **Rev:** Crown above 5-line inscription with OSNABRVC in bracket and date below **Note:** Struck with 1 Thaler dies, KM#37. Prev. KM#1.

Date	Mintage	VG	F	VF	XF	Unc
1633 Rare	—	—	—	—	—	—

CITY

The city of Osnabruck is located northeast of Munster. Although the city owed its original growth to the bishopric it achieved considerable independence from the bishops and joined the Hanseatic League. It had its own local coinage from the early 16th century until 1805. It was absorbed by Hannover in 1803.

MINT OFFICIALS' INITIALS

Initials	Date	Name
CD	1586-1633	Cordt Dellebrugk
HB	1667-82	Hermann Brauwe
	1691-98	Johann Brockmann
IM	1690-98	Jürgen Meyer, die-cutter

REFERENCE
K = Karl Kennepohl, **Die Munzen von Osnabruck**, München, 1938.
Sch = Wolfgang Schulten, ***Deutsche Munzen aus der Zeit Karls V.*** Frankfurt am Main, 1974

REGULAR COINAGE

City coinage is sometimes found countermarked with the Osnabrück wheel, most likely as a validation symbol.

MB# 100 PFENNIG
Copper, 16-18 mm. **Obv:** Osnabrück arms in ornamented shield, date at end of legend **Obv. Legend:** STADT. OSNABRVGK. **Obv. Inscription:** STADT OSNABRVGK **Rev:** Value I in ornamented frame **Mint:** Osnabrück **Note:** K-443, 444. Varieties exist.

Date	Mintage	VG	F	VF	XF	Unc
1622	—	10.00	20.00	40.00	85.00	—

KM# 139.1 PFENNIG
Copper, 17-18 mm. **Obv:** Osnabrück arms in ornamented shield, date at end of legend **Obv. Legend:** STADT. OSNABRVGK. **Rev:** Value I in ornamented frame **Mint:** Osnabrück **Note:** K-464, 467, 468. Varieties exist.

Date	Mintage	VG	F	VF	XF	Unc
1676 HB	8,280	10.00	20.00	40.00	80.00	—
1691	17,000	10.00	20.00	40.00	80.00	—
1698	29,610	10.00	20.00	40.00	80.00	—

KM# 139.2 PFENNIG
Copper, 20x20 mm. **Obv:** Osnabrück arms in ornamented shield, date at end of legend **Obv. Legend:** STADT. OSNABRVGK. **Rev:** Value I in ornamented frame **Mint:** Osnabrück **Note:** K-468b. Klippe.

Date	Mintage	VG	F	VF	XF	Unc
1698	—	—	—	—	—	—

MB# 103 1-1/2 PFENNIG
Copper, 17 mm. **Obv:** Osnabrück arms in ornamented shield, date at end of legend **Obv. Legend:** STADT. OSNABRVGK. **Rev:** Value I over I—I **Mint:** Osnabrück **Note:** K-442, 447.

Date	Mintage	VG	F	VF	XF	Unc
1622	3,192	20.00	35.00	70.00	145	—

KM# 141 1-1/2 PFENNIG
Copper, 18 mm. **Obv:** Osnabrück arms in ornamented shield, date at end of legend **Obv. Legend:** STADT. OSNABRVGK. **Rev:** Value I over I—I **Note:** K-463.

Date	Mintage	VG	F	VF	XF	Unc
1676	55,000	20.00	37.00	75.00	155	—

MB# 107 3 PFENNIG
Copper, 18-19 mm. **Obv:** Osnabrück arms in ornamented shield, date at end of legend **Obv. Legend:** STADT. OSNABRVGK. **Rev:** Value III in ornamented frame **Mint:** Osnabrück **Note:** K-440, 446. Varieties exist.

Date	Mintage	VG	F	VF	XF	Unc
1622 CD	4,200	15.00	30.00	60.00	120	—
1660	—	10.00	20.00	40.00	80.00	—
1670	—	10.00	20.00	40.00	80.00	—

KM# 144 3 PFENNIG
Copper, 18-20 mm. **Obv:** Osnabrück arms in ornamented shield, date at end of legend **Obv. Legend:** STADT. OSNABRVGK. **Rev:** Value III in ornamented frame **Mint:** Osnabrück **Note:** K-460-462. Varieties exist. Examples with CD mintmaster's initials were struck with old reverse dies.

Date	Mintage	VG	F	VF	XF	Unc
1676	Inc. above	10.00	20.00	40.00	80.00	—
1676 CD	125,403	10.00	20.00	40.00	80.00	—
1676 HB	Inc. above	10.00	20.00	40.00	80.00	—

MB# 110 4 PFENNIG
Copper, 20-23 mm. **Obv:** Osnabrück arms in ornamented shield, date at end of legend **Obv. Legend:** STADT. OSNABRVGK. **Rev:** Value IIII in ornamented frame **Mint:** Osnabrück **Note:** K-437 438, 453. Varieties exist.

Date	Mintage	VG	F	VF	XF	Unc
(16)25	—	9.00	18.00	30.00	60.00	—
1670	—	9.00	18.00	30.00	60.00	—

KM# 146 4 PFENNIG
Copper, 20-22 mm. **Obv:** Osnabrück arms in ornamented shield, date at end of legend **Obv. Legend:** STADT. OSNABRVGK. **Rev:** Value IIII in ornamented frame **Mint:** Osnabrück **Note:** K-459, 465, 466. Varieties exist. The issue with '69' is an error for 1690.

Date	Mintage	VG	F	VF	XF	Unc
1676 HB	46,809	10.00	20.00	40.00	80.00	—
(1)69(0) IM	Inc. above	10.00	20.00	40.00	80.00	—
1690 IM	94,013	10.00	20.00	40.00	80.00	—

MB# 91 5 PFENNIG (Stüber)
Copper, 23-26 mm. **Obv:** Osnabrück arms in ornamented circle, date at end of legend **Obv. Legend:** STADT. OSNABRVGK. **Rev:** Value V within wreath **Mint:** Osnabrück **Note:** K-435, 451, 452. Varieties exist.

Date	Mintage	VG	F	VF	XF	Unc
(16)25	—	9.00	17.00	35.00	75.00	—
(16)26	—	9.00	17.00	35.00	75.00	—
1650	—	9.00	17.00	35.00	75.00	—
1660	119,138	9.00	17.00	35.00	75.00	—
1695	18,350	9.00	17.00	35.00	75.00	—

MB# 92 6 PFENNIG
Copper, 25-26 mm. **Obv:** Osnabrück arms in ornamented shield,

date at end of legend **Obv. Legend:** STADT. OSNABRVGK. **Rev:** Value VI in ornamented frame within wreath **Mint:** Osnabrück **Note:** K-434, 450. Varieties exist.

Date	Mintage	VG	F	VF	XF	Unc
(16)25 CD	72,324	15.00	30.00	48.00	95.00	—

MB# 96 8 PFENNIG

Copper, 27 mm. **Obv:** Osnabrück arms in ornamented shield, date at end of legend **Obv. Legend:** STADT. OSNABRVGK. Ao. **Rev:** Value VIII within wreath **Mint:** Osnabrück **Note:** K-432. Varieties exist.

Date	Mintage	VG	F	VF	XF	Unc
1625 CD	—	13.00	25.00	40.00	85.00	—

MB# 97 9 PFENNIG

Copper, 28 mm. **Obv:** Round shield of city arms in ornamented frame, date at end of legend **Obv. Legend:** STADT. OSNABRVGK. Ao **Rev:** Value VIIII in ornamented frame on reverse without wreath **Mint:** Osnabrück **Note:** K-431, 449. Varieties exist.

Date	Mintage	VG	F	VF	XF	Unc
1625 CD	181,336	12.00	25.00	40.00	85.00	—

MB# 112 12 PFENNIG (Schilling)

Copper, 31-32 mm. **Obv:** Osnabrück arms in ornamented shield, date at end of legend **Obv. Legend:** STADT . OSNABRVGK : Ao. **Rev:** Value XII in ornamented circle **Mint:** Osnabrück **Note:** K-436, 445, 448, 454. Varieties exist.

Date	Mintage	VG	F	VF	XF	Unc
1615 CD	—	13.00	27.00	45.00	90.00	—
1623 CD	—	13.00	27.00	45.00	90.00	—
1633 CD	—	13.00	27.00	45.00	90.00	—

OTTINGEN

OTTINGEN-OTTINGEN

This line of Öttingen counts was founded as the Protestant branch in 1557 during the Reformation. The count was granted the rank of prince in 1674. When it became extinct in 1731, its holdings were divided between Öttingen-Wallerstein-Spielberg and Öttingen-Wallerstein-Wallerstein.

RULERS

Gottfried, 1569-1622
Ludwig Eberhard, 1622-1634
Joachim Ernst, 1634-1659
Kraft Ludwig, 1659-1660
Albrecht Ernst I, 1660-1683
Albrecht Ernst II, 1683-1731

MINT OFFICIALS' INITIALS

Initial	Date	Name
CM, ICM	1670-95	Johann Christoph Müller, die-cutter in Stuttgart
GS, S		

COUNTSHIP

REGULAR COINAGE

KM# 26 PFENNIG

Silver **Ruler:** Ludwig Eberhard **Obv:** Two conjoined shields of arms, LEG above, O below **Note:** Uniface.

Date	Mintage	VG	F	VF	XF	Unc
ND(ca.1625)	—	15.00	30.00	60.00	120	—

KM# 5 3 PFENNIG (Dreier)

Silver **Ruler:** Gottfried **Obv:** Arms of Ottingen, date above, titles of Gottfried **Rev:** Imperial eagle, 3 in orb on breast, titles of Ferdinand II

Date	Mintage	VG	F	VF	XF	Unc
1622 Rare	—	—	—	—	—	—

KM# 10 KREUZER

Silver **Ruler:** Ludwig Eberhard **Obv:** Arms divide Z-O, arms with LEG above **Rev:** Imperial orb with value I divdes date **Note:** Varieties exist.

Date	Mintage	VG	F	VF	XF	Unc
1623	—	27.00	60.00	120	240	—
1624	—	27.00	60.00	120	240	—
1625	—	27.00	60.00	120	240	—

KM# 27 KREUZER

Silver **Ruler:** Ludwig Eberhard **Obv:** Oval arms, LEGZO above **Rev:** Value I between two stars, KREYZ / ER* in two lines below **Note:** Varieties exist.

Date	Mintage	VG	F	VF	XF	Unc
ND(ca.1625)	—	27.00	55.00	95.00	190	—

KM# 6 2 KREUZER (1/2 Batzen)

Silver **Ruler:** Gottfried **Obv:** Öttingen arms in ornamented shield, titles of Gottfried **Rev:** Imperial eagle with Z in orb on breast, titles of Ferdinand II

Date	Mintage	VG	F	VF	XF	Unc
ND(ca.1622/3)	—	—	—	—	—	—

KM# 11 2 KREUZER (1/2 Batzen)

Silver **Ruler:** Ludwig Eberhard **Obv:** Oval arms divide date, titles of Ludwig Eberhard **Rev:** Imperial orb with value 2, titles of Ferdinand II **Note:** Varieties exist.

Date	Mintage	VG	F	VF	XF	Unc
(16)23	—	65.00	135	235	475	—

KM# 12 2 KREUZER (1/2 Batzen)

1.0900 g., Silver **Ruler:** Ludwig Eberhard **Obv:** Large X within ornate shield **Obv. Legend:** FERDIN * II * RO * I * S * A **Rev:** Date divided by cross on orb **Rev. Legend:** LVDWIG * EBER : CO * OTING **Note:** Varieties exist.

Date	Mintage	VG	F	VF	XF	Unc
(16)23	—	20.00	45.00	90.00	185	—
(16)24	—	20.00	45.00	90.00	185	—
(16)25	—	20.00	45.00	90.00	185	—
(16)26	—	20.00	45.00	90.00	185	—

KM# 22 2 KREUZER (1/2 Batzen)

Silver **Ruler:** Ludwig Eberhard **Obv:** Large X within ornae shield **Obv. Legend:** FERDIN * II * RO * I * S * A **Rev:** Date divided by cross on orb **Rev. Legend:** LVDWIG * EBER" CO * OTING **Note:** Klippe. Similar to KM#12.

Date	Mintage	VG	F	VF	XF	Unc
(16)24 Rare	—	—	—	—	—	—

KM# 15 3 KREUZER (1 Groschen)

Silver **Ruler:** Ludwig Eberhard **Rev:** Full date above arms

Date	Mintage	VG	F	VF	XF	Unc
1623	—	27.00	60.00	120	230	—

KM# 13 3 KREUZER (1 Groschen)

Silver **Ruler:** Ludwig Eberhard **Obv:** Oval arms in ornamental frame, titles of Ludwig Eberhard **Rev:** Imperial orb with 3 divides date, titles of Ferdinand II **Note:** Varieties exist.

Date	Mintage	VG	F	VF	XF	Unc
(16)23	—	27.00	60.00	120	230	—

KM# 14 3 KREUZER (1 Groschen)

Silver **Ruler:** Ludwig Eberhard **Rev:** Date divided by arms **Note:** Varieties exist.

Date	Mintage	VG	F	VF	XF	Unc
(16)23	—	27.00	60.00	120	230	—

KM# 35 3 KREUZER (1 Groschen)

Silver **Ruler:** Albrecht Ernst I **Obv:** Bust right **Rev:** Crowned arms between two laurel branches, legend, date **Rev. Legend:** DOMINVS PR (3) VIDEBIT

Date	Mintage	VG	F	VF	XF	Unc
1673	—	100	200	375	775	—

KM# 28 4 KREUZER (1 Batzen)

Silver **Ruler:** Ludwig Eberhard **Obv:** Ornate Ottingen arms; value • 1 • 1 • 1 • 1 • above **Rev:** Crowned imperial eagle, date divided by crown at top, titles of Ferdinand II

Date	Mintage	VG	F	VF	XF	Unc
(16)25	—	135	225	425	875	—

KM# 36 12 KREUZER (Zwolfer)

Silver **Ruler:** Albrecht Ernst I **Obv:** Crowned arms between two laurel branches **Obv. Legend:** +ALBERTVS ERNESTVS COMES OTTINGENSIS **Rev:** Hound's head left, value (XII) in margin at bottom, date at end of legend **Rev. Legend:** DOMINVS PRO - VIDEBIT

Date	Mintage	VG	F	VF	XF	Unc
1673	—	60.00	120	200	425	—

KM# 7 24 KREUZER (6 Batzen)

Silver **Ruler:** Gottfried **Obv:** Arms surmounted by dog's head left which divides date, titles of Gottfried **Rev:** Crowned imperial eagle, 24 in orb on breast, titles of Ferdinand II

Date	Mintage	VG	F	VF	XF	Unc
1622 Rare	—	—	—	—	—	—

KM# 8 24 KREUZER (6 Batzen)

Silver **Ruler:** Gottfried **Rev:** Dog's head right

Date	Mintage	VG	F	VF	XF	Unc
1622 Rare	—	—	—	—	—	—

KM# 9 24 KREUZER (6 Batzen)

Silver **Ruler:** Gottfried **Rev:** Two conjoined shield of arms, dog's head, date above, titles of Gottfried **Note:** Varieties exist.

Date	Mintage	VG	F	VF	XF	Unc
1622	—	375	625	1,150	2,200	—

KM# 16 30 KREUZER (1/2 Guldenthaler)

Silver **Ruler:** Gottfried **Obv:** Arms of Ottingen, crowned angel's head above, titles of Gottfried **Rev:** Crowned imperial eagle, 30 in shield on breast, titles of Ferdinand II

Date	Mintage	VG	F	VF	XF	Unc
ND(ca.1620) Rare	—	—	—	—	—	—

KM# 17 30 KREUZER (1/2 Gulden)

Silver **Ruler:** Ludwig Eberhard **Obv:** Titles of Ludwig Eberhard

Date	Mintage	VG	F	VF	XF	Unc
1623 Rare	—	—	—	—	—	—

KM# 19 60 KREUZER (Gulden)

Silver **Ruler:** Ludwig Eberhard **Obv:** Ottingen arms divide date, titles of Ludwig Eberhard

Date	Mintage	VG	F	VF	XF	Unc
1623 Rare	—	—	—	—	—	—

KM# 18 60 KREUZER (Gulden)

Silver **Ruler:** Gottfried **Obv:** Öttingen arms divide date, titles of Gottfried **Rev:** Crowned imperial eagle, 60 in orb on breast, titles of Ferdinand II **Note:** Dav. #102.

Date	Mintage	VG	F	VF	XF	Unc
1623 Rare; posthumous	—	—	—	—	—	—

KM# 37 60 KREUZER (Gulden)

Silver **Ruler:** Albrecht Ernst I **Obv:** Bust right within circle **Obv. Legend:** ALBERTVS ERNESTVS COMES OTTINGENSIS **Rev:** Crowned arms between two laurel branches, value (60) below in margin, date at end of legend **Rev. Legend:** DOMINVS: PRO - VIDEBIT

Date	Mintage	VG	F	VF	XF	Unc
1673	—	625	1,075	1,650	3,100	—

KM# 39 60 KREUZER (Gulden)
Silver **Ruler:** Albrecht Ernst I **Obv:** Bust to right **Obv. Legend:** ALBERTVS • ERNESTVS • COMES • OTTINGENSIS **Rev:** Crowned oval arms in baroque frame, value (60) divides date below **Rev. Legend:** DOMINVS - PROVIDEBIT **Note:** Varieties exist.

Date	Mintage	VG	F	VF	XF	Unc
1674	—	225	525	850	1,500	—
1674 S	—	225	525	850	1,500	—

KM# A39 60 KREUZER (Gulden)
19.4600 g., Silver **Ruler:** Albrecht Ernst I **Obv:** Bust right **Obv. Legend:** ALBERTVS ERNSTVS COMES OTTINGENSIS **Rev:** Crowned squarish arms in sprays, legend above **Rev. Legend:** DOMINVS PROVIDEBIT

Date	Mintage	Good	VG	F	VF	XF
1674	—	27.00	60.00	120	240	—

KM# 29 1/9 THALER
Silver **Ruler:** Ludwig Eberhard **Obv:** Arms, date above **Rev:** Crowned imperial eagle, value 1/9 on breast, titles of Ferdinand II

Date	Mintage	VG	F	VF	XF	Unc
1629 Rare	—	—	—	—	—	—

KM# 23 1/6 THALER
Silver **Ruler:** Ludwig Eberhard **Obv:** Öttingen arms with angel's head above, date divided **Rev:** Crowned imperial eagle, 1/6 in cirlce on breast, titles of Ferdinand II

Date	Mintage	VG	F	VF	XF	Unc
1624 Rare	—	—	—	—	—	—

KM# 24 1/4 THALER
Silver **Ruler:** Ludwig Eberhard **Obv:** Shield of arms with ornate helmet above, dog's head crest divides date **Rev:** Crowned imperial eagle, value 1/4 in orb on breast, titles of Ferdinand II

Date	Mintage	VG	F	VF	XF	Unc
1624 Rare	—	—	—	—	—	—

KM# 41 1/3 THALER (1/2 Gulden)
Silver **Ruler:** Albrecht Ernst I **Obv:** Bust right **Obv. Legend:** ALBERTVS • ERNESTVS • COMES • OTTINGENSIS **Rev:** Crowned arms between two laurel branches, value (1/3) at bottom divides date **Rev. Legend:** DOMINVS • PROVIDEBIT

Date	Mintage	VG	F	VF	XF	Unc
1674	—	—	—	—	—	—

KM# 42 1/3 THALER (1/2 Gulden)
Silver **Ruler:** Albrecht Ernst I **Obv:** Bust to right **Obv. Legend:** ALBERTVS• ERNESTVS • COMES • OTTINGENSIS **Rev:** Crowned oval arms in baroque frame, value (1/3) divides date below **Rev. Legend:** DOMINVS • PROVIDEBIT

Date	Mintage	VG	F	VF	XF	Unc
1674 CM	—	—	—	—	—	—

KM# 43 2/3 THALER (Gulden)
Silver **Ruler:** Albrecht Ernst I **Obv:** Bust to right **Obv. Legend:** ALBERTVS • ERNESTVS • COMES • OTTINGENSIS **Rev:** Crowned arms in laurel wreath, date divided by value (2/3) below **Rev. Legend:** DOMINVS • PROVIDEBIT **Note:** Varieties exist.

Date	Mintage	VG	F	VF	XF	Unc
1674	—	165	300	575	1,150	—

KM# 44 2/3 THALER (Gulden)
Silver **Ruler:** Albrecht Ernst I **Obv:** Bust to right **Obv. Legend:** ALBERTVS•ERNESTVS•COMES•OTTINGENSIS **Rev:** Value 2/3 punched over 60 **Rev. Legend:** DOMINVS • PROVIDEBIT

Date	Mintage	VG	F	VF	XF	Unc
1674 ICM	—	—	—	—	—	—

KM# 20 THALER
Silver **Ruler:** Ludwig Eberhard **Obv:** Shield of arms with ornate helmet above, dog's head crest divides date **Obv. Legend:** * LUDWIG * EBERHARD * COMES * OTING * **Rev:** Crowned imperial eagle **Rev. Legend:** FERDINANDVS • II • ROM • IMP • SE(M)(P) • AVG(VS) **Note:** Dav. #7136.

Date	Mintage	VG	F	VF	XF	Unc
1623	—	85.00	175	375	950	—
1624	—	85.00	175	350	900	—
1625	—	85.00	175	350	900	—

KM# 21 THALER
Silver **Ruler:** Ludwig Eberhard **Obv:** Shield of arms with ornate helmet above, dog's head crest divides date **Obv. Legend:** * LVDWIG * EBERHART * COMES * OTING * **Rev:** Crowned imperial eagle **Rev. Legend:** FERDINANDVS • II • ROM • IMP • SE(M)(P) • AVG(VS) **Note:** Dav. #7136A.

Date	Mintage	VG	F	VF	XF	Unc
1623	—	85.00	175	375	925	—

KM# 25 THALER
Silver **Ruler:** Ludwig Eberhard **Obv:** St. Michael with sword and shield standing on dragon, L • E • G • Z • Ö at left, date at right **Obv. Legend:** DA PACEM DOMINE IN DIEBVS NOSTRIS **Rev:** Crowned imperial eagle **Rev. Legend:** FERDINANDVS • II • ROM • IMP • SEM • AVGVS **Note:** Dav. #7137.

Date	Mintage	VG	F	VF	XF	Unc
1624	—	1,000	1,850	3,750	9,500	—
1625	—	1,000	1,850	3,750	9,500	—

PRINCIPALITY

REGULAR COINAGE

KM# 65 PFENNIG
Silver **Ruler:** Albrecht Ernst II **Obv:** Crown above script monogram AE, date around crown

Date	Mintage	VG	F	VF	XF	Unc
1690	—	—	—	—	—	—

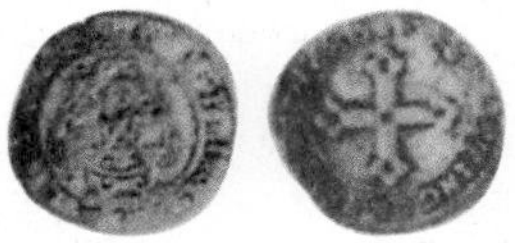

KM# 60 KREUZER
Silver **Ruler:** Albrecht Ernst I **Obv:** Crowned oval shield of arms in baroque frame **Rev:** Cross in circle, date in legend **Rev. Legend:** FVRST: OTTING: KREVTZER

Date	Mintage	VG	F	VF	XF	Unc
1680	—	40.00	75.00	125	240	—

KM# 61 2 KREUZER (1/2 Batzen)
Silver **Ruler:** Albrecht Ernst I **Obv:** Crowned arms **Rev:** Imperial orb with value 2 divides date **Note:** Varieties exist.

Date	Mintage	VG	F	VF	XF	Unc
1680	—	45.00	80.00	140	260	—

KM# 58 3 KREUZER (1 Groschen)
Silver **Ruler:** Albrecht Ernst I **Obv:** Bust to right **Obv. Legend:** ALBERT, ERNEST, D:G. PRINC. OTTING **Rev:** Crowned oval shield of arms in baroque frame, value (3) divides date below **Rev. Legend:** DOMINVS - PROVIDEBIT

Date	Mintage	VG	F	VF	XF	Unc
1675	—	45.00	100	165	360	—

KM# 48 4 KREUZER (1 Batzen)
Silver **Ruler:** Albrecht Ernst I **Obv:** Bust right in circle **Obv. Legend:** ALBERT, ERNEST, D:G. PRINCEPS OTTING **Rev:** Crowned oval arms in baroque frame, value (6) divides date below **Rev. Legend:** DOMINVS - PROVIDEB **Note:** Varieties exist.

Date	Mintage	VG	F	VF	XF	Unc
1675	—	25.00	55.00	110	220	—
1676	—	25.00	55.00	110	220	—
1677	—	25.00	55.00	110	220	—
1678	—	25.00	55.00	110	220	—

KM# 38 30 KREUZER (1/2 Gulden)
Silver **Ruler:** Albrecht Ernst I **Obv:** Bust right **Obv. Legend:** ALBERT, ERNEST, D.G. PRINCEPS. OTTING. **Rev:** Crowned oval arms in baroque frame, value (30) divides date below **Rev. Legend:** PROVIDEBIT - DOMINUS

Date	Mintage	VG	F	VF	XF	Unc
1674	—	55.00	120	200	425	—
1675	—	55.00	120	200	425	—

KM# 40 60 KREUZER (Gulden)

Silver **Ruler:** Albrecht Ernst I **Obv:** Bust to right **Obv. Legend:** ALBERT, ERNEST, PRINCEPS. OTTING. **Rev:** Crowned oval arms in baroque frame, value (60) divides date below **Rev. Legend:** DOMINUS - PROVIDEBIT **Note:** Varieties exist.

Date	Mintage	VG	F	VF	XF	Unc
1674	—	60.00	120	185	360	—
1674 S	—	60.00	120	185	360	—
1674 GS	—	60.00	120	185	360	—
1675	—	60.00	120	185	360	—
1676	—	60.00	120	185	360	—
1677	—	60.00	120	185	360	—
1678	—	60.00	120	185	360	—

KM# 49 60 KREUZER (Gulden)

Silver **Ruler:** Albrecht Ernst I **Obv:** Crowned AEO monogram divides date, value (60) in margin at bottom **Obv. Legend:** DOMINVS. PROVIDEBIT **Rev:** Hound walking left in circle **Rev. Legend:** VIGILANTIA ET FIDELITATE **Note:** Varieties exist. L-321-3; Dav. #737.

Date	Mintage	VG	F	VF	XF	Unc
1675	—	225	375	600	1,100	—

KM# 70 1/4 THALER

Silver **Ruler:** Albrecht Ernst II **Subject:** Death of Eberhardine Sophie, Wife of Christian Eberhard, Prince of Ostfriesland **Obv:** Vintner cutting heavily-laden vine **Rev:** Seven-line inscription with date, death's head below

Date	Mintage	VG	F	VF	XF	Unc
1700 Rare	—	—	—	—	—	—

KM# 50 THALER

Silver **Ruler:** Albrecht Ernst I **Subject:** Albert Ernst I raised to rank of Prince **Obv:** Bust right in circle, legend contains date in chronogram **Obv. Legend:** ALBERTVS • ERNESTVS • FAVENTE • DEI • GRATIA • PRIMVS • ÖTTING: PRINCEPS A **Rev:** Crowned oval shield of arms in baroque frame, legend contains date in chronogram **Rev. Legend:** NVMEN • UNICA • IN TERRIS • SALVS • PROVIDEBIT **Note:** Dav. #7138.

Date	Mintage	VG	F	VF	XF	Unc
1675	—	1,300	2,400	4,000	6,750	12,000

KM# 52 THALER

Silver **Ruler:** Albrecht Ernst I **Obv:** Bust right **Obv. Legend:** ALBERT • ERNEST • D: G: PRINCEPS • OTTINGEN **Rev:** Crowned shield of arms divides date **Rev. Legend:** FVRSTLICH: OTTING: REICHSTHALER **Note:** Dav. #7139.

Date	Mintage	VG	F	VF	XF	Unc
1677	—	1,500	2,750	4,500	7,500	—

KM# 62 THALER

Silver **Ruler:** Albrecht Ernst I **Obv:** Bust to right in circle **Obv. Legend:** ALBERT 9 ERNEST 9 D: G: PRINCEPTS • OTTINGEN **Rev:** Crowned shield of oval arms in baroque frame, date divided at top **Rev. Legend:** FVRSTLICH: OTTING: REICHSTAHALER **Note:** Dav. #7140.

Date	Mintage	VG	F	VF	XF	Unc
1680	—	1,500	2,750	4,500	7,500	16,000

TRADE COINAGE

KM# 45 1/4 DUCAT

0.8750 g., 0.9860 Gold 0.0277 oz. AGW **Ruler:** Albrecht Ernst I **Subject:** Attaining the Rank of Prince **Obv:** Crowned oval arms **Rev:** Allegorical figure standing by altar, arm from clouds with crown

Date	Mintage	VG	F	VF	XF	Unc
ND(1674) Rare	—	—	—	—	—	—

KM# 46 1/4 DUCAT

0.8750 g., 0.9860 Gold 0.0277 oz. AGW **Ruler:** Albrecht Ernst I **Obv:** AE monogram **Rev:** Shield of arms **Note:** Fr. #1955.

Date	Mintage	VG	F	VF	XF	Unc
ND PGN	—	650	1,350	2,700	5,500	—

KM# 47 1/2 DUCAT

1.7500 g., 0.9860 Gold 0.0555 oz. AGW **Ruler:** Albrecht Ernst I **Obv:** AE monogram **Rev:** Crowned and mantled arms **Note:** Klippe. Fr. #1954.

Date	Mintage	VG	F	VF	XF	Unc
ND	—	1,150	2,400	4,800	9,500	—

KM# 51 DUCAT

3.5000 g., 0.9860 Gold 0.1109 oz. AGW **Ruler:** Albrecht Ernst I **Obv:** Bust to right **Rev:** Shield of arms **Note:** Fr. #1952.

Date	Mintage	VG	F	VF	XF	Unc
1675	—	2,650	5,400	9,900	17,500	—

KM# 53 DUCAT

3.5000 g., 0.9860 Gold 0.1109 oz. AGW **Ruler:** Albrecht Ernst I **Obv:** Bust to right **Rev:** Five-line inscription with date above arms **Note:** Fr. #1953.

Date	Mintage	VG	F	VF	XF	Unc
1677 Rare	—	—	—	—	—	—

KM# 55 DUCAT

3.5000 g., 0.9860 Gold 0.1109 oz. AGW **Ruler:** Albrecht Ernst I **Subject:** Peace of Nimwegen **Obv:** Cannon firing right, clouds above **Rev:** Nine-line inscription with date in chronogram

Date	Mintage	VG	F	VF	XF	Unc
1679 Rare	—	—	—	—	—	—

KM# 56 DUCAT

3.5000 g., 0.9860 Gold 0.1109 oz. AGW **Ruler:** Albrecht Ernst II **Obv:** Armored bust to right **Rev:** Crowned and mantled arms **Note:** Fr. #1956.

Date	Mintage	VG	F	VF	XF	Unc
ND	—	2,000	4,000	8,500	14,500	—

KM# 54 2 DUCAT

7.0000 g., 0.9860 Gold 0.2219 oz. AGW **Ruler:** Albrecht Ernst I **Obv:** Bust to right **Rev:** Shield of arms **Note:** Fr. #1951.

Date	Mintage	VG	F	VF	XF	Unc
1677 Rare	—	—	—	—	—	—

KM# 57 2 DUCAT

7.0000 g., 0.9860 Gold 0.2219 oz. AGW **Ruler:** Albrecht Ernst I **Subject:** Peace of Nimwegen **Obv:** Allegorical figure **Rev:** Ten-line inscription with Roman numeral date

Date	Mintage	VG	F	VF	XF	Unc
1679 Rare	—	—	—	—	—	—

PATTERNS

Including off metal strikes

KM#	Date	Mintage	Identification	Mkt Val
Pn1	ND	—	Ducat. Silver. KM#56	—
Pn2	ND(1713)	—	5 Ducat. Silver. KM#75	—
Pn3	ND(1713)	—	10 Ducat. Silver. KM#76	—

OTTINGEN-WALLERSTEIN-WALLERSTEIN

Founded upon the 1602 division of Öttingen-Wallerstein, this line of counts became princes in 1774. Their territories were mediatized in the early 19th century.

RULERS

Ernst II, 1602-1670
Wilhelm IV, 1670-1692 and
Philipp, 1670-1680
Wolfgang IV, 1692-1708 and
Ignaz, 1692-1723

MINT OFFICIALS' INITIALS

Initial	Date	Name
(h)= 2 horseshoes	1668-97	Johann Christoph Holeisen in Augsburg

COUNTSHIP

REGULAR COINAGE

KM# 5 2 KREUZER (1/2 Batzen)

Silver **Ruler:** Wolfgang IV, Ignaz and Karl Anton **Obv:** Oval shield of arms in baroque frame **Obv. Legend:** *WOLF. IGNA. CAR. - ANT. G. Z. ÐTTING. **Rev:** Imperial orb with value 2, date in margin at bottom **Rev. Legend:** VIRTVTE. CONCORDIA. ET. LABORE. **Mint:** Augsburg **Note:** Ref. L-396.

Date	Mintage	VG	F	VF	XF	Unc
1694 (h)	—	100	200	400	775	—

KM# 6 4 KREUZER (Batzen)

Silver **Ruler:** Wolfgang IV, Ignaz and Karl Anton **Obv:** Crowned oval shield of arms in baroque frame **Obv. Legend:** *WOLF. IGNA. CAR. - ANT. G. Z. ÐTTING. **Rev:** Crowned imperial eagle, value '4' in heart-shaped shield on breast, date in margin at bottom **Rev. Legend:** VIRTVTE. CONCO - RDIA. ET. LABORE. **Mint:** Augsburg **Note:** Ref. L-395.

Date	Mintage	VG	F	VF	XF	Unc
1694 (h)	—	125	250	450	775	1,500

KM# 7 THALER

Silver **Ruler:** Wolfgang IV, Ignaz and Karl Anton **Obv:** Crowned ornate shield of arms in baroque frame, 2 Öttingen dogs as supporters at sides **Obv. Legend:** *WOLF. IGNA. CARL - ANT. G. Z. ÖTTING. **Rev:** Crowned imperial eagle, 'LI' in round shield on breast, date in margin at top, '90' (Kreuzer) in frame below **Rev. Legend:** VIRTVTE CONCOR - DIA ET LABORE. **Mint:** Augsburg **Note:** Ref. L-394; Dav. 7141.

Date	Mintage	F	VF	XF	Unc	BU
1694 (h)	—	1,200	2,200	4,250	7,000	—

KM# 8 THALER

Silver **Ruler:** Ignaz **Obv:** Hand from heaven watering flowers, ribbon band around with A SVPREMORE - PENDET **Obv. Legend:** *IGNATIVS COMES - AB ÖTTINGEN+ **Rev:** Ornate helmet with dog's head crest above oval shield of arms, date divided in margin at top, value '90' (Kreuzer) in cartouche at bottom **Rev. Legend:** HINC LABOR - ET OPVS. **Mint:** Augsburg **Note:** Ref. L-393; Dav. 7142.

Date	Mintage	F	VF	XF	Unc	BU
1694 (h)	—	500	1,000	2,000	4,500	7,000

KM# 9 THALER

Silver Weight varies: 28.82-29.03g. **Ruler:** Wolfgang IV **Obv:** Ornate helmet with dog's-head crest above oval shield of arms, date divided in margin at top, value '90' (Kreuzer) in cartouche at bottom **Obv. Legend:** WOLFGANG. C - Z. ÖTTINGEN **Rev:** Crowned imperial eagle, 'LI' in heart-shaped shield on breast **Rev. Legend:** * VIRTVTE - ET LABORE * **Mint:** Augsburg **Note:** Ref. L-392; Dav. 7143.

Date	Mintage	F	VF	XF	Unc	BU
1694 (h)	—	950	1,650	2,750	5,000	—

PADERBORN

One of the principal cities of Westphalia and the seat of a bishopric from its founding by Charlemagne in 795, Paderborn is situated 23 miles (38 kilometers) south-southeast of Bielefeld and about 50 miles (80 kilometers) southeast of Münster. The bishop received the right to strike coins in 1028 and was raised to the rank of Prince of the Empire in about 1100. By the late 12th to early 13th century, the bishops were employing nine different mints in their territories. In 1802, the bishopric was secularized and its domains, as well as the city of Paderborn, were annexed to Prussia. The former bishopric was part of the Kingdom of Westphalia from 1807 to 1813, after which it was returned to Prussia. In addition to the episcopal coinage, the cathedral chapter issued a series of coins in the early 17th century and during the several interregnal years.

The town, and later city, of Paderborn grew up around the cathedral and became a member of the Hanseatic League, but failed to obtain the mint right. Eventually, the townspeople converted to Protestantism and found themselves in opposition to the Catholic bishop. The bishop prevailed and had a series of coins struck for the city in 1605. Paderborn also issued a local coinage during the early period of the Thirty Years' War.

RULERS

Theodor von Fürstenberg, 1585-1618
Ferdinand I, Herzog von Bayern, 1618-50
Theodor Adolf von der Recke, 1650-1661
Ferdinand II von Fürstenberg, 1661-1683
Hermann Werner, Wolff-Metternich zu Gracht,1683-1704

MINT OFFICIALS' INITIALS

Initial	Date	Name
(a)=	1611-	Jacob Pfaler
(b)=	ca. 1616-17	Unknown
(c)=	1652-54, 75-76	Jost Dietrich Koch
(d)= or IDK		
PL	1655-58	Peter Löhr

BISHOPRIC

REGULAR COINAGE

KM# 58 PFENNIG (1/12 Schilling)

Copper **Ruler:** Ferdinand I **Obv:** 4-fold arms of Bavaria and Pfalz in circle **Obv. Legend:** FERD. D. G. A. E. C. E. P. **Rev:** Value I in circle, date at end of legend **Rev. Legend:** ANNO. **Mint:** Unknown **Note:** Ref. S-72; W-620.

Date	Mintage	Good	VG	F	VF	XF
1649	—	—	—	—	—	—

KM# 60 PFENNIG (1/12 Schilling)

Copper, 16 mm. **Ruler:** Theodor Adolf **Obv:** Spanish shield of 4-fold arms of Paderborn and Recke in circle **Obv. Legend:** THE(O). ADO. E(PI). P(A)(D). **Rev:** Value I in circle, date at end of legend **Rev. Legend:** ANNO. **Mint:** Neuhaus **Note:** Ref. S-92, 145, 153; W#635-37. Varieties exist.

Date	Mintage	Good	VG	F	VF	XF
1651	—	16.00	35.00	60.00	100	—
1657	—	16.00	35.00	60.00	100	—
1659	—	16.00	35.00	60.00	100	—

KM# 61 PFENNIG (1/12 Schilling)

Copper, 16 mm. **Ruler:** Theodor Adolf **Obv:** Spanish shield of 4-fold arms of Paderborn and Recke in circle **Obv. Legend:** THEO. ADO. E. P. **Rev:** Value I in circle, date at end of legend **Rev. Legend:** ANN D. **Mint:** Neuhaus **Note:** Ref. W-635e.

Date	Mintage	Good	VG	F	VF	XF
1651	—	16.00	35.00	60.00	125	—

KM# 131 PFENNIG (1/12 Schilling)

Copper, 16 mm. **Ruler:** Ferdinand II **Obv:** Oval shield of 4-fold arms of Paderborn and Pyrmont, with central shield of Fürstenberg, in baroque frame **Obv. Legend:** FER. D. G. E. P. C. M. S. R. I. P. C. P. **Rev:** Value I in ornamented rhombus, date at end of legend **Rev. Legend:** ANNO DOMINI. **Mint:** Neuhaus **Note:** Ref. S-175; W-641.

Date	Mintage	Good	VG	F	VF	XF
1676	27,200	8.00	16.00	35.00	75.00	—

KM# 150 PFENNIG (1/12 Schilling)

Copper, 16-17 mm. **Ruler:** Hermann Werner **Obv:** Oval shield of 4-fold arms of Paderborn and Pyrmont, with central shield of Wolff-Metternich, in baroque frame **Obv. Legend:** HER. WER. D. G. E. P. S. R. I. P. (C.) (P.) **Rev:** Value I in oval baroque frame, date at end of legend **Rev. Legend:** ANNO. DOMINI. **Mint:** Neuhaus **Note:** Ref. S-188, 197; W-650, 651. Prev. C#A4.

Date	Mintage	Good	VG	F	VF	XF
1685	—	7.00	14.00	25.00	55.00	—
1693	—	7.00	14.00	25.00	55.00	70.00

KM# 102 1-1/2 PFENNIG (1/8 Schilling)

Copper, 17 mm. **Ruler:** Theodor Adolf **Obv:** Spanish shield of 4-fold arms of Paderborn and Recke in circle **Obv. Legend:** THE(O). ADO EP. PA(D). **Rev:** Value 1-1/2 expressed as I over horizontal I in circle, date at end of legend **Rev. Legend:** ANNO. **Mint:** Neuhaus **Note:** Ref. S-152; W-634.

Date	Mintage	Good	VG	F	VF	XF
1659	—	20.00	40.00	75.00	150	—

KM# 151 1-1/2 PFENNIG (1/8 Schilling)

Copper, 16.5 mm. **Ruler:** Hermann Werner **Obv:** Oval shield of 4-fold arms of Paderborn and Pyrmont, with central shield of Wolff-Metternich, in baroque frame **Obv. Legend:** HER. WER. D. G. E. P. S. R. I. P. C. P. **Rev:** Value 1-1/2 expressed as I over horizontal I in baroque frame, date at end of legend **Rev. Legend:** ANNO. DOMINI. **Mint:** Neuhaus **Note:** Ref. S-187; W-649.

Date	Mintage	Good	VG	F	VF	XF
1685	—	9.00	20.00	35.00	75.00	—

KM# 62 2 PFENNIG

Copper, 16-18 mm. **Ruler:** Theodor Adolf **Obv:** Spanish shield of 4-fold arms of Paderborn and Recke in circle **Obv. Legend:** THE(O). ADO. EP(I). P(A)(D). **Rev:** Value II in circle, date at end of legend **Rev. Legend:** ANNO. (DO)(M)(I). **Mint:** Neuhaus **Note:** Ref. S-91, 131, 144, 150; W#631-33. Varieties exist.

Date	Mintage	Good	VG	F	VF	XF
1651	—	18.00	40.00	75.00	150	—
1655 Rare	—	—	—	—	—	—
1656	—	200	350	475	725	—
1657	—	18.00	40.00	75.00	150	—
1658	—	18.00	40.00	75.00	150	—

KM# 152 2 PFENNIG

Copper, 19-20 mm. **Ruler:** Hermann Werner **Obv:** Oval shield of 4-fold arms of Paderborn and Pyrmont, with central shield of Wolff-Metternich, in baroque frame **Obv. Legend:** HER. WER. D. G. E(P). P(A). S. R. I. P. C. P. **Rev:** Value II in oval baroque frame, date at end of legend **Rev. Legend:** ANNO. DOMINI. **Mint:** Neuhaus **Note:** Ref. S-186, 196; W-647, 648.

Date	Mintage	Good	VG	F	VF	XF
1685	—	8.00	16.00	35.00	75.00	—
1693	—	8.00	16.00	35.00	75.00	—

KM# 63 3 PFENNING (Dreier=1/4 Schilling)

Copper, 19 mm. **Ruler:** Theodor Adolf **Obv:** Spanish shield of 4-fold arms of Paderborn and Recke in circle **Obv. Legend:** THEO. ADO. EP(I). PA(D)(E)(RB). **Rev:** Value III in circle, date at end of legend **Rev. Legend:** ANNO. D(O)(M)(I)(NI). **Mint:** Neuhaus **Note:** Ref. S-90, 103 149; W#628-30.

Date	Mintage	Good	VG	F	VF	XF
1651	—	18.00	40.00	75.00	150	—
1653	—	18.00	40.00	75.00	150	—
1658	—	18.00	40.00	75.00	150	—

KM# 141 3 PFENNING (Dreier=1/4 Schilling)

Copper, 20 mm. **Ruler:** Hermann Werner **Obv:** Oval shield of 4-fold arms of Paderborn and Pyrmont, with central shield of Wolff-Metternich, in baroque frame **Obv. Legend:** HER. WER. D. G. E(P). P(A)(D). S. R. I. P. C. P. **Rev:** Value III in oval cartouche, date at end of legend **Rev. Legend:** ANNO. DOMINI. **Mint:** Neuhaus **Note:** Ref. S-181, 185, 195; W#644-46.

Date	Mintage	Good	VG	F	VF	XF
1683	—	7.00	14.00	25.00	55.00	—
1685	—	7.00	14.00	25.00	55.00	—
1693	—	7.00	14.00	25.00	55.00	—

KM# 55 4 PFENNING

Copper **Ruler:** Ferdinand I **Obv:** 4-fold arms of Bavaria and Pfalz in circle **Obv. Legend:** FERD. D. G. A. E. C. E. P. **Rev:** Value IIII in circle, date in legend **Rev. Legend:** ANNO. **Mint:** Brakel **Note:** Ref. S-71; W-619. Kipper coinage.

Date	Mintage	Good	VG	F	VF	XF
1622	—	—	—	—	—	—

KM# 64 4 PFENNING

Copper, 20-21 mm. **Ruler:** Theodor Adolf **Obv:** Spanish shield of 4-fold arms of Paderborn and Recke in circle **Obv. Legend:** THEO. ADO(L). EPI. PADE(R)(B). **Rev:** Value IIII in circle, date at end of legend **Rev. Legend:** ANNO. DOM(I)(NI). **Mint:** Neuhaus **Note:** Ref. S-89, 116, 143; W#625-27. Varieties exist.

Date	Mintage	Good	VG	F	VF	XF
1651	—	18.00	40.00	75.00	150	—
1654	—	18.00	40.00	75.00	150	—
1657	—	18.00	40.00	75.00	150	—

KM# 133 4 PFENNING

Copper, 22 mm. **Ruler:** Ferdinand II **Obv:** Oval shield of 4-fold arms of Paderborn and Pyrmont, with central shield of Fürstenberg, in baroque frame **Obv. Legend:** FERD. D. G. EP. PA. CO. MO. S. R. I. PR. CO. PYR. **Rev:** Value IIII in ornamented tablet, date at end of legend **Rev. Legend:** ANNO. DOMINI. **Mint:** Neuhaus **Note:** Ref. S-173; W-639.

Date	Mintage	Good	VG	F	VF	XF
1676	59,700	7.00	14.00	25.00	55.00	—

KM# 156 4 PFENNING

Copper, 20-21 mm. **Ruler:** Hermann Werner **Obv:** Oval shield of 4-fold arms of Paderborn and Pyrmont, with central shield of Wolff-Metternich, in baroque frame **Obv. Legend:** HER. WER. D. G. E(P); P(A)(D). S. R. I. P. C. P. **Rev:** Value IIII in ornamented rectangle, date at end of legend **Rev. Legend:** ANNO. DOMINI. **Mint:** Neuhaus **Note:** Ref. S-190, 194, 199; W-643. Varieties exist.

Date	Mintage	Good	VG	F	VF	XF
1692	—	8.00	16.00	35.00	75.00	—
1693	—	8.00	16.00	35.00	75.00	—
1696	—	8.00	16.00	35.00	75.00	—

KM# 65 6 PFENNING

Copper, 23 mm. **Ruler:** Theodor Adolf **Obv:** Spanish shield of 4-fold arms of Paderborn and Recke in circle **Obv. Legend:** THEO. ADOL. EP(I). PADE(R)(B). **Rev:** Value VI in circle, date at end of legend **Rev. Legend:** SOLI DEO GLORIA. **Mint:** Neuhaus **Note:** Ref. S-86, 102, 142, 148; W-621a-h, 623, 624. Varieties exist.

Date	Mintage	Good	VG	F	VF	XF
1651	—	16.00	25.00	60.00	125	—
1653	—	16.00	25.00	60.00	125	—
1657	—	16.00	25.00	60.00	125	—
1658	—	16.00	25.00	60.00	125	—

KM# 66 6 PFENNING

Copper, 23 mm. **Ruler:** Theodor Adolf **Obv:** Spanish shield of 4-fold arms of Paderborn and Recke in circle **Obv. Legend:** THE(O). ADOL. EP(IS). PADE(R)(P)(B)(OR). **Rev:** Value VI in circle, date at end of legend **Rev. Legend:** ANNO. DOMI(NI). **Mint:** Neuhaus **Note:** Ref. S-87; W-621i-k.

Date	Mintage	Good	VG	F	VF	XF
1651	—	16.00	35.00	60.00	125	—

KM# 67 6 PFENNING

Copper, 23 mm. **Ruler:** Theodor Adolf **Obv:** Spanish shield of 4-fold arms of Paderborn and Recke in circle **Obv. Legend:** PER. CRVCES. AD. ASTRA. **Rev:** Value VI in circle, date at end of legend **Rev. Legend:** ANNO. DOMINI. **Mint:** Unknown **Note:** Ref. S-88; W-622.

Date	Mintage	Good	VG	F	VF	XF
1651	—	16.00	35.00	60.00	125	—

KM# 134 6 PFENNING

Copper, 23 mm. **Ruler:** Ferdinand II **Obv:** Oval shield of 4-fold arms of Paderborn and Pyrmont, with central shield of Fürstenberg in baroque frame **Obv. Legend:** FERD. D. G. EP. PA(D). CO(A). MO(N). S. R. I. PR. CO(M).P(Y)(I)(R). **Rev:** Value VI in ornamented tablet, date at end of legend **Rev. Legend:** ANNO. DOMINI. **Mint:** Neuhaus **Note:** Ref. S-172, 176; W-638. Varieties exist. Some examples countermarked with script FA monogram (Franz Arnold).

Date	Mintage	Good	VG	F	VF	XF
1676	158,700	6.00	12.00	25.00	50.00	—
1677 Rare	—	—	—	—	—	—

KM# 168 6 PFENNING

Copper **Ruler:** Hermann Werner **Obv:** Oval shield of 4-fold arms of Paderborn and Pyrmont, with central shield of Wolff-Metternich, in baroque frame **Obv. Legend:** HER. WER. D. G. EP. PA. S. R. I. P. C. P. **Rev:** Value VI in oval baroque frame, date at end of legend **Rev. Legend:** ANNO. DOMINI. **Mint:** Neuhaus **Note:** Ref. S-202; W-642.

Date	Mintage	Good	VG	F	VF	XF
1700	—	10.00	20.00	40.00	80.00	—

KM# 3 KREUZER

Silver Weight varies: 0.47-0.51g., 15 mm. **Ruler:** Dietrich IV **Obv:** Shield of Fürstenberg arms superimposed on Paderborn cross **Obv. Legend:** THEO. A. FVR. D. G. E. P(A). **Rev:** Crowned imperial eagle, I in oval on breast, date divided below, no legend **Mint:** Paderborn **Note:** Ref. S-26; W-106.

Date	Mintage	VG	F	VF	XF	Unc
1611	—	—	—	—	—	—

KM# 56 MARIENGROSCHEN (1/36 Thaler)

Silver **Ruler:** Ferdinand I **Obv:** 4-fold arms, date above **Obv. Legend:** FER. D. G. EP. PAD. CO. MON. S. R. I. P. C. P. **Rev:** Madonna and Child, rays around **Rev. Legend:** MARIEN - GROSCHE. **Mint:** Brakel **Note:** Ref. S-70; W-120.

Date	Mintage	VG	F	VF	XF	Unc
1622	—	—	—	—	—	—

KM# 71 MARIENGROSCHEN (1/36 Thaler)

1.7320 g., 0.3750 Silver Weight varies: 0.93-1.65g. 0.0209 oz. ASW, 20 mm. **Ruler:** Theodor Adolf **Obv:** 4-line inscription with date **Obv. Legend:** THE. ADO. EP(I). PAD. C. P(I). **Rev:** Madonna and Child, rays around, value (36) in margin at bottom **Rev. Legend:** S. MARIA. - ORA. PRO. NO. **Rev. Inscription:** I / MAR / GRO / (date) **Mint:** Neuhaus **Note:** Ref. S-101, 114; W-146a, 147a. Varieties exist.

Date	Mintage	VG	F	VF	XF	Unc
1653	—	22.00	45.00	95.00	190	—
1654	—	22.00	45.00	95.00	190	—

KM# 72 MARIENGROSCHEN (1/36 Thaler)

1.7320 g., 0.3750 Silver Weight varies: 0.93-1.65g. 0.0209 oz. ASW, 20 mm. **Ruler:** Theodor Adolf **Obv:** 3-line inscription, mintmaster's symbol below, where present, date at end of legend **Obv. Legend:** THE. ADO. EP. PAD(ER). C(O). P(I)(R). **Obv. Inscription:** I / MARI / GRO(S). **Rev:** Madonna and Child, rays around, value (36) in margin at bottom **Rev. Legend:** S. MARIA. (O)(R)(-)R(-)A. PRO. NO(B). **Mint:** Neuhaus **Note:** Ref. S-100 113; W-114b, 147b. Varieties exist. Some examples found with countermark 'P'

Date	Mintage	VG	F	VF	XF	Unc
1653 (c)	—	20.00	45.00	95.00	190	—
1654 (c)	—	20.00	45.00	95.00	190	—
1654	—	20.00	45.00	95.00	190	—

KM# 86.1 MARIENGROSCHEN (1/36 Thaler)

0.3750 Silver Weight varies: 0.93-1.46g., 20 mm. **Ruler:** Theodor Adolf **Obv:** 3-line inscription with value 36 in oval below, all in circle, date at end of legend **Obv. Legend:** THE(O). ADO. EP. PAD(E). CO(M). P(I)(R). **Obv. Inscription:** I / MARI(E) / GRO(S) **Rev:** Madonna and Child, rays around **Rev. Legend:** S. MARIA. O - RA. PRO. NO. **Mint:** Neuhaus **Note:** Ref. S-130, 135; W-148.

Date	Mintage	VG	F	VF	XF	Unc
1655	—	20.00	45.00	95.00	190	—
1656	—	20.00	45.00	95.00	190	—

KM# 86.2 MARIENGROSCHEN (1/36 Thaler)

0.3750 Silver Weight varies: 1.10-1.51g., 20 mm. **Ruler:** Theodor Adolf **Obv:** 3-line inscription in circle, date at end of legend **Obv. Legend:** THE. ADO. EP. PAD. CO. PIR. **Obv. Inscription:** I / MARIE / GRO. **Rev:** Madonna and Child, rays around **Rev. Legend:** S. MARIA. O - RA PRO. NO. **Mint:** Neuhaus **Note:** Ref. S-136.

Date	Mintage	VG	F	VF	XF	Unc
1656	—	20.00	45.00	95.00	190	—

KM# 114 MARIENGROSCHEN (1/36 Thaler)

Silver Weight varies: 1.31-1.67g., 20 mm. **Ruler:** Ferdinand II **Obv:** Oval shield of 4-fold arms of Paderborn and Fürstenberg in baroque frame, date above in margin **Obv. Legend:** FER. D. G. EPS. PAD. S. R. I(M). P. C. P. **Rev:** Madonna and Child, rays around **Rev. Legend:** MARIEN - GROSCHE. **Mint:** Neuhaus **Note:** Ref. S-160; W-158.

Date	Mintage	VG	F	VF	XF	Unc
1666	—	20.00	45.00	95.00	190	—

KM# 123 MARIENGROSCHEN (1/36 Thaler)

Silver Weight varies: 1.25-1.42g., 20 mm. **Ruler:** Ferdinand II **Obv:** Oval shield of 4-fold arms of Paderborn and Pyrmont, with central shield of Fürstenberg, date above, between top of arms and legend **Obv. Legend:** FER. D. G. EP. PAD. CO. MON. S. R. I. P. C. P. **Rev:** Madonna and Child, rays around **Rev. Legend:** MARIEN - GROSCHE. **Mint:** Neuhaus **Note:** Ref. S-165, 166; W-159, 160.

Date	Mintage	VG	F	VF	XF	Unc
1672	—	20.00	45.00	95.00	190	—
1673	—	20.00	45.00	95.00	190	—

KM# 74 2 MARIENGROSCHEN

1.4900 g., 0.9370 Silver Weight varies: 0.78-1.45g. 0.0449 oz. ASW, 19 mm. **Ruler:** Theodor Adolf **Obv:** Oval shield of 4-fold arms of Paderborn and Recke, superimposed on crossed sword and crozier, mitre above **Obv. Legend:** THE. ADO. EP. PA(D). C(O). PI(R). **Rev:** 4-line inscription with date **Rev. Legend:** FORTITER RECTE PIE **Rev. Inscription:** II / MAR(I) / GR(O) / (date) **Mint:** Neuhaus **Note:** Ref. S-94, 107; W-139, 140. Varieties exist. Known with 'P' countermark.

Date	Mintage	VG	F	VF	XF	Unc
1653	—	25.00	50.00	100	210	—
1654	—	25.00	50.00	100	210	—
ND	—	25.00	50.00	100	210	—

KM# 75 2 MARIENGROSCHEN

1.4900 g., 0.9370 Silver 0.0449 oz. ASW, 18.5 mm. **Ruler:** Theodor Adolf **Obv:** TA monogram divides date, miter above **Obv. Legend:** THE. ADO. EP. PA. C. PIR. **Rev:** 4-line inscription with mintmaster's symbol **Rev. Legend:** FORTITER. RECTE. PIE. **Rev. Inscription:** II / MAR / GR(O). / (symbol) **Mint:** Neuhaus **Note:** Ref. S-95; W-141. Varieties exist.

Date	Mintage	VG	F	VF	XF	Unc
1653 (d)	—	25.00	50.00	100	210	—

KM# 79 2 MARIENGROSCHEN

1.4900 g., 0.9370 Silver Weight varies: 0.89-1.12g. 0.0449 oz. ASW, 19 mm. **Ruler:** Theodor Adolf **Obv:** Oval shield of 4-fold arms of Paderborn and Recke, superimposed on crossed sword and crozier, mitre above **Obv. Legend:** THE. ADO. EP. PAD. C. PIR. **Rev:** 3-line inscription, date at end of legend **Rev. Legend:** VON. FEINEM. SILBER. **Rev. Inscription:** II / MARI / GROS **Mint:** Neuhaus **Note:** Ref. S-108; W-140a.

Date	Mintage	VG	F	VF	XF	Unc
1654	—	25.00	50.00	100	210	—

KM# 87 2 MARIENGROSCHEN

Silver Weight varies: 0.87-1.47g., 18 mm. **Ruler:** Theodor Adolf **Obv:** TA monogram divides date, miter above **Obv. Legend:** THE(O). ADO. EP. PAD(E). C. PI. **Rev:** 3-line inscription in circle **Rev. Legend:** FORTITER. RECTE. PIE. **Rev. Inscription:** II / MARI / GRO. **Mint:** Neuhaus **Note:** Ref. S-121; W-142.

Date	Mintage	VG	F	VF	XF	Unc
1655	—	30.00	60.00	120	240	—

KM# 88 2 MARIENGROSCHEN

Silver Weight varies: 0.67-1.46g., 18 mm. **Ruler:** Theodor Adolf **Obv:** TA monogram divides date, miter above **Obv. Legend:** F(V)(U)RS. PAD(E)(B). L(A). MVNT(Z). **Rev:** 3-line inscription in circle **Rev. Legend:** FORTITER. RECT(E). PIE. **Rev. Inscription:** II / MARI / GRO(S). **Mint:** Neuhaus **Note:** Ref. S-122, 123; W-143. Varieties exist.

Date	Mintage	VG	F	VF	XF	Unc
1655	—	30.00	60.00	120	240	—

KM# 89.1 2 MARIENGROSCHEN

1.4900 g., 0.8750 Silver Weight varies: 0.94-0.99g. 0.0419 oz. ASW, 18 mm. **Ruler:** Theodor Adolf **Obv:** DA monogram in circle, date divided at top **Obv. Legend:** FVR. PAD. LAN. MVNT. **Rev:** 3-line inscription **Rev. Legend:** FORTITER RECTE PIE **Rev. Inscription:** II / MARI / GRO **Mint:** Neuhaus **Note:** Ref. S-124; W-144d. Known with 'P' countermark.

Date	Mintage	VG	F	VF	XF	Unc
1655	—	20.00	50.00	100	200	—

KM# 89.2 2 MARIENGROSCHEN

1.4900 g., 0.8750 Silver Weight varies: 0.85-1.34g. 0.0419 oz. ASW, 18 mm. **Ruler:** Theodor Adolf **Obv:** DA monogram in circle, date at end of legend **Obv. Legend:** FVR(S). PAD(E). L(AN)(D). M(VNT). **Rev:** 3-line inscription **Rev. Legend:** FORTITER RECTE PIE. **Rev. Inscription:** II / MARI / GRO **Mint:** Neuhaus **Note:** Ref. S-125; W-144a-c.

Date	Mintage	VG	F	VF	XF	Unc
1655	—	25.00	50.00	100	200	—

KM# 89.3 2 MARIENGROSCHEN

1.4900 g., 0.8750 Silver 0.0419 oz. ASW, 18 mm. **Ruler:** Theodor Adolf **Obv:** DA monogram in circle, mitre above, date at end of legend **Obv. Legend:** FVRS. PADE. L. MVNT. **Rev:** 3-line inscription **Rev. Legend:** FORTITER RECTE PIE. **Rev. Inscription:** II / MARI / GRO **Mint:** Neuhaus **Note:** Ref. S-126.

Date	Mintage	VG	F	VF	XF	Unc
1655	—	25.00	50.00	100	200	—

KM# 89.4 2 MARIENGROSCHEN

1.4900 g., 0.8750 Silver 0.0419 oz. ASW, 18 mm. **Ruler:** Theodor Adolf **Obv:** DA monogram, date below, in circle, mitre above **Obv. Legend:** FVRS. PADE. LANDM. **Rev:** 3-line inscription **Rev. Legend:** FORTITER RECTE PIE. **Rev. Inscription:** II / MARI / GRO **Mint:** Neuhaus **Note:** Ref. S-127.

Date	Mintage	VG	F	VF	XF	Unc
1655	—	25.00	50.00	100	200	—

KM# 90 2 MARIENGROSCHEN

1.4440 g., 0.8750 Silver Weight varies: 0.87-1.43g. 0.0406 oz. ASW, 18 mm. **Ruler:** Theodor Adolf **Obv:** TA monogram divides date, mitre above **Obv. Legend:** FVRS(T). PADE. L. MVNT(Z). **Rev:** 3-line inscription in circle **Rev. Legend:** FORTITER RECTE PIE. **Rev. Inscription:** II / MARI / GRO. **Mint:** Neuhaus **Note:** Ref. S-134; W-145. Known with 'P' countermark.

Date	Mintage	VG	F	VF	XF	Unc
1656	—	25.00	50.00	100	200	—

KM# 77.1 1/28 THALER (Fürstengroschen; 3/4 Schilling)

2.0510 g., 0.4170 Silver Weight varies: 1.20-1.91g. 0.0275 oz. ASW, 20-22 mm. **Ruler:** Theodor Adolf **Obv:** Oval shield of 4-fold arms of Paderborn and Recke in baroque frame, superimposed on crossed sword and crozier, mitre above **Obv. Legend:** T(-)HE(O). ADO. EP. PAD. C(O). P(I)(R). **Rev:** Half-length facing figure of St. Liborius holding crozier, value 28 in exergue, date at end of legend **Rev. Legend:** S. LIBO(RI). PAT(R). PAD(E)(RB). **Mint:** Neuhaus **Note:** Ref. S-96, 98, 110, 111, 112, 128, 129; W-135. Varieties exist.

Date	Mintage	VG	F	VF	XF	Unc
1653	—	12.00	25.00	55.00	110	—
1635 error for 1653	—	—	—	—	—	—
1653 (c)	—	12.00	25.00	55.00	110	—
1654	—	12.00	25.00	55.00	110	—
1655	—	12.00	25.00	55.00	110	—

KM# 77.2 1/28 THALER (Fürstengroschen; 3/4 Schilling)

2.0510 g., 0.4170 Silver Weight varies: 1.36-1.86g. 0.0275 oz. ASW, 22 mm. **Ruler:** Theodor Adolf **Obv:** Oval shield of 4-fold arms of Paderborn and Recke in baroque frame, superimposed on crossed sword and crozier, mitre above **Obv. Legend:** T(-)HE. ADO. EP. PAD. C(O). P(I). **Rev:** Half-length facing figure of St. Liborius holding crozier, value 28 in exergue, date divided at top **Rev. Legend:** S. LIBO. PATR. PADERB. **Mint:** Neuhaus **Note:** Ref. S-97, 99; W-135.

Date	Mintage	VG	F	VF	XF	Unc
1653	—	15.00	30.00	60.00	120	—

KM# 4.1 3 KREUZER (Groschen)

Silver Weight varies: 1.52-1.71g., 20 mm. **Ruler:** Dietrich IV **Obv:** Oval shield of 4-fold arms of Paderborn and Fürstenberg in circle **Obv. Legend:** THEO. A. FURS. - D. G. E. P. E. **Rev:** Imperial orb with 3, date divided by cross at top **Rev. Legend:** RU. II. RO. IM. S. A. **Mint:** Paderborn **Note:** Ref. S-23.

Date	Mintage	VG	F	VF	XF	Unc
1611 (a)	—	80.00	165	250	385	—

KM# 4.2 3 KREUZER (Groschen)

Silver Weight varies: 1.15-1.72g., 20 mm. **Ruler:** Dietrich IV **Obv:** Oval shield of 4-fold arms of Paderborn and Fürstenberg in ornamented frame **Obv. Legend:** THEO. A. FURS. D. G. E. P. E. **Rev:** Crowned imperial eagle, 3 in circle on breast, date divided by crown at top **Rev. Legend:** RU. II. D. G. RO. IM. S. A. **Mint:** Paderborn **Note:** Ref. S-24, 25; W-105a. Varieties exist.

Date	Mintage	VG	F	VF	XF	Unc
1611 (a)	—	80.00	165	250	385	—

KM# 29 3 KREUZER (Groschen)

Silver Weight varies: 0.65-0.71g., 16 mm. **Ruler:** Ferdinand I **Obv:** Spanish shield of 4-fold arms of Bavaria and Pfalz, with central shield of Paderborn, superimposed on crossed sword and crozier, electoral hat above **Obv. Legend:** FER(D). D. G. A. E. E. C. E. P. **Rev:** Value 3 in ornamented inner circle, (III) in margin at bottom **Rev. Legend:** PADERB(O). - LA. GEL(D)T. **Mint:** Brakel **Note:** Ref. S-85. Varieties exist. Kipper coinage.

Date	Mintage	VG	F	VF	XF	Unc
ND(1620-21)	—	—	—	—	—	—

KM# 9 1/24 THALER (Groschen)

0.8270 g., 0.5000 Silver Weight varies: 1.15-1.82g. 0.0133 oz. ASW, 20 mm. **Ruler:** Dietrich IV **Obv:** Oval shield of 4-fold arms of Paderborn and Fürstenberg in baroque frame **Obv. Legend:** THEO. A. F(V)(U)RS. D. G. E. P. E. **Rev:** Imperial orb with Z4, date divided to upper left and right of orb **Rev. Legend:** RUD. II. RO. IM(P). S(E). A(V). **Mint:** Paderborn **Note:** Ref. S-18, 19, 28, 30; W-95, 96. Varieties exist.

Date	Mintage	VG	F	VF	XF	Unc
1611 (a)	—	20.00	30.00	55.00	100	—
161Z (a)	—	20.00	30.00	55.00	100	—
1613 (a)	—	20.00	30.00	55.00	100	—

KM# 8 1/24 THALER (Groschen)

1.8270 g., 0.5000 Silver Weight varies: 1.23-1.93g. 0.0294 oz. ASW, 20-21 mm. **Ruler:** Dietrich IV **Obv:** Oval shield of 4-fold arms of Paderborn and Fürstenberg in baroque frame **Obv. Legend:** THEO. A. FU(RS). D. G. E. P. E(P). **Rev:** Imperial orb with Z4, date divided by top of cross **Rev. Legend:** RU(D). II. RO. IM(P). S. (A)(U). **Mint:** Paderborn **Note:** Ref#20-23; W-95. Varieties exist.

Date	Mintage	VG	F	VF	XF	Unc
1611 (a)	—	18.00	40.00	65.00	110	—

KM# 16.1 1/24 THALER (Groschen)

1.8270 g., 0.5000 Silver Weight varies: 106-1.89g. 0.0294 oz. ASW, 20 mm. **Ruler:** Dietrich IV **Obv:** Oval shield of 4-fold arms of Paderborn and Fürstenberg in baroque frame **Obv. Legend:** THEO. A. FURS. (D.G.) E. P. (E.). **Rev:** Imperial orb with Z4, date divided to upper left and right of orb **Rev. Legend:** MAT(I). I. RO. IM. S. A(U). **Mint:** Paderborn **Note:** Ref. S-29, 31-33; W#96-98. Varieties exist.

Date	Mintage	VG	F	VF	XF	Unc
161Z (a)	—	12.00	25.00	45.00	85.00	—
1613 (a)	—	12.00	25.00	45.00	85.00	—
1614 (a)	—	12.00	25.00	45.00	85.00	—

KM# 9A 1/24 THALER (Groschen)

3.9400 g., 0.5000 Silver 0.0633 oz. ASW, 21x22 mm. **Ruler:** Dietrich IV **Obv:** Oval shield of 4-fold arms of Paderborn and Fürstenberg in baroque frame **Obv. Legend:** THEO. A. FURS. D. G. E. P. E. **Rev:** Imperial orb with Z4, date divided to upper left and right of orb **Rev. Legend:** RUD. II. RO. IM. S. A. **Mint:** Paderborn **Note:** S-28.1. Klippe

Date	Mintage	VG	F	VF	XF	Unc
161Z (a) Rare	—	—	—	—	—	—

KM# 11 1/24 THALER (Groschen)

Silver **Ruler:** Dietrich IV **Obv:** Oval shield of 4-fold arms of Paderborn and Fürstenberg in baroque frame **Obv. Legend:** THEOD. A. FURSTENB. D. G. EP. **Rev:** Imperial orb with Z4 **Rev. Legend:** MAT. I. D. G. R. I. M. S. A. **Mint:** Unknown **Note:** Ref. S-60; W-103.

Date	Mintage	VG	F	VF	XF	Unc
ND(1612-18)	—	—	—	—	—	—

KM# 16.2 1/24 THALER (Groschen)

1.8270 g., 0.5000 Silver Weight varies: 1.15-1.76g. 0.0294 oz. ASW, 20 mm. **Ruler:** Dietrich IV **Obv:** Oval shield of 4-fold arms of Paderborn and Fürstenberg in baroque frame, superimposed on crossed sword and crozier, mitre above **Obv. Legend:** T(H)EO(D). (A. FVRS.) D. G. EP(IS). PA(D). (I). **Rev:** Imperial orb with Z4, date divided to upper left and right of orb **Rev. Legend:** MAT(IAS). I. (D.G.) R(O). I(M)(P). S. A(U)(V). **Mint:** Paderborn **Note:** Ref. S-34, 35, 38; W-99. Varieties exist.

Date	Mintage	VG	F	VF	XF	Unc
1614 (a)	—	12.00	25.00	45.00	85.00	—
1615	—	12.00	25.00	45.00	85.00	—

KM# 16.3 1/24 THALER (Groschen)

1.8270 g., 0.5000 Silver Weight varies: 1.04-1.70g. 0.0294 oz. ASW, 20-21 mm. **Ruler:** Dietrich IV **Obv:** Oval shield of 4-fold arms of Paderborn and Fürstenberg in baroque frame, superimposed on crossed sword and crozier, mitre above **Obv. Legend:** TE(O). A. F(V)(U)(R)(S). D. G. E(P)(I). P(A)(D). **Rev:** Imperial orb with Z4, date divided by top of cross **Rev. Legend:** MAT(I)(AS). I. D. G. R(O). (I)(M). S. A(V)(U). **Mint:** Paderborn **Note:** Ref. S#39-43; W-99, 100. Varieties exist.

Date	Mintage	VG	F	VF	XF	Unc
1615	—	12.00	25.00	45.00	85.00	—
1616	—	12.00	25.00	45.00	85.00	—

KM# 21 1/24 THALER (Groschen)

Silver Weight varies: 1.00-1.53g., 19-20 mm. **Ruler:** Dietrich IV **Obv:** Oval shield of 4-fold arms of Paderborn and Fürstenberg in baroque frame, superimposed on crossed sword and crozier, mitre above **Obv. Legend:** TE(O). A. F(V)(U)(R)(S). D. (G.) E(P)(I). P(A). **Rev:** Imperial orb with Z4, date divided by top of cross **Rev. Legend:** MAT(IAS). I. (D.G.) R(O). I(M). S. A(V). **Mint:** Brakel **Note:** Ref. S#45-48; W-101. Varieties exist.

Date	Mintage	VG	F	VF	XF	Unc
1617	—	18.00	35.00	65.00	120	—
(1)617	—	18.00	35.00	65.00	120	—
1618	—	18.00	35.00	65.00	120	—

KM# 31.1 1/24 THALER (Groschen)

Silver Weight varies: 0.65-1.43g., 17-19 mm. **Ruler:** Dietrich IV **Obv:** Oval shield of 4-fold arms of Paderborn and Fürstenberg in baroque frame, superimposed on crossed sword and crozier, mitre above **Obv. Legend:** T(H)(E)(O). (A.) (F)(V)(U)(R). D. G. E(P). (P)(A). **Rev:** Imperial orb with Z4, date divided by top of cross **Rev. Legend:** MAT(T). I. D. G. R. I(M). S. A(V). **Mint:** Brakel **Note:** Ref. S#52-55, 58; W-102. Varieties exist. Kipper coinage.

Date	Mintage	VG	F	VF	XF	Unc
1618	—	25.00	45.00	90.00	180	—
1619	—	25.00	45.00	90.00	180	—

KM# 31.1A 1/24 THALER (Groschen)

4.6100 g., Silver, 22x23 mm. **Ruler:** Dietrich IV **Obv:** Oval shield of 4-fold arms of Paderborn and Fürstenberg in baroque frame, superimposed on crossed sword and crozier, mitre above **Obv. Legend:** THEO. A. FVR. S. G. E. P. **Rev:** Imperial orb with Z4, date divided by top of cross **Rev. Legend:** MAT. I. D. G. R. IM. S. A. **Mint:** Brakel **Note:** Ref. S-53.1. Kipper coinage. Klippe

Date	Mintage	VG	F	VF	XF	Unc
1618 Rare	—	—	—	—	—	—

KM# 31.2 1/24 THALER (Groschen)

Silver Weight varies: 1.01-1.27g., 19 mm. **Ruler:** Dietrich IV **Obv:** Spanish shield of 4-fold arms of Paderborn and Fürstenberg in baroque frame **Obv. Legend:** TE(O). A. F(V)(R). D. G. EP. PA. **Rev:** Imperial orb with Z4, date divided by top of cross **Rev. Legend:** MAT. I. D. G. R. I. S. A. **Mint:** Brakel **Note:** Ref. S-56, 57. Varieties exist. Kipper coinage.

Date	Mintage	VG	F	VF	XF	Unc
1618	—	—	—	—	—	—

KM# 31.3 1/24 THALER (Groschen)

Silver Weight varies: 0.90-1.02g., 17 mm. **Ruler:** Dietrich IV **Obv:** Oval shield of 4-fold arms of Paderborn and Fürstenberg in baroque frame, superimposed on crossed sword and crozier, mitre above **Obv. Legend:** TEO. A. FVR. D. G. E. P. **Rev:** Imperial orb with Z4, date divided by top of cross **Rev. Legend:** FERD. IIII. D. G. R. I. S. A. **Mint:** Brakel **Note:** Ref. S-59; W-102A. Kipper coinage.

Date	Mintage	VG	F	VF	XF	Unc
1619	—	—	—	—	—	—

KM# 32.1 1/24 THALER (Groschen)

Silver Weight varies: 0.64-0.92g., 16 mm. **Ruler:** Ferdinand I **Obv:** Spanish shield of 4-fold arms of Bavaria and Pfalz, with central shield of Paderborn, superimposed on crossed sword and scepter, electoral hat above **Obv. Legend:** FER(D). D. G. A(RC). E(P). E(C). C(OL). E. P. **Rev:** Imperial orb with Z4, cross on top divides date **Rev. Legend:** FERD. II. (D.G.) R(OM). I(MP). S(E)(M)(P). A(V). **Mint:** Brakel **Note:** Ref. S-61, 67, 69; W-118. Varieties exist. Kipper coinage.

Date	Mintage	VG	F	VF	XF	Unc
1619	—	22.00	50.00	80.00	160	—
16Z0	—	22.00	50.00	80.00	160	—
(1)6Z0	—	22.00	50.00	80.00	160	—
16Z1	—	22.00	50.00	80.00	160	—

KM# 32.2 1/24 THALER (Groschen)

Silver Weight varies: 0.61-1.10g., 17 mm. **Ruler:** Ferdinand I **Obv:** Spanish shield of 4-fold arms of Bavaria and Pfalz, with central shield of Paderborn, superimposed on crossed sword and scepter, electoral hat above **Obv. Legend:** FER(D). D. G. A. E. E. C. E. P(A). **Rev:** Imperial orb with Z4, cross on top divides date, where present **Rev. Legend:** FERD. IIII. D. G. R. I. S. (A). **Mint:** Brakel **Note:** Ref. S-62, 64; W-118. Varieties exist. Kipper coinage.

Date	Mintage	VG	F	VF	XF	Unc
1619	—	22.00	50.00	80.00	160	—
ND(1620-21)	—	22.00	50.00	80.00	160	—

KM# 82 1/24 THALER (Groschen)

Silver **Ruler:** Theodor Adolf **Obv:** Oval shield of 4-fold arms of Paderborn and Recke in baroque frame, superimposed on crossed sword and crozier, mitre above, value (24) below **Obv. Legend:** THE. ADOL - EP. PAD. **Rev:** Facing standing figure of St. Liborius divides date **Rev. Legend:** S. LIBORIVS - PATR. PAD. **Mint:** Neuhaus **Note:** Ref. S-109; W-131.

Date	Mintage	VG	F	VF	XF	Unc
1654	—	—	—	—	—	—

KM# 6 4 KREUZER (Batzen)
Silver Weight varies: 2.00-2.69g, 26 mm. **Ruler:** Dietrich IV **Obv:** Oval shield of 4-fold arms of Paderborn and Fürstenberg in ornamented frame **Obv. Legend:** THEO A. FURST - D. G. E. P. EPIS. **Rev:** Crowned imperial eagle, 4 in circle on breast, date divided in margin at top **Rev. Legend:** RU. II. D.G. RO IMPE. S. AU. **Mint:** Paderborn **Note:** S-17; Saurma 2204.

Date	Mintage	VG	F	VF	XF	Unc
1611 (a)	—	—	—	—	—	—

KM# 36 1/21 THALER (Schilling)
Silver Weight varies: 1.97-3.07g., 26-27 mm. **Ruler:** Ferdinand I **Obv:** Crowned Spanish shield of 4-fold arms of Bavaria and Pfalz, with central shield of Paderborn **Obv. Legend:** FERD(IN). D. G. (ARC.) EP. EC. COL. E. P(A). **Rev:** Crowned imperial eagle, Z1 in orb on breast **Rev. Legend:** FERD. II. D.G. ROM IM. SEMP. AV(G). **Mint:** Brakel **Note:** Ref. S-77. Varieties exist. Kipper coinage.

Date	Mintage	VG	F	VF	XF	Unc
ND(1620-1)	—	40.00	85.00	135	230	—

KM# 37.1 1/21 THALER (Schilling)
Silver Weight varies: 1.65-2.55g., 26 mm. **Ruler:** Ferdinand I **Obv:** Crowned Spanish shield of 4-fold arms of Bavaria and Pfalz, with central shield of Paderborn **Obv. Legend:** FER(D). D. G. ARC(H). EP. (EC.) (EL.) COL. E. P. **Rev:** Crowned imperial eagle, Z1 in orb on breast **Rev. Legend:** PAD. LAND(T). M(U)(V)NTZ XXI. Z(VM). T(H)A(L). **Mint:** Brakel **Note:** Ref. S-76; W-119. Varieties exist. Kipper coinage.

Date	Mintage	VG	F	VF	XF	Unc
ND(1620-1)	—	40.00	85.00	135	240	—

KM# 37.2 1/21 THALER (Schilling)
Silver, 26 mm. **Ruler:** Ferdinand I **Obv:** Crowned Spanish shield of 4-fold arms of Bavaria and Pfalz, with central shield of Paderborn **Obv. Legend:** PAD. LANDT. (MVNTZ) (XXI. ZV) TA. **Rev:** Crowned imperial eagle, Z1 in orb on breast **Rev. Legend:** FERD. (II. D. G. R) O. I(M). **Mint:** Brakel **Note:** Ref. S-80; W-119A. Kipper coinage.

Date	Mintage	VG	F	VF	XF	Unc
ND(1620-1) (b)	—	40.00	85.00	135	240	—

KM# 38 1/21 THALER (Schilling)
Silver, 26 mm. **Ruler:** Ferdinand I **Obv:** Crowned Spanish shield of 4-fold arms of Bavaria and Pfalz, with central shield of Paderborn **Obv. Legend:** LANDT. MVNTZ. XXI. ZV. THAL. **Rev:** Crowned imperial eagle, Z1 in orb on breast **Rev. Legend:** FERD. II. D. G. ROM. IMP. SEM. A. **Mint:** Brakel **Note:** Ref. S-81; W-119B. Kipper coinage.

Date	Mintage	VG	F	VF	XF	Unc
ND(1620-1)	—	40.00	85.00	135	240	—

KM# 39 1/21 THALER (Schilling)
Silver Weight varies: 1.70-2.59g., 26-27 mm. **Ruler:** Ferdinand I **Obv:** Crowned Spanish shield of 4-fold arms of Bavaria and Pfalz, with central shield of Paderborn **Obv. Legend:** PADERB. LAN(D)(T). GEL(D)(T). **Rev:** Crowned imperial eagle, Z1 in orb on breast **Rev. Legend:** FERD. II. D. G. ROM. IMP. SEMP. A(V)(G). **Mint:** Brakel **Note:** Ref. S-78; W-119Ab, 119c. Varieties exist. Kipper coinage.

Date	Mintage	VG	F	VF	XF	Unc
ND(1620-1)	—	40.00	85.00	135	240	—

KM# 40 1/21 THALER (Schilling)
2.6000 g., Silver, 26-27 mm. **Ruler:** Ferdinand I **Obv:** Crowned Spanish shield of 4-fold arms of Bavaria and Pfalz, with central shield of Paderborn **Obv. Legend:** XXI. PADERB. LANDTGELT. **Rev:** Crowned imperial eagle, Z1 in orb on breast **Rev. Legend:** FERD. II. D. G. RO. - IMP. SEMP. AV. **Mint:** Brakel **Note:** Ref. S-79; W-119Aa. Kipper coinage.

Date	Mintage	VG	F	VF	XF	Unc
ND(1620-1)	—	40.00	85.00	135	240	—

KM# 41 1/21 THALER (Schilling)
Silver Weight varies: 2.29-2.48g., 26-29 mm. **Ruler:** Ferdinand I **Obv:** Crowned Spanish shield of 4-fold arms of Bavaria and Pfalz, with central shield of Paderborn **Obv. Legend:** FERD. II. D. G. ROM. IM. SEM. A. **Rev:** Crowned imperial eagle, Z1 in orb on breast **Rev. Legend:** (PA.) LANDT. MVNTZ. XXI. Z(V). THAL. **Mint:** Brakel **Note:** Ref. S-82, 83. Varieties exist. Kipper coinage.

Date	Mintage	VG	F	VF	XF	Unc
ND(1620-1)	—	40.00	85.00	135	240	—

KM# 80 4 MARIENGROSCHEN
Silver Weight varies: 1.88-2.40g., 20 mm. **Ruler:** Theodor Adolf **Obv:** Oval shield of 4-fold arms of Paderborn and Recke in baroque frame, superimposed on crossed sword and crozier, mitre above **Obv. Legend:** THE. ADO. EP. PAD. C. PI. **Rev:** 4-line inscription with date **Rev. Legend:** FORTITER RECTE PIE. **Rev. Inscription:** IIII / MARI / GRO / (date) **Mint:** Neuhaus **Note:** Ref. S-105; W-137.

Date	Mintage	VG	F	VF	XF	Unc
1654	—	—	—	—	—	—

KM# 34 12 KREUZER (Schreckenberger)
Silver Weight varies: 2.08-3.57g., 25-27 mm. **Ruler:** Ferdinand I **Obv:** Spanish shield of 4-fold arms of Bavaria and Pfalz, with central shield of Paderborn, superimposed on crossed sword and crozier, electoral hat above **Obv. Legend:** FERD. (II.) D. G. ARC. (ET.) (EP.) (EC.) (EL.) C(OL). E. (P.) (A). **Rev:** Crowned imperial eagle, 1Z in orb on breast **Rev. Legend:** FERD. II(II). D. G. ROM. IMP. SEM(P). AV. **Mint:** Brakel **Note:** Ref. S#73-75; W-118. Varieties exist. Kipper coinage.

Date	Mintage	VG	F	VF	XF	Unc
ND(1620-21)	—	25.00	55.00	100	200	—

KM# 81 1/14 THALER (2 Fürstengroschen)
2.9980 g., 0.5790 Silver Weight varies: 1.81-3.61g. 0.0558 oz. ASW, 24-25 mm. **Ruler:** Theodor Adolf **Obv:** Oval shield of 4-fold arms of Paderborn and Recke in baroque frame, superimposed on crossed sword and crozier, mitre above **Obv. Legend:** T(-)HE(O)(D). ADO(L). (-) E(P)(I).(-) PA(D)(E)(RB). (ET.) C(O). PI(R). **Rev:** Full-length facing figure of St. Liborious divides date **Rev. Legend:** S. LIBORIVS. (-) PA(-)T(R)(O)(N). PAD(E)(I)(R)(B)(O). **Mint:** Neuhaus **Note:** Ref. S-106, 117, 118, 119, 120, 133; W#132-34. Varieties exist. Some examples have a 'P' countermark.

Date	Mintage	VG	F	VF	XF	Unc
1654	—	55.00	120	235	475	—
1655	—	35.00	85.00	160	325	—
1656	—	35.00	85.00	160	325	—

KM# A22 1/4 THALER (Ortsthaler)
7.2500 g., Silver, 26 mm. **Ruler:** Dietrich IV **Obv:** Oval shield of 4-fold arms of Paderborn and Fürstenberg in baroque frame, superimposed on crossed sword and crozier **Obv. Legend:** THEODOR. A. FVRST. D. G. EP. PADB. **Rev:** Crowned imperial eagle, orb on breast, date divided by crown at top **Rev. Legend:** MATIAS. I. D. G. - RO. IM. S. AVG. **Mint:** Paderborn **Note:** Ref. S-37.

Date	Mintage	VG	F	VF	XF	Unc
1615 Rare	—	—	—	—	—	—

KM# 106 1/4 THALER (Ortsthaler)
Silver Weight varies: 7.01-7.18g., 28 mm. **Ruler:** Ferdinand II **Obv:** Facing robed bust, turned slightly to right **Obv. Legend:** FERD. D. G. EPS. PADER. S. R. I. PRIN. COM. PYRM. **Rev:** Oval shield of 4-fold arms of Paderborn and Pyrmont in baroque frame, superimposed on crossed sword and crozier, hat above, date at end of Greek legend meaning "agreeably and firmly" **Rev. Legend:** ??????OS - ?????OS. **Mint:** Neuhaus **Note:** Ref. S-159; W-155.

Date	Mintage	VG	F	VF	XF	Unc
1663	—	135	250	400	650	—

KM# 127 1/3 THALER (1/2 Gulden)
Silver Weight varies: 9.36-9.40g., 35 mm. **Ruler:** Ferdinand II **Obv:** Robed bust to right **Obv. Legend:** FERDINAND. D. G. EPI. PADER. COADI. MONAST. **Rev:** Crowned oval shield of 4-fold arms of Paderborn and Pyrmont, with central shield of Fürstenberg, in baroque frame, superimposed on crossed sword and crozier, divides date and mintmaster's initials, value (1/3) in oval cartouche below **Rev. Legend:** S. R. I. PRIN. COM. PYRM. - ET. L. B. D. FVRSTENBERG **Mint:** Paderborn **Note:** Ref. S-170; W-157. 12 Groschen.

Date	Mintage	VG	F	VF	XF	Unc
1675 IDK	3,982	—	—	—	—	—

Note: Hanck Auction 21, 3-09, VF realized approximately $17,500.

KM# A23 1/2 THALER
Silver, 30 mm. **Ruler:** Dietrich IV **Obv:** Oval shield of 4-fold arms of Paderborn and Fürstenberg in baroque frame, superimposed on crossed sword and crozier, divides date, mitre above **Obv. Legend:** THEODOR. A. FVRS. D. G. EPI. PA. **Rev:** Crowned imperial eagle, orb on breast **Rev. Legend:** MATTHAIS. I. D. G. ROM. IMP. SEM. AV. **Mint:** Brakel **Note:** Ref. S-44.

Date	Mintage	VG	F	VF	XF	Unc
1617 (b) Rare	—	—	—	—	—	—

KM# B23 1/2 THALER
22.8600 g., Silver, 33x33 mm. **Ruler:** Dietrich IV **Obv:** Oval shield of 4-fold arms of Paderborn and Fürstenberg in baroque frame, superimposed on crossed sword and crozier, divides date, mitre above **Obv. Legend:** THEODOR. A. FVRS. D. G. EPI. PA. **Rev:** Crowned imperial eagle, orb on breast **Rev. Legend:** MATTHIAS. I. D. G. ROM. IMP. SEM. AV. **Mint:** Brakel **Note:** Ref. S-44.1. Klippe.

Date	Mintage	VG	F	VF	XF	Unc
1617 (b) Rare	—	—	—	—	—	—

KM# 95.1 1/2 THALER
Silver Weight varies: 14.43-14.59g., 37 mm. **Ruler:** Theodor Adolf **Obv:** Spanish shield of 4-fold arms of Paderborn and Recke, superimposed on crossed sword and crozier, 3 ornate helmets above, mitre on center helmet **Obv. Legend:** THEOD. ADOL. EP. PADER. C. PIR. **Rev:** Full-length figure of St. Liborius holding crozier divides date, final word of legend to left of crozier **Rev. Legend:** BENEDICTVS ES DOMINE DOCE - ME IVSTIFICATIONES, TVAS **Mint:** Neuhaus **Note:** Ref. S-139; W-126.

Date	Mintage	VG	F	VF	XF	Unc
1657 PL	—	150	275	400	800	—

KM# 95.2 1/2 THALER
14.4600 g., Silver, 37 mm. **Ruler:** Theodor Adolf **Obv:** Spanish shield of 4-fold arms of Paderborn and Recke, superimposed on crossed sword and crozier, 3 ornate helmets above, mitre on center helmet **Obv. Legend:** THEOD. ADOL. EP. PADER. C. PIR. **Rev:** Full-length facing figure of St. Liborius, double legend, date at end of inner legend **Rev. Legend:** Outer: BENEDICT9 ES DNEDO - CE ME IVSTIFICAOES TVAS; Inner: S. LIBORIVS. PATR. - PADERBOR. **Mint:** Neuhaus **Note:** Ref. S-140; W-127a.

Date	Mintage	VG	F	VF	XF	Unc
1657 PL	—	150	275	400	800	—

KM# 96 1/2 THALER
Silver Weight varies: 14.33-14.63g., 37 mm. **Ruler:** Theodor Adolf **Obv:** Spanish shield of 4-fold arms of Paderborn and Recke, superimposed on crossed sword and crozier, 3 ornate helmets above, mitre on center helmet **Obv. Legend:** THEO. ADOL. D. G. EPI. PADERB. CO. PIR. **Rev:** Full-length facing figure of St. Liborius, double legend, date at end of inner legend **Rev. Legend:** Outer: BENEDIT9 ES DNEDO - CE ME IVSTIFICAOES TVAS; Inner: S. LIBORIVS. PATR. - PADEBOR. **Mint:** Neuhaus **Note:** Ref. S-141; W-127b,c.

Date	Mintage	VG	F	VF	XF	Unc
1657 IDK (c)	—	150	275	400	800	—

KM# 100.1 1/2 THALER
Silver Weight varies: 13.86-14.57g., 37 mm. **Ruler:** Theodor Adolf **Obv:** Spanish shield of 4-fold arms of Paderborn and Recke, superimposed on crossed sword and crozier, 3 ornate helmets above, which divide date to left and right **Obv. Legend:** THEO. ADOL. D. G. EPI. PADERB. CO. PIR. **Rev:** Seated facing Madonna with Child, rays around **Rev. Legend:** S. MARIA. SVB. TVVM. PRÆSIDIVM. CONFVGIMVS. **Mint:** Neuhaus **Note:** Ref. S-146; W-128.

Date	Mintage	VG	F	VF	XF	Unc
1658 IDK (c)	—	150	275	400	800	—

KM# 100.2 1/2 THALER
Silver Weight varies: 14.31-14.52g., 35 mm. **Ruler:** Theodor Adolf **Obv:** Spanish shield of 4-fold arms of Paderborn and Recke, superimposed on crossed sword and crozier, 3 ornate helmets above **Obv. Legend:** THEO(DO). ADOL. D. G. EPI. PADERB. C(O). PIR. **Rev:** Seated facing Madonna with Child, rays around **Rev. Legend:** S. MARIA. SVB. TVVM. PRÆSIDIVM. CONFVGIMVS. **Mint:** Neuhaus **Note:** Ref. S-147; W-129. Varieties exist.

Date	Mintage	VG	F	VF	XF	Unc
1658 IDK (c)	—	150	275	400	800	—

KM# 128 2/3 THALER (Gulden)
19.0900 g., 0.7640 Silver Weight varies: 18.80-19.12g. 0.4689 oz. ASW, 38 mm. **Ruler:** Ferdinand II **Obv:** Robed bust to right, motto in band above head in margin **Obv. Legend:** FERDINAND. D. G. EPI. PADER. COAD. MON. S. R. I. P., motto: SVAVITER. ET. FORTITER. **Rev:** Crowned Spanish shield of 4-fold arms of Paderborn and Pyrmont, with central shield of Fürstenberg, superimposed on crossed sword and crozier, divides date and mintmaster's initials, value (2/3) in oval below **Rev. Legend:** COM. PYRMONT. ET. LIB. - BAR. D. FURSTENBERG. **Mint:** Paderborn **Note:** Ref. S-169; W-156b; Dav. 739.

Date	Mintage	VG	F	VF	XF	Unc
1675 IDK	40,787	400	650	850	1,400	—

KM# 129 2/3 THALER (Gulden)
19.0900 g., 0.7640 Silver Weight varies: 16.62-19.16g. 0.4689 oz. ASW, 38 mm. **Ruler:** Ferdinand II **Obv:** Robed bust to right, motto in band above head in margin **Obv. Legend:** FERDINAND. D. G. EPI. PAD(ER). COAD. MON. S. R. I. P., motto: SVAVITER. ET. FORTITER. **Rev:** Crowned oval shield of 4-fold arms of Paderborn and Pyrmont, with central shield of Fürstenberg, in baroque frame, superimposed on crossed sword and crozier, divides date and mintmaster's initials, value (2/3) in oval below **Rev. Legend:** COM. PYRMONT. ET. LIB. - BAR(O). D(E). F(V)(U)R(S)TENBERG. **Mint:** Paderborn **Note:** Ref. S-168, W-156a; Dav. 740.

Date	Mintage	VG	F	VF	XF	Unc
1675 IDK	Inc. above	400	650	850	1,400	—

KM# 162 2/3 THALER (Gulden)
Silver, 40 mm. **Ruler:** Hermann Werner **Obv:** Robed bust to right **Obv. Legend:** D. G. HER. WERNER. EPI. BADERBO. S. R. I. P - C. P. & O. H. **Rev:** Crowned oval shield of 6-fold arms, with central shield of Wolff-Metternich, in baroque frame, superimposed on crossed sword and crozier, value (2/3) in oval below **Rev. Legend:** PROVIDE - ET IVSTE. **Mint:** Neuhaus **Note:** Ref. S-203; Dav. 741.

Date	Mintage	VG	F	VF	XF	Unc
ND(ca1694) Rare	—	—	—	—	—	—

KM# 13 THALER
28.9600 g., Silver, 40 mm. **Ruler:** Dietrich IV **Obv:** Oval shield of 4-fold arms of Paderborn and Fürstenberg in baroque frame **Obv. Legend:** THEOD. A. FVRSTENB. D. G. ECC. PAD. EPIS. **Rev:** Crowned imperial eagle, date divided above claws **Rev. Legend:** RVDOLPHVS. II. - D. G. RO. IMP. S. A. **Mint:** Paderborn **Note:** Ref. S-16; W-87; Dav. 5675.

Date	Mintage	VG	F	VF	XF	Unc
1611 (a) Rare	—	—	—	—	—	—

KM# 18 THALER
Silver Weight varies: 27.18-28.89g., 42 mm. **Ruler:** Dietrich IV **Obv:** Facing bust wearing vestments, turned slightly to right **Obv. Legend:** THEODO. A. FVRSTENB. D. G. EC. PADER. EPIS. **Rev:** Ornate shield of 4-fold arms of Paderborn and Fürstenberg, 3 ornate helmets above, date divided to lower left and right of arms **Rev. Legend:** IVDICIVM. MELIVS. POSTERITATIS. ERIT. **Mint:** Paderborn **Note:** Ref. S-27; W-88; Dav. 5677.

Date	Mintage	VG	F	VF	XF	Unc
1612 Rare	—	—	—	—	—	—

KM# B22 THALER
28.1100 g., Silver, 43 mm. **Ruler:** Dietrich IV **Obv:** Ornate shield of 4-fold arms of Paderborn and Fürstenberg, 3 ornate helmets above **Obv. Legend:** THEODO. A. FVRSTENB. D. G. ECC. PAD. EPIS. **Rev:** Crowned imperial eagle, imperial orb on breast, date divided by tail **Rev. Legend:** MATIAS. I. D. G. ROMA. IMP. E. SEM. AV. **Mint:** Paderborn **Note:** Ref. S-36.

Date	Mintage	VG	F	VF	XF	Unc
1615 Rare	—	—	—	—	—	—

KM# 25A THALER
Silver Weight varies: 28.20-28.88g., 44 mm. **Ruler:** Dietrich IV **Subject:** Death of Dietrich IV **Obv:** Spanish shield of 4-fold arms of Paderborn and Fürstenberg, 3 ornate helmets above, date at end of legend **Obv. Legend:** THEODO. A FVRSTE. D. G. EPISCOPVS. PADER. **Rev:** 7-line inscription with Roman numeral dates **Rev. Legend:** IVDICIVM. MELIVS. POSTERTATIS. ERIT. ANNO. MDCXVIII. **Rev. Inscription:** REXIT / ANNOS. XXXIII / MENS. VI DIES / XXIIX OBIIT. / .IIII. DECEMB. / ANNO / MDCXIIX. **Mint:** Brakel **Note:** Ref. S-51; W-257.

Date	Mintage	VG	F	VF	XF	Unc
1618//MDCXVIII Rare	—	—	—	—	—	—

KM# 23 THALER
Silver Weight varies: 28.07-28.96g., 44 mm. **Ruler:** Dietrich IV **Obv:** Ornate shield of 4-fold arms of Paderborn and Fürstenberg, 3 ornate helmets above **Obv. Legend:** THODO. A. FVRSTENBERG. D. G. EPIS. PADERBOR. **Rev:** Crowned imperial eagle, imperial orb on breast, date divided by claws and tail **Rev. Legend:** MATIAS. I. D. G. RO. IMPER. SEMPER. AVGVST. **Mint:** Brakel **Note:** Ref. S-49; Dav. 5680.

Date	Mintage	VG	F	VF	XF	Unc
1618 Rare	—	—	—	—	—	—

KM# 24 THALER
Silver **Ruler:** Dietrich IV **Obv:** Ornate shield of 4-fold arms of Paderborn and Fürstenberg, 3 ornate helmets above **Obv. Legend:** THEODO. A. FVRSTENBERG. D. G. EPIS. PADERBOR. **Rev:** Crowned imperial eagle, imperial orb on breast, date divided by claws and tail **Rev. Legend:** MATIAS. I. D. G. RO. IMPER. SEMPER. AVGVST. **Mint:** Brakel **Note:** Ref. S-49.2; Dav. 5680a. Klippe.

Date	Mintage	VG	F	VF	XF	Unc
1618 Rare	—	—	—	—	—	—

KM# 25 THALER
Silver Weight varies: 27.88-28.83g., 43 mm. **Ruler:** Dietrich IV **Obv:** Spanish shield of 4-fold arms of Paderborn and Fürstenberg, 3 ornate helmets above, date at end of legend **Obv. Legend:** THEODO. A. FVRSTE. D. G. EPISCOPVS. PADER. **Rev:** Crowned imperial eagle, orb on breast **Rev. Legend:** MATTI. I. D. G. ROMA. IMPERAT. SEMPER. AVGV. **Mint:** Brakel **Note:** Ref. S-50; W-89; Dav. 5681.

Date	Mintage	VG	F	VF	XF	Unc
1618 Rare	—	—	—	—	—	—

KM# 43 THALER
28.8500 g., Silver, 42 mm. **Ruler:** Ferdinand I **Obv:** Robed bust to right in circle **Obv. Legend:** FERDINAND. D. G. ARG. COL. ELE. ADM. HIL. EPI. PADERB. **Rev:** Spanish shield of 4-fold arms of Bavaria and Pfalz, with central shield of Paderborn, in baroque frame, superimposed on crossed sword and crozier, electoral hat above, date at end of legend **Rev. Legend:** FERDINANDVS. II. D. G. ROM. IMP. SEMP. AVG. **Mint:** Brakel **Note:** Ref. S-65; W-112; Dav. 5684. ARG error for ARC in obverse legend.

Date	Mintage	VG	F	VF	XF	Unc
1620 Rare	—	—	—	—	—	—

KM# 44 THALER
29.4000 g., Silver, 42 mm. **Ruler:** Ferdinand I **Obv:** Robed bust to right in circle **Obv. Legend:** FERDINAND. D. G. ARG. COL. EPI. PAD. ET. ADM. HILD. **Rev:** Spanish shield of 4-fold arms of Bavaria and Pfalz, with central shield of Paderborn, in baroque frame, superimposed on crossed sword and crozier, electoral hat above, date at end of legend **Rev. Legend:** FERDINANDVS. II. D. G. ROM. IMP. SEMP. AVGVS. **Mint:** Brakel **Note:** Ref. S-66; Dav. 5685. ARG error for ARC in obverse legend.

Date	Mintage	VG	F	VF	XF	Unc
1620 Rare	—	—	—	—	—	—

KM# 45 THALER
28.2800 g., Silver, 42 mm. **Ruler:** Ferdinand I **Obv:** Full-length facing figure of St. Liborius divides S - L **Obv. Legend:** FERDINAND. D. G. ARG. COL. EPI. PAD. ET. ADM. HIL. **Rev:** Spanish shield of 4-fold arms of Bavaria and Pfalz, with central shield of Paderborn, in baroque frame, superimposed on crossed sword and crozier, electoral hat above, date at end of legend **Rev. Legend:** FERDINANDVS. II. D. G. ROM. IMP. SEMP. AVGVS. **Mint:** Brakel **Note:** Ref. S-64; W-113; Dav. 5686. ARG error for ARC in obverse legend.

Date	Mintage	VG	F	VF	XF	Unc
1620 Rare	—	—	—	—	—	—

KM# 46 THALER
Silver Weight varies: 28.35-28.87g., 42 mm. **Ruler:** Ferdinand I **Obv:** Full-length facing figure of St. Liborius, upward on left SANCTVS, downward at right LIBORIVS **Obv. Legend:** FERDINANDVS. D. G. ARC. COL. EPI. PADERB. V. BAV. DVX. ZC. **Rev:** Spanish shield of 4-fold arms of Bavaria and Pfalz, with central shield of Paderborn, in baroque frame, superimposed on crossed sword and crozier, electoral hat above, date at end of legend **Rev. Legend:** FERDINANDVS. II. D. G. ROM. IMP. SEMP. AVGVSTVS. **Mint:** Brakel **Note:** Ref. S-63; W-114, 115; Dav. 5688.

Date	Mintage	VG	F	VF	XF	Unc
1620 Rare	—	—	—	—	—	—

KM# 84 THALER
28.8700 g., Silver, 44 mm. **Ruler:** Theodor Adolf **Obv:** Robed bust to right **Obv. Legend:** THEODO. ADOL. EPIS. PADERBO. COM. PIRMON. **Rev:** Ornate shield of 4-fold arms of Paderborn and Recke, superimposed on crossed sword and crozier, 3 ornate helmets above, date at end of legend **Rev. Legend:** FORTITER RECTE PIE. **Mint:** Neuhaus **Note:** Ref. S-104; W-123; Dav. 5690.

Date	Mintage	VG	F	VF	XF	Unc
1654 Rare	—	—	—	—	—	—

KM# 92 THALER
Silver Weight varies: 27.77-29.35g., 45 mm. **Ruler:** Theodor Adolf **Obv:** Facing robed bust in circle **Obv. Legend:** THEODO. ADOL. EPIS. PADERBO. COM. PIRMON. **Rev:** Spanish shield of 4-fold arms of Paderborn and Recke, superimposed on crossed sword and crozier, 3 ornate helmets above, mitre on center helmet, date at end of legend **Rev. Legend:** FORTITER * RECTE * PIE * AO • **Mint:** Neuhaus **Note:** Ref. S-132; W-124; Dav. 5692.

Date	Mintage	VG	F	VF	XF	Unc
1656 PL	—	900	1,800	3,900	7,200	—

KM# 98 THALER
Silver Weight varies: 28.47-29.18g., 45 mm. **Ruler:** Theodor Adolf **Obv:** Facing robed bust in circle **Obv. Legend:** THEODO. ADOL. EPIS. PADERBO. COM. PIRMON. **Rev:** Spanish shield of 4-fold arms of Paderborn and Recke, superimposed on crossed sword and crozier, 3 ornate helmets above mitre on center helmet, date at end of legend **Rev. Legend:** FORTITER. RECTE. PIE. ANO. **Mint:** Neuhaus **Note:** REF. S-138; W-125; Dav. 5693.

Date	Mintage	VG	F	VF	XF	Unc
1657 PL	—	1,100	2,200	4,800	8,400	—

KM# 104 THALER
28.8500 g., Silver, 45 mm. **Ruler:** Theodor Adolf **Obv:** Facing robed bust in circle **Obv. Legend:** THEODO. ADOL. EPIS. PADERBO. COM. PIRMON. **Rev:** Spanish shield of 4-fold arms of Paderborn and Recke, superimposed on crossed sword and crozier, 3 ornate helmets above, mitre on center helmet, date divided at lower left and right of arms **Rev. Legend:** THEOD. ADOLP. D. G. EPISC. PADERB. COM. PIRM. **Mint:** Neuhaus **Note:** Ref. S-151; W-130; Dav. 5694.

Date	Mintage	VG	F	VF	XF	Unc
1659	—	1,200	2,400	5,100	9,000	—

KM# 108 THALER
Silver Weight varies: 28.42-29.05g., 44 mm. **Ruler:** Ferdinand II **Obv:** Spanish shield of 4-fold arms of Paderborn and Pyrmont, superimposed on crossed sword and crozier, 3 ornate helmets above **Obv. Legend:** FERDINANDVS. D. G. EPS. PADERB. S. R. I. PRINC. COM. PYRM. **Rev:** Full-length facing figure of St. Meinolphus holding model of church, stag kneeling at lower left, date at end of legend **Rev. Legend:** S. MEINVLPHVS. DIACONVS. PADERBORNENSIS. **Mint:** Neuhaus **Note:** Ref. S-157; Dav. 5696.

Date	Mintage	VG	F	VF	XF	Unc
1663	—	550	1,150	2,100	3,600	—

KM# 110 THALER
Silver Weight varies: 27.73-29.01g., 43 mm. **Ruler:** Ferdinand II **Obv:** Facing robed bust in circle **Obv. Legend:** FERDINANDVS. D. G. EPS. PADERB. S. R. I. P. COM. PYRMON. **Rev:** Spanish shield of 4-fold arms of Paderborn and Pyrmont, superimposed on crossed sword and crozier, 3 ornate helmets above, Roman

numeral date at end of legend **Rev. Legend:** SVAVITER. ET. FORTITER. MDCLXIII. **Mint:** Neuhaus **Note:** Ref. S-158; W-153; Dav. 5698.

Date	Mintage	VG	F	VF	XF	Unc
MDCLXIIII (1663) Rare	—	—	—	—	—	—

KM# 115 THALER

Silver Weight varies: 28.27-29.19g., 43 mm. **Ruler:** Ferdinand II **Obv:** Spanish shield of 4-fold arms of Paderborn and Pyrmont, with central shield of Fürstenberg, superimposed on crossed sword and crozier, 4 ornate helmets above **Obv. Legend:** FERDINANDVS. D. G. EPS. PADERB. COAD. MONAST. S. R. I. P. COM. PYRM. **Rev:** 9-line inscription with Roman numeral dates, thin horizontal line between 6th and 7th lines **Rev. Legend:** COADIVTOR. ET. FVTVRVS. SVCCESSOR. MONASTERIENSIS. **Rev. Inscription:** ELECTVS / AN. MDCLXVII / XIX. IVL / CONFIRMATVS / AN. MDCLXVIII / XXX. APRIL / SVAVITER / ET / FORTITER. **Mint:** Neuhaus **Note:** Ref. S-162; Dav. 5699.

Date	Mintage	VG	F	VF	XF	Unc
MDCLXVIII (1668)	—	575	1,300	2,650	5,000	—

KM# 116 THALER

Silver **Ruler:** Ferdinand II **Obv:** Spanish shield of 4-fold arms of Paderborn and Pyrmont, with central shield of Fürstenberg, superimposed on crossed sword and crozier, 4 ornate helmets above **Obv. Legend:** FERDINANDVS. D. G. EPS. PADERB. COAD. MONAST. S. R. I. P. COM. PYRM. **Rev:** 9-line inscription with Roman numeral dates, thin horizontal line between 6th and 7th lines **Rev. Legend:** COADIVTOR. ET. FVTVRVS. SVCCESOR. MONASTERIENSIS. **Rev. Inscription:** ELECTVS / AN. MDCLXVIII / XXX. APRIL / SVAVITER / ET / FORTITER. **Mint:** Neuhaus **Note:** Ref. S-162.2; Dav. 5699A. Klippe.

Date	Mintage	VG	F	VF	XF	Unc
1668 Rare	—	—	—	—	—	—

KM# 117 THALER

Silver Weight varies: 28.65-28.90g., 43 mm. **Ruler:** Ferdinand II **Obv:** Spanish shield of 4-fold arms of Paderborn and Pyrmont, superimposed on crossed sword and crozier, 3 ornate helmets above **Obv. Legend:** FERDINANDVS • D•G • EPS • PADERB • S • R • I • PRINC • COM • PYRM • **Rev:** 9-line inscription with Roman numeral dates, thin horizontal line between 6th and 7th lines **Rev. Legend:** COADIVTOR • ET • FVTVRVS • SVCCESSOR • MONASTERIENSIS. **Rev. Inscription:** ELECTVS / AN • MDCLXVII / XIX • IVL / CONFIRMATVS / AN • MDCLXVIII / XXX • APRIL / SVAVITER / ET / FORTITER. **Mint:** Neuhaus **Note:** Ref. S-161; Dav. 5700.

Date	Mintage	VG	F	VF	XF	Unc
MDCLXVIII (1668)	—	575	1,300	2,650	5,000	—

KM# 119 THALER

Silver Weight varies: 28.69-29.86g., 48.5 mm. **Ruler:** Ferdinand II **Obv:** Cloaked bust turned 3/4 to right **Obv. Legend:** FERD. D. G. EPISC. PADERB. COAD. M. C. P. **Rev:** Spanish shield of 4-fold arms of Paderborn and Pyrmont, with central shield of Fürstenberg, superimposed on crossed sword and crozier, 4 ornate helmets above, date at end of legend **Rev. Legend:** SVAVITER ET FORTITER. **Mint:** Neuhaus **Note:** Ref. S-163; W-153A; Dav. 5701. Struck on broad flan. Letter E's in legends in script form.

Date	Mintage	VG	F	VF	XF	Unc
1671 Rare	—	—	—	—	—	—

KM# 120 THALER

Silver Weight varies: 28.77-28.95g., 48.5 mm. **Ruler:** Ferdinand II **Obv:** Cloaked bust turned 3/4 to right **Obv. Legend:** FERD. D. G. EPISC. PADERB. COAD. M. C. P. **Rev:** Spanish shield of 4-fold arms of Paderborn and Pyrmont, with central shield of Fürstenberg, superimposed on crossed sword and crozier, 4 ornate helmets above, date divided to lower left and right **Rev. Legend:** SVAVITER ET FORTITER. **Mint:** Neuhaus **Note:** Ref. S-164; W-153Ab; Dav. 5702. Struck on broad flan. Letter E's in legends in script form.

Date	Mintage	VG	F	VF	XF	Unc
1671 Rare	—	—	—	—	—	—

KM# 136 THALER

Silver Weight varies: 27.40-28.86g., 42 mm. **Ruler:** Ferdinand II **Obv:** Robed bust to right. band with motto above head **Obv. Legend:** FERDINAND. D. G. EPI. PAD. COAD. MON. S. R. I. P., motto: SVAVITER. ET. FORTITER. **Rev:** Spanish shield of 4-fold arms of Paderborn and Pyrmont, with central shield of Fürstenberg, superimposed on crossed sword and crozier, 4 ornate helmets above, mintmaster's initials and date divided to lower left and right of arms **Rev. Legend:** COM. PYRMONT. ET. LIB. BARO. D. FVRSTENBERG. **Mint:** Neuhaus **Note:** S-171; W-154; Dav. 5704.

Date	Mintage	VG	F	VF	XF	Unc
1676 IDK	—	1,200	2,100	3,600	6,000	—

KM# 143 THALER

Silver **Ruler:** Hermann Werner **Note:** Dav. 5707. Schwede, p. 315, no. 180, states that only Davenport lists this coin and its existence is doubtful.

Date	Mintage	VG	F	VF	XF	Unc
1683	—	—	—	—	—	—

KM# 145 THALER

Silver Weight varies: 28.22-29.47g., 44 mm. **Ruler:** Hermann Werner **Obv:** Robed bust to right **Obv. Legend:** HERMAN. WERNER. D. G. EPISCOP. PADERB. S. R. I. PRINC. **Rev:** Spanish shield of 4-fold arms of Paderborn and Pyrmont, with central shield of Wolff-Metternich, superimposed on crossed sword and crozier, divides date, 4 ornate helmets above, motto below **Rev. Legend:** COM. PYRMONT. ET. LIB. BARO. WOLF-METTERNNICH.; motto: PROVIDE ET IVSTE. **Mint:** Neuhaus **Note:** Ref. S-183; W-164; Dav. 5709.

Date	Mintage	VG	F	VF	XF	Unc
1684	—	900	1,500	3,000	5,400	—

KM# 154 THALER

Silver Weight varies: 26.53-30.52g., 44-46 mm. **Ruler:** Hermann Werner **Obv:** 3/4-length figure of St. Anthony of Padua at left, turned to right, holding Christchild, St. Mary at right in clouds, holdig wreath over St. Anthony's head, 2-line inscription in exergue **Obv. Legend:** HERMAN. WERNER. D. G. EPS. PADERB. S. R. I. PRINCEPS. **Obv. Inscription:** S. ANTONIVS DE / PADVA. **Rev:** Oval shield of 6-fold arms, with central shield of Wolff-Metternich, in baroque frame, superimposed on crossed sword and crozier, divides date, 5 ornate helmets above, motto curved below **Rev. Legend:** COM. PYRM. PRÆPOS. HILDES. ET. L. B. WOLFF. METTERNICH.; motto: PROVIDE ET IVSTE. **Mint:** Neuhaus **Note:** Ref. S-184, 189, 193; W#165-67; Dav. 5710.

Date	Mintage	VG	F	VF	XF	Unc
1685	—	280	575	1,050	2,000	—
1687 Rare	—	—	—	—	—	—
1693	—	280	575	1,050	2,000	—

KM# 159 THALER

Silver Weight varies: 28.28-28.52g., 44 mm. **Ruler:** Hermann Werner **Obv:** Robed bust to right in circle **Obv. Legend:** HERMAN. WERNER. D - G. EPISCOP. PADERB. S. R. I. PRINC. **Rev:** Oval shield of 6-fold arms, with central shield of Wolff-Metternich, in baroque frame, superimposed on crossed sword and crozier, divides date, 5 ornate helmets above, motto curved below **Rev. Legend:** COM. PYRM. PRÆPOS. HILDES. ET. L. B. WOLFF. METTERNICH.; motto: PROVIDE ET IVSTE. **Mint:** Neuhaus **Note:** Ref. S-192; W-167; Dav. 5712.

Date	Mintage	VG	F	VF	XF	Unc
1693	—	975	1,800	2,500	4,500	—

KM# 163 THALER

Silver Weight varies: 28.99-29.32g., 44 mm. **Ruler:** Hermann Werner **Obv:** Robed bust to right **Obv. Legend:** HERMAN. WERNER. D. G. EPISCOP. PADERB. S. R. I. PRINC. **Rev:** Oval shield of 6-fold arms, with central shield of Wolff-Metternich, in baroque frame, superimposed on crossed sword and crozier, large crown above, motto in large letters to lower left and right, plain date at end of legend **Rev. Legend:** COM. PYRM. PRÆPOS. HILDES. &. L. B. WOLFF. METTERNICH.; motto: PROVIDE - ET IVSTE. **Mint:** Neuhaus **Note:** Ref. S-198; W-168; Dav. 5713.

Date	Mintage	VG	F	VF	XF	Unc
1694	—	500	1,000	1,900	3,150	—

KM# 164 THALER

Silver Weight varies: 28.99-29.32g., 44 mm. **Ruler:** Hermann Werner **Obv:** Robed bust to right **Obv. Legend:** HERMAN. WERNER. D. G. EPISCOP. PADERB. S. R. I. PRINC. **Rev:** Oval shield of 6-fold arms, with central shield of Wolff-Metternich, in baroque frame, superimposed on crossed sword and crozier, crown above, motto in small letters to lower left and right, punctuated date at end of legend **Rev. Legend:** COM. PYRM. PRÆPOS. HILDES. &. L. B. WOLFF. METTERNICH.; motto: PROVIDE - ET IVSTE. **Mint:** Neuhaus **Note:** Ref. S-198; Dav. 5713A.

Date	Mintage	VG	F	VF	XF	Unc
1694	—	575	1,150	2,200	4,400	—

KM# 19 2 THALER

58.2000 g., Silver, 42 mm. **Ruler:** Dietrich IV **Obv:** Facing bust wearing vestments, turned slight to right **Obv. Legend:** THEODO. A. FVRSTENB. D. G. EC. PADER. EPIS. **Rev:** Ornate shield of 4-fold arms of Paderborn and Fürstenberg, 3 ornate helmets above, date divided to lower left and right of arms **Rev. Legend:** IVDICIVM. MELIVS. POSTERITATIS. ERIT. **Mint:** Paderborn **Note:** Ref. S-27.2; W-84; Dav. 5676.

Date	Mintage	VG	F	VF	XF	Unc
1612 Rare	—	—	—	—	—	—

KM# 22 2 THALER

58.2000 g., Silver, 43 mm. **Ruler:** Dietrich IV **Obv:** Ornate shield of 4-fold arms of Paderborn and Fürstenberg, 3 ornate helmets above **Obv. Legend:** THEODO • A • FVRSTENB • D • G • ECC • PAD • EPIS. **Rev:** Crowned imperial eagle, orb on breast, date divided by tail **Rev. Legend:** MATIAS • I • D • G • ROMA • IMP • E • SEM • AV • **Mint:** Paderborn **Note:** Ref. S-36.1; W-85; Dav. 5678.

Date	Mintage	VG	F	VF	XF	Unc
1615 Rare	—	—	—	—	—	—

KM# 26 2 THALER

50.1200 g., Silver, 44 mm. **Ruler:** Dietrich IV **Obv:** Ornate shield of 4-fold arms of Paderborn and Fürstenberg, 3 ornate helmets above **Obv. Legend:** THEODO • A • FVRSTENBERG • D • G • EPIS • PADERBOR. **Rev:** Crowned imperial eagle, orb on breast, date divided by claws and tail **Rev. Legend:** MATIAS • I • D•G • RO: IMPER: SEMPER • AVGVST • **Mint:** Brakel **Note:** Ref. S-49.1; W-86; Dav. 5679.

Date	Mintage	VG	F	VF	XF	Unc
1618 Rare	—	—	—	—	—	—

KM# 27 2 THALER

Silver Weight varies: 59.46-59.61g., 44 mm. **Ruler:** Dietrich IV **Subject:** Death of Dietrich IV **Obv:** Spanish shield of 4-fold arms of Paderborn and Fürstenberg, 3 ornate helmets above, date at end of legend **Obv. Legend:** THEODO. A. FVRSTE. D. G. EPISCOPVS. PADER. **Rev:** 7-line inscription with Roman numeral date, Roman numeral date also at end of legend **Rev. Legend:** IVDICIVM. MELIVS. POSTERITATIS. ERIT. ANNO. MDCXVIII. **Rev. Inscription:** REXIT / ANNOS. XXXIII / MENS. VI DIES / XXIIX OBITT. / .IIII. DECEMB. / ANNO / MDCXIIX. **Mint:** Brakel **Note:** Ref. S-51.1; W-256; Dav. 5682.

Date	Mintage	VG	F	VF	XF	Unc
1618//MDCXVIII Rare	—	—	—	—	—	—

KM# 48 2 THALER

57.6500 g., Silver, 42 mm. **Ruler:** Ferdinand I **Obv:** Robed bust to right in circle **Obv. Legend:** FERDINAND. D. G. ARG. COL. ELE ADM. HIL. EPI. PADERB. **Rev:** Spanish shield of 4-fold arms of Bavaria and Pfalz, with central shield of Paderborn, in baroque frame, superimposed on crossed sword and crozier, electoral hat above, date at end of legend **Rev. Legend:** FERDINANDVS. II. D. G. ROM. IMP. SEMP. AVG. **Mint:** Brakel **Note:** Ref. S-65.1; W-110; Dav. 5683.

Date	Mintage	VG	F	VF	XF	Unc
1620 Rare	—	—	—	—	—	—

KM# 49 2 THALER

Silver Weight varies: 56.22-57.98g., 42 mm. **Ruler:** Ferdinand I **Obv:** Full-length facing figure of St. Liborius, upward on left SANCTVS, downward at right LIBORIVS. **Obv. Legend:** FERDINANDVS. D. G. ARC. COL. EPI. PADERB. V. BAV. DVX. ZC. **Rev:** Spanish shield of 4-fold arms of Bavaria and Pfalz, with central shield of Paderborn, in baroque frame, superimposed on crossed sword and crozier, electoral hat above, date at end of legend **Rev. Legend:** FERDINANDVS. II. D. G. ROM. IMP. SEMP. AVGVSTVS. **Mint:** Brakel **Note:** Ref. S-63.2; W-109; Dav. A5687.

Date	Mintage	VG	F	VF	XF	Unc
1620 Rare	—	—	—	—	—	—

KM# 52 2 THALER

Silver Weight varies: 56.62-57.47g., 65 mm. **Ruler:** Ferdinand I **Obv:** Spanish shield of 4-fold arms of Bavaria and Pfalz, with central shield of Paderborn, in baroque frame, superimposed on crossed sword and crozier, electoral hat above **Obv. Legend:** FERDINANDVS. D. G. ARC. COL. EPI. PADERB. V. BAV. DVX. ZC. **Rev:** Full-length facing figure of St. Liborius, upward on left SANCTVS, downward on right LIBORIVS, date at end of legend **Rev. Legend:** FERDINANDVS. II. D. G. ROM. IMP. SEMP. AVGVSTVS. AN. **Mint:** Brakel **Note:** Ref. S-68; W-111; Dav. 5689. Struck on broad flan.

Date	Mintage	VG	F	VF	XF	Unc
1621 Rare	—	—	—	—	—	—

KM# 93 2 THALER

Silver Weight varies: 57.74-58.92g., 45 mm. **Ruler:** Theodor Adolf **Obv:** Facing robed bust in circle **Obv. Legend:** THEODO. ADOL. EPIS. PADERBO. COM. PIRMON. **Rev:** Spanish shield of 4-fold arms of Paderborn and Recke, superimposed on crossed sword and crozier, 3 ornate helmets above, mitre on center helmet, date at end of legend **Rev. Legend:** FORTITER * RECTE * PIE * AO. **Mint:** Neuhaus **Note:** Ref. S-132.1; W-122; Dav. 5691.

Date	Mintage	VG	F	VF	XF	Unc
1656 PL	—	1,900	3,750	6,600	11,500	—

KM# 109 2 THALER

57.7500 g., Silver, 44 mm. **Ruler:** Ferdinand II **Obv:** Spanish shield of 4-fold arms of Paderborn and Pyrmont, superimposed on crossed sword and crozier, 3 ornate helmets above **Obv. Legend:** FERDINANDVS. D. G. EPS. PADERB. S. R. I. PRINC. COM. PYRM. **Rev:** Full-length facing figure of St. Meinolphus holding model of church, stag kneeling at lower left, date at end of legend **Rev. Legend:** S. MEINVLPHVS. DIACONVS. PADERBORNENSIS. **Mint:** Neuhaus **Note:** Ref. S-157.2; Dav. 5695. Struck from same dies as Thaler, KM#108.

Date	Mintage	VG	F	VF	XF	Unc
1663	—	1,700	3,150	6,100	10,500	—

KM# 111 2 THALER

58.8000 g., Silver, 43 mm. **Ruler:** Ferdinand II **Obv:** Facing robed bust in circle **Obv. Legend:** FERDINANDVS. D. G. EPS. PADERB. S. R. I. P. COM. PYRMON. **Rev:** Spanish shield of 4-fold arms of Paderborn and Pyrmont, superimposed on crossed sword and crozier, 3 ornate helmets above, Roman numeral date at end of legend **Rev. Legend:** SVAVITER. ET. FORTITER. **Mint:** Neuhaus **Note:** Ref. S-158.2; Dav. 5697.

Date	Mintage	VG	F	VF	XF	Unc
MDCLXIII (1663) Rare	—	—	—	—	—	—

KM# 118 2 THALER

57.7000 g., Silver, 43 mm. **Ruler:** Ferdinand II **Obv:** Spanish shield of 4-fold arms of Paderborn and Pyrmont, with central shield of Fürstenberg, superimposed on crossed sword and crozier, 4 ornate helmets above **Obv. Legend:** FERDINANDVS. D. G. EPS. PADERB. COAD. MONAST. S. R. I. P. COM. PYRM. **Rev:** 9-line inscription with Roman numeral dates, thin horizontal line between 6th and 7th lines **Rev. Legend:** COADIVTOR. ET. FVTVRVS. SVCCESSOR. MONASTERIENSIS. **Rev. Inscription:** ELECTVS / AN. MDCLXVII / XIX. IVL / CONFIRMATVS / AN. MDCLXIII / XXX. APRIL . SVAVITER / ET / FORTITER. **Mint:** Neuhaus **Note:** Ref. S-162.1.

Date	Mintage	VG	F	VF	XF	Unc
MDCLXVIII (1668) Rare	—	—	—	—	—	—

KM# 121 2 THALER

57.9100 g., Silver, 48.5 mm. **Ruler:** Ferdinand II **Obv:** Cloaked bust turned 3/4 to right **Obv. Legend:** FERD. D. G. EPISC. PADERB. COAD. M. C. P. **Rev:** Spanish shield of 4-fold arms of Paderborn and Pyrmont, with central shield of Fürstenberg, superimposed on crossed sword and crozier, 4 ornate helmets above, date at end of legend **Rev. Legend:** SVAVITER ET FORTITER. **Mint:** Neuhaus **Note:** Ref. S-163.1; Dav. A5701. Letter E's of legends in script form.

Date	Mintage	VG	F	VF	XF	Unc
1671 Rare	—	—	—	—	—	—

KM# 137 2 THALER

Silver Weight varies: 56.79-57.40g., 42 mm. **Ruler:** Ferdinand II **Obv:** Robed bust to right, band with motto above head **Obv. Legend:** FERDINAND. D. G. EPI. PAD. COAD. MON. S. R. I. P.; motto: SVAVITER. ET. FORTITER. **Rev:** Spanish shield of 4-fold arms of Paderborn and Pyrmont, with central shield of Fürstenberg, superimposed on crossed sword and crozier, mintmaster's initials and date divided to lower left and right of arms **Rev. Legend:** COM. PYRMONT. ET. LIB. BARO. D. FVRSTENBERG. **Mint:** Neuhaus **Note:** Ref. S-171.2; W-151; Dav. 5703.

Date	Mintage	VG	F	VF	XF	Unc
1676 IDK	—	2,150	4,100	7,200	12,500	—

KM# 146 2 THALER

Silver Weight varies: 58.34-58.35g., 44 mm. **Ruler:** Hermann Werner **Obv:** Robed bust to right **Obv. Legend:** HERMAN. WERNER. D. G. EPISCOP. PADERB. S. R. I. PRINC. **Rev:** Spanish shield of 4-fld arms of Paderborn and Pyrmont, with central shield of Wolff-Metternich, superimposed on crossed sword and crozier, divides date, 4 ornate helmets above, motto below **Rev. Legend:** COM. PYRMONT. ET. LIB. BARO. WOLFF-METTERNICH.; motto: PROVIDE ET IVSTE. **Mint:** Neuhaus **Note:** Ref. S-183.2; Dav. 5708.

Date	Mintage	VG	F	VF	XF	Unc
1684 Rare	—	—	—	—	—	—

KM# 158 2 THALER

56.4000 g., Silver, 44 mm. **Ruler:** Hermann Werner **Obv:** 3/4-length figure of St. Anthony at left, turned to right, holding Christchild, St. Mary at right in clouds, holding wreath over St. Anthony's head, 2-line inscription in exergue **Obv. Legend:** HERMAN. WERNER. D. G. EPS. PADERB. S. R. I. PRINCEPS. **Rev:** Oval shield of 6-fold arms, with central shield of Wolff-Metternich, in baroque frame, divides date, superimposed on crossed sword and crozier, 5 ornate helmets above, motto curved below **Rev. Legend:** COM. PYRM. PRÆPOS. HILDES. ET. L. B. WOLFF. METTERNICH.; motto: PROVIDE ET IVSTE. **Mint:** Neuhaus **Note:** Ref. S-193.1.

Date	Mintage	VG	F	VF	XF	Unc
1693 Rare	—	—	—	—	—	—

KM# 160 2 THALER

57.3000 g., Silver, 44 mm. **Ruler:** Hermann Werner **Obv:** Robed bust to right in circle **Obv. Legend:** HERMAN. WERNER. D. G. EPISCOP. PADERB. S. R. I. PRINC. **Rev:** Oval shield of 6-fold arms, with central shield of Wolff-Metternich, in baroque frame, divides date, superimposed on crossed sword and crozier, 5 ornate helmets above, motto curved below **Rev. Legend:** COM. PYRM. PRÆPOS. HILDES. ET. L. B. WOLFF. METTERNICH.; motto: PROVIDE ET IVSTE. **Mint:** Neuhaus **Note:** Ref. S-192.3; Dav. 5711.

Date	Mintage	VG	F	VF	XF	Unc
1693 Rare	—	—	—	—	—	—

KM# 166 2 THALER

Silver **Ruler:** Hermann Werner **Note:** Dav. 5714. Schwede, p. 332, no. 201, doubts the existence of this coin, stating that the date may be misconstrued from 1693.

Date	Mintage	VG	F	VF	XF	Unc
1698 Unknown	—	—	—	—	—	—

KM# 50 3 THALER

Silver, 42 mm. **Ruler:** Ferdinand I **Obv:** Full-length facing figure of St. Liborius, upward on left SANCTVS, downward at right LIBORIVS **Obv. Legend:** FERDINANDVS. D. G. ARC. COL. EPI. PADERB. V. BAV. DVX. ZC. **Rev:** Spanish shield of 4-fold arms of Bavaria and Pfalz, with central shield of Paderborn, in baroque frame, superimposed on crossed sword and crozier, electoral hat above, date at end of legend **Rev. Legend:** FERDINANDVS. II. D. G. ROM. IMP. SEMP. AVGVSTVS. **Mint:** Brakel **Note:** Ref. S-63.1; Dav. 5687.

Date	Mintage	VG	F	VF	XF	Unc
1620 Rare	—	—	—	—	—	—

TRADE COINAGE

KM# 69 DUCAT

3.5000 g., 0.9860 Gold Weight varies: 3.36-3.51g. 0.1109 oz.

AGW, 23 mm. **Ruler:** Theodor Adolf **Obv:** Robed facing bust, turned slightly to right **Obv. Legend:** THE. ADOL. EP. PA. D. CO. PIRM. **Rev:** Oval shield of 4-fold arms of Paderborn and Recke, superimposed on crossed sword and crozier, mitre above divides date **Rev. Legend:** FORTITER. RECTE. PIE. **Mint:** Neuhaus **Note:** Ref. S-93; W-121; Fr. 1958.

Date	Mintage	VG	F	VF	XF	Unc
1653 (c)	—	3,300	6,600	11,000	20,500	—

KM# 107 DUCAT

3.4500 g., Gold, 23 mm. **Ruler:** Ferdinand II **Obv:** Facing robed bust **Obv. Legend:** FERDINANDVS. D. G. EPS. PADERB. **Rev:** Oval shield of 4-fold arms of Paderborn and Fürstenberg, superimposed on crossed sword and crozier, hat above, date at end of legend **Rev. Legend:** S. R. I. PRIN. COM. PYRM. **Mint:** Neuhaus **Note:** Ref. S-156.

Date	Mintage	VG	F	VF	XF	Unc
1663	—	—	—	—	—	—

KM# 125 DUCAT

3.5000 g., 0.9860 Gold Weight varies: 3.15-3.46g. 0.1109 oz. AGW, 23 mm. **Ruler:** Ferdinand II **Obv:** Mantled bust to right, motto in band above head **Obv. Legend:** FERDINAND D. G. EPI. PADERB. COADI. MONAST.; motto: SVAVITER ET FORTITER. **Rev:** Spanish shield of 4-fold arms, with central shield of Fürstenberg, superimposed on crossed sword and crozier, 2 ornate helmets above, date divided at lower left and right of arms **Rev. Legend:** S. R. I. PRINCEPS. COM. PYRMONT. L. B. DE. FURSTENBERG. **Mint:** Neuhaus **Note:** Ref. S-167; W-149; Fr. 1960.

Date	Mintage	VG	F	VF	XF	Unc
1674	—	2,750	5,500	10,500	19,500	—

Note: UBS Auction 55, 9-02, XF realized approximately $15,000.

KM# 147.1 DUCAT

3.5000 g., 0.9860 Gold Weight varies: 3.43-3.45g. 0.1109 oz. AGW, 23 mm. **Ruler:** Hermann Werner **Obv:** Robed bust to right **Obv. Legend:** HERMAN. WERNER. D. G. EPISCOPVS. PADERB. S. R. I. PRINC. **Rev:** Spanish shield of 4-fold arms of Paderborn and Pyrmont, with central shield of Wolff-Metternich, superimposed on crossed sword and crozier, divides date, 4 ornate helmets above, motto curved below **Rev. Legend:** COMES. PYRMONT. ET. LIB. BARO. WOLF. METTERNICH.; motto: PROVIDE ET IVSTE. **Mint:** Neuhaus **Note:** Ref. S-182; W-161; Fr. 1961.

Date	Mintage	VG	F	VF	XF	Unc
1684	—	2,450	5,000	10,000	21,500	—

KM# 147.2 DUCAT

Gold Weight varies: 3.41-3.48g., 23 mm. **Ruler:** Hermann Werner **Obv:** Robed bust to right **Obv. Legend:** HERMAN. WERNER. D. G. EPISCOPVS. PADERB. S. R. I. PRINC. **Rev:** Oval shield of 4-fold arms of Paderborn and Pyrmont, with central shield of Wolff-Metternich, superimposed on crossed sword and crozier, divides date, 4 ornate helmets above, motto curved below **Rev. Legend:** COMES. PYRMONT. ET. LIB. BARO. WOLFF. METTERNICH.; motto: PROVIDE ET IVSTE. **Mint:** Neuhaus **Note:** Ref. S-191, 200; W-162; Fr. 1961.

Date	Mintage	VG	F	VF	XF	Unc
1693	—	2,450	4,750	10,000	21,500	—
1698	—	—	—	—	—	—

Note: Schwede doubts existence of this date.

KM# A114 2 DUCAT

7.6600 g., Gold, 28 mm. **Ruler:** Ferdinand II **Obv:** Facing robed bust, turned slight to right **Obv. Legend:** FERD. D. G. EPS. PADER. S. R. I. PRIN. COM. PYRM. **Rev:** Oval shield of 4-fold arms of Paderborn and Pyrmont in baroque frame, superimposed on crossed sword and crozier, hat above, date at end of Greek legend meaning "agreeably and firmly." **Rev. Legend:** ??????OS - ?????OS. **Mint:** Neuhaus **Note:** Ref. S-159.1. Struck from 1/4 Thaler dies, KM#106.

Date	Mintage	VG	F	VF	XF	Unc
1663 Rare	12	—	—	—	—	—

KM# 112 6 DUCAT

Gold Weight varies: 20.77-20.98g., 44 mm. **Ruler:** Ferdinand II **Obv:** Spanish shield of 4-fold arms of Paderborn and Pyrmont, superimposed on crossed sword and crozier, 3 ornate helmets above **Obv. Legend:** FERDINANDVS. D. G. EPS. PADERB. S. R. I. PRINC. COM. PYRM. **Rev:** Full-length facing figure of St. Meinolphus holdling model of church, stag kneeling at lower left, date at end of legend **Rev. Legend:** S. MEINVLPHVS. DIACONVS. PADERBORNENSIS. **Mint:** Neuhaus **Note:** Ref. S-157.1. Struck from Thaler dies, KM#108.

Date	Mintage	VG	F	VF	XF	Unc
1663 Rare	—	—	—	—	—	—

KM# 113 6 DUCAT

20.7800 g., Gold, 43 mm. **Ruler:** Ferdinand II **Obv:** Facing robed bust in circle **Obv. Legend:** FERDINANDVS. D. G. EPS. PADERB. S. R. I. P. COM. PYRMON. **Rev:** Spanish shield of 4-fold arms of Paderborn and Pyrmont, superimposed on crossed sword and crozier, 3 ornate helmets above, Roman numeral date at end of legend **Rev. Legend:** SVAVITER. ET. FORTITER. **Mint:** Neuhaus **Note:** Ref. S-158.1. Struck from Thaler dies, KM#110.

Date	Mintage	VG	F	VF	XF	Unc
MDCLXIII (1663) Rare	—	—	—	—	—	—

KM# 139 6 DUCAT

21.0000 g., 0.9860 Gold Weight varies: 20.05-22.30g. 0.6657 oz. AGW, 42 mm. **Ruler:** Ferdinand II **Obv:** Robed bust to right, band with motto above head **Obv. Legend:** FERDINAND. D. G. EPI. PAD. COAD. MON. S. R. I. P.; motto: SVAVITER. ET. FORTITER. **Rev:** Spanish shield of 4-fold arms of Paderborn and Pyrmont, with central shield of Fürstenberg, superimposed on crossed sword and crozier, 4 ornate helmets above, mintmaster's initials and date divided to lower left and right of arms **Rev. Legend:** COM. PYRMONT. ET. LIB. BARO. D. FVRSTENBERG. **Mint:** Neuhaus **Note:** Ref. S-171.1; Fr. 1959. Struck from Thaler dies, KM#136.

Date	Mintage	VG	F	VF	XF	Unc
1676 IDK Rare	—	—	—	—	—	—

KM# 148 6 DUCAT

21.0000 g., 0.9860 Gold Weight varies: 20.39-21.00g. 0.6657 oz. AGW, 44 mm. **Ruler:** Hermann Werner **Obv:** Robed bust to right **Obv. Legend:** HERMAN. WERNER. D. G. EPISCOP. PADERB. S. R. I. PRINC. **Rev:** Spanish shield of 4-fold arms of Paderborn and Pyrmont, with central shield of Wolff-Metternich, superimposed on crossed sword and crozier, divides date, 4 ornate helmets above, motto below **Rev. Legend:** COM. PYRMONT. ET. LIB. BARO. WOLF. METTERNICH.; motto: PROVIDE ET IVSTE. **Mint:** Neuhaus **Note:** Ref. S-183.1; Fr. 1960a. Struck from Thaler dies, KM#145.

Date	Mintage	VG	F	VF	XF	Unc
1684 Rare	—	—	—	—	—	—

KM# 161 6 DUCAT

Gold Weight varies: 20.24-21.14g., 44 mm. **Ruler:** Hermann Werner **Obv:** Robed bust to right in circle **Obv. Legend:** HERMAN. WERNER. D. G. EPISCOP. PADERB. S. R. I. PRINC. **Rev:** Oval shield of 6-fold arms, with central shield of Wolff-Metternich, in baroque frame, divides date, superimposed on crossed sword and crozier, 5 ornate helmets above, motto curved below **Rev. Legend:** COM. PYRM. PRÆPOS. HILDES. ET. L. B. WOLFF. METTERNNICH.; motto: PROVIDE ET IVSTE. **Mint:** Neuhaus **Note:** Ref. S-192.2. Struck from Thaler dies, KM#159.

Date	Mintage	VG	F	VF	XF	Unc
1693 Rare	—	—	—	—	—	—

KM# 165 6 DUCAT

21.1400 g., Gold, 44 mm. **Ruler:** Hermann Werner **Obv:** Small robed bust to right in circle **Obv. Legend:** HERMAN. WERNER. D. G. EPISCOP. PADERB. S. R. I. PRINC. **Rev:** Oval shield of 6-fold arms, with central shield of Wolff-Metternich, in baroque frame, superimposed on crossed sword and crozier, crown above, motto in small letters to lower left and right, date at end of legend **Rev. Legend:** COM. PYRM. PRÆPOS. HILDES. &. L. B. WOLFF. METTERNICH.; motto: PROVIDE - ET IVSTE. **Mint:** Neuhaus **Note:** Ref. S-198.2. Struck from Thaler dies, KM#164.

Date	Mintage	VG	F	VF	XF	Unc
1694 Rare	—	—	—	—	—	—

KM# 155 7 DUCAT

24.1600 g., Gold, 45 mm. **Ruler:** Hermann Werner **Obv:** 3/4-length figure of St. Anthony at left, turned to right, holding Christchild, St. Mary at right in clouds, holding wreath over St Anthony's head, 2-line inscription in exergue **Obv. Legend:** HERMAN. WERNER. D. G. EPS. PADERB. S. R. I. PRINCEPS. **Obv. Inscription:** S. ANTONIVS DE / PADVA. **Rev:** Oval shield of 6-fold arms, with central shield of Wolff-Metternich, in baroque frame, divides date, superimposed on crossed sword and crozier, 5 ornate helmets above, motto curved below **Rev. Legend:** COM. PYRM. PRÆPOS. HILDES. ET. L. B. WOLFF. METTERICH.; motto: PROVIDE ET IVSTE. **Mint:** Neuhaus **Note:** Ref. S-184.1. Struck from Thaler dies, KM#154.

Date	Mintage	VG	F	VF	XF	Unc
1685 Rare	—	—	—	—	—	—

KM# A162 7 DUCAT

23.7300 g., Gold, 44 mm. **Ruler:** Hermann Werner **Obv:** Robed bust to right in circle **Obv. Legend:** HERMAN. WERNER. D. G. EPISCOP. PADERB. S. R. I. PRINC. **Rev:** Oval shield of 6-fold arms, with central shield of Wolff-Metternich, in baroque frame, divides date, superimposed on crossed sword and crozier, 5 ornate helmets above, motto curved below **Rev. Legend:** COM. PYRM. PRÆPOS. HILDES. ET. L. B. WOLFF. METTERNICH.; motto: PROVIDE ET IVSTE. **Mint:** Neuhaus **Note:** Ref. S-192.1. Struck from Thaler dies, KM#159.

Date	Mintage	VG	F	VF	XF	Unc
1693 Rare	—	—	—	—	—	—

KM# 20 10 DUCAT

35.0600 g., Gold, 42 mm. **Ruler:** Dietrich IV **Obv:** Facing bust wearing vestments, turned slight to right **Obv. Legend:** THEODO. A. FVRSTENB. D. G. EC. PADER. EPIS. **Rev:** Ornate shield of 4-fold arms of Paderborn and Fürstenberg, 3 ornate helmets above, date divided to lower left and right of arms **Rev. Legend:** IVDICIVM. MELIVS. POSTERITATIS. ERIT. **Mint:** Paderborn **Note:** Ref. S-27.1.

Date	Mintage	VG	F	VF	XF	Unc
1612 Rare	—	—	—	—	—	—

KM# A166 10 DUCAT

34.8500 g., Gold, 44 mm. **Ruler:** Hermann Werner **Obv:** Large robed bust to right in circle **Obv. Legend:** HERMAN. WERNER. D. G. EPISCOP. PADERB. S. R. I. PRINC. **Rev:** Oval shield of 6-fold arms, with central shield of Wolff-Metternich, in baroque frame, superimposed on crossed sword and crozier, large crown above, motto in large letters to lower left and right, date at end of legend **Rev. Legend:** COM. PYRM. PRÆPOS. HILDES. &. L. B. WOLFF. METTERNICH.; motto: PROVIDE - ET IVSTE. **Mint:** Neuhaus **Note:** Ref. S-198.1.

Date	Mintage	VG	F	VF	XF	Unc
1694 Rare	—	—	—	—	—	—

KM# 53 12 DUCAT

42.0000 g., Gold, 65 mm. **Ruler:** Ferdinand I **Obv:** Spanish shield of 4-fold arms of Bavaria and Pfalz, with central shield of Paderborn, in baroque frame, superimposed on crossed sword and crozier, electoral hat above **Obv. Legend:** FERDINANDVS. D. G. ARC. COL. EPI. PADERB. V. BAV. DVX. ZC. **Rev:** Full-length facing figure of St. Liborius, upward on left SANCTVS, downward on right LIBORIVS, date at end of legend **Rev. Legend:** FERDINANDVS. II. D. G. ROM. IMP. SEMP. AVGVSTVS. AN. **Mint:** Brakel **Note:** Ref. S-68.1; W-108. Struck from 2 Thaler dies, KM#52.

Date	Mintage	VG	F	VF	XF	Unc
1621 Rare	—	—	—	—	—	—

CATHEDRAL CHAPTER

REGULAR COINAGE

KM# 303 PFENNIG (1/12 Schilling)

Copper, 15 mm. **Obv:** Bishop's mitre **Obv. Legend:** CAP. PAD. **Rev:** Large I between 2 pellets, date in legend **Rev. Legend:** ANNO. **Mint:** Rietberg **Note:** Ref. S-358; W-687.

Date	Mintage	Good	VG	F	VF	XF
1617 (cc)	127,260	40.00	70.00	125	200	—

KM# 309 PFENNIG (1/12 Schilling)

Copper, 15 mm. **Obv:** Cross in circle of pellets **Obv. Legend:** CAP. PAD. **Rev:** Large I between 2 pellets in circle of pellets **Rev. Legend:** ANNO. **Mint:** Paderborn **Note:** Ref. S-360; W-689.

Date	Mintage	Good	VG	F	VF	XF
1618	—	35.00	60.00	90.00	170	—

KM# 312 PFENNIG (1/12 Schilling)

Copper **Obv:** Half-length figure of St. Liborius, turned 3/4 to right, divides S - L, all in ornamented double circle. **Rev:** Value I in ornamented double circle, small shield with P above, small shield with W below **Mint:** Paderborn **Note:** Ref. W-683.

Date	Mintage	Good	VG	F	VF	XF
ND(ca1627)	—	—	—	—	—	—

KM# 304 3 PFENNING (Dreier=1/4 Schilling)

Copper, 18.5 mm. **Obv:** Bishop's mitre in circle of pellets **Obv. Legend:** CAP. - PAD. **Rev:** Large III in circle of pellets, date in legend **Rev. Legend:** ANNO. **Mint:** Rietberg **Note:** Ref. S-357; W-686.

Date	Mintage	Good	VG	F	VF	XF
1617 (cc)	71,568	40.00	70.00	100	180	—

KM# 310 3 PFENNING (Dreier=1/4 Schilling)

Copper, 18 mm. **Obv:** Cross in circle of pellets **Obv. Legend:** CAP. PADERB. **Rev:** Large III in circle of pellets, date in legend **Rev. Legend:** ANNO. DNI. **Mint:** Paderborn **Note:** Ref. S-359; W-688.

Date	Mintage	Good	VG	F	VF	XF
1618	—	35.00	60.00	90.00	170	—

KM# 313 3 PFENNING (Dreier=1/4 Schilling)

Copper, 21 mm. **Obv:** Half-length figure of St. Liborius, turned 3/4 to right, divides S - L, all i ornamented double circle **Rev:** Value III in ornamented double circle, B to right, I above and PP below **Mint:** Paderborn **Note:** Ref. W-681a.

Date	Mintage	Good	VG	F	VF	XF
ND(ca1627)	—	—	—	—	—	—

KM# 305 4 PFENNING

Copper, 19 mm. **Obv:** Bust of St. Liborius to right in circle of pellets **Obv. Legend:** CAP. PAD. **Rev:** Large IIII in circle of pellets, date in legend **Rev. Legend:** ANNO. **Mint:** Rietberg **Note:** Ref. S-356; W-685. 1/3 Schilling.

Date	Mintage	Good	VG	F	VF	XF
1617 (cc)	66,780	35.00	60.00	90.00	170	—

KM# 306 6 PFENNING

Copper, 23 mm. **Obv:** Bust of St. Liborius to right in circle of pellets **Obv. Legend:** CAPITVLVM. PADE(R)B(O). **Rev:** Large VI in circle of pellets, date in legend **Rev. Legend:** ANNO. **Mint:** Rietberg **Note:** Ref. S-355; W-684. 1/2 Schilling.

Date	Mintage	Good	VG	F	VF	XF
1617 (cc)	81,774	100	200	350	575	—

KM# 314 6 PFENNING

Copper, 29 mm. **Obv:** Half-length figure of St. Liborius, turned 3/4 to right, divides S - L, all in ornamented double circle **Rev:** Value VI in shield, VI : I above, B.P. P below **Mint:** Paderborn **Note:** Ref. W-681. 1/2 Schilling.

Date	Mintage	Good	VG	F	VF	XF
ND(ca1627)	—	—	—	—	—	—

KM# 307 12 PFENNIG (Schilling)

Copper, 28 mm. **Obv:** Bust of St. Liborius to right in circle of pellets **Obv. Legend:** CAPITVLVM. PADER(BO). **Rev:** Large XII in circle of pellets, date in legend **Rev. Legend:** ANNO. **Mint:** Rietberg **Note:** Ref. S-354; W-683.

Date	Mintage	Good	VG	F	VF	XF
1617 (cc)	66,864	200	325	550	900	—

KM# 315 12 PFENNIG (Schilling)

Copper, 30 mm. **Obv:** Half-length figure of St. Liborius, turned 3/4 to right, divides S - L, all in ornamented double circle **Rev:** Value XII in center, with date divided 1.6. above and 2.7. below. **Mint:** Paderborn **Note:** Ref. W-677.

Date	Mintage	Good	VG	F	VF	XF
1627	—	55.00	100	140	275	—

KM# 316 12 PFENNIG (Schilling)

Copper, 30 mm. **Obv:** Half-length figure of St. Liborius, turned 3/4 to right, divides S - L, all in ornamented double circle **Rev:** Value XII in center, countermarks XII : PP above and X - B below center **Mint:** Paderborn **Note:** Ref. W-678.

Date	Mintage	Good	VG	F	VF	XF
ND(ca1627)	—	100	175	325	550	—

KM# 317 12 PFENNIG (Schilling)

Copper, 30 mm. **Obv:** Half-length figure of St. Liborius, turned 3/4 to right, divides S - L, all in ornamented double circle **Rev:** Value BL and X.II countermarks in center **Mint:** Paderborn **Note:** Ref. W-379.

Date	Mintage	Good	VG	F	VF	XF
ND(ca1627)	—	80.00	140	200	375	—

KM# 322 MARIENGROSCHEN (1/36 Thaler)

Silver Weight varies: 1.18-1.54g., 22 mm. **Ruler:** Sede Vacante **Obv:** Facing bust of St. Liborius, date in exergue **Obv. Legend:** S. LIBORIVS. **Rev:** 3-line inscription **Rev. Legend:** CAPIT. PADERB. SEDE. VACAN. **Rev. Inscription:** 36 / EINE / THALER. **Mint:** Unknown **Note:** Ref. S-179; W-252.

Date	Mintage	VG	F	VF	XF	Unc
1683	—	150	275	400	625	—

KM# 318 3 SCHILLING

Copper, 30 mm. **Obv:** Half-length figure of St. Liborius, turned 3/4 to right, divides S - L, all in ornamented double circle **Rev:** Value S.I.I.I. in center, date divided above and below **Mint:** Paderborn **Note:** Ref. W-675.

Date	Mintage	Good	VG	F	VF	XF
1627	—	80.00	140	200	300	—

KM# 319 3 SCHILLING

Copper, 30 mm. **Obv:** Half-length figure of St. Liborius, turned 3/4 to right, divides S - L, all in ornamented double circle **Rev:** Value S.I.I.I. divides PP - B, date divided above and below **Mint:** Paderborn **Note:** Ref. W-676.

Date	Mintage	Good	VG	F	VF	XF
1627	—	80.00	140	200	375	—

KM# 324 THALER

Silver Weight varies: 27.81-29.15g., 44.5 mm. **Ruler:** Sede Vacante **Obv:** Facing 1/2-length figure of St. Liborius holding crozier, 2-line inscription in exergue, date divided in margin at top **Obv. Legend:** CAPITUL. CATHED. PADERB. SEDE. VACANTE. **Obv. Inscription:** S. LIBORIUS / PATRONUS. **Rev:** Facing 1/2-length figure of Charlemagne holding orb and scepter, 2-line inscription in exergue **Rev. Legend:** FUNDATUM - CONSERVA. **Rev. Inscription:** S. CAROL9 MAGNUS / FUNDATOR. **Mint:** Unknown **Note:** Ref. S-178; W-251; Dav. 5706.

Date	Mintage	VG	F	VF	XF	Unc
1683	—	350	750	1,600	2,800	5,500

DAV# 325 2 THALER

57.8000 g., Silver, 44.5 mm. **Ruler:** Sede Vacante **Obv:** Facing 1/2-length figure of St. Liborius holding crozier, 2-line inscription in exergue, date divided in margin at top **Obv. Legend:** CAPITUL. CATHED. PADERB. SEDE. VACANTE. **Obv. Inscription:** S. LIBORIUS / PATRONUS. **Rev:** Facing 1/2-length figure of Charlemagne holding orb and scepter, 2-line inscription in exergue **Rev. Legend:** FUNDATUM - CONSERVA. **Rev. Inscription:** S. CAROL9 MAGNUS / FUNDATOR. **Mint:** Unknown **Note:** Ref. S-178.2; Dav. #5705.

Date	Mintage	VG	F	VF	XF	Unc
1683	—	1,000	1,800	3,600	6,100	—

TRADE COINAGE

KM# 326 6 DUCAT

20.3000 g., Gold, 44.5 mm. **Ruler:** Sede Vacante **Obv:** Facing 1/2-length figure of St. Liborius holding crozier, 2-line inscription in exergue, date divided in margin at top **Obv. Legend:** CAPITUL. CATHED. PADERB. SEDE. VACANTE. **Obv. Inscription:** S. LIBORIUS / PATRONUS. **Rev:** Facing 1/2-length figure of Charlemagne holding orb and scepter, 2-line inscription in exergue **Rev. Legend:** FUNDATUM - CONSERVA. **Rev. Inscription:** S. CAROL9 MAGNUS / FUNDATOR. **Mint:** Unknown **Note:** Ref. S-178.1. Struck from Thaler dies, KM#324.

Date	Mintage	VG	F	VF	XF	Unc
1683 Rare	—	—	—	—	—	—

CITY

REGULAR COINAGE

KM# 353.1 PFENNIG (1/12 Schilling)

Copper, 15 mm. **Obv:** Shield of city arms in circle of pellets **Obv. Legend:** STADT. PAD(E)(I)RBORN. **Rev:** Value • I • in circle, date in legend **Rev. Legend:** T. ?. ANNO. **Mint:** Paderborn **Note:** Ref. S-366; W-697.

Date	Mintage	Good	VG	F	VF	XF
1605	—	7.00	16.00	28.00	55.00	—

KM# 353.2 PFENNIG (1/12 Schilling)

Copper, 15 mm. **Obv:** Shield of city arms in circle of pellets **Obv. Legend:** STADT. PAD(E)(I)RBOR. **Rev:** Value • I • in oval of pellets, date in legend **Rev. Legend:** T. ?. ANNO. **Mint:** Paderborn **Note:** Ref. S-367; W#698-700. Varieties exist.

Date	Mintage	Good	VG	F	VF	XF
1605	—	7.00	16.00	28.00	55.00	—

KM# 353.3 PFENNIG (1/12 Schilling)

Copper, 15 mm. **Obv:** Shield of city arms in circle of pellets **Obv. Legend:** STADT. PADERBORN. **Rev:** Value small • I • in double ornamented oval of pellets, date in legend **Rev. Legend:** T. ?. ANNO. **Mint:** Paderborn **Note:** Ref. S-368; W-701, 703.

Date	Mintage	Good	VG	F	VF	XF
1605	—	7.00	16.00	28.00	55.00	—

KM# 353.4 PFENNIG (1/12 Schilling)

Copper, 15 mm. **Obv:** Shield of city arms in circle of pellets **Obv. Legend:** STADT. PAD(E)(I)RBORN. **Rev:** Value I in pointillate circle, date in legend **Rev. Legend:** T. ?. ANNO. **Mint:** Paderborn **Note:** Ref. S-369; W-702.

Date	Mintage	Good	VG	F	VF	XF
1605	—	7.00	16.00	28.00	55.00	—

KM# 353.5 PFENNIG (1/12 Schilling)

Copper, 15 mm. **Obv:** Shield of city arms in circle of pellets **Obv. Legend:** STADT. PAD(E)(I)RBORN. **Rev:** Value I in center without circle around, date in legend **Rev. Legend:** T. ?. ANNO. **Mint:** Paderborn **Note:** Ref. S-370.

Date	Mintage	Good	VG	F	VF	XF
1605	—	7.00	16.00	28.00	55.00	—

KM# 359 PFENNIG (1/12 Schilling)

Copper, 15 mm. **Obv:** Shield of city arms in circle of pellets **Obv. Legend:** STAD(T). PADERBORN. **Rev:** Value *I* in circle of pellets, date at end of legend **Rev. Legend:** FERDINAND. **Mint:** Paderborn **Note:** Ref. S-374, 375; W-709. Kipper coinage.

Date	Mintage	Good	VG	F	VF	XF
16ZZ	82,404	35.00	60.00	90.00	170	—

KM# 354 2 PFENNIG

Copper, 17 mm. **Obv:** Shield of city arms in baroque frame within circle **Obv. Legend:** STADT. PADERBORN. **Rev:** Value I•I in ornamented square within circle, date in legend **Rev. Legend:** T. ?. ANNO. **Mint:** Paderborn **Note:** Ref. S-365; W-696. 1/6 Schilling.

Date	Mintage	Good	VG	F	VF	XF
1605	—	9.00	20.00	35.00	65.00	—

KM# 355.1 3 PFENNING (Dreier=1/4 Schilling)

Copper, 18 mm. **Obv:** Shield of city arms in circle of pellets **Obv. Legend:** STADT. PAD(E)(I)RBORN. **Rev:** Value III in square within circle of pellets, date in legend **Rev. Legend:** THEO. ?O???. **Mint:** Paderborn **Note:** Ref. S-363; W-695d-f.

Date	Mintage	Good	VG	F	VF	XF
1605	—	9.00	20.00	35.00	65.00	—

KM# 355.2 3 PFENNING (Dreier=1/4 Schilling)

Copper, 18 mm. **Obv:** Shield of city arms in baroque frame within circle of pellets **Obv. Legend:** STADT. PAD(E)(I)RBORN. **Rev:** Value III in ornamented square within circle of pellets, date in legend **Rev. Legend:** THEO. ?O???. **Mint:** Paderborn **Note:** Ref. S-364; W-695a-c.

Date	Mintage	Good	VG	F	VF	XF
1605	—	9.00	20.00	35.00	65.00	—

KM# 361 3 PFENNING (Dreier=1/4 Schilling)
Copper, 18 mm. **Obv:** Ornate shield of city arms in circle of pellets **Obv. Legend:** STADT. PADERBORN. **Rev:** Value III in circle of pellets, date at end of legend **Rev. Legend:** FERDINAND. **Mint:** Paderborn **Note:** Ref. S-373; W-707. Kipper coinage.

Date	Mintage	Good	VG	F	VF	XF
16ZZ	107,520	18.00	40.00	65.00	125	—

KM# 362 4 PFENNING
Copper, 19 mm. **Obv:** Ornate shield of city arms in circle of pellets **Obv. Legend:** STADT. PADERBORN. **Rev:** Value IIII in circle of pellets, date at end of legend **Rev. Legend:** FERDINAND. **Mint:** Paderborn **Note:** Ref. S-371, 372; W-704, 705. Kipper 1/3 Schilling.

Date	Mintage	Good	VG	F	VF	XF
16ZZ	144,967	18.00	40.00	65.00	125	—

KM# 356 6 PFENNING
Copper, 22 mm. **Obv:** Shield of city arms in baroque frame within circle **Obv. Legend:** STADT. PADERBORN. **Rev:** Value VI in ornamented square, date above, all in circle **Rev. Legend:** THEODORI.... **Mint:** Paderborn **Note:** Ref. S-362; W-694.

Date	Mintage	Good	VG	F	VF	XF
1605	—	20.00	45.00	90.00	180	325

KM# 357 12 PFENNIG (Schilling)
Copper, 25 mm. **Obv:** Shield of city arms in baroque frame withiin circle, date at end of legend **Obv. Legend:** STADT. PADERBORN. **Rev:** Value XII i ornamented double circle **Rev. Legend:** THEODORI. ... **Mint:** Paderborn **Note:** Ref. S-361; W-693.

Date	Mintage	Good	VG	F	VF	XF
1605	—	100	175	300	400	575

REGULAR COINAGE

PATTERNS

Including off metal strikes

KM#	Date	Mintage	Identification	Mkt Val
Pn1	ND(1592)	—	Goldgulden. Silver. 4.6300 g. 23x23 mm. MB#3. S-2.1. Klippe.	—
Pn2	1605	—	6 Pfenning. Gold. KM#356.	—
Pn3	1605	—	6 Pfenning. Silver. KM#356.	—
Pn4	1605	—	12 Pfennig. Gold. KM#357.	—
Pn5	1605	—	12 Pfennig. Silver. KM#357.	—
Pn7	1612	—	2 Thaler. Lead. KM#19.	—
Pn6	1612	—	Thaler. Lead. KM#18.	—
Pn8	1620	—	Thaler. Lead. KM#46.	—
Pn9	16ZZ	—	Pfennig. Silver. KM#359.	—
Pn10	16ZZ	—	3 Pfenning. Silver. KM#361.	—
Pn45	16ZZ	—	4 Pfenning. Silver. KM#362.	—
Pn12	1656 PL	—	Thaler. Tin. KM#92.	—
Pn13	1656 PL	—	Thaler. Lead. KM#92.	—
Pn14	1657 IDK (c)	—	1/2 Thaler. Lead. KM#96.	—
Pn15	1658 IDK (c)	—	1/2 Thaler. Lead. KM#100.1.	—
Pn16	1663	—	Thaler. Tin. KM#108.	—
Pn17	1663	—	Thaler. Lead. KM#108.	—
Pn18	MDCLXIII (1663)	—	Thaler. Lead. KM#110.	—
Pn19	1676 IDK	—	Thaler. Lead. KM#136.	—
Pn20	1683	—	Thaler. Lead. KM#324.	—
Pn21	1685	—	Thaler. Lead. KM#154.	—
Pn22	1693	—	3 Pfenning. Silver. KM#141.	—
Pn23	1693	—	Thaler. Lead. KM#159.	—
Pn24	1706	—	6 Pfenning. Silver. KM#173.2.	—
Pn25	1709 JW	—	Thaler. Copper. KM#178.	—
Pn26	1712	—	Mariengroschen. Copper. KM#183.1.	—
Pn27	1712 AP	—	Thaler. Tin. KM#185.1.	—
Pn28	1712 AP	—	Thaler. Lead. KM#185.1.	—
Pn29	1713 AP	—	Thaler. Lead. KM#185.2.	—
Pn26	1714	—	Mariengroschen. Copper. KM#183.1.	—
Pn31	1714 WR	—	Mariengroschen. Copper. KM#183.2.	—
Pn32	1716 AGP	—	Thaler. Tin. KM#191.	—
Pn33	1718 AGP	—	Thaler. Lead. KM#191.	—
Pn34	1719	—	Thaler. Lead. KM#327.	—
Pn35	1719	—	Thaler. Lead. KM#328.	—
Pn36	1761	—	Thaler. Tin. KM#335.	—
Pn37	MDCCLXIII (1763)	—	Thaler. Tin. KM#230.	—
Pn38	MDCCLXIII (1763)	—	Thaler. Lead. KM#230.	—
Pn39	1764 AS	—	2/3 Thaler. Lead. KM#238.	—
Pn40	1765 AS	—	Thaler. Lead. KM#239.	—
Pn43	1766 AS	—	Pfennig. Silver. KM#246.	—
Pn42	1766 AS	—	Thaler. Tin. KM#249	—
Pn43	1767 AS	—	Pfennig. Silver. KM#246.	—
Pn44	1767 AS	—	Thaler. Lead. KM#256.	—
Pn46	1767 AS	—	5 Thaler. Copper. KM#244.	—
	1769 AS	—	5 Thaler. Copper. KM#244.	—
Pn47	1777 AS	—	Ducat. Copper. KM#260.	—
Pn48	1784	—	Ducat. Copper. KM#264.	—

PASSAU

The Bishopric, in Bavaria, near the Austrian border, was established in 738. The bishops obtained the mint right prior to 999 but they originally struck coins jointly at the imperial mint in Passau. Ecclesiastical coinage began in the 12th century. In 1803, Passau was secularized and divided between Bavaria and Salzburg. In 1805 Bavaria absorbed the Salzburg portion.

RULERS

Leopold, Erzherzog von Österreich, 1598-1625
Leopold Wilhelm, Erzherzog von Österreich, 1625-1662
Karl Josef, Erzherzog von Österreich, 1662-1664
Wenzeslaus, Graf von Thun, 1664-1673
Sebastian, Graf von Pötting, 1673-1689
Johann Philipp, Graf von Lamberg, 1689-1712

ARMS

Springing or rampant wolf, usually 1 and w/arms of bishop's own family.

MINT OFFICIALS' INITIALS

Initial	Date	Name
	1622-32	Martin Schall in Gebweiler
	Ca. 1680	Friedrich Schattauer
(a)= Pinecone between 2 horseshoes	1668-97	Johann Christoph Holeisen in Augsburg
M*F or MF	1674-1700	Michael Federer, mintmaster and die-cutter in Regensburg
PHM or (b)= star	1677-1718	Philipp Heinrich Müller, die-cutter in Augsburg
SEIZ	Ca. 1688-1706	V. Seiz, die-cutter in Passau and Salzburg

BISHOPRIC

REGULAR COINAGE

KM# 5 KREUZER
Silver **Obv:** Bust right, titles of Sebastian **Rev:** 5-fold arms, date above **Note:** Prev. KM#1.

Date	Mintage	VG	F	VF	XF	Unc
1674	—	—	—	—	—	—

KM# 7 2 KREUZER
Silver **Obv:** Bust right, value '2' below, titles of Sebastian **Rev:** 5-fold arms, date above **Note:** Prev. KM#2.

Date	Mintage	VG	F	VF	XF	Unc
1674	—	—	—	—	—	—

KM# 30 2 KREUZER
Silver **Obv:** Passau arms divide date, value 2 below, titles of Johann Philipp **Rev:** Crowned 4-fold arms with central shield, titles continued **Note:** Prev. KM#3.

Date	Mintage	VG	F	VF	XF	Unc
1694	—	120	235	475	950	—
1699	—	120	235	475	950	—

KM# 20 3 KREUZER (Groschen)
21.0000 g., 0.9860 Gold 0.6657 oz. AGW **Obv:** 4-fold arms, titles of Sebastian **Rev:** St. Stephen standing behind Passau arms divides date, (3) below **Note:** Prev. KM#5.

Date	Mintage	VG	F	VF	XF	Unc
1682	—	—	—	—	—	—

KM# 9 6 KREUZER
Silver **Obv:** Bust right, (VI) below, titles of Sebastian **Rev:** Ornate 5-fold arms, date in margin at top **Note:** Prev. KM#7.

Date	Mintage	VG	F	VF	XF	Unc
1674	—	—	—	—	—	—

KM# 22 15 KREUZER (1/4 Gulden)
Silver **Obv:** Ornate 4-fold arms, titles of Sebastian **Rev:** St. Stephen standing behind Passau arms divides date, value (15) below **Note:** Prev. KM#8.

Date	Mintage	VG	F	VF	XF	Unc
1682	—	—	—	—	—	—

KM# 25 30 KREUZER (1/2 Reichsguildiner)
Silver **Obv:** Ornate 4-fold arms divides 'Kr', titles of Sebastian **Rev:** St. Stephen standing behind Passau arms divides date, value (30) below **Note:** Prev. KM#9.

Date	Mintage	VG	F	VF	XF	Unc
1682	—	550	1,100	2,100	4,200	—

KM# 2 60 KREUZER (Reichsguildiner)
Silver **Ruler:** Leopold **Obv:** Bust right, date below, titles of Leopold **Rev:** Crowned 3-fold arms, titles continue **Note:** Prev. KM#11.

Date	Mintage	VG	F	VF	XF	Unc
1621	—	325	650	1,300	2,500	—

KM# 3 60 KREUZER (Reichsguildiner)
Silver **Obv:** Bust right, titles of Leopold **Rev:** Crowned 3-fold arms, titles continue **Note:** Prev. KM#12.

Date	Mintage	VG	F	VF	XF	Unc
ND(1623-25)	—	275	550	1,100	2,200	—

KM# 28 60 KREUZER (Reichsguildiner)
Silver **Obv:** Ornate 4-fold arms, value (60) below, titles of Sebastian **Rev:** St. Stephen standing behind Passau arms divides date **Note:** Prev. KM#10.

Date	Mintage	VG	F	VF	XF	Unc
1682	—	—	—	—	—	—

KM# 15 1/2 THALER
Silver **Obv:** Ornate 4-fold arms, titles of Sebastian **Rev:** St. Stephen standing behind Passau arms divides date **Note:** Prev. KM#14.

Date	Mintage	VG	F	VF	XF	Unc
1680	—	—	—	—	—	—
1682	—	550	1,100	2,100	4,200	—

KM# 33 1/2 THALER
Silver **Obv:** Crowned ornate 4-fold arms with central shield, titles of Johann Philipp **Rev:** St. Stephen standing divides date, oval Passau arms below **Note:** Prev. KM#15.

Date	Mintage	VG	F	VF	XF	Unc
1694	—	100	200	425	850	—

KM# 18 THALER
Silver **Ruler:** Sebastian **Obv:** Crowned arms **Rev:** Saint standing with small shield in front dividing date **Note:** Dav. #5715.

Date	Mintage	VG	F	VF	XF	Unc
1680 Rare	—	—	—	—	—	—

KM# 35 THALER
Silver **Ruler:** Johann Philipp **Obv:** Ornate crowned arms **Rev:** Saint with arms outstretched **Note:** Dav. #5716.

Date	Mintage	VG	F	VF	XF	Unc
1694 MF	—	275	550	1,000	1,850	3,000

KM# 39 THALER
Silver **Ruler:** Johann Philipp **Note:** Dav. #5717.

Date	Mintage	VG	F	VF	XF	Unc
1696 PHM/(a)	—	300	600	1,350	2,250	4,200
1697 PHM/MF	—	270	550	1,200	2,200	4,200

TRADE COINAGE

KM# 11 1/6 DUCAT
0.5833 g., 0.9860 Gold 0.0185 oz. AGW **Ruler:** Sebastian **Obv:** Bust of Sebastian right **Rev:** Arms topped by cross, crown and mitre **Note:** Fr. #2067.

Date	Mintage	VG	F	VF	XF	Unc
1674	—	325	825	1,600	3,600	—

KM# 13 1/4 DUCAT
0.8750 g., 0.9860 Gold 0.0277 oz. AGW **Ruler:** Sebastian **Obv:** Bust of Sebastian right **Rev:** Arms topped by cross, crown and mitre **Note:** Fr. #2066.

Date	Mintage	VG	F	VF	XF	Unc
1674	—	425	900	2,000	3,850	—

KM# 42.3 DUCAT
3.5000 g., 0.9860 Gold 0.1109 oz. AGW **Ruler:** Johann Philipp **Obv:** Bust of Johann Philip right **Rev:** Crowned round arms divide date **Note:** Fr#A2069.

Date	Mintage	VG	F	VF	XF	Unc
1698 (b)/(a)	—	650	1,300	2,750	5,500	—

KM# 44.1 2 DUCAT
7.0000 g., 0.9860 Gold 0.2219 oz. AGW **Ruler:** Johann Philipp **Obv:** Bust of Johann Philip right **Rev:** Crowned oval arms, date below **Note:** Fr. #2068.

Date	Mintage	VG	F	VF	XF	Unc
1698 (b)/(a)	—	1,650	3,600	7,200	12,500	—

KM# 37 5 DUCAT
Gold **Obv:** Crowned ornate 4-fold arms with central shield, titles of Johann Philipp **Rev:** St. Stephen standing divides date, oval Passau arms below **Note:** Struck from the same dies as 1/2 Thaler KM#33. Prev. KM#18.

Date	Mintage	VG	F	VF	XF	Unc
1694 Rare	—	—	—	—	—	—

KM# 38 5 DUCAT
17.5000 g., 0.9860 Gold 0.5547 oz. AGW **Ruler:** Johann Philipp **Obv:** Crowned ornate 4-fold arms with central shield, titles of Johann Philipp **Rev:** St. Stephen standing divides date, oval Passau arms below **Note:** Struck with 1/2 Thaler dies. Prev. KM#100.

Date	Mintage	VG	F	VF	XF	Unc
1694 Rare	—	—	—	—	—	—

KM# 41 10 DUCAT
35.0000 g., 0.9860 Gold 1.1095 oz. AGW **Ruler:** Johann Philipp **Obv:** Bust of Johann Philip right, "10" stamped incuse into field at chest line **Rev:** Crowned arms divide date **Note:** Struck with 1 Thaler dies, KM#39. Prev. KM#105.

Date	Mintage	VG	F	VF	XF	Unc
1697 PHM/MF Rare	—	—	—	—	—	—

PFALZ

(Rhenish Palatinate, Rheinpfalz)

The Counts Palatine originally administered and exercised judicial functions over the imperial household of the Holy Roman Emperor, based at the center of Charlemagne's empire, Aachen. They gradually acquired territories in the middle Rhine. From1214 onwards the position was hereditary in the Wittelsbach family, who also controlled Bavaria. For a time the electoral dignity alternated between the Bavarian and Palatinate branches of the Wittelsbach family, until the Golden Bull in1356 settled it upon the Palatinate branch.

When the Protestant nobles in Prague elected Friedrich V, who was also a Protestant, as King of Bohemia in 1618, it precipitated a conflict which became known as the Thirty Years' War. Bohemia had been ruled by the Catholic Habsburg Emperors from Vienna since 1527 and Ferdinand II, was incensed at being rebuffed for the crown. Friedrich V lost his battles with Ferdinand II's armies and had to flee to the Hague and to the protection of his father-in-law, King James I of England. He would forever after be known as "The Winter King" in ridicule of his short reign. As punishment, the electoral dignity was taken from the Pfalz branch of the Wittelsbachs and given to the rival branch, the Catholic Duke of Bavaria. As one of the general conditions set forth in the Peace of Westphalia in 1648-50, an eighth electorship was created for Pfalz and thus the dignity was restored to the family.

The conversion of the electors to Roman Catholicism led to the expulsion of Huguenots and other Protestants from their territories, many of whom made their way to America, founding New Paltz, New York. In the course of the later seventeenth and eighteenth centuries, the various branches of the Palatinate were left without any legitimate heirs, so that Karl The odor was able to combine the thrones of Jülich-Berg, the Palatinate, and Bavaria after the War of the Bavarian Succession.

Karl Theodor was a great Maecenas, whose orchestra at Mannheim was one of the greatest in Europe. He was a patron of Mozart, who wrote *Idomeneo* for the opera house in Munich, and of the chemist Benjamin Thompson, later Count Rumford, who fled Massachusetts when the American Revolution broke out and sought refuge in Bavaria.

The Palatinate was administered as part of Bavaria from1777, and did not mint any separate coins after 1802.The territories which composed the Palatinate were scattered over central Germany, and now form part of the West German states of Bavaria, Baden, Hesse, and Rheinland-Pfalz. The chief industry is bulk chemicals, from the great BASF factory at Ludwigshafen.

In 1753 Bavaria and Austria concluded a monetary convention, reducing the fineness of the thaler to the point that 20 gulden could be coined from a Mark of fine silver. The most important result was that henceforth the gulden, rather than being worth 2/3 of a thaler, was henceforth worth half a thaler. This Convention standard was soon afterwards adopted by most of the states of southwest Germany, including the Palatinate.

The Electors Palatine and the Saxon Elector acted as Vicars of the Empire after the death of a Holy Roman Emperor and before a new one was elected; the Elector Palatine in the areas of Franconian and Suevic law, the Saxon Elector in the areas where Saxon law applied. Both principalities issued coins commemorating the vicariates. Thus the Elector, Palatine Karl Theodor Actedas, Vicar of the Empire in 1790, after the death of Josef II, and again in 1792, after the early death of Leopold II, and issued coins in those two years. These coins are analogous to the "Sede Vacante" coins of ecclesiastical principalities.

PFALZ-ELECTORAL PFALZ

(Rhenish Pfalz, Rheinpfalz, Churpfalz, Kurpfalz)
Line of Succession in the Electoral Dignity

Once the electorship was vested in the Palatine line of the Wittelsbachs, it passed by right of succession through the senior male line until the death of Friedrich II in 1556. His nephew Otto Heinrich then received the dignity, but this failed at his death three years later. The branch of the family with the highest seniority aft this time was that of Pfalz-Simmern and it was to it that the electoral office passed. The electorship was lost, as stated above, in 1623 as a result of Friedrich V's actions and not restored until the end of the Thirty Years' War in 1648 as part of the peace settlement. The royal coinage of Friedrich V for Bohemia is listed under that entity. From 1622 until 1648, the Upper Palatinate and part of the Rhenish Palatinate were administered by Bavaria, which struck coins for use in those territories. See Bavaria for listings of those issues. The Simmern line died out in 1685 and the office of elector fell to Pfalz-Neuburg, the rulers of which were also dukes of Jülich-Berg. The coinage issued of these Pfalz-Neuburg rulers are often confused one with the other and it is sometimes difficult to separate issues for Electoral Pfalz from those of Jülich-Berg, particularly because some issues for one principality were produced or at least the dies were made in the mint of the other territory. The fate of extinction befell the Pfalz-Neuburg line in 1742 and all its lands and titles passed to Pfalz-Sulzbach for one generation. The Elector also became duke and elector in Bavaria when the Wittelsbach line in that principality became extinct and the two branches of the family were finally united after a breach of centuries. Once again the electoral dignity passed to another branch of the Palatine family, this time to Pfalz-Birkenfeld in 1799. With the abolition of the Holy Roman Empire by Napoleon in 1806, the electoral college was no longer needed and passed quietly away.

RULERS
Friedrich IV von Simmern, 1583-1610
Johann Kasimir von Lautern, Regent 1583-92
Friedrich V, "The Winter King", 1610-23, died 1632
Johann II von Zweibrücken, Regent 1610-14
Bavarian Rule, 1622-48
Karl Ludwig von Simmern, 1648-80
Karl von Simmern, 1680-85
Philipp Wilhelm von Neuburg, 1685-90
Johann Wilhelm von Neuburg, 1690-1716

MINT OFFICIALS' INITIALS

HEIDELBERG MINT

Initials	Date	Name
	1620	Johan Ludwig Eichesstein, mintmaster
GP	1650-63	Georg Pfründt, die-cutter in Nürnberg
(a)	1656-59	Johan Kasimir Herman, mintmaster
	1659-76	Johann Kaspar Herman, mintmaster
	1657-?	Michael Koch, warden
ISS	1658-59	Unknown die-cutter
	1659-76	Sebastian Müller, warden
IL, L	1659-1711	Johann Linck, die-cutter and mintmaster
GB	1684-92	Johann Gerhard Bender, mintmaster
IMW, MW	1694-1709	Johann Michael Wunsch, mintmaster

MANNHEIM MINT

Initials	Date	Name
	1607-10	Johann Ludwig Eichelstein, mintmaster

ARMS
Pfalz – rampant lion to left or right
Bavaria or old Wittelsbach – field of lozenges (diamond shapes)
Electorate – blank shield, sometimes shaded with closely spaced horizontal lines or ..arabesques
..- also, an imperial orb

MONETARY SYSTEMS
8 Pfenning = 2 Kreuzer = 1 Albus
16 Pfenning = 4 Kreuzer = 2 Albus = 1 Batzen

ELECTORATE

REGULAR COINAGE

KM# 62 HELLER
Copper **Ruler:** Friedrich V **Obv:** Crowned Bohemian lion right holding orb **Mint:** Amberg **Note:** Kipper. Uniface.

Date	Mintage	VG	F	VF	XF	Unc
ND(1621-22)	—	20.00	40.00	85.00	—	—

KM# 3 PFENNIG
Billon **Ruler:** Friedrich IV **Obv:** Round 4-fold arms, HEIDELBERG, date around **Mint:** Heidelberg **Note:** Uniface. Prev. Pfalz-Simmern KM#6.

Date	Mintage	VG	F	VF	XF	Unc
1608	—	16.00	33.00	75.00	155	—
1609	—	16.00	33.00	75.00	155	—

KM# 28 PFENNIG
Silver **Ruler:** Johann II **Obv:** Shield of 4-fold arms of Pfalz and Bavaria, IAP above (=Johann Admin. Palat.) **Note:** Uniface hohl-type.

Date	Mintage	VG	F	VF	XF	Unc
ND(1610-15)	—	20.00	40.00	85.00	170	—

KM# 58 PFENNIG
Silver **Ruler:** Friedrich V **Obv:** Shield of 3-fold arms with scalloped sides of Pfalz, Electorate and Bavaria divides date, "IC" in ligature above **Mint:** Heidelberg **Note:** Uniface.

Date	Mintage	VG	F	VF	XF	Unc
ND(1615-20)	—	20.00	40.00	85.00	—	—

KM# 64 PFENNIG
Copper **Ruler:** Friedrich V **Obv:** Crowned Bohemian lion to right holding orb **Mint:** Heidelberg **Note:** Kipper, uniface.

Date	Mintage	VG	F	VF	XF	Unc
ND(1621-22)	—	20.00	40.00	85.00	—	—

KM# 77 PFENNIG
Copper **Ruler:** Karl Ludwig **Obv:** Round 3-fold arms in baroque frame, C*L above **Mint:** Heidelberg **Note:** Uniface. Prev. Pfalz-Simmern KM#9.

Date	Mintage	VG	F	VF	XF	Unc
ND(1648-80)	—	25.00	50.00	100	200	—

KM# 101 2 PFENNIG
Silver **Ruler:** Karl Ludwig **Note:** Prev. Pfalz-Simmern KM#107.

Date	Mintage	VG	F	VF	XF	Unc
1662	—	25.00	50.00	100	200	—
ND	—	25.00	50.00	100	200	—

KM# 5 4 PFENNIG (1/2 Albus)
Silver **Ruler:** Friedrich IV **Obv:** Pfalz lion right in circle holding

orb **Obv. Legend:** MO. NO. IIII. NVM. MANHEIM **Rev:** Shield of Wittelsbach arms, date above in circle **Rev. Legend:** C(H)VRF. PFALTS. LANDMVNTZ **Mint:** Mannheim **Note:** Varieties exist. Prev. Pfalz-Simmern KM#10.

Date	Mintage	VG	F	VF	XF	Unc
1608	—	50.00	100	200	400	—
1609	—	50.00	100	200	400	—

KM# 24 4 PFENNIG (1/2 Albus)

Silver **Ruler:** Friedrich IV **Obv:** Bust right in circle, titles of Friedrich IV **Rev:** 4-fold arms, legend, date **Rev. Legend:** MO. NO. IIII. NVM. MAHEM **Mint:** Mannheim

Date	Mintage	VG	F	VF	XF	Unc
1610	—	27.00	55.00	110	—	—

KM# 7 ALBUS

Silver **Ruler:** Friedrich IV **Obv:** Bust right in circle **Obv. Legend:** NOV. ALBVS MANHEIMII CVSVS **Rev:** 3 small shields of arms, 2 above, 1 below which divides date, electoral hat above **Rev. Legend:** CH. FVRST. PFALTZ. LANDMVNZ. **Mint:** Mannheim **Note:** Prev. Pfalz-Simmern KM#13.

Date	Mintage	VG	F	VF	XF	Unc
1608	—	65.00	135	275	550	—

KM# 27 ALBUS

Silver **Ruler:** Friedrich IV **Obv:** Bust right in circle, titles of Friedrich IV **Rev:** 4-fold arms, date **Rev. Legend:** NOV. ALBVS. MANHE. CV. **Mint:** Mannheim

Date	Mintage	VG	F	VF	XF	Unc
(1)610	—	65.00	135	275	550	—

KM# 120 ALBUS

Silver **Ruler:** Karl von Simmern **Obv:** Large script 'C', date divided between crown and 'C' **Rev:** Crowned Pfalz lion left within palm and laurel branches **Mint:** Heidelberg

Date	Mintage	VG	F	VF	XF	Unc
1682	—	55.00	115	235	475	—

KM# 128 ALBUS

Silver **Ruler:** Philipp Wilhelm **Obv:** Bust right with titles of Elector Philipp Wilhelm **Rev:** 3 shields - lion, orb and lozenge, electoral hat above **Note:** Prev. Pfalz-Neuburg KM#40.

Date	Mintage	VG	F	VF	XF	Unc
1685	—	55.00	115	235	475	—

KM# 126 ALBUS

Silver **Ruler:** Philipp Wilhelm **Obv:** Bust right with titles of Elector Philipp Wilhelm **Rev:** 3 shields - lion, orb, and lozenge, electoral hat above **Mint:** Heidelberg **Note:** Prev. Pfalz-Neuburg KM#40.

Date	Mintage	VG	F	VF	XF	Unc
1685	—	55.00	115	235	475	—

KM# 132 ALBUS

Silver **Ruler:** Philipp Wilhelm **Obv:** Crowned Pfalz lion left in circle, titles of Philipp Wilhelm **Rev:** Crowned 8-fold arms with central shield, titles continued ending ALB9 date **Mint:** Heidelberg

Date	Mintage	VG	F	VF	XF	Unc
1688 GB	—	55.00	115	235	475	—

KM# 140 ALBUS

Silver **Ruler:** Johann Wilhelm **Obv:** Crowned Pfalz lion left in circle, titles of Johann Wilhelm **Rev:** Mintmaster's initials, titles cont. and date **Rev. Inscription:** *I* / ALBVS / **Mint:** Heidelberg

Date	Mintage	VG	F	VF	XF	Unc
1691 GB	—	55.00	115	235	475	—

KM# 26 ALBUS (8 Pfennig)

Silver **Ruler:** Friedrich IV **Obv:** Bust right in circle, titles of Friedrich IV **Rev:** 4-fold arms, legend, date **Rev. Legend:** NOV. ALBVS. MA(N)HEMII. C(V) **Mint:** Mannheim **Note:** Prev. Pfalz-Simmern KM#12.

Date	Mintage	VG	F	VF	XF	Unc
1610	—	30.00	50.00	100	210	—

KM# 114 ALBUS (8 Pfennig)

Silver **Ruler:** Karl von Simmern **Obv:** Large script 'C', crown above divides date **Obv. Legend:** SVSTENTANTE DEO. **Rev:** Crowned Pfalz lion left within palm and laurel branches **Mint:** Heidelberg

Date	Mintage	VG	F	VF	XF	Unc
1681	—	25.00	50.00	100	—	—

KM# 144 2 ALBUS

1.7500 g., Billon **Ruler:** Johann Wilhelm **Obv:** Crowned lion rampant left in laurel wreath divides C - P **Rev:** Inscription in laurel wreath **Rev. Inscription:** II / ALBUS / (date) **Note:** Prev. Pfalz-Neuburg KM#51. Varieties exist. Some are counterfeits.

Date	Mintage	VG	F	VF	XF	Unc
1700 IMW	—	40.00	80.00	160	325	—

KM# 9 3-1/4 ALBUS (1/8 Gulden)

Silver **Ruler:** Friedrich IV **Obv:** Bust right in circle, behind III.ALB, in front .II. ... (= 2 Pfennig or 1/4 Albus) **Obv. Legend:** MONE. ARGENT. MANHEMII. CVSA. **Rev:** 3 small shields of arms, 2 above 1 below which divides date, electoral hat above **Rev. Legend:** CHVRF. FVRST. PFALTZ. LANDMVNZ. **Mint:** Mannheim **Note:** Varieties exist.

Date	Mintage	VG	F	VF	XF	Unc
1608	—	—	85.00	165	325	—

KM# 29 3-1/4 ALBUS (1/8 Gulden)

Ruler: Friedrich IV **Obv:** Bust right in circle, titles of Friedrich IV **Rev:** 4-fold arms divide III - 2... **Mint:** Mannheim

Date	Mintage	VG	F	VF	XF	Unc
1610	—	85.00	165	325	—	—

KM# 146 6 ALBUS

Silver **Ruler:** Johann Wilhelm **Obv:** Crowned oval 9-fold arms, titles of Johann Wilhelm **Rev:** Value inscription, date, mintmaster's initials **Rev. Legend:** NACH DEM SCHLUS DER V. STÆND. **Rev. Inscription:** ★ VI ★ / ALBUS/ **Note:** Prev. Pfalz-Neuburg KM#52. Varieties exist.

Date	Mintage	VG	F	VF	XF	Unc
1700 IMW	—	75.00	150	300	600	—

KM# 12 6-1/2 ALBUS

Silver **Ruler:** Friedrich IV **Obv:** Bust right in circle **Obv. Legend:** MON. NO. ARG. VI ... ALB. MANHEMII. CVSA (or variant) **Rev:** 3 small shields of arms, 2 above 1 below which divides date, electoral hat above **Rev. Legend:** CHVRFVRST. PFALTZ. LANDMVNZ. **Mint:** Mannheim **Note:** Klippe.

Date	Mintage	VG	F	VF	XF	Unc
1608	—	—	—	—	—	—

KM# 11 6-1/2 ALBUS

Silver **Ruler:** Friedrich IV **Obv:** Bust right in circle **Obv. Legend:** MON. NO. ARG. VI ... ALB. MANHEMII. CVSA (or variant) **Rev:** 3 small shields of arms, 2 above 1 below which divides date, electoral hat above **Rev. Legend:** CHVRFVRST. PFALTZ. LANDMVNZ. **Mint:** Mannheim **Note:** Prev. Pfalz-Simmern KM#14. Varieties exist.

Date	Mintage	VG	F	VF	XF	Unc
1608	—	80.00	165	300	625	—

KM# 30 6-1/2 ALBUS

Silver **Ruler:** Friedrich IV **Obv:** Bust right in circle, titles of Friedrich IV **Rev:** 4-fold arms divide VI - ... **Mint:** Mannheim

Date	Mintage	VG	F	VF	XF	Unc
1610	—	—	—	—	—	—

KM# 14 13 ALBUS (1/2 Gulden)

Silver **Ruler:** Friedrich IV **Obv:** Bust right in circle, XIII - ALB. behind and in front of bust **Rev:** 3 small shields of arms divide date at bottom, electoral hat above **Mint:** Mannheim **Note:** Prev. Pfalz-Simmern KM#15.

Date	Mintage	VG	F	VF	XF	Unc
1608	—	250	500	1,100	2,000	—

KM# 16 26 ALBUS (Gulden)

Silver **Ruler:** Friedrich IV **Obv:** Bust right divides XXVI at left and ALB at right in inner circle **Rev:** Date divided by lion on top of helmet **Mint:** Mannheim **Note:** Dav.#744. Prev. Pfalz-Simmern KM#16.

Date	Mintage	VG	F	VF	XF	Unc
1608	—	275	550	1,100	2,150	—

KM# 65 KREUZER

Copper, 18 mm. **Ruler:** Friedrich V **Obv:** 2 adjacent shields of arms, Pfalz left, Wittelsbach right, imperial orb between at bottom **Rev:** 4-life inscription with date **Rev. Inscription:** I / KREVTZ / ER / (date) **Mint:** Heidelberg **Note:** Kipper.

Date	Mintage	VG	F	VF	XF	Unc
1621	—	35.00	75.00	155	—	—
1622	—	35.00	75.00	155	—	—

KM# 82 KREUZER

Silver **Ruler:** Karl Ludwig **Obv:** Pfalz lion left in circle, titles of Karl Ludwig **Rev:** Blank oval shield of arms in baroque frame, legend, date **Mint:** Heidelberg **Note:** Prev. Pfalz-Simmern KM#95.

Date	Mintage	VG	F	VF	XF	Unc
1657	—	30.00	60.00	120	—	—
1658	—	30.00	60.00	120	—	—
1663	—	30.00	60.00	120	—	—

KM# 83 KREUZER

Silver **Ruler:** Karl Ludwig **Obv:** Ornate helmet over 3 small shields of arms **Rev:** Inscription in laurel wreath **Rev. Inscription:** I / date / KREVZ / ER **Note:** Prev. Pfalz-Simmern KM#1.

Date	Mintage	VG	F	VF	XF	Unc
1661	—	—	—	—	—	—

KM# 134 KREUZER

Silver **Ruler:** Philipp Wilhelm **Obv:** Crowned Pfalz lion left in circle, titles of Philipp Wilhelm, date in legend **Rev:** Mintmasters' initials in circle, titles cont. **Rev. Inscription:** I / KREV / TZER / **Mint:** Heidelberg **Note:** Prev. Pfalz-Neuburg KM#41.

Date	Mintage	VG	F	VF	XF	Unc
1688 GB	—	—	—	—	—	—

KM# 148 KREUZER

Silver **Ruler:** Johann Wilhelm **Obv:** Pfalz lion left in laurel wreath **Rev:** 3-line inscription, date in laurel wreath **Rev. Inscription:** I / KREU / ZER / **Mint:** Heidelberg **Note:** Prev. Pfalz-Neuburg KM#50.

Date	Mintage	VG	F	VF	XF	Unc
1700	—	60.00	125	250	500	—

KM# 79 2 KREUZER

Billon **Ruler:** Karl Ludwig **Obv:** Crowned rampant lion left in circle, titles of Karl Ludwig **Rev:** Oval blank shield in baroque frame with 2 small points in center, legend, date **Rev. Legend:** S • R • I • EL • & VIC • B • D • DN • PVIDEBIT **Mint:** Heidelberg **Note:** Prev. Pfalz-Simmern KM#91. Vicariat issue.

Date	Mintage	VG	F	VF	XF	Unc
1657 (a)	163,000	50.00	100	200	400	—
1658 (a)	—	50.00	100	200	400	—

KM# 80 2 KREUZER

Billon **Ruler:** Karl Ludwig **Obv:** Crowned rampant lion left in circle, titles of Karl Ludwig **Rev:** Large '2' in ornamented oval, legend, date **Rev. Legend:** DOMINVS PROVIDEBIT **Mint:** Heidelberg **Note:** Prev. Pfalz-Simmern KM#90.

Date	Mintage	VG	F	VF	XF	Unc
1657 (a)	Inc. above	50.00	100	200	400	—

KM# 104 2 KREUZER

Silver **Ruler:** Karl Ludwig **Obv:** Crowned rampant lion left in circle, titles of Karl Ludwig **Obv. Legend:** CAROL • LUD • D • G • DOM ... **Rev:** Oval blank shield in baroque frame **Rev. Legend:** S • R • I • EL • & B • D • DN • PVIDEBIT **Mint:** Heidelberg **Note:** Prev. Pfalz-Simmern KM#108. Varieties exist.

Date	Mintage	VG	F	VF	XF	Unc
1662 (a)	—	40.00	80.00	160	325	—
1663 (a)	—	40.00	80.00	160	325	—
1664 (a)	—	40.00	80.00	160	325	—
1665 (a)	—	40.00	80.00	160	325	—
1667 (a)	—	40.00	80.00	160	325	—
1668 (a)	—	40.00	80.00	160	325	—
1669 (a)	—	40.00	80.00	160	325	—
1670 (a)	—	40.00	80.00	160	325	—
1673 (a)	—	40.00	80.00	160	325	—

KM# 75 4 KREUZER

Copper **Ruler:** Friedrich V **Obv:** Rampant Bohemian lion left **Rev:** Bavarian lozenges divide date, value above **Note:** Prev. Pfalz-Simmern KM#55. Kipper.

Date	Mintage	VG	F	VF	XF	Unc
1622	—	45.00	90.00	185	375	—

KM# 67 12 KREUZER

Billon **Ruler:** Friedrich V **Obv:** Rampant Bohemian lion left **Rev:** 3 shields - lion, orb, and Bavarian lozenge **Mint:** Heidelberg **Note:** Klippe. Pfalz-Simmern KM#44.

Date	Mintage	VG	F	VF	XF	Unc
1621	—	50.00	100	210	425	—

KM# 66 12 KREUZER

Billon **Ruler:** Friedrich V **Obv:** Rampant Bohemian lion left **Rev:** 3 shields - lion, orb, and Bavarian lozenge **Mint:** Heidelberg **Note:** Prev. Pfalz-Simmern KM#43. Kipper.

Date	Mintage	VG	F	VF	XF	Unc
1621	—	50.00	100	210	425	—
1622	—	50.00	100	210	425	—
ND	—	50.00	100	210	425	—

KM# 87 15 KREUZER (1/4 Gulden)

Silver **Ruler:** Karl Ludwig **Obv:** Bust right in circle, titles of Karl Ludwig **Rev:** 3 small shields of arms, 2 above 1, lower shield divides date, electoral hat above all, value (15) at bottom **Rev. Legend:** DOMINVS - PROVIDEBIT **Mint:** Heidelberg **Note:** Prev. Pfalz-Simmern KM#96.

Date	Mintage	VG	F	VF	XF	Unc
1658 (a)	—	55.00	110	200	425	—
1660 (a)	—	55.00	110	200	425	—
1661 (a)	—	55.00	110	200	425	—

KM# 98 15 KREUZER (1/4 Gulden)

Silver **Ruler:** Karl Ludwig **Obv:** Bust right in circle, titles of Karl Ludwig **Rev:** 3 small shields of arms, date divided above middle shield **Rev. Legend:** CHUR FURST LICHER - PFALTZ LANDMUNTZ **Mint:** Heidelberg **Note:** Varieties exist.

Date	Mintage	VG	F	VF	XF	Unc
1661 (a)	—	55.00	110	200	425	—
1662 GP/(a)	—	55.00	110	200	425	—
1666 (a)	—	55.00	110	200	425	—
1668	—	55.00	110	200	425	—
1672	—	55.00	110	200	425	—

KM# 68 24 KREUZER (Sechsbätzner)

Silver **Ruler:** Friedrich V **Obv:** Crowned Bohemian lion rampant left in circle, titles of Friedrich V as king of Bohemia **Rev:** Crown above 3 ornate shields of arms, 2 above 1 below which divides date, titles cont. **Mint:** Heidelberg **Note:** Kipper.

Date	Mintage	VG	F	VF	XF	Unc
1621	—	150	300	600	1,150	—
ND	—	150	300	600	1,150	—

KM# 69 24 KREUZER (Sechsbätzner)

Silver **Ruler:** Friedrich V **Obv:** Crowned Bohemian lion rampant left in circle, titles of Friedrich V as king of Bohemia **Rev:** Crown above 3 ornate shields of arms, 2 above 1 below which divides date, titles cont., legend error REHNI instead of RHENI **Mint:** Heidelberg **Note:** Kipper.

Date	Mintage	VG	F	VF	XF	Unc
ND(1621)	—	150	300	600	1,150	—

KM# 89 30 KREUZER (1/2 Gulden)

Silver **Ruler:** Karl Ludwig **Obv:** Bust right in circle, titles of Karl Ludwig **Rev:** 3 small shields of arms, 2 above 1, lower shield divides date, electoral hat above all, value (30) at bottom **Mint:** Heidelberg **Note:** Prev. Pfalz-Simmern KM#97.

Date	Mintage	VG	F	VF	XF	Unc
1658 (a)	—	80.00	160	300	625	—
1660 (a)	—	80.00	160	300	625	—
1661 (a)	—	80.00	160	300	625	—

KM# 100 30 KREUZER (1/2 Gulden)

Silver **Ruler:** Karl Ludwig **Obv:** Bust right in circle, titles of Karl Ludwig **Rev:** 3 small shields of arms, middle shield divides date, value (30) at bottom **Mint:** Heidelberg **Note:** Prev. Pfalz-Simmern KM#97.

Date	Mintage	VG	F	VF	XF	Unc
1661 (a)	—	80.00	160	300	625	—
1664 (a)	—	80.00	160	300	625	—
1665 (a)	—	80.00	160	300	625	—
1666 (a)	—	80.00	160	300	625	—
1668	—	80.00	160	300	625	—
1672	—	80.00	160	300	625	—
1673	—	80.00	160	300	625	—

KM# 91 60 KREUZER (Gulden)

Silver **Ruler:** Karl Ludwig **Obv:** Armored bust to right in circle **Obv. Legend:** +CAR. LVD. D. G. C. P. R. I. S. R. I. ARCHITHE. ET. F. L. B. D. **Rev:** 3 small shields of arms, ornate helmet above, lion crest on top divides date, value (60) at bottom **Rev. Legend:** +DOMINVS - PROVIDEBIT. **Mint:** Heidelberg **Note:** Prev. Pfalz-Simmern KM#98.

Date	Mintage	VG	F	VF	XF	Unc
1658 ISS	—	100	200	375	775	—
1659 ISS	—	100	200	375	775	—
1660	—	100	200	375	775	—

KM# 95 60 KREUZER (Gulden)

19.2600 g., Silver **Ruler:** Karl Ludwig **Obv:** Armored and draped bust to right in circle **Obv. Legend:** CAR. LVD. D. G. C. P. RH. S. R. I. ARCHITH. ET. BA. DV. **Rev:** 3 small shields of arms, lower shield divides date at bottom, value (60) in margin below **Rev. Legend:** DOMINVS - PROVIDEBIT. **Mint:** Heidelberg **Note:** Ref. Noss I:300, 303; Dav. 745. Prev. Pfalz-Simmern KM#98.

Date	Mintage	VG	F	VF	XF	Unc
1660 (a)	—	100	200	375	775	—
1661 (a)	—	100	200	375	775	—

KM# 96 60 KREUZER (Gulden)

Silver Weight varies: 19.04-19.52g. **Ruler:** Karl Ludwig **Obv:** Bust to right in circle **Obv. Legend:** CAR. L(V)(U)D. D. G. COM. PAL. RH(EN). S. R. I. ARCHITH. (E)(T). EL(E)CT. B. D. **Rev:** 3 small shields of arms, 2 above 1, ornate helmet with seated lion crest divides date above **Rev. Legend:** CH(V)(U)RF(V)(U)RSTLICHER - PFALTZ(:)LANDM(V)(U)NTZ. **Mint:** Heidelberg **Note:** Ref. Noss I:302-312; Dav. 746. Prev. Pfalz-Simmern KM#105. Varieties exist.

Date	Mintage	VG	F	VF	XF	Unc
1660 (a)	—	80.00	185	375	775	—
1661 GP/(a)	—	80.00	185	375	775	—
1662 P/(a)	—	80.00	185	375	775	—
1664	—	80.00	185	375	775	—
1665	—	80.00	185	375	775	—
1666	—	80.00	185	375	775	—
1667 (a)	—	80.00	185	375	775	—
1668 (a)	—	80.00	185	375	775	—
1670 (a)	—	80.00	185	375	775	—
1672	—	80.00	185	375	775	—
1673 (a)	—	80.00	185	375	775	—
1676 (a)	—	80.00	185	375	775	—

KM# 99 60 KREUZER (Gulden)

Silver **Ruler:** Karl Ludwig **Obv:** Large armored bust to right, legend begins at left **Obv. Legend:** CAR: LUD. D. G. C. P. RHE. S. R. I. ARCHITH: EL. BAV. DUX. **Rev:** 3 small shields of arms, ornate helmet above, with lion crest dividing date on top, value '60' below, legend begins at left **Rev. Legend:** DOMINUS - PROVIDEBIT. **Mint:** Heidelberg

Date	Mintage	VG	F	VF	XF	Unc
1661 GP/(a)	—	175	350	600	900	—

KM# 18 GULDEN

Silver **Ruler:** Friedrich III **Obv:** Bust right divides value in circle **Rev:** 3 shields of arms **Mint:** Mannheim

Date	Mintage	VG	F	VF	XF	Unc
1608	—	—	—	—	—	—

KM# 32 1/4 THALER

Silver **Ruler:** Friedrich IV **Obv:** Bust with sword over right shoulder, orb in left hand **Rev:** Crowned arms divide large date **Note:** Klippe. Prev. Pfalz-Simmern KM#26.

Date	Mintage	VG	F	VF	XF	Unc
1610 Rare	—	—	—	—	—	—

KM# 31 1/4 THALER

Silver **Ruler:** Friedrich IV **Obv:** Bust with sword over right shoulder, left hand holds orb right in inner circle **Rev:** Crowned arms divide large date **Note:** Prev. Pfalz-Simmern KM#25.

Date	Mintage	VG	F	VF	XF	Unc
1610	—	—	—	—	—	—

KM# 46 1/4 THALER

Silver **Ruler:** Johann II **Obv:** Bust right in circle, outer legend titles of Johann II **Obv. Legend:** Inner leg. VICARIUS DUX B. CO. V. & SPAN. **Rev:** Crowned imperial eagle, 3-fold arms of Pfalz, Electorate and Bavaria on breast, date at end of legend **Rev. Legend:** VERBUM DOMINI MANET IN ÆTERNUM **Mint:** Heidelberg **Note:** Vicariat issue.

Date	Mintage	VG	F	VF	XF	Unc
161Z	—	—	—	—	—	—

KM# 33 1/2 THALER

Silver **Ruler:** Johann II **Obv:** Bust right in circle, titles of Johann II **Rev:** 3 small shields of arms, 2 above 1, electoral hat above, all in circle, date at end of legend **Rev. Legend:** VERBUM • DOMINI • MANET • IN • ÆTERNVM **Mint:** Heidelberg

Date	Mintage	VG	F	VF	XF	Unc
1610	—	—	—	—	—	—

KM# 48 1/2 THALER

Silver **Ruler:** Johann II **Obv:** Bust right in circle, outer legend, titles of Johann II **Obv. Legend:** Inner leg: VICARIUS DUX B. CO. V. & SPAN **Rev:** Crowned imperial eagle, 3-fold arms of Pfalz, Electorate and Bavaria on breast, date at end of legend **Rev. Legend:** VERBUM DOMINI MANET IN ÆTERN **Mint:** Heidelberg **Note:** Vicariat issue.

Date	Mintage	VG	F	VF	XF	Unc
161Z	—	—	—	—	—	—

KM# 20 THALER

Silver **Ruler:** Friedrich IV **Obv:** Bust with sword and orb right **Rev:** Crowned arms divide date **Mint:** Mannheim **Note:** Dav. #7144. Prev. Pfalz-Simmern KM#17.

Date	Mintage	VG	F	VF	XF	Unc
1608	—	850	1,650	3,750	7,000	—

KM# 37 THALER

Silver **Ruler:** Friedrich IV **Obv:** 1/2-length bust right, sword on right shoulder, orb in left hand in inner circle **Rev:** Crowned arms divide larger date **Mint:** Mannheim **Note:** Dav. #7146. Prev. Pfalz-Simmern KM#28.

Date	Mintage	VG	F	VF	XF	Unc
1610	—	850	1,650	3,750	7,000	12,000

KM# 35 THALER

Silver **Ruler:** Johann II **Obv:** Bust right **Obv. Legend:** IOHAN. D. G. CO. PAL. RH ... **Rev:** 3 shields crowned, date in legend **Note:** Dav. #7180. Prev. Pfalz-Zweibrücken KM#5.

Date	Mintage	VG	F	VF	XF	Unc
1610 Rare	—	—	—	—	—	—

KM# 36 THALER

Silver **Ruler:** Johann II **Obv:** Bust right **Obv. Legend:** IOHAN. D. G. C. PA. RH ... **Rev:** 3 shields crowned, date in legend **Mint:** Heidelberg **Note:** Dav. #7181. Prev. Pfalz-Zweibrücken KM#6.

Date	Mintage	VG	F	VF	XF	Unc
1610 Rare	—	—	—	—	—	—

KM# 41 THALER

Silver **Ruler:** Johann II **Obv:** Bust right **Rev:** 3 shields capped, date below **Mint:** Heidelberg **Note:** Dav. #7182. Prev. Pfalz-Zweibrücken KM#7.

Date	Mintage	VG	F	VF	XF	Unc
1611 Rare	—	—	—	—	—	—

KM# 42 THALER

Silver **Ruler:** Johann II **Obv:** Bust right **Obv. Legend:** IOHAN. D. G. CO. PAL. RH ... **Rev:** 3 shields crowned, scrollwork around date **Mint:** Heidelberg **Note:** Dav. #7182A. Prev. Pfalz-Zweibrücken KM#8.

Date	Mintage	VG	F	VF	XF	Unc
1611 Rare	—	—	—	—	—	—

KM# 43 THALER

Silver **Ruler:** Johann II **Obv:** Bust right **Obv. Legend:** IOHAN. D. G. CO. PAL. RH ... **Rev:** 3 shields crowned, date punctuated 1.6. - .11. **Mint:** Heidelberg **Note:** Dav. #7182B. Prev. Pfalz-Zweibrücken KM#9.

Date	Mintage	VG	F	VF	XF	Unc
1611 Rare	—	—	—	—	—	—

KM# 44 THALER

Silver **Ruler:** Johann II **Obv:** Bust right **Obv. Legend:** IOHAN. D. G. CO. PAL. RH ... **Rev:** 3 shields crowned, date in legend divided by shield **Mint:** Heidelberg **Note:** Dav. #7183. Prev. Pfalz-Zweibrücken KM#10.

Date	Mintage	VG	F	VF	XF	Unc
1611 Rare	—	—	—	—	—	—

KM# 50 THALER

Silver **Ruler:** Johann II **Obv:** Bust right, titles of Johann II **Obv. Legend:** IOHAN • D • G • CO • V • & S • ... **Rev:** Crowned double-headed eagle **Mint:** Heidelberg **Note:** Dav. #7184. Prev. Pfalz-Zweibrücken KM#12. Vicariat issue.

Date	Mintage	VG	F	VF	XF	Unc
161Z	—	950	1,850	4,000	7,500	—

KM# 51 THALER

Silver **Ruler:** Johann II **Obv:** Bust right in inner circle **Obv. Legend:** ... CO. V. & SPANH. **Rev:** Crowned double-headed eagle **Mint:** Heidelberg **Note:** Dav. #7184A. Prev. Pfalz-Zweibrücken KM#13. Vicariat issue.

Date	Mintage	VG	F	VF	XF	Unc
161Z	—	950	1,850	4,000	7,500	—

KM# 52 THALER

Silver **Ruler:** Johann II **Obv:** Bust right **Obv. Legend:** PA: RHE: TVT: ET: AD: DVX **Rev:** Helmeted arms **Rev. Legend:** BAV: CO: VEL: - ET. SPO... **Mint:** Heidelberg **Note:** Dav. #7185. Prev. Pfalz-Zweibrücken KM#14.

Date	Mintage	VG	F	VF	XF	Unc
161Z Rare	—	—	—	—	—	—

KM# 57 THALER

Silver **Ruler:** Friedrich V **Obv:** King standing between shields **Rev:** 5-fold arms **Rev. Legend:** ... LVSA. 1620. **Mint:** Mannheim **Note:** Dav. #7147. Prev. Pfalz-Simmern KM#40.

Date	Mintage	VG	F	VF	XF	Unc
1620 Rare	—	—	—	—	—	—

KM# 59 THALER

Silver **Ruler:** Friedrich V **Obv:** King standing between shields **Rev:** 5-fold arms **Rev. Legend:** ... + LUX. *1620. **Mint:** Mannheim **Note:** Dav. #7147A. Prev. Pfalz-Simmern KM#41.

Date	Mintage	VG	F	VF	XF	Unc
1620 Rare	—	—	—	—	—	—

KM# 60 THALER

Silver **Ruler:** Friedrich V **Obv:** King standing between shields **Rev:** 5-fold arms **Rev. Legend:** ... LVSA.A 1620 **Mint:** Mannheim **Note:** Dav. #7147B. Prev. Pfalz-Simmern KM#42.

Date	Mintage	VG	F	VF	XF	Unc
1620 Rare	—	—	—	—	—	—

KM# 70 THALER

Silver **Ruler:** Friedrich V **Obv:** Crowned Bohemian lion **Rev:** Crown above 3 shields divide date **Mint:** Mannheim **Note:** Dav. #7148. Prev. Pfalz-Simmern KM#46.

Date	Mintage	VG	F	VF	XF	Unc
1621	—	1,250	2,500	4,750	8,500	—

KM# 71 THALER

Silver **Ruler:** Friedrich V **Obv:** Crowned Bohemian lion left **Rev:** Crown above 3 shields, date divided by bottom shield **Mint:** Mannheim **Note:** Dav. #7149. Prev. Pfalz-Simmern KM#47.

Date	Mintage	VG	F	VF	XF	Unc
1621	—	1,000	2,000	4,500	8,000	—

KM# 72 THALER

Silver **Ruler:** Friedrich V **Obv:** Crowned Bohemian lion left, legend has reversed D **Rev:** 3 longer and thinner shields, bottom shield divides date **Mint:** Mannheim **Note:** Dav. #7150. Prev. Pfalz-Simmern KM#48. Varieties exist.

Date	Mintage	VG	F	VF	XF	Unc
1621	—	1,200	2,250	4,250	7,755	—

KM# 84 THALER

Silver **Ruler:** Karl Ludwig **Obv:** 9-line inscription, date **Rev:** Lion above 3 helmeted shields **Mint:** Heidelberg **Note:** Dav. #7151. Prev. Pfalz-Simmern KM#92. Vicariat issue.

Date	Mintage	VG	F	VF	XF	Unc
1657 (a)	—	300	600	1,250	2,750	6,000

KM# 85 THALER

Silver **Ruler:** Karl Ludwig **Obv:** Bust right in inner circle **Obv. Legend:** CAR. LVD. D. G. C. PR. **Rev:** 3 shields of arms, legend, date **Rev. Legend:** DOMINVS PROVIDEBIT. **Mint:** Heidelberg **Note:** Dav. #7152. Prev. Pfalz-Simmern KM#93.

Date	Mintage	VG	F	VF	XF	Unc
1657	—	600	1,200	2,500	4,500	—

KM# 93 THALER

Silver **Ruler:** Karl Ludwig **Obv:** Bust of Karl Ludwig right **Rev:** 3 shields of arms in inner circle, legend, date **Mint:** Heidelberg **Note:** Dav. #7153. Prev. Pfalz-Simmern KM#99.

Date	Mintage	VG	F	VF	XF	Unc
1659	—	235	450	950	1,850	5,000
166Z	—	235	450	950	1,850	5,000
1667	—	235	450	950	1,850	5,000
1669	—	235	450	950	1,850	5,000
1670	—	235	450	950	1,850	5,000

KM# 103 THALER

Silver **Ruler:** Christian August **Obv:** Bust right without inner circle **Rev:** Crowned arms in Order of the Garter Band, date above **Mint:** Heidelberg **Note:** Dav. #7154. Prev. Pfalz-Simmern KM#106.

Date	Mintage	VG	F	VF	XF	Unc
1661	—	600	1,200	2,500	4,500	—

KM# 106 THALER

Silver **Ruler:** Karl Ludwig **Obv:** Facing busts, legend around **Rev:** 5-line inscription, date on 5th line, mint officials' below **Note:** Dav. #7155. Prev. Pfalz-Simmern KM#M1.

Date	Mintage	VG	F	VF	XF	Unc
1671 IL	—	—	—	12,000	20,000	—

Note: Künker Auction 180, 1-11, XF realized approximately $19,170.

KM# 117 THALER

Silver **Ruler:** Karl von Simmern **Obv:** Bust right, dots at shoulder **Rev:** Helmeted and supported arms within Garter Order band, date below **Mint:** Heidelberg **Note:** Dav. #7156. Prev. Pfalz-Simmern KM#115.

Date	Mintage	VG	F	VF	XF	Unc
1681 IL	—	650	1,350	2,750	5,000	—

KM# 118 THALER

Silver **Ruler:** Karl von Simmern **Obv:** Bust right with smaller head, shorter hair, lion's face at shoulder **Mint:** Heidelberg **Note:** Dav. #7156A. Prev. Pfalz-Simmern KM#116.

Date	Mintage	VG	F	VF	XF	Unc
1681	—	600	1,200	2,500	4,750	—

KM# 138 THALER

Silver **Ruler:** Philipp Wilhelm **Obv:** Bust of Philipp Wilhelm right **Obv. Legend:** P. W. C. P. R. ... **Rev:** Crowned arms, date at end of legend **Rev. Legend:** M. D. C. V. S. M. R. & M. D. I. R. **Note:** Dav. #7176. Prev. Pfalz-Neuburg KM#42.

Date	Mintage	VG	F	VF	XF	Unc
1688 Rare	—	—	—	—	—	—

KM# 142 THALER

Silver **Ruler:** Johann Wilhelm **Obv:** Bust of Johann Wilhelm right, legend begins at 8 o'clock **Obv. Legend:** I. W. D. G. C. ... **Rev. Legend:** B. I. C. & M. D ... **Note:** Dav. #7177. Prev. Pfalz-Neuburg KM#46.

Date	Mintage	VG	F	VF	XF	Unc
1694 Rare	—	—	—	—	—	—

Note: Dr. Busso Peus Nachfolger Auction 381, 11-04, XF/Unc realized approximately $35,555

KM# 150 THALER

Silver **Ruler:** Christian August **Obv:** Bust of Christian August right, legend begins at 8 o'clock **Obv. Legend:** I. W. D. G. C. P. R. & ARCHIT & . L. L. **Rev. Legend:** B. I. C. ... M. D. C. V. S. ... **Note:** Dav. #7179. Prev. Pfalz-Neuburg KM#53.

Date	Mintage	VG	F	VF	XF	Unc
1700 IL	—	700	1,400	2,750	5,000	—

KM# 76 1-1/2 THALER

Silver **Ruler:** Bavarian Rule **Obv:** Bust of Maximilian I right **Obv. Legend:** MAXIMILIANVS D:G: COM: PAL: RHENI ... TRI: BAVARIA • DVX • **Rev:** Supported arms **Rev. Legend:** SACRI ROM • IMP • ARCHIDAR ... E • PRINCEPS • ELECTOR **Mint:** Heidelberg **Note:** Dav. #6095. Prev. Pfalz-Simmern KM#77.

Date	Mintage	VG	F	VF	XF	Unc
1627 Rare	—	—	—	—	—	—

KM# 39 2 THALER

Silver **Ruler:** Friedrich IV **Obv:** 1/2-length bust right, sword on right shoulder, orb in left hand **Rev:** 3-fold arms divide date **Mint:** Mannheim **Note:** Dav. #7145. Prev. Pfalz-Simmern KM#29.

Date	Mintage	VG	F	VF	XF	Unc
1610 Rare	—	—	—	—	—	—

KM# 130 2 THALER

Silver **Ruler:** Philipp Wilhelm **Obv:** 3 gothic canopies, St. Peter enthroned under central canopy, Counts Ruprecht I and II kneeling in left and right canopies **Obv. Legend:** VNIVERSITATIS. HEIDELBERG FESTVM. SECVLARE. III **Rev:** 13-line inscription with Roman Numeral date

Date	Mintage	VG	F	VF	XF	Unc
MDCXXCVI (1686) IL Rare	—	—	—	—	—	—

KM# 152 2 THALER
Silver **Ruler:** Johann Wilhelm **Obv:** Bust of Johann Wilhelm right **Rev:** Shield of arms **Note:** Dav. #7178. Prev. Pfalz-Neuburg KM#54.

Date	Mintage	VG	F	VF	XF	Unc
1700 Rare	—	—	—	—	—	—

TRADE COINAGE

KM# 73 GOLDGULDEN
3.5000 g., 0.9860 Gold 0.1109 oz. AGW **Ruler:** Friedrich V **Obv:** Lion **Rev:** Palatine arms in 3 shields **Mint:** Heidelberg **Note:** Fr. #1998. Prev. Pfalz-Simmern KM#52.

Date	Mintage	VG	F	VF	XF	Unc
1621	—	1,100	2,100	4,500	8,400	—

KM# 74 GOLDGULDEN
3.5000 g., 0.9860 Gold 0.1109 oz. AGW **Ruler:** Friedrich IV **Obv:** Rampant lion in inner circle **Mint:** Heidelberg **Note:** Fr. #1999. Prev. Pfalz-Simmern KM#53.

Date	Mintage	VG	F	VF	XF	Unc
1621	—	2,200	4,500	9,000	16,000	—

KM# 22 2-3/4 GOLDGULDEN
3.5000 g., 0.9860 Gold 0.1109 oz. AGW **Ruler:** Friedrich IV **Obv:** 1/2-figure of Friedrich IV w/sword and orb right **Rev:** Crown above 3 shields of arms, date divided below **Mint:** Mannheim **Note:** Fr. #1994. Prev. Pfalz-Simmern KM#18.

Date	Mintage	VG	F	VF	XF	Unc
1608 Rare	—	—	—	—	—	—

KM# 34 10 GOLDGULDEN (Portugalöser)
Gold, 40 mm. **Ruler:** Johann II **Obv:** Bust to right in circle **Obv. Legend:** IOHAN. D.G. CO. PAL. RH. TV. ET. ADMI. EL. PAL. D. BA. C. V. E. S. **Rev:** Three small shields of arms, 2 over 1, crown above, date at end of legend **Rev. Legend:** VERBVM. DOMINI. MANET. IN AETERNVM. A. **Note:** Struck from Thaler dies, KM#35.

Date	Mintage	Good	VG	F	VF	XF
1610 Rare	—	—	—	—	—	—

KM# 110 1/4 DUCAT
0.8750 g., Gold **Ruler:** Karl Ludwig **Obv:** Bust of Karl Ludwig right in inner circle **Rev:** Helmet above 3 shields of arms in inner circle, date in legend **Note:** Fr. #2004. Prev. Pfalz-Simmern KM#111.

Date	Mintage	VG	F	VF	XF	Unc
1674	—	550	1,100	2,400	5,500	—

KM# 108 1/2 DUCAT
1.7500 g., 0.9860 Gold 0.0555 oz. AGW **Ruler:** Karl Ludwig **Obv:** Bust of Karl Ludwig right **Rev:** 3 shields of arms **Note:** Fr. #2003. Prev. Pfalz-Simmern KM#110.

Date	Mintage	VG	F	VF	XF	Unc
1673	—	650	1,500	3,650	6,600	—

KM# 112 1/2 DUCAT
1.7500 g., 0.9860 Gold 0.0555 oz. AGW **Ruler:** Karl Ludwig **Obv:** Bust of Karl Ludwig right in inner circle **Rev:** Date in legend at right **Note:** Fr. #2002. Prev. Pfalz-Simmern KM#112. Rhine Gold.

Date	Mintage	VG	F	VF	XF	Unc
1674	—	550	1,300	2,800	5,500	—

KM# 54 DUCAT
Gold **Ruler:** Friedrich V **Obv:** Full-length facing armored figure holding orb, helmet at feet, titles of Friedrich V **Rev:** 3 small shields of arms, 2 above 1, electoral hat above, all in circle, date at end of legend **Rev. Legend:** MONETA. NOVA. AVREA. ANNO. **Mint:** Heidelberg

Date	Mintage	VG	F	VF	XF	Unc
1612 Rare	—	—	—	—	—	—

KM# 49 DUCAT
3.5000 g., 0.9860 Gold 0.1109 oz. AGW **Ruler:** Friedrich V **Obv:** Equestrian figure of Friedrich V right in inner circle **Rev:** Crown above 3 shields of arms in inner circle, date in legend **Note:** Fr. #1997. Prev. Pfalz-Simmern KM#31.

Date	Mintage	VG	F	VF	XF	Unc
1612	—	3,250	5,900	9,800	—	—

KM# 86 DUCAT
3.5000 g., 0.9860 Gold 0.1109 oz. AGW **Ruler:** Karl Ludwig **Obv:** Bust of Karl Ludwig right in inner circle **Rev:** Crown above 3 shields **Note:** Fr. #2000. Vicariat issue. Prev. Pfalz-Simmern KM#94.

Date	Mintage	VG	F	VF	XF	Unc
1657	—	1,000	2,000	4,600	8,300	—

KM# 94 DUCAT
3.5000 g., 0.9860 Gold 0.1109 oz. AGW **Ruler:** Karl Ludwig **Obv:** Bust of Karl Ludwig right **Rev:** Crowned 3 shields in inner circle **Note:** Fr. #2001. Prev. Pfalz-Simmern KM#100.

Date	Mintage	VG	F	VF	XF	Unc
1659	—	925	2,150	5,100	9,200	—
1662	—	925	2,150	5,100	9,200	—
1673	—	925	2,150	5,100	9,200	—

KM# 122 DUCAT
3.5000 g., 0.9860 Gold 0.1109 oz. AGW **Ruler:** Karl von Simmern **Obv:** Bust of Karl right in inner circle **Note:** Fr. #2005. Prev. Pfalz-Simmern KM#117.

Date	Mintage	VG	F	VF	XF	Unc
1682	—	725	1,500	3,300	6,600	—
1683	—	725	1,500	3,300	6,600	—

KM# 124 DUCAT
3.5000 g., 0.9860 Gold 0.1109 oz. AGW **Ruler:** Johann Wilhelm **Obv:** Bust of Johann Wilhelm right **Rev:** Crowned arms **Note:** Prev. Pfalz-Sulzbach KM#6.

Date	Mintage	VG	F	VF	XF	Unc
1683	—	450	1,000	2,200	4,400	—
1686	—	450	1,000	2,200	4,400	—

KM# 53 2 DUCAT
7.0000 g., 0.9860 Gold 0.2219 oz. AGW **Ruler:** Friedrich V **Obv:** Equestrian figure of Friedrich V right in inner circle **Rev:** Crown above 3 shields of arms in inner circle, date in legend **Note:** Fr. #1996. Prev. Pfalz-Simmern KM#32.

Date	Mintage	VG	F	VF	XF	Unc
1612 Rare	—	—	—	—	—	—

KM# 56 2 DUCAT
Gold **Ruler:** Johann II **Obv:** Bust right in circle, date at end of inner legend, outer legend - titles of Johann II **Obv. Legend:** VICARIVS DVXB. CO. V. & SPAN **Rev:** Crowned imperial eagle, legend divided by crown at top and 3 small shields of arms at left, right and bottom **Rev. Legend:** VERB. - DOMI. - MANI. - ?TER. **Mint:** Heidelberg **Note:** Vicariat issue.

Date	Mintage	VG	F	VF	XF	Unc
161Z Rare	—	—	—	—	—	—

KM# 55 4 DUCAT
14.0000 g., 0.9860 Gold 0.4438 oz. AGW **Ruler:** Friedrich V **Obv:** Equestrian figure of Friedrich V right **Rev:** Crown above 3 shields in inner circle **Note:** Fr. #1995. Prev. Pfalz-Simmern KM#33.

Date	Mintage	VG	F	VF	XF	Unc
1612 Rare	—	—	—	—	—	—

PFALZ-NEUBURG

Pfalz-Neuburg takes its name designation from the town Neuburg on the Danube, 11 miles (18 kilometers) west of Ingolstadt, in the Upper Palatinate (Oberpfalz). It was acquired by Electoral Pfalz from Bavaria-Landshut when the ducal line of that principality became extinct in 1504. Two nephews of the elector ruled in Pfalz-Neuburg jointly, then the survivor continued until he succeeded to the electorate in 1556. In the following year, Wolfgang, the count Palatine (Pfalzgraf) of Pfalz-Zweibrücken purchased Neuburg and Sulzbach. The new line of Pfalz-Neuburg was founded by the eldest son of Wolfgang in the division of 1569. Pfalz-Neuburg acquired Pfalz-Sulzbach in 1604, then divided into Pfalz-Neuburg and Pfalz-Sulzbach in 1614. In 1685, the male line of descent in the Electoral Line from Pfalz-Simmern failed and the electoral dignity passed to Pfalz-Neuburg. See Electoral Pfalz for coinage after 1685.

RULERS
Otto Heinrich, 1507-1556
Philipp the Warlike, 1507-1548
Philipp Ludwig, 1569-1614
Wolfgang-Wilhelm, 1614-1653
Philipp Wilhelm, 1653-1685, died 1690

MINT OFFICIALS' INITIALS

Other than Neuburg itself, mints were opened in four locations during the Kipper Period of the Thirty Years' War. Gundelfingen is a town on the River Brenz close to where it joins the Danube, next to the larger town of Lauingen and about halfway between Ulm and Donauwörth. Höchstädt is a town on the Danube about 12 miles (21km) southwest of Donauwörth. Stockau is a very small village on the River Paar 14 miles (23km) east-southeast of Neuburg and Kallmünz is a village at the junction of the Naab and Vils Rivers, 11 miles (19km) northwest of Regensburg.

Gundelfingen Mint (G)

Initial	Date	Name
	July, 1621	Abraham Jud
(a)= 	1621-22	Heinrich Brandes
(b)= 	Jan. 1622	Johann Rentsch
	Aug. 1622-	Friedrich Gebhardt
	1622	Joachim Friedrich Krauss, warden

Höchstädt Mint (H)

Initial	Date	Name
	Jan. 1622-	Johann Rentsch

Kallmünz Mint (K or C)

Initial	Date	Name
(e)=  or 	1622	Heinrich Brandes
CE	1623-25	Karl Ernst
	1623	Jonas Federer
(f)= 	1626-27	Friedrich held
	Ca. 1629	Christof Resel, die-cutter
(g)=  or 	1625-32	Jörg (Georg) Thomas Paul
ITP/GTP		Jörg (Georg) Thomas paul
(h)= face in half moon to left	1625	Christof Geissler

Stockau Mint (S)

Initial	Date	Name
	Sept. 1621	Abraham Jud
(c)= 	1622	Schottmüller
(d)= 	Jan. 1622	Johann Rentsch

REFERENCE

N = Alfred Noss, *Die pfälzischen Münzen des Hauses Wittelsbach,* **v. 4,** *Pfalz-Veldenz, Pfalz-Neuburg, Pfalz-Sulzbach,* **Munich, 1938.**

PALATINE COUNTSHIP

REGULAR COINAGE

KM# 53 PFENNIG
Silver **Ruler:** Wolfgang-Wilhelm **Obv:** Large 'N' with date above in circle **Rev:** Oval Wittelsbach arms divide mintmaster's initials, 'C' above, all in circle **Mint:** Kallmunz **Note:** Ref. N#341.

Date	Mintage	VG	F	VF	XF	Unc
1624 CE	—	10.00	25.00	50.00	100	—

KM# 62 PFENNIG
Silver **Ruler:** Wolfgang-Wilhelm **Obv:** Large double 'W' **Rev:** Small Spanish shield of Wittelsbach arms in circle **Mint:** Kallmunz **Note:** Ref. N#406-07. Varieties exist.

Date	Mintage	VG	F	VF	XF	Unc
ND(1625-30)	—	10.00	25.00	50.00	100	—

KM# 66 PFENNIG
Silver **Ruler:** Wolfgang-Wilhelm **Obv:** Large double 'W', C.P.R. (Comes Palatinus Rheni) above, date below, all in circle **Rev:** Small spanish shield of Wittelsbach arms in circle **Mint:** Kallmunz **Note:** Ref. N#365.

Date	Mintage	VG	F	VF	XF	Unc
1626	—	10.00	25.00	50.00	100	—

KM# 30 1/2 SCHILLING (1/16 Thaler)
Silver **Ruler:** Wolfgang-Wilhelm **Obv:** Crowned oval 8-fold arms with central shield, all within Order of Golden Fleece **Obv. Legend:** IN DEO MEA - CONSOLATIO **Rev:** 7-line inscription **Rev. Inscription:** HALBER / BAIRISCH. SC. / HILLING. NACH / ALTEM. VALOR / .XVI. FVR. EIN / REICHSDALER / (date) **Mint:** Gundelfingen **Note:** Bavarian standard. Ref. N#279.

Date	Mintage	VG	F	VF	XF	Unc
1622 (a)	—	—	—	—	—	—

KM# 31 1/2 SCHILLING (1/16 Thaler)
Silver **Ruler:** Wolfgang-Wilhelm **Obv:** Crowned oval 8-fold arms with central shield, al within Order of Golden Fleece **Obv. Legend:** IN DEO MEA - CONSOLATIO **Rev:** 7-line inscription, date at end **Rev. Inscription:** HALBER / BAIRISCH. SC. /

HILLING. NACH / ALTEM. VALER / .XVI. FVR. EIN / REISCHSDALER **Mint:** Gundelfingen **Note:** Ref. N#280.

Date	Mintage	VG	F	VF	XF	Unc
1622 (a)	—	—	—	—	—	—

KM# 3 1/2 KREUZER

Billon **Ruler:** Wolfgang-Wilhelm **Obv:** Similar to KM#2 but w/oval 8-fold arms with central shield within Order of Golden Fleece **Mint:** Kallmunz **Note:** Kipper. Ref. N#299.

Date	Mintage	Good	VG	F	VF	XF
ND(1621-22)	—	10.00	20.00	40.00	85.00	—

KM# 2 1/2 KREUZER

Billon **Ruler:** Wolfgang-Wilhelm **Obv:** 3 small adjacent shields of arms with electoral hat above divide date, titles of Wolfgang Wilhelm **Rev:** Inscription in wreath **Rev. Inscription:** 120 / 1/2 K **Mint:** Kallmunz **Note:** Kipper. Ref. N#297-98.

Date	Mintage	VG	F	VF	XF	Unc
1621	—	25.00	50.00	100	—	—
1622	—	25.00	50.00	100	—	—

KM# 8 1/2 KREUZER

Silver **Ruler:** Wolfgang-Wilhelm **Obv:** 3 small shields of arms, 2 above 1, electoral hat above **Obv. Legend:** W ★ W ★ - ★ CP ★ R ★ (Wolfgang Wilhelm Comes Palatinus Rheni) **Mint:** Kallmunz **Note:** Ref. N#320-21. Varieties exist. Uniface.

Date	Mintage	VG	F	VF	XF	Unc
ND(1622-23)	—	27.00	55.00	115	—	—

KM# 38 1/2 KREUZER

Silver **Ruler:** Wolfgang-Wilhelm **Obv:** Hatted 3-fold arms in Spanish shield **Obv. Legend:** W. W. C. P. R. **Rev:** Imperial orb with 1/2 divides date **Mint:** Kallmunz **Note:** Ref. N#330-31. Varieties exist.

Date	Mintage	VG	F	VF	XF	Unc
1623	—	27.00	55.00	115	—	—

KM# 55 1/2 KREUZER

Silver **Ruler:** Wolfgang-Wilhelm **Obv:** 3 small shields of arms, 2 above 1, electoral hat divides date **Mint:** Kallmunz **Note:** Uniface. Ref. N#340, 350, 361-64, 383, 404. Varieties exist.

Date	Mintage	VG	F	VF	XF	Unc
1624	—	15.00	30.00	50.00	100	—
1625	—	15.00	30.00	50.00	100	—
1626	—	15.00	30.00	50.00	100	—
1628	—	15.00	30.00	50.00	100	—
1632	—	15.00	30.00	50.00	100	—

KM# 75 1/2 KREUZER

Silver **Ruler:** Wolfgang-Wilhelm **Obv:** Oval 3-fold arms, electoral hat above divides date, legend around **Obv. Legend:** W. W. C. P. R. **Mint:** Kallmunz **Note:** Ref. N#384. Uniface.

Date	Mintage	VG	F	VF	XF	Unc
1628	—	27.00	55.00	115	—	—

KM# 10 KREUZER

Billon **Ruler:** Wolfgang-Wilhelm **Obv:** 8-fold arms with central shield, electoral hat above divides date, titles of Wolfgang Wilhelm **Rev:** 60/K in wreath **Mint:** Kallmunz **Note:** Ref. N#296. Kipper.

Date	Mintage	VG	F	VF	XF	Unc
1622	—	10.00	20.00	40.00	85.00	—

KM# 68 KREUZER

Silver **Ruler:** Wolfgang-Wilhelm **Obv:** Double-cross in circle, value 'I' in small central shield, date divided at top, titles of Wolfgang Wilhelm **Rev:** Hatted 8-fold arms with central shield, titles continued **Mint:** Kallmunz **Note:** Ref. N#359-60, 376. Varieties exist.

Date	Mintage	VG	F	VF	XF	Unc
1626	—	15.00	30.00	60.00	—	—
1627	—	15.00	30.00	60.00	—	—

KM# 77 KREUZER

Silver **Ruler:** Wolfgang-Wilhelm **Obv:** Cross with lily ends in circle, value 'I' in small central shield, date divided at top, titles of Woldgang Wilhelm **Mint:** Kallmunz **Note:** Ref. N#382.

Date	Mintage	VG	F	VF	XF	Unc
1628 (g)	—	15.00	30.00	60.00	—	—

KM# 41 KREUZER

Billon **Ruler:** Philipp Wilhelm **Obv:** Crowned lion rampant left in circle **Obv. Legend:** P. W. C. P. R. S... **Rev:** 1 KREUTZER **Rev. Legend:** B. I. C. M. D. C...

Date	Mintage	VG	F	VF	XF	Unc
1688 gb	—	20.00	40.00	80.00	160	—

KM# 11 KREUZER (4 Pfennig)

Copper **Ruler:** Wolfgang-Wilhelm **Obv:** Hatted 8-fold arms with central shield divide date, titles of Wolfgang Wilhelm **Rev:** II + II in circle **Mint:** Kallmunz **Note:** Ref. N#300.

Date	Mintage	VG	F	VF	XF	Unc
1622	1,053,000	12.00	25.00	55.00	110	—

KM# 12 KREUZER (4 Pfennig)

Copper **Ruler:** Wolfgang-Wilhelm **Obv:** Hatted oval arms with central shield dividing date, titles of Wolfgang Wilhelm **Rev:** II + II in circle **Mint:** Kallmunz **Note:** Ref. N#301-07. Varieties exist.

Date	Mintage	VG	F	VF	XF	Unc
ND(1622-23)	—	10.00	20.00	40.00	80.00	—

KM# 40 2 KREUZER (1/2 Batzen)

1.0800 g., Silver, 19 mm. **Ruler:** Wolfgang-Wilhelm **Obv:** Hatted 8-fold arms with central shield, titles of Wolfgang Wilhelm **Rev:** Imperial orb with 2 or Z divides date **Rev. Legend:** MON. NOVA. PAL(A)NEOBVRG (or variant) **Mint:** Kallmunz **Note:** Ref. N#326-29, 334-39, 343-49, 353-58, 368-75, 377-81, 387-89, 393-95, 399-403, 405. Varieties exist.

Date	Mintage	VG	F	VF	XF	Unc
1623	—	10.00	18.00	30.00	65.00	—
1623 (a)	—	10.00	18.00	30.00	65.00	—
1624	—	10.00	18.00	30.00	65.00	—
1625	—	10.00	18.00	30.00	65.00	—
1625 (g)	—	20.00	48.00	30.00	65.00	—
1625 (h)	—	10.00	18.00	30.00	65.00	—
1626 (c)	—	10.00	18.00	30.00	65.00	—
1626 (g)	—	10.00	18.00	30.00	65.00	—
1627 (g)	—	10.00	18.00	30.00	65.00	—
1628	—	10.00	18.00	30.00	65.00	—
1628 (g)	—	10.00	18.00	30.00	65.00	—
1629 (g)	—	10.00	18.00	30.00	65.00	—
1630 (g)	—	10.00	18.00	30.00	65.00	—
1631 (g)	—	10.00	18.00	30.00	65.00	—
1632 (g)	—	10.00	18.00	30.00	65.00	—
163Z (g)	—	10.00	18.00	30.00	65.00	—
1634 (g)	—	10.00	18.00	30.00	65.00	—

KM# 42 3 KREUZER (Groschen)

Silver **Ruler:** Wolfgang-Wilhelm **Obv:** Crowned rampant Pfalz lion to left in circle, titles of Wolfgang Wilhelm **Rev:** Imperial orb with 3 divides date, titles continued **Note:** Ref. N#325.

Date	Mintage	VG	F	VF	XF	Unc
1623 (b)	—	—	—	—	—	—

KM# 5 24 KREUZER (Sechsbätzner)

Silver **Ruler:** Wolfgang-Wilhelm **Obv:** Crowned lion rampant left holding ornamented oval with 24 **Obv. Legend:** MONETA. NOVA ... **Rev:** Ornate 8-fold arms with central shield, Order of Golden Fleece around, electoral hat above **Rev. Legend:** IN DEO MEA - CONSOLATIO **Mint:** Gundelfingen **Note:** Ref. N#263. Kipper.

Date	Mintage	VG	F	VF	XF	Unc
ND(1621) (a)	—	200	325	500	950	—

KM# 6 24 KREUZER (Sechsbätzner)

Silver **Ruler:** Wolfgang-Wilhelm **Obv:** Crowned lion rampant left holding ornamented oval, date below with value **Obv. Legend:** MONETA. NOVA ... **Rev:** Ornate 8-fold arms with central shield, Order of Golden Fleece around, electoral hat above **Rev. Legend:** IN DEO MEA - CONSOLATIO **Mint:** Gundelfingen **Note:** Ref. N#264-65, 278. Kipper.

Date	Mintage	VG	F	VF	XF	Unc
1621 (a)	—	150	275	450	925	—
1622 (g)	—	150	275	450	925	—
1622 G	—	150	275	450	925	—

KM# 14 24 KREUZER (Sechsbätzner)

Silver **Ruler:** Wolfgang-Wilhelm **Obv:** Crowned lion rampant left with mint mark 'G' below, ornamented oval with 24 **Obv. Legend:** MONETA. NOVA ... **Rev:** Ornate 8-fold arms with central shield, Order of Golden Fleece around, electoral hat above **Rev. Legend:** IN DEO MEA - CONSOLATIO. **Mint:** Gundelfingen **Note:** Ref. N#266-67, 271-72. Kipper.

Date	Mintage	VG	F	VF	XF	Unc
1622 G	—	150	275	450	925	—
ND G	—	150	275	450	925	—

KM# 15 24 KREUZER (Sechsbätzner)

Silver **Ruler:** Wolfgang-Wilhelm **Obv:** Crowned lion rampant left holding ornamented oval with 24, date at end of legend **Obv. Legend:** MONETA. NOVA **Rev:** Ornate 8-fold arms with central shield, Order of Golden Fleece around, electoral hat above **Rev. Legend:** IN DEO MEA - CONSOLATIO **Mint:** Gundelfingen **Note:** Ref. N#268. Kipper.

Date	Mintage	VG	F	VF	XF	Unc
1622 (b)	—	150	275	450	925	—

KM# 16 24 KREUZER (Sechsbätzner)

Silver **Ruler:** Wolfgang-Wilhelm **Obv:** Crowned lion rampant left holding ornamented oval with 24, mint mark 'G' below lion, date at end of legend **Obv. Legend:** MONETA. NOVA ... **Rev:** Ornate 8-fold arms with central shield, Order of Golden Fleece around, electoral hat above **Rev. Legend:** IN DEO MEA - CONSOLATIO **Mint:** Gundelfingen **Note:** Ref. N#269-70.

Date	Mintage	VG	F	VF	XF	Unc
1622	—	150	275	450	925	—

KM# 17 24 KREUZER (Sechsbätzner)

Silver **Ruler:** Wolfgang-Wilhelm **Obv:** Crowned lion rampant left holding ornamented oval with 24, mint mark 'G' below lion, date by hind leg of lion **Obv. Legend:** MONETA. NOVA ... **Rev:** Ornate 8-fold arms with central shield, Order of Golden Fleece around, electoral hat abaove **Rev. Legend:** IN DEO MEA - CONSOLATIO **Mint:** Gundelfingen **Note:** Kipper. Ref. N#276-77.

Date	Mintage	VG	F	VF	XF	Unc
1622 G	—	150	275	450	925	—

KM# 18 24 KREUZER (Sechsbätzner)

Silver **Ruler:** Wolfgang-Wilhelm **Obv:** Crowned lion rampant left holding ornamented oval with 24 **Obv. Legend:** MONETA. NOVA ... **Rev:** Oval arms, Order of Golden Fleece around, electoral hat above **Rev. Legend:** IN DEO MEA - CONSOLATIO **Mint:** Stockau **Note:** Kipper. Ref. N#284.

Date	Mintage	VG	F	VF	XF	Unc
ND(1622) (c)	—	150	275	450	925	—

KM# 19 24 KREUZER (Sechsbätzner)

Silver **Ruler:** Wolfgang-Wilhelm **Obv:** Crowned lion rampant left holding ornamented oval with 24, 'S' below lion **Obv. Legend:** MONETA. NOVA ... **Rev:** Oval arms, Order of Golden Fleece around, electoral hat above **Rev. Legend:** IN DEO MEA - CONSOLATIO **Mint:** Stockau **Note:** Kipper. Ref. N#285, 287-88. Varieties exist.

Date	Mintage	VG	F	VF	XF	Unc
ND(1622) S	—	150	275	450	925	—
ND(1622) S (d)	—	150	275	450	925	—

KM# 20 24 KREUZER (Sechsbätzner)

Silver **Ruler:** Wolfgang-Wilhelm **Obv:** Crowned lion rampant left holding ornamented oval with 24, mint mark 'S' below lion **Obv. Legend:** MONETA. NOVA ... **Rev:** Oval arms, Order of Golden Fleece around, electoral hat above, date at end of legend **Rev. Legend:** IN DEO MEA - CONSOLATIO **Mint:** Stockau **Note:** Kipper. Ref. N#286.

Date	Mintage	VG	F	VF	XF	Unc
1622 S (d)	—	150	275	450	925	—

KM# 21 24 KREUZER (Sechsbätzner)

Silver **Ruler:** Wolfgang-Wilhelm **Obv:** Crowned lion rampant left holding ornamented oval with 24 **Obv. Legend:** MONETA. NOVA ... **Rev:** Ornate 8-fold arms with central shield, Order of Golden Fleece around, electoral hat above, date at end of legend **Rev. Legend:** IN DEO MEA - CONSOLATIO **Mint:** Hochstadt **Note:** Ref. N#289. Kipper.

Date	Mintage	VG	F	VF	XF	Unc
1622 H	—	150	275	450	925	—

KM# 22 24 KREUZER (Sechsbätzner)

Silver **Ruler:** Wolfgang-Wilhelm **Obv:** Crowned lion rampant left holding ornamented oval with 24, mint mark 'H' engraved over 'G' **Obv. Legend:** MONETA. NOVA ... **Rev:** Ornate 8-fold arms with central shield, Order of Golden Fleece around **Rev. Legend:** IN DEO MEA - CONSOLATIO **Mint:** Hochstadt **Note:** Ref. N#290. Kipper.

Date	Mintage	VG	F	VF	XF	Unc
ND(1622) H	—	150	275	450	925	—

KM# 23 24 KREUZER (Sechsbätzner)

Silver **Ruler:** Wolfgang-Wilhelm **Obv:** Crowned lion rampant left holding ornamental oval with 24, 'K' below lion **Obv. Legend:** MONETA. NOVA ... **Rev:** Ornately shaped arms, Order of Golden Fleece around, electoral hat above **Rev. Legend:** IN DEO MEA - CONSOLATIO **Mint:** Kallmunz **Note:** Ref. N#291-94. Kipper. Varieties exist.

Date	Mintage	VG	F	VF	XF	Unc
1622 K (e)	—	150	275	450	925	—
1622 K	—	150	275	450	925	—

KM# 95 30 KREUZER (1/2 Gulden)

Silver **Ruler:** Philipp Wilhelm **Obv:** Armored bust right, titles of Philip Wilhelm ending with date at top **Rev:** Crowned 8-fold arms with central shield, all in Order of Golden Fleece, value (30) below **Rev. Legend:** MONETA. NOVA ... **Mint:** Kallmunz **Note:** Ref. N#415.

Date	Mintage	VG	F	VF	XF	Unc
1674	—	225	450	625	1,150	—

KM# 25 48 KREUZER

Silver **Ruler:** Wolfgang-Wilhelm **Obv:** Crowned facing lion, seated and holding oval with '48' in paw, head divides date **Obv. Legend:** MONETA. NOVA ... **Rev:** Oval 8-fold arms with central shield, Order of Golden Fleece around, electoral hat above **Rev. Legend:** IN DEO MEA - CONSOLATIO **Mint:** Gundelfingen **Note:** Ref. N#273. Kipper. Varieties exist.

Date	Mintage	VG	F	VF	XF	Unc
1622 (a)	—	—	—	—	—	—

KM# 26 48 KREUZER

Silver **Ruler:** Wolfgang-Wilhelm **Obv:** Crowned facing lion, seated and holding oval with 48 in paw, date at end of legend **Obv. Legend:** MONETA. NOVA ? **Rev:** Oval 8 fold arms with central shield, Order of Golden Fleece around, electoral hat above **Rev. Legend:** IN DEO MEA - CONSOLATIO **Mint:** Gundelfingen **Note:** Ref. N#274. Varieties exist.

Date	Mintage	VG	F	VF	XF	Unc
1622	—	—	—	—	—	—

KM# 27 48 KREUZER

Silver **Ruler:** Wolfgang-Wilhelm **Obv:** Crowned, seated lion 1/2-right holding oval with 48 in paw, mint mark G below, head divides date **Obv. Legend:** MONETA. NOVA ... **Rev:** Oval 8-fold arms with central shield, Order of Golden Fleece around, electoral hat above **Rev. Legend:** IN DEO MEA - CONSOLATIO **Mint:** Gundelfingen **Note:** Ref. N#275.

Date	Mintage	VG	F	VF	XF	Unc
1622 G	—	—	—	—	—	—

KM# 28 48 KREUZER

Silver **Ruler:** Wolfgang-Wilhelm **Obv:** Crowned seated lion 1/2-right holding oval with 48 in paw, 'S' mint mark, no date **Obv. Legend:** MONETA. NOVA ... **Rev:** Oval 8-fold arms with central shield, Order of Golden Fleece around, electoral hat above **Rev. Legend:** IN DEO MEA - CONSOLATIO **Mint:** Stockau **Note:** Ref. N#281-83. Varieties exist.

Date	Mintage	VG	F	VF	XF	Unc
ND(1622) S	—	—	—	—	—	—
ND(1622) S (c)	—	—	—	—	—	—

KM# 97 60 KREUZER (1 Gulden)

Silver **Ruler:** Philipp Wilhelm **Obv:** Armored bust right divides date, titles of Philipp Wilhelm **Rev:** Crowned 8-fold arms with central shield, all within Order of Golden Fleece, value (60) below **Rev. Legend:** MONETA. NOVA ... **Mint:** Stockau **Note:** Dav. #757. Varieties exist.

Date	Mintage	VG	F	VF	XF	Unc
1674	—	125	250	475	925	—

KM# 98 60 KREUZER (1 Gulden)

Silver **Ruler:** Philipp Wilhelm **Obv:** Armored bust right, titles of Philipp Wilhelm ending with date above or divided by crown **Rev:** Crowned 8-fold arms with central shield, all in Order of Golden Fleece, value (60) below arms **Rev. Legend:** MONETA. NOVA ... **Mint:** Stockau **Note:** Dav. #758. Varieties exist.

Date	Mintage	VG	F	VF	XF	Unc
1674	—	100	200	325	675	—
1675	—	100	200	325	675	—

KM# 83 1/6 THALER

Silver **Ruler:** Wolfgang-Wilhelm **Obv:** Bust right in circle, value 1/6 in oval below, titles of Wolfgang Wilhelm **Rev:** Ornate 8-fold arms with central shield within Order of Golden Fleece divide mintmaster's initials, titles continued, date in legend **Mint:** Neuburg **Note:** Ref. N#392.

Date	Mintage	VG	F	VF	XF	Unc
1631 GTP	—	—	—	—	—	—

KM# 88 1/4 THALER

Silver **Ruler:** Wolfgang-Wilhelm **Obv:** Bust right in circle, titles of Wolfgang Wilhelm **Rev:** Ornate 8-fold arms with central shield within Order of Golden Fleece divide mintmaster's initials, titles continued **Mint:** Neuburg **Note:** Ref. N#319.

Date	Mintage	VG	F	VF	XF	Unc
ND(1632-35) (b)	—	—	—	—	—	—

KM# 44 1/2 THALER

Silver **Ruler:** Wolfgang-Wilhelm **Obv:** Collared bust right, outer legend with titles of Wolfgang Wilhelm **Obv. Legend:** IN DEO MEA - CONSOLATIO **Rev:** 8-fold arms with central shield, all within Order of Golden Fleece, crown above divides date, titles continued **Mint:** Neuburg **Note:** Ref. N#313, 318.

Date	Mintage	VG	F	VF	XF	Unc
1623	—	800	1,150	1,600	2,750	—
ND	—	800	1,150	1,600	2,750	—

KM# 57 1/2 THALER

Silver **Ruler:** Wolfgang-Wilhelm **Obv:** Collared bust right, value '1/2' at top, outer legend titles of Wolfgang Wilhelm **Rev:** 8-fold arms with central shield, all within Order of Golden Fleece, crown above, titles continued with date at end **Mint:** Neuburg **Note:** Ref. N#333.

Date	Mintage	VG	F	VF	XF	Unc
1624	—	500	850	1,200	1,950	—

KM# 90 1/2 THALER

Silver **Ruler:** Wolfgang-Wilhelm **Obv:** Armored bust right, titles of Wolfgang Wilhelm **Obv. Legend:** IN DEO MEA - CONSOLATIO **Rev:** 8-fold arms with central shield, all within Order of Golden Fleece, crown above, titles continued, date at end of legend **Mint:** Neuburg **Note:** Ref. N#397.

Date	Mintage	VG	F	VF	XF	Unc
1632 (g)	—	—	—	—	—	—

KM# 33 THALER

Silver **Ruler:** Wolfgang-Wilhelm **Obv:** Ruffled bust right, inside legend **Obv. Legend:** IN. DEO. MEO. CONSOLATIO. **Rev:** Crowned arms divide date **Note:** Dav. #7158. Prev. KM#5.

Date	Mintage	VG	F	VF	XF	Unc
1622	—	270	550	1,000	1,850	—

KM# 35 THALER

Silver **Ruler:** Wolfgang-Wilhelm **Note:** Klippe. Dav. #7158A. Prev. KM#6.

Date	Mintage	VG	F	VF	XF	Unc
1622 Rare	—	—	—	—	—	—

KM# 36 THALER

Silver **Ruler:** Wolfgang-Wilhelm **Obv:** Inside legend **Obv. Legend:** IN. DEO. MEA. CONSLATIO **Note:** Dav. #7159. Prev. KM#7.

Date	Mintage	VG	F	VF	XF	Unc
1622	—	300	600	1,250	2,500	—

KM# 46 THALER

Silver **Ruler:** Wolfgang-Wilhelm **Obv:** Large collar, fuller beard **Rev:** Crowned arms divide date above **Note:** Dav. #7160.

Date	Mintage	VG	F	VF	XF	Unc
1623	—	225	425	850	1,650	—

KM# 47 THALER

Silver **Ruler:** Wolfgang-Wilhelm **Obv. Legend:** WOLF. GVIL. CO. PAL. RH. DVX... **Note:** Dav. #7161. Prev. KM#10.

Date	Mintage	VG	F	VF	XF	Unc
1623	—	225	425	850	1,650	—

KM# 48 THALER

Silver **Ruler:** Wolfgang-Wilhelm **Obv. Legend:** ...CLI. ET. MONT. **Note:** Dav. #7162. Prev. KM#11.

Date	Mintage	VG	F	VF	XF	Unc
1623	—	225	425	850	1,650	—

KM# 49 THALER

Silver **Ruler:** Wolfgang-Wilhelm **Obv:** Larger head **Obv. Legend:** ... MO: **Note:** Dav. #7162A. Prev. KM#12.

Date	Mintage	VG	F	VF	XF	Unc
1623	—	225	425	850	1,650	—

KM# 50 THALER

Silver **Ruler:** Wolfgang-Wilhelm **Obv:** Bust right divides date **Note:** Dav. #7163. Prev. KM#13.

Date	Mintage	VG	F	VF	XF	Unc
1623	—	225	425	850	1,650	—

KM# 51 THALER

Silver **Ruler:** Wolfgang-Wilhelm **Obv:** Ruffled bust divides inner legend **Rev:** Crowned arms **Note:** Dav. #7164. Prev. KM#14.

Date	Mintage	VG	F	VF	XF	Unc
ND (b)	—	225	425	850	1,650	—

KM# 59 THALER

Silver **Ruler:** Wolfgang-Wilhelm **Obv:** Ruffled bust right, ornamented shoulder, inner legend **Rev:** Crowned arms in Order chain **Note:** Dav. #7166. Prev. KM#15.

Date	Mintage	VG	F	VF	XF	Unc
1624 CE	—	225	425	850	1,650	2,500

KM# 64 THALER

Silver **Ruler:** Wolfgang-Wilhelm **Obv:** Plain inner field **Rev:** Crowned ornate arms, date in legend **Note:** Dav. #7167. Prev. KM#17.

Date	Mintage	VG	F	VF	XF	Unc
1625 (h)	—	225	425	850	1,650	—
1626 ITP	—	225	425	850	1,650	—

KM# 70 THALER

Silver **Ruler:** Wolfgang-Wilhelm **Obv:** Bust right in inner circle, titles of Wolfgang-Wilhelm **Rev:** Crowned shield of arms **Note:** Dav. #7168. Prev. KM#18.

Date	Mintage	VG	F	VF	XF	Unc
1626 GTP	—	350	675	1,200	2,250	—

KM# 72 THALER

Silver **Ruler:** Wolfgang-Wilhelm **Rev:** Capped arms in Order chain divide GT-P **Note:** Dav. #7170. Prev. KM#19.

Date	Mintage	VG	F	VF	XF	Unc
1627 GTP Rare	—	—	—	—	—	—

KM# 79 THALER

Silver **Ruler:** Wolfgang-Wilhelm **Obv:** Taller bust **Note:** Dav. #7172. Prev. KM#21.

Date	Mintage	VG	F	VF	XF	Unc
16Z9 GTP	—	350	750	1,350	2,750	—

KM# 81 THALER

Silver **Ruler:** Wolfgang-Wilhelm **Rev:** City view with angels above, NEOBVRG below **Note:** Varieties exist. Dav. #7173. Prev. KM#22. Tiny letters between pillars of bridge G-T-P-M-M-I-C-O-L-M = Georg Thomas Paur Münz Meister in Colmünz and on the bridge itself in tiny letters CHRISTOF RESEL, the name of the die-cutter.

Date	Mintage	VG	F	VF	XF	Unc
16Z9 GTP Rare	—	—	—	—	—	—

KM# 85 THALER

Silver **Ruler:** Wolfgang-Wilhelm **Obv:** Small bust **Obv. Legend:** ...ET: MON. **Rev:** Crowned arms, date in legend **Note:** Dav. #7174. Prev. KM#30.

Date	Mintage	VG	F	VF	XF	Unc
1631 GTP Rare	—	—	—	—	—	—

KM# 86 THALER

Silver **Ruler:** Wolfgang-Wilhelm **Obv. Legend:** ...ET: MO. **Note:** Dav. #7174A. Prev. KM#31.

Date	Mintage	VG	F	VF	XF	Unc
1631 GTP Rare	—	—	—	—	—	—

KM# 92 THALER

Silver **Ruler:** Wolfgang-Wilhelm **Obv. Legend:** ...MONE. **Rev:** Oval arms supported by angels **Note:** Dav. #7175. Prev. KM#32.

Date	Mintage	VG	F	VF	XF	Unc
1632 (g)	—	270	550	950	1,750	—

KM# 93 THALER

Silver **Ruler:** Wolfgang-Wilhelm **Obv. Legend:** ...MONT. **Note:** Dav. #7175A. Prev. KM#33.

Date	Mintage	VG	F	VF	XF	Unc
1632 (g)	—	270	550	950	1,750	—

KM# 34 2 THALER

Silver **Ruler:** Wolfgang-Wilhelm **Obv:** Ruffled bust right, inner legend **Obv. Legend:** IN. DEO. MEO. CONSOLATIO. **Rev:** Crowned arms divide date **Note:** Similar to 1 Thaler, KM#33. Dav. #7157. Prev. KM#8.

Date	Mintage	VG	F	VF	XF	Unc
1622 Rare	—	—	—	—	—	—

KM# 60 2 THALER

Silver **Ruler:** Wolfgang-Wilhelm **Obv:** Ruffled bust right in inner circle, titles of Wolfgang **Obv. Legend:** WOLFG • WIL • D • G • C • PA • RHE • D • BA • CL • EM • T * **Rev:** Crowned shield of arms, date at end of legend **Rev. Legend:** CO. VEL. SP. MAR • RA - MOR • D • RA • **Note:** Klippe. Similar to 1 Thaler, KM#59. Dav. #7165.

Date	Mintage	VG	F	VF	XF	Unc
1624 CE Rare	—	—	—	—	—	—

KM# 73 2 THALER

Silver **Ruler:** Wolfgang-Wilhelm **Note:** Dav. #7169. Prev. KM#20. Similar to 1 Thaler, KM#72.

Date	Mintage	VG	F	VF	XF	Unc
1627 GTP Rare	—	—	—	—	—	—

KM# 80 2 THALER

Silver **Ruler:** Wolfgang-Wilhelm **Obv:** Smaller bust right **Rev:** Crowned arms **Note:** Dav. #7171. Prev. KM#23.

Date	Mintage	VG	F	VF	XF	Unc
16Z9 GTP Rare	—	—	—	—	—	—

PFALZ-SIMMERN

One of the four branches of the Pfalz stemming from the division of 1410, Pfalz-Simmern was itself divided into the Simmern and Zweibrücken lines after one generation in 1459. When the electoral line in the Rhenish Pfalz (Rheinpfalz) came to an end a century later, the electoral dignity passed to the eldest of three brothers in Pfalz-Simmern, while the younger two ruled successively in Simmern. After the last brother died, Pfalz-Simmern was ruled by the electoral line until 1610, at which time the younger brother of the Elector was given the countship there. This final line in Simmern only lasted two generations and reverted to the Elector once again in 1674. However, the Electoral line itself became extinct in 1685 and the Electorate with all its titles passed to Pfalz-Neuburg.

RULERS

Stephan, 1410-1459
Friedrich I, 1459-1480
Johann I der Ältere, 1480-1509
Johann II der Jüngere, 1509-1557
Friedrich III, 1557-1559, Elector until 1576
Georg, 1559-1569
Richard, 1569-1598
Johann Kasimir von Lautern, 1576-1592
Friedrich IV, 1598-1610
Ludwig Philipp, 1610-55
Ludwig Heinrich Moritz, 1655-74

MINT OFFICIALS' INITIALS

Initials	Date	Name
IGP	1661-62	Johann Georg Pfründt in Stromberg

ARMS

Sponheim (associated with Simmern line) – checkerboard
Wittelsbach family – field of lozenges (diamond shapes)

REFERENCES

S = Hugo Frhr. Von Saurma-Jeltsch, ***Die Saurmasche Münzsammlung deutscher, schweizerischer und polnischer Gepräge von etwa dem Beginn der Groschenzeit bis zur Kipperperiode*** , Berlin, 1892.
Sch = Wolfgang Schulten, ***Deutsche Münzen aus dere Zeit Karls V.***, Frankfurt am Main, 1974.

PALATINE COUNTSHIP

REGULAR COINAGE

KM# 3 KREUZER

Silver **Ruler:** Ludwig Heinrich Moritz **Obv:** Ornate helmet over 3 small shields of arms **Rev:** Inscription in laurel wreath **Rev. Inscription:** I/ date/ KREVZ/ ER **Mint:** Stromberg

Date	Mintage	VG	F	VF	XF	Unc
1661	—	—	—	—	—	—

KM# 15 ALBUS (2 Kreuzer)
Silver **Ruler:** Ludwig Heinrich Moritz **Obv:** Ornate helmet above 3 small shields of arms **Rev:** 3-line inscription, date on last line in laurel wreath **Rev. Inscription:** 1/ALBVS/ **Mint:** Stromberg **Note:** Varieties exist.

Date	Mintage	VG	F	VF	XF	Unc
1663	—	45.00	90.00	180	360	—
1667	—	40.00	80.00	160	325	—

KM# 5 15 KREUZER (1/4 Gulden)
Silver **Ruler:** Ludwig Heinrich Moritz **Obv:** Bust right in circle **Rev:** Ornate helmet over 3 small shields of arms, value (15) at bottom, date **Rev. Legend:** MONETA NOVA **Mint:** Stromberg

Date	Mintage	VG	F	VF	XF	Unc
1661 Rare	—	—	—	—	—	—

KM# 7 60 KREUZER (1 Gulden)
Silver **Ruler:** Ludwig Heinrich Moritz **Obv:** Bust right in circle **Rev:** Ornate helmet above 3 small shields of arms, value (60) at bottom, date **Rev. Legend:** MONETA NOVA **Mint:** Stromberg **Note:** Dav. #754.

Date	Mintage	VG	F	VF	XF	Unc
1661 Rare	—	—	—	—	—	—

KM# 8 60 KREUZER (1 Gulden)
Silver **Ruler:** Ludwig Heinrich Moritz **Obv:** Bust right in circle **Rev:** Ornate helmet above 3 small shields of arms divides date, value (60) at bottom **Rev. Legend:** MONETA NOVA... **Mint:** Stromberg

Date	Mintage	VG	F	VF	XF	Unc
1661	—	—	—	—	—	—

KM# 9 60 KREUZER (1 Gulden)
Silver **Ruler:** Ludwig Heinrich Moritz **Obv:** Bust right in circle **Rev:** Ornate helmet above 3 small shields of arms divides date, value (60) at bottom **Rev. Legend:** FVRSTLICHE: PFALTZ — SIMEREN: LANDMVNTZ

Date	Mintage	VG	F	VF	XF	Unc
1661 IGP	—	1,750	3,250	6,500	—	—

KM# 11 60 KREUZER (1 Gulden)
Silver **Ruler:** Ludwig Heinrich Moritz **Obv:** Bust right in circle **Rev:** Ornate helmet above 3 small shields of arms divides date, value (60) at bottom **Rev. Legend:** FVRSTLICHE: PFALTZ — SIMERN. LANDMVNTZ **Mint:** Stromberg **Note:** Dav. #756. Varieties exist

Date	Mintage	VG	F	VF	XF	Unc
1662 IGP	—	1,100	1,800	3,600	7,200	—

TRADE COINAGE

KM# 13 DUCAT
Gold **Ruler:** Ludwig Heinrich Moritz **Obv:** Bust right in circle **Rev:** Ornate helmet over 3 small shields of arms in circle, Roman numeral date **Rev. Legend:** DUCATUS NOVUS SIMERIENSIS **Mint:** Stromberg

Date	Mintage	VG	F	VF	XF	Unc
MDCLXII (1662) Rare	—	—	—	—	—	—

PFALZ-SULZBACH

Originally one of the four lines established in 1569, the first ruler died childless in 1604 and Sulzbach went to the eldest brother in Pfalz-Neuburg. The latter's younger son began a new line in 1614 upon the division of Pfalz-Neuburg. Early in the 18th century, the electoral dignity had passed to Pfalz-Neuburg, but that line also became extinct and all titles, including the electorate, reverted to Pfalz-Sulzbach in 1742 (see Electoral Pfalz for listings after this date).

RULERS
Otto Heinrich, 1569-1604
August, 1614-32
Christian August, 1632-1708

MINT MARKS
All coins struck in Nürnberg mint, but there are no distinguishing marks or symbols.

REFERENCE
N = Alfred Noss, ***Die pfälzischen Münzen des Hauses Wittelsbach***, v. 4, ***Pfalz-Veldenz, Pfalz-Neuburg, Pfalz-Sulzbach***, Munich, 1938.

PALATINE COUNTSHIP

STANDARD COINAGE

KM# 1 THALER
Silver **Ruler:** Christian August **Obv:** Hatted bust right **Rev:** Crowned oval 8-fold arms with central shield of Pfalz in baroque frame, Roman numeral date at end of legend at bottom **Rev. Legend:** SI VIS VINCE - RE PERDE **Mint:** Nurnberg

Date	Mintage	VG	F	VF	XF	Unc
MDCLXV (1665) Rare	—	—	—	—	—	—

TRADE COINAGE

KM# 3 1/4 DUCAT
Gold **Ruler:** Christian August **Obv:** Crowned oval 8-fold arms with central shield in baroque frame **Rev:** Christ rising from grave, mourner to either side **Rev. Legend:** VERBVM CRVCIS VIRTVS DEI **Mint:** Nurnberg **Note:** Fr. #2053.

Date	Mintage	VG	F	VF	XF	Unc
ND(ca1682)	—	650	1,250	2,400	4,950	—

KM# 4 DUCAT
Gold **Ruler:** Christian August **Obv:** Armored bust right **Rev:** Crowned oval 8-fold arms with central shield in baroque frame divide date near bottom **Rev. Legend:** SI VIS VINCE - RE PERDE **Mint:** Nurnberg **Note:** Fr. #2052.

Date	Mintage	VG	F	VF	XF	Unc
1682	—	1,600	3,050	6,100	10,500	—

KM# 2 6 DUCAT
Gold **Ruler:** Christian August **Obv:** Hatted bust right **Rev:** Crowned oval 8-fold arms with central shield of Pfalz in baroque frame, Roman numeral date at bottom **Rev. Legend:** SI VIS VINCE - RE PERDE **Mint:** Numberg **Note:** Struck with Thaler dies, KM#1.

Date	Mintage	VG	F	VF	XF	Unc
MDCLXV (1665) Rare	—	—	—	—	—	—

PATTERNS

Including off metal strikes

KM#	Date	Mintage	Identification	Mkt Val
Pn1	1682	—	Ducat. Silver. KM#4.	250

PFALZ-VELDENZ

This line of Counts Palatine controlled territory centered on Veldenz, overlooking the Mosel River, 20 miles (33km) northeast of Trier. Their principal residence was the castle at Lauterecken on the Glan, some 16 miles (27km) north-northwest of Kaiserslautern. Pfalz-Veldenz was established in 1514 when Pfalz-Zweibrücken-Veldenz was divided into Pfalz-Zweibrücken and Pfalz-Veldenz. However, the younger of the two brothers did not receive full recognition of his rights until 1543. The line of Pfalz-Veldenz fell extinct in 1694, the lands and titles having then been divided by Pfalz-Birkenfeld-Zweibrücken and Pfalz-Sulzbach.

RULERS
Ruprecht, 1514-1544
Georg Johann (Hans) I, 1544-1592
Georg Gustav, 1592-1634
Johann August, 1592-1611, in Lützelstein 1598-1611
Ludwig Philipp, 1592-1601
Georg Johann (Hans) II, 1592-1634, in Lützelstein 1611-54
Leopold Ludwig, 1634-94

MINT OFFICIALS' INITIALS

Initial	Date	Name
(f)= ✱	1600-02	Georg Gustav Preyell in Rockenhausen
(g)= ✱/✱/✱	1603-?	Jakob Dietrich in Rockenhausen
(h)= ⚒ or ⚑ plus HI	1608-09	Hans Jakob in Veldenz
	1608-09	Hans Stumpff in Veldenz
	1619	Johann Jakob Eiselstein in Rothau
	1619	Gümbel G. Wolkenhauer in Rothau
BM	1671-75	Johann Brettmacher in Weinburg

ARMS
Crowned rampant lion left

REFERENCE
N = Alfred Noss, ***Die pfälzischen Münzen des Hauses Wittelsbach***, v. 4, ***Pfalz-Veldenz, Pfalz-Neuburg, Pfalz-Sulzbach***, Munich, 1938.

PALATINE COUNTSHIP

REGULAR COINAGE

KM# 32 HELLER
0.2350 g., Silver, 12 mm. **Ruler:** Leopold Ludwig **Obv:** Uniface schüssel-type: Crowned 4-fold arms of Pfalz and Bavaria with central shield of Veldenz divide date, H below **Mint:** Weinburg **Note:** N#258.

Date	Mintage	Good	VG	F	VF	XF
1673	—	30.00	60.00	120	—	—

KM# 4 PFENNIG
Silver Weight varies: 0.185-0.21g., 13 mm. **Ruler:** Georg Gustav **Obv:** 2-fold arms divided diagonally, Pfalz lion in upper left, Bavarian lozenges in lower right, GGP above (=Georg Gustav Pfalzgraf) **Mint:** Rockenhausen **Note:** Uniface schüssel-type. N#174.

Date	Mintage	Good	VG	F	VF	XF
ND(ca1603-5)	—	25.00	55.00	110	220	—

KM# 34 PFENNIG

0.2500 g., Silver, 19 mm. **Ruler:** Leopold Ludwig **Obv:** Crowned 4-fold arms of Pfalz and Bavaria with central shield of Veldenz divide date **Mint:** Weinburg **Note:** Uniface schüssel-type. N#257.

Date	Mintage	Good	VG	F	VF	XF
1673	—	45.00	90.00	180	—	—

KM# 22 KREUZER

Silver Weight varies: 0.49-0.58g., 17-17.5 mm. **Ruler:** Leopold Ludwig **Obv:** Crowned 4-fold arms of Pfalz and Bavaria with central shield of Veldenz divide date **Rev:** Imperial orb with 1K, legend around, all within laurel wreath **Rev. Legend:** PFALTZ. VELDENTZ. **Mint:** Weinburg **Note:** Varieties exist. N#245, 262.

Date	Mintage	Good	VG	F	VF	XF
1669	—	30.00	60.00	125	200	385
1674 BM	—	30.00	60.00	125	200	385

KM# 24 2 KREUZER (1/2 Batzen)

Silver, 20 mm. **Ruler:** Leopold Ludwig **Obv:** Crowned 4-fold arms of Pfalz and Bavaria with central shield of Veldenz, date divided to left, above and right of crown, all in laurel wreath **Rev:** Imperial orb with 2K in circle **Rev. Legend:** PFALTZ. VELDENTZISCHE. **Mint:** Weinburg **Note:** N#244.

Date	Mintage	Good	VG	F	VF	XF
1669	—	30.00	60.00	120	—	—

KM# 46 2 KREUZER (1/2 Batzen)

1.2200 g., Silver, 20 mm. **Ruler:** Leopold Ludwig **Obv:** Crowned 4-fold arms of Pfalz and Bavaria with central shield of Veldenz divide date, all within laurel wreath **Rev:** Imperial orb with 2K in circle **Rev. Legend:** PFALTZ. VELDENTZISCHE. **Mint:** Weinburg **Note:** N#261.

Date	Mintage	Good	VG	F	VF	XF
1674 BM	—	30.00	60.00	120	—	—

KM# 2 3 KREUZER (Groschen)

Silver Weight varies: 1.38-1.90g., 20.5-22.5 mm. **Ruler:** Georg Gustav **Obv:** 4-fold arms in spanish shield with central shield of Veldenz, date above **Obv. Legend:** GE(OR). GV(S)(T). D.G. C(O). R(A). R(H). D(V). B(A). C(O). V(E). (E.S.). **Rev:** Crowned imperial eagle, 3 in orb on breast **Rev. Legend:** RVDOL. (Z.) (II.) (RO.) IM(-)P. (SE.) AVG. (P.F. DEC.) **Mint:** Rockenhausen **Note:** Varieties exist. N#165-7, 169-70.

Date	Mintage	Good	VG	F	VF	XF
160Z (f)	—	30.00	65.00	100	140	270
1603 (g)	—	30.00	65.00	100	140	270
ND(ca1603) (g)	—	30.00	50.00	90.00	125	230

KM# 7 3 KREUZER (Groschen)

Silver Weight varies: 1.49-1.58g., 22-23 mm. **Ruler:** Georg Gustav **Obv:** Ornately-shaped shield of 4-fold arms of Pfalz and Bavaria with central shield of Veldenz **Obv. Legend:** GE. GVS. D.G. C(O). P(A). R(H). D. B(A). C. V. (E.) (S.). **Rev:** Crowned imperial eagle, 3 in orb on breast **Rev. Legend:** RVDOL. (Z.)(II.) (RO.) IMP. (-) (SE.) AVG. (P. F. DEC). **Mint:** Rockenhausen **Note:** Varieties exist. N#171-3.

Date	Mintage	Good	VG	F	VF	XF
ND(ca1603) (g)	—	40.00	80.00	160	—	—

KM# 6 3 KREUZER (Groschen)

6.8500 g., Silver, 24x25 mm. **Ruler:** Georg Gustav **Obv:** Spanish shield with 4-fold arms of Pfalz and Bavaria with central shield of Veldenz **Obv. Legend:** GE. GV. D.G. CO. PA. RH. DV. BA. CO. V. **Rev:** Crowned imperial eagle, 3 in orb on breast. **Rev. Legend:** RVDOL. II. RO. IMP. AVG. P. F. DEC. **Mint:** Rockenhausen **Note:** Klippe. N#168.

Date	Mintage	Good	VG	F	VF	XF
ND(ca1603) (g)	—	40.00	80.00	160	—	—

KM# 9 3 KREUZER (Groschen)

Silver Weight varies: 1.25-1.80g., 21-22 mm. **Ruler:** Georg Gustav **Obv:** Spanish shield of 4-fold arms of Pfalz and Bavaria with central shield of Veldenz, date above **Obv. Legend:** GE. GVS. D.G. CO. PA. (RH.) D. B. C. V. (E.) ET. S. **Rev:** Crowned imperial eagle, 3 in orb on breast **Rev. Legend:** RVDOL. Z. IMP. AVG. P. F. DEC. **Mint:** Veldenz **Note:** Varieties exist. N#175-7, 180.5.

Date	Mintage	Good	VG	F	VF	XF
(1)608 (h)	—	15.00	30.00	60.00	85.00	160
(1)609 (h)	—	15.00	30.00	60.00	85.00	160

KM# 10 3 KREUZER (Groschen)

Silver Weight varies: 1.59-1.70g., 20.5-22 mm. **Ruler:** Georg Gustav **Obv:** Ornately-shaped shield of 4-fold arms of Pfalz and Bavaria with central shield of Veldenz divide date **Obv. Legend:** GE GVS. D.G(.) CO. PA. RH. D(V). B(A). C. V(.)E. ET. S. **Rev:** Crowned imperial eagle, 3 in orb on breast **Rev. Legend:** RVDOL. Z. IMP. AVG. P. F. DEC **Mint:** Veldenz **Note:** Varieties exist. N#178-80.

Date	Mintage	Good	VG	F	VF	XF
(1)608 (h)	—	15.00	30.00	60.00	85.00	160
(1)609 (h)	—	15.00	30.00	60.00	85.00	160

KM# 12 3 KREUZER (Groschen)

Silver Weight varies: 1.32-1.505g., 22 mm. **Ruler:** Georg Gustav **Obv:** Ornately-shaped shield of 4-fold arms of Pfalz and Bavaria with central shield of Veldenz **Obv. Legend:** GE. GVS(T). D.G. C(O). P. R. D. B. C(O). V. E. S. **Rev:** Crowned imperial eagle, 3 in orb on breast **Rev. Legend:** MATT(H)(IAS). II. RO(M). IMP(ER). S(E). A(VG). **Mint:** Rothau **Note:** Varieties exist. N#224-5.

Date	Mintage	Good	VG	F	VF	XF
ND(ca1619)	—	25.00	40.00	75.00	155	—

KM# 13 3 KREUZER (Groschen)

Silver Weight varies: 1.13-1.93g., 20-22 mm. **Ruler:** Georg Gustav **Obv:** Spanish shield of 4-fold arms of Pfalz and Bavaria with central shield of Veldenz **Obv. Legend:** GE. GVST. D.G. C(O). P. R. D. B. (C)(O). V. E. S. **Rev:** Crowned imperial eagle, 3 in orb on breast **Rev. Legend:** MATT(H)(I)(AS). I(I). RO(M). IM(P)(E)(R). S. A. **Mint:** Rothau **Note:** Varieties exist. N#226-37.

Date	Mintage	Good	VG	F	VF	XF
ND(ca1619)	—	30.00	50.00	90.00	180	—

KM# 15 12 KREUZER (Dreibätzner)

Silver Weight varies: 5.11-5.19g., 27.5 mm. **Ruler:** Georg Gustav **Obv:** Crowned ornately-shaped shield of 4-fold arms of Pfalz and Bavaria with central shield of Veldenz **Obv. Legend:** GEORG GVST. D. G. C. P. R. D. B. C. V. E. S. **Rev:** Imperial eagle with orb on breast, (XII) at top in margin **Rev. Legend:** FERDINAND. II. ROM. IM. P. S. AV. **Mint:** Rothau **Note:** N#238.

Date	Mintage	Good	VG	F	VF	XF
ND(1619-34)	—	120	225	400	650	1,300

KM# 36 12 KREUZER (Dreibätzner)

Silver Weight varies: 4.59-5.16g., 26-28.5 mm. **Ruler:** Leopold Ludwig **Obv:** Crowned shield of 4-fold arms of Pfalz and Bavaria with central shield of Veldenz divides date **Obv. Legend:** LEOP. LVD. D.G. C. P. R. D. B. ET. COM. VELDENTIÆ. **Rev:** Crowned imperial eagle in circle, orb on breast, (XII) in margin at top **Rev. Legend:** LEOPOLDVS. I. ROM. IMP. SEMP AVG. **Mint:** Weinburg **Note:** N#256, 260.

Date	Mintage	Good	VG	F	VF	XF
1673 BM	—	45.00	80.00	160	—	—
1674/3 BM	—	45.00	80.00	160	—	—

KM# 17 12 KREUZER (Schreckenberger)

Silver Weight varies: 2.45-3.02g., 25-26 mm. **Ruler:** Georg Gustav **Obv:** Bust to right in circle **Obv. Legend:** GEORG. GVST. D.G. C(O). P(A). R(H). D. G. C(O). V. E. S. **Rev:** Ornamented Spanish shield of 4-fold arms of Pfalz and Bavaria with central shield of Veldenz, value (12) above, date at end of legend **Rev. Legend:** SOLI. DEO. GLORIA. **Mint:** Rothau **Note:** Kipper Coinage. Varieties exist. N#220-3.

Date	Mintage	Good	VG	F	VF	XF
1621	—	40.00	80.00	160	325	650
1622	—	40.00	80.00	160	325	650

KM# 20 24 KREUZER (Sechsbätzner)

Silver Weight varies: 8.28-8.92g., 31x30, 32x32 mm. **Ruler:** Georg Gustav **Obv:** Armored bust to right in circle **Obv. Legend:** GEORG. GVST. D.G. CO. PA. RH. D. G. C. V. E. S. **Rev:** Crowned shield of 4-fold arms of Pfalz and Bavaria with central shield of Veldenz **Rev. Legend:** SOLI. DEO. GLORIA. **Mint:** Rothau **Note:** Kipper coinage, Klippe. N#181, 206.

Date	Mintage	Good	VG	F	VF	XF
ND(1621-22)	—	55.00	110	225	450	—

KM# 19 24 KREUZER (Sechsbätzner)

Silver Weight varies: 6.98-9.17g., 28-31 mm. **Ruler:** Georg Gustav **Obv:** Armored bust to right in circle **Obv. Legend:** GEORG. GVST. D.G. C(O)(M). R(A). R(H). D. B. C(O). V. E. S. **Rev:** Crowned shield of 4-fold arms of Pfalz and Bavaria with central shield of Veldenz **Rev. Legend:** SOLI. DEO. GLORIA. **Mint:** Rothau **Note:** Kipper coinage, varieties exist. N#181-219.

Date	Mintage	Good	VG	F	VF	XF
ND(1621-22)	—	55.00	110	225	450	—

KM# 26 30 KREUZER (1/2 Gulden)
Silver Weight varies: 9.57-9.88g., 32 mm. **Ruler:** Leopold Ludwig **Obv:** Armored bust to right in circle **Obv. Legend:** LEOPOLD. LVD. D.G. C. P. R. D. B. ET. COM. VELDENTIÆ. **Rev:** Two ornate helmets divide date above shield of 4-fold arms of Pfalz and Bavaria with central shield of Veldenz, (30) below in margin **Rev. Legend:** VERBVM DOMINI MA - NET IN ÆTERNVM. **Mint:** Weinburg **Note:** Varieties exist. N#243, 254.

Date	Mintage	Good	VG	F	VF	XF
1669	—	—	—	—	—	—
1673 BM	—	300	600	1,200	2,400	—

KM# 38 45 KREUZER (3/4 Gulden)
14.5200 g., Silver, 34 mm. **Ruler:** Leopold Ludwig **Obv:** Armored bust to right in circle **Obv. Legend:** LEOPOLD. LVDOVIC. D.G. C. P. R. D. B. ET. COM. VELDENTIÆ. **Rev:** Shield of 4-fold arms of Pfalz and Bavaria with central shield of Veldenz, 2 ornate helmets above divide date, (45) in margin at bottom **Rev. Legend:** VERBVM. DOMINI. - MANET. IN. ÆTERNVM. **Mint:** Weinburg **Note:** N#253.

Date	Mintage	Good	VG	F	VF	XF
1673 BM	—	—	—	—	—	—

KM# 28 60 KREUZER (Gulden)
Silver Weight varies: 18.78-19.29g., 36 mm. **Ruler:** Leopold Ludwig **Obv:** Armored bust to right in circle **Obv. Legend:** LEOPOLD. LVDOVIC. D.G. COM. PAL. RH. D. BAV. ET. COM. VELDENT. **Rev:** Shield of 4-fold arms of Pfalz and Bavaria with central shield of Veldenz, date divided among crests of 2 ornate helmets above, (60) in margin at bottom **Rev. Legend:** + VERBVM. DOMINI - MANET. IN. ÆTERNVM. **Mint:** Weinburg **Note:** Varieties exist. Dav. #759; N#242, 246.

Date	Mintage	Good	VG	F	VF	XF
1669	—	—	—	—	—	—
1670/69	—	—	—	—	—	—

KM# 30 60 KREUZER (Gulden)
19.8200 g., Silver, 35.5 mm. **Ruler:** Leopold Ludwig **Obv:** Large armored bust to right in circle **Obv. Legend:** LEOPOLD. LVDOVIC. D.G. C. P. R. D. B. ET. COM. VELDENTIÆ. **Rev:** Shield of 4-fold arms of Pfalz and Bavaria with central shield of Veldenz, date divided among crests of 2 ornate helmets above, (60) in margin at bottom **Rev. Legend:** VERBVM. DOMINI - MANET. IN. ÆTERNVM. **Mint:** Weinburg **Note:** Dav. #760; N#248.

Date	Mintage	Good	VG	F	VF	XF
1672	—	300	600	1,000	1,500	3,000

KM# 40 60 KREUZER (Gulden)
Silver Weight varies: 18.63-19.45g., 32-37 mm. **Ruler:** Leopold Ludwig **Obv:** Armored bust to right in circle **Obv. Legend:** LEOPOLD. LVD(OV)(W)IC. D.G. C. P. R. D. B. ET. COM. VELDENTIÆ. **Rev:** Shield of 4-fold arms of Pfalz and Bavaria with central shield of Veldenz, date divided by crests of 2 ornate helmets above, (60) in margin at bottom **Rev. Legend:** VERBVM. DOMINI. (-) MA (-) NET. IN ÆTERNVM. **Mint:** Weinburg **Note:** Varieties exist. Dav. #760; N#251-2, 259.

Date	Mintage	Good	VG	F	VF	XF
1673 BM	—	275	500	875	1,200	2,300
1674 BM	—	275	500	875	1,200	2,300

KM# 42 1/4 THALER
7.2300 g., Silver, 31 mm. **Ruler:** Leopold Ludwig **Obv:** Armored bust to right in circle **Obv. Legend:** LEOPOLD. LVD. D.G. C. P. R. D. B. ET. COM. VELDENTIÆ. **Rev:** Shield of 4-fold arms of Pfalz and Bavaria with central shield of Veldenz, date divided by crests of 2 ornate helmets above, (1/4) in margin at bottom **Rev. Legend:** VERBVM. DOMINI MA - NET. IN. ÆTERNVM. **Mint:** Weinburg **Note:** N#255.

Date	Mintage	Good	VG	F	VF	XF
1673 BM	—	300	600	900	1,350	2,600

KM# 39 1/2 THALER
11.8700 g., Silver, 32 mm. **Ruler:** Leopold Ludwig **Obv:** Armored bust to right in circle **Obv. Legend:** LEOPOLD. LVD. D.G. C. P. R. D. B. ET. COM. VELDENTIÆ. **Rev:** Ornate shield of 4-fold arms of Pfalz and Bavaria with central shield of Veldenz, crest on ornate helmet above divides date **Rev. Legend:** VERBVM. DOMINI MA - NET. IN. ÆTERNVM. **Mint:** Weinburg **Note:** Struck from 1/4 Thaler dies, KM#42.

Date	Mintage	Good	VG	F	VF	XF
1673 BM	—	—	1,650	3,000	4,250	7,700

KM# 43 3/4 THALER
14.5300 g., Silver, 33 mm. **Ruler:** Leopold Ludwig **Obv:** Armored bust to right in circle **Obv. Legend:** LEOPOLD. LVD. D.G. C. P. R. D. B. ET. COM. VELDENTIÆ. **Rev:** Ornate shield of 4-fold arms of Pfalz and Bavaria with central shield of Veldenz, crest on ornate helmet above divides date **Rev. Legend:** VERBVM. DOMINI MA - NET. IN. ÆTERNVM. **Mint:** Weinburg **Note:** Struck from 1/4 Thaler dies, KM#42.

Date	Mintage	Good	VG	F	VF	XF
1673 BM Rare	—	—	—	—	—	—

KM# 29 THALER
Silver **Ruler:** Leopold Ludwig **Obv:** Armored and draped bust to right **Obv. Legend:** LEOPOLD. LVDOVIC. D.G. C. P. R. D. B. &. COM. VELDENTIÆ. **Rev:** Ornately-shaped shield of 4-fold arms of Bavaria and Pfalz with central shield of Veldenz, two ornate helmets above divide date **Rev. Legend:** VERBVM. DOMINI. MANET. IN ÆTERNVM. **Mint:** Weinburg **Note:** Dav. #7191; N#247, 250.

Date	Mintage	VG	F	VF	XF	Unc
1671	—	1,350	2,750	5,500	10,000	22,500
1673 MB	—	1,350	2,750	5,500	10,000	22,500

TRADE COINAGE

KM# 44 DUCAT
3.5000 g., 0.9860 Gold 0.1109 oz. AGW, 21 mm. **Ruler:** Leopold Ludwig **Obv:** Armored bust to right, date at end of legend **Obv. Legend:** LEOPOLD. LVD. D.G. C. P. R. D. B. ET. COM. VELDENTIÆ. **Rev:** Shield of 4-fold arms of Bavaria and Pfalz, central shield of Veldenz, 2 helmets above **Rev. Legend:** VERBVM DOMINI MANET IN ÆTERNVM. **Mint:** Weinburg **Note:** FR#2055; N#249.

Date	Mintage	VG	F	VF	XF	Unc
1673 Rare	—	—	—	—	—	—

REGULAR COINAGE

KM#	Date	Mintage	Identification	Mkt Val
Pn1	1621	—	12 Kreuzer. Lead. 26x27 mm. Klippe of KM#17.	400

PFALZ-ZWEIBRUCKEN

This branch of Rhinegraves was established upon the division of Pfalz-Simmern in 1459 and was known first as Pfalz-Zweibrücken-Veldenz until 1514, when a separate line at Veldenz was founded. In 1557, Neuburg and Sulzbach were acquired by purchase from Electoral Pfalz. Four brothers divided their inheritance in 1569 and founded new lines at Neuburg, Sulzbach, Birkenfeld and the continued line of Zweibrücken. The male succession failed several times, once in 1661 when the title passed to a cousin of the Pfalz-Landsberg line, then again in 1731. After more than three years of imperial sequestration, Zweibrücken was acquired by Pfalz-Birkenfeld in 1734, which was known henceforth as Pfalz-Birkenfeld-Zweibrücken. The capital of the principality, Zweibrücken, meaning "Two Bridges", is located not far from the border with France, 17 miles (28km) east of Saarbrücken. The mint town of Meisenheim is on the River Glan, 20 miles (33km) east of Zweibrücken.

RULERS

Ludwig I, 1459-1489
Alexander, 1489-1514
Ludwig II, 1514-1532
Wolfgang, 1532-1569
Johann I der Ältere, 1569-1604
Johann II der Jüngere, 1604-35,
Administrator and Regent in Electoral Pfalz, 1610-15
Friedrich, 1635-61
Friedrich Ludwig von Pfalz-Landsberg, 1661-81
French Occupation, 1677-93
Adolf Johann, 1681-89
Karl XI (King of Sweden), 1681-97
Karl XII (King of Sweden), 1697-1718
Gustav Samuel Leopold von Pfalz-Kleeburg, 1718-1731

MINT OFFICIALS' INITIALS

Initial	Date	Name
(a)=	Ca.1590-1605	Jakob Taglang
	Ca.1592-1604	H. Cunzelmann, die-cutter in Zweibrücken and Meisenheim
	Ca.1600	Balthasar Mey (Meyel)
	1600-07	Johann Ludwig Eichelstein
(b)=	1611-21	Johann Jakob (or Philipp) Mey (May)
(c)=	1611-21	Johann Jakob (or Philipp) Mey (May)
	Ca. 1613	Christoph Peyel, warden
HT/IHT (often in legature)	1621-23	Johann Heinrich Taglang in Meisenheim
	1621-26	In Zweibrücken Hans Tuchmann
(d)=	1623-24	(Christmann Tucher) in Zweibrücken and Meisenheim
(e)=	1624	Paul Dietherr der Jüngere
M	1624-25	Philibert Ludwig Messerschmid

ARMS

Zweibrücken – lion rampant left
Wittelsbach – field of lozenges (Diamond shapes)
Wittelsbach (old) – eagle, head to left

PALATINE COUNTSHIP

REGULAR COINAGE

KM# 4 PFENNIG

Silver **Ruler:** Johann II **Obv:** Shield of Wittelsbach arms divides Z - B, with P above (=Pfalz-Zwei-Brücken) **Note:** Uniface schüssel-type.

Date	Mintage	VG	F	VF	XF	Unc
ND(1604-35)	—	10.00	20.00	45.00	90.00	—

KM# 37 PFENNIG

Ruler: Johann II **Obv:** Shield of Wittelsbach arms divides date, P above **Note:** Uniface hohl-type.

Date	Mintage	VG	F	VF	XF	Unc
(16)22	—	10.00	20.00	45.00	90.00	—

KM# 5 8 PFENNIG

, 17 mm. **Ruler:** Johann II **Obv:** 3-line inscription with value **Obv. Inscription:** M/ VIII/ PF (symbol) **Mint:** Meisenheim **Note:** Uniface. Attribution to Johann II is uncertain.

Date	Mintage	VG	F	VF	XF	Unc
ND(1604-35)	—	10.00	20.00	45.00	90.00	—

KM# 6 2 KREUZER (1/2 Batzen)

0.8600 g., Silver **Ruler:** Johann II **Obv:** Zweibrücken lion rampant to left in circle **Obv. Legend:** IO DG C P R D B IV CL ET MO. **Rev:** 3-line inscription of value **Rev. Legend:** MONETA NOVA BIPONT. **Rev. Inscription:** II / KREVTZ / ER

Date	Mintage	VG	F	VF	XF	Unc
ND(1604-35)	—	20.00	40.00	80.00	160	—

KM# 49 2 KREUZER (1/2 Batzen)

Silver **Ruler:** Johann II **Obv:** Three small shields of arms, 2 above 1, in circle **Obv. Legend:** IOHAN. D.G. CO. PA. RH. DV. BA. C. V. E. S. **Rev:** Imperial orb with Z divides date, large M at top **Rev. Legend:** FERDI. II. RO. IMP. AVG. P. F. DEC. **Mint:** Meisenheim

Date	Mintage	VG	F	VF	XF	Unc
16Z4 M	—	25.00	50.00	100	200	—
16Z5 M	—	25.00	50.00	100	200	—

KM# 2 3 KREUZER (Groschen)

Silver **Ruler:** Johann I **Obv:** 3-fold arms in spanish shield, date above **Obv. Legend:** IOHA. D.G. CO. PA. RH. DV. BA. C. V. E. **Rev:** Crowned imperial eagle, 3 in orb on breast **Rev. Legend:** RVDOL. Z. IMP. AVG. P. F. DE. **Mint:** Zweibrücken **Note:** Varieties exist. S#2013-17.

Date	Mintage	VG	F	VF	XF	Unc
1601	—	16.00	35.00	75.00	155	—
1602	—	16.00	35.00	75.00	155	—
1603	—	16.00	35.00	75.00	155	—
1604	—	16.00	35.00	75.00	155	—

KM# 8 3 KREUZER (Groschen)

Silver **Ruler:** Johann II **Obv:** Three small shields of arms, 2 over 1, date above, all in circle **Obv. Legend:** IOH. D.G. CO. PA. RH. DV. BA. C. V. E. S. **Rev:** Crowned imperial eagle, 3 in orb on breast **Rev. Legend:** RVDOL. Z. RO. IMP. AVG. P. F. DE. **Mint:** Zweibrücken **Note:** Varieties exist. S#2025-29.

Date	Mintage	VG	F	VF	XF	Unc
1604	—	6.00	10.00	20.00	42.00	—
1605	—	6.00	10.00	20.00	42.00	—
1606	—	6.00	10.00	20.00	42.00	—
1607	—	6.00	10.00	20.00	42.00	—
1608	—	6.00	10.00	20.00	42.00	—
ND(ca1610-11)	—	6.00	10.00	20.00	42.00	—

KM# 15 3 KREUZER (Groschen)

1.6400 g., Silver, 21.5 mm. **Ruler:** Johann II **Obv:** 3-fold arms in spanish shield **Obv. Legend:** IOH. D.G. CO. PA. RH. DV. BA. C. V. E. S. **Rev:** Crowned imperial eagle, 3 in orb on breast **Rev. Legend:** RVDOL. Z. RO. IMP. AVG. P. F. DE. **Mint:** Zweibrücken **Note:** S#2030.

Date	Mintage	VG	F	VF	XF	Unc
ND(1611-12) (b)	—	25.00	55.00	110	220	—

KM# 16 3 KREUZER (Groschen)

Silver **Ruler:** Johann II **Obv:** 3-fold arms in spanish shield **Obv. Legend:** IOH. D.G. CO. PA. RH. DV. BA. C. V. E. S. **Rev:** Crowned imperial eagle, 3 in orb on breast **Rev. Legend:** MATHI. I. RO. IMP. AVG. P. F. **Mint:** Zweibrücken **Note:** S#2031.

Date	Mintage	VG	F	VF	XF	Unc
ND(1612-19) (b)	—	25.00	55.00	110	220	—

KM# 33 12 KREUZER (Schreckenberger)

Silver, 27 mm. **Ruler:** Johann II **Obv:** Bust to right in circle **Obv. Legend:** IOHAN. D.G. CO. PA. RHE. DV. BA. CO. VE. ET. S(P). **Rev:** Shield of 4-fold arms of Pfalz and Bavaria with central shield of Zweibrücken divides date, (1Z) above **Rev. Legend:** + VERBVM. DOMINI. MANET. IN ÆTERN(V). **Mint:** Zweibrücken **Note:** Kipper coinage. Varieties exist.

Date	Mintage	VG	F	VF	XF	Unc
16Z0 (b)	—	125	235	325	450	925
16Z1 (b)	—	125	235	325	450	925
16ZZ (c)	—	125	235	325	450	925

KM# 39 12 KREUZER (Schreckenberger)

Silver **Ruler:** Johann II **Obv:** Bust to right in circle **Obv. Legend:** IOHAN. D.G. CO. PA. RHE. DV. BA. CO. VE. ET. S. **Rev:** Shield of 4-fold arms of Pfalz and Bavaria with central shield of Zweibrücken, date at end of legend **Rev. Legend:** VERBVM. DOMINI. MANET. IN AETE. **Note:** Kipper coinage.

Date	Mintage	VG	F	VF	XF	Unc
16ZZ	—	125	235	325	450	925

KM# 57 12 KREUZER (Dreibätzner)

Silver **Ruler:** Johann II **Obv:** Bust to right in circle **Rev:** Shield of 4-fold arms of Pfalz and Bavaria with central shield of Zweibrücken divides date, (1Z) above

Date	Mintage	VG	F	VF	XF	Unc
1627	—	250	350	500	1,025	—

KM# 35 24 KREUZER (Doppelschreckenberger)

Silver Weight varies: 4.69-5.68g., 29 mm. **Ruler:** Johann II **Obv:** Bust to right in circle **Obv. Legend:** IOHAN. D.G. CO. PA. RHE. DV. BA. CO. VE(L). ET. SP(O). **Rev:** Shield of 4-fold arms of Pfalz and Bavaria with central shield of Zweibrücken, date at end of legend **Rev. Legend:** + VERBVM. DOMINI. MANET. IN ÆTE(R)(N). **Mint:** Zweibrücken **Note:** Kipper coinage. Varieties exist.

Date	Mintage	VG	F	VF	XF	Unc
16Z0	—	80.00	135	225	450	—
16Z1	—	80.00	135	225	450	—
16ZZ	—	80.00	135	225	450	—
ND(1621-22)	—	80.00	135	225	450	—

KM# 53 24 KREUZER (Sechsbätzner)

Silver, 31-32 mm. **Ruler:** Johann II **Obv:** Bust to right in circle **Obv. Legend:** IOHAN. D.G. CO. PA. RH. DV. BA. IVL. CLI. ET. MONT. **Rev:** Shield of manifold arms, date above, (XXIIII) in margin at top **Rev. Legend:** CO. VE. SP. MA. ET. RA. DO. IN. RAVEN. **Mint:** Zweibrücken

Date	Mintage	VG	F	VF	XF	Unc
1626 HT Rare	—	—	—	—	—	—

KM# 41 1/8 THALER

Silver, 30-31 mm. **Ruler:** Johann II **Obv:** Ornate shield of manifold arms in circle **Obv. Legend:** IOHANNES DEI GRATIA COMES PALATINVS RHENI BAVARIÆ. **Rev:** Seated lion facing, holding tablet on which is 8.FVR/I.R.T., all in circle, date at end of legend **Rev. Legend:** IVLIÆ. CL. ET BER. DVX CO. VEL. SPO. MAR. ET RA. DO. IN RAV.

Date	Mintage	VG	F	VF	XF	Unc
1623 Rare	—	—	—	—	—	—

KM# 42 1/8 THALER

Silver **Ruler:** Johann II **Obv:** Bust to right in circle **Rev:** Shield of manifold arms, value 1/8 below

Date	Mintage	VG	F	VF	XF	Unc
1623	—	—	—	—	—	—

KM# 18 1/4 THALER

Silver Weight varies: 8.31-8.73g. **Ruler:** Johann II **Obv:** Armored bust to right in circle **Obv. Legend:** IOHAN. D. G. CO(M). PA. RH(E). (-) T (- E). AD. E. P. D. B. C. V. E. S. **Rev:** Shield with 4-fold arms of Pfalz and Bavaria with central shield of Zweibrücken lion, date above **Rev. Legend:** VERBVM. DOM(M)IN(I). MANET. IN. ÆTERN. **Mint:** Heidelberg **Note:** S#2023-24. Varieties exist.

Date	Mintage	VG	F	VF	XF	Unc
1611	—	150	225	450	900	—
161Z	—	150	225	450	900	—
ND(1611)	—	80.00	150	450	900	—

KM# 19 1/4 THALER

Silver **Ruler:** Johann II **Obv:** Armored bust to right in circle **Obv. Legend:** IOHAN. D.G. CO. PA. RHE. DV. BA. CO. VE. ET. SP. **Rev:** Shield of 4-fold arms of Pfalz and Bavaria with central shield of Zweibrücken lion **Rev. Legend:** VERBVM. DOMINI. MANET. IN. ÆTERN. **Mint:** Zweibrücken

Date	Mintage	VG	F	VF	XF	Unc
ND(1616-21) (b)	—	150	300	425	775	—
ND(1616-21) (c)	—	150	300	425	775	—

KM# 47 THALER

Silver, 41-42 mm. **Ruler:** Johann II **Obv:** Bust to right in circle **Obv. Legend:** IOHAN. D.G. CO. PA(L). RHE. DVX. BA. IVL. CLI. ET. MON. **Rev:** Manifold arms, 5 ornate helmets above, date at end of margin **Rev. Legend:** CO. VE. SP. MA. ET. - RA. DO. IN. RAV(E). **Mint:** Meisenheim **Note:** Dav. #7189. Prev. KM#23.

Date	Mintage	Good	VG	F	VF	XF
16Z3	—	—	210	425	775	1,250
16Z4 (e)	—	—	210	425	775	1,250

KM# 44 THALER

Silver, 41 mm. **Ruler:** Johann II **Obv:** Bust to right in circle **Obv. Legend:** IOHAN. D.G. COM. PA. RHE. DVX. PA. IVL. CLI. ET. MONT. **Rev:** Manifold arms, 5 ornate helmets above, date at end of legend **Rev. Legend:** CO. VE. SPO. MAR. ET. RAV. - DO. IN. RAVENST. **Note:** Dav. #7186. Prev. KM#20.

Date	Mintage	VG	F	VF	XF	Unc
16Z3	—	210	425	775	1,250	—

KM# 45 THALER

Silver, 40 mm. **Ruler:** Johann II **Obv:** Bust to right in circle, N's reversed in legend **Obv. Legend:** IOHAN. D.G. CO. PAL. RHE. DVX. BA. IVL. CLI. ET. MON. **Rev:** Manifold arms, 5 ornate helmets above, date at end of legend **Rev. Legend:** CO. VEL. SPOL. MAR. ET RAV. - DO. IN. RAVENS(T). **Note:** Dav. #7187. Prev. KM#21.

Date	Mintage	VG	F	VF	XF	Unc
16Z3	—	125	250	550	1,150	2,250
16Z4	—	125	250	550	1,150	2,250

KM# 46 THALER

Silver, 43 mm. **Ruler:** Johann II **Obv:** Bust to right in circle, N's reversed in legend **Obv. Legend:** IOHAN. D.G. CO. PAL. RHE. DVX. BA. IVL. CLI. ET. MON. **Rev:** Manifold arms, 5 ornate helmets above, date at end of legend **Rev. Legend:** CO.-VE. SP. MA. ET. R. - DO. IN. RAVEN. **Note:** Dav. #7188. Prev. KM#22.

Date	Mintage	VG	F	VF	XF	Unc
16Z3 (d)	—	145	290	525	950	—
16Z4 (d)	—	145	290	525	950	—

KM# 55 THALER

Silver, 42-43 mm. **Ruler:** Johann II **Obv:** Facing armored bust, turned slightly to right, in circle **Obv. Legend:** IOHAN. D.G. COM. PALA. RHE. DVX. BA. IVL. CLI. ET. MONT. **Rev:** Shield of manifold arms, 5 ornate helmets above, date at end of legend near top **Rev. Legend:** CO. - VE. SPO. MAR. ET. R. - AV. DO. IN. RAV. **Mint:** Zweibrücken **Note:** Dav. #7190. Prev. KM#24.

Date	Mintage	VG	F	VF	XF	Unc
16Z6 HT Rare	—	—	—	—	—	—

Note: UBS Auction 65, 9-06, VF-XF realized approximately $10,985.

TRADE COINAGE

KM# 25 GOLDGULDEN

Gold **Ruler:** Johann II **Obv:** 4-fold arms of Pfalz and Bavaria, date above, titles as administrator of Electoral Pfalz **Obv. Legend:** IOH. D.G. C. PA. RHE. T. E. AD. E. P. D. B. C. V. E. S. **Rev:** Crowned imperial eagle, orb on breast **Rev. Legend:** MONE. NOVA. AVREA. BIPONT. **Mint:** Zweibrücken **Note:** FR#2059. Prev. KM#11.

Date	Mintage	VG	F	VF	XF	Unc
1611 (b)	—	500	950	1,750	3,000	—

KM# 27 GOLDGULDEN

3.1000 g., Gold **Ruler:** Johann II **Obv:** 4-fold arms of Pfalz and Bavaria, date above, titles as Administrator of Electoral Pfalz **Obv. Legend:** IOH. D.G. C. PA. RHE. T. E. AD. E. P. D. B. C. V. E. S. **Rev:** Crowned imperial eagle, orb on breast **Rev. Legend:** MONE. NOVA. AVREA. BIPONT. **Mint:** Zweibrücken **Note:** FR#2059.

Date	Mintage	VG	F	VF	XF	Unc
161Z (b)	—	1,500	2,100	3,250	5,500	—

KM# 29 GOLDGULDEN

3.2200 g., Gold **Ruler:** Johann II **Obv:** 4-fold arms of Pfalz and Bavaria in circle **Obv. Legend:** IOHA. D.G. CO. PA. RH. DV. BA. C. V. E. S. **Rev:** Crowned imperial eagle, orb on breast **Rev. Legend:** MONE. NOVA. AVREA. BIPONT. **Mint:** Zweibrücken **Note:** FR#2059.

Date	Mintage	VG	F	VF	XF	Unc
ND(1615-16) (c)	—	1,250	2,200	3,500	6,000	—

KM# 31 GOLDGULDEN

3.1600 g., Gold **Ruler:** Johann II **Obv:** Shield of manifold arms, date above **Obv. Legend:** IOH. D.G. C. P. R. D. B. I. C. ET. M. C. V. SP. M. ET. R. D. I(N). R(A). **Rev:** Crowned imperial eagle, orb on breast **Rev. Legend:** MONET. NOVA. AVREA. BIPONT. **Mint:** Zweibrücken **Note:** FR#2059. Prev. KM#11.

Date	Mintage	VG	F	VF	XF	Unc
1616 (b)	—	225	385	875	2,000	—
1617 (b)	—	225	385	875	2,000	—
1618 (b)	—	225	385	875	2,000	—
1619 (b)	—	225	385	875	2,000	—
1621 (b)	—	225	385	875	2,000	—

KM# 51 GOLDGULDEN

Gold, 22 mm. **Ruler:** Johann II **Obv:** Large shield of manifold arms, date above, M in margin at top **Obv. Legend:** IOH. D.G. C. P. R. D. B. I. C. ET. M. C. V. SP. M. ET. R. D. I. R. **Rev:** Crowned imperial eagle, orb on breast **Rev. Legend:** MONET. NOVA. AVREA. BIPONT. **Mint:** Meisenheim

Date	Mintage	VG	F	VF	XF	Unc
16Z4 M	—	250	550	1,250	2,500	—
16Z5 M	—	250	550	1,250	2,500	—

POMERANIA

(Pommern)

The territory that became Pomerania, stretching along the Baltic coast from the Oder to the Vistula Rivers, was populated by Slavic peoples at least as early as the 5th century. A local ruler named Svantibor took the title of Duke of Pomerania in the late 11th century, thus announcing his claim of independence from Poland. Upon Svantibor's death in 1107, the duchy was divided by his four sons into Inner and Outer Pomerania. In 1181, Pomerania was admitted a constituent state of the Holy Roman Empire. Over the next several centuries, Pomerania underwent several divisions, although that centered on Wolgast emerged as the dominant branch by the early 15th century. Other family members ruled at Barth, Rügenwalde and most importantly, in Stettin, the eventual capital of united Pomerania. Several brothers of the dukes, as well as some dukes themselves, ruled as bishops of Cammin (see) some 20 miles (33km) north-northeast of Stettin.

The line at Wolgast became extinct in 1625 and its territories and titles passed to the Stettin branch, thus united all of Pomerania. The line at Stettin was established in 1569 and lost political power in 1637. The nephew of Bogislaw XIV, Ernst Bogislaw von Croy, was Bishop of Cammin from 1637 until 1650. Upon his death in 1684, the ducal line of almost 700 years came to an end.

Pomerania suffered severely during the Thirty Years' War and when the last duke succeeded to the bishopric of Cammin in 1637, as mentioned above, Sweden annexed the duchy. As part of the terms of the Treaty of Westphalia ending the war, Sweden was forced to pass the eastern part of Pomerania, called Hinter-Pommern, to Brandenburg-Prussia. Sweden did retain Stettin as the capital of its province of West Pomerania and struck a long series of coins specifically for that territory. Swedish control over its portion of Pomerania was continually challenged by the margraves of Brandenburg-Prussia, which succeeded in gaining part of the province in 1679, then all of West Pomerania to the River Peene in 1720. The remaining enclaves of Stralsund, Wolgast and Rügen were awarded to Prussia in 1815.

RULERS

Stettin Line

Barnim XI, 1523-1569 (d. 1573)
Johann Friedrich, 1569-1600
Barnim XII, 1600-1603, in Rügenwalde 1560-1603
Bogislaw XIII, 1603-1606, in Barth 1569-1606
Philip II, 1606-1618
Georg III, in Rügenwalde 1606-1617
Franz, 1618-1620
Bogislaw XIV, 1620-1637, in Rügenwalde 1617-1620

Wolgast Line

Bogislaw X the Great, 1474-1523
Georg I, 1523-1531
Philipp I, 1531-1560
Ernst Ludwig, 1560-1592
Philipp III Julius, 1592-1625

Swedish Occupation

Christian of Sweden, 1632-1654
Karl X of Sweden, 1654-1660
Karl XI of Sweden, 1660-1697
Karl XII of Sweden, 1697-1718
Adolf Fredrik of Sweden, 1751-1771
Gustav III, King of Sweden, 1771-1792
Gustav IV Adolf of Sweden, 1792-1809

MINT OFFICIALS' INITIALS

Stettin

Initial	Date	Name
(a) = stag's antlers	1580-1583	Philipp Kradol
	1583-?	Jürgen Stegen, warden
	1583-?	Sebastian Schoras, warden
(e) = eagle's wings	1594-1596	Gregor Westphalen
(f) = eagle's wing	ca. 1585	Unknown
BA	1681-85	Bastian Altmann
CS	1680-81	Christoph Sucro
DHM	1685-88	David Heinrich Matthaus
DS	1610-1620	Daniel Sailer of Augsburg, die-cutter
DS	1672-76	Daniel Syvertz
GT (some-times in ligature, and/or (z) =	Ca. 1618-1637, 1654	Gottfried Tabbert, die-cutter
HIH, (b)=battle axe	1666-71	Heinrich Johann Hille
HS (sometimes S superimposed on H)	1612-19	Johann (Hans) Schampan
ICA	1695-98	Julius Christian Arensburg
ILA, (c)= crossed battle axes	1688-95	Johann Leonhard Arensburg
IM	1705-10	Johann Memmies
VB	1633-63	Ulrich Butkau

Franzburg

Initial	Date	Name
CR	1608-?	Caspar Rotermund, mint contractor
	1608-?	Joachim Köneke (König)
	1615-?	Michael Martens
HP and/or (d) = acorn	1621-1625	Hans Puls, mint contractor
	1621-1625	Jürgen Stange, warden

Köslin

Initial	Date	Name
CW	ca. 1631	Christian Wilke

ARMS

Pomerania – griffin, usually rampant to left
Barth – rampant griffin to right with two large feathers
Gützkow – St. Andrew's cross with rose in each angle
Rügen – upper half of rampant crowned lion to left over a double set of stairs
Stettin – rampant crowned griffin to right
Wolgast – upper half of rampant griffin to left over checkerboard

COUNTERMARKS

Because of the severe financial hardships brought about by the onset of the Thirty Years' War, Duke Philipp Julius issued an edict in 1622 that effectively devalued the smaller circulating denominations of coins in his realm. In order to revalue the coins in circulation at the time, a series of countermarks was devised for use in the principal towns of the duchy. Most of these countermrks are found on the "Doppelschillinge" pieces and they were henceforth valued at 3 Schilling by the Pomeranian standard or one-1/2 Schilling by the standard of Lübeck. Coins of the same denominations from Pomeranian-Stettin and the Bishopric of Cammin were likewise countermarked. The inflation which continued unabated as the war went on forced a second devaluation in Wolgast in March 1623. The local coinage of 2 Schilling value were reduced to equal only 1 Schilling on the Lübeck standard. It is important to note that the following countermarks were authorized and used by the Duchy of Pomerania-Wolgast, not of the individual towns and cities.

Anklam

c/m – 3 rays connected in point at top, each beginning at bottom with small circle, so whole shaped like an arrowhead (Hildisch GS I)

c/m – 3 rays connected in point at top which divides 'A – 3' (=Anklam – 3 Schilling), each beginning at bottom with small circle, so whole shaped like an arrowhead. (Hildisch GS II)

Demmin

c/m – a double fleur-de-lis (Hildisch GS III)

Franzburg

c/m – Griffin rampant to left. (Hildisch GS IV)
c/m – Griffin rampant to left, 'F' below. (Hildisch GS V)

Greifswald

c/m – 'G3' (Hildisch GS VI)

Stralsund

c/m – 3 rays forming arrowhead shape, central ray begins at bottom with small circle, point surmounted by cross. (Hildisch GS VII)

Wolgast

c/m – Griffin rampant to right. (Hildisch GS VIII)
c/m – Griffin rampant to right, '3' between hind legs. (Hildisch GS IX)

Unknown Place

c/m – 'S' superimposed on 'H', crown above. (Hildisch GS X)

REFERENCES

H = Johannes Hildisch, ***Die Münzen der pommerschen Herzöge***, Cologne/Vienna: Böhlau Verlag, 1980.

S = Hugo Frhr. Von Saurma-Jeltsch, ***Die Saurmasche Münzsammlung deutscher, schweizerischer und polnischer Gepräge von etwa dem Beginn der Groschenzeit bis zur Kipperperiode,*** Berlin, 1892.

Sch = Wolfgang Schulten, ***Deutsche Münzen aus der Zeit Karls V.***, Frankfurt am Main, 1976.

POMERANIA-STETTIN

RULERS

Barnim XII, 1600-1603, in Rügenwalde 1560-1603
Bogislaw XIII, 1603-1606, in Barth 1569-1606
Philip II, 1606-1618
Georg III, in Rügenwalde 1606-1617
Franz, 1618-1620
Bogislaus XIV, 1620-1637, in Rügenwalde 1617-1620

DUCHY

REGULAR COINAGE

KM# 11 3 PFENNIG (Dreier)

0.7400 g., Silver, 16-17 mm. **Ruler:** Philipp II **Obv:** Ornate helmet over small shield of arms, PHD - SPO above **Rev:** Ornate helmet over small shield of arms, date divided near top **Mint:** Stettin **Note:** Varieties exist. H#67-9, 70.

Date	Mintage	Good	VG	F	VF	XF
161Z	—	10.00	20.00	40.00	80.00	—
1613	—	10.00	20.00	40.00	80.00	—
1614	—	10.00	20.00	40.00	80.00	—
1615	—	10.00	20.00	40.00	80.00	—

KM# 97 3 PFENNIG (Dreier)

0.6300 g., Silver, 15-16 mm. **Ruler:** Bogislaw XIV **Obv:** Crowned griffin left holding sword, around B.H. - Z.S.P. **Rev:** Ornate helmet over arms, date divided near top **Mint:** Stettin **Note:** H#138.

Date	Mintage	Good	VG	F	VF	XF
16ZZ	—	10.00	20.00	40.00	80.00	—
(1)6ZZ	—	10.00	20.00	40.00	80.00	—

KM# 94 1/2 GROSCHEN POMMERSCH

0.6000 g., Silver, 14 mm. **Ruler:** Bogislaw XIV **Obv:** Blank shield superimposed on cross in circle **Obv. Legend:** BVGSL. DVX. S. POM. **Rev:** 3-line inscription, date at end of legend **Rev. Legend:** SOLI. PATRIÆ. **Rev. Inscription:** HALB / GROS / POM. **Mint:** Stettin **Note:** H#151.

Date	Mintage	Good	VG	F	VF	XF
16ZZ	—	—	—	—	—	—

KM# 98 WITTEN (4 Pfennig)

0.9500 g., Silver, 16 mm. **Ruler:** Bogislaw XIV **Obv:** Griffin to left in circle with sword **Obv. Legend:** BVGSL. D.G. D. ST. POM. **Rev:** Short cross in circle, date in angles **Rev. Legend:** DEVS. ADIVTOR. MEVS. **Mint:** Stettin **Note:** H#150.

Date	Mintage	Good	VG	F	VF	XF
16ZZ	—	—	—	—	—	—

KM# 61 2 SCHILLING (Doppelschilling)

Silver Weight varies: 1.62-1.90g., 22-23 mm. **Ruler:** Franz **Obv:** Crowned griffin to left in circle holding sword **Obv. Legend:** FRANCIS(C). I. D.G. DVX. S. P(O)(M). **Rev:** Intertwined DS in circle, date at end of legend **Rev. Legend:** ADSIT. AB. ALTO. **Mint:** Stettin **Note:** H#122-4. Prev. Pomerania KM#63.

Date	Mintage	Good	VG	F	VF	XF
1618	—	6.00	10.00	18.00	35.00	70.00
1619	—	6.00	10.00	18.00	35.00	70.00
16Z0	—	6.00	10.00	18.00	35.00	70.00

KM# 84 2 SCHILLING (Doppelschilling)

Silver, 21-21.5 mm. **Ruler:** Bogislaw XIV **Obv:** Crowned griffin to left in circle holding sword **Obv. Legend:** BVGSLAVS. (D.G.) DVX. S. P(OM). **Rev:** Intertwined DS in circle **Rev. Legend:** DEVS. ADIVTOR. MEVS. **Mint:** Stettin **Note:** H#140-1.

Date	Mintage	Good	VG	F	VF	XF
ND(1620-25)	—	15.00	25.00	50.00	100	—

KM# 85 2 SCHILLING (Doppelschilling)

Silver, 23 mm. **Ruler:** Bogislaw XIV **Obv:** Crowned griffin to left in circle **Obv. Legend:** BVGSLAVS. DVX. S. POM. **Rev:** Intertwined DS in circle divides date **Rev. Legend:** DEVS. ADIVTOR. MEVS. **Mint:** Stettin **Note:** H#142-3. Prev. Pomerania KM#63.

Date	Mintage	Good	VG	F	VF	XF
(16)Z0	—	15.00	25.00	50.00	100	—
(16)Z1	—	15.00	25.00	50.00	100	—

KM# 83 2 SCHILLING (Doppelschilling)

1.3100 g., Silver, 22 mm. **Ruler:** Bogislaw XIV **Obv:** Crowned griffin to left in circle **Obv. Legend:** BVGSLAVS. D. G. DVX. S. P. **Rev:** Intertwined DS in circle **Rev. Legend:** DEVS. ADIVTOR. MEVS. **Mint:** Stettin **Note:** H#139.

Date	Mintage	Good	VG	F	VF	XF
ND(1620-25) (z)	—	15.00	25.00	50.00	100	—
ND(1620-25)	—	15.00	25.00	50.00	100	—

KM# 95 2 SCHILLING (Doppelschilling)

1.2600 g., Silver, 21-22 mm. **Ruler:** Bogislaw XIV **Obv:** Crowned griffin to left in circle holding sword **Obv. Legend:** BVGSLAVS. (D.G.) DVX. (X.) S. P(O)(M). **Rev:** Intertwined DS in circle divides date **Rev. Legend:** DEVS. ADIVTOR. MEVS. **Mint:** Stettin **Note:** H#144-9, 366-7. Varieties exist. Prev. Pomerania KM#63.

Date	Mintage	Good	VG	F	VF	XF
(16)Z1 (z)	—	10.00	18.00	30.00	55.00	110
(16)ZZ (z)	—	10.00	18.00	30.00	55.00	110
(16)Z3	—	10.00	18.00	30.00	55.00	110
(16)Z4	—	10.00	18.00	30.00	55.00	110
(16)Z5	—	10.00	18.00	30.00	55.00	110
(16)Z8 (z)	—	10.00	18.00	30.00	55.00	110
(16)Z9 (z)	—	10.00	18.00	30.00	55.00	110

KM# 12 1/24 THALER (Reichsgroschen)

1.4800 g., Silver, 20-21 mm. **Ruler:** Philipp II **Obv:** Crowned griffin to left with sword and book in circle **Obv. Legend:** PHILIPPVS. II. DVX. STE(O). (P)(B)O. **Rev:** Imperial orb with Z4 divides date **Rev. Legend:** CHRI(S)TO. ET. REIPV(B)(R)LI. **Mint:** Stettin **Note:** H#60-66. Varieties exist.

Date	Mintage	Good	VG	F	VF	XF
161Z	—	15.00	30.00	50.00	80.00	160
1613	—	15.00	30.00	50.00	80.00	160
1614	—	15.00	30.00	50.00	80.00	160
1615	—	15.00	30.00	50.00	80.00	160
1616	—	15.00	30.00	50.00	80.00	160
1617	—	15.00	30.00	50.00	80.00	160
1618	—	15.00	30.00	50.00	80.00	160

KM# 62 1/24 THALER (Reichsgroschen)

1.4400 g., Silver, 20 mm. **Ruler:** Franz **Obv:** Crowned griffin to left in circle holding sword **Obv. Legend:** FRANCIS. I. D.G. DVX. S. P. **Rev:** Imperial orb with Z4 **Rev. Legend:** ADSIT. AB. ALTO + **Mint:** Stettin **Note:** H#119.

Date	Mintage	Good	VG	F	VF	XF
ND(1618-20)	—	—	—	—	—	—

KM# 63 1/24 THALER (Reichsgroschen)

1.4400 g., Silver, 19 mm. **Ruler:** Franz **Obv:** Crowned griffin to left in circle holding sword **Obv. Legend:** FRANCIS(C). (I.) D.G. DVX. S. P(O)(M). **Rev:** Imperial or with Z4, date at end of legend **Rev. Legend:** ADSIT. AB. ALTO. **Mint:** Stettin **Note:** H#120-21. Varieties exist. Prev. Pomerania KM#64.

Date	Mintage	Good	VG	F	VF	XF
1618	—	10.00	20.00	40.00	80.00	160
1619	—	10.00	20.00	40.00	80.00	160
(16)19	—	10.00	20.00	40.00	80.00	160

KM# 64 1/24 THALER (Dreipölker)
Silver Weight varies: 0.92-1.40g., 20 mm. **Ruler:** Bogislaw XIV **Obv:** Shield of 4-fold arms, (3) in oval at bottom **Obv. Legend:** BVGSLAV(S). - DVX. S. POM. **Rev:** Imperial orb with Z4 divides date **Rev. Legend:** DEVS. ADIVTOR. MEV(S). **Mint:** Stettin **Note:** Coinage for Rügenwalde. H#283-5. Varieties exist.

Date	Mintage	Good	VG	F	VF	XF
(16)18	—	10.00	20.00	45.00	90.00	180
(16)19	—	10.00	20.00	45.00	90.00	180
(16)Z0	—	10.00	20.00	45.00	90.00	180
(16)0Z error for 1620, value error 4Z in orb	—	10.00	20.00	45.00	90.00	180

KM# 96 1/24 THALER (Dreipölker)
0.8800 g., Silver, 19-20 mm. **Ruler:** Bogislaw XIV **Obv:** Shield of 4-fold arms, value (3) at bottom **Obv. Legend:** BVGSLAV. - DVX. S. POM. **Rev:** Imperial orb with Z4 OR 24 divides date **Rev. Legend:** DEVS. ADIVTOR. MEV(S). **Mint:** Stettin **Note:** H#135-7. Varieties exist.

Date	Mintage	Good	VG	F	VF	XF
(16)Z1	—	10.00	20.00	45.00	90.00	180
(16)ZZ	—	10.00	20.00	45.00	90.00	180
(16)Z3	—	10.00	20.00	45.00	90.00	180
(16)23	—	10.00	20.00	45.00	90.00	180

KM# 100 1/16 THALER (Düttchen)
2.8900 g., Silver, 27-28 mm. **Ruler:** Bogislaw XIV **Obv:** Griffin to left in shield superimposed on long cross **Obv. Legend:** BOGIS. - LAVS. - XIV D.G - DVX. S. P. **Rev:** 4-line inscription with date **Rev. Legend:** REICHS. SC(H)ROT. VND KORN. **Rev. Inscription:** 16. ST./REICHS/TALER/(date) **Mint:** Stettin **Note:** H#362-5. Varieties exist.

Date	Mintage	Good	VG	F	VF	XF
16Z8	—	25.00	45.00	80.00	160	300
16Z9	—	25.00	45.00	80.00	160	300
1630	—	25.00	45.00	80.00	160	300
1631	—	25.00	45.00	80.00	160	300

KM# 99 1/16 THALER (Düttchen)
2.8900 g., Silver, 26-27 mm. **Ruler:** Bogislaw XIV **Obv:** Crowned griffin to left in circle holding sword and book **Obv. Legend:** MONETA. NOVA. BOGISLAI. XIV. D.S. PO. **Rev:** 5-line inscription with date **Rev. Legend:** PRIN. RVG. COM. GVT. TERR. LEOB. E. BV. D(N). **Rev. Inscription:** 16/STVK./EIN. R./TALER/(date). **Mint:** Stettin **Note:** H#361.

Date	Mintage	Good	VG	F	VF	XF
16Z8	—	30.00	50.00	100	200	—
1628	—	30.00	50.00	100	200	—

KM# 31 1/8 THALER (1/2 Reichsort)
3.5800 g., Silver, 25 mm. **Ruler:** Philipp II **Subject:** Death of Anna von Schleswig-Holstein, Widow of Bogislaw XIII **Obv:** Skull above crossed scepter and scythe in circle **Obv. Legend:** OPTIMA PHILOSOPHIA. **Rev:** 5-line inscription with date, floral ornaments at top and bottom **Rev. Inscription:** MEMORIÆ/ FVNEBRI: DN/ ANNÆ DV:/ POM: MAT:/ CARIS. (date). **Mint:** Stettin **Note:** H#91.

Date	Mintage	Good	VG	F	VF	XF
1616	—	—	—	—	—	—

KM# 38 1/8 THALER (1/2 Reichsort)
3.6100 g., Silver, 26 mm. **Ruler:** Philipp II **Subject:** Death of Georg III **Obv:** Wind blowing from clouds at upper right on rose bush below **Obv. Legend:** FLORIS. RAPIT. AVRA. DECOREM. **Rev:** 5-line inscription with Roman numeral date, floral ornaments at top and bottom **Rev. Inscription:** LVCTVS / PVBLICI / MEMORIA / XXVI MAI / AO DCXVII. **Mint:** Stettin **Note:** H#97.

Date	Mintage	Good	VG	F	VF	XF
DCXVII(1617)	—	—	—	—	—	—

KM# 66 1/8 THALER (1/2 Reichsort)
3.5000 g., Silver, 26-27 mm. **Ruler:** Franz **Subject:** Death of Philipp II **Obv:** Rose bush in circle **Obv. Legend:** VT. ROSA RODIMVR OMNES. **Rev:** 5-line inscription with date in wreath **Rev. Inscription:** (date) / CHRISTO / ET / REIPVBLI / CAE. **Mint:** Stettin **Note:** H#111.

Date	Mintage	Good	VG	F	VF	XF
1618	—	—	—	—	—	—

KM# 87 1/8 THALER (1/2 Reichsort)
3.5000 g., Silver, 26-27 mm. **Ruler:** Bogislaw XIV **Subject:** Death of Franz **Obv:** Skull over crossed scepter and scythe, all in wreath **Rev:** 6-line inscription **Rev. Inscription:** PACIFI / CVM RAPV / IT VERVM / NON DEFI / CIT: AL / TER. **Mint:** Stettin **Note:** H#134.

Date	Mintage	Good	VG	F	VF	XF
ND(1620)	—	—	—	—	—	—

KM# 140 1/8 THALER (1/2 Reichsort)
3.4400 g., Silver, 26 mm. **Ruler:** Bogislaw XIV **Obv:** Bust to right in circle, date at end of legend **Obv. Legend:** BOGISLAVS. XIV. D.G. DVX. S. P. **Rev:** 4-line inscription in circle, date at end of legend **Rev. Legend:** DEVS. ADIVTOR. MEVS. (AÕ). **Mint:** Stettin **Note:** H#360.

Date	Mintage	Good	VG	F	VF	XF
1636//1636	—	—	—	—	—	—

KM# 142 1/8 THALER (1/2 Reichsort)
3.5500 g., Silver, 26-27 mm. **Ruler:** Bogislaw XIV **Subject:** Entombment of Bogislaw XIV **Obv:** Tree stump with two young limbs in leaf, view of Stettin behind, sun shining down from upper left divides DEO - DIRIGENTE **Rev:** 11-line inscription with dates in wreath **Rev. Inscription:** NVMMVS / EXEQVIALIS / OPTIMI PRINCI / PIS. BOGISLAI / DVCIS. STET. POME / EIVS NOMINIS. XIV. / ET. VLTIMI / NATI. 31 MART 1580 / DEN. X. MAR 1637 / SEP. 25 MAY / 1654. **Mint:** Stettin **Note:** H#387.

Date	Mintage	Good	VG	F	VF	XF
1654	600	—	—	—	—	—

KM# 2 1/4 THALER (Reichsort)
7.0600 g., Silver, 30 mm. **Ruler:** Philipp II **Obv:** Bust to right in circle **Obv. Legend:** PHILIPPVS. II. D.G. DVX. STET. POM. **Rev:** Skull above crossed scepter and scythe **Rev. Legend:** MEDIT. MORT. OPTIMA. PHILOSOPHIA. **Mint:** Stettin **Note:** H#59.

Date	Mintage	Good	VG	F	VF	XF
ND(1606-18)	—	—	—	—	—	—

KM# 32 1/4 THALER (Reichsort)
7.1500 g., Silver, 30 mm. **Ruler:** Philipp II **Subject:** Death of Anna von Schleswig-Holstein, Widow of Bogislaw XIII **Obv:** Skull above crossed scepter and scythe **Obv. Legend:** MEDIT. MORT. OPTIMA. PHILOSOPHIA. **Rev:** 7-line inscription with Roman numeral date **Rev. Inscription:** MEMORIÆ / FVNEBRI. DÑ / ANNÆ. DVCIS / POM. MATRIS / CARISS. ANNO / MDCXVI. VIII / APRILIS. **Mint:** Stettin **Note:** H#90.

Date	Mintage	Good	VG	F	VF	XF
MDCXVI(1616)	—	—	—	—	—	—

KM# 39 1/4 THALER (Reichsort)
7.1700 g., Silver, 30 mm. **Ruler:** Philipp II **Subject:** Death of Georg III **Obv:** Sun shining on rose bush **Obv. Legend:** REDIENS. SOL. SVSCITAT. HERBAS. **Rev:** 6-line inscription with Roman numeral date **Rev. Inscription:** MEMORI? / GEORGI D PO. / MERAN A FRAT. / PHILIP. II SACRA / TVM. XXVI. MAI / AO. DCXVII. **Mint:** Stettin **Note:** H#96.

Date	Mintage	Good	VG	F	VF	XF
DCXVII(1617)	—	—	—	—	—	—

KM# 67 1/4 THALER (Reichsort)
7.0100 g., Silver, 29.5 mm. **Ruler:** Franz **Subject:** Death of Philipp II **Obv:** Bust to right in ornamented circle **Obv. Legend:** PHILIPPVS. II. D.G. DVX. POM. **Rev:** 7-line inscription with Roman numeral date **Rev. Inscription:** PATRI / PATRIÆ. PIO / PACIFICO MODE / RATO. LITERA / TO. C. LAC. R.P. / AÕ MDCXIIX / XIX MART. **Mint:** Stettin **Note:** H#110.

Date	Mintage	Good	VG	F	VF	XF
MDCXIIX (1618) DS	—	—	—	—	—	—

KM# 88 1/4 THALER (Reichsort)
7.2400 g., Silver, 30-31 mm. **Ruler:** Bogislaw XIV **Subject:** Death of Franz **Obv:** Skull over crossed scepter and scythe, all in wreath **Rev:** 6-line inscription **Rev. Legend:** FRANCISCVS. I. DG. DVX. STETIN. P. **Rev. Inscription:** PACIFI / CVM. RAPV / IT. VERVM / NON. DEFI / CIT: AL / TER. **Mint:** Stettin **Note:** H#133.

Date	Mintage	Good	VG	F	VF	XF
ND(1620) GT	—	—	—	—	—	—

KM# 101 1/4 THALER (Reichsort)
7.1500 g., Silver, 28 mm. **Ruler:** Bogislaw XIV **Obv:** Half-length figure to right divides date in circle **Obv. Legend:** BOGIS. XIV. D.G. DVX. STET. POM. CAS. ET. VAN. **Rev:** Large shield of 9-fold arms in ornate frame within circle **Rev. Legend:** PRIN. RUG. COM. GUTZ. TER. LEOB. ET. BU. DN. **Mint:** Stettin **Note:** H#357.

Date	Mintage	Good	VG	F	VF	XF
16Z8	—	—	—	—	—	—

KM# 102 1/4 THALER (Reichsort)
7.1500 g., Silver, 32 mm. **Ruler:** Bogislaw XIV **Obv:** Bust to right in circle **Obv. Legend:** BOGISLAVS. XIV. D.G. DVX. ST. PO. C. E. V. **Rev:** Ornamented spanish shield of 9-fold arms, date above, in circle **Rev. Legend:** PRIN. RVG. CO. GVT. TER. LEOB. E. BV. DO. **Mint:** Stettin **Note:** H#358.

Date	Mintage	Good	VG	F	VF	XF
16Z8	—	—	—	—	—	—

KM# 135 1/4 THALER (Reichsort)
7.1500 g., Silver, 31 mm. **Ruler:** Bogislaw XIV **Obv:** Small bust to right in circle **Obv. Legend:** BOGISLAVS. XIV. D.G. DVX. STE. POM. **Rev:** 10-fold arms in baroque frame, ducal cap above, date at end of legend **Rev. Legend:** DEVS. ADIVTOR. MEVS. **Mint:** Stettin **Note:** H#359.

Date	Mintage	Good	VG	F	VF	XF
1635	—	—	—	—	—	—

KM# 143 1/4 THALER (Reichsort)
7.1400 g., Silver Weight varies: 7.12-7.14g., 30 mm. **Ruler:** Bogislaw XIV **Subject:** Entombment of Bogislaw XIV **Obv:** Tree stump with two young limbs in leaf, view of Stettin behind, sun shining down from upper left, DEO DIRIGENTE to right of sun **Rev:** 11-line inscription with date within wreath **Rev. Inscription:** NVMMVS. EXEQVIALIS / OPTIMI. PRINCI / PIS. BOGISLAI / DVCIS. STET. POME / EIVS. NOMINIS. XIV / ET VLTIMI / NATI. 31 MART 1580 / DEN. 10. MAR. 1637 / SEP. 25 MAY / 1654. **Mint:** Stettin **Note:** H#386.

Date	Mintage	Good	VG	F	VF	XF
1654	100	300	500	800	1,300	2,000

KM# 3 1/2 THALER
14.0000 g., Silver, 33-34 mm. **Ruler:** Philipp II **Obv:** Bust to right in circle **Obv. Legend:** PHILIPPVS. II. D.G. DVX. POMERANORVM. **Rev:** Crowned griffin to left holding sword in circle, 10 oval shields of arms around, legend in small letters between tops of shields **Rev. Legend:** CR - IS - TO - ET - RE - IP - VB - LI - C - Æ. **Mint:** Stettin **Note:** H#58. Varieties exist.

Date	Mintage	Good	VG	F	VF	XF
ND(1606-18) DS	—	—	—	—	—	—
ND(1606-18)	—	—	—	—	—	—

KM# 40 1/2 THALER
14.6000 g., Silver, 35 mm. **Ruler:** Philipp II **Subject:** Centennial of the Reformation **Obv:** Armored bust wearing ruffed collar to right in circle **Obv. Legend:** PHILIPPVS. II. D.G. DVX. POMERANORVM. **Rev:** Small sailboat, man at tiller, being blown to right by wind from clouds at upper left, legend ends with Roman numeral date **Rev. Legend:** SAPIENTIA NON VIOLENTIA. ANNO. MDCXVII. **Mint:** Stettin **Note:** H#84.

Date	Mintage	Good	VG	F	VF	XF
MDCXVII(1617)	—	—	—	—	—	—

KM# 41 1/2 THALER
14.6000 g., Silver, 35 mm. **Ruler:** Philipp II **Subject:** Centennial of the Reformation **Obv:** Armored bust to right in circle **Obv. Legend:** PHILIPPVS. II. DVX. POMERANORVM. **Rev:** Small sailboat, man at tiller, being blown to right by wind from clouds at upper left, Roman numeral date at end of legend **Rev. Legend:** SAPIENTIA NON VIOLENTIA. ANNO. MDCXVII. **Mint:** Stettin **Note:** H#85.

Date	Mintage	Good	VG	F	VF	XF
MDCXVII(1617)	—	—	—	—	—	—

KM# 42 1/2 THALER
13.8500 g., Silver, 35 mm. **Ruler:** Philipp II **Subject:** Death of Georg III **Obv:** Wildman standing to left of table holding ornately-shaped shield of Pomeranian arms, hourglass, flower and skull on table, the front of which is a square tablet with birth and death dates in Roman numerals **Obv. Inscription:** NATVS / XXX. IAN / M.DLXXXII / OBIIT / XXVII MART / MDCXVII. **Rev:** 9-line inscription with Roman numeral date **Rev. Inscription:** PHILIPPVS / II DVX STETTIN / ET POMERANIÆ. GEORGI III / FRATR DESIDERAT / MEMORIÆ / CVM LACRYM FF / XXVI MAII / MDCXVII. **Mint:** Stettin **Note:** H#95.

Date	Mintage	Good	VG	F	VF	XF
MDCXVII(1617)	—	—	—	—	—	—

KM# 43 1/2 THALER
14.3800 g., Silver, 35 mm. **Ruler:** Philipp II **Subject:** Centennial of the Reformation **Obv:** Samson wrestling with lion, date at end of legend **Obv. Legend:** OBTVRAVIT OS LEONIS. **Rev:** 7-line inscription with Roman numeral date **Rev. Inscription:** IN MEMO / RIAM. IVBILÆI / EVANGELICI / ANNO. M.D.XVII / CELERATI. PHI / LIPPVS. II. DVX / POM. F.F. **Mint:** Stettin **Note:** H#104.

Date	Mintage	Good	VG	F	VF	XF
1617//MDXVII(1517)	—	—	—	—	—	—

KM# 44 1/2 THALER
14.3800 g., Silver, 35 mm. **Ruler:** Philipp II **Subject:** Centennial of the Reformation **Obv:** Samson wrestling with lion on grass, date at end of legend **Obv. Legend:** OBTVRAVIT OS LEONIS. **Rev:** 7-line inscription with Roman numeral date **Rev. Inscription:** IN MEMO / RIAM. IVBILÆI / EVANGELICI / ANNO. M.D.C.XVII / CELEBRATI. PHI / LIPPVS. II. DVX / POM. F.F. **Mint:** Stettin **Note:** H#105.

Date	Mintage	Good	VG	F	VF	XF
1517//MDCXVII(1617)	—	—	—	—	—	—

KM# 68 1/2 THALER
14.1900 g., Silver, 35 mm. **Ruler:** Franz **Subject:** Death of Philipp II **Obv:** Armored bust wearing ruffed collar to right in ornamented circle **Obv. Legend:** PHILIPPVS. II. D.G. DVX. POMERANORVM. **Rev:** 10-line inscription with date **Rev. Inscription:** NVMMVS / MEMOR. FVNEBRI / PHILIPPI. II / DVCIS. STET. POMER / QVI. NATVS. Z8. IVL. AÕ. 1573, DEBAT, 3, FEB, AÕ. 1618/CONSECRATVS/A. FRANC. I. SEDINET/POMER. DVCE. FRAT/ET. SVCCESS. **Mint:** Stettin **Note:** H#109.

Date	Mintage	Good	VG	F	VF	XF
1618	—	—	—	—	—	—

KM# 69 1/2 THALER
14.2100 g., Silver, 35 mm. **Ruler:** Franz **Obv:** Armored bust to right in circle **Obv. Legend:** D.G. FRANCISCVS. I. DVX. SEDINI. POMERAN. CASSVB. ET. VAN. **Rev:** Ornate shield of 9-fold arms supported by 2 wildmen, 3 ornate helmets above **Rev. Legend:** PRINC. RVGIÆ. COM GVTZK. TERR. LEOPOL. ET. BVTOV. DNS. **Mint:** Stettin **Note:** H#117.

Date	Mintage	Good	VG	F	VF	XF
ND(1618-20)	—	—	—	—	—	—

KM# 71 1/2 THALER
14.3300 g., Silver, 35 mm. **Ruler:** Franz **Subject:** Death of Anna Maria von Brandenburg, Widow of Barnim XII **Obv:** Crowned griffin to left holding sword and ornate shield, 10 small shields of arms on wings, standing on ornate tablet which is blank, no legend **Rev:** 10-line inscription with Roman numeral dates **Rev. Inscription:** MEMORIÆ. FVNEB / ANNÆ MARIÆ / IOH. GEORG. EL. BR. FILIÆ / BARNI. XI. DVC. POM. VIDVÆ / NATÆ. M. D. LXVII / DENA. M.DCXIIX / SEP. 17. XB. STET. Ã. EOD / FRANCISCVS. I. DVX. STET. POM / F. F. **Mint:** Stettin **Note:** H#127.

Date	Mintage	Good	VG	F	VF	XF
MDCXIIX(1618)	—	—	—	—	—	—

KM# 70 1/2 THALER
14.2100 g., Silver, 35 mm. **Ruler:** Franz **Obv:** Armored bust to right in circle **Obv. Legend:** D.G. FRANCISCVS. I. DVX. SEDINI. POMERAN. CASSVB. ET. VAN. **Rev:** Ornate shield of 9-fold arms supported by 2 wildmen, 3 ornate helmets above **Rev. Legend:** PRINC. RVGIÆ. COM. GVTZK. TERR. LEOPOL. ET. BVTOV. DN. **Mint:** Stettin **Note:** H#118.

Date	Mintage	Good	VG	F	VF	XF
ND(1618-20) GT	—	—	—	—	—	—

KM# 89 1/2 THALER

13.7500 g., Silver, 35 mm. **Ruler:** Bogislaw XIV **Subject:** Death of Franz **Obv:** Armored bust to right in circle **Obv. Legend:** D.G. FRANCISCVS. I. DVX. SEDINI. POMERAN. CASSVB. ET. VAN. **Rev:** 10-line inscription with dates **Rev. Inscription:** NVMMVS / NOVISSIMO. HONORI / FRANCISCI. I / DVCIS. STET. POM. QVI / NATVS. XXIV. MART. AÕ. 1577 / MORTVVS. XXVII. NOVE / ANNO. 1620. DICATVS / A. BOGISLAO. SIV / FRATRE. ET. SVC / CESSORE. **Mint:** Stettin **Note:** H#132.

Date	Mintage	Good	VG	F	VF	XF
1620 GT	—	—	—	—	—	—

KM# 103 1/2 THALER

13.9400 g., Silver, 36 mm. **Ruler:** Bogislaw XIV **Obv:** Half-length armored figure to right divides date in circle **Obv. Legend:** BOGISLAVS. XIV. D.G. DVX. STE. POM. CASS. ET. VAN. **Rev:** Shield of 9-fold arms in ornate frame within circle **Rev. Legend:** PRINCEPS. RVG. COM. GVTZK. TERR. LEOB. ET. BVT. DN. **Mint:** Stettin **Note:** H#353.

Date	Mintage	Good	VG	F	VF	XF
16Z8	—	—	—	—	—	—

KM# 104 1/2 THALER

13.9400 g., Silver, 36-37 mm. **Ruler:** Bogislaw XIV **Obv:** Large armored half-length figure to right divides date and breaks circle at top **Obv. Legend:** BOGISLAVS. XIV. D.G. DVX. STET. POM. CAS. E. VA. **Rev:** Shield of 9-fold arms in ornate frame within circle **Rev. Legend:** PRINCEPS. RVG. COM. GVTZK. TERR. LEOB. ET. BVT. DN. **Mint:** Stettin **Note:** H#354.

Date	Mintage	Good	VG	F	VF	XF
16Z8	—	—	—	—	—	—

KM# 105 1/2 THALER

13.9400 g., Silver, 33 mm. **Ruler:** Bogislaw XIV **Obv:** Half-length armored figure to right divides date in circle **Obv. Legend:** BOGIS. XIV. D.G. DVX. STET. POM. CASSVB. ET. VANDA. **Rev:** Shield of 9-fold arms in ornate frame within circle **Rev. Legend:** PRINCEPS. RVG. COM. GVTZ. TER. LEOB. ET. BVT. DN. **Mint:** Stettin **Note:** H#355.

Date	Mintage	Good	VG	F	VF	XF
16Z8	—	—	—	—	—	—

KM# 106 1/2 THALER

13.9400 g., Silver, 38 mm. **Ruler:** Bogislaw XIV **Obv:** Bust to right in circle **Obv. Legend:** BOGISLAVS. XIV. D.G. DVX. STE. POM. CAS. E. V. **Rev:** Squarish shield of 9-fold arms, 3 ornate helmets above, date divided at top in margin **Rev. Legend:** PRINC. RVG. COM. GVT. TER. LEOB. E. BV. D. **Mint:** Stettin **Note:** H#356. Varieties exist.

Date	Mintage	Good	VG	F	VF	XF
16Z8	—	—	—	—	—	—
16Z8 error XVI for XIV	—	—	—	—	—	—

KM# 144 1/2 THALER

14.2900 g., Silver, 42 mm. **Ruler:** Bogislaw XIV **Subject:** Entombment of Bogislaw XIV **Obv:** Bust to right in wreath **Obv. Legend:** BOGISLAVS. XIV. D.G. DVX. STET. POM. C. &. V. P. RV. E. C. C. G. T. L. E. B. D. **Rev:** 12-line inscription with dates in wreath **Rev. Inscription:** NVMMVS / EXEQVALIS. / OPTIMI PRINCIPIS / *BOGISLAI* / DVCIS STET. POM EIVS / NOMINIS. 14. ET VLTIMI / NATI. 31. MART. 1580 / DENATI. 10. MART. 1637 / CONDITI. 25. MAI. 1654 / REG. C. R. S. ET. F. W / M. &. E. B. D. P / P.P. **Mint:** Stettin **Note:** H#382.

Date	Mintage	Good	VG	F	VF	XF
1654	200	—	—	—	—	—

KM# 145 1/2 THALER

14.2900 g., Silver, 34 mm. **Ruler:** Bogislaw XIV **Subject:** Entombment of Bogislaw XIV **Obv:** Bust to right in wreath, double legend with dates **Obv. Legend:** IN MEMORIAM VLTIMI EX GRYPHICA STIRPE DVCIS POMERAN BOGISLAI. 14. // NATI. 31. MART. 1580. DENATI. 10. MART. 1637. HVMATI. 25. MAI. 1654. **Rev:** Tree stump with two young limbs in leaf, crowned griffin standing on top, skull below, crowned oval arms of Sweden and Brandenburg at lower left and right, sun shining down from above, all in wreath **Rev. Legend:** GRYPS TRIBUS ECCE CORONIS ET SCEPTRO CEDIT. **Mint:** Stettin **Note:** H#383.

Date	Mintage	Good	VG	F	VF	XF
1654	Inc. above	400	700	1,000	1,600	2,250

KM# 146 1/2 THALER

14.2900 g., Silver, 32 mm. **Ruler:** Bogislaw XIV **Subject:** Entombment of Bogislaw XIV **Obv:** Tree stump with two young limbs in leaf, view of Stettin behind, sun shiniing down from upper left, DEO DIRIGENTE to right of sun **Rev:** 11-line inscription with dates in wreath **Rev. Inscription:** NVMMVS / EXEQVIALIS / OPTIMI PRINCI / PIS BOGISLAI / DVCIS. STET. POME / EIVS. NOMINIS. XIV / ET. VLTIMI / NATI. 31. MART. 1580 / DEN. X. MAR. 1637 / SEP. 25. MAY / 1654. **Mint:** Stettin **Note:** H#384.

Date	Mintage	Good	VG	F	VF	XF
1654	Inc. above	—	—	—	—	—

KM# 147 1/2 THALER

14.2900 g., Silver, 28 mm. **Ruler:** Bogislaw XIV **Subject:** Entombment of Bogislaw XIV **Obv:** Tree stump with two young limbs in leaf, view of Stettin behind, sun shining down from upper left divides DEO - DIRIGENTE. **Rev:** 11-line inscription with dates in wreath **Rev. Inscription:** NVMMVS / EXEQVIALIS / OPTIMI PRINCI / PIS. BOGISLAI / DVCIS. STET. POMER / EIVS. NOMINIS. SIV / ET. VLTIMI / NATI. 31. MART. 1580 / DEN. 10. MAR. 1637 / SEP. 25. MAY / 1654. **Mint:** Stettin **Note:** H#385. Struck on thick flan from 1/8 Thaler dies.

Date	Mintage	Good	VG	F	VF	XF
1654	Inc. above	—	—	—	—	—

KM# 4 THALER

Silver, 40.5-42 mm. **Ruler:** Philipp II **Obv:** Bust to right in ornamented circle **Obv. Legend:** PHILIPPVS. II. D.G. DVX. POMERANORVM **Rev:** Crowned griffin to left holding sword in circle, 10 oval shields of arms around, legend in small letters between tops of shields **Rev. Legend:** CR - IS - TO - ET - RE - IP - VB - LI - C - Æ. **Mint:** Stettin **Note:** Dav. #7215; H#50. Prev. Pomerania KM#40.

Date	Mintage	VG	F	VF	XF	Unc
ND(1606-18) DS	—	700	1,400	2,500	4,250	6,750
ND(1606-18)	—	700	1,400	2,500	4,250	6,750

KM# 5 THALER

28.7100 g., Silver, 41-42 mm. **Ruler:** Philipp II **Obv:** Bust to right in circle **Obv. Legend:** PHILIPPVS. II. DVX. POMERANORVM. **Rev:** Crowned griffin left holding sword in circle, 10 oval shields of arms around, legend in small letters between tops of shields **Rev. Legend:** CR - IS - TO - ET - RE - IP - VB - LI - C - Æ. **Mint:** Stettin **Note:** Dav. #7211; H#51. Prev. Pomerania KM#38.

Date	Mintage	VG	F	VF	XF	Unc
ND(1606-18)	—	1,350	2,750	5,000	8,500	—

KM# 6 THALER

28.7000 g., Silver, 40-41 mm. **Ruler:** Philipp II **Obv:** Bust to right in ornamented circle **Obv. Legend:** PHILIPPVS. II. D.G. DVX. POMERANORVM. **Rev:** Crowned griffin left holding sword and book, 10 small shields of arms on wings, 2-line inscription in ornate tablet below **Rev. Inscription:** CHRISTO. ET. REIP / VBLICÆ. **Mint:** Stettin **Note:** Dav. #7213; H#52. Prev. Pomerania KM#39.

Date	Mintage	VG	F	VF	XF	Unc
ND(1606-18)	—	750	1,500	2,750	4,650	—

KM# 13 THALER

28.7000 g., Silver, 42-43 mm. **Ruler:** Philipp II **Obv:** Bust to right in circle, legend divided by 5 small shields of arms in margin **Obv. Legend:** V. G. G. - PHI. - LIPS - H. Z. S. - POM. **Rev:** Crowned griffin left holding sword and book, legend divided by 5 small shields of arms in margin, date at end of legend **Rev. Legend:** CHRI - STO. ET - REIP - ANNO - (date) **Mint:** Stettin **Note:** Dav. #7205; H#53, 55. Prev. Pomerania KM#23.

Date	Mintage	VG	F	VF	XF	Unc
1613	—	1,400	2,500	4,750	7,750	—
1614	—	1,400	2,500	4,750	7,750	—

KM# 18 THALER

28.7000 g., Silver, 42 mm. **Ruler:** Philipp II **Obv:** Bust to right in circle **Obv. Legend:** PHILIPPVS. II. DVX. POMERANORVM. **Rev:** Shield of 9-fold arms supported by 2 helmeted wildmen, ornate helmet above, date at end of legend **Rev. Legend:** CHRISTO. ET. REIPVBLICÆ. **Mint:** Stettin **Note:** Dav. #7208; H#54, 54. Prev. Pomerania KM#27.

Date	Mintage	VG	F	VF	XF	Unc
1614	—	1,150	2,150	4,250	7,500	—
1616	—	1,150	2,150	4,250	7,500	—

KM# 19 THALER

Silver **Ruler:** Philipp II **Obv:** Bust to right in circle, legend divided by 5 small shields of arms **Obv. Legend:** V. G. G. - PHI. - LIPS - H. A. S. - POM. **Rev:** Crowned griffin to left holding sword and book, legend divided by 5 small shields of arms, date at end of legend **Rev. Legend:** CHRI - STO. ET - REIP - ANNO - (date) **Mint:** Stettin **Note:** Klippe. Dav. #7205A; H#KL55. Prev. Pomerania KM#26.

Date	Mintage	VG	F	VF	XF	Unc
1614 Rare	—	—	—	—	—	—

KM# 25 THALER

Silver, 43 mm. **Ruler:** Philipp II **Obv:** Bust to right in circle, legend divided by 5 small shields of arms **Obv. Legend:** V. G. G. - PHI. - LIPS - H. Z. S. - POM. **Rev:** 11-line inscription with date **Rev. Inscription:** (date) / A. DEO / OMNIA. OR / NAMENTA / REIPVBLICAE. ET / FVNDAMEN / TVM. EIVS / EST. NON / GAVDE / REVA / NIS **Mint:** Stettin **Note:** Dav. #7209; H#56. Prev. Pomerania KM#35.

Date	Mintage	VG	F	VF	XF	Unc
1615 Rare	—	—	—	—	—	—

KM# 33 THALER

27.2600 g., Silver, 42 mm. **Ruler:** Philipp II **Subject:** Death of Anna von Schleswig-Holstein, Widow of Bogislaw XIII **Obv:** Bust to right in circle **Obv. Legend:** PHILIPPVS. II. DVX. POMERANORVM. **Rev:** 9-line inscription with Roman numeral dates **Rev. Inscription:** ANNA FILIA/ IOHAN. DVCIS/ HOLS. VIDVA. BOGIS/ LAI. SEN. DVCIS POM./ MATER CARISS. NATA/ MDLXXVII. VII. OCT/ DENATA. MDCXVI/ XXX IAN. SEPVL/ VIII. APRI. **Mint:** Stettin **Note:** Dav. #7218; H#89. Prev. Pomerania KM#41.

Date	Mintage	VG	F	VF	XF	Unc
MDCXVI(1616)	—	2,100	3,900	7,800	12,000	—

KM# 45 THALER

28.6000 g., Silver, 41 mm. **Ruler:** Philipp II **Subject:** Centennial of the Reformation **Obv:** Bust to right in ornamented circle **Obv. Legend:** PHILIPPVS. II. D.G. DVX. POMERANORVM. **Rev:** Small sailboat, man at tiller, being blown to right by wind from clouds at upper left. Roman numeral date at end of legend **Rev. Legend:** SAPIENTIA NON VIOLENTIA. ANNO. MDCXVII. **Mint:** Stettin **Note:** Dav. #7226; H#82. Prev. Pomerania KM#50.2.

Date	Mintage	VG	F	VF	XF	Unc
MDCXVII(1617)	—	1,800	3,200	5,500	9,500	—

KM# 46 THALER

27.2500 g., Silver, 42 mm. **Ruler:** Philipp II **Subject:** Centennial of the Reformation **Obv:** Bust to right in circle **Obv. Legend:** PHILIPPVS. II. DVX. POMERANORVM. **Rev:** Small sailboat, man at tiller, being blown to right by wind from clouds at upper left, Roman numeral date at end of legend **Rev. Legend:** SAPIENTIA NON VIOLENTIA. ANNO. MDCXVII. **Mint:** Stettin **Note:** Dav. #7224; H#83. Prev. Pomerania KM#50.1.

Date	Mintage	VG	F	VF	XF	Unc
MDCXVII(1617)	—	1,800	3,200	5,500	9,500	—

KM# 47 THALER

28.6100 g., Silver, 43 mm. **Ruler:** Philipp II **Subject:** Death of Georg III **Obv:** Wildman standing to left of table holding ornately-shaped shield of Pomeranian arms, hourglass, flower and skull on table, the front of which is a square tablet with birth and death dates in Roman numerals **Obv. Inscription:** NATVS / XXX. IAN / M.DLXXXII / OBIIT / XXVII MART / MDCXVII. **Rev:** 9-line inscription with Roman numeral date **Rev. Inscription:** PHILIPPVS / II DVX STETTIN / ET POMERANIÆ. GEORGI III / FRATR DESIDERAT / MEMORIÆ / CVM LACRYM FF / XXVI MAII / MDCXVII. **Mint:** Stettin **Note:** Dav. #7221; H#94. Prev. Pomerania KM#49.

Date	Mintage	VG	F	VF	XF	Unc
MDCXVII(1617)	—	1,650	3,000	5,500	9,000	—

KM# 48 THALER

28.4400 g., Silver, 37 mm. **Ruler:** Philipp II **Subject:** Centennial of the Reformation **Obv:** Samson wrestling with lion on grass, date at end of legend **Obv. Legend:** OBTVRAVIT OS LEONIS. **Rev:** 7-line inscription with Roman numeral date **Rev. Inscription:** IN MEMO/ RIAM. IVBILÆI / EVANGELICI / ANNO. M.D.C.XVII / CELEBRATI. PHI / LIPPVS. II. DVX / POM. F.F. **Mint:** Stettin **Note:** Dav. #7229; H#103. Prev. Pomerania KM#51.

Date	Mintage	VG	F	VF	XF	Unc
1517//MDCXVII(1617) Rare	—	—	—	—	—	—

KM# 49 THALER

28.4400 g., Silver, 37 mm. **Ruler:** Philipp II **Subject:** Centennial of the Reformation **Obv:** Samson wrestling with lion, date at end of legend **Obv. Legend:** OBTVRAVIT OS LEONIS. **Rev:** 7-line inscription with Roman numeral date **Rev. Inscription:** IN MEMO / RIAM. IVBILÆI / EVANGELICI / ANNO. M.D.XVII / CELERATI. PHI / LIPPVS. II. DVX / POM. F.F. **Mint:** Stettin **Note:** H#102.

Date	Mintage	VG	F	VF	XF	Unc
1617//MDXVII(1 517) Rare	—	—	—	—	—	—

KM# 72 THALER

28.7400 g., Silver, 43-44 mm. **Ruler:** Franz **Subject:** Death of Philipp II **Obv:** Armored bust wearing ruffed collar to right in ornamented circle **Obv. Legend:** PHILIPPVS. II. D.G. DVX. POMERANORVM. **Rev:** 10-line inscription with dates **Rev. Inscription:** NVMMVS / MEMOR. FVNEBRI / PHILIPPI. II / DVCIS. STET. POMER / QVI. NATVS. Z8. IVL. AÕ.1573, DEBAT, 3, FEB, AÕ. 1618 / CONSECRATVS / A. FRANC. I. SEDINET / POMER. DVCE. FRAT / ET. SVCCESS. **Mint:** Stettin **Note:** Dav. #7232; H#108. Prev. Pomerania KM#65.

Date	Mintage	VG	F	VF	XF	Unc
1618 Rare	—	—	—	—	—	—

KM# 73 THALER

28.7000 g., Silver, 42-43 mm. **Ruler:** Franz **Obv:** Armored bust to right in circle **Obv. Legend:** D.G. FRANCISCVS. I. DVX. SEDINI. POMERAN. CASSVB. ET. VAN. **Rev:** Ornate shield of 9-fold arms supported by 2 wildmen, 3 ornate helmets above **Rev. Legend:** PRINC. RVGIÆ. COM GVTZK. TERR. LEOPOL. ET. BVTOV. DNS. **Mint:** Stettin **Note:** Dav. #7233; H#116. Prev. Pomerania KM#66.

Date	Mintage	VG	F	VF	XF	Unc
ND(1618-20)	—	2,500	4,400	7,300	12,000	—

KM# 74 THALER

28.7000 g., Silver, 42-43 mm. **Ruler:** Franz **Obv:** Armored bust to right in circle **Obv. Legend:** D.G. FRANCISCVS. I. DVX. SEDINI. POMERAN. CASSVB. ET. VAN. **Rev:** Ornate shield of 9-fold arms supported by 2 wildmen, 3 ornate helmets above **Rev. Legend:** PRINC. RVGIÆ. COM. GVTZK. TERR. LEOPOL. ET. BVTOV. DN. **Mint:** Stettin **Note:** Dav. #7233A; H#115.

Date	Mintage	VG	F	VF	XF	Unc
ND(1618-20) GT	—	2,500	4,400	7,300	12,000	—

KM# 75 THALER

28.5900 g., Silver, 42-43 mm. **Ruler:** Franz **Subject:** Death of Anna Maria von Brandenburg, Widow of Barnim XII **Obv:** Crowned griffin to left holding sword and ornate shield, 10 small shields of arms on wings, standing on ornate tablet which is blank, no legend **Rev:** 10-line inscription with Roman numeral dates **Rev. Inscription:** MEMORIÆ. FVNEB / ANNÆ MARIÆ / IOH. GEORG. EL. BR. FILIÆ / BARNI. XI. DVC. POM. VIDVÆ / NATÆ. M.D.LXVII / DENA. M.DCXIIX / SEP. 17. XB. STET. Ã. EOD / FRANCISCVS. I. DVX. STET. POM / F. F. **Mint:** Stettin **Note:** Dav. #7236; H#126. Prev. Pomerania KM#67.

Date	Mintage	VG	F	VF	XF	Unc
MDCXIIX(1618)	—	2,000	3,750	6,600	11,000	—

KM# 90 THALER

29.0500 g., Silver, 43 mm. **Ruler:** Bogislaw XIV **Subject:** Death of Franz **Obv:** Armored bust to right in circle **Obv. Legend:** D.G. FRANCISCVS. I. DVX. SEDINI. POMERAN. CASSVB. ET. VAN. **Rev:** 10-line inscription with dates **Rev. Inscription:** NVMMVS / NOVISSIMO. HONORI / FRANCISCI. I / DVCIS. STET. POM. QVI / NATVS. XXIV. MART. AÕ. 1577 / MORTVVS. XXVII. NOVE / ANNO. 1620. DICATVS / A. BOGISLAO. SIV / FRATRE. ET. SVC / CESSORE. **Mint:** Stettin **Note:** Dav. #7239; H#131. Prev. Pomerania KM#82.

Date	Mintage	VG	F	VF	XF	Unc
1620 GT	—	1,700	3,350	6,000	10,000	—

KM# 115 THALER

Silver **Ruler:** Bogislaw XIV **Obv:** Half-length figure to right, wearing highly ornamented armor, divides date **Obv. Legend:** BOGISLAVS. XIV. D.G. DVX. STET. POM. CAS. ET. VAN. **Rev:** Ornate shield of 9-fold arms with ornate helmet above, supported by 2 wildmen wearing helmets **Rev. Legend:** PRINCEPS. RVG. CO. GVTZK. TERR. LEOB. E. B. D(N). **Mint:** Stettin **Note:** Dav. #7254; H#343-4. Prev. Pomerania KM#110. 1628 not in Hildisch and may not exist.

Date	Mintage	Good	VG	F	VF	XF
1628 Reported, not confirmed	—	—	—	—	—	—
1629/8	—	—	825	1,650	3,000	5,000
1630	—	—	825	1,650	3,000	5,000

KM# 110 THALER

28.5500 g., Silver, 42-43 mm. **Ruler:** Bogislaw XIV **Obv:** Bust to right in circle **Obv. Legend:** BOGISLAVS. XIV. D.G. DVX. STET. POM. CASSVB. ET. VAN. **Rev:** Shield of 9-fold arms, ornate helmet above, supported by 2 wildmen wearing helmets, date divided at top **Rev. Legend:** PRINC. RVG. COM GVTZK. TERR. LEOB. E. BVT. DO. **Mint:** Stettin **Note:** Dav. #7248. Prev. Pomerania KM#105.

Date	Mintage	Good	VG	F	VF	XF
16Z8	—	—	525	1,050	1,800	3,000

KM# 107 THALER
28.5500 g., Silver, 43 mm. **Ruler:** Bogislaw XIV **Obv:** Bust to right divides date in circle **Obv. Legend:** BOGISLAVS. XIV. D.G. DVX. STET. POM. CASSVB. ET. VAN. **Rev:** Griffin to right holding sword in ornate shield, ducal cap above divides date **Rev. Legend:** PRINC. RVG. COM. GVTZK. TERR. LEOBVRG. ET. BVTOV. DN. **Mint:** Stettin **Note:** Dav. #7244. Prev. Pomerania KM#102.

Date	Mintage	VG	F	VF	XF	Unc
16Z8//16Z8 (z)	—	1,150	2,350	4,300	7,200	—

KM# 108 THALER
28.5500 g., Silver, 43 mm. **Ruler:** Bogislaw XIV **Obv:** Bust to right divides date in circle **Obv. Legend:** BOGISLAVS. XIV. D.G. DVX. STET. POM. CASSVB. ET. VAN. **Rev:** Griffin to right holding sword in ornate shield, ducal cap above divides date **Rev. Legend:** PRINC. RVG. COM. GVTZK. TERR. LEOBVRG. ET. BVTO. DN. **Mint:** Stettin **Note:** Dav. #7244A. Prev. Pomerania KM#103.

Date	Mintage	VG	F	VF	XF	Unc
16Z8//16Z8 (z)	—	1,150	2,350	4,300	7,200	—

KM# 109 THALER
28.5500 g., Silver, 43 mm. **Ruler:** Bogislaw XIV **Obv:** Bust to right in circle **Obv. Legend:** BOGISLAVS. XIV. D.G. DVX. STET. POM. CASSVB. ET. VAN. **Rev:** Griffin to right holding sword in ornate shield, ducal cap above divides date **Rev. Legend:** PRINC. RVG. COM. GVTZK. TERR. LEOBVRG. ET. BVTOV. DN. **Mint:** Stettin **Note:** Dav. #7246. Prev. Pomerania KM#104. Varieties exist.

Date	Mintage	VG	F	VF	XF	Unc
16Z8 (z)	—	775	1,550	2,700	4,500	—

KM# 111 THALER
28.5500 g., Silver, 41 mm. **Ruler:** Bogislaw XIV **Obv:** Half-length armored figure to right divides date **Obv. Legend:** BOGISLAVS. XIV. D.G. DVX. STET. POM. CASSVB. ET. VAN. **Rev:** Shield of 9-fold arms with ornate helmet above, supported by 2 wildmen wearing helmets **Rev. Legend:** PRINC. RVGIÆ. COM. GVTZK. TERR. LEOPOL. ET. BVTOV. DN. **Mint:** Stettin **Note:** Dav. #7249. Prev. Pomerania KM#106. Varieties exist.

Date	Mintage	VG	F	VF	XF	Unc
16Z8 GT(z)	—	850	1,700	3,000	5,200	—

KM# 112 THALER
28.5500 g., Silver, 46 mm. **Ruler:** Bogislaw XIV **Obv:** Half-length armored figure to right divides date **Obv. Legend:** BOGISLAVS. XIV. D.G. DVX. STET. POM. CASS. ET. VAN. **Rev:** Ornate shield of 9-fold arms with ornate helmet above, supported by 2 wildmen wearing helmets **Rev. Legend:** PRINCEPS. RVG. COM. GVTZK. TERR. LEOB. ET. BVT. DN. **Mint:** Stettin **Note:** Dav. #7251. Prev. Pomerania KM#107.

Date	Mintage	VG	F	VF	XF	Unc
1628 Rare	—	—	—	—	—	—

KM# 113 THALER
28.5500 g., Silver, 42 mm. **Ruler:** Bogislaw XIV **Obv:** Small and thin half-length armored figure to right divides date **Obv. Legend:** BOGISLAVS. XIV. D.G. DVX. STET. POM. CAS. ET. VAN. **Rev:** Ornate shield of 9-fold arms with ornate helmet above, supported by 2 wildmen wearing helmets **Rev. Legend:** PRINCEPS. RVG. COM. GVTZK. TERR. LEOB. E. B. D. **Mint:** Stettin **Note:** Dav. #7252. Prev. Pomerania KM#108.

Date	Mintage	VG	F	VF	XF	Unc
16Z8	—	1,000	2,050	3,600	6,200	—

KM# 114 THALER
28.5500 g., Silver **Ruler:** Bogislaw XIV **Obv:** Half-length armored figure to right divides date **Obv. Legend:** BOGISLAVS. XIV. D.G. DVX. STETIN. POM. CAS. ET. VAN. **Rev:** Ornate shield of 9-fold arms with ornate helmet above, supported by 2 wildmen wearing helmets **Rev. Legend:** PRINC. RVG. COM. GVTZK. TERR. LEOBVRG. ET. BVTOV. DN. **Mint:** Stettin **Note:** Dav. #7253; H#337. Prev. Pomerania KM#109.

Date	Mintage	VG	F	VF	XF	Unc
16Z8	—	1,000	2,050	3,600	6,200	—

KM# 121 THALER
Silver **Ruler:** Bogislaw XIV **Obv:** Half-length armored figure to right divides date **Obv. Legend:** BOGISLAVS. XIV. D.G. DVX. STET. POM. CAS. ET. VAN. **Rev:** Ornate shield of 9-fold arms with ornate helmet above, supported by 2 wildmen wearing helmets **Rev. Legend:** PRIN. RVG. COM. GVTZK. TERR. LEOB. ET. B. DN. **Mint:** Stettin **Note:** Dav. #7255. Prev. Pomerania KM#128.1.

Date	Mintage	VG	F	VF	XF	Unc
1630	—	1,000	2,050	3,600	6,200	—

KM# 122 THALER
Silver **Ruler:** Bogislaw XIV **Obv:** Half-length armored figure to right divides date **Obv. Legend:** BOGISLAVS. XIV. D.G. DVX. STET. POM. CAS. ET. VAN. **Rev:** Ornate shield of 9-fold arms with ornate helmet above, supported by 2 wildmen wearing helmets **Rev. Legend:** PRINCEPS. RVG. COM. GVTZK. TERR. LEOB. ET. B. DN. **Mint:** Stettin **Note:** Dav. #7255A. Prev. Pomerania KM#128.2.

Date	Mintage	VG	F	VF	XF	Unc
1630	—	1,000	2,050	3,600	6,200	—

KM# 123 THALER
Silver **Ruler:** Bogislaw XIV **Obv:** Half-length armored figure to right divides date **Obv. Legend:** BOGISLAVS. XIV. D.G. DVX. STET. POM. CAS. ET. VAN. **Rev:** Ornate shield of 9-fold arms with ornate helmet above, supported by 2 wildmen wearing helmets **Rev. Legend:** PRIN. RVG. COM. GVTZK. TERR. LEOB. E. T. B. D. **Mint:** Stettin **Note:** Dav. #7255B. Prev. Pomerania KM#128.3.

Date	Mintage	VG	F	VF	XF	Unc
1630	—	1,000	2,050	3,600	6,200	—

KM# 124 THALER
Silver **Ruler:** Bogislaw XIV **Obv:** Half-length armored figure to right divides date **Obv. Legend:** BOGISLAVS. XIV. D.G. SVX. STET. POM. CAS. ET. VAN. **Rev:** Ornate shield of 9-fold arms with ornate helmet above, supported by 2 wildmen wearing helmets **Rev. Legend:** PRIN. RVG. COM. GVTZK. TERR. LEOB. E. G. DN. **Mint:** Stettin **Note:** Dav. #7255C. Prev. Pomerania KM#128.4.

Date	Mintage	VG	F	VF	XF	Unc
1630	—	1,050	2,100	3,800	6,200	—

KM# 126 THALER
Silver, 43-45 mm. **Ruler:** Bogislaw XIV **Obv:** Large half-length armored figure to right **Obv. Legend:** BOGISLAVS. XIV. D.G. DVX. STE. PO. CAS. ET. V. **Rev:** Ornate shield of 9-fold arms with ornate helmet above, supported by 2 wildmen wearing helmets, date divide near top by crest of helmet, where present **Rev. Legend:** PRIN. RVG. COM. GVTZK. TERR. LEOB. ET. B. D(N). **Mint:** Köslin **Note:** Dav. #7256; H#346. Prev. Pomerania KM#146.

Date	Mintage	VG	F	VF	XF	Unc
1631 CW	—	1,250	2,150	3,950	7,000	—
ND(1631)	—	900	1,800	3,250	5,600	—

KM# 127 THALER
Silver **Ruler:** Bogislaw XIV **Obv:** Half-length armored figure to right divides date **Obv. Legend:** BOGISLAVS. XIV. D.G. DVX. STET. POM. CAS. ET. VAN. **Rev:** Ornate shield of 9-fold arms with ornate helmet above, supported by 2 wildmen wearing helmets **Rev. Legend:** PRIN. RVG. COM. GVTZK. TERR. LEOB. ET. B. DN. **Mint:** Stettin **Note:** Dav. #7257; H#347. Prev. Pomerania KM#147.

Date	Mintage	VG	F	VF	XF	Unc
1631	—	600	1,200	2,150	3,600	—

KM# 128 THALER
Silver **Ruler:** Bogislaw XIV **Obv:** Large armored bust to right divides date **Obv. Legend:** BOGISLAVS. XIV. D. G. DVX. STE. PO. CAS. ET. VAND. **Rev:** Ornate shield of 9-fold arms with ornate helmet above, supported by 2 wildmen wearing helmets, date divided by crest of helmet near top **Rev. Legend:** PRIN. RVG. COM. GVTZK. TERR. LEOB. ET. BVT. - DN. **Mint:** Stettin **Note:** Dav. #7258. Prev. Pomerania KM#153.1.

Date	Mintage	VG	F	VF	XF	Unc
163Z/163Z Rare	—	—	—	—	—	—

KM# 129 THALER
Silver **Ruler:** Bogislaw XIV **Obv:** Large armored bust to right divides date **Obv. Legend:** BOGISLAVS. XIV. D.G. DVX. STE. PO. CAS. ET. VAND. **Rev:** Ornate shield of 9-fold arms with ornate helmet above, supported by 2 wildmen wearing helmets, date divided by crest of helmet near top **Rev. Legend:** PRIN. RVG. COM. GVTZK. TERR. LEOB. ET. B. DN. **Mint:** Stettin **Note:** Dav. #7258A; H#348. Prev. Pomerania KM#153.2.

Date	Mintage	VG	F	VF	XF	Unc
163Z//163Z Rare	—	—	—	—	—	—

KM# 130 THALER
Silver **Ruler:** Bogislaw XIV **Obv:** Large armored bust to right breaks circle at top **Obv. Legend:** BOGISLAVS. XIV. D.G. DVX. STE. PO. CAS. E. VAN. **Rev:** Ornate shield of 9-fold arms with ornate helmet above, supported by 2 wildmen wearing helmets, date divided by crest of helmet near top **Rev. Legend:** PRIN. RVG. COM. GVTZK. TERR. LEOB. ET. BVT. DN. **Mint:** Stettin **Note:** Dav. #7259; H#349. Prev. Pomerania KM#157.1.

Date	Mintage	VG	F	VF	XF	Unc
1633	—	875	1,750	3,200	5,200	—

KM# 131 THALER
Silver **Ruler:** Bogislaw XIV **Obv:** Large armored bust to right breaks circle at top **Obv. Legend:** BOGISLAVS. XIV. D.G. DVX. STE. PO. CAS. E. V. **Rev:** Ornate shield of 9-fold arms with ornate helmet above, supported by 2 wildmen wearing helmets, date divided by crest of helmet near top **Rev. Legend:** PRIN. RVG. COM GVTZK. TERR. LEOB. ET. B. DN. **Mint:** Stettin **Note:** Dav. #7259A; H#349. Prev. Pomerania KM#157.2.

Date	Mintage	VG	F	VF	XF	Unc
1633	—	875	1,750	3,200	5,200	—

KM# 134 THALER
Silver **Ruler:** Bogislaw XIV **Obv:** Large armored bust to right breaks circle at top **Obv. Legend:** BOGISLAVS. XIV. D.G. DVX. STE. P. CAS. E(T). VAN. **Rev:** Ornate shield of 9-fold arms with ornate helmet above, supported by 2 wildmen wearing helmets, date divided by crest of helmet near top **Rev. Legend:** PRIN. RVG. CO. GVTZK. TERR. LEOB. ET. BVT. DN. **Mint:** Stettin **Note:** Dav. #7260; H#350. Prev. Pomerania KM#170.

Date	Mintage	VG	F	VF	XF	Unc
1634 Rare	—	—	—	—	—	—
1635 Rare	—	—	—	—	—	—

KM# 136 THALER
Silver **Ruler:** Bogislaw XIV **Obv:** Large armored bust to right breaks circle at top **Obv. Legend:** BOGISLAVS. XIV. D.G. DVX. STE. P. CAS. E(T). VAN. **Rev:** Ornate shield of 9-fold arms with ornate helmet above, supported by 2 wildmen wearing helmets, date divided by crest of helmet near top **Rev. Legend:** PRIN. RVG. CO. GVTZK. TERR. LEOB. ET. B. D. **Mint:** Stettin **Note:** H#351.

Date	Mintage	VG	F	VF	XF	Unc
1635 Rare	—	—	—	—	—	—

KM# 137 THALER
27.1700 g., Silver, 43 mm. **Ruler:** Bogislaw XIV **Obv:** Duke on horseback galloping to right, small oval Pomeranian arms below **Obv. Legend:** BOGISLAVS. XIV - DG. - DVX. S. P. **Rev:** Ornate shield of 10-fold arms with ornate helmet above, supported by 2 wildmen wearing helmets, date above left wildman **Rev. Legend:** CASSVB. ET. VAND. PRINC. RVB. EP. CAM. COM. GVTZK. TER. LEOB. ET. BV. DO. **Mint:** Stettin **Note:** H#370.

Date	Mintage	VG	F	VF	XF	Unc
1635 GT Rare	—	—	—	—	—	—

KM# 141 THALER
Silver **Ruler:** Bogislaw XIV **Obv:** Large armored bust to right breaks circle at top. **Obv. Legend:** BOGISLAVS. XIV. D.G. DVX. STE. P. CAS. ET. VA. **Rev:** Ornate shield of 9-fold arms with ornate helmet above, supported by 2 wildmen wearing helmets, date divided by crest of helmet **Rev. Legend:** PRIN. RVG. COM. GVTZK. TERR. LEOB. E. B. D. **Mint:** Stettin **Note:** Dav. #7261; H#352. Prev. Pomerania KM#178.

Date	Mintage	VG	F	VF	XF	Unc
1636 Rare	—	—	—	—	—	—

KM# 148 THALER
28.8000 g., Silver, 44 mm. **Ruler:** Bogislaw XIV **Subject:** Entombment of Bogislaw XIV **Obv:** Duke on horseback galloping to right, small oval Pomeranian arms below **Obv. Legend:** BOGISLAVS. XIV - DG. - DVX. S. P. **Rev:** Skull within wreath, triple circular legends around **Rev. Legend:** IN MEMORIAM ULTIMI EX GRYPHICA STIRPE DUCIS POMER/ BOGISLAI. XIV. NATI. XXXI. MART. 1580. DENATI. X/ MART. 1637. HVMATI. 25. MAI. 1654. **Mint:** Stettin **Note:** H#378.

Date	Mintage	VG	F	VF	XF	Unc
1654 GT Rare	120	—	—	—	—	—

KM# 149 THALER
28.8000 g., Silver **Ruler:** Bogislaw XIV **Subject:** Entombment of Bogislaw XIV **Obv:** Armored bust to right in wreath **Obv. Legend:** BOGISLAVS. XIV. D.G. DVX. ST. POM. C. &. VAND. P. RV. EP. C. CO. G. T. L. &. B. D. **Rev:** 15-line inscription with dates **Rev. Inscription:** NOVISSIMIS / HONORIBVS / BOGISLAI. DVC. STET / POMER. EIVS. NOMINIS / 14. ET. VLTIMI / NATI. 31. MART. 1637 / HVMATI. 25. MAI. 1654 / CHRISTINA. D. G. SVECOR / GOTHOR. VANDAL. REGI / ET/FRIDERICVS. WILH. / D. G. MARC. &. EL. B/ DVCE. POM / F. F. **Mint:** Stettin **Note:** Dav. #LS372B; H#379. Prev. Pomerania KM#211.

Date	Mintage	VG	F	VF	XF	Unc
1654	Inc. above	—	—	5,700	9,000	—

KM# 150 THALER
28.8000 g., Silver, 45 mm. **Ruler:** Bogislaw XIV **Subject:** Entombment of Bogislaw XIV **Obv:** Large crowned griffin to left standing on tree trunk lying on ground, 10 small shields of arms on wings, small tree to right, skull to lower left, several young branches growing up from it with arms of Sweden and Brandenburg attached, sun shining dow **Rev:** 11-line inscription with date in wreath, triple marginal legend in Gothic letters **Rev. Inscription:** NVMMVS / EXEQVIALIS / OPTIMI.PRINCI / PIS.BOGISLAI / DVCIS.STET.POM / EIVS.NOMINIS.14 / ET.VLTIMI / NATI.31.MAR.1580 / DEN.X.MAR.1637 / SEP.25.MAI / 1654. **Mint:** Stettin **Note:** H#380.

Date	Mintage	VG	F	VF	XF	Unc
1654 GT Rare	Inc. above	—	—	—	—	—

KM# 151 THALER
28.8000 g., Silver, 33 mm. **Ruler:** Bogislaw XIV **Subject:** Entombment of Bogislaw XIV **Obv:** Tree stump with two young limbs in leaf, view of Stettin behind, sun shining down from upper left, DEO DIRIGENTE to right of sun **Rev:** 11-line inscription with dates in wreath **Rev. Inscription:** NVMMVS / EXEQVIALIS / OPTIMI PRINCI / PIS BOGISLAI / DVCIS. STET. POME / EIVS. NOMINIS. XIV / ET. VLTIMI / NATI. 31. MART. 1580 / DEN. X. MAR. 1637 / SEP. 25. MAY / 1654. **Mint:** Stettin **Note:** H#381. Struck from 1/2 Thaler dies, KM#146.

Date	Mintage	Good	VG	F	VF	XF
1654 Rare	Inc. above	—	—	—	—	—

KM# 14 1-1/2 THALER
42.8200 g., Silver, 42 mm. **Ruler:** Philipp II **Obv:** Bust to right in circle, legend divided by 5 small shields of arms in margin **Obv. Legend:** V. G. G. - PHI. - LIPS - H. Z. S. - POM. **Rev:** Crowned griffin left holding sword and book, legend divided by 5 small shields of arms in margin, date at end of legend **Rev. Legend:** CHRI - STO. ET - REIP - ANNO - (date) **Mint:** Stettin **Note:** Dav. #7204; H#49. Prev. Pomerania KM#24.

Date	Mintage	VG	F	VF	XF	Unc
1613 Rare	—	—	—	—	—	—

KM# 15 1-1/2 THALER
Silver **Ruler:** Bogislaw XIV **Obv:** Bust to right in circle, legend divided by 5 small shields of arms in margin **Obv. Legend:** V. G. G. - PHI. - LIPS - H. Z. S. - POM. **Rev:** Crowned griffin left holding sword and book, legend divided by 5 small shields of arms in margin, date at end of legend **Rev. Legend:** CHRI - STO. ET - REIP - ANNO - (date) **Mint:** Stettin **Note:** Klippe. Dav. #7204A; H#KL49.

Date	Mintage	VG	F	VF	XF	Unc
1613 Rare	—	—	—	—	—	—

KM# 7 2 THALER
57.2600 g., Silver, 41 mm. **Ruler:** Philipp II **Obv:** Bust to right in ornamented circle **Obv. Legend:** PHILIPPVS. II. D.G. DVX. POMERANORVM. **Rev:** Crowned griffin left holding sword in circle, 10 oval shields of arms around, legend in small letters between tops of shields **Rev. Legend:** CR - IS - TO - ET - RE - IP - VB - LI - C - Æ. **Mint:** Stettin **Note:** Dav. #7214; H#41. Prev. Pomerania KM#44.

Date	Mintage	VG	F	VF	XF	Unc
ND(1606-18) Rare	—	—	—	—	—	—

KM# 8 2 THALER
57.2600 g., Silver, 41 mm. **Ruler:** Philipp II **Obv:** Bust to right in circle **Obv. Legend:** PHILIPPVS. II. DVX. POMERANORVM. **Rev:** Crowned griffin left holding sword in circle, 10 oval shields of arms around, legend in small letters between tops of shields **Rev. Legend:** CR - IS - TO - ET - RE - IP - VB - LI - C - Æ. **Mint:** Stettin **Note:** Dav. #7210; H#42. Prev. Pomerania KM#42.

Date	Mintage	VG	F	VF	XF	Unc
ND(1606-18) Rare	—	—	—	—	—	—

KM# 9 2 THALER
57.2500 g., Silver, 40-41 mm. **Ruler:** Philipp II **Obv:** Bust to right in ornamented circle **Obv. Legend:** PHILIPPVS. II. D.G. DVX. POMERANORVM. **Rev:** Crowned griffin left holding sword and book, 10 small shields of arms on wings, 2-line inscription in ornate tablet below **Rev. Inscription:** CHRISTO. ET. REIP / VBLICÆ. **Mint:** Stettin **Note:** Dav. #7212; H#43. Prev. Pomerania KM#43.

Date	Mintage	VG	F	VF	XF	Unc
ND(1606-18) Rare	—	—	—	—	—	—

KM# 16 2 THALER
Silver **Ruler:** Philipp II **Obv:** Bust to right in circle, legend divided by 5 small shields of arms in margin **Obv. Legend:** V. G. G. - PHI. - LIPS - H. Z. S. - POM. **Rev:** Crowned griffin left holding sword and book, legend divided by 5 small shields of arms in margin, date at end of legend **Rev. Legend:** CHRI - STO. ET - REIP - ANNO - (date) **Mint:** Stettin **Note:** Dav. #7203; H#44, 46. Prev. Pomerania KM#25.

Date	Mintage	VG	F	VF	XF	Unc
1613 Rare	—	—	—	—	—	—
1614 Rare	—	—	—	—	—	—

KM# 20 2 THALER
Silver **Ruler:** Philipp II **Obv:** Bust to right in circle **Obv. Legend:** PHILIPPVS. II. DVX. POMERANORVM. **Rev:** Shield of 9-fold arms supported by 2 helmeted wildmen, ornate helmet above, date at end of legend **Rev. Legend:** CHRISTO. ET. REIPVBLICÆ. **Mint:** Stettin **Note:** Dav. #7207; H#45, 48. Prev. Pomerania KM#28.

Date	Mintage	VG	F	VF	XF	Unc
1614	—	7,400	11,500	17,000	—	—
1616	—	7,400	11,500	17,000	—	—

KM# 26 2 THALER
Silver, 43 mm. **Ruler:** Philipp II **Obv:** Bust to right in circle, legend divided by 5 small shields of arms **Obv. Legend:** V. G. G. - PHI. - LIPS - H. Z. S. - POM. **Rev:** 11-line inscription with date **Rev. Inscription:** (date) / A. DEO / OMNIA. OR / NAMENTA / REIPVBLICAE. ET / FVNDAMEN / TVM. EIVS / EST. NON / GAVDE / REVA/ NIS **Mint:** Stettin **Note:** Dav. #A7209; H#47.

Date	Mintage	VG	F	VF	XF	Unc
1615 Rare	—	—	—	—	—	—

KM# 34 2 THALER
57.3300 g., Silver, 43 mm. **Ruler:** Philipp II **Subject:** Death of Anna vn Schleswig-Holstein, Widow of Bogislaw XIII **Obv:** Bust to right in circle **Obv. Legend:** PHILIPPVS. II. DVX. POMERANORVM. **Rev:** 9-line inscription with Roman numeral dates **Rev. Inscription:** ANNA FILIA / IOHAN. DVCIS / HOLS. VIDVA. BOGIS / LAI. SEN. DVCIS POM. / MATER CARISS. NATA / MDLXXVII. VII. OCT / DENATA. MDCXVI / XXX IAN. SEPVL / VIII. APRI. **Mint:** Stettin **Note:** Dav. #7217; H#88. Prev. Pomerania KM#45.

Date	Mintage	VG	F	VF	XF	Unc
MDCXVI(1616)	—	5,000	8,300	11,500	17,000	—

KM# 52 2 THALER
57.4200 g., Silver, 43 mm. **Ruler:** Philipp II **Subject:** Death of Georg III **Obv:** Wildman standing to left of table holding ornately-shaped shield of Pomeranian arms, hourglass, flower and skull on table, the front of which is a square tablet with birth and death dates in Roman numerals **Obv. Inscription:** NATVS / XXX. IAN / M.DLXXXII / OBIIT / XXVII MART / MDCXVII. **Rev:** 9-line inscription with Roman numeral date **Rev. Inscription:** PHILIPPVS / II DVX STETTIN / ET POMERANIÆ. GEORGI III / FRATR DESIDERAT / MEMORIÆ / CVM LACRYM FF / XXVI MAII / MDCXVII. **Mint:** Stettin **Note:** Dav. #7220; H#93. Prev. Pomerania KM#52.

Date	Mintage	VG	F	VF	XF	Unc
MDCXVII(1617) 52 Rare	—	—	—	—	—	—

KM# 53 2 THALER
57.7300 g., Silver, 58-59 mm. **Ruler:** Philipp II **Subject:** Centennial of the Reformation **Obv:** Luther kneeling in church pew and holding book **Obv. Legend:** PERIERAT. ET. INVENTVS EST. 1517. **Rev:** Priest placing book on chest inscribed ANNO IVBEL/ 1617. **Rev. Legend:** INVENI QVEM DILIGIT ANIMA MEA **Mint:** Stettin **Note:** Dav. #7228; H#101. Prev. Pomerania KM#55.

Date	Mintage	VG	F	VF	XF	Unc
1617 53 Rare	—	—	—	—	—	—

KM# 50 2 THALER
58.8000 g., Silver, 41 mm. **Ruler:** Philipp II **Subject:** Centennial of the Reformation **Obv:** Bust to right in ornamented circle **Obv. Legend:** PHILIPPVS. II. D.G. DVX. POMERANORVM. **Rev:** Small sailboat, man at tiller, being blown to right by wind from clouds at upper left. Roman numeral date at end of legend **Rev. Legend:** SAPIENTIA NON VIOLENTIA. ANNO. MDCXVII. **Mint:** Stettin **Note:** Dav. #7225; H#80. Prev. Pomerania KM#54.

Date	Mintage	VG	F	VF	XF	Unc
MDCXVII(1617)	—	4,150	7,400	11,500	17,000	—

KM# 51 2 THALER
58.8000 g., Silver, 42 mm. **Ruler:** Philipp II **Subject:** Centennial of the Reformation **Obv:** Bust to right in circle **Obv. Legend:** PHILIPPVS. II. DVX. POMERANORVM. **Rev:** Small sailboat, man at tiller, being blown to right by wind from clouds at upper left, Roman numeral date at end of legend **Rev. Legend:** SAPIENTIA NON VIOLENTIA. ANNO. MDCXVII. **Mint:** Stettin **Note:** Dav. #7223; H#81. Prev. Pomerania KM#53.

Date	Mintage	VG	F	VF	XF	Unc
MDCXVII(1617)	—	4,150	7,400	11,500	17,000	—

KM# 76 2 THALER
58.2000 g., Silver, 43-44 mm. **Ruler:** Franz **Subject:** Death of Philipp II **Obv:** Armored bust wearing ruffed collar to right in ornamented circle **Obv. Legend:** PHILIPPVS. II. D.G. DVX. POMERANORVM. **Rev:** 10-line inscription with dates **Rev. Inscription:** NVMMVS / MEMOR. FVNEBRI / PHILIPPI. II / DVCIS. STET. POMER / QVI. NATVS. Z8. IVL. AÕ.1573, DEBAT, 3, FEB, AÕ. 1618 / CONSECRATVS / A. FRANC. I. SEDINET / POMER. DVCE. FRAT / ET. SVCCESS. **Mint:** Stettin **Note:** Dav. #7231; H#107. Prev. Pomerania KM#68.

Date	Mintage	VG	F	VF	XF	Unc
1618	—	4,150	7,400	11,500	17,000	—

KM# 77 2 THALER
Silver, 42-43 mm. **Ruler:** Franz **Subject:** Death of Anna Maria von Brandenburg, Widow of Barnim XII **Obv:** Crowned griffin to left holding sword and ornate shield, 10 small shields of arms on wings, standing on ornate tablet which is blank, no legend **Rev:** 10-line inscription with Roman numeral dates **Rev. Inscription:** MEMORIÆ. FVNEB / ANNÆ MARIÆ / IOH. GEORG. EL. BR. FILIÆ / BARNI. XI. DVC. POM. VIDVÆ / NATÆ. M.D.LXVII / DENA. M.DCXIIX/ SEP. 17. XB. STET. Ã. EOD / FRANCISCVS. I. DVX. STET. POM / F. F. **Mint:** Stettin **Note:** Dav. #7235. Prev. Pomerania KM#69. Unlisted in Hildisch, existence questionable.

Date	Mintage	VG	F	VF	XF	Unc
MDCXIIX(1618) Rare	—	—	—	—	—	—

KM# 91 2 THALER
Silver, 43 mm. **Ruler:** Bogislaw XIV **Subject:** Death of Franz **Obv:** Armored bust to right in circle **Obv. Legend:** D.G. FRANCISCVS. I. DVX. SEDINI. POMERAN. CASSVB. ET. VAN. **Rev:** 10-line inscription with dates **Rev. Inscription:** NVMMVS / NOVISSIMO. HONORI / FRANCISCI. I / DVCIS. STET. POM. QVI / NATVS. XXIV. MART. AÕ. 1577 / MORTVVS. XXVII. NOVE / ANNO. 1620. DICATVS / A. BOGISLAO. SIV / FRATRE. ET. SVC / CESSORE. **Mint:** Stettin **Note:** Dav. #A7239; H#130.

Date	Mintage	VG	F	VF	XF	Unc
1620 GT Rare	—	—	—	—	—	—

KM# 116 2 THALER
55.4800 g., Silver, 43 mm. **Ruler:** Bogislaw XIV **Obv:** Bust to right in circle **Obv. Legend:** BOGISLAVS. XIV. D.G. DVX. STET. POM. CASSVB. ET. VAN. **Rev:** Griffin to right holding sword in ornate shield, ducal cap above divides date **Rev. Legend:** PRINC. RVG. COM. GVTZK. TERR. LEOBVRG. ET. BVTOV. DN. **Mint:** Stettin **Note:** Dav. #7245; H#334. Prev. Pomerania KM#117.

Date	Mintage	VG	F	VF	XF	Unc
16Z8 (z) Rare	—	—	—	—	—	—

KM# 117 2 THALER
55.4800 g., Silver, 42-43 mm. **Ruler:** Bogislaw XIV **Obv:** Bust to right in circle **Obv. Legend:** BOGISLAVS. XIV. D.G. DVX. STET. POM. CASSVB. ET. VAN. **Rev:** Shield of 9-fold arms, ornate helmet above, supported by 2 wildmen wearing helmets, date divided at top **Rev. Legend:** PRINC. RVG. COM GVTZK. TERR. LEOB. E. BVT. DO. **Mint:** Stettin **Note:** Dav. #7247. Prev. Pomerania KM#118.

Date	Mintage	VG	F	VF	XF	Unc
16Z8 Rare	—	—	—	—	—	—

KM# 118 2 THALER
55.4800 g., Silver, 46 mm. **Ruler:** Bogislaw XIV **Obv:** Half-length armored figure to right divides date **Obv. Legend:** BOGISLAVS. XIV. D.G. DVX. STET. POM. CASS. ET. VAN. **Rev:** Ornate shield of 9-fold arms with ornate helmet above, supported by 2 wildmen wearing helmets **Rev. Legend:** PRINCEPS. RVG. COM. GVTZK. TERR. LEOB. ET. BVT. DN. **Mint:** Stettin **Note:** Dav. #7250. Prev. Pomerania KM#119.

Date	Mintage	VG	F	VF	XF	Unc
1628 Rare	—	—	—	—	—	—

KM# 138 2 THALER
57.0000 g., Silver, 43 mm. **Ruler:** Bogislaw XIV **Obv:** Duke on horseback galloping to right, small oval Pomeranian arms below **Obv. Legend:** BOGISLAVS. XIV - DG. - DVX. S. P. **Rev:** Ornate shield of 10-fold arms with ornate helmet above, supported by 2 wildmen wearing helmets, date above left wildman **Rev. Legend:** CASSVB. ET. VAND. PRINC. RVB. EP. CAM. COM. GVTZK. TER. LEOB. ET. BV. DO. **Mint:** Stettin **Note:** H#369.

Date	Mintage	VG	F	VF	XF	Unc
1635 GT	—	—	—	—	—	—

KM# 152 2 THALER
51.0100 g., Silver **Ruler:** Bogislaw XIV **Subject:** Entombment of Bogislaw XIV **Obv:** Armored bust to right in wreath **Obv. Legend:** BOGISLAVS. XIV. D.G. DVX. ST. POM. C. &. VAND. P. RV. EP. C. CO. G. T. L. &. B. D. **Rev:** 15-line inscription with dates **Rev. Inscription:** NOVISSIMIS / HONORIBVS / BOGISLAI. DVC. STET / POMER. EIVS. NOMINIS / 14. ET. VLTIMI / NATI. 31. MART. 1637 / HVMATI. 25. MAI. 1654 / CHRISTINA. D. G. SVECOR / GOTHOR. VANDAL. REGI / ET / FRIDERICVS. WILH. / D. G. MARC. &. EL. B / DVCE. POM / F. F. **Mint:** Stettin **Note:** Dav. #LS372A; H#377. Prev. Pomerania KM#212.

Date	Mintage	VG	F	VF	XF	Unc
1654	50	—	—	8,000	14,000	—

KM# 17 3 THALER
84.5100 g., Silver, 44 mm. **Ruler:** Philipp II **Obv:** Bust to right in circle, legend divided by 5 small shields of arms in margin **Obv. Legend:** V. G. G. - PHI. - LIPS - H. Z. S. - POM. **Rev:** Crowned griffin left holding sword and book, legend divided by 5 small shields of arms in margin, date at end of legend **Rev. Legend:** CHRI - STO. ET - REIP - ANNO - (date) **Mint:** Stettin **Note:** Dav. #A7203; H#38, 40.

Date	Mintage	VG	F	VF	XF	Unc
1613 Rare	—	—	—	—	—	—
1614 Rare	—	—	—	—	—	—

KM# 21 3 THALER
Silver **Ruler:** Philipp II **Obv:** Bust to right in circle **Obv. Legend:** PHILIPPVS. II. DVX. POMERANORVM. **Rev:** Shield of 9-fold arms supported by 2 helmeted wildmen, ornate helmet above, date at end of legend **Rev. Legend:** CHRISTO. ET. REIPVBLICÆ. **Mint:** Stettin **Note:** Dav. #7206; ;H#39. Prev. Pomerania KM#29.

Date	Mintage	VG	F	VF	XF	Unc
1614 Rare	—	—	—	—	—	—

KM# 54 3 THALER
Silver, 42 mm. **Ruler:** Philipp II **Subject:** Centennial of the Reformation **Obv:** Bust to right in circle **Obv. Legend:** PHILIPPVS. II. DVX. POMERANORVM. **Rev:** Small sailboat, man at tiller, being blown to right by wind from clouds at upper left, Roman numeral date at end of legend **Rev. Legend:** SAPIENTIA NON VIOLENTIA. ANNO. MDCXVII. **Mint:** Stettin **Note:** Dav. #7222; H#79. Prev. Pomerania KM#57.

Date	Mintage	VG	F	VF	XF	Unc
MDCXVII(1617) Rare	—	—	—	—	—	—

KM# 55 3 THALER
86.1600 g., Silver, 44 mm. **Ruler:** Philipp II **Subject:** Death of Georg III **Obv:** Wildman standing to left of table holding ornately-shaped shield of Pomeranian arms, hourglass, flower and skull on table, the front of which is a square tablet with birth and death dates in Roman numerals **Obv. Inscription:** NATVS / XXX. IAN / M.DLXXXII / OBIIT / XXVII MART / MDCXVII. **Rev:** 9-line inscription with Roman numeral date **Rev. Inscription:** PHILIPPVS / II DVX STETTIN / ET POMERANIÆ. GEORGI III / FRATR DESIDERAT / MEMORIÆ / CVM LACRYM FF / XXVI MAII / MDCXVII. **Mint:** Stettin **Note:** Dav. #7219; H#92. Prev. Pomerania KM#56.

Date	Mintage	VG	F	VF	XF	Unc
MDCXVII(1617) Rare	—	—	—	—	—	—

KM# 56 3 THALER
Silver, 49 mm. **Ruler:** Philipp II **Subject:** Centennial of the Reformation **Obv:** Luther kneeling in church pew and hlding book **Obv. Legend:** PERIERAT. ET. INVENTVS EST. 1517. **Rev:** Priest placing book on chest inscribed ANNO IVBEL / 1617. **Rev. Legend:** INVENI QVEM DILIGET ANIMA MEA. **Mint:** Stettin **Note:** Dav. #7227; H#100. Prev. Pomerania KM#58.

Date	Mintage	VG	F	VF	XF	Unc
1617 Rare	—	—	—	—	—	—

KM# 78 3 THALER
86.5500 g., Silver, 43 mm. **Ruler:** Franz **Subject:** Death of Anna Maria von Brandenburg, Widow of Barnim XII **Obv:** Crowned griffin to left holding sword and ornate shield, 10 small shields of arms on wings, standing on ornate tablet which is blank, no legend **Rev:** 10-line inscription with Roman numeral dates **Rev. Inscription:** MEMORIÆ. FVNEB / ANNÆ MARIÆ / IOH. GEORG. EL. BR. FILIÆ / BARNI. XI. DVC. POM. VIDVÆ / NATÆ. M.D.LXVII / DENA. M.DCXIIX / SEP. 17. XB. STET. Ã. EOD / FRANCISCVS. I. DVX. STET. POM / F. F. **Mint:** Stettin **Note:** Dav. #7234; H#125. Prev. Pomerania KM#70.

Date	Mintage	VG	F	VF	XF	Unc
MDCXIIX(1618) Rare	—	—	—	—	—	—

KM# 92 3 THALER
88.4700 g., Silver, 43 mm. **Ruler:** Bogislaw XIV **Subject:** Death of Franz **Obv:** Armored bust to right in circle **Obv. Legend:** D.G. FRANCISCVS. I. DVX. SEDINI. POMERAN. CASSVB. ET. VAN. **Rev:** 10-line inscription with dates **Rev. Inscription:** NVMMVS / NOVISSIMO. HONORI / FRANCISCI. I / DVCIS. STET. POM. QVI / NATVS. XXIV. MART. AÕ. 1577 / MORTVVS. XXVII. NOVE / ANNO. 1620. DICATVS / A. BOGISLAO. SIV / FRATRE. ET. SVC / CESSORE. **Mint:** Stettin **Note:** Dav. #7238; H#129. Prev. Pomerania KM#87.

Date	Mintage	VG	F	VF	XF	Unc
1620 GT Rare	—	—	—	—	—	—

KM# 153 3 THALER
86.9300 g., Silver, 50 mm. **Ruler:** Bogislaw XIV **Subject:** Entombment of Bogislaw XIV **Obv:** Armored bust to right in wreath **Obv. Legend:** BOGISLAVS. XIV. D.G. DVX. ST. POM. C. &. VAND. P. RVG. EP. CAM. COM. GVTZ. TER. LEOB. &. BVTO. DNS. **Rev:** 17-line inscription with Roman numeral dates **Rev. Inscription:** INFERIÆ / OPTIMI. PRINCIP / BOGISLAI / DVCIS. STETINI. POMERA / EIVS. NOMINIS. XIV. ET. VLTIMI / NATI. XXXI. MART. MDLXXX / DENATI. X. MART. MDCXXXVII / CONDITI. XXV. MAI. MDCLIV / ADORNATÆ / A / CHRISTINA. D.G. SVECORVM. GO / THORVM. VANDALORQ. REGI(N)/ ET / FRIDERICO. WIL **Mint:** Stettin **Note:** Dav. #LS371; H#376. Prev. Pomerania KM#213.

Date	Mintage	VG	F	VF	XF	Unc
MDCLIV(1654) GT	36	—	—	17,000	27,500	—

KM# 22 4 THALER
Silver **Ruler:** Philipp II **Obv:** Bust to right in circle **Obv. Legend:** PHILIPPVS. II. DVX. POMERANORVM. **Rev:** Shield of 9-fold arms supported by 2 helmeted wildmen, ornate helmet above, date at end of legend **Rev. Legend:** CHRISTO. ET. REIPVBLICÆ. **Mint:** Stettin **Note:** Dav. #A7206; H#37.

Date	Mintage	VG	F	VF	XF	Unc
1614 Rare	—	—	—	—	—	—

KM# 35 4 THALER
Silver **Ruler:** Philipp II **Subject:** Death of Anna von Schleswig-Holstein, Widow of Bogislaw XIII **Obv:** Bust to right in circle **Obv. Legend:** PHILIPPVS. II. DVX. POMERANORVM. **Rev:** 9-line inscription with Roman numeral dates **Rev. Inscription:** ANNA FILIA / IOHAN. DVCIS / HOLS. VIDVA. BOGIS / LAI. SEN. DVCIS POM. / MATER CARISS. NATA / MDLXXVII. VII. OCT / DENATA. MDCXVI / XXX IAN. SEPVL / VIII. APRI. **Mint:** Stettin **Note:** Dav. #7216; H#87. Prev. Pomerania KM#46.

Date	Mintage	VG	F	VF	XF	Unc
MDCXVI(1616)	—	—	—	21,500	30,000	—

KM# 79 4 THALER
114.6500 g., Silver, 43-44 mm. **Ruler:** Franz **Subject:** Death of Philipp II **Obv:** Armored bust wearing ruffed collar to right in ornamented circle **Obv. Legend:** PHILIPPVS. II. D.G. DVX. POMERANORVM. **Rev:** 10-line inscription with dates **Rev. Inscription:** NVMMVS / MEMOR. FVNEBRI / PHILIPPI. II / DVCIS. STET. POMER / QVI. NATVS. Z8. IVL. AÕ.1573, DEBAT, 3, FEB, AÕ. 1618 / CONSECRATVS / A. FRANC. I. SEDINET / POMER. DVCE. FRAT / ET. SVCCESS. **Mint:** Stettin **Note:** Dav. #7230; H#106. Prev. Pomerania KM#71.

Date	Mintage	VG	F	VF	XF	Unc
1618 Rare	—	—	—	—	—	—

KM# 93 4 THALER
115.2800 g., Silver, 43 mm. **Ruler:** Bogislaw XIV **Subject:** Death of Franz **Obv:** Armored bust to right in circle **Obv. Legend:** D.G. FRANCISCVS. I. DVX. SEDINI. POMERAN. CASSVB. ET. VAN. **Rev:** 10-line inscription with dates **Rev. Inscription:** NVMMVS / NOVISSIMO. HONORI / FRANCISCI. I / DVCIS. STET. POM. QVI / NATVS. XXIV. MART. AÕ. 1577 / MORTVVS. XXVII. NOVE / ANNO. 1620. DICATVS / A. BOGISLAO. SIV / FRATRE. ET. SVC / CESSORE. **Mint:** Stettin **Note:** Dav. #7237; H#128. Prev. Pomerania KM#88.

Date	Mintage	VG	F	VF	XF	Unc
1620 GT Rare	—	—	—	—	—	—

KM# 154 4 THALER
114.8800 g., Silver, 68 mm. **Ruler:** Bogislaw XIV **Subject:** Entombment of Bogislaw XIV **Obv:** Bust to right in wreath **Obv. Legend:** BOGISLAVS. XIV. D.G. DVX. STET. POM. CAS. &. VAND. PR. RV(G). EP. CAM. CO(M). GVTZ. TER. LE(OB). &. BV(TO). DNS. **Rev:** 17-line inscription with Roman numeral dates **Rev. Inscription:** INFERIÆ / OPTIMI. PRINCIP(IS) / BOGISLAI / DVCIS. STETINI. POMERA(N) / EIVS. NOMINIS. XIV.(&) (ET). VLTI(M)(I) / NATI. XXXI. MART. MDLXXX / DENATI. X. MART. MDCXXXVII / CONDITI. XXV. MAI. MDCLIV / ADORNATÆ / A /CHRISTINA. D.G. SVECORVM. GO / THORVM. VANDALORQ. REGI(N)(A) / **Mint:** Stettin **Note:** Dav. #LS370; H#374. Prev. Pomerania KM#214. Varieties exist.

Date	Mintage	VG	F	VF	XF	Unc
MDCLIV(1654) GT Rare	36	—	—	—	—	—

KM# 155 4 THALER
115.0000 g., Silver, 50 mm. **Ruler:** Bogislaw XIV **Subject:** Entombment of Bogislaw XIV **Obv:** Bust to right in wreath **Obv. Legend:** BOGISLAVS. XIV. D.G. DVX. ST. POM. C. &. VAND. P. RV. EP. C. CO. G. T. L. &. B. **Rev:** 15-line inscription with dates **Rev. Inscription:** NOVISSIMIS / HONORIBVS / BOGISLAI. DVC. STET / POMER. EIVS. NOMINIS / 14. ET. VLTIMI / NATI. 31. MART. 1580 / DENATI. 10. MART. 1637 / HVMATI. 25. MAI. 1654 / CHRISTINA. D.G. SVECORV / GOTHOR. VANDAL. REGIN / ET / FRIDERICVS. WILHEL / D.G. MARC. &. EL. BRA / DVCES. POMER / F **Mint:** Stettin **Note:** H#375.

Date	Mintage	VG	F	VF	XF	Unc
1654 Rare	Inc. above	—	—	—	—	—

TRADE COINAGE

KM# A13 GOLDGULDEN
3.1800 g., Gold, 22 mm. **Ruler:** Philipp II **Obv:** Bust to right in circle **Obv. Legend:** PHILIPPVS. II. DVX. STET. POM. **Rev:** Shield of 9-fold arms in circle, date at end of legend **Rev. Legend:** CHRISTO. ET. REIPVBLI. (date). **Mint:** Stettin **Note:** FR#2080; H#30, 31. Prev. Pomerania KM#16.

Date	Mintage	VG	F	VF	XF	Unc
161Z	—	775	1,900	4,600	7,700	—
1613	—	775	1,900	4,600	7,700	—

KM# 23 GOLDGULDEN
Gold Weight varies: 3.16-3.21g., 21.5 mm. **Ruler:** Philipp II **Obv:** Bust to right in circle **Obv. Legend:** PHILIPPVS. II. DVX. STET. POM. **Rev:** Sword vertical superimposed on quill pointed to left, all in circle **Rev. Legend:** ALLES. ZU. SEINER. ZEIT. (date). **Mint:** Stettin **Note:** FR#2083; H#73, 74. Prev. Pomerania KM#30.

Date	Mintage	VG	F	VF	XF	Unc
1614	—	2,600	4,300	6,100	7,400	—
1615	—	2,600	4,300	6,100	7,400	—

KM# 28 GOLDGULDEN
3.2000 g., Gold, 22 mm. **Ruler:** Philipp II **Obv:** Bust to right in circle **Obv. Legend:** PHILIPPVS. II. DVX. STETIN. POMER. **Rev:** Stag standing to left towards cascading falls, date at end of legend **Rev. Legend:** IN. TE. SITIT. ANIMA. MEA. (date). **Mint:** Stettin **Note:** FR#2087; H#32, 33. Prev. Pomerania KM#36.

Date	Mintage	VG	F	VF	XF	Unc
1615	—	725	1,800	4,300	7,200	—
1616	—	725	1,800	4,300	7,200	—

KM# 27 GOLDGULDEN
3.2000 g., Gold, 21.5 mm. **Ruler:** Philipp II **Obv:** Bust to right in circle **Obv. Legend:** PHILIPPVS. II. DVX. STET. POM. **Rev:** Sword vertical superimposed on quill pointed to right, all in circle **Rev. Legend:** ALLES. ZU. SEINER. ZEIT. (date). **Mint:** Stettin **Note:** H#75.

Date	Mintage	VG	F	VF	XF	Unc
1615	—	1,100	2,100	3,950	6,500	—

KM# 36 GOLDGULDEN
3.2000 g., Gold, 22 mm. **Ruler:** Philipp II **Obv:** Bust to right in circle **Obv. Legend:** PHILIPPVS. II. DVX. STETI(N). POM(ER). **Rev:** 4-line inscription with date in palm and laurel wreath **Rev. Inscription:** SOLI / DEO GLO / RIA / (date) **Mint:** Stettin **Note:** FR#2091; H#34-6. Prev. Pomerania KM#47. Varieties exist.

Date	Mintage	VG	F	VF	XF	Unc
1616	—	600	1,500	3,600	6,000	—
1617	—	600	1,500	3,600	6,000	—
1618	—	600	1,500	3,600	6,000	—

KM# 57 GOLDGULDEN
3.2000 g., Gold, 22 mm. **Ruler:** Philipp II **Obv:** Bust to right in circle **Obv. Legend:** PHILIPPVS. II. DVX. STETIN. POMER. **Rev:** Snail gliding over twig to left in cirle, date at end of legend **Rev. Legend:** LENTE. SED. ATTENTE. (date). **Mint:** Stettin **Note:** FR#2089; H#76-8. Prev. Pomerania KM#61. Varieties exist.

Date	Mintage	VG	F	VF	XF	Unc
1617	—	850	2,100	5,000	8,400	—
1618	—	850	2,100	5,000	8,400	—

KM# 58 GOLDGULDEN
3.1700 g., Gold, 21 mm. **Ruler:** Philipp II **Subject:** Enlargement of Stettin Palace **Obv:** Bust to right in circle **Obv. Legend:** PHILIPPVS. II. DVX. STETIN. POMER. **Rev:** 5-line inscription with date **Rev. Inscription:** MEMOR / AMPLIFIC / ARCIS / STETINEN / (date). **Mint:** Stettin **Note:** FR#2094; H#86.

Date	Mintage	VG	F	VF	XF	Unc
1617	—	1,200	2,500	5,000	8,600	—

KM# 59 GOLDGULDEN
3.1700 g., Gold, 22 mm. **Ruler:** Philipp II **Subject:** Centennial of the Reformation **Obv:** The Good Shepherd holding lamb before lion in circle **Obv. Legend:** DE ORE. LEONIS - 1517. **Rev:** 5-line inscription with date **Rev. Inscription:** NVMMVS / SÆCVLARIS / PHILIPPI. II / DVCIS. POM / (date) **Mint:** Stettin **Note:** FR#2093; H#98. Prev. Pomerania KM#60.

Date	Mintage	VG	F	VF	XF	Unc
1617	—	725	1,800	4,300	7,200	—

KM# 60 GOLDGULDEN
3.1700 g., Gold, 22 mm. **Ruler:** Philipp II **Subject:** Centennial of the Reformation **Obv:** Bust to right in circle **Obv. Legend:** PHILIPPVS. II. DVX. STETIN. POMER. **Rev:** 5-line inscription with date **Rev. Inscription:** NVMMVS / SÆCVLARIS / PHILIPPI. II / DVCIS. POM / (date) **Mint:** Stettin **Note:** FR#2092; H#99. Prev. Pomerania KM#59.

Date	Mintage	VG	F	VF	XF	Unc
1617	—	775	1,900	4,600	7,700	—

KM# 80 GOLDGULDEN
3.1800 g., Gold, 22 mm. **Ruler:** Franz **Obv:** Bust to right in circle **Obv. Legend:** FRANCIS. I. D.G. DVX. S. POM. **Rev:** Crowned griffin to left in circle holding sword, date at end of legend **Rev. Legend:** ADSIT. AB. ALTO. (date). **Mint:** Stettin **Note:** FR#2095; H#114. Prev. Pomerania KM#72.

Date	Mintage	VG	F	VF	XF	Unc
1618	—	1,150	2,900	7,000	11,500	—

KM# 119 GOLDGULDEN
3.1400 g., Gold, 21 mm. **Ruler:** Bogislaw XIV **Obv:** Half-length figure to right in circle **Obv. Legend:** BOGISLAVS. XIV. D.G. DVX. STE(T). P(O). **Rev:** Crowned griffin to left holding sword and book in circle, date at end of legend **Rev. Legend:** HIC. REGIT. ILLE. TVETVR. (date). **Mint:** Stettin **Note:** FR#2099; H#288. Prev. Pomerania KM#133.

Date	Mintage	VG	F	VF	XF	Unc
16Z9	—	1,100	2,700	6,500	11,000	—

KM# 24 2 GOLDGULDEN
6.9400 g., Gold, 22 mm. **Ruler:** Philipp II **Obv:** Bust to right in circle **Obv. Legend:** PHILIPPVS. II. DVX. STETIN. POMER. **Rev:** King David facing left, playing harp to flock of sheep, date at end of legend **Rev. Legend:** EGO. TVLI. TE. DE. GREGE. (date). **Mint:** Stettin **Note:** FR#2082; H#71. Prev. Pomerania KM#31.

Date	Mintage	VG	F	VF	XF	Unc
1614 Rare	—	—	—	—	—	—

KM# 29 2 GOLDGULDEN
6.3700 g., Gold, 21 mm. **Ruler:** Philipp II **Obv:** Bust to right in circle **Obv. Legend:** PHILIPPVS. II. DVX. STETIN. POMER. **Rev:** Stag standing to left towards cascading fals, date at end of legend **Rev. Legend:** IN. TE. SITIT. ANIMA. MEA. (date). **Mint:** Stettin **Note:** FR#2086; H#27. Prev. Pomerania KM#37.

Date	Mintage	VG	F	VF	XF	Unc
1615 Rare	—	—	—	—	—	—

KM# 30 2 GOLDGULDEN
6.4000 g., Gold, 22 mm. **Ruler:** Philipp II **Obv:** Bust to right in circle **Obv. Legend:** PHILIPPVS. II. DVX. STETI. POM. **Rev:** Candlestick with burning taper in circle, date at end of legend **Rev. Legend:** OFFICIO. MIHI. OFFICIO. (date). **Mint:** Stettin **Note:** FR#2084; H#72.

Date	Mintage	VG	F	VF	XF	Unc
1615 Rare	—	—	—	—	—	—

KM# 37 2 GOLDGULDEN
6.3300 g., Gold, 22 mm. **Ruler:** Philipp II **Obv:** Armored bust to right in circle **Obv. Legend:** PHILIPPVS. II. DVX. STETIN. POMER. **Rev:** 4-line inscription with date in palm and laurel wreath **Rev. Inscription:** SOLI / DEO GLOR / RIA / (date) **Mint:** Stettin **Note:** FR#2090; H#28, 29. Prev. Pomerania KM#48.

Date	Mintage	VG	F	VF	XF	Unc
1616 Rare	—	—	—	—	—	—
Note: Leu Numismatik AG Auction 85, 10-02, VF realized approximately $8,320						
1617 Rare	—	—	—	—	—	—

KM# 156 1/2 DUCAT
1.7300 g., Gold, 18 mm. **Ruler:** Bogislaw XIV **Subject:** Entombment of Bogislaw XIV **Obv:** 8-line inscription with date **Obv. Inscription:** NVMMVS / EXEQVIALIS / BOGISLAI / DVCIS. STETI / POMERANOR / EIVS. NOMIN / 14.ET.VLT / 1654. **Rev:** Skull in wreath, curved legend above **Rev. Legend:** SPERO VITAM **Mint:** Stettin **Note:** FR#2103; H#373.

Date	Mintage	VG	F	VF	XF	Unc
1654 Rare	50	—	—	—	—	—

KM# 120 DUCAT
3.4300 g., Gold, 23 mm. **Ruler:** Bogislaw XIV **Obv:** Full-length standing figure, head turned to right, divides date **Obv. Legend:** BOGISLAVS. XIV. (-) D.G. - D (-) VX. STETIN. P(OMM). **Rev:** Shield of 9-fold arms in ornamented frame **Rev. Legend:** PRIN. RVG. COM. GVTZ. TERR. LEOB. E. B(V). D. **Mint:** Stettin **Note:** H#292-3. Prev. Pomerania KM#134. Varieties exist.

Date	Mintage	VG	F	VF	XF	Unc
16Z9	—	750	1,500	3,000	5,300	—
1631	—	750	1,500	3,000	5,300	—

KM# 125 DUCAT
3.4300 g., Gold, 23 mm. **Ruler:** Bogislaw XIV **Obv:** Full-length standing figure, head turned to right **Obv. Legend:** BOGISL. XIV - D.G. D. ST. PO. **Rev:** Shield of 9-fold arms, 3 ornate helmets above **Rev. Legend:** MO: NO: - AVREA. **Mint:** Stettin **Note:** FR#2101; H#289.

Date	Mintage	VG	F	VF	XF	Unc
ND(ca1630-5)	—	900	1,800	3,700	6,500	—

KM# 132 DUCAT
3.4400 g., Gold, 24 mm. **Ruler:** Bogislaw XIV **Obv:** Full-length standing figure, head turned to right, divides date **Obv. Legend:** BOGISL. XIV - D.G. D(VX). S(T). P(O). (C. ET. V. P. R.) **Rev:** Shield of 9-fold arms, 3 ornate helmets above **Rev. Legend:** MO: NO: - AVREA. **Mint:** Stettin **Note:** FR#2101; H#295. Prev. Pomerania KM#169.

Date	Mintage	VG	F	VF	XF	Unc
1633	—	900	1,800	3,700	6,500	—

KM# 133 DUCAT
3.4300 g., Gold, 23 mm. **Ruler:** Bogislaw XIV **Obv:** Full-length standing figure, head turned to right, divides date **Obv. Legend:** BOGISLAVS. XIV. - D. - G. DVX. STE. P. C. E. **Rev:** Oval shield of 9-fold arms **Rev. Legend:** P. R. CO. G. TER. LEOB. ET. BVT. DOM. **Mint:** Stettin **Note:** H#296.

Date	Mintage	VG	F	VF	XF	Unc
1633	—	900	1,800	3,700	6,500	—

KM# 157 DUCAT
3.4500 g., Gold, 24 mm. **Ruler:** Bogislaw XIV **Obv:** 11-line inscription with dates **Obv. Inscription:** NVMMVS / EXEQVIALIS / OPTIMI.PRINCI / PIS. BOGISLAI / DVCIS. STET. POM / EIVS. NOMINIS. 14 / ET. ELTIMI / NATI. 31. MAR. 1580 / DEN. 10. MAR. 1637 / SEP. 25. MAY / 1654. **Rev:** Skull, curved legend above, all in wreath **Rev. Legend:** SPERO VITAM **Mint:** Stettin **Note:** FR#2102; H#372.

Date	Mintage	VG	F	VF	XF	Unc
1654 Rare	25	—	—	—	—	—

KM# 10 6 DUCAT
Gold, 42 mm. **Ruler:** Philipp II **Obv:** Bust to right in ornamented circle **Obv. Legend:** PHILIPPVS. II. D.G. DVX. POMERANORVM. **Rev:** Crowned griffin to left holding sword in circle, 10 oval shields of arms around, legend in small letters between tops of shields **Rev. Legend:** CR - IS - TO - ET - RE - IP - VB - LI - C - Æ. **Mint:** Stettin **Note:** H#26. Struck from Thaler dies, KM#4.

Date	Mintage	VG	F	VF	XF	Unc
ND(1606-18) DS Rare	—	—	—	—	—	—

KM# 81 6 DUCAT
20.4800 g., Gold, 42 mm. **Ruler:** Franz **Obv:** Armored bust to right in circle **Obv. Legend:** D.G. FRANCISCVS. I. DVX. SEDINI. POMERAN. CASSVB. ET. VANDAL. **Rev:** Shield of 9-fold arms, ornate helmet above, supported by 2 wildmen wearing helmets **Rev. Legend:** PRINC. RVGIÆ. COM. GVTZK. TERR. LEOPOL. ET. BVTOV. DNS. **Mint:** Stettin **Note:** H#113.

Date	Mintage	VG	F	VF	XF	Unc
ND(1618-20) DS Rare	—	—	—	—	—	—

KM# 82 10 DUCAT (Portugalöser)
34.7900 g., Gold, 42 mm. **Ruler:** Franz **Obv:** Armored bust to right wearing ruffed collar, in circle **Obv. Legend:** D.G. FRANCISCVS. I. DVX. SEDINI. POMERAN. CASSVB. ET. VANDAL. **Rev:** Shield of 9-fold arms with ornate helmet above, supported by 2 wildmen wearing helmets **Rev. Legend:** PRINC. RVGIÆ. COM. GVTZK. TERR. LEOPOL. ET. BVTOV. DNS. **Mint:** Stettin **Note:** FR#2096; H#112.

Date	Mintage	VG	F	VF	XF	Unc
ND(1618-20) DS Rare	—	—	—	—	—	—

KM# 139 10 DUCAT (Portugalöser)
34.5700 g., Gold, 43 mm. **Ruler:** Bogislaw XIV **Obv:** Duke on horseback galloping to right, small oval Pomeranian arms below **Obv. Legend:** BOGISLAVS. XIV - DG. - DVX. S. P. **Rev:** Ornate shield of 10-fold arms with ornate helmet above, supported by 2 wildmen wearing helmets, date above left wildman **Rev. Legend:** CASSVB. ET. VAND. PRINC. RVB. EP. CAM. COM. GVTZK. TER. LEOB. ET. BV. DO. **Mint:** Stettin **Note:** H#368.

Date	Mintage	VG	F	VF	XF	Unc
1635 GT Rare	—	—	—	—	—	—

KM# 158 10 DUCAT (Portugalöser)
34.5000 g., Gold, 43 mm. **Ruler:** Bogislaw XIV **Subject:** Entombment of Bogislaw XIV **Obv:** Duke on horseback galloping to right, small oval Pomeranian arms below **Obv. Legend:** BOGISLAVS. XIV - DG. - DVX. S. P. **Rev:** Skull in wreath, triple marginal legends with dates **Rev. Legend:** IN MEMORIAM ULTIMI EX GRYPHICA STIRPE DUCIS POMER / BOGISLAI. XIV. NATI. XXXI. MART. 1580. DENATI. X / MART. 1637. HVMATI. 25. MAI. 1654. **Mint:** Stettin **Note:** H#371.

Date	Mintage	VG	F	VF	XF	Unc
1654 GT Rare	10	—	—	—	—	—

PATTERNS

Including off metal strikes

KM#	Date	Mintage	Identification	Mkt Val
Pn1	1615	—	Thaler. Bronze. 43 mm. KM# 25. Prev. Pomerania KM#35.	—

POMERANIA-WOLGAST

RULERS
Philip III Julius, 1592-1625

DUCHY

REGULAR COINAGE

KM# 1 PFENNIG
1.0000 g., Copper, 18 mm. **Ruler:** Philipp III Julius **Obv:** 4-line inscription with date **Obv. Inscription:** PHIL / IVLIVS / H.Z.S.P. / (date) **Rev:** Crowned griffin to left **Note:** H#229.

Date	Mintage	Good	VG	F	VF	XF
1609	—	65.00	125	235	475	825

KM# 28 3 PFENNIG (Pommersch)
1.2900 g., Copper, 18 mm. **Ruler:** Philipp III Julius **Obv:** Griffin to left in circle **Obv. Legend:** PHILIPPVS. IVL. H.Z.S.P. **Rev:** 5-line inscription with date **Rev. Inscription:** III / PFEN / NING / POM / (date). **Note:** H#228.

Date	Mintage	Good	VG	F	VF	XF
16ZZ	—	15.00	25.00	55.00	110	—

KM# 18 WITTEN (4 Pfennig)
0.5500 g., Silver, 14-15 mm. **Ruler:** Philipp III Julius **Obv:** Griffin to left in circle **Obv. Legend:** PHILIPPVS. IVLIVS. **Rev:** Short cross in circle, date divided in angles **Rev. Legend:** D.G. SVX. STET. POM. **Note:** H#220.

Date	Mintage	Good	VG	F	VF	XF
1619	—	30.00	65.00	125	225	—

KM# 29 6 PFENNIG (Pommersch)
2.0400 g., Copper, 22 mm. **Ruler:** Philipp III Julius **Obv:** Griffin to left in circle **Obv. Legend:** PHILIPPVS. IVL. H.Z.S.P. **Rev:** 5-line inscription with date **Rev. Inscription:** VI / PFEN / NING / POM(E) / (date). **Note:** H#227.

Date	Mintage	Good	VG	F	VF	XF
16ZZ	—	18.00	30.00	60.00	120	220

KM# 13.1 6 PFENNIG (1/64 Thaler)
1.4900 g., Silver, 20 mm. **Ruler:** Philipp III Julius **Obv:** Griffin to left in circle **Obv. Legend:** PHILIPPVS. IULIUS. **Rev:** Imperial orb with 64 in circle, date at end of legend **Rev. Legend:** HERT. Z. STE. POM. **Note:** H#215, 216.

Date	Mintage	Good	VG	F	VF	XF
(1)610	—	15.00	30.00	60.00	125	—
1615	—	15.00	30.00	60.00	125	—

KM# 13.2 6 PFENNIG (1/64 Thaler)
0.6400 g., Silver, 18 mm. **Ruler:** Philipp III Julius **Obv:** Griffin to left in circle **Obv. Legend:** PHILIPPVS. IVLIVS. **Rev:** Imperial orb with 64 divides date **Rev. Legend:** D.G. DVX. STE(T). P(O)(M). **Note:** H#217-19. Kipper coinage. Varieties exist.

Date	Mintage	Good	VG	F	VF	XF
1619	—	15.00	30.00	60.00	125	—
16Z0	—	15.00	30.00	60.00	125	—
16Z1	—	15.00	30.00	60.00	125	—

KM# 25 SCHILLING (Pommersch)
0.6500 g., Silver, 16-17 mm. **Ruler:** Philipp III Julius **Obv:** Griffin to left in circle **Obv. Legend:** PHILIPPVS. IVL. H.Z.S.P. **Rev:** 5-line inscription with date **Rev. Inscription:** I / SCHIL / LING / POM(E) / (date). **Mint:** Franzburg **Note:** H#222-6. Varieties exist.

Date	Mintage	Good	VG	F	VF	XF
16Z1 (d)	—	12.00	25.00	50.00	100	—
16ZZ (d)	—	12.00	25.00	50.00	100	—
16Z3 (d)	—	12.00	25.00	50.00	100	—
16Z4 (d)	—	12.00	25.00	50.00	100	—
16Z5 (d)	—	12.00	25.00	50.00	100	—

KM# 19 SCHILLING (12 Pfennig Lübisch)
0.9700 g., Silver, 19 mm. **Ruler:** Philipp III Julius **Obv:** Griffin to left in circle **Obv. Legend:** PHILIPPVS. IVLIVS. D.G. **Rev:** Shield of Rügen arms, 1Z P.L. above, date at end of legend **Rev. Legend:** DVX. STET. POM. **Note:** H#213-14.

Date	Mintage	Good	VG	F	VF	XF
16Z0	—	12.00	25.00	50.00	100	—
16Z1	—	12.00	25.00	50.00	100	—

KM# 5 2 SCHILLING (Doppelschilling)
Silver Weight varies: 1.39-2.53g., 24 mm. **Ruler:** Philipp III Julius **Obv:** Shield of 4-fold arms divides date to left, top and right **Obv. Legend:** PHILIPPUS. IU(L)(I)(U)(S). H. Z. S. (P.) **Rev:** Intertwined DS in ornamented shield **Rev. Legend:** RECTE. FACI. NE. METUAS. **Mint:** Franzburg **Note:** H#199-212. Varieties exist, V's instead of U's on some examples.

Date	Mintage	Good	VG	F	VF	XF
1609	—	18.00	30.00	55.00	110	190
1610	—	18.00	30.00	55.00	110	190
1611	—	18.00	30.00	55.00	110	190
161Z	—	18.00	30.00	55.00	110	190
1613	—	18.00	30.00	55.00	110	190
1614	—	18.00	30.00	55.00	110	190
1615	—	18.00	30.00	55.00	110	190
1616	—	18.00	30.00	55.00	110	190
1617	—	18.00	30.00	55.00	110	190
1618	—	18.00	30.00	55.00	110	190
1619	—	18.00	30.00	55.00	110	190
16Z0	—	18.00	30.00	55.00	110	190
16Z1	—	18.00	30.00	55.00	110	190

KM# 2 2 SCHILLING (Doppelschilling)
2.5300 g., Silver, 26 mm. **Ruler:** Philipp III Julius **Obv:** Shield of 9-fold arms in circle **Obv. Legend:** P. I. H. Z. S. P. NEMINEM. METUA. **Rev:** Intertwined DS in ornamented shield **Rev. Legend:** RECTE. FACI. NEM. TIMEAS. **Note:** H#193.

Date	Mintage	Good	VG	F	VF	XF
ND(1609-13)	—	25.00	55.00	110	225	—

KM# 3 2 SCHILLING (Doppelschilling)
2.5300 g., Silver, 26 mm. **Ruler:** Philipp III Julius **Obv:** Shield of 9-fold arms in circle **Obv. Legend:** P. I/ H. Z. S. P. - NEMINEM. METUAS. **Rev:** Intertwined DS in ornamented shield, date at end of legend **Rev. Legend:** RE (-) CTE. (-) FACIE (-) NDO. **Note:** H#195-6. Varieties exist.

Date	Mintage	Good	VG	F	VF	XF
1609	—	25.00	55.00	110	225	—

KM# 4.1 2 SCHILLING (Doppelschilling)
2.5300 g., Silver, 26 mm. **Ruler:** Philipp III Julius **Obv:** Shield of 9-fold arms in circle **Obv. Legend:** P. I. H. Z. S. P. - NEMINEM. MET(U)(V)S. **Rev:** Intertwined DS in ornamented shield which divides date to left, top and right **Rev. Legend:** RECTE. FACIE. NE(MI). MET(U)(V)A(S). **Note:** H#197. Varieties exist.

Date	Mintage	Good	VG	F	VF	XF
1609	—	18.00	30.00	65.00	125	230

KM# 4.2 2 SCHILLING (Doppelschilling)
2.5300 g., Silver, 26 mm. **Ruler:** Philipp III Julius **Obv:** Shield of 9-fold arms in circle **Obv. Legend:** PHILIPPUS. IULIUS. H. Z. S. P. (A.) **Rev:** Intertwined DS in ornamented shield which divides date to left, top and right **Rev. Legend:** RECTE. FAC(I)(E). NE. METUA(S). **Mint:** Franzburg **Note:** H#198.

Date	Mintage	Good	VG	F	VF	XF
1609 CR	—	20.00	35.00	70.00	120	240

KM# 16 2 SCHILLING (Doppelschilling)
2.2300 g., Silver, 23 mm. **Ruler:** Philipp III Julius **Obv:** Shield of 4-fold arms in circle **Obv. Legend:** PHILIPPUS. IUL. H. Z. S. P. **Rev:** Intertwined DS in ornamented shield **Rev. Legend:** RECTE. FA. NE. METVAS. **Note:** H#194.

Date	Mintage	Good	VG	F	VF	XF
ND(1614-17)	—	25.00	45.00	85.00	150	300

KM# 30 2 SCHILLING (Pommersch)
1.0600 g., Silver, 20 mm. **Ruler:** Philipp III Julius **Obv:** Griffin to left in circle **Obv. Legend:** PHILIPPVS. IVL. H. Z. S. P. **Rev:** 5-line inscription with date **Rev. Inscription:** II / SCHILL / ING. POM / MERSCH / (date). **Mint:** Franzburg **Note:** H#221. Varieties exist.

Date	Mintage	Good	VG	F	VF	XF
16ZZ (d)	—	80.00	150	215	275	500

KM# 17 4 SCHILLING
3.6400 g., Silver, 30 mm. **Ruler:** Philipp III Julius **Obv:** Crowned shield of 4-fold arms divides date in circle **Obv. Legend:** PHILIPPVS. IULIUS. V. G. G. HZ. STET. P. **Rev:** Crowned imperial eagle **Rev. Legend:** MATTHIAS. I. D. G. R. I S. AUGUSTU. **Note:** H#187.

Date	Mintage	Good	VG	F	VF	XF
1616	—	—	—	—	—	—

KM# 7 1/24 THALER (Reichsgroschen)
1.6500 g., Silver, 20-21 mm. **Ruler:** Philipp III Julius **Obv:** Shield of 4-fold arms in circle **Obv. Legend:** PHILIP(US). IULI(US). H. Z. S. P(O). **Rev:** Imperial orb with Z4, first half of date divided at top, second half by orb **Rev. Legend:** SI. DEUS. P. N. Q. C(O). NO(S). **Mint:** Franzburg **Note:** H#181-6. Varieties exist.

Date	Mintage	Good	VG	F	VF	XF
1609 CR	—	12.00	25.00	40.00	75.00	150
1610	—	12.00	25.00	40.00	75.00	150
1611	—	12.00	25.00	40.00	75.00	150
161Z	—	12.00	25.00	40.00	75.00	150
1613	—	12.00	25.00	40.00	75.00	150
1616	—	12.00	25.00	40.00	75.00	150

KM# 6 1/24 THALER (Reichsgroschen)
1.6500 g., Silver, 23 mm. **Ruler:** Philipp III Julius **Obv:** Shield of 4-fold arms in circle **Obv. Legend:** PHILIP. IULIUS. D. S(T). P(O). **Rev:** Imperial orb with Z4 divides date **Rev. Legend:** SI. DEUS. P. N. Q. C(O). NOS. **Mint:** Franzburg **Note:** H#180.

Date	Mintage	Good	VG	F	VF	XF
(1)609 CR	—	15.00	30.00	55.00	110	225
1609	—	15.00	30.00	55.00	110	225

KM# 31 1/16 THALER (Düttchen)
3.0900 g., Silver, 27-28 mm. **Ruler:** Philipp III Julius **Obv:** Griffin to left in shield superimposed on long cross **Obv. Legend:** PHILI - PPVS. - IVLIVS. - H.Z.S.P. **Rev:** 7-line inscription with date **Rev. Inscription:** NACH / ALTEN. SC / HROT. VND / KORN. XVI. ST / VCKE. EINEN / REICHS. TA / LER. (date) **Mint:** Franzburg **Note:** H#188.

Date	Mintage	Good	VG	F	VF	XF
16ZZ (d)	—	—	—	—	—	—

KM# 37 1/16 THALER (Düttchen)
3.0900 g., Silver, 27-28 mm. **Ruler:** Philipp III Julius **Obv:** Griffin to left in shield superimposed on long cross **Obv. Legend:** PHILI - PPVS. - IVLIVS. - H.Z.S.P. **Rev:** 4-line inscription with date **Rev. Legend:** REICHS. SCHROT. V(ND) KORN. **Rev. Inscription:** 16. ST / REICHS / TALER / (date). **Mint:** Franzburg **Note:** H#189-90.

Date	Mintage	Good	VG	F	VF	XF
16Z3 (d)	—	30.00	55.00	100	185	375
16Z4 (d)	—	120	225	325	475	850

KM# 38 1/16 THALER (Düttchen)
3.0900 g., Silver, 27-28 mm. **Ruler:** Philipp III Julius **Obv:** Griffin to left in shield, head breaks shield at top, superimposed on long cross **Obv. Legend:** PHILIP - PVS. IV - LIVS. H. - Z.S.P. **Rev:** 4-line inscription with date **Rev. Legend:** REICHS. SCHROT. VND KORN. **Rev. Inscription:** 16. ST / REICHS / TALER / (date). **Mint:** Franzburg **Note:** H#191-2. Varieties exist, U's substituted for V's.

Date	Mintage	Good	VG	F	VF	XF
16Z4 (d)	—	18.00	30.00	55.00	100	200
16Z5 (d)	—	18.00	30.00	55.00	100	200

KM# 32 1/8 THALER (1/2 Reichsort)
3.3100 g., Silver, 24-25 mm. **Ruler:** Philipp III Julius **Obv:** Crowned griffin to left in circle **Obv. Legend:** V. G. G. PHILIPPVS. IVL. H. A. Z. P. **Rev:** 4-line inscription with date **Rev. Legend:** FATA. F. FERAM. P. PATI. PALMAM. **Rev. Inscription:** HALB / REICHS / ORTH / (date). **Note:** H#179.

Date	Mintage	Good	VG	F	VF	XF
16ZZ	—	—	—	—	—	—

KM# 39 1/8 THALER (1/2 Reichsort)
3.6400 g., Silver, 28 mm. **Ruler:** Philipp III Julius **Subject:** Death of Philipp III Julius **Obv:** Bust to right divides date **Obv. Legend:** PHILIPP. IVL. D.G. DVX. STE. POM. **Rev:** Sun shining on flowering plant **Rev. Legend:** ADHVC. MEA. MESSIS. IN. HERBA. **Mint:** Franzburg **Note:** H#234.

Date	Mintage	Good	VG	F	VF	XF
(1)6Z5 (d)	—	—	—	—	—	—

KM# 33 1/4 THALER (Reichsort)
7.0700 g., Silver, 31 mm. **Ruler:** Philipp III Julius **Obv:** Crowned griffin to left in double circle **Obv. Legend:** V. G. G. PHILIPPVS. IVLIVS. H. Z. S. P. **Rev:** 4-line inscription with date **Rev. Legend:** FATA. FER. FE. PART. PATIE. PALMAM. **Rev. Inscription:** REI / CHES.ORTH / (date). **Mint:** Franzburg **Note:** H#178.

Date	Mintage	Good	VG	F	VF	XF
16ZZ (d)	—	—	—	—	—	—

KM# 40 1/4 THALER (Reichsort)

7.0300 g., Silver, 34 mm. **Ruler:** Philipp III Julius **Subject:** Death of Philipp III Julius **Obv:** Bust to right in circle **Obv. Legend:** PHILIPPVS. IVLIVS. D.G. DVX. S. P. C. E. V. **Rev:** Sun shining on flowering plant, date at end of legend **Rev. Legend:** ADHVC. MEA. MESSIS. IN. HERBA. **Mint:** Franzburg **Note:** H#233.

Date	Mintage	Good	VG	F	VF	XF
16Z5 (d)	—	—	—	—	—	—

KM# 34 1/2 THALER

14.1600 g., Silver, 35 mm. **Ruler:** Philipp III Julius **Obv:** Bust with double high ruffed collar to right in circle **Obv. Legend:** PHILIPPVS. IVLIVS. D.G. DVX. STE. POME. **Rev:** Shield of 9-fold arms, ornate helmet above, supported by 2 wildmen wearing helmets, date divided by crest of helmet at upper left **Rev. Legend:** FATA. F. FE. PARI. P. PALM. **Mint:** Franzburg **Note:** H#176.

Date	Mintage	Good	VG	F	VF	XF
16ZZ (d)	—	400	800	1,650	3,000	6,000
(16)ZZ (d)	—	400	800	1,650	3,000	6,000

KM# 35 1/2 THALER

14.1600 g., Silver, 36 mm. **Ruler:** Philipp III Julius **Obv:** Large armored bust to right breaks circle at top **Obv. Legend:** V. G. G. PHILIPPVS. IVLIVS. H. Z. S. PO. **Rev:** Shield of 9-fold arms, ornate helmet above, supported by 2 wildmen wearing helmets, date divided by crests of middle and right helmets **Rev. Legend:** FATA. F. FE. PARI. P. PALM. **Mint:** Franzburg **Note:** H#177.

Date	Mintage	Good	VG	F	VF	XF
16ZZ HP	—	—	—	—	—	—

KM# 41 1/2 THALER

14.4200 g., Silver, 38-39 mm. **Ruler:** Philipp III Julius **Subject:** Death of Philipp III Julius **Obv:** Armored bust to right in circle **Obv. Legend:** PHILIPPVS. IVLIVS. D.G. DVX. STE. POM. CAS. E. VAN. **Rev:** 10-line inscription with dates **Rev. Inscription:** NVMVS. EX / TREMÆ. MEMOR / PHILIPP. IVLII. DV / S.P. NATI. AN. 1584 / Z7. DEC. DENATI. 17Z5.6. FEB. A. PATRUELE / ET. SVCCESSORE / BOGISLAO. 14. DV / STE. POM. CON / SECRATVS. **Mint:** Franzburg **Note:** H#232.

Date	Mintage	Good	VG	F	VF	XF
16Z5 (d)	—	—	—	—	—	—

KM# 8 THALER

28.4100 g., Silver, 41 mm. **Ruler:** Philipp III Julius **Obv:** High-collared bust to right in circle **Obv. Legend:** PHILIPPUS. IULIUS. D.G. DUX. STETIN. POMER. **Rev:** Shield of 9-fold arms, ornate helmet above, supported by 2 wildmen wearing helmets **Rev. Legend:** FATA. FEREN. FE. PARI. PATIEN. PALMAM. **Note:** Dav. #7201; H#168. Prev. Pomerania KM#95.

Date	Mintage	VG	F	VF	XF	Unc
ND(1609-10) Rare	—	—	—	—	—	—

KM# 9 THALER

28.4100 g., Silver, 40 mm. **Ruler:** Philipp III Julius **Obv:** Bust to right in circle divides date **Obv. Legend:** PHILIPPUS. IULIUS. D.G. D. STETIN. POM **Rev:** Shield of 9-fold arms, ornate helmet above, supported by 2 wildmen wearing helmets **Rev. Legend:** FATA. FEREN. FE. PARI. PATIEN. PALMAM. **Mint:** Franzburg **Note:** Dav. #7192; H#169. Prev. Pomerania KM#11.1.

Date	Mintage	VG	F	VF	XF	Unc
(1)609 CR	—	725	1,450	2,650	4,500	—

KM# 10 THALER

28.4100 g., Silver, 40 mm. **Ruler:** Philipp III Julius **Obv:** Bust to right in circle divides date **Obv. Legend:** PHILIPPUS. IULIUS. D.G. D. STETIN. POM. **Rev:** Shield of 9-fold arms, ornate helmet above, supported by 2 wildmen wearing helmets **Rev. Legend:** FATA. FEREN. FE. PARI. PATIEN. PALMAm. **Mint:** Franzburg **Note:** Dav. #7192A. Prev. Pomerania KM#11.2. Second 'M' in PALMAM is small.

Date	Mintage	VG	F	VF	XF	Unc
(1)609 CR	—	725	1,450	2,650	4,500	—

KM# 14 THALER

Silver, 41-42 mm. **Ruler:** Philipp III Julius **Obv:** Armored bust to right in circle divides date **Obv. Legend:** PHILIPPUS. IULIUS. D.G. D. STETIN. POME. **Rev:** Shield of 9-fold arms, ornate helmet above, supported by 2 wildmen wearing helmets **Rev. Legend:** FATA. FEREN. FE. PARI. PATIEN. PALMAM. **Note:** Dav. #7194; H#170-1. Prev. Pomerania 21.

Date	Mintage	VG	F	VF	XF	Unc
1610	—	1,500	3,200	5,700	9,600	—
1611	—	1,500	3,200	5,700	9,600	—
ND(1610-11)	—	1,500	3,200	5,700	9,600	—

KM# 20 THALER

28.4000 g., Silver, 41-42 mm. **Ruler:** Philipp III Julius **Obv:** Bust to right in circle divides date **Obv. Legend:** PHILIPPUS. IULIUS. D.G. D. STET. POMER. **Rev:** Shield of 9-fold arms, ornate helmet above, supported by 2 wildmen wearing helmets **Rev. Legend:** FATA. FEREN. FE. PARI. PATIEN. PALMAM. **Note:** Dav. #7197; H#172. Prev. Pomerania KM#83.

Date	Mintage	VG	F	VF	XF	Unc
16Z0	—	900	1,800	3,500	6,750	—
1620	—	900	1,800	3,500	6,750	—

KM# 21 THALER

28.4000 g., Silver, 43 mm. **Ruler:** Philipp III Julius **Obv:** Armored bust to right in circle **Obv. Legend:** PHILIPPUS. IULIUS. D.G. DUX. STETIN. POMER. **Rev:** Shield of 9-fold arms, ornate helmet above, supported by 2 wildmen wearing helmets, date divided in margin at top **Rev. Legend:** FATA. FEREN. FE. PARI. PATIENT. PALMAM. **Note:** Dav. #7198; H#172-3. Prev. Pomerania KM#84.

Date	Mintage	VG	F	VF	XF	Unc
16Z0 Rare	—	—	—	—	—	—

KM# 26 THALER

28.4000 g., Silver, 40 mm. **Ruler:** Philipp III Julius **Obv:** Bust to right in circle wearing double ruffed collar **Obv. Legend:** PHILIPPUS. IULIUS. D.G. DUX. STETIN. POMER. **Rev:** Shield of 9-fold arms, ornate helmet above, supported by 2 wildmen wearing helmets, date divided in margin at top **Rev. Legend:** FATA. FEREN. FE. PARI. PATIEN. PALMAM. **Note:** Dav. #7200; H#174. Prev. Pomerania KM#89.

Date	Mintage	VG	F	VF	XF	Unc
16Z1	—	550	1,150	2,350	4,500	—
ND(1621)	—	550	1,150	2,350	4,500	—

KM# 36 THALER

28.4000 g., Silver, 41 mm. **Ruler:** Philipp III Julius **Obv:** Bust to right in circle divides date **Obv. Legend:** PHILIPPVS. IVLIVS. D.G. DVX. STETTIN. POMER. **Rev:** Shield of 9-fold arms, ornate helmet above, supported by 2 wildmen wearing helmets **Rev. Legend:** FATA. FEREN. FE. PARI. PATIENT. PALMAM. **Mint:** Franzburg **Note:** Dav. #7201; H#175. Prev. Pomerania KM#95.

Date	Mintage	VG	F	VF	XF	Unc
16ZZ (d) Rare	—	—	—	—	—	—

KM# 42 THALER

28.6500 g., Silver, 49 mm. **Ruler:** Philipp III Julius **Subject:** Death of Philipp III Julius **Obv:** Draped bust to right in circle **Obv. Legend:** PHILIPPVS. IVLIUS. D.G. DVX. STET. POM. CASSV. ET. VAN. **Rev:** 10-line inscription with dates **Rev. Inscription:** NVMVS. EX / TREMÆ. MEMOR / PHILIPPI. IVLII. DV / S. POM. NATI. A. 1584 / Z7. DEC. DENATI. A. 16Z5 / 6. FEB. A. PATRUELE / ET. SVCCESSORE / BOGISLAO. 14. DVC / STE. POM. CON / SECRATVS. **Mint:** Franzburg **Note:** jDav. #7207; H#231. Prev. Pomerania KM#101.

Date	Mintage	VG	F	VF	XF	Unc
16Z5 (d) Rare	—	—	—	—	—	—

KM# 22 1-1/2 THALER

40.6600 g., Silver, 41 mm. **Ruler:** Philipp III Julius **Obv:** Bust to right in circle divides date **Obv. Legend:** PHILIPPUS. IULIUS. D.G. D. STET. POMER. **Rev:** Shield of 9-fold arms, ornate helmet above, supported by 2 wildmen wearing helmets **Rev. Legend:** FATA. FEREN. FE. PARI. PATIEN. PALMAM. **Note:** Dav. #7196; H#167. Prev. Pomerania KM#85.

Date	Mintage	VG	F	VF	XF	Unc
16Z0 Rare	—	—	—	—	—	—

KM# 11 2 THALER

Silver, 40 mm. **Ruler:** Philipp III Julius **Obv:** Bust to right in circle divides date **Obv. Legend:** PHILIPPUS. IULIUS. D.G. D. STETIN. POM. **Rev:** Shield of 9-fold arms, ornate helmet above, supported by 2 wildmen wearing helmets **Rev. Legend:** FATA. FEREN. FE. PARI. PATIEN. PALMAM. **Mint:** Franzburg **Note:** Dav. #A7192.

Date	Mintage	VG	F	VF	XF	Unc
(1)609 CR Rare	—	—	—	—	—	—

KM# 15 2 THALER

57.5800 g., Silver, 42 mm. **Ruler:** Philipp III Julius **Obv:** Bust to rght in circle divides date **Obv. Legend:** PHILIPPUS. IULIUS. D.G. D. STETIN. POME. **Rev:** Shield of 9-fold arms, ornate helmet above, supported by 2 wildmen wearing helmets **Rev. Legend:** FATA. FEREN. FE. PARI. PATIEN. PALMAM. **Note:** Dav. #7193; H#164. Prev. Pomerania KM#22.

Date	Mintage	VG	F	VF	XF	Unc
1610 Rare	—	—	—	—	—	—

KM# 23 2 THALER

57.6000 g., Silver, 43-44 mm. **Ruler:** Philipp III Julius **Obv:** Bust to right in circle divides date **Obv. Legend:** PHILIPPUS. IULIUS. D.G. D. STET. POMER. **Rev:** Shield of 9-fold arms, ornate helmet above, supported by 2 wildmen wearing helmets **Rev. Legend:** FATA. FEREN. FE. PARI. PATIEN(T). PALMAM. **Note:** Dav. #7195; H#165. Prev. Pomerania KM#86.

Date	Mintage	VG	F	VF	XF	Unc
16Z0 Rare	—	—	—	—	—	—
1620 Rare	—	—	—	—	—	—

KM# 24 2 THALER

Silver, 42x44 mm. **Ruler:** Philipp III Julius **Obv:** Bust to right in circle divides date **Obv. Legend:** PHILIPPUS. IULIUS. D.G. D. STET. POMER. **Rev:** Shield of 9-fold arms, ornate helmet above, supported by 2 wildmen wearing helmets **Rev. Legend:** FATA. FEREN. FE. PARI. PATIENT. PALMAM. **Note:** Klippe. Dav. #7195A; H#KL165.

Date	Mintage	VG	F	VF	XF	Unc
16Z0 Rare	—	—	—	—	—	—

KM# 27 2 THALER

57.6000 g., Silver, 40-41 mm. **Ruler:** Philipp III Julius **Obv:** Bust wearing high ruffed collar to right in circle **Obv. Legend:** PHILIPPUS. IULIUS. D.G. DUX. STETIN. POMER. **Rev:** Shield of 9-fold arms, ornate helmet above, supported by 2 wildmen wearing helmets, date divided in margin at top **Rev. Legend:** FATA. FEREN. FE. PARI. PATIEN. PALMAM. **Note:** Dav. #7199; H#166. Prev. Pomerania KM#90.

Date	Mintage	VG	F	VF	XF	Unc
16Z1 Rare	—	—	—	—	—	—

KM# 43 2 THALER

56.8000 g., Silver, 52 mm. **Ruler:** Philipp III Julius **Obv:** Draped bust to right in circle **Obv. Legend:** PHILIPPVS. IVLIVS. D.G. DVX. STET. POM. CASSV. ET. VAN. **Rev:** 10-line inscription with dates **Rev. Inscription:** NVMVS. EX / TREMÆ. MEMOR / PHILIPPI. IVLII. DV / S. POM. NATI. A. 1584 / Z7. DEC. DENATI. A. 16Z5 / 6. FEB. A. PATRUELE / ET. SVCCESSORE / BOGISLAO. 14. DVC / STE. POM. CON / SECRATVS. **Mint:** Franzburg **Note:** Dav. #A7202 and LS368; H#230. Prev. Pomerania KM#102.

Date	Mintage	VG	F	VF	XF	Unc
16Z5 (d) Rare	—	—	—	—	—	—

Note: WAG Auction 52, 2-10, VF+ realized approximately $13,675.

TRADE COINAGE

KM# 12 GOLDGULDEN

3.0600 g., Gold, 23 mm. **Ruler:** Philipp III Julius **Obv:** Bust to right in circle divides date **Obv. Legend:** PHILIPPUS. IULIUS. D.G. D. S. P(O). **Rev:** Shield of 9-fold arms in circle **Rev. Legend:** DESPERAND(U)(V)M. DEO. D(U)(V)CE). NIL. **Mint:** Franzburg **Note:** FR#2079; H#162-3. Prev. Pomerania KM#12. Varieties exist.

Date	Mintage	VG	F	VF	XF	Unc
(1)609	—	1,000	2,250	5,000	9,000	—
(1)609 CR	—	1,000	2,250	5,000	9,000	—
(1)611 CR	—	1,000	2,250	5,000	9,000	—

SWEDISH OCCUPATION

RULERS

Christina of Sweden, 1637-1654
Karl X of Sweden, 1654-1660
Karl XI of Sweden, 1660-1697
Karl XII of Sweden, 1697-1718

REGULAR COINAGE

KM# 207 WITTEN (1/192 Thaler)

Silver **Obv:** Crowned griffin left in inner circle **Obv. Legend:** KRISTINA... **Rev:** Value and date in inner circle

Date	Mintage	VG	F	VF	XF	Unc
1650	—	45.00	90.00	180	360	—
1651	—	45.00	90.00	180	360	—
1654	—	45.00	90.00	180	360	—

KM# 216 WITTEN (1/192 Thaler)

Silver **Obv:** Griffin holding sword **Obv. Legend:** CAROLUS. GUSTAVUS...

Date	Mintage	VG	F	VF	XF	Unc
1655	—	50.00	100	200	425	—
1656	—	50.00	100	200	425	—
1657	—	80.00	165	335	675	—

KM# 238 WITTEN (1/192 Thaler)

Silver **Obv:** Crowned griffin **Obv. Legend:** CAROLUS XI... **Rev:** Value: WITT, date in inner circle

Date	Mintage	VG	F	VF	XF	Unc
1666	—	45.00	90.00	180	360	—

KM# 240 WITTEN (1/192 Thaler)

Silver **Rev:** Value: WIT

Date	Mintage	VG	F	VF	XF	Unc
1668	—	125	250	—	—	—
1670 Rare	—	—	—	—	—	—

KM# 296 WITTEN (1/192 Thaler)

Silver **Rev:** Value: WITTEN

Date	Mintage	VG	F	VF	XF	Unc
1684 Rare	—	—	—	—	—	—

KM# 297 WITTEN (1/192 Thaler)

Silver **Obv:** BA below griffin **Rev:** Value in three lines

Date	Mintage	VG	F	VF	XF	Unc
1684 BA	—	50.00	100	200	425	—

KM# 298 WITTEN (1/192 Thaler)

Silver **Rev:** WITTEN

Date	Mintage	VG	F	VF	XF	Unc
1684 BA Rare	—	—	—	—	—	—
1685 BA	—	50.00	100	200	425	—
1686 BA Rare	—	—	—	—	—	—

KM# 306 WITTEN (1/192 Thaler)

Silver **Obv:** Initials below griffin

Date	Mintage	VG	F	VF	XF	Unc
1686 DHM	—	50.00	100	200	425	—

KM# 315 WITTEN (1/192 Thaler)

Silver **Rev:** Value/initials/date

Date	Mintage	VG	F	VF	XF	Unc
1687 DHM	—	50.00	100	200	425	—

KM# 321 WITTEN (1/192 Thaler)

Silver **Rev:** Value/date/initials

Date	Mintage	VG	F	VF	XF	Unc
1688 DHM	—	50.00	100	200	425	—

KM# 336 WITTEN (1/192 Thaler)

Silver **Rev:** Value / date / initials

Date	Mintage	VG	F	VF	XF	Unc
1690 ILA	—	45.00	90.00	180	360	—

KM# 258 1/192 THALER (Witten)

Silver **Obv:** Crowned griffin left **Rev:** Value in orb, date in legend

Date	Mintage	VG	F	VF	XF	Unc
1673	—	65.00	135	275	550	—
1674	—	60.00	135	275	550	—

KM# 259 1/96 THALER (Sechsling)

Silver

Date	Mintage	VG	F	VF	XF	Unc
1673	—	65.00	135	275	550	—
1674 Rare	—	—	—	—	—	—

KM# 299 1/96 THALER (Sechsling)

Silver **Obv:** Initials below griffin **Rev:** Value, date below

Date	Mintage	VG	F	VF	XF	Unc
1684 BA	—	45.00	90.00	180	360	—
1685 BA Rare	—	—	—	—	—	—
1685 DHM Rare	—	—	—	—	—	—
1687 DHM	—	45.00	90.00	180	360	—

KM# 316 1/96 THALER (Sechsling)

Silver **Rev:** Value, date, initials

Date	Mintage	VG	F	VF	XF	Unc
1687 DHM	—	45.00	90.00	180	360	—
1688 DHM	—	45.00	90.00	180	360	—

KM# 324 1/96 THALER (Sechsling)

Silver **Obv:** Crowned C, date divided by crown **Rev:** Orb dividing initials

Date	Mintage	VG	F	VF	XF	Unc
1689 ILA	—	45.00	90.00	180	360	—
1690 ILA	—	45.00	90.00	180	360	—
1691 ILA	—	45.00	90.00	180	360	—
1692 ILA Rare	—	—	—	—	—	—

KM# 251.1 1/48 THALER (Schilling)

Silver **Obv:** Crowned griffin, initials below in inner circle **Rev:** Value in inner circle, date in legend

Date	Mintage	VG	F	VF	XF	Unc
1661 VB Rare	—	—	—	—	—	—
1670 HIH Rare	—	—	—	—	—	—
1671 HIH Rare	—	—	—	—	—	—
1672 DS	—	15.00	35.00	70.00	145	—
1672 DS	—	15.00	35.00	70.00	145	—
1673 DS	—	15.00	35.00	70.00	145	—
1674 DS Rare	—	—	—	—	—	—
1675 DS Rare	—	—	—	—	—	—
1676 DS Rare	—	—	—	—	—	—
1680 CS Rare	—	—	—	—	—	—
1681 CS	—	25.00	50.00	100	210	—
1681 BA	—	25.00	50.00	100	210	—
1682 BA Rare	—	—	—	—	—	—
1683 BA Rare	—	—	—	—	—	—
1684 BA	—	15.00	35.00	70.00	145	—
1685 BA Rare	—	—	—	—	—	—
1685 BA Rare	—	—	—	—	—	—
1686 DHM Rare	—	—	—	—	—	—
1689 DHM	—	35.00	75.00	150	300	—
1690 ILA	—	20.00	45.00	90.00	180	—
1691 ILA	—	20.00	45.00	90.00	180	—
1692 ILA	—	20.00	45.00	90.00	180	—
1693 ILA	—	35.00	75.00	150	300	—
1694 ILA Rare	—	—	—	—	—	—

KM# 251.2 1/48 THALER (Schilling)

Silver **Rev:** Initials in legend

Date	Mintage	VG	F	VF	XF	Unc
1681 CS	—	15.00	35.00	70.00	145	—

KM# 251.3 1/48 THALER (Schilling)

Silver **Obv:** Initials in legend

Date	Mintage	VG	F	VF	XF	Unc
1687 DHM Rare	—	—	—	—	—	—

KM# 317 1/48 THALER (Schilling)

Silver **Rev:** Value and initials in inner circle

Date	Mintage	VG	F	VF	XF	Unc
1687 DHM	—	20.00	4.00	90.00	180	—
1688 DHM Rare	—	—	—	—	—	—

KM# 224 DOPPEL-SCHILLING (1/16 Thaler)

Silver **Obv:** Griffin holding sword in inner circle **Obv. Legend:** CAROL GVST... **Rev:** DS in inner circle, date in legend

Date	Mintage	VG	F	VF	XF	Unc
1656	—	25.00	50.00	100	200	—
1657	—	25.00	50.00	100	200	—
1658	—	25.00	50.00	100	200	—
1659	—	25.00	50.00	100	200	—
1660	—	25.00	50.00	100	200	—

KM# 241 DOPPEL-SCHILLING (1/16 Thaler)

Silver **Obv. Legend:** CAROL XI...

Date	Mintage	VG	F	VF	XF	Unc
1662	—	25.00	50.00	100	200	—
1666	—	50.00	100	200	425	—
1666 HIH (b)	—	35.00	75.00	150	300	—
1667 (b)	—	25.00	50.00	100	200	—
1668	—	25.00	50.00	100	200	—
1668 (b)	—	25.00	50.00	100	200	—
1669	—	25.00	50.00	100	200	—
1669 (b)	—	25.00	50.00	100	200	—
1670	—	25.00	50.00	100	200	—

KM# 273 DOPPEL-SCHILLING (1/16 Thaler)

Silver **Rev:** Legend begins at bottom

Date	Mintage	VG	F	VF	XF	Unc
1670	—	35.00	75.00	150	300	—

KM# 232 1/24 THALER (Groschen)

Silver **Obv:** Shield in inner circle **Rev:** Orb divides date and initials in inner circle

Date	Mintage	VG	F	VF	XF	Unc
1661 VB	—	135	275	450	900	—
1662 VB	—	165	325	675	1,300	—

KM# 247.1 1/24 THALER (Groschen)
Silver **Obv:** Griffin with sword left **Rev:** Value and initials in inner circle, date in legend

Date	Mintage	VG	F	VF	XF	Unc
1670 HIH	—	30.00	65.00	130	265	—
1671 HIH	—	25.00	50.00	100	210	—
1687 DHM	—	20.00	45.00	90.00	180	—
1688 DHM	—	25.00	50.00	100	210	—

KM# 247.2 1/24 THALER (Groschen)
Silver **Rev:** Without initials

Date	Mintage	VG	F	VF	XF	Unc
1671	—	35.00	75.00	150	300	—

KM# 249.1 1/24 THALER (Groschen)
Silver **Rev:** Initials in legend at top

Date	Mintage	VG	F	VF	XF	Unc
1671 HIH	—	13.00	27.00	55.00	110	—
1675 DS	—	25.00	50.00	100	210	—
1676 DS	—	35.00	75.00	150	300	—
1680 CS Rare	—	—	—	—	—	—
1681 CS	—	10.00	25.00	55.00	110	—

KM# 249.2 1/24 THALER (Groschen)
Silver **Rev:** Initials divide date in legend

Date	Mintage	VG	F	VF	XF	Unc
1671 HIH	—	15.00	35.00	70.00	145	—

KM# 252 1/24 THALER (Groschen)
Silver **Rev:** Initials below griffin in inner circle

Date	Mintage	VG	F	VF	XF	Unc
1672 DS	—	10.00	25.00	50.00	110	—
1681 CS	—	15.00	35.00	70.00	145	—
1681 BA	—	15.00	35.00	70.00	145	—
1682 BA	—	35.00	75.00	150	300	—
1683 BA Rare	—	—	—	—	—	—
1684 BA	—	35.00	75.00	120	300	—

KM# 253 1/24 THALER (Groschen)
Silver **Obv. Legend:** CAROLUS...DS...

Date	Mintage	VG	F	VF	XF	Unc
1672 DS	—	15.00	35.00	70.00	145	—

KM# 254 1/24 THALER (Groschen)
Silver **Obv. Legend:** CAROLUS XI...DS...

Date	Mintage	VG	F	VF	XF	Unc
1672 DS	—	15.00	35.00	70.00	145	—

KM# 282 1/24 THALER (Groschen)
Silver **Obv:** Initials below griffin **Rev:** Mintmaster's initials in legend

Date	Mintage	VG	F	VF	XF	Unc
1681 CS	—	35.00	75.00	150	300	—
1687 DHM Rare	—	—	—	—	—	—

KM# 281 1/24 THALER (Groschen)
Silver, 22 mm. **Ruler:** Karl XI **Obv:** Rampant griffin to left in circle **Obv. Legend:** CAROLUS XI. D.G. REX. SUECIÆ. **Rev:** 4-line inscription, date at end of legend **Rev. Legend:** IN IEHOUA SORS MEA. **Rev. Inscription:** 24 / EINEN / REICHS / DALER **Mint:** Stettin **Note:** Mule.

Date	Mintage	VG	F	VF	XF	Unc
1681 DS//CS	—	25.00	50.00	100	210	—

KM# 302.1 1/24 THALER (Groschen)
Silver **Obv:** Right leg of griffin divides initials

Date	Mintage	VG	F	VF	XF	Unc
1685 BA	—	25.00	50.00	100	210	—

KM# 302.2 1/24 THALER (Groschen)
Silver **Obv:** Initials between hind legs of griffin

Date	Mintage	VG	F	VF	XF	Unc
1685 DHM	—	35.00	75.00	150	300	—
1687 DHM	—	15.00	35.00	70.00	145	—
1688 DHM	—	15.00	35.00	70.00	145	—

KM# 302.3 1/24 THALER (Groschen)
Silver **Obv:** Initials below hind legs of griffin

Date	Mintage	VG	F	VF	XF	Unc
1686 DHM	—	15.00	35.00	70.00	145	—

KM# 312 1/24 THALER (Groschen)
Silver **Obv:** Initials in oval below griffin

Date	Mintage	VG	F	VF	XF	Unc
1686 DHM	—	15.00	35.00	70.00	145	—

KM# 325 1/24 THALER (Groschen)
Silver **Obv:** Crowned shield **Rev:** Value and initials in inner circle, date in legend

Date	Mintage	VG	F	VF	XF	Unc
1689 ILA	—	50.00	100	200	425	—
1690 ILA	—	35.00	75.00	150	300	—
1692 ILA Rare	—	—	—	—	—	—

KM# 283.1 1/12 THALER (2 Groschen)
Silver **Obv:** Crowned griffin in inner circle **Rev:** Value and initials in inner circle, date in legend

Date	Mintage	VG	F	VF	XF	Unc
1681 CS	—	25.00	50.00	100	210	—
1681 3 stars Rare	—	—	—	—	—	—
1681 BA	—	45.00	90.00	180	360	—
1682 BA	—	50.00	100	200	425	—
1688 DHM	—	45.00	90.00	180	360	—

KM# 283.2 1/12 THALER (2 Groschen)
Silver **Obv:** Crowned griffin in small circle **Rev:** Value, date, and initials in inner circle, date in legend

Date	Mintage	VG	F	VF	XF	Unc
1688 DHM Rare	—	—	—	—	—	—

KM# 323 1/12 THALER (2 Groschen)
Silver **Obv:** Crowned straight-sided shield **Rev:** Value and initials in inner circle, date in legend

Date	Mintage	VG	F	VF	XF	Unc
1689 ILA	—	25.00	50.00	100	210	—
1690 ILA	—	20.00	45.00	90.00	180	—
1691 ILA	—	20.00	45.00	90.00	180	—
1692 ILA	—	35.00	75.00	150	300	—
1693 ILA	—	20.00	45.00	90.00	180	—

KM# 337 1/12 THALER (2 Groschen)
Silver **Obv:** Griffin left in coat of arms

Date	Mintage	VG	F	VF	XF	Unc
1690 ILA	—	45.00	90.00	180	360	—
1691 ILA	—	35.00	75.00	150	300	—

KM# 343 1/12 THALER (2 Groschen)
Silver **Obv:** Crowned, curved shield divides initials

Date	Mintage	VG	F	VF	XF	Unc
1693 ILA	—	30.00	60.00	125	250	—
1664 ILA Error for 1694	—	135	275	550	1,160	—
1694 ILA	—	50.00	100	200	425	—
1695 ILA	—	50.00	100	200	425	—
1695 ICA	—	45.00	90.00	180	360	—
1696 ICA	—	65.00	135	275	550	—
1697 ICA	—	65.00	135	275	550	—

KM# 345 1/12 THALER (2 Groschen)
Silver

Date	Mintage	VG	F	VF	XF	Unc
1694 ILA	—	50.00	100	200	425	—

KM# 208 1/8 THALER (1/2 Reichsort)
Silver **Obv:** Christina right in inner circle **Rev:** Value, date below in inner circle

Date	Mintage	VG	F	VF	XF	Unc
1653 Rare	—	—	—	—	—	—

KM# 210 1/8 THALER (1/2 Reichsort)
Silver **Rev:** Value in inner circle, date in legend **Note:** Varieties of reverse exist.

Date	Mintage	VG	F	VF	XF	Unc
1654 Rare	—	—	—	—	—	—

KM# 326.1 1/6 THALER (4 Groschen)
Silver **Obv:** Bust right with chest armor **Rev:** Crowned, supported arms, value below divides date

Date	Mintage	VG	F	VF	XF	Unc
1689 ILA	—	80.00	165	335	675	—

KM# 327 1/6 THALER (4 Groschen)
Silver **Obv:** Bust right with chest armor **Rev:** Value in four lines in inner circle

Date	Mintage	VG	F	VF	XF	Unc
1689 ILA-KMK Unique	—	—	—	—	—	—

KM# 326.2 1/6 THALER (4 Groschen)
Silver **Obv:** Bust right with chest armor and shoulder armor **Rev:** Crowned, supported arms, value below divides date

Date	Mintage	VG	F	VF	XF	Unc
1693 ILA	—	150	360	700	1,400	—

KM# 233 1/4 THALER (Reichsort)
Silver **Obv:** Laureate bust right **Rev:** Shield divides initials in inner circle, date in legend

Date	Mintage	VG	F	VF	XF	Unc
1661 VB Rare	—	—	—	—	—	—

KM# 234 1/4 THALER (Reichsort)
Silver **Obv:** Bust right

Date	Mintage	VG	F	VF	XF	Unc
1661 VB Rare	—	—	—	—	—	—

KM# 221 REICHSORT (1/4 Thaler)
Silver **Obv:** Charles X right in inner circle **Rev:** Arms, date in legend

Date	Mintage	VG	F	VF	XF	Unc
1658 VB Rare	—	—	—	—	—	—

KM# 261 1/3 THALER (1/2 Gulden)
Silver **Obv:** Draped laureate bust with hair locks on chest and back **Rev:** Crowned, supported shield, value and initials below, date in legend

Date	Mintage	VG	F	VF	XF	Unc
1672 DS Rare	—	—	—	—	—	—
1673 DS	—	50.00	100	200	425	—

KM# 255 1/3 THALER (1/2 Gulden)
Silver **Obv:** Draped laureate bust with short wig and shoulder flaps

Date	Mintage	VG	F	VF	XF	Unc
1672 DS Rare	—	—	—	—	—	—
1673 DS	—	80.00	165	335	675	—

KM# 256 1/3 THALER (1/2 Gulden)
Silver **Obv:** Long wig

Date	Mintage	VG	F	VF	XF	Unc
1672 DS Rare	—	—	—	—	—	—
1673 DS	—	65.00	135	275	575	—

KM# 260 1/3 THALER (1/2 Gulden)
Silver **Obv:** Long wig, initials below bust

Date	Mintage	VG	F	VF	XF	Unc
1673 DS	—	45.00	90.00	180	360	—
1674 DS	—	45.00	90.00	180	360	—

KM# 262 1/3 THALER (1/2 Gulden)
Silver **Obv:** Draped bust with hair locks on back, initials below

Date	Mintage	VG	F	VF	XF	Unc
1674 DS	—	50.00	100	200	425	850
1681 CS Rare	—	—	—	—	—	—

KM# 263 1/3 THALER (1/2 Gulden)
Silver **Obv:** Laureate draped bust with hair locks and shoulder armor, initials below

Date	Mintage	VG	F	VF	XF	Unc
1674 DS	—	45.00	90.00	180	360	—
1675 DS	—	45.00	90.00	180	360	—

KM# 268 1/3 THALER (1/2 Gulden)
Silver **Obv:** Laureate draped bust with chest and shoulder armor

Date	Mintage	VG	F	VF	XF	Unc
1674 DS	—	80.00	165	335	675	—

KM# 284 1/3 THALER (1/2 Gulden)
Silver **Obv:** Draped bust **Rev:** Crowned, supported shield divides initials

Date	Mintage	VG	F	VF	XF	Unc
1681 CS Rare	—	—	—	—	—	—

KM# 285 1/3 THALER (1/2 Gulden)
Silver **Obv:** Draped bust with ornamented chest and shoulder armor, initials below

Date	Mintage	VG	F	VF	XF	Unc
1681 CA Rare	—	—	—	—	—	—
1682 BA Rare	—	—	—	—	—	—
1684 BA Rare	—	—	—	—	—	—
1685 DHM Rare	—	—	—	—	—	—
1686 DHM Rare	—	—	—	—	—	—

KM# 294 1/3 THALER (1/2 Gulden)
Silver **Obv:** Draped bust with ornamented chest armor

Date	Mintage	VG	F	VF	XF	Unc
1683 BA Rare	—	—	—	—	—	—

KM# 304 1/3 THALER (1/2 Gulden)
Silver **Obv:** Draped bust with plain chest armor

Date	Mintage	VG	F	VF	XF	Unc
1685 DHM Rare	—	—	—	—	—	—

KM# 328 1/3 THALER (1/2 Gulden)
Silver **Obv:** Draped bust with riveted chest armor, divided legend

Date	Mintage	VG	F	VF	XF	Unc
1689 ILA Rare	—	—	—	—	—	—
1689 ILA - crossed flags Rare	—	—	—	—	—	—
1690 ILA	—	100	200	425	875	—
1690 ILA - crossed flags	—	100	200	425	875	—

KM# 347 1/3 THALER (1/2 Gulden)
Silver **Obv:** Draped bust with ornamented chest and shoulder armor, divided legend **Rev:** Indented, crowned arms

Date	Mintage	VG	F	VF	XF	Unc
1696 ICA Rare	—	—	—	—	—	—

KM# 187 1/2 THALER
Silver **Obv:** Half-length portrait of Christina **Rev:** Christ holding orb above shield dividing date

Date	Mintage	VG	F	VF	XF	Unc
1640 Rare	—	—	—	—	—	—

KM# 189 1/2 THALER
Silver **Obv:** Half-length portrait in ornamental circle

Date	Mintage	VG	F	VF	XF	Unc
1641 Rare	—	—	—	—	—	—

KM# 192 1/2 THALER
Silver **Obv:** Bust left

Date	Mintage	VG	F	VF	XF	Unc
1642 Rare	—	—	—	—	—	—
1646 Rare	—	—	—	—	—	—

KM# 231 1/2 THALER
Silver **Obv:** Laureate bust right **Rev:** Shield divides initials in inner circle, date in legend

Date	Mintage	VG	F	VF	XF	Unc
1661 Unique	—	—	—	—	—	—

KM# 264 2/3 THALER (Gulden)
Silver **Obv:** Draped laureate bust with shoulder flaps right, initials below **Rev:** Crowned, supported arms, value below, date in legend

Date	Mintage	VG	F	VF	XF	Unc
1673 DS	—	135	275	550	1,100	—

KM# 286 2/3 THALER (Gulden)
Silver **Obv:** Draped laureate bust with shoulder armor

Date	Mintage	VG	F	VF	XF	Unc
1681 CS	—	100	200	425	875	—

KM# 287 2/3 THALER (Gulden)
Silver **Obv:** Draped bust

Date	Mintage	VG	F	VF	XF	Unc
1681 CS	—	100	200	425	875	—

KM# 288 2/3 THALER (Gulden)
Silver **Rev:** Arms divide initials

Date	Mintage	VG	F	VF	XF	Unc
1681 CS-CS	—	135	275	550	1,100	—

KM# 289 2/3 THALER (Gulden)
Silver

Date	Mintage	VG	F	VF	XF	Unc
1681 Rare	—	—	—	—	—	—
1681 CS	—	100	200	425	875	—
1684/3 BA	—	100	200	425	875	—
1684 BA	—	100	200	425	875	—

KM# 290 2/3 THALER (Gulden)
Silver

Date	Mintage	VG	F	VF	XF	Unc
1681 BA	—	80.00	160	325	675	—

KM# 291 2/3 THALER (Gulden)
Silver **Obv:** Riveted armor

Date	Mintage	VG	F	VF	XF	Unc
1681 BA	—	90.00	180	360	625	—
1683 BA	—	80.00	165	335	675	—
1685 BA	—	135	275	575	1,150	—
1686 DHM	—	135	275	550	1,100	—
1688 DHM	—	180	325	650	1,300	—

KM# 292 2/3 THALER (Gulden)
Silver **Obv:** Ornamented bust armor

Date	Mintage	VG	F	VF	XF	Unc
1681 BA	—	80.00	160	325	675	—
1682 BA Rare	—	—	—	—	—	—
1683 BA	—	80.00	160	325	675	—
1685 BA	—	135	275	575	1,150	—

KM# 295 2/3 THALER (Gulden)
Silver

Date	Mintage	VG	F	VF	XF	Unc
1683 BA	—	100	200	425	850	—
1684/3 BA	—	80.00	160	325	675	—
1684 BA	—	80.00	160	325	675	—
1685 DHM Rare	—	—	—	—	—	—

KM# 307.1 2/3 THALER (Gulden)
Silver

Date	Mintage	VG	F	VF	XF	Unc
1686 DHM	—	135	275	350	1,100	—
1687 DHM	—	85.00	175	350	700	1,200
1688 DHM Rare	—	—	—	—	—	—
1689	—	135	275	550	1,100	—
1689 ILA	—	60.00	125	250	500	1,000
1689 ILA/(c)	—	65.00	135	275	550	1,100
1690 ILA	—	65.00	135	275	550	1,100
1660 ILA Rare; error for 1690	—	—	—	—	—	—
1690 ILA/(c)	—	60.00	125	250	500	1,000
1691 ILA	—	70.00	150	300	600	1,150
1692 ILA	—	65.00	135	275	550	1,100

KM# 308.1 2/3 THALER (Gulden)

Silver **Obv:** Draped bust with chest armor and shoulder rosette, full legend

Date	Mintage	VG	F	VF	XF	Unc
1686 DHM	—	135	275	550	1,100	—

KM# 308.2 2/3 THALER (Gulden)

Silver **Obv:** Divided legend

Date	Mintage	VG	F	VF	XF	Unc
1686 DHM	—	135	275	550	1,100	—

KM# 319 2/3 THALER (Gulden)

Silver **Obv:** Draped bust with plain chest armor, divided legend

Date	Mintage	VG	F	VF	XF	Unc
1687 DHM	—	100	200	425	850	—
1688 DHM	—	135	275	550	1,100	—

KM# 307.2 2/3 THALER (Gulden)

Silver **Obv:** Without G++V

Date	Mintage	VG	F	VF	XF	Unc
1690 ILA/(c)	—	80.00	160	325	675	—

KM# 341 2/3 THALER (Gulden)

Silver

Date	Mintage	VG	F	VF	XF	Unc
1692 ILA	—	80.00	160	325	675	—
1693 ILA	—	90.00	185	375	775	—
1694 ILA Rare	—	—	—	—	—	—
1695 ILA	—	90.00	185	375	775	—
1695 ICA	—	90.00	185	375	775	—
1695 ICA/(C)	—	90.00	185	375	775	—
1696 ICA beside truncation	—	—	—	—	—	—
1696 ICA below truncation	—	—	—	—	—	—
1697 ICA on truncation	—	80.00	160	325	675	—
1697 ICA beside truncation	—	75.00	150	300	625	—

KM# 188.1 THALER

Silver **Obv:** Half-length portrait in ornamented circle, large crown at left **Rev:** Christ above supported arms **Note:** Dav. #4571.

Date	Mintage	VG	F	VF	XF	Unc
1640	—	600	1,200	2,850	6,000	—
1641	—	600	1,200	2,250	5,000	—

KM# 188.2 THALER

Silver **Obv:** Small crown at left **Note:** Dav. #4571A.

Date	Mintage	VG	F	VF	XF	Unc
1641	—	600	1,200	2,250	5,000	—

KM# 193.2 THALER

Silver **Obv:** Bust with curly hair **Note:** Dav. #4573.

Date	Mintage	VG	F	VF	XF	Unc
164Z	—	400	800	1,750	3,250	—
1644	—	1,450	2,750	4,500	—	—
1647	—	500	1,000	2,000	3,750	—
1654 Rare	—	—	—	—	—	—

KM# 190 THALER

Silver **Obv:** Bust left in ornamented circle **Rev:** Helmeted, supported arms **Note:** Dav. #4575.

Date	Mintage	VG	F	VF	XF	Unc
1642 Rare	—	—	—	—	—	—

KM# 193.1 THALER

Silver **Obv:** Bust with wavy hair in plain circle **Note:** Dav. #A4573.

Date	Mintage	VG	F	VF	XF	Unc
1642	—	450	900	1,850	3,500	—

KM# 217.1 THALER

Silver **Obv:** Karl X **Rev:** Helmeted, supported arms **Note:** Varieties of portraits exist. Dav. #4577.

Date	Mintage	VG	F	VF	XF	Unc
1655	—	850	1,750	3,250	5,500	—

KM# 217.2 THALER

Silver **Obv:** Larger bust **Note:** Portrait varieties exist. Dav. #4577A.

Date	Mintage	VG	F	VF	XF	Unc
1657 VB	—	650	1,250	2,250	4,250	6,500

KM# 265.1 THALER

Silver **Obv:** Laureate bust with hair locks on shoulder and back **Rev:** Crowned, supported straight sided arms, DS below **Note:** Dav. #4578.

Date	Mintage	VG	F	VF	XF	Unc
1673 DS Rare	—	—	—	—	—	—

KM# 265.2 THALER

Silver **Obv:** DS below bust **Note:** Dav. #4578A.

Date	Mintage	VG	F	VF	XF	Unc
1673 DS Rare	—	—	—	—	—	—

Note: Künker Auction 156, 6-09, nearly XF realized approximately $18,240.

KM# 266 THALER

Silver **Obv:** Hair locks on back **Note:** Dav. #4579.

Date	Mintage	VG	F	VF	XF	Unc
1674 DS Rare	—	—	—	—	—	—

Note: Hess-Divo Auction 295, 5-03, XF realized approximately $16,860.

KM# 271 THALER

Silver **Obv:** Hair locks on bust and back **Rev:** Round shield **Note:** Dav. #4580.

Date	Mintage	VG	F	VF	XF	Unc
1675 DS Rare	—	—	—	—	—	—

KM# 310 THALER

Silver **Obv:** Bust with rosette **Rev:** Shield with indented sides **Note:** Dav. #4581.

Date	Mintage	VG	F	VF	XF	Unc
1686 DHM Rare	—	—	—	—	—	—
1687 DHM Rare	—	—	—	—	—	—

KM# 329 THALER

Silver **Obv:** Bust with chest armor **Rev:** Plumes above crowned round arms divide date **Note:** Dav. #4582.

Date	Mintage	VG	F	VF	XF	Unc
1689 ILA-(c) Rare	—	—	—	—	—	—
1690 Rare	—	—	—	—	—	—

KM# 196.2 2 THALER

Silver **Obv:** Bust in plain circle **Note:** Dav. #4572.

Date	Mintage	VG	F	VF	XF	Unc
1642 Rare	—	—	—	—	—	—
1647 Rare	—	—	—	—	—	—

KM# 196.1 2 THALER

Silver **Obv:** Bust of Christina left in ornamented circle **Rev:** Helmeted, supported arms, date in legend **Note:** Dav. #4574.

Date	Mintage	VG	F	VF	XF	Unc
1642 Rare	—	—	—	—	—	—

KM# 218 2 THALER

57.3000 g., Silver **Obv:** Bust of Karl X right in inner circle **Rev:** Plume of helmet on crowned arms divide date **Note:** Dav. #4576.

Date	Mintage	VG	F	VF	XF	Unc
1655 Rare	—	—	—	—	—	—
1657 VB Rare	—	—	—	—	—	—

TRADE COINAGE

KM# 191 DUCAT

3.5000 g., 0.9860 Gold 0.1109 oz. AGW **Obv:** Facing half-figure of Christina in ornate inner circle **Rev:** Christ holding orb above shield of arms in inner circle

Date	Mintage	VG	F	VF	XF	Unc
1641	—	325	750	1,650	2,950	—

KM# 198 DUCAT

3.5000 g., 0.9860 Gold 0.1109 oz. AGW **Obv:** Without ornamentation on inner circle **Rev:** Shield of arms, date in legend

Date	Mintage	VG	F	VF	XF	Unc
1642	—	375	825	2,000	3,300	—

KM# 199.1 DUCAT

3.5000 g., 0.9860 Gold 0.1109 oz. AGW **Obv:** Christina

Date	Mintage	VG	F	VF	XF	Unc
1642	—	275	625	1,400	2,500	—
1653	—	275	625	1,400	2,500	—

KM# 199.2 DUCAT

3.5000 g., 0.9860 Gold 0.1109 oz. AGW **Rev:** Arms in inner circle

Date	Mintage	VG	F	VF	XF	Unc
1646	—	275	625	1,400	2,500	—
1653	—	275	625	1,400	2,500	—
1654	—	275	625	1,400	2,500	—

KM# 215.1 DUCAT

3.5000 g., 0.9860 Gold 0.1109 oz. AGW **Obv:** Karl X standing holding scepter and orb **Rev:** Shield of arms, date in legend

Date	Mintage	VG	F	VF	XF	Unc
1654	—	1,450	3,050	6,100	11,500	—
1656 VB	—	1,450	3,050	6,100	11,500	—
1658 VB	—	1,450	3,050	6,100	11,500	—

KM# 215.2 DUCAT

3.5000 g., 0.9860 Gold 0.1109 oz. AGW **Rev:** Arms in inner circle

Date	Mintage	VG	F	VF	XF	Unc
1659 VB	—	1,450	3,050	6,100	11,500	—

KM# 235 DUCAT

3.5000 g., 0.9860 Gold 0.1109 oz. AGW **Obv:** Laureate bust of Karl XI right in inner circle **Rev:** Crowned shield of arms, date in legend

Date	Mintage	VG	F	VF	XF	Unc
1662	—	875	1,900	4,300	8,600	—

KM# 239.1 DUCAT

3.5000 g., 0.9860 Gold 0.1109 oz. AGW **Obv:** Laureate bust of Karl XI in narrow armor left **Rev:** Shield of arms, date in legend

Date	Mintage	VG	F	VF	XF	Unc
1666 HIH/(b)	—	775	1,750	4,100	8,200	—

KM# 239.2 DUCAT

3.5000 g., 0.9860 Gold 0.1109 oz. AGW **Obv:** Bust in wide armor **Note:** Varieties exist.

Date	Mintage	VG	F	VF	XF	Unc
1666 HIH/(b) Rare	—	—	—	—	—	—

KM# 257.1 DUCAT

3.5000 g., 0.9860 Gold 0.1109 oz. AGW **Obv:** Large laureate bust of Karl XI right **Rev:** Arms topped by helmet with wildmen supporters

Date	Mintage	VG	F	VF	XF	Unc
1672 DS Rare	—	—	—	—	—	—

KM# 257.2 DUCAT

3.5000 g., 0.9860 Gold 0.1109 oz. AGW **Obv:** Small bust

Date	Mintage	VG	F	VF	XF	Unc
1673 DS	—	1,300	3,000	6,600	11,500	—
1674 DS	—	1,300	3,000	6,600	11,500	—

KM# 257.3 DUCAT

3.5000 g., 0.9860 Gold 0.1109 oz. AGW **Rev:** Round shield

Date	Mintage	VG	F	VF	XF	Unc
1675 DS	—	1,300	3,000	6,600	11,500	—

KM# 257.4 DUCAT

3.5000 g., 0.9860 Gold 0.1109 oz. AGW **Obv:** Older bust

Date	Mintage	VG	F	VF	XF	Unc
1682 BA	—	1,300	3,000	6,600	11,500	—

KM# 300.1 DUCAT

3.5000 g., 0.9860 Gold 0.1109 oz. AGW **Obv:** Bust right with ornamented chest armor

Date	Mintage	VG	F	VF	XF	Unc
1684 BA	—	1,300	3,000	6,600	11,500	—

KM# 300.2 DUCAT

3.5000 g., 0.9860 Gold 0.1109 oz. AGW **Obv:** Bust right with plain chest armor

Date	Mintage	VG	F	VF	XF	Unc
1685 BA	—	1,300	3,000	6,600	11,500	—

KM# 313.1 DUCAT

3.5000 g., 0.9860 Gold 0.1109 oz. AGW **Rev:** Full legend

Date	Mintage	VG	F	VF	XF	Unc
1686 DHM Rare	—	—	—	—	—	—

KM# 313.2 DUCAT

3.5000 g., 0.9860 Gold 0.1109 oz. AGW **Rev:** Divided legend

Date	Mintage	VG	F	VF	XF	Unc
1686 DHM Rare	—	—	—	—	—	—

KM# 330 DUCAT

3.5000 g., 0.9860 Gold 0.1109 oz. AGW **Obv:** Bust right with shoulder armor

Date	Mintage	VG	F	VF	XF	Unc
1689 ILA/(c)	—	1,300	3,000	6,600	11,500	—
1690 ILA/(c)	—	1,300	3,000	6,600	11,500	—

KM# 340.1 DUCAT

3.5000 g., 0.9860 Gold 0.1109 oz. AGW **Obv:** Legend divided **Rev:** ILA added

Date	Mintage	VG	F	VF	XF	Unc
1691 ILA/(c)	—	1,300	3,000	6,600	11,500	—
1693 ILA	—	1,300	3,000	6,600	11,500	—
1694 ILA	—	1,300	3,000	6,600	11,500	—

KM# 340.2 DUCAT

3.5000 g., 0.9860 Gold 0.1109 oz. AGW **Obv:** ICA added **Note:** Varieties exist.

Date	Mintage	VG	F	VF	XF	Unc
1695 ICA Rare	—	—	—	—	—	—
1696 ICA	—	1,300	3,000	6,600	11,500	—
1697 ICA	—	1,300	3,000	6,600	11,500	—

KM# 220 1-1/2 DUCAT

5.2500 g., 0.9860 Gold 0.1664 oz. AGW **Obv:** Armored bust of Karl XI **Rev:** Wheat sheaf holding crown, orb and crossed sword and scepter in inner circle

Date	Mintage	VG	F	VF	XF	Unc
ND ILA Unique	—	—	—	—	—	—

KM# 222 2 DUCAT

7.0000 g., 0.9860 Gold 0.2219 oz. AGW **Subject:** Karl X

Date	Mintage	VG	F	VF	XF	Unc
1658 Rare	—	—	—	—	—	—

Note: WAG Auction 46, 2-08, VF realized approximately $17,395.

KM# 236.1 2 DUCAT

7.0000 g., 0.9860 Gold 0.2219 oz. AGW **Subject:** Karl XI

Date	Mintage	VG	F	VF	XF	Unc
1661	—	875	1,950	5,500	12,500	—

KM# 236.2 2 DUCAT
7.0000 g., 0.9860 Gold 0.2219 oz. AGW **Obv:** Plain head of Karl XI

Date	Mintage	VG	F	VF	XF	Unc
1661	—	1,250	2,650	6,300	13,500	—

KM# 301 2 DUCAT
7.0000 g., 0.9860 Gold 0.2219 oz. AGW **Obv:** Armored bust of Karl XI

Date	Mintage	VG	F	VF	XF	Unc
1684 BA	—	1,150	2,300	5,500	12,000	—

KM# 320 2 DUCAT
7.0000 g., 0.9860 Gold 0.2219 oz. AGW **Obv:** Bust with draped shoulder

Date	Mintage	VG	F	VF	XF	Unc
1687 DHM	—	1,150	2,300	5,500	12,000	—

KM# 339 2 DUCAT
7.0000 g., 0.9860 Gold 0.2219 oz. AGW **Obv:** Divided legend **Note:** Varieties exist.

Date	Mintage	VG	F	VF	XF	Unc
1690 ILA	—	1,150	2,300	5,500	12,000	—
1695 ILA	—	1,150	2,300	5,500	12,000	—

KM# 342 2 DUCAT
7.0000 g., 0.9860 Gold 0.2219 oz. AGW **Obv:** Armored bust of Karl XI **Rev:** Wheat sheaf holding crown, orb, crossed sword, and scepter in inner circle **Note:** Varieties exist.

Date	Mintage	VG	F	VF	XF	Unc
1692 ILA	—	1,100	2,250	4,900	10,500	—
1693 ILA	—	1,100	2,250	4,900	10,500	—
1694 ILA	—	1,100	2,250	4,900	10,500	—
1696 ICA	—	700	1,400	3,100	6,500	—
1697 ICA	—	850	1,700	4,200	8,100	—
ND ILA	—	1,100	2,250	4,900	10,500	—

KM# 209 2-1/2 DUCAT
8.7500 g., 0.9860 Gold 0.2774 oz. AGW **Obv:** Laureate bust of Christina right in inner circle **Rev:** Shield of arms, date in legend

Date	Mintage	VG	F	VF	XF	Unc
1653 Rare	—	—	—	—	—	—

KM# 270 3 DUCAT
10.5000 g., 0.9860 Gold 0.3328 oz. AGW **Obv:** Laureate bust of Karl XI right **Rev:** Crowned arms with wildmen supporters, date in legend

Date	Mintage	VG	F	VF	XF	Unc
1674 Unique	—	—	—	—	—	—

PRENZLAU

(Prenzlow)

The town of Prenzlau is in Pomerania, about 28 miles (47km) southwest of Stettin, and appears as a mint for the dukes of Pomerania from the second half of the 12th century. By the mid-13th century, Prenzlau came under the control of the margraves of Brandenburg and was soon producing coins for those rulers. The town had its own coinage in the latter 15th century and again during the Kipper Period of the Thirty Years' War.

PROVINCIAL TOWN

REGULAR COINAGE

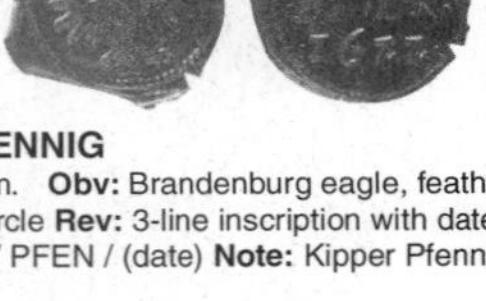

KM# 1 PFENNIG
Copper, 15 mm. **Obv:** Brandenburg eagle, feathered helmet above, all in circle **Rev:** 3-line inscription with date **Rev. Inscription:** I / PFEN / (date) **Note:** Kipper Pfennig. Varieties exist.

Date	Mintage	VG	F	VF	XF	Unc
16Z1	—	18.00	35.00	75.00	150	—
16ZZ	—	18.00	35.00	75.00	150	—
1622	—	18.00	35.00	75.00	150	—

KM# 2 PFENNIG
Silver **Obv:** Brandenburg eagle, feathered helmet above divides date, all in a circle **Note:** Uniface.

Date	Mintage	VG	F	VF	XF	Unc
1622	—	—	—	—	—	—

QUEDLINBURG

The small provincial town of Quedlinburg, 8 miles (13km) south-southeast of Halberstadt and slightly north of the Harz Mountains, was founded in 922. The town itself had its own coinage during the middle of the 17th century, but most of the local coinage was produced in and for the abbey. Near the village in 966, Emperor Otto I the Great (962-73) founded an abbey primarily for princesses of his imperial Saxon family. Otto I's grandson, Otto III (983-1002), established an imperial mint in the town and gave the abbesses the right to strike their own coinage at about the same time. Many of the abbesses were members of the House of Saxony or from noble families closely associated with it. When the Electorate and Duchy of Saxony itself became officially Protestant during the Reformation, Quedlinburg followed the same path in 1539. The coinage of the abbesses came to an end in 1697 when Elector Friedrich August I of Saxony (1694-1733) sold his rights over Quedlinburg to Brandenburg-Prussia in order to become King of Poland. A brief and scarce issue of a few types occurred in 1759, but otherwise the abbesses had only their 40-square mile (65-square km) territory to administer. Even this was secularized and annexed by Prussia in 1803.

RULERS
Anna I von Plauen, 1435-1458
Hedwig von Sachsen, 1458-1511
Magdalena von Anhalt, 1511-1514
Anna II von Stolberg-Königstein, 1514-1574
Elisabeth II von Regenstein-Blankenburg, 1574-1584
Anna III von Stolberg-Wernigerode, 1584-1601
Maria von Sachsen-Weimar, 1601-10
Dorothea von Sachsen, 1610-1617
Dorothea Sophia von Sachsen-Altenburg, 1618-1645
Anna Sophia I von Pfalz-Birkenfeld, 1645-1680
Anna Sophia II von Hessen-Darmstadt, 1681-1683
Anna Dorothea von Sachsen-Weimar, 1684-1704

MINT OFFICIALS' INITIALS

Initials	Date	Name
TE	1615-17	Tobias Eitze, mintmaster
HL	1617-19	Heinrich Löhr, mintmaster
	June-Aug 1619	Heinrich Meyer, mintmaster
	Oct-Dec 1619	Heinrich Oppermann, mintmaster
HL	1620-24, 1633-37	Hans Lauch, mintmaster
	Aug-Nov 1621	Johann Lampe, mintmaster
	1623-25	Georg Koch, mintmaster
AH	1674-76	August Hackeberg, mint director
	1674-80	Heinrich Römer, mint director
GF	1675-77	Georg Fromholtz, warden
	Ca.1675	Martin Müller, die-cutter
HAR	1676-?	Heinricyh Albert Reinecke, mintmaster
	Ca.1685	Johann Arensburger, mintmaster
	Ca.1690?	Philipp Ernst, mintmaster
HCH	1689-1729	Heinrich Christoph Hille, mintmaster in Braunschweig
HIC	1676-?	Henning Jürgen Cammer (Kemmer), warden

ARMS
Two crossed fish, but also sometimes an eagle or a three-towered city gate, or a combination of these.
Electoral and Ducal Saxony arms often appear on coins of abbesses from that family.

REFERENCE
D = Adalbert Düning, ***Übersich über die Münzgeschichte des kaiserlichen freien weltlichen Stifts Quedlinburg***, Quedlinburg, 1886.

ABBEY

REGULAR COINAGE

KM# 23 PFENNIG (Kipper)
Copper **Ruler:** Dorothea Sophia **Obv:** Heart-shaped 2-fold arms of ducal Saxony and Quedlingburg **Rev:** Large 'Q', date below **Note:** Ref. D-33.

Date	Mintage	VG	F	VF	XF	Unc
1620	—	22.00	45.00	90.00	180	—
1621	—	22.00	45.00	90.00	180	—
1622	—	22.00	45.00	90.00	180	—

KM# 24 PFENNIG (Kipper)
Copper **Ruler:** Dorothea Sophia **Obv:** Heart-shaped 2-fold arms of ducal Saxony and Quedlingburg **Note:** Uniface.

Date	Mintage	VG	F	VF	XF	Unc
ND(1620-22)	—	16.00	33.00	65.00	130	—

KM# 25 PFENNIG (Straubpfennig)
Copper **Ruler:** Dorothea Sophia **Obv:** 2-fold arms of ducal Saxony and Quedlinburg **Rev. Legend:** I/ STRAV/ PHEN

Date	Mintage	VG	F	VF	XF	Unc
ND(ca.1620)	—	20.00	40.00	75.00	150	—

KM# 42 PFENNIG (Straubpfennig)
Silver **Ruler:** Dorothea Sophia **Obv:** Heart-shaped 2-fold arms of Ducal and Electoral Saxony divide mintmaster's initials, date divided below. **Note:** Uniface. Ref. D-32.

Date	Mintage	VG	F	VF	XF	Unc
(16)34 HL	—	—	—	—	—	—

KM# 67 PFENNIG (Straubpfennig)
Silver **Ruler:** Anna Sophie I **Obv:** 2-fold arms of Quedlingburg and Pfalz, rampant lion left, divide date. **Note:** Uniface.

Date	Mintage	VG	F	VF	XF	Unc
(16)77	—	—	—	—	—	—

KM# 28 3 PFENNIG (Dreier)
Copper, 16 mm. **Ruler:** Dorothea Sophia **Obv:** Shield 2-fold arms of ducal Saxony and Quedlingburg in baroque frame **Rev:** Imperial orb with '3' divides date

Date	Mintage	VG	F	VF	XF	Unc
(16)Z1	—	16.00	35.00	70.00	145	—

KM# 34 3 PFENNIG (Dreier)
Copper **Ruler:** Dorothea Sophia **Obv:** Crowned 2-fold arms of ducal Saxony and Quedlinburg in baroque frame **Rev:** Complete date over Imperial orb

Date	Mintage	VG	F	VF	XF	Unc
1622	—	20.00	40.00	85.00	170	—

KM# 29 3 PFENNIG (Dreier)
Silver **Ruler:** Dorothea Sophia **Obv:** Ornate 2-fold arms of ducal and electoral Saxony **Rev:** Imperial orb with '3' divides date in baroque frame **Note:** Ref. D-31.

Date	Mintage	VG	F	VF	XF	Unc
1621 HL	—	12.00	25.00	50.00	100	—
1622 HL	—	12.00	25.00	50.00	100	—

KM# 59 3 PFENNIG (Dreier)
Silver **Ruler:** Anna Sophie I **Obv:** Crowned heart-shaped 2-fold arms of Quedlinburg and Pfalz, rampant lion left, within palm branches **Rev:** Imperial orb with '3' divides date **Note:** Ref. D-38.

Date	Mintage	VG	F	VF	XF	Unc
1676	—	100	200	425	—	—
1677	—	—	—	—	—	—

KM# 30 4 GROSCHEN (Schreckenberger)
Silver **Ruler:** Dorothea Sophia **Obv:** Heart-shaped 2-fold arms of ducal Saxony and Quedlinburg in ornate frame, date at top **Obv. Legend:** MO. NO. D-G. DORT. SOPHI **Rev:** Crowned Imperial eagle, '4' in circle on breast **Rev. Legend:** DVCISS. SAX. ABBAT. QVEDLB **Note:** Varieties exist. Ref. D-28.

Date	Mintage	VG	F	VF	XF	Unc
16Z1	—	30.00	60.00	125	250	—

KM# 31 4 GROSCHEN (Schreckenberger)
Silver **Ruler:** Dorothea Sophia **Obv:** Heart-shaped 2-fold arms of ducal Saxony and Quedlinburg in ornate frame, date at top **Obv. Legend:** MO. NO. D-G. DORT. SOPHI **Rev:** Crowned imperial eagle, '4' in circle on breast **Rev. Legend:** DVCISS. SAX. ABBAT. QVEDLB **Note:** Klippe. Ref. D-28

Date	Mintage	VG	F	VF	XF	Unc
16Z1	—	30.00	60.00	125	250	—

KM# 32 12 KREUZER (Schreckenberger)
Silver **Ruler:** Dorothea Sophia **Obv:** Heart-shaped 2-fold arms of ducal Saxony and Quedlingburg, date above **Obv. Legend:** MO. NO. D-G. DORO. SO **Rev:** Crowned imperial eagle, '12' in circle on breast **Rev. Legend:** DUCIS. SA. ABBA. QUE **Note:** Varieties exist. Ref. D-29.

Date	Mintage	VG	F	VF	XF	Unc
1621	—	35.00	70.00	140	—	—

KM# 3 1/24 THALER (Groschen)

Silver **Ruler:** Dorothea **Obv:** 2-fold arms of Ducal and Electoral Saxony in circle **Obv. Legend:** MO. NO. D.G. DOROTHEÆ **Rev:** Imperial orb with Z4, date divided by cross at top **Rev. Legend:** DVC. SAX. AB. QVEDL **Note:** Varieties exist. Ref. D-25.

Date	Mintage	VG	F	VF	XF	Unc
1612	—	18.00	35.00	75.00	150	—
1614	—	18.00	35.00	75.00	150	—
1615 TE	—	18.00	35.00	75.00	150	—
1616 TE	—	18.00	35.00	75.00	150	—
1616	—	18.00	35.00	75.00	150	—
1617	—	18.00	35.00	75.00	150	—
1617/5 TE	—	18.00	35.00	75.00	150	—
1617 TE	—	18.00	35.00	75.00	150	—
1617 HL	—	18.00	35.00	75.00	150	—

KM# 18 1/24 THALER (Groschen)

Silver **Ruler:** Dorothea Sophia **Obv:** 2-fold arms of Ducal and Electoral Saxony in circle. **Obv. Legend:** MO. NO. D.G. DOROTHEÆ **Rev:** Imperial orb with Z4, date divided by cross at top **Rev. Legend:** DVC. SAX. AB. QVEDL **Note:** Varieties exist. Ref. D-30.

Date	Mintage	VG	F	VF	XF	Unc
1618 HL	—	18.00	35.00	75.00	150	—
1619 HL	—	18.00	35.00	75.00	150	—
1620 HL	—	18.00	35.00	75.00	150	—
1621 HL	—	18.00	35.00	75.00	150	—
1622 HL	—	18.00	35.00	75.00	150	—
ND HL	—	18.00	35.00	75.00	150	—

KM# 22 1/24 THALER (Groschen)

Silver **Ruler:** Dorothea Sophia **Obv:** 2-fold arms of ducal and electoral Saxony in circle, titles of Dorothea Sophia **Obv. Legend:** MO. NO. D.G. DOROTHEÆ **Rev:** Imperial orb with Z4, date divided by cross at top **Rev. Legend:** DVC. SAX. AB. QVEDL **Note:** Klippe. Ref. D-30.

Date	Mintage	VG	F	VF	XF	Unc
1620 HL	—	—	—	—	—	—
1622 HL	—	—	—	—	—	—

KM# 45 1/24 THALER (Groschen)

Silver **Ruler:** Anna Sophie I **Obv:** Crowned 6-fold arms with central shield of Quedlinburg divides mintmaster's initials. **Rev:** Imperial orb with 24 divides date **Rev. Legend:** MONETA . NOVA... **Note:** Ref. D-37.

Date	Mintage	VG	F	VF	XF	Unc
1675 GF	—	85.00	175	325	650	—
1676 GF	—	85.00	175	325	650	—

KM# 35 1/4 THALER

Silver, 30 mm. **Ruler:** Dorothea Sophia **Obv:** Manifold arms with central shield of Quedlinburg **Obv. Legend:** MO: NO: D:G: DOR: SOPH: DV: SA: A **Rev:** Crowned imperial eagle, orb on breast, date divided above **Rev. Legend:** FERDI: II. D:G: ROM: IMP: SEM: AVG

Date	Mintage	VG	F	VF	XF	Unc
16Z4	—	185	375	650	1,300	—

KM# 46 1/3 THALER (1/2 Gulden)

Silver **Ruler:** Anna Sophie I **Obv:** Crowned 6-fold arms with central shield of Quedlinburg divide date, value 1/3 in oval **Obv. Legend:** MONETA . NOVA... **Rev:** Crowned ornate script monogram **Rev. Legend:** BESCHAW. DAS. ZIEL. SAGE. NICHT. VIEL

Date	Mintage	VG	F	VF	XF	Unc
1675 GF	—	1,100	2,000	3,500	6,000	—

KM# 47 1/3 THALER (1/2 Gulden)

Silver **Ruler:** Anna Sophie I **Obv:** Bust left, titles of Anna Sophia I **Rev:** 6-fold arms with central shield of Quedlinburg, 3 helmets above, divide date

Date	Mintage	VG	F	VF	XF	Unc
1675 GF	—	1,100	2,000	3,500	6,000	—

KM# 36 1/2 THALER

Silver **Ruler:** Dorothea Sophia **Rev. Legend:** ... QVE **Note:** Dav. #5721. Similar to 1 Thaler, KM#37.2.

Date	Mintage	VG	F	VF	XF	Unc
1623 HL	—	—	—	—	—	—

KM# 48 1/2 THALER

Silver **Ruler:** Anna Sophie I **Obv:** Bust left in sprays **Rev:** Helmeted arms, date divided among helmets. **Note:** Dav. #5726. Similar to 1 Thaler, KM#55.

Date	Mintage	VG	F	VF	XF	Unc
1675 GF	—	—	—	—	—	—

KM# 49 1/2 THALER

Silver **Ruler:** Anna Sophie I **Subject:** 30th Anniversary of the Investiture of Anna Sophia I **Obv:** Bust left in sprays **Rev:** Helmeted arms with helmets dividing date **Note:** Dav. #5727. Similar to 1 Thaler, KM#55.

Date	Mintage	VG	F	VF	XF	Unc
1675	—	—	—	—	—	—

KM# 51 2/3 THALER (Gulden)

Silver **Ruler:** Anna Sophie I **Obv:** Bust left. **Obv. Legend:** ANNA SOPHIA: P:B:R:H:I:B:A:Z:Q:G:Z:V:V:S. **Rev:** 3 helmets above manifold arms, oval with value '2/3' below, date at end of legend. **Rev. Legend:** MONETA. NOVA. ARG. - DIOEC. QVEDLINB. **Note:** Dav. #773.

Date	Mintage	VG	F	VF	XF	Unc
1675 GF	—	250	500	900	1,750	—

KM# 54 2/3 THALER (Gulden)

Silver **Ruler:** Anna Sophie I **Obv:** Crowned ornate script monogram, crossed palm fronds below. **Obv. Inscription:** BESCHAW. DAS. ZIEL. SAGE. NICHT. VIEL. **Rev:** Crowned 6-fold arms with central shield of Quedlinburg, value '2/3' in oval below, date at end of legend. **Rev. Legend:** MONETA NOVA ARG: - DIOEC. QVEDLINB. **Note:** Dav. #776.

Date	Mintage	VG	F	VF	XF	Unc
1675 GF	—	100	200	425	—	—

KM# 52 2/3 THALER (Gulden)

Silver **Ruler:** Anna Sophie I **Obv:** Bust right, titles of Anna Sophia I **Note:** Dav. 774.

Date	Mintage	VG	F	VF	XF	Unc
1675 GF	—	500	900	1,750	—	—
1676 GF	—	500	900	1,750	—	—

KM# 61 2/3 THALER (Gulden)

Silver **Ruler:** Anna Sophie I **Obv:** Bust left, titles of Anna Sophia I **Rev:** Date divided by arms **Note:** Reference Dav. 775B.

Date	Mintage	VG	F	VF	XF	Unc
1676 HAR	—	135	225	325	650	—
1677 HAR	—	135	225	325	650	—

KM# 53 2/3 THALER (Gulden)

Silver **Ruler:** Anna Sophie I **Obv:** Bust left, titles of Anna Sophia I **Rev:** Crowned arms and date divided **Note:** Varieties exist. Reference Dav. 775A.

Date	Mintage	VG	F	VF	XF	Unc
1676 AH	—	135	225	325	650	—
1676 HAR	—	135	225	325	650	—
1676	—	135	225	325	650	—
1677 HAR	—	135	225	325	650	—

KM# 62 2/3 THALER (Gulden)

Silver **Ruler:** Anna Sophie I **Obv:** Crowned ornate script monogram, crossed palm fronds below. **Obv. Legend:** BESCHAW. DAS ZIEL. SAGE NICHT VIEL. **Rev:** Crowned 6-fold arms with central shield of Quedlinburg divide date and mintmaster's initials, value '2/3' in oval below. **Rev. Legend:** MONETA. NOVA. ARG. - DIOEC. QVEDLINB. **Note:** Dav. #777.

Date	Mintage	VG	F	VF	XF	Unc
1676 GF	—	85.00	140	235	475	—
1676 HIC	—	85.00	140	235	475	—

KM# 63 2/3 THALER (Gulden)

Silver **Ruler:** Anna Sophie I **Obv:** Bust right, titles of Anna Sophia I, date divided by arms **Rev:** Crowned ornate script monogram, date above **Rev. Legend:** BESCHAW. DAS. ZIEL. SAGE. NICHT. VIEL **Note:** Dav. #777A.

Date	Mintage	VG	F	VF	XF	Unc
1676 GF	—	—	—	—	—	—

KM# 64 2/3 THALER (Gulden)

Silver **Ruler:** Anna Sophie I **Obv:** Bust right, titles of Anna Sophia I, date divided by arms **Rev:** Crowned ornate script monogram, date above **Rev. Legend:** BESCHAW. DAS. ZIEL. SAGE. NICHT. VIEL **Note:** Mule; 2 different dates.

Date	Mintage	VG	F	VF	XF	Unc
1676//1677 GF	—	—	—	—	—	—

KM# 5 THALER

Silver **Ruler:** Dorothea **Obv:** Crowned imperial eagle with orb on breast, date above in legend **Rev:** Helmeted arms **Note:** Dav. #5718.

Date	Mintage	VG	F	VF	XF	Unc
1615 TE	—	725	1,300	2,300	2,900	—
1617/5 TE Rare	—	—	—	—	—	—

Note: UBS Gold & Numismatics Auction 57, 9-03, XF realized approximately $12,345

Date	Mintage	VG	F	VF	XF	Unc
1617 HL Rare	—	—	—	—	—	—

KM# 9 THALER

Silver **Ruler:** Dorothea **Subject:** Centennial of the Reformation **Obv:** 3 ornate helmets above manifold arms, date divided at top. **Obv. Legend:** DOROTHE: D:G. ABBATIS. - QVEDELB. DVCIS: SAXO. **Rev:** Full-length standing figure of Emperor Heinrich I (918-36) holding sword and orb, town view in background. **Rev. Legend:** HEINR AVG. D.G ROM IM SAX - DVX. ABB: QVEDLB: FVND. **Note:** Dav. #LS374; 28.50 grams - 29.37 grams.

Date	Mintage	VG	F	VF	XF	Unc
1617 HL	—	900	1,500	2,700	4,500	—
1617 HL/IH	—	900	1,500	2,700	4,500	—

KM# 26 THALER

Silver **Ruler:** Dorothea Sophia **Obv. Legend:** MATHI. D. G. ROM-IMP... **Rev. Legend:** MO. NO D. G. DOROT-SOP... **Note:** Dav.#5719.

Date	Mintage	VG	F	VF	XF	Unc
1618 HL	—	550	1,150	2,000	—	—

KM# 37.1 THALER

Silver **Ruler:** Dorothea Sophia **Rev. Legend:** ... QVED **Note:** Similar to KM#37.1.

Date	Mintage	VG	F	VF	XF	Unc
1623	—	600	1,200	2,200	—	—

KM# 37.2 THALER

Silver **Ruler:** Dorothea Sophia **Rev. Legend:** ... QVE **Note:** Dav. #5721.

Date	Mintage	VG	F	VF	XF	Unc
1623 HL	—	475	950	1,900	—	—

KM# 37.3 THALER

Silver **Ruler:** Dorothea Sophia **Obv:** 3 ornate helmets above manifold arms which divide mintmaster's initials. **Obv. Legend:** MO. NO. D.G. DOROT. SOPH. DV. SAX. A. QVED. **Rev:** Crowned imperial eagle, orb on breast, date divided at top. **Rev. Legend:** FERDI. II. D.G. ROM. IMP: SEMP: AVGV. **Note:** Similar to Dav. #5721.

Date	Mintage	VG	F	VF	XF	Unc
1623 HL	—	550	1,000	2,000	—	—

KM# 39 THALER

Silver **Ruler:** Dorothea Sophia **Rev. Legend:** ... AVGVS **Note:** Dav. #5722. Weight varies: 28.50-29.37 grams.

Date	Mintage	VG	F	VF	XF	Unc
1624	—	575	1,150	2,100	—	—
16Z9	—	575	1,150	2,100	—	—

KM# 40 THALER

Silver **Ruler:** Dorothea Sophia **Obv:** Similar to Dav. #5724 but legend: MON. NOV... **Rev:** Crowned arms, date below **Rev. Legend:** DVC. SAX. ABBAT... **Note:** Dav. #5723.

Date	Mintage	VG	F	VF	XF	Unc
1633 HL	—	775	1,400	2,400	—	—

KM# 44 THALER

Silver **Ruler:** Dorothea Sophia **Obv. Legend:** MONET. NOV... **Rev. Legend:** DVCIS. SAXON... **Note:** Dav. #5724.

Date	Mintage	VG	F	VF	XF	Unc
1634 HL	—	350	725	1,150	2,000	—

KM# 55 THALER

Silver **Ruler:** Anna Sophie I **Obv:** Bust left in sprays **Rev:** Helmeted arms with helmets dividing date **Note:** Dav. #5726.

Date	Mintage	VG	F	VF	XF	Unc
1675 GF Rare	—	—	—	—	—	—

KM# 56 THALER

Silver **Ruler:** Anna Sophie I **Subject:** 30th Anniversary of Investiture of Anna Sophia **Obv:** Bust left **Rev:** Nine-line inscription **Note:** Dav. #1675.

Date	Mintage	VG	F	VF	XF	Unc
1675 Rare	—	—	—	—	—	—

KM# 69 THALER

Silver **Ruler:** Anna Sophie I **Obv:** Large crown above shield with Thuringian lion rampant left holding crossed Quedlinburg fish, date divided at left and right. **Obv. Legend:** ANNA. SOPHIA. P: B: R: H: I: B: A: Z: Q: G: Z: V: V: S. **Rev:** Three medallions, 2 above 1, each with tree, town view and legend, floral sprays around. **Note:** Dav. #5728.

Date	Mintage	VG	F	VF	XF	Unc
1677	—	1,150	2,100	3,900	6,600	—

KM# 11 1-1/2 THALER

Silver **Ruler:** Dorothea **Subject:** Centennial of the Reformation **Obv:** 3 ornate helmets above manifold arms, date divided at top **Rev:** Full-length standing figure of Emperor Heinrich I holding sword and orb, town view in background **Note:** Similar to 2 Thaler, Dav. #LS373.

Date	Mintage	VG	F	VF	XF	Unc
1617 HL	—	2,100	3,500	5,600	9,500	—

KM# 12 2 THALER

57.4000 g., Silver **Ruler:** Dorothea **Subject:** Centennial of the Reformation **Obv:** 3 ornate helmets above manifold arms, date divided at top. **Obv. Legend:** DOROTHE. D:G. ABBATIS - QVEDELB. DVCIS: SAXO. **Rev:** Full-length standing figure of Emperor Heinrich I (918-36) holding sword and orb, town view in background. **Rev. Legend:** HEINR: AVG. D:G. RO. IM: SAX - DVX. ABB: QVEDLB: FVND-AT. **Note:** Dav. #LS373. Similar to 1 Thaler, KM#9.

Date	Mintage	VG	F	VF	XF	Unc
1617 HL/IH	—	2,650	4,300	6,600	10,000	—

KM# 57 2 THALER

57.4000 g., Silver **Ruler:** Anna Sophie I **Obv:** Bust left in sprays **Rev:** Helmeted arms with helmet dividing date, G-F below **Note:** Dav. #5725.

Date	Mintage	VG	F	VF	XF	Unc
1675 GF Rare	—	—	—	—	—	—

TRADE COINAGE

KM# 8 DUCAT

Gold **Ruler:** Dorothea **Obv:** Full-length facing figure of St. Servatius divides legend **Obv. Legend:** S — S DOROT. D.G. DVC. — SAX. AB. QVED **Rev:** Manifold arms with central shield of Quedlingburg, date divided at top **Rev. Legend:** V.D.M. — I. Æ **Note:** Klippe. Ref. D-24.

Date	Mintage	VG	F	VF	XF	Unc
1616 Rare	—	—	—	—	—	—

KM# 7 DUCAT

Gold **Ruler:** Dorothea **Obv:** Full-length facing figure of St. Servatius divides legend **Obv. Legend:** S — S DOROT. D.G. DVC. — SAX. AB. QVED **Rev:** Manifold arms with central shield of Quedlingburg, date divided at top **Rev. Legend:** V.D.M. — I. Æ **Note:** Ref. D-24.

Date	Mintage	VG	F	VF	XF	Unc
1616 Rare	—	—	—	—	—	—

KM# 20 DUCAT

3.5000 g., 0.9860 Gold 0.1109 oz. AGW **Ruler:** Dorothea Sophia **Obv:** Crowned arms of Quedlinburg in inner circle, titles of Dorothea Sophia **Rev:** Crowned arms of Saxony in inner circle **Note:** Fr. #2445.

Date	Mintage	VG	F	VF	XF	Unc
ND	—	1,450	2,900	5,000	9,200	—

KM# 14 8 DUCAT

26.6400 g., 0.9860 Gold 0.8445 oz. AGW **Ruler:** Dorothea **Subject:** Centennial of the Reformation **Obv:** Helmeted arms, titles of Dorothea **Rev:** Heinrich I standing with sword and orb, city in background **Note:** Struck with 2 Thaler dies, Dav. #LS373.

Date	Mintage	VG	F	VF	XF	Unc
1617 HL Rare	—	—	—	—	—	—

Note: CNG - Triton X Auction, 1-07, XF realized approximately $29,000. Peus Auction 373, 10-02, VF realized approximately $6,885.

KM# 17 10 DUCAT

35.0000 g., 0.9860 Gold 1.1095 oz. AGW **Ruler:** Dorothea **Subject:** Centennial of the Reformation **Note:** Fr. #2443, similar to 8 Ducat, Fr. #2444. Struck with 2 Thaler dies, KM #12.

Date	Mintage	VG	F	VF	XF	Unc
1617 HL Rare	—	—	—	—	—	—

KM# 16 10 DUCAT

Gold **Ruler:** Dorothea **Subject:** Centennial of the Reformation **Note:** Fr. #2443. Struck from the same dies as 1 Thaler, KM#9.

Date	Mintage	VG	F	VF	XF	Unc
1617 HL Rare	—	—	—	—	—	—

TOWN

REGULAR COINAGE

KM# 70 3 PFENNIG (Dreier)

Copper **Obv:** 'Q' in circle divides date **Rev:** Value 'III' in circle

Date	Mintage	VG	F	VF	XF	Unc
(16)62 Rare	—	—	—	—	—	—

RANTZAU

(Ranzau)

The small county of Rantzau was situated in Holstein and its seat was the castle of Breitenburg, located just a few miles south of Itzehoe and ten miles (17km) north-northeast from Glückstadt on the Elbe River. The ruling family of Rantzau is mentioned in sources as early as 1362, which refer back to a certain Schalko Rantzau who was Burggraf of Leisnig in Saxony in 1283. Meanwhile, the rule of Count Adolf II of Holstein (1128-64) saw the beginnings of a Saxon colonization of his territories. It seems that some members of the Rantzau family relocated to that region during the following century or two. Johann Rantzau (1492-1565) built the castle of Breitenburg, the foundation stone of which bears the date 1501. His great-grandson, Christian, was granted the title of count and the mint right by Emperor Ferdinand III in 1650. The line of counts became extinct in 1734, but other branches of the family continued in widely separate territories – Leisnig, Bohemia, Mecklenburg, Prussia, Hannover, Württemberg, Oldenburg, Denmark and the Netherlands. Breitenburg passed in marriage to Kastell-Rüdenhausen and eventually back to the Rantzau-Ahrensburg branch of the family.

RULERS

Gerhard, 1598-1627
Christian, 1627-1663
Detlef, 1663-1697
Christian Detlef, 1697-1721
Wilhelm Adolf, 1721-1734

Initial	Date	Name
(a)= 	1635-68	Matthias Freude der Ältere in Hamburg

ARMS

Usually 4-fold arms (quartered) with a central shield, Rantzau in quarters 1 and 4, divided vertically with right side shaded; quarters 2 and 3, for Burggrafs of Leisnig, are divided by diagonal bar with six lozenges (Diamonds) on each side of bar; central shield has rampant lion left for lordship of Penik in Bohemia.

REFERENCE

M = Adolph Meyer, ***Die Münzen und Medaillen der Herren von Rantzau***, Vienna, 1882.

COUNTSHIP

REGULAR COINAGE

KM# 4 2/3 THALER (Gulden)

Silver **Ruler:** Detlef **Obv:** Bust right, value '2/3' in oval at bottom. **Obv. Legend:** DETHLEF. S. R. I. C. I. R(ANZOVV). ET(&) L. D. I. B. **Rev:** Large crown above 4-fold arms in baroque frame with central shield of Penik lion, date divided in margin at bottom. **Rev. Legend:** RECTE. FACIENDO. NEMINEM. TIMEAS. **Note:** Dav. #778, Meyer 9-14.

Date	Mintage	VG	F	VF	XF	Unc
1689	—	750	1,200	2,000	3,250	—

KM# 2 THALER

Silver **Ruler:** Christian I **Obv:** Bust right in circle. **Obv. Legend:** CHRISTIAN: COM: IN: RANTZOU. DOM: IN. BREITENB:. **Rev:** 4-fold arms with central shield of Penik lion, mintmaster's symbol at beginning and date at end of legend. **Rev. Legend:** DEO DVCE COMITE FORTVNA. **Note:** Dav. #7290, Meyer 7, 8.

Date	Mintage	VG	F	VF	XF	Unc
1656 (a)	—	4,500	7,500	12,500	22,000	—
1657 (a)	—	4,200	7,200	11,500	20,000	—

TRADE COINAGE

KM# 1 DUCAT

3.5000 g., 0.9860 Gold 0.1109 oz. AGW **Ruler:** Christian I **Obv:** Bust right in circle. **Obv. Legend:** CHRISTIAN. COM. IN RANTZ. DOM. IN BREITENB. **Rev:** 4-fold arms with central shield of Penik lion divide date near bottom, 3 ornate helmets above. **Rev. Legend:** DEO DVCE COMITE FORTVNA. **Note:** Fr. #2449, Meyer 1, 2, 4, 5.

Date	Mintage	VG	F	VF	XF	Unc
1655 (a)	—	1,800	3,750	7,500	12,500	—
1656 (a)	—	1,800	3,750	7,500	12,500	—
1658 (a)	—	1,800	3,750	7,500	12,500	—

KM# 5 DUCAT

3.5000 g., 0.9860 Gold 0.1109 oz. AGW **Ruler:** Detlef **Obv:** Bust right. **Obv. Legend:** DETHLEF. S. R. I. C. R. ET L. D. I. B. **Rev:** 4-fold arms with central shield of Penik lion, 3 ornate helmets above divide date. **Rev. Legend:** RECTE. FACIENDO. NEMINEM. TIMEAS. **Note:** Fr. #2450, Meyer 6.

Date	Mintage	VG	F	VF	XF	Unc
1689 Rare	—	—	—	—	—	—

Note: Künker Auction 112, 6-06, XF realized approximately $38,915.

KM# 3 2 DUCAT

7.0000 g., 0.9860 Gold 0.2219 oz. AGW **Ruler:** Christian I **Obv:** Bust right in circle, titles of Christian I. **Rev:** 4-fold arms with central shield of Penik lion divide date near bottom, 3 ornate helmets above. **Rev. Legend:** DEO DVCE COMITE FORTVNA. **Note:** Fr. #2448, Meyer 3.

Date	Mintage	VG	F	VF	XF	Unc
1656 (a) Rare	—	—	—	—	—	—

RATZEBURG

A countship in Westphalia surrounded by the bishoprics of Minden on the northeast, Osnabruck on the northwest, Munster on the west, the lordships of Rheda and Rechenberg and the countship of Rietberg on the southwest, and the countship of Lippe on the southeast. The dynasty of rulers emerged in the late 11th century. The countship of Berg was obtained through marriage in the early 14th century, then Ravensberg itself passed in marriage to the duchy of Julich later in the same century. In the first part of the 16th century, these territories were joined to the duchy of Cleveland the county of Mark by marriage. The coinage of each of these principalities has been listed elsewhere. When the last ruler of Julich-Cleve-Berg-Mark-Ravensberg died without heir in 1609, it set off the greatest controversy of the age and was one of the disputes leading to the general conflagration known as the Thirty Years' War (1618-1648).Brandenburg-Prussia and Pfalz-Neuburg laid claim to Ravensberg and the two struck a joint coinage for the countship from 1609 until 1614. Brandenburg controlled the countship from 1614 to 1623, striking coins for the territory it regarded as its own. However, from 1623 to 1647, while Brandenburg was occupied with the war against the Empire farther to the east, Pfalz-Neuburg maintained a presence in Ravensberg. Beginning in 1647, Brandenburg obtained permanent control of Ravensberg and struck a separate coinage for the countship until 1667. The chief mint of Ravensberg was Bielefeld.

RULERS

Johann Wilhelm, Herzog von Jülich-Kleve-Berg 1592-1609
Johann Sigismund of Brandenburg-Prussia, 1614-1619
Georg Wilhelm of Brandenburg-Prussia, 1619-1623
Wolfgang Wilhelm, 1623-1647
Friedrich Wilhelm of Brandenburg-Prussia, 1647-1688

MINT OFFICIALS' INITIALS

Bielefeld

Initial	Date	Name
(a)= or	1591-1616	Peter Busch
	?-1614	Ernst Schroder, warden
	1615-22	Anton Hoyer at Emmerich (Cleve)
	1615-38	Henning Brauns, warden
	1616-19, 27-29	Georg Kuhne
	1620-27	Julius Billerbeck
(b)=	1629-54	Jobst Koch
	1654-66	Johann Koch
	1655-56	Jobst Dietrich Koch

ARMS

3 chevrons (Ravensberg), usually in combination with the arms of the other four principalities, Ravensberg is in the lower right-hand division lion rampant left (Pfalz) scepter vertical (Brandenburg), usually with electoral cap above.

REFERENCE

S = Ewald Stange, **Geld- und Münzgeschichte der Grafschaft Ravensberg**, Münster, 1951.

BISHOPRIC

REGULAR COINAGE

KM# 18 3 PFENNIG
Silver, 13 mm. **Ruler:** August **Obv:** Shield of Ratzeburg arms, miter above, crozier behind **Rev:** Imperial orb with 3, cross divides date at upper left and right **Note:** Ref. B-28; W-877. Kipper issue.

Date	Mintage	VG	F	VF	XF	Unc
1620	—	100	225	375	650	—

KM# 19 3 PFENNIG
0.5200 g., Silver, 15-16 mm. **Ruler:** August **Obv:** Shield of 2-fold arms divided vertically, crenelated gate at left, crozier at right, miter above **Rev:** Imperial orb with 3, cross divides date at upper left and right **Note:** Ref. B-29. Kipper issue.

Date	Mintage	VG	F	VF	XF	Unc
1620	—	125	250	375	625	—

KM# 37 1/24 THALER (Groschen)
Silver, 21-22 mm. **Ruler:** Christian I Ludwig **Obv:** Crowned CL monogram in chain of order **Obv. Legend:** FVRSTL RA - TZEBVRGI: **Rev:** 4-line inscription with date, in circle **Rev. Legend:** LANDTMVNTZ. **Rev. Inscription:** 24 / REICHS / DALER / (date) **Mint:** Ratzeburg **Note:** Ref. K-637.

Date	Mintage	VG	F	VF	XF	Unc
1672 (f)	—	70.00	140	275	450	—
1673 (f)	—	70.00	140	275	450	—

KM# 10 2 SCHILLING (1/16 Thaler)
Silver Weight varies: 1.92-1.95g., 23-24 mm. **Ruler:** August **Obv:** Shield of 4-fold arms, with central shield of Ratzeburg, in circle **Obv. Legend:** AVGVSTVS. D. G. P. E. RATZEB. **Rev:** Intertwined DS, date at end of legend **Rev. Legend:** DVX. BRVNOVIC. E. L. **Mint:** Schönberg **Note:** Ref. W-874; B-8, 21, 25. Varieties exist. U's in place of V's on some examples.

Date	Mintage	VG	F	VF	XF	Unc
1617 (c)	—	80.00	165	250	450	—
1618 (c)	—	80.00	165	250	450	—
(16)20 (d)	—	80.00	165	250	450	—
(16)Z0 (d)	—	80.00	165	250	450	—

KM# 11 2 SCHILLING (1/16 Thaler)
Silver, 23 mm. **Ruler:** August **Obv:** Shield of 4-fold arms in circle **Obv. Legend:** AVGVSTVS. D. G. P. E. RATZEB. **Rev:** Intertwined DS, date at end of legend **Rev. Legend:** DVX. BRVNOVIC. E. L. **Mint:** Schönberg **Note:** Ref. W-875.

Date	Mintage	VG	F	VF	XF	Unc
(16)17 (c)	—	65.00	135	200	325	—
(16)18 (c)	—	65.00	135	299	325	—
(16)19 (d)	—	65.00	135	299	325	—

KM# 8 2 SCHILLING (1/16 Thaler)
1.8300 g., Silver, 24 mm. **Ruler:** August **Obv:** Shield of 8-fold arms with central shield of Ratzeburg, 3 ornate helmets above **Obv. Legend:** AVGV - P. E. RA. **Rev:** Intertwined DS, date at the end of legend **Rev. Legend:** DVX. BRVNOVIC. E. L. **Mint:** Schönberg **Note:** Ref. W-871, 872.

Date	Mintage	VG	F	VF	XF	Unc
1617 (a)	—	90.00	175	275	550	—

KM# 9 2 SCHILLING (1/16 Thaler)
Silver, 24 mm. **Ruler:** August **Obv:** Shield of 6-fold arms with central shield of Ratzeburg **Obv. Legend:** AVGV - P. E. RA. **Rev:** Intertwined DS, date at end of legend **Rev. Legend:** DVX. BRVNOVIC. E. L. **Mint:** Schönberg **Note:** Ref. W-873.

Date	Mintage	VG	F	VF	XF	Unc
1617 (c)	—	90.00	175	275	550	—

KM# 20 2 SCHILLING (1/16 Thaler)
Silver, 23 mm. **Ruler:** August **Obv:** Shield of 2-fold arms divided vertically, crenelated gate on left, crozier on right **Rev:** Intertwined DS, date at end of legend **Mint:** Schönberg **Note:** Ref. W-876.

Date	Mintage	VG	F	VF	XF	Unc
1620 (d)	—	90.00	175	275	550	—

KM# 25 1/16 THALER
3.1300 g., Silver, 24 mm. **Ruler:** August **Obv:** Shield of 4-fold arms, with central shield of Ratzeburg, in circle **Obv. Legend:** AVGVSTVS. D: G. P: E: P: RA. D: B. E: LV: **Rev:** 4-line inscription with date in circle **Rev. Legend:** REICHS. SCHROTS. VN. KORNS. **Rev. Inscription:** 16 / REICHS / DALER / (date) **Mint:** Schönberg **Note:** Ref. B-34.

Date	Mintage	VG	F	VF	XF	Unc
1623	—	1,300	1,900	2,500	4,000	—

KM# 27 1/2 REICHSORT (1/8 Thaler)
Silver, 25 mm. **Ruler:** August **Obv:** Ornate helmet with horse crest **Rev:** 4-line inscription with mintmaster's symbol **Mint:** Ratzeburg **Note:** Ref. W-870A.

Date	Mintage	VG	F	VF	XF	Unc
16Z3 (e)	—	—	—	—	—	—

KM# 29 1/2 THALER
Silver Weight varies: 14.27-14.40g., 37 mm. **Ruler:** August **Obv:** Shield of 8-fold arms, with central shield of Ratzeburg, 3 ornate helmets above **Obv. Legend:** AVGVSTVS. D: G. - P. EP. RA: D: B: E: L. **Rev:** Fully-armored figure on horseback to right, date at end of legend, mintmaster's symbol before horse **Rev. Legend:** PATRIIS - VIRTVTIBVS. **Mint:** Ratzeburg **Note:** Ref. W-870.

Date	Mintage	VG	F	VF	XF	Unc
16Z3 (e)	—	1,100	2,000	3,500	—	—

KM# 30 1/2 THALER
14.2700 g., Silver **Ruler:** August **Obv:** 8-fold arms of Brunswick with central shield of Ratzeburg, 3 ornate shields above **Obv. Legend:** AVGVSTVS. D: G. - P. EP. RA: D: B: E: L. **Rev:** Fully-armored figure on horseback to right, date at end of legend, mintmaster's symbol below horse **Rev. Legend:** PATRIIS - VIRTVTIBVS. **Mint:** Ratzeburg **Note:** Ref. Welter 870.

Date	Mintage	VG	F	VF	XF	Unc
16Z3 (e)	—	—	—	—	—	—

KM# 35 2/3 THALER (Gulden)
Silver, 36-37 mm. **Ruler:** Christian I Ludwig **Obv:** Ornate intertwined CLDM monogram, large crown above held by 2 angels, two chains of order suspended below **Obv. Legend:** CHRISTIANUS. - LUDOVICUS. D. G. **Rev:** Large cross in circle, (2/3) in oval below, date at end of legend **Rev. Legend:** PRINCEPS. RATZE. - BURGENSIS. **Mint:** Ratzeburg **Note:** Ref. K-636; Dav. 779.

Date	Mintage	VG	F	VF	XF	Unc
1671 (f)	—	1,800	3,000	4,000	6,000	—
1672 (f)	—	1,800	3,000	4,000	6,000	—

KM# 13 THALER
28.5000 g., Silver, 43 mm. **Ruler:** August **Obv:** Spanish shield of 8-fold arms with central shield of Ratzeburg, 3 ornate helmets above **Obv. Legend:** AVGVSTVS. D: G: - P: EP: RA: D: B: E:L: **Rev:** Fully-armored figure of bishop on horseback riding to right,

date at end of legend under horse's front hooves **Rev. Legend:** PATRIIS - UI - RTUTIBUS. **Mint:** Schönberg **Note:** Ref. W-869; Dav. 5729. Varieties exist.

Date	Mintage	VG	F	VF	XF	Unc
1617 (b)	—	250	450	750	1,250	—
1620 (b)	—	250	450	750	1,250	—

KM# 14 THALER

28.5000 g., Silver, 43 mm. **Ruler:** August **Obv:** Spanish shield of 8-fold arms, with central shield of Ratzeburg, 3 ornate helmets above **Obv. Legend:** AVGVSTVS. D: G: - P: EP: RA: D: B: E: L: **Rev:** Full-armored figure of bishop on horseback galloping to right, date at end of legend, under horse **Rev. Legend:** PATRI - IS - VIRTVTIBVS. - ANNO. **Mint:** Schönberg **Note:** Ref. W-869; Dav. 5730.

Date	Mintage	VG	F	VF	XF	Unc
1617 (b)	—	250	450	750	1,250	—

KM# 31 THALER

28.5000 g., Silver, 43 mm. **Ruler:** August **Obv:** Spanish shield of 8-fold arms, with central shield of Ratzeburg, 3 ornate helmets above **Obv. Legend:** AVGVSTVS. D: G. - P. E: P: RA: D. B: E: L: **Rev:** Fully-armored figure of bishop on horseback riding to right, dated divided between rear and front hooves of horse, mintmaster's symbol below bishop's stirrup **Rev. Legend:** PATRIIS - UI - RTUTIBUS. **Note:** Ref. W-869; Dav. 5731. Varieties exist.

Date	Mintage	VG	F	VF	XF	Unc
1623 (e)	—	275	500	900	1,650	—

KM# 40 THALER

Silver, 44-45 mm. **Ruler:** Christian I Ludwig **Obv:** Draped bust to right **Obv. Legend:** CHRISTIAN: LVDOV: D. G. PRINC: RATZEBVRG: **Rev:** Spanish shield of 6-fold arms, with central shield, 2 chains of order suspended below, angels hold large crown above, which divides date **Rev. Legend:** SI DEVS PRO NOBIS - QVIS CONTRA NOS. **Mint:** Ratzeburg **Note:** Ref. K-635; Dav. 7039.

Date	Mintage	VG	F	VF	XF	Unc
1672 Rare	—	—	—	—	—	—

KM# 41 2 THALER

Silver, 44-45 mm. **Ruler:** Christian I Ludwig **Obv:** Draped bust to right **Obv. Legend:** CHRISTIAN: LVDOV: D. G. PRINC: RATZEBVRG: **Rev:** Spanish shield of 6-fold arms, with central shield, 2 chains of order suspended below, angels hold large crown above, which divides date **Rev. Legend:** SI DEVS PRO NOBIS - QVIS CONTRA NOS. **Mint:** Ratzeburg **Note:** Ref. K-635; Dav. A7039. Struck on thick flan from Thaler dies, KM#40.

Date	Mintage	VG	F	VF	XF	Unc
1672 Rare	—	—	—	—	—	—

TRADE COINAGE

KM# 16 GOLDGULDEN

Gold, 21 mm. **Ruler:** August **Obv:** Bishop on horseback to right **Rev:** Shield of 8-fold arms, date at end of legend **Mint:** Schönberg **Note:** Ref. W-867; Fr. 2451.

Date	Mintage	VG	F	VF	XF	Unc
1618 (c) Rare	—	—	—	—	—	—

KM# 22 DUCAT

3.5000 g., 0.9860 Gold Weight varies: 3.44-3.49g. 0.1109 oz. AGW, 22.5-23 mm. **Ruler:** August **Obv:** Full-length armored figure of bishop holding baton **Obv. Legend:** AUGUST9 D. G. - PO - EPIS. RACEBUR. **Rev:** Crowned oval shield of 8-fold arms with central shield of Ratzeburg **Rev. Legend:** DUX. BRUNSUI. ET. LUNEBURGE. **Note:** Ref. W-868; Fr. 2452.

Date	Mintage	VG	F	VF	XF	Unc
ND(ca1620) HS	—	—	6,500	10,000	15,000	25,000

RAVENSBERG

A countship in Westphalia surrounded by the bishoprics of Minden on the northeast, Osnabruck on the northwest, Munster on the west, the lordships of Rheda and Rechenberg and the countship of Rietberg on the southwest, and the countship of Lippe on the southeast. The dynasty of rulers emerged in the late 11th century. The countship of Berg was obtained through marriage in the early 14th century, then Ravensberg itself passed in marriage to the duchy of Julich later in the same century. In the first part of the 16th century, these territories were joined to the duchy of Cleveland the county of Mark by marriage. The coinage of each of these principalities has been listed elsewhere. When the last ruler of Julich-Cleve-Berg-Mark-Ravensberg died without heir in 1609, it set off the greatest controversy of the age and was one of the disputes leading to the general conflagration known as the Thirty Years' War (1618-1648).Brandenburg-Prussia and Pfalz-Neuburg laid claim to Ravensberg and the two struck a joint coinage for the countship from 1609 until 1614. Brandenburg controlled the countship from 1614 to 1623, striking coins for the territory it regarded as its own. However, from 1623 to 1647, while Brandenburg was occupied with the war against the Empire farther to the east, Pfalz-Neuburg maintained a presence in Ravensberg. Beginning in 1647, Brandenburg obtained permanent control of Ravensberg and struck a separate coinage for the countship until 1667. The chief mint of Ravensberg was Bielefeld.

RULERS

Johann Wilhelm, Herzog von Jülich-Kleve-Berg 1592-1609
Johann Sigismund of Brandenburg-Prussia, 1614-1619
Georg Wilhelm of Brandenburg-Prussia, 1619-1623
Wolfgang Wilhelm, 1623-1647
Friedrich Wilhelm of Brandenburg-Prussia, 1647-1688

MINT OFFICIALS' INITIALS

Bielefeld

Initial	Date	Name
(a)=	1591-1616	Peter Busch
	?-1614	Ernst Schroder, warden
	1615-22	Anton Hoyer at Emmerich (Cleve)
	1615-38	Henning Brauns, warden
	1616-19, 27-29	Georg Kuhne
	1620-27	Julius Billerbeck
(b)=	1629-54	Jobst Koch
	1654-66	Johann Koch
	1655-56	Jobst Dietrich Koch

ARMS

3 chevrons (Ravensberg), usually in combination with the arms of the other four principalities, Ravensberg is in the lower right-hand division lion rampant left (Pfalz) scepter vertical (Brandenburg), usually with electoral cap above.

REFERENCE

S = Ewald Stange, **Geld- und Münzgeschichte der Grafschaft Ravensberg**, Münster, 1951.

COUNTSHIP

REGULAR COINAGE

KM# 20 PFENNIG

0.7520 g., Copper, 15 mm. **Ruler:** Georg Wilhelm **Obv:** Ravensberg arms in ornamented shield **Obv. Legend:** NVMVS RAVENSBERG **Rev:** Value I in ornamented square, date above **Mint:** Bielefeld **Note:** Ref. S-164.

Date	Mintage	VG	F	VF	XF	Unc
1620	—	24.00	45.00	75.00	155	—

KM# 21 PFENNIG

0.7520 g., Copper, 15 mm. **Ruler:** Georg Wilhelm **Obv:** Ravensberg arms in ornamented shield **Obv. Legend:** NVM - RAV **Rev:** Value large I divides date in ornamented circle **Mint:** Bielefeld **Note:** Ref. S-165.

Date	Mintage	VG	F	VF	XF	Unc
16Z0	—	24.00	45.00	75.00	155	—

KM# 22 2 PFENNIG

1.2890 g., Copper, 17 mm. **Ruler:** Georg Wilhelm **Obv:** Ravensberg arms in ornamented shield **Obv. Legend:** NVMMVS RAVENSBERG **Rev:** Value II in ornamented square, date above **Mint:** Bielefeld **Note:** Ref. S-163.

Date	Mintage	VG	F	VF	XF	Unc
1620	—	24.00	45.00	75.00	155	—

KM# 26 2 PFENNIG

1.2890 g., Copper, 17 mm. **Ruler:** Georg Wilhelm **Obv:** Ravensberg arms in ornamented shield **Obv. Legend:** NVMVS RAVENSPVRG **Rev:** Value II divides date in ornamented circle **Mint:** Bielefeld **Note:** Ref. S-169.

Date	Mintage	VG	F	VF	XF	Unc
16Z1	—	24.00	45.00	75.00	155	—

KM# 23 3 PFENNIG

1.7190 g., Copper, 19 mm. **Ruler:** Georg Wilhelm **Obv:** Ravensberg arms in ornamented shield **Obv. Legend:** NVMMVS RAVENSPVRG **Rev:** Value III divides date in ornamented circle **Mint:** Bielefeld **Note:** Ref. S-162.

Date	Mintage	VG	F	VF	XF	Unc
1620	—	27.00	55.00	110	225	—

KM# 27 3 PFENNIG

1.7190 g., Copper, 18 mm. **Ruler:** Georg Wilhelm **Obv:** Ravensberg arms in ornamented shield **Obv. Legend:** NVMMVS RAVENSPVRG **Rev:** Date divided between the letters of the value III, all in ornamented circle **Mint:** Bielefeld **Note:** Ref. S-168.

Date	Mintage	VG	F	VF	XF	Unc
16Z1	—	33.00	65.00	130	260	—

KM# 57 3 PFENNIG

Copper, 20 mm. **Ruler:** Friedrich Wilhelm **Obv:** Scepter with electoral hat above divides date **Obv. Legend:** RAVENSB. LANT. MVN. **Rev:** Value III in ornamented square **Mint:** Bielefeld **Note:** Ref. S-251, 252. Varieties exist.

Date	Mintage	VG	F	VF	XF	Unc
1655	—	20.00	40.00	75.00	155	—

KM# 58 3 PFENNIG

Copper, 20 mm. **Ruler:** Friedrich Wilhelm **Obv:** Scepter with electoral hat above **Obv. Legend:** RAVENSB. LANDT. MVNTZ. **Rev:** Value III in ornamented square **Mint:** Bielefeld

Date	Mintage	VG	F	VF	XF	Unc
ND(1655)	—	16.00	33.00	50.00	100	—

KM# 24 6 PFENNIG

2.5790 g., Copper, 18-20 mm. **Ruler:** Georg Wilhelm **Obv:** Ravensberg arms in ornamented shield **Obv. Legend:** NVMMVS. RAVENSPVRG. **Rev:** Large value VI, date above, in ornamented circle **Mint:** Bielefeld **Note:** Ref. S-161, 167. Varieties exist.

Date	Mintage	VG	F	VF	XF	Unc
1620	—	18.00	35.00	60.00	125	—
16Z1	—	18.00	35.00	60.00	125	—

KM# 59 6 PFENNIG

Copper, 19-21 mm. **Ruler:** Friedrich Wilhelm **Obv:** Scepter, with electoral hat above, divides date **Obv. Legend:** RAVENSB. LANT. MUNT(Z). **Rev:** Value VI in ornamented square **Mint:** Bielefeld **Note:** Ref. S-250.

Date	Mintage	VG	F	VF	XF	Unc
1655	—	18.00	35.00	60.00	125	—

KM# 25 12 PFENNIG (1 Schilling)

4.4060 g., Copper, 26-27 mm. **Ruler:** Georg Wilhelm **Obv:** Ravensberg arms in ornamented shield **Obv. Legend:**

NVMMVS. RAVENSPVRG(ENSI). **Rev:** XII with date above in ornamented circle **Mint:** Bielefeld **Note:** Ref. S-160, 166. Varieties exist.

Date	Mintage	VG	F	VF	XF	Unc
1620	—	40.00	85.00	150	265	—
16Z1	—	30.00	65.00	120	240	—

KM# 60 12 PFENNIG (1 Schilling)

Copper **Ruler:** Friedrich Wilhelm **Obv:** Scepter, with electoral hat above, divides date **Obv. Legend:** RAVENSB. LANT. MVNT(Z). **Rev:** Value XII in ornamented square **Mint:** Bielefeld **Note:** Ref. S#245-49. Varieties exist. Most examples of this type have a small countermark of Ravensberg arms on obverse.

Date	Mintage	VG	F	VF	XF	Unc
1655	—	24.00	45.00	85.00	170	—
1663	—	24.00	45.00	85.00	170	—

KM# 29.1 KORTLING (6 Heller-3 Pfennig-1/4 Mariengroschen)

0.7310 g., 0.1780 Silver Weight varies: 0.45-0.695g. 0.0042 oz. ASW, 17 mm. **Ruler:** Wolfgang Wilhelm **Obv:** Shield of 5-fold arms **Obv. Legend:** MO. N(O). D. (I.) C. E. M. C. RA(V). **Rev:** Imperial orb with 6, date at end of legend **Rev. Legend:** IN. DEO. SP(E)(S). ME(A). **Mint:** Bielefeld **Note:** Ref. S#200-03, 205. Varieties exist.

Date	Mintage	VG	F	VF	XF	Unc
1629 (b)	6,400	27.00	55.00	85.00	190	—
1630 (b)	25,600	27.00	55.00	85.00	190	—
163Z (b)	—	27.00	55.00	85.00	190	—
1634	1,280	27.00	55.00	85.00	190	—
ND(1635)	—	27.00	55.00	85.00	190	—

KM# 29.2 KORTLING (6 Heller-3 Pfennig-1/4 Mariengroschen)

0.6960 g., 0.2050 Silver Weight varies: 0.63-0.685g. 0.0046 oz. ASW, 17 mm. **Ruler:** Wolfgang Wilhelm **Obv:** Shield of 5-fold arms **Obv. Legend:** MO. NO. D. I. C. EMC. RAV. **Rev:** Imperial orb with 6, date at end of legend **Rev. Legend:** IN DEO SPS MEA. **Mint:** Bielefeld **Note:** Ref. S-204.

Date	Mintage	VG	F	VF	XF	Unc
1643 (b)	—	—	—	—	—	—

KM# 30 KORTLING (6 Heller-3 Pfennig-1/4 Mariengroschen)

0.6960 g., 0.2050 Silver Weight varies: 0.455-0.667g. 0.0046 oz. ASW, 17 mm. **Ruler:** Friedrich Wilhelm **Obv:** Shield of 5-fold arms with shield of scepter arms in lower center **Obv. Legend:** MO. NO. EL. BR(A)(N). B. I. C. M. **Rev:** Imperial orb with 6 **Rev. Legend:** S. P. D. CO(.)M. RA. D. IN. R. **Mint:** Bielefeld **Note:** Ref. S#242-44. Varieties exist.

Date	Mintage	VG	F	VF	XF	Unc
ND(1650) (b)	27,552	27.00	55.00	90.00	185	—
ND(1650)	Inc. above	27.00	55.00	90.00	185	—

KM# 35 MATTIER (1/2 Mariengroschen)

0.9750 g., 0.3150 Silver Weight varies: 0.82-0.95g. 0.0099 oz. ASW, 18 mm. **Ruler:** Wolfgang Wilhelm **Obv:** 5-line inscription with date **Obv. Inscription:** EIN / MATTH / IER. RAV / ENSPV / (date) **Rev:** Madonna and Child **Rev. Legend:** MARIA. MA. DOMINI. **Mint:** Bielefeld **Note:** Ref. S-198.

Date	Mintage	VG	F	VF	XF	Unc
1630 (b)	—	—	—	—	—	—

KM# 47 MATTIER (1/2 Mariengroschen)

0.9750 g., 0.3150 Silver Weight varies: 075-0.96g. 0.0099 oz. ASW, 18 mm. **Ruler:** Wolfgang Wilhelm **Obv:** 5-line inscription with date **Obv. Inscription:** EIN / MATIER / RAVEN / SPVRG / (date) **Rev:** Madonna and Child **Rev. Legend:** MARIA. MA. DOMINI. **Mint:** Bielefeld **Note:** Ref. S-199.

Date	Mintage	VG	F	VF	XF	Unc
164Z	—	150	300	600	—	—

KM# 55 MATTIER (1/2 Mariengroschen)

0.9750 g., 0.3150 Silver Weight varies: 0.715-0.95g. 0.0099 oz. ASW, 17.5 mm. **Ruler:** Friedrich Wilhelm **Obv:** Scepter, with electoral hat above, divides date **Obv. Legend:** MO. NO. EL. BRA(N). B. I. C. M. **Rev:** 4-line inscription **Rev. Inscription:** EIN / MATIER / RAVENS / P(U)(V)RG. **Mint:** Bielefeld **Note:** Ref. S#235-41. Varieties exist.

Date	Mintage	VG	F	VF	XF	Unc
1651	—	55.00	95.00	145	260	—
1652	—	225	375	650	—	—
1653	—	55.00	95.00	145	260	—
1660	—	55.00	95.00	145	260	—
1661	—	45.00	80.00	120	275	—
1664	—	45.00	80.00	120	275	—
1665	—	225	375	700	1,100	—

KM# 31 MARIENGROSCHEN (1/36 Thaler)

1.7710 g., 0.3750 Silver Weight varies: 1.33-1.65g. 0.0214 oz. ASW, 22-23 mm. **Ruler:** Wolfgang Wilhelm **Obv:** Shield of 5-fold arms **Obv. Legend:** MO. NO. D. I. CLI. E. MO. C. RAV. **Rev:** Madonna and Child, date at end of legend. **Rev. Legend:** MARIA. M(A). (-) DOM(I)(N)(I). **Mint:** Bielefeld **Note:** Ref. S#189-97. Varieties exist.

Date	Mintage	VG	F	VF	XF	Unc
1629 (b)	—	27.00	55.00	115	230	—
1630 (b)	13,200	27.00	55.00	115	230	—
1631 (b)	2,376	27.00	55.00	115	230	—
163Z (b)	3,564	27.00	55.00	115	230	—
1633 (b)	—	27.00	55.00	115	230	—
1634 (b)	7,260	27.00	55.00	115	230	—
ND(1635) (b)	11,484	27.00	55.00	115	230	—
ND(1635)	Inc. above	27.00	55.00	115	230	—

KM# 51.1 MARIENGROSCHEN (1/36 Thaler)

1.1771 g., 0.3750 Silver Weight varies: 1.33-1.75g. 0.0142 oz. ASW, 22-23 mm. **Ruler:** Friedrich Wilhelm **Obv:** Shield of 5-fold arms with shield of scepter arms in lower center, date at end of legend **Obv. Legend:** MO. NO. EL. BRA. B. I. C. M. **Rev:** Madonna and Child **Rev. Legend:** MARIEN - GROSCHE. **Mint:** Bielefeld **Note:** Ref. S-224, 225.

Date	Mintage	VG	F	VF	XF	Unc
1648 (b)	—	30.00	65.00	115	230	—
1653 (b)	—	30.00	65.00	115	230	—

KM# 51.2 MARIENGROSCHEN (1/36 Thaler)

1.7320 g., 0.3750 Silver Weight varies: 1.105-1.805g. 0.0209 oz. ASW, 22-23 mm. **Ruler:** Friedrich Wilhelm **Obv:** Shield of 5-fold arms with shield of scepter arms in lower center, date at end of legend **Obv. Legend:** MO. NO. EL. BRAN. B. I. C. M. **Rev:** Madonna and Child **Rev. Legend:** MARIEN - GROSCHE. **Mint:** Bielefeld **Note:** Ref. S#226-34. Varieties exist.

Date	Mintage	VG	F	VF	XF	Unc
1660	—	27.00	55.00	115	230	—
1661	—	27.00	55.00	115	230	—
1662	—	27.00	55.00	115	230	—
1663	—	27.00	55.00	115	230	—
1664	—	27.00	55.00	115	230	—
1665	—	27.00	55.00	115	230	—
1666	—	27.00	55.00	115	230	—

KM# 48 2 MARIENGROSCHEN

1.4890 g., 0.9600 Silver Weight varies: 1.11-1.265g. 0.0460 oz. ASW, 19 mm. **Ruler:** Wolfgang Wilhelm **Obv:** Crowned shield of 5-fold arms **Obv. Legend:** MO. NO. D. I. C. E. M. C. RAV. **Rev:** 3-line inscription, date at end of legend **Rev. Legend:** IN. DEO. SPE. MEA. **Rev. Inscription:** II / MAR / GR. **Mint:** Bielefeld **Note:** Ref. S-206, 207. Varieties exist.

Date	Mintage	VG	F	VF	XF	Unc
1644	—	20.00	40.00	80.00	165	—
1646	—	20.00	40.00	80.00	165	—

KM# 49 2 MARIENGROSCHEN

1.4890 g., 0.9600 Silver Weight varies: 0.94-1.28g. 0.0460 oz. ASW, 19 mm. **Ruler:** Friedrich Wilhelm **Obv:** Shield of 5-fold arms, shield of scepter arms in lower center **Obv. Legend:** MO. NO. EL. BRA. B. I. (C.) M. **Rev:** 4-line inscription with date **Rev. Legend:** (S.) P. D. CO. M. RA. D. IN. R. **Mint:** Bielefeld **Note:** Ref. S#211-16, 218-23. Varieties exist.

Date	Mintage	VG	F	VF	XF	Unc
1647	—	40.00	80.00	125	240	—
1647 (b)	—	60.00	115	175	300	—
1649 (b)	—	60.00	115	175	300	—
1653	—	40.00	80.00	125	240	—
1664	—	25.00	50.00	95.00	180	—
1665	—	25.00	50.00	95.00	180	—
1666	—	25.00	50.00	95.00	180	—
1667	—	25.00	50.00	95.00	180	—
ND	—	25.00	50.00	95.00	180	—

KM# 56 2 MARIENGROSCHEN

1.4890 g., 0.9600 Silver Weight varies: 1.01-1.31g. 0.0460 oz. ASW, 19 mm. **Ruler:** Friedrich Wilhelm **Obv:** Shield of 5-fold arms, shield of scepter arms in lower center **Obv. Legend:** MO. NO. EL. BRA. B. IM. **Rev:** 3-line inscription, date at end of legend **Rev. Legend:** SP. D. CO. M. RA. D. IN. R. **Mint:** Bielefeld **Note:** Ref. S-217.

Date	Mintage	VG	F	VF	XF	Unc
1653	—	20.00	40.00	80.00	165	—

KM# 5 1/24 THALER (Reichsgroschen)

2.0890 g., 0.5000 Silver Weight varies: 1.29-2.32g. 0.0336 oz. ASW, 21-23 mm. **Ruler:** Johann Wilhelm **Obv:** Shield of 5-fold arms, three helmets above, small shield of Ravensberg at bottom **Obv. Legend:** DEVS. REF(V)(U)-(V)GI(V)(U)M. (M)(E)(V)(M) **Rev:** Imperial orb with Z4, cross above divides date **Rev. Legend:** MO. NO. D(V)(U)C. I(V)(U)L. CL(I). ET. MO(N). **Mint:** Bielefeld **Note:** Ref. S#108-157. Varieties exist.

Date	Mintage	VG	F	VF	XF	Unc
1601 (a)	30,916	16.00	35.00	70.00	140	—
160Z (a)	26,992	16.00	35.00	70.00	140	—
1603 (a)	30,688	16.00	35.00	70.00	140	—
1604 (a)	6,160	16.00	35.00	70.00	140	—
1605 (a)	21,616	16.00	35.00	70.00	140	—
1606 (a)	20,584	16.00	35.00	70.00	140	—
1607 (a)	8,516	16.00	35.00	70.00	140	—
1608 (a)	11,200	16.00	35.00	70.00	140	—
1609 (a)	7,840	16.00	35.00	70.00	140	—

KM# 15.1 1/24 THALER (Reichsgroschen)

1.3450 g., Silver, 20 mm. **Ruler:** Johann Sigismund **Obv:** Shield of 5-fold arms, 3 helmets above, small shield of Ravensberg arms at bottom **Obv. Legend:** DEVS RE - FVG ME. **Rev:** Imperial orb with Z4, date divided in legend at top **Rev. Legend:** MO NO DVC IVL CLI ET. **Mint:** Bielefeld **Note:** Ref. S-158.

Date	Mintage	VG	F	VF	XF	Unc
1618	—	20.00	40.00	80.00	165	—

KM# 15.2 1/24 THALER (Reichsgroschen)

Silver Weight varies: 0.97-1.23g., 20 mm. **Ruler:** Johann Sigismund **Obv:** Shield of 5-fold arms, 3 helmets above, small shield of Ravensberg arms at bottom **Obv. Legend:** DEVS RE - FV MEV. **Rev:** Imperial orb with Z4, date divided by base of cross inside legend **Rev. Legend:** MO NO D IV(L) CL(I) (E)(T) (M.) **Mint:** Bielefeld **Note:** Ref. S-159.

Date	Mintage	VG	F	VF	XF	Unc
1618	—	28.00	60.00	100	210	—

KM# 28 1/24 THALER (Reichsgroschen)
Silver **Ruler:** Georg Wilhelm **Obv:** Shield of 5-fold arms, 3 helmets above, small shield of Ravensberg arms below **Obv. Legend:** DEVS. REFVG. ME. **Rev:** Imperial orb with Z4 **Rev. Legend:** MO NO IVL CLI ET M. **Mint:** Bielefeld **Note:** Kipper issue.

Date	Mintage	F	VF	XF	Unc	BU
ND(1622-23)	—	—	—	—	—	—

KM# 32 1/24 THALER (Reichsgroschen)
2.0880 g., 0.4930 Silver Weight varies: 1.49-2.15g. 0.0331 oz. ASW, 24 mm. **Ruler:** Wolfgang Wilhelm **Obv:** Crowned shield of 8-fold arms with central shield of Pfalz **Obv. Legend:** WOLF. W. D. G. C. P. R. D. B. I. C. E. M. **Rev:** Imperial orb with Z4, cross divides date **Rev. Legend:** FER(D). II. D. G. RO. IMP. S. AVG. **Mint:** Bielefeld **Note:** Ref. S#180-87; Noss 27. Gute Groschen. Varieties exist.

Date	Mintage	VG	F	VF	XF	Unc
16Z9 (b)	—	85.00	200	300	500	—
1630 (b)	6,160	175	325	450	700	—
1631 (b)	4,928	60.00	100	200	400	—
1632 (b)	7,616	175	325	450	700	—
1635 (b)	—	60.00	100	200	400	—
1635	—	70.00	125	250	450	—
1636	23,403	20.00	40.00	75.00	150	—
1637	11,312	30.00	55.00	95.00	190	—
1638 (b)	—	20.00	40.00	75.00	150	—
ND	—	20.00	55.00	95.00	190	—

KM# 39 1/24 THALER (Reichsgroschen)
2.0880 g., 0.4930 Silver Weight varies: 1.65-1.67g. 0.0331 oz. ASW, 24 mm. **Ruler:** Wolfgang Wilhelm **Obv:** Crowned shield of 8-fold arms with central shield of Pfalz **Obv. Legend:** WOLF. W. D. G. C. P. R. D. B. I. C. E. M. **Rev:** Imperial orb with Z4, cross divides date within legend **Rev. Legend:** FER. III. D. G. RO. IM. S. AVG. **Mint:** Bielefeld **Note:** Ref. S-188.

Date	Mintage	VG	F	VF	XF	Unc
1639 (b)	—	40.00	80.00	150	300	—

KM# A28 24 KREUZER (Doppel-Schreckenberger)
Silver **Ruler:** Georg Wilhelm **Obv:** Shield of Ravensberg arms, date at end of legend **Obv. Legend:** CONSILIO. ET. VIRTUTE. **Rev:** Crowned imperial eagle, Z4 in orb on breast **Rev. Legend:** FERD. II. ... **Mint:** Bielefeld **Note:** Noss 19. Kipper issue.

Date	Mintage	VG	F	VF	XF	Unc
(1)6ZZ	—	—	—	—	—	—

KM# 8 1/4 THALER (Reichsort-Ortstaler-Orter)
Silver, 29 mm. **Ruler:** Johann Wilhelm **Obv:** Half-length bust to right, holding baton **Obv. Legend:** IOAN. GVIL. D. G. DVX. IVL. CLI. ET. MO' &. **Rev:** Shield of 5-fold arms, three helmets above, small shield of Ravensberg arms at bottom, date divided in legend at upper left and top **Rev. Legend:** DEVS. REFVG - IVM. MEVM. **Mint:** Bielefeld **Note:** Ref. S-107.

Date	Mintage	VG	F	VF	XF	Unc
(1)608 (a)	—	—	—	—	—	—

KM# 6 THALER
29.2300 g., 0.8920 Silver Weight varies: 28.35-29.12g. 0.8382 oz. ASW, 40-41 mm. **Ruler:** Johann Wilhelm **Obv:** Half-length armored figure to right, holding sword hilt and baton **Obv. Legend:** IOAN. GVIL. D. G. DVX. IVL. CLI. ET. MON. **Rev:** Ornate shield of 5-fold arms, 3 helmets above, small shield of Ravensberg below, date at end of legend **Rev. Legend:** DEVS. REFVG(I) - (I)(V)M. MEVM. **Mint:** Bielefeld **Note:** Ref. S#100-104; Dav. 9677, 7293.

Date	Mintage	VG	F	VF	XF	Unc
1603 (a)	22,352	1,500	2,500	4,500	7,000	—
1604 (a)	25,864	1,500	2,500	4,500	7,750	—
1608 (a)	9,520	2,000	3,750	7,500	12,500	—
1609 (a)	4,112	2,750	5,500	10,000	16,500	—

KM# 9 THALER
35.8300 g., Silver, 39x40 mm. **Ruler:** Johann Wilhelm **Obv:** Half-length armored figure to right holding baton **Obv. Legend:** IOAN. GVIL. D. G. DVX. IVL. CLI. ET. MON. **Rev:** Ornate shield of 5-fold arms, 3 helmets above, small shield of Ravensberg below, date at end of legend **Rev. Legend:** DEVS. REFVG(I) - (I)(V)M. MEVM. **Mint:** Bielefeld **Note:** Ref. S-103; Dav. 9678A, 7293A. Klippe.

Date	Mintage	VG	F	VF	XF	Unc
1608 (a) Rare	—	—	—	—	—	—

KM# 36 THALER
29.2300 g., 0.8920 Silver Weight varies: 28.43-29.13g. 0.8382 oz. ASW, 42 mm. **Ruler:** Wolfgang Wilhelm **Obv:** Bust to right in circle, inner legend divided by head **Obv. Legend:** Outer: WOLFG. WIL. D. G. C. PA. RHE. D. BA. IVL. CLI. ET. MO.; inner: IN DEO - MEA CONSOLA. **Rev:** Crowned Spanish shield of 8-fold arms, with central shield of Pfalz, Order of the Golden Fleece suspended below, date divided at upper left and right corners of shield **Rev. Legend:** C. VEL. SP. MAR. RA(V) - ET. MORS. DO. IN. RA. **Mint:** Bielefeld **Note:** Ref. S#172-74; Dav. 7294.

Date	Mintage	VG	F	VF	XF	Unc
1630 (b) Rare	352	—	—	—	—	—
163Z (b) Rare	480	—	—	—	—	—

Note: Fritz Rudolf Künker Münzenhandlung Auction 93, 6-04 nearly XF realized approximately $14,510

Date	Mintage	VG	F	VF	XF	Unc
1633 (b) Rare	200	—	—	—	—	—

KM# 38 THALER
Silver Weight varies: 28.20-28.32g., 42-43 mm. **Ruler:** Wolfgang Wilhelm **Obv:** Bust to right in circle, inner legend divided by head **Obv. Legend:** Outer: WOLFG. WIL. D. G. (C.) PA. RHE. D. BA. IVL. CLI. ET. MO.; Inner: IN DEO MEA - CONSOLA. **Rev:** Crowned Spanish shield of 8-fold arms, with central shield of Pfalz, Order of the Golden Fleece suspended below, date divided at upper left and right corners of shield **Rev. Legend:** C. VEL. SP. MAR. RA - ET. MORS. DO. IN RA. **Mint:** Bielefeld **Note:** Ref. S-175, 176; Dav. 7295. Varieties exist.

Date	Mintage	VG	F	VF	XF	Unc
1638 (b) Rare	—	—	—	—	—	—
1640 (b) Rare	—	—	—	—	—	—

Note: Fritz Rudolf Künker Münzenhandlung Auction 93, 6-04, VF realized approximately $7,860

KM# 45 THALER
28.2500 g., Silver, 44-45 mm. **Ruler:** Wolfgang Wilhelm **Obv:** Large bust to right, no circle, inner legend divided by top of head and begins at upper right, ends at upper left **Obv. Legend:** Outer: WOLFG. WILH. D. G. C. PAL. RHEN. D. BAV.; Inner: CONSOLA: - IN DEO. MEA. **Rev:** Spanish shield of 8-fold arms, with central shield of Pfalz, small crown above, Order of the Golden Fleece suspended below, date divided at upper left and right corners of shield **Rev. Legend:** C. VEL. SP. MAR. RA. - ET. MORS. DO. IN. RA. **Mint:** Bielefeld **Note:** Ref. S-177; Dav. 7296.

Date	Mintage	VG	F	VF	XF	Unc
1641 (b)	—	1,800	3,600	6,000	—	—

KM# 46 THALER
28.3200 g., Silver, 42 mm. **Ruler:** Wolfgang Wilhelm **Obv:** Large bust to right breaks inner legend and circle above **Obv. Legend:** Outer: WOLFG. WIL. D. G. C. PA. RHE. D. BA. IVL. CLI. ET. MO.; Inner: IN DEO MEA - CONSOLA. **Rev:** Spanish shield of 8-fold arms, with central shield of Pfalz, small crown above, Order of the Golden Fleece suspended below, date divided at upper left and right corners of shield **Rev. Legend:** C. VEL. SP. MAR. RA - ET. MORS. DO.INRA. **Mint:** Bielefeld **Note:** Ref. S-178, 179; Dav. 7297.

Date	Mintage	VG	F	VF	XF	Unc
1641 (b) Rare	—	—	—	—	—	—
1642 (b) Rare	—	—	—	—	—	—

KM# 10 1-1/2 THALER
43.5400 g., Silver **Ruler:** Johann Wilhelm **Obv. Legend:** IOAN. GVIL. D. G. DVX. IVL. CLI. ET. MON. **Rev. Legend:** DEVS. REFVGI - M. MEVM. **Mint:** Bielefeld **Note:** Similar to 1 Thaler, KM#6 but Klippe. Dav. #7292.

Date	Mintage	VG	F	VF	XF	Unc
1608 (b) Rare	—	—	—	—	—	—

Note: An example in almost XF realized approximately $12,675 in a USB auction, January 2001.

KM# 7 2 THALER
58.0510 g., 0.8920 Silver 1.6647 oz. ASW, 48x48 mm. **Ruler:** Johann Wilhelm **Obv:** Half-length armored figure to right, holding sword hilt and baton **Obv. Legend:** IOAN. GVIL. D. G. DVX. IVL. CLI. ET. MON. **Rev:** Shield of 5-fold arms, 3 helmets above, small shield of Ravensberg arms at bottom, date at end of legend **Rev. Legend:** DEVS. REFVGI - M. MEVM. **Mint:** Bielefeld **Note:** Dav. 7291. Klippe. Illustration reduced.

Date	Mintage	VG	F	VF	XF	Unc
1604 (a) Rare	—	—	—	—	—	—
1608 (a) Rare	—	—	—	—	—	—

TRADE COINAGE

KM# 37 GOLDGULDEN
3.2320 g., 0.7708 Gold 0.0801 oz. AGW, 21.5 mm. **Ruler:** Wolfgang Wilhelm **Obv:** Bust to right, with date below, in circle, inner legend divided by head **Obv. Legend:** Outer: WOLF. WI. DG. C. PA. RE. D. BA. IV. CL. E. M.; Inner: IN DEO - MEA CONS. **Rev:** Crowned shield of 8-fold arms with central shield of Pfalz **Rev. Legend:** VEL. SPMAR. RA. ET. MOR. DO IN R. **Mint:** Bielefeld **Note:** Ref. S-171.

Date	Mintage	VG	F	VF	XF	Unc
1631 Rare	324	—	—	—	—	—

KM# 40 DUCAT
3.4900 g., 0.9860 Gold Weight varlies: 3.373-3.48g. 0.1106 oz. AGW, 24 mm. **Ruler:** Wolfgang Wilhelm **Obv:** Crowned shield of 8-fold arms with central shield of Pfalz, chain of Order around **Obv. Legend:** WOLF. GWIL. C. PAL. R. D. BAV. I. C. ET. M. **Rev:** 5-line inscription with date in ornamented square **Rev. Inscription:** DVCATV(/)S (/) NOVVS / RAVEN(/)S (/) BVR / (date) **Mint:** Bielefeld **Note:** Ref. S-170.

Date	Mintage	VG	F	VF	XF	Unc
1639 2 known	—	—	—	—	—	—
164Z Rare	—	—	—	—	—	—

Note: An example in XF realized approximately $20,300 in a Westfälische A.G. auction September 2004.

KM# 50 DUCAT
3.4900 g., 0.9860 Gold 0.1106 oz. AGW, 23-24 mm. **Ruler:** Friedrich Wilhelm **Obv:** Shield of 5-fold arms with central shield of scepter arms, large electoral hat above **Obv. Legend:** FRID. WIL. M. B. S. R. I. AR. C(.) A. E. E(L). (L.) B. I. C. M. D. **Rev:** 5-line inscription with date **Rev. Inscription:** DUCATU(/)S. / NOVUS. / COM / RAV /ENS. / BERG / (date) **Mint:** Bielefeld **Note:** Ref. S-208, 209. Varieties exist.

Date	Mintage	VG	F	VF	XF	Unc
1647 Rare	—	—	—	—	—	—
1648 Rare	—	—	—	—	—	—

KM# 52 DUCAT
3.4900 g., 0.9860 Gold Weight varies: 3.44-3.49g. 0.1106 oz. AGW, 25 mm. **Ruler:** Friedrich Wilhelm **Obv:** Bust to right wearing electoral hat **Obv. Legend:** FRID. WIL. DG. M. BS. RI. A. C. EE. L. BIC. M. S. P. **Rev:** Shield of 5-fold arms, with central shield of scepter arms, divides date **Rev. Legend:** C. V. C. I. S. E. I. D. B. N. P. R. COM. M. E. RAV. D. I. R. **Mint:** Bielefeld **Note:** Ref. S-210.

Date	Mintage	VG	F	VF	XF	Unc
1648 Rare	—	—	—	—	—	—

Note: An example in XF realized approximately $13,650 in a June 2001 Künker auction.

PATTERNS

Including off metal strikes

KM#	Date	Mintage	Identification	Mkt Val
Pn1	(15)99 (a)	—	Thaler. Lead. KM#6.	—
Pn2	1632	—	Thaler. Pewter. KM-36. Previous KM#Pn1.	100

RAVENSBURG

(Ravenspurg)

Not to be confused with Ravensberg in Westphalia, Ravensburg is located some 13 miles (22 kilometers) north of Lake Constance in lower Swabia. The earliest structures of the city fortifications date from about 750. The city takes its name from the old German personal name Ravan, that is Rabe in modern German, meaning raven or crow, but who this actually refers to is lost to history. By the middle of the 11th century, Ravensburg was a growing town and received the right to hold markets early in the 12th century. Although Ravensburg is mentioned as the site of an imperial mint in the 12th century, then as a mint for the bishops of Constance early in the next century, it did not receive the mint right for municipal coinage until the 14th century. The first city coinages known date from the later 1300s. Ravensburg had been elevated to the rank of an imperial city in 1276. From the inception of its coinage until the early 18th century, Ravensburg produced intermittent issue of coins. The city also had a short-lived joint coinage with Ulm and Überlingen in the early 16th century (see the latter for these). During the Napoleonic Wars, Ravensburg was annexed by Bavaria in 1803 and transferred to Württemberg in 1810.

MINT OFFICIALS' INITIALS

Bielefeld

Initial	Date	Name
DS	1620-1625	Daniel Sailer, die-cutter in Augsburg
	1622	Konrad Beck
	1693	Daniel Sommer

ARMS

City gate with two crenelated towers.

FREE CITY

REGULAR COINAGE

KM# 10 PFENNIG
Silver **Obv:** City arms in circle, date above in margin **Note:** Uniface hohl-type.

Date	Mintage	VG	F	VF	XF	Unc
1624	—	—	—	—	—	—

KM# 15 PFENNIG (1/4 Kreuzer)
Copper **Obv:** City arms, '4' above. **Note:** Uniface.

Date	Mintage	VG	F	VF	XF	Unc
ND (ca1693)	—	13.00	33.00	65.00	130	—

KM# 16 PFENNIG (1/4 Kreuzer)
Copper **Obv:** City arms, '4' above **Note:** Uniface. Klippe.

Date	Mintage	VG	F	VF	XF	Unc
ND(ca1693)	—	18.00	35.00	60.00	115	—

KM# 17 PFENNIG (1/4 Kreuzer)
Copper **Obv:** City arms divide date, '4' above **Note:** Uniface. Varieties exist.

Date	Mintage	VG	F	VF	XF	Unc
1693	—	10.00	25.00	40.00	80.00	—
1694	—	10.00	25.00	40.00	80.00	—
1695	—	10.00	25.00	40.00	80.00	—
1696	—	10.00	25.00	40.00	80.00	—
1697	—	10.00	25.00	40.00	80.00	—
1698	—	10.00	25.00	40.00	80.00	—

KM# 18 1/4 KREUZER (Pfennig)
Billon **Obv:** Imperial eagle, R in oval on breast **Note:** Uniface.

Date	Mintage	VG	F	VF	XF	Unc
ND(ca1693)	—	75.00	150	300	600	—

KM# 19 1/2 KREUZER (2 Pfennig)
Billon **Obv:** 2 adjacent oval arms, imperial eagle in left, city arms in right, 1/2 in oval below **Rev:** Value 1/2

Date	Mintage	VG	F	VF	XF	Unc
ND(ca1693)	—	40.00	80.00	165	325	—

KM# 20 1/2 KREUZER (2 Pfennig)
Billon **Obv:** 2 adjacent oval arms, imperial eagle in left, city arms in right, 1/2 in oval below **Note:** Uniface.

Date	Mintage	VG	F	VF	XF	Unc
ND(ca1693)	—	40.00	80.00	165	325	—

KM# 21 KREUZER (4 Pfennig)
Silver **Obv:** Shield of city arms between 2 stars, '4' above **Note:** Uniface. Kipper Coinage.

Date	Mintage	VG	F	VF	XF	Unc
ND(1622)	—	60.00	125	250	—	—

KM# 22 KREUZER (4 Pfennig)
Silver **Obv:** Ornamented shield of city arms **Rev:** Crowned imperial eagle, 'I' in oval on breast **Note:** Varieties exist.

Date	Mintage	VG	F	VF	XF	Unc
ND(ca1693)	—	25.00	50.00	100	210	—

KM# 23 KREUZER (4 Pfennig)

Silver **Obv:** Ornameted shield of city arms **Rev:** Imperial eagle, 'I' in oval on breast

Date	Mintage	VG	F	VF	XF	Unc
ND(ca1693)	—	25.00	50.00	100	210	—

KM# 24 KREUZER (4 Pfennig)

Silver **Obv:** Ornamented shield of city arms **Rev:** Imperial eagle, 'K' in oval on breast

Date	Mintage	VG	F	VF	XF	Unc
ND(ca1693)	—	25.00	50.00	100	210	—

KM# 25 KREUZER (4 Pfennig)

Billon **Obv:** Ornamented city arms, date above **Rev:** Imperial eagle, 'I' in oval on breast

Date	Mintage	VG	F	VF	XF	Unc
1693	—	30.00	65.00	130	260	—

KM# 28 KREUZER (4 Pfennig)

Silver **Obv:** City arms in baroque frame **Rev:** Crowned imperial eagle, 'K' in oval on breast

Date	Mintage	VG	F	VF	XF	Unc
1700	—	50.00	100	200	400	—

COUNTERMARKED COINAGE

KM# 5 2 KREUZER (Halbbatzen)

Silver **Countermark:** City arms **Note:** Countermark on Montfort 12 Kreuzer, KM#9.

CM Date	Host Date	Good	VG	F	VF	XF
ND	ND(1623)	—	—	—	—	—

REGENSBURG

(Ratisbon)

Both the bishopric and the city of Regensburg issued coinage, but often shared the officials who worked in the mint. Those are listed together here, with separate introductions for each entity to follow.

MINTMASTERS' INITIALS

Initial	Date	Name
HF	1653-73	Hieronymus Federer
MF	1673-1700	Michael Federer
Cinquefoil	1635-37	Christoph Leinmuth
Wing	1639-53	Hans Siegmund Federer
3 ears of grain	1637-38	Hans Putzer
Hat	1623-34	Balthasar Ziegler
Fleur-de-lis	1639-40	Unknown
	1598-ca. 1619	Haubold Lehner

WARDENS

Date	Name
1586-1604	Georg Fraisslich
1637-?	Hans Putzer
1660-85	Friedrich Hungar
1688-?	Johann Gottlieb Stotz
1700-18	Johann Georg Kramer

DIE-CUTTERS and ENGRAVERS

Date	Name
1626	Christoph Pessle
1633	Georg Thomas Paur
1660	Ulrich Gravenauer
1663-89	Georg Sigmundt Renz
1690	Tobias Pannesperger
1691-1706	Johann Adam Seitz

BISHOPRIC

The town of Regensburg, located on the Danube River in Bavaria about 35 miles (57km) northeast of Ingolstadt, became the seat of a bishopric in 470. The first coins of the bishops were joint issues with the dukes of Bavaria from the mid-10th century. In the 11th century, independent episcopal coinage made its appearance. Most of the bishops were members of the local Bavarian nobility. Karl Theodor von Dalberg, the last one with territorial control transferred those lands to Bavaria in 1810, having been raised to the rank of archbishop in 1805. He was given Frankfurt am Main in exchange by Napoleon, who made him a grand duke as well. When Napoleon lost his empire, the bishop was left with only his ecclesiastic title as archbishop of Regensburg.

RULERS

Wolfgang II von Hausen, 1600-1613
Albrecht IV von Törring, 1613-1649
Franz Wilhelm von Wartenberg, 1649-1661
Johann Georg von Herberstein, 1661-1663
Adam Lorenz von Törring, 1663-1666
Guidobald von Thun-Hohnstein, 1666-1668
Albrecht Sigmund, Herzog von Bayern, 1668-1685
Josef Clemens, Herzog von Bayern, 1685-1716

ARMS

Bishopric – diagonal band from upper left to lower right

REFERENCE

E/K = Hubert Emmerig and Otto Kozinowski, **Die Münzen und Medaillen der Regensburger Bishöfe und des Domkapitels seit dem 16. Jahrhundert**, Stuttgart, 1998.

REGULAR COINAGE

KM# 25 THALER

Silver **Obv:** 5-line inscription **Obv. Inscription:** ALBERTVS / .G.D. / EPISCOBVS / RATISBON / ENSIS. **Rev:** Date in inner circle at center of star **Note:** Dav. #5739.

Date	Mintage	VG	F	VF	XF	Unc
1621	—	1,000	2,000	4,000	7,500	—

KM# 144 THALER

Silver **Note:** Similar to KM#145 but with date divided 1-6-5-7 above arms, rosette below arms. Dav. #5740.

Date	Mintage	VG	F	VF	XF	Unc
1657	—	2,500	5,000	9,000	—	—
ND	—	2,500	5,000	9,000	—	—

KM# 145 THALER

Silver **Obv:** Franz Wilhelm **Rev:** Without date above and rosette below arms **Note:** Dav. #5740A.

Date	Mintage	VG	F	VF	XF	Unc
ND	—	2,750	5,500	9,500	—	—

KM# 168 THALER

Silver **Obv:** Capped bust **Rev:** Bishop's cap above oval arms **Note:** Dav. #5741.

Date	Mintage	VG	F	VF	XF	Unc
1661	—	1,500	2,900	5,000	9,000	—

TRADE COINAGE

KM# 414 10 DUCAT

35.0000 g., Gold **Ruler:** Franz Wilhelm **Obv:** Bust of Franz Wilhelm right **Rev:** Date divided 1-6-5-7 above arms, rosette below arms **Note:** Ref. E/K#90.1. Struck from Thaler dies. (Old KM#144.)

Date	Mintage	VG	F	VF	XF	Unc
ND(ca1657) Rare	—	—	—	—	—	—

FREE CITY

The site of Regensburg was settled before the arrival of the Romans, who called the place Ratisbona. After the establishment of a bishopric there in the 5th century, the town was also the chief residence of the early dukes of Bavaria. From the 10th century through the early 13th century, Regensburg contained a mint which produced coins for the dukes and bishops. Regensburg was elevated to a free imperial city in 1180 and obtained the mint right in 1230. A long series of issues dating from 1508 and continuing into the early 19th century ensued.

Regensburg was the site of the Imperial Diet (Reichstag) or Parliament, which met continuously in the Reichssaal of the city hall from 1663 until 1806, when Napoleon dissolved the Holy Roman Empire. The opening of each year's session, attended by the emperor in person, all the secular princes and ecclesiastic rulers of the empire, was a source of great pride and prestige for the city. However, Regensburg lost its independence and was handed over to the bishop in 1803. It came into the possession of Bavaria, along with the bishopric, in 1810.

ARMS

2 crossed keys

REFERENCE

B = Egon Beckenbauer, **Die Münzen der Reichsstadt Regensburg**, Grünwald bei München, 1978.

REGULAR COINAGE

KM# 34 HELLER

Copper **Obv:** Regensburg arms in square **Rev:** .1.

Date	Mintage	VG	F	VF	XF	Unc
ND(1622-23)	—	33.00	80.00	125	225	—

KM# 33 HELLER

Copper **Obv:** Regensburg arms in square **Rev:** "R" in circle of pellets **Note:** Kipper Heller.

Date	Mintage	VG	F	VF	XF	Unc
ND(1622-23)	—	20.00	45.00	80.00	165	—

KM# 192 HELLER

Copper **Note:** Diamond-shaped with rounded corners, Regensburg arms divide date, R above, H below.

Date	Mintage	VG	F	VF	XF	Unc
1677	—	7.00	16.00	35.00	75.00	—
1679	159,000	7.00	16.00	35.00	75.00	—
1681	190,000	7.00	16.00	35.00	75.00	—
1682	374,000	7.00	16.00	35.00	75.00	—

Date	Mintage	VG	F	VF	XF	Unc
1684	296,000	7.00	16.00	35.00	75.00	—
1686	147,000	7.00	16.00	35.00	75.00	—
1687	210,000	7.00	16.00	35.00	75.00	—
1689	289,000	7.00	16.00	35.00	75.00	—
1691	178,000	7.00	16.00	35.00	75.00	—
1692	314,000	7.00	16.00	35.00	75.00	—
1693	336,000	7.00	16.00	35.00	75.00	—
1694	445,000	7.00	16.00	5.00	75.00	—
1695	226,000	7.00	16.00	35.00	75.00	—
1696	605,000	7.00	16.00	35.00	75.00	—
1697	—	7.00	16.00	35.00	75.00	—
1698	411,000	7.00	16.00	35.00	75.00	—
1699	371,000	7.00	16.00	35.00	75.00	—
1700	380,000	7.00	16.00	35.00	75.00	—

KM# 10 PFENNING (1/84 Gulden)

Silver **Obv:** Regensburg arms in ornamented shield **Rev:** Imperial orb with 84 in baroque frame divides date **Note:** Varieties exist.

Date	Mintage	VG	F	VF	XF	Unc
1611	—	33.00	80.00	125	225	—
1613	—	33.00	80.00	125	225	—
ND	—	27.00	60.00	100	200	—

KM# 26 PFENNING (1/84 Gulden)

Billon **Obv:** Regensburg arms, "R" above, date below **Note:** Kipper Pfenning. Uniface.

Date	Mintage	VG	F	VF	XF	Unc
16Z1	—	27.00	60.00	100	210	—

KM# 26a PFENNING (1/84 Gulden)

Copper **Note:** Uniface.

Date	Mintage	VG	F	VF	XF	Unc
16ZZ	—	20.00	45.00	80.00	160	—

KM# 37 PFENNING (1/84 Gulden)

Silver **Obv:** Regensburg arms in ornamented shield, date above **Note:** Uniface.

Date	Mintage	VG	F	VF	XF	Unc
1623	—	9.00	16.00	33.00	65.00	—

KM# 42 PFENNING (1/84 Gulden)

Silver **Obv:** Regensburg arms in plain shield, date above **Note:** Uniface.

Date	Mintage	VG	F	VF	XF	Unc
1624	—	9.00	16.00	33.00	75.00	—
1625	—	9.00	16.00	33.00	75.00	—
1626	—	9.00	16.00	33.00	75.00	—

KM# 53 PFENNING (1/84 Gulden)

Silver **Obv:** Regensburg arms in baroque cartouche-like shield, date above **Note:** Uniface.

Date	Mintage	VG	F	VF	XF	Unc
1627	—	9.00	16.00	33.00	75.00	—
1628	—	9.00	16.00	33.00	75.00	—
1629	—	9.00	16.00	33.00	75.00	—

KM# 60 PFENNING (1/84 Gulden)

Silver **Obv:** Date divided at top by ornament

Date	Mintage	VG	F	VF	XF	Unc
1629	—	9.00	16.00	33.00	65.00	—
1631	—	9.00	16.00	33.00	65.00	—

KM# 92 PFENNING (1/84 Gulden)

Silver **Obv:** Regensburg arms in oval baroque frame, date divided above by ornament **Note:** Varieties exist.

Date	Mintage	VG	F	VF	XF	Unc
1639	—	11.00	22.00	45.00	90.00	—
1640	—	11.00	22.00	45.00	90.00	—
1641	—	12.00	27.00	55.00	110	—
1642	—	12.00	27.00	55.00	110	—
1644	—	12.00	27.00	55.00	110	—
1647	—	11.00	22.00	45.00	90.00	—

KM# 125 PFENNING (1/84 Gulden)

Silver **Obv:** Regensburg arms in heart-shaped shield, date divided above

Date	Mintage	VG	F	VF	XF	Unc
1651	—	11.00	22.00	45.00	90.00	—
1652	—	11.00	22.00	45.00	90.00	—

KM# 132 PFENNING (1/84 Gulden)

Silver **Obv:** Mintmaster's initials below shield

Date	Mintage	VG	F	VF	XF	Unc
1653 HF	—	11.00	22.00	45.00	90.00	—
1656 HF	—	11.00	22.00	45.00	90.00	—

KM# 169 PFENNING (1/84 Gulden)

Silver **Obv:** Regensburg arms in rhombus, date divided to upper left and right

Date	Mintage	VG	F	VF	XF	Unc
1660	—	15.00	30.00	60.00	120	—
1661	—	11.00	22.00	45.00	90.00	—

KM# 175 PFENNING (1/84 Gulden)

Silver **Obv:** Regensburg arms in heart-shaped shield, date above **Note:** Varieties exist.

Date	Mintage	VG	F	VF	XF	Unc
1665	—	8.00	15.00	35.00	75.00	—
1668	—	8.00	15.00	35.00	75.00	—
1673	—	8.00	15.00	35.00	75.00	—
1674	—	8.00	15.00	35.00	75.00	—
1677	—	8.00	15.00	35.00	75.00	—
1680	60,000	8.00	15.00	35.00	75.00	—
1684	—	8.00	15.00	35.00	75.00	—
1685	—	8.00	15.00	35.00	75.00	—
1687	57,000	8.00	15.00	35.00	75.00	—
1691	36,000	8.00	15.00	35.00	75.00	—

KM# 200 PFENNING (1/84 Gulden)

Silver **Obv:** Regensburg arms in oval baroque frame, date above

Date	Mintage	VG	F	VF	XF	Unc
1693	78,000	12.00	25.00	50.00	100	—

KM# 201 PFENNING (1/84 Gulden)

Silver **Obv:** Regensburg arms in wreath-like frame, date above

Date	Mintage	VG	F	VF	XF	Unc
1693	Inc. above	9.00	20.00	40.00	80.00	—

KM# 204 PFENNING (1/84 Gulden)

Silver **Obv:** Regensburg arms in frame of two joined ovals, date above

Date	Mintage	VG	F	VF	XF	Unc
1696	—	9.00	20.00	45.00	90.00	—

KM# 100 1/2 KREUZER (2 Pfennig)

Silver **Obv:** Regensburg arms in heart-shaped frame, value: 1/2 in oval above divides date **Note:** Uniface. Varieties exist.

Date	Mintage	VG	F	VF	XF	Unc
1640	—	11.00	20.00	45.00	90.00	—
1641	—	9.00	16.00	45.00	90.00	—
1644	—	9.00	16.00	45.00	90.00	—
1645	—	9.00	16.00	45.00	90.00	—
1646	—	9.00	16.00	45.00	90.00	—
1647	—	11.00	20.00	45.00	90.00	—
1651	—	11.00	20.00	45.00	90.00	—
1652	—	11.00	20.00	45.00	90.00	—
1653	—	11.00	20.00	45.00	90.00	—

KM# 112 1/2 KREUZER (2 Pfennig)

Silver **Obv:** Imperial eagle, Regensburg arms in shield on breast, all in rhombus, value: 1/2 in circle at top, date divided at upper left and right

Date	Mintage	VG	F	VF	XF	Unc
1647	—	45.00	95.00	175	350	—

KM# 133 1/2 KREUZER (2 Pfennig)

Silver **Obv:** Regensburg arms in cartouche, value 1/2 in circle above divides date

Date	Mintage	VG	F	VF	XF	Unc
1653	—	11.00	20.00	40.00	85.00	—

KM# 156 1/2 KREUZER (2 Pfennig)

Silver **Obv:** Regensburg arms in cartouche, value 1/2 in circle above divides date, mintmaster's initials at bottom

Date	Mintage	VG	F	VF	XF	Unc
1659 HF	—	9.00	20.00	40.00	80.00	150
1666 HF	—	9.00	20.00	40.00	80.00	150

KM# 190 1/2 KREUZER (2 Pfennig)

Silver **Obv:** Regensburg arms in more defined heart shaped-frame than KM#100, bottom closed, value 1/2 in oval above divides date **Note:** Uniface. Varieties exist.

Date	Mintage	VG	F	VF	XF	Unc
1674	—	11.00	20.00	40.00	80.00	—
1680	—	11.00	20.00	40.00	80.00	—
1690	—	11.00	20.00	40.00	80.00	—

KM# 206 1/2 KREUZER (2 Pfennig)

Silver **Obv:** Regensburg arms with value 1/2 above in baroque frame, initial below

Date	Mintage	VG	F	VF	XF	Unc
ND B	—	16.00	35.00	75.00	150	—

KM# 205 1/2 KREUZER (2 Pfennig)

Silver **Obv:** Regensburg arms in cartouche, value: 1/2 in ornament above divides date **Note:** Uniface

Date	Mintage	VG	F	VF	XF	Unc
1696	—	8.00	20.00	40.00	80.00	—

Note: 1/2 Kreuzer dated 1696 reported struck in 1696, 1701 and 1734; Mintage reported only in latter year at 6,048 pieces

KM# 28 KREUZER

Billon **Rev:** Double cross (x on ++), value I in shield in center

Date	Mintage	VG	F	VF	XF	Unc
1621	—	13.00	30.00	65.00	130	—
1622	—	13.00	30.00	65.00	130	—

KM# 27 KREUZER

Billon **Obv:** Regensburg arms in ornamented shield, date above **Rev:** Imperial orb in ornamented shield **Note:** Kipper Kreuzer.

Date	Mintage	VG	F	VF	XF	Unc
1621	—	27.00	80.00	120	240	—

KM# 36 KREUZER

Billon **Obv:** Regensburg arms in ornate shield **Rev:** R in shield superimposed on cross

Date	Mintage	VG	F	VF	XF	Unc
ND(1622-23)	—	16.00	33.00	75.00	150	—

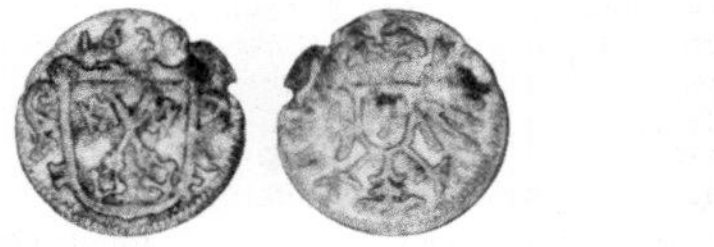

KM# 38 KREUZER

Billon **Obv:** Regensburg arms in ornamented shield, date above **Rev:** Imperial eagle, shield on breast with I **Note:** Varieties exist.

Date	Mintage	VG	F	VF	XF	Unc
1623	—	11.00	20.00	40.00	80.00	—
1624	—	11.00	20.00	40.00	80.00	—
1625	—	11.00	20.00	40.00	80.00	—
1626	—	11.00	20.00	40.00	80.00	—

KM# 54 KREUZER

Billon **Obv:** Crowned imperial eagle, value: I in shield on breast **Rev:** Regensburg arms in rounded shield, date divided by ornament at top **Note:** Varieties exist.

Date	Mintage	VG	F	VF	XF	Unc
1627	—	12.00	25.00	55.00	110	—
1628	—	11.00	20.00	40.00	80.00	—
1631	—	11.00	20.00	40.00	80.00	—
1637 (b)	—	12.00	25.00	55.00	110	—

KM# 93 KREUZER

Billon **Obv:** Regensburg arms in oval baroque frame, date divided by ornament above **Rev:** Double-headed imperial eagle, orb on breast **Note:** Varieties exist.

Date	Mintage	VG	F	VF	XF	Unc
1639	—	11.00	20.00	40.00	80.00	—
1640	—	11.00	20.00	40.00	80.00	—
1641	—	11.00	20.00	40.00	80.00	—
1642	—	11.00	20.00	40.00	80.00	—
1643	—	11.00	20.00	40.00	80.00	—
1644	—	11.00	20.00	40.00	80.00	—
1645	—	11.00	20.00	40.00	80.00	—
1646	—	11.00	20.00	40.00	80.00	—
1647	—	11.00	20.00	40.00	80.00	—
1648	—	11.00	20.00	40.00	80.00	—
1649	—	11.00	20.00	40.00	80.00	—
1650	—	11.00	20.00	40.00	80.00	—
1651	—	11.00	20.00	40.00	80.00	—
1652	—	11.00	20.00	40.00	80.00	—
1653	—	11.00	20.00	40.00	80.00	—
1655 HF	—	11.00	20.00	40.00	80.00	—

KM# 116 KREUZER

Billon **Obv:** Crowned imperial eagle, value: I in orb on breast, titles of Ferdinand III **Rev:** Legend, date **Rev. Legend:** MONE... **Note:** Varieties exist.

Date	Mintage	VG	F	VF	XF	Unc
1648	—	9.00	16.00	35.00	75.00	—
1649	—	11.00	20.00	40.00	80.00	—

KM# 126 KREUZER

Billon **Obv:** Crowned imperial eagle, arms of Austria on breast **Rev:** Regensburg arms in baroque frame, divide date, value I above

Date	Mintage	VG	F	VF	XF	Unc
1651	—	11.00	20.00	40.00	80.00	—

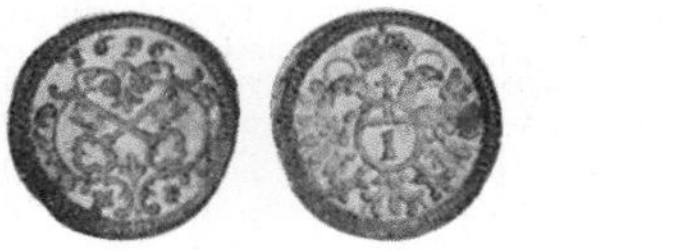

KM# 176 KREUZER

Billon **Obv:** Heart-shaped cartouche encloses arms, date above **Rev:** Crowned imperial eagle, value: I in shield on breast **Note:** Varieties exist.

Date	Mintage	VG	F	VF	XF	Unc
1665 HF	—	9.00	20.00	55.00	110	—
1680 HF	—	9.00	20.00	55.00	110	—
1691 HF	—	9.00	20.00	55.00	110	—
1693 HF	6,600	9.00	20.00	55.00	110	—
1696 MF	—	9.00	20.00	55.00	110	—

KM# 40 2 KREUZER (Halbbatzen)

Silver **Note:** Klippe.

Date	Mintage	VG	F	VF	XF	Unc
1623	—	110	165	240	450	—

KM# 39 2 KREUZER (Halbbatzen)
Silver **Obv:** Regensburg arms in plain shield, date above **Obv. Legend:** MONE... **Rev:** Crowned imperial eagle, Z in shield on breast **Rev. Legend:** DA. PACEM... **Note:** Varieties exist.

Date	Mintage	VG	F	VF	XF	Unc
1623	—	12.00	27.00	55.00	110	—
1624	—	12.00	27.00	55.00	110	—
1625	—	12.00	27.00	55.00	110	—

KM# 46 2 KREUZER (Halbbatzen)
Silver **Obv:** Arms in cartouche, date in legend **Rev:** Crowned double-headed imperial eagle **Note:** Varieties exist.

Date	Mintage	VG	F	VF	XF	Unc
1626	—	13.00	30.00	60.00	120	—
1627	—	13.00	30.00	60.00	120	—
1628	—	9.00	20.00	60.00	120	—
1629	—	9.00	20.00	60.00	120	—
1630	—	9.00	20.00	60.00	120	—
1631	—	9.00	20.00	60.00	120	—

KM# 45 2 KREUZER (Halbbatzen)
Silver **Obv:** Value: 2 in shield **Rev:** Ornamented shield

Date	Mintage	VG	F	VF	XF	Unc
1626	—	13.00	30.00	60.00	120	—

KM# 72 2 KREUZER (Halbbatzen)
Silver **Obv:** Z in circle on eagle's breast

Date	Mintage	VG	F	VF	XF	Unc
1631	—	12.00	27.00	55.00	115	—

KM# 73 2 KREUZER (Halbbatzen)
Silver **Obv:** Z in imperial orb on breast **Note:** Varieties exist.

Date	Mintage	VG	F	VF	XF	Unc
1632	—	12.00	27.00	55.00	115	—
1633	—	12.00	27.00	55.00	115	—
1634	—	12.00	27.00	55.00	115	—

KM# 80 2 KREUZER (Halbbatzen)
Silver **Obv:** Mintmaster's symbol in heart-shaped cartouche at bottom **Rev:** Crowned double-headed eagle, value in orb on breast

Date	Mintage	VG	F	VF	XF	Unc
1634 (a)	—	13.00	30.00	60.00	120	—

Note: Struck in 1635-37

KM# 81 2 KREUZER (Halbbatzen)
Silver **Rev:** Mintmaster's symbol at top

Date	Mintage	VG	F	VF	XF	Unc
1634 (b)	—	16.00	35.00	70.00	140	—

Note: Struck in 1637-38

KM# 82 2 KREUZER (Halbbatzen)
Silver **Rev:** Mintmaster's symbol at bottom

Date	Mintage	VG	F	VF	XF	Unc
1634 (c)	—	15.00	33.00	65.00	130	—

Note: Struck in 1639-40

KM# 165 2 KREUZER (Halbbatzen)
Silver **Obv:** Regensburg arms in oval baroque frame, date in legend **Rev:** Crowned imperial eagle, value: 2 in circle on breast **Rev. Legend:** SERVA. NOBIS...

Date	Mintage	VG	F	VF	XF	Unc
1660	—	20.00	45.00	80.00	155	—

KM# 171 2 KREUZER (Halbbatzen)
Silver **Obv:** Value: 2 on breast, imperial orb

Date	Mintage	VG	F	VF	XF	Unc
1663	—	20.00	40.00	75.00	155	—

KM# 184 2 KREUZER (Halbbatzen)
Silver **Rev:** Heart-shaped arms **Note:** Varieties exist.

Date	Mintage	VG	F	VF	XF	Unc
1668 HF	—	16.00	33.00	65.00	80.00	—
1680 MF	—	16.00	33.00	65.00	80.00	—
1694 MF	31,000	16.00	33.00	65.00	80.00	—

KM# 17 10 KREUZER (1/6 Guldenthaler)
Silver **Obv:** City arms in ornate frame divide date **Obv. Legend:** MONETA. REIPVBLICÆ. RATISBONENSIS. **Rev:** Crowned imperial eagle, orb with '10' on breast **Rev. Legend:** MATHIÆ. ROM. IMP. AVG. P. F. DECRETO.

Date	Mintage	VG	F	VF	XF	Unc
(16)19	—	125	220	320	650	—

KM# 11 30 KREUZER (1/2 Guldenthaler)
Silver **Obv:** Regensburg arms in shield **Rev:** Crowned imperial eagle, 30 in orb on breast, titles of Matthias

Date	Mintage	VG	F	VF	XF	Unc
1613	—	500	825	1,400	2,400	—
ND	—	275	550	1,100	1,800	—

KM# 29 30 KREUZER (1/2 Guldenthaler)
Silver **Obv:** Titles of Ferdinand II

Date	Mintage	VG	F	VF	XF	Unc
(16)Z1	—	500	825	1,400	2,400	—

KM# 70 30 KREUZER (1/2 Guldenthaler)
Silver **Obv:** Oval Regensburg arms in baroque frame, angel above, date in legend **Rev:** Crowned double-headed imperial eagle, value in orb on breast

Date	Mintage	VG	F	VF	XF	Unc
1630	—	2,200	3,000	4,500	7,400	—

KM# 47 1/9 THALER
Silver **Obv:** Crowned imperial eagle, arms of Austria on breast, titles of Ferdinand II **Rev:** Regensburg arms, angel above, value 1/9 in oval below, date in legend

Date	Mintage	VG	F	VF	XF	Unc
1626	—	225	400	750	1,100	—

KM# 61 1/9 THALER
Silver **Obv:** Crowned imperial eagle in circle, value: 1/9 in circle on breast, titles of Ferdinand II and date in legend **Rev:** Regensburg arms in oval shield with point at bottom, angel above

Date	Mintage	VG	F	VF	XF	Unc
16Z9	—	225	400	750	1,150	—

KM# 86 1/9 THALER
Silver **Obv:** Crowned imperial eagle, value: 1/9 in oval at bottom, titles of Ferdinand III **Rev:** Oval Regensburg arms in baroque frame, angel's head above, date in legend **Note:** Varieties exist.

Date	Mintage	VG	F	VF	XF	Unc
1638	—	175	340	700	1,050	—
1641	—	180	375	725	1,075	—
1645	—	210	400	750	1,100	—
1646	—	180	375	725	1,075	—
1647	—	180	375	725	1,075	—

KM# 117 1/9 THALER
Silver **Obv:** Large crowned imperial eagle **Rev:** Without angel at top

Date	Mintage	VG	F	VF	XF	Unc
1648 (c)	—	180	375	725	1,075	—

KM# 139 1/9 THALER
Silver **Obv:** Regensburg arms in oval baroque frame, date in margin **Rev:** Crowned imperial eagle, value 1/9 in orb on breast, titles of Ferdinand III **Note:** Varieties exist.

Date	Mintage	VG	F	VF	XF	Unc
1654 HF	—	180	375	725	1,075	—
1655 HF	—	180	375	725	1,075	—
1656 HF	—	180	375	725	1,075	—
1657 HF	—	180	375	725	1,075	—

KM# 146 1/9 THALER
Silver **Obv:** Titles of Leopold I **Note:** Varieties exist.

Date	Mintage	VG	F	VF	XF	Unc
1657	—	—	—	—	—	—

Note: Coin dated 1657, if it exists, would be a mule of obverse die for KM#139 and reverse die for KM#146; Reported, not confirmed

Date	Mintage	VG	F	VF	XF	Unc
1659 HF	—	185	375	725	1,075	—
1661 HF	—	185	375	725	1,075	—
1662 HF	—	185	375	725	1,075	—
1663 HF	—	185	375	725	1,075	—
1664 HF	—	185	375	725	1,075	—
1665 HF	—	185	375	725	1,075	—
1667 HF	—	185	375	725	1,075	—

KM# 48 1/6 THALER (1/4 Gulden)
Silver **Obv:** Crowned imperial eagle, arms of Austria on breast, titles of Ferdinand II **Rev:** Regensburg arms, angel above, value 1/6 in oval below, date in legend

Date	Mintage	VG	F	VF	XF	Unc
1626	—	450	750	1,150	2,000	—
1627	—	450	750	1,150	2,000	—

KM# 55 1/6 THALER (1/4 Gulden)
Silver **Obv:** Crowned imperial eagle in circle, Austria arms on breast, value 1/6 in oval below, titles of Ferdinand II **Rev:** Ornately-shaped Regensburg arms, angel above, date in legend

Date	Mintage	VG	F	VF	XF	Unc
1627	—	450	750	1,150	2,000	—
1628	—	425	675	975	1,650	—

KM# 87 1/6 THALER (1/4 Gulden)
Silver **Obv:** Value 1/6 below eagle **Note:** Varieties exist.

Date	Mintage	VG	F	VF	XF	Unc
1638 (b)	—	425	675	975	1,650	—
1641 (c)	—	425	675	975	1,650	—

KM# 107 1/6 THALER (1/4 Gulden)
Silver **Obv:** Value 1/6 in orb on eagle's breast **Note:** Varieties exist.

Date	Mintage	VG	F	VF	XF	Unc
1644 (c)	—	425	675	975	1,650	—
1645 (c)	—	425	675	975	1,650	—
1646 (c)	—	425	675	975	1,650	—
1647 (c)	—	425	675	975	1,650	—
1651 (c)	—	425	675	975	1,650	—

KM# 128 1/6 THALER (1/4 Gulden)
Silver **Obv:** Without angel's head above arms **Rev:** Crowned double-headed imperial eagle, value in orb on breast

Date	Mintage	VG	F	VF	XF	Unc
1652 (c)	—	55.00	900	1,350	2,150	—

KM# 134 1/6 THALER (1/4 Gulden)
Silver **Obv:** Without inner circle **Rev:** Without inner circle

Date	Mintage	VG	F	VF	XF	Unc
1653	—	425	675	975	1,650	—
1657 HF	—	425	675	975	1,650	—

KM# 140 1/6 THALER (1/4 Gulden)
Silver **Obv:** Enclosed in circle

Date	Mintage	VG	F	VF	XF	Unc
1654 HF	—	425	675	975	1,650	—
1656 HF	—	425	675	975	1,650	—

KM# 157 1/6 THALER (1/4 Gulden)
Silver **Obv:** Titles of Leopold I **Note:** Varieties exist.

Date	Mintage	VG	F	VF	XF	Unc
1659 HF	—	300	500	925	1,550	—
1662 HF	—	300	500	925	1,550	—
1663 HF	—	300	500	925	1,550	—
1664 HF	—	550	900	1,350	2,150	—

KM# 179 1/6 THALER (1/4 Gulden)
Silver **Rev:** Heart-shaped arms

Date	Mintage	VG	F	VF	XF	Unc
1667 HF	—	425	675	975	1,650	—
1680 MF	—	425	675	975	1,650	—

Note: 1680-dated coins struck from altered 1667 dies

KM# 49 1/4 THALER
Silver **Obv:** Crowned imperial eagle, arms of Austria on breast, titles of Ferdinand II **Rev:** Regensburg arms, angel above, value 1/4 in oval below, date in legend

Date	Mintage	VG	F	VF	XF	Unc
1626	—	600	950	1,500	2,400	—

KM# 50 1/4 THALER
Silver **Obv:** Value 1/4 on bottom, oval **Rev:** Ornately-shaped arms **Note:** Varieties exist.

Date	Mintage	VG	F	VF	XF	Unc
1626	—	475	750	1,150	1,850	—
1627	—	475	750	1,150	1,850	—
1628	—	475	750	1,150	1,850	—

KM# 88 1/4 THALER
Silver **Obv:** Crowned imperial eagle, value 1/4 in oval at bottom, titles of Ferdinand III **Rev:** Oval Regensburg arms in baroque frame, angel's head above, date in legend **Note:** Varieties exist.

Date	Mintage	VG	F	VF	XF	Unc
1638 (b)	—	600	950	1,500	2,400	—
1641 (c)	—	500	775	1,150	1,850	—
1642 (c)	—	500	775	1,150	1,850	—
1645 (c)	—	500	900	1,350	2,200	—
1646 (c)	—	500	900	1,350	2,200	—

KM# 108 1/4 THALER
Silver **Obv:** Ornate arms **Rev:** Crowned double-headed eagle, value in orb on breast

Date	Mintage	VG	F	VF	XF	Unc
1644 (c)	—	500	775	1,150	1,850	—
1646 (c)	—	500	900	1,350	2,200	—
1647 (c)	—	500	900	1,350	2,200	—

KM# 113 1/4 THALER
Silver **Obv:** Modified oval shield **Rev:** Heart-shaped shield with value on eagle's breast

Date	Mintage	VG	F	VF	XF	Unc
1647 (c)	—	550	900	1,400	2,400	—

KM# 129 1/4 THALER
Silver **Obv:** Ornate arms **Rev:** Crowned double-headed eagle, value in orb on breast **Note:** Varieties exist.

Date	Mintage	VG	F	VF	XF	Unc
1652 (c)	—	475	750	1,150	1,900	—
1654	—	475	750	1,150	1,900	—
1655	—	475	750	1,150	1,900	—

KM# 142 1/4 THALER
Silver **Obv:** Without inner circle **Rev:** Without inner circle

Date	Mintage	VG	F	VF	XF	Unc
1656 HF	—	475	750	1,150	1,900	—

KM# 147 1/4 THALER
Silver **Obv:** Ornate oval arms, date in legend **Rev:** Crowned double-headed imperial eagle, value in orb on breast

Date	Mintage	VG	F	VF	XF	Unc
1657 HF	—	475	750	1,150	1,900	—

KM# 158 1/4 THALER
Silver **Obv:** Value: 1/4 in orb, titles of Leopold I **Note:** Varieties exist.

Date	Mintage	VG	F	VF	XF	Unc
1660 HF	—	475	750	1,150	1,900	—
1661 HF	—	475	750	1,150	1,900	—
1662 HF	—	475	750	1,150	1,900	—
1663 HF	—	475	750	1,150	1,900	—
1664 HF	—	475	750	1,150	1,900	—

KM# 177 1/4 THALER
Silver **Obv:** Heart-shaped arms **Rev:** Heart-shaped shield on eagle's breast **Note:** Varieties exist.

Date	Mintage	VG	F	VF	XF	Unc
1665 HF	—	500	900	1,350	2,200	—
1666 HF	—	475	750	1,150	1,900	—
1667 HF	—	475	750	1,150	1,900	—
1672 HF	—	475	750	1,150	1,900	—
1680 HF	—	500	900	1,350	2,200	—

Note: 1680 dated coins struck from altered 1672 dies

KM# 202 1/4 THALER
Silver **Note:** Modified and more ornate oval shield of arms, date divided at top

Date	Mintage	VG	F	VF	XF	Unc
1694 MF	—	550	900	1,400	2,400	—

KM# 110 1/3 THALER (1/2 Gulden)
Silver **Obv:** Modified oval shield **Rev:** Heart-shaped shield with 1/3 on eagle's breast

Date	Mintage	VG	F	VF	XF	Unc
1646 (c)	—	800	1,300	1,750	2,600	—

KM# 130 1/3 THALER (1/2 Gulden)
Silver **Obv:** Without angel's head above arms **Rev:** Crowned double-headed imperial eagle, 1/3 in orb on breast

Date	Mintage	VG	F	VF	XF	Unc
1652 (c)	—	800	1,300	1,750	2,600	—

KM# 141 1/3 THALER (1/2 Gulden)
Silver **Obv:** Ornate arms **Rev:** Crowned double-headed imperial eagle, value in orb on breast **Note:** Varieties exist.

Date	Mintage	VG	F	VF	XF	Unc
1654 HF	—	800	1,300	1,750	2,600	—
1655 HF	—	800	1,300	1,750	2,600	—
1656 HF	—	800	1,300	1,750	2,600	—
1657 HF	—	800	1,300	1,750	2,600	—

KM# 159 1/3 THALER (1/2 Gulden)
Silver **Obv:** Titles of Leopold I **Note:** Varieties exist.

Date	Mintage	VG	F	VF	XF	Unc
1659 HF	—	800	1,300	1,750	2,600	—
1663 HF	—	800	1,300	1,750	2,600	—
1664 HF	—	800	1,300	1,750	2,600	—
1666 HF	—	800	1,300	1,750	2,600	—

KM# 180 1/3 THALER (1/2 Gulden)
Silver **Obv:** Heart-shaped arms **Rev:** Heart-shaped shield with 1/3 in shield on eagle's breast

Date	Mintage	VG	F	VF	XF	Unc
1667 HF	—	500	1,000	1,650	2,400	—
1672 HF	—	700	1,300	1,750	2,600	—
1680 HF	—	700	1,300	1,750	2,600	—

Note: 1680 dated coins struck from altered 1672 dies

KM# 43 1/2 THALER
Silver **Obv:** Cherub above shield **Rev:** Double-headed imperial eagle, shield on breast

Date	Mintage	VG	F	VF	XF	Unc
1625	—	500	750	1,150	1,900	—
1627	—	500	750	1,150	1,900	—

KM# 62 1/2 THALER
Silver **Rev:** Oval Regensburg arms in baroque frame

Date	Mintage	VG	F	VF	XF	Unc
1629	—	500	750	1,150	1,900	—

KM# 63 1/2 THALER
Silver **Obv:** Oval arms pointed at bottom **Rev:** Crowned double-headed imperial eagle, shield on breast

Date	Mintage	VG	F	VF	XF	Unc
1629	—	500	750	1,150	1,900	—

KM# 89 1/2 THALER
Silver **Obv:** Ornate arms **Rev:** Crowned double-headed imperial eagle, shield on breast, without indication of value

Date	Mintage	VG	F	VF	XF	Unc
1638 (b)	—	550	900	1,400	2,500	—
1639	—	600	1,100	1,500	2,600	—

KM# 101 1/2 THALER
Silver **Obv:** Ornate arms **Rev:** Crown above double-headed imperial eagle, shield on breast **Note:** Varieties exist.

Date	Mintage	VG	F	VF	XF	Unc
1640 (c)	—	600	1,100	1,525	2,600	—
1643 (c)	—	600	900	1,400	2,400	—

KM# 105 1/2 THALER
Silver **Obv:** Bust right, titles of Ferdinand III **Rev:** Date divided at top **Note:** Varieties exist.

Date	Mintage	VG	F	VF	XF	Unc
1644 (c)	—	600	900	1,400	2,400	—
1645 (c)	—	600	900	1,400	2,400	—
1646 (c)	—	500	750	1,150	1,900	—

KM# 114 1/2 THALER
Silver **Obv:** Ornate arms **Rev:** Value in shield on eagle's breast **Note:** Varieties exist.

Date	Mintage	VG	F	VF	XF	Unc
1647 (c)	—	575	950	1,450	2,600	—
1653 (c)	—	650	1,100	1,650	2,700	—
1654 HF	—	650	1,100	1,650	2,700	—

KM# 143 1/2 THALER
Silver **Obv:** Ornate arms **Rev:** Value in orb on breast

Date	Mintage	VG	F	VF	XF	Unc
1656 HF	—	550	900	1,400	2,400	—
1657 HF	—	550	900	1,400	2,400	—

KM# 148 1/2 THALER
Silver **Obv:** Arms of Austria on eagle's breast, without indication of value

Date	Mintage	VG	F	VF	XF	Unc
1657	—	—	—	—	—	—

Note: Reported, not confirmed

KM# 152 1/2 THALER
Silver **Obv:** Large ornate oval arms **Rev:** SVB VMBRA ALARUM TVARUM instead of emperor's titles

Date	Mintage	VG	F	VF	XF	Unc
1658 HF	—	1,600	2,300	3,100	4,500	—

KM# 166 1/2 THALER
Silver **Obv:** Ornate arms **Rev:** Value in orb on breast **Note:** Varieties exist.

Date	Mintage	VG	F	VF	XF	Unc
1660 HF	—	550	900	1,400	2,400	—
1661 HF	—	550	900	1,400	2,400	—
1662 HF	—	550	900	1,350	2,300	—

Date	Mintage	VG	F	VF	XF	Unc
1663 HF	—	550	900	1,350	2,300	—
1664 HF	—	550	900	1,350	2,300	—

KM# 178 1/2 THALER
Silver **Obv:** Heart-shaped ornate arms, cherub face and wings above **Rev:** Value in orb on breast **Note:** Varieties exist.

Date	Mintage	VG	F	VF	XF	Unc
1665 HF	—	525	900	1,350	2,200	—
1666/5 HF	—	525	900	1,350	2,200	—
1667 HF	—	525	900	1,350	2,200	—
1672 HF	—	525	900	1,350	2,200	—
1680 MF	—	550	900	1,400	2,400	—
Note: Struck from altered 1672 dies						
1691 MF	—	550	900	1,400	2,400	—
1694 MF	1,245	525	900	1,350	2,200	—
Note: Struck from altered 1672 dies						

KM# 207 1/2 THALER
Silver **Obv:** Ornate modified oval Regensburg arms, date divided at top **Rev:** Crowned imperial eagle, Austrian arms in heart-shaped shield on breast, titles of Leopold I

Date	Mintage	VG	F	VF	XF	Unc
1696 MF	—	500	900	1,350	2,200	—

KM# 111 2/3 THALER (Gulden)
Silver **Obv:** Ornate arms **Rev:** Crowned double-headed eagle, heart shaped shield with value on breast **Note:** Similar to 1/4 Thaler, KM#113, but value: 2/3 in shield on eagle's breast. Dav. #783, 784.

Date	Mintage	VG	F	VF	XF	Unc
1646 (c)	—	1,300	2,100	2,700	3,800	—
1655 HF	—	1,300	2,100	2,700	3,800	—

KM# 149 2/3 THALER (Gulden)
Silver **Obv:** Ornate arms **Rev:** Crowned double-headed imperial eagle, 2/3 in heart shaped shield on eagle's breast **Note:** Similar to 1/3 Thaler, KM#141, but value: 2/3 in heart-shaped shield on eagle's breast. Dav. #785.

Date	Mintage	VG	F	VF	XF	Unc
1657 HF	—	1,200	1,750	2,500	3,900	—

KM# 170 2/3 THALER (Gulden)
Silver **Obv:** Ornate arms **Rev:** Crowned double-headed imperial eagle with 2/3 in orb on breast, titles of Leopold I. **Note:** Dav. #786, 787.

Date	Mintage	VG	F	VF	XF	Unc
1662 HF	—	1,200	1,750	2,400	4,000	—
1663 HF	—	1,200	1,750	2,400	4,000	—
1664 HF	—	1,200	1,750	2,400	4,000	—
1666 HF	—	1,200	1,750	2,400	4,000	—
1667 HF	—	1,200	1,750	2,400	4,000	—
1672 HF	—	1,200	1,750	2,400	4,000	—
1680 HF	—	1,200	1,750	2,400	4,000	—

Note: 1680 dated coins struck from altered 1672 die

KM# 12 GULDENTHALER OF 60 KREUZER
Silver **Obv:** Value: 60 in orb on breast of crowned imperial eagle **Obv. Legend:** MATHIAE * ROM: IMP: AVG: P*F: DECRETO* **Rev:** Arms dividing date **Rev. Legend:** MONETA * REIPVLICAE * RATISPONENSIS * **Note:** Dav. #115.

Date	Mintage	VG	F	VF	XF	Unc
1613	—	900	1,700	2,950	5,500	—

KM# 13 GULDENTHALER OF 60 KREUZER
Silver **Obv:** Simplified eagle **Rev:** Revised arms **Note:** Dav. #115.

Date	Mintage	VG	F	VF	XF	Unc
ND	—	850	1,550	2,600	5,000	—

KM# 14 GULDENTHALER OF 60 KREUZER
Silver **Rev:** Ornate arms **Note:** Dav. #115.

Date	Mintage	VG	F	VF	XF	Unc
ND	—	650	1,200	2,000	3,850	—

KM# 15 GULDENTHALER OF 60 KREUZER
Silver **Rev:** Dots divide legend, simplified arms **Note:** Dav. #115.

Date	Mintage	VG	F	VF	XF	Unc
ND	—	850	1,550	2,600	5,000	—

KM# 18 GULDENTHALER OF 60 KREUZER
Silver **Obv:** City arms divide date encircled by wreath, senators arms with initials around **Rev:** Crowned double-headed imperial eagle, value in orb on breast **Rev. Legend:** MONETA * REIPVBLICAE * RATISPONENSIS * **Note:** Dav. #118.

Date	Mintage	VG	F	VF	XF	Unc
1619	—	1,050	1,950	3,250	5,700	—

KM# 30 GULDENTHALER OF 60 KREUZER
Silver **Obv. Legend:** • MATHIAE • ROM • IMP • AVG:P*F DECRETO* • **Rev:** Arms divide date

Date	Mintage	VG	F	VF	XF	Unc
1621	—	—	—	—	—	—

Note: Reported, not confirmed

KM# 31 GULDENTHALER OF 60 KREUZER
Silver **Obv:** Flower breaks legend at top, arms on shield in inner circle **Rev:** Double-headed eagle, crown above, value in orb on breast, legend around **Rev. Legend:** FERDINANDI • II • ROM • IMP • S:AVG • P • F DECRETO **Note:** Dav. #119.

Date	Mintage	VG	F	VF	XF	Unc
16Z1	—	525	900	1,550	2,900	—

KM# 32 GULDENTHALER OF 60 KREUZER

Silver **Obv:** *'s begin and end legend, revised border on arms **Rev:** Crowned double-headed imperial eagle, value in orb on breast **Note:** Dav. #119.

Date	Mintage	VG	F	VF	XF	Unc
1621	—	525	900	1,550	2,900	—

KM# 71 GULDENTHALER OF 60 KREUZER

Silver **Obv:** Legend, angel above arms **Obv. Legend:** •MONE: REIPVB: -RATISPON: 1640 **Rev:** Crowned double-headed imperial eagle, value in orb on breast **Rev. Legend:** FERDINANDVS • II • ROM: IMP: ABG: P • F • DECRETO **Note:** Dav. #120.

Date	Mintage	VG	F	VF	XF	Unc
1630	—	650	1,150	1,950	3,600	—

KM# 41 THALER

Silver **Obv:** Ornate shield divides date **Rev:** Crowned double-headed imperial eagle, shield on breast, different punctuation **Note:** Dav. #5744.

Date	Mintage	VG	F	VF	XF	Unc
1623	—	275	575	1,250	2,500	—

KM# 44 THALER

Silver **Obv:** Angel holding shield before him **Obv. Legend:** MONETA* REIPVLICAE... **Rev. Legend:** ...AVGVSTVS. **Note:** Dav. #5745.

Date	Mintage	VG	F	VF	XF	Unc
1625	—	275	575	1,250	2,500	—

KM# 51 THALER

Silver **Obv. Legend:** ...D. R. ROM. IMP. SEM... **Rev. Legend:** MONETA. REIPVB... **Note:** Dav. #5746.

Date	Mintage	VG	F	VF	XF	Unc
1626	—	275	575	1,250	2,500	—
1628	—	275	575	1,250	2,500	—

KM# 52 THALER

Silver **Obv:** Angel above ornate shield **Obv. Legend:** MONE... **Rev:** Crown above double-headed imperial eagle, shield on breast, legend, titles of Ferdinand **Note:** Dav. #5747.

Date	Mintage	VG	F	VF	XF	Unc
1626	—	175	350	700	1,350	2,750
1627	—	175	350	700	1,350	2,750

KM# 64 THALER

Silver **Obv:** Angel above ornate egg-shaped shield **Rev:** Crown above double-headed imperial eagle, shield on breast **Note:** Dav. #5748.

Date	Mintage	VG	F	VF	XF	Unc
1629	—	600	1,150	2,250	3,750	—

KM# 74 THALER

Silver **Obv:** Angel above ornate egg-shaped shield **Rev:** Crown above double-headed imperial eagle, shield on breast **Note:** Dav. #5749.

Date	Mintage	VG	F	VF	XF	Unc
1632	—	650	1,200	2,350	4,250	—

Note: Fritz Rudolf Künker Münzenhandlung Auction 113, 6-06, nearly Unc. realized approximately $14,540

KM# 77 THALER

Silver **Subject:** Conquest of Regensburg by Duke Bernhard of Saxony **Note:** Dav. #5750.

Date	Mintage	VG	F	VF	XF	Unc
1633	—	1,000	2,000	4,000	7,000	—

KM# 78 THALER

Silver **Obv:** 7-line inscription within wreath **Rev:** City view in inner circle **Note:** Dav. #5751.

Date	Mintage	VG	F	VF	XF	Unc
1633 Rare	—	—	—	—	—	—

KM# 83 THALER

Silver **Obv:** Angel above ornate egg-shaped shield **Rev:** City view in inner circle **Note:** Dav. #5752.

Date	Mintage	VG	F	VF	XF	Unc
1634 Rare	—	—	—	—	—	—

KM# 90 THALER

Silver **Obv:** Arms in round frame **Rev:** Crowned imperial eagle without sword or scepter, Austrian arms on chest **Note:** Dav. #5754.

Date	Mintage	VG	F	VF	XF	Unc
1638 (b)	—	400	800	1,650	2,850	—

KM# 94 THALER

Silver **Obv:** Angel above ornate egg-shaped shield **Rev:** Crown above double-headed imperial eagle, shield on breast **Note:** Dav. #5755.

Date	Mintage	VG	F	VF	XF	Unc
1639	—	850	1,650	3,250	6,000	—

KM# 102 THALER

Silver **Obv:** Angel head, two eagle heads above arms **Rev:** Crown above imperial eagle, orb between necks, shield on breast **Note:** Dav. #5758.

Date	Mintage	VG	F	VF	XF	Unc
1641 (c)	—	250	500	1,200	2,750	5,000
1642 (c)	—	250	500	1,200	2,750	—

KM# 106 THALER

Silver **Obv:** Crowned imperial eagle with Emperor's bust on breast **Rev:** Angel above arms in frame **Note:** Dav. #5760.

Date	Mintage	VG	F	VF	XF	Unc
1643 (c)	—	350	750	1,500	3,500	—
1644 (c)	—	350	750	1,500	3,500	—

KM# 109 THALER

Silver **Obv. Legend:** ...ROMA: IMP:... **Note:** Dav. #5761.

Date	Mintage	VG	F	VF	XF	Unc
1645 (c)	—	300	650	1,350	2,850	5,250
1646 (c)	—	300	650	1,350	2,850	—
1647 (c)	—	300	650	1,350	2,850	—

KM# 115 THALER

Silver **Rev:** Oval shield without angel **Note:** Dav. #5762.

Date	Mintage	VG	F	VF	XF	Unc
1647 (c)	—	650	1,150	2,250	5,750	—

KM# 118 THALER

Silver **Obv:** Angel above arms **Rev:** Crowned imperial eagle with oval arms on breast **Note:** Dav. #5763.

Date	Mintage	VG	F	VF	XF	Unc
1649 (c)	—	150	375	850	1,750	3,750

KM# 131 THALER

Silver **Obv:** Crowned imperial eagle with emperor's head on breast **Rev:** Angel head above arms in round frame **Note:** Dav. #5764.

Date	Mintage	VG	F	VF	XF	Unc
1652 (c)	—	650	1,250	4,500	7,000	—
1653 (c)	—	650	1,250	4,500	7,000	—
1654 HF	—	—	—	—	—	—

KM# 151 THALER

Silver **Obv:** Angel head above arms in inner circle **Rev:** Crowned imperial eagle with nothing on breast **Note:** Dav. #5766.

Date	Mintage	VG	F	VF	XF	Unc
1656 HF	—	400	800	1,750	3,250	—
1657 HF	—	400	800	1,750	3,250	—

KM# 153 THALER

Silver **Obv:** Arms in frame, HF below **Rev:** Crowned double-headed imperial eagle **Note:** Dav. #5767.

Date	Mintage	VG	F	VF	XF	Unc
1658 HF	—	850	1,600	3,300	5,400	—

KM# 167 THALER

Silver **Obv:** Arms in frame, without inner circle, HF below **Rev:** Crowned imperial eagle with Austrian arms in heart shield **Note:** Dav. #5769.

Date	Mintage	VG	F	VF	XF	Unc
1660 HF	—	400	800	1,750	3,250	—
1661 HF	—	400	800	1,750	3,250	—
1662 HF	—	400	800	1,750	3,250	—
1663 HF	—	400	800	1,750	3,250	—

KM# 172 THALER

Silver **Obv:** Ornate oval shield **Rev:** Crowned imperial eagle with arms on breast **Note:** Dav. #5770.

Date	Mintage	VG	F	VF	XF	Unc
1664 HF	—	400	800	1,750	3,350	—
1665 HF	—	400	800	1,750	3,350	—
1666 HF	—	400	800	1,750	3,350	—
1667 HF	—	600	1,200	1,750	3,350	—
1672 HF	—	600	1,200	1,750	3,350	—

KM# 191 THALER

Silver **Obv:** Crowned imperial eagle without shield on breast **Note:** Dav. #5771.

Date	Mintage	VG	F	VF	XF	Unc
1676 MF Rare	—	—	—	—	—	—

KM# 195 THALER

Silver **Obv:** Eagle with heart-shaped Austrian arms on breast **Rev:** Arms in frame, MF below **Note:** Dav. #5772.

Date	Mintage	VG	F	VF	XF	Unc
1680/72 MF	—	700	1,350	2,750	4,500	—
1680 MF	—	700	1,350	2,750	4,500	—
1681 MF	—	425	850	1,750	3,500	5,500
1691 MF	—	450	900	1,850	3,750	—
1694 MF	6,821	450	900	1,850	3,750	—

KM# 203 THALER

Silver **Rev:** Angel above arms in frame **Note:** Dav. #5773.

Date	Mintage	F	VF	XF	Unc	BU
1694 MF	Inc. above	200	400	850	1,900	—
1696 MF	307	275	575	1,150	2,250	—

KM# 19 1-1/2 GULDENTHALER

Silver **Obv:** City arms divide date encircled by wreath, senators arms with initials around **Rev:** Crowned double-headed imperial eagle, value in orb on breast **Rev. Legend:** MONETA * REIPVBLICAE * RATISPONENSIS *

Date	Mintage	VG	F	VF	XF	Unc
1619	—	4,000	5,300	6,300	9,500	—

KM# 5 1-1/2 THALER

Silver **Obv:** Angel holding imperial and city shields **Rev:** 7-line inscription **Note:** Klippe. Dav. #A5742.

Date	Mintage	VG	F	VF	XF	Unc
1608 Rare	—	—	—	—	—	—

KM# 20 2 GULDENTHALER

Silver **Obv:** City arms divide date encircled by wreath, senators' arms with initials around **Rev:** Crowned double-headed imperial eagle, value in orb on breast **Rev. Legend:** MONETA * REIPVBLICAE * RATISPONENSIS * **Note:** Similar to 1 Guldenthaler, KM#18.

Date	Mintage	VG	F	VF	XF	Unc
1619 Rare	—	—	—	—	—	—

KM# 6 2 THALER

Silver **Obv:** Angle holding imperial and city shields **Rev:** 7-line inscription **Note:** Klippe. Dav. #5742.

Date	Mintage	VG	F	VF	XF	Unc
1608 Rare	—	—	—	—	—	—

TRADE COINAGE

KM# 16 GOLDGULDEN

3.5000 g., 0.9860 Gold 0.1109 oz. AGW **Obv:** Crossed key arms topped by date in inner circle **Rev:** Crowned imperial eagle, titles of Leopold Mathias

Date	Mintage	VG	F	VF	XF	Unc
1617	—	1,450	2,800	4,500	7,500	12,500

Note: UBS Regensburg Auction 60, 9-04, nearly FDC realized $14,170

Date	Mintage	VG	F	VF	XF	Unc
1618	—	1,450	2,800	4,500	7,500	12,500

KM# 209 1/3 DUCAT

1.1666 g., 0.9860 Gold 0.0370 oz. AGW **Obv:** City arms **Rev:** Crowned imperial double-headed eagle

Date	Mintage	VG	F	VF	XF	Unc
1696	—	350	650	1,250	2,250	—

KM# 135 1/2 DUCAT

1.1666 g., 0.9860 Gold 0.0370 oz. AGW **Obv:** Crowned legend **Obv. Legend:** FERDINAND IV... **Rev:** Legend on ribbon **Rev. Legend:** PRO DEO ET...

Date	Mintage	VG	F	VF	XF	Unc
1653	—	150	300	650	1,250	—

KM# 56 DUCAT

3.5000 g., 0.9860 Gold 0.1109 oz. AGW **Obv:** Trinity Church **Rev:** Inscription

Date	Mintage	VG	F	VF	XF	Unc
1627	—	600	1,200	2,250	3,750	—

KM# 75 DUCAT

3.5000 g., 0.9860 Gold 0.1109 oz. AGW **Obv:** Crossed keys in cartouche in inner circle, date divided at top **Rev:** Crowned imperial eagle with arms on breast in inner circle, titles of Ferdinand II

Date	Mintage	VG	F	VF	XF	Unc
1632	—	1,200	2,400	4,800	8,000	—

KM# 79 DUCAT

3.5000 g., 0.9860 Gold 0.1109 oz. AGW **Subject:** Triumphal Entry into City of Bernhard of Saxe-Weimar on Nov. 4, 1633 **Rev:** 6-line inscription

Date	Mintage	VG	F	VF	XF	Unc
1633	—	1,250	2,250	4,250	7,750	—

KM# 84 DUCAT

3.5000 g., 0.9860 Gold 0.1109 oz. AGW **Rev:** City of Regensburg

Date	Mintage	VG	F	VF	XF	Unc
1634	—	1,300	2,600	5,200	9,000	—

KM# 85 DUCAT

3.5000 g., 0.9860 Gold 0.1109 oz. AGW **Subject:** Coronation of Ferdinand III

Date	Mintage	VG	F	VF	XF	Unc
1636	—	1,250	2,500	4,500	—	—

KM# 91 DUCAT

3.5000 g., 0.9860 Gold 0.1109 oz. AGW **Obv:** Crossed keys in cartouche in inner circle, cherub head at top, date in legend **Rev:** Crowned imperial eagle **Note:** Varieties exist.

Date	Mintage	VG	F	VF	XF	Unc
1638 (b)	—	400	850	1,750	3,500	6,500
1639 (b)	—	400	850	1,750	3,500	6,500
1640 (c)	—	400	850	1,750	3,500	6,500
1641 (c)	—	400	850	1,750	3,500	6,500
1642 (c)	—	400	850	1,750	3,500	6,500
1643 (c)	—	400	850	1,750	3,500	6,500
1644 (c)	—	400	850	1,750	3,500	6,500
1645	—	425	900	1,800	4,000	6,750
1646 (c)	—	400	850	1,750	3,500	6,500
1647 (c)	—	400	850	1,750	3,500	6,500
1651	—	450	950	1,850	4,500	8,000
1652	—	400	850	1,750	3,500	6,500
1656 HF	—	400	850	1,750	3,500	6,500
1657 HF	—	450	950	1,850	4,000	6,750

KM# 103 DUCAT

3.5000 g., 0.9860 Gold 0.1109 oz. AGW **Subject:** 200th Anniversary of the Reformation in Regensburg **Obv:** 5-line inscription, arms divide date at top **Rev:** Light and hands

Date	Mintage	VG	F	VF	XF	Unc
1641	—	1,000	2,000	3,600	6,000	—

KM# 104 DUCAT

3.5000 g., 0.9860 Gold 0.1109 oz. AGW **Obv:** 5-line inscription, arms divide date at top **Rev:** Candle above Bible on stand, banner at top

Date	Mintage	VG	F	VF	XF	Unc
1642	—	175	350	725	1,350	2,250

KM# 119 DUCAT

3.5000 g., 0.9860 Gold 0.1109 oz. AGW

Date	Mintage	VG	F	VF	XF	Unc
1649 (c)	—	550	1,100	2,150	3,850	6,500

KM# 127 DUCAT

3.5000 g., 0.9860 Gold 0.1109 oz. AGW **Obv:** 3-line inscription on mantle, divided date below **Rev:** Crowned imperial eagle

Date	Mintage	VG	F	VF	XF	Unc
1651	—	1,800	3,600	7,200	11,500	—

KM# 136 DUCAT

3.5000 g., 0.9860 Gold 0.1109 oz. AGW **Obv:** Crowned legend **Obv. Legend:** FERDINAND IV... **Rev:** Legend on ribbon **Rev. Legend:** PRO DEO ET...

Date	Mintage	VG	F	VF	XF	Unc
1653	—	225	450	850	1,750	—

KM# 137 DUCAT

3.5000 g., 0.9860 Gold 0.1109 oz. AGW **Obv:** Wreath **Rev:** Crowned imperial eagle

Date	Mintage	VG	F	VF	XF	Unc
1653	—	550	1,150	2,000	3,750	—

KM# 154 DUCAT

3.5000 g., 0.9860 Gold 0.1109 oz. AGW **Note:** Similar to KM#160.

Date	Mintage	VG	F	VF	XF	Unc
1658 HF	—	1,200	2,400	4,800	8,000	—

KM# 160 DUCAT

3.5000 g., 0.9860 Gold 0.1109 oz. AGW **Obv:** Crossed keys in cartouche, date in legend, titles of Leopold I **Rev:** Crowned imperial eagle with shield on breast **Note:** Varieties exist.

Date	Mintage	VG	F	VF	XF	Unc
1659 HF	—	750	1,600	3,250	5,500	—
1660 HF	—	750	1,600	3,250	5,500	—
1661 HF	—	750	1,600	3,250	5,500	—
1662 HF	—	750	1,600	3,250	5,500	—
1663 HF	—	750	1,600	3,250	5,500	—
1664 HF	—	750	1,600	3,250	5,500	—
1665 HF	—	750	1,600	3,250	5,500	—
1666 HF	—	750	1,600	3,250	5,500	—
1668 HF	—	750	1,600	3,250	5,500	—
1672 HF	—	750	1,600	3,250	5,500	—
1680 HF	334	750	1,600	3,250	5,500	—
1696 MF	7	—	—	—	—	—

KM# 57 2 DUCAT

7.0000 g., 0.9860 Gold 0.2219 oz. AGW **Obv:** Trinity Church **Rev:** Inscription **Note:** Struck with 1 Ducat dies, KM#56.

Date	Mintage	VG	F	VF	XF	Unc
1627	—	2,400	3,600	6,750	11,500	—

KM# 76 2 DUCAT

7.0000 g., 0.9860 Gold 0.2219 oz. AGW **Obv:** Arms in cartouche, date divided at top **Rev:** Crowned imperial eagle with shield on breast in inner circle **Note:** Struck with 1 Ducat dies, KM#75.

Date	Mintage	VG	F	VF	XF	Unc
1632	—	2,700	5,100	7,800	12,500	—

KM# A39 2 DUCAT

7.0000 g., 0.9860 Gold 0.2219 oz. AGW **Subject:** Centennial of Reformation in Regensburg **Obv:** City arms in cartouche divide date above 5-line inscription **Obv. Inscription:** NVN LEICHT DIS / LICHT VNS 100 IAHR / DASSELB NOCH FORT / VS GOTT BEWAHR / S.P.Q.R. **Rev:** Hands and arms extending from clouds at left and right, holding candle over table on the top of which is S. BIBLIA, and on facing side, CONFES/AVGVST/ANA, inscription in ribbon above V.D.M.I.Æ. **Rev. Legend:** DEN. XV. — OCTOB: **Note:** FR#2467.

Date	Mintage	VG	F	VF	XF	Unc
1642	—	—	—	1,850	3,250	5,500

KM# A53 2 DUCAT

7.0000 g., 0.9860 Gold 0.2219 oz. AGW **Subject:** Coronation of Ferdinand IV as King of Rome **Obv:** Imperial crown and palm fronds to left and right above 6-line inscription **Obv. Inscription:** FERDINAND: IV / HVNG: ET: BOH REX / CORON IN REGEM / ROMANORVM / XVIII. IVNV / MDCLIII. **Rev:** Scepter standing vertically, top reaching into clouds with Eye of God above, palm fronds to lower left and right, ribbon behind with inscription **Rev. Legend:** PRO DEO — ET POPVLO. **Note:** FR#2471a.

Date	Mintage	VG	F	VF	XF	Unc
MDCLIII (1653)	—	—	—	1,350	2,700	5,000

KM# 150 2 DUCAT

7.0000 g., 0.9860 Gold 0.2219 oz. AGW **Obv:** Crossed keys in ornate border **Rev:** Crowned imperial eagle, titles of Leopold I

Date	Mintage	VG	F	VF	XF	Unc
ND(1657-1705) HF	—	1,350	2,750	5,000	8,500	12,500

Note: UBS Regensburg Auction 60, 9-04, XF-nearly FDC realized $10,970

KM# 58 3 DUCAT

10.5000 g., 0.9860 Gold 0.3328 oz. AGW **Obv:** Trinity Church **Rev:** Inscription

Date	Mintage	VG	F	VF	XF	Unc
1627	—	2,500	4,500	7,000	11,500	—

KM# 155 3 DUCAT

10.5000 g., 0.9860 Gold 0.3328 oz. AGW **Obv:** Arms in cartouche **Rev:** Crowned imperial eagle with heart-shaped arms on breast, titles of Leopold I

Date	Mintage	VG	F	VF	XF	Unc
ND(1658-1705) Rare	—	—	—	—	—	—

KM# 173 4 DUCAT

14.0000 g., 0.9860 Gold 0.4438 oz. AGW **Obv:** Crowned imperial eagle, heart shaped shield on breast, titles of Leopold I **Rev:** Ornate arms

Date	Mintage	VG	F	VF	XF	Unc
1664 HF Rare	—	—	—	—	—	—

Note: UBS Regensburg Auction 60, 9-04, FDC realized $21,940

KM# 138 5 DUCAT

17.5000 g., 0.9860 Gold 0.5547 oz. AGW **Obv:** Crowned 5-line inscription: FERDINAND IV... **Rev:** Legend on ribbon **Rev. Legend:** PRO DEO ET...

Date	Mintage	VG	F	VF	XF	Unc
1653	—	2,500	4,000	7,000	12,000	—

KM# 174 5 DUCAT

17.5000 g., 0.9860 Gold 0.5547 oz. AGW **Obv:** Arms **Rev:** Crowned imperial eagle, titles of Leopold I

Date	Mintage	VG	F	VF	XF	Unc
1664 HF Rare	—	—	—	—	—	—

Note: UBS Regensburg Auction 60, 9-04, XF realized $14,625

KM# 181 6 DUCAT

21.0000 g., 0.9860 Gold 0.6657 oz. AGW **Obv:** Arms divide date in cartouche **Rev:** Crowned double-headed imperial eagle, heart shaped shield on breast, titles of Leopold I

Date	Mintage	VG	F	VF	XF	Unc
1667 HF Rare	—	—	—	—	—	—
ND IMF/HF Rare	—	—	—	—	—	—

Note (1667 HF): UBS Regensburg Auction 60, 9-04, XF realized $21,940

KM# 182 8 DUCAT

28.0000 g., 0.9860 Gold 0.8876 oz. AGW **Obv:** Crossed keys divide date in cartouche **Rev:** Crowned imperial eagle with crowned hear-shaped arms on breast

Date	Mintage	VG	F	VF	XF	Unc
1667 HF Rare	—	—	—	—	—	—

KM# 59 10 DUCAT

35.0000 g., 0.9860 Gold 1.1095 oz. AGW **Obv:** Ornate arms **Rev:** Crowned imperial eagle

Date	Mintage	VG	F	VF	XF	Unc
1627 Rare	—	—	—	—	—	—

KM# 183 10 DUCAT

35.0000 g., 0.9860 Gold 1.1095 oz. AGW **Obv:** Ornate arms **Rev:** Crowned imperial eagle, heart shaped shield on breast, titles of Leopold

Date	Mintage	VG	F	VF	XF	Unc
1667 HF Rare	—	—	—	—	—	—
ND IMF/HF Rare	—	—	—	—	—	—

Note (1667 HF): UBS Regensburg Auction 60, 9-04, nearly FDC realized $29,250

Note (ND IMF/HF): UBS Regensburg Auction 60, 9-04, XF realized $43,875

PATTERNS

Including off metal strikes

KM#	Date	Mintage	Identification	Mkt Val
Pn1	1546	—	Guldiner. Pewter. MB#53.	—
Pn2	1547	—	Guldiner. Pewter. MB#53.	—
Pn3	1556	—	Guldiner. Pewter. MB#88. Ref. E/K#42.1.	—
Pn4	1599	—	10 Kreuzer. Gold. MB#194. Weight of 3-3/4 Ducat.	—
Pn5	1619	—	Guldenthaler Of 60 Kreuzer. Gold. 36.6000 g. Klippe. KM#18.	—
Pn6	1640	—	Kreuzer. Gold. KM#93.	1,750
Pn7	1653	—	1/2 Kreuzer. Gold. 1/4 Ducat weight. KM#133.	—
Pn10	1680	—	1/2 Kreuzer. Gold. 1/6 Ducat weight. KM#190.	—
Pn11	1680	—	Kreuzer. Gold. KM#176.	2,250
Pn12	1687	—	Pfennig. Gold. 1/8 Ducat weight. KM#175.	—
Pn13	1691	—	Pfennig. Gold. 1/8 Ducat weight. KM#175.	—

KM#	Date	Mintage	Identification	Mkt Val
Pn16	1693	—	Pfennig. Gold. 1/8 Ducat weight. KM#201.	—
Pn15	1693	—	Pfennig. Gold. 1/10 Ducat weight. KM#200.	1,400
Pn14	1693	—	Heller. Gold. KM#192.	2,250
Pn17	1696	—	Pfennig. Gold. 1/8 Ducat weight. KM#204.	1,400
Pn18	1696	—	Pfennig. Gold. 1/5 Ducat weight. KM#204.	1,850
Pn19	1696	—	Kreuzer. Gold. KM#176.	2,250
Pn20	1699	—	Heller. Gold. KM#192.	2,250

REGENSTEIN

(Reinstein)

The counts of Regenstein trace their line of descent from the younger branch of the counts of Blankenburg from the early 13th century. The seat of power for the early counts was the castle of Regenstein, 12 miles (20km) southwest of the city of Halberstadt. When the counts of Blankenburg became extinct about 1370, those lands and titles passed to Regenstein. The last count of the line died in 1599 and the twin counties were divided by Brunswick and the bishopric of Halberstadt. There followed a succession of rulers until Brunswick and Brandenburg, which had received Halberstadt as part of the settlement stemming from the Peace of Westphalia, divided the two counties between them. Brandenburg (q.v.) subsequently struck coins in and for Regenstein.

RULERS

Johann Ernst, 1597-1599
  to Brunswick and Halberstadt, 1599-1629
Johann von Merode, 1629-1631
  to Brunswick, 1631-1643
Wilhelm Leopold von Tättenbach, 1643-1661
Johann Erasmus von Tättenbach, 1661-1671

NOTE: The copper 3 Pfennig of Brunswick-Wolfenbüttel (q.v.) dated 1621, KM#237, with crowned R, was issued for Regenstein.

COUNTSHIP

REGULAR COINAGE

KM# 1 1/2 THALER

Silver, 34 mm. **Ruler:** Johann Erasmus **Obv:** Bust to right in circle **Obv. Legend:** IOAN. ERAS. S. R. IMP. COM. DE. REINSTEIN. ET. TATTENBACH. **Rev:** Crowned 9-fold arms with small helmeted shield of arms to either side, date at end of legend **Rev. Legend:** SOLI. DEO. GLORIA

Date	Mintage	VG	F	VF	XF	Unc
1663 Rare	—	—	—	—	—	—

KM# 2 THALER

Silver **Ruler:** Johann Erasmus **Obv:** Bust to right in circle **Obv. Legend:** IOHAN. ERAS. S. R. IMP. COMES. DE. REINSTEIN. ET TATTENBACH. **Rev:** Helmeted 9-fold arms with small helmeted shield of arms to either side, date at end of legend **Rev. Legend:** SOLI. DEO. GLORIA. ANNO. **Note:** Dav. 7299.

Date	Mintage	VG	F	VF	XF	Unc
1663 Rare	—	—	—	—	—	—

KM# 3 2 THALER

Silver **Ruler:** Johann Erasmus **Obv:** Bust to right in circle **Obv. Legend:** IOHAN. ERAS. S. R. IMP. COMES. DE. REINSTEIN. ET TATTENBACH. **Rev:** Helmeted 9-fold arms with small helmeted shield of arms to either side, date at end of legend **Rev. Legend:** SOLI. DEO. GLORIA. ANNO. **Note:** Dav. 7298.

Date	Mintage	VG	F	VF	XF	Unc
1663 Rare	—	—	—	—	—	—

REUSS

The Reuss family, whose lands were located in Thuringia, was founded c. 1035. By the end of the 12th century, the custom of naming all males in the ruling house Heinrich had been established. The Elder Line modified this strange practice in the late 17th century to numbering all males from 1 to 100, then beginning over again. The Younger Line, meanwhile, decided to start the numbering of Heinrichs with the first male born in each century. Greiz was founded in 1303. Upper and Lower Greiz lines were founded in 1535 and the territories were divided until 1768. In 1778 the ruler was made a prince of the Holy Roman Empire. The principality endured until 1918.

MINT MARKS

A - Berlin
B – Hannover

MINT OFFICIALS' INITIALS

Initial	Date	Name
ES	1622	Ernst Schultes in Gera
	1623	In Lobenstein
HO	1621-?	Heinrich Oppermann in Moschlitz
IAB	1678-79	Johann Adam Bottcher in Schleiz
ICF	1681	Johann Carl Falkner in Darmstadt
	1692-93	In Eisenach
ILH	1698-1716	Johann Lorenz Holland in Dresden
IS	1624-35	Johann Schneider, known as Weissmantel in Erfurt
MR	1632-73	Martin Reinmann in Saalfeld
SD	1669-75, 78-80	Simon Dannes in Schleiz
TL	1621	Tobias Lippold, mint lessee in Gera
WA	1604-24 (d. 1634	Wolf Albrech in Saalfeld

LORDSHIP

JOINT COINAGE

of Younger Line

KM# 5 1/24 THALER (Groschen)

Silver **Obv:** Crowned heart-shaped 4-fold arms in baroque frame **Rev:** Imperial orb with 24 divides date, legend **Rev. Legend:** OBER SAXSISCHEN KREISSES GROSCH

Date	Mintage	VG	F	VF	XF	Unc
1655	—	200	310	475	725	—

KM# 6 1/4 THALER

Silver **Rev. Legend:** VIVIT POST FVNERA VIRTVS **Note:** Similar to 1 Thaler, KM#7.

Date	Mintage	VG	F	VF	XF	Unc
1655 MR	—	170	250	450	850	—

KM# 7 THALER

Silver **Note:** Dav. #7313

Date	Mintage	VG	F	VF	XF	Unc
MDCLV (1655) MR	—	775	1,650	3,050	5,500	—

REUSS-BURGK

The Elder Line in Untergreiz divided their lands in about1582 and Reuss-Burgk was thus founded. When this branch died out after 3 generations, Burgk reverted to Untergreiz.

RULERS

Heinrich II, 1582-1608
Heinrich II, 1608-1639
Heinrich III, 1639-1640

COUNTSHIP

REGULAR COINAGE

KM# 5 12 KREUZER (3 Batzen)

Silver **Obv:** Crowned imperial eagle, 12 in orb on breast, date divided near bottom, titles of Ferdinand II **Rev:** Crowned arms in ornamented shield divided vertically, lion left and crane right **Rev. Legend:** MO. NO...

Date	Mintage	VG	F	VF	XF	Unc
1621 HO	—	110	220	325	—	—

KM# 6 24 KREUZER (6 Batzen)

Silver **Obv:** Crowned imperial eagle, 24 in orb on breast, titles of Ferdinand II **Rev:** Crowned oval four-fold arms in baroque frame divide date near bottom, titles of Heinrich II

Date	Mintage	VG	F	VF	XF	Unc
1621 HO	—	135	250	350	—	—

KM# 7 24 KREUZER (6 Batzen)

Silver **Rev:** Date divided near bottom

Date	Mintage	VG	F	VF	XF	Unc
1621	—	135	250	350	—	—

KM# 8 24 KREUZER (6 Batzen)

Silver **Obv:** Without titles of Heinrich II **Obv. Legend:** MON. NOV. ARGENT. RVTHENICA BVR. **Note:** Varieties exist.

Date	Mintage	VG	F	VF	XF	Unc
1621	—	135	250	350	—	—
1622	—	135	250	350	—	—

KM# 9 24 KREUZER (6 Batzen)

Silver **Obv:** Crowned imperial eagle, 24 in orb on breast, titles of Ferdinand II **Rev:** Lion rampant left in ornamented oval shield, titles of Heinrich II

Date	Mintage	VG	F	VF	XF	Unc
ND	—	135	250	350	—	—

KM# 15 GROSCHEN

Silver **Subject:** Death of Heinrich II **Obv:** Crowned four-fold arms in ornamented heart-shaped shield, titles of Heinrich II **Obv. Legend:** Six-line inscription with date **Rev:** AN. GottES...

Date	Mintage	VG	F	VF	XF	Unc
1639	—	27.00	55.00	100	180	—

KM# 16 1/4 THALER

Silver **Subject:** Death of Heinrich II **Note:** Similar to 1 Groschen KM#15, but seven-line inscription on reverse.

Date	Mintage	VG	F	VF	XF	Unc
1639 Rare	—	—	—	—	—	—

KM# 17 1/2 THALER

Silver **Subject:** Death of Heinrich II **Obv:** Half-length figure of armored Heinrich right, titles in legend **Rev:** Seven-line inscription with date **Rev. Legend:** AN GOTTES...

Date	Mintage	VG	F	VF	XF	Unc
1639	—	850	1,650	3,000	5,000	—

KM# 10 THALER
Silver **Obv:** Helmeted arms **Rev:** Crowned imperial eagle with orb between necks **Note:** Dav. #7302.

Date	Mintage	VG	F	VF	XF	Unc
1624 WA	—	600	1,200	2,250	3,750	—

KM# 19 THALER
Silver **Rev:** Roman numeral date **Rev. Legend:** ...GREITZ. DECEM... **Note:** Dav. #7303A.

Date	Mintage	VG	F	VF	XF	Unc
MDCXXX9 (1639)	—	1,500	3,250	6,000	—	—

KM# 20 THALER
Silver **Subject:** Death of Heinrich II **Rev:** Seven-line inscription, legend divided by arms **Note:** Dav. #7304.

Date	Mintage	VG	F	VF	XF	Unc
1639 Rare	—	—	—	—	—	—

KM# 18 THALER
Silver **Subject:** Death of Heinrich II **Obv:** Half figure right **Rev:** Crowned shield **Note:** Varieties exist. Dav. #7303.

Date	Mintage	VG	F	VF	XF	Unc
1639 Rare	—	—	—	—	—	—

REUSS-DOLAU

Originally an offshoot of Reuss-Burgk from 1616, it reverted to the main Burgk line in 1636 and was transferred to Reuss-Obergreiz in 1640.

RULERS
Heinrich IV, 1616-1636
Heinrich XVI von Obergreiz, 1681-1698

COUNTSHIP

REGULAR COINAGE

KM# 5 24 KREUZER (6 Batzen)
Silver **Obv:** Crowned imperial eagle, 24 in orb on breast, titles of Ferdinand II **Rev:** Four-fold arms in ornamented frame **Rev. Legend:** MON. NOV. ARGENT. RVTHENICA. DOL. **Note:** Kipper 24 Kreuzer. Varieties exist.

Date	Mintage	VG	F	VF	XF	Unc
ND	—	—	—	—	—	—

KM# 6 1/24 THALER (1 Groschen)
Silver **Obv:** Value: 24 on imperial orb, titles of Ferdinand II **Rev:** Arms of Reuss lion left **Rev. Legend:** MO. NO. AR. RVTHE. D"O. **Note:** Kipper 1/24 Thaler.

Date	Mintage	VG	F	VF	XF	Unc
ND	—	80.00	175	—	—	—

REUSS-GERA

This lordship was founded in 1206 and became extinct in 1550, passing to Greiz. The Younger Line established a new branch in Gera in the same year. In 1635, Gera was divided into the lines of Gera, Lobenstein, Saalburgand Schleiz. Gera fell extinct again in 1802 and the title passed to Schleiz.

RULERS
Heinrich II Posthumous, 1572-1635
Heinrich II the Younger, 1635-1670
Heinrich IV, 1670-1686
Heinrich XVIII, 1686-1735

LORDSHIP

REGULAR COINAGE

KM# 24 3 PFENNIG (Dreier)
Silver **Subject:** Lordship of Lobenstein **Obv:** Imperial orb with 3 **Rev:** Helmet with dog head divides date, LOB above

Date	Mintage	VG	F	VF	XF	Unc
1622 ES	—	40.00	80.00	160	325	—

KM# 41 3 PFENNIG (Dreier)
Silver **Rev. Legend:** LOBENST... **Note:** Varieties exist.

Date	Mintage	VG	F	VF	XF	Unc
16Z3 ES	—	40.00	80.00	160	325	—

KM# 42 3 PFENNIG (Dreier)
Silver **Rev:** Imperial orb in baroque frame

Date	Mintage	VG	F	VF	XF	Unc
16Z3 MR	—	40.00	80.00	160	325	—

KM# 43 3 PFENNIG (Dreier)
Silver **Obv:** Legend around orb **Obv. Legend:** MONETA - RVTHENICA

Date	Mintage	VG	F	VF	XF	Unc
1623	—	—	—	—	—	—

Note: Reported, not confirmed

KM# 44 6 PFENNIG (Sechser)
Silver **Subject:** Lordship of Lobenstein **Obv:** VI in orb **Rev:** Helmet with dog head divides date

Date	Mintage	VG	F	VF	XF	Unc
1623 ES	—	—	—	—	—	—

Note: Reported, not confirmed

KM# 14 3 KREUZER (Groschen)
Silver **Subject:** Lordship of Lobenstein **Obv:** Crowned imperial eagle, 3 in orb on breast, titles of Ferdinand II **Rev:** Lion left in baroque frame **Rev. Legend:** MO. NO. AR. RVTHE. L. **Note:** Kipper 3 Kreuzer.

Date	Mintage	VG	F	VF	XF	Unc
ND	—	65.00	120	180	325	—

KM# 12 12 KREUZER (3 Batzen)
Silver **Subject:** Lordship of Lobenstein **Obv:** Date in legend at top **Rev:** Shield of lion arms, dog head above **Rev. Legend:** HERRSCAFT. LOBENSTEIN **Note:** Varieties exist.

Date	Mintage	VG	F	VF	XF	Unc
16Z0	—	90.00	160	325	650	—

KM# 16 12 KREUZER (3 Batzen)
Silver **Rev:** Legend, date **Rev. Legend:** MO: NO: ARG: RVTHENICA **Note:** Varieties exist.

Date	Mintage	VG	F	VF	XF	Unc
16Z1	—	90.00	160	325	650	—
1621	—	90.00	160	325	650	—

KM# 15 12 KREUZER (3 Batzen)
Silver **Obv:** Crowned imperial eagle, 12 in orb on breast, titles of Ferdinand II **Rev:** Oval lion arms, dog head above divides date

Date	Mintage	VG	F	VF	XF	Unc
1621	—	80.00	150	300	625	—

KM# 13 24 KREUZER (6 Batzen)
Silver **Subject:** Lordship of Lobenstein **Obv:** 24 in orb **Rev:** Shield of lion arms, dog head above **Rev. Legend:** HERRSCHAFT

Date	Mintage	VG	F	VF	XF	Unc
1620	—	—	—	—	—	—

KM# 22 24 KREUZER (6 Batzen)
Silver **Rev:** Arms divide date **Rev. Legend:** MO: NO: ARG: RVTHENICA. DOM. 4

Date	Mintage	VG	F	VF	XF	Unc
1621	—	—	—	—	—	—

KM# 23 24 KREUZER (6 Batzen)
Silver **Rev:** Date in legend

Date	Mintage	VG	F	VF	XF	Unc
1621	—	—	—	—	—	—

KM# 17 24 KREUZER (6 Batzen)
Silver **Obv:** Crowned imperial eagle, 24 in orb on breast, titles of Ferdinand II **Rev:** Ornamented four-fold arms, date and mint mark in legend **Note:** Kipper 24 Kreuzer. Varieties exist.

Date	Mintage	VG	F	VF	XF	Unc
(16)21 G	—	80.00	135	250	500	—
(1)621 G	—	80.00	135	250	500	—
1622 G	—	80.00	135	250	500	—

KM# 18 24 KREUZER (6 Batzen)
Silver **Note:** Klippe.

Date	Mintage	VG	F	VF	XF	Unc
(16)21 G	—	—	—	—	—	—

KM# 19 24 KREUZER (6 Batzen)
Silver **Obv:** Date divided by arms **Obv. Legend:** Ends: GE or GER **Rev:** Double-headed imperial eagle, value in orb on breast **Note:** Varieties exist.

Date	Mintage	VG	F	VF	XF	Unc
1621 TL	—	55.00	115	200	400	—
ND TL	—	55.00	115	200	400	—

KM# 21 24 KREUZER (6 Batzen)
Silver **Rev:** Oval lion arms, dog head left above divides date **Note:** Varieties exist.

Date	Mintage	VG	F	VF	XF	Unc
1621	—	65.00	120	235	475	—
ND	—	65.00	120	235	475	—

KM# 20 24 KREUZER (6 Batzen)
Silver **Rev:** Oval lion arms, plume of helmet above divides date

Date	Mintage	VG	F	VF	XF	Unc
1621	—	65.00	120	235	475	1,000

KM# 25 24 KREUZER (6 Batzen)
Silver **Rev:** Date divided by dog head **Rev. Legend:** Ends: RVTHENICA*L. **Note:** Varieties exist.

Date	Mintage	VG	F	VF	XF	Unc
16ZZ	—	65.00	120	235	475	—
1622	—	65.00	120	235	475	—

KM# 26 24 KREUZER (6 Batzen)
Silver **Note:** Klippe. Mintmaster's initials in two of the corners

Date	Mintage	VG	F	VF	XF	Unc
1622 IS	—	—	—	—	—	—

KM# 27 1/24 THALER (Groschen)
Silver **Subject:** Lordship of Lobenstein **Obv:** Helmet with do head right **Obv. Legend:** ...RVTHEN:L. **Rev:** Imperial orb wi 24 divides date, titles of Ferdinand II **Note:** .55-.65 grams. Kip 1/24 Thaler.

Date	Mintage	VG	F	VF	XF
16ZZ	—	65.00	120	235	475

KM# 28 1/24 THALER (12 Pfennig)

1.2500 g., Silver **Obv:** Lion arms with dog head left **Obv. Legend:** NACH. DEM. AL: SCH: V: KOR: **Rev:** Imperial orb with 1Z divides date

Date	Mintage	VG	F	VF	XF	Unc
16ZZ	—	50.00	100	200	425	—

KM# 29 1/24 THALER (12 Pfennig)

1.2500 g., Silver **Ruler:** Heinrich II Posthumous **Rev:** Imperial orb with 24 divides date, titles of Ferdinand II **Note:** Varieties exist.

Date	Mintage	VG	F	VF	XF	Unc
16ZZ ES	—	55.00	110	225	450	—
16Z3 ES	—	55.00	110	225	450	—
16Z3 MR	—	55.00	110	225	450	—

KM# 55 1/24 THALER (12 Pfennig)

1.2500 g., Silver **Ruler:** Heinrich II Posthumous **Subject:** Death of Heinrich II Posthumous **Obv:** Four-fold arms, titles of Heinrich II **Rev:** 6-line inscription **Rev. Legend:** PIETAS-AD-OMNIA-VTILIS **Rev. Inscription:** I. B. A. G / NAT9IO. IV / NII. Ao 1572 / OBIIIt. 3. DECEMB. Ao / 1635

Date	Mintage	VG	F	VF	XF	Unc
1635	2,410	—	—	—	—	—

KM# 30 1/4 THALER

Silver **Ruler:** Heinrich II Posthumous **Subject:** Lordship of Lobenstein **Obv:** Two helmets with dog head and crane, date above **Rev:** Phoenix rising from flames on short column, imperial orb above, hands from clouds on either side with palm branch and sword

Date	Mintage	VG	F	VF	XF	Unc
16ZZ Rare	—	—	—	—	—	—

KM# 47 1/4 THALER

Silver **Obv:** Crowned imperial eagle, orb on breast, titles of Ferdinand II **Rev:** Two helmets facing forward with dog head and crane, date below

Date	Mintage	VG	F	VF	XF	Unc
16Z4 WA Rare	—	—	—	—	—	—

KM# 56 1/4 THALER

Silver **Ruler:** Heinrich II Posthumous **Subject:** Death of Heinrich II Posthumous **Obv:** Four-fold arms, two helmets with dog head and crane above **Rev:** Six-line inscription I. B. A. G. /NAT910. IV/NII. Ao 1572/OBIIt. 3. DE/CEMB. Ao/1635

Date	Mintage	VG	F	VF	XF	Unc
1635	140	110	1,800	3,000	6,000	—

KM# 31 1/2 THALER (30 Groschen)

20.5400 g., Silver **Obv:** Oval four-fold arms surmounted by two ornate helmets **Rev:** Phoenix rising from flames on short column, orb above, from clouds at left a hand with palm branch, at right with sword, date in legend, value (30) at bottom

Date	Mintage	VG	F	VF	XF	Unc
1622 Rare	—	—	—	—	—	—

KM# 33 1/2 THALER (30 Groschen)

20.5400 g., Silver **Obv:** Squarish four-fold arms, two helmets above with dog head and crane **Rev:** Similar to KM#31 but without indication of value

Date	Mintage	VG	F	VF	XF	Unc
1622 ES Rare	—	—	—	—	—	—

KM# 32 1/2 THALER (30 Groschen)

20.5400 g., Silver **Subject:** Lordship of Lobenstein **Obv:** Crowned imperial eagle, 1Z in orb on breast, titles of Ferdinand II and date in legend **Rev:** Oval four-fold arms, two helmets above with dog head and crane **Note:** Varieties exist.

Date	Mintage	VG	F	VF	XF	Unc
16ZZ ES Rare	—	—	—	—	—	—

KM# 45 1/2 THALER (30 Groschen)

20.5400 g., Silver **Obv:** Similar to KM#32 **Rev:** Heart-shaped four-fold arms, two helmets above

Date	Mintage	VG	F	VF	XF	Unc
1623 Rare	—	—	—	—	—	—

KM# 48 1/2 THALER (30 Groschen)

20.5400 g., Silver **Obv:** Ornamented four-fold arms, two helmets with dog head and crane above **Rev:** Crowned double-headed imperial eagle, orb on breast, titles of Ferdinand II, date in legend

Date	Mintage	VG	F	VF	XF	Unc
16Z4 WA Rare	—	—	—	—	—	—

KM# 57 1/2 THALER (30 Groschen)

20.5400 g., Silver **Ruler:** Heinrich II Posthumous **Subject:** Death of Heinrich II Posthumous **Obv:** Gothic letters in field around head; Ich Bau - auff Gott **Rev:** Eight-line inscription **Note:** Varieties exist.

Date	Mintage	VG	F	VF	XF	Unc
1635	274	450	675	1,100	1,800	—

KM# 10 THALER

Silver **Ruler:** Heinrich II Posthumous **Note:** Varieties exist. Dav. #7308.

Date	Mintage	VG	F	VF	XF	Unc
1620	4,730	600	1,150	2,250	4,000	—

KM# 34 THALER

Silver **Ruler:** Heinrich II Posthumous **Obv:** Oval four-fold arms surmounted by two ornate helmets **Rev:** Phoenix rising from flames on short column, orb above, from clouds at left a hand with palm branch, at right with sword, date in legend, value (60) at bottom **Note:** 60 Kreuzer. Varieties exist.

Date	Mintage	VG	F	VF	XF	Unc
1622	—	500	1,000	2,000	3,500	—

KM# 35 THALER

Silver **Ruler:** Heinrich II Posthumous **Note:** Klippe. Varieties exist.

Date	Mintage	VG	F	VF	XF	Unc
1622 Rare	—	—	—	—	—	—

KM# 36 THALER

Silver **Ruler:** Heinrich II Posthumous **Subject:** Lordship of Lobenstein **Note:** Varieties exist. Dav. 7309

Date	Mintage	VG	F	VF	XF	Unc
1622 ES	—	500	1,000	2,000	3,500	—

KM# 37 THALER

Silver **Ruler:** Heinrich II Posthumous **Rev. Legend:** ...HVNG: ET: BOH: REX:... **Note:** Varieties exist. Dav. 7310. 24 Groschen.

Date	Mintage	VG	F	VF	XF	Unc
1622 ES	—	850	1,700	3,500	6,250	—

KM# 38 THALER

Silver **Ruler:** Heinrich II Posthumous **Obv:** Ornate oval shield **Rev:** Crown above double-headed imperial eagle, value in orb on breast **Rev. Legend:** Error: BON instead of BOH in legend **Note:** Dav. 7310A. 24 Groschen.

Date	Mintage	VG	F	VF	XF	Unc
1622	—	900	1,750	3,650	6,500	—

KM# 46 THALER

Silver **Ruler:** Heinrich II Posthumous **Obv:** Ornate oval shield **Obv. Legend:** ...SEN: RVH: DN: **Rev:** Crowned imperial eagle, value Z4 in orb on breast **Note:** Dav. 7311. 24 Groschen.

Date	Mintage	VG	F	VF	XF	Unc
16Z3 MR	—	650	1,250	2,250	5,000	—

KM# 58 THALER

Silver **Ruler:** Heinrich II Posthumous **Subject:** Death of Heinrich II Posthumous **Rev:** Eight-line inscription **Note:** Dav. #7312.

Date	Mintage	VG	F	VF	XF	Unc
MDCXXXV (1635)	257	300	600	1,250	2,500	—

KM# 59 THALER

Silver **Ruler:** Heinrich II Posthumous **Subject:** Death of Heinrich II Posthumous **Rev:** Ten-line inscription **Note:** Dav. #7312A.

Date	Mintage	VG	F	VF	XF	Unc
MDCXXXV (1635)	Inc. above	350	700	1,450	2,750	—

KM# 11 2 THALER

Silver **Note:** Similar to 1 Thaler, KM#10. Dav. #7307.

Date	Mintage	VG	F	VF	XF	Unc
1620 Rare	—	—	—	—	—	—

TRADE COINAGE

KM# 5 GOLDGULDEN

3.5000 g., 0.9860 Gold 0.1109 oz. AGW **Ruler:** Heinrich II Posthumous **Obv:** Two helmets with dog head and crane **Rev:** Four-fold arms, date above

Date	Mintage	VG	F	VF	XF	Unc
1619 WA	—	1,650	2,750	5,000	9,000	—

KM# 39 GOLDGULDEN

3.5000 g., 0.9860 Gold 0.1109 oz. AGW **Subject:** Lordship of Lobenstein **Obv:** Ornamented four-fold arms, small imperial orb above divides date **Rev:** Two helmets surmounted by dog head and crane, titles of Heinrich II

Date	Mintage	VG	F	VF	XF	Unc
1622	—	1,650	2,750	5,000	9,000	—

KM# 60 GOLDGULDEN

3.5000 g., 0.9860 Gold 0.1109 oz. AGW **Ruler:** Heinrich II Posthumous **Subject:** Death of Heinrich II Posthumous **Note:** Similar to 1/2 Thaler, KM#57.

Date	Mintage	VG	F	VF	XF	Unc
1635	—	—	—	—	—	—

Note: Reported, not confirmed

KM# 40 3 DUCAT

10.5000 g., 0.9860 Gold 0.3328 oz. AGW **Subject:** Lordship of Lobenstein **Obv:** Squarish four-fold arms, two helmets above with dog head and crane **Rev:** Eight-line inscription, date

Date	Mintage	VG	F	VF	XF	Unc
1622 ES Rare	—	—	—	—	—	—

REUSS-GREIZ

RULERS

Heinrich IV von Reuss-Obergreiz and
Heinrich V von Reuss-Untergreiz

LORDSHIP

JOINT COINAGE

1604-29

KM# 5 12 KREUZER (3 Batzen)

Silver **Obv:** Crowned imperial eagle, 12 in orb on breast, titles of Ferdinand II **Rev:** Helmeted oval lion arms, plume of helmet divides date **Note:** Kipper 12 Kreuzer. Varieties exist.

Date	Mintage	VG	F	VF	XF	Unc
1621	—	80.00	140	220	350	—

KM# 6 24 KREUZER (6 Batzen)

Silver **Obv:** Crowned imperial eagle, 24 in orb on breast, titles of Ferdinand II **Rev:** Oval lion arms, helmet and dog head above divide date **Note:** Kipper 24 Kreuzer.

Date	Mintage	VG	F	VF	XF	Unc
1621	—	65.00	120	200	325	—

KM# 8 24 KREUZER (6 Batzen)

Silver **Note:** Klippe. Varieties exist.

Date	Mintage	VG	F	VF	XF	Unc
1621	—	—	—	—	—	—
(16)21	—	—	—	—	—	—
ND	—	—	—	—	—	—

KM# 7 24 KREUZER (6 Batzen)

Silver **Rev:** Crowned four-fold arms, date in legend **Note:** Varieties exist.

Date	Mintage	VG	F	VF	XF	Unc
1621	—	55.00	115	195	350	—
ND	—	55.00	115	195	350	—

KM# 9 THALER

Silver **Obv:** Ornate helmeted arms **Rev:** Crown above double-headed imperial eagle, orb on breast **Note:** Varieties exist. Dav. #7305.

Date	Mintage	VG	F	VF	XF	Unc
1624 WA	—	550	1,150	2,200	3,750	—

JOINT COINAGE

1619

KM# 15 1/2 THALER

14.3600 g., Silver **Obv:** Ornate four-fold arms **Rev:** Phoenix rising from flames on top of short column, imperial orb above from clouds; hand with palm branch on left, sword on right; date in legend

Date	Mintage	VG	F	VF	XF	Unc
1619 WA	—	—	—	—	—	—

KM# 16.1 THALER

Silver **Obv:** Helmeted arms **Obv. Legend:** Ends:...G: C: G: S: ET. L:* **Rev:** Phoenix in flames under orb on pedestal, hand with palm frond at left, sword at right **Note:** Dav. #7301.

Date	Mintage	VG	F	VF	XF	Unc
1619 WA	—	375	750	1,500	2,750	—

KM# 16.2 THALER

Silver **Rev:** Different clouds **Note:** Dav. #7301A.

Date	Mintage	VG	F	VF	XF	Unc
1619 WA	—	375	750	1,500	2,750	—

KM# 16.3 THALER

Silver **Obv. Legend:** Ends:...G: C: G: S: ET.LO. **Note:** Dav. #7301B.

Date	Mintage	VG	F	VF	XF	Unc
1619 WA	—	375	750	1,500	2,750	—

KM# 17 2 THALER

Silver **Note:** Similar to 1 Thaler, KM#16. Dav. #7300.

Date	Mintage	VG	F	VF	XF	Unc
1619 WA Rare	—	—	—	—	—	—

REUSS-OBERGREIZ

The other branch of the division of 1635, Obergreiz went through a number of consolidations and further divisions. Upon the extinction of the Ruess-Untergreiz line in 1768, the latter passed to Reuss-Obergreiz and this line continued on into the 20th century, obtaining the rank of count back in 1673 and that of prince in 1778.

RULERS

Heinrich I, 1580-1607
Heinrich II, 1607-1616
Heinrich IV, 1616-1629
Heinrich I, 1629-1681
Heinrich VI, 1681-1697
Heinrich I, 1697-1714

LORDSHIP

REGULAR COINAGE

KM# 5 HELLER

Copper **Ruler:** Heinrich I **Obv:** 3-line inscription with date **Obv. Inscription:** R/HELLER/(date) **Note:** Uniface. Varieties exist.

Date	Mintage	Good	VG	F	VF	XF
1660	—	10.00	20.00	40.00	80.00	—
1661	—	10.00	20.00	40.00	80.00	—
1667	—	10.00	20.00	40.00	80.00	—
1668	—	10.00	20.00	40.00	80.00	—

KM# 6 HELLER

Copper **Ruler:** Heinrich I **Obv:** Crowned lion **Rev:** Date **Rev. Legend:** R/HELLER **Note:** Varieties exist.

Date	Mintage	Good	VG	F	VF	XF
1660	—	7.00	15.00	30.00	60.00	—
1661	—	7.00	15.00	30.00	60.00	—

KM# 7 HELLER

Copper **Ruler:** Heinrich I **Obv:** Helmet with hound's head crest **Rev:** Date **Rev. Legend:** REISI/HELER

Date	Mintage	Good	VG	F	VF	XF
1661	—	—	—	—	—	—

COUNTSHIP

REGULAR COINAGE

KM# 10 HELLER

Copper **Ruler:** Heinrich I **Obv:** Crowned lion rampant left in shield **Rev:** Date **Rev. Legend:** R/HELLER

Date	Mintage	Good	VG	F	VF	XF
1676	—	—	—	—	—	—

KM# 11 HELLER

Copper **Ruler:** Heinrich I **Obv:** Crowned rampant lion left **Note:** Varieties exist.

Date	Mintage	Good	VG	F	VF	XF
1676	—	6.00	13.00	27.00	55.00	—
1677	—	6.00	13.00	27.00	55.00	—
1678	—	6.00	13.00	27.00	55.00	—

KM# 9 HELLER

Copper **Ruler:** Heinrich I **Obv:** 3-line inscription with date **Obv. Inscription:** R/HELLER/(date) **Note:** Uniface. Varieties exist.

Date	Mintage	Good	VG	F	VF	XF
1676	—	8.00	15.00	30.00	60.00	—
1677	—	8.00	15.00	30.00	60.00	—
1678	—	8.00	15.00	30.00	60.00	—
1681	—	8.00	15.00	30.00	60.00	—

KM# 12 HELLER

Copper **Ruler:** Heinrich I **Obv:** Lion right **Rev:** Date **Rev. Inscription:** R / HE.ER

Date	Mintage	Good	VG	F	VF	XF
1677	—	—	—	—	—	—

KM# 13 HELLER

Copper **Ruler:** Heinrich I **Obv:** Crowned lion rampant left **Rev. Inscription:** Reusisch: / Obergratzi = / sche Heller / date

Date	Mintage	Good	VG	F	VF	XF
1678	—	6.00	13.00	27.00	55.00	—

KM# 14 HELLER

Copper **Ruler:** Heinrich I **Obv:** Helmet with dog head right above **Rev:** Crowned lion rampant left, date spaced around

Date	Mintage	Good	VG	F	VF	XF
ND	—	—	—	—	—	—

KM# 15 HELLER

Copper **Ruler:** Heinrich I **Obv:** Dog head left **Rev:** Similar to KM#5 **Note:** Varieties exist.

Date	Mintage	Good	VG	F	VF	XF
1678	—	6.00	13.00	27.00	55.00	—

KM# 20 HELLER

Copper **Ruler:** Heinrich I **Obv:** Helmet with dog head right above **Rev:** Dog head turned right divides date **Note:** Varieties exist.

Date	Mintage	Good	VG	F	VF	XF
1679	—	6.00	13.00	27.00	55.00	—
1680	—	6.00	13.00	27.00	55.00	—

KM# 22 HELLER

Copper **Ruler:** Heinrich I **Rev. Inscription:** REUSISCH / OBERGRAITZI: / SCHE HELLER **Note:** Varieties exist.

Date	Mintage	Good	VG	F	VF	XF
1679	—	6.00	13.00	27.00	55.00	—
1680	—	6.00	13.00	27.00	55.00	—
1681	—	6.00	13.00	27.00	55.00	—

KM# 21 HELLER

Copper **Ruler:** Heinrich I **Obv:** Dog head right divides date **Rev. Legend:** GR/REUss/heller/O G

Date	Mintage	Good	VG	F	VF	XF
1679	—	8.00	15.00	30.00	60.00	—

KM# 28 HELLER

Copper **Ruler:** Heinrich VI **Obv:** Helmet with hound's head crest **Rev. Inscription:** REIS I / HELER / (date)

Date	Mintage	Good	VG	F	VF	XF
1681	—	—	—	—	—	—

KM# 31 HELLER

Copper **Ruler:** Heinrich VI **Note:** Crowned lion rampant left, space around. Uniface. Varieties exist.

Date	Mintage	Good	VG	F	VF	XF
1686	—	10.00	20.00	40.00	80.00	—
ND	—	10.00	20.00	40.00	80.00	—

KM# 32 HELLER

Copper **Ruler:** Heinrich VI **Obv:** Lion without crown **Note:** Uniface.

Date	Mintage	Good	VG	F	VF	XF
1686	—	—	—	—	—	—

KM# 33 HELLER

Copper **Ruler:** Heinrich VI **Obv:** Lion right **Note:** Uniface.

Date	Mintage	Good	VG	F	VF	XF
ND	—	—	—	—	—	—

KM# 34 HELLER

Copper **Ruler:** Heinrich VI **Obv:** Helmet with dog head right above **Note:** Uniface.

Date	Mintage	Good	VG	F	VF	XF
ND	—	6.00	13.00	27.00	55.00	—

KM# 35 HELLER

Copper **Ruler:** Heinrich VI **Obv:** Dog head left **Note:** Uniface.

Date	Mintage	Good	VG	F	VF	XF
ND	—	—	—	—	—	—

KM# 29 HELLER

Copper **Ruler:** Heinrich VI **Obv:** 3-line inscription with date **Obv. Inscription:** R / HELLER / (date) **Note:** Uniface. Varieties exist.

Date	Mintage	Good	VG	F	VF	XF
1686	—	7.00	15.00	30.00	60.00	—
1691	—	6.00	13.00	27.00	55.00	—

KM# 40 HELLER

Copper **Ruler:** Heinrich VI **Obv. Inscription:** R / HL-LR / date **Note:** Uniface.

Date	Mintage	Good	VG	F	VF	XF
1691	—	6.00	13.00	27.00	55.00	—

KM# 16 PFENNIG

Silver **Ruler:** Heinrich I **Obv:** Crane left **Obv. Legend:** GR. PFENIGE **Note:** Varieties exist.

Date	Mintage	VG	F	VF	XF	Unc
1678	—	10.00	20.00	40.00	80.00	—
1679	—	10.00	20.00	40.00	80.00	—
1680	—	10.00	20.00	40.00	80.00	—

KM# 30 PFENNIG

Silver **Ruler:** Heinrich I **Obv:** Lion rampant left **Obv. Legend:** GR. PFENNIGE **Rev:** Imperial orb with symbol divides date

Date	Mintage	VG	F	VF	XF	Unc
1680	—	16.00	33.00	55.00	115	—

KM# 17 3 PFENNIG

Silver **Ruler:** Heinrich I **Obv. Inscription:** GR / DREYER **Rev:** Value 3 on imperial orb divides date as 1 - 6 / 7 - 8

Date	Mintage	VG	F	VF	XF	Unc
1678	—	12.00	25.00	55.00	110	—

KM# 18 1/84 THALER (3 Pfennig)

Silver **Ruler:** Heinrich I **Obv:** Value: 84 on imperial orb divides date, titles of Heinrich I **Rev:** 3 small shields of arms, 2 above 1 **Note:** Varieties exist.

Date	Mintage	VG	F	VF	XF	Unc
1678	—	27.00	50.00	110	220	—
1680	—	27.00	50.00	110	220	—

KM# 19 1/24 THALER (Groschen)

Silver **Ruler:** Heinrich I **Obv:** Crowned 4-fold arms **Obv. Legend:** AN GOTTES SEGEN... **Rev:** Value: 24 on imperial orb divides date **Rev. Legend:** GR. G. W. REUSISCHE. GROSCHEN **Note:** Varieties exist.

Date	Mintage	VG	F	VF	XF	Unc
1678	—	13.00	30.00	65.00	130	—
1679/78	—	20.00	40.00	80.00	160	—
1679	—	13.00	30.00	65.00	130	—
1680	—	13.00	30.00	65.00	130	—

KM# 23 1/6 THALER (1/4 Gulden)

Silver **Ruler:** Heinrich I **Obv:** Value 1/6 in oval below arms **Rev:** Cross in center with IHS; date **Rev. Legend:** IN HOC VICTORIA CERTA; OMNIA - CUM - DEO **Note:** Varieties exist.

Date	Mintage	VG	F	VF	XF	Unc
1679	—	40.00	80.00	150	300	—

KM# 24 1/6 THALER (1/4 Gulden)

Silver **Ruler:** Heinrich I **Obv:** Date, bust right **Obv. Legend:** OMNIA CUM DEO **Note:** Varieties exist.

Date	Mintage	VG	F	VF	XF	Unc
1679	—	65.00	135	235	475	—

KM# 25 1/3 THALER (1/2 Gulden)
Silver **Ruler:** Heinrich I **Obv:** Titles of Heinrich I

Date	Mintage	VG	F	VF	XF	Unc
1679	—	55.00	110	200	425	—

KM# 26 1/3 THALER (1/2 Gulden)
Silver **Ruler:** Heinrich I **Note:** Similar to 1/6 Thaler, KM#24, but value: 1/3.

Date	Mintage	VG	F	VF	XF	Unc
1679	—	—	—	—	—	—

KM# 27 2/3 THALER (1 Gulden)
Silver **Ruler:** Heinrich I

Date	Mintage	VG	F	VF	XF	Unc
1679	—	200	400	650	1,300	—

KM# 41 THALER
Silver **Ruler:** Heinrich I **Subject:** Internment of Heinrich VI (died 1697, buried 1698) **Note:** Dav. #7306.

Date	Mintage	VG	F	VF	XF	Unc
1698 ILH	—	—	850	1,750	3,000	5,000

TRADE COINAGE

KM# 42 5 DUCAT
17.5000 g., 0.9860 Gold 0.5547 oz. AGW **Ruler:** Heinrich I **Subject:** Internment of Heinrich VI **Obv:** Bust right **Rev:** 11-line inscription, date

Date	Mintage	VG	F	VF	XF	Unc
1698 ILH Rare	—	—	—	—	—	—

Note: Struck with 1 Thaler dies, KM#41

REUSS-ROTHENTHAL

The smallest of the Reuss branches, only Heinrich V of lower Greiz issued coins for this division.

RULER
Heinrich V, 1668-1698

COUNTSHIP

TRADE COINAGE

KM# 5 DUCAT
3.5000 g., 0.9860 Gold 0.1109 oz. AGW **Obv:** Bust of Heinrich right in inner circle **Rev:** Arms in inner circle

Date	Mintage	VG	F	VF	XF	Unc
1679 ICF Rare	—	—	—	—	—	—

REUSS-SCHLEIZ

Originally part of the holdings of Reuss-Gera, Schleiz was ruled separately on and off during the first half of the 16th century. When the Gera line died out in 1550, Schleiz passed to Ober-greiz. Schleiz was reintegrated into a new line of Gera and a separate countship at Schleiz was founded in 1635, only to last one generation. At its extinction in 1666, Schleiz passed to Reuss-Saalburg which thereafter took the name of Reuss-Schleiz.

RULERS
Heinrich II, 1580-1616
Heinrich II Posthumous, 1616-1635
Heinrich IX, 1635-1666
Heinrich I, 1666-1692
Heinrich XI, 1692-1726

LORDSHIP

REGULAR COINAGE

KM# 10 3 PFENNIG
Silver **Ruler:** Heinrich I **Obv:** Dog head above helmet **Obv. Legend:** SCHLAIZER DREIER **Rev:** Value: 84 on imperial orb dividing initials, date above

Date	Mintage	VG	F	VF	XF	Unc
1669 SD	—	22.00	45.00	90.00	180	—

KM# 15 2/3 THALER (Gulden)
Silver **Ruler:** Heinrich I **Obv:** Bust right **Rev:** Crowned arms in round shield, value: 2/3 divides date below **Mint:** Friedenstein bei Gotha

Date	Mintage	VG	F	VF	XF	Unc
1670 SD	—	—	—	—	—	—

COUNTSHIP

REGULAR COINAGE

KM# 30 PFENNIG
Silver **Ruler:** Heinrich I **Obv:** Dog head above helmet **Rev:** Imperial orb with 1 dividing date and initials **Mint:** Friedenstein bei Gotha

Date	Mintage	VG	F	VF	XF	Unc
1680 SD	—	40.00	80.00	160	325	—

KM# 31 PFENNIG
Silver **Ruler:** Heinrich I **Rev:** Imperial orb with 1 dividing R-S and date **Mint:** Friedenstein bei Gotha **Note:** Struck at Friedenstein bei Gotha.

Date	Mintage	VG	F	VF	XF	Unc
1683	—	30.00	65.00	130	260	—

KM# 32 2 PFENNIG
Silver **Ruler:** Heinrich I **Obv:** Dog head above helmet **Rev:** Imperial orb dividing R-S and date **Mint:** Friedenstein bei Gotha

Date	Mintage	VG	F	VF	XF	Unc
1683	—	40.00	80.00	160	325	—

KM# 23 3 PFENNIG
Silver **Ruler:** Heinrich I **Obv. Legend:** SCHLAITZ: DREYER **Rev:** Orb divides date and initials **Mint:** Friedenstein bei Gotha **Note:** Varieties exist.

Date	Mintage	VG	F	VF	XF	Unc
1679 SD	—	22.00	45.00	90.00	180	—

KM# 24 1/24 THALER (Groschen)
Silver **Ruler:** Heinrich I **Obv:** Crowned four-fold arms in palm wreath **Rev:** Value: 24/EINEN/REICHS/THALER/date **Mint:** Friedenstein bei Gotha **Note:** Varieties exist.

Date	Mintage	VG	F	VF	XF	Unc
1679 SD	—	22.00	45.00	90.00	185	—

KM# 16 1/12 THALER
Silver **Ruler:** Heinrich I **Subject:** Death of Heinrich I's Wife, Maximilane von Hardegg **Mint:** Friedenstein bei Gotha **Note:** Similar to 2/3 Thaler KM#19, but obverse with value "2 gl" in oval.

Date	Mintage	VG	F	VF	XF	Unc
1678	—	50.00	100	200	425	—

KM# 17 1/4 THALER
Silver **Ruler:** Heinrich I **Subject:** Death of Heinrich I's Wife, Maximilane von Hardegg **Mint:** Friedenstein bei Gotha **Note:** Similar to 2/3 Thaler KM#19, but obverse with value "2 gl" in oval on obverse replaced by skull.

Date	Mintage	VG	F	VF	XF	Unc
1678	—	100	200	350	675	—

KM# 18 1/3 THALER (1/2 Gulden)
Silver **Ruler:** Heinrich I **Obv:** Bust right **Rev:** Crowned round four-fold arms, value: 1/3 in oval below divides date **Mint:** Friedenstein bei Gotha **Note:** Varieties exist.

Date	Mintage	VG	F	VF	XF	Unc
1678 SD	—	—	—	—	—	—
1679 SD	—	—	—	—	—	—

KM# 19 2/3 THALER (Gulden)
Silver **Ruler:** Heinrich I **Subject:** Death of Heinrich I's Wife, Maximilane von Hardegg **Obv:** Value: 2/3 in oval below frame **Note:** Varieties exist.

Date	Mintage	VG	F	VF	XF	Unc
1678 SD	—	225	300	500	1,000	—

KM# 20 2/3 THALER (Gulden)
Silver **Ruler:** Heinrich I **Mint:** Friedenstein bei Gotha **Note:** Varieties exist.

Date	Mintage	VG	F	VF	XF	Unc
1678 SD	—	135	200	350	675	—
1679 SD	—	135	200	350	675	—

KM# 21 2/3 THALER (Gulden)
Silver **Ruler:** Heinrich I **Rev:** Arm extending from clouds holdin scale, value: 2/3 below, date in legend **Mint:** Friedenstein bei Gotha **Note:** Varieties exist.

Date	Mintage	VG	F	VF	XF
1678 SD	—	275	400	750	1,500

KM# 25 2/3 THALER (Gulden)
Silver **Ruler:** Heinrich I **Obv:** Bust 3/4 right **Rev:** Small oval four-fold arms in crossed oak branches, value: 2/3 in oval divides date **Mint:** Friedenstein bei Gotha **Note:** Varieties exist.

Date	Mintage	VG	F	VF	XF	Unc
1679 SD	—	—	—	—	—	—

KM# 26 THALER
Silver **Ruler:** Heinrich I **Mint:** Schleiz **Note:** Dav. #7314.

Date	Mintage	VG	F	VF	XF	Unc
1679 IAB	—	650	1,150	2,250	4,750	7,500

KM# 27 THALER
Silver **Ruler:** Heinrich I **Mint:** Schleiz **Note:** Dav. #7316.

Date	Mintage	VG	F	VF	XF	Unc
1679 IAB	—	700	1,250	2,450	5,000	—

KM# 28 2 THALER
Silver **Ruler:** Heinrich I **Mint:** Schleiz **Note:** Similar to 1 Thaler, KM#27. Dav. #7315.

Date	Mintage	VG	F	VF	XF	Unc
1679 IAB Rare	—	—	—	—	—	—

PATTERNS

Including off metal strikes

KM#	Date	Mintage	Identification	Mkt Val
Pn1	1678	—	Goldgulden. Silver.	—

REUSS-UNTERGREIZ

Founded in 1535, inherited Burgk in 1550. After several acquisitions and subsequent divisions, the line died out in 1768 and all holdings passed to Reuss-Obergreiz.

RULERS
Heinrich V, 1572-1604
Heinrich III, 1604-1609
Heinrich IV, 1609-1616
Heinrich V, 1609-(1625)-1667
Heinrich II, 1668-1697
Heinrich IV, 1668-1675
Heinrich V, 1668-1698
Heinrich XIII, 1675-1733

LORDSHIP

REGULAR COINAGE

KM# 5 3 PFENNIG (1/84 Thaler)
Silver **Ruler:** Heinrich V **Obv:** Helmet with dog head divides date **Obv. Legend:** OBER SAX: KREISSES **Rev:** Value: 3 on imperial orb divides initials

Date	Mintage	VG	F	VF	XF	Unc
1657 MR	—	35.00	75.00	150	300	—

KM# 6 3 PFENNIG (1/84 Thaler)
Silver **Ruler:** Heinrich V **Obv:** Two ornamented helmets with dog head and crane divide date **Rev:** Value: 3 on imperial orb in ornamental frame

Date	Mintage	VG	F	VF	XF	Unc
1659	—	35.00	75.00	150	300	—

COUNTSHIP

REGULAR COINAGE

KM# 16 6 PFENNIG
Silver **Ruler:** Heinrich II **Obv:** Helmet with dog head left divides G-R **Rev:** Value: 6 on imperial orb divides date **Note:** Sechser. Varieties exist.

Date	Mintage	VG	F	VF	XF	Unc
1690	—	25.00	50.00	100	210	—
1691	—	25.00	50.00	100	210	—

KM# 15 1/48 THALER
Silver **Ruler:** Heinrich II **Obv:** Helmet with dog head left divides GR-DR **Rev:** Value: 84 on imperial orb divides date, all in rhombus

Date	Mintage	VG	F	VF	XF	Unc
1690	—	24.00	50.00	110	220	—
1691	—	24.00	50.00	110	220	—

KM# 10 2/3 THALER (Gulden)
Silver **Ruler:** Heinrich II **Obv:** Bust right, titles of Heinrich II **Rev:** Crowned four-fold arms with central shield, date 16 above crown, rest divided by arms, value: 2/3 in oval below **Note:** Varieties exist.

Date	Mintage	VG	F	VF	XF	Unc
1678	—	350	650	1,200	2,200	—
1683	—	350	650	1,200	2,200	—

RHEINE

(Reine)

Located on the River Ems in Westphalia about 25 miles (42km) west of Osnabrück and 24 miles (39km) northwest of Münster, the town of Rheine received municipal rights from the bishop of the latter city in 1327. The town leaders petitioned Ernst of Bavaria, Administrator of Münster in the late 16th century for permission to issue minor coinage. The request was granted several years later and coins were produced from about 1602 until 1609.

TOWN ARMS

Shield with horizontal band across middle in which are three stars in line.

REFERENCES

D = Wilhelm Döll, ***Die Kupfermünzen und Kupfermarken der Stadt Rheine***, Rheine, 1980.

W = Joseph Weingärtner, ***Beschreibung der Kupfermünzen Westfalens nebst historischen Nachrichten,*** 2 vols., Paderborn, 1872-81.

PROVINCIAL TOWN

REGULAR COINAGE

KM# 1 HELLER
Copper Weight varies: 0.60-1.10g., 14.5-16 mm. **Obv:** Shield of town arms **Obv. Legend:** STADT — REINE **Rev:** 'I' inset with upper half of H, within 2 ornamented circles **Note:** Ref. W-247; Döll 1.

Date	Mintage	Good	VG	F	VF	XF
ND(1602)	—	—	—	—	—	—

KM# 2 PFENNIG
Copper Weight varies: 0.77-1.52g., 14.5-18.5 mm. **Obv:** Shield of town arms **Obv. Legend:** STADT — REINE **Rev:** 'I' in ornamented rhombus with arches in sides, all within a circle **Note:** Ref. W-246; Döll 2.

Date	Mintage	Good	VG	F	VF	XF
ND(1602)	—	175	375	750	1,500	—

KM# 3 2 PFENNIG
Copper Weight varies: 0.96-1.60g., 16-17.5 mm. **Obv:** Lion striding to left, holding shield of town arms in forepaws **Obv. Legend:** STAD — T. R — EINE **Rev:** 'II' in ornamented square **Note:** Ref. W-1058; Döll 3. Varieties exist.

Date	Mintage	Good	VG	F	VF	XF
ND(1602) Rare	—	—	—	—	—	—

KM# 4 3 PFENNIG
Copper Weight varies: 1.07-2.70g., 19.5-21 mm. **Obv:** Shield of town arms, date **Obv. Legend:** STADT . R — EINE **Rev:** 'III' with arabesques around **Note:** Ref. W-245; Döll 4. Varieties exist.

Date	Mintage	Good	VG	F	VF	XF
160Z	—	200	400	525	900	—
1602	—	200	400	525	900	—
1609	—	200	400	525	900	—

KM# 5 4 PFENNIG
Copper Weight varies: 1.06-3.035g., 20-21 mm. **Obv:** Shield of town arms, date **Obv. Legend:** STADT . R — EINE **Rev:** 'IIII' with arabesques around **Note:** Ref. W-244; Döll #5. Varieties exist.

Date	Mintage	Good	VG	F	VF	XF
160Z	—	40.00	85.00	175	350	—
1602	—	40.00	85.00	175	350	—
1609	—	40.00	85.00	175	350	—

KM# 6 6 PFENNIG
Copper Weight varies: 1.40-3.20g., 21-23 mm. **Obv:** Shield of town arms, date **Obv. Legend:** STADT— REINE **Rev:** "VI" in circle, ornamented border of either 20 or 24 small crescents **Note:** Ref. W-243; Döll 6. Varieties exist.

Date	Mintage	Good	VG	F	VF	XF
160Z	—	90.00	175	350	725	—
1602	—	90.00	175	350	725	—

KM# 7 8 PFENNIG
Copper Weight varies: 1.51-2.07g., 21.5-23.5 mm. **Obv:** Ornamented shield of town arms, date **Obv. Legend:** STADT. REINE **Rev:** 'VIII' with arabesques around **Note:** Ref. W-242; Döll 7. Varieties exist.

Date	Mintage	Good	VG	F	VF	XF
160Z	—	110	220	450	900	—
1602	—	120	235	475	950	—

KM# 8 12 PFENNIG
Copper Weight varies: 2.595-8.15g., 29-32 mm. **Obv:** Ornamented shield of town arms, date **Obv. Legend:** STADT . REINE **Rev:** Gothic '12' in circle, outer margin of striations **Note:** Ref. W#241. Varieties exist.

Date	Mintage	Good	VG	F	VF	XF
160Z	—	325	600	1,200	2,400	—

RIETBERG

The counts of Rietberg held lands along the River Ems in Westphalia. Rietberg castle and town are located on the river about 15 miles (25 km) west-northwest of Paderborn. The line of Rietberg counts was established by Heinrich II (1185-1207), the younger brother of Count Gottfried II of Arnsberg (1185-1235). The line in Rietberg had the misfortune to become extinct in the male line more than once. When Konrad IV died in 1439, he was succeeded by his grandson through his daughter. In the mid-16th century, Johann II left only two daughters. Irmgard married first Erich von Hoya, second Simon von Lippe, who ruled Rietberg briefly after his wife died in 1583. Meanwhile, Walburg had married Enno III von Ostfriesland and their daughter Sabina Katharina eventually married her uncle, Johann III von Ostfriesland. Johann III ruled Rietberg and their son was the first of a new line of counts there. When that line became extinct as well in 1690, Rietberg passed in marriage to the counts of Kaunitz. The countship was raised to a principality in 1764 and was mediatized in 1807, passing to Westphalia thereafter.

RULERS
Sabina Katharina, 1600-1618 and
Johann III von Ostfriesland, 1600-1625
Ernst Christof I, 1625-1640
Johann IV, 1640-1660
Friedrich Wilhelm, 1660-1677
Franz Adolf Wilhelm, 1677-1685
Ferdinand Maximilian, 1685-1687
Franz Adolf Wilhelm, again 1687-1690

Maria Ernestine Franziska, 1690-1758
Maximilian Ulrich von Kaunitz, 1699-1746

MINT OFFICIALS'

Mark		Date	Name
(a) =	or	1615-?	Georg Koenen, mintmaster
(b) =	or	1640-ca.1660	Kaspar Hoffmann, mintmaster
(c) = P N or PN =		1680-93	Peter Newers, mintmaster in Cologne
HLO		1699-?	Heinrich Lorenz Odendahl, mintmaster

ARMS

Rietberg – displayed eagle
Esens (lordship) – bear standing on hind legs
Wittmund (lordship) – two crossed whips
Ostfriesland – crowned harpy

REFERENCE

B = W. Buse, ***Münzgeschichte der Grafschaft Rietberg*, Zeitschrift für Numismatik** 29 (1912), pp. 254-362, pls. 6-9.

COUNTSHIP

REGULAR COINAGE

KM# 60 4 PFENNIG
Copper **Ruler:** Johann IV **Obv:** Eagle **Rev:** Denomination: II•II and date

Date	Mintage	VG	F	VF	XF	Unc
1654	—	350	675	—	—	—

KM# 61 6 PFENNIG
Copper **Ruler:** Johann IV **Obv:** Eagle **Rev:** Denomination VI and date

Date	Mintage	VG	F	VF	XF	Unc
1654	—	475	900	—	—	—

KM# 17 SCHILLING
Silver **Ruler:** Sabina Katharina and Johann III von Ostfriesland **Obv:** Crowned arms on St. Andrew's cross **Rev:** Imperial eagle, titles of Matthias

Date	Mintage	VG	F	VF	XF	Unc
1617	—	80.00	150	275	550	—

KM# 18 SCHILLING
Silver, 29 mm. **Ruler:** Johann III von Ostfriesland **Obv:** Crowned shield of 6-fold arms in baroque frame **Obv. Legend:** IOH. COM. ET. DO. FRI. OR. ET. RITBE. **Rev:** Crowned imperial eagle, orb on breast, date divided by crown at top **Rev. Legend:** MATI. D. G. ROM IMP. SEM. AVGVS. **Note:** Several legend varieties exist.

Date	Mintage	VG	F	VF	XF	Unc
1617	—	55.00	110	225	450	—
1618	—	55.00	110	225	450	—

Note: An XF example realized approximately $1,950 in a Westfälische Auktionsgesellschaft auction in February 2010.

Date	Mintage	VG	F	VF	XF	Unc
1619	—	55.00	110	225	450	—

KM# 22 SCHILLING
Silver **Ruler:** Johann III von Ostfriesland **Obv:** Crowned arms **Rev:** Crowned imperial eagle, titles of Ferdinand II

Date	Mintage	VG	F	VF	XF	Unc
1619	—	65.00	135	275	550	—

KM# 21 SCHILLING
11.0000 g., Silver **Ruler:** Johann III von Ostfriesland **Obv:** Crowned shield of 6-fold arms **Rev:** Crowned imperial eagle, orb on breast **Note:** Klippe.

Date	Mintage	VG	F	VF	XF	Unc
ND(1619)	—	—	—	—	—	—

KM# 23 SCHRECKENBERGER
Silver **Ruler:** Johann III von Ostfriesland **Obv:** Arms **Rev:** Crowned imperial eagle, titles of Matthias

Date	Mintage	VG	F	VF	XF	Unc
1618	—	90.00	185	375	775	—
1619	—	90.00	185	375	775	—

KM# 24 SCHRECKENBERGER
Silver **Ruler:** Johann III von Ostfriesland **Obv:** Arms **Rev:** Crowned imperial eagle, titles of Ferdinand II **Note:** Kipper Coinage

Date	Mintage	VG	F	VF	XF	Unc
1619	—	80.00	160	325	650	—

KM# 25 SCHRECKENBERGER
10.8000 g., Silver **Ruler:** Johann III von Ostfriesland **Obv:** Arms **Rev:** Crowned imperial eagle, titles of Ferdinand II **Note:** Klippe.

Date	Mintage	VG	F	VF	XF	Unc
1619	—	—	—	—	—	—

KM# 62 2 MARIENGROSCHEN
1.1150 g., Silver **Ruler:** Johann IV **Obv:** Arms **Rev:** Denomination

Date	Mintage	VG	F	VF	XF	Unc
1654 (b)	—	525	900	—	—	—

KM# 14 1/24 THALER (Groschen)
1.3000 g., Silver **Ruler:** Sabina Katharina and Johann III von Ostfriesland **Obv:** Arms of Rietberg and Ostfriesland **Rev:** Imperial orb, titles of Matthias

Date	Mintage	VG	F	VF	XF	Unc
1615	—	20.00	40.00	80.00	160	325
1616	—	20.00	40.00	80.00	160	325
1616 (a)	—	20.00	40.00	80.00	160	325
1617	—	20.00	40.00	80.00	160	325
1617 (a)	—	20.00	40.00	80.00	160	325
1618	—	20.00	40.00	80.00	160	325
1618 (a)	—	20.00	40.00	80.00	160	325

KM# 15 1/24 THALER (Groschen)
Silver **Ruler:** Sabina Katharina and Johann III von Ostfriesland **Obv:** 2 Shields, legend around **Rev:** Imperial orb, value within **Note:** Klippe.

Date	Mintage	VG	F	VF	XF	Unc
1616 (a)	—	—	—	—	—	—

KM# 19 1/24 THALER (Groschen)
Silver **Ruler:** Johann III von Ostfriesland **Obv:** 2 Shields, legend around **Rev:** Imperial orb, value within **Note:** Smaller, cruder strike with legend varieties. Many varieties exist.

Date	Mintage	VG	F	VF	XF	Unc
1617 (a)	—	20.00	40.00	85.00	170	—
1618 (a)	—	20.00	40.00	85.00	170	—
1619 (a)	—	20.00	40.00	85.00	170	—

KM# 26 1/24 THALER (Groschen)
Silver **Ruler:** Johann III von Ostfriesland **Obv:** 2 Shields, legend around **Rev:** Titles of Ferdinand II **Note:** Kipper Coinage

Date	Mintage	VG	F	VF	XF	Unc
1619	—	25.00	55.00	110	225	—
16Z0	—	25.00	55.00	110	225	—

KM# 35 1/21 THALER (Fürstengroschen)
Silver **Ruler:** Johann III von Ostfriesland **Obv:** Round 2-fold arms of Rietburg and Ostfriesland. **Obv. Legend:** LANTMVNTZ. XXI. ZV R. DALER. **Rev:** Imperial eagle, '1Z' in circle on breast. **Rev. Legend:** FERD. II. D.G. ROM. IM. SEM. AVG. **Note:** Kipper 1/21 Thaler. Many varieties exist.

Date	Mintage	VG	F	VF	XF	Unc
ND	—	33.00	55.00	100	210	—

KM# 36 1/21 THALER (Fürstengroschen)
Silver **Ruler:** Johann III von Ostfriesland **Obv:** Error, 1Z in orb

Date	Mintage	VG	F	VF	XF	Unc
ND	—	33.00	55.00	100	210	—

KM# 37 1/21 THALER (Fürstengroschen)

Silver **Ruler:** Johann III von Ostfriesland **Obv:** Round 2-fold arms of Rietburg and Ostfriesland **Obv. Legend:** IOH. COM. ET DO. FR. OR. ET. RIT. **Rev:** Crowned imperial eagle, 'Z1' in circle on breast. **Rev. Legend:** RITP. MVNTZ. XXI. ZV R. DALER. **Note:** Kipper coinage. Many varieties exist.

Date	Mintage	VG	F	VF	XF	Unc
ND	—	27.00	50.00	100	200	—

KM# 38 1/21 THALER (Fürstengroschen)

Silver **Ruler:** Johann III von Ostfriesland **Obv:** Helmeted arms **Rev:** Crowned imperial eagle, 1Z in orb on eagle's chest, titles of Ferdinand II **Note:** Varieties exist.

Date	Mintage	VG	F	VF	XF	Unc
ND (a)	—	40.00	65.00	120	240	—

KM# 27 1/4 THALER

Silver **Ruler:** Johann III von Ostfriesland **Obv:** Crowned imperial eagle, titles of Matthias **Rev:** Arms **Note:** Legend varieties exist.

Date	Mintage	VG	F	VF	XF	Unc
1619	—	—	—	—	—	—

KM# 28 1/4 THALER

Silver **Ruler:** Johann III von Ostfriesland **Obv:** Crowned imperial eagle, titles of Ferdinand II **Rev:** Arms **Note:** Legend varieties exist.

Date	Mintage	VG	F	VF	XF	Unc
1619	—	—	—	—	—	—

KM# 81 1/3 THALER (Half Gulden)

9.1000 g., Silver **Ruler:** Franz Adolf Wilhelm 2nd reign **Obv:** Crowned arms **Rev:** Denomination and horse countermark

Date	Mintage	VG	F	VF	XF	Unc
1688 (c) Rare	—	—	—	—	—	—

KM# 63 1/2 THALER

13.2000 g., Silver **Ruler:** Johann IV **Obv:** 3-fold shield of arms, 3 ornate helmets above **Rev:** Crowned imperial eagle, date divided below, titles of Ferdinand III

Date	Mintage	VG	F	VF	XF	Unc
1654 (b) Rare	—	—	—	—	—	—

KM# 64 2/3 THALER (Gulden)

Silver **Ruler:** Johann IV **Obv:** Crowned imperial eagle, titles of Ferdinand III, denomination divides date **Rev:** Helmeted arms

Date	Mintage	VG	F	VF	XF	Unc
1654 Rare	—	—	—	—	—	—

KM# 82 2/3 THALER (Gulden)

Silver Weight varies: 18.10-18.70g. **Ruler:** Franz Adolf Wilhelm 2nd reign **Obv:** Crowned arms **Rev:** Denomination and horse countermark

Date	Mintage	VG	F	VF	XF	Unc
1688 Rare	—	—	—	—	—	—
1688 (c)	—	—	—	—	—	—

KM# 90 2/3 THALER (Gulden)

Silver **Ruler:** Maria Ernestine Franziska **Obv:** Regent's portrait **Rev:** Crowned arms

Date	Mintage	VG	F	VF	XF	Unc
1693 PN Rare	—	—	—	—	—	—

KM# 16 THALER

Silver **Ruler:** Sabina Katharina and Johann III von Ostfriesland **Obv:** Crowned imperial eagle with orb on breast, date divided below **Obv. Legend:** MATTIAS. I. D. G. ROMAN… **Rev:** Helmeted arms **Rev. Legend:** IOAN. COM. E-DO… **Note:** Dav. #7317.

Date	Mintage	VG	F	VF	XF	Unc
1616 Rare	—	—	—	—	—	—

KM# 20 THALER

Silver **Ruler:** Johann III von Ostfriesland **Obv:** Date divided by helmets 1-6-1-8 **Obv. Legend:** IOAN: COM: ET: DO: FRI: OR: ET: RIT. **Rev:** Crown above double-headed imperial eagle, orb on breast **Rev. Legend:** MATHI. I. D. G. RA. ROMAN. IMPE. SEM. AVGV. **Note:** Dav. #7318.

Date	Mintage	VG	F	VF	XF	Unc
1618 (a) Rare	—	—	—	—	—	—

KM# 50 THALER

Silver **Ruler:** Johann III von Ostfriesland **Obv:** Arms **Obv. Legend:** IOAN: CO: ET. D - FR. OR. ET. RITP. **Rev:** Crowned imperial eagle, orb on breast **Rev. Legend:** FER* II* D: G* EL* RO* IM* SEM* AVG. **Note:** Dav. 7323.

Date	Mintage	VG	F	VF	XF	Unc
ND(1618-25) Rare	—	—	—	—	—	—

KM# 42 THALER

Silver **Ruler:** Johann III von Ostfriesland **Obv:** Arms, legend around **Rev:** Crowned imperial eagle, orb on breast **Note:** Klippe. Dav. 7320A. Illustration reduced.

Date	Mintage	VG	F	VF	XF	Unc
1621 Rare	—	—	—	—	—	—

KM# 41 THALER

Silver **Ruler:** Johann III von Ostfriesland **Obv:** Arms **Rev:** Crown above double-headed imperial eagle, orb on breast **Note:** Dav. #7320.

Date	Mintage	VG	F	VF	XF	Unc
1621 Rare	—	—	—	—	—	—

KM# 43 THALER

Silver **Ruler:** Johann III von Ostfriesland **Obv:** Arms **Rev:** Crown above double-headed imperial eagle, orb on breast **Rev. Legend:** FERDI*I. I. D: G*EL*ROM*IMP... **Note:** Dav. #7321.

Date	Mintage	VG	F	VF	XF	Unc
1621 Rare	—	—	—	—	—	—
ND(1625) Rare	—	—	—	—	—	—
1625 Rare	—	—	—	—	—	—

KM# 51 THALER

Silver **Ruler:** Johann III von Ostfriesland **Obv:** Spanish shield of arms, 3 ornate helmets above, chain of order around **Obv. Legend:** IOAN. CO. E. D. - FR. OR. ET. RITP. **Rev:** Crowned imperial eagle, orb on breast **Rev. Legend:** FER. II. D:G. EL. RO. IM. SEM. AVG. **Note:** Dav. 7324.

Date	Mintage	VG	F	VF	XF	Unc
ND Rare	—	—	—	—	—	—

KM# 52 THALER

Silver **Ruler:** Johann IV **Obv:** Helmeted arms **Obv. Legend:** IOAN: COM: ET: DO: FRI: OR... **Rev:** Crown above double-headed imperial eagle, orb on breast **Rev. Legend:** FERDINAND: I. I. I. D. GRA... **Note:** Dav. #7325.

Date	Mintage	VG	F	VF	XF	Unc
ND (b) Rare	—	—	—	—	—	—

Note: Dr. Busso Peus Nachfolger Auction 389, 11-06, VF realized approximately $26,830

KM# 53 THALER

Silver **Ruler:** Johann IV **Obv. Legend:** FERDINAND: I. I. I. I... **Note:** Dav. #7325A.

Date	Mintage	VG	F	VF	XF	Unc
ND (b) Rare	—	—	—	—	—	—

KM# 71.2 THALER

Silver Plated Copper **Ruler:** Johann IV **Obv. Legend:** ...EOED RIDTHE. **Note:** Dav. #7326A.

Date	Mintage	VG	F	VF	XF	Unc
1660	—	75.00	150	300	—	—

Note: This coin is a contemporary copy of the then current Netherlands Lowenthaler type struck in Rietberg by Johann IV

KM# 71.3 THALER

Silver Plated Copper **Ruler:** Johann IV **Obv. Legend:** ...EOED RIDTH. **Note:** Dav. #7326B.

Date	Mintage	VG	F	VF	XF	Unc
1660	—	100	200	350	—	—

KM# 72.1 THALER

Silver Plated Copper **Ruler:** Johann IV **Obv. Legend:** +MO ARC FROCN+ - EOFD RIDTHF. **Rev. Legend:** CONFIDENS. DNO. NON. MOVETFVR. **Note:** Dav. 7326C.

Date	Mintage	VG	F	VF	XF	Unc
1660	—	100	200	350	—	—

KM# 71.1 THALER

Silver Plated Copper **Ruler:** Johann IV **Obv:** Knight behind arms **Obv. Legend:** ...EOFD RIDTHF. **Rev:** Lion, date **Note:** 20.00-25.00 grams. Dav. #7326.

Date	Mintage	VG	F	VF	XF	Unc
1660	—	75.00	150	300	—	—

Note: This coin is a contemporary copy of the then current Netherlands Lowenthaler type struck in Rietberg by Johann IV

KM# 72.2 THALER

Silver Plated Copper **Ruler:** Johann IV **Rev. Legend:** ...MOVETVIR **Note:** Additional varieties exist. Some with reversed D's. Dav. #7326D.

Date	Mintage	VG	F	VF	XF	Unc
1660	—	100	200	350	—	—

KM# 39 2 THALER

Silver **Ruler:** Johann III von Ostfriesland **Obv:** Spanish shield of arms, 3 ornate helmets above, chain of order around **Obv. Legend:** *-IOAN: CO: ET* D - :FR * OR * ET * RITP* **Rev:** Crowned imperial eagle, orb on breast **Rev. Legend:** *FERD* II * D* G* EL* RO* IM* SEM* AVG* **Note:** Dav. 7319.

Date	Mintage	VG	F	VF	XF	Unc
1621 Rare	—	—	—	—	—	—

KM# 40 2 THALER

Silver **Ruler:** Johann III von Ostfriesland **Obv:** Spanish shield of arms, 3 ornate helmets above, chain of order around **Obv. Legend:** IOAN: CO: ET. D - FR. OR. ET. RITP. **Rev:** Crowned imperial eagle, orb on breast **Rev. Legend:** FER* II* D:G* EL* RO* IM* SEM* AVG. **Note:** Dav. 7322.

Date	Mintage	VG	F	VF	XF	Unc
ND Rare	—	—	—	—	—	—

TRADE COINAGE

KM# 5 GOLDGULDEN

3.5000 g., 0.9860 Gold 0.1109 oz. AGW **Ruler:** Sabina Katharina and Johann III von Ostfriesland **Obv:** Crowned arms **Rev:** Crowned imperial eagle, titles of Matthias

Date	Mintage	VG	F	VF	XF	Unc
ND(1612-19) Rare	—	—	—	—	—	—

KM# 6 1-1/2 GOLDGULDEN
5.2500 g., 0.9860 Gold 0.1664 oz. AGW **Ruler:** Sabina Katharina and Johann III von Ostfriesland **Obv:** Crowned shield of arms **Rev:** Crowned imperial eagle, orb on breast, titles of Matthias

Date	Mintage	VG	F	VF	XF	Unc
ND(1612-19) Rare	—	—	—	—	—	—

PROVINCIAL TOWN

REGULAR COINAGE

KM# 140 PFENNIG
Copper **Obv:** Eagle, legend around **Rev:** Denomination, date to right

Date	Mintage	VG	F	VF	XF	Unc
1617	—	225	500	1,000	—	—
1626	—	225	500	1,000	—	—
1639	—	225	500	1,000	—	—

KM# 148 PFENNIG
Copper

Date	Mintage	VG	F	VF	XF	Unc
1651	—	225	500	1,000	—	—

KM# 142 3 PFENNIG
Copper **Obv:** Eagle facing left in beaded circle, legend around **Rev:** Tall numerals of denomination in beaded circle

Date	Mintage	VG	F	VF	XF	Unc
1617	—	165	330	675	—	—
1639	—	165	330	675	—	—

KM# 150 3 PFENNIG
Copper **Obv:** Eagle facing right in corded circle, legend around **Rev:** Denomination in corded circle

Date	Mintage	VG	F	VF	XF	Unc
1651	—	180	350	750	—	—

KM# 146 4 PFENNIG
Copper **Obv:** Eagle, legend around **Rev:** Denomination

Date	Mintage	VG	F	VF	XF	Unc
1626	—	350	650	1,250	—	—

KM# 152 4 PFENNIG
Copper

Date	Mintage	VG	F	VF	XF	Unc
1651	—	350	650	1,250	—	—
1654	—	350	650	1,250	—	—

ROSTOCK

The town of Rostock is first mentioned in 1030 and was the seat of a lordship of the same name in the 13th century. It is located just a few miles inland from where the Warnow River enters the Baltic Sea and was an important trading center from earliest times. Although Rostock was usually under some control by the Mecklenburg dukes, it functioned somewhat as a free city, gaining a municipal charter as early as 1218. The city obtained control of its own coinage in 1323 and received the mint right unconditionally in 1361. From 1381, Rostock was a member of the Wendischen Münzverein (Wendish Monetary Union) and joined the Hanseatic League not long afterwards. The city coinage was struck from the 14th century until 1864.

MINTMASTERS' MARKS

Mark	Date	Name
(g)=	1594-1606	Sebastian Schoras
(h)=	1605/6-1609	Joachim Konike (Köneke)
(i)= or or	1609-14	Marcus Hoyer
(j)=	1614-15	Hans Klein
(k)=	1615-16 or 18 1620-23	Hironymus Sulzberger Georg Stange
HD (sometimes in ligature)	1621-22/3 1623-29	Hans Klein, 2nd time Hans Dethloff
(l)=	1629-35	Mathias Freude
(m)=	1635-56	Samuel Timpfe
(n)=	1659-60	Andreas Timpfe
(o)=	1661-70	Johann Freude
(p)= or PE	1670-72	Paul Eggers
(q)= or or AH	1672-79	Arnold Hille
IM	1679-1711	Johann Memmies

ARMS

Griffin, usually rampant to left. Also, shield divided by horizontal band above griffin walking left, below arabesques or sometimes an arrow.

CITY

REGULAR COINAGE

MB# 16 1/2 PFENNIG
Copper **Obv:** Gothic 'r' divides date inside raised circle **Note:** Ref. G#1253-76. Uniface. 1600-09 have a small zero above the Gothic 'r'. Varieties exist.

Date	Mintage	VG	F	VF	XF	Unc
(1)601	—	20.00	45.00	90.00	—	—
(1)602	—	20.00	45.00	90.00	—	—
(1)603	—	20.00	45.00	90.00	—	—
(1)604	—	20.00	45.00	90.00	—	—
(1)606	—	20.00	45.00	90.00	—	—
(1)607	—	20.00	45.00	90.00	—	—
(1)608	—	20.00	45.00	90.00	—	—
(1)609	—	20.00	45.00	90.00	—	—
16Z1	—	20.00	45.00	90.00	—	—
16ZZ	—	20.00	45.00	90.00	—	—
16Z3	—	20.00	45.00	90.00	—	—

KM# 27 PFENNIG
Copper **Obv:** Griffin **Obv. Legend:** CIVIT ROSTOCK **Rev:** Denomination and date **Edge:** Plain

Date	Mintage	VG	F	VF	XF	Unc
1621	—	12.00	25.00	50.00	100	—
1622	—	12.00	25.00	50.00	100	—
1638	—	12.00	25.00	50.00	100	—
1647	—	12.00	25.00	50.00	100	—
1654	—	12.00	25.00	50.00	100	—

KM# A27 PFENNIG
Copper **Obv:** Griffin to left in circle **Obv. Legend:** CIVIT ROSTOCK **Rev. Inscription:** I / date **Note:** Ref. E, pg#410. Varieties exist.

Date	Mintage	VG	F	VF	XF	Unc
16Z1	—	7.00	15.00	25.00	50.00	—
16ZZ	—	7.00	15.00	25.00	50.00	—
1638	—	7.00	15.00	25.00	50.00	—
164Z	—	7.00	15.00	25.00	50.00	—
1647 (m)	—	7.00	15.00	25.00	50.00	—
1654 (m)	—	7.00	15.00	25.00	50.00	—
1658	—	7.00	15.00	25.00	50.00	—
1660	—	7.00	15.00	25.00	50.00	—
166Z	—	7.00	15.00	25.00	50.00	—

KM# 55 PFENNIG
Copper **Obv:** Griffin to left in circle **Obv. Legend:** CIVIT ROSTOCKER **Rev. Inscription:** I / date **Note:** Ref. E pg#410.

Date	Mintage	VG	F	VF	XF	Unc
163Z	—	22.00	45.00	90.00	180	—

KM# 76 PFENNIG
Copper **Obv:** Griffin to left in circle **Obv. Legend:** CIVIT ROSTOCHI **Rev. Inscription:** I / date **Note:** Ref. E pg#410.

Date	Mintage	VG	F	VF	XF	Unc
1638	—	22.00	45.00	90.00	180	—

KM# 95 PFENNIG
Copper **Obv:** Griffin to left in circle **Obv. Legend:** ROSTOCKER **Rev:** Value and date **Rev. Inscription:** I/(date) **Note:** Prev. C#A1.

Date	Mintage	VG	F	VF	XF	Unc
1666 (o)	—	17.00	35.00	75.00	155	—
1682	—	17.00	35.00	75.00	155	—
1689	—	17.00	35.00	75.00	155	—
1699	—	17.00	35.00	75.00	155	—

KM# A28 2 PFENNIG (Zweier)
Copper **Obv:** Griffin left in circle **Obv. Legend:** CIVIT. ROSTOCK. **Rev. Inscription:** II / date **Note:** Ref. E, pg#409.

Date	Mintage	VG	F	VF	XF	Unc
16Z1	—	50.00	100	210	425	—

KM# 28 2 PFENNIG (Zweier)
Copper **Obv:** Griffin **Obv. Legend:** CIVIT ROSTOCK **Rev:** Denomination and date **Edge:** Plain

Date	Mintage	VG	F	VF	XF	Unc
1621	—	55.00	110	225	450	—

KM# A22 3 PFENNIG (Dreiling)
Copper **Obv:** Griffin left in circle **Obv. Legend:** CIVIT: ROSTOCK. **Rev. Inscription:** III / date **Note:** Ref. E pg#405.

Date	Mintage	VG	F	VF	XF	Unc
1615	—	6.00	12.00	22.00	45.00	—
16Z1	—	6.00	12.00	22.00	45.00	—
16ZZ (k)	—	6.00	12.00	22.00	45.00	—
1644	—	6.00	12.00	22.00	45.00	—
1645	—	6.00	12.00	22.00	45.00	—
1647 (m)	—	6.00	12.00	22.00	45.00	—
1654 (m)	—	6.00	12.00	22.00	45.00	—
1655 (m)	—	6.00	12.00	22.00	45.00	—

KM# 22 3 PFENNIG (Dreiling)
Copper **Obv:** Griffin **Obv. Legend:** CIVIT ROSTOCK **Rev:** Denomination and date **Edge:** Plain

Date	Mintage	VG	F	VF	XF	Unc
1621	—	8.00	16.00	36.00	60.00	—
1622	—	8.00	16.00	36.00	60.00	—
1638	—	8.00	16.00	36.00	60.00	—
1647	—	8.00	16.00	36.00	60.00	—
1654	—	8.00	16.00	36.00	60.00	—

KM# 29 3 PFENNIG (Dreiling)
Copper **Obv:** Griffin left in circle **Obv. Legend:** CIVITAS. ROSTOCK. **Rev. Inscription:** III / date **Note:** Ref. E pg#405.

Date	Mintage	VG	F	VF	XF	Unc
16ZZ (k)	—	6.00	12.00	20.00	45.00	—

KM# 85 3 PFENNIG (Dreiling)
Copper **Obv:** Griffin left in circle **Obv. Legend:** CIVITA. — ROSTOC(H)(I). **Rev:** Value and date **Rev. Inscription:** III / (date)

Date	Mintage	VG	F	VF	XF	Unc
1660 (n)	—	8.00	16.00	30.00	60.00	—
1666 (o)	—	8.00	16.00	30.00	60.00	—
1672 PE	—	8.00	16.00	30.00	60.00	—
1673 (q)	—	8.00	16.00	30.00	60.00	—
1686 IM	—	8.00	16.00	30.00	60.00	—
1687 IM	—	8.00	16.00	30.00	60.00	—
1692 IM	—	8.00	16.00	30.00	60.00	—
1695 IM	—	8.00	16.00	30.00	60.00	—
1697 IM	—	8.00	16.00	30.00	60.00	—
1699 IM	—	8.00	16.00	30.00	60.00	—

KM# C31 3 PFENNIG (1/192 Thaler)
Silver **Obv:** Griffin left in circle **Obv. Legend:** MONETA ROSTOCK. **Rev:** Imperial orb with 192 **Rev. Legend:** LEOP: D: G: R.I.S.

Date	Mintage	VG	F	VF	XF	Unc
ND(ca1685)	—	—	—	—	—	—

KM# A31 3 PFENNIG (1/192 Thaler)
Silver **Obv:** Griffin left in circle **Obv. Legend:** MO. NO. ROSTOCK. **Rev:** Imperial orb with 192 **Rev. Legend:** LEOP: D: G: R.I.S. **Note:** Ref. E pg#404.

Date	Mintage	VG	F	VF	XF	Unc
ND(ca1685)	—	—	—	—	—	—

KM# B31 3 PFENNIG (1/192 Thaler)
Silver **Obv:** Griffin left in circle **Obv. Legend:** MONETA ROSTOCK. **Rev:** Imperial orb with 192 **Rev. Legend:** LEOP. D. G. R.I.S. A. **Note:** Ref. E pg#404.

Date	Mintage	VG	F	VF	XF	Unc
ND(ca1685)	—	—	—	—	—	—

KM# 31 3 PFENNIG (1/192 Thaler)
Silver **Obv:** Griffin left in circle **Obv. Legend:** MONETA ROSTOCK. **Rev:** Imperial orb with 192, date divided at top **Rev. Legend:** LEOP: D. G. R.I.S. A. **Note:** Ref. E pg#404.

Date	Mintage	VG	F	VF	XF	Unc
(16)95	—	10.00	20.00	35.00	70.00	—

KM# A81 SECHSLING (1/96 Thaler)
0.8000 g., Silver, 16.5 mm. **Obv:** Gothic 'r' in quatrefoil superimposed on long cross, date at end of legend **Obv. Legend:** MONETA. NOVA. **Rev:** Imperial orb with 96 **Rev. Legend:** CIVIT. ROSTOCH. **Note:** Ref. G#972a.

Date	Mintage	VG	F	VF	XF	Unc
1644 (m)	—	—	—	—	—	—

KM# 86 SECHSLING (1/96 Thaler)
0.8000 g., Silver, 16.5 mm. **Obv:** Griffin to left in circle **Obv. Legend:** ROSTOCKER. **Rev:** Date at end of legend **Rev. Legend:** STADT GELDT **Rev. Inscription:** I / SOES / LIN **Note:** Ref. E pg#402.

Date	Mintage	VG	F	VF	XF	Unc
1661 (o)	—	—	—	—	—	—

KM# 98 SECHSLING (1/96 Thaler)
0.8000 g., Silver, 16.5 mm. **Obv:** Griffin to left in circle **Obv. Legend:** ROSTO(C)KER. **Rev:** Date at end of legend **Rev. Legend:** STAD. + GELD + **Rev. Inscription:** I / SES/ LING **Note:** Ref. E pg#402. Varieties exist.

Date	Mintage	VG	F	VF	XF	Unc
1673 (q)	—	15.00	32.00	60.00	120	—
1675 (q)	—	15.00	32.00	60.00	120	—
1676 (q)	—	15.00	32.00	60.00	120	—

KM# 105 SECHSLING (1/96 Thaler)
Silver **Obv:** Shield of city arms, date at end of legend **Obv. Legend:** MO. NO. ROSTOCH. **Rev:** Imperial orb with 96 **Rev. Legend:** LEOPOL. D. G. R. I. S. A. **Note:** Ref. E pg#402-03. Varieties exist.

Date	Mintage	VG	F	VF	XF	Unc
1687	—	14.00	30.00	55.00	110	—
1694	—	14.00	30.00	55.00	110	—
1696	—	14.00	30.00	55.00	110	—
1697	—	14.00	30.00	55.00	110	—
1699	—	14.00	30.00	55.00	110	—
1700	—	14.00	30.00	55.00	110	—

KM# 107 SECHSLING (1/96 Thaler)
Obv: Griffin left in circle, date at end of legend **Obv. Legend:** MO. NO. ROSTOCH. **Rev:** Imperial orb with 96 **Rev. Legend:** LEOPOL. D. G. R. I. S. A. **Note:** Ref. G#983.

Date	Mintage	VG	F	VF	XF	Unc
1696	—	—	—	—	—	—

KM# 25 SCHILLING (12 Pfennig)
Silver **Obv:** Griffin left in circle **Obv. Legend:** MONE(TA): NOVA. ROSTOC(HI). **Rev:** Gothic 'r' divides date in rose bloom superimposed on cross **Rev. Legend:** SIT - NOM - DNI - BND. **Note:** Ref. E pg#396.

Date	Mintage	VG	F	VF	XF	Unc
(16)20 HD	—	15.00	35.00	75.00	150	—
(16)26 HD	—	15.00	35.00	75.00	150	—

KM# 30 SCHILLING (12 Pfennig)
Silver **Obv:** Griffin left in circle, date at end of legend **Obv. Legend:** MONE: NO: ROSTOCK. **Rev:** Gothic 'r' in rose bloom superimposed on cross **Rev. Legend:** SIT - NOM - DNI - BND. **Note:** Ref. E pg#396-97. Varieties exist.

Date	Mintage	VG	F	VF	XF	Unc
(1)622 (k)	—	15.00	35.00	75.00	150	—
1622 (k)	—	15.00	35.00	75.00	150	—
1637	—	15.00	35.00	75.00	150	—

KM# 35 SCHILLING (12 Pfennig)
Silver **Obv:** Griffin left in circle **Obv. Legend:** MONE(TA): NOVA. ROSTOC(HI). **Rev:** Gothic 'r' in rose bloom superimposed on cross **Rev. Legend:** SIT - NOM - DNI - BND. **Note:** Ref. E pg#395. Varieties exist.

Date	Mintage	VG	F	VF	XF	Unc
ND(1623-29) HD	—	20.00	45.00	80.00	160	—

KM# 65 SCHILLING (12 Pfennig)
Silver **Obv:** Griffin left in circle, date at end of legend **Obv. Legend:** PAX. OPTIMA. RERVM. **Rev. Legend:** PACEM. TE. POSCIMVS. OMNES. **Rev. Inscription:** ROST / OCKER / STADT / GELT. **Note:** Ref. E pg#397, G#735. Varieties exist.

Date	Mintage	VG	F	VF	XF	Unc
(16)34 (l)	—	15.00	35.00	75.00	150	—
1634 (l)	—	15.00	35.00	75.00	150	—
1654	—	15.00	35.00	75.00	150	—

KM# 66 SCHILLING (12 Pfennig)
Silver **Obv:** Griffin left in circle, date at end of legend **Obv. Legend:** PAX. OPTIMA. RERVM. **Rev:** Gothic 'r' divides date in rose bloom superimposed on cross **Rev. Legend:** ST - AD - GE - LD. **Note:** Ref. E pg#397.

Date	Mintage	VG	F	VF	XF	Unc
(16)34 (l)	—	20.00	40.00	80.00	160	—

KM# 83 SCHILLING (12 Pfennig)
Silver **Obv:** Griffin left in circle, date at end of legend **Obv. Legend:** MONE. NO. ROSTOC(K) **Rev:** Gothic 'r' superimposed on cross **Rev. Legend:** SIT. NOM. DNI. BND. **Note:** Ref. E pg#397-98.

Date	Mintage	VG	F	VF	XF	Unc
1651	—	15.00	30.00	60.00	120	—
1653	—	15.00	30.00	60.00	120	—

KM# 87 SCHILLING (12 Pfennig)
Silver **Obv:** Griffin left in circle, date at end of legend **Obv. Legend:** MON(E). NO(V). ROSTOC(K) **Rev:** Gothic 'r' in rose bloom superimposed on cross **Rev. Legend:** SIT. NOM. DNI. BND. **Note:** Ref. E, pg#398-99. Varieties exist.

Date	Mintage	VG	F	VF	XF	Unc
1661 (o)	—	15.00	30.00	55.00	110	—
1663 (o)	—	15.00	30.00	55.00	110	—
1664 (o)	—	15.00	30.00	55.00	110	—
1667 (o)	—	15.00	30.00	55.00	110	—
1669 (o)	—	15.00	30.00	55.00	110	—
1671 (p)	—	15.00	30.00	55.00	110	—
1678	—	12.00	25.00	45.00	90.00	—
1683	—	12.00	25.00	45.00	90.00	—
1685	—	12.00	25.00	45.00	90.00	—
1686	—	12.00	25.00	45.00	90.00	—
1687	—	12.00	25.00	45.00	90.00	—
1692	—	12.00	25.00	45.00	90.00	—
1695	—	12.00	25.00	45.00	90.00	—
1697	—	12.00	25.00	45.00	90.00	—

KM# 1 2 SCHILLING (Doppelschilling)
Silver **Obv:** Griffin to left in circle, date at end of legend **Obv. Legend:** MONETA. NOVA. ROSTOCHIENS **Rev:** Gothic 'r' in ornamented quatrefoil superimposed on long cross **Rev. Legend:** RVDOLP: II: D: G: IMPERA: SEM. AVG. **Note:** Ref. E pg#375.

Date	Mintage	VG	F	VF	XF	Unc
(1)604 (g)	—	100	200	350	725	—

KM# 2 2 SCHILLING (Doppelschilling)
Silver **Obv:** Griffin to left in circle **Obv. Legend:** MONE(TA). NOV(A). ROSTOC(HI)(E)(N)(S)(I). **Rev:** Gothic 'r' in ornamented quatrefoil superimposed on long cross, date at end of legend **Rev. Legend:** SIT. NOMEN DOMINI BEN(E)(D) **Note:** Ref. E pg#385-85, G#294, 299. Varieties exist.

Date	Mintage	VG	F	VF	XF	Unc
(1)605 (h)	—	18.00	35.00	75.00	150	—
(1)606 (h)	—	18.00	35.00	75.00	150	—
1606 (h)	—	18.00	35.00	75.00	150	—
(1)607 (h)	—	18.00	35.00	75.00	150	—
(1)608 (h)	—	18.00	35.00	75.00	150	—

KM# 12 2 SCHILLING (Doppelschilling)
Silver **Obv:** Griffin left in circle **Obv. Legend:** MONET. NOV. ROSTOCHIENS. **Rev:** Intertwinced 'DS' in circle, date at end of legend **Rev. Legend:** SIT. NO. DOMINI. BENEDI. **Note:** Ref. E pg#386.

Date	Mintage	VG	F	VF	XF	Unc
1610	—	20.00	40.00	70.00	145	—

KM# 18 2 SCHILLING (Doppelschilling)
Silver **Obv:** Griffin to left in circle, date at end of legend **Obv. Legend:** MONETA. NO. ROSTOCH. **Rev:** Gothic 'r' superimposed on cross **Rev. Legend:** SIT. NOM(EN) DOM(INI) BE(NE). **Note:** Ref. E pg#386.

Date	Mintage	VG	F	VF	XF	Unc
1613	—	30.00	40.00	70.00	145	—

KM# 19 2 SCHILLING (Doppelschilling)
Silver **Obv:** Griffin to left in circle **Obv. Legend:** MONE(TA) NO(V)(A) ROSTOCH. **Rev:** Gothic 'r' superimposed on cross, date at end of legend **Rev. Legend:** SIT. NOM(EN) DOM(INI) BE(NE) **Note:** Ref. E, pg. #386-88, G#306, 311, 317, 320. Varieties exist.

Date	Mintage	VG	F	VF	XF	Unc
1613	—	20.00	40.00	65.00	120	240
(1)614 (j)	—	20.00	40.00	65.00	120	240
1614	—	20.00	40.00	65.00	120	240
(1)615 (j)	—	20.00	40.00	65.00	120	240
(16)15 (j)	—	20.00	40.00	65.00	120	240
(1)616 (j)	—	20.00	40.00	65.00	120	240
(16)16 (j)	—	20.00	40.00	65.00	120	240
(1)617	—	20.00	40.00	65.00	120	240
(16)17	—	20.00	40.00	65.00	120	240
1617	—	20.00	40.00	65.00	120	240
1618	—	20.00	40.00	65.00	120	240
(1)6Z7	—	20.00	40.00	65.00	120	240

KM# 77 3 SCHILLING
Silver **Obv:** Griffin to left in circle **Obv. Legend:** ROSTOCKER. STADT. GELDT:. **Rev:** Date at end of inscription **Rev. Legend:** REICHS. THALER. SILBER. **Rev. Inscription:** III / SCHIL / LINGE **Note:** Ref. E pg#379.

Date	Mintage	VG	F	VF	XF	Unc
1639 (m)	—	—	—	—	—	—

KM# 88 1/24 THALER (Groschen)
Silver **Obv:** Griffin left in circle **Obv. Legend:** ROSTOCKER STAD(T): GEL(D)(T):. **Rev:** Date at end of inscription **Rev. Legend:** NOBISCVM: CHRIST(E). MANE:. **Rev. Inscription:** 24 / REICHS / DALER **Note:** Ref. E pg#388-89, G#427, 431. Varieties exist.

Date	Mintage	VG	F	VF	XF	Unc
1661 (o)	—	50.00	100	200	425	—
1664 (o)	—	50.00	100	200	425	—
1665 (o)	—	50.00	100	200	425	—
1667 (o)	—	50.00	100	200	425	—
1668 (o)	—	50.00	100	200	425	—
1671 (p)	—	50.00	100	200	425	—
1672 (p)	—	50.00	100	200	425	—
1672 AH	—	50.00	100	200	425	—
1673 AH	—	50.00	100	200	425	—

KM# 96 1/24 THALER (Groschen)
Silver **Obv:** Griffin left in circle **Obv. Legend:** ROSTOCKER STAD(T): GEL(D)(T)(:. **Rev:** Date at end of legend **Rev. Legend:** NOBISCVM: CHRIST(E). MANE. **Rev. Inscription:** 24 / REICHS / DALER. **Note:** Ref. E pg#389. Varieties exist.

Date	Mintage	VG	F	VF	XF	Unc
1668 (o)	—	50.00	100	200	425	—
1670 (p)	—	50.00	100	200	425	—
1671 (p)	—	50.00	100	200	425	—

KM# 26 1/16 THALER (Düttchen = Doppelschilling)
Silver **Obv:** Griffin left in circle **Obv. Legend:** ROSTO(C)HKER STA(D)(T): GELD(T). **Rev:** Date at end of inscription **Rev. Legend:** NOBISCV(M) CHRIST(E). MANETO. **Rev. Inscription:** 16. VFN / REICHS / TALER **Note:** Ref. E pg. #376-78, G#338a, 365a, 370a. Varieties exist.

Date	Mintage	VG	F	VF	XF	Unc
1620 HD	—	40.00	85.00	165	335	—
1625	—	40.00	85.00	165	335	—
1625 HD	—	40.00	85.00	165	335	—
1626 HD	—	40.00	85.00	165	335	—
1627 HD	—	40.00	85.00	165	335	—
1628 HD	—	40.00	85.00	165	335	—
1629 HD	—	40.00	85.00	165	335	—
1630 (l)	—	40.00	85.00	165	335	—
1630 HD	—	40.00	85.00	165	335	—
1631 (l)	—	40.00	85.00	165	335	—

KM# A38 1/16 THALER (1/4 Ortstaler)
Silver **Obv:** Griffin left in circle **Obv. Legend:** MONETA. NOVA. CIVITAS ROSTOCK. **Rev. Inscription:** 16 1/4 22 / REICHS / ORTH. **Note:** Ref. G#271.

Date	Mintage	VG	F	VF	XF	Unc
1622 (k)	—	—	—	—	—	—

KM# B38 1/16 THALER (1/4 Ortstaler)
Silver **Obv:** Griffin left in circle **Obv. Legend:** MON(E). NO(V)(A) ROSTOCHIEN(SI)(S). **Rev:** Date at end of inscription **Rev. Legend:** NOBISCV(M) CHRIST(E). MANETO. **Note:** Ref. B#326-27.

Date	Mintage	VG	F	VF	XF	Unc
1624 HD	—	30.00	60.00	120	240	—

KM# 38 1/16 THALER (1/4 Ortstaler)
Silver **Obv:** Griffin left in circle **Obv. Legend:** ROSTO(C)HKER STA(D)(T): GELD(T). **Rev:** Date at end of legend **Rev. Legend:** NOBISCV(M) CHRIST(E). MANET. **Rev. Inscription:** 16. VFN / REICHS / TALER **Note:** Ref. E pg#378.

Date	Mintage	VG	F	VF	XF	Unc
1630 (l)	—	30.00	60.00	120	240	—

KM# 71 1/16 THALER (1/4 Ortstaler)
Silver **Obv:** City arms in ornamented shield, date at end of legend **Obv. Legend:** MONETA NOVA CIVITA: ROSTOCH. **Rev. Legend:** REICHS DALER SILBER. **Rev. Inscription:** 16. VFN / REICHS / TALER. **Note:** Ref. E pg#379.

Date	Mintage	VG	F	VF	XF	Unc
1636 (m)	—	—	—	—	—	—

KM# 82 1/16 THALER (1/4 Ortstaler)
Silver **Obv:** City arms in ornamented shield **Obv. Legend:** MONETA NO(VA) CIVI(TA) ROSTOC(K)H(I). **Rev:** Date at end of legend **Rev. Legend:** REI(CHS) SILBER. **Rev. Inscription:** XVI / EINEN / REICHES / DALER. **Note:** Ref. E pg#379-83. G#389a, 390a, 401a, 404, 410a.

Date	Mintage	VG	F	VF	XF	Unc
1644 (m)	—	35.00	75.00	150	300	—
1645 (m)	—	35.00	75.00	150	300	—
1646 (m)	—	35.00	75.00	150	300	—
1647 (m)	—	35.00	75.00	150	300	—
1648 (m)	—	35.00	75.00	150	300	—
1649 (m)	—	35.00	75.00	150	300	—
1650 (m)	—	35.00	75.00	150	300	—
1651 (m)	—	35.00	75.00	150	300	—
165Z (m)	—	35.00	75.00	150	300	—
1654 (m)	—	35.00	75.00	150	300	—
1655 (m)	—	35.00	75.00	150	300	—
1656 (m)	—	35.00	75.00	150	300	—
1659 (n)	—	35.00	75.00	150	300	—
1661 (o)	—	35.00	75.00	150	300	—
1673 AH	—	35.00	75.00	150	300	—
1675 AH	—	35.00	75.00	150	300	—

KM# 84 1/16 THALER (1/4 Ortstaler)
Silver **Obv:** Griffin left in circle **Obv. Legend:** MONETA NO(VA) CIVI(TA) ROSTOCK(K)H(I). **Rev:** Date at end of legend **Rev. Legend:** REI(CHS) SILBER. **Rev. Inscription:** XVI / EINEN / REICHES / DALER. **Note:** Ref. E pg#382.

Date	Mintage	VG	F	VF	XF	Unc
1656 (m)	—	—	—	—	—	—

KM# 102 1/16 THALER (1/4 Ortstaler)
Silver **Obv:** City arms in ornamented shield **Obv. Legend:** MONETA NO(VA) CIVI(TA) ROSTOC(K)H(I). **Rev:** Date at end of legend **Rev. Legend:** NOBISC. CHRIST. MANET. **Rev. Inscription:** XVI / EINEN / REICHES / DALER.

Date	Mintage	VG	F	VF	XF	Unc
1677 AH	—	80.00	165	335	—	—

KM# 32 1/8 THALER (Halber Reichsort)
Silver **Obv:** Griffin to left in circle **Obv. Legend:** MONE: NOV: ROSTOCHI:. **Rev:** Date at end of inscription **Rev. Inscription:** HALB / REICHS / ORTH **Note:** Ref. E pg#374.

Date	Mintage	VG	F	VF	XF	Unc
1622 (k)	—	—	—	—	—	—

KM# 33 1/8 THALER (Halber Reichsort)
Silver **Obv:** Griffin to left in circle, date at end of legend **Obv. Legend:** MONE: NOV: ROSTOCHIE(N) **Rev. Inscription:** HALB / REICHS / ORTH. **Note:** Ref. E pg#374.

Date	Mintage	VG	F	VF	XF	Unc
1622 (k)	—	—	—	—	—	—

KM# 67 1/8 THALER (4 Schilling)
Silver **Obv:** Griffin to left in circle, date at end of legend **Obv. Legend:** MON: NOV: CIVI: ROSTOCHIENSIS. **Rev:** Crowned imperial eagle, '4' in orb on breast **Rev. Legend:** FERDINANDUS. II. D: G;: ROMA: IM:L S: AU:. **Note:** Ref. E pg#374-75.

Date	Mintage	VG	F	VF	XF	Unc
1634 (l)	—	325	675	1,350	—	—

KM# 72 1/8 THALER (4 Schilling)
Silver **Obv:** City arms in ornamented shield, date at end of legend **Obv. Legend:** MONETA NOVA CIVITA: ROSTOCH **Rev. Legend:** REICHS DALER SILBER. **Rev. Inscription:** EIN / HALB. R / EICHES / OHRT / HALB. **Note:** Ref. E pg#378.

Date	Mintage	VG	F	VF	XF	Unc
1636 (m)	—	525	1,050	2,100	—	—

KM# 34 1/4 THALER (Reichsort = 8 Schilling)
Silver **Obv:** Griffin left in circle **Obv. Legend:** MONE NOVA - ROSTOCHIEN **Rev:** Date at end of inscription **Rev. Inscription:** REICHS / ORTHS / THALER **Note:** Ref. E pg#373.

Date	Mintage	VG	F	VF	XF	Unc
1622 (k)	—	—	—	—	—	—

KM# 56 1/4 THALER (Reichsort = 8 Schilling)
Silver **Obv:** Griffin left in circle, date at end of legend **Obv. Legend:** MONE. NOVA. ROSTOCKIENSIS. **Rev:** Crowned imperial eagle **Rev. Legend:** FERDINANDVS. II D. G. RO. I. S. AVG. D. P. **Note:** Ref. E pg#373.

Date	Mintage	VG	F	VF	XF	Unc
1632	—	—	—	—	—	—

KM# 68 1/4 THALER (Reichsort = 8 Schilling)
Silver **Obv:** Griffin left in circle, date at end of legend **Obv. Legend:** MONE(T)(A): NOV(A). CIVI(T). ROSTOCHIENSIS: **Rev:** Crowned imperial eagle, '8' in orb on breast **Rev. Legend:** FERDINANDVS II. D. G. ROMA. IM. S(E). A(V). **Note:** Ref. E pg#373-74.

Date	Mintage	VG	F	VF	XF	Unc
1634	—	120	200	425	850	—
1634 (l)	—	120	200	425	850	—

KM# 69 1/4 THALER (Reichsort = 8 Schilling)
Silver **Obv:** Griffin left in circle **Obv. Legend:** MONE(T)(A): NOV(A). CIVI(T). ROSTOCHIENSIS. **Rev:** Crowned imperial eagle, '8' in orb on breast, date at end of legend **Rev. Legend:** FERDINANDVS II. D. G. ROMA. IM. S. A. **Note:** Ref. E pg. #374, G#272.

Date	Mintage	VG	F	VF	XF	Unc
1634 (l)	—	120	200	425	850	—
1636 (m)	—	120	200	425	850	—

KM# 94 1/4 THALER (Reichsort = 8 Schilling)
Silver **Obv:** Griffin to left in circle **Obv. Legend:** MONETA. NOVA. CIVIT: ROSTOCHIE. **Rev:** Crowned imperial eagle, '8' in orb on breast, date at end of legend **Rev. Legend:** LEOPOLDUS D: G: ROM. IM: S: A: **Note:** Ref. E pg#374.

Date	Mintage	VG	F	VF	XF	Unc
1664 (o)	—	—	—	—	—	—

KM# 97 1/3 THALER (16 Schilling = 1/2 Gulden)
Silver **Obv:** Griffin to left in circle, date at end of legend **Obv. Legend:** MONET. NOVA. CIVIT: ROST: **Rev:** Griffin to left above horizontal bar, '16 fls.' below **Rev. Legend:** NOBISCVM. CHRISTE MANETO. **Note:** Ref. G#248.

Date	Mintage	VG	F	VF	XF	Unc
1672 (p)	—	800	1,600	3,250	—	—

KM# 99 1/3 THALER (16 Schilling = 1/2 Gulden)
Silver **Obv:** Griffin to left above horizontal bar in ornamented shield **Obv. Legend:** MONETA NOVA CIVIT. ROSTOCHIENSIS. **Rev:** Inscription in ornamented shield, mintmaster's initials at end of inscription, date at end of legend **Rev. Legend:** NOBISCUM CHRISTE MANETO. ANNO **Rev. Inscription:** 1 / 3 / REICHS / DALER **Note:** Ref. E pg#371-72.

Date	Mintage	VG	F	VF	XF	Unc
1676 AH	—	100	200	425	—	—

KM# 100 1/3 THALER (16 Schilling = 1/2 Gulden)
Silver **Obv:** Griffin to left in circle, date at end of legend **Obv. Legend:** MONETA. NOVA. CIVIT. ROSTOCHIENSIS. **Rev:** Inscription in ornamented shield **Rev. Legend:** NOBISCUM CHRISTE MANETO. **Rev. Inscription:** 1 / 3 / REICHS / THALER **Note:** Ref. E pg#372.

Date	Mintage	VG	F	VF	XF	Unc
1676	—	100	200	425	—	—

KM# 103 1/3 THALER (16 Schilling = 1/2 Gulden)
Silver **Obv:** Griffin to left in circle, date at end of legend **Obv. Legend:** MONETA. NOVA. CIVIT. ROSTOCHIENSIS. **Rev:** Inscription in ornamented shield **Rev. Legend:** NOBISCUM CHRISTE MANETO. **Rev. Inscription:** 1 / 2 / REICHS / DALER. **Note:** Ref. E pg#372.

Date	Mintage	VG	F	VF	XF	Unc
1677 AH	—	80.00	160	325	—	—
1679 IM	—	80.00	160	325	—	—

KM# 104 1/3 THALER (16 Schilling = 1/2 Gulden)
Silver **Obv:** Griffin to left in circle, date at end of legend **Obv. Legend:** MONETA. NOVA. CIVIT. ROSTOCHIENSIS. **Rev:** '1/3' in ornamented shield, date at end of legend **Rev. Legend:** NOBISCUM CHRISTE MANETO. ANNO. **Note:** Ref. E pg#372.

Date	Mintage	VG	F	VF	XF	Unc
1685 IM	—	—	—	—	—	—

MB# 36 1/2 THALER (16 Schilling)
Silver **Obv:** Griffin left in circle, date at end of legend **Obv. Legend:** MON(E)(TA): NOVA: ROSTOCHIENSIS: **Rev:** Crowned imperial eagle, '16' in orb on breast **Rev. Legend:** RVDOL(PHS): II: D: G: RO(MA): SE(M): AVGVS(TO). (P.F.D). **Note:** Ref. G#216-19. Varieties exist.

Date	Mintage	VG	F	VF	XF	Unc
(1)605 (g)	—	650	1,350	2,750	5,500	—
(1)609 (i)	—	650	1,350	2,750	5,500	—
(1)610	—	650	1,350	2,750	5,500	—

KM# 39 1/2 THALER (16 Schilling)
Silver **Obv:** Griffin left in circle, date divided at top **Obv. Legend:** MON(E)(TA): NOVA: ROSTOCHIENSIS. **Rev:** Crowned imperial eagle, '16' in orb on breast **Rev. Legend:** FERDIN(ANDVS). II. D. G. RO(M). I. S. A(VG). D. P. **Note:** Ref. E pg#369.

Date	Mintage	VG	F	VF	XF	Unc
1624	—	700	1,400	2,800	5,600	—
1625/4	—	700	1,400	2,900	5,800	—
1627	—	700	1,400	2,800	5,600	—
1630	—	700	1,400	2,800	5,600	—

KM# 49 1/2 THALER (16 Schilling)
Silver **Obv:** Griffin left in circle, date divided at top **Obv. Legend:** MONE(TA). NO. ROSTOCH(K)IENSIS. **Rev:** Crowned imperial eagle, '16' in orb on breast, date at end of legend **Rev. Legend:** FERDIN(AND). II: D: G: RO. I. S. AV. G. D. P. **Note:** Ref. E pg#369-70, G#226-28.

Date	Mintage	VG	F	VF	XF	Unc
1628 HD	—	700	1,400	2,800	5,600	—
(1)632 (I)	—	700	1,400	2,800	5,600	—
(16)3Z (I)	—	700	1,400	2,800	5,600	—
1633 (I)	—	700	1,400	2,800	5,600	—

KM# 70 1/2 THALER (16 Schilling)
Silver **Obv:** Griffin left in circle, date divided at top, date at end of legend **Obv. Legend:** MONETA NOVA CIVI(TA)(T): ROSTOCH(K)IENSIS. **Rev:** Crowned imperial eagle, '16' in orb on breast **Rev. Legend:** FERDINANDUS II D: G: ROMA(N): I(M)(P)(ER): SE(M)(P): AU(GU):. **Note:** Ref. E pg#370, G#234.

Date	Mintage	VG	F	VF	XF	Unc
1634 (I)	—	250	500	1,000	2,000	—
1635 (I)	—	350	650	1,300	2,600	—
1636 (m)	—	350	650	1,250	2,500	—

KM# 74 1/2 THALER (16 Schilling)
Silver **Obv:** Griffin left in circle, date divided at top, date at end of legend **Obv. Legend:** MONETA NOVA CIVI(TA)(T): ROSTOCH(K)IENSIS. **Rev:** Crowned imperial eagle, '16' in orb on breast **Rev. Legend:** FERDINANDUS. II: D: G: ROM(A): IM(P)(S): S(E)(M): A(U):. **Note:** Ref. E pg#371.

Date	Mintage	VG	F	VF	XF	Unc
1637 (m)	—	400	900	2,000	4,100	—

KM# 92 1/2 THALER (16 Schilling)
Silver **Obv:** Griffin left in circle **Obv. Legend:** MONETA NOVA: CIVIT: ROSTOCHI. **Rev:** Crowned imperial eagle, date at end of legend **Rev. Legend:** LEOPOLDUS. D: G: ROMA: IMP: S: A: **Note:** Ref. E pg#371.

Date	Mintage	VG	F	VF	XF	Unc
1663 (o)	—	—	—	—	—	—

KM# 101 2/3 THALER (Gulden)
Silver **Obv:** Griffin to left above horizontal bar in ornamented shield **Obv. Legend:** MONETA NOVA CIVIT: ROSTOCHIENSIS. **Rev:** Inscription in ornamented shield, mintmaster's initials at end of inscription, date at end of legend **Rev. Legend:** NOBISCUM. CHRISTE MANETO. ANNO. **Rev. Inscription:** 2/3 / REICHS / DALER **Note:** Dav#803. Varieties exist.

Date	Mintage	VG	F	VF	XF	Unc
1676 AH	—	275	550	1,100	—	—
1677 AH	—	275	550	1,100	—	—
1679 IM	—	275	550	1,100	—	—

KM# 110 2/3 THALER (Gulden)
Silver **Obv:** Griffin to left above horizontal bar in ornamented shield **Obv. Legend:** MONETA NOVA CIVIT: ROSTOCHIENSIS. **Rev:** Inscription in ornamented shield, mintmaster's initials at end of inscription, date at end of legend **Rev. Legend:** NACH. DEN. LEIPZIGER FUS. **Rev. Inscription:** 2/3 / REICHS / DALER **Note:** Dav#804.

Date	Mintage	VG	F	VF	XF	Unc
1698 IM	—	—	—	—	—	—

KM# 111 2/3 THALER (Gulden)
Silver **Obv:** Griffin to left above horizontal bar in ornamented shield **Obv. Legend:** MONETA NOVA CIVIT: ROSTOCHIENSIS. **Rev:** Inscription in heart-shaped shield, mintmaster's initials at end of inscription, date at end of legend **Rev. Legend:** NACH DEM LEIPZIGER FUSS. **Rev. Inscription:** 2/3 / REICHS / DALER

Date	Mintage	VG	F	VF	XF	Unc
1698 IM	—	—	—	—	—	—

KM# 3 THALER
Silver **Obv:** Griffin **Rev:** Crowned double-headed imperial eagle, orb on breast **Note:** Dav. #5778; Varieties exist.

Date	Mintage	VG	F	VF	XF	Unc
(1)605 (h)	—	500	1,000	2,150	4,200	—
(1)607 (h)	—	500	1,000	2,150	4,200	—
(1)609 (i)	—	500	1,000	2,150	4,200	—
(1)610 (i)	—	400	900	1,850	4,200	—
(1)611 (i)	—	500	1,000	2,150	4,200	—

KM# 10 THALER
Silver **Obv:** Partial date above eagle **Rev:** Full date in legend **Note:** Dav. #5780.

Date	Mintage	VG	F	VF	XF	Unc
1607//1607 (h)	—	650	1,250	2,750	5,000	—
1609//1609 (i)	—	650	1,250	2,750	5,000	—

KM# 9 THALER
Silver **Rev:** Full dates in legend **Note:** Dav. #5780; Varieties exist.

Date	Mintage	VG	F	VF	XF	Unc
1607 (h)	—	500	1,000	2,150	3,600	—
1608 (h)	—	550	1,100	2,250	4,250	—
1609 (i)	—	550	1,100	2,250	4,250	—
1611 (i)	—	600	1,200	2,500	4,500	—
1612 (i)	—	600	1,200	2,500	4,500	—

KM# 15 THALER
Silver **Subject:** Baptism of Prince Hans Christoph, eldest son of Duke Johann Albrecht II **Obv:** Ornate shield **Rev:** Crown above double-headed imperial eagle, orb on breast **Note:** Dav. #5782.

Date	Mintage	VG	F	VF	XF	Unc
1612 (i)	—	1,500	3,000	5,500	10,000	—

Note: Fritz Rudolf Künker Münzenhandlung Auction 141, 6-08, XF+ realized approximately $13,940

KM# 16 THALER
Silver **Rev:** Date **Rev. Legend:** MONETA: NOVA: ROSTOCHIENSIS **Note:** Dav. #5783.

Date	Mintage	VG	F	VF	XF	Unc
1612 (i) Rare	—	—	—	—	—	—

KM# 17 THALER
Silver **Obv:** Griffin **Rev:** Crown above double-headed imperial eagle, orb on breast **Rev. Legend:** MATTIAS. I. D. G. RO... **Note:** Dav. #5784; Varieties exist.

Date	Mintage	VG	F	VF	XF	Unc
1612 (i)	—	350	750	1,600	3,250	—
1613 (i)	—	350	750	1,600	3,250	—
1618	—	600	1,250	3,000	5,000	—
ND	—	350	750	1,600	5,250	—

KM# 20 THALER
Silver **Obv:** Griffin **Rev:** Crown above double-headed imperial eagle, orb on breast **Rev. Legend:** MATTH. D: G: ROM:-IMP. **Note:** Dav. #5785.

Date	Mintage	VG	F	VF	XF	Unc
1613 (i)	—	450	850	1,750	3,500	—
ND	—	450	850	1,750	3,500	—

KM# 23 THALER

Silver **Subject:** Baptism of Prince Carl Heinrich, second son of Duke Johann Albrecht II! **Note:** Dav. #LS381.

Date	Mintage	VG	F	VF	XF	Unc
1616	—	1,750	3,000	5,000	9,000	—

KM# 36 THALER

Silver **Obv:** Griffin with claws **Rev:** Crowned imperial eagle **Rev. Legend:** FERDINAN: II: D: G: R:... **Note:** Dav. #5786.

Date	Mintage	VG	F	VF	XF	Unc
1623 (k)	—	625	1,250	2,250	4,250	—
1624 HD	—	625	1,250	2,250	4,250	—
1625 HD	—	625	1,250	2,250	4,250	—
1626 HD	—	625	1,250	2,250	4,250	—

KM# 40 THALER

Silver **Subject:** Baptism of Prince Christian, oldest son of Duke Adolph Friedrich I **Note:** Dav. #LS385.

Date	Mintage	VG	F	VF	XF	Unc
1624 HD	—	650	1,200	2,000	3,500	—

KM# 45 THALER

Silver **Obv:** Crowned imperial eagle **Obv. Legend:** FERDINANDVS II... **Rev:** Griffin **Rev. Legend:** MONE. NOVA... **Note:** Dav. #5787.

Date	Mintage	VG	F	VF	XF	Unc
1626 HD	—	625	1,250	2,250	4,250	—
1627 HD	—	625	1,250	2,250	4,250	—

KM# 46 THALER

Silver **Obv:** Griffin **Obv. Legend:** HD*MONETA... **Rev:** Crown above double-headed imperial eagle, orb on breast **Note:** Dav. #5788.

Date	Mintage	VG	F	VF	XF	Unc
1627 HD	—	900	1,850	3,750	6,250	—

KM# 47 THALER

Silver **Obv. Legend:** ...D: G: RO: I: S: A:... **Rev:** Griffin with hooves **Rev. Legend:** ...ROSTOCHIENSIS. **Note:** Dav. #5789.

Date	Mintage	VG	F	VF	XF	Unc
1627 HD	—	300	650	1,350	2,350	—
1628 HD	—	300	650	1,350	2,350	—
1629 HD	—	300	650	1,350	2,350	—
1631 (I)	—	350	700	1,450	2,500	—
1632 (I)	—	350	700	1,450	2,500	—
1633 (I)	—	350	700	1,450	2,500	—

KM# 50 THALER

Silver **Rev. Legend:** ROS. THOCHI. ENSIS. **Note:** Dav. #5789A.

Date	Mintage	VG	F	VF	XF	Unc
1629 HD	—	300	650	1,350	2,350	—

KM# 51 THALER

Silver **Obv:** Crowned imperial eagles with halos, date divided by crown **Obv. Legend:** FERDIN. II. D. G. RO:... **Note:** Dav. #5791.

Date	Mintage	VG	F	VF	XF	Unc
1630 (I)	—	400	750	1,500	2,750	—
1631 (I)	—	400	750	1,500	2,750	—
1632 (I)	—	400	750	1,500	2,750	—
1633 (I)	—	400	750	1,500	2,750	—

KM# 54 THALER

Silver **Obv:** Griffin **Rev:** Crown above double-headed imperial eagle, value in orb on breast **Rev. Legend:** ...D: G: ROMIO: I: S: A:... **Note:** Dav. #5789B.

Date	Mintage	VG	F	VF	XF	Unc
1631 (I)	—	300	650	1,350	2,350	—

KM# 59 THALER

Silver **Obv. Legend:** ...ROSTOCK. IENSIS: **Note:** Dav. #5791A.

Date	Mintage	VG	F	VF	XF	Unc
1633 (I)	—	400	750	1,500	2,750	—

KM# 60 THALER

Silver **Obv:** Eagles without halos **Note:** Dav. #5791B.

Date	Mintage	VG	F	VF	XF	Unc
1633 (I)	—	400	750	1,500	2,750	—

KM# 61 THALER

Silver **Obv. Legend:** FERDINAND: II...IMP: SEMP: **Rev. Legend:** ...ROSTOCK: IENSIS:X. **Note:** Dav. #5792.

Date	Mintage	VG	F	VF	XF	Unc
ND Rare	—	—	—	—	—	—

KM# 62 THALER

Silver **Rev. Legend:** ...ROS. THOCHI: EN. SIS. **Note:** Dav. #5792A.

Date	Mintage	VG	F	VF	XF	Unc
ND Rare	—	—	—	—	—	—

KM# 63 THALER

Silver **Obv. Legend:** ...NOVA. CIVIT:... **Rev:** Crowned imperial eagle without halos **Note:** Dav. #5793.

Date	Mintage	VG	F	VF	XF	Unc
1633 (l)	—	300	650	1,350	2,350	—
1634 (l)	—	300	650	1,350	2,350	—

KM# 64 THALER

Silver **Rev. Legend:** FERDINANDUS. II. ROMA: IMP:... **Note:** Dav. #5794.

Date	Mintage	VG	F	VF	XF	Unc
1633 (l)	—	275	600	1,250	2,150	—
1634 (l)	—	275	600	1,250	2,150	—
1635 (l)	—	275	600	1,250	2,150	—
1636 (m)	—	275	600	1,250	2,150	—
1637 (m)	—	275	600	1,250	2,150	—

KM# 58 THALER

Silver **Rev:** Eagle with halos

Date	Mintage	VG	F	VF	XF	Unc
1633 (l)	—	275	600	1,250	2,150	—

KM# 75 THALER

Silver **Obv:** Griffin **Rev:** Crown above double-headed imperial eagle, value in orb on breast **Rev. Legend:** FERDINANDUS. III... **Note:** Dav. #5795.

Date	Mintage	VG	F	VF	XF	Unc
1637 (m)	—	275	600	1,250	2,150	—
1639 (m)	—	275	600	1,250	2,150	—

KM# 79 THALER

Silver **Obv. Legend:** MON. NOVA:... **Note:** Dav. #5796.

Date	Mintage	VG	F	VF	XF	Unc
1640 (m)	—	275	600	1,250	2,150	—
1657	—	—	—	—	—	—

KM# 80 THALER

Silver **Obv:** Griffin, date in legend **Obv. Legend:** ...CIVITA... **Rev:** Crowned imperial eagle dividing date below **Rev. Legend:** ...ROMANO... **Note:** Dav. #5797.

Date	Mintage	VG	F	VF	XF	Unc
1642//1642	—	450	900	1,850	3,250	—
1643//1642	—	600	1,200	2,250	—	—
1646//1642	—	600	1,200	2,250	—	—

KM# 89 THALER

Silver **Obv. Legend:** LEOPOLDUS. D: G: ROMA: IMP: SE: AUG: **Rev:** Mint mark before griffin **Note:** Dav. #5798.

Date	Mintage	VG	F	VF	XF	Unc
1661 (o)	—	450	1,000	2,000	3,750	—
1664 (o)	—	450	1,000	2,000	3,750	—

KM# 93 THALER

Silver **Obv:** Date **Obv. Legend:** ...ROM: I: M: S: A: **Note:** Dav. #5799.

Date	Mintage	VG	F	VF	XF	Unc
1663 (o)	—	275	525	950	1,850	—

KM# 4 1-1/2 THALER

Silver **Obv:** Helmeted arms **Rev:** Crown above double-headed imperial eagle, orb on breast **Note:** Dav. #LS378.

Date	Mintage	VG	F	VF	XF	Unc
1605 (h) Rare	—	—	—	—	—	—

KM# 41 1-1/2 THALER
Silver **Subject:** Baptism of Prince Adolph Friedrich **Note:** Dav. #LS383.

Date	Mintage	VG	F	VF	XF	Unc
1624 HD	—	1,850	3,250	5,500	9,500	—

KM# 5 2 THALER
Silver **Note:** Similar to 1-1/2 Thaler. Dav. #LS377.

Date	Mintage	VG	F	VF	XF	Unc
1605 (h) Rare	—	—	—	—	—	—

KM# 11 2 THALER
Silver **Note:** Previous Dav.#5779.

Date	Mintage	VG	F	VF	XF	Unc
1609 (i) Rare	—	—	—	—	—	—

KM# 13 2 THALER
Silver **Obv:** Helmeted arms **Rev:** Crowned imperial eagle, orb on breast **Note:** Dav. #LS380.

Date	Mintage	VG	F	VF	XF	Unc
1611 (i) Rare	—	—	—	—	—	—

KM# 24 2 THALER
Silver **Subject:** Baptism of Prince Carl Heinrich, second son of Duke Johann Albrecht II **Note:** Dav. #LS381.

Date	Mintage	VG	F	VF	XF	Unc
1616	—	2,300	4,000	7,500	12,500	—

KM# 42 2 THALER
Silver **Subject:** Baptism of Prince Adolph Friedrich **Note:** Dav. #LS382.

Date	Mintage	VG	F	VF	XF	Unc
1624 HD	—	1,900	3,300	6,000	10,000	—

KM# 43 2 THALER
Silver **Subject:** Baptism of Prince Christian, oldest son of Duke Adolph Friedrich **Note:** Dav. #LS384.

Date	Mintage	VG	F	VF	XF	Unc
1624 HD	—	1,850	3,250	5,500	9,500	—

KM# 48 2 THALER
Silver **Obv:** Griffin with claws, date above in legend **Rev:** Crowned imperial eagle **Rev. Legend:** FERDINANDUS II... **Note:** Dav. #A5787.

Date	Mintage	VG	F	VF	XF	Unc
1627 HD Rare	—	—	—	—	—	—

KM# 52 2 THALER
Silver **Note:** Dav. #5790.

Date	Mintage	VG	F	VF	XF	Unc
1630 (l) Rare	—	—	—	—	—	—

KM# 6 3 THALER
Silver **Note:** Dav. #LS376.

Date	Mintage	VG	F	VF	XF	Unc
1605 (h) Rare	—	—	—	—	—	—

KM# 14 3 THALER
Silver **Note:** Dav. #LS379.

Date	Mintage	VG	F	VF	XF	Unc
1611 (i) Rare	—	—	—	—	—	—

KM# 7 4 THALER
Silver **Note:** Dav. #LS375.

Date	Mintage	VG	F	VF	XF	Unc
1605 (h) Rare	—	—	—	—	—	—

TRADE COINAGE

KM# 8 GOLDGULDEN
3.5000 g., 0.9860 Gold 0.1109 oz. AGW **Obv:** Griffin in inner circle **Rev:** Crowned imperial eagle in inner circle, titles of Rudolf II **Note:** Fr. #2583.

Date	Mintage	VG	F	VF	XF	Unc
1606 (h)	—	1,500	2,800	5,500	9,750	—
1608 (h)	—	1,500	2,800	5,500	9,750	—
1609 (i)	—	1,500	2,800	5,500	9,750	—
1610 (i)	—	1,500	2,800	5,500	9,750	—
1611 (i)	—	1,500	2,800	5,500	9,750	—
ND	—	1,500	2,800	5,500	9,750	—

KM# 21 GOLDGULDEN
3.5000 g., 0.9860 Gold 0.1109 oz. AGW **Obv:** Griffin in inner circle, date in legend **Rev:** Crowned imperial eagle in inner circle, titles of Matthias **Note:** Fr. #2584.

Date	Mintage	F	VF	XF	Unc
1613	—	775	1,550	3,700	5,500	—
1614	—	775	1,550	3,700	5,500	—
1615	—	775	1,550	3,700	5,500	—
1616	—	775	1,550	3,700	5,500	—
1617	—	775	1,550	3,700	5,500	—

KM# 44 GOLDGULDEN
3.5000 g., 0.9860 Gold 0.1109 oz. AGW **Rev:** Crowned imperial eagle in inner circle, titles of Ferdinand II **Note:** Fr. #2586.

Date	Mintage	VG	F	VF	XF	Unc
1625	—	925	1,850	3,500	6,000	—
1626	—	925	1,850	3,500	6,000	—
1627	—	925	1,850	3,500	6,000	—
1629 HD	—	925	1,850	3,500	6,000	—
1630	—	925	1,850	3,500	6,000	—
1631	—	925	1,850	3,500	6,000	—

KM# 37 2 GOLDGULDEN
7.0000 g., 0.9860 Gold 0.2219 oz. AGW **Obv:** Griffin in inner circle, date in legend **Rev:** Crowned imperial eagle in inner circle, titles of Ferdinand II **Note:** Fr. #2585.

Date	Mintage	VG	F	VF	XF	Unc
1623 (k)	—	1,300	2,600	5,500	9,500	—

KM# 109 1/4 DUCAT
0.8750 g., 0.9860 Gold 0.0277 oz. AGW **Obv:** Griffin, titles of Leopold I **Rev:** Value and date **Note:** FR#2594.

Date	Mintage	VG	F	VF	XF	Unc
1696	—	375	800	1,750	3,500	—

KM# 106 1/2 DUCAT
1.7500 g., 0.9860 Gold 0.0555 oz. AGW **Obv:** Griffin, date in legend **Rev:** Crowned imperial eagle, titles of Leopold I **Note:** Fr. #2592.

Date	Mintage	VG	F	VF	XF	Unc
1695	—	750	1,650	3,750	7,250	—

KM# 53 DUCAT
Gold **Obv:** Griffin to left in circle **Obv. Legend:** MON: NOVA: ROSTOCHIEN:. **Rev:** Crowned imperial eagle, orb on breast, date divided at top **Rev. Legend:** FERDINAND. II. D. G. RO. I. S. A.

Date	Mintage	VG	F	VF	XF	Unc
1630 (l) Rare	—	—	—	—	—	—

KM# 57 DUCAT
3.5000 g., 0.9860 Gold 0.1109 oz. AGW **Obv:** Arms in inner circle, date in legend **Rev:** Crowned imperial eagle, titles of Ferdinand II **Note:** Fr. #2587.

Date	Mintage	VG	F	VF	XF	Unc
1632 (l)	—	450	1,000	2,000	4,000	—
1633 (l)	—	450	1,000	2,000	4,000	—
1634 (l)	—	450	1,000	2,000	4,000	—
1636 (m)	—	450	1,000	2,000	4,000	—

KM# 73 DUCAT
3.5000 g., 0.9860 Gold 0.1109 oz. AGW **Obv:** Ornate arms within beaded circle **Rev:** Crowned imperial eagle, titles of Ferdinand III **Note:** Fr. #2589.

Date	Mintage	VG	F	VF	XF	Unc
1636 (m)	—	325	725	1,350	2,650	—
1639 (m)	—	325	725	1,350	2,650	—

Date	Mintage	VG	F	VF	XF	Unc
1646 (m)	—	325	725	1,350	2,650	—
1655 (m)	—	325	725	1,350	2,650	—

KM# 90 DUCAT

3.5000 g., 0.9860 Gold 0.1109 oz. AGW **Obv:** Arms in inner circle, date in legend **Rev:** Crowned imperial eagle in inner circle, titles of Leopold I **Note:** Fr. #2591. Varieties exist.

Date	Mintage	VG	F	VF	XF	Unc
1661 (o)	—	975	1,900	4,000	7,500	—
1664 (o)	—	975	1,900	4,000	7,500	—
1665 (o)	—	975	1,900	4,000	7,500	—
1672 (q)	—	975	1,900	4,000	7,500	—
1677 AH	—	975	1,900	4,000	7,500	—
1682 IM	—	975	1,900	4,000	7,500	—
1694 IM	—	975	1,900	4,000	7,500	—

KM# 78 2 DUCAT

7.0000 g., 0.9860 Gold 0.2219 oz. AGW **Obv:** Oval arms divides date within square disign with inscription **Rev:** Crowned imperial eagle, titles of Ferdinand III **Note:** Fr. #2588.

Date	Mintage	VG	F	VF	XF	Unc
1639 (m)	—	750	1,350	2,750	5,000	—

KM# 81 2 DUCAT

7.0000 g., 0.9860 Gold 0.2219 oz. AGW **Obv:** Arms in inner circle, date in legend **Rev:** Crowned imperial eagle, titles of Leopold I **Note:** Fr. #2590.

Date	Mintage	VG	F	VF	XF	Unc
1661	—	1,300	2,500	5,000	9,000	—
1695 IM	—	1,300	2,500	5,000	9,000	—

KM# 91 2 DUCAT

Gold **Obv:** Shield of city arms of griffin left over horizontal bar, date at end of legend **Obv. Legend:** DUCATUS - NOVS - CIVITATIS - ROSTOCHI - EN - EN - SIS **Rev:** Crowed imperial eagle **Rev. Legend:** LEOPOLDUS. D: G: ROMAN: IMP. SEMP. AUG. **Note:** Fr#2590.

Date	Mintage	VG	F	VF	XF	Unc
1661 (o) Rare	—	—	—	—	—	—

KM# 108 2 DUCAT

Gold **Obv:** Oval shield of city arms of griffin left over horizontal bar, date divided above, curved inscription over all **Obv. Legend:** MO: NO: - CIVITATIS - ROSTOCH. **Obv. Inscription:** DEUS PROTECTOR NOSTER. **Rev:** Crowned imperial eagle, orb on breast **Rev. Legend:** LEOPOLDUS. D: G: ROM: IMP: S: AUG. **Note:** Fr#2590.

Date	Mintage	VG	F	VF	XF	Unc
1695 IM Rare	—	—	—	—	—	—

ROTHENBURG

A city located in Bavaria on the Tauber River southeast of Wurzburg. Population: 11,882. Exports include soap and textiles.

Nobles of Rothenburg, whose castle lay in the Harz Mountains, were the cadet line of the counts of Beichlingen. Founded by Friedrich IV (1252-1313) the city became an imperial city in 1274 and reached the height of its prosperity at the end of the 14th century.

CITY

TRADE COINAGE

KM# 4 DUCAT

3.5000 g., 0.9860 Gold 0.1109 oz. AGW **Subject:** 100th Anniversary of Reformation **Obv:** Castle and legend **Rev:** Inscription **Note:** Date as chronogram.

Date	Mintage	VG	F	VF	XF	Unc
MIVLVVLID (1617)	—	1,500	2,750	5,000	9,000	—

PATTERNS

Including off metal strikes

KM#	Date	Mintage	Identification	Mkt Val
Pn1	1617	—	Ducat. Silver. KM#4.	450
Pn2	1717	—	Ducat. Silver. KM#5.	150
Pn3	1717	—	Ducat. Silver. KM#6.	180
Pn4	1717	—	2 Ducat. Silver. KM#7.	200
Pn5	1744	—	Ducat. Silver. KM#8.	100
Pn6	1792	—	Ducat. Silver. KM#9.	180

ROTTWEIL

The city of Rottweil is located on the upper Neckar River, northwest of the Swabian Alps and about 32 miles (53km) southsouthwest of Tübingen. The place was first mentioned in records as early as 771 and became an established market town from about 1140. During the third quarter of the 12th century, bracteates with the eagle arms of the town were struck in Rottweil. Subsequent issues appeared in the 13th century prior to its elevation to the status of a Free City of the Empire in 1268. The earliest seal with the eagle city arms is known from 1280. The first mint right was granted by the Count of Zähringen in 1218, but the imperial concession was made in 1285. A new mint privilege was granted by Emperor Maximilian I in 1512, although some coins had been struck in and for the city prior to that date. Only a few issues were struck during the 16th century and a few more were issued by the city in the early period of the Thirty Years' War. Records show that the last coins minted in Rottweil were Kreuzers in the year 1701, but none are known to exist. The city lost its free status during the Napoleonic Wars and in 1803, Rottweil was absorbed by Württemberg.

Initial	Date	Name
IM	1623-24	Johann Martin
	1623-24	Thomas Linckh von Zug, warden

ARMS

Eagle with wings spread

REFERENCES

N = Elisabeth Nau, **Die Münzen und Medaillen des oberschwäbischen Städte**, Freiburg im Breisgau, 1964.

Sch = Wolfgang Schulten, **Deutsche Münzen aus der Zeit Karls V.**, Frankfurt am Main, 1976.

FREE CITY

REGULAR COINAGE

KM# 12 KREUZER

Silver, 14 mm. **Obv:** City arms in circle **Rev:** Double-cross with 'I' in circle in center **Note:** Nau 29.

Date	Mintage	VG	F	VF	XF	Unc
ND(ca1623)	—	—	—	—	—	—

KM# 2 3 KREUZER (Groschen)

Silver Weight varies: 0.70-1.59g., 17-18.5 mm. **Obv:** City eagle arms, '3' in circle on breast **Obv. Legend:** MO. NO. ROTWILENSIS. **Rev:** Latin cross divides date **Rev. Legend:** SALVE. CRVX. SANCTA. **Note:** Kipper; varieties exist. Nau 26.

Date	Mintage	VG	F	VF	XF	Unc
16ZZ	—	100	200	375	775	—

KM# 3 3 KREUZER (Groschen)

Silver Weight varies: 0.70-1.59g., 17-18.5 mm. **Obv:** City arms in circle, date at end of legend **Obv. Legend:** MONE. NO. ROTWILENSI **Rev:** Crowned imperial eagle, value '3' in circle on breast **Rev. Legend:** FERDINAND. II IM. S. AV. **Note:** Varieties of design and legend exist. Nau 27.

Date	Mintage	VG	F	VF	XF	Unc
16ZZ	—	150	300	550	1,100	—

KM# 4 3 KREUZER (Groschen)

Silver Weight varies: 0.70-1.59g., 17-18.5 mm. **Obv:** City arms in circle **Obv. Legend:** MONE. ROTWILENSIS. **Rev:** Crowned imperial eagle, value '3' in circle on breast **Rev. Legend:** FERDINA(N)D. II. I(M). S. AV. **Note:** Kipper. Nau 28.

Date	Mintage	VG	F	VF	XF	Unc
16ZZ	—	125	250	450	900	—

KM# 5 6 KREUZER

Silver Weight varies: 1.59-2.91g., 24 mm. **Obv:** City arms in circle **Obv. Legend:** MONETA. NOVA. ROTWILENSIS.6. **Rev:** Latin cross divides date in circle **Rev. Legend:** SALVE. CRVX. SANCTA. **Note:** Kipper; varieties exist. Nau 24-25.

Date	Mintage	VG	F	VF	XF	Unc
16ZZ	—	175	350	650	1,200	—

KM# 1 12 KREUZER (Dreibätzner)

Silver Weight varies: 2.30-3.37g., 26 mm. **Obv:** City eagle arms with '12' in circle on breast **Obv. Legend:** MONETA. NOVA. ROTWILENSIS **Rev:** Latin cross divides date in circle **Rev. Legend:** SALVE. CRVX. SANCTA. **Note:** Kipper; varieties exist. Nau 16, 19.

Date	Mintage	VG	F	VF	XF	Unc
16Z1	—	300	600	1,100	—	—
16ZZ	—	300	600	1,100	—	—

KM# 6 12 KREUZER (Dreibätzner)

Silver, 26 mm. **Obv:** City eagle arms, small shield with cross on breast, date at end of legend **Obv. Legend:** MONE. NO. ROTWILENSIS. **Rev:** Crowned imperial eagle, value '12' in circle on breast **Rev. Legend:** FERDINAND: II. IMPER. S. AVG. **Note:** Kipper; varieties exist; weight varies 2.09 - 3.19 grams.

Date	Mintage	VG	F	VF	XF	Unc
16ZZ	—	800	1,600	3,250	—	—

KM# 7 24 KREUZER (Sechsbätzner = Dicken)

Silver, 26-28 mm. **Obv:** City eagle arms in circle **Obv. Legend:** MONETA. NOVA. ROTWILENSIS. **Rev:** Latin cross divides date in circle **Rev. Legend:** SALVE. CRVX. SANCTA. **Note:** Kipper; varieties exist. Nau 17-18.

Date	Mintage	VG	F	VF	XF	Unc
16ZZ	—	450	900	1,800	3,600	—

KM# 8 THALER

29.9000 g., Silver, 30x30 mm. **Obv:** City eagle arms in circle **Obv. Legend:** MONETA. NOVA. ROTWILENSIS. **Rev:** Latin cross divides date in circle **Rev. Legend:** SALVE. CRVX. SANCTA. **Note:** Klippe; struck on square flan with same dies as KM#6.

Date	Mintage	VG	F	VF	XF	Unc
16ZZ Rare	—	—	—	—	—	—

KM# 9 THALER

Silver **Obv:** Displayed eagle in circle, date at end of legend **Obv. Legend:** MONETA: NOVA: ROTWILENSIS **Rev:** Crowned imperial eagle **Rev. Legend:** FERDINANDVS: II: ROM: IMP: SEMPE: AVG. **Note:** Dav. #5803.

Date	Mintage	VG	F	VF	XF	Unc
1623 IM Rare	—	—	—	—	—	—

Note: Fritz Rudolf Künker Münzenhandlung Auction 69, 10-01, nearly XF realized approximately $10,655

KM# 10 THALER
Silver **Obv:** Displayed eagle in circle, date at end of legend **Obv. Legend:** MONETA. NOVA. ROTVVILENSIS. **Rev:** Crowned imperial eagle within circle **Rev. Legend:** FERDINANDVS. II. ROM. IMP. SEMPER. AVGVSTVS. **Note:** Dav. #5804.

Date	Mintage	VG	F	VF	XF	Unc
1623 Rare	—	—	—	—	—	—

Note: Künker Auction 170, 6-10, XF realized approximately $14,235. Auktionshaus Meister & Sonntag Auction 5, 9-07, XF realized approximately $15,355; Fritz Rudolf Künker Münzenhandlung Auction 113, 6-06, VF-XF realized approximately $8,220

KM# 11 1-1/4 THALER
Silver **Obv:** Displayed eagle in circle, date at end of legend **Obv. Legend:** MONETA. NOVA. ROTWILENSIS. **Rev:** Crowned imperial eagle **Rev. Legend:** FERDINANDVS. II. ROM. IMP. SEMPE. AV. **Note:** Dav. #5803A. Klippe.

Date	Mintage	VG	F	VF	XF	Unc
1623 IM Rare	—	—	—	—	—	—

Note: Auktionshaus Meister & Sonntag Auction 5, 9-07, XF realized approximately $55,835

SALM

The earliest rulers of this county, with widely scattered territories in the border region of present-day Germany, France and Belgium, descended from the counts of Luxembourg in the second half of the 11th century. The patrimony was divided between two succeeding sons about 1130-35. Lower Salm was located in the Ardenne region of France and became extinct in 1416 with the death of Heinrich VI. It passed by marriage to the lord of Reifferscheidt who in turn established the line of Salm-Reifferscheidt in 1455. The other division of old Salm was Upper Salm and was located in the Vosges to the southwest of Strassburg. This line underwent several divisions, one of which died out and passed to Lorraine in 1503. Another branch subdivided and half passed to as on who left the area and established himself as progenitor of the Salm-Neuburg line in Austria. The remaining half of Salm went to the older son and was inherited through marriage upon his death in 1475 by a ruler styled Wild and Rhinegrave. This latter individual was well-established in lands which stretched along the Rhine between Trier and Mainz. Thus, the early modern lines of Salm and its subdivisions in Germany came into being. The old castle of Salm, seat of the earliest counts, is located southwest of Strassburg, but the dynastic name was transferred to the Rhineland counts, who became from that point on, the Wild- and Rhinegraves of Salm. Two main lines were founded in 1499.

ARMS

Salm - 2 fish (salmon) standing on tails
Rhinegraves - lion with double tail
Wildgraves - crowned lion
Kyrburg - 3 lions, 2 above 1

REFERENCE

J = Paul Joseph, **Die Medaillen und Münzen der Wild- und Rheingrafen Fürsten zu Salm**, Frankfurt am Main, 1914.

SALM-DHAUN

(Salm-Daun)

The seat of this branch was at Dhaun (Daun), about 37 miles (62 km) east of Trier, near Kirn an der Nahe. It was further divided in 1561 into three lines: Salm-Neuweiler, Salm-Dhaun and Salm-Grumbach. Salm-Dhaun has a final division in 1697 into Salm-Dhaun and Salm-Püttlingen. The last count died and Püttlingen passed by marriage to Lowenstein-Wertheim-Rochefort in 1750.

RULERS

Adolf Heinrich, 1561-1606
Wolfgang Friedrich, 1606-1638
under guardianship of his mother Juliane, 1606-1617
Johann Ludwig, 1638-1673
Johann Philipp, 1673-1693
Karl, 1693-1733

MINT OFFICIALS' INITIALS

Meddersheim Mint

Symbol	Date	Name
	ca. 1605	Andreas Wachsmuth
	ca. 1605	Georg Müller
	ca. 1612	Wilhelm Schreiner, warden
	ca. 1613	Henning Kissel
H	ca. 1615-18	Peter Hex
(a) =	ca. 1619-?	Christian Ulmen

COUNTSHIP

REGULAR COINAGE

KM# 17 PFENNIG
Silver **Ruler:** Wolfgang Friedrich **Obv:** DAVN above 2-fold arms **Mint:** Meddersheim **Note:** Uniface schüssel-type.

Date	Mintage	VG	F	VF	XF	Unc
ND(ca1607-12)	—	15.00	30.00	60.00	115	—

KM# 25 ALBUS (8 Heller)
Silver **Ruler:** Wolfgang Friedrich **Obv:** Crowned lion left **Obv. Legend:** CVRATEL . DAVN . COMITVM **Rev. Legend:** SILVESTRIS... **Rev. Inscription:** ALB / NOVVS / date / 8 **Mint:** Meddersheim **Note:** Varieties exist.

Date	Mintage	VG	F	VF	XF	Unc
1610	9,420	45.00	90.00	—	—	—

KM# 26 ALBUS (8 Heller)
Silver **Ruler:** Wolfgang Friedrich **Obv:** Crowned lion left **Obv. Legend:** CVRATEL . DAVN . COMITVM **Rev:** Date at end of inscription **Rev. Legend:** SILVESTRIS... **Rev. Inscription:** ALB / NOVVS **Mint:** Meddersheim **Note:** Varieties exist. Mintage numbers for 1610 included with KM#25 numbers.

Date	Mintage	VG	F	VF	XF	Unc
1610	—	35.00	75.00	150	300	—
1611	36,000	35.00	75.00	150	300	—

KM# 4 3 KREUZER (Groschen)
Silver **Ruler:** Adolf Heinrich **Obv:** 4-fold arms with central shield, date above, titles of Adolf Heinrich around **Rev:** Crowned imperial eagle, 3 in orb on breast, titles of Rudolf II around **Mint:** Meddersheim **Note:** Varieties exist.

Date	Mintage	VG	F	VF	XF	Unc
160Z	—	—	—	—	—	—

KM# 5 3 KREUZER (Groschen)
Silver **Ruler:** Adolf Heinrich **Obv:** 4-fold arms with central shield, date above, titles of Adolf Heinrich around **Rev:** Crowned imperial eagle, 3 in orb on breast, titles of Rudolf II around **Mint:** Meddersheim **Note:** Klippe.

Date	Mintage	VG	F	VF	XF	Unc
160Z	—	—	—	—	—	—

KM# 10 3 KREUZER (Groschen)
Silver **Ruler:** Adolf Heinrich **Obv:** 3 small shields of arms, 2 above 1, crown above, titles of Adolf Heinrich around **Rev:** Crowned imperial eagle, 3 in circle on breast, titles of Rudolf II around **Mint:** Meddersheim

Date	Mintage	VG	F	VF	XF	Unc
ND(ca1605)	—	25.00	50.00	90.00	180	—

KM# 9 3 KREUZER (Groschen)
Silver **Ruler:** Adolf Heinrich **Obv:** 4-fold arms with central shield, titles of Adolf Heinrich around **Rev:** Crowned imperial eagle, 3 in circle on breast, titles of Rudolf II around **Mint:** Meddersheim **Note:** Varieties exist.

Date	Mintage	VG	F	VF	XF	Unc
ND(ca1605)	—	25.00	50.00	90.00	180	—

KM# 11 3 KREUZER (Groschen)
Silver **Ruler:** Adolf Heinrich **Obv:** 3 small shields of arms, 2 above 1, titles of Adolf Heinrich around **Rev:** Crowned imperial eagle, 3 in circle on breast, titles of Rudolf II around **Mint:** Meddersheim **Note:** Varieties exist.

Date	Mintage	VG	F	VF	XF	Unc
ND(ca1605)	—	25.00	50.00	90.00	180	—

KM# 13 3 KREUZER (Groschen)
Silver **Ruler:** Adolf Heinrich **Obv:** 3 small shields of arms, 2 above 1, date above, titles of Adolf Heinrich around **Rev:** Crowned imperial eagle, 3 in circle on breast, titles of Rudolf II around **Mint:** Meddersheim **Note:** Varieties exist.

Date	Mintage	VG	F	VF	XF	Unc
1606	32,000	30.00	65.00	135	275	—

KM# 14 3 KREUZER (Groschen)
Silver **Ruler:** Wolfgang Friedrich **Obv:** 4-fold arms with central shield **Obv. Legend:** RHEIN GRAF. DAVN. CVRATEL (or variant) **Rev:** Crowned imperial eagle, 3 in circle on breast, titles of Rudolf II around **Mint:** Meddersheim **Note:** Varieties exist.

Date	Mintage	VG	F	VF	XF	Unc
ND(1606-12)	—	20.00	45.00	90.00	180	—

KM# 15 3 KREUZER (Groschen)
Silver **Ruler:** Wolfgang Friedrich **Obv:** 3 small shields of arms in trefoil arrangement **Obv. Legend:** RHEINGRAF... **Rev:** Crowned imperial eagle, 3 in circle on breast, titles of Rudolf II around **Mint:** Meddersheim

Date	Mintage	VG	F	VF	XF	Unc
ND(1606-12)	—	20.00	45.00	90.00	180	—

KM# 18 3 KREUZER (Groschen)
Silver **Ruler:** Wolfgang Friedrich **Obv:** 4-fold arms with central shield, date above arms **Obv. Legend:** RHEIN GRAF. DAVN. CVRATEL (or variant) **Rev:** Crowned imperial eagle, 3 in circle on breast, titles of Rudolf II around **Mint:** Meddersheim **Note:** Varieties exist.

Date	Mintage	VG	F	VF	XF	Unc
1607	—	30.00	65.00	135	275	—

KM# 19 3 KREUZER (Groschen)
Silver **Ruler:** Wolfgang Friedrich **Obv:** 3 small shields of arms, 2 above 1, date above, titles of Adolf Heinrich around **Obv. Legend:** REINGRAF DAVN CVRATEL. **Rev:** Crowned imperial eagle, 3 in circle on breast, titles of Rudolf II around **Mint:** Meddersheim **Note:** Varieties exist.

Date	Mintage	VG	F	VF	XF	Unc
(1)608	329,000	20.00	40.00	85.00	170	—

KM# 20 3 KREUZER (Groschen)
Silver **Ruler:** Wolfgang Friedrich **Obv:** 3 small shields of arms, 2 above 1, crown above, titles of Adolf Heinrich **Obv. Legend:** REINGRAF DAVN CVRATEL. **Rev:** Crowned imperial eagle, 3 in circle on breast, titles of Rudolf II around **Mint:** Meddersheim **Note:** Varieties exist.

Date	Mintage	VG	F	VF	XF	Unc
ND(ca1608)	91,000	20.00	45.00	90.00	180	—

KM# 24 3 KREUZER (Groschen)

Silver **Ruler:** Wolfgang Friedrich **Obv:** 3 small shields of arms, 2 above 1, crown above, titles of Adolf Heinrich around **Obv. Legend:** CVRATEL. DAVN. COMIT. **Rev:** Crowned imperial eagle, 3 in circle on breast, titles of Rudolf II around **Mint:** Meddersheim **Note:** Klippe.

Date	Mintage	VG	F	VF	XF	Unc
ND(ca1608)	—	—	—	—	—	—

KM# 22 3 KREUZER (Groschen)

Silver **Ruler:** Wolfgang Friedrich **Obv:** 3 small shields of arms, 2 above 1, crown above, titles of Adolf Heinrich around **Obv. Legend:** CVR: DAVN: COMITVM: RHE (or variant) **Rev:** Crowned imperial eagle, 3 in circle on breast, titles of Rudolf II around **Mint:** Meddersheim **Note:** Mintage numbers included with KM#20.

Date	Mintage	VG	F	VF	XF	Unc
ND(ca1608)	—	20.00	45.00	90.00	180	—

KM# 23 3 KREUZER (Groschen)

Silver **Ruler:** Wolfgang Friedrich **Obv:** 3 small shields of arms, 2 above 1, crown above, titles of Adolf Heinrich around **Obv. Legend:** CVRATEL. DAVN. COMIT. **Rev:** Crowned imperial eagle, 3 in circle on breast, titles of Rudolf II around **Mint:** Meddersheim **Note:** Mintage numbers included with KM#20.

Date	Mintage	VG	F	VF	XF	Unc
ND(ca1608)	—	20.00	45.00	90.00	180	—

KM# 21 3 KREUZER (Groschen)

Silver **Ruler:** Wolfgang Friedrich **Obv:** 3 small shields of arms, 2 above 1, titles of Adolf Heinrich around **Obv. Legend:** CVR: DAVN: COMITVM: RHE (or variant) **Rev:** Crowned imperial eagle, 3 in circle on breast, titles of Rudolf II around **Mint:** Meddersheim **Note:** Varieties exist. Mintage numbers included with KM#20.

Date	Mintage	VG	F	VF	XF	Unc
ND(ca1608)	—	20.00	45.00	90.00	180	—

KM# 28 3 KREUZER (Groschen)

Silver **Ruler:** Wolfgang Friedrich **Obv:** 3 small shields of arms, 2 above 1, crown above, titles of Adolf Heinrich around **Obv. Legend:** CVR: DAVN: COMITVM: RHE (or variant) **Rev:** Crowned imperial eagle, 3 in circle on breast, titles of Rudolf II around, date **Mint:** Meddersheim

Date	Mintage	VG	F	VF	XF	Unc
1611	6,213	35.00	75.00	150	300	—

KM# 29 3 KREUZER (Groschen)

Silver **Ruler:** Wolfgang Friedrich **Obv:** 3 small shields of arms, 2 above 1, titles of Adolf Heinrich around **Obv. Legend:** CVRATEL. DAVN. COMIT. **Rev:** Crowned imperial eagle, 3 in circle on breast, titles of Rudolf II around, date at end **Mint:** Meddersheim **Note:** Varieties exist. Mintage numbers for 1611 and 161Z included with KM#28. Known dated 1611 struck on double-thickness flan, 3.01 g.

Date	Mintage	VG	F	VF	XF	Unc
1611	—	35.00	70.00	135	270	—
(1)61Z	16,000	35.00	70.00	135	270	—
161Z	—	35.00	70.00	135	270	—

KM# 30 3 KREUZER (Groschen)

Silver **Ruler:** Wolfgang Friedrich **Obv:** 3 small shields of arms, 2 above 1, titles of Adolf Heinrich around **Obv. Legend:** CVRATEL. DAVN. COMIT. **Rev:** Crowned imperial eagle, 3 in circle on breast, titles of Matthias around **Mint:** Meddersheim **Note:** Varieties exist. Mintage numbers for 161Z included with KM#29.

Date	Mintage	VG	F	VF	XF	Unc
ND(1612-17)	—	35.00	70.00	135	270	—
161Z	—	35.00	70.00	135	270	—

KM# 33 3 KREUZER (Groschen)

Silver **Ruler:** Wolfgang Friedrich **Obv:** 3 small shields of arms, 2 above 1, titles of Adolf Heinrich around, date in margin **Obv. Legend:** CVRATEL. DAVN. COMIT. **Rev:** Crowned imperial eagle, 3 in circle on breast, titles of Matthias around **Mint:** Meddersheim **Note:** Varieties exist.

Date	Mintage	VG	F	VF	XF	Unc
(1)615	36,000	32.00	65.00	135	270	—
1616	—	32.00	65.00	135	270	—
1617	14,000	32.00	65.00	135	270	—
1617 H	Inc. above	32.00	65.00	135	270	—

KM# 37 3 KREUZER (Groschen)

Silver **Ruler:** Wolfgang Friedrich **Obv:** 4-fold arms with central shield **Obv. Legend:** MON. REINGR . DAVNENSI. **Rev:** Crowned imperial eagle, 3 in orb on breast, titles of Matthias around **Mint:** Meddersheim **Note:** Varieties exist.

Date	Mintage	VG	F	VF	XF	Unc
ND(1618)	65,000	40.00	80.00	150	300	—
ND(1619) (a)	52,000	40.00	80.00	150	300	—

KM# 39 3 KREUZER (Groschen)

Silver **Ruler:** Wolfgang Friedrich **Obv:** 4-fold arms with central shield **Rev:** Crowned imperial eagle, 3 in orb on breast, titles of Ferdinand II **Mint:** Meddersheim **Note:** Mintage numbers included with KM#37.

Date	Mintage	VG	F	VF	XF	Unc
ND(1619) (a)	—	40.00	80.00	150	300	—

KM# 27 12 KREUZER (Dreibatzner)

Silver **Ruler:** Wolfgang Friedrich **Obv:** Ornate 4-fold arms with central shield **Rev:** Crowned imperial eagle, 1Z in orb on breast, titles of Rudolf II and date around **Mint:** Meddersheim **Note:** Varieties exist.

Date	Mintage	VG	F	VF	XF	Unc
1610	25,000	—	—	—	—	—

KM# 34 12 KREUZER (Dreibatzner)

Silver **Ruler:** Wolfgang Friedrich **Obv:** 4-fold arms with central shield, date at end of legend **Obv. Legend:** CVRATEL . DAVNEN COMITVM **Rev:** Crowned imperial eagle, 1Z in orb on breast, titles of Matthias **Mint:** Meddersheim

Date	Mintage	VG	F	VF	XF	Unc
1617 H	4,471	—	—	—	—	—

KM# 12 DICKEN (Teston = 1/4 Thaler)

Silver **Ruler:** Adolf Heinrich **Obv:** 4-fold arms with central shield, 3 helmets above, titles of Adolf Heinrich around **Rev:** Holy lamb left with flag on staff **Rev. Legend:** ECCE AGNVS DEI... **Mint:** Meddersheim **Note:** Also known struck on thick flan at 1/2 Thaler weight, ca. 1 g.

Date	Mintage	VG	F	VF	XF	Unc
ND(ca1605)	—	—	—	—	—	—

KM# 32 DICKEN (Teston = 1/4 Thaler)

Silver **Ruler:** Wolfgang Friedrich **Obv:** 4-fold arms with central shield **Obv. Legend:** CVRATEL DAVNEN . COMITVM. **Rev:** Crowned imperial eagle, orb on breast, titles of Matthias around **Mint:** Meddersheim **Note:** Klippe.

Date	Mintage	VG	F	VF	XF	Unc
ND(ca1612-')	—	—	—	—	—	—

KM# 31 DICKEN (Teston = 1/4 Thaler)

Silver **Ruler:** Wolfgang Friedrich **Obv:** 4-fold arms with central shield **Obv. Legend:** CVRATEL DAVNEN . COMITVM. **Rev:** Crowned imperial eagle, orb on breast, titles of Matthias around **Mint:** Meddersheim

Date	Mintage	VG	F	VF	XF	Unc
ND(ca1611 7)	—	—	—	—	—	—

KM# DICKEN (Teston = 1/4 Thaler)

Silver **Ruler:** Wolfgang Friedrich **Obv:** 4-fold arms with central shield, date at end of legend **Obv. Legend:** CVRATEL DAVNEN . COMITVM. **Rev:** Crowned imperial eagle, orb on breast, titles of Matthias around **Mint:** Meddersheim **Note:** Varieties exist.

Date	Mintage	VG	F	VF	XF	Unc
1617	1,156	125	250	500	1,000	2,000
1617	Inc. above	125	250	500	1,000	2,000
(1)61	Inc. above	175	350	650	1,200	2,400

K 38 DICKEN (Teston = 1/4 Thaler)

S **Ruler:** Wolfgang Friedrich **Obv:** 4-fold arms with central s d, date at end of legend **Obv. Legend:** MON . RHEINGR . NENSIVM **Rev:** Crowned imperial eagle, orb on breast, titles atthias around **Mint:** Meddersheim **Note:** Varieties exist.

[	Mintage	VG	F	VF	XF	Unc
18	Inc. above	175	250	450	950	1,900
3	1,305	175	250	450	950	1,900
9	26,000	175	350	650	1,000	2,000
9 (a)	Inc. above	175	350	650	1,000	2,000

1# 41 DICKEN (Teston = 1/4 Thaler)

ver **Ruler:** Wolfgang Friedrich **Obv:** 4-fold arms with central eld, date at end of legend **Obv. Legend:** MON . RHEINGR . VNENSIVM **Rev:** Crowned imperial eagle, orb on breast, titles Ferdinand II around **Mint:** Meddersheim **Note:** Varieties exist.

te	Mintage	VG	F	VF	XF	Unc
620 (a)	—	175	350	650	1,200	—
20 (a)	—	175	350	650	1,200	—

KM# 42 DICKEN (Teston = 1/4 Thaler)

Silver **Ruler:** Wolfgang Friedrich **Obv:** 4-fold arms with central shield, arms divide date **Obv. Legend:** MON . RHEINGR . DAVNENSIVM **Rev:** Crowned imperial eagle, orb on breast, titles of Ferdinand II around **Mint:** Meddersheim

Date	Mintage	VG	F	VF	XF	Unc
1620 (a)	—	175	350	650	1,200	—

KM# 43 DICKEN (Teston = 1/4 Thaler)

Silver **Ruler:** Wolfgang Friedrich **Obv:** 4-fold arms with central shield, date above arms **Rev:** Crowned imperial eagle, orb on breast, titles of Ferdinand II around **Mint:** Meddersheim

Date	Mintage	VG	F	VF	XF	Unc
1620 (a)	—	175	350	650	1,200	—

KM# 1 THALER

Silver **Obv:** Crowned imperial eagle, orb on breast, date **Obv. Legend:** RVDOLP * II * IMP * AVG * P * **Rev:** Helmeted arms **Rev. Legend:** AD. HE. CO:SI.-E. **Mint:** Meddersheim **Note:** Dav. #7330.

Date	Mintage	VG	F	VF	XF	Unc
1601 Rare	—	—	—	—	—	—

KM# 2 2 THALER

Silver **Obv:** Crowned imperial eagle, orb on breast, date **Obv. Legend:** RVDOLP * II * IMP AVG * P * **Rev:** Helmeted arms **Rev. Legend:** AD. HE. CO:SI.-E. **Note:** Dav. #7329.

Date	Mintage	VG	F	VF	XF	Unc
1601 Rare	—	—	—	—	—	—

KM# 3 2 THALER

Silver **Obv. Legend:** RVDOLF. II. ROM... **Rev. Legend:** AD. HEIN. SYLVES. RHENIQ... **Note:** Dav. #7331.

Date	Mintage	VG	F	VF	XF	Unc
1601 Rare	—	—	—	—	—	—

KM# 6 2 THALER

Silver **Obv. Legend:** * RVDOLP * II * ROM *... **Rev. Legend:** AD: HEIN: SYL-VES: RHENIQ... **Note:** Dav. #7332.

Date	Mintage	VG	F	VF	XF	Unc
1602 Rare	—	—	—	—	—	—

KM# 7 2 THALER

Silver **Obv. Legend:** RVDOLF... **Note:** Dav. #7332A.

Date	Mintage	VG	F	VF	XF	Unc
1602 Rare	—	—	—	—	—	—

KM# 8 2 THALER

Silver **Obv:** Legend, date **Obv. Legend:** RVDOLP * II * IMP * AVG * P * F * DECRE **Rev:** Helmeted oval arms **Note:** Dav. #7333.

Date	Mintage	VG	F	VF	XF	Unc
1604 Rare	2,567	—	—	—	—	—

KM# 16 2 THALER

Silver **Obv. Legend:** RVDOLF: ROM: IMP: AVGVSTVS... **Rev:** Helmeted arms **Rev. Legend:** REINGRAFSCHA-FT... **Note:** Dav. #7334.

Date	Mintage	VG	F	VF	XF	Unc
ND(1606-12) Rare	—	—	—	—	—	—

TRADE COINAGE

KM# 36 GOLDGULDEN

3.5000 g., 0.9860 Gold 0.1109 oz. AGW **Obv:** Crowned imperial eagle in inner circle, titles of Matthias **Rev:** Arms in inner circle **Note:** Fr. #2602.

Date	Mintage	VG	F	VF	XF	Unc
(1)617 Rare	360	—	—	—	—	—

KM# 40 GOLDGULDEN

3.5000 g., 0.9860 Gold 0.1109 oz. AGW **Note:** Fr. #2603.

Date	Mintage	VG	F	VF	XF	Unc
1619 Rare	—	—	—	—	—	—

SALM-GRUMBACH

Located just to the west of Lauterecken on the River Glan and 11 miles (19 kilometers) south of Dhaun, Grumbach was one result of the 1561 division of Salm-Dhaun. A branch line was founded in 1668 at Rheingrafenstein (Grehweiler), but it became extinct in the early 19th century. Descendants of the Salm-Grumbach line continued well into the 20th century, although the lands were mediatized in 1806.

RULERS

Johann, 1585-1630
Adolf, 1585-1626
Adolf (alone), 1630-1648
Leopold Philipp Wilhelm, 1648-1719
Friedrich Wilhelm von Rheingrafenstein, 1648-1688 (1706)

MINT OFFICIALS' INITIALS

Alzenz Mint

Symbol	Date	Name
(a) =	ca. 1607-1609	Anthoni Eisenbein
or	ca. 1609-?	Georg Gustav Preuel von Lautereck
	ca. 1609-?	Georg Wolkenhauer von Stockau bei Hannover, warden

COUNTSHIP

STANDARD COINAGE

KM# 5 PFENNIG

Silver **Ruler:** Johann **Obv:** IR above 2-fold arms **Mint:** Alzenz **Note:** Uniface schüssel-type. Varieties exist.

Date	Mintage	VG	F	VF	XF	Unc
ND(1626-30)	—	20.00	45.00	90.00	180	—

KM# 4 ALBUS

Silver **Ruler:** Johann and Adolf **Obv:** 3 shields of arms, 2 above 1, titles of Johann and Adolf around **Rev:** Standing figure of St. Laurentius divides date **Rev. Legend:** S: LAVRE - NTIVS. I . ALB. **Mint:** Alzenz

Date	Mintage	VG	F	VF	XF	Unc
(1)609	—	—	—	—	—	—

KM# 1 3 KREUZER (Groschen)

Silver **Ruler:** Johann and Adolf **Obv:** 4-fold arms with central shield, date above, titles of Johann and Adolf around **Rev:** Crowned imperial eagle, 3 in circle on breast, titles of Rudolf II around **Mint:** Alzenz

Date	Mintage	VG	F	VF	XF	Unc
1607 (a)	—	—	—	—	—	—

KM# 2 3 KREUZER (Groschen)

Silver **Ruler:** Johann and Adolf **Obv:** Crown above 3 shields of arms, 2 above 1, titles of Johann and Adolf around **Rev:** Crowned imperial eagle, 3 in circle on breast, titles of Rudolf II around **Mint:** Alzenz **Note:** Varieties exist.

Date	Mintage	VG	F	VF	XF	Unc
ND(ca1607-09)	—	25.00	55.00	110	225	—

KM# 3 3 KREUZER (Groschen)

Silver **Ruler:** Johann and Adolf **Obv:** 4-fold arms with central shield, titles of Johann and Adolf around **Rev:** Crowned imperial eagle, 3 in circle on breast, titles of Rudolf II around **Mint:** Alzenz **Note:** Varieties exist.

Date	Mintage	VG	F	VF	XF	Unc
ND(ca1607-09) (a)	—	25.00	50.00	100	210	—
ND(ca1609-12)	—	25.00	50.00	100	210	—

SALM-KYRBURG

Founded in 1499, this branch took its name from Kyrburg Castle, the ruins of which are located three miles (5 km) west-southwest of Dhaun. A further subdivision was made in 1607, resulting in the lines of Salm-Kyrburg,Salm-Mörchingen and Salm-Tronecken, the latter lasting only one generation. The main line became extinct in 1681 and fell to Salm-Mörchingen, which in turn ended in the male line in 1688. All Salm-Kyrburg lands and titles then reverted to Salm-Salm. After several subdivisions of that senior branch, a new line of Salm-Kyrburg was established from Salm-Neuweiler-Lenze in 1738. The count was raised to the rank of Prince of the Empire in 1742. All territories of the family were mediatized in 1806, but the Salm-Kyrburg line has survived down to modern times.

RULERS

Otto I, 1548-1607
Johann Kasimer, 1607-1651
with Johann IX von Salm-Mörchingen, 1607-1623
and Otto II von Salm-Tronecken, 1607-1637
then Johann Philipp von Salm-Mörchingen,
1623-1638 and Otto Ludwig von Salm-Mörchingen, 1623-1634
George Friedrich, 1651-1681

COUNTSHIP

REGULAR COINAGE

KM# 3 3 KREUZER (Groschen)

Silver **Ruler:** Otto I **Obv:** 4-fold arms with central shield, date above, titles of Otto I around **Rev:** Crowned imperial eagle, 3 in circle on breast, titles of Rudolf II around **Note:** Klippe.

Date	Mintage	VG	F	VF	XF	Unc
160Z	—	40.00	90.00	180	—	—

KM# 2 3 KREUZER (Groschen)

Silver **Ruler:** Otto I **Obv:** 4-fold arms with central shield, date above, titles of Otto I around **Rev:** Crowned imperial eagle, 3 in circle on breast, titles of Rudolf II around **Note:** Varieties exist.

Date	Mintage	VG	F	VF	XF	Unc
160Z (c/b)	—	45.00	90.00	180	—	—
1603 (c/b)	—	45.00	90.00	180	—	—
ND (c/b)	—	45.00	90.00	180	—	—
ND (c)	—	45.00	90.00	180	—	—
ND	—	45.00	90.00	180	—	—

KM# 6 3 KREUZER (Groschen)

Silver **Ruler:** Otto I **Obv:** 3 small shields of arms, 2 above 1, date above all 3, titles of Otto I around **Rev:** Crowned imperial eagle, 3 in circle on breast, titles of Rudolf II around **Note:** Varieties exist.

Date	Mintage	VG	F	VF	XF	Unc
1606 (c)	—	—	—	—	—	—
ND (c)	—	—	—	—	—	—

KM# 7 3 KREUZER (Groschen)

Silver **Ruler:** Otto I **Obv:** 3 small shields in trefdl arrangement with bottom of each to center, date above all 3, ttles of Otto I around **Rev:** Crowned imperial eagle, 3 in circle n breast, titles of Rudolf II around

Date	Mintage	VG	F	VF	XF	Unc
ND(ca1606) (c)	—	—	—	—	—	—

KM# 5 THALER

Silver **Ruler:** Otto I **Obv:** Helmeted armsCrownedmperial eagle with orb on breast, date divided below **Obv. Legend:** OT-TO. CO: SILV.-E:... **Rev:** Crowned imperial eagle with rb on breast, date divided below **Rev. Legend:** RVDOL. II. ROM. **Note:** Dav. #7328.

Date	Mintage	VG	F	VF	XF	Unc
1604 (c) Rare	—	—	—	—	—	—

KM# 4 2 THALER

Silver **Ruler:** Otto I **Obv:** Helmeted armsCrowned imerial eagle with orb on breast, date divided below **Obv. Legen** OT-TO. CO: SILV-E... **Rev:** Crowned imperial eagle with orbn breast, date divided below **Rev. Legend:** RVDOL. II. ROM...T-TO. CO: SILV-E... **Note:** Dav. #7327.

Date	Mintage	VG	F	VF	XF	Unc
1602 (c) Rare	—	—	—	—	—	—
1604 (c) Rare	—	—	—	—	—	—

JOINT COINAGE

KM# 10 2 KREUZER (1/2 Batzen = Halbbazen)

Silver **Ruler:** Johann Kasimir, Otto II, Johann Philippnd Otto Ludwig **Obv:** Double-tailed lion arms (Rhinegraves) **v. Legend:** MO . NO . SIL ET RH CO IN KV. **Rev:** Titles of rdinand II **Rev. Inscription:** II / KREUTZ / ER

Date	Mintage	VG	F	VF	XF	Unc
ND(ca1623-30)	—	—	—	—	—	—

KM# 13 2 KREUZER (1/2 Batzen = Halbbatz)

Silver **Ruler:** Johann Kasimir, Otto II, Johann Philipp anOtto Ludwig **Obv:** Double-tailed lion arms (Rhinegraves), date ove arms **Obv. Legend:** MO . NO . SIL ET RH CO IN KV. **Rev:** les of Ferdinand II **Rev. Inscription:** II / KREVTZ / ER **Mint:** Diemeringen **Note:** Varieties exist.

Date	Mintage	VG	F	VF	XF	Unc
1631 (e)	—	40.00	80.00	160	325	—
163Z (e)	—	40.00	80.00	160	325	—
1633	—	40.00	80.00	160	325	—
1633 (e)	—	40.00	80.00	160	325	—
1634 (e)	—	40.00	80.00	160	325	—

KM# 8 3 KREUZER (Groschen)

Silver, 20.3 mm. **Ruler:** Johann Kasimir, Johann IX and Otto **Obv:** 4-fold arms with central shield, titles of 3 brothers aroun **Rev:** Crowned imperial eagle, 3 in circle on breast, titles of Rudc II around **Note:** Varieties exist.

Date	Mintage	VG	F	VF	XF	Unc
ND(ca1607-09) (c)	—	45.00	90.00	180	—	—

KM# 12 12 KREUZER (Dreibatzner)

Silver **Ruler:** Johann Kasimir, Otto II, Johann Philipp and Otto Ludwig **Obv:** 4-fold arms with central shield, date above **Rev:** Crowned imperial eagle, orb on breast, (XII) in margin at top, titles of Ferdinand II around

Date	Mintage	VG	F	VF	XF	Unc
16Z9 (d)	—	650	1,250	2,250	4,500	—

TRADE COINAGE

KM# 11 GOLDGULDEN

3.5000 g., 0.9860 Gold 0.1109 oz. AGW **Ruler:** Johann Kasimer **Obv:** Lion with shield of arms in inner circle **Rev:** Crowned imperial eagle in inner circle **Note:** Fr. #2605.

Date	Mintage	VG	F	VF	XF	Unc
ND(1623-30) (d) Rare	—	—	—	—	—	—

SALM-SALM

This branch resulted from a division of Salm-Neuweiler in 1608. The count was given the rank of Prince of the Empire in 1623. His grandson inherited the defunct Salm-Kyrburg lands and titles in 1688, but the main line became extinct as well in 1738. The lands and titles then reverted to Salm-Neuweiler. The latter took on the name as the new Salm-Salm line, sold Neuweiler to France in 1751 and continued past mediatization in 1806 and down to the present day.

RULERS

Philipp Otto, 1608-1634, Prince 1623
Leopold Philipp, 1634-1663
Karl Theodor Otto, 1663-1710

MINT OFFICIALS

Initials	Date	Name
	1639-ca. 1664	Simon Rhode, mintmaster in Badenweiler
	ca. 1640-60	Segerus Wendel, mintmaster in Anholt

PRINCIPALITY

REGULAR COINAGE

KM# 5 STUBER

Silver **Ruler:** Leopold Philipp **Obv:** Crowned 4-fold arms divide I - S, titles of Leopold Philipp around **Rev:** Ornate cross forming diamond in center **Rev. Legend:** MON - NOV - ANH - CVS. **Mint:** Anholt

Date	Mintage	VG	F	VF	XF	Unc
ND(1634-63)	—	100	200	350	650	—

KM# 6 STUBER

Silver **Ruler:** Leopold Philipp **Obv:** Crowned 4-fold arms divide I - S, titles of Leopold Philipp around **Rev:** Ornate cross forming diamond in center **Rev. Legend:** MON - ARG - ANH - CVS. **Mint:** Anholt **Note:** Varieties exist.

Date	Mintage	VG	F	VF	XF	Unc
ND(1634-63)	—	100	200	350	650	—

KM# 1 2 KREUZER (1/2 Batzen)

Silver **Ruler:** Philipp Otto **Obv:** II • K above 4-fold arms, titles of Philipp Otto around **Rev:** Crowned imperial eagle, orb on breast, titles of Ferdinand II around

Date	Mintage	VG	F	VF	XF	Unc
ND(1623-34)	—	—	—	—	—	—

KM# 8 GROSCHEN (3 Kreuzer)

Silver **Ruler:** Leopold Philipp **Obv:** Eagle, titles of Leopold Philipp around **Rev:** Crowned arms of Salm **Rev. Legend:** MONETA . NOVA . BA . CVSA. **Mint:** Badenweiler **Note:** Varieties exist.

Date	Mintage	VG	F	VF	XF	Unc
ND(ca1639-42)	—	—	—	—	—	—

KM# 10 2 GROSCHEN (Doppelgroschen)

Silver **Ruler:** Leopold Philipp **Obv:** Crowned imperial eagle, titles of Leopold Philipp around **Rev:** Crowned 4-fold arms with central shield, date at top **Rev. Legend:** MONETA . NOV . BAD . CVSA.

Date	Mintage	VG	F	VF	XF	Unc
1641	—	—	—	—	—	—

KM# 2 12 KREUZER (Dreibätzner)

Silver **Ruler:** Philipp Otto **Obv:** Crowned 4-fold arms with central shield, titles of Philipp Otto around **Rev:** Crowned imperial eagle, 12 in orb on breast **Rev. Legend:** SVB: VMB: ALA: TVA: PROT: NO.

Date	Mintage	VG	F	VF	XF	Unc
ND(ca1623-34)	—	—	—	—	—	—

KM# 3 12 KREUZER (Dreibätzner)

Silver **Ruler:** Philipp Otto **Obv:** Crowned 4-fold arms with central shield, titles of Philipp Otto around **Rev:** Crowned imperial eagle, 2 in orb on breast **Rev. Legend:** SVB: VMB: ALA: TVA: PROT: O. **Note:** Klippe.

Date	Mintage	VG	F	VF	XF	Unc
(ca1623-34)	—	—	—	—	—	—

KM# 7 SCHILLING (6 Stüber)

Silver **Ruler:** Leopold Philipp **Obv:** Crowned 8-fold arms superimposed on Burgundian cross, titles of Leopold Philipp around **Rev:** Lion rampart left holding oval shield **Rev. Legend:** MO . NO . AN . AD . LEGEM IMPERIAL ... **Mint:** Anholt

Date	Mintage	VG	F	VF	XF	Unc
ND(1634-63)	—	—	—	—	—	—

KM# 4 DICKEN (Teston; 1/3 Thaler)

Silver **Ruler:** Philipp Otto **Obv:** Bust right, titles of Philipp Otto around **Rev:** Crowned imperial eagle, orb on breast, titles of Ferdinand II around

Date	Mintage	VG	F	VF	XF	Unc
ND(ca1623-34)	—	—	—	—	—	—

KM# 9 DICKEN (Teston; 1/3 Thaler)

Silver **Ruler:** Leopold Philipp **Obv:** Young bust left, titles of Leopold PHilipp around **Rev:** Crowned 4-fold arms with central shield, date divided at top by points of crown **Rev. Legend:** MONETA . NOVA . BAD . CVSA. **Mint:** Badenweiler

Date	Mintage	VG	F	VF	XF	Unc
1639	—	—	—	—	—	—

KM# 11 DICKEN (Teston; 1/3 Thaler)

Silver **Ruler:** Leopold Philipp **Obv:** Older bust right, titles of Leopold Philipp around **Rev:** Crowned 4-fold arms with central shield, date divided at top by points of crown **Rev. Legend:** MONETA . NOVA . BAD . CVSA. **Mint:** Badenweiler **Note:** Varieties exist.

Date	Mintage	VG	F	VF	XF	Unc
1641	—	750	1,500	2,700	5,500	—
1642	—	—	—	—	—	—

TRADE COINAGE

KM# 12 2 DUCAT

6.6100 g., Gold **Ruler:** Leopold Philipp **Obv:** Older bust right, titles of Leopold Philipp around **Rev:** Crowned 4-fold arms with central shield, date divided at top by points of crown **Rev. Legend:** MONETA . NOVA . BAD . CVSA. **Note:** Struck using same dies as Dicken, KM#11.

Date	Mintage	VG	F	VF	XF	Unc
1642 Rare	—	—	—	—	—	—

SANKT BLASIEN

The Benedictine abbey of Sankt Blasien, located in the Black Forest, 18 miles (30 kilometers) southeast of Freiburg im Breisgau, was founded in the 9th century. It is not to be confused with the monastery of St. Blasien in Northeim, which issued coins in the 12-13th centuries. In 1694, Abbot Roman had several coins struck to pay the workers of the iron furnace at Guttenberg. These are the only issues known of the place.

RULERS

Roman, 1672-1695

ABBEY

STANDARD COINAGE

KM# 1 KREUZER

Copper, 20 mm. **Ruler:** Roman **Obv:** 4-line inscription **Obv. Inscription:** BERG / WERKS. ZV / GVTEN / BVRG **Rev:** 3-line inscription with date **Rev. Inscription:** I / CREVZER / (date) **Mint:** Sankt Blasien

Date	Mintage	VG	F	VF	XF	Unc
1694	—	1,000	2,000	3,500	—	—

KM# 2 3 KREUZER

1.5400 g., Copper **Ruler:** Roman **Obv:** 4-line inscription **Obv. Inscription:** BERG / WERKS. ZV / GVTEN / BVRG **Rev:** 3-line inscription with date **Rev. Inscription:** III / CREVZER / (date) **Mint:** Sankt Blasien

Date	Mintage	VG	F	VF	XF	Unc
1694	—	100	200	450	875	—

KM# 3 15 KREUZER (1/4 Gulden)

4.2200 g., Copper **Ruler:** Roman **Obv:** Flaming iron furnace in circle **Obv. Legend:** EX. DVRO. LIQVIDVM. REDDITVR. QVIS. RE. **Rev:** 3-line inscription with date **Rev. Legend:** BVRGWERKS. ZV. GVTENBVRG. **Rev. Inscription:** XV / CREVZER / (date) **Mint:** Sankt Blasien

Date	Mintage	VG	F	VF	XF	Unc
1694	—	100	210	475	950	—

KM# 4 GULDEN (60 Kreuzer)

11.4100 g., Copper, 33 mm. **Ruler:** Roman **Obv:** Flaming iron furnace in circle **Obv. Legend:** DVROS. INFERRVM. LAPIDES. CONVERTO. LIQVESCES. **Rev:** 3-line inscription with date **Rev. Legend:** BVRGWERKS. ZV. GVTENBVRG. **Rev. Inscription:** 1 / GVLDEN / (date) **Mint:** Sankt Blasien **Note:** Prev. KM#6.

Date	Mintage	VG	F	VF	XF	Unc
1694	—	250	650	1,350	2,250	—

SAXONY

(Sachsen)

From about the time of Charlemagne, the term Saxony covered most of what is the northwestern part of modern day Germany. It roughly covered the area between the River Ems, the North Sea, the Eider and Elbe Rivers, extending to the southern slopes of the Harz Mountains, bordering Franconia, but not as far as the Rhine. The early Saxon tribes were pagans who, upon conquest by the Franks, became the nucleus of a buffer state between that empire and the heathen Slav peoples to the east.

The first Margrave of Saxony was Ludolf, named in 850 to defend the frontier, and recognized as founder of the Liudolfinger dynasty. His grandson acquired Thuringia (Thüringen) in 908 and was raised to the rank of duke in 911. The dynasty furnished the Saxon line of German kings and emperors beginning with Heinrich I the Fowler in 919 and up to Heinrich II, who died in 1024. A relative of the dynasty was delegated to rule Saxony and founded the Billung dynasty of dukes in 961. In 1260, Saxony was divided into Saxe-Lauenburg (Northern or Lower Saxony, which see) and Saxe-Wittenberg, also known as Upper Saxony, the southern part of the territory ruled by the Billungers.

INDEX

SAXE-LAUENBURG

(Sachsen-Lauenburg)

One of older branches of the Saxon house, founded in 1260 by Johann I, the line became extinct in 1689 with the death of Julius Franz.. Lauenburg passed to Brunswick-Luneburg, then to Hannover, then Prussia, Denmark and finally, back to Prussia in 1864.

RULERS

Magnus II, 1581-1603
Moritz, 1581-1612
Franz II, 1581-1619
August II, 1619-1656
Julius Heinrich, 1656-1665
Franz Erdmann, 1665-1666
Julius Franz, 1666-1689

MINT OFFICIALS' INITIALS and MARKS

Initial or Mark	Date	Name
IG (monogram)	1609-19	Jonas Georgens
(a)	Clenchedfist holdingingot hook	Christoph Feustel
(b)	1620-24	Barthold Bartels
(c)	1645-46	Simon Timpe
IS	1656	Johann Schultze
(d)	1657-62	Matthias Freude
(e) or HI	1670-71	Henning Jiders
IW	1672-73	Johann Wagner, mintmaster in Ratzeburg
(f)	1673	Georg Nürnberger der Jüngere
(g) = 3 small stars, usually in triangle pattern	1678-89	Lorenz Wagner, mintmaster in Elbschifferstadt

REFERENCE

D = Bruno Dorfmann, **Die Münzen und Medaillen der Herzöge von Sachsen-Lauenburg**, Ratzeburg, 1940.

DUCHY

REGULAR COINAGE

KM# 64 2 PFENNIG

Copper **Ruler:** August II **Obv:** Oval Saxon arms, legend around **Obv. Legend:** DVRA. PATI. VIRT. **Rev. Inscription:** II / PEN / NING / (date) **Note:** Kipper 2 Pfennig.

Date	Mintage	Good	VG	F	VF	XF
16Z1	—	18.00	40.00	65.00	130	—

KM# 54 DREILING (3 Pfennig)

Silver **Ruler:** August II **Obv:** Oval Saxon arms, helmet above divides date **Rev:** Imperial orb with 3 in baroque frame **Mint:** Otterndorf

Date	Mintage	VG	F	VF	XF	Unc
16Z0	—	25.00	50.00	100	—	—

KM# 55 DREILING (3 Pfennig)

Silver **Ruler:** August II **Obv:** A: H: above 4-fold arms which divide Z - S. **Rev:** Imperial orb with 3 in baroque frame **Mint:** Otterndorf

Date	Mintage	VG	F	VF	XF	Unc
ND(ca.1620)	—	25.00	50.00	100	—	—

KM# 65 3 PFENNIG

Copper **Ruler:** August II **Obv:** 4-fold arms, titles of August II around **Rev:** Value, date **Rev. Inscription:** III / PFEN / NING / **Mint:** Lauenburg **Note:** Kipper 3 Pfennig. Varieties exist.

Date	Mintage	Good	VG	F	VF	XF
16Z1 (b)	—	18.00	40.00	65.00	130	—

KM# 57 SECHSLING (6 Pfennig; 1/2 Schilling)

Silver **Ruler:** August II **Obv:** Oval Saxon arms, titles of August II around **Rev:** Cross in circle, value 6 - 4 in 2 upper angles, date in margin **Mint:** Otterndorf

Date	Mintage	VG	F	VF	XF	Unc
(1)6Z0	—	125	250	450	900	—

KM# 80 6 PFENNIG

Copper **Ruler:** August II **Obv:** 3 helmets above 4-fold arms, titles of August II around **Rev:** Value, date **Rev. Inscription:** IIIIII / PFENN / ING: / **Mint:** Lauenburg **Note:** Kipper 6 Pfennig.

Date	Mintage	Good	VG	F	VF	XF
(1)6ZZ (b)	—	22.00	50.00	90.00	180	—

KM# 125 SECHSLING (1/96 Thaler)

Silver **Ruler:** Julius Franz **Obv:** Crowned eagle in circle, titles of Julius Franz around **Rev:** Value 96 between 2 branches, date at end of legend **Rev. Legend:** LANDT. MVNTZ ... **Mint:** Elbschifferstadt

Date	Mintage	VG	F	VF	XF	Unc
1679 (g)	—	65.00	135	275	550	—

KM# 15 SCHILLING (1/32 Thaler)

Silver **Ruler:** Franz II **Obv:** Crowned helmet above Saxon arms, value (32) below, titles of Franz II around **Rev:** 4-fold arms, date above **Mint:** Lauenburg

Date	Mintage	VG	F	VF	XF	Unc
1610 IG	—	—	—	—	—	—

KM# 113 SCHILLING (1/48 Thaler)

Silver **Ruler:** Julius Franz **Obv:** Crowned eagle, arms of Saxony on breast, titles of Julius Franz around **Rev:** Inscription with value, date and mintmaster's initials, legend around **Rev. Legend:** LANDT. MVNTZ **Rev. Inscription:** 48 / REICHS / DALER / ... **Mint:** Ratzeburg

Date	Mintage	VG	F	VF	XF	Unc
1672 IW	—	60.00	120	225	450	—

KM# 119 SCHILLING (1/48 Thaler)

Silver **Ruler:** Julius Franz **Obv:** Crowned eagle in circle, titles of Julius Franz around **Rev:** Inscription with value 48 between 2 branches, legend around with date **Rev. Legend:** MONET • NOVA • ARGENT • **Mint:** Elbschifferstadt

Date	Mintage	VG	F	VF	XF	Unc
1678 (g)	—	60.00	120	240	—	—
1679 (g)	—	60.00	120	240	—	—

KM# 66 2 SCHILLING

Silver **Ruler:** August II **Obv:** Oval Saxon arms, Z / S-L above, titles of August II around **Rev:** Date, inscription **Rev. Inscription:** ... / RICKES / DALER / SVLVER **Mint:** Lauenburg

Date	Mintage	VG	F	VF	XF	Unc
1621 (b)	—	—	—	—	—	—

KM# 67 2 SCHILLING

Silver **Ruler:** August II **Obv:** Oval Saxon arms, Z / S-L above, titles of August II around **Rev:** Inscription, date at end **Rev. Inscription:** RICKES / DALER / SVLVER / ... **Mint:** Lauenburg

Date	Mintage	VG	F	VF	XF	Unc
1621 (b)	—	—	—	—	—	—

KM# 42 SCHRECKENBERGER
(3 Zinsgroschen = 4 Groschen)

Silver **Ruler:** Franz II **Obv:** Angel above 4-fold arms, titles of Franz II around **Rev:** Crowned imperial eagle, 4 in orb on breast, titles of Matthias around **Mint:** Lauenburg

Date	Mintage	VG	F	VF	XF	Unc
ND(1615-17) IG	—	65.00	135	275	550	—

KM# 45 SCHRECKENBERGER
(3 Zinsgroschen = 4 Groschen)

Silver **Ruler:** Franz II **Obv:** Bust right, titles of Franz II around **Rev:** Crowned imperial eagle, value 4... in orb on breast, titles of Matthias around

Date	Mintage	VG	F	VF	XF	Unc
ND(1615-17)	—	65.00	135	275	550	—

KM# 43 SCHRECKENBERGER
(3 Zinsgroschen = 4 Groschen)

Silver **Ruler:** Franz II **Obv:** 4-fold arms in ornamented shield, titles of Franz II around **Rev:** Crowned imperial eagle, 4... in orb on breast, titles of Matthias around **Mint:** Lauenburg **Note:** Varieties exist.

Date	Mintage	VG	F	VF	XF	Unc
ND(1615-17) IG	—	65.00	135	275	550	—

KM# 44 SCHRECKENBERGER
(3 Zinsgroschen = 4 Groschen)

Silver **Ruler:** Franz II **Obv:** 4-fold shield of arms without ornaments, titles of Franz II around **Rev:** Crowned imperial eagle, value 4 ... in orb on breast, titles of Matthias around **Mint:** Lauenburg **Note:** Varieties exist.

Date	Mintage	VG	F	VF	XF	Unc
ND(1615-17)	—	65.00	135	275	550	—
ND(1615-17) IG	—	65.00	135	275	550	—

KM# 58 SCHRECKENBERGER
(4 Groschen = 12 Kreuzer)

Silver **Ruler:** August II **Obv:** Helmeted oval eagle arms **Obv. Legend:** DVRA • PATI • VIRTVS **Rev:** Crowned imperial eagle, value 4G on breast, titles of Ferdinand II and date around **Note:** Varieties exist.

Date	Mintage	VG	F	VF	XF	Unc
1620	—	65.00	125	250	500	—
(1)621	—	65.00	125	250	500	—

KM# 68 SCHRECKENBERGER
(4 Groschen = 12 Kreuzer)

Silver **Ruler:** August II **Obv:** Helmeted oval eagle arms, titles of August II around **Rev:** Crowned imperial eagle, value 4G on breast, titles of Ferdinand II and date around **Mint:** Lauenburg **Note:** Kipper Schreckenberger. Varieties exist.

Date	Mintage	VG	F	VF	XF	Unc
(1)6Z1 (b)	—	65.00	125	250	500	—
(16)Z1	—	65.00	125	250	500	—
(16)Z1 (b)	—	65.00	125	250	500	—

KM# 69 SCHRECKENBERGER
(4 Groschen = 12 Kreuzer)

Silver **Ruler:** August II **Obv:** Helmeted oval eagle arms, date in margin **Obv. Legend:** DVRA • PATI • VIRTVS **Rev:** Crowned imperial eagle, value 4G on breast, titles of Ferdinand II around **Mint:** Lauenburg **Note:** Kipper Schreckenberger. Varieties exist.

Date	Mintage	VG	F	VF	XF	Unc
(1)6Z1//(1)621	—	85.00	175	275	550	—
(1)6Z1//(16)Z1	—	85.00	175	275	550	—
---/ (16)Z1	—	85.00	175	275	550	—

KM# 70 SCHRECKENBERGER
(4 Groschen = 12 Kreuzer)

Silver **Ruler:** August II **Obv:** Helmeted oval eagle arms, legend around, date at end **Obv. Legend:** DVRA • PATI • VIRTVS **Rev:** Crowned imperial eagle, value 4G on breast, titles of Ferdinand II around **Note:** Varieties exist.

Date	Mintage	VG	F	VF	XF	Unc
ND(ca1621)	—	65.00	125	250	500	—

KM# 73 1/24 THALER (Groschen)

Silver **Ruler:** August II **Obv:** Helmeted eagle arms **Obv. Legend:** DURA • PA • VIRT (or variant) **Rev:** Imperial orb with value Z4, titles of August II around

Date	Mintage	VG	F	VF	XF	Unc
1621	—	60.00	120	240	—	—

KM# 74 1/24 THALER (Groschen)

Silver **Ruler:** August II **Obv:** Eagle in inner circle, titles of August II around **Rev:** Imperial orb with value Z4, titles of Ferdinand II, date around **Mint:** Lauenburg

Date	Mintage	VG	F	VF	XF	Unc
(16)Z1 (b)	—	60.00	120	240	—	—

KM# 76 1/24 THALER (Groschen)

Silver **Ruler:** August II **Obv:** Crowned Saxon arms, around DVRA ... **Rev:** Imperial orb with value Z4, titles of Ferdinand II, date around

Date	Mintage	VG	F	VF	XF	Unc
ND(c.1621)	—	50.00	100	210	—	—

KM# 71 1/24 THALER (Groschen)

Silver **Ruler:** August II **Obv:** Crowned 4-fold arms, titles of August II around **Rev:** Imperial orb with value Z4, titles of Ferdinand II, date around **Mint:** Lauenburg **Note:** Kipper 1/24 Thaler.

Date	Mintage	VG	F	VF	XF	Unc
(16)21 (b)	—	60.00	120	240	—	—
(16)Z1 (b)	—	60.00	120	240	—	—

KM# 72 1/24 THALER (Groschen)

Silver **Ruler:** August II **Obv:** Helmeted eagle arms, titles of August II around **Rev:** Imperial orb with value Z4, titles of Ferdinand II, date around **Mint:** Lauenburg **Note:** Varieties exist.

Date	Mintage	VG	F	VF	XF	Unc
(16)21 (b)	—	60.00	120	240	—	—
(16)Z1 (b)	—	60.00	120	240	—	—
ND (b)	—	60.00	120	240	—	—

KM# 75 1/24 THALER (Groschen)

Silver **Ruler:** August II **Obv:** Eagle in inner circle **Obv. Legend:** DVRA • PATI • VIRTVS. **Rev:** Imperial orb with value Z4, titles of Ferdinand II, date around **Mint:** Lauenburg **Note:** Varieties exist.

Date	Mintage	VG	F	VF	XF	Unc
(16)Z1 (b)	—	60.00	120	240	—	—
(16)Z6 (b)	—	60.00	120	240	—	—
ND (b)	—	60.00	120	240	—	—

KM# 77 1/24 THALER (Groschen)

Silver **Ruler:** August II **Obv:** Crowned Saxon arms, titles of August II around **Rev:** Imperial orb with value Z4, titles of Ferdinand II, date around **Mint:** Lauenburg **Note:** Varieties exist.

Date	Mintage	VG	F	VF	XF	Unc
(16)Z1	—	60.00	120	240	—	—
(16)Z1 (b)	—	60.00	120	240	—	—

KM# 81 1/24 THALER (Groschen)

Silver **Ruler:** August II **Obv:** Shield of water lily arms **Obv. Legend:** DURA • PATI • VIRT • **Rev:** Imperial orb with value Z4, titles of Ferdinand II, date around **Note:** Varieties exist.

Date	Mintage	VG	F	VF	XF	Unc
(16)22	—	60.00	120	240	—	—
ND	—	60.00	120	240	—	—

KM# 110 1/24 THALER (Groschen)

Silver **Ruler:** Julius Franz **Obv:** Crowned eagle, arms of Saxony on breast, titles of Julius Franz around **Rev:** Value in inscription, legend around **Rev. Legend:** LANDT. MVNTZ **Rev. Inscription:** 24 / Reichs / Daler / date / mintmaster's initials **Mint:** Ratzeburg **Note:** Varieties exist.

Date	Mintage	VG	F	VF	XF	Unc
1671 HI	—	35.00	75.00	150	300	—
1672 IW	—	35.00	75.00	150	300	—
1673 IW	—	35.00	75.00	150	300	—

KM# 120 1/24 THALER (Groschen)

Silver **Ruler:** Julius Franz **Obv:** Crowned eagle, arms of Saxony on breast, titles of Julius Franz around **Rev:** Imperial orb with 24, legend around **Rev. Legend:** MONETA NOVA ARGENTEA **Mint:** Elbschifferstadt

Date	Mintage	VG	F	VF	XF	Unc
ND(1678-89) (g)	—	40.00	80.00	160	325	—

KM# 3 1/16 THALER (Doppelschilling)

Silver **Ruler:** Franz II **Obv:** 3 helmets above 4-fold arms, titles of Franz II around **Rev:** Crowned imperial eagle, orb with 16 on breast, titles of Rudolf II around, date around **Mint:** Lauenburg **Note:** Varieties exist.

Date	Mintage	VG	F	VF	XF	Unc
(1)609 IG	—	30.00	65.00	100	200	—

KM# 4 1/16 THALER (Doppelschilling)

Silver **Ruler:** Franz II **Obv:** 3 helmets above 4-fold arms, titles of Franz II around **Rev:** Crowned imperial eagle, orb on breast, titles of Rudolf II, date around **Mint:** Lauenburg

Date	Mintage	VG	F	VF	XF	Unc
1609 IG	—	40.00	75.00	115	230	—

KM# 16 1/16 THALER (Doppelschilling)

Silver **Ruler:** Franz II **Obv:** Bust right, titles of Franz II around **Rev:** Helmeted 4-fold arms, date in margin **Mint:** Lauenburg

Date	Mintage	VG	F	VF	XF	Unc
1610 IG	—	—	—	—	—	—

KM# 37 1/16 THALER (Doppelschilling)

Silver **Ruler:** Franz II **Obv:** 4-fold arms divide date, 3 helmets above, titles of Franz II around **Rev:** Crowned imperial eagle, 16 in orb on breast, titles of Matthias around **Mint:** Lauenburg **Note:** Varieties exist.

Date	Mintage	VG	F	VF	XF	Unc
1613 IG	—	80.00	180	360	—	—
1614 IG	—	80.00	180	360	—	—
ND IG	—	80.00	180	360	—	—

KM# 40 1/16 THALER (Doppelschilling)

Silver **Ruler:** Franz II **Obv:** 4-fold arms, 3 helmets above, titles of Franz II around **Rev:** Crowned imperial eagle, 16 in orb on breast, date in legend, titles of Matthias around **Mint:** Lauenburg **Note:** Varieties exist.

Date	Mintage	VG	F	VF	XF	Unc
1614 IG	—	85.00	170	340	—	—
1615 IG	—	85.00	170	340	—	—
1616 IG	—	85.00	170	340	—	—
(1)617	—	85.00	170	340	—	—
1617	—	85.00	170	340	—	—
1619	—	85.00	170	340	—	—

KM# 59 1/16 THALER (Doppelschilling)

Silver **Ruler:** August II **Obv:** 3 helmets above 4-fold arms, titles of August II around, imperial orb at top **Rev:** Intertwined DS, date in margin **Mint:** Lauenburg **Note:** Varieties exist.

Date	Mintage	VG	F	VF	XF	Unc
ND (a)	—	65.00	135	275	550	—
(1)6Z0 (a)	—	65.00	135	275	550	—
(16)Z0 (a)	—	65.00	135	275	550	—
16Z0 (b)	—	65.00	135	275	550	—
(1)6Z0 (b)	—	65.00	135	275	550	—
ND (b)	—	65.00	135	275	550	—
(1)620 (b)	—	65.00	135	275	550	—
1620 (b)	—	65.00	135	275	550	—
(1)6Z1	—	65.00	135	275	550	—
(16)Z1 (b)	—	65.00	135	275	550	—
(1)621 (b)	—	65.00	135	275	550	—
(16)21 (b)	—	65.00	135	275	550	—
(16)21	—	65.00	135	275	550	—

KM# 60 1/16 THALER (Doppelschilling)

Silver **Ruler:** August II **Obv:** 3 helmets above 4-fold arms, date divided to left, top and right of arms, titles of August II around, imperial orb at top **Rev:** Intertwined DS **Mint:** Lauenburg

Date	Mintage	VG	F	VF	XF	Unc
16Z0 (b)	—	—	—	—	—	—

KM# 121 1/16 THALER (3 Schilliing - Dütchen)

Silver **Ruler:** Julius Franz **Obv:** Bust right, titles of Julius Franz around **Rev:** Inscription, date at end of legend **Rev. Legend:** MONETA • NOVA • ARGENT **Rev. Inscription:** IVI / REICH / TALE (THAL) **Mint:** Elbschifferstadt **Note:** Varieties exist.

Date	Mintage	VG	F	VF	XF	Unc
1678 (g)	—	35.00	75.00	150	300	—

KM# 28 1/8 THALER (3-1/2 Groschen)

Silver **Ruler:** Franz II **Obv:** Bust right, titles of Franz II, date around, value 3-1/2 at bottom **Rev:** 3 helmets above 4-fold arms

Date	Mintage	VG	F	VF	XF	Unc
1611	—	—	—	—	—	—

KM# 29 1/8 THALER (3-1/2 Groschen)

Silver **Ruler:** Franz II **Obv:** Bust right, titles of Franz II, date around **Rev:** 3 helmets above 4-fold arms

Date	Mintage	VG	F	VF	XF	Unc
1611	—	—	—	—	—	—

KM# 47 1/8 THALER (3-1/2 Groschen)

Silver **Ruler:** Franz II **Subject:** Death of Franz II **Obv:** Bust right, titles around **Rev:** 7-line inscription with dates **Mint:** Lauenburg

Date	Mintage	VG	F	VF	XF	Unc
1619 IG	—	—	—	—	—	—

KM# 82 1/8 THALER (1/2 Reichsort)

Silver **Ruler:** August II **Obv:** Bust right, titles of August II around **Rev:** 4-line inscription, date at end of legend **Rev. Legend:** DURA PATI VIRTUS **Rev. Inscription:** EIN / HALBEN / RICKES / ORT **Mint:** Lauenburg

Date	Mintage	VG	F	VF	XF	Unc
16ZZ (b)	—	—	—	—	—	—

KM# 83 1/8 THALER (1/2 Reichsort)

Silver **Ruler:** August II **Obv:** 3 helmets above 4-fold arms, titles of August II around **Rev:** Inscription, date at end of legend **Rev. Legend:** DURA PATI VIRTUS **Rev. Inscription:** EIN / HALBEN / RICKES / ORT **Note:** Varieties exist.

Date	Mintage	VG	F	VF	XF	Unc
16ZZ	—	—	—	—	—	—

KM# 85 1/8 THALER (1/2 Reichsort)

Silver **Ruler:** August II **Subject:** Death of Prince Franz August **Obv:** Bust right, titles of August II around **Rev:** 6-line inscription with dates **Mint:** Lauenburg

Date	Mintage	VG	F	VF	XF	Unc
16Z4 (b)	—	—	—	—	—	—

KM# 17 1/4 THALER

Silver **Ruler:** Franz II **Obv:** Small bust right within circle, titles of Franz II around **Rev:** 4-fold arms, 3 helmets above separate each numeral of date **Mint:** Lauenburg

Date	Mintage	VG	F	VF	XF	Unc
1610 IG	—	—	—	—	—	—
1611	—	—	—	—	—	—

KM# 18 1/4 THALER

Silver **Ruler:** Franz II **Obv:** Large bust breaks circle, date divided in top margin by head **Rev:** 4-fold arms, 3 helmets above **Mint:** Lauenburg

Date	Mintage	VG	F	VF	XF	Unc
1610 IG	—	—	—	—	—	—

KM# 48 1/4 THALER

Silver **Ruler:** Franz II **Subject:** Death of Franz II **Obv:** Bust right, titles around **Rev:** 8-line inscription with dates **Mint:** Lauenburg

Date	Mintage	VG	F	VF	XF	Unc
1619 IG	—	—	—	—	—	—

KM# 86 1/4 THALER

Silver **Ruler:** August II **Obv:** Bust to right **Rev:** Shield of 4-fold arms, ornate helmets above, date at end of legend **Rev. Legend:** DURA • PAT • VIRTUS (or variant) **Mint:** Lauenburg **Note:** Varieties exist.

Date	Mintage	VG	F	VF	XF	Unc
(1)6Z4 (b)	—	—	—	—	—	—
16Z4 (b)	—	—	—	—	—	—

KM# 5 1/2 THALER

Silver **Ruler:** Franz II **Obv:** Bust right, titles of Franz II around **Rev:** 3 helmets above 4-fold arms, date at end of legend **Rev. Legend:** PROPI • DEO • SECUR • AGO **Mint:** Lauenburg

Date	Mintage	VG	F	VF	XF	Unc
(1)609	—	—	—	—	—	—

KM# 19 1/2 THALER

Silver **Ruler:** Franz II **Obv:** Bust right, titles of Franz II around **Rev:** 3 helmets above 4-fold arms which divide date **Rev. Legend:** PROPITIO • DEO • SECU • RUS • AGO **Mint:** Lauenburg

Date	Mintage	VG	F	VF	XF	Unc
1610 IG	—	—	—	—	—	—

KM# 38 1/2 THALER

Silver **Ruler:** Franz II **Obv:** Bust right, titles of Franz II around **Rev:** 3 helmets above 4-fold arms, helmets separate date **Rev. Legend:** PROPITIO • DEO • SECU • RUS • AGO **Mint:** Lauenburg

Date	Mintage	VG	F	VF	XF	Unc
1613	—	—	—	—	—	—
1617 IG	—	—	—	—	—	—

KM# 49 1/2 THALER

Silver **Ruler:** Franz II **Subject:** Death of Franz II **Obv:** Bust right, titles around **Rev:** 10-line inscription **Mint:** Lauenburg

Date	Mintage	VG	F	VF	XF	Unc
1619 IG	—	—	—	—	—	—

KM# 61 1/2 THALER

Silver **Ruler:** August II **Obv:** Bust right, titles of August II around **Rev:** 3 helmets above 4-fold arms, date at end of legend **Rev. Legend:** DURA • PAT • VIRTUS (or variant) **Mint:** Lauenburg **Note:** Varieties exist.

Date	Mintage	VG	F	VF	XF	Unc
(1)6Z0 (b)	—	—	—	—	—	—
(1)6Z4	—	—	—	—	—	—
16Z4	—	—	—	—	—	—

KM# 111 2/3 THALER (Gulden; Doppelmarken)

Silver **Ruler:** Julius Franz **Obv:** Crown aabove elaborate JF monogram, 2/3 in oval below, titles of Julius Franz around **Rev:** Crowned eagle, Saxon arms on breast, date at end of legend **Rev. Legend:** MONETA • NOVA • ARGENTEA **Note:** Dav. #603.

Date	Mintage	VG	F	VF	XF	Unc
1671 (e)	—	—	—	—	—	—

KM# 122 2/3 THALER (Gulden; Doppelmarken)

Silver **Ruler:** Julius Franz **Obv:** Bust right, titles of Julius Franz around **Rev:** Crowned 4-fold arms divide 2/3 - T, date at end of legend **Rev. Legend:** THV • RECHT • RECHT • SCHEV • NIMANDT **Mint:** Elbschifferstadt **Note:** Dav. #604.

Date	Mintage	VG	F	VF	XF	Unc
1678 (g)	—	65.00	120	200	425	—

KM# 123 2/3 THALER (Gulden; Doppelmarken)

Silver **Ruler:** Julius Franz **Obv:** Bust right, titles of Julius Franz around **Rev:** Crowned 4-fold arms, value 2/3 below, date at end of legend **Rev. Legend:** THV • RECHT • RECHT • SCHEV • NIMANDT **Mint:** Elbschifferstadt **Note:** Dav. #604A. Varieties exist.

Date	Mintage	VG	F	VF	XF	Unc
1678 (g)	—	65.00	100	180	360	—

KM# 6 THALER

Silver **Ruler:** Franz II **Obv:** Duke on horseback to left **Rev:** Helmeted arms, date at end of legend **Note:** Dav. 7336.

Date	Mintage	Good	VG	F	VF	XF
(1)609 IG	—	600	1,200	2,300	3,600	6,500

KM# 7 THALER

Silver **Ruler:** Franz II **Obv:** Bust with ruffed collar to right **Obv. Legend:** FRANC: II: D: G: DUX: SAXO:... **Rev:** Date in legend **Note:** Dav. 7337.

Date	Mintage	Good	VG	F	VF	XF
(1)609 IG	—	600	1,200	2,300	3,600	—

KM# 30 THALER

Silver **Ruler:** Franz II **Obv. Legend:** FRANCIS:...SAX **Rev:** Arms with straight sides **Note:** Dav. 7338.

Date	Mintage	Good	VG	F	VF	XF
(1)611 IG	—	450	900	1,650	2,600	—

KM# 31 THALER

Silver **Ruler:** Franz II **Obv. Legend:** ...SAXO: ANGA:... **Rev:** Helmeted arms break legend and divide date at bottom **Note:** Dav. 7339.

Date	Mintage	Good	VG	F	VF	XF
1611	—	375	750	1,450	2,250	—

KM# 32 THALER

Silver **Ruler:** Franz II **Obv:** Bust right with lion head on shoulder **Obv. Legend:** FRANC: II:... **Note:** Dav. 7340.

Date	Mintage	Good	VG	F	VF	XF
1611	—	375	750	1,450	2,250	—

KM# 39 THALER

Silver **Ruler:** Franz II **Obv:** Head to right **Obv. Legend:** FRANCIS: II. D: G:...WEST **Rev:** Helmeted arms with date divided by helmets **Note:** Dav. 7342.

Date	Mintage	Good	VG	F	VF	XF
1613 IG	—	300	600	1,150	2,000	4,000
1617 IG	—	350	700	1,300	2,500	—
1619 IG	—	350	700	1,300	2,500	—

KM# 35 THALER

Silver **Ruler:** Franz II **Obv:** Duke on horseback to right **Rev:** Helmeted arms **Note:** Dav. 7341.

Date	Mintage	Good	VG	F	VF	XF
ND IG Rare	—	—	—	—	—	—

KM# 50 THALER

Silver **Ruler:** Franz II **Subject:** Death of Franz II **Obv:** Head to right **Rev:** 10-line inscription **Note:** Dav. 7343.

Date	Mintage	Good	VG	F	VF	XF
1619 IG Rare	—	—	—	—	—	—

KM# 51 THALER

29.0000 g., Silver **Ruler:** Franz II **Subject:** Death of Franz II **Obv:** Armored 1/2 length figure to right with scepter, helmet in front **Rev:** 10-line inscription with dates, 3 lines in exergue **Note:** Dav. #LS433.

Date	Mintage	VG	F	VF	XF	Unc
1619 IG	—	1,300	2,200	3,600	6,300	—

KM# 62 THALER

29.0000 g., Silver **Ruler:** August II **Obv:** Armored and draped bust to right **Rev:** Helmeted arms **Note:** Dav. 7344.

Date	Mintage	Good	VG	F	VF	XF
1620 (b)	—	190	375	675	1,200	—
1621 (b)	—	190	375	675	1,200	—
1622 (b)	—	190	375	675	1,200	—
1624 (b)	—	155	325	575	1,000	—

KM# 87 THALER

29.0000 g., Silver **Ruler:** August II **Rev:** 8-line inscription **Note:** Dav. 7345.

Date	Mintage	Good	VG	F	VF	XF
1624 (b)	—	400	800	1,600	3,000	6,500

KM# 94 THALER

29.0000 g., Silver **Ruler:** August II **Obv:** Armored and collared bust to right in circle **Obv. Legend:** AUGUSTUS. D: G: DUX. SAXON: ANGAR. ET. WEST. **Rev:** Crowned imperial eagle, 32 in orb on breast **Rev. Legend:** FERDINANDUS. II. D G. ROM. IMP. SE. AV. **Note:** Dav. 7349. 32 Schilling.

Date	Mintage	Good	VG	F	VF	XF
ND (b)	—	400	725	1,250	2,000	—

KM# 89 THALER

29.0000 g., Silver **Ruler:** August II **Obv:** Facing bust divides date **Rev:** Helmeted arms **Note:** Dav. 7347.

Date	Mintage	Good	VG	F	VF	XF
1645 (c)	—	500	1,000	1,800	3,200	—

KM# 92 THALER

29.0000 g., Silver **Ruler:** August II **Subject:** Death of Johann Adolph, Son of August II **Obv:** Helmeted arms **Rev:** 6-line inscription **Note:** Dav. 7348.

Date	Mintage	Good	VG	F	VF	XF
1646 (c) Rare	—	—	—	—	—	—

KM# 95 THALER

29.0000 g., Silver **Ruler:** August II **Obv:** 3/4-length figure right, helmet in front **Rev:** Helmeted arms **Note:** Dav. #LS437.

Date	Mintage	VG	F	VF	XF	Unc
ND (b) Rare	—	1,150	2,200	4,500	—	—

KM# 100 THALER

29.0000 g., Silver **Ruler:** August II **Subject:** Death of August II **Obv:** Helmeted arms **Rev:** 9-line inscription **Note:** Dav. 7351.

Date	Mintage	VG	F	VF	XF	Unc
1656 (d) Rare	—	—	—	—	—	—

KM# 99 THALER

Silver **Ruler:** Julius Heinrich **Obv:** Bust right, titles of Julius Heinrich around **Rev:** 3 helmets above 4-fold arms, date at end of legend **Rev. Legend:** OMNE • SOLUM • FORT • PATRIA • ANNO

Date	Mintage	VG	F	VF	XF	Unc
1656 IS Rare	—	—	—	—	—	—

KM# 107 THALER

29.0000 g., Silver **Ruler:** Julius Heinrich **Subject:** Death of Julius Heinrich **Obv:** Bust right **Rev:** Church

Date	Mintage	VG	F	VF	XF	Unc
1665 Rare	—	—	—	—	—	—

KM# 109 THALER

29.0000 g., Silver **Ruler:** Julius Franz **Obv:** Draped and armored bust to right **Rev:** Eagle above, crown in sprays at center **Note:** Dav. 7353.

Date	Mintage	VG	F	VF	XF	Unc
1670	—	900	1,800	3,350	6,000	—

KM# 115 THALER

29.0000 g., Silver **Ruler:** Julius Franz **Obv:** Bust right **Rev:** Capped arms divide date **Note:** Dav. 7354.

Date	Mintage	VG	F	VF	XF	Unc
1673 (f) Rare	—	—	—	—	—	—

KM# 116 THALER

29.0000 g., Silver **Ruler:** Julius Franz **Obv:** Armored bust to right **Rev:** Helmeted arms **Note:** Dav. 7355.

Date	Mintage	VG	F	VF	XF	Unc
1673 (f) Rare	—	—	—	—	—	—

KM# 124 THALER

29.0000 g., Silver **Ruler:** Julius Franz **Rev:** Crowned arms **Note:** Dav. 7356.

Date	Mintage	VG	F	VF	XF	Unc
1678 Rare	—	—	—	—	—	—

KM# 126 THALER

29.0000 g., Silver **Ruler:** Julius Franz **Obv:** Large bust right **Note:** Dav. 7358.

Date	Mintage	VG	F	VF	XF	Unc
1679	—	900	1,800	3,300	5,500	—

KM# 128 THALER

29.0000 g., Silver **Ruler:** Julius Franz **Obv:** Armored and draped bust to right **Rev:** Shield of 4-fold arms, 3 ornate helmets above divide date **Note:** Dav. 7359.

Date	Mintage	VG	F	VF	XF	Unc
1680	—	650	1,250	2,750	4,750	—

KM# 130 THALER

Silver, 40 mm. **Ruler:** Julius Franz **Note:** Small flan. Dav. 7359A.

Date	Mintage	VG	F	VF	XF	Unc
1683	—	650	1,250	2,750	4,750	—

KM# 20 1-1/4 THALER

25.0000 g., Silver **Ruler:** Franz II **Rev:** Helmeted arms, date in legend **Note:** Dav. #LS430.

Date	Mintage	VG	F	VF	XF	Unc
1610	—	1,450	2,350	3,750	6,600	—

KM# 21 1-1/4 THALER

25.0000 g., Silver **Ruler:** Franz II **Obv:** Bust right, helmet in front **Rev:** Helmeted arms **Note:** Dav. #LS431B.

Date	Mintage	VG	F	VF	XF	Unc
ND Rare	—	—	—	—	—	—

KM# 96 1-1/4 THALER

25.0000 g., Silver **Ruler:** August II **Note:** Dav. #LS436. Similar to 1 Thaler, KM#95.

Date	Mintage	VG	F	VF	XF	Unc
ND Rare	—	—	—	—	—	—

KM# 8 1-1/2 THALER

Silver **Ruler:** Franz II **Obv:** Circle within triangle, within double circles **Rev:** Triangle within double circles **Note:** Dav. #LS427A.

Date	Mintage	VG	F	VF	XF	Unc
ND	—	2,250	4,050	6,800	—	—

KM# 22 1-1/2 THALER

Silver **Ruler:** Franz II **Note:** Dav. #LS429. Similar to 1-1/4 Thaler, KM#20.

Date	Mintage	VG	F	VF	XF	Unc
1610	—	2,400	4,050	6,800	11,500	—

KM# 23 1-1/2 THALER

Silver **Ruler:** Franz II **Note:** Dav. #LS431A. Similar to 1-1/4 Thaler, KM#21.

Date	Mintage	VG	F	VF	XF	Unc
ND Rare	—	—	—	—	—	—

KM# 97 1-1/2 THALER

Silver **Ruler:** August II **Note:** Dav. #LS435. Similar to 1 Thaler, KM#95.

Date	Mintage	VG	F	VF	XF	Unc
ND Rare	—	—	—	—	—	—

KM# 9 2 THALER

Silver **Ruler:** Franz II **Note:** Dav. #7336. Similar to 1 Thaler, KM#6.

Date	Mintage	VG	F	VF	XF	Unc
1609 Rare	—	—	—	—	—	—

KM# 10 2 THALER

57.0000 g., Silver **Ruler:** Franz II **Note:** Dav. #LS427. Similar to 1-1/2 Thaler, KM#8.

Date	Mintage	VG	F	VF	XF	Unc
ND	—	2,350	4,150	7,500	13,000	—

KM# 24 2 THALER

57.0000 g., Silver **Ruler:** Franz II **Note:** Dav. #LS428. Similar to 1-1/4 Thaler, KM#20.

Date	Mintage	VG	F	VF	XF	Unc
1610	—	1,900	3,400	5,600	9,000	—

KM# 25 2 THALER

57.0000 g., Silver **Ruler:** Franz II **Note:** Dav. #LS431. Similar to 1-1/4 Thaler, KM#21.

Date	Mintage	VG	F	VF	XF	Unc
ND Rare	—	—	—	—	—	—

KM# 52 2 THALER

57.0000 g., Silver **Ruler:** Franz II **Subject:** Death of Franz II **Obv:** 1/2-lengh armored figure to right holding scepter, helmet at right **Rev:** 10-line inscription with dates, 3 lines in exergue **Note:** Dav. #LS433. Similar to 1 Thaler, KM#51.

Date	Mintage	VG	F	VF	XF	Unc
1619	—	2,200	3,600	5,300	11,000	—

KM# 90 2 THALER

57.0000 g., Silver **Ruler:** August II **Rev:** Helmeted arms **Note:** Dav. 7346.

Date	Mintage	VG	F	VF	XF	Unc
1645 (c) Rare	—	—	—	—	—	—

Note: Fritz Rudolf Künker Münzenhandlung Auction 80, 3-03, XF realized approximately $61,355

KM# 101 2 THALER

57.0000 g., Silver **Ruler:** August II **Subject:** Death of August II **Obv:** Helmeted arms **Rev:** 9-line inscription **Note:** Dav. 7350.

Date	Mintage	VG	F	VF	XF	Unc
1656 (d) Rare	—	—	—	—	—	—

KM# 11 3 THALER

86.0000 g., Silver **Ruler:** Julius Heinrich **Note:** Dav. #LS426. Similar to 1-1/2 Thaler, KM#8.

Date	Mintage	VG	F	VF	XF	Unc
ND Rare	—	—	—	—	—	—

KM# 98 3 THALER
86.0000 g., Silver **Ruler:** August II **Note:** Dav. #LS434. Similar to 1 Thaler, KM#98.

Date	Mintage	VG	F	VF	XF	Unc
ND Rare	—	—	—	—	—	—

KM# 12 4 THALER
Silver **Ruler:** Julius Heinrich **Note:** Dav. #LS425. Similar to 1-1/2 Thaler, KM#8.

Date	Mintage	VG	F	VF	XF	Unc
ND Rare	—	—	—	—	—	—

KM# 13 5 THALER
143.0000 g., Silver **Ruler:** Julius Heinrich **Note:** Dav. #LS424. Similar to 1-1/2 Thaler, KM#8.

Date	Mintage	VG	F	VF	XF	Unc
ND Rare	—	—	—	—	—	—

TRADE COINAGE

KM# 33 GOLDGULDEN
3.5000 g., 0.9860 Gold 0.1109 oz. AGW **Ruler:** Franz II **Obv:** Bust to right in circle **Rev:** Helmeted arms in circle **Note:** Fr. 2982.

Date	Mintage	VG	F	VF	XF	Unc
1611 IG	—	1,600	3,100	6,100	11,500	—

KM# 26 8 GOLDGULDEN
28.0000 g., 0.9860 Gold 0.8876 oz. AGW **Ruler:** Franz II **Obv:** Equestrian figure to right **Rev:** Helmeted arms in circle **Note:** Fr. 2983.

Date	Mintage	VG	F	VF	XF	Unc
ND IG Rare	—	—	—	—	—	—

KM# 102 DUCAT
3.5000 g., 0.9860 Gold 0.1109 oz. AGW **Ruler:** Julius Heinrich **Obv:** Bust to right in circle **Rev:** Helmeted arms in circle **Note:** Fr. 2985.

Date	Mintage	VG	F	VF	XF	Unc
1657 (d)	—	2,200	4,200	7,500	12,500	—
1662 (d)	—	2,200	4,200	7,500	12,500	—

KM# 104 DUCAT
3.5000 g., 0.9860 Gold 0.1109 oz. AGW **Ruler:** Julius Heinrich **Rev:** Madonna and child in circle **Note:** Fr. 2986.

Date	Mintage	VG	F	VF	XF	Unc
1659 (d)	—	2,400	4,600	8,300	14,500	—

KM# 108 DUCAT
3.5000 g., 0.9860 Gold 0.1109 oz. AGW **Ruler:** Julius Franz **Obv:** Bust to right **Rev:** Cap and sprays in large trefoil **Note:** Fr. 2988.

Date	Mintage	VG	F	VF	XF	Unc
1670	—	1,550	3,250	6,500	11,000	—
1673	—	1,550	3,250	6,500	11,000	—
ND	—	1,550	3,250	6,500	11,000	—

KM# 106 2 DUCAT
7.0000 g., 0.9860 Gold 0.2219 oz. AGW **Ruler:** Julius Heinrich **Obv:** Bust to right in circle **Rev:** Helmeted arms in circle **Note:** Fr. 2984.

Date	Mintage	VG	F	VF	XF	Unc
1662 (d) Rare	—	—	—	—	—	—

KM# 117 2 DUCAT
7.0000 g., 0.9860 Gold 0.2219 oz. AGW **Ruler:** Julius Franz **Obv:** Bust to right **Rev:** Cap and sprays in large trefoil **Note:** Fr. 2987.

Date	Mintage	VG	F	VF	XF	Unc
1673	—	3,300	5,500	10,500	18,000	—
1678	—	3,300	5,500	10,500	18,000	—
1680	—	3,300	5,500	10,500	18,000	—
1681	—	3,300	5,500	10,500	18,000	—
1683	—	3,300	5,500	10,500	18,000	—
ND	—	3,300	5,500	10,500	18,000	—

SAXONY-ALBERTINE

(Sachsen-Albertinische Linie)

The younger of the two branches of the Billung dynasty, which ruled in Upper Saxony and Meissen, this line founded by Friedrich II's son, Albrecht, in 1485, first ruled in Meissen as dukes of Saxony. As a result of the conflict between Johann Friedrich I and Emperor Karl V (see Ernestine Line), the Albertine Line acquired the electoral dignity in 1547. The elector also became King of Poland in 1696 and permanently in 1709. As a result of the Napoleonic Wars (1792-1815), the elector was made King of Saxony in 1806, but lost half his territory to Prussia in 1813. The last king was forced to abdicate at the end of World War I.

RULERS

Friedrich Wilhelm von Saxe-Altenburg, Regent, 1591-1601
Christian II, Johann Georg I and August, jointly 1591-1611
Johann Georg I and August, jointly 1611-1615
Johann Georg I, alone 1615-1656
Johann Georg II, 1656-1680
Johann Georg III, 1680-1691
Johann Georg IV, 1691-1694
Friedrich August I, 1694-1733

MINT MARKS

L - Leipzig

MINT OFFICIALS' INITIALS

Annaberg Mint

Initial	Date	Name
Acorn on twig	1621-23	Michael Rothe

Bautzen Mint

CR	1640-78	Constantin Rothe in Dresden for Bautzen
HI	1666-67	Hennig Idlers

Bitterfeld Mint

Acorn w/o twig	1621	Barthel Eckardt

Chemnitz Mint

K in shield	1621-22	Christoph Sundtheim

Dresden Mint

CF, 2 fish	1678-86	Christoph Fischer
CM	1635	Cornelius Meide
CR, acorn	1640-78	Constantin Rothe
HB ligate	1556-1604	Hans Biener
HvR ligate, swan	1605-24	Heinrich von Rehnen
HI	1624-35	Hans Jacob
IK, 2 crossed arrows	1688-98	Johann Koch
ILH	1698-1716	Johann Lorenz Holland
SD	1635-40	Sebald Dierleber

Eckartsberga Mint

	1621	Christian Gerlach
EB	1621-22	Bernhard Hillard

Ehrenfriedersdorf Mint

Finger ring w/tapered stone	1622	Unknown

Eilenburg Mint

E in shield	1621	Unknown

Gommern Mint

6-pointed star	1621-22	Paul Lieber Paus

Grossenhain Mint

MB and/or 3-pointed rosette	1621-22	Marcus Brun

Grunthal Mint

	1621-23	August Rothe

Langensalza Mint

3 towers	1621	Andreas Becker

Leipzig Mint

EPH, fish	1693-1714	Ernst Peter Hecht
SL, as monogram in shield or w/hunting horn between 2 stag's antlers	1621-22	Stadt Leipzig Reichard Jager

Liebenwerda Mint

LW	1621	Jobst Wenighausen

Lutzen Mint

WQ and/or 4 L's in shape of cross	1621	Wilhelm Quendal

Merseburg Mint

MB and/or rooster	1621-22	Georg Sommerling

Naumburg Mint

N w/ or w/o heart	June 1621	Georg Oppermann
	Summer 1621	Curt Marquardt
	September 1621	Sebastian Hartel
	October 1621	Friedrich Ulm

Neustadt an der Orla Mint

N and/or HT monogram	1621-22	Hans Treuttner
	1621-22	Christoph Krafft

Pirna Mint

GS monogram w/pear on twig	1621-22	Georg Stange

Sangerhausen Mint

S	1621	Heinrich Ulm

Schkeuditz Mint

HVS monogram	1621	Heinrich Ulm

Taucha Mint

T in shield	1621	Matthias von Neuss and David Wolke

Tennstedt Mint

Tree	1621	Unknown

Weida Mint

W (sometimes in shield)	1621-22	Christoph Sundtheim

Zwickau Mint

Anchor and/or 3 swans	1621-22	Adam Prellhoff, Jacob Cern, die-cutter

ARMS

Saxony (ducal) – ten bars of alternating shade, crown opened
diagonally across from upper left to lower right
Saxony (electoral) – two crossed swords on background dividedhorizontally

ELECTORATE

REGULAR COINAGE

MB# 316 PFENNIG
Silver **Ruler:** Christian II, Johann Georg I and August **Obv:** 2-fold spade-shaped arms of electoral and ducal Saxony **Rev:** Imperial orb in ornamented frame divides date **Mint:** Dresden **Note:** Varieties exist.

Date	Mintage	VG	F	VF	XF	Unc
1601 HB	—	30.00	60.00	90.00	170	—

KM# 5.1 PFENNIG
Silver **Ruler:** Christian II, Johann Georg I and August **Obv:** 2-fold arms of Saxony divided diagonally, date abaove, mintmaster's initials below **Rev:** Imperial orb in plain field **Note:** Varieties exist. Prev. KM#5.

Date	Mintage	VG	F	VF	XF	Unc
1601 HB	—	7.00	15.00	30.00	60.00	—
160Z HB	—	7.00	15.00	30.00	60.00	—

KM# 5.2 PFENNIG

Silver **Ruler:** Christian II, Johann Georg I and August **Obv:** 2-fold arms divided vertically in ornamented frame, mintmaster's initials above **Rev:** Imperial orb in cartouche divides date **Mint:** Dresden

Date	Mintage	VG	F	VF	XF	Unc
(1)60Z HB	—	10.00	20.00	40.00	80.00	—

KM# 5.3 PFENNIG

Silver **Ruler:** Christian II, Johann Georg I and August **Obv:** 2-fold arms divided vertically in plain shield, mintmaster's initials above **Rev:** Imperial orb in cartouche divides date **Mint:** Dresden

Date	Mintage	VG	F	VF	XF	Unc
(1)603 HB	—	10.00	20.00	40.00	80.00	—
(1)604 HB	—	10.00	20.00	40.00	80.00	—
(1)605 HB	—	10.00	20.00	40.00	80.00	—

KM# 5.4 PFENNIG

Silver **Ruler:** Christian II, Johann Georg I and August **Obv:** Oval arms in cartouche between 2 rosettes **Rev:** Imperial orb in ornamented rhombus divides date **Mint:** Dresden

Date	Mintage	VG	F	VF	XF	Unc
1606 HvR	—	10.00	20.00	40.00	80.00	—
(16)07 HvR	—	10.00	20.00	40.00	80.00	—
1607 HvR	—	10.00	20.00	40.00	80.00	—

KM# 5.5 PFENNIG

Silver **Ruler:** Christian II, Johann Georg I and August **Obv:** Plain arms in cartouche between 2 rosettes, mintmaster's initials above **Rev:** Imperial orb in cartouche divides date **Mint:** Dresden

Date	Mintage	VG	F	VF	XF	Unc
(16)09 HvR	—	—	—	—	—	—

KM# 65 PFENNIG

Silver **Ruler:** Johann Georg I and August **Obv:** 2-fold arms divided vertically in ornamented frame, mintmaster's symbol above **Rev:** Imperial orb in cartouche divides date **Mint:** Dresden

Date	Mintage	VG	F	VF	XF	Unc
1613 swan	—	7.00	15.00	30.00	60.00	—
1615 swan	—	7.00	15.00	30.00	60.00	—

KM# 130.1 PFENNIG

Silver **Ruler:** Johann Georg I **Obv:** 3 small shields of arms, 1 above 2, divide date, mintmaster's symbol below **Rev:** Imperial orb in baroque frame **Mint:** Dresden **Note:** Prev. KM#130.

Date	Mintage	VG	F	VF	XF	Unc
16Z0 swan	—	7.00	15.00	30.00	60.00	—
16Z1 HvR	—	7.00	15.00	30.00	60.00	—
16ZZ HvR	—	7.00	15.00	30.00	60.00	—
1623 HvR	—	7.00	15.00	30.00	60.00	—
1624 HvR	—	7.00	15.00	30.00	60.00	—
1625 HI	—	7.00	15.00	30.00	60.00	—
1626 HI	—	7.00	15.00	30.00	60.00	—
1627 HI	—	7.00	15.00	30.00	60.00	—
1628 HI	—	7.00	15.00	30.00	60.00	—
1629 HI	—	7.00	15.00	30.00	60.00	—
1630 HI	—	7.00	15.00	30.00	60.00	—
1631 HI	—	7.00	15.00	30.00	60.00	—
1632 HI	—	7.00	15.00	30.00	60.00	—
1636 SD	—	7.00	15.00	30.00	60.00	—
1637 SD	—	7.00	15.00	30.00	60.00	—
1638 SD	—	7.00	15.00	30.00	60.00	—
1639 SD	—	7.00	15.00	30.00	60.00	—
1640 CR	—	7.00	15.00	30.00	60.00	—
1640 SD	—	7.00	15.00	30.00	60.00	—
1641 CR	—	7.00	15.00	30.00	60.00	—
1642 CR	—	7.00	15.00	30.00	60.00	—
1643 CR	—	7.00	15.00	30.00	60.00	—
1644 CR	—	7.00	15.00	30.00	60.00	—
1645 CR	—	7.00	15.00	30.00	60.00	—
1646 CR	—	7.00	15.00	30.00	60.00	—
1647 CR	—	7.00	15.00	30.00	60.00	—
1648 CR	—	7.00	15.00	30.00	60.00	—
1649 CR	—	7.00	15.00	30.00	60.00	—
1650 CR	—	7.00	15.00	30.00	60.00	—
1651 CR	—	7.00	15.00	30.00	60.00	—
1652 CR	—	7.00	15.00	30.00	60.00	—
1653 CR	—	7.00	15.00	30.00	60.00	—
1654 CR	—	7.00	15.00	30.00	60.00	—
1654 CR	—	7.00	15.00	30.00	60.00	—

Note: Varieties exist

KM# 137 PFENNIG

Copper **Ruler:** Johann Georg I **Obv:** Oval Saxony arms in baroque frame, date above **Mint:** Grunthal **Note:** Kipper coinage. Uniface. Varieties exist.

Date	Mintage	VG	F	VF	XF	Unc
1621	—	6.00	13.00	27.00	55.00	—
16Z1	—	6.00	13.00	27.00	55.00	—
1622	—	6.00	13.00	27.00	55.00	—

KM# 138 PFENNIG

Copper **Ruler:** Johann Georg I **Obv:** Date divided above arms **Note:** Uniface. Varieties exist.

Date	Mintage	VG	F	VF	XF	Unc
16Z1	—	6.00	13.00	27.00	45.00	—
16ZZ	—	6.00	13.00	27.00	55.00	—
16Z3	—	6.00	13.00	27.00	55.00	—

KM# 139 PFENNIG

Copper **Ruler:** Johann Georg I **Obv:** Heart-shaped Saxony arms in ornamented frame, date divided above, S - L divided below **Mint:** Leipzig

Date	Mintage	VG	F	VF	XF	Unc
16Z1 SL	—	3.00	13.00	27.00	55.00	—

KM# 140 PFENNIG

Copper **Ruler:** Johann Georg I **Obv:** Oval shield of Saxony arms

Date	Mintage	VG	F	VF	XF	Unc
16Z1 SL	—	6.00	13.00	27.00	55.00	—

KM# 130.2 PFENNIG

Silver **Ruler:** Johann Georg I **Obv:** Oval 2-fold arms of electoral and ducal Saxony in baroque frame, mintmaster's symbol below **Rev:** Imperial orb in baroque frame divides date **Mint:** Dresden

Date	Mintage	VG	F	VF	XF	Unc
16Z3 swan	—	10.00	25.00	50.00	100	—
16Z4 swan	—	10.00	25.00	50.00	100	—

KM# 455.1 PFENNIG

Copper **Ruler:** Johann Georg II **Obv:** Round 2-fold arms in baroque frame, date below **Rev:** Imperial orb with symbol (Pfennig), legend, mintmaster's symbol **Rev. Legend:** OBER. SAX. KREISS **Mint:** Dresden **Note:** Prev. KM#455.

Date	Mintage	VG	F	VF	XF	Unc
1657 acorn	—	7.00	15.00	30.00	60.00	—
1658 acorn	—	7.00	15.00	30.00	60.00	—

KM# 455.2 PFENNIG

Silver **Ruler:** Johann Georg II **Obv:** Round 2-fold arms in baroque frame, date below **Rev:** Imperial orb with symbol (pfennig), mintmaster's initials divided at top **Rev. Legend:** OBER. SAX. KREISS **Mint:** Dresden

Date	Mintage	VG	F	VF	XF	Unc
1659 CR	—	7.00	15.00	30.00	60.00	—
1660 CR	—	7.00	15.00	30.00	60.00	—
1661 CR	—	7.00	15.00	30.00	60.00	—

KM# 455.3 PFENNIG

Silver **Ruler:** Johann Georg II **Obv:** Round 2-fold arms in baroque frame, date below **Rev:** Imperial orb with symbol (pfennig), mintmaster's initials divided by date **Rev. Legend:** OBER. SAX. KREISS. **Mint:** Dresden

Date	Mintage	VG	F	VF	XF	Unc
1662 CR	—	7.00	15.00	30.00	60.00	—
1663 CR	—	7.00	15.00	30.00	60.00	—
1664 CR	—	7.00	15.00	30.00	60.00	—
1665 CR	—	7.00	15.00	30.00	60.00	—
1666 CR	—	7.00	15.00	30.00	60.00	—
1667 CR	—	7.00	15.00	30.00	60.00	—

KM# 519 PFENNIG

Billon **Obv:** Oval Saxony arms in ornamented frame, initials below **Rev:** Imperial orb in shield divides date **Note:** Varieties exist.

Date	Mintage	VG	F	VF	XF	Unc
1667 CR	—	7.00	15.00	30.00	60.00	—
1668 CR	—	7.00	15.00	30.00	60.00	—
1669 CR	—	7.00	15.00	30.00	60.00	—
1670 CR	—	7.00	15.00	30.00	60.00	—
1671 CR	—	7.00	15.00	30.00	60.00	—
1672 CR	—	7.00	15.00	30.00	60.00	—
1673 CR	—	7.00	15.00	30.00	60.00	—
1674 CR	—	7.00	15.00	30.00	60.00	—
1675 CR	—	7.00	15.00	30.00	60.00	—
1676 CR	—	7.00	15.00	30.00	60.00	—
1677 CR	—	7.00	15.00	30.00	60.00	—
1679 CF	—	7.00	15.00	30.00	60.00	—

KM# 573 PFENNIG

Billon **Obv:** Crowned Saxony arms between 2 palm branches, initials divided below **Note:** Varieties exist.

Date	Mintage	VG	F	VF	XF	Unc
1681 CF	—	7.00	15.00	30.00	60.00	—
1682 CF	—	7.00	15.00	30.00	60.00	—
1683 CF	—	7.00	15.00	30.00	60.00	—
1684 CF	—	7.00	15.00	30.00	60.00	—
1685 CF	—	7.00	15.00	30.00	60.00	—
1686/5	—	7.00	15.00	30.00	60.00	—
1686 CF	—	7.00	15.00	30.00	60.00	—
1687	—	7.00	15.00	30.00	60.00	—
1689 IK	—	7.00	15.00	30.00	60.00	—
1691 IK	—	7.00	15.00	30.00	60.00	—

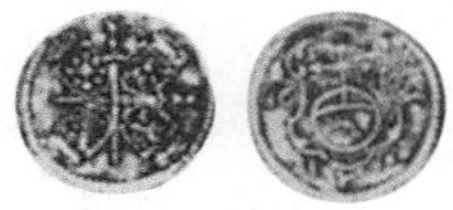

KM# 623 PFENNIG

Billon **Obv:** 4 small crowned shields of arms, 1 in each angle of 2 crossed swords **Rev:** Initials divided at bottom

Date	Mintage	VG	F	VF	XF	Unc
1692 IK	—	7.00	15.00	30.00	60.00	—

KM# 636 PFENNIG

Billon **Obv:** 2 adjacent oval arms in baroque frame, crown above **Note:** Varieties exist.

Date	Mintage	VG	F	VF	XF	Unc
1693 IK	—	7.00	15.00	30.00	60.00	—
1694 EPH	—	7.00	15.00	30.00	60.00	—
1694 IK	—	7.00	15.00	30.00	60.00	—

KM# 663 PFENNIG

Billon **Ruler:** Johann Georg IV **Rev:** Initials at bottom **Mint:** Dresden **Note:** Varieties exist.

Date	Mintage	VG	F	VF	XF	Unc
1694 IK	—	7.00	15.00	30.00	60.00	—
1695 EPH	—	7.00	15.00	30.00	60.00	—
1695 IK	—	7.00	15.00	30.00	60.00	—
1695 EPH	—	7.00	15.00	30.00	60.00	—
1696 IK	—	7.00	15.00	30.00	60.00	—
1697 IK	—	7.00	15.00	30.00	60.00	—
1698 IK	—	7.00	15.00	30.00	60.00	—

KM# 674 PFENNIG

Billon **Obv:** Initials at bottom

Date	Mintage	VG	F	VF	XF	Unc
1696 EPH	—	7.00	15.00	30.00	60.00	—
1697 EPH	—	7.00	15.00	30.00	60.00	—

KM# 702 PFENNIG

Billon, 13.1 mm. **Ruler:** Friedrich August I **Obv:** Crowned 4-fold arms with central shield within palm branches **Rev:** Imperial orb in cartouche divides date

Date	Mintage	VG	F	VF	XF	Unc
1698 ILH	—	7.00	13.00	30.00	60.00	—
1698 LIH	—	7.00	13.00	30.00	60.00	—
1699 ILH	—	7.00	13.00	30.00	60.00	—
1700 ILH	—	7.00	13.00	30.00	60.00	—

KM# 720 PFENNIG

Billon **Obv:** Crowned 4-fold arms with central shild between palm branches **Rev:** Imperial orb in cartouche, date above

Date	Mintage	VG	F	VF	XF	Unc
1700 ILH	—	10.00	20.00	40.00	80.00	—

MB# 307 3 PFENNIG (Dreier)

Silver, 15-16 mm. **Ruler:** Christian II, Johann Georg I and August **Obv:** 3 small shields of arms, 1 above 2, upper shield divides date, mintmaster's initials below **Rev:** Imperial orb in baroque frame **Mint:** Dresden **Note:** Varieties exist.

Date	Mintage	VG	F	VF	XF	Unc
1601	—	14.00	22.00	40.00	85.00	—

KM# 6.2 3 PFENNIG (Dreier)

Silver **Ruler:** Christian II, Johann Georg I and August **Obv:** 2-fold arms of Saxony in baroque frame **Rev:** Imperial orb in baroque frame divides date **Mint:** Dresden

Date	Mintage	VG	F	VF	XF	Unc
1606 HvR	—	—	—	—	—	—
(16)07 HvR	—	—	—	—	—	—
(16)08 HvR	—	—	—	—	—	—
(16)09 HvR	—	—	—	—	—	—

KM# 48.2 3 PFENNIG (Dreier)

Silver **Ruler:** Christian II, Johann Georg I and August **Obv:** 3 small ornate shields of arms, 1 above 2, upper shield divides date **Rev:** Imperial orb in ornamented rhombus **Mint:** Dresden

Date	Mintage	VG	F	VF	XF	Unc
1614 swan	—	—	—	—	—	—

KM# 385.1 3 PFENNIG (Dreier)
Silver **Ruler:** Johann Georg I **Obv:** 3 small ornate shields of arms, 1 above 2, upper arms divide date, mintmaster's initials below **Rev:** Imperial orb in ornamented rhombus **Mint:** Dresden **Note:** Varieties exist.

Date	Mintage	VG	F	VF	XF	Unc
16Z3 HvR	—	9.00	25.00	40.00	85.00	—
16Z4 HvR	—	9.00	25.00	40.00	85.00	—

KM# 385.2 3 PFENNIG (Dreier)
Silver **Ruler:** Johann Georg I **Obv:** 3 small ornate shields of arms, 1 above 2, upper arms divide date, mintmaster's initials at bottom **Rev:** Imperial orb in ornamented rhombus **Mint:** Dresden

Date	Mintage	VG	F	VF	XF	Unc
16Z4 HI	—	5.00	10.00	25.00	55.00	—
16Z5 HI	—	5.00	10.00	25.00	55.00	—
16Z6 HI	—	5.00	10.00	25.00	55.00	—
16Z7 HI	—	5.00	10.00	25.00	55.00	—
16Z8 HI	—	5.00	10.00	25.00	55.00	—
16Z9 HI	—	5.00	10.00	25.00	55.00	—
1630 HI	—	5.00	10.00	25.00	55.00	—
1631 HI	—	5.00	10.00	25.00	55.00	—
1632 HI	—	5.00	10.00	25.00	55.00	—
1633 HI	—	5.00	10.00	25.00	55.00	—
1634 HI	—	5.00	10.00	25.00	55.00	—
1635 HI	—	5.00	10.00	25.00	55.00	—
1636 SD	—	5.00	10.00	25.00	55.00	—
1637 SD	—	5.00	10.00	25.00	55.00	—
1638 SD	—	5.00	10.00	25.00	55.00	—
1639 SD	—	5.00	10.00	25.00	55.00	—

KM# 385.3 3 PFENNIG (Dreier)
Silver **Ruler:** Johann Georg I **Obv:** 3 small ornate shields of arms, 1 above 2, upper arms divide date, mintmaster's initials at bottom **Rev:** Imperial orb in baroque frame **Mint:** Dresden

Date	Mintage	VG	F	VF	XF	Unc
1641 CR	—	5.00	10.00	25.00	55.00	—
1642 CR	—	5.00	10.00	25.00	55.00	—
1643 CR	—	5.00	10.00	25.00	55.00	—
1645 CR	—	5.00	10.00	25.00	55.00	—
1647 CR	—	5.00	10.00	25.00	55.00	—
1648 CR	—	5.00	10.00	25.00	55.00	—
1649 CR	—	5.00	10.00	25.00	55.00	—
1651 CR	—	5.00	10.00	25.00	55.00	—
1652 CR	—	5.00	10.00	25.00	55.00	—
1654 CR	—	5.00	10.00	25.00	55.00	—

KM# 6.1 3 PFENNIG
Silver **Obv:** 3 small ornate shields of arms, 1 above 2, divide date, mintmasters initials monogram below **Rev:** Imperial orb in baroque frame **Note:** Varieties exist.

Date	Mintage	VG	F	VF	XF	Unc
(16)01 HB	—	13.00	30.00	65.00	130	—
(16)02 HB	—	13.00	30.00	65.00	130	—
(16)03 HB	—	13.00	30.00	65.00	130	—
(16)04 HB	—	13.00	30.00	65.00	130	—
(16)04 HvR	—	13.00	30.00	65.00	130	—
(16)05 HB	—	13.00	30.00	65.00	130	—
(16)06 HvR	—	13.00	30.00	65.00	130	—
(16)07 HvR	—	13.00	30.00	65.00	130	—
(16)08 HvR	—	13.00	30.00	65.00	130	—
(16)09 HvR	—	13.00	30.00	65.00	130	—

Note: Varieties exist

KM# 48.1 3 PFENNIG
Silver **Obv:** Oval 2-fold arms in baroque frame, mintmaster's symbol below **Rev:** Imperial orb in baroque frame divides date **Note:** Varieties exist.

Date	Mintage	VG	F	VF	XF	Unc
161Z swan	—	16.00	35.00	70.00	145	—
1613 swan	—	16.00	35.00	70.00	145	—

KM# 131 3 PFENNIG
Silver **Ruler:** Johann Georg I **Rev:** Imperial orb in baroque frame **Mint:** Dresden **Note:** Kipper coinage.

Date	Mintage	VG	F	VF	XF	Unc
1620 (swan)	—	13.00	30.00	60.00	125	—

KM# 141 3 PFENNIG
Silver **Ruler:** Johann Georg I **Obv:** 3 small shields of arms, 1 above 2 **Rev:** Imperial orb with 3 divides date **Mint:** Grossenhain

Date	Mintage	VG	F	VF	XF	Unc
1621	—	13.00	30.00	60.00	125	—

KM# 142 3 PFENNIG
Silver **Ruler:** Johann Georg I **Obv:** Ornate 2-fold arms, angel's head above, mintmaster's symbol in margin at top **Rev:** 3 in imperial orb, date divided in legend at top **Mint:** Merseburg

Date	Mintage	VG	F	VF	XF	Unc
1621 (rooster)	—	13.00	30.00	55.00	105	—

KM# 144 3 PFENNIG
Silver **Ruler:** Johann Georg I **Obv:** 2 adjacent leaf-shaped shields of arms, 5-petaled rosettes above, 3 below **Rev:** 3 in imperial orb divdes date, all in rhombus

Date	Mintage	VG	F	VF	XF	Unc
(16)21	—	9.00	25.00	60.00	125	—

KM# 145 3 PFENNIG
Silver **Ruler:** Johann Georg I **Obv:** Ornate 2-fold arms, 6-petaled rosette divides date above **Rev:** 3 in imperial orb, 6-petaled rosette at left and right, date divided by cross above

Date	Mintage	VG	F	VF	XF	Unc
(16)21//(16)21	—	9.00	25.00	55.00	110	—

KM# 146 3 PFENNIG
Silver **Ruler:** Johann Georg I **Obv:** Ornate shield of 2-fold arms **Rev:** 3 in imperial orb, 6-petaled rosette at left and right, date divided by cross above

Date	Mintage	VG	F	VF	XF	Unc
(16)21	—	9.00	25.00	55.00	110	—

KM# 147 3 PFENNIG
Silver **Ruler:** Johann Georg I **Obv:** Ornate shield of 2-fold arms between two 6-petaled rosettes, value III above divides date

Date	Mintage	VG	F	VF	XF	Unc
1621	—	9.00	25.00	55.00	110	—

KM# 148 3 PFENNIG
Silver **Ruler:** Johann Georg I **Obv:** Ornate shield of 2-fold arms divides date

Date	Mintage	VG	F	VF	XF	Unc
16Z1	—	9.00	25.00	55.00	110	—

KM# 149 3 PFENNIG
Silver **Ruler:** Johann Georg I **Obv:** Ornate shield of 2-fold arms between two 6-petaled rosettes, value III above

Date	Mintage	VG	F	VF	XF	Unc
(16)Z1	—	9.00	25.00	55.00	110	—

KM# 152 3 PFENNIG
Silver **Ruler:** Johann Georg I **Obv:** Ornately-shaped 2-fold arms in baroque frame, date above

Date	Mintage	VG	F	VF	XF	Unc
1621	—	9.00	25.00	55.00	110	—

KM# 150 3 PFENNIG
Silver **Ruler:** Johann Georg I **Obv:** Heart-shaped 2-fold arms in baroque frame, value III above divides date **Note:** Uniface.

Date	Mintage	VG	F	VF	XF	Unc
1621	—	9.00	25.00	55.00	110	—

KM# 151 3 PFENNIG
Silver **Ruler:** Johann Georg I **Obv:** Heart-shaped 2-fold arms in baroque frame, value III above

Date	Mintage	VG	F	VF	XF	Unc
ND(1621)	—	9.00	25.00	55.00	110	—

KM# 153 3 PFENNIG
Silver **Ruler:** Johann Georg I **Rev:** Value III replaces date **Note:** Varieties exist.

Date	Mintage	VG	F	VF	XF	Unc
ND(1621)	—	9.00	25.00	55.00	110	—

KM# 143 3 PFENNIG
Silver **Ruler:** Johann Georg I **Obv:** 3 ornate shields of arms, 1 above 2, divide date **Rev:** 2 crossed swords above 3 in baroque frame

Date	Mintage	VG	F	VF	XF	Unc
1622	—	13.00	30.00	60.00	125	—

KM# 344 3 PFENNIG
Silver **Ruler:** Johann Georg I **Obv:** Ornate 2-fold arms **Rev:** Value: 3 on imperial orb divides date

Date	Mintage	VG	F	VF	XF	Unc
1622	—	9.00	25.00	55.00	110	—

KM# 345 3 PFENNIG
Silver **Ruler:** Johann Georg I **Obv:** 2 ornamented adjoining shields of arms **Rev:** Imperial orb in baroque frame divides date

Date	Mintage	VG	F	VF	XF	Unc
(16)22	—	9.00	25.00	55.00	110	—

KM# 445 3 PFENNIG
Silver **Obv:** Ornate oval 2-fold arms divide initials, date below **Rev:** Imperial orb with 3 **Rev. Legend:** OBER. SAX. KREISSES **Note:** Varieties exist.

Date	Mintage	VG	F	VF	XF	Unc
1656 CR	—	9.00	25.00	55.00	110	—
1659 CR	—	9.00	25.00	55.00	110	—
1660 CR	—	9.00	25.00	55.00	110	—
1661 CR	—	9.00	25.00	55.00	110	—
1662 CR	—	9.00	25.00	55.00	110	—
1663 CR	—	9.00	25.00	55.00	110	—
1664 CR	—	9.00	25.00	55.00	110	—
1665 CR	—	9.00	25.00	55.00	110	—

KM# 508 3 PFENNIG
Silver **Obv:** Angular shield of arms

Date	Mintage	VG	F	VF	XF	Unc
1665 CR	—	9.00	25.00	55.00	110	—

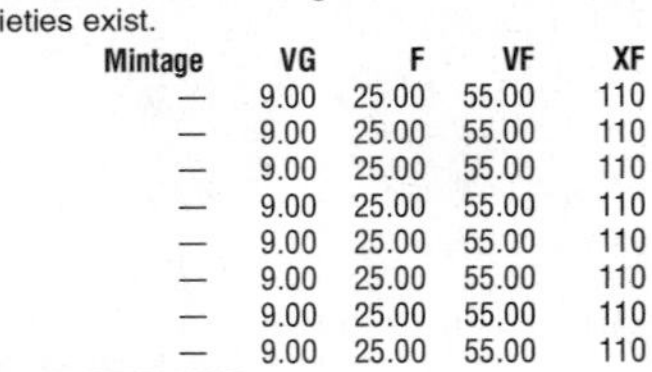

KM# 523 3 PFENNIG
Silver **Obv:** Oval 2-fold arms in baroque frame, date divided by acorn at bottom **Rev:** Imperial orb in baroque frame divides initials **Note:** Varieties exist.

Date	Mintage	VG	F	VF	XF	Unc
1669 CR	—	9.00	25.00	55.00	110	—
1679 CF	—	9.00	25.00	55.00	110	—

KM# 574 3 PFENNIG
Silver **Ruler:** Johann Georg III **Obv:** Crowned 2-fold arms between palm branches, date divided by 2 small fish below **Rev:** Imperial orb with 3 in baroque frame divides mintmaster's initials

Date	Mintage	VG	F	VF	XF	Unc
1681 CF	—	15.00	30.00	60.00	120	—
1682 CF	—	15.00	30.00	60.00	120	—

KM# 605 3 PFENNIG
Silver **Obv:** 2 adjacent oval arms in baroque frames, crown above divides initials **Rev:** Imperial orb with 3 in baroque frame divides date, crossed arrows below

Date	Mintage	VG	F	VF	XF	Unc
1690 IK	—	9.00	25.00	40.00	85.00	—
1691 IK	—	9.00	25.00	40.00	85.00	—

KM# 624 3 PFENNIG
Silver **Ruler:** Johann Georg IV **Obv:** 4 small crowned shields of arms, 1 in each angle of 2 crossed swords

Date	Mintage	VG	F	VF	XF	Unc
1692 IK	—	9.00	25.00	55.00	110	—
1693 IK	—	9.00	25.00	55.00	110	—

KM# 637 3 PFENNIG
Silver **Obv:** Initials in between arms, near bottom

Date	Mintage	VG	F	VF	XF	Unc
1693 IK	—	9.00	25.00	45.00	90.00	—
1694 IK	—	9.00	25.00	45.00	90.00	—

KM# 665 3 PFENNIG
Silver **Obv:** Crowned oval 2-fold arms between palm branches **Rev:** Imperial orb with 3 in baroque frame divides date, initials below

Date	Mintage	VG	F	VF	XF	Unc
1695 EPH	—	13.00	30.00	65.00	130	—
1696 EPH	—	13.00	30.00	65.00	130	—

KM# 664 3 PFENNIG
Silver **Obv:** Initials between arms near bottom **Note:** Similar to KM#637.

Date	Mintage	VG	F	VF	XF	Unc
1695 IK	—	9.00	25.00	45.00	90.00	—
1696 IK	—	9.00	25.00	45.00	90.00	—
1697 IK	—	9.00	25.00	45.00	90.00	—

KM# 711 3 PFENNIG
Silver, 18 mm. **Ruler:** Friedrich August I **Obv:** Crowned round 4-fold arms with central shield of 2-fold arms between 2 palm branches, initials below **Rev:** Value: 3 on imperial orb in baroque frame, date at top

Date	Mintage	VG	F	VF	XF	Unc
1699 ILH	—	15.00	30.00	60.00	120	—
1700 ILH	—	15.00	30.00	60.00	120	—

KM# 509 6 PFENNIG (Sechser)
Silver **Obv:** Crowned 2-fold arms in ornamented frame, date below **Rev:** Imperial orb with 6 divides initials **Rev. Legend:** OBER SAX KREISS

Date	Mintage	VG	F	VF	XF	Unc
1665 CR	—	33.00	60.00	100	210	—

KM# 155 3 KREUZER
Silver **Ruler:** Johann Georg I **Obv:** Heart-shaped arms

Date	Mintage	VG	F	VF	XF	Unc
ND(1621) (acorn)	—	33.00	65.00	130	275	—

KM# 163 3 KREUZER
Silver **Ruler:** Johann Georg I **Obv:** Oval shield of 2-fold arms **Rev:** Crowned imperial eagle, 3 in orb on breast, date divided by crown at top

Date	Mintage	VG	F	VF	XF	Unc
1621 SL	—	33.00	65.00	135	275	—

KM# 164 3 KREUZER
Silver **Ruler:** Johann Georg I **Obv:** Oval shield of 2-fold arms in baroque frame, angel's head above **Rev:** Crowned imperial eagle, 3 in orb on breast, date in legend **Mint:** Merseburg

Date	Mintage	VG	F	VF	XF	Unc
1621 (rooster)	—	33.00	65.00	130	265	—

KM# 165 3 KREUZER
Silver **Ruler:** Johann Georg I **Obv:** Round shield of 2-fold arms in baroque frame, angel's head above **Rev:** Crowned imperial eagle, 3 in orb on breast, date divided above crown

Date	Mintage	VG	F	VF	XF	Unc
(16)21	—	30.00	60.00	120	240	—
(16)Z1	—	30.00	60.00	120	240	—

KM# 166 3 KREUZER
Silver **Ruler:** Johann Georg I **Obv:** Round shield of 2-fold arms in plain circle, angel's head above **Rev:** Crowned imperial eagle, 3 on breast, date in legend

Date	Mintage	VG	F	VF	XF	Unc
(16)Z1	—	30.00	60.00	120	240	—

KM# 168 3 KREUZER
Silver **Ruler:** Johann Georg I **Obv:** Shield of 2 fold arms, date divided at top **Rev:** Crowned imperial eagle, 3 in orb on breast, date divided above

Date	Mintage	VG	F	VF	XF	Unc
(16)Z1//(16)Z1	—	30.00	60.00	120	240	—

KM# 169 3 KREUZER
Silver **Ruler:** Johann Georg I **Obv:** Oval shield of 2-fold arms in baroque frame **Rev:** Crowned imperial eagle, 3 in orb on breast, date divided by crown

Date	Mintage	VG	F	VF	XF	Unc
16Z1	—	30.00	60.00	120	240	—

KM# 154 3 KREUZER
Silver **Ruler:** Johann Georg I **Obv:** 2-fold arms in baroque frame **Rev:** Crowned imperial eagle, 3 in orb on breast, date above **Mint:** Bitterfeld **Note:** Kipper coinage.

Date	Mintage	VG	F	VF	XF	Unc
(16)21 (acorn)	—	25.00	50.00	100	200	—
ND(1621) (acorn)	—	25.00	50.00	100	200	—

KM# 156 3 KREUZER
Silver **Ruler:** Johann Georg I **Obv:** 2-fold arms in baroque frame **Rev:** Crowned imperial eagle, 3 in orb on breast, date divided above **Mint:** Eckartsberga **Note:** Kipper coinage.

Date	Mintage	VG	F	VF	XF	Unc
16Z1 EB	—	33.00	65.00	130	265	—

KM# 158 3 KREUZER
Silver **Ruler:** Johann Georg I **Obv:** 2-fold arms in baroque frame, date above **Rev:** Crowned imperial eagle, 3 in orb on breast, HAIN above **Mint:** Grossenhain **Note:** Kipper coinage.

Date	Mintage	VG	F	VF	XF	Unc
1621 (rosette)	—	33.00	65.00	135	275	—

KM# 160 3 KREUZER
5.0400 g., Silver **Ruler:** Johann Georg I **Note:** Kipper coinage.

Date	Mintage	VG	F	VF	XF	Unc
(16)21 (rosette)	—	40.00	75.00	150	300	—

KM# 161 3 KREUZER
Silver **Ruler:** Johann Georg I **Obv:** Oval shield of 2-fold arms **Rev:** Oval arms of Cleve with 3 **Note:** Kipper coinage.

Date	Mintage	VG	F	VF	XF	Unc
ND(1621) (rosette)	—	33.00	65.00	135	265	—

KM# 157 3 KREUZER
Silver **Ruler:** Johann Georg I **Obv:** 2-fold arms in baroque frame **Rev:** Crowned imperial eagle, 3 in orb on breast, date divided above **Mint:** Gommern **Note:** Kipper coinage. Varieties exist.

Date	Mintage	VG	F	VF	XF	Unc
(16)Z1 (star)	—	33.00	65.00	130	265	—
16Z1 (star)	—	33.00	65.00	130	265	—
1621 (star)	—	33.00	65.00	130	265	—
ND(1621) (star)	—	33.00	65.00	130	265	—

KM# 167 3 KREUZER
Silver **Ruler:** Johann Georg I **Obv:** Round shield of 2-fold arms in plain circle, angel's head above **Rev:** Crowned imperial eagle, 3 in orb on breast, date divided above **Note:** Klippe.

Date	Mintage	VG	F	VF	XF	Unc
(16)Z1	—	33.00	65.00	130	265	—

KM# 162 3 KREUZER
Silver **Ruler:** Johann Georg I **Obv:** Round shield of 2-fold arms **Rev:** Crowned imperial eagle, 3 in orb on breast, date in legend **Mint:** Leipzig **Note:** Kipper coinage.

Date	Mintage	VG	F	VF	XF	Unc
16Z1 SL	—	33.00	65.00	130	265	—
1621 SL	—	33.00	65.00	130	265	—

KM# 159 3 KREUZER
Silver **Ruler:** Johann Georg I **Obv:** Shield of 2-fold arms in baroque frame divides date **Rev:** Crowned imperial eagle, 3 in orb on breast **Note:** Kipper coinage.

Date	Mintage	VG	F	VF	XF	Unc
(16)21 (rosette)	—	33.00	65.00	135	275	—
ND(1621) (rosette)	—	33.00	65.00	135	275	—

KM# 512 3 KREUZER
Silver **Obv:** Bust right **Rev:** 3 in oval at bottom **Mint:** Bautzen **Note:** Coinage for Oberlausitz. Similar to 15 Kreuzer, KM#514.

Date	Mintage	VG	F	VF	XF	Unc
1666 HI	—	65.00	135	275	550	—

KM# 446 GROSCHEN (1/24 Thaler)
Silver **Subject:** Death of Johann Georg I **Obv:** Bust right holding sword over right shoulder **Rev:** 8-line inscription with Roman numeral dates

Date	Mintage	VG	F	VF	XF	Unc
MDCLVI (1656)	—	20.00	35.00	75.00	155	—

KM# 478 GROSCHEN (1/24 Thaler)
Silver **Subject:** Death of Johann Georg II's Mother, Magdalene Sibylle **Obv:** 7-line inscription **Rev:** 6-line inscription with Roman numeral dates

Date	Mintage	VG	F	VF	XF	Unc
1659 (acorn)	—	33.00	65.00	135	265	—

KM# 592 GROSCHEN (1/24 Thaler)
Silver **Subject:** Death of Johann Georg III's Mother, Magdalene Sibylle **Obv:** MANET in wreath, SOLA. SPES. MEA in band at top **Rev:** 7-line inscription with dates

Date	Mintage	VG	F	VF	XF	Unc
1687	—	30.00	55.00	110	220	—

KM# 608 GROSCHEN (1/24 Thaler)
Silver **Subject:** Death of Johann Georg III **Obv:** Arms from clouds holding partly furled flag **Obv. Legend:** IEHOVA VEXILLVM MEVM **Rev:** 7-line inscription with RN dates, value (symbol) in small circle at bottom **Mint:** Dresden

Date	Mintage	VG	F	VF	XF	Unc
MDCXCI (1691) IK	—	27.00	55.00	100	210	—

KM# 643 GROSCHEN (1/24 Thaler)
Silver **Subject:** Death of Johann Georg IV **Obv:** Pyramid with crowned shields of arms on 2 sides **Rev:** 6-line inscription with Roman numeral dates, 1 in small circle below

Date	Mintage	VG	F	VF	XF	Unc
MDCXCIV (1694) IK	—	27.00	55.00	100	210	—

MB# 309 1/24 THALER (Groschen)
Silver **Ruler:** Christian II, Johann Georg I and August **Obv:** 2 adjacent shields of ducal Saxony and Meissen arms, imperial orb above divides date, titles of the 3 brothers **Rev:** Helmeted electoral Saxony arms, titles continued **Mint:** Dresden **Note:** Varieties exist.

Date	Mintage	VG	F	VF	XF	Unc
(16)01 (HB)	—	32.00	60.00	100	200	—

KM# 11.2 1/24 THALER (Groschen)
Silver **Ruler:** Christian II, Johann Georg I and August **Obv:** 2 adjacent shields of arms (ducal Saxony and Thuringia), titles of 3 brothers **Rev:** Ornate helmet above arms of electoral Saxony, titles continued **Mint:** Dresden

Date	Mintage	VG	F	VF	XF	Unc
1603 HB	—	45.00	90.00	180	—	—
1604 HB	—	45.00	90.00	180	—	—

KM# 11.3 1/24 THALER (Groschen)
Silver **Ruler:** Christian II, Johann Georg I and August **Obv:** Ornate helmet above arms of electoral Saxony, titles of 3 brothers begin **Rev:** 2 adjacent shields of arms (ducal Saxony and Thuringia), small imperial orb above divides date, titles continued **Mint:** Dresden **Note:** Varieties exist.

Date	Mintage	VG	F	VF	XF	Unc
1605 HvR	—	35.00	70.00	140	—	—
1606 HvR	—	35.00	70.00	140	—	—
1607 HvR	—	35.00	70.00	140	—	—
1608 HvR	—	35.00	70.00	140	—	—
1610 HvR	—	35.00	70.00	140	—	—

KM# 11.4 1/24 THALER (Groschen)
Silver **Ruler:** Christian II, Johann Georg I and August **Obv:** Ornate helmet above arms of electoral Saxony, shortened titles of 3 brothers begin **Rev:** 2 adjacent shields of arms (ducal Saxony and Thuringia), small imperial orb above divides date, titles continued **Mint:** Dresden

Date	Mintage	VG	F	VF	XF	Unc
1610 swan	—	10.00	20.00	40.00	85.00	—
1611 swan	—	10.00	20.00	40.00	85.00	—

KM# 610A 1/24 THALER (Groschen)
Silver **Ruler:** Johann Georg IV **Obv:** 2 adjacent oval arms, crown above, mintmaster's initials below **Rev:** Value, date **Rev. Inscription:** 24 / EINEN / THAL ... **Mint:** Dresden

Date	Mintage	VG	F	VF	XF	Unc
1693 IK	—	8.00	15.00	35.00	70.00	—
1694 IK	—	8.00	15.00	35.00	70.00	—

KM# 513 6 KREUZER
Silver **Obv:** Bust right **Mint:** Bautzen **Note:** Coinage for Oberlausitz. Similar to 15 Kreuzer, KM#514 but VI in oval at bottom.

Date	Mintage	VG	F	VF	XF	Unc
1666 HI	—	—	—	—	—	—

KM# 242 2 GROSCHEN (1/12 Thaler)
Silver **Ruler:** Johann Georg I **Obv:** Ornate 2-fold arms **Rev:** 3 shields of arms, small imperial orb above, date divided at top **Mint:** Dresden **Note:** Kipper 2 Groschen.

Date	Mintage	VG	F	VF	XF	Unc
1621 (swan) Rare	—	—	—	—	—	—

KM# 609 2 GROSCHEN (1/12 Thaler)
Silver **Subject:** Death of Johann Georg III **Rev:** Value 2 in oval, symbol for Groschen

Date	Mintage	VG	F	VF	XF	Unc
MDCXCI (1691) IK	—	27.00	55.00	110	220	—

KM# 644 2 GROSCHEN (1/12 Thaler)
Silver **Subject:** Death of Johann Georg IV

Date	Mintage	VG	F	VF	XF	Unc
1694 IK	—	27.00	55.00	110	220	—
MDCXCIV (1694) IK	—	27.00	55.00	110	220	—

KM# 190 12 KREUZER
Silver **Ruler:** Johann Georg I **Rev:** 12 in orb on breast

Date	Mintage	VG	F	VF	XF	Unc
16Z1 NN	—	40.00	80.00	160	325	—

KM# 191 12 KREUZER
Silver **Ruler:** Johann Georg I **Obv:** Heart-shaped arms

Date	Mintage	VG	F	VF	XF	Unc
16Z1	—	45.00	90.00	180	360	—

KM# 192 12 KREUZER
Silver **Ruler:** Johann Georg I **Obv:** Oval arms

Date	Mintage	VG	F	VF	XF	Unc
16Z1	—	40.00	80.00	160	325	—

KM# 171 12 KREUZER
Silver **Ruler:** Johann Georg I **Obv:** Ornamented heart-shaped shield of arms **Rev:** Value (12) at bottom **Mint:** Grossenhain **Note:** Kipper coinage.

Date	Mintage	VG	F	VF	XF	Unc
1621 (rosette)	—	45.00	95.00	190	385	—

KM# 174 12 KREUZER
Silver **Ruler:** Johann Georg I **Rev:** Value 12 at bottom **Mint:** Langensalza **Note:** Kipper coinage.

Date	Mintage	VG	F	VF	XF	Unc
1621 (3 towers)	—	45.00	95.00	190	385	—

KM# 175 12 KREUZER
Silver **Ruler:** Johann Georg I **Obv:** Shield of arms nearly flat on top, rounded on bottom, value (1Z) below **Mint:** Merseburg **Note:** Kipper coinage.

Date	Mintage	VG	F	VF	XF	Unc
1621 (rooster)	—	45.00	90.00	180	360	—

KM# 173 12 KREUZER
Silver **Ruler:** Johann Georg I **Obv:** Oval shield of 2-fold arms, angel above **Rev:** 3 small shields of arms, 1 above 2, upper shield divides date

Date	Mintage	VG	F	VF	XF	Unc
ND(1621) (rosette)	—	45.00	90.00	180	360	—

KM# 185 12 KREUZER
Silver **Ruler:** Johann Georg I **Obv:** Heart-shaped arms **Rev:** T in shield at top

Date	Mintage	VG	F	VF	XF	Unc
1621 T	—	45.00	95.00	190	385	—

KM# 186 12 KREUZER
Silver **Ruler:** Johann Georg I **Rev:** Tree between 2 lower arms **Mint:** Tennstedt

Date	Mintage	VG	F	VF	XF	Unc
1621 (tree)	—	45.00	85.00	135	275	—

KM# 170 12 KREUZER
Silver **Ruler:** Johann Georg I **Obv:** Oval shield of 2-fold arms, angel above **Rev:** Crowned imperial eagle, 1Z in orb on breast, date in legend **Mint:** Bitterfeld **Note:** Kipper coinage. Varieties exist.

Date	Mintage	VG	F	VF	XF	Unc
16Z1 (acorn)	—	45.00	90.00	180	360	—

KM# 179 12 KREUZER
Silver **Ruler:** Johann Georg I **Obv:** Date above angel **Mint:** Pirna **Note:** Kipper coinage.

Date	Mintage	VG	F	VF	XF	Unc
1621 GS	—	45.00	90.00	180	360	—

KM# 182 12 KREUZER
Silver **Ruler:** Johann Georg I **Rev:** Without value indicated **Mint:** Schkeuditz **Note:** Kipper coinage.

Date	Mintage	VG	F	VF	XF	Unc
1621 SVH	—	45.00	90.00	180	360	—

KM# 176 12 KREUZER
Silver **Ruler:** Johann Georg I **Mint:** Langensalza **Note:** Klippe.

Date	Mintage	VG	F	VF	XF	Unc
1621 (rooster)	—	—	—	—	—	—

KM# 181 12 KREUZER
Silver **Ruler:** Johann Georg I **Mint:** Schkeuditz **Note:** Klippe.

Date	Mintage	VG	F	VF	XF	Unc
1621 SVH	—	—	—	—	—	—

KM# 183 12 KREUZER
Silver **Ruler:** Johann Georg I **Obv:** Oval arms **Mint:** Schkeuditz **Note:** Kipper coinage.

Date	Mintage	VG	F	VF	XF	Unc
1621 SVH	—	45.00	90.00	180	360	—
16Z1 SVH	—	45.00	90.00	180	360	—

KM# 172 12 KREUZER
Silver **Ruler:** Johann Georg I **Obv:** Oval arms **Rev:** With value **Note:** Kipper coinage. Varieties exist.

Date	Mintage	VG	F	VF	XF	Unc
1621 (rosette)	—	45.00	90.00	180	360	—
ND(1621) (rosette)	—	45.00	90.00	180	360	—

KM# 180 12 KREUZER
Silver **Ruler:** Johann Georg I **Rev:** 2 angels behind upper arms, date above, 12 in legend at bottom **Mint:** Schkeuditz **Note:** Kipper coinage. Varieties exist.

Date	Mintage	VG	F	VF	XF	Unc
1621 SVH	—	45.00	90.00	180	360	—
ND(1621) SVH	—	45.00	90.00	180	360	—

KM# 184 12 KREUZER
Silver **Ruler:** Johann Georg I **Rev:** T in small shield in legend at top divides date, where present **Mint:** Taucha **Note:** Kipper coinage. Varieties exist.

Date	Mintage	VG	F	VF	XF	Unc
1621 T	—	45.00	95.00	190	385	—
ND(1621) T	—	45.00	95.00	190	385	—

KM# 187 12 KREUZER
Silver **Ruler:** Johann Georg I **Rev:** Value (12) in legend at bottom

Date	Mintage	VG	F	VF	XF	Unc
1621 (tree)	—	45.00	95.00	190	385	—
16Z1 (tree)	—	45.00	95.00	190	385	—

KM# 188 12 KREUZER
Silver **Ruler:** Johann Georg I **Obv:** Heart-shaped arms **Rev:** Crowned imperial eagle, orb on breast with 1Z, date in legend **Mint:** Weida

Date	Mintage	VG	F	VF	XF	Unc
ND W	—	45.00	95.00	190	385	—

KM# 189 12 KREUZER
Silver **Ruler:** Johann Georg I **Obv:** 2-fold arms, angel above **Note:** Varieties exist.

Date	Mintage	VG	F	VF	XF	Unc
ND NN	—	40.00	80.00	160	325	—

KM# 177 12 KREUZER
Silver **Ruler:** Johann Georg I **Obv:** Crowned ornamented shield of 2-fold arms **Rev:** 3 small shields of arms, 1 above 2, upper shield divides date **Note:** Kipper coinage.

Date	Mintage	VG	F	VF	XF	Unc
1622 MB	—	45.00	90.00	180	360	—
1622 (rooster)	—	45.00	90.00	180	360	—

KM# 178 12 KREUZER
Silver Varieties exist. **Ruler:** Johann Georg I **Obv:** Heart-shaped shield of arms, angel above **Rev:** Crowned imperial eagle, 1Z in orb on breast, date in legend **Mint:** Naumburg **Note:** Kipper coinage.

Date	Mintage	VG	F	VF	XF	Unc
ND(1622) N	—	45.00	90.00	180	360	—

KM# 224 SCHRECKENBERGER (12 Kreuzer)
Silver **Ruler:** Johann Georg I **Obv:** Heart-shaped arms **Rev:** 2 angels behind upper arms, date above **Mint:** Dresden **Note:** Kipper coinage.

Date	Mintage	VG	F	VF	XF	Unc
1620 (swan)	—	100	200	375	775	—
1621 (swan)	—	100	200	375	775	—

KM# 225 SCHRECKENBERGER (12 Kreuzer)
Silver **Ruler:** Johann Georg I **Obv:** Arms almost oval **Mint:** Dresden **Note:** Kipper coinage.

Date	Mintage	VG	F	VF	XF	Unc
1620 (swan)	—	85.00	180	325	675	—
1621 (swan)	—	85.00	180	325	675	—

KM# 226 SCHRECKENBERGER (12 Kreuzer)
Silver **Ruler:** Johann Georg I **Obv:** Round arms **Mint:** Dresden **Note:** Kipper coinage.

Date	Mintage	VG	F	VF	XF	Unc
1621 (swan)	—	85.00	180	325	675	—
1622 (swan)	—	85.00	180	325	675	—

KM# 227 SCHRECKENBERGER (12 Kreuzer)
Silver **Ruler:** Johann Georg I **Obv:** Arms almost oval **Mint:** Eilenburg **Note:** Kipper coinage.

Date	Mintage	VG	F	VF	XF	Unc
1621 E	—	—	—	—	—	—
16Z1 E	—	—	—	—	—	—

KM# 228 SCHRECKENBERGER (12 Kreuzer)
Silver **Ruler:** Johann Georg I **Mint:** Gommern

Date	Mintage	VG	F	VF	XF	Unc
16Z1 (star)	—	—	—	—	—	—

KM# 223 SCHRECKENBERGER (12 Kreuzer)
Silver **Ruler:** Johann Georg I **Obv:** Oval 2-fold arms, angel above **Rev:** 3 small shields of arms, 1 above 2, upper shield divides date **Mint:** Bitterfeld **Note:** Kipper coinage. Varieties exist.

Date	Mintage	VG	F	VF	XF	Unc
1621 (acorn)	—	85.00	180	325	675	—
ND(1621) (acorn)	—	85.00	180	325	675	—

KM# 193 15 KREUZER (1/6 Thaler)
Silver **Ruler:** Johann Georg I **Mint:** Chemnitz **Note:** Kipper issue. Similar to 20 Groschen, KM#187 but 15 in small orb at top on reverse.

Date	Mintage	VG	F	VF	XF	Unc
1621 K	—	—	—	—	—	—

KM# 514 15 KREUZER (1/6 Thaler)
Silver **Ruler:** Johann Georg II **Mint:** Bautzen **Note:** Coinage for Oberlausitz.

Date	Mintage	VG	F	VF	XF	Unc
1666 HI	—	90.00	190	325	675	—
1667 HI	—	90.00	190	325	675	—

KM# 524 15 KREUZER (1/6 Thaler)
Silver **Note:** Coinage for Meissen. Struck at Leipzig. Similar to 60 Kreuzer, KM#526, but 15 in legend at bottom on reverse.

Date	Mintage	VG	F	VF	XF	Unc
1669	—	80.00	240	325	650	—

KM# A587 1/6 THALER
Silver, 27 mm. **Ruler:** Johann Georg III **Obv:** Armored bust to right **Obv. Legend:** IOH. GEORG. III. D. G. DUX. SAX. I. C. & M. **Rev:** Shield of 2-fold arms between 2 palm branches, date over electoral hat above, value (1/6) in oval below **Rev. Legend:** SAC. ROM. IIMP. AR - CHIM. ET ELECT. **Mint:** Dresden **Note:** Ref. Kohl 290.

Date	Mintage	VG	F	VF	XF	Unc
1682 CF	—	40.00	80.00	125	240	—

KM# 247 4 GROSCHEN
Silver **Ruler:** Johann Georg I **Obv:** Squarish arms **Rev:** 2 angels behind upper arms, date above **Note:** Kipper coinage.

Date	Mintage	VG	F	VF	XF	Unc
ND(1621) (4L)	—	30.00	60.00	125	255	—

KM# 251 4 GROSCHEN
Silver **Ruler:** Johann Georg I **Rev:** Mint symbol in legend at top **Note:** Kipper coinage.

Date	Mintage	VG	F	VF	XF	Unc
1621	—	30.00	60.00	120	240	—

KM# 244 4 GROSCHEN
Silver **Ruler:** Johann Georg I **Obv:** Oval 2-fold arms, angel above **Rev:** Crowned imperial eagle, orb with 4 on breast, date in legend **Mint:** Liebenwerda **Note:** Kipper coinage. Varieties exist.

Date	Mintage	VG	F	VF	XF	Unc
(16)Z1 LW	—	—	—	—	—	—

KM# 245 4 GROSCHEN
Silver **Ruler:** Johann Georg I **Obv:** Heart-shaped arms **Mint:** Liebenwerda **Note:** Kipper coinage. Varieties exist.

Date	Mintage	VG	F	VF	XF	Unc
(16)Z1 LW	—	—	—	—	—	—

KM# 248 4 GROSCHEN
Silver **Ruler:** Johann Georg I **Obv:** Date above angel **Rev:** Crowned imperial eagle, 4 in orb on eagle's breast **Mint:** Pirna **Note:** Varieties exist.

Date	Mintage	VG	F	VF	XF	Unc
1621 GS	—	35.00	75.00	150	300	—

KM# 246 4 GROSCHEN
Silver **Ruler:** Johann Georg I **Rev:** 3 small shields of arms, 1 above 2, upper shield divides date **Mint:** Lutzen **Note:** Kipper coinage. Varieties exist.

Date	Mintage	VG	F	VF	XF	Unc
1621 (4L) WQ	—	35.00	75.00	150	300	—
1621 (4L)	—	35.00	75.00	150	300	—
ND(1621) (4L)	—	35.00	75.00	150	300	—

KM# 249 4 GROSCHEN
Silver **Ruler:** Johann Georg I **Mint:** Zwickau **Note:** Similar to 8 Groschen, KM#359, but value 4 gr at bottom on reverse. Kipper coinage.

Date	Mintage	VG	F	VF	XF	Unc
1622 (anchor & 3 swans)	—	35.00	75.00	150	300	—

KM# 243 4 GROSCHEN
Silver **Ruler:** Johann Georg I **Obv:** Crowned ornamented 2-fold arms, value 4 gr. below **Rev:** 3 small shields of arms, 1 above 2, upper shield divides date **Mint:** Leipzig

Date	Mintage	VG	F	VF	XF	Unc
1622 SL	—	35.00	75.00	150	300	—

KM# 250 4 GROSCHEN
Silver **Ruler:** Johann Georg I **Mint:** Grossenhain

Date	Mintage	VG	F	VF	XF	Unc
1622 (rosette)	—	30.00	60.00	125	250	—

KM# 252 5 GROSCHEN
Silver **Ruler:** Johann Georg I **Obv:** Heart-shaped 2-fold arms in baroque frame, angel below **Rev:** 3 small arms, 1 above 2, angels at left and right of upper shield, date above, value 5 at bottom **Mint:** Dresden **Note:** Kipper 5 Groschen. Similar to 20 Groschen, KM#253.

Date	Mintage	VG	F	VF	XF	Unc
1622 (swan)	—	—	—	—	—	—

MB# 310 1/4 THALER
Silver **Ruler:** Christian II, Johann Georg I and August **Obv:** 1/2-length facing figures of 3 brothers in circle, head of middle figure divides date, small imperial orb above, titles in legend **Rev:** Spade-shaped 2-fold arms of electoral and ducal Saxony in ornate frame, titles continued **Mint:** Dresden **Note:** Varieties exist.

Date	Mintage	VG	F	VF	XF	Unc
1601	—	30.00	55.00	110	220	—

KM# 449.2 1/4 THALER
Silver **Ruler:** Johann Georg II **Obv:** Bust right without sword **Rev:** Crowned oval 2-fold arms in baroque frame divide mintmaster's initials near bottom, titles continued in legend ending with date in upper left **Mint:** Dresden

Date	Mintage	VG	F	VF	XF	Unc
1670 CR	—	—	—	—	—	—
1671 CR	—	—	—	—	—	—

KM# 230 2 SCHRECKENBERGER (24 Kreuzer)
Silver **Ruler:** Johann Georg I **Obv:** Oval 2-fold arms, angel above **Rev:** Crowned imperial eagle, orb on breast, date in legend **Mint:** Eilenburg

Date	Mintage	VG	F	VF	XF	Unc
1621 E	—	30.00	65.00	130	265	—

KM# 231 2 SCHRECKENBERGER (24 Kreuzer)
Silver **Ruler:** Johann Georg I **Obv:** Arms almost oval **Rev:** 2 angels behind upper arms, date above. **Mint:** Gommern

Date	Mintage	VG	F	VF	XF	Unc
16Z1 (star)	—	30.00	65.00	130	265	—
(16)Z1 (star)	—	30.00	65.00	130	265	—

KM# 232 2 SCHRECKENBERGER (24 Kreuzer)
Silver **Ruler:** Johann Georg I **Obv:** Heart-shaped arms **Mint:** Leipzig

Date	Mintage	VG	F	VF	XF	Unc
(16)Z1 (4L)	—	30.00	65.00	130	265	—
16Z1 (4L)	—	30.00	65.00	130	265	—

KM# 234 2 SCHRECKENBERGER (24 Kreuzer)
Silver **Ruler:** Johann Georg I **Obv:** Heart-shaped arms **Rev:** 3 small shields of arms, 1 above 2, upper shield divides date **Mint:** Sangerhausen

Date	Mintage	VG	F	VF	XF	Unc
1621 S	—	30.00	60.00	120	220	—

KM# 237 2 SCHRECKENBERGER (24 Kreuzer)
Silver **Ruler:** Johann Georg I **Obv:** Oval 2-fold arms, angel above **Mint:** Zwickau

Date	Mintage	VG	F	VF	XF	Unc
1621 (anchor/3 swans)	—	30.00	65.00	130	265	—

KM# 229 2 SCHRECKENBERGER (24 Kreuzer)
Silver **Ruler:** Johann Georg I **Obv:** Ornamented heart-shaped 2-fold arms, angel above **Rev:** 3 small arms, 1 above 2, angels left and right of upper shield, date divided by lower 2 shields **Mint:** Chemnitz **Note:** Kipper 2 Schreckenberger.

Date	Mintage	VG	F	VF	XF	Unc
1621 K	—	30.00	65.00	130	265	—

KM# 233 2 SCHRECKENBERGER (24 Kreuzer)
Silver **Ruler:** Johann Georg I **Obv:** Arms almost oval **Mint:** Pirna **Note:** Kipper coinage.

Date	Mintage	VG	F	VF	XF	Unc
1621 GS	—	30.00	65.00 130,265		220	—

KM# 235 2 SCHRECKENBERGER (24 Kreuzer)
Silver **Ruler:** Johann Georg I **Obv:** Ornamented heart-shaped 2-fold arms, angel above **Rev:** 3 small arms, 1 above 2, angels left and right of upper shield, date above arms **Note:** Kipper coinage.

Date	Mintage	VG	F	VF	XF	Unc
16Z1 W	—	30.00	65.00	130	265	—

KM# 236 2 SCHRECKENBERGER (24 Kreuzer)
Silver **Ruler:** Johann Georg I **Obv:** Heart-shaped arms, angel above **Rev:** 3 small shields of arms, 1 above 2, upper shield divides date **Note:** Kipper coinage.

Date	Mintage	VG	F	VF	XF	Unc
16Z1 W	—	30.00	65.00	130	265	—

KM# 238 2 SCHRECKENBERGER (24 Kreuzer)
Silver **Ruler:** Johann Georg I **Obv:** Heart-shaped arms **Rev:** 2 angels behind upper arms, date in legend **Note:** Kipper coinage.

Date	Mintage	VG	F	VF	XF	Unc
16Z1	—	30.00	60.00	120	240	—

KM# 240 2 SCHRECKENBERGER (24 Kreuzer)
Silver **Ruler:** Johann Georg I **Rev:** 3 small shields of arms, 1 above 2, upper shield divides date **Note:** Kipper coinage.

Date	Mintage	VG	F	VF	XF	Unc
1621	—	30.00	65.00	135	275	—

KM# 241 2 SCHRECKENBERGER (24 Kreuzer)
Silver **Ruler:** Johann Georg I **Rev:** 3 arms are round **Note:** Kipper coinage.

Date	Mintage	VG	F	VF	XF	Unc
ND(1621) (3 small rings)	—	27.00	55.00	115	230	—

KM# 239 2 SCHRECKENBERGER (24 Kreuzer)
Silver **Ruler:** Johann Georg I **Rev:** 2 angels behind upper arms, date above **Note:** Kipper coinage. Varieties exist.

Date	Mintage	VG	F	VF	XF	Unc
16Z1 (bear above shield)	—	30.00	60.00	125	255	—
1621	—	30.00	60.00	125	255	—
ND(1621)	—	30.00	60.00	125	255	—

KM# 202 24 KREUZER (8 Groschen)
Silver **Ruler:** Johann Georg I **Obv:** Value (24) in legend at bottom **Mint:** Sangerhausen

Date	Mintage	VG	F	VF	XF	Unc
1621	—	45.00	90.00	200	385	—
1621 S	—	45.00	90.00	200	385	—

KM# 207 24 KREUZER (8 Groschen)
Silver **Ruler:** Johann Georg I **Obv:** Heart-shaped arms, angel above **Rev:** 3 small shields of arms, 1 above 2, upper shield divides date, tree between lower shields **Mint:** Tennstedt

Date	Mintage	VG	F	VF	XF	Unc
1621 (tree)	—	65.00	135	275	550	—

KM# 208 24 KREUZER (8 Groschen)
Silver **Ruler:** Johann Georg I **Obv:** Arms almost oval **Rev:** 2 angels behind upper arms, date above **Mint:** Weida

Date	Mintage	VG	F	VF	XF	Unc
ND W	—	45.00	95.00	190	385	—
16Z1 W	—	45.00	95.00	190	385	—

KM# 194 24 KREUZER (8 Groschen)
Silver **Ruler:** Johann Georg I **Obv:** Oval 2-fold arms, angel above. **Rev:** Crowned imperial eagle, orb on breast **Mint:** Bitterfeld **Note:** Kipper 24 Kreuzer.

Date	Mintage	VG	F	VF	XF	Unc
16Z1 (acorn)	—	55.00	110	220	425	—

KM# 195 24 KREUZER (8 Groschen)
Silver **Ruler:** Johann Georg I **Rev:** 3 small shield of arms, 1 above 2 **Note:** Kipper coinage.

Date	Mintage	VG	F	VF	XF	Unc
ND (acorn)	—	—	—	—	—	—

KM# 198 24 KREUZER (8 Groschen)
Silver **Ruler:** Johann Georg I **Obv:** Heart-shaped arms **Note:** Kipper coinage.

Date	Mintage	VG	F	VF	XF	Unc
1621 (3 towers)	—	60.00	120	235	475	—

KM# 204 24 KREUZER (8 Groschen)
Silver **Ruler:** Johann Georg I **Rev:** Date in legend **Note:** Kipper coinage.

Date	Mintage	VG	F	VF	XF	Unc
(16)21 SVH	—	45.00	90.00	200	385	—

KM# 209 24 KREUZER (8 Groschen)
Silver **Ruler:** Johann Georg I **Obv:** Heart-shaped arms, angel above **Rev:** Crowned imperial eagle, orb on breast with Z4, date in legend **Note:** Kipper coinage.

Date	Mintage	VG	F	VF	XF	Unc
ND(1621) NN	—	40.00	80.00	160	325	—

KM# 205 24 KREUZER (8 Groschen)
Silver **Ruler:** Johann Georg I **Obv:** Value (24) at bottom **Rev:** Without angels **Note:** Kipper coinage. Varieties exist.

Date	Mintage	VG	F	VF	XF	Unc
1621 SVH	—	45.00	90.00	200	385	—
1622 SVH	—	45.00	90.00	200	385	—

KM# 210 24 KREUZER (8 Groschen)
Silver **Ruler:** Johann Georg I **Obv:** Mule. **Rev:** Mule **Note:** Obverse of KM#194. Kipper coinage.

Date	Mintage	VG	F	VF	XF	Unc
ND cross with 2 points above	—	40.00	80.00	160	325	—

KM# 201 24 KREUZER (8 Groschen)
Silver **Ruler:** Johann Georg I **Obv:** Ornamented heart-shaped 2-fold arms, angel above **Rev:** Date above arms, value Z4 in small orb at top in legend **Mint:** Naumburg **Note:** Varieties exist.

Date	Mintage	VG	F	VF	XF	Unc
ND N	—	45.00	90.00	200	385	—
1621 N	—	45.00	90.00	200	385	—
16Z1 N	—	45.00	90.00	200	385	—

KM# 203 24 KREUZER (8 Groschen)
Silver **Ruler:** Johann Georg I **Obv:** Heart-shaped arms, angel above **Rev:** 2 angels behind upper arms, date above **Mint:** Schkeuditz **Note:** Varieties exist.

Date	Mintage	VG	F	VF	XF	Unc
ND SVH	—	45.00	90.00	200	385	—
(16)21 SVH	—	45.00	90.00	200	385	—
1621 SVH	—	45.00	90.00	200	385	—

KM# 206 24 KREUZER (8 Groschen)
Silver **Ruler:** Johann Georg I **Obv:** Oval 2-fold arms, angel above **Rev:** Date divided at top **Mint:** Taucha **Note:** Varieties exist.

Date	Mintage	VG	F	VF	XF	Unc
1621 T	—	65.00	135	275	550	—

KM# 196 24 KREUZER (8 Groschen)
Silver **Ruler:** Johann Georg I **Obv:** Ornamented heart-shaped arms, angel above **Rev:** 2 angels behind upper arms, date above, 24 in legend **Mint:** Grossenhain

Date	Mintage	VG	F	VF	XF	Unc
1621 (rooster)	—	65.00	135	275	475	—
1621 MB	—	65.00	135	275	475	—

KM# 197 24 KREUZER (8 Groschen)
Silver **Ruler:** Johann Georg I **Obv:** Oval 2-fold arms, angel above **Rev:** 3 small shields of arms, 1 above 2, upper shield divides date, value (24) at bottom **Mint:** Langensalza

Date	Mintage	VG	F	VF	XF	Unc
1621 (3 towers)	—	60.00	120	235	475	—

KM# 199 24 KREUZER (8 Groschen)
Silver **Ruler:** Johann Georg I **Obv:** Arms nearly flat on top, rounded on bottom, and (Z4) below **Mint:** Merseburg

Date	Mintage	VG	F	VF	XF	Unc
1622 (rooster)	—	55.00	110	210	425	—

KM# 200 24 KREUZER (8 Groschen)
Silver **Ruler:** Johann Georg I **Obv:** Crowned ornamented 2-fold arms, value (24) below **Note:** Kipper coinage.

Date	Mintage	VG	F	VF	XF	Unc
1622 (rooster)	—	55.00	110	210	425	—
ND(1622) (rooster)	—	55.00	110	210	425	—

KM# 212 30 KREUZER (1/3 Thaler)
Silver **Ruler:** Johann Georg I **Rev:** Value 30 in small orb at top **Mint:** Grossenhain

Date	Mintage	VG	F	VF	XF	Unc
1621 (rosette)	—	45.00	90.00	180	360	—

KM# 213 30 KREUZER (1/3 Thaler)
Silver **Ruler:** Johann Georg I **Obv:** Ornamented heart-shaped 2-fold arms, angel above, value 30 in orb **Rev:** 3 small shields of arms, 1 above 2, angels at sides of upper shield, date divided by lower 2 shields **Mint:** Naumburg

Date	Mintage	VG	F	VF	XF	Unc
1621 N	—	45.00	95.00	190	385	—

KM# 214 30 KREUZER (1/3 Thaler)
Silver **Ruler:** Johann Georg I **Obv:** Ornamented heart-shaped arms **Rev:** 2 arms above 1, lower arms divides date **Mint:** Pirna

Date	Mintage	VG	F	VF	XF	Unc
1621 GS	—	45.00	95.00	190	385	—

KM# 215 30 KREUZER (1/3 Thaler)
Silver **Ruler:** Johann Georg I **Obv:** Oval 2-fold arms, angel above, value 30 in legend **Rev:** 3 small shields of arms, 1 above 2, upper shield divides date **Mint:** Sangerhausen

Date	Mintage	VG	F	VF	XF	Unc
1621 S	—	45.00	90.00	180	360	—

KM# 216 30 KREUZER (1/3 Thaler)
Silver **Ruler:** Johann Georg I **Obv:** Heart-shaped arms **Rev:** 2 arms above 1, lower arms divide date **Mint:** Schkeuditz

Date	Mintage	VG	F	VF	XF	Unc
1621 SH-S	—	55.00	110	200	425	—

KM# 217 30 KREUZER (1/3 Thaler)
Silver **Ruler:** Johann Georg I **Obv:** Oval 2-fold arms, angel above **Rev:** Crowned imperial eagle, orb with 30 on breast, date in legend **Mint:** Taucha

Date	Mintage	VG	F	VF	XF	Unc
1621 T	—	45.00	90.00	180	385	—

KM# 218 30 KREUZER (1/3 Thaler)
Silver **Ruler:** Johann Georg I **Obv:** Heart-shaped arms, angel above **Rev:** 3 small shields of arms, 1 above 2, upper shield divides date, 30 in legend at top **Mint:** Tennstedt

Date	Mintage	VG	F	VF	XF	Unc
1621 (tree)	—	55.00	110	200	425	—

KM# 219 30 KREUZER (1/3 Thaler)
Silver **Ruler:** Johann Georg I **Rev:** Crowned imperial eagle, orb with 30 on breast, date in legend

Date	Mintage	VG	F	VF	XF	Unc
ND(1621)	—	33.00	65.00	135	275	—

KM# 211 30 KREUZER (1/3 Thaler)
Silver **Ruler:** Johann Georg I **Obv:** Oval arms, angel above. **Rev:** Crowned imperial eagle with 30 in orb on breast, date in legend **Mint:** Eilenburg **Note:** Kipper 30 Kreuzer.

Date	Mintage	VG	F	VF	XF	Unc
1621 E	—	45.00	90.00	180	360	—

KM# 220 30 KREUZER (1/3 Thaler)
Silver **Ruler:** Johann Georg I **Note:** Similar to KM#217.

Date	Mintage	VG	F	VF	XF	Unc
ND(1621)	—	33.00	65.00	135	275	—

KM# 525.1 30 KREUZER (1/3 Thaler)
Silver **Obv:** Bust right **Rev:** Shields of arms **Mint:** Leipzig **Note:** Coinage for Meissen.

Date	Mintage	VG	F	VF	XF	Unc
1669	—	60.00	120	235	475	—

KM# 525.2 30 KREUZER (1/3 Thaler)
Silver **Ruler:** Johann Georg II **Obv:** Bust right **Rev:** Shields of arms, date below **Mint:** Leipzig **Note:** Coinage for Meissen.

Date	Mintage	VG	F	VF	XF	Unc
1669	—	—	—	—	—	—

KM# 525.3 30 KREUZER (1/3 Thaler)
Silver **Ruler:** Johann Georg II **Obv:** Bust right **Rev:** Date divided by hat above arms **Mint:** Leipzig **Note:** Coinage for Meissen.

Date	Mintage	VG	F	VF	XF	Unc
1669	—	—	—	—	—	—

KM# 352 8 GROSCHEN (1/3 Thaler)
Silver **Ruler:** Johann Georg I **Obv:** Crowned 2-fold arms in baroque frame, value at bottom in legend **Mint:** Annaberg **Note:** Kipper coinage.

Date	Mintage	VG	F	VF	XF	Unc
1622 (acorn)	—	30.00	60.00	120	240	—
1623 (acorn)	—	30.00	60.00	120	240	—
16Z3 (acorn)	—	30.00	60.00	120	240	—

KM# 356 8 GROSCHEN (1/3 Thaler)
Silver **Ruler:** Johann Georg I **Rev:** Value at bottom **Mint:** Naumburg **Note:** Kipper coinage.

Date	Mintage	VG	F	VF	XF	Unc
16ZZ N	—	30.00	60.00	125	255	—

KM# 361 8 GROSCHEN (1/3 Thaler)
Silver **Ruler:** Johann Georg I **Note:** Kipper coinage.

Date	Mintage	VG	F	VF	XF	Unc
16ZZ (rosette)	—	20.00	45.00	90.00	185	—
1622 (rosette)	—	20.00	45.00	90.00	185	—
16ZZ (rosette/star)	—	20.00	45.00	90.00	185	—
1622 (:8:)	—	20.00	45.00	90.00	155	—

KM# 349 8 GROSCHEN (1/3 Thaler)
Silver **Ruler:** Johann Georg I **Mint:** Annaberg **Note:** Kipper coinage. Similar to 20 Groschen, KM#253, but value (8gr) at bottom of obverse.

Date	Mintage	VG	F	VF	XF	Unc
1622 (acorn)	—	30.00	60.00	120	240	—

KM# 357 8 GROSCHEN (1/3 Thaler)
Silver **Ruler:** Johann Georg I **Obv:** Large, ornately-shaped arms. **Mint:** Naumburg **Note:** Kipper coinage. Varieties exist.

Date	Mintage	VG	F	VF	XF	Unc
16ZZ N	—	30.00	65.00	130	265	—

KM# 347 8 GROSCHEN (1/3 Thaler)
Silver **Ruler:** Johann Georg I **Mint:** Leipzig **Note:** Klippe.

Date	Mintage	VG	F	VF	XF	Unc
1622 SL	—	—	—	—	—	—

KM# 354 8 GROSCHEN (1/3 Thaler)
3.7500 g., Silver, 28 mm. **Ruler:** Johann Georg I **Obv:** Crowned ornate shield of 2-fold arms in baroque frame **Obv. Legend:** IOHA: GEORG. D: G .DVX. S. IV. G. E. **Rev:** 3 small shields of arms, 1 above 2, upper shield divides date, value '8 gl' below in margin **Rev. Legend:** SA. ROM. IMPE.: - :.ARC. M. ET ELE. **Mint:** Ehrenfriedersdorf **Note:** Rahneführer 188. Kipper coinage. Varieties exist.

Date	Mintage	VG	F	VF	XF	Unc
1622 (ring)	—	55.00	100	175	325	—

KM# 355 8 GROSCHEN (1/3 Thaler)
Silver **Ruler:** Johann Georg I **Mint:** Neustadt an der Orla **Note:** Similar to KM#359, but value at bottom on obverse.

Date	Mintage	VG	F	VF	XF	Unc
1622 N - HT	—	30.00	60.00	125	255	—

KM# 358 8 GROSCHEN (1/3 Thaler)
Silver **Ruler:** Johann Georg I **Mint:** Pirna **Note:** Similar to KM#359.

Date	Mintage	VG	F	VF	XF	Unc
1622 GS	—	30.00	65.00	130	265	—

KM# 346 8 GROSCHEN (1/3 Thaler)
Silver **Ruler:** Johann Georg I **Obv:** Crowned ornamented 2-fold arms, value 8 gr below **Rev:** 3 small shields of arms, 1 above 2, upper shield divides date **Mint:** Leipzig **Note:** Varieties exist.

Date	Mintage	VG	F	VF	XF	Unc
1622 SL	—	35.00	75.00	155	315	—
16ZZ SL	—	35.00	75.00	155	315	—

KM# 353 8 GROSCHEN (1/3 Thaler)
Silver **Ruler:** Johann Georg I **Obv:** Crowned ornamented 2-fold arms, value 8 gr below **Mint:** Chemnitz **Note:** Varieties exist.

Date	Mintage	VG	F	VF	XF	Unc
1622 K	—	30.00	60.00	125	255	—
16ZZ K	—	30.00	60.00	125	255	—

KM# 359 8 GROSCHEN (1/3 Thaler)
Silver **Ruler:** Johann Georg I **Mint:** Weida **Note:** Varieties exist.

Date	Mintage	VG	F	VF	XF	Unc
16ZZ W	—	30.00	60.00	125	255	—

KM# 348 8 GROSCHEN (1/3 Thaler)
Silver **Ruler:** Johann Georg I **Obv:** Value 8 at top **Mint:** Leipzig

Date	Mintage	VG	F	VF	XF	Unc
1622 SL	—	35.00	75.00	155	315	—

KM# 360 8 GROSCHEN (1/3 Thaler)
Silver **Ruler:** Johann Georg I **Mint:** Zwickau

Date	Mintage	VG	F	VF	XF	Unc
1622 (anchor/3 swan)	—	30.00	60.00	125	255	—

KM# 350 8 GROSCHEN (1/3 Thaler)
Silver **Ruler:** Johann Georg I **Rev:** Value at bottom **Mint:** Annaberg **Note:** Kipper coinage.

Date	Mintage	VG	F	VF	XF	Unc
1622 (acorn)	—	30.00	60.00	120	240	—

KM# 351 8 GROSCHEN (1/3 Thaler)
Silver **Ruler:** Johann Georg I **Obv:** Crowned ornamented 2-fold arms **Rev:** 3 small shields, 1 above 2, upper shield divides date **Mint:** Annaberg **Note:** Kipper coinage.

Date	Mintage	VG	F	VF	XF	Unc
1622 (acorn)	—	30.00	60.00	120	240	—
16ZZ (acorn)	—	30.00	60.00	120	240	—

KM# 527.2 8 GROSCHEN (1/3 Thaler)
Silver **Ruler:** August I **Obv:** Bust right in inner circle **Rev:** Date divided by crown above arms

Date	Mintage	VG	F	VF	XF	Unc
1669	—	—	—	—	—	—

KM# 527.1 8 GROSCHEN (1/3 Thaler)
Silver **Obv:** Bust right in inner circle **Rev:** Value (8gr) and date below arms **Mint:** Leipzig **Note:** Coinage for Meissen. Prev. KM#527.

Date	Mintage	VG	F	VF	XF	Unc
1669	—	135	275	475	950	—

KM# A362 10 GROSCHEN
Silver **Note:** Kipper 10 Groschen. Struck at Annaberg. Similar to 20 Groschen, KM#253, but value (10gr) on obverse. Prev. KM#362.

Date	Mintage	VG	F	VF	XF	Unc
1622 (acorn)	—	45.00	90.00	180	360	—

KM# A363 10 GROSCHEN
Silver **Obv:** Round arms **Mint:** Dresden **Note:** Prev. KM#363.

Date	Mintage	VG	F	VF	XF	Unc
1622 (swan)	—	45.00	90.00	180	360	—
16ZZ (swan)	—	45.00	90.00	180	360	—
1623 (swan)	—	45.00	90.00	180	360	—

KM# A364 10 GROSCHEN
Silver **Obv:** Round arms **Note:** Similar to 8 Groschen, KM#359, but value: 10gr. Prev. KM#364.

Date	Mintage	VG	F	VF	XF	Unc
1622 (swan)	—	45.00	90.00	180	360	—
1623 (swan)	—	45.00	90.00	180	360	—

KM# 221 60 KREUZER (2/3 Thaler)
Silver **Ruler:** Johann Georg I **Obv:** Heart-shaped 2-fold arms, angel above (60) at bottom **Rev:** 3 small shields of arms, 1 above 2, date divided by upper arms, T in shield at bottom **Mint:** Taucha **Note:** Kipper coinage.

Date	Mintage	VG	F	VF	XF	Unc
1621 T	—	—	—	—	—	—

KM# 526 60 KREUZER (2/3 Thaler)
Silver **Mint:** Leipzig **Note:** Coinage for Meissen.

Date	Mintage	VG	F	VF	XF	Unc
1669	—	100	200	375	775	—
1670	—	100	200	375	775	—

KM# 256 20 GROSCHEN
Silver **Ruler:** Johann Georg I **Obv:** Heart-shaped 2-fold arms **Mint:** Dresden **Note:** Kipper coinage.

Date	Mintage	VG	F	VF	XF	Unc
1620 (swan)	—	55.00	115	235	475	—

KM# 257 20 GROSCHEN
Silver **Ruler:** Johann Georg I **Obv:** Arms nearly flat on top, curved on bottom **Mint:** Dresden **Note:** Varieties exist.

Date	Mintage	VG	F	VF	XF	Unc
1620 (swan)	—	35.00	75.00	150	300	—
1621 (swan)	—	35.00	75.00	150	300	—
16Z1 (swan)	—	35.00	75.00	150	300	—
1622 (swan)	—	35.00	75.00	150	300	—

KM# 253 20 GROSCHEN
Silver **Ruler:** Johann Georg I **Obv:** Heart-shaped 2-fold arms in baroque frame, angel below, value: 20gr in legend at bottom **Rev:** 3 small arms, 1 above 2, angels at left and right of upper shield, date above **Mint:** Annaberg **Note:** Kipper coinage.

Date	Mintage	VG	F	VF	XF	Unc
1621 (acorn)	—	45.00	90.00	180	360	—

KM# 258 20 GROSCHEN
Silver **Ruler:** Johann Georg I **Obv:** Without indication of value. Hybrid strike **Mint:** Dresden **Note:** Kipper coinage.

Date	Mintage	VG	F	VF	XF	Unc
1621 (swan)	—	35.00	75.00	150	300	—

KM# 260 20 GROSCHEN
Silver **Ruler:** Johann Georg I **Obv:** Arms nearly flat on top, curved on bottom divide date **Mint:** Merseburg **Note:** Kipper coinage.

Date	Mintage	VG	F	VF	XF	Unc
1621 (rooster)	—	45.00	90.00	180	360	—

KM# 261 20 GROSCHEN
Silver **Ruler:** Johann Georg I **Rev:** 3 small arms, 1 above 2, angels at left and right of upper shield, date above **Mint:** Merseburg **Note:** Kipper coinage.

Date	Mintage	VG	F	VF	XF	Unc
1621 (rooster)	—	45.00	90.00	180	360	—

KM# 263 20 GROSCHEN
Silver **Ruler:** Johann Georg I **Mint:** Pirna **Note:** Kipper coinage.

Date	Mintage	VG	F	VF	XF	Unc
1621 GS	—	55.00	115	235	475	—

KM# 264 20 GROSCHEN
Silver **Ruler:** Johann Georg I **Obv:** Value in legend at top **Mint:** Zwickau **Note:** Kipper coinage.

Date	Mintage	VG	F	VF	XF	Unc
1621 (anchor & 3 swans)	—	35.00	75.00	150	300	—
1622 (anchor & 3 swans)	—	35.00	75.00	150	300	—

KM# 265 20 GROSCHEN
Silver **Ruler:** Johann Georg I **Mint:** Zwickau **Note:** Kipper coinage. Klippe.

Date	Mintage	VG	F	VF	XF	Unc
1621 (anchor & 3 swans)	—	—	—	—	—	—

KM# 254 20 GROSCHEN
Silver **Ruler:** Johann Georg I **Obv:** Arms nearly flat on top , curved on bottom **Mint:** Annaberg **Note:** Kipper coinage. Varieties exist.

Date	Mintage	VG	F	VF	XF	Unc
1621 (acorn)	—	45.00	90.00	180	360	—
1622 (acorn)	—	45.00	90.00	180	360	—

KM# 262 20 GROSCHEN
Silver **Ruler:** Johann Georg I **Obv:** Arms nearly flat on top, curved on bottom **Mint:** Naumburg **Note:** Kipper coinage.

Date	Mintage	VG	F	VF	XF	Unc
1621 N	—	55.00	115	235	475	—
16Z1 N	—	55.00	115	235	475	—

KM# 259 20 GROSCHEN
Silver **Ruler:** Johann Georg I **Obv:** Oval 2-fold arms in baroque frame, angel below, value 20 gr in legend at bottom **Rev:** 3 small arms, 1 above 2, angels at left and right of upper shield, date above **Mint:** Leipzig **Note:** Similar to KM#253, but oval arms on obverse. Kipper coinage.

Date	Mintage	VG	F	VF	XF	Unc
1622 SL	—	55.00	115	235	475	—

KM# 255 20 GROSCHEN
Silver **Ruler:** Johann Georg I **Mint:** Chemnitz **Note:** Kipper coinage.

Date	Mintage	VG	F	VF	XF	Unc
1622 K	—	55.00	115	235	475	—

KM# 272 30 GROSCHEN
Silver **Ruler:** Johann Georg I **Mint:** Naumburg **Note:** Kipper coinage.

Date	Mintage	VG	F	VF	XF	Unc
1621 N	—	45.00	90.00	180	360	—

KM# 277 30 GROSCHEN
Silver **Ruler:** Johann Georg I **Rev:** T in small shield **Mint:** Taucha **Note:** Kipper coinage.

Date	Mintage	VG	F	VF	XF	Unc
1621 T	—	60.00	120	235	475	—

KM# 273 30 GROSCHEN
Silver **Ruler:** Johann Georg I **Note:** Kipper coinage. Klippe.

Date	Mintage	VG	F	VF	XF	Unc
1621 N	—	—	—	—	—	—

KM# 266 30 GROSCHEN
Silver **Ruler:** Johann Georg I **Obv:** Arms nearly flat on top, curved on bottom, angel above, value (30 gr) in legend at bottom **Rev:** Similar to 20 Groschen, KM#253. 3 small arms, 1 above 2, angels at left and right of upper shield, date above **Mint:** Annaberg **Note:** Kipper coinage. Varieties exist.

Date	Mintage	VG	F	VF	XF	Unc
1621 (acorn)	—	45.00	90.00	180	300	—
1622 (acorn)	—	45.00	90.00	180	300	—
1623 (acorn)	—	45.00	90.00	180	300	—

KM# 274 30 GROSCHEN
Silver **Ruler:** Johann Georg I **Rev:** N in small shield at top **Note:** Kipper coinage. Varieties exist.

Date	Mintage	VG	F	VF	XF	Unc
16Z1 N	—	45.00	90.00	180	360	—
16ZZ N	—	45.00	90.00	180	360	—

KM# 280 30 GROSCHEN
Silver **Ruler:** Johann Georg I **Note:** Kipper coinage. Klippe.

Date	Mintage	VG	F	VF	XF	Unc
1622 (anchor & 3 swans)	—	65.00	120	210	425	—

KM# 268 30 GROSCHEN

Silver **Ruler:** Johann Georg I **Obv:** Heart-shaped 2-fold arms in baroque frame, angel below, value 30gr in legend at bottom **Rev:** 3 small arms, 1 above 2, angels at left and right of upper shield, date above **Mint:** Dresden **Note:** Kipper coinage. Similar to 20 Groschen, KM#253. Varieties exist.

Date	Mintage	VG	F	VF	XF	Unc
1622 (swan)	—	45.00	90.00	180	360	—
1623 (swan)	—	45.00	90.00	180	360	—

KM# 278 30 GROSCHEN

Silver **Ruler:** Johann Georg I **Rev:** W at top **Mint:** Weida **Note:** Kipper coinage. Varieties exist.

Date	Mintage	VG	F	VF	XF	Unc
1622 W	—	60.00	120	235	475	—

KM# 279 30 GROSCHEN

Silver **Ruler:** Johann Georg I **Mint:** Zwickau **Note:** Kipper coinage.

Date	Mintage	VG	F	VF	XF	Unc
1622 (anchor & 3 swans)	—	45.00	90.00	180	360	—

KM# 275 30 GROSCHEN

Silver **Ruler:** Johann Georg I **Obv:** Arms almost round **Note:** Kipper coinage.

Date	Mintage	VG	F	VF	XF	Unc
16ZZ N	—	40.00	90.00	180	360	—

KM# 267 30 GROSCHEN

Silver **Ruler:** Johann Georg I **Rev:** K in shield at top **Mint:** Chemnitz **Note:** Kipper coinage.

Date	Mintage	VG	F	VF	XF	Unc
1622 K	—	60.00	120	235	475	—

KM# 270 30 GROSCHEN

Silver **Ruler:** Johann Georg I **Obv:** Arms nearly flat on top, curved on bottom **Note:** Kipper coinage.

Date	Mintage	VG	F	VF	XF	Unc
1622 SL	—	55.00	95.00	190	385	—

KM# 271 30 GROSCHEN

Silver **Ruler:** Johann Georg I **Mint:** Merseburg **Note:** Kipper coinage.

Date	Mintage	VG	F	VF	XF	Unc
1622 (rooster)	—	60.00	120	235	475	—

KM# 269 30 GROSCHEN

Silver **Ruler:** Johann Georg I **Obv:** Oval arms **Mint:** Leipzig **Note:** Kipper coinage.

Date	Mintage	VG	F	VF	XF	Unc
1622 SL	—	55.00	95.00	190	385	—
16ZZ SL	—	55.00	95.00	190	385	—

KM# 276 30 GROSCHEN

Silver **Ruler:** Johann Georg I **Obv:** Arms nearly flat on top, curved on bottom **Mint:** Pirna **Note:** Kipper coinage. Varieties exist.

Date	Mintage	VG	F	VF	XF	Unc
1622 GS	—	60.00	120	235	475	—
16ZZ GS	—	60.00	120	235	475	—

KM# 284 40 GROSCHEN

Silver **Ruler:** Johann Georg I **Mint:** Dresden **Note:** Kipper coinage. Varieties exist.

Date	Mintage	VG	F	VF	XF	Unc
1620 (swan)	—	55.00	110	225	450	—
1621 (swan)	—	55.00	110	225	450	—
16Z1 (swan)	—	55.00	110	225	450	—
1622 (swan)	—	55.00	110	225	450	—

KM# 291 40 GROSCHEN

Silver **Ruler:** Johann Georg I **Obv:** 2-fold arms with angel above and behind, value in legend below **Rev:** Shield divides 2 half-length men in inner circle, legend around **Mint:** Pirna **Note:** Kipper coinage. Varieties exist.

Date	Mintage	VG	F	VF	XF	Unc
1621 GS	—	55.00	110	225	450	—
1622 GS	—	55.00	110	225	450	—

KM# 295 40 GROSCHEN

Silver **Ruler:** Johann Georg I **Obv:** 2-fold arms with angel above and behind, value in legend below **Rev:** Shield divides 2 half-length men in inner circle, legend around, W in shield at top **Mint:** Weida **Note:** Kipper coinage. Varieties exist.

Date	Mintage	VG	F	VF	XF	Unc
16Z1 W	—	55.00	110	225	450	—
16Z1 W	—	55.00	110	225	450	—
16ZZ W	—	55.00	110	225	450	—

KM# 286 40 GROSCHEN

Silver **Ruler:** Johann Georg I **Obv:** Date divided by arms **Mint:** Merseburg **Note:** Kipper coinage.

Date	Mintage	VG	F	VF	XF	Unc
1621 (rooster)	—	80.00	160	300	600	—

KM# 289 40 GROSCHEN

Silver **Ruler:** Johann Georg I **Obv:** 2-fold arms with angel above and behind, value in legend below **Rev:** Shield divides 2 half-length men in inner circle, legend around **Mint:** Naumburg **Note:** Kipper coinage.

Date	Mintage	VG	F	VF	XF	Unc
1621 N	—	65.00	135	275	550	—

KM# 290 40 GROSCHEN

Silver **Ruler:** Johann Georg I **Obv:** Large oval 2-fold arms in baroque frame, value (40) in legend at bottom. **Rev:** N in small shield at top **Mint:** Naumburg **Note:** Kipper coinage.

Date	Mintage	VG	F	VF	XF	Unc
16Z1 N	—	65.00	135	275	575	—

KM# 293 40 GROSCHEN

Silver **Ruler:** Johann Georg I **Obv:** Oval arms **Rev:** Date below T in shield at top **Mint:** Taucha **Note:** Kipper coinage.

Date	Mintage	VG	F	VF	XF	Unc
1621 T	—	80.00	160	300	600	—

KM# 294 40 GROSCHEN

Silver **Ruler:** Johann Georg I **Obv:** Half-length armored figure to right, with sword over shoulder, value (40) below **Rev:** 2-fold arms in baroque frame, T in shield below **Mint:** Taucha **Note:** Kipper coinage.

Date	Mintage	VG	F	VF	XF	Unc
ND(1621-22) T	—	80.00	160	300	600	—

KM# 296 40 GROSCHEN

Silver **Ruler:** Johann Georg I **Obv:** Crowned nearly oval 2-fold arms in baroque frame, value 40 gr in legend at top **Rev:** 3 shields of arms, 1 above 2, upper arms divide date **Note:** Kipper coinage.

Date	Mintage	VG	F	VF	XF	Unc
1621 (anchor & 3 swans)	—	45.00	80.00	150	300	—

KM# 297 40 GROSCHEN

Silver **Ruler:** Johann Georg I **Obv:** 2-fold shield of arms, angel behind, value in legend at top **Rev:** Shield divides 2 half-length men in inner circle, legend around **Note:** Kipper coinage.

Date	Mintage	VG	F	VF	XF	Unc
1621 (anchor & 3 swans)	—	45.00	80.00	165	330	—
1622 (anchor & 3 swans)	—	45.00	80.00	165	330	—

KM# 298 40 GROSCHEN

Silver **Ruler:** Johann Georg I **Obv:** Date divided by arms **Note:** Kipper coinage.

Date	Mintage	VG	F	VF	XF	Unc
1621 (anchor & 3 swans)	—	33.00	65.00	130	265	—

KM# 299 40 GROSCHEN

Silver **Ruler:** Johann Georg I **Obv:** Value (40 gr) in legend at bottom **Note:** Kipper coinage.

Date	Mintage	VG	F	VF	XF	Unc
1621 (anchor & 3 swans)	—	35.00	65.00	130	265	—

KM# 288 40 GROSCHEN

Silver **Ruler:** Johann Georg I **Obv:** Similar to 40 Groschen KM#286 **Rev:** Similar to 40 Groschen KM#287 **Mint:** Merseburg **Note:** Kipper coinage. Hybrid Strike.

Date	Mintage	VG	F	VF	XF	Unc
1621/1621 (rooster)	—	80.00	160	300	600	—
1622/1622 (rooster)	—	80.00	160	300	600	—

KM# 300 40 GROSCHEN

Silver **Ruler:** Johann Georg I **Rev:** Similar to 40 Groschen KM#297 **Note:** Kipper coinage. Hybrid Strike.

Date	Mintage	VG	F	VF	XF	Unc
1621/1621 (anchor & 3 swans)	—	33.00	65.00	130	265	—

KM# 281 40 GROSCHEN

Silver **Ruler:** Johann Georg I **Obv:** 2-fold arms with angel above and behind, value in legend below **Rev:** Shield divides 2 half-length men in inner circle, legend around **Mint:** Annaberg **Note:** Kipper coinage. Varieties exist.

Date	Mintage	VG	F	VF	XF	Unc
1621 (acorn)	—	65.00	135	275	575	—
1622 (acorn)	—	65.00	135	275	575	—

KM# 287 40 GROSCHEN

Silver **Ruler:** Johann Georg I **Obv:** Date above arms **Mint:** Merseburg **Note:** Kipper coinage.

Date	Mintage	VG	F	VF	XF	Unc
1621 (rooster)	—	80.00	160	300	600	—
16Z1 (rooster)	—	80.00	160	300	600	—

KM# 292 40 GROSCHEN

Silver **Ruler:** Johann Georg I **Rev:** Date divided by T in shield at top **Mint:** Taucha **Note:** Varieties exist.

Date	Mintage	VG	F	VF	XF	Unc
1621 T	—	80.00	160	300	600	—
ND(1621) T	—	80.00	160	300	600	—

KM# 283 40 GROSCHEN

Silver **Ruler:** Johann Georg I **Obv:** Full-length armored figure with sword over shoulder, value: 40 gr between feet **Rev:** 3-line inscription in cartouche, electoral hat above, within 20 small shields of arms **Rev. Inscription:** CHVRSACHS / SENLANDT / MVNTZE **Mint:** Dresden

Date	Mintage	VG	F	VF	XF	Unc
ND(1621-2) Rare	—	—	—	—	—	—

KM# 282 40 GROSCHEN

Silver **Ruler:** Johann Georg I **Obv:** Heart-shaped arms **Rev:** 2 arms above 1, K in shield at top, lower shield divides date **Mint:** Chemnitz **Note:** Kipper coinage.

Date	Mintage	VG	F	VF	XF	Unc
1622 K	—	55.00	165	300	600	—

KM# 285 40 GROSCHEN

Silver **Ruler:** Johann Georg I **Obv:** Oval arms **Mint:** Leipzig **Note:** Kipper coinage.

Date	Mintage	VG	F	VF	XF	Unc
1622 SL	—	85.00	165	300	600	—

KM# 301 40 GROSCHEN

Silver **Ruler:** Johann Georg I **Obv:** 2-fold arms with angel above and behind, value in legend below **Rev:** Shield divides 2 half-length men in inner circle, legend around **Note:** Kipper coinage.

Date	Mintage	VG	F	VF	XF	Unc
1622 (anchor & 3 swans)	—	33.00	65.00	130	265	—

KM# 369 60 GROSCHEN

Silver **Ruler:** Johann Georg I **Mint:** Naumburg **Note:** Kipper coinage.

Date	Mintage	VG	F	VF	XF	Unc
1621 N	—	45.00	85.00	165	325	—

KM# 370 60 GROSCHEN

Silver **Ruler:** Johann Georg I **Rev:** N in small shield at top **Mint:** Neustadt an der Orla **Note:** Kipper coinage.

Date	Mintage	VG	F	VF	XF	Unc
16Z1 N	—	45.00	85.00	165	325	—
16ZZ N	—	45.00	85.00	165	325	—
16ZZ N - HT	—	45.00	85.00	165	325	—

KM# 375 60 GROSCHEN

Silver **Ruler:** Johann Georg I **Obv:** Heart-shaped arms **Rev:** T in shield bottom **Mint:** Taucha **Note:** Kipper coinage.

Date	Mintage	VG	F	VF	XF	Unc
1621 T	—	325	525	1,000	1,950	—

KM# 371 60 GROSCHEN

Silver **Ruler:** Johann Georg I **Mint:** Neustadt an der Orla **Note:** Kipper coinage. Klippe.

Date	Mintage	VG	F	VF	XF	Unc
16Z1 N	—	—	—	—	—	—

KM# 376 60 GROSCHEN

Silver **Ruler:** Johann Georg I **Rev:** W at top **Mint:** Weida **Note:** Kipper coinage. Varieties exist.

Date	Mintage	VG	F	VF	XF	Unc
16Z1 W	—	60.00	120	225	450	—
16ZZ W	—	60.00	120	225	450	—

KM# 380 60 GROSCHEN

Silver **Ruler:** Johann Georg I **Note:** Kipper coinage. Varieties exist.

Date	Mintage	VG	F	VF	XF	Unc
1622 (flying bird)	—	40.00	80.00	160	325	—
1622 (trefoil)	—	40.00	80.00	160	325	—

KM# 373 60 GROSCHEN

Silver **Ruler:** Johann Georg I **Obv:** Arms nearly flat on top, curved at bottom **Mint:** Pirna **Note:** Kipper coinage. Varieties exist.

Date	Mintage	VG	F	VF	XF	Unc
1622 GS	—	45.00	85.00	165	325	—

KM# 374 60 GROSCHEN

Silver **Ruler:** Johann Georg I **Mint:** Pirna **Note:** Kipper coinage. Klippe.

Date	Mintage	VG	F	VF	XF	Unc
1622 GS	—	—	—	—	—	—

KM# 379 60 GROSCHEN

Silver **Ruler:** Johann Georg I **Mint:** Zwickau **Note:** Kipper coinage. Klippe.

Date	Mintage	VG	F	VF	XF	Unc
1622 (anchor & 3 swans)	—	—	—	—	—	—

KM# 365 60 GROSCHEN

Silver **Ruler:** Johann Georg I **Obv:** Heart-shaped 2-fold arms in baroque frame, angel below, value 60gr in legend at bottom **Rev:** 3 small arms, 1 above 2, angels at left and right of upper shield, date above **Mint:** Leipzig **Note:** Kipper coinage. Similar to 20 Groschen, KM#253.

Date	Mintage	VG	F	VF	XF	Unc
1622 SL	—	45.00	85.00	165	325	—

KM# 362 60 GROSCHEN

Silver **Ruler:** Johann Georg I **Obv:** Arms nearly flat on top, curved at bottom, value (60 gr) in legend at bottom **Rev:** 3 shields of arms, 1 above 2, upper arms divide date **Mint:** Annaberg **Note:** Kipper coinage. Varieties exist.

Date	Mintage	VG	F	VF	XF	Unc
1622 (acorn)	—	45.00	85.00	165	325	—
1623 (acorn)	—	45.00	85.00	165	325	—

KM# 364 60 GROSCHEN

Silver **Ruler:** Johann Georg I **Rev:** Without initial in shield at top **Mint:** Dresden **Note:** Kipper coinage. Varieties exist.

Date	Mintage	VG	F	VF	XF	Unc
1622 (swan)	—	45.00	85.00	165	325	—
1623 (swan)	—	45.00	85.00	165	325	—

KM# 377 60 GROSCHEN

Silver **Ruler:** Johann Georg I **Obv:** Arms nearly flat on top, curved at bottom, value in legend at top **Mint:** Zwickau **Note:** Kipper coinage.

Date	Mintage	VG	F	VF	XF	Unc
1622 (anchor & 3 swans)	—	55.00	100	200	385	—

KM# 378 60 GROSCHEN

Silver **Ruler:** Johann Georg I **Obv:** Value in legend at bottom **Mint:** Zwickau **Note:** Kipper coinage.

Date	Mintage	VG	F	VF	XF	Unc
1622 (anchor & 3 swans)	—	45.00	85.00	165	325	—

KM# 368 60 GROSCHEN

Silver **Ruler:** Johann Georg I **Mint:** Merseburg **Note:** Kipper coinage. Klippe.

Date	Mintage	VG	F	VF	XF	Unc
1622 MB/(rooster)	—	—	—	—	—	—

KM# 372 60 GROSCHEN

Silver **Ruler:** Johann Georg I **Obv:** Heart-shaped arms **Mint:** Neustadt an der Orla **Note:** Kipper coinage.

Date	Mintage	VG	F	VF	XF	Unc
16ZZ N	—	—	—	—	—	—

KM# 363 60 GROSCHEN

Silver **Ruler:** Johann Georg I **Rev:** K in shield at top **Mint:** Chemnitz **Note:** Kipper coinage.

Date	Mintage	VG	F	VF	XF	Unc
1622 K	—	60.00	120	225	450	—

KM# 367 60 GROSCHEN

Silver **Ruler:** Johann Georg I **Obv:** Arms nearly flat on top, curved at bottom, (60 gr) in legend at bottom **Rev:** 3 shields of arms, 1 above 2, upper arms divide date **Mint:** Merseburg **Note:** Kipper coinage.

Date	Mintage	VG	F	VF	XF	Unc
1622 MB/ (rooster)	—	45.00	85.00	165	325	—
1622 (rooster)	—	45.00	85.00	165	325	—

KM# 366 60 GROSCHEN

Silver **Ruler:** Johann Georg I **Obv:** Arms nearly flat on top, curved on bottom, value (60 gr) **Mint:** Dresden **Note:** Kipper coinage. Varieties exist.

Date	Mintage	VG	F	VF	XF	Unc
1622 SL	—	45.00	85.00	165	325	—
16ZZ SL	—	45.00	85.00	165	325	—

KM# 625 1/48 THALER (1/2 Groschen)

Silver **Obv:** Mintmasters initials at bottom **Rev:** Value, titles of Johann Georg IV **Rev. Inscription:** 48 / EINEN / THAL / date

Date	Mintage	VG	F	VF	XF	Unc
1692 IK	—	8.00	16.00	35.00	75.00	—

KM# 666 1/48 THALER (1/2 Groschen)

Silver **Obv:** Crowned 2-fold arms between palm branches, initials divided near bottom **Note:** Varieties exist.

Date	Mintage	VG	F	VF	XF	Unc
1695 EPH	—	8.00	16.00	35.00	75.00	—
1695 IK	—	8.00	16.00	35.00	75.00	—
1696 EPH	—	8.00	16.00	35.00	75.00	—
1696 IK	—	8.00	16.00	35.00	75.00	—

KM# 703 1/48 THALER (1/2 Groschen)

Silver **Ruler:** Friedrich August I **Obv:** Small branch at sides of arms **Rev:** Crossed palm fronds

Date	Mintage	VG	F	VF	XF	Unc
1698 ILH	—	8.00	16.00	35.00	75.00	—

KM# 712 1/48 THALER (1/2 Groschen)

Silver **Ruler:** Johann Georg IV **Obv:** Crowned round 4-fold arms with crowned central shield of 2-fold arms, between 2 crossed palm branches, initials below **Rev:** Value and date in palm wreath

Date	Mintage	VG	F	VF	XF	Unc
1699 ILH	—	8.00	16.00	35.00	75.00	—
1700 ILH	—	8.00	16.00	35.00	75.00	—

KM# 7 1/24 THALER (Groschen)

Silver **Obv:** 2 ornate adjacent shields of arms, small imperial orb divides date above, titles of 3 brothers **Rev:** Ornate helmet above arms of crossed swords, titles continued

Date	Mintage	VG	F	VF	XF	Unc
1601 HB	—	45.00	90.00	180	360	—

KM# 11.1 1/24 THALER (Groschen)

Silver **Ruler:** Christian II, Johann Georg I and August **Obv:** Ornate helmet above arms of electoral Saxony, titles of 3 brothers begin **Rev:** 2 adjacent shields of arms, (ducal Saxony and Thuringia), small imperial orb above divides date, titles continued **Mint:** Dresden **Note:** Varieties exist.

Date	Mintage	VG	F	VF	XF	Unc
1601 HB	—	35.00	75.00	150	300	—
160Z HB	—	35.00	75.00	150	300	—
1604 HB	—	35.00	75.00	150	300	—
1605 HB	—	35.00	75.00	150	300	—

KM# 37 1/24 THALER (Groschen)

Silver **Ruler:** Johann Georg I and August **Obv:** 2 small adjacent shields of arms, small orb above divides date, titles of Johann Georg I **Rev:** 3 small shields of arms, 1 above 2, titles of August **Mint:** Dresden

Date	Mintage	VG	F	VF	XF	Unc
1610 (swan) Error for 1611	—	40.00	80.00	160	325	—
1611 (swan)	—	40.00	80.00	160	325	—
1612 (swan)	—	40.00	80.00	160	325	—
161Z (swan)	—	40.00	80.00	160	325	—

KM# 49 1/24 THALER (Groschen)

Silver **Ruler:** Johann Georg I and August **Subject:** Vicariat Issue **Obv:** 2-fold arms in baroque frame divide date, small orb above, titles of Johann Georg I **Rev:** 4-fold arms, vicariat titles **Mint:** Dresden

Date	Mintage	VG	F	VF	XF	Unc
161Z (swan)	—	40.00	75.00	120	240	—

KM# 66 1/24 THALER (Groschen)

Silver **Ruler:** Johann Georg I and August **Obv:** Ornamented 2-fold arms divide date, small orb above, titles of Johann Georg I **Rev:** Ornamented 4-fold arms, titles of August **Mint:** Dresden

Date	Mintage	VG	F	VF	XF	Unc
161Z	—	—	—	—	—	—
1613 (swan)	—	40.00	80.00	160	325	—
1614 (swan)	—	40.00	80.00	160	325	—

KM# 70 1/24 THALER (Groschen)

Silver **Obv:** Oval 2-fold arms in baroque frame, titles of Johann Georg I **Rev:** 3 small ornately-shaped shields of arms, 2 above 1, small orb divides date at top, titles of August

Date	Mintage	VG	F	VF	XF	Unc
1614 (swan)	—	35.00	75.00	150	300	—
1615 (swan)	—	35.00	75.00	150	300	—

KM# 71 1/24 THALER (Groschen)

Silver **Obv:** Titles of Johann Georg I **Note:** Kipper 1/24 Thaler. All Kipper groschen are of a small module, usually under 20 mm in diameter. Varieties exist.

Date	Mintage	VG	F	VF	XF	Unc
1614 (swan)	—	35.00	75.00	150	300	—
1616 (swan)	—	35.00	75.00	150	300	—
1619 (swan)	—	35.00	75.00	150	300	—
1620 (swan)	—	35.00	75.00	150	300	—
1621 (swan)	—	35.00	75.00	150	300	—
1622 (swan)	—	35.00	75.00	150	300	—
1623 (swan)	—	35.00	75.00	150	300	—
1624 (swan)	—	35.00	75.00	150	300	—
1624 HI	—	35.00	75.00	150	300	—
1625 HI	—	35.00	75.00	150	300	—
1626 HI	—	35.00	75.00	150	300	—
1627 HI	—	35.00	75.00	150	300	—
1628 HI	—	35.00	75.00	150	300	—
1629 HI	—	35.00	75.00	150	300	—
1630 HI	—	35.00	75.00	150	300	—
1631 HI	—	35.00	75.00	150	300	—
1632 HI	—	35.00	75.00	150	300	—
1633 HI	—	35.00	75.00	150	300	—
1634 HI	—	35.00	75.00	150	300	—
1635 CM	—	35.00	75.00	150	300	—
1635 HI	—	35.00	75.00	150	300	—
1635 SD	—	35.00	75.00	150	300	—
1636 SD	—	35.00	75.00	150	300	—
1637 SD	—	35.00	75.00	150	300	—
1638 SD	—	35.00	75.00	150	300	—
1639 SD	—	35.00	75.00	150	300	—
1640 CR	—	35.00	75.00	150	300	—
1640 SD	—	35.00	75.00	150	300	—
1641 CR	—	35.00	75.00	150	300	—
1642 CR	—	35.00	75.00	150	300	—
1643 CR	—	35.00	75.00	150	300	—
1644 CR	—	35.00	75.00	150	300	—
1645 CR	—	35.00	75.00	150	300	—
1646 CR	—	35.00	75.00	150	300	—
1648 CR	—	35.00	75.00	150	300	—
1649 CR	—	35.00	75.00	150	300	—
1650 CR	—	35.00	75.00	150	300	—
1651 CR	—	35.00	75.00	150	300	—
1652 CR	—	35.00	75.00	150	300	—
1653 CR	—	35.00	75.00	150	300	—
1655 CR	—	35.00	75.00	150	300	—

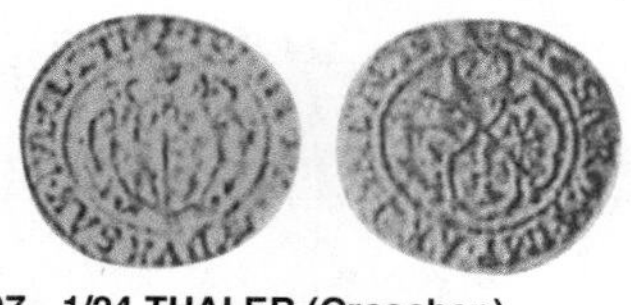

KM# 307 1/24 THALER (Groschen)

Silver **Ruler:** Johann Georg I **Obv:** Oval 2-fold arms in baroque frame, angel's head and wings above **Rev:** 3 small, ornately-shaped shields of arms, 2 above 1, imperial orb with 24 at top divides date **Mint:** Dresden **Note:** Kipper coinage. Varieties exist.

Date	Mintage	VG	F	VF	XF	Unc
1620 (swan)	—	30.00	65.00	135	275	—
1621 (swan)	—	30.00	65.00	135	275	—
16Z1 (swan)	—	30.00	65.00	135	275	—

KM# 308 1/24 THALER (Groschen)

Silver **Ruler:** Johann Georg I **Rev:** Value: 24 on imperial orb divides date **Note:** Kipper coinage. Varieties exist.

Date	Mintage	VG	F	VF	XF	Unc
16Z1 (swan)	—	30.00	65.00	135	275	—

Date	Mintage	VG	F	VF	XF	Unc
16ZZ (swan)	—	30.00	65.00	135	275	—
16Z3 (swan)	—	30.00	65.00	135	275	—

KM# 302 1/24 THALER (Groschen)
Silver **Ruler:** Johann Georg I **Obv:** 2-fold arms in baroque frame, angel's head and wings above **Rev:** Imperial orb with 24 divides date **Mint:** Annaberg **Note:** Kipper coinage. Varieties exist.

Date	Mintage	VG	F	VF	XF	Unc
16Z1 (acorn)	—	35.00	75.00	150	300	—

KM# 337 1/24 THALER (Groschen)
Silver **Ruler:** Johann Georg I **Obv:** Large 2-fold arms **Rev:** Rampant lion right **Note:** Kipper coinage.

Date	Mintage	VG	F	VF	XF	Unc
ND(1621)	—	15.00	30.00	70.00	145	—

KM# 338 1/24 THALER (Groschen)
Silver **Ruler:** Johann Georg I **Rev:** Round arms, date at top **Rev. Legend:** ARCHIM. E. ELECT. **Note:** Kipper coinage.

Date	Mintage	VG	F	VF	XF	Unc
16Z1 (trefoil)	—	15.00	35.00	75.00	155	—

KM# 327 1/24 THALER (Groschen)
Silver **Ruler:** Johann Georg I **Mint:** Zwickau **Note:** Kipper coinage. Klippe.

Date	Mintage	VG	F	VF	XF	Unc
1621 (3 swans)	—	35.00	75.00	150	300	—

KM# 311 1/24 THALER (Groschen)
Silver **Ruler:** Johann Georg I **Mint:** Gommern **Note:** Kipper coinage. Varieties exist.

Date	Mintage	VG	F	VF	XF	Unc
ND(1621) (star)	—	30.00	65.00	130	265	—

KM# 313 1/24 THALER (Groschen)
Silver **Ruler:** Johann Georg I **Rev:** Date divided in legend at top **Mint:** Leipzig **Note:** Kipper coinage. Varieties exist.

Date	Mintage	VG	F	VF	XF	Unc
16Z1 SL	—	30.00	65.00	135	275	—
1622 SL	—	30.00	65.00	135	275	—

KM# 333 1/24 THALER (Groschen)
Silver **Ruler:** Johann Georg I **Rev:** 24 in orb **Rev. Legend:** SA. RO... **Note:** Kipper coinage. Varieties exist.

Date	Mintage	VG	F	VF	XF	Unc
1621 (flying bird)	—	15.00	35.00	75.00	155	—
(16)21 (flying bird)	—	15.00	35.00	75.00	155	—
(16)22 (cross)	—	15.00	35.00	75.00	155	—
1622 (5-petaled rosette)	—	15.00	35.00	75.00	155	—
ND(1621) (crown)	—	15.00	35.00	75.00	155	—

KM# 334 1/24 THALER (Groschen)
Silver **Ruler:** Johann Georg I **Rev. Legend:** SA. ROMANI... **Note:** Kipper coinage. Varieties exist.

Date	Mintage	VG	F	VF	XF	Unc
16Z1 (5-petaled rosette)	—	15.00	35.00	75.00	155	—
ND(1621) (4-petaled rosette)	—	15.00	35.00	75.00	155	—

KM# 335 1/24 THALER (Groschen)
Silver **Ruler:** Johann Georg I **Rev:** Titles of Johann Georg I **Rev. Legend:** SA. RO... **Note:** Kipper coinage. Varieties exist.

Date	Mintage	VG	F	VF	XF	Unc
ND(1621)	—	15.00	35.00	75.00	155	—
ND(1621) 4-petaled rosette	—	15.00	35.00	75.00	155	—

KM# 336 1/24 THALER (Groschen)
Silver **Ruler:** Johann Georg I **Obv:** 3 small shields of arms, 1 above 2 **Rev:** Imperial orb with 24 **Rev. Legend:** SA. R..., date divided at top **Note:** Kipper coinage. Varieties exist.

Date	Mintage	VG	F	VF	XF	Unc
1621 (cross)	—	15.00	35.00	75.00	155	—
ND(1621) (cross)	—	15.00	35.00	75.00	155	—
1621	—	15.00	35.00	75.00	155	—
ND(1621)	—	15.00	35.00	75.00	155	—

KM# 303 1/24 THALER (Groschen)
Silver **Ruler:** Johann Georg I **Obv:** 2-fold arms **Rev:** Imperial orb with Z4, date divided in legend at top **Mint:** Bitterfeld **Note:** Kipper coinage.

Date	Mintage	VG	F	VF	XF	Unc
16Z1 (acorn)	—	35.00	75.00	150	300	—

KM# 305 1/24 THALER (Groschen)
Silver **Ruler:** Johann Georg I **Obv:** Angel's head and wings above arms **Mint:** Chemnitz **Note:** Kipper coinage.

Date	Mintage	VG	F	VF	XF	Unc
ND K	—	30.00	65.00	130	265	—

KM# 309 1/24 THALER (Groschen)
Silver **Ruler:** Johann Georg I **Obv:** Plain 2-fold arms between E - B **Mint:** Eckartsberga **Note:** Kipper coinage.

Date	Mintage	VG	F	VF	XF	Unc
16Z1 EB	—	35.00	75.00	150	300	—

KM# 312 1/24 THALER (Groschen)
Silver **Ruler:** Johann Georg I **Rev:** Without date, Z4 in orb **Mint:** Grossenhain **Note:** Kipper coinage.

Date	Mintage	VG	F	VF	XF	Unc
ND(1621) (rosette)	—	30.00	65.00	130	265	—

KM# 314 1/24 THALER (Groschen)
Silver **Ruler:** Johann Georg I **Obv:** 3 small ornately-shaped shields, 2 above 1 **Mint:** Leipzig **Note:** Kipper coinage.

Date	Mintage	VG	F	VF	XF	Unc
1621 SL	—	30.00	65.00	135	275	—

KM# 328 1/24 THALER (Groschen)
Silver **Ruler:** Johann Georg I **Rev:** Imperial orb with 24, date divided at top **Mint:** Zwickau **Note:** Kipper coinage.

Date	Mintage	VG	F	VF	XF	Unc
1621 (3 swans)	—	35.00	75.00	150	300	—
1622 (3 swans)	—	35.00	75.00	150	300	—

KM# 304 1/24 THALER (Groschen)
Silver **Ruler:** Johann Georg I **Obv:** Ornately-shaped 2-fold arms **Rev:** Imperial orb with Z4, titles of Ferdinand II **Mint:** Chemnitz **Note:** Varieties exist.

Date	Mintage	VG	F	VF	XF	Unc
ND(1621-22) K	—	35.00	75.00	150	300	—
ND(1621-22)	—	35.00	75.00	150	300	—

KM# 326 1/24 THALER (Groschen)
Silver **Ruler:** Johann Georg I **Obv:** Ornate 2-fold arms **Rev:** 3 small shields of arms, 1 above 2, divide date **Mint:** Zwickau **Note:** Kipper coinage.

Date	Mintage	VG	F	VF	XF	Unc
1621 (3 swans)	—	35.00	75.00	150	300	—
16Z1 (3 swans)	—	35.00	75.00	150	300	—

KM# 332 1/24 THALER (Groschen)
Silver **Ruler:** Johann Georg I **Rev:** Round arms and date at top **Note:** Kipper coinage. Varieties exist.

Date	Mintage	VG	F	VF	XF	Unc
1621 (lily)	—	15.00	35.00	75.00	155	—
1621 (double-lily)	—	15.00	35.00	75.00	155	—
ND(1621)	—	15.00	35.00	75.00	155	—

KM# 330 1/24 THALER (Groschen)
Silver **Ruler:** Johann Georg I **Rev:** Date undivided at end of legend **Mint:** Zwickau **Note:** Kipper coinage.

Date	Mintage	VG	F	VF	XF	Unc
1622 (3 swans)	—	35.00	75.00	150	300	—

KM# 324 1/24 THALER (Groschen)
Silver **Ruler:** Johann Georg I **Obv:** W in legend at top **Mint:** Weida **Note:** Kipper coinage.

Date	Mintage	VG	F	VF	XF	Unc
1622 W	—	35.00	75.00	150	300	—

KM# 325 1/24 THALER (Groschen)
Silver **Ruler:** Johann Georg I **Rev:** Z4 in orb **Mint:** Weida **Note:** Kipper coinage.

Date	Mintage	VG	F	VF	XF	Unc
1622 W	—	35.00	75.00	150	300	—

KM# 315 1/24 THALER (Groschen)
Silver **Ruler:** Johann Georg I **Rev:** Date undivided at end of legend **Mint:** Leipzig **Note:** Kipper coinage.

Date	Mintage	VG	F	VF	XF	Unc
1622 SL	—	30.00	65.00	135	275	—

KM# 316 1/24 THALER (Groschen)
Silver **Ruler:** Johann Georg I **Obv:** 2-fold arms in baroque frame, angel's head and wings above **Rev:** Imperial orb with Z4, date divided in legend at top **Mint:** Merseburg **Note:** Kipper coinage.

Date	Mintage	VG	F	VF	XF	Unc
1622 (rooster)	—	30.00	65.00	135	275	—

KM# 319 1/24 THALER (Groschen)
Silver **Ruler:** Johann Georg I **Obv:** Oval 2-fold arms in baroque frame, small N below **Rev:** Imperial orb with Z4 **Mint:** Neustadt an der Orla **Note:** Kipper coinage. Varieties exist.

Date	Mintage	VG	F	VF	XF	Unc
ND(1622) N	—	30.00	65.00	130	265	—

KM# 321 1/24 THALER (Groschen)
Silver **Ruler:** Johann Georg I **Obv:** N above arms **Mint:** Neustadt an der Orla **Note:** Kipper coinage. Varieties exist.

Date	Mintage	VG	F	VF	XF	Unc
ND(1622) N	—	30.00	65.00	130	265	—

KM# 322 1/24 THALER (Groschen)
Silver **Ruler:** Johann Georg I **Rev:** Date divided in legend at top **Note:** Kipper coinage. Varieties exist.

Date	Mintage	VG	F	VF	XF	Unc
16ZZ N	—	35.00	75.00	150	300	—

KM# 323 1/24 THALER (Groschen)
Silver **Ruler:** Johann Georg I **Obv:** Ornate 2-fold arms **Rev:** Imperial orb with 24, date divided at top **Mint:** Pirna **Note:** Kipper coinage. Varieties exist.

Date	Mintage	VG	F	VF	XF	Unc
1622 GS	—	35.00	75.00	150	300	—

KM# 329 1/24 THALER (Groschen)
Silver **Ruler:** Johann Georg I **Mint:** Zwickau **Note:** Kipper coinage. Klippe.

Date	Mintage	VG	F	VF	XF	Unc
1622 (3 swans)	—	35.00	75.00	150	300	—

KM# 320 1/24 THALER (Groschen)
Silver **Ruler:** Johann Georg I **Mint:** Neustadt an der Orla **Note:** Kipper coinage. Klippe.

Date	Mintage	VG	F	VF	XF	Unc
ND(1622) N	—	33.00	65.00	135	275	—

KM# 306 1/24 THALER (Groschen)
Silver **Ruler:** Johann Georg I **Rev:** Date divided by orb **Rev. Legend:** SA ROM I M... **Note:** Kipper coinage. Varieties exist.

Date	Mintage	VG	F	VF	XF	Unc
16ZZ	—	30.00	65.00	135	275	—

KM# 310 1/24 THALER (Groschen)
Silver **Ruler:** Johann Georg I **Obv:** 2-fold arms **Mint:** Ehrenfriedersdorf **Note:** Kipper coinage. Varieties exist.

Date	Mintage	VG	F	VF	XF	Unc
16ZZ (finger ring)	—	35.00	75.00	150	300	—
ND(1622) (finger ring)	—	35.00	75.00	150	300	—

KM# 331 1/24 THALER (Groschen)
Silver **Ruler:** Johann Georg I **Obv:** Heart-shaped 2-fold arms, mint symbol at top **Rev:** Imperial orb with Z4, titles of Ferdinand II, date at top, when present **Note:** Kipper coinage. Varieties exist.

Date	Mintage	VG	F	VF	XF	Unc
16ZZ (lily)	—	15.00	35.00	75.00	155	—
ND(1622) (lily)	—	15.00	35.00	75.00	155	—
ND(1622) (4-petaled rosette)	—	15.00	35.00	75.00	155	—
1622 (trefoil)	—	15.00	35.00	75.00	155	—

KM# 317 1/24 THALER (Groschen)
Silver **Ruler:** Johann Georg I **Obv:** Without angel's head and wings **Rev:** 24 in orb **Mint:** Merseburg **Note:** Kipper coinage.

Date	Mintage	VG	F	VF	XF	Unc
1622 (rooster)/MD	—	30.00	65.00	135	275	—
1622 (rooster)	—	30.00	65.00	135	275	—

KM# 318 1/24 THALER (Groschen)
Silver **Ruler:** Johann Georg I **Obv:** Oval 2-fold arms in baroque frame **Rev:** Imperial orb with 24 or Z4 **Mint:** Naumburg **Note:** Kipper coinage.

Date	Mintage	VG	F	VF	XF	Unc
ND(1622) N	—	30.00	65.00	130	265	—
ND(1622)	—	30.00	65.00	130	265	—

KM# 471 1/24 THALER (Groschen)
Silver **Obv:** Oval 2-fold arms in baroque frame, titles of Johann Georg II **Rev:** Imperial orb with 24 divides date and initials **Rev. Legend:** OBER SAXSISCH KREISSES GROSCH **Note:** Varieties exist.

Date	Mintage	VG	F	VF	XF	Unc
1658 CR	—	11.00	25.00	55.00	110	—
1659 CR	—	11.00	25.00	55.00	110	—
1660 CR	—	11.00	25.00	55.00	110	—
1661 CR	—	11.00	25.00	55.00	110	—
1662 CR	—	11.00	25.00	55.00	110	—
1663 CR	—	11.00	25.00	55.00	110	—
1664 CR	—	11.00	25.00	55.00	110	—
1665 CR	—	11.00	25.00	55.00	110	—
1666 CR	—	11.00	25.00	55.00	110	—
1667 CR	—	11.00	25.00	55.00	110	—
1668 CR	—	11.00	25.00	55.00	110	—

KM# 520 1/24 THALER (Groschen)
Silver **Rev. Legend:** SAC. ROM... **Note:** Varieties exist.

Date	Mintage	VG	F	VF	XF	Unc
1667 CR	—	11.00	25.00	55.00	110	—
1668 CR	—	11.00	25.00	55.00	110	—
1669 CR	—	11.00	25.00	55.00	110	—
1670 CR	—	11.00	25.00	55.00	110	—
1671 CR	—	11.00	25.00	55.00	110	—
1672 CR	—	11.00	25.00	55.00	110	—
1673 CR	—	11.00	25.00	55.00	110	—
1674 CR	—	11.00	25.00	55.00	110	—
1677 CR	—	11.00	25.00	55.00	110	—
1678 CF	—	11.00	25.00	55.00	110	—
1678 CR	—	11.00	25.00	55.00	110	—
1679 CF	—	11.00	25.00	55.00	110	—
1680 CF	—	11.00	25.00	55.00	110	—

KM# 570 1/24 THALER (Groschen)

Silver **Obv:** Crowned 2-fold arms between 2 palm branches **Note:** Varieties exist.

Date	Mintage	VG	F	VF	XF	Unc
1680 CF	—	11.00	25.00	55.00	110	—
1681 CF	—	11.00	25.00	55.00	110	—
1682 CF	—	11.00	25.00	55.00	110	—
1683 CF	—	11.00	25.00	55.00	110	—
1684 CF	—	11.00	25.00	55.00	110	—
1685 CF	—	11.00	25.00	55.00	110	—
1686 CF	—	11.00	25.00	55.00	110	—
1687	—	11.00	25.00	55.00	110	—
1688	—	11.00	25.00	55.00	110	—
1688 IK	—	11.00	25.00	55.00	110	—
1689 IK	—	11.00	25.00	55.00	110	—
1690 IK	—	11.00	25.00	55.00	110	—
1691 IK	—	11.00	25.00	55.00	110	—

KM# 610 1/24 THALER (Groschen)

Silver **Obv:** Titles of Johann Georg IV **Rev:** Inscription, date **Rev. Legend:** SAC. ROM... **Rev. Inscription:** 24 / EINEN / THAL

Date	Mintage	VG	F	VF	XF	Unc
1691 IK	—	11.00	25.00	55.00	110	—
1692 IK	—	11.00	25.00	55.00	110	—
1693 IK	—	11.00	25.00	55.00	110	—

KM# A645 1/24 THALER (Groschen)

Silver **Obv:** 2 ornamented heraldic shields

Date	Mintage	VG	F	VF	XF	Unc
1693 IK	—	11.00	25.00	55.00	110	—

KM# 645 1/24 THALER (Groschen)

Silver **Obv:** Crowned round 2-fold arms in crossed palm branches, mintmaster's initials below **Note:** Varieties exist.

Date	Mintage	VG	F	VF	XF	Unc
1694 IK	—	11.00	25.00	55.00	110	—
1695 EPH	—	11.00	25.00	55.00	110	—
1695 IK	—	11.00	25.00	55.00	110	—
1696 EPH	—	11.00	25.00	55.00	110	—
1696 IK	—	11.00	25.00	55.00	110	—
1696 EPH	—	11.00	25.00	55.00	110	—
1697 EPH	—	11.00	25.00	55.00	110	—
1697 IK	—	11.00	25.00	55.00	110	—
1698 EPH	—	11.00	25.00	55.00	110	—
1699 EPH	—	11.00	25.00	55.00	110	—

KM# 682 1/24 THALER (Groschen)

Silver **Ruler:** Johann Georg IV **Obv:** Crowned round 4-fold arms with crowned central shield of 2-fold arms **Rev:** Value in palm wreath **Rev. Inscription:** 24 / EINEN / THAI / date **Note:** Varieties exist.

Date	Mintage	VG	F	VF	XF	Unc
1697 IK	—	11.00	25.00	55.00	110	—
1697 ILH	—	11.00	25.00	55.00	110	—
1698 ILH	—	11.00	25.00	55.00	110	—
1699 ILH	—	11.00	25.00	55.00	110	—
1700 ILH	—	11.00	25.00	55.00	110	—

KM# 515 1/15 THALER

Silver **Obv:** 2 ornately-shaped shields of arms above small city arms of Bautzen, divide date **Rev:** Value **Rev. Legend:** MONETA NOVA ... **Rev. Inscription:** XV / EIN / REICHS / THAL / initials

Date	Mintage	VG	F	VF	XF	Unc
1666 HI	—	—	—	—	—	—

KM# 606 1/12 THALER (Doppelgroschen)

Silver **Obv:** Crowned 3-fold arms between palm branches, titles of Johann Georg III **Rev:** Value, date, titles continued **Rev. Inscription:** 12 / EINEN / THAL / ...

Date	Mintage	VG	F	VF	XF	Unc
1690 IK	—	10.00	25.00	55.00	115	—
1691 IK	—	10.00	25.00	55.00	115	—

KM# 611 1/12 THALER (Doppelgroschen)

Silver **Note:** Varieties exist.

Date	Mintage	VG	F	VF	XF	Unc
1691 IK	—	15.00	35.00	75.00	150	—
1692 IK	—	15.00	35.00	75.00	150	—
1693 IK	—	15.00	35.00	75.00	150	—

KM# 638 1/12 THALER (Doppelgroschen)

Silver **Obv:** 2 adjacent oval arms in baroque frames, crown above, initials below, where present **Rev:** Value, date **Rev. Inscription:** 12 / EINEN / THAL / ... **Note:** Varieties exist.

Date	Mintage	VG	F	VF	XF	Unc
1693	—	15.00	35.00	75.00	150	—
1693 IK	—	15.00	35.00	75.00	150	—
1693 EPH	—	15.00	35.00	75.00	150	—
1694 IK	—	15.00	35.00	75.00	150	—
1694 EPH	—	15.00	35.00	75.00	150	—

KM# 646 1/12 THALER (Doppelgroschen)

Silver **Obv:** Crowned oval 2-fold arms framed by crossed palm branches, initials below **Note:** Varieties exist.

Date	Mintage	VG	F	VF	XF	Unc
1694 EPH	—	15.00	35.00	75.00	150	—
1694 IK	—	15.00	35.00	75.00	150	—
1695 EPH	—	15.00	35.00	75.00	150	—
1695 IK	—	15.00	35.00	75.00	150	—
1696 EPH	—	15.00	35.00	75.00	150	—
1696 IK	—	15.00	35.00	75.00	150	—
1697 EPH	—	15.00	35.00	75.00	150	—
1698 EPH	—	15.00	35.00	75.00	150	—

KM# A683 1/12 THALER (Doppelgroschen)

Silver

Date	Mintage	VG	F	VF	XF	Unc
1697 EPH	—	15.00	35.00	75.00	150	—
1698 EPH	—	15.00	35.00	75.00	150	—
1699 ILH	—	15.00	35.00	75.00	150	—

KM# 12 1/8 THALER

Silver **Ruler:** Christian II, Johann Georg I and August **Obv:** Bust of Christian II right, small imperial orb above, shield of electoral Saxony arms below, titles of 3 brothers **Rev:** Busts of Johann Georg I and August facing each other, small shield of ducal Saxony arms above, titles continued, date

Date	Mintage	VG	F	VF	XF	Unc
1601	—	75.00	140	225	450	—

KM# 35 1/8 THALER

Silver **Ruler:** Christian II, Johann Georg I and August **Obv:** Oval Electoral Saxony arms in baroque frame, titles of three brothers **Rev:** Oval ducal Saxony arms in baroque frame, titles continued and date in legend **Mint:** Dresden

Date	Mintage	VG	F	VF	XF	Unc
1610 (swan)	—	—	—	—	—	—
1611 (swan)	—	—	—	—	—	—

KM# 50 1/8 THALER

Silver **Obv:** Titles of Johann Georg I and August only

Date	Mintage	VG	F	VF	XF	Unc
1612 (swan)	—	—	—	—	—	—

KM# 51 1/8 THALER

Silver **Obv:** 1/2-length crowned bust of Johann Georg I right holding sword over right shoulder **Rev:** Ornate 4-fold arms with central shield of electoral Saxony, date divided above

Date	Mintage	VG	F	VF	XF	Unc
1612 (swan)	—	75.00	150	300	625	—

KM# 93 1/8 THALER

Silver **Subject:** Reformation Centennial **Obv:** 1/2-length figure holding sword over right shoulder divides IOH - GEOR, 4-fold arms with central shield below, date divided at bottom **Rev:** 1/2-length figure holding sword over right shoulder divides FRID - III, 2-fold arms of Saxony below, 15 - 17 at bottom

Date	Mintage	VG	F	VF	XF	Unc
1617	—	40.00	80.00	160	325	—

KM# 115 1/8 THALER

Silver **Ruler:** Johann Georg I **Obv:** Elector on horseback to right, with sword over right shoulder, divides date, oval shield of 2-fold arms of electoral and ducal Saxony below **Obv. Legend:** PRO LEGE - ET GREGE **Rev:** 12-line inscription **Note:** Vicariat Issue.

Date	Mintage	VG	F	VF	XF	Unc
1619	—	55.00	115	235	475	—

KM# 386 1/8 THALER

Silver **Ruler:** Johann Georg I **Obv:** 1/2-length armored figure right with sword over right shoulder, titles of Johann Georg I begin with small imperial orb **Rev:** Ornate 4-fold arms with central shield of electoral Saxony, date divided in top margin by mintmaster's symbol, titles continued **Mint:** Dresden

Date	Mintage	VG	F	VF	XF	Unc
16Z3 (swan)	—	100	200	375	775	—
16Z4 (swan)	—	100	200	375	775	—

KM# 387 1/8 THALER

Silver **Ruler:** Johann Georg I **Rev:** 3-fold arms **Note:** Varieties exist.

Date	Mintage	VG	F	VF	XF	Unc
1624 HI	—	20.00	45.00	95.00	190	—
1625 HI	—	20.00	45.00	95.00	190	—
1627 HI	—	20.00	45.00	95.00	190	—
1628 HI	—	20.00	45.00	95.00	190	—
1629 HI	—	20.00	45.00	95.00	190	—
1630 HI	—	20.00	45.00	95.00	190	—
1635 HI	—	20.00	45.00	95.00	190	—
1635 SD	—	20.00	45.00	95.00	190	—
1636 SD	—	20.00	45.00	95.00	190	—
1637 SD	—	20.00	45.00	95.00	190	—
1638 SD	—	20.00	45.00	95.00	190	—
1639 SD	—	20.00	45.00	95.00	190	—
1640 CR	—	20.00	45.00	95.00	190	—
1640 SD	—	20.00	45.00	95.00	190	—
1641 CR	—	20.00	45.00	95.00	190	—
1642 CR	—	20.00	45.00	95.00	190	—

Date	Mintage	VG	F	VF	XF	Unc
1643 CR	—	20.00	45.00	95.00	190	—
1644 CR	—	20.00	45.00	95.00	190	—
1645 CR	—	20.00	45.00	95.00	190	—
1646 CR	—	20.00	45.00	95.00	190	—
1647 CR	—	20.00	45.00	95.00	190	—
1648 CR	—	20.00	45.00	95.00	190	—
1649 CR	—	20.00	45.00	95.00	190	—
1650 CR	—	20.00	45.00	95.00	190	—
1651 CR	—	20.00	45.00	95.00	190	—
1652 CR	—	20.00	45.00	95.00	190	—
1653 CR	—	20.00	45.00	95.00	190	—
1654 CR	—	20.00	45.00	95.00	190	—
1655 CR	—	20.00	45.00	95.00	190	—
1656 CR	—	20.00	45.00	95.00	190	—

KM# 405 1/8 THALER

Silver **Ruler:** Johann Georg I **Subject:** Centennial of Augsburg Confession **Obv:** 1/2-length figure of Johann Georg I, sword over right shoulder, divides IOH - GEO, oval 4-fold arms with central shield below, full date divided by head **Rev:** 1/2-length figure of Duke Johann, sword over right shoulder, divides IOH - NES, 4 small shields of arms around, full date (1530) divided by head

Date	Mintage	VG	F	VF	XF	Unc
1630	—	45.00	90.00	180	360	—

KM# 447 1/8 THALER

Silver **Subject:** Death of Johann Georg I **Obv:** Bust facing slightly right, sword over shoulder **Rev:** 8-line inscription with Roman numeral date

Date	Mintage	VG	F	VF	XF	Unc
MDCLVI (1656)	—	60.00	120	235	475	—

KM# 456 1/8 THALER

Silver **Obv:** Duke on horseback, with sword over shoulder, oval 2-fold arms below, date in legend **Rev:** 10-line inscription **Note:** Vicariat Issue.

Date	Mintage	VG	F	VF	XF	Unc
1657	—	45.00	90.00	180	360	—

KM# 472 1/8 THALER

Silver **Obv:** Bust right with sword over right shoulder **Rev:** 3-fold arms, mintmasters initials below **Note:** Varieties exist.

Date	Mintage	VG	F	VF	XF	Unc
1658 CR	—	30.00	60.00	120	240	—
1659 CR	—	30.00	60.00	120	240	—
1660 CR	—	30.00	60.00	120	240	—
1661 CR	—	30.00	60.00	120	240	—
1662 CR	—	30.00	60.00	120	240	—
1663 CR	—	30.00	60.00	120	240	—
1664 CR	—	30.00	60.00	120	240	—
1665 CR	—	30.00	60.00	120	240	—
1666 CR	—	30.00	60.00	120	240	—
1667 CR	—	30.00	60.00	120	240	—
1668 CR	—	30.00	60.00	120	240	—
1673 CR	—	30.00	60.00	120	240	—
1674 CR	—	30.00	60.00	120	240	—
1675 CR	—	30.00	60.00	120	240	—
1676 CR	—	30.00	60.00	120	240	—
1678 CR	—	30.00	60.00	120	240	—
1680 CR	—	30.00	60.00	120	240	—

KM# 575 1/8 THALER

Silver **Obv:** 1/2-length figure right with sword over shoulder **Rev:** 3-fold arms, date in legend **Note:** Varieties exist.

Date	Mintage	VG	F	VF	XF	Unc
1681 CF	—	80.00	160	325	650	—
1688 IK	—	80.00	160	325	650	—

KM# 593 1/8 THALER

Silver **Ruler:** Johann Georg III **Subject:** Death of Johann Georg III's Mother, Magdalene Sibylle **Obv:** MANET in wreath, SOLA. SPES. MEA in band at top **Rev:** 7-line inscription w/dates

Date	Mintage	VG	F	VF	XF	Unc
1687	—	50.00	85.00	160	325	—

KM# 647 1/8 THALER

Silver **Obv:** Large bust right **Rev:** Crowned 3-fold arms divide mintmasters initials, date in legend **Note:** Varieties exist.

Date	Mintage	VG	F	VF	XF	Unc
1694 IK	—	27.00	55.00	110	225	—
1695 IK	—	27.00	55.00	110	225	—
1696 IK	—	27.00	55.00	110	225	—
1697 IK	—	27.00	55.00	110	225	—

KM# 721 1/8 THALER

Silver **Ruler:** Johann Georg IV **Obv:** Large bust right **Rev:** Crowned flat top 2-fold arms between palm branches divides initials, date in legend **Note:** Varieties exist.

Date	Mintage	VG	F	VF	XF	Unc
1700 ILH	—	20.00	45.00	90.00	185	—

KM# 516 1/6 THALER (1/4 Gulden)

Silver **Mint:** Bautzen **Note:** Coinage for Oberlausitz. Varieties exist.

Date	Mintage	VG	F	VF	XF	Unc
1666 HI	—	45.00	90.00	180	360	—
1667 HI	—	45.00	90.00	180	360	—
1668 CR	—	45.00	90.00	180	360	—

KM# 521 1/6 THALER (1/4 Gulden)

Silver **Obv:** Bust right **Rev:** Crowned 4-fold arms with central shield of electoral Saxony divide initials, 1/6 in oval below, date at top in legend

Date	Mintage	VG	F	VF	XF	Unc
1668 CR	—	45.00	90.00	180	360	—
1669 CR	—	45.00	90.00	180	360	—
1672 CR	—	45.00	90.00	180	360	—
1673 CR	—	45.00	90.00	180	360	—
1674 CR	—	45.00	90.00	180	360	—

KM# 558 1/6 THALER (1/4 Gulden)

Silver **Ruler:** Johann Georg II **Obv:** Small bust right **Rev:** Crowned oval 2-fold arms between 2 palm branches, value 1/6 in oval below, date in legend at top **Mint:** Bautzen

Date	Mintage	VG	F	VF	XF	Unc
1675 CR	—	40.00	80.00	160	325	—
1676 CR	—	40.00	80.00	160	325	—
1677 CR	—	40.00	80.00	160	325	—
1678 CF	—	40.00	80.00	160	325	—
1679 CF	—	40.00	80.00	160	325	—
1680 CF	—	40.00	80.00	160	325	—

KM# 576 1/6 THALER (1/4 Gulden)

Silver **Obv:** Bust right **Rev:** Crowned 2-fold arms between 2 palm branches, value 1/6 in oval below, date in legend at top **Note:** Varieties exist.

Date	Mintage	VG	F	VF	XF	Unc
1681 CF	—	40.00	80.00	160	325	—
1682 CF	—	40.00	80.00	160	325	—
1683 CF	—	40.00	80.00	160	325	—
1684 CF	—	40.00	80.00	160	325	—
1685 CF	—	40.00	80.00	160	325	—
1686 CF	—	40.00	80.00	160	325	—
1687	—	40.00	80.00	160	325	—
1688	—	40.00	80.00	160	325	—
1688 IK	—	40.00	80.00	160	325	—
1689 IK	—	40.00	80.00	160	325	—
1690 IK	—	40.00	80.00	160	325	—
1691 IK	—	40.00	80.00	160	325	—

KM# 612 1/6 THALER (1/4 Gulden)

Silver **Subject:** Death of Johann Georg III **Obv:** Arms from clouds holding partly furled flag **Obv. Legend:** IEHOVA VEXILLIVM MEVM **Rev:** 7-line inscription with RN dates, value 1/6 in small circle at bottom **Note:** Similar to 1 Groschen, KM#608.

Date	Mintage	VG	F	VF	XF	Unc
1691 IK	—	55.00	110	200	385	—
MDCXCI (1691) IK	—	55.00	110	200	385	—

KM# 626 1/6 THALER (1/4 Gulden)

Silver **Ruler:** Johann Georg IV **Rev:** 4 small crowned shields of arms, 1 in each angle of 2 crossed swords, date divided at top and value 1/6 divided in upper and lower angles of crossed swords **Mint:** Dresden

Date	Mintage	VG	F	VF	XF	Unc
1692 IK	—	50.00	95.00	190	385	—
1693 IK	—	50.00	95.00	190	385	—

KM# 648 1/6 THALER (1/4 Gulden)

Silver **Subject:** Death of Johann Georg IV **Obv:** Pyramid with crowned shields of arms on 2 sides **Rev:** 9-line inscription and value 1/6 in oval at bottom

Date	Mintage	VG	F	VF	XF	Unc
MDCXCIV (1694) IK	—	80.00	140	275	575	—

KM# 667 1/6 THALER (1/4 Gulden)

Silver **Rev:** Crowned oval 2-fold arms between 2 palm branches, date divided above, value: 1/6 in oval below **Note:** Varieties exist.

Date	Mintage	VG	F	VF	XF	Unc
1695 IK	—	40.00	80.00	160	325	—
1696 IK	—	40.00	80.00	160	325	—
1696 EPH	—	40.00	80.00	160	325	—

KM# 704 1/6 THALER (1/4 Gulden)

Silver **Rev:** 2 adjacent shields of arms **Note:** Varieties exist.

Date	Mintage	VG	F	VF	XF	Unc
1698 ILH	—	40.00	80.00	160	325	—
1698 EPH	—	40.00	80.00	160	325	—
1699 ILH	—	40.00	80.00	160	325	—
1699 EPH	—	40.00	80.00	160	325	—
1699 EPH EPH	—	40.00	80.00	160	325	—
1700 ILH	—	40.00	80.00	160	325	—

KM# 722 1/6 THALER (1/4 Gulden)

Silver **Ruler:** Friedrich August I **Rev:** 2 adjacent shields between palm branches, with 4-fold arms, with central shield of electoral Saxony, large crown above, value: 1/6 in oval below, date in legend

Date	Mintage	VG	F	VF	XF	Unc
1700 ILH	—	40.00	80.00	160	325	—

KM# 8 1/4 THALER

Silver **Obv:** 3 facing 1/2-length figures, date divided above, small imperial orb at top **Rev:** Ornate 2-fold arms in baroque frame

Date	Mintage	VG	F	VF	XF	Unc
1601 HB	—	55.00	115	235	475	—

KM# 13 1/4 THALER

Silver **Ruler:** Christian II, Johann Georg I and August **Obv:** Half-length bust, with sword over right shoulder divides date, small crossed swords arms below **Rev:** 2 busts facing each other, small open-crown arms below **Mint:** Dresden **Note:** Varieties exist.

Date	Mintage	VG	F	VF	XF	Unc
1601 HB	—	55.00	115	235	475	—
1602 HB	—	55.00	115	235	475	—
1603 HB	—	55.00	115	235	475	—
1604 HB	—	55.00	115	235	475	—
1605 HB	—	55.00	115	235	475	—
1605 HvR	—	55.00	115	235	475	—
1606 HvR	—	55.00	115	235	475	—
1607 HvR	—	55.00	115	235	475	—
1608 HvR	—	55.00	115	235	475	—
1609 HvR	—	55.00	115	235	475	—
1610 HvR	—	55.00	115	235	475	—
1611 (swan)	—	55.00	115	235	475	—
1611 HvR	—	55.00	115	235	475	—

KM# 40 1/4 THALER

Silver **Ruler:** Johann Georg I and August **Obv:** 1/2-length bust of Johann Georg I right with sword over right shoulder divides date, crossed swords arms below **Rev:** 1/2-length bust of August right, 4 small shields of arms in legend **Mint:** Dresden **Note:** Varieties exist.

Date	Mintage	VG	F	VF	XF	Unc
1611 (swan)	—	80.00	160	325	650	—
1612 (swan)	—	80.00	160	325	650	—
1613 (swan)	—	80.00	160	325	650	—
1614 (swan)	—	80.00	160	325	650	—
1615 (swan)	—	80.00	160	325	650	—
1616 (swan)	—	80.00	160	325	650	—

KM# 38 1/4 THALER

Silver **Ruler:** Johann Georg I and August **Subject:** Death of Christian II **Obv:** 9-line inscription with Roman numeral date **Rev:** 6-line inscription

Date	Mintage	VG	F	VF	XF	Unc
MDCXI (1611)	—	65.00	135	275	575	—

KM# 39 1/4 THALER

Silver **Ruler:** Johann Georg I **Subject:** Accession of Johann Georg I **Obv:** Full-length figure of Johann Georg I with sword and scepter **Rev:** Bear and ape by tree

Date	Mintage	VG	F	VF	XF	Unc
ND	—	—	—	—	—	—

KM# 52 1/4 THALER

Silver **Obv:** 1/2-length crowned bust of Johann Georg I right holding sword over right shoulder **Rev:** Ornate 4-fold arms with central shield of electoral Saxony, date divided above **Note:** Vicariat Issue.

Date	Mintage	VG	F	VF	XF	Unc
1612 (swan)	—	125	250	500	1,000	—

KM# 77 1/4 THALER

Silver **Subject:** Death of August II **Obv:** 1/2-length armored figure right holding baton, titles in legend **Rev:** 4-line inscription, RN dates in legend **Rev. Inscription:** TIMEDEVM / ET / HONORACÆ / SAREM

Date	Mintage	VG	F	VF	XF	Unc
MDCXV (1615)	—	100	175	300	600	—

KM# 78 1/4 THALER

Silver **Obv:** 1/2-length armored figure right with sword over right shoulder, titles of Johann Georg I begin with small imperial orb **Rev:** Oval 4-fold arms in baroque frame, date divided in top margin by mintmaster's symbol, titles continued

Date	Mintage	VG	F	VF	XF	Unc
1615 (swan)	—	65.00	125	235	475	—
1616 (swan)	—	65.00	125	235	475	—
1617 (swan)	—	65.00	125	235	475	—

KM# 88 1/4 THALER

Silver **Obv:** 1/2-length armored figure right with sword over right shoulder, titles of Johann Georg I begin with small imperial orb **Rev:** Squarish 4-fold arms with central shield of electoral Saxony, date divided in top margin by mintmaster's symbol, titles continued **Note:** Varieties exist.

Date	Mintage	VG	F	VF	XF	Unc
1616 (swan)	—	75.00	150	300	600	—
1617 (swan)	—	75.00	150	300	600	—
1618 (swan)	—	75.00	150	300	600	—
1619 (swan)	—	75.00	150	300	600	—
1620 (swan)	—	75.00	150	300	600	—
1621 (swan)	—	75.00	150	300	600	—
1622 (swan)	—	75.00	150	300	600	—
1623 (swan)	—	75.00	150	300	600	—
1624 (swan)	—	75.00	150	300	600	—

KM# 94 1/4 THALER

Silver **Subject:** Reformation Centennial **Obv:** Standing figure before seated king **Obv. Legend:** VT SALOMON..., date **Rev:** Mailed hands holding up severed arms

Date	Mintage	VG	F	VF	XF	Unc
1617	—	80.00	160	325	650	—

KM# 95 1/4 THALER

Silver **Obv:** Johann Georg I standing before his mother **Obv. Legend:** HONOR... **Rev:** Hands between 2 cornucopia, date in legend

Date	Mintage	VG	F	VF	XF	Unc
1617	—	100	185	375	750	—

KM# 96 1/4 THALER

Silver **Subject:** Reformation Centennial **Obv:** 1/2-length figure holding sword over right shoulder divides IOH - GEOR, 4-fold arms with central shield below, date divided at bottom **Rev:** 1/2-length figure holding sword over right shoulder divides FRID - III, 2-fold arms of Saxony below, 15 - 17 at bottom

Date	Mintage	VG	F	VF	XF	Unc
1617	—	100	185	375	750	—

KM# 116 1/4 THALER

Silver **Ruler:** Johann Georg I **Obv:** Elector on horseback to right, with sword over right shoulder, divides date, oval shield of 2-fold arms of electoral and ducal Saxony below **Obv. Legend:** PRO LEGE - ET GREGE **Rev:** 12-line inscription **Note:** Vicariat Issue.

Date	Mintage	VG	F	VF	XF	Unc
1619	—	75.00	150	300	625	—

KM# 117 1/4 THALER

Silver **Ruler:** Johann Georg I **Obv:** Elector on horseback to right, with sword over right shoulder, divides date, oval shield of 2-fold arms of electoral and ducal Saxony below **Obv. Legend:** PRO LEGE - ET GREGE **Rev:** 12-line inscription **Note:** Thick flan. Vicariat issue.

Date	Mintage	VG	F	VF	XF	Unc
1619	—	—	—	—	—	—

KM# 388 1/4 THALER

Silver **Ruler:** Johann Georg I **Obv:** Bust right with sword on shoulder **Rev:** 4-fold arms with central shield on reverse **Note:** Similar to KM#407.

Date	Mintage	VG	F	VF	XF	Unc
1623	—	65.00	135	275	575	—
1624 HI	—	65.00	135	275	575	—
1625 HI	—	65.00	135	275	575	—
1627 HI	—	65.00	135	275	575	—

KM# 407 1/4 THALER

Silver **Ruler:** Johann Georg I **Obv:** Bust right with sword on shoulder **Rev:** 3-fold arms, date at top **Note:** Varieties exist.

Date	Mintage	VG	F	VF	XF	Unc
1626 HI	—	65.00	135	275	575	—
1627 HI	—	65.00	135	275	575	—
1628 HI	—	65.00	135	275	575	—
1629 HI	—	65.00	135	275	575	—
1630 HI	—	65.00	135	275	575	—
1631 HI	—	65.00	135	275	575	—
1632 HI	—	65.00	135	275	575	—
1633 HI	—	65.00	135	275	575	—
1634 HI	—	65.00	135	275	575	—
1635 CM	—	65.00	135	275	575	—
1635 HI	—	65.00	135	275	575	—
1635 SD	—	65.00	135	275	575	—
1636 SD	—	65.00	135	275	575	—
1637 SD	—	65.00	135	275	575	—
1638 SD	—	65.00	135	275	575	—
1639 SD	—	65.00	135	275	575	—
1640 SD	—	65.00	135	275	575	—
1640 SD	—	65.00	135	275	575	—
1640 CR	—	65.00	135	275	575	—
1641 CR	—	65.00	135	275	575	—
1642 CR	—	65.00	135	275	575	—
1643 CR	—	65.00	135	275	575	—
1644 CR	—	65.00	135	275	575	—
1645 CR	—	65.00	135	275	575	—
1646 CR	—	65.00	135	275	575	—
1647 CR	—	65.00	135	275	575	—
1648 CR	—	65.00	135	275	575	—
1649 CR	—	65.00	135	275	575	—
1650 CR	—	65.00	135	275	575	—
1651 CR	—	65.00	135	275	575	—
1652 CR	—	65.00	135	275	575	—
1653 CR	—	65.00	135	275	575	—
1654 CR	—	65.00	135	275	575	—
1655 CR	—	65.00	135	275	575	—
1656 CR	—	65.00	135	275	575	—

KM# 406 1/4 THALER

Silver **Ruler:** Johann Georg I **Subject:** Augsburg Confession Centennial

Date	Mintage	VG	F	VF	XF	Unc
1630	—	75.00	150	300	600	—

KM# 448 1/4 THALER

Silver **Subject:** Death of Johann Georg I

Date	Mintage	VG	F	VF	XF	Unc
MDCLVI (1656)	—	85.00	165	300	625	—

KM# 449.1 1/4 THALER

Silver **Ruler:** Johann Georg II **Obv:** Titles of Johann Georg II **Mint:** Dresden **Note:** Prev. KM#449. Varieties exist.

Date	Mintage	VG	F	VF	XF	Unc
1656 CR	—	65.00	135	275	575	—
1658 CR	—	65.00	135	275	575	—
1659 CR	—	65.00	135	275	575	—
1660 CR	—	65.00	135	275	575	—
1661 CR	—	65.00	135	275	575	—
1662 CR	—	65.00	135	275	575	—
1663 CR	—	65.00	135	275	575	—
1664 CR	—	65.00	135	275	575	—
1665 CR	—	65.00	135	275	575	—
1666 CR	—	65.00	135	275	575	—
1667 CR	—	65.00	135	275	575	—
1668 CR	—	65.00	135	275	575	—
1675 CR	—	65.00	135	275	575	—
1677 CR	—	65.00	135	275	575	—

Date	Mintage	VG	F	VF	XF	Unc
1679 CF	—	65.00	135	275	575	—
1680 CF	—	65.00	135	275	575	—

KM# 457 1/4 THALER
Silver **Ruler:** Johann Georg II **Obv:** Duke on horseback right with sword over shoulder, oval 2-fold arms below, date in legend **Rev:** 12-line inscription **Mint:** Dresden **Note:** Vicariat Issue.

Date	Mintage	VG	F	VF	XF	Unc
1657 (acorn)	—	75.00	150	300	625	—

KM# 535 1/4 THALER
Silver **Subject:** Wechsel Succession **Obv:** Bust of Johann Georg II right **Rev:** Crowned oval 2-fold arms in baroque frame, WECHSEL THALER below, date in legend

Date	Mintage	VG	F	VF	XF	Unc
1670 CR	—	—	—	—	—	—

KM# 577 1/4 THALER
Silver **Obv:** Bust right with sword on shoulder, titles of Johann Georg III **Rev:** 3-fold arms, date at top **Note:** Similar to KM#407. Varieties exist.

Date	Mintage	VG	F	VF	XF	Unc
1681 CF	—	75.00	150	300	600	—
1683 CF	—	75.00	150	300	600	—
1687	—	75.00	150	300	600	—
1688 IK	—	75.00	150	300	600	—
1690 IK	—	75.00	150	300	600	—
1691 IK	—	75.00	150	300	600	—

KM# 594 1/4 THALER
Silver **Subject:** Death of Johann Georg III's Mother, Magdalene Sibylle **Obv:** MANET in wreath, SOLA. SPES. MEA in band at top **Rev:** 7-line inscription with dates

Date	Mintage	VG	F	VF	XF	Unc
1687	—	60.00	100	200	425	—

KM# 639 1/4 THALER
Silver **Obv:** Bust right with sword on shoulder, titles of Johann Georg IV **Rev:** Electoral hat above 3-fold arms, date at top **Note:** Similar to KM#407. Varieties exist.

Date	Mintage	VG	F	VF	XF	Unc
1692 IK	—	75.00	150	300	600	—
1693 IK	—	75.00	150	300	600	—
1694 EPH	—	75.00	150	300	600	—
1694 IK	—	75.00	150	300	600	—

KM# 650 1/4 THALER
Silver **Obv:** Bust right with sword on shoulder, titles of Friedrich August I **Rev:** Electoral hat above 3-fold arms, date at top **Note:** Similar to KM#639. Varieties exist.

Date	Mintage	VG	F	VF	XF	Unc
1694 IK	—	75.00	150	300	600	—
1695 IK	—	75.00	150	300	600	—
1696 IK	—	75.00	150	300	600	—
1697 IK	—	75.00	150	300	600	—

KM# 649 1/4 THALER
Silver **Subject:** Homage of Dresden to Friedrich August I **Obv:** 4 crowned double-F monograms in cruciform, A in each angle, crossed-swords arms in center **Rev:** Hand in center holding up 2 fingers, curved inscription below, all in wreath, outer marginal inscription with Roman numeral date

Date	Mintage	VG	F	VF	XF	Unc
1694	—	—	—	—	—	—

KM# 676 1/4 THALER
Silver **Obv:** Crowned bust right **Rev:** Crowned 4-fold arms of Poland and Lithuania with central shield of Saxony arms divide 1-8, date in margin

Date	Mintage	VG	F	VF	XF	Unc
1698	—	—	—	—	—	—

Note: Struck for circulation in Poland

KM# 705 1/4 THALER
Silver **Ruler:** Friedrich August I **Obv:** Large bust right **Rev:** Round arms between palm branches dividing initials **Note:** Varieties exist.

Date	Mintage	VG	F	VF	XF	Unc
1698 ILH	—	65.00	135	275	575	—
1699 ILH	—	65.00	135	275	575	—
1700 ILH	—	65.00	135	275	575	—

KM# 517 1/3 THALER (1/2 Gulden)
Silver **Mint:** Bautzen **Note:** Coinage for Oberlaustiz.

Date	Mintage	VG	F	VF	XF	Unc
1666 HI	—	65.00	135	275	550	—
1667 HI	—	65.00	135	275	550	—
1668 CR	—	65.00	135	275	550	—

KM# 522 1/3 THALER (1/2 Gulden)
Silver **Obv:** Bust right **Rev:** Crowned 4-fold arms with central shield of electoral Saxony divide initials, 1/3 in oval below, date at top in legend **Note:** Varieties exist.

Date	Mintage	VG	F	VF	XF	Unc
1668 CR	—	55.00	110	225	450	—
1669 CR	—	55.00	110	225	450	—
1670 CR	—	55.00	110	225	450	—

KM# 547 1/3 THALER (1/2 Gulden)
Silver **Obv:** Bust right **Rev:** Crowned 4-fold arms with central shield of crossed swords divide mintmasters initials, value: 1/3 in oval below **Note:** Varieties exist.

Date	Mintage	VG	F	VF	XF	Unc
1672 CR	—	45.00	90.00	180	360	—
1673 CR	—	45.00	90.00	180	360	—
1674 CR	—	45.00	90.00	180	360	—
1675 CR	—	45.00	90.00	180	360	—
1680 CR	—	45.00	90.00	180	360	—

KM# 548 1/3 THALER (1/2 Gulden)
Silver **Obv:** Bust right **Rev:** Crowned oval 2-fold arms in palm branches, date in legend at top, value: 1/3 in oval below **Note:** Varieties exist.

Date	Mintage	VG	F	VF	XF	Unc
1675 CR	—	50.00	100	200	425	—
1676 CR	—	50.00	100	200	425	—
1677 CR	—	50.00	100	200	425	—
1678 CR	—	50.00	100	200	425	—
1678 CF	—	50.00	100	200	425	—
1679 CF	—	50.00	100	200	425	—
1680 CF	—	50.00	100	200	425	—

KM# 578 1/3 THALER (1/2 Gulden)
Silver **Rev:** Squarish arms **Note:** Varieties exist.

Date	Mintage	VG	F	VF	XF	Unc
1681 CF	—	50.00	100	200	425	—
1682 CF	—	50.00	100	200	425	—
1683 CF	—	50.00	100	200	425	—
1684 CF	—	50.00	100	200	425	—
1685 CF	—	50.00	100	200	425	—
1686 CF	—	50.00	100	200	425	—
1687	—	50.00	100	200	425	—
1688 IK	—	50.00	100	200	425	—
1689 IK	—	50.00	100	200	425	—
1690 IK	—	50.00	100	200	425	—
1691 IK	—	50.00	100	200	425	—

KM# 613 1/3 THALER (1/2 Gulden)
Silver **Subject:** Death of Johann Georg III

Date	Mintage	VG	F	VF	XF	Unc
MDCXCI (1691) IK	—	55.00	110	225	450	—

KM# 627 1/3 THALER (1/2 Gulden)
Silver **Obv:** Bust right **Rev:** Similar to obverse of 1 Pfennig, KM#623, but date divided at top and value: 1/3 divided in upper and lower angles of crossed swords

Date	Mintage	VG	F	VF	XF	Unc
1692 IK	—	45.00	95.00	190	385	—
1693 IK	—	55.00	110	225	450	—

KM# 640 1/3 THALER (1/2 Gulden)
Silver **Obv:** Bust right **Rev:** 2 adjacent oval arms in baroque frame, crown above divides date, value 1/3 in oval below without mintmaster's initials **Note:** Varieties exist.

Date	Mintage	VG	F	VF	XF	Unc
1693 IK	—	85.00	160	325	650	—
1694 EPH	—	85.00	160	325	650	—
1694 IK	—	85.00	160	325	650	—

KM# 652 1/3 THALER (1/2 Gulden)
Silver **Obv:** Bust right **Rev:** Crowned oval 2-fold arms between 2 palm branches, date divided above, value 1/3 in oval below **Note:** Varieties exist.

Date	Mintage	VG	F	VF	XF	Unc
1694 IK	—	—	—	—	—	—
1695 EPH	—	45.00	95.00	190	385	—
1695 IK	—	45.00	95.00	190	385	—
1696 EPH	—	45.00	95.00	190	385	—
1696 IK	—	45.00	95.00	190	385	—
1697 EPH	—	45.00	95.00	190	385	—
1697 IK	—	45.00	95.00	190	385	—

KM# 651 1/3 THALER (1/2 Gulden)
Silver **Subject:** Death of Johann Georg IV

Date	Mintage	VG	F	VF	XF	Unc
MDCXCIV (1694) IK	—	55.00	110	225	450	—

KM# 706 1/3 THALER (1/2 Gulden)
Silver **Rev:** 2 adjacent shields of arms **Note:** Varieties exist.

Date	Mintage	VG	F	VF	XF	Unc
1698 EPH	—	40.00	80.00	160	325	—
1698 ILH	—	40.00	80.00	160	325	—
1699 EPH	—	40.00	80.00	160	325	—
1699 ILH	—	40.00	80.00	160	325	—
1700 ILH	—	40.00	80.00	160	325	—

KM# 723 1/3 THALER (1/2 Gulden)
Silver **Ruler:** Friedrich August I **Obv:** Armored bust right **Rev:** Crown above two shields, value below **Note:** Varieties exist.

Date	Mintage	VG	F	VF	XF	Unc
1700 ILH	—	55.00	110	225	450	—

KM# 14 1/2 THALER

Silver **Ruler:** Christian II, Johann Georg I and August **Mint:** Dresden **Note:** Varieties exist.

Date	Mintage	VG	F	VF	XF	Unc
1601 HB	—	75.00	150	300	625	—
1602 HB	—	75.00	150	300	625	—
1603 HB	—	75.00	150	300	625	—
1604 HB	—	75.00	150	300	625	—
1605 HvR	—	75.00	150	300	625	—
1606 HvR	—	75.00	150	300	625	—
1607 HvR	—	75.00	150	300	625	—
1608 HvR	—	75.00	150	300	625	—
1609 HvR	—	75.00	150	300	625	—
1610 HvR	—	75.00	150	300	625	—
1611 (swan)	—	75.00	150	300	625	—
1611 HvR	—	75.00	150	300	625	—

MB# 318 1/2 THALER

Silver **Ruler:** Christian II, Johann Georg I and August **Obv:** Smaller 1/2-length facing figures of 3 brothers in circle, head of middle figure divides date, small imperial orb above, titles in legend **Rev:** 4-fold arms with central shield of electoral Saxony in ornate frame, titles continued **Mint:** Dresden **Note:** Varieties exist.

Date	Mintage	VG	F	VF	XF	Unc
1601 HB	—	50.00	85.00	140	275	—

MB# 319 1/2 THALER

Silver **Ruler:** Christian II, Johann Georg I and August **Obv:** Smaller 1/2-length facing figures of 3 brothers in circle, head of middle figure divides date, small imperial orb above, titles in legend **Rev:** Heart-shaped 2-fold arms of electoral and ducal Saxony in ornate frame, titles continued **Mint:** Dresden **Note:** Varieties exist.

Date	Mintage	VG	F	VF	XF	Unc
1601 HB	—	50.00	85.00	140	275	—

KM# 22 1/2 THALER

Silver **Ruler:** Christian II, Johann Georg I and August **Note:** Thick flan.

Date	Mintage	VG	F	VF	XF	Unc
1602 HB	—	135	275	525	1,050	—
1609 HvR	—	135	275	525	1,050	—
1610 HvR	—	135	275	525	1,050	—
1611 (swan)	—	135	275	525	1,050	—

KM# 42.1 1/2 THALER

Silver **Subject:** Accession of Johann Georg I **Obv:** Full-length figure of Johann Georg I with sword and scepter **Rev:** Bear and ape by tree

Date	Mintage	VG	F	VF	XF	Unc
1611	—	—	—	—	—	—

KM# 42.2 1/2 THALER

Silver **Ruler:** Johann Georg I and August **Subject:** Accession of Johann Georg I **Obv:** 10-line inscription **Rev:** Bear and ape by tree

Date	Mintage	VG	F	VF	XF	Unc
MDCXI (1611)	—	—	—	—	—	—

KM# 41 1/2 THALER

Silver **Ruler:** Johann Georg I and August **Subject:** Death of Christian II **Note:** Similar to 1/4 Thaler, KM#38.

Date	Mintage	VG	F	VF	XF	Unc
MDCXI (1611)	—	100	200	375	750	—

KM# 53 1/2 THALER

Silver

Date	Mintage	VG	F	VF	XF	Unc
1612 (swan)	—	55.00	115	235	475	—
1613 (swan)	—	55.00	115	235	475	—
1614 (swan)	—	55.00	115	235	475	—
1615 (swan)	—	55.00	115	235	475	—
1616 (swan)	—	55.00	115	235	475	—

KM# 54 1/2 THALER

Silver **Note:** Vicariat Issue.

Date	Mintage	VG	F	VF	XF	Unc
1612 (swan)	—	80.00	165	325	675	—

KM# 79 1/2 THALER

Silver **Ruler:** Johann Georg I **Obv:** 1/2-length bust of Johann Georg I right w/sword over right shoulder divides date, crossed swords arms below **Rev:** 1/2-length bust of August right, 4 small shields of arms in legend **Mint:** Dresden **Note:** Struck on thick flan using same dies as 1/4 Thaler, KM#40.

Date	Mintage	VG	F	VF	XF	Unc
1615 (swan)	—	—	—	—	—	—

KM# 80 1/2 THALER

Silver **Ruler:** Johann Georg I **Subject:** Death of August II **Obv:** Bust right with baton and helmet **Rev:** 4-line inscription

Date	Mintage	VG	F	VF	XF	Unc
MDCXV (1615)	—	275	450	900	1,800	—

KM# 81 1/2 THALER

Silver **Obv:** Bust right with sword and helmet, band over left shoulder **Rev:** Helmeted arms divide date at top

Date	Mintage	VG	F	VF	XF	Unc
1615 (swan)	—	65.00	135	275	575	—
1616 (swan)	—	65.00	135	275	575	—

KM# 81A 1/2 THALER

Silver **Ruler:** Johann Georg I **Obv:** Bust right, sword over shoulder **Rev:** Round 2-fold arms **Mint:** Dresden **Note:** Struck on thick flan using same dies as 1/4 Thaler, KM#78.

Date	Mintage	VG	F	VF	XF	Unc
1616 (swan)	—	—	—	—	—	—

KM# 98 1/2 THALER

Silver **Note:** Thick flan.

Date	Mintage	VG	F	VF	XF	Unc
1617	—	—	—	—	—	—

KM# 101 1/2 THALER

Silver, 35 mm. **Ruler:** Johann Georg I **Subject:** Centenary of Protestant Reformation **Obv:** Half-length figure to right, wearing rob and electoral hat, holding sword over right shoulder, divides IOH - GEOR, shield of 4-fold arms, with central shield of electoral Saxony in front divides date **Obv. Legend:** VERBVM DOMINI MANET IN ÆTERNVM. **Rev:** Half-length figure to right, wearing rob and electoral hat, holding sword over right shoulder, divides FRID - III, shield of 2-fold arms of electoral and ducal Saxony in front divides 15 - 17 **Rev. Legend:** SECVLVM LVTHERANVM. **Note:** Thick flan.

Date	Mintage	VG	F	VF	XF	Unc
1617	—	—	—	—	—	—

KM# 102 1/2 THALER

Silver, 36 mm. **Ruler:** Johann Georg I **Obv:** Half-length armored figure to right, holding sword over right shoulder, small imperial orb above **Obv. Legend:** IOHAN. GEORG. D. G. DVX SAX. IVL. CLIV. ET. MONTI. **Rev:** Spanish shield of 4-fold arms, with central shield of electoral Saxony, in baroque frame, date divided by mintmaster's symbol at top **Rev. Legend:** SACRI. ROMANI. IMP. ARCHIMAR. ET ELECT. **Note:** Varieties exist.

Date	Mintage	VG	F	VF	XF	Unc
1617 (swan)	—	65.00	135	275	575	—
1618 (swan)	—	65.00	135	275	575	—
1619 (swan)	—	65.00	135	275	575	—
16Z0 (swan)	—	65.00	135	275	575	—
16Z1 (swan)	—	65.00	135	275	575	—
16Z3 (swan)	—	65.00	135	275	575	—
16Z4 (swan)	—	65.00	135	275	575	—

KM# 97 1/2 THALER

Silver, 34 mm. **Ruler:** Johann Georg I **Subject:** Centenary of Protestant Reformation **Obv:** Woman seated at left, King Solomon with scepter standing at right, date at end of legend **Obv. Legend:** VT SALOMON SIC ECO MATREM. **Rev:** Pair of praying hands extended up to 'Jehovah' in Hebrew in clouds above **Rev. Legend:** MATERNIS PRECIBVS NIHIL FORTIVS.

Date	Mintage	VG	F	VF	XF	Unc
1617	—	200	400	700	1,350	—

KM# 99 1/2 THALER

Silver

Date	Mintage	VG	F	VF	XF	Unc
1617	—	100	200	350	675	—

KM# 100 1/2 THALER

Silver, 37 mm. **Ruler:** Johann Georg I **Subject:** Centenary of Protestant Reformation **Obv:** Half-length figure to right, wearing rob and electoral hat, holding sword over right shoulder, divides IOH - GEOR, shield of 4-fold arms, with central shield of electoral Saxony in front divides date **Obv. Legend:** VERBVM DOMINI MANET IN ÆTERNVM. **Rev:** Half-length figure to right, wearing rob and electoral hat, holding sword over right shoulder, divides FRID - III, shield of 2-fold arms of electoral and ducal Saxony in front divides 15 - 17 **Rev. Legend:** SECVLVM LVTHERANVM.

Date	Mintage	VG	F	VF	XF	Unc
1617	—	100	200	350	675	—

KM# 118 1/2 THALER

Silver **Ruler:** Johann Georg I **Obv:** Elector on horseback to right, with sword over right shoulder, divides date, oval shield of 2-fold arms of electoral and ducal Saxony below **Obv. Legend:** PRO LEGE - ET GREGE **Rev:** 12-line inscription **Note:** Vicariat Issue.

Date	Mintage	VG	F	VF	XF	Unc
1619	—	85.00	165	325	650	—

KM# 381 1/2 THALER

Silver **Ruler:** Johann Georg I **Obv:** Bust right with sword over shoulder, band over right shoulder **Rev:** 4-fold arms with central shield of crossed swords in ornamented frame **Mint:** Dresden **Note:** Similar to 1 Thaler, KM#90.

Date	Mintage	VG	F	VF	XF	Unc
1622 (swan)	—	65.00	135	275	575	—
1623 (swan)	—	65.00	135	275	575	—
16Z6 HI	—	65.00	135	275	575	—

KM# 389 1/2 THALER

Silver **Ruler:** Johann Georg I **Obv:** Bust right with sword over shoulder **Rev:** Helmeted arms **Note:** Varieties exist.

Date	Mintage	VG	F	VF	XF	Unc
1624 HI	—	65.00	135	275	550	—
1625 HI	—	65.00	135	275	550	—
1626 HI	—	65.00	135	275	550	—
1627 HI	—	65.00	135	275	550	—
1628 HI	—	65.00	135	275	550	—
1629 HI	—	65.00	135	275	550	—

KM# 410 1/2 THALER

Silver **Ruler:** Johann Georg I **Rev:** Without helmets above 4-fold arms, central shield of crossed swords **Note:** Varieties exist.

Date	Mintage	VG	F	VF	XF	Unc
1630 HI	—	65.00	135	275	550	—
1631 HI	—	65.00	135	275	550	—
1632 HI	—	65.00	135	275	550	—
1633 HI	—	65.00	135	275	550	—
1634 HI	—	65.00	135	275	550	—
1635 CM	—	65.00	135	275	550	—
1635 HI	—	65.00	135	275	550	—
1635 SD	—	65.00	135	275	550	—
1636 SD	—	65.00	135	275	550	—
1637 SD	—	65.00	135	275	550	—
1638 SD	—	65.00	135	275	550	—
1639 SD	—	65.00	135	275	550	—
1640 CR	—	65.00	135	275	550	—
1641 CR	—	65.00	135	275	550	—
1642 CR	—	65.00	135	275	550	—
1644 CR	—	65.00	135	275	550	—
1645 CR	—	65.00	135	275	550	—
1646 CR	—	65.00	135	275	550	—
1647 CR	—	65.00	135	275	550	—
1648 CR	—	65.00	135	275	550	—
1649 CR	—	65.00	135	275	550	—
1650 CR	—	65.00	135	275	550	—
1651 CR	—	65.00	135	275	550	—
1652 CR	—	65.00	135	275	550	—
1653 CR	—	65.00	135	275	550	—
1654 CR	—	65.00	135	275	550	—
1655 CR	—	65.00	135	275	550	—
1656 CR	—	65.00	135	275	550	—

KM# 409 1/2 THALER

Silver **Ruler:** Johann Georg I **Note:** Thick flan.

Date	Mintage	VG	F	VF	XF	Unc
1630	—	—	—	—	—	—

KM# 408 1/2 THALER

Silver **Ruler:** Johann Georg I **Subject:** Augsburg Confession Centennial

Date	Mintage	VG	F	VF	XF	Unc
1630	—	65.00	135	275	575	—

KM# 450 1/2 THALER

Silver **Subject:** Death of Johann Georg I

Date	Mintage	VG	F	VF	XF	Unc
MDCLVI (1656)	—	65.00	135	275	575	—

KM# 459 1/2 THALER

Silver **Obv:** Duke on horseback with sword over right shoulder to right, oval 2-fold arms below, date in legend **Rev:** 12-line inscription **Note:** Struck on thick flan using same dies as 1/8 Thaler, KM#456.

Date	Mintage	VG	F	VF	XF	Unc
1657 (acorn)	—	30.00	450	925	1,850	—

KM# 458 1/2 THALER

Silver **Obv:** Duke on horseback w/sword over right shoulder to right, oval 2-fold arms below, date in legend **Rev:** 12-line inscription **Note:** Vicariat Issue.

Date	Mintage	VG	F	VF	XF	Unc
1657 (acorn)	—	65.00	135	275	575	—
1658 (acorn)	—	65.00	135	275	575	—

KM# 473 1/2 THALER

Silver

Date	Mintage	VG	F	VF	XF	Unc
1658 CR	—	65.00	135	275	575	—
1659 CR	—	65.00	135	275	575	—
1660 CR	—	65.00	135	275	575	—
1661 CR	—	65.00	135	275	575	—
1662 CR	—	65.00	135	275	575	—
1663 CR	—	65.00	135	275	575	—
1665 CR	—	65.00	135	275	575	—

KM# 479 1/2 THALER

Silver **Subject:** Death of Johann Georg II's Mother, Magdalene Sibylle **Obv:** 7-line inscription **Rev:** 6-line inscription with R.N. dates

Date	Mintage	VG	F	VF	XF	Unc
MDCLIX (1659) Rare	—	—	—	—	—	—

KM# 495.1 1/2 THALER

Silver **Ruler:** Johann Georg II **Obv:** Bust right with sword over right shoulder **Rev:** 3-fold arms, mintmaster's initials below, date in legend **Mint:** Bautzen **Note:** Struck on thick flan using same dies as 1/8 Thaler, KM#472.

Date	Mintage	VG	F	VF	XF	Unc
1659 CR	—	165	325	650	1,300	—
1660 CR	—	165	325	650	1,300	—
1661 CR	—	165	325	650	1,300	—
1666 CR	—	165	325	650	1,300	—

KM# 495.2 1/2 THALER

Silver **Ruler:** Johann Georg II **Obv:** Bust right with sword over right shoulder in inner circle, titles of Johann Georg II **Rev:** 3-fold arms **Mint:** Bautzen **Note:** Struck on thick flan using same dies as 1/4 Thaler, KM#449.1.

Date	Mintage	VG	F	VF	XF	Unc
1659 CR	—	—	—	—	—	—
1660 CR	—	—	—	—	—	—

KM# 510 1/2 THALER

Silver **Obv:** Elector in armor to right with sword over shoulder **Rev:** 4-fold arms with central shield **Note:** Similar to KM#473. Varieties exist.

Date	Mintage	VG	F	VF	XF	Unc
1665 CR	—	80.00	165	335	675	—
1666 CR	—	80.00	165	335	675	—
1667 CR	—	80.00	165	335	675	—
1671 CR	—	80.00	165	335	675	—
1672 CR	—	80.00	165	335	675	—
1673 CR	—	80.00	165	335	675	—
1679 CR	—	80.00	165	335	675	—

KM# 518 1/2 THALER

Silver **Obv:** Johann Georg II galloping on horseback right, small oval 2-fold arms below **Rev:** 9-line inscription with date **Note:** Show 1/2 Thaler. Struck at Bautzen.

Date	Mintage	VG	F	VF	XF	Unc
1666	—	—	—	—	—	—

KM# 536 1/2 THALER

Silver **Subject:** Wechsel Succession **Obv:** Different bust right **Rev:** WECHSEL • THALER below arms **Note:** Similar to 1 Thaler, KM#538.

Date	Mintage	VG	F	VF	XF	Unc
1670 CR	—	135	275	525	1,050	—

KM# 579 1/2 THALER

Silver **Note:** Similar to KM#473, but titles of Johann George III.

Date	Mintage	VG	F	VF	XF	Unc
1681 CF	—	55.00	90.00	165	425	—
1683 CF	—	55.00	90.00	165	425	—
1684 CF	—	55.00	90.00	165	425	—
1686 CF	—	55.00	90.00	165	425	—
1687	—	55.00	90.00	165	425	—
1688 IK	—	55.00	90.00	165	425	—
1689 IK	—	55.00	90.00	165	425	—
1690 IK	—	55.00	90.00	165	425	—
1691 IK	—	55.00	90.00	165	425	—

Note: Varieties exist

KM# 595 1/2 THALER

Silver **Subject:** Death of Johann Georg III's Mother, Magdalene Sibylla **Obv:** MANET in wreath, SOLA. SPES. MEA in band at top **Rev:** 7-line inscription with dates **Note:** Similar to 1 Groschen, KM#592.

Date	Mintage	VG	F	VF	XF	Unc
1687	—	—	—	—	—	—

KM# 614 1/2 THALER

Silver **Obv:** Elector in armor with sword over right shoulder to right, titles of Johann Georg IV **Rev:** Crowned 4-fold arms in inner circle **Note:** Similar to 1/2 Thaler, KM#510.

Date	Mintage	VG	F	VF	XF	Unc
1691 IK	—	300	550	1,000	2,000	—
1692 IK	—	300	550	1,000	2,000	—
1693 IK	—	300	550	1,000	2,000	—
1694 IK	—	300	550	1,000	2,000	—

Note: Varieties exist

KM# 653 1/2 THALER

Silver **Obv:** Bust right with sword over right shoulder to right, helmet in front **Rev:** Helmeted arms separating initials, date divided at top

Date	Mintage	VG	F	VF	XF	Unc
1694 EPH	—	425	600	1,200	2,300	—

KM# A668 1/2 THALER

Silver **Ruler:** Johann Georg IV **Obv:** Bust right with sword over right shoulder to right, titles of Johann Georg IV **Rev:** 3-fold arms, electoral hat above **Mint:** Leipzig **Note:** Struck on thick flan using same dies as 1/4 Thaler, KM#639.

Date	Mintage	VG	F	VF	XF	Unc
1694 EPH Rare	—	—	—	—	—	—

KM# 668 1/2 THALER

Silver, 37 mm. **Ruler:** Friedrich August I **Obv:** Long-haired 1/3 length figure to right holding upright sword, small imperial orb in margin above, titles of Friedrich August I **Obv. Legend:** FR - ID. AUGUST. DG. DUX. SAX. I. C. M. ANGR. ET. WESTPH. **Rev:** Electoral hat above ornate shield of 4-fold arms with central shield of Electoral Saxony arms, date in margin at top **Rev. Legend:** SAC. ROMANI. IMP. ARCHIMARS. ET. ELECT. X. **Mint:** Dresden

Date	Mintage	VG	F	VF	XF	Unc
1695 IK	—	250	450	925	1,850	—
1696 IK	—	250	450	925	1,850	—
1697 IK	—	250	450	925	1,850	—

KM# 724 1/2 THALER

Silver **Ruler:** Friedrich August I **Obv:** Laureate bust right **Obv. Legend:** DG.FRID.AUG.REX.POL — DUX SAX. I.C.M.A & W. **Rev:** Crowned, round 4-fold arms with crowned central shield of 2-fold arms, between 2 palm branches crossed at bottom, date at top **Rev. Legend:** SAC. ROMANI. IMP. ARCHIMARS. ET. ELECT. **Note:** Varieties exist.

Date	Mintage	VG	F	VF	XF	Unc
1698 ILH	—	90.00	200	375	775	—
1700 ILH	—	90.00	200	375	775	—

KM# 549 2/3 THALER (Gulden)

Silver **Note:** Varieties exist.

Date	Mintage	VG	F	VF	XF	Unc
1675 CR	—	55.00	100	210	425	—
1676 CR	—	55.00	100	210	425	—
1677 CR	—	55.00	100	210	425	—
1678 CR	—	55.00	100	210	425	—

KM# 559 2/3 THALER (Gulden)

Silver **Obv:** Smaller bust right **Rev:** 3-fold arms **Note:** Varieties exist.

Date	Mintage	VG	F	VF	XF	Unc
1678 CF	—	55.00	100	210	425	—
1679 CF	—	55.00	100	210	425	—
1680 CF	—	55.00	100	210	425	—
1681 CF	—	55.00	100	210	425	—

Note: Posthumous error.

KM# 571 2/3 THALER (Gulden)

Silver **Note:** Varieties exist. Dav. #810.

Date	Mintage	VG	F	VF	XF	Unc
1680 CF	—	55.00	100	210	425	—
1681 CF	—	55.00	100	210	425	—
1682 CF	—	55.00	100	210	425	—
1683 CF	—	55.00	100	210	425	—
1684 CF	—	55.00	100	210	425	—
1685 CF	—	55.00	100	210	425	—
1686 CF	—	55.00	100	210	425	—
1687	—	55.00	100	210	425	—
1688	—	55.00	100	210	425	—
1688 IK	—	55.00	100	210	425	—
1689	—	55.00	100	210	425	—
1689 IK	—	55.00	100	210	425	—
1690 IK	—	55.00	100	210	425	—
1691 IK	—	55.00	100	210	425	—

KM# 596 2/3 THALER (Gulden)

Silver **Subject:** Death of Johann Georg III's Mother, Magdalene Sibylle

Date	Mintage	VG	F	VF	XF	Unc
1687	—	70.00	120	235	475	—

KM# 615 2/3 THALER (Gulden)

Silver **Subject:** Death of Johann Georg III

Date	Mintage	VG	F	VF	XF	Unc
MDCXCI (1691) IK	—	65.00	135	275	550	—

KM# 628 2/3 THALER (Gulden)

Silver

Date	Mintage	VG	F	VF	XF	Unc
1692 IK	—	35.00	75.00	150	300	—
1693 (2 crossed arrows)	—	35.00	75.00	150	300	—
1693 IK	—	35.00	75.00	150	300	—

KM# 641 2/3 THALER (Gulden)

Silver

Date	Mintage	VG	F	VF	XF	Unc
1693	—	35.00	75.00	150	300	—
1693 IK	—	35.00	75.00	150	300	—
1693 SD	—	40.00	75.00	150	300	—
1693 EPH	—	40.00	75.00	150	300	—
1694 IK	—	35.00	75.00	150	300	—
1694 EPH	—	40.00	75.00	150	300	—

KM# 654 2/3 THALER (Gulden)

Silver **Subject:** Death of Johann Georg IV

Date	Mintage	VG	F	VF	XF	Unc
MDCXCIV (1694) IK	—	65.00	135	275	575	—

KM# 655 2/3 THALER (Gulden)

Silver **Note:** Varieties exist.

Date	Mintage	VG	F	VF	XF	Unc
1694 IK	—	35.00	75.00	150	315	—
1694 EPH	—	45.00	90.00	180	360	—
1695 IK	—	35.00	75.00	150	315	—
1695 EPH	—	45.00	90.00	180	360	—
1696 IK	—	35.00	75.00	150	315	—
1696 EPH	—	45.00	90.00	180	360	—
1697 IK	—	35.00	75.00	150	315	—
1697 EPH	—	45.00	90.00	180	360	—

KM# 685 2/3 THALER (Gulden)

Silver **Ruler:** Friedrich August I **Obv:** Armored, laureate bust right **Obv. Legend:** DG • FRID • AUGUST • REX POLONIARUM **Rev:** Crown above two shields, value below **Rev. Legend:** DUX • SAX • I • C • M • A • & • W • S • R • I • ... **Note:** Similar to 1 Thaler, KM#707, but value: 2/3 on reverse. Dav.#819.

Date	Mintage	VG	F	VF	XF	Unc
1697 EPH	—	35.00	75.00	150	315	—
1697 IK	—	35.00	75.00	150	315	—
1698 EPH	—	35.00	75.00	150	315	—
1698 ILH	—	35.00	75.00	150	315	—
1699 EPH	—	35.00	75.00	150	315	—
1699 ILH	—	35.00	75.00	150	315	—
1700 EPH	—	35.00	75.00	150	315	—
1700 ILH	—	35.00	75.00	150	315	—

MB# 314 THALER

Silver **Ruler:** Christian II, Johann Georg I and August **Obv:** 1/2-length facing figures of 3 brothers in circle, head of middle figure divides date, small imperial orb above, titles in legend **Rev:** 13-fold arms with central shield of electoral Saxony breaks legend at bottom **Rev. Legend:** FRAT. ET. DV - CES. SAXON **Mint:** Dresden **Note:** Dav. #9820. Varieties exist.

Date	Mintage	VG	F	VF	XF	Unc
1601 HB	—	70.00	145	240	425	600

KM# 15 THALER

Silver, 42 mm. **Ruler:** Christian II, Johann Georg I and August **Obv:** 3 half-length facing figures, date divided above, small imperial orb at top **Obv. Legend:** CHRISTIAN. IOHAN: GEORG. ET. AVGVSTVS. **Rev:** Shield of 12-fold arms, with central shield of electoral Saxony, 3 ornate helmets above **Rev. Legend:** FRAT: ET. DV - CES. SAXON. **Note:** Ref. Dav. 7557.

Date	Mintage	VG	F	VF	XF	Unc
1601 HB	—	110	205	270	425	—

KM# 16 THALER

28.7700 g., Silver, 42 mm. **Ruler:** Christian II, Johann Georg I and August **Obv:** Half-length armored figure to right, holding sword over right shoulder and helmet with left hand, head divides date, small imperial orb at top, small shield of electoral Saxony arms at botttom **Obv. Legend:** CHRISTIAN. II. D. G. SA. RO - IMP. ARCHIMAR. ET. ELEC. **Rev:** 2 small facing busts in circle, 14 small shields of arms around, shield of ducal Saxony at top **Rev. Legend:** IOHAN: GEORG. ET. AVGVST: FRAT. ET. DVCES. SAXON+. **Note:** Ref. Dav. 7561.

Date	Mintage	VG	F	VF	XF	Unc
1601 HB	—	115	220	295	450	—
160Z HB	—	115	220	295	450	—
1603 HB	—	115	220	295	450	—
1604 HB	—	115	220	295	450	—
1605 HB	—	115	220	295	450	—

KM# 24 THALER

Silver **Ruler:** Christian II, Johann Georg I and August **Obv:** Bust right with sword and helmet divide date **Rev:** Busts facing one another **Mint:** Dresden **Note:** Dav. 7566.

Date	Mintage	VG	F	VF	XF	Unc
1604 HR	—	115	220	295	450	—
1605 HR	—	115	220	295	450	—
1606 HR	—	115	220	295	450	—
1607 HR	—	115	220	295	450	—
1608 HR	—	115	220	295	450	—
1609 HR	—	115	220	295	450	—
1610 HR	—	115	220	295	450	—
1611 HR	—	115	220	295	450	—

KM# 43 THALER

Silver **Subject:** Death of Christian II **Obv:** Bust right, 2 rows of legends around **Rev:** 6-line inscription **Note:** Dav. #7569.

Date	Mintage	VG	F	VF	XF	Unc
1611	—	400	750	1,350	2,300	—

KM# 44 THALER

Silver **Obv:** Bust right with sword and helmet dividing date **Rev:** Circle of 18 shields around bust right **Note:** Dav. #7573.

Date	Mintage	VG	F	VF	XF	Unc
1611 swan	—	100	185	250	375	—
1612 swan	—	160	295	375	600	—
1613 swan	—	100	185	250	375	—
1614 swan	—	160	295	375	600	—
1615 swan	—	160	295	375	600	—
1616 swan	—	100	185	250	375	—

KM# 125 THALER

Silver **Ruler:** Johann Georg I **Subject:** Accession After the Settlement of the Ducal Succession in Julich **Obv:** Standing figure with sword **Rev:** Bear and ape by tree **Note:** Dav. #7575.

Date	Mintage	VG	F	VF	XF	Unc
1611 Rare	—	—	—	—	—	—

Note: Fritz Rudolf Künker Münzenhandlung Auction 119, 2-07, XF realized approximately $13,025

KM# 55 THALER

Silver **Subject:** Death of Emperor Rudolf **Obv:** Capped bust with sword **Rev:** Shield dividing date **Note:** Dav. #7579.

Date	Mintage	VG	F	VF	XF	Unc
1612 swan	—	155	325	875	1,900	—

KM# 56 THALER

Silver **Rev:** Arms dividing date at top **Note:** Dav. #7580.

Date	Mintage	VG	F	VF	XF	Unc
1612 swan	—	1,000	2,000	3,750	6,500	—

KM# 72 THALER

Silver **Subject:** Baptism of August, Son of Johann Georg **Obv:** 1/2 figure right with baton and helmet **Rev:** Crowned crossed swords in branches **Note:** Klippe. Dav. #7583.

Date	Mintage	VG	F	VF	XF	Unc
1614	—	300	550	950	1,750	—

KM# 82 THALER

Silver **Subject:** Baptism of Christian, Son of Johann Georg **Obv:** 1/2 figure in different armor right with baton and helmet **Note:** Klippe. Dav. #7587.

Date	Mintage	VG	F	VF	XF	Unc
1615	—	215	425	800	2,250	—

KM# 83 THALER

Silver **Subject:** Death of August, Administrator of Naumburg **Obv:** Bust right with baton and helmet **Rev:** 4-line inscription **Note:** Dav. #7588.

Date	Mintage	VG	F	VF	XF	Unc
1615	—	215	425	850	2,400	—

KM# 89 THALER

Silver **Obv:** Bust right with sword and helmet, band over left shoulder **Rev:** Helmeted arms divide date at top **Note:** Dav. #7589.

Date	Mintage	VG	F	VF	XF	Unc
1616 swan	—	200	400	500	750	—

KM# 90 THALER

Silver **Obv:** Bust right with sword and helmet, band over right shoulder **Note:** Dav. #7591.

Date	Mintage	VG	F	VF	XF	Unc
1616 swan	—	130	250	325	500	1,150
1617 swan	—	130	250	325	500	1,150
1618 swan	—	130	250	325	500	1,150
1619 swan	—	130	250	325	500	1,150
1620 swan	—	130	250	325	500	1,150

KM# 103 THALER

Silver, 42 mm. **Ruler:** Johann Georg I **Subject:** Centenary of Protestant Reformation **Obv:** Half-length figure to right, wearing rob and electoral hat, holding sword over right shoulder, divides IOH - GEOR, shield of 4-fold arms, with central shield of electoral Saxony in front divides date **Obv. Legend:** VERBVM DOMINI MANET IN ÆTERNVM. **Rev:** Half-length figure to right, wearing rob and electoral hat, holding sword over right shoulder, divides FRID - III, shield of 2-fold arms of electoral and ducal Saxony in front divides 15 - 17 **Rev. Legend:** SECVLVM LVTHERANVM. **Note:** Ref. Dav. 7595.

Date	Mintage	VG	F	VF	XF	Unc
1617	—	195	375	675	1,150	—

KM# 119 THALER

Silver **Ruler:** Johann Georg I **Obv:** Elector on horseback to right, with sword over right shoulder, divides date, oval shield of 2-fold arms of electoral and ducal Saxony below **Obv. Legend:** PRO LEGE - ET GREGE **Rev:** 12-line inscription **Note:** Ref. Dav. 7597. Vicariat issue.

Date	Mintage	VG	F	VF	XF	Unc
1619	—	150	300	550	950	—

KM# 132 THALER

Silver, 42-43 mm. **Ruler:** Johann Georg I **Obv:** Half-length armored figure to right, holding sword over right shoulder and helmet in left hand **Obv. Legend:** IOHAN. GEORG. D. G. DVX SAX. IVL. CLIV. ET. MONTI. **Rev:** Spanish shield of manifold arms, with central shield of electoral Saxony, 6 ornate helmets above divide date to upper left and right **Rev. Legend:** SA. ROM. IMP. ARCHIM. ET ELECT. **Note:** Ref. Dav. 7601. Either letter V or U in legends. Varieties exist.

Date	Mintage	VG	F	VF	XF	Unc
1620 HvR swan	—	70.00	175	325	500	900
1621 HvR swan	—	70.00	175	325	500	900
1622 HvR swan	—	70.00	175	325	500	900
1623 HvR swan	—	70.00	175	325	500	900
1624 HI	—	70.00	175	325	500	900
1625 HI	—	70.00	175	325	500	900
1626 HI	—	70.00	175	325	500	900
1627 HI	—	70.00	175	325	500	900
1628 HI	—	70.00	175	325	500	900
1629 HI	—	70.00	175	325	500	900
1630 HI	—	70.00	175	325	500	900
1631 HI	—	70.00	175	325	500	900
1632 HI	—	70.00	175	325	500	900
1633 HI	—	70.00	175	325	500	900
1634 HI	—	70.00	175	325	475	900
1635 CM	—	70.00	175	325	500	900
1635 HI	—	70.00	175	325	500	900
1635 SD	—	70.00	175	325	500	900
1636 SD	—	70.00	175	325	500	900
1637 SD	—	70.00	175	325	500	900
1638 SD	—	70.00	175	325	500	900

KM# 339 THALER

Silver **Ruler:** Johann Georg I **Mint:** Merseburg **Note:** Kipper coinage. Similar to 20 Groschen, KM#253, but oval arms and without indication of value.

Date	Mintage	VG	F	VF	XF	Unc
1621 (rooster)	—	—	—	—	—	—
ND(1621) (rooster)	—	—	—	—	—	—

KM# 340 THALER

Silver **Ruler:** Johann Georg I **Mint:** Merseburg **Note:** Kipper coinage. Similar to 20 Groschen, KM#253, but arms nearly flat on top, curved on bottom without indication of value.

Date	Mintage	VG	F	VF	XF	Unc
1622 (rooster)	—	—	—	—	—	—
1622 MB/(rooster)	—	—	—	—	—	—

KM# 394 THALER

Silver **Ruler:** Johann Georg I **Obv:** Elector on horseback to right, Dresden and Elbe River bridge below **Rev:** Helmeted arms divide date **Note:** Similar to 2 Thaler, KM#392. Dav. LS390.

Date	Mintage	VG	F	VF	XF	Unc
1628 Rare	—	—	—	—	—	—

KM# 411 THALER

Silver **Ruler:** Johann Georg I **Subject:** Centennial of Augsburg Confession **Obv:** Capped bust holding sword with two hands right **Obv. Legend:** ...EXHIBITAE... **Note:** Dav. 7605.

Date	Mintage	VG	F	VF	XF	Unc
1630	—	100	190	350	700	—

KM# 412 THALER

Silver **Ruler:** Johann Georg I **Subject:** Centennial of Augsburg Confession **Obv:** Capped bust holding sword with one hand **Note:** Dav. 7605A.

Date	Mintage	VG	F	VF	XF	Unc
1630	—	130	250	450	900	—

KM# 413 THALER

Silver **Ruler:** Johann Georg I **Subject:** Centennial of Augsburg Confession **Obv:** 25 Juny-1630 below in legend **Obv. Legend:** ...EXHIBIT... **Rev:** 25 Juny-1530 divided below in legend **Note:** Dav. 7606.

Date	Mintage	VG	F	VF	XF	Unc
1630	—	130	250	450	850	—

KM# 414 THALER

Silver **Ruler:** Johann Georg I **Subject:** Marriage of Maria Elisabeth, Daughter of Johann Georg, to Friedrich III **Obv:** Clasped and chained hands **Note:** Dav. 7609.

Date	Mintage	VG	F	VF	XF	Unc
MDCXXX (1630)	—	270	500	900	1,850	3,000

KM# 425 THALER

Silver **Rev:** 8 helmets above shield dividing date **Note:** Dav. #7612.

Date	Mintage	VG	F	VF	XF	Unc
1638 SD	—	80.00	155	250	375	750
1639 SD	—	80.00	155	250	375	750
1640 CR	—	80.00	155	250	375	750
1640 SD	—	80.00	155	250	375	750
1641 CR	—	80.00	155	250	375	750
1642 CR	—	80.00	155	250	375	750
1643 CR	—	80.00	155	250	375	750
1644 CR	—	80.00	155	250	375	750
1645 CR	—	80.00	155	250	375	750
1646 CR	—	80.00	155	250	375	750
1647 CR	—	80.00	155	250	375	750
1648 CR	—	80.00	155	250	375	750
1649 CR	—	80.00	155	250	375	750
1650 CR	—	80.00	155	250	375	750
1651 CR	—	80.00	155	250	375	750
1652 CR	—	80.00	155	250	375	750
1653 CR	—	80.00	155	250	375	750
1654 CR	—	80.00	155	250	375	750
1655 CR	—	80.00	155	250	375	750
1656 CR	—	80.00	155	250	375	750

KM# 451 THALER

Silver **Subject:** Death of Johann Georg I **Obv:** Facing bust within 2 outer legends **Rev:** 10-line inscription **Note:** Dav. #7614.

Date	Mintage	VG	F	VF	XF	Unc
1656	—	155	300	550	900	—

KM# 481 THALER

Silver **Subject:** Death of Emperor Ferdinand III **Obv. Legend:** DEO ET - PATRIAE begins at 2 o'clock **Note:** Dav. #7630.

Date	Mintage	VG	F	VF	XF	Unc
1657 acorn	—	100	210	450	900	—
1658 acorn	—	100	210	450	900	—

KM# 480 THALER

Silver **Subject:** Death of the Emperor Ferdinand III **Obv. Legend:** DEO ET-PATRIAE **Note:** Similar to Dav. #7630 but obverse legend begins at 9 o'clock. Dav. #7628.

Date	Mintage	VG	F	VF	XF	Unc
1657 acorn	—	110	215	475	950	—

KM# 474 THALER

Silver **Obv:** Bust with sword right, cap in front **Rev:** Helmeted arms, date divided by helmets **Note:** Dav. #7617.

Date	Mintage	VG	F	VF	XF	Unc
1658 CR	—	130	250	425	625	—
1659 CR	—	130	250	425	625	—
1660 CR	—	130	250	425	625	—
1661 CR	—	130	250	425	625	—
1662 CR	—	130	250	425	625	—
1663 CR	—	130	250	425	625	—
1664 CR	—	130	250	425	625	—
1665 CR	—	130	250	425	625	—
1666 CR	—	130	250	425	625	—
1667 CR	—	130	250	425	625	—
1678 CR	—	130	250	425	625	—
1679 CR	—	130	250	425	625	—
1680 CR	—	130	250	425	625	—

KM# 476 THALER

Silver **Obv:** Bust in armor, helmet in front **Note:** Dav. #7617.

Date	Mintage	VG	F	VF	XF	Unc
1658 CR	—	130	250	425	625	—
1659 CR	—	130	250	425	625	—
1660 CR	—	130	250	425	625	—
1664 CR	—	130	250	425	625	—
1665 CR	—	130	250	425	625	—
1666 CR	—	130	250	425	625	—
1667 CR	—	130	250	425	625	—
1668 CR	—	130	250	425	625	—

KM# 482 THALER

Silver **Subject:** Death of Magdalena Sibylla, Wife of Johann Georg I **Obv:** 10-line inscription **Rev:** 11-line inscription **Note:** Dav. #7615.

Date	Mintage	VG	F	VF	XF	Unc
1659	—	140	270	500	850	—

KM# 475 THALER

Silver **Note:** Thick flan. Dav. #7617A. Struck with 1/4 Thaler dies, KM#449.

Date	Mintage	VG	F	VF	XF	Unc
1660 CR	—	130	250	450	650	—
1661 CR	—	130	250	450	650	—
1662 CR	—	130	250	450	650	—
1666 CR	—	130	250	450	650	—

KM# 500 THALER

Silver **Subject:** Marriage of Erdmuthe Sophie, Daughter of Johann Georg, to Christian Ernst **Obv:** Arms with wreath from clouds above pillars and monument **Rev:** 9-line inscription, arms in four corners **Note:** Klippe. Dav. #7631. Illustration reduced.

Date	Mintage	VG	F	VF	XF	Unc
1662	—	200	400	900	1,850	3,750

KM# 502 THALER

Silver **Subject:** Confessional Issue **Obv:** Standing figure of Johann Georg II facing, table at left and right with fancy cloth **Note:** Similar to 2 Thaler, KM#504.

Date	Mintage	VG	F	VF	XF	Unc
1663	—	—	—	—	—	—

KM# 528 THALER

Silver **Subject:** Birth of Johann Georg IV, Grandson of Johann Georg II **Obv:** IG4 monogram **Rev:** Young Hercules in a cradle grasping a snake, date in corners **Note:** Klippe. Dav. #7632. Illustration reduced.

Date	Mintage	VG	F	VF	XF	Unc
1669	—	—	600	1,200	2,000	—

KM# 537 THALER

Silver **Obv:** Bust right **Rev:** Capped arms in frame **Note:** Dav. #7621.

Date	Mintage	VG	F	VF	XF	Unc
1670 CR	—	130	250	475	750	—
1671 CR	—	130	250	475	750	—

KM# 538 THALER

Silver **Obv:** Different bust right **Rev:** WECHSEL., THALER below arms **Note:** Dav. #7625.

Date	Mintage	VG	F	VF	XF	Unc
1670 CR	—	135	275	550	1,000	—
1671 CR	—	135	275	550	1,000	—

KM# 565 THALER

22.4800 g., Silver **Subject:** Election to the Order of the Garter **Obv:** St. George slaying the dragon **Rev:** 9-line inscription in laurel wreath **Note:** Dav. #7633.

Date	Mintage	VG	F	VF	XF	Unc
MDCLXXI (1671)	—	130	250	500	1,250	3,750
MDCLXXVIII (1678)	—	130	250	500	1,250	3,750

KM# 544 THALER

Silver **Obv:** Larger bust **Rev:** Oval shield and different frame **Note:** Dav. #7624.

Date	Mintage	VG	F	VF	XF	Unc
1671 CR	—	125	250	500	900	—

KM# 550 THALER

Silver **Obv:** Heavier bust **Rev:** Differently shaped shield **Note:** Dav. #7626.

Date	Mintage	VG	F	VF	XF	Unc
1675 CR	—	250	550	1,250	2,250	—
1676 CR	—	250	550	1,250	2,250	—
1677 CR	—	250	550	1,250	2,250	—
1678 CR	—	250	550	1,250	2,250	—

KM# 560 THALER

Silver **Obv:** Thinner bust with long hair **Rev:** Differently shaped shield dividing C-F **Note:** Dav. #7627.

Date	Mintage	VG	F	VF	XF	Unc
1678 CF	—	250	550	1,250	2,250	—
1679 CF	—	250	550	1,250	2,250	—
1680 CF	—	250	550	1,250	2,250	—

KM# 561 THALER

Silver **Subject:** Shooting Match at Dresden **Obv:** Bust right, arms in corners **Rev:** 7-line inscription in wreath, arms in corners **Note:** Klippe. Dav. #7635.

Date	Mintage	VG	F	VF	XF	Unc
1678	—	300	625	1,250	2,150	—

KM# 562 THALER

21.8800 g., Silver **Subject:** Shooting Match at Dresden **Obv:** Capped arms in Order band with motto, arms in corners **Rev:** Hercules standing with club date in Roman numerals **Note:** Klippe. Dav. #7636.

Date	Mintage	VG	F	VF	XF	Unc
MDC-LXXVIII (1678)	—	300	625	1,250	2,500	—

KM# 564 THALER

Silver **Subject:** Peace of Nijmegen **Obv:** 6-line inscription in wreath, arms in corners **Rev:** Hand from cloud with wreath above Hercules on a cloud **Note:** Klippe. Dav.#7637.

Date	Mintage	VG	F	VF	XF	Unc
1679	—	200	375	650	1,250	—

KM# 572 THALER

Silver **Subject:** Death of Johann Georg II **Obv:** Fama above capped shields, Saturn below **Rev:** 16-line inscription **Note:** Dav.#7638.

Date	Mintage	VG	F	VF	XF	Unc
1680	—	300	625	1,250	2,200	—

KM# 580 THALER

Silver **Obv:** Bust right with helmet in front **Rev:** Helmeted arms separating initials, date divided at top **Note:** Dav. #7640.

Date	Mintage	VG	F	VF	XF	Unc
1681 CF	—	125	300	625	1,150	2,000
1682 CF	—	125	300	625	1,150	2,000
1683 CF	—	125	300	625	1,150	2,000
1684 CF	—	125	300	625	1,150	2,000
1685 CF	—	125	300	625	1,150	2,000
1686 CF	—	125	300	625	1,150	2,000
1687	—	125	300	625	1,150	2,000
1688	—	125	300	625	1,150	2,000
1688 IK	—	125	300	625	1,150	2,000
1689 IK	—	125	300	625	1,150	2,000

KM# 599 THALER

Silver **Subject:** Relief of Turkish Siege of Vienna **Obv:** Helmeted and armored bust of Johann Georg III right **Rev:** Elector's hat above field marshall's staff, dividing city view below, crossed swords between arms of Saxony, turban at right below arms **Designer:** Johann Höhn

Date	Mintage	VG	F	VF	XF	Unc
ND(1683) Rare	—	—	—	—	—	—

Note: Baldwin's Auctions Ltd Auction 41, 5-05, good VF realized approximately $6,090

KM# 597 THALER

Silver **Subject:** Death of Johann Georg II's Wife, Magdalena Sibylla of Brandenburg-Bayreuth **Obv:** 9-line inscription **Obv. Inscription:** +/ D • G •/ MAGDALENA/ SIBYLLA • ELECTRIX •/ SAXONIÆ • E • PROSAP •/ MARCH • BRANDENB •/ NAT • 1612 • DENAT • 1687/ DIE • 20 MART •/ + **Rev:** Large crown above 4-banded rainbow beneath which a 2-line inscription, all in laurel wreath **Rev. Inscription:** SOLA •/ SPES• MEA • **Note:** Dav# 7641.

Date	Mintage	VG	F	VF	XF	Unc
1687	—	700	1,500	3,000	5,000	—

KM# 607 THALER

Silver **Rev:** Helmeted arms **Note:** Dav. #7642.

Date	Mintage	VG	F	VF	XF	Unc
1690 IK	—	225	450	950	1,750	—
1691 IK	—	225	450	950	1,750	—

KM# 616 THALER

Silver **Subject:** Death of Johann Georg III **Obv:** Arm from clouds holding flag **Rev:** 11-line inscription **Note:** Dav. #7643.

Date	Mintage	VG	F	VF	XF	Unc
1691 IK	—	125	275	600	1,000	—

KM# 617 THALER

Silver **Subject:** Death of Johann Georg III **Obv:** Bust right in center, 3 legends around **Rev:** 15-line inscription **Note:** Dav. #7645.

Date	Mintage	VG	F	VF	XF	Unc
1691 IK	—	300	600	1,200	2,350	—

KM# 618 THALER

Silver **Obv:** Bust right, helmet in front **Rev:** Helmeted arms separating initials, date divided at top **Note:** Dav. #7647.

Date	Mintage	VG	F	VF	XF	Unc
1691 IK	—	500	900	2,000	6,000	8,500
1692 IK	—	500	900	2,000	6,000	8,500
1693 IK	—	500	900	2,000	6,000	8,500
1694 IK	—	500	900	2,000	6,000	8,500

KM# 642 THALER

Silver **Subject:** Johann Georg IV Receiving the Order of the Garter **Obv:** JG4 monogram in Garter band, arms in corners **Rev:** Capped wreath with crossed swords, arms in corners **Note:** Klippe. Dav. #7649.

Date	Mintage	VG	F	VF	XF	Unc
1693	—	150	300	700	1,100	1,850

KM# 656 THALER

Silver **Rev:** Capped arms dividing initials, date in legend **Note:** Dav. #7648.

Date	Mintage	VG	F	VF	XF	Unc
1694 EP-H	—	725	1,450	2,400	4,200	—

KM# 657 THALER

Silver **Subject:** Death of Johann Georg IV **Obv:** Pyramid with arms on 2 sides, churches in background **Rev:** Pyramid with 14-line inscription, tents and guns in background, flags and cannons in foreground **Note:** Dav. #7650.

Date	Mintage	VG	F	VF	XF	Unc
1694 IK	—	200	400	900	1,800	—

KM# 658 THALER

Silver **Subject:** Death of Johann Georg IV **Obv:** Bust right, 3 legends around **Rev:** 16-line inscription **Note:** Dav. #7651.

Date	Mintage	VG	F	VF	XF	Unc
1694 IK	—	270	550	1,150	2,250	4,050

KM# 669 THALER

Silver **Obv:** Bust right, sword and helmet in front **Rev:** Helmeted arms divide initials, date divided above **Note:** Dav. #7652.

Date	Mintage	VG	F	VF	XF	Unc
1695 IK	—	300	750	1,650	4,500	—
1696 IK	—	300	750	1,650	4,500	—
1697 IK	—	300	750	1,650	4,500	—
1698 IK	—	300	750	1,650	4,500	—

KM# 675 THALER

Silver **Subject:** Birth of Friedrich August II **Obv:** Knight holding large shield, door in background **Rev:** FAS in cloud above city view of Dresden **Note:** Dav. #7653.

Date	Mintage	VG	F	VF	XF	Unc
1696 IK	—	—	—	7,500	12,500	18,500

KM# 686 THALER

Silver **Obv:** Crowned FAC monogram in sprays, date divided above **Rev:** Hand with wreath from cloud above Hercules on a cloud **Note:** Klippe. Dav. #7654.

Date	Mintage	VG	F	VF	XF	Unc
1697	—	175	350	750	1,850	—

KM# 707 THALER

Silver **Ruler:** Friedrich August I **Rev:** 2 shields crowned between palm branches **Note:** Dav. #7656.

Date	Mintage	F	VF	XF	Unc	BU
1698 IK	—	600	1,200	2,500	4,000	6,000
1698 ILH	—	600	1,200	2,500	4,000	6,000
1699 ILH	—	600	1,200	2,500	4,000	6,000
1700 ILH	—	600	1,200	2,500	4,000	6,000

KM# 713 THALER

Silver **Ruler:** Friedrich August I **Obv:** Crowned A in sprays, date divided above **Rev:** Hand with wreath from cloud above Hercules on a cloud **Rev. Legend:** VIRTUTE PARATA **Shape:** 4-Sided **Note:** Klippe. Dav. #7657 and Dav. #2648. Illustration reduced.

Date	Mintage	F	VF	XF	Unc	BU
1699	—	400	800	1,350	2,250	—

KM# 222 120 KREUZER

Silver **Ruler:** Johann Georg I **Obv:** Heart-shaped 2-fold arms, angel above, (120) at bottom **Rev:** 3 small shields of arms, 1 above 2, 2 angels flank upper arms, date above **Mint:** Taucha **Note:** Kipper coinage.

Date	Mintage	VG	F	VF	XF	Unc
1621 T	—	—	—	—	—	—
16Z1 T	—	—	—	—	—	—
(1621) T	—	—	—	—	—	—

KM# 395 1-1/2 THALER

Silver **Ruler:** Johann Georg I **Obv:** Elector on horseback to right, Dresden and Elbe River bridge below **Rev:** Helmeted arms divide date **Note:** Dav. LS389. Illustration reduced.

Date	Mintage	VG	F	VF	XF	Unc
16Z8	—	925	1,800	3,050	—	—

KM# 503 1-1/2 THALER

Silver **Subject:** For the Confession **Obv:** Full-length figure holding sword, table at left and right **Note:** Dav. #LS405.

Date	Mintage	VG	F	VF	XF	Unc
1663	—	825	1,400	2,150	3,600	—

KM# 18 2 THALER
Silver, 43 mm. **Ruler:** Christian II, Johann Georg I and August **Obv:** Half-length armored figure to right, holding sword over right shoulder and helmet with left hand, head divides date, small imperial orb above, small shield of electoral Saxony at bottom **Obv. Legend:** CHRISTIAN. II. D. G. SA. RO - IMP. ARCHIMAR. ET. ELEC. **Rev:** Two small facing busts in circle, 14 small shields of arms around, shield of ducal Saxony at top **Rev. Legend:** IOHAN: GEORG. ET. AVGVST: FRAT. ET. DVCES. SAXON+. **Note:** Ref. Dav. 7560.

Date	Mintage	VG	F	VF	XF	Unc
1601 HB	—	400	700	1,150	2,200	—
160Z HB	—	400	700	1,150	2,200	—
1603 HB	—	400	700	1,150	2,200	—
1604 HB	—	400	700	1,150	2,200	—
1605 HB	—	400	700	1,150	2,200	—

KM# 26 2 THALER
Silver **Ruler:** Christian II, Johann Georg I and August **Obv:** Bust right with sword and helmet divide date **Rev:** Busts facing one another **Note:** Dav. 7565.

Date	Mintage	VG	F	VF	XF	Unc
1605 HvR	—	400	700	1,150	2,200	—
1606 HvR	—	400	700	1,150	2,200	—
1607 HvR	—	400	700	1,150	2,200	—
1608 HvR	—	400	700	1,150	2,200	—
1609 HvR	—	400	700	1,150	2,200	—
1610 HvR	—	400	700	1,150	2,200	—
1611 HvR	—	400	700	1,150	2,200	—

KM# 45 2 THALER
Silver **Subject:** Death of Christian II **Obv:** Bust right, 2 rows of legends around **Rev:** 6-line inscription **Note:** Dav. #7568.

Date	Mintage	VG	F	VF	XF	Unc
1611	—	1,250	2,500	4,750	—	—

KM# 46 2 THALER
Silver **Obv:** Bust right with sword and helmet dividing date **Rev:** Circle of 18 shields around bust right **Note:** Dav. #7572.

Date	Mintage	VG	F	VF	XF	Unc
1611	—	550	1,100	1,750	3,000	—
1612	—	550	1,100	1,750	3,000	—
1613	—	550	1,100	1,750	3,000	—
1614	—	550	1,100	1,750	3,000	—
1615	—	550	1,100	1,750	3,000	—

KM# 124 2 THALER
Silver **Ruler:** Johann Georg I **Subject:** Accession After the Settlement of the Ducal Succession in Julich **Obv:** Standing figure with sword **Rev:** Bear and ape by tree **Note:** Dav. #7574.

Date	Mintage	VG	F	VF	XF	Unc
1611 Rare	—	—	—	—	—	—

KM# 57 2 THALER
Silver **Ruler:** Johann Georg I and August **Subject:** Death of Emperor Rudolph **Obv:** Capped bust with sword **Rev:** Shield dividing date **Note:** Dav. #7578.

Date	Mintage	VG	F	VF	XF	Unc
1612 swan	—	750	1,500	2,800	—	—

KM# 73 2 THALER
Silver **Subject:** Baptism of August, Son of Johann Georg I **Obv:** Bust right with staff **Rev:** Sword pointing to last A in AMONA **Note:** Klippe. Dav. #7582.

Date	Mintage	VG	F	VF	XF	Unc
1614	—	650	1,200	2,400	4,250	—

KM# 74 2 THALER
Silver **Subject:** Baptism of August, Son of Johann Georg I **Rev:** Sword pointing to S in SVIS **Note:** Klippe. Dav. #7582A.

Date	Mintage	VG	F	VF	XF	Unc
1614	—	600	1,200	2,450	4,250	—

KM# 84 2 THALER
Silver **Subject:** Baptism of Christian, Son of Johann Georg I **Obv:** Different armor **Note:** Klippe. Dav. #7586.

Date	Mintage	VG	F	VF	XF	Unc
1615	—	650	1,250	2,500	4,500	—

KM# 91 2 THALER
Silver **Ruler:** Johann Georg I **Obv:** Bust right with sword and helmet, band over right shoulder **Rev:** Helmeted arms **Note:** Dav. #7590A.

Date	Mintage	VG	F	VF	XF	Unc
1616 swan	—	500	1,000	2,250	3,850	—
1617 swan	—	500	1,000	2,250	3,850	—
1618 swan	—	500	1,000	2,250	3,850	—
1619 swan	—	500	1,000	2,250	3,850	—

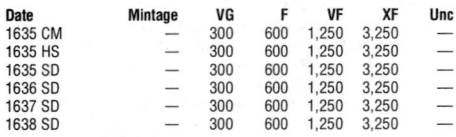

KM# 104 2 THALER

Silver, 42 mm. **Ruler:** Johann Georg I **Subject:** Centenary of Protestant Reformation **Obv:** Half-length figure to right, wearing rob and electoral hat, holding sword over right shoulder, divides IOH - GEOR, shield of 4-fold arms, with central shield of electoral Saxony in front divides date **Obv. Legend:** VERBVM DOMINI MANET IN ÆTERNVM. **Rev:** Half-length figure to right, wearing rob and electoral hat, holding sword over right shoulder, divides FRID - III, shield of 2-fold arms of electoral and ducal Saxony in front divides 15 - 17 **Rev. Legend:** SECVLVM LVTHERANVM. **Note:** Ref. Dav. 7594.

Date	Mintage	VG	F	VF	XF	Unc
1617	—	850	1,750	3,500	6,000	—

KM# 120 2 THALER

Silver **Ruler:** Johann Georg I **Obv:** Elector on horseback to right, with sword over right shoulder, divides date, oval shield of 2-fold arms of electoral and ducal Saxony below **Obv. Legend:** PRO LEGE - ET GREGE **Rev:** 12-line inscription **Note:** Ref. Dav. 7596. Vicariat issue.

Date	Mintage	VG	F	VF	XF	Unc
1619	—	950	1,850	3,750	6,500	—

KM# 133 2 THALER

Silver **Ruler:** Johann Georg I **Obv:** 1/2-length bust with sword to right **Rev:** Helmeted arms **Note:** Dav. #7600.

Date	Mintage	VG	F	VF	XF	Unc
1620 HR	—	300	600	1,250	3,250	—
1621 HR	—	300	600	1,250	3,250	—
1623 HR	—	300	600	1,250	3,250	—
1625 HS	—	300	600	1,250	3,250	—
1626 HS	—	300	600	1,250	3,250	—
1627 HS	—	300	600	1,250	3,250	—
1628 HS	—	300	600	1,250	3,250	—
1629 HS	—	300	600	1,250	3,250	—
1631	—	300	600	1,250	3,250	—
1632 HS	—	300	600	1,250	3,250	—
1633 HS	—	300	600	1,250	3,250	—
1634 HS	—	300	600	1,250	3,250	—

Date	Mintage	VG	F	VF	XF	Unc
1635 CM	—	300	600	1,250	3,250	—
1635 HS	—	300	600	1,250	3,250	—
1635 SD	—	300	600	1,250	3,250	—
1636 SD	—	300	600	1,250	3,250	—
1637 SD	—	300	600	1,250	3,250	—
1638 SD	—	300	600	1,250	3,250	—

KM# 342 2 THALER

Silver **Ruler:** Johann Georg I **Mint:** Merseburg **Note:** Kipper coinage. Also dated above angels on reverse.

Date	Mintage	VG	F	VF	XF	Unc
1621/1621 (rooster)	—	—	—	—	—	—

KM# 341 2 THALER

Silver **Ruler:** Johann Georg I **Obv:** Heart-shaped 2-fold arms in baroque frame, angel below with date at bottom **Rev:** 3 small arms, 1 above 2, angels at left and right of upper shield **Mint:** Merseburg **Note:** Kipper coinage. Similar to 20 Groschen, KM#253.

Date	Mintage	VG	F	VF	XF	Unc
1621 (rooster)	—	—	—	—	—	—

KM# 343 2 THALER

Silver **Ruler:** Johann Georg I **Mint:** Merseburg **Note:** Kipper coinage. Date only above angels on reverse.

Date	Mintage	VG	F	VF	XF	Unc
1622 MB/(rooster)	—	—	—	—	—	—
1622 (rooster)	—	—	—	—	—	—

KM# 392 2 THALER

Silver **Ruler:** Johann Georg I **Obv:** Elector on horseback, Dresden and Elbe River bridge below **Rev:** Helmeted arms divide date **Note:** Illustration reduced. Dav. LS388.

Date	Mintage	VG	F	VF	XF	Unc
1626 HI	—	1,200	2,400	4,200	—	—
1627 HI	—	1,200	2,400	4,200	—	—
1628 HI	—	1,200	2,400	4,200	—	—

KM# 391 2 THALER

Silver **Ruler:** Johann Georg I **Obv:** Bust in cloak with sword right **Rev:** Capped arms divide date at top **Note:** Dav. 7602.

Date	Mintage	VG	F	VF	XF	Unc
1626 HI	—	900	1,800	3,400	5,600	—
1627 HI	—	900	1,800	3,400	5,600	—
1628 HI	—	900	1,800	3,400	5,600	—

KM# 415 2 THALER

Silver **Ruler:** Johann Georg I **Subject:** Centennial of Augsburg Confession **Obv:** Johann Georg with sword in 2 hands **Note:** Dav. 7604.

Date	Mintage	VG	F	VF	XF	Unc
1630	—	500	1,000	2,000	3,750	—

KM# 416 2 THALER

Silver **Subject:** Centennial of Augsburg Confession **Note:** Similar to 1 Thaler, KM#412. Dav. #7604A.

Date	Mintage	VG	F	VF	XF	Unc
1630	—	500	1,000	2,000	3,750	—

KM# 417 2 THALER
Silver **Subject:** Marriage of Maria Elisabeth, Daughter of Johann Georg, and Friedrich III **Rev:** Clasped and chained hands **Note:** Dav. #7608.

Date	Mintage	VG	F	VF	XF	Unc
1630	—	950	1,850	3,500	5,750	—

KM# 430 2 THALER
Silver **Obv:** 1/2-length figure holding sword to right **Rev:** 8 helmets above shield dividing date **Note:** Similar to 1 Thaler, KM#425. Dav. #7611.

Date	Mintage	VG	F	VF	XF	Unc
1645 CR	—	450	900	1,750	3,000	—
1646 CR	—	450	900	1,750	3,000	—
1654 CR	—	450	900	1,750	3,000	—
1655 CR	—	450	900	1,750	3,000	—

KM# 435 2 THALER
58.0000 g., Silver **Subject:** Peace of Westphalia **Note:** Similar to 3 Thaler, KM#436. Dav. #LS395.

Date	Mintage	VG	F	VF	XF	Unc
1650 CR	—	1,800	2,950	4,500	6,600	—

KM# 443 2 THALER
Silver **Obv:** 1/2 figure facing with sword **Rev:** 8 helmets above shield **Note:** Dav. #7613.

Date	Mintage	VG	F	VF	XF	Unc
1652 CR	—	1,000	2,000	4,000	7,000	—
1653 CR	—	1,000	2,000	4,000	7,000	—

KM# 460 2 THALER
Silver, 51 mm. **Subject:** Death of Emperor Ferdinand III **Obv:** Duke on horseback, arms below **Rev:** 12-line inscription **Note:** Dav. #LS398.

Date	Mintage	VG	F	VF	XF	Unc
1657 acorn	—	1,200	2,400	4,200	6,000	—
1658 acorn	—	1,200	2,400	4,200	6,000	—

KM# 496 2 THALER
Silver, 64 mm. **Ruler:** Johann Georg II **Subject:** Chapel at Moritzburg **Note:** Illustration reduced. Dav. #LS401.

Date	Mintage	VG	F	VF	XF	Unc
1661 acorn	—	600	1,100	2,100	3,300	—

KM# 499 2 THALER
Silver **Obv:** Bust with sword right, cap in front **Rev:** Helmeted arms **Note:** Dav. #7616.

Date	Mintage	VG	F	VF	XF	Unc
1662 CR	—	650	1,150	2,200	3,750	—
1677 CR	—	650	1,150	2,200	3,750	—

KM# 504 2 THALER
58.0000 g., Silver **Subject:** For the Confession **Note:** Illustration reduced. Dav. #LS404.

Date	Mintage	VG	F	VF	XF	Unc
1663 CR	—	1,250	2,100	3,250	4,750	—

KM# 511 2 THALER
Silver **Note:** Similar to 1 Thaler, KM#476. Dav. #7618.

Date	Mintage	VG	F	VF	XF	Unc
1665 CR	—	1,300	2,500	4,150	6,600	—

KM# 539 2 THALER
Silver **Note:** Similar to 1 Thaler, KM#537. Dav. #7620.

Date	Mintage	VG	F	VF	XF	Unc
1670 CR	—	1,300	2,500	4,150	6,600	—

KM# 545 2 THALER
58.0000 g., Silver **Rev:** Capped oval shield in frame **Note:** Dav. #7623.

Date	Mintage	VG	F	VF	XF	Unc
1671 CR	—	1,300	2,500	4,150	6,600	—

KM# 598 2 THALER
Silver **Note:** Similar to 1 Thaler, KM#580. Dav. #7639.

Date	Mintage	VG	F	VF	XF	Unc
1687	—	1,450	2,550	4,250	7,000	—

KM# 619 2 THALER

Silver **Subject:** Death of Johann Georg III **Obv:** Bust right in center of circle, 3 rows of legend around **Rev:** 15-line inscription **Note:** Dav. #7644.

Date	Mintage	VG	F	VF	XF	Unc
1691 IK	—	1,150	2,250	3,750	6,300	—

KM# 629 2 THALER

Silver **Note:** Similar to 1 Thaler, KM#618. Dav. #7646.

Date	Mintage	VG	F	VF	XF	Unc
1692 IK Rare	—	—	—	—	—	—

KM# 708 2 THALER

Silver **Rev:** 2 shields crowned between palm branches, date divided at top **Note:** Dav. #7655.

Date	Mintage	VG	F	VF	XF	Unc
1698 ILH Rare	—	—	—	—	—	—
1699 ILH Rare	—	—	—	—	—	—

KM# 554 2-1/2 THALER

Silver **Subject:** Dedication of Spire at Dresden Palace **Obv:** View of palace with spire in center **Rev:** 15-line inscription with Roman numeral date **Note:** Show 2-1/2 Thaler.

Date	Mintage	VG	F	VF	XF	Unc
1676 Rare	—	—	—	—	—	—

KM# 25 3 THALER

Silver **Ruler:** Christian II, Johann Georg I and August **Obv:** Bust right with sword and helmet, date divided above **Rev:** 2 facing busts in circle of 14 shields **Mint:** Dresden **Note:** Similar to 1 Thaler, KM#16. Dav. #7559.

Date	Mintage	VG	F	VF	XF	Unc
1604 HB	—	1,550	2,800	4,650	7,100	—

KM# 27 3 THALER

Silver **Ruler:** Christian II, Johann Georg I and August **Obv:** Bust right with sword and helmet divide date **Rev:** 2 busts facing **Note:** Similar to 1 Thaler, KM#24. Dav. #7564.

Date	Mintage	VG	F	VF	XF	Unc
1606 HvR	—	1,550	2,800	4,650	7,100	—
1610 HvR	—	1,550	2,800	4,650	7,100	—

KM# 47 3 THALER

Silver **Subject:** Death of Christian II **Obv:** Bust right, 2 rows of legends around **Rev:** 6-line inscription **Note:** Similar to 1 Thaler, KM#43. Dav. #7567.

Date	Mintage	VG	F	VF	XF	Unc
1611 Rare	—	—	—	—	—	—

KM# 67 3 THALER

Silver **Obv:** Bust right with sword and helmet dividing date **Rev:** Circle of 18 shields around bust right **Note:** Similar to 1 Thaler, KM#44. Dav. #7571.

Date	Mintage	VG	F	VF	XF	Unc
1613	—	1,550	2,800	4,650	7,100	—
1614	—	1,550	2,800	4,650	7,100	—

KM# 75 3 THALER

Silver **Subject:** Baptism of August, Son of Johann Georg **Obv:** 1/2-figure right with baton and helmet **Rev:** Crowned crossed swords in branches **Note:** Klippe. Similar to 1 Thaler, KM#72. Dav. #7581.

Date	Mintage	VG	F	VF	XF	Unc
1614 Rare	—	—	—	—	—	—

KM# 85 3 THALER

Silver **Subject:** Baptism of Christian, Son of Johann Georg **Obv:** 1/2-figure in different armor right with baton and helmet **Rev:** Crossed swords **Note:** Klippe. Similar to 1 Thaler, KM#82. Dav. #7585.

Date	Mintage	VG	F	VF	XF	Unc
1615 Rare	—	—	—	—	—	—

KM# 105 3 THALER

Silver, 43 mm. **Ruler:** Johann Georg I **Subject:** Centenary of Protestant Reformation **Obv:** Half-length figure to right, wearing rob and electoral hat, holding sword over right shoulder, divides IOH - GEOR, shield of 4-fold arms, with central shield of electoral Saxony in front divides date **Obv. Legend:** VERBVM DOMINI MANET IN ÆTERNVM. **Rev:** Half-length figure to right, wearing rob and electoral hat, holding sword over right shoulder, divides FRID - III, shield of 2-fold arms of electoral and ducal Saxony in front divides 15 - 17 **Rev. Legend:** SECVLVM LVTHERANVM. **Note:** Ref. Dav. 7593.

Date	Mintage	VG	F	VF	XF	Unc
1617	—	1,550	2,800	4,650	7,100	—

KM# 393 3 THALER

87.0000 g., Silver **Ruler:** Johann Georg I **Note:** Similar to 2 Thaler, KM#392. Dav. LS387.

Date	Mintage	VG	F	VF	XF	Unc
1626 HI	—	1,800	3,200	4,800	6,700	—
1627 HI	—	1,800	3,200	4,800	6,700	—
1628 HI	—	1,800	3,200	4,800	6,700	—

KM# 396 3 THALER

87.0000 g., Silver **Ruler:** Johann Georg I **Note:** Similar to 1 Thaler, KM#132. Dav. #7599.

Date	Mintage	VG	F	VF	XF	Unc
1628 HS	—	1,550	2,800	4,650	7,100	—
1629 HS	—	1,550	2,800	4,650	7,100	—

KM# 418 3 THALER

87.0000 g., Silver **Subject:** Centennial of the Augsburg Confession **Note:** Similar to 1 Thaler, KM#411. Dav. #7603.

Date	Mintage	VG	F	VF	XF	Unc
1630 Rare	—	—	—	—	—	—

KM# 419 3 THALER

87.0000 g., Silver **Subject:** Marriage of Maria Elisabeth, Daughter of Johann Georg to Friedrich III **Note:** Klippe. Similar to 1 Thaler, KM#415. Dav. #7607.

Date	Mintage	VG	F	VF	XF	Unc
1630 Rare	—	—	—	—	—	—

KM# 436 3 THALER

Silver **Subject:** Peace of Westphalia **Note:** Illustration reduced. Dav. #LS394.

Date	Mintage	VG	F	VF	XF	Unc
1650 CR	—	1,400	2,700	5,400	9,000	—

KM# 452 3 THALER

Silver **Note:** Similar to 1 Thaler, KM#425. Dav. #7610.

Date	Mintage	VG	F	VF	XF	Unc
1656 CR	—	1,550	2,800	4,650	7,100	—

KM# 461 3 THALER

88.0000 g., Silver **Note:** Similar to 2 Thaler, KM#460. Dav. #LS397. Illustration reduced.

Date	Mintage	VG	F	VF	XF	Unc
1657 acorn	—	1,800	3,600	7,200	11,500	—

KM# 497 3 THALER
87.0000 g., Silver **Subject:** Chapel at Moritzburg **Note:** Similar to 2 Thaler, KM#496. Dav. #LS400. Illustration reduced.

Date	Mintage	VG	F	VF	XF	Unc
1661 acorn	—	2,150	3,600	5,500	7,800	—

KM# 505 3 THALER
Silver **Subject:** For the Confession **Note:** Similar to 2 Thaler, KM#504. Dav. #LS403. Illustration reduced.

Date	Mintage	VG	F	VF	XF	Unc
1663 CR	—	2,800	4,750	7,300	10,500	—

KM# 555 3 THALER
Silver **Subject:** Shooting Festival at Dresden, Magdalena Sybil as Queen **Note:** Klippe. Illustration reduced. Dav. #LS409.

Date	Mintage	VG	F	VF	XF	Unc
1676 Rare	—	—	—	—	—	—

KM# 23 4 THALER
Silver **Ruler:** Christian II, Johann Georg I and August **Mint:** Dresden **Note:** Similar to 1 Thaler, KM#16. Dav. #7558.

Date	Mintage	VG	F	VF	XF	Unc
1603 HB Rare	—	—	—	—	—	—
1604 HB Rare	—	—	—	—	—	—

KM# 28 4 THALER
Silver **Ruler:** Christian II, Johann Georg I and August **Mint:** Dresden **Note:** Similar to 1 Thaler, KM#24. Dav. #7563.

Date	Mintage	VG	F	VF	XF	Unc
1606 HvR	—	2,800	4,950	7,800	—	—
1608 HvR	—	2,800	4,950	7,800	—	—
1609 HvR	—	2,800	4,950	7,800	—	—
1610 HvR	—	2,800	4,950	7,800	—	—
1611 HvR	—	2,800	4,950	7,800	—	—

KM# 68 4 THALER
Silver **Subject:** Death of Emperor Rudolph **Note:** Similar to 1 Thaler, KM#55. Dav. #7577.

Date	Mintage	VG	F	VF	XF	Unc
1612 (swan)	—	3,400	5,600	9,100	—	—

KM# 69 4 THALER
Silver **Note:** Similar to 1 Thaler, KM#44. Dav. #7570.

Date	Mintage	VG	F	VF	XF	Unc
1613	—	2,550	4,500	7,800	12,500	—
1614	—	2,550	4,500	7,800	12,500	—
1615	—	2,550	4,500	7,800	12,500	—

KM# 86 4 THALER
Silver **Subject:** Baptism of Christian, Son of Johann Georg **Note:** Klippe. Similar to 1 Thaler, KM#82. Dav. #7584.

Date	Mintage	VG	F	VF	XF	Unc
1615 Rare	—	—	—	—	—	—

KM# 106 4 THALER
Silver, 43 mm. **Ruler:** Johann Georg I **Subject:** Centenary of Protestant Reformation **Obv:** Half-length figure to right, wearing rob and electoral hat, holding sword over right shoulder, divides IOH - GEOR, shield of 4-fold arms, with central shield of electoral Saxony in front divides date **Obv. Legend:** VERBVM DOMINI MANET IN ÆTERNVM. **Rev:** Half-length figure to right, wearing rob and electoral hat, holding sword over right shoulder, divides FRID - III, shield of 2-fold arms of electoral and ducal Saxony in front divides 15 - 17 **Rev. Legend:** SECVLVM LVTHERANVM. **Note:** Ref. Dav. 7592.

Date	Mintage	VG	F	VF	XF	Unc
1617 Rare	—	—	—	—	—	—

KM# 114 4 THALER
Silver **Ruler:** Johann Georg I **Note:** Ref. Dav. 7590. Similar to Thaler, KM#90.

Date	Mintage	VG	F	VF	XF	Unc
1618 (swan) Rare	—	—	—	—	—	—

KM# 397 4 THALER
Silver **Ruler:** Johann Georg I **Note:** Similar to 1 Thaler, KM#132. Dav. #7598.

Date	Mintage	VG	F	VF	XF	Unc
1628 HS Rare	—	—	—	—	—	—

KM# 398 4 THALER
Silver **Ruler:** Johann Georg I **Note:** Similar to 1 Thaler, KM#392. Dav. LS386. Illustration reduced.

Date	Mintage	VG	F	VF	XF	Unc
1628 HI	—	3,250	5,400	8,500	12,000	—

KM# 437 4 THALER

Silver **Subject:** Peace of Westphalia **Note:** Similar to 3 Thaler, KM#436. Dav. #LS393.

Date	Mintage	VG	F	VF	XF	Unc
1650 CR Rare	—	—	—	—	—	—

KM# 462 4 THALER

Silver, 67 mm. **Obv:** Duke mounted with sword right **Obv. Legend:** PATRIAE DEO ET **Rev:** 12-line inscription **Note:** Dav. #LS396. Illustration reduced.

Date	Mintage	VG	F	VF	XF	Unc
1657 (acorn) Rare	—	—	—	—	—	—

KM# 498 4 THALER

87.0000 g., Silver **Subject:** Chapel at Moritzburg **Note:** Similar to 2 Thaler, KM#496. Dav. #LS399.

Date	Mintage	VG	F	VF	XF	Unc
1661 (acorn) Rare	—	—	—	—	—	—

KM# 506 4 THALER

87.0000 g., Silver **Subject:** For the Confession **Note:** Similar to 2 Thaler, KM#504. Dav. #LS402.

Date	Mintage	VG	F	VF	XF	Unc
1663 CR Rare	—	—	—	—	—	—

KM# 546 4 THALER

87.0000 g., Silver **Note:** Similar to 1 Thaler, KM#544. Dav. #7622.

Date	Mintage	VG	F	VF	XF	Unc
1671 CR Rare	—	—	—	—	—	—

KM# 556 4 THALER

87.0000 g., Silver **Subject:** Shooting Festival at Dresden **Note:** Klippe. Similar to 3 Thaler, KM#555. Dav. #LS408.

Date	Mintage	VG	F	VF	XF	Unc
1676 Rare	—	—	—	—	—	—

KM# 563 4 THALER

87.0000 g., Silver **Subject:** Shooting Match at Dresden **Note:** Klippe. Similar to 1 Thaler, KM#561. Dav. #7634.

Date	Mintage	VG	F	VF	XF	Unc
1678 Rare	—	—	—	—	—	—

KM# 30 5 THALER

Silver **Ruler:** Christian II, Johann Georg I and August **Mint:** Dresden **Note:** Similar to 1 Thaler, KM#24. Dav. #7562.

Date	Mintage	VG	F	VF	XF	Unc
1609 HvR Rare	—	—	—	—	—	—

KM# 58 5 THALER

Silver **Subject:** Death of Emperor Rudolph **Note:** Similar to 1 Thaler, KM#55. Dav. #7576.

Date	Mintage	VG	F	VF	XF	Unc
1612 swan Rare	—	—	—	—	—	—

KM# 438 5 THALER

Silver **Subject:** Peace of Westphalia **Note:** Similar to 3 Thaler, KM#436. Dav. #LS392.

Date	Mintage	VG	F	VF	XF	Unc
1650 CR Rare	—	—	—	—	—	—

KM# 439 6 THALER

Silver **Subject:** Peace of Westphalia **Note:** Similar to 3 Thaler, KM#436. Dav. #LS391.

Date	Mintage	VG	F	VF	XF	Unc
1650 CR Rare	—	—	—	—	—	—

KM# 557 6 THALER

Silver **Note:** Klippe. Similar to 3 Thaler, KM#555. Dav. #LS407

Date	Mintage	VG	F	VF	XF	Unc
1676 Rare	—	—	—	—	—	—

KM# 399 9 THALER

Silver **Ruler:** Johann Georg I **Note:** Similar to 2 Thaler, KM#392. Dav. LS-A386

Date	Mintage	VG	F	VF	XF	Unc
1628 HI Rare	—	—	—	—	—	—

TRADE COINAGE

KM# 87 GOLDGULDEN

3.5000 g., 0.9860 Gold 0.1109 oz. AGW **Obv:** 1/2 figure of Johann Georg I right with sword and helmet in inner circle **Rev:** Arms in inner circle, date divided at top in legend **Mint:** Dresden

Date	Mintage	VG	F	VF	XF	Unc
1615 HR ligate	—	525	1,200	2,650	5,900	—
1616 HR ligate	—	525	1,200	2,650	5,900	—
1618 (swan)	—	525	1,200	2,650	5,900	—
1619 (swan)	—	525	1,200	2,650	5,900	—
1620 (swan)	—	525	1,200	2,650	5,900	—
1625 HI	—	525	1,200	2,650	5,900	—
1632 HI	—	525	1,200	2,650	5,900	—
1641 CR	—	525	1,200	2,650	5,900	—

KM# 540 GOLDGULDEN

3.5000 g., 0.9860 Gold 0.1109 oz. AGW **Obv:** Bust right **Rev:** Crowned 3-fold arms divide date **Rev. Legend:** MONETA ARGENTEA MISNICA **Mint:** Leipzig **Note:** Coinage for Meissen.

Date	Mintage	VG	F	VF	XF	Unc
1670	—	1,050	2,100	4,250	8,800	—

KM# 134 2 GOLDGULDEN

7.0000 g., 0.9860 Gold 0.2219 oz. AGW **Ruler:** Johann Georg I **Obv:** Half-length armored figure to right, holding sword over right shoulder and helmet in left hand **Rev:** Shield of arms in inner circle, date divided at top in legend **Mint:** Dresden

Date	Mintage	VG	F	VF	XF	Unc
1620 (swan)	—	1,400	2,800	5,800	11,500	—
1651 CR	—	1,400	2,800	5,800	11,500	—

KM# A678 1/12 DUCAT

0.2900 g., 0.9860 Gold 0.0092 oz. AGW **Obv:** Bust of Friedrich August I right **Rev:** Arm holding sword

Date	Mintage	VG	F	VF	XF	Unc
ND(1694-1733)	—	—	—	—	—	—

KM# 59 1/8 DUCAT

0.4375 g., 0.9860 Gold 0.0139 oz. AGW **Obv:** Bare-headed bust right **Rev:** Oval 4-fold arms with central shield of crossed swords in baroque frame, date below **Note:** Vicariat Issue.

Date	Mintage	VG	F	VF	XF	Unc
1612	—	—	—	—	—	—

KM# 60 1/4 DUCAT

0.8750 g., 0.9860 Gold 0.0277 oz. AGW **Obv:** Bare-headed bust right **Rev:** Oval 4-fold arms with central shield of crossed swords in baroque frame, date below **Note:** Vicariat Issue.

Date	Mintage	VG	F	VF	XF	Unc
1612	—	—	—	—	—	—

KM# 441 1/4 DUCAT

0.8750 g., 0.9860 Gold 0.0277 oz. AGW **Obv:** 1/2 figure of Johann Georg I right with sword and helmet in inner circle **Rev:** Arms in inner circle, date divided at top in legend **Mint:** Dresden

Date	Mintage	VG	F	VF	XF	Unc
1651 CR	—	210	425	725	1,450	—

KM# 541 1/4 DUCAT

0.8750 g., 0.9860 Gold 0.0277 oz. AGW **Obv:** Bust right **Rev:** Crowned 3-fold arms divide date **Rev. Legend:** MONETA ARGENTEA MISNICA **Mint:** Leipzig **Note:** Coinage for Meissen.

Date	Mintage	VG	F	VF	XF	Unc
1670	—	—	—	—	—	—

KM# 678 1/4 DUCAT

0.8750 g., 0.9860 Gold 0.0277 oz. AGW **Obv:** Bust of Friedrich August I right

Date	Mintage	VG	F	VF	XF	Unc
1696 IK	—	115	235	500	1,150	—

KM# 687 1/4 DUCAT

0.8750 g., 0.9860 Gold 0.0277 oz. AGW **Obv:** Equestrian figure of Friedrich August I right **Rev:** Crowned and mantled arms, date divided at top **Mint:** Leipzig

Date	Mintage	VG	F	VF	XF	Unc
1697	—	115	235	500	1,150	—

KM# 725 1/4 DUCAT

0.8750 g., 0.9860 Gold 0.0277 oz. AGW **Ruler:** Friedrich August I **Obv:** Bust right **Rev:** Crowned arms **Mint:** Dresden

Date	Mintage	VG	F	VF	XF	Unc
1700 ILH	—	165	300	575	1,250	—

KM# 61 1/2 DUCAT

1.7500 g., 0.9860 Gold 0.0555 oz. AGW **Obv:** Bare-headed bust right **Rev:** Oval 4-fold arms with central shield of crossed swords in baroque frame, date below **Note:** Vicariat Issue.

Date	Mintage	VG	F	VF	XF	Unc
1612	—	—	—	—	—	—

KM# 442 1/2 DUCAT

1.7500 g., 0.9860 Gold 0.0555 oz. AGW **Obv:** John George I standing in inner circle **Rev:** Arms in cartouche in inner circle, date divided at top **Mint:** Dresden

Date	Mintage	VG	F	VF	XF	Unc
1651 CR	—	230	525	1,150	2,450	—
1652 CR	—	230	525	1,150	2,450	—
1653 CR	—	230	525	1,150	2,450	—
1655 CR	—	230	525	1,150	2,450	—

KM# 483 1/2 DUCAT

1.7500 g., 0.9860 Gold 0.0555 oz. AGW **Obv:** Robed 1/2 figure of Johann Georg II holding sword and elector's hat in inner circle **Rev:** Arms in cartouche in inner circle, date divided at top

Date	Mintage	VG	F	VF	XF	Unc
1659 acorn	—	175	400	975	2,050	—
1660 acorn	—	175	400	975	2,050	—
1662 acorn	—	175	400	975	2,050	—
1664 acorn	—	175	400	975	2,050	—
1665 acorn	—	175	400	975	2,050	—
1666 acorn	—	175	400	975	2,050	—

KM# 587 1/2 DUCAT

1.7500 g., 0.9860 Gold 0.0555 oz. AGW **Obv:** Robed 1/2 figure of Johann Georg III holding sword and elector's hat in inner circle **Rev:** Crowned arms in palm branches, date at top

Date	Mintage	VG	F	VF	XF	Unc
1683 CF	—	165	350	825	1,650	—
1684 CF	—	165	350	825	1,650	—
1686 CF	—	165	350	825	1,650	—
1688	—	165	350	825	1,650	—
1690 IK	—	165	350	825	1,650	—
1691 IK	—	165	350	825	1,650	—

KM# 630 1/2 DUCAT

1.7500 g., 0.9860 Gold 0.0555 oz. AGW **Obv:** Robed 1/2 figure of Johann Georg IV holding sword and elector's hat in inner circle **Rev:** Crowned arms in cartouche, date at top

Date	Mintage	VG	F	VF	XF	Unc
1692 IK	—	195	425	1,000	2,150	—
1693 IK	—	195	425	1,000	2,150	—
1694 IK	—	195	425	1,000	2,150	—

KM# 679 1/2 DUCAT

1.7500 g., 0.9860 Gold 0.0555 oz. AGW **Obv:** Bust of Friedrich August I right in inner circle **Rev:** Lion holding upraised sword and shield of arms, date at top

Date	Mintage	VG	F	VF	XF	Unc
1696 IK	—	145	290	725	1,650	—

KM# 688 1/2 DUCAT

1.7500 g., 0.9860 Gold 0.0555 oz. AGW **Obv:** Equestrian figure of Friedrich August I right in inner circle **Rev:** Crowned and mantled arms, date divided at top **Mint:** Leipzig

Date	Mintage	VG	F	VF	XF	Unc
1697 EPH	—	145	290	725	1,650	—

KM# 689 1/2 DUCAT

1.7500 g., 0.9860 Gold 0.0555 oz. AGW **Subject:** Coronation of Friedrich August I as August II of Poland **Obv:** Bust of Friedrich August I right, titles as king of Poland **Rev:** Crown **Rev. Legend:** A DEO

Date	Mintage	VG	F	VF	XF	Unc
ND	—	125	255	625	1,450	—

KM# 690 1/2 DUCAT

1.7500 g., 0.9860 Gold 0.0555 oz. AGW **Rev. Legend:** HANC DEVS IPSE DEDIT

Date	Mintage	VG	F	VF	XF	Unc
ND	—	125	255	625	1,450	—

KM# 714 1/2 DUCAT

1.7500 g., 0.9860 Gold 0.0555 oz. AGW **Ruler:** Friedrich August I **Obv:** Bust right **Rev:** Date in legend **Mint:** Dresden

Date	Mintage	VG	F	VF	XF	Unc
1699 ILH	—	175	375	925	1,900	—

KM# 542 3/4 DUCAT
2.6250 g., 0.9860 Gold 0.0832 oz. AGW **Obv:** Bust right **Rev:** crowned 3-fold arms divide date **Rev. Legend:** MONETA ARGENTEA MISNICA **Mint:** Leipzig **Note:** Coinage for Meissen.

Date	Mintage	VG	F	VF	XF	Unc
1670	—	—	—	—	—	—

KM# 19 DUCAT
3.5000 g., 0.9860 Gold 0.1109 oz. AGW **Ruler:** Christian II, Johann Georg I and August **Note:** Similar to 1 Thaler, KM#15.

Date	Mintage	VG	F	VF	XF	Unc
1601 Rare	—	—	—	—	—	—

KM# 62 DUCAT
3.5000 g., 0.9860 Gold 0.1109 oz. AGW **Obv:** Bare-headed bust right **Rev:** Oval 4-fold arms with central shield of crossed swords in baroque frame, date below **Note:** Vicariat Issue.

Date	Mintage	VG	F	VF	XF	Unc
1612	—	—	—	—	—	—

KM# 126 DUCAT
3.5000 g., 0.9860 Gold 0.1109 oz. AGW, 25 mm. **Ruler:** Johann Georg I **Subject:** Baptism of Children and Christmas **Obv:** Large SC monogram superimposed on 2 crossed swords (electoral Saxony), electoral hat above **Obv. Legend:** WOL DEM DER FREUD AN SEIN KIND: ERLEPT. **Rev:** "Eye of God" in rays above IHS monogram, dove with spread wings below, date at end of legend **Rev. Legend:** HILF DV HEILIGE DREYFALTIGKEIT. **Mint:** Dresden **Note:** Ref. M-771; Fr. 2642. Sophiendukat. This coin was restruck periodically until 1872 and most examples offered are late 18th and early 19th c. restrikes or imitations. See KM#X5.

Date	Mintage	VG	F	VF	XF	Unc
1616	—	190	290	425	575	—

KM# 108 DUCAT
3.5000 g., 0.9860 Gold 0.1109 oz. AGW **Ruler:** Johann Georg I **Note:** Similar to 1/2 Thaler, KM#99.

Date	Mintage	VG	F	VF	XF	Unc
1617	—	425	900	1,800	3,500	—

KM# 107 DUCAT
3.5000 g., 0.9860 Gold 0.1109 oz. AGW, 23 mm. **Ruler:** Johann Georg I **Subject:** Centenary of Protestant Reformation **Obv:** Woman seated at left, King Solomon holding scepter standing at right, date at end of legend **Obv. Legend:** VT SALOMON SIC ECO MATREM. **Rev:** Pair of praying hands extended upwards to 'Jehovah' in Hebrew in clouds above **Rev. Legend:** MATERNIS PRECIBVS NIHIL FORTIVS.

Date	Mintage	VG	F	VF	XF	Unc
1617	—	500	1,050	2,050	3,450	—

KM# 109 DUCAT
3.5000 g., 0.9860 Gold 0.1109 oz. AGW, 24 mm. **Ruler:** Johann Georg I **Subject:** Centenary of Protestant Reformation **Obv:** Half-length figure to right, wearing rob and electoral hat, holding sword over right shoulder, divides IOH - GEOR, shield of 4-fold arms, with central shield of electoral Saxony in front divides date **Obv. Legend:** VERBVM DNI MANET IN ÆTERNVM. **Rev:** Half-length figure to right, wearing rob and electoral hat, holding sword over right shoulder, divides FRID - III, shield of 2-fold arms of electoral and ducal Saxony in front divides 15 - 17 **Rev. Legend:** SECVLVM LVTHERANVM.

Date	Mintage	VG	F	VF	XF	Unc
1617	—	195	400	850	1,900	—

KM# 121 DUCAT
3.5000 g., 0.9860 Gold 0.1109 oz. AGW, 24 mm. **Ruler:** Johann Georg I **Obv:** Elector on horseback to right, with sword over right shoulder, divides date, oval shield of 2-fold arms of electoral and ducal Saxony below **Obv. Legend:** PRO LEGE - ET GREGE **Rev:** 12-line inscription **Note:** Vicariat Issue.

Date	Mintage	VG	F	VF	XF	Unc
1619	—	400	725	1,450	2,850	—

KM# 135 DUCAT
3.5000 g., 0.9860 Gold 0.1109 oz. AGW **Ruler:** Johann Georg I **Subject:** Military Campaign in Oberlausitz **Obv:** Oval 4-fold arms with central shield of crossed swords in baroque frame, date divided date **Rev:** Arms and armor in center **Rev. Legend:** ZVM GLVCKLICHEN ANFANG VND GVTEM ENDE

Date	Mintage	VG	F	VF	XF	Unc
1620	—	—	—	—	—	—

KM# 382 DUCAT
3.5000 g., 0.9860 Gold 0.1109 oz. AGW **Ruler:** Johann Georg I **Subject:** Baptism of Prince Heinrich **Obv:** Crowned shield of arms **Rev:** St. George slaying the dragon

Date	Mintage	VG	F	VF	XF	Unc
1622	—	500	900	1,800	3,400	—

KM# 383 DUCAT
3.5000 g., 0.9860 Gold 0.1109 oz. AGW **Ruler:** Johann Georg I **Obv:** Johann Georg I **Mint:** Dresden

Date	Mintage	VG	F	VF	XF	Unc
1622 (swan)	—	300	550	1,150	2,100	—

KM# 390 DUCAT
3.5000 g., 0.9860 Gold 0.1109 oz. AGW **Ruler:** Johann Georg I

Date	Mintage	VG	F	VF	XF	Unc
1625 HI	—	245	425	825	1,300	—
1627 HI	—	245	425	825	1,300	—
1628 HI	—	245	425	825	1,300	—
1629 HI	—	245	425	825	1,300	—
1632 HI	—	245	425	825	1,300	—
1633 HI	—	245	425	825	1,300	—
1634 HI	—	245	425	825	1,300	—
1635 CM	—	425	650	1,300	2,000	—
1635 SD	—	245	425	825	1,300	—
1636 SD	—	245	425	825	1,300	—
1637 SD	—	245	425	825	1,300	—
1638 SD	—	245	425	825	1,300	—
1639 SD	—	245	425	825	1,300	—
1640 SD	—	245	425	825	1,300	—
1640 CR	—	285	450	900	1,500	—
1641 CR	—	285	450	900	1,500	—
1642 CR	—	285	450	900	1,500	—
1643 CR	—	285	450	900	1,500	—
1644 CR	—	285	450	900	1,500	—
1645 CR	—	285	450	900	1,500	—
1646 CR	—	285	450	900	1,500	—
1648 CR	—	285	450	900	1,500	—
1649 CR	—	285	450	900	1,500	—
1650 CR	—	285	450	900	1,500	—
1652 CR	—	285	450	900	1,500	—
1653 CR	—	285	450	900	1,500	—
1655 CR	—	285	450	900	1,500	—

KM# 420 DUCAT
3.5000 g., 0.9860 Gold 0.1109 oz. AGW **Ruler:** Johann Georg I **Subject:** Centennial of the Augsburg Confession **Obv:** Bust of Johann Georg I right **Rev:** Bust of Johann right

Date	Mintage	VG	F	VF	XF	Unc
1630	—	260	450	975	1,800	—

KM# 424 DUCAT
3.5000 g., 0.9860 Gold 0.1109 oz. AGW **Ruler:** Johann Georg I **Subject:** Peace of Prague

Date	Mintage	VG	F	VF	XF	Unc
1635	—	295	575	1,100	2,100	—

KM# 444 DUCAT
3.5000 g., 0.9860 Gold 0.1109 oz. AGW **Subject:** Birth of Johann Georg I's Granddaughter, Erdmuthe Sophie **Obv:** Three small flames in wreath, inscription around **Rev:** Plant with 3 blossoms, date in legend

Date	Mintage	VG	F	VF	XF	Unc
1654	—	350	650	1,200	2,200	—

KM# 463 DUCAT
3.5000 g., 0.9860 Gold 0.1109 oz. AGW **Obv:** Equestrian figure of Johann Georg II right **Rev:** 6-line inscription **Note:** Vicariat Issue.

Date	Mintage	VG	F	VF	XF	Unc
1657	—	400	775	1,550	2,850	—

KM# 484 DUCAT
3.5000 g., 0.9860 Gold 0.1109 oz. AGW **Subject:** Death of Johann Georg II's Mother, Magdalene Sibylle **Obv:** 7-line inscription **Rev:** 6-line inscription with Roman numeral date

Date	Mintage	VG	F	VF	XF	Unc
1659 (acorn)	—	—	—	—	—	—

KM# 485 DUCAT
3.5000 g., 0.9860 Gold 0.1109 oz. AGW **Obv:** Johann Georg II

Date	Mintage	VG	F	VF	XF	Unc
1659 CR	—	500	1,000	2,100	3,650	—
1660 CR	—	500	1,000	2,100	3,650	—
1662 CR	—	500	1,000	2,100	3,650	—
1664 CR	—	500	1,000	2,100	3,650	—
1665 CR	—	500	1,000	2,100	3,650	—
1672 CR	—	550	1,100	2,300	4,050	—

KM# 529 DUCAT
3.5000 g., 0.9860 Gold 0.1109 oz. AGW **Obv:** Equestrian figure of Johann Georg II above arms in inner circle **Rev:** Sword and quill behind shield on ornamental column, date at sides

Date	Mintage	VG	F	VF	XF	Unc
1669	—	675	1,350	2,850	4,900	—

KM# 543 DUCAT
3.5000 g., 0.9860 Gold 0.1109 oz. AGW **Obv:** Bust right **Rev:** Crowned 3-fold arms divide date **Rev. Legend:** MONETA ARGENTEA MISNICA **Mint:** Leipzig **Note:** Coinage for Meissen.

Date	Mintage	VG	F	VF	XF	Unc
1670	—	—	—	—	—	—

KM# 581 DUCAT
3.5000 g., 0.9860 Gold 0.1109 oz. AGW **Obv:** Robed 1/2 figure of Johann Georg III right with sword and elector's cap in inner circle **Rev:** Crowned arms in palm branches, date at top

Date	Mintage	VG	F	VF	XF	Unc
1681 CF	—	425	850	1,800	3,100	—
1683 CF	—	425	850	1,800	3,100	—
1684 CF	—	425	850	1,800	3,100	—
1686 CF	—	425	850	1,800	3,100	—
1687	—	425	850	1,800	3,100	—
1690 IK	—	425	850	1,800	3,100	—
1691 IK	—	425	850	1,800	3,100	—

KM# 591 DUCAT
3.5000 g., 0.9860 Gold 0.1109 oz. AGW **Obv:** Bust of Johann Georg III right in inner circle **Rev:** Crossed swords with shields of arms in angles

Date	Mintage	VG	F	VF	XF	Unc
1686	—	450	900	1,900	3,250	—

KM# 620 DUCAT
3.5000 g., 0.9860 Gold 0.1109 oz. AGW **Subject:** Death of Johann Georg III **Obv:** 6-line inscription **Rev:** Banner held by arm from clouds

Date	Mintage	VG	F	VF	XF	Unc
1691	—	450	900	1,900	3,250	—

KM# 621 DUCAT
3.5000 g., 0.9860 Gold 0.1109 oz. AGW **Obv:** Bust of Johann Georg IV holding sword to right in inner circle **Rev:** Crowned arms, date at top

Date	Mintage	VG	F	VF	XF	Unc
1691 IK	—	1,050	2,300	3,900	6,900	—
1692 IK	—	1,050	2,300	3,900	6,900	—
1693 IK	—	1,050	2,300	3,900	6,900	—
1694 IK	—	1,050	2,300	3,900	6,900	—

KM# 659 DUCAT

3.5000 g., 0.9860 Gold 0.1109 oz. AGW **Mint:** Leipzig

Date	Mintage	VG	F	VF	XF	Unc
1694 EPH	—	400	775	1,650	2,850	—

KM# 660 DUCAT

3.5000 g., 0.9860 Gold 0.1109 oz. AGW **Obv:** Bust of Friedrich August I with sword to right in inner circle **Rev:** Crowned arms, date at top **Mint:** Dresden

Date	Mintage	VG	F	VF	XF	Unc
1694 IK	—	450	900	1,900	3,250	—

KM# 670 DUCAT

3.5000 g., 0.9860 Gold 0.1109 oz. AGW **Subject:** Hungarian Campaign **Obv:** Friedrich August I

Date	Mintage	VG	F	VF	XF	Unc
ND	—	295	625	1,300	2,400	—
1695	—	295	625	1,300	2,400	—

KM# 671 DUCAT

3.5000 g., 0.9860 Gold 0.1109 oz. AGW **Obv:** Robed 1/2 figure of Friedrich August I to right with sword and elector's hat in inner circle **Rev:** Lion holding upraised sword and shield of arms, date at top

Date	Mintage	VG	F	VF	XF	Unc
1695 IK	—	450	900	1,900	3,250	—
1696 IK	—	450	900	1,900	3,250	—
1697 IK	—	450	900	1,900	3,250	—

KM# 691 DUCAT

3.5000 g., 0.9860 Gold 0.1109 oz. AGW **Obv:** Equestrian figure of Friedrich August I right **Rev:** Draped arms **Mint:** Leipzig

Date	Mintage	VG	F	VF	XF	Unc
1697 EPH	—	350	675	1,250	2,300	—

KM# 692 DUCAT

3.5000 g., 0.9860 Gold 0.1109 oz. AGW **Note:** Struck with 1/2 Ducat dies, KM #688.

Date	Mintage	VG	F	VF	XF	Unc
1697	—	350	675	1,250	2,300	—

KM# 693 DUCAT

3.5000 g., 0.9860 Gold 0.1109 oz. AGW **Note:** Struck with 1/4 Ducat dies.

Date	Mintage	VG	F	VF	XF	Unc
1697 EPH	—	400	825	1,650	2,800	—

KM# 694 DUCAT

3.5000 g., 0.9860 Gold 0.1109 oz. AGW **Subject:** Coronation of Friedrich August I as August II of Poland **Mint:** Dresden

Date	Mintage	VG	F	VF	XF	Unc
1697	—	235	450	950	1,550	—

KM# 695 DUCAT

3.5000 g., 0.9860 Gold 0.1109 oz. AGW

Date	Mintage	VG	F	VF	XF	Unc
1697 IK	—	235	450	950	1,550	—

KM# 696 DUCAT

3.5000 g., 0.9860 Gold 0.1109 oz. AGW **Subject:** Coronation of Friedrich August I as August II of Poland **Obv:** Bust of Friedrich August I right **Rev:** Large crown at center

Date	Mintage	VG	F	VF	XF	Unc
1697	—	235	450	950	1,550	—

KM# 697 DUCAT

3.5000 g., 0.9860 Gold 0.1109 oz. AGW **Subject:** Coronation of Friedrich August I as King of Poland in 1697 **Obv:** Friedrich August I mounted on horse right **Note:** Struck with 1/2 Ducat dies.

Date	Mintage	VG	F	VF	XF	Unc
ND	—	325	650	1,300	2,350	—

KM# 709 DUCAT

3.5000 g., 0.9860 Gold 0.1109 oz. AGW **Ruler:** Friedrich August I **Obv:** Draped bust right **Obv. Legend:** D • G • FRID: AUG: REX POL DUX SAX: .. **Rev:** Crowned arms within branches

Date	Mintage	VG	F	VF	XF	Unc
1698 ILH	—	375	725	1,900	3,200	—
1699 ILH	—	375	725	1,900	3,200	—
1700 ILH	—	375	725	1,900	3,200	—

KM# 582 1-1/2 DUCAT

5.2500 g., 0.9860 Gold 0.1664 oz. AGW **Obv:** Armored bust of Johann Georg III right **Rev:** Crowned arms in palm branches, date divided at top

Date	Mintage	VG	F	VF	XF	Unc
1681 CF	—	450	1,000	2,200	3,900	—
1683 CF	—	450	1,000	2,200	3,900	—
1684 CF	—	450	1,000	2,200	3,900	—
1688	—	450	1,000	2,200	3,900	—
1690 IK	—	450	1,000	2,200	3,900	—

KM# 631 1-1/2 DUCAT

5.2500 g., 0.9860 Gold 0.1664 oz. AGW **Obv:** Bust of Johann Georg IV right **Rev:** Crossed swords with shields of arms in angles

Date	Mintage	VG	F	VF	XF	Unc
1692 IK	—	450	1,000	2,200	3,900	—
1693 IK	—	450	1,000	2,200	3,900	—
1694 IK	—	450	1,000	2,200	3,900	—

KM# 698 1-1/2 DUCAT

5.2500 g., 0.9860 Gold 0.1664 oz. AGW **Obv:** Equestrian figure of Friedrich August I right **Rev:** Draped arms

Date	Mintage	VG	F	VF	XF	Unc
1697 EPH	—	350	725	1,550	3,250	—

KM# 20 2 DUCAT

7.0000 g., 0.9860 Gold 0.2219 oz. AGW **Ruler:** Christian II, Johann Georg I and August **Note:** Similar to 1 Thaler, KM#15.

Date	Mintage	VG	F	VF	XF	Unc
1601 HB Rare	—	—	—	—	—	—

KM# 63 2 DUCAT

7.0000 g., 0.9860 Gold 0.2219 oz. AGW **Obv:** Bare-headed bust right **Rev:** Oval 4-fold arms with central shield of crossed swords in baroque frame, date below **Note:** Vicariat Issue.

Date	Mintage	VG	F	VF	XF	Unc
1612	—	—	—	—	—	—

KM# 92 2 DUCAT

7.0000 g., 0.9860 Gold 0.2219 oz. AGW **Obv:** 1/2 figure of Johann Georg I right with sword and helm in inner circle **Mint:** Dresden

Date	Mintage	VG	F	VF	XF	Unc
1616 (swan)	—	950	1,900	3,750	6,600	—
1625 HI	—	950	1,900	3,750	6,600	—

KM# 127 2 DUCAT

7.0000 g., 0.9860 Gold 0.2219 oz. AGW **Ruler:** Johann Georg I **Subject:** Baptism of Children and Christmas **Obv:** Large SC monogram superimposed on 2 crossed swords (electoral Saxony), electoral hat above **Obv. Legend:** WOL DEM DER FREUD AN SEIN KIND: ERLEPT. **Rev:** "Eye of God" in rays above IHS monogram, dove with spread wings below, date at end of legend **Rev. Legend:** HILF DV HEILIGE DREYFALTIGKEIT. **Mint:** Dresden

Date	Mintage	VG	F	VF	XF	Unc
1616	—	1,050	2,200	4,400	7,500	—

KM# 110 2 DUCAT

7.0000 g., 0.9860 Gold 0.2219 oz. AGW, 24 mm. **Ruler:** Johann Georg I **Subject:** Centenary of Protestant Reformation **Obv:** Woman seated at left, King Solomon holding scepter standing at right, date at end of legend **Obv. Legend:** VT SALOMON SIC ECO MATREM. **Rev:** Pair of hands praying extended upwards towards 'Jehovah' in Hebrew in clouds above **Rev. Legend:** MATERNIS PRECIBVS NIHIL FORTIVS.

Date	Mintage	VG	F	VF	XF	Unc
1617	—	525	1,050	2,150	3,600	—

KM# 111 2 DUCAT

7.0000 g., 0.9860 Gold 0.2219 oz. AGW **Ruler:** Johann Georg I **Note:** Similar to 1/2 Thaler, KM#99.

Date	Mintage	VG	F	VF	XF	Unc
1617 Rare	—	—	—	—	—	—

KM# 112 2 DUCAT

7.0000 g., 0.9860 Gold 0.2219 oz. AGW, 24 mm. **Ruler:** Johann Georg I **Subject:** Centenary of Protestant Reformation **Obv:** Half-length figure to right, wearing rob and electoral hat, holding sword over right shoulder, divides IOH - GEOR, shield of 4-fold arms, with central shield of electoral Saxony in front divides date **Obv. Legend:** VERBVM DNI MANET IN ÆTERNVM. **Rev:** Half-length figure to right, wearing rob and electoral hat, holding sword over right shoulder, divides FRID - III, shield of 2-fold arms of electoral and ducal Saxony in front divides 15 - 17 **Rev. Legend:** SECVLVM LVTHERANVM.

Date	Mintage	VG	F	VF	XF	Unc
1617	—	575	975	1,750	3,100	—

KM# 122 2 DUCAT

7.0000 g., 0.9860 Gold 0.2219 oz. AGW **Ruler:** Johann Georg I **Obv:** Elector on horseback to right, with sword over right shoulder, divides date, oval shield of 2-fold arms of electoral and ducal Saxony below **Obv. Legend:** PRO LEGE - ET GREGE **Rev:** 12-line inscription **Note:** Vicariat Issue.

Date	Mintage	VG	F	VF	XF	Unc
1619	—	575	1,150	2,750	4,900	—

KM# 136 2 DUCAT

7.0000 g., 0.9860 Gold 0.2219 oz. AGW **Ruler:** Johann Georg I

Date	Mintage	VG	F	VF	XF	Unc
1620 (swan)	—	775	1,550	3,150	5,600	—

KM# 384 2 DUCAT

7.0000 g., 0.9860 Gold 0.2219 oz. AGW **Ruler:** Johann Georg I **Subject:** Baptism of Prince Heinrich **Obv:** Crowned shield of arms **Rev:** St. George slaying the dragon

Date	Mintage	VG	F	VF	XF	Unc
1622 Rare	—	—	—	—	—	—

KM# 400 2 DUCAT

7.0000 g., 0.9860 Gold 0.2219 oz. AGW, 26 mm. **Ruler:** Johann Georg I **Obv:** Full-length standing armored figure, head turned to right, holding sword over right shoulder **Obv. Legend:** IOH. GEORG. D. G. - DVX SAX. I. C. ET M. **Rev:** Oval shield of 4-fold arms, with central shield of electoral Saxony, in baroque frame, date above **Rev. Legend:** SA. ROM(ANI). IMP(ERI) - ARCHIM. ET ELE. **Note:** Varieties exist.

Date	Mintage	VG	F	VF	XF	Unc
1628 HI	—	500	975	2,350	3,900	—
1629 HI	—	500	975	2,350	3,900	—
1632 HI	—	500	975	2,350	3,900	—
1635 CM	—	575	1,150	2,750	4,900	—
1636 SD	—	550	875	2,150	3,450	—
1637 SD	—	550	875	2,150	3,450	—
1638 SD	—	550	875	2,150	3,450	—
1639 SD	—	550	875	2,150	3,450	—
1640 CR	—	550	875	2,150	3,450	—
1641 CR	—	550	875	2,150	3,450	—
1642 CR	—	550	875	2,150	3,450	—
1643 CR	—	550	875	2,150	3,450	—
1644 CR	—	550	875	2,150	3,450	—
1645 CR	—	550	875	2,150	3,450	—
1646 CR	—	550	875	2,150	3,450	—
1652 CR	—	550	875	2,150	3,450	—
1654 CR	—	550	875	2,150	3,450	—

KM# 421 2 DUCAT

7.0000 g., 0.9860 Gold 0.2219 oz. AGW **Subject:** Centennial of the Augsburg Confession **Obv:** Bust of Johann Georg I right **Rev:** Bust of Johann right

Date	Mintage	VG	F	VF	XF	Unc
1630	—	425	850	1,700	2,950	—

KM# 464 2 DUCAT
7.0000 g., 0.9860 Gold 0.2219 oz. AGW **Obv:** Johann Georg II **Note:** Vicariat Issue.

Date	Mintage	VG	F	VF	XF	Unc
1657	—	525	1,050	1,950	3,600	—

KM# 486 2 DUCAT
7.0000 g., 0.9860 Gold 0.2219 oz. AGW **Obv:** Robed 1/2 figure of Johann Georg II with sword and elector's cap in inner circle **Rev:** Arms in cartouche, date at top

Date	Mintage	VG	F	VF	XF	Unc
1659 CR	—	875	1,750	3,950	6,300	—
1660 CR	—	875	1,750	3,950	6,300	—
1662 CR	—	875	1,750	3,950	6,300	—

KM# 507 2 DUCAT
7.0000 g., 0.9860 Gold 0.2219 oz. AGW **Note:** Confessional Issue. Similar to 2 Thaler, KM#504.

Date	Mintage	VG	F	VF	XF	Unc
1663	—	—	—	—	—	—

KM# 551 2 DUCAT
7.0000 g., 0.9860 Gold 0.2219 oz. AGW **Obv:** Armored bust of Johann Georg II right **Rev:** Crowned arms in palm branches, date at top

Date	Mintage	VG	F	VF	XF	Unc
1675 CR	—	700	1,500	3,250	5,300	—
1676 CR	—	700	1,500	3,250	5,300	—

KM# 583 2 DUCAT
7.0000 g., 0.9860 Gold 0.2219 oz. AGW **Obv:** Armored bust of Johann Georg III right **Rev:** Crowned arms in palm branches, date divided at top

Date	Mintage	VG	F	VF	XF	Unc
1681 CF	—	700	1,500	3,250	5,300	—
1683 CF	—	700	1,500	3,250	5,300	—
1684 CF	—	700	1,500	3,250	5,300	—
1686 CF	—	700	1,500	3,250	5,300	—
1688	—	700	1,500	3,250	5,300	—
1689 IK	—	700	1,500	3,250	5,300	—
1691 IK	—	700	1,500	3,250	5,300	—

KM# 590 2 DUCAT
7.0000 g., 0.9860 Gold 0.2219 oz. AGW **Obv:** 1/2 length figure of Johann Georg III with sword and elector's cap in inner circle **Rev:** Crowned arms in inner circle

Date	Mintage	VG	F	VF	XF	Unc
1685 F	—	850	1,700	3,750	6,000	—

KM# 622 2 DUCAT
7.0000 g., 0.9860 Gold 0.2219 oz. AGW **Obv:** Bust of Johann Georg III with sword and helmet **Rev:** Crowned arms

Date	Mintage	VG	F	VF	XF	Unc
1691 IK	—	700	1,500	3,250	5,300	—

KM# 632 2 DUCAT
7.0000 g., 0.9860 Gold 0.2219 oz. AGW **Obv:** Bust of Johann Georg IV right **Rev:** Crossed swords with shields of arms in angles

Date	Mintage	VG	F	VF	XF	Unc
1692 IK	—	700	1,500	3,250	5,300	—
1693 IK	—	700	1,500	3,250	5,300	—
1694 IK	—	700	1,500	3,250	5,300	—

KM# 661 2 DUCAT
7.0000 g., 0.9860 Gold 0.2219 oz. AGW **Mint:** Leipzig

Date	Mintage	VG	F	VF	XF	Unc
1694 EPH	—	600	1,250	2,750	4,500	—

KM# 672 2 DUCAT
7.0000 g., 0.9860 Gold 0.2219 oz. AGW **Obv:** Bust of Friedrich August I with sword in inner circle **Rev:** Crowned arms in inner circle **Mint:** Dresden

Date	Mintage	VG	F	VF	XF	Unc
1695 IK	—	850	1,700	3,750	6,000	—

KM# 673 2 DUCAT
7.0000 g., 0.9860 Gold 0.2219 oz. AGW **Subject:** Hungarian Campaign **Obv:** Equestrian figure of Friedrich August I right **Rev:** Draped arms

Date	Mintage	VG	F	VF	XF	Unc
1695	—	425	825	1,800	3,450	—

KM# 680 2 DUCAT
7.0000 g., 0.9860 Gold 0.2219 oz. AGW **Obv:** Friedrich August I standing right beside desk **Rev:** 2 shields of arms topped by elector's cap

Date	Mintage	VG	F	VF	XF	Unc
1696	—	650	1,300	2,750	4,950	—

KM# 681 2 DUCAT
7.0000 g., 0.9860 Gold 0.2219 oz. AGW **Obv:** Friedrich August I standing **Rev:** Altar

Date	Mintage	VG	F	VF	XF	Unc
1696	—	500	875	1,950	3,900	—

KM# 699 2 DUCAT
7.0000 g., 0.9860 Gold 0.2219 oz. AGW **Subject:** Coronation of Friedrich August I as August II of Poland **Obv:** Friedrich August I

Date	Mintage	VG	F	VF	XF	Unc
1697	—	325	650	1,500	2,850	—

KM# 700 2 DUCAT
7.0000 g., 0.9860 Gold 0.2219 oz. AGW **Subject:** Coronation of Friedrich August I as August II of Poland **Obv:** Bust of Friedrich August I right **Obv. Legend:** FRID. AUG... **Rev:** Large crown at center

Date	Mintage	VG	F	VF	XF	Unc
1697	—	450	975	2,150	4,250	—

KM# 701 2 DUCAT
7.0000 g., 0.9860 Gold 0.2219 oz. AGW **Obv. Legend:** FRIDERICUS AUGUST...

Date	Mintage	VG	F	VF	XF	Unc
1697	—	300	625	1,250	2,400	—

KM# 710.1 2 DUCAT
7.0000 g., 0.9860 Gold 0.2219 oz. AGW **Ruler:** Friedrich August I **Obv:** Armored, laureate bust right **Obv. Legend:** D G FRID AUG REX POL - DUX ... **Rev:** Date above crown **Note:** Some dates struck from 1/2 Thaler dies, KM# 724.

Date	Mintage	VG	F	VF	XF	Unc
1698 ILH	—	1,000	2,400	5,100	9,400	—
1700 ILH	—	1,000	2,400	5,100	9,400	—

KM# 739 2 DUCAT
7.0000 g., 0.9860 Gold 0.2219 oz. AGW **Ruler:** Friedrich August I **Obv:** Bust right **Rev:** Crowned round 4-fold arms with central shield of 2-fold arms, flanked by 2 palm branches crossed at bottom, date at top **Note:** Struck from 1/8 Thaler dies, KM# 721.

Date	Mintage	VG	F	VF	XF	Unc
1700 ILH	—	750	1,800	3,750	7,000	—

KM# A422 3 DUCAT
10.5000 g., 0.9860 Gold 0.3328 oz. AGW **Subject:** Centennial of the Augsburg Confession **Obv:** Bust of Johann Georg right **Rev:** Bust of Johann right

Date	Mintage	VG	F	VF	XF	Unc
1630	—	975	1,900	3,450	6,300	—

KM# 465 3 DUCAT
10.5000 g., 0.9860 Gold 0.3328 oz. AGW **Obv:** Equestrian figure of Johann Georg II right **Rev:** 6-line inscription

Date	Mintage	VG	F	VF	XF	Unc
1657 (acorn)	—	—	—	—	—	—
1658 (acorn)	—	—	—	—	—	—

KM# 552 3 DUCAT
10.5000 g., 0.9860 Gold 0.3328 oz. AGW **Obv:** Armored bust of Johann Georg II right **Rev:** Crowned arms in palm branches, date at top

Date	Mintage	VG	F	VF	XF	Unc
1675 CR	—	975	2,000	4,250	7,500	—
1679 CF	—	975	2,000	4,250	7,500	—

KM# 584 3 DUCAT
10.5000 g., 0.9860 Gold 0.3328 oz. AGW

Date	Mintage	VG	F	VF	XF	Unc
1681 CF	—	950	1,900	4,650	7,500	—
1683 CF	—	950	1,900	4,650	7,500	—
1684 CF	—	950	1,900	4,650	7,500	—
1686 CF	—	950	1,900	4,650	7,500	—
1688 IK	—	950	1,900	4,650	7,500	—
1689 IK	—	950	1,900	4,650	7,500	—
1690 IK	—	950	1,900	4,650	7,500	—
1691 IK	—	950	1,900	4,650	7,500	—

KM# 633 3 DUCAT
10.5000 g., 0.9860 Gold 0.3328 oz. AGW **Obv:** Johann Georg IV

Date	Mintage	VG	F	VF	XF	Unc
1692 IK	—	1,050	2,250	4,500	7,500	—

KM# 726 3 DUCAT
10.5000 g., 0.9860 Gold 0.3328 oz. AGW **Obv:** Bust right **Rev:** Crowned round 4-fold arms with central shield of 2-fold arms between 2 palm branches crossed at bottom, date at top **Note:** Struck with 1/2 Thaler dies, KM#724.

Date	Mintage	VG	F	VF	XF	Unc
1700 ILH	—	—	—	—	—	—

KM# 21 4 DUCAT
14.0000 g., 0.9860 Gold 0.4438 oz. AGW **Ruler:** Christian II, Johann Georg I and August **Obv:** 3 half-figures facing with date divided above **Rev:** Helmeted arms

Date	Mintage	VG	F	VF	XF	Unc
1601 HB Rare	—	—	—	—	—	—

KM# A123 4 DUCAT
13.8600 g., Gold **Obv:** Equestrian figure of Johann Georg I right **Obv. Legend:** PROLEGE-ET GREGE **Rev:** 12-line inscription **Note:** Vicariat issue. Fr#2673.

Date	Mintage	VG	F	VF	XF	Unc
1619	—	—	—	—	20,000	—

KM# A421 4 DUCAT
14.0000 g., 0.9860 Gold 0.4438 oz. AGW **Subject:** Centennial of the Augsburg Confession **Obv:** Bust of Johann Georg I right **Rev:** Bust of Johann right

Date	Mintage	VG	F	VF	XF	Unc
1630	—	1,050	2,150	4,250	7,800	—

KM# 466 4 DUCAT
14.0000 g., 0.9860 Gold 0.4438 oz. AGW **Note:** Vicariat Issue. Similar to 1 Ducat, KM#463.

Date	Mintage	VG	F	VF	XF	Unc
1657 (acorn)	—	—	—	—	—	—
1658 (acorn)	—	—	—	—	—	—

KM# 553 4 DUCAT
14.0000 g., 0.9860 Gold 0.4438 oz. AGW **Obv:** Armored bust of Johann Georg II right **Rev:** Crowned arms in palm branches, date at top

Date	Mintage	VG	F	VF	XF	Unc
1675 CR	—	—	—	—	—	—

KM# 585.1 4 DUCAT
14.0000 g., 0.9860 Gold 0.4438 oz. AGW **Obv:** Johann Georg II **Mint:** Dresden

Date	Mintage	VG	F	VF	XF	Unc
1681 CF	—	1,500	2,850	6,500	11,500	—
1683 CF	—	1,250	2,450	5,700	9,800	—
1684 CF	—	1,250	2,450	5,700	9,800	—
1685 CF	—	1,500	2,850	6,500	11,500	—
1688	—	1,250	2,450	5,700	9,800	—

KM# 585.2 4 DUCAT
14.0000 g., 0.9860 Gold 0.4438 oz. AGW **Obv:** Draped armored bust of Johann Georg II

Date	Mintage	VG	F	VF	XF	Unc
1690 IK	—	975	2,200	4,900	8,200	—
1691 IK	—	1,150	2,450	5,700	9,000	—

KM# 634 4 DUCAT
14.0000 g., 0.9860 Gold 0.4438 oz. AGW **Note:** Similar to 3 Ducat, KM#633.

Date	Mintage	VG	F	VF	XF	Unc
1692 IK	—	1,500	2,850	6,100	10,500	—

KM# 662 4 DUCAT
14.0000 g., 0.9860 Gold 0.4438 oz. AGW **Obv:** Bust of Johann Georg IV holding sword right in inner circle **Rev:** Crowned arms, date at top

Date	Mintage	VG	F	VF	XF	Unc
1694 Rare	—	—	—	—	—	—

KM# A674 4 DUCAT
14.0000 g., 0.9860 Gold 0.4438 oz. AGW, 37 mm. **Ruler:** Friedrich August I **Obv:** Long-haired 1/3 figure to right holding upright sword, small imperial orb in margin above **Obv. Legend:** FR - ID. AUGUST. DG. DUX. SAX. I. C. M. ANGR. ET. WESTPH. **Rev:** Electoral hat above ornate shield of 4-fold arms with central shield of Electoral Saxony arms, date in margin at top **Rev. Legend:** SAC. ROMANI. IMP. ARCHIMARS. ET. ELECT. X. **Mint:** Dresden **Note:** Struck from 1/2 Thaler dies, KM#668.

Date	Mintage	VG	F	VF	XF	Unc
1696 IK	—	—	—	—	—	—

Note: An example in XF realized approximately $25,000 in Feb 2009 Künker auction.

KM# 64 5 DUCAT (1/2 Portugalöser)
17.5000 g., 0.9860 Gold 0.5547 oz. AGW **Obv:** Bare-headed bust right **Rev:** Oval 4-fold arms with central shield of crossed swords in baroque frame, date below **Note:** Vicariat Issue.

Date	Mintage	VG	F	VF	XF	Unc
1612 Rare	—	—	—	—	—	—

KM# 76 5 DUCAT (1/2 Portugalöser)
17.5000 g., 0.9860 Gold 0.5547 oz. AGW **Obv:** 1/2 length figure of Johann Georg with sword and helmet in inner circle **Rev:** Cross within inner circle of 19 shields of arms **Mint:** Dresden

Date	Mintage	VG	F	VF	XF	Unc
1614 Rare	—	—	—	—	—	—

KM# 123 5 DUCAT (1/2 Portugalöser)
17.5000 g., 0.9860 Gold 0.5547 oz. AGW **Ruler:** Johann Georg I **Obv:** Elector on horseback to right, with sword over right shoulder, oval shield of 2-fold arms of electoral and ducal Saxony below, date at end of legend **Obv. Legend:** PRO LEGE - ET GREGE **Rev:** 12-line inscription **Note:** Vicariat Issue.

Date	Mintage	VG	F	VF	XF	Unc
1619 Rare	—	—	—	—	—	—

KM# 422 5 DUCAT (1/2 Portugalöser)
17.5000 g., 0.9860 Gold 0.5547 oz. AGW **Subject:** Centennial of the Augsburg Confession **Obv:** Johann Georg I **Rev:** Johann

Date	Mintage	VG	F	VF	XF	Unc
1630	—	775	1,600	3,300	5,400	—

KM# 453 5 DUCAT (1/2 Portugalöser)
17.5000 g., 0.9860 Gold 0.5547 oz. AGW **Subject:** Death of Johann Georg I **Obv:** Facing bust within 2 outer legends **Rev:** 10-line inscription **Note:** Similar to 1 Thaler, KM#451. Struck from same dies.

Date	Mintage	VG	F	VF	XF	Unc
1656 Rare	—	—	—	—	—	—

KM# 467 5 DUCAT (1/2 Portugalöser)
17.5000 g., 0.9860 Gold 0.5547 oz. AGW **Obv:** Equestrian figure of Johann Georg II right **Rev:** 6-line inscription **Note:** Vicariat Issue.

Date	Mintage	VG	F	VF	XF	Unc
1657 (acorn)	—	—	—	—	—	—
1658 (acorn)	—	—	—	—	—	—

KM# 586 5 DUCAT (1/2 Portugalöser)
17.5000 g., 0.9860 Gold 0.5547 oz. AGW **Obv:** Bust of Johann Georg III right **Rev:** Crowned shield of arms, date above

Date	Mintage	VG	F	VF	XF	Unc
1681 CF Rare	—	—	—	—	—	—
1688 Rare	—	—	—	—	—	—

KM# 635 5 DUCAT (1/2 Portugalöser)
17.5000 g., 0.9860 Gold 0.5547 oz. AGW **Obv:** Bust of Johann Georg IV right, legend around **Rev:** Crossed swords with shields in divided fields

Date	Mintage	VG	F	VF	XF	Unc
1692 IK Rare	—	—	—	—	—	—

KM# 727 5 DUCAT (1/2 Portugalöser)
17.5000 g., 0.9860 Gold 0.5547 oz. AGW **Obv:** Bust right **Rev:** Crowned round 4-fold arms with central shield of 2-fold arms between 2 palm branches crossed at bottom, date at top **Note:** Struck with 1 Thaler dies, KM#707.

Date	Mintage	VG	F	VF	XF	Unc
1700 OLH	—	—	—	—	—	—

KM# 113 6 DUCAT
21.0000 g., 0.9860 Gold 0.6657 oz. AGW **Ruler:** Johann Georg I **Subject:** Centenary of Protestant Reformation **Obv:** Half-length figure to right, wearing rob and electoral hat, holding sword over right shoulder, divides IOH - GEOR, shield of 4-fold arms, with central shield of electoral Saxony in front divides date **Obv. Legend:** VERBVM DOMINI MANET IN ÆTERNVM. **Rev:** Half-length figure to right, wearing rob and electoral hat, holding sword over right shoulder, divides FRID - III, shield of 2-fold arms of electoral and ducal Saxony in front divides 15 - 17 **Rev. Legend:** SECVLVM LVTHERANVM.

Date	Mintage	VG	F	VF	XF	Unc
1617 Rare	—	—	—	—	—	—

KM# A423 6 DUCAT
21.0000 g., 0.9860 Gold 0.6657 oz. AGW **Subject:** Centennial of the Augsburg Confession **Obv:** Bust of Johann Georg right **Rev:** Bust of Johann right **Note:** Similar to 10 Ducat, KM#423.

Date	Mintage	VG	F	VF	XF	Unc
1630	—	2,300	3,900	6,500	10,500	—

KM# 468 6 DUCAT
21.0000 g., 0.9860 Gold 0.6657 oz. AGW **Obv:** Equestrian figure of Johann Georg II right **Rev:** 12-line inscription **Note:** Vicariat Issue. Similar to 1 Ducat, KM#463.

Date	Mintage	VG	F	VF	XF	Unc
1657 (acorn) Rare	—	—	—	—	—	—

KM# 588 6 DUCAT
21.0000 g., 0.9860 Gold 0.6657 oz. AGW **Obv:** Half-length bust right **Rev:** Helmeted 8-fold arms

Date	Mintage	VG	F	VF	XF	Unc
1684 Rare	—	—	—	—	—	—
1685 Rare	—	—	—	—	—	—
1690 Rare	—	—	—	—	—	—

KM# 589 6 DUCAT
21.0000 g., 0.9860 Gold 0.6657 oz. AGW **Obv:** Bust of Johann Georg III right **Rev:** Crowned arms, date above

Date	Mintage	VG	F	VF	XF	Unc
1685 CF Rare	—	—	—	—	—	—

KM# B423 7 DUCAT
24.5000 g., 0.9860 Gold 0.7766 oz. AGW **Subject:** Centennial of the Augsburg Confession **Obv:** Bust of Johann Georg right **Rev:** Bust of Johann right

Date	Mintage	VG	F	VF	XF	Unc
1630	—	2,150	4,250	7,800	11,500	—

KM# A418 8 DUCAT
28.0000 g., 0.9860 Gold 0.8876 oz. AGW **Obv:** 1/2-length bust with sword **Rev:** Arms

Date	Mintage	VG	F	VF	XF	Unc
1628 Rare	—	—	—	—	—	—

KM# C423 8 DUCAT
28.0000 g., 0.9860 Gold 0.8876 oz. AGW **Subject:** Centennial of the Augsburg Confession **Obv:** Bust of Johann Georg right **Rev:** Bust of Johann right

Date	Mintage	VG	F	VF	XF	Unc
1630	—	2,600	4,550	8,500	12,500	—

KM# 469 8 DUCAT
28.0000 g., 0.9860 Gold 0.8876 oz. AGW **Obv:** Equestrian figure of Johann Georg II right **Rev:** Multiple line inscription **Note:** Vicariat Issue. Similar to 1 Ducat, KM#463.

Date	Mintage	VG	F	VF	XF	Unc
1657 (acorn) Rare	—	—	—	—	—	—

KM# D423 9 DUCAT
31.5000 g., 0.9860 Gold 0.9985 oz. AGW **Subject:** Centennial of the Augsburg Confession **Obv:** Bust of Johann Georg right **Rev:** Bust of Johann right **Note:** Similar to 10 Ducat, KM#423.

Date	Mintage	VG	F	VF	XF	Unc
1630	—	3,750	5,600	9,400	20,500	—

KM# 29 10 DUCAT (Portugalöser)
35.0000 g., 0.9860 Gold 1.1095 oz. AGW **Ruler:** Christian II, Johann Georg I and August **Obv:** Bust of Friedrich August I right **Rev:** 2 shields crowned between palm branches **Note:** Struck with 1 Thaler dies, KM#707.

Date	Mintage	VG	F	VF	XF	Unc
1606 Rare	—	—	—	—	—	—

KM# B123 10 DUCAT (Portugalöser)
35.0000 g., 0.9860 Gold 1.1095 oz. AGW **Obv:** Equestrian figure of Johann Georg I right **Rev:** 12-line inscription **Note:** Vicariat Issue. Struck with 1 Thaler dies, KM#119. Prev. KM#A123.

Date	Mintage	VG	F	VF	XF	Unc
1619 Rare	—	—	—	—	—	—

KM# B418 10 DUCAT (Portugalöser)
35.0000 g., 0.9860 Gold 1.1095 oz. AGW **Obv:** 1/2-length bust with sword **Rev:** Arms

Date	Mintage	VG	F	VF	XF	Unc
1628 Rare	—	—	—	—	—	—

KM# 423 10 DUCAT (Portugalöser)
35.0000 g., 0.9860 Gold 1.1095 oz. AGW **Subject:** Centennial of the Augsburg Confession **Obv:** Bust of Johann Georg right **Rev:** Bust of Johann right

Date	Mintage	VG	F	VF	XF	Unc
1630	—	—	—	14,500	20,000	—

KM# 470 10 DUCAT (Portugalöser)
35.0000 g., 0.9860 Gold 1.1095 oz. AGW **Note:** Vicariat Issue. Similar to 1 Ducat, KM#463. Struck with 1 Thaler dies, KM#481.

Date	Mintage	VG	F	VF	XF	Unc
1657 (acorn) Rare	—	—	—	—	—	—

KM# 487 10 DUCAT (Portugalöser)
35.0000 g., 0.9860 Gold 1.1095 oz. AGW **Subject:** Death of Johann Georg II's Mother, Magdalene Sibylle **Obv:** 7-line inscription **Rev:** 6-line inscription with Roman numeral date **Note:** Similar to 1 Ducat, KM#484. Struck with 1 Thaler dies, KM#482.

Date	Mintage	VG	F	VF	XF	Unc
1659 (acorn) Rare	—	—	—	—	—	—

KM# 501 10 DUCAT (Portugalöser)
35.0000 g., 0.9860 Gold 1.1095 oz. AGW **Subject:** Marriage of Erdmuthe Sophie to Christian Ernst **Note:** Struck with 1 Thaler dies, KM#500.

Date	Mintage	VG	F	VF	XF	Unc
1662 Rare	—	—	—	—	—	—

KM# 530 10 DUCAT (Portugalöser)
35.0000 g., 0.9860 Gold 1.1095 oz. AGW **Subject:** Birth of Johann Georg IV **Note:** Struck with 1 Thaler dies, KM#528.

Date	Mintage	VG	F	VF	XF	Unc
1669 Rare	—	—	—	—	—	—

KM# A424 12 DUCAT
42.0000 g., 0.9860 Gold 1.3314 oz. AGW **Subject:** Centennial of the Augsburg Confession **Obv:** Bust of Johann Georg right **Rev:** Bust of Johann right **Note:** Similar to 10 Ducat, KM#423.

Date	Mintage	VG	F	VF	XF	Unc
1630 Rare	—	—	—	—	—	—

KM# A419 16 DUCAT
57.0000 g., 0.9860 Gold 1.8069 oz. AGW **Obv:** Equestrian figure on horse in front of Dresden city view **Rev:** 6-fold helmeted arms

Date	Mintage	VG	F	VF	XF	Unc
1627 Rare	—	—	—	—	—	—

KM# 36 20 DUCAT (Doppel Portugalöser)
70.0000 g., 0.9860 Gold 2.2190 oz. AGW **Ruler:** Christian II, Johann Georg I and August **Obv:** Bust right with sword and helmet divide date **Rev:** Busts facing one another **Note:** Struck with 2 Thaler dies, KM#26.

Date	Mintage	VG	F	VF	XF	Unc
1610 Rare	—	—	—	—	—	—

KM# B419 20 DUCAT (Doppel Portugalöser)
70.0000 g., 0.9860 Gold 2.2190 oz. AGW **Obv:** Equestrian figure on horse in front of Dresden city view **Rev:** 6-fold helmeted arms

Date	Mintage	VG	F	VF	XF	Unc
1628 Rare	—	—	—	—	—	—

KM# 454 20 DUCAT (Doppel Portugalöser)
70.0000 g., 0.9860 Gold 2.2190 oz. AGW **Subject:** Death of Johann Georg I **Note:** Struck with 1 Thaler dies, KM#451.

Date	Mintage	VG	F	VF	XF	Unc
1656 Rare	—	—	—	—	—	—

KM# 477 20 DUCAT (Doppel Portugalöser)
70.0000 g., 0.9860 Gold 2.2190 oz. AGW **Note:** Vicariat Issue. Struck with 2 Thaler dies, KM#489.

Date	Mintage	VG	F	VF	XF	Unc
1658 (acorn) Rare	—	—	—	—	—	—

KM# 488 20 DUCAT (Doppel Portugalöser)
70.0000 g., 0.9860 Gold 2.2190 oz. AGW **Subject:** Death of Johann Georg II's Mother, Magdalene Sibylle **Note:** Struck with 1 Thaler dies, KM#482.

Date	Mintage	VG	F	VF	XF	Unc
1659 (acorn) Rare	—	—	—	—	—	—

KM# C419 25 DUCAT
87.5000 g., 0.9860 Gold 2.7737 oz. AGW **Obv:** Equestrian figure on horse in front of Dresden city view **Rev:** 6-fold helmeted arms

Date	Mintage	VG	F	VF	XF	Unc
1628 Rare	—	—	—	—	—	—

MEDALLIC COINAGE

PATTERNS

Including off metal strikes

KM#	Date	Mintage	Identification	Mkt Val
Pn1	1630	—	10 Ducat. Silver. 34.7000 g. KM423.	—
PnA2	1694	—	Pfennig. Gold. KM636.	—
Pn2	1700 ILH	—	2 Ducat. Silver. KM710.	—
Pn3	1701	—	Ducat. Silver. KM729.	—
Pn4	1702 ILH	—	2 Ducat. Silver. KM710.	—
Pn5	1703 ILH	—	2 Ducat. Silver. KM710.	—
Pn6	1704 ILH	—	2 Ducat. Silver. KM710.	—
PnA6	1704 ILH	—	2/3 Thaler. Gold. KM# 685.	—
Pn8	1708	—	1/3 Thaler. Gold. KM768.	—
Pn7	1708 ILH	—	1/3 Thaler. Copper. KM768.	—
Pn9	1708 ILH	—	Thaler. Lead. KM769.	—
Pn10	1709	—	Ducat. Silver. KM729.	—
Pn12	1709	—	Ducat. Silver. Leipzig Univ., KM778.	—
Pn11	1709 ILH	—	Ducat. Silver. KM771.	—
Pn14	1710	—	1/4 Ducat. Silver. KM793.	—
Pn17	1710	—	Ducat. Copper. KM793.	—
Pn18	1710	—	Ducat. Silver. KM796.	—
Pn13	1710 ILH	—	1/4 Ducat. Silver. KM725.	—
Pn15	1710 ILH	—	1/2 Ducat. Copper. KM795.	—
Pn16	1710 ILH	—	1/2 Ducat. Silver. KM795.	—
Pn20	1711 ILH	—	1/4 Thaler. Copper. KM801.	—
Pn21	1711	—	Ducat. Silver. KM806.	125
Pn22	1711 OLH	—	2 Ducat. Silver. KM807.	135
Pn19	1711 ILH	—	Pfennig. Gold. KM702.	325
Pn23	1711	—	3 Ducat. Silver. KM811.	350
Pn24	1711	—	4 Ducat. Silver. KM814.	375
Pn25	1712 ILH	—	Pfennig. Gold. KM702.	325
Pn26	1714	—	Ducat. Silver. Mining, KM779.	125
Pn27	1715	—	Ducat. Silver. Lublin, KM821.	—
Pn28	1717	—	Ducat. Silver. KM830.	—
Pn29	1717	—	Ducat. Silver. KM831.	95.00
Pn30	1717	—	2 Ducat. Silver. KM832.	125
Pn31	1721	—	Pfennig. Silver. KM850.	—
Pn32	1721	—	Pfennig. Gold. KM850.	—
Pn33	1735 FWoF	—	2 Ducat. Silver. KM888.	125
Pn34	1738 FWoF	—	3 Ducat. Silver. KM892.	175
Pn35	1738 FWoF	—	4 Ducat. Silver. KM893.	200
PnA36	1739 FWoF	—	2 Ducat. Copper. KM888.	—
Pn36	1739 FWoF	—	2 Ducat. Silver. KM888.	125
Pn38	1742 FWoF	—	2 Ducat. Silver. KM888.	125
Pn39	1743 FWoF	—	2 Ducat. Silver. KM888.	125
Pn40	1744 FWoF	—	Pfennig. Gold. KM894.	600
PnA41	1753	—	Thaler. Silver.	—
Pn41	1763	—	Ducat. Silver. Hubertusburg Peace.	—
Pn42	1764 C	—	Pfennig. Gold. KM964.	400
Pn44	1765 C	—	3 Pfennig. Billon. KM965.	65.00
Pn43	1765 C	—	Pfennig. Gold. KM980.	400
Pn45	1772 C	—	Pfennig. Silver. KM1000.	85.00
Pn49	1779	—	Pfennig. Gold. KM1000.	—
Pn46	1779	—	Heller. Silver. KM1002.	45.00
Pn48	1779	—	Pfennig. Silver. KM1000.	85.00
Pn47	1779 C	—	Heller. Gold. KM1002.	1,350
Pn50	1780	—	Heller. Silver. KM1002.	45.00
Pn52	1781	—	3 Pfennig. Gold. KM965.	—
Pn51	1781	—	Pfennig. Silver. KM1000.	85.00
Pn53	1782	—	Pfennig. Silver. KM1000.	85.00
Pn54	1783	—	Heller. Silver. KM1002.	45.00
Pn55	1783	—	Pfennig. Silver. KM1000.	85.00
Pn56	1785	—	Pfennig. Silver. KM1000.	85.00
Pn57	1798	—	Pfennig. Silver. KM1000.	85.00
Pn58	1799	—	3 Pfennig. Silver. KM1037.	—
Pn59	1800	—	Pfennig. Silver. KM1000.	85.00
Pn61	1804	—	Pfennig. Gold. KM1000.	—
Pn60	1804	—	Heller. Gold. KM1002.	1,350
Pn62	1805	—	Pfennig. Gold. KM1000.	—
Pn63	1808 H	—	Pfennig. Gold. KM1057.	—
Pn64	1808 SGH	—	Thaler. Silver.	3,000
Pn65	1813 H	—	Heller. Silver. KM1072.	500
Pn66	1813 IGS	—	Thaler. Silver.	8,000
Pn67	1814	—	Thaler.	10,000
Pn68	1814 IGS	134	Ducat. Gold.	7,000
Pn69	1816	—	1/24 Thaler. Gold. KM1075.	—
Pn71	183x G	—	3 Pfennig.	—
Pn70	1832 S	—	3 Pfennig. Silver.	1,200
Pn73	185x	—	1/6 Thaler.	—
Pn72	1857 F	—	5 Pfennig. Copper.	—
Pn74	1873 E	—	10 Mark. Copper. KM1235. KM1232. Plain edge.	—
Pn75	1873 E	—	20 Mark. Copper. KM1233. KM1236. Plain edge.	—
Pn76	1875 E	—	5 Mark. Zinc. Plain edge, KM1237.	—
Pn77	1876 E	—	10 Mark. Silver. Plain edge, KM1235.	—
Pn78	1902 E	—	5 Mark. Silver. KM1258.	—
PnA78	1905E	—	20 Mark. Copper. 4.0600 g.	—
PnB78	1905E	—	20 Mark. Copper. 4.8900 g. Bust in uniform.	—
Pn79	1913	—	3 Mark. Silver.	—
Pn80	1917 E	—	3 Mark. Aluminum. KM1267.	—

SAXE-WEISSENFELS

(Sachsen-Weissenfels)

Branch of the Albertine Saxon house, which was created in 1656 for August, 2nd son of the Elector of Saxony, Johann Georg I. The line became extinct with the death of Johann Adolf II in 1746 and the territories reverted to Electoral Saxony.

RULERS

August, 1656-1680
Johann Adolf I, 1680-1697
Johann Georg, 1697-1712

MINT OFFICIALS' INITIALS

Initials	Date	Name
IHF or HHF	1669-1670	Johann (Hans) Heinrich Friese, mintmaster in Halle
SQ	1686	Samuel Querfurt, mintmaster in Weissenfels

REFERENCE

M = Otto Merseburger, **Sammlung Otto Merseburger umfassend Münzen und Medaillen von Sachsen**, Leipzig, 1894.

DUCHY

STANDARD COINAGE

KM# 5 GROSCHEN (1/24 Thaler)

Silver, 23 mm. **Ruler:** August **Subject:** Death of August's First Wife, Anna Maria von Mecklenburg-Schwerin **Obv:** Crowned AM monogram in palm branches **Obv. Legend:** DEVM QVI HABET OMNIA HABET. **Rev:** 7-line inscription with dates **Rev. Inscription:** NATA. / SVER. 1. IVL. 1627. / DENAT. / HAL. 10. DEC. 1669 / ÆTAT. / XLII. M.5. D. / 10. **Mint:** Halle **Note:** Ref. M-2319.

Date	Mintage	VG	F	VF	XF	Unc
1669 HHF	—	40.00	80.00	160	325	—

KM# 17 GROSCHEN (1/24 Thaler)

Silver, 23 mm. **Ruler:** Johann Adolf I **Subject:** Death of Johann Adolf I's Wife, Johanna Magdalena von Sachsen-Altenburg **Obv:** Crowned intertwined script JA and JM monograms **Rev:** 8-line inscription with dates **Rev. Inscription:** NAT. / ALTENB:14 / IAN: Ao. 1656. / DEN: LEUCOPE= / TRÆ. 22. IAN: Ao. 1686. ÆTAT / XXX. D. IX. / S.Q. **Mint:** Weissenfels **Note:** Ref. M-2327.

Date	Mintage	VG	F	VF	XF	Unc
1686 SQ	—	45.00	90.00	180	360	—

KM# 7 1/4 THALER

7.2500 g., Silver **Ruler:** August **Subject:** Death of August's First Wife, Anna Maria von Mecklenburg-Schwerin **Obv:** Crowned AM monogram in palm branches **Obv. Legend:** DEVM. QVI. HABET. OMNIA. HABET. **Rev:** 7-line inscription with dates **Rev. Inscription:** NATA / SVER. 1. IVL. 1627. / DENAT. / HAL. 11. DEC. 1669 / ÆTAT. / XLII. M. 5. D. / 10. **Mint:** Halle **Note:** M#2318.

Date	Mintage	VG	F	VF	XF	Unc
1669 HHF	—	40.00	80.00	160	325	—

KM# 18 1/4 THALER

Silver **Ruler:** Johann Adolf I **Subject:** Death of Johann Adolf I's Wife, Johanna Magdalena von Sachsen-Altenburg **Obv:** Crowned script JM monogram **Obv. Legend:** + PROVIDENTIA. DOMINI. SUFFICIENTIA MIHI. **Rev:** 8-line inscription with dates **Mint:** Weissenfels

Date	Mintage	VG	F	VF	XF	Unc
1686 SQ	—	175	350	700	1,200	—

KM# 8 1/2 THALER

14.5800 g., Silver **Ruler:** August **Subject:** Death of August's First Wife, Anna Maria von Mecklenburg-Schwerin **Obv:** Jacob wrestling with the archangel **Obv. Legend:** DEVM. QVI. HABET. OMNIA. HABET. **Rev:** 11-line inscription with dates **Rev. Legend:** + D.G. ANNA MARIA. DUX. SAX. IUL. CLIV. ET. MONT. **Rev. Inscription:** NAT. / E. DOM. MEG. / SVER. 1. IUL. 1627. / NUPTA / IBID. 23. NOV. 1647. / DENATA / HAL. 11. DEC. 1669 / VIXIT / ANNOS. XLII. / MENS. 5. D. 10. / IH. F. **Mint:** Halle **Note:** M#2317.

Date	Mintage	VG	F	VF	XF	Unc
1669 IHF	—	75.00	150	300	600	—

KM# 19 1/2 THALER

Silver **Ruler:** Johann Adolf I **Subject:** Death of Johann Adolf I's Wife, Johanna Magdalena von Sachsen-Altenburg **Obv:** Figure of Jesus as the Good Shepherd, carrying staff, with lamb over shoulders **Obv. Legend:** + PROVIDENTIA. DOMINI. SUFFICIENTIA. MIHI. **Rev:** 8-line inscription with dates **Rev. Legend:** + D.G. IOHANNA. MAGDALENA. D. S. I. C. & M. **Rev. Inscription:** NATA / ALTENBURGI / 14. IAN: Ao. 1656. / DENAT: LEUCOPE= / TRÆ. 22. IAN: Ao. / 1686, ÆTAT: / XXX. D. IX. / S.Q. **Mint:** Weissenfels **Note:** M#2326.

Date	Mintage	VG	F	VF	XF	Unc
1686 SQ	—	75.00	150	300	600	—

KM# 3 THALER

Silver **Ruler:** August **Subject:** Laying Foundation Stone of New Palace Church **Obv:** IESUS above altar, hands in prayer and Bible with inscriptions **Obv. Legend:** SANCTA TRINITAS MEA HEREDITAS. **Rev:** 12-line inscription with date **Mint:** Halle **Note:** Dav. #7658

Date	Mintage	VG	F	VF	XF	Unc
1663	—	150	300	525	1,200	2,000

KM# 9 THALER

29.0700 g., Silver, 40 mm. **Ruler:** August **Subject:** Death of August's First Wife, Anna Maria von Mecklenburg-Schwerin **Obv:** Jacob wrestling with the archangel **Obv. Legend:** DEVM. QVI. HABET. OMNIA. HABET. **Rev:** 11-line inscription with dates **Rev. Legend:** + D.G. ANNA MARIA. DUX. SAX. IUL. CLIV. ET. MONT.

Rev. Inscription: NAT. / E. DOM. MEG. / SVER. 1. IUL 1627. / NUPTA / IBID 23. NOV. 1647. / DENATA / HAL 11. DEC. 1669 / VIXIT / ANNOS. XLIIL / MENS. 5. D. / IH. 10. F. **Mint:** Halle **Note:** Ref. Dav. 7659.

Date	Mintage	VG	F	VF	XF	Unc
1669 IHF	—	200	400	950	2,000	5,500

KM# 10 THALER

Silver **Ruler:** August **Subject:** Death of August's First Wife, Anna Maria von Mecklenburg-Schwerin **Obv:** Jacob wrestling with the archangel **Obv. Legend:** DEUM. QVI. HABET. OMNIA. HABET. **Rev:** 11-line inscription with dates **Rev. Legend:** + D.G. ANNA MARIA. DUX. SAX. IUL. CLIV. ET. MONT. **Rev. Inscription:** NAT. / E. DOM. MEG. / SVER. 1. IUL 1627. / NUPTA / IBID 23. NOV. 1647. / DENATA / HAL 11. DEC. 1669 / VIXIT / ANNOS. XLIIL / MENS. 5. D. 10 / HHF. **Mint:** Halle **Note:** Ref. Dav. 7659A.

Date	Mintage	VG	F	VF	XF	Unc
1669 HHF	—	200	400	900	1,850	—

KM# 13 THALER

Silver **Ruler:** Johann Adolf I **Subject:** Birth of Prince Adolf **Obv:** Crowned JA's in palm sprays, shields in corners **Obv. Legend:** AUF DER NEUEN AUGUSTUS BURG ZU WEISSENFELS **Rev:** Sun above child in cradle, Roman numeral date divided in corners **Rev. Legend:** BUCHSEN SCHIESSEN BEY DER PRINZLICHEN EINSEGNUNG **Note:** Klippe. Dav. #7662.

Date	Mintage	VG	F	VF	XF	Unc
MDCLXXXV(1685)	—	700	1,400	2,800	4,900	—

KM# 20 THALER

Silver **Ruler:** Johann Adolf I **Subject:** Death of Johann Adolf I's Wife, Johanna Magdalena von Sachsen-Altenburg **Obv:** Figure of Jesus as the Good Shepherd, holding staff, with lamb on shoulders **Obv. Legend:** + PROVIDENTIA DOMINI SUFFICIENTIA MIHI **Rev:** 8-line inscription with dates **Rev. Legend:** + D.G. IOHANNA. MAGDALENA. D.S.I.C. &. M. **Rev. Inscription:** NATA/ALTENBURGI./14. IAN: Ao. 1656./DENAT. LEUCOPE=/TR. E. 22. IANUAR:/Ao. 1686. ÆTATE:/Ao. XXX. DIE./S. IX. Q. **Mint:** Weissenfels **Note:** Dav. #7663.

Date	Mintage	VG	F	VF	XF	Unc
1686 SQ	—	240	550	1,150	2,100	—

KM# 25 THALER (Shooting)

Silver **Ruler:** Johann Georg **Obv:** Cross in center of 8-rayed star, ribbon with Order of the Elephant around **Rev:** Large crown above two adjacent oval shields, ducal Saxony in left, JG monogram in right, R.N. date divided in corners **Rev. Legend:** + SCHIESEN BEY DEM CARNEVAL AUF DER NEUEN AUGUSTUSBURG Z. WE. **Note:** Klippe. Dav. #7664.

Date	Mintage	VG	F	VF	XF	Unc
MDCIC(1699)	—	1,650	2,750	—	—	—

Note: Baldwin's Auctions Ltd., Auction 49, 9-06, ex-mounted, tooled, otherwise VF realized approximately $2,565

KM# 28 THALER (Shooting)

Silver **Ruler:** Johann Georg **Obv:** Cross in 8-pointed star, ribbon of Order of the Elephant around **Rev:** Crown over two adjacent oval shields, ducal Saxony in left, JG monogram in right, R.N. date divided in corners **Rev. Legend:** + SCHIESEN BEY SR. HOCHF. DURCHL. GEBURTSTAG. AUF. DER NEUEN AUGUSTUSB. Z. WEISENF. **Note:** Klippe. Dav. #7665.

Date	Mintage	VG	F	VF	XF	Unc
MDCC(1700)	—	1,250	2,150	4,300	7,200	—

KM# 14 1-1/2 THALER

Silver **Ruler:** Johann Adolf I **Subject:** Birth of Prince Adolf **Obv:** Crowned JA's in palm sprays, shields in corners **Obv. Legend:** AUF DER NEUEN AUGUSTUS BURG ZU WEISSENFELS **Rev:** Sun above child in cradle, Roman numeral date divided in corners **Rev. Legend:** RINGEL RENNEN BEY DER PRINZLICHEN EINSEGNUNG **Note:** Klippe. Dav. #7661.

Date	Mintage	VG	F	VF	XF	Unc
MDCLXXXV(1685) Rare	—	—	—	—	—	—

KM# 15 2 THALER

Silver **Ruler:** Johann Adolf I **Subject:** Birth of Prince Adolf **Obv:** Crowned JA's in palm sprays, shields in corners **Obv. Legend:** AUF DER NEUEN AUGUSTUS BURG ZU WEISSENFELS **Rev:** Sun above child in cradle, Roman numeral date divided in corners **Rev. Legend:** RINGEL RENNEN BEY DER PRINZLICHEN EINSEGNUNG **Note:** Klippe. Dav. #7660.

Date	Mintage	VG	F	VF	XF	Unc
MDCLXXXV(1685) Rare	—	—	—	—	—	—

TRADE COINAGE

KM# 11 DUCAT

Gold **Ruler:** August **Subject:** Death of August's First Wife, Anna Maria von Mecklenburg-Schwerin **Obv:** Crowned AM monogram in palm branches **Obv. Legend:** DEVM. QVI. HABET. OMNIA. HABET. **Rev:** 7-line inscription with dates **Rev. Inscription:** NATA. / SVER. 1. IVL. 1627. / DENAT. / HAL. 11. DEC. 1669 / ÆTAT. / XLII. M. 5. D. / 10. **Mint:** Halle **Note:** Struck from Groschen dies, KM #5; FR#1561.

Date	Mintage	VG	F	VF	XF	Unc
1669 HHF	—	950	1,900	3,800	6,400	—

KM# 21 DUCAT

3.5000 g., 0.9860 Gold 0.1109 oz. AGW **Ruler:** Johann Adolf I **Subject:** Death of Johanna Magdalena, Wife of Johann Adolf **Obv:** Capped JA monogram **Rev:** 8-line inscription **Mint:** Weissenfels **Note:** FR#3044.

Date	Mintage	VG	F	VF	XF	Unc
1686 SQ	—	950	1,900	3,700	5,900	—

KM# 23 DUCAT

3.5000 g., 0.9860 Gold 0.1109 oz. AGW **Ruler:** Johann Georg **Subject:** Denmark's Order of the Elephant Conferred upon Johann Georg **Obv:** Full-length figure of duke to right with hand on altar **Rev:** Round Saxony arms in baroque frame, date divided below, surrounded by Order of the Elephant, crown above **Note:** FR#3045.

Date	Mintage	VG	F	VF	XF	Unc
1698	—	1,550	3,100	6,200	11,000	—

KM# 24 2 DUCAT

Gold **Ruler:** Johann Georg **Subject:** Marriage of Johann Georg and Friderike Elisabeth von Sachsen-Eisenach **Obv:** Two hearts on altar, arms of Saxony infront, rays streaming down from clouds above **Obv. Legend:** COELESTIBVS - IGNIBVS ARDENT **Rev:** 10-line inscription with date

Date	Mintage	VG	F	VF	XF	Unc
1698 Rare	—	—	—	—	—	—

KM# 26 2 DUCAT

Gold **Ruler:** Johann Georg **Subject:** Homage of Langensalza **Obv:** Flaming altar, legend curved above in Gothic letters, 2-line Gothic inscription in exergue **Obv. Legend:** Ein ewiger - Saltz = Bund. **Rev:** 9-line inscription in Gothic letters with date

Date	Mintage	VG	F	VF	XF	Unc
1699 CW Rare	—	—	—	—	—	—

SAXE-ZEITZ-NAUMBURG

(Sachsen-Zeitz-Naumburg)

Saxe-Zeitz was created at the same time as Saxe-Weissenfels for the fourth son of the elector Johann Georg I. Moritz, was also administrator of the bishopric of Naumburg-Zeitz and a part of Henneberg. At the death of his son Moritz-Wilhelm, a Catholic, in 1718, this line became extinct and reverted to the electoral line.

RULER

Moritz, 1656-1681

DUCHY

STANDARD COINAGE

DAV# 7666 THALER

28.9900 g., Silver **Ruler:** Moritz **Obv:** Bust of Moritz facing **Rev:** Mauritzburg Castle

Date	Mintage	VG	F	VF	XF	Unc
1667	—	650	1,250	2,500	4,500	—

DAV# 7666A 2 THALER

52.1000 g., Silver **Ruler:** Moritz **Obv:** Bust of Mortiz facing **Rev:** Mauritzburg Castle

Date	Mintage	VG	F	VF	XF	Unc
1667	—	1,900	3,200	4,800	7,500	—

SAXE-BARBY

(Sachsen-Barby)

When the line of counts of Barby (q.v.) became extinct in 1659, the lands of that county fell to Electoral Saxony. In 1680, a separate line of Saxe-Barby was established by a son of the duke of Saxe-Weissenfels. It was short-lived, however, and reverted to Saxe-Weissenfels in 1739. The latter also became extinct in 1746 and Barby was integrated from that time into the kingdom of Saxony.

RULER

Heinrich, 1680-1728
Georg Albrecht, 1728-1739

DUCHY

REGULAR COINAGE

KM# 1 2/3 THALER (Gulden)

Silver Weight varies: 17.51-17.78g., 39 mm. **Ruler:** Heinrich **Obv:** Armored bust to right **Obv. Legend:** HENRIC. D.G. DUX SAX. IU. C.& M. C. I. B. **Rev:** Crowned shield of 4-fold arms, with central shield of Barby, divide date, value 2/3 in oval below **Rev. Legend:** MONETA NOVA - ARGENTEA **Note:** Dav.#834.

Date	Mintage	VG	F	VF	XF	Unc
1687 Rare	—	3,500	5,200	8,500	13,500	—

Note: Fritz Rudolf Künker Münzenhandlung Auction 80, 3-03, VF realized approximately $13,265

SAXE-OLD-GOTHA

(Sachsen-Alt-Gotha)

In the aftermath of the religious struggles of the first half of the 16th century, Ernestine Saxony was ruled jointly, divided, and ruled jointly again in relentless succession. The sons of Johann Friedrich I effected a division of the domains in 1565. When the older brother was imprisoned two years later, Gotha reverted to Saxe-Old Weimar. Gotha was ceded in 1572 by Weimar to the Coburg branch of the family, but reverted to the former again in 1638. Upon its extinction in the latter year, Gotha fell to Weimar a third time, from which a new Gotha line was established in 1640.

RULERS

Johann Friedrich II, 1565-1567(d.1595)
And Johann Wilhelm, 1565-1567
Johann Wilhelm, 1565-1567
And Johann Ernst II von Eisenach, 1572-1638

MINT OFFICIALS' INITIALS

Initial	Date	Name
WA	1604-12	Wolf Albrecht der Jüngere in Coburg
	1612-20, 23-32	Wolf Albrecht der Jüngere in Saalfeld
(c)=	1578-1603	Gregor Bechstedt (Bechstädt) in Saalfeld
(d)=	1603-04	Barther Bechstedt in Saalfeld
(e)= ☿ or WF	1620-April 1621	Wolfgang Frömell in Coburg (Ehrenburg)
	April-Dec. 1621	In Hildburghausen
	Early 1622	In Gotha
	1622-23	In Coburg
	1622	Tobias Rentsch in Neustadt an der Heide
(f)= ♀	1622	Johann Stopffel in Gotha
	1622	Hans Brauer (Brawer) in Hildburghausen
(g)= or	1620-21	Johann Ziessler in Eisenach
(h)=	1621-22	Hans Schmidt in Körner (Amt Volkenroda)
(i)= or MR	1633-39	Martin Reimann in Saalfeld
(j)= arm with sickle or EF/EFS E	1636-72	Ernst Friedrich Schneider in Coburg Ehrenburg mint in Coburg

DUCHY

REGULAR COINAGE

KM# 23 PFENNIG

Silver, 11 mm. **Ruler:** Johann Casimir and Johann Ernst II **Obv:** Saxony arms in ornamented shield, 'C' above **Mint:** Neustadt an der Heide **Note:** Ref. KOR-218. Kipper coinage. Uniface.

Date	Mintage	VG	F	VF	XF	Unc
ND(1620-22)	—	—	—	—	—	—

KM# 173 PFENNIG

Silver, 13 mm. **Ruler:** Johann Ernst II **Obv:** Oval shield of ducal Saxony arms in baroque frame **Rev:** Imperial orb divides date, COBVRG above, mintmaster's symbol below **Mint:** Coburg **Note:** Ref. KOR-363.

Date	Mintage	VG	F	VF	XF	Unc
1637 (j)	—	—	—	—	—	—

KM# A90.1 3 PFENNIG (Dreier)

Silver, 16-17 mm. **Ruler:** Johann Casimir and Johann Ernst II **Obv:** Oval shield of ducal Saxony arms in baroque frame divides FE - VV **Rev:** Imperial orb with 3 divides date in ornamented rhombus **Mint:** Neustadt an der Heide **Note:** Ref. KOR-259, 264-5. Varieties exist.

Date	Mintage	VG	F	VF	XF	Unc
16ZZ	—	—	—	—	—	—
16Z3	—	—	—	—	—	—

KM# A90.2 3 PFENNIG (Dreier)

Silver, 17 mm. **Ruler:** Johann Casimir and Johann Ernst II **Obv:** Spanish shield of ducal Saxony arms in baroque frame, FE - VV above **Rev:** Imperial orb with 3 divides date in ornamented rhombus **Mint:** Neustadt an der Heide **Note:** Ref. KOR-260. Varieties exist.

Date	Mintage	VG	F	VF	XF	Unc
16ZZ	—	—	—	—	—	—

KM# A90.3 3 PFENNIG (Dreier)

Silver, 17 mm. **Ruler:** Johann Casimir and Johann Ernst II **Obv:** Spanish shield of ducal Saxony arms in baroque frame, FE - VV above **Rev:** Imperial orb with 3 divides date at upper left and right, garland curved below **Mint:** Neustadt an der Heide **Note:** Ref. KOR-261.

Date	Mintage	VG	F	VF	XF	Unc
16ZZ	—	—	—	—	—	—

KM# A90.4 3 PFENNIG (Dreier)

Silver, 16 mm. **Ruler:** Johann Casimir and Johann Ernst II **Obv:** Spanish shield of ducal Saxony arms in baroque frame divides FE - VV **Rev:** Imperial orb with 3 divides date in ornamented rhombus **Mint:** Neustadt an der Heide **Note:** Ref. KOR-262.1.

Date	Mintage	VG	F	VF	XF	Unc
16ZZ	—	—	—	—	—	—

KM# A90.5 3 PFENNIG (Dreier)

Silver, 17 mm. **Ruler:** Johann Casimir and Johann Ernst II **Obv:** Spanish shield of ducal Saxony arms divides FE - VV, date divided at top **Rev:** Imperial orb with 3 in ornamented rhombus **Mint:** Neustadt an der Heide **Note:** Ref. KOR-262.2.

Date	Mintage	VG	F	VF	XF	Unc
16ZZ	—	—	—	—	—	—

KM# A93 3 PFENNIG (Dreier)

Silver, 17 mm. **Ruler:** Johann Casimir and Johann Ernst II **Obv:** Spade-shaped shield of ducal Saxony arms in baroque frame, FE - VV divided above **Rev:** Imperial orb with 3 divides date in ornamented rhombus **Mint:** Neustadt an der Heide **Note:** Ref. KOR-263.

Date	Mintage	VG	F	VF	XF	Unc
16Z3	—	—	—	—	—	—

KM# 175 3 PFENNIG (Dreier)

Silver, 16-17 mm. **Ruler:** Johann Ernst II **Obv:** Oval shield of ducal Saxony arms in baroque frame, COBVRG above, date divided below **Rev:** 4 small shields of arms around small imperial orb, value 3 below **Mint:** Coburg **Note:** Ref. KOR-361, 362.

Date	Mintage	VG	F	VF	XF	Unc
1636 (j)	—	—	—	—	—	—
1637 (j)	—	—	—	—	—	—

KM# 25 KREUZER

Silver, 15 mm. **Ruler:** Johann Casimir and Johann Ernst II **Obv:** Ornate shield of ducal Saxony arms between 2 stars **Rev:** Imperial orb with 'C' divides FE - VV to upper left and right **Mint:** Neustadt an der Heide **Note:** Ref. KOR-217. Kipper Coinage.

Date	Mintage	VG	F	VF	XF	Unc
ND(1620-22)	—	—	—	—	—	—

KM# 47 KREUZER

Silver, 12-13 mm. **Ruler:** Johann Casimir and Johann Ernst II **Obv:** Spanish shield of ducal Saxony arms in baroque frame, FE - VV divided to upper left and right **Rev:** Imperial orb with 'C' divides date **Mint:** Neustadt an der Heide **Note:** Ref. KOR-215. Varieties exist. Kipper coinage.

Date	Mintage	VG	F	VF	XF	Unc
1621	—	—	—	—	—	—

KM# 48 KREUZER

Silver, 11-13 mm. **Ruler:** Johann Casimir and Johann Ernst II **Obv:** Spanish shield of ducal Saxony arms in baroque frame, F - E - V - V divided near top around arms **Rev:** Imperial orb with 'C' divides date **Mint:** Neustadt an der Heide **Note:** Ref. KOR-216. Varieties exist. Kipper coinage.

Date	Mintage	VG	F	VF	XF	Unc
1621	—	—	—	—	—	—

KM# 49.1 KREUZER

Silver, 12-13 mm. **Ruler:** Johann Casimir and Johann Ernst II **Obv:** Oval shield of ducal Saxony arms in baroque frame, mintmaster's symbol above divides FE - VV. **Rev:** Imperial orb with 'C' divides date **Mint:** Neustadt an der Heide **Note:** Ref. KOR-214.1. Varieties exist. Kipper coinage.

Date	Mintage	VG	F	VF	XF	Unc
1621 (e)	—	—	—	—	—	—

KM# 49.2 KREUZER

Silver, 11-12 mm. **Ruler:** Johann Casimir and Johann Ernst II **Obv:** Oval shield of ducal Saxony arms in baroque frame, FE - VV divided to upper left and right **Rev:** Imperial orb with 'C' divides date **Mint:** Neustadt an der Heide **Note:** Ref. KOR-214.2. Varieties exist. Kipper coinage.

Date	Mintage	VG	F	VF	XF	Unc
1621	—	—	—	—	—	—

KM# 26 3 KREUZER (Groschen)

Silver, 16-18 mm. **Ruler:** Johann Casimir and Johann Ernst II **Obv:** Spanish shield of ducal Saxony arms in baroque frame **Obv. Legend:** D. G. IOH. CAS. ET. IOH. ER. FR(A)(T). **Rev:** Imperial orb with 'C', value (3) at bottom **Rev. Legend:** DV(C). SAX. (-) IV(L) (-) CL(I). ET. M(ON). **Mint:** Neustadt an der Heide **Note:** Ref. KOR#206-10. Kipper coinage. Varieties exist.

Date	Mintage	VG	F	VF	XF	Unc
ND(1620-21) (e)	—	—	—	—	—	—
ND(1620-21)	—	—	—	—	—	—

KM# 27 3 KREUZER (Groschen)

Silver, 16 mm. **Ruler:** Johann Casimir and Johann Ernst II **Obv:** Shield of oval ducal Saxony arms in baroque frame **Obv. Legend:** D. G. IOH. CAS. ET. IOH. ER. FR. **Rev:** Imperial orb with 'C', value (3) at bottom **Rev. Legend:** DV. SAX. IV - CL. ET. MO. **Mint:** Neustadt an der Heide **Note:** Ref. KOR-211. Kipper coinage.

Date	Mintage	VG	F	VF	XF	Unc
ND(1620-21) (e)	—	—	—	—	—	—

KM# 53 3 KREUZER (Groschen)

Billon, 17 mm. **Ruler:** Johann Casimir and Johann Ernst II **Obv:** Shield of ducal Saxony arms with concave sides, small imperial orb above **Obv. Legend:** D. G. IOH. CAS. ET. IOH. ERN. **Rev:** Crowned imperial eagle, 3 in circle on breast **Rev. Legend:** DVC. SAX. IVL. CLI. ET. MO. **Mint:** Eisenach **Note:** Ref. KOR-241. Kipper coinage.

Date	Mintage	VG	F	VF	XF	Unc
ND(1621)	—	—	—	—	—	—

KM# 54 3 KREUZER (Groschen)

Silver, 16-17 mm. **Ruler:** Johann Casimir and Johann Ernst II **Obv:** Oval shield of ducal Saxony arms in baroque frame, small imperial orb above **Obv. Legend:** D G. IOH. CAS. ET. IOH. ER(N). (F) **Rev:** Crowned imperial eagle, 3 in circle on breast **Rev. Legend:** DVC. SAX. IVL. CLI. ET. MO(N). **Mint:** Eisenach **Note:** Ref. KOR-242, 243. Kipper coinage. Varieties exist.

Date	Mintage	VG	F	VF	XF	Unc
ND(1621)	—	75.00	150	300	—	—

KM# 51 3 KREUZER (Groschen)

Billon **Ruler:** Johann Casimir and Johann Ernst II **Obv:** Flat-topped Saxony arms in baroque frame, titles of 2 dukes **Rev:** Imperial orb with 'C' engraved over HH monogram **Mint:** Hildburghausen **Note:** Kipper coinage.

Date	Mintage	VG	F	VF	XF	Unc
ND(1621) (e)	—	—	—	—	—	—

KM# 52 3 KREUZER (Groschen)

Billon **Ruler:** Johann Casimir and Johann Ernst II **Obv:** Oval Saxony arms in baroque frame, titles of 2 dukes **Rev:** Imperial orb with 'C' engraved over HH monogram **Mint:** Hildburghausen **Note:** Kipper coinage.

Date	Mintage	VG	F	VF	XF	Unc
ND(1621)	—	—	—	—	—	—

KM# 76 3 KREUZER (Groschen)

Billon **Ruler:** Johann Casimir and Johann Ernst II **Obv:** Saxony arms with curved top divides O - O, small imperial orb above divides FE - VV **Rev:** Crowned imperial eagle, 3 in circle on breast, date in legend **Mint:** Ostheim **Note:** Kipper coinage.

Date	Mintage	VG	F	VF	XF	Unc
1622	—	—	—	—	—	—

KM# 79 3 KREUZER (Groschen)

Billon **Ruler:** Johann Casimir and Johann Ernst II **Obv:** Oval Saxony arms in ornamented rhombus divide FE - VV or VV - FE **Rev:** Imperial orb with 3 divides date in ornamented rhombus **Mint:** Coburg **Note:** Kipper coinage.

Date	Mintage	VG	F	VF	XF	Unc
16ZZ	—	80.00	160	325	—	—

KM# 80 3 KREUZER (Groschen)

Billon **Ruler:** Johann Casimir and Johann Ernst II **Obv:** Saxony arms in ornamented shield with slightly curved top, FE - VV divided above **Rev:** Imperial orb with 3 divides date in ornamented rhombus **Mint:** Coburg **Note:** Kipper coinage.

Date	Mintage	VG	F	VF	XF	Unc
16ZZ	—	80.00	160	325	—	—

KM# 81 3 KREUZER (Groschen)

Billon **Ruler:** Johann Casimir and Johann Ernst II **Obv:** Saxony arms in ornamented shield with flat top divides FE - VV **Rev:** Imperial orb with 3 divides date in ornamented rhombus **Mint:** Coburg **Note:** Kipper coinage.

Date	Mintage	VG	F	VF	XF	Unc
1622	—	80.00	160	325	—	—

KM# 82 3 KREUZER (Groschen)

Billon **Ruler:** Johann Casimir and Johann Ernst II **Obv:** Oval saxony arms in ornamented frame, FE - VV and date divided above **Rev:** Imperial orb with 3 in ornamented rhombus **Mint:** Coburg **Note:** Kipper coinage.

Date	Mintage	VG	F	VF	XF	Unc
1622	—	80.00	160	325	—	—

KM# 78 3 KREUZER (Groschen)

Silver, 16 mm. **Ruler:** Johann Casimir and Johann Ernst II **Obv:** Ornate shield of ducal Saxony arms divides FE - VV, small imperial orb above **Obv. Legend:** D. G. IOH. CAS. ET. IOH. E(R). F. **Rev:** Crowned imperial eagle, 3 in circle on breast, crown divides date at top **Rev. Legend:** DVC. SAX. IVL. CL. E. M. **Mint:**

Körner (Volkenroda) **Note:** Ref. KOR-257. Kipper coinage. Varieties exist.

Date	Mintage	VG	F	VF	XF	Unc
16ZZ	—	—	—	—	—	—

KM# 74.1 3 KREUZER (Groschen)

Silver, 15 mm. **Ruler:** Johann Casimir and Johann Ernst II **Obv:** Spanish shield of ducal Saxony arms in circle, value 3 in oval at bottom **Obv. Legend:** D G. IOH. CA - ET. IOH. ER* **Rev:** Imperial orb with 'G' **Rev. Legend:** DVC. SAX. IVL. CLI. E. **Mint:** Gotha **Note:** Ref. KOR-229. Kipper coinage.

Date	Mintage	VG	F	VF	XF	Unc
ND(1622)	—	—	—	—	—	—

KM# 77.1 3 KREUZER (Groschen)

Silver, 18-19 mm. **Ruler:** Johann Casimir and Johann Ernst II **Obv:** Shield of ducal Saxony arms with curved top divides OO, small imperial orb above divides FE - VV **Obv. Legend:** D. G. IOH. CAS. ET. IOH. ERN. F. **Rev:** Crowned imperial eagle, 3 in circle on breast, date at end of legend **Rev. Legend:** DVC. SAX. IVL. CLI. ET. M. **Mint:** Ostheim **Note:** Ref. KOR-249. Kipper coinage.

Date	Mintage	VG	F	VF	XF	Unc
1622	—	—	—	—	—	—

KM# 77.2 3 KREUZER (Groschen)

Silver, 17 mm. **Ruler:** Johann Casimir and Johann Ernst II **Obv:** Ornate shield of ducal Saxony arms divides FE - VV, O-O above, small imperial orb at top **Obv. Legend:** D. G. IOH. CAS. ET. IOH. ERN. F. **Rev:** Crowned imperial eagle, 3 in circle on breast, date at end of legend **Rev. Legend:** DVC. SAX. IVL. CLI. ET. M. **Mint:** Ostheim **Note:** Ref. KOR-250. Kipper coinage.

Date	Mintage	VG	F	VF	XF	Unc
1622	—	—	—	—	—	—

KM# 74.2 3 KREUZER (Groschen)

Silver, 16-18 mm. **Ruler:** Johann Casimir and Johann Ernst II **Obv:** Spade-shaped shield of ducal Saxony arms **Obv. Legend:** D G IOH. CAS. ET. IO ER F **Rev:** Imperial orb with 'G' **Rev. Legend:** DVC. SAX. IVL. CLI. ET. MO. **Mint:** Gotha **Note:** Ref. KOR-227. Kipper coinage.

Date	Mintage	VG	F	VF	XF	Unc
ND(1622) (e)	—	—	—	—	—	—

KM# 75 3 KREUZER (Groschen)

Billon, 16-17 mm. **Ruler:** Johann Casimir and Johann Ernst II **Obv:** Spade-shaped shield of ducal Saxony arms in baroque frame **Obv. Legend:** D. G. IOH. CAS. ET. IOH. ER FR. **Rev:** Imperial orb with 'G,' value (3) in oval below **Rev. Legend:** DV. SAX. IV - CL. ET. MO* **Mint:** Gotha **Note:** Ref. KOR-228. Kipper coinage.

Date	Mintage	VG	F	VF	XF	Unc
ND(1622)	—	—	—	—	—	—

KM# 91 3 KREUZER (Groschen)

Billon **Ruler:** Johann Casimir and Johann Ernst II **Obv:** Oval Saxony arms divide FE - VV or VV - FE **Rev:** Imperial orb with 3 divides date in ornamented rhombus **Mint:** Coburg **Note:** Kipper coinage.

Date	Mintage	VG	F	VF	XF	Unc
16Z3	—	—	—	—	—	—

KM# 92 3 KREUZER (Groschen)

Billon **Ruler:** Johann Casimir and Johann Ernst II **Obv:** Oval Saxony arms in ornamented frame, FE - VV divided above and date divided below arms **Rev:** Imperial orb with 3 in ornamented rhombus **Mint:** Coburg **Note:** Kipper coinage.

Date	Mintage	VG	F	VF	XF	Unc
16Z3	—	—	—	—	—	—

KM# 126 3 KREUZER (Groschen)

Silver, 22-23 mm. **Ruler:** Johann Ernst II **Subject:** Death of Johann Casimir **Obv:** Ornate shield of 4-fold arms, with central shield of ducal Saxony, divides mintmaster's initials, small imperial orb above, value (3) in oval below **Obv. Legend:** D. G. IOH. CAS(I). DV(X). - SAX. IVL. CLI. ET MO **Rev:** 6-line inscription with dates in circle **Rev. Legend:** *ELEND NICHT SCHADT. WER TVGED HAT. **Rev. Inscription:** NATVS / 12. IVNII. / Ao. 1564 / OBIIT 16. / IVLII. Ao / 1633 **Mint:** Saalfeld **Note:** Ref. KOR-317. Varieties exist.

Date	Mintage	VG	F	VF	XF	Unc
1633 MR	—	—	—	—	—	—

KM# 161 3 KREUZER (Groschen)

Silver, 23-24 mm. **Ruler:** Johann Ernst II **Obv:** Oval shield of ducal Saxony arms in baroque frame **Obv. Legend:** D. G. IOHAN. ERNST. DVX. SAX. IVL. CLI. ET MONT. **Rev:** Spanish shield of 4-fold arms in baroque frame divide mintmaster's initials, date divided by small imperial orb at top **Rev. Legend:** LAN. THV. MAR. MIS. CO(M). MAR. ET. RA. D. IN RA. **Mint:** Coburg **Note:** Ref. KOR-358.

Date	Mintage	VG	F	VF	XF	Unc
1636 EFS(j)	—	—	—	—	—	—

KM# 162 3 KREUZER (Groschen)

Silver, 23 mm. **Ruler:** Johann Ernst II **Obv:** Oval shield of ducal Saxony arms in baroque frame **Obv. Legend:** D. G. IOHANN. ERNST. D. SAX. IV(L). CL(I). ET MO(N). **Rev:** Spanish shield of 4-fold arms in baroque frame, date divided by small imperial orb at top **Rev. Legend:** GOTT BESSERE DIE ZEIT VND LEVT. **Mint:** Coburg **Note:** Ref. KOR-359, 360. Spruchgroschen.

Date	Mintage	VG	F	VF	XF	Unc
1636 (j)	—	—	—	—	—	—
1637 (j)	—	—	—	—	—	—

KM# 182 3 KREUZER (Groschen)

Silver, 23 mm. **Ruler:** Johann Ernst II **Subject:** Death of Johann Ernst II **Obv:** Oval shield of ducal Saxony arms in baroque frame, small imperial orb above **Obv. Legend:** DEI. GRATIA. IOHAN. ERNEST. III. **Rev:** 6-line inscription with dates in circle **Rev. Legend:** ET NATV MAXIMVS. D. S. I. C. M. **Rev. Inscription:** GENIT: / 9. IVL: / ANNO 1566 / OBIIT 23. / OCTOB: / Ao 1638. **Mint:** Coburg **Note:** Ref. KOR-368.

Date	Mintage	VG	F	VF	XF	Unc
1638 EF EF//(j)	—	—	—	—	—	—

KM# 90 1/24 THALER (Groschen)

Silver, 21-22 mm. **Ruler:** Johann Casimir and Johann Ernst II **Obv:** Imperial orb with 24 divides date **Obv. Legend:** D. G. IOH. CAS. ET. IOH. ER. FRA(T). **Rev:** Spanish shield of ducal Saxony arms in baroque frame divides mintmaster's initials, FE - VV above **Rev. Legend:** DVC. SAX. IVL. CLI. ET. MONTANIÆ. **Mint:** Neustadt an der Heide **Note:** Ref. KOR-258. Varieties exist.

Date	Mintage	VG	F	VF	XF	Unc
16ZZ WF	—	—	—	—	—	—

KM# 128 1/8 THALER

Silver, 26 mm. **Ruler:** Johann Ernst II **Subject:** Death of Johann Casimir **Obv:** Armored bust to right, small shield of ducal Saxony arms below **Obv. Legend:** D. G. IOHAN. CASIMI. - DVX. SAX. IV. CL. ET MO. **Rev:** 6-line inscription with dates in circle, two small shields of arms at left and right of inscription **Rev. Legend:** *ELEND NICHT SCHADT. WER TVGEND HAT. **Rev. Inscription:** NATVS / 12. IVNII. Ao / 1564 / OBIIT / 16. IVLII. Ao / 1633 **Mint:** Saalfeld **Note:** Ref. KOR-316.

Date	Mintage	VG	F	VF	XF	Unc
1633 (i)	—	40.00	85.00	165	325	—

KM# 164 1/8 THALER

Silver, 25-26 mm. **Ruler:** Johann Ernst II **Obv:** Half-length armored figure to right in circle, small imperial orb above **Obv. Legend:** D. G. IOHAN. ERNST. DVX. SAX. IVL. CLI. ET MON **Rev:** Spanish shield of 4-fold arms, with central shield of ducal Saxony, divides mintmaster's initials, date above **Rev. Legend:** LAN. THV. MAR. MIS. COM. MAR. ET RA. DO. IN RA. **Mint:** Coburg **Note:** Ref. KOR-356, 357.

Date	Mintage	VG	F	VF	XF	Unc
1636 EFS (j)	—	—	—	—	—	—
1637 EFS (j)	—	—	—	—	—	—

KM# 31 12 KREUZER (Dreibätzner)

Silver, 26-27 mm. **Ruler:** Johann Casimir and Johann Ernst II **Obv:** Ornate shield with concave sides of ducal Saxony arms, FEVV above, value 12 (or 1Z) in circle below **Obv. Legend:** D. G. IOH. CAS. - ET. IOH. ERN. F. **Rev:** 3 small shields of arms, 2 above 1, 'E' in center, small imperial orb above, date at end of legend **Rev. Legend:** DVC. SAX. IVL. CLI. ET. MON. **Mint:** Eisenach **Note:** Ref. KOR#238-40. Kipper coinage. Varieties exist.

Date	Mintage	VG	F	VF	XF	Unc
1620	—	—	—	—	—	—
16Z1 (g)	—	—	—	—	—	—

KM# 29 12 KREUZER (Dreibätzner)

Silver, 25-26 mm. **Ruler:** Johann Casimir and Johann Ernst II **Obv:** Angel behind oval shield of ducal Saxony arms in ornamented frame **Obv. Legend:** D. G. IOHN. CASI(.) ET(.) IOHAN. ER(N). FRA(T). **Rev:** 3 small ornately shaped shields of arms, 2 above 1, lower shield divides FE - VV, 'C' in center, imperial orb above with 1Z **Rev. Legend:** DVC. SAX. IVL. (-) CLI. ET MONT. **Mint:** Neustadt an der Heide **Note:** Ref. KOR-203, 204. Kipper coinage. Varieties exist.

Date	Mintage	VG	F	VF	XF	Unc
ND(1620-21) (e)	—	—	—	—	—	—

KM# 30 12 KREUZER (Dreibätzner)

Silver, 25 mm. **Ruler:** Johann Casimir and Johann Ernst II **Obv:** Angel behind oval Saxony arms in ornamented frame **Obv. Legend:** D. G. IOHAN. CAS - ET. IOH. ERN. FRA. **Rev:** 3 small oval shields of arms, 2 above 1, orb divides FE - VV, 'C' in center, imperial orb above with 1Z **Rev. Legend:** DVC(ES). SAX(ON). IVL* - *CLIVI(Æ). ET. MON(TA). **Mint:** Neustadt an der Heide **Note:** Ref. KOR-205. Kipper coinage. Varieties exist.

Date	Mintage	VG	F	VF	XF	Unc
ND(1620-21) (e)	—	—	—	—	—	—

KM# 56 12 KREUZER (Dreibätzner)

Silver, 25 mm. **Ruler:** Johann Casimir and Johann Ernst II **Obv:** Ornate shield of ducal Saxony arms, FEVV above, value 12 in circle below **Obv. Legend:** D. G. IOH. CAS - ET. IOH. ER FR. **Rev:** 3 small shields of arms, 2 above 1, 'O' in center, small imperial orb above, date at end of legend **Rev. Legend:** DVC. SAX. IVL. CLI. ET. MON. **Mint:** Ostheim **Note:** Ref. KOR-247. Kipper coinage.

Date	Mintage	VG	F	VF	XF	Unc
1621	—	375	750	1,500	—	—

KM# 57 12 KREUZER (Dreibätzner)

Silver, 25 mm. **Ruler:** Johann Casimir and Johann Ernst II **Obv:** Ornate shield of ducal Saxony arms, FEVV above **Obv. Legend:** D. G. IOH. CAS. ET. IOH. ERN. FR. **Rev:** 3 small shields of arms, 2 above 1, 'O' in center, small imperial orb above, date at end of legend **Rev. Legend:** DVC. SAX. IVL. CLI. ET. MON. **Mint:** Ostheim **Note:** Ref. KOR-246. Kipper coinage.

Date	Mintage	VG	F	VF	XF	Unc
16Z1	—	375	750	1,500	—	—

KM# 83 12 KREUZER (Dreibätzner)

Silver, 25 mm. **Ruler:** Johann Casimir and Johann Ernst II **Obv:** Ornate shield of ducal Saxony arms, FEVV above **Obv. Legend:** D. G. IOH. CAS. ET. IOH. ERN. FRA. **Rev:** 3 small shields of arms, 2 above one, 'O' in center, small imperial orb with 12 at top, date at end of legend **Rev. Legend:** DVC. SAX. IVL. CLI. ET. MON. **Mint:** Ostheim **Note:** Ref. KOR-248. Kipper coinage.

Date	Mintage	VG	F	VF	XF	Unc
1622	—	—	—	—	—	—

KM# 3 1/4 THALER (6 Groschen)

Silver, 26-27 mm. **Ruler:** Johann Casimir and Johann Ernst II **Obv:** 1/2-length figures facing each other, small imperial orb above, letters F.E and V.V at upper left and right **Obv. Legend:** D. G. IOH. CASI. ET. IOH. ERNS. FRA. DVCES. SAXO. **Rev:** Shield of ducal Saxony arms in circle, date above, divides C - O, 13 small shields of arms around **Rev. Legend:** LANTG. THVRI. ET. MARCHIO. MISN. MO. IM. **Mint:** Coburg **Note:** Ref. KOR#132-135. Varieties exist.

Date	Mintage	VG	F	VF	XF	Unc
1601 (c)	—	135	275	550	1,100	—
1602 (c)	—	135	275	550	1,100	—
1603 (c)	—	135	275	550	1,100	—
1604 (d)	—	135	275	550	1,100	—

KM# 9 1/4 THALER (6 Groschen)

Silver, 26-27 mm. **Ruler:** Johann Casimir and Johann Ernst II **Obv:** 1/2-length figures facing each other, small imperial orb above, letters F.E and V.V at upper left and right **Obv. Legend:** D.G. IOH. CASI. ET. IOH. ERNS. FRA. DVCES. SAX(O). **Rev:** Shield of ducal Saxony arms divides C - O in circle, date above, 13 small shields of arms around **Rev. Legend:** LANTG. THVRI. ET. MARCHIO. MIS(N). MO. I(M)(P). **Mint:** Coburg **Note:** Ref. KOR#136-44. Varieties exist.

Date	Mintage	VG	F	VF	XF	Unc
(1)604 WA	—	125	250	475	975	—
1605 WA	—	125	250	475	975	—
1606 WA	—	125	250	475	975	—
1607 WA	—	125	250	475	975	—
1608 WA	—	125	250	475	975	—
1609 WA	—	125	250	475	975	—
1610 WA	—	125	250	475	975	—
1611 WA	—	125	250	475	975	—

KM# 14 1/4 THALER (6 Groschen)

Silver, 27-28 mm. **Ruler:** Johann Casimir and Johann Ernst II **Obv:** Two 1/2-length figures facing each other, small imperial orb above, letters F.E and V.V at upper left and right **Obv. Legend:** D.G. IOH. CASI. ET. IOH. ERN. FRA. DV. SAX. IVL(I)Æ. CLI. ET. MON(T). **Rev:** Knight on horseback to left in circle, date divided at front and back of horse, 16 small shields of arms around **Rev. Legend:** LANDG. TRV. MAR. MIS. COM. MAR. ET. RAVENS. DN. IN. RA(V)(E). **Mint:** Coburg **Note:** Ref. KOR#169-76. Varieties exist.

Date	Mintage	VG	F	VF	XF	Unc
161Z WA	—	85.00	165	300	600	—
1613/Z	—	85.00	165	300	600	—
1613 WA	—	85.00	165	300	600	—
1614 WA	—	85.00	165	300	600	—
1615 WA	—	85.00	165	300	600	—
1616 WA	—	85.00	165	300	600	—
1617 WA	—	85.00	165	300	600	—
1618 WA	—	85.00	165	300	600	—
1619 WA	—	85.00	165	300	600	—

KM# 94 1/4 THALER (6 Groschen)

Silver, 32-34 mm. **Ruler:** Johann Casimir and Johann Ernst II **Obv:** 1/2-length figure of Johann Casimir right divides FE - VV, 6 small shields of arms divide legend **Obv. Legend:** D - G - IO. CA - ET. IO(H) - ERN. F - D. SAX - IV. CL **Rev:** 1/2-length figure of Johann Ernst II to left divides date **Rev. Legend:** ET. MON. LAN. THV. MAR. MIS. COM. MAR. ET. R(A). D. IN. R(A). **Mint:** Saalfeld **Note:** Ref. KOR#283-88. Varieties exist.

Date	Mintage	VG	F	VF	XF	Unc
1624 WA	—	110	220	400	775	—
1625 WA	—	110	220	400	775	—
1626 WA	—	110	220	400	775	—
1627 WA	—	110	220	400	775	—
1628 WA	—	110	220	400	775	—
1629 WA	—	110	220	400	775	—

KM# 95 1/4 THALER (6 Groschen)

Silver, 40 mm. **Ruler:** Johann Casimir and Johann Ernst II **Obv. Legend:** D G - IO - CASIM - ET. IOH - ERNES - FR . DVC - SAX. IV **Rev. Legend:** CLI. ET. MON. LAN. THV. MAR. MIS. COM. MAR. ET. RA. D. IN. RAV. **Mint:** Saalfeld **Note:** Ref. KOR-282. Struck on thin flan with 1/2 Thaler dies, KM#96.

Date	Mintage	VG	F	VF	XF	Unc
1624 WA	—	—	—	—	—	—

KM# 131 1/4 THALER (6 Groschen)

Silver, 32 mm. **Ruler:** Johann Ernst II **Obv:** Half-length armored figure to right in circle, small shield of arms, small imperial orb above **Obv. Legend:** D. G. IOHANN. ERNEST. DVX. SAX. IVL. CLI. ET MONT. **Rev:** Fully armored knight on horseback to left between 2 small shields of arms in circle, 16 small shields of arms around, date at end of legend **Rev. Legend:** LANDG. THV. MAR. MIS. COM MAR. ET RAV. DOM. IN RAV. **Mint:** Saalfeld **Note:** Ref. KOR-351.

Date	Mintage	VG	F	VF	XF	Unc
1633 MR (i)	—	—	—	—	—	—

KM# 130 1/4 THALER (6 Groschen)

Silver, 31-32 mm. **Ruler:** Johann Ernst II **Subject:** Death of Johann Casimir **Obv:** Armored bust to right, small shield of ducal Saxony arms below **Obv. Legend:** D. G. IOHAN. CASIM. D. - SAX. IVL. CLI. ET MO: **Rev:** 6-line inscription with dates in circle, two small shields of arms at left and right of inscription **Rev. Legend:** *ELEND NICHT SCHADT * WER TVGEND HAT. **Rev. Inscription:** NATVS / 12. IVNII. (/) Ao: (/) 1564. / OBIIT. (/) 16. (/) IVLII. Ao. / 1633 **Mint:** Saalfeld **Note:** Ref. KOR-315. Varieties exist.

Date	Mintage	VG	F	VF	XF	Unc
1633 (i)	—	—	—	—	—	—
1633 M(i)R	—	—	—	—	—	—

KM# 148 1/4 THALER (6 Groschen)
Silver, 29 mm. **Ruler:** Johann Ernst II **Subject:** 69th Birthday of Johann Ernst II **Obv:** Eagle flying left toward the sun with small ducal Saxony arms in beak, AQVILÆ SENECTA curved above **Obv. Legend:** *MEM. NAT. IOH. ERN. D. SAX. IX. IVL. LXIX. ÆT. AN. INGR. SACR. **Rev:** Rampant lion striding left holding open book, date below **Rev. Legend:** WEISHEIT - GEHT - VOR - STERCK* **Mint:** Coburg **Note:** Ref. KOR-323. Struck from 2 Ducat dies, KM#150.

Date	Mintage	VG	F	VF	XF	Unc
1634 (j)	—	90.00	200	300	500	—

KM# 166 1/4 THALER (6 Groschen)
Silver, 35-36 mm. **Ruler:** Johann Ernst II **Obv:** Half-length armored figure to right in circle, small imperial orb above **Obv. Legend:** D. G. IOHANN. ERN(E)ST. DVX. SAX. IVL. CLI. ET MO(N)(T). **Rev:** Shield of manifold arms, with central shield of electoral Saxony, divides date and mintmaster's initials, 6 ornate helmets above **Rev. Legend:** LAN(DG). THV. MAR. MIS. COM. MAR. ET R(A)(V). D(O). IN. (RA)(VE). **Mint:** Coburg **Note:** Ref. KOR#352-55. Varieties exist.

Date	Mintage	VG	F	VF	XF	Unc
1635 (j)	—	—	—	—	—	—
1636 EFS (j)	—	—	—	—	—	—
1637 EF (j)	—	—	—	—	—	—
1638 EF (j)	—	—	—	—	—	—

KM# 184 1/4 THALER (6 Groschen)
Silver, 31 mm. **Ruler:** Johann Ernst II **Subject:** Death of Johann Ernst II **Obv:** Half-length armored figure to right in circle, small imperial orb above **Obv. Legend:** D. G. IOHANN. ERNST. DVX. SAX. IVL. CLI. ET MON. **Rev:** 6-line inscription with dates, mintmaster's initials below, 3 small shields of arms above **Rev. Legend:** IOHAN. ERNEST. III. ET NATV MAX. D. S. I. C. M. **Rev. Inscription:** GENITVS / 9. IVLII / ANNO. 1566. / OBIIT 23. / OCTOBRIS / Ao. 1638 / (initials) **Mint:** Coburg **Note:** Ref. KOR-367.

Date	Mintage	VG	F	VF	XF	Unc
1638 EFS	—	—	—	—	—	—

KM# 38 24 KREUZER (Sechsbätzner)
Silver, 27-28 mm. **Ruler:** Johann Casimir and Johann Ernst II **Obv:** Spanish shield of ducal Saxony arms with ornamentation at sides, FEVV above **Obv. Legend:** D. G. IOH. CAS. ET. IOH. ERN. FRA(T). **Rev:** 3 small shields of arms, 2 above 1, 'E' in center, small imperial orb above, date at end of legend **Rev. Legend:** DVC. SAX. IVL. CLI. ET. MON. **Mint:** Eisenach **Note:** Ref. KOR#232-4. Kipper coinage. Varieties exist.

Date	Mintage	VG	F	VF	XF	Unc
16Z0	—	185	375	775	—	—
16Z0 (g)	—	185	375	775	—	—
16Z1 (g)	—	185	375	775	—	—

KM# 33 24 KREUZER (Sechsbätzner)
Silver, 27 mm. **Ruler:** Johann Casimir and Johann Ernst II **Obv:** Spanish shield of ducal Saxony arms in baroque frame divides VV - FE **Obv. Legend:** D. G. IOHAN. CAS. ET. IOH. ERN. FRAT. **Rev:** 3 small asymmetrical oval shields of arms, 2 above 1, imperial orb above with 24 **Rev. Legend:** DVC. SAX. IVLI. - .CLI. ET. MONT* **Mint:** Neustadt an der Heide **Note:** Ref. KOR-202. Kipper coinage.

Date	Mintage	VG	F	VF	XF	Unc
ND(1620-21)	—	160	325	650	—	—

KM# 34 24 KREUZER (Sechsbätzner)
Silver, 26 mm. **Ruler:** Johann Casimir and Johann Ernst II **Obv:** Oval shield of ducal Saxony arms in baroque frame divides VV - FE **Obv. Legend:** D. G. IOHAN. CAS. ET. IOH. ER. FRAT. **Rev:** 3 small round shields of arms in baroque frames, 2 above 1, lower one divides C - B **Rev. Legend:** DVC. SAX. IVL* - *CLI. ET. MONT* **Mint:** Neustadt an der Heide **Note:** Ref. KOR-192, 193. Kipper coinage.

Date	Mintage	VG	F	VF	XF	Unc
ND(1620-21)	—	160	325	650	—	—

KM# 35 24 KREUZER (Sechsbätzner)
Silver, 27-29 mm. **Ruler:** Johann Casimir and Johann Ernst II **Obv:** Oval shield of ducal Saxony arms in baroque frame **Obv. Legend:** D. G. IOH(AN). CAS(IM). (-) ET. IOH(AN). ER(N)(EST). FRA(T). **Rev:** 3 small shields of arms, 2 above 1, 'C' in center, imperial orb above with 24 divides VV - FE or FE - VV **Rev. Legend:** DVCES. SAXON. (-) IV(L)(I). (-) .CLI. ET. MO(N)(T)(A). **Mint:** Neustadt an der Heide **Note:** Ref. KOR#186-190, 197-9. Kipper coinage. Varieties exist.

Date	Mintage	VG	F	VF	XF	Unc
ND(1620-21) (e)	—	160	325	650	—	—
ND(1620-22)	—	160	325	650	—	—

KM# 36 24 KREUZER (Sechsbätzner)
Silver, 27 mm. **Ruler:** Johann Casimir and Johann Ernst II **Obv:** Oval shield of ducal Saxony arms in baroque frame divide VV - FE, 'C' in circle above **Obv. Legend:** D. G. IOH. CASIM. ET. IOHAN. ER. FRA. **Rev:** 3 small spade shaped shields of arms, 2 above 1, imperial orb above with 24 **Rev. Legend:** DVC. SAX. IVL.* - *CLI. ET. MONT. **Mint:** Neustadt an der Heide **Note:** Ref. KOR-191. Kipper coinage.

Date	Mintage	VG	F	VF	XF	Unc
ND(1620-21)	—	160	325	650	—	—

KM# 37 24 KREUZER (Sechsbätzner)
Silver, 28-29 mm. **Ruler:** Johann Casimir and Johann Ernst II **Obv:** Ornate shield with concave sides of ducal Saxony arms **Obv. Legend:** D. G. IOHAN. CAS(I). ET. IOHAN. ERN. FRA(T). **Rev:** 3 small shields of arms with concave sides, 2 above 1, lower one divides FE - VV, imperial orb above with 24 **Rev. Legend:** DVC. SAX. IVL. CLI. ET(.) MONT. **Mint:** Neustadt an der Heide **Note:** Ref. KOR-200, 201. Kipper coinage.

Date	Mintage	VG	F	VF	XF	Unc
ND(1620-21) (e)	—	160	325	650	—	—

KM# 61 24 KREUZER (Sechsbätzner)
Silver, 27-29 mm. **Ruler:** Johann Casimir and Johann Ernst II **Obv:** Ornate shield with concave sides of ducal Saxony arms, FEVV above **Obv. Legend:** D. G. IOH. CAS. ET. IOH. ERN. F(R)(A). **Rev:** 3 small shields of arms, 2 above 1, 'E' in center, small imperial orb above, date at end of legend **Rev. Legend:** DVC. SAX. IVL. CLI. ET. M(ON). **Mint:** Eisenach **Note:** Ref. KOR#235-7. Kipper coinage. Varieties exist.

Date	Mintage	VG	F	VF	XF	Unc
16Z1 (g)	—	180	360	725	—	—
1622	—	180	360	725	—	—

KM# 62 24 KREUZER (Sechsbätzner)
Silver, 28-29 mm. **Ruler:** Johann Casimir and Johann Ernst II **Obv:** Ornate shield of ducal Saxony arms, FEVV above **Obv. Legend:** D. G. IOH. CAS. ET. IOH. (+) ERN. FRA(T). **Rev:** 3 small shields of arms, 2 above 1, 'O' in center, small imperial orb above, date at end of legend **Rev. Legend:** DVC. SAX. IVL. CLI. ET. MON. **Mint:** Ostheim **Note:** Ref. KOR-244, 245. Kipper coinage. Varieties exist.

Date	Mintage	VG	F	VF	XF	Unc
1621 HK	—	—	—	—	—	—
1622	—	—	—	—	—	—

KM# 64.1 24 KREUZER (Sechsbätzner)
Silver, 26-28 mm. **Ruler:** Johann Casimir and Johann Ernst II **Obv:** Ornate shield of ducal Saxony arms, FEVV above **Obv. Legend:** D. G. IOH. CAS. ET. IOH. ERN. F. **Rev:** 3 small shields of arms, 2 above 1, 'V' in center, small imperial orb above, date at end of legend **Rev. Legend:** DVC. SAX. IVL. CLI. ET. M(ON). **Mint:** Körner (Volkenroda) **Note:** Ref. KOR-254.1, 256a,b. Kipper coinage. Varieties exist.

Date	Mintage	VG	F	VF	XF	Unc
1621 (h)	—	90.00	180	360	—	—
1622 (h)	—	90.00	180	360	—	—

KM# 63 24 KREUZER (Sechsbätzner)
Silver, 28-29 mm. **Ruler:** Johann Casimir and Johann Ernst II **Obv:** Ornate shield of ducal Saxony arms, FEVV above **Obv. Legend:** D. G. IOH. CAS. ET. IOH. ERN. F(R). **Rev:** 3 small shields of arms, 2 above 1, 'K' in center, small imperial orb above, date at end of legend **Rev. Legend:** DVC. SAX. IVL. CLI. ET. MO(N). **Mint:** Körner (Volkenroda) **Note:** Ref. KOR-252, 253. Kipper coinage. Varieties exist.

Date	Mintage	VG	F	VF	XF	Unc
16Z1 (g)	—	90.00	180	360	—	—
1621 (h)	—	90.00	180	360	—	—

KM# 59.1 24 KREUZER (Sechsbätzner)
Silver, 27 mm. **Ruler:** Johann Casimir and Johann Ernst II **Obv:** Spanish shield of ducal Saxony arms in baroque frame divides VV - FE **Obv. Legend:** D. G. IOHAN. CASIM. ET. IOH. ER. FRAT. **Rev:** 3 small shields of arms, 2 above 1, imperial orb above with 24, lower arms divide H - H **Rev. Legend:** DVC. SAX. IVLI* - *CLI. ET MONT. **Mint:** Hildburghausen **Note:** Ref. KOR-221. Kipper coinage.

Date	Mintage	VG	F	VF	XF	Unc
ND(1621) (e)	—	—	—	—	—	—

KM# 59.2 24 KREUZER (Sechsbätzner)
Silver, 26 mm. **Ruler:** Johann Casimir and Johann Ernst II **Obv:** Spanish shield of ducal Saxony arms in baroque frame **Obv. Legend:** D. G. IOHAN. CASIM. ET. IOH ERN. FR. **Rev:** 3 small shields of arms, 2 above 1, imperial orb above with 24, lower arms divide H - H **Rev. Legend:** DVC, SAX. IVLI* - *CLI. ET. MONTA* **Mint:** Hildburghausen **Note:** Ref. KOR-222. Kipper coinage.

Date	Mintage	VG	F	VF	XF	Unc
ND(1621) (e)	—	—	—	—	—	—

KM# 60 24 KREUZER (Sechsbätzner)
Silver, 27 mm. **Ruler:** Johann Casimir and Johann Ernst II **Obv:** Spanish shield of ducal Saxony arms in baroque frame divides VV - FE **Obv. Legend:** D. G. IOHAN. CASIM. ET. IOH. ER. FRA. **Rev:** 3 small shields of arms, 2 above 1, imperial orb divides H - H at top **Rev. Legend:** DVC. SAX. IVL. - CLI. ET. MON. **Mint:** Hildburghausen **Note:** Ref. KOR-220. Kipper coinage.

Date	Mintage	VG	F	VF	XF	Unc
ND(1621) (e)	—	—	—	—	—	—

KM# 64.2 24 KREUZER (Sechsbätzner)
Silver, 28 mm. **Ruler:** Johann Casimir and Johann Ernst II **Obv:** Spanish shield of ducal Saxony arms in baroque frame, FEVV above **Obv. Legend:** D. G. IOH. CAS. ET. IOH. ERN. FR. **Rev:** 3 small shields of arms, 2 above 1, 'V' in center, small imperial orb above, date at end of legend **Rev. Legend:** DVC. SAX. IVL. CLI. ET. M. **Mint:** Körner (Volkenroda) **Note:** Ref. KOR-255.

Date	Mintage	VG	F	VF	XF	Unc
1621 (h)	—	—	—	—	—	—

KM# 65 24 KREUZER (Sechsbätzner)
15.9000 g., Silver, 29x30 mm. **Ruler:** Johann Casimir and Johann Ernst II **Obv:** Ornate shield of ducal Saxony arms, FEVV above **Obv. Legend:** D. G. IOH. CAS. ET. IOH. ERN. FR. **Rev:** 3 small shields of arms, 2 above 1, 'V' in center, small imperial orb above, date at end of legend **Rev. Legend:** DVC. SAX. IVL. CLI. ET. M. **Mint:** Körner (Volkenroda) **Note:** Ref. KOR-254.2. Kipper coinage. Klippe.

Date	Mintage	VG	F	VF	XF	Unc
1621 (h)	—	90.00	180	360	—	—

KM# 88 24 KREUZER (Sechsbätzner)
Silver, 28 mm. **Ruler:** Johann Casimir and Johann Ernst II **Obv:** Ornate shield of ducal Saxony arms, FEVV above **Obv. Legend:** D. G. IOH. CAS. ET. IOH. ERN F. **Rev:** 3 small shields of arms, 2 above 1, 'V' in center, small imperial orb above, lower shield divides 2 - 4, date at end of legend **Rev. Legend:** DVC. SAX. IVL. CLI. ET. M. **Mint:** Körner (Volkenroda) **Note:** Ref. KOR-256. Kipper coinage.

Date	Mintage	VG	F	VF	XF	Unc
1622	—	—	—	—	—	—

KM# 87 24 KREUZER (Sechsbätzner)
Silver **Ruler:** Johann Casimir and Johann Ernst II **Obv:** Imperial orb with 24 divides date, titles of 2 dukes **Rev:** Saxony arms in ornamented frame divides mintmaster's initials, FE - VV divided above, titles of 2 dukes continued **Mint:** Coburg **Note:** Kipper coinage.

Date	Mintage	VG	F	VF	XF	Unc
16ZZ WF	—	—	—	—	—	—
16Z3 WF	—	—	—	—	—	—

KM# 84 24 KREUZER (Sechsbätzner)
Silver, 28 mm. **Ruler:** Johann Casimir and Johann Ernst II **Obv:** Spanish shield of ducal Saxony arms in baroque frame **Obv. Legend:** D. G. IOHAN. CASI* - *ET. IOH. ERN. FRAT. **Rev:** 3 small round shields of arms, 2 above 1, 'G' in center, imperial orb divides FE - VV at top **Rev. Legend:** DVCES. SAXONI* - *IVL. CLI. ET. MON* **Mint:** Gotha **Note:** Ref. KOR-226. Kipper coinage.

Date	Mintage	VG	F	VF	XF	Unc
ND(1622)	—	—	—	—	—	—

KM# 85 24 KREUZER (Sechsbätzner)
Silver, 26-28 mm. **Ruler:** Johann Casimir and Johann Ernst II **Obv:** Angel behind oval shield of ducal Saxony arms in baroque frame **Obv. Legend:** D. G. IOHAN. CAS(I) - ET. IOH. ERN. FRAT. **Rev:** 3 small oval shields of arms, 2 above 1, 'G' in center, imperial orb divides FE - VV at top **Rev. Legend:** DVCES. SAXONI(A) - IVL. CLI. ET. MON(T). **Mint:** Gotha **Note:** Ref. KOR-224, 225. Kipper coinage. Varieties exist.

Date	Mintage	VG	F	VF	XF	Unc
ND(1622) (e)	—	—	—	—	—	—
ND(1622)	—	—	—	—	—	—

KM# 86 24 KREUZER (Sechsbätzner)
Silver, 28 mm. **Ruler:** Johann Casimir and Johann Ernst II **Obv:** Angel behind Spanish shield of ducal Saxony arms divides date **Obv. Legend:** D. G. IOHAN. CAS. ET. IOHAN. ERN. FRAT. **Rev:** 3 small ornate shields of arms with concave sides, 2 above 1, 'G' in center, lower shield divides FE - VV, imperial orb with 24 at top **Rev. Legend:** DVC. SAX. IVL - CLI. ET. MONT. **Mint:** Gotha **Note:** Ref. KOR-225. Kipper coinage.

Date	Mintage	VG	F	VF	XF	Unc
16ZZ (f)	—	—	—	—	—	—

KM# 4 1/2 THALER
Silver, 35 mm. **Ruler:** Johann Casimir and Johann Ernst II **Obv:** 1/2-length figures facing each other, small imperial orb above, double legend **Obv. Legend:** Outer - D. G. IOHA. CASI. E. IOH. ERNS. FRA. DVCES. SAXON; Inner - FRID. ERNEHRT - UNFRID. VER. ZEHRT. **Rev:** Shield of ducal Saxony arms divides C - O in circle, date above, 13 small shields of arms around **Rev. Legend:** LANTG. THVRI. ET. MARCHIO. MISN. MON. IMP(E). **Mint:** Coburg **Note:** Ref. KOR#119-22. Varieties exist.

Date	Mintage	VG	F	VF	XF	Unc
1601 (c)	—	80.00	160	325	650	—
160Z (c)	—	80.00	160	325	650	—
1603 (c)	—	80.00	160	325	650	—
1604 (d)	—	80.00	160	325	650	—

KM# 10 1/2 THALER
Silver, 35-37 mm. **Ruler:** Johann Casimir and Johann Ernst II **Obv:** 1/2-length figures facing each other, small imperial orb above, double legend **Obv. Legend:** Outer - D. G. IOHA. CASI. E. IOH. ERNS. FRA. DVCES. SAXON; Inner - FRID. ERNEHRT - VNFRID. VER. ZEHRT. **Rev:** Shield of ducal Saxony arms divides C - O in circle, date above, 13 small shields of arms around **Rev. Legend:** LANTG. THVRI. ET. MARCHHIO. MISN. MO(N). IM(P). **Mint:** Coburg **Note:** Ref. KOR#123-31. Varieties exist.

Date	Mintage	VG	F	VF	XF	Unc
1604 WA	—	60.00	120	235	475	—
1605 WA	—	60.00	120	235	475	—
1606 WA	—	60.00	120	235	475	—
1607 WA	—	60.00	120	235	475	—
1608 WA	—	60.00	120	235	475	—
1609 WA	—	60.00	120	235	475	—
1610 WA	—	60.00	120	235	475	—

Date	Mintage	VG	F	VF	XF	Unc
1611 WA	—	60.00	120	235	475	—
161Z WA	—	60.00	120	235	475	—

KM# 15 1/2 THALER

Silver, 35-37 mm. **Ruler:** Johann Casimir and Johann Ernst II **Obv:** 1/2-length figures facing each other, small imperial orb above, double legend **Obv. Legend:** Outer - D. G. IOH. CASI. ET. IOH. ERN. FRA. DV. SAX. IVLIÆ. CLI. ET. MO(N).; Inner - FRID. ERNEHRT - VNFRID. VERZEHRT. **Rev:** Knight on horseback to left in circle, date divided at front and rear of horse, 13 small shields of arms around **Rev. Legend:** LANDG. THV. MAR. MIS. COM. MAR. ET. RAVENS. DN. IN. RA(V). **Mint:** Coburg **Note:** Ref. KOR#161-68. Varieties exist.

Date	Mintage	VG	F	VF	XF	Unc
161Z WA	—	65.00	125	240	480	—
1613 WA	—	65.00	125	240	480	—
1614 WA	—	65.00	125	240	480	—
1615 WA	—	65.00	125	240	480	—
1616 WA	—	65.00	125	240	480	—
1617 WA	—	65.00	125	240	480	—
1618 WA	—	65.00	125	240	480	—
1619 WA	—	65.00	125	240	480	—

KM# 96 1/2 THALER

Silver, 38-40 mm. **Ruler:** Johann Casimir and Johann Ernst II **Obv:** 1/2-length figure of Johann Casimir, head divides FRIED - ERNEHRT, 6 small shields of arms **Obv. Legend:** D G - IO - CAS(IM) (-) ET. IO(.)(H) (-) ERN(ES) - FR. DV(C)(X) - SAX. IV. (- CL. ET. M) **Rev:** 1/2-length figure of Johann Ernst II to left divides VNFRIED - VERZEHRT **Rev. Legend:** (CLI. ET. MON.) LAN(TG). THV. MAR(G). MIS. COM. MAR. ET. RA(V). D(O). IN. R(A)(V). **Mint:** Saalfeld **Note:** Ref. KOR#277-81. Varieties exist.

Date	Mintage	VG	F	VF	XF	Unc
1624 WA	—	90.00	185	375	775	—
1625 WA	—	90.00	185	375	775	—
1626 WA	—	90.00	185	375	775	—
1627 WA	—	90.00	185	375	775	—
1629 WA	—	90.00	185	375	775	—

KM# 117 1/2 THALER

Silver **Ruler:** Johann Casimir and Johann Ernst II **Obv:** 1/2-length figure of Johann Casimir right, head divides FRIED - ERNEHRT, 6 small shields of arms **Rev:** 1/2-length figure of Johann Ernst II to left divides VNFRIED - VERZEHRT

Date	Mintage	VG	F	VF	XF	Unc
1629 WA	—	—	—	—	—	—

KM# 133 1/2 THALER

Silver, 38 mm. **Ruler:** Johann Ernst II **Subject:** Death of Johann Casimir **Obv:** Armored bust to right, 6 small shields of arms divide legend **Obv. Legend:** D - G - IOHA - CASI - DVX - SAX IV. CL - ET MO **Rev:** 6-line inscription with dates, 3 small shields of arms above, a small shield to left and right of inscription **Rev. Legend:** ELEND NICHT SCHADT * WER TVGEND HAT. **Rev. Inscription:** NATVS / 12. IVNII. Ao. / 1564. / OBIIT / 16. IVLII. Ao. / 1633. **Mint:** Saalfeld **Note:** Ref. KOR-314.

Date	Mintage	VG	F	VF	XF	Unc
1633 M(i)R	—	—	—	—	—	—

KM# 134 1/2 THALER

Silver, 37 mm. **Ruler:** Johann Ernst II **Obv:** Half-length armored figure to right in circle, small imperial orb above **Obv. Legend:** D. G. IOHAN. ERNEST. DVX. SAX. IVL. CLI. ET MONT. **Rev:** Fully armored knight on horseback to left, divides two small shields of arms and date, in circle, 16 small shields of arms around **Rev. Legend:** LANDG. THV. MAR. MIS. COM. MAR. ET RA. D. IN RAV. **Mint:** Saalfeld **Note:** Ref. KOR-346.

Date	Mintage	VG	F	VF	XF	Unc
1633 (i)	—	—	—	—	—	—

KM# 153 1/2 THALER

Silver, 37 mm. **Ruler:** Johann Ernst II **Obv:** Half-length armored figure to right in circle, small imperial orb above **Obv. Legend:** D. G. IOHAN. ERNEST. DVX. SAX. IVL. CLI. ET MONT. **Rev:** Fully armored knight on horseback to left, divides 2 small shields of arms and date, in circle, 16 small shields of arms around **Rev. Legend:** LANDG. THV. MAR. MIS. COM. MAR. ET RA. D. IN RAV. **Mint:** Coburg **Note:** Ref. KOR-347.1.

Date	Mintage	VG	F	VF	XF	Unc
1635 (j)	—	—	—	—	—	—

KM# 154 1/2 THALER

Silver, 37-38 mm. **Ruler:** Johann Ernst II **Obv:** Half-length armored figure to right in circle, small imperial orb above **Obv. Legend:** D. G. IOHAN(N). ERNEST. DVX. SAX. IVL. CLI. ET MONT. **Rev:** Shield of manifold arms, with central shield of ducal Saxony, divides mintmaster's initials and date, 6 ornate helmets above **Rev. Legend:** LAN(D)(G). THV. MAR. MIS. CO(M). M(AR). ET R(A). D(O). IN (R)(A)(V). **Mint:** Coburg **Note:** Ref. KOR-247.2, 348, 349. Varieties exist.

Date	Mintage	VG	F	VF	XF	Unc
1635 EFS (j)	—	275	550	1,100	—	—
1636 EF (j)	—	275	550	1,100	—	—
1636 EFS (j)	—	275	550	1,100	—	—
1637 EF (j)	—	275	550	1,100	—	—

KM# 186 1/2 THALER

Silver, 38-39 mm. **Ruler:** Johann Ernst II **Obv:** Half-length armored figure to right in circle, small imperial orb above **Obv. Legend:** D. G. IOHAN. ERNST. DVX. SAX. IVL. CLI. ET MONT. **Rev:** Shield of manifold arms, with central shield of ducal Saxony, divides date and mintmaster's initials, 6 ornate helmets above, additional legend around lower part of arms inside partial beaded circle **Rev. Legend:** Outer: LAN. THV. MAR. MIS. COM. M. ET RA. D. IN RA.; Inner: GOTT BESSERE DIE ZEIT. V. LEVT. **Mint:** Coburg **Note:** Ref. KOR-350. 1/2 Spruchthaler. Varieties exist.

Date	Mintage	VG	F	VF	XF	Unc
1638 EF (j)	—	1,000	2,100	4,200	8,400	—

KM# 187 1/2 THALER

Silver, 38 mm. **Ruler:** Johann Ernst II **Subject:** Death of Johann Ernst II **Obv:** Half-length armored figure to right in circle, small imperial orb above **Obv. Legend:** D. G. IOHAN. ERNST. DVX. SAX. IVL. CLI. ET MONT. **Rev:** 6-line inscription, with mintmaster's initials below, in circle, legend surrounded by 19 shields around border **Rev. Legend:** IOHAN. ERNEST. III. ET NATV MAXIMVS. D. S. I. C. M. **Rev. Inscription:** GENITVS / 9. IVLII / ANNO 1566. / OBIIT 23. OCTOBRIS / Ao: 1638 / (initials) **Mint:** Coburg **Note:** Ref. KOR-366.

Date	Mintage	VG	F	VF	XF	Unc
1638 EFS (j)	—	250	500	950	2,850	5,600

KM# 40 20 GROSCHEN (Guldenthaler)

Silver, 35 mm. **Ruler:** Johann Casimir and Johann Ernst II **Obv:** Oval shield of ducal Saxony arms in baroque frame, FE - VV divided at upper left and right, value '20 - gl' divided at botom **Obv. Legend:** D. G. IOH. CASIMIR. ET. IOH. ERNESTVS. FRA. **Rev:** 'C' in small shield superimposed on foliated cross, 4 small shields of arms in angles of cross **Rev. Legend:** DVCES. SAXONIÆ. IVL. CLIV. ET. MONTAN. **Mint:** Coburg **Note:** Ref. KOR-184. Kipper coinage.

Date	Mintage	VG	F	VF	XF	Unc
ND(1620-21) (e)	—	—	—	—	—	—

KM# 41 20 GROSCHEN (Guldenthaler)

Silver, 35 mm. **Ruler:** Johann Casimir and Johann Ernst II **Obv:** Spanish shield of ducal Saxony arms in baroque frame, second legend around within circle, value 'Z0 gl' in cartouche at bottom **Obv. Legend:** Outer: D. G. IOHAN. CASI. ET IOHAN. ERN. FRAT.; Inner: FRIED. ERNEHRD. VNFRIED. VERZEHRT. **Rev:** 4 small arms in cartouches around 'C' in center **Rev. Legend:** DVCES. SAXON. IVL(IÆ). CLIV. ET MONT. **Mint:** Neustadt an der Heide **Note:** Ref. KOR-185. Kipper coinage. Varieties exist.

Date	Mintage	VG	F	VF	XF	Unc
ND(1620-21) (e)	—	—	—	—	—	—

KM# 5 THALER

Silver **Ruler:** Johann Casimir and Johann Ernst II **Obv:** Facing busts **Rev:** Date above center shield dividing C-O in circle of thirteen shields **Mint:** Coburg **Note:** Dav. 7426.

Date	Mintage	VG	F	VF	XF	Unc
1601 (c)	—	75.00	165	325	600	—
160Z (c)	—	75.00	165	325	600	—
1603 (c)	—	75.00	165	325	600	—
1604 (d)	—	75.00	165	325	600	—
1604 WA	—	75.00	165	325	600	—
1605 WA	—	75.00	165	325	600	—
1606 WA	—	75.00	165	325	600	—
1607 WA	—	75.00	165	325	600	—
1608 WA	—	75.00	165	325	600	—
1609 WA	—	75.00	165	325	600	—
1610 WA	—	75.00	165	325	600	—
1611 WA	—	75.00	165	325	600	—
1612 WA	—	75.00	165	325	600	—

KM# 16 THALER

Silver **Ruler:** Johann Casimir and Johann Ernst II **Rev:** Sixteen shields around knight on horseback, date below horse **Mint:** Coburg **Note:** Dav. 7427.

Date	Mintage	VG	F	VF	XF	Unc
1612 WA	—	300	600	1,000	—	—

KM# 17 THALER

Silver **Ruler:** Johann Casimir and Johann Ernst II **Rev:** Knight on horse dividing date **Mint:** Saalfeld **Note:** Dav. 7429.

Date	Mintage	VG	F	VF	XF	Unc
1612 WA	—	80.00	175	350	900	—
1613 WA	—	80.00	175	350	900	—
1614 WA	—	80.00	175	350	900	—
1615 WA	—	80.00	175	350	900	—
1616 WA	—	80.00	175	350	900	—
1617 WA	—	80.00	175	350	900	—
1618 WA	—	80.00	175	350	900	—
1619 WA	—	80.00	175	350	900	—

KM# 93 THALER

Silver, 43 mm. **Ruler:** Johann Casimir and Johann Ernst II **Obv:** Bust right divides date; Ligate WA appears either below or after VERZEHRT at right **Rev:** Bust left with arm at left and right **Mint:** Saalfeld **Note:** Ref. KOR#269-75; Dav. 7431. Varieties exist.

Date	Mintage	VG	F	VF	XF	Unc
1623 WA	—	85.00	170	350	800	—
1624 WA	—	85.00	170	350	800	—
1625 WA	—	85.00	170	350	800	—
1626 WA	—	85.00	170	350	800	—
1627 WA	—	85.00	170	350	800	—
1628 WA	—	85.00	170	350	800	—
1629 WA	—	85.00	170	350	800	—

KM# 100 THALER

Silver **Ruler:** Johann Casimir and Johann Ernst II **Note:** Struck from same dies as 2 Thaler, KM#99 on broad flan.

Date	Mintage	VG	F	VF	XF	Unc
1624 WA	—	—	—	—	—	—

KM# 119 THALER

Silver **Ruler:** Johann Casimir and Johann Ernst II **Obv:** Duke on horseback right, tree clump below **Rev:** Helmeted arms divide date and W-A below

Date	Mintage	VG	F	VF	XF	Unc
1629 WA	—	—	—	—	—	—

KM# 135 THALER

Silver, 42 mm. **Ruler:** Johann Casimir and Johann Ernst II **Obv:** Larger and thicker bust, without date **Rev:** Shorter and thicker bust, date in field behind bust **Mint:** Saalfeld **Note:** Ref. KOR-276; Dav. 7432.

Date	Mintage	VG	F	VF	XF	Unc
1633 MR(i)	—	325	650	1,300	2,200	—

KM# 136 THALER

Silver, 43 mm. **Ruler:** Johann Ernst II **Subject:** Death of Johann Casimir **Obv:** Armored bust to right, 9 small shields of arms divide legend **Obv. Legend:** D - G - IOHA - CASI - DVX - SAX - IVL - CLI - ET. M **Rev:** 6-line inscription with dates, 3 small shields of arms above, 2 over 1, small shield to left and right of inscription, 5 other small shields divide legend **Rev. Legend:** ELEND - NICHT - SCHADT - WER - TVGEND - HAT **Rev. Inscription:** NATVS / 12. IVNII. Ao. / 1564. / OBIIT / 16. IVLII. Ao. / 1633. **Mint:** Saalfeld **Note:** Ref. KOR-313; Dav. 7433.

Date	Mintage	VG	F	VF	XF	Unc
1633 MR	—	425	825	1,650	2,750	—

KM# 139 THALER

Silver, 43-44 mm. **Ruler:** Johann Ernst II **Obv:** Half-length armored figure to right in circle, small imperial orb above **Obv. Legend:** D. G. IOHANN. ERNEST. DVX. SAX. IVLI. CLIVI. ET MONT. **Rev:** Fully armored knight on horseback to left, divides 2 small shields of arms and date, in circle, 16 small shields of arms around **Rev. Legend:** LANDG. THV. MAR. MIS. COM. MAR. ET RVENS. DO. IN RAVEN. **Mint:** Saalfeld **Note:** Ref. KOR-332. Dav. 7434. Varieties exist.

Date	Mintage	VG	F	VF	XF	Unc
1633 MR (i)	—	525	925	1,950	3,100	—

KM# 140 THALER

Silver, 43 mm. **Ruler:** Johann Ernst II **Obv:** Half-length armored figure to right in circle, small imperial orb above **Obv. Legend:** D:G: IOHANN. ERNEST. DVX: SAX: IVLI. CLIVI. ET MONT. **Rev:** Shield of manifold arms, with central shield of ducal Saxony, divides date near bottom, six ornate helmets above **Rev. Legend:** LANDG: THV: MAR: MIS: COM: MAR: ET RAVENS: DO: IN RAVE: **Mint:** Saalfeld **Note:** Ref. KOR-333; Dav. A7435.

Date	Mintage	VG	F	VF	XF	Unc
1633 MR (i)	—	500	975	1,650	2,750	—

KM# 155 THALER

Silver, 44 mm. **Ruler:** Johann Ernst II **Obv:** Half-length armored figure to right in circle, small imperial orb above **Obv. Legend:** D. G. IOHANN. ERNST. DVX. SAX. IVLI. CLIVI. ET MONT. **Rev:** Fully armored knight on horseback to left, divides 2 small shields of arms and date, in circle, 6 small shields of arms around **Rev. Legend:** LANDG. THV. MAR. MIS. COM. MAR. ET RAVENS. DO. IN RAVEN. **Mint:** Coburg **Note:** Ref. KOR-334; Dav. 7434.

Date	Mintage	VG	F	VF	XF	Unc
1635 MR (j)	—	—	—	—	—	—

KM# 156 THALER

Silver, 41 mm. **Ruler:** Johann Ernst II **Obv:** Half-length facing armored figure in circle, small imperial orb above **Obv. Legend:** D. G. IOHANN ERNST. DVX. SAX. IVL. CLI. ET MONT. **Rev:** Shield of manifold arms, with central shield of ducal Saxony, divides date near bottom, 6 ornate helmets above **Rev. Legend:** LAND. THV. MAR. MIS. COM. MAR. ET RAVENS. DO. IN RAVE. **Mint:** Coburg **Note:** Ref. KOR-336; Dav. 7435.

Date	Mintage	VG	F	VF	XF	Unc
1635 EFS (j)	—	425	825	1,600	2,650	—

KM# 157 THALER

Silver, 43 mm. **Ruler:** Johann Ernst II **Obv:** Half-length armored figure to right in circle, small imperial orb above **Obv. Legend:** D. G. IOHANN. ERNST. DVX. SAX. IVLI. CLIVI. ET MONT. **Rev:** Shield of manifold arms, with central shield of ducal Saxony, divides date near bottom, 6 ornate helmets above divide mintmaster's initials and symbol **Rev. Legend:** LAND. THV. MAR. MIS. COM. MAR. ET RAVENS. DO. IN RAVE. **Mint:** Coburg **Note:** Ref. KOR-335; Dav. 7436.

Date	Mintage	VG	F	VF	XF	Unc
1635 EFS (j)	—	425	825	1,600	2,650	—

KM# 169 THALER

Silver, 41-44 mm. **Ruler:** Johann Ernst II **Obv:** Small half-length armored figure to right in circle, small imperial orb above **Obv. Legend:** D. G. IOHANN. ERN(E)ST. DVX. SAX. IVL. CLI. ET MONT(IVM). **Rev:** Shield of manifold arms, with central shield of ducal Saxony, divides date and mintmaster's intials, 6 ornate helmets above **Rev. Legend:** LANDG. THV. MAR. MIS. COM. MAR. ET RAVEN. DO(MI). IN RAV(EN)(S). **Mint:** Coburg **Note:** Ref. KOR-338.1a, 341-2; Dav. 7437.

Date	Mintage	VG	F	VF	XF	Unc
1636 EFS (j)	—	425	825	1,600	2,650	—
1637 EFS (j)	—	425	825	1,600	2,650	—

KM# 168 THALER

Silver, 41-44 mm. **Ruler:** Johann Ernst II **Obv:** Half-length armored figure to right in circle, small imperial orb above **Obv. Legend:** D. G. IOHANN. ERNEST. DVX. SAX. IVL. CLI. ET MONTIVM. **Rev:** Shield of manifold arms, with central shield of ducal Saxony, divides date (where present) and mintmaster's initials near bottom, 6 ornate helmets above, all in circle **Rev. Legend:** LAND(G). THV. MAR. MIS. COM. MAR. ET RAVEN(S). DO. IN RAV(E)(N). **Mint:** Coburg **Note:** Ref. KOR-337, 338. Dav. 7437. Varieties exist.

Date	Mintage	VG	F	VF	XF	Unc
1636 EFS (j)	—	425	825	1,600	2,650	—
ND(1636) EFS (j)	—	—	—	—	—	—

KM# 177 THALER

Silver, 42 mm. **Ruler:** Johann Ernst II **Obv:** Half-length armored figure to right in circle, small imperial orb above, date at end of legend **Obv. Legend:** D. G. IOHANN. ERNST. DVX. SAX. IVL. CLI. ET MONT. **Rev:** Shield of manifold arms, with central shield of ducal Saxony, divides mintmaster's initials **Rev. Legend:** LANDG. THV. MAR. MIS. COM. MAR. ET RAV. DO(MI). IN RAV(ENS). **Mint:** Coburg **Note:** Ref. KOR-340, 344; Dav. 7438. Varieties exist.

Date	Mintage	VG	F	VF	XF	Unc
1637 EFS (j)	—	425	825	1,600	2,650	—
1638 EFS (j)	—	425	825	1,600	2,650	—

KM# 178 THALER

Silver, 42-44 mm. **Ruler:** Johann Ernst II **Obv:** Half-length armored figure to right in circle, small imperial orb above **Obv. Legend:** D. G. IOHANN. ERNST. DVX. SAX. IVL. CLI. ET MONTIVM. **Rev:** Shield of manifold arms, with central shield of ducal Saxony, divides date and mintmaster's initials, 6 ornate helmets above, additional inner inscription within partial beaded circle **Rev. Legend:** Outer: LAN. THV. MAR. MIS. COM. M(AR). ET RA. DO. IN RA(V)(E).; Inner: GOTT BESSERE DIE ZEIT UND LE(V)(I)T. **Mint:** Coburg **Note:** Ref. KOR-343; 345; Dav. 7439. Varieties exist. Spruchthaler.

Date	Mintage	VG	F	VF	XF	Unc
1637 EF (j)	—	325	650	1,300	2,200	—
1638 EF (j)	—	325	650	1,300	2,200	—

KM# 189 THALER

Silver, 42 mm. **Ruler:** Johann Ernst II **Subject:** Death of Johann Ernst II **Obv:** Half-length armored figure to right in circle, small imperial orb above **Obv. Legend:** D. G. IOHANN. ERNEST. DVX. SAX. IVL. CLI. ET MONT. **Rev:** 6-line inscription in circle, legend surrounded by 19 shields of arms around border **Rev. Legend:** IOHAN. ERNEST. III. ET NATV MAX. D. S. I. C. M. **Rev. Inscription:** GENITVS / 9. IVLII / ANNO. 1566 / OBIIT 23. / OCTOBRIS / Ao. 1638. **Mint:** Coburg **Note:** Ref. KOR-365; Dav. 7440.

Date	Mintage	VG	F	VF	XF	Unc
1638 EFS (j)	—	425	700	1,400	2,350	—

KM# 67.1 40 GROSCHEN (Doppelguldenthaler)

Silver, 41 mm. **Ruler:** Johann Casimir and Johann Ernst II **Obv:** Oval shield of ducal Saxony arms in baroque frame, value '40 gl' in cartouche below, VV - FE divided to upper left and right **Obv. Legend:** D. G. IOHAN. CASI. ET. - IOHAN. ERNEST. FRA. **Rev:** Gothic 'C' in small oval superimposed on thin-armed cross with lily ends, all in ornamented circle **Rev. Legend:** DVC * SAXONIÆ * IVLIÆ * CLIVIÆ * ET MON* **Mint:** Coburg **Note:** Ref. KOR-178. Kipper coinage. Known with date 16-Z1 punched at left and right of arms on obverse.

Date	Mintage	VG	F	VF	XF	Unc
ND(1620) (e)	—	950	1,900	3,400	—	—

KM# 67.1A 40 GROSCHEN (Doppelguldenthaler)

Silver, 54x55 mm. **Ruler:** Johann Casimir and Johann Ernst II **Obv:** Oval shield of ducal Saxony arms in baroque frame, value '40 gl' in oval cartouche below, VV - FE divided to upper left and right **Obv. Legend:** D. G. IOHA. CASI. ET - IOHANN. ERNEST. FRA. **Rev:** Gothic 'C' in small oval superimposed on thin-armed foliated cross, all in ornamented circle **Rev. Legend:** DVCES. SAXONIÆ. IVL. CLI. ET. MONTANI. **Mint:** Coburg **Note:** Ref. KOR-177. Kipper coinage. Klippe.

Date	Mintage	VG	F	VF	XF	Unc
ND(1620)	—	950	1,900	3,400	—	—

KM# 67.2 40 GROSCHEN (Doppelguldenthaler)

Silver, 41 mm. **Ruler:** Johann Casimir and Johann Ernst II **Obv:** Oval shield of ducal Saxony arms in baroque frame, value '40 gl' in oval cartouche below, second legend inside circle around arms **Obv. Legend:** Outer: D. G. IOHAN. CAS. ET. - IOHAN. EREST. FRA.; Inner: FRIED. ERNEHRT* - VNFRIED: VERZEHR. **Rev:** Gothic 'C' in center surrounded by 4 small shields of arms, all in ornamented circle **Rev. Legend:** DVC* SAXONIÆ* IVLIÆ* CLIVIÆ* ET* MONT* **Mint:** Coburg **Note:** Ref. KOR-179. Kipper coinage.

Date	Mintage	VG	F	VF	XF	Unc
AH(1620) (e)	—	950	1,900	3,400	—	—

KM# 67.3 40 GROSCHEN (Doppelguldenthaler)

Silver, 42 mm. **Ruler:** Johann Casimir and Johann Ernst II **Obv:** Oval shield of ducal Saxony arms in baroque frame, value '40-gl' in cartouche at bottom, second legend within circle around arms **Obv. Legend:** Outer: D. G. IOHAN. CASIM(I). ET - IOHAN. ERNEST. FRAT.; Inner: FRIED: ERNEHRDT. - VNFRIED: VERZEHRT. **Rev:** Large 'C' in small spade shaped shild superimposed on thin-armed cross with lily ends, all in ornamented circle **Rev. Legend:** DVCES. SAX(X)ONIÆ* IVLIÆ* CLIVIÆ* ET MONT(AN). **Mint:** Neustadt an der Heide **Note:** Ref. KOR-180, 183. Kipper coinage.

Date	Mintage	VG	F	VF	XF	Unc
ND(1621) (e)	—	950	1,900	3,400	—	—
1621	—	950	1,900	3,400	—	—

KM# 68 40 GROSCHEN (Doppelguldenthaler)

Silver, 41 mm. **Ruler:** Johann Casimir and Johann Ernst II **Obv:** Oval shield of ducal Saxony arms in baroque frame, V - V - F - E divided to upper left and right, value '40 - gl' in oval cartouche at bottom **Obv. Legend:** D. G. IOHAN. CASI. ET - IOHAN. ERNEST. FRA. **Rev:** Letter 'C' in center, surrounded by 4 small shields of arms, all in ornamented circle **Rev. Legend:** DVCES. SAXONIÆ. IVLIÆ. CLIVIÆ. ET MONTA. **Mint:** Neustadt an der Heide **Note:** Ref. KOR-181. Kipper coinage.

Date	Mintage	VG	F	VF	XF	Unc
ND(1621) (e)	—	950	1,900	3,400	—	—

KM# 69 40 GROSCHEN (Doppelguldenthaler)

Silver, 41-42 mm. **Ruler:** Johann Casimir and Johann Ernst II **Obv:** Oval shield of ducal Saxony arms in baroque frame, value '40 - gl' in oval cartouche at bottom, inner legend around arms **Obv. Legend:** Outer: D. G. IOHAN. CASIM(I)(R). ET - IOHAN. ERNEST. FRAT.; Inner: FRIED: ERNEHR(D)T. - VNFRIED: VERZEH(RT). **Rev:** Letter 'C' in small oval superimposed on thin-armed cross with lily ends, 4 small shields of arms in angles of cross, all in ornamented circle **Rev. Legend:** DVCES. SAXONIÆ. IVLI(Æ). CLIVIÆ. ET. MONT(AN)(I)(Æ). **Mint:** Neustadt an der Heide **Note:** Ref. KOR-180a, b, 182. Kipper coinage. Varieties exist.

Date	Mintage	VG	F	VF	XF	Unc
ND(1621) (e)	—	950	1,900	3,400	—	—

KM# 70 40 GROSCHEN (Doppelguldenthaler)

Silver, 40 mm. **Ruler:** Johann Casimir and Johann Ernst II **Obv:** Oval shield of ducal Saxony arms in baroque frame, V - V - F - E divided at upper left and right, value '40 - gl' in oval cartouche at bottom **Obv. Legend:** D. G. IOHAN. CASIM. - ET IOH. ERN. FRAT. **Rev:** Ornamented square with small arms in each of four quadrants formed by superimposed cross, 'HH' in oval in center **Rev. Legend:** DVCES. SAXONIÆ. IVLI. CLIV. ET. MONTAN. **Mint:** Hildburghausen **Note:** Ref. KOR-219. Kipper coinage.

Date	Mintage	VG	F	VF	XF	Unc
ND(1621) (e)	—	1,100	2,100	3,600	—	—

KM# 89 40 GROSCHEN (Doppelguldenthaler)

Silver, 42 mm. **Ruler:** Johann Casimir and Johann Ernst II **Obv:** Oval shield of ducal Saxony arms in baroque frame, date divided below, value '40 - gl' in oval cartouche at bottom, second legend inside circle around arms **Obv. Legend:** Outer: D. G. IOHAN. CASIM. ET. - IOHAN. ERNEST. FRAT.; Inner: FRIED: ERNEHRT. - VNFRIED: VERZEHR - T. **Rev:** Crowned 'G' in small shield superimposed on foliated cross, 4 small shields of arms in angles of cross **Rev. Legend:** DVCES* SAXONIÆ. IVL* - *CLI* ET* MONTANIÆ* **Mint:** Gotha **Note:** Ref. KOR-223. Kipper coinage.

Date	Mintage	VG	F	VF	XF	Unc
16ZZ (f)	—	1,100	2,100	3,600	—	—

KM# 72 40 GROSCHEN (120 Kreuzer)

Silver, 41 mm. **Ruler:** Johann Casimir and Johann Ernst II **Obv:** Oval shield of ducal Saxony arms in baroque frame, value '1Z0 K' in oval cartouche at bottom, second legend around arms within circle **Obv. Legend:** Outer: D. G. IOHAN. CASIMIR - ET. IOHAN. ERN. FRA.; Inner: FRID: ERNERT. - VNFRIED: VERZERT **Rev:** 4 small ornately shaped shields of arms arranged around 'E' in center, date at end of legend **Rev. Legend:** DVCES. SAXON. IVL. CLIV. ET. MONT. **Mint:** Eisenach **Note:** Ref. KOR-230. Kipper coinage.

Date	Mintage	VG	F	VF	XF	Unc
16Z1 (g)	—	800	1,600	2,850	—	—

KM# 7 2 THALER

Silver **Ruler:** Johann Casimir and Johann Ernst II **Obv:** Facing busts **Rev:** Date above center shield dividing C-O in circle of 13 shields **Mint:** Coburg **Note:** Dav. 7425.

Date	Mintage	VG	F	VF	XF	Unc
1603 (c)	—	1,650	3,000	5,400	—	—
1604 WA	—	1,650	3,000	5,400	—	—
1610 WA	—	1,650	3,000	5,400	—	—
1611 WA	—	1,650	3,000	5,400	—	—

KM# 21 2 THALER

Silver **Ruler:** Johann Casimir and Johann Ernst II **Obv:** 2 1/2-length busts facing **Rev:** Knight on horse dividing date **Mint:** Saalfeld **Note:** Dav. 7428.

Date	Mintage	VG	F	VF	XF	Unc
1613 WA	—	1,650	3,000	5,400	—	—
1614 WA	—	1,650	3,000	5,400	—	—
1615 WA	—	1,650	3,000	5,400	—	—

KM# 97 2 THALER

Silver **Ruler:** Johann Casimir and Johann Ernst II **Obv:** Bust righth divides date **Rev:** Bust left with arms at left and right **Mint:** Saalfeld **Note:** Dav. 7430.

Date	Mintage	VG	F	VF	XF	Unc
1624 WA	—	1,050	1,950	3,600	6,000	—
1625 WA	—	1,050	1,950	3,600	6,000	—

KM# 99 2 THALER

58.0000 g., Silver **Ruler:** Johann Casimir **Obv:** Castle below duke on horseback **Mint:** Saalfeld **Note:** Dav. LS413. Illustration reduced.

Date	Mintage	VG	F	VF	XF	Unc
1624 WA	—	1,000	1,650	2,950	—	—
1625 WA	—	1,000	1,650	2,950	—	—
1626 WA	—	1,000	1,650	2,950	—	—

KM# 98 2 THALER

Silver, 59-61 mm. **Ruler:** Johann Casimir **Obv:** Duke on horseback right, grass below **Obv. Legend:** D: G. IOHA. CASI. DVX. - .SAXON. IV. CL. ET. MO **Rev:** Helmeted arms divide date, W-A divided below **Rev. Legend:** ELEND. - NICHT. SCHAD. WER. - THVGENT. HAT. **Mint:** Saalfeld **Note:** Ref. KOR-289b; Dav. LS411. Illustration reduced.

Date	Mintage	VG	F	VF	XF	Unc
1624 WA	—	1,800	3,250	6,000	—	—

KM# 105 2 THALER

58.0000 g., Silver **Ruler:** Johann Casimir **Rev:** Without inner circle **Mint:** Saalfeld **Note:** Dav. LS415.

Date	Mintage	VG	F	VF	XF	Unc
1625 WA	—	875	1,550	2,500	—	—
1626 WA	—	875	1,550	2,500	—	—

KM# 109 2 THALER

58.0000 g., Silver **Ruler:** Johann Casimir **Obv:** Duke on horseback looking back, without inner circle **Mint:** Saalfeld **Note:** LS416.

Date	Mintage	VG	F	VF	XF	Unc
1626 WA Rare	—	—	—	—	—	—

KM# 114 2 THALER

58.0000 g., Silver **Ruler:** Johann Casimir **Obv:** Bust right in medallion, eighteen shields around **Rev:** Duke on horseback right **Note:** Dav. A7433.

Date	Mintage	VG	F	VF	XF	Unc
1627 Rare	—	—	—	—	—	—

KM# 115 2 THALER

58.0000 g., Silver **Ruler:** Johann Casimir **Obv:** Duke on horseback right, tree clump below **Rev:** Helmeted arms divide date and W-A below **Mint:** Saalfeld **Note:** Dav. LS417. Illustration reduced.

Date	Mintage	VG	F	VF	XF	Unc
1627 WA	—	900	1,600	2,900	4,750	—
1629 WA	—	900	1,600	2,900	4,750	—

KM# 121 2 THALER

57.8000 g., Silver **Ruler:** Johann Casimir **Obv:** Duke looks back, castle and date below horse **Rev:** W-A divided by helmeted arms **Mint:** Saalfeld **Note:** Dav. LS418.

Date	Mintage	VG	F	VF	XF	Unc
1629 WA	—	2,000	4,000	6,000	9,500	—

KM# 122 2 THALER

58.0000 g., Silver **Ruler:** Johann Casimir **Obv:** Duke on horseback looks right, without castle below **Mint:** Saalfeld **Note:** Dav. LS419.

Date	Mintage	VG	F	VF	XF	Unc
1629 WA	—	2,000	4,000	6,500	10,000	—

KM# 141 2 THALER

58.0000 g., Silver **Ruler:** Johann Ernst II **Obv:** Flowers below duke on horseback, date in exergue **Rev:** Helmeted arms divide M-R **Mint:** Saalfeld **Note:** Dav. LS420.

Date	Mintage	VG	F	VF	XF	Unc
1633 MR-(i) Rare	—	—	—	—	—	—

Note: WAG Auction 39, 9-06, nearly XF realized approximately $10,750.

KM# 171 2 THALER

58.0000 g., Silver **Ruler:** Johann Ernst II **Obv:** Facing 1/2-figure **Rev:** Helmeted shield within inner circle divides date **Rev. Legend:** DO: IN RAV: **Mint:** Coburg **Note:** Dav. 7435B.

Date	Mintage	VG	F	VF	XF	Unc
1636 EFS-(j) Rare	—	—	—	—	—	—

KM# 103 3 THALER

87.0000 g., Silver **Ruler:** Johann Casimir **Obv:** Castle below duke on horseback **Rev:** Helmeted arms divide date **Mint:** Saalfeld **Note:** Dav. LS412.

Date	Mintage	VG	F	VF	XF	Unc
1624 WA Rare	—	—	—	—	—	—
1625 WA Rare	—	—	—	—	—	—

KM# 102 3 THALER

86.5000 g., Silver, 61 mm. **Ruler:** Johann Casimir **Obv:** Duke on horseback right, grass below **Obv. Legend:** D: G. IOHA. CASI. DVX. - .SAXON. IV. CL. ET. MO **Rev:** Helmeted arms divide date, W-A divided below **Rev. Legend:** ELEND. - NICHT. SCHAD. WER. - THVGENT. HAT. **Mint:** Saalfeld **Note:** Ref. KOR-289a; Dav. LS410.

Date	Mintage	VG	F	VF	XF	Unc
1624 WA Rare	—	—	—	—	—	—

KM# 112 3 THALER

87.0000 g., Silver **Ruler:** Johann Casimir **Obv:** Duke on horseback looking back, without inner circle **Rev:** Helmeted arms divide date without inner circle **Mint:** Saalfeld **Note:** Dav. LS-A416.

Date	Mintage	VG	F	VF	XF	Unc
1626 WA Rare	—	—	—	—	—	—

KM# 111 3 THALER

87.0000 g., Silver **Ruler:** Johann Casimir **Obv:** Duke on horseback, castle and hills and grass below horse **Rev:** Helmeted arms divide date, without inner circle **Mint:** Saalfeld **Note:** Dav. LS414.

Date	Mintage	VG	F	VF	XF	Unc
1626 WA Rare	—	—	—	—	—	—

KM# 124 3 THALER

87.2000 g., Silver **Ruler:** Johann Casimir **Obv:** Duke on horseback looks right, without castle **Rev:** Helmeted arms **Mint:** Saalfeld **Note:** Dav. LS419A.

Date	Mintage	VG	F	VF	XF	Unc
1629 WA Rare	—	—	—	—	—	—

KM# 143 3 THALER

87.2000 g., Silver **Ruler:** Johann Ernst II **Obv:** Duke on horseback looks right, without castle below **Rev:** Helmeted arms divide M-R **Mint:** Saalfeld **Note:** Dav. LS420A.

Date	Mintage	VG	F	VF	XF	Unc
1633/1629 MR-(i)	—	—	—	—	—	—

TRADE COINAGE

KM# 137 DUCAT
Gold **Ruler:** Johann Ernst II **Obv:** Armored bust to right, small shield of ducal Saxony arms below **Obv. Legend:** D. G. IOHAN. CASIMI. - DVX. SAX. IV. CL. ET MO. **Rev:** 6-line inscription with dates in circle, two small shields of arms at left and right of inscription **Rev. Legend:** *ELEND NICHT SCHADT. WER TVGED HAT. **Rev. Inscription:** NATVS / 12. IVNII. Ao / 1564. / OBIIT / 16. IVLII. Ao / 1633. **Mint:** Saalfeld **Note:** Ref. KOR-312; Fr. 2942. Struck on thick flan from 1/8 Thaler dies, KM#128.

Date	Mintage	VG	F	VF	XF	Unc
1633 (i)	—	—	—	—	—	—

KM# 159 DUCAT
3.5000 g., 0.9860 Gold 0.1109 oz. AGW, 23-24 mm. **Ruler:** Johann Ernst II **Obv:** Facing armored bust in circle **Obv. Legend:** D. G. IOHANN. ERNST. DVX. SAX. IVL. CLI. ET M(ONT). **Rev:** Shield of manifold arms, with central shield of ducal Saxony, divides date **Rev. Legend:** LAN. T. M. M. (-) C. - M. (-) ET. R. D. IN R(AV). **Mint:** Coburg **Note:** Ref. KOR-325, 326. Fr. 2944. Varieties exist.

Date	Mintage	VG	F	VF	XF	Unc
1635 (j)	—	750	1,500	3,250	6,000	—
1636 (j)	—	750	1,500	3,250	6,000	—

KM# 176 DUCAT
Gold, 24 mm. **Ruler:** Johann Ernst II **Obv:** Facing armored bust in circle **Obv. Legend:** D. G. IOHANN. ERNST. DVX. SAX. IVL. CLI. ET. MO. **Rev:** Shield of manifold arms, with central shield of ducal Saxony arms, divides date, 6 ornate helmets above **Rev. Legend:** LANDG. THV. M. MIS. - C. MAR. ET RA. D. IN R. **Mint:** Coburg **Note:** Ref. KOR-326.3.

Date	Mintage	VG	F	VF	XF	Unc
1636 (j)	—	—	—	—	—	—

KM# 180 DUCAT
3.5000 g., 0.9860 Gold 0.1109 oz. AGW, 23-24 mm. **Ruler:** Johann Ernst II **Obv:** Facing armored bust in circle **Obv. Legend:** D. G. IOHANN. ERNST. D(VX). SAX. IVL. CLI. ET M(ON). **Rev:** Shield of manifold arms, with central shield of ducal Saxony, divides date, 6 ornate helmets above **Rev. Legend:** GOTT BES(S). - D. Z. V. LEVT. **Mint:** Coburg **Note:** Ref. KOR-327, 328. Fr. 2945. Varieties exist. Spruchdukat.

Date	Mintage	VG	F	VF	XF	Unc
1637 (j)	—	750	1,500	3,250	6,000	—
1638 EF	—	750	1,500	3,250	6,000	—

KM# 191 DUCAT
3.5000 g., 0.9860 Gold 0.1109 oz. AGW, 23 mm. **Ruler:** Johann Ernst II **Subject:** Death of Johann Ernst II **Obv:** Facing armored bust in circle **Obv. Legend:** DEI. GRATIA. IOHAN. ERNEST. III. **Rev:** 6-line inscription with dates in circle **Rev. Legend:** ET NATV MAXIMVS. D. S. I. C. M. **Rev. Inscription:** GENIT: / 9 IVL: / ANNO 1566 / OBIIT 23. / OCTOB: / Ao 1638. **Mint:** Coburg **Note:** Ref. KOR-364; Fr. 2946.

Date	Mintage	VG	F	VF	XF	Unc
1638 (j)	—	800	1,900	4,000	7,000	—

KM# 8 2 DUCAT
Gold **Ruler:** Johann Casimir and Johann Ernst II **Obv:** 1/2-length figures facing each other, small imperial orb above **Rev:** Saxony arms in circle with date divided above, center shield divides C - O, 13 small shields of arms around **Note:** Struck using same dies as 1/4 Thaler, KM#3.

Date	Mintage	VG	F	VF	XF	Unc
1603 (c) Rare	—	—	—	—	—	—

KM# 12 2 DUCAT
Gold **Ruler:** Johann Casimir and Johann Ernst II **Obv:** 1/2-length figures facing each other, small imperial orb above **Obv. Legend:** D.G. IOH. CASI. ET. IOH. ERNS. FRA. DVCES. SAX. **Rev:** Saxony arms in circle with date divided above and at sides, 13 small shields of arms, center shield divides C - O **Rev. Legend:** LANTG. THVRI. ET. MARCHIO. MISN. MO. IM. **Note:** Struck using same dies as 1/4 Taler, KM#9.

Date	Mintage	VG	F	VF	XF	Unc
1608 WA Rare	—	—	—	—	—	—
1610 WA Rare	—	—	—	—	—	—

KM# 19 2 DUCAT
Gold **Ruler:** Johann Casimir and Johann Ernst II **Obv:** 1/2-length figures facing each other, small imperial orb above **Rev:** Knight on horseback left in circle, date divided at front and back of horse, 16 small shields of arms around **Rev. Legend:** LANDG: TRV... **Note:** Struck using same dies as 1/4 Thaler, KM#14. The 1615 and 1619 coins have retrograde dates.

Date	Mintage	VG	F	VF	XF	Unc
1612 WA Rare	—	—	—	—	—	—
1614 WA Rare	—	—	—	—	—	—
1615 WA Rare	—	—	—	—	—	—
1619 WA Rare	—	—	—	—	—	—

KM# 104 2 DUCAT
Gold, 32-34 mm. **Ruler:** Johann Casimir and Johann Ernst II **Obv:** Half-length armored figure to right, head divides F.E. - V.V., 6 small shields of arms divide legend **Obv. Legend:** D - G - IO. CA - ET. IO - ERN. F - D. SAX - IV. CL **Rev:** Half-length armored figure to left, head divides date **Rev. Legend:** ET. MON. LAN. THV. MAR. MIS. COM. MAR. ET. R(A). D. IN. R(A). **Mint:** Saalfeld **Note:** Ref. KOR-267, 268. Struck from 1/4 Thaler dies, KM#94. Varieties exist.

Date	Mintage	VG	F	VF	XF	Unc
1624	—	—	—	—	—	—
1625 WA	—	—	—	—	—	—

KM# 138 2 DUCAT
7.0000 g., 0.9860 Gold 0.2219 oz. AGW, 31 mm. **Ruler:** Johann Ernst II **Subject:** Death of Johann Casimir **Obv:** Armored bust to right, small shield of ducal Saxony arms below **Obv. Legend:** D. G. IOHAN. CASIM. D. - SAX. IVL. CLI. ET MO: **Rev:** 6-line inscription with dates in circle, two small shields of arms at left and right of inscription **Rev. Legend:** *ELEND NICHT SCHADT 8 WER TVGEND HAT **Rev. Inscription:** NATVS / 12. IVNII. Ao. / 1564. / OBIIT / 16. IVLII. Ao. / 1633. **Mint:** Saalfeld **Note:** Ref. KOR-311; Fr. 2942. Struck from 1/4 Thaler dies, KM#130. Prev. KM#145.

Date	Mintage	VG	F	VF	XF	Unc
1633 M(i)R	—	2,500	5,000	9,500	15,000	—

KM# 146 2 DUCAT
Gold, 32 mm. **Ruler:** Johann Ernst II **Obv:** Half-length armored figure to right in circle, small imperial orb above **Obv. Legend:** D. G. IOHANN. ERNEST. DVX. SAX. IVL. CLI. ET MONT. **Rev:** Fully armored knight on horseback to left between 2 small shields of arms in circle, 16 small shields of arms around, date at end of legende **Rev. Legend:** LANDG. THV. MAR. MIS. COM. MAR. ET RAV. DOM. IN RAV. **Mint:** Saalfeld **Note:** Ref. KOR-324; Fr. 2943. Struck with 1/4 Thaler dies, KM#131.

Date	Mintage	VG	F	VF	XF	Unc
1633 MR (i) Rare	—	—	—	—	—	—

KM# 150 2 DUCAT
Gold, 29 mm. **Ruler:** Johann Ernst II **Subject:** 69th Birthday of Johann Ernst II **Obv:** Eagle flying left toward the sun with small ducal Saxony arms in beak, AQVILÆ SENECTA curved above **Obv. Legend:** *MEM. NAT. IOH. ER. D. SAX. IX. IVL. LXIX. ÆT. AN. INGR. SACR. **Rev:** Rampant lion striding left holding open book, date below **Rev. Legend:** WEISHEIT - GEHT - VOR - STERCK* **Mint:** Coburg **Note:** Ref. KOR-322.

Date	Mintage	VG	F	VF	XF	Unc
1634 (j) Rare	—	—	—	—	—	—

KM# 151 3 DUCAT
Gold, 29 mm. **Ruler:** Johann Ernst II **Subject:** 69th Birthday of Johann Ernst II **Obv:** Eagle flying left toward the sun with small ducal Saxony arms in beak, AQVILÆ SENECTA curved above **Obv. Legend:** *MEM. NAT. IOH. ERN. D. SAX. IX. IVL. LXIX. ÆT. AN. INGR. SACR. **Rev:** Rampant lion striding left holding open book, date below **Rev. Legend:** WEISHEIT - GEHT - VOR - STERCK* **Mint:** Coburg **Note:** Ref. KOR-321. Struck from 2 Ducat dies, KM#150.

Date	Mintage	VG	F	VF	XF	Unc
1634 (j) Rare	—	—	—	—	—	—

KM# 6 4 DUCAT
14.0000 g., Gold, 35 mm. **Ruler:** Johann Casimir and Johann Ernst II **Obv:** Half-length figures of 2 dukes of Saxe-Weimar facing each other, small imperial orb above **Obv. Legend:** D. G. FRID. WIL. ADM. ET. IOHAN. FRA. DVC. SAX. **Rev:** Half-length figures of 2 dukes facing each other, small imperial orb above, double legend **Rev. Legend:** Outer - D. G. IOHA. CASI. E. IOH. ERNS. FRA. DVCES. SAXON; inner - FRID. ERNEHRT - VNFRID. VER. ZEHRT. **Mint:** Saalfeld **Note:** Ref. KOR-76.2. Struck from 1/2 Thaler dies.

Date	Mintage	VG	F	VF	XF	Unc
ND(1601) Rare	—	—	—	—	—	—

KM# 107 5 DUCAT
Gold, 39-40 mm. **Ruler:** Johann Casimir and Johann Ernst II **Obv:** 1/2-length figure of Johann Casimir right divides FE - VV, 6 small shields of arms divide legend **Rev:** 1/2-length figure of Johann Ernst II to left divides date **Mint:** Saalfeld **Note:** Struck using 1/2 Thaler dies, KM#96.

Date	Mintage	VG	F	VF	XF	Unc
1625 WA Rare	—	—	—	—	—	—

KM# A7 7 DUCAT
22.6000 g., Gold, 36 mm. **Ruler:** Johann Casimir and Johann Ernst II **Obv:** Half-length figures of 2 dukes of Saxe-Weimar facing each other, small imperial orb above **Obv. Legend:** D. G. FRID. WIL. ADM. ET. IOHANN. FRA. DVC. SAX. **Rev:** Half-length figures of 2 dukes of facing each other, small imperial orb above, double legend **Rev. Legend:** Outer - D. G. IOHA. CASI. E. IOH. ERNS. FRA. DVCES. SAXON; Inner - FRID. ERNEHRT - VNFRID. VER. ZEHRT. **Mint:** Saalfeld **Note:** Ref. KOR-76.1. Struck from 1/2 Thaler dies.

Date	Mintage	VG	F	VF	XF	Unc
ND(1601) Rare	—	—	—	—	—	—

SAXE-OLD-WEIMAR

(Sachsen-Alt Weimar)

After the loss of the electoral dignity by Johann Friedrich I in 1547 (see Saxony-Ernestine Line) and his death in 1554, his sons ruled jointly in Wittenberg and Thuringia (Thüringen) until 1565. Weimar and Altenburg were separated and ruled by Johann Friedrich's second son, who also appropriated Gotha in 1567. In 1573, the lines of Saxe-Old-Altenburg and Saxe-Middle-Weimar were founded, but the two sons ruled together and issued a series of joint coinages.

RULERS

Friedrich Wilhelm I of Altenburg, 1573-1602
and Johann III of Weimar, 1573-1605

MINT OFFICIALS

Mark	Date	Name
(c)= [mark]	1578-1603	Gregor Bechstedt (Bechstädt) in Saalfeld
(e)= flower or WA (ligature)	1604-12	Wolf Albrecht der Jüngere in Coburg
	161612-20, 1623-32	Wolf Albrecht der Jüngere in Saalfeld

DUCHY

STANDARD COINAGE

KM# 17 PFENNIG
Copper **Ruler:** Johann III **Subject:** Death of Johann III **Obv:** Ornate 9-fold arms with central shield of Saxony **Rev:** Arabesque, date **Rev. Inscription:** OMNIA / CONANDO / DOCILISSO / LERTIA. VI= / NCIT

Date	Mintage	VG	F	VF	XF	Unc
1605	—	—	—	—	—	—

KM# 18 SCHRECKENBERGER (1/8 Thaler)
Silver **Ruler:** Johann III **Subject:** Death of Johann III **Obv:** 1/2-length figure of angel behind S arms, titles of Johann III **Rev:** 8-line inscription with dates **Rev. Legend:** DOMINE DIRIGE. ME. IN. VERBO. TVO

Date	Mintage	VG	F	VF	XF	Unc
1605 WA	—	45.00	85.00	160	325	—

KM# 9 1/4 THALER
Silver **Ruler:** Johann III **Subject:** Death of Friedrich Wilhelm I **Obv:** Saxony arms in ornate frame, titles of Friedrich Wilhelm I **Rev:** 8-line inscription with dates in circle **Rev. Legend:** DOMINE CONSERVA...

Date	Mintage	VG	F	VF	XF	Unc
160Z	—	—	—	—	—	—

KM# 19 1/4 THALER
Silver **Ruler:** Johann III **Subject:** Death of Johann III **Obv:** Bust right in circle **Rev:** 8-line inscription with dates **Rev. Legend:** DOMINE DIRIGE. ME. IN. VERBO. TVO

Date	Mintage	VG	F	VF	XF	Unc
1605 WA	—	175	350	650	1,300	—

KM# 10 1/2 THALER
Silver **Ruler:** Johann III **Subject:** Death of Friedrich Wilhelm I **Obv:** Saxony arms in ornate frame, titles of Friedrich I **Rev:** 8-line inscription with dates in circle **Rev. Legend:** DOMINE CONSERVA...

Date	Mintage	VG	F	VF	XF	Unc
160Z WA	—	125	225	425	875	—

KM# 20 1/2 THALER
Silver **Ruler:** Johann III **Obv:** Bust of Johann III **Rev:** Helmeted arms

Date	Mintage	VG	F	VF	XF	Unc
1605 WA	—	400	800	1,600	—	—

KM# 21 1/2 THALER
Silver **Ruler:** Johann III **Subject:** Death of Johann III **Obv:** Bust right in circle **Rev:** 8-line inscription with dates **Rev. Legend:** DOMINE DIRIGE. ME. IN. VERBO. TVO

Date	Mintage	VG	F	VF	XF	Unc
1605 WA	—	150	300	600	—	—

KM# 5 THALER

Silver **Ruler:** Johann III **Obv:** Two 1/2-length figures of dukes facing each other, small imperial orb above, titles around **Rev:** Saxony arms in ornate shield with date above in circle, 12 small shields around, legend in outer margin **Rev. Legend:** LANTG. THURI. ET. MARCHIO **Note:** Dav. #7515.

Date	Mintage	VG	F	VF	XF	Unc
1601 (c)	—	80.00	175	325	700	—

KM# 6 THALER

Silver **Ruler:** Johann III **Obv:** Two 1/2-length figures of dukes facing each other, small imperial orb above, titles around **Rev:** 3 helmets above 11-fold arms, bottom of shield divides date **Note:** Dav. #7517.

Date	Mintage	VG	F	VF	XF	Unc
1601 (c)	—	80.00	150	275	650	—
160Z (c)	—	80.00	150	275	650	—

KM# 11 THALER

Silver **Ruler:** Johann III **Subject:** Death of Friedrich Wilhelm **Obv:** 1/2-length armored bust right, titles of Friedrich Wilhelm **Rev:** 7-line inscription with dates **Rev. Legend:** DOMINE CONSERVA **Note:** Dav.#7518.

Date	Mintage	VG	F	VF	XF	Unc
160Z (c)	—	200	400	700	1,150	—
160Z WA	—	200	400	700	1,150	—
160Z	—	200	400	700	1,150	—

KM# 14 THALER

Silver **Ruler:** Johann III **Obv:** Bust of Johann III right **Obv. Legend:** ... SAXONIAE. LANDT: THUR **Rev:** Helmeted arms **Note:** Dav. #7519.

Date	Mintage	VG	F	VF	XF	Unc
(1)604 WA	—	155	325	650	1,150	—
1604	—	155	325	650	1,150	—
1605 WA	—	155	325	650	1,150	—

KM# 15 THALER

Silver **Ruler:** Johann III **Obv:** Armored bust of Johann III right **Obv. Legend:** ... SAXONIAE. LANDT: THUR **Rev:** Helmeted arms **Note:** Dav. #7519A.

Date	Mintage	VG	F	VF	XF	Unc
1604	—	155	325	650	1,150	—

KM# 22 THALER

Silver **Ruler:** Johann III **Subject:** Death of Johann III **Obv:** Bust right **Rev:** Eight-line inscription in inner circle **Note:** Dav. #7520.

Date	Mintage	VG	F	VF	XF	Unc
1605	—	150	300	600	1,000	2,750

KM# 7 2 THALER

Silver **Ruler:** Johann III **Obv:** Two 1/2-length figures of dukes with batons in hand, facing each other, small imperial orb above, titles around **Rev:** 3 helmets above 11-fold arms, bottom of shield divides date

Date	Mintage	VG	F	VF	XF	Unc
1601 (c) Rare	—	—	—	—	—	—

KM# 12 2 THALER

Silver **Ruler:** Johann III **Obv:** Two 1/2-length figures of dukes facing each other, small imperial orb above, titles around **Rev:** 3 helmets above 11-fold arms, bottom of shield divides date **Note:** Dav. #7516.

Date	Mintage	VG	F	VF	XF	Unc
160Z (c) Rare	—	—	—	—	—	—

JOINT COINAGE

MB# 84 1/4 THALER

Silver **Ruler:** Friedrich Wilhelm I and Johann III **Obv:** 5 small shields of arms, 4 arranged around one in center, upper and lower shields divide date, titles of two dukes **Rev:** 2 angels holding Saxony arms, PS:33 above, text in margin **Mint:** Saalfeld

Date	Mintage	VG	F	VF	XF	Unc
160Z (c)	—	120	225	375	725	—

MB# 79 THALER

Silver **Ruler:** Friedrich Wilhelm I and Johann III **Obv:** Two 1/2-length figures of dukes facing each other, small imperial orb above **Obv. Legend:** D.G. FRIDE. WILH. ADM. ET. IOHAN. FRA. DVCES. SAXO. **Rev:** Saxony arms in ornate shield with date above in circle, 12 small shields around, legend in outer margin **Rev. Legend:** LANTG. THVRI. ET. MARCHIO. MISN. MON. IMPERI. **Mint:** Saalfeld **Note:** Dav. 9779. Koppe 106-15. Prev. KM#3. Varieties exist.

Date	Mintage	VG	F	VF	XF	Unc
1601 (c)	—	90.00	200	375	700	—

SAXE-MIDDLE-WEIMAR

(Sachsen-Mittel-Weimar)

Upon the death of Johann III of Saxe-Old-Weimar in 1605, his eight sons ruled the duchy together. Both Eisenach and Gotha were acquired from Saxe-Old Gotha when Johann Ernst II died in 1638. By 1640, three brothers alone remained and they divided the territory into Saxe-(New)-Weimar, Saxe-Eisenach and Saxe-(Middle) Gotha.

RULERS

Joint Rule, 1605-1640
- Johann Ernst IV, 1605-1626
- Friedrich VII, 1605-1622
- Wilhelm IV, 1605-1640
- Albrecht II, 1605-1640
- Johann Friedrich VI, 1605-1628
- Ernst III the Pious, 1605-1640
- Friedrich Wilhelm, 1605-1619
- Bernhard the Great, 1605-1639, Duke of Franconia 1633-1634

MINT OFFICIALS' INITIALS

Initial	Date	Name
WA	1604-12	Wolf Albrecht der Jüngere, in Coburg
	1612-20, 23-32	in Saalfeld
CVL	1616-20	Cyriacus von Lehr, in Weimar
	1622	in Hornstein
GA	1620-24	Georg Andreae (known as Gabriel Andresse), in Weimar
	?-1622	Franz Saalfelder, warden in Weimar
CF	1621-23	Caspar Fochtmann, mintmaster and warden in Reinhardtsbrunn
BB	1622	Barthel Bechstein, in Ichtershausen
(a)=	1622	Georg Zapf, die-cutter in Weimar
EF or EFS	1636-72	Ernst Friedrich Schneider, in Coburg
B	Kipper Period	Berka an der Ilm mint
I or IH	Kipper Period	Ichtershausen mint
K	Kipper Period	Königsberg in Franconia mint (also possible Krahwinkel)
RB	Kipper Period	Reinhardtsbrunn mint
RS	Kipper Period	Rotenstein mint
SB	Kipper Period	Saalborn mint

DUCHY

STANDARD COINAGE

KM# 32 HELLER

Copper **Ruler:** Joint Rule **Obv:** Elongated shield of Saxony arms **Mint:** Weimar **Note:** Uniface. Kipper coinage.

Date	Mintage	VG	F	VF	XF	Unc
ND(1620-22)	—	—	—	—	—	—

KM# 33 HELLER

Copper **Ruler:** Joint Rule **Obv:** Oval Saxony arms **Mint:** Weimar **Note:** Uniface. Kipper coinage.

Date	Mintage	VG	F	VF	XF	Unc
ND(1620-22)	—	—	—	—	—	—

KM# 35 HELLER

Copper **Ruler:** Joint Rule **Obv:** Saxony arms divide date, W above **Mint:** Weimar **Note:** Uniface. Kipper coinage.

Date	Mintage	VG	F	VF	XF	Unc
(16)21	—	—	—	—	—	—

KM# 36 3 FLITTER

Copper **Ruler:** Joint Rule **Obv:** Saxony arms **Rev:** Date at end of inscription **Rev. Inscription:** III **Mint:** Weimar **Note:** Kipper coinage.

Date	Mintage	VG	F	VF	XF	Unc
1621	—	—	—	—	—	—

KM# 7 PFENNIG

Copper **Ruler:** Joint Rule **Obv:** 11-fold arms with central shield of Saxony in ornate frame **Rev:** Date at end of inscription, which is all in wreath **Rev. Inscription:** I+C / SALVS / POPVLI / SVPREMA / LEX ESTO / ANNO

Date	Mintage	VG	F	VF	XF	Unc
1610	—	12.00	20.00	40.00	85.00	—
1616	—	12.00	20.00	40.00	85.00	—

KM# 37 PFENNIG

Copper **Ruler:** Joint Rule **Obv:** Ornate Saxony arms, W above **Rev:** Date at end of inscription **Rev. Inscription:** I **Mint:** Weimar

Date	Mintage	VG	F	VF	XF	Unc
1621	—	15.00	20.00	40.00	85.00	—

KM# 53 PFENNIG

Silver **Ruler:** Joint Rule **Obv:** Saxony arms, 'WEIMAR' below **Rev:** Imperial orb with 1 divides date **Mint:** Weimar **Note:** Kipper coinage.

Date	Mintage	VG	F	VF	XF	Unc
(16)ZZ GA	—	15.00	30.00	60.00	120	—

KM# 38 2 PFENNIG (Zweier)

Copper **Ruler:** Joint Rule **Obv:** Ornate Saxony arms, W above **Rev:** Date at end of inscription **Rev. Inscription:** II **Mint:** Weimar **Note:** Kipper coinage.

Date	Mintage	VG	F	VF	XF	Unc
1621 W	—	15.00	20.00	40.00	85.00	—

KM# 39 2 PFENNIG (Zweier)

Copper **Ruler:** Joint Rule **Obv:** Shield of Saxony arms, RB above **Rev:** Date at end of inscription **Rev. Inscription:** I • I • **Mint:** Reinhardtsbrunn **Note:** Kipper coinage.

Date	Mintage	VG	F	VF	XF	Unc
1621 RB	—	15.00	20.00	40.00	85.00	—

KM# 42 3 PFENNIG (Dreier)

Copper **Ruler:** Joint Rule **Obv:** Shield of Saxony arms, 'IH' above **Rev:** Imperial orb with 3 divides date **Mint:** Ichtershausen **Note:** Kipper coinage.

Date	Mintage	VG	F	VF	XF	Unc
1621 I	—	16.00	28.00	45.00	90.00	—
1621 IH	—	16.00	28.00	45.00	90.00	—

KM# 40 3 PFENNIG (Dreier)

Copper **Ruler:** Joint Rule **Obv:** Shield of Saxony armd, RB above **Rev:** Date at end of inscription **Rev. Inscription:** III **Mint:** Reinhardtsbrunn **Note:** Kipper coinage.

Date	Mintage	VG	F	VF	XF	Unc
1621 RB	—	15.00	20.00	40.00	85.00	—

KM# 41 3 PFENNIG (Dreier)

Copper **Ruler:** Joint Rule **Obv:** Shield of Saxony arms, RB above **Rev:** Imperial orb with 3 **Mint:** Reinhardtsbrunn **Note:** Kipper coinage.

Date	Mintage	VG	F	VF	XF	Unc
ND(1621-22) RB	—	16.00	28.00	45.00	90.00	—

KM# 55 3 PFENNIG (Dreier)

Copper **Ruler:** Joint Rule **Obv:** Shield of Saxony arms, 'B' above **Rev:** Imperial orb with 3 divides date **Mint:** Berka **Note:** Kipper coinage.

Date	Mintage	VG	F	VF	XF	Unc
1622 B	—	16.00	28.00	45.00	90.00	—

KM# 54 3 PFENNIG (Dreier)

Copper **Ruler:** Joint Rule **Obv:** Ornate Saxony arms, W above **Rev:** Imperial orb with 3 divides date **Mint:** Weimar **Note:** Kipper coinage.

Date	Mintage	VG	F	VF	XF	Unc
16ZZ W	—	16.00	28.00	45.00	90.00	—

KM# 56 3 PFENNIG (Dreier)

Copper, 23 mm. **Ruler:** Joint Rule **Obv:** Shield of Saxony arms, 'K' above **Rev:** Date at end of inscription **Rev. Inscription:** III **Mint:** Königsberg **Note:** Kipper coinage.

Date	Mintage	VG	F	VF	XF	Unc
1622 K	—	20.00	32.00	55.00	100	—

KM# 57 3 PFENNIG (Dreier)

Copper **Ruler:** Joint Rule **Obv:** Shield of Saxony arms, 'K' above **Rev:** Date at end of inscription **Rev. Inscription:** III **Mint:** Königsberg **Note:** Kipper coinage.

Date	Mintage	VG	F	VF	XF	Unc
1622 K	—	20.00	32.00	55.00	100	—

KM# 58 3 PFENNIG (Dreier)

Copper **Ruler:** Joint Rule **Obv:** 3 small shields of arms, 1 above 2, date divided by upper shield **Rev:** Imperial orb with 3 **Mint:** Königsberg **Note:** Kipper coinage.

Date	Mintage	VG	F	VF	XF	Unc
(16)22 WA	—	20.00	35.00	60.00	110	—
1622 WA	—	20.00	35.00	60.00	90.00	—

KM# 59 3 PFENNIG (Dreier)

Copper **Ruler:** Joint Rule **Obv:** 3 small shields of arms, 1 above 2, date divided by upper shield **Rev:** 'WEI - MAR' divided **Mint:** Königsberg **Note:** Kipper coinage.

Date	Mintage	VG	F	VF	XF	Unc
1622	—	20.00	35.00	60.00	110	—

KM# 60 3 PFENNIG (Dreier)

Copper **Ruler:** Joint Rule **Obv:** 3-fold arms **Rev:** Imperial orb with 3 **Mint:** Königsberg **Note:** Kipper coinage.

Date	Mintage	VG	F	VF	XF	Unc
1622	—	20.00	35.00	60.00	110	—
1623	—	20.00	35.00	60.00	110	—

KM# 80 3 PFENNIG (Dreier)

Copper **Ruler:** Joint Rule **Obv:** 3 small shields of arms, 1 above 2 **Rev:** Imperial orb with 3 divides date **Mint:** Königsberg **Note:** Kipper coinage.

Date	Mintage	VG	F	VF	XF	Unc
1623 WA	—	20.00	35.00	60.00	110	—

KM# 81 3 PFENNIG (Dreier)

Copper **Ruler:** Joint Rule **Obv:** 3 small shields of arms, 1 above 2, 'WEI - MAR' **Rev:** Imperial orb with 3, in cartouche, divides date **Mint:** Königsberg **Note:** Kipper coinage.

Date	Mintage	VG	F	VF	XF	Unc
1623 GA	—	20.00	35.00	65.00	125	—

KM# 104 3 PFENNIG (Dreier)

Copper **Ruler:** Joint Rule **Obv:** Saxony arms **Rev:** Imperial orb with 3 **Mint:** Königsberg **Note:** Kipper coinage.

Date	Mintage	VG	F	VF	XF	Unc
1637	—	20.00	35.00	65.00	125	—
1639	—	20.00	35.00	65.00	125	—

KM# 43 6 PFENNIG (Sechser)

Copper **Ruler:** Joint Rule **Obv:** Shield of Saxony arms divides I - H **Rev:** Imperial orb with 6, date below **Mint:** Ichtershausen **Note:** Kipper coinage.

Date	Mintage	VG	F	VF	XF	Unc
1621 IH	—	16.00	28.00	45.00	90.00	—

KM# 44 6 PFENNIG (Sechser)

Copper **Ruler:** Joint Rule **Obv:** Saxony arms, 'IH' above **Rev:** Imperial orb with 6, date below **Mint:** Ichtershausen **Note:** Kipper coinage.

Date	Mintage	VG	F	VF	XF	Unc
1621 IH	—	16.00	28.00	45.00	90.00	—
1622 IH	—	16.00	28.00	45.00	90.00	—

KM# 45 6 PFENNIG (Sechser)

Copper **Ruler:** Joint Rule **Obv:** Saxony arms divide S - B **Rev:** Imperial orb with 6 **Mint:** Saalborn **Note:** Kipper coinage.

Date	Mintage	VG	F	VF	XF	Unc
ND(1621-22)	—	16.00	28.00	45.00	90.00	—

KM# 61 6 PFENNIG (Sechser)

Copper **Ruler:** Joint Rule **Obv:** Ornate Saxony arms, 'W' above **Rev:** Imperial orb with 6 divides date **Mint:** Weimar **Note:** Kipper coinage.

Date	Mintage	VG	F	VF	XF	Unc
1622 W	—	16.00	28.00	45.00	90.00	—

KM# 62 6 PFENNIG (Sechser)

Copper **Ruler:** Joint Rule **Obv:** Saxony arms divide R - B **Rev:** Imperial orb with 6 divides date **Mint:** Reinhardtsbrunn **Note:** Kipper coinage.

Date	Mintage	VG	F	VF	XF	Unc
1622 RB	—	16.00	28.00	45.00	90.00	—

KM# 63 6 PFENNIG (Sechser)

Copper **Ruler:** Joint Rule **Obv:** Shield of Saxony arms, VI above **Rev:** Imperial orb with 'B' divides date **Mint:** Berka **Note:** Kipper coinage.

Date	Mintage	VG	F	VF	XF	Unc
1622 B	—	16.00	28.00	45.00	90.00	—

KM# 64 6 PFENNIG (Sechser)

Copper, 18 mm. **Ruler:** Joint Rule **Obv:** Saxony arms divide S - B **Rev:** Imperial orb with VI divides date **Mint:** Saalborn **Note:** Kipper coinage.

Date	Mintage	VG	F	VF	XF	Unc
1622 SB	—	16.00	28.00	45.00	90.00	—

KM# 65 6 PFENNIG (Sechser)

Copper **Ruler:** Joint Rule **Obv:** Shield of Saxony arms, 'K' above **Rev:** Value VI, date at end of inscription **Rev. Inscription:** III **Mint:** Königsberg **Note:** Kipper coinage.

Date	Mintage	VG	F	VF	XF	Unc
1622 K	—	22.00	35.00	60.00	110	—

KM# 21 1/24 THALER (Groschen)

Silver **Ruler:** Joint Rule **Obv:** Saxony arms **Rev:** Imperial orb with 24

Date	Mintage	VG	F	VF	XF	Unc
1615	—	—	—	—	—	—

KM# 23 1/24 THALER (Groschen)

Silver **Ruler:** Joint Rule **Subject:** Death of Dorothea Marie, Widow of Johann III **Obv:** Crowned 8-fold arms with central shield of Saxony **Rev:** 7-line inscription with date

Date	Mintage	VG	F	VF	XF	Unc
1617 WA	—	—	—	—	—	—

KM# 46 1/24 THALER (Groschen)

Silver **Ruler:** Joint Rule **Obv:** Saxony arms **Rev:** Imperial orb with 24 **Mint:** Weimar **Note:** Kipper coinage.

Date	Mintage	VG	F	VF	XF	Unc
1621	—	—	—	—	—	—
1622	—	—	—	—	—	—

KM# 68 1/24 THALER (Groschen)

Silver, 24 mm. **Ruler:** Joint Rule **Obv:** Shield of 4-fold arms divides mintmaster's initials, date above, titles of 6 dukes **Obv. Legend:** MON: FRATER: DVC. SAX. LIN: VINA: **Rev:** Imperial orb with 24 **Rev. Legend:** NACH DEM ALTEN SCHROT V(ND). KORN. **Mint:** Weimar **Note:** Ref. Koppe 232. Varieties exist.

Date	Mintage	VG	F	VF	XF	Unc
1622 GA	—	15.00	30.00	55.00	100	—
1623 GA	—	15.00	30.00	55.00	100	—
1624 GA	—	15.00	30.00	55.00	100	—

KM# 67 1/24 THALER (Groschen)

Silver **Ruler:** Joint Rule **Obv:** 3-fold arms, titles of 6 dukes, date **Rev:** Imperial orb with 24 **Rev. Legend:** NACH DEM ALTEN SCHROT V. KORN (or variant) **Mint:** Weimar **Note:** Varieties exist.

Date	Mintage	VG	F	VF	XF	Unc
1622 CF	—	15.00	30.00	55.00	100	—
1623 CF	—	15.00	30.00	55.00	100	—
1624 CF	—	15.00	30.00	55.00	100	—

KM# 66 1/24 THALER (Groschen)

Silver **Ruler:** Joint Rule **Subject:** Death of Friedrich VII **Obv:** Saxony arms in laurel wreath, titles of Friedrich VII **Rev:** 7-line inscription with dates **Mint:** Weimar

Date	Mintage	VG	F	VF	XF	Unc
1622	—	35.00	75.00	150	300	—

KM# 89 1/24 THALER (Groschen)

Silver **Ruler:** Joint Rule **Subject:** Death of Wilhelm IV's Son, Wilhelm **Obv:** Harp to left of young sapling, inner margin legend in script **Obv. Legend:** Versa est in lachrymas (inner legend); WIL. IVN. D.S. FILIOLO. PRIMVLO. VNICO. (outer legend) **Rev:** 5-line inscription with dates, titles of Wilhelm IV **Mint:** Weimar

Date	Mintage	VG	F	VF	XF	Unc
1626	—	25.00	50.00	85.00	170	—

KM# 90 1/24 THALER (Groschen)

Silver **Ruler:** Joint Rule **Subject:** Death and Interment of Johann Ernst IV **Obv:** Inscription in wreath, titles of Johann Ernst IV **Obv. Inscription:** SAPIEN / TERET / CONSTAN / TER **Rev:** 8-line inscription with dates **Mint:** Weimar **Note:** Although Johann Ernst IV died in Hungary in December 1626, he was not buried in Weimar until July 1627.

Date	Mintage	VG	F	VF	XF	Unc
1626-27	—	—	—	—	—	—

KM# 95 1/24 THALER (Groschen)

Silver **Ruler:** Joint Rule **Subject:** Centenary of the Augsburg Confession **Obv:** Open Bible in circle **Obv. Legend:** EXHIBITA CAROLO V... **Rev:** 7-line inscription with date in wreath **Mint:** Weimar

Date	Mintage	VG	F	VF	XF	Unc
1630	—	—	—	—	—	—

KM# 97 1/24 THALER (Groschen)

Silver **Ruler:** Joint Rule **Subject:** Death of Johann Bernhard von Bozheim, Marschall zu Weimar **Obv:** 7-line inscription with date, titles of Wilhelm IV **Rev:** Inscription in wreath, date at end **Rev. Inscription:** TREW HERR / TREW KNECHT **Mint:** Weimar

Date	Mintage	VG	F	VF	XF	Unc
1631	—	25.00	50.00	85.00	155	—

KM# 105 1/24 THALER (Groschen)

Silver, 24 mm. **Ruler:** Joint Rule **Obv:** Shield of 4-fold arms in baroque frame divides mintmaster's initials, date above **Obv. Legend:** MON: FRATER: DVC. SAX. LIN: VINARIE: **Rev:** Imperial orb with 24 **Rev. Legend:** NACH. DEM. ALTEN. SCHROT. VND. KORN. **Mint:** Weimar **Note:** Ref. Koppe 262.

Date	Mintage	VG	F	VF	XF	Unc
1637 DW	—	18.00	40.00	60.00	100	—
1639 DW	—	18.00	40.00	60.00	100	—
1642	—	18.00	40.00	60.00	100	—

KM# 107 1/24 THALER (Groschen)

Silver **Ruler:** Joint Rule **Subject:** Death of Wilhelm IV's Son, Johann Wilhelm **Obv:** 2 arms bound together holding wreath with IWHZD (Johann Wilhelm Herzog zu Sachsen), initials of parents on ribbon ends tying arms **Rev:** 8-line inscription, titles of Wilhelm IV **Mint:** Weimar

Date	Mintage	VG	F	VF	XF	Unc
ND(1639)	—	25.00	50.00	85.00	170	—

KM# 47 20 GROSCHEN

Silver **Ruler:** Joint Rule **Obv:** Saxony arms **Rev:** 3 small shields of arms, 1 above 2, divide R - B **Mint:** Reinhardtsbrunn **Note:** Kipper coinage.

Date	Mintage	VG	F	VF	XF	Unc
1621 RB	—	—	—	—	—	—

KM# 34 12 KREUZER (Schreckenberger)

Silver **Ruler:** Joint Rule **Obv:** Ornate Saxony arms, small imperial orb above **Obv. Legend:** MONETA NOVA... **Rev:** 3 small shields of arms, 1 above divides date, 2 below **Rev. Legend:** FRATRVM... **Mint:** Weimar **Note:** Kipper coinage.

Date	Mintage	VG	F	VF	XF	Unc
1620 GA	—	—	—	—	—	—

KM# 69 12 KREUZER (Schreckenberger)

Silver **Ruler:** Joint Rule **Obv:** 1/2-length figure of angel behind Saxony arms **Rev:** 3 small shields of arms, 1 above divides date, 2 below, 'BB' at bottom **Rev. Legend:** FRATRVM... **Mint:** Ichtershausen **Note:** Kipper coinage.

Date	Mintage	VG	F	VF	XF	Unc
1622 BB	—	—	—	—	—	—

KM# 29 24 KREUZER (Doppelschreckenberger)

Silver **Ruler:** Joint Rule **Obv:** Large Saxony arms, crown and imperial orb above **Obv. Legend:** MONETA NOVA... **Rev:** 3 small ornate shields of arms, 1 above 2, Z4 below, upper arms divide date, intertwined mintmaster's initials below **Rev. Legend:** FRATRVM... **Mint:** Weimar **Note:** Kipper coinage.

Date	Mintage	VG	F	VF	XF	Unc
1619 CVL	—	80.00	160	325	—	—

KM# 30 24 KREUZER (Doppelschreckenberger)

Silver **Ruler:** Joint Rule **Obv:** Large Saxony arms, crown and imperial orb above **Obv. Legend:** MONETA NOVA... **Rev:** 3 small ornate shields of arms, 1 above 2, Z4 below, upper arms divide date, mintmaster's initials below **Rev. Legend:** FRATRVM... **Mint:** Weimar **Note:** Kipper coinage. Varieties exist.

Date	Mintage	VG	F	VF	XF	Unc
1619 CVL	—	80.00	160	325	—	—
1620 CVL	—	80.00	160	325	—	—
1620 GA	—	80.00	160	325	—	—
1621 GA	—	80.00	160	325	—	—

KM# 48 24 KREUZER (Doppelschreckenberger)

Silver **Ruler:** Joint Rule **Obv:** Oval Saxony arms in baroque frame divide R - S, date at end of legend **Obv. Legend:** MONETA NOVA... **Rev:** 3 small ornate shields of arms, 1 above 2, Z4 below **Rev. Legend:** FRATRVM... **Mint:** Rotenstein **Note:** Kipper coinage.

Date	Mintage	VG	F	VF	XF	Unc
1621 RS	—	90.00	180	360	—	—

KM# 49 24 KREUZER (Doppelschreckenberger)

Silver **Ruler:** Joint Rule **Obv:** Large Saxony arms, crown and imperial orb above **Obv. Legend:** MONETA NOVA... **Rev:** 4-fold arms in ornamented frame divide date **Rev. Legend:** FRATRVM... **Mint:** Weimar **Note:** Kipper coinage.

Date	Mintage	VG	F	VF	XF	Unc
1621 GA	—	90.00	180	360	—	—

KM# 70 24 KREUZER (Doppelschreckenberger)

Silver **Ruler:** Joint Rule **Obv:** Large Saxony arms, crown and imperial orb above **Obv. Legend:** MONETA NOVA... **Rev:** 3 small ornate shields of arms, 1 above 2, Z4 at top, upper arms divide date, intertwined mintmaster's initials below **Rev. Legend:** FRATRVM... **Mint:** Weimar **Note:** Kipper coinage.

Date	Mintage	VG	F	VF	XF	Unc
1622	—	90.00	180	360	—	—

KM# 50 60 KREUZER (Gulden = 2/3 Thaler)

Silver **Ruler:** Joint Rule **Obv:** Saxony arms **Rev:** 3 small shields of arms, 1 above 2, divide R - B **Mint:** Reinhardtsbrunn **Note:** Kipper coinage.

Date	Mintage	VG	F	VF	XF	Unc
1621 RB	—	—	—	—	—	—

KM# 51 60 KREUZER (Gulden = 2/3 Thaler)

Silver **Ruler:** Joint Rule **Obv:** Saxony arms **Rev:** 5 small shields of arms, mintmaster's initials below **Mint:** Weimar **Note:** Kipper coinage.

Date	Mintage	VG	F	VF	XF	Unc
1621 GA	—	—	—	—	—	—

KM# 71 60 KREUZER (Gulden = 2/3 Thaler)

Silver **Ruler:** Joint Rule **Obv:** Saxony arms **Rev:** 5 small shields of arms, 'W' at top, mintmaster's initials below **Mint:** Weimar **Note:** Kipper coinage.

Date	Mintage	VG	F	VF	XF	Unc
1622 GA	—	175	350	700	1,400	—

KM# 72 60 KREUZER (Gulden = 2/3 Thaler)

Silver **Ruler:** Joint Rule **Obv:** 1/2-length figure of angel behind Saxony arms **Rev:** Manifold arms in ornate shield **Mint:** Weimar **Note:** Kipper coinage.

Date	Mintage	VG	F	VF	XF	Unc
1622 GA	—	175	350	700	1,400	—

KM# 96 60 KREUZER (Gulden = 2/3 Thaler)

Silver **Ruler:** Joint Rule **Subject:** Centenary of the Augsburg Confession **Obv:** Open Bible in circle **Obv. Legend:** EXHIBITA CAROLO V... **Rev:** Church with 3 angles around, inscription in exergue, date at end **Rev. Inscription:** JUBILÆUM **Mint:** Weimar **Note:** Kipper coinage.

Date	Mintage	VG	F	VF	XF	Unc
1630	—	—	—	—	—	—

KM# 3 1/4 THALER

Silver **Ruler:** Joint Rule **Obv:** 4 half-figures facing, inscription below **Obv. Inscription:** MON: NOV: ARG: ... **Rev:** 4 half-figures facing, 2-line inscription below, date below **Rev. Inscription:** LINEASE VINA / RIENSIS. **Note:** Dav#7523. Varieties exist.

Date	Mintage	VG	F	VF	XF	Unc
1608 WA	—	30.00	60.00	120	240	—
1609 WA	—	30.00	60.00	120	240	—
1610 WA	—	30.00	60.00	120	240	—
1611 WA	—	30.00	60.00	120	240	—

KM# 13 1/4 THALER

Silver **Ruler:** Joint Rule **Obv:** Inscription below figures **Obv. Inscription:** DISCORDIÆ / FOMES INNRIA **Rev:** Inscription above figures **Rev. Inscription:** 8 FRAT. DVC: SAXON: / IVL: CLI: MOT: **Note:** Dav#7525.

Date	Mintage	VG	F	VF	XF	Unc
1613 WA	—	30.00	60.00	120	240	—

KM# 14 1/4 THALER

Silver **Ruler:** Joint Rule **Obv:** 4 half-figures facing, scrollwork below **Note:** Dav#7527. Varieties exist.

Date	Mintage	VG	F	VF	XF	Unc
1613 WA	—	30.00	60.00	120	240	—
1614 WA	—	30.00	60.00	120	240	—
1615 WA	—	30.00	60.00	120	240	—

KM# 24 1/4 THALER

Silver **Ruler:** Joint Rule **Subject:** Death of Dorothea Marie, Widow of Johann III **Obv:** Crowned 8-fold arms with central shield of Saxony **Rev:** 8-line inscription with date

Date	Mintage	VG	F	VF	XF	Unc
1617 WA	—	—	—	—	—	—

KM# 73 1/4 THALER

Silver **Ruler:** Joint Rule **Subject:** Death of Friedrich VII **Obv:** Saxony arms in laurel wreath, titles of Friedrich VII **Rev:** 7-line inscription with dates **Rev. Legend:** IN. COELO...

Date	Mintage	VG	F	VF	XF	Unc
1622 (a)	—	125	250	450	900	—

KM# 74 1/4 THALER (6 Groschen)

Silver **Ruler:** Joint Rule **Obv:** Pallas standing with spear and shield, looking right, date divided by helmet at top **Obv. Legend:** MONETA FRATRVM... **Rev:** 4 small arms around central small shield in cruciform, mintmaster's initials and value 6gl divided by upper and lower shields **Rev. Legend:** NACH. DEM. ALTEN. SCHROT. VND. KORN.

Date	Mintage	VG	F	VF	XF	Unc
1622 CF	—	—	—	—	—	—

KM# 98 1/4 THALER (6 Groschen)

Silver **Ruler:** Joint Rule **Subject:** Death of Johann Bernhard von Bozheim, Marschall zu Weimar **Obv:** 7-line inscription with date, titles of Wilhelm IV **Rev:** Inscription in wreath, date at end **Rev. Inscription:** TREW HERR / TREW KNECHT

Date	Mintage	VG	F	VF	XF	Unc
1631	—	40.00	85.00	135	230	—

KM# 4 1/2 THALER

Silver **Ruler:** Joint Rule **Obv:** 4 half-figures facing, inscription below **Obv. Inscription:** MON: NOV: ARG: ... **Rev:** 4 half-figures facing, 2-line inscription below, date below **Rev. Inscription:** LINEASE VINA / RIENSIS. **Note:** Dav#7523. Varieties exist.

Date	Mintage	VG	F	VF	XF	Unc
1608 WA	—	35.00	75.00	150	300	—
1609 WA	—	35.00	75.00	150	300	—
1610 WA	—	35.00	75.00	150	300	—
1611 WA	—	35.00	75.00	150	300	—

KM# 8 1/2 THALER

Silver **Ruler:** Joint Rule **Obv:** 4 half-figures facing, inscription below **Obv. Inscription:** MON: NOV: ARG: ... **Rev:** 4 half-figures facing, 2-line inscription below, date below **Rev. Inscription:** LINEASE VINA / RIENSIS. **Note:** Dav#7523. Struck on a broad, thin flan from Thaler dies.

Date	Mintage	VG	F	VF	XF	Unc
1610 WA	—	35.00	75.00	150	300	—

KM# 15 1/2 THALER

Silver **Ruler:** Joint Rule **Obv:** Inscription below figures **Obv. Inscription:** DISCORDIÆ / FOMES INNRIA **Rev:** Inscription above figures **Rev. Inscription:** 8 FRAT. DVC: SAXON: / IVL: CLI: MOT: **Note:** Dav#7525.

Date	Mintage	VG	F	VF	XF	Unc
1613 WA	—	35.00	75.00	150	300	—

KM# 16 1/2 THALER

Silver **Ruler:** Joint Rule **Obv:** 4 half-figures facing, scrollwork below **Note:** Dav#7527. Varieties exist.

Date	Mintage	VG	F	VF	XF	Unc
1613 WA	—	35.00	75.00	150	300	—
1614 WA	—	35.00	75.00	150	300	—
1615 WA	—	35.00	75.00	150	300	—

KM# 25 1/2 THALER

Silver **Ruler:** Joint Rule **Subject:** Death of Dorothea Marie, Widow of Johann III **Obv:** Crowned 8-fold arms with central shield of Saxony **Rev:** 10-line inscription with date

Date	Mintage	VG	F	VF	XF	Unc
1617 WA	—	—	—	—	—	—

KM# 75 1/2 THALER

Silver **Ruler:** Joint Rule **Subject:** Death of Friedrich VII **Obv:** Arms above 7-line inscription **Mint:** Weimar **Note:** Dav#7530.

Date	Mintage	VG	F	VF	XF	Unc
1622 (a)	—	150	300	575	1,150	—

KM# 83 1/2 THALER

Silver **Ruler:** Joint Rule **Obv:** Figure of Pallas standing with spear and shield, spear divides date **Rev:** Helmeted spears **Note:** Dav#7531.

Date	Mintage	VG	F	VF	XF	Unc
1623 GA	—	300	600	1,200	—	—

KM# 92 1/2 THALER

Silver **Ruler:** Joint Rule **Subject:** Death of Johann Ernst IV **Obv:** Bust right **Rev:** 10-line inscription **Note:** Dav#7533.

Date	Mintage	VG	F	VF	XF	Unc
1626 WA	—	200	350	750	1,500	—

KM# 109 1/2 THALER

Silver **Ruler:** Joint Rule **Subject:** Death of Johann Wilhelm, Son of Wilhelm IV **Obv:** 9-line inscription **Rev:** 2 arms bound together holding a wreath with initials of the duke, duchess and dead son **Note:** Dav#7540.

Date	Mintage	VG	F	VF	XF	Unc
1639	—	325	650	1,200	2,400	—

KM# 1 THALER

Silver **Ruler:** Joint Rule **Obv:** 4 half-figures facing, 3-line inscription below **Obv. Inscription:** MON: NOV: ARG: ... **Rev:** 4 half-figures facing, 3-line inscription with date below **Rev. Inscription:** LINEASE VINA / RIENSIS. **Note:** Dav. 7523. "8 Brothers" design.

Date	Mintage	VG	F	VF	XF	Unc
1607 WA	—	75.00	150	300	600	1,850
1608 WA	—	75.00	150	300	600	1,850
1609 WA	—	75.00	150	300	600	1,850
1610 WA	—	75.00	150	300	600	1,850
1611 WA	—	75.00	150	300	600	1,850
1612 WA	—	75.00	150	300	600	1,850

KM# 11 THALER

Silver **Ruler:** Joint Rule **Obv:** 4 half-figures facing, scrollwork below **Note:** Dav. 7527.

Date	Mintage	VG	F	VF	XF	Unc
1612 WA	—	75.00	150	300	600	1,850
1613 WA	—	75.00	150	300	600	1,850
1614 WA	—	75.00	150	300	600	1,850
1615 WA	—	75.00	150	300	600	1,850
1616 WA	—	75.00	150	300	600	1,850

KM# 10 THALER

Silver **Ruler:** Joint Rule **Obv:** Inscription below figures **Obv. Inscription:** DISCORDIAE / FOMES INNRIA **Rev:** Inscription above figures **Rev. Inscription:** 8 FRAT. DVC: SAXON: / IVL: CLI: MOT: **Note:** Dav. #7525.

Date	Mintage	VG	F	VF	XF	Unc
1612 WA	—	75.00	150	300	600	1,850
1613 WA	—	75.00	150	300	600	1,850

KM# A22 THALER

Silver **Ruler:** Joint Rule **Obv:** Figure right with 7 busts around **Rev:** Helmeted arms divide date **Note:** Dav. 7529.

Date	Mintage	VG	F	VF	XF	Unc
1616 WA	—	85.00	165	375	650	—
1617 WA	—	85.00	165	375	650	—
1618 WA	—	85.00	165	375	650	—
1619 WA	—	85.00	165	375	650	—

KM# 26 THALER

Silver **Ruler:** Joint Rule **Subject:** Death of Dorothea Marie, Widow of Johann III **Obv:** Crowned heart-shaped arms **Rev:** 12-line inscription with date **Note:** Dav. 7521.

Date	Mintage	VG	F	VF	XF	Unc
1617 WA	—	350	700	1,250	2,250	—

KM# 77 THALER

Silver **Ruler:** Joint Rule **Subject:** Death of Frederick VII **Rev:** Arms above 7-line inscription **Note:** Dav. 7530.

Date	Mintage	VG	F	VF	XF	Unc
1622 (a)	—	150	300	650	1,250	—

KM# 76 THALER

28.9400 g., Silver **Ruler:** Joint Rule **Obv:** Figure of Pallas standing with spear and shield, spear divides date **Rev:** Helmeted spears **Note:** Dav. 7531. "6 Brothers" design.

Date	Mintage	VG	F	VF	XF	Unc
1622 GA	—	120	250	500	900	—
1623 GA	—	120	250	500	900	—

KM# 84 THALER

Silver **Ruler:** Joint Rule **Obv:** Wreath in field, helmet on Pallas divides date **Rev:** Helmeted arms divide letters at bottom **Note:** Dav. 7532.

Date	Mintage	VG	F	VF	XF	Unc
1623 CF	—	100	200	425	850	—
1623 GA	—	100	200	425	850	—

KM# 85 THALER

Silver **Ruler:** Joint Rule **Obv:** Rough wreath, helmet divides date **Note:** Dav. 7532A.

Date	Mintage	VG	F	VF	XF	Unc
1623 CF	—	100	200	425	850	—

KM# 93 THALER

Silver **Ruler:** Joint Rule **Subject:** Death of Johann Ernst IV **Obv:** Bust right **Rev:** 10-line inscription **Note:** Dav. 7533.

Date	Mintage	VG	F	VF	XF	Unc
1626 WA Rare	—	—	—	—	—	—

KM# 100 THALER

Silver **Obv:** Bust of Gustavus Adolphus right **Rev:** Crowned oval 4-fold arms with central shield in ornate frame, date in margin **Note:** Dav. 4557. Swedish issue.

Date	Mintage	VG	F	VF	XF	Unc
1631 GA Rare	—	—	—	—	—	—

KM# 111 THALER

Silver **Ruler:** Joint Rule **Obv:** Bust right **Rev:** 2 busts **Note:** Dav. 7536. "3 Brothers" design.

Date	Mintage	VG	F	VF	XF	Unc
1639 EF Rare	—	—	—	—	—	—

KM# 110 THALER

Silver **Ruler:** Joint Rule **Subject:** Death of Johann Wilhelm, Son of Wilhelm IV **Obv:** 9-line inscription **Rev:** 2 arms bound together holding a wreath with initials of the duke, duchess and dead son **Note:** Dav. 7540.

Date	Mintage	VG	F	VF	XF	Unc
1639 Rare	—	—	—	—	—	—

KM# 2 2 THALER

Silver **Ruler:** Joint Rule **Note:** Dav. 7522. "8 Brothers" design. Similar to 1 Thaler, KM#1.

Date	Mintage	VG	F	VF	XF	Unc
1607 WA	—	550	1,100	2,000	3,250	—
1608 WA	—	550	1,100	2,000	3,250	—
1609 WA	—	550	1,100	2,000	3,250	—

KM# 18 2 THALER

Silver **Ruler:** Joint Rule **Obv:** 4 half figures facing, DISCORDIAE/... below **Rev:** 4 half figures facing, 8 FRAT. DVC:... above **Note:** Dav. 7524.

Date	Mintage	VG	F	VF	XF	Unc
1613 WA	—	550	1,100	2,000	3,250	—
1614 WA	—	550	1,100	2,000	3,250	—

KM# 17 2 THALER

Silver **Ruler:** Joint Rule **Note:** Dav. #7526. Similar to 1 Thaler, KM#11.

Date	Mintage	VG	F	VF	XF	Unc
1613 WA	—	550	1,100	2,000	3,250	—
1614 WA	—	550	1,100	2,000	3,250	—

KM# 27 2 THALER

Silver **Ruler:** Joint Rule **Note:** Dav. 7528. Similar to 1 Thaler, KM#A22.

Date	Mintage	VG	F	VF	XF	Unc
1617 WA	—	775	1,450	2,400	4,050	—
1619 WA	—	775	1,450	2,400	4,050	—

KM# 78 2 THALER
Silver **Ruler:** Joint Rule **Obv:** 1/2-length figure of angel behind Saxony arms **Rev:** Manifold arms **Mint:** Weimar **Note:** Kipper coinage.

Date	Mintage	VG	F	VF	XF	Unc
1622	—	—	—	—	—	—

TRADE COINAGE

KM# 19 GOLDGULDEN
3.5000 g., 0.9860 Gold 0.1109 oz. AGW **Ruler:** Joint Rule **Obv:** Facing busts of 4 brothers, ornament below in exergue, legend divided by 3 sets of 2 and one set of 3 small shields of arms **Obv. Legend:** MONETA - NO(V). AVREA - FRAT. - SAX. **Rev:** Facing bust of 4 additional brothers, date divided by mintmaster's initials in exergue, legend divided by 3 sets of 2 and one set of 3 small shields of arms **Rev. Legend:** LINEÆ - VINAR - IVL. CLIVI - ET. MONTI. **Mint:** Coburg and Saalfeld **Note:** Fr. 3014. Varieties exist.

Date	Mintage	VG	F	VF	XF	Unc
1613 WA	—	300	600	1,200	2,350	—
1614 WA	—	300	600	1,200	2,350	—
1615 WA	—	300	600	1,200	2,350	—
1617 WA	—	300	600	1,200	2,350	—
1619 WA	—	300	600	1,200	2,350	—

KM# 87 GOLDGULDEN
3.5000 g., 0.9860 Gold 0.1109 oz. AGW **Ruler:** Joint Rule **Obv:** Shield of 6-fold arms in ornate frame, with central shield, divides mintmaster's initials **Obv. Legend:** FRATRVM. DVC: SAXON: LIN: VIN: **Rev:** Crowned ornate shield of ducal Saxony arms in wreath, date divided in margin at top **Rev. Legend:** MONETA. NOVA. AVREA. **Mint:** Weimar **Note:** Fr. 3015.

Date	Mintage	VG	F	VF	XF	Unc
1623 GA	—	825	1,750	4,150	6,800	—

KM# 9 2 GOLDGULDEN
6.7700 g., Gold, 30 mm. **Ruler:** Joint Rule **Obv:** Busts of 4 brothers facing, legend divided by 4 small shields of arms, 3-line inscription in exergue **Obv. Legend:** D.G. IO: ERN. - FRIDERI: - WILHELM. - ALBERT. **Obv. Inscription:** MON. NOV. ARG / VIII. FRAT. / DVX. SAX. **Rev:** Busts fo 4 brothers facing, legend divided by 4 small shields of arms, 3-line inscription with date in exergue **Rev. Legend:** IO: FRIDE - ERNEST9 - FRID: WIL. - BERNHAR: **Rev. Inscription:** LINEÆ. VINA / RIENSIS / 16 WA 08. **Mint:** Coburg and Saalfeld **Note:** Fr. 3013c. Struck from 1/4 Thaler dies, KM #3.

Date	Mintage	VG	F	VF	XF	Unc
1608 WA	—	2,750	3,850	8,300	13,000	—
1611 WA	—	2,750	3,850	8,300	13,000	—
1614 WA	—	2,750	3,850	8,300	13,000	—

KM# 5 3 GOLDGULDEN
Gold **Ruler:** Joint Rule **Obv:** Busts of 4 brothers facing, legend divided by 4 small shields of arms, 3-line inscription in exergue **Obv. Legend:** D.G. IO: ERN. - FRIDERI: - WILHELM. - ALBERT. **Obv. Inscription:** MON. NOV. ARG. / VIII. FRAT. / DVC. SAX. **Rev:** Busts of 4 brothers facing, legend divided by 4 small shields of arms, 3-line inscription with date in exergue **Rev. Legend:** IO: FRIDE - ERNEST9 - FRID: WIL. - BERNHAR: **Rev. Inscription:** LINEÆ. VINA / RIENSIS / 16 WA 08. **Mint:** Coburg **Note:** Fr. 3013b. Struck from 1/4 Thaler dies, KM #3.

Date	Mintage	VG	F	VF	XF	Unc
1608 WA Rare	—	—	—	—	—	—

KM# 79 4 DUCAT
Gold **Ruler:** Joint Rule **Subject:** Death of Friedrich VII **Obv:** Half-length armored figure to right holding helmet at right **Obv. Legend:** FRIDERICVS SENIOR DVX SAXON. IVL. CLI. MONT. LIN. VIN. **Rev:** 7-line inscription with Roman numeral date, small shield of ducal Saxony arms in wreath above **Rev. Legend:** IN. COELO. PATRIVM - BENE - .TRANSIT. HABET. **Rev. Inscription:** NAT9. I. MART. AN. / MDXCVI. / TRANSIT PER ME / DIOS HOSTES AD / CVLMINA COELI / XIX. AVG. AN / MDC.XXII. **Mint:** Weimar **Note:** Fr. 1314a. Struck from 1/2 Thaler dies, KM #75.

Date	Mintage	VG	F	VF	XF	Unc
MDCXXII (1622) (a) Rare	—	—	—	—	—	—

KM# 22 5 DUCAT
Gold **Ruler:** Joint Rule **Obv:** Facing busts of 4 brothers, legend divided by 3 sets of 2 small shields of arms and one set of 3 at bottom, 2-line inscription in exergue **Obv. Legend:** D:G: IO: ERN - FRIDERIC9 - WILHELM9. - ALBERTVS. **Obv. Inscription:** DISCORDIÆ / FOMES. INIVRIA. **Rev:** Facing busts of 4 brothers, legend divided by 3 sets of 2 small shields of arms and one set of 3 at bottom, 3-line inscription with date in exergue **Rev. Legend:** IO: FRIDERI: - ERNESTVS - FRID: WIL: - BERNHARD9. **Rev. Inscription:** LINEÆ. VINA / RIENSIS / 16 WA 15. **Mint:** Saalfeld **Note:** Fr. 3013a. Struck from 1/2 Thaler dies, KM #16.

Date	Mintage	VG	F	VF	XF	Unc
1615 WA Rare	—	—	—	—	—	—

SAXE-WEIMAR

(Sachsen-Neu-Weimar)

Founded from Saxe-Middle-Weimar in 1640, the division ended the joint rule of the duchy begun by all eight sons of Johann III. In 1662, the four sons of Wilhelm IV divided their inheritance into the lines of Saxe-(New)-Weimar, Saxe-Eisenach, Saxe-Marksuhl and Saxe-Jena. When the line in Eisenach became extinct in 1741, that territory and titles reverted to Weimar, which became known from that time on as Saxe-Weimar-Eisenach

RULERS
Wilhelm IV, 1640-1662
Johann Ernst II (V), 1662-1683
Wilhelm Ernst, 1683-1728

MINT OFFICIALS' INITIALS

Initial	Date	Name
(a) arm with sickle or EF or EFS	1636-72	Ernst Friedrich Schneider in Coburg
	1639-69	Andreas Ulrich, mintmaster in Weimar
	1669-72	Johann Friedrich, mintmaster in Weimar
ID	1652-62	Johann Christoph Dürr, die-cutter in Weimar
GFS	1673-76	George Friedrich Staude, mintmaster in Weimar
	1677-81	in Gotha
ICD	1677-84	Johann Christoph Dürr, mintmaster in Weimar
ICS	1684-86	Johann Christoph Staude, mintmaster in Weimar
BA	1687-91-1702	Bastian Altmann, mintmaster in Weimar
CW, W	1688-1739	Christian Wermuth, die-cutter in Gotha

REFERENCE
K = Lothar Koppe, **Die Münzen des Hauses Sachsen-Weimar**, 1573 bis 1918, Regenstauf, 2007.

DUCHY

STANDARD COINAGE

KM# 8 PFENNIG
Silver **Ruler:** Wilhelm IV **Subject:** Repair and Rebuilding of the Ducal Palace at Weimar **Obv:** Crowned Saxony arms in wreath, titles of Wilhelm IV **Rev:** Hebrew 'Jehovah' with rays at top, 5-line inscription with dates **Mint:** Weimar **Note:** Spruch.

Date	Mintage	VG	F	VF	XF	Unc
1651	—	—	—	—	—	—

KM# 17 PFENNIG
Silver **Ruler:** Wilhelm IV **Subject:** Rebuilding of the Ducal Palace **Obv:** Crowned Saxony arms, W. H. - Z. S., date below **Rev:** Hebrew 'Jehovah' with rays at top, 4-line inscription **Rev. Inscription:** CONDITUR ... **Mint:** Weimar **Note:** Spruch.

Date	Mintage	VG	F	VF	XF	Unc
1652	—	—	—	—	—	—

KM# 38 PFENNIG
Silver **Ruler:** Wilhelm IV **Subject:** Interment of Duke Bernhard in Weimar **Obv:** BH over Z/S in wreath **Rev:** 6-line inscription with dates **Mint:** Weimar **Note:** Spruch.

Date	Mintage	VG	F	VF	XF	Unc
1655	—	—	—	—	—	—

KM# 57 PFENNIG
Silver **Ruler:** Wilhelm IV **Subject:** Dedication of Wilhelmsburg **Obv:** Crowned Saxony arms **Rev:** 4-line inscription, date below **Mint:** Weimar **Note:** Spruch.

Date	Mintage	VG	F	VF	XF	Unc
1658	—	—	—	—	—	—

KM# 69 PFENNIG
Silver **Ruler:** Wilhelm IV **Obv:** Saxony arms **Rev:** Imperial orb **Mint:** Weimar

Date	Mintage	VG	F	VF	XF	Unc
1660	—	15.00	30.00	60.00	—	—
1661	—	15.00	30.00	60.00	—	—

KM# 101 PFENNIG
Silver **Ruler:** Johann Ernst II (V) **Obv:** Saxony arms **Rev:** Imperial orb **Mint:** Weimar

Date	Mintage	VG	F	VF	XF	Unc
1676 GFS	—	15.00	30.00	60.00	—	—
1681	—	15.00	30.00	60.00	—	—

KM# 122 PFENNIG
Silver **Ruler:** Wilhelm Ernst **Obv:** 3 small shields of arms **Rev:** Imperial orb **Mint:** Weimar

Date	Mintage	VG	F	VF	XF	Unc
1685 ICS	—	—	—	—	—	—

KM# 9 3 PFENNIG (Dreier)
Silver **Ruler:** Wilhelm IV **Subject:** Commencement of Rebuilding Ducal Palace at Weimar **Obv:** Crowned Saxony arms, H. H. Z. S - G. C. U. B, date below **Rev:** 4-line inscription **Rev. Inscription:** Vin. Aul. Rudera ... **Mint:** Weimar **Note:** Spruch.

Date	Mintage	VG	F	VF	XF	Unc
1651	—	20.00	45.00	90.00	180	—

KM# 18 3 PFENNIG (Dreier)
Silver **Ruler:** Wilhelm IV **Subject:** Rebuilding of the Ducal Palace **Obv:** Crowned Saxony arms, W. H. - Z. S., date below **Rev:** Hebrew 'Jehovah' with rays at top, 4-line inscription **Rev. Inscription:** CONDITUR... **Mint:** Weimar **Note:** Spruch.

Date	Mintage	VG	F	VF	XF	Unc
1652	—	20.00	35.00	75.00	150	—

KM# 22 3 PFENNIG (Dreier)
Silver **Ruler:** Wilhelm IV **Obv:** Crowned Saxony arms, W. H. - Z. S., date below **Rev:** Hebrew 'Jehovah' with rays at top, 5-line inscription with dates **Rev. Inscription:** Cæpta Deus ... **Mint:** Weimar **Note:** Spruch.

Date	Mintage	VG	F	VF	XF	Unc
1653	—	20.00	35.00	75.00	150	—

KM# 23 3 PFENNIG (Dreier)
Silver **Ruler:** Wilhelm IV **Obv:** Crowned Saxony arms, W. H. - Z. S., date below **Rev:** Hebrew 'Jehovah' in center with rays, inscription in script around in triangle **Rev. Inscription:** Cæpta Deus ... **Mint:** Weimar **Note:** Spruch.

Date	Mintage	VG	F	VF	XF	Unc
1653	—	10.00	20.00	40.00	85.00	—

KM# 24 3 PFENNIG (Dreier)
Silver **Ruler:** Wilhelm IV **Subject:** Death of Wilhelm IV's Daughter, Wilhelmine Eleonore **Obv:** Cross with 'Wilhelmina / Eleonora' on arms, FIL - WIL - DVX - SAX. **Rev:** 6-line inscription with date **Mint:** Weimar **Note:** Spruch.

Date	Mintage	VG	F	VF	XF	Unc
1653	—	10.00	20.00	40.00	85.00	—

KM# 32 3 PFENNIG (Dreier)
Silver **Ruler:** Wilhelm IV **Subject:** Commencement of Rebuilding Ducal Palace at Weimar **Obv:** Crowned Saxony arms, H. H. Z. S - G. C. U. B, date below **Rev. Inscription:** Cum Deo / Bene - faci ... **Mint:** Weimar **Note:** Spruch. Varieties exist.

Date	Mintage	VG	F	VF	XF	Unc
1654	—	10.00	20.00	40.00	85.00	—
1656	—	10.00	20.00	40.00	85.00	—

KM# 39 3 PFENNIG (Dreier)
Silver **Ruler:** Wilhelm IV **Subject:** Interment of Duke Bernhard in Weimar **Obv:** B H over Z / S in wreath **Rev:** 6-line inscription with dates **Mint:** Weimar **Note:** Spruch.

Date	Mintage	VG	F	VF	XF	Unc
1655	—	25.00	45.00	90.00	180	—

KM# 49 3 PFENNIG (Dreier)
Silver **Ruler:** Wilhelm IV **Subject:** Death of Wilhelm IV's Son, Friedrich **Obv:** Large crowned F monogram **Obv. Legend:** WILHELMI. DUC. SAX. F. **Rev:** Cross with name FRIDERICVS

on arms, inscription and dates between arms **Mint:** Weimar **Note:** Spruch dreier.

Date	Mintage	VG	F	VF	XF	Unc
1656	—	30.00	60.00	120	240	—

KM# 58 3 PFENNIG (Dreier)

Silver **Ruler:** Wilhelm IV **Subject:** Dedication of Wilhelmsburg **Obv:** Crowned Saxony arms, in script Zu gedächtnis ... **Rev:** Inscription, date divided below **Rev. Inscription:** Und / Seiner / Wilhelms / burg **Mint:** Weimar **Note:** Spruch.

Date	Mintage	VG	F	VF	XF	Unc
1658	—	10.00	20.00	40.00	85.00	—

KM# 59 3 PFENNIG (Dreier)

Silver **Ruler:** Wilhelm IV **Obv:** 3 small shields, 1 above 2, upper shield divides W. H. - Z. S., date at bottom **Rev:** Imperial orb with 3 in cartouche **Mint:** Weimar

Date	Mintage	VG	F	VF	XF	Unc
1658	—	15.00	25.00	55.00	110	—
1660 ID	—	15.00	25.00	55.00	110	—
1661	—	15.00	25.00	55.00	110	—

KM# 70 3 PFENNIG (Dreier)

Silver **Ruler:** Wilhelm IV **Subject:** Votive Offering of Wilhelm IV **Obv:** Imperial orb with 3 in baroque frame, titles of Wilhelm IV **Rev. Inscription:** PRO / MEMO / RIA / date **Mint:** Weimar

Date	Mintage	VG	F	VF	XF	Unc
1660	—	—	—	—	—	—

KM# 77 3 PFENNIG (Dreier)

Silver **Ruler:** Wilhelm IV **Subject:** Death of Wilhelm IV **Obv:** 2 arms from clouds holding 4 arrows with ribbon, crown above, FRATR ... **Rev:** 7-line inscription with date in chronogram **Mint:** Weimar

Date	Mintage	VG	F	VF	XF	Unc
1662	—	—	—	—	—	—

KM# 89 3 PFENNIG (Dreier)

Silver **Ruler:** Johann Ernst II (V) **Subject:** Death of Eleonora Dorothea, Widow of Wihelm IV **Obv:** Heart on which JESUS. E. D. H. Z. S. above, G. F. Z. A. below **Rev:** 6-line inscription with dates **Mint:** Weimar

Date	Mintage	VG	F	VF	XF	Unc
1665	—	18.00	35.00	65.00	120	—

KM# 99 3 PFENNIG (Dreier)

Silver **Ruler:** Johann Ernst II (V) **Obv:** 3 small shields of arms, crown above divides date where present **Rev:** Imperial orb with 3 in cartouche **Mint:** Weimar

Date	Mintage	VG	F	VF	XF	Unc
1675 GFS	—	15.00	25.00	55.00	110	—
1676 GFS	—	15.00	25.00	55.00	110	—
1677	—	15.00	25.00	55.00	110	—
1681	—	15.00	25.00	55.00	110	—
1682	—	15.00	25.00	55.00	110	—

KM# 107 3 PFENNIG (Dreier)

Silver **Ruler:** Johann Ernst II (V) **Subject:** Death of Christiane Elisaeth, Wife of Johann Ernst II **Obv:** Crowned CE monogram in palm branches **Rev:** 6-line inscription with dates **Mint:** Weimar

Date	Mintage	VG	F	VF	XF	Unc
1679	—	35.00	70.00	135	275	—

KM# 114 3 PFENNIG (Dreier)

Silver **Ruler:** Johann Ernst II (V) **Obv:** Crowned script JE monogram **Rev:** 6-line inscription with dates **Mint:** Weimar

Date	Mintage	VG	F	VF	XF	Unc
1683	—	—	—	—	—	—

KM# 115 3 PFENNIG (Dreier)

Silver **Ruler:** Wilhelm Ernst **Obv:** 3 small shields of arms **Rev:** Imperial orb with 3 **Mint:** Weimar **Note:** Varieties exist.

Date	Mintage	VG	F	VF	XF	Unc
1683	—	15.00	25.00	55.00	110	—
1684	—	15.00	25.00	55.00	110	—
1685 ICS	—	15.00	25.00	55.00	110	—
1686 ICS	—	15.00	25.00	55.00	110	—

Date	Mintage	VG	F	VF	XF	Unc
1687 BA	—	15.00	25.00	55.00	110	—
1688 BA	—	15.00	25.00	55.00	110	—
1689 BA	—	15.00	25.00	55.00	110	—

KM# 25 6 PFENNIG (Sechser)

Silver **Ruler:** Wilhelm IV **Obv:** Crowned Saxony arms, W. H. Z. S. - G. C. V. B., date below **Rev:** Hebrew 'Jehovah' in center with rays, inscription in script around triangle **Rev. Inscription:** Cæpta Deus **Mint:** Weimar **Note:** Spruch.

Date	Mintage	VG	F	VF	XF	Unc
1653	—	—	—	—	—	—

KM# 120 6 PFENNIG (Sechser)

Silver **Ruler:** Wilhelm Ernst **Obv:** Crowned shield of Saxony arms between 2 branches **Rev:** Imperial orb with 6 between 2 branches **Mint:** Weimar

Date	Mintage	VG	F	VF	XF	Unc
1684 ICS	—	—	—	—	—	—

KM# 3 1/24 THALER (GROSCHEN)

Silver **Ruler:** Wilhelm IV **Subject:** Peace of Westphalia **Obv:** Crowned oval Saxony arms, sword left, olive branch right, date below **Rev:** 3 hands clasped above sword, inscription above and below **Mint:** Weimar

Date	Mintage	VG	F	VF	XF	Unc
1650	—	40.00	70.00	110	200	—

KM# 10 1/24 THALER (GROSCHEN)

Silver **Ruler:** Wilhelm IV **Subject:** Repair and Rebuilding of the Ducal Palace at Weimar **Obv:** Imperial orb with 24, titles of Wilhelm IV **Rev:** Hebrew 'Jehovah' in rays above 5-line inscription with date **Rev. Inscription:** VIN. AUL. ... **Mint:** Weimar **Note:** Spruch.

Date	Mintage	VG	F	VF	XF	Unc
1651	—	20.00	40.00	80.00	160	—
1653	—	20.00	40.00	80.00	160	—

KM# 19 1/24 THALER (GROSCHEN)

Silver **Ruler:** Wilhelm IV **Subject:** Rebuilding the Ducal Palace **Obv:** Imperial orb with 24, titles of Wilhelm IV **Rev:** Hebrew 'Jehovah' in rays above 5-line inscription with date **Rev. Inscription:** Conditor ... **Mint:** Weimar

Date	Mintage	VG	F	VF	XF	Unc
1652	—	—	—	—	—	—

KM# 26 1/24 THALER (GROSCHEN)

Silver **Ruler:** Wilhelm IV **Subject:** Death of Wilhelm IV's Daughter, Wilhelmine Eleonore **Obv:** Cross on which IESUS, titles of Wilhelm IV, inscription with dates between arms of cross **Rev:** W/E in wreath, crown above, Saxony arms below divide date **Rev. Legend:** QUIESCIT AD GLORI - AM SURRECTURA. **Mint:** Weimar

Date	Mintage	VG	F	VF	XF	Unc
1653	—	30.00	70.00	135	275	—

KM# 40 1/24 THALER (GROSCHEN)

Silver **Ruler:** Wilhelm IV **Obv:** Imperial orb with Z4 **Obv. Legend:** D. G. WILHELM9 DVX SAX. IVL. CLIV. ET. MONT. **Rev:** 4-line inscription on mantle in center, Cum Deo ..., date above, war trophies around **Mint:** Weimar

Date	Mintage	VG	F	VF	XF	Unc
1655	—	30.00	60.00	100	180	—

KM# 41 1/24 THALER (GROSCHEN)

Silver **Ruler:** Wilhelm IV **Subject:** Interment of Duke Bernhard in Weimar **Obv:** Half-length bust, turned 3/4 to right, in circle **Obv. Legend:** D. G. BERNHARDUS. DUX. SAX. IUL. CL. & M. **Rev:** 9-line inscription with dates **Mint:** Weimar

Date	Mintage	VG	F	VF	XF	Unc
1655	—	45.00	90.00	180	360	—

KM# 42 1/24 THALER (GROSCHEN)

Silver **Ruler:** Wilhelm IV **Obv:** Ornate shield of manifold Saxony arms **Rev:** 9-line inscription with dates **Mint:** Weimar

Date	Mintage	VG	F	VF	XF	Unc
1655	—	20.00	45.00	90.00	180	—

KM# 50 1/24 THALER (GROSCHEN)

Silver **Ruler:** Wilhelm IV **Subject:** Death of Wilhelm IV's Son, Friedrich **Obv:** Cross on which IESUS, titles of Wilhelm IV, inscription with dates pertaining to Friedrich between arms of cross **Obv. Legend:** WILHELMI. IV. DUC, SAX. VIN. FILI9 NATU-MINIM9 **Rev:** Clouds with rays above, 'Orietur' above, 4-line inscription with date below, titles of Friedrich **Rev. Legend:** +FRIDERICUS SENIOR DUX SAX. IUL. CLIU. ET. MONT. **Mint:** Weimar

Date	Mintage	VG	F	VF	XF	Unc
1656	—	30.00	60.00	120	240	—

KM# 60 1/24 THALER (GROSCHEN)

Silver **Ruler:** Wilhelm IV **Subject:** Dedication of Wilhelmsburg **Obv:** Crowned manifold arms divide date, titles of Wilhelm IV **Rev:** 'Zu Gedächtnis ... **Mint:** Weimar **Note:** Spruch.

Date	Mintage	VG	F	VF	XF	Unc
1658	—	15.00	30.00	60.00	120	—

KM# 61 1/24 THALER (GROSCHEN)

Silver **Ruler:** Wilhelm IV **Obv:** Crowned shield with concave sides of manifold arms divides date **Obv. Legend:** D. G. WILHELMUS DUX SAX. IUL. CL. & M. **Rev:** 7-line inscription beginning 'SIC bene ... ' **Mint:** Weimar **Note:** Spruch.

Date	Mintage	VG	F	VF	XF	Unc
1658	—	15.00	30.00	60.00	120	—

KM# 71 1/24 THALER (GROSCHEN)

Silver **Ruler:** Wilhelm IV **Obv:** Saxony arms **Rev:** Imperial orb with 24 **Mint:** Weimar

Date	Mintage	VG	F	VF	XF	Unc
1660	—	—	—	—	—	—

KM# 78 1/24 THALER (GROSCHEN)

Silver **Ruler:** Wilhelm IV **Subject:** Death of Wilhelm IV **Obv:** 2 arms from clouds holding 4 arrows with ribbon, crown above, FRATR ... **Rev:** 7-line inscription with date in chronogram **Mint:** Weimar

Date	Mintage	VG	F	VF	XF	Unc
1662	—	—	—	—	—	—

KM# 90 1/24 THALER (GROSCHEN)

Ruler: Johann Ernst II (V) **Subject:** Death of Eleonora Dorothea, Widow of Wilhelm IV **Obv:** Arms from clouds hold crown above heart on which JESUS **Rev:** 7-line inscription with dates **Mint:** Weimar

Date	Mintage	VG	F	VF	XF	Unc
1665	—	45.00	90.00	180	—	—

KM# 94 1/24 THALER (GROSCHEN)

Silver **Ruler:** Johann Ernst II (V) **Obv:** Crowned Saxony arms divide date **Rev:** Imperial orb with 24 **Mint:** Weimar

Date	Mintage	VG	F	VF	XF	Unc
1674 GFS	—	15.00	30.00	60.00	120	—
1675 GFS	—	15.00	30.00	60.00	120	—
1677 ICD	—	15.00	30.00	60.00	120	—

KM# 108 1/24 THALER (GROSCHEN)

Silver **Ruler:** Johann Ernst II (V) **Subject:** Death of Christiane Elisabeth, Wife of Johann Ernst II **Obv:** Winged heart flying from earth to sun **Rev:** 9-line inscription with dates **Mint:** Weimar

Date	Mintage	VG	F	VF	XF	Unc
1679	—	—	—	—	—	—

KM# 116 1/24 THALER (GROSCHEN)

Silver **Ruler:** Johann Ernst II (V) **Subject:** Death of Johann Ernst II **Obv:** Sun shining down on goddess with wreath and Roman soldier, altar between **Obv. Legend:** PIETAS. DOM. - SAXON. **Rev:** 8-line inscription with dates **Mint:** Weimar

Date	Mintage	VG	F	VF	XF	Unc
1683	—	—	—	—	—	—

KM# 124 1/24 THALER (GROSCHEN)

Silver **Ruler:** Wilhelm Ernst **Obv:** Crowned shield of 4-fold Saxony arms **Rev:** Imperial orb with 24 divides date in cartouche **Mint:** Weimar

Date	Mintage	VG	F	VF	XF	Unc
1685 ICS	—	15.00	30.00	60.00	120	—
1687 BA	—	15.00	30.00	60.00	120	—

Date	Mintage	VG	F	VF	XF	Unc
1688 BA	—	15.00	30.00	60.00	120	—
1689 BA	—	15.00	30.00	60.00	120	—
1690 BA	—	15.00	30.00	60.00	120	—

KM# 4 1/4 THALER

Silver **Ruler:** Wilhelm IV **Subject:** Peace of Westphalia **Obv:** Crowned oval Saxony arms, sword left, olive branch right, date below **Rev:** 3 hands clasped above sword, inscription above and below **Mint:** Weimar

Date	Mintage	VG	F	VF	XF	Unc
1650	—	—	—	—	—	—

KM# 27 1/4 THALER

Silver **Ruler:** Wilhelm IV **Subject:** Death of Wilhelm IV's Daughter, Wilhelmine Eleonore **Obv:** Cross on which IESUS, titles of Wilhelm IV, inscription with dates between arms below divine date **Obv. Legend:** QUIESCIT AD GLORI - AM SURRECTURA **Rev:** W/E in wreath, crown above, Saxony arms below divide date **Mint:** Weimar

Date	Mintage	VG	F	VF	XF	Unc
1653	—	70.00	140	285	575	—

KM# 33 1/4 THALER

Silver **Ruler:** Wilhelm IV **Obv:** Bust of Wilhelm IV **Mint:** Weimar

Date	Mintage	VG	F	VF	XF	Unc
1654	—	125	250	450	900	—

KM# 43 1/4 THALER

Silver **Ruler:** Wilhelm IV **Subject:** Intermant of Duke Bernhard in Weimar **Obv:** Facing 1/2-length bust **Rev:** 9-line inscription with dates **Mint:** Weimar

Date	Mintage	VG	F	VF	XF	Unc
1655	—	115	235	475	950	—

KM# 51 1/4 THALER

Silver **Ruler:** Wilhelm IV **Subject:** Death of Wilhelm IV's Son, Friedrich **Obv:** Cross on which FRIDERICUS, titles of Wilhelm IV, inscriptions with dates between arms of cross **Rev:** 'Occidit. ast. orietur' above clouds **Mint:** Weimar

Date	Mintage	VG	F	VF	XF	Unc
1656	—	—	—	—	—	—

KM# 62 1/4 THALER

Silver **Ruler:** Wilhelm IV **Subject:** Dedication of Wilhelmsburg **Obv:** Bust of Wilhelm IV facing 1/4 to left, date in margin **Rev:** 7-line inscription with date in chronogram **Mint:** Weimar

Date	Mintage	VG	F	VF	XF	Unc
1658	—	90.00	175	350	725	—

KM# 79 1/4 THALER

Silver **Ruler:** Wilhelm IV **Subject:** Death of Wilhelm IV **Obv:** Obelisk with ribbons **Rev:** 2 arms from clouds tying 4 arrows together below a crown **Mint:** Weimar

Date	Mintage	VG	F	VF	XF	Unc
1662	—	90.00	150	225	360	—

KM# 80 1/4 THALER

Silver **Ruler:** Wilhelm IV **Obv:** Obelisk with ribbons **Rev:** 2 arms from clouds tying 4 arrows together below a crown **Mint:** Weimar

Date	Mintage	VG	F	VF	XF	Unc
1662	—	—	—	—	—	—

KM# 91 1/4 THALER

Silver **Ruler:** Johann Ernst II (V) **Subject:** Death of Eleonora Dorothea, Widow of Wilhelm IV **Obv:** Arms from clouds hold crown above heart on which JESUS **Rev:** 7-line inscription with dates **Mint:** Weimar

Date	Mintage	VG	F	VF	XF	Unc
1665	—	50.00	100	180	360	—

KM# 109 1/4 THALER

Silver **Ruler:** Johann Ernst II (V) **Subject:** Death of Christiane Elisabeth, Wife of Johann Ernst II **Obv:** Winged heart flying from earth to sun **Rev:** 10-line inscription with dates **Mint:** Weimar

Date	Mintage	VG	F	VF	XF	Unc
1679	—	—	—	—	—	—

KM# 117 1/4 THALER

Silver **Ruler:** Johann Ernst III (VI) **Subject:** Death of Johann Ernst II **Obv:** Bust right above 4-line inscription with R.N. date **Rev:** 8-line inscription with dates **Mint:** Weimar

Date	Mintage	VG	F	VF	XF	Unc
MDCLXXXIII (1683)	—	200	375	550	900	—

KM# 5 1/2 THALER

Silver **Ruler:** Wilhelm IV **Subject:** Peace of Westphalia **Obv:** 2 hands holding wreath above coat of arms, sword at left, olive branch at right **Rev:** 3 clasped hands above a sword, date in chronogram **Mint:** Weimar

Date	Mintage	VG	F	VF	XF	Unc
1650	—	—	—	—	—	—

KM# 28 1/2 THALER

Silver **Ruler:** Wilhelm IV **Subject:** Death of Wilhelm IV's Daughter, Wilhelmine Eleonore **Obv:** Cross on which IESUS, titles of Wilhelm IV, inscription with dates between arms of cross **Rev:** W/E in wreath, crown above, Saxony arms below divide date **Rev. Legend:** QUIESCIT AD GLORI - AM SURRECTURA **Mint:** Weimar

Date	Mintage	VG	F	VF	XF	Unc
1653	—	150	300	600	1,200	—

KM# 44 1/2 THALER

Silver **Ruler:** Wilhelm IV **Obv:** Facing 1/2-length bust **Rev:** 9-line inscription with dates **Mint:** Weimar

Date	Mintage	VG	F	VF	XF	Unc
1655	—	375	750	1,500	—	—

KM# 52 1/2 THALER

Silver **Ruler:** Wilhelm IV **Subject:** Death of Wilhelm IV's Son, Friedrich **Obv:** FRIDERICUS on arms of cross, titles of Wilhelm IV, inscription with dates pertaining to Friedrich **Rev:** W/E in wreath, crown above, Saxony arms below divide R.N. date **Rev. Legend:** QUIESCIT AD GLORI - AM SURRECTURA **Mint:** Weimar

Date	Mintage	VG	F	VF	XF	Unc
MDCLVI (1656)	—	—	—	—	—	—

KM# 63 1/2 THALER

Silver **Ruler:** Wilhelm IV **Subject:** Dedication of Wilhelmsburg **Obv:** Bust 1/2 right **Rev:** Palace, 5-line inscription below **Mint:** Weimar

Date	Mintage	VG	F	VF	XF	Unc
1658	—	175	350	700	1,400	2,250

KM# 81 1/2 THALER

Silver **Ruler:** Wilhelm IV **Subject:** Death of Wilhelm IV **Obv:** Obelisk with ribbons **Rev:** 2 arms from clouds tying 4 arrows together below a crown **Mint:** Weimar

Date	Mintage	VG	F	VF	XF	Unc
1662	—	—	—	—	—	—

KM# 82 1/2 THALER

Silver **Ruler:** Wilhelm IV **Subject:** Death of Wilhelm IV **Obv:** Obelisk with ribbons, without 4-line inscription on base **Rev:** 2 arms from clouds tying 4 arrows together below a crown **Mint:** Weimar

Date	Mintage	VG	F	VF	XF	Unc
1662	—	—	—	—	—	—

KM# 92 1/2 THALER

Silver **Ruler:** Johann Ernst II (V) **Subject:** Death of Eleonora Dorothea, Widow of Wilhelm IV **Obv:** 8-line inscription **Rev:** Hands from clouds holding crown above heart inscribed JESUS **Mint:** Weimar

Date	Mintage	VG	F	VF	XF	Unc
1665	—	225	450	900	—	—

KM# 110 1/2 THALER

Silver **Ruler:** Johann Ernst II (V) **Subject:** Death of Christiane Elisabeth, Wife of Johann Ernst II **Obv:** "JEHOVAH" in Hebrew above in sun with clouds, moon and earth below **Rev:** 13-line inscription **Mint:** Weimar

Date	Mintage	VG	F	VF	XF	Unc
1679	—	—	—	—	—	—

KM# 118 1/2 THALER

Silver **Ruler:** Wilhelm Ernst **Subject:** Death of Johann Ernst II **Obv:** Bust right in laurel branches **Rev:** 8-line inscription below crowned arms on tomb, R.N. date **Mint:** Weimar

Date	Mintage	VG	F	VF	XF	Unc
MDCLXXXIII (1683)	—	—	—	—	—	—

KM# 95 2/3 THALER (Gulden)

Silver **Ruler:** Johann Ernst II (V) **Obv:** Bust right, titles of Johann Ernst II **Rev:** Crowned 3-fold arms, value 2/3 in oval below **Mint:** Weimar **Note:** Dav. #886.

Date	Mintage	VG	F	VF	XF	Unc
ND(ca1674) GFS	—	—	—	—	—	—

KM# 96 2/3 THALER (Gulden)

Silver **Ruler:** Johann Ernst II (V) **Obv:** Bust right, titles of Johann Ernst II **Rev:** Crowned 4-fold arms divide date, value 2/3 in oval below **Mint:** Weimar **Note:** Dav. #887.

Date	Mintage	VG	F	VF	XF	Unc
1674 GFS	—	100	200	350	725	—
1675 GFS	—	100	200	350	725	—

KM# 97 2/3 THALER (Gulden)

Silver **Ruler:** Johann Ernst II (V) **Obv:** Bust right, titles of Johann Ernst II **Rev:** Palm branches to either side of crowned 4-fold arms, date above, value 2/3 in oval below **Mint:** Weimar **Note:** Dav. #888.

Date	Mintage	VG	F	VF	XF	Unc
1674 GFS	—	100	200	350	725	—

KM# 100 2/3 THALER (Gulden)

Silver **Ruler:** Johann Ernst II (V) **Obv:** Bust right, titles of Johann Ernst II **Rev:** Crowned 4-fold arms, value 2/3 in circle at bottom **Mint:** Weimar **Note:** Dav. #889. Varieties exist.

Date	Mintage	VG	F	VF	XF	Unc
1675 GFS	—	100	200	350	725	—
1676 GFS	—	100	200	350	725	—

KM# 102 2/3 THALER (Gulden)

Silver **Ruler:** Johann Ernst II (V) **Obv:** Bust right, titles of Johann Ernst II, legend ends in MONT. **Rev:** Crowned 4-fold arms, value in circle at bottom **Mint:** Weimar **Note:** Dav. #890. Varieties exist.

Date	Mintage	VG	F	VF	XF	Unc
1676	—	100	200	350	725	—

KM# 104 2/3 THALER (Gulden)

Silver **Ruler:** Johann Ernst II (V) **Obv:** Bust right in inner circle, titles of Johann Ernst II, legend ends in MONT. **Rev:** Small crown above 4-fold arms , value 2/3 in circle at bottom **Mint:** Gotha **Note:** Dav. #891. Varieties exist.

Date	Mintage	VG	F	VF	XF	Unc
1677	—	100	200	350	725	—
1678	—	100	200	350	725	—
1679	—	100	200	350	725	—

KM# 105 2/3 THALER (Gulden)

Silver **Ruler:** Johann Ernst II (V) **Obv:** Armored and draped bust to right **Obv. Legend:** D: G. IOHAN. ERNEST. D: S: I: C: ET. MONT. **Rev:** Crowned shield of 4-fold arms divides date, value (2/3) in oval below **Rev. Legend:** PRUDENTER. ET - CONSTANTER. **Mint:** Weimar **Note:** Ref. Dav. 892.

Date	Mintage	VG	F	VF	XF	Unc
1677	—	40.00	75.00	125	240	—
1678	—	40.00	75.00	125	240	—

KM# 125 16 GROSCHEN (2/3 Thaler)

Silver **Ruler:** Wilhelm Ernst **Obv. Legend:** MONETA. NOVA ... **Obv. Inscription:** XVI / GROSCHEN / ANNO / date **Rev:** Crowned Saxony arms **Mint:** Weimar **Note:** Dav. #893.

Date	Mintage	VG	F	VF	XF	Unc
1690 BA	—	—	—	—	—	—

KM# 126 16 GROSCHEN (2/3 Thaler)

Silver **Ruler:** Wilhelm Ernst **Obv. Inscription:** * XVI * / GROSCHEN / D. MR. / FEIN A: / 12 TH B#A. **Rev:** Crowned arms divide date, all in wreath **Mint:** Weimar **Note:** Dav. #894.

Date	Mintage	VG	F	VF	XF	Unc
1690 BA	—	—	—	—	—	—

KM# 6 THALER

Silver **Ruler:** Wilhelm IV **Subject:** Peace in Weimar **Obv:** Two hands holding wreath above coat of arms, sword at left, olive branch at right **Rev:** Three clasped hands above a sword, date in chronogram **Note:** Dav. #7541.

Date	Mintage	VG	F	VF	XF	Unc
1650	—	800	1,600	3,300	5,400	—

KM# 20 THALER

Silver **Ruler:** Wilhelm IV **Subject:** Rebuilding the Palace at Weimar **Obv:** View of the newly rebuilt palace, date in margin at top **Obv. Legend:** D. G. WILHELM. DVX SAXONIÆ. IULIÆ. CLIVIÆ. et MONT. **Rev:** View of the palace on fire **Rev. Legend:** AULA VINARIENSIS. 1618. ITA CONCREMATA. **Note:** Dav. #7542.

Date	Mintage	VG	F	VF	XF	Unc
1652	—	1,150	2,250	4,750	9,000	14,500

KM# 29 THALER

Silver **Ruler:** Wilhelm IV **Obv. Legend:** ... SAXON. IVL. CLIV. &MONT. **Rev:** Legend starts at lower left **Rev. Legend:** AULA... **Note:** Dav. #7543.

Date	Mintage	VG	F	VF	XF	Unc
1653	—	1,250	2,500	5,000	10,000	—

KM# 30 THALER

Silver **Ruler:** Wilhelm IV **Subject:** Death of Wilhelmina Eleonora, Daughter of Wilhelm IV **Obv:** IESUSEI both ways in a cross, biographical data in field **Obv. Legend:** Crowned wreath with W E inside, WILHELMINA-ELEONORA at sides **Note:** Dav.#7544.

Date	Mintage	VG	F	VF	XF	Unc
1653 Rare	—	—	—	—	—	—

KM# 34 THALER

Silver **Ruler:** Wilhelm IV **Subject:** Duke Bernhard Assuming the Rectorship of Jena University **Obv:** Two crowned hearts with bust of Johann Friedrich and two shields at center **Rev:** Two busts in center of Johann Friedrich and Johann Wilhelm **Note:** Dav.#7545.

Date	Mintage	VG	F	VF	XF	Unc
1654	—	750	1,500	3,000	5,100	—

KM# 45 THALER

Silver **Ruler:** Wilhelm IV **Subject:** Entombment of Bernhard in Weimar **Rev:** Nine-line inscription **Note:** Dav.#7537.

Date	Mintage	VG	F	VF	XF	Unc
1655	—	650	1,300	2,700	4,800	—

KM# 53 THALER

Silver **Ruler:** Wilhelm IV **Subject:** Death of Friedrich, Son of Wilhelm IV **Obv:** FRIDERICVS both ways on a cross, biographical data in field **Obv. Legend:** WILHELMI. IV. DUX. SAX. VIN. FILI9 NATU-MINIM9 **Rev:** Sun behind clouds, biographical data below **Rev. Legend:** +FRIDERICUS SENIOR DUX SAX. IUL. CLIV. ET. MONTIUM. **Note:** Dav.#7546.

Date	Mintage	VG	F	VF	XF	Unc
1656	—	700	1,350	2,750	5,500	9,000

KM# 64 THALER

Silver **Ruler:** Wilhelm IV **Subject:** New Palace of Wilhelmsburg **Obv:** Facing armored bust, date at end of legend **Obv. Legend:** D. G. WILHELMUS. DUX SAX. IUL. CLIV. ET MONTIUM. **Rev:** View of palace, five-line inscription below **Note:** Dav.#7547.

Date	Mintage	VG	F	VF	XF	Unc
1658	—	575	1,150	2,350	3,850	6,500

KM# 83 THALER

Silver **Ruler:** Wilhelm IV **Obv:** Bust right **Rev:** Wilhelmsburg Castle at Weimar **Note:** Dav.#7549.

Date	Mintage	VG	F	VF	XF	Unc
1662 Rare	—	—	—	—	—	—

KM# 84.1 THALER

Silver **Ruler:** Wilhelm IV **Subject:** Death of Wilhelm IV **Obv:** Obelisk with ribbons, 4-line inscription on base **Rev:** Two arms from clouds tying four arrows together below a crown **Note:** Dav.#7550. Varieties exist.

Date	Mintage	VG	F	VF	XF	Unc
1662	—	150	300	700	1,750	4,500

KM# 84.2 THALER

Silver **Ruler:** Wilhelm IV **Subject:** Death of Wilhelm IV **Obv:** Obelisk with ribbons, 3-line inscription on base **Rev:** 2 arms from clouds tying 4 arrows together below a crown **Mint:** Weimar **Note:** Dav. #7550.2.

Date	Mintage	VG	F	VF	XF	Unc
1662	—	125	275	600	1,850	—

KM# 84.3 THALER

Silver **Ruler:** Wilhelm IV **Subject:** Death of Wilhelm IV **Obv:** Obelisk with ribbons, without inscription on base **Rev:** 2 arms from clouds tying 4 arrows together below a crown **Mint:** Weimar **Note:** Dav. #7550.3.

Date	Mintage	VG	F	VF	XF	Unc
1662	—	—	—	—	—	—

KM# 87 THALER
Silver **Ruler:** Johann Ernst II (V) **Obv:** Armored bust to right **Obv. Legend:** D. G. IOHAN ERNEST. DVX. SAX. I. C. ET. MONT. **Rev:** Female figure seated by column with staff, palace behind **Rev. Legend:** PRUDENTER. CONSTANTER. **Note:** Dav.#7552.

Date	Mintage	VG	F	VF	XF	Unc
ND(1663)	—	2,000	4,000	7,250	—	—

KM# 93 THALER
Silver **Ruler:** Johann Ernst II (V) **Subject:** Death of Eleonora Dorothea, Widow of Wilhelm IV **Obv:** Eight-line inscription **Rev:** Hands from clouds holding crown above heart inscribed JESUS **Note:** Dav.#7551.

Date	Mintage	VG	F	VF	XF	Unc
1665	—	175	350	750	1,650	4,250

KM# 111 THALER
Silver **Ruler:** Johann Ernst II (V) **Subject:** Death of Christiane Elisabeth, Wife of Johann Ernst **Obv:** "JEHOVAH" in Hebrew above in sun with clouds, moon, and earth below **Rev:** Twelve-line inscription **Note:** Dav.#7554.

Date	Mintage	VG	F	VF	XF	Unc
1679	—	1,250	2,500	5,750	—	—

KM# 119 THALER
Silver **Ruler:** Johann Ernst II (V) **Subject:** Death of Johann Ernst II **Obv:** Armored bust to right in laurel branches **Obv. Legend:** IOHANNES ERNESTUS. D. G. - DUX SAX. IUL. CLIV. ET MONT. **Rev:** 8-line inscription below crowned arms on tomb, Roman numeral date **Note:** Dav.#7555.

Date	Mintage	VG	F	VF	XF	Unc
MDCLXXXIII (1683) PP Rare	—	—	—	—	—	—

Note: Westfälische Auktionsgesellschaft Auction 40, 2-07, nearly XF realized approximately $8,940.

KM# 46 1-1/4 THALER
Silver **Ruler:** Wilhelm IV **Subject:** Entombment of Bernhard in Weimar **Note:** Dav.#7537A. Similar to 1 Thaler, KM#45.

Date	Mintage	VG	F	VF	XF	Unc
1655 Rare	—	—	—	—	—	—

KM# 112 1 1/2 THALER
Silver **Ruler:** Johann Ernst II (V) **Obv:** Bust **Rev:** Arms **Mint:** Weimar **Note:** Dav.#7553. Prev. listed in Saxe-Middle-Weimer.

Date	Mintage	VG	F	VF	XF	Unc
1679 Rare	—	—	—	—	—	—

KM# 47 3 THALER
Silver **Ruler:** Wilhelm IV **Subject:** Entombment of Bernhard in Weimar **Note:** Dav.#7537B. Similar to 1 Thaler, KM#45.

Date	Mintage	VG	F	VF	XF	Unc
1655 Rare	—	—	—	—	—	—

TRADE COINAGE

KM# 11 1/4 DUCAT
0.8750 g., 0.9860 Gold 0.0277 oz. AGW **Ruler:** Wilhelm IV **Obv:** Crowned arms **Rev:** "Jehovah" in Hebrew and legend **Note:** Fr.#3019.

Date	Mintage	VG	F	VF	XF	Unc
1651	—	175	350	700	1,300	—

KM# 65 1/4 DUCAT
0.8750 g., 0.9860 Gold 0.0277 oz. AGW **Ruler:** Wilhelm IV **Obv:** Saxon arms in branches **Rev:** "Jehovah" at top, four-line inscription, date at bottom **Note:** FR#3024.

Date	Mintage	VG	F	VF	XF	Unc
1658	—	230	450	900	1,800	—

KM# 85 1/4 DUCAT
0.8750 g., 0.9860 Gold 0.0277 oz. AGW **Ruler:** Wilhelm IV **Obv:** Draped bust to right right **Obv. Legend:** W H Z - S G C V B. **Rev:** Crowned oval shield of ducal Saxony arms, date divided below **Note:** Ref. Fr. 3029.

Date	Mintage	VG	F	VF	XF	Unc
1662	—	270	500	1,050	2,100	—

KM# 12 1/2 DUCAT
1.7500 g., 0.9860 Gold 0.0555 oz. AGW **Ruler:** Wilhelm IV **Obv:** Crowned arms **Rev:** "Jehovah" and legend **Note:** Fr.#3018.

Date	Mintage	VG	F	VF	XF	Unc
1651	—	265	550	1,100	2,150	—
1652	—	265	550	1,100	2,150	—

KM# 13 1/2 DUCAT
1.7500 g., 0.9860 Gold 0.0555 oz. AGW **Ruler:** Wilhelm IV **Obv:** Saxon arms in branches in inner circle **Rev:** "Jehovah" at top, four-line inscription, date at bottom **Note:** Fr.#3023.

Date	Mintage	VG	F	VF	XF	Unc
1651	—	265	550	1,100	2,150	—
1656	—	265	550	1,100	2,150	—

KM# 35 1/2 DUCAT
1.7500 g., 0.9860 Gold 0.0555 oz. AGW **Ruler:** Wilhelm IV **Obv:** Wilhelm **Note:** Fr.#3021.

Date	Mintage	VG	F	VF	XF	Unc
1654	—	265	475	1,050	2,100	—

KM# 14 DUCAT
3.5000 g., 0.9860 Gold 0.1109 oz. AGW **Ruler:** Wilhelm IV **Obv:** Crowned arms **Rev:** "Jehovah" and legend **Note:** Ref. Fr. 3017.

Date	Mintage	VG	F	VF	XF	Unc
1651	—	475	900	1,800	3,000	—

KM# 15 DUCAT
3.5000 g., 0.9860 Gold 0.1109 oz. AGW **Ruler:** Wilhelm IV **Rev:** "Jehovah" at top **Note:** Ref. Fr. 3022.

Date	Mintage	VG	F	VF	XF	Unc
1651	—	600	1,150	2,300	4,500	—

KM# 74 DUCAT
3.5000 g., 0.9860 Gold 0.1109 oz. AGW **Ruler:** Wilhelm IV **Obv:** Bust of Wilhelm right in inner circle **Rev:** Jena Castle **Note:** Ref. Fr. 3028.

Date	Mintage	VG	F	VF	XF	Unc
1661	—	1,200	2,400	4,550	9,100	—

KM# 73 DUCAT
3.5000 g., 0.9860 Gold 0.1109 oz. AGW **Ruler:** Wilhelm IV **Obv:** Arms of Henneberg-Ilmenau **Rev:** Five-line inscription **Note:** Fr.#3026.

Date	Mintage	VG	F	VF	XF	Unc
1661	—	1,200	2,400	4,550	9,100	—

KM# 36 2 DUCAT
7.0000 g., 0.9860 Gold 0.2219 oz. AGW **Ruler:** Wilhelm IV **Obv:** Bust of Wilhelm **Rev:** 4-line inscription on banner before military trophies, date at top **Mint:** Weimar **Note:** Fr.#3020. Prev. listed in Saxe-Middle-Weimer.

Date	Mintage	VG	F	VF	XF	Unc
1654	—	2,700	5,400	10,000	18,000	—

KM# 65b 2 DUCAT
Gold **Ruler:** Wilhelm IV **Obv:** Bust in circle turned slightly to left, date at top in margin **Obv. Legend:** D.G. WILHELM. DVX. SAX. IVL. CLIV. & MONT. **Rev:** 7-line inscription with date in chronogram **Rev. Inscription:** SIC BENE / WILHELMVS / FECIT FACIET / QVE BENE VLTRA. / VT RATA VERIF DVO / EST ELLOGIO / GENITRIX **Note:** Fr. #3024b.

Date	Mintage	VG	F	VF	XF	Unc
1658 Unique	—	—	—	—	—	—

Note: Künker Auction 68, 10-01, VF realized approximately $7,980.

KM# 75 2 DUCAT
Gold **Ruler:** Wilhelm IV **Obv:** Armored bust to right, legend in Gothic script **Rev:** Crown above 2 small ornate shields of arms divides date, 5-line inscription below **Note:** Fr. #3027.

Date	Mintage	VG	F	VF	XF	Unc
1661 Rare	—	—	—	—	—	—

KM# 65d 3 DUCAT
Gold **Ruler:** Wilhelm IV **Obv:** Armored bust turned slightly to right, date at top in margin **Obv. Legend:** D.G. WILHELM, DVX SAX. IVL. CLIV. ET MONT. **Rev:** View of courtyard of palace, Wilhelms=Burg in Gothic letters in ribbon above, 5-line inscription with chronogram below **Rev. Inscription:** SIC bene WILheLMVs feClt / faCletaVe VLtra / Vt rata VerIfLVo / est eLLogio / genItrIX **Note:** Fr. 3024d.

Date	Mintage	VG	F	VF	XF	Unc
1658 Rare	—	—	—	—	—	—

SAXE-EISENACH

(Sachsen-Eisenach)

One of the Ernestine Saxon duchies in Thuringia (Thüringen), Saxe-Eisenach was first ruled separately by one of eight brothers beginning in 1640. It reverted back to Saxe-Middle-Weimar in 1644, but a new line was established by the second son of Duke Wilhelm IV as Saxe-(New)-Weimar in 1622. This second line became extinct very shortly thereafter and Eisenach passed to Wilhelm IV's third son in 1671. Sayn-Altenkirchen (q.v.) was added to the duke's possessions through marriage in 1686. Again, the line passed out of existence and Eisenach was returned to Saxe-Weimar in 1741. See Saxe-Weimar-Eisenach for subsequent coinages.

RULERS

Albrecht II, 1640-1644
Adolph Wilhelm, 1662-1668
Johann Georg I, 1671-1686
Johann Georg II, 1686-1698
Johann Wilhelm, 1698-1729

MINT OFFICIALS' INITIALS

Initial	Date	Name
CW	1688-1739	Christian Wermuth, die-cutter in Gotha
HCM/HGM w/or w/o two crossed ingot hooks	1689-90	Heinrich Christian Müller
HD	1693-?	Hubertus Dönnigke
ICF	1692-93	Johann Carl Falkner
	1692-?	Johann Matthias Obermüller
IEK	1689-90	Johann Esaias Krauel (Grauel)
IGW	1683-90	Johann Gottfried Wichmannshausen in Gotha
SC	1700-01	Simon Conradi

DUCHY

REGULAR COINAGE

KM# 32 HELLER

Copper **Ruler:** Johann Wilhelm **Obv:** Crowned Saxony arms between palm branches **Rev. Inscription:** 1 / HELLER / F. E. L., date

Date	Mintage	VG	F	VF	XF	Unc
1700	—	13.00	27.00	55.00	110	—

KM# 33 2 PFENNIG (Leuchte)

Silver **Ruler:** Johann Wilhelm **Obv:** 3 small oval shields of arms, crown above **Rev. Inscription:** 2 / LEUCHTE / PFENN / F. E. L. M., date

Date	Mintage	VG	F	VF	XF	Unc
1700	—	12.00	27.00	55.00	115	—

KM# 34 3 PFENNIG (Dreier)

Silver **Ruler:** Johann Wilhelm **Obv:** Crowned script 'IW' monogram divides date **Rev:** Imperial orb with 3 **Rev. Legend:** NACH DEM LEIPZIGER FUS

Date	Mintage	VG	F	VF	XF	Unc
1700	—	30.00	60.00	125	250	—

KM# 15 GROSCHEN

Silver **Ruler:** Johann Georg I **Subject:** Death of Johann Georg I's Son, Friedrich August **Obv:** Bust left **Rev:** 6-line inscription, Roman numeral dates in legend

Date	Mintage	VG	F	VF	XF	Unc
MDCLXXXIV (1684)	—	30.00	60.00	150	240	—

KM# 35 GROSCHEN

Silver **Ruler:** Johann Wilhelm **Obv:** Bust right **Rev:** 4 small crowned shields of arms in cruciform divide date, 1/GROS in center circle **Rev. Legend:** NACH - LEIPZ - FUS

Date	Mintage	VG	F	VF	XF	Unc
1700 SC	—	25.00	50.00	100	210	—

KM# 36 GROSCHEN

Silver **Ruler:** Johann Wilhelm **Obv:** Bust left **Rev:** 4 small crowned shields of arms in cruciform divide date, 1/GROS in center circle **Rev. Legend:** NACH - DEM - LEIPZ - FUS

Date	Mintage	VG	F	VF	XF	Unc
1700 SC	—	25.00	50.00	100	210	—

KM# 26 1/12 THALER (Doppelgroschen)

Silver **Ruler:** Johann Georg II **Obv:** Arms of Saxony **Rev:** 12/EINEN, date

Date	Mintage	VG	F	VF	XF	Unc
1692	—	25.00	50.00	100	210	—
1693	—	25.00	50.00	100	210	—

KM# 27 1/6 THALER (1/4 Gulden)

Silver **Ruler:** Johann Georg II **Obv:** Bust right **Rev:** Crowned arms in center of 4 crowned IG monograms within palm branches forming quatrefoil, value 1/6 in oval below divided date

Date	Mintage	VG	F	VF	XF	Unc
1693 ICF	—	35.00	75.00	150	300	—
1694 HD	—	35.00	75.00	150	300	—

KM# 3 1/4 THALER

Silver **Ruler:** Albrecht II **Subject:** Death and Interment of Albrecht II **Obv:** Jehovah's name in rayed sun above palm sprays with W.H.Z.S. A.H.Z.S.E.H.Z.S. **Rev:** 8-line inscription

Date	Mintage	VG	F	VF	XF	Unc
1644-45	—	—	—	—	—	—

KM# 37 1/3 THALER (1/2 Gulden)

Silver **Ruler:** Johann Wilhelm **Obv:** Bust right **Rev:** 4 small crowned IW monograms with palm branches in cruciform, Saxony arms in center, value 1/3 in oval below divides date

Date	Mintage	VG	F	VF	XF	Unc
1700 SC	—	—	—	—	—	—

KM# 16 1/2 THALER

Silver **Ruler:** Johann Georg I **Subject:** Death of Johann Georg I's Son, Friedrich August **Obv:** Bust left **Rev:** 7-line inscription in palm wreath

Date	Mintage	VG	F	VF	XF	Unc
1684 IGW	—	—	—	—	—	—

KM# 13 2/3 THALER (Gulden)

Silver **Ruler:** Johann Georg I **Obv:** Crowned manifold arms with date **Rev:** 2/3 in wreath **Rev. Legend:** DOMINVS PROVIDEBIT **Note:** Dav. #839.

Date	Mintage	VG	F	VF	XF	Unc
1682	—	—	—	—	—	—

KM# 14 2/3 THALER (Gulden)

Silver **Ruler:** Johann Georg I **Obv:** Crowned manifold arms, titles of Johann Georg I **Rev:** Large 2/3 in circle **Rev. Legend:** DOMINVS PROVIDEBIT **Note:** Dav. #840.

Date	Mintage	VG	F	VF	XF	Unc
ND(ca.1682)	—	—	—	—	—	—

KM# 19 2/3 THALER (Gulden)

Silver **Ruler:** Johann Georg II **Obv:** Bust right **Rev:** Crowned and ornamented manifold arms, 2/3 in oval cartouche divides date below

Date	Mintage	VG	F	VF	XF	Unc
1689 IEK	—	95.00	190	385	—	—

KM# 20 2/3 THALER (Gulden)

Silver **Ruler:** Johann Georg II **Obv:** Bust right **Rev:** Crowned manifold arms in palm branches divide date, value 2/3 in oval below

Date	Mintage	VG	F	VF	XF	Unc
1690 HCM	—	45.00	75.00	150	300	—
1690 HGM	—	45.00	75.00	150	300	—

KM# 21 2/3 THALER (Gulden)

Silver **Ruler:** Johann Georg II **Obv:** Bust right within circle **Rev:** Crowned manifold arms in palm branches divide date, value 2/3 in oval below, all in circle

Date	Mintage	VG	F	VF	XF	Unc
1690 HGM	—	45.00	75.00	150	300	—

KM# 22 2/3 THALER (Gulden)

Silver **Ruler:** Johann Georg II **Obv:** Bust right **Rev:** Crowned manifold arms in palm branches , value 2/3 in oval below divides date

Date	Mintage	VG	F	VF	XF	Unc
1690 HCM	—	80.00	150	220	425	—

KM# 23 2/3 THALER (Gulden)

Silver **Ruler:** Johann Georg II **Obv:** Crowned ornate, intertwined JGS monogram, value 2/3 in center, date divided to upper left and right **Rev:** Sailing ship to right, FORTUNA & ZEPHYRO

Date	Mintage	VG	F	VF	XF	Unc
1690	—	—	—	—	—	—

KM# 25 2/3 THALER (Gulden)

Silver **Ruler:** Johann Georg II **Obv:** Bust right **Rev:** Crowned manifold arms in palm branches, date divided by value in oval at bottom **Note:** Dav. #844.

Date	Mintage	VG	F	VF	XF	Unc
1691	—	80.00	150	220	425	—

KM# 38 2/3 THALER (Gulden)

Silver **Ruler:** Johann Wilhelm **Obv:** Bust right **Rev:** 4 small crowned IW monograms within palm branches in cruciform, Saxony arms in center, value 2/3 in oval below divided date

Date	Mintage	VG	F	VF	XF	Unc
1700 SC	—	—	—	—	—	—

KM# 28 2/3 THALER

Silver **Ruler:** Johann Georg II **Obv:** Bust right **Rev:** Crowned arms in center of 4 crowned IG monograms within palm branches forming quatrefoil, value 2/3 in oval below divided date **Note:** Dav. #845.

Date	Mintage	VG	F	VF	XF	Unc
1693 ICF	—	75.00	150	300	—	—

KM# 4 THALER

Silver **Ruler:** Albrecht II **Subject:** Death and Interment of Albrecht II. **Obv:** Jehovah's name in rayed sun above palm sprays. **Obv. Legend:** W.H.Z.S., A.H.Z.S.E.H.Z.S. **Rev:** 8-line inscription. **Note:** Dav# 7414.

Date	Mintage	Good	VG	F	VF	XF
1645	—	550	1,100	2,200	4,600	7,400

KM# 5 THALER

Silver **Ruler:** Albrecht II **Subject:** Death and Interment of Albrecht II. **Obv:** Jehovah's name in rayed sun above bust of Albrecht, inner initials. **Obv. Legend:** A.H.Z.-S.I.C.V.B. **Note:** Dav# 7415.

Date	Mintage	Good	VG	F	VF	XF
1645	—	550	1,000	2,100	4,500	7,200

KM# 11 THALER

Silver **Ruler:** Adolph Wilhelm **Subject:** Death of Adolph Wilhelm **Obv:** Facing bust of Adolph Wilhelm **Rev:** 21-line inscription **Note:** Dav# 7416

Date	Mintage	VG	F	VF	XF	Unc
1668 Rare	—	—	—	—	—	—

KM# 17 THALER

Silver **Ruler:** Johann Georg I **Subject:** Death of Friedrich August, son of Johann Georg I **Obv:** Bust left **Rev:** Seven-line inscription **Note:** Dav# 7417.

Date	Mintage	VG	F	VF	XF	Unc
1684 IGW	—	1,100	2,200	4,600	7,400	—

KM# 18 THALER

Silver **Ruler:** Johann Georg I **Subject:** Death of Johann Georg I **Obv:** Bust right **Rev:** 24-line inscription **Note:** Dav# 7418.

Date	Mintage	VG	F	VF	XF	Unc
1686 Rare	—	—	—	—	—	—

KM# 30 THALER

Silver **Ruler:** Johann Georg II **Subject:** Death of Johann Georg II **Obv:** Bust right **Rev:** 23-line inscription **Note:** Dav# 7419.

Date	Mintage	VG	F	VF	XF	Unc
1698 Rare	—	—	—	—	—	—

KM# 6 1-1/4 THALER

Silver **Ruler:** Albrecht II **Subject:** Death and Interment of Albrecht II **Obv:** Jehovah's name in rayed sun above palm sprays w/initials. **Obv. Legend:** W.H.Z.S., A.H.Z.S., E.H.Z.S. **Rev:** 8-line inscription. **Note:** Dav# 7413.

Date	Mintage	VG	F	VF	XF	Unc
1645 Rare	—	—	—	—	—	—

KM# 7 1-1/4 THALER

Silver **Ruler:** Albrecht II **Subject:** Death and Interment of Albrecht II **Note:** Klippe. Dav#7413A.

Date	Mintage	VG	F	VF	XF	Unc
1645 Rare	—	—	—	—	—	—

TRADE COINAGE

KM# 8 DUCAT

3.5000 g., 0.9860 Gold 0.1109 oz. AGW **Ruler:** Albrecht II **Subject:** Death and Interment of Albrecht II **Obv:** Jehovah's name in rayed sun above bust, inner initials: A.H.Z.-S.I.C.V.B.

Date	Mintage	VG	F	VF	XF	Unc
1644-45 Rare	—	—	—	—	—	—

KM# 9 DUCAT

3.5000 g., 0.9860 Gold 0.1109 oz. AGW **Ruler:** Albrecht II **Subject:** Death and Interment of Albrecht II **Obv:** Jehovah's name in rayed sun above palm sprays with W.H.Z.S. A.H.Z.S.E.H.Z.S. **Rev:** 8-line inscription

Date	Mintage	VG	F	VF	XF	Unc
1644-45 Rare	—	—	—	—	—	—

KM# 39 DUCAT

3.5000 g., 0.9860 Gold 0.1109 oz. AGW **Ruler:** Johann Wilhelm **Obv:** Bust of Johann Wilhelm right **Rev:** Monograms in script letters

Date	Mintage	VG	F	VF	XF	Unc
1700 CW Rare	—	—	—	—	—	—

KM# 40 DUCAT

3.5000 g., 0.9860 Gold 0.1109 oz. AGW **Ruler:** Johann Wilhelm **Obv:** Bust of Johann Wilhelm right **Rev:** 4 crowned cruciform JW monograms with small oval arms of ducal Saxony in center **Note:** Fr# 2916.

Date	Mintage	VG	F	VF	XF	Unc
1700 CW	—	3,000	4,800	7,800	12,500	—

SAXE-JENA

(Sachsen-Jena)

As a branch of the Ernestine line of Saxony, the duchy of Saxe-Jena was established upon the division of Saxe-Weimar-Eisenach in 1662. The Saxe-Jena branch only lasted for two generations, becoming extinct in 1690, and its lands reverted to Saxe-Eisenach.

RULERS

Bernhard II, 1662-1678
Johann Wilhelm, 1678-1690

MINT OFFICIALS' INITIALS

Initials	Date	Name
ABC/ABK	1667-80	Anton Bernhard Koburger in Eisleben
HIW		Hans Jacob Wolrab, die-cutter in Nuremberg

REFERENCE

F = Lothar Frede, **Geld- und Münzwesen im Herzogtum Sachsen-Jena**, Jena, 1942.

DUCHY

REGULAR COINAGE

KM# 17 3 PFENNIG (Dreier)

Silver **Ruler:** Bernhard II **Subject:** Interment of Bernhard II **Obv:** Crowned oval arms of Saxony in baroque frame **Rev:** Six-line inscription with dates

Date	Mintage	VG	F	VF	XF	Unc
1678	—	—	—	—	—	—

KM# 25 3 PFENNIG (Dreier)

Silver **Ruler:** Johann Wilhelm **Subject:** Death of Marie, Wife of Bernhard II **Obv:** Crowned M, ribbons trailing down each side **Rev:** Seven-line inscription with dates

Date	Mintage	VG	F	VF	XF	Unc
1682	—	20.00	40.00	85.00	175	—

KM# 35 3 PFENNIG (Dreier)

Silver **Ruler:** Johann Wilhelm **Subject:** Interment of Johann Wilhelm III **Obv:** Intertwined JW monogram, crown above, cross below **Rev:** 6-line inscription with date

Date	Mintage	VG	F	VF	XF	Unc
1691	—	—	—	—	—	—

KM# 18 GROSCHEN (1/24 Thaler)

Silver **Ruler:** Bernhard II **Subject:** Interment of Bernhard II **Obv:** Crowned oval arms of Saxony in baroque frame **Rev:** Seven-line inscription with dates

Date	Mintage	VG	F	VF	XF	Unc
1678	—	65.00	125	250	475	—

KM# 26 GROSCHEN (1/24 Thaler)

Silver **Ruler:** Johann Wilhelm **Subject:** Death of Marie, Wife of Bernhard II **Obv:** Crowned M, ribbons trailing down each side **Rev:** Seven-line inscription with dates

Date	Mintage	VG	F	VF	XF	Unc
1682	—	40.00	80.00	160	325	—

KM# 30 GROSCHEN (1/24 Thaler)

Silver **Ruler:** Johann Wilhelm **Subject:** Acceptance of the Chancellorship of Jena University for Johann Wilhelm III **Obv:** Six-line inscription with date **Rev:** Six-line inscription with titles

Date	Mintage	VG	F	VF	XF	Unc
1688	—	30.00	65.00	135	275	—

KM# 36 GROSCHEN (1/24 Thaler)

Silver **Ruler:** Johann Wilhelm **Subject:** Interment of Johann Wilhelm III **Obv:** Crowned arms of Saxony, inscriptions above and below in arcs **Rev:** 9-line inscription, Roman numeral dates, titles in legend

Date	Mintage	VG	F	VF	XF	Unc
ND(1691)	—	24.00	45.00	90.00	185	—

KM# 5 1/8 THALER

Silver **Ruler:** Bernhard II **Subject:** Completion of Jena Palace **Obv:** Bust to right **Rev:** View of palace, date above, legend around

Date	Mintage	VG	F	VF	XF	Unc
1661	—	—	—	—	—	—

KM# 6 1/4 THALER

Silver **Ruler:** Bernhard II **Subject:** Completion of Jena Palace **Obv:** Bust to right **Rev:** View of palace, date above, legend around

Date	Mintage	VG	F	VF	XF	Unc
1661	—	—	—	—	—	—

KM# 19 1/4 THALER

Silver **Ruler:** Bernhard II **Subject:** Interment of Bernhard II **Obv:** Wigged bust right **Rev:** 9-line inscription, R.N., crown above

Date	Mintage	VG	F	VF	XF	Unc
ND(1678)	—	—	—	—	—	—

KM# 27 1/4 THALER

Silver **Ruler:** Johann Wilhelm **Subject:** Death of Marie, Wife of Bernhard II **Obv:** Bust turned 1/4 right, titles and date in legend **Rev:** Rectangular altar, 7-line inscription on side

Date	Mintage	VG	F	VF	XF	Unc
1682	—	90.00	160	275	575	—

KM# 31 1/4 THALER

Silver **Ruler:** Johann Wilhelm **Subject:** Acceptance of the Chancellorship of Jena University for Johann Wilhelm III **Obv:** Winged cadeuceus surmounted with crowned arms of Saxony, view of Jena in background, rays streaming from sun above, legend at sides **Obv. Legend:** TUETUR - ET ORNAT **Rev:** 9-line inscription with date

Date	Mintage	VG	F	VF	XF	Unc
1688	—	125	250	475	975	—

KM# 37 1/4 THALER

Silver **Ruler:** Johann Wilhelm **Subject:** Interment of Johann Wilhelm III **Obv:** Epitaph on tablet in five lines **Obv. Legend:** NON PERITVRA NECE **Rev:** 5-line inscription, R.N. dates within two palm branches

Date	Mintage	VG	F	VF	XF	Unc
ND(1691)	—	190	375	750	1,500	—

KM# 10 1/3 THALER (1/2 Gulden)

Silver **Ruler:** Bernhard II **Obv:** Bust right **Rev:** Crowned oval manifold arms, branches at sides, value 1/3 in oval below, date in legend **Mint:** Eisleben **Note:** Varieties exist.

Date	Mintage	VG	F	VF	XF	Unc
1673 ABK	—	225	400	800	1,600	—
1673 ABC	—	225	400	800	1,600	—
1674 ABC	—	225	400	800	1,600	—

KM# 20 1/2 THALER

Silver **Ruler:** Bernhard II **Subject:** Interment of Bernhard II **Obv:** Wigged bust right **Rev:** 10-line inscription, R.N. dates, crown above

Date	Mintage	VG	F	VF	XF	Unc
ND(1678)	—	—	—	—	—	—

KM# 28 1/2 THALER

Silver **Ruler:** Johann Wilhelm **Subject:** Death of Marie, Wife of Bernhard II **Obv:** Bust turned 1/4 right, titles and date in legend **Rev:** Rectangular seven-line inscription on side

Date	Mintage	VG	F	VF	XF	Unc
1682	—	—	—	—	—	—

KM# 32 1/2 THALER

Silver **Ruler:** Johann Wilhelm **Subject:** Acceptance of the Chancellorship of Jena University for Johann Wilhelm III **Obv:** Winged cadeuceus surmounted with crowned arms of Saxony, view of Jena in background, rays streaming from sun above, legend at sides **Obv. Legend:** TUETUR - ET ORNAT **Rev:** 9-line inscription with date **Mint:** Nürnberg

Date	Mintage	VG	F	VF	XF	Unc
1688 HIW	—	90.00	190	375	775	—

KM# 38 1/2 THALER

Silver **Ruler:** Johann Wilhelm **Subject:** Interment of Johann Wilhelm III **Obv:** Facing wigged bust, turned slightly to right **Rev:** 9-line inscription with R.N. date on tablet, crown above **Note:** Varieties exist.

Date	Mintage	VG	F	VF	XF	Unc
ND(1691)	—	250	425	750	1,500	—

KM# 11 2/3 THALER (Gulden)

Silver **Ruler:** Bernhard II **Obv:** Bust right in circle **Rev:** Crowned arms of Saxony between two branches, date at top, value 2/3 at bottom **Mint:** Eisleben **Note:** Varieties exist.

Date	Mintage	VG	F	VF	XF	Unc
1673 ABC	—	225	375	700	1,500	—
1674 ABC	—	225	375	700	1,500	—

KM# 16 2/3 THALER (Gulden)

Silver **Ruler:** Bernhard II **Obv:** Bust not in circle **Mint:** Eisleben **Note:** Varieties exist.

Date	Mintage	VG	F	VF	XF	Unc
1674 ABC	—	225	375	700	1,500	—

KM# 12 THALER

Silver **Ruler:** Bernhard II **Obv:** Bust right **Rev:** Crowned arms divide date and AB-C **Mint:** Eisleben **Note:** Dav. 7492.

Date	Mintage	VG	F	VF	XF	Unc
1673 ABC Rare	—	—	—	—	—	—

KM# 13 THALER

Silver **Ruler:** Bernhard II **Rev:** Date above crowned arms **Mint:** Eisleben **Note:** Dav. 7493.

Date	Mintage	VG	F	VF	XF	Unc
1673 ABK	—	2,500	5,000	9,000	15,000	—

KM# 14 THALER

Silver **Ruler:** Bernhard II **Rev:** Smaller letters, BANCO THALER added in inner row **Mint:** Eisleben **Note:** Dav. 7494.

Date	Mintage	VG	F	VF	XF	Unc
1673 ABK Rare	—	—	—	—	—	—

KM# 21 THALER

Silver **Ruler:** Bernhard II **Subject:** Interment of Bernhard II **Obv:** Bust right **Rev:** Eleven-line inscription **Note:** Dav. 7495.

Date	Mintage	VG	F	VF	XF	Unc
1678 Rare	—	—	—	—	—	—

KM# 29 THALER

Silver **Ruler:** Johann Wilhelm **Subject:** Death of Marie, Wife of Bernhard II **Obv:** Facing laureate bust, turned slightly to right **Rev:** Seven-line inscription on tablet with rope border **Note:** Dav. 7496.

Date	Mintage	VG	F	VF	XF	Unc
1682	—	1,250	2,500	4,750	8,500	—

KM# 33 THALER

Silver **Ruler:** Johann Wilhelm **Subject:** Acceptance of the Chancellorship of Jena University for Johann Wilhelm III **Obv:** Winged cadeuceus surmounted with crowned arms of Saxony, view of Jena in background, rays streaming from sun above, legend at sides **Obv. Legend:** TUETUR - ET ORNAT **Rev:** 9-line inscription with date **Note:** Varieties exist.

Date	Mintage	VG	F	VF	XF	Unc
1688	—	725	1,450	3,000	5,500	—

KM# 39 THALER

Silver **Ruler:** Johann Wilhelm **Subject:** Interment of Johann Wilhelm III **Obv:** Bust to right **Rev:** 10-line inscription with dates on tablet, crown above **Note:** Dav. 7497.

Date	Mintage	VG	F	VF	XF	Unc
1691	—	900	1,800	3,350	6,000	—

KM# 15 1-1/2 THALER

Silver **Ruler:** Bernhard II **Subject:** 35th Birthday of Bernhard II **Obv:** Two-masted ship sailing right towards rocks, 2-line inscription in curved band above **Rev:** 10-line inscription with R.N. date **Mint:** Eisleben

Date	Mintage	VG	F	VF	XF	Unc
ND(1673) ABK Rare	—	—	—	—	—	—

TRADE COINAGE

KM# A16 5 DUCAT

17.5000 g., 0.9860 Gold 0.5547 oz. AGW **Ruler:** Bernhard II **Obv:** Bust to right **Rev:** Crowned arms in sprays **Mint:** Eisleben **Note:** Struck with Thaler dies, KM#14.

Date	Mintage	VG	F	VF	XF	Unc
1673 ABK Unique	—	—	—	—	—	—

KM# B16 10 DUCAT

35.0000 g., 0.9860 Gold 1.1095 oz. AGW **Ruler:** Bernhard II **Subject:** 35th Birthday of Bernhard II **Obv:** 2-masted sailing ship right, two-line inscription in curved band above **Rev:** 10-line inscription, R.N. date **Mint:** Eisleben **Note:** Struck with 1-1/2 Thaler dies, KM#15.

Date	Mintage	VG	F	VF	XF	Unc
ND(1673) ABK Rare	—	—	—	—	—	—

PATTERNS

Including off metal strikes

KM#	Date	Mintage	Identification	Mkt Val
Pn1	1661	—	1/8 Thaler. Tin. KM#5	—
Pn2	1661	—	1/8 Thaler. Gold. KM#5	—

SAXE-NEW-GOTHA

(Sachsen-Neu-Gotha)

Short-lived branch of the Ernestine Saxon house which was created for Ernst III, 6th son of Johann III of Saxe-Middle-Weimar. When Ernst died in 1675 his seven sons ruled jointly until 1680 and then divided their holdings into seven ducal lines.

RULERS

Ernst I (III) the Pious, 1640-1675
Joint Rule of Seven Brothers, 1675-1680
- Friedrich I of Altenburg
- Albrecht III of Middle-Coburg
- Bernhard III of Meiningen
- Heinrich III of Römhild
- Christian of Eisenberg
- Ernst IV of Hildburghausen
- Johan Ernst VIII of Saalfeld

MINT OFFICIALS' INITIALS

Initials	Date	Name
MR	1630-73	Martin Reimann, mintmaster in Saalfeld
IB	Sept-Dec 1650	Johann Braun, mintmaster in Gotha
	ca. 1650-65	Wendel Elias Freund, die-cutter in Gotha
ICF	ca. 1665-75?	Johann Christian Freund, die-cutter in Gotha
ABK	1667-80	Anton Bernhard Koburger, mintmaster in Eisleben
	ca. 1675	Martin Müller, die-cutter in Zellerfeld
GFS	1677-80	Georg Friedrich Staude, mintmaster in Gotha
F	1688-90	Christian Fischer, warden in Gotha

DUCHY

REGULAR COINAGE

KM# 50 HELLER

Copper, 13-16 mm. **Ruler:** Ernst I **Obv:** Oval shield of ducal Saxony arms in baroque frame **Rev:** Rose stem divides Gothic C - H (= Coburger Heller) and date **Mint:** Gotha and Saalfeld **Note:** Ref. KOR#467-69. Coinage for Coburg. Varieties exist.

Date	Mintage	VG	F	VF	XF	Unc
1673	—	10.00	20.00	40.00	85.00	—
1674	—	10.00	20.00	40.00	85.00	—
1675	—	10.00	20.00	40.00	85.00	—

KM# 60.3 HELLER

Copper, 14-15 mm. **Ruler:** Friedrich I **Obv:** Oval shield of ducal Saxony arms in baroque frame **Rev:** 4-line inscription with date in Gothic letters **Rev. Inscription:** Co / burger / Heller / (date) **Mint:** Coburg **Note:** Ref. KOR#514-19. Varieties exist. Mintage numbers for 1676 and 1678 included with KM#61.1.

Date	Mintage	VG	F	VF	XF	Unc
1675	—	7.00	12.00	27.00	55.00	—
1676	—	7.00	12.00	27.00	55.00	—
1677	27,924	7.00	12.00	27.00	55.00	—
1678	—	7.00	12.00	27.00	55.00	—
1679	—	7.00	12.00	27.00	55.00	—
1680	—	7.00	12.00	27.00	55.00	—

KM# 60.1 HELLER

Copper, 14-15 mm. **Ruler:** Friedrich I **Obv:** Modified Spanish shield of ducal Saxony arms, legend around in Gothic letters, date at end of legend **Obv. Legend:** Coburger • Heller • (Ao •) (or AD) **Mint:** Gotha **Note:** Ref. KOR#521, 521b-27. Coinage for Coburg. Uniface. Varieties exist.

Date	Mintage	VG	F	VF	XF	Unc
1675	84,840	8.00	15.00	30.00	60.00	—
1676	108,284	8.00	15.00	30.00	60.00	—
1677	—	8.00	15.00	30.00	60.00	—
1678	25,068	8.00	15.00	30.00	60.00	—
1679	—	8.00	15.00	30.00	60.00	—
1680	—	8.00	15.00	30.00	60.00	—
1681	—	8.00	15.00	30.00	60.00	—

KM# 60.2 HELLER

Copper, 15 mm. **Ruler:** Friedrich I **Obv:** Shield of ducal Saxony arms, Gothic legend around **Obv. Legend:** Coburger Heller **Mint:** Gotha **Note:** Ref. KOR-520. Uniface.

Date	Mintage	Good	VG	F	VF	XF
ND(1675)	—	—	—	—	—	—

KM# 88 HELLER

Copper **Ruler:** Joint Rule **Obv:** Ornamented Saxony arms divide mintmaster's initials **Rev:** Flower divides script C - H (= Coburger Heller) and date **Mint:** Gotha **Note:** Coinage for Coburg. Mintage numbers included with KM#61.

Date	Mintage	VG	F	VF	XF	Unc
1678 GFS	—	8.00	15.00	30.00	60.00	—

KM# 52 PFENNIG

Billon **Ruler:** Ernst I **Obv:** Oval shield of ducal Saxony arms, date divided below **Rev:** 4-line inscription in Gothic letters **Rev. Inscription:** Gott givts, / Jesus erwirbts / der Glaube / nimbts G **Mint:** Gotha **Note:** Ref. KOR-463, 466. Coinage for Coburg.

Date	Mintage	VG	F	VF	XF	Unc
1673	—	25.00	50.00	100	210	—
1675	—	25.00	50.00	100	210	—

KM# 51 PFENNIG

Copper, 13-15 mm. **Ruler:** Ernst I **Obv:** Oval shield of ducal Saxony arms in baroque frame **Rev:** Rose stem divides Gothic C - H (= Coburger Heller) and date **Mint:** Gotha and Saalfeld **Note:** Ref. KOR-464, 465. Coinage for Coburg. Struck on thick flan from Heller dies, KM#50.

Date	Mintage	VG	F	VF	XF	Unc
1673	—	10.00	20.00	45.00	90.00	—
1674	—	10.00	20.00	45.00	90.00	—

KM# 89 PFENNIG

Billon, 13 mm. **Ruler:** Friedrich I **Obv:** Crowned F in palm branches, date divided below **Rev:** Oval shield of ducal Saxony arms, (1) in oval below divides mintmaster's initials **Mint:** Gotha **Note:** Ref. KOR#511-13. Coinage for Coburg.

Date	Mintage	VG	F	VF	XF	Unc
1678 GFS	—	12.00	25.00	55.00	110	—
1679 GFS	—	12.00	25.00	55.00	110	—
ND(1680) GFS	—	12.00	25.00	55.00	110	—

KM# 98 PFENNIG

Billon **Ruler:** Joint Rule **Obv:** Oval shield of ducal Saxony arms in baroque frame **Rev:** Imperial orb with 1 divides date and mintmaster's initials **Mint:** Gotha **Note:** Coinage for Coburg.

Date	Mintage	VG	F	VF	XF	Unc
1680 GFS	—	15.00	30.00	60.00	125	—

KM# 53 2 PFENNIG (Zweier)

Billon, 15 mm. **Ruler:** Ernst I **Obv:** Oval shield of ducal Saxony arms in baroque frame, princely crown above, value 2 - (symbol for Pfennig) below **Rev:** 6-line inscription in Gothic letters, with date **Rev. Inscription:** Das / Heÿl gott gibt, / Jesus erwirbt / der Glaube / nimbt Goth / (date) **Mint:** Gotha **Note:** Ref. KOR-461.2, 462.

Date	Mintage	VG	F	VF	XF	Unc
1673	—	35.00	75.00	150	300	—
1675	—	35.00	75.00	150	300	—

KM# 54 2 PFENNIG (Zweier)

Billon, 15 mm. **Ruler:** Ernst I **Obv:** Oval shield of ducal Saxony arms in baroque frame, princely crown above, value (2) in circle at bottom **Rev:** 6-line inscription in Gothic letters, with date **Rev. Inscription:** Das / Haÿl gott givt, / Jesus erwirbt / der Glaube / nimbt Goth / (date) **Mint:** Gotha **Note:** Ref. KOR-461.1.

Date	Mintage	VG	F	VF	XF	Unc
1673	—	10.00	20.00	45.00	90.00	—

KM# 100 2 PFENNIG (Zweier)

Billon **Ruler:** Joint Rule **Obv:** Oval Saxony arms in baroque frame **Rev:** Imperial orb with 2 divides date and mintmaster's initials **Mint:** Gotha

Date	Mintage	VG	F	VF	XF	Unc
1680 GFS	—	10.00	25.00	50.00	100	—

KM# 99 2 PFENNIG (Zweier)

Billon, 14-15 mm. **Ruler:** Friedrich I **Obv:** Crowned F in palm branches, date divided below **Rev:** Oval shield of ducal Saxony arms, (2) in oval below divides mintmaster's initials **Mint:** Gotha **Note:** Ref. KOR-510.

Date	Mintage	VG	F	VF	XF	Unc
1680 GFS	—	10.00	25.00	50.00	100	—

KM# 90 3 PFENNIG (Dreier)

Billon, 17-18 mm. **Ruler:** Friedrich I **Obv:** Crowned F monogram between 2 palm branches, date divided below **Rev:** Oval shield of ducal Saxony arms, (3) in oval below divides mintmaster's initials **Mint:** Gotha **Note:** Ref. KOR#506-509. Varieties exist.

Date	Mintage	VG	F	VF	XF	Unc
1678 GFS	—	15.00	30.00	60.00	125	—
ND(1678-9) GFS	—	15.00	30.00	60.00	125	—
1679 GFS	—	15.00	30.00	60.00	125	—
1680 GFS	—	15.00	30.00	60.00	125	—

KM# 101 3 PFENNIG (Dreier)

Billon **Ruler:** Joint Rule **Obv:** Arms, date divided below **Rev:** Saxony arms, '3' in oval below divides mintmaster's initials **Mint:** Gotha

Date	Mintage	VG	F	VF	XF	Unc
1680	—	15.00	30.00	60.00	125	—

KM# 102 3 PFENNIG (Dreier)

Billon **Ruler:** Joint Rule **Obv:** Oval Saxony arms in baroque frame **Rev:** Imperial orb with 3 divides date and mintmaster's initials **Mint:** Gotha

Date	Mintage	VG	F	VF	XF	Unc
1680 GFS	—	15.00	30.00	60.00	125	—

KM# 3 1/24 THALER (Groschen)

Silver **Ruler:** Ernst I **Subject:** Peace of Westphalia **Obv:** Small Saxony arms between palm branches above 5-line inscription **Rev:** Small imperial orb with 24 divides date above 6-line inscription **Mint:** Gotha

Date	Mintage	VG	F	VF	XF	Unc
1650 IB	15,000	35.00	65.00	135	275	—

KM# 20 1/24 THALER (Groschen)

Silver **Ruler:** Ernst I **Subject:** Death of Ernst's Son, Johann Ernst **Obv:** IESVS in rays above 5-line inscription in flaming heart, titles around **Rev:** Ornate crowned Saxony arms, 2 inscriptions around with R.N. dates **Mint:** Gotha

Date	Mintage	VG	F	VF	XF	Unc
1657 (MDCLVII)	—	—	—	—	—	—

KM# 61 1/24 THALER (Groschen)

Silver, 24 mm. **Ruler:** Joint Rule **Subject:** Death of Ernst I, the Pious **Obv:** Draped bust to right **Obv. Legend:** D. G. ERNESTUS SAX IUL. CL. & MONT. DUX. **Rev:** 10-line inscription with dates **Rev. Inscription:** NATUS / AO: 1601. D. 25. / DECEMBR: / DENATUS / 1675. D. 26. MARTII / REGIMINIS. 35. / ÆTAT. 73. MENS. 3. D. I. / HUMATUS / D: 4. JUNY. D: / A: 1675. **Mint:** Gotha **Note:** Ref. KOR-484. Struck from Ducat dies, KM#73.

Date	Mintage	VG	F	VF	XF	Unc
1675	—	—	—	—	—	—

KM# 62 1/24 THALER (Groschen)

Silver, 22 mm. **Ruler:** Joint Rule **Subject:** Death of Ernst I, the Pious **Obv:** Draped and armored bust to right **Obv. Legend:** D. G. ERNEST, S. I. CL. &. MONT. D. **Rev:** 9-line inscription with dates **Rev. Legend:** LANDG. THUR. MARCH. MIS. PR. H. COM. MAR. & R. DYN. IN RAV. **Rev. Inscription:** NATUS / 1601. 25 DEC. / DENATUS / 1675. D. 26. MART. / REGIMINIS 35. / ÆTAT. 73. M. 3. DI. / HUMAT. / D. 4. JUNII / 1675. **Mint:** Gotha **Note:** Ref. KOR-483.

Date	Mintage	VG	F	VF	XF	Unc
1675	6,728	25.00	50.00	100	175	325

KM# 83 1/24 THALER (Groschen)

Silver, 22-23 mm. **Ruler:** Friedrich I **Obv:** Crowned oval shield of ducal Saxony arms in baroque frame, between 2 palm branches **Rev:** 5-line inscription in Gothic letters, value 24 in oval divides date below **Rev. Inscription:** Fürstl. S. / Gotha. Alten / burg. und Co / burger Land / muntze. / (date) **Mint:** Gotha **Note:** Ref. KOR-502, 503. Varieties exist.

Date	Mintage	VG	F	VF	XF	Unc
1677 GFS	—	12.00	25.00	55.00	110	—
1678 GFS	—	12.00	25.00	55.00	110	—

KM# 84 1/24 THALER (Groschen)

Silver, 23 mm. **Ruler:** Friedrich I **Obv:** Crowned F between 2 palm branches, 24 in oval below **Obv. Legend:** AD ASPRA - PER ASTRA. **Rev:** Oval shield of ducal Saxony arms in baroque frame, mintmaster's initials below **Rev. Legend:** F. S. GOTHA. ALTENB. U. COB. L. M. **Mint:** Gotha **Note:** Ref. KOR-504, 505. Varieties exist.

Date	Mintage	VG	F	VF	XF	Unc
1678 GFS	—	25.00	50.00	100	210	—
ND(1678-9) GFS	—	25.00	50.00	100	210	—

KM# 103 1/24 THALER (Groschen)

Silver **Ruler:** Friedrich I **Obv:** Oval 4-fold arms in baroque frame, titles of Friedrich I **Rev:** Imperial orb with 24 divides date and mintmaster's initials **Rev. Legend:** NACH. DEM. OBER. SACHS. CREYS. SCHLUS. **Mint:** Gotha

Date	Mintage	VG	F	VF	XF	Unc
1680 GFS	—	20.00	40.00	80.00	160	—

KM# 63 1/12 THALER (Doppelgroschen)

Silver, 25 mm. **Ruler:** Joint Rule **Subject:** Death of Ernst I, the Pious **Obv:** Draped bust to right **Obv. Legend:** D. G. ERNESTUS. SAX. IUL. CL & MONT. DUX. **Rev:** 10-line inscription with dates **Rev. Inscription:** NATUS / AO: 1601. D. 25. DECEMBR: / DENATUS / 1675. D. 26. MARTII / REGIMINIS. 35. / ÆTAT. 73. MENS. 3. D. I. / HUMATUS / D: 4. JUNY. D: / A: 1675. **Mint:** Gotha **Note:** Ref. KOR-482.

Date	Mintage	VG	F	VF	XF	Unc
1675	—	—	—	—	—	—

KM# 4 1/4 THALER

Silver **Ruler:** Ernst I **Subject:** Peace of Westphalia **Obv:** Saxon arms divide date **Rev:** 5-line inscription, Hebrew letters in sun above **Mint:** Gotha **Note:** Dav#7442, 7444. Struck in 1672-75.

Date	Mintage	VG	F	VF	XF	Unc
1650	—	—	—	—	—	—

KM# 64 1/4 THALER

Silver, 30 mm. **Ruler:** Joint Rule **Subject:** Death of Ernst I, the Pious **Obv:** Draped and armored bust to right **Obv. Legend:** D: G: ERNESTUS SAX IUL: CLIV: ET MONTIUM DUX. **Rev:** 10-line inscription with dates **Rev. Inscription:** NATUS / AO. 1601. D: 25 / DECEMBR: / DENATUS / 1675. D. 26. MARTII / REGIMINIS. 35 / ÆTAT: 73 MENS. 3. D. I / HUMATUS / D: 4. JUNY D: / A 1675. **Mint:** Gotha **Note:** Ref. KOR-481.

Date	Mintage	VG	F	VF	XF	Unc
1675	—	165	325	600	1,200	—

KM# 85 1/3 THALER (1/2 Gulden)
Silver, 34 mm. **Ruler:** Friedrich I **Obv:** Crowned shield of manifold arms, with central shield of ducal Saxony, divides mintmaster's initials and date, (1/3) in oval below **Obv. Legend:** FRIEDERICUS. DUX. SAX - IUL. CLIV. ET. MONTIUM. **Rev:** Crowned F between 2 palm branches, 4 small shields of arms in margin divide legend **Rev. Legend:** PER - ASPERA - AD - ASTRA **Mint:** Gotha **Note:** Ref. KOR-498.

Date	Mintage	VG	F	VF	XF	Unc
1677 GFS	—	—	—	—	—	—

KM# 91 1/3 THALER (1/2 Gulden)
Silver, 33 mm. **Ruler:** Friedrich I **Obv:** Crowned shield of manifold arms, with central shield of ducal Saxony, divides mintmaster's initials and date, (1/3) in oval below **Obv. Legend:** FRIEDERIC. DUX. SA - X. IUL. CLIV. ET MON. **Rev:** Crowned F between 2 palm branches, 4 small shields of arms in margin divide legend **Rev. Legend:** PER - ASPERA - AD - ASTRA. **Mint:** Gotha **Note:** Ref. KOR-499.

Date	Mintage	VG	F	VF	XF	Unc
1678 GFS	—	—	—	—	—	—

KM# 92 1/3 THALER (1/2 Gulden)
Silver, 32 mm. **Ruler:** Friedrich I **Obv:** Crowned ornate shield of 4-fold arms, with central shield of ducal Saxony, divides date and mintmaster's initials, (1/3) in oval below **Obv. Legend:** FRIDERIC: DUX. - SAX. IUL. CL. ET. M. **Rev:** Crowned F between two palm branches, 4 small shields of arms divide legend **Rev. Legend:** PER - ASPERA - AD - ASTRA. **Mint:** Gotha **Note:** Ref. KOR-500.

Date	Mintage	VG	F	VF	XF	Unc
1678 GFS	—	—	—	—	—	—

KM# 94 1/3 THALER (1/2 Gulden)
Silver, 32 mm. **Ruler:** Friedrich I **Obv:** Crowned shield of manifold arms, with central shield of ducal Saxony, divides date and mintmaster's initials, (1/3) in oval below **Obv. Legend:** FRIDERIC: D: G: DUX - SAX: IUL: CL: ET: M: **Rev:** Crowned F between 2 palm branches, 4 small shields of arms in margin divide legend **Rev. Legend:** PER - ASPERA - AD - ASTRA. **Mint:** Gotha **Note:** Ref. KOR-501.

Date	Mintage	VG	F	VF	XF	Unc
1679 GFS	—	—	—	—	—	—

KM# 5 1/2 THALER
Silver **Ruler:** Ernst I **Subject:** Peace of Westphalia **Obv:** Saxon arms divide date **Rev:** 5-line inscription, Hebrew letters in sun above **Mint:** Gotha **Note:** Struck in 1672-75 on thin flan from same dies.

Date	Mintage	VG	F	VF	XF	Unc
1650	—	—	—	—	—	—

KM# 65 1/2 THALER
Silver, 30 mm. **Ruler:** Joint Rule **Subject:** Death of Ernst I, the Pious **Obv:** Draped and armored bust to right **Obv. Legend:** D: G: ERNESTUS SAX IUL: CLIV: ET MONTIUM DUX. **Rev:** 10-line inscription with dates **Rev. Inscription:** NATUS / AO. 1601. D: 25 / DECEMBR: / DENATUS / 1675. D. 26. MARTII / REGIMINIS. 35 / ÆTAT: 73 MENS. 3. D. I / HUMATUS / D: 4. JUNY D: / A 1675. **Mint:** Gotha **Note:** Ref. KOR-480. Struck on thick flan with 1/4 Thaler dies, KM#64.

Date	Mintage	VG	F	VF	XF	Unc
1675	—	—	—	—	—	—

KM# 55 2/3 THALER (Gulden)
Silver, 39 mm. **Ruler:** Friedrich I **Obv:** Crowned shield of 4-fold arms divides date and mintmaster's initials **Obv. Legend:** FRIDERICUS. D. G. DUX. SAX - IUL. CLIV. ET. MONTIUM **Rev:** 4-line inscription within 2 palm branches **Rev. Inscription:** CHI S' ARMA / DI VERTU VIN / CE OGNI / FORZA **Mint:** Saalfeld **Note:** Ref. KOR-490; Dav. 853.

Date	Mintage	VG	F	VF	XF	Unc
1673 MR	—	—	—	—	—	—

KM# 66 2/3 THALER (Gulden)
Silver, 38-39 mm. **Ruler:** Friedrich I **Obv:** Crowned shield of manifold arms, with central shield of ducal Saxony, divides date, (2/3) in oval below. **Obv. Legend:** FRIDERIC(US). (D.G.) DUX. (-) SAX(ON)(IÆ) - I(UL)(II). C(LIVII). (ET.) (&.) MONT(IUM). **Rev:** Crowned F between 2 palm branches, 4 small shields of arms in margin divide legend **Rev. Legend:** PER - ASPERA - AD - ASTRA. **Mint:** Gotha **Note:** Ref. KOR-491, 492; Dav. 854. Varieties exist.

Date	Mintage	VG	F	VF	XF	Unc
1675	365	—	—	—	—	—
1676	86	—	—	—	—	—
1676 GFS	Inc. above	—	—	—	—	—

KM# 87 2/3 THALER (Gulden)
Silver, 38-39 mm. **Ruler:** Friedrich I **Obv:** Shield of 4-fold arms, with central shield of ducal Saxony, divides date **Obv. Legend:** FRIDERIC: D(U)(V)X - SAX. I(UL). C(L). ET. M. **Rev:** Crowned F between 2 palm branches, 4 small shields of arms in margin divide legend **Rev. Legend:** PER - ASPERA - AD - ASTRA. **Mint:** Gotha **Note:** Ref. KOR-493, 497; Dav. 856. Varieties exist. The 1679 date was struck until the end of 1690.

Date	Mintage	VG	F	VF	XF	Unc
1678 GFS	—	35.00	75.00	150	300	—
1679	—	35.00	75.00	150	300	—

KM# 93 2/3 THALER (Gulden)
Silver, 37-39 mm. **Ruler:** Friedrich I **Obv:** Crowned shield of manifold arms, with central shield of ducal Saxony, divides date and mintmaster's intials, where present, (2/3) in oval below **Obv. Legend:** FRIDERIC. D. G. DUX - SAX. IUL. CL. ET. M. **Rev:** Crowned F between 2 palm branches, 4 small shields of arms in margin divide legend **Rev. Legend:** PER - ASPERA - AD - ASTRA. **Mint:** Gotha **Note:** Ref. KOR-494, 495. Dav. 855. Varieties exist. The 1678 date was struck until the end of 1690.

Date	Mintage	VG	F	VF	XF	Unc
1678	—	35.00	75.00	150	300	—
1679 GFS	—	35.00	75.00	150	300	—

KM# 95 2/3 THALER (Gulden)
Silver, 36 mm. **Ruler:** Friedrich I **Obv:** Crowned ornate shield of manifold arms, with central shield of ducal Saxony, divides date and mintmaster's intials, (2/3) in oval below **Obv. Legend:** FRIDERIC: D: G. DUX - SAX IUL. CL: ET M: **Rev:** 4-line inscription within laurel and palm branches **Rev. Inscription:** NACH / DEM OBER / SACH: CREIS / SCHLUS. **Mint:** Gotha **Note:** Ref. KOR-496; Dav. 857.

Date	Mintage	VG	F	VF	XF	Unc
1679 GFS	—	—	—	—	—	—

KM# 104 2/3 THALER (Gulden)
Silver **Ruler:** Joint Rule **Obv:** Bust right **Rev:** Inscription in laurel and palm branches **Rev. Legend:** NACH / DEM OBER / SACH. CREIS / SCHLUS **Mint:** Saalfeld **Note:** Dav#858.

Date	Mintage	VG	F	VF	XF	Unc
1680 GFS	—	—	—	—	—	—

KM# 32 3/4 THALER
Silver **Ruler:** Ernst I **Subject:** On the Catechism **Obv:** Three lines around sun, nine beams radiating from the sun with qualities of God **Rev:** 10-line inscription **Mint:** Eisleben **Note:** Struck on thin flan from Thaler dies, KM#23.

Date	Mintage	VG	F	VF	XF	Unc
1671 ABK Rare	—	—	—	—	—	—

KM# 34 3/4 THALER
Silver **Ruler:** Ernst I **Subject:** Baptism of Friedrich I's Second Daughter **Obv:** Baptism scene with eleven-line inscription in field **Rev:** 10-line inscription **Mint:** Eisleben **Note:** Struck on thin flan from Thaler dies, KM#36.

Date	Mintage	VG	F	VF	XF	Unc
1671 ABK Rare	—	—	—	—	—	—

KM# 33 3/4 THALER
Silver **Ruler:** Ernst I **Subject:** On the Catechism **Obv:** JESUS in sun above crown, inverted heart with eight-line inscription **Rev:** 10-line inscription **Mint:** Eisleben **Note:** Struck on thin flan from Thaler dies, M#24.

Date	Mintage	VG	F	VF	XF	Unc
1671 ABK Rare	—	—	—	—	—	—

KM# 6 THALER
Silver **Ruler:** Ernst I **Subject:** Peace of Westphalia **Obv:** Saxon arms divide date **Rev:** 5-line inscription, Hebrew letters in sun above **Note:** Dav. #7442. Struck in 1672-75.

Date	Mintage	VG	F	VF	XF	Unc
1650	—	240	475	850	1,450	—

KM# 7 THALER
Silver **Ruler:** Ernst I **Subject:** Peace of Westphalia **Obv:** Saxon arms divide date **Rev:** 4-line inscription, Hebrew letters in sun above **Note:** Dav. #7444. Struck in 1672-75.

Date	Mintage	VG	F	VF	XF	Unc
1650	—	240	475	850	1,450	—

KM# 21 THALER
Silver **Ruler:** Ernst I **Subject:** Death of Johann Ernst, Son of Ernst **Obv:** JE-SVS, 4-line inscription within heart **Rev:** Crowned oval shield of ducal Saxony arms, double legend **Note:** Dav. #7445.

Date	Mintage	VG	F	VF	XF	Unc
MDCLVII (1657)	—	450	850	1,400	2,400	—

KM# 23 THALER

Silver **Ruler:** Ernst I **Subject:** The Catechism **Obv:** Three lines of text around sun, nine sun rays, each with a quality of God **Rev:** 10-line inscription **Mint:** Gotha **Note:** Dav. #7447.

Date	Mintage	VG	F	VF	XF	Unc
1668 ICF	258	240	475	850	1,450	—
1671 ABK	—	240	475	850	1,450	—

KM# 24 THALER

Silver **Ruler:** Ernst I **Obv:** JESUS in sun above crown, inverted heart with eight-line inscription **Rev:** 10-line inscription **Mint:** Gotha **Note:** Dav. #7448.

Date	Mintage	VG	F	VF	XF	Unc
1668	204	280	575	1,000	1,700	—
1671 ABK	1,300	280	575	1,000	1,700	—

KM# 25 THALER

Silver **Ruler:** Ernst I **Subject:** Marriage of Friedrich and Magdalena Sybilla **Obv:** "JEHOVAH" with rays descending on wedding couple **Rev:** 12-line inscription **Note:** Dav. #7449.

Date	Mintage	VG	F	VF	XF	Unc
1669	747	265	475	775	1,400	—

KM# 27 THALER

Silver **Ruler:** Ernst I **Subject:** Baptism of Princess Anna Sophia, Oldest Daughter of Prince Friedrich **Obv:** Baptismal scene with twelve-line inscription in field **Rev:** Ten-line inscription **Note:** Dav. #7450.

Date	Mintage	VG	F	VF	XF	Unc
1670	—	325	600	950	1,700	—

KM# 35 THALER

Silver **Ruler:** Ernst I **Subject:** Marriage of Bernhard and Maria Hedwig **Obv:** "JEHOVAH" with rays descending on wedding couple **Rev:** 12-line inscription **Mint:** Eisleben **Note:** Dav. #7451.

Date	Mintage	VG	F	VF	XF	Unc
1671 ABK	700	265	475	775	1,400	—

KM# 36 THALER

Silver **Ruler:** Ernst I **Subject:** Baptism of Daughter of Prince Friedrich **Obv:** Baptism scene with eleven-line inscription in field **Rev:** 10-line inscription **Mint:** Eisleben **Note:** Dav. #7453.

Date	Mintage	VG	F	VF	XF	Unc
1671 ABK	—	240	475	1,000	1,800	—

KM# 44 THALER

Silver **Ruler:** Ernst I **Subject:** The "Happiness" Thaler **Obv:** 11-line inscription **Rev:** 10-line inscription **Note:** Dav. #A7454.

Date	Mintage	VG	F	VF	XF	Unc
1672	405	230	450	850	1,400	—

KM# 45 THALER

Silver **Ruler:** Ernst I **Subject:** The "Happiness" Thaler **Obv:** Considerable modifications **Rev:** Considerable modifications **Note:** Dav. #B7454. Mintage included with KM#44.

Date	Mintage	VG	F	VF	XF	Unc
1672	—	350	725	1,450	2,400	—

KM# 56 THALER

Silver, 45 mm. **Ruler:** Friedrich I **Subject:** Transfer of Rule over Altenburg to Friedrich I in 1672 **Obv:** Large crowned Spanish shield of manifold arms, with central shield of ducal Saxony, divides mintmaster's initials, date above **Obv. Legend:** FRIDERICUS. D. G. DUX. SAXON. IULIÆ. CLIVIÆ. ET. MONTIUM. **Rev:** Man in center of landscape, inscription in band to left above man's head **Rev. Inscription:** DUC ME SEQVAR **Mint:** Saalfeld **Note:** Ref. KOR-488; Dav. 7459 prev. listed in Saxe-Gotha-Altenburg.

Date	Mintage	VG	F	VF	XF	Unc
1673 MR	—	475	950	1,800	3,000	—

KM# 67 THALER

Silver, 42 mm. **Ruler:** Joint Rule **Subject:** Death of Ernst I, the Pious **Obv:** Draped and armored bust to right **Obv. Legend:** D. G. ERNEST. SAX. IUL. CLIV. ET. MONTIUM. DUX. **Rev:** 9-line inscription with dates, 19 small shields of arms around, one at top is ducal Saxony, with princely crown **Rev. Legend:** LANDG. THUR. MARCH. MISN. PRINC. HEN. COM. MAR. ET RAV. DYN IN RAVENST. **Rev. Inscription:** NATUS / 1601. 25. DECEM. / DENATUS. / 1675. 26. MARTII / REGIMINIS 35. / ÆTAT. 73.

MENS. 3. D. I / HUMATUS / D. 4. JUNII 1675. / GOTHA. **Mint:** Gotha **Note:** Ref. KOR-478; Dav. 7455.

Date	Mintage	VG	F	VF	XF	Unc
1675	—	210	350	600	1,000	—

KM# 68 THALER

Silver, 49-50 mm. **Ruler:** Joint Rule **Subject:** Death of Ernst I, the Pious **Obv:** Draped and armored bust to right **Obv. Legend:** D: G: ERNESTUS SAX: IUL: CLIV: ET MONTIUM DUX. **Rev:** 9-line inscription with dates, 19 small shields of arms around, one at top is larger, crowned shield of ducal Saxony arms **Rev. Legend:** LANDG: THUR: MARCH: MISN: PRINC: HEN: COM: MAR: & RAV: DYNAST: IN(:) RAVE(N). **Rev. Inscription:** NATUS / 1601. 25. DECEMBR(.) / DENATUS / 1675. D. 26. MARTII / REGIMINIS. 35(.) / ÆTAT: 73. MENS. 3. D. I. / HUMATUS / D: 4(.) JUNY(.) D: / A: 1675. **Mint:** Gotha **Note:** Ref. KOR-479; Dav. 7458. Varieties exist.

Date	Mintage	VG	F	VF	XF	Unc
1675	—	250	450	825	1,800	3,300

KM# 96.1 THALER

Silver, 51 mm. **Ruler:** Friedrich I **Subject:** Investiture of Friedrich I with the Danish Order of the Elephant **Obv:** Draped and armored bust to right **Obv. Legend:** D. G. FRIDERIC. - DVX. SAX. I. C. ET. M. **Rev:** Crowned ornate manifold arms, with central shield of ducal Saxony, in baroque frame, divides date, Order of Elephant suspended below divides mintmaster's initials **Rev. Legend:** PER ASPERA - AD ASTRA. **Mint:** Gotha **Note:** Ref. KOR-489.1.

Date	Mintage	VG	F	VF	XF	Unc
1679 GFS	—	—	—	—	—	—

KM# 96.2 THALER

Silver, 51 mm. **Ruler:** Friedrich I **Subject:** Investiture of Friedrich I with Danish Order of the Elephant **Obv:** Draped and armored bust to right **Obv. Legend:** D. G. FRIDERIC. - DVX. SAX. I. C. ET. M. **Rev:** Crowned ornate manifold arms, with central shield of ducal Saxony, in baroque frame, divides mintmaster's initials, Order of Elephant suspended below divides date **Rev. Legend:** PER ASPERA - AD ASTRA. **Mint:** Gotha **Note:** Ref. KOR-489.2.

Date	Mintage	VG	F	VF	XF	Unc
1679 GFS Rare	—	—	—	—	—	—

KM# 37 1-1/2 THALER

Silver **Ruler:** Ernst I **Subject:** Marriage of Bernhard III and Maria Hedwig von Hessen-Darmstadt **Obv:** "JEHOVAH" with rays descending on wedding couple **Rev:** 12-line inscription **Mint:** Eisleben **Note:** Struck from same Thaler dies, KM#35.

Date	Mintage	VG	F	VF	XF	Unc
1671 ABK Rare	—	—	—	—	—	—

KM# 38 1-1/2 THALER

Silver **Ruler:** Ernst I **Subject:** Baptism of Friedrich I's Second Daughter **Obv:** Baptism scene with eleven-line inscription in field **Rev:** 10-line inscription **Mint:** Eisleben **Note:** Struck from same Thaler dies, KM#36.

Date	Mintage	VG	F	VF	XF	Unc
1671 ABK Rare	—	—	—	—	—	—

KM# 69.1 1-1/2 THALER

Silver, 53 mm. **Ruler:** Joint Rule **Subject:** Death of Ernst I, the Pious **Obv:** Draped and armored bust to right **Obv. Legend:** D: G: ERNESTUS SAX: IUL: CLIV: ET MONTIUM DUX. **Rev:** 9-line inscription with dates, 19 small shields of arms around, one at top larger, crowned shield of ducal Saxony arms **Rev. Legend:** LANDG: THUR: MARCH: MISN: PRINC: HEN: COM: MAR: & RAV: DYNAST: IN: RAVE: **Rev. Inscription:** NATUS / 1601. 25. DECEMBR. / DENATUS / 1675. D: 26. MARTII / REGIMINIS. 35 / ÆTAT: 73. MENS. 3. D: I. / HUMATUS / D: 4. JUNY D: / A: 1675. **Mint:** Gotha **Note:** Ref. KOR-477.1; Dav. 7457. Struck from Thaler dies, KM#68.

Date	Mintage	VG	F	VF	XF	Unc
1675 Rare	—	—	—	—	—	—

KM# 69.2 1-1/2 THALER

Silver, 53 mm. **Ruler:** Joint Rule **Subject:** Death of Ernst I, the Pious **Obv:** Draped and armored bust to right **Obv. Legend:** D: G: ERNESTUS SAX: IUL: CLIV: ET. MONTIUM. DX. **Rev:** 9-line inscription with dates, 19 small shields of arms around, one at top larger, crowned shield of ducal Saxony arms **Rev. Legend:** LANDG: THUR: MARCH: MISN: PRINC: HEN: COM: MAR: & RAV: DYNAST: IN: RAVE: **Rev. Inscription:** NATUS / 1601. 25. DECEMBR. / DENATUS / 1675. D: 26. MARTII / REGIMINIS. 35 / ÆTAT: 73. MENS. 3. D: I. / HUMATUS / D: 4. JUNY D: / A: 1675. **Mint:** Gotha **Note:** Ref. KOR-477.2.

Date	Mintage	VG	F	VF	XF	Unc
1675	—	—	—	—	—	—

KM# 8 2 THALER

Silver **Ruler:** Ernst I **Subject:** Peace of Westphalia **Note:** Dav. #7441. Similar to Thaler, KM#6.

Date	Mintage	VG	F	VF	XF	Unc
1650 Rare	—	—	—	—	—	—

Note: Struck in 1672-75

KM# 9 2 THALER

Silver **Ruler:** Ernst I **Subject:** Peace of Westphalia **Obv:** Saxon arms at top divide date **Rev:** 4-line inscription, Hebrew letters in sun above **Note:** Ref. Dav. 7443.

Date	Mintage	VG	F	VF	XF	Unc
1650 Rare	—	—	—	—	—	—

Note: Struck in 1672-75; Fritz Rudolf Künker Münzenhandlung Auction 98, 3-05, VF realized approximately $12,680

KM# 18 2 THALER

Silver **Ruler:** Ernst I **Subject:** Marriage of Ernst I and Elisabeth Sophia **Obv:** Full-length figures of Ernst the Pious and Elisabeth Sophia, dove with rays above **Obv. Legend:** QUOS DEUS... **Rev:** Marriage feast at Cana **Rev. Legend:** IESUS CHRISTUS MACHT... **Mint:** Gotha

Date	Mintage	VG	F	VF	XF	Unc
ND(1653) Rare	—	—	—	—	—	—

KM# 39 2 THALER

Silver **Ruler:** Ernst I **Subject:** On the Catechism **Obv:** Three lines around sun, nine beams radiating from the sun with qualities of God **Rev:** 10-line inscription **Mint:** Eisleben **Note:** Struck from same Thaler dies, KM#23.

Date	Mintage	VG	F	VF	XF	Unc
1671 ABK Rare	—	—	—	—	—	—

KM# 40 2 THALER

Silver **Ruler:** Ernst I **Subject:** Baptism of Friedrich I's Second Daughter **Obv:** Baptism scene with eleven-line inscription in field **Rev:** 10-line inscription **Mint:** Eisleben **Note:** Struck from same Thaler dies, KM#36.

Date	Mintage	VG	F	VF	XF	Unc
1671 ABK Rare	—	—	—	—	—	—

KM# 46 2 THALER

Silver **Ruler:** Ernst I **Subject:** "Happiness" Thaler **Obv:** 11-line inscription **Rev:** 10-line inscription **Mint:** Eisleben **Note:** Struck from same Thaler dies, KM#.

Date	Mintage	VG	F	VF	XF	Unc
1672 Rare	—	—	—	—	—	—

KM# 71 2 THALER

Silver, 49 mm. **Ruler:** Joint Rule **Subject:** Death of Ernst I, the Pious **Obv:** Draped and armored bust to right **Obv. Legend:** D: G: ERNESTUS SAX: IUL: CLIV: ET MONTIUM DUX. **Rev:** 9-line inscription with dates, 19 small shields of arms around, one at top is larger, crowned shield of ducal Saxony arms **Rev. Legend:** LANDG: THUR: MARCH: MISN: PRINC: HEN: COM: MAR: & RAV: DYNAST: IN RAVEN: **Rev. Inscription:** NATUS / 1601. 25. DECEMBR / DENATUS / 1675. D. 26. MARTII / REGIMINIS. 35. / ÆTAT. 73. MENS. 3. D. I. / HUMATUS / D: 4. JUNY. D: / A: 1675. **Mint:** Gotha **Note:** Ref. KOR-476; Dav. 7456. Struck on thick flan with Thaler dies, KM#68. The type reportedly struck with KM#67 dies, Dav. 7454, does not exist.

Date	Mintage	VG	F	VF	XF	Unc
1675 Rare	—	—	—	—	—	—

KM# 41 3 THALER

Silver **Ruler:** Ernst I **Subject:** Baptism of Daughter of Prince Friedrich **Mint:** Eisleben **Note:** Dav. #7452. Similar to 1 Thaler, KM#36.

Date	Mintage	VG	F	VF	XF	Unc
1671 ABK Rare	—	—	—	—	—	—

TRADE COINAGE

KM# 72 1/4 DUCAT

0.8750 g., 0.9860 Gold 0.0277 oz. AGW, 12 mm. **Ruler:** Ernst I **Obv:** Oval shield of ducal Saxony arms in baroque frame, date divided below **Rev:** 4-line inscription in Gothic letters **Rev. Inscription:** Gott gibts, / Jesus erwirbts / der Glaube / nimbts G **Mint:** Gotha **Note:** Ref. KOR-460; Fr. 2953. Struck from Pfennig dies, KM#52.

Date	Mintage	VG	F	VF	XF	Unc
1675	—	400	625	1,300	2,650	—

KM# 10 1/2 DUCAT

1.7500 g., 0.9860 Gold 0.0555 oz. AGW **Ruler:** Ernst I **Subject:** Peace of Westphalia **Obv:** 5-line inscription in Gothic letters **Rev:** 5-line inscription in Gothic letters, date above **Note:** Fr. #2949.

Date	Mintage	VG	F	VF	XF	Unc
1650	—	275	550	1,200	2,200	—

Note: Struck in 1672-73

KM# 57 1/2 DUCAT

1.7500 g., 0.9860 Gold 0.0555 oz. AGW **Ruler:** Ernst I **Obv:** Oval Saxon arms **Rev:** 5-line inscription **Note:** Ref. Fr. 2952.

Date	Mintage	VG	F	VF	XF	Unc
1673	—	425	1,000	2,000	4,200	—

KM# 11 DUCAT

3.5000 g., 0.9860 Gold 0.1109 oz. AGW **Ruler:** Ernst I **Subject:** Peace of Westphalia **Obv:** 5-line inscription **Rev:** 5-line inscription, date above **Mint:** Gotha **Note:** Fr. #2948.

Date	Mintage	VG	F	VF	XF	Unc
1650 IB	1,278	525	1,100	2,150	3,450	—

KM# 13 DUCAT

Gold **Ruler:** Ernst I **Obv:** 5-line inscription **Rev:** 5-line inscription, date above **Mint:** Eisleben **Note:** Inscriptions in Gothic letters.

Date	Mintage	VG	F	VF	XF	Unc
1650	—	525	1,100	2,150	3,450	—

KM# 12 DUCAT

Gold **Ruler:** Ernst I **Obv:** 5-line inscription **Rev:** 5-line inscription, date above **Mint:** Eisleben **Note:** Struck in 1672-73 without mintmaster's initials.

Date	Mintage	VG	F	VF	XF	Unc
1650	—	525	1,100	2,150	3,450	—

KM# 58 DUCAT

3.5000 g., 0.9860 Gold 0.1109 oz. AGW, 22 mm. **Ruler:** Friedrich I **Subject:** Transfer of Rule over Altenburg to Friedrich I in 1672 **Obv:** Crowned F divides date, four small shields of arms divide legend **Obv. Legend:** DUX - SAX. - IUL. CL. - ET MON. **Rev:** Crowned MS monogram (Magdalene Sibylla) divides mintmaster's initials, 4 small shields of arms divide legend **Rev. Legend:** DUCISS - SAXON - IUL. CLI. - ET MON. **Mint:** Saalfeld **Note:** Ref. KOR-487.

Date	Mintage	VG	F	VF	XF	Unc
1673 MR Rare	—	—	—	—	—	—

KM# 73 DUCAT

3.5000 g., 0.9860 Gold 0.1109 oz. AGW, 25 mm. **Ruler:** Joint Rule **Subject:** Death of Ernst I, the Pious **Obv:** Draped bust to right **Obv. Legend:** D: G: ERNESTUS SAX IUL. CLI & MONT. DUX. **Rev:** 10-line inscription with dates **Rev. Inscription:** NATUS / AO: 1601. D. 25. / DECEMBR: / DENATUS / 1675. D. 26. MARTII / REGIMINIS. 35. / ÆTAT. 73. MENS. 3. D. I. / HUMATUS / D: 4. JUNY. D: / A: 1675. **Mint:** Gotha **Note:** Ref. KOR-475; Fr. 2955.

Date	Mintage	VG	F	VF	XF	Unc
1675	143	900	1,800	3,500	7,000	—

KM# 14 2 DUCAT

7.0000 g., 0.9860 Gold 0.2219 oz. AGW **Ruler:** Ernst I **Subject:** Peace of Westphalia **Obv:** 5-line inscription **Rev:** 5-line inscription, date above **Note:** Fr. #2947.

Date	Mintage	VG	F	VF	XF	Unc
1650	—	1,400	2,700	5,100	10,000	—

KM# 74.1 2 DUCAT

7.0000 g., 0.9860 Gold 0.2219 oz. AGW, 30 mm. **Ruler:** Joint Rule **Subject:** Death of Ernst I, the Pious **Obv:** Draped and armored bust to right **Obv. Legend:** D: G: ERNESTUS SAX IUL: CLIV: ET MONTIUM DUX. **Rev:** 10-line inscription with dates **Rev. Inscription:** NATUS / AO. 1601. D: 25 / DECEMBR: / DENATUS / 1675. D. 26. MARTII / REGIMINIS. 35 / ÆTAT: 73 MENS. 3. D. I / HUMATUS / D: 4. JUNY D: / A 1675. **Mint:** Gotha **Note:** Ref. KOR-473. Struck from 1/4 Thaler dies, KM#64.

Date	Mintage	VG	F	VF	XF	Unc
1675	—	2,400	4,800	8,400	14,500	—

KM# 74.2 2 DUCAT

7.0000 g., 0.9860 Gold 0.2219 oz. AGW, 25 mm. **Ruler:** Joint Rule **Subject:** Death of Ernst I, the Pious **Obv:** Draped bust to right **Obv. Legend:** D. G. ERNESTUS. SAX. IUL. CL & MONT. DUX. **Rev:** 10-line inscription with dates **Rev. Inscription:** NATUS / AP: 1601. D. 25. DECEMBR: / DENATUS / 1675. D. 26. MARTII / REGIMINIS. 35. / ÆTAT. 73. MENS. 3. D. I. / HUMATUS / D: 4. JUNY. D: / A: 1675. **Mint:** Gotha **Note:** Ref. KOR-474; Fr. 2954. Struck from 1/12 Thaler dies, KM#63.

Date	Mintage	VG	F	VF	XF	Unc
1675	—	—	—	—	—	—

KM# 86 2 DUCAT

Gold **Ruler:** Joint Rule **Obv:** Bust right, titles of Friedrich I **Rev:** Crowned oval 4-fold arms in baroque frame within palm branches **Rev. Legend:** AD ASTRA PER ASTRA. **Mint:** Gotha

Date	Mintage	VG	F	VF	XF	Unc
ND(1677-80) GFS Rare	—	—	—	—	—	—

KM# 75 3 DUCAT
10.5000 g., 0.9860 Gold 0.3328 oz. AGW, 30 mm. **Ruler:** Joint Rule **Subject:** Death of Ernst I, the Pious **Obv:** Draped and armored bust to right **Obv. Legend:** D: G: ERNESTUS SAX IUL: CLIV: ET MONTIUM DUX. **Rev:** 10-line inscription with dates **Rev. Inscription:** NATUS / AO. 1601. D: 25 / DECEMBR: / DENATUS / 1675. D. 26. MARTII / REGIMINIS. 35 / ÆTAT: 73 MENS. 3. D. I / HUMATUS / D: 4. JUNY D: / A 1675. **Mint:** Gotha **Note:** Ref. KOR-472. Struck from 1/4 Thaler dies, KM#64.

Date	Mintage	VG	F	VF	XF	Unc
1675 Rare	—	—	—	—	—	—

KM# 76 4 DUCAT
14.0000 g., 0.9860 Gold 0.4438 oz. AGW, 30 mm. **Ruler:** Joint Rule **Subject:** Death of Ernst I, the Pious **Obv:** Draped and armored bust to right **Obv. Legend:** D: G: ERNESTUS SAX IUL: CLIV: ET MONTIUM DUX. **Rev:** 10-line inscription with dates **Rev. Inscription:** NATUS / AO. 1601. D: 25 / DECEMBR: / DENATUS / 1675. D. 26. MARTII / REGIMINIS. 35 / ÆTAT: 73 MENS. 3. D. I / HUMATUS / D: 4. JUNY D: / A 1675. **Mint:** Gotha **Note:** Ref. KOR-471. Struck from 1/4 Thaler dies, KM#64.

Date	Mintage	VG	F	VF	XF	Unc
1675 Rare	—	—	—	—	—	—

KM# 77 5 DUCAT
17.5000 g., 0.9860 Gold 0.5547 oz. AGW, 38 mm. **Ruler:** Friedrich I **Obv:** Crowned shield of manifold arms, with central shield of ducal Saxony, divides date, (5) in oval below **Obv. Legend:** FRIDERICUS DUX SAXONIÆ - IULII. CLIVII. ET. MONTIUM. **Rev:** Crowned F between 2 palm branches, 4 small shields of arms in margin divide legend **Rev. Legend:** PER - ASPERA - AD - ASTRA. **Mint:** Gotha **Note:** Ref. KOR-486; Fr. 2956. Struck from 2/3 Thaler dies, KM#66.

Date	Mintage	VG	F	VF	XF	Unc
1675 Rare	—	—	—	—	—	—

KM# 28 6 DUCAT
Gold **Ruler:** Ernst I **Subject:** Baptism of Friedrich I's Daughter, Anna Sophia **Obv:** Baptismal scene with twelve-line inscription in field **Rev:** 10-line inscription **Mint:** Gotha **Note:** Struck from same Thaler dies, KM#27.

Date	Mintage	VG	F	VF	XF	Unc
1670 Rare	—	—	—	—	—	—

KM# 30 8 DUCAT
28.0000 g., 0.9860 Gold 0.8876 oz. AGW **Ruler:** Ernst I **Subject:** Baptism of Princess Anna Sophia **Obv:** Baptismal scene, counterstamp small "8K" **Rev:** Ten-line inscription **Note:** Struck with Thaler dies, KM#27.

Date	Mintage	VG	F	VF	XF	Unc
1670 Rare	—	—	—	—	—	—

KM# 15 10 DUCAT
Gold **Ruler:** Ernst I **Subject:** Peace of Westphalia **Obv:** Saxon arms divide date **Rev:** 5-line inscription, Hebrew letters in sun above **Mint:** Gotha **Note:** Struck in 1672-75 from same Thaler dies, KM#6.

Date	Mintage	VG	F	VF	XF	Unc
1650 Rare	—	—	—	—	—	—

KM# A30 10 DUCAT
Gold **Ruler:** Ernst I **Subject:** Baptism of Friedrich I's Daughter, Anna Sophia **Obv:** Baptismal scene with twelve-line inscription in field **Rev:** 10-line inscription **Mint:** Gotha **Note:** Struck from same Thaler dies, KM#27.

Date	Mintage	VG	F	VF	XF	Unc
1670 Rare	—	—	—	—	—	—

KM# 42 10 DUCAT
Gold **Ruler:** Ernst I **Subject:** On the Catechism **Obv:** Three lines around sun, nine beams radiating from the sun with qualities of God **Rev:** 10-line inscription **Mint:** Eisleben **Note:** Struck from same Thaler dies, KM#23.

Date	Mintage	VG	F	VF	XF	Unc
1671 ABK Rare	—	—	—	—	—	—

KM# 59 10 DUCAT
35.0000 g., 0.9860 Gold 1.1095 oz. AGW, 45 mm. **Ruler:** Friedrich I **Subject:** Transfer of Rule over Altenburg to Friedrich I in 1672 **Obv:** Large crowned shield of manifold arms, with central shield of ducal Saxony, in baroque frame, divides mintmaster's initials, date above **Obv. Legend:** FRIDERICUS. D. G. DUX. SAXON. IULIÆ. CLIVIÆ. ET. MONTIUM. **Rev:** Man in center of landscape, inscription in band above and to left of man's head **Rev. Inscription:** DUC ME SEQVAR **Mint:** Saalfeld **Note:** Ref. KOR-485; Fr. 2956. Struck from Thaler dies, KM#56.

Date	Mintage	VG	F	VF	XF	Unc
1673 MR Rare	—	—	—	—	—	—

KM# 78 10 DUCAT
35.0000 g., 0.9860 Gold 1.1095 oz. AGW, 49 mm. **Ruler:** Joint Rule **Subject:** Death of Ernst I, the Pious **Obv:** Draped and armored bust to right **Obv. Legend:** D: G: ERNESTUS SAX: IUL: CLIV: ET MONTIUM DUX. **Rev:** 9-line inscription with dates, 19 small shields of arms around, one at top is larger, crowned shield of ducal Saxony arms **Rev. Legend:** LANDG: THUR: MARCH: MISN: PRINC: HEN: COM: MAR: & RAV: DYNAST: IN RAVEN: **Rev. Inscription:** NATUS / 1601. 25. DECEMBR / DENATUS / 1675. D. 26. MARTII / REGIMINIS. 35. / ÆTAT. 73. MENS. 3. D. I. / HUMATUS / D: 4. JUNY. D: / A: 1675. **Mint:** Gotha **Note:** Ref. KOR-470. Struck from Thaler dies, KM#68.

Date	Mintage	VG	F	VF	XF	Unc
1675 Rare	—	—	—	—	—	—

KM# 48 18 DUCAT
Gold **Ruler:** Ernst I **Subject:** Happiness **Obv:** Considerable modifications **Rev:** Considerable modifications **Mint:** Gotha **Note:** Struck from same Thaler dies, KM#45.

Date	Mintage	VG	F	VF	XF	Unc
1672 Rare	—	—	—	—	—	—

KM# 16 20 DUCAT
Gold **Ruler:** Ernst I **Subject:** Peace of Westphalia **Obv:** Saxon arms divide date **Rev:** 5-line inscription, Hebrew letters in sun above **Mint:** Gotha **Note:** Struck in 1672-75 from same Thaler dies, KM#6.

Date	Mintage	VG	F	VF	XF	Unc
1650 Rare	—	—	—	—	—	—

PATTERNS

Including off metal strikes

KM#	Date	Mintage	Identification	Mkt Val
Pn1	1675	—	Ducat. Silver. KM#58.	—
Pn2	ND(1677-89) GFS	—	Ducat. Silver. KM#86.	—

SAXE-GOTHA-ALTENBURG

(Sachsen-Gotha-Altenburg)

When the seven sons of Ernst the Pious of Saxe-New-Gotha divided the lands of their father in 1680, the eldest established the line of Saxe-Gotha-Altenburg. The line became extinct in 1825 and the following year witnessed the division of the territory which resulted in a general reorganization of the Thuringian duchies. Altenburg itself was inherited by the duke of Saxe-Hildburghausen, who transferred Hildburghausen to Saxe-Meiningen and became the founder of a new line of Saxe-Altenburg. Saxe-Meiningen also received Saalfeld from Saxe-Coburg, which in turn had acquired Gotha as part of the proceedings. The line of Saxe-Coburg-Gotha was established as a result. See under each of the foregoing regarding developments after the realignment of 1826. For a short period of time, from 1688 to 1692, the duke leased the abbey of Walkenried from Brunswick-Wolfenbüttel and struck a series of coins for that district.

RULERS

Friedrich I, 1680-1691
Friedrich II, 1691-1732
Jointly with brother Johann Wilhelm, 1691-1707

MINT OFFICIALS' INITIALS

Initials	Date	Name
GFS	1677-80	Georg Friedrich Staude, mintmaster in Gotha
HM	1681-83	Henning Müller, mintmaster in Gotha
CF or F	1681-88	Christian Fischer, warden in Gotha
	1688-90	mintmaster
IGS	1681-87	Johann Georg Sorberger, die-cutter in Gotha
IGW	1683-90	Johann Gottfried Wichmannshausen, mintmaster in Gotha
ICB	1688-89	Johann Christoph Bähr, mintmaster in Walkenried
	1690-93	warden in Gotha
	1693-96	mintmaster
CW or W	1688-1739	Christian Wermuth, die-cutter in Gotha
IT	1690-1723	Johann Thun, mintmaster in Gotha

DUCHY

REGULAR COINAGE

KM# 6 HELLER
Copper **Ruler:** Friedrich I **Obv:** Oval Saxony arms in baroque frame **Rev. Inscription:** GOTHA / ISCHE / HELLER / date

Date	Mintage	VG	F	VF	XF	Unc
1681	—	15.00	30.00	60.00	—	—

KM# 25 HELLER
Copper **Ruler:** Friedrich I **Obv:** Oval Saxony arms in baroque frame **Rev:** GOTHA / ISCHER / HELLER

Date	Mintage	VG	F	VF	XF	Unc
1682	—	15.00	30.00	60.00	—	—

KM# 122 HELLER
Copper **Ruler:** Friedrich II **Obv:** Crowned squarish Saxony arms in palm branches **Rev. Inscription:** GOTH= / U. ALTENB: / HELLER. / date

Date	Mintage	VG	F	VF	XF	Unc
1692	—	12.00	25.00	45.00	90.00	—

KM# 137 HELLER
Copper **Ruler:** Friedrich II **Obv:** Crowned round Saxony arms in baroque frame **Rev. Inscription:** GOTHA. / UND. / ALTENB: / HELLER. / date in laurel wreath

Date	Mintage	VG	F	VF	XF	Unc
1693	—	8.00	17.00	35.00	70.00	—

KM# 147 HELLER
Copper **Ruler:** Friedrich II **Obv:** Crowned squarish Saxony arms in palm branches **Rev. Inscription:** GOTHA. / UNS. / ALTENB: / HELLER. / date in laurel wreath

Date	Mintage	VG	F	VF	XF	Unc
1695	—	8.00	17.00	35.00	70.00	—
1696	—	8.00	17.00	35.00	70.00	—

KM# 7 PFENNIG
Silver **Ruler:** Friedrich I **Obv:** Crowned oval Saxony arms in cartouche, date below **Rev:** Imperial orb with 1 in cartouche

Date	Mintage	VG	F	VF	XF	Unc
1681	—	15.00	25.00	45.00	90.00	—

KM# 8 PFENNIG
Silver **Ruler:** Friedrich I **Obv:** Crowned script 'F' divides date **Rev:** Oval Saxony arms in baroque frame

Date	Mintage	VG	F	VF	XF	Unc
1681	—	10.00	20.00	40.00	80.00	—
1684	—	10.00	20.00	40.00	80.00	—
1685	—	10.00	20.00	40.00	80.00	—
1686	—	10.00	20.00	40.00	80.00	—

KM# 9 PFENNIG
Silver **Ruler:** Friedrich I **Obv:** Oval Saxony arms in baroque frame **Rev:** Imperial orb with 1 divides date and mintmaster's initials **Mint:** Gotha

Date	Mintage	VG	F	VF	XF	Unc
1681 HM	—	25.00	55.00	110	225	—

KM# 123 PFENNIG
Silver **Ruler:** Friedrich II **Obv:** Crowned script 'F' divides date **Rev:** Crowned oval Saxony arms in palm branches

Date	Mintage	VG	F	VF	XF	Unc
1692	—	15.00	30.00	60.00	—	—

KM# 138 PFENNIG
Silver **Ruler:** Friedrich II **Obv:** 4 small crowned shields of arms in cruciform, date divided in angles **Rev:** Imperial orb with 1 divides mintmaster's initials **Note:** Varieties exist.

Date	Mintage	VG	F	VF	XF	Unc
1693	305,000	8.00	17.00	35.00	—	—
1697	Inc. above	8.00	17.00	35.00	—	—

KM# 148 PFENNIG
Silver **Ruler:** Friedrich II **Obv:** Crowned ornately-shaped shield of Saxony arms **Rev:** Imperial orb with 1 divides date **Mint:** Gotha

Date	Mintage	VG	F	VF	XF	Unc
1695 IT	—	—	—	—	—	—

KM# 54 2 PFENNIG (Zweier)
Silver **Ruler:** Friedrich I **Obv:** Crowned oval Saxony arms in baroque frame **Rev:** Imperial orb with 2 divides date and mintmaster's initials **Mint:** Gotha

Date	Mintage	VG	F	VF	XF	Unc
1686 IGW	—	15.00	30.00	60.00	120	—

KM# 55 2 PFENNIG (Zweier)
Silver **Ruler:** Friedrich I **Obv:** Crowned oval Saxony arms in baroque frame **Rev:** Imperial orb with 2 divides date

Date	Mintage	VG	F	VF	XF	Unc
1686	—	15.00	20.00	60.00	120	—

KM# 124 2 PFENNIG (Zweier)
Silver **Ruler:** Friedrich II **Obv:** Crowned Saxony arms in palm branches **Rev:** F. S. G. V. A. L. M. curved above imperial orb with 2 divides date and mintmaster's initials **Mint:** Gotha

Date	Mintage	VG	F	VF	XF	Unc
1692 IT	—	15.00	20.00	60.00	120	—

KM# 10 3 PFENNIG (Dreier)

Silver **Ruler:** Friedrich I **Obv:** Oval Saxony arms in baroque frame **Rev:** Imperial orb with 3 divides date and mintmaster's initials **Mint:** Gotha

Date	Mintage	VG	F	VF	XF	Unc
1681	—	10.00	25.00	50.00	100	—

KM# 26 3 PFENNIG (Dreier)

Silver **Ruler:** Friedrich I **Obv:** Crowned oval Saxony arms in baroque frame **Rev:** Imperial orb with 3 divides date and mintmaster's initials **Mint:** Gotha **Note:** Varieties exist.

Date	Mintage	VG	F	VF	XF	Unc
1682 HM	—	10.00	20.00	40.00	80.00	—
1683 HM	—	10.00	20.00	40.00	80.00	—
1683 IGW	—	10.00	20.00	40.00	80.00	—
1684 IGW	—	10.00	20.00	40.00	80.00	—
1687 IGW	—	10.00	20.00	40.00	80.00	—
1688 IGW	—	10.00	20.00	40.00	80.00	—

KM# 49 3 PFENNIG (Dreier)

Silver **Ruler:** Friedrich I **Obv:** Crowned oval Saxony arms in baroque frame **Rev:** Lower part of imperial orb divides date **Rev. Legend:** N. D. OBERS. C. S. **Mint:** Gotha

Date	Mintage	VG	F	VF	XF	Unc
1685 IGW	—	10.00	25.00	50.00	100	—

KM# 64 3 PFENNIG (Dreier)

Silver **Ruler:** Friedrich I **Obv:** Crowned script 'F' divides date and mintmaster's initials **Rev:** Imperial orb with 3, curved above F. S. ST. - date - W(R). M. **Mint:** Walkenried **Note:** Coinage for Abbey of Walkenried.

Date	Mintage	VG	F	VF	XF	Unc
1688 ICB	—	10.00	25.00	50.00	100	—

KM# 109 3 PFENNIG (Dreier)

Silver **Ruler:** Friedrich II **Obv:** Crowned oval 4-fold arms in palm branches **Rev:** Imperial orb with 3 divides date and mintmaster's initials, curved above F. S. G - A. L. M. **Mint:** Gotha

Date	Mintage	VG	F	VF	XF	Unc
1691 IT	—	10.00	25.00	50.00	100	—

KM# 125 3 PFENNIG (Dreier)

Silver **Ruler:** Friedrich II **Obv:** Crowned oval 4-fold arms in palm branches **Rev:** Imperial orb with 3 divides date and mintmaster's initials, curved above F. S. G. V. A. L. M. or variant **Mint:** Gotha **Note:** Varieties exist.

Date	Mintage	VG	F	VF	XF	Unc
1692 IT	—	10.00	25.00	50.00	100	—

KM# 149 3 PFENNIG (Dreier)

Silver **Ruler:** Friedrich II **Obv:** Helmet above Saxony arms, titles of Friedrich II **Rev:** Imperial orb with 3 divides date and mintmaster's initials **Rev. Legend:** NACH DEM LEIPZIG FUS **Mint:** Gotha **Note:** Varieties exist.

Date	Mintage	VG	F	VF	XF	Unc
1695 IT	—	10.00	18.00	30.00	60.00	—
1696 IT	—	10.00	18.00	30.00	60.00	—
1697 IT	—	10.00	18.00	30.00	60.00	—

KM# 126 6 PFENNIG (Sechser)

Silver **Ruler:** Friedrich II **Obv:** Crowned 4-fold arms in palm branches **Rev. Inscription:** 6 / PF. S. GOTH. / U. ALTENB. / LANDMUNZ / date / mintmaster's initials **Mint:** Gotha

Date	Mintage	VG	F	VF	XF	Unc
1692 IT	—	—	—	—	—	—

KM# 11 1/24 THALER (Groschen)

Silver **Ruler:** Friedrich I **Obv:** 4-fold arms in baroque frame, titles of Friedrich I **Rev:** Imperial orb with 24 divides date and mintmaster's initials **Rev. Legend:** NACH DEM OBER SACHS CREYS SCHLUS **Mint:** Gotha

Date	Mintage	VG	F	VF	XF	Unc
1681 HM	—	20.00	45.00	90.00	180	—

KM# 12 1/24 THALER (Groschen)

Silver **Ruler:** Friedrich I **Subject:** Death of Friedrich I's First Wife, Magdalene Sibylla von Sachsen-Weissenfels **Obv:** Bust right **Rev:** Castle, date below

Date	Mintage	VG	F	VF	XF	Unc
MDCLXXXI (1681)	—	—	—	—	—	—

KM# 50 1/24 THALER (Groschen)

Silver **Ruler:** Friedrich I **Obv:** Crowned 4-fold arms in baroque frame, titles of Friedrich I **Rev:** Imperial orb with 24 divides date and mintmaster's initials **Rev. Legend:** NACH DEM OBER SACHS CREYS SCHLUS **Mint:** Gotha **Note:** Varieties exist.

Date	Mintage	VG	F	VF	XF	Unc
1685 IGW	—	—	—	—	—	—

KM# 66 1/24 THALER (Groschen)

Silver **Ruler:** Friedrich I **Obv:** Crowned 4-fold arms in baroque frame, titles of Friedrich I **Rev:** Imperial orb with 24 divides date and mintmaster's initials **Rev. Legend:** FVRSTL. SACHS. GOTA. V. ALTENB. LAND. MVNTZ. **Mint:** Gotha **Note:** Varieties exist.

Date	Mintage	VG	F	VF	XF	Unc
1688 CF	—	12.00	25.00	55.00	110	—

KM# 67 1/24 THALER (Groschen)

Silver **Ruler:** Friedrich I **Obv:** Bust right, titles of Friedrich I **Rev:** Imperial orb divides date and mintmaster's initials **Rev. Legend:** FURSTL. SACHS. STIFT. WALCKENR. **Mint:** Walkenried **Note:** Coinage for Abbey of Walkenried.

Date	Mintage	VG	F	VF	XF	Unc
1688 ICB	—	15.00	35.00	75.00	150	—
1689 ICB	—	15.00	35.00	75.00	150	—

KM# 110 1/24 THALER (Groschen)

Silver **Ruler:** Friedrich I **Obv:** Crowned 4-fold arms in palm branches, titles of Friedrich I **Rev:** Imperial orb with 24 divides date and mintmaster's initials **Rev. Legend:** FVRSTL. SACHS. GOTA. V. ALTENB. LAND. MVNTZ. **Mint:** Gotha **Note:** Varieties exist.

Date	Mintage	VG	F	VF	XF	Unc
1691 ICB	—	20.00	40.00	85.00	170	—
1691 IT	—	20.00	40.00	85.00	170	—

KM# 111 1/24 THALER (Groschen)

Silver **Ruler:** Friedrich I **Subject:** Death of Friedrich I **Obv:** Bust right **Rev:** 8-line inscription with dates **Mint:** Gotha

Date	Mintage	VG	F	VF	XF	Unc
1691 IT	—	25.00	50.00	100	210	—

KM# 127 1/24 THALER (Groschen)

Silver **Ruler:** Friedrich II and Johann Wilhelm **Subject:** Homage of Gotha to the Regents **Obv:** Facing busts of Bernhard and Heinrich, regents for Friedrich and Johann Wilhelm **Mint:** Gotha

Date	Mintage	VG	F	VF	XF	Unc
1692 IT	2,400	—	—	—	—	—

KM# 128 1/24 THALER (Groschen)

Silver **Ruler:** Friedrich II **Obv:** Crowned oval 4-fold arms **Rev:** Imperial orb with 24 divides date and mintmaster's initials **Rev. Legend:** FURSTL. SACHS. ... **Mint:** Gotha

Date	Mintage	VG	F	VF	XF	Unc
1692 IT	—	—	—	—	—	—

KM# 139 1/24 THALER (Groschen)

Silver **Ruler:** Friedrich II **Obv:** Bust right, titles of Friedrich II **Rev:** 4 small crowned shields of arms in cruciform, date divided in angles, 1. GROS. in circle in center **Rev. Legend:** NACH - DEM - LEIPZ. - FUES. **Mint:** Gotha

Date	Mintage	VG	F	VF	XF	Unc
1693 IT	—	—	—	—	—	—

KM# 32 1/12 THALER (Doppelgroschen)

Silver **Ruler:** Friedrich I **Obv:** Crowned oval 4-fold arms in baroque frame, titles of Friedrich I **Rev:** Date divides mintmaster's initials, all in palm branches below inscription **Rev. Inscription:** 12 / EINEN / REICHS / THALER **Mint:** Gotha **Note:** Varieties exist.

Date	Mintage	VG	F	VF	XF	Unc
1683	—	12.00	25.00	55.00	110	—
1683 HM	—	12.00	25.00	55.00	110	—
1683 IGW	—	12.00	25.00	55.00	110	—
1684 IGW	—	12.00	25.00	55.00	110	—

KM# 112 1/12 THALER (Doppelgroschen)

Silver **Ruler:** Friedrich I **Obv:** Crowned oval 4-fold arms in palm branches, titles of Friedrich I **Rev:** Legend around **Rev. Legend:** FURSTL. SACHS. GOHT. U. ALTENB. LAND. M. **Rev. Inscription:** 12 / EINEN / THALR / date in circle **Mint:** Gotha **Note:** Varieties exist.

Date	Mintage	VG	F	VF	XF	Unc
1691 IT	—	12.00	25.00	55.00	110	—
1691 ICB	—	15.00	30.00	65.00	130	—

KM# 129 1/12 THALER (Doppelgroschen)

Silver **Ruler:** Friedrich II **Obv:** Bust right, titles of Friedrich II **Rev:** 4 small crowned shields of arms in cruciform, date divided in angles, 2 / GROS in oval center **Rev. Legend:** NACH - DEM - LEIPZ. - FUES **Mint:** Gotha

Date	Mintage	VG	F	VF	XF	Unc
1692 IT	—	15.00	30.00	60.00	120	—

KM# 28 1/6 THALER

Silver **Ruler:** Friedrich I **Obv:** Armored and draped bust right, titles of Friedrich I **Rev:** Crossed sword and palm branch, curved above UTROQUE OPUS, in exergue V. FEIN SILVER / 1/6 in oval dividing date and mintmaster's initials **Rev. Legend:** NACH DEM OBER SA CHS. CREYS SCHLUS. **Mint:** Gotha

Date	Mintage	VG	F	VF	XF	Unc
1682 HM	—	125	250	450	900	—

KM# 68 1/6 THALER

Silver **Ruler:** Friedrich I **Obv:** Armored and draped bust right, titles of Friedrich I **Rev:** Crowned oval 4-fold arms divide date as 1-6/8-8, 1/6 in oval below, NACH DEM etc. **Mint:** Gotha

Date	Mintage	VG	F	VF	XF	Unc
1688 CF	—	115	235	475	—	—

KM# 69 1/6 THALER

Silver **Ruler:** Friedrich I **Obv:** Armored and draped bust right, titles of Friedrich I **Rev:** Date divided by crossed sword and palm branch, 1/6 in oval at bottom **Mint:** Gotha

Date	Mintage	VG	F	VF	XF	Unc
1688 CF	—	115	235	475	—	—

KM# 94 1/6 THALER

Silver **Ruler:** Friedrich I **Obv:** Armored and draped bust right, titles of Friedrich I **Rev:** Date divided by crossed sword and palm branch, curved above UTROQUE OPUS, in exergue V. FEIN SILVER / 1/6 in oval dividing date and mintmaster's initials **Rev. Legend:** MONETA. NOVA. ARGENTEA. **Mint:** Gotha

Date	Mintage	VG	F	VF	XF	Unc
1690 IT	—	20.00	40.00	75.00	150	—

KM# 65 6 MARIENGROSCHEN (1/4 Thaler)

Ruler: Friedrich I **Obv:** Bust right, titles of Friedrich I **Rev. Legend:** FURSTL. SACHS. STIFTS. WALCKENRID MUNTZ. **Rev. Inscription:** VI / MARIEN / GROSCH / date / mintmaster's initials **Mint:** Walkenried **Note:** Coinage for Abbey of Walkenried.

Date	Mintage	VG	F	VF	XF	Unc
1688 ICB	—	—	—	—	—	—

KM# 86 1/4 THALER

Silver **Ruler:** Friedrich I **Subject:** Dedication of Friedrichswerth Castle **Obv:** Bust right **Rev:** View of castle, ARCEM TEMPLVM FRIDERICHS WERTHE, in exergue INAVGVRARI FECIT / date **Mint:** Gotha

Date	Mintage	VG	F	VF	XF	Unc
1689 F	—	100	200	375	775	—

KM# 113 1/4 THALER

Silver **Ruler:** Friedrich I **Subject:** Death of Friedrich I **Obv:** Bust right **Rev:** 9-line inscription with dates **Mint:** Gotha

Date	Mintage	VG	F	VF	XF	Unc
1691 IT	—	—	—	—	—	—

KM# 13 1/3 THALER

Silver **Ruler:** Friedrich I **Obv:** Bust right **Rev:** Crowned manifold arms divide date and mintmaster's initials, value 1/3 in oval at bottom, NACH DEM ... **Mint:** Gotha **Note:** Varieties exist.

Date	Mintage	VG	F	VF	XF	Unc
1681 HM	—	—	—	—	—	—
1685 IGW	—	—	—	—	—	—

KM# 70 1/3 THALER

Silver **Ruler:** Friedrich I **Obv:** Armored and draped bust right, titles of Friedrich I **Rev:** Crowned oval 4-fold arms divide date as 1-6/8-8, 1/3 in oval below, NACH DEM ... **Mint:** Gotha

Date	Mintage	VG	F	VF	XF	Unc
1688 CF	—	—	—	—	—	—

KM# 95 1/3 THALER

Silver **Ruler:** Friedrich I **Obv:** Armored and draped bust right, titles of Friedrich I **Rev:** Crowned oval 4-fold arms divide date , 1/3 in oval below **Rev. Legend:** MONETA NOV - A ARGENTEA **Mint:** Gotha

Date	Mintage	VG	F	VF	XF	Unc
1690 IT	—	300	600	1,200	—	—

KM# 140 1/3 THALER

Silver **Ruler:** Friedrich II **Obv:** Bust right, titles of Friedrich II **Rev:** Crowned oval 4-fold arms with central shield in palm branches, value 1/3 in oval below divides date and mintmaster's initials **Rev. Legend:** NACH DEM - LEIPZ. FUES. **Mint:** Gotha

Date	Mintage	VG	F	VF	XF	Unc
1693 IT	—	—	—	—	—	—
1694 IT	—	—	—	—	—	—

KM# 14 1/2 THALER
Silver **Ruler:** Friedrich I **Obv:** Draped bust right, titles of Friedrich I **Rev:** Ornate manifold arms, 6 helmets above, date in lower right margin **Mint:** Gotha

Date	Mintage	VG	F	VF	XF	Unc
1681 HM	—	—	—	—	—	—

KM# 15 1/2 THALER
Silver **Ruler:** Friedrich I **Subject:** Death of Friedrich I's First Wife, Magdalene Sibylla von Sachsen-Weissenfels **Obv:** Bust right **Rev:** Castle, date below

Date	Mintage	VG	F	VF	XF	Unc
MDCLXXXI (1681)	—	—	—	—	—	—

KM# 33 1/2 THALER
Silver **Ruler:** Friedrich I **Obv:** Bust right **Rev:** Scales on pillow, 1/2 in oval punched in above date on reverse **Mint:** Gotha **Note:** Struck on thin flan with same dies as Thaler, KM#34.

Date	Mintage	VG	F	VF	XF	Unc
1683 IGW	—	300	600	1,200	2,400	—

KM# 57 1/2 THALER
Silver **Ruler:** Friedrich I **Obv:** Draped bust right, titles of Friedrich I **Rev:** Ornate manifold arms in circle, 6 helmets above, divided date near bottom **Mint:** Gotha

Date	Mintage	VG	F	VF	XF	Unc
1687/2 IGW	—	550	1,100	2,100	—	—

KM# 87 1/2 THALER
Ruler: Friedrich I **Subject:** Dedication of Friedrichwswerth Castle **Obv:** Bust right **Rev:** Different view of castle than KM#86, inscription in exergue below **Rev. Legend:** ARCEM TEMPLVM FRIDERICHS WERTHE **Rev. Inscription:** INA VGVRARI FECIT / date **Mint:** Gotha

Date	Mintage	VG	F	VF	XF	Unc
1689 F	—	300	600	1,200	—	—

KM# 114 1/2 THALER
Silver **Ruler:** Friedrich I **Subject:** Death of Friedrich I **Obv:** Bust right **Rev:** 9-line inscription, not in circle, arms above with 19 shields around **Mint:** Gotha

Date	Mintage	VG	F	VF	XF	Unc
1691 IT	—	175	350	700	1,350	1,850

KM# 27 16 GUTE GROSCHEN (2/3 Thaler)
Silver **Ruler:** Friedrich I **Obv:** Bust right, titles of Friedrich I **Rev. Inscription:** XVI / GUTE / GROSCH: / VON FEINEM / SILBER / date / mintmaster's initials and symbol **Mint:** Gotha

Date	Mintage	VG	F	VF	XF	Unc
1682 HM	—	—	—	—	—	—

KM# 16 2/3 THALER (Gulden)
Silver **Ruler:** Friedrich I **Obv:** Bust right **Rev:** Crowned manifold arms divide date and mintmaster's initials, value 2/3 in oval at bottom, NACH DEM ... **Mint:** Gotha

Date	Mintage	VG	F	VF	XF	Unc
1681 HM	—	—	—	—	—	—
1685 IGW	—	—	—	—	—	—
1692 HM	—	—	—	—	—	—

KM# 29 2/3 THALER (Gulden)
Silver **Ruler:** Friedrich I **Obv:** Armored and draped bust right, titles of Friedrich I **Rev:** Crossed sword and palm branch, curved above UTROQUE OPUS, in exergue V. FEIN SILVER / 2/3 in oval dividing date and mintmaster's initials **Rev. Legend:** NACH DEM OBER SA CHS. CREYS SCHLUS **Mint:** Gotha **Note:** Dav. #859.

Date	Mintage	VG	F	VF	XF	Unc
1682 HM	—	275	550	1,100	2,100	—

KM# 58 2/3 THALER (Gulden)
Silver **Ruler:** Friedrich I **Obv:** Bust right **Rev:** Crowned manifold arms divide mintmaster's initials, value 2/3 in oval at bottom **Rev. Legend:** MONETA. NOVA. - ARGENTEA, date **Mint:** Gotha

Date	Mintage	VG	F	VF	XF	Unc
1687 IGW	—	—	—	—	—	—

KM# 71 2/3 THALER (Gulden)
Silver **Ruler:** Friedrich I **Subject:** Coinage for Abbey of Walkenried **Obv:** Bust right **Rev:** Manifold arms, 6 helmets above divide mintmaster's initials, value 2/3 below divides date **Rev. Legend:** FURSTL. SACHS. STIFTS WALCKENRID. MUNTZ. **Mint:** Walkenried **Note:** Dav. #860.

Date	Mintage	VG	F	VF	XF	Unc
1688 ICB	—	—	—	—	—	—

KM# 96 2/3 THALER (Gulden)
Silver **Ruler:** Friedrich I **Obv:** Bust right **Rev:** Manifold arms, 6 helmets above divide mintmaster's initials, value 2/3 below divides date **Mint:** Gotha **Note:** Dav. #861. Varieties exist.

Date	Mintage	VG	F	VF	XF	Unc
1690 CF	—	—	—	—	—	—
1690 IT	—	—	—	—	—	—
1691 IT	—	—	—	—	—	—

KM# 97 2/3 THALER (Gulden)
Silver **Ruler:** Friedrich I **Obv:** Armored and draped bust right, titles of Friedrich I, arms in palm branches **Rev:** Crowned oval 4-fold arms divide date, value 2/3 bottom **Rev. Legend:** ... ET W. ... **Mint:** Gotha **Note:** Dav. 862-63. Varieties exist.

Date	Mintage	VG	F	VF	XF	Unc
1690 IT	—	50.00	100	200	425	—
1691 IT	—	50.00	100	200	425	—
1692 IT	—	50.00	100	200	425	—

KM# 115 2/3 THALER (Gulden)
Silver **Ruler:** Friedrich II **Obv:** Armored and draped bust right, titles of Friedrich II **Rev:** Crowned oval 4-fold arms divide date, 2/3 in oval below **Mint:** Gotha **Note:** Dav. #864.

Date	Mintage	VG	F	VF	XF	Unc
1691 IT	—	65.00	125	250	475	—
1692 IT	—	65.00	125	250	475	—

KM# 130 2/3 THALER (Gulden)
Silver **Ruler:** Friedrich II **Obv:** Bust right, titles of Friedrich II **Rev:** Crowned ornate manifold arms divide date, value 2/3 in oval with crossed palm fronds behind **Rev. Legend:** MONETA NOVA. - ARGENTEA. **Mint:** Gotha

Date	Mintage	VG	F	VF	XF	Unc
1692 IT	—	—	—	—	—	—

KM# 141 2/3 THALER (Gulden)
Silver **Ruler:** Friedrich II **Obv:** Armored and draped bust right, titles of Friedrich II **Rev:** Crowned oval 4-fold arms divide date farther apart at bottom **Mint:** Gotha **Note:** Dav. #865.

Date	Mintage	VG	F	VF	XF	Unc
1693 IT	—	50.00	100	200	425	—
1694 IT	—	50.00	100	200	425	—

KM# 2 3/4 THALER
Silver **Ruler:** Friedrich I **Subject:** Laying Foundation Stone for Friedrichswerth Castle **Obv:** Bust right **Rev:** Castle, date below **Mint:** Gotha

Date	Mintage	VG	F	VF	XF	Unc
1680 GFS	—	—	—	—	—	—

KM# 98 3/4 THALER
Silver **Ruler:** Friedrich I **Obv:** 6 medallions with busts either left or right around central medallion with bust right **Obv. Legend:** DVCES - SAXON - IVL. - CLIV. - ET - MONT: **Rev:** 6 helmeted manifold arms divide mintmaster's initials in middle, date near bottom **Rev. Legend:** LANDG: TH: MARCH: M: PRINC: DIC: HENN: **Mint:** Gotha **Note:** Struck on thin flan from same dies as 1 Thaler, KM#75.

Date	Mintage	VG	F	VF	XF	Unc
1690 IT	—	—	—	—	—	—
1691 IT	—	—	—	—	—	—

KM# 4 THALER
Silver **Ruler:** Friedrich I **Obv:** Bust right, titles of Friedrich I **Rev:** Crowned and supported arms, date below **Rev. Legend:** CONSILIO. — ET. ARMIS **Note:** Dav. #7461.

Date	Mintage	VG	F	VF	XF	Unc
1680 Rare	—	—	—	—	—	—
1681 Rare	—	—	—	—	—	—

Note: Edge inscription: IMERAT. IN. TOTO. REGINA. PECVNIA.

KM# 3 THALER
Silver **Ruler:** Friedrich I **Subject:** Building of the Castle in Friedrichswerth **Obv:** Bust right **Rev:** Castle, date below **Note:** Dav. 7460.

Date	Mintage	VG	F	VF	XF	Unc
1680	—	1,250	2,500	4,750	8,250	—

KM# 18 THALER
Silver **Ruler:** Friedrich I **Obv:** Draped bust right, titles of Friedrich I **Rev:** Ornate manifold arms, 6 helmets above, date in lower right margin **Mint:** Gotha **Note:** Struck on thick flan from same dies as 1/2 Thaler, KM#14.

Date	Mintage	VG	F	VF	XF	Unc
1681 HM	—	—	—	—	—	—

KM# 17 THALER
Silver **Ruler:** Friedrich I **Obv:** Draped and armored bust right **Rev:** Manifold Saxony arms, 6 helmets above, date in lower right margin **Mint:** Gotha **Note:** Dav. #7462.

Date	Mintage	VG	F	VF	XF	Unc
1681 HM Rare	—	—	—	—	—	—

KM# 19 THALER
Silver **Ruler:** Friedrich I **Subject:** Death of Magdalena Sybilla, First Wife of Friedrich **Obv:** Bust of Magdalena left, date in R.N. **Rev:** 8-line inscription on pedestal between palm sprays **Note:** Dav. #7463.

Date	Mintage	VG	F	VF	XF	Unc
MDCLXXXI (1681)	—	1,000	2,000	4,000	—	—

KM# 34 THALER
Silver **Ruler:** Friedrich I **Rev:** Scales on pillow, date in legend **Note:** Dav. 7464.

Date	Mintage	VG	F	VF	XF	Unc
1683 IGW	—	2,500	4,500	7,500	10,000	—

KM# 51 THALER
Silver **Ruler:** Friedrich I **Obv:** Bust right in circle, legend unbroken at top **Rev:** Helmeted arms dividing date and IG-W **Mint:** Gotha **Note:** Dav. #7465.

Date	Mintage	VG	F	VF	XF	Unc
1685 Rare	—	—	—	—	—	—

KM# A59 THALER
Silver **Ruler:** Friedrich I **Obv:** Bust right in circle, legend unbroken at top **Rev:** Helmeted arms dividing date and IG-W **Note:** Dav. #7465A. Similar to KM#51.

Date	Mintage	VG	F	VF	XF	Unc
1687 Rare	—	—	—	—	—	—

KM# 60 THALER
Silver **Ruler:** Friedrich I **Subject:** Test of Alchemy **Obv:** Laureate bust right **Rev:** Hexagram in rays and clouds, sun to left, moon to right above A. NUMINE. LUMEN, below crowned phoenix holding disk in beak with alchemical symbols, curved at bottom SUSCIPIO. GOT date ET. REDDO. **Mint:** Gotha

Date	Mintage	VG	F	VF	XF	Unc
1687 IGW Rare	—	—	—	—	—	—

KM# 59 THALER

Silver **Ruler:** Friedrich I **Obv:** Draped bust right, titles of Friedrich I **Rev:** Ornate manifold arms in circle, 6 helmets above, divided date near bottom **Mint:** Gotha **Note:** Struck on thick flan with same dies as 1/2 Thaler, KM#57.

Date	Mintage	VG	F	VF	XF	Unc
1687/2 IGW Rare	—	—	—	—	—	—

KM# 72 THALER

Silver **Ruler:** Friedrich I **Obv:** Bust right breaks legend at top and bottom, without inner circle **Rev:** Helmeted arms within circle at top, date in legend at bottom divided by arms **Note:** Dav. 7466.

Date	Mintage	VG	F	VF	XF	Unc
1688 IGW Rare	—	—	—	—	—	—

KM# 73 THALER

Silver **Ruler:** Friedrich I **Obv:** 6 medallions with busts either left or right around center medallion of bust turned 3/4 to left, D-S-I-&-M in margin **Rev:** 6-helmeted manifold arms divide mintmaster's initials in middle, date near bottom **Rev. Legend:** LANDG: TH: MARCH: M: PRINC: DIC: HENN: **Note:** Dav. 7468.

Date	Mintage	VG	F	VF	XF	Unc
1688 IGW Rare	—	—	—	—	—	—

KM# 75 THALER

Silver **Ruler:** Friedrich I **Obv:** 6 medallions with busts either left or right around center medallion of bust right **Obv. Legend:** DUCES-SAXON-IVL.-CLIV.-ET-MONT: **Rev:** 6-helmeted manifold arms divide date **Rev. Legend:** LANDG: TH: MARCH: M: PRINC: DIC: HENN: **Note:** Dav. 7470. Varieties exist.

Date	Mintage	VG	F	VF	XF	Unc
1688 IGW	—	—	275	475	850	1,650
1690 IT	—	—	275	475	850	1,650
1691 IT	—	—	275	475	850	1,650

KM# 76 THALER

Silver **Ruler:** Friedrich I **Obv:** 6 medallions with busts either left or right around center medallion of bust right **Rev:** Helmeted arms in inner circle, date in legend below **Rev. Legend:** LANDG: TH: MARCH: M: PRINC: DIC: HENN: **Note:** Dav. 7471.

Date	Mintage	VG	F	VF	XF	Unc
1688 IGW	—	—	300	600	1,150	2,000

KM# 74 THALER

Silver **Ruler:** Friedrich I **Obv:** 6 medallions with busts either left or right around central medallion of bust turned 3/4 to left **Obv. Legend:** D - S - I - & - M **Rev:** 6-helmeted manifold arms divide date **Rev. Legend:** FRATRES LINIÆ GOTHANÆ **Mint:** Gotha

Date	Mintage	VG	F	VF	XF	Unc
1688 IGW	—	275	550	1,100	1,950	—

KM# 78 THALER

Silver **Ruler:** Friedrich I **Subject:** Remembrance of Friedrich I's First Wife, Magdalene Sibylla von Sachsen-Weissenfels **Obv:** Laureate bust of Magdalene Sibylla to left **Rev:** Square tablet with 12-line inscription and R.N. date, issue date in arabesque above **Mint:** Gotha

Date	Mintage	VG	F	VF	XF	Unc
1688 CW//CF	—	450	900	1,700	2,850	—
1689 CW//CF	—	450	900	1,700	2,850	—

KM# 77 THALER

Silver **Ruler:** Friedrich I **Obv:** Seven busts facing left and right **Rev:** Date divided at top **Note:** Dav. #7473.

Date	Mintage	F	VF	XF	Unc	BU
1688 IGW	—	800	1,750	3,300	5,500	—
1690 IT	—	800	1,750	3,300	5,500	—

KM# A73 THALER

Silver **Ruler:** Friedrich I **Obv:** 6 medallions with busts either left or right around center medallion of bust turned 3/4 to left, D-S-I-&-M in margin **Rev:** 6-helmeted manifold arms divide date **Note:** Dav. #7468A.

Date	Mintage	VG	F	VF	XF	Unc
1688 Rare	—	—	—	—	—	—

KM# 88 THALER

Silver **Ruler:** Friedrich I **Subject:** Inauguration of the Castle **Rev:** Castle, date below **Note:** Dav. 7474.

Date	Mintage	F	VF	XF	Unc	BU
1689 W	—	2,250	4,500	8,500	—	—

KM# 35 THALER

Silver **Ruler:** Friedrich I **Note:** Dav. #LS421B. Similar to 1-1/2 Thaler, KM#37.

Date	Mintage	VG	F	VF	XF	Unc
ND	—	—	1,550	2,900	6,000	—

KM# 36 THALER

Silver **Ruler:** Friedrich I **Note:** Dav. #LS422A. Similar to 1-1/2 Thaler, KM#38.

Date	Mintage	VG	F	VF	XF	Unc
ND	—	—	1,550	2,900	6,000	—

KM# 116 THALER

Silver **Ruler:** Friedrich I **Subject:** Death of Friedrich **Rev:** 9-line inscription, arms above with 19 shields around **Note:** Dav. #7475.

Date	Mintage	VG	F	VF	XF	Unc
1691 IT	—	—	975	1,800	3,750	6,000

KM# 117 THALER

Silver, 46 mm. **Ruler:** Friedrich II **Note:** Dav. 7476.

Date	Mintage	VG	F	VF	XF	Unc
1691 IT Rare	—	—	—	—	—	—

KM# 131 THALER

Silver **Ruler:** Friedrich II and Johann Wilhelm **Subject:** Allegiance of Gotha **Obv:** Two busts left and two busts right **Rev:** Helmeted round arms, date below **Note:** Dav. 7477.

Date	Mintage	VG	F	VF	XF	Unc
1692 IT	—	—	875	1,950	3,450	—

KM# 132 THALER

Silver **Ruler:** Friedrich II **Obv:** Armored bust to right **Rev:** Crowned arms of Saxony in center, 5 crowned shields of arms around, double mirror-image FF monograms between shields, palm branches at bottom containing 32/ divide date **Note:** Dav. #7478. Speciestaler of 32 Groschen.

Date	Mintage	VG	F	VF	XF	Unc
1692 IT	—	—	2,050	3,600	6,600	—

KM# A132 THALER

Silver **Ruler:** Friedrich II **Obv:** Armored bust to right **Rev:** Crowned quartered round arms of Saxony in center, 5 crowned shields of arms around, double mirror-image FF monograms between shields, palm branches at bottom containing 32 divide date **Note:** Dav. #7478A. Similar to KM#132.

Date	Mintage	VG	F	VF	XF	Unc
1692	—	—	2,050	3,600	6,600	—

KM# 133 THALER

Silver **Ruler:** Friedrich II **Subject:** Baptismal Thaler **Obv:** John the Baptist baptising Christ in Jordan **Obv. Legend:** DIS IST MEIN LEIBER ... **Rev:** 9-line inscription, large ornament above, crossed palm branches below divide date **Mint:** Gotha

Date	Mintage	VG	F	VF	XF	Unc
1692 W//IT Rare	300	—	—	—	—	—

KM# 142 THALER

Silver **Ruler:** Friedrich II **Obv:** Armored bust right **Rev:** Crowned oval 4-fold arms with central shield of Saxony in palm branches, braided circle at bottom with 32/ divides date **Mint:** Gotha **Note:** Speciestaler of 32 Groschen.

Date	Mintage	VG	F	VF	XF	Unc
1693 IT	—	1,800	3,600	6,300	—	—

KM# 144 THALER
Silver **Ruler:** Friedrich II **Rev:** Helmeted arms divide date and I-T **Note:** Dav. 7479.

Date	Mintage	VG	F	VF	XF	Unc
1694 IT	—	—	750	1,350	2,250	—

KM# 153 THALER
Silver **Ruler:** Friedrich II **Obv:** Crowned wreath with 7-line inscription, shields in corners **Rev:** 19-line inscription **Note:** Dav. 7480.

Date	Mintage	F	VF	XF	Unc	BU
1699 CW Rare	—	—	—	—	—	—

KM# 20 1-1/2 THALER
Silver **Ruler:** Friedrich I **Obv:** Rural scene **Rev:** 4-line inscription, value 1-1/2 punched in near bottom **Mint:** Gotha **Note:** Varieties exist.

Date	Mintage	VG	F	VF	XF	Unc
ND(1681-83) IGS//HM	—	—	—	—	—	—
ND(1683-88) IGS//IGW	—	—	—	—	—	—
ND(1683-88) IGW	—	—	—	—	—	—

KM# 39 1-1/2 THALER
Silver **Ruler:** Friedrich I **Obv:** Bust right **Rev:** Crown surmounted by imperial orb **Mint:** Gotha

Date	Mintage	VG	F	VF	XF	Unc
(1683-88) IGW	—	—	—	—	—	—

KM# 37 1-1/2 THALER
32.5000 g., Silver **Ruler:** Friedrich I **Note:** Dav. #LS421A.

Date	Mintage	VG	F	VF	XF	Unc
ND(1683-88) IGW	—	—	—	3,750	6,800	—

KM# 38 1-1/2 THALER
Silver **Ruler:** Friedrich I **Note:** Dav. #LS422. Similar to 2 Thaler, KM#41.

Date	Mintage	VG	F	VF	XF	Unc
ND(1683-88) IGW	—	—	—	4,500	7,500	—

KM# 118 1-1/2 THALER
Silver **Ruler:** Friedrich I **Obv:** Bust right **Rev:** Large ornate script monogram between palm fronds, crown above, date divided to lower left and right **Rev. Legend:** PIETATE - PRVDENTIA - IVSTITIA **Mint:** Gotha

Date	Mintage	VG	F	VF	XF	Unc
1691 IT	—	—	—	—	—	—

KM# 21 2 THALER
Silver **Ruler:** Friedrich I **Subject:** Admission into the Pegnitzschafer Order **Obv:** Rural scene **Rev:** 4 lines in scroll, value punched near bottom **Note:** Dav. #LS423. Varieties exist with and without 2 stamped at lower reverse.

Date	Mintage	VG	F	VF	XF	Unc
ND(1681-83) IGW//HM	—	—	—	—	—	—
ND(1683-88) IGS//IGW	—	—	—	—	—	—
ND(1683-88) IGW	—	—	—	—	—	—
ND	—	—	—	7,500	13,000	—

KM# 41 2 THALER
44.0000 g., Silver **Ruler:** Friedrich I **Note:** Dav. #LS-A422.

Date	Mintage	VG	F	VF	XF	Unc
ND(1683-90) IGW	—	1,800	3,000	4,650	6,600	—

KM# A40 2 THALER
Silver **Ruler:** Friedrich I **Obv:** Bust right **Rev:** Scales on pillow, date in legend **Note:** Dav. #A7464. Similar to 1 Thaler, KM#34.

Date	Mintage	VG	F	VF	XF	Unc
1683	—	—	—	—	—	—

KM# 42 2 THALER
Silver **Ruler:** Friedrich I **Obv:** Bust right **Rev:** Crown surmounted by imperial orb **Mint:** Gotha

Date	Mintage	VG	F	VF	XF	Unc
ND(1683-88) IGW	—	—	—	—	—	—

KM# 44 2 THALER
Silver **Ruler:** Friedrich I **Obv:** Bust right **Rev:** Scales on pillow, date in legend **Mint:** Gotha

Date	Mintage	VG	F	VF	XF	Unc
1683 IGW	—	—	—	—	—	—

KM# 40 2 THALER
43.3000 g., Silver **Ruler:** Friedrich I **Note:** Dav. #LS421. Similar to 1-1/2 Thaler, KM#37.

Date	Mintage	VG	F	VF	XF	Unc
ND(1683-88) IGW	—	—	—	5,300	8,300	—

KM# 61 2 THALER

Silver **Ruler:** Friedrich I **Obv:** Laureate bust right **Rev:** Hexagram in rays and clouds, sun to left, moon to right, above A. NUMINE. LUMEN, below crowned phoenix holding disk in beak with alchemical symbols, curved at bottom SUSCIPIO. GOT date ET. REDDO. **Mint:** Gotha

Date	Mintage	VG	F	VF	XF	Unc
1687 IGW	—	—	—	—	—	—

KM# 81 2 THALER

Silver **Ruler:** Friedrich I **Obv:** 6 medallions with busts either left or right around central medallion with bust right **Rev:** 6-helmeted manifold arms divide mintmaster's initials in middle, date near bottom **Rev. Legend:** LANDG: TH: MARCH: M: PRINC: DIC: HENN: **Mint:** Gotha

Date	Mintage	VG	F	VF	XF	Unc
1688 IGW	—	—	—	—	—	—

KM# 79 2 THALER

Silver **Ruler:** Friedrich I **Obv:** Six medalluions with busts either left or right aroud central medallion of bust turned 3/4 to left **Obv. Legend:** D-S-I-C-&-M **Rev:** 6-helmeted manifold arms divide mintmaster's initials in middle, date near bottom **Rev. Legend:** LANDG: TH: MARCH: M: PRINC: DIC: HENN: **Mint:** Gotha **Note:** Dav. #7467.

Date	Mintage	VG	F	VF	XF	Unc
1688 IGW Rare	—	—	—	—	—	—

KM# 80 2 THALER

Silver **Ruler:** Friedrich I **Obv:** 6 medallions with busts either left or right around center medallion of bust right **Rev:** 6-helmeted manifold arms divide date **Note:** Dav. #7469. Similar to 1 Thaler, KM#75.

Date	Mintage	VG	F	VF	XF	Unc
1688 IGW Rare	—	—	—	—	—	—
1691 IT Rare	—	—	—	—	—	—

KM# A82 2 THALER

Silver **Ruler:** Friedrich I **Obv:** 6 medallions with busts either left or right around center medallion of bust right **Rev:** Helmeted arms in inner circle, date in legend below **Note:** Dav. #A7471. Similar to 1 Thaler, KM#76.

Date	Mintage	VG	F	VF	XF	Unc
1688 Rare	—	—	—	—	—	—

KM# 82 2 THALER

Silver **Ruler:** Friedrich I **Obv:** 7 busts facing left and right **Rev:** Date divided at top **Note:** Dav. 7472. Similar to 1 Thaler, KM#77.

Date	Mintage	VG	F	VF	XF	Unc
1688 IGW Rare	—	—	—	—	—	—

KM# 22 3 THALER

Silver **Ruler:** Friedrich I **Obv:** Rural scene **Rev:** Value 3 punched in near bottom **Mint:** Gotha **Note:** Varieties exist.

Date	Mintage	VG	F	VF	XF	Unc
ND(1681-83) IGS//HM	—	—	—	—	—	—
ND(1683-88) IGS//IGW	—	—	—	—	—	—
ND(1683-88) IGW	—	—	—	—	—	—

KM# 45 4 THALER

Silver **Ruler:** Friedrich I **Note:** Dav. #LS-A421. Similar to 1-1/2 Thaler, KM#37.

Date	Mintage	VG	F	VF	XF	Unc
ND(1683-90) IGW Rare	—	—	—	—	—	—

TRADE COINAGE

KM# 47 GOLDGULDEN

3.5000 g., 0.9860 Gold 0.1109 oz. AGW **Ruler:** Friedrich I **Obv:** Crowned 4-fold arms in inner circle **Rev:** Figure of Fortune on globe **Note:** Fr. 2959.

Date	Mintage	VG	F	VF	XF	Unc
1684 IGW	—	1,900	4,050	7,400	12,500	—

KM# 30 1/4 DUCAT

0.8750 g., 0.9860 Gold 0.0277 oz. AGW **Ruler:** Friedrich I **Obv:** Bust to right **Rev:** Crowned oval arms **Note:** Fr. 2966.

Date	Mintage	VG	F	VF	XF	Unc
1682 HIM	—	240	600	1,100	2,000	—
1684 IGW	—	240	600	1,100	2,000	—

KM# 89 1/2 DUCAT

1.7500 g., 0.9860 Gold 0.0555 oz. AGW **Ruler:** Friedrich I **Obv:** Bust to right **Rev:** Cruciform arms with F in angles **Note:** Fr. 2961.

Date	Mintage	VG	F	VF	XF	Unc
1689	—	450	900	1,950	3,500	—
1690	—	450	900	1,950	3,500	—

KM# 99 1/2 DUCAT

1.7500 g., 0.9860 Gold 0.0555 oz. AGW **Ruler:** Friedrich I **Rev:** Ship at sea **Note:** Fr. 2963.

Date	Mintage	VG	F	VF	XF	Unc
1690	—	750	1,500	3,000	5,500	—

KM# 23 DUCAT

3.5000 g., 0.9860 Gold 0.1109 oz. AGW **Ruler:** Friedrich I **Obv:** Bust to right **Rev:** Crowned oval manifold arms in baroque frame, date in legend at upper left **Note:** Fr. #2957.

Date	Mintage	VG	F	VF	XF	Unc
1681 HM	—	1,150	2,300	4,500	9,500	—
1683 IGW	—	1,150	2,300	4,500	9,500	—

KM# 24 DUCAT

3.5000 g., 0.9860 Gold 0.1109 oz. AGW **Ruler:** Friedrich I **Subject:** Death of Magdalena Sybilla, Wife of Friedrich I **Obv:** Laureate head of Magdalena Sybilla left **Rev:** 6-line inscription **Note:** Fr. 2958.

Date	Mintage	VG	F	VF	XF	Unc
1681	—	950	1,900	3,850	7,500	—

KM# 90 DUCAT

3.5000 g., 0.9860 Gold 0.1109 oz. AGW **Ruler:** Friedrich I **Obv:** Bust to right **Rev:** Cruciform arms with F in angles **Note:** Fr. 2960.

Date	Mintage	VG	F	VF	XF	Unc
1689 F	—	850	1,700	3,600	7,000	—

KM# 100 DUCAT

3.5000 g., 0.9860 Gold 0.1109 oz. AGW **Ruler:** Friedrich I **Rev:** Ship at sea **Note:** Fr. 2962.

Date	Mintage	VG	F	VF	XF	Unc
1690	—	1,450	3,150	6,000	10,500	—

KM# 101 DUCAT

3.5000 g., 0.9860 Gold 0.1109 oz. AGW **Ruler:** Friedrich I **Subject:** Friedrich I Awarded Danish Order of Danneborg **Obv:** Head to right **Rev:** Star of Danneborg flanked by cruciform arms with F in angles **Note:** Fr. 2965.

Date	Mintage	VG	F	VF	XF	Unc
1690 F	—	900	1,850	3,600	7,000	—

KM# 120 DUCAT

3.5000 g., 0.9860 Gold 0.1109 oz. AGW **Ruler:** Friedrich I **Subject:** Death of Friedrich I **Obv:** Armored bust to right **Rev:** 8-line inscription in palm branches **Note:** Fr. 2967.

Date	Mintage	VG	F	VF	XF	Unc
1691 IT	—	525	1,150	2,550	5,000	—

KM# 119 DUCAT

Gold **Ruler:** Friedrich I **Subject:** Friedrich I Awarded Danish Order of Danneborg **Obv:** Head of Friedrich I right **Rev:** Star of Dannenborg flanked by 4 oval arms

Date	Mintage	VG	F	VF	XF	Unc
1691	—	—	—	—	—	—

Note: Künker Auction 144, 10-08, Unc realized approximately $19,575.

KM# 134 DUCAT

3.5000 g., 0.9860 Gold 0.1109 oz. AGW **Ruler:** Friedrich II and Johann Wilhelm **Subject:** Homage of the City of Gotha **Obv:** Bernhard and Heinrich, regents for Friedrich and Johann Wilhelm **Note:** Fr. 2968.

Date	Mintage	VG	F	VF	XF	Unc
1692	115	525	1,050	2,200	3,850	—

KM# 135 DUCAT

3.5000 g., 0.9860 Gold 0.1109 oz. AGW **Ruler:** Friedrich II and Johann Wilhelm **Obv:** Bust with high coiffure facing right **Rev:** Crowned oval manifold arms in baroque frame **Rev. Legend:** LANDGR. TH. etc. **Note:** Fr. #2970.

Date	Mintage	VG	F	VF	XF	Unc
1692	—	650	1,450	3,250	6,750	—

KM# 145 DUCAT

Gold **Ruler:** Friedrich II **Obv:** Bust with high coiffure facing right **Rev:** Manifold arms with concave sides divide date near bottom, 6 helmets above **Rev. Legend:** LANDG. TH. ... **Mint:** Gotha **Note:** Fr. #2970.

Date	Mintage	VG	F	VF	XF	Unc
1694 IT	100	1,000	2,000	4,000	7,750	—

KM# 151 DUCAT

Gold **Ruler:** Friedrich II **Obv:** Bust with high coiffure facing right **Rev:** Manifold oval arms divide date near bottom, 6 helmets above, AMORE ET PRVDENTIA curved above **Mint:** Gotha **Note:** Fr. #2970.

Date	Mintage	VG	F	VF	XF	Unc
1698 CS//IT	Inc. above	1,000	2,000	4,000	7,750	—
1698 IT	1,224	1,000	2,000	4,000	7,750	—
1699 CS	—	1,000	2,000	4,000	7,750	—

KM# 102 1-1/2 DUCAT

Gold **Ruler:** Friedrich I **Obv:** Laureate bust of Friedrich I right **Rev:** Busts of princes Friedrich (II) and Johann Wilhelm right in circle, date below

Date	Mintage	VG	F	VF	XF	Unc
1690 Rare	—	—	—	—	—	—

KM# 91 2 DUCAT

Gold **Ruler:** Friedrich I **Subject:** Dedication of Friedrichswerth Castle **Obv:** Bust right **Rev:** View of castle **Rev. Legend:** ARCEM TEMPLVM FRIDERICHS WERTHE **Rev. Inscription:** INA VGVRARI FECIT / date **Note:** Fr. #2959a prev. listed in Saxe-New-Gotha. Struck using same dies as 1/4 Thaler, KM#86.

Date	Mintage	VG	F	VF	XF	Unc
1689 F Rare	—	—	—	—	—	—

KM# 103 2 DUCAT

7.0000 g., 0.9860 Gold 0.2219 oz. AGW **Ruler:** Friedrich I **Obv:** Laureate bust to right **Rev:** Busts of princes Friedrich II and Johann Wilhelm right **Note:** Fr. 2967a. Struck from same dies as 1-1/2 Ducat, KM#102.

Date	Mintage	VG	F	VF	XF	Unc
1690	—	850	1,600	3,300	6,250	—

KM# 104 2 DUCAT

Gold **Ruler:** Friedrich I **Subject:** Friedrich I Awarded Danish Order of Danneborg **Obv:** Head of Friedrich I right **Rev:** Star of Danneborg flanked by cruciform arms with 'F' in angles **Mint:** Gotha

Date	Mintage	VG	F	VF	XF	Unc
1690 F	—	2,000	3,500	6,000	10,000	—

KM# 155 2 DUCAT

Gold **Ruler:** Friedrich II **Obv:** Bust with high coiffure facing right **Rev:** Manifold oval arms, AMORE ET PRVDENTIA curved above **Mint:** Gotha

Date	Mintage	VG	F	VF	XF	Unc
1699 CW Rare	—	—	—	—	—	—

KM# 92 3 DUCAT

Gold **Ruler:** Friedrich I **Subject:** Dedication of Friedrichswerth Castle **Obv:** Bust right **Rev:** View of castle, in exergue INA VGVRARI FECIT / date **Rev. Legend:** ARCEM TEMPLVM FRIDERICS WERTHE **Note:** Struck from same dies as 1/4 Thaler, KM#86.

Date	Mintage	VG	F	VF	XF	Unc
1689 F Rare	—	—	—	—	—	—

KM# 106 6 DUCAT

Gold **Ruler:** Friedrich I **Obv:** 6 medallions with busts either left or right around central medallion of bust turned right **Obv. Legend:** DVCES - SAXON - IVL. - CLIV. - ET - MONT: **Rev:** 6-helmeted manifold arms divide mintmaster's initials in middle, date near bottom **Rev. Legend:** LANDG: TH: MARCH: M: PRINC: DIC: HENN: **Mint:** Gotha **Note:** Struck from same dies as Thaler, KM#75.

Date	Mintage	VG	F	VF	XF	Unc
1690 IT Rare	—	—	—	—	—	—

KM# 52 10 DUCAT

Gold **Ruler:** Friedrich I **Obv:** Bust right in circle, legend unbroken at top **Rev:** Helmeted arms dividing date and IG-W **Mint:** Gotha **Note:** Struck from same dies as Thaler, KM#51.

Date	Mintage	VG	F	VF	XF	Unc
1685 IGW Rare	—	—	—	—	—	—

KM# 62 10 DUCAT

Gold **Ruler:** Friedrich I **Subject:** Test of Alchemy **Obv:** Laureate bust right **Rev:** Hexagram in rays and clouds, sun to left, moon to right, above A. NUMINE. LUMEN, below crowned phoenix holding disk in beak with alchemical symbols, curved at bottom SUSCIPIO. GOT date ET. REDDO. **Mint:** Gotha **Note:** Struck from same dies as Thaler, KM#60.

Date	Mintage	VG	F	VF	XF	Unc
1687 IGW Rare	—	—	—	—	—	—

KM# 84 10 DUCAT

Gold **Ruler:** Friedrich I **Subject:** Remembrance of Friedrich I's First Wife, Magdalene Sibylla von Sachsen-Weissenfels **Obv:** Laureate bust of Magdalene Sibylla to left **Rev:** Square tablet with 12-line inscription and R.N. date, issue date in arabesque above **Mint:** Gotha **Note:** Struck from same dies as Thaler, KM#78.

Date	Mintage	VG	F	VF	XF	Unc
1688 CW//CF Rare	—	—	—	—	—	—

PATTERNS

Including off metal strikes

KM#	Date	Mintage	Identification	Mkt Val
Pn1	1680 GFS	—	Thaler. Tin. KM#3.	—
Pn2	1689	—	1/2 Ducat. Silver. KM#89.	—
Pn3	1689	—	Ducat. Silver. KM#90.	—
Pn4	1690	—	1/2 Ducat. Silver. KM#99.	—
Pn5	1690	—	Ducat. Silver. KM#101.	—
Pn6	1690	—	2 Ducat. Silver. KM#103.	—
Pn7	1691	—	1/4 Thaler. Tin. KM#113.	—
Pn8	1698 IT	—	Ducat. Silver. KM#151. (1/12 Thaler?)	—

SAXE-COBURG

(Sachsen-Coburg)

Coburg, a town in southern Thuringia (Thüringen) – now belonging to Bavaria - came to the Wettin dukes of Saxony and Thuringia thru a marriage in the fourteenth century. In the division of the Wettin territories into two lines in 1485, Coburg was vested in the Ernestine branch. It was ruled by Johann Ernst I (1542-1553), younger brother of Johann Friedrich I, passing successively to Old-Gotha, Old-Altenburg, and finally to the New-Gotha line. In 1680, Coburg was created a separate duchy for Albrecht III, the second son of Ernst the Pious. At his death in 1699, there was vehement contention among his surviving brothers. The duke of Saxe-Meiningen controlled most of the Coburg territories at first, but eventually they were assigned to the youngest brother, Johann Ernst VIII of Saalfeld.

RULER

Albrecht III, 1680-1699

MINT OFFICIALS' INITIALS

Initial	Date	Name
SM	1674-95	Sebastian Müller, mintmaster in Hanau
RA	1676-1690?	Johann Reinhart Arnold, warden in Hanau
GFS	1677-80	Georg Friedrich Staude, mintmaster in Gotha
(a = and/or PFC	1686-1714	Paul Friedrich Crumm, warden and mintmaster in Coburg
HEA	1686-1705	Heinrich Ernst Angerstein, mintmaster in Coburg

DUCHY

REGULAR COINAGE

KM# A1 HELLER

Copper, 15 mm. **Ruler:** Albrecht III **Obv:** Crowned A between 2 palm branches **Rev:** 4-line inscription with date in Gothic letters **Rev. Inscription:** Co / burger / Heller / (date) **Mint:** Coburg **Note:** Ref. KOR-578. Mule of obverse die of KM#2 with reverse die of Saxe-New-Gotha, KM#60.3.

Date	Mintage	Good	VG	F	VF	XF
1679	—	—	—	—	—	—

KM# 2 HELLER

Copper **Ruler:** Albrecht III **Obv:** Capped A between 2 palm branches **Rev:** 4-line inscription with date **Rev. Inscription:** CO / BURGER / HELLER / (date) **Mint:** Coburg **Note:** Ref. KOR#579-85. Previous KM#5. Varieties exist.

Date	Mintage	VG	F	VF	XF	Unc
1680	—	—	—	—	—	—
Note: Reported, not confirmed.						
1681	—	10.00	20.00	40.00	80.00	—
1682	—	10.00	20.00	40.00	80.00	—
1683	—	10.00	20.00	40.00	80.00	—
1684	—	10.00	20.00	40.00	80.00	—
1685	—	10.00	20.00	40.00	80.00	—
1686	—	10.00	20.00	40.00	80.00	—
1689	—	10.00	20.00	40.00	80.00	—

KM# A5 HELLER

Copper, 15 mm. **Ruler:** Albrecht III **Obv:** Oval shield of ducal Saxony arms in baroque frame **Rev:** Rose stem divides Gothic C - H and date **Mint:** Gotha **Note:** Ref. KOR-577.

Date	Mintage	Good	VG	F	VF	XF
1683	—	—	—	—	—	—

KM# 18 HELLER

Copper, 14-15 mm. **Ruler:** Albrecht III **Obv:** Thin capped A between 2 palm branches **Rev:** Small 4-line inscription with date **Rev. Inscription:** CO / BURGER / HELLER / date **Mint:** Coburg **Note:** Ref. KOR#586-92. Varieties exist.

Date	Mintage	Good	VG	F	VF	XF
1691	—	6.00	10.00	22.00	45.00	—
1692	—	6.00	10.00	22.00	45.00	—
1693	—	6.00	10.00	22.00	45.00	—
1694	—	6.00	10.00	22.00	45.00	—
1695	—	6.00	10.00	22.00	45.00	—
1696	—	6.00	10.00	22.00	45.00	—
1697	—	6.00	10.00	22.00	45.00	—

KM# 30 HELLER

Copper **Ruler:** Albrecht III **Obv:** Thin capped A between 2 palm branches **Rev:** 4-line inscription with date, top and bottom lines bracketed by stars **Rev. Inscription:** ★ CO ★ / BURGER / HELLER / ★ date ★ **Mint:** Coburg **Note:** Ref. KOR-593.

Date	Mintage	Good	VG	F	VF	XF
1699	—	8.00	15.00	30.00	60.00	—

KM# 10 3 PFENNIG (Dreier)

Billon, 15-17 mm. **Ruler:** Albrecht III **Obv:** Oval shield of ducal Saxony arms in baroque frame, princely hat divides date above **Rev:** Imperial orb with 3 divides mintmaster's initials, legend curved above **Rev. Legend:** A. H - Z. S. **Mint:** Coburg **Note:** Ref. KOR#564-569, 571, 573. Varieties exist.

Date	Mintage	VG	F	VF	XF	Unc
1685 PFC	—	7.00	15.00	35.00	70.00	140
1686 PFC	—	7.00	15.00	35.00	70.00	140
1687 PFC	—	7.00	15.00	35.00	70.00	140
1688 PFC	—	7.00	15.00	35.00	70.00	140
1689 PFC	—	7.00	15.00	35.00	70.00	140
1690 PFC	—	7.00	15.00	35.00	70.00	140
1691 PFC	—	7.00	15.00	35.00	70.00	140

KM# 17 3 PFENNIG (Dreier)

0.9700 g., 0.1875 Billon 0.0058 oz., 16-18 mm. **Ruler:** Albrecht III **Obv:** Large oval shield of ducal Saxony arms in baroque frame, princely cap divides date above **Rev:** Imperial orb with 3 divides mintmaster's initials, legend curved above **Rev. Legend:** A. H - Z. S. **Mint:** Coburg **Note:** Ref. KOR#570, 572, 574, 575. Varieties exist.

Date	Mintage	VG	F	VF	XF	Unc
1689 HEA	—	10.00	22.00	45.00	90.00	170
1690 HEA	—	10.00	22.00	45.00	90.00	170
1691 HEA	—	10.00	22.00	45.00	90.00	170
1692 HEA	—	10.00	22.00	45.00	90.00	170

KM# 27 3 PFENNIG (Dreier)

0.9700 g., 0.1875 Billon 0.0058 oz., 16 mm. **Ruler:** Albrecht III **Obv:** Capped oval shield of ducal Saxony arms within palm branches **Rev:** Imperial orb with 3 divides mintmaster's initials, date at end of legend **Rev. Legend:** A. H. Z. S. I. C. M. A. & W. **Mint:** Coburg **Note:** Ref. KOR-576.

Date	Mintage	VG	F	VF	XF	Unc
1695 HEA	—	12.00	25.00	50.00	100	—

KM# 28 6 PFENNIG (Sechser)

1.5000 g., 0.2500 Billon 0.0121 oz., 19 mm. **Ruler:** Albrecht III **Obv:** Oval shield of ducal Saxony arms in baroque frame divides date at top, princely hat above **Rev:** Imperial orb with 6 divides mintmaster's initials **Rev. Legend:** D. G. ALBERTUS III DUX SAX. I. C. M. A. & W. **Mint:** Coburg **Note:** Ref. KOR-562, 563.

Date	Mintage	VG	F	VF	XF	Unc
1695 HEA	—	115	235	775	—	—
1697 HEA	—	—	—	—	—	—

KM# 3 1/24 THALER (Groschen)

Silver, 21 mm. **Ruler:** Albrecht III **Obv:** Shield of 4-fold arms, with central shield of ducal Saxony, divides date, princely hat above **Obv. Legend:** D. G. ALBERTUS. DUX. SAX. I. C. E. MON. **Rev:** Imperial orb with 24 **Rev. Legend:** NACH DEM ZINNISCHEM VERGLEICH **Mint:** Gotha **Note:** Ref. KOR-557.

Date	Mintage	VG	F	VF	XF	Unc
1681	—	—	—	—	—	—

KM# 4 1/24 THALER (Groschen)

Silver, 20-21 mm. **Ruler:** Albrecht III **Obv:** Shield of 4-fold arms, with central shield of ducal Saxony, divides date, princely hat above **Obv. Legend:** D. G. ALBERTUS. DUX. SAX. I. C. E. MON. **Rev:** Imperial orb with 24 **Rev. Legend:** NACH DEM OBER(.)SACHS CREYS SCHLUS **Mint:** Gotha **Note:** Ref. KOR-558, 559. Varieties exist.

Date	Mintage	VG	F	VF	XF	Unc
1681	—	—	—	—	—	—
1682	—	75.00	150	275	—	—

KM# 22 1/24 THALER (Groschen)

1.9700 g., 0.4160 Silver 0.0263 oz. ASW, 22-23 mm. **Ruler:** Albrecht III **Obv:** Cross in circle, 4 small capped shields of arms in angles **Obv. Legend:** D. G. ALBERTUS III. - DVX. S. I. C. M. A. & W. **Rev:** 6-line inscription with date and mintmaster's initials/symbol **Rev. Legend:** NACH DEM LEIP ZIGER FVS. **Rev. Inscription:** 24 / EINEN / REICHS / THALER / (date) / (initials) **Mint:** Coburg **Note:** Ref. KOR-560, 561. Varieties exist.

Date	Mintage	VG	F	VF	XF	Unc
1693 HEA (a)	—	10.00	25.00	55.00	110	—
1694 HEA (a)	—	—	—	—	—	—
Note: Reported, not confirmed.						
1695 HEA (a)	—	10.00	25.00	55.00	110	—

KM# 5 1/12 THALER (Doppelgroschen)

Silver, 24-25 mm. **Ruler:** Albrecht III **Obv:** Armored bust to right divides date to lower left and right **Obv. Legend:** D. G. ALBERTUS. DUX. SAX. I. C. &. M. **Rev:** Oval shield of 4-fold arms in baroque frame, princely hat above **Rev. Legend:** XII. EIN(EN) REICHS THALER **Mint:** Gotha **Note:** Ref. KOR-545, 546. Varieties exist.

Date	Mintage	VG	F	VF	XF	Unc
1683	—	100	200	345	675	—

KM# 7 1/12 THALER (Doppelgroschen)

Silver, 24-26 mm. **Ruler:** Albrecht III **Obv:** Oval shield of 4-fold arms in baroque frame, princely hat above **Obv. Legend:** D. G. ALBERTUS. DUX. SAX. I. C. E. MO. **Rev:** 6-line inscription with date and mintmaster's initials within palm branches **Rev. Inscription:** 12 / EINEN / REICHS / THALER / (date) / (initials) **Mint:** Hanau **Note:** Ref. KOR-548, 549. Varieties exist.

Date	Mintage	VG	F	VF	XF	Unc
1684 SM	—	50.00	100	200	425	—
1685 SM	—	50.00	100	200	425	—

KM# 6 1/12 THALER (Doppelgroschen)

Silver, 25 mm. **Ruler:** Albrecht III **Obv:** Crowned script ADSC monogram divides date, mintmaster's initials below **Obv. Legend:** D. G. ALBERTUS. DUX. SAX. I. C. E. MO. **Rev:** Oval shield of 4-fold arms in baroque frame, princely hat above **Rev. Legend:** XII. EINEN. REICHS THALER **Mint:** Hanau **Note:** Ref. KOR-547.

Date	Mintage	VG	F	VF	XF	Unc
1684 SM	—	50.00	100	200	425	—

KM# 12 1/12 THALER (Doppelgroschen)

Silver **Ruler:** Albrecht III **Subject:** Death of Marie Elisabeth von Braunschweig-Wolfenbüttel, Wife of Albrecht III **Obv:** Bust to right **Obv. Legend:** MARIA. ELISABETHA. DUC. SAX. IUL. **Rev:** 8-line inscription, with dates, in circle **Rev. Legend:** *CLIV. & MONT. NATA DU (-) C (-) BRUNSV. & LUNEBURG. **Rev. Inscription:** NATA / BRUNSVIG. / Z7 IAN 1638. / DENAT. COBUR / 15 FEBR 1687 / ÆTAT. AN 49. / DIE 19 / (initials) **Mint:** Coburg **Note:** Ref. KOR#594-96. Varieties exist.

Date	Mintage	VG	F	VF	XF	Unc
1687 PFC	—	—	—	—	—	—
1687 HEA (a)	—	70.00	140	250	475	—
1687 HEA	—	80.00	165	300	600	—

KM# 16 1/12 THALER (Doppelgroschen)

Silver, 26-27 mm. **Ruler:** Albrecht III **Obv:** Oval shield of 4-fold arms in baroque frame, princely hat above **Obv. Legend:** D. G. ALBERTUS. DUX. SAX. I. C. E. MO. **Rev:** 5-line inscription with date in palm branches **Rev. Inscription:** 12 / EINEN / REICHS / THALER / (date) **Mint:** Hanau **Note:** Ref. KOR#550-552. Varieties exist.

Date	Mintage	VG	F	VF	XF	Unc
1688	—	50.00	100	200	425	—
1689	—	50.00	100	200	425	—
1689 RA	—	50.00	100	200	425	—
1690	—	50.00	100	200	425	—

KM# 20.1 1/12 THALER (Doppelgroschen)

3.1500 g., 0.5000 Silver 0.0506 oz. ASW, 26 mm. **Ruler:** Albrecht III **Obv:** Cross superimposed on shield of 4-fold arms in circle, princely hat above **Obv. Legend:** D. G. ALBERT. III - DUX. S. I. C. M. A & W. **Rev:** 6-line inscription with date and mintmaster's intials in circle **Rev. Legend:** L. THVR. M. MISN. C. P. HENNE(B). C. M. & R. D. R. **Rev. Inscription:** 12 / EINEN / REICHS / THALER / (date) / (initials) **Mint:** Coburg **Note:** Ref. KOR-553.

Date	Mintage	VG	F	VF	XF	Unc
1692 HEA	—	—	—	—	—	—

KM# 20.2 1/12 THALER (Doppelgroschen)

3.1500 g., 0.5000 Silver 0.0506 oz. ASW, 25 mm. **Ruler:** Albrecht III **Obv:** Cross superimposed on 4-fold arms in circle, princely hat above **Obv. Legend:** ALBERTUS III. D - G. DUX. S. I. C. M. A. & W. **Rev:** 6-line inscription with date and mintmaster's intials in circle **Rev. Legend:** NACH DEN OBERSACHS: INT: CREYS FUS: A. **Rev. Inscription:** 12 / EINEN / REICHS / THALE / R (date) / (initials) **Mint:** Coburg **Note:** Ref. KOR-554.

Date	Mintage	VG	F	VF	XF	Unc
1692 HEA	—	15.00	35.00	75.00	150	—

KM# 23.2 1/12 THALER (Doppelgroschen)

3.1500 g., 0.5000 Silver 0.0506 oz. ASW, 26-27 mm. **Ruler:** Albrecht III **Obv:** Cross in circle, 4 small shields of arms in angles **Obv. Legend:** D. G. ALBERTUS III - D(U)(V)X. S. I. C. M. A. & W. **Rev:** 6-line inscription with date and mintmaster's initials/symbol in circle **Rev. Legend:** NACH DEM LEIP ZIGER F(V)(U)S. **Rev. Inscription:** 12 / EINEN / REICHS / THALER / (date) / (initials) **Mint:** Coburg **Note:** Ref. KOR-555.2, 556.

Date	Mintage	VG	F	VF	XF	Unc
1693 HEA	—	25.00	50.00	100	200	—
1695 HEA	—	25.00	50.00	100	200	—

KM# 23.1 1/12 THALER (Doppelgroschen)

3.1500 g., 0.5000 Silver 0.0506 oz. ASW, 26 mm. **Ruler:** Albrecht III **Obv:** Cross in circle, 4 small capped shields of arms in angles, date at end of legend **Obv. Legend:** D. G. ALBERTUS III. - DVX. S. I. C. M. A. & W. **Rev:** 5-line inscription with mintmaster's initials in circle **Rev. Legend:** NACH DEM LEIP ZIGER FUS **Rev. Inscription:** 12 / EINEN / REICHS / THALER / date / (initials) **Mint:** Coburg **Note:** Ref. KOR-555.1.

Date	Mintage	VG	F	VF	XF	Unc
1693 HEA (a)	—	25.00	50.00	100	200	—

KM# 24 1/6 THALER (4 Groschen)

4.3300 g., 0.7500 Silver 0.1044 oz. ASW, 28-29 mm. **Ruler:** Albrecht III **Obv:** Draped bust to right, value (1/6) in oval on shoulder **Obv. Legend:** ALBERTUS. III. - D. G. D. S. I. C. M. A. A. & W. **Rev:** Cross in circle, 4 small shields of capped arms in angles, date divided by foot of cross **Rev. Legend:** NACH DEN LEIPZIGER FUS. **Mint:** Coburg **Note:** Ref. KOR-542, 543.

Date	Mintage	VG	F	VF	XF	Unc
1693 HEA (a)	—	20.00	40.00	80.00	160	—
1693 HEA	—	20.00	40.00	80.00	160	—

KM# 25 1/6 THALER (4 Groschen)

4.3300 g., 0.7500 Silver 0.1044 oz. ASW, 29-30 mm. **Ruler:** Albrecht III **Obv:** Armored bust to right **Obv. Legend:** D. G. ALBERT(V)(U)S III. DVX. SAX. I. C. M. A. & W. **Rev:** Cross in circle, 4 small capped shields of arms in angles, date at beginning of legend, value (1/6) in oval at top, mintmaster's initials and symbol at end of legend **Rev. Legend:** NACH DEM LEIP - ZIGER FVS: **Mint:** Coburg **Note:** Ref. KOR-544. Varieties exist.

Date	Mintage	VG	F	VF	XF	Unc
1694 HEA (a)	—	30.00	65.00	125	240	—

KM# 1 2/3 THALER (Gulden)

Silver, 40 mm. **Ruler:** Albrecht III **Obv:** Crowned shield of 4-fold arms, with central shield of ducal Saxony, divides date and mintmaster's initials, value (2/3) in oval below **Obv. Legend:** ALBERT. D. G. DUX. - SAX. IUL. CL. &. MON. **Rev:** Crown above ornate ADS monogram, legend in cursive lettering **Rev. Legend:** Point de Couronne Sans Peine **Mint:** Gotha **Note:** Ref. KOR-532; Dav. 835.

Date	Mintage	VG	F	VF	XF	Unc
1679 GFS	—	25.00	50.00	100	200	—

KM# 11 2/3 THALER (Gulden)

Silver, 38-40 mm. **Ruler:** Albrecht III **Obv:** Armored bust to right **Obv. Legend:** D. G. ALBERTUS DUX. SAX. I(U)(L). C(L). &(.) M. **Rev:** Crowned Spanish shield of 4-fold arms, with central shield of ducal Saxony, between 2 palm fronds, divides date and mintmaster's initials, value (2/3) below in oval **Rev. Legend:** POINT DE COURO - NNE SANS PEINE **Mint:** Coburg **Note:** Ref. KOR#533-39; Dav. 836. Varieties exist.

Date	Mintage	VG	F	VF	XF	Unc
1685 PFC	—	100	225	325	625	—
1686/5 PFC	—	100	225	325	625	—
1686 PFC	—	100	225	325	625	—
1687 PFC	—	100	225	325	625	—
1688 PFC	—	100	225	325	625	—
1688 HEA	—	100	225	325	625	—
1689 PFC	—	100	225	325	625	—
1689 HEA	—	100	225	325	625	—

KM# 19 2/3 THALER (Gulden)

17.3300 g., 0.7500 Silver 0.4179 oz. ASW, 40 mm. **Ruler:** Albrecht III **Obv:** Armored bust to right in circle, value (2/3) in oval below **Obv. Legend:** D. G. ALBERTUS III. DUX. SAX. IUL. CL. MON. AN. & WES. **Rev:** Cross superimposed on shield of 4-fold arms, large crown above, date at end of legend **Rev. Legend:** NACH DEN SACHS - CR(A)(E)YS FUS. **Mint:** Coburg **Note:** Ref. KOR-540; Dav. 837.

Date	Mintage	VG	F	VF	XF	Unc
1691 HEA	—	—	—	—	—	—

KM# 21 2/3 THALER (Gulden)

17.3300 g., 0.7500 Silver 0.4179 oz. ASW, 37 mm. **Ruler:** Albrecht III **Obv:** Armored bust to right **Obv. Legend:** D. G. ALBERTUS III. DUX. SAX. I. C. M. A & W. **Rev:** Cross superimposed on shield of 4-fold arms, crown above, date divided by arms, value 2/3 at end of legend **Rev. Legend:** NACH DEM LEI - PZIGER FUS * 2/3 * **Mint:** Coburg **Note:** Ref. KOR-541; Dav. 838.

Date	Mintage	VG	F	VF	XF	Unc
1692 HEA	—	—	—	—	—	—
1694 HEA	—	—	—	—	—	—

Note: Reported, not confirmed.

KM# 8 THALER

Silver, 41 mm. **Ruler:** Albrecht III **Subject:** Albrecht III Awarded Danish Order of the Elephant **Obv:** Armored bust to right **Obv. Legend:** D.G. ALBERTUS III - DUX. SAX. I.C. & M. **Rev:** Arm from clouds with crown above eagle on rose bush, mintmaster's initials and symbol in exergue **Rev. Legend:** POINT DE - COURONNE SANS PEINE **Mint:** Coburg **Note:** Dav. 7410. Referred to as a Schauthaler in KOR.

Date	Mintage	VG	F	VF	XF	Unc
ND(1684) HEA (a)	—	350	650	1,100	1,650	—

KM# 13 THALER

Silver, 43 mm. **Ruler:** Albrecht III **Obv:** Armored bust to right **Obv. Legend:** D: G. ALBERTUS III. DUX. SAX. I.C. &. M. **Rev:** Small shield of 4-fold arms in center of cross superimposed on mantled shield of manifold arms, crown above divides date **Rev. Legend:** POINT DE COURONNE SANS PEINE. **Mint:** Coburg **Note:** Ref. KOR-530; Dav. 7411.

Date	Mintage	VG	F	VF	XF	Unc
1687 PFC	—	800	1,500	2,750	4,500	—

KM# 26 THALER

Silver, 44 mm. **Ruler:** Albrecht III **Obv:** Armored bust to right **Obv. Legend:** D. G. ALBERTUS III. DUX. SAX. I. C. M. A. ET W. **Rev:** Small shield of 4-fold arms in center of cross superimposed on crowned and mantled shield of manifold arms, mintmaster's initials and symbol at end of legend, date in edge legend **Rev. Legend:** POINT DE COURONNE SANS PEINE **Edge Lettering:** NACH DEM ALTEN REICHS SCHROT UND KORN. (date). **Mint:** Coburg **Note:** Ref. KOR-531; Dav. 7412. Known with and without edge legend

Date	Mintage	VG	F	VF	XF	Unc
1694 HEA (a)	—	800	1,500	2,750	4,500	—
ND(1694) HEA (a)	—	800	1,500	2,750	4,500	—

TRADE COINAGE

KM# 14 DUCAT

3.5000 g., 0.9860 Gold 0.1109 oz. AGW, 23 mm. **Ruler:** Albrecht III **Obv:** Armored bust to right **Obv. Legend:** D. G. ALBERT. III. DUX. SAX. I. C & M: **Rev:** Small shield of 4-fold arms in center of cross superimposed on mantled shield of manifold arms, crown above divides date **Rev. Legend:** POINT DE COURONNE SANS PEINE. **Mint:** Coburg **Note:** Ref. KOR-529. Prev. KM #30.

Date	Mintage	VG	F	VF	XF	Unc
1687 PFC Rare	—	—	—	—	—	—

KM# 15 2 DUCAT

7.0000 g., 0.9860 Gold 0.2219 oz. AGW, 23 mm. **Ruler:** Albrecht III **Obv:** Armored bust to left **Obv. Legend:** D. G. ALBERT. III. DUX. SAX. I. C & M: **Rev:** Small shield of 4-fold arms in center of cross superimposed on mantled shield of manifold arms, crown above divides date **Rev. Legend:** POINT DE COURONNE SANS PEINE. **Mint:** Coburg **Note:** Ref. KOR-528. Struck on thick flan from Ducat dies, KM#14.

Date	Mintage	VG	F	VF	XF	Unc
1687 PFC Rare	—	—	—	—	—	—

SAXE-MEININGEN

(Sachsen-Meiningen)

The duchy of Saxe-Meiningen was located in Thuringia, sandwiched between Saxe-Weimar-Eisenach on the west and north and the enclave of Schmalkalden belonging to Hesse-Cassel on the east. It was founded upon the division of the Ernestine line in Saxe-Gotha in 1680. In 1735, due to an exchange of some territory, the duchy became known as Saxe-Coburg-Meiningen. In 1826, Saxe-Coburg-Gotha assigned Saalfeld to Saxe-Meiningen. The duchy came under the strong influence of Prussia from 1866, when Bernhard II was forced to abdicate because of his support of Austria. The monarchy ended with the defeat of Germany in 1918.

RULERS

Bernhard, 1680-1706
Ernst Ludwig I, 1706-1724
Ernst Ludwig II, 1724-1729
Karl Friedrich, 1729-1743
Friedrich Wilhelm, 1743-1746
Anton Ulrich, 1746-1763
August Friedrich Karl, under Regency of

Charlotte Amalie, 1763-1775
Alone as Karl, 1775-1782
Georg I, 1782-1803
Bernhard Erich Freund, under Regency of Louise Eleonore, 1803-1821
Bernhard II, 1821-1866
Georg II, 1866-1914
Bernhard III, 1914-1918

MINT OFFICIALS' INITIALS

Initial	Date	Name
CW, W	1688-1739	Christian Wermuth, die-cutter in Gotha
F. HELFRICHT	d. 1892	Ferdinand Helfricht, die-cutter and chief medailleur
GFA	1673-76	Georg Friedrich Staude in Weimar
	1677-80	In Gotha
	1687	In Meiningen
	1687	In Erfurt
HEA	1686-1705	Heinrich Ernst Angerstein, mintmaster in Coburg
	1687-1714	Ernst Friedrich Angerstein in Coburg
HMO	1714-17	Heinrich Ernst Obermuller in Meiningen
ICK	1765-94	Johann Christian Knaust
IGS	1689-90	Johann Georg Sorberger in Meiningen
IT	1690-1723	Johann Thun in Gotha
K	1835-37	Georg Krell, warden then mintmaster
L	1803-33	Georg Christoph Loewel
PFC	1685-1714	Paul Friedrich Crum in Coburg
SNR	1760-74	Siegmund Scholz, warden and
	1764-93	Georg Nikolaus Riedner, mintmaster
VOIGT		J. C. Voigt, die-cutter and medailleur

NOTE: Between 1691 and 1703, Saxe-Meiningen struck coins in various denominations for its part of Henneberg-Ilmenau.

REFERENCE
G = Ludwig Grobe, **Die Münzen des Herzogtums Sachsen-Meiningen**, Meiningen, 1891.

DUCHY

REGULAR COINAGE

KM# 32.1 HELLER
Copper **Ruler:** Bernhard I **Obv:** Crowned arms **Rev:** Value, date **Rev. Legend:** MEIN/HELLER

Date	Mintage	VG	F	VF	XF	Unc
1699	—	5.00	12.00	27.00	55.00	—

KM# 32.2 HELLER
Copper **Ruler:** Bernhard I **Rev:** Value, date **Rev. Legend:** M/HELLER

Date	Mintage	VG	F	VF	XF	Unc
1699	—	5.00	12.00	27.00	55.00	—

KM# 5 GROSCHEN
Silver **Ruler:** Bernhard I **Subject:** Death of Bernhard's First Wife, Marie Hedwig of Hesse-Darmstadt **Obv:** Intertwined M and H, ducal crown above, titles of Marie Hedwig in legend **Rev:** 7-line inscription with dates

Date	Mintage	VG	F	VF	XF	Unc
1680	—	60.00	115	200	425	—

KM# 26 GROSCHEN
Silver **Ruler:** Bernhard I **Obv:** Armored bust of Bernhard right in inner circle **Rev:** View of Meiningen castle

Date	Mintage	VG	F	VF	XF	Unc
1692	—	27.00	45.00	80.00	160	—

KM# 27 GROSCHEN
Silver **Ruler:** Bernhard I **Subject:** Homage of Gotha **Obv:** 2 conjoined busts right, titles in legend **Rev:** 2 joined hands ending in lozenges, MVTVA FIDE above, 4-line inscription with Roman numeral date below

Date	Mintage	VG	F	VF	XF	Unc
1692 IT Rare	—	—	—	—	—	—

KM# 19 1/12 THALER (Doppelgroschen)
Silver **Ruler:** Bernhard I **Obv:** Crowned oval 4-fold arms in baroque frame **Rev:** Value, date and initials **Rev. Legend:** 12/EINEN/REICHS/THALER

Date	Mintage	VG	F	VF	XF	Unc
1689 IGS	—	27.00	55.00	110	220	—
1690 IGS	—	27.00	55.00	110	220	—

KM# 6 1/4 THALER
Silver **Ruler:** Bernhard I **Subject:** Death of Bernhard's First Wife, Marie Hedwig of Hesse-Darmstadt **Obv:** Intertwined M and H, ducal crown above, legend titles of Marie Hedwig **Rev:** 8-line inscription with dates

Date	Mintage	VG	F	VF	XF	Unc
1680 Rare	—	—	—	—	—	—

KM# 9 1/3 THALER (1/2 Gulden)
Silver **Ruler:** Bernhard I **Obv:** Bust right **Rev:** Crowned 4-fold arms in palm branches, value 1/3 below, date in legend

Date	Mintage	VG	F	VF	XF	Unc
1687 GFS	—	—	—	—	—	—

KM# 10 1/3 THALER (1/2 Gulden)
Silver **Ruler:** Bernhard I **Obv:** Date divided at bottom by bust

Date	Mintage	VG	F	VF	XF	Unc
1687	—	—	—	—	—	—

KM# 7 1/2 THALER
Silver **Ruler:** Bernhard I **Subject:** Death of Bernhard's First Wife, Marie Hedwig of Hesse-Darmstadt

Date	Mintage	VG	F	VF	XF	Unc
1680 Rare	—	—	—	—	—	—

KM# 11 2/3 THALER (Gulden)
Silver **Ruler:** Bernhard I **Obv:** Bust right **Rev:** Crowned 4-fold arms in palm branches, value 2/3 below, date in legend

Date	Mintage	VG	F	VF	XF	Unc
1687 GFS	—	45.00	90.00	190	385	—

KM# 14 2/3 THALER (Gulden)
Silver **Ruler:** Bernhard I **Obv:** Bust right **Rev:** Helmeted ornate 18-fold arms, value 2/3 below, date in legend

Date	Mintage	VG	F	VF	XF	Unc
1687 Rare	—	—	—	—	—	—

KM# 15 2/3 THALER (Gulden)
Silver **Ruler:** Bernhard I **Obv:** Crowned intertwined BHZS monogram, value 2/3 below, date in legend **Rev:** Crowned 4-fold arms in palm branches

Date	Mintage	VG	F	VF	XF	Unc
1687	—	225	375	650	1,300	—

KM# 16 2/3 THALER (Gulden)
Silver **Ruler:** Bernhard I **Rev:** Figure seated on stone holding a ring high

Date	Mintage	VG	F	VF	XF	Unc
1687	—	200	325	575	1,150	—

KM# 12 2/3 THALER (Gulden)
Silver **Ruler:** Bernhard I **Obv:** Date divided by bust at bottom and reads facing outwards **Note:** Varieties exist.

Date	Mintage	VG	F	VF	XF	Unc
1687 GFS	—	45.00	90.00	190	385	—
1689 IGS	—	45.00	90.00	190	385	—

KM# 13 2/3 THALER (Gulden)
Silver **Ruler:** Bernhard I **Obv:** Date reads inwards **Note:** Varieties exist.

Date	Mintage	VG	F	VF	XF	Unc
1687 GFS	—	45.00	90.00	190	385	—
1689/7 IGS	—	45.00	90.00	190	385	—
1689 IGS	—	45.00	90.00	190	385	—
1689	—	45.00	90.00	190	385	—

KM# 25 2/3 THALER (Gulden)
Silver **Ruler:** Bernhard I

Date	Mintage	VG	F	VF	XF	Unc
1691 IGS	—	45.00	90.00	190	385	—

KM# 8 THALER
Silver **Ruler:** Bernhard I **Subject:** Death of Bernhard's First Wife, Maria Hedwig of Hesse-Darmstadt **Rev:** Crowned arms above 8-line inscription, 11 arms around **Note:** Dav. #7498.

Date	Mintage	VG	F	VF	XF	Unc
1680	—	1,000	2,000	4,000	7,000	11,500

KM# 28 THALER
Silver **Ruler:** Bernhard I **Subject:** Homage of Gotha **Obv:** 2 conjoined busts right **Rev:** Large helmeted ornate 18-fold arms w/round shield, without value shown **Note:** Dav. #--.

Date	Mintage	VG	F	VF	XF	Unc
1692 Rare	—	—	—	—	—	—

KM# 24 THALER
29.2100 g., Silver, 40 mm. **Ruler:** Bernhard I **Subject:** Dedication of the Chapel at Elisabethenburg Palace **Obv:** Draped and armored bust with long wig to right **Obv. Legend:** BERNHARD9 D. - G. D. S. I. C. M. A. ET. W. **Rev:** Frontal view of palace, "Jehovah" in sun above, double legend, with date at end of outer legend **Rev. Legend:** Outer: TEMPL. SS. TRIN. ELISABETHÆBVRGI. CONSECR. D. LX. NOV. 1692; Inner: TVRRIS. FORTISSIMA. NOMEN. DOMINI. **Mint:** Saalfeld **Note:** Grobe 28; Dav. 7500.

Date	Mintage	VG	F	VF	XF	Unc
1692	—	400	850	1,750	3,250	—

KM# 32 THALER

Silver **Ruler:** Bernhard I **Rev:** Helmeted arms **Note:** Dav. #7501.

Date	Mintage	VG	F	VF	XF	Unc
1694 Rare	—	—	—	—	—	—

TRADE COINAGE

KM# 18 DUCAT

3.5000 g., 0.9860 Gold 0.1109 oz. AGW **Ruler:** Bernhard I **Obv:** Armored bust of Bernhard right in inner circle **Rev:** Arms in inner circle

Date	Mintage	VG	F	VF	XF	Unc
1687	—	800	1,600	2,900	4,600	—
1688	—	800	1,600	2,900	4,600	—

KM# 29 DUCAT

3.5000 g., 0.9860 Gold 0.1109 oz. AGW **Ruler:** Bernhard I **Subject:** Homage of Gotha **Obv:** 2 conjoined busts right, titles in legend **Rev:** 2 joined hands ending in lozenges, MVTVA FIDE above, 4-line inscription with Roman numeral date below

Date	Mintage	VG	F	VF	XF	Unc
1692 IT	—	450	925	1,800	3,050	—

KM# 30 DUCAT

3.5000 g., 0.9860 Gold 0.1109 oz. AGW **Ruler:** Bernhard I **Rev:** View of Meiningen castle

Date	Mintage	VG	F	VF	XF	Unc
1692	—	650	1,300	2,650	4,250	—

KM# 31 2 DUCAT

7.0000 g., 0.9860 Gold 0.2219 oz. AGW **Ruler:** Bernhard I **Obv:** Armored bust of Bernhard right in inner circle **Rev:** View of Meiningen castle

Date	Mintage	VG	F	VF	XF	Unc
1692	—	1,300	2,650	5,300	8,600	—

KM# A25 10 DUCAT

35.0000 g., 0.9860 Gold 1.1095 oz. AGW **Ruler:** Bernhard I **Subject:** Dedication of the Chapel at Elizabethenburg Palace **Obv:** Bust of Bernhard right **Rev:** Jehovah in Hebrew above castle **Note:** Struck with 1 Thaler dies, KM#24.

Date	Mintage	VG	F	VF	XF	Unc
1692 Rare	—	—	—	—	—	—

SAXE-ROMHILD

(Sachsen-Römhild)

Short-lived branch of the Ernestine Saxon house which was created for Heinrich III, 4th son of Ernst the Pious of Saxe-Gotha. The line became extinct in 1710 at Heinrich's death and properties were divided by Gotha, Meiningen and Saalfeld.

RULER

Heinrich III, 1680-1710

MINT OFFICIALS' INITIALS and MARKS

Initial or Mark	Date	Name
ML	ca. 1692	Unknown

DUCHY

REGULAR COINAGE

KM# 1 HELLER

Copper **Ruler:** Heinrich III **Obv:** Crowned 'H' between palm branches **Rev:** Gothic letters **Rev. Inscription:** Rombi / heller / date

Date	Mintage	Good	VG	F	VF	XF
1690	—	100	200	450	1,000	—

KM# A2 3 PFENNIG

0.5600 g., Silver, 17 mm. **Ruler:** Heinrich III **Obv:** Oval shield of ducal Saxony arms in baroque frame, electoral hat above divides date **Rev:** Imperial orb with 3, cross on orb divides H.H. - Z.S. at upper left and right **Mint:** Römhild

Date	Mintage	VG	F	VF	XF	Unc
1690	—	125	250	400	600	—

KM# 3 1/84 GULDEN (Körtling)

Silver **Ruler:** Heinrich III **Obv:** 3 small shields of arms **Rev:** Imperial orb with 84

Date	Mintage	VG	F	VF	XF	Unc
1691	—	35.00	75.00	150	300	650

KM# 5 6 PFENNIG

Silver **Ruler:** Heinrich III **Obv:** 3 small shields of arms **Rev:** Imperial orb with 6

Date	Mintage	VG	F	VF	XF	Unc
1691	—	90.00	190	375	775	—

KM# 4 6 PFENNIG

Silver **Ruler:** Heinrich III **Obv:** Saxony arms **Rev:** Imperial orb with 6 **Note:** Varieties exist.

Date	Mintage	VG	F	VF	XF	Unc
1691	—	100	200	425	850	—

KM# B2 1/42 THALER

Silver, 20 mm. **Ruler:** Heinrich III **Obv:** Shield of ducal Saxony arms between 2 palm branches, electoral hat above **Obv. Legend:** H. H. Z. S. I. C. R. E. M. **Rev:** Imperial orb with 42 divides date within ornamented circle **Mint:** Römhild

Date	Mintage	VG	F	VF	XF	Unc
1690	—	300	650	900	1,250	—

KM# 2 2/3 THALER (Gulden)

Silver **Ruler:** Heinrich III **Obv:** Large armored and wigged bust to right, inward-facing date divided in margin by bottom of bust **Obv. Legend:** D. G. H. D. S. I. C. M. A. &. W. **Rev:** Shield of 4-fold arms between 2 palm branches, electoral hat above, value (2/3) in oval at bottom **Rev. Legend:** SI. DEUS. PRO. NOBIS. - QUIS. CONTRA. NOS. **Mint:** Römhild **Note:** Ref. Dav. 879.

Date	Mintage	VG	F	VF	XF	Unc
1690	—	90.00	180	375	550	—

KM# 6 2/3 THALER (Gulden)

Silver **Ruler:** Heinrich III **Obv:** Bust right, titles of Heinrich III, inward-facing date divided in margin by bottom of bust **Rev:** Smaller crowned 4-fold arms in palm branches, 2/3 in oval at bottom **Note:** Dav. #880.

Date	Mintage	VG	F	VF	XF	Unc
1691	—	115	225	475	—	—

KM# 7 2/3 THALER (Gulden)

Silver **Ruler:** Heinrich III **Obv:** Bust right in inner circle, titles of Heinrich III, inward-facing date divided in margin by bottom of bust **Rev:** Crowned 4-fold arms in palm branches in inner circle, 2/3 in oval at bottom **Note:** Dav. #880A.

Date	Mintage	VG	F	VF	XF	Unc
1691	—	100	200	400	—	—

KM# 8 2/3 THALER (Gulden)

Silver **Ruler:** Heinrich III **Obv:** Bust right, titles of Heinrich III, outward-facing date divided in margin by bottom of bust **Rev:** Crowned 4-fold arms in palm branches, 2/3 in oval at bottom **Note:** Dav. #881.

Date	Mintage	VG	F	VF	XF	Unc
1691	—	85.00	175	365	—	—

KM# 9 THALER

Silver **Ruler:** Heinrich III **Obv:** Armored bust to right **Obv. Legend:** HENRIC'. D.G. - D. S. I. C. M. A. ET. W. **Rev:** Oval shield of manifold arms, 6 ornate helmets above, date divided below **Rev. Legend:** PRINC. D. C. HENN. - LANDG. TH. MAR M. **Note:** Dav. 7502.

Date	Mintage	VG	F	VF	XF	Unc
1692 ML	—	1,400	2,700	4,850	8,200	—

TRADE COINAGE

KM# 10 DUCAT

3.5000 g., 0.9860 Gold 0.1109 oz. AGW **Ruler:** Heinrich III **Obv:** Armored bust to right **Obv. Legend:** HENRICVS. D. - G. DVX. SAX. I. C. M. A. & W. **Rev:** Crowned shield of 4-fold arms, with central shield, divides date as 1- 6 / 9 - 8, suspended Order of the Elephant below, legend begins at lower left **Rev. Legend:** SI DEVS PRO NOBIS - QVIS CONTRA NOS. **Note:** Fr. 2997.1.

Date	Mintage	VG	F	VF	XF	Unc
1698	—	2,050	4,200	8,400	14,500	—

KM# 11 DUCAT

Gold **Ruler:** Heinrich III **Obv:** Armored bust to right **Obv. Legend:** HENRICVS. D. - G. DVX. SAX. I. C. M. A. & W. **Rev:** Crowned oval shield of manifold arms, Order of Elephant around, date divided at bottom, legend begins at upper right **Rev. Legend:** SI DEVS PRO NOBIS - QVIS CONTRA NOS. **Note:** Fr. 2997.2.

Date	Mintage	VG	F	VF	XF	Unc
1698	—	1,700	3,600	6,500	10,500	—

KM# 12 DUCAT

Gold **Ruler:** Heinrich III **Obv:** Armored bust to right **Obv. Legend:** HENRICVS. D. - G. DVX. SAX. I. C. M. A. & W. **Rev:** Small shield of Saxony arms in center of cross superimposed on larger shield of 4-fold arms, suspended Order of the Elephant divides date below, legend begins at upper right **Rev. Legend:** SI DEVS PRO NOBIS - QVIS CONTRA NOS. **Note:** Fr. 2997.3.

Date	Mintage	VG	F	VF	XF	Unc
1698	—	1,700	3,600	6,500	10,500	—

SAXE-EISENBERG

(Sachsen-Eisenberg)

Short-lived branch of the Ernestine Saxon house which was created for Christian, fifth son of Ernst the Pious of Saxe-Gotha. The line became extinct with the death of Christian in 1707 and passed to Saxe-Hildburghausen.

RULER

Christian, 1680-1707

MINT OFFICIALS' INITIALS

Initials	Date	Name
HM	1681-1683	Christian Henning Müller, mintmaster in Gotha
IA	1692-1706	Julius Angerstein, die-cutter and mintmaster in Eisenberg

DUCHY

REGULAR COINAGE

KM# 17 8 PFENNIG

Silver **Ruler:** Christian **Obv:** Facing bust **Obv. Legend:** CHRISTIAN. D.G. DUX. SAX: I. CL. &. MON. **Rev:** Crowned 4-fold arms of Saxony in baroque frame, value (8) in oval at bottom, date at end of legend **Rev. Legend:** VON FEINEM — SILBER **Mint:** Eisenberg

Date	Mintage	VG	F	VF	XF	Unc
1683	—	65.00	110	140	270	—

KM# 38 1/24 THALER (16 Pfennig)

Silver **Ruler:** Christian **Obv:** Armored bust to right **Obv. Legend:** D:G. CHRISTIAN; S. I. C. M. A. &. W. D: **Rev:** Imperial orb with 24 divides date and mintmaster's initials **Rev. Legend:** NACH REICHS SCHROTT U. KORN **Mint:** Eisenberg

Date	Mintage	VG	F	VF	XF	Unc
1698 IA	—	—	—	—	—	—

KM# 39 1/24 THALER (16 Pfennig)

Silver **Ruler:** Christian **Obv:** Helmeted oval arms of ducal Saxony **Obv. Legend:** D:G. CHRISTIANUS SAX. I. C. M. A. &. W. DUX **Rev:** Imperial orb with 24 divides date and mintmaster's initials **Rev. Legend:** NACH REICHS SCHROTT UND KORN **Mint:** Eisenberg

Date	Mintage	VG	F	VF	XF	Unc
1698 IA	—	40.00	80.00	165	325	—

KM# 2 1/4 THALER

Silver **Ruler:** Christian **Subject:** Death of Christian's Wife, Christiane von Sachsen-Merseburg **Obv:** 8-line inscription with dates **Rev:** Cherub on scroll with flower and incense urn **Mint:** Gotha

Date	Mintage	VG	F	VF	XF	Unc
1679	—	500	875	1,350	2,600	—

KM# 3 1/2 THALER

Silver **Ruler:** Christian **Subject:** Death of Christian's Wife, Christiane von Sachsen-Merseburg **Obv:** 9-line inscription with dates **Obv. Legend:** +NUMM. EXEQ: CHRISTIANÆ. D:G. DUC S. I. C. &. MON. PIÆ. MEM **Obv. Inscription:** QUÆ / NATA. MARTISB. / d. 1. IUN. A. 1659. / DESPONSATA / IBID. d. 13 FEBRU. 1677. / DENATA / d. 13. MART. ET. MOR / HUMATA. d. 29. / APR. 1679 **Rev:** Child sitting on skull playing flute, vase with flowers at lower left, smoking urn at lower right, arms from clouds hold ribbon with inscription above **Rev. Inscription:** OMNIA VANITAS

Date	Mintage	VG	F	VF	XF	Unc
1679	—	—	—	—	—	—

KM# 26 1/2 THALER

Silver **Ruler:** Christian **Obv:** Armored bust to right **Obv. Legend:** D:G. CHRISTIAN'. SAX. I. C. M. A. &. W. DUX: **Rev:** Small crowned arms of ducal Saxony in center between palm fronds, four small crowned shields of arms around in cruciform wtih palm fronds, 4 crowned double-C monograms with palm fronds in angles, date divided at top **Rev. Legend:** DE — O — PAT — RIÆ — PROX — IMO — SAC — RUM.

Date	Mintage	VG	F	VF	XF	Unc
1692	—	1,200	1,600	2,500	4,300	—

KM# 31 1/2 THALER

Silver **Ruler:** Christian **Obv:** Bust to right **Rev:** Helmeted oval manifold arms of Saxony, date divided to either side of helmets in margin

Date	Mintage	VG	F	VF	XF	Unc
1697 IA	—	—	—	—	—	—

KM# 10 2/3 THALER (Gulden)

19.3400 g., Silver **Ruler:** Christian **Obv:** Bust right in circle **Obv. Legend:** CHRISTIANUS. D.G. DUX. SAX. IUL. CLIV. ET. MONT **Rev:** Heart on altar, arms from clouds above hold shield and palm branch, inscription curved in band at top, value 2/3 in oval at bottom, date at end of legend **Rev. Legend:** NACH DEM OBER-SACH — CREYS SCHLUS **Rev. Inscription:** DEO PROTECTORI MEO **Mint:** Gotha **Note:** Dav# 850.

Date	Mintage	VG	F	VF	XF	Unc
1682 HM	—	225	400	650	1,225	—

KM# 23 2/3 THALER (Gulden)

19.0200 g., Silver **Ruler:** Christian **Obv:** Bust right in circle **Obv. Legend:** CHRISTIANUS. D.G. DUX. SAX. IUL. CLIV. ET. MONT **Rev:** Table with ducal hat set upon crossed sword and palm branch, oval 4-fold arms in baroque frame divide date below in front, 2/3 in oval at bottom **Rev. Legend:** AD. LEGEM. IMP. IN UTROQUE DEO. MON. NOV. ARG. **Mint:** Gotha **Note:** Dav# 851.

Date	Mintage	VG	F	VF	XF	Unc
1686	—	1,600	2,250	3,000	6,000	—

Note: Only 2 reportedly known

KM# 27 2/3 THALER (Gulden)

Silver **Ruler:** Christian **Obv:** Bust right **Obv. Legend:** D.G. CHRISTIAN9 SAX. I. C. M. A. &. W. DVX **Rev:** Crowned oval arms between palm branches, value 2/3 below, date at end of legend **Rev. Legend:** NACH DEM LEIPZIGER FUS **Mint:** Eisenberg **Note:** Dav# 852.

Date	Mintage	VG	F	VF	XF	Unc
1692 Rare	—	—	—	—	—	—

KM# 4 THALER

Silver Weight varies: 28.92-29.03g. **Ruler:** Christian **Subject:** Death of Christian's Wife, Christiane von Sachsen-Merseburg **Obv:** Twelve-line inscription **Obv. Legend:** + D.G. CHRISTIANÆ. D. SAX. I. C. &. M. L. TH. M. MIS. &. VT: LUS. PR. HEN. C. M. &. R. DN. INI RAV. **Obv. Inscription:** HOC / MONUMENTUM / AMORIS POSITUM. / QUÆ NATA. / MARTISB. 1. IUN. A. 1659. / DESPONSATA / IBID. d. 13 FEBRU. 1677./DENATA POSTPACTUM/FILIOLÆ d. 13. MARTIJ./ET. HUMATA./MARTISB. d. 29. APR./1679 **Rev:** Child sitting on skull playing flute, vase with flowers at lower left, smoking urn at lower right, arms from clouds hold ribbon with inscription above **Rev. Inscription:** OMNIA VANITAS **Mint:** Gotha **Note:** Dav# 7421.

Date	Mintage	VG	F	VF	XF	Unc
1679	—	375	750	1,450	2,650	4,200

KM# 12 THALER

Silver **Ruler:** Christian **Obv:** Youthful armored bust to right **Obv. Legend:** CHRISTIANUS. D.G. DUX SAX. IUL. CLIV. ET. MONT. **Rev:** Shield of manifold arms with concave sides, 6 ornate helmets above divide date to left and right **Rev. Legend:** DEO. PROTECTORI. MEO. **Mint:** Gotha **Note:** Dav# 7422.

Date	Mintage	VG	F	VF	XF	Unc
1682 HM	—	750	1,500	2,750	5,000	—

KM# 24 THALER

Silver **Ruler:** Christian **Obv:** Armored bust to right **Obv. Legend:** CHRISTIANUS • D • G • D U X • SAX • IUL • CLIV • ET • MONTIUM **Rev:** Ducal hat set upon crossed sword and scepter, oval shield of 4-fold arms divides date in baroque frame between 2 palm branches below **Rev. Legend:** NOV • ARGENT **Mint:** Gotha **Note:** Dav. 7422A.

Date	Mintage	VG	F	VF	XF	Unc
1686	—	750	1,500	2,750	5,000	—

KM# 29 THALER

29.1400 g., Silver **Ruler:** Christian **Obv:** Armored bust to right **Obv. Legend:** D:G. CHRISTIAN'. SAX. I. U. CL. M. A. & W. DUX. **Rev:** Crowned shield of ducal Saxony arms, between 2 palm branches, in center, 4 small shields of crowned arms in cruciform, crowned intertwined double-C monograms, date divided near top **Rev. Legend:** DEO PATRIÆ PROXIMO SACRUM **Mint:** Eisenberg **Note:** Dav# 7423.

Date	Mintage	VG	F	VF	XF	Unc
1692	—	750	1,500	2,750	5,000	—

KM# 32 THALER

29.0900 g., Silver **Ruler:** Christian **Obv:** Armored bust to right **Obv. Legend:** D:G. CHRISTIAN: SAX. I. C. M. A. &. W. DUX. **Rev:** Large oval manifold arms, 8 small ornate helmets above, date divided to left and right of helmets in margin **Rev. Legend:** DEO PATRIÆ PROXIMO SACRUM **Mint:** Eisenberg **Note:** Dav# 7424.

Date	Mintage	VG	F	VF	XF	Unc
1697 IA	—	700	1,400	2,500	4,750	—
1699 IA	—	700	1,400	2,500	4,750	—

KM# 5 2 THALER

Silver **Ruler:** Christian **Subject:** Death of Christian's Wife, Christiane von Sachsen-Merseburg **Obv:** 12-line inscription **Rev:** Child sitting on skull playing flute, vase with flowers at lower left, smoking urn at lower right, arms from clouds hold ribbon with inscription above **Note:** Dav# 7420. Similar to Thaler, KM# 4.

Date	Mintage	VG	F	VF	XF	Unc
1679 Rare	—	—	—	—	—	—

TRADE COINAGE

KM# 22 GOLDGULDEN

3.5000 g., 0.9860 Gold 0.1109 oz. AGW, 23 mm. **Ruler:** Christian **Obv:** Shield of 4-fold arms in baroque frame, crown above divides date **Obv. Legend:** CHRISTIANUS. D.G. DUX. SAX. I. C. & MONT. **Rev:** Standing palm tree in circle **Rev. Legend:** SAT. CITO. QUIA. SAT. BENE. FLOR. AUR. SAX. GOTH. **Mint:** Eisenberg **Note:** Fr. 2926.

Date	Mintage	VG	F	VF	XF	Unc
1684	—	4,950	9,400	16,500	—	—

Note: An example in VF realized $15,700 in a Peus auction, April 2009.

KM# 19 1/4 DUCAT

0.8750 g., 0.9860 Gold 0.0277 oz. AGW, 22 mm. **Ruler:** Christian **Obv:** Facing armored bust **Obv. Legend:** + CHRISTIAN: D.G. DUX. SAX: I. C. ET. MONT. **Rev:** Crowned 4-fold arms of Saxony in baroque frame, 1/4 in oval at bottom, date at end of legend **Rev. Legend:** DEO PROTEC — TORI MEO **Mint:** Gotha **Note:** Fr# 2921.

Date	Mintage	VG	F	VF	XF	Unc
1683	—	475	825	1,250	2,000	—
ND	—	475	825	1,250	2,000	—

KM# 20 1/2 DUCAT

1.7500 g., 0.9860 Gold 0.0555 oz. AGW **Ruler:** Christian **Obv:** Bust of Christian right **Rev:** Crowned arms in branches, value below **Note:** Fr# 2920.

Date	Mintage	VG	F	VF	XF	Unc
1683	—	425	750	1,500	2,500	—

KM# 34 1/2 DUCAT

1.7500 g., 0.9860 Gold 0.0555 oz. AGW **Ruler:** Christian **Rev:** Crowned and mantled arms **Note:** Fr# 2925.

Date	Mintage	VG	F	VF	XF	Unc
ND	—	475	800	1,600	2,650	—

KM# 14 DUCAT

3.5000 g., 0.9860 Gold 0.1109 oz. AGW **Ruler:** Christian **Obv:** Facing armored bust **Obv. Legend:** CHRISTIANUS. D.G. DUX. SAX. IUL. CLIV. ET. MONT. **Rev:** Heart on altar, crossed arms and hands from clouds above holding symbols, date in margin at top **Rev. Legend:** DEO — PROTECTORI — MEO. **Mint:** Gotha **Note:** Fr# 2918.

Date	Mintage	VG	F	VF	XF	Unc
1682	—	1,150	1,950	4,150	7,200	—

KM# 25 DUCAT

3.5000 g., 0.9860 Gold 0.1109 oz. AGW **Ruler:** Christian **Rev:** Table holding palm and sword **Note:** Fr# 2922.

Date	Mintage	VG	F	VF	XF	Unc
1686	—	1,000	1,950	3,600	6,600	—

KM# 35 DUCAT

3.5000 g., 0.9860 Gold 0.1109 oz. AGW **Ruler:** Christian **Obv:** Bust of Christian right **Rev:** Crowned and mantled arms, date divided at top **Note:** Fr# 2924.

Date	Mintage	VG	F	VF	XF	Unc
1697	—	1,100	2,200	3,950	6,900	—

KM# 15 2 DUCAT

7.0000 g., 0.9860 Gold 0.2219 oz. AGW **Ruler:** Christian **Obv:** Christian **Note:** Fr# 2919.

Date	Mintage	VG	F	VF	XF	Unc
ND(1682) Rare	—	—	—	—	—	—

KM# 36 2 DUCAT

7.0000 g., 0.9860 Gold 0.2219 oz. AGW **Ruler:** Christian **Rev:** Crowned and mantled arms, date divided at top **Note:** Fr# 2923. Struck on thick planchet from Ducat dies, KM# 35.

Date	Mintage	VG	F	VF	XF	Unc
1697 Rare	—	—	—	—	—	—

KM# 7 4 DUCAT

14.0000 g., 0.9860 Gold 0.4438 oz. AGW **Ruler:** Christian **Subject:** Death of Christian's Wife, Christiane von Sachsen-Merseburg **Obv:** 9-line inscription with dates **Obv. Legend:** +NUMM. EXEQ: CHRISTIANÆ. D:G. DUC S. I. C. &. MON. PIÆ. MEM **Obv. Inscription:** QUÆ / NATA. MARTISB. / d. 1. IUN. A. 1659. / DESPONSATA / IBID. d. 13 FEBRU. 1677. / DENATA / d. 13. MART. ET. MOR / HUMATA. d. 29. / APR. 1679 **Rev:** Child sitting on skull playing flute, vase with flowers at lower left, smoking urn at lower right, arms from clouds hold ribbon with inscription above **Rev. Inscription:** OMNIA VANITAS **Mint:** Gotha **Note:** Struck from 1/2 Thaler dies, KM# 3.

Date	Mintage	VG	F	VF	XF	Unc
1679 Rare	—	—	—	—	—	—

KM# 8 10 DUCAT

35.0000 g., 0.9860 Gold 1.1095 oz. AGW **Ruler:** Christian **Subject:** Death of Christian's Wife, Christiane von Sachsen-Merseburg **Obv:** 12-line inscription with dates **Obv. Legend:** + D.G. CHRISTIANÆ. D. SAX. I. C. &. M. L. TH. M. MIS. &. VT: LUS. PR. HEN. C. M. &. R. DN. INI RAV. **Obv. Inscription:** HOC / MONUMENTUM / AMORIS POSITUM. / QUÆ NATA. / MARTISB. 1. IUN. A. 1659. / DESPONSATA / IBID. d. 13 FEBRU. 1677. / DENATA POSTPACTUM / FILIOLÆ d. 13. MARTIJ. / ET. HUMATA. / MARTISB. d. 29. APR. / 1679 **Rev:** Child sitting on skull playing flute, vase with flowers at lower left, smoking urn at lower right, arms from clouds hold ribbon with inscription above **Rev. Inscription:** OMNIA VANITAS **Mint:** Gotha **Note:** Struck from Thaler dies, KM# 4.

Date	Mintage	VG	F	VF	XF	Unc
1679 Rare	—	—	—	—	—	—

PATTERNS

Including off metal strikes

KM#	Date	Mintage	Identification	Mkt Val
Pn1	1682	—	Ducat. Silver. KM# 14.	—

SAXE-SAALFELD

(Sachsen-Saalfeld)

Saalfeld was purchased by Saxony from Meissen-Thuringia in 1389. As a branch of the Ernestine line, it was created as a duchy for Johann Ernst VIII, 7th son of Ernst the Pious of Saxe-Gotha. Coburg was added to the holdings in 1735 and thereafter the dukes took the name of Saxe-Coburg-Saalfeld. Coinage after that date is listed under the latter entity.

RULER

Johann Ernst VIII, 1680-1729

REFERENCE

G = Walter Grasser, **Münz- und Geldgeschichte von Coburg 1265-1923**, Frankfurt am Main, 1979.

DUCHY

REGULAR COINAGE

KM# 3 HELLER

Copper **Ruler:** Johann Ernst VIII **Obv:** Crowned Saxon arms **Rev:** Date at end of inscription **Rev. Inscription:** SAAL / FELD. HEL / LER/ **Mint:** Saalfeld

Date	Mintage	Good	VG	F	VF	XF
1685	—	6.00	10.00	20.00	40.00	—

KM# 8 HELLER

Copper **Ruler:** Johann Ernst VIII **Obv:** Crowned Saxon arms **Rev:** Inscription in Gothic letters, date at end of inscription **Mint:** Saalfeld

Date	Mintage	Good	VG	F	VF	XF
1688	—	5.00	10.00	20.00	40.00	—
1695	—	5.00	10.00	20.00	40.00	—
1696	—	5.00	10.00	20.00	40.00	—

KM# 18 HELLER

Copper, 14 mm. **Ruler:** Johann Ernst VIII **Obv:** Crowned shield of ducal Saxony arms **Rev:** 3-line inscription with date **Rev. Inscription:** SAALF. / HELLER / (date) **Mint:** Saalfeld **Note:** Ref. KOR#690-96. Varieties exist, especially in shape of shield of arms.

Date	Mintage	Good	VG	F	VF	XF
1692	—	4.00	8.00	15.00	30.00	—
1693	—	4.00	8.00	15.00	30.00	—
1696	—	4.00	8.00	15.00	30.00	—
1698	—	4.00	8.00	15.00	30.00	—
1699	—	4.00	8.00	15.00	30.00	—
1700	—	4.00	8.00	15.00	30.00	—

KM# 30 HELLER

Copper, 14 mm. **Ruler:** Johann Ernst VIII **Obv:** Crowned shield of ducal Saxony arms **Rev:** 4-line inscription with date **Rev. Inscription:** SAAL / FELD / HELLER / (date) **Mint:** Saalfeld **Note:** Ref. KOR-690b, 691b.

Date	Mintage	Good	VG	F	VF	XF
1699	—	—	—	—	—	—
1700	—	—	—	—	—	—

KM# 20 2 GROSCHEN

Silver **Ruler:** Johann Ernst VIII **Obv:** Crowned script JE monogram **Rev:** Crowned oval arms, value below **Mint:** Saalfeld

Date	Mintage	VG	F	VF	XF	Unc
1694	—	—	—	—	—	—

KM# 11 1/2 THALER

Silver **Ruler:** Johann Ernst VIII **Subject:** Marriage of Johann Ernst VIII and Charlotte Johanne von Waldeck **Obv:** Accolated busts right **Rev:** Arms in sprays, date below **Mint:** Saalfeld

Date	Mintage	VG	F	VF	XF	Unc
1690	—	—	—	—	—	—

KM# 4 2/3 THALER (Gulden)

Silver **Ruler:** Johann Ernst VIII **Obv:** Bust right **Rev:** Crowned manifold arms, date in margin, 2/3 below **Rev. Legend:** VON FEINEM SILBER **Mint:** Saalfeld **Note:** Dav#882.

Date	Mintage	VG	F	VF	XF	Unc
1685	—	—	—	—	—	—
1687	—	—	—	—	—	—

KM# 9 2/3 THALER (Gulden)

Silver **Ruler:** Johann Ernst VIII **Obv:** Bust right **Rev:** Crowned and supported manifold arms, dat ein margin, 2/3 below **Rev. Legend:** VON FEINEM SILBER **Mint:** Saalfeld **Note:** Dav#883.

Date	Mintage	VG	F	VF	XF	Unc
1688	—	—	—	—	—	—

KM# 16 2/3 THALER (Gulden)

Silver **Ruler:** Johann Ernst VIII **Obv:** Bust right **Rev:** Crowned and supported manifold arms, date in margin, 2/3 below **Rev. Legend:** MON. NOVA. SAALF. **Mint:** Saalfeld **Note:** Dav#884.

Date	Mintage	VG	F	VF	XF	Unc
1691	—	—	—	—	—	—

KM# 17 2/3 THALER (Gulden)

Silver **Ruler:** Johann Ernst VIII **Obv:** Bust right **Rev:** Crowned and supported manifold arms, date in margin, 2/3 below **Rev. Legend:** DEO GRATIA MON. NOV. SAALF. **Mint:** Saalfeld **Note:** Dav#885.

Date	Mintage	VG	F	VF	XF	Unc
1691	—	—	—	—	—	—
1692	—	—	—	—	—	—

KM# 5 THALER

Silver **Ruler:** Johann Ernst VIII **Rev:** Helmeted arms **Mint:** Saalfeld **Note:** Dav. 7505

Date	Mintage	VG	F	VF	XF	Unc
1687	—	575	1,150	2,150	3,500	—

KM# 12 THALER

Silver **Ruler:** Johann Ernst VIII **Subject:** Marriage of Johann Ernst VIII and Charlotte Johanna **Obv:** Accolated busts right **Rev:** Arms in sprays, date below **Mint:** Saalfeld **Note:** Dav. 7508.

Date	Mintage	VG	F	VF	XF	Unc
1690	—	675	1,350	2,500	4,150	—

KM# 13 THALER

Silver **Ruler:** Johann Ernst VIII **Obv:** Bust right **Rev:** Helmeted arms, date divided below **Mint:** Saalfeld **Note:** Dav. 7509.

Date	Mintage	VG	F	VF	XF	Unc
1690 Rare	—	—	—	—	—	—
1691 Rare	—	—	—	—	—	—

KM# 19 THALER

Silver **Ruler:** Johann Ernst VIII **Obv:** Bust right, helmet in front **Rev:** City view **Mint:** Saalfeld **Note:** Dav. 7510.

Date	Mintage	VG	F	VF	XF	Unc
1692 Rare	—	—	—	—	—	—

KM# 22 THALER
Silver **Ruler:** Johann Ernst VIII **Obv:** Bust right, helmet in front **Rev:** Helmeted oval arms **Mint:** Saalfeld **Note:** Dav. 7511.

Date	Mintage	VG	F	VF	XF	Unc
1694	—	450	850	1,500	2,500	4,500

KM# 24 THALER
Silver **Ruler:** Johann Ernst VIII **Obv:** Similar to Dav. #7511 **Rev:** Hand from clouds with wreath above city view **Mint:** Saalfeld **Note:** Dav. 7513.

Date	Mintage	VG	F	VF	XF	Unc
1697 Rare	—	—	—	—	—	—
1698 Rare	—	—	—	—	—	—

KM# 29 THALER
Silver **Ruler:** Johann Ernst VIII **Obv:** Large bust right, helmet in front **Rev:** Helmeted arms divide date below **Mint:** Saalfeld **Note:** Dav. 7514.

Date	Mintage	VG	F	VF	XF	Unc
1698 Rare	—	1,650	2,850	5,000	9,000	—

KM# 6 1-1/2 THALER
Silver **Ruler:** Johann Ernst VIII **Mint:** Saalfeld **Note:** Dav. 7504.

Date	Mintage	VG	F	VF	XF	Unc
1687	—	1,750	3,500	6,500	10,000	—

KM# 14 1-1/2 THALER
Silver **Ruler:** Johann Ernst VIII **Subject:** Marriage of Johann Ernst and Charlotte Johanna **Mint:** Saalfeld **Note:** Dav. 7507.

Date	Mintage	VG	F	VF	XF	Unc
1690 Rare	—	—	—	—	—	—

KM# 25 1-1/2 THALER
Silver **Ruler:** Johann Ernst VIII **Obv:** Bust right **Rev:** Hand from clouds with wreath above city view, Roman numeral date below **Mint:** Saalfeld **Note:** Dav. 7512.

Date	Mintage	VG	F	VF	XF	Unc
1697 Rare	—	—	—	—	—	—

KM# 7 2 THALER
Silver **Ruler:** Johann Ernst VIII **Rev:** Helmeted arms **Mint:** Saalfeld **Note:** Dav. 7503.

Date	Mintage	VG	F	VF	XF	Unc
1687 Rare	—	—	—	—	—	—

Note: Rauch Auction 85, 11-09, VF realized approximately $28,600.

KM# 15 2 THALER
Silver **Ruler:** Johann Ernst VIII **Subject:** Marriage of Johann Ernst and Charlotte Johanna **Mint:** Saalfeld **Note:** Dav. 7506.

Date	Mintage	VG	F	VF	XF	Unc
1690 Rare	—	—	—	—	—	—

TRADE COINAGE

KM# 26 DUCAT
3.5000 g., 0.9860 Gold 0.1109 oz. AGW, 23 mm. **Ruler:** Johann Ernst VIII **Obv:** Youthful armored bust to right in circle **Rev:** Shield of manifold arms, with central shield of ducal Saxony, 6 ornate helmets above, date divided below **Mint:** Saalfeld **Note:** Fr. 3000

Date	Mintage	VG	F	VF	XF	Unc
1698	—	2,000	4,000	7,500	12,000	—

KM# 27 2 DUCAT
7.0000 g., 0.9860 Gold 0.2219 oz. AGW **Ruler:** Johann Ernst VIII **Obv:** Bust of Johann Ernst VIII right **Rev:** Oval manifold arms, six helmets above, date divided at bottom **Mint:** Saalfeld **Note:** Fr. 2999.

Date	Mintage	VG	F	VF	XF	Unc
1698 Rare	—	—	—	—	—	—

KM# 28 6 DUCAT
21.0000 g., 0.9860 Gold 0.6657 oz. AGW **Ruler:** Johann Ernst VIII **Obv:** Bust of Johann Ernst VIII right **Rev:** Crowned arms **Mint:** Saalfeld **Note:** Fr. 2998. Struck with Thaler dies, Dav. #7514.

Date	Mintage	VG	F	VF	XF	Unc
1698 Rare	—	—	—	—	—	—

SAYN-ALTENKIRCHEN

The younger daughter of Ernest of Sayn-Wittgenstein-Sayn (1623-32) founded the line of Sayn-Altenkirchen at the end of the Thirty Years' War, having married Duke Johann Georg I of Saxe-Eisenach (1662-86). When Saxe-Eisenach (see) fell extinct in 1741, Sayn-Altenkirchen passed in marriage to the Margraves of Brandenburg-Ansbach, then to Prussia in 1791 and finally to Nassau in 1803. Altenkirchen is in the Westerwald 16 miles (27 kilometers) north of Sayn.

RULERS
Johannetta, 1648-1661
Johann Georg I, Herzog von Sachsen-Eisenach, 1662-1686
Johann Wilhelm, Herzog von Sachsen-Eisenach, 1686-1729
Wilhelm Heinrich, Herzog von Sachsen-Eisenach, 1729-1741
Karl Wilhelm Friedrich, Markgraf von Brandenburg-Ansbach, 1741-1757
Christian Friedrich Karl Alexander, Markgraf von Brandenburg-Ansbach, 1757-1791

COUNTSHIP

STANDARD COINAGE

KM# 4 ALBUS
Silver **Ruler:** Johann Wilhelm **Obv:** Crowned oval arms of Ducal Saxony, palm branch to left and right **Obv. Legend:** I. W. D. G. D. S. I. C. M. A. & W. C. S. & W. **Rev:** 3-line inscription with date **Rev. Legend:** NACH DEM SCHLVS DER. V. STÄND. **Rev. Inscription:** I / ALBUS / 1693. **Mint:** Friedewald **Note:** Prev. KM#3. Ref. M/V#407a.

Date	Mintage	VG	F	VF	XF	Unc
1693	—	—	—	—	—	—

KM# 5 ALBUS
Silver **Ruler:** Johann Wilhelm **Obv:** Crowned oval arms of Ducal Saxony, palm branch to left and right **Obv. Legend:** I. W. H. Z. S. G. Z. S. **Rev:** 3-line inscription with date **Rev. Legend:** NACH DEM FRANCKF. SCHLVS. **Rev. Inscription:** I / ALBUS / 1693. **Mint:** Friedewald **Note:** Prev. KM#4. Ref. M/V#407b.

Date	Mintage	VG	F	VF	XF	Unc
1693	—	—	—	—	—	—

KM# 7 2 ALBUS
Silver **Ruler:** Johann Wilhelm **Obv:** Crowned oval arms of Ducal Saxony, palm branch to left and right **Obv. Legend:** I. W. H. ZV SACHSEN G. Z. S. **Rev:** 3-line inscription with date **Rev. Legend:** NACH DEM FRANCKF. SCHLUS. **Rev. Inscription:** II / ALBUS / 1693. **Mint:** Friedewald **Note:** Prev. KM#6. Ref. M/V#407a.

Date	Mintage	VG	F	VF	XF	Unc
1693	—	—	—	—	—	—

KM# 9 15 KREUZER
Silver **Ruler:** Johann Wilhelm **Obv:** Armored bust of Johann Wilhelm left in inner circle **Obv. Legend:** I. W. D. G. D. S. I. C. M. - A. & W. C. S. & W. **Rev:** Crowned oval arms of Ducal Saxony left and Sayn right between 2 palm fronds, electoral hat above, value 'XV' in cartouche below, date in margin at top **Rev. Legend:** FURSTL. SACHS. SEYN. LANDMUNZ. **Mint:** Friedewald **Note:** Prev. KM#8. Ref. M/V#405.

Date	Mintage	VG	F	VF	XF	Unc
1693	—	175	350	750	1,500	—

KM# 10 15 KREUZER
Silver **Obv:** Armored bust left **Obv. Legend:** I. W. D. G. D. S. I. C. M. - A. & W. C. S. & W. **Rev:** 2 adjacent oval arms, Ducal Saxony left and Sayn right between 2 palm fronds, electoral hat aabove, value 'XV' in cartouche below, date at end of legend **Rev. Legend:** FURSTL. SACHS. SEYN. LANDMUNTZ. **Note:** Prev. KM#9. Ref. M/V#405a.

Date	Mintage	VG	F	VF	XF	Unc
1693	—	175	350	750	1,500	—

KM# 11 1/6 THALER
Silver **Ruler:** Johann Wilhelm **Obv:** Armored bust of Johann Wilhelm left **Rev:** 1/6 with date in angles in inner circle **Mint:** Friedewald

Date	Mintage	VG	F	VF	XF	Unc
1692	—	—	—	—	—	—

KM# 2 1/6 THALER
Silver **Ruler:** Johann Wilhelm **Obv:** Armored bust left **Obv. Legend:** I. W. D. G. D. S. I. C. M. - A. & W. C. S. & W. **Rev:** Large '1/6' which divides date aabove and below dividing line as 1-6/9-2 **Rev. Legend:** CONSTANTER ET VIGILANTER **Mint:** Friedewald **Note:** Ref. M/V#402.

Date	Mintage	VG	F	VF	XF	Unc
1692	—	—	—	—	—	—

KM# 12 2/3 THALER
Silver **Ruler:** Johann Wilhelm **Obv:** Armored bust of Johann Wilhelm to left in inner circle **Rev:** Large 2 adjacent oval shields of arms between 2 palm branches, Ducal Saxony left, Sayn right, large crown above, value '2/3' in oval below, date in margin at top **Rev. Legend:** FURSTL: SACHS: SEYN: LANDMUNTZ. **Mint:** Friedewald **Note:** Dav. #847. Prev. KM#13. Ref. M/V#403.

Date	Mintage	VG	F	VF	XF	Unc
1693	—	—	—	—	—	—

SAYN-WITTGENSTEIN-BERLEBURG

COUNTSHIP

STANDARD COINAGE

KM# 2 PFENNIG (Bombe)
Silver **Ruler:** Georg V **Obv:** Three boars' heads (Freusburg) in raised circle **Note:** Uniface, hohl-type. Kipper coinage. Prev. KM#5. Ref. M/V#51.

Date	Mintage	VG	F	VF	XF	Unc
ND(ca.1620-22)	—	27.00	45.00	90.00	185	—

KM# 3 PFENNIG (Bombe)
Silver **Ruler:** Georg V **Obv:** 2-fold arms divided vertically, Freusburg on left, Wittgenstein on right, 'H' above **Mint:** Homburg **Note:** Uniface schüssel-type, kipper coinage. Prev. KM#6. Ref. M/V#52.

Date	Mintage	VG	F	VF	XF	Unc
ND(ca1620-22)	—	27.00	45.00	90.00	185	—

KM# 4 PFENNIG (Bombe)
Billon **Ruler:** Georg V **Obv:** 2-fold arms divided vertically, 4 pellets in left, Sayn lion in right, 'H' above **Mint:** Homburg **Note:** Uniface schüssel-type, kipper coinage. Prev. KM#7. Ref. M/V#53.

Date	Mintage	VG	F	VF	XF	Unc
ND(ca1620-22)	—	27.00	45.00	90.00	185	—

KM# 5 PFENNIG (Bombe)
Silver **Ruler:** Georg V **Obv:** 2-fold arms divided vertically, Wittgenstein on left, Sayn at right, 'H' above **Mint:** Homburg **Note:** Uniface schüssel-type, kipper coinage. Prev. KM#8. Ref. M/V#54.

Date	Mintage	VG	F	VF	XF	Unc
ND(ca1620-22)	—	27.00	45.00	90.00	185	—

KM# 6 PFENNIG (Bombe)
Silver **Ruler:** Georg V **Obv:** 2-fold arms divided vertically, Wittgenstein at left, Sayn at right, arrow right above **Mint:** Homburg **Note:** Uniface schüssel-type, kipper coinage. Prev. KM#9. Ref. M/V#55.

Date	Mintage	VG	F	VF	XF	Unc
ND(ca1620-22)	—	27.00	45.00	90.00	185	—

KM# 56 PFENNIG (Bombe)
Silver **Ruler:** Georg Wilhelm **Obv:** Crowned 'GW' monogram in circle of pellets **Mint:** Homburg **Note:** Uniface schüssel-type. Ref. M/V#98. Prev. KM#10.

Date	Mintage	VG	F	VF	XF	Unc
ND(ca1681-84)	—	27.00	45.00	90.00	185	—

KM# 33 4 GUTE PFENNIG
0.7700 g., Silver **Ruler:** Georg **Obv:** Large crowned Gothic 'G' divides date **Rev:** Value **Rev. Inscription:** + / +IIII+ / G + PEN / + **Mint:** Berleburg **Note:** Prev. KM#40. Ref. M/V#56.

Date	Mintage	VG	F	VF	XF	Unc
1660	—	—	—	—	—	—

KM# 8 3 KREUZER (1/8 Thaler)
Silver **Ruler:** Georg V **Obv:** Homburg arms in circle, date at end of legend **Obv. Legend:** G. G. Z. S. V. W. H. Z. H. **Rev:** Crowned imperial eagle, '3' in orb on breast **Rev. Legend:** FER. II. D. G. R. I. S. A. **Mint:** Berleburg **Note:** Kipper coinage. Prev. KM#20. Ref. M/V#32.

Date	Mintage	VG	F	VF	XF	Unc
16ZZ	—	—	—	—	—	—

KM# 9 3 KREUZER (1/8 Thaler)
Silver **Ruler:** Georg V **Obv:** Ornately-shaped 4-fold arms with central shield of Sayn, date at end of legend **Obv. Legend:** G. G. Z. S. V. W. H. Z. HO. **Rev:** Crowned imperial eagle, '3' in orb on breast **Rev. Legend:** FER. II. D. G. ROM. IM. S. A. **Mint:** Berleburg **Note:** Prev. KM#21. Ref. M/V#32a.

Date	Mintage	VG	F	VF	XF	Unc
16ZZ	—	—	—	—	—	—

KM# 10 3 KREUZER (1/8 Thaler)
Silver **Ruler:** Georg V **Obv:** Ornately-shaped 4-fold arms with central shield of Sayn **Obv. Legend:** GEORG. COM. I. S. &. W. D. I. H. **Rev:** Crowned imperial eagle, '3' in orb on breast **Rev. Legend:** FERDI. Z. D. G. ROM. IM. S. A. **Mint:** Berleburg **Note:** Ref. M/V#33.

Date	Mintage	VG	F	VF	XF	Unc
ND(1622)	—	—	—	—	—	—

KM# 12 12 KREUZER (1/2 Thaler)
Silver **Ruler:** Georg V **Obv:** Sayn lion left in circle **Obv. Legend:** G. G. Z. S. V. W. H. Z. H. **Rev:** Crowned imperial eagle, '1Z' in orb on breast **Rev. Legend:** FERD. II. D. G. R. O. IM. S. A. **Mint:** Berleburg **Note:** Kipper coinage. Prev. KM#11. Ref. M/V#31.

Date	Mintage	VG	F	VF	XF	Unc
ND(1622)	—	—	—	—	—	—

KM# 14 24 KREUZER (1 Thaler)
Silver **Ruler:** Georg V **Obv:** Bust of Georg right in inner circle, date at end of legend **Obv. Legend:** G. G. Z. S. V. W. H. Z. HOM(B). **Rev:** Crowned imperial eagle, 'Z4' in orb on breast **Rev. Legend:** FERD. II. D. G. RO(M). IM(P). S(E)(M). A(V). **Mint:** Berleburg **Note:** Kipper coinage. Prev. KM#22. Ref. M/V#28-30. Varieties exist.

Date	Mintage	VG	F	VF	XF	Unc
16ZZ	—	—	—	—	—	—

KM# 35 30 KREUZER (1/2 Gulden)
Silver **Ruler:** Georg Wilhelm **Obv:** Large bust of Georg Wilhelm right, '30' below **Obv. Legend:** GEORG. W. G. Z. S. V. W. H. Z. H. V. N. **Rev:** Crowned ornamented shield of 4-fold arms with central shield of Sayn divide mintmaster's initials (where present), date at end of legend **Rev. Legend:** AD INSTAR. GRUIS. **Mint:** Berleburg **Note:** Prev. KM#45. Ref. M/V#92-93, 93a. Varieties exist.

Date	Mintage	VG	F	VF	XF	Unc
1675	—	325	675	1,300	2,600	—
1675 IB	—	325	675	1,300	2,600	—

KM# 37 30 KREUZER (1/2 Gulden)
Silver **Ruler:** Georg Wilhelm **Obv:** Small bust of Georg Wilhelm right, value '30' below **Obv. Legend:** GEORG. W. G. Z. S. V. W. H. Z. H. V. N. **Rev:** Crowned ornamented shield of 4-fold arms with central shield of Sayn divide mintmaster's initials, date at end of legend **Rev. Legend:** AD INSTAR. GRUIS. **Mint:** Berleburg **Note:** Prev. KM#46. Ref. M/V#95-95a.

Date	Mintage	VG	F	VF	XF	Unc
1675 IB	—	250	500	975	1,950	—

KM# 36 30 KREUZER (1/2 Gulden)
Silver **Ruler:** Georg Wilhelm **Obv:** Large bust right, '30' below **Obv. Legend:** GEORG. WILHELM. G. Z. S. W. H. Z. H. V. N. **Rev:** Crowned 4-fold arms with central shield of Sayn between palm branches divide mintmaster's initials, dat at end of legend **Rev. Legend:** AD INSTAR. GRUIS. **Mint:** Berleburg **Note:** Ref. M/V#94.

Date	Mintage	VG	F	VF	XF	Unc
1675 IB	—	—	—	—	—	—

KM# 42 30 KREUZER (1/2 Gulden)
Silver **Ruler:** Georg Wilhelm **Obv:** Large bust right, '30' below **Obv. Legend:** GEORG. W. G. Z. S. V. W. H. Z. H. V. N. **Rev:** Crowned 4-fold arms with central shield of Sayn between palm branches, date at end of legend **Rev. Legend:** AD INSTAR(.) GRUIS. **Mint:** Berleburg **Note:** Prev. KM#55. Ref. M/V#96-97. Varieties exist.

Date	Mintage	VG	F	VF	XF	Unc
1676	—	325	675	1,300	2,600	—

KM# 39 60 KREUZER (Gulden)
16.3400 g., Silver **Ruler:** Georg Wilhelm **Obv:** Small bust to right, value '60' below **Obv. Legend:** GEORG. WILHELM. G. Z. S. W. H. Z. H. V. N. **Rev:** Large crowned 4-fold arms with central shield of Sayn divide mintmaster's initials, date at end of legend **Rev. Legend:** AD(.) INSTAR(.) GRUIS. **Mint:** Berleburg **Note:** Dav. #899. Ref. M/V#58-62, 67-75. Prev. KM#47-54. Varieties exist.

Date	Mintage	VG	F	VF	XF	Unc
1675	—	150	250	425	850	—

KM# 40 60 KREUZER (Gulden)
16.3400 g., Silver **Ruler:** Georg Wilhelm **Obv:** Large bust to right, value '60' below **Obv. Legend:** GEORG. WILHELM. G. Z. S. W. H. Z. H. V. N. **Rev:** Smaller crowned 4-fold arms with central shield of Sayn divide mintmaster's initials, date at end of legend **Rev. Legend:** AD(.) INSTAR(.) GRUIS. **Mint:** Berleburg **Note:** Dav. #900. Ref. M/V #63-66, 78-79. Prev. KM#47-56. Varieties exist.

Date	Mintage	VG	F	VF	XF	Unc
1675 IB	—	150	300	550	1,100	—
1676 IB	—	150	300	550	1,100	—

KM# 47 60 KREUZER (Gulden)
16.3400 g., Silver **Ruler:** Georg Wilhelm **Obv:** Large bust to right, '60' in oval cartouche below **Obv. Legend:** GEORG WILHELM. G. - Z. S. W. H. Z. H. V. N. **Rev:** Large crowned shield of 4-fold arms with central shield of Sayn between 2 palm branches, date at end of legend with stops between numerals **Rev. Legend:** AD INSTAR. GRUIS. **Mint:** Berleburg **Note:** Dav. #902a. Ref. M/V#86-89.

Date	Mintage	VG	F	VF	XF	Unc
1676 I(c)VB	—	—	—	—	—	—

KM# 48 60 KREUZER (Gulden)
16.3400 g., Silver **Obv:** Different bust of Georg Wilhelm right in inner circle, value '60' in oval cartouche below **Obv. Legend:** GEORG WILHELM. G. - Z. S. W. H. Z. H. V. N. **Rev:** Round 4-fold arms in baroque frame, date in legend **Rev. Legend:** SOLI. DEO - GLORIA. **Note:** Dav. #903. Ref. M/V#90. Prev. KM#60.

Date	Mintage	VG	F	VF	XF	Unc
1676 (b)	—	120	240	475	975	—

KM# 44 60 KREUZER (Gulden)
16.3400 g., Silver **Ruler:** Georg Wilhelm **Obv:** Large bust right, value '60' below **Obv. Legend:** GEORG. WILHELM. G. Z. S. W. H. Z. H. V. N. **Rev:** Large crowned shield of 4-fold arms with central shield of Sayn between 2 palm branches, date at end of legend **Rev. Legend:** AD INSTAR. GRUIS. ANNO. **Mint:** Berleburg **Note:** Prev. KM#57. Dav. #901. Ref. M/V#80.

Date	Mintage	VG	F	VF	XF	Unc
1676	—	120	240	475	975	—

KM# 45 60 KREUZER (Gulden)
16.3400 g., Silver **Ruler:** Georg Wilhelm **Obv:** Large bust to right, value '60' below **Obv. Legend:** GEORG. WILHELM. G. Z. S. W. H. Z. H. V. N. **Rev:** Large crowned shield of 4-fold arms with central shield of Sayn between 2 palm branches, date at end of legend **Rev. Legend:** AD INSTAR. GRUIS. **Mint:** Berleburg **Note:** Prev. KM#58. Dav. #901A. Ref. M/V#81.

Date	Mintage	VG	F	VF	XF	Unc
1676	—	120	240	475	975	—

KM# 46 60 KREUZER (Gulden)
Silver **Ruler:** Georg Wilhelm **Obv:** Large bust right, '60' in oval cartouche below **Obv. Legend:** GEORG WILHELM. G. - Z. S. W. H. Z. H. V. N. **Rev:** Large crowned shield of 4-fold arms with central shield of Sayn between 2 palm branches, date at end of legend **Rev. Legend:** AD INSTAR. GR(V)(U)IS. **Mint:** Berleburg **Note:** Prev. KM#59. Dav. #902. Ref. M/V#82-85.

Date	Mintage	VG	F	VF	XF	Unc
1676 I(c)VB	—	120	240	475	975	—
1676 IV(c)B	—	120	240	475	975	—

KM# 50 24 MARIENGROSCHEN (Gulden)
Silver **Ruler:** Georg Wilhelm **Obv:** Bust right in circle, value '60' below shoulder in margin **Obv. Legend:** GEORG. WILHELM. G. - Z. S. W. H. Z. H. V. N. **Rev:** 4-line inscription with date, mintmaster's symbol below **Rev. Legend:** GLORIA in EXCELSIS DEO **Rev. Inscription:** XXIIII / MARIEN / GROSCH / 1676. **Mint:** Berleburg **Note:** Dav. #906. Ref. M/V#91. Prev. KM#61.

Date	Mintage	VG	F	VF	XF	Unc
1676 (b)	—	400	750	1,400	2,750	—

KM# 28 1/2 THALER
Silver **Ruler:** Georg V **Obv:** 4-fold arms with central shield of Sayn in ornamented frame **Obv. Legend:** GEORG. COM. IN. SAYN. ET. WITG. DOM. IN. H. **Rev:** Crowned imperial eagle, orb on breast, date at end of legend **Rev. Legend:** FERDIN. II. D. G. ROM. IMP. SEMP. AUG. **Mint:** Berleburg **Note:** Prev. KM#23. Ref. M/V#27.

Date	Mintage	VG	F	VF	XF	Unc
(16)Z5 (a)	—	—	—	—	—	—

KM# 52 2/3 THALER
16.0900 g., Silver **Ruler:** Georg Wilhelm **Obv:** Bust of Gustav of Sayn-Wittgenstein-Wittgenstein right breaks circle at bottom **Obv. Legend:** GEORG. WILHELM. G. Z. S. W. H. Z. H. V. N. **Rev:** Crowned 4-fold arms with central shield of Sayn, value '2/3' in oval below, date at end of legend **Rev. Legend:** AD INSTAR - GRUIS. **Mint:** Berleburg **Note:** Dav. #898. Ref. M/V#76-77. Prev. KM#62. Varieties exist.

Date	Mintage	VG	F	VF	XF	Unc
1676	—	450	800	1,350	2,200	—

KM# 26 THALER
Silver **Ruler:** Georg V **Obv:** 4-fold arms with central shield of Sayn, 3 ornate helmets above **Obv. Legend:** + GEORG: COM: IN. SAYN. ET: WITG: DOM: IN: HOMB: + **Rev:** Crowned imperial eagle with orb on breast in inner circle, date at end of legend **Rev. Legend:** + FERDIN: II" D:G: ROM: IMP: SEMP: AVGVS: + **Mint:** Berleburg **Note:** Prev. Dav. #7667. Ref. M/V#23-24.

Date	Mintage	VG	F	VF	XF	Unc
16Z4	—	5,600	9,400	15,000	—	—
16Z5	—	5,600	9,400	15,000	—	—

KM# 31 THALER
Silver **Ruler:** Georg V **Obv:** 4-fold arms with central shield of Sayn in ornamented shield **Obv. Legend:** + GEORG: COMES: IN. SAYN. ET. WITG: DOM: IN: HOMB: + **Rev:** Crowned imperial eagle, orb on breast, date at end of legend **Rev. Legend:** + FERDINAND: II: D: G: ROM: IMP: SEMP: AUG: G: H: B: R: **Mint:** Berleburg **Note:** Prev. Dav. #7667A/B.

Date	Mintage	VG	F	VF	XF	Unc
(1)6Z5	—	5,600	9,400	15,000	—	—

KM# 30 THALER
Silver **Ruler:** Georg V **Obv:** Bust of Georg right in inner circle, date at end oflegend **Obv. Legend:** + G: C: I: S: E: W: D: I: H + M: G: V: K + **Rev:** Crowned imperial eagle, orb on breast **Rev. Legend:** ++ FERDINA + Z + D: G + ROM + IMP + SEMP + AUG + **Mint:** Berleburg **Note:** Prev. Dav. #7668. Ref. M/V#25.

Date	Mintage	VG	F	VF	XF	Unc
16Z5 H(a)S Rare	—	—	—	—	—	—

KM# 54 THALER
Silver **Ruler:** Georg Wilhelm **Obv:** Bust of Georg Wilhelm right in inner circle, final 'N' reversed in legend **Obv. Legend:** GEORG WILHELM. G. Z. S. V. W. H. Z. H. V. N. **Rev:** 4-fold arms with central shield of Sayn, 3 ornate helmets above, date at end of legend **Rev. Legend:** VIRTUTE ET LABORE. **Mint:** Berleburg **Note:** Dav. #7669. Ref. M/V#57.

Date	Mintage	VG	F	VF	XF	Unc
1678 IV(b)B Rare	—	—	—	—	—	—

TRADE COINAGE

KM# 16 GOLDGULDEN
Gold **Ruler:** Georg V **Obv:** 4-fold arms with central shield of Sayn in ornamented shield **Obv. Legend:** + MON(E). NOVA. A(V)(U)RI. COM. IN. (S.E.) W(I)(T). **Rev:** Crowned imperial eagle, imperial orb on breast **Rev. Legend:** FERDI. II. D. G. RO. IM(P). S. AU(G). G. H. B. REX. **Mint:** Berleburg **Note:** Fr. #3050a. Ref. M/V#21, 34-36. Weight varies: 2.89-3.23 g. Varieties exist.

Date	Mintage	VG	F	VF	XF	Unc
ND(1623-26) Rare	—	—	—	—	—	—

KM# 17 GOLDGULDEN
3.5000 g., 0.9860 Gold 0.1109 oz. AGW **Obv:** 3 small round shields of arms in form of cloverleaf **Obv. Legend:** + MO. NOV(A). AUR. COM. IN. WITGENSTE. **Rev:** Crowned imperial eagle in inner circle, orb on breast **Rev. Legend:** FERDI. II. D. G. RO. IMP. S. AUG. G. H. B. R(EX). **Note:** Prev. Fr. #3054. Ref. M/V#38-40.

Date	Mintage	VG	F	VF	XF	Unc
ND(1623-26) Rare	—	900	1,800	3,600	6,400	—

KM# 18 GOLDGULDEN
3.5000 g., 0.9860 Gold 0.1109 oz. AGW **Obv:** 3 small Spanish shields of arms, tops towards center in which a rosette **Obv. Legend:** + MON. NOV. AURI. COM. IN. S. E. WI. **Rev:** Imperial orb in cartouche **Rev. Legend:** + FERDIN. D. G. ROM. IMP. SEMP. AUG. **Note:** Prev. Fr. #3056. Ref. M/V#41.

Date	Mintage	VG	F	VF	XF	Unc
ND(1623-26) Rare	—	775	1,800	3,850	6,700	—

KM# 19 GOLDGULDEN
Gold **Ruler:** Georg V **Obv:** 3 small Spanish shields of arms, tops towards center in which a rosette **Obv. Legend:** + MON. NOV. AURI. COM. IN. S. E. WI. **Rev:** Crowned imperial eagle, orb on breast **Rev. Legend:** FERDI. II. D. G. RO. IMP. S. AUG. G. H. B. REX. **Mint:** Berleburg **Note:** Ref. M/V#42. Weight varies: 2.89-3.23 g.

Date	Mintage	VG	F	VF	XF	Unc
ND(1623-26) Rare	—	—	—	—	—	—

KM# 20 GOLDGULDEN
3.5000 g., 0.9860 Gold 0.1109 oz. AGW **Obv:** 2 adjacent shields of arms attached by looped hanger **Obv. Legend:** + MON: NOV: AVR: COM: IN. WITG **Rev:** Crowned imperial eagle, orb on breast **Rev. Legend:** FEER: II. D: RO: IMP: SE: A. **Note:** Prev. Fr. #3051. Ref. M/V#43.

Date	Mintage	VG	F	VF	XF	Unc
ND(1623-26) Rare	—	1,550	3,100	6,200	10,000	—

KM# 21 GOLDGULDEN
3.5000 g., 0.9860 Gold 0.1109 oz. AGW **Ruler:** Georg V **Obv:** 2 adjacent shields of arms attached by looped hanger **Obv. Legend:** + MON: NO(V): A(V)(U)R: CO(M). IN. WITG(N): **Rev:** Imperial orb in pointed trefoil **Rev. Legend:** + FER(D): II. D: G: RO(M): IMP: SE(MP): A(V)(G): **Mint:** Berleburg **Note:** Prev. Fr. #3057. Ref. M/V#44-48.

Date	Mintage	VG	F	VF	XF	Unc
ND(1623-26) Rare	—	775	1,800	3,850	6,700	—

KM# 22 GOLDGULDEN
3.5000 g., 0.9860 Gold 0.1109 oz. AGW **Ruler:** Georg V **Obv:** 2 adjacent shields of arms, arabesques above and below **Obv. Legend:** + MON. NOVA. AURI. COMES. IN. WIT. **Rev:** Imperial orb in pointed trefoil **Rev. Legend:** + FERDI. II. D. G. RO. IMP. S. AUG. G. H. B. REX. **Mint:** Berleburg **Note:** Prev. Fr. #3053. Ref. M/V#49.

Date	Mintage	VG	F	VF	XF	Unc
ND(1623-26) Rare	—	1,250	2,700	5,000	8,200	—

KM# 23 GOLDGULDEN
Gold **Ruler:** Georg V **Obv:** 2 adjacent shields of arms, arabesques above and below **Obv. Legend:** + MONETA. NOVA. AURI: COM: IN: WIT. **Rev:** Crowned imperial eagle, orb on breast **Rev. Legend:** FERDI. II. D. G. RO. IMP. S. AUG. G. H. B. REX. **Mint:** Berleburg **Note:** Ref. M/V#50.

Date	Mintage	VG	F	VF	XF	Unc
ND(1623-26) Rare	—	—	—	—	—	—

KM# 24 GOLDGULDEN
3.5000 g., 0.9860 Gold 0.1109 oz. AGW **Ruler:** Georg V **Obv:** 4-fold arms with central shield of Sayn in ornamented shield **Obv. Legend:** + MON: NO: AVR. CO: IN: WITGN: **Rev:** Imperial orb in pointed trefoil **Rev. Legend:** + MON: NO: AVR: COM: IN: WITGEN: **Mint:** Berleburg **Note:** Prev. Fr. #3052. Ref. M/V#37.

Date	Mintage	VG	F	VF	XF	Unc
ND(1623-26) Rare	—	1,050	2,400	5,300	8,600	—

KM# 80 GOLDGULDEN
3.5000 g., 0.9860 Gold 0.1109 oz. AGW **Rev:** Helmeted arms in inner circle

Date	Mintage	VG	F	VF	XF	Unc
1624 Rare	—	—	—	—	—	—

KM# 27 GOLDGULDEN
Gold **Ruler:** Georg V **Obv:** Ornate shield of 4-fold arms with central shield of Sayn, 3 helmets above **Obv. Legend:** GEORG. G. Z. S. U. W. H. Z. H: B. **Rev:** Crowned imperial eagle, imperial orb on breast, date at end of legend **Rev. Legend:** + MO: NOV. AU. CO: I: WI: + **Mint:** Berleburg **Note:** Ref. M/V#22.

Date	Mintage	VG	F	VF	XF	Unc
(16)Z4 Rare	—	—	—	—	—	—

SAYN-WITTGENSTEIN-HOMBURG

Established as a cadet branch of Sayn-Wittgenstein-Berleburg in 1631, Sayn-Wittgenstein-Homburg lasted only three generations and fell extinct in 1743. A single coin type was struck for this branch of Sayn.

RULERS
Ernst, 1631-1649
Wilhelm Friedrich, 1649-1698
Friedrich Karl, 1698-1743

COUNTSHIP

STANDARD COINAGE

KM# 5 1/6 THALER
5.8200 g., Silver **Ruler:** Wilhelm Friedrich **Obv:** Armored bust to right in circle **Obv. Legend:** W.I.L.H.E.L.M - FRIE: D: G. Z. H. V. U. N. **Rev:** 4-line inscription with date in circle **Rev. Legend:** CUM. DEO. ET. LABORE. **Rev. Inscription:** VI / I REICHS / THALER / 1689. **Mint:** Homburg **Note:** Ref. M/V#396.

Date	Mintage	VG	F	VF	XF	Unc
1689	—	—	—	—	—	—

SAYN-WITTGENSTEIN-SAYN

(Sayn-Hachenberg-Altenkirchen)

The eldest son of Ludwig III married Anna Elisabeth, the heiress of the main line of Sayn, and the result was a branch known variously as Sayn-Wittgenstein-Sayn and Sayn-Hachenberg-Altenkirchen. It soon fell extinct in the male line, but the daughters of Ernest divided the title into the lines of Sayn-Hachenberg and Sayn-Altenkirchen. Joint coinage for the death of Ernest's widow and in commemoration of the succeeding rulers who married their daughters was struck in 1670.

RULERS
Wilhelm III, 1605-1623
Ernest, 1623-1632
Ernestine Salentine, 1632-1648
Johanetta, 1632-1648

COUNTSHIP

STANDARD COINAGE

KM# 3 PFENNIG
Silver **Ruler:** Wilhelm III **Obv:** Shield of 4-fold arms quartered Sayn and Wittgenstein, 'VV' above, all in circle of pellets **Note:** Ref. M/V#398. Uniface, schüssel-type.

Date	Mintage	VG	F	VF	XF	Unc
ND(ca1610-15)	—	—	—	—	—	—

KM# 2 PFENNIG
Silver **Ruler:** Wilhelm III **Obv:** Shield of 4-fold arms quartered Sayn and Wittgenstein, 'W' above, all in circle of pellets **Note:** Uniface, schüssel-type. Prev. KM#5. Ref. M/V#397.

Date	Mintage	VG	F	VF	XF	Unc
ND(ca. 1610-15)	—	35.00	75.00	150	290	—

KM# 5 1/16 THALER
Silver **Subject:** Death of Luise Juliane von Erbach, Widow of Count Ernest **Obv:** 6-line inscription **Obv. Inscription:** MONE / FAMÆ. IM / MORT. DNÆ / LOŸSÆ. IVLI / ANÆ. COMIT / SAIN. **Rev:** 6-line inscription with dates **Rev. Inscription:** DE / STEMM AT. / ERBACENS / NAT. Ao. 1604 / DEFVNCT. / Ao. 1670. **Mint:** Dortmund **Note:** Prev. KM#16. Ref. M/V#401.

Date	Mintage	VG	F	VF	XF	Unc
1670	300	110	200	375	775	—

KM# 6 1/16 THALER
Silver **Subject:** Joint Issue of Saxe-Eisenach and Manderscheid as Successors to Sayn-Wittgenstein-Sayn **Obv:** Small shield of Sayn arms divides date, XVI above, I. REICHS / T below **Obv. Legend:** MON. SAXO. ET. MANDERS. SEINE. **Rev:** Laureate bust of emperor right in circle **Rev. Legend:** LEOPOLD. D. G. ROM. IMP. S. AVG. **Mint:** Dortmund **Note:** Prev. KM#17. Ref. M/V#402.

Date	Mintage	VG	F	VF	XF	Unc
1670	11,620	—	—	—	—	—
1671	Inc. above	—	—	—	—	—

KM# 8 1/4 THALER
7.2100 g., Silver **Subject:** Death of Luise Juliane von Erbach, Widow of Count Ernest **Obv:** 8-line inscription with dates **Obv. Inscription:** IN / MEMORIAM / DNÆ. LOŸSÆ. IVL. / COMITISS. SAIN. / DE. STEMM. ER / BAC. NAT. 1604 / DEFVNCTÆ. / Ao. 1670. **Rev:** The countess in sailboat on sea right, radiant sun from clouds in upper left, all in circle **Rev. Legend:** INVENI. PORTVM. SPES. ET. FORTVNA. VALETE. **Mint:** Dortmund **Note:** Prev. KM#18. Ref. M/V#400.

Date	Mintage	VG	F	VF	XF	Unc
1670	200	325	525	950	1,800	—

KM# 10 1/2 THALER
14.5000 g., Silver **Subject:** Death of Luise Juliane von Erbach, Widow of Count Ernest **Obv:** 8-line inscription with dates **Obv. Inscription:** IN / MEMORIAM. / DNÆ. LOŸSÆ. IVL. / IANÆ. COMITISS. / SAIN. DE. STEMM. / ERBAC. NAT. Ao. / 1604. DEFVNCT. / ANNO. 1670. **Rev:** The countess in sailboat on sea to right, radiant sun from clouds in upper left, all in circle **Rev. Legend:** INVENI. PORTVM. SPES. ET. FORTVNA. VALETE. **Mint:** Dortmund **Note:** Prev. Sayn-Hachenberg-Altenkirchen KM#19. Ref. M/V#399.

Date	Mintage	VG	F	VF	XF	Unc
1670	100	450	850	1,400	2,650	—

SAYN-WITTGENSTEIN-WITTGENSTEIN

The middle line of Sayn-Wittgenstein was founded in 1605. Count Johann VIII was a chief minister of the Elector of Brandenburg-Prussia during te Thirty Years' War. At the conclusion of the war after the Peace of Westphalia, Johann was given Clettenberg and Lohra in Hohnstein for services. He was also the governor of Minden and had coins struck especially for use in that town. His son was notorious for issuing a wide variety of poor value coinage, including counterfeits, fakes and forgeries until the Elector of Brandenburg was forced to close his mint at Elrich and repossess the Hohnstein territories. In 1804, the count was raised to the rank of prince.

RULERS
Ludwig II, 1605-1634
Johann VIII, 1634-1657
Gustav, 1657-1701
Ludwig Christian, 1657-1683

COUNTSHIP

STANDARD COINAGE

KM# 103 8 HELLER
0.6200 g., Silver **Ruler:** Gustav **Obv:** Shield of Sayn arms, date at end of legend **Obv. Legend:** GUSTAV: H. Z. S. W. E. H. **Rev:** 2-line inscription in circle **Rev. Legend:** MONETA. WITIGE. **Rev. Inscription:** VIII / ICF **Mint:** Berleburg **Note:** Ref. M/V#221. Prev. KM#83.

Date	Mintage	VG	F	VF	XF	Unc
1681 ICF	14,670	30.00	60.00	120	240	—

KM# 104 8 HELLER
0.6200 g., Silver **Ruler:** Gustav **Obv:** Shield of Sayn arms divides mintmaster's symbols **Obv. Legend:** GUSTAV. H. Z. S. W. E. H. **Rev:** 2-line inscription, date at end of legend **Rev. Legend:** MONETA. WITTIGENS. **Rev. Inscription:** VIII / ICF **Mint:** Berleburg **Note:** Ref. M/V#222. Prev. KM#83.

Date	Mintage	VG	F	VF	XF	Unc
1682 ICF	61,335	30.00	60.00	120	240	—

KM# 105 8 HELLER
0.6200 g., Silver **Ruler:** Gustav **Obv:** Shield of Sayn arms **Obv. Legend:** GVSTAV. H. Z. S. W. E. H. G. V. **Rev:** 2-line inscription, date at end of legend **Rev. Legend:** MONETA. WITIGENS. **Rev. Inscription:** VIII / IC **Mint:** Berleburg **Note:** Ref. M/V#223. Prev. KM#83.

Date	Mintage	VG	F	VF	XF	Unc
(16)82 IC	Inc. above	15.00	35.00	70.00	145	—

KM# 106 8 HELLER
0.6200 g., Silver **Ruler:** Gustav **Obv:** Shield of Sayn arms divides mintmaster's symbols **Obv. Legend:** GUSTAV. G. Z. S. W. E. H. **Rev:** 2-line inscription in circle **Rev. Legend:** MONETA. WITIGENS **Rev. Inscription:** VIII / ICF **Mint:** Berleburg **Note:** Ref. M/V#224. Prev. KM#83.

Date	Mintage	VG	F	VF	XF	Unc
ND(ca1682) ICF	Inc. above	35.00	75.00	150	300	—

KM# 19 3 PFENNIG (DREIER)
0.5200 g., Silver **Ruler:** Gustav **Obv:** Crowned G divides date **Rev:** Imperial orb with 3 near bottom **Mint:** Elrich **Note:** Ref. M/V#198. Prev. KM#20.

Date	Mintage	VG	F	VF	XF	Unc
167Z	—	45.00	90.00	180	360	—

KM# 20 3 PFENNIG (DREIER)
0.5200 g., Silver **Ruler:** Gustav **Obv:** 2-fold arms in ornamented shield, divided vertically, Hohnstein on left, Lauterburg on right, date above **Rev:** Imperial orb with '3'. **Mint:** Elrich **Note:** Ref. M/V#199. Prev. KM#21.

Date	Mintage	VG	F	VF	XF	Unc
167Z	—	45.00	90.00	180	360	—

KM# 108 KREUZER (4 Pfennig)
Silver **Ruler:** Gustav **Obv:** Shield of Sayn arms divides mintmaster's symbols, all in palm wreath **Rev:** 5-line inscription with date in palm wreath **Rev. Inscription:** I / KREU / TZER / 1682 / ICF **Mint:** Schwarzenau **Note:** Ref. M/V#226, 237. Prev. KM#80.

Date	Mintage	VG	F	VF	XF	Unc
1682 ICF	353,520	30.00	60.00	125	240	—
1686 ICF	—	30.00	60.00	125	240	—

KM# 112 KREUZER (4 Pfennig)
Silver **Ruler:** Gustav **Obv:** Shield of Sayn arms in palm wreath **Rev:** 5-line inscription with date in palm wreath **Rev. Inscription:** I / KREU / TZER / 1683 / IVB **Mint:** Schwarzenau **Note:** Ref. M/V#227-230. Prev. KM#80.

Date	Mintage	VG	F	VF	XF	Unc
1683 (b)IVB	—	60.00	115	200	425	—
1683 IUB	—	60.00	115	200	425	—
1684 IVB	—	60.00	115	200	425	—
1684 IUB	—	60.00	115	200	425	—

KM# 122 KREUZER (4 Pfennig)
Billon **Ruler:** Gustav **Obv:** Shield of Sayn arms in palm wreath **Rev:** 5-line inscription with date in palm wreath **Rev. Inscription:** I / KREU / TZER / 1682 / HM. **Mint:** Wittgenstein **Note:** Ref. M/V#233-236, 238-39. Prev. KM#81. Varieties exist.

Date	Mintage	VG	F	VF	XF	Unc
1685 (b)IVB	Inc. above	—	—	—	—	—
1685 HM	391,824	60.00	115	200	425	—
1685 HCM	Inc. above	60.00	115	200	425	—
1685 IVB(b)	Inc. above	60.00	115	200	425	—
1686	—	—	—	—	—	—
1686 IL?	—	60.00	115	200	425	—

KM# 14 ALBUS (2 Kreuzer, 1/32 Thaler)
Silver **Ruler:** Johann VIII **Obv:** 4-fold arms of Sayn and Wittgenstein, 'W' above, all in wreath **Rev:** Value and large date in 3 lines **Rev. Inscription:** I / ALBVS / 1657 **Mint:** Wittgenstein **Note:** Ref. M/V#146. Prev. KM#5.

Date	Mintage	VG	F	VF	XF	Unc
1657 Large date	—	100	200	425	—	—
1657 Small date	—	100	200	425	—	—

KM# 15 ALBUS (2 Kreuzer, 1/32 Thaler)
Silver **Ruler:** Johann VIII **Obv:** 4-fold arms of Sayn and Wittgenstein, 'W' above, all in wreath **Rev:** Value and small date in 3 lines **Rev. Inscription:** I / ALBVS / 1657 **Mint:** Wittgenstein **Note:** Ref. M/V#147. Prev. KM#5.

Date	Mintage	VG	F	VF	XF	Unc
1657	—	—	—	—	—	—

KM# 100 ALBUS (2 Kreuzer, 1/32 Thaler)
Silver **Ruler:** Gustav **Obv:** Shield of Sayn arms, mintmaster's symbols above, all in palm wreath **Rev:** 3-line inscription with date, mintmaster's initials at left, above, and right of numeral 'I'. **Rev. Inscription:** I / ALBVS / 1681 **Mint:** Berleburg **Note:** Ref. M/V#220. Prev. KM#82.

Date	Mintage	VG	F	VF	XF	Unc
1681 (e)/ICF	32,080	65.00	135	275	550	—

KM# 124 ALBUS (2 Kreuzer, 1/32 Thaler)
Silver **Ruler:** Gustav **Obv:** Shield of Sayn arms in palm wreath **Rev:** 3-line inscription with date in palm wreath **Rev. Inscription:** I / ALBUS / 1686 **Mint:** Wittgenstein **Note:** Ref. M/V#232.

Date	Mintage	VG	F	VF	XF	Unc
1686	—	—	—	—	—	—

KM# 152 2 ALBUS (4 Kreuzer, 1/16 Thaler)
Silver **Ruler:** Gustav **Obv:** 6-fold arms with central shield of Sayn, rosette above, all in palm wreath **Rev:** 3-line inscription with date in palm wreath **Rev. Inscription:** II / ALBUS / 1692. **Mint:** Homburg **Note:** Ref. M/V#240. Prev. KM#105.

Date	Mintage	VG	F	VF	XF	Unc
1692	—	85.00	160	300	575	—

KM# 10 MARIENGROSCHEN (8 Pfennig)
Silver **Ruler:** Johann VIII **Obv:** Sayn lion in inner circle, date at end of legend **Obv. Legend:** I. G. Z. S. W. V. H. H. Z. H. V. N. L. V. C. **Rev:** Radiant figure of Madonna holding child in inner circle **Rev. Legend:** MARI(A)(.) M(-) A (-) (.) (T) (ER) (.) DOMI(N). **Mint:** Minden **Note:** Ref. M/V#141-145. Prev. KM#6. Weight varies: .812-1.69 g. Legend varieties.

Date	Mintage	VG	F	VF	XF	Unc
1655	—	45.00	80.00	150	300	—
1656	—	45.00	80.00	150	300	—
1657	—	45.00	80.00	150	300	—

KM# 22 MARIENGROSCHEN (8 Pfennig)
Silver **Ruler:** Gustav **Obv:** Crowned 'G' divides date **Obv. Legend:** G. G. Z. S. W. V. H. H. Z. H. (V)(U). N. L. V. C. L. **Rev:** Without inner circle **Rev. Legend:** MO. NO. HON - STEINENS. **Mint:** Elrich **Note:** Ref. M/V#190,193-95. Weight varies: 1.17-1.50 g. Varieties exist.

Date	Mintage	VG	F	VF	XF	Unc
1672	—	33.00	60.00	110	220	—
1673	—	33.00	60.00	110	220	—

KM# 23 MARIENGROSCHEN (8 Pfennig)
Silver **Ruler:** Gustav **Obv:** Crowned 4-fold arms divided vertically, Hohnstein on left, Wittgenstein on right, divide date **Obv. Legend:** G. G. Z. S. W. V. H. H. Z. H. (V)(U). N. L. V. C. L. **Rev:** Radiant Madonna and Child **Rev. Legend:** MARIA - MAT. DOM(I). **Mint:** Elrich **Note:** Ref. M/V#191-92. Weight varies: 1.17-1.50.

Date	Mintage	VG	F	VF	XF	Unc
1672	—	40.00	65.00	135	275	—

KM# 7 2 MARIENGROSCHEN (1/18 Thaler)
Silver **Ruler:** Johann VIII **Obv:** Crowned shield of Sayn arms divides date in inner circle **Obv. Legend:** I. G. Z. S. W. V. H. H. Z. H. V. N. L. V. C. **Rev:** 3-line inscription **Rev. Legend:** VON. FEINEM. SILBER. **Rev. Inscription:** II / MARI / GRO. **Mint:** Minden **Note:** Ref. M/V#126-139. Weight varies: .841-1.59 g. Prev. KM#7. Punctuation varieties.

Date	Mintage	VG	F	VF	XF	Unc
1654	—	20.00	45.00	90.00	185	—
1655	—	20.00	45.00	90.00	185	—
1650 (error for 1656)	—	20.00	45.00	90.00	185	—

KM# 12 4 MARIENGROSCHEN (1/9 Thaler)
Silver, 22 mm. **Ruler:** Johann VIII **Obv:** Crowned shield of Sayn arms divides date in inner circle **Obv. Legend:** I. G. Z. S. W. V. H. H. Z. H. V. N. L. V. C. **Rev:** 3-line inscription **Rev. Legend:** MONETA. NOVA. ARGEN(E)(A). **Rev. Inscription:** IIII / MARIE / GRO(S). **Mint:** Minden **Note:** Ref. M/V#105-125. Prev. KM#8. Ornamentation varieties exist.

Date	Mintage	VG	F	VF	XF	Unc
1655	—	45.00	90.00	180	360	—
1656	—	45.00	90.00	180	360	—
1657	—	45.00	90.00	180	360	—

KM# 128 6 MARIENGROSCHEN (4 Gute Groschen, 1/6 Thaler)
5.0700 g., Silver **Ruler:** Gustav **Obv:** Draped bust of Gustav right **Obv. Legend:** GUS. G. Z. S. (V)(W). U. H. H. Z. H. V. N. L. (V)(U). C. **Rev:** Value in 4-line inscription with date **Rev. Legend:** MONETA. NOVA. ARGENTEA. **Rev. Inscription:** VI / MARIEN / GRO / 1688 **Mint:** Stettin **Note:** Ref. M/V#257-59. Prev. KM#84. Varieties exist.

Date	Mintage	VG	F	VF	XF	Unc
1688	—	50.00	100	200	425	—
1689	—	50.00	100	200	425	—

KM# 25 12 MARIENGROSCHEN (1/3 Thaler, 1/2 Gulden)
Silver **Ruler:** Gustav **Obv:** Stag left in circle (Lohra & Klettenberg arms) **Obv. Legend:** G. G. Z. S. W. V. H. H. Z. H. V. N. L. V. CL. **Rev:** 3-line inscription, date at end of legend **Rev. Legend:** PIE ET. CAUTE. **Rev. Inscription:** XII / MARIA / GROS **Mint:** Elrich **Note:** Ref. M/V#183. Prev. KM#24.

Date	Mintage	VG	F	VF	XF	Unc
167Z	—	200	375	775	—	—

KM# 26 12 MARIENGROSCHEN (1/3 Thaler, 1/2 Gulden)
Silver **Ruler:** Gustav **Obv:** Stag left in circle (Lohra & Klettenberg arms) **Obv. Legend:** GUSTAV. G. Z. S. W. V. HONSTEIN. H. Z. H. V. N. L. V. CL. **Rev:** 3-line inscription, mintmasters' initials and symbol below (where present), date at end of legend **Rev. Legend:** PIE ET CAUTE **Rev. Inscription:** XII / MARIEN / GROSCH **Mint:** Elrich **Note:** Ref. M/V#184-86. Prev. KM#25. Varieties exist.

Date	Mintage	VG	F	VF	XF	Unc
167Z	—	200	375	775	—	—
1673 IZ(f)W	—	200	375	775	—	—

KM# 31 12 MARIENGROSCHEN (1/3 Thaler, 1/2 Gulden)
Silver **Ruler:** Gustav **Obv:** Draped bust of Gustav right **Obv. Legend:** GUSTAV. G. Z. S. W. V. HO(N). H. Z. H. V. N. L. V. CL. **Rev:** 3-line inscription, mintmasters' initials and symbol below (where present), date at end of legend **Rev. Legend:** PIE ET CAUTE **Rev. Inscription:** XII / MARIEN / GROSCH. **Mint:** Elrich **Note:** Ref. M/V#187-89. Prev. KM#26. Varieties exist.

Date	Mintage	VG	F	VF	XF	Unc
1673	—	235	475	950	—	—
1673 IZ(f)W	—	235	475	950	—	—
1674 IZ(f)W	—	235	475	950	—	—

KM# 59 60 KREUZER (2/3 Thaler, Gulden)
Silver **Ruler:** Gustav **Obv:** Crowned monogram divides date, mintmaster's initials and symbol, value '60' in oval below, all in wreath, no legend **Rev:** 6-fold arms with central shield of Sayn, 2 ornate helmets above **Rev. Legend:** AD. INSTAR. GRUIS. **Mint:** Berleburg **Note:** Dav. #904. Ref. M/V#201-02. Weight varies: 17.93-19.00 g. Prev. KM#55.

Date	Mintage	VG	F	VF	XF	Unc
1675 IW(f)	—	750	1,500	3,000	—	—

KM# 55 60 KREUZER (2/3 Thaler, Gulden)
Silver **Ruler:** Gustav **Obv:** Draped bust right, value '60' below **Obv. Legend:** G. G. Z. S. W. V. HO. H. Z. H. N. L. V. CL. **Rev:** Crowned 6-fold arms with central shield of Sayn divide mintmaster's initials, date at end of legend **Rev. Legend:** MONETA NOVA - ARGENTEA **Mint:** Berleburg **Note:** Dav. #924. Ref. M/V#203-04. Weight varies: 17.93-19.00. Prev. KM#56. Varieties exist.

Date	Mintage	VG	F	VF	XF	Unc
1675 IB	—	—	—	—	—	—

KM# 57 60 KREUZER (2/3 Thaler, Gulden)
Silver **Ruler:** Gustav **Obv:** Draped bust of Gustav right **Obv. Legend:** GUSTAV. G. Z. S. W. V. HON. H. Z. H. V. N. L. V. C. **Rev:** Crowned 6-fold arms with central shield of Sayn divides mintmaster's initials, value '60' in oval at bottom, date at end of legend **Rev. Legend:** MONETA NNOVA - ARGENTEA **Mint:** Berleburg **Note:** Dav. #925. Ref. M/V#205-06. Weight varies: 17.93-19.00. Prev. KM#56.

Date	Mintage	VG	F	VF	XF	Unc
1675 IB	—	80.00	165	335	675	—

KM# 58 60 KREUZER (2/3 Thaler, Gulden)
Silver **Ruler:** Gustav **Obv:** Draped bust of Gustav right. **Obv. Legend:** G. C. DE. S. W. ET. H. (D.) (O.) AT. H. N. L. E. C. **Rev:** Crowned 6-fold arms with central shield of Sayn divide mintmaster's initials, value '60' in oval at bottom, date at end of legend **Rev. Legend:** MONETA. NOVA. ANNO. **Mint:** Berleburg **Note:** Dav. #926. Ref. M/V#207-14. Weight varies: 17.93-19.00 g. Prev. KM#57. Varieties exist.

Date	Mintage	VG	F	VF	XF	Unc
1675 IB	—	80.00	165	335	675	—
1676 IB	—	80.00	165	335	675	—

KM# 73 60 KREUZER (2/3 Thaler, Gulden)
Silver **Ruler:** Gustav **Obv:** Crowned monogram above date and value '60', all in wreath, no legend **Rev:** 4-fold arms with central shield of Sayn, 2 ornate helmets above, no legend **Mint:** Berleburg **Note:** Dav. #905. Ref. M/V#215-16. Weight varies: 17.93-19.00. Prev. KM#58.

Date	Mintage	VG	F	VF	XF	Unc
1676	—	—	—	—	—	—

KM# 52 16 GUTE GROSCHEN (2/3 Thaler)
Silver **Ruler:** Gustav **Obv:** Crowned 6-fold arms with central shield of Sayn between 2 palm branches, value '2/3' in oval below, date in legend **Obv. Legend:** PER ASPERA - AD ASTRA **Rev:** 4-line inscription with date in circle **Rev. Legend:** AD INSTAR GRUIS **Rev. Inscription:** XVI / GVDE / GROSCH / 1675 **Note:** Dav. #923. Ref. M/V#379. Weight varies: 14.54-16.80. Prev. KM#28.

Date	Mintage	VG	F	VF	XF	Unc
1675//1675	—	200	400	800	1,600	—

KM# 51 16 GUTE GROSCHEN (2/3 Thaler)
Silver **Obv:** Stag left in circle (Lohra & Klettenberg arms). **Obv. Legend:** GUSTAV. G. Z. S. W. V. HONSTEIN. Z. H. V. N. L. V. CLET. **Rev:** 4-line inscription with date in circle **Rev. Legend:** C. D. S. W. ET. H. DO. D. H. V. N. L. ET. CLET. **Rev. Inscription:** 16 / GUTE / GROSCH / 16 EN 75 **Note:** Dav. #937. Ref. M/V#378. Weight varies: 14.54-16.80. Prev. KM#27.

Date	Mintage	VG	F	VF	XF	Unc
1675	—	250	500	1,000	2,000	—

KM# 53 16 GUTE GROSCHEN (2/3 Thaler)
Silver **Ruler:** Gustav **Obv:** 4-line inscription with date in circle **Obv. Legend:** GVSTAV. G. Z. S. W. V. HON. H. Z. H. V. N. L. V. C. **Obv. Inscription:** XVI / GVDE / GROSCH / 1675 **Rev:** Crowned 6-fold arms with central shield of Sayn between 2 palm branches **Rev. Legend:** AD. INSTAR. GRUIS. **Note:** Dav. #938. Ref. M/V#380. Weight varies: 14.54-16.80. Prev. KM#29.

Date	Mintage	VG	F	VF	XF	Unc
1675	—	200	400	800	1,600	—

KM# 54 16 GUTE GROSCHEN (2/3 Thaler)
Silver **Ruler:** Gustav **Obv:** 4-line inscription with date in circle **Obv. Legend:** GVSTAV. G. Z. S. W. V. HON. H. Z. H. V. N. L. V. C. **Obv. Inscription:** XVI / GVDE / GROSCH / 1675 **Rev:** Crowned 6-fold arms with central shield of Sayn between 2 palm branches in ornamented shield **Rev. Legend:** AD. INSTAR. GRUIS. **Note:** Dav. #938A. Ref. M/V#381. Weight varies: 14.54-16.80. Prev. KM#29.

Date	Mintage	VG	F	VF	XF	Unc
1675	—	—	—	—	—	—

KM# 68 16 GUTE GROSCHEN (2/3 Thaler)
Silver **Obv:** 6-fold arms with central shield of Sayn, 4 ornate helmets above **Obv. Legend:** GVSTAV. G. Z. S. W. V. HON. H. Z. H. V. N. L. V. C. (LE). **Rev:** 3-line inscription in circle, R.N. date at end of legend **Rev. Legend:** TANDEM FORTVNA OBSTETRICE. Ao. **Rev. Inscription:** 16 / GUTE / GROSCH **Note:** Dav. #940. Ref. M/V#382-84. Weight varies: 14.54-16.80. Prev. KM#30. Varieties exist.

Date	Mintage	VG	F	VF	XF	Unc
MDCLXXVI (1676)	—	115	200	325	675	—

KM# 69 16 GUTE GROSCHEN (2/3 Thaler)
Silver **Ruler:** Gustav **Obv:** 6-fold arms with central shield of Sayn, 4 ornate helmets above **Obv. Legend:** GVSTAV. G. Z. S. W. V. ON. H. Z. H. V. N. L. CLET. **Rev:** 4-line inscription in circle **Rev. Legend:** TANDEM FORTVNA OBSTETRICE **Rev. Inscription:** 16 / GUTE / GROSCH / EN **Note:** Dav. #941. Weight varies: 14.54-16.80.

Date	Mintage	VG	F	VF	XF	Unc
ND(1676)	—	—	—	—	—	—

KM# 70 16 GUTE GROSCHEN (2/3 Thaler)
Silver **Ruler:** Gustav **Obv:** Stag left in circle (Lohra & Klettenberg arms). **Obv. Legend:** GUSTAV9. C. IN. S. W. & HON. H. Z. H. V. N. L. & CLET. **Rev:** 4-line inscription with R.N. date **Rev. Legend:** AD PALMAM PRÆSSA LÆTIUS RESURGO **Rev. Inscription:** XVI / GUTE / GROSCHEN / M.DC.LXXVI. **Mint:** Elrich **Note:** Dav. #942. Ref. M/V#385. Weight varies: 14.54-16.80 g. Prev. KM#31.

Date	Mintage	VG	F	VF	XF	Unc
MDCLXXVI(1676)	—	175	350	700	1,400	—

KM# 71 16 GUTE GROSCHEN (2/3 Thaler)
Silver **Ruler:** Gustav **Obv:** 4-line inscription with R.N. date **Obv. Legend:** GUSTAV. G. Z. S. W. V. HON. H. Z. H. V. N. L. V. CLETT. **Obv. Inscription:** XVI / GUTE / GROSCHEN / MDCLXXVI **Rev:** Walking stag left in inner circle (Lohra & Klettenberg arms) **Rev. Legend:** AD PALMAM PRÆSSA LÆTIUS RESURGO **Mint:** Elrich **Note:** Dav. #943. Ref. M/V#386. Weight varies: 14.54-16.80. Prev. KM#32.

Date	Mintage	VG	F	VF	XF	Unc
MDCLXXVI (1676)	—	180	375	750	1,500	—

KM# 95 16 GUTE GROSCHEN (2/3 Thaler)
Silver **Obv:** Stag leaping left in circle (Lohra & Klettenberg arms) **Obv. Legend:** GUSTAV. G. Z. S. W. V. HON. H. Z. H. V. N. L. V. C. **Rev:** 5-line inscription with date in circle **Rev. Legend:** TANDEM. FORTUNA. OBSTETRICE. **Rev. Inscription:** 16 / GUTE / GROSCH / EN / 1677 **Note:** Dav. #944. Ref. M/V#387. Weight varies: 14.54-16.80. Prev. KM#33.

Date	Mintage	VG	F	VF	XF	Unc
1677	—	185	375	775	1,550	—

KM# 96 16 GUTE GROSCHEN (2/3 Thaler)
Silver **Obv:** Draped bust of Gustav right **Obv. Legend:** GUSTAV. G. Z. S. W. V. HON. H. Z. H. V. N. L. V. C. **Rev:** 5-line inscription with date in circle **Rev. Legend:** IUSTE - PIE - & - CAUTE **Rev. Inscription:** 16 / GUTE / GROSH / EN / 1677 **Note:** Dav. #945. Ref. M/V#388. Weight varies: 14.54-16.80. Prev. KM#34.

Date	Mintage	VG	F	VF	XF	Unc
1677	—	200	400	800	1,600	—

KM# 33 24 MARIENGROSCHEN (2/3 Thaler)
Silver **Ruler:** Gustav **Obv:** Stag left in circle (Lohra & Klettenberg arms) **Obv. Legend:** GUSTAV. G. Z. S. W. V. HONSTEIN. Z. H. V. N. L. V. CL. **Rev:** 3-line inscription, mintmaster's initials and symbol below, date at end of legend **Rev. Legend:** PIE. ET. CAUTE. **Rev. Inscription:** XXIIII / MARIEN / GROSCH. **Mint:** Elrich **Note:** Dav. #(927). Ref. M/V#178. Prev. KM#35.

Date	Mintage	VG	F	VF	XF	Unc
1673 IZ(f)W	—	115	235	475	975	—
1675	—	115	235	475	975	—

KM# 34 24 MARIENGROSCHEN (2/3 Thaler)
Silver **Ruler:** Gustav **Obv:** Draped bust of Gustav right **Obv. Legend:** GUSTAV. G. Z. S. W. V. HON(ST). H. Z. H. V. N. L. V. C(L). **Rev:** 3-line inscription, mintmaster's initials and symbol below, date at end of legend **Rev. Legend:** PIE. ET. CAUTE. **Rev. Inscription:** XXIIII / MARIEN / GROSCH. **Mint:** Elrich **Note:** Dav. #(928). Ref. M/V#179-80. Prev. KM#36. Varieties exist.

Date	Mintage	VG	F	VF	XF	Unc
1673 IZ(f)W	—	—	—	—	—	—

KM# 38 24 MARIENGROSCHEN (2/3 Thaler)
Silver **Ruler:** Gustav **Obv:** Draped bust of Gustav right **Obv. Legend:** GUSTAV. G. Z. S. W. V. HON. H. Z. H. V. N. L. V. C(L). **Rev:** 3-line inscription, mintmasters' initials and symbol below, date at end of legend **Rev. Legend:** PIE. ET. CAUTE(.) ANNO **Rev. Inscription:** XXIIII / MARIEN / GROSCH. **Mint:** Elrich **Note:** Dav. #(928). Ref. M/V#181-82. Prev. KM#36. Varieties exist.

Date	Mintage	VG	F	VF	XF	Unc
1674 IZ(f)W	—	335	675	1,350	—	—

KM# 39 24 MARIENGROSCHEN (2/3 Thaler)
Silver **Ruler:** Gustav **Obv:** Draped bust of Gustav right in circle **Obv. Legend:** GUSTAV. G. Z. S. W. V. HON. H. Z. H. V. N. L. V. C. **Rev:** 3-line inscription, R.N. date at end of legend **Rev. Legend:** PIE ET. CAUTE(.) ANNO. **Rev. Inscription:** XXIIII / MARIEN / GROSCH. **Note:** Dav. #929. Ref. M/V#362-63. Prev. KM#37.

Date	Mintage	VG	F	VF	XF	Unc
MDCLXXIIII (1674)	—	40.00	100	190	385	—

KM# 49 24 MARIENGROSCHEN (2/3 Thaler)
Silver **Obv:** Stag left in inner circle (Lohra & Klettenberg arms) **Obv. Legend:** GUSTAV. G. Z. S. W. V. HON(STEIN). H. Z. H. V. N. L. V. C(LET). **Rev:** 3-line inscription, mintmasters' initials and symbol below, date at end of legend **Rev. Legend:** PIE. ET. CAUTE. **Rev. Inscription:** XXIIII / MARIEN / GROSCH. **Note:** Dav. #(927). Ref. M/V#364-66. Prev. KM#38. Varieties exist.

Date	Mintage	VG	F	VF	XF	Unc
1675	—	65.00	135	235	475	—

KM# 48 24 MARIENGROSCHEN (2/3 Thaler)
Silver **Ruler:** Gustav **Obv:** Draped bust of Gustav right in inner circle **Obv. Legend:** GUSTAV. G. Z. S. W. V. HON. H. Z. H. V. N. L. V. C. **Rev:** 4-line inscription with date in circle **Rev. Legend:** VERBIUM. DOMINI. MANET. IN. AETERNUM. **Rev. Inscription:** XXIIII / MARIEN / GROSCHEN / 1675 **Note:** Dav. #930. Ref. M/V#367. Prev. KM#39.

Date	Mintage	VG	F	VF	XF	Unc
1675	—	200	400	775	1,550	—

KM# 65 24 MARIENGROSCHEN (2/3 Thaler)
Silver **Ruler:** Gustav **Obv:** Draped bust of Gustav right in circle **Obv. Legend:** GUSTAV. G. Z. S. W. V. HON. H. Z. H. V. N. L. V. C. **Rev:** 4-line inscription with date in circle **Rev. Legend:** AD PALMAM PRÆSSA LÆTIUS RESURGO **Rev. Inscription:** XXIIII / MARIEN / GROSCHEN / 1676 **Note:** Dav. #931. Ref. M/V#371-72. Prev. KM#41.

Date	Mintage	VG	F	VF	XF	Unc
1676	—	45.00	100	190	385	—

KM# 66 24 MARIENGROSCHEN (2/3 Thaler)
Silver **Ruler:** Gustav **Obv:** 6-fold arms with central shield of Sayn, 4 ornate helmets above **Obv. Legend:** G(U)(V)STAV. G. Z. S. W. V. HON. H. Z. H. V. N. L. V. C. **Rev:** 3-line inscription in circle, R.N. date at end of legend **Rev. Legend:** TANDEM FORTUNA OBSTETRICE. (A)(N)(o) **Rev. Inscription:** XXIV / MARIEN / GROSCH **Note:** Dav. #932. Ref. M/V#368-70, 373. Prev. KM#40. Varieties exist.

Date	Mintage	VG	F	VF	XF	Unc
MDCLXXVI (1676)	—	185	375	750	1,500	—
MDCLXXVII (1677)	—	185	375	750	1,500	—

KM# 93 24 MARIENGROSCHEN (2/3 Thaler)
Silver **Ruler:** Gustav **Obv:** Draped bust of Gustav right in inner circle **Obv. Legend:** GUSTAV. G. Z. S. W. V. HON. H. Z. H. V. N. L. V. C. **Rev:** 4-line inscription, date at end of legend **Rev. Legend:** PIE. ET. CAUTE. **Rev. Inscription:** XXIIII / MARIE / GROSCH / EN **Note:** Dav. #929. Ref. M/V#374. Prev. KM#42.

Date	Mintage	VG	F	VF	XF	Unc
1677	—	65.00	135	235	475	—

KM# 135 24 MARIENGROSCHEN (2/3 Thaler)
Silver **Ruler:** Gustav **Obv:** Draped bust right **Obv. Legend:** GUS. G. Z. S. W. U. H. H. Z. H. V. N. L. U. C. **Rev:** 3-line inscription in circle, date at end of legend **Rev. Legend:** MONETA NOVA ARGENTEA **Rev. Inscription:** XXIIII / MARIEN / GROS. **Note:** Dav. #933. Ref. M/V#375. Prev. KM#85.

Date	Mintage	VG	F	VF	XF	Unc
1689	—	275	575	1,150	—	—

KM# 140 24 MARIENGROSCHEN (2/3 Thaler)
Silver **Ruler:** Gustav **Obv:** 6-fold arms with central shield of Sayn, 4 ornate helmets above **Obv. Legend:** GUSTAV. G. Z. S. W. V. HON. H. Z. H. V. N. L. V. CLET. **Rev:** 3-line inscription, R.N. date at end of legend **Rev. Legend:** AD PALMAM PRESSA LÆTIUS RESURGO **Rev. Inscription:** XXIV / MARIEN / GROSCH **Note:** Dav. #934.

Date	Mintage	VG	F	VF	XF	Unc
MDCXC (1690)	—	—	—	—	—	—

KM# 142 24 MARIENGROSCHEN (2/3 Thaler)
Silver **Ruler:** Gustav **Obv:** 6-fold arms with central shield of Sayn, 4 ornate helmets above **Obv. Legend:** GUSTAV. G. Z. S. W. V. HON. H. Z. H. V. N. L. V. C. **Rev:** 4-line inscription in circle **Rev. Legend:** TANDEM FORTUNA OBSTETRICE **Rev. Inscription:** XXIIII / MARIE / GROSCH / EN **Note:** Dav. #(935).Ref. M/V#377, 392-93. Prev. KM#107.

Date	Mintage	VG	F	VF	XF	Unc
ND(1690)	—	200	400	775	1,550	—

KM# 141 24 MARIENGROSCHEN (2/3 Thaler)
Silver **Ruler:** Gustav **Obv:** 6-fold arms with central shield of Sayn, 4 ornate helmets above **Obv. Legend:** GUSTAV. G. Z. S. W. V. HON. H. Z. H. V. N. L. V. CLET. **Rev:** Stag leaping left in circle, R.N. date at end of legend **Rev. Legend:** AD PALMAM PRESSA LÆTIUS RESURGO. **Note:** Ref. M/V#376. Prev. KM#106.

Date	Mintage	VG	F	VF	XF	Unc
MDCLXXXX(1690)	—	175	375	775	—	—

KM# 147 24 MARIENGROSCHEN (2/3 Thaler)
Silver **Ruler:** Gustav **Obv:** Draped bust right in circle **Obv. Legend:** GVSTAV. G. Z. S. W. V. HON. H. Z. H. V. N. L. V. C. **Rev:** 3-line inscription in circle, R.N. date at end of legend **Rev. Legend:** TANDEM FORTUNA OBSTETRICE. **Rev. Inscription:** XXIV / MARIEN / GROSCH. **Mint:** Stettin **Note:** Ref. M/V#256. Prev. KM#104.

Date	Mintage	VG	F	VF	XF	Unc
MDCLXXXXI (1691)	—	225	450	900	1,800	—

KM# 28 1/24 THALER (Groschen)
Silver **Ruler:** Gustav **Obv:** Stag right in circle (Lohra & Klettenberg arms) **Obv. Legend:** G. G. Z. S. W. V. H. H. Z. H. V. N. L. V. CL. **Rev:** Imperial orb with 24 in inner circle, titles of Gustav in legend **Rev. Legend:** G. G. Z. S. W. V. H. H. Z. H. V. N. L. V. CL. **Mint:** Elrich **Note:** Ref. M/V#196. Prev. KM#43. Weight varies: 1.60-1.68.

Date	Mintage	VG	F	VF	XF	Unc
ND(1672)	—	80.00	160	275	550	—

KM# 29 1/24 THALER (Groschen)
Silver **Ruler:** Gustav **Obv:** Stag right in circle (Lohra & Klettenberg arms) **Obv. Legend:** G. G. Z. S. W. V. H. H. Z. H. V. N. L. V. CL. **Rev:** Imperial orb with 24 in circle, date at end of legend **Rev. Legend:** PIE. ET. CAUTE **Mint:** Elrich **Note:** Ref. M/V#197. Prev. KM#44. Weight varies 1.60-1.68.

Date	Mintage	VG	F	VF	XF	Unc
1672	—	65.00	135	235	475	—

KM# 118 1/24 THALER (Groschen)
Silver **Ruler:** Gustav **Obv:** Crowned 6-fold arms with central shield of Sayn divides mintmasters' initials **Obv. Legend:** GUSTAV. G. Z. S. W. U. HONST. **Rev:** Imperial orb with 24 divides date as 1-6/8-4 in circle **Rev. Legend:** H. Z. H. V. N. L. U. CLETTENBERG. **Mint:** Klettenberg **Note:** Ref. M/V#200c. Weight varies: 1.60-1.68 g. Prev. KM#A45.

Date	Mintage	VG	F	VF	XF	Unc
1684 DF/(g)	—	65.00	135	275	550	—

KM# 113 1/16 THALER (Duttchen)
Silver **Ruler:** Gustav **Obv:** Crowned ornate 'G' monogram between 2 palm branches **Obv. Legend:** GUS. G. Z. S. W. U. H. H. Z. H. V. N. L. U. C. **Rev:** Value in 3-line inscription in inner circle, date st end of legend **Rev. Legend:** MONETA. NOVA. ARGENTEA. **Rev. Inscription:** XVI / REICHS / THAL. **Note:** Ref. M/V#254. Prev. KM#86.

Date	Mintage	VG	F	VF	XF	Unc
1683	—	—	—	—	—	—

KM# 114 1/16 THALER (Duttchen)
Silver **Ruler:** Gustav **Obv:** Bust of Gustav right in circle **Obv. Legend:** GUS. G. Z. S. W. U. H. H. Z. H. V. N. L. U. C. **Rev:** 3-line inscription in circle, date at end of legend **Rev. Legend:** MONETA. NOVA. ARGENTEA. **Rev. Inscription:** XVI / REICHS / THAL. **Note:** Ref. M/V#255. Prev. KM#87.

Date	Mintage	VG	F	VF	XF	Unc
1683	—	175	350	700	1,400	—

KM# 120 1/12 THALER (Doppelgroschen)
Silver **Ruler:** Gustav **Obv:** Crowned 6-fold arms with central shield of Sayn divides date as 1-6/8-4 **Obv. Legend:** GUST. G. Z. S. W. U. HON. H. Z. H. U. N. L. (U.C.) **Rev:** 5-line inscription in circle, mintmaster's symbol and / or initials in margin at top **Rev. Legend:** MONETA NOVA ARGENTEA **Rev. Inscription:** 12 / EINEN / REICHS / THAL / ER **Mint:** Klettenberg **Note:** Prev. KM#88, 90. Ref. M/V#200-200b, 360-61. Weight varies: 2.61-3.32 g. Varieties exist.

Date	Mintage	VG	F	VF	XF	Unc
1684 (g)	—	85.00	165	300	600	—
1684 D(g)F	—	85.00	165	300	600	—

KM# 138 1/12 THALER (Doppelgroschen)
Silver **Ruler:** Gustav **Obv:** Crowned 6-fold arms with central shield of Sayn **Obv. Legend:** GUS. G. Z. S. W. U. H. H. Z. H. V. N. L. U. C. **Rev:** 4-line inscription in circle, date at end of legend **Rev. Legend:** MONETA. NOV. ARGENT. **Rev. Inscription:** 12 / EINEN / REICHS / THAL. **Mint:** Klettenberg **Note:** Ref. M/V#252. Weight varies: 2.61-3.32 g. Prev. KM#89.

Date	Mintage	VG	F	VF	XF	Unc
1689	—	—	—	—	—	—

KM# 137 1/12 THALER (Doppelgroschen)
Silver **Ruler:** Gustav **Obv:** Crowned 6-fold arms with central shield of Sayn **Obv. Legend:** GUS. G. Z. S. W. U. H. H. Z. H. V. N. L. U. C. **Rev:** 5-line inscription in circle, date at end of legend **Rev. Legend:** MONETA NOVA ARGENTEA **Rev. Inscription:** 12 / EINEN / REICHS / THAL / ER **Mint:** Klettenberg **Note:** Ref. M/V#253. Weight varies: 2.61-3.32 g. Prev. KM#89.

Date	Mintage	VG	F	VF	XF	Unc
1689	—	115	200	425	—	—

KM# 102 1/8 THALER
3.3000 g., Silver **Ruler:** Gustav **Obv:** Armored bust of Gustav right **Obv. Legend:** IGUSTAV. C. IN. S. W. E. H. D. IN. H. V. N. L. E. C. **Rev:** 6-fold arms with central shield of Sayn, 4 ornate helmets above, date over crests of 2 middle helmets **Rev. Legend:** A. SOLO. IEHOVA. SAPEINTIA. VERA. **Mint:** Berleburg **Note:** Ref. M/V#219.

Date	Mintage	VG	F	VF	XF	Unc
1681 ICF/(e)	—	—	—	—	—	—

KM# 130 1/6 THALER (1/4 Gulden)
Silver **Ruler:** Gustav **Obv:** Draped bust of Gustav right **Obv. Legend:** GUS. G. Z. S. W. U. H. H. Z. H. N. V. L. U. C. **Rev:** Value in 4-line inscription in circle, date at end of legend **Rev. Legend:** MONETA. NOVA. ARGENTEA. **Rev. Inscription:** VI / EINEN / REICHS / THAL. **Note:** Ref. M/V#248, 250. Prev. KM#91, 93. Varieties exist.

Date	Mintage	VG	F	VF	XF	Unc
1688	—	275	575	1,100	2,150	—
1689	—	275	575	1,100	2,150	—

KM# 131 1/6 THALER (1/4 Gulden)
Silver **Ruler:** Gustav **Obv:** Armored and draped bust right **Obv. Legend:** D: G: G: Z: - S: W: H: G: **Rev:** Value in 5-line inscription with date in circle **Rev. Legend:** MONETA. NOVA. ARGENTEA. **Rev. Inscription:** VI / EINEN / REICHS / THAL / (1688; 1689) **Note:** Ref. M/V#249, 251. Prev. KM#92, 94, 95. Varieties exist.

Date	Mintage	VG	F	VF	XF	Unc
1688	—	275	575	1,100	2,150	—

KM# 75 1/4 THALER (6 Gute Groschen)
Silver, 26 mm. **Obv:** Bust of Gustav right in inner circle **Obv. Legend:** GUSTAV: C. IN. S. W. ET. HON. D. IN. H. V. N. L. ET. CLETTENB. **Rev:** Sailing ship left in ocean, setting or rising sun on horizon, legend curved above, 2-line inscription in exergue **Rev. Legend:** LONGINQUO. VENIENS. VEHO. **Rev. Inscription:** FLUMINE. FLUMI / NA. GANGIS. **Mint:** Elrich **Note:** Ref. M/V#359. Prev. KM#45. Struck from dies of unissued 2 Ducat coin with silver from the East Indies, hence the reference to the River Ganges in the reverse exergue.

Date	Mintage	VG	F	VF	XF	Unc
ND(ca1676)	—	—	—	—	—	—

Note: Struck from dies of unknown double ducat and with silver from the Netherlands East Indies

KM# 41 1/3 THALER (1/2 Gulden)
Silver **Ruler:** Gustav **Obv:** Draped bust of Gustav right **Obv. Legend:** GUSTAV. G. Z. S. W. V. HO(N). H. Z. H. V. N. L. V. CL. **Rev:** Crowned 6-fold arms with central shield of Sayn divide mintmasters' symbol and initials, value '1/3' in oval below, date at end of legend **Rev. Legend:** UT PRESSA - PALM9 **Mint:** Elrich **Note:** Ref. M/V#171-77. Prev. KM#46.

Date	Mintage	VG	F	VF	XF	Unc
1674 IZW(f)	—	100	200	375	775	—
1676 PL	—	100	200	375	775	—

KM# 42 1/3 THALER (1/2 Gulden)
Silver **Ruler:** Gustav **Obv:** Draped bust of Gustav right **Obv. Legend:** GUSTAV. G. Z. S. W. V. HO(N). H. Z. H. V. N. L. V. CL. **Rev:** Crowned 6-fold arms with central shield of Sayn divide mintmasters' symbols and initials, value '1/3' in oval below, date at end of legend **Rev. Legend:** PIE ET CAUTE-ANNO **Mint:** Elrich **Note:** Ref. M/V#172a. Prev. KM#47. Weight varies: 8.98-9.07.

Date	Mintage	VG	F	VF	XF	Unc
1674 ZIW(f)	—	100	200	375	775	—

KM# 77 1/3 THALER (1/2 Gulden)
Silver **Ruler:** Gustav **Obv:** Draped bust of Gustav right **Obv. Legend:** G: G. Z. S. W. V. HO. H. Z. H. V. N. L. V. CL. **Rev:** Crowned 6-fold arms with central shield of Sayn divide mintmasters' initials, value '1/3' in oval below, date at end of legend **Rev. Legend:** UT PRESSA - PALMUS **Mint:** Elrich **Note:** Ref. M/V#173. Weight varies: 8.98-9.07 g. Prev. KM#48.

Date	Mintage	VG	F	VF	XF	Unc
1676 PL	—	100	200	375	775	—

KM# 78 1/3 THALER (1/2 Gulden)
Silver **Ruler:** Gustav **Obv:** Draped bust of Gustav right **Obv. Legend:** GUSTAV. G. Z. S. W. V. HON. H. Z. H. V. N. L. V. CL. **Rev:** Crowned 6-fold arms with central shield of Sayn divide mintmasters' initials, value '1/3' in oval below, date at end of legend **Rev. Legend:** TANDEM FORTUNA - OBSTETRILE **Mint:** Elrich **Note:** Ref. M/V#174. Weight varies: 8.98-9.07. Prev. KM#49.

Date	Mintage	VG	F	VF	XF	Unc
1676 PL	—	90.00	185	375	750	—

KM# 79 1/3 THALER (1/2 Gulden)
Silver **Ruler:** Gustav **Obv:** Draped bust of Gustav right **Obv. Legend:** GUSTAV. G. Z. S. W. V. HON. H. Z. H. V. N. L. V. CL. **Rev:** Crowned 6-fold arms with central shield of Sayn divide date and mintmasters' initials, value '1/3' in oval below **Rev. Legend:** TANDEM FORTUNA - OBSTETRICE **Mint:** Elrich **Note:** Ref. M/V#175. Weight varies: 8.98-9.07 g. Prev. KM#49.

Date	Mintage	VG	F	VF	XF	Unc
1676 PL	—	100	200	375	775	—

KM# 81 1/3 THALER (1/2 Gulden)
Silver **Ruler:** Gustav **Obv:** Draped bust of Gustav right **Obv. Legend:** GUSTAV. G. Z. S. W. V. HON. H. Z. H. V. N. L. V. CL. **Rev:** Crowned 6-fold arms with central shield of Sayn divide date, value '1/3' in oval below **Rev. Legend:** TANDEM FORTUNA - OBSTETRICE. **Mint:** Elrich **Note:** Ref. M/V#176. Weight varies: 8.98-9.07. Prev. KM#49.

Date	Mintage	VG	F	VF	XF	Unc
1676	—	100	200	375	775	—

KM# 80 1/3 THALER (1/2 Gulden)
Silver **Ruler:** Gustav **Obv:** Draped bust of Gustav right **Obv. Legend:** GUSTAV. G. Z. S. W. V. HON. H. Z. H. V. N. L. V. CL. **Rev:** Crowned 6-fold arms with central shield of Sayn divide date and mintmasters' initials, value '1/3' in oval below **Rev. Legend:** TANDEM FORTU - NA. OBSTETRICE. **Mint:** Elrich **Note:** Ref. M/V#177. Weight varies: 8.98-9.07 g. Prev. KM#49.

Date	Mintage	VG	F	VF	XF	Unc
1676 PL	—	100	200	375	775	—

KM# 98 1/3 THALER (1/2 Gulden)
Silver **Ruler:** Gustav **Obv:** Draped bust of Gustav right **Obv. Legend:** GUSTAV. G. Z. S. W. V. HON. H. Z. H. V. N. L. V. CL. **Rev:** Crowned 6-fold arms with central shield of Sayn, value '1/3' in oval below, date at end of legend **Rev. Legend:** TANDEM: FORTUNA - OBSTETRICE. **Mint:** Elrich **Note:** Ref. M/V#177a. Weight varies: 8.98-9.07 g. Prev. KM#49.

Date	Mintage	VG	F	VF	XF	Unc
1677	—	—	—	—	—	—

KM# 36 2/3 THALER (60 Kreuzer)
Silver **Ruler:** Gustav **Obv:** Bust of Gustav right **Obv. Legend:** GVSTAV. G. Z. S. W. V. H. Z. H. V. N. L. V. CL. **Rev:** Crowned 6-fold arms with central shield of Sayn, value '2/3' in oval below, date at end of legend **Rev. Legend:** PIE ★ ET ★ CAVTE ★ **Mint:** Elrich **Note:** Ref. M/V#151. Weight varies: 13.66-18.90. Prev. KM#50.1.

Date	Mintage	VG	F	VF	XF	Unc
1673	—	110	225	450	900	—

KM# 45 2/3 THALER (60 Kreuzer)
Silver **Ruler:** Gustav **Obv:** Draped bust of Gustav right **Obv. Legend:** GUSTAV. G. Z. S. W. V. HON. H. Z. H. V. N. L. V. C(L). **Rev:** Crowned 6-fold arms with central shield of Sayn divides mintmasters' initials and symbol, value '2/3' in oval below, date at end of legend **Rev. Legend:** UT PRESSA - PALM9 **Mint:** Elrich **Note:** Dav. #(908). Ref. M/V#154-63. Weight varies: 13.66-18.90. Prev. KM#51-52. Varieties exist.

Date	Mintage	VG	F	VF	XF	Unc
1674 IZW(f)	—	80.00	165	335	675	—
1675 IZW(f)	—	80.00	165	335	675	—
1676 PL	—	80.00	165	335	675	—

KM# 46 2/3 THALER (60 Kreuzer)

Silver **Ruler:** Gustav **Obv:** Draped bust of Gustav right **Obv. Legend:** GUSTAV. G. Z. S. W. V. HON. H. Z. H. V. N. L. V. C(L). **Rev:** Crowned 6-fold arms with central shield of Sayn, date at end of legend **Rev. Legend:** UT PRESSA - PALM **Note:** Dav. #(908). Ref. M/V#260. Weight varies: 13.66-18.90 g.

Date	Mintage	VG	F	VF	XF	Unc
1674	—	90.00	180	360	725	—

KM# 44 2/3 THALER (60 Kreuzer)

Silver **Obv:** Draped bust of Gustav right **Obv. Legend:** GUSTAV. G. Z. S. W. V. HON. H. Z. H. V. N. L. V. CL. **Rev:** Crowned 6-fold arms with central shield of Sayn divide mintmasters' initials and symbol, value '2/3' in oval below, date at end of legend **Rev. Legend:** PIE ET CAUTE. - ANNO. **Note:** Dav. #907. Ref. M/V#152-53. Weight varies: 13.66-18.90. Prev. KM#50.2.

Date	Mintage	VG	F	VF	XF	Unc
1674 IZW(f)	—	80.00	165	335	675	—

KM# 61 2/3 THALER (60 Kreuzer)

Silver **Ruler:** Gustav **Obv:** Draped bust of Gustav right **Obv. Legend:** GUSTAV. G. Z. S. W. V. HON. H. Z. H. V. N. L. V. CL. **Rev:** Crowned 6-fold arms with central shield of Sayn divide mintmaster's initials, value '2/3' in oval below, date at end of legend **Rev. Legend:** UT PRESSA - PALMUS **Mint:** Elrich **Note:** Dav. #909. Ref. M/V#164-66, 169. Weight varies: 13.66-18.90. Prev. KM#53. Varieties exist.

Date	Mintage	VG	F	VF	XF	Unc
1675 PL	—	80.00	165	335	675	—
1676 PL	—	80.00	165	335	675	—

KM# 63 2/3 THALER (60 Kreuzer)

Silver **Ruler:** Gustav **Obv:** Draped bust of Gustav right in inner circle **Obv. Legend:** G(U)(V)STAV. G. Z. S. W. V. HON. H. Z. H. V. N. L. V. CL. **Rev:** Crowned 6-fold arms with central shield of Sayn divide date, value '2/3' in oval below **Rev. Legend:** TENDEM. FORT(U)(V)(-) N (-) A (-) OBSTETRICE. **Note:** Dav. #916. Ref. M/V#261, 263, 269-90, 293-96, 333-50, 352, 354, 389-91. Weight varies: 13.66-18.90. Prev. KM#60, 62, 64-68, 72, 73, 78, 108. Varieties exist.

Date	Mintage	VG	F	VF	XF	Unc
1675	—	90.00	165	335	675	—
1676	—	90.00	165	335	675	—
1677	—	90.00	165	335	675	—
1678	—	90.00	165	335	675	—
1679	—	90.00	165	335	675	—
1688	—	90.00	165	335	675	—
1690	—	90.00	165	335	675	—
ND	—	90.00	165	335	675	—

KM# 62 2/3 THALER (60 Kreuzer)

Silver **Ruler:** Gustav **Obv:** Large monogram between rosettes, large crown above, date below. **Obv. Legend:** AD. ASTRA. PER. ASPERA. **Rev:** Large '2/3' in inner circle **Rev. Legend:** MODERATA - DURANT. **Note:** Dav. #920. Ref. M/V#241. Weight varies: 13.66-18.90. Prev. KM#59.

Date	Mintage	VG	F	VF	XF	Unc
1675	—	1,500	3,000	6,000	—	—

KM# 91 2/3 THALER (60 Kreuzer)

Silver **Ruler:** Gustav **Obv:** Draped bust of Gustav right in circle **Obv. Legend:** G(U)(V)STAV. G. Z. s. W. V. HON. H. Z. H. V. N. L. V. C. **Rev:** Crowned 6-fold arms with central shield of Sayn divide date, value '2/3' in oval below **Rev. Legend:** TANDEM FORT(U)(V)(=)(-)NA(.)(-) OBSTETRICE **Note:** Dav. #918. Ref. M/V#310-29. Weight varies: 13.66-18.90. Varieties exist.

Date	Mintage	VG	F	VF	XF	Unc
1676	—	40.00	80.00	150	300	—

KM# 84 2/3 THALER (60 Kreuzer)

Silver **Obv:** Draped bust of Gustav right **Obv. Legend:** GUSTAV. G. Z. S. W. V. HON. H. Z. H. V. N. L. V. CL. **Rev:** Crowned six-fold arms with central shield of Sayn divide mintmasters' initials, , value 2/3 in oval below, date at end of legend **Rev. Legend:** TANDEM FORTUNA - OBSTETRICE **Note:** Dav. #915. Ref. M/V#170. Prev. KM#A55. Weight varies: 13.66-18.90 g.

Date	Mintage	VG	F	VF	XF	Unc
1676 PL	—	110	225	450	900	—

KM# 85 2/3 THALER (60 Kreuzer)

Silver **Ruler:** Gustav **Obv:** Draped bust of Gustav right **Obv. Legend:** GVSTAV. G. Z. S. W. V. H(.)ON. H. Z. H. V. N. L. U. C. **Rev:** 6-fold arms with central shield of Sayn, 4 ornate helmets above, value '2/3' in oval below, date at end of legend **Rev. Legend:** UT PRESSA - PALM **Note:** Dav. #910. Ref. M/V#291-92. Weight varies 13.66-18.90.

Date	Mintage	VG	F	VF	XF	Unc
1676	—	70.00	135	250	450	—

KM# 83 2/3 THALER (60 Kreuzer)

Silver **Ruler:** Gustav **Obv:** Draped bust right **Obv. Legend:** GUSTAV. G. Z. S. W. V. HON. H. Z. H. V. N. L. V. CL. **Rev:** Crowned 6-fold arms with central shield of Sayn divides mintmaster's initials and date, value '2/3' in oval below **Rev. Legend:** AD • PALMUM • PRES-SA • LÆTIUS • SURGIT • **Mint:** Elrich **Note:** Dav. #911. Ref. M/V#167-68. Prev. KM#54.

Date	Mintage	VG	F	VF	XF	Unc
1676 PL	—	80.00	165	335	675	—

KM# 86 2/3 THALER (60 Kreuzer)

Silver **Ruler:** Gustav **Obv:** Older bust of Gustav right in inner circle, value '2/3' in oval below **Obv. Legend:** GUSTAV. G. Z. S. W. & HON. D. I. H. V. N. L. & CLETT. **Rev:** Crowned 4-fold arms with central shield of Sayn in inner circle, date at top in margin **Rev. Legend:** AD PALMAM PR(Æ)(E)SSA L(Æ)(A)TIUS RESIRGO. **Note:** Dav. #912. Ref. M/V#262, 351, 353. Weight varies: 13.66-18.90. Prev. KM#61, 98. Varieties exist.

Date	Mintage	VG	F	VF	XF	Unc
1676	—	110	200	375	750	—
1680	—	110	200	375	750	—
1689	—	110	200	375	750	—

KM# 90 2/3 THALER (60 Kreuzer)

Silver **Ruler:** Gustav **Obv:** Draped bust of Gustav right in inner circle **Obv. Legend:** GUSTAV. G. Z. S. W. V. HON. H. Z. H. V. N. L. V. C. **Rev:** Crowned 6-fold arms with central shield of Sayn divide date, value '2/3' in oval below **Rev. Legend:** AD PALMAM PRÆSSA LÆTIUS RESURGO **Note:** Dav. #913. Ref. M/V#310. Weight varies: 13.66-18.90. Prev. KM#70. Varieties exist.

Date	Mintage	VG	F	VF	XF	Unc
1676	—	50.00	100	190	385	—
1677	—	50.00	100	190	385	—

KM# 87 2/3 THALER (60 Kreuzer)

Silver **Ruler:** Gustav **Obv:** Draped bust of Gustav right **Obv. Legend:** GUSTAV. G. z. S. W. V. HON. H. Z. H. V. N. L. V. C. **Rev:** Crowned 6-fold arms with central shield of Sayn divide date, value '2/3' in oval below **Rev. Legend:** AD PALMAM. PRÆS - SA. LÆT(9)(US) RESURGO **Note:** Dav. #(912). Ref. M/V#264-68. Weight varies: 13.66-18.90.

Date	Mintage	VG	F	VF	XF	Unc
1676	—	110	200	375	750	—

KM# 88 2/3 THALER (60 Kreuzer)

Silver **Ruler:** Gustav **Obv:** Draped bust to right **Obv. Legend:** GUSTAV. G. Z. S. W. V. HON. H. Z. H. V. N. L. V. CL. **Rev:** Crowned 6-fold arms with central shield of Sayn, value '2/3' in oval below, date at end of legend **Rev. Legend:** TANDEM FORT(U)(V)NA - OBSTETRICE **Note:** Dav. #(917). Ref. M/V#297-300, 302-09, 312-13, 330-32. Weight varies: 13.66-18.90. Prev. KM#71, 77, 79. Varieties exist.

Date	Mintage	VG	F	VF	XF	Unc
1676	—	80.00	165	335	475	—
1677	—	80.00	165	335	475	—

KM# 89 2/3 THALER (60 Kreuzer)
Silver **Ruler:** Gustav **Obv:** Draped bust of Gustav right with plume below **Obv. Legend:** GUSTAV. G. Z. S. W. V. HON. H. Z. H. V. N. L. V. CL. **Rev:** 4-fold arms with central shield of Sayn divide date, 4 ornate helmets above, value '2/3' in oval below **Rev. Legend:** TANDEM FORTUNA - OBSTETRICE **Note:** Dav. #(917). Ref. M/V#301. Weight varies: 13.66-18.90 g. Prev. KM#69.

Date	Mintage	VG	F	VF	XF	Unc
1676	—	65.00	135	235	475	—

KM# 116 2/3 THALER (60 Kreuzer)
Silver **Ruler:** Gustav **Obv:** Draped bust of Gustav right **Obv. Legend:** GUS. G. Z. S. W. U. H. H. Z. H. V. N. L. U. C. **Rev:** Crowned shield of Sayn arms in inner circle, value '2/3' in oval below, date at end of legend **Rev. Legend:** MONETA. NOVA - ARGENTEA. **Note:** Dav. #921. Ref. M/V#242-45. Weight varies: 13.66-18.90. Prev. KM#96.

Date	Mintage	VG	F	VF	XF	Unc
1683	—	275	525	900	1,800	—
1684	162,495	300	600	1,000	2,000	—
1686	—	300	600	1,000	2,000	—
1687	—	300	600	1,000	2,000	—

KM# 117 2/3 THALER (60 Kreuzer)
Silver **Ruler:** Gustav **Obv:** Older draped bust of Gustav right **Obv. Legend:** GUS. G. Z. S. W. U. H. H. Z. H. V. N. L. U. C. **Rev:** Large 2/3 in inner circle, date in legend **Rev. Legend:** MONETA. NOVA. ARGENTEA. **Note:** Dav. #921. Ref. M/V#246-47. Weight varies: 13.66-18.90. Prev. KM#97.

Date	Mintage	VG	F	VF	XF	Unc
1688	—	300	600	1,000	2,000	—
1689	—	300	600	1,000	2,000	—

KM# 145 2/3 THALER (60 Kreuzer)
Silver **Ruler:** Gustav **Obv:** Draped bust to right in circle **Obv. Legend:** GUSTAV. G. Z. S. W. V. HON. H. Z. H. V. N. L. V. C. **Rev:** 6-fold arms with central shield of Sayn, 4 ornate helmets above, date at end of legend **Rev. Legend:** AD PALMAM PRESSA LÆTIUS RESURGO **Note:** Dav. #914. Ref. M/V#355. Prev. KM#109. Weight varies: 13.66-18.90 g.

Date	Mintage	VG	F	VF	XF	Unc
1690	—	135	275	525	1,050	—

KM# 149 2/3 THALER (60 Kreuzer)
Silver **Ruler:** Gustav **Obv:** Draped bust right in circle **Obv. Legend:** GVSTA(V). G. Z. S. W. V. HON. H. Z. H. V. N. L. V. C. **Rev:** 6-fold arms with central shield of Sayn, 4 ornate helmets above, vlaue '2/3' in oval below, date at end of legend **Rev. Legend:** TANDEM FORTVN - A OBSTETRICE. **Note:** Dav. #(919). Ref. M/V#356-57. Prev. KM#110. Weight varies: 13.66-18.90 g.

Date	Mintage	VG	F	VF	XF	Unc
1691	—	135	275	525	1,050	—

KM# 150 2/3 THALER (60 Kreuzer)
Silver **Ruler:** Gustav **Obv:** Draped bust of Gustav right in circle **Obv. Legend:** GVSTA(V). G. Z. S. W. V. HON. H. Z. H. V. N. L. V. C. **Rev:** 6-fold arms with central shield of Sayn divide date, 4 ornate helmets above, value '2/3' in oval below **Rev. Legend:** TANDEM FORTVN - A OBSTETRICE **Note:** Dav. #(919). Ref. M/V#358.

Date	Mintage	VG	F	VF	XF	Unc
1691	—	150	300	550	1,100	—

KM# 5 THALER
Silver **Obv:** Armored bust of Johann VIII right in inner circle **Obv. Legend:** IOHAN. GRAF. Z. SA. WIT. V. HO(M). HER(R). Z. H. V. N. L. V. C. **Rev:** 6-fold arms with central shield of Sayn, 4 ornate helmets above, ribbon at top with TANDEM, date divided at bottom **Rev. Legend:** N(V)(U)LL. SIMULAT - DIUTURNUM. **Note:** Dav. #7670. Ref. M/V#100-100a, 102-04. Varieties exist.

Date	Mintage	VG	F	VF	XF	Unc
1654	—	—	—	—	—	—
1654 (d)	—	1,350	2,500	5,250	8,500	—
1656 (d)	—	1,350	2,500	5,250	8,500	—

KM# 6 THALER
Silver **Ruler:** Johann VIII **Obv:** Armored bust of Johann VIII facing in ornamented circle **Obv. Legend:** IOHAN: GRAF: Z: SA: WIT: V: HO: HERR. Z: V: N: L: V: C: **Rev:** 6-fold arms with central shield of Sayn, 4 ornate helmets above, ribbon at top with TANDEM, date divided at bottom **Rev. Legend:** NVLL. SIMULAT - DIUTURNUM. **Mint:** Minden **Note:** Dav. #A7671. Ref. M/V#101.

Date	Mintage	VG	F	VF	XF	Unc
1654 Rare	—	—	—	—	—	—

KM# 17 THALER
Silver **Ruler:** Ludwig Christian **Obv:** Draped bust right **Obv. Legend:** LUDWIG. CHRISTIAN. GRAF. ZU. SAYN: WITGEN: V: HOHNST: ... **Rev:** 6-fold arms with central shield of Sayn divide date near bottom, 4 ornate helmets above **Rev. Legend:** CUM DEO - ET LABORE. **Mint:** Wittgenstein **Note:** Dav. #7671. Ref. M/V#150.

Date	Mintage	VG	F	VF	XF	Unc
1667	—	1,250	2,250	5,000	8,000	—

KM# 110 THALER
Silver **Ruler:** Gustav **Obv:** Armored and draped bust of Gustav right in inner circle **Obv. Legend:** GUSTAV. C. IN. S. W. E. H. D. IN. H. U. NL. ET. C: **Rev:** 6-fold arms with central shield of Sayn, 4 ornate helmets above, date at end of legend **Rev. Legend:** A. SOLO. IEHOUA. SAPIENTIA. VERA. **Mint:** Schwarzenau **Note:** Dav. #7672. Ref. M/V#225.

Date	Mintage	VG	F	VF	XF	Unc
1682 ICF/(e) Rare	—	—	—	—	—	—

TRADE COINAGE

KM# 8 DUCAT
0.9860 Gold **Ruler:** Johann VIII **Obv:** Armored bust of Johann right, top of head breaks circle **Obv. Legend:** IO. GR. Z. S. W. V. H. H. Z. H. V. N. L. V. C. **Rev:** Shield of 6-fold arms with central shield of Sayn divides date, 4 ornate helmets above **Rev. Legend:** NULL: SI - MU: DIUT: **Mint:** Minden **Note:** Fr#3058. Ref. M/V#99. Weight varies: 3.40-3.445.

Date	Mintage	VG	F	VF	XF	Unc
1654 Rare	—	—	—	—	—	—

KM# 9 DUCAT
Silver **Ruler:** Gustav **Obv:** Armored bust of Gustav right in inner circle **Rev:** Helmeted arms with date above in inner circle **Mint:** Berleburg **Note:** Prev. KM#112. Ducat struck in silver only.

Date	Mintage	VG	F	VF	XF	Unc
1681 Rare	—	—	—	—	—	—

KM# 126 2 DUCAT
7.0000 g., 0.9860 Gold 0.2219 oz. AGW **Ruler:** Gustav **Obv:** Draped bust right **Obv. Legend:** GUSTAVUS. C. IN. S. W. & H. D. IN. H. V. L. & C. **Rev:** Mountain goat on rocky promontory by ruin, stream with rapids below, date divided at end and beginning of legend **Rev. Legend:** SVPER GRESSUS **Mint:** Wittgenstein **Note:** Fr. #3059.

Date	Mintage	VG	F	VF	XF	Unc
1687 IS Rare	—	—	—	—	—	—

SCHAUMBURG-HESSEN

Located in northwest Germany, Schaumburg-Hessen was founded in 1640 when Schaumburg-Gehmen was divided between Hesse-Cassel and Lippe-Alverdissen. The acquired territories were renamed Schaumburg-Hessen and Schaumburg-Lippe respectively. Cassel struck coins for Schaumburg-Hessen well into the 19th century. By agreement between the rulers of the two divisions of Schaumburg, who themselves were related by marriage, many of the issues struck by the landgraves of Hesse-Cassel were for use in both Schaumburg-Hessen and Schaumburg-Lippe.

RULERS
Wilhelm VI (of Hesse-Cassel), 1640-1663
Wilhelm VII (of Hesse-Cassel), 1663-1670
Karl (of Hesse-Cassel), 1670-1730

Mint Officials

Initials	Date	Name
	1637-57	Arnold Gall, mintmaster Cassel
IGB	1657-80	Johann Georg Büttner, mintmaster Cassel
IHH and/or	1680-81	Johann Hinrich Hoffmann, mintmaster Cassel
(a) =		

Arms:
Nettleleaf of Schaumburg

MONETARY SYSTEM
8 Gute Pfennig = 1 Mariengroschen

REFERENCES:
H = Jakob Christoph Hoffmeister, **Historische-kritische Beschreibung aller bis jetzt bekannt gewordenen hessischen Münzen, Medaillen und Marken**, 4 v. in 3, Leipzig & Hannover, 1862-1880.
S = Artur Schütz, **Die Hessischen Münzen des Hauses Brabant, Teil III, Gesamthessen Hessen-Marburg und Hessen-Kassel 1509-1670**, Frankfurt, 1997.
W = Paul Weinmeister, "Die schaumburgischen Münzen des 17. Jahrhunderts nach der Teilung der Grafschaft," **Blätter für Münzfreunde** 41 (1906), col. 3540ff.
PA = Prince Alexander von Hessen, **Hessisches Münzcabinet**, Darmstadt, 1877-85.

COUNTSHIP

STANDARD COINAGE

KM# 4 PFENNIG
Silver **Ruler:** Wilhelm VI **Obv:** Shield of Schaumburg arms **Mint:** Cassel **Note:** Uniface.

Date	Mintage	VG	F	VF	XF	Unc
ND(1656-59)	—	225	450	900	—	—

KM# 15 PFENNIG
Silver **Ruler:** Wilhelm VII **Obv:** Shield of Schaumburg arms, date above **Mint:** Cassel **Note:** Ref. S#1192. Uniface.

Date	Mintage	VG	F	VF	XF	Unc
1665	251,172	—	—	—	—	—

KM# 22 PFENNIG
Silver, 11 mm. **Ruler:** Karl **Obv:** Schaumburg arms **Mint:** Cassel **Note:** Uniface.

Date	Mintage	VG	F	VF	XF	Unc
ND(1676-77)	120,384	100	200	400	775	—

KM# 28 PFENNIG
Silver **Ruler:** Karl **Obv:** Schaumburg arms, date divided below **Mint:** Cassel **Note:** Ref. H#1507-08. Uniface.

Date	Mintage	VG	F	VF	XF	Unc
1680	53,796	125	250	500	1,000	—

KM# 10 2 PFENNIG
0.5400 g., Silver, 13-14 mm. **Ruler:** Wilhelm VI **Obv:** Crowned Hessian lion striding left holding Schaumburg arms in right paw **Rev:** 2-line inscription, date at end of legend **Rev. Legend:** SCHAVENB. L. M. **Rev. Inscription:** II / PF. **Mint:** Cassel **Note:** Ref. S#1116.

Date	Mintage	VG	F	VF	XF	Unc
1657	—	100	200	425	850	—

KM# 16 2 PFENNIG
Silver Weight varies: 0.43-0.47g., 15 mm. **Ruler:** Wilhelm VII **Obv:** Shield of Schaumburg arms between 2 palm branches, date above **Rev:** 2-line inscription **Rev. Legend:** SCHAVENB. LAND. M. **Rev. Inscription:** II / PFEN **Mint:** Cassel **Note:** Ref. S#1191; H-1428.

Date	Mintage	VG	F	VF	XF	Unc
1665	—	125	250	475	—	—

KM# 18 2 PFENNIG
Silver **Ruler:** Wilhelm VII **Obv:** Shield of Schaumburg arms, date above **Rev:** 2-line inscription **Rev. Legend:** SCHAVENB. LAND. M. **Rev. Inscription:** II / PFEN. **Mint:** Cassel **Note:** Ref. S#1196A.

Date	Mintage	VG	F	VF	XF	Unc
1667	116,484	—	—	—	—	—

KM# 21 2 PFENNIG
Silver, 15 mm. **Ruler:** Karl **Obv:** Shield of Schaumburg arms, date above **Rev:** 2-line inscription **Rev. Legend:** SCHAUMB. LAND. M. **Rev. Inscription:** II / PFEN. **Mint:** Cassel **Note:** Ref. H#1470.

Date	Mintage	VG	F	VF	XF	Unc
1674	—	—	—	—	—	—

KM# 26 2 PFENNIG (Gute)
Silver, 12 mm. **Ruler:** Karl **Obv:** Schaumburg arms **Obv. Legend:** SCHAUEN. B. LAND. M. **Rev:** 3-line inscription **Rev. Inscription:** II / GU. TE / PF. **Mint:** Cassel **Note:** Ref. H#1870.

Date	Mintage	VG	F	VF	XF	Unc
ND(1677)	46,944	—	—	—	—	—

KM# 29 2 PFENNIG (Gute)
Silver, 12 mm. **Ruler:** Karl **Obv:** Schaumburg arms in baroque frame, date divided at four points around **Rev:** 2-line inscription **Rev. Legend:** SCHAVMB. LAND. M. **Rev. Inscription:** II / PFEN. **Mint:** Cassel

Date	Mintage	VG	F	VF	XF	Unc
1680	36,096	100	250	360	675	—

KM# 6 MATTIER (4 Pfennig = 1/72 Thaler)
Silver Weight varies: 0.66-0.87g., 15-16 mm. **Ruler:** Wilhelm VI **Obv:** Crowned Hessian lion striding to left holding Schaumburg arms in right paw **Rev:** 5-line inscription with date **Rev. Inscription:** EIN / MATIER / SCHA(V)(U)(E) / (E)NB: L. M: / (date) **Mint:** Cassel **Note:** Ref. S#1099, 1114, 1127; H-1292-3, 1306-7, 1327.

Date	Mintage	VG	F	VF	XF	Unc
1656	—	100	225	450	900	—
1657	—	100	225	450	900	—
1659	—	100	225	450	900	—

KM# 11 MATTIER (4 Pfennig = 1/72 Thaler)
Silver Weight varies: 0.66-0.87g., 15-16 mm. **Ruler:** Wilhelm VI **Obv:** Crowned Hessian lion striding left holding Schaumburg arms in right paw **Rev:** 4-line inscription with date **Rev. Inscription:** I / MATIER / SCHAUENB. L. M. / (date) **Mint:** Cassel **Note:** Ref. S#1119.

Date	Mintage	VG	F	VF	XF	Unc
1658	—	—	—	—	—	—

KM# 17 MATTIER (4 Pfennig = 1/72 Thaler)
Silver Weight varies: 0.65-0.73g., 15-17 mm. **Ruler:** Wilhelm VII **Obv:** Schaumburg arms in oval baroque frame within palm wreath **Rev:** 5-line inscription with date **Rev. Inscription:** I / MATIER / SCHAVENB: / LAND. M. / (date) **Mint:** Cassel **Note:** Ref. S#1190, 1196.

Date	Mintage	VG	F	VF	XF	Unc
1665	—	100	210	425	—	—
1667	63,783	100	210	425	—	—

KM# 30 MATTIER (4 Pfennig = 1/72 Thaler)
Silver **Ruler:** Karl **Obv:** Schaumburg arms in baroque frame **Rev:** 5-line inscription with date, which is divided by mintmaster's initials **Rev. Inscription:** I / MATIER / SCHAVMB / LAND. M. / (date) **Mint:** Cassel **Note:** Ref. H#1506.

Date	Mintage	VG	F	VF	XF	Unc
1680 IGB	25,600	70.00	150	300	600	—

KM# 1 4 PFENNIG
Copper Weight varies: 1.42-3.30g., 20 mm. **Ruler:** Wilhelm VI **Obv:** Crowned Hessian lion striding left between 2 floral branches, value 'IIII' below **Rev:** Schaumburg arms in 4 concentric circles, value 'IIII' breaks circles at bottom **Mint:** Rinteln **Note:** Ref. S#1150; H-1367-8. This was a joint coinage with Schaumburg-Lippe.

Date	Mintage	VG	F	VF	XF	Unc
ND(1648)	—	25.00	45.00	75.00	150	—

KM# 24 4 PFENNIG (Gute)
Silver, 16 mm. **Ruler:** Karl **Obv:** Schaumburg arms **Obv. Legend:** SCHA(V)(U)EN(.)B: LAND. M. **Rev:** 4-line inscription with date **Rev. Inscription:** IIII / GUTE / PF / (date) **Mint:** Rinteln **Note:** Ref. H#1481-83.

Date	Mintage	VG	F	VF	XF	Unc
1676	25,056	—	—	—	—	—
1677	5,040	—	—	—	—	—

KM# 2 6 PFENNIG
Copper Weight varies: 1.81-3.20g., 23 mm. **Ruler:** Wilhelm VI **Obv:** Crowned Hessian lion striding left between 2 floral branches, value 'VI' below **Rev:** Schaumburg arms within braided circle and wreath, value 'VI' below **Mint:** Rinteln **Note:** Ref. S#1149; H-1366. This was a joint coinage with Schaumburg-Lippe.

Date	Mintage	VG	F	VF	XF	Unc
ND(1648)	—	28.00	50.00	85.00	170	—

KM# 8 MARIENGROSCHEN
(8 Pfennig = 1/36 Thaler)
Silver Weight varies: 1.00-1.19g., 20 mm. **Ruler:** Wilhelm VI **Obv:** Hessian lion striding to left holding Schaumburg arms in right paw within palm wreath **Rev:** 4-line inscription, date at end of legend **Rev. Legend:** SCHAVENB. LANDT(.) MUNTZ. **Rev. Inscription:** I / MARI / GRO / 36. **Mint:** Cassel **Note:** Ref. S#1096, 1107; H-1096, 1107, 1288-9, 1299, 6195. Varieties exist.

Date	Mintage	VG	F	VF	XF	Unc
1656	—	175	350	725	—	—
1657	—	175	350	725	—	—

KM# 12 MARIENGROSCHEN
(8 Pfennig = 1/36 Thaler)
Silver Weight varies: 1.05-1.29g., 19 mm. **Ruler:** Wilhelm VI **Obv:** Crowned Hessian lion striding left holding Schaumburg arms in right paw within floral wreath **Rev:** 4-line inscription, date at end of legend **Rev. Legend:** SCHAUM. LANDTMUNTZ. **Rev. Inscription:** I / MARI / GRO / 36. **Mint:** Cassel **Note:** Ref. S#1125, 1130.

Date	Mintage	VG	F	VF	XF	Unc
1656	—	250	475	950	—	—
1659	—	250	475	950	—	—
1660	—	250	475	950	—	—

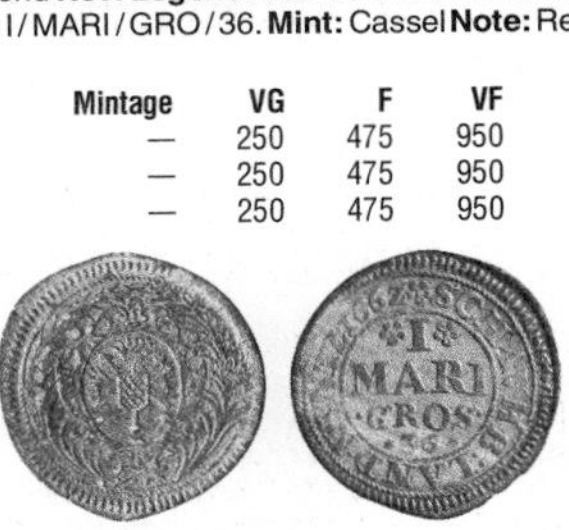

KM# 13 MARIENGROSCHEN
(8 Pfennig = 1/36 Thaler)
1.6500 g., Silver, 18 mm. **Ruler:** Wilhelm VI **Obv:** Schaumburg arms in ornamented frame between 2 palm fronds **Rev:** 4-line inscription, date at end of legend **Rev. Legend:** SCHAV (MB) (EN). LAND. MVNTZ. **Rev. Inscription:** I / MARI / GROS / 36. **Mint:** Cassel **Note:** Ref. S#1140.

Date	Mintage	VG	F	VF	XF	Unc
166Z	—	200	425	850	—	—

KM# 14 MARIENGROSCHEN
(8 Pfennig = 1/36 Thaler)
Silver Weight varies: 1.00-1.21g., 19-20 mm. **Ruler:** Wilhelm VII **Obv:** Schaumburg arms in oval cartouche within palm wreath **Rev:** 4-line inscription, date at end of legend **Rev. Legend:** SCHAV(EN)(M)B. LAND(T). M(V)(U)N(TZ). **Rev. Inscription:** I / MARI / GROS / 36. **Mint:** Cassel **Note:** Ref. S#1183, 1189, 1195, 1202. Varieties exist.

Date	Mintage	VG	F	VF	XF	Unc
1663	—	250	475	950	—	—
1665	—	250	475	950	—	—
1667	77,580	250	475	950	—	—
1669	—	250	475	950	—	—

KM# 20 MARIENGROSCHEN
(8 Pfennig = 1/36 Thaler)
Silver **Ruler:** Karl **Obv:** Schaumburg arms in baroque frame between 2 palm branches **Rev:** 4-line inscription, date at end of legend **Rev. Legend:** SCHAVENB. LAND. MVNTZ. **Rev. Inscription:** I / MARI / GROS / 36. **Mint:** Cassel **Note:** Ref. W, col. 3574

Date	Mintage	VG	F	VF	XF	Unc
1673	—	135	275	550	1,100	—

KM# 31 MARIENGROSCHEN
(8 Pfennig = 1/36 Thaler)
Silver, 17.5 mm. **Ruler:** Karl **Obv:** Schaumburg arms in baroque frame **Rev:** Date at end of legend **Rev. Legend:** SCHAVMB. LAND. MVN. **Rev. Inscription:** IGB / I / MARI / GROS / 36. **Mint:** Cassel **Note:** Ref. H#1501.

Date	Mintage	VG	F	VF	XF	Unc
1680 IGB	126,787	40.00	80.00	150	300	—

KM# 32 MARIENGROSCHEN
(8 Pfennig = 1/36 Thaler)
Silver, 17.5 mm. **Ruler:** Karl **Obv:** Schaumburg arms in baroque frame **Rev:** Date at end of legend **Rev. Legend:** SCHAVMB. LAND. MVN. **Rev. Inscription:** I / MARI / GROS / 36. **Mint:** Cassel **Note:** Ref. H#1502-04.

Date	Mintage	VG	F	VF	XF	Unc
1680	Inc. above	60.00	100	200	425	—

PATTERNS

Including off metal strikes

KM#	Date	Mintage	Identification	Mkt Val
Pn1	1680	—	Pfennig. Copper. KM#28. Ref. H#4733.	—

SCHAUMBURG-LIPPE

The tiny countship of Schaumburg-Lippe, with an area of only 131 square miles (218 square kilometers) in northwest Germany, was surrounded by the larger states of Brunswick-Lüneburg-Calenberg, an enclave of Hesse-Cassel, and the bishopric of Minden (part of Brandenburg-Prussia from 1648). It was founded in 1640 when Schaumburg-Gehmen was divided between Hesse-Cassel and Lippe-Alverdissen. The two became known as Schaumburg-Hessen and Schaumburg-Lippe. Philipp II, the youngest son of Count Simon VI of Lippe came into the possession of Alverdissen and Lipperode upon his father's death in 1613. In 1640, he also inherited half of Schaumburg-Bückeburg, becoming the first Count of Schaumburg-Lippe. A separate line of Schaumburg-Alverdissen was established in 1681 and, upon the extinction of the elder line in 1777, the lands and titles devolved onto Alverdissen, becoming the ruling line in the countship. In 1807, the count was raised to the rank of prince and Schaumburg-Lippe was incorporated into the Rhine Confederation. It became a part of the German Confederation in 1815 and joined the North German Confederation in 1866. The principality became a member state in the German Empire in 1871. The last sovereign prince resigned as a result of World War I.

See Schaumburg-Hessen for coinage which also circulated in Schaumburg-Lippe.

RULERS
Philipp I, 1644-1681
Friedrich Christian, 1681-1728

MINT OFFICIALS

Initial or mark	Date	Name
PL	1659-60	Peter Löhr, mintmaster Bückeburg
IHH or	1676-77	Johann Hinrich Hoffmann, mintmaster Bückeburg
A =		

REFERENCE

W = Paul Weinmeister, "Die Münzen und Medaillen von Schaumburg-Lippe," **Blätter für Münzfreunde** 42 (1907), col. 3615ff.

COUNTSHIP

REGULAR COINAGE

KM# 1 6 PFENNIG

Copper Weight varies: 1.81-3.20g., 23 mm. **Ruler:** Philipp I **Obv:** Crowned Hessian lion striding to left between 2 floral branches, value VI below **Rev:** Schaumburg arms within braided circle and wreath, value VI below **Mint:** Rinteln **Note:** W-1; S#1149; H-1366. Joint issue, see Schaumburg-Hessen, KM#2.

Date	Mintage	Good	VG	F	VF	XF
ND(1648)	—	28.00	50.00	85.00	175	—

KM# 3 MARIENGROSCHEN

Silver **Ruler:** Philipp I **Obv:** Schaumburg arms in laurel wreath **Rev:** 4-line inscription, date at end of legend **Rev. Legend:** SCHAUENB. LAND. MUN. (date) **Rev. Inscription:** 1 / MARI / GROS. / 36. **Note:** Ref. W#20.

Date	Mintage	VG	F	VF	XF	Unc
1667	—	—	—	—	—	—

KM# 4 MARIENGROSCHEN

Silver, 20 mm. **Ruler:** Philipp I **Obv:** Schaumburg arms in laurel wreath, value '36' below **Rev:** 3-line inscription, 'I' in first line divides mintmastwer's initials and symbol, date at end of legend **Rev. Legend:** SCHAUEN. B. LAND. MU. **Rev. Inscription:** I / MARI / GROS. **Mint:** Bückeburg **Note:** Ref. W#24, 27.

Date	Mintage	VG	F	VF	XF	Unc
1676 IHH (a)	9,252	200	425	850	—	—
1677 IHH (a)	20,952	135	275	550	—	—

KM# 2 THALER

28.9000 g., Silver, 46 mm. **Ruler:** Philipp I **Obv:** Facing armored bust turned slightly to right **Obv. Legend:** V. G. G. PHILIP. GRAF. ZU. SCHAUMB. LIPP. V. STERNB. **Rev:** Ornate shield of 4-fold arms with central shield of Schaumburg, 3 ornate helmets above divide date to left and right in margin **Rev. Legend:** DURCH GOTTES SEGEN. **Mint:** Bückeburg **Note:** Dav. #7673.

Date	Mintage	VG	F	VF	XF	Unc
1660 PL	200	2,000	3,500	6,500	10,000	—

SCHAUMBURG-PINNEBERG

(Schauenburg-Pinneberg)

County in northwest Germany. First count in 1030. In 1106 it became part of Holstein, which remained for over 2 centuries. Many churchmen came from this house. Raised to the rank of prince in 1620. Senior line died out in 1622 and title reverted to Holstein-Schauenburg-Gehmen branch, which had been established in 1581. Gehmen itself became extinct in 1640 and Holstein-Schauenburg was divided among various states. Pinneberg was given to Denmark, Buckeburg was split between Hesse-Cassel and Lippe-Alverdissen and renamed Schaumburg-Hessen and Schaumburg-Lippe respectively. Gehmen went to Limburg-Styrum.

RULERS

Adolf XIII, 1576-1601
Ernst III, 1601-1622
Jobst Hermann, 1622-1635
Otto VI, 1635-1640

MINT OFFICIALS' INITIALS

Rineteln Mint

Initial	Date	Name
(a)=	1603-04	Henning Hanses
(b)=	1618-20	Julius Bilderbeck

Oldendorf Mint

Initial	Date	Name
(c)=	1604-05	Henning Hanses
(d)=	1609-11	Kaspar Kohl
(e)=	1611-17	Christoph Feistell
(f)=	1617-18	Julius Bilderbeck
(g), (h)=	1620-21	Kaspar Kohl
(i), (j)=	1621-22	Justus Arnoldi
(k)=	1622-23	Ernst Beissner
(l)=	1623-24	Kaspar Gieseler
(m)=	1624-25	Christoph Feistell
(n)=	1635-40	Kaspar Kohl

Altona Mint

Initial	Date	Name
(o)=	1592-1600	Klaus Isenbehn
(p)=	1599-1605	Daniel Kostede
(q), (r), (s)= ... or ... or ...	1605-18	Henning Hanses
(t), (u)=	1618-20	Christoph Feistell
	1621	Henning Hanses
(v)=	1621-24	Thomas Eisenbein
(w)=	1624-40	Christoph Feistell

ARMS

Nettleleaf, often as central shield in 4-fold arms.

REFERENCES

W = Paul Weinmeister, ***"Münzgeschichte der Grafschaft Holstein-Schauenburg,"*** Zeitschrift für Numismatik 26 (1908), pp. 348-481 and 27 (1909), pp. 278-83.

S = Hugo Frhr. Von Saurma-Jeltsch, **Die Saurmasche Münzsammlung deutscher, schweizerischer und polnischer Gepräge von etwa dem Beginn der Groschenzeit bis zur Kipperperiode**, Berlin, 1892.

COUNTSHIP

STANDARD COINAGE

KM# A135 PFENNIG

0.3000 g., Silver, 13-14 mm. **Ruler:** Jobst Hermann **Obv:** Shield of Schaumburg arms, date above **Note:** W-374, 375. Uniface hohl-type. Prev. Schleswig-Holstein-Gottorp KM#89.

Date	Mintage	VG	F	VF	XF	Unc
16Z4	—	27.00	60.00	110	200	—
16Z5	—	27.00	60.00	110	200	—

KM# 139B PFENNIG

0.3000 g., Silver, 13-14 mm. **Ruler:** Jobst Hermann **Obv:** Shield of Schaumburg arms, date divided at top and to left and right **Note:** W-376-9. Uniface hohl-type. Prev. Schleswig-Holstein-Gottorp KM#A96.

Date	Mintage	VG	F	VF	XF	Unc
16Z6	—	27.00	60.00	110	225	—
16Z7	—	27.00	60.00	110	225	—
(16)Z7	—	27.00	60.00	110	225	—
ND(1628)	—	27.00	60.00	110	225	—

KM# 148 PFENNIG

0.3000 g., Silver, 13 mm. **Ruler:** Otto VI **Obv:** Shield of Schaumburg arms divide date **Note:** W-386. Uniface hohl-type. Prev. Schleswig-Holstein-Gottorp KM#A105.

Date	Mintage	VG	F	VF	XF	Unc
(16)38	—	—	—	—	—	—

KM# 152 PFENNIG

0.3000 g., Silver, 13 mm. **Ruler:** Otto VI **Obv:** Shield of Schaumburg arms, date above **Note:** W-387. Uniface hohl-type. Prev. Schleswig-Holstein-Gottorp KM#A110.

Date	Mintage	VG	F	VF	XF	Unc
1640	—	—	—	—	—	—

KM# 85 PFENNIG (1/12 Groschen)

Copper, 13 mm. **Ruler:** Ernst III **Obv:** Arms, value '1Z' above **Rev:** 'I' in square **Note:** W-317.

Date	Mintage	Good	VG	F	VF	XF
ND(ca.1620)	—	30.00	60.00	125	250	—

KM# 86 1-1/2 PFENNIG (1/8 Groschen)

Copper, 15 mm. **Ruler:** Ernst III **Obv:** Arms divide date, where present, value '8' above **Rev:** Ornamented square with value '1-1/2' **Note:** W-315, 316.

Date	Mintage	Good	VG	F	VF	XF
16Z0	—	40.00	85.00	160	325	—
ND(1620)	—	40.00	85.00	160	325	—

KM# 87 3 PFENNIG

Copper, 16-17 mm. **Ruler:** Ernst III **Obv:** Arms, value '3' above **Rev:** Value 'III' in ornamented square within circle of pellets **Note:** W-314.

Date	Mintage	Good	VG	F	VF	XF
ND(ca.1620)	—	75.00	150	235	475	—

KM# 123 3 PFENNIG

Silver Weight varies: 0.8-0.9g., 17-19 mm. **Ruler:** Jobst Hermann **Obv:** Shield of 4-fold arms with central shield **Obv. Legend:** I H G Z H S V S H Z G **Rev:** Imperial orb with '3' divides date **Note:** W-373.

Date	Mintage	VG	F	VF	XF	Unc
16ZZ	—	80.00	160	325	—	—

KM# 88 4 PFENNIG

Copper, 17-18 mm. **Ruler:** Ernst III **Obv:** Arms with value '4' above divide date, where present **Rev:** Value 'IIII' in ornamented square **Note:** W-311, 313.

Date	Mintage	Good	VG	F	VF	XF
(16)Z0	—	50.00	115	160	325	—
ND(1620)	—	50.00	115	160	325	—

KM# 89 4 PFENNIG

Copper, 17-18 mm. **Ruler:** Ernst III **Obv:** Arms, value '4' above divides date **Rev:** Value 'IV' in ornamented square **Note:** W-312.

Date	Mintage	Good	VG	F	VF	XF
(16)Z0	—	50.00	115	160	325	—

KM# 90 6 PFENNIG

Copper, 18 mm. **Ruler:** Ernst III **Obv:** Arms, value '6' above **Rev:** Value 'VI' in ornamented square within circle **Note:** W-310.

Date	Mintage	Good	VG	F	VF	XF
ND(ca.1620)	—	65.00	135	210	425	—

KM# 91 12 PFENNIG (Fürstengroschen)

Silver Weight varies: 1.5-1.9g., 22-25 mm. **Ruler:** Ernst III **Obv:** Shield of 4-fold arms with central shield **Obv. Legend:** E. D. G. P. - C. H. (S)(C). (F.) (E.) S. D. (I)G. **Rev:** Crowned imperial eagle, orb on breast **Rev. Legend:** F. LANDT. MVN(T). ZV. IZ. **Note:** W-300-302. Kipper issue. Varieties exist.

Date	Mintage	VG	F	VF	XF	Unc
ND (after 1620)	—	40.00	80.00	150	300	—

KM# 92 12 PFENNIG (Fürstengroschen)

Silver Weight varies: 1.5-1.9g., 22-25 mm. **Ruler:** Ernst III **Obv:** Large crown above shield of 4-fold arms with central shield, all superimposed on cross **Obv. Legend:** ER - NES. - D. G. P. F. - C. H(O). (-) (E.) S. **Rev:** Crowned imperial eagle, orb on breast **Rev. Legend:** LANDT. MVNZE. ZV. 1Z. PN. **Note:** W-303, 304. Kipper issue. Varieties exist.

Date	Mintage	VG	F	VF	XF	Unc
ND (after 1620)	—	40.00	80.00	150	300	—

KM# 93 12 PFENNIG (Fürstengroschen)

Silver Weight varies: 1.5-1.9g., 22-25 mm. **Ruler:** Ernst III **Obv:** Large crown above shield of 4-fold arms with central shield, all superimposed on cross **Obv. Legend:** ER - NES - D. G. P. F. - C. H(O). - E. S. **Rev:** Crowned imperial eagle, 1Z in orb on breast **Rev. Legend:** FVR. SCHAV. LAN. MV(N). **Note:** W-305, 306. Kipper issue. Varieties exist.

Date	Mintage	VG	F	VF	XF	Unc
ND (after 1620)	—	40.00	80.00	150	300	—

KM# 94 12 PFENNIG (Fürstengroschen)

Silver Weight varies: 1.5-1.9g., 22-25 mm. **Ruler:** Ernst III **Obv:** 3 small shields of arms, one above two **Obv. Legend:** ERNESTVS. D. G. P. E. C. H. E. S. **Rev:** Crowned imperial eagle, 1Z in orb on breast **Rev. Legend:** FVR. SCHAV. LAN. MVN. **Note:** W-307. Kipper issue.

Date	Mintage	VG	F	VF	XF	Unc
ND (after 1620)	—	40.00	85.00	175	350	—

KM# 95 12 PFENNIG (Fürstengroschen)

Silver Weight varies: 1.5-1.9g., 22-25 mm. **Ruler:** Ernst III **Obv:** Large ornate helmet in circle **Obv. Legend:** ERNESTVS. D. G. P. E. C. H. E. S. **Rev:** Crowned imperial eagle, 1Z in orb on breast **Rev. Legend:** FVR. SCHAV. LAN. MV. **Note:** W-308. Kipper issue.

Date	Mintage	VG	F	VF	XF	Unc
ND (after 1620)	—	40.00	80.00	150	300	—

KM# 96 12 PFENNIG (Fürstengroschen)

Silver Weight varies: 1.5-1.9g., 22-25 mm. **Ruler:** Ernst III **Obv:** Large ornate helmet in circle **Obv. Legend:** ERNESTVS. D. G. P. E. C. H. E. S. **Rev:** Crowned imperial eagle, 1Z in orb on breast **Rev. Legend:** LANT - MVNZE. ZV. 1Z. **Note:** W-309. Kipper issue.

Date	Mintage	VG	F	VF	XF	Unc
ND (after 1620)	—	40.00	80.00	150	300	—

KM# A134 2 MARIENGROSCHEN

1.3000 g., Silver, 19 mm. **Ruler:** Jobst Hermann **Obv:** Crowned nettle leaf arms divide date as 1-6/Z-4 **Obv. Legend:** IVS. HER. D. G. C. H. S. E. S. D. G. E. B. **Rev:** 3-line inscription **Rev. Legend:** LANDT. MVNZ. V. FEIN. SIL(B). **Rev. Inscription:** II / MARI / GRO **Note:** W-349, 350. Prev. KM#134.

Date	Mintage	VG	F	VF	XF	Unc
1624	—	45.00	85.00	160	325	—
1626	—	45.00	85.00	160	325	—

KM# 135 4 MARIENGROSCHEN

2.4000 g., Silver, 22 mm. **Ruler:** Jobst Hermann **Obv:** Crowned nettle leaf arms divide date as 1-6/Z-4 **Obv. Legend:** I(V)(U)S(T). HE(R). D. G. C. H. S. E. S. D. G. E. B. **Rev:** 3-line inscription **Rev. Legend:** LANDT. M(V)(U)NTZ. V. FEIN. SIL. **Rev. Inscription:** IIII / MARI / GRO **Note:** W-347, 348.

Date	Mintage	VG	F	VF	XF	Unc
16Z4	—	65.00	110	200	425	—

KM# 76 SCHRECKENBERGER (12 Kreuzer)

Silver, 32x32 mm. **Ruler:** Ernst III **Obv:** Crowned shield of 4-fold arms with central shield, superimposed on cross, ends of cross divide legend **Obv. Legend:** ERN - ES. D - G. CO. H - O. S. E. S - D. G. **Rev:** Crowned imperial eagle **Rev. Legend:** MATTHIAS. D. G. RO. IM. SEM. AV. **Note:** W-193. Klippe.

Date	Mintage	VG	F	VF	XF	Unc
ND(1616-19)	—	—	—	—	—	—

KM# 75 SCHRECKENBERGER (12 Kreuzer)

Silver Weight varies: 5-6g., 29-30 mm. **Ruler:** Ernst III **Obv:** Crowned 4-fold arms with central shield, superimposed on cross, ends of cross divided legend **Obv. Legend:** ERN(E)(S) - (E)(ST). D. G. - C(O). HOL(S). - (S.) ET. S. - D. G. **Rev:** Crowned imperial eagle **Rev. Legend:** MATTHIAS. D. G. RO. IM(P). SEM. A(V)(G). **Note:** W-167-195. Varieties exist. Struck at Oldendorf and Altona mints.

Date	Mintage	VG	F	VF	XF	Unc
ND(1616-19)	—	30.00	60.00	120	220	—
ND(1616-19) (e)	—	30.00	60.00	120	220	—
ND(1616-19) (t)	—	30.00	60.00	120	220	—

KM# 114 SCHRECKENBERGER (4 Groschen)

Silver Weight varies: 5-6g., 29-30 mm. **Ruler:** Ernst III **Obv:** Crowned shield of 4-fold arms with central shield, superimposed on cross, ends of cross divide legend **Obv. Legend:** ER. PR - ET. C. H. S. - E. S. D. G. **Rev:** Crowned imperial eagle, value '4G' in orb on breast, date at end of legend **Rev. Legend:** FERDINAN(DVS). D. G. R. IM. S. AV. **Note:** W-196, 197, 198a. Varieties exist.

Date	Mintage	VG	F	VF	XF	Unc
(1)6Z1	—	100	200	425	—	—
(16)Z1	—	100	200	425	—	—
ND	—	100	200	425	—	—

KM# 115 SCHRECKENBERGER (4 Groschen)

Silver, 28x28 mm. **Ruler:** Ernst III **Obv:** Crowned shield of 4-fold arms with central shield, superimposed on cross, ends of cross divide legend **Obv. Legend:** ER. PRI. - ET. C. H. S. - E. S. D. G. **Rev:** Crowned imperial eagle, value '4G' in orb on breast, date at end of legend **Rev. Legend:** FERDINANDVS. D. G. R. IM. S. AV. **Note:** W-198. Klippe.

Date	Mintage	VG	F	VF	XF	Unc
(16)Z1	—	—	—	—	—	—

MB# 12 1/24 THALER (Groschen)

1.8000 g., Silver, 22-23 mm. **Ruler:** Adolf XIII **Obv:** 4-fold arms with central shield of Schaumburg **Obv. Legend:** AD(OL). D. G. C(O). HO(L)(I). S(C). E. S(T). D. (I.) G(H). **Rev:** Imperial orb with Z4 divides date **Rev. Legend:** RVDOL. II. (D.G.) RO(M). I(M)(P). S(E)(M). A(V)(G). **Mint:** Altona **Note:** Ref. W#42-51, 54-56. Varieties exist. Also struck at Rinteln mint.

Date	Mintage	VG	F	VF	XF	Unc
(1)601 (p)	—	12.00	20.00	35.00	65.00	—

MB# 14 1/24 THALER (Groschen)

1.8000 g., Silver, 22-23 mm. **Ruler:** Adolf XIII **Obv:** 4-fold arms with central shield of Schaumburg, 3 helmets above, I-G between helmets **Obv. Legend:** A(D). D. G. (-) D.(O). (-) (O). H. S. E. S. D(O). **Rev:** Imperial orb with 4 divides date **Rev. Legend:** RVDO(L)(I)(P). II. (D.G.) RO(M)(P). S(E)(M). A(V)(G). **Mint:** Altona **Note:** Ref. W#57-78, S#3165, 3168. Varieties exist. Also struck at Rinteln mint.

Date	Mintage	VG	F	VF	XF	Unc
(1)601 (p)	—	12.00	20.00	35.00	75.00	—

KM# 7 1/24 THALER (Groschen)

Silver Weight varies: 1.5-1.9g., 21 mm. **Ruler:** Ernst III **Obv:** Shield of 4-fold arms with central shield of Schaumburg **Obv. Legend:** ERNE. (D.G. C.) HOL. S(C). E. S(T). D(O). (I.) G(E). **Rev:** Imperial orb with Z4 divides date **Rev. Legend:** R(V)(U)DOL. II. D. G. RO. I. S. A. **Note:** W-232-7. Varieties exist. Struck at Altona and Oldendorf mints.

Date	Mintage	VG	F	VF	XF	Unc
(1)601 (p)	—	16.00	27.00	50.00	100	—
(1)60Z (p)	—	16.00	27.00	50.00	100	—
(1)603 (p)	—	16.00	27.00	50.00	100	—
(1)604 (p)	—	16.00	27.00	50.00	100	—
1604 (p)	—	16.00	27.00	50.00	100	—
(1)1604 (c)	—	16.00	27.00	50.00	100	—

KM# 8 1/24 THALER (Groschen)

Silver Weight varies: 1.5-1.9g., 21 mm. **Ruler:** Ernst III **Obv:** Shield of 4-fold arms with central shield of Schaumburg, 3 helmets above **Obv. Legend:** E D G C (H) - (H) S E S (D) (I) (G). **Rev:** Imperial orb with Z4 divides date **Rev. Legend:** R(V)(U)DOL. II. (D.G) R(O). I(MP). (S)(EM). A(U)(V). **Mint:** Altona **Note:** W238-67. Varieties exist. Also struck at Rinteln mint.

Date	Mintage	VG	F	VF	XF	Unc
(1)601 (p)	—	16.00	27.00	50.00	100	—
(1)60Z (p)	—	16.00	27.00	50.00	100	—
(1)603 (p)	—	16.00	27.00	50.00	100	—
1603 (a)	—	16.00	27.00	50.00	100	—
(1)604 (p)	—	16.00	27.00	50.00	100	—
(1)604 (a)	—	16.00	27.00	50.00	100	—
1604 (a)	—	16.00	27.00	50.00	100	—
(1)605 (a)	—	16.00	27.00	50.00	100	—
(1)606 (c)	—	16.00	27.00	50.00	100	—
1606 (q)	—	16.00	27.00	50.00	100	—
(1)607 (p)	—	16.00	27.00	50.00	100	—
(1)607 (q)	—	16.00	27.00	50.00	100	—
(1)608 (q)	—	16.00	27.00	50.00	100	—
(1)609 (q)	—	16.00	27.00	50.00	100	—

KM# 73 1/24 THALER (Groschen)

Silver Weight varies: 1.5-1.9g., 20 mm. **Ruler:** Ernst III **Obv:** Shield of 4-fold arms with central shield of Schaumburg, 3 ornate helmets above **Obv. Legend:** E D G (C) H (S) - (S) E S (C) D G. **Rev:** Imperial orb with Z4, date divided at top **Rev. Legend:** MAT(T)(IAS). I. (D.G.) R(O). I)M). S. A(U)(V). **Mint:** Oldendorf **Note:** W-264-86. Varieties exist.

Date	Mintage	VG	F	VF	XF	Unc
1614	—	16.00	27.00	50.00	100	—
1614 (e)	—	16.00	27.00	50.00	100	—
1615 (e)	—	16.00	27.00	50.00	100	—
1616 (e)	—	16.00	27.00	50.00	100	—
1616	—	16.00	27.00	50.00	100	—
1617	—	16.00	27.00	50.00	100	—
1617 (e)	—	16.00	27.00	50.00	100	—
1618	—	16.00	27.00	50.00	100	—
1618 (e)	—	16.00	27.00	50.00	100	—
(1)618 (e)	—	16.00	27.00	50.00	100	—
1619	—	16.00	27.00	50.00	100	—
1619 (e)	—	16.00	27.00	50.00	100	—
(!)619 (e)	—	16.00	27.00	50.00	100	—
(16)19 (e)	—	16.00	27.00	50.00	100	—
16Z0	—	16.00	27.00	50.00	100	—
16Z0 (e)	—	16.00	27.00	50.00	100	—

KM# 99 1/24 THALER (Groschen)

0.8000 g., Silver, 18 mm. **Ruler:** Ernst III **Obv:** Shield of 4-fold arms with central shield of Schaumburg, 3 ornate helmets above **Obv. Legend:** E D G H S - E S C D (G). **Rev:** Imperial orb with Z4, date at end of legend **Rev. Legend:** FERD(I). (Z.)(II.) D. G. R. I. S. A(V). **Note:** W-287-92. Kipper issue. Varieties exist.

Date	Mintage	VG	F	VF	XF	Unc
(1)6Z0	—	16.00	27.00	50.00	100	—
(16)Z0	—	16.00	27.00	50.00	100	—
ND(1620)	—	16.00	27.00	50.00	100	—

KM# 124 1/24 THALER (Groschen)

1.7000 g., Silver, 23-24 mm. **Ruler:** Jobst Hermann **Obv:** Shield of 4-fold arms with central shield, 3 ornate helmets above **Obv. Legend:** I. H. G. Z. H. S. (V.) - (V.) S. H. Z. G. V. B. **Rev:** Imperial orb with Z4 divides date **Rev. Legend:** FERD(I). II. D. G. RO(M). I(M). S(E). A(V)(G). **Mint:** Oldendorf **Note:** W-352-72. Varieties exist.

Date	Mintage	VG	F	VF	XF	Unc
16ZZ	—	27.00	60.00	100	210	—
16ZZ (k)	—	27.00	60.00	100	210	—
16Z3 (k)	—	27.00	60.00	100	210	—
16Z4 (l)	—	27.00	60.00	100	210	—
16Z5 (m)	—	27.00	60.00	100	210	—
16Z6 (m)	—	27.00	60.00	100	210	—
16Z6	—	27.00	60.00	100	210	—
16Z7 (m)	—	27.00	60.00	100	210	—
1630 (m)	—	27.00	60.00	100	210	—
1631 (m)	—	27.00	60.00	100	210	—
163Z (m)	—	27.00	60.00	100	210	—
1633 (m)	—	27.00	60.00	100	210	—
1635 (m)	—	27.00	60.00	100	210	—

KM# 150 1/24 THALER (Groschen)

1.7000 g., Silver, 23 mm. **Ruler:** Otto VI **Obv:** Shield of 4-fold arms with central shield, 3 ornate helmets above **Obv. Legend:** OT. G. Z. H. S. (V.) - (V.) S. H. Z. G. V. B. **Rev:** Imperial orb with Z4 divides date **Rev. Legend:** FER(D). III. D. G. RO(M). I(M). S(E). (A)(V). **Mint:** Oldendorf **Note:** W-380-85. Varieties exist.

Date	Mintage	VG	F	VF	XF	Unc
1638 (n)	—	27.00	60.00	100	210	—
(16)38 (n)	—	27.00	60.00	100	210	—
(16)39 (n)	—	27.00	60.00	100	210	—

KM# 64.1 1/24 THALER (Adlergroschen)
Silver Weight varies: 1.5-1.9g., 21 mm. **Ruler:** Ernst III **Obv:** Shield of 4-fold arms with central shield of Schaumburg, 3 ornate helmets above **Obv. Legend:** E D G C - H S E S D **Rev:** Crowned imperial eagle, Z4 in orb on breast, date at end of legend **Rev. Legend:** RVDOL. II. D.G. R. IM. S. A. **Mint:** Altona **Note:** W-293.

Date	Mintage	VG	F	VF	XF	Unc
(1)611	—	25.00	40.00	80.00	160	—

KM# 64.2 1/24 THALER (Adlergroschen)
Silver Weight varies: 1.0-1.9g., 20-21 mm. **Ruler:** Ernst III **Obv:** Shield of 4-fold arms with central shield of Schaumburg, 3 ornate helmets above **Obv. Legend:** E D G L - H S E S D **Rev:** Crowned imperial eagle, Z4 in orb on breast, date divided at top **Rev. Legend:** MAT(TH)IAS. (D. G.) RO. IM. S. A. **Mint:** Altona **Note:** W-294-97. Varieties exist

Date	Mintage	VG	F	VF	XF	Unc
1612	—	20.00	33.00	55.00	110	—
1614	—	20.00	33.00	55.00	110	—
1615 (e)	—	20.00	33.00	55.00	110	—
1616	—	20.00	33.00	55.00	110	—
(1)618 (t)	—	20.00	33.00	55.00	110	—

KM# 97 3 KREUZER (Groschen)
0.7800 g., Silver, 17 mm. **Ruler:** Ernst III **Obv:** Crowned 4-fold arms with central shield **Obv. Legend:** E. D. G. P. E. C. HO. E. S. **Rev:** Crowned imperial eagle, 3 in circle on breast **Rev. Legend:** FERD. II. D. G. R. I. S. AV. **Note:** W-299. Kipper issue.

Date	Mintage	VG	F	VF	XF	Unc
ND(1620)	—	40.00	80.00	150	300	—

KM# 116 1/21 THALER (1-1/2 Schilling)
Silver Weight varies: 2.0-2.3g., 26-28 mm. **Ruler:** Ernst III **Obv:** Crowned shield of 4-fold arms with central shield, superimposed on cross **Obv. Legend:** ER - NES. - D. G. P. E. - C. HO. - E. S. **Rev:** Crowned imperial eagle, Z1 in orb on breast **Rev. Legend:** XXI THO EINEM. THALER **Note:** W-228. Kipper issue. Also called a Fürstengroschen.

Date	Mintage	VG	F	VF	XF	Unc
ND(1621)	—	65.00	135	225	425	—

Note: This issue was struck for the Westphalian part of the county

KM# 117 1/21 THALER (1-1/2 Schilling)
Silver Weight varies: 2.0-2.3g., 26-28 mm. **Ruler:** Ernst III **Obv:** Crowned shield of 4-fold arms with central shield, superimposed on cross **Obv. Legend:** ER - NES - D. G. P. (E)(F). - C. HO - E. S. **Rev:** Crowned imperial eagle, Z1 in orb on breast **Rev. Legend:** XXI ZV. EINEM. T(H)AL(L)ER. **Mint:** Oldendorf **Note:** W-229-31. Kipper issue. Also called a Fürstengroschen.

Date	Mintage	VG	F	VF	XF	Unc
ND(1621)	—	65.00	135	225	425	—

Note: This issue was struck for the Westphalian part of the county

KM# 66 1/18-1/2 THALER (Schilling)
6.5000 g., Silver, 27x27 mm. **Ruler:** Ernst III **Obv:** Shield of 4-fold arms with central shield, 3 ornate helmets above **Obv. Legend:** E. D. G. C. - H. S. E. S. D. **Rev:** Crowned imperial eagle, 18-1/2 in orb on breast, date at end of legend **Rev. Legend:** R(V)(U)DOL. II. D. G. RO. I. S. A. **Mint:** Altona **Note:** W-202. Klippe.

Date	Mintage	VG	F	VF	XF	Unc
(1)611 (q)	—	115	225	450	900	—

KM# 65 1/18-1/2 THALER (Schilling)
2.6000 g., Silver, 26 mm. **Ruler:** Ernst III **Obv:** Shield of 4-fold arms with central shield, 3 ornate helmets above **Obv. Legend:** E. D. G. C. - H. S. E. S. D. **Rev:** Crowned imperial eagle, 18-1/2 in orb on breast, date at end of legend **Rev. Legend:** R(V)(U)DOL. II. D. G. R(O). I. S. A. **Mint:** Altona **Note:** W-202-204. Varieties exist.

Date	Mintage	VG	F	VF	XF	Unc
(1)611 (q)	—	27.00	55.00	100	210	—
(1)61Z (q)	—	27.00	55.00	100	210	—
(1)613 (q)	—	27.00	55.00	100	210	—

KM# 72 1/18-1/2 THALER (Schilling)
2.6000 g., Silver, 24-25 mm. **Ruler:** Ernst III **Obv:** Shield of 4-fold arms with central shield, 3 ornate helmets above **Obv. Legend:** E. D. G. C. - H. S. E. S. D. IG. **Rev:** Crowned imperial eagle, 18-1/2 in orb on breast, date at end of legend **Rev. Legend:** MATT(H)IAS. (I.) D. - G. R. I. S. A. **Mint:** Altona **Note:** W-205-209. Varieties exist.

Date	Mintage	VG	F	VF	XF	Unc
(1)613 (q)	—	33.00	60.00	125	250	—
(1)614 (q)	—	33.00	60.00	125	250	—
(1)615 (q)	—	33.00	60.00	125	250	—
(1)616 (q)	—	33.00	60.00	125	250	—

KM# 47 1/16 THALER (2 Schilling)
2.6000 g., Silver, 26 mm. **Ruler:** Ernst III **Obv:** Shield of 4-fold arms with central shield, 3 ornate helmets above **Obv. Legend:** E. D. G. C. - H. S. E. S. D. **Rev:** Crowned imperial eagle, value 16 in orb on breast, date at end of legend **Rev. Legend:** R(U)(V)DOL. II. D. G. R(O). I. S. A(U). **Mint:** Altona **Note:** W-199-201. Varieties exist.

Date	Mintage	VG	F	VF	XF	Unc
(1)608 (q)	—	20.00	45.00	90.00	185	—
(1)609 (q)	—	20.00	45.00	90.00	185	—
(1)611	—	20.00	45.00	90.00	185	—

KM# 77 1/16 THALER (2 Schilling)
Silver Weight varies: 1.5-1.8g., 22-25 mm. **Ruler:** Ernst III **Obv:** Shield of 4-fold arms with central shield, 3 ornate helmets above **Obv. Legend:** E. D. G. C. (H). - (H.) S. E. S. D. (G). **Rev:** Crowned imperial eagle, value 16 in orb on breast, date at end of legend **Rev. Legend:** MATTHIA(S). D. G. R(O). I(M). S. (A). **Note:** W-210-17. Varieties exist. Struck at Altona and Oldendorf mints.

Date	Mintage	VG	F	VF	XF	Unc
(1)616 (f)	—	27.00	55.00	100	210	—
(1)617 (f)	—	27.00	55.00	100	210	—
(1)617 (q)	—	27.00	55.00	100	210	—
(1)618 (t)	—	27.00	55.00	100	210	—
(1)619 (t)	—	27.00	55.00	100	210	—
(1)6Z0 (t)	—	27.00	55.00	100	210	—

KM# 100 1/16 THALER (2 Schilling)
Silver Weight varies: 1.5-1.6g., 22 mm. **Ruler:** Ernst III **Obv:** Shield of 4-fold arms with central shield, 3 ornate helmets above **Obv. Legend:** E(R)(NESTVS). D. G. P(RI)(N). E(). (-) C. H. S. (E.) S. (D.) (G). **Rev:** Crowned imperial eagle, value 16 in orb on breast, date at end of legend **Rev. Legend:** FERDINAN(DVS). D. G. R(O). IM. S(EM). A(VG). **Note:** W-218, 219, 223. Kipper issue. Struck at Oldendorf and Rinteln mints.

Date	Mintage	VG	F	VF	XF	Unc
(1)6Z0	—	27.00	55.00	100	210	—
(1)6Z0 (b)	—	27.00	55.00	100	210	—
(1)6Z1 (i)	—	27.00	55.00	100	210	—

KM# 101 1/16 THALER (2 Schilling)
Silver **Ruler:** Ernst III **Obv:** Shield of 4-fold arms with central shield, 3 ornate helmets above **Obv. Legend:** E. D. G. P. E. - C. H. S. E. S. D. **Rev:** Crowned imperial eagle, value 16 in orb on breast, date at end of legend **Rev. Legend:** FERDINAN. D. G. R. IM. S. A. **Note:** W-219. Klippe.

Date	Mintage	VG	F	VF	XF	Unc
(1)6Z0	—	115	225	450	900	—

KM# 118 1/16 THALER (2 Schilling)
2.6000 g., Silver, 25-26 mm. **Ruler:** Ernst III **Obv:** Shield of 4-fold arms with central shield divides date, 3 ornate helmets above **Obv. Legend:** ERNES(T). D. G. P. E. C. HO. E. S. **Rev:** Crowned imperial eagle, value 1-6 divided below, date at end of legend **Rev. Legend:** FERD(I). (Z.) D. G. RO. IM SE. A(V). **Mint:** Oldendorf **Note:** W-220, 221. Varieties exist.

Date	Mintage	VG	F	VF	XF	Unc
16Z1//16Z1 (h)	—	30.00	60.00	110	220	—

KM# 120 1/16 THALER (2 Schilling)
2.6000 g., Silver, 25-26 mm. **Ruler:** Ernst III **Obv:** Shield of 4-fold arms with central shield, date at left, 3 ornate helmets above **Obv. Legend:** ERNES D. G. P. E. C. HO. E. S. **Rev:** Crowned imperial eagle, no indication of value **Rev. Legend:** FERD. Z. D. G. RO. IM. SEM. AVG. **Note:** W-222a.

Date	Mintage	VG	F	VF	XF	Unc
(16)Z1	—	30.00	60.00	110	220	—

KM# 119 1/16 THALER (2 Schilling)
2.6000 g., Silver, 25-26 mm. **Ruler:** Ernst III **Obv:** Shield of 4-fold arms with central shield, date to left, 3 ornate helmets above **Obv. Legend:** ERNES. D. G. P. E. C. HO. E. S. **Rev:** Crowned imperial eagle, value 1-6 divided below, date at end of legend **Rev. Legend:** FERD. Z. D. G. RO. IM .SEM. AVG. **Note:** W-222b.

Date	Mintage	VG	F	VF	XF	Unc
(16)Z1//16Z1	—	30.00	60.00	110	220	—

KM# 121 1/16 THALER (2 Schilling)
2.6000 g., Silver, 25-26 mm. **Ruler:** Ernst III **Obv:** Shield of 4-fold arms with central shield, 3 ornate helmets above **Obv. Legend:** ERNES. D. G. P. F. C. HO. E. S. **Rev:** Crowned imperial eagle, date at end of legend, no indication of value **Rev. Legend:** FERDI. Z. D. G. RO. IM. S. **Mint:** Oldendorf **Note:** W-224.

Date	Mintage	VG	F	VF	XF	Unc
16Z1 (h)	—	30.00	60.00	110	220	—

KM# 122 1/16 THALER (2 Schilling)
2.6000 g., Silver, 25-26 mm. **Ruler:** Ernst III **Obv:** Shield of 4-fold arms with central shield, 3 ornate helmets above **Obv. Legend:** ERNES. D. G. (D. E.) (P.) C. H(OL). (E.) S. **Rev:** Crowned imperial eagle, value 1-6 divided below, date divided at top by crown **Rev. Legend:** FERDI. Z. D. G. RO(M). IM. S(E). A(V). **Mint:** Oldendorf **Note:** W-225-7. Varieties exist.

Date	Mintage	VG	F	VF	XF	Unc
16Z1 (h)	—	27.00	55.00	100	210	—
ND(1621) (h)	—	27.00	55.00	100	210	—

KM# 136 1/16 THALER (2 Schilling)
2.6000 g., Silver, 26 mm. **Ruler:** Jobst Hermann **Obv:** Shield of 4-fold arms with central shield, 3 ornate helmets above **Obv. Legend:** I. H. D. G. C. - H S E S D. G. **Rev:** Crowned imperial eagle, value 16 in orb on breast, date at end of legend **Rev. Legend:** FER. D II. D. - G. Ro. IM. S. A. **Note:** W-351.

Date	Mintage	VG	F	VF	XF	Unc
1624	—	35.00	75.00	150	300	—

KM# 48 1/4 THALER
7.0000 g., Silver, 30 mm. **Ruler:** Ernst III **Obv:** Shield of 4-fold arms with central shield, 3 ornate helmets above **Obv. Legend:** ERNESTUS. D. G. H. S. E. S. C. D. G. **Rev:** Crowned imperial eagle, orb on breast, date at end of legend **Rev. Legend:** RUDOL. II. D. G. RO. I. S. AUG. P. F. D. **Note:** W-164.

Date	Mintage	VG	F	VF	XF	Unc
(1)608	—	500	1,000	1,800	3,400	—

KM# 57 1/4 THALER

7.1000 g., Silver, 30 mm. **Ruler:** Ernst III **Obv:** Shield of 4-fold arms with central shield divides date, where present, 3 ornate helmets above **Obv. Legend:** ERNES(TVS). HO(L). S(C). E. S. CO. D. G(EM). **Rev:** Crowned imperial eagle, orb on breast **Rev. Legend:** R(U)(V)DOL(P). II. (D.G.) RO(M). IM(P). SEM. A(VGV). **Mint:** Altona **Note:** W-165, 166. Varieties exist.

Date	Mintage	VG	F	VF	XF	Unc
(1)610 (q)	—	500	1,000	1,800	3,400	—
ND(1610)	—	500	1,000	1,800	3,400	—

KM# 126 1/4 THALER

7.0000 g., Silver, 31 mm. **Ruler:** Jobst Hermann **Obv:** Shield of 4-fold arms with central shield break legend at bottom **Obv. Legend:** IVS. H. D. G. - C. H. S. E. S. D. G. **Rev:** Crowned imperial eagle, orb on breast, date at end of legend **Rev. Legend:** FERDINANDVS. II. D. G. RO. I. S. A. **Note:** W-345.

Date	Mintage	VG	F	VF	XF	Unc
(1)6ZZ	—	500	1,000	1,800	3,400	—

KM# 125 1/4 THALER (8 Groschen)

7.0000 g., Silver, 31 mm. **Ruler:** Ernst III **Obv:** Shield of 4-fold arms with central shield, three helmets above **Obv. Legend:** IVS. H. D. G. - C. H. S. E. S. D. G. **Rev:** Crowned imperial eagle, value '8' in orb on breast **Rev. Legend:** FERDINAN. II. D. G. ROM. IM. S. A. **Note:** W-346.

Date	Mintage	VG	F	VF	XF	Unc
ND(ca.1622)	—	135	275	550	—	—

KM# 58 1/2 THALER

Silver Weight varies: 14-15g., 36 mm. **Ruler:** Ernst III **Obv:** Shield of 4-fold arms with central shield, 3 ornate helmets above, date divided among helmets **Obv. Legend:** ERNESTUS. HOLS. E. S. CO. D(O). G. **Rev:** Crowned imperial eagle, orb on breast **Rev. Legend:** RUDOL. II. D. G. RO. - IMP. SEMP. AUGU. **Mint:** Altona **Note:** W-155, 157. Varieties exist.

Date	Mintage	VG	F	VF	XF	Unc
1610 (q)	—	850	1,600	2,500	4,400	—
1613 (q)	—	850	1,600	2,500	4,400	—

KM# 69 1/2 THALER

Silver Weight varies: 14-15g., 36 mm. **Ruler:** Ernst III **Obv:** Shield of 4-fold arms with central shield divides date, 3 ornate helmets above **Obv. Legend:** ERNESTVS. HOL. S. E. S. CO. D. GE. **Rev. Legend:** RVDOL. II. D. G. RO. IMP. SEMP. AUGU. **Note:** W-156.

Date	Mintage	VG	F	VF	XF	Unc
(1)61Z	—	850	1,600	2,500	4,400	—

KM# 102 1/2 THALER

14.2000 g., Silver, 36 mm. **Ruler:** Ernst III **Obv:** Bust to right **Obv. Legend:** ERNESTUS. D. G. PRINC. ET COM. HOL. SCHAW. **Rev:** Shield of 4-fold arms with central shield, 3 ornate helmets above, date divided among helmets **Rev. Legend:** COMES. STERNB. DOM(I). GE(H)M(Æ). **Note:** W-158, 159. Varieties exist.

Date	Mintage	VG	F	VF	XF	Unc
(16)Z0	—	—	—	—	—	—
ND(1620)	—	—	—	—	—	—

KM# 103 1/2 THALER

14.5000 g., Silver, 45 mm. **Ruler:** Ernst III **Obv:** Shield of 4-fold arms with central shield, 3 ornate helmets above **Obv. Legend:** ERNESTVS. D. G. - C. HO. S. E. ST. D. I. G. **Rev:** Count on horseback galloping to right, legend enclosed in garland **Rev. Legend:** HATS. GODT. VO - RSEHN. SO. WI - RTS. GESCHEN. **Mint:** Altona **Note:** W-160.

Date	Mintage	VG	F	VF	XF	Unc
ND(1620) Rare	—	—	—	—	—	—

KM# 104 1/2 THALER

15.0000 g., Silver, 45 mm. **Ruler:** Ernst III **Obv:** Representation of the Miracle in the Wedding at Cana, the turning of water into wine **Obv. Legend:** IESUS CHRISTUS MACHET WASSER ZU WEINN IN CANA. GA. IO. II. **Rev:** Count on horseback galloping to right **Rev. Legend:** HATS. GODT. VO - RSEHN. SO WI - RTS. GESCHEN. **Mint:** Altona **Note:** W-161.

Date	Mintage	VG	F	VF	XF	Unc
ND(1620) Rare	—	—	—	—	—	—

KM# 105 1/2 THALER

15.0000 g., Silver, 45 mm. **Ruler:** Ernst III **Obv:** Scene from Cana - the seven-headed dragon of Babylon with one head severed **Obv. Legend:** DIE ROTE HVR DE. DRACH: REIT. - DE KELC DS GIF: U: GREWELS. TREIT. **Rev:** Count on horseback galloping to right **Rev. Legend:** HATS. GODT. VO - RSEHN. SO WI - RTS. GESCHEN. **Mint:** Altona **Note:** W-162.

Date	Mintage	VG	F	VF	XF	Unc
ND(1620) (t) Rare	—	—	—	—	—	—

KM# 127 1/2 THALER

14.0000 g., Silver, 36 mm. **Ruler:** Ernst III **Subject:** Death of Ernst III **Obv:** Shield of 4-fold arms with central shield in ornamented frame, all within circle **Obv. Legend:** ERNEST. D. G. S. R. I. PRIN. COM. HOLS. SCHAU. D. G. **Rev:** 9-line inscription with Roman numeral date **Rev. Inscription:** OBIIT / AN: CHRI: MDCXXII / DIE. XVII. IAN(U)(VA). INTE / VII ET VIII. MATVTIN / C(U)(VM) VIXISSET. A. LII. / MEN. III. DIES. XXIV. H. I. / IN REGIMINE VERO / ANOS. XX. M. VI. / D. XV. H. IV. **Note:** W-163.

Date	Mintage	VG	F	VF	XF	Unc
MDCXXII (1622) Rare	—	—	—	—	—	—

KM# 128.1 1/2 THALER

14.5000 g., Silver, 36 mm. **Ruler:** Jobst Hermann **Obv:** Shield of oval 4-fold arms with central shield in baroque frame, 3 ornate helmets above **Obv. Legend:** I(U)(V)S(T)(VS). HER. (-) (D.G.) C(O). - H(OL). (C.) (E.) (S.) S. D. G. (E. B). **Rev:** Crowned imperial eagle, orb on breast, date at end of legend, where present **Rev. Legend:** FERDINAND(V)(U)S. II. D. G. RO(M)(A). IM(P). S(E). A(V). **Mint:** Altona **Note:** W-340, 342, 343. Varieties exist.

Date	Mintage	VG	F	VF	XF	Unc
(1)6ZZ	—	850	1,600	2,500	4,400	—
ND(1622)	—	850	1,600	2,500	4,400	—
1618 Error for 1628	—	850	1,600	2,500	4,400	—

KM# 128.2 1/2 THALER

14.5000 g., Silver, 36 mm. **Ruler:** Jobst Hermann **Obv:** 4-fold arms in Spanish shield, with central shield, 3 ornate helmets above **Obv. Legend:** IUST. HER. D. G. CO. H. S. E. S. D. G. E. B. **Rev:** Crowned imperial eagle, orb on breast, date at end of legend **Rev. Legend:** FERDINANDVS. II. D. G. ROM. IM. S. A. **Mint:** Altona

Date	Mintage	VG	F	VF	XF	Unc
(1)6ZZ	—	1,650	2,500	3,500	6,000	—

KM# 137 1/2 THALER

14.5000 g., Silver, 36 mm. **Ruler:** Jobst Hermann **Obv:** Shield of 4-fold arms with central shield, 3 ornate helmets above **Obv. Legend:** IUST, HERMA, D. G. C. H. S. E. S. D. G. ET. B. **Rev:** Crowned imperial eagle, orb on breast, date divided below **Rev. Legend:** FERDINANDVS. II. D. G. RO. IM. SEM. AVG. **Note:** W-341.

Date	Mintage	VG	F	VF	XF	Unc
16Z4	—	850	1,600	2,500	4,400	—

KM# 98 1/2 THALER (16 Groschen)

14.5000 g., Silver, 36 mm. **Ruler:** Ernst III **Obv:** Shield of 4-fold arms with central shield, 3 ornate helmets above **Obv. Legend:** IUST. HER. C. - H. S. E. S. D. G. E. B. **Rev:** Crowned imperial eagle, value '16' in orb on breast **Rev. Legend:** FERDINANDUS. II. D. G. ROM. IM. S. A. **Note:** W-344.

Date	Mintage	VG	F	VF	XF	Unc
ND(1622)	—	80.00	160	325	—	—

KM# 17 THALER

Silver Weight varies: 28-29g., 41-43 mm. **Ruler:** Ernst III **Obv:** Shield of 4-fold arms with central shield divides date, 3 ornate helmets above **Obv. Legend:** ERNESTUS. HOL. SC. E. ST. CO. DOM. GEMMÆ. **Rev:** Crowned imperial eagle with orb on breast **Rev. Legend:** RVDOLP. II. ROM. IMP. SEMP. AVGVST. **Mint:** Altona **Note:** Dav. #3723. Ref. W-108.

Date	Mintage	VG	F	VF	XF	Unc
1602 (p)	—	525	900	1,650	3,350	—

KM# 18 THALER

Silver Weight varies: 28-29g., 41-43 mm. **Ruler:** Ernst III **Obv:** Shield of 4-fold arms with central shield divides date near bottom, 3 ornate helmets above **Obv. Legend:** ERNESTUS. HOL. S(C). E. S. CO. D. GEMM. **Rev:** Crowned imperial eagle, orb on breast **Rev. Legend:** RVDOLP. II. ROM. IMP. SEMP. AVGVST. **Mint:** Altona **Note:** Dav. #3724.

Date	Mintage	VG	F	VF	XF	Unc
1602 (p)	—	525	900	1,650	3,350	—

KM# 19 THALER

Silver Weight varies: 28-29g., 41-43 mm. **Ruler:** Ernst III **Obv:** Shield of 4-fold arms with central shield divides date near bottom, 3 ornate helmets above **Obv. Legend:** ERNESTUS. HOL. SC. E. ST. CO. D. GEMMÆ. **Rev:** Crowned imperial eagle, orb on breast **Rev. Legend:** RUDOL. II. D. G. RO. IM. SEM. AVGVST. **Mint:** Altona **Note:** Dav. #3725.

Date	Mintage	VG	F	VF	XF	Unc
1602 (p)	—	525	900	1,650	3,350	—

KM# 20 THALER

Silver Weight varies: 28-29g., 41-43 mm. **Ruler:** Ernst III **Obv:** Shield of 4-fold arms with central shield, 3 ornate helmets above **Obv. Legend:** ERNESTUS. D. G. HOL. SC. E. ST. CO. D: G. **Rev:** Crowned imperial eagle, orb on breast, date divided by tail **Rev. Legend:** RUDOL. II. D. G. ROMA. IMPER. SEMPER AVGVS. **Mint:** Rinteln **Note:** Dav. #3726. Ref. W-110.

Date	Mintage	VG	F	VF	XF	Unc
1603 (a)	—	525	900	1,650	3,350	—

KM# 21 THALER

Silver Weight varies: 28-29g., 41-43 mm. **Ruler:** Ernst III **Obv:** Shield of 4-fold arms with central shield, 3 ornate helmets above **Obv. Legend:** ERNESTUS. D. G. HOL. SC. E. ST. CO. D. G. **Rev:** Crowned imperial eagle, orb on breast, date divided by tail **Rev. Legend:** RUDOL. II. ROMA. IMP. SEMPER AUGUS. **Mint:** Rinteln **Note:** Dav. #3726A.

Date	Mintage	VG	F	VF	XF	Unc
1603 (a)	—	525	900	1,650	3,350	—

KM# 22 THALER

Silver Weight varies: 29-30g., 57-59 mm. **Ruler:** Ernst III **Obv:** Shield of 4-fold arms with central shield, 3 ornate helmets above, date at end of legend, above crest of left helmet **Obv. Legend:** ERNES. D. G. C. H. - S. E. ST. DO. I. GHE. **Rev:** Count on horseback galloping to right **Rev. Legend:** HATS - GOT: VORSEN: SO: WIR - TS - WOL: GESCHE - N. **Note:** Dav. #LS465. Ref. W-147.

Date	Mintage	VG	F	VF	XF	Unc
1603 Rare	—	—	—	—	—	—

KM# 28 THALER

Silver Weight varies: 28-29g., 41-43 mm. **Ruler:** Ernst III **Obv:** Shield of 4-fold arms with central shield, 3 ornate helmets above **Obv. Legend:** ERNESTUS. D. G. HOL. SC. E. ST. CO. D. G(E). **Rev:** Crowned imperial eagle, orb on breast, date divided by tail **Rev. Legend:** RUDOL. II. D. G. ROMA. IMPER. SEMPER. AVGVS. **Mint:** Rinteln **Note:** Dav. #3727. Ref. W-111, 112.

Date	Mintage	VG	F	VF	XF	Unc
1604 (a)	—	525	900	1,650	3,350	—

KM# 29 THALER

Silver Weight varies: 29-30g., 57-59 mm. **Ruler:** Ernst III **Obv:** Shield of 4-fold arms with central shield, 3 ornate helmets above, date at end of legend, above crest of left helmet **Obv. Legend:** ERNESTVS. D. G. - H. S. E. S. C. D. G. **Rev:** Count on horseback galloping to right **Rev. Legend:** HATS. GOT. VORSIN. SO. WIR - TS. - WOL. GESCHEN. **Note:** Dav. #LS467. Ref. W-148.

Date	Mintage	VG	F	VF	XF	Unc
1606 Rare	—	—	—	—	—	—

KM# 46 THALER

Silver Weight varies: 28-29g., 41-43 mm. **Ruler:** Ernst III **Obv:** Shield of 4-fold arms with central shield, 3 ornate helmets above, date divided near bottom **Obv. Legend:** ERNESTUS. HOL. SC. E. ST. CO. DO: GEM. **Rev:** Crowned imperial eagle, orb on breast **Rev. Legend:** RUDOLP. II. D. G. ROM. IMP. SEMP. AUGUSTUS. **Mint:** Altona **Note:** Dav. #3728. Ref. W-113.

Date	Mintage	VG	F	VF	XF	Unc
1607 (q)	—	525	900	1,650	3,350	—

KM# 30 THALER

Silver Weight varies: 29-30g., 57-59 mm. **Ruler:** Ernst III **Obv:** Shield of 4-fold arms with central shield, 3 ornate helmets above **Obv. Legend:** ERNESTUS: D: G: HOL: SCA: E: STE: C: D: G. **Rev:** Count on horseback galloping to right **Rev. Legend:** HATS - GOT: UORSEN: SO: WIRTS - WOL - GESCHEN. **Note:** Dav. #LS474. Ref. W-150.

Date	Mintage	VG	F	VF	XF	Unc
ND(1607)	—	2,400	3,750	5,900	8,500	—

KM# 31 THALER

Silver Weight varies: 29-30g., 57-59 mm. **Ruler:** Ernst III **Obv:** Shield of 4-fold arms with central shield, 3 ornate helmets above **Obv. Legend:** ERNEST: D: G: PRINC: E: OM: HOLSAT: SCHAWENB: COM: STERNB:DOM: GEH: **Rev:** Count on horseback galloping to right **Rev. Legend:** HATS + GODT + VERSEHN + SO. WIRDTS + GESCHEN+ **Note:** Dav. #LS483. Ref. W-151.

Date	Mintage	VG	F	VF	XF	Unc
ND(1607) Rare	—	—	—	—	—	—

KM# 49 THALER

Silver Weight varies: 28-29g., 41-43 mm. **Ruler:** Ernst III **Obv:** Helmeted arms **Obv. Legend:** ERNESTUS. HO(L). SC. E. ST. CO. DO. GEM(M). **Rev:** Double-headed imperial eagle, orb on breast **Rev. Legend:** RVDOL. II. D: G. RO: IM: SEM. AVGVST. P. F. D. **Mint:** Altona **Note:** Dav. #3729. Ref. W-116, 125.

Date	Mintage	VG	F	VF	XF	Unc
1608 (q)	—	—	—	—	—	—
ND(1608)	—	525	900	1,650	3,350	—

KM# 50 THALER

Silver Weight varies: 28-29g., 41-43 mm. **Ruler:** Ernst III **Obv:** Shield of 4-fold arms with central shield, 3 ornate helmets above, date divided among helmets **Obv. Legend:** ERNESTVS. D. G. HOL. SE. S: CO. D(O): GE. **Rev:** Crowned imperial eagle, orb on breast **Rev. Legend:** RVDOL. II. D. G. ROMA. - IMPER: SEMPER: AVG. **Mint:** Altona **Note:** Dav. #3730. Ref. W-114, 117, 123, 124.

Date	Mintage	VG	F	VF	XF	Unc
1608 (q)	—	800	1,650	3,000	5,000	—
1609 (q)	—	800	1,650	3,000	5,000	—
1611 (q)	—	800	1,650	3,000	5,000	—
1613 (q)	—	800	1,650	3,000	5,000	—

KM# 51 THALER

Silver Weight varies: 28-29g., 41-43 mm. **Ruler:** Ernst III **Obv:** Shield of 4-fold arms with central shield, 3 ornate helmets above, date divided among helmets **Obv. Legend:** ERNESTVS. D. G. HOL. S. E. S. CO. D. GE. **Rev:** Crowned imperial eagle, orb on breast **Rev. Legend:** RVDOL. II. D. G. RO. IM. SEM. AVGVST. P. F. D. **Mint:** Altona **Note:** Dav. #3730A. Ref. W-115.

Date	Mintage	VG	F	VF	XF	Unc
1608 (q)	—	800	1,650	3,000	5,000	—

KM# 59 THALER

Silver Weight varies: 28-29g., 41-43 mm. **Ruler:** Ernst III **Obv:** Shield of oval 4-fold arms with central shield, 3 ornate helmets above, date divided near bottom **Obv. Legend:** ERNESTUS. D. G. - H. S. E. CO. D. G. **Rev:** Crowned imperial eagle, orb on breast **Rev. Legend:** RUDOL. II. D. G. ROMAN. IMPER. SEMPER. AUGV. **Mint:** Altona **Note:** Dav. #3731.

Date	Mintage	VG	F	VF	XF	Unc
1610 (q)	—	625	1,050	1,950	4,300	—

KM# 62 THALER

Silver Weight varies: 28-29g., 41-43 mm. **Ruler:** Ernst III **Obv:** Shield of 4-fold arms with central shield, 3 ornate helmets above, date at end of legend **Obv. Legend:** ERNESTUS. D. G. HOL. S(C). E. S. CO. D. G(E). **Rev:** Crowned imperial eagle, orb on breast **Rev. Legend:** RUDOL. II. D. G. ROMA. IMPER. SEM. AUG. P. F. D. **Mint:** Altona **Note:** Dav. #3733. Ref. W-120.

Date	Mintage	VG	F	VF	XF	Unc
1610 (q)	—	850	1,650	3,000	5,000	—
1611 (q)	—	850	1,650	3,000	5,000	—

KM# 61 THALER

Silver Weight varies: 28-29g., 41-43 mm. **Ruler:** Ernst III **Obv:** Shield of 4-fold arms with central shield, 3 ornate helmets above, date divided among helmets **Obv. Legend:** ERNESTUS. D. G. HOL. SC. E. S. CO. D. GE. **Rev:** Crowned imperial eagle, orb on breast **Rev. Legend:** RUDOL. II. D. G. ROMA. IMPER. SEM. AUG. P. F. D. **Mint:** Altona **Note:** Dav. #3732. Ref. W-121.

Date	Mintage	VG	F	VF	XF	Unc
1610 (q)	—	850	1,650	3,000	5,000	—

KM# 68 THALER

Silver Weight varies: 28-29g., 41-43 mm. **Ruler:** Ernst III **Obv:** Bust to right in circle **Obv. Legend:** ERNESTUS. D. G. HOLSATIÆ. SCHAWENBVRGI. ET. STER. **Rev:** Shield of 4-fold arms with central shield, 3 ornate helmets above, date divided among the helmets **Rev. Legend:** NEBERGÆ. COMES - DOMINUS. GEHMÆ. **Mint:** Altona **Note:** Dav. #3737. Ref. W-126-29, 132, 137, 140, 141. Varieties with U's and V's interchangeable.

Date	Mintage	VG	F	VF	XF	Unc
1611 (q)	—	450	900	1,850	3,500	—
1614 (q)	—	450	900	1,850	3,500	—
(1)614 (s)	—	450	900	1,850	3,500	—
1614 (s)	—	450	900	1,850	3,500	—
6141 (q) error for 1614	—	450	900	1,850	3,500	—
1615 (q)	—	450	900	1,850	3,500	—
1616 (q)	—	450	900	1,850	3,500	—
1618 (q)	—	450	900	1,850	3,500	—
ND (q)	—	450	900	1,850	3,500	—
ND (s)	—	450	900	1,850	3,500	—

KM# 74 THALER

Silver Weight varies: 28-29g., 41-43 mm. **Ruler:** Ernst III **Obv:** Bust to right in circle **Obv. Legend:** ERNESTUS. D. G. HOLSATIÆ. SCHAWENBVR(GI). ET. STER. **Rev:** Shield of 4-fold arms with central shield, 3 ornate helmets above, date divided near bottom **Rev. Legend:** NEBERGÆ. COMES - DOMI(NUS). GEHMÆ. **Mint:** Altona **Note:** Dav. #3738. Ref. W-130-1, 133-6, 138, 139, 142. Varieties with U's and V's interchangeable.

Date	Mintage	VG	F	VF	XF	Unc
1615 (q)	—	450	900	1,850	3,500	—
1617	—	450	900	1,850	3,500	—
1618	—	450	900	1,850	3,500	—
1618 (q)	—	450	900	1,850	3,500	—
1618 (u)	—	450	900	1,850	3,500	—
1619 (u)	—	450	900	1,850	3,500	—
1619	—	450	900	1,850	3,500	—
ND(1619) (u)	—	450	900	1,850	3,500	—

KM# 79 THALER

Silver, 44x44 mm. **Ruler:** Ernst III **Obv:** Bust to right in circle **Obv. Legend:** ERNESTUS. D. G. HOLSATIÆ. SCHAWERBUR. ET. STER. **Rev:** Shield of 4-fold arms with central shield, 3 ornate helmets above, date divided near bottom **Rev. Legend:** NEBERGÆ. COMES - DOMINUS. GEHMÆ. **Mint:** Altona **Note:** Klippe. Dav. #3738A. Ref. W-133, 134.

Date	Mintage	VG	F	VF	XF	Unc
1617 Rare	—	—	—	—	—	—
1618 Rare	—	—	—	—	—	—

KM# 106 THALER

Silver Weight varies: 28-29g., 41-43 mm. **Ruler:** Ernst III **Obv:** Bust to right in circle **Obv. Legend:** ERNESTUS. D. G. HOLSATIÆ. SCHAWENBVRGI. ET. STER. **Rev:** Shield of 4-fold arms with central shield, 3 ornate helmets above, date at end of legend **Rev. Legend:** NEBERGÆ. COM. DOMINUS. GE. **Mint:** Oldendorf **Note:** Dav. #3739.

Date	Mintage	VG	F	VF	XF	Unc
(1)6Z0 (g)	—	750	1,200	2,200	4,200	—

KM# 107 THALER

Silver Weight varies: 28-29g., 41-43 mm. **Ruler:** Ernst III **Obv:** Bust to right in circle **Obv. Legend:** ERNESTUS. D. G. PRINC. ET. COMES. HOLSA. SCHAW+ **Rev:** Shield of 4-fold arms with central shield, 3 ornate helmets above, date divided near bottom **Rev. Legend:** NEBERGÆ. COMES. DOMINUS. GEHMÆ. **Note:** Dav. #3740. Ref. W-146. Mule of obverse die of KM#108 and reverse die of KM#74.

Date	Mintage	VG	F	VF	XF	Unc
(1620)//(16)19	—	750	1,200	2,200	4,200	—

KM# 108 THALER

Silver Weight varies: 28-29g., 41-43 mm. **Ruler:** Ernst III **Obv:** Bust to right in circle **Obv. Legend:** ERNESTUS: D. G. PRINC: ET. COMES: HOLS(A)(T): SCHAW(EN). **Rev:** Shield of 4-fold arms with central shield, 3 ornate helmets above, date at end of legend **Rev. Legend:** COMES: STERNB: DOMINVS: GE. **Mint:** Oldendorf **Note:** Dav. #3741.

Date	Mintage	VG	F	VF	XF	Unc
(1)6Z0 (g)	—	400	650	1,150	1,900	—

KM# 109 THALER

Silver Weight varies: 28-29g., 41-43 mm. **Ruler:** Ernst III **Obv:** Bust to right in circle **Obv. Legend:** ERNESTUS. D. G. PRINC. ET. COMES. HOLS. SCHAWEN. **Rev:** Shield of 4-fold arms with central shield, 3 ornate helmets above, date at end of legend **Rev. Legend:** COM: STERNB: DOM: GEHM. **Mint:** Oldendorf **Note:** Dav. #3741A.

Date	Mintage	VG	F	VF	XF	Unc
(1)6Z0 (g)	—	400	650	1,150	1,900	—

KM# 110 THALER

Silver Weight varies: 28-29g., 41-43 mm. **Ruler:** Ernst III **Obv:** Bust to right in circle **Obv. Legend:** ERNESTUS. D. G. PRINC. ET. COMES: HOLS(A): SCHAW(E)(N). **Rev:** Shield of 4-fold arms with central shield, 3 ornate helmets above, first part of date at end of legend and rest divided by crest of central helmet **Rev. Legend:** COMES. STERNB. DOMIN: GEHM. **Note:** Dav. #3742. Ref. W-145.

Date	Mintage	VG	F	VF	XF	Unc
16Z0	—	400	650	1,150	1,900	—

KM# 111 THALER

Silver Weight varies: 28-29g., 41-43 mm. **Ruler:** Ernst III **Obv:** Bust to right in circle **Obv. Legend:** EERNESTVS. D. G. PRINCE. ET. COMES. HOLSA. SCHAW. **Rev:** Shield of 4-fold arms with central shield, 3 ornate helmets above, date divided by crest of central helmet **Rev. Legend:** COMES. STERNB. DOMIN. GEHM. **Mint:** Oldendorf **Note:** Dav. #3742A.

Date	Mintage	VG	F	VF	XF	Unc
(16)Z0 (g)	—	400	650	1,150	1,900	—

KM# 129 THALER

28.0000 g., Silver, 43 mm. **Ruler:** Ernst III **Subject:** Death of Ernest III **Obv:** Shield of 4-fold arms, with central shield, in ornamented frame **Obv. Legend:** ERNEST: D: G: S: R: I. PRINC. CO: HOLS: SCHAUMB: STER: D: G: **Rev:** Nine-line inscription with Roman numeral date **Rev. Inscription:** OBIIT / AN: CHRI: MDCXXII / DIE. XVII. IANUAR: INT: / VII. ET: VIII: MATUTINAM / CUM. VIXISSET. ANOS: LII / MENS: III. DIES. XXIV. H: I / IN. REGIMINE: VERO. / ANNOS. XX. ME. VI. / DIE: XV. HO. IV **Note:** Dav. #3745. Ref. W-153.

Date	Mintage	VG	F	VF	XF	Unc
MDCXXII (1622)	—	1,000	2,000	3,500	6,000	—

KM# 134 THALER

Silver Weight varies: 28-29g., 43 mm. **Ruler:** Jobst Hermann **Obv:** Shield of 4-fold arms with central shield, 3 ornate helmets above **Obv. Legend:** IUST. HER. D.G. CO. H. S. E(T). S. D. G. ET. B(ER). **Rev:** Crowned imperial eagle, orb on breast, date at end of legend **Rev. Legend:** FERDINANDU(S): (II). D. G. R(O)(M). IM(P). S(EM). AU(G). **Note:** Dav. #3749.

Date	Mintage	VG	F	VF	XF	Unc
16ZZ	—	125	275	675	1,750	—
(1)6ZZ	—	125	275	675	1,750	—
16Z3	—	125	275	675	1,750	—
ND	—	125	275	675	1,750	—

KM# 130 THALER

28.0000 g., Silver, 43 mm. **Ruler:** Ernst III **Subject:** Death of Ernest III **Obv:** Shield of 4-fold arms, with central shield, in ornamented frame **Obv. Legend:** ERNEST. D. G. S. R. I. PRINC. CO(M): HOLS(AT). SCHAVMB. STER(NB). D(N): G(EH). **Rev:** 9-line inscription with Roman numeral date **Rev. Inscription:** OBIIT / AN: CHR: MDCXXII / DI: XVII. IANUA. INT: / VII. ET. VII. MATUTIN / CUM: VIXISSET. AN: LII / MEN: III. DIE: XXIV: H: I: / IN REGIMINE: VER: ANOS XX. M: VI. / D: XV. H: IV. **Note:** Dav. #3746. Ref. W-154.

Date	Mintage	VG	F	VF	XF	Unc
MDCXXII (1622)	—	650	1,250	2,500	4,000	—

KM# 131 THALER

Silver Weight varies: 28-29g., 43 mm. **Ruler:** Jobst Hermann **Obv:** Shield of 4-fold arms with central shield, 3 ornate helmets above **Obv. Legend:** IOBST. HERMAN. - D. G. CO. H. E. S. D. G. **Rev:** Crowned imperial eagle, orb on breast, date at end of legend **Rev. Legend:** FERDINANDUS. II. D. G. ROMA. IM. S. A. **Note:** Dav. #3747.

Date	Mintage	VG	F	VF	XF	Unc
(1)6ZZ	—	375	750	1,350	2,200	—

KM# 132 THALER

Silver Weight varies: 28-29g., 43 mm. **Ruler:** Jobst Hermann **Obv:** Shield of 4-fold arms with central shield, 3 ornate helmets above **Obv. Legend:** IUSTUS. HARM. - D. G. C. H. S. (E.) S. D. G. **Rev:** Crowned imperial eagle, orb on breast, date at end of legend **Rev. Legend:** FERDINANDUS. II. D. G. ROM(A). IM(P). S. A. **Note:** Dav. #3748.

Date	Mintage	VG	F	VF	XF	Unc
16ZZ	—	375	750	1,350	2,200	—

KM# 133 THALER

Silver Weight varies: 28-29g., 43 mm. **Ruler:** Jobst Hermann **Obv:** Shield of 4-fold arms with central shield, 3 ornate helmets above **Obv. Legend:** IUSTUS. HARM. - D. G. C. H. S. S. D. G. **Rev:** Crowned imperial eagle, orb on breast, date at end of legend **Rev. Legend:** FERDINANDUS. II. D. G. ROMA. IM. S. A. **Note:** Dav. #3748A.

Date	Mintage	VG	F	VF	XF	Unc
(1)6ZZ	—	375	750	1,350	2,200	—

KM# 139 THALER

Silver Weight varies: 28-29g., 43 mm. **Ruler:** Jobst Hermann **Obv:** Shield of 4-fold arms with central shield, 3 ornate helmets above **Obv. Legend:** IVST. HERM. D. G. C. H. S. E. S. D. G. ET. BE. **Rev:** Crowned imperial eagle, orb on breast, date divided by tail at bottom **Rev. Legend:** FERDINANDVS. II. - DG. RO. IM. SEM. AV(G). **Note:** Dav. #3751.

Date	Mintage	VG	F	VF	XF	Unc
16Z4	—	375	750	1,350	2,200	—

KM# 138 THALER

Silver Weight varies: 28-29g., 43 mm. **Ruler:** Jobst Hermann **Obv:** Shield of 4-fold arms with central shield, 3 ornate helmets above **Obv. Legend:** IVST. HERM. D. G. C. H. S. E. S. D. G. ET. B(E)(R). **Rev:** Crowned imperial eagle, orb on breast, date at end of legend **Rev. Legend:** FERDINANDUS. II. D. G. RO. IM. S. AU. **Note:** Dav. #3750.

Date	Mintage	VG	F	VF	XF	Unc
16Z4	—	375	750	1,350	2,200	—

KM# 140 THALER

Silver Weight varies: 28-29g., 43 mm. **Ruler:** Jobst Hermann **Obv:** Shield of 4-fold arms with central shield, 3 ornate helmets above **Obv. Legend:** IUS. HER. D. G. CO. HOL. S. ET. S. D. G. ET. B. **Rev:** Crowned imperial eagle, orb on breast, date at end of legend **Rev. Legend:** FERDINANDUS. II. D. G. RO(M). IM(P). S(EM). AU. **Note:** Dav. #3752.

Date	Mintage	VG	F	VF	XF	Unc
16Z8	—	375	750	1,300	2,200	—
ND	—	375	750	1,300	2,200	—

KM# 141 THALER

Silver Weight varies: 28-29g., 43 mm. **Ruler:** Jobst Hermann **Obv:** Shield of 4-fold arms with central shield, 3 ornate helmets above **Obv. Legend:** IUS. HER. D. G. CO. HOL. S. ET. S. D. G. ET. B. **Rev:** Crowned imperial eagle, orb on breast, date at end of legend **Rev. Legend:** FERDINANDUS. II. D. G. RO. IM. S. AV. **Note:** Dav. #3752A.

Date	Mintage	VG	F	VF	XF	Unc
16Z8	—	375	750	1,350	2,200	—

KM# 143 THALER

Silver Weight varies: 28-29g., 43 mm. **Ruler:** Jobst Hermann **Obv:** Shield of 4-fold arms with central shield, 3 ornate helmets above **Obv. Legend:** IUS. HER. D. G. CO. HOL. S. ET. S. D. G. ET. B. **Rev:** Crowned imperial eagle, orb on breast, date divided by tail at bottom **Rev. Legend:** FERDINANDUS. II. D. G. R(O). IM. SEM. AV(G). **Note:** Dav. #3753.

Date	Mintage	VG	F	VF	XF	Unc
16Z8	—	200	400	675	1,450	—

KM# 55 THALER (28 Groschen)

Silver Weight varies: 28-29g., 41-43 mm. **Ruler:** Ernst III **Obv:** 4-fold arms with central shield, three helmets above **Obv. Legend:** ERNESTUS. D.G. - H. S. E. S. CO. D. G. **Rev:** Crowned imperial eagle, 'Z8' in orb on breast, date divided below **Rev. Legend:** RUDOL II. D.G. ROMA. IMPER. SEMPER. AUG. **Mint:** Altona **Note:** Dav. 3731A. Ref. W-119.

Date	Mintage	VG	F	VF	XF	Unc
1610 (q)	—	265	475	800	1,650	—

KM# 63 THALER (28 Groschen)

Silver Weight varies: 28-29g., 41-43 mm. **Ruler:** Ernst III **Obv:** Shield of 4-fold arms with central shield of nettle leaf, 3 ornate helmets above, date at end of legend **Obv. Legend:** ERNESTUS. D: G. HOL: S: E: S: CO: D. G. **Rev:** Crowned imperial eagle, 'Z8' in orb on breast **Rev. Legend:** RUDOL. II. D.G. ROMA. IMPER: SEMPER. AUG. **Mint:** Altona **Note:** Dav. 3734. Ref. W-122.

Date	Mintage	VG	F	VF	XF	Unc
1611 (q)	—	265	475	800	1,650	—

KM# 70 THALER (28 Groschen)

Silver Weight varies: 28-29g., 41-43 mm. **Ruler:** Ernst III **Obv:** Shield of 4-fold arms with central shield, 3 ornate helmets above, date divided among helmets **Obv. Legend:** ERNESTVS. D. G. HOL. S. E. S. C. D. G. **Rev:** Crowned imperial eagle, value Z8 in orb on breast **Rev. Legend:** RUDOL. II. D. G. ROMA. IMPER. SEMPER. AVG. **Mint:** Altona **Note:** Dav. #3735.

Date	Mintage	VG	F	VF	XF	Unc
1612 (q)	—	280	475	875	1,900	—

KM# 71 THALER (28 Groschen)
Silver Weight varies: 28-29g., 41-43 mm. **Ruler:** Ernst III **Obv:** Shield of 4-fold arms with central shield, 3 ornate helmets above **Obv. Legend:** ERNESTUS. D. G. - H. S. E. S. CO. D. G. **Rev:** Crowned imperial eagle, value Z8 in orb on breast **Rev. Legend:** RUDOL. II. D. G. ROMA - IMPER. SEMPER. AUG. **Mint:** Altona **Note:** Dav. #3736.

Date	Mintage	VG	F	VF	XF	Unc
ND(1613) (q)	—	350	725	1,050	2,000	—

KM# 142 THALER (32 Schilling)
Silver Weight varies: 28-29g., 43 mm. **Ruler:** Jobst Hermann **Obv:** 4-fold arms with central shield of nettle leaf, 3 ornate helmets above **Obv. Legend:** IUS. HER. D.G. CO. HOL. S. ET. - S. D. G. ET. - B. **Rev:** Crowned imperial eagle, '3Z' in orb on breast **Rev. Legend:** FERDINANDVS. II. D:G: ROM: IMP: S. AU: **Note:** Dav. #3752B. Ref. W-339.

Date	Mintage	VG	F	VF	XF	Unc
ND(1628)	—	200	400	725	1,450	—

KM# 23 1-1/2 THALER
Silver **Ruler:** Ernst III **Obv:** Shield of 4-fold arms with central shield, 3 ornate helmets above **Obv. Legend:** ERNEST, COM. - HOL. SCHAWENB. **Rev:** Count on horseback galloping to right **Rev. Legend:** HATS - GOT : VORSEN; SO : WIR - TS WOL: GESCHEN. **Note:** Dav. #LS463. Ref. W-103.

Date	Mintage	VG	F	VF	XF	Unc
(1)603 Rare	—	—	—	—	—	—

KM# 32 1-1/2 THALER
Silver **Ruler:** Ernst III **Obv:** Shield of 4-fold arms with central shield, 3 ornate helmets above **Obv. Legend:** ERNEST. D. G. PRINC. E. COM. HOLSAT. SCHAWENB. COM. STERNB. DOM. GEH. **Rev:** Count on horseback galloping to right **Rev. Legend:** HATS. - GODT. VERSEHN. SO. WIRDTS. - GESCHEN. **Note:** Dav. #LS466. Ref. W-105.

Date	Mintage	VG	F	VF	XF	Unc
ND(1603) Rare	—	—	—	—	—	—

KM# 33 1-1/2 THALER
43.0500 g., Silver **Ruler:** Ernst III **Obv:** Shield of 4-fold arms with central shield, 3 ornate helmets above **Obv. Legend:** ERNESTUS. D. G. HOL. SC(H)A. E. ST(E). C. D. G. **Rev:** Count on horseback galloping to right **Rev. Legend:** HATS. - GOT. (V)(U)ORSEN. SO. WIRTS. WOL. - GESCHEN. **Note:** Dav. #LS473. Ref. W-104.

Date	Mintage	VG	F	VF	XF	Unc
ND(1603)	—	1,450	2,450	4,100	6,400	—

KM# 34 1-1/2 THALER
43.0000 g., Silver **Ruler:** Ernst III **Obv:** Shield of 4-fold arms with central shield, 3 ornate helmets above **Obv. Legend:** ERNES. D. G. C. H. - S. E. ST. E. DO. I. G. **Rev:** Count on horseback galloping to right **Rev. Legend:** HATS. GOT. VORSE. SO. WIR - TS - WOL. GESCHEN. **Note:** Dav. #LS476.

Date	Mintage	VG	F	VF	XF	Unc
ND(1603) Rare	—	—	—	—	—	—

KM# 35 1-1/2 THALER
43.0000 g., Silver **Ruler:** Ernst III **Obv:** Shield of 4-fold arms with central shield, 3 ornate helmets above **Obv. Legend:** ERNST: D: G: PRINC: E. COM. HOLSAT: SCHAWENB: COM: STERNB: DOM: GEH: **Rev:** Count on horseback galloping to right **Rev. Legend:** HATS + - GODT + VERSEHN + SO. WIRDTS + GESCHEN + **Note:** Dav. #LS482. Ref. W-106.

Date	Mintage	VG	F	VF	XF	Unc
ND(1603)	—	2,700	4,500	7,200	11,000	—

KM# 9 2 THALER
58.0000 g., Silver **Ruler:** Ernst III **Obv:** Helmeted arms **Rev:** Horseman **Note:** Dav. #LS458.

Date	Mintage	VG	F	VF	XF	Unc
1601 Rare	—	—	—	—	—	—

KM# 11 2 THALER
58.0000 g., Silver **Ruler:** Ernst III **Obv. Legend:** ERNST: D: G: CH... **Note:** Dav. #LS460.

Date	Mintage	VG	F	VF	XF	Unc
(1)601	—	3,600	6,400	10,000	14,000	—
(1)602	—	3,600	6,400	10,000	14,000	—

KM# 10 2 THALER
58.0000 g., Silver **Obv. Legend:** ADOLP. D: G. COM. HOL. SCH... **Note:** Dav. #LS549.

Date	Mintage	VG	F	VF	XF	Unc
ND Rare	—	—	—	—	—	—

KM# 24 2 THALER
58.0000 g., Silver **Ruler:** Ernst III **Obv:** Helmeted arms **Rev:** Horseman right **Note:** Dav. #LS462.

Date	Mintage	VG	F	VF	XF	Unc
(1)603	—	2,700	4,500	7,200	11,000	—

KM# 25 2 THALER

58.0000 g., Silver **Ruler:** Ernst III **Obv:** Helmeted arms **Rev:** Horseman **Note:** Dav. #LS464.

Date	Mintage	VG	F	VF	XF	Unc
(1)603 Rare	—	—	—	—	—	—

KM# 113 2 THALER

58.0000 g., Silver, 43 mm. **Ruler:** Ernst III **Obv:** Shield of 4-fold arms with central shield, 3 ornate helmets above **Obv. Legend:** ERNESTVS. DG: HOL: SCA: E: STE: C: D: G: **Rev:** Count on horseback galloping to right **Rev. Legend:** HATS: - GOT : VORSEN. SO. WIRTS. - WOL. GESCHEN. **Note:** Dav. #3744. Ref. W-102. Struck on thick, narrow flan.

Date	Mintage	VG	F	VF	XF	Unc
ND Rare	—	—	—	—	—	—

KM# 112 2 THALER

58.0000 g., Silver, 43 mm. **Ruler:** Ernst III **Obv:** Shield of 4-fold arms with central shield, 3 ornate helmets above **Obv. Legend:** ERNESTVS. D: G: C: HO: S: E: ST: D: I: G: **Rev:** Count on horseback galloping to right **Rev. Legend:** HATS: - GOT : VORSEN. SO. WIRTS. - WOL. GESCHEN. **Note:** Dav. #3743. Ref. W-101. Struck on thick, narrow flan.

Date	Mintage	VG	F	VF	XF	Unc
ND Rare	—	—	—	—	—	—

KM# 36 2 THALER

58.0000 g., Silver **Ruler:** Ernst III **Rev:** Without decoration below horse, only ground **Note:** Dav. #LS468.

Date	Mintage	VG	F	VF	XF	Unc
(1)606 Rare	—	—	—	—	—	—

KM# 37 2 THALER

58.0000 g., Silver **Ruler:** Ernst III **Rev:** Horseman with ground below **Note:** Dav. #LS470.

Date	Mintage	VG	F	VF	XF	Unc
(1)606 Rare	—	—	—	—	—	—

KM# 38 2 THALER

58.0000 g., Silver **Ruler:** Ernst III **Obv:** Shield of arms **Rev:** Horseman right, ground below **Mint:** Altona **Note:** Dav. #LS472. Illustration reduced.

Date	Mintage	VG	F	VF	XF	Unc
ND	—	1,750	2,950	4,900	7,800	—

KM# 39 2 THALER

58.0000 g., Silver **Ruler:** Ernst III **Obv:** Helmeted arms **Rev:** Horseman **Note:** Dav. #LS475. Illustration reduced.

Date	Mintage	VG	F	VF	XF	Unc
ND	—	2,700	4,500	7,200	11,000	—

KM# 40 2 THALER

58.0000 g., Silver **Ruler:** Ernst III **Obv:** Helmeted oval arms within circle **Rev:** Horseman within circle **Note:** Dav. #LS479. Illustration reduced.

Date	Mintage	VG	F	VF	XF	Unc
ND	—	3,600	6,400	10,000	14,000	—

KM# 41 2 THALER

58.0000 g., Silver **Ruler:** Ernst III **Obv:** Helmeted arms **Obv. Legend:** ERNEST: D: G: PRINC: E:... **Rev:** Horseman right **Note:** Dav. #LS481.

Date	Mintage	VG	F	VF	XF	Unc
ND Rare	—	—	—	—	—	—

KM# 12 2-1/2 THALER

Silver **Ruler:** Ernst III **Obv:** Helmeted oval arms within circle **Rev:** Horseman within circle **Note:** Dav. #LS478.

Date	Mintage	VG	F	VF	XF	Unc
ND Rare	—	—	—	—	—	—

KM# 26 3 THALER

87.0000 g., Silver **Ruler:** Ernst III **Obv:** Helmeted arms **Rev:** Horseman **Note:** Dav. #LS461.

Date	Mintage	VG	F	VF	XF	Unc
(1)603 Rare	—	—	—	—	—	—
ND	—	—	—	—	—	—

KM# 42 3 THALER

87.0000 g., Silver **Ruler:** Ernst III **Rev:** Horseman with ground below **Note:** Dav. #LS469.

Date	Mintage	VG	F	VF	XF	Unc
(1)606 Rare	—	—	—	—	—	—

KM# 43 3 THALER

87.0000 g., Silver **Ruler:** Ernst III **Obv:** Helmeted arms within circle **Rev:** Horseman right above ground **Note:** Dav. #LS471.

Date	Mintage	VG	F	VF	XF	Unc
ND	—	2,700	4,500	6,700	10,000	—

KM# 44 3 THALER

87.0000 g., Silver **Ruler:** Ernst III **Obv:** Helmeted oval arms within circle **Rev:** Horseman within circle **Note:** Dav. #LS477.

Date	Mintage	VG	F	VF	XF	Unc
ND Rare	—	—	—	—	—	—

KM# 45 3 THALER

87.0000 g., Silver **Ruler:** Ernst III **Obv:** Helmeted arms within circle **Obv. Legend:** IVSTVS... **Rev:** Horseman right within inner circle **Note:** Dav. #LS485.

Date	Mintage	VG	F	VF	XF	Unc
ND Rare	—	—	—	—	—	—

KM# 13 5 THALER

146.0000 g., Silver **Ruler:** Ernst III **Obv:** Helmeted arms **Rev:** Horseman **Note:** Dav. #LS480.

Date	Mintage	VG	F	VF	XF	Unc
ND Rare	—	—	—	—	—	—

TRADE COINAGE

KM# 27 GOLDGULDEN

Gold, 22-23.5 mm. **Ruler:** Ernst III **Obv:** Shield of 4-fold arms with central shield, 3 ornate helmets above **Obv. Legend:** M. AV. E. D. G. H. (-) S. E. S. C. E. D. G. **Rev:** Crowned imperial eagle in circle, date at end of legend **Rev. Legend:** RVDOL. II. ROM. IM(P). SEM. A(V). **Note:** Fr. 3062. Ref. W-82-87. Struck at Altona and Rinteln mints.

Date	Mintage	VG	F	VF	XF	Unc
1603 (a)	—	650	1,450	3,050	6,200	—
1604 (a)	—	650	1,450	3,050	6,200	—
1608 (q)	—	650	1,450	3,050	6,200	—
1610 (q)	—	650	1,450	3,050	6,200	—
161Z (q)	—	650	1,450	3,050	6,200	—
161Z	—	650	1,450	3,050	6,200	—

KM# 78 GOLDGULDEN

Gold **Ruler:** Ernst III **Obv:** Shield of 4-fold arms with central shield, 3 ornate helmets above **Obv. Legend:** M. AV. E. D. G. H. S. E. S. C. E. D. G. **Rev:** Crowned imperial eagle in circle, date at end of legend **Rev. Legend:** MATTHIA. D. G. R. I. S. A. **Note:** Fr. 3063. Ref. W-88.

Date	Mintage	VG	F	VF	XF	Unc
1616	—	775	1,750	3,350	6,700	—

KM# 139A 4 DUCAT

14.5200 g., Gold, 42 mm. **Ruler:** Jobst Hermann **Obv:** 4-fold arms with Schaumburg arms in center, but not in shield, 3 ornate helmets above **Obv. Legend:** IVST9 HERM9 D: G. C. H. S. E. S. D. G. E. B. **Rev:** Crowned imperial eagle, orb on breast, date divided by eagle's claws **Rev. Legend:** FERDINANDVS. II. - D G. RO. IM. SEM. AV. **Note:** Ref. Ch. Lange, Berliner Münzblätter, 1910, p.469. Struck from Thaler dies, KM#139.

Date	Mintage	VG	F	VF	XF	Unc
16Z4 Rare	—	—	—	—	—	—

KM# 14 5 DUCAT (1/2 Portugalöser)

Gold, 45 mm. **Ruler:** Ernst III **Obv:** Shield of 4-fold arms with central shield, 3 ornate helmets above **Obv. Legend:** ERNESTVS. D. G. C. HO. S. E. ST. D. I. G. **Rev:** Count on horseback galloping to right, legend enclosed in garland **Rev. Legend:** HATS GODT VORSEHN SO WIRTS GESCHEN. **Note:** Fr. 3067. Ref. W-81. Struck from 1/2 Taler dies, KM#103.

Date	Mintage	VG	F	VF	XF	Unc
ND Rare	—	—	—	—	—	—

KM# 15.1 10 DUCAT (Portugalöser)

Gold, 45 mm. **Ruler:** Ernst III **Obv:** Shield of oval 4-fold arms with central shield, 3 ornate helmets above **Obv. Legend:** ERNESTVS. D: G: - C: HO. S. E. ST. D: I: G. **Rev:** Count on horseback galloping to right, garland around legend **Rev. Legend:** HATS. GOT. VOR - SEN. SO. WIRT - S. WOL. GESCHEN **Note:** Fr. 3066.

Date	Mintage	VG	F	VF	XF	Unc
ND Rare	—	—	—	—	—	—

KM# 15.2 10 DUCAT (Portugalöser)

Gold, 51 mm. **Ruler:** Ernst III **Obv:** Shield of 4-fold arms with central shield, 3 ornate helmets above **Obv. Legend:** ERNEST: D: G: PRINC: E. COM: HOLSAT: SCHAW: COM: STER: DN: G: **Rev:** Count on horseback galloping to right **Rev. Legend:** HATS. GODT. VERSEHN + SO. WIRDTS. GESCHEN + **Note:** Fr. 3066. Ref. W-80.

Date	Mintage	VG	F	VF	XF	Unc
ND Rare	—	—	—	—	—	—

KM# 16 20 DUCAT (2 Portugalöser)

Gold, 45 mm. **Ruler:** Ernst III **Obv:** Scene from Cana - the 7-headed dragon of Babylon with one head severed **Obv. Legend:** DIE ROTE HVR DE. DRACH: REIT. - DE KELC DS GIF: U: GREWELS. TREIT. **Rev:** Count on horseback galloping to right **Rev. Legend:** HATS. GODT. VO - RSEHN. SO. WI - RTS. GESCHEN. **Note:** Fr. 3064. Ref. W-79. Struck from 1/2 Taler dies, KM#105.

Date	Mintage	VG	F	VF	XF	Unc
ND Unique	—	—	—	—	—	—

KM# A17 20 DUCAT (2 Portugalöser)

Gold, 45 mm. **Ruler:** Ernst III **Obv:** Shield of oval 4-fold arms with central shield, 3 ornate helmets above **Obv. Legend:** ERNESTVS. D. G. - C. HO. S. E. ST. D: I: G: **Rev:** Count on horseback galloping to right **Rev. Legend:** HATS. GOT. VOR. SEN. SO. WIRT - S. WOL. GESCHEN. **Note:** Fr. 3065.

Date	Mintage	VG	F	VF	XF	Unc
ND Rare	—	—	—	—	—	—

SCHLESWIG-HOLSTEIN-GLUCKSBURG

Established upon the division of Schleswig-Holstein-Sonderburg in 1622, the duchy of Schleswig-Holstein-Glücksburg existed for about one and a half centuries. When the line became extinct in 1779, the lands and titles passed to Denmark.

RULERS

Philipp, 1622-1663
Christian, 1663-1698
Philipp Ernst, 1698-1729

DUCHY

STANDARD COINAGE

KM# 5 THALER

Silver **Obv:** Philip right **Rev:** Helmeted arms, date in legend **Note:** Dav. #3718.

Date	Mintage	VG	F	VF	XF	Unc
1632 Rare	—	—	—	—	—	—
ND Rare	—	—	—	—	—	—

Note: UBS Gold & Numismatics Auction 53, 1-2002, VF realized approximately $6,295.

TRIAL STRIKES

KM#	Date	Mintage	Identification	Mkt Val
TS1	ND	—	Thaler. Lead. Uniface, Christian.	—

SCHLESWIG-HOLSTEIN-GOTTORP

The line of Gottorp was established in 1533 as a territorial domain for the youngest son of Friedrich I, King of Denmark and Duke of Schleswig-Holstein. Many members of this line and a cadet line founded in 1702 became bishops of Lübeck (see). Duke Karl Peter Ulrich, whose father, Karl Friedrich, had married Anna of Russia, became Czar Peter III in 1762, but was killed shortly after his accession to the throne. His son, Paul, traded Gottorp to Denmark for Oldenburg in 1773 (see Oldenburg) and ruled Russia as Czar Paul I (1798-1901).

RULERS

Johann Adolf, 1590-1616
Friedrich III, 1616-1659
Christian Albrecht, 1659-1694
Land occupied by Danes, 1675-79 and 1683-89
Friedrich IV, 1694-1702

NOTE: For mint officials and arms, see Schleswig-Holstein.

Reference:

L = Christian Lange, ***Chr. Lange's Sammlun schleswig-holsteinischer Münzen und Medaillen.*** 2 vols., Berlin, 1908-12.

DUCHY

REGULAR COINAGE

KM# 139 SECHSLING (6 Pfennig)

Silver **Ruler:** Christian Albrecht **Obv:** Crowned arms of Schleswig in circle, titles of Christian Albrecht **Rev:** Inscription in circle, titles continued and date **Rev. Inscription:** I / SOSL.ING **Note:** Ref. L#408. Varieties exist.

Date	Mintage	VG	F	VF	XF	Unc
1682	—	7.00	15.00	35.00	70.00	—

KM# 149 SECHSLING (6 Pfennig)

Silver **Ruler:** Christian Albrecht **Obv:** Crowned 'CA' monogram divides date **Rev:** Oval Schleswig arms in cartouche, crown above, value **Rev. Inscription:** I. SOSLING **Note:** Ref. L#409a-409b.

Date	Mintage	VG	F	VF	XF	Unc
1693	—	—	—	—	—	—
1693 SC	—	—	—	—	—	—

KM# 131 SCHILLING

Silver **Ruler:** Christian Albrecht **Obv:** Crowned Schleswig arms in circle, titles of Christian Albrecht in legend **Rev. Inscription:** I / SCHIL / LING / LVBECS / (date) / C.M.B. **Note:** Ref. L#406.

Date	Mintage	VG	F	VF	XF	Unc
1681 C.M.B.	—	20.00	40.00	80.00	160	—

KM# 140 SCHILLING

Silver **Ruler:** Christian Albrecht **Obv:** Crowned Schleswig arms in circle, titles of Christian Albrecht in legend **Rev:** Inscription, initials or symbol, titles cont. and date **Rev. Inscription:** I / SCHIL / LVBES **Note:** Ref. L#407a-407b.

Date	Mintage	VG	F	VF	XF	Unc
1682	—	15.00	30.00	60.00	120	—
1682 CMB	—	15.00	30.00	60.00	120	—

KM# 150 SCHILLING

Silver **Ruler:** Christian Albrecht **Obv:** Crowned 'CA' monogram divides date **Rev:** Crowned oval Schleswig arms in cartouche **Rev. Inscription:** I. SCHILLING. LUBES. **Note:** Ref. L#407A.

Date	Mintage	VG	F	VF	XF	Unc
1693 SC	—	—	—	—	—	—

KM# 52 2 SCHILLING

Silver **Ruler:** Friedrich III **Obv:** Duke on horseback to left, Z SL below **Rev:** Titles of Friedrich III in 6-line inscription **Note:** Ref. L#359.

Date	Mintage	VG	F	VF	XF	Unc
ND(1616-59)	—	20.00	45.00	70.00	145	—

KM# 132 2 SCHILLING
Silver **Ruler:** Christian Albrecht **Obv:** Crowned Schleswig arms in circle, titles of Christian Albrecht in legend **Rev. Inscription:** II / SCHIL / LING / LVBECS / (date) **Note:** Ref. L#404A, 405.

Date	Mintage	VG	F	VF	XF	Unc
1681 CMB	—	70.00	135	250	475	—
1682	—	70.00	135	250	475	—

KM# 151 2 SCHILLING
Silver **Ruler:** Christian Albrecht **Obv:** Crowned 'CA' monogram divides date **Rev:** Oval Schleswig arms in cartouche, crown above **Rev. Inscription:** II. SCHILLING. LUBES **Note:** Ref. L#405A.

Date	Mintage	VG	F	VF	XF	Unc
1693 SC	—	—	—	—	—	—

KM# 157 2 SCHILLING
Silver **Ruler:** Friedrich IV **Obv:** Crowned double mirror-image 'F' monogram **Obv. Legend:** CONSTANTIA. ET. LABORE. **Rev. Inscription:** II / SCHIL / LING / (date) **Note:** Ref. L#439.

Date	Mintage	VG	F	VF	XF	Unc
1696	—	15.00	30.00	60.00	120	—
1697	—	15.00	30.00	60.00	120	—
1698	—	15.00	30.00	60.00	120	—
1699	—	15.00	30.00	60.00	120	—

KM# 44 4 SCHILLING
Silver **Ruler:** Friedrich III **Obv:** Duke on horseback to left, 4 SL below **Rev:** Titles of Friedrich III in 6 line inscription **Note:** Ref. L#358E. Varieties exist.

Date	Mintage	VG	F	VF	XF	Unc
ND(1616-59)	—	—	—	—	—	—

KM# 155 4 SCHILLING
Silver **Ruler:** Friedrich IV **Obv:** Crowned double mirror-image 'F' monogram **Obv. Legend:** CONSTANTIA. ET. LABORE. **Rev:** Crowned oval Schleswig arms in cartouche **Rev. Inscription:** IIII. SCHILLING. (date) **Note:** Ref. L#431-32, 434, 436-38; Schön#1 for 1702.

Date	Mintage	VG	F	VF	XF	Unc
1695	—	12.00	30.00	55.00	115	—
1696	—	12.00	30.00	55.00	115	—
1697	—	12.00	30.00	55.00	115	—
1698	—	12.00	30.00	55.00	115	—
1699	—	12.00	30.00	55.00	115	—
1700	—	12.00	30.00	55.00	115	—

KM# 158 4 SCHILLING
Silver **Ruler:** Friedrich IV **Obv:** Bust right, titles of Friedrich IV in legend **Rev:** Crowned oval arms of Schleswig in cartouche divide 4 - S **Rev. Legend:** CONSTANTIA - ET. LABORE. **Note:** Ref. L#433.

Date	Mintage	VG	F	VF	XF	Unc
1696	—	18.00	35.00	75.00	150	—
1697	—	18.00	35.00	75.00	150	—
1698	—	18.00	35.00	75.00	150	—

KM# 163 4 SCHILLING
Silver **Ruler:** Friedrich IV **Obv:** Crowned shield of Schleswig arms **Obv. Legend:** MONETA. SLESVICENSIS. **Rev:** Plan of the Stapelholm fortifications **Rev. Legend:** SVPREMVS. LABOR. IN CONSTANTIA. (date) **Note:** Ref. L#435. Struck from 1 Ducat dies, KM#168.

Date	Mintage	VG	F	VF	XF	Unc
1698	—	65.00	100	150	300	—

KM# 164 8 SCHILLING
Silver **Ruler:** Friedrich IV **Obv:** Crowned shield of Schleswig arms **Obv. Legend:** MONETA. SLESVICENSIS. **Rev:** Plan of the Stapelholm fortifications **Rev. Legend:** SVPREMVS. LABOR, IN CONSTANTIA. (date) **Note:** Ref. L#430B. Struck from 1 Ducat dies, KM#168.

Date	Mintage	VG	F	VF	XF	Unc
1698	—	—	—	—	—	—

KM# 91 1/192 THALER (Dreiling)
0.4600 g., Silver **Ruler:** Friedrich III **Obv:** Schleswig arms in circle, titles of Friedrich III in legend **Rev:** Value '192' in cartouche, titles continued, date **Note:** Ref. L#358CIV, 358D, 358DI, 358DII. Varieties exist.

Date	Mintage	VG	F	VF	XF	Unc
164Z HG	—	25.00	45.00	90.00	180	—
1645 (k)	—	25.00	45.00	90.00	180	—
1646 (k)	—	25.00	45.00	90.00	180	—
1653 (k)	—	25.00	45.00	90.00	180	—

KM# 104 1/192 THALER (Dreiling)
Silver **Ruler:** Christian Albrecht **Obv:** Two lions walking left **Rev:** 192 in sunburst **Note:** Prev. KM#50.

Date	Mintage	VG	F	VF	XF	Unc
1661	—	27.00	55.00	100	200	—
1662	—	27.00	55.00	100	200	—
1663	—	27.00	55.00	100	200	—
1668	—	27.00	55.00	100	200	—
1670	—	27.00	55.00	100	200	—
1671	—	27.00	55.00	100	200	—
1675	—	27.00	55.00	100	200	—

KM# 81 1/128 THALER
Silver **Ruler:** Friedrich III **Obv:** Schleswig arms in circle, titles of Friedrich III in legend **Rev:** Value '1Z8' in cartouche, titles continued, date **Note:** Ref. L#358CI-358CIII. Varieties exist.

Date	Mintage	VG	F	VF	XF	Unc
1632	—	20.00	45.00	90.00	180	—
1636	—	20.00	45.00	90.00	180	—
1642	—	20.00	45.00	90.00	180	—

KM# 55 1/96 THALER (Sechsling)
Silver **Ruler:** Friedrich III **Obv:** Schleswig arms in circle, titles of Friedrich III in legend **Rev:** Small circle with '96' superimposed on cross, titles continued, date **Note:** Ref. L#354a-354b, 356. Varieties exist.

Date	Mintage	VG	F	VF	XF	Unc
(1)621	—	15.00	35.00	70.00	145	—
1621	—	15.00	35.00	70.00	145	—
16Z4 ST	—	15.00	35.00	70.00	145	—

KM# 59 1/96 THALER (Sechsling)
Silver **Ruler:** Friedrich III **Obv:** Holstein arms in quatrefoil superimposed on cross, titles of Friedrich III in legend **Rev:** Imperial orb with value '96', titles continued, date **Note:** Ref. L#354A, 355A. Varieties exist.

Date	Mintage	VG	F	VF	XF	Unc
(1)6ZZ ST	—	15.00	35.00	70.00	145	—
16Z3 ST	—	15.00	35.00	70.00	145	—

KM# 68 1/96 THALER (Sechsling)
Silver **Ruler:** Friedrich III **Obv:** Holstein arms in quatrefoil superimposed on cross, titles of Friedrich III in legend **Rev:** Imperial orb with value '96' **Rev. Legend:** VIRT: GLORIA. M:, (date) **Note:** Ref. L#355.

Date	Mintage	VG	F	VF	XF	Unc
(1)6Z3 ST	—	—	—	—	—	—

KM# 92 1/96 THALER (Sechsling)
Silver **Ruler:** Friedrich III **Obv:** Holstein arms in trefoil, titles of Friedrich III in legend **Rev:** Small shield with value '96' in circle, titles continued and date in legend **Note:** Ref. L#357.

Date	Mintage	VG	F	VF	XF	Unc
164Z HG	—	—	—	—	—	—

KM# 96 1/96 THALER (Sechsling)
Silver **Ruler:** Friedrich III **Obv:** Holstein arms in circle, titles of Friedrich III in legend **Rev:** Small shield with value '96' in circle, titles continued and date in legend **Note:** Ref. L#357A-357B, 358-358C. Varieties exist.

Date	Mintage	VG	F	VF	XF	Unc
1646 (k)	—	15.00	30.00	60.00	120	—
1647 (k)	—	15.00	30.00	60.00	120	—
1650 (k)	—	15.00	30.00	60.00	120	—
1652 (k)	—	15.00	30.00	60.00	120	—
1653 (k)	—	15.00	30.00	60.00	120	—
1657 (k)	—	15.00	30.00	60.00	120	—

KM# 105 1/96 THALER (Sechsling)
Silver **Ruler:** Christian Albrecht **Obv:** Three arrows and nine rays with ball ends around shield **Rev:** 96 in sunburst **Note:** Prev. KM#51.

Date	Mintage	VG	F	VF	XF	Unc
1661	—	45.00	90.00	165	325	—
1662	—	45.00	90.00	165	325	—
1663	—	45.00	90.00	165	325	—

KM# 111 1/96 THALER (Sechsling)
Silver **Ruler:** Christian Albrecht **Obv:** Three arrows and 11 thick wedges around shield **Rev:** 96 in center **Note:** Prev. KM#55.

Date	Mintage	VG	F	VF	XF	Unc
1668	—	16.00	35.00	75.00	155	—
1670	—	16.00	35.00	75.00	155	—
1671	—	16.00	35.00	75.00	155	—
1672	—	16.00	35.00	75.00	155	—
1675	—	16.00	35.00	75.00	155	—
1676	—	16.00	35.00	75.00	155	—

KM# 4 1/64 THALER
Silver **Ruler:** Johann Adolf **Obv:** Shield of Schleswig arms divides date, titles of Johann Adolf in legend **Rev:** Value '64' in shield superimposed on cross in circle **Rev. Legend:** MO. NO. SCLESWICEN (or variant), (date) **Note:** Ref. L#307-312. Varieties exist.

Date	Mintage	VG	F	VF	XF	Unc
(1)60Z (c)	—	15.00	35.00	75.00	150	300
(1)604 (c)	—	15.00	35.00	75.00	150	300

KM# 174 1/48 THALER
Silver **Ruler:** Friedrich IV **Obv:** Crowned double mirror-image script 'F' monogram **Obv. Legend:** CONSTANTIA. ET. LABORE. **Rev. Inscription:** 48 / I: REICHS / THALER / (date) **Note:** Ref. L#439A, 440-441; Sch?n #2 for 1699. Varieties exist.

Date	Mintage	VG	F	VF	XF	Unc
1699	—	10.00	25.00	50.00	100	—
1700	—	10.00	25.00	50.00	100	—

KM# 6 1/32 THALER (Schilling)
Silver **Ruler:** Johann Adolf **Obv:** Schleswig arms in circle, titles of Johann Adolf in legend **Rev:** Value '3Z' in shield superimposed on cross in circle **Rev. Legend:** MO. NO. SCLESWICEN (or variant), (date) **Note:** Ref. L#304-305A. Varieties exist.

Date	Mintage	VG	F	VF	XF	Unc
(1)601 (c)	—	18.00	35.00	55.00	100	—

KM# 8 1/24 THALER (Groschen)
Silver **Ruler:** Johann Adolf **Obv:** 4-fold arms with central shield, 3 helmets above, titles of Johann Adolf in legend **Rev:** Imperial orb with value 24 or Z4 divides date **Rev. Legend:** MONETA. NOVA. HOLST (or variant) **Note:** Ref. L#295A, 298-300, 301, 303A. Varieties exist.

Date	Mintage	VG	F	VF	XF	Unc
(1)601 (c)	—	12.00	30.00	50.00	100	—
(1)60Z (c)	—	12.00	30.00	50.00	100	—
(1)603 (c)	—	12.00	30.00	50.00	100	—

KM# 7 1/24 THALER (Groschen)
Silver **Ruler:** Johann Adolf **Obv:** 4-fold arms with central shield, 3 helmets above, titles of Johann Adolf in legend **Rev:** Imperial orb with value 24 or Z4 divides date, titles of Rudolf II in legend **Note:** Ref. L#295B, 296-297, 302, 302d, 303. Varieties exist.

Date	Mintage	VG	F	VF	XF	Unc
(1)601 (f)	—	12.00	30.00	50.00	100	—
(1)60Z (f)	—	12.00	30.00	50.00	100	—
160Z	—	12.00	30.00	50.00	100	—
1603 (g)	—	12.00	30.00	50.00	100	—

KM# 40 1/18-1/2 THALER (2 Schilling)

Silver **Ruler:** Johann Adolf **Obv:** 4-fold arms with central shield, 3 helmets above, titles of Johann Adolf in legend **Rev:** Crowned imperial eagle, value 18-1/2 in orb on breast, titles of Matthias and date in legend **Note:** Ref. L#293-94. Varieties exist.

Date	Mintage	VG	F	VF	XF	Unc
(1)614 MP	—	18.00	40.00	65.00	130	—
(1)615 (e)	—	18.00	40.00	65.00	130	—

KM# 5 1/16 THALER

Silver **Ruler:** Johann Adolf **Obv:** Round Schleswig arms, titles of Johann Adolf in legend **Rev:** Small shield with value '16' superimposed on floriated cross **Rev. Legend:** MONETA. NOVA. SCHLESWI (or variant), (date) **Note:** Ref. L#280-290; Slg. Roeper #3069 for 1594. Varieties exist.

Date	Mintage	VG	F	VF	XF	Unc
(1)601 (c)	—	14.00	28.00	55.00	115	—
(1)60Z (c)	—	14.00	28.00	55.00	115	—
(1)603 (c)	—	14.00	28.00	55.00	115	—
(1)604 (c)	—	14.00	28.00	55.00	115	—
(1)605 (c)	—	14.00	28.00	55.00	115	—

KM# 12 1/16 THALER

Silver **Ruler:** Johann Adolf **Obv:** 6-fold arms with central shield, 3 helmets above, titles of Johann Adolf in legend **Rev:** Imperial orb with value '16' superimposed on floriated cross, titles of Rudolf II and date in legend **Note:** Ref. L#287A, 288b, 289Aa, 289Ab, 291-92. Varieties exist.

Date	Mintage	VG	F	VF	XF	Unc
160Z (g)	—	12.00	25.00	50.00	100	—
1603 (g)	—	12.00	25.00	50.00	100	—
(1)604 (g)	—	12.00	25.00	50.00	100	—
1604 (g)	—	12.00	25.00	50.00	100	—
(1)607 (g)	—	12.00	25.00	50.00	100	—
(1)608 (g)	—	12.00	25.00	50.00	100	—

KM# 42 1/16 THALER

Silver **Ruler:** Johann Adolf **Obv:** 5-fold arms with central shield, 3 helmets above, titles of Johann Adolf in legend **Rev:** Imperial orb with value '16' superimposed on floriated cross, titles of Matthias and date in legend **Note:** Ref. L#292A.

Date	Mintage	VG	F	VF	XF	Unc
(1)615 (e)	—	20.00	45.00	90.00	180	—

KM# 46 1/16 THALER

Silver **Ruler:** Friedrich III **Obv:** 5-fold arms with central shield Schleswig, 3 helmets above, titles of Friedrich III in legend **Rev:** Value '16' in circle within quatrefoil superimposed on cross, titles cont. and date in legend **Note:** Ref. L#339, 339C.

Date	Mintage	VG	F	VF	XF	Unc
(1)617	—	20.00	40.00	80.00	160	—
(1)619	—	20.00	40.00	80.00	160	—

KM# 46a 1/16 THALER

Silver **Ruler:** Friedrich III **Obv:** Shield of 5-fold arms with central shield of Schleswig **Obv. Legend:** FRIDERICVS. D. G. HER. NOR. **Rev:** 3 ornate helmets in circle, value '16' below, date at end of legend **Rev. Legend:** DVX. SCHLES: H. HOLSA. **Note:** Ref. L#339Aa.

Date	Mintage	VG	F	VF	XF	Unc
1617	—	20.00	45.00	90.00	180	—

KM# 69 1/16 THALER

Silver **Ruler:** Friedrich III **Obv:** Bust right in circle, titles of Friedrich III in legend **Rev:** Inscription in circle **Rev. Legend:** VIRTUT GLORIA MERC. (date) **Rev. Inscription:** XVI / REIS / DAL (or variant) **Note:** Ref. L#340a-c, 341, 341A, 341B. Varieties exist.

Date	Mintage	VG	F	VF	XF	Unc
(1)6Z3 ST	—	15.00	27.00	55.00	110	—
16Z3 ST	—	15.00	27.00	55.00	110	—
(1)6Z4 ST	—	15.00	27.00	55.00	110	—
(1)625 ST	—	15.00	27.00	55.00	110	—
(16)Z8	—	15.00	27.00	55.00	110	—

KM# 93 1/16 THALER

Silver **Ruler:** Friedrich III **Obv:** Large bust right, titles of Friedrich III in legend **Rev:** Value inscription within circle **Rev. Legend:** VIRTVT GLORIA MERC, (date) **Rev. Inscription:** XVI / I. REIC / HS: DA (or variant) **Note:** Ref. L#342-353. Varieties exist.

Date	Mintage	VG	F	VF	XF	Unc
164Z HG	—	15.00	27.00	55.00	110	—
1645 (k)	—	15.00	27.00	55.00	110	—
1646 (k)	—	15.00	27.00	55.00	110	—
1647 (k)	—	15.00	27.00	55.00	110	—
1648 (k)	—	15.00	27.00	55.00	110	—
1649 (k)	—	15.00	27.00	55.00	110	—
1650 (k)	—	15.00	27.00	55.00	110	—
1651 (k)	—	15.00	27.00	55.00	110	—
1652 (k)	—	15.00	27.00	55.00	110	—
1653 (k)	—	15.00	27.00	55.00	110	—
1657 (k)	—	15.00	27.00	55.00	110	—
1658 (k)	—	15.00	27.00	55.00	110	—

KM# 106 1/16 THALER

Silver **Ruler:** Christian Albrecht **Obv:** Tall bust right breaks inner circle at top **Rev:** Value within legend **Note:** Reichs 1/16 Thaler. Prev. KM#52.

Date	Mintage	VG	F	VF	XF	Unc
1661	—	27.00	55.00	90.00	185	—
1662	—	27.00	55.00	90.00	185	—
1663	—	27.00	55.00	90.00	185	—
1664	—	27.00	55.00	90.00	185	—
1665	—	27.00	55.00	90.00	185	—

KM# 112 1/16 THALER

Silver **Ruler:** Christian Albrecht **Obv:** Tall bust right breaks inner circle at bottom **Note:** Prev. KM#56.

Date	Mintage	VG	F	VF	XF	Unc
1668	—	27.00	55.00	90.00	185	—
1669	—	27.00	55.00	90.00	185	—

KM# 113 1/16 THALER

Silver **Ruler:** Christian Albrecht **Obv:** Short bust right within inner circle **Note:** Prev. KM#57.

Date	Mintage	VG	F	VF	XF	Unc
1669	—	33.00	55.00	90.00	185	—
1670	—	33.00	55.00	90.00	185	—
1671	—	33.00	55.00	90.00	185	—
1675	—	33.00	55.00	90.00	185	—

KM# 126 1/16 THALER

Silver **Ruler:** Christian Albrecht **Obv:** Short bust right without inner circle **Note:** Prev. KM#68.

Date	Mintage	VG	F	VF	XF	Unc
1675	—	27.00	55.00	90.00	185	—

KM# 60 1/8 THALER

Silver **Ruler:** Friedrich III **Obv:** Bust right in circle, titles of Friedrich III in legend **Rev:** Crowned 5-fold arms with central shield, titles continued and date **Note:** Ref. L#335.

Date	Mintage	VG	F	VF	XF	Unc
(16)ZZ ST	—	90.00	180	360	—	—

KM# 75 1/8 THALER

Silver **Ruler:** Friedrich III **Obv:** Bust right in circle, titles of Friedrich III in legend **Rev:** Value inscription in circle **Rev. Legend:** VIRTVTIS. GLORIA. MERCES (or variant), (date) **Rev. Inscription:** VIII / EINEN / REICHS / DALER **Note:** Ref. L#336-338A. Varieties exist.

Date	Mintage	VG	F	VF	XF	Unc
(1)625 ST	—	30.00	65.00	130	265	—
1626	—	30.00	65.00	130	265	—
1635 PT	—	30.00	65.00	130	265	—
1636 PT	—	30.00	65.00	130	265	—
1656 (k)	—	30.00	65.00	130	265	—
1657 (k)	—	30.00	65.00	130	265	—

KM# 24 1/4 THALER

Silver **Ruler:** Johann Adolf **Obv:** Bust right in circle, titles of Johann Adolf in legend **Rev:** 5-fold arms with central shield, 3 helmets above, date divided below, titles continued in legend **Note:** Ref. L#277B, 278A, 279.

Date	Mintage	VG	F	VF	XF	Unc
1609	—	—	—	—	—	—
161Z	—	—	—	—	—	—
1617	—	—	—	—	—	—

Note: Posthumous

KM# 32 1/4 THALER

Silver **Ruler:** Johann Adolf **Obv:** Bust right breaks legend at top, titles of Johann Adolf in legend **Rev:** 5-fold arms with central shield, 3 helmets above, date divided below, titles continued **Note:** Ref. L#277A, 278.

Date	Mintage	VG	F	VF	XF	Unc
ND(1611)	—	550	1,000	1,800	3,250	—
1611 MP	—	550	1,000	1,800	3,250	—

KM# 61 1/4 THALER

Silver **Ruler:** Friedrich III **Obv:** Bust right in circle, titles of Friedrich III in legend **Rev:** 5-fold arms with central shield, 3 helmets above **Rev. Legend:** VIRT: GLOR: - MERCES. (date) **Note:** Ref. L#333.

Date	Mintage	VG	F	VF	XF	Unc
(16)ZZ ST	—	110	200	350	725	—

KM# 70 1/4 THALER

Silver **Ruler:** Friedrich III **Obv:** Bust right in circle, titles of Friedrich III in legend **Rev:** 5-fold arms with central shield, 3 helmets above dividing date **Rev. Legend:** VIRT: GLOR: - MERCES. **Note:** Ref. L#334-334A.

Date	Mintage	VG	F	VF	XF	Unc
16Z3 ST	—	—	—	—	—	—
16Z4 ST	—	—	—	—	—	—

KM# 127 1/4 THALER
Silver **Ruler:** Christian Albrecht **Obv:** Bust right **Rev:** Shield of six parts **Note:** Prev. KM#69.

Date	Mintage	VG	F	VF	XF	Unc
1675	—	350	700	1,300	2,600	—
1676	—	350	700	1,300	2,600	—

KM# 14 1/2 THALER
Silver **Ruler:** Johann Adolf **Obv:** 1/2-length armored figure to right, titles of Johann Adolf in legend **Rev:** 6-fold arms with cross of L&#65533;beck in center divide date as 1-6 / 0-6, 3 helmets above, titles continued in legend **Note:** Ref. L#275A, 275B.

Date	Mintage	VG	F	VF	XF	Unc
1606 IG	—	—	—	—	—	—
1607 IG	—	—	—	—	—	—

KM# 20 1/2 THALER
Silver **Ruler:** Johann Adolf **Obv:** 1/2-length armored figure to right, titles of Johann Adolf in legend **Rev:** 5-fold arms with central shield, date divided among 3 helmets above, titles continued in legend **Note:** Ref. L#275C.

Date	Mintage	VG	F	VF	XF	Unc
1608 HP	—	—	—	—	—	—

KM# 25 1/2 THALER
Silver **Ruler:** Johann Adolf **Obv:** Bearded bust right, titles of Johann Adolf in legend **Rev:** 5-fold arms with central shield, 3 helmets above, titles continued and date in legend **Note:** Ref. L#276-77.

Date	Mintage	VG	F	VF	XF	Unc
1609	—	225	400	650	1,225	—
1611	—	225	400	650	1,225	—
1612	—	475	750	1,000	2,000	—

KM# 62 1/2 THALER
Silver **Ruler:** Friedrich III **Obv:** Bust right in circle, titles of Friedrich III in legend **Rev:** 5-fold arms with central shield, 3 helmets above **Rev. Legend:** VIRT: GLOR: - MERCES. (date) **Note:** Ref. L#329, 331a.

Date	Mintage	VG	F	VF	XF	Unc
(16)ZZ (t)	—	275	550	1,100	—	—
(1)6Z6 ST	—	275	550	1,100	—	—

KM# 71 1/2 THALER
Silver **Ruler:** Friedrich III **Obv:** Bust right in circle, titles of Friedrich III in legend **Rev:** 5-fold arms with central shield, 3 helmets above divide date **Rev. Legend:** VIRT: GLOR: - MERCES. **Note:** Ref. L#330, 331b, 332, 332A. Varieties exist.

Date	Mintage	VG	F	VF	XF	Unc
16Z3 ST	—	175	250	350	675	—
(1)626 ST	—	175	250	350	675	—
1627 ST	—	175	250	350	675	—
16Z8 (j)	—	175	250	350	675	—

KM# 117 1/2 THALER
Silver **Ruler:** Christian Albrecht **Obv:** Armored and draped bust right **Rev:** Crowned shield between palm branches **Note:** Prev. KM#61.

Date	Mintage	VG	F	VF	XF	Unc
1673	—	750	1,400	2,700	5,300	—

KM# 115 2/3 THALER
Silver **Ruler:** Christian Albrecht **Obv:** Crowned CA monogram **Rev:** Crowned shield, value below **Note:** Prev. KM#60.

Date	Mintage	VG	F	VF	XF	Unc
1672	—	200	400	750	1,500	—

KM# 129 2/3 THALER
Silver **Ruler:** Christian Albrecht **Rev:** Crowned shield, mintmaster's initials below **Note:** Prev. KM#70.

Date	Mintage	VG	F	VF	XF	Unc
1676	—	1,000	1,650	3,000	6,000	—

KM# 130 2/3 THALER
Silver **Ruler:** Christian Albrecht **Obv:** Armored and draped bust right **Rev:** Crowned shield between palm branches **Note:** Prev. KM#71.

Date	Mintage	VG	F	VF	XF	Unc
1676	—	—	—	—	—	—

KM# 143 2/3 THALER
Silver **Ruler:** Christian Albrecht **Rev:** Crowned shield divides date **Note:** Prev. KM#79.

Date	Mintage	VG	F	VF	XF	Unc
1683	—	1,000	1,650	3,000	6,000	—
1688	—	1,000	1,650	3,000	6,000	—

KM# 145 2/3 THALER
Silver **Ruler:** Christian Albrecht **Obv:** Value in oval below armored and draped bust right **Rev:** Crowned shield **Note:** Prev. KM#80.

Date	Mintage	VG	F	VF	XF	Unc
1689	—	1,000	1,650	3,000	6,000	—

KM# 16 THALER
Silver **Ruler:** Johann Adolf **Obv:** 6-fold arms with central shield, date divided near bottom, 3 ornate helmets above, titles of Johann Adolf in legend **Rev:** 1/2-length armored figure to right holding mace **Rev. Legend:** ★ STOR: ... **Note:** Ref. L#264c.

Date	Mintage	VG	F	VF	XF	Unc
1607 Rare	—	—	—	—	—	—

KM# 21 THALER
Silver **Ruler:** Johann Adolf **Obv:** Bust right **Obv. Legend:** IOHAN: ADOLPH: D: G: HERES * NORWEGI. **Rev:** Helmeted arms in cartouche design, date divided in helmets **Rev. Legend:** DVX. SLE. HO. S. - E: DI. CO: O: E. DE. **Note:** Dav. #3682. Prev. KM#5.

Date	Mintage	VG	F	VF	XF	Unc
1608 HP Rare	—	—	—	—	—	—
Note: Künker Auction 176, 9-10, XF realized approximately $10,160.						
1609 Rare	—	—	—	—	—	—

KM# 22 THALER
Silver **Ruler:** Johann Adolf **Obv:** Half-length armored figure to right holding field marshall's baton **Obv. Legend:** IOHAN • ADOLF • D:G • HERES • NORV • DVX • SL **Rev:** Shield of 6-fold arms, 3 ornate helmets above with date spaced between them **Rev. Legend:** D S H S E DI - C O E D M N S. **Note:** Ref. Dav. 3683. Prev. KM#6.

Date	Mintage	VG	F	VF	XF	Unc
1608 MP Rare	—	—	—	—	—	—

KM# 27 THALER
Silver **Ruler:** Johann Adolf **Obv:** Older bust with beard **Obv. Legend:** IOH. ADOL. D. G. HAER • **Rev:** Helmeted arms wider at bottom, date **Rev. Legend:** E DITM. COM. OLDENB. & DELMENHOR **Note:** Ref. Dav. 3687. Prev. KM#8.

Date	Mintage	VG	F	VF	XF	Unc
1609 Rare	—	—	—	—	—	—

KM# 26 THALER
Silver **Ruler:** Johann Adolf **Obv:** Bust right **Obv. Legend:** IOHAN • ADOLF • NORWEGI **Rev. Legend:** D. S. H. S. E. DI. - C. O. E. D. M. N. S. **Note:** Dav. 3684. Prev. KM#7.

Date	Mintage	VG	F	VF	XF	Unc
1609 Rare	—	—	—	—	—	—

KM# 33 THALER
Silver **Ruler:** Johann Adolf **Obv. Legend:** IOHAN * ADOLPH * D * G * HERES ... **Rev. Legend:** SLEIS • HOL • ST. - DIT • CO • O. E. DE. **Note:** Some coins have an orb above the duke's head in the legend. Dav. 3688. Prev. KM#12.

Date	Mintage	VG	F	VF	XF	Unc
1611 MP	—	190	325	575	1,000	—
1612 MP	—	190	325	575	1,000	—
1615	—	190	325	575	1,000	—

KM# 34 THALER
28.7100 g., Silver **Ruler:** Johann Adolf **Rev:** Date divided at bottom by arms **Note:** Ref. Dav. 3689. Prev. KM#13.

Date	Mintage	VG	F	VF	XF	Unc
1611	—	190	325	575	1,000	—
1612	—	190	325	575	1,000	—

KM# 35 THALER

Silver **Ruler:** Johann Adolf **Rev. Legend:** ...E: DI: CO: O: E. DE. **Note:** Ref. Dav. 3690. Prev. KM#14.

Date	Mintage	VG	F	VF	XF	Unc
1611 MP	—	400	850	1,750	3,500	—

KM# 38 THALER

Silver **Ruler:** Johann Adolf **Obv:** Bust with ruff **Obv. Legend:** • NORWEGIAE: DVX **Rev:** Date divided in helmets **Note:** Ref. Dav. 3691. Prev. KM#15.

Date	Mintage	VG	F	VF	XF	Unc
1613 Rare	—	—	—	—	—	—

KM# 41 THALER

Silver **Ruler:** Johann Adolf **Obv:** Bust right **Rev. Legend:** • DIT. CO: O: E: DEL. **Note:** Dav. #3692. Prev. KM#16.

Date	Mintage	VG	F	VF	XF	Unc
1614	—	475	950	1,900	4,000	—

KM# 47 THALER

Silver **Ruler:** Friedrich III **Rev:** Date divided below arms **Rev. Legend:** D: C: O: E: CE: **Note:** Ref. Dav. 3693. Prev. KM#17.

Date	Mintage	VG	F	VF	XF	Unc
1617	—	475	950	1,900	4,000	—

KM# 49 THALER

Silver **Ruler:** Friedrich III **Obv:** Bust of Frederik right **Obv. Legend:** FRIDERICUS • D: G: HAERES • NORWEGIAE **Rev:** Helmeted arms, date divided in helmets **Rev. Legend:** DVX • SLES: HOL • - ST: DIT: C: OE: DE: **Note:** Ref. Dav. 3695. Prev. KM#18.

Date	Mintage	VG	F	VF	XF	Unc
1618	—	575	1,200	2,400	4,200	—
1620	—	575	1,200	2,400	4,200	—

KM# 57 THALER

Silver **Ruler:** Friedrich III **Obv. Legend:** • G: DUX. SLES: ET. HOLSA: **Rev. Legend:** VIRTUTIS GLOR - RIA MERCES 6Z1 **Note:** Ref. Dav. 3696. Prev. KM#25.

Date	Mintage	VG	F	VF	XF	Unc
1621 (t)	—	575	1,200	2,400	4,200	—

KM# 63 THALER

Silver **Ruler:** Friedrich III **Obv. Legend:** FRIDERICH • D: G: HERES • NORWE: DVX **Rev:** Date in helmets above arms **Rev. Legend:** SLEIS. HOL • **Note:** Ref. Dav. 3697. Prev. KM#26.

Date	Mintage	VG	F	VF	XF	Unc
1622	—	575	1,000	1,750	2,850	—

KM# 64 THALER

Silver **Ruler:** Friedrich III **Obv:** Bust in wide lace collar **Obv. Legend:** FRIDERICUS • D: G • DVS • **Rev:** Helmeted arms with date in helmets **Rev. Legend:** VIRTUT: GLO - RIA. MER. **Note:** Ref. Dav. 3698. Prev. KM#27.

Date	Mintage	VG	F	VF	XF	Unc
1622 ST	—	225	375	700	1,250	—
1623 ST	—	225	375	700	1,250	—
1624 ST	—	225	375	700	1,250	—
1625 ST	—	225	375	700	1,250	—
1626 ST	—	225	375	700	1,250	—

KM# 65 THALER

Silver **Ruler:** Friedrich III **Rev:** Date in legend **Note:** Ref. Dav. 3698A.

Date	Mintage	VG	F	VF	XF	Unc
1622	—	250	400	800	1,500	—

KM# 66 THALER

Silver **Ruler:** Friedrich III **Rev:** Date by lower arms **Note:** Ref. Dav. 3698B. Prev. KM#29.

Date	Mintage	VG	F	VF	XF	Unc
1622	—	250	400	800	1,500	—

KM# 78 THALER

Silver **Ruler:** Friedrich III **Obv:** Bust right with pointy beard, thin lace collar **Rev:** Differently shaped shield **Note:** Ref. Dav. 3699. Prev. KM#30.

Date	Mintage	VG	F	VF	XF	Unc
1626 ST	—	225	375	700	1,250	—
1627 ST	—	225	375	700	1,250	—
1628	—	225	375	700	1,250	—

KM# 83 THALER

Silver **Ruler:** Friedrich III **Obv:** Bust right **Obv. Legend:** ...HERES * NORWEGIAE. DUX. **Rev:** Date in legend **Rev. Legend:** SLES: E: HOL - SATIAE **Note:** Ref. Dav. 3700. Prev. KM#35.

Date	Mintage	VG	F	VF	XF	Unc
1634 PT	—	750	1,500	2,750	4,750	—
1636 PT	—	750	1,500	2,750	4,750	—
1637	—	750	1,500	2,750	4,750	—

KM# 98 THALER

Silver **Ruler:** Friedrich III **Obv. Legend:** ... H: N: DUX: SLES: ET: HOLSA **Rev:** Legend, date **Rev. Legend:** VIRTUT: GLORIA: MERC: **Note:** Ref. Dav. 3701. Prev. KM#40.

Date	Mintage	VG	F	VF	XF	Unc
1647 (k) Rare	—	—	—	—	—	—

KM# 99 THALER

Silver **Ruler:** Friedrich III **Subject:** Death of Frederik III **Obv:** Old bust right **Rev:** 9-line inscription **Rev. Inscription:** ... DECMR. and MXM ... **Note:** Ref. Dav. 3702. Prev. KM#45.

Date	Mintage	VG	F	VF	XF	Unc
1659 (k)	—	1,000	2,000	3,500	6,000	—

KM# 100 THALER

Silver **Ruler:** Friedrich III **Subject:** Death of Friedrich III **Rev:** 9-line inscription **Rev. Inscription:** ... DECEMB ... **Note:** Ref. Dav. 3702A. Prev. KM#46.

Date	Mintage	VG	F	VF	XF	Unc
1659 (k)	—	1,000	2,000	3,500	6,000	—

KM# 101 THALER

Silver **Ruler:** Friedrich III **Subject:** Death of Friedrich III **Rev:** 9-line inscription **Rev. Inscription:** ... MXM ... **Note:** Ref. Dav. 3702B. Prev. KM#47.

Date	Mintage	VG	F	VF	XF	Unc
1659	—	1,000	2,000	3,500	6,000	—

KM# 118 THALER

Silver **Ruler:** Christian Albrecht **Obv:** Bust to right **Rev:** M-F above arms, date in legend **Note:** Ref. Dav. 3703. Prev. KM#62.

Date	Mintage	VG	F	VF	XF	Unc
1673 MF	—	2,250	4,750	8,500	15,000	—
1674 MF	—	2,250	4,750	8,500	15,000	—

KM# 120 THALER

Silver **Ruler:** Christian Albrecht **Obv:** Bust to right, different drapery **Note:** Ref. Dav. 3704. Prev. KM#63.

Date	Mintage	VG	F	VF	XF	Unc
1674 AH	—	2,250	4,750	8,500	15,000	—

KM# 121 THALER

Silver **Ruler:** Christian Albrecht **Obv:** Bust to right, legend is unbroken and starts at top **Note:** Ref. Dav. 3705. Prev. KM#64.

Date	Mintage	VG	F	VF	XF	Unc
1674 AH	—	2,250	4,750	8,500	15,000	—

KM# 137 THALER

Silver **Ruler:** Christian Albrecht **Rev:** Helmeted arms with rounded bottom, date above, CI - MB below **Note:** Ref. Dav. 3706. Prev. KM#77.

Date	Mintage	VG	F	VF	XF	Unc
1681 CIMB Rare	—	—	—	—	—	—

KM# 141 THALER

Silver **Ruler:** Christian Albrecht **Rev:** Helmeted arms with flat bottom divide date at bottom **Note:** Ref. Dav. 3707. Prev. KM#78.

Date	Mintage	VG	F	VF	XF	Unc
1682 CMB Rare	—	—	—	—	—	—

KM# 153 THALER

Silver **Ruler:** Christian Albrecht **Rev:** S.C. 1693 in cartouche below arms **Note:** Dav. #3708. Prev. KM#85.

Date	Mintage	VG	F	VF	XF	Unc
1693 Rare	—	—	—	—	—	—

KM# 160 THALER
Silver **Ruler:** Friedrich IV **Obv:** Bust of Frederik IV right **Rev:** Crowned arms with six shields around, flag behind **Note:** Dav. #3710. Prev. KM#86.

Date	Mintage	VG	F	VF	XF	Unc
1697 Rare	—	—	—	—	—	—

KM# 167 THALER
Silver **Ruler:** Friedrich IV **Rev:** Crowned arms with six shields around in decoration **Note:** Ref. Dav. 3711. Prev. KM#88.

Date	Mintage	VG	F	VF	XF	Unc
1698	—	2,250	4,750	8,500	—	—

KM# 176 THALER
Silver **Ruler:** Friedrich IV **Rev:** Crowned arms in palm branches **Note:** Ref. Dav. 3712. Prev. KM#95.

Date	Mintage	VG	F	VF	XF	Unc
1700	—	2,000	4,000	7,500	12,500	—

KM# 88 1-1/2 THALER
43.5000 g., Silver **Ruler:** Friedrich III **Obv:** 1/2-length armored figure to right holding commander's baton in right hand, helmet at right on pedestal, titles of Friedrich III in legend **Rev:** Ornate 5-fold arms with 4-fold central shield, 3 ornate helmets above **Rev. Legend:** VIRTUTIS GLOR - RIA MERCES **Note:** Ref. L#319.

Date	Mintage	VG	F	VF	XF	Unc
ND(ca1640) Rare	—	—	—	—	—	—

KM# 17 2 THALER
Silver **Ruler:** Johann Adolf **Obv:** 6-fold arms with central shield, date divided near bottom, 3 ornate helmets above, titles of Johann Adolf in legend **Rev:** Busts of duke and duchess facing each other in circle, continued titles **Rev. Legend:** STO * ... **Note:** Ref. L#264B.

Date	Mintage	VG	F	VF	XF	Unc
1607 G Rare	—	—	—	—	—	—

KM# 23 2 THALER
Silver, 40 mm. **Ruler:** Johann Adolf **Obv:** Half-length armored figure to right holding field marshall's baton **Obv. Legend:** IOHAN • ADOLF • D:G • HERES • NORV • DVX • SL **Rev:** Shield of 6-fold arms, 3 ornate helmets above with date spaced between them **Rev. Legend:** D S H S E DI - C O E D MNS. **Note:** Struck on thick flan from Thaler dies, KM#22.

Date	Mintage	VG	F	VF	XF	Unc
1608 MP One known	—	—	—	—	—	—

Note: An example in VF realized approximately $29,900 in a Westfälische Auktionsgesellschaft sale of February 2004.

KM# 28 2 THALER
Silver **Ruler:** Johann Adolf **Obv:** Bust of Johann Adolf right **Rev:** Helmeted arms with H-P above and date divided in helmets **Note:** Ref. Dav. 3681. Prev. KM#9.

Date	Mintage	VG	F	VF	XF	Unc
1609 MP Rare	—	—	—	—	—	—

KM# 29 2 THALER
Silver **Ruler:** Johann Adolf **Obv:** Older bust right **Rev:** Helmeted arms, date in legend **Note:** Ref. Dav. 3686. Prev. KM#10.

Date	Mintage	VG	F	VF	XF	Unc
1609 Rare	—	—	—	—	—	—

KM# 50 2 THALER
Silver **Ruler:** Friedrich III **Obv:** Bust of Frederik right **Rev:** Helmeted arms with date divided by helmets **Note:** Ref. Dav. 3694. Prev. KM#19.

Date	Mintage	VG	F	VF	XF	Unc
1618 Rare	—	—	—	—	—	—

KM# 122 2 THALER
Silver **Ruler:** Christian Albrecht **Obv:** Bust to right **Rev:** Crowned oval arms in wreath **Note:** Ref. Dav. A3705. Prev. KM#65.

Date	Mintage	VG	F	VF	XF	Unc
1674 AH Rare	—	—	—	—	—	—

KM# 161 2 THALER
Silver **Ruler:** Friedrich IV **Obv:** Bust to right **Rev:** Crowned arms with six shields around, flags behing **Note:** Ref. Dav. 3709. Prev. KM#87.

Date	Mintage	VG	F	VF	XF	Unc
1697 Rare	—	—	—	—	—	—

KM# 18 3 THALER
Silver **Ruler:** Johann Adolf **Obv:** 6-fold arms with central shield, date divided near bottom, 3 ornate helmets above, titles of Johann Adolf in legend **Rev:** Busts of duke and duchess facing each other in circle, titles continued in legend **Rev. Legend:** STOR: ... **Note:** Ref. L#264A.

Date	Mintage	VG	F	VF	XF	Unc
1607 IG Rare	—	—	—	—	—	—

KM# 11 3 THALER
Silver **Ruler:** Johann Adolf **Obv:** Bust of Johann Adolf right **Rev:** Helmeted arms, date in legend **Note:** Ref. Dav. 3685.

Date	Mintage	VG	F	VF	XF	Unc
1609 Rare	—	—	—	—	—	—

KM# 89 3-1/2 THALER
102.1600 g., Silver **Ruler:** Friedrich III **Obv:** 1/2-length armored figure to right holding commander's baton in right hand, helmet at right on pedestal, titles of Friedrich III in legend **Rev:** Ornate 5-fold arms with 4-fold central shield, 3 ornate helmets above **Rev. Legend:** VIRTUTIS GLOR - RIA MERCES. **Note:** Ref. L#318A.

Date	Mintage	VG	F	VF	XF	Unc
ND(ca1640) Rare	—	—	—	—	—	—

KM# 133 MARK
Silver **Ruler:** Christian Albrecht **Obv:** Wreath around shield design **Rev:** Value within legend **Note:** Prev. KM#75.

Date	Mintage	VG	F	VF	XF	Unc
1681 Rare	—	—	—	—	—	—

Note: Künker Auction 165, 3-10, XF realized approximately $13,610.

KM# 165 MARK
Silver **Ruler:** Friedrich IV **Obv:** Bust right, titles of Friedrich IV in legend **Rev:** Schleswig arms in oval baroque frame divide I - M (= 1 Mark), large crown above divides date **Rev. Legend:** CONSTANTIA. ET. LABORE. **Note:** Ref. L#430A.

Date	Mintage	VG	F	VF	XF	Unc
1698	—	450	700	950	1,250	—

KM# 134 2 MARK
Silver **Ruler:** Christian Albrecht **Obv:** Large crown over double mirror-image 'CA' monogram, 2/MAR below titles of Christian Albrecht in legend **Rev:** Crowned 5-fold arms with 4-fold central shield, palm frond to either side **Rev. Legend:** PER: ASPERA: AD - ASTRA, (date) **Note:** Dav. #576. Ref. L#402.

Date	Mintage	VG	F	VF	XF	Unc
1681 CIMB	—	900	1,750	3,250	6,000	—

KM# 136 2 MARK
Silver **Ruler:** Christian Albrecht **Obv:** Large crown over double mirror-image 'CA' monogram in circle, titles of Christian Albrecht in legend **Rev:** Crowned shield of Schleswig arms **Rev. Legend:** II. MARCK - LVB. (date) **Note:** Dav. #577. Ref. L#400, 401, 403. Varieties exist. The second 1681 CMB has III. MARCK and CMMB in error.

Date	Mintage	VG	F	VF	XF	Unc
1681 CIMB	—	650	1,350	2,750	5,000	—
1681 CMB	—	650	1,350	2,750	5,000	—
168Z	—	650	1,350	2,750	5,000	—

KM# 135 2 MARK
Silver **Ruler:** Christian Albrecht **Obv:** Crowned monogram, value below **Rev:** Crowned shield between palm branches **Note:** Prev. KM#76.

Date	Mintage	VG	F	VF	XF	Unc
1681 CIMB	—	175	350	650	—	—

KM# 152 2 MARK
Silver **Ruler:** Christian Albrecht **Obv:** Bust right, titles of Christian Albrecht **Rev:** Schleswig arms in oval baroque frame, large crown above, mintmaster's initials and date in small oval below **Rev. Legend:** PER ASPERA AD ASTRA" II. MARCK LUBS **Note:** Dav. #578. Ref. L#403A.

Date	Mintage	VG	F	VF	XF	Unc
1693 SC	—	—	—	—	—	—

KM# 166 2 MARK
Silver **Ruler:** Friedrich IV **Obv:** Bust right, titles of Friedrich IV in legend **Rev:** Schleswig arms in oval baroque frame divide 2 - M, large crown above divides date **Rev. Legend:** CONSTANTIA. ET. LABORE **Note:** Dav. #579. Ref. L#430AA.

Date	Mintage	VG	F	VF	XF	Unc
1698	—	—	—	—	—	—

TRADE COINAGE

KM# 53 GOLDGULDEN
3.5000 g., 0.9860 Gold 0.1109 oz. AGW **Ruler:** Friedrich III **Obv:** Bust of Friedrich III right in inner circle **Rev:** Arms topped by three helmets, date in legend **Note:** Prev. KM#24.

Date	Mintage	VG	F	VF	XF	Unc
1619	—	1,650	3,300	6,600	11,000	—

KM# 79 GOLDGULDEN
3.5000 g., 0.9860 Gold 0.1109 oz. AGW **Ruler:** Friedrich III **Obv:** Friedrich III standing right in inner circle **Note:** Prev. KM#34.

Date	Mintage	VG	F	VF	XF	Unc
1627	—	1,050	2,250	4,150	6,600	—

KM# 108 GOLDGULDEN

3.5000 g., 0.9860 Gold 0.1109 oz. AGW **Ruler:** Christian Albrecht **Obv:** Bust of Christian Albrecht right in inner circle **Rev:** Orb at center **Note:** Prev. KM#53.

Date	Mintage	VG	F	VF	XF	Unc
1664	—	1,450	2,950	5,400	9,100	—

KM# 10 DUCAT

3.5000 g., 0.9860 Gold 0.1109 oz. AGW **Ruler:** Johann Adolf **Obv:** Full-length armored figure turned slightly right, titles of Johann Adolf in legend **Rev:** Crowned shield of Schleswig arms divide date **Rev. Legend:** MONETA. NOVA. DVCAT. SCHLES. **Note:** Prev. KM#4. Fr. #3075.

Date	Mintage	VG	F	VF	XF	Unc
(1)601 Rare	—	—	—	—	—	—

KM# 94 DUCAT

3.5000 g., 0.9860 Gold 0.1109 oz. AGW **Ruler:** Friedrich III **Obv:** Bust of Friedrich III right in inner circle **Rev:** Arms topped by 3 helmets in inner circle **Note:** Prev. KM#39.

Date	Mintage	VG	F	VF	XF	Unc
1642 HG	—	825	1,700	3,300	5,500	—

KM# 109 DUCAT

3.5000 g., 0.9860 Gold 0.1109 oz. AGW **Ruler:** Christian Albrecht **Rev:** Crowned oval arms **Note:** Prev. KM#54.

Date	Mintage	VG	F	VF	XF	Unc
1664	—	2,000	4,050	7,200	12,000	—

KM# 123 DUCAT

3.5000 g., 0.9860 Gold 0.1109 oz. AGW **Ruler:** Christian Albrecht **Obv:** Smaller bust, without inner circle **Note:** Prev. KM#66.

Date	Mintage	VG	F	VF	XF	Unc
1674 AH	—	2,000	4,050	7,200	12,000	—

KM# 146 DUCAT

3.5000 g., 0.9860 Gold 0.1109 oz. AGW **Ruler:** Christian Albrecht **Rev:** Crowned shield, date below **Note:** Prev. KM#81.

Date	Mintage	VG	F	VF	XF	Unc
1689 HHL Rare	—	—	—	—	—	—

KM# 147 DUCAT

3.5000 g., 0.9860 Gold 0.1109 oz. AGW **Ruler:** Christian Albrecht **Rev:** Crowned mountain, date in cartouche at bottom **Note:** Prev. KM#82.

Date	Mintage	VG	F	VF	XF	Unc
1689 HHL	—	900	1,800	3,650	6,400	—

KM# 169 DUCAT

3.5000 g., 0.9860 Gold 0.1109 oz. AGW **Ruler:** Friedrich IV **Obv:** Bust to right **Note:** Prev. KM#90.

Date	Mintage	VG	F	VF	XF	Unc
1698	—	825	1,650	3,300	5,800	—

KM# 170 DUCAT

3.5000 g., 0.9860 Gold 0.1109 oz. AGW **Ruler:** Friedrich IV **Rev:** Crowned shield with lions at center **Note:** Prev. KM#91.

Date	Mintage	VG	F	VF	XF	Unc
1698	—	825	1,650	3,300	5,800	—
1700	—	825	1,650	3,300	5,800	—

KM# 171 DUCAT

3.5000 g., 0.9860 Gold 0.1109 oz. AGW **Ruler:** Friedrich IV **Rev:** Shield with lions surrounded by six shields of arms **Note:** Prev. KM#92.

Date	Mintage	VG	F	VF	XF	Unc
1698	—	1,050	2,250	4,150	6,600	—

KM# 73 DUCAT

3.5000 g., 0.9860 Gold 0.1109 oz. AGW **Ruler:** Friedrich IV **Obv:** Crowned shield with lions **Rev:** View of Holm fortress with guidance from above, date at top **Note:** Prev. KM#A89.

Date	Mintage	VG	F	VF	XF	Unc
1698	—	1,150	2,350	4,400	7,000	—

KM# 172 DUCAT

Gold **Ruler:** Friedrich IV **Obv:** Crowned shield of Schleswig arms **Obv. Legend:** MONETA. SLESVICENSIS. **Rev:** Plan of the Stapelholm fortifications **Rev. Legend:** SVPREMVS. LABOR. IN CONSTANTIA., (date) **Note:** Fr. #3083.

Date	Mintage	VG	F	VF	XF	Unc
1698	—	—	—	—	—	—

KM# 36 5 DUCAT

17.5000 g., 0.9860 Gold 0.5547 oz. AGW **Ruler:** Johann Adolf **Obv:** 5-fold arms with central shield, date divided at bottom, 3 helmets above, titles of Johann Adolf in legend **Rev:** Portuguese cross in circle, outer legend has continued titles **Rev. Legend:** Inner: NACH PORTUGALI: SCHROT: UND: KORN **Note:** Ref. L#263.

Date	Mintage	VG	F	VF	XF	Unc
1611 (c) Rare	—	—	—	—	—	—

KM# 124 5 DUCAT

17.5000 g., 0.9860 Gold 0.5547 oz. AGW **Ruler:** Christian Albrecht **Note:** Prev. KM#67.

Date	Mintage	VG	F	VF	XF	Unc
1674 AH Rare	—	—	—	—	—	—

PATTERNS

Including off metal strikes

KM#	Date	Mintage	Identification	Mkt Val
Pn1	1698	—	Ducat. Silver. KM#169.	350
Pn2	1698	—	Ducat. Copper. KM#169.	—
Pn3	1698	—	Ducat. Copper. KM#170.	—

SCHLESWIG-HOLSTEIN-NORBURG

Established upon the division of Schleswig-Holstein-Sonderburg in 1622. The first line became extinct after two generations and passed to Schleswig-Holstein-Plön, from which a second line was begun in 1679. When the Plön branch of the family died out in 1706, Norburg acquired the lands and titles. Schleswig-Holstein-Norburg passed to Denmark in 1761.

RULER

August, 1676-1699

REFERENCE

L = Christian Lange, ***Chr. Lange's Sammlung schleswig-holsteinischer Münzen und Medaillen***. 2 vols, Berlin, 1908-12.

DUCHY

REGULAR COINAGE

KM# 5 THALER

Silver **Subject:** Conclusion of Oldensburg Succession Dispute **Obv:** Helmeted shield, date flanking in straight line, 16 - 76 **Note:** Dav. #3722.

Date	Mintage	VG	F	VF	XF	Unc
1676 CP	—	350	750	1,500	2,750	—

KM# 6 THALER

Silver **Subject:** Conclusion of Oldensburg Succession Dispute **Obv:** Helmeted shield, date below on a curve **Note:** Dav. #3722A.

Date	Mintage	VG	F	VF	XF	Unc
1676 GP	—	600	1,200	2,500	4,000	—

TRADE COINAGE

KM# 7 3 DUCAT

10.5000 g., 0.9860 Gold 0.3328 oz. AGW **Subject:** Conclusion of Oldenburg's Succession Dispute **Obv:** 5-fold arms with central shield, 3 ornate helmets above, date divided near bottom, titles of August **Rev:** Eagle flying above view of mining scene, carrying a scale in his claws, sun shining with rays from above **Rev. Legend:** DIVINA BENEDICTIONE ET CÆSAREA IUSTITIA **Note:** Ref. L#766.

Date	Mintage	VG	F	VF	XF	Unc
1676 CP Rare	—	—	—	—	—	—

KM# 8 4 DUCAT

14.0000 g., 0.9860 Gold 0.4438 oz. AGW **Subject:** Conclusion of Oldenburg's Succession Dispute **Obv:** 5-fold arms with central shield, 3 ornate helmets above, date divided near bottom, titles of August **Rev:** Eagle in flight holding scales above mining scene,sun shining with rays from above **Rev. Legend:** DIVINA BENEDICTIONE ET CÆSAREA IUSTITIA **Note:** Ref. L#766.

Date	Mintage	VG	F	VF	XF	Unc
1676 CP Rare	—	—	—	—	—	—

SCHLESWIG-HOLSTEIN-PLOEN

One of the branches of Schleswig-Holstein founded upon the division of Schleswig-Holstein-Sonderburg in 1622. It fell extinct in 1706 and all lands and titles reverted to Schleswig-Holstein-Norburg.

RULERS
Joachim Ernst, 1622-1671
Johann Adolf, 1671-1704

REFERENCE
L = Christian Lange, ***Chr. Lange's Sammlung schleswig-holsteinischer Münzen und Medaillen***. 2 vols, Berlin, 1908-12.

DUCHY

REGULAR COINAGE

KM# 10 2 MARK (Lübsch)
Silver **Ruler:** Johann Adolf **Obv:** Crowned 5-fold arms with central shield divide date, titles of Johann Adolf **Rev. Legend:** Palm tree divides mintmaster's initials, large stone resting in branches

Date	Mintage	VG	F	VF	XF	Unc
1677 CR	—	85.00	175	375	750	—

KM# 11 1/16 THALER
Silver **Ruler:** Johann Adolf **Obv:** Draped bust right **Rev:** Value, date within legend

Date	Mintage	VG	F	VF	XF	Unc
1677 CR	—	75.00	160	300	625	—

KM# 13 1/12 THALER
Silver **Ruler:** Johann Adolf **Obv:** Crowned shield **Rev:** Value within legend

Date	Mintage	VG	F	VF	XF	Unc
1690	—	65.00	135	245	550	—

KM# 14 2/3 THALER
Silver **Ruler:** Johann Adolf **Obv:** Draped, armored bust right, value in oval below **Rev:** Crowned shield between palm branches

Date	Mintage	VG	F	VF	XF	Unc
1690	—	85.00	160	300	600	—

KM# 15 2/3 THALER
Silver **Ruler:** Johann Adolf **Rev:** Crowned shield

Date	Mintage	VG	F	VF	XF	Unc
1690	—	75.00	150	275	550	—

KM# 16 2/3 THALER
Silver **Ruler:** Johann Adolf **Obv:** Large armored bust right **Rev:** Crowned shield in circle, value below

Date	Mintage	VG	F	VF	XF	Unc
1690	—	65.00	135	275	550	—

KM# 17 2/3 THALER
Silver **Ruler:** Johann Adolf **Rev:** Fraction within legend

Date	Mintage	VG	F	VF	XF	Unc
1690	—	65.00	135	275	550	—

KM# 5 THALER
Silver **Ruler:** Joachim Ernst **Obv:** Bust of Joachim Ernst right **Rev:** Helmeted arms, date in legend **Note:** Dav.#3719.

Date	Mintage	VG	F	VF	XF	Unc
1625 MA Rare	—	—	—	—	—	—

KM# 6 THALER
Silver **Ruler:** Joachim Ernst **Obv:** Helmeted arms **Rev:** Crowned, double-headed eagle, orb with 32 on breast **Note:** Dav. #3720.

Date	Mintage	VG	F	VF	XF	Unc
1625 MA Rare	—	—	—	—	—	—

KM# 18 THALER
Silver **Ruler:** Johann Adolf **Obv:** Bust of Johann Adolf right, date below **Rev:** Helmeted arms

Date	Mintage	VG	F	VF	XF	Unc
1690 Rare	—	—	—	—	—	—

TRADE COINAGE

KM# 12 DUCAT
3.5000 g., 0.9860 Gold 0.1109 oz. AGW **Ruler:** Johann Adolf **Obv:** Arms in inner circle **Rev:** Crowned JA monogram

Date	Mintage	VG	F	VF	XF	Unc
1677 CR	—	1,250	2,250	4,500	7,500	—

KM# 19 DUCAT
3.5000 g., 0.9860 Gold 0.1109 oz. AGW **Ruler:** Johann Adolf **Obv:** Bust of Johann Adolf right in inner circle **Rev:** Arms in inner circle

Date	Mintage	VG	F	VF	XF	Unc
1690	—	1,750	3,250	5,750	9,500	—

PATTERNS

(Including off metal strikes)

KM#	Date	Mintage	Identification	Mkt Val
Pn2	1677	—	Ducat. Copper. KM#12; 10-sided klippe.	—
Pn1	1690	—	Thaler. Tin. KM#18.	—

SCHLESWIG-HOLSTEIN-SONDERBURG

Sonderburg was split away from Schleswig-Holstein in 1559 and created as a separate duchy for a younger son of King Christian III of Denmark. Divisions of Schleswig-Holstein-Sonderburg occurred in 1622 and again in 1627. The first division resulted in the branches of Glücksburg, Norburg and Plön, all of which were acquired by Denmark in the second half of the 18th century.

RULERS
Johann der Jüngere, 1559-1622
Alexander, 1622-1627

MINT OFFICIALS' INITIALS

Initial	Date	Name
PH	1608-	P. Hanssen in Sonderburg
(r)= R	1618-1620	Tobias Reinhardt in Reinfeld
	1620	Christoph Mittelbach in Reinfeld
= 	1625-27	Johann Lilienthal in Sonderburg and Reinfeld

DUCHY

REGULAR COINAGE

KM# 4 2 SCHILLING (Lübsch)
Silver **Ruler:** Johann **Obv:** Rider on horse leaping to left, value: Z SL below **Rev:** Titles of Johann in 6-line inscription **Note:** Ref. L#540.

Date	Mintage	VG	F	VF	XF	Unc
ND(1618-22)	—	16.00	40.00	75.00	155	—

KM# 11 2 SCHILLING (Lübsch)
Silver **Ruler:** Johann **Obv:** Nettle leaf of Holstein divides value: 2 - L or Z - L, date above **Rev:** Titles of Johann in 6-line inscription **Note:** Ref. L#541-42, 547-48. Varieties exist.

Date	Mintage	VG	F	VF	XF	Unc
16Z0	—	16.00	40.00	75.00	155	—
16Z1	—	16.00	40.00	75.00	155	—
16Z3 Posthumous	—	16.00	40.00	75.00	155	—
16Z5 Posthumous	—	16.00	40.00	75.00	155	—

KM# 5 2 SCHILLING (Doppelschilling)
Silver **Ruler:** Johann **Obv:** 5-fold arms with central shield, titles of Johann in legend **Rev:** Large intertwined 'DS' in circle, small imperial orb above, titles continued in legend, date **Note:** Ref. L#535a, 535b, 536. Varieties exist.

Date	Mintage	VG	F	VF	XF	Unc
(16)18	—	60.00	110	180	325	—
(16)18 (r)	—	60.00	110	180	325	—
(16)19 (r)	—	60.00	110	180	325	—

KM# 13 4 SCHILLING (Lübsch)
Silver **Ruler:** Johann **Obv:** Rider on horse leaping to left, value: 4 SL below **Rev:** Titles of Johann in 6-line inscription **Note:** Ref. L#539.

Date	Mintage	VG	F	VF	XF	Unc
ND(1618-22)	—	65.00	135	300	550	—

KM# 12 4 SCHILLING (Lübsch)
Silver **Ruler:** Johann **Obv:** Rider on horse leaping to left, value: 4 SL below **Rev:** Titles of Johann in 7-line inscription, date in last line **Note:** Ref. L#539A.

Date	Mintage	VG	F	VF	XF	Unc
16ZZ	—	85.00	165	300	625	—

KM# 14 1/96 THALER (Sechsling)
Silver **Ruler:** Johann **Obv:** Quatrefoil superimposed on floriated cross, titles of Johann **Rev:** Imperial orb with 96, date **Rev. Legend:** SLES. E. HOLS **Note:** Ref. L#538.

Date	Mintage	VG	F	VF	XF	Unc
(1)622	—	—	—	—	—	—

KM# 8 1/64 THALER (Sechsling)
Silver **Ruler:** Johann **Obv:** Shield of lion rampant left (Norway) superimposed on cross, titles of Johann in legend **Rev:** Imperial orb with 64, titles and date in legend

Date	Mintage	VG	F	VF	XF	Unc
(1)619 (r)	—	65.00	135	275	550	—

KM# 3 1/16 THALER

Silver **Ruler:** Johann **Obv:** 16 within orb **Rev:** Helmeted shield **Note:** Previous KM#5.

Date	Mintage	VG	F	VF	XF	Unc
1604	—	135	275	575	1,150	—

KM# 6 1/16 THALER

Silver **Obv:** Group of shields **Rev:** 16 within orb **Note:** Prev. KM#10.

Date	Mintage	VG	F	VF	XF	Unc
1618 (r)	—	160	325	650	1,300	—
1619 (r)	—	160	325	650	1,300	—

KM# 9 1/16 THALER

Silver **Obv:** Helmeted shield **Rev:** Eagle with 16 on breast **Note:** Previous KM#11.

Date	Mintage	VG	F	VF	XF	Unc
1619 (r)	—	160	325	650	1,300	—
1620 (r)	—	160	325	650	1,300	—

KM# 25 1/16 THALER

Silver **Subject:** Alexander

Date	Mintage	VG	F	VF	XF	Unc
(1)6Z5 (s)	—	180	350	725	—	—

KM# 7 1/4 THALER

Silver **Obv:** Bust right **Rev:** Helmeted shield **Note:** Previous KM#15.

Date	Mintage	VG	F	VF	XF	Unc
ND(1618-22) (r)	—	—	—	—	—	—

KM# 16 1/4 THALER

Silver **Subject:** Death of Johann

Date	Mintage	VG	F	VF	XF	Unc
1622	—	650	1,150	2,200	4,200	—

KM# 27 1/4 THALER

Silver **Subject:** Death of Alexander

Date	Mintage	VG	F	VF	XF	Unc
1627	—	—	—	—	—	—

KM# 17 1/2 THALER

Silver **Subject:** Death of Johann

Date	Mintage	VG	F	VF	XF	Unc
1622	—	1,000	1,800	3,300	6,500	—

KM# 18 THALER

Silver **Obv:** Bust of Johann right **Rev:** Helmeted arms **Note:** Dav. #3714.

Date	Mintage	VG	F	VF	XF	Unc
(1)622	—	1,250	2,500	4,500	—	—

KM# 19 THALER

Silver **Rev:** Narrower shield **Note:** Dav. #3714A.

Date	Mintage	VG	F	VF	XF	Unc
(1)622	—	2,500	4,500	7,500	—	—

KM# 20 THALER

Silver **Obv:** Bow knot on duke's shoulder **Note:** Dav. #3714B.

Date	Mintage	VG	F	VF	XF	Unc
(1)622 (r)	—	2,500	4,500	7,500	—	—

KM# 21 THALER

Silver **Subject:** Death of Johann **Note:** Similar to 2 Thaler, KM#23. Dav. #3715.

Date	Mintage	VG	F	VF	XF	Unc
1622	—	1,800	3,500	6,500	9,500	—

KM# 26 THALER

Silver **Obv:** Bust of Alexander right **Rev:** Helmeted arms **Note:** Dav. #3716.

Date	Mintage	VG	F	VF	XF	Unc
(1)626 (s)	—	1,600	3,300	5,400	—	—

KM# 28 THALER

Silver **Subject:** Death of Alexander **Obv:** 8-line inscription inside inner circle **Rev:** Helmeted arms, date (1)626 **Note:** Dav. #3717.

Date	Mintage	VG	F	VF	XF	Unc
1627 (s)	—	2,000	4,000	7,000	10,000	—

KM# 22 2 THALER

Silver **Obv:** Bust of Johann right **Rev:** Helmeted arms **Note:** Dav. #3713.

Date	Mintage	VG	F	VF	XF	Unc
1622 Rare	—	—	—	—	—	—

KM# 23 2 THALER

Silver **Subject:** Death of Johann **Note:** Dav. #A3715.

Date	Mintage	VG	F	VF	XF	Unc
1622 Rare	—	—	—	—	—	—

Note: Künker Auction 176, 9-10, VF realized approximately $40,635.

TRADE COINAGE

KM# 10 GOLDGULDEN

3.5000 g., 0.9860 Gold 0.1109 oz. AGW **Obv:** Bust of Johann right in inner circle **Rev:** Orb in inner circle **Note:** Prev. KM#12. Fr#3099.

Date	Mintage	VG	F	VF	XF	Unc
1619 (r)	—	1,500	3,000	5,000	9,000	—

KM# 24 GOLDGULDEN

3.5000 g., 0.9860 Gold 0.1109 oz. AGW **Obv:** Crowned shields in inner circle **Note:** Fr#3100.

Date	Mintage	VG	F	VF	XF	Unc
1624	—	1,150	2,250	4,000	7,000	—

SCHMALKALDEN

This lordship, centered on the town of the same name, became the property of Hesse-Cassel in 1583. The landgraves issued a series of copper coins for Schmalkalden during the first half of the 18th century.

LORDSHIP

STANDARD COINAGE

KM# 1 PFENNIG

Copper **Ruler:** Karl **Obv:** Crowned 'CL' monogram divides date as 1 - 6/8 - 4 **Rev. Inscription:** S. PF.

Date	Mintage	VG	F	VF	XF	Unc
1684	—	25.00	55.00	80.00	160	—

SCHWARZBURG

The countship of Schwarzburg had its beginnings in central Thuringia (Thüringen) and the ruling family eventually held numerous small territories from northern to central Thuringia. The earliest rulers known with any historical certainty were counts of Käfernburg in the 12th century. The line was divided into Käfernburg and Schwarzburg in the early 13th century, but when that of Käfernburg became extinct in 1385, most of its territories reverted to Schwarzburg. Several divisions of the countship took place during the next several centuries and at the beginning of the 16th century, there existed the branches of Schwarzburg-Arnstadt, Schwarzburg-Blankenburg and Schwarzburg-Leutenberg. The rulers of the various lines usually struck a joint coinage during the 16th century, but some of the counts issued coins in their own right as well. In 1526, the lines of Schwarzburg-Frankenhausen and Schwarzburg-Sondershausen were established from Schwarzburg-Blankenburg. Frankenhausen only lasted for one generation, but Schwarzburg-Sondershausen was further divided into Schwarzburg-Arnstadt, Schwarzburg-Rudolstadt and Schwarzburg-Sondershausen in 1552 (see separate listings for each of these). The Arnstadt line also failed after a single generation, but was reestablished as a branch of Schwarzburg-Sondershausen in 1642.

RULERS

Joint Rule

Joint Coinage I
 Günther XXXIX der Bremer, 1488-1531
 Heinrich XXXI, 1484-1526

Joint Coinage II
 Balthasar II zu Leutenberg, 1463-1525
 Günther XXXIX der Bremer, 1488-1531
 Heinrich XXXI, 1484-1526

Joint Coinage III
 Günther XL zu Arnstadt, 1526-1552
 Heinrich XXXIII, 1526-1528
 Heinrich XXXIV zu Frankenhausen, 1526-1547

Joint Coinage IV
 Heinrich XXXII, 1531-1538
 Günther XL zu Arnstadt, 1526-1552

Joint Coinage V
 Günther XLI der Streitbare zu Arnstadt, 1552-1583
 Johann Günther I zu Sondershausen, 1552-1586

Joint Coinage VI
 Albrecht VII von Rudolstadt, 1586-1605
 Günther XLII von Sondershausen, 1586-1643
 Anton Heinrich von Sondershausen, 1586-1638
 Johann Günther II von Sondershausen, 1586-1631
 Christian Günther I von Sondershausen, 1586-1642

Joint Coinage VII
 Karl Günther von Rudolstadt, 1605-1630Ludwig Günther von Rudolstadt, 1605-1646Albrecht Günther von Rudolstadt, 1605-1634Günther XLII von Sondershausen, 1586-1643Anton Heinrich von Sondershausen, 1586-1638Johann Günther II von Sondershausen, 1586-1631Christian Günther I von Sondershausen, 1586-1642

MINT OFFICIALS

Initial or mark	Date	Name
(b) = 	1597-1606	Florian Gruber, mintmaster in Erfurt
	Ca.1597-1606	Hans Weber, warden in Erfurt
HG	1606-09	Hieronymus Gronberger, mintmaster in Erfurt
WA	Ca.1611-13	Wolf Albrecht, mintmaster in Saalfeld

ARMS

Schwarzburg – (1) early arms, a crowned lion, often to right, (2) the symbols of a two-tined fork and a comb are often found as part of the arms, usually at the bottom of the main body of the arms, (3) the imperial eagle with arms on breast were adopted by all branches of the family who became princes of the empire in the late 17th and early 18th centuries
Arnstadt – eagle
Hohnstein – checkerboard
Klettenberg – striding deer
Lutterberg – crowned striding lion above four horizontal bars
Sondershausen – deer antlers

REFERENCES

F = Ernst Fischer, **Die Münzen des Hauses Schwarzburg**, Heidelberg, 1904.
R = Ernst Helmuth von Betha, **Schwarzburger Münzen und Medaillen: Sammlung des Schlossmuseums in Rudolstadt**, Halle (Saale), 1903.

COUNTSHIP

STANDARD COINAGE

KM# 5 PFENNIG

0.3200 g., Silver **Ruler:** Joint Coinage IV **Obv:** 2 adjacent shields of arms, Schwarzburg on left, Hohnstein on right, date above, fork below. **Note:** Uniface. Ref. F# 169-171. Size varies: 12-13 mm

Date	Mintage	VG	F	VF	XF	Unc
1602	—	—	—	—	—	—
160Z	—	200	425	850	—	—
1605	—	—	—	—	—	—

KM# 10 PFENNIG

0.3200 g., Silver **Ruler:** Joint Coinage IV **Obv:** 2 adjacent shields of arms, Schwarzburg on left, Hohnstein on right, date above, mintmaster's symbol below **Mint:** Erfurt **Note:** Uniface. Ref. F#172. Size varies: 12-13 mm.

Date	Mintage	VG	F	VF	XF	Unc
1605 (b)	—	200	425	850	—	—

KM# 13 PFENNIG

0.3200 g., Silver **Ruler:** Joint Coinage VII **Obv:** 2 adjacent shields of arms, Schwarzburg on left, Hohnstein on right, date and fork above **Note:** Uniface. Ref. F#192. Size varies: 12-13 mm. Varieties exist.

Date	Mintage	VG	F	VF	XF	Unc
1606	—	600	1,100	2,000	—	—

KM# 6 3 PFENNIG (DREIER)

Silver **Obv:** 3 small shields of arms in shape of cloverleaf, date above upper 2 shields, ork to left and right of lower shield, mintmaster's symbol in center **Note:** Ref. F#448. Size varies: 17-19 mm.

Date	Mintage	VG	F	VF	XF	Unc
160Z (b)	—	—	—	—	—	—

KM# 7 GROSCHEN (12 Pfennig)

2.2000 g., Silver, 23.5 mm. **Ruler:** Joint Coinage VI **Obv:** Ornate shield of 4-fold arms with central shield of Schwarzburg divides date **Obv. Legend:** MON. COMI. IN. SCWARZ. ET. HONS. **Rev:** Imperial orb with 1Z in baroque frame **Rev. Legend:** RVDOLPH. II. ROMA. IMPE. SE. AVB. **Note:** Ref. F#167.

Date	Mintage	VG	F	VF	XF	Unc
(16)0Z (B)	5,424	—	—	—	—	—

KM# 14 1/4 TALER

Silver, 30-31 mm. **Ruler:** Joint Coinage VII **Obv:** Ornate shield of manifold arms, date above **Obv. Legend:** GVN. AN. HEI. CAR. GVN. HA(N). GVN. CHRI GV(N). **Rev:** St. Martin on horseback to right, imperial orb above **Rev. Legend:** LVD. GVN. ALB. GVN. CO(M). I. SCHWAR. E. HONS. **Mint:** Erfurt **Note:** Ref. F#190-191.

Date	Mintage	VG	F	VF	XF	Unc
1606 (b)	—	—	—	—	—	—
1608 HG	—	—	—	—	—	—

KM# 2 1/2 THALER

14.1000 g., Silver, 36 mm. **Ruler:** Joint Coinage VI **Obv:** 4-fold arms with central shield of Schwarzburg divide date, supported by wildman and woman holding pennants, 3 ornate helmets above **Obv. Legend:** AL. GVN. A. HE. HA. GVNT. CH. - .GVN. COM. A. SCHWARZ. E. HON. **Rev:** Crowned imperial eagle with orb on breast, in circle **Rev. Legend:** RVDOL. II. ROMAN. IMPERA. SEMPER. AVGVSTVS. **Mint:** Erfurt **Note:** Ref. F#166.

Date	Mintage	VG	F	VF	XF	Unc
1601 (b)	—	—	—	—	—	—

KM# 11 1/2 THALER

Silver, 38 mm. **Ruler:** Joint Coinage VII **Obv:** 4-fold arms with central shield of Schwarzburg, supported by wildman and woman holding pennants, 3 ornate helmets above, date divided by crest of middle helmet **Obv. Legend:** GVN. AN. HEIN. CAR. - GVN. HA. GVN. CH GV. **Rev:** St. Martin on horseback to right, imperial orb above **Rev. Legend:** LVD. GVN. ALBV. GVN. COM. I. SCHWAR. E. HONS. **Mint:** Erfurt **Note:** Ref. #R490, F189, R493a. Varieties exist.

Date	Mintage	VG	F	VF	XF	Unc
1605 (b)	—	110	220	435	975	—
1606 (b)	—	—	—	—	—	—
1608 (b)	—	—	—	—	—	—

KM# 3 THALER

Silver **Ruler:** Joint Coinage VI **Obv:** Helmeted and supported arms, divided date above **Obv. Legend:** ALB. GVN. AN. HE. HA. GV. CH... **Rev:** Crowned double eagle wtih orb and cross **Rev. Legend:** RUDOLPH... **Mint:** Erfurt **Note:** Dav. #7674.

Date	Mintage	VG	F	VF	XF	Unc
1601 (b)	1,539	375	725	1,150	1,900	—
1602 (b)	—	375	725	1,150	1,900	—
1603 (b)	3,572	375	725	1,150	1,900	—
1604 (b)	3,700	375	725	1,150	1,900	—
1605 (b)	—	375	725	1,150	1,900	—

KM# 12 THALER

Silver **Ruler:** Joint Coinage VII **Obv:** Helmeted and supported arms **Obv. Legend:** GVNT: AN. HEIN: CAR... **Rev:** St. Martin and beggar, orb above divides date **Mint:** Erfurt **Note:** Dav. #7675.

Date	Mintage	VG	F	VF	XF	Unc
1605 (b)	—	350	625	1,000	1,700	—

KM# 15 THALER

Silver **Ruler:** Joint Coinage VII **Obv:** Helmeted and supported arms divide date **Rev:** St. Martin and beggar, orb above divides date **Mint:** Erfurt **Note:** Dav. #7676.

Date	Mintage	VG	F	VF	XF	Unc
1606//1606 (b)	—	375	725	1,150	1,900	—

KM# 16 THALER

Silver **Ruler:** Joint Coinage VII **Rev:** St. Martin and seated beggar **Mint:** Erfurt **Note:** Dav. #7677.

Date	Mintage	VG	F	VF	XF	Unc
1606 (b)	—	350	625	1,000	1,700	—
1607 HG	13,166	350	625	1,000	1,700	—
1608 HG	—	350	625	1,000	1,700	—
1609 HG	—	350	625	1,000	1,700	—

KM# 17 THALER

Silver **Ruler:** Joint Coinage VII **Rev:** Beggar reclining **Mint:** Erfurt **Note:** Dav. #7677A.

Date	Mintage	VG	F	VF	XF	Unc
1606 HG	—	350	625	1,000	1,700	—
1608 HG	—	350	625	1,000	1,700	—

KM# 18 THALER
Silver **Ruler:** Joint Coinage VII **Obv:** Helmeted arms with date in helmets **Rev:** Similar to KM #17 **Mint:** Erfurt **Note:** Dav. #7678.

Date	Mintage	VG	F	VF	XF	Unc
1606 (b)	—	375	725	1,150	1,900	—

KM# 21 THALER
Silver **Ruler:** Joint Coinage VII **Rev:** Beggar seated right **Mint:** Erfurt **Note:** Dav. #7677B.

Date	Mintage	VG	F	VF	XF	Unc
1608 HG	13,166	375	725	1,150	1,900	—

KM# 23 THALER
Silver **Ruler:** Joint Coinage VII **Rev:** Date appears: AN. 16-09 **Mint:** Erfurt **Note:** Dav. #7677C.

Date	Mintage	VG	F	VF	XF	Unc
1609 HG	—	375	725	1,150	1,900	—

KM# 25 THALER
Silver **Ruler:** Joint Coinage VII **Obv:** Date above helmets **Mint:** Saalfeld **Note:** Dav. #7679.

Date	Mintage	VG	F	VF	XF	Unc
1613 WA	510	450	850	1,450	2,350	—

TRADE COINAGE

KM# 8 GOLDGULDEN
Gold **Ruler:** Joint Coinage VI **Obv:** Shield of Schwarzburg lion arms, ornate helmet above divides date **Obv. Legend:** MON: COMIT: IN. SCHWARTZ: ET. HONST. **Rev:** 2 ornate adjacent shields of arms, Hohnstein on left, Klettenberg on right, small imperial orb above, fork at bottom **Rev. Legend:** DO: IN. ARNS: SOND. LEVT. LOR. ET. CLETTEN. **Note:** Ref. R#447. Coin only known in silver, may not exist in gold; probably a die trial.

Date	Mintage	VG	F	VF	XF	Unc
1603	—	—	—	—	—	—

KM# 9 GOLDGULDEN
Ruler: Joint Coinage VI **Obv:** 3 helmets over comb and fork, date divided above **Obv. Legend:** MONE. AVRE. COMI. IN SCHWARTZ. ET HON. **Rev:** 4-fold arms with central shield of Schwarzburg, helmet above **Rev. Legend:** OM. IN ARNS. SOND. LEV. LOHR. ET CLET. **Note:** Ref. F#159.

Date	Mintage	VG	F	VF	XF	Unc
1604 Rare	—	—	—	—	—	—

KM# 19 GOLDGULDEN
Gold **Ruler:** Joint Coinage VII **Obv:** 3 ornate helmets, date divided above, comb and fork below **Obv. Legend:** MONETA AVREA COMITUMIN SCHWARZBVRG ET HOHNSTEIN **Rev:** Schwarzburg arms in circle **Rev. Legend:** DOM. IN ARNST. SOND. LEV. LOHR. ET CLET. **Mint:** Erfurt **Note:** Fr#3101.

Date	Mintage	VG	F	VF	XF	Unc
1606 (b) Rare	—	—	—	—	—	—

KM# 20 GOLDGULDEN
Gold **Ruler:** Joint Coinage VII **Obv:** 3 ornate helmets, date divided above, comb and fork below **Obv. Legend:** MONETA AVREA COMITVMIN SCHWARZBVRG ET HOHNSTEIN. **Rev:** Small shield of Schwarzburg arms superimposed on cross with lily ends at right, bottom and left, with imperial orb at end of upper arm, 4 small shields of arms in angles **Rev. Legend:** DOM. IN ARNS. SOND(H). LIV (or LEV). LOHR. ET. CLET. **Mint:** Erfurt **Note:** Fr#3102.

Date	Mintage	VG	F	VF	XF	Unc
1606 (b) Rare	—	—	—	—	—	—
1608 HG Rare	676	—	—	—	—	—

KM# 22 GOLDGULDEN
Gold **Ruler:** Joint Coinage VII **Obv:** 3 ornate helmets, date divided above, comb and fork below **Obv. Legend:** MONE. AVRE. COMI. IN SCHWARZ. ET. HON. **Rev:** 4-fold arms with central shield of Schwarzburg **Rev. Legend:** DOM. IN ARNS. SOND. LEV. LOH. ET. CLET. **Note:** Ref. F#175.

Date	Mintage	VG	F	VF	XF	Unc
1608 Rare	Inc. above	—	—	—	—	—

KM# 24 GOLDGULDEN
Gold **Ruler:** Joint Coinage VII **Obv:** 3 ornate helmets, date divided above, comb and fork below **Obv. Legend:** MONE. AVRE COM(I) IN. SCHWARTZ. ET. HON. **Rev:** Small shield of Schwarzburg arms superimposed on cross with lily ends at right, bottom and left, with imperial orb at end of upper arm, 4 small shields of arms in angles **Rev. Legend:** DOM. IN. ARNS. SOND. LEV. LOHR. ET. CLE(T). **Note:** Dav#3103. Ref. F#177-80; R#460 for 1616 date. Varieties exist.

Date	Mintage	VG	F	VF	XF	Unc
1611 WA WA	10,098	900	1,750	3,300	5,400	—
1613	Inc. above	900	1,750	3,300	5,400	—
1613 WA WA	Inc. above	900	1,750	3,300	5,400	—
1616 WA WA	1,278	900	1,750	3,300	5,400	—
1618 WA WA	3,167	900	1,750	3,300	5,400	—

SCHWARZBURG-ARNSTADT

The seat of this branch of Schwarzburg is located about 10 miles (16 kilometers) south of Erfurt. The town, castle and surrounding territory were acquired by the counts of Schwarzburg in the early 14th century and a line was soon established separate from Schwarzburg-Blankenburg. The latter fell extinct in the mid-14th century and passed to Arnstadt. Generations later, the lines of Schwarzburg-Sondershausen and Schwarzburg-Rudolstadt were founded and Arnstadt was absorbed by the former, only to reemerge as a separate line in 1642. The last count of Schwarzburg-Arnstadt was raised to the rank of prince in 1709, but died without heirs in 1716.

RULERS

Christian Günther I zu Sondershausen, 1586-1642
Christian Günther II, 1642-1666
Johann Günther IV, 1666-1669
Anton Günther II, 1669-1716, Prince 1709

MINT OFFICIALS

Initial or mark	Date	Name
HM+	1675-81	Henning Müller, mintmaster in Sondershausen
(a)=	1676-78	Henning Müller, mintmaster in Keula
HCH	1685-89	Heinrich Christoph Hille, mintmaster in Arnstadt

Arms: See under Schwarzburg

CROSS REFERENCES:

F = **Ernst Fischer,** *Die Münzen des Hauses Schwarzburg,* **Heidelberg, 1904.**

R = **Ernst Helmuth von Bethe,** *Schwarzburger Münzen und Medaillen: Sammlung des Schlossmuseums in Rudolstadt,* **Halle (Saale), 1903.**

COUNTSHIP

REGULAR COINAGE

KM# 31 3 PFENNIG (DREIER)
Silver, 16-18 mm. **Ruler:** Anton Günther II **Obv:** Crowned intertwined 'AG' monogram **Rev:** Imperial orb with 3 divides date and mintmaster's initials **Mint:** Arnstadt **Note:** Ref. F#380. Weight varies: .82-1.05 g.

Date	Mintage	VG	F	VF	XF	Unc
1685 HCH	—	—	—	—	—	—

KM# 2 GROSCHEN
Silver, 23 mm. **Ruler:** Christian Günther II **Subject:** Death of Christian Günther II **Obv:** Crowned manifold arms **Obv. Legend:** CHRISTIAN GUNTH E. IV. COM. COM IN SCHW. ET H. **Rev. Legend:** SYMB: PATIENTER. ET CONSTANTER. **Rev. Inscription:** NATVS / 1. APRIL. AN / 1616 MORT. 10 / 7BRIS. AN. 1666 / HOR XI. ME / RID. **Note:** Ref. F#266.

Date	Mintage	VG	F	VF	XF	Unc
1666	—	—	—	—	—	—

KM# 17 1/16 THALER
Silver, 18-19 mm. **Ruler:** Anton Günther II **Obv:** Draped bust to left **Obv. Legend:** ANTHPN: GVNTER. **Rev:** Date at end of legend **Rev. Legend:** E. IV. COM. I. C. D. S. E. H. **Rev. Inscription:** XVI / EINEN / REICHS / THAL. **Note:** Ref. R#896-97. Varieties exist.

Date	Mintage	VG	F	VF	XF	Unc
1676	—	—	—	—	—	—

KM# 32 6 MARIENGROSCHEN (1/4 Gulden)
Silver, 25 mm. **Ruler:** Anton Günther II **Obv:** Armored bust to right **Obv. Legend:** ANTHON: GUNTHER: E: IV: COM: IMP. **Rev. Legend:** NACH DEM OBER SACH CREUSSCHLUS. **Rev. Inscription:** ★ VI ★ / MARIE: / ★ GROS ★ / FEIN. SILV. / date / mintmaster's initials. **Mint:** Arnstadt **Note:** Ref. F#379.

Date	Mintage	VG	F	VF	XF	Unc
1685 HCH	—	—	—	—	—	—

KM# 18 1/6 THALER
Silver, 26.5 mm. **Ruler:** Anton Günther II **Obv:** Bust to left **Obv. Legend:** ANTHON: GVNTHER: E. IV. COM. I. **Rev:** Crowned shield of arms, lion left above fork and comb, divides date and mintmaster's initials, value (1/6) below **Rev. Legend:** COM. DE. SCHWAR - ET - HONSTEIN **Mint:** Sondershausen **Note:** Ref. F# 896-97. Varieties exist.

Date	Mintage	VG	F	VF	XF	Unc
1676 HM	—	—	—	—	—	—

KM# 3 1/4 THALER
7.0000 g., Silver, 30 mm. **Ruler:** Christian Günther II **Subject:** Death of Christian Günther II **Obv:** Ornate shield of manifold arms, crown above, comb below **Obv. Legend:** CHRISTIAN GUNTH. E. IV. COM. COM. IN. SCHWARZB. ET. HONST. **Rev:** 6-line inscription in laurel wreath **Rev. Legend:** SYMB: PATIENT - ER - ET CONSTANTER **Rev. Inscription:** NATVS. / 1. APRIL. AN. / 1616. MORT 10 / 7BRIS. AN. 1666 / HOR. X. 1. ME: / RID. **Note:** Ref. R#656.

Date	Mintage	VG	F	VF	XF	Unc
1666	—	—	—	—	—	—

KM# 5 1/4 THALER
7.0000 g., Silver, 34 mm. **Ruler:** Johann Günther IV **Subject:** Death of Johann Günther IV **Obv:** Crowned ornamented shield of manifold arms, comb below **Obv. Legend:** IOHAN. GUNTH. E. IV. COM. S.R.I. COM. IN. SCHW. ET. HONST.DVN. A.S.L. L. ET. C. **Rev:** 9-line inscription in laurel wreath **Rev. Legend:** SYMBOL. PIETATE - ET IUSTITIA. **Rev. Inscription:** NATUS. / ARNST. 30 IUN: / 1654. BEATE. DEFUNCT / TUBING. IN. ILL. / COLL. 29. AUGUST. / 1669. HOR. MED. 2. / MATUT. ÆTAT: / ANN. 15. MENS. / 2. DIES. 2. **Note:** Ref. F#268.

Date	Mintage	VG	F	VF	XF	Unc
1669	—	—	—	—	—	—

KM# 33 12 MARIENGROSCHEN (1/2 Gulden)
Silver, 32 mm. **Ruler:** Anton Günther II **Obv:** Armored bust to right **Obv. Legend:** ANTHON: GUNTHER: E: IV: COM: IMP. **Rev. Legend:** NACH DEM OBERSACH CREUSSCHLUS **Rev. Inscription:** XII / MARIEN / GROSCH: / V. FEIN. SILB. / date / mintmaster's initials. **Mint:** Arnstadt **Note:** Ref. F#377-378.

Date	Mintage	VG	F	VF	XF	Unc
1685 HCH	—	—	—	—	—	—
Reported, not confirmed						
1686/5 HCH	—	—	—	—	—	—

KM# 7 24 MARIENGROSCHEN (Gulden)
Silver, 39 mm. **Ruler:** Anton Günther II **Obv:** Armored bust to left **Obv. Legend:** ANTHON. GVNTH: E. IV. COM. I. CO. DE. **Rev. Legend:** SCHWARTZ. E. HON. DYN. I. ARN. SON. LEV. ET CL. **Rev. Inscription:** XXIIII / MARIEN / GROSCHEN / date / mintmaster's initials. **Mint:** Sondershausen **Note:** Dav#966. Ref. F#363.

Date	Mintage	VG	F	VF	XF	Unc
1675 HM	—	500	1,000	2,000	3,900	—

KM# 9 60 KREUZER (Gulden)
Silver, 36.5-38.5 mm. **Ruler:** Anton Günther II **Obv:** Bust to right **Obv. Legend:** ANTHON. GVNTH: E: IV. COM. I. CO. DE. **Rev:** Manifold arms supported by wildman and woman holding pennants, 3 ornate helmets above, value (60) below **Rev. Legend:** DYN. I. AR. SON. L.L. ET CL. - SCHWARTZ. E. HON., date **Mint:** Sondershausen **Note:** Dav#965. Ref. F#349.

Date	Mintage	VG	F	VF	XF	Unc
1675 HM	—	400	800	1,600	3,250	—

KM# 11 60 KREUZER (Gulden)
Silver, 36.5-38.5 mm. **Ruler:** Anton Günther II **Obv:** Bust to left **Obv. Legend:** ANTHON. GVNTH: E: IV. COM. I. CO. DE. **Rev:** Manifold arms supported by wildman and woman holding pennants, 3 ornate helmets above, date divided by crests of helmets, value (60) below **Rev. Legend:** DYN. I. AR. SON. L.L. ET CL. - CO. DE. SCHWARTZ. E. HON. **Mint:** Sondershausen **Note:** Ref. F#346.

Date	Mintage	VG	F	VF	XF	Unc
1675 HM	—	400	800	1,600	3,250	—

KM# 12 60 KREUZER (Gulden)
Silver, 36.5-38.5 mm. **Ruler:** Anton Günther II **Obv:** Bust to left **Obv. Legend:** ANTHON. GVNTH: E: IV. COM. I. CO. DE. **Rev:** Manifold arms supported by wildman and woman holding pennants, 3 ornate helmets above, date divided by crests of helmets, value (60) below **Rev. Legend:** DYN. I. AR. SON. L.L. ET CL. - SCHWARTZ. E. HON. **Mint:** Sondershausen **Note:** Ref. F#347-348. Varieties exist.

Date	Mintage	VG	F	VF	XF	Unc
1675 HM	—	400	800	1,600	3,250	—

KM# 10 60 KREUZER (Gulden)
Silver, 36.5-38.5 mm. **Ruler:** Anton Günther II **Obv:** But to right **Obv. Legend:** ANTHON. GVNTH: E: IV. COM. I. CO. DE. **Rev:** Manifold arms supported by wildman and woman holding pennants, 3 ornate helmets above, date divided by crests of helmets, value (60) below **Rev. Legend:** DYN. . AR. SON. L.L. ET CL. - CO. DE. SCHWARTZ. E. HON. **Mint:** Sondershausen **Note:** Ref. F#350. Known with c/m of Franconian Circle.

Date	Mintage	VG	F	VF	XF	Unc
1675 HM	—	400	800	1,600	3,250	—

KM# 14 2/3 THALER
Silver, 38.5 mm. **Ruler:** Anton Günther II **Obv:** Draped bust right **Obv. Legend:** ANTHON: GVNTH: E. IV. COM. I. CO. DE. SCHWAR. **Rev:** Crowned shield of rectangular Schwarzburg lion arms over fork and comb, supported by wildman and woman holding pennants, value 2/3 in oval below **Rev. Legend:** E. HON. DYN. IN. ARN - SON. LEV. LOH. ET. CL. **Mint:** Sondershausen **Note:** Ref. F#352; 355.

Date	Mintage	VG	F	VF	XF	Unc
1675 HM	—	225	450	900	1,860	—

KM# 16 2/3 THALER

Silver, 38 mm. **Ruler:** Anton Günther II **Obv:** Draped bust right **Obv. Legend:** ANTHON: GUNTHER. E. IV. COM: IMP. **Rev:** Crowned shield with concave sides of Schwarzburg lion arms over fork and comb, supported by wildman and woman holding pennants, date above, value 2/3 in oval below **Rev. Legend:** DE SCHWAR. E. HON - DYN. I. ARN. SON. L. L. E. CL. **Mint:** Sondershausen **Note:** Ref. F#356.

Date	Mintage	VG	F	VF	XF	Unc
1675 HM	—	225	450	900	1,800	—

KM# 13 2/3 THALER

Silver, 38.5 mm. **Ruler:** Anton Günther II **Obv:** Draped bust right **Obv. Legend:** ANTHON: GVNTHER: E. IV. COM. I. **Rev:** Crowned shield of rectangular Schwarzburg ion arms over fork and comb, supported by wildman and woman holding pennants, date above, value 2/3 in oval below **Rev. Legend:** COM. DE. SCHWAR. E. HON - DYN. I. ARN. SON. LEV. L. E. CL. **Mint:** Sondershausen **Note:** Dav#958. Ref. F#353, 354.

Date	Mintage	VG	F	VF	XF	Unc
1675 HM	—	250	500	1,000	1,950	—

KM# 15 2/3 THALER

Silver, 36 mm. **Ruler:** Anton Günther II **Obv:** Draped bust right. **Obv. Legend:** ANTHON: GVNTHER: E. IV. COM. I. COM. **Rev:** Crowned shield of rectangular Schwarzburg lion arms over fork and comb, supported by wildman and woman holding pennants, date above, value 2/3 in oval below **Rev. Legend:** DE SCHWAR. E. HON - DYN. I. ARN. SON. L. L. E. CL. **Mint:** Sondershausen **Note:** Dav#959. Ref. F#356 (1676 date).

Date	Mintage	VG	F	VF	XF	Unc
1675 HM	—	135	275	375	775	—
1676 HM	—	135	275	375	775	—

KM# 19 2/3 THALER

Silver, 36 mm. **Ruler:** Anton Günther II **Obv:** Draped bust right **Obv. Legend:** ANTHON. GUNTER: IV. COM: IMP:. **Rev:** Crowned shield with concave sides of Schwarzburg lion arms over fork and comb, supported by wildman and woman holding pennants, date above, value 2/3 in oval below **Rev. Legend:** COM: DE. SCHWARTZ. - ET. HON STEIN **Mint:** Sondershausen **Note:** Dav#960. Ref. F#359.

Date	Mintage	VG	F	VF	XF	Unc
1676 HM	—	75.00	150	300	600	—

KM# 25 2/3 THALER

Silver, 38 mm. **Ruler:** Anton Günther II **Obv:** Bust left **Obv. Legend:** ANTHON. GUNTE. COM. IMP:. **Rev:** Crowned shield with concave sides of Schwarzburg ion arms over fork and comb, supported by wildman and woman holding pennants, date above, value 2/3 in oval below **Rev. Legend:** COM: DE. SCHWARTZ. - ET. HON STEIN **Mint:** Sondershausen **Note:** Dav#961.

Date	Mintage	VG	F	VF	XF	Unc
1676 HM	—	85.00	175	375	750	1,500

KM# A27 2/3 THALER

Silver, 36 mm mm. **Ruler:** Anton Günther II **Obv:** Draped bust right **Obv. Legend:** ANTHON: GUNTHER: E. IV. COM. I. COM. **Rev:** Crowned triangular shield of Schwarzburg lion arms with curved top and small scallops in sides, over fork and comb, supported by wildman and woman holding pennants, date above, value 2/3 in oval below **Rev. Legend:** DE SCHWAR. E. HON. DYN. I. ARN. SON. L.L. E. CL. **Mint:** Sondershausen **Note:** Dav#962.

Date	Mintage	VG	F	VF	XF	Unc
1676 HM	—	85.00	175	375	775	—

KM# 27 2/3 THALER

Silver, 36 mm mm. **Ruler:** Anton Günther II **Obv:** Crowned shield of rectangular Schwarzburg lion arms over fork and comb, supported by wildman and woman holding pennants, date above **Obv. Legend:** ANTHON: GVNTHER: E. IV. COM. I. COM. **Rev. Legend:** DE SCHWAR. E. HON. DYN. I. ARN. SON. LEV.L. E. CL. **Mint:** Sondershausen **Note:** Dav#963. Ref. F#351.

Date	Mintage	VG	F	VF	XF	Unc
1676 HM	—	85.00	175	375	775	—

KM# 26 2/3 THALER

Silver, 36 mm. **Ruler:** Anton Günther II **Obv:** Draped bust right **Obv. Legend:** ANTHON: GVNTHER. E. IV. COM. I. COM. **Rev:** Crowned shield with concave sides of Schwarzburg lion arms over fork and comb, supported by wildman and woman holding pennants, date above, value 2/3 in oval below **Rev. Legend:** .DE. SCHWAR. E. HON. - DYN. I. ARN. SON. L.L. E. CL. **Mint:** Sondershausen **Note:** Ref. F#358.

Date	Mintage	VG	F	VF	XF	Unc
1676 HM	—	85.00	175	375	775	—

KM# 20 2/3 THALER

Silver, 35.5-38 mm. **Ruler:** Anton Günther II **Obv:** Draped bust right **Obv. Legend:** ANTHON: GUNTHER: E: IV. COM: IMP. **Rev:** Crowned shield with concave sides of Schwarzburg lion arms over fork and comb, supported by wildman and woman holding pennants, date above, value 2/3 in oval below **Rev. Legend:** COM: DE. SCHWARTZ. - ET HONSTEIN. **Note:** Ref. F#360-61, 366, 370, 372-73. Struck at either Sondershausen or Keula mints. Varieties exist.

Date	Mintage	VG	F	VF	XF	Unc
1676 (a)	—	35.00	75.00	150	310	—
1676 HM	—	35.00	75.00	150	310	—
1678 (a) large letters	—	35.00	75.00	150	310	—
1678 (a) small letters	—	35.00	75.00	150	310	—

KM# 21 2/3 THALER

Silver, 38 mm. **Ruler:** Anton Günther II **Obv:** Draped bust right **Obv. Legend:** ANTHON: GUNTHER: E: IV. COM: IMP. **Rev:** Crowned shield with concave sides of Schwarzburg lion arms over fork and comb, supported by wildman and woman holding pennants, date above, value 2/3 in oval below **Rev. Legend:** COM. DE. SCHWA - RTZ. - ET - HONST - EIN. **Mint:** Keula **Note:** Ref. F#367.

Date	Mintage	VG	F	VF	XF	Unc
1676 (a)	—	40.00	80.00	160	325	—

KM# 22 2/3 THALER

Silver, 38.5 mm mm. **Ruler:** Anton Günther II **Obv:** Draped bust right **Obv. Legend:** ANTHON: GUNTHER: E: IV. COM: IMP:. **Rev:** Crowned shield with concave sides of Schwarzburg lion arms over fork and comb, supported by wildman and woman holding pennants, date above, value 2/3 in oval below **Rev. Legend:** COM: DE. SCHWARTZ. - ET - HONSTEIN **Mint:** Keula **Note:** Ref. F#368.

Date	Mintage	VG	F	VF	XF	Unc
1676 (a)	—	40.00	80.00	160	325	—

KM# 23 2/3 THALER

Silver, 38.5 mm mm. **Ruler:** Anton Günther II **Obv:** Draped bust right **Obv. Legend:** ANTHON: GUNTHER: E: IV. COM: IMP. **Rev:** Crowned shield with concave sides of Schwarzburg lion arms over fork and comb, supported by wildman and woman holding pennants, date above, value 2/3 in oval below **Rev. Legend:** COM: DE. SCHWARTZ. - ET HONSTEIN **Mint:** Keula **Note:** Ref. F#369.

Date	Mintage	VG	F	VF	XF	Unc
1676 (a)	—	40.00	80.00	160	325	—

KM# 24 2/3 THALER

Silver, 38 mm mm. **Ruler:** Anton Günther II **Obv:** Draped bust rght **Obv. Legend:** ANTHON: GUINTHER: E: IV. COM: IMP. **Rev:** Crowned shield with concave sides of Schwarzburg lion arms over fork and comb, supported by wildman and woman holding pennants, date above, value 2/3 in oval below **Rev. Legend:** COM: DE. SCHWARTZ. - ET. HON STEIN. **Mint:** Keula **Note:** Ref. F#371.

Date	Mintage	VG	F	VF	XF	Unc
1676 (a)	—	40.00	80.00	160	325	—

KM# 28 2/3 THALER

Silver, 36 mm mm. **Ruler:** Anton Günther II **Obv:** Small bust right in circle **Obv. Legend:** ANTHON: GUNTER: E. IV: COM: IMPER. **Rev:** Crowned squarish shield of Schwarzburg lion arms, fork and comb in large pediment below lion, supported by wildman and woman holding pennants, date above, value 2/3 in oval below **Rev. Legend:** COM. DE. SCHWARTZ. E. HON - DYN. I. AR. SON. L. L. E. CL. **Mint:** Keula **Note:** Dav#964.

Date	Mintage	VG	F	VF	XF	Unc
1679 (a)	—	40.00	80.00	160	325	—

KM# 4 THALER

Silver **Ruler:** Christian Günther II **Subject:** Death of Christian Günther II **Obv:** Helmeted and supported arms **Rev:** Five-line inscription within wreath **Note:** Prev. Dav#7686.

Date	Mintage	VG	F	VF	XF	Unc
1666	—	1,000	2,000	4,000	6,500	—

KM# 6 THALER

Silver **Ruler:** Johann Günther IV **Subject:** Death of Johann Günther IV **Obv:** Helmeted and supported arms **Rev:** Nine-line inscription within wreath **Note:** Prev. Dav#7687.

Date	Mintage	VG	F	VF	XF	Unc
1669	—	1,000	2,000	4,000	6,500	—

KM# 30 THALER

Silver, 44 mm. **Ruler:** Anton Günther II **Obv:** Draped bust right **Obv. Legend:** ANTHON. GUNTHER. E. IV. COM: IMP:. **Rev:** Ornately manifold arms supported by wildman and woman holding pennants, 3 ornate helmets above **Rev. Legend:** COM: DE. SCHWARTZ - B: ET. HONSTEIN, date. **Mint:** Sondershausen **Note:** Dav#7692.

Date	Mintage	VG	F	VF	XF	Unc
1681 HM Rare	—	—	—	—	—	—

Note: Künker Auction 100, 6-05, VF+ realized approximately $13,960.

Date	Mintage	VG	F	VF	XF	Unc
1682 HM Rare	—	—	—	—	—	—

KM# 34 THALER

Silver, 47 mm mm. **Ruler:** Anton Günther II **Obv:** Armored bust right **Obv. Legend:** ANTHON: GUNTHER: E: IV. COM: IMP. **Rev:** Ornately manifold arms supported by wildman and woman holding pennants, 3 ornate helmets aboe **Rev. Legend:** COM: DE SCHWARTZB: ET HONSTEIN, date. **Mint:** Arnstadt **Note:** Dav#7693. Date at end of reverse legend.

Date	Mintage	VG	F	VF	XF	Unc
1686 HCH Rare	—	—	—	—	—	—

TRADE COINAGE

KM# 29 DUCAT

3.5000 g., 0.9860 Gold 0.1109 oz. AGW, 21.5 mm. **Ruler:** Anton Günther II **Obv:** Armored bust to left **Obv. Legend:** ANTHON. GUNTHER. E. IV. COM. IMP:. **Rev:** Manifold arms supported by wildman and woman, 3 ornate helmets above, date at end of legend **Rev. Legend:** COM. DE. SCHVVARTZB: — ET HONSTEIN. (date). **Note:** Fr#3108.

Date	Mintage	VG	F	VF	XF	Unc
1680 HM	—	2,500	4,000	7,500	12,500	—

SCHWARZBURG-RUDOLSTADT

Established upon the division of Schwarzburg-Sondershausen in 1552, the younger main branch of Schwarzburg, centered on the castle and town of Rudolstadt, 17 miles (29 kilometers) south of Weimar, flourished until the end of World War I. The count was raised to the rank of prince in 1711. The three sons of Albrecht VII, the first Count of Schwarzburg-Rudolstadt, ruled and issued coinage jointly, followed by a long succession of sole rulers descended from the middle son, Ludwig Günther I.

RULERS

Albrecht VII, 1552-1605

Joint Rule:

Karl Günther zu Kranichfeld, 1605-1630

Ludwig Günther I zu Rudolstadt, 1605-1646

Albrecht Günther zu Stadtilm, 1605-1634

Albrecht Anton, 1646-1710

MINTMARKS AND MINT OFFICIALS' INITIALS

Initials	Date	Name
R	1621-1623	Rudolstadt mint
BB	1621, 1622-1625	Barthel Bechstett (or Bechstein), mintmaster in Rudolstadt
	1621	Christoph Carpe, mintmaster in Rudolstadt
F	1621-1622	Friedeburg mint
Z	1621-1623	Heinrich Abel Ziegenmeier, mintmaster in Friedeburg
K, KS	1621-1622	Königsee mint
	1620-1621	Heinrich Meyer von Halle, mintmaster in Königsee
S	1621-1623	Peter Schrader von Magdeburg, mintmaster in Königsee

L	1621-1622	Leutenberg mint
P	1621-1623	Johann Pabst, mintmaster in Leutenberg
	1621-1622	Wolf Albrecht, mintmaster in Leutenberg
	1622	Barthel Bechstett (or Bechstein), mintmaster in Kranichfeld
	1622	Caspar Urleben, mintmaster in Kranichfeld

Arms: See under Schwarzburg

REFERENCES:

F = Ernst Fischer, ***Die Münzen des Hauses Schwarzburg***, Heidelberg, 1904.

R = Ernst Helmuth von Bethe, ***Schwarzburger Münzen und Medaillen: Sammlung des Schlossmuseums in Rudolstadt***, Halle (Saale), 1903.

COUNTSHIP

REGULAR COINAGE

KM# 6 3 PFENNIG (DREIER)

Copper, 17 mm. **Ruler:** Karl Günther; Ludwig Günther and Albrecht Günther **Obv:** Heart-shaped shield of arms divided vertically, Schwarzburg lion left, Arnstadt eagle right, comb below, mantle draped ot lower left, bottom and right **Rev:** Shield of arms divided horizontally, Hohnstein above, Klettenberg below, various mintmarks and symbols to left and right of shield, III above **Mint:** Friedeburg **Note:** Ref. F#477a-c. Varieties exist.

Date	Mintage	VG	F	VF	XF	Unc
ND(1621-23) P	—	100	200	425	—	—
ND(1621-23) S	—	100	200	425	—	—
ND(1621-23) Z	—	100	200	425	—	—

KM# 7 3 PFENNIG (DREIER)

Copper, 18 mm. **Ruler:** Karl Günther; Ludwig Günther and Albrecht Günther **Obv:** 3 small shields of arms, 1 above 2, comb below **Obv. Legend:** MO. NO. CO. CHW. R. L. **Rev:** Imperial orb with 3 **Rev. Legend:** FERD. II. ROM. M. A. **Mint:** Leutenberg **Note:** Ref. R#1135a.

Date	Mintage	VG	F	VF	XF	Unc
ND(1621-23)	—	100	200	425	—	—

KM# 45 3 PFENNIG (DREIER)

Silver, 17-18 mm. **Ruler:** Karl Günther; Ludwig Günther and Albrecht Günther **Obv:** 3 small shields of arms, 1 at top, others to left and right, 'R' in center, comb below **Obv. Legend:** A. GG. K. Z. S. V. H. **Rev:** Imperial orb with 3 divides date, mintmark above, all in ornamented oval **Mint:** Konigsee **Note:** Ref. R#1156. Weight varies: .55-.61 g.

Date	Mintage	VG	F	VF	XF	Unc
1622 K	—	—	—	—	—	—

KM# 40 3 PFENNIG (DREIER)

Silver, 17-18 mm. **Ruler:** Karl Günther; Ludwig Günther and Albrecht Günther **Obv:** 3 small shields of arms, 1 at top, others to left and right, 'R' in center, comb below **Obv. Legend:** A. G. G. Z. S. V. H. **Rev:** Imperial orb with 3 divides date, mintmark above, all in ornamented oval **Mint:** Konigsee **Note:** Ref. F#508, 517. Weight varies: .55-.61 g. Varieties exist.

Date	Mintage	VG	F	VF	XF	Unc
1622 K	—	200	400	650	1,150	—
1623 K	—	200	400	650	1,150	—

KM# 41 3 PFENNIG (DREIER)

Silver, 17-18 mm. **Ruler:** Karl Günther; Ludwig Günther and Albrecht Günther **Obv:** 3 small shields of arms, 1 at top, others to left and right, 'R' in center, comb below **Obv. Legend:** A. G. G. Z. S. V. H. **Rev:** Imperial orb with 3 divides date, mintmark above **Mint:** Konigsee **Note:** Ref. F#509. Weight varies: .55-.61 g.

Date	Mintage	VG	F	VF	XF	Unc
1622 K	—	—	—	—	—	—

KM# 42 3 PFENNIG (DREIER)

Silver, 17-18 mm. **Ruler:** Karl Günther; Ludwig Günther and Albrecht Günther **Obv:** 3 small shields of arms, 1 at top, others to left and right, 'R' in center, comb below **Obv. Legend:** A. G. G. Z. S. V. H. **Rev:** Imperial orb with 3, date divided by mintmark in arc above **Mint:** Konigsee **Note:** Ref. F#510. Weight varies: .55-.61 g.

Date	Mintage	VG	F	VF	XF	Unc
16ZZ K	—	—	—	—	—	—

KM# 43 3 PFENNIG (DREIER)

Silver, 17-18 mm. **Ruler:** Karl Günther; Ludwig Günther and Albrecht Günther **Obv:** 3 small shields of arm, 1 at top, others to left and right, 'R' in center, comb below **Obv. Legend:** A. G. G. Z. S. V. H. **Rev:** Imperial orb with 3, date divided by mintmark in arc above, all in ornamented oval **Mint:** Konigsee **Note:** Ref. F#511. Weight varies: .55-.61 g.

Date	Mintage	VG	F	VF	XF	Unc
1622 K	—	—	—	—	—	—

KM# 44 3 PFENNIG (DREIER)

Silver, 17-18 mm. **Ruler:** Karl Günther; Ludwig Günther and Albrecht Günther **Obv:** 3 small shields of arms, 1 at top, others to left and right, 'R' in center, comb below **Obv. Legend:** A. G ★ K ★ G. Z. S. **Rev:** Imperial orb with 3 divides date **Mint:** Konigsee **Note:** Ref. F#512. Weight varies: .55-.61 g.

Date	Mintage	VG	F	VF	XF	Unc
1622 K	—	—	—	—	—	—

KM# 66 3 PFENNIG (DREIER)

Silver, 17-18 mm. **Ruler:** Karl Günther; Ludwig Günther and Albrecht Günther **Obv:** 3 small shields of arms, 1 above 2, comb below **Obv. Legend:** A. G. G. Z. S. V. H. **Rev:** Imperial orb with 3 divides K - S, date divided above **Mint:** Konigsee **Note:** Ref. F#513. Weight varies: .55-.61 g.

Date	Mintage	VG	F	VF	XF	Unc
1623 KS	—	—	—	—	—	—

KM# 67 3 PFENNIG (DREIER)

Silver, 17-18 mm. **Ruler:** Karl Günther; Ludwig Günther and Albrecht Günther **Obv:** 3 small shields of arms, 1 above 3, comb below **Obv. Legend:** A. G. G. Z. S. V. H. **Rev:** '3' in heart-shaped shield which divides date, mintmark above **Mint:** Konigsee **Note:** Ref. F#514. Weight varies: .55-.61 g.

Date	Mintage	VG	F	VF	XF	Unc
1623 K	—	90.00	180	360	—	—

KM# 68 3 PFENNIG (DREIER)

Silver, 17-18 mm. **Ruler:** Karl Günther; Ludwig Günther and Albrecht Günther **Obv:** 3 small shields of arms, 1 above 2, comb below **Obv. Legend:** A. G. G. Z. S. V. H. **Rev:** Imperial orb with 3 in ornamented oval, date divided by mintmark in arc at sides and above **Mint:** Konigsee **Note:** Ref. F#515. Weight varies: .55-.61 g.

Date	Mintage	VG	F	VF	XF	Unc
1623 K	—	115	225	400	775	—

KM# 69 3 PFENNIG (DREIER)

Silver, 17-18 mm. **Ruler:** Karl Günther; Ludwig Günther and Albrecht Günther **Obv:** Shield of 4-fold arms, comb below, mintmark aboe **Rev:** IMperial orb with 3 divides date in ornamented rhombus **Rev. Legend:** A. G. G. Z. S. V. H. **Mint:** Konigsee **Note:** Ref. F#516. Weight varies: .55-.61 g.

Date	Mintage	VG	F	VF	XF	Unc
1623 K	—	115	235	475	—	—

KM# 63 3 PFENNIG (DREIER)

Silver, 16.5 mm. **Ruler:** Karl Günther; Ludwig Günther and Albrecht Günther **Obv:** 3 small shields of arms, 1 at top, others to left and right, 'R' in center, comb below, mintmaster's initials at bottom **Rev:** Imperial orb with 3 divides date within ornamented rhombus **Mint:** Rudolstadt **Note:** Ref. F#464-66. Kipper coinage. Weight varies: .57-.72 g. Varieties exist.

Date	Mintage	VG	F	VF	XF	Unc
16Z3 R-BB	—	65.00	135	275	550	—

KM# 64 3 PFENNIG (DREIER)

Silver, 16.5 mm. **Ruler:** Karl Günther; Ludwig Günther and Albrecht Günther **Obv:** 3 small shields of arms, 1 at top, others to left and right, 'R' in center, comb below, mintmaster's initials at bottom **Rev:** Imperial orb with 3 divides date within ornamented rhombus **Mint:** Rudolstadt **Note:** Ref. F#467. Kipper coinage. Weight varies: .57-.72 g.

Date	Mintage	VG	F	VF	XF	Unc
16Z3 R-S	—	—	—	—	—	—

KM# 13 12 KREUZER (Schreckenberger)

Silver, 26 mm. **Ruler:** Karl Günther; Ludwig Günther and Albrecht Günther **Obv:** Ornamented shield of 4-fold arms with central shield of Schwarzburg, mintmark above **Obv. Legend:** MO. NO: COMIT: SCHWARTZB: ET. H: RUD: OL* **Rev:** Imperial eagle with 12 on breast, date at end of legend **Rev. Legend:** FERD: II: ROM: IMPER: SEMP: AUG: **Mint:** Leutenberg **Note:** Ref. F#481.

Date	Mintage	VG	F	VF	XF	Unc
1621 L	—	—	—	—	—	—

KM# 80 GROSCHEN

Silver **Ruler:** Karl Günther; Ludwig Günther and Albrecht Günther **Subject:** Death of Karl Günther **Obv:** 4-line inscription in wreath **Obv. Legend:** CAROL: GVNTH: S. R. I. QVAT: COM. SCHVARTZB. E. H. D. A. S. L. L. [symbol] CAP. WAL. ADM: +. **Obv. Inscription:** Jesu / Christ: Blut / Mein / Pestes Gut **Rev. Inscription:** Natus 8: Noue: / Anno 1576 / Obiit in Arce Cranichf: / Sup. 24. Sep: An. 1630 / Dondeb: Rudol: / 1. Noue: An. Eiusb. **Note:** Ref. F#493. All lettering except obverse outer legend in script.

Date	Mintage	VG	F	VF	XF	Unc
1630	—	45.00	90.00	180	360	—

KM# 82 GROSCHEN

Silver, 22 mm. **Ruler:** Karl Günther; Ludwig Günther and Albrecht Günther **Subject:** Death of Albrecht Günther **Obv:** 5-line inscription in wreath **Obv. Legend:** ALBRECHT. GINT. S. R. I. QVAT. COM. SCHWARTZB. E. H. D. A. S. L. L. C. **Obv. Inscription:** ALLEIN / BEI CHRI / SDO EWI / GE GREI / DE. **Rev. Inscription:** NATVS ANNI / .1582. 8. AVGV. / MARTVVS. ERFV. / 20. IAN. AN. 1634 / CONDEBATVR RV / DOLPHS. 18. MA / EIVS. D. ANN. **Note:** Ref. F#506.

Date	Mintage	VG	F	VF	XF	Unc
1634	—	—	—	—	—	—

KM# 86 GROSCHEN

Silver, 24 mm. **Ruler:** Karl Günther; Ludwig Günther and Albrecht Günther **Subject:** Death of Ludwig Günther I **Obv:** 5-line inscription in wreath **Obv. Legend:** LUDW. GUNTH. S. R. I. QVAT. COM. IN. SCHWARTZB. E.H. **Obv. Inscription:** SYM / BOLUM. / VIVIT POST / FUNERA / VIRTUS / [symbol] **Rev. Inscription:** NATUS / IN ARCE RUDEL / STAD. XXVII. IUN / AN. M.D.LXXXI. / OBIIT IBIDEM IV / NOVEMBRIS. AN: / M.DC.XXXXVI/[symbol] **Note:** Ref. F#500.

Date	Mintage	VG	F	VF	XF	Unc
1646	—	80.00	160	325	—	—

KM# 90 GROSCHEN

Silver, 22 mm. **Ruler:** Albrecht Anton **Subject:** Death of Anna Sophie von Anhalt, wife of Karth Günther **Obv:** Ornamented heart-shaped shield of Anhalt arms divides date, 7-line inscription below **Obv. Inscription:** MEMOR. ILLV / STRISS. PR. ANNÆ. SO / PHIÆ. PR. ANHALT. / COMIT. SCHWARTZ / BVRG. VIDVÆ SO / ROR. ET CO / GNAT **Rev. Inscription:** 24 / HONOR. / NATÆ. DESSAVI / Æ. XV. IVN. HOR XII. / MDLXXXIV. DE / NAT. IN ARCE / KRANCHFELT / SVP. IX. IVN. / MDCLII. **Note:** Ref. F#497.

Date	Mintage	VG	F	VF	XF	Unc
1652	—	80.00	160	325	—	—

KM# 92 GROSCHEN

Silver, 24 mm. **Ruler:** Albrecht Anton **Subject:** Death of Emilie von Oldenburg-Demenhorst, wife of Ludwig Günther I. **Obv:** Crowned 'Æ' monogram, 2-line inscription below **Obv. Legend:** C: IN SCHW. ET HOHN: NAT: CO: ET. D ★. **Obv. Inscription:** IN. TE. D. / CON:. **Rev. Inscription:** NATA / IN CASTEL / DELMENH: / D: XV. IUN 16 / 14 DENAT: ★ / LEUTENB. D. / 4. DEC. ★ / .1670. **Note:** Ref. F#503.

Date	Mintage	VG	F	VF	XF	Unc
1670	—	275	500	1,025	—	—

KM# 81 THALER

Silver **Ruler:** Ludwig Günther I and Albrecht Günther **Subject:** Death of Karl Günther **Rev:** 8-line inscription **Note:** Dav #7694.

Date	Mintage	VG	F	VF	XF	Unc
1630	—	1,100	2,100	3,850	7,200	—

KM# 85 THALER
Silver **Ruler:** Ludwig Günther I **Subject:** Death of Albrecht Günther **Rev:** 8-line inscription **Note:** Dav #7698.

Date	Mintage	VG	F	VF	XF	Unc
1634 Rare	—	—	—	—	—	—

KM# 88 THALER
Silver **Ruler:** Ludwig Günther I **Subject:** Death of Ludwig Günther I **Rev:** Crowned arms **Note:** Dav #7696.

Date	Mintage	VG	F	VF	XF	Unc
1646	—	850	1,550	2,800	5,000	—

KM# 89 THALER
Silver **Ruler:** Ludwig Günther I **Obv:** Order of Johann cross on right breast **Note:** Dav #7696A.

Date	Mintage	VG	F	VF	XF	Unc
1646	—	850	1,550	2,800	5,000	—

KM# 91 THALER
Silver **Ruler:** Albrecht Anton **Subject:** Death of Anna Sophia, Wife of Karl Günther **Obv:** Crowned arms of Anhalt and Schwarzburg **Rev:** 11-line inscription **Note:** Dav #7695.

Date	Mintage	VG	F	VF	XF	Unc
1652	—	1,300	2,400	4,300	7,200	—

KM# 95 THALER
Silver **Ruler:** Albrecht Anton **Subject:** Death of Emilie, Wife of Ludwig Günther **Obv:** 2 crowned shields **Rev:** Cross with hearts at top and base **Note:** Dav #7697.

Date	Mintage	VG	F	VF	XF	Unc
1670	—	1,500	2,700	4,950	8,300	—

JOINT COINAGE

Karl Günther; Ludwig Günther I; Albrecht Günther

KM# 11 12 KREUZER (Schreckenberger)
Silver, 26 mm. **Ruler:** Karl Günther; Ludwig Günther and Albrecht Günther **Obv:** Ornamented shield of 4-fold arms, mintmark divides date above, comb below **Obv. Legend:** MO. NO: COMIT: SCHWARTZB: ET. H: RVDO: F. **Rev:** Crowned imperial eagle, large imperial orb on breast with 1Z **Rev. Legend:** FERDINAND II. ROM. IMPER: SEMP: AVG. **Mint:** Friedeburg **Note:** Ref. F#475.

Date	Mintage	VG	F	VF	XF	Unc
16Z1 F	—	—	—	—	—	—

KM# 12 12 KREUZER (Schreckenberger)
Silver, 26 mm. **Ruler:** Karl Günther; Ludwig Günther and Albrecht Günther **Obv:** Ornamented shield of 4-fold arms, mintmark divides date above, comb below **Obv. Legend:** MO. NO: COMIT: SCHWARTZB: ET. H: RVDOL: L(I): ✠ **Rev:** Crowned imperial eagle, large imperial orb on breast with 1Z **Rev. Legend:** FERDINA(N)D: II. ROM. IMPER: SEMP: AVG. **Mint:** Leutenberg **Note:** Ref. F#480.

Date	Mintage	VG	F	VF	XF	Unc
16Z1 L	—	—	—	—	—	—

KM# 14 12 KREUZER (Schreckenberger)
Silver, 26 mm. **Ruler:** Karl Günther; Ludwig Günther and Albrecht Günther **Obv:** Shield of 4-fold arms, comb below **Obv. Legend:** MON. NOV. COM. SCHWAR. RVD. L(I). **Rev:** Imperial eagle, 12 in orb on breast **Rev. Legend:** FERD. II. D:F. ROM(A). IM(P). SEM. A(V)(G). **Note:** Ref. F#488. Varieties exist.

Date	Mintage	VG	F	VF	XF	Unc
ND(1621-22)	—	—	—	—	—	—

KM# 9 12 KREUZER (Schreckenberger)
Silver, 27 mm. **Ruler:** Karl Günther; Ludwig Günther and Albrecht Günther **Obv:** Shield of 4-fold arms, comb below **Obv. Legend:** MO: NO: COM: SCHWARTZB. E.H.L. **Rev:** Crowned imperial eagle, orb on breast with 1Z, date at end of legend **Rev. Legend:** FERD. II. ROM. IMP. SEM. A **Mint:** Rudolstadt **Note:** Ref. R#1102a. Kipper coinage.

Date	Mintage	VG	F	VF	XF	Unc
16Z1	—	60.00	120	240	—	—

KM# 17 24 KREUZER (Doppelschreckenberger)
Silver, 25-30 mm. **Ruler:** Karl Günther; Ludwig Günther and Albrecht Günther **Obv:** Ornamented shield of 4-fold arms, date and mint mark at end of legend **Obv. Legend:** MO. NO. COM. SCHW(Z)R. RU. L. **Rev:** Imperial eagle, orb on breast with Z4 **Rev. Legend:** FERD. II. D.G. ROM. IM. SEM. AUG(U). **Mint:** Konigsee **Note:** Ref. F#444; R#1088. Kipper coinage.

Date	Mintage	VG	F	VF	XF	Unc
16Z1 K	—	75.00	150	300	—	—
16ZZ K	—	75.00	150	300	—	—

KM# 18 24 KREUZER (Doppelschreckenberger)
Silver, 25-30 mm. **Ruler:** Karl Günther; Ludwig Günther and Albrecht Günther **Obv:** Ornamented shield of 4-fold arms **Obv. Legend:** MO. NO. COM. SCHWAR. RU. L. **Rev:** Crowned imperial eagle, orb on breast with Z4 **Rev. Legend:** FERD. II. D.G. RO. IM. SEM. AUG. **Mint:** Konigsee **Note:** Ref. F#445. Kipper coinage.

Date	Mintage	VG	F	VF	XF	Unc
16Z1 K	—	—	—	—	—	—

KM# 19 24 KREUZER (Doppelschreckenberger)
Silver, 25-30 mm. **Ruler:** Karl Günther; Ludwig Günther and Albrecht Günther **Obv:** Ornamented shield of 4-fold arms with central shield of Schwarzburg, date and mint mark at end of leg. **Obv. Legend:** MO. NO. COM. SCHWAR. RU. L. **Rev:** Imperial eagle, orb on breast with 24 **Rev. Legend:** FERD. II. D.G. ROM. IM. SEM. AUG. **Mint:** Konigsee **Note:** Ref. F#446. Kipper coinage.

Date	Mintage	VG	F	VF	XF	Unc
1621 K	—	—	—	—	—	—

KM# 20 24 KREUZER (Doppelschreckenberger)
Silver, 25-30 mm. **Ruler:** Karl Günther; Ludwig Günther and Albrecht Günther **Obv:** Ornamented shield of 4-fold arms, 'K' above **Obv. Legend:** MO. NO. COMIT. SCHWARTZB. ET. HO. RVDE. L. **Rev:** IMperial eagle, orb on breast with 24, date divided at top **Rev. Legend:** FERDINA. I.I. ROM. IMPE. SEMP. AVG. **Mint:** Konigsee **Note:** Ref. F#447. Kipper coinage.

Date	Mintage	VG	F	VF	XF	Unc
16Z1 K	—	—	—	—	—	—

KM# 22 24 KREUZER (Doppelschreckenberger)
Silver, 25-30 mm. **Ruler:** Karl Günther; Ludwig Günther and Albrecht Günther **Obv:** Ornamented shield of 4-fold arms, comb in bottom, date at end of legend **Obv. Legend:** MO. NO(U). COM(IT). SCHWAR. RU(D). L(I). **Rev:** Imperial eagle under princely crown, large orb on breast with Z4 **Rev. Legend:** FERD(INA). II. D.G. RO(M). IM. SEM. A(U)(G)(U)(S). **Mint:** Konigsee **Note:** Ref. F#448, 450-51. Kipper coinage.

Date	Mintage	VG	F	VF	XF	Unc
16Z1 K	—	—	—	—	—	—
16ZZ	—	235	475	950	—	—
16ZZ K	—	235	475	950	—	—

KM# 23 24 KREUZER (Doppelschreckenberger)
Silver, 25-30 mm. **Ruler:** Karl Günther; Ludwig Günther and Albrecht Günther **Obv:** Ornamented shield of 4-fold arms, comb in bottom, date and mintmark at end of legend **Obv. Legend:** MO. NO. COM. SCHWAR. RU. L. **Rev:** Crowned imperial eagle, orb on breast with 24 **Rev. Legend:** FERD. II. D.G. ROM. IM. SEM. AUGU. **Mint:** Konigsee **Note:** Ref. F#449. Kipper coinage.

Date	Mintage	VG	F	VF	XF	Unc
1621 K	—	—	—	—	—	—

KM# 24 24 KREUZER (Doppelschreckenberger)
Silver, 28.5-29 mm. **Ruler:** Karl Günther; Ludwig Günther and Albrecht Günther **Obv:** Square ornamented shield of 4-fold arms, mintmark above, comb below **Obv. Legend:** MO: NO: COMI: SCHWART. E.H.I ★. **Rev:** Crowned imperial eagle, large orb on breast with 24, date at end of legend **Rev. Legend:** FERD. II. ROM. IMP. S(EM). A. **Mint:** Rudolstadt **Note:** Ref. F#454, 459a. Kipper coinage.

Date	Mintage	VG	F	VF	XF	Unc
1621 R	—	—	—	—	—	—
1622 R	—	285	550	1,100	—	—

KM# 25 24 KREUZER (Doppelschreckenberger)
Silver, 28.5-29 mm. **Ruler:** Karl Günther; Ludwig Günther and Albrecht Günther **Obv:** Shield of 4-fold arms, mintmark above **Obv. Legend:** MO: NO: COM(I). SCHWART. E.H.L. **Rev:** Crowned imperial eagle, large orb on breast with 24, date at end of legend **Rev. Legend:** FERD. II. ROM. IMP. S(E)(M). A. **Mint:** Rudolstadt **Note:** Ref. F#455, 459b. Kipper coinage.

Date	Mintage	VG	F	VF	XF	Unc
1621 R	—	—	—	—	—	—
1622 R	—	275	500	950	—	—

KM# 26 24 KREUZER (Doppelschreckenberger)
Silver, 28.5-29 mm. **Ruler:** Karl Günther; Ludwig Günther and Albrecht Günther **Obv:** Square ornamented shield of 4-fold arms, mintmark above, comb below **Obv. Legend:** MO: NO: COMI: SCHWAR. T:E.HI. **Rev:** Crowned imperial eagle, large orb on breast with 24, date at end of legend **Rev. Legend:** FERD. II. ROM. IMP. S.E.A. **Mint:** Rudolstadt **Note:** Ref. F#456. Kipper coinage.

Date	Mintage	VG	F	VF	XF	Unc
1621 R	—	—	—	—	—	—

KM# 27 24 KREUZER (Doppelschreckenberger)
Silver, 29 mm. **Ruler:** Karl Günther; Ludwig Günther and Albrecht Günther **Obv:** Ornamented shield of 4-fold arms, date divided by mintmark above, comb below **Obv. Legend:** MO: NO: COMIT: SCHWARTZB: ET. H. RVDOL: F. **Rev:** Crowned imperial eagle, orb on breast with Z4 **Rev. Legend:** FERDINAND: II: ROM: IMPER: SEMP(ER). AVG. **Mint:** Friedeburg **Note:** Ref. F#468. Kipper coinage.

Date	Mintage	VG	F	VF	XF	Unc
16Z1 F	—	200	425	850	—	—

KM# 28 24 KREUZER (Doppelschreckenberger)
Silver, 29 mm. **Ruler:** Karl Günther; Ludwig Günther and Albrecht Günther **Obv:** Shield of 4-fold arms, date above, mintmark between date and legend, comb below **Obv. Legend:** MO: NO: COMIT: SCHWARTZB: ET. H: RVDO **Rev:** Crowned imperial eagle, large orb on breast with Z4 **Rev. Legend:** FERDINAND: II: ROM: IMPER: SEMP: AVG. **Mint:** Friedeburg **Note:** Ref. F#469. Kipper coinage.

Date	Mintage	VG	F	VF	XF	Unc
16Z1 F	—	—	—	—	—	—

KM# 29 24 KREUZER (Doppelschreckenberger)
Silver, 29 mm. **Ruler:** Karl Günther; Ludwig Günther and Albrecht Günther **Obv:** Ornamented shield of 4-fold arms, comb below **Obv. Legend:** MO: NO: COMIT: SCHWARTZB: ET: RVDOL: zF1. **Rev:** Crowned imperial eagle, large orb on beast with Z4 **Rev. Legend:** FERDINAND: II: ROM: IMPER: SEMP. AVGV:. **Mint:** Friedeburg **Note:** Ref. F#470. Kipper coinage.

Date	Mintage	VG	F	VF	XF	Unc
(16)Z1 F	—	—	—	—	—	—

KM# 30 24 KREUZER (Doppelschreckenberger)
Silver, 29 mm. **Ruler:** Karl Günther; Ludwig Günther and Albrecht Günther **Obv:** Shield of 4-fold arms, mintmark divides date above, comb below **Obv. Legend:** MONE: NO: COMIT: SCHWARTZB. ET. H: RVDOL. LI. ✠ **Rev:** Imperial eagle, orb on breast with Z4 **Rev. Legend:** FERDINAND: II. ROM. IMPER: SEMP: AVG:. **Mint:** Leutenberg **Note:** Ref. F#478. Kipper coinage.

Date	Mintage	VG	F	VF	XF	Unc
16Z1 L	—	—	—	—	—	—

KM# 31 24 KREUZER (Doppelschreckenberger)
Silver, 29 mm. **Ruler:** Karl Günther; Ludwig Günther and Albrecht Günther **Obv:** Shield of ornamented 4-fold arms, mintmark divides date above, comb below **Obv. Legend:** + MONE: NO: COMIT: SCHWARTZB. ET. H: RVDOL. LI. **Rev:** Crowned imperial eagle, orb on breast with Z4 **Rev. Legend:** FERDINAND: II. ROM. IMP: SEMP: AVG:. **Mint:** Leutenberg **Note:** Ref. F#479. Kipper coinage.

Date	Mintage	VG	F	VF	XF	Unc
16Z1 L	—	—	—	—	—	—

KM# 32 24 KREUZER (Doppelschreckenberger)
Silver, 26-30 mm. **Ruler:** Karl Günther; Ludwig Günther and Albrecht Günther **Obv:** Ornamented shield of 4-fold arms, comb below **Obv. Legend:** MON NO COMIT. SCHWARTZB. R. VD[symbol]. **Rev:** Imperial eagle, large orb on breast with 24, date at end of legend **Rev. Legend:** FERDI. II. ROM. IMP. S. A. **Note:** Ref. F#485. Kipper coinage.

Date	Mintage	VG	F	VF	XF	Unc
1621	—	—	—	—	—	—

KM# 33 24 KREUZER (Doppelschreckenberger)
Silver, 26-30 mm. **Ruler:** Karl Günther; Ludwig Günther and Albrecht Günther **Obv:** Shield of 4-fold arms, comb below **Obv. Legend:** MO. NO. COM. SCHWARZB. ET. H. **Rev:** Imperial eagle with 24 on breast, date at end of legend **Rev. Legend:** FERDI. II. ROM. IMP. S. A. **Note:** Ref. F#486. Kipper coinage.

Date	Mintage	VG	F	VF	XF	Unc
1621	—	—	—	—	—	—

KM# 59 24 KREUZER (Doppelschreckenberger)
Silver, 26-30 mm. **Ruler:** Karl Günther; Ludwig Günther and Albrecht Günther **Obv:** Shield of 4-fold arms, date above **Obv. Legend:** MO: NO: COMIT: SCHWART. ET. RVD. **Rev:** Imperial eagle with 24 on breast **Rev. Legend:** FERDINAND: II: ROM. IMP: SE: AV. **Note:** Ref. F#487. Kipper coinage.

Date	Mintage	VG	F	VF	XF	Unc
1622	—	—	—	—	—	—

KM# 60 24 KREUZER (Doppelschreckenberger)
Silver **Ruler:** Karl Günther; Ludwig Günther and Albrecht Günther **Obv:** 2 floriated oval frames in which arms of Schwarzburg lion and Klettenberg deer, date above and intertwined initials **Obv. Legend:** CARL. GUNTH: COM: SCHWARTZ: E. HONS **Obv. Inscription:** A / GS / I / AG (An Gottes Segen ist alles gelegen). **Rev:** Imperial eagle, orb with Z4 on breast, princely crown above **Rev. Legend:** FERDIN: II. D: G: RONAN (sic): IM: SEM: AUG. **Mint:** Kranichfeld **Note:** Ref. F#494. Kipper coinage.

Date	Mintage	VG	F	VF	XF	Unc
1622	—	—	—	—	—	—

KM# 55 24 KREUZER (Doppelschreckenberger)
Silver, 29 mm. **Ruler:** Karl Günther; Ludwig Günther and Albrecht Günther **Obv:** Ornamented shiled of 4-fold arms, comb below **Obv. Legend:** MONETA NO: COMIT: SCH: ET: RVD 16Fzz. **Rev:** Crowned imperial eagle, large orb on breast with Z4 **Rev. Legend:** FERDINAND: II: ROM: IMP: SEM(P): A(V). **Mint:** Friedeburg **Note:** Ref. F#471; R#1123. Kipper coinage.

Date	Mintage	VG	F	VF	XF	Unc
(1)6ZZ F	—	—	—	—	—	—
16ZZ F	—	275	550	1,100	—	—

KM# 56 24 KREUZER (Doppelschreckenberger)
Silver, 29 mm. **Ruler:** Karl Günther; Ludwig Günther and Albrecht Günther **Obv:** Ornamented shield of 4-fold arms, comb below **Obv. Legend:** MONETA: NOV. CO: SCHW. E. R. 6Fzz. **Rev:** Crowned imperial eagle, large orb on breast with Z4 **Rev. Legend:** FERDINAND: II: ROM: IMP: SEM(P): A(V). **Mint:** Friedeburg **Note:** Ref. F#472. Kipper coinage.

Date	Mintage	VG	F	VF	XF	Unc
(1)6ZZ F	—	—	—	—	—	—

KM# 57 24 KREUZER (Doppelschreckenberger)
Silver, 29 mm. **Ruler:** Karl Günther; Ludwig Günther and Albrecht Günther **Obv:** Square ornamented shield of 4-fold arms, date divided by mintmark above, comb below **Obv. Legend:** [iron cross] MO: NO: COMIT: SCHWAR: ET. RVDO:. **Rev:** Crowned imperial eagle, orb on breast with Z4 **Rev. Legend:** FERDIN: II. ROM: IMPL SEM: AVG:. **Mint:** Friedeburg **Note:** Ref. F#473. Kipper coinage.

Date	Mintage	VG	F	VF	XF	Unc
16ZZ F	—	—	—	—	—	—

KM# 58 24 KREUZER (Doppelschreckenberger)
Silver, 29 mm. **Ruler:** Karl Günther; Ludwig Günther and Albrecht Günther **Obv:** Square ornamented shield of 4-fold arms, date above, comb below **Obv. Legend:** F: MO: NO: COMIT: SCHWART: ET: RVD:. **Rev:** Crowned imperial eagle, orb on breast with Z4 **Rev. Legend:** FERDINAND: II: ROM: IMP: SEM. A. **Mint:** Friedeburg **Note:** Ref. F#474. Kipper coinage.

Date	Mintage	VG	F	VF	XF	Unc
16ZZ F	—	—	—	—	—	—

KM# 54 24 KREUZER (Doppelschreckenberger)
Silver, 29 mm. **Ruler:** Karl Günther; Ludwig Günther and Albrecht Günther **Obv:** Ornamented shield of 4-fold arms, date above **Obv. Legend:** MONETA. NOV: CO: SCHWAR: ET. RVD: F. **Rev:** Crowned imperial eagle, orb on breast with Z4 **Rev. Legend:** FERDINAND: II: ROM: IMP: SEM: AV. **Mint:** Friedeburg **Note:** Ref. R#1129. Kipper coinage.

Date	Mintage	VG	F	VF	XF	Unc
(1)6ZZ F	—	—	—	—	—	—

KM# 49 24 KREUZER (Doppelschreckenberger)
Silver, 28.5-29 mm. **Ruler:** Karl Günther; Ludwig Günther and Albrecht Günther **Obv:** Square ornamented shield of 4-fold arms, mintmark above, comb below **Obv. Legend:** MO NO COMI SCHWART ET H I* **Rev:** Crowned imperial eagle, large orb on breast with 24, date at end of legend **Rev. Legend:** FERD. II. ROM. IMP. S(EM). A. **Mint:** Rudolstadt **Note:** Ref. F#457. Kipper coinage.

Date	Mintage	VG	F	VF	XF	Unc
1622 R	—	—	—	—	—	—

KM# 50 24 KREUZER (Doppelschreckenberger)
Silver, 29 mm. **Ruler:** Karl Günther; Ludwig Günther and Albrecht Günther **Obv:** Ornamented shield of 4-fold arms, comb at bottom, date and mintmark at end of legend **Obv. Legend:** MON. NOU. COM. SCHWART. RUL. L. **Rev:** Imperial eagle under princely crown, large orb on breast with Z4 **Rev. Legend:** FERDIN. II. D G. ROM. IM: SEM. AUGUST **Mint:** Rudolstadt **Note:** Ref. F#458. Kipper coinage.

Date	Mintage	VG	F	VF	XF	Unc
16ZZ R	—	—	—	—	—	—

KM# 51 24 KREUZER (Doppelschreckenberger)
Silver, 29 mm. **Ruler:** Karl Günther; Ludwig Günther and Albrecht Günther **Obv:** Shield of 4-fold arms, mintmark and date above **Obv. Legend:** MO: NO: CO: SCHWAR: RVD:. **Rev:** Imperial eagle with 24 on breast **Rev. Legend:** FERD: II: D: G: ROM: IM: SEM: AVGV:. **Mint:** Rudolstadt **Note:** Ref. F#460. Kipper coinage.

Date	Mintage	VG	F	VF	XF	Unc
1622 R	—	—	—	—	—	—

KM# 52 24 KREUZER (Doppelschreckenberger)
Silver, 29 mm. **Ruler:** Karl Günther; Ludwig Günther and Albrecht Günther **Obv:** Shield of 4-fold arms, mintmark below **Obv. Legend:** MO: NO: COM: SCHWART: E: H: L:. **Rev:** Imperial eagle with 24 on breast, date at end of legend **Rev. Legend:** FERD: II: ROM: IMP. S: A. **Mint:** Rudolstadt **Note:** Ref. F#461. Kipper coinage.

Date	Mintage	VG	F	VF	XF	Unc
1622 R	—	—	—	—	—	—

KM# 53 24 KREUZER (Doppelschreckenberger)
Silver, 29 mm. **Ruler:** Karl Günther; Ludwig Günther and Albrecht Günther **Obv:** Shield of 4-fold arms divides date on sides as 1-6, Z-Z, mintmark above, comb below **Obv. Legend:** MONETA: NOV. COMIT SCHWA ET RVD. **Rev:** Crowned imperial eagle, large orb on breast with Z4 **Rev. Legend:** FERDINAND ROM IMPER: SEMP AV. **Mint:** Rudolstadt **Note:** Ref. F#462. Kipper coinage.

Date	Mintage	VG	F	VF	XF	Unc
16ZZ R	—	—	—	—	—	—

KM# 47 24 KREUZER (Doppelschreckenberger)
Silver, 25-30 mm. **Ruler:** Karl Günther; Ludwig Günther and Albrecht Günther **Obv:** Ornamented shield of 4-fold arms, comb at bottom **Obv. Legend:** MONETA NOV: COMIT: SCHWA: ET RVDO: zKz **Rev:** Imperial eagle, orb on breast with Z4 **Rev. Legend:** FERDINAND: II ROM: IMPER: SEMPER AV: **Mint:** Konigsee **Note:** Ref. F#452a. Kipper coinage.

Date	Mintage	VG	F	VF	XF	Unc
(16)ZZ K	—	—	—	—	—	—

KM# 46 24 KREUZER (Doppelschreckenberger)
Silver, 25-30 mm. **Ruler:** Karl Günther; Ludwig Günther and Albrecht Günther **Obv:** Ornamented shield of 4-fold arms, comb at bottom, date at end of legend **Obv. Legend:** MO. NO. COM. SCHWA. RU. L. **Rev:** Imperial eagle, orb on breast with Z4 **Rev. Legend:** FERD. II. D.G. ROM. IM. SEM. AUG(U). **Mint:** Konigsee **Note:** Ref. F#452b. Kipper coinage.

Date	Mintage	VG	F	VF	XF	Unc
1622 K	—	—	—	—	—	—

KM# 48 24 KREUZER (Doppelschreckenberger)
Silver, 25-30 mm. **Ruler:** Karl Günther; Ludwig Günther and Albrecht Günther **Obv:** Squarish ornamented shield of 4-fold arms, date above, comb below **Obv. Legend:** MONETA. NOV: COMIT: SCHWA: ET. RVDO (K). **Rev:** Crowned imperial eagle, large orb on breast with Z4 **Rev. Legend:** FERDINAND: II: ROM: IMPER: SEMPER. AV. **Mint:** Konigsee **Note:** Ref. F#453. Kipper coinage.

Date	Mintage	VG	F	VF	XF	Unc
16ZZ K	—	—	—	—	—	—

KM# 21 24 KREUZER (Doppelschreckenberger)
Silver, 25-30 mm. **Ruler:** Karl Günther; Ludwig Günther and Albrecht Günther **Obv:** Ornamented shield of 4-fold arms, 'K' above **Obv. Legend:** MO. NO. COMIT. SCHWARTZB. ET. HO. RVDE. L. **Rev:** Crowned imperial eagle, orb on breast with Z4, date at end of legend **Rev. Legend:** FERD II. ROM. IMPE. SEM. AVG. **Mint:** Konigsee **Note:** Ref. R#1086. Kipper coinage.

Date	Mintage	VG	F	VF	XF	Unc
1621 K	—	—	—	—	—	—

KM# 83 GULDEN
Silver **Ruler:** Ludwig Günther I and Albrecht Günther **Subject:** Death of Albrecht Günther **Obv:** Facing bust turned slightly to left **Obv. Legend:** ALBRECHT GINTHER. S.R.I. QVAT. COM. SCHWARTZB. E.H.D.A.S.L.L.C* **Rev:** 2 small shields of arms at top, Schwarzburg on left, Klettenberg on right, AL - BC - EF at left, middle and right (Allein bei Christo ewige Freude), 7-line inscription below **Rev. Inscription:** NATVS. ANNO. 1582. / .8 AVGVSTI / PLACI. I. DOMI. EXPIR. / ERFVR. 20. IAN. 1634 / CONDEBA. RVDOL PS / TADI .18. MARTI. / EGVSD. ANNI. **Note:** Ref. F#505. Kipper coinage.

Date	Mintage	VG	F	VF	XF	Unc
1634	—	—	—	—	—	—

KM# 4 1/24 THALER (Groschen)
Silver, 16 mm. **Ruler:** Karl Günther; Ludwig Günther and Albrecht Günther **Obv:** 3 small shields of arms (Schwarzburg, Klettenberg, Arnstadt) in shape of cloverleaf, comb below **Obv. Legend:** MO. NO. CO(M). SCHW. R(V)(D). **Rev:** Imperial orb with Z4 in circle. Date at end of legend. **Rev. Legend:** FER. II. D. G. R(O). I(M). S. A(V). **Note:** Ref. F#443b. Klippe. Kipper coinage. Weight varies: .65-.85 g.

Date	Mintage	VG	F	VF	XF	Unc
16Z0	—	50.00	100	200	—	—

KM# 3 1/24 THALER (Groschen)
Silver, 16 mm. **Ruler:** Karl Günther; Ludwig Günther and Albrecht Günther **Obv:** 3 small shields of arms (Schwarzburg, Klettenberg, Arnstadt) in shape of cloverleaf, comb below **Obv. Legend:** MO. NO. CO(M). SCHW. R(V)(D). **Rev:** Imperial orb with Z4 in circle. Date at end of legend. **Rev. Legend:** FER. II. D. G. R(O). I(M). S. A(V). **Note:** Ref. F#505. Weight varies: .65-.85 g. Kipper coinage.

Date	Mintage	VG	F	VF	XF	Unc
16Z0	—	20.00	45.00	90.00	180	—

KM# 36 1/24 THALER (Groschen)
0.4200 g., Silver, 15.5-16 mm. **Ruler:** Karl Günther; Ludwig Günther and Albrecht Günther **Obv:** 3 small shields of arms (Schwarzburg, Klettenberg, Arnstadt) in shape of cloverleaf, comb at bottom **Obv. Legend:** MO: NO. COM: SCHW:R. **Rev:** Imperial orb with 24 **Rev. Legend:** FER: II. ROM: IM: S: A:. **Note:** Ref. F#490. Kipper coinage.

Date	Mintage	VG	F	VF	XF	Unc
ND(1621-22)	—	—	—	—	—	—

KM# 37 1/24 THALER (Groschen)
0.4200 g., Silver, 15.5-16 mm. **Ruler:** Karl Günther; Ludwig Günther and Albrecht Günther **Obv:** 3 small shields of arms (Schwarzburg, Klettenberg, Arnstadt) in shape of cloverleaf, comb at bottom **Obv. Legend:** MO NO COM. SCHW. R. L. **Rev:** Imperial orb with Z4 **Rev. Legend:** FERD. II. ROM. IM. S. A. **Note:** Ref. F#491. Kipper coinage.

Date	Mintage	VG	F	VF	XF	Unc
ND(1621-22)	—	—	—	—	—	—

KM# 34 1/24 THALER (Groschen)
Silver, 17 mm. **Ruler:** Karl Günther; Ludwig Günther and Albrecht Günther **Obv:** 3 small shields of arms (Schwarzburg, Klettenberg, Arnstadt) in shape of cloverleaf, 'F' below, comb at bottom **Obv. Legend:** MO: NO: CO: SCHW. E: H: R: F. **Rev:** IMPERIAL ORB WITH Z4, DATE DIVIDED IN MARGIN AT TOP **Rev. Legend:** FERD II ROM: IM: SE: A:. **Mint:** Friedeburg **Note:** Ref. F#476. Weight varies: .65-.85 g. Kipper coinage.

Date	Mintage	VG	F	VF	XF	Unc
16Z1 F	—	—	—	—	—	—

KM# 35 1/24 THALER (Groschen)
Silver, 16-18 mm. **Ruler:** Karl Günther; Ludwig Günther and Albrecht Günther **Obv:** 3 small shields of arms (Schwarzburg, Klettenberg, Arnstadt) in shape of cloverleaf, 'L' below, comb at bottom **Obv. Legend:** MO: NO: CO: SCH(W): E(T): H: R: (L). **Rev:** Imperial orb with Z4 or 24, date divided at top **Rev. Legend:** FER(D): II. RO(M): IM(P): S(E)(M): A:. **Mint:** Leutenberg **Note:** Ref. F#482-83, 484a-b; R#1143. Weight varies: .65-.85 g. Kipper coinage. Varieties exist.

Date	Mintage	VG	F	VF	XF	Unc
16Z1 L	—	70.00	140	250	475	—
1622 L	—	70.00	140	250	475	—
16ZZ L	—	70.00	140	250	475	—
ND L	—	70.00	140	250	475	—

KM# 73 1/24 THALER (Groschen)
0.4200 g., Silver, 15.5-16 mm. **Ruler:** Karl Günther; Ludwig Günther and Albrecht Günther **Obv:** 3 small shields of arms (Schwarzburg, Klettenberg, Arnstadt) in shape of cloverleaf, comb at bottom **Obv. Legend:** MON: NOV: COM: S.C.R. **Rev:** Small imperial orb with Z4, cross on orb divides date **Rev. Legend:** FER: II ROM: IM: S: AV. **Note:** Ref. F#489. Kipper coinage.

Date	Mintage	VG	F	VF	XF	Unc
(16)ZZ	—	—	—	—	—	—

KM# 72 1/24 THALER (Groschen)
Silver, 17.5 mm. **Ruler:** Karl Günther; Ludwig Günther and Albrecht Günther **Obv:** 3 small shields of arms (Schwarzburg, Klettenberg, Arnstadt) in shape of cloverleaf, "R" below, comb at bottom **Obv. Legend:** MO NO CO - SCH E H L★ **Rev:** Imperial orb with Z4, cross on orb divides date **Rev. Legend:** FER. II. ROM I S A. **Mint:** Rudolstadt **Note:** Ref. F#463. Weight varies: .65-.85 g. Kipper coinage.

Date	Mintage	VG	F	VF	XF	Unc
1622 R	—	—	—	—	—	—

KM# 74 1/24 THALER (Groschen)
Silver, 23 mm. **Ruler:** Karl Günther; Ludwig Günther and Albrecht Günther **Obv:** Ornamented shield of Schwarzburg lion arms, date divided above **Obv. Legend:** MON(E): CAR: GVN: COM: IN: SCHW(A): E: HON. **Rev:** Imperial orb with Z4 **Rev. Legend:** NACH. DEM. ALTN. SCHROT. V: KORN. **Mint:** Rudolstadt **Note:** Ref. F#495. Kipper coinage.

Date	Mintage	VG	F	VF	XF	Unc
1622	—	—	—	—	—	—

KM# 84 1/4 THALER
Silver, 30.5 mm. **Ruler:** Karl Günther; Ludwig Günther and Albrecht Günther **Subject:** Death of Albrecht Günther **Obv. Legend:** ALBRECHT GINTHER. S.R.I. QVAT. COM. SCHWARTZB. E.H.D.A.S.L.L.C* **Rev:** 2 small shields of arms on top, Schwarzburg on left, Klettenberg on right, AL - BC 0 EF at left, middle and right (Allein bei Christo ewige Freude), 7-line inscription below **Rev. Inscription:** NATVS. ANNO. 1582. / .8. AVGVSTI / PLACI. I. DOMI. EXPIR. / ERFVR. 20. IAN. 1634 / CONDEBA. RVDOL PS / TADI .18. MARTI. / EGVSD. ANNI. **Note:** Ref. R#1191. Kipper coinage.

Date	Mintage	VG	F	VF	XF	Unc
1634	—	175	375	775	—	—

KM# 87 1/2 THALER
15.0000 g., Silver, 39 mm. **Ruler:** Karl Günther; Ludwig Günther and Albrecht Günther **Subject:** Death of Ludwig Günther I **Obv:** Facing bust turned slightly to right. **Obv. Legend:** LUDW. GUNTH. S.R.I. QVAT. COM. I. SCHWARTZB. ET. H. DOM. AR. S.L.L.ET CL* **Rev:** Ornamented heart-shaped shield of manifold arms with fork and comb in bottom, large crown above **Rev. Legend:** NAT: IN. AR: RUDELS. XXVII. IUN. M.D.LXXXI. OBI. IBI. D. VI. NO. M.D C.XXXXVI ★ **Note:** Ref. F#499. Kipper coinage. Date of death engraved VI in error instead of IV (November).

Date	Mintage	VG	F	VF	XF	Unc
1646	—	—	—	—	—	—

KM# 93 1/2 THALER
15.0000 g., Silver, 35-37 mm. **Ruler:** Karl Günther; Ludwig Günther and Albrecht Günther **Subject:** Death of Emilie von Oldenburg-Delmenhorst, Wife of Ludwig Günther I **Obv:** 2 ornate adjacent shields of arms, manifold arms of Schwarzburg on left, 4-fold arms of Oldenburg on right, large crown above, cartouche with 2-line inscription below **Obv. Legend:** ÆMILIA. C.S.E.H. NAT. C. OLD. DELM. 15. IVN. 1614. OB. LEVTENB. 4.XB. 1670. Æ. 56 1/2. **Obv. Inscription:** AVF DICH HERR / TRAV ICH **Rev:** Cross with heart in which IESVS, another heart at food with 4 branches growing out of top and bottom, SVB - CRVCE along 2 upper branches. 9-line double margin legend in laurel wreath. **Rev. Legend:** Inner: HOC DVCE - NON SINE LUCE. Outer: Æ. MEMOR. ET GLOR. DN. MATR. DESIDERATISS. BN. MER. GRAT. C.H. MON. F.F. FILI9★ **Note:** Ref. F#502. Kipper coinage.

Date	Mintage	VG	F	VF	XF	Unc
1670	—	500	1,000	2,000	3,900	—

KM# 94 THALER
30.0000 g., Silver, 35 mm. **Ruler:** Karl Günther; Ludwig Günther and Albrecht Günther **Subject:** Death of Emilie von Oldenburg-Delmenhorst, Wife of Ludwig Günther I **Obv:** 2 ornate adjacent shields of arms, manifold arms of Schwarzburg on left, 4-fold arms of Oldenburg on right, large crown above, cartouche with 2-line inscription below **Obv. Legend:** ÆMILIA. C.S.E.H. NAT. C. OLD. DELM. 15. IVN. 1614. OB. LEVTENB. 4.XB. 1670. Æ. 56 1/2. **Obv. Inscription:** AVF DICH HERR / TRAV ICH **Rev:** Cross with heart in which IESVS, another heart at foot with 4 branches growing out on top and bottom, SVB - CRVCE along 2 upper branches. 9-line double margin legend in laurel wreath. **Rev. Legend:** Inner: HOC DVCE - NON SINE LUCE. Outer: Æ. MEMOR. ET GLOR. DN. MATR. DESIDERATISS. BN. MER. GRAT. C.H. MON. F.F. FILI9★. **Note:** Ref. R#1181. Struck on thick flan from 1/2 Thaler dies, KM#93.

Date	Mintage	VG	F	VF	XF	Unc
1670	—	1,900	3,350	5,700	9,000	—

SCHWARZBURG-SONDERSHAUSEN

As the elder main line of Schwarzburg established in 1552, the counts of Schwarzburg-Sondershausen controlled their scattered territories from the castle of Sondershausen in northern Thuringia (Thüringen), 10 miles (16 kilometers) southeast of Nordhausen. Count Christian Wilhelm I was raised to the rank of prince in 1697 and the line descended from him until it finally became extinct in 1909. All titles and territories then passed to Schwarzburg-Rudolstadt.

RULERS

Joint Coinage (1619-23):
Günther XLII, 1586-1643
Anton Heinrich, 1586-1638,
Johann Günther II, 1586-1631
Christian Günther I, 1586-1642
Anton Günther I, 1642-1666
Ludwig Günther II zu Ebeleben, 1642-1681
Christian Wilhelm I, 1666-1721, Prince 1697
Jointly with Anton Günther II zu Arnstadt, 1677-1679

MINTMARKS AND MINT OFFICIALS' INITIALS

Initial	Date	Name
A, AR	1621-22	Arnstadt mint
WF	1621	Wolfgang Fröhmel, mintmaster in Arnstadt
G, GR	1621-22	Greussen mint
CO	1620-22	Claus Oppermann, mintmaster in Greussen
HHO	1622-23	Hans Heinrich Otte, mintmaster in Greussen;
	1622-23	In Hohnstein
(b)=  or HE	1620-22	Hans von Eck, mintmaster in Clingen
	1621-22	Volkmar Happe, mintmaster in Keula
LW	1621-22	Lipold Wefer, mintmaster in Lohra or Kelbra(?)
SH	1621-22	Sondershausen mint
	1624	Johann Schulthess, mintmaster in Sondershausen
IBM	1631-50	Joachim Blum (Monetarius), die-cutter in Bremen
HM	1675-82	Henning Müller, mintmaster in Sondershausen
(a)= 	1676-79	Henning Müller, mintmaster in Arnstadt and Keula
IH	ca1683-84	Johann Hercher, mintmaster in Sondershausen
IT	1684-89 or 1690	Johann Thun, mintmaster in Sondershausen
W	ca1677, 1686-88	Christian Wermuth, die-cutter in Sondershausen

ARMS: See under Schwarzburg

CROSS REFERENCES:

F = Ernst Fischer, *Die Münzen des Hauses Schwarzburg,* **Heidelberg, 1904.**

R = Ernst Helmuth von Bethe, *Schwarzburger Münzen und Medaillen: Sammlung des Schlossmuseums in Rudolstadt,* **Halle (Saale), 1903.**

COUNTSHIP

JOINT COINAGE

KM# 26 3 FLITTER
Copper **Ruler:** Günther XLII, Anton Heinrich, Johann Günther II and Christian Günther I **Obv:** Shield of 2-fold arms divided horizontally, Schwarzburg lion above, fork over comb below **Rev:** Date at end of inscription **Rev. Inscription:** III / FLITTER **Note:** Ref. F#233. Kipper coinage.

Date	Mintage	VG	F	VF	XF	Unc
1621	—	36.00	65.00	120	240	—

KM# 23 PFENNIG
Copper **Ruler:** Günther XLII, Anton Heinrich, Johann Günther II and Christian Günther I **Obv:** 'S' between 2 rosettes, comb and fork below **Rev. Inscription:** * I * / PFEN / NI(N)G / • * • **Note:** Ref. F#236-37. Kipper coinage. Varieties exist.

Date	Mintage	VG	F	VF	XF	Unc
ND(1621-22)	—	36.00	65.00	120	240	—

KM# 24 2 PFENNIG (Zweier)
Copper, 12 mm. **Ruler:** Günther XLII, Anton Heinrich, Johann Günther II and Christian Günther I **Obv:** ★ S ★, comb and fork below **Rev. Inscription:** [flower] II [flower] / PFEN / NING / [bullet] [flower] [bullet] **Note:** Ref. F#234-35. Kipper coinage. Varieties exist.

Date	Mintage	VG	F	VF	XF	Unc
ND(1621-22)	—	30.00	50.00	110	225	—

KM# 25 3 PFENNIG
0.5600 g., Silver, 17 mm. **Ruler:** Günther XLII, Anton Heinrich, Johann Günther II and Christian Günther I **Obv:** Shield of 4-fold arms, fork below **Obv. Legend:** MO. NO. AR. CO. SCH(W). **Rev:** Imperial orb with 3, date at end of legend **Rev. Legend:** FRAT: L: SOND(E). **Note:** Ref. 198, 201-02. Kipper coinage. Varieties exist.

Date	Mintage	VG	F	VF	XF	Unc
1621	—	—	—	—	—	—
1622	—	—	—	—	—	—

KM# 45 3 PFENNIG
0.5800 g., Silver, 18 mm. **Ruler:** Günther XLII, Anton Heinrich, Johann Günther II and Christian Günther I **Obv:** 3 small shields of arms, 1 above 2, date divided by upper shield, fork below **Rev:** Imperial orb with 3 in ornamented oval frame **Note:** Ref. F#247. Kipper coinage.

Date	Mintage	VG	F	VF	XF	Unc
16ZZ	—	—	—	—	—	—

KM# 46 3 PFENNIG
0.5800 g., Silver, 18 mm. **Ruler:** Günther XLII, Anton Heinrich, Johann Günther II and Christian Günther I **Obv. Inscription:** COMIT / SCHWAR / TZBVRGK / LIN. ARN / STAT. **Rev:** Imperial orb with 3 in ornamented oval frame, date divided above **Note:** Ref. F#248-49. Kipper coinage.

Date	Mintage	VG	F	VF	XF	Unc
1622	—	—	—	—	—	—
16ZZ	—	—	—	—	—	—

KM# 54 3 PFENNIG
Silver, 16.5 mm. **Ruler:** Günther XLII, Anton Heinrich, Johann Günther II and Christian Günther I **Obv:** Ornamented shield of 4-fold arms, fork below **Rev:** Imperial orb with 3 divides date within ornamented rhombus **Note:** Ref. F#243a-b. Kipper coinage.

Date	Mintage	VG	F	VF	XF	Unc
1623	—	—	—	—	—	—
16Z3	—	—	—	—	—	—

KM# 47 3 KREUZER (Groschen)
Silver, 16 mm. **Ruler:** Günther XLII, Anton Heinrich, Johann Günther II and Christian Günther I **Obv:** Shield of 4-fold arms **Obv. Legend:** MO: NO: AR. CO. SCHWAR. **Rev:** Imperial eagle, circle on breast with 3, crown above divides date **Rev. Legend:** FRAT. LIN. SON. AR. **Note:** Ref. F#213. Kipper coinage.

Date	Mintage	VG	F	VF	XF	Unc
16ZZ	—	—	—	—	—	—

KM# 48 3 KREUZER (Groschen)
Silver, 16 mm. **Ruler:** Günther XLII, Anton Heinrich, Johann Günther II and Christian Günther I **Obv:** Shield of 4-fold arms, fork below **Obv. Legend:** MO: NO: AR. CO. SCHWAR(T). **Rev:** Imperial eagle, circle on breast with 3, crown above divides date **Rev. Legend:** FRAT. LIN. SON. AR(N). **Note:** Ref. F#230a-b. Kipper coinage.

Date	Mintage	VG	F	VF	XF	Unc
1622	—	—	—	—	—	—
16ZZ	—	—	—	—	—	—

KM# 49 3 KREUZER (Groschen)
Silver, 16 mm. **Ruler:** Günther XLII, Anton Heinrich, Johann Günther II and Christian Günther I **Obv:** Shield of 4-fold arms, fork below **Obv. Legend:** MO. NO. AR. CO. SCH(W). **Rev:** Imperial eagle, 3 in circle on breast, date at end of legend **Rev. Legend:** FRAT. L. SOND. **Note:** Ref. F#231. Kipper coinage.

Date	Mintage	VG	F	VF	XF	Unc
1622	—	225	450	—	—	—

KM# 2 1/24 THALER (Groschen)
Silver, 17-18.5 mm. **Ruler:** Günther XLII, Anton Heinrich, Johann Günther II and Christian Günther I **Obv:** Shield of 4-fold arms, fork at bottom **Obv. Legend:** MO. NO. AR. CO. SCHW. **Rev:** Imperial orb with Z4, date divided at top **Rev. Legend:** MATI. D.G.R.I.S.A. **Note:** Ref. F#193, 199. Weight varies: .80-.97 g. Varieties exist.

Date	Mintage	VG	F	VF	XF	Unc
1619	—	50.00	100	180	360	—

KM# 3 1/24 THALER (Groschen)
Silver, 17-18.5 mm. **Ruler:** Günther XLII, Anton Heinrich, Johann Günther II and Christian Günther I **Obv:** Shield of 4-fold arms, fork at bottom **Obv. Legend:** MO. NO. AR. CO. SCHW. **Rev:** Imperial orb with Z4 or 24, date divided at top **Rev. Legend:** FRAT. L. SONDH. **Note:** Ref. F#194, 195-97. Weight varies: .80-.97 g. Varieties exist.

Date	Mintage	VG	F	VF	XF	Unc
1619	—	20.00	40.00	85.00	175	340
16Z0	—	20.00	40.00	85.00	175	340

KM# 52 1/24 THALER (Groschen)
Silver, 22 mm. **Ruler:** Günther XLII, Anton Heinrich, Johann Günther II and Christian Günther I **Obv:** Imperial orb with 24 divides date **Obv. Legend:** MON(ETA). NOV(A). ARGENT. FRAT. **Rev:** 3 small ornamented shields of arms, 1 above 2, upper arms divide mintmaster's initials, fork below **Rev. Legend:** COM(IT). SCHWARTZB(VRG). LI(N). ARN(S). **Mint:** Arnstadt **Note:** Ref. F#245-46.

Date	Mintage	VG	F	VF	XF	Unc
1622 WF	—	—	—	—	—	—
16Z3 WF	—	—	—	—	—	—

KM# 56 1/24 THALER (Groschen)
1.8800 g., Silver, 23.5 mm. **Ruler:** Günther XLII, Anton Heinrich, Johann Günther II and Christian Günther I **Obv:** Imperial orb with 24 divides date. **Obv. Legend:** MON. NOVA. ARGENT. FRAT. **Rev:** Ornamented shield of 4-fold arms, fork below **Rev. Legend:** COM. SCHWARTZB. LI. ARNS. **Note:** Ref. F#242a-c.

Date	Mintage	VG	F	VF	XF	Unc
1623	—	—	—	—	—	—
16Z3	—	—	—	—	—	—

KM# 5 12 KREUZER (Schreckenberger)
2.8500 g., Silver, 26-28 mm. **Ruler:** Günther XLII, Anton Heinrich, Johann Günther II and Christian Günther I **Obv:** 3

small shields of arms, 1 above 2, fork below **Obv. Legend:** FRAT. COM. SCHWAR. L. SONDH(A). **Rev:** Imperial eagle, empty orb on breast, crown above divides date **Rev. Legend:** FERD: II. D:G. I. RO. SEM. A(V). **Mint:** Greussen **Note:** Ref. F#206, 208. Kipper coinage.

Date	Mintage	VG	F	VF	XF	Unc
16Z0	—	35.00	75.00	150	300	600
16Z0 CO	—	35.00	75.00	150	300	600

KM# 6 12 KREUZER (Schreckenberger)

2.8500 g., Silver, 28 mm. **Ruler:** Günther XLII, Anton Heinrich, Johann Günther II and Christian Günther I **Obv:** 3 small shields of arms, 1 above 2, fork below **Obv. Legend:** FRAT. COM. SCHWAR. L. SONDH(A). **Rev:** Crowned imperial eagle, 1Z in orb on breast, date divided above **Rev. Legend:** FERD: II. D:G. I. RO. SEM. A(V). **Note:** Ref. F#207, 210. Kipper coinage.

Date	Mintage	VG	F	VF	XF	Unc
16Z0	—	70.00	145	—	—	—
16Z1	—	70.00	145	—	—	—

KM# 7 12 KREUZER (Schreckenberger)

Silver, 28 x 28 mm. **Ruler:** Günther XLII, Anton Heinrich, Johann Günther II and Christian Günther I **Obv:** 3 small shields of arms, 1 above 2, fork below **Obv. Legend:** FRAT. COM. SCHWAR. L. SONDH(A). **Rev:** Crowned imperial eagle, 1Z in orb on breast, date divided above **Rev. Legend:** FERD: II. D:G. I. RO. SEM. A(V). **Note:** Ref. F#209. Klippe. Kipper coinage.

Date	Mintage	VG	F	VF	XF	Unc
16Z0	—	—	—	—	—	—

KM# 8 12 KREUZER (Schreckenberger)

1.7000 g., Silver, 25-28 mm. **Ruler:** Günther XLII, Anton Heinrich, Johann Günther II and Christian Günther I **Obv:** 3 small shields of arms, 1 above 2, fork below **Obv. Legend:** FRAT. COM. SCHWAR. L(I)(N). SO(N)(D)(H)(A). **Rev:** Crowned imperial eagle, 12 in orb on breast **Rev. Legend:** FERD(IN): II. D. G. RO(M)(A). IM(P)(ER). SEM(P). AV(G). **Note:** Ref. F#212, 226-27. Kipper coinage.

Date	Mintage	VG	F	VF	XF	Unc
ND(1620-22)	—	—	—	—	—	—

KM# 9 12 KREUZER (Schreckenberger)

1.7000 g., Silver, 26 mm. **Ruler:** Günther XLII, Anton Heinrich, Johann Günther II and Christian Günther I **Obv:** 3 small shields of arms, 1 above 2, upper shield divides S-H, fork below **Obv. Legend:** FRAT. COM: SCHWARTZ(Z)(B). LI. SO. **Rev:** Crowned imperial eagle, 1Z in orb on breast **Rev. Legend:** FERDI (or E)NANDVS. II: D: G. ROM. I(M): (P): S: A:. **Mint:** Sondershausen **Note:** Ref. F#214. Kipper coinage.

Date	Mintage	VG	F	VF	XF	Unc
ND(1620-22) SH	—	—	—	—	—	—

KM# 10 12 KREUZER (Schreckenberger)

1.7000 g., Silver, 26 mm. **Ruler:** Günther XLII, Anton Heinrich, Johann Günther II and Christian Günther I **Obv:** 3 small shields of arms, 1 above 2, upper shield divides S-H, fork below **Obv. Legend:** FRAT. COM: SCHWARZ(Z)(B). LI. SO. **Rev:** Crowned imperial eagle, 1Z in orb on breast **Rev. Legend:** FERDINANDVS II. D. G. I. R. S. A. **Mint:** Sondershausen **Note:** Ref. F#214d. Kipper coinage.

Date	Mintage	VG	F	VF	XF	Unc
ND(1620-22) SH	—	—	—	—	—	—

KM# 11 12 KREUZER (Schreckenberger)

1.7000 g., Silver, 26 mm. **Ruler:** Günther XLII, Anton Heinrich, Johann Günther II and Christian Günther I **Obv:** 3 small shields of arms, 1 above 2, upper shield divides S-H, fork below **Obv. Legend:** FRAT: COM: SCHW: L.S **Rev:** Crowned imperial eagle, 1Z in orb on breast **Rev. Legend:** FERD: II: D. G. RO: IM: S: AV. **Mint:** Sondershausen **Note:** Ref. F#214e. Kipper coinage.

Date	Mintage	VG	F	VF	XF	Unc
ND(1620-22) SH	—	—	—	—	—	—

KM# 12 12 KREUZER (Schreckenberger)

1.7000 g., Silver, 26 mm. **Ruler:** Günther XLII, Anton Heinrich, Johann Günther II and Christian Günther I **Obv:** 3 small shields of arms, 1 above 2, fork below **Obv. Legend:** FRAT. COM. SCHWARTZB. L. SON. **Rev:** Crowned imperial eagle, 1Z in orb on breast, date divided above **Rev. Legend:** FERD: II. D:G. I. RO. SEM. A. A. **Note:** Ref. F#215. Kipper coinage.

Date	Mintage	VG	F	VF	XF	Unc
16Z0	—	—	—	—	—	—

KM# 13 12 KREUZER (Schreckenberger)

1.7000 g., Silver, 27.5 mm. **Ruler:** Günther XLII, Anton Heinrich, Johann Günther II and Christian Günther I **Obv:** 3 small shields of arms, 1 above 2, upper shield divides S-H, fork below **Obv. Legend:** FRAT: COM: SCHW: L. SOND. **Rev:** Crowned imperial eagle, 1Z in orb on breast **Rev. Legend:** FERD: I:I: D: G ROMA IMPER: S MA V **Note:** Ref. F#218. Kipper coinage.

Date	Mintage	VG	F	VF	XF	Unc
ND(1620-22)	—	115	235	475	—	—

KM# 34 12 KREUZER (Schreckenberger)

1.7000 g., Silver, 26 mm. **Ruler:** Günther XLII, Anton Heinrich, Johann Günther II and Christian Günther I **Obv:** 3 small shields of arms, 1 above 2, fork below **Obv. Legend:** FRAT(R)(V). COM. SCHVVART. L. S. **Rev:** Crowned imperial eagle, 12 in orb on breast, date at end of legend **Rev. Legend:** FERDINAND. II. D.G. R. I. S. (A). **Mint:** Clingen **Note:** Ref. F#221. Kipper coinage.

Date	Mintage	VG	F	VF	XF	Unc
1621 (b)	—	70.00	140	225	450	—

KM# 35 12 KREUZER (Schreckenberger)

1.7000 g., Silver, 23-25 mm. **Ruler:** Günther XLII, Anton Heinrich, Johann Günther II and Christian Günther I **Obv:** 3 small shields of arms, 1 above 2, upper shield divides S-H, fork below **Obv. Legend:** FRATR. COM. SCHWART. L. (S). **Rev:** Crowned imperial eagle, 1Z in orb on breast, date at end of legend **Rev. Legend:** FERDIN. II. ROM. IM. (S.A.) **Note:** Ref. F#222-23. Kipper coinage.

Date	Mintage	VG	F	VF	XF	Unc
16Z1	—	65.00	125	225	450	—
16ZZ	—	65.00	125	225	450	—

KM# 36 12 KREUZER (Schreckenberger)

1.7000 g., Silver, 28 mm. **Ruler:** Günther XLII, Anton Heinrich, Johann Günther II and Christian Günther I **Obv:** 3 small shields of arms, 1 above 2, upper shield divides S-H, fork below **Obv. Legend:** FRAT. COM. SCHWARTZB. LI. SON. **Rev:** Crowned imperial eagle, 1Z in orb on breast, date at end of legend **Rev. Legend:** FERD: II D.G: RO. - IM: SE: AV: **Note:** Ref. F#224. Kipper coinage.

Date	Mintage	VG	F	VF	XF	Unc
16Z1	—	175	375	775	—	—

KM# 37 12 KREUZER (Schreckenberger)

1.7000 g., Silver, 28 mm. **Ruler:** Günther XLII, Anton Heinrich, Johann Günther II and Christian Günther I **Obv:** 3 small shields of arms, 1 above 2, upper shield divides S-H, fork below **Obv. Legend:** FRAT. COM. SCHWARTZB. LIN. SONDH. **Rev:** Crowned imperial eagle, 12 in orb on breast, date divided above **Rev. Legend:** FERD: II D.G: ROM. IMP: SEMPER. AV. **Note:** Ref. F#225. Kipper coinage.

Date	Mintage	VG	F	VF	XF	Unc
1621	—	175	375	775	—	—

KM# 29 12 KREUZER (Schreckenberger)

1.7000 g., Silver, 23 mm. **Ruler:** Günther XLII, Anton Heinrich, Johann Günther II and Christian Günther I **Obv:** 3 small shields of arms, 1 above 2, 'A' under 2 lower shields, fork at bottom **Obv. Legend:** FRAT. COM. SCHW. LIN. SONDH. **Rev:** Crowned imperial eagle, 12 in orb on breast, date divided at top **Rev. Legend:** FERD. II. D. G. ROM. IMP. SEM. A. **Mint:** Arnstadt **Note:** Ref. F#551. Kipper coinage.

Date	Mintage	VG	F	VF	XF	Unc
1621 A	—	—	—	—	—	—

KM# 28 12 KREUZER (Schreckenberger)

1.7000 g., Silver, 25 mm. **Ruler:** Günther XLII, Anton Heinrich, Johann Günther II and Christian Günther I **Obv:** 3 small shields of arms, 1 above 2, upper shield divides A - R, fork below **Obv. Legend:** FRAT. COM. SCHWARTZB. LIN. SONDH. **Rev:** Crowned imperial eagle, 12 in orb on breast, date at end of legend **Rev. Legend:** FERD. II. D. G. ROM. IMP. SEMP. AV. **Mint:** Arnstadt **Note:** Ref. R#550. Kipper coinage.

Date	Mintage	VG	F	VF	XF	Unc
1621 AR	—	—	—	—	—	—

KM# 32 12 KREUZER (Schreckenberger)

1.7000 g., Silver, 28 mm. **Ruler:** Günther XLII, Anton Heinrich, Johann Günther II and Christian Günther I **Obv:** 3 small shields of arms, 1 above 2, upper shield divides date, fork below **Obv. Legend:** FRAT. COM. SCHWARTZ: L: S:. **Rev:** Crowned imperial eagle, 1Z in orb on breast **Rev. Legend:** FERD. II: D: G: ROMA: IM: PE: SE: AV:. **Note:** Ref. R#555. Kipper coinage.

Date	Mintage	VG	F	VF	XF	Unc
16Z1	—	200	400	800	—	—

KM# 30 12 KREUZER (Schreckenberger)

1.7000 g., Silver, 23 mm. **Ruler:** Günther XLII, Anton Heinrich, Johann Günther II and Christian Günther I **Obv:** 3 small shields of arms, 1 above 2, fork below **Obv. Legend:** FRAT. COM. SCHWARTZB. LIN. SONDH. **Rev:** Crowned imperial eagle, 12 in orb on breast, date at end of legend **Rev. Legend:** FERD. II. D. G. ROM. IMP: SEM: AV. **Note:** Ref. F#216. Kipper coinage.

Date	Mintage	VG	F	VF	XF	Unc
1621	—	200	400	800	—	—

KM# 31 12 KREUZER (Schreckenberger)

1.7000 g., Silver, 25 mm. **Ruler:** Günther XLII, Anton Heinrich, Johann Günther II and Christian Günther I **Obv:** 3 small shields of arms, 1 above 2, fork below **Obv. Legend:** FRAT. COM. SCHWAR. LI. SOND. **Rev:** Crowned imperial eagle, 1Z in orb on breast, date divided above **Rev. Legend:** FER. II. D. G. ROM. IMP. SEM. AV. **Note:** Ref. F#217. Kipper coinage.

Date	Mintage	VG	F	VF	XF	Unc
16Z1	—	200	400	800	—	—

KM# 27 12 KREUZER (Schreckenberger)

1.7000 g., Silver, 27.5 mm. **Ruler:** Günther XLII, Anton Heinrich, Johann Günther II and Christian Günther I **Obv:** 3 small shields of arms, 1 above 2, fork below **Obv. Legend:** FRAT. COM. SCHWARTZB. LIN. SONDH. **Rev:** Crowned imperial eagle, 12 in orb on breast, date divided above **Rev. Legend:** FERD. II. D. G. ROM. IMP: SEMPER. AV. **Note:** Ref. F#211. Kipper coinage.

Date	Mintage	VG	F	VF	XF	Unc
1621	—	200	400	800	—	—

KM# 33 12 KREUZER (Schreckenberger)

1.7000 g., Silver, 27 mm. **Ruler:** Günther XLII, Anton Heinrich, Johann Günther II and Christian Günther I **Obv:** 3 small shields of arms, 1 above 2, fork below **Obv. Legend:** FRAT. COM. SCHWARTZ: LI. S:. **Rev:** Crowned imperial eagle, 1Z in orb on breast **Rev. Legend:** FERD. II: D G. ROMA: IMP PER: SE: AV. **Note:** Ref. R#556. Kipper coinage.

Date	Mintage	VG	F	VF	XF	Unc
ND(1621-22)	—	—	—	—	—	—

KM# 16 24 KREUZER (Doppelschreckenberger)

Silver, 29 mm. **Ruler:** Günther XLII, Anton Heinrich, Johann Günther II and Christian Günther I **Obv:** Ornamented shield of 4-fold arms, 'G' above, fork below **Obv. Legend:** FRAT. COM. SCHWARTZB. LIN. SON. **Rev:** Crowned imperial eagle, orb on breast with 24 **Rev. Legend:** FERDIN. II. D. G - ROM: IMP. SEM. A. **Note:** Ref. F#205. Kipper coinage.

Date	Mintage	VG	F	VF	XF	Unc
ND(1620-22) G	—	—	—	—	—	—

KM# 19 24 KREUZER (Doppelschreckenberger)

Silver, 26 x 25 mm. **Ruler:** Günther XLII, Anton Heinrich, Johann Günther II and Christian Günther I **Obv:** Ornamented shield of 4-fold arms, 'GR' above, fork below **Obv. Legend:** FRAT. COM. SCHWARTZB. LIN. SONDH. **Rev:** Crowned imperial eagle, orb on breast with 24 **Rev. Legend:** FERDIN: II. D. G ROM. IMP: SEM: AV. **Mint:** Greussen **Note:** Ref. R#585. Klippe. Kipper coinage.

Date	Mintage	VG	F	VF	XF	Unc
ND(1620-22) GR	—	—	—	—	—	—

KM# 18 24 KREUZER (Doppelschreckenberger)

Silver, 29 mm. **Ruler:** Günther XLII, Anton Heinrich, Johann Günther II and Christian Günther I **Obv:** Ornamented shield of 4-fold arms, 'GR' above, fork below **Obv. Legend:** FRAT. COM. SCHWARTZB. LIN. SONDH. **Rev:** Crowned imperial eagle, orb on breast with 24 **Rev. Legend:** FERDIN: II. D. G ROM. IMP: SEM: AV. **Mint:** Greussen **Note:** Ref. R#586. Kipper coinage.

Date	Mintage	VG	F	VF	XF	Unc
ND(1620-22) GR	—	—	—	—	—	—

KM# 17 24 KREUZER (Doppelschreckenberger)

Silver, 29 mm. **Ruler:** Günther XLII, Anton Heinrich, Johann Günther II and Christian Günther I **Obv:** Ornamented shield of 4-fold arms divides G-R, fork below **Obv. Legend:** FRAT. COM. SCHWARTZB. LIN. SOND. **Rev:** Crowned imperial eagle, orb on breast with 24 **Rev. Legend:** FERD: II. D. G. RO - IMP. SEMPER. AV. **Mint:** Greussen **Note:** Ref. R#587. Kipper coinage.

Date	Mintage	VG	F	VF	XF	Unc
ND(1620-22) GR	—	—	—	—	—	—

KM# 38 24 KREUZER (Doppelschreckenberger)

Silver, 29 mm. **Ruler:** Günther XLII, Anton Heinrich, Johann Günther II and Christian Günther I **Obv:** Shield of 4-fold arms, date at end of legend **Obv. Legend:** FRA. COMITVM. SCHWAR. LI. SOND: **Rev:** Imperial eagle, orb on breast with 24 **Rev. Legend:** FERDINAND. II. D. G. ROM. IMPER. SEMP: A:. **Note:** Ref. F#203. Kipper coinage.

Date	Mintage	VG	F	VF	XF	Unc
(16)21	—	—	—	—	—	—

KM# 39 24 KREUZER (Doppelschreckenberger)

Silver, 26 mm. **Ruler:** Günther XLII, Anton Heinrich, Johann Günther II and Christian Günther I **Obv:** Square ornamented shield of 4-fold arms, date above, fork below **Obv. Legend:** FRAT. COM. SCHWAR. LIN. SON. ARN. **Rev:** Imperial eagle, 24 in orb on breast **Rev. Legend:** FERD II. D: G. ROM IMP. SEMP. AVGV. **Note:** Ref. F#204. Kipper coinage.

Date	Mintage	VG	F	VF	XF	Unc
1621	—	—	—	—	—	—

KM# 40 24 KREUZER (Doppelschreckenberger)

Silver, 26 mm. **Ruler:** Günther XLII, Anton Heinrich, Johann Günther II and Christian Günther I **Obv:** 3 small shields of arms, 1 above 2, date divided by upper shield **Obv. Legend:** FRATRVM: COM. SCHWART. L.S. **Rev:** Imperial eagle with 24 on breast **Rev. Legend:** FERDINAND. II. D.G. ROM. IMP. A. S. **Note:** Ref. F#219. Kipper coinage.

Date	Mintage	VG	F	VF	XF	Unc
1621	—	125	250	450	900	—

KM# 42 24 KREUZER (Doppelschreckenberger)

Silver, 26 mm. **Ruler:** Günther XLII, Anton Heinrich, Johann Günther II and Christian Günther I **Obv:** 3 small shields of arms, 1 above 2, date divided by upper shield **Obv. Legend:** FRATRVM: COM. SCHVVART. L. (S). **Rev:** Crowned imperial eagle with 24 in orb on breast **Rev. Legend:** FERDINAND. II. D.G. ROM. IM. S. AV(G). **Note:** Ref. F#220. Kipper coinage.

Date	Mintage	VG	F	VF	XF	Unc
1621	—	125	250	450	900	—

KM# 41 24 KREUZER (Doppelschreckenberger)

Silver, 26 mm. **Ruler:** Günther XLII, Anton Heinrich, Johann Günther II and Christian Günther I **Obv:** 3 small shields of arms, 1 above 2, upper shield divides S - H. **Obv. Legend:** FRAT: COM. SCHWART. L. SO. **Rev:** Imperial eagle with Z4 on breast **Rev. Legend:** FERDINANDVS: II: D: G: ROM. IM. S: AV. **Mint:** Sondershausen **Note:** Ref. R#557. Kipper coinage.

Date	Mintage	VG	F	VF	XF	Unc
ND(1621-22) SH	—	—	—	—	—	—

KM# 50 24 KREUZER (Doppelschreckenberger)

Silver, 26 mm. **Ruler:** Günther XLII, Anton Heinrich, Johann Günther II and Christian Günther I **Obv:** Shield of 4-fold arms, date above **Obv. Legend:** +FRAT. COM. SCHWAR(Z). LIN. SON. ARN. **Rev:** Imperial eagle, orb on breast with 24 **Rev. Legend:** FERD II. D G ROM. IMP. SEMP. **Note:** Ref. F#228-29. Kipper coinage.

Date	Mintage	VG	F	VF	XF	Unc
1622	—	—	—	—	—	—

KM# 51 24 KREUZER (Doppelschreckenberger)

Silver, 26 mm. **Ruler:** Günther XLII, Anton Heinrich, Johann Günther II and Christian Günther I **Obv:** Shield of 4-fold arms **Obv. Legend:** FRATRVM. COM: SCHWAR: LI: SONG: zLWz. **Rev:** Imperial eagle, orb on breast with 24. **Rev. Legend:** FERDINAND: II: DEO G: ROM: SEM: A. **Note:** Ref. F#232. Kipper coinage. Struck at either the Lohra or Kelbra mint.

Date	Mintage	VG	F	VF	XF	Unc
(16)ZZ LW	—	—	—	—	—	—

KM# 21 1/2 THALER
Silver, 31 x 31 mm. **Ruler:** Günther XLII, Anton Heinrich, Johann Günther II and Christian Günther I **Obv:** 3 small ornate shields of arms, 1 above 2, upper shield divides mintmaster's initials, fork below, letters G - A - R - L stamped into 4 corners of flan **Obv. Legend:** FRAT. COM. SCHWAR. L. SONH. **Rev:** Crowned imperial eagle, imperial orb on breast, date divided at top **Rev. Legend:** FERD: II. D: G. I. RO: SEM. A. **Mint:** Greussen **Note:** Ref. R#535. Klippe.

Date	Mintage	VG	F	VF	XF	Unc
16Z0 CO	—	—	—	—	—	—

KM# 58 1/2 THALER
Silver, 36-40 mm. **Ruler:** Günther XLII, Anton Heinrich, Johann Günther II and Christian Günther I **Obv:** Ornate shield of 4-fold arms divides date (where present) **Obv. Legend:** GVNT. ANT. HEIN. HANS GVNT. ET. CHR. GVNT. **Rev:** St. Martin on horseback to right, beggar below, mintmaster's initials in exergue **Rev. Legend:** COM. IN. SCHWARTZB. ET HONS. LIN. ARN ET. SON. **Mint:** Greussen **Note:** Ref. F#240-41. Weight varies: 14-15 g.

Date	Mintage	VG	F	VF	XF	Unc
1623 HHO	—	—	—	—	—	—
ND HHO	—	—	—	—	—	—

KM# 59 1/2 THALER
14.4300 g., Silver, 34 mm. **Ruler:** Günther XLII, Anton Heinrich, Johann Günther II and Christian Günther I **Obv:** Ornate shield of manifold arms, date above, fork and comb below **Obv. Legend:** GVN. ANT. HE. HA. GV. CH. CV - FR: CO: SCHW. ET. HO LI: AR:. **Rev:** Crowned imperial eagle, orb on breast **Rev. Legend:** FERDINANDVS. II. D: G - ROM. IMPL SEMP. AVGVS. **Mint:** Arnstadt **Note:** Ref. F#244.

Date	Mintage	VG	F	VF	XF	Unc
16Z3 WF	—	450	900	1,800	—	—

KM# 106 1/2 THALER
15.0000 g., Silver, 37.5 mm. **Ruler:** Christian Wilhelm I and Anton Günther II **Obv:** Horse galloping right over falls, hand and arm from cloud holding wreath in which TAN/DEM. Date at end of legend. **Obv. Legend:** CHRISTIAN: WILH. &. ANTHON: GUNTH: **Rev:** Ornate shield of manifold arms supported by wildman and woman holding pennants, 3 ornate helmets above **Rev. Legend:** E. IV. COM: IMP. COM: IN - SCHWARTZB: & HONST. **Mint:** Sondershausen **Note:** Ref. F#279.

Date	Mintage	VG	F	VF	XF	Unc
1679 HM	—	—	—	—	—	—

REGULAR COINAGE

KM# 123 PFENNIG
Silver, 12 mm. **Ruler:** Christian Wilhelm I **Obv:** Crowned shield of 2-fold arms, Schwarzburg lion over fork and comb, divides date as 1 - 6/8 - 6 **Rev:** Imperial orb with '1' in baroque frame **Note:** Ref. F#338-39.

Date	Mintage	VG	F	VF	XF	Unc
1686	—	—	—	—	—	—
1687	—	—	—	—	—	—

KM# 114 3 PFENNIG
Silver, 16.5 mm. **Ruler:** Christian Wilhelm I **Obv:** Crowned "CW" monogram **Rev:** Imperial orb with 3 divides date and mintmaster's initials **Note:** Ref. F#337.

Date	Mintage	VG	F	VF	XF	Unc
1683 IH	—	—	—	—	—	—

KM# 116 6 PFENNIG
Silver, 18.5-19 mm. **Ruler:** Christian Wilhelm I **Obv:** Crowned 'CW' monogram between 2 palm branches **Rev:** Imperial orb with 6 divides date **Note:** Ref. F#335. Kipper coinage.

Date	Mintage	VG	F	VF	XF	Unc
1684	—	50.00	100	210	—	—

KM# 117 6 PFENNIG
Silver, 18.5-19 mm. **Ruler:** Christian Wilhelm I **Obv:** Crowned 'CW' monogram between 2 laurel branches **Rev:** Imperial orb with 6 divides date **Note:** Ref. F#336; R#843.

Date	Mintage	VG	F	VF	XF	Unc
1684	—	50.00	100	210	—	—
1685	—	75.00	150	300	—	—

KM# 65 GROSCHEN
Silver, 24-26 mm. **Ruler:** Günther XLII **Subject:** Death of Johann Günther II **Obv:** 3-line inscription in wreath **Obv. Legend:** IOH. GVN. S.R.I. QVAT. COM. SWARTZ. E. HON. DN. A. S. L. (L). E. CL. **Obv. Inscription:** SIMB. (or SYMB) / EX. DVRIS / GLORIA. **Rev. Inscription:** NAT9 I. / MAII. 1577 / OBIIT XVI. XBR / ANN. 1631. COND / SONG. IV. MART. / 1631. **Note:** Ref. F#257. Varieties exist.

Date	Mintage	VG	F	VF	XF	Unc
1631	—	135	275	575	—	—

KM# 66 GROSCHEN
Silver, 23.5-24 mm. **Ruler:** Günther XLII **Subject:** Death of Anton Heinrich **Obv:** 3-line inscription in wreath **Obv. Legend:** ANT. HEINR. E. IV. S.R.I. COMIT. ET. DOM. IN. SCHWARTZB ET. HONST. **Obv. Inscription:** SPES / MEA [iron cross] / CHRS. **Rev. Inscription:** NATUS [iron cross] / 7.OctoB. 1571 / OBIIT 10. AUGUST. & (C) / SEPULTUS. DIE / NATAL / ANNO 1638 / [iron cross] **Note:** Ref. F#255a. Varieties exist.

Date	Mintage	VG	F	VF	XF	Unc
1638	—	120	250	475	—	—

KM# 67 GROSCHEN
Silver, 23.5-24 mm. **Ruler:** Günther XLII **Subject:** Death of Anton Heinrich **Obv:** 3-line inscription in wreath **Obv. Legend:** ANT. HEINR. E. IV. S.R.I. COMIT. COM. IN. SCHWARTZB ET. HONST. **Obv. Inscription:** SPES / MEA [iron cross] / CHRS. **Rev. Inscription:** NATUS [iron cross] / 7.OCTOB. 1571 / OBIIT 10. AUGUSTI. / SEPULTUS + DIE + / NATALI + / ANNO 1638 **Note:** Ref. F#255b.

Date	Mintage	VG	F	VF	XF	Unc
1638	—	120	250	475	—	—

KM# 69 GROSCHEN
Silver, 23-24 mm. **Ruler:** Günther XLII **Subject:** Death of the Four Counts' Sister, Anna **Obv:** 8-line inscription, 2 small shields of Schwarzburg and Klettenberg arms above **Obv. Inscription:** GUNTHER. E. IV. / S.R. IMP. COM. COMES / IN SCHWARTZB. / ET. HONST &c SOROR / CARISS. FRAT. / AMOR ET. MEM. E / .F.F. / A. VG. G.W.E. **Rev. Inscription:** ANNA. IOH. / GUNTHERI. E: IV / S:R:I. COM. COMIT, / IN SCHWARTZB, / FILIA: NATA 19: 8BR / HOR: 3: MAR. A. 15 / 74. MORT. 3[symbol]9BR. / HOR. I. MAT. A. / 16.40. **Note:** Ref. F#263.

Date	Mintage	VG	F	VF	XF	Unc
1640	—	135	275	550	—	—

KM# 70 GROSCHEN
Silver, 23-24 mm. **Ruler:** Günther XLII **Subject:** Death of the Four Counts' Sister, Anna **Obv:** 8-line inscription, 2 small shields of Schwarzburg and Klettenberg arms above **Obv. Inscription:** GUNTHER. E. IV. S.R. / IMP. COM. COMES: IN. / SCHWARTZB. ET. HON,, / &C SORORI: CARISS. / FRAT. AMOR. ET. / MEM. E.F.F. / A.V.G: G: W: E. **Rev. Inscription:** ANNA. IOH. / GUNTHERI. E: IV / S:R:I. COM. COMIT, / IN SCHWARTZB, FILIA: NATA. 19: 8BR / HOR: 3: MAR. A. 15 / 74. MORT. 3 9BR. / HOR. I. MAT. A. / 16.40. **Note:** Ref. F#654.

Date	Mintage	VG	F	VF	XF	Unc
1640	—	—	—	—	—	—

KM# 73 GROSCHEN
Silver, 23.5 mm. **Ruler:** Günther XLII **Subject:** Death of Christian Günther I **Obv:** 3-line inscription in wreath, 2 small shields of Schwarzburg and Klettenberg above **Obv. Inscription:** DURUM / PATIENTIA / MOLLIT **Rev. Inscription:** CHRISTIAN / GUNTR. S.R.I. / QUATUORU COM. IN / SCHW. &c HONST / NATUS. 11. MAI 1. / 1578. DENATUS / Z5. 9BZ. / 1.6.4Z **Note:** Ref. F#260.

Date	Mintage	VG	F	VF	XF	Unc
1642	—	120	250	475	—	—

KM# 75 GROSCHEN
Silver, 22-23 mm. **Ruler:** Ludwig Günther II **Subject:** Death of Günther XLII **Obv:** 3-line inscription in wreath **Obv. Legend:** GVNT. E. IV. S.R. IMP. COMIT. COM. IN. SCHWARTZB. ET. HON:. **Obv. Inscription:** PIETATE / ET / IUSTITIA. **Rev. Inscription:** NATVS / SONDERSH. VII / .MERID. A. MDLXX. / ET. DENATVS. / ARNSTETI. CIRCA / HOR. XII. ET. NOCT. / QVAE. SEQEBATUR / VII. IANVARI / ANNO. / MDCXLIII. **Note:** Ref. F#253.

Date	Mintage	VG	F	VF	XF	Unc
1643	—	100	200	425	—	—

KM# 80 GROSCHEN
Silver, 22 mm. **Ruler:** Christian Wilhelm I **Subject:** Death of Anton Günther I **Obv:** Crowned shield of manifold Schwarzburg arms **Obv. Legend:** ANTHON GUNTH: E. IV. COMIT. IMP. C. DE SCHW. ET. H. **Rev. Inscription:** NAT: / EBELEB: I. IAN. / 16Z0. DENAT. SON: / DERSCH: 19 AUG: 1666 / HOR: 5 VESP: VIXIT / ANN: 46 MENS. 7. / DIES. 10. **Note:** Ref. F#271-72. Weight varies: 2.11-2.18 g. Varieties exist.

Date	Mintage	VG	F	VF	XF	Unc
1666	—	42.00	85.00	120	230	—

KM# 110 GROSCHEN
2.0400 g., Silver, 22 mm. **Ruler:** Christian Wilhelm I **Subject:** Death of Ludwig Günther II zu Ebeleben **Obv:** Crowned shield of manifold Schwarzburg arms divide mintmaster's initials **Obv. Legend:** SAPIENTER - E - T - FORTITER. **Rev. Inscription:** LUDOVIC9. / GVNTHER VS / E. IV. C.I.C.DE. S. / ET. H.D. IN. A.S. L.L. / ET. CLETT: / NATVS EBELEB: II. MAR / TI MDCXXI. DENAT' / ARN: XX. IVL. MDCLXXXI / HORA XI. MERID: / VIX. ANN. LX M. IV. D. XVIII. **Mint:** Sondershausen **Note:** Ref. F#267-77. Varieties exist.

Date	Mintage	VG	F	VF	XF	Unc
1681 HM	—	55.00	110	160	250	—

KM# 119 1/24 THALER (Groschen)
Silver, 21 mm. **Ruler:** Christian Wilhelm I **Obv:** Crowned 'CW' monogram **Obv. Legend:** ANNO. 1684. **Rev:** Imperial orb with Z4 divides mintmaster's initials **Rev. Legend:** MONETA NOVA ARGENTEA **Mint:** Sondershausen **Note:** Ref. F#333-34.

Date	Mintage	VG	F	VF	XF	Unc
1684 IH	—	75.00	150	300	—	—
1684 IT	—	75.00	150	300	—	—

KM# 94 1/16 THALER
Silver, 19-20 mm. **Ruler:** Christian Wilhelm I **Obv:** Bust right in circle **Obv. Legend:** CHRI(S)T: WILHELM. **Rev:** Date at end of legend **Rev. Legend:** E. IV. COM. I. C. D. S. E. H. **Rev. Inscription:** XVI / EINEN / REICHS / THAL. **Mint:** Sondershausen **Note:** Ref. F#307-08.

Date	Mintage	VG	F	VF	XF	Unc
1676	—	—	—	—	—	—

KM# 95 1/16 THALER
Silver, 19-20 mm. **Ruler:** Christian Wilhelm I **Obv:** Bust let in circle **Obv. Legend:** CHRI(S)T: WILHELM. **Rev:** Date at end of legend **Rev. Legend:** E. IV. COM. I. C. D. S. E. H. **Rev. Inscription:** XVI / EINEN / REICHS / THAL. **Mint:** Sondershausen **Note:** Ref. F#309.

Date	Mintage	VG	F	VF	XF	Unc
1676	—	200	400	825	—	—

KM# 120 1/12 THALER (Doppelgroschen)
Silver **Ruler:** Christian Wilhelm I **Obv:** Crowned shield of arms, Schwarzburg lion over fork and comb, divides date **Obv. Legend:** CHR: WILH: E: IV: C: I: C: D: S: E: HONSTEIN. **Rev:** 5-line inscription in wreath, mintmaster's initials at end of inscription **Rev. Inscription:** 12 / EINEN / REICHS / THALER **Mint:** Sondershausen **Note:** Ref. F#332.

Date	Mintage	VG	F	VF	XF	Unc
1684 IT	—	20.00	45.00	75.00	150	—

KM# 122 6 MARIENGROSCHEN (1/6 Thaler)
Silver **Ruler:** Christian Wilhelm I **Obv:** Draped bust right in circle **Obv. Legend:** CHRISTIAN: WILH: E. IV: COM: IMP. **Rev:** Date at end of inscription **Rev. Legend:** NACH DEM OBER SÄCH CREUSCHLUS **Rev. Inscription:** VI / MARIEN / GROS / FEIN SILB. **Mint:** Sondershausen **Note:** Ref. F#331.

Date	Mintage	VG	F	VF	XF	Unc
1685 IT	—	—	—	—	—	—

KM# 96 1/6 THALER (1/4 Gulden)
Silver, 27 mm. **Ruler:** Christian Wilhelm I **Obv:** Armored bust left in circle **Obv. Legend:** CHRISTIAN9 WILHELM9 E. IV. COM. I. **Rev:** Crowned ornamented shield of 2-fold arms divided horizontally, Schwarzburg lion above, fork over comb below, date and mintmaster's initials divided to left and right, value 1/6 in oval at bottom **Rev. Legend:** COM. DE. SCHWAR - ET. HONSTEIN. **Mint:** Sondershausen **Note:** Ref. F#305-06. Varieties exist.

Date	Mintage	VG	F	VF	XF	Unc
1676	—	—	—	—	—	—

KM# 71 1/4 THALER
7.0000 g., Silver, 32 mm. **Ruler:** Günther XLII **Subject:** Death of the Four Counts' Sister, ANNA **Obv. Inscription:** ANNA, IOH., / GUNTHERI, E. IV. S. / R. IMP. COM. COMIT. IN / SCHWARTZB. FILIA: / NATA. XIX. IIXBR: H: / III. MAT. A. MDLXXIV. / MORT. III.IXBR. H. IX / MAT. A: MDCXL. **Rev:** 8-line inscription, 2 adjacent shields of Schwarzburg and Klettenberg arms above **Rev. Inscription:** GUNTERH E: / IV. S.R. IMP 6. COM. / COMES IN SCHWA / RTZB. ET. HONST. &C / SORORI CARISS. / FRAT. AMOR. ET. / MEM. E.F.F. / A: V.G.G.W.E. **Note:** Ref. F#262.

Date	Mintage	VG	F	VF	XF	Unc
1640	—	—	—	—	—	—

KM# 74 1/4 THALER
7.0000 g., Silver, 32 mm. **Ruler:** Ludwig Günther II **Subject:** Death of Christian Günther I **Obv. Legend:** CHRIST. GUNT. ANTON. GUNT. LVDVV. GUNT. DE. IV. S.R.I. COM. **Obv. Inscription:** IN / HONOR. / ET MEMOR. / PATRIS / DESIDERA / TISS. **Rev. Inscription:** DN / CHRISTIANI / GUNT. COM. IN / SCHWARTZB. ET / HONST. NATI. / II MAII. A. 1.5.78 / ET. Z5.9DZ. A. 164Z / PIE DEFUNCTI / F.F. / .D.P.M. **Note:** Ref. F#259.

Date	Mintage	VG	F	VF	XF	Unc
164Z	—	1,750	3,250	6,000	11,750	—

KM# 76 1/4 THALER

Silver, 33.5 mm. **Ruler:** Ludwig Günther II **Subject:** Death of Günther XLII **Obv:** Ornamented shield of manifold Schwarzburg arms, curved inscription below **Obv. Legend:** GUNT. E. IV. S.R. IMP. COMIT. IN SCHWARTZB. ET. HONST. **Obv. Inscription:** PIETATE ET IUSTITIA. **Rev. Legend:** NATUS / SONDERSH. / VII. VIIBR CIRCA. XII / MERID. Ao MDLXX. ET / DENATUS ARNSTETI / CIRCA. HOR. XII. ET NOCT / QU / E. SEQUEBATUR / VII. IANUARI. / ANNO / QUÆ. **Note:** Ref. F#252.

Date	Mintage	VG	F	VF	XF	Unc
1643	—	350	700	1,250	2,500	4,800

KM# 81 1/4 THALER

Silver, 31 mm. **Ruler:** Christian Wilhelm I **Subject:** Death of Anton Günther I **Obv:** Ornamented shield of manifold arms, crown above **Obv. Legend:** ANTHON G¨UNTH. E. IV. COMIT. IMP. C. DE SCHW. ET. HON:. **Rev:** 8-line inscription with dates in laurel wreath **Rev. Legend:** SYMB: PRO ARIS ET FOCIS **Rev. Inscription:** NAT / EBELEB. I. / IAN. 1620. DE / NAT. SONDERSH / 19. AUG 1666. HOR / 5. VESP. VIXIT / ANN. 46. MEN / 7. DIES. 10. **Note:** Ref. F#270. Weight varies: 6.85-7.0 g.

Date	Mintage	VG	F	VF	XF	Unc
1666	—	135	275	475	950	—

KM# 111 1/4 THALER

7.0000 g., Silver, 32.5-33 mm. **Ruler:** Christian Wilhelm I **Subject:** Death of Ludwig Günther zu Ebeleben **Obv:** Crowned shield of 4-fold arms divides mintmaster's initials **Obv. Legend:** SAPIENTER - E - T - FORTITER. **Rev. Inscription:** LUDOVIC / GVNTHERUS / E. IV. COM: IMP: COM: DE. / SCHW: ET. HONST: DYN: IN / ARNST SOND: LEUT: LOHR / ET. CLETT: NATUS EBELEB: / II. MARCY. MDCXXI DENA: / ARNST XX IULY. MDCLXXXI / HORA. XI. MERID: / VIXIT ANNOS LX. MENSES. IV. D. / XVIII. **Mint:** Sondershausen **Note:** Ref. F#274. Kipper coinage.

Date	Mintage	VG	F	VF	XF	Unc
1681 HM	—	135	275	550	—	—

KM# 118 12 MARIENGROSCHEN (1/3 Thaler)

Silver, 32 mm. **Ruler:** Christian Wilhelm I **Obv:** Draped bust right in circle **Obv. Legend:** CHRISTIAN: WILH: E. IV: COM: IMP. **Rev:** Date at end of inscription **Rev. Legend:** NACH DEM OBER SACH: CREUS SCHLUS **Rev. Inscription:** XII / MARIEN / GROSCH: / V. FEIN SILBER **Mint:** Sondershausen **Note:** Ref. F#330.

Date	Mintage	VG	F	VF	XF	Unc
1684 IT	—	—	—	—	—	—

KM# 85 60 KREUZER (2/3 Thaler)

Silver **Ruler:** Christian Wilhelm I **Obv:** Bust right **Obv. Legend:** CHRISTIAN9 WILHELM9 E. IV. COM. I. **Rev:** Shield of manifold Schwarzburg arms, supported by wildman and woman, divide date, 3 ornate helmets above, value (60) below **Rev. Legend:** DE. SCHWARZ. E. HON. DYN. I. AR. SON. L.L. ET CL. **Note:** Dav#952.

Date	Mintage	VG	F	VF	XF	Unc
1675	—	—	—	—	—	—

KM# 86 60 KREUZER (2/3 Thaler)

Silver, 38 mm. **Ruler:** Christian Wilhelm I **Obv:** Armored bust to left **Obv. Legend:** CHRISTIAN9 WILHELM9 E. IV. COM. I. **Rev:** Shield of manifold Schwarzburg arms, supported by wildman and woman, date divided between 3 ornate helmets above, value (60) below **Rev. Legend:** CO. DE. SCHWARTZ. E. HON - DYN. I. AR(N). SON. L.L. ET. CL. **Mint:** Sondershausen **Note:** Dav#953.

Date	Mintage	VG	F	VF	XF	Unc
1675 HM	—	—	—	—	—	—

KM# 87 60 KREUZER (2/3 Thaler)

Silver, 38-39.5 mm. **Ruler:** Christian Wilhelm I **Obv:** Facing bust **Obv. Legend:** CHRISTIAN9 WILHELM9 E. IV. COM: R. **Rev:** Shield of manifold Schwarzburg arms, supported by wildman and woman, 3 ornate helmets above, date divided between crests of helmets, value (60) below **Rev. Legend:** I. C(O). DE. SCHWARZ. E. H(ON). DYN. I. AR(N): SON: L(EV): L. E(T). C(L). **Mint:** Sondershausen **Note:** Dav#954.

Date	Mintage	VG	F	VF	XF	Unc
1675 HM	—	600	1,200	2,400	4,500	—

KM# 88 60 KREUZER (2/3 Thaler)

Silver, 39.5 mm. **Ruler:** Christian Wilhelm I **Obv:** Armored bust to left **Obv. Legend:** CHRISTIAN9 WILHELM9 E. IV. COM. I. **Rev:** Squarish shield of 4-fold arms, supported by wildman and woman, 3 ornate helmets above, value (60) below, date inserted after 'HON.' in legend. **Rev. Legend:** SCHWARZ. E. HON. - DYN. I. AR. SON. L.L. ET CL. **Mint:** Sondershausen **Note:** Dav#955.

Date	Mintage	VG	F	VF	XF	Unc
1675 HM	—	—	—	—	—	—

KM# 89 24 MARIENGROSCHEN (2/3 Thaler)

Silver **Ruler:** Christian Wilhelm I **Obv:** Armored bust to left **Obv. Legend:** CHRISTIAN9 WILHELM9 E. IV. COM. I. **Rev:** Date and mintmaster's initials at end of inscription **Rev. Legend:** CO. DE. SCHWARTZ. E. HON. DYN. I. AR. SON. L. L. ET CL. **Rev. Inscription:** XXIIII / MARIEN / GROSCHEN **Mint:** Sondershausen **Note:** Dav#956.

Date	Mintage	VG	F	VF	XF	Unc
1675 HM	—	—	—	—	—	—

KM# 115 24 MARIENGROSCHEN (2/3 Thaler)

Silver **Ruler:** Christian Wilhelm I **Obv:** Bust **Obv. Legend:** CHRIST. WILH. E. IV. C.I.C.D.S. & HONSTEIN. **Rev:** Date at end of inscription **Rev. Legend:** NACH DEM OBRE SÄCH. CREYS SCHLUS. **Rev. Inscription:** 24 / MARIEN / GROSCH. / V. FEIN. SILBER **Mint:** Sondershausen **Note:** Dav#957.

Date	Mintage	VG	F	VF	XF	Unc
1683 IH	—	—	—	—	—	—

KM# 91 2/3 THALER (Gulden)

Silver, 38.5-40 mm. **Ruler:** Christian Wilhelm I **Obv:** Armored bust to left **Obv. Legend:** CHRISTIAN9 WILHELM9 E. IV. CO(M). (I). **Rev:** Crowned ornamented shield of 2-fold arms divided horizontally, Schwarzburg lion above, fork over comb below, supported by wildman and woman, date above crown, mintmaster's initials divided to left and right, value 2/3 in oval at bottom **Rev. Legend:** COM. DE. SCHWAR. E: HO(N0> - DYN. I. ARN. SON. LEV. L. E. CL. **Mint:** Sondershausen **Note:** Dav#946.

Date	Mintage	VG	F	VF	XF	Unc
1675 HM	—	—	—	—	—	—

KM# 92 2/3 THALER (Gulden)

Silver, 36-40 mm. **Ruler:** Christian Wilhelm I **Obv:** Armored bust to right **Obv. Legend:** CHRISTIAN9 WILHELM9 E. IV. COM. I. COM. **Rev:** Crowned ornamented shield of 2-fold arms divided horizontally, Schwarzburg lion above, fork over comb below, supported by wildman and woman, date above crown, mintmaster's initials divided to left and right, value 2/3 in oval at bottom **Rev. Legend:** DE. SCHWAR(T). E: HO(N). - DYN. I. ARN. SON. L. L. E. CL. **Mint:** Sondershausen **Note:** Dav#948.

Date	Mintage	VG	F	VF	XF	Unc
1675 HM	—	60.00	110	180	360	—
1676 HM	—	60.00	110	180	360	—

KM# 93 2/3 THALER (Gulden)

Silver, 35-37 mm. **Ruler:** Christian Wilhelm I **Obv:** Crowned ornamented shield of 2-fold arms divided horizontally, Schwarzburg lion above, fork over comb below, supported by wildman and woman, date above crown, mintmaster's initials divided to left and right, value 2/3 in oval at bottom **Obv. Legend:** CHRISTIAN9 WILHELM9 E. IV. COM. I. COM **Rev:** Large '2/3' in circle **Rev. Legend:** DE. SCHWAR. E: HO(N). - DYN. I. ARN. SON. LEV. L. E. CL. **Mint:** Sondershausen **Note:** Dav#949.

Date	Mintage	VG	F	VF	XF	Unc
1675 HM	—	120	215	275	575	—

KM# 97 2/3 THALER (Gulden)

Silver, 35-40 mm. **Ruler:** Christian Wilhelm I **Obv:** Armored bust to right **Obv. Legend:** CHRISTIAN: WILH: E. IV. COM. IMP. **Rev:** Crowned ornamented shield of 2-fold arms divided horizontally, Schwarzburg lion above, fork over comb below, supported by wildman and woman, date above crown, mintmaster's initials divided to left and right, value 2/3 in oval at bottom **Rev. Legend:** COM: DE. SCHWARTZ. - ET HON - STEIN **Note:** Dav#950. Varieties exist. Struck at either Sondershausen, Arnstadt or Keula mints.

Date	Mintage	VG	F	VF	XF	Unc
1676 (a)	—	45.00	80.00	135	275	550
1676 HM	—	45.00	80.00	135	275	550
1678 (a)	—	45.00	80.00	135	275	550
1679 (a)	—	45.00	80.00	135	275	550

KM# 98 2/3 THALER (Gulden)

Silver, 37.5-38 mm. **Ruler:** Christian Wilhelm I **Obv:** Armored bust to right **Obv. Legend:** CHRISTIAN: WILHE(L)M: IV. COM: IMPER. **Rev:** Crowned ornamented shield of 2-fold arms divided horizontally, Schwarzburg lion above, fork over comb below, supported by wildman and woman, date above crown, mintmaster's initials divided to left and right, value 2/3 in oval at bottom **Rev. Legend:** COM: DE. SCHWARTZ. - ET HONSTEIN. **Note:** Dav#951. Struck at either Sondershausen, Arnstadt or Keula mints.

Date	Mintage	VG	F	VF	XF	Unc
1676 (a)	—	75.00	145	275	550	—
1676 HM	—	75.00	145	275	550	—
1678 HM	—	75.00	145	275	550	—

KM# 99 2/3 THALER (Gulden)

Silver, 37.5 mm. **Ruler:** Christian Wilhelm I **Obv:** Armored bust to right **Obv. Legend:** CHRISTIAN9 WILHELM9 E. IV. COM. I. COM. **Rev:** Crowned ornamented shield of 2-fold arms divided horizontally, Schwarzburg lion above, fork over comb below, supported by wildman and woman, date above crown, mintmaster's initials divided to left and right, value 2/3 in oval at bottom **Rev. Legend:** COM: DE SCHWART. - Z ET HONSTEIN. **Mint:** Sondershausen **Note:** Ref. F#299.

Date	Mintage	VG	F	VF	XF	Unc
1676 HM	—	125	250	450	900	—

KM# 100 2/3 THALER (Gulden)

Silver, 37.5-38 mm. **Ruler:** Christian Wilhelm I **Obv:** Armored bust to right **Obv. Legend:** CHRISTIAN: WILH: E. IV. COM. IMP. **Rev:** Crowned ornamented shield of 2-fold arms divided horizontally, Schwarzburg lion above, fork over comb below, supported by wildman and woman, date divided above crown (where present), mintmaster's initials divided to left and right, value 2/3 in oval **Rev. Legend:** COM - DE SCHWA RTZ - ET HONST - EIN. **Mint:** Arnstadt **Note:** Varieties exist. Struck at either Arnstadt or Keula mints.

Date	Mintage	VG	F	VF	XF	Unc
1676	—	35.00	60.00	100	200	—
1676 (a)	—	35.00	60.00	100	200	—
ND	—	35.00	60.00	100	200	—

KM# 61 THALER

Silver **Ruler:** Karl Günther, Ludwig Günther, Albrecht Günther, Günther XLII, Anton Heinrich, Johann Günther, Christian Günther **Obv:** Helmeted arms divide date at helmets **Obv. Legend:** GVNT. ANT. HEIN. HAN-S ... **Rev:** St. Martin and beggar above legend **Rev. Legend:** HH ++ O ++ **Mint:** Greussen **Note:** Dav.#7680. Prev. Schwarzburg KM#61.

Date	Mintage	VG	F	VF	XF	Unc
1623 HHO	—	240	450	750	1,350	—

KM# 62 THALER

Silver **Ruler:** Karl Günther, Ludwig Günther, Albrecht Günther, Günther XLII, Anton Heinrich, Johann Günther, Christian Günther **Rev. Legend:** LIN ++ ARN ++ ER ++ SONND **Mint:** Greussen **Note:** Dav.#7680B. Prev. Schwarzburg KM#62.

Date	Mintage	VG	F	VF	XF	Unc
1623 HHO	—	240	450	750	1,350	—

KM# 63 THALER
Silver **Ruler:** Karl Günther, Ludwig Günther, Albrecht Günther, Günther XLII, Anton Heinrich, Johann Günther, Christian Günt her **Obv. Legend:** HEIN. HANSGVNT ... **Mint:** Greussen **Note:** Dav.#7680C. Prev. Schwarzburg KM#63.

Date	Mintage	VG	F	VF	XF	Unc
1623 HHO	—	240	450	750	1,350	—

KM# A65 THALER
Silver **Ruler:** Karl Günther, Ludwig Günther, Albrecht Günther, Günther XLII, Anton Heinrich, Johann Günther, Christian Günth er **Subject:** Death of Johann Günther II **Obv:** Facing bust **Rev:** 11-line inscription **Note:** Dav.#7681. Prev. Schwarzburg KM#65.

Date	Mintage	VG	F	VF	XF	Unc
1632	—	600	1,100	1,850	3,100	—

KM# 68 THALER
Silver **Ruler:** Karl Günther, Ludwig Günther, Albrecht Günther, Günther XLII, Anton Heinrich, Johann Günther, Christian Günth er **Subject:** Death of Anton Heinrich **Obv:** Helmeted arms **Rev:** 7-line inscription **Note:** Dav.#7682. Prev. Schwarzburg KM#68.

Date	Mintage	VG	F	VF	XF	Unc
1638 IBM	—	1,300	2,750	5,200	8,500	—

KM# 72 THALER
Silver **Ruler:** Karl Günther, Ludwig Günther, Albrecht Günther, Günther XLII, Anton Heinrich, Johann Günther, Christian Günth er **Subject:** Death of Anna, sister of the 4 Counts **Obv:** 10-line inscription **Rev:** 8-line inscription **Note:** Dav. #7683. Prev. Schwarzburg KM#72.

Date	Mintage	VG	F	VF	XF	Unc
1640 Rare	—	—	—	—	—	—

KM# 77 THALER
Silver **Ruler:**
Karl Günther, Ludwig Günther, Albrecht Günther, Günther XLII, Anton Heinrich, Johann Günther, Christian Günther **Subject:** Memorial Thaler for Christian Günther I **Obv:** Helmeted arms, legend above **Obv. Legend:** DVRVM PATIETIA MOLLIT **Rev:** 9-line inscription **Note:** Dav.#7684. Prev. Schwarzburg KM#77.

Date	Mintage	VG	F	VF	XF	Unc
1643 Rare	—	—	—	—	—	—

KM# 78 THALER
Silver **Ruler:**
Karl Günther, Ludwig Günther, Albrecht Günther, Günther XLII, Anton Heinrich, Johann Günther, Christian Günther **Subject:** Death of Günther XLII **Obv:** Helmeted and supported arms **Obv. Legend:** PIETATE ET. IUSTITIA **Note:** Dav.#7685. Prev. Schwarzburg KM#78.

Date	Mintage	VG	F	VF	XF	Unc
1643 Rare	—	—	—	—	—	—

KM# 82 THALER
Silver **Ruler:** Anton Günther I **Subject:** Death of Anton Günther I **Obv:** Helmeted and supported arms **Rev:** 8-line inscription in wreath **Note:** Dav #7688.

Date	Mintage	VG	F	VF	XF	Unc
1666	—	1,100	2,000	3,600	6,000	—

KM# 102 THALER
Silver **Ruler:** Christian Wilhelm I and Anton Günther II **Obv:** Horse in landscape **Rev:** Ornate shield of manifold arms divide mintmaster's initials, 3 ornate helmets above **Mint:** Sondershausen **Note:** Dav #7689. Prev. KM #M1.

Date	Mintage	VG	F	VF	XF	Unc
1677 HM	—	700	1,500	3,000	5,000	—

KM# 103 THALER
Silver **Ruler:** Christian Wilhelm I and Anton Günther II **Obv:** Horse in different landscape **Mint:** Sondershausen **Note:** Dav #7690. Prev. KM#M2.

Date	Mintage	VG	F	VF	XF	Unc
1677 HM/W	—	900	1,750	3,250	5,500	—

KM# 104 2 THALER
51.0800 g., Silver **Ruler:**
Christian Wilhelm I and Anton Günther II **Mint:** Sondershausen **Note:** Dav #7690A. Prev. KM #M3.

Date	Mintage	VG	F	VF	XF	Unc
1677 HM/W	—	1,850	3,250	5,750	9,500	—

TRADE COINAGE

KM# 105 10 DUCAT
34.0000 g., Gold, 45 mm. **Ruler:** Christian Wilhelm I and Anton Günther II **Obv:** Horse galloping right over falls, hand and arm from cloud holding wreath in which TAN/DEM. Date at end of legend. **Obv. Legend:** CHRISTIAN: WILHELM & ANTHON GUNTHER **Rev:** Ornate shield of manifold arms supported by wildman and woman holding pennants, 3 ornate helmets above **Rev. Legend:** E. IV. COM: IMP. COM: IN - SCHWARTZB: & HONST:. **Mint:** Sondershausen **Note:** Ref. F#278. Struck from Thaler dies, KM#102 (Dav#7689).

Date	Mintage	VG	F	VF	XF	Unc
1677 HM Rare	—	—	—	—	—	—

PRINCIPALITY

REGULAR COINAGE

KM# 112 THALER
Silver **Ruler:** Christian Wilhelm I **Subject:** Death of Ludwig Günther II **Note:** Similar to 2 Thaler, KM# 113. Previous Dav #LS486A.

Date	Mintage	VG	F	VF	XF	Unc
1681 HM	—	1,750	3,000	5,000	8,100	—

KM# 124 THALER

Silver **Ruler:** Christian Wilhelm I **Obv:** Bust of Christian Wilhelm right **Rev:** Helmeted and supported arms, I-T below **Mint:** Sondershausen **Note:** Dav #7691.

Date	Mintage	VG	F	VF	XF	Unc
1687 IT Rare	—	—	—	—	—	—

KM# 113 2 THALER

Silver **Ruler:** Christian Wilhelm I and Anton Günther II **Subject:** Death of Ludwig Günther II **Obv:** 13-line inscription **Rev:** Helmeted and supported arms **Mint:** Sondershausen **Note:** Dav #LS486.

Date	Mintage	VG	F	VF	XF	Unc
1681 HM	—	2,500	4,400	7,100	12,000	—

TRADE COINAGE

KM# 121 1/4 DUCAT

0.8750 g., 0.9860 Gold 0.0277 oz. AGW **Ruler:** Christian Wilhelm I and Anton Günther II **Obv:** Bust of Christian Wilhelm right **Rev:** Shield of arms **Mint:** Sondershausen **Note:** Fr#3106.

Date	Mintage	VG	F	VF	XF	Unc
1684 IT	—	285	575	1,150	2,150	—
1686 IT	—	285	575	1,150	2,150	—

KM# 107 DUCAT

3.5000 g., 0.9860 Gold 0.1109 oz. AGW **Ruler:** Christian Wilhelm I and Anton Günther II **Obv:** Bust of Christian Wilhelm right **Rev:** Crowned arms with wild man and wild woman supporters **Mint:** Sondershausen **Note:** Fr#3107.

Date	Mintage	VG	F	VF	XF	Unc
1679 HM	—	825	1,650	3,250	5,700	—
1684	—	825	1,650	3,250	5,700	—
1689 IT	—	825	1,650	3,250	5,700	—

PATTERNS

Including off metal strikes

KM#	Date	Mintage	Identification	Mkt Val
Pn1	1643	—	1/4 Thaler. Lead. KM#76.	—
Pn2	1901A	—	2 Mark. Silver. Y209.	3,000
Pn3	1901A	—	2 Mark. Silver. Y211.	3,000
Pn4	1909A	—	3 Mark. Silver.	3,500

SCHWARZENBERG

The princes of Schwarzenberg based their land holdings in Franconia after Erkinger I of Stefansberg bought the lordship of Schwarzenberg sometime between 1405 and 1411. He became a member of the Imperial Diet in 1429 and upon his death in 1437, his two sons founded the lines of Schwarzenberg-Stefansberg and Schwarzenberg-Hohenlandsberg. The younger line, which was raised to the rank of count in 1566, became extinct in 1646. Its lands and titles reverted to Stefansberg, which attained the countship in 1599. In 1670, the count of Schwarzenberg was made a prince and, a generation later, the territories of Sulz and Kettgau were added to the family holdings through marriage, followed by Krumau in 1719. Having acquired Gimborn earlier, the prince sold that county to Wallmoden in 1783. Klettgau was sold to Baden in 1813, but not before the principality in Franconia was mediatized to Bavaria when the Holy Roman Empire came to an end in 1806. Members of the family retained their titles and held extensive lands in Bavaria, Austria and Bohemia/Czechoslovakia well into the 20th century. Several princes von Schwarzenberg distinguished themselves in both civil and military service to Austria.

RULERS

Schwarzenberg-Hohenlandsberg
Georg Ludwig, 1596-1646
Schwarzenberg-Stefansberg
Adam, 1599-1641
Johann Adolf, 1641-1683, prince 1670
Ferdinand Wilhelm Eusebius, 1683-1703

MINT OFFICIALS' INITIALS

Cologne Mint

Initials	Date	Name
PN	1680-98	Peter Newers
	ca. 1697	Martin Brunner, die-cutter

Kremnitz Mint

MIM	ca. 1696	Martin Josef Mayerl, warden
	ca. 1696 (1650-1736)	Johann Michael Hofmann, die-cutter

Nuremberg Mint

(n)		Nuremberg mint (either struck or dies from there)
VM	1569-1603 (died 1603)	Valentin Maler, die-cutter
GFN	1677-1716	Georg Friedrich Nürnberg, mintmaster
	ca. 1696	Martin Brunner, die-cutter

Vienna Mint

(a) =	1648-ca. 1682	Johann (Hans) Konrad Richthausen, mintmaster
	ca. 1682-? (1650-1736)	Johann Michael Hofmann, die-cutter
(b) or MM	1679-99	Matthias Mittermayer von Waffenberg, mintmaster

REFERENCE

T = Karl Tannich, "Die Münzen und Medaillen der Fürsten zu Schwarzenberg," **Schwarzenbergisches Jahrbuch**, Budweis, 1938.

PRINCIPALITY

REGULAR COINAGE

KM# 5 THALER

Silver **Ruler:** Johann Adolf **Obv:** Bust of Johann Adolf right **Rev:** Crowned arms **Mint:** Vienna **Note:** Dav# 7699.

Date	Mintage	VG	F	VF	XF	Unc
1682 (a)	—	325	700	1,500	2,750	4,500

KM# 12 THALER

Silver **Ruler:** Ferdinand Wilhelm Eusebius **Obv:** Bust right **Rev:** Crowned arms in Order chain **Mint:** Nürnberg **Note:** Dav# 7700.

Date	Mintage	VG	F	VF	XF	Unc
1696 GF-N	—	400	900	1,800	3,000	—

KM# 16 THALER

Silver **Ruler:** Ferdinand Wilhelm Eusebius **Obv:** Conjoined busts of Ferdinand and Maria Anna **Rev:** Two crowned and mantled shields, date above, legend begins at top **Rev. Legend:** PRINCEPS. A... **Mint:** Vienna **Note:** Dav# 7701.

Date	Mintage	VG	F	VF	XF	Unc
1696 MM	—	100	255	425	700	—

KM# 17 THALER

Silver **Ruler:** Ferdinand Wilhelm Eusebius **Obv:** Conjoined busts of Ferdinand and Maria Anna to right **Rev:** 2 crowned and mantled shields, date above, legend begins at bottom **Rev. Legend:** D: G: PRINC. A... **Mint:** Kremnitz **Note:** Dav# 7702.

Date	Mintage	VG	F	VF	XF	Unc
1696 MIM	—	85.00	215	375	675	—

KM# 18 THALER
Silver **Ruler:** Ferdinand Wilhelm Eusebius **Obv:** Bust of Ferdinand right **Rev:** Crowned arms **Mint:** Cologne **Note:** Dav# 7703.

Date	Mintage	VG	F	VF	XF	Unc
1697 P-N	—	425	775	1,400	2,350	—

TRADE COINAGE

KM# 7 DUCAT
3.5000 g., 0.9860 Gold 0.1109 oz. AGW **Ruler:** Johann Adolf **Obv:** Bust of Johann Adolf right **Rev:** Capped arms in Order collar **Mint:** Vienna **Note:** Prev. Fr# 92.

Date	Mintage	VG	F	VF	XF	Unc
1682 (a)	—	725	1,750	3,600	5,400	—

KM# 10 DUCAT
3.5000 g., 0.9860 Gold 0.1109 oz. AGW **Ruler:** Ferdinand Wilhelm Eusebius **Obv:** Bust of Ferdinand Wilhelm Eusebius right **Rev:** Capped arms in Order collar **Mint:** Vienna **Note:** Fr# 94.

Date	Mintage	VG	F	VF	XF	Unc
1693 (b)	—	500	1,000	2,050	3,600	—
1695 (b)	—	500	1,000	2,050	3,600	—

KM# 14 10 DUCAT
35.0000 g., 0.9860 Gold 1.1095 oz. AGW **Ruler:** Ferdinand Wilhelm Eusebius **Obv:** Draped and armored bust to right **Obv. Legend:** FERDINAND. D.G. PR. — A SCHWARTZENBERG. **Rev:** Crowned shield of 4-fold arms in chain of order divides date **Rev. Legend:** DOM. IN HOHEN LANDSBERG. GIMB. MUR. WIT. ET FRAUENBERG. **Mint:** Nürnberg **Note:** Struck with Thaler dies, KM# 12 (Dav #7700). Prev. KM# 60.

Date	Mintage	VG	F	VF	XF	Unc
1696 GFN Rare	—	—	—	—	—	—

SCHWEIDNITZ

The town of Schweidnitz was the seat of a Silesian duchy from about the year 1290. The line of dukes fell extinct in 1392 and the small principality fell to Bohemia until 1526. It passed along with all Bohemian possessions to the Habsburgs until the Prussian conquest and annexation of large parts of Silesia in the 1740s.

The town itself was founded in the 11th century and obtained civic rights in 1250. The town purchased the mint right from the reigning duke in 1351 and began producing a steady stream of coins until the right was taken away by the imperial court. The town revolted at this usurpation of its prerogatives and the mint right was soon restored. Coinage continued, thereafter, until the Kipper Period of the Thirty Years' War.

MINT OFFICIAL'S INITIALS

Initial	Date	Name
SK	1621-22	Samuel Kirchner, mint contractor

ARMS:

Usually 4-fold, with crown in upper left and lower right quarters, griffin to left in upper right quarter, boar in lower left quarter.

REFERENCES:

F/S = Ferdinand Friedensburg and Hans Seger, ***Schlesiens Münzen und Medaillen der Neueren Zeit***, Breslau, 1901 (reprint Frankfurt/Main, 1976).

S = Hugo Frhr. Von Saurma-Jeltsch, ***Die Saurmasche Münzsammlung Deutscher, Schweizerischer und Polnischer Gepräge von etwa dem Beginn der Groschenzeit bis zur Kipperperiode***, Berlin, 1892.

S/Sch = Hugo Frhr. Von Saurma-Jeltsch, ***Schlesische Münzen und Medaillen***, Breslau, 1883.

Sch = Wolfgang Schulten, ***Deutsche Münzen aus der Zeit Karls V***. Frankfurt am Main, 1974.

PROVINCIAL CITY

STANDARD COINAGE

KM# 8 3 HELLER
Copper **Obv:** 3 oval shields of arms, 1 above 2, upper arms divide date, value 'III' below **Note:** Ref. F/S#3621. Uniface. Kipper coinage.

Date	Mintage	VG	F	VF	XF	Unc
1622	—	—	—	—	—	—

KM# 10 KREUZER
Silver **Obv:** Silesian eagle in circle **Obv. Legend:** FER. II. R. I. S. A. G. H. B. R. E. DV. S. **Rev:** Crown in circle, date at end of legend **Rev. Legend:** MO. NOVA. CIVI. SWIDN. **Note:** Ref. F/S#3620; S/Sch#146. Kipper coinage.

Date	Mintage	VG	F	VF	XF	Unc
(1)6ZZ	—	—	—	—	—	—
1622	—	—	—	—	—	—

KM# 3 3 KREUZER (Groschen)
Silver **Obv:** Bust right in circle, value '3' in oval below **Obv. Legend:** FER. II. RO. I. S. A. - G. H. BO. R. DV. S. **Rev:** Ornamented Spanish shield of 4-fold arms in circle, date at end of legend **Rev. Legend:** MON. NOV. CIVI SWIDNIC. **Note:** Ref. F/S#3603, 3615. Kipper coinage.

Date	Mintage	VG	F	VF	XF	Unc
1621	—	40.00	75.00	150	—	—
1622	—	40.00	75.00	150	—	—

KM# 4 3 KREUZER (Groschen)
Silver **Obv:** Silesian eagle in circle, value '3' in oval below **Obv. Legend:** FER. II. RO. I. S. A. - G. H. BO. R. DV. S. **Rev:** Ornately-shaped 4-fold arms in circle, date at end of legend **Rev. Legend:** MON. NOVA. CIVI. SWIDNIC. **Note:** Ref. F/S#3602, 3616-19. Kipper coinage. Varieties exist.

Date	Mintage	VG	F	VF	XF	Unc
1621 SK	—	20.00	40.00	75.00	150	—
1622 SK	—	20.00	40.00	75.00	150	—
1622	—	20.00	40.00	75.00	150	—

KM# 12 3 KREUZER (Groschen)
Silver **Obv:** Bust right in circle, value '3' in oval below **Obv. Legend:** FER. II. R. IM. S. A. - G. H. BO. R. DV. S. **Rev:** Silesian eagle in circle, date at end of legend **Rev. Legend:** MON. NOVA. CIVI. SWIDNIC. **Note:** Ref. F/S#3614. Kipper coinage.

Date	Mintage	VG	F	VF	XF	Unc
1622	—	—	—	—	—	—

KM# 14 6 KREUZER (Weissgroschen)
Silver **Obv:** Bust right in circle, value (VI) below **Obv. Legend:** FERD. II. R. IMP. S. A. - G. H. BO. REX. DVX. **Rev:** Oval 4-fold arms in baroque frame, date at end of legend **Rev. Legend:** GROSSVS. CIVITATIS. SWIDNIC. **Note:** Ref. F/S#3613. Kipper coinage.

Date	Mintage	VG	F	VF	XF	Unc
1622 SK	—	—	—	—	—	—

KM# 16 12 KREUZER (Schreckenberger)
Silver **Obv:** Bust right in circle, value (12) below **Obv. Legend:** FERD. II. R. IMP. S. A. - G. H. BO. REX. DV. S. **Rev:** Oval 4-fold arms in baroque frame, date at end of legend **Rev. Legend:** GROSSVS. CIVITATIS. SWIDNIC. **Note:** Ref. F/S#3611. Kipper coinage.

Date	Mintage	VG	F	VF	XF	Unc
1622 SK	—	35.00	75.00	150	—	—

KM# 17 12 KREUZER (Schreckenberger)
Silver **Obv:** Bust right in circle, value (12) below **Obv. Legend:** FERD. II. R. IMP. S. A. - G. H. BO. REX. DV. S. **Rev:** Oval 4-fold arms in baroque frame, date at end of legend **Rev. Legend:** GROSS. TRIPL. CIVI. SWIDNICEN. **Note:** Ref. F/S#3612. Kipper coinage.

Date	Mintage	VG	F	VF	XF	Unc
1622 SK	—	70.00	140	250	525	—

KM# 6 24 KREUZER (Vierundzwanziger)
Silver **Obv:** Silesian eagle in circle, value (24) below in margin **Obv. Legend:** FERD. II. RO. IM. S. AV. - G. H. BO. REX. DV. SI. **Rev:** Crowned bust of St. Wenceslaus with banner to right in circle, curved ribbon below with S. WENCESLAVS, date at end of legend **Rev. Legend:** GROS. DVODECVPL. CIVI. SWIDN(I). **Note:** Ref. F/S#3601, 3608. Kipper coinage.

Date	Mintage	VG	F	VF	XF	Unc
1621 SK	—	40.00	80.00	160	325	—
1622 SK	—	40.00	80.00	160	325	—

KM# 21 24 KREUZER (Vierundzwanziger)
Silver **Obv:** Laureate bust right in circle, value (24) below in margin **Obv. Legend:** FERD. II. R. IMP. S. A. - G. H. BO. REX. DV. S. **Rev:** Spanish shield with 4-fold arms in baroque frame, date at end of legend **Rev. Legend:** GROS. DVODECVPL. CIVI. SWIDN. **Note:** Ref. F/S#3604, 3607. Kipper coinage.

Date	Mintage	VG	F	VF	XF	Unc
1622	—	35.00	75.00	150	300	—
1622 SK	—	35.00	75.00	150	300	—

KM# 22 24 KREUZER (Vierundzwanziger)
Silver **Obv:** Laureate bust right in circle, value (24) below in margin **Obv. Legend:** FERD. II. R. IMP. S. A. - G. H. BO. REX. DV. S. **Rev:** Spanish shield with 4-fold arms in baroque frame, date at end of legend **Rev. Legend:** GROS. DVODECVPL. CIVI. SWIDN. **Note:** Ref. F/S#3605. Klippe.

Date	Mintage	VG	F	VF	XF	Unc
1622	—	—	—	—	—	—

KM# 23 24 KREUZER (Vierundzwanziger)
Silver **Obv:** Laureate bust right in circle, no value shown **Obv. Legend:** FERD. II. R. IMP. S. A. - G. H. BO. REX. DV. S. **Rev:** Spanish shield with 4-fold arms in baroque frame, date at end of legend **Rev. Legend:** GROS. DVODECVPL. CIVI. SWIDN. **Note:** Ref. F/S#3606. Kipper coinage.

Date	Mintage	VG	F	VF	XF	Unc
1622	—	80.00	160	325	—	—

KM# 19 24 KREUZER (Vierundzwanziger)
Silver **Obv:** Crowned bust of St. Wenceslaus right in circle, curved ribbon below with S. WENCESLAVS, value (24) below in margin **Obv. Legend:** FERD. II. R. IMP. S. A. - G. H. BO. REX. DVX. S. **Rev:** Spanish shield with 4-fold arms in baroque frame, date at end of legend **Rev. Legend:** GROS. DVODECVPL. CIVI. SWIDNIC. **Note:** Ref. F/S#3609. Kipper coinage.

Date	Mintage	VG	F	VF	XF	Unc
1622 SK	—	40.00	80.00	160	325	—

KM# 20 24 KREUZER (Vierundzwanziger)
Silver **Obv:** Silesian eagle in circle, value (24) below in margin **Obv. Legend:** FERD. II. R. IMP. S. A. - G. H. BO. REX. DVX. S. **Rev:** Bust of St. Wenceslaus right in circle, curved ribbon below with S. WENCESL, date at end of legend **Rev. Legend:** GROS. DVODECVPL. CIVI. SWIDN. **Note:** Ref. F/S#3610. Kipper coinage.

Date	Mintage	VG	F	VF	XF	Unc
1622	—	—	—	—	—	—

SCHWEINFURT

Schweinfurt was a Free City located in Lower Franconia some 27 miles northeast of Würzburg. It was first mentioned in 790, became a Free City in the 13th century. Immediately after becoming free, Schweinfurt was the site of a short-lived royal bracteate mint.

The only Schweinfurt local coinage appeared in 1622, though a 1717 series of Reformation commemoratives may have passed as coins.

In 1803 the town was annexed to Bavaria.

FREE CITY

REGULAR COINAGE

KM# 1 1/84 GULDEN

1.2300 g., Copper **Obv:** City arms divide date, "S-S-M" (Schweinfurt Stadt Münz) at left, top and right **Rev:** Denomination "84" in wreath **Note:** Size varies 17.4 - 17.8mm.

Date	Mintage	Good	VG	F	VF	XF
1622	—	—	25.00	45.00	90.00	180

KM# 2 KREUZER

Copper **Obv:** City arms **Rev. Inscription:** I / KREUZ / ER/ date

Date	Mintage	Good	VG	F	VF	XF
1622	—	—	45.00	75.00	145	225

SILESIA

The territory of Silesia was historically located between Bohemia and Poland, but was Germanic in character from an early period. The first ruling dynasty, that of the Piasts, was descended from the Polish royal line and soon had divided Silesia into a number of smaller entities. Silesia proper became a part of the Holy Roman Empire in the 14th century and came under the influence of Bohemia, which began striking coins for that territory. After the mid-14th century, Breslau (see) became the capital and the principal mint of the duchy. In 1526, Silesia, along with Bohemia, came into the possession of the Habsburg imperial family. The Austrian-style coinage of Silesia was struck from that time until 1740, with few gaps, most notably during the Thirty Years' War, when the estates struck a series of emergency coinage. All during the period of Habsburg domination, the various semi-independent small duchies, in all their branches, continued to strike their own coins. The bishops of Breslau and a number of towns and cities also issued coinages in their own names (see under Breslau and the town names).

In the 1740's, Prussia conquered the greater portion of Silesia and established a mint in Breslau which struck coins within the Prussian system from 1743 until 1797 (see under Prussia). Silesia remained a province of Prussia throughout the 18th and 19th centuries, only to be divided and partly awarded to Poland after World War I. Following the Second World War, the rest of Silesia was united with Poland and remains as part of that country up to the present day.

RULERS

Habsburg Dynasty

Rudolf II, 1576-1612
Matthias, 1612-1619
Ferdinand II, 1619-1637
Ferdinand III, 1637-1657
Leopold I, 1657-1705

MINT MARKS

A - Berlin
B - Breslau
W - Wratislawia (i.e. Breslau)

MINT OFFICIALS' INITIALS

BRESLAU MINT

(Wroclaw, Vratislav)
(in Silesia)

Coat of arms sometimes at top center of crowned shield. Other times just Austrian arms on imperial eagle's breast. Legend usually ends: DVX S, SI or SIL.

MINT OFFICIALS' INITIALS

Initials	Dates	Names
BZ	1623-24	B. Zwirner
FBDL	1664	Franz Baron de Lisola
FBL	1664-65	Franz Baron de Lisola
GFH, G	1678-79, 1709	George Franz Hoffmann, die-cutter
HR	1624-35	Hans Riedel, warden
HT	1623-24	H. Tuchmann
HZ	1632-35	Hans Ziesler
IE	Ca.1683	Jan Engelhart
IZ	1630-34	Johann Ziesler
IZHZ	1631-34	Hans Ziesler
MI	1637-46	Michael Jan, warden
MMW	1692-1702	M.M.v. Wackerl
SHS, SH	1664-91	Salomon Hammerschmidt, warden

MINT OFFICIALS' PRIVY MARKS

Privy Mark	Description	Dates	Names
AT	Stylized AT	1625-26	Andreas Tschorr
(b) -	Metal hook	1627, 1635-36	Johann Ziesler
(bh) - HZ	H battle axe Z	1635-37	Hans Ziesler
(cb) -	Crossed halberd	1627-33, 1636	Johan Ziesler
(2ch)	2 crossed halberds		
(3ch)	3 crossed halberds		
(cbh)	HZ, crossed halberd	1636	Hans Ziesler
(f) -	Flags	1628-34	Johann Ziesler
(fa) - H-Z	HZ above flags	1633-36	Hans Ziesler
(fb) - H Z	Flags between H and Z	1636	Hans Ziesler
(fl) -	GH, double fleur de lis in circle	1648-64	Georg Hubner, warden
(g) - GR	Goose in circle	1637-67	Georg Reichart
(h)	HR monogram		
(ha)	Halberd		
(hp)	HP monogram		
(ht)	HT monogram		
(p)	PH monogram		

BRIEG MINT

(Breh, Brzeg)
(in Silesia)

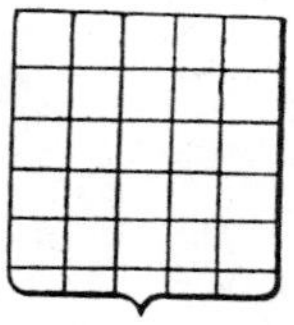

Coat of arms in legend.

MINT MARKS

Initials	Dates	Name
MB	1693-1702	
MBL	1665	

MINT OFFICIALS' INITIALS

Initials	Dates	Name
CB	1677-1713	Christoph Brettschneider

GLOGAU MINT

(Glogow, Hlohov)
(in Silesia)

Large coat of arms, like Vienna, on imperial eagle's breast. Legend usually ends MO.

MINT MARK

G - Glogau, 1623

MINT OFFICIALS' INITIALS

Initials	Dates	Names
BZ	1623	B. Zwirner
HR, ligate HR	-	Hans Riedel
IH, IIH	1623	J. J. Huser
II	1625	J. Jamnitzer

MINT OFFICIALS' PRIVY MARKS

Privy Mark	Description	Dates	Names
(m) -	4 above M	-	Matthaus Jachtmann
(p) -	ZP monogram	-	Zacharius Petzold

NEISSE MINT

(Nysa, Nisa)
(in Silesia)

Large coat of arms, like Vienna, on imperial eagle's breast. Legend usually ends MO.CO.T.

MINT OFFICIALS' INITIALS

Initials	Dates	Names
BZ	1623-24	Balthasar Zwirner
DVB	1624-25	D. V. Bren

MINT OFFICIALS' PRIVY MARKS

Privy Mark	Description	Dates	Names
(dt)	Double trefoil		-
(f)	Varieties of fleur de lis	1622-25	-
(s)	Star & star in crescents	1622-24	-

OELS MINT

(Olesnica, Olesnice)
(in Silesia)

Revolutionary types of Friedrich von der Pfalz

MINT OFFICIALS' PRIVY MARKS

Privy mark	Description	Date	Name
HT -	Ligate HT	1621	Hans Tuchmann

OPPELN MINT

(Opole, Opoli)
(in Silesia)

Large coat of arms, like Vienna, on imperial eagle's breast or coat of arms, like Breslau, on minor types without eagle. Legend usually ends CO.T or CO.TY.

MINT MARKS

(f) - - double fleur de lis

MINT OFFICIALS' INITIALS

Initials	Dates	Names
FIK	1673-85	Franz Ignaz Kirschenhofer, Warden
FN	1699-1705	Franz Nowak, warden
SF	1625	Salomon Franzel, warden

MINT OFFICIALS' PRIVY MARKS

Privy Marks	Description	Dates	Names
MMW M MW	MMW	1685-99	Martin Max. v. Wackerl, warden

RATIBOR MINT

(Raciborz)
(in Silesia)

Large coat of arms, like Vienna on imperial eagle's breast. Legend ends TY.

MINT OFFICIALS' INITIALS

Initials	Dates	Names
DR, R	1624-25	D. Raschke
SD	1624-25	S. Dyringer

SAGAN MINT

(Zagan, Zahan)
(in Silesia)

Large coat of arms, like Vienna on imperial eagle's breast. Legend ends CO.TY.

MINT OFFICIALS' INITIALS

Initials	Dates	Names
GE	-	Gottfried Ehrlich, warden
HDM	1625	-

MINT OFFICIALS' PRIVY MARKS

Privy Marks	Description	Dates	Names
VM VM	VM	1625	
HZ, IZ	3 crossed metal hooks	1628-29	Jan Ziesler
(f) -	Metal hook	1629-31	Jan Henryk Jacob
(h)	Halberd		

SCHWEIDNITZ MINT

MINT OFFICIALS' INITIALS

Initial	Date	Name
	1525-28	Paul Monau and Konrad Saurman
AE, AHE	1743-51	Adam Heinrich von Ehrenberg
D	1735-67	Ignaz Donner, die-cutter and medailleur

ARMS:

Eagle with crescent on breast, sometimes with small cross on crescent.

REFERENCES

Ferdinand Friedensburg and Hans Seger, ***Schlesiens Münzen und Medaillen der Neueren Zeit***, Breslau, 1901 (reprint Frankfurt/Main)

Norbert Jaschke and Fritz P. Maercker, ***Schlesische Münzen und Medaillen***, Ihringen, 1985.

Viktor Miller zu Aichholz, A. Loehr, E. Holzmaair, ***Österreichische Münzprägungen 1519-1938***, 2 vols., 2nd edn., Chicago, 1981

Hugo Frhr. Von Saurma-Jeltsch, Die Saurmasche Münzsammlung deutscher, schweizerischer und polnischer Gepräge von etwa dem Beginn der Groschenzeit bis zur Kipperperiode, Berlin, 1892

Hugo Frhr. Von Saurma-Jeltsch, ***Schlesische Münzen und Medaillen***, Breslau, 1883.

Wolfgang Schulten, ***Deutsche Münzen aus der Zeit Karls V.***, Frankfurt am Main, 1974

DUCHY

STANDARD COINAGE

MB# 62 HELLER

Silver **Ruler:** Rudolf II **Obv:** Crowned 'M' divides date **Mint:** Breslau **Note:** Uniface. S/Sch#82-83, 90-99.

Date	Mintage	VG	F	VF	XF	Unc
160Z	—	7.00	15.00	25.00	50.00	—
1603	—	7.00	15.00	25.00	50.00	—
1604	—	7.00	15.00	25.00	50.00	—

KM# 1 HELLER

Silver **Ruler:** Rudolf II **Obv:** Crowned 'R' divides mint marks, date below **Mint:** Breslau **Note:** Uniface. S/Sch.# 101-102, 104-106. Varieties exist.

Date	Mintage	VG	F	VF	XF	Unc
1605 RB	—	7.00	15.00	30.00	65.00	—
1606	—	7.00	15.00	30.00	65.00	—
1608	—	7.00	15.00	30.00	65.00	—
1609	—	7.00	15.00	30.00	65.00	—
1610	—	7.00	15.00	30.00	65.00	—

KM# 2 HELLER

Silver **Ruler:** Matthias **Obv:** Crowned 'M' divides B-B or R-B, date below **Mint:** Breslau **Note:** Uniface. S/Sch#107-109.

Date	Mintage	VG	F	VF	XF	Unc
1613	—	8.00	16.00	35.00	75.00	—
1614	—	8.00	16.00	35.00	75.00	—
1617	—	8.00	16.00	35.00	75.00	—

KM# 3 HELLER

Silver **Ruler:** Ferdinand II **Obv:** Crowned FII divides R - B, date below **Mint:** Breslau **Note:** Uniface. S/Sch#114.

Date	Mintage	VG	F	VF	XF	Unc
1619	—	10.00	25.00	55.00	110	—

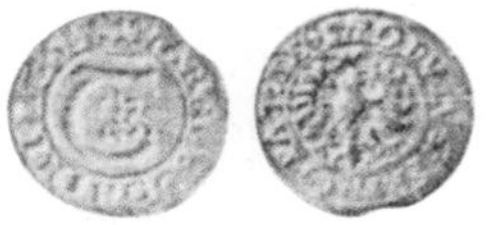

KM# 377 HELLER

Billon **Ruler:** Ferdinand III **Obv:** Crowned Gothic Y in center circle **Rev:** Crowned eagle in inner circle, date in legend **Mint:** Teschen **Note:** Prev. Austria KM#970 (1690). Varieties exist.

Date	Mintage	VG	F	VF	XF	Unc
1650	—	6.00	13.00	27.00	55.00	—
1651	—	6.00	13.00	27.00	55.00	—
1652	—	6.00	13.00	27.00	55.00	—
1653	—	6.00	13.00	27.00	55.00	—
1654	—	6.00	13.00	27.00	55.00	—
1655	—	6.00	13.00	27.00	55.00	—

KM# 510 4 HELLER (Vierer)

Billon **Ruler:** Leopold I **Obv:** Crown divides date above two shields of arms, value below **Mint:** Oppeln **Note:** Prev. Austria #1277 (KM#1276). Varieties exist.

Date	Mintage	VG	F	VF	XF	Unc
1674	—	11.00	22.00	45.00	90.00	—
1675	—	11.00	22.00	45.00	90.00	—
1676	—	11.00	22.00	45.00	90.00	—
1677 FIK	—	11.00	22.00	45.00	90.00	—
1678	—	11.00	22.00	45.00	90.00	—
1679	—	11.00	22.00	45.00	90.00	—
1681	—	11.00	22.00	45.00	90.00	—
1684	—	11.00	22.00	45.00	90.00	—
1686	—	11.00	22.00	45.00	90.00	—
1689	—	11.00	22.00	45.00	90.00	—
1691	—	11.00	22.00	45.00	90.00	—

KM# 534 4 HELLER (Vierer)

Billon **Ruler:** Leopold I **Obv:** Date divided at bottom **Mint:** Oppeln **Note:** Prev. Austria KM#1300 (KM#1278).

Date	Mintage	VG	F	VF	XF	Unc
1678	—	20.00	40.00	80.00	—	—

KM# 540 4 HELLER (Vierer)

Billon **Ruler:** Leopold I **Mint:** Oppeln **Note:** Prev. Austria KM#1301 (KM#1277). Klippe of Austria KM#1277.

Date	Mintage	VG	F	VF	XF	Unc
1679	—	20.00	40.00	80.00	—	—

KM# 648 4 HELLER (Vierer)

Billon **Ruler:** Leopold I **Obv:** Orb with value **Mint:** Oppeln **Note:** Prev. Austria KM#1396 (KM#1275).

Date	Mintage	VG	F	VF	XF	Unc
1699	—	20.00	40.00	80.00	—	—

KM# 72 PFENNIG

Billon **Ruler:** Ferdinand II **Obv:** Straight-sided shield divides date in diamond, F above shield, HR below **Mint:** Breslau **Note:** Uniface. Prev. Austria KM#465 (KM#10).

Date	Mintage	VG	F	VF	XF	Unc
1624 W-(h)	—	12.50	25.00	45.00	85.00	—
1624 HR-W	—	12.50	25.00	45.00	85.00	—
1624 (h)	—	12.50	25.00	45.00	85.00	—
1624 W	—	12.50	25.00	45.00	85.00	—
1625 (h)	—	12.50	25.00	45.00	85.00	—

KM# 162 PFENNIG

Billon **Ruler:** Ferdinand II **Obv:** Shield with concave sides **Mint:** Breslau **Note:** Uniface. Prev. Austria KM#561 (KM#11).

Date	Mintage	VG	F	VF	XF	Unc
1625 (h)	—	12.50	25.00	40.00	85.00	—

KM# 54 2 PFENNIG

Billon **Ruler:** Ferdinand II **Obv:** Crown with arabesque below, above two shields, crown divides date **Mint:** Neisse **Note:** Uniface. Varieties exist. Prev. Austria KM#436 (KM#1195).

Date	Mintage	VG	F	VF	XF	Unc
1623 (dt)	—	25.00	50.00	100	200	—
1624 (dt)	—	25.00	50.00	100	200	—
1625 (dt)	—	25.00	50.00	100	200	—

KM# 75 2 PFENNIG

Billon **Ruler:** Ferdinand II **Obv:** Crown above two shields, in trilobe, crown divides date **Mint:** Breslau **Note:** Uniface. Varieties exist. Prev. Austria KM#468 (KM#12).

Date	Mintage	VG	F	VF	XF	Unc
1624 HR	—	15.00	30.00	55.00	110	—

KM# 78 2 PFENNIG

Billon **Ruler:** Ferdinand II **Obv:** Date above crown **Mint:** Breslau **Note:** Prev. Austria KM#469 (KM#13).

Date	Mintage	VG	F	VF	XF	Unc
1624 W	—	15.00	30.00	55.00	110	—

KM# 81 2 PFENNIG

Billon **Ruler:** Ferdinand II **Rev:** "IIH" **Mint:** Neisse **Note:** Prev. Austria KM#470 (KM#1196).

Date	Mintage	VG	F	VF	XF	Unc
1624 (dt)	—	25.00	50.00	100	200	—

KM# 165 2 PFENNIG

Billon **Ruler:** Ferdinand II **Obv:** Crown above two shields tilted inward **Mint:** Breslau **Note:** Prev. Austria KM#562 (KM#14).

Date	Mintage	VG	F	VF	XF	Unc
1625 HR	—	12.50	27.50	50.00	100	—

KM# 168 2 PFENNIG

Billon **Ruler:** Ferdinand II **Obv:** Arabesque below crown, shields tilted slightly **Mint:** Breslau **Note:** Prev. Austria KM#563 (KM#15).

Date	Mintage	VG	F	VF	XF	Unc
1625 HR	—	12.50	27.50	50.00	100	—
1627 W (h)	—	12.50	27.50	50.00	100	—
1628 IIH	—	12.50	27.50	50.00	100	—
1643 MI	—	12.50	27.50	50.00	100	—

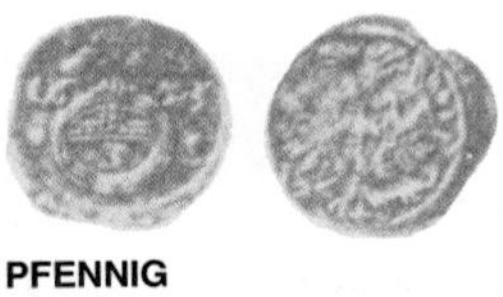

KM# 93 3 PFENNIG

Billon **Ruler:** Ferdinand II **Obv:** Orb with value within, date divided by orb **Rev:** Imperial eagle **Mint:** Glogau **Note:** Prev. Austria KM#472 (KM#325). Varieties exist with and without dots in and around orb.

Date	Mintage	VG	F	VF	XF	Unc
1624	—	7.00	15.00	30.00	60.00	—
1625 II	—	7.00	15.00	30.00	60.00	—
1625 DR	—	7.00	15.00	30.00	60.00	—

KM# 84.1 3 PFENNIG

Billon **Ruler:** Ferdinand II **Obv:** Orb with value within divides date **Rev:** Imperial eagle with arms on breast **Mint:** Breslau **Note:** Prev. Austria KM#471.1 (KM#16.1).

Date	Mintage	VG	F	VF	XF	Unc
1624	—	15.00	32.50	60.00	125	—

KM# 84.2 3 PFENNIG

Billon **Ruler:** Ferdinand II **Mint:** Breslau **Note:** Prev. Austria KM#471.2 (KM#16.2). Privy mark on obverse and reverse.

Date	Mintage	VG	F	VF	XF	Unc
1624 (h)	—	15.00	32.50	60.00	125	—

KM# 84.3 3 PFENNIG

Billon **Ruler:** Ferdinand II **Mint:** Breslau **Note:** Prev. Austria KM#471.3 (KM#16.3). Privy mark on obverse.

Date	Mintage	VG	F	VF	XF	Unc
1624 (h)	—	15.00	32.50	60.00	125	—
1625 (h)	—	15.00	32.50	60.00	125	—

KM# 96 3 PFENNIG

Billon **Ruler:** Ferdinand II **Obv:** Orb with value wihtin divides date **Rev:** Imperial eagle **Mint:** Neisse **Note:** Prev. Austria KM#473 (KM#1197).

Date	Mintage	VG	F	VF	XF	Unc
1624 (dt)	—	25.00	50.00	100	200	—
1624 IIH	—	25.00	50.00	100	200	—

Note: Dots may appear in top quarter of orb or in field

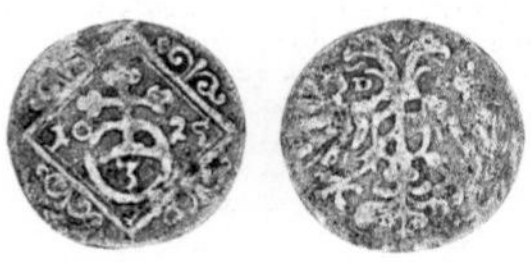

KM# 183 3 PFENNIG

Billon **Ruler:** Ferdinand II **Obv:** Orb with value within divides date in diamond **Mint:** Neisse **Note:** Prev. Austria KM#567 (KM#1198). Varieties exist.

Date	Mintage	VG	F	VF	XF	Unc
1625 DVB	—	25.00	50.00	100	200	—

KM# 186 3 PFENNIG

Billon **Ruler:** Ferdinand II **Obv:** Orb with value within, date divided by orb **Rev:** Crowned imperial eagle **Mint:** Oppeln **Note:** Prev. Austria KM#568 (KM#1265). Varieties exist.

Date	Mintage	VG	F	VF	XF	Unc
1625 SF Rare	—	—	—	—	—	—

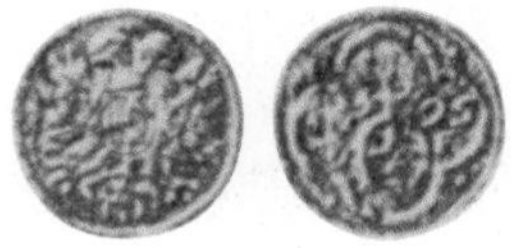

KM# 189 3 PFENNIG

Billon **Ruler:** Ferdinand II **Obv:** Orb with value within divides date in quatrefoil **Mint:** Oppeln **Note:** Prev. Austria KM#569 (KM#1266). Varieties exist.

Date	Mintage	VG	F	VF	XF	Unc
1625 SF Rare	—	—	—	—	—	—

KM# 192 3 PFENNIG

Billon, 16.5 mm. **Ruler:** Ferdinand II **Obv:** Imperial eagle **Rev:** Orb with value within, arched date divided by orb **Mint:** Sagan **Note:** Prev. Austria KM#570 (KM#1580).

Date	Mintage	VG	F	VF	XF	Unc
1625 (h) Rare	—	—	—	—	—	—

KM# 195 3 PFENNIG

Billon **Ruler:** Ferdinand II **Obv:** Straight date divided by orb **Mint:** Sagan **Note:** Prev. Austria KM#571 (KM#1581).

Date	Mintage	VG	F	VF	XF	Unc
1625 (h) Rare	—	—	—	—	—	—

KM# 198 3 PFENNIG

Billon **Ruler:** Ferdinand II **Obv:** Orb with value within, arched date divided by orb, all in diamond **Mint:** Sagan **Note:** Prev. Austria KM#572 (KM#1582).

Date	Mintage	VG	F	VF	XF	Unc
1625 VM Rare	—	—	—	—	—	—

KM# 84.4 3 PFENNIG

Billon **Ruler:** Ferdinand II **Rev:** Two dots and two crosses **Mint:** Breslau **Note:** Prev. Austria KM#471.4 (KM#16.4).

Date	Mintage	VG	F	VF	XF	Unc
1625 AT	—	15.00	32.50	60.00	125	—

KM# 84.5 3 PFENNIG

Billon **Ruler:** Ferdinand II **Rev:** Four dots **Mint:** Breslau **Note:** Prev. Austria KM#471.5 (KM#16.5).

Date	Mintage	VG	F	VF	XF	Unc
1625 AT	—	15.00	32.50	60.00	125	—

KM# 84.6 3 PFENNIG

Billon **Ruler:** Ferdinand II **Rev:** Four crosses **Mint:** Breslau **Note:** Prev. Austria KM#471.6 (KM#16.6).

Date	Mintage	VG	F	VF	XF	Unc
1625 AT	—	15.00	32.50	60.00	125	—

KM# 84.7 3 PFENNIG

Billon **Ruler:** Ferdinand II **Rev:** Four rosettes **Mint:** Breslau **Note:** Prev. Austria KM#471.7 (16.7).

Date	Mintage	VG	F	VF	XF	Unc
1625 AT	—	15.00	32.50	60.00	125	—

KM# 372 3 PFENNIG

Billon **Ruler:** Ferdinand III **Obv:** Displayed eale with arms on breast **Rev:** Orb with value within; date divided at sides **Mint:** Teschen **Note:** Prev. Austria KM#965 (KM#1691). Varieites exist.

Date	Mintage	VG	F	VF	XF	Unc
1649	—	6.00	12.00	27.00	55.00	—
1650	—	6.00	12.00	27.00	55.00	—

KM# 378 3 PFENNIG

Billon **Ruler:** Ferdinand III **Obv:** Orb divides date in diamond; ornamentation in outer fields **Mint:** Teschen **Note:** Prev. Austria KM#971 (KM#1692).

Date	Mintage	VG	F	VF	XF	Unc
1650	—	6.00	12.00	27.00	55.00	—
1651	—	6.00	12.00	27.00	55.00	—
1652	—	6.00	12.00	27.00	55.00	—
1653	—	6.00	12.00	27.00	55.00	—
1654	—	6.00	12.00	27.00	55.00	—
1655	—	6.00	12.00	27.00	55.00	—

KM# 438 3 PFENNIG

Billon **Ruler:** Leopold I **Obv:** Orb with value within divides date, ornamentation at sides **Mint:** Oppeln **Note:** Prev. Austria KM#1279, (1184). Varieties exist.

Date	Mintage	VG	F	VF	XF	Unc
1661	—	12.00	27.00	55.00	110	—
1663	—	12.00	27.00	55.00	110	—
1668	—	12.00	27.00	55.00	110	—
1669	—	12.00	27.00	55.00	110	—
1670	—	12.00	27.00	55.00	110	—
1671	—	12.00	27.00	55.00	110	—
1672	—	12.00	27.00	55.00	110	—
1673	—	12.00	27.00	55.00	110	—
1674	—	12.00	27.00	55.00	110	—
1679	—	12.00	27.00	55.00	110	—
1680	—	12.00	27.00	55.00	110	—
1681	—	12.00	27.00	55.00	110	—
1682	—	12.00	27.00	55.00	110	—
1683	—	12.00	27.00	55.00	110	—
1684	—	12.00	27.00	55.00	110	—
1686	—	12.00	27.00	55.00	110	—
1687	—	12.00	27.00	55.00	110	—
1688	—	12.00	27.00	55.00	110	—
1689	—	12.00	27.00	55.00	110	—
1690	—	12.00	27.00	55.00	110	—
1691	—	12.00	27.00	55.00	110	—
1692	—	12.00	27.00	55.00	110	—
1693	—	12.00	27.00	55.00	110	—
1694	—	12.00	27.00	55.00	110	—
1695	—	12.00	27.00	55.00	110	—
1696	—	12.00	27.00	55.00	110	—
1697	—	12.00	27.00	55.00	110	—

KM# 594 3 PFENNIG

Silver **Ruler:** Leopold I **Obv:** Imperial eagle with arms on breast **Rev:** Value within orb dividing date **Mint:** Brieg **Note:** Prev. Austria KM#170 (KM#1365). Varieties exist.

Date	Mintage	VG	F	VF	XF	Unc
1693MB	—	10.00	25.00	50.00	100	—
1694MB	—	10.00	25.00	50.00	100	—
1695MB	—	10.00	25.00	50.00	100	—
1696MB	—	10.00	25.00	50.00	100	—
1697MB	—	10.00	25.00	50.00	100	—

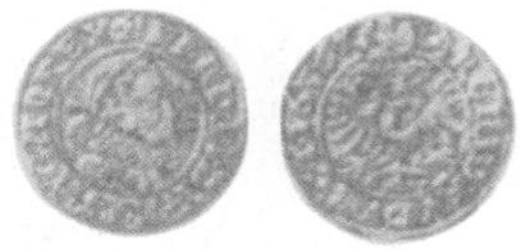

KM# 99 KREUZER

Silver **Ruler:** Ferdinand II **Obv:** Laureate bust right in inner circle **Rev:** Crowned imperial eagle with value on breast in inner circle, date in legend **Mint:** Breslau **Note:** Prev. Austira KM#477 (KM#19).

Date	Mintage	VG	F	VF	XF	Unc
1624 W	—	10.00	20.00	40.00	80.00	—
1625 W	—	10.00	20.00	40.00	80.00	—

KM# 102 KREUZER

Silver **Ruler:** Ferdinand II **Rev:** Privy mark added **Mint:** Breslau **Note:** Prev. Austria KM#478 (KM#20). Varieties exist.

Date	Mintage	VG	F	VF	XF	Unc
1624 W-HR	—	10.00	20.00	40.00	80.00	—
1625 W-(h)	—	10.00	20.00	40.00	80.00	—
1625 W-HR	—	10.00	20.00	40.00	80.00	—
1626 W-(h)	—	10.00	20.00	40.00	80.00	—
1627 W-(h)	—	10.00	20.00	40.00	80.00	—
1627 W(ha)-(h)	—	10.00	20.00	40.00	80.00	—
1632 W-HZ	—	10.00	20.00	40.00	80.00	—
1632 W-(3ch)	—	10.00	20.00	40.00	80.00	—
1633 W-(3ch)	—	10.00	20.00	40.00	80.00	—
1633 HZ-(3ch)	—	10.00	20.00	40.00	80.00	—
1633 W-HZ	—	10.00	20.00	40.00	80.00	—
1633 HZ-HZ	—	10.00	20.00	40.00	80.00	—
1635 (ha)	—	10.00	20.00	40.00	80.00	—
1636 (ha)	—	10.00	20.00	40.00	80.00	—

KM# 111 KREUZER

Silver **Ruler:** Ferdinand II **Obv:** Laureate bust right in inner circle **Rev:** Crowned imperial eagle with value on breast in inner circle; dates in legend **Mint:** Ratibor **Note:** Prev. Austria KM#485 (KM#1565).

Date	Mintage	VG	F	VF	XF	Unc
1624 SD Rare	—	—	—	—	—	—
1625 SD Rare	—	—	—	—	—	—

KM# 105 KREUZER

Silver **Ruler:** Ferdinand II **Obv:** Laureate bust right in inner circle **Rev:** Crowned imperial eagle with value on breast in inner circle, date in legend **Mint:** Neisse **Note:** Prev. Austria KM#482 (KM#1199).

Date	Mintage	VG	F	VF	XF	Unc
1624 BZ	—	20.00	40.00	80.00	160	—
1624 BZ/dt)	—	20.00	40.00	80.00	160	—
1624 (dt) BZ	—	20.00	40.00	80.00	160	—
1624 IIH	—	20.00	40.00	80.00	160	—
1624 DVB/(dt)	—	20.00	40.00	80.00	160	—
1624 DVB	—	20.00	40.00	80.00	160	—

KM# 108 KREUZER

Silver **Ruler:** Ferdinand II **Rev:** Coat of arms below eagle **Mint:** Neisse **Note:** Prev. Austria KM#483 (KM#1200).

Date	Mintage	VG	F	VF	XF	Unc
1624 BZ	—	20.00	40.00	80.00	160	—
1624 BZ/(dt)	—	20.00	40.00	80.00	160	—

KM# 207 KREUZER

Silver **Ruler:** Ferdinand II **Rev:** Shield of arms on cross in inner circle, date in legend **Mint:** Oppeln **Note:** Prev. Austria KM#579 (KM#1268).

Date	Mintage	VG	F	VF	XF	Unc
1625 SF Rare	—	—	—	—	—	—

KM# 210 KREUZER

Silver **Ruler:** Ferdinand II **Obv:** Shield of arms on cross in inner circle; date in legend **Mint:** Ratibor **Note:** Prev. Austria KM#580 (KM#1566). Varieties exist.

Date	Mintage	VG	F	VF	XF	Unc
1625 SD Rare	—	—	—	—	—	—

KM# 201 KREUZER

Silver **Ruler:** Ferdinand II **Rev:** Value on imperial eagle shield on double cross **Mint:** Neisse **Note:** Prev. Austria KM#576 (KM#1201).

Date	Mintage	VG	F	VF	XF	Unc
1625 DVB	—	15.00	30.00	60.00	120	—
1625 DVB/(dt)	—	15.00	30.00	60.00	120	—

KM# 204 KREUZER

Silver **Ruler:** Ferdinand II **Obv:** Laureate bust right in inner circle **Rev:** Crowned imperial eagle with value on breast, date in legend **Mint:** Oppeln **Note:** Prev. Austria KM#578 (KM#1267). Varieties exist.

Date	Mintage	VG	F	VF	XF	Unc
1625 (dt) Rare	—	—	—	—	—	—
1625 SF Rare	—	—	—	—	—	—

KM# 333 KREUZER

Silver **Ruler:** Ferdinand III **Mint:** Breslau **Note:** Prev. Austria KM#828 (KM#60). Varieties exist.

Date	Mintage	VG	F	VF	XF	Unc
1637	—	10.00	20.00	45.00	90.00	—
1638	—	10.00	20.00	45.00	90.00	—
1639	—	10.00	20.00	45.00	90.00	—
1640	—	10.00	20.00	45.00	90.00	—
1641	—	10.00	20.00	45.00	90.00	—
1642	—	10.00	20.00	45.00	90.00	—
1643	—	10.00	20.00	45.00	90.00	—
1644	—	10.00	20.00	45.00	90.00	—
1649	—	10.00	20.00	45.00	90.00	—
1651	—	10.00	20.00	45.00	90.00	—
1652	—	10.00	20.00	45.00	90.00	—
1653	—	10.00	20.00	45.00	90.00	—
1654	—	10.00	20.00	45.00	90.00	—

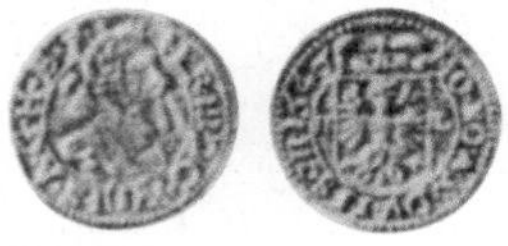

KM# 363 KREUZER

Silver **Ruler:** Ferdinand III **Obv:** Laureate bust in inner circle, value below **Rev:** Crowned arms in inner circle, date in legend **Mint:** Teschen **Note:** Prev. Austria KM#919 (KM#1693). Varieties exist.

Date	Mintage	VG	F	VF	XF	Unc
1644	—	10.00	20.00	40.00	80.00	—
1645	—	10.00	20.00	40.00	80.00	—
1646	—	10.00	20.00	40.00	80.00	—
1647	—	10.00	20.00	40.00	80.00	—
1648	—	10.00	20.00	40.00	80.00	—
1649	—	10.00	20.00	40.00	80.00	—

KM# 405 KREUZER

Silver **Ruler:** Leopold I **Obv:** Laureate bust right in inner circle **Rev:** Crowned imperial eagle with value on breast, date in legend **Mint:** Breslau **Note:** Prev. Austria KM#1132 (KM#75). Varieties exist.

Date	Mintage	VG	F	VF	XF	Unc
1659 G-H	—	10.00	25.00	55.00	115	—
1660 G-H	—	10.00	25.00	55.00	115	—
1661 G-H	—	10.00	25.00	55.00	115	—
1665 S-H	—	10.00	25.00	55.00	115	—

KM# 498 KREUZER
Silver **Ruler:** Leopold I **Rev:** Crown divides date **Mint:** Breslau **Note:** Prev. Austria KM#1267 (KM#76). Varieties exist.

Date	Mintage	VG	F	VF	XF	Unc
1670	—	10.00	20.00	40.00	80.00	—
1671	—	10.00	20.00	40.00	80.00	—
1672	—	10.00	20.00	40.00	80.00	—
1698	—	10.00	20.00	40.00	80.00	—
1699	—	10.00	20.00	40.00	80.00	—

KM# 606 KREUZER
Silver **Ruler:** Leopold I **Obv:** Laureate bust right in inner circle **Rev:** Crowned imperial eagle with value on breast, crown divides date **Mint:** Brieg **Note:** Prev. Austria KM#171 (1373). Varieties exist.

Date	Mintage	VG	F	VF	XF	Unc
1694 CB	—	10.00	25.00	50.00	100	—
1696 CB	—	10.00	25.00	50.00	100	—
1697 CB	—	10.00	25.00	50.00	100	—
1698 CB	—	10.00	25.00	50.00	100	—
1699 CB	—	10.00	25.00	50.00	100	—
1700 CB	—	10.00	25.00	50.00	100	—

KM# 612 KREUZER
Silver **Ruler:** Leopold I **Obv:** Bust right in inner circle **Obv. Legend:** LEOPOLDVS • D • G • R • I • S • ... **Rev:** Crowned imperial eagle with value on breast in inner circle, crown divides date **Mint:** Oppeln **Note:** Prev. Austria KM#1280 (1382). Varieties exist.

Date	Mintage	VG	F	VF	XF	Unc
1695	—	15.00	30.00	60.00	120	—
1697	—	15.00	30.00	60.00	120	—
1698	—	15.00	30.00	60.00	120	—
1698 FN	—	15.00	30.00	60.00	120	—
1699 FN	—	15.00	30.00	60.00	120	—
1700 FN	—	15.00	30.00	60.00	120	—

KM# 639 KREUZER
Silver **Ruler:** Leopold I **Obv:** Without inner circle **Mint:** Brieg **Note:** Prev. Austria KM#1394 (KM#172).

Date	Mintage	VG	F	VF	XF	Unc
1697 CB	—	—	—	—	—	—

KM# 36 3 KREUZER
Silver **Ruler:** Ferdinand II **Mint:** Breslau **Note:** Prev. Austria KM#385 (KM#21).

Date	Mintage	VG	F	VF	XF	Unc
1622	—	15.00	30.00	50.00	100	—
1623	—	15.00	30.00	50.00	100	—

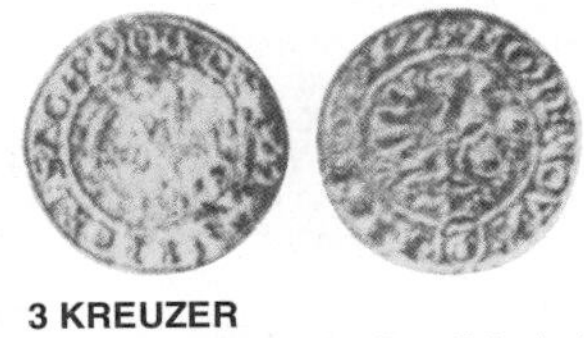

KM# 39 3 KREUZER
Silver **Ruler:** Ferdinand II **Obv:** Orb **Rev:** Value below Silesian eagle **Mint:** Breslau **Note:** Prev. Austria KM#386 (KM#22).

Date	Mintage	VG	F	VF	XF	Unc
1622	—	15.00	30.00	50.00	100	—

KM# 42 3 KREUZER
Silver **Ruler:** Ferdinand II **Mint:** Neisse **Note:** 3 Kipper Kreuzer. Similar to KM#495. Prev. Austria KM#392 (KM#1202).

Date	Mintage	VG	F	VF	XF	Unc
1622	—	15.00	30.00	60.00	120	—

KM# 114 3 KREUZER
Silver **Ruler:** Ferdinand II **Obv:** Laureate bust right in inner circle **Rev:** Crowned imperial eagle in inner circle, date in legend, value at bottom **Mint:** Breslau **Note:** Prev. Austria KM#491 (KM#23). Varieties exist.

Date	Mintage	VG	F	VF	XF	Unc
1624	—	12.00	25.00	50.00	100	—
1624 HR	—	12.00	25.00	50.00	100	—
1624 BZ	—	12.00	25.00	50.00	100	—
1624 W	—	12.00	25.00	50.00	100	—
1624 BZ-HT	—	12.00	25.00	50.00	100	—
1624 BZ-HR	—	12.00	25.00	50.00	100	—
1625	—	12.00	25.00	50.00	100	—
1625 AT	—	12.00	25.00	50.00	100	—
1625 W	—	12.00	25.00	50.00	100	—
1625 HR	—	12.00	25.00	50.00	100	—
1626 HR	—	12.00	25.00	50.00	100	—
1627 HR	—	12.00	25.00	50.00	100	—
1627 (ch)-HR	—	12.00	25.00	50.00	100	—
1627 (h)-HR	—	12.00	25.00	50.00	100	—
1628 (ch)-(h)	—	12.00	25.00	50.00	100	—
1629 (ch)-(h)	—	12.00	25.00	50.00	100	—
1630 (2ch)-HR	—	12.00	25.00	50.00	100	—
1630 (3ch)-HR	—	12.00	25.00	50.00	100	—
1631 (3ch)-HR	—	12.00	25.00	50.00	100	—
1632 (3ch)-HR	—	12.00	25.00	50.00	100	—
1632 (3ch)-HZ	—	12.00	25.00	50.00	100	—
1633 (3ch)-HZ	—	12.00	25.00	50.00	100	—
1634 (3ch)-HZ	—	12.00	25.00	50.00	100	—
1635 HZ	—	12.00	25.00	50.00	100	—
1635 H(ha)-Z	—	12.00	25.00	50.00	100	—
1636 H(3ch)-Z	—	12.00	25.00	50.00	100	—
1636 H(ha)-Z	—	12.00	25.00	50.00	100	—
1637 H(ha)-Z	—	12.00	25.00	50.00	100	—
ND HR	—	12.00	25.00	50.00	100	—

KM# 117 3 KREUZER
Silver **Ruler:** Ferdinand II **Obv:** Without privy mark or denomination **Rev:** Without privy mark or denomination **Mint:** Breslau **Note:** Prev. Austria KM#492 (KM#25).

Date	Mintage	VG	F	VF	XF	Unc
1624	—	—	—	—	—	—

KM# 120 3 KREUZER
Silver **Ruler:** Ferdinand II **Mint:** Neisse **Note:** Prev. Austria KM#495 (KM#1203). Varieties exist.

Date	Mintage	VG	F	VF	XF	Unc
1624 BZ	—	15.00	30.00	60.00	120	—
1624 IIH	—	15.00	30.00	60.00	120	—
1624 DVB/(dt)	—	15.00	30.00	60.00	120	—
1624 DVB	—	15.00	30.00	60.00	120	—
1625 DVB/(dt)	—	15.00	30.00	60.00	120	—
1625 DVB	—	15.00	30.00	60.00	120	—

KM# 213 3 KREUZER
Silver **Ruler:** Ferdinand II **Obv:** Value below bust **Mint:** Breslau **Note:** Prev. Austria KM#581 (KM#27). Varieties exist.

Date	Mintage	VG	F	VF	XF	Unc
1625 HR	—	15.00	30.00	60.00	120	—
1626 HR	—	15.00	30.00	60.00	120	—
1627 HR	—	15.00	30.00	60.00	120	—
1629	—	15.00	30.00	60.00	120	—
1630	—	15.00	30.00	60.00	120	—
1631	—	15.00	30.00	60.00	120	—
1632	—	15.00	30.00	60.00	120	—
1633	—	15.00	30.00	60.00	120	—
1634	—	15.00	30.00	60.00	120	—
1635	—	15.00	30.00	60.00	120	—
1636	—	15.00	30.00	60.00	120	—
1637	—	15.00	30.00	60.00	120	—

KM# 216 3 KREUZER
Silver **Ruler:** Ferdinand II **Obv:** Laureate bust right in inner circle, value below **Rev:** Crowned imperial eagle in inner circle, date in legend **Mint:** Oppeln **Note:** Prev. Austria KM#585 (KM#1269). Varieties exist.

Date	Mintage	VG	F	VF	XF	Unc
1625 SF Rare	—	—	—	—	—	—

KM# 222 3 KREUZER
Silver **Ruler:** Ferdinand II **Obv:** Laureate bust right in inner circle **Rev:** Crowned imperial eagle in inner circle, value below, date in legend **Mint:** Ratibor **Note:** Prev. Austria KM#587 (KM#1567). Varieties exist.

Date	Mintage	VG	F	VF	XF	Unc
1625 SD Rare	—	—	—	—	—	—

KM# 225 3 KREUZER
Silver **Ruler:** Ferdinand II **Obv:** Laureate bust right in inner circle **Rev:** Crowned imperial eagle in inner circle; value below, date in legend **Mint:** Sagan **Note:** Prev. Austria KM#588 (KM#1583). Varieties exist.

Date	Mintage	VG	F	VF	XF	Unc
1625 (h) Rare	—	—	—	—	—	—
1625 HDM Rare	—	—	—	—	—	—

KM# 219 3 KREUZER
Silver **Ruler:** Ferdinand II **Rev:** Three shields, one above two - points together, ornamentation between in inner circle, date in legend **Mint:** Oppeln **Note:** Prev. Austria KM#586 (KM#1270). Varieties exist.

Date	Mintage	VG	F	VF	XF	Unc
1625 (dt)-SF Rare	—	—	—	—	—	—
1625 SF Rare	—	—	—	—	—	—

KM# 282 3 KREUZER
Silver **Ruler:** Ferdinand II **Obv:** Date below bust in inner circle **Mint:** Breslau **Note:** Prev. Austria KM#691 (KM#28).

Date	Mintage	VG	F	VF	XF	Unc
1628 (ch)-HR	—	—	—	—	—	—

KM# 288 3 KREUZER
Silver **Ruler:** Ferdinand II **Mint:** Breslau **Note:** Prev. Austria KM#708 (KM#24). Klippe.

Date	Mintage	VG	F	VF	XF	Unc
1629 (ch)-HR	—	—	—	—	—	—

KM# 297 3 KREUZER
Silver **Ruler:** Ferdinand II **Obv:** Bust with plain collar **Mint:** Breslau **Note:** Prev. Austria KM#742 (KM#26). Varieties exist.

Date	Mintage	VG	F	VF	XF	Unc
1630 (p)	—	—	—	—	—	—

KM# 336 3 KREUZER
Silver **Ruler:** Ferdinand III **Obv:** Ferdinand III **Rev:** Date in legend **Mint:** Breslau **Note:** Prev. Austria KM#831 (KM#61). Varieties exist.

Date	Mintage	VG	F	VF	XF	Unc
1637	—	12.00	25.00	50.00	100	—
1638	—	12.00	25.00	50.00	100	—
1639	—	12.00	25.00	55.00	100	—
1640	—	12.00	25.00	50.00	100	—
1641	—	12.00	25.00	50.00	100	—
1642	—	12.00	25.00	50.00	100	—
1643	—	12.00	25.00	50.00	100	—
1644	—	12.00	25.00	50.00	100	—
1645	—	12.00	25.00	50.00	100	—
1646	—	12.00	25.00	50.00	100	—
1647	—	12.00	25.00	50.00	100	—
1648	—	12.00	25.00	50.00	100	—
1649	—	12.00	25.00	50.00	100	—
1650	—	12.00	25.00	50.00	100	—
1651	—	12.00	25.00	50.00	100	—
1652	—	12.00	25.00	50.00	100	—
1653	—	12.00	25.00	50.00	100	—
1654	—	12.00	25.00	50.00	100	—
1655	—	12.00	25.00	50.00	100	—

Date	Mintage	VG	F	VF	XF	Unc
1656	—	12.00	25.00	50.00	100	—
1657 GH	—	12.00	25.00	50.00	100	—

KM# 354 3 KREUZER

Silver **Ruler:** Ferdinand III **Obv:** Laureate bust right in inner circle, value below **Rev:** Crowned arms in inner circle, date in legend **Mint:** Teschen **Note:** Prev. Austria KM#907 (KM#1694).

Date	Mintage	VG	F	VF	XF	Unc
1642 DR	—	10.00	25.00	50.00	100	—
1644 HL	—	10.00	25.00	50.00	100	—
1646 HL	—	10.00	25.00	50.00	100	—
1647 H	—	10.00	25.00	50.00	100	—
1647 DR	—	10.00	25.00	50.00	100	—
1648 HL	—	10.00	25.00	50.00	100	—
1648 LB	—	10.00	25.00	50.00	100	—
1649 HL	—	10.00	25.00	50.00	100	—
1649 LB	—	10.00	25.00	50.00	100	—

KM# 357 3 KREUZER

Silver **Ruler:** Ferdinand III **Rev:** Eagle **Mint:** Teschen **Note:** Prev. Austria KM#917 (KM#1695).

Date	Mintage	VG	F	VF	XF	Unc
1643 HL	—	10.00	25.00	50.00	100	—
1649 GG	—	10.00	25.00	50.00	100	—
1652 GG	—	10.00	25.00	50.00	100	—

KM# 369 3 KREUZER

Silver **Ruler:** Ferdinand III **Obv:** Crowned bust of Wladislaus IV right in inner circle **Rev:** Crowned arms, date right of arms **Note:** Prev. Poland-Silesia KM#5.

Date	Mintage	VG	F	VF	XF	Unc
1647 Rare	—	—	—	—	—	—

KM# 390 3 KREUZER

Silver **Ruler:** Leopold I **Obv:** Laureate of John Casimir right in inner circle, value below **Rev:** Displayed eagle in inner circle, date in legend **Note:** Prev. Poland-Silesia KM#10.

Date	Mintage	VG	F	VF	XF	Unc
1657 Rare	—	—	—	—	—	—

KM# 402 3 KREUZER

Silver **Ruler:** Leopold I **Rev:** Without AT **Note:** Prev. Poland-Silesia KM#11.

Date	Mintage	VG	F	VF	XF	Unc
1658 Rare	—	—	—	—	—	—

KM# 399 3 KREUZER

Silver **Ruler:** Ferdinand III **Mint:** Breslau **Note:** Prev. Austria KM#1113 (KM#62). Posthumous issue.

Date	Mintage	VG	F	VF	XF	Unc
1658 GH	—	—	—	—	—	—

KM# 408 3 KREUZER

Silver **Ruler:** Leopold I **Obv:** Crowned bust holding septer and orb right in inner circle, value below **Rev:** Crowned imperial eagle in inner circle, date in legend **Mint:** Breslau **Note:** Prev. Austria KM#1138 (KM#77).

Date	Mintage	VG	F	VF	XF	Unc
1659 G-H	—	—	—	—	—	—

KM# 411.1 3 KREUZER

Silver **Ruler:** Leopold I **Obv:** Laureate bust right in inner circle, value below **Mint:** Breslau **Note:** Prev. Austria KM#1139.1 (KM#78.1). Varieties exist.

Date	Mintage	VG	F	VF	XF	Unc
1659 G-H	—	10.00	20.00	40.00	80.00	—
1660 G-H	—	10.00	20.00	40.00	80.00	—
1661 G-H	—	10.00	20.00	40.00	80.00	—
1662 G-H	—	10.00	20.00	40.00	80.00	—
1663 G-H	—	10.00	20.00	40.00	80.00	—
1664 G-H	—	10.00	20.00	40.00	80.00	—
1665 S-H	—	10.00	20.00	40.00	80.00	—

KM# 426 3 KREUZER

Silver **Ruler:** Leopold I **Rev:** Crowned displayed eagle in inner circle, date in legend **Note:** Prev. Poland-Silesia KM#15.

Date	Mintage	VG	F	VF	XF	Unc
1660 TT Rare	—	—	—	—	—	—
1661 Rare	—	—	—	—	—	—
1661 TT Rare	—	—	—	—	—	—

KM# 411.2 3 KREUZER

Silver **Ruler:** Leopold I **Obv:** Value inverted **Mint:** Breslau **Note:** Prev. Austria KM#1139.2 (KM#78.2).

Date	Mintage	VG	F	VF	XF	Unc
1664	—	10.00	20.00	45.00	90.00	—

KM# 471 3 KREUZER

Silver **Ruler:** Leopold I **Obv:** Bust right **Obv. Legend:** LEOPOLDUS • D • G • R • I • ... **Rev:** Crowned double, eagle, crown divides date **Mint:** Breslau **Note:** Varieties exist. Prev. Austria KM#79 (KM#1230).

Date	Mintage	VG	F	VF	XF	Unc
1665 FBL	—	10.00	25.00	50.00	100	—
1665 SHS	—	10.00	25.00	50.00	100	—
1666 SHS	—	10.00	25.00	50.00	100	—
1667 SHS	—	10.00	25.00	50.00	100	—
1668 SHS	—	10.00	25.00	50.00	100	—
1669 SHS	—	10.00	25.00	50.00	100	—
1670 SHS	—	10.00	25.00	50.00	100	—
1672	—	10.00	25.00	50.00	100	—
1693	—	10.00	25.00	50.00	100	—
1695	—	10.00	25.00	50.00	100	—
1696	—	10.00	25.00	50.00	100	—
1697	—	10.00	25.00	50.00	100	—
1698	—	10.00	25.00	50.00	100	—

KM# 504 3 KREUZER

Silver **Ruler:** Leopold I **Obv:** Laureate bust right in inner circle, value below **Rev:** Crowned imperial eagle in inner circle, crown divides date **Mint:** Oppeln **Note:** Prev. Austria KM#1281 (KM#1273). Varieties exist.

Date	Mintage	VG	F	VF	XF	Unc
1672	—	10.00	20.00	40.00	80.00	—
1673	—	10.00	20.00	40.00	80.00	—
1673 FIK	—	10.00	20.00	40.00	80.00	—
1674 FIK	—	10.00	20.00	40.00	80.00	—
1675 FIK	—	10.00	20.00	40.00	80.00	—
1699 FN	—	10.00	20.00	40.00	80.00	—
1699 F-N	—	10.00	20.00	40.00	80.00	—
1700 FN	—	10.00	20.00	40.00	80.00	—

KM# 516 3 KREUZER

Silver, 21.3 mm. **Ruler:** Leopold I **Obv:** Laureate bust right in inner circle, value below **Rev:** Crowned imperial eagle in inner circle, crown divides date **Mint:** Brieg **Note:** Prev. Austria KM#173 (KM#1287). Varieties exist.

Date	Mintage	VG	F	VF	XF	Unc
1676 CB	—	10.00	25.00	55.00	115	—
1695 CB	—	10.00	25.00	55.00	115	—
1696 CB	—	10.00	25.00	55.00	115	—
1697 CB	—	10.00	25.00	55.00	115	—
1698 CB	—	10.00	25.00	55.00	115	—
1699 CB	—	10.00	25.00	55.00	115	—
1700 CB	—	10.00	25.00	55.00	115	—

KM# 381 3 KREUZER

Silver **Ruler:** Ferdinand III **Obv:** Crowned bust facing in inner circle **Rev:** Crowned eagle in inner circle, date in legend **Mint:** Teschen **Note:** Prev. Austria KM#981 (KM#1696).

Date	Mintage	VG	F	VF	XF	Unc
1683	—	10.00	25.00	55.00	110	—

KM# 474 6 KREUZER

Silver **Ruler:** Leopold I **Obv:** Laureate bust right in inner circle, vialue in Roman numerals below **Rev:** Crowned imperial eagle in inner circle, date in legend **Mint:** Breslau **Note:** Prev. Austria KM#1232 (KM#81).

Date	Mintage	VG	F	VF	XF	Unc
1665 S-H	—	10.00	20.00	45.00	90.00	—
1666 S-H	—	10.00	20.00	45.00	90.00	—
1666 SHS	—	10.00	20.00	45.00	90.00	—

KM# 507 6 KREUZER

Silver **Ruler:** Leopold I **Rev:** Crown divides date **Mint:** Breslau **Note:** Prev. Austria KM#1274 (KM#82). Varieties exist.

Date	Mintage	VG	F	VF	XF	Unc
1672 SHS	—	10.00	20.00	40.00	85.00	—
1673 SHS	—	10.00	20.00	40.00	85.00	—
1674 SHS	—	10.00	20.00	40.00	85.00	—
1675 SHS	—	10.00	20.00	40.00	85.00	—
1676 SHS	—	10.00	20.00	40.00	85.00	—
1677 SHS	—	10.00	20.00	40.00	85.00	—
1678 SHS	—	10.00	20.00	40.00	85.00	—
1679 SHS	—	10.00	20.00	40.00	85.00	—
1680 SHS	—	10.00	20.00	40.00	85.00	—
1681 SHS	—	10.00	20.00	40.00	85.00	—
1682 SHS	—	10.00	20.00	40.00	85.00	—
1683 SHS	—	10.00	20.00	40.00	85.00	—
1684 SHS	—	10.00	20.00	40.00	85.00	—
1685 SHS	—	10.00	20.00	40.00	85.00	—
1686 SHS	—	10.00	20.00	40.00	85.00	—
1687 SHS	—	10.00	20.00	40.00	85.00	—
1688 SHS	—	10.00	20.00	40.00	85.00	—
1689 SHS	—	10.00	20.00	40.00	85.00	—
1690 SHS	—	10.00	20.00	40.00	85.00	—
1691 SHS	—	10.00	20.00	40.00	85.00	—
1692	—	10.00	20.00	40.00	85.00	—
1693	—	10.00	20.00	40.00	85.00	—

KM# 517 6 KREUZER

Silver **Ruler:** Leopold I **Mint:** Oppeln **Note:** Prev. Austria KM#1278 (KM#1282). Varieties exist.

Date	Mintage	VG	F	VF	XF	Unc
1675 FIK	—	20.00	45.00	90.00	180	—
1676 FIK	—	20.00	45.00	90.00	180	—
1677 FIK	—	20.00	45.00	90.00	180	—
1678 FIK	—	20.00	45.00	90.00	180	—
1679 FIK	—	20.00	45.00	90.00	180	—
1681 FIK	—	20.00	45.00	90.00	180	—
1682 FIK	—	20.00	45.00	90.00	180	—
1683 FIK	—	20.00	45.00	90.00	180	—
1685	—	20.00	45.00	90.00	180	—
1686	—	20.00	45.00	90.00	180	—
1688	—	20.00	45.00	90.00	180	—
1689	—	20.00	45.00	90.00	180	—
1690	—	20.00	45.00	90.00	180	—

KM# 522 6 KREUZER

Silver **Ruler:** Leopold I **Obv:** Laureate bust right in inner circle, value below **Rev:** Crowned imperial eagle in inner circle, crown divides date **Mint:** Brieg **Note:** Prev. Austria KM#1297 (KM#174). Varieties exist.

Date	Mintage	VG	F	VF	XF	Unc
1677 CB	—	25.00	50.00	100	200	—

KM# 57 15 KREUZER

Silver **Ruler:** Ferdinand II **Mint:** Glogau **Note:** Prev. Austria KM#439 (KM#326). Varieties exist.

Date	Mintage	VG	F	VF	XF	Unc
1623 IH	—	9.00	20.00	40.00	80.00	—
1623 G/BZ	—	9.00	20.00	40.00	80.00	—

KM# 414 15 KREUZER
Silver **Ruler:** Leopold I **Obv:** Laureate bust right in inner circle, value below **Rev:** Crowned imperial ealge in inner circle, date in legend **Mint:** Breslau **Note:** Prev. Austria KM#1143 (KM#83). Varieties exist.

Date	Mintage	VG	F	VF	XF	Unc
1659 G-H	—	10.00	25.00	55.00	115	—
1660 G-H	—	10.00	25.00	55.00	115	—
1661 G-H	—	10.00	25.00	55.00	115	—
1662 G-H	—	10.00	25.00	55.00	115	—
1663 G-H	—	10.00	25.00	55.00	115	—
1664 G-H	—	10.00	25.00	55.00	115	—
1664 S-HS	—	10.00	25.00	55.00	115	—

KM# 462 15 KREUZER
Silver **Ruler:** Leopold I **Obv:** Crown divides date **Mint:** Breslau **Note:** Prev. Austria KM#1218 (KM#84). Varieties exist.

Date	Mintage	VG	F	VF	XF	Unc
1664 FBDL	—	10.00	25.00	55.00	115	—
1664 FBL	—	10.00	25.00	55.00	115	—
1664 SH	—	10.00	25.00	55.00	115	—
1665 FBL	—	10.00	25.00	55.00	115	—
1665 SH	—	10.00	25.00	55.00	115	—
1674 SHS	—	10.00	25.00	55.00	115	—
1675 SHS	—	10.00	25.00	55.00	115	—
1676 SHS	—	10.00	25.00	55.00	115	—
1692	—	10.00	25.00	55.00	115	—
1693	—	10.00	25.00	55.00	115	—
1694	—	10.00	25.00	55.00	115	—
1695	—	10.00	25.00	55.00	115	—
1696	—	10.00	25.00	55.00	115	—

KM# 465 15 KREUZER
Silver **Ruler:** Leopold I **Obv:** Laureate bust of John Casimir right in inner circle, value below **Rev:** Crowned displayed eagle in inner circle, date in legend **Note:** Prev. Poland-Silesia KM#16.

Date	Mintage	VG	F	VF	XF	Unc
1664 AT Rare	—	—	—	—	—	—

KM# 525 15 KREUZER
Silver **Ruler:** Leopold I **Obv:** Laureate bust right in inner circle, value below **Rev:** Crowned imperial eagle in inner circle, crown divides date **Mint:** Brieg **Note:** Prev. Austria KM#1298 (KM#175). Varieties exist.

Date	Mintage	VG	F	VF	XF	Unc
1677 CB	—	40.00	80.00	160	325	—
1693 CB	—	40.00	80.00	160	325	—
1694 CB	—	40.00	80.00	160	325	—

KM# 393 18 KREUZER
Silver **Ruler:** Leopold I **Obv:** Crowned arms divide value in inner circle **Mint:** Breslau **Note:** Prev. Austria KM#1001 (KM#85).

Date	Mintage	VG	F	VF	XF	Unc
1657 G-H	—	—	—	—	—	—

KM# 9 24 KREUZER
Silver **Ruler:** Friedrich **Mint:** Oels **Note:** Prev. KM#304 (KM#1225).

Date	Mintage	VG	F	VF	XF	Unc
1621 HT monogram Rare	—	—	—	—	—	—

KM# 45 24 KREUZER
Silver **Ruler:** Ferdinand II **Obv:** Silesian eagle **Mint:** Breslau **Note:** Prev. Austria KM#396 (KM#29).

Date	Mintage	VG	F	VF	XF	Unc
1622	—	—	—	—	—	—

KM# 48 24 KREUZER
Silver **Ruler:** Ferdinand II **Mint:** Neisse **Note:** Prev. Austria KM#398. 24 Kipper Kreuzer. Varieties exist.

Date	Mintage	VG	F	VF	XF	Unc
1622	—	25.00	50.00	100	200	—
1623 BZ	—	25.00	50.00	100	200	—
1623 (dt)	—	25.00	50.00	100	200	—
1624 BZ	—	25.00	50.00	100	200	—

KM# 60 24 KREUZER
Silver **Ruler:** Ferdinand II **Mint:** Breslau **Note:** Prev. Austria KM#440 (KM#30). 24 Kipper Kreuzer.

Date	Mintage	VG	F	VF	XF	Unc
1623 BZ	—	14.00	30.00	60.00	120	—
1623 HT	—	14.00	30.00	60.00	120	—
1623 BZ-HT	—	14.00	30.00	60.00	120	—

KM# 63 24 KREUZER
Silver **Ruler:** Ferdinand II **Mint:** Glogau **Note:** Prev. Austria KM#441 (KM#327). 24 Kipper Kreuzer.

Date	Mintage	VG	F	VF	XF	Unc
1623 G/BZ	—	9.00	22.00	40.00	80.00	—
1623 IH	—	9.00	22.00	40.00	80.00	—
1623 IIH	—	9.00	22.00	40.00	80.00	—

KM# 12 30 KREUZER
Silver **Ruler:** Ferdinand II **Obv:** Four-line denomination in rectangle **Rev:** Silesian eagle **Mint:** Breslau **Note:** Prev. Austria KM#308 (KM#31).

Date	Mintage	VG	F	VF	XF	Unc
1621 HR	—	—	—	—	—	—

KM# 15 48 KREUZER
Silver **Ruler:** Friedrich **Mint:** Oels **Note:** Prev. Austria KM#258 (KM#1226). Similar to 24 Kreuzer KM#239.

Date	Mintage	VG	F	VF	XF	Unc
1621 Ht monogram Rare	—	—	—	—	—	—

KM# 51 150 KREUZER
Silver **Ruler:** Ferdinand II **Mint:** Neisse **Note:** Prev. Austria KM#421 (KM#1205). Varieties exist.

Date	Mintage	VG	F	VF	XF	Unc
1622 (dt) Rare	—	—	—	—	—	—
1623 (dt) Rare	—	—	—	—	—	—

KM# 123 1/4 THALER
Silver **Ruler:** Ferdinand II **Obv:** Laureate bust right in inner circle **Rev:** Crowned imperial eagle in inner circle, date in legend **Mint:** Neisse **Note:** Prev. Austria KM#505 (KM#1206).

Date	Mintage	VG	F	VF	XF	Unc
1624 BZ Rare	—	—	—	—	—	—

KM# 348 1/4 THALER
Silver **Ruler:** Ferdinand III **Obv:** Crowned bust right in inner circle **Rev:** Crowned imperial eagle in inner circle, date in legend **Mint:** Breslau **Note:** Prev. Austria KM#894 (KM#63). Varieties exist.

Date	Mintage	VG	F	VF	XF	Unc
1641	—	15.00	30.00	65.00	130	—
1642	—	15.00	30.00	65.00	130	—
1643	—	15.00	30.00	65.00	130	—
1644	—	15.00	30.00	65.00	130	—
1645	—	15.00	30.00	65.00	130	—
1646	—	15.00	30.00	65.00	130	—
1648	—	15.00	30.00	65.00	130	—
1649	—	15.00	30.00	65.00	130	—
1650	—	15.00	30.00	65.00	130	—
1651	—	15.00	30.00	65.00	130	—
1653	—	15.00	30.00	65.00	130	—
1654	—	15.00	30.00	65.00	130	—
1655	—	15.00	30.00	65.00	130	—
1657	—	15.00	30.00	65.00	130	—

KM# 429 1/4 THALER
Silver **Ruler:** Leopold I **Obv:** Laureate bust right in inner circle **Rev:** Crowned imperial eagle in inner circle, crown divides date **Mint:** Breslau **Note:** Prev. Austria KM#1171 (KM#86). Varieties exist.

Date	Mintage	VG	F	VF	XF	Unc
1660 G-H	—	20.00	40.00	65.00	130	—
1662 G-H	—	20.00	40.00	65.00	130	—
1664 G-H	—	20.00	40.00	65.00	130	—
1666 S-HS	—	20.00	40.00	65.00	130	—
1695	—	20.00	40.00	65.00	130	—

KM# 432 1/4 THALER
Silver **Ruler:** Leopold I **Obv:** Crowned bust holding septer **Rev:** Heart-shaped arns on double eagle **Mint:** Breslau **Note:** Prev. Austria KM#1172 (KM#87).

Date	Mintage	VG	F	VF	XF	Unc
1660 GH	—	25.00	50.00	100	200	—

KM# 126 1/2 THALER
Silver **Ruler:** Ferdinand II **Obv:** Laureate bust right in inner circle **Rev:** Crowned imperial eagle in inner circle, date in legend **Mint:** Neisse **Note:** Prev. Austria KM#512 (KM#1207).

Date	Mintage	VG	F	VF	XF	Unc
1624 (dt) - BZ Rare	—	—	—	—	—	—

KM# 228 1/2 THALER
Silver **Ruler:** Ferdinand II **Obv:** Bust right **Rev:** Heraldic double eagle **Mint:** Oppeln **Note:** Prev. Austria KM#593 (KM#1271).

Date	Mintage	VG	F	VF	XF	Unc
1625 SF Rare	—	—	—	—	—	—

KM# 231 1/2 THALER
Silver **Ruler:** Ferdinand II **Obv:** Laureate bust right in inner circle **Rev:** Crowned imperial eagle in inner circle, date in legend **Mint:** Ratibor **Note:** Prev. Austria KM#594 (KM#1568).

Date	Mintage	VG	F	VF	XF	Unc
1625 DR-SD Rare	—	—	—	—	—	—

KM# 285 1/2 THALER
Silver **Ruler:** Ferdinand II **Mint:** Breslau **Note:** Prev. Austria KM#697(KM#32). Varieties exist.

Date	Mintage	VG	F	VF	XF	Unc
1628 W-(3ch)	—	125	250	425	850	—
1631 W/HR-(3ch)IZ	—	125	250	425	850	—
1632 W-(3ch)/IZ	—	125	250	425	850	—

KM# 318 1/2 THALER
Silver **Ruler:** Ferdinand II **Mint:** Breslau **Note:** Prev. Austria KM#781 (KM#33). Varieties exist.

Date	Mintage	VG	F	VF	XF	Unc
1632 W/HR-(3ch)/IZ	—	125	250	425	850	—

KM# 340 1/2 THALER
Silver **Ruler:** Ferdinand III **Obv:** Bust right in inner circle **Rev:** Inner circle added **Mint:** Breslau **Note:** Prev. Austria KM#853 (KM#64). Varieties exist.

Date	Mintage	VG	F	VF	XF	Unc
1638	—	30.00	65.00	135	275	—
1639	—	30.00	65.00	135	275	—
1641	—	30.00	65.00	135	275	—
1642	—	30.00	65.00	135	275	—
1643	—	30.00	65.00	135	275	—
1644	—	30.00	65.00	135	275	—
1645	—	30.00	65.00	135	275	—
1646	—	30.00	65.00	135	275	—
1648	—	30.00	65.00	135	275	—
1651	—	30.00	65.00	135	275	—
1653	—	30.00	65.00	135	275	—
1654	—	30.00	65.00	135	275	—
1655	—	30.00	65.00	135	275	—
1657	—	30.00	65.00	135	275	—

KM# 366 1/2 THALER
Silver **Ruler:** Ferdinand III **Mint:** Breslau **Note:** Prev. Austria KM#928 (KM#65).

Date	Mintage	VG	F	VF	XF	Unc
1646	—	45.00	95.00	190	385	—
1650	—	45.00	95.00	190	385	—

KM# 417 1/2 THALER
Silver **Ruler:** Leopold I **Mint:** Breslau **Note:** Prev. Austria KM#1146 (KM#88).

Date	Mintage	VG	F	VF	XF	Unc
1659 G-H	—	300	500	800	1,550	—
1660 G-H	—	300	500	800	1,550	—
1662 G-H	—	300	500	800	1,550	—
1663 G-H	—	300	500	800	1,550	—
1664 G-H	—	300	500	800	1,550	—

KM# 477 1/2 THALER
Silver **Ruler:** Leopold I **Obv:** Laureate bust **Rev:** Crowned imperial eagle in inner circle, crown divides date **Mint:** Breslau **Note:** Varieties exist. Prev. Austria KM#89 (KM#1236).

Date	Mintage	VG	F	VF	XF	Unc
1665 SH	—	135	275	425	850	—
1670 SHS	—	135	275	425	850	—
1672 SHS	—	135	275	425	850	—
1677 SHS	—	135	275	425	850	—
1679 SHS	—	135	275	425	850	—
1689 SHS	—	135	275	425	850	—
1695	—	135	275	425	850	—
1696	—	135	275	425	850	—

KM# 579 1/2 THALER
Silver **Ruler:** Leopold I **Obv:** Laureate bust right in inner circle **Rev:** Crowned imperial eagle in inner circle, crown divides date **Mint:** Oppeln **Note:** Prev. Austria KM#1347 (KM#1283). Varieties exist.

Date	Mintage	VG	F	VF	XF	Unc
1690 Rare	—	—	—	—	—	—
1700 FN Rare	—	—	—	—	—	—

KM# 615 1/2 THALER
Silver **Ruler:** Leopold I **Obv:** Laureate bust right in inner circle **Rev:** Crowned imperial eagle in inner circle, crown divides date **Mint:** Brieg **Note:** Prev. Austria KM#176 (KM#1384).

Date	Mintage	VG	F	VF	XF	Unc
1695 CB	—	200	400	675	1,300	—

KM# 18 3/4 THALER
Silver **Ruler:** Ferdinand II **Obv:** Silesian eagle within legend; M, HR, and SP monograms in corners **Mint:** Glogau **Note:** Prev. Austria KM#332 (KM#328). Uniface. Klippe.

Date	Mintage	VG	F	VF	XF	Unc
1621 Rare	—	—	—	—	—	—

KM# 129.1 THALER
Silver **Ruler:** Ferdinand II **Obv:** Bust right **Obv. Legend:** FERDINANDVS. II. D: G. R. IM. S. A. G. H. B. REX. DV. X. S. **Rev:** Crowned double eagle **Rev. Legend:** NEC NON ARCHID (W) AV. DVX. BV. M. M. C. T. **Mint:** Breslau **Note:** Prev. Austria KM#516.1 (KM#34.1, Dav.#3151).

Date	Mintage	VG	F	VF	XF	Unc
ND W/(3ch)	—	400	700	1,200	2,000	—
ND W/(2ch)	—	400	700	1,200	2,000	—
ND W	—	400	700	1,200	2,000	—

KM# 144 THALER

Silver **Ruler:** Ferdinand II **Mint:** Neisse **Note:** Prev. Austria KM#524 (Dav.#3164, KM#1209). Varieties exist.

Date	Mintage	VG	F	VF	XF	Unc
1624 BZ	—	1,150	2,250	4,500	7,500	—
1624 (dt)-BZ	—	1,150	2,250	4,500	7,500	—
1624 BZ-BZ	—	1,150	2,250	4,500	7,500	—
1624 BZ	—	1,150	2,250	4,500	7,500	—
Note: Strike mark on reverse						
1624 (dt)	—	1,150	2,250	4,500	7,500	—

KM# 129.2 THALER

Silver **Ruler:** Ferdinand II **Obv. Legend:** D: G. RO. IM. S. AV. GER. HV. BOH. REX. **Rev. Legend:** ARCHIDVX. AVSTRI. DVX. BVRG. SILESIAE **Mint:** Breslau **Note:** Prev. Austria KM#516.2 (KM#34.2, Dav.#3152).

Date	Mintage	VG	F	VF	XF	Unc
1624 BZ/HR	—	400	700	1,200	2,000	—

KM# 129.3 THALER

Silver **Ruler:** Ferdinand II **Rev. Legend:** ARCHIDVX. AVS. DVX. BVR. MAR. MO. CO. TYR. **Mint:** Breslau **Note:** Prev. Austria KM#516.3 (Dav.#3153, KM#34.3).

Date	Mintage	VG	F	VF	XF	Unc
1624 BZ	—	400	700	1,000	1,800	—

KM# 129.4 THALER

Silver **Ruler:** Ferdinand II **Rev. Legend:** ARCHIDVX. AVS. DVX. BVR. MAR. MO. CO. TYR. **Mint:** Breslau **Note:** Prev. Austria KM#516.4 (Dav.#3154, KM#34.4)

Date	Mintage	VG	F	VF	XF	Unc
1624 BZ/BZ	—	3,000	5,700	9,300	—	—

KM# 141 THALER

Silver **Ruler:** Ferdinand II **Obv:** Laureate half-figure right holding orb and scepter in inner circle **Rev:** Crowned imperial eagle with round arms on breast in inner circle, date in legend **Mint:** Neisse **Note:** Prev. Austria KM#523 (Dav.#3165, KM#1208).

Date	Mintage	VG	F	VF	XF	Unc
1624 (dt) Rare	—	—	—	—	—	—

KM# 234 THALER

Silver **Ruler:** Ferdinand II **Obv:** Ferdinand II right in ornamented inner circle **Mint:** Breslau **Note:** Prev. Austria KM#595 (KM#36, Dav.#A.3155). Thick planchet.

Date	Mintage	VG	F	VF	XF	Unc
1625 HR Rare	—	—	—	—	—	—

KM# 237 THALER

Silver **Ruler:** Ferdinand II **Obv:** Ferdinand II in plain inner circle, date below legend **Obv. Legend:** ...D: G. R. I. S. A. G. H. B. REX. DV. S **Rev:** Crowned arms in Order chain **Rev. Legend:** NEC NON ARCHIDVX - A. DVX. BVR. M. M. C. TY - R. **Mint:** Breslau **Note:** Prev. Austria KM#596 (KM#37, Dav.#3155).

Date	Mintage	VG	F	VF	XF	Unc
1625 Rare	—	—	—	—	—	—

KM# 240 THALER

Silver **Ruler:** Ferdinand II **Mint:** Oppeln **Note:** Prev. Austria KM#597 (KM#1272, Dav.#3166).

Date	Mintage	VG	F	VF	XF	Unc
1625 SF Rare	—	—	—	—	—	—

KM# 246 THALER

Silver **Ruler:** Ferdinand II **Obv:** Facing bust with scepter and orb **Rev:** Soldiers and city view **Mint:** Breslau **Note:** Prev. Austria KM#627 (KM#38).

Date	Mintage	VG	F	VF	XF	Unc
1626 HR Rare	—	—	—	—	—	—

KM# 129.5 THALER

Silver **Ruler:** Ferdinand II **Obv:** Date below legend **Obv. Legend:** D: G. R. IMP. S .A. GER. H: B: REX. DVX. SIL **Rev. Legend:** NEC NON ARCHIN (W) AV. DV. BV. MA. MO. C. T. **Mint:** Breslau **Note:** Prev. Austria KM#516.5 (KM#34.5, Dav.#3156).

Date	Mintage	VG	F	VF	XF	Unc
1627 W/(2ch)	—	400	700	1,200	2,000	—

KM# 129.6 THALER

Silver **Ruler:** Ferdinand II **Rev. Legend:** ... ARCHIDVX (W) AVS. DVX. BVR. M. M. C. T. **Mint:** Breslau **Note:** Prev. Austria KM#516.6 (KM#34.6, Dav.#3156A).

Date	Mintage	VG	F	VF	XF	Unc
1627 W/(2ch) Rare	—	—	—	—	—	—

KM# 276 THALER

Silver **Ruler:** Ferdinand II **Mint:** Breslau **Note:** Prev. Austria KM#674 (KM#35). Klippe. Similar to KM#129.5.

Date	Mintage	VG	F	VF	XF	Unc
1627 W/(2ch) Rare	—	—	—	—	—	—

KM# 129.7 THALER

Silver **Ruler:** Ferdinand II **Obv. Legend:** ... IM. S. A. G. H. B. REX. DV. X. S. **Rev:** Eagle divides date at bottom **Mint:** Breslau **Note:** Prev. Austria KM#516.7 (KM#34.7, Dav.#3157).

Date	Mintage	VG	F	VF	XF	Unc
1629 W/(2ch)	—	260	450	775	1,250	—

KM# 300 THALER

Silver **Ruler:** Ferdinand II **Obv. Legend:** ... D. G. ROM. IMP. S. A. G. H. B. REX. **Rev:** Date divided below eagle **Rev. Legend:** AR: AV: D. BV: MA: MO (W) DVX SILESIAE & PH **Mint:** Breslau **Note:** Prev. Austria KM#745 (KM#34.8, Dav.#3158).

Date	Mintage	VG	F	VF	XF	Unc
1630 W/(p)	—	400	700	1,200	2,000	—

KM# 315 THALER

Silver **Ruler:** Ferdinand II **Obv. Legend:** ... D. G. R. IM. S. A. G. H. B. REX. DVX. SI **Rev. Legend:** NEC NON ARCHIDVX. (W) AVS. DVX. BVR. M. M. C. T. **Mint:** Breslau **Note:** Prev. Austria KM#767 (KM#34.9, Dav.#3159).

Date	Mintage	VG	F	VF	XF	Unc
1631 W/IZ(3ch)	—	400	700	1,200	2,000	—
1631 IZ/(3ch)	—	400	700	1,200	2,000	—

KM# 129.10 THALER

Silver **Ruler:** Ferdinand II **Obv. Legend:** ...DVX. S. **Rev:** Date in legend **Rev. Legend:** ARCHIDVX, AVST. DVX. (W)BVFRG. SILE ze **Mint:** Breslau **Note:** Prev. Austria KM#516.10 (KM#34.10, Dav.#3160).

Date	Mintage	VG	F	VF	XF	Unc
1632 W/IZ/(3ch)	—	400	700	1,200	2,000	—

KM# 129.11 THALER

Silver **Ruler:** Ferdinand II **Rev:** Date after legend **Rev. Legend:** ....AVSTRI. DVX. BVR(G) SILESI. ze **Mint:** Breslau **Note:** Prev. Austria KM#516.11 (KM#34.11, Dav.#3161).

Date	Mintage	VG	F	VF	XF	Unc
1632 IZ/(3ch)	—	350	875	1,350	2,500	—

KM# 129.12 THALER

Silver **Ruler:** Ferdinand II **Obv. Legend:** D: G(W)R. I. CS. A. G. HVNG. BO. REX **Rev:** Date after legend **Rev. Legend:** ...AVSTRIDVX. BVRG. SILESI. ze **Mint:** Breslau **Note:** Prev. Austria KM#516.12 (KM#34.12, Dav.#3162).

Date	Mintage	VG	F	VF	XF	Unc
1632 IZ/(3ch) Rare	—	—	—	—	—	—

KM# 345.1 THALER

Silver **Ruler:** Ferdinand III **Obv:** Crowned bust right in inner circle **Rev:** Crowned imperial eagle in inner circle, date in legend **Mint:** Breslau **Note:** Prev. Austria KM#875.1 (KM#66.1, Dav.#3219). Legend varieties exist.

Date	Mintage	VG	F	VF	XF	Unc
1639 M-I	—	275	550	1,250	2,350	—
1641 M-I	—	275	550	1,250	2,350	—
1642 M-I	—	275	550	1,250	2,350	—
1643 M-I	—	275	550	1,250	2,350	—
1645 M-I	—	275	550	1,250	2,350	—
1646 M-I	—	275	550	1,250	2,350	—
1648 M-I	—	275	550	1,250	2,350	—
1650 G-I	—	275	550	1,250	2,350	—
1651 G-I	—	275	550	1,250	2,350	—
1653 G-I	—	275	550	1,250	2,350	—
1654 G-I	—	275	550	1,250	2,350	—
1655	—	275	550	1,250	2,350	—

KM# 375 THALER

Silver **Ruler:** Ferdinand III **Obv:** Laureate bust right with wide lace collar in inner circle **Mint:** Breslau **Note:** Prev. Austria KM#966 (KM#67, Dav.#3220).

Date	Mintage	VG	F	VF	XF	Unc
1649 G-H	—	2,000	3,900	6,600	—	—

KM# 384 THALER

Silver **Ruler:** Ferdinand III **Obv:** Narrow laureate bust right in inner circle **Mint:** Breslau **Note:** Prev. Austria KM#991 (KM#68, Dav.#3221).

Date	Mintage	VG	F	VF	XF	Unc
1655 G-H Rare	—	—	—	—	—	—
1656 G-H Rare	—	—	—	—	—	—

KM# 345.2 THALER

Silver **Ruler:** Ferdinand III **Rev:** Modified arms **Mint:** Breslau **Note:** Prev. Austria KM#875.2 (KM#66.2, Dav.#3222).

Date	Mintage	VG	F	VF	XF	Unc
1656	—	275	550	1,250	2,350	—
1657 G-H	—	275	550	1,250	2,350	—

KM# 420 THALER

Silver **Ruler:** Leopold I **Mint:** Breslau **Note:** Prev. Austria KM#1155 (KM#90, Dav.#3285).

Date	Mintage	VG	F	VF	XF	Unc
1659 G-H Rare	—	—	—	—	—	—
1660 G-H Rare	—	—	—	—	—	—

KM# 435.1 THALER

Silver **Ruler:** Leopold I **Obv:** Young laureate bust right **Obv. Legend:** ...BOHEN.ZC.REX. **Rev:** Eagle with arms in Order collar on breast, date **Rev. Legend:** BURGUND.COMES.TYR **Mint:** Breslau **Note:** Prev. Austria KM#1174.1 (KM#92.1, Dav#3286).

Date	Mintage	VG	F	VF	XF	Unc
1660 GH Rare	—	—	—	—	—	—

KM# 447 THALER

Silver **Ruler:** Leopold I **Rev:** Sword and scepter in eagle claws **Mint:** Breslau **Note:** Prev. Austria KM#1199 (KM#91, Dav.#3287).

Date	Mintage	VG	F	VF	XF	Unc
1662 GH Rare	—	—	—	—	—	—
1663 GH Rare	—	—	—	—	—	—

KM# 435.2 THALER

Silver **Ruler:** Leopold I **Obv. Legend:** ...BO.H.ETC.REX **Rev:** Date after legend **Rev. Legend:** ...BURG.COM TYROL **Mint:** Breslau **Note:** Prev. Austria KM#1174.2 (KM#92.2, Dav.#A3288).

Date	Mintage	VG	F	VF	XF	Unc
1663 GH Rare	—	—	—	—	—	—

KM# 480.1 THALER

Silver **Ruler:** Leopold I **Mint:** Breslau **Note:** Prev. Austria KM#1221.1 (KM#93.1, Dav.#3288).

Date	Mintage	VG	F	VF	XF	Unc
1664 GH Rare	—	—	—	—	—	—
1665 SH	—	2,100	3,900	6,600	—	—

KM# 480.2 THALER

Silver **Ruler:** Leopold I **Mint:** Breslau **Note:** Prev. Austria KM#1221.2 (KM#93.2, Dav.#3288A).

Date	Mintage	VG	F	VF	XF	Unc
1665 Rare	—	—	—	—	—	—

KM# 483.1 THALER

Silver **Ruler:** Leopold I **Obv:** Laureate bust **Obv. Legend:** LEOPOLDVS. D: G. EL. RO. LSE. AVG. GER. HV. BO: REX. **Rev. Legend:** ARCHI. DVX. AVST. SHS DVX. BURG. ET. SIL... **Mint:** Breslau **Note:** Prev. Austria KM#1244.1 (KM#94.1, Dav.#3289).

Date	Mintage	VG	F	VF	XF	Unc
1666 shs	—	1,150	2,300	4,600	7,500	—

KM# 483.2 THALER

Silver **Ruler:** Leopold I **Obv:** Lion's head on shoulder **Mint:** Breslau **Note:** Prev. Austria KM#1244.2 (KM#94.2, Dav.#3290).

Date	Mintage	VG	F	VF	XF	Unc
1668 SHS	—	1,150	2,300	4,600	7,500	—
1669 SHS	—	1,150	2,300	4,600	7,500	—

KM# 483.3 THALER

Silver **Ruler:** Leopold I **Obv. Legend:** ...R. LSE. AVG. GE... **Rev. Legend:** ...ET. SILE: **Mint:** Breslau **Note:** Prev. Austria KM#1244.3 9KM#94.3, Dav.#3291).

Date	Mintage	VG	F	VF	XF	Unc
1670 SHS	—	875	1,750	3,450	5,800	—
1672 SHS	—	875	1,750	3,450	5,800	—
1673 SHS	—	875	1,750	3,450	5,800	—
1674 SHS	—	875	1,750	3,450	5,800	—

KM# 483.4 THALER

Silver **Ruler:** Leopold I **Obv. Legend:** ...ROM IMP: SE: AV: GE: HV: BO: REX. **Rev. Legend:** ARCHIDVX... **Mint:** Breslau **Note:** Prev. Austria KM#1244.4 (KM#94.4, Dav.#3292).

Date	Mintage	VG	F	VF	XF	Unc
1677 SHS	—	875	1,750	3,450	5,800	—

KM# 483.5 THALER

Silver **Ruler:** Leopold I **Obv:** Bust with GFH on shoulder **Obv. Legend:** ...DG: EL... GER... **Rev. Legend:** ...BVR. ET. SILESIAE. **Mint:** Breslau **Note:** Prev. Austria KM#1244.5 (KM#94.5, Dav.#3293).

Date	Mintage	VG	F	VF	XF	Unc
1678 SHS	—	875	1,750	3,450	5,800	—
1679 SHS	—	875	1,750	3,450	5,800	—

KM# 483.7 THALER

Silver **Ruler:** Leopold I **Obv. Legend:** ...HV. & BO. REX. **Mint:** Breslau **Note:** Prev. Austria KM#1244.7 (KM#94.7, Dav.#3295).

Date	Mintage	VG	F	VF	XF	Unc
1683 SHS	—	1,100	2,000	4,050	6,900	—
1684 SHS	—	1,100	2,000	4,050	6,900	—

KM# 483.6 THALER

Silver **Ruler:** Leopold I **Obv. Legend:** ...DG. ROM. IMP. SE. AVE. GER. HV. BO **Rev. Legend:** ...SILES **Mint:** Breslau **Note:** Prev. Austria KM#1244.6 (KM#94.6, Dav.#3294).

Date	Mintage	VG	F	VF	XF	Unc
1683 SHS	—	750	1,450	2,900	5,500	—

KM# 483.8 THALER

Silver **Ruler:** Leopold I **Obv:** Bust right with lion's head on arm **Obv. Legend:** ...SEM: AVG:. **Rev. Legend:** ... AVSTRI: SHSDVX. BVRG: ET. SILE. **Mint:** Breslau **Note:** Prev. Austria KM#1224.8 (KM#9438, Dav.#3296).

Date	Mintage	VG	F	VF	XF	Unc
1685 SHS	—	925	1,850	3,750	6,300	—
1686 SHS	—	925	1,850	3,750	6,300	—
1687 SHS	—	925	1,850	3,750	6,300	—
1688 SHS	—	925	1,850	3,750	6,300	—

KM# 483.9 THALER

Silver **Ruler:** Leopold I **Obv:** Armored bust **Mint:** Breslau **Note:** Prev. Austria KM#1224.9 (KM#94.9, Dav.#3296A).

Date	Mintage	VG	F	VF	XF	Unc
1686 SHS	—	925	1,850	3,750	6,300	—

KM# 483.10 THALER

Silver **Ruler:** Leopold I **Obv. Legend:** ...D: G: ROM... **Mint:** Breslau **Note:** Prev. Austria KM#1224.10 (KM#94.10, Dav.#3297).

Date	Mintage	VG	F	VF	XF	Unc
1689 SHS	—	675	1,350	3,000	5,000	—
1690 SHS	—	675	1,350	3,000	5,000	—

KM# 483.11 THALER

Silver **Ruler:** Leopold I **Obv. Legend:** ...DG. ROM...HVN & BOH. REX **Rev. Legend:** AVSTRIAE MMW DVX. BVRG & SILESIAE. **Mint:** Breslau **Note:** Prev. Austria KM#1224.11 (KM#94.11, Dav.#3298).

Date	Mintage	VG	F	VF	XF	Unc
1691 SHS	—	675	1,350	3,000	5,000	—
1692	—	675	1,350	3,000	5,000	—
1693	—	675	1,350	3,000	5,000	—

KM# 483.12 THALER

Silver **Ruler:** Leopold I **Obv:** Bust divides legend **Obv. Legend:** ...AV. GE. H. B. REX. **Rev. Legend:** ...AVST. MMW...& SILE. **Mint:** Breslau **Note:** Prev. Austria KM#1224.12 (KM#94.12, Dav.#3299).

Date	Mintage	VG	F	VF	XF	Unc
1694	—	800	1,600	3,700	6,500	—

KM# 483.13 THALER

Silver **Ruler:** Leopold I **Obv:** Thin bust **Obv. Legend:** ...D: G:... AVG: GERM: HU: & BO: REX. **Rev. Legend:** AVSTRIAE... SILESIAE. **Mint:** Breslau **Note:** Prev. Austria KM#1224.13 (KM#94.13, Dav.#3300).

Date	Mintage	VG	F	VF	XF	Unc
1695	—	725	1,450	3,300	5,500	—
1696	—	725	1,450	3,300	5,500	—

KM# 621.1 THALER

Silver **Ruler:** Leopold I **Obv:** Laureate bust right separates inner circle **Rev:** Crowned imperial eagle in inner circle, crown divides date **Mint:** Brieg **Note:** Prev. Austria KM#1386.1 (KM#177.1, Dav.#3304).

Date	Mintage	VG	F	VF	XF	Unc
1695 CB	—	575	1,250	2,700	4,500	—

KM# 621.2 THALER

Silver **Ruler:** Leopold I **Obv:** Laureate bust right in inner circle **Obv. Legend:** LEOPOLDUS. DG: ROM: IMPERATOR ... **Mint:** Brieg **Note:** Prev. KM#1386.2 (KM#177.2, Dav.#3305)

Date	Mintage	VG	F	VF	XF	Unc
1696 CB	—	575	1,250	2,700	4,500	—
1697 CB	—	575	1,250	2,700	4,500	—

KM# 483.14 THALER

Silver **Ruler:** Leopold I **Obv:** Armored bust right without inner circle **Obv. Legend:** LEOPOLDUS. DG: ROM: IMP: SE: AV: GE:... **Rev. Legend:** Ends: SILESI **Mint:** Breslau **Note:** Prev. Austria KM#1224.14 (KM#94.14, Dav.#3301).

Date	Mintage	VG	F	VF	XF	Unc
1697	—	800	1,600	3,700	6,500	—
1698	—	800	1,600	3,700	6,500	—

KM# 651.1 THALER

Silver **Ruler:** Leopold I **Obv:** Laureate armored bust right **Obv. Legend:** LEOPOLDUS • D • G • ROM: IMP: SEM: AVG: GER: HU: BO: REX • **Rev:** Crowned imperial eagle with arms on breast **Rev. Legend:** ARCHIDUX • AVSTRIAE DUX • BVRG •... **Mint:** Oppeln **Note:** Dav. #3303. Prev. Austria KM#1284.1 (KM#1398.1).

Date	Mintage	VG	F	VF	XF	Unc
1699 Rare	—	—	—	—	—	—
1700 FN	—	675	1,350	3,000	5,000	—

KM# 21 1-1/2 THALER

Silver **Ruler:** Ferdinand II **Obv:** Silesian eagle within legend ; M. HR, and SP monograms in corners **Mint:** Glogau **Note:** Prev. Austria KM#351 (KM#329). Klippe. Uniface.

Date	Mintage	VG	F	VF	XF	Unc
1621 Rare	—	—	—	—	—	—

KM# 249 1-1/2 THALER

Silver **Ruler:** Ferdinand II **Obv:** Laureate bust half right holding orb and scepter **Rev:** City view of Breslau with horseman and companion in foreground in inner circle **Mint:** Breslau **Note:** Prev. Austria KM#635 (KM#39).

Date	Mintage	VG	F	VF	XF	Unc
1626 (h) Rare	—	—	—	—	—	—

KM# 4.1 2 THALER

Silver **Ruler:** Ferdinand II **Obv:** Laureate bust right in inner circle **Obv. Legend:** FERNINANDVS. II. D: G. R. IM. S. A. G. H. B. REX. DV. X. S **Rev:** Crowned imperial eagle with date divided below in inner circle **Rev. Legend:** NEC NON ARCHIS (W) AV. DVX. BV. M. M. C. T. **Mint:** Breslau **Note:** Prev. Austria KM#269.1 (KM#40.1, Dav.#3150).

Date	Mintage	VG	F	VF	XF	Unc
ND W/(2ch) Rare	—	—	—	—	—	—

KM# 6 2 THALER

Silver **Ruler:** Ferdinand II **Mint:** Breslau **Note:** Prev. Austria KM#270 (KM#41). Klippe.

Date	Mintage	VG	F	VF	XF	Unc
ND Rare	—	—	—	—	—	—

KM# 147 2 THALER

Silver **Ruler:** Ferdinand II **Obv:** Laureate bust right in inner circle **Rev:** Crowned imperial eagle in inner circle, date in legend **Mint:** Neisse **Note:** Prev. Austria KM#543 (KM#1210, Dav.#A3163).

Date	Mintage	VG	F	VF	XF	Unc
1624 BZ Rare	—	—	—	—	—	—

KM# 252 2 THALER

Silver **Ruler:** Ferdinand II **Obv:** Laureate bust half right holding orb and scepter in inner circle **Rev:** City view of Breslau with horseman and companion in foreground in inner circle **Mint:** Breslau **Note:** Prev. Austria KM#638 (KM#42).

Date	Mintage	VG	F	VF	XF	Unc
1626 (h) Rare	—	—	—	—	—	—

KM# 40.2 2 THALER

Silver **Ruler:** Ferdinand II **Obv:** Date below bust **Obv. Legend:** ...IMP. S. A. GER. H: B. RX. DVX. SIL **Rev. Legend:** DV. BV. MA. MO. C. T. **Mint:** Breslau **Note:** Prev. Austria KM#269.2 (KM#40.2, Dav.#A3156).

Date	Mintage	VG	F	VF	XF	Unc
1627 W/(2ch) Rare	—	—	—	—	—	—

KM# 40.3 2 THALER

Silver **Ruler:** Ferdinand II **Obv. Legend:** IM. S. A. G. H. B. REX. DV. X. S. **Rev:** Date divied by eagle **Rev. Legend:** ARCHIDVX (W) AVX. DVX. BVR. M. M. C. T. **Mint:** Breslau **Note:** Prev. Austria KM#269.3 (KM#40.3, Dav.#A3157).

Date	Mintage	VG	F	VF	XF	Unc
1629 W/(2ch) Rare	—	—	—	—	—	—

KM# 40.4 2 THALER

Silver **Ruler:** Ferdinand II **Obv. Legend:** ...D. G. ROM. IMP. S. A. G. H. B. REX. **Rev:** Date below legend **Rev. Legend:** AR: AV: D. BV: MA: MO (W) DVX SILESIAE & PH **Mint:** Breslau **Note:** Prev. Austria KM#269.4 (KM#40.4, Dav.#A3158). Varieties exist.

Date	Mintage	VG	F	VF	XF	Unc
1630 W/(hp) Rare	—	—	—	—	—	—

KM# 360.1 2 THALER

Silver **Ruler:** Ferdinand III **Obv:** Crowned bust right in inner circle **Rev:** Crowned imperial eagle in inner circle, date in legend **Mint:** Breslau **Note:** Prev. Austria KM#918.1 (KM#69.1, Dav.#3218). Legend varieties exist.

Date	Mintage	VG	F	VF	XF	Unc
1643 M-I Rare	—	—	—	—	—	—
1646 M-I Rare	—	—	—	—	—	—
1650 G-H Rare	—	—	—	—	—	—

KM# 396 2 THALER

Silver **Ruler:** Ferdinand III **Rev:** Modified arms **Mint:** Breslau **Note:** Prev. Austria KM#1006 (KM#69.2, Dav.#A3222).

Date	Mintage	VG	F	VF	XF	Unc
1657 G-H Rare	—	—	—	—	—	—

KM# 450 2 THALER

Silver **Ruler:** Leopold I **Obv:** Young laureate bust right in inner circle **Rev:** Crowned imperial eagle in inner circle, date in legend **Mint:** Breslau **Note:** Prev. Austria KM#1201 (KM#95, Dav.#A3287).

Date	Mintage	VG	F	VF	XF	Unc
1662 GH Rare	—	—	—	—	—	—

KM# 24 3 THALER

12.2800 g., Silver **Ruler:** Ferdinand II **Mint:** Glogau **Note:** Prev. Austria KM#358 (KM#330). Struck with 3/4 Thaler dies KM#332. Uniface. Klippe.

Date	Mintage	VG	F	VF	XF	Unc
1621 Rare	—	—	—	—	—	—

KM# 150 3 THALER

86.0300 g., Silver **Ruler:** Ferdinand II **Obv:** Laureate bust right in inner circle **Rev:** Crowned imperial eagle in inner circle, date in legend **Mint:** Neisse **Note:** Prev. Austria KM#548 (KM#1211, Dav.#3163).

Date	Mintage	VG	F	VF	XF	Unc
1624 BZ/(dt) Rare	—	—	—	—	—	—

KM# 153 3 THALER

86.0300 g., Silver **Ruler:** Ferdinand II **Mint:** Neisse **Note:** Prev. Austria KM#549 (KM#1212, Dav.#3163A). Octagonal klippe.

Date	Mintage	VG	F	VF	XF	Unc
1624 BZ Rare	—	—	—	—	—	—

KM# 255 3 THALER

Silver **Ruler:** Ferdinand II **Obv:** Laureate bust half right holding orb and scepter in inner circle **Rev:** City view of Breslau with horseman and companion in foreground in inner circle **Mint:** Breslau **Note:** Prev. Austria KM#646 (KM#43).

Date	Mintage	VG	F	VF	XF	Unc
1626 (h) Rare	—	—	—	—	—	—

KM# 258 4 THALER

115.2000 g., Silver **Ruler:** Ferdinand II **Obv:** Laureate bust half right holding orb and scepter in inner circle **Rev:** City view of Breslau with horseman and companion in foreground in inner circle **Mint:** Breslau **Note:** Prev. Austria KM#655 (KM#44).

Date	Mintage	VG	F	VF	XF	Unc
1626 (h) Rare	—	—	—	—	—	—

KM# 27 6 THALER

24.3200 g., Silver **Ruler:** Ferdinand II **Obv:** Silesian eagle within legend; M, HR, and SP monograms in corners **Mint:** Glogau **Note:** Prev. Austria KM#360 (KM#331). Uniface. Klippe.

Date	Mintage	VG	F	VF	XF	Unc
1621 Rare	—	—	—	—	—	—

KM# 33 25 THALER

Silver **Ruler:** Ferdinand II **Obv:** Five-line denomination in rectangle **Rev:** Silesian eagle **Mint:** Breslau **Note:** Prev. Austria KM#45.

Date	Mintage	VG	F	VF	XF	Unc
1621 HR Rare	—	—	—	—	—	—

TRADE COINAGE

KM# 543 1/12 DUCAT

0.2917 g., 0.9860 Gold 0.0092 oz. AGW **Ruler:** Leopold I **Obv:** Laureate bust of Leopold right in inner circle, value at shoulder **Rev:** Crowned imperial eagle in inner circle **Mint:** Breslau **Note:** Prev. Austria KM#1310 (KM#96).

Date	Mintage	VG	F	VF	XF	Unc
1681	—	75.00	160	235	450	—
1682	—	75.00	160	235	450	—
1683	—	75.00	160	235	450	—
1687	—	75.00	160	235	450	—
1688	—	75.00	160	235	450	—
1690	—	75.00	160	235	450	—
ND	—	75.00	160	235	450	—

KM# 585 1/12 DUCAT

0.2917 g., 0.9860 Gold 0.0092 oz. AGW **Ruler:** Leopold I **Obv:** Tall laureate bust right, value at shoulder **Mint:** Breslau **Note:** Prev. Austria KM#1357 (KM#97).

Date	Mintage	VG	F	VF	XF	Unc
1692	—	75.00	160	255	475	—
1693	—	75.00	160	255	475	—
1694	—	75.00	160	255	475	—
1695	—	75.00	160	255	475	—
1696	—	75.00	160	255	475	—
1698	—	75.00	160	255	475	—

KM# 654 1/12 DUCAT

0.2917 g., 0.9860 Gold 0.0092 oz. AGW **Ruler:** Leopold I **Obv:** Laureate head right, value at shoulder **Rev:** Crowned imperial eagle in inner circle **Mint:** Oppeln **Note:** Prev. Austria KM#1399 (KM#1285).

Date	Mintage	VG	F	VF	XF	Unc
1699	—	130	230	475	1,000	—

KM# 564 1/8 DUCAT

0.4375 g., 0.0139 Gold 0.0002 oz. AGW **Ruler:** Leopold I **Obv:** Crown divides date above two shields, value below **Mint:** Breslau **Note:** Prev. Austria KM#1339 (KM#98). Uniface.

Date	Mintage	VG	F	VF	XF	Unc
1686	—	120	235	450	1,000	—
1690	—	120	235	450	1,000	—
1694	—	120	235	450	1,000	—
1698	—	120	235	450	1,000	—

KM# 573 1/8 DUCAT

0.4375 g., 0.9860 Gold 0.0139 oz. AGW **Ruler:** Leopold I **Rev:** Crowned imperial eagle **Mint:** Breslau **Note:** Prev. Austria KM#1345 (KM#99).

Date	Mintage	VG	F	VF	XF	Unc
1688 SHS	—	120	235	450	1,000	—
1690 SHS	—	120	235	450	1,000	—
1693	—	120	235	450	1,000	—
1695	—	120	235	450	1,000	—
1696	—	120	235	450	1,000	—
1697	—	120	235	450	1,000	—

KM# 657 1/8 DUCAT

0.5834 g., 0.9860 Gold 0.0185 oz. AGW **Ruler:** Leopold I **Obv:** Laureate head right, value at shoulder **Rev:** Crowned imperial eagle in inner circle **Mint:** Oppeln **Note:** Prev. Austria KM#1400 (KM#1286).

Date	Mintage	VG	F	VF	XF	Unc
1699	—	200	350	525	1,050	—

KM# 492 1/6 DUCAT

0.5834 g., 0.9860 Gold 0.0185 oz. AGW **Ruler:** Leopold I **Mint:** Breslau **Note:** Prev. Austria KM#1259 (KM#100).

Date	Mintage	VG	F	VF	XF	Unc
1669 SHS	—	65.00	120	225	475	—
1670 SHS	—	65.00	120	225	475	—
1671 SHS	—	65.00	120	225	475	—
1673 SHS	—	65.00	120	225	475	—
1674 SHS	—	65.00	120	225	475	—
1675 SHS	—	65.00	120	225	475	—
1676 SHS	—	65.00	120	225	475	—
1677 SHS	—	65.00	120	225	475	—
1679 SHS	—	65.00	120	225	475	—
1681 SHS	—	65.00	120	225	475	—
1682 SHS	—	65.00	120	225	475	—

KM# 567 1/6 DUCAT

0.5834 g., 0.9860 Gold 0.0185 oz. AGW **Ruler:** Leopold I **Obv:** Lauerate bust right, value at shoulder **Rev:** Crowned imperial eagle **Mint:** Breslau **Note:** Prev. Austria KM#1342 (KM#101).

Date	Mintage	VG	F	VF	XF	Unc
1687 SHS	—	65.00	120	225	475	—
1688 SHS	—	65.00	120	225	475	—
1690 SHS	—	65.00	120	225	475	—
1691 SHS	—	65.00	120	225	475	—
1693	—	65.00	120	225	475	—
1694	—	65.00	120	225	475	—
1695	—	65.00	120	225	475	—
1696	—	65.00	120	225	475	—
1698	—	65.00	120	225	475	—

KM# 495 1/4 DUCAT

0.8750 g., 0.9860 Gold 0.0277 oz. AGW **Ruler:** Leopold I **Obv:** Laureate bust right in inner circle **Rev:** Crowned imperial eagle in inner circle **Mint:** Breslau **Note:** Prev. Austria KM#1260 (KM#102).

Date	Mintage	VG	F	VF	XF	Unc
1669 SHS	—	105	265	475	1,000	—
1671 SHS	—	105	265	475	1,000	—
1675 SHS	—	105	265	475	1,000	—
1676 SHS	—	105	265	475	1,000	—
1678 SHS	—	105	265	475	1,000	—
1679 SHS	—	105	265	475	1,000	—
1680 SHS	—	105	265	475	1,000	—
1681 SHS	—	105	265	475	1,000	—
1682 SHS	—	105	265	475	1,000	—
1683 SHS	—	105	265	475	1,000	—
1684 SHS	—	105	265	475	1,000	—

KM# 570 1/4 DUCAT

1.7500 g., 0.9860 Gold 0.0555 oz. AGW **Ruler:** Leopold I **Obv:** Standing figure right between two shields **Rev:** Heraldic imperial eagle **Mint:** Breslau **Note:** Prev. Austria KM#1343 (KM#103).

Date	Mintage	VG	F	VF	XF	Unc
1687 SHS	—	105	265	475	1,000	—
1688 SHS	—	105	265	475	1,000	—
1689 SHS	—	105	265	475	1,000	—
1690 SHS	—	105	265	475	1,000	—
1691 SHS	—	105	265	475	1,000	—

KM# 597 1/4 DUCAT

0.8750 g., 0.9860 Gold 0.0277 oz. AGW **Ruler:** Leopold I **Obv:** Laureate bust right in inner circle, value at shoulder **Rev:** Crowned imperial eagle without inner circle **Mint:** Breslau **Note:** Prev. Austria KM#1369 (KM#104)

Date	Mintage	VG	F	VF	XF	Unc
1693	—	105	265	475	1,000	—
1694	—	105	265	475	1,000	—
1696	—	105	265	475	1,000	—
1698	—	105	265	475	1,000	—

KM# 660 1/4 DUCAT

0.8750 g., 0.9860 Gold 0.0277 oz. AGW **Ruler:** Leopold I **Obv:** Laureate bust right in inner circle, value at shoulder **Rev:** Crowned imperial eagle **Mint:** Oppeln **Note:** Prev. Austria KM#1401 (KM#1287).

Date	Mintage	VG	F	VF	XF	Unc
1699	—	265	475	800	1,600	—

KM# 441 1/3 DUCAT

1.7500 g., 0.9860 Gold 0.0555 oz. AGW **Ruler:** Leopold I **Obv:** Crowned bust right in inner circle **Rev:** Oval arms on crowned imperial eagle in inner circle **Mint:** Breslau **Note:** Prev. Austria KM#1188 (KM#106).

Date	Mintage	VG	F	VF	XF	Unc
1661 GH	—	200	350	600	1,200	—
1663 GH	—	200	350	600	1,200	—

KM# 468 1/3 DUCAT

1.7500 g., 0.9860 Gold 0.0555 oz. AGW **Ruler:** Leopold I **Mint:** Breslau **Note:** Prev. Austria KM#1222 (KM#107).

Date	Mintage	VG	F	VF	XF	Unc
1664 GH	—	200	350	600	1,200	—

KM# 486 1/3 DUCAT

1.7500 g., 0.9860 Gold 0.0555 oz. AGW **Ruler:** Leopold I **Obv:** Laureatebust right in inner circle **Rev:** Shield of arms on crowned imperial eagle in inner circle **Mint:** Breslau **Note:** Prev. Austria KM#1249 (KM#108).

Date	Mintage	VG	F	VF	XF	Unc
1667 SHS	—	165	295	550	1,100	—
1668 SHS	—	165	295	550	1,100	—
1669 SHS	—	165	295	550	1,100	—
1670 SHS	—	165	295	550	1,100	—
1671 SHS	—	165	295	550	1,100	—
1674 SHS	—	165	295	550	1,100	—
1675 SHS	—	165	295	550	1,100	—
1676 SHS	—	165	295	550	1,100	—
1677 SHS	—	165	295	550	1,100	—
1678 SHS	—	165	295	550	1,100	—
1679 SHS	—	165	295	550	1,100	—
1680 SHS	—	165	295	550	1,100	—
1681 SHS	—	165	295	550	1,100	—
1682 SHS	—	165	295	550	1,100	—
1683 SHS	—	165	295	550	1,100	—
1684 SHS	—	165	295	550	1,100	—
1686 SHS	—	165	295	550	1,100	—
1687 SHS	—	165	295	550	1,100	—
1688 SHS	—	165	295	550	1,100	—
1689 SHS	—	165	295	550	1,100	—
1690 SHS	—	165	295	550	1,100	—
1691 SHS	—	165	295	550	1,100	—

KM# 546 1/3 DUCAT

1.1667 g., 0.9860 Gold 0.0370 oz. AGW **Ruler:** Leopold I **Obv:** Laureate bust right in inner circle, value at shoulder **Rev:** Crowned imperial eagle in inner circle **Mint:** Breslau **Note:** Prev. Austria KM#1311 (KM#105).

Date	Mintage	VG	F	VF	XF	Unc
1681 SHS	—	130	295	525	1,100	—
1683 SHS	—	130	295	525	1,100	—
1688 SHS	—	130	295	525	1,100	—
1690 SHS	—	130	295	525	1,100	—

KM# 600 1/3 DUCAT

1.1667 g., 0.9860 Gold 0.0370 oz. AGW **Ruler:** Leopold I **Mint:** Breslau **Note:** Prev. Austria KM#1370 (KM#A106).

Date	Mintage	VG	F	VF	XF	Unc
1693	—	130	295	525	1,100	—
1694	—	130	295	525	1,100	—
1696	—	130	295	525	1,100	—
1698	—	130	295	525	1,100	—

KM# 603 1/3 DUCAT

1.7500 g., 0.9860 Gold 0.0555 oz. AGW **Ruler:** Leopold I **Mint:** Breslau **Note:** Prev. Austria KM#1371 (KM#A109).

Date	Mintage	VG	F	VF	XF	Unc
1693	—	165	295	550	1,100	—
1694	—	165	295	550	1,100	—
1696	—	165	295	550	1,100	—
1698	—	165	295	550	1,100	—

KM# 330 1/2 DUCAT

Gold **Ruler:** Ferdinand II **Obv:** Standing figure right between two shields **Rev:** Heraldic imperial eagle **Mint:** Breslau **Note:** Prev. Austria KM#818 (KM#46).

Date	Mintage	VG	F	VF	XF	Unc
1636 HZ/(2ch)	—	—	—	—	—	—
Note: Reported, not confirmed						
1636 HZ above (2ch)	—	220	375	825	2,150	—

KM# 66 DUCAT

3.5000 g., 0.9860 Gold 0.1109 oz. AGW **Ruler:** Ferdinand II **Obv:** Laureate bust **Rev:** Silesian eagle **Mint:** Breslau **Note:** Prev. Austria KM#458 (KM#47).

Date	Mintage	VG	F	VF	XF	Unc
1623	—	700	1,400	2,550	4,150	—

KM# 69 DUCAT

3.5000 g., 0.9860 Gold 0.1109 oz. AGW **Ruler:** Ferdinand II **Obv:** Ferdinand II standing right divides date in inner circle **Rev:** Crowned imperial eagle in inner circle **Mint:** Breslau **Note:** Prev. Austria KM#459 (KM#48).

Date	Mintage	VG	F	VF	XF	Unc
1623 (ht)	—	205	300	700	2,150	—
1625 W-(h)	—	205	300	700	2,150	—

KM# 261 DUCAT

3.5000 g., 0.9860 Gold 0.1109 oz. AGW **Ruler:** Ferdinand II **Obv:** Crowned shield of arms added at each side of standing figure **Rev:** Date in legend **Mint:** Breslau **Note:** Prev. Austria KM#656(KM#49).

Date	Mintage	VG	F	VF	XF	Unc
1626 W-(h)	—	205	300	700	2,150	—
1629 W-(h)	—	205	300	700	2,150	—
1630 W-(hp)	—	205	300	700	2,150	—
1633 W(3ch)IZ	—	205	300	700	2,150	—
1633 W-HZ above (3ch)	—	205	300	700	2,150	—

KM# 306 DUCAT

3.5000 g., 0.9860 Gold 0.1109 oz. AGW **Ruler:** Ferdinand II **Obv:** Bust right **Mint:** Breslau **Note:** Prev. Austria KM#755 (KM#50).

Date	Mintage	VG	F	VF	XF	Unc
1630 W/(3ch)/IZ	—	—	—	—	—	—

KM# 309 DUCAT

3.5000 g., 0.9860 Gold 0.1109 oz. AGW **Ruler:** Ferdinand II **Obv:** Crowned bust in inner circle **Mint:** Breslau **Note:** Prev. Austria KM#756 (KM#51).

Date	Mintage	VG	F	VF	XF	Unc
1630 W/(3ch)/IZ	—	—	—	—	—	—
1631 W(3ch)IZ	—	275	450	975	2,350	—

Date	Mintage	VG	F	VF	XF	Unc
1632 W(3ch)IZ	—	275	450	975	2,350	—
1635 HZ-(2ch)	—	275	450	975	2,350	—
1636 HZ-(2ch)	—	275	450	975	2,350	—

KM# 339 DUCAT

3.5000 g., 0.9860 Gold 0.1109 oz. AGW **Ruler:** Ferdinand III **Obv:** Crowned bust right in inner circle **Rev:** Crowned imperial eagle in inner circle, date in legend **Mint:** Breslau **Note:** Prev. Austria KM#842 (KM#70).

Date	Mintage	VG	F	VF	XF	Unc
1637	—	220	450	825	2,150	4,150
1638	—	220	450	825	2,150	4,150
1639	—	220	450	825	2,150	4,150
1640	—	220	450	825	2,150	4,150
1641	—	220	450	825	2,150	4,150
1642	—	220	450	825	2,150	4,150
1643	—	220	450	825	2,150	4,150
1644	—	220	450	825	2,150	4,150
1645	—	220	450	825	2,150	4,150
1646	—	220	450	825	2,150	4,150
1647	—	220	450	825	2,150	4,150
1648	—	220	450	825	2,150	4,150
1649	—	220	450	825	2,150	4,150
1650	—	220	450	825	2,150	4,150
1651	—	220	450	825	2,150	4,150
1652	—	220	450	825	2,150	4,150
1653	—	220	450	825	2,150	4,150
1654	—	220	450	825	2,150	4,150
1655	—	220	450	825	2,150	4,150
1656	—	220	450	825	2,150	4,150
1657	—	220	450	825	2,150	4,150

KM# 423 DUCAT

3.5000 g., 0.9860 Gold 0.1109 oz. AGW **Ruler:** Leopold I **Obv:** Crowned bust right in inner circle **Rev:** Crowned imperial eagle in inner circle, date in legend **Mint:** Breslau **Note:** Prev. Austria KM#1157 (KM#109).

Date	Mintage	VG	F	VF	XF	Unc
1659 GH	—	240	525	1,050	2,200	4,400
1660 GH	—	240	525	1,050	2,200	4,400
1661 GH	—	240	525	1,050	2,200	4,400
1663 GH	—	240	525	1,050	2,200	4,400
1664 GH	—	240	525	1,050	2,200	4,400
1665 GH	—	240	525	1,050	2,200	4,400

KM# 497 DUCAT

3.5000 g., 0.9860 Gold 0.1109 oz. AGW **Ruler:** Leopold I **Obv:** Laureate bust right in inner circle **Rev:** Crowned imperial eagle in inner circle, crown divides date **Mint:** Breslau **Note:** Prev. Austria KM#1262 (KM#110).

Date	Mintage	VG	F	VF	XF	Unc
1669 SHS	—	200	450	925	1,800	3,300
1673 SHS	—	200	450	925	1,800	3,300
1674 SHS	—	200	450	925	1,800	3,300
1675 SHS	—	200	450	925	1,800	3,300
1676 SHS	—	200	450	925	1,800	3,300
1677 SHS	—	200	450	925	1,800	3,300
1678 SHS	—	200	450	925	1,800	3,300
1679 SHS	—	200	450	925	1,800	3,300
1680 SHS	—	200	450	925	1,800	3,300
1681 SHS	—	200	450	925	1,800	3,300
1682 SHS	—	200	450	925	1,800	3,300
1684 SHS	—	200	450	925	1,800	3,300
1685 SHS	—	200	450	925	1,800	3,300
1688 SHS	—	200	450	925	1,800	3,300
1689 SHS	—	200	450	925	1,800	3,300
1690 SHS	—	200	450	925	1,800	3,300
1691 SHS	—	200	450	925	1,800	3,300

KM# 531 DUCAT

3.5000 g., 0.9860 Gold 0.1109 oz. AGW **Ruler:** Leopold I **Obv:** Laureate bust right in inner circle **Rev:** Crowned imperial eagle in inner circle, crown divides date **Mint:** Brieg **Note:** Prev. Austria KM#1299 (KM#178).

Date	Mintage	VG	F	VF	XF	Unc
1677 CB	—	220	450	975	2,200	—

KM# 588 DUCAT

3.5000 g., 0.9860 Gold 0.1109 oz. AGW **Ruler:** Leopold I **Obv:** Fuller laureate bust right in inner circle **Rev:** Crowned imperial eagle, crown divides date **Mint:** Breslau **Note:** Prev. Austria KM#111 (KM#1358).

Date	Mintage	VG	F	VF	XF	Unc
1692	—	200	525	1,100	2,200	—
1693	—	200	525	1,100	2,200	—

Date	Mintage	VG	F	VF	XF	Unc
1694	—	200	525	1,100	2,200	—
1696	—	200	525	1,100	2,200	—
1697	—	200	525	1,100	2,200	—
1698	—	200	525	1,100	2,200	—

KM# 636 DUCAT

3.5000 g., 0.9860 Gold 0.1109 oz. AGW **Ruler:** Leopold I **Obv:** Smaller bust right in inner circle **Rev:** Crowned imperial eagle in inner circle, date in legend **Mint:** Brieg **Note:** Prev. Austria KM#1393 (KM#179)

Date	Mintage	VG	F	VF	XF	Unc
1696 CB	—	200	525	1,100	2,300	—
1697 CB	—	200	525	1,100	2,300	—

KM# 666 DUCAT

3.5000 g., 0.9860 Gold 0.1109 oz. AGW **Ruler:** Leopold I **Obv:** Laureate armored bust right in inner circle **Rev:** Crowned arms in Order collar in inner circle **Mint:** Oppeln **Note:** Prev. Austria KM#1409 (KM#1288)

Date	Mintage	VG	F	VF	XF	Unc
1700 FN	—	500	1,450	3,050	5,800	—

KM# 312 2 DUCAT

7.0000 g., 0.9860 Gold 0.2219 oz. AGW **Ruler:** Ferdinand II **Obv:** Crowned bust right **Rev:** Heraldic imperial eagle **Mint:** Breslau **Note:** Prev. Austria KM#759 (KM#52).

Date	Mintage	VG	F	VF	XF	Unc
1630 W-IZ	—	450	875	2,200	5,500	—

KM# 351 2 DUCAT

7.0000 g., 0.9860 Gold 0.2219 oz. AGW **Ruler:** Ferdinand III **Obv:** Crowned bust right in inner circle **Rev:** Crowned imperial eagle **Mint:** Breslau **Note:** Prev. Austria KM#898 (KM#71). Legend varieties exist.

Date	Mintage	VG	F	VF	XF	Unc
1641	—	375	925	2,400	5,700	—
1642	—	375	925	2,400	5,700	—
1643	—	375	925	2,400	5,700	—
1645	—	375	925	2,400	5,700	—

KM# 444 2 DUCAT

7.0000 g., 0.9860 Gold 0.2219 oz. AGW **Ruler:** Leopold I **Obv:** Crowned bust right in inner circle **Rev:** Crowned imperial eagle in inner circle, date in legend **Mint:** Breslau **Note:** Prev. Austria KM#1189 (KM#112)

Date	Mintage	VG	F	VF	XF	Unc
1661	—	500	1,000	2,950	7,300	—
1665 SH	—	500	1,000	2,950	7,300	—
1669 SHS	—	500	1,000	2,950	7,300	—
1671 SHS	—	500	1,000	2,950	7,300	—
1672 SHS	—	500	1,000	2,950	7,300	—
1673 SHS	—	500	1,000	2,950	7,300	—
1679 SHS	—	500	1,000	2,950	7,300	—
1684 SHS	—	500	1,000	2,950	7,300	—
1687 SHS	—	500	1,000	2,950	7,300	—
1692	—	500	1,000	2,950	7,300	—

KM# 663 2 DUCAT

7.0000 g., 0.9860 Gold 0.2219 oz. AGW **Ruler:** Leopold I **Obv:** Laureate bust right in inner circle **Rev:** Crowned eagle with wreath around head in inner circle **Mint:** Oppeln **Note:** Prev. Austria KM#1402 (KM#1289).

Date	Mintage	VG	F	VF	XF	Unc
1699 FN	—	725	1,400	3,600	10,500	—

KM# 456 3 DUCAT

10.5000 g., 0.9860 Gold 0.3328 oz. AGW **Ruler:** Leopold I **Obv:** Crowned bust right in inner circle **Rev:** Crowned imperial eagle in inner circle, date in legend **Mint:** Breslau **Note:** Prev. Austria KM#1213 (KM#113).

Date	Mintage	VG	F	VF	XF	Unc
1663 GH	—	800	1,750	6,700	11,500	—
1665/3 SH	—	800	1,750	6,700	11,500	—
1667 SHS	—	800	1,750	6,700	11,500	—

KM# 513 3 DUCAT

10.5000 g., 0.9860 Gold 0.3328 oz. AGW **Ruler:** Leopold I **Obv:** Laureate bust right in inner circle **Rev:** Crowned imperial eagle in inner circle, crown divides date **Mint:** Breslau **Note:** Prev. Austria KM#1285 (KM#114).

Date	Mintage	VG	F	VF	XF	Unc
1675 SHS	—	625	1,150	3,950	7,900	—
1684 SHS	—	625	1,150	3,950	7,900	—
1689 SHS	—	625	1,150	3,950	7,900	—

KM# 624 3 DUCAT

10.5000 g., 0.9860 Gold 0.3328 oz. AGW **Ruler:** Leopold I **Mint:** Breslau **Note:** Prev. Austria KM#1390 (KM#A115).

Date	Mintage	VG	F	VF	XF	Unc
1695 MMW	—	625	1,150	3,950	7,900	—
1696 MMW	—	625	1,150	3,950	7,900	—

KM# 669 3 DUCAT

10.5000 g., 0.9860 Gold 0.3328 oz. AGW **Ruler:** Leopold I **Obv:** Laureate bust right in inner circle **Rev:** Crowned imperial eagle in inner circle **Mint:** Oppeln **Note:** Prev. Austria KM#1411 (KM#1290)

Date	Mintage	VG	F	VF	XF	Unc
1700 FN	—	725	1,450	4,850	10,500	—

KM# 519 4 DUCAT

14.0000 g., 0.9860 Gold 0.4438 oz. AGW **Ruler:** Leopold I **Obv:** Laureate bust right in inner circle **Rev:** Crowned imperial eagle in inner circle **Mint:** Breslau **Note:** Prev. Austria KM#1291 (KM#115).

Date	Mintage	VG	F	VF	XF	Unc
1676 SHS	—	1,200	2,400	7,200	12,000	—

KM# 591 4 DUCAT

14.0000 g., 0.9860 Gold 0.4438 oz. AGW **Ruler:** Leopold I **Mint:** Breslau **Note:** Prev. Austria KM#1359 (KM#A116).

Date	Mintage	VG	F	VF	XF	Unc
1692 MMW	—	1,200	2,400	7,300	12,000	—
1695 MMW	—	1,200	2,400	7,300	12,000	—

KM# 627 4 DUCAT

14.0000 g., 0.9860 Gold 0.4438 oz. AGW **Ruler:** Leopold I **Obv:** Older bust **Mint:** Breslau **Note:** Prev. Austria KM#1391 (KM#116).

Date	Mintage	VG	F	VF	XF	Unc
1695	—	2,200	4,400	9,400	15,000	—

KM# 264 5 DUCAT

17.5000 g., 0.9860 Gold 0.5547 oz. AGW **Ruler:** Ferdinand II **Obv:** Laureate bust right in inner circle **Rev:** Crowned imperial eagle in inner circle **Mint:** Breslau **Note:** Prev. Austria KM#658 (KM#53).

Date	Mintage	VG	F	VF	XF	Unc
1626 HR	—	1,000	1,750	3,650	7,900	—
1627 HR	—	1,000	1,750	3,650	7,900	—
1628	—	1,000	1,750	3,650	7,900	—
1629	—	1,000	1,750	3,650	7,900	—

KM# 342 5 DUCAT

17.5000 g., 0.9860 Gold 0.5547 oz. AGW **Ruler:** Ferdinand III **Obv:** Laureate bust right in inner circle **Rev:** Crowned imperial eagle **Mint:** Breslau **Note:** Prev. Austria KM#862 (KM#72).

Date	Mintage	VG	F	VF	XF	Unc
1638	—	1,000	1,400	3,450	7,400	—
1643	—	1,000	1,400	3,450	7,400	—

KM# 555 5 DUCAT

17.5000 g., 0.9860 Gold 0.5547 oz. AGW **Ruler:** Leopold I **Obv:** Laureate bust right in inner circle **Rev:** Crowned imperial eagle in inner circle **Mint:** Breslau **Note:** Prev. Austria KM#1328 (KM#117).

Date	Mintage	VG	F	VF	XF	Unc
1684 SHS	—	1,000	1,800	5,200	9,900	—
1690 SHS	—	1,000	1,800	5,200	9,900	—

KM# 630 5 DUCAT

17.5000 g., 0.9860 Gold 0.5547 oz. AGW **Ruler:** Leopold I **Obv:** Laureate bust right in inner circle **Rev:** Crowned imperial eagle in inner circle **Mint:** Brieg **Note:** Prev. Austria KM#1392 (KM#180).

Date	Mintage	VG	F	VF	XF	Unc
1695 CB	—	1,100	2,000	5,200	9,900	—

KM# 645 5 DUCAT

17.5000 g., 0.9860 Gold 0.5547 oz. AGW **Ruler:** Leopold I **Mint:** Breslau **Note:** Prev. Austria KM#1395 (KM#A118).

Date	Mintage	VG	F	VF	XF	Unc
1698	—	1,000	1,800	5,200	9,900	—

KM# 156 6 DUCAT

21.0000 g., 0.9860 Gold 0.6657 oz. AGW **Ruler:** Ferdinand II **Obv:** Bust right **Rev:** Heraldic imperial eagle **Mint:** Breslau **Note:** Prev. Austria KM#554 (KM#54).

Date	Mintage	VG	F	VF	XF	Unc
1624 BZ/HR Rare	—	—	—	—	—	—

KM# 159 10 DUCAT

35.0000 g., 0.9860 Gold 1.1095 oz. AGW **Ruler:** Ferdinand II **Mint:** Neisse **Note:** Prev. Austria KM#555 (KM#1214). Struck with 1 Thaler dies of KM#599.

Date	Mintage	VG	F	VF	XF	Unc
1624 (dt) - BZ Rare	—	—	—	—	—	—

KM# 243 10 DUCAT
35.0000 g., 0.9860 Gold 1.1095 oz. AGW **Ruler:** Ferdinand II **Obv:** Bust right **Rev:** Heraldic imperial eagle **Mint:** Oppeln **Note:** Prev. Austria KM#621 (KM#1273).

Date	Mintage	VG	F	VF	XF	Unc
1625 SF Rare	—	—	—	—	—	—

KM# 267 10 DUCAT
35.0000 g., 0.9860 Gold 1.1095 oz. AGW **Ruler:** Ferdinand II **Obv:** Frontal portrait with scepter and orb **Rev:** Soldiers with city view in background **Mint:** Breslau **Note:** Prev. Austria KM#663 (KM#55).

Date	Mintage	VG	F	VF	XF	Unc
1626 (h) Rare	—	—	—	—	—	—

PATTERNS

Including off metal strikes

KM#	Date	Mintage	Identification	Mkt Val
PnA1	1584	—	Heller. Gold. MLH. MB#68.	—
PnBR1	ND(1649)	—	Kreuzer. Gold.	—
PnBR2	ND(1652)	—	Kreuzer. Gold.	—
PnBR3	ND(1653)	—	Kreuzer. Gold.	—
PnOP2	ND(1680)	—	3 Pfennig. Gold.	—
PnOP3	ND(1686)	—	3 Pfennig. Gold.	—
PnOP4	ND(1687)	—	3 Pfennig. Gold.	—
PnOP5	ND(1688)	—	3 Pfennig. Gold.	—
PnOP6	ND(1689)	—	3 Pfennig. Gold.	—
PnOP7	ND(1690)	—	3 Pfennig. Gold.	—
PnOP8	ND(1693)	—	3 Pfennig. Gold.	—
PnOP9	ND(1694)	—	3 Pfennig. Gold.	—
PnOP10	ND(1695)	—	4 Heller. Gold.	—
PnOP11	ND(1696)	—	3 Pfennig. Gold.	—
PnOP12	ND(1699)	—	4 Heller. Gold.	—
PnOP13	ND(1699)	—	3 Pfennig. Gold.	—
Pn1	1755B	—	Groschel. Gold. KM#972.	550
Pn2	1756B	—	Kreuzer. Gold. Crowned eagle. KM#960.1.	750
Pn3	1756B	—	3 Kreuzer. Gold. KM#966.	—
Pn4	1756B	—	6 Kreuzer. Gold. KM#981.	—
Pn5	1756B	—	Groschel. Gold. KM#972.	550
Pn6	1757B	—	Kreuzer. Gold. Crowned eagle. KM#960.1.	750
Pn7	1757B	—	Groschel. Gold. KM#972.	550

SILESIA-LIEGNITZ-BRIEG

One of the major divisions of Silesia and notably having two administrative centers, Silesia-Liegnitz-Brieg went through periods when its two parts were ruled separately by various family members. Liegnitz is northwest of the traditional Silesian capital of Breslau and separated from it by the territory of Neumarkt. Brieg is southwest of Breslau, with the district of Ohlau separating the two entities.

The seemingly numerous divisions of Silesia-Liegnitz-Brieg in reality were not an alienation of the various components of the duchy, but rather a division of the administration by members of the ruling family. Therefore, all parts of Silesia-Liegnitz-Brieg were under a single ruler during some years, whereas the districts of Liegnitz, Brieg, Ohlau, Lüben, Wohlau and Goldberg-Haynau had their own individual dukes during other periods. The rulers sometimes issued joint coinages under this system.

When the last duke died childless in 1675, Silesia-Liegnitz-Brieg passed to the control of the Habsburg emperors as Kings of Bohemia. The duchy finally was acquired by Prussia through force of arms in the 1740's, along with most of the rest of Silesia.

RULERS

Friedrich IV, Liegnitz with
  Anna von Württemberg, Haynau, 1594-1616
Joachim Friedrich, in Brieg, 1586-1602
  in Liegnitz, 1596-1602
  Anna Maria von Anhalt-Dessau, Ohlau, 1602-1605
Georg Rudolph, Liegnitz & Goldberg, 1602-1653
Johann Christian, in Brieg, 1602-1639
Georg III, in Brieg, 1639-1664
Ludwig IV, in Liegnitz, 1653-1663
  Anna Sophie von Mecklenburg, Parchwitz, 1663-1667
Christian, in Liegnitz, 1663-1672
  in Brieg, 1664-1672
  in Ohlau, 1639-1672
  Louise von Anhalt, in Ohlau, 1672-1680, regent for Georg Wilhelm, in Liegnitz-Brieg, 1672-1675

MINT OFFICIALS' INITIALS or MARKS

Brieg Mint

Initial or Mark	Date	Name
BH (sometimes in ligature)	1616-22	Burkhard Hase, also Kreuzburg
	1621-?	Joachim Stein, mint contractor
	? – 1623	Caspar Wecker, mintmaster
	1623	Blasius Pförtner, mintmaster
EW	1657-73	Elilas Weiss, warden & mintmaster
CB, CBS	1668-1713	Christoph Brettschneider, warden and Mintmaster
SK	1674-75	Samuel Koller, goldsmith and medailleur

Breslau Mint

Initial or Mark	Date	Name
HR	1614-35	Hans Rieger, warden and die-cutter, also in Ohlau and Reichenstein
(fs)= or FS	1625	Friedrich Schönau, die-cutter
GH	1645-65	Georg Hübner, imperial warden
DVF, VOGT	1659-63	D. Vogt, medailleur
GFH	1666-1706	Georg Franz Hoffmann, die-cutter

Haynau Mint

Initial or Mark	Date	Name
(mt)= or MT	1620-23	Markus Täubner

Liegnitz Mint

Initial or Mark	Date	Name
(c) = or CC	1612-21	Christoph Cantor
GH	1612-23	Georg Heinecke (Heinke)
(mt) = or MT	1620-21	Markus Täubner

Liegnitz and Brieg Mints

Initial or Mark	Date	Name
(d)=	1607-10	Christoph Tuchmann
(e)=	1602-05, 1621-22	Unknown
AK	1621	Unknown
IB	1638-70	Johann Bensheim, die-cutter
VT	1651-52	Unknown warden
(pf)= or or	1652-65	Christian Pfahler
ER	Ca. 1673-74	Unknown die-cutter

Wohlau Mint

Initial or Mark	Date	Name
IK	1621-23	Johann Knoblauch

ARMS

Silesia – eagle with crescent on breast
Brieg – checkerboard
Liegnitz-Brieg – 4-fold, quartered with arms of Silesia and Brieg

REFERENCES

B = Walter Baum, ***Zur Geschichte der Liegnitzer Münze***, **Lorch**, Württemberg, 1981.

F/S = Ferdinand Friedensburg and Hans Seger, ***Schlesiens Münzen und Medaillen der neueren Zeit***, Breslau, 1901 (reprint Frankfurt/Main, 1976).

J/M = Norbert Jaschke and Fritz P. Maercker, ***Schlesische Münzen und Medaillen***, Ihringen, 1985.

S = Hugo Frhr. Von Saurma-Jeltsch, ***Die Saurmasche Münzsammlung deutscher, schweizerischer und polnischer Gepräge von etwa dem Beginn der Groschenzeit bis zur Kipperperiode***, Berlin, 1892.

S/Sch = Hugo Frhr. Von Saurma-Jeltsch, ***Schlesische Münzen und Medaillen***, Breslau, 1883.

Sch = Wolfgang Schulten, ***Deutsche Münzen aus der Zeit Karls V***,. Frankfurt am Main, 1974.

DUCHY

REGULAR COINAGE

KM# 5 HELLER
Silver **Ruler:** Anna Maria **Obv:** 2 adjacent shields of arms, Ahalt left, Brieg right, suspension loop above, Gothic 'O' below **Mint:** Ohlau **Note:** Uniface. Ref. S/Sch#51.

Date	Mintage	VG	F	VF	XF	Unc
ND(1602-05)	—	20.00	40.00	85.00	—	—

KM# 6 HELLER
Silver **Ruler:** Anna Maria **Obv:** 2 adjacent shields of arms, Anhalt left, Brieg right, suspension loop above, lily below **Mint:** Ohlau **Note:** Uniface. Ref. S/Sch#52.

Date	Mintage	VG	F	VF	XF	Unc
ND(1602-05)	—	20.00	40.00	85.00	—	—

KM# 221 HELLER
Copper **Ruler:** Johann Christian **Obv:** Silesian eagle with arms of Brieg on breast **Obv. Legend:** IO: C - D. L. B. **Mint:** Ohlau **Note:** Uniface. F/S#1609.

Date	Mintage	VG	F	VF	XF	Unc
ND(1621-39)	—	18.00	37.00	75.00	—	—

KM# 220 HELLER
Silver **Ruler:** Johann Christian **Obv:** Silesian eagle, arms of Brieg on breast, divides L - B **Mint:** Ohlau **Note:** Uniface. Ref. F/S#1608.

Date	Mintage	VG	F	VF	XF	Unc
ND(1621-39)	—	15.00	35.00	70.00	—	—

KM# 222 HELLER
Copper **Ruler:** Johann Christian **Obv:** 2 adjacent shields of arms, Silesian eagle left, Brieg right, LB below, inscription in straight line above **Obv. Legend:** IO. C. D. L. B. **Mint:** Ohlau **Note:** Uniface. Ref. F/S#1610.

Date	Mintage	VG	F	VF	XF	Unc
ND(1621-39)	—	18.00	37.00	75.00	—	—

KM# 223 HELLER
Copper **Ruler:** Johann Christian **Obv:** 2 adjacent shields of arms, Silesian eagle left, Brieg right, inscription in curved arc above **Mint:** Ohlau **Note:** Uniface. Ref. F/S#1611.

Date	Mintage	VG	F	VF	XF	Unc
ND(1621-39)	—	18.00	37.00	75.00	—	—

KM# 292 3 HELLER
Copper **Ruler:** Johann Christian **Obv:** Crown above 2-line inscription with date **Obv. Inscription:** M. BREG / 3 H. 16ZZ. **Mint:** Brieg **Note:** Uniface, Kipper Coinage. Ref. F/S#1589.

Date	Mintage	VG	F	VF	XF	Unc
16ZZ	—	—	—	—	—	—

KM# 293 3 HELLER
Copper **Ruler:** Johann Christian **Obv:** Crown above 2-line inscription with date **Obv. Inscription:** M. BREG / 3 H. **Mint:** Brieg **Note:** Uniface. Ref. F/S#1590. Kipper coinage.

Date	Mintage	VG	F	VF	XF	Unc
ND(1622-23)	—	—	—	—	—	—

KM# 294 3 HELLER
Copper **Ruler:** Georg Rudolf **Obv:** Trefoil with crown in upper lobe, 2 small shields of arms in lower lobes, Silesian eagle in left, Brieg in right, value III below, date divided by upper lobe **Note:** Uniface. Ref. F/S#1653, 1660.

Date	Mintage	VG	F	VF	XF	Unc
(16)22	—	20.00	45.00	90.00	—	—
(16)23	—	20.00	45.00	90.00	—	—

KM# 295 3 HELLER
Copper **Ruler:** Georg Rudolf **Obv:** Trefoil with crown in upper lobe, 2 small shields of arms in lower lobes, Silesian eagle in left, Brieg in right, date divided by upper lobe **Note:** Uniface. Ref. F/S#1654, 1661.

Date	Mintage	VG	F	VF	XF	Unc
(16)22	—	20.00	45.00	90.00	—	—
(16)23	—	20.00	45.00	90.00	—	—

KM# 68 3 PFENNIG (DREIER)
Silver **Ruler:** Johann Christian and Georg Rudolph **Obv:** 2 adjacent shields of arms, Silesian eagle at left, Brieg at right, crown above, '84' below **Rev:** Large Silesian eagle divides date **Note:** Ref. F/S#1443, 1478, 1485. Varieties exist.

Date	Mintage	VG	F	VF	XF	Unc
1609	—	20.00	45.00	90.00	180	—
1611	—	20.00	45.00	90.00	180	—
161Z	—	20.00	45.00	90.00	180	—

KM# 91 3 PFENNIG (DREIER)
Silver **Ruler:** Johann Christian and Georg Rudolph **Obv:** 2 adjacent shields of arms, Silesian eagle at left, Brieg at right, crown above, '84' below **Rev:** Silesian eagle in oval baroque frame, date divided near bottom, where present **Note:** Ref. F/S#1461-62.

Date	Mintage	VG	F	VF	XF	Unc
ND(1610) Reported, not confirmed	—	—	—	—	—	—
1610 Reported, not confirmed	—	—	—	—	—	—

KM# 121 3 PFENNIG (DREIER)
Silver **Ruler:** Johann Christian and Georg Rudolph **Obv:** 2 adjacent shields of arms, Silesian eagle at left, Brieg at right, crown above, '84' below **Rev:** Silesian eagle in ornate baroque frame divides date **Note:** Ref. F/S#1479.

Date	Mintage	VG	F	VF	XF	Unc
1611	—	25.00	55.00	115	—	—

KM# 186 3 PFENNIG (DREIER)

Silver **Ruler:** Johann Christian and Georg Rudolph **Obv:** 2 small shields of arms in lower lobes of trefoil, crown in upper lobe, date divided outside upper lobe **Note:** Uniface. Ref. F/S#1538.

Date	Mintage	VG	F	VF	XF	Unc
(16)19	—	25.00	55.00	115	—	—

KM# 297 3 PFENNIG (DREIER)

Silver **Ruler:** Johann Christian **Obv:** Silesian eagle divides date and L - B, III ... below **Note:** Uniface. Ref. F/S#1607.

Date	Mintage	VG	F	VF	XF	Unc
16ZZ	—	25.00	55.00	115	—	—

KM# 502 3 PFENNIG (DREIER)

Silver **Ruler:** Christian zu Liegnitz **Obv:** Silesian eagle divides mintmaster's initials **Rev:** 2 ornately shaped adjacent shields of arms, crown above, date below **Note:** Ref. F/S#1933, 1938.

Date	Mintage	VG	F	VF	XF	Unc
1669 CB	—	15.00	35.00	70.00	145	—
1670 CB	—	15.00	35.00	70.00	145	—

KM# 510 3 PFENNIG (DREIER)

Silver **Ruler:** Christian zu Liegnitz **Obv:** Silesian eagle divides mintmaster's initials **Rev:** 2 adjacent oval arms in baroque frame, crown above divides date **Note:** Ref. F/S#1954.

Date	Mintage	VG	F	VF	XF	Unc
1673 CB	—	15.00	35.00	70.00	145	—

KM# 511 3 PFENNIG (DREIER)

Silver **Ruler:** Christian zu Ohlau **Obv:** Silesian eagle divides mintmaster's initials **Rev:** 2 ornately shaped adjacent shields of arms, crown above, date below where present **Note:** Ref: F/S#1955-57.

Date	Mintage	VG	F	VF	XF	Unc
1673	—	15.00	30.00	65.00	130	—
1673 CB	—	15.00	30.00	65.00	130	—
ND ER	—	15.00	30.00	65.00	130	—

KM# 35 GROSCHEN

Silver **Ruler:** Friedrich II **Subject:** Death of Joachim Friedrich's Widow, Anna Maria von Anhalt **Obv:** Crowned shield of 4-fold arms **Obv. Legend:** MEM. ANNÆ. MAR. PR. ANHAL. DVCI. SIL. **Rev:** 4-line inscription with R.N. date, circular marginal legend **Rev. Legend:** + LEG. BREG. FILII. MOESTIS. F.F. ZVÆ(PIA). **Rev. Inscription:** OBIIT / M. NOV. DIE. / XIV. ANNO / M.D.C.V. **Mint:** Liegnitz **Note:** Ref. F/S#1397.

Date	Mintage	VG	F	VF	XF	Unc
MDCV (1605)	—	—	—	—	—	—

KM# 300 3 GROSCHEL (Almosengroschen)

Silver **Ruler:** Georg Rudolf **Obv:** Large crown above 2 adjacent shields of arms, Silesian eagle on left, Brieg on right, value '3' in oval below **Rev:** 3-line incription above date which is divided by small angel's head **Rev. Inscription:** FVRST = / LICH. / ALMOS. **Mint:** Liegnitz **Note:** Ref. F/S#1699.

Date	Mintage	VG	F	VF	XF	Unc
16ZZ	—	—	—	—	—	—

KM# 299 3 GROSCHEL (Almosengroschen)

Silver **Ruler:** Johann Christian **Obv:** Large crown above 2 adjacent shields of arms, Silesian eagle on left, Brieg on right, value '3' in oval below **Rev:** 3-line inscription above date which is divided by mintmaster's symbol in oval **Rev. Inscription:** FVRST = / LICH. / ALMOS. **Mint:** Liegnitz **Note:** Ref. S/Sch#209.

Date	Mintage	VG	F	VF	XF	Unc
16ZZ (e)	—	—	—	—	—	—

KM# 302 3 GROSCHER (Dreigroscher)

Silver **Ruler:** Johann Christian **Obv:** Bust right with large ruffed collar **Obv. Legend:** D. G. IOHA. CHRIST. DVX. SI(L). **Rev:** 3-turreted city gate, value 'III' above, Silesian eagle left, shield of Brieg arms at right, date divided between the 3 symbols, 3-line inscription below **Rev. Inscription:** GROS. ARGE / TRIPL. CRV / CIBVRG. **Mint:** Kreuzburg **Note:** Ref. F/S#1602.

Date	Mintage	VG	F	VF	XF	Unc
1622 BH	—	—	—	—	—	—

KM# 368 KREUZER

Silver, 16.6 mm. **Ruler:** Georg III, Ludwig IV and Christian **Obv:** 3 facing 1/2-length figures, small imperial orb above **Obv. Legend:** D.G. GEORG • LUD • ET • CHRI • FRAT • **Rev:** Silesian eagle in circle, (I) below, date at end of legend **Rev. Legend:** DUCES • SI • LIG • - ET • BREG • **Mint:** Kreuzburg **Note:** Ref: F/S#1712, 1722-23.

Date	Mintage	VG	F	VF	XF	Unc
1651	—	15.00	30.00	60.00	120	—
165Z	—	15.00	30.00	60.00	120	—
165Z GH	—	15.00	30.00	60.00	120	—

KM# 386 KREUZER

Silver **Ruler:** Georg III, Ludwig IV and Christian **Obv:** 3 facing 1/2-length figures, small imperial orb above, date at end of legend **Obv. Legend:** D. G. GEORG. LUDOVI. & CHRIST. **Rev:** Silesian eagle in circle, (I) below, date at end of legend **Rev. Legend:** FRAT. DUC. SIL. - LIG. BREG. **Mint:** Kreuzburg **Note:** Ref: F/S#1732, 1738, 1744.

Date	Mintage	VG	F	VF	XF	Unc
165Z//1653	—	15.00	35.00	70.00	145	—
165Z//1654	—	15.00	35.00	70.00	145	—
1654//1655	—	15.00	35.00	70.00	145	—

KM# 393 KREUZER

Silver **Ruler:** Georg III, Ludwig IV and Christian **Obv:** 3 facing 1/2-length figures, small imperial orb above, date at end of legend where present **Obv. Legend:** D. G. GEORG. LUDOVI. & CHRIST. **Rev:** Silesian eagle in circle, (I) below **Rev. Legend:** FRAT. DUC. SIL. - LIG. BREG. **Mint:** Kreuzburg **Note:** Ref: F/S#1728, 1730, 1734.

Date	Mintage	VG	F	VF	XF	Unc
ND(1653-54) GH	—	15.00	35.00	70.00	145	—
1653	—	15.00	35.00	70.00	145	—
1653 GH	—	15.00	35.00	70.00	145	—

KM# 392 KREUZER

Silver **Ruler:** Georg III, Ludwig IV and Christian **Obv:** 3 facing 1/2-length figures, small imperial orb above **Obv. Legend:** D. G. GEORG. LUDOVI. & CHRIST. (FRAT.) **Rev:** Silesian eagle in circle, (I) below, date at end of legend, where present **Rev. Legend:** FRAT. DUC. SIL - LIG. BREG. **Mint:** Kreuzburg **Note:** Ref: F/S#1729, 1737, 1743, 1733, 1782. Varieties exist.

Date	Mintage	VG	F	VF	XF	Unc
ND(1653-55)	—	8.00	15.00	30.00	60.00	—
1653	—	8.00	15.00	30.00	60.00	—
1654	—	8.00	15.00	30.00	60.00	—
1655	—	8.00	15.00	30.00	60.00	—
1659 EW	—	8.00	15.00	30.00	60.00	—

KM# 482 KREUZER

Silver **Ruler:** Christian zu Ohlau **Obv:** Bust right **Obv. Legend:** D. G. CHRISTIAN. DUX. S. L. B. & W. **Rev:** Silesian eagle, value (I) below, date at end of legend **Rev. Legend:** MONETA. NOVA. - ARGENT. **Mint:** Kreuzburg **Note:** Ref: F/S#1919, 1929-30, 1932, 1937. Varieties exist.

Date	Mintage	VG	F	VF	XF	Unc
1665	—	5.00	9.00	15.00	35.00	—
1668	—	5.00	9.00	15.00	35.00	—
1668 CB	—	5.00	9.00	15.00	35.00	—
1669 CB	—	5.00	9.00	15.00	35.00	—
1670 CB	—	5.00	9.00	15.00	35.00	—

KM# 3 3 KREUZER (Groschen)

Silver **Ruler:** Joachim Friedrich zu Liegnitz **Obv:** Bust right, '3' in oval below **Obv. Legend:** MO NO ARGEN IOA - CHIMI FRIDERICI **Rev:** 4-fold arms, date at end of legend **Rev. Legend:** DVCIS LEGNICEN. ET BREGEN. **Mint:** Kreuzburg **Note:** Ref: F/S#1382, 1385.

Date	Mintage	VG	F	VF	XF	Unc
1601	—	35.00	55.00	75.00	150	—
160Z	—	35.00	55.00	75.00	150	—

KM# 8 3 KREUZER (Groschen)

Ruler: Joachim Friedrich zu Liegnitz **Subject:** Death of Joachim Friedrich **Obv:** Collared bust right, '3' in wedge below **Obv. Legend:** ⊕ MEMOR. IOACH. FRID. - DVCIS. SLE. LEG. BREG. **Rev:** 5-line inscription with R.N. date, ornaments above and below **Rev. Inscription:** PLACIDIS. / OBIIT. AN. M. / D. C II. M. MART. / DIE. XXV. HO / RA. VI. P.M. **Mint:** Kreuzburg **Note:** Ref: F/S#1390.

Date	Mintage	VG	F	VF	XF	Unc
MDCII (1602)	—	—	—	—	—	—

KM# 25 3 KREUZER (Groschen)

Silver **Ruler:** Johann Christian and Georg Rudolph **Obv:** Silesian eagle with '3' in shield on breast **Obv. Legend:** IOHAN. CHRIST. ET. GEORG. RVDOL. D. G. **Rev:** Ornate helmet with Silesian eagle crest, date below **Rev. Legend:** FRATRVM. DVC. SIL. LIG. ET. BREG. MO. AR. **Mint:** Kreuzburg **Note:** Ref. F/S#1398.

Date	Mintage	VG	F	VF	XF	Unc
(1)603	—	20.00	40.00	85.00	170	—

KM# 28 3 KREUZER (Groschen)

Silver **Ruler:** Johann Christian and Georg Rudolph **Obv:** Silesian eagle with '3' in oval on breast, large crown above **Obv. Legend:** D. G. IOAN. CHR. ET. GEOR. RVD. FR. **Rev:** Ornamented shield of Brieg arms, date at end of legend **Rev. Legend:** ⊕ DVC. SIL. LEGNI. ET. BREG. **Mint:** Kreuzburg **Note:** Klippe. Ref. F/S#1402.

Date	Mintage	VG	F	VF	XF	Unc
1604	—	20.00	40.00	85.00	170	—

KM# 30 3 KREUZER (Groschen)

Silver **Ruler:** Johann Christian and Georg Rudolph **Obv:** Silesian eagle with '3' in oval on breast, large crown above **Obv. Legend:** D. G. IOAN. CHR. ET. GEOR. RVD. FR. **Rev:** Ornate 4-fold arms divide date, crown above **Rev. Legend:** DVC. SIL. LIGNICEN. ET. BREG. **Mint:** Kreuzburg **Note:** Klippe. Ref: F/S#1403.

Date	Mintage	VG	F	VF	XF	Unc
1604	—	20.00	40.00	85.00	170	—

KM# 27 3 KREUZER (Groschen)

Silver **Ruler:** Johann Christian and Georg Rudolph **Obv:** Silesian eagle, '3' below **Obv. Legend:** MO. NO. ARGEN. IO - AN. CHRIS. GEOR. R. **Rev:** Crowned shield of Brieg arms divides date **Rev. Legend:** DVCVM. LIGNICEN. ET. BREG. FRA. **Mint:** Kreuzburg **Note:** Ref: F/S#1401.

Date	Mintage	VG	F	VF	XF	Unc
1604	—	20.00	40.00	85.00	170	—

KM# 37 3 KREUZER (Groschen)

Silver **Ruler:** Johann Christian and Georg Rudolph **Obv:** Silesian eagle with '3' in oval on breast, large crown above **Obv. Legend:** D. G. IOAN. CHR. ET. GEOR. RVD. FR. **Rev:** Ornamented shield of Brieg arms, date at end of legend **Rev. Legend:** ⊕ DVC. SIL. LEGNI. ET. BREG. **Mint:** Kreuzburg **Note:** Ref. F/S#1406.

Date	Mintage	VG	F	VF	XF	Unc
1605	—	20.00	40.00	85.00	170	—

KM# 38 3 KREUZER (1/24 Thaler)

Silver **Ruler:** Johann Christian and Georg Rudolph **Obv:** Silesian eagle, '3' in oval below **Obv. Legend:** + D. G. IOAN. CHR. - ET. GEOR. RVD. FR. **Rev:** 2 adjacent shields of arms, Silesian eagle left, Brieg right, large crown above, 'Z$' in oval below, date at end of legend **Rev. Legend:** DVC. SIL. LEG. ET. BREG. **Mint:** Kreuzburg **Note:** Ref. F/S#1407, 1411, 1418, 1426, 1441-42, 1459-60, 1477, 1484. Varieties exist.

Date	Mintage	VG	F	VF	XF	Unc
1605	—	12.00	18.00	30.00	60.00	—
1606	—	12.00	18.00	30.00	60.00	—
1607	—	12.00	18.00	30.00	60.00	—
1608	—	12.00	18.00	30.00	60.00	—
1609	—	12.00	18.00	30.00	60.00	—
1609 (d)	—	12.00	18.00	30.00	60.00	—
1610	—	12.00	18.00	30.00	60.00	—
1610 (d)	—	12.00	18.00	30.00	60.00	—
1611	—	12.00	18.00	30.00	60.00	—
161Z	—	12.00	18.00	30.00	60.00	—

KM# 144 3 KREUZER (1/24 Thaler)

Silver **Ruler:** Johann Christian and Georg Rudolph **Obv:** Silesian eagle **Obv. Legend:** D. G. IOAN. CHRI. ET. GEOR. RVD. FRA. **Rev:** 2 adjacent shields of arms, Silesian eagle left, Brieg right, large crown above, '3' in oval below, date at end of legend **Rev. Legend:** DVC. SIL. LIG. ET. BREG. **Mint:** Kreuzburg **Note:** Ref. F/S#1483, 1487.

Date	Mintage	VG	F	VF	XF	Unc
161Z (c)	—	18.00	32.00	60.00	120	—
1613 (c)	—	18.00	32.00	60.00	120	—

KM# 165 3 KREUZER (1/24 Thaler)

Silver **Ruler:** Johann Christian and Georg Rudolph **Obv:** Silesian eagle **Obv. Legend:** IO. CHR. ET. GEO. RVD. DVC. SIL. L. B. **Rev:** 2 adjacent shields of arms, Silesian eagle left, Brieg right, large crown above, '3' in oval below, date at end of legend **Rev. Legend:** MO. NOV. ARG. REICHST. **Mint:** Reichenstein **Note:** Klippe. Ref. F/S#1504.

Date	Mintage	VG	F	VF	XF	Unc
1616 BH	—	18.00	32.00	60.00	120	—

KM# 211 3 KREUZER (1/24 Thaler)

Silver **Ruler:** Georg Rudolf **Obv:** Silesian eagle in circle **Obv. Legend:** D. G. GEO. RVD. DVC. SIL. LI. ET. B. **Rev:** 2 adjacent shields of arms, crown above, '3' in oval below, mintmaster's initials and date at end of legend **Rev. Legend:** MON. NOV. ARGENT. **Mint:** Haynau **Note:** Ref: F/S#1662.

Date	Mintage	VG	F	VF	XF	Unc
(1)6Z0 (mt)	—	20.00	35.00	55.00	115	—

KM# 230 3 KREUZER (1/24 Thaler)

Silver **Ruler:** Georg Rudolf **Obv:** 2 adjacent shields of arms, crown above, '3' in partial oval below **Obv. Legend:** D. G. GEO. RU. DU. SI. LI. & B. **Rev:** Silesian eagle, date at end of legend **Rev. Legend:** MO. NO. ARGE. SILESI. **Note:** Ref: F/S#1627.

Date	Mintage	VG	F	VF	XF	Unc
16Z1	—	20.00	35.00	55.00	115	—

KM# 231 3 KREUZER (1/24 Thaler)

Silver **Ruler:** Georg Rudolf **Obv:** Bust right **Obv. Legend:** D. G. GEO. RVD. DVX. SIL. LI. ET B. **Rev:** Crowned shield of 4-fold arms, value '3' in oval below, date at end of legend **Rev. Legend:** MON. NOVA. ARGENT. **Note:** Ref: F/S#1628, 1642.

Date	Mintage	VG	F	VF	XF	Unc
16Z1	—	18.00	30.00	60.00	120	—
16ZZ	—	18.00	30.00	60.00	120	—

KM# 227 3 KREUZER (1/24 Thaler)

Silver **Ruler:** Johann Christian **Obv:** Crown over 2 adjacent shields of arms, Silesian eagle left, Brieg right, value '3' below **Obv. Legend:** D. G. IO. CHR. DVX. SIL. LI. & B. **Rev:** Silesian eagle in circle, date at end of legend **Rev. Legend:** MO. NO. ARGENT. REICHEN. **Mint:** Reichenstein **Note:** Kipper coinage. Ref: F/S#1605.

Date	Mintage	VG	F	VF	XF	Unc
16Z1 HR	—	18.00	30.00	60.00	120	—

KM# 229 3 KREUZER (1/24 Thaler)

Silver **Ruler:** Georg Rudolf **Obv:** Silesian eagle, '3' in oval below **Obv. Legend:** D. G. GEO. RVD. - DVX. SI. LI. ET B. **Rev:** Crowned rounded 4-fold arms with incut sides, date at end of legend **Rev. Legend:** MON. NOV. ARGENT. **Note:** Kipper coinage. Ref: F/S#1626, 1646.

Date	Mintage	VG	F	VF	XF	Unc
16Z1	—	25.00	45.00	90.00	180	—
16ZZ	—	25.00	45.00	90.00	180	—

KM# 225 3 KREUZER (1/24 Thaler)

Silver **Ruler:** Johann Christian **Obv:** Crown over 2 adjacent shields of arms, Silesian eagle left, Brieg right, value '3' below **Obv. Legend:** D. G. IO. CHR. DVX. SIL. LI(G). & B **Rev:** Silesian eagle in circle, date at end of legend **Rev. Legend:** MO. NO(V). ARGENT. OLAV. **Mint:** Ohlau **Note:** Kipper coinage. Ref. F/S#1569, 1577-78, 1581. Varieties exist.

Date	Mintage	VG	F	VF	XF	Unc
16Z1 HR	—	25.00	45.00	90.00	180	—
16ZZ HR	—	25.00	45.00	90.00	180	—
16Z3 HR	—	25.00	45.00	90.00	180	—

KM# 226 3 KREUZER (1/24 Thaler)
Silver **Ruler:** Johann Christian **Obv:** Crown over 2 adjacent shields of arms, Silesian eagle left, Brieg right, value '3' below **Obv. Legend:** D. G. IO. CHR. DV. SIL. LI. & B. **Rev:** Silesian eagle in circle, date at end of legend **Rev. Legend:** MO. NO(V). ARGENT. BREG. **Mint:** Brieg **Note:** Kipper coinage. Ref. F/S#1582, 1587-88. Varieties exist.

Date	Mintage	VG	F	VF	XF	Unc
16Z1 BH	—	25.00	45.00	90.00	180	—
16ZZ BH	—	25.00	45.00	90.00	180	—

KM# 228 3 KREUZER (1/24 Thaler)
Silver **Ruler:** Georg Rudolf **Obv:** Silesian eagle, '3' in oval below **Obv. Legend:** D. G. GEO. RVD. - DVC. SIL. LI. ET B. **Rev:** Crowned round 4-fold arms with scalloped sides, mintmaster's initials and date at end of legend. **Rev. Legend:** MON. NOV. ARGENT. **Mint:** Haynau **Note:** Kipper coinage. Ref: F/S#1677.

Date	Mintage	VG	F	VF	XF	Unc
(1)6Z1 (mt)	—	28.00	55.00	110	220	—

KM# 305 3 KREUZER (1/24 Thaler)
Silver **Ruler:** Georg Rudolf **Obv:** Bust right, '3' below in oval **Obv. Legend:** D. G. GEO. RV. DV. - SIL. LIG. ET. BR. **Rev:** Crowned ornately shaped 4-fold arms, date at end of legend **Rev. Legend:** MO. NO. ARGENT. HERNS. **Mint:** Herrnstadt **Note:** Kipper coinage. Ref: F/S#1678.

Date	Mintage	VG	F	VF	XF	Unc
16ZZ	—	28.00	50.00	100	210	—

KM# 307 3 KREUZER (1/24 Thaler)
Silver **Ruler:** Georg Rudolf **Obv:** Bust right **Obv. Legend:** D. G. GEO. RV. DV. **Rev:** 2 adjacent shields of arms, crown above, '3' in oval below, mintmaster's symbol at bottom, date at end of legend **Rev. Legend:** MONE. NOVA. - ARG. **Mint:** Liegnitz **Note:** Kipper coinage. Ref: F/S#1695.

Date	Mintage	VG	F	VF	XF	Unc
1622 (e)	—	28.00	50.00	100	210	—

KM# 308 3 KREUZER (1/24 Thaler)
Silver **Ruler:** Georg Rudolf **Obv:** Silesian eagle, mintmaster's symbol at bottom **Obv. Legend:** D. G. GEO. RVD. - D. SI. LI. E. B. **Rev:** 2 adjacent shields of arms, crown above, '3' in oval below, date at end of legend **Rev. Legend:** MONE. NOVA. ARGE. **Mint:** Liegnitz **Note:** Kipper coinage. Ref: F/S#1696-97.

Date	Mintage	VG	F	VF	XF	Unc
1622 (e)	—	28.00	50.00	100	210	—

KM# 304 3 KREUZER (1/24 Thaler)
Silver **Ruler:** Johann Christian **Obv:** Crown over 2 adjacent shields of arms, Silesian eagle left, Brieg right, value '3' below **Obv. Legend:** D. G. IO. CHR. DVX. SIL. LI. & B **Rev:** Silesian eagle in circle, date at end of legend **Rev. Legend:** MO. NO. ARGENT. CRVCIBV. **Mint:** Kreuzburg **Note:** Kipper coinage. Ref. F/S#1603-04. Varieties exist.

Date	Mintage	VG	F	VF	XF	Unc
16ZZ BH	—	28.00	50.00	100	210	—

KM# 306 3 KREUZER (1/24 Thaler)
Silver **Ruler:** Georg Rudolf **Obv:** Silesian eagle in circle **Obv. Legend:** D. G. GEO. RVD. DVC. SIL. LI. ET. B. **Rev:** 2 adjacent shields of arms, crown above, '3' in oval below, date at end of legend **Rev. Legend:** MON. NOV. ARGENT. **Mint:** Herrnstadt **Note:** Kipper coinage. Ref. F/S#1679.

Date	Mintage	VG	F	VF	XF	Unc
16ZZ	—	28.00	50.00	100	210	—

KM# 310 3 KREUZER (1/24 Thaler)
Silver **Ruler:** Georg Rudolf **Obv:** 2 adjacent shields of arms, crown above, '3' in partial oval below **Obv. Legend:** D. G. GEO. RVD. DVX. SIL. L. & BR. **Rev:** Silesian eagle, date at end of legend **Rev. Legend:** + MONETA. NOVA. ARG. OL. **Mint:** Ohlau **Note:** Kipper coinage. Ref: F/S#1651.

Date	Mintage	VG	F	VF	XF	Unc
1622	—	28.00	55.00	110	220	—

KM# 314 3 KREUZER (1/24 Thaler)
Silver **Ruler:** Georg Rudolf **Obv:** Large bust right, value '3' in oval below **Obv. Legend:** D. G. GEO. RVD. - D. SI. LI. E. B. **Rev:** Crowned ornately shaped 4-fold arms, date at end of legend **Rev. Legend:** MONE. NOVA. ARGEN. **Note:** Klippe. Ref: F/S#1645.

Date	Mintage	VG	F	VF	XF	Unc
1622	—	—	—	—	—	—

KM# 311 3 KREUZER (1/24 Thaler)
Silver **Ruler:** Georg Rudolf **Obv:** Silesian eagle, '3' in oval below **Obv. Legend:** D. G. GEO. RVD. - DVX. SI. LI. ET B. **Rev:** Crowned rounded 4-fold arms with incut sides, date at end of legend **Rev. Legend:** MON. NOV. ARGENT. **Note:** Klippe. Ref: F/S#1647.

Date	Mintage	VG	F	VF	XF	Unc
16ZZ	—	—	—	—	—	—

KM# 316 3 KREUZER (1/24 Thaler)
Silver **Ruler:** Georg Rudolf **Obv:** Silesian eagle **Obv. Legend:** D. G. GEO. RVD. - D. SI. LI. E. B. **Rev:** 2 adjacent shields of arms, crown above, '3' in oval below, date at end of legend **Rev. Legend:** MONE. NOVA. ARGE. **Note:** Klippe. Ref: F/S#1652.

Date	Mintage	VG	F	VF	XF	Unc
1622	—	—	—	—	—	—

KM# 312 3 KREUZER (1/24 Thaler)
Silver **Ruler:** Georg Rudolf **Obv:** Large bust right **Obv. Legend:** D. G. GEO. RVD. DVX. SIL. LI. ET BR. **Rev:** 2 adjacent shields of arms, crown above, '3' in oval below, date at end of legend **Rev. Legend:** MO. NO. ARGENT. **Note:** Ref: F/S#1643.

Date	Mintage	VG	F	VF	XF	Unc
1622	—	28.00	50.00	100	210	—

KM# 313 3 KREUZER (1/24 Thaler)
Silver **Ruler:** Georg Rudolf **Obv:** Large bust right, value '3' in oval below **Obv. Legend:** D. G. GEO. RVD. - D. SI. LI. E. B. **Rev:** Crowned ornately shaped 4-fold arms, date at end of legend **Rev. Legend:** MONE. NOVA. ARGEN. **Note:** Ref: F/S#1644.

Date	Mintage	VG	F	VF	XF	Unc
1622	—	28.00	50.00	100	210	—

KM# 315 3 KREUZER (1/24 Thaler)
Silver **Ruler:** Georg Rudolf **Obv:** Silesian eagle **Obv. Legend:** D. G. GEO. RVD. - D. SI. LI. E. B. **Rev:** 2 adjacent shields of arms, crown above, '3' in oval below, date at end of legend **Rev. Legend:** MONE. NOVA. ARGE. **Note:** Ref: F/S#1648.

Date	Mintage	VG	F	VF	XF	Unc
1622	—	28.00	50.00	100	210	—

KM# 317 3 KREUZER (1/24 Thaler)
Silver **Ruler:** Georg Rudolf **Obv:** Silesian eagle, value '3' at bottom **Obv. Legend:** D. G. GEO. RVD. - D. SI. LI. E. B. **Rev:** 2 adjacent shields of arms, crown above, '3' also in oval below, date at end of legend **Rev. Legend:** MONE. NOVA. ARGE. **Note:** Ref: F/S#1649.

Date	Mintage	VG	F	VF	XF	Unc
1622	—	28.00	50.00	100	210	—

KM# 318 3 KREUZER (1/24 Thaler)
Silver **Ruler:** Georg Rudolf **Obv:** 2 adjacent shields of arms, crown above, '3' in partial oval below **Obv. Legend:** D. G. GEO. RVD. DV. SIL. LI. & B. **Rev:** Silesian eagle, date at end of legend **Rev. Legend:** MON. NOVA. ARGENT. **Note:** Ref: F/S#1650, 1659.

Date	Mintage	VG	F	VF	XF	Unc
1622	—	28.00	50.00	100	210	—
1623	—	28.00	50.00	100	210	—

KM# 309 3 KREUZER (1/24 Thaler)
Silver **Ruler:** Georg Rudolf **Obv:** 2 adjacent arms in ornately shaped shields, crown above, '3' in oval below **Obv. Legend:** D. G. GEO. RVD. - DVX. SI. LI. E. B. **Rev:** Silesian eagle, crossed keys in small circle below, date at end of legend **Rev. Legend:** MONET. NOVA. - ARGENT. **Mint:** Liegnitz **Note:** Kipper coinage. Ref: S/Sch#267.

Date	Mintage	VG	F	VF	XF	Unc
16ZZ	—	28.00	50.00	100	210	—

KM# 364 3 KREUZER (1/24 Thaler)
Silver **Ruler:** Georg Rudolf **Obv:** Bust right **Obv. Legend:** D. G. GEOR. RVD. DVX. SI. LIG. ET. B. **Rev:** 2 adjacent shields of arms, crown above, '3' in oval below, date at end of legend **Rev. Legend:** MONE. NOV. ARGENT. **Mint:** Liegnitz **Note:** Kipper coinage. Ref: F/S#1700.

Date	Mintage	VG	F	VF	XF	Unc
1623 GH	—	28.00	50.00	100	210	—

KM# 395 3 KREUZER (1/24 Thaler)
Silver, 20 mm. **Ruler:** Georg III, Ludwig IV and Christian **Obv:** 3 facing 1/2-length figures, small imperial orb at top, value '3' in oval below **Obv. Legend:** D. G. GEORG. LV - DO. & CHRIST. **Rev:** Silesian eagle in circle, date at end of legend **Rev. Legend:** FRAT. DVC. SIL. - LIG. BREG. **Note:** Ref: F/S#1727, 1736, 1741-42, 1751-52, 1760-61, 1772, 1781. Varieties exist.

Date	Mintage	VG	F	VF	XF	Unc
1653 (pf)	—	6.00	10.00	25.00	50.00	—
1654 (pf)	—	6.00	10.00	25.00	50.00	—
1655 (pf)	—	6.00	10.00	25.00	50.00	—
1656 (pf)	—	6.00	10.00	25.00	50.00	—
1657 (pf)	—	6.00	10.00	25.00	50.00	—
1657 (pf)-EW	—	6.00	10.00	25.00	50.00	—
1658 (pf)-EW	—	6.00	10.00	25.00	50.00	—
1659 (pf)-EW	—	6.00	10.00	25.00	50.00	—

KM# 425 3 KREUZER (1/24 Thaler)
Silver, 22 mm. **Ruler:** Georg III **Obv:** Mantled bust right, value '3' in oval below **Obv. Legend:** D.G. GEORGI • DVX • - SIL • L(IGN) • & BREG • **Rev:** Silesian eagle in circle, date at end of legend **Rev. Legend:** MONETA • NOVA - ARGENT • **Note:** Ref: F/S#1834, 1843, 1850-51, 1854-55. Varieties exist.

Date	Mintage	VG	F	VF	XF	Unc
1659 (pf)	—	12.00	25.00	55.00	115	—
1660 (pf) - EW	—	12.00	25.00	55.00	115	—
1661 (pf)	—	12.00	25.00	55.00	115	—
1661 (pf) - EW	—	12.00	25.00	55.00	115	—
1662 (pf)	—	12.00	25.00	55.00	115	—
1662 EW	—	12.00	25.00	55.00	115	—

KM# 424 3 KREUZER (1/24 Thaler)
Silver **Ruler:** Georg III **Obv:** Mantled bust right, value '3' in oval below **Obv. Legend:** D. G. GEORG. DU - X. SIL. LIGN. & B. **Rev:** Silesian eagle in circle, date at end of legend **Rev. Legend:** MONETA. NOVA. ARGENT. **Note:** Ref: F/S#1835.

Date	Mintage	VG	F	VF	XF	Unc
1659	—	—	—	—	—	—

KM# 427 3 KREUZER (1/24 Thaler)
Silver **Ruler:** Christian zu Ohlau **Obv:** Mantled bust right, value '3' in oval below **Obv. Legend:** D. G. CHRIST. DVX. - SIL. L. B. & WOLAV. **Rev:** Silesian eagle, date at end of legend **Rev. Legend:** MONETA. NOVA. - ARGENT. **Note:** Ref: F/S#1894, 1899-1900, 1907-08, 1911-13, 1916, 1918, 1927. Varieties exist.

Date	Mintage	VG	F	VF	XF	Unc
1659 (pf)	—	6.00	10.00	25.00	50.00	—
1660 (pf)	—	6.00	10.00	25.00	50.00	—
1660 (pf)-EW	—	6.00	10.00	25.00	50.00	—
1661	—	6.00	10.00	25.00	50.00	—
1661 (pf)-EW	—	6.00	10.00	25.00	50.00	—
1662	—	6.00	10.00	25.00	50.00	—
1662 (pf)	—	6.00	10.00	25.00	50.00	—
1662 EW	—	6.00	10.00	25.00	50.00	—
1664 (pf)	—	6.00	10.00	25.00	50.00	—
1665 (pf)	—	6.00	10.00	25.00	50.00	—
1668 CB	—	6.00	10.00	25.00	50.00	—

KM# 426 3 KREUZER (1/24 Thaler)
Silver **Ruler:** Ludwig IV **Obv:** Mantled bust right, value '3' in oval below **Obv. Legend:** D.G. LUDOV (IC) • DUX • - SIL • L • B • & GOLDB. **Rev:** Silesian eagle in circle, date at end of legend **Rev. Legend:** MONETA. NOVA - ARGENT. **Note:** Ref. F/S#1870, 1872-73, 79-80, 1884-86. Varieties exist.

Date	Mintage	VG	F	VF	XF	Unc
1659 (pf)	—	12.00	25.00	55.00	115	—
1660 (pf)	—	12.00	25.00	55.00	115	—
1660 (pf) - EW	—	12.00	25.00	55.00	115	—
1661 EW	—	12.00	25.00	55.00	115	—
1661 (pf) - EW	—	12.00	25.00	55.00	115	—
1662	—	12.00	25.00	55.00	115	—
1662 (pf)	—	12.00	25.00	55.00	115	—
1662 EW	—	12.00	25.00	55.00	115	—

KM# 513 3 KREUZER (1/24 Thaler)
Silver **Ruler:** Louise **Obv:** Silesian eagle, crown above, '3' below **Obv. Legend:** MONETA. NOV. AR - GENT. DVC. SIL. **Rev:** 2 adjacent ornately shaped arms, crown above, date at top in margin **Rev. Legend:** LIGNICENS. BREGENS. &. WOLAV. **Note:** Ref: F/S#1952-53.

Date	Mintage	VG	F	VF	XF	Unc
1673	—	—	—	—	—	—
1673 CB	—	—	—	—	—	—

KM# 518 3 KREUZER (1/24 Thaler)
Silver **Ruler:** Georg Wilhelm **Obv:** Armored and mantled bust right, '3' below shoulder **Obv. Legend:** GEORG. WILHELM. - D. G. DVX. SI. **Rev:** Silesian eagle, crown above divides date in margin **Rev. Legend:** LIGNIC. BREGENS. & WOLAV. **Note:** Ref: F/S#1961, 1971.

Date	Mintage	VG	F	VF	XF	Unc
1674 CB	—	12.00	20.00	35.00	70.00	—
1675 CB	—	12.00	20.00	35.00	70.00	—

KM# 519 3 KREUZER (1/24 Thaler)
Silver **Ruler:** Georg Wilhelm **Obv:** Large armored and mantled bust right, '3' below shoulder **Obv. Legend:** GEORG. WILHELM. - D. G. DVX. SIL. **Rev:** Silesian eagle, crown above divides date in margin **Rev. Legend:** LIGNIC. BREGENS. & WOLAVI. **Note:** Ref. #J/M-139.

Date	Mintage	VG	F	VF	XF	Unc
1674 CB	—	—	—	—	—	—

KM# 150 3 KREUZER
Silver **Ruler:** Johann Christian and Georg Rudolph **Obv:** Silesian eagle **Obv. Legend:** IO. CHR. ET. GEO. RVD. DVC. SIL. L. B. **Rev:** 2 adjacent shields of arms, Silesian eagle left, Brieg right, large crown above, 3 in oval below, date at end of legend **Rev. Legend:** MO. NOV. ARG. REICHST. **Mint:** Reichenstein **Note:** Varieties exist. Ref: F/S#1493, 1496, 1500-01, 1503, 1514-15, 1518, 1537, 1545-46, 1556, J/M#114.

Date	Mintage	VG	F	VF	XF	Unc
1614 (c)	—	20.00	27.00	50.00	100	—
1615 (c)	—	20.00	27.00	50.00	100	—
1616	—	20.00	27.00	50.00	100	—
1616 (c)	—	20.00	27.00	50.00	100	—
1616 BH	—	20.00	27.00	50.00	100	—
1617 BH	—	20.00	27.00	50.00	100	—
1617 HR	—	20.00	27.00	50.00	100	—
1618 HR	—	20.00	27.00	50.00	100	—
168 HR (error)	—	20.00	27.00	50.00	100	—
1619 HR	—	20.00	27.00	50.00	100	—
16Z0 HR	—	20.00	27.00	50.00	100	—
16Z1 HR	—	20.00	27.00	50.00	100	—

KM# 370 3 KREUZER

Silver **Ruler:** Georg III, Ludwig IV and Christian **Obv:** 3 facing 1/2-length figures, value 3 in oval below **Obv. Legend:** D.G. GEORG. LUDW - ET. CHRISTIAN. **Rev:** Silesian eagle in circle, date at end of legend **Rev. Legend:** FRAT. DUC. SIL. - LIG. BREG. **Note:** Ref: F/S#1711, 1720-21.

Date	Mintage	VG	F	VF	XF	Unc
1651 (pf) - VT	—	15.00	30.00	60.00	120	—
1652	—	15.00	30.00	60.00	120	—
1652 GH	—	15.00	30.00	60.00	120	—

KM# 500 3 KREUZER

Silver **Ruler:** Christian zu Ohlau **Obv:** Mantled bust right, value '3' in oval below **Obv. Legend:** CHRISTIANVS ? - ? D?G ? DVX ? SIL **Rev:** Silesian eagle, crown above divides date in margin **Rev. Legend:** LIGNIC ? BREGENS ? & ? WOLAV. **Note:** Ref. F/S#1928, 1931, 1936.

Date	Mintage	VG	F	VF	XF	Unc
1668 CB	—	8.00	15.00	30.00	60.00	120
1669 CB	—	8.00	15.00	30.00	60.00	120
1670 CB	—	8.00	15.00	30.00	60.00	120

KM# 484 6 KREUZER

Silver **Ruler:** Christian zu Ohlau **Obv:** Armored bust right, VI below **Obv. Legend:** D. G. CHRIST. DUX. SIL. - L. B. & WOLAV. **Rev:** Silesian eagle in circle, date at end of legend **Rev. Legend:** MONETA. NOVA. - ARGENTEA. **Note:** Ref: F/S#1917.

Date	Mintage	VG	F	VF	XF	Unc
1665 (pf)	—	—	—	—	—	—

KM# 515 6 KREUZER

Silver **Ruler:** Louise **Obv:** 2 adjacent ornately shaped arms, crown above, value 'VI' below **Obv. Legend:** MON. NO. ARG. DVC. SIL. LIGNIC. **Rev:** Silesian eagle, crown above, date at end of legend **Rev. Legend:** BREGENSIS. ET. WOLAVIEN. **Note:** Ref: F/S#1949.

Date	Mintage	VG	F	VF	XF	Unc
1673 CB	—	—	—	—	—	—

KM# 516 6 KREUZER

Silver **Ruler:** Louise **Obv:** Silesian eagle, crown above, (VI) below **Obv. Legend:** MONETA NOV. AR - GENT. DUC. SIL(E) **Rev:** 2 adjacent oval arms in baroque frame, crown above, date at top in margin **Rev. Legend:** LIGN(ICENS). BREG(ENS). (ET) (&). WOLA(V) (U) IE (NSIS). **Note:** Ref. F/S#1950-51. Varieties exist.

Date	Mintage	VG	F	VF	XF	Unc
1673	—	—	—	—	—	—
1673 CB	—	9.00	15.00	30.00	60.00	—

KM# 521 6 KREUZER

Silver **Ruler:** Georg Wilhelm **Obv:** Armored and mantled bust right **Obv. Legend:** GEORG. WILHELM. D.G. DVX. SIL. **Rev:** Silesian eagle, crown above divides date in margin, (VI) below **Rev. Legend:** LIGNIC. BREGE - NS. & WOLAVI. **Note:** Ref. F/S#1960.

Date	Mintage	VG	F	VF	XF	Unc
1674 CB	—	30.00	42.00	60.00	115	—

KM# 233 12 KREUZER (Zwolfer)

Silver **Ruler:** Johann Christian and Georg Rudolph **Obv:** Silesian eagle in circle **Obv. Legend:** + IOHAN. CHRIST. & GEOR. RUDO. DUC. SIL. **Rev:** 2 ornate adjacent shields of arms, Silesia on left, Brieg on right, large crown above, 'IZ' below, date at end of legend **Rev. Legend:** MONE. NOUA. ARGEN. REICHST. **Mint:** Reichenstein **Note:** Kipper coinage. Ref: F/S#1555.

Date	Mintage	VG	F	VF	XF	Unc
1621 HR	—	50.00	100	210	—	—

KM# 234 12 KREUZER (Zwolfer)

Silver **Ruler:** Georg Rudolf **Obv:** Bust right, small imperial orb above, value '1Z' in oval below **Obv. Legend:** D. G. GEOR. RVD - DVX. SI. LI. ET. B. **Rev:** Crowned 4-fold arms in baroque frame, date at end of legend **Rev. Legend:** GROSSVS. ARGENT. SEXD. **Mint:** Haynau **Note:** Kipper coinage. Ref: F/S#1671.

Date	Mintage	VG	F	VF	XF	Unc
16Z1 MT	—	50.00	100	210	—	—

KM# 237 12 KREUZER (Zwolfer)

Silver **Ruler:** Georg Rudolf **Obv:** Bust right, small imperial orb above, value '1Z' in oval below **Obv. Legend:** D. G. GEORG. RVD. DVC. SIL. LI. ET. B. **Rev:** Crowned squarish 4-fold arms in baroque frame, date at end of legend **Rev. Legend:** GROSSVS. ARGENT. SEXD. **Mint:** Haynau **Note:** Kipper coinage. Ref: F/S#1674.

Date	Mintage	VG	F	VF	XF	Unc
16Z1 MT	—	50.00	100	210	—	—

KM# 238 12 KREUZER (Zwolfer)

Silver **Ruler:** Georg Rudolf **Obv:** Silesian eagle in circle, value '1Z' in oval at bottom **Obv. Legend:** D. G. GEORG. RVD. - DVC. SIL. LI. ET. B **Rev:** Crowned ornate 4-fold arms, date at end of legend **Rev. Legend:** GROSSVS. ARGENT. SEXD. **Mint:** Haynau **Note:** Kipper coinage. Ref: F/S#1675.

Date	Mintage	VG	F	VF	XF	Unc
16Z1 MT	—	50.00	100	210	—	—

KM# 235 12 KREUZER (Zwolfer)

Silver **Ruler:** Georg Rudolf **Obv:** Bust right, small imperial orb above, value '1Z' in oval below **Obv. Legend:** D. G. GEOR. RVD - DVX. SI. LI. ET. B. **Rev:** Ornately shaped 4-fold arms, crown above, date at end of legend **Rev. Legend:** GROSSVS. ARGENT. SEXD. **Mint:** Haynau **Note:** Klippe. Kipper coinage. Ref: F/S#1672.

Date	Mintage	VG	F	VF	XF	Unc
16Z1 MT	—	—	—	—	—	—

KM# 236 12 KREUZER (Zwolfer)

Silver **Ruler:** Georg Rudolf **Obv:** Bust right, small imperial orb above, value '1Z' in oval below **Obv. Legend:** D. G. GEORG. RVD. DVC. SIL. LI. ET. B. **Rev:** Ornately shaped 4-fold arms, crown above, date at end of legend **Rev. Legend:** GROSSVS. ARGENT. SEXD. **Mint:** Haynau **Note:** Klippe. Kipper coinage. Ref: F/S#1673.

Date	Mintage	VG	F	VF	XF	Unc
16Z1 MT	—	—	—	—	—	—

KM# 239 12 KREUZER (Zwolfer)

Silver **Ruler:** Georg Rudolf **Obv:** Bust right breaks circle at top **Obv. Legend:** D. G. GEO. RUD. DUX. SIL. LI. E. B. **Rev:** Crowned ornate 4-fold arms, date at end of legend **Rev. Inscription:** GROSS. ARG. / XII / CRUCI. **Mint:** Haynau **Note:** Kipper coinage. Ref. F/S#1676.

Date	Mintage	VG	F	VF	XF	Unc
16Z1 MT	—	50.00	100	210	—	—

KM# 319 12 KREUZER (Zwolfer)

Silver **Ruler:** Georg Rudolf **Obv:** Bust right breaks circle at top **Obv. Legend:** D. G. GEO. RUD. DUX. SIL. LI. E. B. **Rev:** 2 small shields of arms divide date and mintmaster's initials, crown above, 3 line inscription below **Rev. Inscription:** GROSS. ARG. / XII / CRUCI **Mint:** Liegnitz **Note:** Kipper coinage. Ref. F/S#1694.

Date	Mintage	VG	F	VF	XF	Unc
16ZZ (e)	—	50.00	100	210	—	—

KM# 320 12 KREUZER (Zwolfer)

Silver **Ruler:** Georg Rudolf **Obv:** Bust right in circle, small imperial orb at top **Obv. Legend:** D. G. GEO. RVD. DVX. SIL. LEG. & BRE. **Rev:** 2 small shields of arms divide date, crown above, 3-line inscription below **Rev. Inscription:** GROSS. ARG. / XII / CRVCI. **Note:** Kipper coinage. Ref. F/S#1641.

Date	Mintage	VG	F	VF	XF	Unc
16ZZ	—	50.00	100	210	—	—

KM# 429 15 KREUZER (1/6 Thaler)

Silver **Ruler:** Georg III **Obv:** Armored bust to right, value 'XV' below **Obv. Legend:** D. G. GEORGIUS. DUX. - SIL. LIGN. ET. BREG. **Rev:** Crowned 4-fold arms in baroque frame, date at end of legend **Rev. Legend:** MONETA. NOVA. - ARGENTEA. **Note:** Ref. F/S#1831-32.

Date	Mintage	VG	F	VF	XF	Unc
1659 (pf)	—	35.00	75.00	150	—	—
1659 EW	—	35.00	75.00	150	—	—

KM# 430 15 KREUZER (1/6 Thaler)

, 28 mm. **Ruler:** Georg III **Obv:** Armored bust to right, value (XV) below **Obv. Legend:** D.G. GEORGIUS. DUX. - SIL. LIGN. ET. BREG. **Rev:** Silesian eagle in circle, date at end of legend **Rev. Legend:** MONETA. NOVA. - ARGENTEA. **Note:** Ref. F/S#1833, 1842, 1848-49, 1852-53, 1856, 1860. Varieties exist.

Date	Mintage	VG	F	VF	XF	Unc
1659 (pf)	—	30.00	65.00	135	275	—
1660 (pf) - EW	—	30.00	65.00	135	275	—
1661 (pf) - EW	—	30.00	65.00	135	275	—
1661 EW	—	30.00	65.00	135	275	—
1662 (pf)	—	30.00	65.00	135	275	—
1662 EW	—	30.00	65.00	135	275	—
1663 (pf)	—	30.00	65.00	135	275	—
1664 (pf)	—	30.00	65.00	135	275	—

KM# 431 15 KREUZER (1/6 Thaler)

Silver **Ruler:** Ludwig IV **Obv:** Mantled bust to right, value 'XV' below **Obv. Legend:** D. G. LUDOVIC. DUX. SIL. - LIGN. BREG & GOLDB. **Rev:** Crowned 4-fold arms in baroque frame, date at end of legend **Rev. Legend:** MONETA. NOVA. ARGENTEA. **Note:** Ref. F/S#1868.

Date	Mintage	VG	F	VF	XF	Unc
1659 EW	—	40.00	75.00	150	300	—

KM# 432 15 KREUZER (1/6 Thaler)

Silver **Ruler:** Ludwig IV **Obv:** Mantled bust to right, value 'XV' below **Obv. Legend:** D. G. LUDOVIC. DUX. SIL. - LIGN. BREG & GOLDB. **Rev:** Silesian eagle in circle, date at end of legend **Rev. Legend:** MONETA. NOVA. - ARGENTEA. **Note:** Ref. F/S#1869, 1871, 1877-78, 1882-83, 1887. Varieties exist.

Date	Mintage	VG	F	VF	XF	Unc
1659 (pf)	—	30.00	65.00	130	265	—
1660 (pf)-EW	—	30.00	65.00	130	265	—
1661 (pf)-EW	—	30.00	65.00	130	265	—
1661 EW	—	30.00	65.00	130	265	—
1662 (pf)	—	30.00	65.00	130	265	—
1662 EW	—	30.00	65.00	130	265	—
1663 (pf)	—	30.00	65.00	130	265	—

KM# 433 15 KREUZER (1/6 Thaler)

Silver **Ruler:** Christian zu Ohlau **Obv:** Mantled bust to right, value 'XV' below **Obv. Legend:** D. G. CHRISTIAN. DUX. SIL. - LIGN. BREG & WOLAV. **Rev:** Crowned 4-fold arms in baroque frame, date at end of legend **Rev. Legend:** MONETA. NOVA. - ARGENTEA. **Note:** Ref. F/S#1891-92.

Date	Mintage	VG	F	VF	XF	Unc
1659 (pf)	—	30.00	65.00	130	265	—
1659 EW	—	30.00	65.00	130	265	—

KM# 434 15 KREUZER (1/6 Thaler)

Silver **Ruler:** Christian zu Ohlau **Obv:** Armored bust to right, value 'XV' below **Obv. Legend:** D. G. CHRIST. DUX. SIL. - L. B. & WOLAV. **Rev:** Silesian eagle in circle, date at end of legend **Rev. Legend:** MONETA. NOVA. - ARGENTEA. **Note:** Ref. F/S#1893, 1898, 1905-06, 1909-10, 1914-15. Varieties exist.

Date	Mintage	VG	F	VF	XF	Unc
1659 (pf)	—	12.00	20.00	40.00	85.00	—
1660 (pf)-EW	—	12.00	20.00	40.00	85.00	—
1661 (pf)-EW	—	12.00	20.00	40.00	85.00	—
1661 EW	—	12.00	20.00	40.00	85.00	—
1662 (pf)	—	12.00	20.00	40.00	85.00	—
1662 EW	—	12.00	20.00	40.00	85.00	—
1663 (pf)	—	12.00	20.00	40.00	85.00	—
1664 (pf)	—	12.00	20.00	40.00	85.00	—

KM# 527 15 KREUZER (1/6 Thaler)

Silver **Ruler:** Georg Wilhelm **Obv:** Armored and mantled bust right, 'XV' below shoulder **Obv. Legend:** GEORGIVS. WILHELM. - D. G. DVX. SILESI. **Rev:** Silesian eagle, crown above divides date in margin **Rev. Legend:** LIGNICENS. BREGENS. & WOLAVIENS. **Note:** Ref. F/S#1969-70.

Date	Mintage	VG	F	VF	XF	Unc
1675 CB	—	—	—	—	—	—

KM# 248 24 KREUZER (Vierundzwanziger)

Silver **Ruler:** Georg Rudolf **Obv:** Armored bust right in circle, small imperial orb at top in margin **Obv. Legend:** D. G. GEO. RVD. DVX. SIL. LIG. BR. ET. GOL. **Rev:** Ornately shaped 4-fold arms, crown above, date at end of legend **Rev. Legend:** MON. NOV. ARGENT. **Mint:** Haynau **Note:** Kipper coinage. Ref. F/S#1668. Saurma calls this coin a 1/4 Thaler.

Date	Mintage	VG	F	VF	XF	Unc
16Z1 MT	—	—	—	—	—	—

KM# 249 24 KREUZER (Vierundzwanziger)

Silver **Ruler:** Georg Rudolf **Obv:** Armored bust right in circle, small imperial orb at top in margin **Obv. Legend:** D. G. GEO. RVD. DVX. SIL. LIG. BR. ET. GOL. **Rev:** Crowned squarish 4-fold arms in baroque frame, date at end of legend **Rev. Legend:** MON. NOV. ARGENT. **Mint:** Haynau **Note:** Kipper coinage. Ref. F/S#1669.

Date	Mintage	VG	F	VF	XF	Unc
16Z1 MT	—	30.00	50.00	100	175	—

KM# 250 24 KREUZER (Vierundzwanziger)
Silver **Ruler:** Georg Rudolf **Obv:** Armored bust right in circle, small imperial orb at top in margin **Obv. Legend:** D. G. GEO. RVD. DVX. SIL. LIG. BR. ET. GOL. **Rev:** Crowned squarish 4-fold arms in baroque frame, date at end of legend **Rev. Legend:** MON. NOV. ARGENT. **Mint:** Haynau **Note:** Kipper coinage. Ref. F/S#1670. Klippe.

Date	Mintage	VG	F	VF	XF	Unc
16Z1 MT	—	—	—	—	—	—

KM# 251 24 KREUZER (Vierundzwanziger)
Silver **Ruler:** Georg Rudolf **Obv:** 1/2-length armored figure to right, small imperial orb at top, '24' at bottom **Obv. Legend:** D. G. GEO. RVD. DVC. - SIL. LIG. ET. BRIG. **Rev:** Squarish 4-fold arms in baroque frame, crown above in margin, date at end of legend **Rev. Legend:** MONETA. NOVA. ARGENTEA. **Mint:** Ohlau **Note:** Kipper coinage. Ref. F/S#1681.

Date	Mintage	VG	F	VF	XF	Unc
1621 IK	—	30.00	50.00	100	210	—

KM# 252 24 KREUZER (Vierundzwanziger)
Silver **Ruler:** Georg Rudolf **Obv:** Armored bust to right, small imperial orb at top, '24' below **Obv. Legend:** D. G. GEO. RVD. DVX. - SIL. LIG. BRI. ET. G. **Rev:** Squarish 4-fold arms in baroque frame, crown aabove in margin, date at end of legend **Rev. Legend:** MONETA. NOVA. ARGENTEA. **Mint:** Ohlau **Note:** Kipper coinage. Ref. F/S#1682.

Date	Mintage	VG	F	VF	XF	Unc
1621 IK	—	25.00	45.00	80.00	160	—

KM# 253 24 KREUZER (Vierundzwanziger)
Silver **Ruler:** Georg Rudolf **Obv:** Armored bust to right, small imperial orb at top, 24 below **Obv. Legend:** D. G. GEO. RVD. DVX. - SIL. LIG. BR. ET. GOLT. **Rev:** Crowned Spanish shield of 4-fold arms in baroque frame, dat at end of legend **Rev. Legend:** MON. NOV. ARGENT. **Mint:** Liegnitz **Note:** Kipper coinage. Ref. F/S#1683.

Date	Mintage	VG	F	VF	XF	Unc
1621 (c)	—	20.00	35.00	75.00	150	—

KM# 254 24 KREUZER (Vierundzwanziger)
Silver **Ruler:** Georg Rudolf **Obv:** Armored bust to riht, small imperial orb at top, '24' below **Obv. Legend:** D. G. GEO. RUD. DUX. - SIL. LIG. BR. (ET) (&). GOLT. **Rev:** Crowned 4-fold arms in oval baroque frame, date at end of legend **Rev. Legend:** MON. NOU. ARGENT. **Mint:** Liegnitz **Note:** Kipper coinage. Ref. F/S#1684.

Date	Mintage	VG	F	VF	XF	Unc
1621 (c)	—	25.00	45.00	80.00	160	—

KM# 255 24 KREUZER (Vierundzwanziger)
Silver **Ruler:** Georg Rudolf **Obv:** Armored bust to right, small imperial orb at top, '24' below **Obv. Legend:** D. G. GEO. RUD. DUX. - SIL. LIG. BR. (ET &). GOLT. **Rev:** Crowned 4-fold arms in squarish baroque frame, date at end of legend **Rev. Legend:** MON. NOU. ARGENT. **Mint:** Liegnitz **Note:** Kipper coinage. Ref. F/S#1685.

Date	Mintage	VG	F	VF	XF	Unc
1621 (c)	—	25.00	45.00	80.00	160	—

KM# 256 24 KREUZER (Vierundzwanziger)
Silver **Ruler:** Georg Rudolf **Obv:** Large armored bust to right, small imperial orb at top, '24' below. **Obv. Legend:** D. G. GEO. RVD. DVX. - SIL. LIG. BR. ET. GOLT. **Rev:** Crowned Spanish shield of 4-fold arms in baroque frame, date at end of legend **Rev. Legend:** MON. NOV. ARGENT. **Mint:** Liegnitz **Note:** Kipper coinage. Ref. F/S#1686.

Date	Mintage	VG	F	VF	XF	Unc
1621 (c)	—	25.00	45.00	80.00	160	—

KM# 257 24 KREUZER (Vierundzwanziger)
Silver **Ruler:** Georg Rudolf **Obv:** Armored bust to left, small imperial orb at top, '24' below **Obv. Legend:** D. G. GEO. RVD. DVX. - SIL. LIG. BR. ET. GOL. **Rev:** Crowned Spanish shield of 4-fold arms in baroque frame, date at end of legend **Rev. Legend:** MON. NOV. ARGENT. **Mint:** Liegnitz **Note:** Kipper coinage. Ref. F/S#1687.

Date	Mintage	VG	F	VF	XF	Unc
1621 (c)	—	—	—	—	—	—

KM# 258 24 KREUZER (Vierundzwanziger)
Silver **Ruler:** Georg Rudolf **Obv:** Armored bust to right, small imperial orb at top in margin **Obv. Legend:** D. G. GEO. RVD. DVX. SIL. LIG. BR. ET. GOL. **Rev:** Ornately shaped 4-fold arms, crown above, date at end of legend **Rev. Legend:** MON. NOV. ARGENT. **Mint:** Liegnitz **Note:** Kipper coinage. Ref. F/S#1689, 1693.

Date	Mintage	VG	F	VF	XF	Unc
16Z1 (e)	—	45.00	75.00	120	210	—
16ZZ (e)	—	45.00	75.00	120	210	—

KM# 259 24 KREUZER (Vierundzwanziger)
Silver **Ruler:** Georg Rudolf **Obv:** Armored bust right in circle, small imperial orb at top in margin **Obv. Legend:** D. G. GEO. RVD. DVX. SIL. LIG. BR. ET. GOL. **Rev:** Ornately shaped 4-fold arms, crown above, date at end of legend **Rev. Legend:** MON. NOV. ARGENT. **Note:** Kipper coinage. Ref: F/S#1621-22, 1636.

Date	Mintage	VG	F	VF	XF	Unc
16Z1	—	45.00	75.00	120	210	—
16Z1 AK	—	45.00	75.00	120	210	—
1622	—	45.00	75.00	120	210	—

KM# 260 24 KREUZER (Vierundzwanziger)
Silver **Ruler:** Georg Rudolf **Obv:** Armored bust right in circle, small imperial orb at top in margin **Obv. Legend:** D. G. GEO. RVD. DVX. SIL. LIG. BR. ET. GOL. **Rev:** Crowned squarish 4-fold arms in baroque frame, date at end of legend **Rev. Legend:** MON. NOV. ARGENT. **Note:** Kipper coinage. Ref: F/S#1623.

Date	Mintage	VG	F	VF	XF	Unc
1621	—	25.00	45.00	90.00	180	—

KM# 261 24 KREUZER (Vierundzwanziger)
Silver **Ruler:** Georg Rudolf **Obv:** Large armored bust right in circle, small imperial orb at top in margin **Obv. Legend:** D. G. GEO. RVD. DVX. SIL. LIG. BR. ET. GOL. **Rev:** Crowned squarish 4-fold arms in baroque frame, date at end of legend **Rev. Legend:** MON. NOV. ARGENT. **Note:** Kipper coinage. Ref: F/S#1624.

Date	Mintage	VG	F	VF	XF	Unc
1621	—	24.00	45.00	90.00	180	—

KM# 262 24 KREUZER (Vierundzwanziger)
Silver **Ruler:** Georg Rudolf **Obv:** Armored 1/2-length figure right, small imperial orb at top, '24' at bottom **Obv. Legend:** D. G. GEO. RVD. DVC. - SIL. LIG. ET. BRIG. **Rev:** Squarish 4-fold arms in baroque frame, crown above in margin, date at end of legend **Rev. Legend:** MONETA. NOVA. ARGENTEA. **Note:** Kipper coinage. Ref: F/S#1625, 1633.

Date	Mintage	VG	F	VF	XF	Unc
1621	—	35.00	60.00	95.00	185	—
1622	—	35.00	60.00	95.00	185	—

KM# 241 24 KREUZER (Vierundzwanziger)
Silver **Ruler:** Johann Christian and Georg Rudolph **Obv:** Crowned and ornamented 4-fold arms **Obv. Legend:** D. G. IO. CHRIST. ET GEOR. RVD. FRATR. **Rev:** Silesian eagle, date in margin at top, value '24' at bottom **Rev. Legend:** DVC. SIL. LIGNI. - ET. BREGENSIS. **Note:** Kipper coinage. Ref. F/S#1554.

Date	Mintage	VG	F	VF	XF	Unc
1621 HR	—	25.00	50.00	100	200	—

KM# 242 24 KREUZER (Vierundzwanziger)
Silver **Ruler:** Johann Christian **Obv:** Crowned 4-fold arms in oval baroque frame **Obv. Legend:** D. G. IO. CHR. DVC. SIL. LIG. ET. BR. **Rev:** Silesian eagle in circle, date in margin at top, value '24' at bottom **Rev. Legend:** MO. NO. ARG - ENT. OLAU. **Mint:** Ohlau **Note:** Kipper coinage. Ref. F/S#1565.

Date	Mintage	VG	F	VF	XF	Unc
1621 HR	—	25.00	50.00	100	200	—

KM# 243 24 KREUZER (Vierundzwanziger)
Silver **Ruler:** Johann Christian **Obv:** Crowned 4-fold arms in squarish baroque frame **Obv. Legend:** D. G. IO. CHR. DVC. SIL. LIG. ET. BR. **Rev:** Silesian eagle in circle, date in margin at top, value '24' at bottom **Rev. Legend:** MO. NO. ARG - ENT. OLAU. **Mint:** Ohlau **Note:** Kipper coinage. Ref. F/S#1566.

Date	Mintage	VG	F	VF	XF	Unc
1621 HR	—	—	—	—	—	—

KM# 244 24 KREUZER (Vierundzwanziger)
Silver **Ruler:** Johann Christian **Obv:** Bust right, small imperial orb at top in margin **Obv. Legend:** D. G. IO. CHRIST. D(U)(V)X. SIL. LIG(E). (&)(ET). B(R)(IGEN). **Rev:** 4-fold arms in oval baroque frame, large crown above in margin, date at end of legend, value '24' at bottom **Rev. Legend:** MO(N). NO(VA). ARG - ENT. OLA(VU). **Mint:** Ohlau **Note:** Kipper coinage. Ref. F/S#1567, 1574-76, 1579-80. Varieties exist.

Date	Mintage	VG	F	VF	XF	Unc
1621 HR	—	35.00	60.00	85.00	160	—
(1)622 HR	—	35.00	60.00	85.00	160	—
1622	—	35.00	60.00	85.00	160	—
(1)623 HR	—	65.00	100	145	265	—
1623	—	35.00	60.00	85.00	265	—

KM# 245 24 KREUZER (Vierundzwanziger)
Silver **Ruler:** Johann Christian **Obv:** Bust right, small imperial orb at top in margin **Obv. Legend:** D. G. IO. CHRIST. DV. SIL. LIG. E. B. **Rev:** 4-fold arms in oval baroque frame, value 'Z4' at bottom, date at end of legend **Rev. Legend:** MO. NO. ARGE. - CRVCIB. **Mint:** Kreuzburg **Note:** Kipper coinage. Ref. F/S#1591-92.

Date	Mintage	VG	F	VF	XF	Unc
(1)621 (fs)	—	25.00	45.00	80.00	160	—
(1)621 FS	—	25.00	45.00	80.00	160	—

KM# 246 24 KREUZER (Vierundzwanziger)
Silver **Ruler:** Johann Christian **Obv:** Bust right, small imperial orb at top in margin **Obv. Legend:** D. G. IO. CHRISTI. DV. SIL. LIG. E. B. **Rev:** Silesian eagle in circle, 'Z4' below in margin, date at end of legend **Rev. Legend:** MONE. NO. ARGE. - CRVCIBVR. **Mint:** Kreuzburg **Note:** Kipper coinage. Ref. F/S#1593-94.

Date	Mintage	VG	F	VF	XF	Unc
16Z1	—	25.00	45.00	80.00	160	—
16Z1 FS	—	25.00	45.00	80.00	160	—

KM# 247 24 KREUZER (Vierundzwanziger)
Silver **Ruler:** Johann Christian **Obv:** Small armored bust right, small imperial orb at top in margin **Obv. Legend:** D. G. IOHAN. CHRIST. DVX. SIL. LIG. ET. BR. **Rev:** Silesian eagle in circle, 'Z4' below in margin, date at end of legend **Rev. Legend:** MONE. NO. ARGE. - CRVCIBVR. **Mint:** Kreuzburg **Note:** Kipper coinage. Ref. F/S#1595.

Date	Mintage	VG	F	VF	XF	Unc
16Z1	—	25.00	45.00	80.00	160	—

KM# 366 24 KREUZER (Vierundzwanziger)
Silver **Ruler:** Georg Rudolf **Obv:** Armored bust to right, small imperial orb at top, 'Z4' below **Obv. Legend:** D. G. GEO. RVD. DVX. - SI. LIG. & BREG. **Rev:** Crowned ornate 4-fold arms, date at end of legend where present **Rev. Legend:** MONETA. NOUA. ARGENTEA. **Note:** Kipper coinage. Ref: F/S#1658, 1617.

Date	Mintage	VG	F	VF	XF	Unc
ND(1621-23)	—	40.00	65.00	100	200	—
16Z3	—	40.00	65.00	100	200	—

KM# 327 24 KREUZER (Vierundzwanziger)
Silver **Ruler:** Johann Christian **Obv:** Large armored bust right, small imperial orb at top in margin **Obv. Legend:** D. G. IOHAN. CHRIST. DVX. SIL. LIG. ET. BR. **Rev:** Squarish 4-fold arms in baroque frame, crown above in margin, value 'Z4' below in margin, date at end of legend **Rev. Legend:** MO. NO. ARGENT - CRVCIBVR. **Mint:** Kreuzburg **Note:** Kipper coinage. Ref. F/S#1600.

Date	Mintage	VG	F	VF	XF	Unc
1622 BH	—	25.00	45.00	80.00	160	—

KM# 328 24 KREUZER (Vierundzwanziger)
Silver **Ruler:** Johann Christian **Obv:** Armored and mantled bust right, small imperial orb at top in margin **Obv. Legend:** D. G. IOHAN. CHRIST. DVX. SIL. LIG. ET. BR. **Rev:** Squarish 4-fold arms in baroque frame, crown above in margin, value 'Z4' below in margin, date at end of legend **Rev. Legend:** MO. NO. ARGENT - CRVCIBVR. **Mint:** Kreuzburg **Note:** Kipper coinage. Ref. F/S#1601-1601a.

Date	Mintage	VG	F	VF	XF	Unc
1622	—	32.00	60.00	95.00	185	—
1622 FS	—	32.00	60.00	95.00	185	—

KM# 322 24 KREUZER (Vierundzwanziger)
Silver **Ruler:** Johann Christian **Obv:** Bust right, small imperial orb at top in margin **Obv. Legend:** D. G. IO. CHRIST. DVX. SIL. LIG. ET. BR. **Rev:** 4-fold arms in oval baroque frame, large crown above in margin, date at end of legend **Rev. Legend:** MON. NOVA. ARGENT. OLAV. **Mint:** Ohlau **Note:** Kipper coinage. Ref. F/S#1568.

Date	Mintage	VG	F	VF	XF	Unc
1622 HR	—	25.00	45.00	80.00	160	—

KM# 323 24 KREUZER (Vierundzwanziger)
Silver **Ruler:** Johann Christian **Obv:** Bust right, small imperial orb at top in margin **Obv. Legend:** D. G. IO. CHRIST. DUX. SIL. LIG. & BR. **Rev:** 4-fold arms in squarish baroque frame, large crown above in margin, date at end of legend, value '24' at bottom **Rev. Legend:** MON. NOVA. ARG - ENT. OLAV. **Mint:** Ohlau **Note:** Kipper coinage. Ref. F/S#1573.

Date	Mintage	VG	F	VF	XF	Unc
1622 HR	—	—	—	—	—	—

KM# 324 24 KREUZER (Vierundzwanziger)
Silver **Ruler:** Johann Christian **Obv:** Bust right, small imperial orb at top in margin **Obv. Legend:** D. G. IO. CHRIST. DUX. SIL. LIG. ET. BR. **Rev:** 4-fold arms in oval baroque frame, large crown above in margin, date at end of legend, value '24' at bottom **Rev. Legend:** MON. NO(VA). ARG - ENT. BREG. **Mint:** Brieg **Note:** Kipper coinage. Ref. F/S#1583.

Date	Mintage	VG	F	VF	XF	Unc
1622 BH	—	25.00	45.00	80.00	160	—

KM# 325 24 KREUZER (Vierundzwanziger)
Silver **Ruler:** Johann Christian **Obv:** Bust right, small imperial orb at top in margin **Obv. Legend:** D. G. IO. CHRIST. DUX. SIL. LIG. ET. BR. **Rev:** 4-fold arms in oval baroque frame, large crown above in margin, date at end of legend, value '24' at bottom **Rev. Legend:** MON. NO(VA). ARG - ENT. BREG. **Mint:** Brieg **Note:** Kipper coinage. Ref. F/S#1584. Klippe.

Date	Mintage	VG	F	VF	XF	Unc
1622 BH	—	—	—	—	—	—

KM# 326 24 KREUZER (Vierundzwanziger)
Silver **Ruler:** Johann Christian **Obv:** Bust right, small imperial orb at top in margin **Obv. Legend:** D. G. IO. CHRIST. DUX. SIL. LIG. & BR. **Rev:** 4-fold arms in squarish baroque frame, large crown above in margin, date at end of legend, value '24' at bottom **Rev. Legend:** MON. NOVA. ARG - ENT. BREG. **Mint:** Brieg **Note:** Kipper coinage. Ref. F/S#1585-86.

Date	Mintage	VG	F	VF	XF	Unc
1622	—	25.00	45.00	80.00	160	—
1622 BH	—	25.00	45.00	80.00	160	—

KM# 329 24 KREUZER (Vierundzwanziger)
Silver **Ruler:** Georg Rudolf **Obv:** Large bust right, small imperial orb at top, 'Z4' below **Obv. Legend:** D. G. GEO. RUD. DUX. - SIL. LIG. BR. & GOL. **Rev:** Crowned Spanish shield of 4-fold arms in baroque frame, date at end of legend **Rev. Legend:** MONE. NOUA. ARGENT. **Note:** Kipper coinage. Ref: F/S#1634.

Date	Mintage	VG	F	VF	XF	Unc
1622	—	20.00	35.00	65.00	130	—

KM# 330 24 KREUZER (Vierundzwanziger)
Silver **Ruler:** Georg Rudolf **Obv:** Large bust right, small imperial orb at top, 'Z4' below **Obv. Legend:** D. G. GEO. RVD. D - SIL. LIG. ET. BR. **Rev:** Crowned Spanish shield of 4-fold arms in baroque frame, date at end of legend **Rev. Legend:** MONETA. NOVA. ARGENT. **Note:** Kipper coinage. Ref: F/S#1635.

Date	Mintage	VG	F	VF	XF	Unc
1622	—	20.00	40.00	70.00	145	—

KM# 331 24 KREUZER (Vierundzwanziger)
Silver **Ruler:** Georg Rudolf **Obv:** Large bust right, small imperial orb at top, 'Z4' below **Obv. Legend:** D. G. GEO. RVD. D. - SIL. LIG. ET. BR. **Rev:** Crowned 4-fold arms in oval baroque frame, date at end of legend **Rev. Legend:** MONETA. NOVA. ARGENT. **Note:** Kipper coinage. Ref: F/S#1637.

Date	Mintage	VG	F	VF	XF	Unc
1622	—	20.00	40.00	70.00	145	—

KM# 332 24 KREUZER (Vierundzwanziger)
Silver **Ruler:** Georg Rudolf **Obv:** Armored bust to left, small imperial orb at top, '24' below **Obv. Legend:** D. G. GEO. RVD. DVX. - SIL. LIG. BR. ET. G. **Rev:** Crowned 4-fold arms in oval baroque frame, date at end of legend **Rev. Legend:** MONETA. NOVA. ARGENT. **Note:** Kipper coinage. Ref: F/S#1638.

Date	Mintage	VG	F	VF	XF	Unc
1622	—	20.00	40.00	70.00	145	—

KM# 333 24 KREUZER (Vierundzwanziger)
Silver **Ruler:** Georg Rudolf **Obv:** Armored bust right, small imperial orb at top, '24' below **Obv. Legend:** D. G. GEO. RVD. DVX. - SIL. LIG. BR. ET. GOLT. **Rev:** Crowned 4-fold arms in oval baroque frame, date at end of legend **Rev. Legend:** MONETA. NOVA. ARGENT. **Note:** Kipper coinage. Ref: F/S#1639.

Date	Mintage	VG	F	VF	XF	Unc
1622	—	20.00	40.00	70.00	145	—

KM# 334 24 KREUZER (Vierundzwanziger)
Silver **Ruler:** Georg Rudolf **Obv:** Armored bust to right, small imperial orb at top, '24' below **Obv. Legend:** D. G. GEO. RVD. DVX. - SIL. LIG. BR. ET. G. **Rev:** Squarish 4-fold arms in baroque frame, crown above in margin, date at end of legend **Rev. Legend:** MONETA. NOVA. ARGENTEA. **Note:** Kipper coinage. Ref: F/S#1640.

Date	Mintage	VG	F	VF	XF	Unc
1622	—	20.00	35.00	65.00	130	—

KM# 264 48 KREUZER (Achtundvierziger)
Silver **Ruler:** Johann Christian and Georg Rudolph **Obv:** Crowned and ornamented 4-fold arms **Obv. Legend:** D. G. IO. CHRIST. ET GEOR. RVD. FRATR. **Rev:** Silesian eagle, date in margin at top, value '48' at bottom **Rev. Legend:** DVC. SIL. LIGNI. - ET. BREGENSIS. **Note:** Kipper coinage. Ref: F/S#1553.

Date	Mintage	VG	F	VF	XF	Unc
16Z1 HR	—	—	—	—	—	—

KM# 336 1/8 THALER
Silver **Ruler:** Johann Christian and Georg Rudolph **Subject:** Death of Georg Rudolph's Wife, Sophia Elisabeth von Anhalt-Dessau **Obv:** Crowned 9-fold arms in baroque frame divides date **Rev:** 7-line inscription with R. N. date **Rev. Inscription:** SOPHIA / ELISABETHA / PRINC. ANH. / DVC. LIG. BREG / OB / A. M. DCXXII / IX. FEB. **Note:** Kipper coinage. Ref. F/S#1656.

Date	Mintage	VG	F	VF	XF	Unc
16ZZ	—	—	—	—	—	—

KM# 397 1/8 THALER
Silver **Ruler:** Johann Christian and Georg Rudolph **Obv:** Facing bust, turned slightly to right **Obv. Legend:** D.G. GEORG. RUDOLPH. DUX. SIL. LIG. BREG & GOLDBE. **Rev:** 6-line inscription with dates **Rev. Legend:** S. CÆS. MAI. VICAR. REG. SUPR. PRÆF. PER. UTRAM & SIL. **Rev. Inscription:** NATUS / 22. IANUARII / ANNO 1595 / OBIIT 14 / IANUARII / 1653 **Note:** Ref. F/S#1702.

Date	Mintage	VG	F	VF	XF	Unc
1653	—	150	250	350	650	—

KM# 436 1/8 THALER (1/2 Reichsort)
Silver **Ruler:** Johann Christian and Georg Rudolph **Subject:** Death of Sophie Katharina von Münsterberg-Öls, Wife of Georg III **Obv:** Round 4-fold arms with central shield of Münsterberg-Öls, 3 helmets above **Obv. Legend:** SOPHIA CATHARINA DUCISS. SILES. LIGN. BREG. **Rev:** 8-line inscription with dates **Rev. Legend:** PENULTIMAE STIRPE DUC. MONSTERB. OLSN. COMIT. GLAC. **Rev. Inscription:** NATA / A° 1601. D. 2. SEPT. / NUPTA / 1638. D. 22 FEBR. / DENATA / 1659. D. 21 MART / EIN HALB REICHS / ORTH. **Note:** Ref: F/S#1837.

Date	Mintage	VG	F	VF	XF	Unc
1659	—	50.00	95.00	150	300	—

KM# 468 1/8 THALER (1/2 Reichsort)
Silver **Ruler:** Johann Christian and Georg Rudolph **Subject:** Death of Ludwig IV **Obv:** Round 4-fold arms in baroque frame, 3 helmets above **Obv. Legend:** LUDOVICUS. DUX. SILESI?. LIGNIC. BREG. ET. GOLD. **Rev:** 6-line inscription with dates **Rev. Legend:** CONSILIVM IEHOV? STABIT. **Rev. Inscription:** NATUS / A. 1616. D. 19. APR. / DENATUS / A. 1663. D. 24 NOV. / ?TAT. 47. HEBD. / 31. **Note:** Ref: F/S#1889.

Date	Mintage	VG	F	VF	XF	Unc
1663	—	—	—	—	—	—

KM# 472 1/8 THALER (1/2 Reichsort)
Silver **Ruler:** Johann Christian and Georg Rudolph **Subject:** Death of Elisabeth Maria Charlotte von der Pfalz **Obv:** Crowned and ornamented 4-fold arms of Bavaria-Pfalz with central shield of Brieg **Obv. Legend:** MEM. ELISABETH?. CHARLOTT?. PALAT RHEN. **Rev:** 6-line inscription with R. N. date **Rev. Legend:** DUC. SIL. LIGN. BREG. EXEMPL. CASTITAT. **Rev. Inscription:** OBIIT. / MDCLXIV. / M. MAI O. D. XIX / ?T. AN. XXV. / MENS. VI. / D. XXIIX. **Note:** Ref: F/S#1862.

Date	Mintage	VG	F	VF	XF	Unc
1664	—	—	—	—	—	—

KM# 473 1/8 THALER (1/2 Reichsort)
Silver **Ruler:** Johann Christian and Georg Rudolph **Subject:** Death of Georg III **Obv:** Facing long-haired bust **Obv. Legend:** GEORGIUS. III. DUX. SILES. LIGN. BREG. SUPR. CAP. SIL. **Rev:** 6-line inscription with date **Rev. Legend:** DEO. PATRI? ET C?SARI. **Rev. Inscription:** NATUS / A. 1611. D. 4. SEP. / DENATUS / A. 1664. D. 14. IUL. / ?TAT. 5Z. MENS. / X. DIE. X. **Note:** Ref: F/S#1865.

Date	Mintage	VG	F	VF	XF	Unc
1664	—	—	—	—	—	—

KM# 70 1/4 THALER
Silver **Ruler:** Johann Christian and Georg Rudolph **Obv:** Two 1/2-length figures facing each other **Obv. Legend:** D. G. IOAN. CHRIST. ET. GEORG. RVD. FRA. **Rev:** 4-fold arms, 3 ornate helmets above, date at end of legend **Rev. Legend:** DVC. SIL. LIG. - ET. BREG. **Note:** Ref: F/S#1440.

Date	Mintage	VG	F	VF	XF	Unc
(1)609 (d)	—	70.00	110	175	325	—

KM# 123 1/4 THALER
Silver **Ruler:** Johann Christian and Georg Rudolph **Obv:** Draped bust right, legend begins at bottom divided by 2 small shields of arms at left and right **Obv. Legend:** D. G. IO - HANN. CHRISTI. - AN. ET. **Rev:** Draped bust to left divides date, legend begins at upper left, 2 small shields of arms at left and right **Rev. Legend:** GEOR. RVD. FR. D. - SI. LIG. ET. BREG. **Note:** Ref: F/S#1476.

Date	Mintage	VG	F	VF	XF	Unc
1611	—	—	—	—	—	—

KM# 167 1/4 THALER
Silver **Ruler:** Johann Christian and Georg Rudolph **Obv:** Bust right, legend begins at upper left divided by 2 small shields of arms at left and right **Obv. Legend:** D. G. IOH. CHR - ET. GEO. RVD. FR. **Rev:** Bust left, legends ends with date, 2 small shields of arms at left and right **Rev. Legend:** DVX. SIL. LI. - ET. BRE. **Note:** Ref: F/S#1513, 1535, 1552.

Date	Mintage	VG	F	VF	XF	Unc
1617 BH	—	—	—	—	—	—
1619 HR	—	—	—	—	—	—
1621 HR	—	—	—	—	—	—

KM# 188 1/4 THALER
Silver **Ruler:** Johann Christian and Georg Rudolph **Obv:** Bust right, legend begins at upper left, divided by 2 small shields of arms at left and right **Obv. Legend:** D. G. IOH. CHR - ET. GEO. RVD. FR. **Rev:** Bust left, legend ends with date, 2 small shields of arms at left and right **Rev. Legend:** DVX. SIL. LI. - ET. BRE. **Note:** Ref: F/S#1536. Klippe.

Date	Mintage	VG	F	VF	XF	Unc
1619 HR	—	500	750	900	1,550	—

KM# 338 1/4 THALER
Silver **Ruler:** Georg Rudolf **Obv:** Large bust right **Obv. Legend:** D. G. GEORG. RVDOL. DVX. SLESIÆ **Rev:** 4-fold arms, 3 ornate helmets above, date at end of legend **Rev. Legend:** LIGNICE. ET * BREG'. **Note:** Ref: F/S#1631; J/M#124.

Date	Mintage	VG	F	VF	XF	Unc
16ZZ	—	—	—	—	—	—

KM# 339 1/4 THALER
Silver **Ruler:** Georg Rudolf **Obv:** Small bust right, small imperial orb at top **Obv. Legend:** D. G. GEORG. RVDOL. DVX. SILE. LIG. BR. & GOL. **Rev:** 4-fold arms, 3 ornate helmets above, date at end of legend **Rev. Legend:** MONE. NOV. - ARGEN. **Note:** Ref: F/S#1632. Klippe.

Date	Mintage	VG	F	VF	XF	Unc
16ZZ	—	—	—	—	—	—

KM# 340 1/4 THALER
Silver **Ruler:** Georg Rudolf **Subject:** Death of Georg Rudolph's Wife, Sophia Elisabeth von Anhalt-Dessau **Obv:** Ornate 9-fold arms, 3 helmets above divide date **Rev:** 12-line inscription with R.N. dates **Rev. Inscription:** NVM. ARG / IN SEP. / DNAE / SOPHIÆ. ELISABETAE / PRINC. ANHALT. / DVCISS. LIGIO. BREGE. / NATÆ / AN. MDLXXXIX. M. F. / D. X. / MORT. LIG. A. MDCXXII / M. F. D. IX. H. IX. AM / CVSVS. **Note:** Ref: F/S#1655.

Date	Mintage	VG	F	VF	XF	Unc
16ZZ	—	—	—	—	—	—

KM# 372 1/4 THALER
Silver **Ruler:** Georg III, Ludwig IV and Christian **Obv:** 3 facing 1/2-length figures, horizontal line below with arabesques in exergue, small imperial orb at top **Obv. Legend:** D. G. GEORG. LUDOVIC. ET. CHRISTIAN. FRATRES **Rev:** 3 helmets above ornate 4-fold arms, date at end of legend **Rev. Legend:** DUCES. SILESIÆ. LIGN. - ET. BREGENES. **Note:** Ref. F/S#1710, 1719.

Date	Mintage	VG	F	VF	XF	Unc
1651 (pf)-VT	—	125	175	250	—	—
165Z (pf)-VT	—	125	175	250	—	—

KM# 399 1/4 THALER
Silver **Ruler:** Georg III, Ludwig IV and Christian **Obv:** 3 facing armored 1/2-length figures, small imperial orb at top, arabesques in exergue **Obv. Legend:** D. G. GEORGIUS. LUDOVICUS. & CHRISTIANUS. FRATRES. **Rev:** 3 helmets above ornate 4-fold arms, date at end of legend **Rev. Legend:** DUCES. SILESIÆ. LIGNIC - ENSES. ET. BREGENSES. **Note:** Ref. F/S#1726, 1771, 1780. Varieties exist.

Date	Mintage	VG	F	VF	XF	Unc
1653 (pf)	—	—	—	—	—	—
1658 (pf)	—	—	—	—	—	—
1659 (pf)-EW	—	—	—	—	—	—

KM# 438 1/4 THALER (Reichsort)
Silver **Ruler:** Georg III, Ludwig IV and Christian **Subject:** Death of Sophie Katharina von Münsterberg-Öls, Wife of Georg III **Obv:** Round 4-fold arms with central shield of Münsterberg-Öls, 3 helmets above **Obv. Legend:** SOPHIA CATHARINA DUCISS. SILES. LIGN. BREG. **Rev:** 8-line inscription with dates **Rev. Legend:** PENULTIMAE STIRPE DUC. MONSTERB. OLSN. COMIT. GLAC. **Rev. Inscription:** NATA / A° 1601. D. 2. SEPT. / NUPTA / 1638. D. 22. FEBR. / DENATA / 1659. D. 21. MART / EIN REICHS / ORTH. **Note:** Ref. F/S#1836.

Date	Mintage	VG	F	VF	XF	Unc
1659	—	35.00	60.00	115	230	—

KM# 470 1/4 THALER (Reichsort)
Silver **Ruler:** Georg III, Ludwig IV and Christian **Subject:** Death of Ludwig IV **Obv:** Round 4-fold arms in baroque frame, 3 helmets above **Obv. Legend:** LUDOVICUS. DUX. SILESIÆ. LIGNIC. BREG. ET. GOLD. **Rev:** 6-line inscription with dates **Rev. Legend:** CONSILIVM IEHOV Æ STABIT. **Rev. Inscription:** NATUS / A. 1616. D. 19. APR. / DENATUS / A. 1663. D. 24 NOV. / ÆTAT. 47. HEBD. / 31. **Note:** Ref. F/S#1888.

Date	Mintage	VG	F	VF	XF	Unc
1663	—	—	—	—	—	—

KM# 475 1/4 THALER (Reichsort)
Silver **Ruler:** Georg III, Ludwig IV and Christian **Subject:** Death of Elisabeth Maria Charlotte von der Pfalz **Obv:** Crowned and ornamented 4-fold arms of Bavaria-Pfalz with central shield of Brieg **Obv. Legend:** MEM. ELISABETHÆ. MARIÆ. CHARLOTTÆ. PALAT RHEN. **Rev:** 6-line inscription with R.N. date **Rev. Legend:** DUC. SIL. LIGN. BREG. EXEMPL. CASTITAT. **Rev. Inscription:** OBIIT. / MDCLXIV. / M. MAI O. D. XIX / ÆT. AN. XXV. / MENS. VI. / D. XXIIX. **Note:** Ref. F/S#1861.

Date	Mintage	VG	F	VF	XF	Unc
1664	—	—	—	—	—	—

KM# 476 1/4 THALER (Reichsort)
Silver **Ruler:** Georg III, Ludwig IV and Christian **Subject:** Death of Georg III **Obv:** Facing long-haired bust **Obv. Legend:** GEORGIUS. III. DUX. SILES. LIGN. BREG. SUPR. CAP. SIL. **Rev:** 6-line inscription with date **Rev. Legend:** DEO. PATRIÆ ET CÆSARI. **Rev. Inscription:** NATUSA / A. 1611. D. 4. SEP. / DENATUS / A. 1664. D. 14. IUL. / ÆTAT. 5Z. MENS. / X. DIE. X. **Note:** Ref. F/S#1864.

Date	Mintage	VG	F	VF	XF	Unc
1664	—	80.00	125	200	360	—

KM# 486 1/4 THALER (Reichsort)
Silver **Ruler:** Christian zu Ohlau **Obv:** Armored and mantled bust to right **Obv. Legend:** CHRISTIANVS. D. G. DVX. SILESIÆ. LIGNICE. **Rev:** Silesian eagle, crown above divides date in margin, mintmaster's initials in oval at bottom **Rev. Legend:** BREGENSIS. ET. ET. - WOLAVIENSIS. **Note:** Ref. F/S#1926.

Date	Mintage	VG	F	VF	XF	Unc
1666 CBS	—	—	—	—	—	—

KM# 504 1/4 THALER (Reichsort)
Silver **Ruler:** Christian zu Ohlau **Subject:** Death of Christian **Obv:** Armored and mantled bust right **Obv. Legend:** CONSTANTER. ET. SINCERE. **Rev:** 6-line inscription with R. N. dates, arabesques above and below **Rev. Legend:** CHRISTIANVS. D. B. DVX. SIL. LIG. BREG. ET. WOL. **Rev. Inscription:** NAT. OLAV. / A. C. MDCXIIX. / XIX. APRIL / DENAT. LIGNICI. / A. C. MDCLXXII / XXIX. FEBR. **Note:** Ref. F/S#1948.

Date	Mintage	VG	F	VF	XF	Unc
1672	—	90.00	150	275	575	—

KM# 529 1/4 THALER (Reichsort)
Silver **Ruler:** Christian zu Ohlau **Obv:** Armored and mantled bust right **Obv. Legend:** GEORG. WILH. D. G. DVX. SILE. LIGN. BREG. & WOL. **Rev:** 10-line inscription with R.N. dates **Rev. Inscription:** PIASTE? / REG. FAM. ULTIM / VIRTUTI. INT> PRI. MOS / ANIMAM. / D. XXIX. SEPT. MDCLX / ACCEPT AM / DEO. ITA. IUBENTI / D XXI. NOV. MDCLXXV / ILLACHYM. SILES / REDDIDIT. **Note:** Ref. F/S#1975.

Date	Mintage	VG	F	VF	XF	Unc
MDCLXXV (1675)	—	90.00	150	275	575	—

KM# 10 1/2 THALER
Silver **Ruler:** Friedrich II **Subject:** Death of Joachim Friedrich **Obv:** Armored and collared bust right **Obv. Legend:** ✠ MEMOR. IOACH. FRID. DVCIS. SILES. LEGN. BREGENSIS. **Rev:** 10-line inscription with R. N. dates **Rev. Inscription:** ✠ / DEO. OPT. / MAX. IN. ?TERN. / VIVENS. SVM. PATR. / LVCIV. PLACIDE. OBI / IT. AN. M.D.C II. M. MA / RT. XX. V. HORA. P. MER / VI. CVM. VIRISSET / AN. LI. MEN. S. V / DIES. XXVI. **Note:** Ref. F/S#1386.

Date	Mintage	VG	F	VF	XF	Unc
MDCII (1602)	—	100	175	275	550	—

KM# 11 1/2 THALER
Silver **Ruler:** Friedrich II **Obv:** Armored and collared bust to right **Obv. Legend:** ✠ MEMOR. IOACH. FRID. DVCIS. SILES. LEGN. BREGENSIS. **Rev:** 10-line inscription with R. N. dates **Rev. Inscription:** ✠ / DEO. OPT. / MAX. IN. ?TERN. / VIVENS. SVM. PATR. / LVCIV. PLACIDE. OBI / IT. AN. M.D.CII. M. MA / RT. XX. V. HORA. P. MER / VI. CVM. VIRISSET / AN. LI. MEN. S. V / DIES. XXVI. **Note:** Ref. F/S#1387. Klippe.

Date	Mintage	VG	F	VF	XF	Unc
MDCII (1602)	—	—	—	—	—	—

KM# 12 1/2 THALER
Silver **Ruler:** Friedrich II **Obv:** Armored and collared bust right **Obv. Legend:** ✠ MEMOR. IOACH. FRID. DVCIS. SILES. LEGN. BREGENSIS. **Rev:** 8-line inscription with R.N. date, circular marginal inscription. **Rev. Legend:** ✠ DEO. OPT. MAX. IN. ?TERN. VIVENs. SVM. PATR. **Rev. Inscription:** OBIIT. AN / NO. M.D. C II. / M. MART. XXV. / HORA. P. MER. VI / CVM. / VIXISSMI. / AN. LI. MENS. V / DIES. XXVI. / ✠ **Note:** Ref. F/S#1389.

Date	Mintage	VG	F	VF	XF	Unc
MDCII (1602)	—	75.00	115	150	300	—

KM# 40 1/2 THALER
Silver **Ruler:** Johann Christian and Georg Rudolph **Subject:** Death of Joachim Friedrich's widow, Ann Maria von Anhalt **Obv:** Crowned 4-fold arms **Obv. Legend:** IO. CHR. ET. GE. RVD. FR. DVC. SL. LIG. ET. BREG. **Rev:** Crowned shield of 8-fold arms with central shield of Anhalt, double marginal legends with R. N. date **Rev. Legend:** Outer leg: MEM. IL. MAT. ANN?. MAR. PR. ANHAL. DVCI. SIL. LEG. BREG. QV?.; Inner leg: PIA. OBIIT. M. NOV. DIE. XIV. M.D.C.V. F.F. **Note:** Ref. F/S#1396.

Date	Mintage	VG	F	VF	XF	Unc
MDCV (1605)	—	—	—	—	—	—

KM# 57 1/2 THALER
Silver **Ruler:** Johann Christian and Georg Rudolph **Obv:** 2 busts facing each other, date below **Obv. Legend:** D. G. IOHAN. CHRIST. ET. GEOR. RVD. FRA. **Rev:** 4-fold arms, 3 ornate helmets above **Rev. Legend:** DVC. SIL. LIG. - ET. BREGEN. **Note:** Ref. F/S#1417.

Date	Mintage	VG	F	VF	XF	Unc
(1)607	—	—	—	—	—	—

KM# 72 1/2 THALER
Silver **Ruler:** Johann Christian and Georg Rudolph **Obv:** Two 1/2-length figures facing each other **Obv. Legend:** D. G. IOAN. CHRIST. ET. GEORG. RVD. FRA. **Rev:** 4-fold arms, 3 ornate helmets above, date at end of legend **Rev. Legend:** DVC. SIL. LIG. - ET. BREG. **Note:** Ref. F/S#1439, 1458.

Date	Mintage	VG	F	VF	XF	Unc
(1)609 (d)	—	—	—	—	—	—
(1)610 (d)	—	—	—	—	—	—

KM# 93 1/2 THALER
Silver **Ruler:** Johann Christian and Georg Rudolph **Obv:** Two 1/2-length figures facing each other behind flat surface with arabesques in exergue **Obv. Legend:** D. G. IOHAN. CHRIST. ET. GEORG. RVD. FRA. **Rev:** 4-fold arms, 3 ornate helmets above, date at end of legend **Rev. Legend:** DVC. SIL. LIG. - ET. BREG. **Note:** Ref. F/S#1457.

Date	Mintage	VG	F	VF	XF	Unc
(1)610 (d)	—	—	—	—	—	—

KM# 125 1/2 THALER
Silver **Ruler:** Johann Christian and Georg Rudolph **Obv:** Draped bust to right, legend begins at bottom divided by 2 small shields of arms at left and right **Obv. Legend:** D. G. IO - HANN. CHRISTI. - AN. ET. **Rev:** Draped bust to left divides date, legend begins at upper left, 2 small shields of arms at left and right **Rev. Legend:** GEOR. RVD. FR. D. - SI. LIG. ET. BREG. **Note:** Ref. F/S#1474.

Date	Mintage	VG	F	VF	XF	Unc
1611	—	—	—	—	—	—

KM# 126 1/2 THALER
Silver **Ruler:** Johann Christian and Georg Rudolph **Obv:** Draped bust to right, legend begins at bottom **Obv. Legend:** D. G. IO - HANN. CHRISTI. - AN. ET. **Rev:** Draped bust to left divides date, legend begins at upper left, 2 small shields of arms at left and right **Rev. Legend:** GEOR. RVD. FR. D. - SI. LIG. ET. BREG. **Note:** Ref. F/S#1475. Klippe.

Date	Mintage	VG	F	VF	XF	Unc
1611	—	—	—	—	—	—

KM# 152 1/2 THALER
Silver **Ruler:** Johann Christian and Georg Rudolph **Obv:** Bust right, legend begins at upper left, divided by 2 small shields of arms at left and right **Obv. Legend:** D. G. IO. CHR. ET. G - EO. RVD. DVX. SI. L. B. **Rev:** Bust left, legend ends with date, 2 small shields of arms at left and right **Rev. Legend:** MON. NOV. ARGE. - REICHST. **Mint:** Reichenstein **Note:** Ref. F/S#1499; S/Sch#128. Klippe.

Date	Mintage	VG	F	VF	XF	Unc
1614	—	900	1,750	—	—	—
1615	—	900	1,750	—	—	—
1616	—	900	1,750	—	—	—

KM# 190 1/2 THALER
Silver **Ruler:** Johann Christian and Georg Rudolph **Obv:** Bust right, legend begins at upper left, divided by 2 small shields of arms at tlet right **Obv. Legend:** D. G. IOHA. CHRI. ET. - GEORG. RVD. FRA. **Rev:** Bust left, legend ends with date, 2 small shields of arms at left and right **Rev. Legend:** DVX. SIL. LIGNI. ET. - BREGEN. **Mint:** Reichenstein **Note:** Ref. F/S#1533, 1543.

Date	Mintage	VG	F	VF	XF	Unc
1619 HR	—	—	—	—	—	—
1620 HR	—	—	—	—	—	—

KM# 191 1/2 THALER
Silver **Ruler:** Johann Christian and Georg Rudolph **Obv:** Bust right, legend begins at upper left **Obv. Legend:** D. G. IOHA. CHRI. ET. - GEORG. RVD. FRA. **Rev:** Bust left, legend ends with date, 2 small shields of arms at left and right **Rev. Legend:** DVX. SIL. LIGNI. ET. - BREGEN. **Mint:** Reichenstein **Note:** Ref. F/S#1534, 1544. Klippe.

Date	Mintage	VG	F	VF	XF	Unc
1619 HR	—	—	—	—	—	—
1620 HR	—	—	—	—	—	—

KM# 343 1/2 THALER
Silver **Ruler:** Johann Christian **Obv:** Bust right, small imperial orb at top in margin **Obv. Legend:** D. G. IOHAN. CHRIST. DVX. SIL. LIG. ET. B. **Rev:** 4-fold arms, 3 helmets above, date at end of legend **Rev. Legend:** MONETA. NOVA. CRVCIBVRGENSIS **Mint:** Kreuzburg **Note:** Ref. F/S#1599.

Date	Mintage	VG	F	VF	XF	Unc
1622	—	—	—	—	—	—

KM# 374 1/2 THALER
Silver **Ruler:** Georg III, Ludwig IV and Christian **Obv:** 3 facing 1/2-length figures, horizontal line below with arabesques in exergue, small imperial orb at top **Obv. Legend:** D. G. GEORG. LUDOVIC. ET. CHRISTIAN. FRATRES. **Rev:** 3 helmets above ornate 4-fold arms, date at end of legend **Rev. Legend:** DUCES. SILESI?. LIGN. - ET. BREGENES. **Mint:** Kreuzburg **Note:** Ref. F/S#1709, 1717; J/M#129.

Date	Mintage	VG	F	VF	XF	Unc
1651 (pf)-VT	—	125	175	250	475	—
165Z (pf)-VT	—	125	175	250	475	—
165Z/1 (pf)-VT	—	125	175	250	475	—

KM# 487 1/2 THALER
Silver **Ruler:** Georg III, Ludwig IV and Christian **Obv:** 3 facing armored 1/2-length figures, small imperial orb at top, arabesques in exergue **Obv. Legend:** D. G. GEORGIUS. LUDOVICUS. & CHRISTIANUS. FRATRES. **Rev:** 3 helmets above ornate 4-fold arms, date at end of legend **Rev. Legend:** DUCES. SILESIÆ. LIGNIC - ENSES. ET. BREGENSES. **Mint:** Kreuzburg **Note:** Ref. F/S#1750, 1770, 1779. Varieties exist.

Date	Mintage	VG	F	VF	XF	Unc
1656 ;(pf)	—	—	—	—	—	—
1658 (pf)	—	—	—	—	—	—
1659 (pf)-EW	—	—	—	—	—	—

KM# 488 1/2 THALER
Silver **Ruler:** Christian zu Ohlau **Obv:** Armored and mantled bust to right **Obv. Legend:** CHRISTIANVS. D. G. DVX. SILESIÆ. LIGNICE. **Rev:** Silesian eagle, crown above divides date in margin, mintmaster's initials in oval at bottom **Rev. Legend:** BREGENSIS. ET. - WOLAVIENSIS. **Mint:** Kreuzburg **Note:** Ref. F/S#1925, 1942.

Date	Mintage	VG	F	VF	XF	Unc
1666 GFH/CBS	—	375	550	750	1,150	—
1671 CBS	—	375	550	750	1,150	—

KM# 506 1/2 THALER
Silver **Ruler:** Georg Wilhelm **Subject:** Death of Christian **Obv:** Armored and mantled bust to right **Obv. Legend:** CONSTANTER. ET. SINCERE. **Rev:** 6-line inscription with Roman numeral dates, arabesques above and below **Rev. Legend:** CHRISTIANVS. D.B. DVX. SIL. LIG. BREG. ET. WOL. **Rev. Inscription:** NAT. OLAV. / A.C. MDCXIIX. / XIX. APRIL / DENAT. LIGNICI. / A.C. MDCLXXII / XXIX. FEBR. **Note:** Ref. F/S#1947.

Date	Mintage	VG	F	VF	XF	Unc
1672	—	—	—	—	—	—

KM# 531 1/2 THALER
Silver **Ruler:** Georg Wilhelm **Obv:** Armored bust to right **Obv. Legend:** GEORGIVS. WILHELM. D. G. DVX. SILESI. **Rev:** Silesian eagle, crown above divides date in margin at top **Rev. Legend:** LIGNIC. BREGENS. ET. WOLAVIENS. **Note:** Ref. F/S#1968.

Date	Mintage	VG	F	VF	XF	Unc
1675 CBS	—	—	—	—	—	—

KM# 532 1/2 THALER
Silver **Subject:** Death of Georg Wilhelm **Obv:** Mantled bust to right **Obv. Legend:** GEORG. WILHELM. D.G. DVX. SILESIÆ. **Rev:** 10-line inscription with dates **Rev. Inscription:** PIASTEÆ / REG. FAM. ULTIM. / VIRTUTE. PRIMUS. / ANIMAM. / DIE. 20. SEPTEMB. 1660. / ACCEPTAM / DEO. ITA. IUBENTI. / D. 21. NOVEMB. 1675 / ILLACHRYM. SILES. / REDDIDIT. **Note:** Ref. F/S#1974.

Date	Mintage	VG	F	VF	XF	Unc
1675 SK	—	65.00	100	150	300	—

KM# 14 THALER
Silver **Ruler:** Joachim Friedrich zu Liegnitz **Obv:** Armored bust with high collar to right **Obv. Legend:** IOACH. FRID. HERZ. I. SCHL. Z. L. V. B. T. Z. M. **Rev:** Bust right of Anna Marie von Anhalt wearing ruffed collar and small cap, date at top **Rev. Legend:** A. MARIA. G. F. Z. AN. HERZ. I. SCHL. Z. L. V. B. **Note:** Dav. #7705. Ref. F/S#1384.

Date	Mintage	VG	F	VF	XF	Unc
160Z Rare	—	—	—	—	—	—

KM# 15 THALER
Silver **Subject:** Death of Joachim Friedrich **Obv:** Armored and collared bust to right **Obv. Legend:** ✠ MEMOR. IOACH. FRID. DVCIS. SILES. LEGN. BREGENSIS **Rev:** 10-line inscription with Roman numeral dates **Rev. Inscription:** ✠ / DEO. OPT. / MAX. IN. ÆTERN. / VIVENS. SVM. PATR. / LVCIV. PLACIDE. OBI / IT. AN. M.D.C II. M. MA / RT. XX. V. HORA. P. MER / VI. CVM. VIRISSET / AN. LI. MEN. S.V / DIES. XXVI. **Note:** Ref. F/S#1388. Struck on thick flan from 1/2 Thaler dies, KM#10.

Date	Mintage	VG	F	VF	XF	Unc
MDCII (1602) Rare	—	—	—	—	—	—

KM# 42 THALER
Silver **Ruler:** Johann Christian and Georg Rudolph **Subject:** Death of Anna Maria von Anhalt, Widow of Joachim Friedrich **Obv:** Crowned 4-fold arms **Obv. Legend:** IO. CHR. ET. GE. RVD. FR. DVC. SL. LIG. ET. BREG. **Rev:** Crowned shield of 8-fold arms within central shield of Anhalt, double marginal legends with Roman numeral date **Rev. Legend:** Outer leg: MEM. IL. MAT. ANNÆ. MAR. PR. ANHAL. DVCI. SIL. LEG. BREG. QVÆ. Inner leg: PIA. OBIIT. M. NOV. DIE. XIV. M.D.C.V.F.F. **Note:** Dav. #7706. Ref. F/S#1395. Struck on thick flan from 1/2 Thaler dies, KM#40.

Date	Mintage	VG	F	VF	XF	Unc
MDCV (1605) Rare	—	—	—	—	—	—

KM# 53 THALER
Silver **Ruler:** Johann Christian and Georg Rudolph **Obv:** Two 1/2-length figures facing each other behind flat surface with arabesques in exergue **Obv. Legend:** D.G. IOHAN. CHRIST. ET. GEOR(G). RVD. FRA **Rev:** 4-fold arms, 3 ornate helmets above, date at end of legend **Rev. Legend:** DVC. SIL. LIG. - ET. BREG. **Note:** Dav. #7708. Ref. F/S#1410, 1416, 1420, 1424, 1438, 1456.

Date	Mintage	VG	F	VF	XF	Unc
(1)606	—	240	600	1,300	2,650	—
(1)607	—	240	600	1,300	2,650	—
(1)607 (d)	—	240	600	1,300	2,650	—
(1)608 (d)	—	240	600	1,300	2,650	—
(1)609 (d)	—	240	600	1,300	2,650	—
(1)610 (d)	—	240	600	1,300	2,650	—

KM# 63 THALER
Silver **Ruler:** Johann Christian and Georg Rudolph **Obv:** Two 1/2-length figures facing each other **Obv. Legend:** D.G. IOAN. CHRIST. ET. GEORG. RVD. FRA. **Rev:** Ornately shaped shield of 4-fold arms, 3 helmets above, date at end of legend **Rev. Legend:** DVC. SIL. LIG. - ET. BREG. **Note:** Dav. #7710. Ref. F/S#1425, 1436.

Date	Mintage	VG	F	VF	XF	Unc
(1)608 (d)	—	400	800	1,850	3,700	—
(1)609 (d)	—	400	800	1,850	3,700	—

KM# 64 THALER
Silver **Ruler:** Johann Christian and Georg Rudolph **Obv:** Two 1/2-length figures facing each other **Obv. Legend:** D.G. IOAN. CHRIST. ET. GEORG. RVD. FRA. **Rev:** Shield of 4-fold arms with flat top, 3 helmets above, date at end of legend **Rev. Legend:** DVC. SIL. LIG. - ET. BREG. **Note:** Dav. #7710A.

Date	Mintage	VG	F	VF	XF	Unc
(1)608 (d)	—	400	800	1,850	3,700	—

KM# 74 THALER
Silver **Ruler:** Johann Christian and Georg Rudolph **Obv:** Two 1/2-length figures facing each other, ornamented fillet below **Obv. Legend:** D.G. IOAN. CHRIST. ET. GEORG. RVD. FRA. **Rev:** Shield of 4-fold arms with flat top, 3 helmets above, date at end of legend **Rev. Legend:** DVC. DIL. LIG. - ET. BREG. **Note:** Dav. #7710B. Ref. F/S#1437.

Date	Mintage	VG	F	VF	XF	Unc
(1)609 (d)	—	450	900	2,000	4,000	—

KM# 76 THALER
Silver **Ruler:** Johann Christian and Georg Rudolph **Obv:** Two 1/2-length figures facing each other, wearing different armor, nothing below **Obv. Legend:** D.G. IOHAN. CHRIST. ET. GEORG. RVD. FRA. **Rev:** Oval shield of 4-fold arms, 3 helmets above, date at end of legend **Rev. Legend:** DVC. SIL. LIG. - ET. BREG. **Note:** Dav. #7713.

Date	Mintage	VG	F	VF	XF	Unc
(1)609 (d)	—	400	800	1,850	3,700	—
(1)610 (d)	—	400	800	1,850	3,700	—

KM# 75 THALER
Silver **Ruler:** Johann Christian and Georg Rudolph **Obv:** Two 1/2-length figures facing each other over horizontal line below **Obv. Legend:** D.G. IOHAN. CHRIST. ET. GEORG. RVD. FRA. **Rev:** Flat shield with rounded bottom of 4-fold arms, 3 helmets above, date at end of legend **Rev. Legend:** DVC. SIL. LIG. - ET. BREG. **Note:** Dav. #7712.

Date	Mintage	VG	F	VF	XF	Unc
(1)609 (d)	—	500	1,000	2,300	4,500	—

KM# 95 THALER
Silver **Ruler:** Johann Christian and Georg Rudolph **Obv:** Two 1/2-length figures facing each other **Obv. Legend:** D.G. IOAN. CHRIST. ET. GEORG. RVD. FRA. **Rev:** Oval shield of 4-fold arms, 3 helmets above, date at end of legend **Rev. Legend:** DVC. SIL. LIG. - ET. BREG. **Note:** Dav. #7713A.

Date	Mintage	VG	F	VF	XF	Unc
(1)610 (d)	—	400	800	1,850	3,700	—

KM# 128 THALER
Silver **Ruler:** Johann Christian and Georg Rudolph **Obv:** Draped bust to right, legend begins at bottom, divided by 2 small shields of arms at left and right, small imperial orb in circle at bottom **Obv. Legend:** D.G. IO - HANN. CHRISTI. - AN. ET. **Rev:** Draped bust to left divides date, legend begins at upper left, 2 small shields of arms at left and right **Rev. Legend:** GEOR. RVD. FRA. D. - SIL. LIG. ET. BREG. **Note:** Dav. #7715. Ref. F/S#1472.

Date	Mintage	VG	F	VF	XF	Unc
1611	—	450	900	1,900	3,750	—

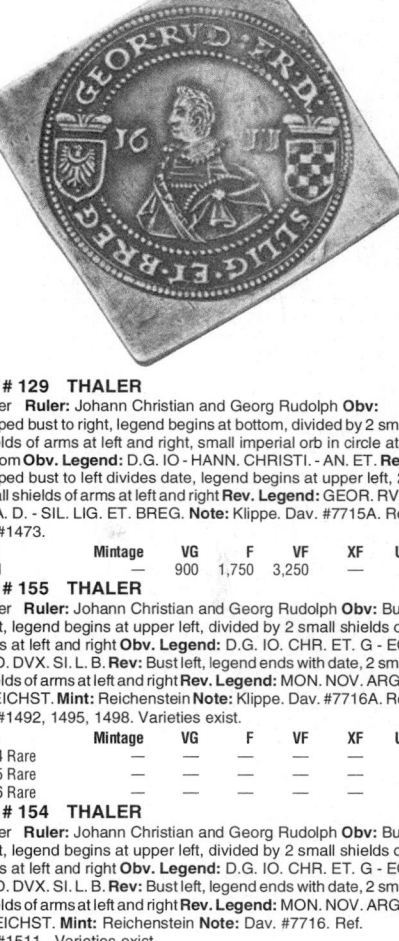

KM# 129 THALER
Silver **Ruler:** Johann Christian and Georg Rudolph **Obv:** Draped bust to right, legend begins at bottom, divided by 2 small shields of arms at left and right, small imperial orb in circle at bottom **Obv. Legend:** D.G. IO - HANN. CHRISTI. - AN. ET. **Rev:** Draped bust to left divides date, legend begins at upper left, 2 small shields of arms at left and right **Rev. Legend:** GEOR. RVD. FRA. D. - SIL. LIG. ET. BREG. **Note:** Klippe. Dav. #7715A. Ref. F/S#1473.

Date	Mintage	VG	F	VF	XF	Unc
1611	—	900	1,750	3,250	—	—

KM# 155 THALER
Silver **Ruler:** Johann Christian and Georg Rudolph **Obv:** Bust right, legend begins at upper left, divided by 2 small shields of arms at left and right **Obv. Legend:** D.G. IO. CHR. ET. G - EO. RVD. DVX. SI. L. B. **Rev:** Bust left, legend ends with date, 2 small shields of arms at left and right **Rev. Legend:** MON. NOV. ARGE. - REICHST. **Mint:** Reichenstein **Note:** Klippe. Dav. #7716A. Ref. F/S#1492, 1495, 1498. Varieties exist.

Date	Mintage	VG	F	VF	XF	Unc
1614 Rare	—	—	—	—	—	—
1615 Rare	—	—	—	—	—	—
1616 Rare	—	—	—	—	—	—

KM# 154 THALER
Silver **Ruler:** Johann Christian and Georg Rudolph **Obv:** Bust right, legend begins at upper left, divided by 2 small shields of arms at left and right **Obv. Legend:** D.G. IO. CHR. ET. G - EO. RVD. DVX. SI. L. B. **Rev:** Bust left, legend ends with date, 2 small shields of arms at left and right **Rev. Legend:** MON. NOV. ARGE. - REICHST. **Mint:** Reichenstein **Note:** Dav. #7716. Ref. F/S#1511. Varieties exist.

Date	Mintage	VG	F	VF	XF	Unc
1614 Rare	—	—	—	—	—	—
1615 Rare	—	—	—	—	—	—
1616 Rare	—	—	—	—	—	—
1617 Rare	—	—	—	—	—	—

KM# 169 THALER

Silver **Ruler:** Johann Christian and Georg Rudolph **Obv:** 2 armored 1/2-length figures facing each other, horizontal line with ornamentation below **Obv. Legend:** D.G. IOHAN. CHRIS(T). ET. GEORG. RVDO. FRAT(R). **Rev:** Shield with flat top and rounded bottom of 4-fold arms, 3 ornate helmets above, date at end of legend **Rev. Legend:** DVC. SIL. LIGNIC. ET. BREGE. **Mint:** Reichenstein **Note:** Dav. #7718. Ref. F/S#1512, 1531, 1542. Varieties exist.

Date	Mintage	VG	F	VF	XF	Unc
1617 HR	—	600	1,200	2,500	5,750	—
1618 HR	—	600	1,200	2,500	5,750	—
1619 HR	—	600	1,200	2,500	5,750	—
16Z0 HR	—	750	1,500	3,000	6,500	—
1621 HR	—	750	1,500	3,000	6,500	—
1621	—	750	1,500	3,000	6,500	—

KM# 184 THALER

Silver **Ruler:** Johann Christian and Georg Rudolph **Obv:** 2 armored 1/2-length figures facing each other, horizontal line with ornamentation below **Obv. Legend:** D.G. IOHAN. CHRIS(T). ET. GEORG. RVDO. FRAT(R). **Rev:** Shield with flat top and rounded bottom of 4-fold arms, 3 ornate helmets above, date at end of legend **Rev. Legend:** DVC. SIL. LIGNIC. ET. BREGE. **Mint:** Reichenstein **Note:** Klippe. Dav. #7718B. Ref. F/S#1517, 1532.

Date	Mintage	VG	F	VF	XF	Unc
1618 HR	—	1,850	3,500	6,500	—	—
1619 HR	—	1,850	3,500	6,500	—	—
1621	—	1,850	3,500	6,500	—	—

KM# 193 THALER

Silver **Ruler:** Johann Christian and Georg Rudolph **Obv:** 2 armored 1/2-length figures facing each other **Obv. Legend:** D.G. IOHAN. CHRIS(T). ET. GEORG. RVDO. FRAT(R). **Rev:** Shield with flat top and rounded bottom of 4-fold arms, 3 ornate helmets above, date at end of legend **Rev. Legend:** DVC. SIL. LIGNIC. ET. BREGE. **Mint:** Reichenstein **Note:** Dav. #7718A. Ref. F/S#1517, 1532.

Date	Mintage	VG	F	VF	XF	Unc
1619	—	600	1,200	2,500	5,750	—

KM# 266 THALER

Silver **Ruler:** Johann Christian **Obv:** Armored bust to right **Obv. Legend:** D.G. IOHAN. CHRISTIAN. DVX. SIL. **Rev:** 4-fold arms, 3 helmets above, date at top in margin **Rev. Legend:** LIGN. ET. BREG. SVP. CAPVT. SIL. **Mint:** Ohlau **Note:** Dav. #7719. Ref. F/S#1562.

Date	Mintage	VG	F	VF	XF	Unc
16Z1 HR Rare	—	—	—	—	—	—

KM# 270 THALER

Silver **Ruler:** Georg Rudolf **Obv:** Armored bust right, small imperial orb at top **Obv. Legend:** D.G. GEORG. RVDOLPHVS. DVC. SILESIÆ. **Rev:** 4-fold arms, 3 helmets above, date at end of legend **Rev. Legend:** LIGNICEN. ET. - BREGEN **Mint:** Liegnitz **Note:** Dav. #7724. Ref. F/S#1688, 1692.

Date	Mintage	VG	F	VF	XF	Unc
16Z1 (e)	—	—	—	—	—	—
16ZZ (e)	—	1,850	3,500	6,750	—	—

KM# 267 THALER

Silver **Ruler:** Johann Christian **Obv:** Armored bust to right divides date, small imperial orb at top in margin **Obv. Legend:** D. G. IOHANES • CHRISTIANVS • DVX **Rev:** 4-fold arms, 3 helmets above **Rev. Legend:** SIL. LIGNI. - ET. BREGE. **Mint:** Ohlau **Note:** Dav. #7720. Ref. F/S#1563.

Date	Mintage	VG	F	VF	XF	Unc
1621 HR Rare	—	—	—	—	—	—

Note: Fritz Rudolf Künker Münzenhandlung Auction 135, 1-08, near XF realized approximately $7,750

KM# 268 THALER

Silver **Ruler:** Johann Christian **Obv:** Armored bust to right divides date, small imperial orb at top in margin **Obv. Legend:** D.G. IOHANES. CHRISTIANVS. DVX. **Rev:** 4-fold arms, 3 helmets above **Rev. Legend:** SIL. LIGNI. - ET. BREGE. **Mint:** Ohlau **Note:** Klippe. Dav. #7720A. Ref. F/S#1564.

Date	Mintage	VG	F	VF	XF	Unc
1621 HR Rare	—	—	—	—	—	—

KM# 269 THALER

Silver **Ruler:** Georg Rudolf **Obv:** Armored bust right, small imperial orb at top **Obv. Legend:** D.G. GEORG. RVDOLPHVS. DVC. SILES. **Rev:** 4-fold arms, 3 helmets above, date at end of legend **Rev. Legend:** LIGNIC • ET • BREG • **Mint:** Haynau **Note:** Dav. #7723.

Date	Mintage	VG	F	VF	XF	Unc
16Z1 MT Rare	—	—	—	—	—	—

KM# 345 THALER

Silver **Ruler:** Johann Christian **Obv:** Armored and mantled bust to right, small imperial orb at top in margin **Obv. Legend:** D: G. IOHAN. CHRISTIAN. DVX. SILES. LIGNI. ET. BREG. **Rev:** 4-fold arms, 3 helmets above, date at end of legend **Rev. Legend:** MONETA • NOVA • CRVCIBVRGENSIS. **Mint:** Kreuzburg **Note:** Dav. #7721. Ref. F/S#1598.

Date	Mintage	VG	F	VF	XF	Unc
1622 (fs) Rare	—	—	—	—	—	—

Note: Fritz Rudolf Künker Münzenhandlung Auction 135, 1-08, XF realized approximately $38,395

KM# 346 THALER

Silver **Ruler:** Georg Rudolf **Obv:** 1/2-length armored figure to right, legend begins with small imperial orb **Obv. Legend:** D.G. GEORGIVS. RVDOLPHVS. DVX. SILESIÆ. **Rev:** 4-fold arms, 3 helmets above, date divided at top **Rev. Legend:** LIGNICENSIS. ET. - BREGENSIS. **Mint:** Liegnitz **Note:** Dav. #7725. Ref. F/S#1690.

Date	Mintage	VG	F	VF	XF	Unc
16ZZ (e) Rare	—	—	—	—	—	—

KM# 347 THALER

Silver **Ruler:** Georg Rudolf **Obv:** 1/2-length armored figure to right, legend begins with small imperial orb **Obv. Legend:** D.G. GEORGIVS. RVDOLPHVS. DVX. SILESIÆ. **Rev:** City view of Liegnitz with battlements in foreground, date at end of legend **Rev. Legend:** SI. DEVS. PRO. NOBIS. QVIS. CONTRA. NOS. **Mint:** Liegnitz **Note:** Dav. #7726. Ref. F/S#1691.

Date	Mintage	VG	F	VF	XF	Unc
16ZZ (e) Rare	—	—	—	—	—	—

KM# 376 THALER

Silver **Ruler:** Georg III, Ludwig IV and Christian **Obv:** Three facing 1/2-length figures, horizontal line below with arabesques in exergue, small imperial orb at top **Obv. Legend:** D.G. GEORG. LUDOVIC. ET. CHRISTIAN. FRATRES. **Rev:** 3 helmets above ornate 4-fold arms, date at end of legend **Rev. Legend:** DUCES. SILESIÆ. LIGN. - ET. BREGENES. **Note:** Dav. #7727. Ref. F/S#1707-08, 1716.

Date	Mintage	VG	F	VF	XF	Unc
1651 (pf)	—	300	600	1,150	2,250	—
1651 (pf)-VT	—	750	1,500	3,000	6,250	—
165Z (pf)-VT	—	1,250	2,500	5,500	10,000	—

KM# 388 THALER

Silver **Ruler:** Georg III, Ludwig IV and Christian **Obv:** 3 facing 1/2-length figures, horizontal line below with arabesques in exergue, small imperial orb at top **Obv. Legend:** D.G. GEORG. LUDOVIC. ET. CHRISTIAN. FRATRES. **Rev:** 3 helmets above ornate 4-fold arms, date at end of legend **Rev. Legend:** DUCES. SILESI?. LIGN. - ET. BREGENES. **Note:** Ref. F/S#1718. Struck on thick flan from 1/2 Thaler dies, KM#374.

Date	Mintage	VG	F	VF	XF	Unc
165Z (pf)-VT	—	—	—	—	—	—

KM# 407.1 THALER

Silver **Ruler:** Georg III, Ludwig IV and Christian **Obv:** 3 facing 3/4-length figures, horizontal line below with arabesques in exergue, small imperial orb at top **Obv. Legend:** D.G. GEORGIVS. LUDOVICVS. ET. CHRISTIANVS. FRATR. **Rev:** 3 helmets above ornate 4-fold arms, date at end of legend **Rev. Legend:** DVCES. SILESI. LIGNI. BR - EGENES. ET. WOLAV. **Note:** Dav. #7729. Ref. F/S#1749. Varieties exist.

Date	Mintage	VG	F	VF	XF	Unc
1656 (pf)	—	1,200	2,250	4,500	7,500	—

KM# 407.2 THALER

Silver **Ruler:** Georg III, Ludwig IV and Christian **Obv:** 3 facing 1/2 length figures, horizontal line below, batons at waist **Obv. Legend:** D.G. GEORGIVS. LUDOVICVS. ET. CHRISTIANVS. FRATR. **Rev:** 3 helmets above ornate 4-fold arms, date at end of legend. **Rev. Legend:** DVCES. SILESI. LIGNI. BR - EGENES. ET. WOLAV. **Note:** Dav. #7729A. Ref. F/S#1749. Varieties exist.

Date	Mintage	VG	F	VF	XF	Unc
1656 (pf)	—	1,250	2,500	4,750	7,750	—

KM# 414.1 THALER

Silver **Ruler:** Georg III, Ludwig IV and Christian **Obv:** 3 facing armored 1/2-length figures, small imperial orb at top, arabesques in exergue **Obv. Legend:** D.G. GEORGIUS. LUDOVICVS. & CHRISTIANVS. FRATRES. **Rev:** 3 helmets above oval 4-fold arms, date at end of legend, EW below **Rev. Legend:** DVCES. SILESIÆ. LIGNIC. BRE - GENS. ET. WOLAVIENSES. **Note:** Dav. #7731. Ref. F/S#1759, 1768-69, 1778. Varieties exist.

Date	Mintage	VG	F	VF	XF	Unc
1657 (pf)-EW	—	450	1,100	2,750	6,500	—
1658 (pf)-EW	—	450	1,100	2,750	6,500	—
1659 (pf)-EW	—	450	1,100	2,750	6,500	—

KM# 414.2 THALER

Silver **Ruler:** Georg III, Ludwig IV and Christian **Obv:** 3 facing 1/2-length figures, horizontal line below with arabesques in exergue, small imperial orb at top **Obv. Legend:** D.G. GEORGIVS. LUDOVICVS. & CHRISTIANVS. FRATRES. **Rev:** 3 helmets above oval 4-fold arms, date at end of legend, no EW below **Rev. Legend:** DVCES. SILESIÆ. LIGNIC. BRE - GENS. ET. WOLAVIENSES **Note:** Dav. #7731. Ref. F/S#1759, 1768-69, 1778. Varieties exist.

Date	Mintage	VG	F	VF	XF	Unc
1657 (pf)	—	450	1,100	2,750	6,500	—
1658 (pf)	—	450	1,100	2,750	6,500	—

KM# 413 THALER

Silver **Ruler:** Georg III, Ludwig IV and Christian **Obv:** 3 facing armored 1/2-length figures, small imperial orb at top, arabesques in exergue **Obv. Legend:** D.G. GEORGIUS. LUDOVICUS. & CHRISTIANUS. FRATRES. **Rev:** 3 helmets above ornate 4-fold arms, date at end of legend **Rev. Legend:** DUCES. SILESI?. LIGNIC - ENSES. ET. BREGENSES. **Note:** Ref. F/S#1757-58.

Date	Mintage	VG	F	VF	XF	Unc
1657 (pf)	—	500	1,200	3,000	7,000	—
1657 (pf)-EW	—	500	1,200	3,000	7,000	—

KM# 444 THALER

Silver **Ruler:** Christian zu Ohlau **Obv:** Mantled bust to right, crown in margin at top **Obv. Legend:** D.G. CHRISTIANUS. DUX. SILESIÆ. LIGNIC. BREG. ET. WOL. **Rev:** Round 4-fold arms in baroque frame, 3 ornate helmets above, date at end of legend **Rev. Legend:** SUFFICIT MIHI GRA - TIA TUA DOMINE A. **Note:** Dav. #7739. Ref. F/S#1894, 1904.

Date	Mintage	VG	F	VF	XF	Unc
1660 (pf)-EW	—	2,000	4,000	7,000	12,500	—
1661 (pf)-EW	—	2,000	4,000	7,000	12,500	—

KM# 445 THALER

Silver **Ruler:** Christian zu Liegnitz **Obv:** Mantled bust to right, crown in margin at top **Obv. Legend:** D.G. CHRISTIANUS. DUX. SILESIÆ. LIGNIC. BREG. ET. WOL. **Rev:** Round 4-fold arms in baroque frame, 3 ornate helmets above, date at end of legend **Rev. Legend:** CONSILIUM IEHOVÆ STABIT. AN. **Note:** Dav. #7740. Ref. F/S#1897, 1903.

Date	Mintage	VG	F	VF	XF	Unc
1660 (pf)-EW	—	1,150	2,250	4,500	8,000	—
1661 EW	—	1,150	2,250	4,500	8,000	—

KM# 442 THALER

Silver **Ruler:** Georg III, Ludwig IV and Christian **Obv:** 3 facing 1/2-length figures, horizontal line below with arabesques in exergue, small imperial orb at top **Obv. Legend:** D.G. GEORGIVS. LUDOVICVS. & CHRISTIANVS. FRATRES. **Rev:** 3 helmets above oval 4-fold arms, date at end of legend **Rev. Legend:** SUFFICIT MIHI GRA - TIA TUA DOMINE A. **Note:** Dav. #7732. Ref. F/S#1786.

Date	Mintage	VG	F	VF	XF	Unc
1660 (pf)-EW	—	450	1,100	2,750	6,500	—

KM# 443 THALER

Silver **Ruler:** Georg III **Obv:** Mantled bust right, crown in margin at top **Obv. Legend:** D.G. GEORGIUS. DUX. SILESIÆ. LIGNIC. ET. BREGEN. **Rev:** Round 4-fold arms in baroque frame, 3 ornate helmets above, date at end of legend **Rev. Legend:** SORS MEA A-DOMINO AN. **Note:** Dav. #7735. Ref. F/S#1840-41.

Date	Mintage	VG	F	VF	XF	Unc
1660 (pf)-EW	—	1,000	2,000	4,200	7,000	—
1660	—	1,000	2,000	4,200	7,000	—

KM# 452 THALER

Silver **Ruler:** Georg III, Ludwig IV and Christian **Obv:** 3 facing 1/2 length figures, horizontal line below with arabesques in exergue, small imperial orb at top **Obv. Legend:** D.G. GEORGIVS. LUDOVICVS. & CHRISTIANVS. FRATRES. **Rev:** 3 helmets above oval 4-fold arms, date at end of legend **Rev. Legend:** CONSILIUM IEHOVÆ STABIT. AN. **Note:** Dav. #7733. Ref. F/S#1789.

Date	Mintage	VG	F	VF	XF	Unc
1661 EW	—	1,200	2,300	4,750	8,500	—

KM# 453 THALER

Silver **Ruler:** Georg III **Obv:** Mantled bust right, crown in margin at top **Obv. Legend:** D.G. GEORGIUS. DUX. SILESIÆ. LIGNIC. ET. BREGEN. **Rev:** 3 helmets above oval 4-fold arms, date at end of legend **Rev. Legend:** CONSILIUM IEHOVÆ STABIT. AN. **Note:** Dav. #7736. Ref. F/S#1847.

Date	Mintage	VG	F	VF	XF	Unc
1661 EW	—	2,000	4,000	7,000	12,500	—

KM# 454 THALER

Silver **Ruler:** Ludwig IV **Obv:** Crown above bust right of LudwigMantled bust right, crown in margin at top **Obv. Legend:** D.G. LUDOVICUS. DUX. SILESIÆ. LIGNIC. BREG. ET. GOLDBER. **Rev:** Round 4-fold arms in baroque frame, 3 ornate helmets above, date at end of legend **Rev. Legend:** CONSILIUM IEHOVÆ STABIT. AN. **Note:** Dav. #7738. Ref. F/S#1876.

Date	Mintage	VG	F	VF	XF	Unc
1661 EW	—	700	1,500	3,250	7,500	—

KM# 490 THALER

Silver **Ruler:** Christian zu Liegnitz **Obv:** Armored and mantled bust to right **Obv. Legend:** CHRISTIANVS. D.G. DVX. SILESIÆ. LIGNICE(NSIS). **Rev:** Silesian eagle, crown above divides date in margin, mintmaster's initials in oval at bottom **Rev. Legend:** BREGENSIS. E(T). - WOLAVIENSIS. **Note:** Dav. #7741. Ref. F/S#1924, 1940-41, 1946. Varieties exist.

Date	Mintage	VG	F	VF	XF	Unc
1666 GFH/CBS	—	550	950	1,600	2,700	—
1671 GFH/CBS	—	550	950	1,600	2,700	—
1671 CBS	—	475	875	1,500	2,450	—
1672 CBS	—	475	875	1,500	2,450	—

KM# 534 THALER

Silver **Ruler:** Georg Wilhelm **Obv:** Armored bust to right **Obv. Legend:** + GEORGIVS. WILHELM. D.G. DVX. SILESIAE **Rev:** Silesian eagle, date divided by head, large crown above **Rev. Legend:** LIGNICENSIS. BREGENSIS. ET. WOLAVIENSIS. **Note:** Dav. #7742. Ref. F/S#1967.

Date	Mintage	VG	F	VF	XF	Unc
1675 CB	—	650	1,500	3,600	7,200	14,000

KM# 536 1-1/4 THALER

Silver **Subject:** Death of Georg Wilhelm **Rev:** Sixteen-line inscription **Note:** Dav. #LS488. Ref. F/S-1973. Weight varies: 33.00-34.00 grams.

Date	Mintage	VG	F	VF	XF	Unc
1675	—	1,500	3,000	6,000	10,000	16,000

KM# 538 1-1/2 THALER

Silver **Ruler:** Georg Wilhelm **Subject:** Death of Georg Wilhelm **Obv:** Armored and mantled bust turned 3/4 right **Obv. Legend:** + GEORG + WILHELM + D.G + DVX + SILESIAE + LIGN + BREG + & WOLAVIENS + **Rev:** 16-line inscription with Roman numeral dates **Rev. Inscription:** PIASTI • / ET NARCIIÆ POLONIÆ / ULTIMUS. NEPOS. PRIN(ceps) / XV. VIX. ANNOS. NAT. SEDTA(men) / DIE. XXI. NOVEMB. A. MDCLXXV. / SIBI. REGIÆ FAMILIÆ. / NOVEMQ' SECULORUM. SENIO. / FATALEM. FIGIT. TERMINUM. / AMBIGENTE. SILESIA / NUM. PIASTI. NATA. LIB, (PL), **Note:** Dav.#LS487 (F/S-1973). Illustration reduced.

Date	Mintage	VG	F	VF	XF	Unc
MDCLXXV (1675) SK	—	1,800	3,600	6,600	10,500	17,000

KM# 17 2 THALER

Silver **Ruler:** Joachim Friedrich zu Liegnitz **Obv:** Armored bust with high collar to right **Obv. Legend:** IOACH. FRID. HERZ. I. SCHL. Z. L. V. B. T. Z. M. **Rev:** Bust right of Anna Marie von Anhalt wearing ruffed collar and small cap, date at top **Rev. Legend:** A. MARIA. G. F. Z. AN. HERZ. I. SCHL. Z. L. V. B. **Note:** Dav. #7704. Ref. F/S-1415.

Date	Mintage	VG	F	VF	XF	Unc
160Z Rare	—	—	—	—	—	—

KM# 59 2 THALER

Silver **Ruler:** Johann Christian and Georg Rudolph **Obv:** Two 1/2-length figures facing each other behind flat surface with arabesques in exergue **Obv. Legend:** D. G. IOHAN. CHRIST. ET. GEOR(G). RVD. FRA. **Rev:** 4-fold arms, 3 ornate helmets above, date at end of legend **Rev. Legend:** DVC. SIL. LIG. - ET. BREG. **Note:** Dav. #7707. Ref. F/S-1415.

Date	Mintage	VG	F	VF	XF	Unc
(1)607 Rare	—	—	—	—	—	—
(1)607 (d) Rare	—	—	—	—	—	—

KM# 78 2 THALER

Silver **Ruler:** Johann Christian and Georg Rudolph **Obv:** Two 1/2-length figures facing **Obv. Legend:** D. G. IOHAN. CHRIST. ET. GEOR(G). RVD. FRA. **Rev:** 4-fold arms, 3 ornate helmets above, date at end of legend **Rev. Legend:** DVC. SIL. LIG. - ET. BREG. **Note:** Dav. #7709.

Date	Mintage	VG	F	VF	XF	Unc
(1)609 (d) Rare	—	—	—	—	—	—

KM# 79 2 THALER

Silver **Ruler:** Johann Christian and Georg Rudolph **Obv:** Two 1/2-length figures facing behind flat surface with ornamented fillet below **Obv. Legend:** D. G. IOHAN. CHRIST. ET. GEOR(G). RVD. FRA. **Rev:** 4-fold arms, 3 ornate helmets above, date at end of legend **Rev. Legend:** DVC. SIL. LIG. - ET. BREG. **Note:** Dav. #7709A. Ref. F/S-1434.

Date	Mintage	VG	F	VF	XF	Unc
(1)609 (d) Rare	—	—	—	—	—	—

KM# 80 2 THALER

Silver **Ruler:** Johann Christian and Georg Rudolph **Obv:** Two 1/2-length figures facing each other behind flat surface with ornamented fillet below **Obv. Legend:** D. G. IOHAN. CHRIST. ET. GEOR(G). RVD. FRA. **Rev:** 4-fold arms, 3 ornate helmets above, date at end of legend **Rev. Legend:** DVC. SIL. LIG. - ET. BREG. **Note:** Klippe. Dav. #7709B. Ref. F/S-1435.

Date	Mintage	VG	F	VF	XF	Unc
(1)609 (d) Rare	—	—	—	—	—	—

KM# 81 2 THALER

Silver **Ruler:** Johann Christian and Georg Rudolph **Obv:** Two 1/2-length figures facing each other over horizontal line below **Obv. Legend:** D. G. IOHAN. CHRIST. ET. GEORG. RVD. FRA. **Rev:** Flat shield with rounded bottom of 4-fold arms, 3 helmets above, date at end of legend **Rev. Legend:** DVC. SIL. LIG. - ET. BREG. **Note:** Dav. #7711.

Date	Mintage	VG	F	VF	XF	Unc
(1)609 Rare	—	—	—	—	—	—

KM# 131 2 THALER

Silver **Ruler:** Johann Christian and Georg Rudolph **Obv:** Draped bust to right, legend begins at bottom, divided by 2 small shields of arms at left and right, small imperial orb in circle at bottom **Obv. Legend:** D. G. IO - HANN. CHRISTI. - AN. ET. **Rev:** Draped bust to left divides date, legend begins at upper left, 2 small shields of arms at left and right **Rev. Legend:** GEOR. RVD. FRA. D. - SIL. LIG. ET. BREG. **Note:** Dav. #7714. Ref. F/S-1470.

Date	Mintage	VG	F	VF	XF	Unc
1611 Rare	—	—	—	—	—	—

KM# 132 2 THALER

Silver **Ruler:** Johann Christian and Georg Rudolph **Obv:** Draped bust to right, legend begins at bottom, divided by 2 small shields of arms at left and right, small imperial orb in circle at bottom **Obv. Legend:** D. G. IO - HANN. CHRISTI. - AN. ET. **Rev:** Draped bust to left divides date, legend begins at upper left, 2 small shields of arms at left and right **Rev. Legend:** GEOR. RVD. FRA. D. - SIL. LIG. ET. BREG. **Note:** Klippe. Dav. #7714A. Ref. F/S-1471.

Date	Mintage	VG	F	VF	XF	Unc
1611 Rare	—	—	—	—	—	—

KM# 195 2 THALER

Silver **Ruler:** Johann Christian and Georg Rudolph **Obv:** 2 armored 1/2-length figures facing each other, horizontal line with ornamentation below **Obv. Legend:** D. G. IOHAN. CHRIS(T). ET. GEORG. RVDO. FRAT(R). **Rev:** Shield with flat top and rounded bottom of 4-fold arms, 3 ornate helmets above, date at end of legend **Rev. Legend:** DVC. SIL. LIGNIC. ET. BREGE. **Note:** Klippe. Dav. #7717. Ref. F/S-1530.

Date	Mintage	VG	F	VF	XF	Unc
1619 HR Rare	—	—	—	—	—	—
1621 Rare	—	—	—	—	—	—

KM# 272 2 THALER

Silver **Ruler:** Johann Christian and Georg Rudolph **Obv:** 2 armored 1/2-length figures facing each other, horizontal line with ornamentation below **Obv. Legend:** D. G. IOHAN. CHRIS(T). ET. GEORG. RVDO. FRAT(R). **Rev:** Shield with flat top and rounded bottom of 4-fold arms, 3 ornate helmets above, date at end of legend **Rev. Legend:** DVC. SIL. LIGNIC. ET. BREGE. **Note:** Klippe. Dav. #7717A. Ref. F/S-1548.

Date	Mintage	VG	F	VF	XF	Unc
1621 Rare	—	—	—	—	—	—

KM# 273 2 THALER
Silver **Ruler:** Georg Rudolf **Obv:** Armored bust right, small imperial orb at top **Obv. Legend:** D. G. GEORG. RVDOLPHVS. DVX. SILESI. **Rev:** 4-fold arms, 3 helmets above, date at end of legend **Rev. Legend:** LIGNIC. ET. BEG. HERNS. **Note:** Dav. #7722. Ref. F/S-1680.

Date	Mintage	VG	F	VF	XF	Unc
1621 IK Rare	—	—	—	—	—	—

KM# 349 2 THALER
Silver **Ruler:** Georg Rudolf **Obv:** 1/2-length armored figure to right, legend begins with small imperial orb **Obv. Legend:** D. G. GEORGIVS. RVDOLPHVS. DVX. SILESIÆ. **Rev:** 4-fold arms, 3 helmets above, date divided at top **Rev. Legend:** LIGNICENSIS. ET. - BREGENSIS. **Mint:** Liegnitz **Note:** Dav. #A7725. Ref. J/M-123.

Date	Mintage	VG	F	VF	XF	Unc
16ZZ (e) Rare	—	—	—	—	—	—

KM# 409 2 THALER
Silver **Ruler:** Georg III, Ludwig IV and Christian **Obv:** 3 facing 3/4-lentth figures, horizontal line abelow with arabesques in exergue, small imperial orb at top **Obv. Legend:** D. G. GEORGIVS. LUDOVICVS. ET. CHRISTIANVS. FRATR. **Rev:** 3 helmets above ornate 4-fold arms, date at end of legend **Rev. Legend:** DVCES. SILESI. LIGNI. BR - EGENES. ET. WOLAV. **Note:** Dav. #7728. Ref. F/S-1748.

Date	Mintage	VG	F	VF	XF	Unc
1656 (pf) Rare	—	—	—	—	—	—

KM# 416 2 THALER
Silver **Ruler:** Georg III, Ludwig IV and Christian **Obv:** 3 facing armored 1/2-length figures, small imperial orb at top, arabesques in exergue **Obv. Legend:** D. G. GEORGIUS. LUDOVICUS. & CHRISTIANUS. FRATRES. **Rev:** 3 helmets above ornate 4-fold arms, date at end of legend **Rev. Legend:** DUCES. SILESIÆ. LIGNIC - ENSES. ET. BREGENSES. **Note:** Ref. F/S #1756.

Date	Mintage	VG	F	VF	XF	Unc
1657 (pf)	—	—	—	—	—	—

KM# 418 2 THALER
Silver **Ruler:** Georg III, Ludwig IV and Christian **Obv:** 3 facing 1/2-length figures, horizontal line below with arabesques in exergue, small imperial orb at top **Obv. Legend:** D. G. GEORGIVS. LUDOVICVS. & CHRISTIANVS. FRATRES. **Rev:** 3 helmets above oval 4-fold arms, date at end of legend **Rev. Legend:** DVCES. SILESIÆ. LIGNIC. BRE - GENS. ET. WOLAVIENSES. **Note:** Dav. #7730. Ref. F/S-1777, J/M-132.

Date	Mintage	VG	F	VF	XF	Unc
1658 (pf) Rare	—	—	—	—	—	—
1659 (pf)-EW Rare	—	—	—	—	—	—

KM# 447 2 THALER
Silver **Ruler:** Georg III **Obv:** Mantled bust to right, crown in margin at top **Obv. Legend:** D. G. GEORGIUS. DUX. SILESIÆ. LIGNIC. ET. BREGEN. **Rev:** Round 4-fold arms in baroque frame, 3 ornate helmets above, date at end of legend **Rev. Legend:** SORS MEA A - DOMINO AN. **Note:** Dav. #7734. Ref. F/S-1839.

Date	Mintage	VG	F	VF	XF	Unc
1660 (pf)-EW Rare	—	—	—	—	—	—

KM# 456 2 THALER
Silver **Ruler:** Ludwig IV **Obv:** Mantled bust right, crown in margin at top **Obv. Legend:** D. G. LUDOVICUS. DUX. SILESIÆ. LIGNIC. BREG. ET. GOLDBER. **Rev:** Round 4-fold arms in baroque frame, 3 ornate helmets above, date at end of legend **Rev. Legend:** CONSILIUM IEHOVÆ STABIT. AN. **Note:** Dav. #7737. Ref. F/S-1875.

Date	Mintage	VG	F	VF	XF	Unc
1661 EW Rare	—	—	—	—	—	—

TRADE COINAGE

KM# 97 1/4 DUCAT
0.8750 g., 0.9860 Gold 0.0277 oz. AGW **Ruler:** Johann Christian and Georg Rudolph **Obv:** Crowned ornate 4-fold arms divide date **Rev:** 6-line inscription **Rev. Inscription:** MO. / AVR. D.G. IO. / CHR. ET. GE. / RVD. FR. D. SL. / LIG. ET. BRE / GEN. **Mint:** Liegnitz

Date	Mintage	VG	F	VF	XF	Unc
1610	—	—	—	—	—	—

KM# 197 1/4 DUCAT
0.8750 g., 0.9860 Gold 0.0277 oz. AGW **Obv:** 2 adjacent oval arms of Silesian eagle and Brieg in baroque frames, crown above **Rev:** 4-line inscription with date **Rev. Inscription:** MONE / TA. NOVA. / AVREA. / 1619. **Note:** Fr. #3174.

Date	Mintage	VG	F	VF	XF	Unc
1619	—	180	350	600	1,300	—

KM# 198 1/4 DUCAT
0.8750 g., 0.9860 Gold 0.0277 oz. AGW **Obv:** 2 adjacent oval arms of Silesian eagle and Brieg in baroque frames, crown above **Rev:** 4-line inscription with date **Rev. Inscription:** MONE / TA. NOVA. / AVREA. / 1619. **Note:** Fr. #3175. Klippe.

Date	Mintage	VG	F	VF	XF	Unc
1619	—	240	550	950	1,800	—

KM# 213 1/4 DUCAT
0.8750 g., 0.9860 Gold 0.0277 oz. AGW **Ruler:** Johann Christian and Georg Rudolph **Obv:** 2 busts facing each other, legend begins with small imperial orb **Obv. Legend:** D.G. IOH. CHRI. ET. GEORG. RVD. FRA. **Rev:** 4-fold arms, 3 ornate helmets above, date divided at top **Rev. Legend:** MO. AV. DVC. SI. LI. ET. BRE. **Mint:** Liegnitz

Date	Mintage	VG	F	VF	XF	Unc
16Z0	—	—	—	—	—	—

KM# 523 1/4 DUCAT
0.8750 g., 0.9860 Gold 0.0277 oz. AGW **Ruler:** Louise **Obv:** Facing bust of Louise slightly right, mother of Georg Wilhelm, in inner circle **Obv. Legend:** + LOVISE. D.G. DVC. SIL. LIG. BREG. E. WOLAV. **Rev:** 2 adjacent oval arms in baroque frame, crown above divides date **Rev. Legend:** NAT. PD. ANH. CO. ASC. DO. SER. ET. RER. TV. ET. GV. **Note:** Fr. #3214.

Date	Mintage	VG	F	VF	XF	Unc
1674	—	300	600	1,150	2,400	—

KM# 540 1/4 DUCAT
0.8750 g., 0.9860 Gold 0.0277 oz. AGW **Ruler:** Georg Wilhelm **Obv:** Armored bust of Georg Wilhelm right in inner circle **Obv. Legend:** GEORG. WILHELM. D.G. DVX. SIL. **Rev:** Crowned Silesian eagle in inner circle, crown divides date in margin at top **Rev. Legend:** LIGNIC. BREGENS. ET. WOLAVIEN. **Note:** Fr. #3217.

Date	Mintage	VG	F	VF	XF	Unc
167 CB (error)	—	—	—	—	—	—
1675 CB	—	180	350	600	1,000	—

KM# 99 1/2 DUCAT
1.7500 g., 0.9860 Gold 0.0555 oz. AGW **Ruler:** Johann Christian and Georg Rudolph **Obv:** Crowned ornate 4-fold arms divide date **Rev:** 6-line inscription **Rev. Inscription:** MO. / AVR. D.G. IO. / CHR. ET. GE. / RVD. FR. D. SL. / LIG. ET. BRE / GEN. **Note:** Fr. #3168.

Date	Mintage	VG	F	VF	XF	Unc
1610	—	210	425	850	1,400	—

KM# 100 1/2 DUCAT
1.7500 g., 0.9860 Gold 0.0555 oz. AGW **Ruler:** Johann Christian and Georg Rudolph **Obv:** Crowned ornate 4-fold arms divide date **Rev:** 5-line inscription **Rev. Inscription:** MO. / AVR. D.G. IO. / CHR. ET. GE. / RVD. FR. D. SL. / LIG. ET. BREGEN. **Note:** Fr. #3169.

Date	Mintage	VG	F	VF	XF	Unc
1610	—	210	425	850	1,400	—

KM# 200 1/2 DUCAT
1.7500 g., 0.9860 Gold 0.0555 oz. AGW **Ruler:** Johann Christian and Georg Rudolph **Obv:** Facing busts of Johann Christian and Georg Rudolf in inner circle, 2 adjacent oval arms in baroque frame in exergue **Rev:** 7-line inscription with date **Rev. Inscription:** MO. / AVR. D.G. IO. / CHR. ET. GEO. / RVD. FRA. D / SIL. LIGNI. / ET. BREG. / 1619. **Note:** Fr. #3172.

Date	Mintage	VG	F	VF	XF	Unc
1619	—	210	425	850	1,400	—

KM# 201 1/2 DUCAT
1.7500 g., 0.9860 Gold 0.0555 oz. AGW **Ruler:** Johann Christian and Georg Rudolph **Obv:** 1/2-length busts of Johann Christian and Georg Rudolf facing in inner circle, 2 adjacent oval arms in baroque frame in exergue **Rev:** 7-line inscription with date **Rev. Inscription:** MO. / AVR. D.G. IO. / CHR. ET. GEO. / RVD. FRA. D / SIL. LIGNI. / ET. BREG. / 1619. **Note:** Fr. #3173. Klippe.

Date	Mintage	VG	F	VF	XF	Unc
1619	—	325	750	1,450	2,450	—

KM# 19 1/2 DUCAT
1.7500 g., 0.9860 Gold 0.0555 oz. AGW **Ruler:** Johann Christian and Georg Rudolph **Obv:** Facing 1/2-length busts of Johann Christian and Georg Rudolf facing each other in inner circle, legend begins with small imperial orb **Obv. Legend:** D.G. IOH. CHRI ET. GEOR. RVD. FRA. **Rev:** Crowned ornate 4-fold arms in inner circle **Rev. Legend:** MO. AV. D. - S. L. BR. **Note:** Fr. #3146.

Date	Mintage	VG	F	VF	XF	Unc
ND(1602-21)	—	250	500	850	1,500	—

KM# 215 1/2 DUCAT
1.7500 g., 0.9860 Gold 0.0555 oz. AGW **Ruler:** Johann Christian and Georg Rudolph **Obv:** Busts of Johann Christian and Georg Rudolph facing, legend begins with small imperial orb **Obv. Legend:** D.G. IOH. CHRI. ET. GEORG. RVD. FRA. **Rev:** 4-fold arms, 3 ornate helmets above, date divided at top **Rev. Legend:** MO. AV. DVC. SI. LI. ET. BRE. **Note:** Fr. #3155.

Date	Mintage	VG	F	VF	XF	Unc
1620	—	250	500	850	1,500	—

KM# 216 1/2 DUCAT
1.7500 g., 0.9860 Gold 0.0555 oz. AGW **Ruler:** Johann Christian and Georg Rudolph **Obv:** Busts of Johann Christian and Georg Rudolph facing, legend begins with small imperial orb **Obv. Legend:** D.G. IOH. CHRI. ET. GEORG. RVD. FRA. **Rev:** 4-fold arms, 3 ornate helmets abaove, date divided at top **Rev. Legend:** MO. AV. DVC. SI. LI. ET. BRE. **Note:** Klippe.

Date	Mintage	VG	F	VF	XF	Unc
16Z0	—	—	—	—	—	—

KM# 378 1/2 DUCAT
1.7500 g., 0.9860 Gold 0.0555 oz. AGW **Ruler:** Georg III, Ludwig IV and Christian **Obv:** Facing 1/2-length figures of Georg, Ludwig, and Christian in inner circle, horizontal line below with arabesques in exergue, small imperial orb at top **Obv. Legend:** D:G • GEORG • LUDOVIC • ET • CHRISTIAN • FRATRES • **Rev:** Ornate 4-fold arms topped by three helmets in inner circle, date at end of legend **Rev. Legend:** DUCES • SILESIÆ • LIGN • - ET • BREGENES • **Note:** Fr. #3201. Ref. F/S #1706, 1715.

Date	Mintage	VG	F	VF	XF	Unc
1651	—	230	450	800	1,550	—
1652	—	230	450	800	1,550	—
1656	—	230	450	800	1,550	—

KM# 400 1/2 DUCAT
1.7500 g., 0.9860 Gold 0.0555 oz. AGW **Ruler:** Georg III, Ludwig IV and Christian **Obv:** 3 armored 1/2-length figures of Georg, Ludwig and Christian in inner circle, small imperial orb at top, arabesques in exergue **Obv. Legend:** D:G • GEORGIUS • LUDOVICUS • & CHRISTIANUS • FRATRES • **Rev:** 3 helmets above ornate 4-fold arms, date at end of legend **Rev. Legend:** DUCES • SILESIÆ • LIGNIC - ENSES • ET • BREGENSES. **Note:** Fr. #3201.

Date	Mintage	VG	F	VF	XF	Unc
1653/2/1	—	180	350	725	1,250	—
1653/Z	—	180	350	725	1,250	—
1654/Z	—	180	350	725	1,250	—
1656	—	180	350	725	1,250	—

KM# 542 1/2 DUCAT
1.7500 g., 0.9860 Gold 0.0555 oz. AGW **Ruler:** Georg Wilhelm **Obv:** Armored bust of Georg Wilhelm facing right in inner circle **Obv. Legend:** GEORG. WILHELM. D.G. DVX. SI. **Rev:** Crowned Silesian eagle in inner circle, crown above divides date in margin at top **Rev. Legend:** LIGNIC. BREGENS. ET. WOLAVI. **Mint:** Brieg **Note:** Fr. #3219.

Date	Mintage	VG	F	VF	XF	Unc
1675 CB	—	325	650	1,250	2,300	—

KM# 1 DUCAT
3.5000 g., 0.9860 Gold 0.1109 oz. AGW **Ruler:** Joachim Friedrich zu Liegnitz **Obv:** Collared bust of Joachim Friedrich right in inner circle **Obv. Legend:** (flower) MO. NO. AVR. IOACHIMI. FRIDERICI. **Rev:** Crowned 4-fold arms in inner circle, date at end of legend **Rev. Legend:** DVCIS. LEGNICEN. ET BREGEN. **Note:** Fr. #3139.

Date	Mintage	VG	F	VF	XF	Unc
1601	—	300	600	1,400	3,100	—

KM# 32 DUCAT
3.5000 g., 0.9860 Gold 0.1109 oz. AGW **Ruler:** Johann Christian and Georg Rudolph **Obv:** Facing busts of Johann Christian and Georg Rudolf in inner circle, horizontal line below, date in exergue **Obv. Legend:** MON. NOVA. AVR. IOAN. CHRIS. GEORG. RV. **Rev:** Crowned 4-fold arms **Rev. Legend:** DVCVM. LIGNI. ET. BREGEN. FRA. **Note:** Fr. #3142.

Date	Mintage	VG	F	VF	XF	Unc
1604	—	350	725	1,700	3,700	—

KM# 33 DUCAT
3.5000 g., 0.9860 Gold 0.1109 oz. AGW **Ruler:** Johann Christian and Georg Rudolph **Obv:** Large facing busts of Johann Christian & Georg Rudolph **Obv. Legend:** MO. NO. AVR. IOA. CHR. ET. GEOR. RV. FR. **Rev:** Crowned ornate 4-fold arms divide date **Rev. Legend:** DVC. SIL. LIGNICEN. ET. BREG. **Note:** Fr. #3142.

Date	Mintage	VG	F	VF	XF	Unc
1604	—	350	725	1,700	3,700	—

KM# 44 DUCAT

3.5000 g., 0.9860 Gold 0.1109 oz. AGW **Ruler:** Johann Christian and Georg Rudolph **Obv:** Large facing busts of Johann Christian and Georg Rudolph **Obv. Legend:** MO. NO. AVR. IOAN. CHR. ET. GEOR. RVD. FRA. **Rev:** Crowned ornate 4-fold arms, date at end of legend **Rev. Legend:** DVC. SIL. LEG. ET. BREG. **Note:** Fr. #3142.

Date	Mintage	VG	F	VF	XF	Unc
1605	—	350	725	1,700	3,700	—
1606	—	350	725	1,700	3,700	—

KM# 55 DUCAT

3.5000 g., 0.9860 Gold 0.1109 oz. AGW **Ruler:** Johann Christian and Georg Rudolph **Obv:** Small facing busts of John Christian and Georg Rudolf **Obv. Legend:** MO • AVR • IOAN • CHR • ET • GEOR • RVD • FR(A) • **Rev:** Crowned 4-fold arms, date at end of legend **Rev. Legend:** DVC • SIL • LIG • - ET • BREG • **Note:** Fr. #3145.

Date	Mintage	VG	F	VF	XF	Unc
1606	—	350	725	1,700	3,350	5,500
1607	—	350	725	1,700	3,350	5,500
1608	—	350	725	1,700	3,350	5,500
1609	—	350	725	1,700	3,350	5,500
1609 (d)	—	350	725	1,700	3,350	5,500

KM# 102 DUCAT

3.5000 g., 0.9860 Gold 0.1109 oz. AGW **Ruler:** Johann Christian and Georg Rudolph **Obv:** Armored bust of Johann Christian right in inner circle, legend divided by 2 small shields of arms **Obv. Legend:** MO. AVREA. D.G. - IOHAN. CHR. ET. **Rev:** Armored bust of Georg Rudolf left divides date in inner circle, legend divided by 2 small shields of arms **Rev. Legend:** GEOR. RVD. FR. D. - SL. LIG. ET. BRE. **Note:** Fr. #3166.

Date	Mintage	VG	F	VF	XF	Unc
1610 (d)	—	265	550	1,300	2,450	—
1611	—	265	550	1,300	2,450	—

KM# 103 DUCAT

3.5000 g., 0.9860 Gold 0.1109 oz. AGW **Ruler:** Johann Christian and Georg Rudolph **Obv:** Crowned, ornate 4-fold arms divide date **Rev:** 6-line inscription **Rev. Inscription:** MO. / AVR. D.G. IO. / CHR. ET. GE. / RVD. FR. D. SL. / LIG. ET. BRE / GEN. **Note:** Thick planchet. Fr. #3167. Struck on thick flan with 1/2 Ducat dies, KM#99.

Date	Mintage	VG	F	VF	XF	Unc
1610	—	450	900	2,100	3,850	—

KM# 146 DUCAT

3.5000 g., 0.9860 Gold 0.1109 oz. AGW **Ruler:** Johann Christian and Georg Rudolph **Obv:** Armored 1/2-length busts of Johann Christian and Georg Rudolf facing each other **Obv. Legend:** MO • AVR • IOAN • CHR • ET • GEOR • RVD • FRA • **Rev:** 2 adjacent shields of arms, Silesian eagle left, Brieg right, large crown above, date below **Rev. Legend:** DVC • SIL • LIGNI • ET • BREGEN • **Note:** Fr. #3170.

Date	Mintage	VG	F	VF	XF	Unc
161Z	—	300	625	1,550	3,100	—

KM# 156 DUCAT

3.5000 g., 0.9860 Gold 0.1109 oz. AGW **Ruler:** Johann Christian and Georg Rudolph **Obv:** Armored bust of Johann Christian right, legend divided by 2 small shields of arms **Obv. Legend:** D.G. IO. - CH. ET. GE. RV. DV - SIL. L. B. **Rev:** Armored bust of Georg Rudolph left, legend divided by 2 small shields of arms which ends with date **Rev. Legend:** MO. NOV. - AVR. REICHST. - (date). **Mint:** Reichenstein **Note:** Fr. #3178. Ref. F/S#1491.

Date	Mintage	VG	F	VF	XF	Unc
1614	—	425	875	2,050	3,700	—

KM# 205 DUCAT

3.5000 g., 0.9860 Gold 0.1109 oz. AGW **Ruler:** Johann Christian and Georg Rudolph **Obv:** 1/2-length figures of Johann Christian and Georg Rudolph facing each other, 2 adjacent oval arms in baroque frame in exergue **Rev:** 7-line inscription with date **Rev. Inscription:** MO. / AVR. D.G. IO. / CHR. ET. GEO. / RVD. FRA. D / SIL. LIGNI. / ET. BREG. / 1619. **Mint:** Reichenstein **Note:** Fr. #3171. Struck on thick flan with 1/2 Ducat dies, KM#200.

Date	Mintage	VG	F	VF	XF	Unc
1619	—	400	750	1,750	3,550	—

KM# 204 DUCAT

3.5000 g., 0.9860 Gold 0.1109 oz. AGW **Ruler:** Johann Christian and Georg Rudolph **Obv:** Small armored bust of Johann Christian right, legend divided by 2 small shields of arms **Obv. Legend:** D.G. I - OH. CHR. ET. GEO. - RV. FR. **Rev:** Small armored bust of Georg Rudolph left, legend divided by 2 small shields of arms which ends with date **Rev. Legend:** MO. AV. - DVX. SI. LI. ET. BR - EG. **Mint:** Reichenstein **Note:** Fr. #3166.

Date	Mintage	VG	F	VF	XF	Unc
1619	—	230	450	1,050	1,950	—

KM# 203 DUCAT

3.5000 g., 0.9860 Gold 0.1109 oz. AGW **Ruler:** Johann Christian and Georg Rudolph **Obv:** Large armored bust of Johann Christian right, legend divided by 2 small shields of arms **Obv. Legend:** D.G. I - OH. CHR. ET. GEO. - RV. FR. **Rev:** Large armored bust of Georg Rudolph left, legend divided by 2 small shields of arms which ends with date **Rev. Legend:** MO. AV. - DVX. SI. LI. ET. BR - EG. **Mint:** Reichenstein **Note:** Fr. #3166. Ref. F/S#1523.

Date	Mintage	VG	F	VF	XF	Unc
1619	—	300	600	1,450	2,800	—

KM# 218 DUCAT

3.5000 g., 0.9860 Gold 0.1109 oz. AGW **Ruler:** Johann Christian and Georg Rudolph **Obv:** Busts of Johann Christian and Georg Rudolph facing each other, legend begins with small imperial orb **Obv. Legend:** D.G. IOHA. CHRI. ET. GEORG. RVD. FRAT. **Rev:** 4-fold arms, 3 ornate helmets above, date divided at top **Rev. Legend:** MO. AVR. DVC. SIL. LE. ET. BRE. **Mint:** Reichenstein **Note:** Fr. #3154.

Date	Mintage	VG	F	VF	XF	Unc
16Z0	—	265	550	1,300	2,600	—

KM# 275 DUCAT

3.5000 g., 0.9860 Gold 0.1109 oz. AGW **Ruler:** Georg Rudolf **Obv:** High-collared bust of Georg Rudolf right in inner circle **Obv. Legend:** D.G. GEOR. RVD. DVC. SI. LI. ET. BR. **Rev:** 3 helmets above 4-fold arms, date at end of legend **Rev. Legend:** MONETA. AVREA. **Mint:** Haynau **Note:** Fr. #3194.

Date	Mintage	VG	F	VF	XF	Unc
16Z1 MT	—	290	575	1,400	2,850	—

KM# 276 DUCAT

3.5000 g., 0.9860 Gold 0.1109 oz. AGW **Ruler:** Georg Rudolf **Obv:** High-collared bust of Georg Rudolph right **Obv. Legend:** D.G. GEOR. RVD. DVC. SI. LI. ET. BR. **Rev:** 3 helmets above 4-fold arms, date at end of legend **Rev. Legend:** MONETA. AVREA. **Note:** Fr. #3194.

Date	Mintage	VG	F	VF	XF	Unc
16Z1	—	400	775	1,800	3,350	—

KM# 277 DUCAT

3.5000 g., 0.9860 Gold 0.1109 oz. AGW **Ruler:** Georg Rudolf **Obv:** Armored bust of Georg Rudolph right **Obv. Legend:** D.G. GEOR. RVD. DVC. SI. LI. ET. BR. **Rev:** 3 helmets above 4-fold arms, date at end of legend **Rev. Legend:** MONETA. AVREA. **Note:** Fr. #3194.

Date	Mintage	VG	F	VF	XF	Unc
16Z1	—	400	775	1,800	3,350	—

KM# 351 DUCAT

3.5000 g., 0.9860 Gold 0.1109 oz. AGW **Ruler:** Georg Rudolf **Obv:** Armored bust of Georg Rudolph right, small imperial orb at top **Obv. Legend:** D.G. GEORG. RVDO. DVX. SIL. LI. & BRE. **Rev:** Crowned ornamented 4-fold arms, date at end of legend **Rev. Legend:** MONETA. AVREA. ANNO.

Date	Mintage	VG	F	VF	XF	Unc
1622	—	400	775	1,800	3,350	—

KM# 380 DUCAT

3.5000 g., 0.9860 Gold 0.1109 oz. AGW **Ruler:** Georg III, Ludwig IV and Christian **Obv:** 1/2-length busts of Georg III, Ludwig IV & Christian facing, horizontal line below with arabesques in exergue, small imperial orb at top **Obv. Legend:** D.G. GEORG. LUDOVIC. ET. CHRISTIAN. FRATRES. **Rev:** 3 helmets above ornate 4-fold arms, date at end of legend **Rev. Legend:** DUCES. SILESIÆ. LIGN. - ET. BREGENES. **Note:** Fr. #3200. Struck at either Liegnitz or Brieg mint.

Date	Mintage	VG	F	VF	XF	Unc
1651 VT	—	200	325	650	1,050	—
165Z VT	—	200	325	650	1,050	—
165Z/1 VT	—	200	325	650	1,050	—

KM# 401 DUCAT

3.5000 g., 0.9860 Gold 0.1109 oz. AGW **Ruler:** Georg III, Ludwig IV and Christian **Obv:** Armored 1/2-length busts of Georg, Ludwig, and Christian facing, small imperial orb at top, arabesques in exergue **Obv. Legend:** D.G. GEORGIUS. LUDOVICUS. & CHRISTIANUS. FRATRES. **Rev:** 3 helmets above ornate 4-fold arms, date at end of legend **Rev. Legend:** DUCES. SILESIÆ. LIGNIC - ENSES. ET. BREGENSES. **Note:** Fr. #3200. Struck at Liegnitz or Brieg mint. Varieties exist.

Date	Mintage	VG	F	VF	XF	Unc
1653 (pf)	—	200	325	650	1,200	2,000
1654	—	200	325	650	1,200	2,000
1655	—	200	325	650	1,200	2,000
1656 (pf)	—	—	—	—	—	—
1657 (pf)	—	—	—	—	—	—
1657 (pf) - EW	—	200	325	650	1,200	2,000
1658 (pf)	—	—	—	—	—	—
1658 (pf) - EW	—	200	325	650	1,200	2,000
1659 (pf) - EW	—	200	325	650	1,200	2,000
1660 (pf)	—	—	—	—	—	—
1660 (pf) - EW	—	200	325	650	1,200	2,000
1661	—	200	325	650	1,200	2,000
1662 EW	—	200	325	650	1,200	2,000

KM# 449 DUCAT

3.5000 g., 0.9860 Gold 0.1109 oz. AGW **Ruler:** Georg III **Obv:** Mantled bust of Georg III right in inner circle, crown in margin at top **Obv. Legend:** D.G. GEORGIUS. DUX. SILESIÆ. LIGNIC. ET. BREGEN. **Rev:** Round 4-fold arms in baroque frame, 3 ornate helmets above, date at end of legend **Rev. Legend:** SORS MEA A - DOMINO AN. **Note:** Fr. #3202. Struck at either Liegnitz or Brieg mints.

Date	Mintage	VG	F	VF	XF	Unc
1660 (pf) - EW	—	700	1,400	2,750	5,000	8,500

KM# 450 DUCAT

3.5000 g., 0.9860 Gold 0.1109 oz. AGW **Ruler:** Christian zu Ohlau **Obv:** Mantled bust of Christian right in inner circle, crown above in margin **Obv. Legend:** D.G. CHRISTIANUS. DUX. SIL. L. BREG. & W. **Rev:** 3 helmets above ornate 4-fold arms, date at end of legend **Rev. Legend:** DUCES. SILESIÆ. LIGNIC - ENSES. ET. BREGENSES. **Note:** Fr. #3207. Struck at Liegnitz or Brieg mints.

Date	Mintage	VG	F	VF	XF	Unc
1660 (pf) - EW	—	400	750	1,750	3,550	—

KM# 462 DUCAT

3.5000 g., 0.9860 Gold 0.1109 oz. AGW **Ruler:** Christian zu Ohlau **Obv:** Mantled bust of Christian right, crown above in margin **Obv. Legend:** D.G. CHRISTIANUS. DUX. SIL. L. BREG. & W. **Rev:** Round 4-fold arms in baroque frame, 3 ornate helmets above, date at end of legend **Rev. Legend:** CONSILIUM IEHOVÆ STABIT. AN. **Mint:** Brieg **Note:** Fr. #3208.

Date	Mintage	VG	F	VF	XF	Unc
1661 EW	—	325	700	1,600	2,950	—

KM# 461 DUCAT

3.5000 g., 0.9860 Gold 0.1109 oz. AGW **Ruler:** Christian zu Ohlau **Obv:** Armored and mantled bust of Christian right, crown above in margin **Obv. Legend:** D.G. CHRISTIANUS. DUX. SIL. L. BREG. & WOL. **Rev:** Round 4-fold arms in baroque frame, 3 ornate helmets above, date at end of legend **Rev. Legend:** SUFFICIT MIHI GRA - TIA TUA DOMINE A. **Note:** Fr. #3208. Struck at either Liegnitz or Brieg mints.

Date	Mintage	VG	F	VF	XF	Unc
1661 (pf) - EW	—	400	750	1,750	3,200	—

KM# 460 DUCAT

3.5000 g., 0.9860 Gold 0.1109 oz. AGW **Ruler:** Ludwig IV **Obv:** Mantled bust of Ludwig right in inner circle, crown in margin at top **Obv. Legend:** D.G. LUDOVICUS. DUX. SIL. LIGNIC. B. & GOLD. **Rev:** Round 4-fold arms in baroque frame, 3 ornate helmets above, date at end of legend **Rev. Legend:** CONSILIUM IEHOVÆ STABIT. AN. **Mint:** Brieg **Note:** Fr. #3205.

Date	Mintage	VG	F	VF	XF	Unc
1661 EW	—	400	750	1,750	3,550	—

KM# 458 DUCAT

3.5000 g., 0.9860 Gold 0.1109 oz. AGW **Ruler:** Georg III, Ludwig IV and Christian **Obv:** Armored 1/2-length figures of Georg III, Ludwig IV & Christian facing, small imperial orb at top, arabesques in exergue **Obv. Legend:** D.G. GEORGIUS. LUDOVICUS. & CHRISTIANUS. FRATRES. **Rev:** 3 helmets above ornate 4-fold arms, date at end of legend. **Rev. Legend:** SUFFICIT MIHI GRA - TIA TUA DOMINE A. **Note:** Fr. #3200.

Date	Mintage	VG	F	VF	XF	Unc
1661 (pf) - EW	—	220	425	1,000	1,450	—

KM# 459 DUCAT

3.5000 g., 0.9860 Gold 0.1109 oz. AGW **Ruler:** Georg III, Ludwig IV and Christian **Obv:** Armored 1/2-length figures of Georg III, Ludwig IV & Christian facing, small imperial orb at top, arabesques in exergue **Obv. Legend:** D.G. GEORGIUS. LUDOVICUS. & CHRISTIANUS. FRATRES. **Rev:** 3 helmets above ornate 4-fold arms, date at end of legend. **Rev. Legend:** CONSILIUM IEHOVÆ STABIT. AN. **Mint:** Brieg **Note:** Fr. #3200.

Date	Mintage	VG	F	VF	XF	Unc
1661 EW	—	220	425	1,000	1,450	—

KM# 466 DUCAT

3.5000 g., 0.9860 Gold 0.1109 oz. AGW **Ruler:** Ludwig IV **Obv:** Mantled bust of Ludwig IV right, crown in margin at top **Obv. Legend:** D.G. LUDOVICUS. DUX. SIL. LIGNIC. B. & GOLD. **Rev:** 3 helmets above ornate 4-fold arms, date at end of legend **Rev. Legend:** DUCES. SILESIÆ. LIGNIC - ENSES. ET. BREGENSES. **Mint:** Brieg **Note:** Fr. #3206.

Date	Mintage	VG	F	VF	XF	Unc
1662 EW	—	300	600	1,400	2,850	—

KM# 477 DUCAT

3.5000 g., 0.9860 Gold 0.1109 oz. AGW **Ruler:** Georg III **Obv:** Bust of Georg III right, crown above in margin **Obv. Legend:** D.G. GEORGIUS. DUX. SIL. LIGN. & BREG. **Rev:** Round 4-fold arms, 3 helmets above, date at end of legend **Rev. Legend:** MONETA. AVRE. NOVA. REICHSTENIENSI. **Mint:** Reichenstein **Note:** Fr. #3203.

Date	Mintage	VG	F	VF	XF	Unc
1664	—	700	1,400	3,150	5,300	—

KM# 492 DUCAT

3.5000 g., 0.9860 Gold 0.1109 oz. AGW **Ruler:** Christian zu Liegnitz **Obv:** Armored and mantled bust of Christian right in inner circle **Obv. Legend:** CHRISTIANVS. D.G. DVX. SILESIÆ. LIGNICE. **Rev:** Crowned Silesian eagle in inner circle, crown above divides date in margin, mintmaster's initials in oval at bottom **Rev. Legend:** BREGENSIS. ET. - WOLAVIENSIS. **Mint:** Brieg **Note:** Fr. #3213.

Date	Mintage	VG	F	VF	XF	Unc
1666 CBS	—	400	750	1,800	3,550	—
1670 CB	—	400	750	1,800	3,550	—
1672 CB	—	400	750	1,800	3,550	—
1672 CBS	—	400	750	1,800	3,550	—

KM# 525 DUCAT

3.5000 g., 0.9860 Gold 0.1109 oz. AGW **Ruler:** Georg Wilhelm **Obv:** Armored bust of Georg Wilhelm right **Obv. Legend:** GEORG. WILHELM. D.G. DVX. SIL. **Rev:** Silesian eagle, crown above divides date in margin at top **Rev. Legend:** LIGNIC. BREG. & WOLAVIEN. **Mint:** Brieg **Note:** Fr. #3216.

Date	Mintage	VG	F	VF	XF	Unc
1674	—	425	850	2,050	3,900	—
1675 CB	—	425	850	2,050	3,900	—

KM# 544 DUCAT

3.5000 g., 0.9860 Gold 0.1109 oz. AGW **Ruler:** Georg Wilhelm **Obv:** Armored, facing bust of Georg Wilhelm right in inner circle **Obv. Legend:** GEORG. WILHELM. D.G. DVX. SI. **Rev:** Silesian eagle, crown above divides date in margin at top **Rev. Legend:** LIGNIC. BREGENS. ET. WOLAVI. **Mint:** Brieg **Note:** Struck on thick flan with 1/2 Ducat dies, KM#542. Fr. #3218.

Date	Mintage	VG	F	VF	XF	Unc
1675	—	575	1,150	2,800	4,900	—

KM# 21 2 DUCAT

7.0000 g., 0.9860 Gold 0.2219 oz. AGW **Subject:** Death of Joachim Friedrich **Obv:** Armored and collared bust of Joachim Friedrich right in inner circle **Obv. Legend:** ✠ MEMOR. IOACH. FRID. DVCIS. SILES. LEGN. BREGENSIS. **Rev:** 8-line inscription with R.N. date, circular marginal inscription **Rev. Legend:** ✠ DEO. OPT. MAX. IN. ÆTERN. VIVENS. SVM. PATR. **Rev. Inscription:** OBIIT. AN / NO. M.D. C II. / M. MART. XXV. / HORA. P. MER. VI / CVM. / VIXISSMI. / AN. LI. MENS. V / DIES. XXVI. / ✠. **Note:** Fr. #3141. Struck with 1/2 Thaler dies, KM#12.

Date	Mintage	VG	F	VF	XF	Unc
MDCII (1602)	—	775	1,550	3,900	7,400	—

KM# 66 2 DUCAT

7.0000 g., 0.9860 Gold 0.2219 oz. AGW **Ruler:** Johann Christian and Georg Rudolph **Obv:** Small busts of Johann Christian & Georg Rudolph slightly facing each other **Obv. Legend:** MO. AVR. IOAN. CHR. ET. GEOR. RVD. FR(A). **Rev:** Crowned 4-fold arms, date at end of legend **Rev. Legend:** DVC. SIL. LIG. - ET. BREG. **Note:** Klippe. Fr. #3143.

Date	Mintage	VG	F	VF	XF	Unc
1608	—	1,000	1,900	4,250	7,700	—

KM# 83 2 DUCAT

7.0000 g., 0.9860 Gold 0.2219 oz. AGW **Ruler:** Johann Christian and Georg Rudolph **Obv:** Small facing busts of Johann Christian and Georg Rudolf in inner circle **Obv. Legend:** MO. AVR. IOAN. CHR. ET. GEOR. RVD. FR(A). **Rev:** Crowned oval shield of 4-fold arms, date at end of legend **Rev. Legend:** DVC. SIL. LIG. - ET. BREG. **Note:** Fr. #3144.

Date	Mintage	VG	F	VF	XF	Unc
1609	—	650	1,300	3,300	6,300	—

KM# 84 2 DUCAT

7.0000 g., 0.9860 Gold 0.2219 oz. AGW **Ruler:** Johann Christian and Georg Rudolph **Obv:** Armored bust of Johann Christian right, legend begins at lower left, divided by 2 small shields of arms **Obv. Legend:** D.G. IO - HANN. CHRISTI - AN. ET. **Rev:** Armored bust of Georg Rudolf left divides date, legend begins at upper left, divided by 2 small shields of arms **Rev. Legend:** GEOR. RVD. FR. D. - SL. LIG. ET. BREG. **Note:** Fr. #3164. Struck at either Liegnitz or Brieg mints.

Date	Mintage	VG	F	VF	XF	Unc
1609 (d)	—	575	1,150	2,800	5,300	—
1609	—	575	1,150	2,800	5,300	—
1610 (d)	—	575	1,150	2,800	5,300	—

KM# 105 2 DUCAT

7.0000 g., 0.9860 Gold 0.2219 oz. AGW **Ruler:** Johann Christian and Georg Rudolph **Obv:** Armored bust of Johann Christian right, legend begins at lower left, divided by 2 small shields of arms **Obv. Legend:** D.G. IO - HANN. CHRISTI - AN. ET. **Rev:** Armored bust of Georg Rudolph left divides date, legend begins at upper left, divided by 2 small shields of arms. **Rev. Legend:** GEOR. RVD. FR. D. - SL. LIG. ET. BREG. **Note:** Klippe. Struck at either Liegnitz or Brieg mints. Fr. #3165.

Date	Mintage	VG	F	VF	XF	Unc
1610 (d)	—	750	1,500	3,500	6,400	—
1611	—	750	1,500	3,500	6,400	—

KM# 157 2 DUCAT

7.0000 g., 0.9860 Gold 0.2219 oz. AGW **Ruler:** Johann Christian and Georg Rudolph **Obv:** Armored bust of Johann Christian right, legend divided by 2 small shields of arms **Obv. Legend:** D.G. IO. - CH. ET. GE. RV. DV - SIL. L. B. **Rev:** Armored bust of Georg Rudolph left, legend divided by 2 small shields of arms which ends with date **Rev. Legend:** MO. NOV. - AVR. REICHST. - (date). **Mint:** Reichenstein **Note:** Fr. #3177.

Date	Mintage	VG	F	VF	XF	Unc
1614	—	1,750	3,350	7,400	14,000	—

KM# 353 2 DUCAT

7.0000 g., 0.9860 Gold 0.2219 oz. AGW **Ruler:** Georg Rudolf **Obv:** Armored bust of Georg Rudolf right in inner circle, small imperial orb at top **Obv. Legend:** D.G. GEO. RVD. DVX. SIL. LIG. & BRE. **Rev:** Crowned ornamented 4-fold arms in inner circle, date at end of legend **Rev. Legend:** MONETA. AVREA. ANNO. **Note:** Fr. #3190.

Date	Mintage	VG	F	VF	XF	Unc
16ZZ	—	800	1,600	3,800	6,800	—

KM# 382 2 DUCAT

7.0000 g., 0.9860 Gold 0.2219 oz. AGW **Ruler:** Georg III, Ludwig IV and Christian **Obv:** 1/2-length figures of Georg III, Ludwig IV & Christian facing, horizontal line below with arabesques in exergue, small imperial orb at top **Obv. Legend:** D.G. GEORG. LUDOVIC. ET. CHRISTIAN. FRATRES. **Rev:** 3 helmets above ornate 4-fold arms, date at end of legend **Rev. Legend:** DUCES. SILESIÆ. LIGN. - ET. BREGENES. **Note:** Fr. #3199.

Date	Mintage	VG	F	VF	XF	Unc
1651 (pf)	—	550	1,050	2,500	4,700	—

KM# 402 2 DUCAT

7.0000 g., 0.9860 Gold 0.2219 oz. AGW **Subject:** Death of Georg Rudolf **Obv:** Facing bust of Georg Rudolf right in inner circle **Obv. Legend:** D.G. GEORG. RUDOLPH. DUX. SIL. LIG. BREG & GOLDBE. **Rev:** 6-line inscription with date in inner circle **Rev. Legend:** S. CÆS. MAI. VICAR. REG. SUPR. PRÆF. PER. UTRAM & SIL. **Rev. Inscription:** NATUS / 22. IANUARII / ANNO 1595 / OBIIT 14 / IANUARII / 1653. **Note:** Fr. #3195.

Date	Mintage	VG	F	VF	XF	Unc
1653	—	1,150	2,400	5,000	9,200	—

KM# 403 2 DUCAT

7.0000 g., 0.9860 Gold 0.2219 oz. AGW **Ruler:** Georg III, Ludwig IV and Christian **Obv:** Armored facing 1/2-length busts of Georg, Ludwig, and Christian, small imperial orb at top, arabesques in exergue **Obv. Legend:** D.G. GEORGIUS. LUDOVICUS. & CHRISTIANUS. FRATRES. **Rev:** 3 helmets above ornate 4-fold arms, date at end of legend **Rev. Legend:** DUCES. SILESIÆE. LIGNIC - ENSES. ET. BREGENSES. **Note:** Struck at either Liegnitz or Brieg mints. Varieties exist. Fr. #3199.

Date	Mintage	VG	F	VF	XF	Unc
1653 (pf)	—	500	1,000	2,500	4,600	—
1657 (pf) - EW	—	500	1,000	2,500	4,600	—
1658 (pf)	—	500	1,000	2,500	4,600	—
1659 (pf) - EW	—	500	1,000	2,500	4,600	—

KM# 480 2 DUCAT

7.0000 g., 0.9860 Gold 0.2219 oz. AGW **Subject:** Death of Georg III **Obv:** Facing long-haired bust of Georg III in inner circle **Obv. Legend:** GEORGIUS. III. DUX. SILES. LIGN. BREG. SUPR. CAP. SIL. **Rev:** 6-line inscription and date in inner circle **Rev. Legend:** DEO. PATRIÆ ET CÆSARI. **Rev. Inscription:** NATUS / A. 1611. D. 4. SEP. / DENATUS / A. 1664. D. 14. IUL. / ÆTAT. 5Z. MENS. / X. DIE. X. **Note:** Fr. #3204. Struck with 1/4 Thaler dies, KM#476.

Date	Mintage	VG	F	VF	XF	Unc
1664	—	1,150	2,400	5,000	9,200	—

KM# 494 2 DUCAT

7.0000 g., 0.9860 Gold 0.2219 oz. AGW **Ruler:** Christian zu Liegnitz **Obv:** Armored and mantled bust of Christian right in inner circle **Obv. Legend:** CHRISTIANVS. D.G. DVX. SILESIÆ. LIGNICE. **Rev:** Crowned Silesian eagle in inner circle, crown above divides date in margin, mintmaster's initials in oval at bottom **Rev. Legend:** BREGENSIS. ET. - WOLAVIENSIS. **Mint:** Brieg **Note:** Fr. #3212.

Date	Mintage	VG	F	VF	XF	Unc
1666 CBS	—	900	1,800	4,200	8,100	—
1670 CBS	—	900	1,800	4,200	8,100	—
1672 CBS	—	900	1,800	4,200	8,100	—

KM# 546 2 DUCAT

7.0000 g., 0.9860 Gold 0.2219 oz. AGW **Ruler:** Georg Wilhelm **Obv:** Armored bust of Georg Wilhelm right in inner circle **Obv. Legend:** + GEORGIVS. WILHELM. D.G. DVX. SILESIAE. **Rev:** Silesian eagle, date divided by crown in margin at top **Rev. Legend:** LIGNICENSIS. BREGENSIS. ET. WOLAVIENSIS. **Mint:** Brieg **Note:** Fr. #3215.

Date	Mintage	VG	F	VF	XF	Unc
1675 CBS	—	900	1,800	4,550	8,700	—

KM# 547 2 DUCAT

7.0000 g., 0.9860 Gold 0.2219 oz. AGW **Subject:** Death of Georg Wilhelm **Obv:** Armored and mantled bust of Georg Wilhelm right **Obv. Legend:** GEORG. WILH. D.G. DVX. SILE. LIGN. BREG. & WOL. **Rev:** 10-line inscription with R.N. dates in inner circle **Rev. Inscription:** PIASTEÆ / REG. FAM. ULTIM / VIRTUTI. INT. PRI. MOS / ANIMAM. / D. XXIX. SEPT. MDCLX / ACCEPTAM / DEO. ITA. IUBENTI / DXXI. NOV. MDCLXXV / ILLACHRYM. SILES / REDDIDIT. **Note:** Fr. #3221. Struck with 1/4 Thaler dies, KM#529.

Date	Mintage	VG	F	VF	XF	Unc
MDCLXXV (1675)	—	875	1,750	4,400	8,300	—

KM# 47 3 DUCAT

10.5000 g., 0.9860 Gold 0.3328 oz. AGW **Ruler:** Johann Christian and Georg Rudolph **Subject:** Death of Joachim Friedrich's Widow, Anna Maria von Anhalt **Obv:** Crowned 4-fold arms **Obv. Legend:** IO. CHR. ET. GE. RVD. FR. DVC. SL. LIG. ET. BREG. **Rev:** Crowned shield of 8-fold arms with central shield of Anhalt, double marginal legends with R.N. date **Rev. Legend:** Outer: MEM. IL. MAT. ANNÆ. MAR. PR. ANHAL. DVCI. SIL. LEG. BREG. QVÆ. Inner: PIA. OBIIT. M. NOV. DIE. XIV. M.D.C.V. F.F. **Note:** Klippe.

Date	Mintage	VG	F	VF	XF	Unc
MDCV (1605) Rare	—	—	—	—	—	—

KM# 46 3 DUCAT

10.5000 g., 0.9860 Gold 0.3328 oz. AGW **Ruler:** Johann Christian and Georg Rudolph **Subject:** Death of Joachim Friedrich's Widow, Anna Maria von Anhalt **Obv:** Crowned 4-fold arms **Obv. Legend:** IO. CHR. ET. GE. RVD. FR. DVC. SL. LIG. ET. BREG **Rev:** Crowned shield of 8-fold arms with central shield of Anhalt, double marginal legends with R.N. dates **Rev. Legend:** Outer: MEM. IL. MAT. ANNÆ. MAR. PR. ANHAL. DVCI. SIL. LEG. BREG. QVÆ. Inner: PIA. OBIIT. M. NOV. DIE. XIV. M.D.C. V. F.F. **Note:** Struck with 1/2 Thaler dies, KM#40.

Date	Mintage	VG	F	VF	XF	Unc
MDCV (1605) Rare	—	—	—	—	—	—

KM# 108 3 DUCAT

10.5000 g., 0.9860 Gold 0.3328 oz. AGW **Ruler:** Johann Christian and Georg Rudolph **Obv:** 1/2-length figures of Johann Christian and Georg Rudolf facing each other behind flat surface with arabesques in exergue **Obv. Legend:** D:G • IOHAN • CHRIST • ET • GEORG • RVD • FRA • **Rev:** 4-fold arms, 3 ornate helmets above, date at end of legend **Rev. Legend:** DVC • SIL • LIG • - ET • BREG • **Note:** Fr. #3153. Struck with 1/2 Thaler dies, KM#93. Struck at either Liegnitz or Brieg mints.

Date	Mintage	VG	F	VF	XF	Unc
(1)610 (d)	—	800	1,600	3,800	6,700	—
1613	—	800	1,600	3,800	6,700	—

KM# 107 3 DUCAT

10.5000 g., 0.9860 Gold 0.3328 oz. AGW **Ruler:** Johann Christian and Georg Rudolph **Obv:** Armored bust of Johann Christian right, legend divided by 2 small shields of arms **Obv. Legend:** MO. AVREA. D.G. - IOHAN. CHR. ET. **Rev:** Armored bust of Georg Rudolph left divides date, legend divided by 2 small shields of arms **Rev. Legend:** GEOR. RVD. FR. D. - SL. LIG. ET. BRE. **Note:** Klippe. Fr. #3163. Struck at either Liegnitz or Brieg mints.

Date	Mintage	VG	F	VF	XF	Unc
1610 (d)	—	1,200	2,450	5,300	9,500	—

KM# 134 3 DUCAT

10.5000 g., 0.9860 Gold 0.3328 oz. AGW **Ruler:** Johann Christian and Georg Rudolph **Obv:** Draped bust of Christian right in inner circle, legend begins at bottom, divided by 2 small crowned shields of arms at left and right **Obv. Legend:** D:G • IO - HANN • CHRISTI • - AN • ET • **Rev:** Draped bust of Georg Rudolf to left divides date in inner circle, legend begins at upper left, 2 small crowned shields of arms at left and right **Rev. Legend:** GEOR • RVD • FR • D • - SI • LIG • ET • BREG • **Note:** Fr. #3162. Struck with 1/2 Thaler dies, KM#125.

Date	Mintage	VG	F	VF	XF	Unc
1611	—	850	1,700	3,900	7,000	—

KM# A135 3 DUCAT

10.5000 g., 0.9860 Gold 0.3328 oz. AGW **Ruler:** Johann Christian and Georg Rudolph **Obv:** 1/2-length armored figures of Johann Christian & Georg Rudolph facing each other **Obv. Legend:** MO. AVR. IOAN. CHR. ET. GEOR. RVD. FRA. **Rev:** Ornate 4-fold arms, 3 helmets above, date at end of legend **Rev. Legend:** DVC. SIL. LIGN. ET. BREG. **Mint:** Liegnitz **Note:** Fr. #3153.

Date	Mintage	VG	F	VF	XF	Unc
1613 CC	—	725	1,450	3,500	6,300	—

KM# 171 3 DUCAT

10.5000 g., 0.9860 Gold 0.3328 oz. AGW **Ruler:** Johann Christian and Georg Rudolph **Obv:** Bust of Johann Christian right, legend begins at upper left, divided by 2 small crowned shields of arms at left and right **Obv. Legend:** D.G. IOHA. CHRI. ET. - GEORG. RVD. FRA. **Rev:** Bust of Georg Rudolph left, legend ends with date, 2 small crowned shields of arms at left and right **Rev. Legend:** DVX. SIL. LIGNI. ET. - BREGEN. **Mint:** Breslau **Note:** Fr. #3162. Struck with 1/2 Thaler dies, KM#190.

Date	Mintage	VG	F	VF	XF	Unc
1617 HR	—	750	1,500	3,500	6,300	—

KM# 207 3 DUCAT

10.5000 g., 0.9860 Gold 0.3328 oz. AGW **Ruler:** Johann Christian and Georg Rudolph **Obv:** Bust of Johann Christian right, legend begins at upper left, divided by 2 small crowned shields of arms at left and right **Obv. Legend:** D.G. IOH. CHR - ET. GEO. RVD. FR. **Rev:** Bust of Georg Rudolph left, legend ends with date, 2 small crowned shields of arms at left and right **Rev. Legend:** DVX. SIL. LI. - ET. BRE. **Mint:** Breslau **Note:** Fr. #3162. Struck with 1/4 Thaler dies, KM#167.

Date	Mintage	VG	F	VF	XF	Unc
1619 HR	—	750	1,500	3,500	6,300	—

KM# 279 3 DUCAT

10.5000 g., 0.9860 Gold 0.3328 oz. AGW **Ruler:** Georg Rudolf **Obv:** Bust of Johann Christian right, legend begins at upper left, divided by 2 small shields of arms at left and right **Obv. Legend:** D.G. IOH. CHR - ET. GEO. RVD. FR. **Rev:** Bust Georg Rudolph left, legend ends with date, 2 small shields of arms at left and right **Rev. Legend:** DVX. SIL. LI. - ET. BRE. **Mint:** Liegnitz **Note:** Struck with 24 Kreuzer dies, KM#248.

Date	Mintage	VG	F	VF	XF	Unc
16Z1 MT Rare	—	—	—	—	—	—

KM# 355 3 DUCAT

10.5000 g., 0.9860 Gold 0.3328 oz. AGW **Ruler:** Johann Christian **Obv:** Armored bust of Johann Christian right in inner circle, date at lower right within the circle around bust, small imperial orb at top **Obv. Legend:** D.G. IOHANNES. CHRISTIANUS. DUX. **Rev:** Oval 4-fold arms topped by three helmets in inner circle **Rev. Legend:** SIL. LIGN. - ET. BREG. **Mint:** Ohlau **Note:** Fr. #3186.

Date	Mintage	VG	F	VF	XF	Unc
16ZZ HR Rare	—	—	—	—	—	—

KM# 356 3 DUCAT

10.5000 g., 0.9860 Gold 0.3328 oz. AGW **Ruler:** Johann Christian **Mint:** Ohlau **Note:** Klippe. Fr. #3187.

Date	Mintage	VG	F	VF	XF	Unc
16ZZ HR Rare	—	—	—	—	—	—

KM# 357 3 DUCAT

10.5000 g., 0.9860 Gold 0.3328 oz. AGW **Ruler:** Georg Rudolf **Obv:** Armored bust of Georg Rudolf right in inner circle, small imperial orb at top **Obv. Legend:** D.G. GEO. RVD. DVX. SIL. LIG. & BRE. **Rev:** Crowned ornamented 4-fold arms in inner circle, date at end of legend **Rev. Legend:** MONETA. AVREA. ANNO. **Note:** Fr. #3189.

Date	Mintage	VG	F	VF	XF	Unc
16ZZ	—	2,100	3,800	7,400	12,000	—

KM# 384 3 DUCAT

10.5000 g., 0.9860 Gold 0.3328 oz. AGW **Ruler:** Georg III, Ludwig IV and Christian **Obv:** Facing 1/2-figures of Georg, Ludwig, and Christian in inner circle, horizontal line below with arabesques in exergue, small imperial orb at top **Obv. Legend:** D.G. GEORG LUDOVIC. ET. CHRISTIAN. FRATRES. **Rev:** Ornate 4-fold arms topped by three helmets in inner circle, date at end of legend **Rev. Legend:** DUCES. SILESIÆ. LIGN. - ET. BREGENES. **Note:** Fr. #3198. Struck at Liegnitz or Brieg mints.

Date	Mintage	VG	F	VF	XF	Unc
1651 (pf) - VT	—	750	1,500	3,500	6,300	—

KM# 420 3 DUCAT

10.5000 g., 0.9860 Gold 0.3328 oz. AGW **Ruler:** Georg III, Ludwig IV and Christian **Obv:** Armored 1/2-length figures of Georg, Ludwig & Christian facing **Obv. Legend:** D.G. GEORGIUS. LUDOVICUS. & CHRISTIANUS. FRATRES. **Rev:** 3 helmets above ornate 4-fold arms, date at end of legend **Rev. Legend:** DUCES. SILESIÆ. LIGNIC - ENSES. ET. BREGENSES. **Note:** Fr. #3198. Struck at Liegnitz or Brieg mints.

Date	Mintage	VG	F	VF	XF	Unc
1658 (pf)	—	750	1,500	3,500	6,300	—
1660 (pf) - EW	—	750	1,500	3,500	6,300	—

KM# 464 3 DUCAT

10.5000 g., 0.9860 Gold 0.3328 oz. AGW **Ruler:** Georg III, Ludwig IV and Christian **Obv:** Armored 1/2-length figures of Georg, Ludwig & Christian facing, small imperial orb at top, arabesques in exergue **Obv. Legend:** D.G. GEORGIUS. LUDOVICUS. & CHRISTIANUS. FRATRES. **Rev:** 3 helmets above ornate 4-fold arms, date at end of legend **Rev. Legend:** SUFFICIT MIHI GRA - TIA TUA DOMINE A **Note:** Struck at either Liegnitz or Brieg mints.

Date	Mintage	VG	F	VF	XF	Unc
1661 (pf) - EW	—	—	—	—	—	—

KM# 496 3 DUCAT

10.5000 g., 0.9860 Gold 0.3328 oz. AGW **Ruler:** Christian zu Ohlau **Obv:** Armored and mantled bust of Georg Wilhelm right in inner circle **Obv. Legend:** CHRISTIANVS • D:G • DVX • SILESIÆ • LIGNICE • **Rev:** Crowned Silesian eagle in inner circle, crown divides date in margin, mintmaster's initials in oval at bottom **Rev. Legend:** BREGENSIS • ET • - WOLAVIENSIS • **Mint:** Brieg **Note:** Fr. #3211.

Date	Mintage	VG	F	VF	XF	Unc
1666 CBS	—	2,150	3,950	7,600	12,000	—

KM# 49 4 DUCAT

14.0000 g., 0.9860 Gold 0.4438 oz. AGW **Ruler:** Johann Christian and Georg Rudolph **Obv:** Small 1/2-length figures of Johann Christian and Georg Rudolf facing each other behind flat surface with arabesques in exergue **Obv. Legend:** D:G • IOHAN • CHRIST • ET • GEOR(G) • RVD • FRA • **Rev:** 4-fold arms topped by three helmets, date at end of legend **Rev. Legend:** DVC • SIL • LIG • - ET • BREG • **Note:** Fr. #3152. Struck with Thaler dies, KM#53. Struck at either Liegnitz or Brieg mints.

Date	Mintage	VG	F	VF	XF	Unc
(1)605	—	1,200	2,450	5,300	9,100	—
(1)607	—	1,200	2,450	5,300	9,100	—
(1)607 (d)	—	1,200	2,450	5,300	9,100	—
(1)609	—	1,200	2,450	5,300	9,100	—
(1)610	—	1,200	2,450	5,300	9,100	—

KM# 110 4 DUCAT

14.0000 g., 0.9860 Gold 0.4438 oz. AGW **Ruler:** Johann Christian and Georg Rudolph **Obv:** 1/2-length figures of Johann Christian & Georg Rudolph facing each other behind flat surface with arabesques in exergue **Obv. Legend:** D:G • IOHAN • CHRIST • ET • GEORG • RVD • FRA • **Rev:** 4-fold arms, 3 ornate helmets above, date at end of legend **Rev. Legend:** DVC • SIL • LIG • - ET • BREG • **Note:** Fr. #3152. Struck with 1/2 Thaler dies, KM#93. Struck at either Liegnitz or Brieg mints.

Date	Mintage	VG	F	VF	XF	Unc
(1)610 (d)	—	1,200	2,450	5,300	9,100	—

KM# 111 4 DUCAT

14.0000 g., 0.9860 Gold 0.4438 oz. AGW **Ruler:** Johann Christian and Georg Rudolph **Obv:** Armored bust of Johann Christian right, legend divided by 2 small shields of arms **Obv. Legend:** MO. AVREA. D.G. - IOHAN. CHR. ET. **Rev:** Armored bust of Georg Rudolph left divides date, legend divided by 2 small shields of arms **Rev. Legend:** GEOR. RVD. FR. D. - SL. LIG. ET. BRE. **Note:** Klippe. Struck at either Liegnitz or Brieg mints on thick, square flan with Ducat dies, KM#102. Fr. #3161.

Date	Mintage	VG	F	VF	XF	Unc
1610 (d)	—	1,800	3,600	8,400	13,500	—
1611	—	1,800	3,600	8,400	13,500	—

KM# 136 4 DUCAT

14.0000 g., 0.9860 Gold 0.4438 oz. AGW **Ruler:** Johann Christian and Georg Rudolph **Obv:** Draped bust of Johann Christian right, legend begins at bottom divided by 2 small shields of arms at left and right **Obv. Legend:** D:G • IO - HANN • CHRISTI • - AN • ET • **Rev:** Draped bust of Georg Rudolf left divides date, legend begins at upper left, 2 small shields of arms at left and right **Rev. Legend:** GEOR • RVD • FR • D • - SI • LIG • ET • BREG • **Note:** Fr. #3160. Struck with 1/2 Thaler dies, KM#134.

Date	Mintage	VG	F	VF	XF	Unc
1611	—	1,200	2,450	5,300	9,100	—

KM# 159 4 DUCAT

14.0000 g., 0.9860 Gold 0.4438 oz. AGW **Ruler:** Johann Christian and Georg Rudolph **Obv:** Armored bust of Johann Christian right, legend divided by 2 small shields of arms **Obv. Legend:** D.G. IO. - CH. ET. GE. RV. DV - SIL. L. B. **Rev:** Armored bust of Georg Rudolph left, legend divided by 2 small shields of arms which ends with date **Rev. Legend:** MO. NOV. - AVR. REICHST. - (date). **Mint:** Reichenstein **Note:** Fr. #3176.

Date	Mintage	VG	F	VF	XF	Unc
1614 Rare	—	—	—	—	—	—

KM# 173 4 DUCAT

14.0000 g., 0.9860 Gold 0.4438 oz. AGW **Ruler:** Johann Christian and Georg Rudolph **Obv:** Draped bust of Johann Christian right, legend begins at bottom, divided by 2 small shields of arms at left and right **Obv. Legend:** D.G. IO - HANN. CHRISTI. - AN. ET. **Rev:** Draped bust of Georg Rudolph left divides date, legend begins at upper left, 2 small shields of arms at left and right **Rev. Legend:** GEOR. RVD. FR. D. - SI. LIG. ET. BREG. **Mint:** Breslau

Date	Mintage	VG	F	VF	XF	Unc
1617 HR Rare	—	—	—	—	—	—

KM# 359 4 DUCAT

14.0000 g., 0.9860 Gold 0.4438 oz. AGW **Ruler:** Johann Christian **Obv:** Armored bust of Johann Christian right, date at lower right within the circle around bust, small imperial orb at top **Obv. Legend:** D.G. IOHANNES. CHRISTIANUS. DUX. **Rev:** Oval 4-fold arms topped by three helmets in inner circle **Rev. Legend:** SIL. LIGN. - ET. BREG. **Mint:** Ohlau **Note:** Fr. #3185.

Date	Mintage	VG	F	VF	XF	Unc
16ZZ HR Rare	—	—	—	—	—	—

KM# 390 4 DUCAT

14.0000 g., 0.9860 Gold 0.4438 oz. AGW **Ruler:** Georg III, Ludwig IV and Christian **Obv:** Facing 1/2-length figures of Georg, Ludwig, and Christian in inner circle, horizontal line below with arabesques in exergue, small imperial orb at top **Obv. Legend:** D.G. GEORG. LUDOVIC. ET. CHRISTIAN. FRATRES. **Rev:** 3 helmets above ornate 4-fold arms, date at end of legend **Rev. Legend:** DUCES. SILESIÆ. LIGN. - ET. BREGENES. **Note:** Fr. #3197. Struck with 1/2 Thaler dies, KM#374. Struck at either Liegnitz or Brieg mints.

Date	Mintage	VG	F	VF	XF	Unc
165Z (pf) - VT	—	1,200	2,450	5,300	9,100	—

KM# 422 4 DUCAT

14.0000 g., 0.9860 Gold 0.4438 oz. AGW **Ruler:** Georg III, Ludwig IV and Christian **Obv:** Facing, armored 1/2-length figures of Georg, Ludwig & Christian, small imperial orb at top, arabesques in exergue **Obv. Legend:** D.G. GEORGIUS. LUDOVICUS. & CHRISTIANUS. FRATRES. **Rev:** 3 helmets above ornate 4-fold arms, date at end of legend **Rev. Legend:** DUCES. SILESIÆ. LIGNIC - ENSES. ET. BREGENSES. **Note:** Fr. #3197. Struck at either Liegnitz or Brieg mints. Struck with 1/4 Thaler dies, KM#399.

Date	Mintage	VG	F	VF	XF	Unc
1658 (pf)	—	1,200	2,450	5,300	9,100	—
1659 (pf) - EW	—	1,200	2,450	5,300	9,100	—

KM# 23 5 DUCAT

17.5000 g., 0.9860 Gold 0.5547 oz. AGW **Subject:** Death of Joachim Friedrich **Obv:** Armored and collared bust of Joachim Friedrich right in inner circle **Obv. Legend:** ✠ MEMOR. IOACH. FRID. DVCIS. SILES. LEGN. BREGENSIS. **Rev:** 8-line inscription with R.N. date, circular marginal inscription **Rev. Legend:** ✠ DEO. OPT. MAX. IN. ÆTERN. VIVENS. SVM. PATR. **Rev. Designer:** OBIIT. AN / NO. M.D. C II. / M. MART. XXV. / HORA. P. MER. VI / CVM. / VIXISSMI. / AN. LI. MENS. V / DIES. XXVI. / ✠. **Note:** Fr. #3140. Struck from 1/2 Thaler dies, KM#12.

Date	Mintage	VG	F	VF	XF	Unc
MDCII (1602) Rare	—	—	—	—	—	—

KM# 67 5 DUCAT

17.5000 g., 0.9860 Gold 0.5547 oz. AGW **Ruler:** Johann Christian and Georg Rudolph **Obv:** Small busts of Johann Christian and Georg Rudolf facing each other, date below **Obv. Legend:** D.G. IOHAN. CHRIST. ET. GEOR. RVD. FRA. **Rev:** 4-fold arms, 3 ornate helmets above **Rev. Legend:** DVC. SIL. LIG. - ET. BREGEN. **Note:** Fr. #3151. Struck with 1/2 Thaler dies, KM#57. Struck at either Liegnitz or Brieg mints.

Date	Mintage	VG	F	VF	XF	Unc
(1)608 (d)	—	1,750	3,500	7,500	12,500	—

KM# 86 5 DUCAT

17.5000 g., 0.9860 Gold 0.5547 oz. AGW **Ruler:** Johann Christian and Georg Rudolph **Obv:** 1/2-length figures of Johann Christian & Georg Rudolph facing each other **Obv. Legend:** D:G • IOAN • CHRIST • ET • GEORG • RVD • FRA • **Rev:** 4-fold arms, 3 ornate helmets above, date at end of legend **Rev. Legend:** DVC • SIL • LIG • - ET • BREG • **Note:** Fr. #3151. Struck with 1/2 Thaler dies, KM#72.

Date	Mintage	VG	F	VF	XF	Unc
(1)609 (d)	—	1,700	3,200	6,600	11,500	—

KM# 113 5 DUCAT

17.5000 g., 0.9860 Gold 0.5547 oz. AGW **Ruler:** Johann Christian and Georg Rudolph **Obv:** 1/2-length figures of Johann Christian & Georg Rudolph facing each other behind flat surface with arabesques in exergue **Obv. Legend:** D.G. IOHAN. CHRIST. ET. GEOR(G). RVD. FRA. **Rev:** 4-fold arms, 3 ornate helmets above, date at end of legend **Rev. Legend:** DVC. SIL. LIG. - ET. BREG. **Note:** Fr. #3151. Struck with Thaler dies, KM#53.

Date	Mintage	VG	F	VF	XF	Unc
(1)610 (d)	—	1,700	3,200	6,600	11,500	—

KM# 138 5 DUCAT

17.5000 g., 0.9860 Gold 0.5547 oz. AGW **Ruler:** Johann Christian and Georg Rudolph **Obv:** Draped bust of Johann Christian right in inner circle, legend begins at bottom, divided by 2 small shields of arms at left and right **Obv. Legend:** D.G. IO - HANN. CHRISTI. - AN. ET. **Rev:** Draped bust of Georg Rudolf left divides date in inner circle, legend begins at upper left, 2 small shields of arms at left and right **Rev. Legend:** GEOR. RVD. FR. D. - SI. LIG. ET. BREG. **Note:** Fr. #3159. Struck with 1/2 Thaler dies, KM#134.

Date	Mintage	VG	F	VF	XF	Unc
1611	—	1,750	3,500	7,500	12,500	—

KM# 161 5 DUCAT

17.5000 g., 0.9860 Gold 0.5547 oz. AGW **Ruler:** Johann Christian and Georg Rudolph **Obv:** Bust of Johann Christian right, legend begins at upper left, divided by 2 small shields of arms at left and right **Obv. Legend:** D.G. IO. CHR. ET. G - EO. RVD. DVX. SI. L. B. **Rev:** Bust of Georg Rudolph left, legend ends with date, 2 small shields of arms at left and right **Rev. Legend:** MON. NOV. ARGE. - REICHST. **Mint:** Reichenstein **Note:** Fr. #3182. Struck with Thaler dies, KM#154.

Date	Mintage	VG	F	VF	XF	Unc
1615 Rare	—	—	—	—	—	—
1616 Rare	—	—	—	—	—	—

KM# 175 5 DUCAT

17.5000 g., 0.9860 Gold 0.5547 oz. AGW **Ruler:** Johann Christian and Georg Rudolph **Obv:** Bust of Johann Christian right, legend begins at upper left, divided by 2 small shields of arms at left and right **Obv. Legend:** D.G. IOHA. CHRI. ET. - GEORG. RVD. FRA. **Rev:** Bust of Georg Rudolph left, legend ends with date, 2 small shields of arms at left and right **Rev. Legend:** DVX. SIL. LIGNI. ET. - BREGEN. **Mint:** Reichenstein **Note:** Fr. #3159. Struck with 1/2 Thaler dies, KM#190.

Date	Mintage	VG	F	VF	XF	Unc
1617 HR	—	1,700	3,500	6,800	11,500	—

KM# 209 5 DUCAT

17.5000 g., 0.9860 Gold 0.5547 oz. AGW **Ruler:** Johann Christian and Georg Rudolph **Obv:** Armored, 1/2-length figures of Johann Christian and Georg Rudolph facing each other, horizontal line with ornamentation below **Obv. Legend:** D.G. IOHAN. CHRIS(T). ET. GEORG. RVDO. FRAT(R). **Rev:** Shield with flat top and rounded bottom of 4-fold arms, 3 ornate helmets above, date at end of legend **Rev. Legend:** DVC. SIL. LIGNIC. ET. BREGE. **Mint:** Reichenstein **Note:** Fr. #3151. Struck with Thaler dies, KM#169.

Date	Mintage	VG	F	VF	XF	Unc
1619 HR	—	1,900	3,850	7,000	13,500	—

KM# 281 5 DUCAT

17.5000 g., 0.9860 Gold 0.5547 oz. AGW **Ruler:** Georg Rudolf **Obv:** Armored bust of Georg Rudolph right, small imperial orb at top in margin **Obv. Legend:** D.G. GEOR. RVD. DVX. SIL. LIG. BRI. ET. GO. **Rev:** Crowned Spanish shield of 4-fold arms in baroque frame, date at end of legend **Rev. Legend:** MONETA. NOVA. AVREA. **Note:** Fr. #3188.

Date	Mintage	VG	F	VF	XF	Unc
1621 Rare	—	—	—	—	—	—

KM# 362 5 DUCAT

17.5000 g., 0.9860 Gold 0.5547 oz. AGW **Ruler:** Johann Christian **Obv:** Armored and mantled bust of Johann Christian right, small imperial orb at top in margin **Obv. Legend:** D.G. IOHAN. CHRIST. DVX. SIL. LIG. ET. B. **Rev:** 4-fold arms, 3 helmets above, date at end of legend **Rev. Legend:** MONETA. NOVA. CRVCIBVRGENSIS. **Mint:** Kreuzburg **Note:** Fr. #3184.

Date	Mintage	VG	F	VF	XF	Unc
1622 FS Rare	—	—	—	—	—	—

KM# 361 5 DUCAT

17.5000 g., 0.9860 Gold 0.5547 oz. AGW **Ruler:** Johann Christian **Obv:** Bust of Johann Christian right in inner circle, small imperial orb at top in margin **Obv. Legend:** D.G. IOHAN. CHRIST. DVX. SIL. LIG. ET. B. **Rev:** 4-fold arms topped by three helmets in inner circle, date at end of legend **Rev. Legend:** MONETA. NOVA. CRVCIBVRGENSIS. **Mint:** Kreuzburg **Note:** Fr. #3184. Struck with 1/2 Thaler dies, KM#343.

Date	Mintage	VG	F	VF	XF	Unc
1622 FS Rare	—	—	—	—	—	—

KM# 411 5 DUCAT

17.5000 g., 0.9860 Gold 0.5547 oz. AGW **Ruler:** Georg III, Ludwig IV and Christian **Obv:** Armored 1/2-length figures of Georg, Ludwig, and Christian facing, small imperial orb at top, arabesques in exergue **Obv. Legend:** D.G. GEORGIUS. LUDOVICUS. & CHRISTIANUS. FRATRES. **Rev:** 3 helmets above ornate 4-fold arms, date at end of legend **Rev. Legend:** DUCES. SILESIÆ. LIGNIC - ENSES. ET. BREGENSES. **Note:** Fr. #3196. Struck with 1/2 Thaler dies, KM#305 at either Liegnitz or Brieg mints. Varieties exist.

Date	Mintage	VG	F	VF	XF	Unc
1656 (pf)	—	1,200	2,500	5,900	10,000	—
1658 (pf)	—	1,050	2,100	5,000	9,400	—
1659 (pf) - EW	—	1,050	2,100	5,000	9,400	—

KM# 508 5 DUCAT

17.5000 g., 0.9860 Gold 0.5547 oz. AGW **Ruler:** Christian zu Brieg **Obv:** Armored and mantled bust of Christian right in inner circle **Obv. Legend:** CHRISTIANVS. D.G. DVX. SILESIÆ. LIGNICE. **Rev:** Crowned Silesian eagle in inner circle, crown divides date in margin, mintmaster's initials in oval at bottom **Rev. Legend:** BREGENSIS. ET. - WOLAVIENSIS. **Mint:** Brieg **Note:** Fr. #3210.

Date	Mintage	VG	F	VF	XF	Unc
1672 CBS Rare	—	—	—	—	—	—

FR# 3220 5 DUCAT

17.5000 g., 0.9860 Gold 0.5547 oz. AGW **Subject:** Death of Georg Wilhelm **Note:** Similar to 2 Ducat, Fr. #3221.

Date	Mintage	VG	F	VF	XF	Unc
1675 Rare	—	—	—	—	—	—

FR# A3150 6 DUCAT

21.0000 g., 0.9860 Gold 0.6657 oz. AGW **Obv:** Small busts of Johann Christian and Georg Rudolf **Note:** Struck with 1/2 Thaler dies.

Date	Mintage	VG	F	VF	XF	Unc
1605 Rare	—	—	—	—	—	—

KM# 61 6 DUCAT

21.0000 g., 0.9860 Gold 0.6657 oz. AGW **Ruler:** Johann Christian and Georg Rudolph **Obv:** 1/2-length figures of Johann Christian & Georg Rudolph facing each other behind flat surface with arabesques in exergue **Obv. Legend:** D.G. IOHAN. CHRIST. ET. GEOR. RVD. FRA. **Rev:** 4-fold arms, 3 ornate helmets above, date at end of legend **Rev. Legend:** DVC. SIL. LIG. - ET. BREGEN. **Note:** Fr. #3150. Struck with Thaler dies, KM#53.

Date	Mintage	VG	F	VF	XF	Unc
(1)607 Rare	—	—	—	—	—	—

KM# 115 6 DUCAT

21.0000 g., 0.9860 Gold 0.6657 oz. AGW **Ruler:** Johann Christian and Georg Rudolph **Obv:** 1/2-length figures of Johann Christian & Georg Rudolph facing each other behind flat surface with arabesques in exergue **Obv. Legend:** D.G. IOHAN. CHRIST. ET. GEOR(G). RVD. FRA. **Rev:** 4-fold arms, 3 ornate helmets above, date at end of legend **Rev. Legend:** DVC. SIL. LIG. - ET. BREG. **Note:** Fr. #3150. Struck at either Liegnitz or Brieg mints.

Date	Mintage	VG	F	VF	XF	Unc
(1)610 (d) Rare	—	—	—	—	—	—

KM# 140 6 DUCAT

21.0000 g., 0.9860 Gold 0.6657 oz. AGW **Ruler:** Johann Christian and Georg Rudolph **Obv:** Draped bust of Johann Christian right in inner circle, legend begins at bottom, divided by 2 small shields of arms at left and right, small imperial orb in circle at bottom **Obv. Legend:** D.G. IO - HANN. CHRISTI. - AN. ET. **Rev:** Draped bust of Georg Rudolf left divides date in inner circle, legend begins at upper left, 2 small shields of arms at left and right **Rev. Legend:** GEOR. RVD. FRA. D. - SIL. LIG. ET. BREG. **Note:** Fr. #3158. Struck with Thaler dies, KM#128.

Date	Mintage	VG	F	VF	XF	Unc
1611 Rare	—	—	—	—	—	—

KM# 163 6 DUCAT

21.0000 g., 0.9860 Gold 0.6657 oz. AGW **Ruler:** Johann Christian and Georg Rudolph **Obv:** Bust of Johann Christian right, legend begins at upper left, divided by 2 small shields of arms at left and right **Obv. Legend:** D.G. IO. CHR. ET. G - EO. RVD. DVX. SI. L. B. **Rev:** Bust of Georg Rudolph left, legend ends with date, 2 small shields of arms at left and right **Rev. Legend:** MON. NOV. ARGE. - REICHST. **Mint:** Reichenstein **Note:** Fr. #3181. Struck with Thaler dies, KM#154. Specimen dated 1616 sold at auction in 1983 as XF for SFr 30,500.

Date	Mintage	VG	F	VF	XF	Unc
1615 Rare	—	—	—	—	—	—
1616 Rare	—	—	—	—	—	—

KM# 177 6 DUCAT
21.0000 g., 0.9860 Gold 0.6657 oz. AGW **Ruler:** Johann Christian and Georg Rudolph **Obv:** Armored 1/2-length figures of Johann Christian and Georg Rudolf facing each other, horizontal line with ornamentation below **Obv. Legend:** D.G. IOHA(N). CHRIS(T). ET. GEOR(G). RVDO. FRAT(R). **Rev:** Shield with flat top and rounded bottom of 4-fold arms, 3 ornate helmets above, date at end of legend **Rev. Legend:** DVC. SIL. LIGNIC. ET. BREGE. **Mint:** Reichenstein **Note:** Fr. #3150. Struck with Thaler dies, KM#169.

Date	Mintage	VG	F	VF	XF	Unc
1616 Rare	—	—	—	—	—	—
1617 HR Rare	—	—	—	—	—	—
1619 HR Rare	—	—	—	—	—	—
1621 Rare	—	—	—	—	—	—

KM# 283 6 DUCAT
21.0000 g., 0.9860 Gold 0.6657 oz. AGW **Ruler:** Georg Rudolf **Obv:** Armored bust of Georg Rudolph right in inner circle, small imperial orb at top **Obv. Legend:** D.G. GEORG. RVDOLPHVS. DVC. SILES. **Rev:** 4-fold arms topped by three helmets in inner circle, date at end of legend **Rev. Legend:** LIGNIC. ET. BREG. **Mint:** Haynau **Note:** Fr. #3193. Struck with Thaler dies, KM#269.

Date	Mintage	VG	F	VF	XF	Unc
16Z1 MT Rare	—	—	—	—	—	—

KM# 117 7 DUCAT
24.5000 g., 0.9860 Gold 0.7766 oz. AGW **Ruler:** Johann Christian and Georg Rudolph **Obv:** 1/2-length figures of Johann Christian and Georg Rudolf facing each other behind flat surface with arabesques in exergue **Obv. Legend:** D.G. IOHAN. CHRIST. ET. GEOR(G). RVD. FRA. **Rev:** 4-fold arms, 3 ornate helmets above, date at end of legend **Rev. Legend:** DVC. SIL. LIG. - ET. BREG. **Note:** Fr. #3149. Struck with Thaler dies, KM#53 at either Liegnitz or Brieg mints.

Date	Mintage	VG	F	VF	XF	Unc
(1)610 (d) Rare	—	—	—	—	—	—

KM# 285 7 DUCAT
24.5000 g., 0.9860 Gold 0.7766 oz. AGW **Ruler:** Johann Christian **Obv:** Armored bust of Johann Christian right **Obv. Legend:** D.G. IOHAN. CHRISTIAN. DVX. SIL. **Rev:** 4-fold arms, 3 helmets above, date at top in margin **Rev. Legend:** LIGN. ET. BREG. SVP. CAPVT. SIL. **Mint:** Ohlau **Note:** Fr. #3183. Struck with Thaler dies, KM#266.

Date	Mintage	VG	F	VF	XF	Unc
16Z1 HR Rare	—	—	—	—	—	—

KM# 286 7 DUCAT
24.5000 g., 0.9860 Gold 0.7766 oz. AGW **Ruler:** Georg Rudolf **Obv:** Armored bust of Georg Rudolph right, small imperial orb at top **Obv. Legend:** D.G. GEORG. RVDOLPHVS. DVC. SILES. **Rev:** 4-fold arms, 3 helmets above, date at end of legend **Rev. Legend:** LIGNIC. ET. BREG. **Mint:** Haynau **Note:** Fr. #3192. Struck with Thaler dies, KM#269.

Date	Mintage	VG	F	VF	XF	Unc
16Z1 MT Rare	—	—	—	—	—	—

KM# 179 8 DUCAT
28.0000 g., 0.9860 Gold 0.8876 oz. AGW **Ruler:** Johann Christian and Georg Rudolph **Obv:** Large bust of Johann Christian right, legend begins at upper left, divided by 2 small shields of arms at left and right **Obv. Legend:** D.G. IO. CHR. ET. G - EO. RVD. DVX. SI. L. B. **Rev:** Large bust of Georg Rudolph left, legend ends with date, 2 small shields of arms at left and right **Rev. Legend:** MON. NOV. ARGE. - REICHST. **Mint:** Reichenstein **Note:** Fr. #3180. Struck with Thaler dies, KM#154.

Date	Mintage	VG	F	VF	XF	Unc
1617 Rare	—	—	—	—	—	—

KM# 288 8 DUCAT
28.0000 g., 0.9860 Gold 0.8876 oz. AGW **Ruler:** Georg Rudolf **Obv:** Armored bust of Georg Rudolph right, small imperial orb at top **Obv. Legend:** D.G. GEORG. RVDOLPHVS. DVC. SILES. **Rev:** 4-fold arms, 3 helmets above, date at end of legend **Rev. Legend:** LIGNIC. ET. BREG. **Mint:** Haynau **Note:** Fr. #3191. Struck with Thaler dies, KM#269.

Date	Mintage	VG	F	VF	XF	Unc
16Z1 MT Rare	—	—	—	—	—	—

KM# 51 10 DUCAT
35.0000 g., 0.9860 Gold 1.1095 oz. AGW **Ruler:** Johann Christian and Georg Rudolph **Subject:** Death of Joachim Friedrich's Widow, Anna Maria von Anhalt **Obv:** Facing bust wearing small hat **Rev:** Crowned shield of 8-fold arms within central shield of Anhalt, double marginal legends with R.N. date. **Rev. Legend:** Outer: MEM. IL. MAT. ANNÆ. MAR. PR. ANHAL. DVCI. SIL. LEG. BREG. QVÆ.; Inner: PIA. ORIIT. M. NOV. DIE. XIV. M.D.C.V. F.F.

Date	Mintage	VG	F	VF	XF	Unc
MDCV (1605) Rare	—	—	—	—	—	—

KM# 89 10 DUCAT
35.0000 g., 0.9860 Gold 1.1095 oz. AGW **Ruler:** Johann Christian and Georg Rudolph **Obv:** Small busts of Johann Christian and Georg Rudolf facing each other **Obv. Legend:** D.G. IOAN. CHRIST. ET. GEORG. RVD. FRA. **Rev:** Ornately shaped shield of 4-fold arms, 3 helmets above, date at end of legend **Rev. Legend:** DVC. SIL. LIG. - ET. BREG. **Note:** Fr. #3148. Struck with Thaler dies, KM#269 at either Liegnitz or Brieg mints.

Date	Mintage	VG	F	VF	XF	Unc
(1)609 (d) Rare	—	—	—	—	—	—

KM# 88 10 DUCAT
35.0000 g., 0.9860 Gold 1.1095 oz. AGW **Ruler:** Johann Christian and Georg Rudolph **Obv:** 3/4-length armored figure to right divides date, small imperial orb at top, 2 small shields of arms below **Obv. Legend:** D.G. IOHANN - CHRISTIAN. ET. **Rev:** 3/4-length armored figure to left, 2 small shields of arms below **Rev. Legend:** (Large cross) GEORG. RVD. FRAT - DVC. SIL. LIG. ET. BRE. **Note:** Fr. #3156.

Date	Mintage	VG	F	VF	XF	Unc
1609 Rare	—	—	—	—	—	—

KM# 119 10 DUCAT
35.0000 g., 0.9860 Gold 1.1095 oz. AGW **Ruler:** Johann Christian and Georg Rudolph **Obv:** Small 1/2-length figures facing each other behind flat surface with arabesques in exergue **Obv. Legend:** D.G. IOHAN. CHRIST. ET. GEOR(G). RVD. FRA. **Rev:** 4-fold arms, 3 ornate helmets above, date at end of legend **Rev. Legend:** DVC. SIL. LIG. - ET. BREG. **Note:** Fr. #3148. Struck with Thaler dies, KM#53 at either Liegnitz or Brieg mints.

Date	Mintage	VG	F	VF	XF	Unc
(1)610 (d) Rare	—	—	—	—	—	—

KM# 142 10 DUCAT
35.0000 g., 0.9860 Gold 1.1095 oz. AGW **Ruler:** Johann Christian and Georg Rudolph **Obv:** Draped bust of Johann Christian right, legend begins at bottom, divided by 2 small shields of arms at left and right, small imperial orb in circle at bottom **Obv. Legend:** D.G. IO - HANN. CHRISTI. - AN. ET. **Rev:** Draped bust of Georg Rudolph left divides date, legend begins at upper left, 2 small shields of arms at left and right **Rev. Legend:** GEOR. RVD. FRA. D. - SIL. LIG. ET. BREG. **Note:** Fr. #3157. Struck with Thaler dies, KM#128.

Date	Mintage	VG	F	VF	XF	Unc
1611 Rare	—	—	—	—	—	—

KM# 181 10 DUCAT
35.0000 g., 0.9860 Gold 1.1095 oz. AGW **Ruler:** Johann Christian and Georg Rudolph **Obv:** Large bust of Johann Christian right, legend begins at upper left, divided by 2 small shields of arms at left and right **Obv. Legend:** D.G. IO. CHR. ET. G - EO. RVD. DVX. SI. L. B. **Rev:** Large bust of Georg Rudolph left, legend ends with date, 2 small shields of arms at left and right **Rev. Legend:** MON. NOV. ARGE. - REICHST. **Mint:** Reichenstein **Note:** Fr. #3179. Struck with Thaler dies, KM#154.

Date	Mintage	VG	F	VF	XF	Unc
1617 Rare	—	—	—	—	—	—

KM# 182 10 DUCAT
35.0000 g., 0.9860 Gold 1.1095 oz. AGW **Ruler:** Johann Christian and Georg Rudolph **Obv:** Armored 1/2-length figures of Johann Christian and Georg Rudolph facing each other, horizontal line with ornamentation below **Obv. Legend:** D.G. IOHAN. CHRIS(T). ET. GEORG. RVDO. FRAT(R). **Rev:** Shield with flat top and rounded bottom of 4-fold arms, 3 ornate helmets above, date at end of legend **Rev. Legend:** DVC. SIL. LIGNIC. ET. BREGE. **Mint:** Reichenstein **Note:** Fr. #3148. Struck with Thaler dies, KM#169.

Date	Mintage	VG	F	VF	XF	Unc
1617 HR Rare	—	—	—	—	—	—
1619 HR Rare	—	—	—	—	—	—

KM# 290 10 DUCAT
35.0000 g., 0.9860 Gold 1.1095 oz. AGW **Ruler:** Georg Rudolf **Obv:** Armored bust of Georg Rudolph right, small imperial orb at top **Obv. Legend:** D.G. GEORG. RVDOLPHVS. DVC. SILES. **Rev:** 4-fold arms, 3 helmets above, date at end of legend **Rev. Legend:** LIGNIC. ET. BREG. **Mint:** Haynau **Note:** Struck with Thaler dies, KM#269.

Date	Mintage	VG	F	VF	XF	Unc
16Z1 MT Rare	—	—	—	—	—	—

KM# 498 10 DUCAT
35.0000 g., 0.9860 Gold 1.1095 oz. AGW **Ruler:** Christian zu Brieg **Obv:** Armored and mantled bust of Christian right **Obv. Legend:** CHRISTIANVS. D.G. DVX. SILESIÆ. LIGNICE(NSIS). **Rev:** Silesian eagle, crown above divides date in margin, mintmaster's initials in oval at bottom **Rev. Legend:** BREGENSIS. E(T). - WOLAVIENSIS. **Note:** Fr. #3209. Struck with Thaler dies, KM#490 at Brieg or Breslau mints.

Date	Mintage	VG	F	VF	XF	Unc
1666 GFH/CBS Rare	—	—	—	—	—	—

KM# 440 12 DUCAT
42.0000 g., 0.9860 Gold 1.3314 oz. AGW **Ruler:** Georg III, Ludwig IV and Christian **Obv:** 1/2-length figures of Georg, Ludwig & Christian facing, horizontal line below with arabesques in exergue, small imperial orb at top **Obv. Legend:** D.G. GEORGIVS. LUDOVICVS. & CHRISTIANVS. FRATRES. **Rev:** 3 helmets above oval 4-fold arms, date at end of legend **Rev. Legend:** DVCES. SILESIÆ. LIGNIC. BRE - GENS. ET. WOLAVIENSES. **Note:** Struck with Thaler dies, KM#414 at either Liegnitz or Brieg mints.

Date	Mintage	VG	F	VF	XF	Unc
1659 (pf) - EW Rare	—	—	—	—	—	—

KM# 183 20 DUCAT
70.0000 g., 0.9860 Gold 2.2190 oz. AGW **Obv:** Small busts of Johann Christian and Georg Rudolf **Note:** Fr. #3147.

Date	Mintage	VG	F	VF	XF	Unc
1617 Rare	—	—	—	—	—	—

CITY

REGULAR COINAGE

KM# A5 2 HELLER
Copper **Obv:** Two crossed keys divide G- H, L above, II below **Note:** Uniface.

Date	Mintage	VG	F	VF	XF	Unc
ND GH	—	6.00	12.00	27.00	55.00	—

KM# A6 3 HELLER
Copper, 14.8 mm. **Obv:** Bohemian lion striding left towards two crossed keys at left, L above, G III H below **Note:** Uniface.

Date	Mintage	VG	F	VF	XF	Unc
ND GH	—	6.00	12.00	27.00	55.00	—

KM# A7 3 HELLER
Copper **Obv:** Trefoil with L in top lobe dividing G - H, crossed keys lower left, Bohemian lion lower right, III below.

Date	Mintage	VG	F	VF	XF	Unc
ND GH	—	6.00	12.00	27.00	55.00	—
ND	—	6.00	12.00	20.00	45.00	—

KM# A8 3 HELLER
Copper **Obv:** Trefoil with L in top lobe dividing date, lion lower left, crossed keys lower right, III below

Date	Mintage	VG	F	VF	XF	Unc
16ZZ GH	—	6.00	12.00	27.00	55.00	—

KM# A9 3 HELLER
Copper **Obv:** Crossed keys below L divide G - H **Note:** Uniface.

Date	Mintage	VG	F	VF	XF	Unc
16ZZ GH	—	6.00	12.00	25.00	50.00	—

PATTERNS

Including off metal strikes

KM#	Date	Mintage	Identification	Mkt Val
Pn1	1610	—	3 Pfennig (Dreier). Gold. KM#91. Ref. F/S#(1461).	—
Pn2	16ZZ	—	1/4 Thaler. Gold. KM#339. Ref. F/S#1631a.	—
Pn3	1664	—	1/4 Thaler. Tin. Ref. J/M-#134. KM#476.	—

SOEST

Soest is a town in Westphalia, 27 miles (46 km) east of Dortmund. It was important in trade and as an imperial mint from at least the 11th-12th centuries. After Westphalia, for the most part, came under the control of the archbishops of Cologne and Soest grew in its role as a member of the Hanseatic League, the two came into increasing conflict. By the mid-15th century, Soest sought protection from the duke of Cleves. The town produced its own coinage in the late 15th century and then from the second half of the 16th until the mid-18th centuries. Prussia annexed Soest in 1813.

MINT OFFICIALS

Date	Name
1601-12	Heinrich Holtkamp, die-cutter
1616-354	Gottfried Nase, die-cutter
1637	Jorgen in dem Brande, die-cutter
1654	Hermann Schoneberg, die-cutter
1662-83	Johann Schotte, die-cutter
1680, 1703	Goswin Schönberg, die-cutter
ca. 1700	Georg Harnold

ARMS

A key, usually with ornate tabs, standing vertically.

REFERENCES

K = Hans Krusy, "Beiträge zur Münzgeschichte der Stadt Soest," **Soester Zeitschrift** 87 (1975), pp. 5-17; 88 (1976), pp. 28-46; 89 (1977), pp. 78-95; 91 (1979), pp. 71-131.

W = Joseph Weingärtner, **Beschreibung der Kupfermünzen Westfalens**, 2 vols., Paderborn, 1872-75.

PROVINCIAL TOWN

REGULAR COINAGE

KM# 6 HELLER (1/2 Pfennig)

Copper **Obv:** Vertical key, date at end of legend **Obv. Legend:** SVSATE - NSIS **Rev:** •I•••I• in circle **Note:** Ref. K#47.

Date	Mintage	Good	VG	F	VF	XF
1607	864	—	—	—	—	—

KM# 14 PFENNIG

Copper **Obv:** Vertical key in circle **Rev:** I in ornamented rhombus **Note:** Ref. K#54.

Date	Mintage	Good	VG	F	VF	XF
ND(1612-15)	4,992	—	—	—	—	—

KM# 17 PFENNIG

Copper **Obv:** Vertical key, I below tabs **Obv. Legend:** SVS - ATENSIS. **Rev:** I in ornamented rhombus **Note:** Ref. K#64.

Date	Mintage	Good	VG	F	VF	XF
ND(1620-21)	7,776	12.00	25.00	35.00	75.00	—

KM# 7 2 PFENNIG

Copper **Obv:** Vertical key, date at end of legend **Obv. Legend:** SVSAT - ENSIS **Rev:** •I•I• in ornamented circle **Note:** Ref. K#46.

Date	Mintage	Good	VG	F	VF	XF
1607	2,304	12.00	25.00	35.00	75.00	—

KM# 12 2 PFENNIG

Copper **Obv:** Vertical key **Obv. Legend:** SVSA - TNESIS **Rev:** I•••I in ornamented square **Note:** Ref. K#52.

Date	Mintage	Good	VG	F	VF	XF
ND(1610-11)	1,800	—	—	—	—	—

KM# 15 2 PFENNIG

Copper **Obv:** Vertical key, date at end of legend **Obv. Legend:** SVSA - TENSIS **Rev:** • I • I • in ornamented circle **Note:** Ref. K#54.

Date	Mintage	Good	VG	F	VF	XF
1612 3594	—	—	—	—	—	—

KM# 1 3 PFENNIG

Copper **Obv:** Vertical key, date at end of legend **Obv. Legend:** SVSA - TENSIS. **Rev:** III in ornamented border **Note:** Ref. K#44.

Date	Mintage	Good	VG	F	VF	XF
1604	2,016	12.00	25.00	35.00	75.00	—

KM# 11 3 PFENNIG

Copper **Obv:** Vertical key **Obv. Legend:** SVSATENSIS. **Rev:** •I•I•I• in heart-shaped ornamented shield **Note:** Ref. K#51.

Date	Mintage	Good	VG	F	VF	XF
ND(1609-13)	960	—	—	—	—	—

KM# 19 3 PFENNIG

Copper **Obv:** Vertical key, III below tabs, date at end of legend **Obv. Legend:** SVSA - TENSIS **Rev:** III in ornamented square **Note:** Ref. K#59-61. Varieties exist.

Date	Mintage	Good	VG	F	VF	XF
(16)20	17,000	—	—	—	—	—

KM# 20 3 PFENNIG

Copper **Obv:** Vertical key, III below tabs **Obv. Legend:** SVSA - TENSIS **Rev:** III in ornamented square **Note:** Ref. K#62. Varieties exist. Mintage numbers included with KM#19.

Date	Mintage	Good	VG	F	VF	XF
ND(1620)	—	7.00	12.00	25.00	50.00	—

KM# 21 3 PFENNIG

Copper **Obv:** Vertical key **Obv. Legend:** SVSAT - EN **Rev:** III in ornamented square **Note:** Ref. K#63. Mintage numbers included with KM#19.

Date	Mintage	Good	VG	F	VF	XF
ND(1620)	—	—	—	—	—	—

KM# 35 3 PFENNIG

Copper **Obv:** Vertical key **Rev:** o I•I•I o in ornamented frame **Note:** Ref. K#71.

Date	Mintage	Good	VG	F	VF	XF
ND(1625-35)	14,000	—	—	—	—	—

KM# 41 3 PFENNIG

Copper **Obv:** Vertical key **Obv. Legend:** 1 - 6 - 6 - Z. **Rev:** III in ornamented square **Note:** Ref. K#74, 76. Varieties exist.

Date	Mintage	Good	VG	F	VF	XF
166Z	16,000	35.00	75.00	150	—	—
1670	37,000	35.00	75.00	150	—	—

KM# 42 3 PFENNIG

Copper **Obv:** Vertical key **Obv. Legend:** 1 - 6 - 6 - Z **Rev:** III in wreath **Note:** Ref. K#75. Mintage numbers included with KM#41.

Date	Mintage	Good	VG	F	VF	XF
166Z	—	—	—	—	—	—

KM# 45 3 PFENNIG

Copper **Obv:** Vertical key **Rev:** III in circle of pellets and small ornaments in field **Note:** Ref. K#78.

Date	Mintage	Good	VG	F	VF	XF
1673	14,000	—	—	—	—	—

KM# 47 3 PFENNIG

Copper **Obv:** Vertical key **Rev:** III in circle of pellets and small ornaments in field **Note:** Ref. K#79-80, 82-93. Varieties exist.

Date	Mintage	Good	VG	F	VF	XF
ND(1676-92)	94,000	135	275	575	1,150	—

KM# 13 4 PFENNIG

Copper **Obv:** Vertical key, date at end of legend **Obv. Legend:** SVSATEN - SIS **Rev:** IIII in ornamented circle **Note:** Ref. K#53.

Date	Mintage	Good	VG	F	VF	XF
1611	2,772	—	—	—	—	—

KM# 2 6 PFENNIG

Copper **Obv:** Vertical key **Obv. Legend:** SVSA - TENSIS. **Rev:** VI in ornamented circle **Note:** Ref. K#43.

Date	Mintage	Good	VG	F	VF	XF
1604	20,000	100	210	425	—	—

KM# 23 6 PFENNIG

Copper **Obv:** Vertical key, VI under tabs **Obv. Legend:** SVS - ATENSIS. **Rev:** VI in wide ornamented margin **Note:** Ref. K#65.

Date	Mintage	Good	VG	F	VF	XF
ND(1620-38)	314,000	12.00	25.00	35.00	75.00	—

KM# 24 6 PFENNIG

Copper **Obv:** Vertical key, VI under tabls **Obv. Legend:** SVS - ATENSIS. **Rev:** III in ornamented square **Note:** Ref. K#66. Mule.

Date	Mintage	Good	VG	F	VF	XF
ND(1620)	—	—	—	—	—	—

KM# 25 6 PFENNIG

Copper **Obv:** Vertical key, VI under tabs **Obv. Legend:** SVSA - TENSIS. **Rev:** VI in wide ornamented margin **Note:** Ref. K#67. Varieties exist. Mintage numbers included with KM#23.

Date	Mintage	Good	VG	F	VF	XF
ND(1620-38)	—	12.00	25.00	40.00	85.00	—

KM# 26 6 PFENNIG

Copper **Obv:** Vertical key, VI under tables **Obv. Legend:** SVSAT - ENSIS. **Rev:** VI in wide ornamented margin **Note:** Ref. K#68. Varieties exist. Mintage numbers included with KM#23.

Date	Mintage	Good	VG	F	VF	XF
ND(1620-38)	—	12.00	25.00	40.00	85.00	—

KM# 27 6 PFENNIG

Copper **Obv:** Vertical key, VI under tabs **Obv. Legend:** SVSATE - NSIS. **Rev:** VI in wide ornamented margin **Note:** Ref. K#69. Mintage numbers included with KM#23.

Date	Mintage	Good	VG	F	VF	XF
ND(1620-38)	—	12.00	25.00	40.00	85.00	—

KM# 28 6 PFENNIG

Copper **Obv:** Vertical key, VI under tabs **Obv. Legend:** SVSATEN - SIS. **Rev:** VI in wide ornamented margin **Note:** Ref. K#70. Mintage numbers included with KM#23.

Date	Mintage	Good	VG	F	VF	XF
ND(1620-38)	—	12.00	25.00	40.00	85.00	—

KM# 37 6 PFENNIG

Copper **Obv:** Vertical key, VI under tabs **Obv. Legend:** SVSA - TENSIS. **Rev:** o I • I • I o in ornamented frame **Note:** Ref. K#72. Mule.

Date	Mintage	Good	VG	F	VF	XF
ND(1625-35)	—	15.00	30.00	55.00	110	—

KM# 39 6 PFENNIG

Copper **Obv:** Vertical key, handle of key is a trefoil, VI under tabs **Obv. Legend:** SVSA - TENSIS. **Rev:** VI in wide ornamented margin **Note:** Ref. K#73.

Date	Mintage	Good	VG	F	VF	XF
ND(ca1654)	—	15.00	30.00	55.00	110	—

KM# 43 6 PFENNIG

Copper **Obv:** Vertical key, VI under tabs **Obv. Legend:** SVSA - TENSIS **Rev:** III in ornamented square **Note:** Ref. K#77.

Date	Mintage	Good	VG	F	VF	XF
ND(ca1670)	—	15.00	30.00	55.00	110	—

KM# 48 6 PFENNIG

Copper **Obv:** Vertical key, III below tabs **Rev:** III in circle of pellets and small ornaments in field **Note:** Ref. K#81. Mule.

Date	Mintage	Good	VG	F	VF	XF
ND(1676-92)	—	15.00	30.00	55.00	110	—

KM# 3 12 PFENNIG

Copper **Obv:** Vertical key in ornamented square, angel's head and wings above, date at end of legend **Obv. Legend:** SVSATENSIS **Rev:** XII in ornamented square within ornamented circle **Note:** Ref. K#41.

Date	Mintage	Good	VG	F	VF	XF
1604	—	15.00	30.00	60.00	125	—

KM# 4 12 PFENNIG

Copper **Obv:** Vertical key **Obv. Legend:** SVSA - TENSIS. **Rev:** XII in ornamented circle **Note:** Ref. K#42, 45, 48, 50. Varieties exist.

Date	Mintage	Good	VG	F	VF	XF
1604	—	120	235	475	950	—
1605	3,852	15.00	30.00	60.00	125	—
1608	11,000	15.00	30.00	60.00	125	—
1610	8,916	15.00	30.00	60.00	125	—

KM# 9 12 PFENNIG

Copper **Obv:** Vertical key **Obv. Legend:** SVSATEN - SIS **Rev:** XII in ornamented circle **Note:** Ref. K#49. Mintage numbers included with KM#4.

Date	Mintage	Good	VG	F	VF	XF
1608	—	120	235	475	850	—

KM# 30 12 PFENNIG

Copper **Obv:** Vertical key with 12 below tabs in oval baroque frame, date at top in margin **Obv. Legend:** SVSATE - NSIS **Rev:** XII in ornamented circular margin **Note:** Ref. K#57.

Date	Mintage	Good	VG	F	VF	XF
1620	174,000	12.00	25.00	35.00	75.00	—

KM# 31 12 PFENNIG

Copper **Obv:** Vertical key with 12 below tabs in oval baroque frame, date in margin at top **Obv. Legend:** SVSATE - NSIS **Rev:** VI in wide ornamented margin **Note:** Ref. K#58. Mule.

Date	Mintage	Good	VG	F	VF	XF
1620	—	15.00	30.00	60.00	125	—

KM# 33 2 SCHILLING

Copper **Obv:** Soest arms in oval baroque frame, date divided above **Obv. Legend:** SVSATENSIS. **Rev:** Large 'II' in ornate circular margin, (S) at top **Note:** Prev KM#5.

Date	Mintage	VG	F	VF	XF	Unc
1620	686,000	13.00	27.00	55.00	110	—

SOLMS-BRAUNFELS

Established in the first division of Solms in 1409, Solms-Braunfels was further divided in 1592 into Solms-Braunfels, Solms-Greiffenstein and Solms-Hungen. Braunfels is located just 1.5 miles (3 km) south of Burgsolms (Hohensolms). Greiffenstein is a small village 7 miles (12 km) northwest of Burgsolms, whereas Hungen is further away, being 12.5 miles (21 km) southeast of Giessen or 22 miles (36 km) east-southeast of Burgsolms. The direct line of Solms-Braunfels became extinct in 1693 and passed to Greiffenstein, which was known as Braunfels from that date onwards count wa.

RULERS

Johann Albrecht I, 1592-1623
jointly with Wilhelm I von
Solms-Greiffenstein, 1602-1635
Reinhard von Solms-Hungen, 1610-1630
Johann Albrecht II, 1623-1648
Heinrich Trajectinus, 1648-1693
Wilhelm Moritz von Solms-Greiffenstein, 1693-1724

MINTMASTER INITIALS

Initial	Date	Name
(a)= 	Ca. 1623	

COUNTSHIP

REGULAR COINAGE

KM# 15 ALBUS

Silver **Obv:** Helmeted arms of Solms **Obv. Legend:** SOLMS - GREIFSTEIN **Rev:** Value **Rev. Legend:** NACH. DEM. F FURTER. SCHLVS. **Rev. Inscription:** I / ALBUS / date

Date	Mintage	VG	F	VF	XF	Unc
1693	—	125	250	500	1,000	—

KM# 16 ALBUS

Silver **Obv:** Similar to KM#15 **Rev. Legend:** NACH DEM . FRANCFVRTER. SCHLVS. **Note:** Varieties exist.

Date	Mintage	VG	F	VF	XF	Unc
1693	—	125	250	500	1,000	—

KM# 17 2 ALBUS

Silver **Obv:** Helmeted Solms arms **Obv. Legend:** SOLMS .

GREIFFENSTEIN. **Rev. Legend:** NACH. DEM. FRANCFURTER SCHLUS. **Rev. Inscription:** II / ALBUS / date **Note:** Varieties exist.

Date	Mintage	VG	F	VF	XF	Unc
1693	—	150	300	600	1,150	—

KM# 9 15 KREUZER (1/4 Gulden)

Silver **Obv:** Bust right, value "XV" below **Obv. Legend:** Titles of Wilhelm Moritz around **Rev:** Crowned eight-fold arms divide date **Rev. Legend:** Titles continued around

Date	Mintage	VG	F	VF	XF	Unc
1691	—	500	1,000	2,000	—	—

KM# 12 15 KREUZER (1/4 Gulden)

Silver **Obv:** Bust right, titles of Wilhelm Moritz around **Rev:** Crowned eight-fold arms with central shield divide date, value "XV" in oval below, titles continued

Date	Mintage	VG	F	VF	XF	Unc
1692	—	500	1,000	2,000	—	—

KM# 3 1/4 THALER

Silver **Obv:** Helmeted arms of Solms **Obv. Legend:** SOLMS - GREIFSTEIN **Rev:** Value **Rev. Legend:** NACH. DEM. F FURTER. SCHLVS. **Rev. Inscription:** I / ALBUS / date **Note:** Mining Thaler. Similar to KM#15.

Date	Mintage	VG	F	VF	XF	Unc
1623 (a)	—	—	—	—	—	—

KM# 4 1/2 THALER

Silver **Obv:** 3 helmets in decoration above HOINGEN, date below **Obv. Legend:** *MO: NO: EX: PRI: SOL: WILH: ET: REINH: CO: SOL: FR(A) **Rev:** Crowned imperial eagle with orb on breast **Rev. Legend:** FERDIN • II • D • G • ROM • IMP **Note:** Mining Thaler. Similar to KM#5.

Date	Mintage	VG	F	VF	XF	Unc
1623 (a)	—	2,100	4,200	8,400	—	—

KM# 10 2/3 THALER (Gulden)

Silver **Obv:** Bust right **Obv. Legend:** Titles of Heinrich Trajectinus around **Rev:** Oval eight-fold arms, crown above divides date **Rev. Legend:** Titles continued

Date	Mintage	VG	F	VF	XF	Unc
1691	—	—	—	—	—	—

KM# 11 2/3 THALER (Gulden)

Silver **Obv:** Bust right **Obv. Legend:** Titles of Wilhelm Moritz around **Rev:** Crowned eight-fold arms with central shield divide date **Rev. Legend:** Titles continued

Date	Mintage	VG	F	VF	XF	Unc
1691	—	—	—	—	—	—

KM# 13 2/3 THALER (Gulden)

Silver **Obv:** Similar to KM#11 **Rev:** Arms supported by two griffins, value "2/3" in oval below divides date

Date	Mintage	VG	F	VF	XF	Unc
1692	—	—	—	—	—	—

KM# 6 THALER

Silver **Obv:** Similar to KM#5 **Rev:** Crowned imperial eagle with orb on breast **Rev. Legend:** FERDIN • II • DEI • GR • RO • IMP... **Note:** Dav.#7744.

Date	Mintage	VG	F	VF	XF	Unc
1623//1625 (a)	—	2,000	4,000	7,500	12,500	—

KM# 5 THALER

Silver **Obv:** Three helmets in decoration above HOINGEN, date below **Obv. Legend:** *MO: NO: EX: PRI: SOL: WILH: ET: REINH: CO: SOL: FR(A) **Rev:** Crowned imperial eagle with orb on breast **Rev. Legend:** FERDIN • II • D • G • ROM • IMP... **Note:** Many varieties in abbreviations and punctuation exist. Dav.#7743.

Date	Mintage	VG	F	VF	XF	Unc
1623 (a)	—	1,750	3,000	6,500	11,500	—

SOLMS-HERULETZ

(Neuheroletz)

Established as a separate line from Solms-Lich in 1590, it did not acquire a distinctive name until the count, an officer in the service of the emperor, purchased the confiscated Bohemian lordships of Heruletz and Humpolezin in 1623. Marriage brought other Bohemian properties into the count's holdings. It appears that coinage for this distant branch of the dynasty was all struck in the Lich mint. The line only lasted for two generations and reverted to Solms-Lich upon extinction in 1670.

RULERS

Philipp II, 1590-1631
Philipp Adam, 1631-1670

MINT OFFICIALS' INITIALS

Lich Mint

Initial	Date	Name
(a)= Z ꝑ or (b)= ⌒ꝑ	1613-14	Georg Arnes (Arends)
(c)= ꝑ or ꝑK or ꝑB or tree trunk	1614-21	Ernst Knorr
	1613-21	Hieronymous Pinck, die-cutter

COUNTSHIP

REGULAR COINAGE

KM# 3 PFENNIG

Silver **Ruler:** Philipp II **Obv:** Four-fold arms, SL above **Note:** Uniface schussel type.

Date	Mintage	VG	F	VF	XF	Unc
ND(ca.1612)	—	15.00	35.00	65.00	130	—

KM# 12 PFENNIG

Silver **Ruler:** Philipp II **Obv:** 4-fold arms, P above **Note:** Similar to KM#3. Uniface schüssel-type.

Date	Mintage	VG	F	VF	XF	Unc
ND(ca.1615)	—	15.00	30.00	60.00	120	—

KM# 29 PFENNIG

Silver **Ruler:** Philipp II **Obv:** 4-fold arms divide date **Note:** Similar to KM#3. Uniface, schüssel-type.

Date	Mintage	VG	F	VF	XF	Unc
(16)Z8	—	—	—	—	—	—

KM# 4 3 KREUZER (Groschen)

Silver **Ruler:** Philipp II **Obv:** Four-fold arms, titles of Philipp around **Obv. Legend:** ...SOLMS. SOL. **Rev:** Crowned imperial eagle, circle with 3 on breast, titles of Matthias, date around **Mint:** Hohensolms

Date	Mintage	VG	F	VF	XF	Unc
161Z	—	45.00	95.00	190	385	—

KM# 6.1 3 KREUZER (Groschen)

Silver **Ruler:** Philipp II **Obv:** First half of date divided by arms **Obv. Legend:** ...SOLMS. LICH. **Mint:** Lich **Note:** Similar to KM#4. Varieties exist.

Date	Mintage	VG	F	VF	XF	Unc
1613 (a)	—	27.00	55.00	110	225	—
16/1613 (a)	—	27.00	55.00	110	225	—
1613 (b)	—	27.00	55.00	110	225	—
1614 (a)	—	27.00	55.00	110	225	—
1614 (c)	—	27.00	55.00	110	225	—
16/1614 (c)	—	27.00	55.00	110	225	—
1616 (c)	—	27.00	55.00	110	225	—

KM# 7 3 KREUZER (Groschen)

Silver **Ruler:** Philipp II **Rev:** Date in legend **Note:** Similar to KM#6.1. Varieties exist.

Date	Mintage	VG	F	VF	XF	Unc
1614 (c)	—	27.00	55.00	110	220	—
1615 (c)	—	27.00	55.00	110	220	—
165 (c) Error	—	27.00	55.00	110	220	—
1616 (c)	—	27.00	55.00	110	220	—
1618 (c)	—	27.00	55.00	110	220	—
(16)18	—	27.00	55.00	110	220	—
(16)19	—	27.00	55.00	110	220	—
ND	—	27.00	55.00	110	220	—

KM# 8 3 KREUZER (Groschen)

Silver **Ruler:** Philipp II **Note:** Klippe.

Date	Mintage	VG	F	VF	XF	Unc
1615 (c)	—	—	—	—	—	—

KM# 6.2 3 KREUZER (Groschen)

Silver **Ruler:** Philipp II **Mint:** Lich **Note:** Klippe.

Date	Mintage	VG	F	VF	XF	Unc
1616 (c)	—	—	—	—	—	—

KM# 16 3 KREUZER (Groschen)

Silver **Ruler:** Philipp II **Obv:** Date divided by arms **Note:** Similar to KM#15. Varieties exist.

Date	Mintage	VG	F	VF	XF	Unc
(16)17 (c)	—	33.00	65.00	135	275	—
(16)18 (c)	—	33.00	65.00	135	275	—

KM# 15 3 KREUZER (Groschen)

Silver **Ruler:** Philipp II **Note:** Similar to KM#6.1 but date on both sides.

Date	Mintage	VG	F	VF	XF	Unc
(16)17 (c)	—	33.00	65.00	135	275	—

KM# 14 3 KREUZER (Groschen)

Silver **Ruler:** Philipp II **Note:** Similar to KM#6.1 but first part of date on reverse, second part on obverse.

Date	Mintage	VG	F	VF	XF	Unc
1617 (c)	—	33.00	65.00	135	275	—

KM# 18 3 KREUZER (Groschen)

Silver **Ruler:** Philipp II **Obv:** Date divided by arms **Rev. Legend:** Titles of Ferdinand II **Note:** Varieties exist. Similar to KM#16.

Date	Mintage	VG	F	VF	XF	Unc
(16)19	—	20.00	45.00	90.00	180	—
(16)Z0	—	20.00	45.00	90.00	180	—
ND	—	20.00	45.00	90.00	180	—

KM# 21 3 KREUZER (Groschen)

Silver **Ruler:** Philipp II **Obv:** Date divided by arms **Note:** Similar to KM#18 but smaller and lighter. Kipper coinage.

Date	Mintage	VG	F	VF	XF	Unc
(16)Z1	—	—	—	—	—	—
(16)ZZ	—	—	—	—	—	—
ND	—	—	—	—	—	—

KM# 22 6 KREUZER

Silver **Ruler:** Philipp II **Obv:** Four-fold arms, date above, titles of Philipp II and 6 K in margin **Rev:** Crowned imperial eagle, orb on breast, titles of Ferdinand II around **Note:** Varieties exist. Kipper coinage.

Date	Mintage	VG	F	VF	XF	Unc
16Z1	—	—	—	—	—	—

KM# 9.1 12 KREUZER (Dreibätzner)

Silver **Ruler:** Philipp II **Obv:** Four-fold arms, titles of Philipp II **Rev:** Crowned imperial eagle, 1Z in orb on breast, titles of Matthias, date in margin

Date	Mintage	VG	F	VF	XF	Unc
1614 (c)	—	—	—	—	—	—

KM# 9.2 12 KREUZER (Dreibätzner)

Silver **Ruler:** Philipp II **Note:** Klippe.

Date	Mintage	VG	F	VF	XF	Unc
1614 (c)	—	—	—	—	—	—

KM# 19 12 KREUZER (Dreibätzner)

Silver **Ruler:** Philipp II **Obv:** Similar to KM#9.1 **Rev:** Titles of Ferdinand II **Note:** Kipper coinage.

Date	Mintage	VG	F	VF	XF	Unc
(16)Z0	—	200	375	725	—	—

KM# 24 1/8 THALER

Silver **Ruler:** Philipp II **Obv:** Oval four-fold arms, date above, titles of Philipp II **Rev:** Crowned imperial eagle, 1/8 in orb on breast, titles of Ferdinand II

Date	Mintage	VG	F	VF	XF	Unc
16Z4	—	—	—	—	—	—

KM# 25 1/4 THALER

Silver **Ruler:** Philipp II **Obv:** Oval four-fold arms, first half of date, titles of Philipp II **Rev:** Crowned imperial eagle, 1/4 in orb on breast, second half of date, titles of Ferdinand II

Date	Mintage	VG	F	VF	XF	Unc
16Z4	—	925	1,800	3,500	—	—

KM# 26 1/2 THALER

Silver, 36 mm. **Ruler:** Philipp II **Obv:** Oval shield of 4-fold arms, in baroque frame, divides 1 - 6, 3 ornate helmets with crests above **Obv. Legend:** PHILIPS. CO. - SOLM: LICH. **Rev:** Crowned imperial eagle, 1/z in orb on breast, final 2 digits of date at end of legend **Rev. Legend:** FERDIN. II. D. G. ROM. IMP. S. AUG. G. H. B. REX. **Mint:** Lich **Note:** Ref. Joseph 176.

Date	Mintage	VG	F	VF	XF	Unc
16Z4 Rare	—	—	—	—	—	—

Note: An example in VF realized approximately $10,300 in a Künker auction of January 2011.

KM# 27 1/2 THALER

Silver **Ruler:** Philipp II **Obv:** Oval shield of 4-fold arms, in baroque frame, divides 1 - 6, 3 ornate helmets with crests above **Obv. Legend:** PHILIPS. CO. - SOLM: LICH. **Rev:** Crowned imperial eagle, 1/z in orb on breast, final 2 digits of date at end of legend **Rev. Legend:** FERDIN. II. D. G. ROM. IMP. S. AUG. G. H. B. REX. **Mint:** Lich **Note:** Klippe.

Date	Mintage	VG	F	VF	XF	Unc
16Z4 Rare	—	—	—	—	—	—

KM# 5A THALER

39.9800 g., Silver, 42x42 mm. **Ruler:** Philipp II **Obv:** Spanish shield of 8-fold arms, 3 ornate helmets with crests above **Obv. Legend:** PHILIPPUS. COMES. IN SOLMS: LICH. **Rev:** Crowned imperial eagle, orb on breast, date divided by tail below **Rev. Legend:** MATTHIAS. I. D. G. RO: IMP. SE. AUG. G. G. H: BO: REX. **Mint:** Lich **Note:** Joseph 128. Klippe.

Date	Mintage	VG	F	VF	XF	Unc
1613 Rare	—	—	—	—	—	—

Note: An example in XF realized approximately $15,500 in the Künker auction of January 2010.

KM# 5 THALER

Silver, 40 mm. **Ruler:** Philipp II **Obv:** Spanish shield of 8-fold arms, in baroque frame, 3 ornate helmets with crests above **Obv. Legend:** PHILIPPUS. COMES. IN SOLMS: LICH. **Rev:** Crowned imperial eagle, orb on breast, date divided by tail below **Rev. Legend:** MATTHIAS. I. D. G. RO: IMP. SE. AUG. G. G. H: BO: REX. **Mint:** Lich **Note:** Ref. Dav. 7747. Prev. Solms-Lich KM#24.

Date	Mintage	VG	F	VF	XF	Unc
1613 Rare	—	—	—	—	—	—
1616 Rare	—	—	—	—	—	—

SOLMS-HOHENSOLMS

Centered on the ancestral castle of Hohensolms (the modern Burgsolms), the line was originally known as Solms-Lich and Hohensolms from the division of 1409. A second division into Solms-Lich-Hohensolms and Solms-Laubach was effected before Philipp I's death in 1544. Shortly thereafter, in 1562, Hohensolms and Lich were the objects of separate lines. Hohensolms reacquired Lich in 1718 when the latter fell extinct, revising the name to Solms-Hohensolms-Lich. One count became the Danish king's viceroy in Wolfenbüttel during the Thirty Years' War and a later descendant was raised to the rank of prince in 1792. Solms-Hohensolms-Lick was mediatized during the Napoleonic Era, but counts of this line were still in existence in the 20th century. Most of the early 17th century coins for Solms-Hohensolms were struck at the small village of Nieder-Weisel, just to the southeast of Butzbach, itself about 10 miles (16 km) southeast of Wetzlar.

RULERS

Hermann Adolf, 1562-1613
Philipp Reinhard I, 1613-1635
as governor of Braunschweig-Wolfenbüttel for Christian IV of Denmark, 1627-1634
Philipp Reinhard II, 1635-1665
Karl Ludwig, 1665-1668
Johann Heinrich Christian, 1668
Ludwig, 1668-1707

MINT OFFICIALS' INITIALS

Nieder-Weisel Mint

Date	Name
1612-13	Henning Kiessel
1613-15	Hans Ziesler von Molsheim
1612-15	Hans Kapphaus, warden
1615-20	Hans Kapphaus, mintmaster
1620	Hans Jakob Ayrer

Butzbach Mint

1620-22	Hans Jakob Ayrer

Hohensolms Mint

IB	1675	Johann Bostelmann
ICB	ca. 1675	Johann Christoph Bähr
IA or 	1676	Jürgen Ahrens (Jörg Arens)
IIF	1690-1719	Johann Jeremias Freitag in Frankfurt am Main
PPP	1676	Peter Paul Peckstein
H	1683	Paul Heuser
	ca. 1691	Wilhelm Lender
FA	1693	Fredrich Arnoldt

COUNTSHIP

REGULAR COINAGE

KM# 63 HELLER (Fettmannchen)

Copper **Ruler:** Philipp Reinhard I **Obv:** Two-fold arms **Obv. Legend:** NVMMVS. CON. SOL. **Rev:** Value: VIII **Rev. Legend:** NVMMVS. COM. SOLM. **Mint:** Wolfenbüttel **Note:** Varieties exist. Prev. KM#65.

Date	Mintage	VG	F	VF	XF	Unc
ND(ca.1627)	—	—	—	—	—	—

KM# 4 PFENNIG

Billon **Obv:** 2-fold arms of Solms and Wildenfels with H above **Note:** Uniface schüssel-type. Varieties exist.

Date	Mintage	VG	F	VF	XF	Unc
ND(1610-15)	—	12.00	27.00	55.00	110	—

KM# 2 PFENNIG

Billon **Obv:** Crowned oval two-fold arms of Solms and Wildenfels **Note:** Uniface, schüssel-type.

Date	Mintage	VG	F	VF	XF	Unc
ND(1610-15)	—	12.00	27.00	55.00	110	—

KM# 3 PFENNIG

Billon **Obv:** Two-fold arms of Solms and Wildenfels **Note:** Uniface, schüssel-type.

Date	Mintage	VG	F	VF	XF	Unc
ND(1610-15)	—	12.00	27.00	55.00	110	—

KM# 5 PFENNIG

Billon **Obv:** 2-fold arms, H below arms **Note:** Uniface, schüssel-type.

Date	Mintage	VG	F	VF	XF	Unc
ND(1610-15)	—	12.00	27.00	55.00	110	—

KM# 6 PFENNIG

Billon **Obv:** 2-fold arms, I above **Note:** Uniface, schüssel-type.

Date	Mintage	VG	F	VF	XF	Unc
ND(1610-15)	—	12.00	27.00	55.00	110	—

KM# 8 PFENNIG

Billon **Obv:** 2-fold arms divide B - H **Note:** Uniface, schüssel-type.

Date	Mintage	VG	F	VF	XF	Unc
ND(1610-15)	—	12.00	27.00	55.00	110	—

KM# 10 PFENNIG

Billon **Obv:** 2-fold arms, BH on left, rampant lion left on right **Note:** Uniface, schüssel-type.

Date	Mintage	VG	F	VF	XF	Unc
ND(1610-15)	—	12.00	27.00	55.00	110	—

KM# 11 PFENNIG

Billon **Obv:** 2-fold arms, BH above lion left **Note:** Uniface, schüssel-type.

Date	Mintage	VG	F	VF	XF	Unc
ND(1610-15)	—	12.00	27.00	55.00	110	—

KM# 12 PFENNIG

Billon **Obv:** 2-fold arms, H above arms **Note:** Uniface, schüssel-type.

Date	Mintage	VG	F	VF	XF	Unc
ND(1610-15)	—	12.00	27.00	55.00	110	—

KM# 13 PFENNIG

Billon **Obv:** 2-fold arms, lion above BH **Note:** Uniface, schüssel-type.

Date	Mintage	VG	F	VF	XF	Unc
ND(1610-15)	—	12.00	27.00	55.00	110	—

KM# 14 PFENNIG

Billon **Obv:** 2-folds arms, Minzenberg above lion left, arms divide P - H **Note:** Uniface, schüssel-type.

Date	Mintage	VG	F	VF	XF	Unc
ND(1610-15)	—	12.00	27.00	55.00	110	—

KM# 15 PFENNIG

Billon **Obv:** Lion to right, H below head **Note:** Uniface, schüssel-type.

Date	Mintage	VG	F	VF	XF	Unc
ND(1610-15)	—	12.00	27.00	55.00	110	—

KM# 17 PFENNIG

Billon **Obv:** Lion right in shield, crown above **Note:** Uniface, schüssel-type.

Date	Mintage	VG	F	VF	XF	Unc
ND(1610-15)	—	12.00	27.00	55.00	110	—

KM# 20 PFENNIG

Billon **Obv:** Lion right, H near head **Note:** Uniface, schüssel-type.

Date	Mintage	VG	F	VF	XF	Unc
ND(1610-15)	—	12.00	27.00	55.00	110	—

KM# 21 PFENNIG

Billon **Obv:** Lion to left in shield **Note:** Uniface, schüssel-type.

Date	Mintage	VG	F	VF	XF	Unc
ND(1610-15)	—	12.00	27.00	55.00	110	—

KM# 22 PFENNIG

Billon **Obv:** Lion to left in shield of arms, H above **Note:** Uniface, schüssel-type.

Date	Mintage	VG	F	VF	XF	Unc
ND(1610-15)	—	12.00	27.00	55.00	110	—

KM# 24 PFENNIG

Billon **Obv:** Rose arms of Wildenfels **Note:** Uniface, schüssel-type.

Date	Mintage	VG	F	VF	XF	Unc
ND(1610-15)	—	12.00	27.00	55.00	110	—

KM# 25 PFENNIG

Billon **Obv:** H above rose arms **Note:** Uniface, schüssel-type.

Date	Mintage	VG	F	VF	XF	Unc
ND(1610-15)	—	12.00	27.00	55.00	110	—

KM# 27 PFENNIG

Billon **Obv:** Maltese cross in shield **Note:** Uniface, schüssel-type.

Date	Mintage	VG	F	VF	XF	Unc
ND(1610-15)	—	12.00	27.00	55.00	110	—

KM# 28 PFENNIG

Billon **Obv:** H over large crown in circle **Note:** Uniface, schüssel-type.

Date	Mintage	VG	F	VF	XF	Unc
ND(1610-15)	—	12.00	27.00	55.00	110	—

KM# 29 PFENNIG

Billon **Obv:** Eagle, head to left **Note:** Uniface, schüssel-type.

Date	Mintage	VG	F	VF	XF	Unc
ND(1610-15)	—	12.00	27.00	55.00	110	—

KM# 30 PFENNIG

Billon **Obv:** Goat in shield divides I - P **Note:** Uniface, schüssel-type.

Date	Mintage	VG	F	VF	XF	Unc
ND(1610-15)	—	12.00	27.00	55.00	110	—

KM# 31 PFENNIG

Billon **Obv:** Lion rampant left **Note:** Uniface, schüssel-type.

Date	Mintage	VG	F	VF	XF	Unc
ND(1610-15)	—	15.00	30.00	60.00	120	—

KM# 32 PFENNIG

Billon **Obv:** Lion rampant right **Note:** Uniface, schüssel-type.

Date	Mintage	VG	F	VF	XF	Unc
ND(1610-15)	—	15.00	30.00	60.00	120	—

KM# 33 PFENNIG

Billon **Obv:** B H, animal head above and below **Note:** Uniface, schüssel-type.

Date	Mintage	VG	F	VF	XF	Unc
ND(1610-15)	—	15.00	30.00	60.00	120	—

KM# 34 PFENNIG

Billon **Obv:** Three animal heads, one above the other **Note:** Uniface, schüssel-type.

Date	Mintage	VG	F	VF	XF	Unc
ND(1610-15)	—	15.00	30.00	60.00	120	—

KM# 35 PFENNIG

Billon **Obv:** Three crowns, one above the other **Note:** Uniface, schüssel-type.

Date	Mintage	VG	F	VF	XF	Unc
ND(1610-15)	—	15.00	30.00	60.00	120	—

KM# 7 PFENNIG

Billon **Ruler:** Hermann Adolf **Obv:** H above two-fold arms of Wildenfels and Solms **Note:** Uniface, schüssel-type. Varieties exist.

Date	Mintage	VG	F	VF	XF	Unc
ND(1610-15)	—	12.00	27.00	55.00	110	—

KM# 9 PFENNIG

Billon **Obv:** 2-fold arms, no letter above **Note:** Uniface, schüssel-type. Varieties exist.

Date	Mintage	VG	F	VF	XF	Unc
ND(1610-15)	—	12.00	27.00	55.00	110	—

KM# 16 PFENNIG

Billon **Obv:** H above arms with lion to right **Note:** Uniface, schüssel-type. Varieties exist.

Date	Mintage	VG	F	VF	XF	Unc
ND(1610-15)	—	12.00	27.00	55.00	110	—

KM# 18 PFENNIG

Billon **Obv:** Shield of lion right, H between paws **Note:** Uniface, schüssel-type. Varieties exist.

Date	Mintage	VG	F	VF	XF	Unc
ND(1610-15)	—	12.00	27.00	55.00	110	—

KM# 19 PFENNIG

Billon **Obv:** Lion right in shield **Note:** Uniface, schüssel-type. Varieties exist.

Date	Mintage	VG	F	VF	XF	Unc
ND(1610-15)	—	12.00	27.00	55.00	110	—

KM# 23 PFENNIG

Billon **Obv:** Crowned lion left in shield **Note:** Uniface, schüssel-type. Varieties exist.

Date	Mintage	VG	F	VF	XF	Unc
ND(1610-15)	—	12.00	27.00	55.00	110	—

KM# 26 PFENNIG

Billon **Obv:** Rose in circle **Note:** Uniface, schüssel-type. Varieties exist.

Date	Mintage	VG	F	VF	XF	Unc
ND(1610-15)	—	12.00	27.00	55.00	110	—

KM# 1 PFENNIG

Copper **Obv:** 2 small shields of arms, 1 above 2, value "• I •" between 2 lower arms **Note:** Uniface. Varieties exist.

Date	Mintage	VG	F	VF	XF	Unc
ND(1610-15)	—	15.00	30.00	60.00	120	—

KM# 64 12 PFENNIG

Copper **Ruler:** Philipp Reinhard I **Obv. Inscription:** 12 • / WOLFEB / GARNIS / date. **Mint:** Wolfenbüttel **Note:** Uniface. Varieties exist.

Date	Mintage	VG	F	VF	XF	Unc
1627 Rare	—	—	—	—	—	—

KM# 65 GROSCHEN

Silver **Ruler:** Philipp Reinhard I **Obv:** Crowned cipher (C4) of Christian IV of Denmark **Obv. Legend:** QVID. NON. PRO. RELIGIO(NE). **Rev. Legend:** NACH. REICHS. SCHROT. V. K. **Rev. Inscription:** I / GVTER / GROS(CH) / date **Mint:** Wolfenbüttel **Note:** Varieties exist. Prev. KM#66.

Date	Mintage	VG	F	VF	XF	Unc
1627 Rare	—	—	—	—	—	—

KM# 102 ALBUS

Silver **Obv:** Lion rampant left in shield, crowned helmet above **Obv. Legend:** SOLMS. HOH - EN. SOLMS. **Rev:** Mintmaster's initials **Rev. Legend:** NACH. DEM. SCHLVS. DER. V. STAND. **Rev. Inscription:** I / ALBUS / date

Date	Mintage	VG	F	VF	XF	Unc
1693 FA	—	—	—	—	—	—

KM# 106 ALBUS

Silver **Obv:** Crowned shield of lion rampant left, arms between palm branches **Obv. Legend:** SOLMS - HOCH - SOLMS **Rev. Legend:** NACH DEN FVNF STAENDEN **Rev. Inscription:** I / ALBVS / date

Date	Mintage	VG	F	VF	XF	Unc
1694	—	—	—	—	—	—

KM# 103 2 ALBUS

Silver **Obv:** Lion rampant left in shield, crowned helmet above **Obv. Legend:** SOLMS. HOH - EN. SOLMS. **Rev:** Mintmaster's initials **Rev. Legend:** NACH DEM. SCHLVS. DER. V. STAND. **Rev. Inscription:** II / ALBUS / date

Date	Mintage	VG	F	VF	XF	Unc
1693 FA	—	—	—	—	—	—

KM# 104 6 ALBUS

Silver **Obv:** Lion rampant left on crowned eight-fold arms **Obv. Legend:** Titles of Ludwig **Rev:** Mintmaster's initials **Rev. Inscription:** VI / ALBUS / date

Date	Mintage	VG	F	VF	XF	Unc
1693 FA	—	—	—	—	—	—

KM# 42 3 KREUZER (Groschen)

Silver **Obv:** 4-fold arms, titles of Philipp Reinhard I **Rev:** Crowned imperial eagle, 3 in circle on breast **Note:** Varieties exist.

Date	Mintage	VG	F	VF	XF	Unc
161Z	—	10.00	20.00	40.00	80.00	—
(1)61Z	—	10.00	20.00	40.00	80.00	—
1615	—	10.00	20.00	40.00	80.00	—
1616	—	10.00	20.00	40.00	80.00	—
1617	—	10.00	20.00	40.00	80.00	—
(16)17	—	10.00	20.00	40.00	80.00	—
ND	—	10.00	20.00	40.00	80.00	—

KM# 40 3 KREUZER (Groschen)

Silver **Obv:** Four-fold arms, titles of Herman Adolf around **Rev:** Crowned imperial eagle, 3 in circle on breast, titles of Rudolf II, date around **Note:** Varieties exist.

Date	Mintage	VG	F	VF	XF	Unc
161Z	—	10.00	20.00	45.00	90.00	—

KM# 41 3 KREUZER (Groschen)

Silver, 21.4 mm. **Obv:** 4-fold arms, titles around **Rev:** Titles of Matthias **Note:** Varieties exist.

Date	Mintage	VG	F	VF	XF	Unc
161Z	—	10.00	20.00	40.00	80.00	—
1612	—	10.00	20.00	40.00	80.00	—

KM# 43 3 KREUZER (Groschen)

Silver **Obv:** 4-fold arms, titles of Philipp Reinhard K **Rev:** Crowned imperial eagle, 3 in circle on breast **Note:** Klippe.

Date	Mintage	VG	F	VF	XF	Unc
ND(1612-17)	—	—	—	250	450	—

KM# 46 3 KREUZER (Groschen)

Silver **Obv:** 4-fold arms with date above **Rev:** Crowned imperial eagle, 3 in circle on breast

Date	Mintage	VG	F	VF	XF	Unc
1614	—	10.00	20.00	45.00	90.00	—

KM# 48 3 KREUZER (Groschen)

Silver **Obv:** 4-fold arms divide date **Rev:** Crowned imperial eagle, 3 in circle on breast

Date	Mintage	VG	F	VF	XF	Unc
(16)17	—	10.00	20.00	45.00	90.00	—
(16)18	—	10.00	20.00	45.00	90.00	—

KM# 49 3 KREUZER (Groschen)

Silver **Obv:** 4-fold arms divide date, date also in margin **Rev:** Crowned imperial eagle, 3 in circle on breast

Date	Mintage	VG	F	VF	XF	Unc
(16)17	—	9.00	20.00	45.00	90.00	—

KM# 51 3 KREUZER (Groschen)

Silver **Obv:** 4-fold arms **Rev:** Crowned imperial eagle, 3 in circle on breast, titles of Ferdinand II in legend

Date	Mintage	VG	F	VF	XF	Unc
(16)19	—	—	—	—	—	—

KM# 57 3 KREUZER (Groschen)

Silver **Note:** Klippe.

Date	Mintage	VG	F	VF	XF	Unc
(16)Z0	—	—	—	—	—	—
(16)Z1	—	—	—	—	—	—

KM# 56 3 KREUZER (Groschen)

Silver **Obv:** 4-fold arms **Rev:** Crowned imperial eagle, 3 in orb on breast **Note:** Reduced size and weight. Varieties exist.

Date	Mintage	VG	F	VF	XF	Unc
(16)Z0	—	10.00	20.00	40.00	80.00	—
(16)Z1	—	10.00	20.00	40.00	80.00	—
(16)ZZ	—	10.00	20.00	40.00	80.00	—

KM# 59 3 KREUZER (Groschen)

Silver **Ruler:** Philipp Reinhard I **Obv:** 4-fold arms **Obv. Legend:** ... BUT **Rev:** Crowned imperial eagle, 3 in circle on breast **Mint:** Butzbach **Note:** Prev. KM#60.

Date	Mintage	VG	F	VF	XF	Unc
(16)Z1	—	—	—	—	—	—

KM# 58 12 KREUZER (Dreibätzner)

Silver **Obv:** Four-fold arms, titles of Philipp Reinhard I around **Rev:** Crowned imperial eagle, 1Z in orb on breast, date, titles of Ferdinand II **Note:** Varieties exist.

Date	Mintage	VG	F	VF	XF	Unc
(16)Z0	—	180	360	725	—	—
(16)Z1	—	180	360	725	—	—

KM# 61 12 KREUZER (Dreibätzner)

Silver **Ruler:** Philipp Reinhard I **Obv:** 4-fold arms, titles of Philipp Reinhard I around **Obv. Legend:** ... BUTZB(A) **Rev:** Crowned imperial eagle, 1Z in orb on breast, date, titles of Feerdinand II **Mint:** Butzbach **Note:** Klippe. Prev. KM#62.

Date	Mintage	VG	F	VF	XF	Unc
(16)Z1	—	—	—	—	—	—

KM# 60 12 KREUZER (Dreibätzner)

Silver **Ruler:** Philipp Reinhard I **Obv:** 4-fold arms, titles of Philipp Reinhard I around **Obv. Legend:** ... BUTZB(A) **Rev:** Crowned imperial eagle, 1Z in orb on breast, date, titles of Ferdinand II **Mint:** Butzbach **Note:** Prev. KM#61.

Date	Mintage	VG	F	VF	XF	Unc
(16)Z1	—	—	—	—	—	—

KM# 45 DICKEN (Teston)

Silver **Obv:** Four-fold arms

Date	Mintage	VG	F	VF	XF	Unc
ND(ca.1613-19)	—	—	—	—	—	—

KM# 54 DICKEN (Teston)

Silver **Obv:** Four-fold arms divide date, titles of Philipp Reinhard I **Rev:** Crowned imperial eagle, orb on breast, titles of Ferdinand II

Date	Mintage	VG	F	VF	XF	Unc
1619	—	—	—	—	—	—

KM# 52 DICKEN (Teston)

Silver **Obv:** Crowned eight-fold arms, titles of Philipp Reinhard I **Rev:** Crowned imperial eagle, orb on breast, titles of Matthias, date **Note:** Varieties exist.

Date	Mintage	VG	F	VF	XF	Unc
1619	—	1,000	1,900	3,600	—	—

KM# 53 DICKEN (Teston)

Silver **Obv:** Similar to KM#52, but date above crown **Rev:** Similar to KM#52 **Note:** Varieties exist.

Date	Mintage	VG	F	VF	XF	Unc
1619	—	1,000	1,900	3,600	—	—

KM# 74 1/3 THALER (1/2 Gulden)

Silver **Ruler:** Ludwig **Obv:** Bust right, titles of Ludwig **Rev:** Three helmets over eight-fold arms, value (30) below, date divided at top **Rev. Legend:** MONETA... **Note:** Previous KM#68.

Date	Mintage	VG	F	VF	XF	Unc
1675	—	—	—	—	—	—

KM# 76 1/3 THALER (1/2 Gulden)

Silver **Ruler:** Ludwig **Obv:** Bust right, value (30) below, titles of Ludwig **Rev:** Crowned 8-fold arms between palm branches, date **Rev. Legend:** MONETA... **Note:** Prev. KM#74.

Date	Mintage	VG	F	VF	XF	Unc
1676	—	—	—	—	—	—

KM# 90 2/3 THALER (Gulden)

Silver **Obv:** Armored bust right, value (60) below **Obv. Legend:** *LUDWIG • G • ZU • S • H • ZU • M • W • U • S* **Rev:** Crowned arms divide date **Note:** Dav.#984.

Date	Mintage	VG	F	VF	XF	Unc
1671 IA(a)	—	85.00	165	335	675	—

KM# 75 2/3 THALER (Gulden)

Silver **Ruler:** Ludwig **Obv:** Armored bust right, value (60) below **Obv. Legend:** * L * G * Z * (H) * S * H * Z * M * W * V * S * **Rev:** Crowned eight-fold arms, date **Rev. Legend:** MONETA. NOVA. ARGENTEA. **Mint:** Hohensolms **Note:** Varieties exist.

Date	Mintage	VG	F	VF	XF	Unc
ICB	—	90.00	175	325	675	—
1675 IB	—	90.00	175	325	675	—

KM# 77 2/3 THALER (Gulden)

Silver **Obv:** Armored bust right in inner circle, value (60) in margin at bottom **Obv. Legend:** * LVTWIG • G • Z • S • (=) H • Z • M • (W) • V • S * **Rev:** Crowned ornate arms, date divided in top margin **Note:** Dav. #970. Varieties exist.

Date	Mintage	VG	F	VF	XF	Unc
1676 (a)	—	80.00	160	325	650	—

KM# 78 2/3 THALER (Gulden)

Silver **Obv:** Armored bust right in inner circle **Obv. Legend:** * LVTWIG • G • Z • S • H • Z • M • W • V • S * **Rev:** Crowned arms with palm branches in inner circle **Note:** Dav.#971.

Date	Mintage	VG	F	VF	XF	Unc
1676 (a)	—	80.00	160	325	650	—

KM# 79 2/3 THALER (Gulden)

Silver **Obv:** Armored bust right in inner circle, value (60) in margin below **Obv. Legend:** LVTWIG • G • Z • S - H • Z • M • W • V • S **Rev:** Crowned arms with palm branches in inner circle **Note:** Dav.#972. Varieties exist.

Date	Mintage	VG	F	VF	XF	Unc
1676 (a)	—	115	235	475	950	—

KM# 80 2/3 THALER (Gulden)

Silver **Obv:** Youthful armored bust right in inner circle **Rev:** With either branches or ornaments to either side of crowned arms in inner circle **Note:** Dav.#973. Varieties exist.

Date	Mintage	VG	F	VF	XF	Unc
1676 LVTWIG	—	65.00	135	275	575	—
1676 LUDWIG	—	65.00	135	275	575	—
1676 PXP	—	65.00	135	275	575	—

KM# 81 2/3 THALER (Gulden)

Silver **Obv:** Older armored bust right **Obv. Legend:** LUDWIG • G • ZU • S • H • Z • M • W • U • S * **Rev:** Ornately-shaped crowned arms divide date **Note:** Dav.#974. Varieties exist.

Date	Mintage	VG	F	VF	XF	Unc
1676 IA	—	65.00	135	275	550	—
1676 (a)	—	65.00	135	275	550	—
1677 IA	—	65.00	135	275	550	—
1677 IA(a)	—	65.00	135	275	550	—

KM# 82 2/3 THALER (Gulden)

Silver **Obv:** Armored bust right, value (60) on shoulder **Obv. Legend:** LUDWIG • G • ZU • S • H • Z(U) • M • W • U • S • **Rev:** Crowned ornate arms, date below **Note:** Dav.#975. Varieties exist.

Date	Mintage	VG	F	VF	XF	Unc
1676 IA	—	60.00	120	235	475	—
1677 IA(a)	—	60.00	120	235	475	—

KM# 83 2/3 THALER (Gulden)

Silver **Obv:** Armored bust right, value (60) on shoulder **Rev:** Ornately-shaped crowned arms divide date **Note:** Dav.#976. Varieties exist.

Date	Mintage	VG	F	VF	XF	Unc
1676 IA (a)	—	80.00	160	325	650	—

KM# 84 2/3 THALER (Gulden)

Silver **Obv:** Crowned ornate eight-fold arms divide date **Rev:** Ornately-shaped crowned arms divide date **Rev. Inscription:** HERR / NACH / DEINEM / WILLEN / 60 (in sprays) **Note:** Dav.#977. Varieties exist.

Date	Mintage	VG	F	VF	XF	Unc
1676	—	75.00	150	300	600	—
1676 IA	—	75.00	150	300	600	—
1676 IA(a)	—	75.00	150	300	600	—

KM# 85 2/3 THALER (Gulden)

Silver **Obv. Legend:** MONETA*NOVA*ARGENTEA*date **Rev. Inscription:** HERRE/NACHDEINE/M WILLEN/60 in sprays **Note:** Dav.#979.

Date	Mintage	VG	F	VF	XF	Unc
1676	—	60.00	120	235	475	—

KM# 86 2/3 THALER (Gulden)

Silver **Obv:** Armored bust right, date divided below **Obv. Legend:** *LUDWIG • G • Z • S • H • Z • M • W • U • S* **Rev:** Crowned eight-fold arms, palm branch to either side, 2/3 in oval at bottom **Rev. Legend:** MONETA.NOV-A.ARGENTEA **Note:** Dav.#968.

Date	Mintage	VG	F	VF	XF	Unc
1676	—	80.00	160	325	650	—

KM# 87 2/3 THALER (Gulden)

Silver **Obv:** Armored bust right, value (60) below **Obv. Legend:** *LUDWIG • G • ZU • S • H • Z(U) • M • W • U • S* **Rev:** Crowned arms divide date **Note:** Dav.#981.

Date	Mintage	VG	F	VF	XF	Unc
1676 (a)	—	60.00	120	235	475	—
1677 (a)	—	60.00	120	235	475	—

KM# 92 2/3 THALER (Gulden)

Silver **Obv:** Facing bust, value (60) in oval below **Obv. Legend:** *LUDWIG G•Z(U)•S•-H•Z(U)•M•W•V•S• **Rev. Inscription:** HERR. / NACH / DEINEM. / WILLEN / 60 (in sprays) **Note:** Dav.#978. Varieties exist.

Date	Mintage	VG	F	VF	XF	Unc
ND(1676)	—	275	525	1,050	—	—

KM# 89 2/3 THALER (Gulden)

Silver **Obv:** Older armored bust right, legend begins at top **Obv. Legend:** LUDWIG • G • ZU • S • H • Z • M • W • U • S * **Rev:** Ornately-shaped crowned arms divide date **Note:** Dav.#983.

Date	Mintage	VG	F	VF	XF	Unc
1677	—	85.00	165	325	650	—

KM# 91 2/3 THALER (Gulden)

Silver **Obv:** Crowned arms divide date **Obv. Legend:** MONETA . NOVA . ARGENTA . **Rev:** Inscription in sprays **Rev. Inscription:** HERR. / NACH / DEINEM. / WILLEN / 60 **Note:** Dav.#980.

Date	Mintage	VG	F	VF	XF	Unc
1677	—	65.00	125	250	500	—

KM# 93 2/3 THALER (Gulden)
Silver **Obv:** Armored bust right **Rev:** Inscription in sprays **Rev. Inscription:** HERR / NACH / DEINEM / WILLEN

Date	Mintage	VG	F	VF	XF	Unc
ND(1677)	—	—	—	—	—	—

KM# 94 2/3 THALER (Gulden)
Silver **Obv:** Armored bust right **Obv. Legend:** MONETA NOUA **Note:** Dav.#985.

Date	Mintage	VG	F	VF	XF	Unc
ND(1677) (a)	—	—	—	—	—	—

KM# 95 2/3 THALER (Gulden)
Silver **Obv:** Armored bust right, value (60) on shoulder **Obv. Legend:** *LUDWIG • G • Z • S • H • Z • M • W • V • S* **Rev:** Three helmets above eight-fold arms **Note:** Dav.#986.

Date	Mintage	VG	F	VF	XF	Unc
ND(1677) IIF	—	175	325	650	1,300	—
ND(1677)	—	175	325	650	1,300	—

KM# 96 2/3 THALER (Gulden)
Silver **Obv:** Armored bust in inner circle **Obv. Legend:** *LVDWIG G • Z • S • H • Z • M • W • V • S • **Rev:** Crowned eight-fold arms in inner circle, 60 in oval at bottom **Rev. Legend:** MONETA NOVA ARGENTEA **Note:** Dav.#987.

Date	Mintage	VG	F	VF	XF	Unc
ND(1677)	—	60.00	120	235	475	—

KM# 100 2/3 THALER (Gulden)
Silver **Obv:** Armored bust right, value (60) below **Obv. Legend:** LVDWIG : G : ZV : S = H • ZV : M : W : V : S(ON) : **Rev:** Crowned eight-fold arms in inner circle, 60 in oval at bottom **Rev. Legend:** • MONETA • NOVA • ARGENTEA **Note:** Similar to KM#71. Dav.#988.

Date	Mintage	VG	F	VF	XF	Unc
1686	—	—	—	—	—	—

KM# 62 THALER
Silver **Ruler:** Philipp Reinhard I **Obv:** Ornate shield of 8-fold arms, 3 ornate helmets above divide 1 - 6 **Obv. Legend:** PHILIPS. REINHART. CO. IN. SOL(MS). DO. I. M(I). **Rev:** Crowned imperial eagle, orb on breast. date at end of legend **Rev. Legend:** FERDIN(AN). II. D.(G). RO(M). IMP. S(E). AUG. G. H. B. RE(X). **Note:** Dav. 7755.

Date	Mintage	VG	F	VF	XF	Unc
16Z4 Rare	—	—	—	—	—	—

Note: Künker Auction 163, 1-10, VF realized approximately $16,850.

KM# 66 THALER
Silver **Ruler:** Philipp Reinhard I **Obv:** Crowned shield of 8-fold arms in ornate frame **Obv. Legend:** MONET. R. D. N. VIC: PHIL: REINH: C: S: **Rev:** Crowned C4 cipher for Christian IV of Denmark, date at end of legend **Rev. Legend:** QUID. NON. PRO. RELIGIONE. Ao. **Mint:** Wolfenbüttel **Note:** Dav. 7758.

Date	Mintage	VG	F	VF	XF	Unc
1627	—	725	1,450	2,700	4,750	—

KM# 67 THALER
Silver **Ruler:** Philipp Reinhard I **Obv:** Crowned shield of 8-fold arms **Obv. Legend:** MONET. R. D. N. VIC: REINH: C: S: **Rev:** Crowned C4 cipher, for Christian IV of Denmark, divides date **Rev. Legend:** QVID * NON * PRO * RELIGIONE * **Mint:** Wolfenbüttel **Note:** Dav. 7759.

Date	Mintage	VG	F	VF	XF	Unc
1627	—	950	1,800	3,700	6,100	—

KM# 68 THALER
Silver **Ruler:** Philipp Reinhard I **Obv:** Crowned shield of 8-fold arms in baroque frame divides date **Obv. Legend:** MONET: REGIS. DAN: NORW: VICARII. PHILIP. REINH: COM: S: **Rev:** Crowned C4 cipher for Christian IV of Denmark in circle **Rev. Legend:** QVID - NON - PRO - RELIGIONE **Mint:** Wolfenbüttel **Note:** Dav. 7760.

Date	Mintage	VG	F	VF	XF	Unc
1627	—	1,200	2,100	4,050	6,800	—

KM# 69 THALER
Silver **Ruler:** Philipp Reinhard I **Obv:** Crowned shield of 8-fold arms in baroque frame **Obv. Legend:** MONET: REGIS. DAN: NORW: VICARII. PHILIP. REINH: COM: S: **Rev:** Crowned C4 cipher, for Christian IV of Denmark, divides date in circle **Rev. Legend:** QVID - NON - PRO - RELIGIONE **Mint:** Wolfenbüttel **Note:** Dav. 7761.

Date	Mintage	VG	F	VF	XF	Unc
1627	—	1,200	2,100	4,050	6,800	—

KM# A63 2 THALER
Silver **Ruler:** Philipp Reinhard I **Obv:** Ornate shield of 8-fold arms, 3 ornate helmets above divide 1 - 6 **Obv. Legend:** PHILIPS. REINHART. CO. IN. SOL(MS). DO. I. M(I). **Rev:** Crowned imperial eagle, orb on breast, date at end of legend **Rev. Legend:** FERDIN(AN). II. D.(G). RO(M). IMP. S(E). AUG. G. H. B. RE(X). **Note:** Dav. 7754.

Date	Mintage	VG	F	VF	XF	Unc
(16)Z4 Rare	—	—	—	—	—	—

KM# 70 2 THALER
Silver **Ruler:** Philipp Reinhard I **Obv:** Crowned shield of 8-fold arms in ornate frame **Obv. Legend:** MONET. R. D. N. VIC: PHIL: REINH: C: S: **Rev:** Crowned C4 cipher for Christian IV of Denmark, date at end of legend **Rev. Legend:** QVID. NON. PRO. RELIGIONE. Ao. **Mint:** Wolfenbüttel **Note:** Dav. 7757.

Date	Mintage	VG	F	VF	XF	Unc
1627 Rare	—	—	—	—	—	—

KM# 71 3 THALER
Silver **Ruler:** Philipp Reinhard I **Obv:** Crowned shield of 8-fold arms in ornate frame **Obv. Legend:** MONET: REGIS. DAN: NORW: VICARII. PHILIP. (REIN)H: COM: S. **Rev:** Crowned C4 cipher for Christian IV of Denmark, date at end of legend **Rev. Legend:** QVID. NON(.) PRO. RELIGIONE. A(o). **Mint:** Wolfenbüttel **Note:** Dav. 7756.

Date	Mintage	VG	F	VF	XF	Unc
1627 Rare	—	—	—	—	—	—

TRADE COINAGE

KM# 72 DUCAT
3.5000 g., 0.9860 Gold 0.1109 oz. AGW **Ruler:** Philipp Reinhard I **Obv:** Crowned shield of 8-fold arms in ornate frame **Rev:** Crowned C4 cipher for Christian IV of Denmark **Mint:** Wolfenbüttel **Note:** Fr. 3300.

Date	Mintage	VG	F	VF	XF	Unc
1627	—	3,000	5,900	9,600	15,500	—

KM# 73 2 DUCAT
7.0000 g., 0.9860 Gold 0.2219 oz. AGW **Ruler:** Philipp Reinhard I **Obv:** Crowned shield of 8-fold arms in ornate frame **Rev:** Crowned C4 cipher for Christian IV of Denmark **Mint:** Wolfenbüttel **Note:** Fr. 3299.

Date	Mintage	VG	F	VF	XF	Unc
1627 Rare	—	—	—	—	—	—

SOLMS-LAUBACH

Founded by a younger son of Philipp I of Solms-Lich and Hohensolms prior to 1522 and seated at the town of Laubach some 14 miles (23 km) east-southeast of Giessen, this branch lasted until at least the 20th century. The first division in 1561 resulted in the two lines of Solms-Laubach and Solms-Sonnenwalde. The next division occurred when Solms-Laubach, Solms-Baruth, Solms-Sonnenwalde and Solms-Rödelheim were established in 1600. The first Solms-Laubach died out in 1676 and titles passed to Solms-Wildenfels, from which a second line was constituted in 1696. As was the case with all other branches of Solms, Laubach was mediatized around 1806.

RULERS
Albrecht Otto I, 1600-1610
Albrecht Otto II, 1610-1639, 1610-1631
under guardianship of mother and three uncles
Karl Otto, 1639-1676
Johann Friedrich von Solms-Wildenfels, 1676-1696
Friedrich Ernst, 1696-1723

COUNTY

REGULAR COINAGE

KM# 3 3 KREUZER (Groschen)
Silver **Obv:** Four-fold arms, TUT. AL. OT. etc., around **Rev:** Crowned imperial eagle, 3 in circle on breast, titles of Ferdinand II, date around **Note:** Varieties exist.

Date	Mintage	VG	F	VF	XF	Unc
(16)Z0	—	45.00	90.00	180	360	—
(16)Z1	—	45.00	90.00	180	360	—
(16)ZZ	—	45.00	90.00	180	360	—

KM# 7.1 6 KREUZER
Silver **Obv:** Four-fold arms, date above **Obv. Legend:** TUT. ALB. OT... **Rev:** Crowned imperial eagle, 6 in orb on breast **Rev. Legend:** Titles of Ferdinand II **Note:** Kipper coinage. Varieties exist.

Date	Mintage	VG	F	VF	XF	Unc
16Z1	—	—	—	—	—	—

KM# 7.2 6 KREUZER
Silver **Obv:** 4-fold arms, date above **Rev:** Crowned imperial eagle, 6 in orb on breast, titles of Ferdinand II **Note:** Kipper klippe.

Date	Mintage	VG	F	VF	XF	Unc
16Z1	—	—	—	—	—	—

KM# 8 6 KREUZER
Silver **Ruler:** Albrecht Otto II **Obv:** 4-fold arms, date above, value "6K" at end of margin **Rev:** Crowned imperial eagle, 6 in orb on breast, titles of Ferdinand II **Note:** Varieties exist.

Date	Mintage	VG	F	VF	XF	Unc
16Z1	—	200	400	775	—	—

KM# 9 6 KREUZER
Silver **Obv:** 4-fold arms, date above, value "6K" in oval at top **Rev:** Crowned imperial eagle **Note:** Varieties exist.

Date	Mintage	VG	F	VF	XF	Unc
16Z1	—	—	—	—	—	—

KM# 4.2 12 KREUZER (Dreibätzner)
Silver

Date	Mintage	VG	F	VF	XF	Unc
(16)Z0	—	—	—	—	—	—

KM# 4.1 12 KREUZER (Dreibätzner)
Silver **Obv:** Four-fold arms **Obv. Legend:** TUT. AL. OT... **Rev:** Crowned imperial eagle, value "1Z" in orb on breast **Rev. Legend:** Titles of Ferdinand II, date around **Note:** Varieties exist.

Date	Mintage	VG	F	VF	XF	Unc
(16)Z0	—	150	300	625	—	—
(16)Z1	—	150	300	625	—	—

KM# 12 12 KREUZER (Dreibätzner)
Silver **Obv:** 4-fold arms, date above arms **Rev:** Crowned imperial eagle, value 1Z in orb on breast, titles of Ferdinand II

Date	Mintage	VG	F	VF	XF	Unc
16Z1	—	200	400	750	—	—

KM# 14 1/2 THALER
Silver **Obv:** Crowned eight-fold arms **Obv. Legend:** TVT. ALBART. OTT **Rev:** Crowned imperial eagle, orb on breast, titles of Ferdinand II, date

Date	Mintage	VG	F	VF	XF	Unc
16Z3	—	—	—	—	—	—

KM# 15 THALER

Silver **Obv:** Crowned ornate arms **Obv. Legend:** *:TVT: ALB: OTT: COM: IN: SOLMS: D: I: M: W: E: S: **Rev:** Crowned imperial eagle **Rev. Legend:** *FERDINANDVS: II • D:G: ROM. IMP... **Note:** Dav. #7763.

Date	Mintage	VG	F	VF	XF	Unc
16Z3	—	850	1,650	3,000	5,000	—

SOLMS-LICH

One of the original two divisions of Solms in 1409, with its seat at Lich, just 7 miles (12 km) southeast of Giessen, Solms-Lich was joined with Hohensolms (Burgsolms) until a further division in 1562. The branch of Solms-Heruletz was established from Solms-Lich in 1590, but the parent line fell extinct in 1718.The Lich lands and titles reverted to Solms-Hohensolms in the latter year.

RULERS

Ernst I
With George Eerhard, 1596-1602
Ernst II, 1602-1619
Otto Sebastian, 1619-1640
Ludwig Christoph, 1640-1650
Hermann Adolf Moritz, 1650-1718

Joint Coinage

II - Eberhard (d.1600), Hermann Adolf, Reinhard II, George Eberhard,
Ernest II and Philipp, 1590-1610
III - Otto Sebastian and Ludwig Christoph, under guardianship of Friedrich zu Solms-Rodelheim and Joachim Friedrich zu Mansfeld, 1619-1623

MINT OFFICIALS' INITIALS

Lich Mint

Initial	Date	Name
(a)=	1589-93, 1602-08	Peter Arnsburger
	Ca. 1605	(Amtmann) Sprenger

Södel Mint

Initial	Date	Name
	1612	Georg Kupper
(b)=	1612-19	Hans Schmidt von Bielefeld
	1613-?	Michael Loth von Giessen
(c)=	1620-21	Sebastian Reess
	1621-?	Hartmann Diel

COUNTSHIP

JOINT COINAGE

KM# 18 PFENNIG

Silver **Ruler:** Ernst II **Obv:** 4-fold arms **Obv. Legend:** S D G (SOLI DEO GLORIA) **Note:** Uniface schüssel-type.

Date	Mintage	VG	F	VF	XF	Unc
ND(1612)	74,000	65.00	125	250	—	—

KM# 13.2 3 KREUZER (Groschen)

Silver **Ruler:** Ernst II **Note:** Klippe.

Date	Mintage	VG	F	VF	XF	Unc
1611	—	—	—	—	—	—

KM# 13.1 3 KREUZER (Groschen)

Silver **Ruler:** Ernst II **Obv:** 4-fold arms, titles of Ernst II around **Rev:** Crowned imperial eagle, 3 in circle on breast, titles of Rudolf II, date around **Note:** Varieties exist.

Date	Mintage	VG	F	VF	XF	Unc
1611	—	35.00	75.00	150	300	—
1612	—	35.00	75.00	150	300	—
ND	—	35.00	75.00	150	300	—

KM# 19 3 KREUZER (Groschen)

Silver **Ruler:** Ernst II **Obv:** 4-fold arms, titles of Ernst II around **Rev:** Crowned imperial eagle, 3 in circle on breast, titles of Matthias in margin **Note:** Varieties exist.

Date	Mintage	VG	F	VF	XF	Unc
ND(1612)	—	30.00	65.00	135	275	—
1612	—	30.00	65.00	135	275	—
161Z	—	30.00	65.00	135	275	—
1613	—	30.00	65.00	135	275	—
1613 (b)	—	30.00	65.00	135	275	—
1615 (b)	—	30.00	65.00	135	275	—
(1)615 (b)	—	30.00	65.00	135	275	—
(16)15 (b)	—	30.00	65.00	135	275	—
1616 (b)	—	30.00	65.00	135	275	—
(16)16	—	30.00	65.00	135	275	—
1617 (b)	—	30.00	65.00	135	275	—
(16)17 (b)	—	30.00	65.00	135	275	—
(1)617 (b)	—	30.00	65.00	135	275	—
(16)18 (b)	—	30.00	65.00	135	275	—
1618 (b)	—	30.00	65.00	135	275	—
(16)19 (b)	—	30.00	65.00	135	275	—
(16)19	—	30.00	65.00	135	275	—
ND (b)	—	30.00	65.00	135	275	—

KM# 21 3 KREUZER (Groschen)

Silver **Ruler:** Ernst II **Obv:** 4-fold arms divide first half of date, titles of Ernst II around **Rev:** Crowned imperial eagle, 3 in circle on breast, titles of Rudolf II **Note:** Varieties exist.

Date	Mintage	VG	F	VF	XF	Unc
16/1613	—	30.00	65.00	135	275	—
1613	—	30.00	65.00	135	275	—
1613 (b)	—	30.00	65.00	135	275	—
1614 (b)	—	30.00	65.00	135	275	—
1616 (b)	—	30.00	65.00	135	275	—
1617 (b)	—	30.00	65.00	135	275	—
16/1617 (b)	—	30.00	65.00	135	275	—
17/1617 (b)	—	30.00	65.00	135	275	—
1618 (b)	—	30.00	65.00	135	275	—

KM# 20 3 KREUZER (Groschen)

Silver **Ruler:** Ernst II **Note:** Klippe.

Date	Mintage	VG	F	VF	XF	Unc
(16)13 (b)	—	800	1,650	3,000	—	—

KM# 23 3 KREUZER (Groschen)

Silver **Ruler:** Ernst II **Obv:** 4-fold arms, first half of date in margin **Rev:** Crowned imperial eagle, 3 in circle on breast

Date	Mintage	VG	F	VF	XF	Unc
1613 (b)	—	35.00	75.00	150	290	—

KM# 22 3 KREUZER (Groschen)

Silver **Ruler:** Ernst II **Note:** Klippe.

Date	Mintage	VG	F	VF	XF	Unc
1617 (b)	—	—	—	—	—	—

KM# 38 3 KREUZER (Groschen)

Silver **Ruler:** Ernst II **Note:** Klippe.

Date	Mintage	VG	F	VF	XF	Unc
(16)19	—	—	—	—	—	—

KM# 37 3 KREUZER (Groschen)

Silver **Ruler:** Ernst II **Obv:** 4-fold arms **Rev:** Crowned imperial eagle, 3 in circle on breast, titles of Ferdinand II **Note:** Varieties exist.

Date	Mintage	VG	F	VF	XF	Unc
(16)19	—	35.00	75.00	150	300	—
(16)Z0	—	35.00	75.00	150	300	—

KM# 41 3 KREUZER (Groschen)

Silver **Ruler:** Ernst II **Note:** Klippe.

Date	Mintage	VG	F	VF	XF	Unc
ND (c)	—	—	—	—	—	—

KM# 40 3 KREUZER (Groschen)

Silver **Ruler:** Ernst II **Obv:** Four-fold arms around ILLUST. TUT. CO. I. SOL. LICH (or variant) **Rev:** Crowned imperial eagle, 3 in circle on breast, titles of Ferdinand II around

Date	Mintage	VG	F	VF	XF	Unc
ND(ca.1620)	—	—	—	—	—	—

KM# 42 3 KREUZER (Groschen)

Silver **Ruler:** Ernst II **Obv:** 4-fold arms around ILLUS. TUT. CO. SOLMS. LICH (or variant) **Rev:** Crowned imperial eagle, 3 in circle on breast, titles of Ferdinand II around **Note:** Varieties exist.

Date	Mintage	VG	F	VF	XF	Unc
(16)Z1	—	45.00	95.00	190	385	—
(16)ZZ	—	45.00	95.00	190	385	—

KM# 43 6 KREUZER

Silver **Ruler:** Ernst II **Obv:** Four-fold arms, date above, around ILLUST. TUT. CO(M). SOLMS. LICH 6•K **Rev:** Crowned imperial eagle, orb on breast, titles of Ferdinand II around **Note:** Varieties exist.

Date	Mintage	VG	F	VF	XF	Unc
16Z1	—	—	—	—	—	—

KM# 14 ALBUS

Silver **Ruler:** Ernst II **Obv:** 4-fold arms, titles of Ernst II around **Rev:** Inscription **Rev. Inscription:** NOVVS / ALBVS / date, SOLI DEO GLORIA around **Note:** Varieties exist.

Date	Mintage	VG	F	VF	XF	Unc
1611	—	—	—	—	—	—

KM# 15 12 KREUZER (Dreibätzner)

Silver **Ruler:** Ernst II **Obv:** Four-fold arms, titles of Ernst II around **Rev:** Crowned imperial eagle, 12 in circle on breast, titles of Rudolf II, date around

Date	Mintage	VG	F	VF	XF	Unc
1611	—	1,000	1,800	3,600	—	—

KM# 16 12 KREUZER (Dreibätzner)

Silver **Ruler:** Ernst II **Note:** Klippe.

Date	Mintage	VG	F	VF	XF	Unc
1611	—	—	—	—	—	—

KM# 27 12 KREUZER (Dreibätzner)

Silver **Ruler:** Ernst II **Obv:** Eight-fold arms in ornamented shield, first half of date above, titles of Ernst II around **Rev:** Crowned imperial eagle, 1Z in orb on breast, tail of eagle divides second half of date, titles of Matthias around

Date	Mintage	VG	F	VF	XF	Unc
1614 (b)	—	—	—	—	—	—

KM# 39 12 KREUZER (Dreibätzner)

Silver **Ruler:** Ernst II **Obv:** four-fold arms, around ILLUSTR. TUT. COME. SOLMS. LICH **Rev:** Crowned imperial eagle, 1Z in orb on breast, titles of Ferdinand II, date around **Note:** Varieties exist.

Date	Mintage	VG	F	VF	XF	Unc
(16)19	—	900	1,800	3,600	—	—
(16)Z0	—	900	1,800	3,600	—	—
ND (c)	—	900	1,800	3,600	—	—

KM# 44 12 KREUZER (Dreibätzner)

Silver **Ruler:** Ernst II **Obv:** Date above arms **Note:** Similar to KM#39.

Date	Mintage	VG	F	VF	XF	Unc
16Z1	—	950	1,900	3,700	—	—

KM# 3 DICKEN (Teston)

Silver **Ruler:** Ernst II **Obv:** Oval four-fold arms in ornate frame, date above, MO. ARG. COM... around **Rev:** Crowned imperial eagle, orb on breast, titles of Rudolf II around

Date	Mintage	VG	F	VF	XF	Unc
1601	—	1,100	2,200	4,300	—	—

KM# 5 1/2 THALER

Silver **Obv:** Oval four-fold arms divide date, two helmets above, legend around **Obv. Legend:** MO. ARG. CO - SOLM • LICH **Rev:** Crowned imperial eagle, orb on breast, titles of Rudolf II around

Date	Mintage	VG	F	VF	XF	Unc
1601 Rare	—	—	—	—	—	—

KM# 28 THALER

Silver **Obv:** Crowned imperial eagle with orb on breast, date 1-6-1-4 below tail feathers **Obv. Legend:** ERNESTUS• COM • IN • SOLMS • LICH • L.D.G. **Rev:** Helmeted arms **Rev. Legend:** MATTHIAS • I • D • G • RO • IMP... **Note:** Dav. #7745.

Date	Mintage	VG	F	VF	XF	Unc
1614 Rare	—	—	—	—	—	—

KM# 48 THALER

Silver **Obv:** Helmeted oval arms **Obv. Legend:** • MO • ARG • CO • SOLM : LICH **Rev:** Crowned imperial eagle with orb on breast, 2-3 next to neck or by claws of eagle **Rev. Legend:** • FERDINAN • II • D : G • ROM • IMP... **Note:** Dav. #7746.

Date	Mintage	VG	F	VF	XF	Unc
16Z3 Rare	—	—	—	—	—	—
ND Rare	—	—	—	—	—	—

KM# 35 2 THALER

Silver **Obv:** Helmeted arms **Obv. Legend:** PHILIPPUS. COMES. IN: SOLMS: LICH **Rev:** Crowned imperial eagle with orb on breast, date divided by tail **Rev. Legend:** MATTHIAS: D: G: RO: IMP... **Note:** Klippe. Dav. #7748.

Date	Mintage	VG	F	VF	XF	Unc
1618 Rare	—	—	—	—	—	—

KM# 53 2 THALER

Silver **Obv:** Helmeted ornate oval arms **Obv. Legend:** PHILIPS • COM • SOLM • LICH **Rev:** Crowned imperial eagle **Rev. Legend:** FERDIN • II • D • G • ROM • IMP... **Note:** Dav. #7752.

Date	Mintage	VG	F	VF	XF	Unc
1624 Rare	—	—	—	—	—	—

KM# 46 2 GULDEN

21.5000 g., Silver **Obv:** Helmeted arms **Obv. Legend:** FERDI. II...REX IZ0 **Note:** Dav, #7750.

Date	Mintage	VG	F	VF	XF	Unc
16ZZ Rare	—	—	—	—	—	—

KM# 49 2 GULDEN

21.5000 g., Silver **Obv:** Helmeted arms **Obv. Legend:** PHILIPS • COM • SOLM • LICH **Rev:** Crowned imperial eagle, neck divides Z-3 **Note:** Dav.#7751.

Date	Mintage	VG	F	VF	XF	Unc
(16)Z3	—	1,750	3,100	5,100	9,500	—

KM# 52 2 GULDEN

21.5000 g., Silver **Obv:** Helmeted arms **Obv. Legend:** PHILIPS • COM • SOLM • LICH **Rev:** Crowned imperial eagle **Rev. Legend:** FERDIN • II • D • G • ROM • IMP... Z4 **Note:** Dav.#7753.

Date	Mintage	VG	F	VF	XF	Unc
(16)Z4	—	1,750	3,100	5,100	9,500	—

KM# 45 4 GULDEN

24.0000 g., Silver **Obv:** Helmeted arms **Obv. Legend:** PHILIPPUS • COMES • IN : SOLMS: LICH **Rev:** Date divided by necks of crowned imperial eagle **Rev. Legend:** FERDIN II... REX.IV FL **Note:** Dav.#7749

Date	Mintage	VG	F	VF	XF	Unc
16ZZ Rare	—	—	—	—	—	—

TRADE COINAGE

KM# 7 GOLDGULDEN

3.5000 g., 0.9860 Gold 0.1109 oz. AGW **Ruler:** Joint Coinage II **Obv:** Arms in inner circle **Rev:** Crowned imperial eagle in inner circle, titles of Rudolf II **Note:** Fr.#3294.

Date	Mintage	VG	F	VF	XF	Unc
1601 Rare	—	—	—	—	—	—

KM# 30 GOLDGULDEN

3.5000 g., 0.9860 Gold 0.1109 oz. AGW **Ruler:** Joint Coinage II **Obv:** Arms **Rev:** Crowned imperial eagle, titles of Matthias **Note:** Fr.#3295.

Date	Mintage	VG	F	VF	XF	Unc
1615 (b) Rare	—	—	—	—	—	—

Note: Künker Auction 100, 6-05, VF-XF realized approximately $10,440.

KM# 31 GOLDGULDEN

3.5000 g., 0.9860 Gold 0.1109 oz. AGW **Ruler:** Joint Coinage II **Obv:** Arms **Rev:** Crowned imperial eagle **Note:** Fr.#3296.

Date	Mintage	VG	F	VF	XF	Unc
1616	—	1,850	3,500	6,500	10,000	—

KM# 50 GOLDGULDEN

3.5000 g., 0.9860 Gold 0.1109 oz. AGW **Ruler:** Joint Coinage II **Obv:** Arms **Rev:** Crowned imperial eagle, titles of Ferdinand II **Note:** Fr.#3297.

Date	Mintage	VG	F	VF	XF	Unc
1623	—	2,500	5,000	8,500	—	—

KM# 25 DUCAT

3.5000 g., 0.9860 Gold 0.1109 oz. AGW **Ruler:** Joint Coinage II **Obv:** Arms in inner circle **Rev:** Emperor Matthias standing in inner circle **Note:** Fr.#3298.

Date	Mintage	VG	F	VF	XF	Unc
1613	—	2,000	4,000	7,500	12,500	—

KM# 10 6 DUCAT

20.0900 g., 0.9860 Gold 0.6368 oz. AGW **Obv:** Oval four-fold arms divide date, two helmets above, legend around **Obv. Legend:** MO. ARG. CO -SOLM • LICH **Rev:** Crowned imperial eagle, orb on breast, titles of Rudolf II around

Date	Mintage	VG	F	VF	XF	Unc
1601 Rare	—	—	—	—	—	—

SOLMS-ROEDELHEIM

COUNTSHIP

REGULAR COINAGE

KM# 16 KREUZER

Silver **Ruler:** Ludwig **Obv:** Crowned arms of Solms divides S - R, all between two branches **Rev. Inscription:** I/KREU/TZER/date/LBM

Date	Mintage	VG	F	VF	XF	Unc
1686 LBM	—	80.00	165	335	675	—

KM# 3 3 KREUZER (Groschen)

Silver **Ruler:** Friedrich **Obv:** Four-fold arms, titles of Friedrich **Rev:** Crowned imperial eagle, 3 in circle on breast, titles of Ferdinand II, date **Note:** Varieties exist.

Date	Mintage	VG	F	VF	XF	Unc
1622	—	165	335	675	—	—
ND	—	150	335	675	—	—

KM# 4 1/4 THALER

Silver **Ruler:** Friedrich **Obv:** Facing bust, value 1/4 on right, titles of Friedrich **Rev:** Crowned eight-fold arms divide date, titles continue

Date	Mintage	VG	F	VF	XF	Unc
1622	—	—	—	—	—	—

KM# 5 1/4 THALER

Silver **Ruler:** Friedrich **Obv:** Crowned eight-fold arms, titles of Ferdinand II, date **Rev:** Crowned imperial eagle, orb on breast, titles of Ferdinand II, date

Date	Mintage	VG	F	VF	XF	Unc
16ZZ	—	—	—	—	—	—

KM# 11 2/3 THALER (Gulden)

Silver **Ruler:** Johann August **Obv:** Bust right, titles of Johann August **Rev:** Crowned 8-fold arms with palm branches at sides, date below, value 60 at bottom **Note:** Dav. #989.

Date	Mintage	VG	F	VF	XF	Unc
1675 SM	—	135	275	575	1,175	—

KM# 10 2/3 THALER (Gulden)

Silver **Ruler:** Johann August **Obv:** Bust right, titles of Johann August **Rev:** Crowned eight-fold arms, date below, value (60) at bottom **Rev. Legend:** PER ANGUSTA - AD AVGVSTA **Note:** Dav. #989. Varieties exist.

Date	Mintage	VG	F	VF	XF	Unc
1675 SM	—	135	275	575	1,175	—
1676 SM	—	135	275	575	1,175	—

KM# 12 2/3 THALER (Gulden)

Silver **Ruler:** Johann August **Rev:** Similar to KM#10 but date divided by arms **Note:** Dav. #990. Varieties exist.

Date	Mintage	VG	F	VF	XF	Unc
1676	—	160	325	—	—	—
1676 SM/IIF	—	160	325	—	—	—

JOINT COINAGE

1635-1665

KM# 7 ALBUS

Silver **Ruler:** Johann August, Johann Friedrich, Friedrich Sigismund, and Jo hann George III **Obv:** Crowned heart-shaped two-fold arms of Solms and Wildenfels **Obv. Legend:** R. G. S. SOLMS... **Rev:** Value between two branches **Rev. Inscription:** I/ALBVS/date/MG **Note:** Varieties exist.

Date	Mintage	VG	F	VF	XF	Unc
1655 MG	—	55.00	110	200	425	—
1656 MG	—	55.00	110	200	425	—
1657 MG	—	55.00	110	200	425	—
1657 BM	—	55.00	110	200	425	—
1657 SM	—	55.00	110	200	425	—
1658 SM	—	55.00	110	200	425	—

KM# 6 1/2 THALER

Silver **Ruler:** Johann August, Johann Friedrich, Friedrich Sigismund, and Jo hann George III **Obv:** Crowned eight-fold arms divide date, titles of Friedrich **Rev:** Crowned imperial eagle, orb on breast, titles of Leopold I around

Date	Mintage	VG	F	VF	XF	Unc
1658 SM	—	1,500	3,000	6,000	—	—

TRADE COINAGE

KM# 8 DUCAT

3.5000 g., 0.9860 Gold 0.1109 oz. AGW **Ruler:** Johann August, Johann Friedrich, Friedrich Sigismund, and Jo hann George III **Obv:** Arms in inner circle **Rev:** Value and date in wreath **Note:** Fr.#3301.

Date	Mintage	VG	F	VF	XF	Unc
1656 Rare	—	—	—	—	—	—

KM# 14 DUCAT

3.5000 g., 0.9860 Gold 0.1109 oz. AGW **Ruler:** Johann August **Obv:** Bust of Johann August right in inner circle **Rev:** Arms in inner circle **Note:** Fr.#3302.

Date	Mintage	VG	F	VF	XF	Unc
1680 Rare	—	—	—	—	—	—

SORAU

The oldest town of Lower Lusatia, Sorau was founded at least by 840 and was the property of the abbey of Fulda until the mid-13th century. It was the seat of the Lords of Döben (Dewin) from 1154 to 1280, then under the Lords of Pack until 1355, at which time it passed to Biberstein. The latter obtained the mint right in 1414. When the Biberstein line died out in 1551, it fell to Brandenburg, which sold it almost immediately to Promnitz. The Lord of Promnitz later struck coins in league with the Elector of Saxony at Sorau during the Kipper Period of the Thirty Years' War.

MINT OFFICIALS

Initial	Date	Name
FS	1621-23	Friedrich von Stierbitz, mintmaster
	1621-23	Sebald Lindelbach, mintmaster
	1621-23	Johann Jacob Huser, mintmaster
	1621-23	Johann Merkel, mintmaster

PROVINCIAL TOWN

STANDARD COINAGE

KM# 1 PFENNIG

Copper **Obv:** Large W, S above divides date **Note:** Uniface. Kipper Coinage. Varieties exist.

Date	Mintage	VG	F	VF	XF	Unc
1621	—	35.00	75.00	150	300	—
16Z1	—	35.00	75.00	150	300	—
1622	—	35.00	75.00	150	300	—
16ZZ	—	35.00	75.00	150	300	—

KM# 5 PFENNIG

Copper **Obv:** Shield with arrow between 2 star, date above **Note:** Uniface. Kipper Pfennig. Varieties exist.

Date	Mintage	VG	F	VF	XF	Unc
16ZZ	—	40.00	80.00	160	325	—

KM# 8 3 PFENNIG (Drier)

Copper **Obv:** Ornate shield with arrow between 2 stars **Rev:** Large W, S above divides date **Note:** Kipper 3 Pfennig.

Date	Mintage	VG	F	VF	XF	Unc
16ZZ	—	45.00	90.00	185	375	—

KM# 12 3 PFENNIG (Drier)

Copper **Obv:** Ornate shield with arrow between 2 stars **Rev:** Large W with III value below, S above divides date **Note:** Kipper 3 Pfennig. Varieties exist.

Date	Mintage	VG	F	VF	XF	Unc
16ZZ	—	45.00	90.00	185	375	—

KM# 13 3 PFENNIG (Drier)

Copper **Obv:** Oval arms in baroque frame **Rev:** Large W with III value below, S above divides date **Note:** Kipper 3 Pfennig. Varieties exist.

Date	Mintage	VG	F	VF	XF	Unc
1622	—	45.00	90.00	185	375	—

KM# 16 3 KREUZER (Groschen)

Silver **Obv:** 3-fold arms of Promnitz, date divided by orb above, value (3) below, legend **Obv. Legend:** MO•NOVA SORAVI. **Rev:** Crowned imperial eagle, titles of Ferdinand II **Note:** Kipper 3 Kreuzer. Varieties exist.

Date	Mintage	VG	F	VF	XF	Unc
1622 FS Retrograde	—	—	—	—	—	—

KM# 17 3 KREUZER (Groschen)

Silver **Obv:** 3-fold arms of Promnitz, date divided by orb above, value (3) below, legend **Rev:** Bust of Ferdinand II right in circle, titles around **Note:** Kipper 3 Kreuzer. Varieties exist.

Date	Mintage	VG	F	VF	XF	Unc
1622 FS	—	—	—	—	—	—

KM# 19 3 KREUZER (Groschen)

Silver **Obv:** Bust of emperor right, circle around, legend, date **Rev:** Crowned imperial eagle, titles of Ferdinand II **Note:** Kipper 3 Kreuzer. Varieties exist.

Date	Mintage	VG	F	VF	XF	Unc
1622	—	—	—	—	—	—

KM# 20 3 KREUZER (Groschen)

Silver **Obv:** Bust of emperor to right, barely breaks circle at top, value (3) below, titles of Ferdinand II **Rev:** Crowned imperial eagle, Austria arms on breast, titles continued around and dat **Note:** Kipper 3 Kreuzer. Varieties exist.

Date	Mintage	VG	F	VF	XF	Unc
1622	—	—	—	—	—	—
1623	—	—	—	—	—	—

KM# 18 3 KREUZER (Groschen)

Silver **Obv:** Bust of emperor right, head breaks circle, legend, date **Obv. Legend:** MO . NOVA . SORAVIE **Rev:** Crowned imperial eagle, arms of Austria on breast, value (3) below, titles of Ferdinand II **Note:** Kipper 3 Kruezer. Varieties exist.

Date	Mintage	VG	F	VF	XF	Unc
1622	—	—	—	—	—	—
1623	—	—	—	—	—	—

KM# 3 1/24 THALER (Groschen)

Silver **Obv:** 3-fold arms of Promnitz, legend, date **Obv. Legend:** MONETA CIVIT . SORAV **Rev:** Crowned imperial eagle, titles of Ferdinand II **Note:** Kipper 1/24 Thaler.

Date	Mintage	VG	F	VF	XF	Unc
1621	—	100	200	425	—	—

KM# 25 1/24 THALER (Groschen)
Silver **Obv:** Promnitz lion rampant left, legend **Obv. Legend:** DO . PROT . NOST. **Rev:** Imperial orb with 24, date above, legend **Rev. Legend:** MO: NO: CIVI . SORA. **Note:** Kipper coinage. Prev. KM#25.1.

Date	Mintage	VG	F	VF	XF	Unc
1622	—	100	200	425	—	—

KM# 26 1/24 THALER (Groschen)
Silver, 18 mm. **Obv:** Shield of 3-fold arms of Promnitz, date divided above **Obv. Legend:** MO: NOVA - SORAVI. **Rev:** Imperial orb with 24 divides mintmaster's initials **Rev. Legend:** FERD. II. D: G: R. IM: SEM: AVG. **Note:** Bahrfeldt 223. Kipper coinage.

Date	Mintage	VG	F	VF	XF	Unc
(16)22 FS	—	85.00	200	300	475	—

KM# 27 1/24 THALER (Groschen)
Silver **Obv:** Shield of 3-fold arms of Promnitz, date divided above **Obv. Legend:** MO: NOVA - SORAVI. **Rev:** Imperial orb with 24 divides mintmaster's initials **Rev. Legend:** FERD. II. D: G: R. IM: SEM: AVG. **Note:** Klippe, Kipper coinage. Varieties exist. Prev. KM#25.2.

Date	Mintage	VG	F	VF	XF	Unc
(16)22 FS	—	—	—	—	—	—

SPEYER

(Spires)

City and bishopric spanning the Rhine 15 miles south of Mannheim. The bishopric was founded in the 4th century, destroyed by barbarians and re-established in 610. The city received the mint right in 1111 and became the site of the imperial mint. It became a free city of the empire in 1294 and was taken by France from 1801 to 1814. In the latter year, Speyer passed into the possession of Bavaria.

BISHOPRIC

RULERS

Eberhard von Dienheim, 1581-1610
Philipp Christof von Sötern, 1610-1652
Lothar Friedrich von Metternich-Burscheid, 1652-1675
Johann Hugh von Orsbeck, 1677-1711

MINT OFFICIALS' INITIALS

Initial	Date	Name
LS	1616-24	Lorenz Schneider at Koblenz
I-A	1624-27	Hans Jakob Ayrer at Koblenz
HL	1625-27	Heinrich Lambert at Koblenz
MS	1627-52	Matthias Stein at Koblenz
MF	Ca. 1665-83	Matthias Fischer at Bruchsal
DZ	1678-91	Dietrich Zimmermann at Bruchsal
A	Ca. 1680	

ARMS

Cross w/middle line between outer line of each arm.

Residence of the bishops was at Bruchsal, about 14 miles (24km) southeast of Speyer, at which place the mint was also located.

REGULAR COINAGE

KM# 21 PFENNIG
0.2500 g., Silver **Ruler:** Philipp Christof **Obv:** 2-fold arms, divided horizontally on cross of Speyer, divide date **Note:** Uniface schüssel-type.

Date	Mintage	VG	F	VF	XF	Unc
(16)24	—	75.00	150	300	—	—
(16)26	—	75.00	150	300	—	—

KM# 37 ALBUS (Rheinish Standard)
0.8500 g., Silver **Ruler:** Lothar Friedrich **Obv:** 4-fold arms with central shield **Rev:** Inscription and date in wreath **Rev. Inscription:** I / ALBVS **Mint:** Bruchsal

Date	Mintage	VG	F	VF	XF	Unc
1665	—	—	—	—	—	—

KM# 45 ALBUS (Rheinish Standard)
0.8500 g., Silver **Ruler:** Johann Hugh **Obv:** Heart-shaped 4-fold arms with central shield between branches **Rev:** Inscription, date and mintmaster's initials all in laurel wreath **Rev. Inscription:** I / ALBVS **Mint:** Bruchsal

Date	Mintage	VG	F	VF	XF	Unc
1678 DZ	—	20.00	45.00	90.00	180	—
1679 DZ	—	20.00	45.00	90.00	180	—

KM# 46 ALBUS (Rheinish Standard)
0.8500 g., Silver **Ruler:** Johann Hugh **Obv:** 3 small shields of arms, 2 above 1, all between laurel branches **Rev:** Inscription, date and mintmaster's initials all in laurel wreath **Mint:** Bruchsal

Date	Mintage	VG	F	VF	XF	Unc
1678 DZ	—	20.00	45.00	90.00	180	—
1679 DZ	—	20.00	45.00	90.00	180	—

KM# 49 ALBUS (Rheinish Standard)
0.8500 g., Silver **Ruler:** Johann Hugh **Obv:** 3 small shields of arms, 2 above 1, all between laurel branches **Rev:** Date at end of inscritpion **Mint:** Bruchsal

Date	Mintage	VG	F	VF	XF	Unc
1680 A	—	—	—	—	—	—

KM# 12 1/2 KREUZER (2 Pfennig)
0.3300 g., Silver **Ruler:** Philipp Christof **Obv:** 2-fold arms of Weissenburg above Prüm, superimposed on cross of Speyer **Note:** Uniface.

Date	Mintage	VG	F	VF	XF	Unc
ND(ca1623)	—	—	—	—	—	—

KM# 11 KREUZER (4 Pfennig)
Billon **Ruler:** Philipp Christof **Obv:** Cross of Speyer, PCPZS above **Rev:** 2 adjacent shields of arms, value 4 above **Note:** Kipper coinage. Weight varies: .45-.50 g. Varieties exist.

Date	Mintage	VG	F	VF	XF	Unc
ND(ca1621)	—	—	—	—	—	—

KM# 13 KREUZER (4 Pfennig)
Silver **Ruler:** Philipp Christof **Obv:** Arms of Trier, CPZS above **Rev:** Arms of Speyer, LSN above **Note:** Kipper coinage. Weight varies: .45-.50 g. Philipp Christof was also archbishop of Trier, 1623-52.

Date	Mintage	VG	F	VF	XF	Unc
ND(ca1623)	—	—	—	—	—	—

KM# 23 2 KREUZER (Halbbatzen)
Silver **Ruler:** Philipp Christof **Obv:** 4-fold arms with central shield **Rev:** Imperial orb with Z, cross divides date above **Note:** Weight varies: 1.05-1.20 g. Varieties exist.

Date	Mintage	VG	F	VF	XF	Unc
1625	—	60.00	120	240	—	—
1628	—	60.00	120	240	—	—

KM# 27 2 KREUZER (Halbbatzen)
Silver **Ruler:** Philipp Christof **Obv:** 4-fold arms with central shield, date in margin **Rev:** Imperial orb with Z, cross divides date above **Note:** Weight varies: 1.05-1.20 g.

Date	Mintage	VG	F	VF	XF	Unc
1632	—	—	—	—	—	—

KM# 3 3 KREUZER (Groschen)
Silver **Ruler:** Philipp Christof **Obv:** 4-fold arms, 3 helmets above **Rev:** Crowned imperial eagle, 3 in circle on breast, titles of Matthias, date in margin

Date	Mintage	VG	F	VF	XF	Unc
1612	—	—	—	—	—	—

KM# 7 3 KREUZER (Groschen)
Silver **Ruler:** Philipp Christof **Obv:** 3 shields of arms, 2 above 1 **Rev:** Crowned imperial eagle, 3 in orb on breast, titles of Ferdinand II

Date	Mintage	VG	F	VF	XF	Unc
ND(after 1619)	—	—	—	—	—	—

KM# 28 10 KREUZER
4.3500 g., Silver **Ruler:** Philipp Christof **Obv:** 4-fold arms with central shield, date divided around **Rev:** 1/2-length figure of St. Philip, value 10 below **Mint:** Philipsburg

Date	Mintage	VG	F	VF	XF	Unc
1632	—	—	—	—	—	—

KM# 8 12 KREUZER (Dreibätzner)
1.3300 g., Silver **Ruler:** Philipp Christof **Obv:** 4-fold arms with central shield **Rev:** Crowned imperial eagle, 12 in orb on breast, titles of Ferdinand II around **Note:** Kipper coinage.

Date	Mintage	VG	F	VF	XF	Unc
ND(ca1620)	—	—	—	—	—	—

KM# 9 12 KREUZER (Dreibätzner)
1.3300 g., Silver **Ruler:** Philipp Christof **Obv:** 3 shields of arms, 2 above 1 **Rev:** Crowned imperial eagle, 12 in orb on breast, titles of Ferdinand II around **Note:** Kipper coinage.

Date	Mintage	VG	F	VF	XF	Unc
ND(ca1620)	—	—	—	—	—	—

KM# 10 24 KREUZER (Dicken)
Silver **Ruler:** Philipp Christof **Obv:** 3 shields of arms, 2 above 1 **Rev:** Crowned imperial eagle, orb on breast, titles of Ferdinand II around **Note:** Kipper coinage. 3.8-4.4 g.

Date	Mintage	VG	F	VF	XF	Unc
ND(ca1620)	—	350	750	1,250	—	—

KM# 25 30 KREUZER (1/2 Gulden)
Silver **Ruler:** Philipp Christof **Obv:** Crowned 4-fodl arms with central shield divide date **Rev:** 1/2-length figure of St. Philip, value 30 below **Mint:** Philipsburg

Date	Mintage	VG	F	VF	XF	Unc
1630	—	—	—	—	—	—

KM# 47 30 KREUZER (1/2 Gulden)
Silver **Ruler:** Johann Hugh **Obv:** Bust right **Rev:** 4-fold arms with central shield divide date, value 30 below in margin **Mint:** Philipsburg

Date	Mintage	VG	F	VF	XF	Unc
1679 DZ	—	—	—	—	—	—

KM# 38 60 KREUZER (Gulden)
Silver **Ruler:** Lothar Friedrich **Obv:** Bust of Lothar Friedrich to righ **Rev:** Mitered 4-fold arms with central shield, date in margin

Date	Mintage	VG	F	VF	XF	Unc
1665	—	—	—	—	—	—

KM# 39 60 KREUZER (Gulden)
Silver **Ruler:** Lothar Friedrich **Obv:** Bust of Lothar Friedrich to right **Rev:** Mitered 4-fold arms with central shield, value 60 at bottom and date in margin **Note:** Dav#991.

Date	Mintage	VG	F	VF	XF	Unc
1665 MF	—	125	250	475	950	—
1671 MF	—	—	—	—	—	—

KM# 43 60 KREUZER (Gulden)
Silver **Ruler:** Lothar Friedrich **Obv:** Bust of Lothar Friedrich to right **Rev:** Mitered 4-fold arms with central shield, value 60 at bottom and date in margin **Note:** Dav#992. Varieties exist.

Date	Mintage	VG	F	VF	XF	Unc
1672	—	125	250	500	900	—
1672 MF	—	125	250	500	900	—

KM# 48 60 KREUZER (Gulden)
Silver **Ruler:** Johann Hugh **Obv:** Bust right **Rev:** 4-fold arms with central shield divide date, value 60 above in margin **Note:** Dav#993.

Date	Mintage	VG	F	VF	XF	Unc
1679 DZ	—	—	—	—	—	—

KM# 14 1/4 THALER
Silver **Ruler:** Philipp Christof **Obv:** 4-fold arms with central shield, 3 helmets above **Rev:** Full-length standing figure of St. Philip with crozier divides date

Date	Mintage	VG	F	VF	XF	Unc
1623	—	350	700	—	—	—

KM# 30 1/4 THALER
7.3200 g., Silver **Ruler:** Philipp Christof **Obv:** 4-fold arms with central shield divide date **Rev:** Madonna and child, crescent below, rays around **Mint:** Philipsburg **Note:** Klippe.

Date	Mintage	VG	F	VF	XF	Unc
1632	—	1,200	2,500	4,000	—	—

KM# 15 1/2 THALER
Silver **Ruler:** Philipp Christof **Obv:** 4-fold arms with central shield in ornate frame **Rev:** Full-length standing figure of St. Philip with crozier divides date **Mint:** Philipsburg

Date	Mintage	VG	F	VF	XF	Unc
1623	—	—	—	—	—	—

KM# 16 THALER
Silver **Ruler:** Philipp Christof **Subject:** Changing the Name of Udenheim to Phillipsburg **Obv:** Helmeted arms **Obv. Legend:** EP * SPIR * PRAEP * **Rev:** Saint standing **Rev. Legend:** S * PHILIPPVS * PATRONVS * **Note:** Dav. #5806.

Date	Mintage	VG	F	VF	XF	Unc
1623 Rare	—	—	—	—	—	—

Note: Rauch Auction 85, 11-09, XF realized approximately $46,675.

KM# 17 THALER
Silver **Ruler:** Philipp Christof **Obv. Legend:** ... ARCHI. TREVIR. PRINC. ELECT* **Rev:** Standing saint divides date **Rev. Legend:** EPIS. SPIRENSIS. AD. PRVM. PRAEP. WEISSENB. **Note:** Dav. #5807.

Date	Mintage	VG	F	VF	XF	Unc
1623 Rare	—	—	—	—	—	—

KM# 18 THALER
Silver **Ruler:** Philipp Christof **Note:** Klippe. Dav. 5807A.

Date	Mintage	VG	F	VF	XF	Unc
1623 Rare	—	—	—	—	—	—

KM# 19 2 THALER
Silver **Ruler:** Philipp Christof **Subject:** Changing the Name of Udenheim to Phillipsburg **Obv:** Helmeted arms **Rev:** Saint standing **Note:** Dav. #5805.

Date	Mintage	VG	F	VF	XF	Unc
1623 Rare	—	—	—	—	—	—

TRADE COINAGE

KM# 33 GOLDGULDEN
Gold **Ruler:** Philipp Christof **Mint:** Philipsburg **Note:** Klippe. Prev. KM#A16.

Date	Mintage	VG	F	VF	XF	Unc
1632 Rare	—	—	—	—	—	—

KM# 32 GOLDGULDEN
Gold **Ruler:** Philipp Christof **Obv:** Crowned 4-fold arms with central shield dividing date **Rev:** Madonna and child on crescent, rays around **Mint:** Philipsburg **Note:** Prev. KM#A15.

Date	Mintage	VG	F	VF	XF	Unc
1632	—	—	—	—	—	—

KM# 5 2 GOLDGULDEN
7.0000 g., 0.9860 Gold 0.2219 oz. AGW **Ruler:** Philipp Christof **Obv:** Helmeted 4-fold arms **Rev:** Madonna and child **Note:** Prev. FR#3304.

Date	Mintage	VG	F	VF	XF	Unc
1612 Rare	—	—	—	—	—	—

KM# 41 DUCAT
3.5000 g., 0.9860 Gold 0.1109 oz. AGW **Ruler:** Lothar Friedrich **Obv:** Bust right **Rev:** Crowned arms **Note:** Prev. FR#3305.

Date	Mintage	VG	F	VF	XF	Unc
1665	—	1,300	2,600	5,200	8,500	—

CITY

Although the city of Speyer received the mint right in 1111, very few coins were struck on its behalf over the centuries. Special coins were minted for the first and second hundred years of the Protestant Reformation There are also a few notable counter-marked coins dating from the early phase of the Thirty Years' War.

REGULAR COINAGE

KM# 87 PFENNIG

0.1800 g., Silver **Obv:** View of cathedral divides I - P, date above **Note:** Uniface schüssel-type.

Date	Mintage	VG	F	VF	XF	Unc
1624	—	—	—	—	—	—

KM# 88 ALBUS (2 Kreuzer)

Silver **Obv:** Crowned imperial eagle, 2 in orb on breast, titles of Ferdinand **Rev:** Crowned oval 4-fold arms w/central shield (cross), date in legend **Note:** Weight varies: .65-1.32 g. Varieties exist. Issue of Johann Ludwig von Leiningen-Dagsburg-Falkenburg (KM#13), counter-marked with ornate S of Speyer

Date	Mintage	VG	F	VF	XF	Unc
1624	—	—	—	—	—	—

KM# 86 2 STUBER (Groschen)

2.1000 g., Silver **Obv:** Crowned 4-fold arms with central shield **Rev:** Ornate cross **Note:** Issue of Philip the Fair of Holland (1482-1506), counter-marked with ornate S of Speyer

Date	Mintage	VG	F	VF	XF	Unc
ND(ca1620)	—	—	—	—	—	—

KM# 80 GROSCHEN

1.8500 g., Silver **Subject:** Centennial of the Reformation **Obv:** View of cathedral, inscription around **Rev:** 8-line inscription with Roman numeral dates **Note:** Klippe.

Date	Mintage	VG	F	VF	XF	Unc
1617	—	—	—	—	—	—

KM# 81 GROSCHEN

1.8500 g., Silver **Obv:** 6-line inscription **Rev:** 8-line inscription with Roman numeral dates **Note:** Varieties exist.

Date	Mintage	VG	F	VF	XF	Unc
1617	—	—	—	—	—	—

KM# 82 1/4 THALER

Silver **Subject:** Centennial of the Reformation **Obv:** View of cathedral, inscription around within wreath **Rev:** 4-line inscription with Roman numeral date, inscription with Roman numeral date around, all within wreath **Note:** Klippe. Weight varies: 7.2-8.5 g.

Date	Mintage	VG	F	VF	XF	Unc
1617 Rare	30	—	—	—	—	—

KM# 83 1/2 THALER

Silver **Subject:** Centennial of the Reformation **Obv:** View of cathedral, inscription around within wreath **Rev:** 4-line inscription with Roman numeral date, inscription with Roman numeral date around, all within wreath **Note:** Klippe. Weight varies: 15-17 g.

Date	Mintage	VG	F	VF	XF	Unc
1617 Rare	88	—	—	—	—	—

TRADE COINAGE

KM# 84 GOLDGULDEN

3.2000 g., 0.9860 Gold 0.1014 oz. AGW **Subject:** Centennial of the Reformation **Obv:** 6-line inscription **Rev:** 8-line inscription with R. N. date **Note:** Klippe. Prev. KM#5.

Date	Mintage	VG	F	VF	XF	Unc
ND(1617) Rare	—	—	—	—	—	—

KM# 85 GOLDGULDEN

3.4000 g., Gold **Subject:** Centennial of the Reformation **Obv:** View of cathedral, inscription around **Rev:** 8-line inscription with Roman numeral dates

Date	Mintage	VG	F	VF	XF	Unc
1617 Rare	—	—	—	—	—	—

PHILLIPSBURG

TRADE COINAGE

KM# 1 2 GOLDGULDEN

0.9860 Gold **Obv:** Madonna and child with rays, crescent moon below, inscription around **Obv. Inscription:** MONETA. NOVA. AVREA. PHILLIPPSBVRG. **Rev:** 10-line inscription **Rev. Inscription:** AO' / 1635.D' / Z4. IANVAR / 1ST, PHILIPS / BVRG DVRCH / D. KAY: OBRISTEN / BAVMBERGER / MIT. STVRM / ER. OBERT. WORD / EN /(Translation: Year 1635, the 24th of January, Phillipsburg was taken by st **Note:** Weight varies: 7.08-7.32 grams.

Date	Mintage	VG	F	VF	XF	Unc
1635 Rare	—	—	—	—	—	—

KM# 2 2 GOLDGULDEN

0.9860 Gold **Note:** Klippe. Uniface.

Date	Mintage	VG	F	VF	XF	Unc
1635	—	1,500	3,500	5,500	—	—

PATTERNS

Including off-metal strikes

KM#	Date	Mintage	Identification	Mkt Val
Pn1	1617	—	Groschen. Lead. 3.5000 g. KM#81.	—

STADE

First mentioned as early as about 1000AD, Stade is located along the Elbe River about 16 miles (27km) west of Hamburg and downstream from that city. Yet, from the mid-11th century, the town was the site for a mint of the archbishops of Bremen. By 1168, Stade was completely under the control of Bremen, but was given the right to strike its own local coinage beginning in 1272. The city struck a series of issues until the late 17th century. Stade was included in the Duchy of Bremen and Werden from 1644 until 1719, then was made a part of Hannover in the latter year.

MINT OFFICIALS' INITALS

Initials	Date	Name
	1497-ca1515	Hinrik Holtorp, mintmaster
(a)= 	1614-21	Simon Timpfe, mintmaster
HB (ligature)	ca 1621	unknown
(b)=  or PT	1638-43	Peter Timpfe, mintmaster
	1649	Heinrich Timke, warden
	1657-60	Johann Schulze, mintmaster
	1660-70	Michael Müller, mintmaster
AH	1670-76	Andreas Hille, mintmaster
IS	1660-80	Jacob Schröder, as warden
	1680-95	as mintmaster
IS	1695-1706	Diedrich Jürgen Schröder, mintmaster

ARMS

Key, as that of Bremen

REFERENCES

B = Max Bahrfeldt, ***Die Münzen der Stadt Stade***, Vienna, 1879.

S = Hugo Frhr. von Saurma-Jeltsch, *Die Saurmasche Münzsammlung deutscher, schweizerischer und polnischer Gepräge von etwa dem Beginn der Groschenzeit bis zur Kipperperiode*, **Berlin, 1892.**

PROVINCIAL CITY

REGULAR COINAGE

KM# 20 3 PFENNIG (Dreiling)

0.5100 g., Silver, 15 mm. **Obv:** Shield of city arms in circle **Obv. Legend:** MO. NO. CIVI. STADENS. **Rev:** Date at end of inscription **Rev. Legend:** DEVS. EST. OMNIPOT. **Rev. Inscription:** 3 / PEN **Note:** Ref. B#37.

Date	Mintage	VG	F	VF	XF	Unc
(1)640	—	—	—	—	—	—

KM# 5 SECHSLING (1/96 Thaler)

Silver **Obv:** Key within circle of branches **Rev:** Value in inner circle, date in legend

Date	Mintage	VG	F	VF	XF	Unc
1676	—	25.00	50.00	100	200	—

KM# 3 SECHSLING (1/64 Thaler)

Silver **Obv:** Oval city arms supported by 2 griffins **Obv. Legend:** MON. NO. CI. STADENSIS. **Rev:** Cross in circle, date divided in angles **Rev. Legend:** DEVS. EST. OMNIPOTENS. **Note:** Ref. S#3397. Klippe.

Date	Mintage	VG	F	VF	XF	Unc
1615 (a)	—	180	360	725	—	—

KM# 10 SECHSLING (1/64 Thaler)

Silver, 17 mm. **Obv:** Shield of city arms in circle, date at end of legend **Obv. Legend:** MO. NO. CI. STADEN **Rev:** Cross in circle, small annulets in upepr angles, 6 - 4 in lower 2 angles **Rev. Legend:** DEVS. EST. OMNIPOTENS. **Note:** Ref. B#25. Kipper coinage. Weight varies: .63-.65 g.

Date	Mintage	VG	F	VF	XF	Unc
(16)Z0 (a)	—	—	—	—	—	—

KM# 13 SECHSLING (1/64 Thaler)

Silver, 15 mm. **Obv:** Shield of city arms in circle, date at end of legend **Obv. Legend:** MO. NO. CIV(I). STADE. **Rev. Legend:** DEVS. EST. OMNIPOTE(N)(S). **Rev. Inscription:** I / SOES / LING. **Note:** Ref. B#31. Weight varies: .50-.60 g.

Date	Mintage	VG	F	VF	XF	Unc
(16)Z1	—	80.00	150	240	450	—

KM# 14 SECHSLING (1/64 Thaler)

Silver **Obv:** Key in dotted circle, date at end of legend **Obv. Legend:** MO. NO. CIV(I). STADE. **Rev. Legend:** DEVS. EST. OMNIPOTE(N)(S). **Rev. Inscription:** I / SOES / LING. **Note:** Ref. B#32.

Date	Mintage	VG	F	VF	XF	Unc
(16)Z1	—	85.00	175	375	775	—

KM# 21 SECHSLING (1/64 Thaler)

Silver **Obv:** Shield of city arms in circle **Obv. Legend:** MO. NO. CI(V). STADENSIS. **Rev:** Cross in circle, date divided in angles **Rev. Legend:** DEUS. EST. OMNIPOTENS. **Note:** Ref. B#36.

Date	Mintage	VG	F	VF	XF	Unc
1640 (b)	—	—	—	—	—	—

KM# 25 SECHSLING (1/64 Thaler)

Silver, 15 mm. **Obv:** Key in wreath of 2 palm branches **Obv. Legend:** STADER **Rev:** Date at end of legend **Rev. Legend:** STADT. GELDT. **Rev. Inscription:** I / SECH / S. LIN / AH. **Note:** Ref. B#39. Weight varies: .45-.50 g.

Date	Mintage	VG	F	VF	XF	Unc
1676 AH	—	18.00	35.00	60.00	120	—

KM# A6 GROSCHEN

Silver, 24 mm. **Obv:** Oval city arms supported by 2 griffins, date at end of legend **Obv. Legend:** MON: NO: CIVI: STADENSIS: **Rev:** Crowned imperial eagle, imperial orb on breast **Rev. Legend:** MATTHIAS. D.G. RO. IM. SE: AV. **Note:** Ref. B#19.

Date	Mintage	VG	F	VF	XF	Unc
1616 (a)	—	—	—	—	—	—

KM# 15 2 SCHILLING (Doppelschilling)

Silver, 16-17 mm. **Obv:** 2-line inscription over small keys, all in circle, date at end of legend **Obv. Legend:** MO: NO: CIV - STADE. **Obv. Inscription:** Z / SCHILL. **Rev. Inscription:** REICHS / TALER / SILBER. **Note:** Ref. B#28. Kipper coinage. Weight varies: .91-1.0 g.

Date	Mintage	VG	F	VF	XF	Unc
(16)Z1	—	—	—	—	—	—

KM# 16 2 SCHILLING (Doppelschilling)

Silver, 16-17 mm. **Obv:** 2-line inscription over small keys, all in circle **Obv. Legend:** MO. NO. CIVI - STADEN(S). **Obv. Inscription:** Z / SCHILL. **Rev. Inscription:** REICHS / TALER. S / ILBER. **Note:** Ref. B#29. Kipper coinage. Weight varies: .91-1.0 g.

Date	Mintage	VG	F	VF	XF	Unc
ND(ca1621-22)	—	—	—	—	—	—

KM# 17 2 SCHILLING (Doppelschilling)

Silver, 16-17 mm. **Obv:** Small key above single-line inscription **Obv. Legend:** MO. NO. CIVI - STADEN(S). **Obv. Inscription:** Z / SL. **Rev. Inscription:** RICHS. D / ALDER. S / ILVER. **Note:** Ref. B#30. Kipper coinage. Weight varies: .91-1.0 g.

Date	Mintage	VG	F	VF	XF	Unc
ND(ca1621-22) HB	—	—	—	—	—	—

KM# 22 2 SCHILLING (Doppelschilling)

Silver, 23 mm. **Obv:** Oval city arms supported by 2 griffins in circle, date at end of legend **Obv. Legend:** MON. NO(V). CIV. STADENSIS. **Rev:** Crowned imperial eagle, pellet in orb on breast **Rev. Legend:** FERDINANDUS. III. D.G.R(O). I(M). S. A. **Note:** Ref. B#35a-d. Weight varies: 1.46-2.0 g.

Date	Mintage	VG	F	VF	XF	Unc
1640 (b)	—	—	—	—	—	—
1640 PT	—	100	200	425	—	—

KM# 26 1/48 THALER (Schilling = 1/2 Groschen)

Silver, 18 mm. **Obv:** Key in wreath of 2 palm branches **Obv. Legend:** STADER. **Rev:** Date at end of legend **Rev. Legend:** STADT. GELDT. **Rev. Inscription:** 48 / E. REIC / HS. TAL (or DAL) / A.H. **Note:** Ref. B#38. Weight varies: .82 - .91 g. Varieties exist.

Date	Mintage	VG	F	VF	XF	Unc
1676 AH	—	35.00	75.00	150	300	—

KM# 1 1/16 THALER (Duttchen = Doppelschilling)

2.1800 g., Silver, 25 mm. **Obv:** Oval city arms supported by 2 griffins **Obv. Legend:** MON: NOV: CIV: STADENSIS. **Rev:** Crowned imperial eagle, 16 in orb on breast **Rev. Legend:** MATTHIAS. D:G: R(O): IM: SE: AV. **Note:** Ref. B#10.

Date	Mintage	VG	F	VF	XF	Unc
ND(1612-19) (a)	—	85.00	150	300	600	1,200

KM# 2 1/16 THALER (Duttchen = Doppelschilling)

Silver **Obv:** Oval city arms supported by 2 griffins, date at end of legend **Obv. Legend:** MO(N): NO(V): CI(VI): STADENSIS. **Rev:** Crowned imperial eagle, 16 in orb on breast **Rev. Legend:** MATTHIAS. D:G: R(O)(M): I(M): S(E): A(V) or (U):. **Note:** Ref. B#13, 18. Weight varies: 2.01-2.45 g. Varieties exist.

Date	Mintage	VG	F	VF	XF	Unc
1614 (a)	—	200	350	500	1,025	—
1615 (a)	—	100	175	300	1,025	—
1616 (a)	—	100	175	300	1,025	—

KM# 4 1/16 THALER (Duttchen = Doppelschilling)

Silver **Obv:** Oval city arms supported by 2 griffins, date at end of legend **Obv. Legend:** MO(N): NO(V): CI(VI): STADENSIS., **Rev:** Crowned imperial eagle, 16 in orb on breast **Rev. Legend:** MATTHIAS. D:G: R(O)(M): I(M): S(E): A(V) or (U):. **Note:** Ref. B#12, 16. Klippe. Weight varies 4.93-7.308 g.

Date	Mintage	VG	F	VF	XF	Unc
1615 (a)	—	—	—	—	—	—
1616 (a)	—	—	—	—	—	—

KM# 7 1/16 THALER (Duttchen = Doppelschilling)
Silver **Obv:** Oval city arms supported by 2 griffins **Obv. Legend:** MO(N). NO(V). CIV(I). STADEN(S)(I)(S). **Rev:** Crowned imperial eagle, 16 in orb on breast, date at end of legend **Rev. Legend:** MATT(HIAS). D.G. R(O). I(M). S. A(V). **Note:** Ref. B#17, 20, 20g, 20i; 21, 21a, 21e; 22, 22d, 22e. Varieties exist.

Date	Mintage	VG	F	VF	XF	Unc
(1)616 (a)	—	35.00	70.00	125	225	—
(1)617 (a)	—	35.00	70.00	125	225	—
1617 (a)	—	35.00	70.00	125	225	—
(1)618 (a)	—	35.00	70.00	125	225	—
(16)18 (a)	—	35.00	70.00	125	225	—
1618 (a)	—	35.00	70.00	125	225	—
(1)619 (a)	—	35.00	70.00	125	225	—
(16)19 (a)	—	35.00	70.00	125	225	—

KM# 11 1/16 THALER (Duttchen = Doppelschilling)
Silver, 23 mm. **Obv:** Oval city arms supported by 2 griffins **Obv. Legend:** MO: (NO). CIVI: STADE(N)(S)(IS). **Rev:** Crowned imperial eagle, 16 in orb on breast, date at end of legend **Rev. Legend:** FERDIN: D:G: R. IM. S. A. **Note:** Ref. B#24. Kipper coinage. Weight varies: 1.28-1.67 g.

Date	Mintage	VG	F	VF	XF	Unc
(1)6Z0	—	40.00	80.00	135	240	—

KM# 23 1/16 THALER (Duttchen = Doppelschilling)
Silver, 19 mm. **Obv:** City arms in oval ornamented shield, date at end of legend **Obv. Legend:** CIVITA(S): STADENSIS. **Rev. Legend:** MONET(A). NOVA. ARGENTEA. **Rev. Inscription:** XVI / E. REIS / DAL. **Note:** Ref. B#34. Weight varies: 1.54-1.75 g.

Date	Mintage	VG	F	VF	XF	Unc
1640 (b)	—	42.00	85.00	140	250	—

KM# 12 1/12 THALER (Schreckenberger = Doppelgroschen)
Silver, 20 mm. **Obv:** Shield of arms in circle **Obv. Legend:** MO. NO. CIVI. STADENS. **Rev:** Crowned imperial eagle, 1Z in orb on breast, date at end of legend **Rev. Legend:** FERDIN. D.G. R. I. S. A. **Note:** Ref. B#23. Kipper coinage.

Date	Mintage	VG	F	VF	XF	Unc
(1)6Z0 (a)	—	—	—	—	—	—

KM# A5 1/2 THALER (16 Schilling)
14.3000 g., Silver, 35 mm. **Obv:** Oval city arms supported by 2 griffins **Obv. Legend:** MONETA. NOVA. CIVITA: STADENSIS. **Rev:** Crowned imperial eagle, 16 in orb on breast, date at end of legend **Rev. Legend:** MATTHIAS. D:G: ROM: IM: SE: AVG: **Note:** Ref. B#11.

Date	Mintage	VG	F	VF	XF	Unc
1615 (a)	—	—	—	—	—	—

KM# 8 THALER
28.7100 g., Silver **Obv:** Oval city arms supported by 2 griffins, date at end of legend **Obv. Legend:** MONETA. NOVA. CIVITATIS. STADENSIS **Rev:** Crowned imperial eagle, orb on breast **Rev. Legend:** MATTHIAS. D.G. ROM. IMP. SEMP. AVG(VST or AUG) **Note:** Dav. #5810.

Date	Mintage	VG	F	VF	XF	Unc
1616 (a)	—	4,500	6,000	10,000	—	—

KM# 18 THALER
Silver **Obv:** Supported city arms, key left (reversed) on arms **Rev:** 32 in orb on breast of eagle, titles of Ferdinand II **Note:** Dav# 5811.

Date	Mintage	VG	F	VF	XF	Unc
16Z1 HB	—	1,000	1,650	3,250	6,000	—

KM# 19 THALER
Silver **Rev:** 23 in orb on eagle's breast **Note:** Dav# 5811A.

Date	Mintage	VG	F	VF	XF	Unc
1621 HB	—	1,000	1,750	3,500	6,500	—

KM# 24 THALER
Silver **Rev:** Plain orb on eagle's breast, titles of Ferdinand III **Rev. Legend:** ... IMP: S: A: **Note:** Dav# 5812.

Date	Mintage	VG	F	VF	XF	Unc
1640 (b) Rare	—	—	—	—	—	—

KM# 27 THALER
Silver, 44 mm. **Obv:** City arms in oval baroque frame supported by 2 griffins, date at end of legend **Obv. Legend:** MONETA. NOVA. CIVITATIS. STADENSIS **Rev:** Crowned imperial eagle, orb on breast **Rev. Legend:** LEOPOLDUS. D.G. ROM: IMP: SE: AUG. **Note:** Dav. #5814. Weight varies: 29.20-29.30 g.

Date	Mintage	VG	F	VF	XF	Unc
1686 IS	—	1,800	3,000	5,250	9,000	—

KM# 9 2 THALER
Silver, 41 mm. **Obv:** Oval city arms supported by 2 griffins, date at end of legend **Obv. Legend:** MONETA. NOVA. CIVITATIS. STADENSIS. **Rev:** Crowned imperial eagle, orb on breast **Rev. Legend:** MATTHIAS. D.G. ROM. IMP. SEMP. AVG (VST or AUG) **Note:** Dav. #5809. Weight varies: 57.80-59. g.

Date	Mintage	VG	F	VF	XF	Unc
1616 (a) Rare	—	—	—	—	—	—

KM# 28 2 THALER
58.5000 g., Silver, 44 mm. **Obv:** City arms in oval baroque frame supported by 2 griffins, date at end of legend **Obv. Legend:** MONETA. NOVA. CIVITATIS. STADENSIS. **Rev:** Crowned imperial eagle, orb on breast **Rev. Legend:** LEOPOLDUS. D.G. ROM: IMP: SE: AUG. **Note:** Dav. #5813.

Date	Mintage	VG	F	VF	XF	Unc
1686 IS Rare	—	—	—	—	—	—

Note: WAG Auction 24, 2-04, XF realized approximately $43,855.

STENDAL

Albrecht the Bear (1134-1170) founded the provincial town of Stendal, 65 miles (107 km) west of Berlin, in 1151. It became an important mint town for the margraves of Brandenburg by the turn of the 12-13th centuries and struck coins for the increasingly powerful principality through the 16th century. The town gained the right to mint its own coinage in 1488, but only produced a few small silver coins. Again, during the Kipper Period of the early phase of the Thirty Years' War, Stendal had a local copper coinage. The town's arms appear on all its coins: The left half of the Brandenburg eagle and either three ofr four small diamonds, representing stones.

PROVINCIAL TOWN

STANDARD COINAGE

KM# 1 SCHERF (1/2 Pfennig)
Copper **Obv:** Stendal arms in shield with scalloped sides, date above **Note:** Uniface. Kipper coinage.

Date	Mintage	VG	F	VF	XF	Unc
16Z1	—	37.00	75.00	150	300	—

KM# 2 SCHERF (1/2 Pfennig)
Copper **Obv:** Stendal arms in shield with straight sides, date above **Note:** Uniface. Kipper coinage.

Date	Mintage	VG	F	VF	XF	Unc
16Z1	—	37.00	75.00	150	300	—

STOLBERG

The castle of Stolberg, located on the southern slopes of the Harz Mountains, 9 miles (15 km) northeast of Nordhausen, is the ancestral home of the counts of that name. The dynasty has a recognized line of succession from count Heinrich I (1210-1239), but the family claimed descent from Otto Colonna, an Italian noble of the 6th century. The column in the family arms signifies this supposed connection, whether historically accurate or not. Count Heinrich was the younger brother of the count of Hohnstein whose castle lay just 6 miles away. Whatever the origin of the earlier counts of Stolberg, they came to an end and the line founded by Heinrich I began in about 1222. The long series of coins, based on the rich Harz silver mine holdings of the family, began at this time. Various territories, some scattered a distance from the family home, were added to the Stolberg lands and two brothers established separate lines in 1538, Stolberg-Stolberg and Stolberg-Wernigerode. Another brother succeeded to the Dietz portion of Königstein in1574.

RULERS

Wolf Ernst in Stolberg, 1552-1606
Johann in Stolberg, 1606-1612
Heinrich XXII, 1552-1615
Ludwig Georg in Ortenberg, 1572-1618
Christof II in Schwarze (Wernigerode), 1572-1638
Wolfgang Georg in Stolberg, 1612-1631
Heinrich Volrad in Ortenberg, 1618-1641

From 1498 to 1638, various combinations of the above counts-brothers, uncles, nephew and cousins-issued extensive coinages jointly in their names. Because the many counts were rulers in their own right in parts of the Stolberg possessions, their jointly issued coinages are treated together under Stolberg. Individual issues are listed under that particular branch of the countship. The joint issue groupings are given designations to avoid repetition of the names in the following manner:

XII - Wolf Ernst, Johann, Heinrich XXII, Ludwig George Christof II, 1587-1606
XIII - Johann, Heinrich XXII, Ludwig Georg, Christof II, 1606
XIV - Johann and Heinrich XXII, 1607-1612
XV - Heinrich XXII and Wolfgang Georg, 1612-1615
XVI - Christof II and Heinrich Volrad, 1618-1638

MINT OFFICIALS' INITIALS

The output of the Harz silver mines belonging to the counts of Stolberg was often beyond the capacity of their several mints to turn into coins. Production of many coins were frequently farmed out to mints in other territories, such as neighboring Mansfeld, or to city mints in Frankfurt am Main, Augsburg, etc. Sometimes mintmasters and die engravers were invited to work in Stolberg mints on a temporary basis. Over the centuries a bewildering number of people worked in and for Stolberg mints and many left their symbols and initials on the coins.

Erfurt Mint

(z)=	1605-07	Florian Gruber
	1605	Hans Weber, warden
(bb)=	1607-08	Hieronymus Grunenberger

Frankfurt am Main Mint

(hh)=	1619? – 1629	Lorenz Schilling

Gedern Mint

	1622-24	Simon Wefel
	1624-27	Kaspar Pan

Nordhausen Mint

DZ	1622	Daniel Zunder
	ca.1660	Hans König
	1660-?	Johann Krieg

Ortenberg Mint

(dd)=	1597-1605?	Daniel Ludwig von Weiersdorf
	1607	Henning Kiesel
	1617-23	Hans Heinrich Schlehenbusch (Schlebusch)
	1621	Jost Arnold
	1621-22	Simon Wefel (Wevel, Wewell)
	1622	Bartholomäus Simon
	1622-23	Hans Georg Dornwaldt

Ranstadt Mint

	1604-06	Peter Arenburg (Arnburch)
(gg)= or	1605, 1609, 1615-?	Georg Kipper (Kupper)
	1610	Hans Meyer or Schmidt
	1610	Michaël Lodt, warden
(cc)=	1610-12	Daniel Ayrer
(ee)=	1612-14	Paul Lachendress (Lachentriss)
(ff)=	1614	Thomas Isebein
	1615	Hermann Liebert
	1617	Henning Kiesel
	1617-22	Hans Heinrich Schlehenbusch (Schlebusch)
	1622	Simon Wefel (Wevel, Wewell)

Stolberg Mint

(aa)=	1607	Andreas Lafferts
	1607	Hans Kreuper (Krueper)
GM	1609-12	Georg Meinhart in Eisleben (Mansfeld)
	1619	Thomas N-?, die-cutter
	1621	Baldwin Köln
	1621	Hans Lauch
	1621	Hans Lapp, die-cutter
	1621	Valentin Reich, die-cutter
	1621	Ernst Stam, die-cutter
CZ	1623-26, 1632	Christof Ziegenhorn
UZ / VZ	1644-?	Volkmar Ziegenhorn
IPK	1663	Johann Philipp Koburger in Eisleben (Mansfeld
IA	1668-69	Johann Arensberger von Halberstadt in Rottleberode
	1669	Ernst Kaspar Dürre von Nordhausen, die-cutter
ABK	1669	Anton Bernhard Koburger in Eisleben and Rottleberode
	1623	Bartholomäus Reuke (Renke), warden
IK	1645-60	Johann Krieg
IT	1690-1723	Johann Thun in Gotha
JAS	1692-1706	Julius Angerstein (Sculpsit=engraved), mintmaster and die-cutter in Eisenberg
W/CW	1700-1730	Christian Wermuth, medailleur/die-cutter in Gotha

Wernigerode Mint

AL	1612-15	Andreas Lafferts
IH	1612	Isaak Henniges (Henniger), die-cutter
CZ	1618-20	Christof Ziegenhorn
BB	1620-21	Braun Block
IK	1620-21	Jürgen Korll (Kröll)
HL (ligature)	1621-22	Hans Lauch
IK	1622-?	Andreas Weber
HB	1659-60	Hans Becker
IB	1671-74	Johann Bostelmann
	1671-74	Johann Arendsburg (Ahrensbergk), warden
	1674	Steffen Berger, die-cutter
	1674	Jürgen Bode, die-cutter
	1674	Johann Fischer, die-cutter
	1674	Gottfried Hasse, die-cutter
	1674	Dittrich Hefering, die-cutter
	1674	Bernt Hermann, die-cutter

ARMS

Stolberg - stag, usually to left, sometimes to right, antlers extend backwards
Wernigerode - one or two fish (trout) standing on tails
Königstein - lion left
Rochefort - eagle
Eppstein - three chevrons
Minzenberg - horizontal bar
Mark - checkerboard in horizontal bar
Agimont - five horizontal bars
Lohra - lion rampant left
Wertheim - top half of eagle above three roses
Breuberg - two horizontal bars
Hohnstein - checkerboard
Klettenberg - stag left, but antlers extend upwards

COUNTSHIP

REGULAR COINAGE

KM# 36 PFENNIG

Silver **Ruler:** Joint Coinage XVI **Obv:** 4-fold arms in ornamented shield **Mint:** Stolberg **Note:** Uniface hohl-type.

Date	Mintage	VG	F	VF	XF	Unc
ND(1618-38)	—	—	—	—	—	—

KM# 3 3 PFENNIG (1/96 Thaler)

Silver **Ruler:** Joint Coinage XII **Obv:** 3 small shields of arms, Stolberg above Wernigerode and Hohnstein, date divided by bottom of upper shield **Rev:** Imperial orb with 69 (error for 96) in ornamented rhombus **Mint:** Stolberg

Date	Mintage	VG	F	VF	XF	Unc
1605	—	—	—	—	—	—

KM# 14 3 PFENNIG (1/96 Thaler)

Silver **Ruler:** Joint Coinage XV **Obv:** 4-fold arms with central shield of Stolberg **Rev:** Imperial orb with 3 divides mintmaster's initials **Mint:** Wernigerode

Date	Mintage	VG	F	VF	XF	Unc
ND(1612-15) AL	—	—	—	—	—	—

KM# 37 3 KREUZER (Groschen)

Silver **Ruler:** Joint Coinage XVI **Obv:** 4-fold arms, titles of 2 counts **Rev:** Crowned imperial eagle, 3 in orb on breast, titles of Matthias **Mint:** Stolberg

Date	Mintage	VG	F	VF	XF	Unc
ND(1618-19)	—	8.00	15.00	30.00	60.00	—

KM# 38 3 KREUZER (Groschen)

Silver **Ruler:** Joint Coinage XVI **Obv:** 4-fold arms, titles of 2 counts **Rev:** Crowned imperial eagle, 3 in orb on breast, titles of Ferdinand II **Mint:** Stolberg **Note:** Varieties exist.

Date	Mintage	VG	F	VF	XF	Unc
ND(1619-37)	—	8.00	15.00	30.00	60.00	—

KM# 41 6 KREUZER

Silver **Ruler:** Joint Coinage XVI **Obv:** 4-fold arms, titles of 2 counts, value (6 K) in margin **Rev:** Crowned imperial eagle, orb on breast, titles of Ferdinand II **Mint:** Stolberg **Note:** Kipper coinage. Varieties exist.

Date	Mintage	VG	F	VF	XF	Unc
ND(1621/2)	—	—	—	—	—	—

KM# 42 24 KREUZER (8 Groschen = 1/3 Thaler)

Silver **Ruler:** Joint Coinage XVI **Obv:** 3 ornate shields of arms, 1 above 2, small cross in center, upper arms divide date, value 24 between lower 2 arms, titles of 2 counts **Rev:** Stag left, small orb above, titles continued **Mint:** Stolberg **Note:** Kipper coinage.

Date	Mintage	VG	F	VF	XF	Unc
16ZZ DZ	—	—	—	—	—	—

KM# 30 GROSCHEN (1/24 Thaler)

Silver **Ruler:** Joint Coinage XV **Obv:** 4-fold arms with central shield, titles of 2 brothers **Rev:** Imperial orb with Z4, orb divides date, titles continued **Mint:** Wernigerode

Date	Mintage	VG	F	VF	XF	Unc
1613 AL	—	12.00	25.00	60.00	100	200

KM# 31 GROSCHEN (1/24 Thaler)

Silver **Ruler:** Joint Coinage XV **Obv:** 4-fold arms with central shield, titles of 2 brothers **Rev:** Imperial orb with Z4, orb divides date, titles continued **Mint:** Wernigerode **Note:** Klippe.

Date	Mintage	VG	F	VF	XF	Unc
1613 AL	—	12.00	25.00	50.00	100	200

KM# 29 GROSCHEN (1/24 Thaler)

Silver **Ruler:** Joint Coinage XV **Obv:** 4-fold arms with central shield, titles of 2 brothers **Rev:** Imperial orb with Z4, date divided at top, titles continued **Mint:** Wernigerode **Note:** Varieties exist.

Date	Mintage	VG	F	VF	XF	Unc
1613 AL	185,000	12.00	25.00	50.00	100	200
1614	302,000	12.00	25.00	50.00	100	200
1614 AL	Inc. above	12.00	25.00	50.00	100	200
1615 AL	32,000	12.00	25.00	50.00	100	200
ND AL	—	12.00	25.00	50.00	100	200

KM# 43 GROSCHEN (1/24 Thaler)

Silver **Ruler:** Joint Coinage XVI **Obv:** Stag left **Obv. Legend:** MO. ON. CO. S.R. 16. F. ZZ. **Rev:** Imperial orb with Z4, titles of Ferdinand II **Note:** The significance of the large F in the obv legend is unclear. It is perhaps a Frankenhausen mint.

Date	Mintage	VG	F	VF	XF	Unc
16ZZ	—	20.00	40.00	80.00	—	—

KM# 15 GROSCHEN (1/28 Thaler)

Silver **Ruler:** Joint Coinage XIV **Obv:** 4-fold arms with central shield, titles of 2 brothers **Rev:** Imperial orb with Z8 divides date **Mint:** Wernigerode

Date	Mintage	VG	F	VF	XF	Unc
161Z AL	—	20.00	40.00	85.00	—	—

KM# 18 GROSCHEN (1/28 Thaler)

Silver **Ruler:** Joint Coinage XV **Obv:** Stag left in front of column, titles of 2 brothers **Rev:** Imperial orb with Z8, titles continued with date in margin **Mint:** Wernigerode

Date	Mintage	VG	F	VF	XF	Unc
161Z AL	164,000	20.00	40.00	80.00	—	—

KM# 16 GROSCHEN (1/28 Thaler)
Silver **Ruler:** Joint Coinage XIV **Obv:** Stag left in front of column, titles of 2 brothers **Rev:** Imperial orb with Z8, titles continued with date in margin **Mint:** Wernigerode **Note:** Varieties exist.

Date	Mintage	VG	F	VF	XF	Unc
161Z AL	—	20.00	40.00	80.00	—	—

KM# 17 GROSCHEN (1/28 Thaler)
Silver **Ruler:** Joint Coinage XIV **Obv:** Stag left in front of column, titles of 2 brothers **Rev:** Imperial orb with Z8, orb divides date, titles continued **Mint:** Wernigerode **Note:** Varieties exist.

Date	Mintage	VG	F	VF	XF	Unc
161Z AL	—	20.00	40.00	80.00	—	—

KM# 19 GROSCHEN (1/28 Thaler)
Silver **Ruler:** Joint Coinage XV **Obv:** Stag left, titles of 2 brothers **Rev:** Imperial orb with Z8, titles continued with date in margin **Mint:** Wernigerode **Note:** Varieties exist. Mintage numbers for 1612 date included in KM#18.

Date	Mintage	VG	F	VF	XF	Unc
161Z AL	—	20.00	40.00	80.00	—	—
1613 AL	83,000	20.00	40.00	80.00	—	—

KM# 28 GROSCHEN (1/28 Thaler)
Silver **Ruler:** Joint Coinage XV **Obv:** 4-fold arms with central shield, titles of 2 brothers **Rev:** Imperial orb with Z8, date divided at top, titles continued **Mint:** Wernigerode **Note:** Mintage numbers included with 1613 date in KM#19.

Date	Mintage	VG	F	VF	XF	Unc
1613 AL	—	20.00	40.00	85.00	—	—

KM# 20 1/4 THALER (Ortstaler)
Silver **Ruler:** Joint Coinage XV **Obv:** 3 helmets above 11-fold arms, date divided by feathers on middle helmet, titles of 2 brothers **Rev:** Stag left, small imperial orb above in margin, titles continued **Mint:** Wernigerode

Date	Mintage	VG	F	VF	XF	Unc
161Z AL	—	—	—	—	—	—

KM# 47 1/2 THALER
Silver **Ruler:** Joint Coinage XVI **Obv:** 3 helmets above 11-fold arms, date divided among feathers on helmets, titles of 2 counts **Rev:** Stag left, small orb above, titles continued **Mint:** Stolberg

Date	Mintage	VG	F	VF	XF	Unc
163Z CZ	—	—	—	—	—	—

KM# 4 THALER
Silver **Ruler:** Joint Coinage XII **Obv:** Ornate 11-fold arms, 3 helmets above, names of 5 counts **Rev:** Stag left, date between legs, titles of counts in margin **Mint:** Erfurt **Note:** Dav#7765.

Date	Mintage	VG	F	VF	XF	Unc
1605 (z)	—	300	600	1,150	—	—

KM# 5 THALER
Silver **Ruler:** Joint Coinage XIII **Obv:** Ornate 11-fold arms, 3 helmets above, date divided by tops of helmets, names of 4 counts **Rev:** Stag left, date between legs, titles of counts in margin **Mint:** Erfurt **Note:** Dav#7766.

Date	Mintage	VG	F	VF	XF	Unc
1606 (z) Rare	—	—	—	—	—	—

KM# 7 THALER
Silver **Ruler:** Joint Coinage XIV **Obv:** Ornate 11-fold arms, 3 helmets above, names of 2 brothers, date in margin **Rev:** Stag left, date between legs, titles of counts in margin **Mint:** Erfurt **Note:** Dav#7767.

Date	Mintage	VG	F	VF	XF	Unc
1608 (bb)	—	—	—	—	—	—
ND (bb)	—	425	825	1,500	—	—

KM# 24 THALER
Silver **Ruler:** Joint Coinage XV **Obv:** Ornate 11-fold arms, 3 helmets above, names of 2 brothers, date in margin **Rev:** Stag left, date between legs, column behind stag, titles of counts in margin **Mint:** Wernigerode **Note:** Dav#7771. Mintage numbers included with KM#22.

Date	Mintage	VG	F	VF	XF	Unc
161Z AL//IH	—	350	675	1,300	—	—

KM# 22 THALER
Silver **Ruler:** Joint Coinage XV **Obv:** Ornate 11-fold arms, 3 helmets above, names of 2 brothers, date in margin **Rev:** Stag left, date between legs, titles of counts in margin **Mint:** Wernigerode **Note:** Dav#7771A.

Date	Mintage	VG	F	VF	XF	Unc
161Z AL/?IH	1,590	350	675	1,300	—	—

KM# 23 THALER
Silver **Ruler:** Joint Coinage XV **Obv:** Ornate 11-fold arms, 3 helmets above, names of 2 brothers, date in margin **Rev:** Stag left, date between legs, titles of counts in margin **Rev. Legend:** ...ET. CL. **Mint:** Wernigerode **Note:** Dav#7771B. Mintage numbers included with KM#22.

Date	Mintage	VG	F	VF	XF	Unc
161Z AL//IH	—	350	675	1,300	—	—

KM# 32 THALER
Silver **Ruler:** Joint Coinage XV **Obv:** Ornate 11-fold arms, 3 helmets above, date divided above helmets, names of 2 brothers **Rev:** Stag left, date between legs, titles of counts in margin **Mint:** Wernigerode **Note:** Dav#7772. Varieties exist.

Date	Mintage	VG	F	VF	XF	Unc
1613 AL//IH	1,621	350	675	1,300	—	—

KM# 44 THALER
Silver **Ruler:** Joint Coinage XVI **Obv:** Stag left in wreath-like circle, date below, titles of 2 counts **Rev:** 3 helmets above 11-fold arms, titles continued **Mint:** Stolberg **Note:** Dav#7779.

Date	Mintage	VG	F	VF	XF	Unc
16ZZ Rare	—	—	—	—	—	—

KM# 45 THALER
Silver **Ruler:** Joint Coinage XVI **Obv:** Stag left in wreath-like circle, date below, titles of 2 counts **Rev:** Crowned imperial eagle, orb on breast, titles of Ferdinand II **Mint:** Stolberg **Note:** Dav#7780.

Date	Mintage	VG	F	VF	XF	Unc
1623 Rare	—	—	—	—	—	—

KM# 48 THALER
Silver **Ruler:** Joint Coinage XVI **Obv:** 3 helmets above 11-fold arms, date divided among feathers on helmets, titles of 2 counts **Rev:** Stag left, small orb above, titles continued **Mint:** Stolberg **Note:** Dav#7781.

Date	Mintage	VG	F	VF	XF	Unc
163Z CZ	—	750	1,500	2,750	4,750	—

TRADE COINAGE

KM# 6 GOLDGULDEN
Gold **Ruler:** Joint Coinage XIV **Obv:** Stag left, date between legs, titles of 2 brothers **Rev:** 11-fold arms, titles continued **Mint:** Stolberg **Note:** Fr#3316.

Date	Mintage	VG	F	VF	XF	Unc
1607 (aa)	—	2,000	4,050	6,900	11,500	—
1609 (aa)	—	2,000	4,050	6,900	11,500	—

KM# 25 GOLDGULDEN
Gold **Ruler:** Joint Coinage XIV **Obv:** Stag left in front of column, titles of 2 brothers, date in margin **Rev:** 11-fold arms, titles continued **Mint:** Wernigerode **Note:** Fr#3317.

Date	Mintage	VG	F	VF	XF	Unc
1612 AL	792	1,750	3,450	5,800	10,500	—

KM# 26 GOLDGULDEN
Gold **Ruler:** Joint Coinage XIV **Obv:** Stag left in front of column, titles of 2 brothers, date in margin **Rev:** 11-fold arms, titles continued **Mint:** Wernigerode **Note:** Mintage numbers included with KM#25.

Date	Mintage	VG	F	VF	XF	Unc
161Z AL	—	2,300	4,300	7,500	13,000	—

KM# 33 GOLDGULDEN
Gold **Ruler:** Joint Coinage XV **Obv:** Stag left, neck or head divides date, titles of 2 brothers **Rev:** 11-fold arms, titles continued **Mint:** Wernigerode **Note:** Fr#3319. Varieties exist.

Date	Mintage	VG	F	VF	XF	Unc
1613 AL	4,959	2,000	4,050	6,900	11,500	—
1614 AL	984	2,000	4,050	6,900	11,500	—
ND AL	Inc. above	2,000	4,050	6,900	11,500	—

KM# 39 GOLDGULDEN
Gold **Ruler:** Joint Coinage XVI **Obv:** Stag left, titles of 2 counts **Rev:** Crowned imperial eagle, orb on breast, titles of Matthias, date **Mint:** Wernigerode **Note:** Fr#3321.

Date	Mintage	VG	F	VF	XF	Unc
1619 Rare	—	—	—	—	—	—

KM# 49 4 GOLDGULDEN
12.8000 g., Gold **Ruler:** Joint Coinage XVI **Obv:** 3 helmets above 11-fold arms, date divided among feathers on helmets, titles of 2 counts **Rev:** Stag left, small orb above, titles continued **Mint:** Stolberg

Date	Mintage	VG	F	VF	XF	Unc
163Z CZ Rare	—	—	—	—	—	—

KM# 34 DUCAT
Gold **Ruler:** Joint Coinage XV **Obv:** Stag left, date above, titles of 2 brothers **Rev:** 11-fold arms, titles continued **Mint:** Wernigerode

Date	Mintage	VG	F	VF	XF	Unc
1613 AL Rare	—	—	—	—	—	—

STOLBERG-ORTENBERG

Established in 1572 when Stolberg-Wernigerode was divided by two surviving sons, Ortenberg became a separate branch of the countship. Its seat was at the castle of Ortenberg, 13 miles (22 kilometers) east-northeast of Friedberg in the Wetterau. Stolberg-Ortenberg inherited Königstein in 1581, but sold half of the Königstein-Eppstein territories to Mainz in 1590. The rest followed in 1635 and the line fell extinct in 1641. What remained of its holdings passed to Stolberg-Schwarze (Wernigerode).

RULERS
Ludwig Georg, 1572-1618
Heinrich Volrad, 1618-1641

COUNTSHIP

REGULAR COINAGE

KM# 7 PFENNIG
Silver **Ruler:** Ludwig Georg **Obv:** 4-fold arms, L G above **Note:** Uniface höhl-type.

Date	Mintage	VG	F	VF	XF	Unc
ND(ca1606-18)	—	—	—	—	—	—

KM# 10 ALBUS (Weisspfennig = 2 Kreuzer - Halbbatzen)

Silver **Ruler:** Ludwig Georg **Obv:** Stag left in circle, titles of Ludwig Georg **Rev:** Date at beginning of inscription, titles continued **Rev. Inscription:** NOVVS / ALBVS **Mint:** Ranstadt

Date	Mintage	VG	F	VF	XF	Unc
(1)610	—	45.00	90.00	180	—	—

KM# 11 ALBUS (Weisspfennig = 2 Kreuzer - Halbbatzen)

Silver **Ruler:** Ludwig Georg **Obv:** Stag left in circle, titles of Ludwig Georg **Rev:** Date at end of inscription, titles continued **Rev. Inscription:** ALB / VIII & **Mint:** Ranstadt

Date	Mintage	VG	F	VF	XF	Unc
1610	—	45.00	90.00	180	—	—

KM# 9 ALBUS (Weisspfennig = 2 Kreuzer - Halbbatzen)

Silver **Ruler:** Ludwig Georg **Obv:** Stag left in circle, titles of Ludwig Georg **Rev:** Date at end of inscription, titles continued **Rev. Inscription:** NOVVS / ALBVS **Mint:** Ranstadt **Note:** Varieties exist.

Date	Mintage	VG	F	VF	XF	Unc
(1)610 (cc)	—	40.00	80.00	160	—	—

KM# 12 ALBUS (Weisspfennig = 2 Kreuzer - Halbbatzen)

Silver **Ruler:** Ludwig Georg **Obv:** Stag left in circle, titles of Ludwig Georg **Rev:** Various symbols and ornaments above and/or below inscription **Rev. Inscription:** NOVVS / ALBVS **Mint:** Ranstadt **Note:** Varieties exist.

Date	Mintage	VG	F	VF	XF	Unc
ND(1610) (cc)	—	30.00	65.00	160	—	—

KM# 4 3 KREUZER (Groschen)

Silver **Ruler:** Ludwig Georg **Obv:** 4-fold arms, date divided to sides and above, titles of Ludwig Georg **Rev:** Crowned imperial eagle, 3 in orb on breast, titles of Rudolf II **Mint:** Ortenberg

Date	Mintage	VG	F	VF	XF	Unc
1605 (dd)	—	—	—	—	—	—

KM# 5 3 KREUZER (Groschen)

Silver **Ruler:** Ludwig Georg **Obv:** 4-fold arms, date above, titles of Ludwig Georg **Rev:** Crowned imperial eagle, 3 in orb on breast, titles of Rudolf II **Mint:** Ortenberg

Date	Mintage	VG	F	VF	XF	Unc
1605 (dd)	—	—	—	—	—	—

KM# 6 3 KREUZER (Groschen)

Silver **Ruler:** Ludwig Georg **Obv:** 4-fold arms, titles of Ludwig Georg **Rev:** Crowned imperial eagle, 3 in orb on breast, titles of Rudolf II **Mint:** Ortenberg

Date	Mintage	VG	F	VF	XF	Unc
ND(ca1605) (dd)	—	8.00	15.00	30.00	60.00	—

KM# 13 3 KREUZER (Groschen)

Silver **Ruler:** Ludwig Georg **Obv:** 4-fold arms, titles of Ludwig Georg **Rev:** Crowned imperial eagle, 3 in orb on breast, titles of Rudolf II **Mint:** Ranstadt

Date	Mintage	VG	F	VF	XF	Unc
ND(1610-12) (cc)	—	8.00	15.00	30.00	60.00	—

KM# 15 3 KREUZER (Groschen)

Silver **Ruler:** Ludwig Georg **Obv:** 4-fold arms, titles of Ludwig Georg **Rev:** Crowned imperial eagle, 3 in orb on breast, titles of Matthias, date **Mint:** Ranstadt **Note:** Varieties exist.

Date	Mintage	VG	F	VF	XF	Unc
161Z (ee)	—	10.00	20.00	40.00	85.00	—
1613 (ee)	—	10.00	20.00	40.00	85.00	—

KM# 16 3 KREUZER (Groschen)

Silver **Ruler:** Ludwig Georg **Obv:** 4-fold arms, titles of Ludwig George **Rev:** Crowned imperial eagle, 3 in orb on breast, titles of Matthias **Mint:** Ranstadt **Note:** Varieties exist.

Date	Mintage	VG	F	VF	XF	Unc
ND(1612-16)	—	10.00	20.00	40.00	85.00	—

KM# 18 3 KREUZER (Groschen)

Silver **Ruler:** Ludwig Georg **Obv:** 4-fold arms, titles of Ludwig George **Rev:** Crowned imperial eagle, 3 in orb on breast, latter half of date in margin, titles of Matthias **Mint:** Ranstadt **Note:** Varieties exist. Mule.

Date	Mintage	VG	F	VF	XF	Unc
16//1613 (ee)	—	70.00	145	—	—	—
16//1616 (gg)	—	70.00	145	—	—	—

KM# 17 3 KREUZER (Groschen)

Silver, 20.5 mm. **Ruler:** Ludwig Georg **Obv:** 4-fold arms, first half of date divided by arms, titles of Ludwig George **Rev:** Crowned imperial eagle, 3 in orb on breast, second half of date in margin, titles of Matthias **Mint:** Ranstadt **Note:** Varieties exist.

Date	Mintage	VG	F	VF	XF	Unc
1613 (ee)	—	8.00	15.00	30.00	60.00	—
1614 (ff)	—	8.00	15.00	30.00	60.00	—
1615 (gg)	—	8.00	15.00	30.00	60.00	—
1616 (gg)	—	8.00	15.00	30.00	60.00	—

KM# 21 3 KREUZER (Groschen)

Silver **Ruler:** Heinrich Volrad **Obv:** 4-fold arms, titles of Heinrich Volrad **Rev:** Crowned imperial eagle, 3 in orb on breast, titles of Matthias **Mint:** Frankfurt

Date	Mintage	VG	F	VF	XF	Unc
ND(1618-19) (hh)	—	8.00	15.00	30.00	60.00	—

KM# 22 3 KREUZER (Groschen)

Silver **Ruler:** Ludwig Georg **Obv:** 4-fold arms, titles of Heinrich Volrad **Rev:** Crowned imperial eagle, 3 in orb on breas,t titles of Matthias **Mint:** Frankfurt **Note:** Kipper coinage. Smaller and lighter than KM#21, approx .5 g.

Date	Mintage	VG	F	VF	XF	Unc
ND(ca1619) (hh)	—	40.00	80.00	160	—	—

KM# 24 3 KREUZER (Groschen)

Silver **Ruler:** Heinrich Volrad **Obv:** 4-fold arms, arms divide date, titles of Heinrich Volrad **Rev:** Crowned imperial eagle, 3 in orb on breast, titles of Ferdinand II **Mint:** Frankfurt **Note:** Kipper coinage. Smaller and lighter than KM#21,m approx. .5 g.

Date	Mintage	VG	F	VF	XF	Unc
16Z1	—	—	—	—	—	—

KM# 25 6 KREUZER

Silver **Ruler:** Heinrich Volrad **Obv:** 4-fold arms, titles of Heinrich Volrad **Rev:** Crowned imperial eagle, 6 in orb on breast, titles of Ferdinand II **Mint:** Frankfurt **Note:** Kipper coinage.

Date	Mintage	VG	F	VF	XF	Unc
ND(ca1621/2) (hh)	—	80.00	160	325	—	—

KM# 26 6 KREUZER

Silver **Ruler:** Heinrich Volrad **Obv:** 4-fold arms, titles of Heinrich Volrad, value (6K) at end of margin **Rev:** Crowned imperial eagle, titles of Ferdinand II **Mint:** Frankfurt **Note:** Kipper coinage.

Date	Mintage	VG	F	VF	XF	Unc
ND(ca1621/2)	—	80.00	160	325	—	—

KM# 14 12 KREUZER (Dreibatzner)

Silver **Ruler:** Ludwig Georg **Obv:** 4-fold arms in ornate shield, titles of Ludwig Georg **Rev:** Crowned imperial eagle, 12 in orb on breast, titles of Rudolf II, date in margin **Mint:** Frankfurt

Date	Mintage	VG	F	VF	XF	Unc
1610	—	—	—	—	—	—

KM# 2 THALER

Silver **Ruler:** Ludwig Georg **Obv:** Stag left in triple-circle divides date, titles of Ludwig Georg **Rev:** 3 helmets above manifold arms, titles continued **Mint:** Ranstadt **Note:** Dav#7764.

Date	Mintage	VG	F	VF	XF	Unc
1604 Rare	—	—	—	—	—	—

KM# 27 THALER

Silver **Ruler:** Heinrich Volrad **Obv:** Crowned 11-fold arms, titles of Heinrich Volrad **Rev:** Crowned imperial eagle, orb on breast, titles of Ferdinand II, date **Mint:** Frankfurt **Note:** Dav#7782.

Date	Mintage	VG	F	VF	XF	Unc
16Z3 (hh)	—	2,750	4,750	8,000	—	—

TRADE COINAGE

KM# 20 GOLDGULDEN

Gold **Ruler:** Ludwig Georg **Obv:** 11-fold arms, date above, titles of Ludwig Georg **Rev:** Stag to left behind crowned column on pedestal **Rev. Legend:** NULLIS FRAUS TUTA LATEBRIS. **Mint:** Ranstadt **Note:** Fr#3353.

Date	Mintage	VG	F	VF	XF	Unc
1617	—	1,000	2,000	4,000	6,500	—

STOLBERG-STOLBERG

The old line of counts was divided into the senior (Wernigerode) and junior (Stolberg) branches in 1638. The junior branch was divided again in 1704 into Stolberg-Stolberg and Stolberg-Rossla. The two lines issued a large series of coins, mostly as joint issues, throughout the 18th century. There were still counts of Stolberg-Stolberg into the early 20th century.

RULERS

Johann, 1606-1612
Wolfgang Georg, 1612 (1615)-1631
Johann Martin I, 1638-1669
Friedrich Wilhelm, 1669-1684
Christof Ludwig I, 1684-1704

COUNTSHIP

REGULAR COINAGE

KM# 38 PFENNIG

Silver **Ruler:** Wolfgang Georg **Obv:** Stag left divides C - Z, date below **Mint:** Stolberg **Note:** Uniface höhl-type. Varieties exist.

Date	Mintage	VG	F	VF	XF	Unc
(16)Z3 CZ	105,000	30.00	60.00	120	—	—
(16)Z4 CZ	713,000	30.00	60.00	120	—	—

KM# 40 PFENNIG

Silver **Ruler:** Wolfgang Georg **Obv:** Stag left in ornamented oval shield divides C - Z, date above **Mint:** Stolberg **Note:** Uniface höhl-type. Varieties exist.

Date	Mintage	VG	F	VF	XF	Unc
(16)Z3 CZ	—	30.00	60.00	120	—	—

KM# 39 PFENNIG

Silver **Ruler:** Wolfgang Georg **Obv:** Stag left divides C - Z, date below **Mint:** Stolberg **Note:** Uniface. Mintage numbers included with KM#38.

Date	Mintage	VG	F	VF	XF	Unc
(16)Z3 CZ	—	30.00	60.00	120	—	—

KM# 30 3 PFENNIG

Copper **Ruler:** Wolfgang Georg **Obv:** Stag left in ornamented shield **Obv. Legend:** PFENNING **Rev:** Imperial orb with 3 **Mint:** Stolberg **Note:** Kipper coinage.

Date	Mintage	VG	F	VF	XF	Unc
ND(ca1621/2)	—	60.00	120	240	—	—

KM# 42 3 PFENNIG

Silver **Ruler:** Wolfgang Georg **Obv:** Stag left **Obv. Legend:** STO - LBE **Rev:** Imperial orb with 3 divides date **Mint:** Stolberg **Note:** Varieties exist.

Date	Mintage	VG	F	VF	XF	Unc
16Z3 CZ	38,000	—	—	—	—	—

KM# 43 3 PFENNIG

Silver **Ruler:** Wolfgang Georg **Obv:** Stag left **Obv. Legend:** STO - LBE **Rev:** Imperial orb with 3 in ornamented rhombus divides date **Mint:** Stolberg **Note:** Varieties exist. Mintage numbers included with KM#42.

Date	Mintage	VG	F	VF	XF	Unc
16Z3 CA	—	—	—	—	—	—

KM# 65 3 PFENNIG

Copper **Ruler:** Johann Martin I **Obv:** Stag left **Obv. Legend:** STO - LBE **Rev:** Imperial orb with 3 in ornamented rhombus divides date **Mint:** Stolberg

Date	Mintage	VG	F	VF	XF	Unc
1644 VZ	—	—	—	—	—	—

KM# 12 1/28 THALER (Groschen)

Silver **Ruler:** Johann **Obv:** Stag left in rhombus, titles of Johann **Rev:** 3 small shields of arms with bottoms to center divide date/Z8/mintmaster's initials, small orb at top, titles continued **Mint:** Stolberg

Date	Mintage	VG	F	VF	XF	Unc
1611 GM	51,000	—	—	—	—	—

KM# 13 1/28 THALER (Groschen)

Silver **Ruler:** Johann **Subject:** Death of Johann **Obv:** Stag left, titles of Johann **Rev:** 5-line inscription with date **Rev. Inscription:** OBIIT / 30. IVLII / ANNO 1612 / ÆTATIS: / 63.

Date	Mintage	VG	F	VF	XF	Unc
161Z AL	—	—	—	—	—	—

KM# 17 1/24 THALER (Groschen)

Silver **Ruler:** Wolfgang Georg **Subject:** Death of Johann **Obv:** Stag left, titles of Johann **Rev. Inscription:** OBIIT / 30.IVLII / ANNO 1612 / ÆTATIS: / 63. **Mint:** Wernigerode

Date	Mintage	VG	F	VF	XF	Unc
1614 AL	—	—	—	—	—	—
1615 AL	—	—	—	—	—	—

KM# 18 1/24 THALER (Groschen)

Silver **Ruler:** Wolfgang Georg **Obv:** Stag left in circle **Obv. Legend:** WOLF. GEOR. COM. IN. STO. **Rev:** Imperial orb with 'Z4,' cross on orb divides date and mintmaster's initials at top **Rev. Legend:** KON. WER. ET. HON. **Note:** Varieties exist.

Date	Mintage	VG	F	VF	XF	Unc
1618 CZ	—	12.00	25.00	45.00	90.00	180
1619 CZ	—	12.00	25.00	45.00	90.00	180
16Z0 CZ	—	12.00	25.00	45.00	90.00	180
16Z3 CZ	17,000	12.00	25.00	45.00	90.00	180
16Z4 CZ	—	12.00	25.00	45.00	90.00	180
16Z5 CZ	5,994	12.00	25.00	45.00	90.00	180

KM# 28 1/24 THALER (Groschen)

Silver **Ruler:** Wolfgang Georg **Obv:** Stag left in circle, titles of Wolfgang Georg **Rev:** Imperial orb with Z4, titles continued, date divided at top **Mint:** Wernigerode **Note:** Kipper coinage. Varieties exist. Reduced size and weight from KM#18 (.5-.8 g.)

Date	Mintage	VG	F	VF	XF	Unc
16Z0	—	12.00	25.00	45.00	90.00	180
16Z0 BB	—	12.00	25.00	45.00	90.00	180
16Z0 IK	—	12.00	25.00	45.00	90.00	180
16Z1 IK	—	12.00	25.00	45.00	90.00	180

KM# 67 1/24 THALER (Groschen)

Silver **Ruler:** Johann Martin I **Obv:** Stag left in front of crowned column, titles of Johann Martin I **Rev:** Imperial orb with 24, titles continued, date divided at top **Mint:** Wernigerode **Note:** Kipper coinage. Varieties exist. The inscriptions on most of the above are in archail uncial letters.

Date	Mintage	VG	F	VF	XF	Unc
1644 VZ	—	12.00	25.00	45.00	90.00	180
1646 IK	—	12.00	25.00	45.00	90.00	180
1648 IK	—	12.00	25.00	45.00	90.00	180
165Z IK	—	12.00	25.00	45.00	90.00	180

KM# 10 1/21 THALER (Groschen)

Silver **Ruler:** Johann **Obv:** Stag left in front of column, titles of Johann **Rev:** Imperial orb with Z1 divides date, 3 small shields of arms arranged around center **Mint:** Stolberg

Date	Mintage	VG	F	VF	XF	Unc
1611 GM	—	—	—	—	—	—

KM# 11 1/21 THALER (Groschen)

Silver **Ruler:** Johann **Obv:** Stag left in front of column, titles of Johann **Rev:** Imperial orb with Z1 divides date, 3 small shields with tops to center **Mint:** Stolberg

Date	Mintage	VG	F	VF	XF	Unc
1611 GM	—	—	—	—	—	—

KM# 36 12 KREUZER (Schreckenberger)

Silver, 27-28 mm. **Ruler:** Wolfgang Georg **Obv:** Three shields of arms, Stolberg above Wernigerode and Hohnstein, upper arms divide date, value IZ below. **Obv. Legend:** WOLF. GEOR. GR. IN STOLB. K. R. **Rev:** Stag to left in circle, mintmaster's initials between legs **Rev. Legend:** ET. HON. DO. I. EP. M. B. LO. CL. **Note:** Kipper Coinage. F #865.

Date	Mintage	VG	F	VF	XF	Unc
16Z1 HL	—	40.00	75.00	150	300	—
16ZZ HL	—	40.00	75.00	150	300	—

KM# 34 4 GROSCHEN (1/6 Thaler)

Silver **Ruler:** Wolfgang Georg **Obv:** 3 shields of arms, Stolberg above Wernigerode and Hohnstein, upper arms divide date, crown above, titles of Wolfgang Georg **Rev:** Stag left in circle, small orb above, titles continued **Mint:** Wernigerode

Date	Mintage	VG	F	VF	XF	Unc
16Z1	—	—	—	—	—	—

KM# 33 4 GROSCHEN (1/6 Thaler)

Silver **Ruler:** Wolfgang Georg **Obv:** 3 shields of arms, Stolberg above Wernigerode and Hohnstein, upper arms divide date, crown above, value 4 below, titles of Wolfgang Georg **Rev:** Stag left in circle, small orb above, titles continued **Mint:** Wernigerode **Note:** Klippe.

Date	Mintage	VG	F	VF	XF	Unc
16Z1	—	—	—	—	—	—

KM# 32 4 GROSCHEN (1/6 Thaler)

Silver **Ruler:** Wolfgang Georg **Obv:** 3 shields of arms, Stolberg above Wernigerode and Hohnstein, upper arms divide date, crown above, value 4 below, titles of Wolfgang Georg **Rev:** Stag left in circle, small orb above, titles continued **Mint:** Wernigerode **Note:** Varieties exist.

Date	Mintage	VG	F	VF	XF	Unc
16Z1	—	80.00	160	325	—	—

KM# 92 4 GROSCHEN (Gute)

Silver **Ruler:** Johann Martin I **Obv:** Stag left, crowned column behind, small orb above, titles of Johann Martin I **Rev:** Titles continued **Rev. Inscription:** 1111 / GVTE / GROSCH / 16EN68 **Mint:** Wernigerode

Date	Mintage	VG	F	VF	XF	Unc
1668 IA	—	—	—	—	—	—

KM# 93 4 GROSCHEN (Gute)

Silver **Ruler:** Johann Martin I **Obv:** Stag left, crowned column behind, titles of Johann Martin I **Rev:** Small inscription, titles continued **Rev. Inscription:** 1111 / GVTE / GROSCH / 16EN68 **Mint:** Wernigerode

Date	Mintage	VG	F	VF	XF	Unc
1668 IA	—	—	—	—	—	—
1669 IA	—	—	—	—	—	—

KM# 44 1/4 THALER

Silver **Ruler:** Wolfgang Georg **Obv:** 11-fold arms, 3 helmets above, date divided by feathers on helmets, titles of Wolfgang Georg **Rev:** Stag left in circle, small orb above, titles continued **Mint:** Stolberg **Note:** Varieties exist.

Date	Mintage	VG	F	VF	XF	Unc
16Z3 CZ	—	—	—	—	—	—
16Z4 CZ	—	—	—	—	—	—
16Z5 CZ	—	—	—	—	—	—
16Z6 CZ	—	—	—	—	—	—

KM# 74 1/4 THALER

Silver **Ruler:** Johann Martin I **Obv:** Stag left in front of crowned column **Obv. Legend:** IOHAN. MART: COM: IN. STOLB. K. R. W. E. HO. **Rev:** 11-fold arms divide mintmaster's initials, date divided at top **Rev. Legend:** DOM. IN. EPS: MVN: BR: LOR: E. CLETT. **Note:** Varieties exist.

Date	Mintage	VG	F	VF	XF	Unc
1646 IK	—	—	—	—	—	—
1649 IK	—	—	—	—	—	—

KM# 94 8 GROSCHEN (1/3 Thaler)

Silver **Ruler:** Johann Martin I **Obv:** Stag left, crowned column behind, small orb above, titles of Johann Martin I **Rev:** Titles continued **Rev. Inscription:** VIII / GVTE / GROSCH / 16EN68 **Mint:** Wernigerode

Date	Mintage	VG	F	VF	XF	Unc
1668 IA	—	—	—	—	—	—

KM# 95 8 GROSCHEN (1/3 Thaler)

Silver **Ruler:** Johann Martin I **Obv:** Stag left, crowned column behind, titles of Johann Martin I **Rev:** Titles continued **Rev. Inscription:** VIII / GVTE / GROSCH / 16EN68 **Mint:** Wernigerode

Date	Mintage	VG	F	VF	XF	Unc
1668 IA	—	—	—	—	—	—

KM# 96 8 GROSCHEN (1/3 Thaler)

Silver **Ruler:** Johann Martin I **Obv:** Stag left, cronwed column behind, titles of Johann Martin I **Rev:** Titles continued, date at end of inscription **Rev. Inscription:** VIII / GVTE / GROSCHEN **Mint:** Wernigerode

Date	Mintage	VG	F	VF	XF	Unc
1669 IA	—	—	—	—	—	—

KM# 98 1/3 THALER (1/2 Gulden)

Silver **Ruler:** Johann Martin I **Obv:** Stag left, crowned column behind, titles of Johann Martin I **Rev:** Crowned 11-fold arms, value 1/3 in oval below, titles continued, date divided at top **Mint:** Stolberg **Note:** Varieties exist.

Date	Mintage	VG	F	VF	XF	Unc
1669 ABK	—	—	—	—	—	—
1669 IA	—	—	—	—	—	—

KM# 3 1/2 THALER

Silver **Ruler:** Johann **Obv:** Ornate shield with stag left in front of column, titles of Johann **Rev:** 11-fold arms, date divided above, titles continued **Mint:** Stolberg

Date	Mintage	VG	F	VF	XF	Unc
1609 GM	—	—	—	—	—	—

KM# 45 1/2 THALER

Silver **Ruler:** Wolfgang Georg **Obv:** 11-fold arms, 3 helmets above, date divided by arms, titles of Wolfgang Georg **Rev:** Stag left in circle, small orb above, titles continued **Mint:** Stolberg **Note:** Varieties exist.

Date	Mintage	VG	F	VF	XF	Unc
16Z3 CZ	—	—	—	—	—	—

KM# 50 1/2 THALER

Silver **Ruler:** Wolfgang Georg **Obv:** 11-fold arms divide mintmaster's initials, 3 ornate helmets above, date divided among crests of helmets **Obv. Legend:** WOLF. GEORG. CO. IN. STOLB. K. **Rev:** Stag left in circle **Rev. Legend:** WERN. ET. HO: DO. IN. EP. MIN. B. LOR. ET. C. **Note:** Varieties exist.

Date	Mintage	VG	F	VF	XF	Unc
16Z4 CZ	—	—	—	—	—	—
16Z5 CZ	—	—	—	—	—	—
16Z6 CZ	—	—	—	—	—	—

KM# 76 1/2 THALER

Silver **Ruler:** Johann Martin I **Obv:** Stag left, crowned column behind, orb at top, titles of Johann Martin I **Rev:** 11-fold arms, 3 helmets above arms, date divided by feathers of helmets, titles continued **Mint:** Stolberg

Date	Mintage	VG	F	VF	XF	Unc
1646 IK	—	—	—	—	—	—

KM# 6 THALER

Silver **Ruler:** Johann **Obv:** Crowned stag in frame **Rev:** Helmeted arms dividing date in helmets **Note:** Dav# 7770.

Date	Mintage	VG	F	VF	XF	Unc
1609 GM	Inc. above	1,000	2,000	3,500	6,500	—
1610 GM	4,478	1,000	2,000	3,500	6,500	—
1611 GM	1,484	1,000	2,000	3,500	6,500	—

KM# 5 THALER

Silver **Ruler:** Johann **Obv:** Crowned stag in frame separating date **Rev:** Helmeted arms **Rev. Legend:** DOM: IN. EPST. MVN:... **Note:** Dav# 7768.

Date	Mintage	VG	F	VF	XF	Unc
1609 GM	1,961	1,350	2,750	5,000	8,500	—

KM# 20 THALER

Silver **Ruler:** Wolfgang Georg **Obv:** Helmeted arms, C-Z in field **Obv. Legend:** WOLF. GEORG. COM IN. STOLBER. KON. **Rev:** Stag left **Rev. Legend:** ... LORA. ET. CLE. **Note:** Dav# 7775.

Date	Mintage	VG	F	VF	XF	Unc
1619 CZ	—	1,650	3,250	6,000	9,500	—

KM# 47 THALER

Silver **Ruler:** Wolfgang Georg **Obv:** Helmeted arms, date divided above and C-Z beside **Rev:** Stag left **Rev. Legend:** LOR: ET. CLE(T). **Note:** Dav# 7776.

Date	Mintage	VG	F	VF	XF	Unc
16Z3 CZ	—	325	550	900	1,550	—

KM# 52 THALER

Silver **Ruler:** Wolfgang Georg **Rev:** Flowers and grass under stag left **Rev. Legend:** LO. (R). E. C. **Note:** Legend varieties exist. Dav# 7778.

Date	Mintage	VG	F	VF	XF	Unc
16Z4 CZ	—	120	250	500	950	—
16Z5 CZ	—	120	250	500	950	—
16Z6 CZ	—	120	250	500	950	—

KM# 57 THALER

Silver **Ruler:** Wolfgang Georg **Obv:** Helmeted arms, date above **Rev:** Flowers and grass under stag left **Rev. Legend:** LO. (r). E. C. **Note:** Klippe. Dav# 7778A.

Date	Mintage	VG	F	VF	XF	Unc
16Z5 CZ Rare	—	—	—	—	—	—

KM# 69 THALER

Silver **Ruler:** Johann Martin I **Note:** Dav# 7784. Similar to 2 Thaler, Dav# 7783.

Date	Mintage	VG	F	VF	XF	Unc
1644 UZ Rare	—	—	—	—	—	—

KM# 72 THALER

Silver **Ruler:** Johann Martin I **Obv:** Stag left against a pillar **Obv. Legend:** IOHAN: MART:... **Rev:** Helmeted arms with date divided in helmets and I-K below **Rev. Legend:** ...MVN: BREV(B): LOR: ET. CLETE. **Note:** Dav# 7786.

Date	Mintage	VG	F	VF	XF	Unc
1645 IK	—	195	375	800	2,100	3,500
1646 IK	—	195	375	800	2,100	3,500
1647 IK	—	195	375	800	2,100	3,500
1649 IK	—	195	375	800	2,100	3,500
1650 IK	—	195	375	800	2,100	3,500
1650 IK	—	195	375	800	2,100	3,500
Note: Error: RON for KON in legend						
1652 IK	—	195	375	800	2,100	3,500
1652/3 IK	—	195	375	800	2,100	3,500
1653 IK	—	195	375	800	2,100	3,500
1654 IK	—	195	375	800	2,100	3,500
Note: Legend varieties exist for 1654 date strikes						
1655 IK	—	195	375	800	2,100	3,500
1660 IK	—	195	375	800	2,100	3,500
1663 IK	—	195	375	800	2,100	3,500

KM# 88 THALER

Silver **Ruler:** Johann Martin I **Rev. Legend:** ... MIN: BR:LOR: ET: KLETTENB:. **Note:** Dav# 7786A.

Date	Mintage	VG	F	VF	XF	Unc
1660 IK	—	205	400	1,150	2,200	—

KM# 90 THALER

Silver **Ruler:** Johann Martin I **Rev. Legend:** ... PREVP: LOR: ET: KLETTEN. **Note:** Dav# 7786B.

Date	Mintage	VG	F	VF	XF	Unc
1663 IK	—	205	400	1,150	2,200	—

KM# 100 THALER

Silver **Ruler:** Christof Ludwig I **Obv:** Stag left in front of column, trees at sides **Obv. Legend:** CHRISTOPHORVS LUDOVICVS COMES STOLBERGENSIS **Rev:** Helmeted arms, divided date above, JA-S below **Rev. Legend:** KON: ROCH: WER: & HON: DN: EP: MUNZ: BR: AIR: & CL: **Note:** Dav# 7789.

Date	Mintage	VG	F	VF	XF	Unc
1693 JAS Rare	—	—	—	—	—	—
1695 JAS/IT Rare	—	—	—	—	—	—
Note: With edge inscription						

KM# 102 THALER

Silver **Ruler:** Christof Ludwig I **Obv:** Shield of manifold arms, 3 ornate helmets above, legend in Gothic letters with Roman numeral date **Obv. Legend:** CHRISTOPH LUDWIG GRAF ZU STOLBERG. K. R. W. V. H. H. Z. E. M. B. U. L. U. C. ANNO MDCC. **Rev:** Mining scene, "Jehovah" in Hebrew in cloud above, legend in Gothic letters **Rev. Legend:** GOTT SEEGNE DIE STOLLBERGISCHEN BERGWERKE. DENN AN GOTTES SEEGEN IST ALLES GELEGEN. **Note:** Mining Thaler. Dav# 7791.

Date	Mintage	VG	F	VF	XF	Unc
MDCC (1700) IT	—	800	1,650	3,250	5,750	—

KM# 8 2 THALER

Silver **Ruler:** Johann **Note:** Dav# 7769. Similar to 1 Thaler, Dav. #7770.

Date	Mintage	VG	F	VF	XF	Unc
1609 GM Rare	—	—	—	—	—	—

KM# 21 2 THALER

Silver **Ruler:** Wolfgang Georg **Obv:** Helmeted arms with date in helmets, C-Z divided by shield **Rev:** Stag left **Rev. Legend:** ... LOR. ET. CL **Note:** Dav# 7773.

Date	Mintage	VG	F	VF	XF	Unc
1619 CZ Rare	—	—	—	—	—	—

KM# 22 2 THALER

Silver **Ruler:** Wolfgang Georg **Obv:** Date in legend **Rev. Legend:** ... LOR. ET. CLE*. **Note:** Dav# 7774.

Date	Mintage	VG	F	VF	XF	Unc
1619 CZ Rare	—	—	—	—	—	—

KM# 53 2 THALER

Silver **Ruler:** Wolfgang Georg **Obv:** Stag left in circle **Rev:** Manifold arms divide mintmaster's initials, 3 ornate helmets above, date divided among crests **Note:** Dav# 7777. Varieties exist.

Date	Mintage	VG	F	VF	XF	Unc
1624 CZ	—	1,250	2,500	4,750	8,750	—
1625 CZ	—	1,250	2,500	4,750	8,750	—

KM# 70 2 THALER

Silver **Ruler:** Johann Martin I **Obv:** Manifold arms, 3 ornate helmets above divide mintmaster's initials, date at end of legend **Obv. Legend:** IOHAN: MARTIN: COMES. AN: **Rev:** Stag left in front of column **Rev. Legend:** IN. STOLBERG. KON: RUT: WERN: ET. HONS: **Note:** Dav# 7783. Varieties exist.

Date	Mintage	VG	F	VF	XF	Unc
1644 UZ Rare	—	—	—	—	—	—

KM# 78 2 THALER

Silver **Ruler:** Johann Martin I **Obv:** Stag left in front of column **Rev:** Helmeted arms with date divided in helmets, I-K below **Note:** Dav# 7785.

Date	Mintage	VG	F	VF	XF	Unc
1646 IK	—	1,000	2,000	3,750	6,500	—
1649 IK	—	1,000	2,000	3,750	6,500	—
1652 IK	—	1,000	2,000	3,750	6,500	—
1653 IK	—	1,000	2,000	3,750	6,500	—
1654 IK	—	1,000	2,000	3,750	6,500	—
1655 IK	—	1,000	2,000	3,750	6,500	—
1660 IK	—	1,000	2,000	3,750	6,500	—

KM# 103 2 THALER

Silver **Ruler:** Christof Ludwig I **Obv:** Shield of manifold arms, 3 ornate helmets above, legend in Gothic letters with Roman numeral date **Obv. Legend:** CHRISTOPH LUDWIG GRAF ZU STOLBERG. K. R. W. V. H. H. Z. E. M. B. U. L. U. C. ANNO MDCC. **Rev:** Mining scene, "Jehovah" in Hebrew in cloud above, legend in Gothic letters **Rev. Legend:** GOTT SEEGNE DIE STOLLBERGISCHEN BERGWERKE. DENN AN GOTTES SEEGEN IST ALLES GELEGEN. **Note:** Struck from Taler dies, KM# 102. Dav# 7790.

Date	Mintage	VG	F	VF	XF	Unc
1700 IT Rare	—	—	—	—	—	—

TRADE COINAGE

KM# 15 GOLDGULDEN

3.5000 g., 0.9860 Gold 0.1109 oz. AGW **Ruler:** Johann **Subject:** Death of Johann **Obv:** Stag left in inner circle, titles of Johann **Rev:** 5-line inscription with date **Rev. Inscription:** OBIIT / 30. IVLII / ANNO 1612 / ÆTATIS: / 63. **Note:** Struck from same dies as 1/28 Thaler, KM# 13. Fr# 3318.

Date	Mintage	VG	F	VF	XF	Unc
161Z AL	—	1,000	2,150	4,300	8,600	—

KM# 24 GOLDGULDEN

3.5000 g., 0.9860 Gold 0.1109 oz. AGW **Ruler:** Wolfgang Georg **Obv:** 11-fold arms, titles of Wolfgang Georg **Rev:** Stag left, date divided among legs, titles continued **Note:** Fr# 3320 variety.

Date	Mintage	VG	F	VF	XF	Unc
1619 CZ	—	575	1,300	2,900	5,800	—

KM# 59 GOLDGULDEN

Gold **Ruler:** Wolfgang Georg **Obv:** 11-fold arms, titles of Wolfgang Georg **Rev:** Stag left, half date between legs, titles continued **Note:** Fr# 3320 variety.

Date	Mintage	VG	F	VF	XF	Unc
(16)Z5 CZ	234	575	1,300	2,900	5,800	—

KM# 61 GOLDGULDEN

Gold **Ruler:** Wolfgang Georg **Obv:** 11-fold arms, titles of Wolfgang Georg **Rev:** Stag left, date divided to left and right of stag, titles continued **Note:** Fr# 3320 variety.

Date	Mintage	VG	F	VF	XF	Unc
16Z6 CZ	3,295	575	1,300	2,900	5,800	—

KM# 26 4 GOLDGULDEN

12.7800 g., Gold **Ruler:** Wolfgang Georg **Obv:** Helmeted arms with date in helmets, C-Z divided by shield **Rev:** Stag left **Rev. Legend:** ... LOR ET. CL **Mint:** Stolberg

Date	Mintage	VG	F	VF	XF	Unc
1619 CZ Rare	—	—	—	—	—	—

KM# 55 5 GOLDGULDEN

17.2500 g., Gold **Ruler:** Wolfgang Georg **Obv:** 11-fold arms divide mintmaster's initials, 3 ornate helmets above, date divided among crests of helmets **Obv. Legend:** WOLF. GEORG. CO. IN. STOLB. K. **Rev:** Stag left in circle **Rev. Legend:** WERN. ET. HO: DO. IN. EP. MIN. B. LOR. ET. C. **Mint:** Stolberg

Date	Mintage	VG	F	VF	XF	Unc
16Z4 CZ Rare	—	—	—	—	—	—

KM# 63 10 GOLDGULDEN

34.3500 g., Gold **Ruler:** Wolfgang Georg **Rev:** Flowers and grass under stag left **Rev. Legend:** LO. (R). E. C. **Mint:** Stolberg

Date	Mintage	VG	F	VF	XF	Unc
16Z6 CZ Rare	—	—	—	—	—	—

KM# 82 DUCAT

3.5000 g., 0.9860 Gold 0.1109 oz. AGW **Ruler:** Johann Martin I **Obv:** Stag in front of column **Rev:** Value and date in tablet **Note:** Fr# 3323.

Date	Mintage	VG	F	VF	XF	Unc
1647 IK	—	500	1,000	2,150	3,850	—
1649/7 IK	—	500	1,000	2,150	3,850	—

KM# 86 DUCAT

Gold **Ruler:** Johann Martin I **Obv:** Stag in front of column **Rev:** Value in tablet, date in margin **Mint:** Stolberg

Date	Mintage	VG	F	VF	XF	Unc
1653 IK	—	—	—	—	—	—

KM# 80 2 DUCAT

7.0000 g., 0.9860 Gold 0.2219 oz. AGW **Ruler:** Johann Martin I **Note:** Fr# 3322.

Date	Mintage	VG	F	VF	XF	Unc
1646 IK	—	900	1,800	4,500	7,800	—
1649 IK	—	900	1,800	4,500	7,800	—

KM# 105 10 DUCAT

35.0000 g., 0.9860 Gold 1.1095 oz. AGW 1.1095 oz. AGW, 45 mm. **Ruler:** Christof Ludwig I **Obv:** Shield of manifold arms, 3 ornate helmets above, legend in Gothic letters with Roman numeral date **Obv. Legend:** CHRISTOPH LUDWIG GRAF ZU STOLBERG. K. R. W. V. H. H. Z. E. M. B. U. L. U. C. ANNO MDCC. **Rev:** Mining scene, "Jehovah" in Hebrew in cloud above, legend in Gothic letters **Rev. Legend:** GOTT SEEGNE DIE STOLLBERGISCHEN BERGWERKE. DENN AN GOTTES SEEGEN IST ALLES GELEGEN. **Note:** Struck from Thaler dies, KM# 102.

Date	Mintage	VG	F	VF	XF	Unc
1700 IT Rare	—	—	—	—	—	—

STOLBERG-WERNIGERODE

The castle of Wernigerode is situated across the Harz Mountains to the north of Stolberg castle, some 12 miles (20 km) west-southwest of Halberstadt. An early division of the old Stolberg line in 1538 resulted in a separate line in Wernigerode. A second division in 1572 established Stolberg-Ortenberg and Stolberg-Schwarza (Wernigerode) and the latter was divided further into 1876 divided further into the senior branch of Stolberg-Wernigerode and the junior branch of Stolberg-Stolberg.Once again, Stolberg-Wernigerode was the foundation of three separate lines at Gedern, Schwarza and Wernigerode in 1710. The first two fell extinct within a century, but Stolberg-Wernigerode lasted into the 20th century.

RULERS

Heinrich XXI, 1538-1572
Christof II, 1572-1638
Heinrich Ernst I, 1638-1672
Ernst von Stolberg-Wernigerode-Ilsenburg,1672-1710
and Ludwig Christian, 1672-1710

COUNTSHIP

REGULAR COINAGE

KM# 7 PFENNIG

Silver **Ruler:** Christof II **Obv:** 4-fold arms divide Z - S, C G above (Christof Graf zu Stolberg) **Note:** Uniface höhl-type.

Date	Mintage	VG	F	VF	XF	Unc
ND(ca1622)	—	—	—	—	—	—

KM# 21 3 PFENNIG (DREIER)

Silver **Ruler:** Heinrich Ernst I **Obv:** Stag left, date below **Rev:** Imperial orb with 3 divides mintmaster's initials

Date	Mintage	VG	F	VF	XF	Unc
1671 IB	—	30.00	60.00	120	240	—

KM# 35 3 PFENNIG (DREIER)

Silver **Ruler:** Ernst and Ludwig Christian **Obv:** 2-fold arms, date above **Rev:** Imperial orb with 3

Date	Mintage	VG	F	VF	XF	Unc
1673	—	15.00	35.00	75.00	150	300

KM# 36 3 PFENNIG (DREIER)

Silver **Ruler:** Ernst and Ludwig Christian **Obv:** 5-fold arms, date above **Rev:** Imperial orb with 3 divides mintmaster's initials

Date	Mintage	VG	F	VF	XF	Unc
1673 IB	—	—	—	—	—	—

KM# 43 3 PFENNIG (DREIER)

Silver **Ruler:** Ernst and Ludwig Christian **Obv:** 4-fold arms, around left, top and right **Obv. Legend:** 16. STOL . B. B.74. **Rev:** Imperial orb with 3 divides mintmaster's initials

Date	Mintage	VG	F	VF	XF	Unc
1674 IB	—	—	—	—	—	—

KM# 44 3 PFENNIG (DREIER)

Silver **Ruler:** Ernst and Ludwig Christian **Obv:** Stag left **Rev:** Imperial orb with 3 divides date

Date	Mintage	VG	F	VF	XF	Unc
1674	—	30.00	60.00	120	240	—
ND	—	30.00	60.00	120	240	—

KM# 9 3 KREUZER (Groschen)

Silver **Ruler:** Christof II **Obv:** 4-fold arms divide date, titles of Christof II **Rev:** Crowned imperial eagle, 3 in orb on breast, titles of Ferdinand II

Date	Mintage	VG	F	VF	XF	Unc
16Z1	—	—	—	—	—	—
16ZZ	—	—	—	—	—	—

KM# 23 1/24 THALER (Groschen)

Silver **Ruler:** Heinrich Ernst I **Obv:** Imperial orb with 24 divides date, titles of Heinrich Ernst **Rev:** Stag left, titles continued **Note:** Varieties exist.

Date	Mintage	VG	F	VF	XF	Unc
1671 IB	—	45.00	90.00	180	—	—
1676 IB	—	45.00	90.00	180	—	—

KM# 39 1/24 THALER (Groschen)

Silver **Ruler:** Ernst and Ludwig Christian **Obv:** 6-fold arms, imperial orb with 24 divides dates, titles of Ernst and Ludwig Christian **Rev:** 9-fold arms, titles continued **Note:** Varieties exist.

Date	Mintage	VG	F	VF	XF	Unc
1673 IB	—	—	—	—	—	—
1674 IB	—	—	—	—	—	—

KM# 38 1/24 THALER (Groschen)

Silver **Ruler:** Ernst and Ludwig Christian **Obv:** Imperial orb with 24 divides date, titles of Ernst and Ludwig Christian **Rev:** 9-fold arms, titles continued

Date	Mintage	VG	F	VF	XF	Unc
1673 IB	—	—	—	—	—	—

KM# 40 1/24 THALER (Groschen)

Silver **Ruler:** Ernst and Ludwig Christian **Obv:** 5-fold arms, imperial orb with 24 divides date, titles of Ernst and Ludwig Christian **Rev:** 9-fold arms, titles continued

Date	Mintage	VG	F	VF	XF	Unc
1673 IB	—	—	—	—	—	—

KM# 41 1/24 THALER (Groschen)

Silver **Ruler:** Ernst and Ludwig Christian **Obv:** Imperial orb with 24 divides date, titles of Ernst and Ludwig Christian **Rev:** Stag left, titles continued

Date	Mintage	VG	F	VF	XF	Unc
1673 IB	—	45.00	90.00	180	—	—

KM# 25 1/6 THALER (1/4 Gulden)

Silver **Ruler:** Heinrich Ernst I **Obv:** Crown above 11-fold arms divides date, value 1/6 in oval below, titles of Heinrich Ernst **Rev:** Stag left, titles continued **Note:** Varieties exist.

Date	Mintage	VG	F	VF	XF	Unc
1671 IB	—	80.00	165	335	—	—
1672 IB	—	80.00	165	335	—	—

KM# 11 1/4 THALER

Silver **Ruler:** Heinrich Ernst I **Obv:** Stag left, small orb above, titles of Heinrich Ernst **Rev:** 11-fold arms, date divided above, titles continued

Date	Mintage	VG	F	VF	XF	Unc
1659 HB	—	—	—	—	—	—

KM# 28 8 GUTE GROSCHEN (1/3 Thaler)

Silver **Ruler:** Heinrich Ernst I **Obv:** Titles of Heinrich Ernst, date in margin **Obv. Inscription:** VIII / mintmaster's initials / GVTE / GROSS **Rev:** Stag left, titles continued

Date	Mintage	VG	F	VF	XF	Unc
1671 IB	—	350	700	1,350	—	—

KM# 27 8 GUTE GROSCHEN (1/3 Thaler)

Silver **Ruler:** Heinrich Ernst I **Obv:** 5-line inscription with date and mintmaster's initials **Obv. Legend:** HEINR. ERNST. CO. IN. STOL. KON. RI. **Obv. Inscription:** VIII / GUTE / GROSS. / (date) / (mintmaster's initials) **Rev:** Stag left in circle **Rev. Legend:** WERN. ET. HO. DOM. IN. EP. MIN. B. LOR. ET. CLET. **Note:** Varieties exisit.

Date	Mintage	VG	F	VF	XF	Unc
1671 IB	—	—	—	—	—	—
1672 IB	—	—	—	—	—	—

KM# 46 8 GUTE GROSCHEN (1/3 Thaler)

Silver **Ruler:** Ernst and Ludwig Christian **Obv:** Date and mintmaster's initials at end of inscription, titles of Ernst Ludwig Christian **Obv. Inscription:** VIII / GUTE / GROSS **Rev:** 3 helmets above 11-fold arms, titles continued **Note:** Varieties exist.

Date	Mintage	VG	F	VF	XF	Unc
1674 IB	—	135	275	550	1,100	—

KM# 30 1/3 THALER (1/2 Gulden)
Silver **Ruler:** Heinrich Ernst I **Obv:** Crown above 11-fold arms divides date, value 1/3 in oval below, titles of Heinrich Ernst **Rev:** Stag left, titles continued **Note:** Varieties exist. Some of the above dated 1671 are known with countermark of Salzburg dated 1681.

Date	Mintage	VG	F	VF	XF	Unc
1671 IB	—	35.00	75.00	150	310	—
1672 IB	—	35.00	75.00	150	310	—

KM# 31 1/3 THALER (1/2 Gulden)
Silver **Ruler:** Ernst and Ludwig Christian **Obv:** Manifold arms divide mintmaster's initials, crown above divides date, value 1/3 in oval below **Obv. Legend:** ERNST ET LVDO - VICH CHRISTIA' **Rev:** Stag left in circle **Rev. Legend:** CO. IN. S. KO. R. WER. ET. D. IN. EP. M. B. E. LOR. E. CLE. **Note:** Varieties exist.

Date	Mintage	VG	F	VF	XF	Unc
1672 IB	—	35.00	75.00	150	310	—
1673 IB	—	35.00	75.00	150	310	—

KM# 13 1/2 THALER
Silver **Ruler:** Heinrich Ernst I **Obv:** Stag left, small orb above, titles of Heinrich Ernst **Rev:** 11-fold arms, date divided above, titles continued

Date	Mintage	VG	F	VF	XF	Unc
1659 HB	—	—	—	—	—	—

KM# 47 16 GUTE GROSCHEN (2/3 Thaler = Gulden)
Silver **Ruler:** Ernst and Ludwig Christian **Obv:** Date and mintmaster's initials at the end of inscription, titles of Ernst Ludwig Christian **Obv. Inscription:** XVI / GUTE / GROSS **Rev:** 3 helmets above 11-fold arms, titles continued **Note:** Dav#996. Varieties exist.

Date	Mintage	VG	F	VF	XF	Unc
1674 IB	—	275	550	950	1,950	—

KM# 15 THALER
Silver **Ruler:** Heinrich Ernst I **Obv:** Stag left in circle **Obv. Legend:** HEINR: ERNST. COM: IN. STOLBERG. KON: RV: WERN: E. HONS. **Rev:** Manifold arms divide mintmaster's initials, 3 ornate helmets above, date divided among crests **Rev. Legend:** DOM: IN. EPS: MVN: BREVB: LOR: ET. KLETTEN:. **Note:** Dav# 7787.

Date	Mintage	VG	F	VF	XF	Unc
1659 HB	—	1,000	2,000	4,000	7,000	—

KM# 33 THALER
Silver **Ruler:** Heinrich Ernst I **Subject:** Death of Heinrich Ernst I **Obv:** 8-line inscription with R.N. dates, below in two upwardly-curved lines HOC ERGASTULO CONFRACTO / SUBLIMIS VIVO **Obv. Legend:** HEINRICH * ERNST * COMES * IN * STOL * KONIG * RIT * WERNIGE ***. **Rev:** Stag left, mintmaster's initials by legs **Rev. Legend:** ET * HOHEN * DO * IN * EPSTEIN * MIN * BREI * EICH * LOR * ET * CLETT *. **Note:** Dav# 7788.

Date	Mintage	VG	F	VF	XF	Unc
1672 IB	—	2,500	4,500	7,500	—	—

KM# 49 THALER
Silver **Ruler:** Ludwig Christian **Subject:** Count Ernst's First Ten Years of Rule **Obv:** Bust to right, titles of Ernst **Rev:** Ornamented 11-fold arms divide date, 3 ornate helmets above **Rev. Legend:** POTITVS. REGIMEN. ANNO. 1672. Æ. TATIS. XXXII.

Date	Mintage	VG	F	VF	XF	Unc
1682	—	—	—	—	—	—

TRADE COINAGE

KM# 5 GOLDGULDEN
3.5000 g., 0.9860 Gold 0.1109 oz. AGW **Ruler:** Christof II **Obv:** Shield of arms **Rev:** Six-line inscription and date **Note:** Fr# 3353.

Date	Mintage	VG	F	VF	XF	Unc
1617	—	1,050	2,100	4,600	7,700	—

KM# 19 DUCAT
3.5000 g., 0.9860 Gold 0.1109 oz. AGW **Ruler:** Heinrich Ernst I **Obv:** Stag left **Rev:** Crowned shield of arms **Note:** Fr# 3354.

Date	Mintage	VG	F	VF	XF	Unc
1661 HB	—	1,250	2,500	5,500	9,600	—

KM# 17 2 DUCAT
Gold **Ruler:** Heinrich Ernst I **Obv:** Stag left, small orb above, titles of Heinrich Ernst **Rev:** 11-fold arms, date divided above, titles continued

Date	Mintage	VG	F	VF	XF	Unc
1659 HB	—	—	—	—	—	—

STRALSUND

The town of Stralsund, founded about the year 1200 on the mainland opposite the island of Rügen in the Baltic Sea, obtained the rights of a Germanic city in 1234. Stralsund later joined the Hanseatic League and remained strong enough to maintain its independence from the dukes of Pomerania, who struck coins in that place during the 13th century. In 1325, the city purchased the right to coin its own money from the duke and began a series which continued until 1763. The city fell under the rule of Sweden from 1637 until 1815, then passed to Prussia along with the rest of Swedish Pomerania.

MINT OFFICIALS INITIALS OR MARKS

Initials or Marks	Date	Name
	1606-?	Sebastian Schoras
(a)= or	1610-23	Matthias Howe, Sr. and Jr.
(c)=	1623-28	Asmus Riekhof
(d)= or HP (sometimes in ligature)	1625-35	Hans Puls
(e)=	1632	Herman Sander (Zander)
(f)=	1632	Hans Staude
	1633	Heinrich Kleinkamp
CS	1636-62	Casper Sievers
(b)= or HIH	1662-1705	Heinrich Johann Hille
DHM	1689-91	David Heinrich Mathäus

ARMS
An arrowhead pointed upwards.

REFERENCES
B = P. Bratring, "Über das Münzwesen der Stadt Stralsund in neueren Zeiten," **Berliner Münzblätter**, N.F. 28 (1907), pp. 509ff.
Sch = Wolfgang Schulten, ***Deutsche Münzen aus der Zeit Karls V.***, Frankfurt am Main, 1974.

CITY

REGULAR COINAGE

KM# 2 PFENNIG
1.3700 g., Copper, 16 mm. **Obv:** City arms divide date in striated circle **Note:** Ref. B#14, 20. Uniface.

Date	Mintage	VG	F	VF	XF	Unc
1607	—	30.00	65.00	100	200	—

KM# 18 3 PFENNIG (Dreier)
Copper **Obv:** City arms in circle **Obv. Legend:** MONETA NOV STR(AL). **Rev:** 5-line inscription with date **Rev. Inscription:** III / PFEN. / NING. / SVND / (date) **Note:** Ref. B#37a, b, 42. Varieties exist.

Date	Mintage	VG	F	VF	XF	Unc
16ZZ	—	—	—	—	—	—
16Z3	—	—	—	—	—	—

KM# 20 6 PFENNIG (Sechser)
Copper **Obv:** City arms in circle **Obv. Legend:** MON NO STRAL. S. **Rev:** 5-line inscription with date **Rev. Inscription:** VI / PHEN / NING / SVND / (date) **Note:** Ref. B#36a.

Date	Mintage	VG	F	VF	XF	Unc
16ZZ	—	10.00	20.00	40.00	85.00	—

KM# 21 6 PFENNIG (Sechser)
Copper **Obv:** City arms in circle **Obv. Legend:** MON NO STRAL. S. **Rev:** 4-line inscription with date **Rev. Inscription:** VI / PHEN. / N. SVND / (date) **Note:** Ref. B#36b.

Date	Mintage	VG	F	VF	XF	Unc
16ZZ	—	10.00	20.00	40.00	85.00	—

KM# 77 WITTEN (1/2 Schilling)
Silver **Obv:** Shield of city arms in circle **Obv. Legend:** STADT GELDT. **Rev:** 2-line inscription, date in legend **Rev. Legend:** ANNO (date) **Rev. Inscription:** I / WIT. **Note:** Ref. B#65.

Date	Mintage	VG	F	VF	XF	Unc
1633 (f)	—	—	—	—	—	—

KM# 125 WITTEN (1/2 Schilling)
Silver, 12-13 mm. **Obv:** City arms in circle **Obv. Legend:** STRAL. STAT. GELDT. **Rev:** Value, 1 / WITT within circle, date at end of legend **Rev. Legend:** GOTT MIT UNS **Note:** Prev. KM#30.

Date	Mintage	VG	F	VF	XF	Unc
1657	—	50.00	100	200	425	—
1666	—	45.00	90.00	180	360	—
1671	—	30.00	65.00	135	275	—
1682	—	20.00	45.00	90.00	180	—
1682 HIH	—	30.00	65.00	130	265	—
1685 HIH	—	30.00	65.00	130	265	—
1689 HIH	—	—	—	—	—	—
1691 HIH	—	30.00	65.00	130	265	—

KM# 83 WITTEN (1/192 Thaler)
0.5700 g., Silver, 14 mm. **Obv:** Ornately-shaped shield of city arms in circle **Obv. Legend:** STADT. GELDT **Rev:** 2-line inscription of value, date in legend **Rev. Legend:** ANNO. (date) **Rev. Inscription:** I / WIT **Note:** Prev. KM#7.

Date	Mintage	VG	F	VF	XF	Unc
1637 (f)	—	35.00	65.00	125	210	—
1638	—	65.00	135	275	550	—
1667	—	75.00	150	300	625	—

KM# 113 WITTEN (1/192 Thaler)
Silver **Obv:** City arms in inner circle **Note:** Prev. KM#22.

Date	Mintage	VG	F	VF	XF	Unc
1646	—	50.00	100	200	425	—
1647 CS	—	50.00	100	200	425	—
1648 CS	—	—	—	—	—	—

KM# 190 WITTEN (1/192 Thaler)
Silver, 12-14 mm. **Obv:** City arms above cross in circle **Obv. Legend:** STRALS. STAT. GELT. **Rev:** 3-line inscription with mintmaster's initials, date at end of legend **Rev. Legend:** GOTT. MIT. UNS. **Rev. Inscription:** I / WITT / HIH (ligature) **Note:** Prev. KM#58.

Date	Mintage	VG	F	VF	XF	Unc
1692 HIH	—	30.00	65.00	135	275	—
1694 HIH	—	20.00	45.00	90.00	180	—
1696 HIH	—	20.00	45.00	90.00	180	—
1698 HIH	—	20.00	45.00	90.00	180	—

KM# 23 SCHILLING
Silver **Obv:** City arms in circle **Obv. Legend:** MONE: NO. SVNDENS. **Rev:** Cross in circle, date divided in angles **Rev. Legend:** DEV. IN. NO. TV: SALV. **Note:** Ref. B#35.

Date	Mintage	VG	F	VF	XF	Unc
16ZZ (a)	—	—	—	—	—	—

KM# 34 SCHILLING
Silver **Obv:** City arms in circle **Obv. Legend:** MO: NO: STRALSVND. **Rev:** Cross in circle, date divided in angles **Rev. Legend:** DEV. IN. NO. TVO: SALV. **Note:** Ref. B#41a.

Date	Mintage	VG	F	VF	XF	Unc
16Z3	—	—	—	—	—	—

KM# 35 SCHILLING
Silver **Obv:** City arms in circle **Obv. Legend:** MO: NO: STRALSVND. **Rev:** Cross in circle, date divided in angles **Rev. Legend:** OL: IN. NO. TV. SALV. DEVS. **Note:** Ref. B#41b, 47.

Date	Mintage	VG	F	VF	XF	Unc
16Z3	—	—	—	—	—	—
16Z7	—	—	—	—	—	—

KM# 89 SCHILLING
0.6800 g., Silver, 17 mm. **Obv:** City arms in circle **Obv. Legend:** MONE. NOVA. STRAL. **Rev:** Cross in circle, date at end of legend **Rev. Legend:** EIN. SCHIL. SVND. **Note:** Ref. B#75a.

Date	Mintage	VG	F	VF	XF	Unc
1638	—	35.00	80.00	150	275	—

KM# 90 SCHILLING
Silver **Obv:** City arms in circle **Obv. Legend:** MONE. NOVA. STRAL. **Rev:** Cross in circle, date divided in angles **Rev. Legend:** EIN. SCHILLING: SVNDIS. **Note:** Ref. B#75b.

Date	Mintage	VG	F	VF	XF	Unc
1638	—	30.00	65.00	125	240	—

KM# 4 GROSCHEN (Kreuzgroschen)
Silver Weight varies: 2.47-2.73g., 24-25 mm. **Obv:** City arms in circle **Obv. Legend:** MONET(A) NO. STRALSVN(D). **Rev:** Cross in circle **Rev. Legend:** IN. NOM. TV. SALVA. NOS. DEV(S). **Note:** Varieties exist; U's are engraved instead of V's on some coins. Ref. B#23, 25-28.

Date	Mintage	VG	F	VF	XF	Unc
1610 (a)	—	35.00	70.00	125	210	—
(1)611 (a)	—	35.00	70.00	125	210	—
(1)61Z (a)	—	35.00	70.00	125	210	—
(1)613 (a)	—	35.00	70.00	125	210	—
(1)614 (a)	—	35.00	70.00	125	210	—

KM# 16 GROSCHEN (Kreuzgroschen)
Silver **Obv:** City arms divide date in circle **Obv. Legend:** MONE. NO. STRALSUND. **Rev:** Cross in circle **Rev. Legend:** IN. NOM. T. SALU. N. DEUS. **Note:** Ref. B#29.

Date	Mintage	VG	F	VF	XF	Unc
1614 (a)	—	25.00	40.00	70.00	145	—

KM# 115 1/96 THALER (Sechsling)
Silver **Rev:** Cross pattee **Note:** Prev. KM#23.

Date	Mintage	VG	F	VF	XF	Unc
1646	—	35.00	75.00	150	300	—
1646 CS	—	35.00	75.00	150	300	—
1647	—	35.00	75.00	150	300	—
1647 CS	—	35.00	75.00	150	300	—

KM# 149 1/96 THALER (Sechsling)
Silver **Obv:** City arms in inner circle **Rev:** Value in inner circle, date in legend **Note:** Prev. KM#45.

Date	Mintage	VG	F	VF	XF	Unc
1674 HIH	—	15.00	35.00	70.00	145	—
1682	—	30.00	65.00	130	265	—
1685 HIH	—	20.00	45.00	90.00	180	—

KM# 181 1/96 THALER (Sechsling)
Silver **Obv:** City arms above cross, HIH at top **Note:** Prev. KM#70.

Date	Mintage	VG	F	VF	XF	Unc
1685	—	15.00	35.00	70.00	145	—
1691 HIH	—	15.00	35.00	70.00	145	—
1692 HIH	—	45.00	90.00	180	360	—

KM# 130 1/48 THALER (Schilling or 1/2 Groschen)
Silver **Obv:** City arms in ornamented shield **Obv. Legend:** MONETA. NOVA. STRALSVNDENSIS. **Rev:** Imperial orb with 48 in circle divides date near top. **Rev. Legend:** STRAL SVNDISCHE. STAT. GELT. **Note:** Ref. B#111.

Date	Mintage	VG	F	VF	XF	Unc
1662 HIH(b)	—	—	—	—	—	—

KM# 142 1/48 THALER (Schilling or 1/2 Groschen)
Silver **Obv:** City arms in oval shield **Rev:** Value, date in legend in circle **Rev. Legend:** 48 EINEN **Note:** Prev. KM#36.

Date	Mintage	VG	F	VF	XF	Unc
1663 HIH	—	15.00	35.00	70.00	145	—
1663 HIH(b)	—	15.00	35.00	70.00	145	—

KM# 143 1/48 THALER (Schilling or 1/2 Groschen)
Silver **Rev:** Date below value in circle **Note:** Prev. KM#37.

Date	Mintage	VG	F	VF	XF	Unc
1663 HIH(b)	—	15.00	35.00	70.00	145	—

KM# 145 1/48 THALER (Schilling or 1/2 Groschen)
Silver **Obv:** City arms in curved shield **Rev:** 48 in orb, date above in inner circle **Note:** Prev. KM#42.

Date	Mintage	VG	F	VF	XF	Unc
1666 HIH(b)	—	20.00	45.00	90.00	180	—

KM# 151 1/48 THALER (Schilling or 1/2 Groschen)
Silver Weight varies: 0.88-1.06g., 17-18 mm. **Obv:** City arms above cross in circle **Obv. Legend:** STRALSUNDISCH. **Rev:** 4-line inscription with mintmaster's initials, date at end of legend **Rev. Legend:** STADT. GELDT. **Rev. Inscription:** 48 / REICHS / TALER / HIH (ligature) **Note:** Prev. KM#46.

Date	Mintage	VG	F	VF	XF	Unc
1674 HIH	—	20.00	45.00	90.00	180	—
1677 HIH	—	20.00	45.00	90.00	180	—
1678 HIH Rare	—	—	—	—	—	—
1681 HIH	—	15.00	35.00	70.00	145	—
1683 HIH	—	15.00	35.00	70.00	145	—
1684 HIH	—	25.00	50.00	100	210	—
1685 HIH	—	25.00	50.00	100	210	—
1686 HIH	—	25.00	50.00	100	210	—
1689 HIH Rare	—	—	—	—	—	—
1691 HIH	—	35.00	80.00	150	300	—
1692 HIH	—	35.00	80.00	150	300	—

KM# 171 1/48 THALER (Schilling or 1/2 Groschen)
Silver **Obv:** Legend starts at bottom **Note:** Prev. KM#62.

Date	Mintage	VG	F	VF	XF	Unc
1683 HIH	—	25.00	50.00	100	210	—

KM# 132 1/24 THALER (Groschen)
1.8400 g., Silver, 23 mm. **Obv:** Shield of city arms in ornamented frame, date above **Obv. Legend:** STRALSVNDISCH. STAT. GELT. **Rev:** Crowned imperial eagle, 24 in circle on breast **Rev. Legend:** MONETA. NOVA. STRALSVNDENSIS. **Note:** Prev. KM#38.

Date	Mintage	VG	F	VF	XF	Unc
1662 HIH	—	20.00	45.00	90.00	180	—
1662 HIH(b)	—	25.00	50.00	100	210	—
1663 HIH(b)	—	—	—	—	—	—
1666 HIH(b)	—	25.00	50.00	100	210	—
1667 HIH	—	20.00	45.00	90.00	180	—
1667 (b)	—	20.00	45.00	90.00	180	—
1668 HIH(b)	—	20.00	45.00	90.00	180	—

KM# 153 1/24 THALER (Groschen)
Silver Weigh varies: 1.66-1.83g., 23 mm. **Obv:** City arms above cross in inner circle **Obv. Legend:** STRALSUNDISCH. **Rev:** 3-line inscription in circle, date and mintmaster's initials at end of legend **Rev. Legend:** STADT. GELDT. **Rev. Inscription:** 24 / REICHS / DALER **Note:** Prev. KM#47.

Date	Mintage	VG	F	VF	XF	Unc
1674 HIH	—	30.00	60.00	120	240	—
1677 HIH	—	35.00	75.00	150	290	—
1684 HIH	—	45.00	90.00	180	360	—
1686/4 HIH	—	20.00	45.00	90.00	180	—

KM# 154 1/24 THALER (Groschen)
Silver **Rev:** Legend begins at bottom **Note:** Prev. KM#48.

Date	Mintage	VG	F	VF	XF	Unc
1674 HIH	—	35.00	75.00	150	290	—

KM# 186 1/24 THALER (Groschen)
Silver, 23 mm. **Obv:** City arms in circle **Obv. Legend:** STRALSUNDISCH **Rev:** 5-line inscription with mintmaster's initials, date at end of legend **Rev. Legend:** STADT. GELDT. **Rev. Inscription:** 24 / EINEN / REICHS / TALER / HIH **Note:** Prev. KM#74.

Date	Mintage	VG	F	VF	XF	Unc
1688 HIH	—	20.00	45.00	90.00	180	—
1689 HIH	—	20.00	45.00	90.00	180	—
1691 HIH	—	25.00	50.00	100	210	—

KM# 188 1/24 THALER (Groschen)
Silver **Obv:** City arms above cross in round shield **Note:** Prev. KM#75.

Date	Mintage	VG	F	VF	XF	Unc
1691 DHM	—	25.00	50.00	100	210	—

KM# 37 1/16 THALER (Düttchen)
3.0400 g., Silver, 26-27 mm. **Obv:** City arms above cross in circle **Obv. Legend:** DER. STAD. STRALSVND. GELD. **Rev:** 4-line inscription with date **Rev. Legend:** REICHS. SCHROT. VND KORN. **Rev. Inscription:** 16 / REICHS / TALER / (date) **Note:** Ref. B#40, 45-46.

Date	Mintage	VG	F	VF	XF	Unc
16Z3 (c)	—	15.00	30.00	55.00	110	—
16Z6 (c)	—	15.00	30.00	55.00	110	—
16Z7 (c)	—	15.00	30.00	55.00	110	—

KM# 38 1/16 THALER (Düttchen)
Silver **Obv:** City arms above cross in circle **Obv. Legend:** DER. STAD. STRALSVND. GELT. **Rev:** 4-line inscription with date **Rev. Legend:** REICHS. SCHROT. VND KORN. **Rev. Inscription:** 16 / REICHS / TALER / (date) **Note:** Ref. B#40a. Klippe.

Date	Mintage	VG	F	VF	XF	Unc
16Z3 (c)	—	20.00	35.00	65.00	120	—

KM# 46 1/16 THALER (Düttchen)
Silver Weight varies: 2.63-3.20g., 26-27 mm. **Obv:** City arms above cross in circle **Obv. Legend:** DER. STAD. STRALSVND. GELT. **Rev:** 4-line inscription with date **Rev. Legend:** REICHS. SCHROT. VND KORN. **Rev. Inscription:** 16 / REICHS / TALER / (date) **Note:** Ref. B#43-44, 46, 51a, 57, 59, 63. Varieties exist.

Date	Mintage	VG	F	VF	XF	Unc
16Z4 (c)	—	15.00	30.00	60.00	115	—
16Z5 (c)	—	15.00	30.00	60.00	115	—
16Z7 (c)	—	15.00	30.00	60.00	115	—
16Z8 (d)	—	15.00	30.00	60.00	115	—
1630 (d)	—	15.00	30.00	60.00	115	—
1631 (d)	—	15.00	30.00	60.00	115	—
163Z (d)	—	15.00	30.00	60.00	115	—

KM# 48 1/16 THALER (Düttchen)
3.1300 g., Silver, 27-29 mm. **Obv:** City arms above cross in circle **Obv. Legend:** DER. STAD. STRALSVND. (GE). **Rev:** 4-line inscription with date **Rev. Legend:** REICHS. SCHROT. VND KORN. **Rev. Inscription:** 16 / REICHS / TALER / (date) **Note:** Ref. B#51b, 55.

Date	Mintage	VG	F	VF	XF	Unc
16Z8 (d)	—	20.00	35.00	65.00	120	—
16Z9 (d)	—	20.00	35.00	65.00	120	—

KM# 67 1/16 THALER (Düttchen)
Silver **Obv:** City arms divide date in circle **Obv. Legend:** D. STADT. STRALSVND GELT. **Rev:** 4-line inscription with mintmaster's symbol **Rev. Legend:** REICHS. SCHROT. VND. KORN. **Rev. Inscription:** 16 / REICHS / TALER / (mintmaster's symbol)

Date	Mintage	VG	F	VF	XF	Unc
1632 (e)	—	25.00	40.00	75.00	150	—

KM# 117 1/16 THALER (Düttchen)
Silver **Obv:** City arms in oval shield **Rev:** Value in inner circle, date in legend **Note:** Prev. KM#24.

Date	Mintage	VG	F	VF	XF	Unc
1646 CS	—	35.00	75.00	150	290	—

KM# 118 1/16 THALER (Düttchen)

1.6100 g., Silver, 25-26 mm. **Obv:** City arms in baroque frame **Obv. Legend:** MONE(TA). NO. CIVIT. STRAL(LS)SVND. **Rev:** 5-line inscription with mintmaster's initials **Rev. Legend:** REICHS. DALER. SILBER. **Rev. Inscription:** XVI. / EINEN / REICHS / DALER / CS **Note:** Prev. KM#25.

Date	Mintage	VG	F	VF	XF	Unc
1646 CS	—	25.00	50.00	100	210	—
1647 CS	—	20.00	45.00	90.00	180	—
(1)647 CS	—	25.00	50.00	100	210	—
1648 CS	—	35.00	75.00	150	290	—
1658 CS	—	25.00	50.00	100	210	—
1659 CS	—	25.00	50.00	100	210	—
1660 CS	—	25.00	50.00	100	210	—

KM# 128 1/16 THALER (Düttchen)

Silver **Rev:** Value divides CS **Note:** Prev. KM#33.

Date	Mintage	VG	F	VF	XF	Unc
1659 CS	—	45.00	90.00	180	360	—

KM# 25 1/8 THALER (1/2 Reichsort)

Silver **Obv:** City arms above cross in circle **Obv. Legend:** MONETA. NOVA. STRALSV. **Rev:** 5-line inscription with date, top line flanked by two 6-pointed stars **Rev. Inscription:** 1/8 / HALB. / REICHS / ORTH / (date) **Note:** Ref. B#34.

Date	Mintage	VG	F	VF	XF	Unc
16ZZ (a)	—	—	—	—	—	—

KM# 92 1/8 THALER (4 Schilling)

Silver **Obv:** Round shield of city arms **Rev:** Crowned imperial eagle, 4 in orb on breast **Note:** Prev. KM#10.

Date	Mintage	VG	F	VF	XF	Unc
1638 CS Unique	—	—	—	—	—	—

KM# 27 1/4 THALER (8 Schilling)

Silver, 29 mm. **Obv:** City arms above cross divide date, all in circle **Obv. Legend:** MONETA. NOVA. STRAL. SVNDE. **Rev:** Crowned imperial eagle, 8 in orb on breast **Rev. Legend:** FERDINAN. II. D:G. RO: IM. SE. AVG. **Note:** Ref. B#33.

Date	Mintage	VG	F	VF	XF	Unc
16ZZ (a)	—	—	—	—	—	—

KM# 94 1/4 THALER (8 Schilling)

Silver **Obv:** Round shield of city arms **Rev:** Crowned imperial eagle, 8 in orb on breast **Note:** Prev. KM#11.

Date	Mintage	VG	F	VF	XF	Unc
1638 CS / (d) Rare	—	—	—	—	—	—
1639 CS Rare	—	—	—	—	—	—
1640 CS Rare	—	—	—	—	—	—

KM# 155 1/3 THALER (1/2 Gulden)

9.6400 g., Silver, 30-31 mm. **Obv:** City arms, value "1/3" below, all in circle, date at end of legend **Obv. Legend:** MONETA NOVA STRALSUNDENSIS. **Rev:** Cross with spear-tip ends in circle **Rev. Legend:** IN NOMINE TUO SALA NOS DEUS **Note:** Prev. KM#49.

Date	Mintage	VG	F	VF	XF	Unc
1677 HIH	—	80.00	150	300	600	—

KM# 156 1/3 THALER (1/2 Gulden)

Silver **Rev:** Cross Moline **Note:** Prev. KM#50.

Date	Mintage	VG	F	VF	XF	Unc
1677 HIH	—	85.00	175	275	575	—

KM# 173 1/3 THALER (1/2 Gulden)

Silver **Rev:** Greek cross **Note:** Prev. KM#63.

Date	Mintage	VG	F	VF	XF	Unc
1683 HIH	—	80.00	165	335	675	—

KM# 174 1/3 THALER (1/2 Gulden)

Silver **Rev:** Greek cross with trefoils **Note:** Prev. KM#64.

Date	Mintage	VG	F	VF	XF	Unc
1683 HIH	—	100	210	425	850	—

KM# 6 1/2 THALER (16 Schilling)

Silver **Obv:** City arms over cross divides date, all in circle **Obv. Legend:** MONETA NOVA. STRALSVNDENSIS. **Rev:** Crowned imperial eagle, 16 in orb on breast **Rev. Legend:** RVDOLPHV. II. D:G. ROMA. IMPE. SE. AVGVS. **Note:** Ref. B#22.

Date	Mintage	VG	F	VF	XF	Unc
1610 (a)	—	—	—	—	—	—

KM# 29 1/2 THALER (16 Schilling)

Silver Weight varies: 14.01-14.52g., 34-35 mm. **Obv:** City arms over cross divides date, all in circle **Obv. Legend:** MONETA NOVA. STRALSVNDENSIS. **Rev:** Crowned imperial eagle, 16 in orb on breast **Rev. Legend:** FERDINAN(DVS). II. D:G. RO: IM(P). S(EM). A(VGVS). **Note:** Ref. B#32, 39, 50, 54. Varieties exist.

Date	Mintage	VG	F	VF	XF	Unc
16ZZ (a)	—	450	800	1,275	2,400	—
16Z3 (c)	—	450	800	1,275	2,400	—
16Z8 (d)	—	450	800	1,275	2,400	—
16Z9/8 (d)	—	4,800	6,500	8,000	13,500	—

KM# 85 1/2 THALER (16 Schilling)

Silver **Obv:** City arms in oval frame ornamented with angels facing outwards, all in circle **Obv. Legend:** MONETA. NOVA. CIVITATIS: STRALSVNDENSIS. **Rev:** Crowned imperial eagle, 16 in orb on breast, date at end of legend **Rev. Legend:** FERDINANDUS. II. D:G: ROMA: IMP: SE: AU: **Note:** Ref. B#69a.

Date	Mintage	VG	F	VF	XF	Unc
1637 CS	—	—	—	—	—	—

KM# 96 1/2 THALER (16 Schilling)

Silver **Obv:** City arms in oval frame ornamented with angels facing outwards, all in circle **Obv. Legend:** MONETA. NOVA. CIVITATIS: STRALSVNDENSIS. **Rev:** Crowned imperial eagle, 16 in orb on breast, date at end of legend **Rev. Legend:** FERDINANDUS. III. D:G. ROM: IMP: SE. AU. **Note:** Ref. B#73.

Date	Mintage	VG	F	VF	XF	Unc
1638 CS	—	—	—	—	—	—

KM# 103 1/2 THALER (16 Schilling)

14.3800 g., Silver, 35-36 mm. **Obv:** City arms in oval baroque frame, date at end of legend **Obv. Legend:** MON. NOVA. CIVIT. STRALSUNDENSIS. **Rev:** Crowned imperial eagle, orb on breast **Rev. Legend:** FERDINANDUS. III. D. G. ROMANO. IMP. S. A. **Note:** B-82. Prev. KM#16.

Date	Mintage	VG	F	VF	XF	Unc
1640 CS	—	1,000	1,800	3,000	6,000	—
164Z CS	—	1,000	1,800	3,000	6,000	—

KM# 158 2/3 THALER (1 Gulden)

Silver, 36-37 mm. **Obv:** City arms, value "2/3" below, in circle, date at end of legend **Obv. Legend:** MONETA NOVA STRALSUNDENSIS. **Rev:** Cross with spear-tip ends in circle **Rev. Legend:** IN NOMINE TUO SALVA NOS DEUS. **Note:** Dav. 1008. Prev. KM#51.

Date	Mintage	VG	F	VF	XF	Unc
1677 HIH	—	85.00	115	235	475	—

KM# 159 2/3 THALER (1 Gulden)

Silver, 38 mm. **Obv:** City arms, value "2/3" below, in circle, date at end of legend **Obv. Legend:** MONETA NOVA STRALSUNDENSIS. **Rev:** Narrow cross moline with trefoils at ends **Rev. Legend:** IN NOMINE TUO SALVA NOS DEUS. **Note:** Dav. 1009. Prev. KM#52.

Date	Mintage	VG	F	VF	XF	Unc
1677 HIH	—	65.00	135	275	575	—
1678 HIH	—	80.00	165	335	675	—
1679 HIH	—	135	275	550	1,100	—
1680 HIH	—	65.00	135	275	575	—

KM# 160 2/3 THALER (1 Gulden)

Silver, 38 mm. **Obv:** City arms, value "2/3" below, in circle **Obv. Legend:** MONETA NOVA STRALSUNDENSIS. **Rev:** Wide cross moline in circle, date at end of legend **Rev. Legend:** IN NOMINE TUO SALVA NOS DEUS. **Note:** Dav. 1010. Prev. KM#53.

Date	Mintage	VG	F	VF	XF	Unc
1677 HIH	—	65.00	135	275	575	—
1680 HIH	—	65.00	135	275	575	—

KM# 164 2/3 THALER (1 Gulden)

Silver, 39-40 mm. **Obv:** City arms, value "2/3" below, in circle, date at end of legend **Obv. Legend:** MONETA NOVA STRALSUNDENSIS. **Rev:** Greek cross in circle **Rev. Legend:** IN NOMINE TUO SALVA NOS DEUS. **Note:** Dav. 1011. Prev. KM#55.

Date	Mintage	VG	F	VF	XF	Unc
1680 HIH	—	50.00	100	200	400	—
1683 HIH	—	45.00	90.00	180	360	—
1688 HIH	—	65.00	135	275	550	—

KM# 166 2/3 THALER (1 Gulden)

18.8000 g., Silver, 39-40 mm. **Obv:** City arms, value "2/3" below, all in circle **Obv. Legend:** MONETA NOVA STRALSUNDENSIS. **Rev:** Greek cross in circle, date and mintmaster's initials at end of legend **Rev. Legend:** IN NOMINE T(V)(U)O SALVA NOS DE(V)(U)S **Note:** Dav. 1010. Prev. KM#60. Varieties exist.

Date	Mintage	VG	F	VF	XF	Unc
1681 HIH	—	65.00	135	275	550	—
1683 HIH	—	45.00	90.00	180	360	—

KM# 167 2/3 THALER (1 Gulden)

Silver, 38-39 mm. **Obv:** City arms, value "2/3" below, all in circle **Obv. Legend:** MONETA NOVA STRALSUNDENSIS. **Rev:** Maltese cross, mintmaster's initials below, in circle, date at end of legend **Rev. Legend:** IN NOMINE DUO SALVA NOS DEUS **Note:** Dav. 1010. Prev. KM#61.

Date	Mintage	VG	F	VF	XF	Unc
1681 HIH	—	65.00	135	275	550	—
1683 HIH	—	45.00	90.00	180	360	—

KM# 176 2/3 THALER (1 Gulden)

Silver, 37-38 mm. **Obv:** City arms, value "2/3" below, in circle **Obv. Legend:** MONETA NOVA STRALSUNDENSIS. **Rev:** Greek cross, mintmaster's initials below, in circle **Rev. Legend:** IN NOMINE TUO SALVA NOS DEUS. **Note:** Prev. KM#65.

Date	Mintage	VG	F	VF	XF	Unc
1683 HIH	—	45.00	90.00	180	360	—

KM# 177 2/3 THALER (1 Gulden)

Silver, 38 mm. **Obv:** City arms, value "2/3" below, all in circle, date at end of legend **Obv. Legend:** MONETA NOVA STRALSUNDENSIS. **Rev:** Greek cross in circle, mintmaster's initials in oval cartouche above in margin **Rev. Legend:** IN NOMINE TUO SALVA NOS DEUS. **Note:** Prev. KM#66.

Date	Mintage	VG	F	VF	XF	Unc
1683 HIH	—	45.00	90.00	180	360	—

KM# 178 2/3 THALER (1 Gulden)

Silver, 37-38 mm. **Obv:** City arms, value "2/3" below, in circle **Obv. Legend:** MONETA NOVA STRALSUNDENSIS. **Rev:** Greek cross with trefoils, date at end of legend **Rev. Legend:** IN NOMINE TUO SALVA NOS DEUS. **Note:** Prev. KM#67.

Date	Mintage	VG	F	VF	XF	Unc
1683 HIH	—	45.00	90.00	180	360	—

KM# 179 2/3 THALER (1 Gulden)

Silver, 39 mm. **Obv:** City arms, value "2/3" below, date at end of legend **Obv. Legend:** MONETA NOVA STRALSUNDENSIS. **Rev:** Greek cross in circle, small trefoil at each end, mintmaster's initials in margin at top **Rev. Legend:** IN NOMINE TUO SALVA NOS DEUS. **Note:** Prev. KM#68.

Date	Mintage	VG	F	VF	XF	Unc
1683 HIH	—	45.00	90.00	180	360	—

KM# 184 2/3 THALER (1 Gulden)

Silver, 39-40 mm. **Obv:** City arms, value "2/3" below, enclosed in palm branches, date at end of legend **Obv. Legend:** MONETA NOVA STRALSUNDENSIS. **Rev:** Greek cross in circle, mintmaster's initials in oval cartouche at bottom **Rev. Legend:** IN NOMINE TUO - SALVA NOS DEUS. **Note:** Prev. KM#73.

Date	Mintage	VG	F	VF	XF	Unc
1687 HIH	—	80.00	165	335	675	—

KM# 183 2/3 THALER (1 Gulden)

Silver, 40-41 mm. **Obv:** City arms, value "2/3" below, all within palm branches, date at end of legend **Obv. Legend:** MONETA NOVA STRALSUNDENSIS. **Rev:** Greek cross in circle **Rev. Legend:** IN NOMINE TUO SALVA NOS DEUS **Note:** Dav. 1011. Prev. KM#72.

Date	Mintage	VG	F	VF	XF	Unc
1687 HIH	—	90.00	175	325	650	—
1688 HIH	—	250	425	650	1,100	—

KM# 12 THALER

Silver **Obv:** Ornate shield of city arms in circle, date in outer legend **Rev:** Large cross in cartouche within circle **Note:** Dav. #LS493.

Date	Mintage	VG	F	VF	XF	Unc
1611 (a) Rare	—	—	—	—	—	—

KM# 52 THALER

Silver **Obv:** City arms in wreath **Obv. Legend:** + DEO. OPTIM. MAXIM. IMPEER. ROMANO. FOEDERI. POSTERISQ. **Rev:** 14-line inscription with R.N. date **Note:** Under Siege by Wallenstein. Dav. #LS496.

Date	Mintage	VG	F	VF	XF	Unc
MDCXXVIII(1628) Rare	—	—	—	—	—	—

KM# 53 THALER

Silver **Obv:** City arms in wreath **Obv. Legend:** DEO. OPTIM. MAXIM. IMPEER. ROMANO. FOEDERI. POSTERISQ. **Rev:** 14-line inscription with R.N. date **Note:** Under Siege by Wallenstein. Dav. #LS500.

Date	Mintage	VG	F	VF	XF	Unc
MDCXXVIII(1628) Rare	—	—	—	—	—	—

KM# 50 THALER

Silver **Obv:** City arms in laurel wreath **Obv. Legend:** DEO. OPTIMI. MAXIM. IMPER. ROMANO. FOEDERI. POSTERISQ. **Rev:** 12-line inscription with Roman numeral date **Rev. Inscription:** MEMORIÆ / URBIS. STRALSUN: / DAE. AN. MDCXXVIII. / DIE. XII. MAY. A: MILITE / CÆSARIA: NO. CINCTÆ. ALI / QVOTIES. OPPUGNATÆ. / SED. DEI. GRATIA. ET. OPE. / INCLYTOR. REGUM. SE / PTENTRIONAL. DIE / XXIII. IULI: OBSIDIO / NE. LIBERATÆ. / S: P: Q: S: P: P: **Note:** Dav. #5823.

Date	Mintage	VG	F	VF	XF	Unc
MDCXXVIII(1628)	—	1,650	2,600	4,250	6,500	—

KM# 8 THALER (32 Schilling)

Silver, 41 mm. **Obv:** City arms, cross below divides date **Obv. Legend:** MONETA. NOVA. STRALSVNDENSIS. **Rev:** Crowned imperial eagle, 3Z in orb on breast **Rev. Legend:** RVDOLPHVS. II. D.G. RO. IMP. SEMP. AUGUS. **Note:** Dav. #5816.

Date	Mintage	VG	F	VF	XF	Unc
1610 (a)	—	1,500	3,000	5,250	—	—

KM# 11 THALER (32 Schilling)

Silver, 41 mm. **Obv:** City arms over cross divide date **Obv. Legend:** MONETA. NOVA. STRALSVNDENSIS. **Rev:** Crowned imperial eagle, value 3Z in orb on breast **Rev. Legend:** RVDOLPHVS. II. D. G. RO: IMP. SEM. AVGVS. **Note:** Dav. #5817.

Date	Mintage	VG	F	VF	XF	Unc
1611 (a)	—	650	1,250	2,500	—	—

KM# 31.1 THALER (32 Schilling)
Silver **Obv:** City arms over cross divide date **Obv. Legend:** MONETA. NOVA. STRALSVNDENSIS. **Rev:** Crowned imperial eagle, 3Z in orb on breast **Rev. Legend:** FERDINANDVS. II. D: G. RO: IMP. SEMP. AVGVS. **Note:** Dav. #5818.

Date	Mintage	VG	F	VF	XF	Unc
16ZZ (a)	—	500	1,000	2,000	—	—

KM# 31.2 THALER (32 Schilling)
Silver, 41 mm. **Obv:** City arms above cross divide date **Obv. Legend:** MONETA. NOVA. STRALSVNDENSIS. **Rev:** Crowned imperial eagle, value 3Z in orb on breast **Rev. Legend:** FERDINANDVS. II. D: G. ROMA. IMPER. SE. AVG. **Note:** Dav. 5818A.

Date	Mintage	VG	F	VF	XF	Unc
16ZZ (a)	—	500	1,000	2,000	—	—

KM# 32 THALER (32 Schilling)
Silver, 41-42 mm. **Obv:** City arms above cross divide date **Obv. Legend:** MONETA. NOVA. STRALSVNDENSIS. **Rev:** Crowned imperial eagle, value 3Z in orb without cross on breast **Rev. Legend:** FERDINANDVS. D: G. ROM: IMP: SEMP: AVGVS: **Note:** Dav. #5819.

Date	Mintage	VG	F	VF	XF	Unc
16ZZ (a)	—	650	1,250	2,500	—	—

KM# 40 THALER (32 Schilling)
Silver, 42 mm. **Obv:** City arms divide date above cross **Obv. Legend:** MONETA. - NOVA. - STRALSVNDENSIS. **Rev:** Crowned imperial eagle, 3Z in orb on breast **Rev. Legend:** FERDINANDVS. II. D: G: ROM: IMP: SEM: AVG. **Note:** Dav. #5820.

Date	Mintage	VG	F	VF	XF	Unc
16Z3 (c)	—	425	850	1,750	3,000	—

KM# 41.1 THALER (32 Schilling)
Silver, 41-42 mm. **Obv:** City arms divide date over cross **Obv. Legend:** MONETA. - NOVA. - STRALSVNDENSIS. **Rev:** Crowned imperial eagle, 3Z in orb on breast **Rev. Legend:** FERDINANDVS. II. D: G: ROM: IMP: SEM: AVG: **Note:** Dav. #5821.

Date	Mintage	VG	F	VF	XF	Unc
1623 (c)	—	425	850	1,750	3,000	—

KM# 41.2 THALER (32 Schilling)
Silver, 41-42 mm. **Obv:** City arms divided date above cross **Obv. Legend:** MONETA. - NOVA. - STRALSVNDENSIS. **Rev:** Crowned imperial eagle, value 3Z in orb without cross on breast **Rev. Legend:** FEDINANDVS: I.I. D: G: ROM: IMP: SEM: AVG: **Note:** Dav. 5821A.

Date	Mintage	VG	F	VF	XF	Unc
16Z3 (c)	—	425	850	1,750	3,000	—

KM# 42 THALER (32 Schilling)
Silver, 45x44 mm. **Obv:** City arms divide date over cross **Obv. Legend:** MONETA. - NOVA. - STRALSVNDENSIS. **Rev:** Crowned imperial eagle, 3Z in orb without cross on breast **Rev. Legend:** FERDINANDVS. II. D: G: ROM: IMP: SEM: AVG: **Note:** Klippe. Dav. #5821B.

Date	Mintage	VG	F	VF	XF	Unc
16Z3 (c) Rare	—	—	—	—	—	—

Note: Fritz Rudolf Künker Münzenhandlung Auction 141, 6-08, VF-XF realized approximately $17,040

KM# 51 THALER (32 Schilling)
Silver Weight varies: 28.11-29.20g., 41-42 mm. **Obv:** City arms above cross **Obv. Legend:** MONETA. NOVA. STRALSVNDENSIS. **Rev:** Crowned imperial eagle, 3Z in orb on breast, date divided by tail **Rev. Legend:** FERDINANDVS. II. D. G. ROM. IMP. SEM. A(VG). **Note:** Dav. #5824. Varieties exist.

Date	Mintage	VG	F	VF	XF	Unc
16Z8 (c)	—	650	1,350	2,750	5,000	—
16Z9 (d)	—	650	1,350	2,750	5,000	—
1630 (d)	—	650	1,350	2,750	5,000	—
1639/Z9 (d)	—	2,200	4,000	5,500	7,500	—

KM# A51 THALER (32 Schilling)
Silver **Obv:** City arms above cross in circle **Obv. Legend:** MONETA. NOVA. STRALSVNDENSIS. **Rev:** Crowned imperial eagle divides date, 3Z in orb on breast **Rev. Legend:** FERDINANDVS. II. DG. ROM. IMP: SEM: AVG. **Note:** Dav. #5824A.

Date	Mintage	VG	F	VF	XF	Unc
16Z8 (c)	—	650	1,350	2,750	5,000	—

KM# 65 THALER (32 Schilling)
Silver **Obv:** City arms above cross **Obv. Legend:** MONETA. NOVA. STRALSVNDENSIS. **Rev:** Crowned imperial eagle, 3Z in orb on breast **Rev. Legend:** FERDINANDVS. II. D.G. ROM. IMP. SEM. AVG. **Note:** Dav. #5825.

Date	Mintage	VG	F	VF	XF	Unc
ND(1630) (d)	—	1,950	3,250	6,500	—	—

KM# 69 THALER (32 Schilling)
Silver **Obv:** Small oval shield of city arms in baroque frame, head and wings of angel above, date below **Obv. Legend:** MONETA. NOVA. CIVITA. STRALSVNDEN. **Rev:** Crowned imperial eagle, 32 in orb on breast **Rev. Legend:** FERDINAND. II. D.G. ROM. IMPER. S. AVG. **Note:** Dav. #5826.

Date	Mintage	VG	F	VF	XF	Unc
1632 (e)	—	1,650	3,250	6,000	—	—

KM# 70 THALER (32 Schilling)
Silver **Obv:** Oval city arms in baroque frame, date divided below **Obv. Legend:** MONETA. NOVA. CIVITA. STRALSVNDEN. **Rev:** Crowned imperial eagle, 32 in orb on breast **Rev. Legend:** FERDINAND. II. D.G. ROM. IMPER. S. AVG. **Note:** Dav. #5827.

Date	Mintage	VG	F	VF	XF	Unc
1632 (e)	—	1,450	2,850	5,250	8,750	—

KM# 71 THALER (32 Schilling)
Silver **Obv:** Oval city arms in baroque frame, date divided below **Obv. Legend:** MONETA. NOVA. CIVITA. STRALSVNDEN. **Rev:** Crowned imperial eagle, 32 in orb on breast **Rev. Legend:** FERDINAND. II. D.G. ROM. IMPER. S. AVG. **Note:** Klippe. Dav. #5827A.

Date	Mintage	VG	F	VF	XF	Unc
1632 (e) Rare	—	—	—	—	—	—

KM# 79 THALER (32 Schilling)
Silver **Obv:** Large oval shield of city arms in baroque frame, small angels at upper left and right, date at end of legend **Obv. Legend:** MONET. NOVA. CIVITAT. STRALSUNDENSIS. **Rev:** Crowned imperial eagle, 32 in orb on breast **Rev. Legend:** FERDINANDUS. II. D.G. ROMA. IMP. SE. AUG. **Note:** Dav. #5828.

Date	Mintage	VG	F	VF	XF	Unc
1633 (f)	—	1,250	2,050	3,150	—	—

KM# 81 THALER (32 Schilling)
Silver **Obv:** Oval city arms in baroque frame, small angels at upper left and right, date at end of legend **Obv. Legend:** MONETA. NOVA. CIVITAT. STRALSVNDENSIS. **Rev:** Crowned imperial eagle, 32 in orb on breast **Rev. Legend:** FERDINANDUS. II. D.G. ROM. IMP. S. AU. **Note:** Dav. #5829.

Date	Mintage	VG	F	VF	XF	Unc
1635 (d)	—	1,150	2,250	4,000	—	—

KM# 87 THALER (32 Schilling)
Silver **Obv:** Oval shield of city arms in baroque frame, small angel supports at left and right, date at end of legend **Obv. Legend:** MON. NOVA. CIVITA. STRALSUNDENSIS. **Rev:** Crowned imperial eagle, 3Z in orb on breast **Rev. Legend:** FERDINANDUS. II. D.G. ROMA. IM. SE. AU. **Note:** Dav. #5830.

Date	Mintage	VG	F	VF	XF	Unc
1637 CS	—	550	1,150	2,500	—	—

KM# 100 THALER (32 Schilling)
28.2500 g., Silver, 40-41 mm. **Obv:** Oval city arms in baroque frame supported by ornate angels, date at end of legend **Obv. Legend:** MON. NOVA. CIVIT(A). STRALSUNDENSIS. **Rev:** Crowned imperial eagle, 3Z in orb on breast **Rev. Legend:** FERDINANDUS. III. D.G. ROMA. IM(P). SE. A. **Note:** Prev. KM#13.3. Dav. #5831B.

Date	Mintage	VG	F	VF	XF	Unc
1638 CS	—	800	1,400	2,500	3,750	—
1639 CS	—	800	1,400	2,500	3,750	—

KM# 98 THALER (32 Schilling)
Silver, 44 mm. **Obv:** Oval shield of city arms in baroque frame, date at end of legend **Obv. Legend:** MON. NOVA. CIVITA. STRALSVNDEN. **Rev:** Small crown above imperial eagle, 3Z in orb on breast **Rev. Legend:** FERDINANDUS. III. D.G. ROM. IM. SE. AU. **Note:** Prev. KM#13.1. Dav. #5831.

Date	Mintage	VG	F	VF	XF	Unc
1638 CS	—	500	1,000	2,000	3,500	—

KM# 99 THALER (32 Schilling)
Silver, 44 mm. **Obv:** City arms in oval baroque frame, date at end of legend **Obv. Legend:** MON. NOVA. CIVITA. STRASUNDENSIS. **Rev:** Large crown above imperial eagle, value 3Z in orb on breast **Rev. Legend:** FERDINANDUS. III. D. G. ROMA. IMP. SE. AU. **Note:** Prev. KM#13.2. Dav. #5831A.

Date	Mintage	VG	F	VF	XF	Unc
1638 CS	—	750	1,250	2,250	3,750	—

KM# 106 THALER (32 Schilling)
Silver **Obv:** Oval shield of city arms in baroque frame, date at end of legend **Obv. Legend:** MON. NOVA. CIVIT. STRALSVNDENSIS. **Rev:** Crowned imperial eagle, 32 in orb on breast **Rev. Legend:** FERDINANDUS. III. D.G. ROMANO. IMP. S. A. **Note:** Prev. KM#15. Dav. #5835.

Date	Mintage	VG	F	VF	XF	Unc
1640 CS	—	250	650	1,500	3,000	—
1642 CS	—	500	900	2,000	4,000	—
1644 CS Rare	—	—	—	—	—	—
1645 CS Rare	—	—	—	—	—	—
1646 CS	—	500	900	2,000	4,000	—
1648 CS Rare	—	—	—	—	—	—
1649	—	950	1,800	3,500	7,000	—
1652 CS Rare	—	—	—	—	—	—
1655 CS Rare	—	—	—	—	—	—
1657 CS	—	950	1,800	3,500	7,000	—

KM# 104 THALER (32 Schilling)
Silver, 43 mm. **Obv:** City arms within 3 legends, date at end of outer legend **Obv. Legend:** Outer: MONETA. NOVA. CIVITATIS. STRALSUN. Middle: PRÆSIDIUM. PORTÆ. NOSTRÆ. ET. PAX. Inner: +CHRISTUS - IESUS. C.S. **Rev:** Crowned imperial eagle, 3Z in orb on breast **Rev. Legend:** FERDINANDUS. III. D. G. ROM. IM: SE: AU: **Note:** Prev. KM#17. Dav. #5832.

Date	Mintage	VG	F	VF	XF	Unc
1640 CS	—	650	1,350	2,750	4,500	—

KM# 105 THALER (32 Schilling)

Silver, 40 mm. **Obv:** City arms within 3 legends, mintmaster's initials after date in outer legend **Obv. Legend:** Outer: MONETA. NOVA. STRALSVN. Middle: PRÆSIDIUM. PORTÆ. NOSTRÆ. ET. PAX: Inner: +CHRISTUS - IESUS. **Rev:** Crowned imperial eagle, value 3Z in orb on breast **Rev. Legend:** FERDINANDUS. III. D: G: ROM: IMP: S: A: **Note:** Prev. KM#18. Dav. #5833.

Date	Mintage	VG	F	VF	XF	Unc
1640 CS	—	650	1,350	2,750	4,500	—

KM# 134 THALER (32 Schilling)

Silver **Obv:** City arms in baroque frame, date at end of legend **Obv. Legend:** MONETA. NOVA. CIVITATIS. STRALSVNDEN. **Rev:** Crowned imperial eagle, 32 in orb on breast **Rev. Legend:** LEOPOLDVS. D.G. ROMANORVM. IMPE. SEM. A. **Note:** Dav. #5836. Prev. KM#35.

Date	Mintage	VG	F	VF	XF	Unc
1662 HIH	—	950	1,850	3,750	6,250	—

KM# 13 1-1/2 THALER

Silver, 53-54 mm. **Obv:** City arms in baroque frame within circle, 2 legends, date at end of outer legend **Obv. Legend:** Outer: MONETA. NOVA. STRALSVNDENSIS. ANNO. Inner: DA. IST. KEIN. GELVCK. ZV. KEINER. ERIST. **Rev:** Large cross in baroque frame within circle, 2 legends **Rev. Legend:** Outer: RVDOLPHVS. II. D. G. ROMANO. IMPERATOR. SEMPER. AVGVST. Inner: WO. KEIN. TRVW. NOCH. NICHEIT. IST. **Note:** Dav. #LS492. Illustration reduced.

Date	Mintage	VG	F	VF	XF	Unc
1611 (a)	—	3,750	6,200	9,600	—	—

KM# 44 1-1/2 THALER

Silver, 45x45 mm. **Obv:** City arms divide date over cross **Obv. Legend:** MONETA. - NOVA. - STRALSVNDENSIS. **Rev:** Crowned imperial eagle, 3Z in orb on breast **Rev. Legend:** FERDINANDVS. II. D: G: ROM: IMP: SEM: AVG: **Note:** Klippe. Dav. #5821C. Struck from Thaler dies, KM#41.1.

Date	Mintage	VG	F	VF	XF	Unc
16Z3 (c) Rare	—	—	—	—	—	—

KM# 54 1-1/2 THALER

43.4000 g., Silver **Obv:** City arms in wreath **Obv. Legend:** + DEO. OPTIM. MAXIM. IMPER. ROMANO. FOEDERI. POSTERISQ. **Rev:** 14-line inscription with R.N. date **Rev. Inscription:** MEMORIÆ / URBIS. STRAL / SUNDÆ. AO. MDCXX. / VIII. DIE XII. MAII. A. MILI / TÆ CÆSARIA. NO. CINCTÆ / ALIQUOTIES OPPUGNA / TÆ. SED DEI GRATIA ET / OPE INCLYTORUM. RE / GUM. SEPTENTRIO. / NALIUM. DIE XXIV. / IULII OBSIDIONE / LIBERATÆ. / S: P: Q: S: / F: F: **Note:** Under Siege by Wallenstein. Dav. #LS495; B-9.

Date	Mintage	VG	F	VF	XF	Unc
MDCXXVIII (1628)	—	3,300	6,000	9,000	15,000	—

KM# 55 1-1/2 THALER

Silver **Obv:** City arms in wreath **Obv. Legend:** DEO. OPTIM. MAXIM. IMPEER. ROMANO. FOEDERI. POSTERISQ. **Rev:** 14-line inscription with R.N. date **Note:** Under Siege by Wallenstein. Dav. #LS499.

Date	Mintage	VG	F	VF	XF	Unc
MDCXXVIII (1628) Rare	—	—	—	—	—	—

KM# 73 1-1/2 THALER

Silver **Obv:** Oval city arms in baroque frame, date divided below **Obv. Legend:** MONETA. NOVA. CIVITA. STRALSVNDEN. **Rev:** Crowned imperial eagle, 32 in orb on breast **Rev. Legend:** FERDINAND. II. D.G. ROM. IMPER. S. AVG. **Note:** Struck from Thaler dies, KM#70. Dav. #5827B.

Date	Mintage	VG	F	VF	XF	Unc
1632 (e) Rare	—	—	—	—	—	—

KM# 9 2 THALER

Silver, 42 mm. **Obv:** City arms above cross divide date **Obv. Legend:** MONETA NOVA: STRALSVNDENSIS. **Rev:** Crowned imperial eagle, "3Z" in orb on breast **Rev. Legend:** RVDOLPHVS. II. D: G. RO: IMP. SEMP. AUGUS. **Note:** Prev. Dav. #5815. Struck on thick flan from Thaler dies, KM #8.

Date	Mintage	VG	F	VF	XF	Unc
1610 (a) Rare	—	—	—	—	—	—

Note: Frankfurter Munzhandlung E. Button #124 3-77 VF realized $9,200

KM# 14 2 THALER

Silver **Obv:** City arms in cartouche within circle, 2 legends, date at end of outer legend **Obv. Legend:** Outer: MONETA. NOVA. STRALSVNDENSIS. ANNO. Inner: DA. IST. KEIN. GELVCK. ZV. KEINER. ERIST. **Rev:** Large cross in cartouche within circle, 2 legends **Rev. Legend:** Outer: RVDOLPHVS. II. D. G. ROMANO. IMPERATOR. SEMPER. AVGVST. Inner: WO. KEIN. TRVW. NOCH. NICHEIT. IST. **Shape:** 53-54 **Note:** Dav. #LS491. Struck from 1-1/2 Thaler dies, KM #13.

Date	Mintage	VG	F	VF	XF	Unc
1611 (a) Rare	—	—	—	—	—	—

KM# 57 2 THALER

Silver, 53-54 mm. **Obv:** City arms in wreath **Obv. Legend:** +DEO. OPTIM. MAXIM. IMPER. ROMANO. FOEDERI. POSTERISQ. **Rev:** 14-line inscription with R.N. date **Rev. Inscription:** MEMORIÆ / URBIS. STRAL / SUNDÆ. AO. MDCXX. / VIII. DIE XII. MAII. A. MILI / TÆ CÆSARIA. NO. CINCTÆ / ALIQUOTIES OPPUGNA / TÆ. SED DEI GRATIA ET / OPE INCLYTORUM. RE / GUM. SEPTENTRIO. / NALIUM. DIE XXIV. / IULII OBSIDIONE / LIBERATÆ. / S: P: Q: S: / F: F: **Note:** Under Siege by Wallenstein. Dav. #LS494. Struck with 1-1/2 Thaler dies, KM #54.

Date	Mintage	VG	F	VF	XF	Unc
MDCXXVIII (1628) Rare	—	—	—	—	—	—

Note: Künker Auction 141, 6-08, XF realized approximately $18,620.

KM# 58 2 THALER
Silver **Obv:** City arms in wreath **Obv. Legend:** DEO. OPTIM. MAXIM: IMPER: ROMANO: FOEDERI. POSTERISq. **Rev:** 14-line inscription with R.N. date **Rev. Inscription:** MEMORIÆ / VRBIS. STRAL / SVNDÆ. AO. MDC / XXVIII. DIE XII. MAI. / A. MILITE. CÆSARIA. / NO. CINCTÆ. ALIQUO / TIES. OPPVGNATÆ. SED / DEI. GRATIA. ET. OPE IN / CLYTOR. REGVM. SE / PTENTRIONAL. DIE. / XXIII. IVLI. OBSIDI / ONE. LIBERATÆ. / S: P: Q: S: / F: F: **Note:** Under Siege by Wallenstein. Dav. #LS498.

Date	Mintage	VG	F	VF	XF	Unc
MDCXXVIII (1628) Rare	—	—	—	—	—	—

Note: H.D. Rauch Auction, 1-09, VF realized approximately $13,000. Künker Auction 141, 6-08, VF realized approximately $14,740.

KM# 59 2 THALER
Silver **Obv:** City arms in laurel wreath **Obv. Legend:** DEO. OPTIM. MAXIM. IMPER. ROMANO. FOEDERI. POSTERISQ. **Rev:** 12-line inscription with R.N. date **Rev. Inscription:** MEMORIÆ / URBIS. STRALSUN: / DAE. AN. MDCXXVIII. / DIE. XII. MAY. A: MILITE / CÆSARIA: NO. CINCTÆ. ALI / QVOTIES. OPPUGNATÆ. / SED. DEI. GRATIA. ET. OPE./ INCLYTOR. REGUM. SE / PTENTRIONAL. DIE / XXIII. IULI: OBSIDIO / NE. LIBERATÆ. / S: P: Q: S: P: P: **Note:** Dav. #5822.

Date	Mintage	VG	F	VF	XF	Unc
MDCXXVIII (1628)	—	3,400	5,600	9,600	14,500	—

KM# 108 2 THALER
Silver, 42-43 mm. **Obv:** Oval city arms in baroque frame with angel supporters, date at end of legend **Obv. Legend:** MON. NOVA. CIVIT. STRALSUNDENSIS. **Rev:** Crowned imperial eagle, value "32" in orb on breast **Rev. Legend:** FERDINANDUS. III. D.G. ROMANO. IMP. S.A. **Note:** Struck on thick flan from Thaler dies, KM#106. Dav. #5834.

Date	Mintage	VG	F	VF	XF	Unc
1642 CS Rare	—	—	—	—	—	—

KM# 61 3 THALER
Silver **Obv:** City arms in wreath **Obv. Legend:** DEO. OPTIM. MAXIM. IMPER. ROMANO. FOEDERI. POSTERISQ. **Rev:** 14-line inscription with R.N.I date **Rev. Inscription:** MEMORIÆ / URBIS. STRAL / SUNDÆ. AO. MDCXX. / VIII. DIE XII. MAII. A. MILI / TÆ CÆSARIA. NO. CINCTÆ / ALIQUOTIES OPPUGNA / TÆ. SED DEI GRATIA ET / OPE INCLYTORUM. RE / GUM. SEPTENTRIO. / NALIUM. DIE XXIV. / IULII OBSIDIONE / LIBERATÆ. / S: P: Q: S: / F: F: **Note:** Under siege by Wallenstein. Dav. #LS497.

Date	Mintage	VG	F	VF	XF	Unc
MDCXXVIII (1628) Rare	—	—	—	—	—	—

KM# 15 4 THALER
Silver **Obv:** City arms in cartouche within circle, 2 legends, date at end of outer legend **Obv. Legend:** Outer: MONETA. NOVA. STRALSVNDENSIS. ANNO. Inner: DA. IST. KEIN. GELVCK. ZV. KEINER. ERIST. **Rev:** Large cross in cartouche within circle, 2 legends **Rev. Legend:** Outer: RVDOLPHVS. II. D. G. ROMANO. IMPERATOR. SEMPER. AVGVST. Inner: WO. KEIN. TRVW. NOCH. NICHEIT. IST. **Note:** Dav. #LS490.

Date	Mintage	VG	F	VF	XF	Unc
1611 (a) Rare	—	—	—	—	—	—

TRADE COINAGE

KM# 64.1 GOLDGULDEN
Gold, 22 mm. **Obv:** Cross below city arms divides date **Obv. Legend:** MO. NO. AVR. STRALSVNDENSIS. **Rev:** Imperial orb in ornamented circle **Rev. Legend:** FERDINAN. II. D.G. ROM. IM. S. A. **Note:** Prev. KM#3.

Date	Mintage	VG	F	VF	XF	Unc
16Z8 HP Rare	—	—	—	—	—	—

KM# 64.2 GOLDGULDEN
3.2300 g., Gold, 22 mm. **Obv:** City arms above cross in oval baroque frame **Obv. Legend:** MON. NO. AVR. CIV STRALSVN. **Rev:** Imperial orb divides date in circle **Rev. Legend:** FERDINAND. II. D. G. RO. IM. S. (A.) **Note:** Fr. 3366; B-52.

Date	Mintage	VG	F	VF	XF	Unc
16Z9 HP Rare	—	—	—	—	—	—

Note: Künker Auction 141, 6-08, VF-XF realized approximately $12,415.

KM# 66 GOLDGULDEN
Gold Weight varies: 3.19-3.23g., 22 mm. **Obv:** City arms above cross in oval baroque frame **Obv. Legend:** MO. NO. AVR. CIV. STRALSVND. **Rev:** Imperial orb in octafoil within circle, date at end of legend **Rev. Legend:** FERDINAND. II. D. G. R. I. S. A.

Date	Mintage	VG	F	VF	XF	Unc
1630 HP	—	2,250	3,500	5,000	9,000	—
1631 HP	—	3,800	6,000	8,000	12,500	—

KM# 74 DUCAT
3.5200 g., Gold, 23 mm. **Obv:** City arms in wreath, 'S' below, date at end of legend **Obv. Legend:** AVREVS. STRALSVNDENS. **Rev:** Crowned imperial eagle in circle **Rev. Legend:** FERDINAND. II. D. G. RO. IM. S: A: **Note:** Fr. 3367; B-60.

Date	Mintage	VG	F	VF	XF	Unc
1632	—	2,200	4,000	6,000	9,500	—

KM# 75 DUCAT
3.5000 g., 0.9860 Gold 0.1109 oz. AGW **Obv:** City arms in wreath **Obv. Legend:** AUREUS. NOVUS. STRALSUNDEN. **Rev:** Crowned imperial eagle **Rev. Legend:** FERDINANDUS. II. D.G. ROM. IM. SE. AU. **Note:** Prev. KM#5.

Date	Mintage	VG	F	VF	XF	Unc
1632	—	800	1,750	3,450	6,300	—
1633	—	800	1,750	3,450	6,300	—
1635	—	800	1,750	3,450	6,300	—
ND(1637) CS	—	800	1,750	3,450	6,300	—

KM# 102 DUCAT
3.5000 g., 0.9860 Gold 0.1109 oz. AGW, 23 mm. **Obv:** City arms divided date in wreath, mintmaster's initials at end of legend, where present **Obv. Legend:** AVREVS. NOVVS. STRALSVNDEN(SIS). **Rev:** Crowned imperial eagle in circle **Rev. Legend:** FERDINANDVS. III. D.G. ROM. IM. S. AV. **Note:** Prev. KM#14.

Date	Mintage	VG	F	VF	XF	Unc
1638	—	350	750	1,300	2,900	—
1638 CS	—	350	750	1,300	2,900	—
1640 CS	—	350	750	1,300	2,900	—
1641 CS	—	1,050	1,850	2,900	4,050	—

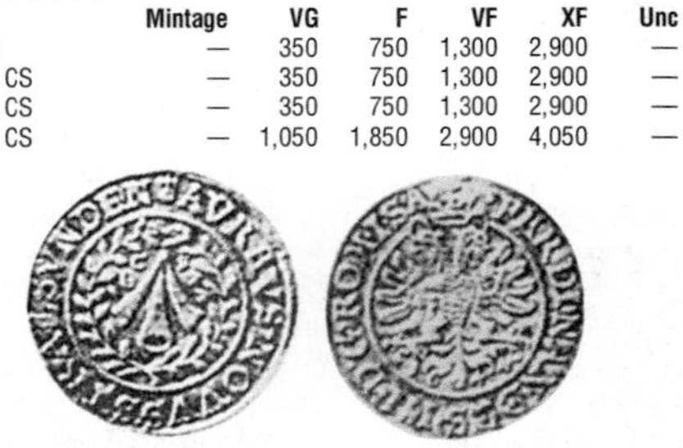

KM# 110 DUCAT
3.5000 g., 0.9860 Gold 0.1109 oz. AGW, 23 mm. **Obv:** City arms divided mintmaster's initials and date in wreath **Obv. Legend:** AVREVS. NOVVS. STRALSVNDEN. **Rev:** Crowned imperial eagle **Rev. Legend:** FERDINANDVS. III. D.G. ROM. I. S. A. **Note:** Prev. KM#19.

Date	Mintage	VG	F	VF	XF	Unc
1644 CS	—	1,400	2,300	3,700	5,200	—

KM# 111 DUCAT
3.5000 g., 0.9860 Gold 0.1109 oz. AGW, 23 mm. **Obv:** City arms divide mintmaster's initials and date within wreath **Obv. Legend:** AVREVS. NOVVS. STRALSVNDEN. **Rev:** Crowned imperial eagle, date divided below tail **Rev. Legend:** FERDINANDUS. III. D.G. ROM. I. S. A. **Note:** Prev. KM#20.

Date	Mintage	VG	F	VF	XF	Unc
1644//1644 CS	—	1,600	2,550	4,050	5,800	—

KM# 122 DUCAT
3.5000 g., 0.9860 Gold 0.1109 oz. AGW, 23 mm. **Obv:** City arms divided date and mintmaster's initials within wreath **Obv. Legend:** AVREVS. NOVUS. STRALSVNDENS. **Rev:** Crowned imperial eagle in circle **Rev. Legend:** FERDINANDUS. III. D: G. ROM. I. S. A. **Note:** B-100. Prev. KM#27.

Date	Mintage	VG	F	VF	XF	Unc
1655 CS	—	400	900	1,850	3,500	—

KM# 123 DUCAT
3.5000 g., 0.9860 Gold 0.1109 oz. AGW, 23 mm. **Obv:** City arms divide date and mintmaster's initials within wreath **Obv. Legend:** AVREVS. NOVUS. STRALSVNDENS. **Rev:** Crowned imperial eagle, date divided below tail **Rev. Legend:** FERDINANDVS. III. D. G. ROM. IM. S. AV. **Note:** Mule dated on both sides. Prev. KM#28.

Date	Mintage	VG	F	VF	XF	Unc
1655//1655 CS	—	1,150	2,050	3,150	5,200	—

KM# 136 DUCAT
3.5000 g., 0.9860 Gold 0.1109 oz. AGW **Obv:** City arms divide date in wreath **Obv. Legend:** AVREVS. NOVVS. STRALSVNDEN. **Rev:** Crowned imperial eagle in circle **Rev. Legend:** LEOPOL. D.G. ROMANO. IMPE. SEM. A. **Note:** Prev. KM#39.

Date	Mintage	VG	F	VF	XF	Unc
1662 HIH(b)	—	600	1,150	2,250	4,000	—
1664 HIH(b) Rare	—	—	—	—	—	—
1666 HIH(b) Rare	—	—	—	—	—	—

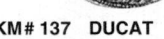

KM# 137 DUCAT
3.4700 g., Gold, 23 mm. **Obv:** City arms in wreath within circle, mintmaster's initials above in margin **Obv. Legend:** AURIUS: NOVUS: STRALSUNDT: **Rev:** Crowned imperial eagle in circle, date at end of legend **Rev. Legend:** LEOPOLDUS. D. G. ROM. I. S. AU. **Note:** Fr. 3370.

Date	Mintage	VG	F	VF	XF	Unc
1666 HIH	—	1,750	2,750	3,750	6,000	—

KM# 147 DUCAT
3.5000 g., 0.9860 Gold 0.1109 oz. AGW **Rev:** Date divided by moneyers initials at top of legend **Note:** Prev. KM#44.

Date	Mintage	VG	F	VF	XF	Unc
1671 HIH Rare	—	—	—	—	—	—

KM# 162 DUCAT

3.5000 g., 0.9860 Gold 0.1109 oz. AGW, 22 mm. **Obv:** City arms within wreath and circle, mintmaster's initials at top in margin **Obv. Legend:** AUREUS NOVUS. STRALSUNDT. **Rev:** Crowned imperial eagle, date at end of legend **Rev. Legend:** LEOPOLDUS. D: G: ROM. I. S. A: **Note:** Fr. 3370. Prev. KM#54.

Date	Mintage	VG	F	VF	XF	Unc
1677 HIH	—	825	1,700	2,650	4,000	—

KM# 169 DUCAT

3.5000 g., 0.9860 Gold 0.1109 oz. AGW, 23 mm. **Obv:** City arms in wreath **Obv. Legend:** AUREUS NOVUS. STRALSUND. **Rev:** Crowned imperial eagle, date at end of legend **Rev. Legend:** LEOPOLDUS. D: G: ROM. I: S: A: **Note:** Prev. KM#56.

Date	Mintage	VG	F	VF	XF	Unc
1681 HIH Rare	—	—	—	—	—	—

Note: Künker Auction 141, 6-08, XF realized approximately $11,250.

KM# 138 6 DUCAT

21.0000 g., 0.9860 Gold 0.6657 oz. AGW, 41-42 mm. **Obv:** Shield of city arms in oval baroque frame, mintmaster's initials at left, date at end of legend **Obv. Legend:** MONETA. NOVA. CIVITATIS. STRALSVNDEN. **Rev:** Crowned Imperial eagle, value "32" in orb on breast **Rev. Legend:** LEOPOLDVS. D: G. ROMANORVM. IMPE. SEM. A. **Note:** Prev. KM#40. Struck with Thaler dies, KM#134.

Date	Mintage	VG	F	VF	XF	Unc
1662 HIH Rare	—	—	—	—	—	—

KM# 63 10 DUCAT (Portugalöser)

Gold, 57 mm. **Obv:** City arms in wreath **Obv. Legend:** +DEO. OPTIM. MAXIM: IMPER: ROMANO: FOEDERI. POSTERISQ. **Rev:** 14-line inscription with Roman numeral date **Rev. Inscription:** MEMORIÆ / URBIS. STRAL / SUNDÆ. AO. MDCXX. / VIII. DIE XII. MAII. A. MILI / TÆ CÆSARIA. NO. CINCTÆ / ALIQUOTIES OPPUGNA / TÆ. SED DEI GRATIA ET / OPE INCLYTORUM. RE / GUM. SEPTENTRIO. / NALIUM. DIE XXIV. / IULII OBSIDIONE / LIBERATÆ. / S: P: Q: S: / F: F: **Note:** Ref. B#7. Under siege by Wallenstein. Struck from 2 Thaler dies, KM#57.

Date	Mintage	VG	F	VF	XF	Unc
MDCXXVIII (1628) Rare	—	—	—	—	—	—

KM# 120 10 DUCAT (Portugalöser)

Gold, 42 mm. **Obv:** City arms in oval frame ornamented with angels facing outwards, all in circle, date at end of legend **Obv. Legend:** MON. NOVA. CIVIT. STRALSVNDENSIS. **Rev:** Crowned imperial eagle, 32 in orb on breast **Rev. Legend:** FERDINANDUS. III. D:G. ROMANO. IMP. S. A. **Note:** Ref. B#98b. Struck from Thaler dies, KM#106.

Date	Mintage	VG	F	VF	XF	Unc
1649 CS Rare	—	—	—	—	—	—

KM# 140 10 DUCAT (Portugalöser)

35.0000 g., 0.9860 Gold 1.1095 oz. AGW, 41 mm. **Obv:** Shield of city arms in oval baroque frame. **Obv. Legend:** MONETA. NOVA. CIVITATIS. STRALSVNDEN. **Rev:** Crowned imperial eagle, value "32" in orb on breast **Rev. Legend:** LEOPOLDVS. D: G. ROMANORVM. IMPE. SEM. A. **Note:** Prev. KM#41. Struck from Thaler dies, KM#134.

Date	Mintage	VG	F	VF	XF	Unc
1662 HIH Unique	—	—	—	—	—	—

PATTERNS

Including off metal strikes

KM#	Date	Mintage	Identification	Mkt Val
Pn1	1607	—	Pfennig. Silver. KM#2.	—

STRASSBURG

The capital and principal city of Alsace, Strassburg is located very near the Rhine, 55 miles (92 km) southeast of Saarbrucken. It was an early Celtic settlement, then the Roman town of Argentoratum, from which is derived its name as found on many of Strassburg's coins. The first mention of a bishopric existing in the place dates from the 6th century. The city was both home to the bishops and the site of an imperial mint, the latter which functioned from the 9th to the 11th centuries. The bishops had received the right to coin their own money in 873, but it was not until Strassburg was made a free imperial city in the early 13th century that the townspeople came into conflict with them. When bishop Walter von Hohengeroldseck (1260-1263) tried to reassert authority over the town, the populace rose up and soundly defeated him at the Battle of Oberhausbergen in 1262. The power of the bishopric never recovered, then the city grew in importance and Strassburg city received the mint right in 1334, even though coins were struck in its name locally beginning in 1296. Strassburg's coinage continued until beyond the annexation of the city in 1681, whereas issues by the bishops continued until 1773. The bishopric was finally secularized and annexed by France in 1789.

ARMS

Strassburg - diagonal bar from upper left to lower right, often a fleur-de-lis appears on city coinage as well.

Alsace - similar diagonal bar with 6 crowns, 3 on each side along bar.

Lorraine - similar diagonal bar with 3 small eagles within it.

BISHOPRIC

REGULAR COINAGE

KM# 58 KREUZER

Silver **Ruler:** Franz Egon **Obv:** Arms of Fürstenberg, titles of Franz Egon **Rev:** Arms of Alsace, I.K. above **Note:** Varieties exist.

Date	Mintage	VG	F	VF	XF	Unc
ND(1663-1682)	—	—	—	—	—	—

KM# 94 2 KREUZER

Silver **Ruler:** Leopold Wilhelm **Obv:** Arms of Alsace **Obv. Legend:** MON NOV. ... **Rev:** Inscription in circle, titles of Ferdinand II **Rev. Inscription:** II / KREUTZER **Note:** Varieties exist.

Date	Mintage	VG	F	VF	XF	Unc
ND(1624-32)	—	—	—	—	—	—

KM# 121 3 KREUZER

Silver **Ruler:** Georg **Obv:** 4-fold arms with central shield, titles of Karl, date above arms **Rev:** Crowned imperial eagle, 3 in orb on breast **Note:** Varieties exist.

Date	Mintage	VG	F	VF	XF	Unc
1601	—	—	10.00	25.00	50.00	100
1603	—	—	10.00	25.00	50.00	100
1604	—	—	10.00	25.00	50.00	100
1605	—	—	10.00	25.00	50.00	100
1606	—	—	10.00	25.00	50.00	100
1607	—	—	10.00	25.00	50.00	100

KM# 124 3 KREUZER

Silver **Ruler:** Georg **Obv:** 4-fold arms with central shield, cardinal's hat above arms, no date

Date	Mintage	VG	F	VF	XF	Unc
ND	—	—	—	—	—	—

KM# 138 10 KREUZER

Silver **Ruler:** Franz Egon **Obv:** Bust right, titles of Franz Egon **Rev:** Crowned and mitered 4-fold arms, value (X) above, date below **Note:** Varieties exist.

Date	Mintage	VG	F	VF	XF	Unc
1665	—	250	500	1,200	2,400	—
1666	—	250	500	1,200	2,400	—
1667	—	250	500	1,200	2,400	—

KM# 153.1 12 KREUZER

Silver **Ruler:** Leopold Wilhelm **Obv:** Madonna and child divide date, arms of Alsace below in front, value (XII) at top **Obv. Legend:** MON: NOVA ... **Rev:** Crowned 4-fold arms with central shield

Date	Mintage	VG	F	VF	XF	Unc
1631	—	30.00	65.00	135	275	—

KM# 153.2 12 KREUZER

Silver **Ruler:** Leopold Wilhelm **Obv:** Madonna and child divide date, arms of Alsace below in front, value (XII) at top **Obv. Legend:** MON: NOVA ... **Rev:** Crowned 4-fold arms with central shield **Note:** Klippe.

Date	Mintage	VG	F	VF	XF	Unc
1631	—	30.00	65.00	135	275	—

KM# 156 12 KREUZER

Silver **Ruler:** Franz Egon **Obv:** Bust right, titles of Franz Egon **Rev:** Crowned and mitered 4-fold arms divide date, value (XII) above

Date	Mintage	VG	F	VF	XF	Unc
1666	—	—	—	—	—	—

KM# 194 60 KREUZER

Silver **Ruler:** Wilhelm Egon **Obv:** Bust right, titles of Franz Egon **Rev:** Crowned and mitered 4-fold arms with central shield divide date, crossed sword and crozier behind, titles continued **Note:** Ref. M & M#530.

Date	Mintage	VG	F	VF	XF	Unc
1668	—	—	—	—	—	—

KM# 244 1/3 THALER

Silver **Ruler:** Karl **Obv:** Bust left, date below, titles of Karl **Obv. Legend:** CAROL. D. G. CARD. LOTH. EP. ARGENT. ET. MET **Rev:** 4-fold arms with central shield, cardinal's hat above **Rev. Legend:** ALSAS. LANGRA. ... **Note:** Varieties exist.

Date	Mintage	VG	F	VF	XF	Unc
1602	—	25.00	50.00	100	200	—
1603	—	25.00	50.00	100	200	—
1604	—	25.00	50.00	100	200	—
1605	—	25.00	50.00	100	200	—
1606	—	25.00	50.00	100	200	—
1607	—	25.00	50.00	100	200	—
ND	—	25.00	50.00	100	200	—

KM# 300 THALER
Silver **Ruler:** Karl **Obv:** Crowned imperial eagle **Obv. Legend:** RVDOLP. II. ROM: IMP:... **Rev:** Capped arms **Rev. Legend:** CAROL. D: G: CARD: LOT: EPICS:... **Note:** Dav. #5837.

Date	Mintage	VG	F	VF	XF	Unc
ND Rare	—	—	—	—	—	—

KM# 303 THALER
Silver **Ruler:** Karl **Rev:** Six shields with shield of Lorraine at center **Rev. Legend:** CAR. D: G: CARD. LOT. EPS... **Note:** Dav. #5839.

Date	Mintage	VG	F	VF	XF	Unc
1605 Rare	—	—	—	—	—	—

KM# A303 THALER
Silver **Ruler:** Karl **Rev. Legend:** ... ARGEN • E • ME •... **Note:** Dav. #5839A.

Date	Mintage	VG	F	VF	XF	Unc
1605 Rare	—	—	—	—	—	—

OBSIDIONAL (SIEGE) COINAGE

KM# 185 40 KREUZER
Silver **Ruler:** Leopold Wilhelm **Obv:** Bust right, titles of Leopold Wilhelm **Rev:** Crowned and mitered 4-fold arms with central shield

Date	Mintage	VG	F	VF	XF	Unc
ND(1632-62)	—	—	—	—	—	—

TRADE COINAGE

KM# 415 1/2 DUCAT
1.7500 g., 0.9860 Gold 0.0555 oz. AGW **Ruler:** Franz Egon **Obv:** Bust right, titles of Franz Egon **Rev:** Crowned, mitered four-fold arms with central shield divide date, titles continued **Note:** FR #250.

Date	Mintage	VG	F	VF	XF	Unc
1666	—	—	—	—	—	—

KM# 418 DUCAT
3.5000 g., 0.9860 Gold 0.1109 oz. AGW **Ruler:** Leopold Wilhelm **Obv:** Madonna and child divide date, arms of Alsace below in front **Rev:** Crowned four-fold arms with central chield **Note:** FR #251.

Date	Mintage	VG	F	VF	XF	Unc
ND(1626-32)	—	600	1,200	2,250	3,750	—

KM# 421 DUCAT
3.5000 g., 0.9860 Gold 0.1109 oz. AGW **Ruler:** Leopold Wilhelm **Obv:** Madonna and child in inner circle **Rev:** Arms, with lion supporters **Note:** Fr. #238.

Date	Mintage	VG	F	VF	XF	Unc
1632	—	350	800	1,500	3,000	—

KM# 437 4 DUCAT
14.0000 g., 0.9860 Gold 0.4438 oz. AGW **Ruler:** Leopold Wilhelm **Note:** FR.#236.

Date	Mintage	VG	F	VF	XF	Unc
ND Rare	—	—	—	—	—	—

CITY

REGULAR COINAGE

KM# 36 PFENNIG
Silver **Obv:** Fleur-de-lis 2-stem base like an H flanked by 2 dots **Note:** Uniface.

Date	Mintage	VG	F	VF	XF	Unc
1601	—	8.00	15.00	35.00	70.00	—

KM# 212 1/2 GROSCHEN (Semissis)
Silver, 23 mm. **Obv:** Similar to MB#209.1 but small shield of city arms in center of cross on reverse

Date	Mintage	VG	F	VF	XF	Unc
ND(1620-96)	—	45.00	90.00	150	250	475

MB# 218 GROSCHEN
Silver **Obv:** Fleur-de-lis in ornamented quatrelobe **Obv. Legend:** ASSIS. REIP. ARGENTORATENS. **Rev:** 2 marginal legends, cross in center divides inner legend **Rev. Legend:** Inner leg: ETIN - TER - R★ - PAX; Outer leg: GLORIA • **Note:** Ref. M & M#591.

Date	Mintage	VG	F	VF	XF	Unc
ND	—	—	—	—	—	—

KM# 52 KREUZER
Silver **Obv:** Similar to KM#46.1 but lis on each side in quatrelobe

Date	Mintage	VG	F	VF	XF	Unc
ND	—	10.00	20.00	40.00	85.00	—

KM# 55 KREUZER
Silver **Rev:** Similar to KM#46.1 but has cross with fleur-de-lis arms in circle

Date	Mintage	VG	F	VF	XF	Unc
ND	—	10.00	20.00	40.00	85.00	—

KM# 61 KREUZER
Silver **Obv:** City arms in ornate shield, I.K. above **Obv. Legend:** MON: NOV • **Rev:** Fleur-de-lis in circle **Rev. Legend:** GLORIA • IN • EXCELS • DEO •

Date	Mintage	VG	F	VF	XF	Unc
ND	—	10.00	20.00	40.00	85.00	—

KM# 147 12 KREUZER
Silver **Obv:** Ornate city arms, XII above **Obv. Legend:** MON • NOV • REIP ... **Rev:** Fleur-de-lis in circle **Rev. Legend:** GLORIA ...

Date	Mintage	VG	F	VF	XF	Unc
ND	—	30.00	60.00	120	240	—

KM# 150 12 KREUZER
Silver **Obv:** Fleur-de-lis in circle **Obv. Legend:** ASSIS • REIP • ARGENT • DVPLEX **Rev:** Cross within circle **Rev. Legend:** GLORIA * IN * EXCELSIS * DEO *

Date	Mintage	VG	F	VF	XF	Unc
ND(1615-23)	—	30.00	65.00	135	275	—

KM# 159 12 KREUZER
Silver **Obv:** Ornate city arms, XII above **Obv. Legend:** MON. NOV. CIVITAT ... **Rev:** Fleur-de-lis in circle

Date	Mintage	VG	F	VF	XF	Unc
ND	—	30.00	60.00	120	240	—

KM# 172 24 KREUZER
Silver **Obv:** Ornate city arms, value (XXIII) above arms **Obv. Legend:** MON • NOV • REIP • ... **Rev:** Fleur-de-lis in circle **Rev. Legend:** GLORIA ...

Date	Mintage	VG	F	VF	XF	Unc
ND	—	35.00	75.00	150	300	—

MB# 168 24 KREUZER
Silver **Obv:** City arms **Obv. Legend:** MON. NOV. REIPVB ... **Rev:** Fleur-de-lis in circle **Rev. Legend:** GLORIA ...

Date	Mintage	VG	F	VF	XF	Unc
ND	—	75.00	150	300	600	—

KM# 178 30 KREUZER
Silver **Obv:** City arms, XXX.K. above **Obv. Legend:** MONETA • NOVA • • **Rev:** Large fleur-de-lis **Rev. Legend:** GLORIA •

Date	Mintage	VG	F	VF	XF	Unc
ND	—	300	600	1,200	—	—

KM# 197 60 KREUZER
Silver **Obv:** City arms, LX.K. above arms **Obv. Legend:** MONETA • NOVA • • **Rev:** Large fleur-de-lis **Rev. Legend:** GLORIA

Date	Mintage	VG	F	VF	XF	Unc
ND	—	50.00	100	200	425	—

KM# 235 1/4 THALER
Silver **Obv:** Ornate city arms with 2 lion supporters **Obv. Legend:** INSIG. REIP. ARGENTORATENSIS **Rev:** Large fleur-de-lis **Rev. Legend:** GLORIA. IN. ALTISSIMIS. DEO.

Date	Mintage	VG	F	VF	XF	Unc
ND	—	—	—	—	—	—

KM# 306 THALER
Silver **Obv:** Legend around lions supporting lis above shield **Obv. Legend:** NVMMVS * REIP *... **Rev:** Legend around ornate fleur-de-lis **Rev. Legend:** * SOLIVS * VIRTVTIS **Note:** Dav.#5842.

Date	Mintage	VG	F	VF	XF	Unc
ND	—	100	200	400	700	—

KM# A306 THALER
28.3000 g., Silver **Note:** Klippe. Struck with 1/2 Thaler dies. Dav.#5842A.

Date	Mintage	VG	F	VF	XF	Unc
ND Rare	—	—	—	—	—	—

KM# 309 THALER
Silver **Obv:** Date divided by lis above shield **Note:** Dav.#5844.

Date	Mintage	VG	F	VF	XF	Unc
1617 Rare	—	—	—	—	—	—

KM# 312.1 THALER
Silver **Subject:** Centennial of Reformation **Rev:** With ornamentation above "PRO" **Note:** Dav.#5846.

Date	Mintage	VG	F	VF	XF	Unc
1617	—	275	575	1,150	2,250	3,500

KM# 312.2 THALER
Silver **Rev:** Without ornamentation above "PRO" **Note:** Dav.#5846A.

Date	Mintage	VG	F	VF	XF	Unc
1617	—	750	1,250	2,500	3,750	—

KM# 312.3 THALER
Silver **Note:** Klippe. Dav.#5846B.

Date	Mintage	VG	F	VF	XF	Unc
1617	—	375	850	1,350	2,750	—

KM# 315 THALER
Silver **Subject:** Peace of Nymegen **Obv:** Date in chronogram **Rev:** Noah's Ark within legend **Note:** Dav.#5847.

Date	Mintage	VG	F	VF	XF	Unc
ND(1679)	—	325	675	1,350	2,250	3,750

KM# 345 2 THALER
Silver **Obv:** Legend around lions supporting lis above shield **Rev:** Legend around ornate fleur-de-lis **Note:** Dav.#A5841. Similar to 1 Thaler, KM#306.

Date	Mintage	VG	F	VF	XF	Unc
ND Rare	—	—	—	—	—	—

KM# 348 2 THALER
Silver **Subject:** Centennial of Reformation **Note:** Dav.#A5845.

Date	Mintage	VG	F	VF	XF	Unc
1617	—	1,150	2,250	3,750	6,500	—

KM# 354 3 THALER
Silver **Obv:** Legend around lions supporting lis above shield **Rev:** Legend around ornate fleur-de-lis **Note:** Dav.#B5841. Similar to 1 Thaler KM#306.

Date	Mintage	VG	F	VF	XF	Unc
ND Rare	—	—	—	—	—	—

KM# 357 3 THALER
81.8600 g., Silver **Subject:** Centennial of Reformation **Obv:** Shield of arms within inner circle, legends around **Rev:** 10-line inscription **Rev. Inscription:** PRO / RELIGIONIS • / CENTVM • ANTE • / ANNOS • DIVINITVS / RESTITVTÆ • MEMO / RIA • NOVIQVE • SECV • / LI • FELICI • AVSPIGIO / S • P • Q • ARGENTOR • / F • F • A° MDCXVII / CAL • NOVEMB **Note:** Dav.#B5845.

Date	Mintage	VG	F	VF	XF	Unc
1617	—	3,500	6,500	10,000	—	—

KM# 363 5 THALER
Silver **Obv:** Legend around lions supporting lis aabove shield **Rev:** Legend around ornate fleur-de-lis **Note:** Dav.#5841. Similar to 1 Thaler KM#306.

Date	Mintage	VG	F	VF	XF	Unc
ND Rare	—	—	—	—	—	—

KM# 396 6 THALER
Silver **Subject:** Centennial of Reformation **Rev:** With ornamentation above "PRO" **Note:** Dav.#5845. Similar to 1 Thaler KM#312.1.

Date	Mintage	VG	F	VF	XF	Unc
1617 Rare	—	—	—	—	—	—

TRADE COINAGE

KM# 424 DUCAT
Gold **Obv:** Helmeted arms with lion supporters **Rev:** 4-line inscription **Rev. Inscription:** DVCATVS / REIPVBLCÆ ... **Note:** FR#237.

Date	Mintage	VG	F	VF	XF	Unc
ND(1650)	—	270	500	800	1,650	—

KM# 424.1 DUCAT
Gold **Rev:** 4-line inscription in square **Note:** FR#A237.

Date	Mintage	VG	F	VF	XF	Unc
ND(1650)	—	270	500	800	1,650	—

KM# 424.2 DUCAT
Gold **Rev:** Inscription within cartouche **Note:** FR#B237.

Date	Mintage	VG	F	VF	XF	Unc
ND(1650)	—	270	500	800	1,650	—

KM# 424.3 DUCAT
Gold **Obv:** Oval arms **Rev:** 4-line inscription in open branches **Note:** FR#C237.

Date	Mintage	VG	F	VF	XF	Unc
ND(1650)	—	270	500	800	1,650	—

KM# 424.4 DUCAT

Gold **Obv:** Oval arms **Obv. Legend:** GLORIA IN EXCELSIS DEO **Rev:** 4-line inscription within palm branches **Rev. Inscription:** DVCATVS / ... **Note:** FR#D237.

Date	Mintage	VG	F	VF	XF	Unc
ND(1650)	—	270	500	800	1,650	—

KM# 427 2 DUCAT

7.0000 g., 0.9860 Gold 0.2219 oz. AGW **Obv:** Helmeted arms with lion supporters **Rev. Inscription:** DVCATVS / REIPVBLCÆ **Note:** FR#252. Similar to 1 Ducat, KM#424.

Date	Mintage	VG	F	VF	XF	Unc
ND(1650) Rare	—	—	—	—	—	—

KM# 430 3 DUCAT

10.5000 g., 0.9860 Gold 0.3328 oz. AGW **Obv:** Helmeted arms with lion supporters **Rev. Inscription:** DVCATVS / CIVITATIS... **Note:** FR#253.

Date	Mintage	VG	F	VF	XF	Unc
ND(1650) Rare	—	—	—	—	—	—

KM# 433 3 DUCAT

10.5000 g., 0.9860 Gold 0.3328 oz. AGW **Obv:** Oval arms **Rev:** 4-line inscription **Note:** FR#254.

Date	Mintage	VG	F	VF	XF	Unc
ND(1681) Rare	—	—	—	—	—	—

KM# 440 4 DUCAT

14.0000 g., 0.9860 Gold 0.4438 oz. AGW **Obv:** Helmeted arms with lion supporters **Rev. Inscription:** DVCATVS / REIPVBLCÆ **Note:** FR#255. Similar to 1 Ducat, KM#424.

Date	Mintage	VG	F	VF	XF	Unc
ND(1650) Rare	—	—	—	—	—	—

KM# 443 6 DUCAT

21.0000 g., 0.9860 Gold 0.6657 oz. AGW **Obv:** Helmeted arms with lion supporters **Rev. Inscription:** DVCATVS / REIPVBLCÆ **Note:** FR#256. Similar to 1 Ducat, KM#424.

Date	Mintage	VG	F	VF	XF	Unc
ND(1650) Rare	—	—	—	—	—	—

STRIEGAU

PROVINCIAL TOWN

A town in Silesia, northwest of Schweidnitz, Striegau issued a few coins during the Kipper Period of the Thirty Years' War.

MINT OFFICIAL'S INITIALS

DA = Unknown, ca. 1622.

REFERENCES:

F/S = Ferdinand Friedensburg and Hans Seger, ***Schlesiens Münzen und Medaillen der Neueren Zeit,*** Breslau, 1901 (reprint Frankfurt/Main, 1976).

S = Hugo Frhr. Von Saurma-Jeltsch, ***Die Saurmasche Münzsammlung Deutscher, Schweizerischer und Polnischer Gepräge von etwa dem Beginn der Groschenzeit bis zur Kipperperiode***, Berlin, 1892.

S/Sch = Hugo Frhr. Von Saurma-Jeltsch, ***Schlesische Münzen und Medaillen***, Breslau, 1883.

PROVINCIAL TOWN

STANDARD COINAGE

KM# 3 3 KREUZER (Groschen)

Silver **Obv:** Laureate bust right in circle **Obv. Legend:** FER. II. R. IM. S. A. G. H. BO. RE. D. SIL. **Rev:** Silesian eagle, '3' in oval on breast, date at end of legend **Rev. Legend:** MONE. NOVA. ARBE. STRIG. **Note:** Ref. F/S#3626. Kipper coinage.

Date	Mintage	VG	F	VF	XF	Unc
16ZZ DA	—	90.00	180	360	—	—

KM# 4 3 KREUZER (Groschen)

Silver **Obv:** Silesian eagle in circle **Obv. Legend:** FER. II. RO. IM. S. AV. HV. BO. RE. DV. SI. **Rev:** Shield of city arms in circle, value '3' below, date at end of legend **Rev. Legend:** MO. NO. AR. CI - VIT. STRI. **Note:** Ref. F/S#3627-28. Kipper coinage. Varieties exist.

Date	Mintage	VG	F	VF	XF	Unc
16ZZ DA	—	90.00	180	360	—	—

KM# 5 3 KREUZER (Groschen)

Silver **Obv:** Silesian eagle in circle **Obv. Legend:** FER. II. RO. IM. S. AV. HV. BO. RE. DV. SI. **Rev:** Intertwined 'ST' monogram in circle, value '3' in small shield below, date at end of legend **Rev. Legend:** MONE. NOV. A - RGENT. **Note:** Ref. F/S#3629. Kipper coinage.

Date	Mintage	VG	F	VF	XF	Unc
16ZZ DA	—	90.00	180	360	—	—

KM# 7 12 KREUZER (Schreckenberger)

Silver **Obv:** Silesian eagle in circle, value '12' below **Obv. Legend:** FER. II. R. IM. S. AUG. - HU. BO. REX. DU. SI. **Rev:** Shield of city arms in circle, date at end of legend **Rev. Legend:** MO. NO. ARGENT. CIUITA. STRIG. **Note:** Ref. F/S#3625. Kipper coinage.

Date	Mintage	VG	F	VF	XF	Unc
1622 DA	—	—	—	—	—	—

KM# 9 24 KREUZER (Vierundzwanziger)

Silver **Obv:** Laureate bust right in circle, value 'Z4' below **Obv. Legend:** FER(DI). II. R. IMP. S. AV - G. H. B(O). REX. DV(X). S(IL). **Rev:** Silesian eagle in circle, date at end of legend **Rev. Legend:** MONETA. NOVA. ARGENT(EA). ST(RI). **Note:** Ref. F/S#3624. Kipper coinage. Varieties exist.

Date	Mintage	VG	F	VF	XF	Unc
16ZZ DA	—	—	—	—	—	—

SULZ

The counts of this Swabian territory became landgraves of Klettgau in Baden around 1425. They apparently struck no coins until the 17th century when Alwig VII and his brother Karl Ludwig had a small coinage. Maria Anna, daughter and heiress of the last of the line, Johann Ludwig (1648-87), married Ferdinand Wilhelm of Schwarzenberg and the lands passed to that house.

RULERS

Karl Ludwig I, 1572-1617
Rudolf VII, 1572-1617
Alwig VII, 1617-1632
Karl Ludwig II Ernst, 1617-1648
Ulrich, 1648-50
Johann Ludwig, 1648-87
Maria Anna, 1687-96

MINT OFFICIALS' INITIALS

Initial	Date	Name
PM	1612-21	possibly Johann Philipp May in Zweibrücken
MS	1622-55	Matthäus Schaffer der Jüngere, die-cutter in Nuremberg
	Ca. 1675	Johann Georg Gilly (Gyllin), mintmaster in Tiengen

The mint for Sulz usually operated at Tiengen.

ARMS

Old Sulz - 3 points (or pointed mountains)
Klettgau – 3 sheaves
Brandis – knotty pine limb, sometimes with flame at one end
Abbey of Rheinau – curved fish

REFERENCE

K = Ulrich Klein, **Münzen der Grafen von Sulz**, Freiburg im Bresgau, 1990

COUNTSHIP

REGULAR COINAGE

KM# 48 3 HELLER

Silver **Ruler:** Karl Ludwig Ernst **Obv:** 3 small arms of Klettgau, old Sulz and Brandis, 1 above 2 in trefoil **Note:** Uniface. Varieties exist.

Date	Mintage	VG	F	VF	XF	Unc
ND(ca1635)	—	—	—	—	—	—

KM# 22 4 HELLER (1/2 Kreuzer)

Copper **Ruler:** Karl Ludwig Ernst **Obv:** Crowned arms of old Sulz, titles of Karl Ludwig Ernst around **Rev:** Value IIII in laurel wreath **Note:** Kipper coinage. Weight varies: .57-.87 g. Known in both 14 mm and 17 mm sizes.

Date	Mintage	VG	F	VF	XF	Unc
ND(ca1622)	—	60.00	90.00	170	—	—

KM# 36 PFENNIG

Silver **Ruler:** Alwig VII **Obv:** A (for Alwig) above curved fish, all in shield, date above **Note:** Uniface.

Date	Mintage	VG	F	VF	XF	Unc
(1)623	—	400	800	1,600	—	—

KM# 16 KREUZER

Silver **Ruler:** Alwig VII **Obv:** Rose, curved fish below **Obv. Legend:** ALB: CO: IN SVL. IN. CL. (or variant) **Rev:** Bust of saint to right, date when present at end of legend **Rev. Legend:** S. FINDANVS **Note:** Varieties exist.

Date	Mintage	VG	F	VF	XF	Unc
ND(ca1621/22)	—	400	800	1,600	—	—
(1)622	—	400	800	1,600	—	—
1622	—	400	800	1,600	—	—

KM# 23 KREUZER

Silver **Ruler:** Alwig VII **Obv:** Arms of Rheinau (fish), titles of Alwig around **Rev:** Bust of saint, date in legend **Rev. Legend:** S. FINDANVS **Note:** Varieties exist.

Date	Mintage	VG	F	VF	XF	Unc
(1)622	—	400	800	1,600	—	—

KM# 37 KREUZER

Silver **Ruler:** Alwig VII **Obv:** 4-fold arms superimposed on double-cross, fish below in margin **Rev:** Crowned imperial eagle, titles of Ferdinand II and date in margin **Note:** Varieties exist.

Date	Mintage	VG	F	VF	XF	Unc
1623	—	350	700	1,350	—	—

KM# 38 KREUZER

Silver **Ruler:** Alwig VII **Obv:** 4-fold arms superimposed on double-cross **Rev:** Crowned imperial eagle, titles of Ferdinand II and date in margin

Date	Mintage	VG	F	VF	XF	Unc
1623	—	350	700	1,350	—	—

KM# 39 KREUZER

Silver **Ruler:** Alwig VII **Obv:** 4-fold arms, titles of Alwig and date in margin **Rev:** Double-cross, value I in center, titles of Ferdinand II around

Date	Mintage	VG	F	VF	XF	Unc
1623	—	350	700	1,350	—	—

KM# 40 2 KREUZER (Halbbatzen)

Silver **Ruler:** Alwig VII **Obv:** 4-fold arms with central shield, titles of Alwig around **Rev:** Imperial orb with 2, titles of Ferdinand II, date in margin

Date	Mintage	VG	F	VF	XF	Unc
1623	—	—	—	—	—	—

KM# 41 2 KREUZER (Halbbatzen)

Silver **Ruler:** Alwig VII **Obv:** 4-fold arms, fish in margin **Rev:** Imperial orb with 2, titles of Ferdinand II, date in margin

Date	Mintage	VG	F	VF	XF	Unc
1623	—	—	—	—	—	—

KM# 42 2 KREUZER (Halbbatzen)

Silver **Ruler:** Alwig VII **Obv:** 4-fold arms with central shield, titles of Alwig around **Rev:** Imperial eagle, titles of ferdinand II, date in margin

Date	Mintage	VG	F	VF	XF	Unc
1623	—	—	—	—	—	—

KM# 43 2 KREUZER (Halbbatzen)

Silver **Ruler:** Alwig VII **Obv:** 4-fold arms **Rev:** Imperial orb with Z, cross divides date, titles of Ferdinand II around

Date	Mintage	VG	F	VF	XF	Unc
1623	—	—	—	—	—	—

KM# 4 3 KREUZER (Groschen)

Silver **Ruler:** Karl Ludwig Ernst **Obv:** 3 small shields of arms, 2 abnove 1, large crown above, titles of Karl Ludwig Ernst around **Rev:** Crowned imperial eagle, 3 in orb on breast, titles of Ferdinand II around **Note:** Weight varies: .77-1.2 g. Varieties exist.

Date	Mintage	VG	F	VF	XF	Unc
ND(ca1620)	—	300	600	1,200	—	—

KM# 5 3 KREUZER (Groschen)

Silver **Ruler:** Karl Ludwig Ernst **Obv:** Crowned arms of old Sulz, titles of Karl Ludwig Ernst around **Rev:** Crowned imperial eagle, 3 in orb on breast, titles of Ferdinand II around **Note:** Wieight varies: .77-1.2 g.

Date	Mintage	VG	F	VF	XF	Unc
ND(ca1620)	—	300	600	1,200	—	—

KM# 3 4 KREUZER (Batzen)

Silver **Ruler:** Alwig VII **Obv:** Crowned arms of old Sulz, value 4 K above **Obv. Legend:** ALVICVS... **Rev:** Crowned imperial eagle, orb on breast, titles of Ferdinand II

Date	Mintage	VG	F	VF	XF	Unc
ND(ca1619-32)	—	—	—	—	—	—

KM# 50 4 KREUZER (Batzen)

Silver **Ruler:** Karl Ludwig Ernst **Obv:** Crowned imperial eagle, titles of Karl Ludwig Ernst around **Rev:** Large cross **Rev. Legend:** IN. OMNEM TERR. EXIV SONg EOR.

Date	Mintage	VG	F	VF	XF	Unc
ND(ca1635)	—	—	—	—	—	—

KM# 49 4 KREUZER (Batzen)

Silver **Ruler:** Karl Ludwig Ernst **Obv:** Crowned arms of old Sulz, titles of Karl Ludwig Ernst around **Rev:** Crowned imperial eagle, titles of Ferdinand II around **Note:** Varieties exist.

Date	Mintage	VG	F	VF	XF	Unc
ND(ca1635)	—	—	—	—	—	—

KM# 6 6 KREUZER

Silver **Ruler:** Karl Ludwig Ernst **Obv:** Crowned 3-fold arms, titles of Karl Ludwig Ernst and value 6 K in margin **Rev:** Imperial eagle, titles of Ferdinand II around

Date	Mintage	VG	F	VF	XF	Unc
ND(ca1620)	—	—	—	—	—	—

KM# 44 10 KREUZER

Silver **Ruler:** Alwig VII **Obv:** Bust right, titles of Alwig and date around **Rev:** Crowned imperial eagle, value 10 on breast, titles of Ferdinand II around **Note:** Kipper coinage.

Date	Mintage	VG	F	VF	XF	Unc
1623	—	—	—	—	—	—

KM# 7 12 KREUZER (Dreibätzner)

Silver **Ruler:** Alwig VII **Obv:** 4-fold arms of old Sulz and Brandis **Obv. Legend:** ALVICVS... **Rev:** Imperial eagle, 12 on breast, titles of Ferdinand II in margin **Note:** Kipper coinage.

Date	Mintage	VG	F	VF	XF	Unc
ND(ca1620/21)	—	—	—	—	—	—

KM# 8 12 KREUZER (Dreibätzner)

Silver **Ruler:** Alwig VII **Obv:** Armored 1/2-length bust of count holding staff in right hand **Rev:** Imperial eagle, 12 on breast, titles of Ferdinand II in margin **Note:** Kipper coinage.

Date	Mintage	VG	F	VF	XF	Unc
ND(ca1620/21)	—	—	—	—	—	—

KM# 9 12 KREUZER (Dreibätzner)

Silver **Ruler:** Alwig VII **Obv:** Armored 1/2-length bust of count holding staff in left hand **Rev:** Imperial eagle, 12 on breast, titles of Ferdinand II in margin **Note:** Kipper coinage.

Date	Mintage	VG	F	VF	XF	Unc
ND(ca1620/21)	—	—	—	—	—	—

KM# 17 12 KREUZER (Dreibätzner)

Silver **Ruler:** Karl Ludwig Ernst **Obv:** Crowned 4-fold arms, titles of Karl Ludwig Ernst around **Rev:** Crowned imperial eagle, 12 in circle on breast, titles of Ferdinand II in margin **Note:** Kipper coinage. Varieties exist.

Date	Mintage	VG	F	VF	XF	Unc
ND(ca1621/22)	—	—	—	—	—	—

KM# 24 12 KREUZER (Dreibätzner)

Silver **Ruler:** Alwig VII **Obv:** Armored 1/2-length bust of count holding staff in left hand, date in margin **Rev:** Imperial eagle, 12 on breast, titles of Ferdinand II in margin **Note:** Kipper coinage.

Date	Mintage	VG	F	VF	XF	Unc
1622	—	—	—	—	—	—

KM# 26 15 KREUZER (1/4 Gulden)

Silver **Ruler:** Alwig VII **Obv:** Bust right holding staff **Rev:** Imperial eagle, value 15 in margin at top, titles of Ferdinand II and date around **Note:** Kipper coinage. Weight varies: 1.12-1.55 g.

Date	Mintage	VG	F	VF	XF	Unc
(1)622	—	250	450	900	—	—

KM# 25 15 KREUZER (1/4 Gulden)

Silver **Ruler:** Alwig VII **Obv:** Armored bust to right, fish below **Rev:** Imperial eagle, 15 on breeast, titles of Ferdinand II and date in margin **Note:** Kipper coinage. Weight varies: 1.12-1.55 g. Varieties exist.

Date	Mintage	VG	F	VF	XF	Unc
(1)622	—	250	450	900	—	—

KM# 55 15 KREUZER (1/4 Gulden)

Silver **Ruler:** Johann Ludwig **Obv:** Bust right, titles of Johann Ludwig Ernst around **Rev:** Crowned 4-fold arms with central shield between palm branches, value (15) divides date below **Rev. Legend:** LABOR OMNIA VINCIT. **Note:** Weight varies: 5.52-5.76 g. Varieties exist.

Date	Mintage	VG	F	VF	XF	Unc
1675	—	135	275	575	—	—

KM# 18 24 KREUZER (Sechsbätzner)

5.6500 g., Silver **Ruler:** Karl Ludwig Ernst **Obv:** Crowned 4-fold arms, titles of Karl Ludwig Ernst around **Rev:** Crowned imperial eagle, orb on breast, titles of Ferdinand II in margin **Note:** Kipper coinage.

Date	Mintage	VG	F	VF	XF	Unc
ND(ca1621/22)	—	—	—	—	—	—

KM# 19 48 KREUZER

10.2500 g., Silver **Ruler:** Karl Ludwig Ernst **Obv:** Crowned 4-fold arms, titles of Karl Ludwig Ernst around **Rev:** Crowned imperial eagle, value 48 in orb on breast, titles of Ferdinand II in margin **Note:** Kipper coinage.

Date	Mintage	VG	F	VF	XF	Unc
ND(ca1621/22)	—	—	—	—	—	—

KM# 10 60 KREUZER (Gulden)

Silver **Ruler:** Alwig VII **Obv:** Armored bust to right, holding staff, curved fish below, titles of Alwig around **Rev:** Imperial eagle, orb with 60 on breast, titles of Ferdinand II in margin

Date	Mintage	VG	F	VF	XF	Unc
ND(1620/21)	—	—	—	—	—	—

KM# 27 1/30 THALER

Copper **Ruler:** Alwig VII **Obv:** Bust right holding staff, titles of Alwig around **Rev:** Imperial eagle, value (30) at top, titles of Ferdinand II and date in margin **Note:** Kipper coinage.

Date	Mintage	VG	F	VF	XF	Unc
16ZZ	—	—	—	—	—	—

KM# 29 1/24 THALER (Groschen)

Billon **Ruler:** Alwig VII **Obv:** Bust right **Rev:** Imperial eagle, value 24 in margin at top, titles of Ferdinand II and date in margin **Note:** Kipper coinage. Weight varies: .96-1.0 g.

Date	Mintage	VG	F	VF	XF	Unc
(1)622	—	1,100	2,200	4,200	—	—

KM# 28 1/24 THALER (Groschen)

Billon **Ruler:** Alwig VII **Obv:** Bust right, holding staff **Rev:** Imperial eagle, value 24 in margin at top, titles of Ferdinand II and date in margin **Note:** Kipper coinage. Weight varies: .96-1.0 g. Varieties exist.

Date	Mintage	VG	F	VF	XF	Unc
1622	—	—	—	—	—	—

KM# 30 1/24 THALER (Groschen)

Billon **Ruler:** Alwig VII **Obv:** Bust right, holding staff **Rev:** Imperial eagle, value 24 on eagle's breast, titles of Ferdinand II and date in margin **Note:** Kipper coinage. Weight varies: .96-1.0 g. Varieties exist.

Date	Mintage	VG	F	VF	XF	Unc
1622	—	—	—	—	—	—

KM# 53 2/3 THALER (Gulden)

Silver **Ruler:** Johann Ludwig **Obv:** Bust right, titles of Johann Ludwig Ernst around **Rev:** Crowned 40-fold arms with central shield between palm branches, value 2/3 below **Rev. Legend:** LABOR OMNIA VINCIT. **Note:** Dav#1015.

Date	Mintage	VG	F	VF	XF	Unc
ND(ca1670)	—	—	—	—	—	—

KM# 56 2/3 THALER (Gulden)

Silver **Ruler:** Johann Ludwig **Obv:** Large bust right, titles of Johann Ludwig Ernst around **Rev:** Crowned 4-fold arms with central shield between palm branches, value 2/3 divides date below **Rev. Legend:** LABOR OMNIA VINCIT. **Note:** Dav#1016. Varieties exist.

Date	Mintage	VG	F	VF	XF	Unc
1675	—	350	750	1,500	—	—

KM# 12 THALER

Silver **Obv:** Bust **Rev:** Crowned double eagle with orb, Q-M **Note:** Dav. #7792.

Date	Mintage	VG	F	VF	XF	Unc
ND(ca1620) Rare	—	—	—	—	—	—

KM# 21 THALER

Silver **Obv:** Crowned arms dividing date **Obv. Legend:** CAROL... **Note:** Dav. #7797

Date	Mintage	VG	F	VF	XF	Unc
1621 Rare	—	—	—	—	—	—

KM# 13 THALER

Silver **Obv:** Bust right **Rev:** Crowned double eagle with orb, M-S **Note:** Dav. #7793.

Date	Mintage	VG	F	VF	XF	Unc
ND Rare	—	—	—	—	—	—

KM# 32 THALER

Silver **Obv:** Crowned bust of Saint right, date in outer legend **Obv. Legend:** Inner: SANCTVS-FINDANVS **Note:** Dav. #7794.

Date	Mintage	VG	F	VF	XF	Unc
1622 Rare	—	—	—	—	—	—

KM# 46 THALER

Silver **Obv:** Bust right **Rev:** Crowned double eagle, date in legend at top **Note:** Dav. #7795.

Date	Mintage	VG	F	VF	XF	Unc
1623 Rare	—	—	—	—	—	—

KM# 14 THALER

Silver **Obv:** Crowned arms **Obv. Legend:** CAROLVS LVD... **Note:** Dav. #7796.

Date	Mintage	VG	F	VF	XF	Unc
ND Rare	—	—	—	—	—	—

TRADE COINAGE

KM# 34 GOLDGULDEN

3.5000 g., 0.9860 Gold 0.1109 oz. AGW **Obv:** Crowned 4-fold arms in ornamented shield, titles of Karl Ludwig Ernst and date in margin **Obv. Legend:** FERDINAND: II: D: G:... **Rev:** Crowned ornate arms **Rev. Legend:** CAR: LV: E: CO: IN: SVLZ: **Note:** Prev. KM#20.

Date	Mintage	VG	F	VF	XF	Unc
1622 Rare	—	—	—	—	—	—

Note: Note: Leu Numismatik auction 5-98, XF realized $37,500.

SWABIAN CIRCLE

An area in Swabia maintained as an imperial administrative district from 1500 to 1806. Constance and Württemberg were the usual administrators over this occasional coin issuer.

IMPERIAL CIRCLE

REGULAR COINAGE

KM# 3 THALER

Silver **Obv:** Oval lion arms within branches, date divided below **Rev:** 2 Shields; one with crown and one with mitre **Rev. Legend:** ...LUDOV: DVX WURT: ET... RUDOL: EPISC:... **Note:** Dav. #7798. Similar to Dav. #7799 with different legend.

Date	Mintage	VG	F	VF	XF	Unc
1694	—	850	1,650	2,750	—	—

KM# 1 THALER

Silver **Obv:** Arms in frame and sprays, date divided below **Rev:** 2 Shields; one with crown and one with mitre **Note:** Dav. #7799.

Date	Mintage	VG	F	VF	XF	Unc
1694	—	750	1,350	2,250	3,500	5,500

KM# 2 THALER

Silver **Obv:** Smaller shield **Rev:** Smaller shields **Note:** Dav. #7800.

Date	Mintage	VG	F	VF	XF	Unc
1694	—	800	1,450	2,500	4,250	—

TELGTE

A town in Westphalia 6.5 miles (11km) east-northeast of Münster. A few local issues were reportedly struck in the early period of the Thirty Years' War, but all are very rare.

PROVINCIAL TOWN

REGULAR COINAGE

KM# 1 3 PFENNIG

Copper **Obv:** Tree with 5 branches in circle **Obv. Legend:**

STADT - TELGTE (or TELGET) **Rev:** Value III, date above, all in circle **Note:** Weingärtner 249.

Date	Mintage	VG	F	VF	XF	Unc
1620	—	275	550	1,100	—	—

KM# 2 4 PFENNIG

Copper **Obv:** Tree with 5 branches in circle **Obv. Legend:** STADT - TELGTE (or TELGET) **Rev:** Date; II.II in double circle

Date	Mintage	VG	F	VF	XF	Unc
1620 Rare	—	—	—	—	—	—

TESCHEN

The Duchy of Teschen constituted part of Upper Silesia, the southern region of Silesia proper. The ruling family of medieval Silesia, as vassals of the kings of Bohemia, underwent several divisions. The branch from which the dukes of Teschen descended was established in 1288. The last duke died in 1625 and was succeeded for a time by his sister before Teschen passed to Bohemia and thus, into the hands of the Habsburgs.

RULERS

Kasimir IV, 1468-1524
Wenzel III Adam, 1524-1579
Friedrich Kasimir zu Freistadt, 1563-1571
Adam Wenzel, 1579-1617
Friedrich Wilhelm, 1617-1625
Ellisabeth Lucretia, 1625-1653
Ferdinand IV von Habsburg, King of the Romans 1653-1654

MINT OFFICIALS' INITIALS

Initial	Date	Name
(a) =	1559	Hans Endres, mintmaster
(b) =	ca. 1591-92	Unknown
or		
(c) =	1596-97	Caspar Rietker, mintmaster
(d) =	1603-11	Valentin Janus, mintmaster
(e) =	1608-10	Hans Tuchmann der Ältere, mintmaster
or		
DR	1611-14	Dietrich Rund, mintmaster first time
CC	1611-12	Christoph Cantor, mintmaster
HL	1620-49	Hans Lorenz, minmaster
DR	1621-22	Daniel Raschke, mint contractor at Skotschau
S	1622	Skotschau mint
DR	1642-47	Dietrich Rund, mintmaster second time
LB	1648-49	Unknown warden
GG	1649-55	Gabriel Görloff, mintmaster

ARMS

Silesian eagle, usually crowned

REFERENCES

F/S = Ferdinand Friedensburg and Hans Seger, ***Schlesiens Münzen und Medaillen der neueren Zeit***, Breslau, 1901 (reprint Frankfurt/Main, 1976).

J/M = Norbert Jaschke and Fritz P. Maercker, ***Schlesische Münzen und Medaillen***, Ihringen, 1985.

S = Hugo Frhr. Von Saurma-Jeltsch, ***Die Saurmasche Münzsammlung deutscher, schweizerischer und polnischer Gepräge von etwa dem Beginn der Groschenzeit bis zur Kipperperiode***, Berlin, 1892.

S/Sch = Hugo Frhr. Von Saurma-Jeltsch, ***Schlesische Münzen und Medaillen***, Breslau, 1883.

Sch = Wolfgang Schulten, ***Deutsche Münzen aus der Zeit Karls V***,. Frankfurt am Main, 1974.

DUCHY

REGULAR COINAGE

KM# 20 HELLER

Silver **Ruler:** Adam Wenzel **Obv:** Crowned 'AW' monogram, date above **Rev:** Silesian eagle **Note:** Ref. F/S#3033-34, 3041-43; S/S#69. Varieties exist.

Date	Mintage	VG	F	VF	XF	Unc
1611	—	45.00	95.00	175	325	—
1611 CC	—	45.00	95.00	175	325	—
161Z	—	45.00	95.00	175	325	—
161Z CC	—	45.00	95.00	175	325	—
161Z DR	—	45.00	95.00	175	325	—
1613 CC	—	45.00	95.00	175	325	—

KM# 46 HELLER

Silver **Ruler:** Elisabeth Lucretia **Obv:** Silesian eagle in circle **Obv. Legend:** OBOLVS... **Rev:** Crown above large Gothic 'T' in circle, date at end of legend **Rev. Legend:** ANNO. DOMINE. **Note:** Ref. F/S#3096-98, 3100, 3104.

Date	Mintage	VG	F	VF	XF	Unc
1650	—	30.00	60.00	120	—	—
1651	—	30.00	60.00	120	—	—
1652	—	30.00	60.00	120	—	—

KM# 53 HELLER

Silver **Ruler:** Elisabeth Lucretia **Obv:** Silesian eagle in circle, date at end of legend **Obv. Legend:** OBOLVS... **Rev:** Crown above large Gothic 'T' in circle, date at end of legend **Rev. Legend:** ANNO. DOMINE. **Note:** Ref. F/S#3101.

Date	Mintage	VG	F	VF	XF	Unc
1651//1651	—	—	—	—	—	—

KM# 54 HELLER

Silver **Ruler:** Ferdinand IV **Obv:** Silesian eagle in circle **Obv. Legend:** OBOLVS... **Rev:** Crown above large Gothic 'T' in circle, date at end of legend **Rev. Legend:** ANNO. DOMINE. **Note:** Ref. F/S#3109.

Date	Mintage	VG	F	VF	XF	Unc
1653	—	25.00	55.00	110	—	—

KM# 55 HELLER

Silver **Ruler:** Ferdinand IV **Obv:** Silesian eagle in circle **Obv. Legend:** OBOLVS... **Rev:** Crown above large Gothic 'T' in circle, date at end of legend **Rev. Legend:** SILESIÆ ANNO. **Note:** Ref. F/S#3110, 3112.

Date	Mintage	VG	F	VF	XF	Unc
1653	—	25.00	50.00	100	—	—
1654	—	25.00	50.00	100	—	—

MB# 23 3 PFENNIG (Ternar, Dreier)

Silver **Ruler:** Adam Wenzel **Obv:** Silesian eagle in ornately shaped shield **Rev:** Ornate helmet, Silesian eagle divides date above **Note:** Ref. F/S#2986, 2993, 2995, 2997, 3000, 3018. Varieties exist.

Date	Mintage	VG	F	VF	XF	Unc
1604	—	15.00	35.00	70.00	145	—
1605	—	15.00	35.00	70.00	145	—
1606	—	15.00	35.00	70.00	145	—
1607	—	15.00	35.00	70.00	145	—
1609 HT	—	15.00	35.00	70.00	145	—

KM# 18 3 PFENNIG (Ternar, Dreier)

Silver **Ruler:** Adam Wenzel **Obv:** Large Silesian eagle **Rev:** Ornate helmet, Silesian eagle divides date above **Note:** Ref. F/S#3020.

Date	Mintage	VG	F	VF	XF	Unc
1610 HT	—	—	—	—	—	—

KM# 19 3 PFENNIG (Ternar, Dreier)

Silver **Ruler:** Adam Wenzel **Obv:** Silesian eagle in oval baroque frame **Rev:** Ornate helmet, Silesian eagle divides date above **Note:** Ref. F/S#3021, 3029-32, 3040.

Date	Mintage	VG	F	VF	XF	Unc
1610 HT	—	15.00	35.00	70.00	145	—
1611	—	15.00	35.00	70.00	145	—
1611 (d)	—	15.00	35.00	70.00	145	—
1611 CC	—	15.00	35.00	70.00	145	—
1611 DR	—	15.00	35.00	70.00	145	—

KM# 26 3 PFENNIG (Ternar, Dreier)

Silver **Ruler:** Adam Wenzel **Obv:** Silesian eagle in oval baroque frame **Rev:** Imperial orb with '3' divides date **Note:** Ref. S/S#70.

Date	Mintage	VG	F	VF	XF	Unc
1616	—	—	—	—	—	—

KM# 30 3 PFENNIG (Ternar, Dreier)

Silver **Ruler:** Friedrich Wilhelm **Obv:** Shield of Silesian eagle arms in baroque frame **Rev:** Imperial orb with '3' divides date **Note:** Ref. S/S#82, 84. Kipper coinage.

Date	Mintage	VG	F	VF	XF	Unc
16ZZ	—	—	—	—	—	—
16Z3	—	—	—	—	—	—

KM# 44 3 PFENNIG (Gröschel)

Silver **Ruler:** Elisabeth Lucretia **Obv:** Silesian eagle with shield on breast **Rev:** Imperial orb with '3' divides date **Note:** Ref. F/S#3089-90, 3095.

Date	Mintage	VG	F	VF	XF	Unc
1649	—	10.00	20.00	40.00	80.00	—
1649 GG	—	10.00	20.00	40.00	80.00	—
1650 GG	—	10.00	20.00	40.00	80.00	—

KM# 47 3 PFENNIG (Gröschel)

Silver **Ruler:** Elisabeth Lucretia **Obv:** Silesian eagle with shield on breast **Rev:** Imperial orb with '3' divides date in ornamented rhombus **Note:** Ref. F/S#3094, 3099, 3103.

Date	Mintage	VG	F	VF	XF	Unc
1650 GG	—	10.00	20.00	40.00	80.00	—
1651 GG	—	10.00	20.00	40.00	80.00	—
1652 GG	—	10.00	20.00	40.00	80.00	—

KM# 48 3 PFENNIG (Gröschel)

Silver **Ruler:** Elisabeth Lucretia **Obv:** Silesian eagle in circle **Rev:** Imperial orb in ornamented rhombus **Note:** Ref. S/S#113.

Date	Mintage	VG	F	VF	XF	Unc
ND(ca1650)	—	—	—	—	—	—

KM# 49 3 PFENNIG (Gröschel)

Silver **Ruler:** Elisabeth Lucretia **Obv:** Silesian eagle in oval baroque frame **Rev:** Imperial orb in ornamented rhombus **Note:** Ref. S/S#114.

Date	Mintage	VG	F	VF	XF	Unc
ND(ca1650)	—	—	—	—	—	—

KM# 58 3 PFENNIG (Gröschel)

Silver **Ruler:** Ferdinand IV **Obv:** Crowned imperial eagle, shield of Austria-Burgundy arms on breast **Rev:** Imperial orb with '3' divides date **Note:** Ref. F#3108, 3113.

Date	Mintage	VG	F	VF	XF	Unc
1653 GG	—	—	—	—	—	—
1655 GG	—	—	—	—	—	—

KM# 56 3 PFENNIG (Gröschel)

Silver **Ruler:** Ferdinand IV **Obv:** Silesian eagle with shield on breast **Rev:** Imperial orb with '3' divides date **Note:** Ref. F/S#3106.

Date	Mintage	VG	F	VF	XF	Unc
1653 GG	—	—	—	—	—	—

KM# 57 3 PFENNIG (Gröschel)

Silver **Ruler:** Ferdinand IV **Obv:** Silesian eagle with shield of Austria-Burgundy on breast **Rev:** Imperial orb with '3' divides date **Note:** Ref. F/S#3107, 3111.

Date	Mintage	VG	F	VF	XF	Unc
1653 GG	—	—	—	—	—	—
1654 GG	—	—	—	—	—	—

KM# 35 3 GROSCHER (Dreigröscher)

Silver **Ruler:** Friedrich Wilhelm **Obv:** High-collared bust right **Obv. Legend:** FRI. W. D.G. I. S. T. E. M. G. D. **Rev:** Small Silesian eagle divides date III above, 4-line inscription below, mintmaster's initials at end of inscription **Rev. Inscription:** GROS. ARG / TRIP. DVC / TESSINE **Note:** Ref. F/S#3063.

Date	Mintage	VG	F	VF	XF	Unc
1624 HL	—	60.00	120	275	575	—

KM# 42 KREUZER

Silver **Ruler:** Elisabeth Lucretia **Obv:** Silesian eagle in shield, crown above divides date **Obv. Legend:** MO. NO. AR. DV. TESH. **Rev:** Laureate bust right in circle **Rev. Legend:** FERD. III. D.G. R (I)I. S. A. G. H. E. B. R. **Note:** Ref. F/S#3071.

Date	Mintage	VG	F	VF	XF	Unc
1644 HL	—	—	—	—	—	—

KM# 43 KREUZER

Silver **Ruler:** Elisabeth Lucretia **Obv:** Silesian eagle in crowned shield, date at end of legend **Obv. Legend:** MO. NO. AR. DV. TESH. **Rev:** Laureate bust right in circle **Rev. Legend:** FERD. III. D.G. R (I)I. S. A. G. H. E. B. R. **Note:** Ref. F/S#3072-74, 76, 79, 82-83, 87-88; J/M#233. Varieties exist.

Date	Mintage	VG	F	VF	XF	Unc
1644 HL	—	10.00	20.00	40.00	80.00	—
1644 DR	—	10.00	20.00	40.00	80.00	—
1645 HL	—	10.00	20.00	40.00	80.00	—
1645 LB	—	10.00	20.00	40.00	80.00	—
1646 HL	—	10.00	20.00	40.00	80.00	—
1647 HL	—	10.00	20.00	40.00	80.00	—
1648 LB	—	10.00	20.00	40.00	80.00	—
1648 HL	—	10.00	20.00	40.00	80.00	—
1649 HL	—	10.00	20.00	40.00	80.00	—
1649 LB	—	10.00	20.00	40.00	80.00	—

KM# 4 2 KREUZER

Silver **Ruler:** Adam Wenzel **Obv:** Crowned bust right in circle, value (Z) below **Obv. Legend:** A. W. D.G. I. - S. T. E. M. G. D. **Rev:** Crowned Silesian eagle in shield within circle, large crown above, date at end of legend **Rev. Legend:** GROS. ARG. II. CRV. **Note:** Ref. F/S#2999.

Date	Mintage	VG	F	VF	XF	Unc
(1)607	—	—	—	—	—	—

KM# 1 3 KREUZER (Groschen)

Silver **Ruler:** Adam Wenzel **Obv:** Head right in circle, value (3) below **Obv. Legend:** A: W: D:G. I: SIL. TES. E. MA. GLO: T. **Rev:** Crowned Silesian eagle in circle, value (3) above, date at end of legend **Rev. Legend:** GROS. ARG. CRVCI: **Note:** Ref. F/S#2990.

Date	Mintage	VG	F	VF	XF	Unc
1603 (d)	—	—	—	—	—	—

KM# 2 3 KREUZER (Groschen)

Silver **Ruler:** Adam Wenzel **Obv:** Bust right in circle, value (3) below **Obv. Legend:** A: WE: D.G. I. SI. TE. E: M: G: D. **Rev:** Shield of Silesian eagle arms, ornate helmet surmounted by eagle above, date at end of legend **Rev. Legend:** GROS: ARG - III. CRV: **Note:** Ref. F/S#2991.

Date	Mintage	VG	F	VF	XF	Unc
1603	—	—	—	—	—	—

KM# 3 3 KREUZER (Groschen)
Silver **Ruler:** Adam Wenzel **Obv:** Large bust right breaks circle at top, value '3' in oval below **Obv. Legend:** A. W. D: G. I. S. - T. E. M. G. D. **Rev:** Shield of Silesian eagle arms, ornate helmet surmounted by eagle above, date at end of legend **Rev. Legend:** GROS. ARG. - III. CRV. **Note:** Ref. F/S#2992, 2994, 2996, 2998, 3001. Varieties exist.

Date	Mintage	VG	F	VF	XF	Unc
(1)604	—	25.00	55.00	110	225	—
(1)605	—	25.00	55.00	110	225	—
(1)606	—	25.00	55.00	110	225	—
(1)607	—	25.00	55.00	110	225	—
(1)608	—	25.00	55.00	110	225	—

KM# 6 3 KREUZER (Groschen)
Silver **Ruler:** Adam Wenzel **Obv:** Large bust right breaks circle at top, value '3' in oval below **Obv. Legend:** A. W. D. G. I. S. - T. E. M. G. D. **Rev:** Shield of Silesian eagle arms, ornate helmet surmounted by eagle above, date at end of legend **Rev. Legend:** GROS. AR. - III. CR. **Note:** Ref. F/S#3011, 14, 24-25, 27-28, 35, 37, 45; S/S#63. Varieties exist.

Date	Mintage	VG	F	VF	XF	Unc
(1)609	—	25.00	55.00	110	225	—
(1)609 (e)	—	25.00	55.00	110	225	—
(1)611 DR	—	25.00	55.00	110	225	—
(1)611 (e)	—	25.00	55.00	110	225	—
(1)611 CC	—	25.00	55.00	110	225	—
(1)611	—	25.00	55.00	110	225	—
(1)61Z	—	25.00	55.00	110	225	—
(1)61Z DR	—	25.00	55.00	110	225	—
(1)61Z CC	—	25.00	55.00	110	225	—
(1)613 DR	—	25.00	55.00	110	225	—

KM# 7 3 KREUZER (Groschen)
Silver **Ruler:** Adam Wenzel **Obv:** Large bust right breaks circle at top, value '3' in oval below **Obv. Legend:** A. W. D. G. I. S. - T. E. M. G. D. **Rev:** Shield of Silesian eagle arms, ornate helmet surmounted by eagle above, date at end of legend **Rev. Legend:** GRO: AR - III. CRV. **Note:** Ref. F/S#3012.

Date	Mintage	VG	F	VF	XF	Unc
(1)609	—	25.00	50.00	100	210	—
(1)609 HT	—	25.00	50.00	100	210	—
(1)610 HT	—	25.00	50.00	100	210	—
(1)611 HT	—	25.00	50.00	100	210	—

KM# 9 3 KREUZER (Groschen)
Silver **Ruler:** Adam Wenzel **Obv:** Large bust right breaks circle at top, value '3' in oval below **Obv. Legend:** A. W. D. G. I. S. - T. E. M. G. D. **Rev:** Crowned Silesian eagle in circle, date at end of legend **Rev. Legend:** GROSSVS. ARG. (mintmaster's symbol) TRIP. CRV. **Note:** Ref. F/S#3017.

Date	Mintage	VG	F	VF	XF	Unc
(1)609 (e)	—	30.00	65.00	135	275	—

KM# 8 3 KREUZER (Groschen)
Silver **Ruler:** Adam Wenzel **Obv:** Large bust right breaks circle at top, value '3' in oval below **Obv. Legend:** A. W. D. G. I. S. - T. E. M. G. D. **Rev:** Crowned Silesian eagle, '3' in shield on breast, all in circle, date at end of legend **Rev. Legend:** GROSSVS. ARG. (mintmaster's symbol) TRIP. CRV. **Note:** Ref. T/S#3015-16.

Date	Mintage	VG	F	VF	XF	Unc
(1)609 (e)	—	30.00	65.00	135	275	—

KM# 24 3 KREUZER (Groschen)
Silver **Ruler:** Adam Wenzel **Obv:** Large bust right breaks circle at top, value '3' in oval below **Obv. Legend:** A. W. D. G. I. S. - T. E. M. G. D. **Rev:** Shield of Silesian eagle arms, ornate helmet surmounted by eagle above, date at end of legend **Rev. Legend:** GROS. AR. - III. CR. **Note:** Ref. F/S#3036, 39. Klippe.

Date	Mintage	VG	F	VF	XF	Unc
(1)61Z	—	15.00	35.00	70.00	—	—
(1)61Z DR	—	15.00	35.00	70.00	—	—

KM# 27 3 KREUZER (Groschen)
Silver **Ruler:** Friedrich Wilhelm **Obv:** Bust right breaks circle at top, value '3' in oval below **Obv. Legend:** FRI. WIL. D. - G. D. SI. TE. **Rev:** Shield of Silesian eagle arms, ornate helmet surmounted by eagle above, date at end of legend **Rev. Legend:** MON. NOV. - III. CRV. **Note:** Ref. F/S#3048, 51-52, 59.

Date	Mintage	VG	F	VF	XF	Unc
16Z0	—	20.00	40.00	80.00	160	—
16Z1	—	20.00	40.00	80.00	160	—
16ZZ	—	20.00	40.00	80.00	160	—

KM# 31 3 KREUZER (Groschen)
Silver **Ruler:** Friedrich Wilhelm **Obv:** Silesian eagle in circle, value '3' in circle below **Obv. Legend:** FRI. WIL. D - G. D. SI. TE. **Rev:** Shield of Silesian eagle arms, ornate helmet surmounted by eagle above, date at end of legend **Rev. Legend:** MON. NOV. - III. CRV. **Note:** Ref. F/S#3056-58.

Date	Mintage	VG	F	VF	XF	Unc
1622 S/DR	—	25.00	50.00	100	210	—
1622	—	25.00	50.00	100	210	—

KM# 32 3 KREUZER (Groschen)
Silver **Ruler:** Friedrich Wilhelm **Obv:** 2 adjacent shields of arms, crown above, (3) below **Obv. Legend:** FRI. WIL. D:G. I. S. T. E. MG. D. **Rev:** Silesian eagle in circle, date at end of legend **Rev. Legend:** MONE. NOVA. III. CRV. **Note:** Ref. F/S#3060, 62.

Date	Mintage	VG	F	VF	XF	Unc
1622	—	25.00	50.00	100	210	—
1623	—	25.00	50.00	100	210	—

KM# 36 3 KREUZER (Groschen)
Silver **Ruler:** Elisabeth Lucretia **Obv:** Laureate bust right in circle, value '3' in circle below **Obv. Legend:** FERD: III. D:G: R: I: - S: A: G. H: BO: REX. **Rev:** Crowned Silesian eagle in shield within circle, crown above divides date or to left of crown **Rev. Legend:** MON: NO: ARG. DVC: TESCH:. **Note:** Ref. F/S#3064, 70, 75, 77-78, 80-81, 85-86. Varieties exist.

Date	Mintage	VG	F	VF	XF	Unc
1642 DR	—	12.00	25.00	45.00	90.00	—
1644 HL	—	12.00	25.00	45.00	90.00	—
1646 HL	—	12.00	25.00	45.00	90.00	—
1647 DR	—	12.00	25.00	45.00	90.00	—
1647 HL	—	12.00	25.00	45.00	90.00	—
1648 HL	—	12.00	25.00	45.00	90.00	—
1648 LB	—	12.00	25.00	45.00	90.00	—
1649 HL	—	12.00	25.00	45.00	90.00	—
1649 LB	—	12.00	25.00	45.00	90.00	—

KM# 37 3 KREUZER (Groschen)
Silver **Ruler:** Elisabeth Lucretia **Obv:** Large laureate bust right breaks circle at top, value '3' in circle below **Obv. Legend:** FERD. III. D:G. R. I. - S. A. G. H. B. R. REX. **Rev:** Crowned Silesian eagle in circle, date at top **Rev. Legend:** MON. NOV. ARG. TESCHINENS. **Note:** Ref. F/S#3069.

Date	Mintage	VG	F	VF	XF	Unc
1643 HL	—	—	—	—	—	—

KM# 45 3 KREUZER (Groschen)
Silver **Ruler:** Elisabeth Lucretia **Obv:** Large laureate bust right breaks circle at top, value '3' in circle below **Obv. Legend:** FERDI. III. D: G: R - I. S: A: G: H: B: R. **Rev:** Silesian eagle with shield on breast in circle, crown at top, date at end of legend **Rev. Legend:** MO: NO: AR: DV: TESCH: **Note:** Ref. F/S#3084, 3102.

Date	Mintage	VG	F	VF	XF	Unc
1649 GG	—	—	—	—	—	—
165Z GG	—	—	—	—	—	—

KM# 59 3 KREUZER (Groschen)
Silver **Ruler:** Ferdinand IV **Obv:** Crowned facing bust turned slightly to left in circle, value (3) below **Obv. Legend:** FERD: IIII: D: - G: R: H: B. REX. **Rev:** Crowned Silesian eagle, Austro-Burgundy arms in shield on breast, date at end of legend **Rev. Legend:** MO: NO: DVC: TES: SIL: **Note:** Ref. F/S#3105.

Date	Mintage	VG	F	VF	XF	Unc
1653 GG	—	—	—	—	—	—

KM# 28 12 KREUZER (Zwölfer = Schreckenberger)
Silver **Ruler:** Friedrich Wilhelm **Obv:** Bust right in circle, value '12' in oval below **Obv. Legend:** FRIDERICVS - WILHEL D. G. D. **Rev:** Small shield with Silesian eagle at bottom, ornate helmet surmounted by crowned Silesian eagle above, date at end of legend **Rev. Legend:** MON(E). NOVA - TESCHI. **Note:** Ref. F/S#3047, 50, 53. Kipper coinage.

Date	Mintage	VG	F	VF	XF	Unc
1620 HL	—	125	275	575	1,150	—
1621 HL	—	125	275	575	1,150	—
16Z1 DR	—	125	275	575	1,150	—

KM# 29 24 KREUZER (Vierundzwanziger)
Silver **Ruler:** Friedrich Wilhelm **Obv:** Bust right in circle, value '24' in oval below **Obv. Legend:** FRIDERICVS - WILHEL D. G. D. **Rev:** Small shield with Silesian eagle at bottom, ornate helmet surmounted by crowned Silesian eagle above, date at end of legend **Rev. Legend:** MONE. NOVA - TESCHI. **Note:** Ref. F/S#3049, 54-55. Kipper coinage.

Date	Mintage	VG	F	VF	XF	Unc
1621 HL	—	80.00	160	325	650	—
16ZZ DR/S	—	80.00	160	325	650	—

KM# 10 1/2 THALER
Silver **Ruler:** Adam Wenzel **Obv:** Bust right in circle divides date **Obv. Legend:** ADAMVS. WENCESLAVS. **Rev:** Crowned shield of Silesian eagle arms **Rev. Legend:** D: G: IN. SIL: TES. E. MA. G. D. **Note:** Ref. F/S#3009. Klippe.

Date	Mintage	VG	F	VF	XF	Unc
1609	—	—	—	—	—	—

KM# 11 1/2 THALER
Silver **Ruler:** Adam Wenzel **Obv:** Bust right in circle **Obv. Legend:** ADAMVS. WENCESLAVS. **Rev:** Crowned shield of Silesian eagle arms, date at end of legend **Rev. Legend:** D: G: IN. SIL: TES. E. MA. G. D. **Note:** Ref. F/S#3010.

Date	Mintage	VG	F	VF	XF	Unc
1609	—	—	—	—	—	—

KM# 12 THALER
Silver **Ruler:** Adam Wenzel **Obv:** 1/2-length armored figure to right, head breaks top of circle **Obv. Legend:** ADAMVS: WENCESLAVS. DVX. TESCHEN. **Rev:** Crowned Silesian eagle in circle, date at end of legend **Rev. Legend:** SAPIENTE. DIFFIDENTIA **Note:** Dav#7807.

Date	Mintage	VG	F	VF	XF	Unc
1609 (e) Rare	—	—	—	—	—	—

Note: Künker Auction 135, 1-08, VF realized approximately $13,610.

KM# 13 THALER
Silver **Ruler:** Adam Wenzel **Obv:** Large 1/2-length armored figure to right, head breaks top of circle **Obv. Legend:** ADAMVS: WENC - ESLAVS. D: G. DVX. **Rev:** Shield of Silesian eagle arms, ornate helmet surmounted by crowned Silesian eagle which divides date **Rev. Legend:** TESCHENENSIS - ET. MAI. GLOG. **Note:** Dav#7807. Klippe.

Date	Mintage	VG	F	VF	XF	Unc
1609 (e) Rare	—	—	—	—	—	—

KM# 21 THALER
Silver **Ruler:** Wenzel III **Obv:** Large 1/2-length armored figure to right, head breaks top of circle **Obv. Legend:** ADAMVS: WENC - ESLAVS. D:G. DVX. **Rev:** Shield of Silesian eagle arms, ornate helmet surmounted by crowned Silesian eagle which divides date **Rev. Legend:** TESCHENENSIS - ET. MAI. GLOG. **Note:** Dav#7808.

Date	Mintage	VG	F	VF	XF	Unc
1611 DR Rare	—	—	—	—	—	—

KM# 22 THALER
Silver **Ruler:** Wenzel III **Obv:** Large 1/2-length armored figure to right, head breaks top of circle **Obv. Legend:** ADAMVS: WENC - ESLAVS. D:G. DVX. **Rev:** Shield of Silesian eagle arms, ornate helmet surmounted by crowned Silesian eagle which divides date **Rev. Legend:** TESCHENENSIS - ET. MAI. GLOG. **Note:** Dav#7808. Klippe.

Date	Mintage	VG	F	VF	XF	Unc
1611 DR Rare	—	—	—	—	—	—

KM# 33 THALER
Silver **Ruler:** Friedrich Wilhelm **Obv:** Bust right in circle **Obv. Legend:** FRID: GVIL. D:G. IN. SIL. TES. ET. MAI. GLOG. DVX. **Rev:** Crowned Silesian eagle in circle, date at end of legend **Rev. Legend:** IN: DEO: MEO: TRANSGRED. AR: MVRVM: HL: **Note:** Dav#7809.

Date	Mintage	VG	F	VF	XF	Unc
16Z3 HL Rare	—	—	—	—	—	—

Note: Künker Auction 135, 1-08, XF realized approximately $26,635.

KM# 34 THALER
Silver **Ruler:** Friedrich Wilhelm **Obv:** Bust right in circle **Obv. Legend:** FRID: GVIL. D:G. IN. SIL. TES. ET. MAI. GLOG. DVX. **Rev:** Crowned Silesian eagle in circle, date at end of legend **Rev. Legend:** IN: DEO: MEO: TRANSGRED. AR: MVRVM: HL: **Note:** Ref. J/M#232. Klippe.

Date	Mintage	VG	F	VF	XF	Unc
16Z3 HL Rare	—	—	—	—	—	—

KM# 38 THALER
Silver **Ruler:** Elisabeth Lucretia **Obv:** Shield of Silesian eagle arms divides date to lower left and right, ornate helmet surmounted by Silesian eagle above, all in circle **Obv. Legend:** MONETA. NOVA. ARGENTEA. TESSCHINENSIS. **Rev:** 8-line inscription in circle, wreath border, mintmaster's initials at end of inscription **Rev. Inscription:** ELISAB: / LVCRET: D: G. / IN. SIL. TESCH: / ET. M: GLOGO. DV / CISA. PRINC: / D: LICHTEN / STEIN **Note:** Dav#7813.

Date	Mintage	VG	F	VF	XF	Unc
1643 HL Rare	—	—	—	—	—	—

KM# 50 THALER
Silver **Ruler:** Elisabeth Lucretia **Obv:** Facing bust turned slightly to left in circle **Obv. Legend:** ELISA: LVCRA. D G: IN SILE: TESCH: ET M: GLO: DVCIS: PRIN: D LICHT. **Rev:** Ornate shield of Silesian eagle arms divides date, large crown above **Rev. Legend:** SI DEVS. PRO. NOBIS. QVIS. CONTRA NOS. **Note:** Dav#7814.

Date	Mintage	VG	F	VF	XF	Unc
1650 Rare	—	—	—	—	—	—

KM# 5 2 THALER
Silver **Ruler:** Adam Wenzel **Obv:** 1/2-length armored figure to right, head breaks top of circle **Obv. Legend:** ADAMVS: WENCESLAVS. DVX. TESCHEN. **Rev:** Crowned Silesian eagle in circle, date at end of legend **Rev. Legend:** SAPIENTE. DIFFIDENTIA **Note:** Dav#7806.

Date	Mintage	VG	F	VF	XF	Unc
1608 (e) Rare	—	—	—	—	—	—
1609 (e) Rare	—	—	—	—	—	—

KM# 39 2 THALER
Silver **Ruler:** Elisabeth Lucretia **Obv:** Shield of Silesian eagle arms divides date to lower left and right, ornate helmet surmounted by Silesian eagle above, all in circle **Obv. Legend:** MONETA. NOVA. ARGENTEA. TESSCHINENSIS. **Rev:** 8-line inscription in circle, wreath border, mintmaster's initials at end of inscription **Rev. Inscription:** ELISAB: / LVCRET: D: G. / IN. SIL. TESCH: / ET. M: GLOGO DV / CISA. PRINC: / D: LICHTEN / STEIN **Note:** Dav#7812.

Date	Mintage	VG	F	VF	XF	Unc
1643 HL Rare	—	—	—	—	—	—

KM# 14 3 THALER
Silver **Ruler:** Adam Wenzel **Obv:** 1/2-length armored figure to right, head breaks top of circle **Obv. Legend:** ADAMVS: WENCESLAVS. DVX. TESCHEN. **Rev:** Crowned Silesian eagle in circle, date at end of legend **Rev. Legend:** SAPIENTE. DIFFIDENTIA **Note:** Dav#7805.

Date	Mintage	VG	F	VF	XF	Unc
1609 (e) Rare	—	—	—	—	—	—

KM# 15 3 THALER
Silver **Ruler:** Adam Wenzel **Obv:** 1/2-length armored figute to right, head breaks top of circle **Obv. Legend:** ADAMVS: WENCESLAVS. DVX. TESCHEN. **Rev:** Crowned Silesian eagle in circle, date at end of legend **Rev. Legend:** SAPIENTE. DIFFIDENTIA **Note:** Dav#7805. Klippe.

Date	Mintage	VG	F	VF	XF	Unc
1609 (e) Rare	—	—	—	—	—	—

KM# 40 4 THALER
Silver **Ruler:** Elisabeth Lucretia **Obv:** Shield of Silesian eagle arms divides date to lwer left and right, ornate helmet surmounted by Silesian eagle above, all in circle **Obv. Legend:** MONETA. NOVA. ARGENTEA. TESSCHINENSIS. **Rev:** 8-line inscription in circle, wreath border, mintmaster's initials at end of inscription **Rev. Inscription:** ELSAB: / LVCRET: D: G. / IN. SIL. TESCH: / ET. M: GLOGO. DV / CISA. PRINC: / D: LICHTEN / STEIN **Note:** Dav#7811.

Date	Mintage	VG	F	VF	XF	Unc
1643 HL Rare	—	—	—	—	—	—

KM# 41 5 THALER
Silver **Ruler:** Elisabeth Lucretia **Obv:** Shield of Silesian eagle armd divides date to lower left and right, ornate helmet surmounted by Silesian eagle above, all in circle **Obv. Legend:** MONETA. NOVA. ARGENTEA. TESSCHINENSIS. **Rev:** 8-line inscription in circle, wreath border, mintmaster's initials at end of inscription **Rev. Inscription:** ELSAB: / LVCRET: D: G. / IN. SIL. TESCH: / ET. M: GLOGO. DV / CISA. PRINC: / D: LICHTEN / STEIN **Note:** Dav#7810.

Date	Mintage	VG	F	VF	XF	Unc
1643 HL Rare	—	—	—	—	—	—

TRADE COINAGE

KM# 25 3 DUCAT
Gold **Ruler:** Adam Wenzel **Obv:** Bust right in circle **Obv. Legend:** ADAM. WENCES... **Rev:** Silesian eagle in circle, crown at top **Rev. Legend:** PATIAR VT POTIAR. **Note:** Fr#3269. Klippe.

Date	Mintage	VG	F	VF	XF	Unc
1613 Rare	—	—	—	—	—	—

KM# 16 5 DUCAT (1/2 Portugalöser)
Gold **Ruler:** Adam Wenzel **Obv:** 1/2-length armored figure to right, head breaks top of circle **Obv. Legend:** ADAMVS: WENCESLAVS. DVX. TESCHEN. **Rev:** Crowned Silesian eagle in circle, date at end of legend **Rev. Legend:** SAPIENTE. DIFFIDENTIA **Note:** Fr#3268. Struck from Thaler dies, KM#12.

Date	Mintage	VG	F	VF	XF	Unc
1609 (e) Rare	—	—	—	—	—	—

KM# 23 5 DUCAT (1/2 Portugalöser)
Gold **Ruler:** Adam Wenzel **Obv:** Large 1/2-length armored figure ot right, head breaks top of circle **Obv. Legend:** ADAMVS: WENC - ESLAVS. D:G. DVX. **Rev:** Shield of Silesian eagle arms, ornate helmet surmounted by crowned Silesian eagle which divides date **Rev. Legend:** TESCHENENSIS - ET. MAI. GLOG. **Note:** Fr#3266. Struck from Thaler dies, KM#21.

Date	Mintage	VG	F	VF	XF	Unc
1611 DR Rare	—	—	—	—	—	—

KM# 51 5 DUCAT (1/2 Portugalöser)
Gold **Ruler:** Elisabeth Lucretia **Obv:** Facing bust turned slightly to left in circle **Obv. Legend:** ELISA : LVCRA. D G: IN SILE: TESCH: ET M: GLO: DVCIS: PRIN: D LICHT. **Rev:** Ornate shield of Silesian eagle arms divides date, large crown above **Rev. Legend:** SI DEVS. PRO. NOBIS. QVIS. CONTRA NOS. **Note:** Fr#3271. Struck from Thaler dies, KM#50.

Date	Mintage	VG	F	VF	XF	Unc
1650 Rare	—	—	—	—	—	—

KM# 17 8 DUCAT
Gold **Ruler:** Adam Wenzel **Obv:** 1/2-length armored figure to right, head breaks top of circle **Obv. Legend:** ADAMVS: WENCESLAVS. DVX. TESCHEN. **Rev:** Crowned Silesian eagle in circle, date at end of legend **Rev. Legend:** SAPIENTE. DIFFIDENTIA **Note:** Fr#3267. Struck from Thaler dies, KM#12.

Date	Mintage	VG	F	VF	XF	Unc
1609 (e) Rare	—	—	—	—	—	—

KM# 52 10 DUCAT (Portugalöser)
Gold **Ruler:** Elisabeth Lucretia **Obv:** Facing bust turned slightly to left in circle **Obv. Legend:** ELISA: LVCRA. D G: IN SILE: TESCH: ET M: GLO: DVCIS: PRIN: D LICHT. **Rev:** Ornate shield of Silesian eagle arms divides date, large crown above **Rev. Legend:** SI DEVS. PRO. NOBIS. QVIS. CONTRA NOS. **Note:** Fr#3270. Struck from Thaler dies, KM#50.

Date	Mintage	VG	F	VF	XF	Unc
1650 Rare	—	—	—	—	—	—

TEUTONIC ORDER

Deutscher Orden

The Order of Knights was founded during the Third Crusade in 1198. They acquired considerable territory by conquest from the heathen Prussians in the late 13th and early 14th centuries. The seat of the Grand Master moved from Acre to Venice and in 1309 to Marienburg, Prussia. The Teutonic Order began striking coins in the late 13th century. In 1355 permission was granted to strike hellers at Mergentheim. However, the bulk of the Order's coinage until 1525 was schillings and half schoters minted in and for Prussia. In 1809 the Order was suppressed and Mergentheim was annexed to Württemberg.

RULERS

Friedrich, Herzog von Sachsen, 1498-1510
Albrecht, Markgraf von Brandenburg, 1511-1525
Walter von Kronberg, 1527-1543
Wolfgang Schutzbar-Milchling, 1543-1566
Georg Hund von Wenkheim, 1566-1572
Heinrich von Bobenhausen, 1572-1588
Maximilian of Austria, 1588-1618
Karl of Austria, 1618-1624
Johann Eustach von Westernach, 1625-1627
Johann Caspar von Stadion, 1627-1641
Leopold Wilhelm of Austria, 1641-1662
Karl Josef of Austria, 1662-1664
Johann Caspar II von Ampringen, 1664-1684
Ludwig Anton von Pfalz-Neuburg, 1684-1694
Ludwig Franz von Pfalz-Neuburg, 1694-1732
Clemens August von Bayern, 1732-1761
Karl Alexander of Lorraine, 1761-1780.
Max Franz of Austria, 1780-1801
Karl Ludwig of Austria, 1801-1804
Anton Victor of Austria, 1804-1809

ARMS

Grand Master: Cross, shield w/eagle in ctr., shield is often w/double outline. Later versions include family and territorial arms in angles of cross.
Order Arms: Long cross superimposed, usually on empty shield, sometimes w/eagle in ctr.

NOTE: Coinage up to 1525 was struck in Königsberg, in or for Mergentheim thereafter.

MINT OFFICIALS' INITIALS

Initials	Date	Name
CO / CÖ	ca. 1612-16	Christoph Örber in Hall, Tyrol
	ca. 1666	Heinrich Moller, die-cutter in Nürnberg
MF	1669-89	Michael Faber in Frankfurt am Main
CB / B	1687-89	Conrad Bechtmann
GFN	1689-1724	Georg Friedrich Nürnberger, mintmaster in Nürnberg
LPH	1678-1701	Leonhard Paul Haller, mintmaster in Neisse (Breslau)
SS	1701-17	Siegmund Strasser, warden in Breslau
CGL	1746-55	Carl Gottlieb Laufer, mintmaster in Nürnberg
W(W)E or WE/W	1765-77	Weber, warden and Eberhard, mintmaster, in Wertheim

KNIGHTLY ORDER

REGULAR COINAGE

KM# 52 PFENNIG
Copper **Ruler:** Karl of Austria **Obv:** Arms of Order divide T-O and date, value I above **Note:** Kipper coinage. Uniface.

Date	Mintage	Good	VG	F	VF	XF
1622	—	60.00	120	235	475	—

KM# 68 PFENNIG
Copper **Ruler:** Johann Caspar **Obv:** 2 shields of arms above 1, Grand Master's arms (Stadion arms / Order arms) **Note:** Uniface.

Date	Mintage	VG	F	VF	XF	Unc
ND(ca1627-41)	—	60.00	120	240	—	—

KM# 81 PFENNIG
Silver **Ruler:** Leopold Wilhelm **Obv:** 2 shields of arms (crowned imperial eagle, Austria-Burgundy) above arms of Order **Rev. Inscription:** PHENI / date **Note:** Uniface.

Date	Mintage	Good	VG	F	VF	XF
1652	—	50.00	100	200	425	—

KM# 83 PFENNIG
Silver **Ruler:** Leopold Wilhelm **Obv:** Shield of crowned imperial eagle above 2 arms of Austria-Burgundy and Order, date divided to left and right **Note:** Uniface.

Date	Mintage	VG	F	VF	XF	Unc
1662	—	—	—	—	—	—

KM# 53 2 PFENNIG
Copper **Ruler:** Karl of Austria **Obv:** Arms of Order divide T-O and date, value II above **Note:** Kipper coinage. Uniface.

Date	Mintage	Good	VG	F	VF	XF
1622	—	65.00	115	180	325	—

KM# 54 3 PFENNIG (Dreier = 1/84 Gulden)
Copper **Ruler:** Karl of Austria **Obv:** Arms of order divide date, T.O. above **Rev:** III in wreath **Note:** Kipper coinage.

Date	Mintage	Good	VG	F	VF	XF
1622	—	20.00	40.00	80.00	160	325

KM# 97 3 PFENNIG (Dreier = 1/84 Gulden)

Copper **Ruler:** Johann Caspar II **Obv:** 3 shields of arms, 2 above 1, TO in center, date above **Rev:** Imperial orb with 84, all in ornamented rhombus **Note:** Varieties exist.

Date	Mintage	VG	F	VF	XF	Unc
1666	—	7.00	15.00	40.00	80.00	—
1668	—	7.00	15.00	40.00	80.00	—
1669	—	7.00	15.00	40.00	80.00	—
1670	—	7.00	15.00	40.00	80.00	—
1680	—	7.00	15.00	40.00	80.00	—
1681	—	7.00	15.00	40.00	80.00	—

KM# 122 3 PFENNIG (Dreier = 1/84 Gulden)

Copper **Ruler:** Ludwig Anton **Obv:** Long cross, Grand Master's arms in center, date divided by angles of cross **Rev:** Imperial orb with 84, all in ornamented rhombus

Date	Mintage	VG	F	VF	XF	Unc
1688	—	20.00	45.00	90.00	180	—
1689 CB	—	20.00	45.00	90.00	180	—

KM# 123 3 PFENNIG (Dreier = 1/84 Gulden)

Copper **Ruler:** Ludwig Anton **Obv:** 3 shields of arms, 2 above 1, TO in center, date above **Rev:** Imperial orb with 84, all in ornamented rhombus **Note:** Varieties exist.

Date	Mintage	VG	F	VF	XF	Unc
1689	—	10.00	20.00	45.00	90.00	—
1690	—	10.00	20.00	45.00	90.00	—
1690 B	—	10.00	20.00	45.00	90.00	—
1691	—	10.00	20.00	45.00	90.00	—
1692	—	10.00	20.00	45.00	90.00	—

KM# 86 GROSCHEN (3 Kreuzer)

1.4000 g., Silver, 21 mm. **Ruler:** Johann Caspar II **Obv:** 3 shields of arms, 2 above 1, date above all **Rev:** Imperial orb with 3, titles of Leopold I around **Note:** Varieties exist.

Date	Mintage	VG	F	VF	XF	Unc
1666	—	30.00	60.00	135	275	—
1668	—	30.00	60.00	135	275	—
1670	—	30.00	60.00	135	275	—
1680	—	30.00	60.00	135	275	—

KM# 125 GROSCHEN (3 Kreuzer)

Silver **Ruler:** Ludwig Franz **Subject:** Death of Ludwig Anton von Pfalz-Neuburg **Obv:** Crowned manifold arms divided by cross of Order **Rev:** 7-line inscription with dates, imperial orb with 3 below

Date	Mintage	VG	F	VF	XF	Unc
1694	—	200	400	750	1,500	—

KM# 55 KREUZER

Copper **Ruler:** Karl of Austria **Obv:** Arms of Order, T.O. above **Rev:** Date at end of inscription **Rev. Inscription:** I / KREUTZ / ER **Note:** Kipper coinage. Known countermarked with "Cross of the Order."

Date	Mintage	Good	VG	F	VF	XF
1622	—	35.00	80.00	120	240	—

KM# 87 KREUZER

Copper **Ruler:** Johann Caspar II **Obv:** 3 shields of arms, 2 above 1, TO in center, date above **Rev:** Imperial orb with I

Date	Mintage	VG	F	VF	XF	Unc
1666	—	—	—	—	—	—

KM# 56 2 KREUZER (Halbbatzen)

Silver **Ruler:** Karl of Austria **Obv:** Arms of Order, TO above **Rev:** Date at end of inscription **Rev. Inscription:** II / KREUTZ / ER **Note:** Kipper coinage.

Date	Mintage	VG	F	VF	XF	Unc
1622	—	—	—	—	—	—

KM# 59 2 KREUZER (Halbbatzen)

Silver **Ruler:** Karl of Austria **Obv:** Grand Master's arms divide date, value 2 above, titles of Karl around **Rev:** Crowned arms of Austria, titles of Ferdinand II around

Date	Mintage	VG	F	VF	XF	Unc
1623	—	—	—	—	—	—

KM# 100 2 KREUZER (Halbbatzen)

1.0600 g., Silver, 18.5 mm. **Ruler:** Johann Caspar II **Obv:** 3 shields of arms, 2 above 1, date above all **Rev:** Imperial orb with 2, titles of Leopold I around **Note:** Varieties exist.

Date	Mintage	VG	F	VF	XF	Unc
1669	—	65.00	135	275	—	—
1670	—	65.00	135	275	—	—
1679	—	65.00	135	275	—	—
1680	—	65.00	135	275	—	—

KM# 88 4 KREUZER (Batzen)

Silver **Ruler:** Johann Caspar II **Obv:** 3 shields of arms, 2 above 1, IIII K. above, titles of Johann Caspar II around **Rev:** Madonna & Child, rays around, date in margin **Note:** Varieties exist.

Date	Mintage	VG	F	VF	XF	Unc
1666	—	45.00	90.00	180	—	—
1667	—	45.00	90.00	180	—	—
1668	—	45.00	90.00	180	—	—
1670	—	45.00	90.00	180	—	—

KM# 113 4 KREUZER (Batzen)

Silver **Ruler:** Ludwig Anton **Subject:** Death of Johann Caspar II von Ampringen **Obv:** Crowned 4-fold arms with central shield of Order, palm branches to either side **Rev:** 6-line inscription with dates, imperial orb with 4 below

Date	Mintage	VG	F	VF	XF	Unc
1684	—	—	—	—	—	—

KM# 114 6 KREUZER

Silver **Ruler:** Ludwig Anton **Subject:** Death of Johann Caspar II von Ampringen **Obv:** Crowned 4-fold arms with central shield of Order, palm branches to either side **Rev:** 6-line inscription with dates, imperial orb with 6 below

Date	Mintage	VG	F	VF	XF	Unc
1684	—	—	—	—	—	—

KM# 45 24 KREUZER

Silver **Ruler:** Karl of Austria **Obv:** Bust right, value Z4 below, titles of Karl around **Rev:** Crowned manifold arms, titles continued around **Note:** Kipper coinage.

Date	Mintage	VG	F	VF	XF	Unc
ND(ca1620-21)	—	45.00	90.00	180	—	—

KM# 50 24 KREUZER

Silver **Ruler:** Karl of Austria **Obv:** Small bust right, date and value 24 below, titles of Karl around **Rev:** Crowned manifold arms, titles continued around **Note:** Kipper coinage. Varieties exist.

Date	Mintage	VG	F	VF	XF	Unc
1621	—	30.00	60.00	120	240	—
1622	—	30.00	60.00	120	240	—

KM# 118 1/12 THALER (2 Groschen)

Silver **Ruler:** Ludwig Anton **Obv:** Long cross, Grand Master's arms in center **Rev:** Date at end of inscription **Rev. Inscription:** 12 / EINEN / REICHS / THALER **Note:** Varieties exist.

Date	Mintage	VG	F	VF	XF	Unc
1687 CB	—	30.00	65.00	135	275	—
1688 CB	—	30.00	65.00	135	275	—

KM# 69 1/8 THALER (Breiter Batzen)

Silver **Ruler:** Johann Caspar **Subject:** Death of Johann Eustach von Westernach **Obv:** 3 helmets above 4-fold arms with central shield of Grand Master's arms **Rev:** 8-line inscription with dates, value (1/8) below

Date	Mintage	VG	F	VF	XF	Unc
1627	—	100	200	425	850	—

KM# 75 1/8 THALER (Breiter Batzen)

Silver **Ruler:** Leopold Wilhelm **Subject:** Death of Johann Caspar von Stadion **Obv:** 3 helmets above 4-fold arms with central shield of Grand Master's arms **Rev:** 6-line inscription with dates, value (1/8) below

Date	Mintage	VG	F	VF	XF	Unc
1641	—	125	250	500	1,025	—

KM# 16 1/4 THALER

Silver **Ruler:** Maximilian **Obv:** Standing Maximilian 3/4 facing, sword in right hand resting on ground **Rev:** Emperor on horseback in circle of shields **Mint:** Hall **Note:** Prev. KM#1; Similar to KM#38 but obervse legend broken.

Date	Mintage	VG	F	VF	XF	Unc
1612 CO	—	45.00	95.00	190	385	—
1614 CO	—	—	—	—	—	—

Note: Reported not confirmed

KM# 38 1/4 THALER

Silver **Ruler:** Maximilian **Obv:** Continuous legend **Obv. Legend:** MAXIMIL: DG: ARC: AV:... **Mint:** Hall **Note:** Prev. KM#2.

Date	Mintage	VG	F	VF	XF	Unc
ND(ca.1615) CO	—	45.00	95.00	190	385	—

KM# 39 1/4 THALER

Silver **Ruler:** Maximilian **Obv:** Broken legend, supported shield at left **Obv. Legend:** MAX: DG: AR-AV-... **Mint:** Hall **Note:** Prev. KM#3.

Date	Mintage	VG	F	VF	XF	Unc
ND(ca.1615) CO	—	45.00	95.00	190	385	—

KM# 116 1/4 THALER (8 Groschen = 12 Schilling)

Silver **Ruler:** Ludwig Anton **Subject:** Death of Johann Caspar II von Ampringen **Obv:** Crowned 4-fold arms with central shield of Order, palm branches to either side **Rev:** 7-line inscription with dates, imperial orb below

Date	Mintage	VG	F	VF	XF	Unc
1684	—	—	—	—	—	—

KM# 126 1/4 THALER (8 Groschen = 12 Schilling)

Silver **Ruler:** Ludwig Franz **Subject:** Death of Ludwig Anton von Pfalz-Neuburg **Obv:** Crowned manifold arms divided by cross of Order **Rev:** 6-line inscription with dates, mintmaster's initials at bottom

Date	Mintage	VG	F	VF	XF	Unc
1694 GFN	—	—	—	—	—	—

KM# 17 1/2 THALER (16 Groschen = 24 Schilling)

Silver **Ruler:** Maximilian **Obv:** Standing Maximilian half facing left with sword in right hand **Rev:** Mounted Maximilian to right, shields of arms form circle around **Mint:** Hall **Note:** Prev. KM#6.

Date	Mintage	VG	F	VF	XF	Unc
1612 CO	—	100	200	425	875	—
ND CO	—	100	200	425	875	—

KM# 28 1/2 THALER (16 Groschen = 24 Schilling)
Silver **Ruler:** Maximilian **Obv:** Supported shield at right **Rev:** Maximilian mounted to right, shields of arms form circle around **Mint:** Hall **Note:** Prev. KM#7.

Date	Mintage	VG	F	VF	XF	Unc
1614 CO	—	100	200	425	875	—

KM# 41 1/2 THALER (16 Groschen = 24 Schilling)
Silver **Ruler:** Maximilian **Obv:** Supported shield at left **Rev:** Maximilian mounted to right, shields of arms form circle around **Mint:** Hall **Note:** Prev. KM#8.

Date	Mintage	VG	F	VF	XF	Unc
1616	—	100	200	425	875	—
1616 CO	—	100	200	425	875	—

KM# 111 1/2 THALER (16 Groschen = 24 Schilling)
Silver **Ruler:** Johann Caspar II **Obv:** Bust of Johann Caspar II to right **Rev:** Madonna & Child above crowned 4-fold arms with central shield of Order, date in margin

Date	Mintage	VG	F	VF	XF	Unc
1680 MF	—	—	—	—	—	—

KM# 3 THALER (32 Groschen)
Silver **Ruler:** Maximilian **Obv:** Master standing on ground, arms at left, helmet at right **Rev:** Emperor on horseback in circle of shields, date below **Note:** Dav. #5848.

Date	Mintage	VG	F	VF	XF	Unc
1603	—	120	200	375	950	2,250

KM# 10 THALER (32 Groschen)
Silver **Ruler:** Maximilian **Rev:** Rear legs of horse lower, date divided by spear and rider's foot **Note:** Dav. #5849.

Date	Mintage	VG	F	VF	XF	Unc
1610	—	225	450	950	1,850	—

KM# 11 THALER (32 Groschen)
Silver **Ruler:** Maximilian **Obv:** Feet, arms, and helmet all break legend **Obv. Legend:** ...ADMIN. **Note:** Dav. #5850.

Date	Mintage	VG	F	VF	XF	Unc
1611	—	120	200	375	950	—

KM# 12 THALER (32 Groschen)
Silver **Ruler:** Maximilian **Obv:** Maximilian standing 3/4 left, sword in right hand **Obv. Legend:** ...ADM. **Rev:** Maximilian on horseback to right, shields all around **Note:** Dav. #5850A.

Date	Mintage	VG	F	VF	XF	Unc
1611	—	120	200	375	950	—

KM# 18 THALER (32 Groschen)
Silver **Ruler:** Maximilian **Obv. Legend:** MAX: DG: AR-AV: D: BV:-M-AG:... **Note:** Dav. #5851.

Date	Mintage	VG	F	VF	XF	Unc
1612	—	120	200	375	950	—

KM# 19 THALER (32 Groschen)
Silver **Ruler:** Maximilian **Obv. Legend:** ...ARC-AV: D: BV... **Note:** Dav. #5851A.

Date	Mintage	VG	F	VF	XF	Unc
1612	—	120	200	375	950	—

KM# 25 THALER (32 Groschen)
Silver **Ruler:** Maximilian **Note:** Dav. #5853.

Date	Mintage	VG	F	VF	XF	Unc
1613	—	115	175	375	950	—

KM# 61 THALER (32 Groschen)
Silver **Ruler:** Karl of Austria **Obv:** Facing bust dividing date **Rev:** Crowned arms **Note:** Dav. #5855.

Date	Mintage	VG	F	VF	XF	Unc
1623	—	200	350	750	1,500	3,750

KM# 63 THALER (32 Groschen)
Silver **Ruler:** Karl of Austria **Obv:** Bust right dividing date in inner circle **Rev:** Crowned shield of arms **Note:** Dav. #5856.

Date	Mintage	VG	F	VF	XF	Unc
1624	—	200	375	750	1,350	2,750

KM# 64 THALER (32 Groschen)
Silver **Ruler:** Johann Eustach **Obv:** Helmeted arms **Rev:** Madonna and child in radiant oval **Note:** Dav. #5857.

Date	Mintage	VG	F	VF	XF	Unc
1625	—	150	300	600	1,200	2,750

KM# 77 THALER (32 Groschen)
Silver **Ruler:** Johann Caspar **Subject:** Death of Johann Kaspar I **Obv:** Helmeted arms **Rev:** 6-line inscription **Note:** Dav. #5858.

Date	Mintage	VG	F	VF	XF	Unc
1641	—	2,000	3,250	6,000	9,500	—

KM# 90 THALER (32 Groschen)
Silver **Ruler:** Johann Caspar II **Obv:** Helmeted arms **Rev:** Madonna and child in radiant oval **Note:** Dav. #5859.

Date	Mintage	VG	F	VF	XF	Unc
1666	—	200	400	800	1,450	2,850
1668	—	200	400	800	1,450	2,850

KM# 102 THALER (32 Groschen)
Silver **Ruler:** Karl of Austria **Obv:** Bust of Karl right **Rev:** Madonna and child above arms **Mint:** Frankfurt am Main **Note:** Dav. #5861.

Date	Mintage	VG	F	VF	XF	Unc
1673 MF	—	250	500	900	1,600	5,000

KM# 120 THALER (32 Groschen)
Silver **Ruler:** Ludwig Anton **Obv:** Bust of Ludwig right **Rev:** Hatted and supported arms **Note:** Dav. #5862.

Date	Mintage	VG	F	VF	XF	Unc
1687	—	—	4,400	6,900	9,400	—

KM# 26 2 THALER
Silver **Ruler:** Maximilian **Obv:** Standing Maximilian 1/2 left **Rev:** Maximilian mounted to right, shields of arms form circle around **Note:** Dav. #5852.

Date	Mintage	VG	F	VF	XF	Unc
1613	—	450	850	1,650	3,000	—

KM# 30 2 THALER
Silver **Ruler:** Maximilian **Obv:** Grand Master of the Order standing with sword, date in exergue **Rev:** Maximilian mounted on horse surrounded by circle of shields of arms **Note:** Dav. #A5854.

Date	Mintage	VG	F	VF	XF	Unc
1614	—	425	775	1,400	2,400	—

KM# 31 2 THALER
Silver **Ruler:** Maximilian **Obv:** Date in exergue below standing Maximilian 3/4 to left holding sword **Rev:** Mounted Maximilian to right in circle of shields around **Note:** Klippe. Dav. #C5854.

Date	Mintage	VG	F	VF	XF	Unc
1614 Rare	—	—	—	—	—	—

KM# 57 2 THALER
Silver **Ruler:** Karl of Austria **Obv:** High-collared bust to right in circle **Obv. Legend:** CAROL • D: G • ARCHIDVX • AVSTRI • ADM • **Rev:** Crown above large manifold arms, small oval mitered arms at left and right, date divided below **Rev. Legend:** M • GEN • PRVS • M • ORD • TEV • EPV • BR • ET • W • **Note:** Klippe. Dav. #A5855.

Date	Mintage	VG	F	VF	XF	Unc
16ZZ Rare	—	—	—	—	—	—

KM# 103 2 THALER
Silver **Ruler:** Johann Caspar II **Obv:** Bust of Johann Caspar II to right **Rev:** Madonna and Child above arms **Mint:** Frankfurt am Main **Note:** Dav. #5860.

Date	Mintage	VG	F	VF	XF	Unc
1673 MF	—	1,800	3,000	5,100	—	—

KM# 32 3 THALER

86.2000 g., Silver **Ruler:** Maximilian **Obv:** Grand Master of the Order standing holding sword, date in exergue **Rev:** Knight on horseback in circle of shields **Note:** Dav. #B5854.

Date	Mintage	VG	F	VF	XF	Unc
1614	—	775	1,400	2,400	4,200	—

KM# 33 3 THALER

86.2000 g., Silver **Ruler:** Maximilian **Obv:** Date in exergue below Maximilian below **Rev:** Emperor on horseback in circle of shields **Note:** Dav. #D5854. Klippe.

Date	Mintage	VG	F	VF	XF	Unc
1614 Rare	—	—	—	—	—	—

KM# 34 5 THALER

Silver **Ruler:** Maximilian **Obv:** Date in exergue below master **Rev:** Emperor on horseback in circles of shields **Note:** Dav. #5854.

Date	Mintage	VG	F	VF	XF	Unc
1614 Rare	—	—	—	—	—	—

TRADE COINAGE

KM# 20 DUCAT

3.5000 g., 0.9860 Gold 0.1109 oz. AGW **Ruler:** Maximilian **Obv:** Maximilian standing **Rev:** Shield of arms **Note:** Fr. #3379.

Date	Mintage	VG	F	VF	XF	Unc
ND(ca1612)	—	1,150	2,700	5,200	8,900	—

KM# 47 DUCAT

3.5000 g., 0.9860 Gold 0.1109 oz. AGW **Ruler:** Karl of Austria **Obv:** Head of Karl right in inner circle **Rev:** Three shields of arms in inner circle **Note:** Fr. #3380.

Date	Mintage	VG	F	VF	XF	Unc
ND(ca.1620)	—	1,100	2,150	4,300	7,600	—

KM# 66 DUCAT

3.5000 g., 0.9860 Gold 0.1109 oz. AGW **Ruler:** Johann Eustach **Obv:** Three shields of arms in inner circle **Rev:** Crowned double-headed eagle **Note:** Fr. #3382.

Date	Mintage	VG	F	VF	XF	Unc
1626 Rare	—	—	—	—	—	—

KM# 71 DUCAT

3.5000 g., 0.9860 Gold 0.1109 oz. AGW **Ruler:** Johann Caspar II **Obv:** Crowned arms in inner circle, titles of Johann Caspar I **Rev:** Madonna and child in inner circle **Note:** Fr. #3383.

Date	Mintage	VG	F	VF	XF	Unc
ND(ca.1627) Rare	—	—	—	—	—	—

KM# 92 DUCAT

3.5000 g., 0.9860 Gold 0.1109 oz. AGW **Ruler:** Johann Caspar II **Obv:** Crowned arms in inner circle **Rev:** Madonna and child in inner circle **Note:** Fr. #3386.

Date	Mintage	VG	F	VF	XF	Unc
1666	—	725	1,600	3,400	6,400	—

KM# 105 DUCAT

3.5000 g., 0.9860 Gold 0.1109 oz. AGW **Ruler:** Johann Caspar II **Obv:** Armored bust of Johann Kaspar II right in inner circle **Mint:** Frankfurt am Main **Note:** Fr. #3384.

Date	Mintage	VG	F	VF	XF	Unc
1673 MF	—	1,450	2,900	5,800	10,000	—

KM# 128 DUCAT

3.5000 g., 0.9860 Gold 0.1109 oz. AGW **Ruler:** Ludwig Franz **Obv:** Bust of Franz Ludwig right in inner circle **Rev:** Crowned arms in inner circle **Note:** Fr. #3388.

Date	Mintage	VG	F	VF	XF	Unc
1696	—	1,200	2,750	5,300	9,000	—

KM# 130 DUCAT

3.5000 g., 0.9860 Gold 0.1109 oz. AGW **Ruler:** Ludwig Franz **Obv:** Armored bust right **Rev:** Cruciform arms **Mint:** Neisse **Note:** Fr. #3389.

Date	Mintage	VG	F	VF	XF	Unc
1699 LPH	—	1,600	3,800	7,800	4,300	—

KM# 21 2 DUCAT

7.0000 g., 0.9860 Gold 0.2219 oz. AGW **Ruler:** Maximilian **Obv:** Maximilian standing in inner circle **Rev:** Crowned arms in inner circle **Note:** Fr. #3378.

Date	Mintage	VG	F	VF	XF	Unc
ND(ca1612)	—	1,150	2,300	4,500	7,600	—

KM# 48 2 DUCAT

7.0000 g., 0.9860 Gold 0.2219 oz. AGW **Ruler:** Karl of Austria **Obv:** Armored bust of Karl right in inner circle **Note:** Fr. #3381.

Date	Mintage	VG	F	VF	XF	Unc
ND(ca1620)	—	2,400	4,200	9,000	14,000	—

KM# 93 2 DUCAT

7.0000 g., 0.9860 Gold 0.2219 oz. AGW **Ruler:** Johann Caspar II **Obv:** Crowned arms in inner circle **Rev:** Madonna and child in inner circle **Note:** Fr. #3385.

Date	Mintage	VG	F	VF	XF	Unc
1666	—	2,400	4,200	9,000	14,000	—

KM# 22 3 DUCAT

10.5000 g., 0.9860 Gold 0.3328 oz. AGW **Ruler:** Maximilian **Obv:** Maximilian standing facing with sword **Obv. Legend:** MAX. DGAR: (supported shield)... **Rev:** Equestrian figure right in circle of shields, order arms below **Note:** Fr. #3379a.

Date	Mintage	VG	F	VF	XF	Unc
1612 Rare	—	—	—	—	—	—

KM# 23 3 DUCAT

10.5000 g., 0.9860 Gold 0.3328 oz. AGW **Ruler:** Maximilian **Obv. Legend:** MAX. D (supported shield) G: AR... **Note:** Fr. #A3379a.

Date	Mintage	VG	F	VF	XF	Unc
1612	—	1,900	3,900	6,800	11,500	—

KM# A23 3 DUCAT

Gold **Ruler:** Maximilian **Obv:** Madonna & Child with rays around in margin 4 small shields of Brandenburg, Nürnberg, Hohenzollerna dn Pomerania, titles of Albrecht around **Rev:** Ornate cross, eagle arms in center, date in margin **Note:** Struck using 1/4 Thaler dies, KM#16.

Date	Mintage	VG	F	VF	XF	Unc
1612 CO	—	2,000	3,900	6,900	11,500	—
1614 CO	—	2,000	3,900	6,900	11,500	—

KM# 40 3 DUCAT

Gold **Ruler:** Maximilian **Obv:** Maximilian standing 1/2 left holding sword **Rev:** Maximilian mounted on horse to right, shields form circle around **Note:** Struck using 1/4 Thaler dies, KM#38.

Date	Mintage	VG	F	VF	XF	Unc
ND(ca1615) CO Rare	—	—	—	—	—	—

KM# 43 4 DUCAT

Gold **Ruler:** Maximilian **Obv:** Maximilian standing 1/2 left holding sword, supported shield at left **Rev:** Maximilian mounted on horse to right, shields form circle around **Note:** Struck using same dies as 1/2 Thaler, KM#41.

Date	Mintage	VG	F	VF	XF	Unc
1616 Rare	—	—	—	—	—	—

KM# 107 4 DUCAT

Gold **Ruler:** Johann Caspar II **Obv:** Bust right **Rev:** Madonna & Child above arms **Mint:** Frankfurt am Main **Note:** Struck using same dies as 1 Thaler, KM#102.

Date	Mintage	VG	F	VF	XF	Unc
1673 MF Rare	—	—	—	—	—	—

KM# 5 5 DUCAT

Gold **Ruler:** Maximilian **Obv:** Maximilian standing on ground, arms at left, helmet at right **Rev:** Emperor on horse back in circle of shields, date below **Note:** Struck using same dies as 1 Thaler, KM#3.

Date	Mintage	VG	F	VF	XF	Unc
1603 Rare	—	—	—	—	—	—

KM# 95 5 DUCAT

17.5000 g., 0.9860 Gold 0.5547 oz. AGW **Ruler:** Johann Caspar II **Obv:** Helmeted ornate arms **Rev:** Madonna with child in flaming oval **Note:** Prev. KM#10.

Date	Mintage	VG	F	VF	XF	Unc
1666 Rare	—	—	—	—	—	—

KM# 98 5 DUCAT

17.5000 g., 0.9860 Gold 0.5547 oz. AGW **Ruler:** Johann Caspar II **Obv:** Helmeted ornate arms **Rev:** Madonna with child in flaming oval, large flames **Note:** Prev. KM#11. Struck using same dies as 1 Thaler, KM#90.

Date	Mintage	VG	F	VF	XF	Unc
1668 Rare	—	—	—	—	—	—

KM# 6 6 DUCAT

21.0000 g., 0.9860 Gold 0.6657 oz. AGW **Ruler:** Maximilian **Obv:** Maximilian standing facing with sword **Rev:** Equestrian figure right in circle of shields, arms of the Order below **Note:** Prev. KM#12.

Date	Mintage	VG	F	VF	XF	Unc
1603 Rare	—	—	—	—	—	—

KM# 8 10 DUCAT
35.0000 g., 0.9860 Gold 1.1095 oz. AGW **Ruler:** Maximilian **Obv:** Maximilian standing facing with sword **Rev:** Equestrian figure right in circle of shields, Order arms below **Note:** Struck with 1 Thaler dies, KM#3. Prev. KM#13.

Date	Mintage	VG	F	VF	XF	Unc
1603 Rare	—	—	—	—	—	—

KM# 13 10 DUCAT
Gold **Ruler:** Maximilian **Obv:** Feet, arms and helmet all break legend **Obv. Legend:** ...ADMIN. **Rev:** Maximilian on horseback to right, shields form circle around **Note:** Struck using same dies as 1 Thaler, KM#11.

Date	Mintage	VG	F	VF	XF	Unc
1611 Rare	—	—	—	—	—	—

KM# 14 10 DUCAT
35.0000 g., 0.9860 Gold 1.1095 oz. AGW **Ruler:** Maximilian **Note:** Struck with 1 Thaler dies, Dav. #5850A.

Date	Mintage	VG	F	VF	XF	Unc
1611 Rare	—	—	—	—	—	—

KM# 36 10 DUCAT
Gold **Ruler:** Maximilian **Obv:** Date in exergue below master **Rev:** Maximilian on horseback to right, shields form circle around **Note:** Struck using same dies as 2 Thaler, KM#30.

Date	Mintage	VG	F	VF	XF	Unc
1614 Rare	—	—	—	—	—	—

KM# 15 10 DUCAT
35.0000 g., 0.9860 Gold 1.1095 oz. AGW **Ruler:** Johann Caspar II **Obv:** Helmeted ornate arms **Rev:** Madonna with child in flaming oval **Note:** Struck with 1 Thaler dies, Dav. #5859.

Date	Mintage	VG	F	VF	XF	Unc
1666 Rare	—	—	—	—	—	—

KM# 109 10 DUCAT
Gold **Ruler:** Johann Caspar II **Obv:** Bust right **Rev:** Madonna and Child above arms **Mint:** Frankfurt am Main **Note:** Struck using same dies as 1 Thaler, KM#102.

Date	Mintage	VG	F	VF	XF	Unc
1673 MF Rare	—	—	—	—	—	—

THANN

Located just 8 miles (14km) west-northwest of Mühlhausen in Alsace, the town of Thann was raised to the rank of free imperial city in 1383. Bracteats were minted there in the 13th century and it had a proper city coinage during the late 15th to 17th centuries. At the conclusion of the Thirty Years' War in 1648, France acquired the town in the general peace settlement.

ARMS

2-fold, divided vertically, single horizontal bar (usually shaded) on left, pine tree on right.

FREE CITY

REGULAR COINAGE

KM# 1 KREUZER
Silver **Obv:** City arms in circle **Obv. Legend:** MO. NO. TANNENSIS **Rev:** Cross in circle **Rev. Legend:** SALVE. CRVX. SANC.

Date	Mintage	VG	F	VF	XF	Unc
ND(1622-24)	—	33.00	55.00	110	220	—

KM# 2 KREUZER
Silver **Obv:** City arms in circle, date at end of margin **Obv. Legend:** MO. NO. TANNENSIS **Rev:** Cross in circle **Rev. Legend:** SALVE. CRVX. SANC.

Date	Mintage	VG	F	VF	XF	Unc
1622	—	27.00	50.00	100	210	—
1623	—	27.00	50.00	100	210	—

KM# 5 2 KREUZER (Halbbatzen)
Silver **Obv:** City arms, T (Z) S below **Obv. Legend:** MO. NO. TANNENSIS **Rev:** Bust of St. Theobald, date below

Date	Mintage	VG	F	VF	XF	Unc
1622	—	40.00	65.00	135	275	—
1623	—	40.00	65.00	135	275	—
1624	—	40.00	65.00	135	275	—

KM# 7 BATZEN
Silver **Obv:** City arms in trilobe, date **Obv. Legend:** MO NO... **Rev:** Facing bust of St. Theobald

Date	Mintage	VG	F	VF	XF	Unc
1623	—	50.00	100	220	—	—
1624	—	50.00	100	220	—	—

KM# 10 2 BATZEN (Doppelbätzner)
Silver **Obv:** City arms in hexalobe, value (Z) below **Obv. Legend:** MONETA NOVA **Rev:** St. Theobald seated facing forward, date in margin

Date	Mintage	VG	F	VF	XF	Unc
1623	—	90.00	180	360	—	—
1624	—	90.00	180	360	—	—

KM# 11 2 BATZEN (Doppelbätzner)
Silver **Obv:** City arms in pentalobe, value: (Z) below **Obv. Legend:** MONETA NOVA **Rev:** St. Theobald seated facing, date in margin

Date	Mintage	VG	F	VF	XF	Unc
1624	—	95.00	190	385	—	—

TRIER

The city of Trier, located on the Mosel River just a few miles from the border with Luxembourg, was an important place from Roman times up to the modern era. Tradition holds that the Emperor Claudius founded the city as Augusta Trevirorum (imperial city of the Treviri, a Belgian tribe of that locale). Even today, Trier contains more Roman antiquities than any other city in northern Europe and was one of the earliest centers of Christianity north of the Alps. Some parts of the 4th century basilica built by Valentinian I (364-75) are extant in the present cathedral, which dates from the 11th to 13th centuries. Trier was the western capital of the Roman Empire until it was taken by the Franks in 464. A bishopric was established there at the dawn of the Middle Ages and was raised to an archbishopric under Bishop Hetto (814-47). The earliest archiepiscopal coinage dates from the end of the 10th century. The importance of Trier grew during the High Middle Ages as the city became one of the ecclesiastic electorates of the German Empire under Baldwin of Luxembourg (1307-54). That lofty status was confirmed by the Golden Bull of 1356, which permanently established the seven electorates of the Empire. The wealth, power and prestige of the archbishops continued through the Late Middle Ages and withstood the Protestant Reformation in the 16th century. The economy of Trier was severely circumscribed by the hyper-inflation of the early period of the Thirty Years' War, and the city never regained its former position. Trier was taken by the French in 1794 and the last archbishop fled from his domains. In 1802, the archbishopric was secularized and divided between Nassau and France, but Prussia obtained most of Trier's territory in 1815, following the conclusion of the Napoleonic Wars.

RULERS

Lothar von Metternich, 1599-1623
Philipp Christof von Sötern, 1623-1652
Karl Kaspar von der Leyen, 1652-1676
Johann Hugo von Orsbeck, 1676-1711

MINT OFFICIALS' INITIALS

Initial	Date	Name
AL	1678-83	Adam Longerich
B	?	Philip Christoph Becker, die-cutter
CL	1683-93	Kaspar Longerich
FS	1693-95	Friedrich Schrattauer
GG	1698-1734	Gerhardt Godt
HA	1624-27	Hans Jacob Ayrer
HE	1669-75	Heinrich Eberskirchen
HL	1625-27	Heinrich Lambert
ICB	1659-66	Johann Christoph Buchsmeyer
IL	1680-90	Joseph Longerich
LS	1616-24	Lorenz Schneider
MS	1627-52	Matthias Stein

ARMS

Cross, usually displayed in conjunction with the family arms of the archbishop

REFERENCES

N = Alfred Noss, **Die Münzen von Trier**, v. I, pt. 2, **Beschreibung der Münzen 1307-1556**, Bonn, 1916.
S = Friedrich von Schrötter, **Die Münzen von Trier**, v. II, **Beschreibung der neuzeitlichen Münzen 1556-1794**, Bonn, 1908.
Sch = Wolfgang Schulten, **Deutsche Münzen aus der Zeit Karls V.**, Frankfurt am Main, 1974.

ARCHBISHOPRIC

REGULAR COINAGE

KM# 1 HELLER
Billon **Obv:** Orsbeck arms divide A-L in pearl circle **Note:** Uniface.

Date	Mintage	VG	F	VF	XF	Unc
ND(1678-83) AL	—	10.00	25.00	55.00	110	—

KM# 5 PFENNIG
Billon **Obv:** Arms divide last two digits of date, T above arms

Date	Mintage	VG	F	VF	XF	Unc
ND	—	10.00	20.00	40.00	80.00	—
(16)24	—	10.00	20.00	40.00	80.00	—
(16)25	—	10.00	20.00	40.00	80.00	—
(16)26	—	10.00	20.00	40.00	80.00	—
(16)33	—	10.00	20.00	40.00	80.00	—

KM# A5 PFENNIG
Silver **Ruler:** Philipp Christof **Obv:** Shield of Sötern arms superimposed on cross of Trier, all in a circle of pellets **Note:** Uniface schüssel-type.

Date	Mintage	VG	F	VF	XF	Unc
(1623-52)	—	—	—	—	—	—

KM# 2 PFENNIG
Billon **Obv:** Quartered arms with T above **Note:** Uniface.

Date	Mintage	VG	F	VF	XF	Unc
ND	—	10.00	20.00	40.00	80.00	—

KM# 3 PFENNIG
Billon **Obv:** Shield of Trier-Metternich arms with L above

Date	Mintage	VG	F	VF	XF	Unc
ND	—	10.00	20.00	40.00	80.00	—

KM# 4 PFENNIG
Billon **Obv:** L.A.T. above shield

Date	Mintage	VG	F	VF	XF	Unc
ND	—	10.00	20.00	40.00	80.00	—

KM# 6 PFENNIG
Billon **Obv:** Leyen arms on Trier arms in inner circle

Date	Mintage	VG	F	VF	XF	Unc
ND	—	10.00	20.00	40.00	80.00	—

KM# 7 PFENNIG
Billon **Obv:** Quartered shield in inner circle

Date	Mintage	VG	F	VF	XF	Unc
ND	—	10.00	20.00	40.00	80.00	—

KM# 8 PFENNIG
Billon **Obv:** Shield of arms divides C L

Date	Mintage	VG	F	VF	XF	Unc
ND(1683-93) CL	—	10.00	20.00	40.00	80.00	—

KM# 9 PFENNIG
Billon **Obv:** Shield of arms divides F S

Date	Mintage	VG	F	VF	XF	Unc
ND(1693-95) FS	—	10.00	20.00	40.00	80.00	—

KM# 93 4 PFENNIG (1/2 Albus)
Silver **Obv:** Arms in inner circle, titles of Philipp **Rev:** Standing figure

Date	Mintage	VG	F	VF	XF	Unc
1648	—	15.00	35.00	70.00	145	—

KM# 106 4 PFENNIG (1/2 Albus)
Silver **Obv:** Arms in inner circle **Rev:** Standing figure of St. Peter with key and book

Date	Mintage	VG	F	VF	XF	Unc
1652	—	15.00	35.00	70.00	145	—

KM# 107 4 PFENNIG (1/2 Albus)
Silver **Obv:** Shield of arms with date above in inner circle

Date	Mintage	VG	F	VF	XF	Unc
1652	—	15.00	30.00	60.00	120	—
1653	—	15.00	30.00	60.00	120	—
1654	—	15.00	30.00	60.00	120	—
1655	—	15.00	30.00	60.00	120	—
1656	—	15.00	30.00	60.00	120	—

KM# 121 4 PFENNIG (1/2 Albus)
Silver **Obv:** Oval arms topped by elector's hat **Rev:** Date in legend in Roman numerals

Date	Mintage	VG	F	VF	XF	Unc
ND	—	15.00	30.00	60.00	120	—
1657	—	15.00	30.00	60.00	120	—
1658	—	15.00	30.00	60.00	120	—

Date	Mintage	VG	F	VF	XF	Unc
1659	—	15.00	30.00	60.00	120	—
1660	—	15.00	30.00	60.00	120	—
1661	—	15.00	30.00	60.00	120	—
1662	—	15.00	30.00	60.00	120	—
1663	—	15.00	30.00	60.00	120	—
1666	—	15.00	30.00	60.00	120	—

KM# 122 4 PFENNIG (1/2 Albus)

Billon

Date	Mintage	VG	F	VF	XF	Unc
1663	—	8.00	20.00	40.00	80.00	—
1664	—	8.00	20.00	40.00	80.00	—
1665	—	8.00	20.00	40.00	80.00	—
1667	—	8.00	20.00	40.00	80.00	—
1668	—	8.00	20.00	40.00	80.00	—
1669	—	8.00	20.00	40.00	80.00	—
1670	—	8.00	20.00	40.00	80.00	—
1672	—	8.00	20.00	40.00	80.00	—
1674	—	8.00	20.00	40.00	80.00	—
1676	—	8.00	20.00	40.00	80.00	—

KM# 123 4 PFENNIG (1/2 Albus)

Billon **Obv:** Halved arms in wreath

Date	Mintage	VG	F	VF	XF	Unc
1665	—	8.00	20.00	45.00	90.00	—

KM# 127 4 PFENNIG (1/2 Albus)

Silver **Rev:** Date in legend in Arabic numerals

Date	Mintage	VG	F	VF	XF	Unc
1667	—	15.00	30.00	60.00	120	—
1668	—	15.00	30.00	60.00	120	—
1669	—	15.00	30.00	60.00	120	—
1670	—	15.00	30.00	60.00	120	—
1671	—	15.00	30.00	60.00	120	—
1672	—	15.00	30.00	60.00	120	—
1673	—	15.00	30.00	60.00	120	—
1674	—	15.00	30.00	60.00	120	—
1675	—	15.00	30.00	60.00	120	—
1676	—	15.00	30.00	60.00	120	—

KM# 138 4 PFENNIG (1/2 Albus)

Silver **Obv:** Round arms topped by elector's cap **Rev:** Standing figure of St. Peter with key, date in legend

Date	Mintage	VG	F	VF	XF	Unc
1677	—	15.00	35.00	70.00	145	—
1678	—	15.00	35.00	70.00	145	—
1679	—	15.00	35.00	70.00	145	—
1680	—	15.00	35.00	70.00	145	—
1681	—	15.00	35.00	70.00	145	—

KM# 126 4 PFENNIG (1/2 Albus)

Billon **Obv:** Orsbeck arms on Trier shield in wreath **Rev:** Value and date in wreath

Date	Mintage	VG	F	VF	XF	Unc
1677	—	10.00	20.00	45.00	90.00	180
1679 AL	—	10.00	20.00	45.00	90.00	180
1680	—	10.00	20.00	45.00	90.00	180

KM# 146 4 PFENNIG (1/2 Albus)

Billon **Obv:** Orsbeck arms on Trier shield, date above **Rev:** Value in wreath

Date	Mintage	VG	F	VF	XF	Unc
1680 AL	—	10.00	20.00	45.00	90.00	—

KM# 150 4 PFENNIG (1/2 Albus)

Billon **Rev:** Value **Rev. Inscription:** IIII / PFEN / TRIER

Date	Mintage	VG	F	VF	XF	Unc
1681 AL	—	10.00	20.00	40.00	85.00	—
1683 AL	—	10.00	20.00	40.00	85.00	—
1683 CL	—	10.00	20.00	40.00	85.00	—

KM# 154 4 PFENNIG (1/2 Albus)

Silver **Obv:** Arms cover inner circle

Date	Mintage	VG	F	VF	XF	Unc
1682	—	10.00	25.00	50.00	110	—
1683	—	10.00	25.00	50.00	110	—
1684	—	10.00	25.00	50.00	110	—
1686	—	10.00	25.00	50.00	110	—
1687	—	10.00	25.00	50.00	110	—
1688	—	10.00	25.00	50.00	110	—
1689	—	10.00	25.00	50.00	110	—

KM# 156 4 PFENNIG (1/2 Albus)

Billon **Rev:** Value **Rev. Inscription:** IIII / PHENN / TRIER

Date	Mintage	VG	F	VF	XF	Unc
1683	—	10.00	20.00	40.00	80.00	—

KM# A8 ALBUS

Silver **Obv:** Standing figure of St. Peter with key and book **Rev:** Quartered arms in inner circle **Mint:** Koblenz

Date	Mintage	VG	F	VF	XF	Unc
ND	—	45.00	80.00	150	300	—

KM# A9 ALBUS

Silver **Obv:** Standing figure of St. Helena with cross and nail **Mint:** Trier

Date	Mintage	VG	F	VF	XF	Unc
ND	—	45.00	80.00	150	300	—

KM# 10 ALBUS

Silver **Rev:** Arms divide value **Note:** Klippe.

Date	Mintage	VG	F	VF	XF	Unc
ND	—	—	—	—	—	—

KM# 45 ALBUS (8 Pfennig)

Silver **Obv:** Arms in inner circle **Rev:** Date in inner circle **Rev. Inscription:** VIII / PFENIG / 1622

Date	Mintage	VG	F	VF	XF	Unc
1622	—	33.00	65.00	135	275	—

KM# 46 ALBUS (8 Pfennig)

Silver **Rev:** Value: VIII and date

Date	Mintage	VG	F	VF	XF	Unc
1622	—	33.00	65.00	135	275	—

KM# 44 ALBUS (8 Pfennig)

Silver **Obv:** Standing figure of St. Peter with VIII right in inner circle **Rev:** Date above shield of arms in inner circle **Note:** Kipper 8 Pfennig.

Date	Mintage	VG	F	VF	XF	Unc
1622	—	33.00	65.00	135	275	—

KM# 11 ALBUS (9 Pfennig)

Silver **Obv:** Partial figure of St. Peter in inner circle with key and book **Rev:** Quartered shield of arms in inner circle **Mint:** Koblenz

Date	Mintage	VG	F	VF	XF	Unc
ND	—	33.00	65.00	135	275	—

KM# 12 ALBUS (9 Pfennig)

Silver **Obv:** Smaller figure of St. Peter

Date	Mintage	VG	F	VF	XF	Unc
ND	—	33.00	65.00	135	275	—

KM# 41 ALBUS (9 Pfennig)

Silver **Rev:** Date above shield in inner circle

Date	Mintage	VG	F	VF	XF	Unc
1621	—	33.00	65.00	135	275	—
1622	—	33.00	65.00	135	275	—
1623	—	33.00	65.00	135	275	—

KM# 66 ALBUS (New Standard)

Silver **Obv:** Date above arms in inner circle **Rev:** Standing figure of St. Peter with key **Note:** Large size, approximately 20 milimeters.

Date	Mintage	VG	F	VF	XF	Unc
ND	—	15.00	30.00	60.00	120	—
1625	—	—	—	—	—	—

KM# 67 ALBUS (New Standard)

Silver **Note:** Small size, approximately 17mm.

Date	Mintage	VG	F	VF	XF	Unc
1625	—	15.00	30.00	60.00	120	—
1627	—	15.00	30.00	60.00	120	—

KM# 74 ALBUS (New Standard)

Silver **Obv:** 27 above shield **Note:** Klippe.

Date	Mintage	VG	F	VF	XF	Unc
1627	—	—	—	—	—	—

KM# 72 ALBUS (New Standard)

Silver **Obv:** Oval arms, two-digit date at sides

Date	Mintage	VG	F	VF	XF	Unc
1627	—	15.00	30.00	60.00	120	—
1628	—	15.00	30.00	60.00	120	—

KM# 75 ALBUS (New Standard)

Silver **Obv:** Flat-topped shield with date above

Date	Mintage	VG	F	VF	XF	Unc
1628	—	15.00	30.00	60.00	120	—
1629	—	15.00	30.00	60.00	120	—
1630	—	15.00	30.00	60.00	120	—

KM# 76 ALBUS (New Standard)

Silver **Obv:** Date above shield **Note:** Klippe.

Date	Mintage	VG	F	VF	XF	Unc
1629	—	—	—	—	—	—

KM# 92 ALBUS (New Standard)

Silver **Obv:** 16 above shield, 47 at sides **Rev:** Standing figure of St. Philip with cross and book

Date	Mintage	VG	F	VF	XF	Unc
1647	—	15.00	30.00	65.00	130	—

KM# 94 ALBUS (New Standard)

Silver **Obv:** 16 above shield, other two digits at sides **Rev:** Standing figure of St. Philip

Date	Mintage	VG	F	VF	XF	Unc
1648	—	15.00	30.00	60.00	120	—
1649	—	15.00	30.00	60.00	120	—

KM# 100 ALBUS (New Standard)

Silver **Obv:** Date above shield

Date	Mintage	VG	F	VF	XF	Unc
1649	—	15.00	30.00	60.00	120	—
1650	—	15.00	30.00	60.00	120	—
1651	—	15.00	30.00	60.00	120	—
1652	—	15.00	30.00	60.00	120	—

KM# 56 3 ALBUS

Billon **Obv:** Standing figure of St. Peter with key, value right **Rev:** Shield of arms with date above in inner circle **Note:** Kipper 3 Albus.

Date	Mintage	VG	F	VF	XF	Unc
1622	—	85.00	175	350	725	—

KM# 48 6 ALBUS

Billon **Obv:** Standing figure of St. Peter with key and book, value right in inner circle **Rev:** Shield of arms with date above in inner circle **Note:** Kipper 6 Albus.

Date	Mintage	VG	F	VF	XF	Unc
1622	—	115	200	325	650	—

KM# 186 1/2 PETERMENGER

Billon **Ruler:** Johann Hugo **Obv:** Date above arms **Rev:** Value **Rev. Inscription:** 1/2 / PETER / MENGEN

Date	Mintage	VG	F	VF	XF	Unc
1698 GG	—	7.00	15.00	30.00	65.00	—
1699 GG	—	7.00	15.00	30.00	65.00	—
1700 GG	—	7.00	15.00	30.00	65.00	—

KM# 158 3 PETERMENGER (3 Albus)

Silver **Ruler:** Johann Hugo **Obv:** Shield of arms topped by elector's hat, date divided at bottom **Rev:** Bust of St. Peter with key and book in clouds, value below

Date	Mintage	VG	F	VF	XF	Unc
1689	—	20.00	40.00	90.00	180	—

KM# 159 3 PETERMENGER (3 Albus)

Silver **Ruler:** Johann Hugo **Obv:** Round arms cover inner circle, date in legend

Date	Mintage	VG	F	VF	XF	Unc
1689	—	20.00	45.00	90.00	180	—

KM# 176 3 PETERMENGER (3 Albus)

Silver **Rev:** Date divided above St. Peter

Date	Mintage	VG	F	VF	XF	Unc
1691	—	10.00	25.00	55.00	115	—
1692	—	10.00	25.00	55.00	115	—
1693	—	10.00	25.00	55.00	115	—
1694	—	10.00	25.00	55.00	115	—
1695	—	10.00	25.00	55.00	115	—

KM# A174 60 KREUZER (2/3 Thaler)

Silver **Ruler:** Johann Hugo **Obv:** Bust to right **Obv. Legend:** IOAN. HUGO. D.G. ARCH. TREV: S. R. I. P. E. E. S. **Rev:** Oval 4-fold arms with central shield of Orsbeck in baroque frame, crossed sword and crozier behind, electoral hat above, date at end of legend **Rev. Legend:** MONE. NOVA. TREVI — RENSIS. ANNI. (date) **Note:** Dav# 1024.

Date	Mintage	VG	F	VF	XF	Unc
1690 CL	—	375	750	1,500	2,900	—

KM# 68 1/8 THALER

Silver **Obv:** Bust of Archbishop right in inner circle, date below shoulder **Rev:** Value above arms in inner circle

Date	Mintage	VG	F	VF	XF	Unc
1625 IA	—	450	800	1,350	2,600	—

KM# 77 1/8 THALER

Silver **Obv:** Standing figure of St. Peter with key and book in inner circle, date in R.N. in legend **Rev:** Value in four lines in inner circle **Note:** Varieties exist.

Date	Mintage	VG	F	VF	XF	Unc
MDCLIX (1659)	—	85.00	165	325	650	—
MDCLX (1660)	—	85.00	165	325	650	—
MDCLXIII (1663)	—	85.00	165	325	650	—
MDCLXV (1665)	—	85.00	165	325	650	—
MDCLXVIII (1668)	—	85.00	165	325	650	—

KM# 52 1/4 THALER

Silver **Obv:** Bust of Archbishop right in inner circle, date below shoulder **Rev:** Shield of arms in inner circle

Date	Mintage	VG	F	VF	XF	Unc
1624	—	525	950	1,800	3,600	—

KM# 136 1/3 THALER

Silver **Obv:** Bust of Archbishop right in inner circle, value in oval below **Rev:** Crowned heart-shaped arms in inner circle, date in legend

Date	Mintage	VG	F	VF	XF	Unc
1675	—	600	1,200	2,000	3,900	—

KM# 147 1/3 THALER

Silver **Obv:** Bust of Archbishop right in inner circle **Rev:** Crowned oval arms divides date in inner circle, value in oval below

Date	Mintage	VG	F	VF	XF	Unc
1680	—	600	1,200	2,000	3,900	—

KM# 17 1/2 THALER

Silver **Obv:** Standing figure of St. Peter left with key and book in inner circle **Rev:** Shield of arms in inner circle, date in legend

Date	Mintage	VG	F	VF	XF	Unc
1602	—	2,200	3,600	6,000	10,000	—

KM# 18 1/2 THALER

Silver **Obv:** Standing figure of St. Peter right with key above shoulder and book in inner circle **Note:** Klippe.

Date	Mintage	VG	F	VF	XF	Unc
1602	—	2,650	4,300	9,500	—	—

KM# 42 1/2 THALER

Silver **Obv:** Figure of St. Peter walking right with key right and book in inner circle **Rev:** Shield of arms in inner circke, date at top in legend

Date	Mintage	VG	F	VF	XF	Unc
1621	—	1,350	2,400	4,500	8,750	—

KM# 53 1/2 THALER

Silver **Obv:** Bust of Archbishop right in inner circle, date below shoulder **Rev:** Helmeted arms, date divided at top in inner circle

Date	Mintage	VG	F	VF	XF	Unc
1624	—	800	1,350	2,700	5,500	—
1627 MS / IA	—	800	1,350	2,700	5,500	—

KM# 54 1/2 THALER

Silver **Rev:** Without date **Note:** Klippe.

Date	Mintage	VG	F	VF	XF	Unc
1624	—	1,000	1,650	3,300	6,200	—
1627 MS / IA	—	1,000	1,650	3,300	6,200	—

KM# 124 1/2 THALER

Silver **Obv:** Archbishop

Date	Mintage	VG	F	VF	XF	Unc
1666 ICB	—	700	1,350	2,750	5,500	—

KM# 137 2/3 THALER

Silver

Date	Mintage	VG	F	VF	XF	Unc
1675	—	300	600	1,200	2,300	—

KM# 148 2/3 THALER

Silver **Obv:** Bust of Archbishop right in inner circle **Rev:** Crowned oval arms divide date in inner circle, value in oval below

Date	Mintage	VG	F	VF	XF	Unc
1680 AL	—	525	950	1,800	3,600	—

KM# 174 2/3 THALER

Silver

Date	Mintage	VG	F	VF	XF	Unc
1690 CL	—	325	650	1,300	2,600	—
1691 CL	—	325	650	1,300	2,600	—
1692 CL	—	—	—	—	—	—

KM# 173 2/3 THALER

Silver **Note:** Varieties exist, including divided date in legend.

Date	Mintage	VG	F	VF	XF	Unc
1690 CL	—	350	700	1,400	2,750	—
1691 CL	—	350	700	1,400	2,750	—

KM# 178 2/3 THALER

Silver

Date	Mintage	VG	F	VF	XF	Unc
1694 FS	—	350	700	1,400	2,750	—

KM# 73 3/4 THALER

Silver **Obv:** Bust of Archbishop right in inner circle **Rev:** Helmeted arms with date at top in inner circle

Date	Mintage	VG	F	VF	XF	Unc
1627 IA	—	2,700	4,500	8,900	—	—

KM# 14 THALER

Silver **Obv:** Helmeted arms in inner circle **Rev:** Facing figure of St. Helena holding cross and nail in inner circle **Mint:** Trier **Note:** Dav. #5865.

Date	Mintage	VG	F	VF	XF	Unc
ND	—	5,900	9,500	15,000	—	—

KM# 19 THALER

Silver **Obv:** Standing figure of St. Peter left holding key and book in inner circle **Rev:** Helmeted arms in inner circle, date in legend **Mint:** Koblenz **Note:** Dav. #5867.

Date	Mintage	VG	F	VF	XF	Unc
1602	—	5,900	9,500	15,000	—	—

KM# 22 THALER

Silver **Obv:** Helmeted arms in inner circle, two-digit date divided by helmet 6-7 **Rev:** Facing figure of St. Helena holding cross and nail in inner circle **Mint:** Trier **Note:** Dav. #5869.

Date	Mintage	VG	F	VF	XF	Unc
1607	—	5,900	9,500	15,000	—	—

KM# 23 THALER

Silver **Obv:** Full four-digit date divided by helmet **Note:** Varieties exist. Dav. #5871.

Date	Mintage	VG	F	VF	XF	Unc
1608	—	4,400	7,100	11,000	—	—
1609	—	4,400	7,100	11,000	—	—
1610	—	4,400	7,100	11,000	—	—
1611	—	4,400	7,100	11,000	—	—
1612	—	4,400	7,100	11,000	—	—

KM# 25 THALER

Silver **Mint:** Koblenz **Note:** Similar to Dav. #5867, but date divided by helmet on reverse. Varieties exist. Dav. #5873.

Date	Mintage	VG	F	VF	XF	Unc
1609	—	2,000	3,650	7,600	11,000	—
1610	—	2,000	3,650	7,600	11,000	—
1613	—	2,000	3,650	7,600	11,000	—
1615	—	2,000	3,650	7,600	11,000	—

KM# 29 THALER

Silver **Obv:** Helmeted arms in inner circle, date divided by helmet **Rev:** Facing figure of St. Peter holding key and book in inner circle **Mint:** Trier **Note:** Varieties exist. Dav. #5876.

Date	Mintage	VG	F	VF	XF	Unc
1612 Rare	—	—	—	—	—	—

KM# 30 THALER

Silver **Obv:** Obverse of Dav. #5871 **Rev:** Reverse of Dav. #5876 **Note:** Mule. Dav. #5877.

Date	Mintage	VG	F	VF	XF	Unc
1612 Rare	—	—	—	—	—	—

KM# 31 THALER

Silver **Rev:** Radiant Madonna and child in inner circle, date in legend **Mint:** Koblenz **Note:** Dav. #5879.

Date	Mintage	VG	F	VF	XF	Unc
1615 Rare	—	—	—	—	—	—

Note: Künker Auction 51, 9-09, VF realized approximately $27,790.

KM# 33 THALER

Silver **Obv:** Bust of Archbishop right in inner circle **Rev:** Helmeted arms in inner circle, date in legend **Note:** Dav. #5882.

Date	Mintage	VG	F	VF	XF	Unc
1616 LS Rare	—	—	—	—	—	—
1617 LS Rare	—	—	—	—	—	—

KM# 34 THALER

Silver **Note:** Klippe. Dav. #5882A.

Date	Mintage	VG	F	VF	XF	Unc
1616 LS Rare	—	—	—	—	—	—
1617 LS Rare	—	—	—	—	—	—

KM# 35 THALER

Silver **Rev:** Radiant Madonna and child in inner circle, date in legend **Note:** Dav. #5883.

Date	Mintage	VG	F	VF	XF	Unc
1616 Rare	—	—	—	—	—	—

KM# 38 THALER

Silver **Rev:** Helmeted arms in inner circle, two-digit date (17) in legend **Note:** Dav. #5884.

Date	Mintage	VG	F	VF	XF	Unc
1617 Rare	—	—	—	—	—	—

KM# 43 THALER

Silver **Rev:** Date divided below arms in inner circle **Note:** Dav. #5885.

Date	Mintage	VG	F	VF	XF	Unc
1621	—	1,550	2,800	4,400	7,500	—

KM# 59 THALER

Silver **Obv:** Bust of Archbishop right in inner circle, date below shoulder **Rev:** Helmeted arms in inner circle **Note:** Varieties exist. Dav. #5887.

Date	Mintage	VG	F	VF	XF	Unc
1624	—	550	1,150	2,000	4,000	—

KM# 60 THALER

Silver **Note:** Klippe. Dav. #5887A.

Date	Mintage	VG	F	VF	XF	Unc
1624 Rare	—	—	—	—	—	—

Note: Dr. Busso Peus Nachfolger Auction 379, 4-04, XF realized approximately $23,885

KM# 61 THALER

Silver **Rev:** Date divided by helmet **Note:** Dav. #5889.

Date	Mintage	VG	F	VF	XF	Unc
1624	—	1,250	2,250	4,750	8,500	—

KM# 62 THALER

Silver **Obv:** Bust right with LS and date on shoulder **Note:** Dav. #5890.

Date	Mintage	VG	F	VF	XF	Unc
1624	—	1,250	2,250	4,750	8,500	—

KM# 69 THALER

Silver **Obv:** Bust of Archbishop right divides date in inner circle **Rev:** Helmeted arms in inner circle **Note:** Dav. #5891.

Date	Mintage	VG	F	VF	XF	Unc
1625 0	—	1,600	2,900	5,500	9,000	—

KM# 70 THALER

Silver **Note:** Klippe. Dav. #5891A.

Date	Mintage	VG	F	VF	XF	Unc
1625 Rare	—	—	—	—	—	—

KM# 109 THALER

Silver **Obv:** Arms topped by elector's hat in inner circle **Rev:** Radiant Madonna and child in inner circle, date in Roman numerals in legend **Note:** Dav. #5894.

Date	Mintage	VG	F	VF	XF	Unc
1657 Rare	—	—	—	—	—	—

Note: Künker Auction 180, 1-11, VF-XF realized approximately $32,865.

KM# 111 THALER

Silver **Obv:** 3/4 right facing bust of Archbishop in inner circle **Rev:** Arms topped by elector's hat in inner circle, date in legend **Note:** Varieties exist. Dav. #5896.

Date	Mintage	VG	F	VF	XF	Unc
1659 ICB Rare	—	—	—	—	—	—

Note: Fritz Rudolf Künker Münzenhandlung Auction 90, 3-04, VF-XF realized approximately $14,265.

KM# 112 THALER

Silver **Obv:** 3/4 right facing bust of Archbishop in inner circle **Note:** Dav. #5897.

Date	Mintage	VG	F	VF	XF	Unc
1659 ICB Rare	—	—	—	—	—	—

KM# 125 THALER

Silver **Obv:** Larger head left **Note:** Dav. #5898.

Date	Mintage	VG	F	VF	XF	Unc
1666 ICB Rare	—	—	—	—	—	—

KM# 135 THALER

Silver **Obv:** 3/4 right facing bust of Archbishop in inner circle **Rev:** Heart-shaped arms topped by elector's hat in inner circle, date in legend **Note:** Dav. #5899.

Date	Mintage	VG	F	VF	XF	Unc
1671 Rare	—	—	—	—	—	—

KM# 151 THALER

Silver **Obv:** Bust of Archbishop right in inner circle **Rev:** Helmeted arms in inner circle, date in legend **Note:** Dav. #5901.

Date	Mintage	VG	F	VF	XF	Unc
1681 Rare	—	—	—	—	—	—

KM# 152 THALER

Silver **Obv:** Without inner circle **Note:** Dav. #5902.

Date	Mintage	VG	F	VF	XF	Unc
1681 Rare	—	—	—	—	—	—

KM# A63 1-1/2 THALER

Silver **Ruler:** Lothar **Obv:** 4-fold arms of Trier and Metternich with central shield of Prüm, ornate helmet above with crest of Metternich arms dividing date, titles of Lothar **Rev:** Full-length facing figure of St. Helena with cross **Rev. Legend:** MONETA. NOVA **Note:** S #124a.

Date	Mintage	VG	F	VF	XF	Unc
1611 Rare	—	—	—	—	—	—

KM# 63 1-1/2 THALER

Silver **Obv:** Bust of Archbishop right in inner circle **Rev:** Helmeted arms in inner circle, date divided by helmet **Mint:** Koblenz **Note:** Dav. #A5888.

Date	Mintage	VG	F	VF	XF	Unc
1624 Rare	—	—	—	—	—	—

KM# 64 1-1/2 THALER

Silver **Mint:** Koblenz **Note:** Klippe. Dav. #B5888.

Date	Mintage	VG	F	VF	XF	Unc
1624 Rare	—	—	—	—	—	—

KM# 15 2 THALER

Silver **Obv:** Helmeted arms in inner circle, date divided by helmet **Rev:** Facing figure of St. Helena holding cross and nail in inner circle **Mint:** Trier **Note:** Dav. #B5864

Date	Mintage	VG	F	VF	XF	Unc
ND Rare	—	—	—	—	—	—

KM# 20 2 THALER

Silver **Ruler:** Lothar **Obv:** Standing figure of St. Peter left holding key and book in inner circle **Rev:** Helmeted arms in inner circle, date in legend **Mint:** Koblenz **Note:** Dav. #5866

Date	Mintage	VG	F	VF	XF	Unc
1602 Rare	—	—	—	—	—	—

KM# 21 2 THALER

Silver **Ruler:** Lothar **Obv:** Facing figure of St. Helena holding cross and nail in inner circle **Rev:** Helmeted arms with date above in inner circle **Note:** Dav. #5868.

Date	Mintage	VG	F	VF	XF	Unc
1606 Rare	—	—	—	—	—	—

KM# 24 2 THALER

Silver **Obv:** Helmeted arms in inner circle, date divided by helmet **Rev:** Facing figrue of St. Helena holding cross and nail in inner circle **Mint:** Trier **Note:** Dav. #5870

Date	Mintage	VG	F	VF	XF	Unc
1608 Rare	—	—	—	—	—	—
1609 Rare	—	—	—	—	—	—
1610 Rare	—	—	—	—	—	—

KM# 27 2 THALER

Silver **Mint:** Koblenz **Note:** Klippe. Similar to Dav. #5866, but date divided by helmet on reverse. Dav. #5872.

Date	Mintage	VG	F	VF	XF	Unc
1610 Rare	—	—	—	—	—	—

KM# 28 2 THALER

Silver **Note:** Klippe. Dav. #5870A.

Date	Mintage	VG	F	VF	XF	Unc
1611 Rare	—	—	—	—	—	—

KM# 32 2 THALER

Silver **Obv:** Helmeted arms in inner circle, date divided by helmet **Rev:** Radiant Madonna and child in inner circle, date in legend **Note:** Klippe. Mining 2 Thaler. Dav. #5878.

Date	Mintage	VG	F	VF	XF	Unc
1615	—	8,100	12,500	19,000	—	—

KM# 36 2 THALER

Silver **Note:** Dav. #5880.

Date	Mintage	VG	F	VF	XF	Unc
1616/15 Rare	—	—	—	—	—	—

KM# 37 2 THALER

Silver **Obv:** Bust of Archbishop right in inner circle **Rev:** Helmeted arms in inner circle, date in legend **Note:** Dav. #5881.

Date	Mintage	VG	F	VF	XF	Unc
1616 Rare	—	—	—	—	—	—

KM# 39 2 THALER

Silver **Note:** Klippe. Dav. #5881A.

Date	Mintage	VG	F	VF	XF	Unc
1617 Rare	—	—	—	—	—	—

KM# 55 2 THALER

Silver **Obv:** Bust of Archbishop right in inner circle, date below shoulder **Rev:** Helmeted arms in inner circle **Note:** Dav. #A5886.

Date	Mintage	VG	F	VF	XF	Unc
1624 Rare	—	—	—	—	—	—

KM# A56 2 THALER

Silver **Note:** Klippe. Dav. #B5886.

Date	Mintage	VG	F	VF	XF	Unc
1624 Rare	—	—	—	—	—	—

KM# 57 2 THALER

Silver **Rev:** Date divided by helmet **Note:** Dav. #5888.

Date	Mintage	VG	F	VF	XF	Unc
1624 Rare	—	—	—	—	—	—

KM# 58 2 THALER

Silver **Note:** Klippe. Dav. #5888A.

Date	Mintage	VG	F	VF	XF	Unc
1624 Rare	—	—	—	—	—	—

KM# 110 2 THALER

Silver **Obv:** Arms topped by elector's hat in inner circle **Rev:** Radiant Madonna and child in inner circle, date in roman numerals in legend **Note:** Dav. #5893.

Date	Mintage	VG	F	VF	XF	Unc
1657 Rare	—	—	—	—	—	—

KM# 113 2 THALER

Silver **Note:** Dav. #5895.

Date	Mintage	VG	F	VF	XF	Unc
1659 ICB Rare	—	—	—	—	—	—

KM# 153 2 THALER

Silver **Obv:** Bust of Archbishop right in inner circle **Rev:** Helmeted arms in inner circle, date in legend **Note:** Dav. #5900.

Date	Mintage	VG	F	VF	XF	Unc
1681 Rare	—	—	—	—	—	—

KM# 175 3 THALER

Silver **Obv:** Bust of Archbishop right in inner circle, date below shoulder **Rev:** Helmeted arms in inner circle **Mint:** Koblenz **Note:** Dav. #5886.

Date	Mintage	VG	F	VF	XF	Unc
1624 Rare	—	—	—	—	—	—

TRADE COINAGE

KM# 16 GOLDGULDEN

3.5000 g., 0.9860 Gold 0.1109 oz. AGW **Obv:** Arms topped by Christ on throne **Rev:** Three shields in trefoil with arms at center **Mint:** Koblenz **Note:** Fr#3459.

Date	Mintage	VG	F	VF	XF	Unc
1601	—	1,000	2,000	4,000	6,500	—
1605	—	1,000	2,000	4,000	6,500	—
1608	—	1,000	2,000	4,000	6,500	—
1609	—	1,000	2,000	4,000	6,500	—
1613	—	1,000	2,000	4,000	6,500	—
1617	—	1,000	2,000	4,000	6,500	—
1618	—	1,000	2,000	4,000	6,500	—
1619	—	1,000	2,000	4,000	6,500	—
ND	—	1,000	2,000	4,000	6,500	—

KM# 26 GOLDGULDEN

3.5000 g., 0.9860 Gold 0.1109 oz. AGW **Obv:** St. Helen standing **Rev:** Four shields in quatrefoil with arms at center **Mint:** Trier **Note:** Fr#3462.

Date	Mintage	VG	F	VF	XF	Unc
1608	—	850	1,700	3,150	5,500	—
1610	—	850	1,700	3,150	5,500	—
1611	—	850	1,700	3,150	5,500	—

KM# 40 GOLDGULDEN

3.5000 g., 0.9860 Gold 0.1109 oz. AGW **Obv:** Arms topped by bust of St. Peter **Mint:** Koblenz **Note:** Fr#3460.

Date	Mintage	VG	F	VF	XF	Unc
1619	—	650	1,250	2,750	5,000	—

KM# 85 GOLDGULDEN

3.5000 g., 0.9860 Gold 0.1109 oz. AGW **Obv:** Arms in inner circle **Rev:** Madonna and child in inner circle **Mint:** Philipsburg **Note:** Fr#3463.

Date	Mintage	VG	F	VF	XF	Unc
1632 Rare	—	—	—	—	—	—

KM# 165 GOLDGULDEN

3.5000 g., 0.9860 Gold 0.1109 oz. AGW **Ruler:** Johann Hugo **Obv:** Bust of St. Peter, value below **Rev:** Three shields of arms **Note:** Fr#3471.

Date	Mintage	VG	F	VF	XF	Unc
1684 CL	—	1,750	3,500	7,500	12,000	—
1694	—	1,750	3,500	7,500	12,000	—
1700	—	1,750	3,500	7,500	12,000	—

KM# 91 1/2 DUCAT

1.7500 g., 0.9860 Gold 0.0555 oz. AGW **Obv:** Bust of Johann Hugo right **Rev:** Crowned arms **Note:** Fr#3469.

Date	Mintage	VG	F	VF	XF	Unc
ND	—	1,350	1,800	3,000	6,300	—

KM# 108 DUCAT

1.7500 g., 0.9860 Gold 0.0555 oz. AGW **Obv:** Karl Caspar **Note:** Fr#3465.

Date	Mintage	VG	F	VF	XF	Unc
1654	—	2,000	3,500	6,500	11,000	—
1656	—	2,000	3,500	6,500	11,000	—

KM# 149 DUCAT

1.7500 g., 0.9860 Gold 0.0555 oz. AGW **Obv:** Johann Hugo **Note:** Fr#3468.

Date	Mintage	VG	F	VF	XF	Unc
1680 AL	—	1,150	2,500	5,000	9,000	—
1684 CL	—	1,150	2,500	5,000	9,000	—
1691	—	1,150	2,500	5,000	9,000	—
1692 CL	—	1,150	2,500	5,000	9,000	—
1699	—	1,150	2,500	5,000	9,000	—

KM# 179 DUCAT

1.7500 g., 0.9860 Gold 0.0555 oz. AGW **Rev:** Three shields of arms **Note:** Fr#3470.

Date	Mintage	VG	F	VF	XF	Unc
1690	—	2,250	4,500	9,000	15,000	—

KM# A114 6 DUCAT

21.0000 g., 0.9860 Gold 0.6657 oz. AGW **Obv:** 3/4 bust of Karl Kaspar right **Rev:** Capped ornate arms **Note:** Struck with 1 Thaler dies, KM#111.

Date	Mintage	VG	F	VF	XF	Unc
1659 Unique	—	—	—	—	—	—

PATTERNS

Including off metal strikes

KM#	Date	Mintage	Identification	Mkt Val
PnA1	(15)89	—	Pfennig. Gold. MB#86.	—
Pn1	1625	—	Thaler. Lead.	1,000
Pn2	1677	—	Petermenger. Gold.	1,200
Pn3	1678	—	Petermenger. Gold.	1,200
Pn4	1681	—	Petermenger. Gold.	1,200
Pn5	1684	—	Petermenger. Gold.	1,200
Pn6	1689	—	3 Petermenger. Gold.	2,250
PnA7	1691	—	Ducat. Silver. KM#149	1,500

ULM

A free city on the Danube located about 60 miles southeast of Stuttgart, Ulm is known from documents to have existed at least from the mid-9th century. During the 11th century, Ulm rose to prominence as the chief urban center of Swabia. The city was granted the distinction of a free imperial city in 1155. The right to mint its own coinage was given to the city in 1398. After a period of jointly issued coins with the cities of Ravensburg and Überlingen, Ulm struck a long series on its own beginning in 1546. Local city coinage ended in 1773, but it was not until 1803 that its free status ended, at which time Ulm became part of Bavaria. Ulm passed permanently to Württemberg in 1809.

MINT MARKS

G - Günzburg

MINT OFFICIALS' INITIALS

Initials	Date	Name
	1620-23	Franz Philipp Kling of Augsburg
	1623	Moritz Lang of Augsburg
	June-Oct., 1626	Friedrich held Hagelsheimer
HL	1635-40	Hans Ludwig der Jüngere
MK	1635-40	Marx Kienlin
HLK	1635-40	Ludwig and Kienlin
HL / HLK	1663-70	Hans Ludwig der Jüng-Jüngere and Hans Adam Kielin
M	1671-1704	Johann Bartholomäus Müller

ARMS

2-fold, divided horizontally, upper half usually shaded cross-hatching or other pattern.

REFERENCE

H = Adolf Häberle, Ulmer **Münz= und Geldgeschichte des XVI.-XIX. Jahrhunderts**, Ulm, 1937.

FREE CITY

REGULAR COINAGE

KM# 7 HELLER

Copper **Obv:** City arms with notched sides **Note:** Uniface. Varieties exist.

Date	Mintage	VG	F	VF	XF	Unc
ND(ca1620/21)	—	10.00	20.00	45.00	90.00	—

KM# 75 HELLER

Silver **Obv:** City arms in half-round shield **Note:** Uniface. Varieties exist.

Date	Mintage	VG	F	VF	XF	Unc
ND(late 17th c)	—	7.00	15.00	35.00	70.00	—

KM# 9a PFENNIG

Copper, 13 mm. **Obv:** City arms with notched sides, suares with pellets in half of shield **Note:** Uniface. Varieties exist.

Date	Mintage	VG	F	VF	XF	Unc
ND(ca 1620-21)	—	—	—	—	—	—

KM# 9b PFENNIG

Copper, 15 mm. **Obv:** City arms with notched sides, diagonial lines in top half of shield **Note:** Uniface.

Date	Mintage	F	VF	XF	Unc	BU
ND(ca 1620-21)	—	—	—	—	—	—

KM# 22 PFENNIG (1/240 Gulden)

Copper **Obv:** City arms, flanked by 2 rosettes, date above **Rev:** Inscription in wreath **Rev. Inscription:** CC / XXXX **Note:** Square flan.

Date	Mintage	VG	F	VF	XF	Unc
16Z1	—	30.00	60.00	120	240	—

KM# 21 PFENNIG (1/240 Gulden)

Copper **Obv:** City arms, date above **Rev:** Inscription in wreath **Rev. Inscription:** CC / XXXX **Note:** Square flan. Varieties exist.

Date	Mintage	VG	F	VF	XF	Unc
16Z1	—	30.00	60.00	120	240	—

KM# 79 PFENNIG (1/240 Gulden)

Copper **Obv:** Oval city arms in ornamented frame **Note:** Round flan. Uniface. Varieties exist.

Date	Mintage	VG	F	VF	XF	Unc
ND(late 17th c)	—	—	—	—	—	—

KM# 19 4 HELLER (Vierer = 2 Pfennig = Kreuzer)

Copper **Obv:** Oval city arms in ornamented frame, 4 above **Note:** Uniface. Varieties exist.

Date	Mintage	VG	F	VF	XF	Unc
ND(1621/22)	—	25.00	55.00	115	—	—

KM# 77 4 HELLER (Vierer = 2 Pfennig = Kreuzer)

Copper **Obv:** Oval city arms in ornamented frame **Note:** Uniface. Varieties exist.

Date	Mintage	VG	F	VF	XF	Unc
ND(late 17th c)	—	25.00	55.00	115	—	—

KM# 40 2 PFENNIG (Zweier)

Silver **Obv:** City arms in spade-shaped frame divide date, value 2 above **Note:** Uniface. Varieties exist.

Date	Mintage	VG	F	VF	XF	Unc
(16)24	—	35.00	70.00	145	—	—

KM# 11 KREUZER

Silver **Obv:** City arms **Rev:** Crowned imperial eagle, I in orb on breast, titles of Ferdinand II

Date	Mintage	VG	F	VF	XF	Unc
ND(ca1620/21)	—	10.00	20.00	45.00	90.00	—

KM# 42 KREUZER

Silver **Obv:** Ornamented city arms, date above **Rev:** Crowned imperial eagle, I in orb on breast

Date	Mintage	VG	F	VF	XF	Unc
1624	—	15.00	35.00	75.00	150	—

KM# 43 KREUZER

Silver **Obv:** Ornamented city arms divide date **Rev:** Crowned imperial eagle, I in orb on breast

Date	Mintage	VG	F	VF	XF	Unc
1624	—	15.00	30.00	60.00	120	—
(16)24	—	15.00	30.00	60.00	120	—

KM# 70 KREUZER

Silver **Obv:** Round city arms in baroque frame **Rev:** Crowned imperial eagle, I in orb on breast

Date	Mintage	VG	F	VF	XF	Unc
ND(after 1681)	—	10.00	20.00	45.00	90.00	—

KM# 38 2 KREUZER (1/2 Batzen)

Silver **Obv:** City arms divide date **Rev:** Crowned imperial eagle, 2 in orb on breast, titles of Ferdinand II **Note:** Varieties exist.

Date	Mintage	VG	F	VF	XF	Unc
(16)23	—	12.00	25.00	55.00	115	—
(16)24	—	12.00	25.00	55.00	115	—

KM# 66 2 KREUZER (1/2 Batzen)

Silver **Obv:** City arms **Rev:** Crowned imperial eagle, 2 in oval on eagle, titles of Leopold I

Date	Mintage	VG	F	VF	XF	Unc
ND(ca1660-80)	—	—	—	—	—	—

KM# 73 2 KREUZER (1/2 Batzen)

Silver **Obv:** City arms in baroque frame, arms divide ST - M **Rev:** Crowned imperial eagle, 2 in orb on breast

Date	Mintage	VG	F	VF	XF	Unc
ND(after 1692)	—	—	—	—	—	—

KM# 72 2 KREUZER (1/2 Batzen)

Silver **Obv:** City arms in baroque frame **Obv. Legend:** STATT MYNTZ **Rev:** Crowned imperial eagle, 2 in orb on breast **Note:** Varieties exist.

Date	Mintage	VG	F	VF	XF	Unc
ND(after 1692)	—	7.00	15.00	30.00	60.00	120

KM# 68 4 KREUZER (Batzen)

Silver **Obv:** City arms in baroque frame **Rev:** Crowned imperial eagle, 4 in oval on eagle

Date	Mintage	VG	F	VF	XF	Unc
ND(ca1660-80)	—	40.00	85.00	175	—	—

KM# 17 6 KREUZER

Silver **Obv:** City arms in ornamented shield **Rev:** Crowned iomperial eagle, value (6) at bottom, titles of Ferdinand II around **Note:** Varieties exist.

Date	Mintage	VG	F	VF	XF	Unc
ND(after 1620)	—	80.00	160	325	650	—

KM# 28 6 KREUZER

Silver **Obv:** City arms divide date **Rev:** Ornament at end of inscription **Rev. Inscription:** VI / STADT / MVNTZ

Date	Mintage	VG	F	VF	XF	Unc
1622	—	95.00	190	385	—	—

KM# 13 12 KREUZER (Dreibätzner)

Silver **Obv:** City arms in baroque frame, date in margin **Rev:** Crowned imperial eagle, 12 in orb on breast, titles of Ferdinand II around

Date	Mintage	VG	F	VF	XF	Unc
1620	—	—	—	—	—	—

KM# 24 12 KREUZER (Dreibätzner)

Silver **Obv:** City arms in baroque frame **Rev:** Crowned imperial eagle, 12 in orb on breast, titles of Ferdinand II around **Note:** Varieties exist.

Date	Mintage	VG	F	VF	XF	Unc
ND(ca1621/22)	—	—	—	—	—	—

KM# 30 12 KREUZER (Stadtmünz)

Silver **Obv:** City arms divide date **Rev:** Ornament at end of inscription **Rev. Inscription:** XII / STADT / MINTZ

Date	Mintage	VG	F	VF	XF	Unc
1622	—	—	—	—	—	—

KM# 32 15 KREUZER (Stadtmünz)

Silver **Obv:** City arms divide date **Rev:** Ornament at end of inscription **Rev. Inscription:** XV K / STADT / MINTZ

Date	Mintage	VG	F	VF	XF	Unc
1622	—	—	—	—	—	—

KM# 26 24 KREUZER (Sechsbätzner)

Silver **Obv:** City arms in baroque frame **Rev:** Crowned imperial eagle, titles of Ferdinand II around **Note:** Varieties exist.

Date	Mintage	VG	F	VF	XF	Unc
ND(ca 1621/22)	—	250	500	1,000	2,000	—

KM# 1 30 KREUZER (1/2 Guldenthaler)

Silver **Obv:** City arms, date in margin **Rev:** Crowned imperial eagle, 30 in orb on breast, titles of Rudolf II around

Date	Mintage	VG	F	VF	XF	Unc
1606	—	1,000	2,000	4,000	7,700	—

KM# 34 30 KREUZER (Stadtmünz)

Silver **Obv:** City arms divide date **Rev:** Ornament at end of inscription **Rev. Inscription:** XXX / STADT MINTZ (or MVNTZ) **Note:** Varieties exist.

Date	Mintage	VG	F	VF	XF	Unc
1622	—	450	900	1,800	3,600	—
1623	—	—	—	—	—	—

KM# 3 60 KREUZER (Guldenthaler)

Silver **Obv:** City arms, date in margin **Rev:** Crowned imperial eagle, 60 in orb on breast, titles of Rudolf II **Note:** Dav#138.

Date	Mintage	VG	F	VF	XF	Unc
1606	—	1,800	3,600	7,200	—	—

KM# 36 60 KREUZER (Stadtmünz)

Silver **Obv:** City arms divide date **Rev:** Ornament at end of inscription **Rev. Inscription:** LX (in cartouche) / STADT / MVNTZ

Date	Mintage	VG	F	VF	XF	Unc
1622	—	—	—	—	—	—

KM# 15 THALER

Silver **Obv:** Large Spanish arms **Rev:** Crowned double-headed imperial eagle **Note:** Dav.#5903.

Date	Mintage	VG	F	VF	XF	Unc
1620	—	—	325	650	1,250	2,300
1623	—	—	350	725	1,300	2,400
1624	—	—	400	775	1,450	2,950

KM# 47 THALER

Silver **Note:** Dav.#5903A. Klippe.

Date	Mintage	VG	F	VF	XF	Unc
1624 Rare	—	—	—	—	—	—

KM# 49 THALER

Silver **Obv:** Angel head above pointed shield, flowers and cornucopia beside, HL below **Rev:** Crown above double-headed imperial eagle **Rev. Legend:** FERDINAND...SEMP.AVG **Note:** Dav.#5904.

Date	Mintage	VG	F	VF	XF	Unc
1635 HL	—	1,250	2,500	5,000	9,000	—

KM# 50 THALER

Silver **Rev:** Round bottom shield, M below **Note:** Dav.#5904A.

Date	Mintage	VG	F	VF	XF	Unc
1635 M	—	1,250	2,500	5,000	9,000	—

KM# 51 THALER

Silver **Obv. Legend:** FERDINANDVS...SEMPER.AVGVSTV **Rev:** Altered frame for arms **Note:** Dav.#5905.

Date	Mintage	VG	F	VF	XF	Unc
1635	—	—	1,550	3,250	5,900	—

KM# 52 THALER

Silver **Rev:** Angel head with wings above pointed shield without flower or mint mark below **Note:** Dav.#5906.

Date	Mintage	VG	F	VF	XF	Unc
1635	—	—	1,200	2,400	4,800	—

KM# 56 THALER

Silver **Obv:** Angel head with wings above straight topped and rounded bottom shield, M below **Rev:** Crown above double-headed imperial eagle **Rev. Legend:** FERDINAND II **Note:** Dav.#5907.

Date	Mintage	VG	F	VF	XF	Unc
1636 M	—	—	1,550	3,250	5,900	—

KM# 57 THALER

Silver **Obv:** Angel head with wings above highly ornamented oval shield with HL-K below **Note:** Dav.#5908.

Date	Mintage	VG	F	VF	XF	Unc
1636 HLK	—	—	2,700	5,300	9,000	—
1637 HK	—	—	2,700	5,300	9,000	—

KM# 58 THALER

Silver **Rev:** Angel head without wings above highly ornamented oval shield with HL-K below **Note:** Dav.#5908A.

Date	Mintage	VG	F	VF	XF	Unc
1636 HLK	—	—	2,700	5,300	9,000	—

KM# 61 THALER

Silver **Obv:** Angel above oval ornate arms **Rev:** Crown above double-headed imperial eagle **Note:** Similar to Thaler, KM# 60. Dav.#5909.

Date	Mintage	VG	F	VF	XF	Unc
1637 Rare	—	—	—	—	—	—
1638 M Rare	—	—	—	—	—	—
1640 HLK Rare	—	—	—	—	—	—

KM# 60 THALER

Silver **Obv:** Angel above oval ornate arms **Rev:** Crown above double-headed imperial eagle **Rev. Legend:** FERDINAND.III... **Note:** Varieties exist. Dav.#5910.

Date	Mintage	VG	F	VF	XF	Unc
1637 M	—	—	2,500	4,700	9,500	—
1638 M	—	—	2,500	4,700	9,500	—
1638 HLK	—	—	2,500	4,700	9,500	—
1639 M	—	—	2,500	4,700	9,500	—
1639 HLK	—	—	2,500	4,700	9,500	—
1640 HLK	—	—	2,500	4,700	9,500	—

TRADE COINAGE

KM# 54 DUCAT

3.5000 g., 0.9860 Gold 0.1109 oz. AGW **Rev:** Five line legend in cartouch or ornamental square. **Note:** Fr#3480.

Date	Mintage	VG	F	VF	XF	Unc
1635 HL	—	2,500	3,500	5,500	—	—
1635 M	—	2,500	3,500	5,500	—	—
Note: Hauch & Aufhäuser Auction 18, 10-4, VF realized approximately $20,850						
1636 HLK	—	3,000	5,000	8,000	—	—
1636 MK	—	3,000	5,000	8,000	—	—
1637 HLK	—	3,000	5,000	8,000	—	—
Note: Künker Auction 171, 6-10, VF-XF realized approximately $21,495						
1638 HLK	—	—	—	—	—	—
1638 MK	—	3,000	5,000	8,000	—	—
ND	—	3,000	5,000	8,000	—	—

FR# 3482 DUCAT

3.5000 g., 0.9860 Gold 0.1109 oz. AGW **Rev:** 5-line inscription in wreath

Date	Mintage	VG	F	VF	XF	Unc
1639 HLK Rare	—	—	—	—	—	—
Note: Künker Auction 171, 6-10, XF realized approximately $27,024						

KM# 5 2 DUCAT

7.0000 g., 0.9860 Gold 0.2219 oz. AGW **Subject:** Centennial of the Reformation **Note:** Fr#3479.

Date	Mintage	VG	F	VF	XF	Unc
1617 Rare	—	—	—	—	—	—

KM# 63 2 DUCAT

7.0000 g., 0.9860 Gold 0.2219 oz. AGW **Rev:** 5-line inscription in wreath **Note:** Fr#3481.

Date	Mintage	VG	F	VF	XF	Unc
1639 HLK Rare	—	—	—	—	—	—

KM# 45 10 DUCAT

Gold **Obv:** Crowned double eagle **Rev:** Large Spanish arms **Note:** Struck on double-thick flan from same dies as Thaler, Dav#5903.

Date	Mintage	VG	F	VF	XF	Unc
1624 3 known	—	—	—	—	—	—

PATTERNS

Including off metal strikes

KM#	Date	Mintage	Identification	Mkt Val
Pn1	1617	—	2 Ducat. Silver. KM#5.	750
Pn2	1635	—	Ducat. Copper. KM#54.	100
Pn3	1717	—	1/2 Ducat. Silver. KM#105.	125
Pn4	1717	—	Ducat. Silver. KM#107.	275
Pn5	1730	—	Ducat. Silver. KM#112.	150
Pn6	1730	—	2 Ducat. Silver. KM#111.	200
Pn7	ND(1772)	—	Heller. Gold. Oval city arms. KM#128.	1,250

VERDEN

The bishopric of Verden was established by Charlemagne in 785 on the Aller River, 22 miles (36 km) southeast of Bremen. Emperor Otto III (983-1002) gave the mint right to Bishop Erpo (976-993) in 985, but the first identifiable Episcopal coinage did not appear until the first half of the 14th century. The bishopric underwent the Reformation and became a Protestant see in the mid-16th century. As part of the settlement folllowing the Thiry Years' War, Verden was awarded to Sweden and, having been joined to Bremen in 1644, became part of a secular duchy in 1648 (see Bremen & Verden). The bishops struck a few intermittent issues and the cathedral chapter supplemented those during the early part of the the 17th century.

RULERS

Philipp Sigmund, Herzog von Braunschweig-Lüneburg, 1586-1623

Friedrich II, Prinz von Dänemark, 1623-1629

Friedrich Wilhelm, Graf von Wartenberg, 1630-1631

Johann Friedrich, Herzog von Schleswig-Holstein-Gottorp, Administrator 1631-1634

Friedrich II, restored, 1635-1644

ARMS

Cross

REFERENCES

G = Herman Grote, "Die Münzen des Bisthums Verden," **Münzstudien** 5 (1865), pp. 53-80, 508-16.

K = Wilhelm Kraaz, **Münzen der deutschen Kipperzeig**, Halle, 1924.

Sch = Wolfgang Schulten, **Deutsche Münzen aus der Zeit Karls V.**, Frankfurt am Main, 1974.

BISHOPRIC

REGULAR COINAGE

KM# 2 PFENNIG

Copper, 16 mm. **Ruler:** Philipp Sigmund **Obv:** Shield of 3-fold arms **Note:** Ref. G#22. Uniface.

Date	Mintage	VG	F	VF	XF	Unc
ND(1620-21)	—	20.00	50.00	70.00	135	—

KM# 4 SCHWAREN

Copper, 15 mm. **Ruler:** Philipp Sigmund **Obv:** 'PS' monogram between 2 rosettes **Rev:** Verden arms in ornamented shield, date at end of legend **Rev. Legend:** 1. VERDER. SCHWARE. **Note:** Ref. G#21.

Date	Mintage	VG	F	VF	XF	Unc
1621	—	18.00	40.00	65.00	120	—

KM# 6 1/2 GROTE

Copper, 18 mm. **Ruler:** Philipp Sigmund **Obv:** Crowned 'PS' monogram between 2 arabesques in ornamented circle **Rev:** Verden rms in baroque frame, value (1/2) in oval above, date at end of legend **Rev. Inscription:** VERDER. GROTE. **Note:** Ref. G#20.

Date	Mintage	VG	F	VF	XF	Unc
1621	—	18.00	40.00	65.00	120	—

KM# 8 GROTE

Copper, 20 mm. **Ruler:** Philipp Sigmund **Obv:** Crowned 'PS' monogram between 2 branches with blooms **Rev:** Verden arms in baroque frame, date at end of legend **Rev. Legend:** 1. VERDER. GROTE. **Note:** Ref. G#19. Sometimes found with countermark 'VD' (in ligature) = Verdener Domkapitel (Cathedral Chapter).

Date	Mintage	VG	F	VF	XF	Unc
1621	—	18.00	40.00	65.00	120	—

KM# 10 2 SCHILLING (Doppelschilling)

Copper, 27 mm. **Ruler:** Philipp Sigmund **Obv:** Crowned 'PS' monogram in ornamented circle **Rev:** Verden arms in baroque frame, date at end of legend **Rev. Legend:** 1. VERDER DOBBELSCHILLING. **Note:** Ref. G#18. Sometimes found with countermark 'VD' (in ligature) = Verdener Domkapitel (Cathedral Chapter).

Date	Mintage	VG	F	VF	XF	Unc
1621	—	45.00	80.00	125	240	—

CATHEDRAL CHAPTER

REGULAR COINAGE

KM# 17 SCHWAREN

Copper **Obv:** Madonna and Child in circle **Obv. Legend:** MONETA NOVA. **Rev:** Shield of Verden arms **Rev. Legend:** CAPIT. VERDENS. **Note:** Ref. G#17.

Date	Mintage	VG	F	VF	XF	Unc
ND(1620-21)	—	—	—	—	—	—

KM# 24 12 KREUZER (Schreckenberger)

Silver **Obv:** Crowned shield of 4-fold arms, date divided at top **Obv. Legend:** MONE. NO. C. VE. **Rev:** Crowned imperial eagle, '1Z' in orb on breast **Rev. Legend:** FERDINAND. II. D. G. R. I. **Note:** Ref. K#58. Kipper coinage.

Date	Mintage	VG	F	VF	XF	Unc
16Z1	—	55.00	90.00	125	210	—

KM# 19 1/48 THALER (Grote)

Silver **Obv:** Verden arms in ornamented shield, value (1 GR.) below **Obv. Legend:** CAPIT - VERD. **Rev:** Imperial orb with 48 **Rev. Legend:** MONETA. NO. **Note:** Ref. G#16. Kipper coinage.

Date	Mintage	VG	F	VF	XF	Unc
ND(1620-21)	—	—	—	—	—	—

KM# 15 1/24 THALER (Groschen)

Silver, 18-20 mm. **Obv:** Cross in shield within ornamented frame **Obv. Legend:** MO. N(O). CAP(I)(T)(T)(V)(U). V(U)(E)(R)(D)(E)(NS)(I). **Rev:** Imperial orb with Z4, date divided at top **Rev. Legend:** MAT(T)(E)(H)(I). I. D. G. R. I(M). S. A(V). **Note:** Ref. G#13. Kipper coinage. Varieties exist.

Date	Mintage	VG	F	VF	XF	Unc
(1)618	—	25.00	50.00	75.00	150	—
1618	—	25.00	50.00	75.00	150	—
(1)619	—	25.00	50.00	75.00	150	—
1619	—	25.00	50.00	75.00	150	—

KM# 21 1/24 THALER (Groschen)

Silver, 16 mm. **Obv:** Cross in shield within ornamented frame **Obv. Legend:** MO(N). NO. CAPIT. VERD(E). **Rev:** Imperial orb with Z4, date divided at top **Rev. Legend:** FER. D. G. R. IM. S. A. **Note:** Ref. G#14. Varieties exist.

Date	Mintage	VG	F	VF	XF	Unc
(16)Z0	—	20.00	45.00	70.00	135	—

KM# 22 1/24 THALER (Groschen)

Silver **Obv:** 4-fold arms in ornamented shield **Obv. Legend:** MONETA. NOVA. C: V. **Rev:** Imperial orb with Z4, date divided at top **Rev. Legend:** FER. D. G. R IM S A. **Note:** Ref. Sch#3358.

Date	Mintage	VG	F	VF	XF	Unc
(16)Z0	—	—	—	—	—	—

KM# 26 1/12 THALER (Doppelgroschen)
Silver, 25 mm. **Obv:** Crowned shield of 4-fold arms, date divided at top **Obv. Legend:** MONE. NOVA. C. V(E). **Rev:** Crowned imperial eagle, '1Z' in orb on breast **Rev. Legend:** FERD(I)NAND. II. D. G. R(O). I(M). (S.A.). **Note:** Ref. G#15. Kipper coinage. Varieties exist.

Date	Mintage	VG	F	VF	XF	Unc
16Z1	—	—	—	—	—	—

WALDBURG-FRIEDBERG-SCHEER

COUNTSHIP

REGULAR COINAGE

KM# 1 3 PFENNIG
0.7500 g., Silver **Ruler:** Otto **Obv:** Sunface with rays between palm branches **Rev:** Imperial orb with 3 divides date

Date	Mintage	VG	F	VF	XF	Unc
1657	—	—	—	—	—	—

KM# 2 3 PFENNIG
Silver **Ruler:** Maximilian Wunibald **Obv:** Smaller sunface **Rev:** Cross on orb divides date

Date	Mintage	VG	F	VF	XF	Unc
1675	—	—	—	—	—	—

WALDECK

The former Countship of Waldeck was located in the western part of the German Empire, bordered by the Landgraviate of Hesse-Cassel on the east and south, the Duchy of Westphalia on the west and the Bishopric of Paderborn on the north. Arolsen was the seat of the counts and they traced their line of descent from a branch of the counts of Schwalenberg beginning in the early 11th century. Waldeck underwent several divisions over the centuries, the first such significant occurrence having taken place in 1474 with the establishment of Waldeck-Wildungen and Waldeck-Eisenberg. The latter was further divided into Waldeck-Eisenberg and Waldeck-Neu-Landau in 1539, but the former inherited Wildungen when the elder branch of the family became extinct in 1598. The line at Neu-Landau failed after two generations and reverted to Eisenberg the previous year (1597). A new line at Wildungen was established from Eisenberg in 1598 as well, but this, too, fell extinct in 1692, only ten years after the count having been raised to the rank of prince.

Waldeck-Eisenberg had received the Countship of Pyrmont in 1625 and became known as Waldeck-Pyrmont (see) upon the permanent unification of the two countships in 1668.

RULERS

Waldeck-Wildungen

Wolrad IV, 1598-1640
Philipp Dietrich, 1640-1645
Heinrich Wolrad V, 1645-1664
Georg Friedrich, 1664-1692, Prince 1682

Waldeck-Eisenberg

Christian, 1588-1638
Philipp VII, 1638-1645
Christian Ludwig, 1645-1668
(continued as Waldeck-Pyrmont)

Waldeck-Neu-Landau

Johann II, 1638-1668

Mint Official's Initials

Initials or Mark	Date	Name
(c) =	1590-1622	Caspar Huxer (Hextor), mintmaster Niederwildungen
(d) =		
(e) =		
	ca.1609	Henrich Gernhardt, die-cutter in Cassel
RAS	ca. 1617	Unknown,
IS	1621-1625	Johann Schmille of Alsfeld, mintmaster in Niederwildungen
	ca.1622	Martin Toell, die-cutter in Warburg
	ca.1622	Valentin Schirmer, mint director
GK	ca.1624-1625	Georg Küpper, mintmaster Niederwildungen
VF	1652-1654	Urban Felgenhauer (Felgenhewer), mintmaster
	1693-95	Johann Hoffmann, mintmaster
FW	1695	Friedrich Wendels, mintmaster

Arms:
6-pointed (early) or 8-pointed (later) star

NOTE:
Many of the 17th century copper coins exist with a small Waldeck star countermark.

REFERENCE:
S = Hugo Frhr. Von Saurma-Jeltsch, ***Die Saurmasche Münzsammlung***, Berlin, 1892.
W = Joseph Weingärtner, ***Beschreibung dr Kupfermünzen Westfalens nebst historischen Nacrichten***, 2 vols., Paderborn, 1872-81.

COUNTSHIP

REGULAR COINAGE

KM# 85 4 HELLER (2 Pfennig)
Silver **Ruler:** Christian and Wolrad IV **Obv:** Waldeck arms in circle **Obv. Legend:** WALDECKISCH **Rev:** 'IIII' in circle, date **Rev. Legend:** LANTMVNTZ **Note:** Ref. S#2308. Kipper coinage.

Date	Mintage	VG	F	VF	XF	Unc
16Z0	—	—	—	—	—	—
(16)Z1	—	200	425	850	—	—

KM# 92 8 HELLER (4 Pfennig)
Silver **Ruler:** Christian and Wolrad IV **Obv:** Waldeck arms in shield within circle **Obv. Legend:** WALDECKISCH **Rev:** Value 'VIII' in ornamented rectangle within circle, date **Rev. Legend:** LANT MVNTZE **Note:** Kipper coinage.

Date	Mintage	VG	F	VF	XF	Unc
16Z1	—	65.00	135	275	550	—

KM# 95 PFENNIG
Copper **Ruler:** Christian and Wolrad IV **Obv:** Waldeck arms in circle, date around **Obv. Legend:** WALDECK **Rev:** 'I' in center **Rev. Legend:** LANTMVNTZ **Note:** Ref. W#739.

Date	Mintage	Good	VG	F	VF	XF
16ZZ	—	18.00	40.00	65.00	120	—

KM# 128 PFENNIG
Copper **Ruler:** Wolrad IV, Philipp VII and Johann II **Obv:** Waldeck arms in center, titles of the 3 counts **Rev:** 'I' in center, legend (or variant), date **Rev. Legend:** WALD. LANTMV **Note:** Ref. W#741. Varieties exist.

Date	Mintage	Good	VG	F	VF	XF
1638	—	15.00	30.00	55.00	110	—

KM# 99 3 PFENNIG (Dreier)
Copper **Ruler:** Christian and Wolrad IV **Obv:** Waldeck arms in circle, date around **Obv. Legend:** WALDECK **Rev:** 'III' in center **Rev. Legend:** LANTMVNTZ **Note:** Ref. W#738. Kipper coinage.

Date	Mintage	Good	VG	F	VF	XF
16ZZ	—	18.00	40.00	65.00	120	—

KM# 131 3 PFENNIG (Dreier)
Copper **Ruler:** Wolrad IV, Philipp VII and Johann II **Obv:** Waldeck arms in center, titles of the 3 counts **Rev:** 'III' in center, legend (or variant), date **Rev. Legend:** WALD. LANTMV **Note:** Ref. W#740. Kipper coinage.

Date	Mintage	Good	VG	F	VF	XF
1638	—	12.00	28.00	45.00	90.00	—

KM# 102 4 PFENNIG
Copper **Ruler:** Christian and Wolrad IV **Obv:** Waldeck arms in circle, date around **Obv. Legend:** WALDECK **Rev:** 'IIII' in center **Rev. Legend:** LANTMVNTZ **Note:** Ref. W#737. Varieties exist.

Date	Mintage	Good	VG	F	VF	XF
16ZZ	—	45.00	95.00	190	385	550

KM# 107 6 PFENNIG
Copper **Ruler:** Christian and Wolrad IV **Obv:** Waldeck arms in circle, date around **Obv. Legend:** WALDECK **Rev:** 'VI' in center **Rev. Legend:** LANTMVNTZ **Note:** Ref. W#736. Varieties exist.

Date	Mintage	Good	VG	F	VF	XF
16ZZ	—	16.00	35.00	55.00	115	—

KM# 54 3 KREUZER (Groschen)
Silver **Ruler:** Christian and Wolrad IV **Obv:** Date divided by feathered ornaments on helmet above Waldeck arms, titles of the 2 counts **Rev:** Crowned imperial eagle, 3 in orb on breast, titles of Rudolf II, date **Mint:** Niederwildungen **Note:** Ref. S#2298-2300.

Date	Mintage	VG	F	VF	XF	Unc
1608 (c)	—	40.00	85.00	175	350	—
1609 (c)	—	40.00	85.00	175	350	—

KM# 52 3 KREUZER (Groschen)
Silver **Ruler:** Christian and Wolrad IV **Obv:** Date divided by feathered ornaments on helmet above Waldeck arms, titles of the 2 counts **Rev:** Crowned imperial eagle, 3 in orb on breast, titles of Matthias **Mint:** Niederwildungen **Note:** Ref. S#2301-05. Varieties exist.

Date	Mintage	VG	F	VF	XF	Unc
1615	—	30.00	65.00	135	275	—
1616	—	30.00	65.00	135	275	—
1616 (e)	—	30.00	65.00	135	275	—
1618	—	30.00	65.00	135	275	—
ND (e)	—	30.00	65.00	135	275	—

KM# 69 3 KREUZER (Groschen)
Silver **Ruler:** Christian and Wolrad IV **Obv:** Shield of Waldeck arms in circle, titles of the 2 counts **Rev:** Crowned imperial eagle, 3 in orb on breast, titles of Matthias, date in legend **Mint:** Waldeck **Note:** Ref. S#2307.

Date	Mintage	VG	F	VF	XF	Unc
1615	—	45.00	90.00	180	—	—

KM# 88 3 KREUZER (Groschen)
Silver **Ruler:** Christian and Wolrad IV **Obv:** Date divided by feathered ornaments on helmet above Waldeck arms, titles of the 2 counts **Rev:** Crowned imperial eagle, 3 in orb on breast, titles of Ferdinand II **Mint:** Niederwildungen **Note:** Ref. S#2306.

Date	Mintage	VG	F	VF	XF	Unc
1620 (e)	—	—	—	—	—	—

KM# 138.1 2 MARIENGROSCHEN (1/18 Thaler)
Silver **Ruler:** Georg Friedrich, Johann II and Heinrich Wolrad V **Obv:** Waldeck arms, titles of the 3 counts **Rev. Inscription:** II / MARIEN / GROS / (date or variant) **Mint:** Waldeck

Date	Mintage	VG	F	VF	XF	Unc
1653 VF	—	30.00	60.00	120	240	—
1654 VF	—	30.00	60.00	120	240	—

KM# 138.2 2 MARIENGROSCHEN (1/18 Thaler)

Silver, 18 mm. **Ruler:** Georg Friedrich, Johann II and Heinrich Wolrad V **Obv:** Waldeck arms, titles of the 3 counts **Rev:** Date divided at top in margin **Rev. Inscription:** II / MARIEN / GROS **Mint:** Waldeck

Date	Mintage	VG	F	VF	XF	Unc
1654 VF	—	30.00	60.00	120	240	—

KM# 146 4 MARIENGROSCHEN (1/9 Thaler)

Silver **Ruler:** Georg Friedrich, Johann II and Heinrich Wolrad V **Obv:** Waldeck arms, titles of the 3 counts **Rev. Inscription:** IIII / MARIEN / GROS / date (or variant) **Mint:** Waldeck

Date	Mintage	VG	F	VF	XF	Unc
1654 VF	—	20.00	45.00	90.00	180	—

KM# 81 1/4 THALER

Silver **Ruler:** Christian and Wolrad IV **Obv:** Ornate helmet above oval Waldeck arms in circle, titles of the 2 counts **Rev:** Crowned imperial eagle, orb on breast, date **Rev. Legend:** LIBERTAS. OPTIMA. **Mint:** Niederwildungen **Note:** Ref. S#2297.

Date	Mintage	VG	F	VF	XF	Unc
1618 (e) Rare	—	—	—	—	—	—

KM# 62 THALER

Silver **Note:** Dav. #7817.

Date	Mintage	VG	F	VF	XF	Unc
1613 Rare	—	—	—	—	—	—

KM# 78 THALER

Silver **Obv:** Date **Obv. Legend:** MATTHIAS. D: G... **Rev. Legend:** CHRISTI: ET. WOLF: FR: COM... **Note:** Dav. #7818.

Date	Mintage	VG	F	VF	XF	Unc
1617 Rare	—	—	—	—	—	—

KM# 111 THALER

Silver **Obv:** Helmeted arms **Obv. Legend:** CHR. ET...I. WALDEC... **Rev:** Date, crowned imperial eagle with orb on breast **Rev. Legend:** FERDINAND: II... **Note:** Dav. #7819.

Date	Mintage	VG	F	VF	XF	Unc
16ZZ Rare	—	—	—	—	—	—
1623 Rare	—	—	—	—	—	—

KM# 119 THALER

Silver **Obv:** Helmeted arms separating J-6 above 2-4 below **Obv. Legend:** CHRIST: ET: WOLRA... **Rev. Legend:** FERDI: II... **Note:** Dav. #7820.

Date	Mintage	VG	F	VF	XF	Unc
1624 Rare	—	—	—	—	—	—

KM# 124 THALER

Silver **Obv:** Helmeted arms divide date below **Obv. Legend:** CHRI: ET: WLRA... **Rev. Legend:** FERDI: II... **Note:** Dav. #7821.

Date	Mintage	VG	F	VF	XF	Unc
1625 Rare	—	—	—	—	—	—

Note: Künker Auction 170, 6-10, VF realized approximately $21,045.

KM# 135 THALER

Silver **Ruler:** Johann II **Subject:** George Friedrich, Johann and Wolrad **Obv:** Helmeted arms **Obv. Legend:** GEORG * FRIDE * JOHAN * WOLRADT ... **Rev:** Palm tree with stone dividing date and VF below **Note:** Dav. #7822.

Date	Mintage	VG	F	VF	XF	Unc
1653 VF	—	3,750	6,500	9,500	—	—

KM# 58 2 THALER

Silver **Obv:** Crowned imperial eagle **Obv. Legend:** RUDOLP. II... **Rev:** Helmeted arms **Rev. Legend:** CHRISTI. ET. WOLRA. CO... **Note:** Dav. #7815.

Date	Mintage	VG	F	VF	XF	Unc
1608 Rare	—	—	—	—	—	—

TRADE COINAGE

KM# 73 GOLDGULDEN

Gold **Ruler:** Christian and Wolrad IV **Obv:** Ornate helmet above shield of Waldeck arms in circle, date at end of legend **Obv. Legend:** MON. NOV. AUR. COM. WALDEC. **Rev:** Crowned imperial eagle, orb on breast, titles of Matthias **Mint:** Niederwildungen **Note:** Fr. #3492.

Date	Mintage	VG	F	VF	XF	Unc
1615 (d) Rare	—	—	—	—	—	—
1616 (d) Rare	—	—	—	—	—	—
1617 (d) Rare	—	—	—	—	—	—

KM# 115 GOLDGULDEN

Gold **Ruler:** Christian and Wolrad IV **Obv:** Ornate helmet above shield of Waldeck arms in circle, date at end of legend **Obv. Legend:** CHR • E • WOLR • F • C • I • WALDECK **Rev:** Crowned imperial eagle, orb on breast, titles of Ferdinand II **Rev. Legend:** MON. NOV. AUR. COI. WALDOO. **Mint:** Niederwildungen **Note:** Fr. #3492.

Date	Mintage	VG	F	VF	XF	Unc
(1)6ZZ (e) Rare	—	—	—	—	—	—

KM# 149 DUCAT

3.5000 g., 0.9860 Gold 0.1109 oz. AGW **Ruler:** Georg Friedrich **Subject:** Johann II and Heinrich Wolrad **Obv:** Elaborately helmeted arms in inner circle **Rev:** Luxurious palm tree divides date in inner circle **Note:** Prev. Fr#3493.

Date	Mintage	VG	F	VF	XF	Unc
1654 Rare	—	—	—	—	—	—

PRINCIPALITY

REGULAR COINAGE

KM# 55 THALER

Silver **Subject:** Christian and Wolrad IV **Obv:** Crowned imperial eagle **Obv. Legend:** RUDOLP \ II... **Rev:** Helmeted arms **Rev. Legend:** CHRISTI. ET. WOLRA. CO.. **Note:** Dav#7816.

Date	Mintage	VG	F	VF	XF	Unc
1608 Rare	—	—	—	—	—	—

KM# 153 THALER

Silver **Subject:** Christian Ludwig **Obv:** Bust right **Rev:** Palm tree divides date and FW **Note:** Dav. #7824.

Date	Mintage	VG	F	VF	XF	Unc
1695 FW Rare	—	—	—	—	—	—

WALDECK-PYRMONT

The Count of Waldeck-Eisenberg inherited the Countship of Pyrmont, located between Lippe and Hannover, in 1625, thus creating an entity which encompassed about 672 square miles (1120 square kilometers). Waldeck and Pyrmont were permanently united in 1668, thus continuing the Eisenberg line as Waldeck-Pyrmont from that date. The count was raised to the rank of prince in 1712 and the unification of the two territories was confirmed in 1812. Waldeck-Pyrmont joined the German Confederation in 1815 and the North German Confederation in 1867. The prince renounced his sovereignty on 1 October of that year and Waldeck-Pyrmont was incorporated into Prussia. However, coinage was struck into the early 20th century for Waldeck-Pyrmont as a member of the German Empire. The hereditary territorial titles were lost along with the war in 1918. Some coins were struck for issue in Pyrmont only in the 18th through 20th centuries and those are listed separately under that name.

RULERS

Christian Ludwig, 1668-1706

MINT OFFICIALS' INITIALS

Initial	Date	Name
	1693-1695	Johann Hoffmann, mintmaster

ARMS

6-pointed (early) or 8-pointed (later) star.

REFERENCE:

W = Joseph Weingärtner, **Beschreibung dr Kupfermünzen Westfalens nebst historischen Nacrichten**, 2 vols., Paderborn, 1872-81.

COUNTSHIP

REGULAR COINAGE

KM# 3 PFENNIG

Copper **Ruler:** Christian Ludwig **Obv:** Oval 4-fold arms with central shield of Waldeck in ornamented frame, titles of Christian Ludwig **Rev:** 'I' in ornamented oval, date at end of inscription **Rev. Inscription:** ANNO DOMINI **Note:** Ref. W#746.

Date	Mintage	Good	VG	F	VF	XF
1693	—	6.00	14.00	30.00	65.00	—

KM# 6 2 PFENNIG

Copper **Ruler:** Christian Ludwig **Obv:** Oval 4-fold arms with central shield of Waldeck in ornamented frame, titles of Christian

Ludwig **Rev:** 'II' in ornamented oval, date at end of inscription **Note:** Ref. W#745.

Date	Mintage	Good	VG	F	VF	XF
1693	—	10.00	20.00	40.00	90.00	—

KM# 8 3 PFENNIG

Copper **Ruler:** Christian Ludwig **Obv:** Oval 4-fold arms with central shield of Waldeck in ornamented frame, titles of Christian Ludwig **Rev:** 'III' in ornamented oval, date **Rev. Inscription:** ANNO DOMINI **Note:** Ref. W#744.

Date	Mintage	Good	VG	F	VF	XF
1693	—	7.00	16.00	35.00	80.00	—

KM# 11 4 PFENNIG

Copper **Ruler:** Christian Ludwig **Obv:** Oval 4-fold arms with central shield of Waldeck in ornamented frame, titles of Christian Ludwig **Rev:** 'IIII' in ornamented rectangle, date **Rev. Inscription:** ANNO DOMINI **Note:** Ref. W#743.

Date	Mintage	Good	VG	F	VF	XF
1693	—	10.00	20.00	45.00	100	—

KM# 13 6 PFENNIG

Copper **Ruler:** Christian Ludwig **Obv:** Oval 4-fold arms with central shield of Waldeck in ornamented frame, titles of Christian Ludwig **Rev:** 'VI' in ornamented rectangle, date **Rev. Inscription:** ANNO DOMINI **Note:** Ref. W#742.

Date	Mintage	Good	VG	F	VF	XF
1693	—	10.00	20.00	40.00	90.00	—

WARBURG

A town in Westphalia 23 miles (38 km) southeast of Paderborn. Control of the town was transferred by Count Dedico von Wartberch to the Bishopric of Paderborn in 1020. Warburg remained under the administration of the bishops, having been the site of an episcopal mint in the 13th century, until secularization in 1803, when it passed to Prussia. It was included in the Kingdom of Westphalia from 1807 to 1813, but was returned to Prussia in the latter year. Warburg was garrisoned by various armies during the Thirty Years' War, which occasioned a short-lived issue of copper coins authorized by the bishop, Ferdinand of Bavaria (1618-50).

PROVINCIAL TOWN

REGULAR COINAGE

KM# 1 PFENNIG

Copper **Obv:** Double lily in center, around legend **Obv. Legend:** STAT. WARBVRG. **Rev:** Value 1 in center, ANNO and date **Note:** Kipper Pfennig. Varieties exist.

Date	Mintage	Good	VG	F	VF	XF
16ZZ	—	45.00	100	160	275	—

KM# 2 PFENNIG

Copper **Obv:** Double lily in center, around STAT. WARBVRG **Rev:** Value 1 in center, FERD. EPS., date **Note:** Kipper Pfennig. Varieties exist.

Date	Mintage	Good	VG	F	VF	XF
16ZZ	—	85.00	120	170	285	—

KM# 3 3 PFENNIG

Copper **Obv:** Double lily in center, around STAT. WARBVRG. **Rev:** Value III in center, ANNO and date **Note:** Kipper 3 Pfennig. Varieties exist.

Date	Mintage	Good	VG	F	VF	XF
16ZZ	—	18.00	35.00	65.00	120	—

KM# 4 4 PFENNIG

Copper **Obv:** Double lily in center, around STAT. WARBVRG. **Rev:** Value IIII in center, ANNO and date **Note:** Kipper 4 Pfennig. Varieties exist.

Date	Mintage	Good	VG	F	VF	XF
16ZZ	—	18.00	35.00	65.00	120	—

KM# 5 4 PFENNIG

Copper **Obv:** Double lily in center, around STAT. WARBVRG. **Rev:** Value IIII in center, FERDINAND. EPS., date **Note:** Kipper 4 Pfennig. Varieties exist.

Date	Mintage	Good	VG	F	VF	XF
16ZZ	—	85.00	120	150	240	—
16Z3	—	85.00	120	150	240	—

WARENDORF

This town in Westphalia is 14 miles (24 km) east of Münster and was included in the territory of that bishopric. It had its own coinage in the 16th and 17th centuries.

Arms:
A portcullis
Patron saint: St. Lawrence

PROVINCIAL TOWN

STANDARD COINAGE

KM# 27 PFENNIG

Copper **Obv:** Standing figure of St. Lawrence holding palm branch divides S - L, city arms to right **Obv. Legend:** MO. CIVITATIS - WARENDORP **Rev:** Within circle of palm branches, date divided by value I **Mint:** no mint

Date	Mintage	Good	VG	F	VF	XF
1690	—	35.00	80.00	150	275	550

KM# 29 PFENNIG

Copper **Obv:** City arms in center, legend around **Obv. Legend:** MON. CIVITA. WARENDORPIEN **Rev:** Within circle of palm branches, date divided by value I **Mint:** no mint

Date	Mintage	Good	VG	F	VF	XF
1690	—	35.00	80.00	150	275	—

KM# 30 PFENNIG

Copper **Obv:** City arms, date at end of legend **Obv. Legend:** STADT WARENDORP. A. **Rev:** Within circle of palm branches, date divided by value I **Mint:** no mint **Note:** Varieties exist.

Date	Mintage	Good	VG	F	VF	XF
1690	—	35.00	80.00	150	275	—

KM# 32 2 PFENNIG

Copper **Obv:** Standing figure of St. Lawrence holding palm branch divides S - L, city arms to right **Obv. Legend:** MO. CIVITATIS - WARENDORP **Rev:** Within circle of palm ranches, date divided by value 'II' **Mint:** no mint

Date	Mintage	Good	VG	F	VF	XF
1690	—	35.00	80.00	150	275	—

KM# 34 3 PFENNIG

Copper, 20.5 mm. **Obv:** Standing figure of St. Lawrence holding palm branch divides S - L, city arms to right **Obv. Legend:** MO. CIVITATIS - WARENDORP **Rev:** Within circle of palm branches, date divided by value III **Mint:** no mint **Note:** Varieties exist.

Date	Mintage	Good	VG	F	VF	XF
1690	—	15.00	32.00	60.00	120	—

KM# 36 4 PFENNIG

Copper **Obv:** Standing figure of St. Lawrence holding palm branch divides S - L, city arms to right **Obv. Legend:** MO. CIVITATIS - WARENDORP **Rev:** Within circle of palm branches, date divided by value 'IIII' **Mint:** no mint **Note:** Varieties exist.

Date	Mintage	Good	VG	F	VF	XF
1690	—	12.00	25.00	40.00	85.00	—

KM# 21 6 PFENNIG

Copper **Obv:** City arms, date at end of legend **Obv. Legend:** STADT: WARENDORP. - AN° **Rev:** Value VI in ornamented frame **Mint:** no mint

Date	Mintage	Good	VG	F	VF	XF
1613	—	30.00	60.00	100	200	—

KM# 23 12 PFENNIG

Copper **Obv:** City arms in baroque frame **Obv. Legend:** STADT: WARENDORP. **Rev:** Within ornamented frame, date and value as 1 X 6 I 1 I 3 **Mint:** no mint

Date	Mintage	Good	VG	F	VF	XF
1613	—	35.00	80.00	150	275	—

KM# 25 3 SCHILLING

Copper **Obv:** City arms **Obv. Legend:** STADT : WARENDORP **Rev:** Ornamented square with value and date at 1 I 6 I 1 I 3, 'W' in oval above, 'S' in square below **Mint:** no mint

Date	Mintage	Good	VG	F	VF	XF
1613	—	60.00	125	200	450	—

WEISSENBURG

(Wissembourg)

A town in the Lower Alsace, 42 miles northeast of Strassburg. It grew up around a Benedictine Abbey founded in the 7th century. It became a free imperial city in 1305, but had a very limited coinage. It went with the rest of Alsace to France in 1648 and shared the subsequent adventures of that province.

FREE CITY

REGULAR COINAGE

KM# 5 HELLER

Silver **Obv:** City arms, crown above **Note:** Uniface.

Date	Mintage	Good	VG	F	VF	XF
ND(ca.1622-24)	—	—	—	—	—	—

KM# 25 PFENNIG

Silver **Obv:** City arms divide date, W above **Note:** Uniface.

Date	Mintage	Good	VG	F	VF	XF
1624	—	—	—	—	—	—

KM# 33 GROSCHEN

Silver **Obv:** City arms **Obv. Legend:** CIVIT. WEISSENBVRG. AM. RHEIN. **Rev. Legend:** Titles of Ferdinand II **Rev. Inscription:** + / RAHTS / GELT /

Date	Mintage	Good	VG	F	VF	XF
1627	—	—	40.00	80.00	160	250

KM# 7 KREUZER

Silver **Obv:** City arms, W above **Rev. Inscription:** I / KREVTZ / ER / (date)

Date	Mintage	Good	VG	F	VF	XF
16ZZ	—	—	45.00	90.00	180	360

KM# 27 KREUZER
Silver **Obv:** City arms divide date **Obv. Legend:** WEISSENBVRG. AM. RHEIN. **Rev:** Imperial orb with value I, titles of Ferdinand II

Date	Mintage	Good	VG	F	VF	XF
1624	—	—	—	—	—	—

KM# 9 2 KREUZERS
Billon **Obv:** Gate arms **Obv. Legend:** MON. NO. IMP. CIV. WISSEMBVRG. **Rev:** Crowned imperial eagle **Rev. Legend:** FERDINAND. II ... **Note:** Prev. KM#3.

Date	Mintage	Good	VG	F	VF	XF
1622	—	10.00	25.00	50.00	100	210

KM# 29 2 KREUZER (Vierer = Halbbatzen)
Silver **Obv:** City arms divide date **Obv. Legend:** WEISSENBVRG. AM. RHEIN. **Rev:** Imperial orb with value 'Z'

Date	Mintage	Good	VG	F	VF	XF
16Z4	—	10.00	25.00	50.00	100	210
16Z6	—	10.00	25.00	50.00	100	210

KM# 35 2 KREUZER (Vierer = Halbbatzen)
Silver **Obv:** City arms divide date **Rev:** Value **Rev. Inscription:** II / KREUTZ / ER **Note:** Varieties exist.

Date	Mintage	Good	VG	F	VF	XF
16Z9	—	5.00	15.00	30.00	65.00	130
1630	—	5.00	15.00	30.00	65.00	130
1631	—	5.00	15.00	30.00	65.00	130
163Z	—	5.00	15.00	30.00	65.00	130
1633	—	5.00	15.00	30.00	65.00	130

KM# 3 12 KREUZER (Dreibätzner = Schrechenberger)
Silver **Obv:** City arms divide date **Obv. Legend:** WEISSENBVRG. AM. RHEIN. **Rev:** Crowned imperial eagle, XII in orb on breast, titles of Ferdinand II **Note:** Varieties exist.

Date	Mintage	Good	VG	F	VF	XF
1616	—	—	—	—	—	—
1618	—	—	—	—	—	—
1622	—	—	55.00	90.00	180	360
1623	—	—	55.00	90.00	180	360
1624	—	—	55.00	90.00	180	360
1626	—	—	55.00	90.00	180	360

KM# 11 12 KREUZER (Dreibätzner = Schrechenberger)
Silver **Obv:** City arms divide date **Obv. Legend:** M. NO. IMP... **Rev:** Crowned imperial eagle, 12 in orb on breast **Rev. Legend:** IN. DEO. SPER. NON. CON. IN. AETER. **Note:** Varieties exist.

Date	Mintage	Good	VG	F	VF	XF
1622	—	—	60.00	100	190	385

KM# 12 12 KREUZER (Dreibätzner = Schrechenberger)
Silver **Obv:** City arms **Rev:** Crowned imperial eagle, titles of Ferdinand II

Date	Mintage	Good	VG	F	VF	XF
1622	—	—	55.00	90.00	190	385

KM# 13 12 KREUZER (Dreibätzner = Schrechenberger)
Silver **Obv:** City arms **Rev:** Crowned imperial eagle, titles of Ferdinand II

Date	Mintage	Good	VG	F	VF	XF
ND(1622)	—	—	55.00	95.00	190	385

KM# 31 12 KREUZER (Dreibätzner = Schrechenberger)
Silver **Obv:** City arms divide date **Obv. Legend:** WEISEMBVRG * AM * RHEIN **Rev:** Value XII above crowned imperial eagle

Date	Mintage	Good	VG	F	VF	XF
1626	—	70.00	120	200	425	—
1628	—	70.00	120	200	425	—

KM# 14 12 KREUZER (Dreibätzner = Schrechenberger)
Silver **Obv:** 2-towered city gate divides date in circle **Obv. Legend:** + WEISSENBVRG * AM * RHEIN: **Rev:** Crowned imperial eagle, orb on breast, (XII) at top **Rev. Legend:** FERDINAND • II • ROM • IMP • SE • AV:

Date	Mintage	Good	VG	F	VF	XF
1626	—	35.00	75.00	150	275	450

KM# 30 24 KREUZER (Sechsbätzner - Doppelschreckenberger)
Silver **Obv:** City arms in ornamented oval frame, date divided above **Obv. Legend:** MON. NOV. IMP... **Rev:** Crowned imperial eagle, 24 in orb on breast **Rev. Legend:** Titles of Ferdinand II

Date	Mintage	Good	VG	F	VF	XF
1624	—	—	—	—	—	—

KM# 15 1/2 THALER
Silver **Obv:** City arms in circle **Obv. Legend:** MON. NOV. IMP... **Rev:** Crowned imperial eagle, plain orb on breast **Rev. Legend:** Titles of Ferdinand II

Date	Mintage	Good	VG	F	VF	XF
ND(1623-32)	—	—	—	—	—	—

KM# 17 THALER
Silver **Obv:** Gate arms in oval shield in wreath border **Obv. Legend:** ✠ MON * NOV * IMP * CIVIT * WEISSEMBVRG * AM * RHEI * **Rev:** Crowned imperial eagle in wreath border, titles of Ferdinand II **Rev. Legend:** *FERDINANDVS * II * D * G * ROM * IMP * SEM* AVG **Note:** Dav. #5915. Prev. KM#5.

Date	Mintage	Good	VG	F	VF	XF
ND(1623-32) Rare	—	—	—	—	—	—

KM# 19 THALER
Silver **Rev:** Large gate arms **Note:** Dav. #5916. Prev. KM#7.

Date	Mintage	Good	VG	F	VF	XF
ND(1623-32) Rare	—	—	—	—	—	—

Note: Auktionshaus H.D. Rauch GmbH Auction 77, 4-06, near XF realized approximately $59,315

KM# 18 THALER
Silver **Obv:** Without wreath borders **Rev:** Without wreath borders **Note:** Dav. #5917. Prev. KM#6.

Date	Mintage	Good	VG	F	VF	XF
ND(1623-32) Rare	—	—	—	—	—	—

KM# 21 2 THALER
Silver **Obv:** Crowned imperial eagle in wreath border **Rev:** Gate arms on oval shield in wreath border **Note:** Dav. #A5914. Prev. KM#8.

Date	Mintage	Good	VG	F	VF	XF
ND(1623-32) Rare	—	—	—	—	—	—

Note: Künker Auction 100, 6-05, realized approximately $24,885

KM# 23 4 THALER
Silver **Obv:** Gate arms on oval shield in wreath border **Rev:** Crowned imperial eagle in wreath border **Note:** Dav. #5914. Prev. KM#9.

Date	Mintage	Good	VG	F	VF	XF
ND(1623-32) Rare	—	—	—	—	—	—

WERDEN & HELMSTEDT

Abbeys

Bishop Ludger of Münster (791-809) founded the monasteries of Werden and Helmstedt early in his tenure as bishop. Werden is located on the River Ruhr six miles (10 kilometers) south of Essen, whereas Helmstedt is situated 20 miles (34 kilometers) east of Braunschweig in Niedersachsen. The abbot obtained the right to mint coins at Werden and at Lüdinghausen from Emperor Otto II (973-83) in 974, but the earliest known coins of the two monasteries date from the 11th century. A small, but fairly steady stream of issues were produced from the 16th century through the middle of the 18th century. In 1803, Werden and

Helmstedt were secularized and their fifty square miles of territory were annexed to Prussia.

RULERS

Heinrich III Duden, 1573-1601
Conrad II Kloet, 1601-1614
Hugo Preutäus von Assindia, 1614-1646
Heinrich IV Dücker, 1646-1667
Adolf IV von Borken, 1667-1670
Ferdinand von Erwitte, 1670-1706

Arms: (early type) – two crossed crosiers.

(later type) – two crossed crosiers in small shield superimposed on cross in larger shield

Imperial eagle - sometimes included to signify that the abbeys had imperial support and sanction.

CROSS REFERENCES:

G = Hermann Grote, "Die Münzen der Abtei Werden," **Münzstudien**, v. 3 (1862-63), pp. 411-445.
S = Hugo Frhr. Von Saurma-Jeltsch, **Die Saurmasche Münzsammlung deutscher, schweizerischer und polnischer Gepräge von etwa dem Beginn der Groschenzeit bis zur Kipperperiode**, Berlin, 1892.

ABBEY

REGULAR COINAGE

KM# 46 5 HELLER
0.3800 g., Silver, 14.5 mm. **Ruler:** Heinrich IV Dücker **Obv:** Shield of early arms superimposed on cross in circle, small crown in margin at top **Obv. Legend:** ABBAT. WERDENS. **Rev:** Value 'V' in circle, date at end of legend **Rev. Legend:** MONETA. NOVA. **Note:** Ref. G#44.

Date	Mintage	VG	F	VF	XF	Unc
(1)659	—	50.00	100	200	425	—

KM# 4 8 HELLER (Fettmannchen)
0.7600 g., Silver, 18 mm. **Ruler:** Konrad II Kloet **Obv:** 2-line inscription within circle **Obv. Legend:** MON. NO. REV. DOM. CON. **Obv. Inscription:** LXX / IIII **Rev:** Value 'VIII' in circle, date at end of legend (where present) **Rev. Legend:** ABB. IN .WERD. ET. HEL. **Note:** Ref. G#24-25.

Date	Mintage	VG	F	VF	XF	Unc
(1)614	—	—	—	—	—	—
ND	—	—	—	—	—	—

KM# 33 8 HELLER (Fettmannchen)
0.7100 g., Silver, 16.5 mm. **Ruler:** Heinrich IV Dücker **Obv:** 2-line inscription within circle **Obv. Legend:** NVMMVS. ABBA. WE. **Obv. Inscription:** LXX / VIII **Rev:** Value 'VIII' in circle, date at end of legend **Rev. Legend:** VERDENSIS. **Note:** Ref. G#39.

Date	Mintage	VG	F	VF	XF	Unc
1646	—	—	—	—	—	—

KM# 38 8 HELLER (Fettmannchen)
0.7100 g., Silver, 16.5 mm. **Ruler:** Heinrich IV Dücker **Obv:** 2-line inscription within circle **Obv. Legend:** NVMMVS. ABBATIAE. **Obv. Inscription:** LXX / VIII **Rev:** Value 'VIII' in circle, date at end of legend **Rev. Legend:** WERDINENSIS. **Note:** Ref. G#40-41. Varieties exist.

Date	Mintage	VG	F	VF	XF	Unc
1647	—	12.00	25.00	50.00	100	—
1648	—	12.00	25.00	50.00	100	—

KM# 48 8 HELLER (Fettmannchen)
0.7100 g., Silver, 16.5 mm. **Ruler:** Heinrich IV Dücker **Obv:** Shield of later arms in circle **Obv. Legend:** ABBATIAE (Æ). WERDENS(')(IS). **Rev:** Value 'VIII' in circle, date at end of legend (where present) **Rev. Legend:** MONETA. NOVA. **Note:** Ref. G#42-43.

Date	Mintage	VG	F	VF	XF	Unc
(1)659	—	25.00	50.00	85.00	170	—
1659	—	25.00	50.00	85.00	170	—
ND	—	25.00	50.00	85.00	170	—

KM# 59 8 HELLER (Fettmannchen)
0.5300 g., Silver, 16 mm. **Ruler:** Ferdinand **Obv:** Shield of later arms in circle **Obv. Legend:** ABBATIÆ. WERDENSIS. **Rev:** Value 'VIII' in circle, date at end of legend (where present) **Rev. Legend:** MONETA NOVA. **Note:** Ref. G#52.

Date	Mintage	VG	F	VF	XF	Unc
1676	—	—	—	—	—	—

KM# 1 SCHILLING
5.0000 g., Silver, 29 mm. **Ruler:** Konrad II Kloet **Obv:** Shield of later arms of Werden and Helmstedt, mitre above **Obv. Legend:** MO. NO. A. R. D. CONRA. AB WERD. HEL(M). **Rev:** Crowned imperial eagle, orb on breast **Rev. Legend:** MATTH. I. D: G. ELEC. ROM. IM. SEM. AV. **Note:** Ref. G#22.

Date	Mintage	VG	F	VF	XF	Unc
ND(1612-14)	—	200	400	750	1,500	—

KM# 5 SCHILLING (Dreibätzner)
Silver, 28.5-31 mm. **Ruler:** Hugo Preutäus **Obv:** 6-fold arms, mitre above **Obv. Legend:** MON - NO ARG - R. D. H. AB - IN .W ET - HEL. **Rev:** Crowned imperial eagle in circle **Rev. Legend:** MATH. D G. ELEC. ROM. IMP. SEMP. AVGV(S). **Note:** Ref. G#32. Weight varies: 4.45-4.92 g.

Date	Mintage	VG	F	VF	XF	Unc
ND(1614-19)	—	65.00	120	180	360	—

KM# 6 SCHILLING (Dreibätzner)
Silver, 28.5-31 mm. **Ruler:** Hugo Preutäus **Obv:** 4-fold arms, mitre above **Obv. Legend:** MO. NO. AR. R. D. HV. AB. IN. W. ET. HEL. I SCHIL. **Rev:** Crowned imperial eagle in circle **Rev. Legend:** MATH. I. D G. ELEC. ROM. IMP. SEMP. AVG. **Note:** Ref. G#33. Weight varies: 4.45-4.92 g.

Date	Mintage	VG	F	VF	XF	Unc
ND(1614-19)	—	—	—	—	—	—

KM# 7 SCHILLING (Dreibätzner)
Silver, 28.5-31 mm. **Ruler:** Hugo Preutäus **Obv:** 2 fold arms divided vertically, later Werden and Helmstedt arms at left, abbot's family arms (3 cloverleafs) at right, mitre above **Obv. Legend:** MO. NO. A. R. D. HVGON. ABB IN WE(R)D. HEL. **Rev:** Crowned imperial eagle in circle **Rev. Legend:** MATH. I. D G. ELEC. ROM. IM. SEM. AV(S). **Note:** Ref. G#34. Weight varies: 4.45-4.92 g.

Date	Mintage	VG	F	VF	XF	Unc
ND(1614-19)	—	—	—	—	—	—

KM# 8 SCHILLING (Dreibätzner)
Silver, 28.5-31 mm. **Ruler:** Hugo Preutäus **Obv:** 4-fold arms with upper left and lower right fields themselves 4-fold arms, all superimposed on floriated St. Andrew's cross, mitre above **Obv. Legend:** MO - NOV. ARG - R. D. H. AB - IN. W. E. H - EL. **Rev:** Crowned imperial eagle in circle **Rev. Legend:** MATH. I. D G. ELEC. RO. IMP: SEMP: AVGVS. **Note:** Ref. G#35. Weight varies: 4.45-4.92 g.

Date	Mintage	VG	F	VF	XF	Unc
ND(1614-19)	—	30.00	60.00	120	—	—

KM# 2 1/24 THALER (Groschen)
1.7100 g., Silver, 20 mm. **Ruler:** Konrad II Kloet **Obv:** Spanish shield of later Werden and Helmstedt arms with mitre above, in circle **Obv. Legend:** MO. A. R. D. CON. AB. IN. W. E. HEL. **Rev:** Imperial orb with Z4 divides date **Rev. Legend:** MATT. RO. IM. SEM. AV. **Note:** Ref. S#2905.

Date	Mintage	VG	F	VF	XF	Unc
ND(1612-14)	—	150	300	575	1,150	—

KM# 12 1/24 THALER (Groschen)
1.7100 g., Silver, 20 mm. **Ruler:** Konrad II Kloet **Obv:** Ornate shield of later Werden and Helmstedt arms with mitre above, in circle **Obv. Legend:** MO. NO. R. D: CON. ABB. IN. W. E. H. **Rev:** Imperial orb with Z4 divides date **Rev. Legend:** MATTHI. ROM. IMP. SEM. AVG(V). **Note:** Ref. G#23.

Date	Mintage	VG	F	VF	XF	Unc
1614	—	—	—	—	—	—

KM# 52 1/16 THALER (5 Albus)
1.5700 g., Silver, 22 mm. **Ruler:** Adolf IV **Obv:** Shield of early arms superimposed on cross which quarters larger background shield of 4-fold arms, imperial eagle in upper left and lower right quarters, Borken family arms (crowned winged heart) in upper right and lower left, mitre above **Obv. Legend:** ADOLPHVS. D. G. ABBAS. **Rev:** 4-line inscription with date, in circle **Rev. Legend:** MON. ARG. ABBAT. WERD &. H. **Rev. Inscription:** XVI. / I. REICHS / THALER / 1670. **Note:** Ref. G#47.

Date	Mintage	VG	F	VF	XF	Unc
1670	—	—	—	—	—	—

KM# 53 1/16 THALER (5 Albus)
Silver, 21 mm. **Ruler:** Ferdinand **Obv:** Crowned shield of early arms superimposed on cross which quarters larger background shield of 4-fold arms, imperial eagle in upper left and lower right quarters, family arms (crowned rampant lion to left on background of 7 horizontal bars) in upper r **Obv. Legend:** FERDIN. - D G. ABB. **Rev:** 4-line inscription with date, in circle **Rev. Legend:** MON. ARG. ABBAT. WERD. &. H. **Rev. Inscription:** XVI. / I. REICHS / THALER / 1670. **Note:** Ref. G#50-51. Weight varies: 1.62-1.63 g.

Date	Mintage	VG	F	VF	XF	Unc
1670	—	40.00	85.00	150	250	—
1689 Reported, not confirmed	—	—	—	—	—	—

KM# 10A 1/4 GULDEN
4.3500 g., Silver, 19 x 19 mm. **Ruler:** Hugo Preutäus **Obv:** Ornamented shield of later Werden and Helmstedt arms, mnitre above **Obv. Legend:** HVGO. D: G. WER. Z. HEL. A. **Rev:** Full-length facing figure of St. Ludger holding model of abbey and crozier **Rev. Legend:** S LVTGE - RVS. EPIS. **Note:** Ref. G#31. Klippe. KM#10 and #10A may have been struck from dies intended for a Ducat, but none are known in gold.

Date	Mintage	VG	F	VF	XF	Unc
ND(1614-46)	—	—	—	—	—	—

KM# 10 1/4 GULDEN
4.1100 g., Silver, 20 mm. **Ruler:** Hugo Preutäus **Obv:** Ornamented shield of later Werden and Helmstedt arms, mitre above **Obv. Legend:** HVGO. D: G. WER. Z. HEL. A. **Rev:** Full-length facing figure of St. Ludger holding model fo abbey and crozier **Rev. Legend:** S LVTGE - RVS. EPIS. **Note:** Ref. G#31. KM#10 and #10A may have been struck from dies intended for a Ducat, but none are known in gold.

Date	Mintage	VG	F	VF	XF	Unc
ND(1614-46)	—	—	—	—	—	—

KM# 20 1/2 THALER
Silver, 34 mm. **Ruler:** Hugo Preutäus **Obv:** Ornate shield of 6-fold arms, mitre above **Obv. Legend:** MO. NO. ARG. REV. D. HVGONIS. ABBA. IN. WERDI. ET. HELM. **Rev:** Crowned imperial eagle, orb on breast **Rev. Legend:** FERDINANDVS. II. D: G. RO. IMP. SEMP. AVGVS. **Note:** Ref. G#27.

Date	Mintage	VG	F	VF	XF	Unc
ND(1619-37) Rare	—	—	—	—	—	—

KM# 42 1/2 THALER
Silver, 38 mm. **Ruler:** Hugo Preutäus **Obv:** Bust right in circle **Obv. Legend:** HENRI: D: G: IMP. MONAS. WERD. ET. HELM. ABBA. **Rev:** Shield of early arms superimposed on cross which quarters larger background shield of 4-fold arms, imperial eagle in upper left and lower right quarters, Dücker family arms (5 horizontal bars) in upper right and lower left, mitre above, date at end o **Rev. Legend:** DVRI. PATIENTIA. VIGTRIX **Note:** Ref. G#38. Klippe. Weight varies: 13.70-17.36 g. Struck on thin flan from Thaler dies, KM#44.

Date	Mintage	VG	F	VF	XF	Unc
1650 Rare	—	—	—	—	—	—

Note: Peus Auction 383, 4-05, VF realized approximately $33,695.

KM# 22 THALER
Silver, 34 mm. **Ruler:** Hugo Preutäus **Obv:** Ornate shield of 6-fold arms, mitre above **Obv. Legend:** MO. NO. ARG. REV. D. HVGONIS. ABBA. IN. WERDI. ET. HELM. **Rev:** Crowned imperial eagle, orb on breast **Rev. Legend:** FERDINANDVS. II. D: G. RO. IMP. SEMP. AVGVS. **Note:** Ref. ex-G#27. Klippe. Struck from 1/2 Thaler dies, KM#20.

Date	Mintage	VG	F	VF	XF	Unc
ND(1619-37) Rare	—	—	—	—	—	—

KM# 28 THALER
Silver, 47 mm. **Ruler:** Hugo Preutäus **Obv:** Cowled bust to right, small date just inside circle to left of back of head, small shield of mitred later arms at bottom **Obv. Legend:** HVGO. D: G. WERDINENSI - VM. ET. HELMONS. ABBAS. **Rev:** Crowned imperial eagle, orb on breast **Rev. Legend:** FERDINANDVS. II. D: G. ROM. IMP. SEMPER. AVGVSTVS. **Note:** Dav#5923, G#29.

Date	Mintage	VG	F	VF	XF	Unc
1636 Rare	—	—	—	—	—	—

KM# 31 THALER
Silver, 46 mm. **Ruler:** Hugo Preutäus **Obv:** Smaller robed bust to right, small date just inside circle to left of back of head, small shield of mitred later arms at bottom **Obv. Legend:** HVGO. D: G. WERDINENS - E. HELMONST. ABBAS. **Rev:** Crowned imperial eagle, orb on breast **Rev. Legend:** FERDINAND. I.I.I. D: G. ROM. IMP. SEMP. AVGVST. **Note:** Dav#5924, G#30.

Date	Mintage	VG	F	VF	XF	Unc
1645 Rare	—	—	—	—	—	—

KM# 35 THALER

Silver, 42 mm. **Ruler:** Adolf IV **Obv:** Shield of early arms superimposed on cross which quarters larger background shield of 4-fold arms, imperial eagle in upper left and lower right quarters, Dücker arms (5 horizontal bars) in upper right **Obv. Legend:** HENRICVS. D: G. MONAST: WERDI: ET. HELMON: ABBAS. **Rev:** Crowned imperial eagle, orb on breast **Rev. Legend:** FERDINAND. I.I.I. D: G. ROM. IMP. SEMP. AVGVST. **Note:** Dav#5925, G#37.

Date	Mintage	VG	F	VF	XF	Unc
1646 Rare	—	—	—	—	—	—

KM# 36 THALER

Silver, 42 mm. **Ruler:** Heinrich IV Dücker **Obv:** Shield of early arms superimposed on cross which quarters larger background shield of 4-fold arms, imperial eagle in upper left and lower right quarters, Dücker arms (5 horizontal bars) in upper right and lower left, mitre above all divides date **Obv. Legend:** HENRICUS. D. G. MONASTE. WERDI. ET HEL. MON. ABB. **Rev:** Crowned imperial eagle, orb on breast **Rev. Legend:** FERDINAND. I.I.I. D: G. ROM. IMP. SEMP. AVGVST. **Note:** Dav#5925A.

Date	Mintage	VG	F	VF	XF	Unc
1646 Rare	—	—	—	—	—	—

KM# 44 THALER

28.2300 g., Silver, 38x38 mm. **Ruler:** Heinrich IV Dücker **Obv:** Bust to right in circle **Obv. Legend:** HENRI: D: G: IMP. MONAS. WERD. ET. HELM. ABBA. **Rev:** Shield of early arms superimposed on cross which quarters larger background shield of 4-fold arms, imperial eagle in upper left and lower right quarters, Dücker arms (5 horizontal bars) in upper right and lower left, mitre above, date at end of legen **Rev. Legend:** DVRI. PATIENTIA. VIGTRIX. **Note:** Klippe; Dav#5926, G#38.

Date	Mintage	VG	F	VF	XF	Unc
1650 Rare	—	—	—	—	—	—

Note: Peus Auction 383, 4-05, VF realized approximately $33,695.

KM# 45 THALER

Silver, 43 mm. **Ruler:** Adolf IV **Obv:** Shield of early arms superimposed on cross which quarters larger background shield of 4-fold arms, imperial eagle in upper left and lower right quarters, Borken arms (crowned winged heart) in upper ri **Obv. Legend:** MO. ADOLPHI. ABB. WERDIN. ET. HELMSTÆD. **Rev:** Full-length facing figure of St. Ludger holding crozier and model of monastery church, date divided by mitre at top **Rev. Legend:** SANCTVS. LVDGE - RVS. EPISCOP. **Note:** Dav#5927, G#45.

Date	Mintage	VG	F	VF	XF	Unc
1667 Rare	—	—	—	—	—	—

KM# 55 THALER

Silver, 48 mm. **Ruler:** Adolf IV **Obv:** Shield of early arms superimposed on cross which quarters larger background shield of 4-fold arms, imperial eagle in upper left and lower right quarters, Borken arms (crowned winged heart) in upper right and lower left, mitre above **Obv. Legend:** MON. ADOLPHI. LIB. IMP. - ABB. WERD. &. HELMST. **Rev:** Full-length facing figure of St. Ludger holding crozier and model of monastery church, date divided by mitre at top **Rev. Legend:** SANCTVS. LVDGE - RVS. EPISCOP. **Note:** Dav#5929, G#46.

Date	Mintage	VG	F	VF	XF	Unc
1670 Rare	—	—	—	—	—	—

KM# 61 THALER

Silver, 43 mm. **Ruler:** Ferdinand **Obv:** Four-fold arms, imperial eagle in upper left and lower right quarters, family arms (crowned rampant lion to left on background of 7 horizontal bars) in upper right and lower left, in oval baroque fram **Obv. Legend:** FERDINANDVS: D: G: ABBAS: WERDIN - ET: HELMSTAD. **Rev:** Full-length fcing figure of St. Ludger holding crozier and model of monastery church, mitre above **Rev. Legend:** SANCTVS: LVDGERVS: - EPISCOPVS FVNDATOR. **Note:** Dav#5930, G#48.

Date	Mintage	VG	F	VF	XF	Unc
1696 Rare	—	—	—	—	—	—

KM# 62 THALER

Silver, 42 mm. **Ruler:** Ferdinand **Obv:** Four-fold arms, imperial eagle in upper left and lower right quarters, family arms (crowned rampant lion to left on background of 7 horizontal bars) in upper right and lower left, in round baroque frame, mitre divides date in margin at top **Obv. Legend:** FERDINANDd. D.G. ABBAS. WERDIN. ET. HELMSTAD. **Rev:** Full-length facing figure of St. Mary standing on crescent moon, stars around head, all in circle with arch in it over head **Rev. Legend:** VIRGO IMMACULATA IVGITER SIT PATRONA. **Note:** Dav#5931, G#49.

Date	Mintage	VG	F	VF	XF	Unc
1698	—	450	900	1,650	3,000	—

KM# 24 1-1/4 THALER

Silver **Ruler:** Hugo Preutäus **Obv:** Ornate shield of 6-fold arms, mitre above **Obv. Legend:** MO. NO. ARG. REV. D. GVGONIS. ABBA. IN. WERDI. ET. HELM. **Rev:** Crowned imperial eagle, orb on breast **Rev. Legend:** FERDINANDVS. II. D: G. RO. IMP. SEMP. AVGVS. **Note:** Klippe, struck from 1/2 Thaler dies, KM#20; G#ex27.

Date	Mintage	VG	F	VF	XF	Unc
ND (1619-37) Rare	—	—	—	—	—	—

KM# 13 1-1/2 THALER

Silver, 45x45 mm. **Ruler:** Hugo Preutäus **Obv:** Ornate shield of 6-fold arms, mitre above **Obv. Legend:** MO. NO. ARG. REV. D. HVGONIS. ABB. IN. WERDEN. ET. HELMS. **Rev:** Crowned imperial eagle, orb on breast **Rev. Legend:** MATTHIAS. I. D. ELEC. RO. IMP. SEM. AVGV. **Note:** Klippe; Dav#A5918, G#26.

Date	Mintage	VG	F	VF	XF	Unc
ND (1614-19) Rare	—	—	—	—	—	—

KM# 17 2 THALER

Silver, 41 mm. **Ruler:** Hugo Preutäus **Obv:** Two-fold arms divided vertically, later Werden and Helmstedt arms at left, Preutäus arms (3 cloverleafs) at right, mitre above, date downwards along right side of shield **Obv. Legend:** MO. NO. A. R. D. HVGON AB. WERDEN. & HELM. **Rev:** Crowned imperial eagle, orb on breast **Rev. Legend:** MATTH. I. D: G. ELE. ROM IM. SEMPER. AVG. **Note:** Dav#5919.

Date	Mintage	VG	F	VF	XF	Unc
1615 Rare	—	—	—	—	—	—

KM# 18 2 THALER

Silver **Ruler:** Hugo Preutäus **Obv:** Two-fold arms divided vertically, later Werden and Helmstedt arms at left, Preutäus arms (3 cloverleafs) at right, mitre above, date downwards along right side of shield **Obv. Legend:** MO. NO. A. R. D. HVGON AB. WERDEN. & HELM. **Rev:** Crowned imperial eagle, orb on breast **Rev. Legend:** MATTH. I. D: G. ELE. ROM. IM. SEMPER. AVG. **Note:** Klippe; Dav#5919A.

Date	Mintage	VG	F	VF	XF	Unc
1616 Rare	—	—	—	—	—	—

KM# 29 2 THALER

Silver **Ruler:** Hugo Preutäus **Obv:** Cowled bust to right, small date just inside circle to left of back of head, small shield of mitred later arms at bottom **Obv. Legend:** HVGO. D: G. WERDINENSI - VM. ET. HELMONS. ABBAS. **Rev:** Crowned imperial eagle, orb on breast **Rev. Legend:** FERDINANDVS. II. D: G. ROM. IMP. SEMPER. AVGVSTVS. **Note:** Dav#5922, G#29.

Date	Mintage	VG	F	VF	XF	Unc
1636 Rare	—	—	—	—	—	—
ND Rare	—	—	—	—	—	—

KM# 57 2 THALER

Silver, 48 mm. **Ruler:** Adolf IV **Obv:** Shield of early arms superimposed on cross which quarters larger background shield of 4-fold arms, imperial eagle in upper left and lower right quarters, Borken arms (crowned winged heart) in upper ri **Obv. Legend:** MON. ADOLPHI. KIB. IMP. - ABB. WERD. &. HELMST. **Rev:** Full-length facing figure of St. Ludger holding crozier and model of monastery church, date divided by mitre at top **Rev. Legend:** SANCTVS. LVDGE - RVS. EPISCOP. **Note:** Dav#5928, G#ex46.

Date	Mintage	VG	F	VF	XF	Unc
1670 Rare	—	—	—	—	—	—

KM# 15 2-1/2 THALER

Silver, 45x45 mm. **Ruler:** Hugo Preutäus **Obv:** Ornate shield of 6-fold arms, mitre above **Obv. Legend:** MO. NO. ARG. REV. D. HVGONIS. ABB. IN. WERDEN. ET. HELMS. **Rev:** Crowned imperial eagle, orb on breast **Rev. Legend:** MATTHIAS. I. D. ELEC. RO. IMP. SEM. AVGV. **Note:** Klippe; Dav#5918, G#26.

Date	Mintage	VG	F	VF	XF	Unc
ND (1614-19) Rare	—	—	—	—	—	—

KM# 25 3 THALER

Silver **Ruler:** Hugo Preutäus **Obv:** Ornate shield of 6-fold arms, mitre above **Obv. Legend:** MO. NO. ARG. REV. D. HVGONIS. ABBA. IN. WERDI. ET. HELM. **Rev:** Crowned imperial eagle, orb on breast **Rev. Legend:** FERDINANDVS. II. D: G. RO. IMP. SEMP. AVGVS. **Note:** Klippe, struck from 1/2 Thaler dies, KM#20; G#ex27.

Date	Mintage	VG	F	VF	XF	Unc
ND (1619-37) Rare	—	—	—	—	—	—

TRADE COINAGE

KM# 40 DUCAT

3.5000 g., 0.9860 Gold 0.1109 oz. AGW, 24 mm. **Ruler:** Heinrich IV Dücker **Obv:** Shield of early arms superimposed on cross which quarters larger background shield of 4-fold arms, imperial eagle in upper left and lower right quarters, Dücker arms (5 horizontal bars) in upper right **Obv. Legend:** HENRIC9. D. ABBAS. WERD. ET. HELM. **Rev:** Five-line inscription with date between laurel and palm branches **Rev. Inscription:** DVCAT / VS. NOV. 9. / ABBATIAE / WERDIN. / (date). **Note:** Fr#3510, G#36.

Date	Mintage	VG	F	VF	XF	Unc
1647 Rare	—	—	—	—	—	—

Note: Dr. Busso Peus Nachfolger Auction 385, 11-05, VF realized approximately $14,475; Dr. Busso Peus Nachfolger Auction 383, 4-05, VF realized approximately $20,095; Dr. Busso Peus Nachfolger Auction 383, 4-05, VF realized approximately $8,035

PATTERNS

Including off metal strikes

KM#	Date	Mintage	Identification	Mkt Val
Pn1	(1)659	—	8 Heller. Gold. KM#48.	—
Pn2	1724 HK	—	Thaler. Copper. 42 mm.	—

WERL

This town in Westphalia, about halfway between Unna and Soest, was a mint for Cologne in the 15th and 16th centuries. Werl had its own local coinage during the late 16th and early 17th centuries.

MINT OFFICIAL

Mark	Date	Name
(a)=	1608-10	Engelhard Hussmann, mintmaster

REFERENCES

K = Hans Krusy, ***Die Münzen von Werl***, Werl, 1979.

W = Joseph Weingärtner, ***Beschreibung dr Kupfermünzen Westfalens nebst historischen Nachrichten***, 2 vols., Paderborn, 1872-81.

PROVINCIAL TOWN

STANDARD COINAGE

KM# 4 PFENNIG

Silver **Obv:** Town arms, 'W' above, date (where present) below **Note:** Ref. K#82-83. Uniface schüssel-type.

Date	Mintage	VG	F	VF	XF	Unc
(16)1Z	—	—	—	—	—	—
ND	—	—	—	—	—	—

KM# 6 3 PFENNIG

Copper **Obv:** Upright key superimposed on cross in circle **Rev:** Value in circle **Note:** Ref. W#454.

Date	Mintage	Good	VG	F	VF	XF
ND	—	150	300	600	—	—

KM# 7 6 PFENNIG

Copper **Obv:** Upright key superimposed on cross in circle **Rev:** Value */ V/ */ I/ * in circle **Note:** Ref. W#453.

Date	Mintage	Good	VG	F	VF	XF
ND	—	28.00	60.00	120	240	—

KM# 9 12 PFENNIG

Copper **Obv:** Upright key superimposed on cross in circle **Obv. Legend:** STADT. - WERLL **Rev:** Value in circle **Note:** Ref. W#452.

Date	Mintage	Good	VG	F	VF	XF
ND	—	100	200	450	1,200	2,400

KM# 1 1/24 THALER (Groschen)

Silver **Obv:** 3 small shields of arms arranged in trilobe, flat tops forming triangle in center **Obv. Legend:** MO - NOV. C - IV: WER - L: **Rev:** Imperial orb with Z (error for Z4), cross divides date, titles of Rudolf II **Note:** Ref. K#64.

Date	Mintage	VG	F	VF	XF	Unc
1608 (a)	—	—	—	—	—	—

KM# 2 1/24 THALER (Groschen)

Silver **Obv:** 3 shields with bottoms to center **Obv. Legend:** MO. NOVA. ... **Rev:** Imperial orb with 'Z4', cross divides date, titles of Rudolf II **Note:** Ref. K#65-68. Varieties exist.

Date	Mintage	VG	F	VF	XF	Unc
1608 (a)	—	—	—	—	—	—
1609 (a)	—	75.00	165	325	650	—

WERNE

A town in Westphalia about 8 miles (13km) west of Hamm. In 1385, Werne received rights as an independant town from the bishop of Münster, but did not strike coins of its own until the early 17th century.

ARMS

Dark horizontal band (cross-hatching on coins) across center of shield, open fields above and below

PROVINCIAL TOWN

REGULAR COINAGE

KM# 1 2 PFENNIG

Copper **Obv:** Town arms in circle **Obv. Legend:** STADT WERNE ... **Rev:** Value "II" in ornamented circle

Date	Mintage	Good	VG	F	VF	XF
ND(c.1602)	—	75.00	150	300	600	—

KM# 2 3 PFENNIG

Copper **Obv:** Town arms in circle, date in legend **Rev:** Value "III"

Date	Mintage	Good	VG	F	VF	XF
1602	—	85.00	175	350	725	—

KM# 3 6 PFENNIG

Copper **Obv:** Town arms in circle **Obv. Legend:** STADT WERNE ... **Rev:** Value 'VI' in ornamented circle

Date	Mintage	Good	VG	F	VF	XF
ND(c.1602)	—	75.00	150	300	600	—

KM# 4 12 PFENNIG

Copper **Obv:** Eagle behind town arms in ornamented circle **Rev:** Value "XII" in rectangle, ornaments above and below, M below, all in ornamented circle

Date	Mintage	Good	VG	F	VF	XF
ND(c.1602)	—	85.00	175	350	725	—

KM# 5 12 PFENNIG

Copper **Obv:** Town arms in circle, date in legend **Rev:** Value 'XII' in ornamented circle

Date	Mintage	Good	VG	F	VF	XF
1602	—	85.00	175	350	725	—

KM# 6 12 PFENNIG

Copper **Obv:** Town arms in circle, date in legend **Obv. Legend:** STADT WERNE ... **Rev:** Value 'XII' with 'W' above **Note:** Varieties exist.

Date	Mintage	Good	VG	F	VF	XF
1610	—	85.00	175	350	725	—

WESTPHALIA

The Duchy of Westphalia was very early the western part of the old Duchy of Saxony. In 1180, most of Westphalia fell to the archbishops of Cologne who added "Duke of Westphalia" to their titles. When Cologne was secularized in 1801, the duchy was administered by Hesse-Darmstadt until 1814 when it was annexed by Prussia. Coins were struck by the archbishops at the beginning of the 17th century and during the early years of the Thirty Years' War specifically for use in the duchy. For the names of the dukes and archbishops, see Cologne.

MINT OFFICIALS' INITIALS and MARKS

Initial or mark	Date	Name
VF/VFH	1631-50	Urban Felgenhauer (Felgenhewer in Arnsberg
(a) = 	1655-?	Jürgen Hartmann in Geseke
(b) = 	Ca.1655-68	Unknown, Dorsten mint
(c)= 	Ca.1663	?Niessmann, mintmaster in Recklinghausen

DUCHY

REGULAR COINAGE

KM# 3 PFENNIG

Silver **Obv:** Westphalian horse springing to left in circle **Obv. Legend:** ERN. D. G. E. E. COLON. **Note:** Uniface schüssel-type.

Date	Mintage	VG	F	VF	XF	Unc
ND(ca1610)	—	—	—	—	—	—

KM# 14 PFENNIG

Silver **Obv:** Westphalian horse springing to left in circle **Obv. Legend:** FERDINAND. D:G. A. E. C. **Note:** Uniface schüssel-type.

Date	Mintage	VG	F	VF	XF	Unc
ND(ca1631)	—	—	—	—	—	—

KM# 6 3 PFENNIG

Copper **Obv:** Westphalian horse left in circle **Obv. Legend:** :MO. III DVC: III WES: III TPH III **Rev:** Value 'III' in ornamented rectangle **Note:** Kipper coinage. Varieties exist.

Date	Mintage	Good	VG	F	VF	XF
ND(1620)	—	30.00	65.00	100	210	—

KM# 7 6 PFENNIG

Copper **Obv:** Westphalian horse left in circle **Obv. Legend:** :MO. III DVC: III WES: III TPH III. **Rev:** Value 'VI' in ornamented rectangle **Note:** Kipper coinage. Varieties exist.

Date	Mintage	Good	VG	F	VF	XF
ND(1620)	—	30.00	65.00	100	210	—

KM# 5 12 PFENNIG

Copper **Obv:** Westphalian horse left in circle **Obv. Legend:** :MO. III DVC: III DVC: III WES: III TPH III. **Rev:** Value 'XII' in ornamented rectangle with date below (where present) **Note:** Kipper coinage. Varieties exist.

Date	Mintage	Good	VG	F	VF	XF
1619	—	18.00	35.00	60.00	120	—
1620	—	18.00	35.00	60.00	120	—
ND	—	18.00	35.00	60.00	120	—

KM# 8 12 PFENNIG

Copper **Obv:** Westphalia horse left in circle **Obv. Legend:** M. NO. DVCA. WESTPHAL. **Rev:** Value 'XII' in baroque frame **Note:** Kipper coinage.

Date	Mintage	Good	VG	F	VF	XF
ND(ca1620)	—	28.00	60.00	90.00	175	—

KM# 9 12 PFENNIG

Copper **Obv:** Crowned oval shield with Westphalian horse to left **Rev:** 'XII' in center, 'PFENNIG' around **Note:** Kipper coinage.

Date	Mintage	Good	VG	F	VF	XF
ND(ca1620)	—	28.00	60.00	90.00	175	—

KM# 10 12 PFENNIG

Copper **Obv:** Crowned oval shield with Westphalian horse to left **Rev:** Imperial orb with 'XII,' 'PFENNING' around **Note:** Kipper coinage.

Date	Mintage	Good	VG	F	VF	XF
ND(ca1620)	—	28.00	60.00	90.00	175	—

KM# 35 8 HELLER (Fettmännchen = 4 Pfennig)

Silver **Obv:** 4-fold arms of Bavaria and Pfalz, titles of Maximili9an Heinrich **Rev:** VIII/date in circle, small town arms (key) at bottom **Rev. Legend:** NVMMVS CVSVS DVRST. **Mint:** Dorsten

Date	Mintage	VG	F	VF	XF	Unc
1653	—	—	—	—	—	—

KM# 36 8 HELLER (Fettmännchen = 4 Pfennig)

Silver **Obv:** 4-fold arms of Bavaria and Pfalz, titles of Maximilian Heinrich **Rev:** VIII in center, date at end of legend **Rev. Legend:** DVSVS. DVRST. **Mint:** Dorsten **Note:** Varieties exist.

Date	Mintage	VG	F	VF	XF	Unc
1653	—	12.00	25.00	55.00	110	—
1654	—	12.00	25.00	55.00	110	—
1655	—	12.00	25.00	55.00	110	—
1656	—	12.00	25.00	55.00	110	—
1657	—	12.00	25.00	55.00	110	—
1659	—	12.00	25.00	55.00	110	—
1661	—	12.00	25.00	55.00	110	—
1662	—	12.00	25.00	55.00	110	—
ND	—	12.00	25.00	55.00	110	—

KM# 63 8 HELLER (Fettmännchen = 4 Pfennig)

Silver **Obv:** 4-fold arms of Bavaria and Pfalz, titles of Maximilian Heinrich **Rev:** Episcopal Cologne arms in circle, small 3-towered church above, date at end of legend **Rev. Legend:** NVM. RICHLINGHVS. **Mint:** Recklinghausen **Note:** Varieties exist.

Date	Mintage	VG	F	VF	XF	Unc
1662	—	25.00	50.00	100	210	—
1663 (c)	—	25.00	50.00	100	210	—
ND	—	25.00	50.00	100	210	—

KM# 62 8 HELLER (Fettmännchen = 4 Pfennig)

Silver **Obv:** 4-fold arms of Bavaria and Pfalz, titles of Maximilian Heinrich **Rev:** Episcopal Cologne arms in circle, date divided by 4 angles of cross, small 3-towered church above **Rev. Legend:** NVM. RICHLINGHVS. **Mint:** Recklinghausen

Date	Mintage	VG	F	VF	XF	Unc
1662	—	25.00	50.00	100	210	—

KM# 53 MATHIER (1/72 Thaler = 1/2 Mariengroschen = 4 Pfennig)

Silver **Obv:** Crowned oval 4-fold arms of Bavaria and Pfalz with central shield of episcopal Cologne, titles of Maximilian Heinrich **Rev:** Date at end of inscription **Rev. Inscription:** EIN / MATI / ER **Mint:** Geseke

Date	Mintage	VG	F	VF	XF	Unc
1657	—	—	—	—	—	—

KM# 54 MATHIER (1/72 Thaler = 1/2 Mariengroschen = 4 Pfennig)

Silver **Obv:** Crowned oval 4-fold arms of Bavaria and Pfalz with central shield of episcopal Cologne, shield has flat top and sides with rounded bottom, titles of Maximilian Heinrich **Rev:** Date at end of inscription **Rev. Inscription:** EIN / MATI / ER **Mint:** Geseke **Note:** Varieties exist.

Date	Mintage	VG	F	VF	XF	Unc
1657	—	—	—	—	—	—

KM# 66 1/2 STUBER (1/108 Thaler)

0.6500 g., Silver **Obv:** 4-fold arms of Bavaria and Pfalz in circle, titles of Maximilian Heinrich **Rev:** Westphalian horse leaping left **Rev. Legend:** FVR. WES - LAN. MVN. **Mint:** Dorsten **Note:** Varieties exist.

Date	Mintage	VG	F	VF	XF	Unc
ND(ca1668)	—	60.00	120	240	—	—
ND(ca1668) (b)	—	60.00	120	240	—	—

KM# 67 STUBER (1/54 Thaler)

1.3000 g., Silver **Obv:** 4-fold arms of Bavaria and Pflaz in circle, titles of Maximilian Heinrich **Rev:** Westphalian horse leaping left, '54' below horse **Rev. Legend:** FVRST. WEST - LAND. MVNZ. **Mint:** Dorsten

Date	Mintage	VG	F	VF	XF	Unc
ND(ca1668) (b)	—	45.00	90.00	185	360	—

KM# 64 2 ALBUS

Silver **Obv:** 4-fold arms of Bavaria and Pfalz in circle, '2AL' at bottom, titles of Maximilian Heinrich **Rev:** Episcopal Cologne arms in circle, date divided by 4 angles of cross, small 3-towered church above **Rev. Legend:** NVM. RICHLINGHVS. **Mint:** Recklinghausen

Date	Mintage	VG	F	VF	XF	Unc
1662	—	—	—	—	—	—

KM# 21 1/3 SCHILLING (1/84 Thaler = 4 Pfennig)

Silver **Obv:** Arms of episcopal Cologne (cross in shield) in circle divide date, '84' at bottom, titles of Ferdinand of Bavaria **Rev:** 4-fold arms of Bavaria and Pfalz in circle, 3 above arms, titles continued

Date	Mintage	VG	F	VF	XF	Unc
ND(ca1637)	—	—	—	—	—	—

KM# 20 1/3 SCHILLING (1/84 Thaler = 4 Pfennig)

Silver **Obv:** Arms of episcopal Cologne (cross in shield) in circle divide date, '84' at bottom, titles of Ferdinand of Bavaria **Rev:** 4-fold arms of Bavaria and Pfalz in circle, (3) at top, titles continued **Mint:** Recklinghausen **Note:** Varieties exist.

Date	Mintage	VG	F	VF	XF	Unc
(16)37	—	—	—	—	—	—
ND	—	—	—	—	—	—

KM# 22 SCHILLING (1/28 Thaler)

Silver **Obv:** 4-fold arms of Bavaria and Pfalz superimposedon cross, titles of Ferdinand of Bavaria **Rev:** Crowned imperial eagle, 'Z8' in orb on breast, dated divided at top, titles of Ferdinand II **Note:** Weight varies: 1.9-2.1 g. Varieties exist.

Date	Mintage	VG	F	VF	XF	Unc
1637 VF	—	—	—	—	—	—
1638 VF	—	—	—	—	—	—

KM# 38 SCHILLING (1/28 Thaler)

Silver **Obv:** Crowned oval 4-fold arms of Bavaria and Pfalz, titles of Maximilian Heinrich, '28' at bottom **Rev:** St. Peter enthroned facing, value '28' below **Rev. Legend:** S. PETRVS... **Mint:** Geseke

Date	Mintage	VG	F	VF	XF	Unc
ND(ca1655)	—	60.00	120	240	—	—

KM# 39 SCHILLING (1/28 Thaler)

Silver **Obv:** Crowned oval 4-fold arms of Bavaria and Pfalz, titles of Maximilian Heinrich, '28' at bottom **Rev:** St. Peter entrhoned facing, value '28' below, date at end of legend **Rev. Legend:** S. PETRVS... **Mint:** Geseke

Date	Mintage	VG	F	VF	XF	Unc
1655	—	60.00	120	240	—	—

KM# 50 SCHILLING (1/28 Thaler)
Silver **Obv:** Crowned oval 4-fold arms of Bavaria and Pfalz, titles of Maximilian Heinrich, '28' at bottom **Rev:** St. Peter enthroned facing which divides date, value '28' below **Rev. Legend:** S. PETRVS... **Mint:** Geseke **Note:** Varieties exist.

Date	Mintage	VG	F	VF	XF	Unc
1656	—	35.00	75.00	150	—	—
1656 (s)	—	25.00	55.00	110	—	—

KM# 12 2 SCHILLING
Copper **Obv:** Westphalian horse left in circle **Obv. Legend:** :MO. III DVC: III DVC: III WES: III TPH III. **Rev:** Value 'II' in ornamented rectangle **Note:** Kipper coinage. Varieties exist.

Date	Mintage	Good	VG	F	VF	XF
ND(ca1620)	—	28.00	60.00	90.00	160	—

KM# 40 2 SCHILLING (1/14 Thaler)
Silver **Obv:** Crowned oval 4-fold arms of Bavaria and Pfalz with central shield of episcopal Cologne, value (14) at bottom, titles of Maximilian Heinrich **Rev:** Full-length facing figure of St. Peter divides date **Rev. Legend:** S. PETRVS... **Note:** Varieties exist.

Date	Mintage	VG	F	VF	XF	Unc
1655	—	75.00	150	300	—	—
1656	—	75.00	150	300	—	—

KM# 23 MARIENGROSCHEN (1/36 Thaler)
Silver **Obv:** Inscription in circle with date at end, (36) at bottom, titles of Ferdinand of Bavaria **Obv. Inscription:** I / MARIE / GROS **Rev:** 4-fold arms of Bavaria and Pfalz superimposed on cross, titles continued **Note:** Varieties exist.

Date	Mintage	VG	F	VF	XF	Unc
1637 VF	—	45.00	90.00	180	—	—
1638 VF	—	45.00	90.00	180	—	—
1639 VF	—	45.00	90.00	180	—	—
1644 VF	—	45.00	90.00	180	—	—

KM# 28 MARIENGROSCHEN (1/36 Thaler)
Silver **Obv:** Crowned 4-fold arms of Bavaria and Pfalz, titles of Ferdinand of Bavaria **Rev:** Date divided at top **Rev. Legend:** VON. FEINEM. SILB. **Rev. Inscription:** I / MA / G

Date	Mintage	VG	F	VF	XF	Unc
(16)39	—	—	—	—	—	—

KM# 41 MARIENGROSCHEN (1/36 Thaler)
Silver **Obv:** Westphalian horse leaping left in circle, date below, titles of Maximilian Heinrich **Rev:** Madonna and child in rays **Rev. Legend:** CLYP. OMNI - IN TE SPE. **Mint:** Geseke

Date	Mintage	VG	F	VF	XF	Unc
1655	—	—	—	—	—	—

KM# 29 2 MARIENGROSCHEN (1/18 Thaler)
Silver **Obv:** Crowned 4-fold arms of Bavaria and Pfalz, titles of Ferdinand of Bavaria **Obv. Inscription:** I / MA / G **Rev:** Date divided at top **Rev. Legend:** VON. FEINEM. SILB. **Note:** Varieties exist.

Date	Mintage	VG	F	VF	XF	Unc
1639	—	12.00	25.00	60.00	120	—
1640	—	12.00	25.00	60.00	120	—
1641	—	12.00	25.00	60.00	120	—
164Z	—	12.00	25.00	60.00	120	—
1643	—	12.00	25.00	60.00	120	—
1644	—	12.00	25.00	60.00	120	—
1645	—	12.00	25.00	60.00	120	—
1646	—	12.00	25.00	60.00	120	—
1647	—	12.00	25.00	60.00	120	—
1649	—	12.00	25.00	60.00	120	—
1650	—	12.00	25.00	60.00	120	—

KM# 42 2 MARIENGROSCHEN (1/18 Thaler)
Silver **Obv:** Crowned MHA monogram (Maximilianus Henricus Archiepiscopus) in circle **Obv. Legend:** CHVRF. COL. W. L. MVNT. **Rev:** Date (where present) at top **Rev. Legend:** PIETATE... **Rev. Inscription:** II / MARIE / GRO **Note:** Varieties exist.

Date	Mintage	VG	F	VF	XF	Unc
ND(ca1655) (a)	—	12.00	25.00	55.00	115	—
1655	—	12.00	25.00	55.00	115	—

KM# 44 2 MARIENGROSCHEN (1/18 Thaler)
Silver **Obv:** Crowned MHA monogram (Maximilianus Henricus Archiepiscopus) in circle **Obv. Legend:** CHVRF. COL. W. L. MVNT. **Rev:** Date at end of legend **Rev. Legend:** PRO. DEO. ET. PATRIA **Rev. Inscription:** II / MARIE / GRO **Note:** Varieties exist.

Date	Mintage	VG	F	VF	XF	Unc
1655 (a)	—	10.00	20.00	40.00	85.00	—
1656	—	10.00	20.00	40.00	85.00	—
1656 (a)	—	10.00	20.00	40.00	85.00	—

KM# 43 2 MARIENGROSCHEN (1/18 Thaler)
Silver **Obv:** Crowned MHA monogram (Maximilianus Henricus Archiepiscopus) in circle **Obv. Legend:** CHVRF. COL. W. L. MVNT. **Rev:** Date at end of inscription **Rev. Legend:** PIETATE... **Rev. Inscription:** II / MARI / GRO

Date	Mintage	VG	F	VF	XF	Unc
1655	—	10.00	20.00	40.00	85.00	—
1656	—	10.00	20.00	40.00	85.00	—

KM# 51 2 MARIENGROSCHEN (1/18 Thaler)
Silver **Obv:** Crowned MHA monogram (Maximilianus Henricus Archiepiscopus) in circle **Obv. Legend:** CHVRF. COL. W. L. MVNT. **Rev:** Date at end of inscription **Rev. Legend:** PRO. DEO. ET. PATRIA **Rev. Inscription:** II / MARI / GROS

Date	Mintage	VG	F	VF	XF	Unc
1656	—	10.00	20.00	40.00	85.00	—

KM# 45 4 MARIENGROSCHEN
Silver **Obv:** Crowned MHA monogram (Maximilianus Henricus Archiepiscopus) in circle **Obv. Legend:** CHVRF. COL. W. L. MVNT. **Rev:** Date at end of legend **Rev. Legend:** PRO. DEO. ET. PATRIA **Rev. Inscription:** IIII / MARIE / GROS.

Date	Mintage	VG	F	VF	XF	Unc
1655	—	—	—	—	—	—

KM# 69 1/16 THALER
Silver **Obv:** Crowned heart-shaped 4-fold arms of episcopal Cologne with 4-fold central shield of Bavaria and Pfalz, titles of Maximilian Heinrich **Rev:** Date at end of inscription, titles continued **Rev. Inscription:** XVI / I. REICHS / THALER **Mint:** Dorsten

Date	Mintage	VG	F	VF	XF	Unc
1671	—	—	—	—	—	—

KM# 46 1/8 THALER (Brabanter Schilling)
4.4500 g., Silver **Obv:** Rampant lion left holding oval episcopal Cologne arms, value '8' between hind legs, titles of Maximilian Heinrich **Rev:** 4-fold arms with central shield of 4-fold arms divide sideways date, titles continued **Mint:** Geseke

Date	Mintage	VG	F	VF	XF	Unc
1655	—	—	—	—	—	—

KM# 15 THALER
Silver **Obv:** Bust right in circle, titles of Ferdinand of Bavaria **Rev:** Crowned 4-fold arms with central shield of 4-fold arms of Bavaria and Pfalz divide date, titles continued **Note:** Dav#5138.

Date	Mintage	VG	F	VF	XF	Unc
1631 VFH	—	825	1,550	3,150	5,000	—

KM# 18 THALER
Silver **Obv:** Bust right in circle, titles of Ferdinand of Bavaria **Rev:** Crowned 4-fold arms with central shield of 4-fold arms of Bavaria and Pfalz divide date at higher point, titles continued **Note:** Dav#5139.

Date	Mintage	VG	F	VF	XF	Unc
1635 VFH	—	2,500	5,000	9,000	—	—

KM# 25 THALER
Silver **Obv:** Large bust right in circle, titles of Ferdinand of Bavaria **Rev:** Crowned 4-fold arms with central shield of 4-fold arms of Bavaria and Pfalz divide date, titles continued **Note:** Dav#5141.

Date	Mintage	VG	F	VF	XF	Unc
1637 VFH Rare	—	—	—	—	—	—

KM# 33 THALER
Silver **Obv:** Bust right in circle, top of bust breaks circle, titles of Ferdinand of Bavaria **Rev:** Crowned 4-fold arms with central shield of smaller, finer shield of 4-fold arms of Bavaria and Pfalz divide date near bottom, titles continued **Note:** Dav#5145.

Date	Mintage	VG	F	VF	XF	Unc
1649 VFH Rare	—	—	—	—	—	—

KM# 57 THALER
Silver **Obv:** Bust right in mantle **Obv. Legend:** ... COL. PR. EL. EP. LEOD. HILD. ADM. BERCH. **Rev:** Capped arms divide date **Rev. Legend:** VTR. BAV. WEST: ANG... COM. PAL. RHE. LAND. LEV. **Note:** Dav.#5149. Prev. Cologne, KM#53.

Date	Mintage	VG	F	VF	XF	Unc
1657 Rare	—	—	—	—	—	—

KM# 58 THALER
Silver **Rev. Legend:** ...BVL. COM. PAL. RHE. LAN: L. **Note:** Dav.#5150. Prev. Cologne, KM#54.

Date	Mintage	VG	F	VF	XF	Unc
1657 Rare	—	—	—	—	—	—

KM# 59 THALER
Silver **Obv. Legend:** ...EP: HIL: LEOD: A: BER: **Rev. Legend:** LAND: LEV: VTR: BA: WEST: AN: B: DVX: CO: PA. RHE: **Note:** Dav.#5151. Prev. Cologne KM#58.

Date	Mintage	VG	F	VF	XF	Unc
1657 Rare	—	—	—	—	—	—

KM# 26 2 THALER

Silver **Obv:** Larger bust right in circle, titles of Ferdinand of Bavaria **Rev:** Crowned 4-fold arms with central shield of 4-fold arms of Bavaria and Pfalz divide date, titles continued **Note:** Dav#5140.

Date	Mintage	VG	F	VF	XF	Unc
1637 VFH Rare	—	—	—	—	—	—

KM# 60 2 THALER

Silver **Obv:** Bust of Maximillian right **Rev:** Capped arms divide date **Note:** Dav.#5148. Prev. Cologne, KM#59.

Date	Mintage	VG	F	VF	XF	Unc
1657 Rare	—	—	—	—	—	—

TRADE COINAGE

KM# 17 GOLDGULDEN

Gold **Obv:** 4-fold arms of Bavaria and Pfalz in ornamented shield, crown above, titles of Ferdinand of Bavaria **Rev:** 4-fold arms of episcopal Cologne in ornamented shield, date above, titles continued **Note:** Fr#820. Varieties exist.

Date	Mintage	VG	F	VF	XF	Unc
1634	—	1,000	2,000	3,600	6,000	—
1637	—	1,000	2,000	3,600	6,000	—

KM# 31 DUCAT

Gold **Obv:** Crowned 4-fold arms of Bavaria and PFalz, titles of Ferdinand of Bavaria **Rev:** Inscription with date at end in ornamented square within circle, titles continued **Rev. Inscription:** DVC / ATVS **Note:** Fr#822.

Date	Mintage	VG	F	VF	XF	Unc
1640	—	1,200	2,400	4,800	7,800	—

KM# 48 DUCAT

Gold **Obv:** Bust right, titles of Maximilian Heinrich **Rev:** Crowned round 4-fold arms with central shield of 4-fold arms of Bavaria and Pfalz **Rev. Legend:** BAVARI. WESTPH - ANGARI. DUX. **Mint:** Dorsten

Date	Mintage	VG	F	VF	XF	Unc
ND(ca1655) (b)	—	800	1,600	3,300	5,400	—

WIEDENBRUCK

The parish church of St. Aegidius in Wiedenbrück was home to a seminary from 1259 until 1810. It was closely tied to the bishopric of Osnabrück (which see). However, the town is located on the upper Ems River, next to Rheda and about 55 miles (90 kilometers) south-southeast of Osnabrück. At various times, Wiedenbrück served as a mint site for the bishops, but it also issued a series of coins for local use from 1596 to 1716.

MINT OFFICIAL

AS	ca. 1716	Unknown

ARMS OR SYMBOL OF TOWN

The wheel of Osnabrück, showing the close association it had with that city and bishopric.

PROVINCIAL TOWN

TOWN COINAGE

KM# 13 HELLER

Copper **Obv:** Wheel around inscription **Obv. Inscription:** MO CIVI WIDENBRVG **Rev:** Small 1 above H

Date	Mintage	Good	VG	F	VF	XF
ND(ca.1630-40)	—	—	—	—	—	—

MB# 5 PFENNIG

Copper **Obv:** Wheel of Osnabr?ck around inscription **Rev:** Value I divides date as 1 - 5/9 - 6. **Note:** Varieties exist.

Date	Mintage	Good	VG	F	VF	XF
1615	—	18.00	37.00	75.00	150	—
1619	—	18.00	37.00	75.00	150	—

KM# 17 PFENNIG

Copper **Obv:** Wheel around inscription, date **Obv. Inscription:** MO. WIDENBRVG(E) **Rev:** Value I in ornamented frame **Note:** Varieties exist.

Date	Mintage	Good	VG	F	VF	XF
ND(ca.1630-40)	—	15.00	30.00	60.00	120	—
1634	—	15.00	30.00	60.00	120	—
1636	—	15.00	30.00	60.00	120	—

KM# 21 PFENNIG

Copper **Obv:** Wheel, inscription around **Obv. Inscription:** MO. WIDENBRVGE (or variant) around **Rev:** Value I divides date as 1 - 6/3 - 6 **Note:** Varieties exist.

Date	Mintage	Good	VG	F	VF	XF
1636	—	12.00	25.00	50.00	100	200
1641	—	12.00	25.00	50.00	100	200
1642	—	12.00	25.00	50.00	100	200
1643	—	12.00	25.00	50.00	100	200
1650	—	12.00	25.00	50.00	100	200
1653	—	12.00	25.00	50.00	100	200
1655	—	12.00	25.00	50.00	100	200
1663	—	12.00	25.00	50.00	100	200
1668	—	12.00	25.00	50.00	100	200
1670	—	12.00	25.00	50.00	100	200
1674	—	12.00	25.00	50.00	100	200
1678	—	12.00	25.00	50.00	100	200
1692	—	12.00	25.00	50.00	100	200
1694	—	12.00	25.00	50.00	100	200

KM# 24 PFENNIG

Copper **Obv:** Wheel around inscription but date also in margin **Rev:** Value I divides date

Date	Mintage	Good	VG	F	VF	XF
1653	—	15.00	30.00	65.00	130	—
1655	—	15.00	30.00	65.00	130	—

KM# 30 PFENNIG

Copper **Obv:** Wheel around inscription **Rev:** Value I divides date as 1 - 7/6 - 0

Date	Mintage	Good	VG	F	VF	XF
1670	—	15.00	30.00	50.00	90.00	—

KM# 32 PFENNIG

Copper **Obv:** Wheel around inscription **Obv. Inscription:** MO. CIVI WI. DENB **Rev:** Value I divides date as 16 'I' 83

Date	Mintage	Good	VG	F	VF	XF
1683	—	15.00	30.00	65.00	130	—

KM# 7 3 PFENNIG

Copper **Obv:** Wheel of Osnabrück around inscription, date **Rev:** Value • I • I • I • **Note:** Varieties exist.

Date	Mintage	Good	VG	F	VF	XF
(1)619	—	16.00	30.00	60.00	120	—
1619	—	16.00	30.00	60.00	120	—

KM# 15 3 PFENNIG

Copper **Obv:** Wheel around inscription **Obv. Inscription:** M. CIVI. WIDENBRVG.

Date	Mintage	Good	VG	F	VF	XF
(ca.1630-40)	—	20.00	40.00	80.00	160	—

KM# 19 3 PFENNIG

Copper **Obv:** Wheel around inscription, date **Rev:** Value III in ornamented frame

Date	Mintage	Good	VG	F	VF	XF
1634	—	18.00	35.00	70.00	145	—

KM# 22 3 PFENNIG

Copper **Obv:** Wheel around inscription, date **Rev:** Value divides date as 1 I 6 I 3 I 6. **Note:** Mule.

Date	Mintage	Good	VG	F	VF	XF
1636	—	18.00	35.00	70.00	145	—

KM# 26 3 PFENNIG

Copper **Obv:** Wheel, inscription (or variant), date around **Rev:** Value III **Note:** Varieties exist.

Date	Mintage	Good	VG	F	VF	XF
1653	—	15.00	25.00	55.00	110	—
1655	—	15.00	25.00	55.00	110	—
1661	—	15.00	25.00	55.00	110	—
1663	—	15.00	25.00	55.00	110	—
1668	—	15.00	25.00	55.00	110	—
(16)69	—	15.00	25.00	55.00	110	—
1670	—	15.00	25.00	55.00	110	—
1671	—	15.00	25.00	55.00	110	—
(16)7Z	—	15.00	25.00	55.00	110	—
167Z	—	15.00	25.00	55.00	110	—
1673	—	15.00	25.00	55.00	110	—
1674	—	15.00	25.00	55.00	110	—
(16)77	—	15.00	25.00	55.00	110	—
1677	—	15.00	25.00	55.00	110	—
1678	—	15.00	25.00	55.00	110	—
ND(1680-1700)	—	15.00	25.00	55.00	110	—
1681	—	15.00	25.00	55.00	110	—
1683	—	15.00	25.00	55.00	110	—
1684	—	15.00	25.00	55.00	110	—
1686	—	15.00	25.00	55.00	110	—
1688	—	15.00	25.00	55.00	110	—
1690	—	15.00	25.00	55.00	110	—
1691	—	15.00	25.00	55.00	110	—
1692	—	15.00	25.00	55.00	110	—
169Z	—	15.00	25.00	55.00	110	—
1693	—	15.00	25.00	55.00	110	—

KM# 28 3 PFENNIG

Copper **Obv:** Wheel, inscription around **Obv. Inscription:** M. CIVI. WIDENBRVG **Rev:** Value III

Date	Mintage	Good	VG	F	VF	XF
ND(ca.1663)	—	18.00	35.00	70.00	145	—

KM# 9 6 PFENNIG

Copper **Obv:** Wheel of Osnabr?ck around inscription, date **Obv. Inscription:** SI DEVS PRO NOBIS. QVIS TRANOS. **Rev:** Value VI **Note:** Varieties exist.

Date	Mintage	Good	VG	F	VF	XF
1610	—	30.00	60.00	120	240	—

KM# 11 6 PFENNIG

Copper **Obv:** Wheel of Osnabr?ck in ornamented circle around inscription, date **Obv. Inscription:** MO: CIVIT: WIDENBRVGGE (or variant) ANNO, date **Rev:** Value VI in ornamental frame **Note:** Varieties exist.

Date	Mintage	Good	VG	F	VF	XF
1619	—	25.00	50.00	90.00	200	—
1663	—	25.00	50.00	90.00	200	—

WISMAR

A seaport on the Baltic, the city of Wismar is said to have obtained municipal rights from Mecklenburg in 1229. It was an important member of the Hanseatic League in the 13th and 14th centuries. Their coinage began at the end of the 13th century and terminated in 1854. They belonged to Sweden from 1648 to 1803. A special plate money was struck by the Swedes in 1715 when the town was under siege. In 1803, Sweden sold Wismar to Mecklenburg-Schwerin. The transaction was confirmed in 1815.

RULERS

Swedish, 1648-1803
Friedrich Franz I, 1785-1837
Paul Friedrich, 1837-1842
Friedrich Franz II, 1842-1883

MINT OFFICIALS' INITIALS

Initial	Date	Name
	1582-1602	Hans Rode, warden
(f)= or JM (ligature)	1594-1600	Jürgen (Georg) Martens der Ältere
(g)=	1601-12	Michael Martens
	1602-06	Andrew Reimers, warden
	1607-19	Cyriacus Klein (Kilian Klehne), warden
	1612	Johann Marten
(h)=	1613-18	Simon Lüdemann
	1618-19	Johann (Hans) Schroeder
	1620-22	Jürgen Martens der Jüngere
(i)=	1622-24	Jacob Mauche (Maucke)
(j)=	1624-37	Johann (Hans) Dase
	1629-30	Hans Jobst (Jost), warden
	1633-45	David Jost, warden
	1636-42	Johann Scheffel, warden
	1643-60	Daniel Hertzberg, warden
(k)=	1647-50	Simon Timpe (Timpffe, Dimpe)
(l)= or BK+	1650-60	Barthold (Balthasar) Krause
(m)= or HS+	1661-70	Henning Stör
	1661-62	Jürgen Maass, warden
(n)=mailed arm holding sword or HR+ plus mailed arm holding sword	1670-74	Hans Ritter (Ridder)
	1671-74	Johann Birek, warden
GS	1675-80	Gregory (Gregor) Sesemann
	1675-80	Heinrich Reimers, warden
IM	1685-1702	Johann Memmies in Rostock

ARMS

2-fold arms divided vertically, half of bull's head of Mecklenburg on left, four alternating light and dark horizontal bars on right. In coin designs, the darker bars are usually designated by cross-hatching or other filler. Some designs show only the four-bar arms in a shield and these are designated "single Wismar arms."

CITY

REGULAR COINAGE

MB# 60 1/2 PFENNIG (Scherf)

Copper **Obv:** City arms, date above **Rev:** SCH / ARF in circle **Note:** Varieties exist.

Date	Mintage	VG	F	VF	XF	Unc
(1)601	—	20.00	45.00	90.00	180	—
(1)60Z	—	20.00	45.00	90.00	180	—
(1)603	—	20.00	45.00	90.00	180	—

Date	Mintage	VG	F	VF	XF	Unc
(1)604	—	20.00	45.00	90.00	180	—
1608	—	20.00	45.00	90.00	180	—
1611	—	20.00	45.00	90.00	180	—
(16)15	—	20.00	45.00	90.00	180	—
ND	—	20.00	45.00	90.00	180	—

KM# 47 PFENNIG

Copper **Obv:** City arms in ornamented shield **Rev:** Date at end of inscription **Rev. Inscription:** I / PHEN / NING **Note:** Kipper coinage.

Date	Mintage	VG	F	VF	XF	Unc
1622	—	—	—	—	—	—

KM# 48 2 PFENNIG (Blaffert)

Copper **Obv:** City arms **Obv. Legend:** MONET NOVA WISMAR **Rev:** Date at end of inscription **Rev. Inscription:** II / PHEN / NING **Note:** Kipper coinage.

Date	Mintage	Good	VG	F	VF	XF
1622	—	8.00	14.00	22.00	43.00	—

KM# 49 2 PFENNIG (Blaffert)

Copper **Obv:** City arms in ornamented shield **Rev:** Date at end of inscription **Rev. Inscription:** II / PHEN / NING **Note:** Kipper coinage.

Date	Mintage	Good	VG	F	VF	XF
16ZZ	—	8.00	14.00	22.00	43.00	—

KM# 45 3 PFENNIG (Dreiling)

Copper **Obv:** City arms **Obv. Legend:** MONET NOVA WISMAR **Rev:** Date at end of inscription **Rev. Inscription:** III / PHEN / NING **Note:** Kipper coinage. Varieties exist.

Date	Mintage	Good	VG	F	VF	XF
1621	—	45.00	90.00	180	360	—
1622	—	45.00	90.00	180	360	—
16ZZ	—	45.00	90.00	180	360	—

KM# 17 2 SCHILLING (Doppelschilling)

Silver **Obv:** City arms **Obv. Legend:** MONETA... **Rev:** Intertwined DS in ornate shield divides date at sides and bottom, orb at top, titles of Rudolf II

Date	Mintage	VG	F	VF	XF	Unc
1610	—	—	—	—	—	—

KM# 18 2 SCHILLING (Doppelschilling)

Silver **Obv:** City arms superimposed on long cross **Obv. Legend:** MONETA... **Rev:** Intertwined DS in ornate shield divides date at sides and bottom, orb at top, titles of Rudolf II

Date	Mintage	VG	F	VF	XF	Unc
ND(ca1610)	—	20.00	45.00	90.00	180	—
1610	—	20.00	45.00	90.00	180	—

KM# 50 4 SCHILLING (1/8 Thaler)

Silver **Obv:** St. Lawrence standing behind city arms, date divided below **Rev:** Corwned imperial eagle, 4 in orb on breast, titles of Ferdinand II

Date	Mintage	VG	F	VF	XF	Unc
1622 (i)	—	175	350	725	—	—

KM# 51 4 SCHILLING (1/8 Thaler)

Silver **Obv:** St. Lawrence standing behind city arms, date in margin **Rev:** Crowned imperial eagle, 4 in orb on breast, titles of Ferdinand II **Note:** Varieties exist.

Date	Mintage	VG	F	VF	XF	Unc
1622 (i)	—	160	325	650	—	—
(16)24	—	—	—	—	—	—

KM# 3 8 SCHILLING (1/4 Thaler)

Silver **Obv:** St. Lawrence standing behind city arms, date in margin **Obv. Legend:** MONETA... **Rev:** Crowned imperial eagle, orb with 8 on breast divides date, titles of Rudolf II **Note:** Varieties exist.

Date	Mintage	VG	F	VF	XF	Unc
(1)603 (g)	—	—	—	—	—	—
ND(ca1604-08)	—	—	—	—	—	—

KM# 53 8 SCHILLING (1/4 Thaler)

Silver **Obv:** St. Lawrence standing behind city arms, date at bottom to right of arms **Rev:** Crowned imperial eagle, 8 in orb on breast, titles of Ferdinand II **Note:** Varieties exist.

Date	Mintage	VG	F	VF	XF	Unc
1622 (i)	—	375	750	1,500	4,200	—
1624 (i)	—	375	750	1,500	4,200	—

KM# 52 8 SCHILLING (1/4 Thaler)

Silver **Obv:** St. Lawrence standing behind city arms, date in margin left of saint's head **Rev:** Crowned imperial eagle, 8 in orb on breast, titles of Ferdinand II

Date	Mintage	VG	F	VF	XF	Unc
(1)622 (i)	—	275	550	1,100	—	—

KM# 1 16 SCHILLING (1/2 Thaler)

Silver **Obv:** St. Lawrence standing behind city arms, date in margin **Obv. Legend:** MONETA... **Rev:** Crowned imperial eagle, orb with 16 on breast, titles of Rudolf II **Note:** Varieties exist.

Date	Mintage	VG	F	VF	XF	Unc
1606 (g)	—	375	750	1,500	—	—
ND(ca1607-08)	—	200	425	850	—	—

KM# 35 16 SCHILLING (1/2 Thaler)

Silver **Obv:** St. Lawrence standing behind city arms **Obv. Legend:** MONETA... **Rev:** Crowned imperial eagle, orb with 16 on breast, date in margin, titles of Matthias

Date	Mintage	VG	F	VF	XF	Unc
(1)615 (h)	—	45.00	90.00	180	—	—

KM# 55 16 SCHILLING (1/2 Thaler)

Silver **Obv:** St. Lawrence standing behind city arms, date in margin left of saint's head **Rev:** Crowned imperial eagle, 16 in orb on breast, titles of Ferdinand II **Note:** Varieties exist.

Date	Mintage	VG	F	VF	XF	Unc
(1)622 (j)	—	—	—	—	—	—
(1)624 (j)	—	600	1,200	2,400	—	—
ND(1624-37) (j)	—	550	1,100	2,250	—	—

KM# 71 1/192 THALER (Dreiling)

Silver **Obv:** City arms, date at end of legend **Obv. Legend:** MO NO WISMAR **Rev:** Imperial orb with 192, titles of Ferdinand II **Note:** Varieties exist.

Date	Mintage	VG	F	VF	XF	Unc
(16)Z9 (j)	—	20.00	45.00	90.00	180	—
(16)37 (j)	—	20.00	45.00	90.00	180	—
ND(1637/8) (j)	—	20.00	45.00	90.00	180	—

KM# 20 1/96 THALER (1 Sechsling)

Silver **Obv:** City arms divides date **Obv. Legend:** MO NO WISMAR **Rev:** Imperial orb with 96, titles of Ferdinand II **Note:** Varieties exist.

Date	Mintage	VG	F	VF	XF	Unc
(16)11 (i)	—	—	—	—	—	—
(16)24 (j)	—	—	—	—	—	—

KM# 54 1/96 THALER (1 Sechsling)

Silver **Obv:** City arms, date at end of legend **Obv. Legend:** MO NO WISMAR **Rev:** Imperial orb with 96, titles of Ferdinand II **Note:** Varieties exist.

Date	Mintage	VG	F	VF	XF	Unc
(16)22	—	7.00	15.00	35.00	70.00	—
(16)22 (i)	—	7.00	15.00	35.00	70.00	—
(16)ZZ (i)	—	7.00	15.00	35.00	70.00	—
(16)24 (j)	—	7.00	15.00	35.00	70.00	—
1637 (j)	—	7.00	15.00	35.00	70.00	—

KM# 111 1/96 THALER (1 Sechsling)

Silver **Obv:** City arms divides date **Obv. Legend:** MO NO WISMAR **Rev:** Imperial with 96, titles of Leopold I **Note:** Klippe.

Date	Mintage	VG	F	VF	XF	Unc
ND(1697-99)	—	—	—	—	—	—

MB# 79 1/64 THALER (Sechsling)

Silver **Obv:** City arms **Obv. Legend:** MONE NO WISMARI (or variant) **Rev:** Imperial orb with 64, date in margin, titles of Rudolf II **Note:** Varieties exist.

Date	Mintage	VG	F	VF	XF	Unc
(1)60Z	—	15.00	30.00	60.00	120	—

KM# 8 1/64 THALER (Sechsling)

Silver **Obv:** City arms **Obv. Legend:** MONE NO WISMARI (or variant) **Rev:** Imperial orb with 64, date above

Date	Mintage	VG	F	VF	XF	Unc
1606	—	—	—	—	—	—

KM# 67 1/48 THALER

Silver, 18.7 mm. **Obv:** City arms **Obv. Legend:** MONETA NOVA WISMAR **Rev:** Imperial orb with 48 divides date, titles of Ferdinand II **Note:** Varieties exist.

Date	Mintage	VG	F	VF	XF	Unc
(16)26 (j)	—	20.00	45.00	90.00	180	—
1626 (j)	—	20.00	45.00	90.00	180	—
(16)27 (j)	—	20.00	45.00	90.00	180	—
(16)28 (j)	—	20.00	45.00	90.00	180	—
ND(1636) (j)	—	20.00	45.00	90.00	180	—

KM# 75 1/48 THALER

Silver **Obv:** City arms, date in margin **Obv. Legend:** MONETA NOVA WISMAR **Rev:** Imperial orb with 48, titles of Ferdinand II

Date	Mintage	VG	F	VF	XF	Unc
(16)37 (j)	—	—	—	—	—	—

KM# 108 1/48 THALER

Silver **Obv:** City arms **Obv. Legend:** MONETEA NOVA WISMAR **Rev:** Imperial orb with 48, date in margin, titles of Leopold I **Note:** Klippe.

Date	Mintage	VG	F	VF	XF	Unc
1692	—	12.00	25.00	50.00	100	—

KM# 2 1/16 THALER (Doppelschilling)

Silver **Obv:** St. Lawrence standing behind city arms at bottom, date at end of legend **Obv. Legend:** MON NOVA... **Rev:** Crowned imperial eagle orb with 16 on breast, superimposed on long cross, titles of Rudolf II **Rev. Inscription:** CIVIT - AS M - AGNO - POL9 **Note:** Varieties exist.

Date	Mintage	VG	F	VF	XF	Unc
(1)601 (g)	—	25.00	55.00	110	225	—
1601 (g)	—	25.00	55.00	110	225	—
(1)602 (g)	—	25.00	55.00	110	225	—
(1)60Z (g)	—	25.00	55.00	110	225	—
(1)603 (g)	—	25.00	55.00	110	225	—
(1)604 (g)	—	25.00	55.00	110	225	—
(1)605 (g)	—	25.00	55.00	110	225	—
(1)606 (g)	—	25.00	55.00	110	225	—

KM# 9 1/16 THALER (Doppelschilling)

Silver **Obv:** St. Lawrence standing behind city arms at bottom, date at end of legend **Obv. Legend:** MON NOVA... **Rev:** Crowned imperial eagle, orb with 16 on breast **Rev. Inscription:** CIVIT - AS M - AGNO - POL9 **Note:** Varieties exist.

Date	Mintage	VG	F	VF	XF	Unc
(1)606	—	25.00	55.00	110	225	—
(1)606 (g)	—	25.00	55.00	110	225	—
ND(1606-12)	—	25.00	55.00	110	225	—
ND(1606-12) (g)	—	25.00	55.00	110	225	—

KM# 29 1/16 THALER (Doppelschilling)

Silver **Obv:** St. Lawrence standing behind city arms at bottom, date at end of legend **Obv. Legend:** MON NOVA... **Rev:** Crowned imperial eagle, orb on breast, titles of Matthias **Note:** Varieties exist.

Date	Mintage	VG	F	VF	XF	Unc
ND(1614) (h)	—	25.00	55.00	110	225	—
1614 (h)	—	25.00	55.00	110	225	—
(1)615 (h)	—	25.00	55.00	110	225	—
(16)15 (h)	—	25.00	55.00	110	225	—
1615	—	25.00	55.00	110	225	—
1615 (h)	—	25.00	55.00	110	225	—
(1)616 (h)	—	25.00	55.00	110	225	—
(16)16 (h)	—	25.00	55.00	110	225	—
1616 (h)	—	25.00	55.00	110	225	—
(1)617 (h)	—	25.00	55.00	110	225	—
(16)17 (h)	—	25.00	55.00	110	225	—
1617 (h)	—	25.00	55.00	110	225	—
(1)618 (h)	—	25.00	55.00	110	225	—
(16)18 (h)	—	25.00	55.00	110	225	—
1618 (h)	—	25.00	55.00	110	225	—

KM# 62 1/16 THALER (Dütchen)

Silver **Obv:** Crowned imperial eagle, titles of Ferdinand II **Rev:** Date, small city below **Rev. Legend:** MONETA... **Rev. Inscription:** 16 / STVCK / EIN REICHS / THALER (or variant) **Note:** Varieties exist.

Date	Mintage	VG	F	VF	XF	Unc
1624 (j)	—	30.00	60.00	125	250	500
1625 (j)	—	30.00	60.00	125	250	500
1628 (j)	—	30.00	60.00	125	250	500
1629 (j)	—	30.00	60.00	125	250	500
1630 (j)	—	30.00	60.00	125	250	500
1631 (j)	—	30.00	60.00	125	250	500

KM# 11A THALER

Silver **Obv:** St. Lawrence standing behind city arms, arms divide date **Obv. Legend:** MONETA... **Rev:** Crowned imperial eagle, 3Z in orb on breast, titles of Rudolf II **Note:** Dav#5932.

Date	Mintage	VG	F	VF	XF	Unc
(1)606 (g) Rare	—	—	—	—	—	—

KM# 22 THALER

28.0000 g., Silver **Subject:** Treaty of Pahrenholz **Obv:** Arms within double legend **Rev:** St. Laurentius with grill and palm spray, shield in front **Note:** Dav. #LS510.

Date	Mintage	VG	F	VF	XF	Unc
ND(1611) Rare	—	—	—	—	—	—

KM# 40 THALER

Silver **Obv:** Date below St. Laurentius **Note:** Dav. #LS514.

Date	Mintage	VG	F	VF	XF	Unc
1617 (h) Rare	—	—	—	—	—	—

KM# 4 THALER (32 Schilling)

Silver **Obv:** St. Laurentius with griddle in right hand and palm spray in left **Rev:** Crown above double-headed imperial eagle, value in orb on breast **Rev. Legend:** RVDOLPHVS... **Note:** Dav. #A5936.

Date	Mintage	VG	F	VF	XF	Unc
ND(1604-05)	—	850	1,600	2,750	—	—

KM# 15 THALER (32 Schilling)

Silver **Obv. Legend:** RUDOL... **Rev:** St. Laurentius with griddle in left hand and palm spray in right **Note:** Dav. #5936.

Date	Mintage	VG	F	VF	XF	Unc
ND(1604-05)	—	700	1,300	2,200	—	—

KM# 11 THALER (32 Schilling)

Silver **Obv:** Crowned imperial eagle **Rev:** St. Laurentius **Note:** Dav. #5932.

Date	Mintage	VG	F	VF	XF	Unc
1606	—	775	1,450	2,600	—	—

KM# 12 THALER (32 Schilling)

Silver **Obv:** St. Laurentius with grill, arms in front, date divided above **Rev:** Crowned imperial eagle with orb and 32 on breast **Note:** Dav. #5933.

Date	Mintage	VG	F	VF	XF	Unc
1606 (g)	—	650	1,200	2,150	4,750	—
1607 (g)	—	650	1,200	2,150	4,750	—

KM# 13 THALER (32 Schilling)

Silver **Obv:** Standing St. above small shield **Obv. Legend:** MONETA NOV*... **Rev:** Crown above douible-headed imperial eagle, value in orb on breast **Rev. Legend:** RVDOL: D. II. D. G... **Note:** Dav. #5934.

Date	Mintage	VG	F	VF	XF	Unc
1607 (g)	—	650	1,200	2,250	—	—

KM# 14 THALER (32 Schilling)

Silver **Obv:** Date divided in field **Obv. Legend:** MONETA NOVA... **Rev:** Crown above double-headed imperial eagle, value in orb on breast **Rev. Legend:** RVDOL: II. D. G.-IMP. SE. A: G: S. **Note:** Dav. #5935. Varieties exist.

Date	Mintage	VG	F	VF	XF	Unc
1608	—	650	1,200	2,250	4,000	—

KM# 31 THALER (32 Schilling)

Silver **Obv. Legend:** MATTHIAS*D. G. -ROMAN... **Rev:** Legend, date **Rev. Legend:** Y MONETA*NOVA*... **Note:** Dav. #5937.

Date	Mintage	VG	F	VF	XF	Unc
1614 (h)	—	1,250	2,500	4,500	—	—

KM# 39 THALER (32 Schilling)

Silver **Obv:** Date divided at top **Obv. Legend:** MONETA. NOVA... **Rev. Legend:** MATTHIAS D. G. ROMA... **Note:** Dav. #5938.

Date	Mintage	VG	F	VF	XF	Unc
1617 (h)	—	1,250	2,500	4,500	—	—

KM# 57 THALER (32 Schilling)
Silver **Obv:** Date divided by shield at bottom **Rev:** Crown above double-headed imperial eagle, value in orb on breast **Rev. Legend:** FERDINDNA. II... **Note:** Dav. #5939.

Date	Mintage	VG	F	VF	XF	Unc
1622 (i)	—	525	975	3,200	—	—
1623 (i)	—	525	975	3,200	—	—

KM# 59 THALER (32 Schilling)
Silver **Obv:** Date divided by St. Laurentius **Rev. Legend:** FERDINAND: II. D. G. RO... **Note:** Dav. #5940.

Date	Mintage	VG	F	VF	XF	Unc
1623 (i)	—	525	975	1,650	3,200	—
1624 (j)	—	525	975	1,650	3,200	—

KM# 60 THALER (32 Schilling)
Silver **Rev:** Date left of St. Laurentius **Note:** Dav. #5941.

Date	Mintage	VG	F	VF	XF	Unc
1623	—	525	975	1,650	—	—
1624	—	525	975	1,650	—	—

KM# 64 THALER (32 Schilling)
Silver **Obv:** Date divided by St. Laurentius **Rev:** Crowned double-headed imperial eagle, date left of crown **Note:** Dav. #5942.

Date	Mintage	VG	F	VF	XF	Unc
1624//16Z4 (j)	—	400	725	1,350	—	—
1624//1625 (j)	—	400	725	1,350	—	—

KM# 65 THALER (32 Schilling)
Silver **Obv:** St. Laurentius without date **Rev:** Crowned double-headed imperial eagle **Note:** Dav. #5943.

Date	Mintage	VG	F	VF	XF	Unc
1625 (j)	—	450	900	1,750	—	—
16Z6 (j)	—	450	900	1,750	—	—
1627 (j)	—	450	900	1,750	—	—
1628 (j)	—	450	900	1,750	—	—

KM# 73 THALER (32 Schilling)
Silver **Rev:** Crown above imperial eagle divides date **Note:** Dav. #5944.

Date	Mintage	VG	F	VF	XF	Unc
1629 (j)	—	425	800	1,400	—	—
1630 (j)	—	425	800	1,400	—	—
1631 (j)	—	425	800	1,400	—	—
1632 (j)	—	425	800	1,400	—	—
1635 (j)	—	425	800	1,400	—	—
1637 (j)	—	425	800	1,400	—	—

KM# 77 THALER (32 Schilling)
Silver **Obv:** Standing St. above small shield **Rev:** Crowned double-headed imperial eagle, value in orb on breast, date in legend **Rev. Legend:** FERDINAN. III... **Note:** Dav. #5945.

Date	Mintage	VG	F	VF	XF	Unc
1640 (j)	—	500	950	1,850	—	—
1641 (j)	—	500	950	1,850	—	—
1645 (j)	—	1,750	3,500	7,500	—	—

KM# 78 THALER (32 Schilling)
Silver **Obv:** Standing St. above small shield **Rev:** Crowned double-headed imperial eagle, value in orb on breast **Rev. Legend:** FERDINANDUS III. D. Q. ROMA: IMP: S: AU: **Note:** Dav. #5946.

Date	Mintage	VG	F	VF	XF	Unc
ND(ca.1640) (j)	—	550	1,000	2,000	—	—
ND(ca.1645-47) (j)	—	—	—	—	—	—

KM# 23 1-1/2 THALER
43.3000 g., Silver **Subject:** Treaty of Pahrenholz **Obv:** Arms within double legend **Rev:** St. Laurentius with grill and palm spray, shield in front **Note:** Dav. #LS509.

Date	Mintage	VG	F	VF	XF	Unc
ND(1601)	—	1,600	3,300	6,600	11,000	—

KM# 41 1-1/2 THALER
Silver **Rev:** Date below St. Laurentius **Note:** Dav. #LS513.

Date	Mintage	VG	F	VF	XF	Unc
1617 (h) Rare	—	—	—	—	—	—

KM# 24 2 THALER
60.0000 g., Silver **Subject:** Treaty of Pahrenholz **Obv:** Arms within double legend **Rev:** St. Laurentius with grill and palm spray, shield in front **Note:** Dav. #LS508.

Date	Mintage	VG	F	VF	XF	Unc
ND(1611) Rare	—	—	—	—	—	—

KM# 42 2 THALER
Silver **Rev:** Date below St. Laurentius **Note:** Dav. #LS512.

Date	Mintage	VG	F	VF	XF	Unc
1617 (h) Rare	—	—	—	—	—	—

KM# 25 2-1/2 THALER
Silver **Subject:** Treaty of Pahrenholz **Obv:** Arms within double legend **Rev:** St. Laurentius with grill and palm spray, shield in front **Note:** Dav. #LS507.

Date	Mintage	VG	F	VF	XF	Unc
ND(1611) Rare	—	—	—	—	—	—

KM# 26 3 THALER
Silver **Subject:** Treaty of Pahrenholz **Obv:** Arms within double legend **Rev:** St. Laurentius w/grill and palm spray, shield in front **Note:** Dav. #LS506.

Date	Mintage	VG	F	VF	XF	Unc
ND(1611) Rare	—	—	—	—	—	—

KM# 43 3 THALER
Silver **Rev:** Date below St. Laurentius **Note:** Dav. #LS511.

Date	Mintage	VG	F	VF	XF	Unc
1617 (h) Rare	—	—	—	—	—	—

KM# 27 4 THALER
Silver **Subject:** Treaty of Pahrenholz **Obv:** Arms within double legend **Rev:** St. Laurentius with grill and palm spray, shield in front **Note:** Dav. #LS505.

Date	Mintage	VG	F	VF	XF	Unc
ND(1611) Rare	—	—	—	—	—	—

TRADE COINAGE

MB# 76 GOLDGULDEN
Gold **Obv:** St. Lawrence standing behind city arms **Obv. Legend:** MONE NO A V... **Rev:** Crowned imperial eagle, titles of Rudolf II, date **Note:** Varieties exist.

Date	Mintage	VG	F	VF	XF	Unc
(1)604 (g)	—	2,200	3,850	8,300	16,500	—
ND(ca1605) (g)	—	2,200	3,850	8,300	16,500	—

KM# 6 GOLDGULDEN
Gold **Obv:** St. Lawrence standing behind city arms **Obv. Legend:** MONE NOVA WISMARI **Rev:** Crowned imperial eagle, titles of Rudolf II, date **Note:** Varieties exist.

Date	Mintage	VG	F	VF	XF	Unc
ND(1605-11) (g) Rare	—	—	—	—	—	—

KM# 33 GOLDGULDEN
Gold **Obv:** St. Lawrence standing behind city arms, date at end of legend **Obv. Legend:** MONE NOVA WISMAR **Rev:** Crowned imperial eagle, titles of Matthias

Date	Mintage	VG	F	VF	XF	Unc
(1)614 (h) Rare	—	—	—	—	—	—

KM# 37 GOLDGULDEN
3.5000 g., 0.9860 Gold 0.1109 oz. AGW **Obv:** St. Laurentius standing holding gridiron with left hand **Note:** FR#3527.

Date	Mintage	VG	F	VF	XF	Unc
(16)16 (h)	—	2,650	5,300	10,500	17,500	—

KM# 69 GOLDGULDEN
3.5000 g., 0.9860 Gold 0.1109 oz. AGW **Note:** FR#3528.

Date	Mintage	VG	F	VF	XF	Unc
(16)26 (j)	—	2,150	4,500	7,800	14,500	—
1629	—	2,150	4,500	7,800	14,500	—
1632 (j)	—	2,150	4,500	7,800	14,500	—

SWEDISH ADMINISTRATION

REGULAR COINAGE

KM# 95 4 SCHILLING (1/8 Thaler)
Silver **Obv:** Crowned imperial eagle, 4 in orb on breast **Rev:** St. Laurentius with gridiron in inner circle, shield at bottom **Note:** Prev. KM#3.

Date	Mintage	VG	F	VF	XF	Unc
1662 HS Rare	—	—	—	—	—	—

KM# 96 8 SCHILLING (1/4 Thaler)
Silver **Obv:** Crowned imperial eagle, 8 in orb on breast **Rev:** St. Laurentius with gridiron in inner circle, shield at bottom **Note:** Prev. KM#4.

Date	Mintage	VG	F	VF	XF	Unc
1662 HS Rare	—	—	—	—	—	—

KM# 99 16 SCHILLING (1/2 Thaler)
Silver **Obv:** Crowned imperial eagle, 16 in orb on breast **Rev:** St. Laurentius with gridiron in inner circle, shield at bottom **Note:** Prev. KM#5.

Date	Mintage	VG	F	VF	XF	Unc
1668 HS Rare	—	—	—	—	—	—

KM# 100 16 SHILLING (1/3 Thaler)
Silver **Obv:** Shield on cross **Rev:** St. Laurentius with cowl reaching to the feet **Note:** Prev. KM#6.

Date	Mintage	VG	F	VF	XF	Unc
1671 (n)	—	—	—	—	—	—
1672 (n)	—	75.00	150	300	600	—

KM# 101 16 SHILLING (1/3 Thaler)
Silver **Rev:** St. Laurentius with cowl reaching to the knees **Note:** Prev. KM#7.

Date	Mintage	VG	F	VF	XF	Unc
1672	—	75.00	150	300	600	—

KM# 90 1/192 THALER (Witten)
Silver **Obv:** City arms **Obv. Legend:** MO. NO. WISMAR. **Rev:** Imperial orb with 192, titles of Leopold I, date **Rev. Legend:** LEOP. D.G. R. I. S. **Note:** Prev. KM#9, 10. Varieties exist.

Date	Mintage	VG	F	VF	XF	Unc
ND(1661-70) (m)	—	13.00	33.00	55.00	110	—
ND(1671-74) (a)	—	13.00	33.00	55.00	110	—
ND(1675-80) GS	—	13.00	33.00	55.00	110	—
ND(1686, 1697-99) IM	—	13.00	33.00	55.00	110	—

KM# 84 1/192 THALER (Dreiling)
Silver **Obv:** City arms **Obv. Legend:** MO NO WISMAR **Rev:** Imperial orb with 192, titles of Ferdinand III, date **Rev. Legend:** FERD. III... **Note:** Prev. KM#8. Varieties exist.

Date	Mintage	VG	F	VF	XF	Unc
ND(1650-57) (l)	—	—	—	—	—	—
(16)51 (l)	—	—	—	—	—	—
(16)5Z (l)	—	—	—	—	—	—
(16)53 (l)	—	—	—	—	—	—

KM# 82 1/96 THALER (1 Sechsling)
Silver **Obv:** City arms, date **Obv. Legend:** MO NO WISMAR **Rev:** Imperial orb with 96, titles of Ferdinand III **Rev. Legend:** FERD. III... **Note:** Prev. KM#11.

Date	Mintage	VG	F	VF	XF	Unc
ND(1650-57) (l)	—	27.00	55.00	110	220	—

KM# 88 1/96 THALER (1 Sechsling)
Silver **Obv:** City arms, date **Obv. Legend:** MO NO WISMAR **Rev:** Imperial orb with 96, titles of Leopold I **Rev. Legend:** LEOP... **Note:** Prev. KM#12. Varieties exist.

Date	Mintage	VG	F	VF	XF	Unc
ND(ca1650) (c)	—	—	—	—	—	—
ND(1657-60) (l)	—	—	—	—	—	—
ND(1661-70) HS	—	—	—	—	—	—
1666 (m)	—	—	—	—	—	—
ND(1671-74) (n)	—	13.00	30.00	45.00	90.00	—
ND(1675-80) GS	—	13.00	30.00	45.00	90.00	—
ND(1697-99)	—	13.00	30.00	45.00	90.00	—

KM# 92 1/48 THALER
Silver **Obv:** City arms **Obv. Legend:** MONETA NOVA WISMAR **Rev:** Imperial orb with 48 divides date, titles of Leopold I **Note:** Prev. KM#14.

Date	Mintage	VG	F	VF	XF	Unc
1661 (m)	—	13.00	30.00	55.00	110	—
1663 (m)	—	13.00	30.00	55.00	110	—

KM# 94 1/48 THALER
Silver **Obv:** City arms in baroque frame **Obv. Legend:** MONETA. NOVA. WISMAR. **Rev:** Imperial orb with 48, titles of Leopold I, date **Rev. Legend:** LEOPOL: D:G: R: I: S: A: **Note:** Prev. KM#15. Varieties exist.

Date	Mintage	VG	F	VF	XF	Unc
1662 (m)	—	—	—	—	—	—
1663 (m)	—	13.00	30.00	55.00	110	—
1664 (m)	—	13.00	30.00	55.00	110	—
1665 (m)	—	13.00	30.00	55.00	110	—
1666 (m)	—	13.00	30.00	55.00	110	—
1667 (m)	—	13.00	30.00	55.00	110	—
1668 (m)	—	13.00	30.00	55.00	110	—
1669 (m)	—	13.00	30.00	55.00	110	—
1692	—	13.00	30.00	55.00	110	—
1695	—	20.00	45.00	90.00	180	—

KM# 80 1/24 THALER (1 Groschen)
Silver **Obv:** Crowned imperial eagle, city arms on breast **Obv. Legend:** MONETA ... **Rev:** Inscription, date at end **Rev. Legend:** WISMARSCH STADTGELDT (or variant) **Rev. Inscription:** 24 / REICHS / DALER / ... **Note:** Prev. KM#16. Varieties exist

Date	Mintage	VG	F	VF	XF	Unc
1648 (k)	—	—	—	—	—	—
1650 (l)	—	—	—	—	—	—
1650 (k)	—	15.00	35.00	70.00	145	—
1651 (l)	—	20.00	45.00	90.00	180	—
1652 (l)	—	15.00	35.00	70.00	145	—
1653 (l)	—	15.00	35.00	70.00	145	—
1654 (l)	—	15.00	35.00	70.00	145	—
1655 (l)	—	15.00	35.00	70.00	145	—
1656 (l)	—	15.00	35.00	70.00	145	—

Date	Mintage	VG	F	VF	XF	Unc
1657 (l)	—	15.00	35.00	70.00	145	—
1658 (l)	—	15.00	35.00	70.00	145	—
1659 (l)	—	15.00	35.00	70.00	145	—
1661 (m)	—	13.00	33.00	60.00	120	—
1662 (m)	—	13.00	33.00	60.00	120	—
1663 (m)	—	13.00	33.00	60.00	120	—
1664 (m)	—	13.00	33.00	60.00	120	—
1665 (m)	—	13.00	33.00	60.00	120	—
1666 (m)	—	13.00	33.00	60.00	120	—
1667 (m)	—	13.00	33.00	60.00	120	—
1668 (m)	—	13.00	33.00	60.00	120	—
1669 (m)	—	13.00	33.00	60.00	120	—
1670 (m)	—	20.00	45.00	90.00	180	—
1670 (n)	—	13.00	33.00	60.00	120	—
1671 (n)	—	13.00	33.00	60.00	120	—
1672 (n)	—	13.00	33.00	60.00	120	—

KM# 86 THALER (32 Schilling)
Silver **Obv:** St. Laurentius standing with gridiron in inner circle **Rev:** Crowned imperial eagle, 32 in orb on breast in inner circle **Rev. Legend:** FERDINANDUS III... **Note:** Dav. #5947.

Date	Mintage	VG	F	VF	XF	Unc
1653 BK	—	2,000	3,250	6,000	9,500	—

KM# 97 THALER (32 Schilling)
Silver **Rev. Legend:** LEOPOLDUS... **Note:** Dav. #5948.

Date	Mintage	VG	F	VF	XF	Unc
1662 HS	—	2,200	4,500	8,000	—	—
1666 HS	—	2,200	4,500	8,000	—	—
1668 HS Rare	—	—	—	—	—	—
1671/68 HR Rare	—	—	—	—	—	—

Note: Künker Auction 185, 3-11, XF realized approximately $32,020

KM# 105 THALER (32 Schilling)
Silver **Obv:** H-R divided by shield below saint **Rev:** Crowned double-headed imperial eagle, value in orb on breast **Note:** Dav. #5949.

Date	Mintage	VG	F	VF	XF	Unc
1673 HR	—	1,250	2,750	5,000	—	—

KM# 106 THALER (32 Schilling)
Silver **Obv:** Standing St. above small shield, without inner circle **Rev:** Crowned double-headed imperial eagle, value in orb on breast, without inner circle **Note:** Dav. #5950. With and without edge inscription.

Date	Mintage	VG	F	VF	XF	Unc
1674 (n)	—	1,800	3,000	6,500	9,500	—

TRADE COINAGE

KM# 103 DUCAT
3.5000 g., 0.9860 Gold 0.1109 oz. AGW **Obv:** Ornate arms **Obv. Legend:** CIVTATIS + WISMARIEN **Rev:** Crowned imperial eagle **Rev. Legend:** MONETA + AVREA **Note:** FR#3529.

Date	Mintage	VG	F	VF	XF	Unc
1672 (n)	—	2,400	4,200	7,800	11,500	—
1676 GS	—	2,400	4,200	7,800	11,500	—

PATTERNS

Including off metal strikes

KM#	Date	Mintage	Identification	Mkt Val
Pn1	1684	—	2/3 Thaler. Silver. KM#17. Proposed coinage for "Lordship of Wismar".	—
Pn2	1692	—	1/48 Thaler. Copper. Klippe.	—
Pn3	1743	—	Ducat. Copper. Fr. 3530.	—
Pn4	1799 FL	—	3 Pfennig. Silver. C#1a.	1,000

WOLGAST

A port city situated at the Baltic coast and the mouth of the Peene River. They received their civic rights in 1247. During the 14th century the dukes of Pomerania struck debased denars at Wolgast. In the late 16th century the city had its own local coinage. When the last duke died in1625, Pomerania became united under Bogislaus XIV, who died in 1637. Coins were probably struck in his name in Wolgast as well as in Stettin.

The Swedes occupied Pomerania during the Thirty-Years War, and Bogislaus was obliged to become an ally. From 1630, Wolgast was a part of Swedish Pomerania until it was ceded to Prussia in 1815. Coins were struck for the Swedish authorities only in 1633, in memory of King Gustavus II Adolphus.

RULERS
Swedish, 1633-1634

CITY

MEDALLIC COINAGE

Largesse Money

KM# M1 1/4 THALER
Silver, 76 mm. **Subject:** Death of Gustavus Adolphus **Obv:** Grapevine growing out of skull resting on ground, two legends around with date **Rev:** Crowned 4-fold arms with central shield, two legens around, date divided by crown

Date	Mintage	VG	F	VF	XF	Unc
1633	—	160	325	650	1,325	—

Note: Dies possibly also used in Erfurt

KM# M2 1/2 THALER
Silver, 37.5 mm. **Subject:** Death of Gustavus Adolphus **Obv:** Gustavus Adolphus lying in state with battle in backgournd **Rev:** King in chariot crushing enemies below

Date	Mintage	VG	F	VF	XF	Unc
1633	—	325	650	1,300	—	—
1634	—	325	650	1,300	—	—

KM# M3 THALER
Silver **Subject:** Death of Gustavus Adolphus **Obv:** Gustavus Adolphus lying in state with battle in backgournd **Rev:** King in chariot crushing enemies below

Date	Mintage	VG	F	VF	XF	Unc
1633	—	750	1,500	3,000	5,000	—

KM# M15 1-1/2 THALER
Silver **Note:** Similar to 2 Thaler, KM#M4. Dav. #LS275.

Date	Mintage	VG	F	VF	XF	Unc
1633	—	825	1,650	3,150	5,500	—

KM# M4 2 THALER
56.8000 g., Silver **Subject:** Death of Gustavus Adolphus **Obv:** Gustavus Adolphus lying in state with battle in background **Rev:** King in chariot crushing enemies below **Note:** Dav. #LS274.

Date	Mintage	VG	F	VF	XF	Unc
1633	—	825	1,650	3,150	5,500	—

KM# M6 3 THALER
Silver, 60 mm.

Date	Mintage	VG	F	VF	XF	Unc
1633	—	—	—	—	—	—

Note: Reported, not confirmed

KM# M5 3 THALER
83.7000 g., Silver **Subject:** Death of Gustavus Adolphus **Obv:** Gustavus Adolphus lying in state with battle in background **Rev:** King in chariot crushing enemies below **Note:** Dav. #LS273.

Date	Mintage	VG	F	VF	XF	Unc
1633	—	1,300	2,500	5,000	8,000	—

KM# M8 4 THALER
Silver, 60 mm. **Note:** Illustration reduced.

Date	Mintage	VG	F	VF	XF	Unc
1633	—	—	—	—	—	—

Note: Reported, not confirmed

KM# M7 4 THALER
116.0000 g., Silver, 76 mm. **Subject:** Death of Gustavus Adolphus **Obv:** Gustavus Adolphus lying in state with battle in background **Rev:** King in chariot crushing enemies below **Note:** Dav. #LS272.

Date	Mintage	VG	F	VF	XF	Unc
1663	—	2,400	4,400	7,000	10,000	—

TRADE COINAGE

KM# M9 2 DUCAT
7.0000 g., 0.9860 Gold 0.2219 oz. AGW **Subject:** Death of Gustavus Adolphus **Obv:** Grapevine growing out of skull resting on ground, two legends around with date **Rev:** Crowned 4-fold arms with central shield, two legends around, date divided by crown

Date	Mintage	VG	F	VF	XF	Unc
1633 Rare	—	—	—	—	—	—

KM# M10 4 DUCAT
14.0000 g., 0.9860 Gold 0.4438 oz. AGW **Subject:** Death of Gustavus Adolphus **Obv:** Gustavus Adolphus lying in state with battle in background **Rev:** King in chariot crushing emenies below

Date	Mintage	VG	F	VF	XF	Unc
1633 Rare	—	—	—	—	—	—
1634 Rare	—	—	—	—	—	—

KM# M11 5 DUCAT
17.5000 g., 0.9860 Gold 0.5547 oz. AGW **Subject:** Death of Gustavus Adolphus **Obv:** Gustavus Adolphus lying in state with battle in background **Rev:** King in chariot crushing emenies below

Date	Mintage	VG	F	VF	XF	Unc
1634 Rare	—	—	—	—	—	—

KM# M12 10 DUCAT
35.0000 g., 0.9860 Gold 1.1095 oz. AGW **Subject:** Death of Gustavus Adolphus **Obv:** Gustavus Adolphus lying in state with battle in background **Rev:** King in chariot crushing emenies below

Date	Mintage	VG	F	VF	XF	Unc
1633 Rare	—	—	—	—	—	—

KM# M13 20 DUCAT
70.0000 g., 0.9860 Gold 2.2190 oz. AGW **Subject:** Death of Gustavus Adolphus **Obv:** Gustavus Adolphus lying in state with battle in background **Rev:** King in chariot crushing emenies below

Date	Mintage	VG	F	VF	XF	Unc
1633 Rare	—	—	—	—	—	—

KM# M14 60 DUCAT
210.0000 g., 0.9860 Gold 6.6569 oz. AGW **Subject:** Death of Gustavus Adolphus **Obv:** Gustavus Adolphus lying in state with battle in background **Rev:** King in chariot crushing emenies below

Date	Mintage	VG	F	VF	XF	Unc
1633 Unique	—	—	—	—	—	—

WOLLWARTH

Only one member of this family of free barons, a city councilman of Nuremberg, struck coins in the early 17th century.

RULER
Hans Sigmund von Wöllwarth-Fachsenfeld, 1546-1622

LORDSHIP

STANDARD COINAGE

KM# 1 6 KREUZER (Sechser)
Silver **Ruler:** Hans Sigmund **Obv:** Family arms (crescent in shield), helmet above, legend around **Obv. Legend:** HANS * SIGMVND * VON * WELLWARDT. **Rev:** 5-line inscription **Rev. Inscription:** + HERR + / MEINEN. GEIST / BEVELH. ICH / IN. DEIE. HAD (or HED) / (6) **Note:** Varieties exist.

Date	Mintage	VG	F	VF	XF	Unc
ND(ca.1608)	1,160	—	—	—	—	—

WORMS

A bishopric was founded at this town site on the rhine in the 4th century and then destroyed by the Hun invasion during the 5th century. The second founding of the ecclesiastic seat occurred in the early 7th century and a long line of bishops ensued. By the Napoleonic era, the bishopric of Worms had been reduced to two enclaves outside of and south of the city, on either bank of the Rhine. The part on the west bank was annexed by France in 1801, while Hesse-Darmstadt obtained the secularized portion east of the Rhine in 1803. The part originally taken by France went to Hesse-Darmstadt in 1815.

RULERS
Philipp I von Rotenstein, 1595-1604
Philipp II Kratz von Scharfenstein, 1604
Wilhelm I von Effern, 1604-1616
Georg Friedrich von Greiffenklau zu Vollraths, 1616-1629
Georg Anton von Rotenstein, 1629-1652
Hugo Eberhard Kratz von Scharfenstein, 1654-1663
Johann Philipp I von Schonborn, 1663-1673
Lothar Friedrich von Metternich, 1673-1675
Damian Hartard von der Leyen, 1675-1678
Karl Heinreich von Metternich, 1679
Franz Emerich Kaspar,
Frhr. von Waldbott-Bassenhein, 1679-1683
Johann Karl, Frhr. von Frankenstein, 1683-1691
Ludwig Anton, Graf von Pfalz-Neuburg, 1691-1694
Franz Ludwig, Graf von Pfalz-Neuburg, 1694-1732

Reference:
J = Paul Joseph, ***Die Münzen von Worms nebst einer münzgeschichtlichen Einleitung,*** Darmstadt, 1906.

BISHOPRIC

REGULAR COINAGE

KM# 30 4 KREUZER (Batzen)
Silver **Ruler:** Franz Emerich Kaspar **Subject:** Death of Franz Emerich Kaspar **Obv:** Bishop's mitre above 4-fold arms between palm fronds, titles of Franz Emerich Kaspar around **Rev:** 8-line inscription with dates

Date	Mintage	VG	F	VF	XF	Unc
1683	—	—	—	—	—	—

FREE IMPERIAL CITY

REGULAR COINAGE

KM# 66 4 HELLER
Billon **Obv:** City arms, W above **Rev:** III in ornamented circle or heart shape **Note:** Kipper 4 Heller. Varieties exist.

Date	Mintage	VG	F	VF	XF	Unc
ND(c.1621)	—	60.00	100	200	400	—

KM# 35 PFENNIG
Silver **Obv:** Double-lined Spanish shield of city arms, W above **Note:** Uniface schussel-type.

Date	Mintage	VG	F	VF	XF	Unc
ND(1614-18)	—	10.00	20.00	40.00	85.00	—

KM# 44 PFENNIG
Silver **Obv:** City arms divide S - G **Note:** Uniface schüssel-type. Known only struck on thick flans of four times normal weight (0.8-1.0 grams).

Date	Mintage	VG	F	VF	XF	Unc
1616	—	10.00	20.00	40.00	85.00	—
1617	—	10.00	20.00	40.00	85.00	—
1620	—	10.00	20.00	40.00	85.00	—

KM# 50 PFENNIG
1.8000 g., Silver **Obv:** City arms divide S - G **Note:** Uniface klippe.

Date	Mintage	VG	F	VF	XF	Unc
1617	—	—	—	—	—	—
1618	—	—	—	—	—	—

KM# 85 PFENNIG
Silver **Obv:** City arms divide R - G (=Rentengeld), W divides date above **Note:** Uniface schüssel-type.

Date	Mintage	VG	F	VF	XF	Unc
1626	—	10.00	20.00	40.00	85.00	—

KM# 121 PFENNIG
Silver **Obv:** Key upright (Worms arms) in circle of pellets **Note:** Uniface.

Date	Mintage	VG	F	VF	XF	Unc
ND(c.1681)	—	8.00	22.00	45.00	90.00	—

KM# 122 2 PFENNIG
Silver **Obv:** Key of Worms, W nearby **Note:** Uniface.

Date	Mintage	VG	F	VF	XF	Unc
ND(c.1681)	—	15.00	30.00	60.00	120	—

KM# 67 12 HELLER (2-1/2 Pfennig)
Billon **Obv:** City arms, W above **Rev:** XII in ornamented border or heart shape **Note:** Kipper 12 Heller.

Date	Mintage	VG	F	VF	XF	Unc
ND(1621)	—	45.00	90.00	180	360	—

KM# 86 ALBUS
Silver **Obv:** I / ALB, around RENTEN. GELT. DER., mintmaster's initials **Rev:** City arms, around STATTWORMBS, date **Note:** Varieties exist.

Date	Mintage	VG	F	VF	XF	Unc
1626 HIA	—	10.00	22.00	45.00	90.00	—
1628 HIA	—	10.00	22.00	45.00	90.00	—

KM# 95 ALBUS
Silver **Note:** Joint coinage of Mainz and Hesse-Darmstadt (KM#684), with city arms countermark of Worms on reverse.

Date	Mintage	VG	F	VF	XF	Unc
1638	—	30.00	65.00	135	275	—
1639	—	30.00	65.00	135	275	—

KM# 100 ALBUS
Silver **Obv:** City arms, legend around **Obv. Legend:** STAAT WORMBS **Rev. Inscription:** I / ALBVS / date **Note:** Varieties exist.

Date	Mintage	VG	F	VF	XF	Unc
1649 (a)	—	11.00	22.00	45.00	90.00	—
1650 (a)	—	11.00	22.00	45.00	90.00	—
1651 (a)	—	11.00	22.00	45.00	90.00	—
1652 DS	—	11.00	22.00	45.00	90.00	—
1653 DS	—	11.00	22.00	45.00	90.00	—
1654	—	11.00	22.00	45.00	90.00	—
1654 HS	—	11.00	22.00	45.00	90.00	—
1655 HS	—	11.00	22.00	45.00	90.00	—
1656 HS	—	11.00	22.00	45.00	90.00	—
1657	—	11.00	22.00	45.00	90.00	—
1657 HS	—	11.00	22.00	45.00	90.00	—
1658 HS	—	11.00	22.00	45.00	90.00	—

KM# 120 ALBUS
Silver **Obv:** Dragon turned to right over city arms **Rev:** Inscsription in wreath **Rev. Inscription:** I / ALBVS / date / mintmaster's initials or symbol **Note:** Varieties exist.

Date	Mintage	VG	F	VF	XF	Unc
1680 MK	—	11.00	22.00	45.00	90.00	—
1680 (b)	—	11.00	22.00	45.00	90.00	—
1681 MK	—	11.00	22.00	45.00	90.00	—
1681 (b)	—	11.00	22.00	45.00	90.00	—

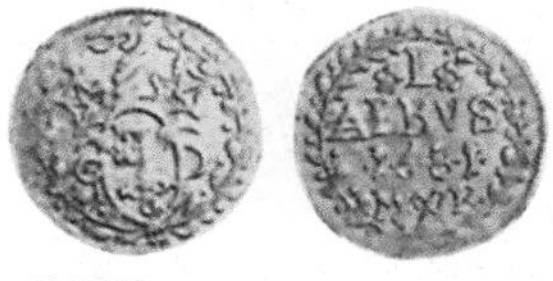

KM# 123 ALBUS
Silver **Obv:** Dragon turned left over city arms **Rev:** Inscription in wreath **Rev. Inscription:** I / ALBVS / date / mintmaster's initials or symbol **Note:** Varieties exist.

Date	Mintage	VG	F	VF	XF	Unc
1681 MK	—	11.00	22.00	45.00	90.00	—
1682 MK	—	11.00	22.00	45.00	90.00	—

KM# 124 KREUZER
Silver **Obv:** City arms in wreath **Rev:** Value, date, mintmaster's initials, all in wreath **Rev. Inscription:** I / KRVTZ,

Date	Mintage	VG	F	VF	XF	Unc
1681 MK	—	12.00	25.00	55.00	110	—

KM# 125 KREUZER
Silver **Obv:** City arms in wreath, W above **Rev:** Value, date, mintmaster's initials in wreath **Rev. Inscription:** I / KRVTZ / ... **Note:** Varieties exist.

Date	Mintage	VG	F	VF	XF	Unc
1681 MK	—	12.00	25.00	55.00	110	—
1682 MK	—	12.00	25.00	55.00	110	—

KM# 36 3 KREUZER (Groschen)

Silver **Obv:** Crowned imperial eagle, 3 in orb on breast, titles of Matthias **Rev:** City arms, date above **Note:** Varieties exist.

Date	Mintage	VG	F	VF	XF	Unc
1614	—	15.00	35.00	70.00	145	—
1615	—	15.00	35.00	70.00	145	—
1616	—	15.00	35.00	70.00	145	—
1617	—	15.00	35.00	70.00	145	—
1618	—	15.00	35.00	70.00	145	—

KM# 43 3 KREUZER (Groschen)

Silver **Obv:** Crowned imperial eagle, 3 in orb on breast, titles of Matthias **Rev:** City arms, date above **Note:** Klippe.

Date	Mintage	VG	F	VF	XF	Unc
1615	—	35.00	65.00	135	265	—

KM# 46 12 KREUZER (Dreibatzner)

Silver **Obv:** City arms **Rev:** Crowned imperial eagle, IZ in orb on breast, date in margin **Note:** Varieties exist.

Date	Mintage	VG	F	VF	XF	Unc
1616	—	45.00	95.00	190	385	—
1617	—	45.00	95.00	190	385	—
1618	—	45.00	95.00	190	385	—
1619	—	45.00	95.00	190	385	—
16Z0	—	45.00	95.00	190	385	—
1620	—	45.00	95.00	190	385	—

KM# 69 12 KREUZER (Dreibatzner)

Silver **Obv:** City arms divide date **Rev:** Dragon standing to right, WORMB...STADT MINTZ around

Date	Mintage	VG	F	VF	XF	Unc
16Z1	—	30.00	65.00	135	275	—
16ZZ	—	30.00	65.00	135	275	—

KM# 68 12 KREUZER (Dreibatzner)

Silver **Obv:** City arms divide date **Rev:** Crowned imperial eagle, 1Z in orb on breast **Note:** Kipper 12 Kreuzer.

Date	Mintage	VG	F	VF	XF	Unc
16Z1	—	30.00	65.00	135	275	—

KM# 70 12 KREUZER (Dreibatzner)

Silver **Obv:** City arms divide date **Rev:** Inscription above heart-shaped baroque frame with IZ **Rev. Inscription:** WORMBS / ISCHE. ST / AT. MVNTZ

Date	Mintage	VG	F	VF	XF	Unc
16Z1	—	30.00	65.00	135	275	—

KM# 71 12 KREUZER (Dreibatzner)

Silver **Obv:** City arms divide S - M and date **Rev:** Crowned imperial eagle, orb with 1Z on breast

Date	Mintage	VG	F	VF	XF	Unc
16Z1	—	30.00	65.00	135	275	—
16ZZ	—	30.00	65.00	135	275	—

KM# 72 12 KREUZER (Dreibatzner)

Silver **Obv:** City arms divided S. - M. and date **Rev:** Heart-shaped baroque frame with IZ, 3-line inscription above **Rev. Inscription:** WORMBS / ISCHE . ST / AT . MVNTZ

Date	Mintage	VG	F	VF	XF	Unc
16Z1	—	30.00	65.00	135	275	—

KM# 75 12 KREUZER (Dreibatzner)

Silver **Obv:** City arms divide date **Rev:** Crowned imperial eagle, 12 in orb on breast, titles of Ferdinand II around **Note:** Varieties exist.

Date	Mintage	VG	F	VF	XF	Unc
1622	—	30.00	65.00	135	275	—
16ZZ	—	30.00	65.00	135	275	—
16Z3	—	30.00	65.00	135	275	—

KM# 74 12 KREUZER (Dreibatzner)

Silver **Obv:** City arms divide date **Rev:** Dragon standing to left **Rev. Inscription:** WORMB ... STADT MINTZ

Date	Mintage	VG	F	VF	XF	Unc
16ZZ	—	30.00	65.00	135	275	—

KM# 38 DICKEN (Teston)

Silver **Obv:** City arms in ornamented shield **Rev:** Crowned imperial eagle, orb on breast, date in margin **Note:** Klippe. Varieties exist.

Date	Mintage	VG	F	VF	XF	Unc
1614	—	550	1,100	2,200	4,300	—
1616	—	550	1,100	2,200	4,300	—
1617	—	550	1,100	2,200	4,300	—

KM# 37 DICKEN (Teston)

Silver **Obv:** City arms in ornamented shield **Rev:** Crowned imperial eagle, orb on breast, date in margin **Note:** Varieties exist.

Date	Mintage	VG	F	VF	XF	Unc
1614	—	65.00	135	275	550	—
1615	—	65.00	135	275	550	—
1616	—	65.00	135	275	550	—
1617	—	65.00	135	275	550	—
1618	—	65.00	135	275	550	—
1619	—	65.00	135	275	550	—
16Z0	—	65.00	135	275	550	—

KM# 78 1/4 THALER

Silver **Obv:** City arms, date in margin **Rev:** Crowned imperial eagle, orb on breast with 1/4

Date	Mintage	VG	F	VF	XF	Unc
1624 HIA	—	150	250	425	850	—

KM# 40 1/2 THALER

Silver **Obv:** Dragon with city arms **Rev:** Crowned imperial eagle, orb on breast, date in margin

Date	Mintage	VG	F	VF	XF	Unc
1614	—	—	—	—	—	—

KM# 45 GULDENTHALER (60 Kreuzer)

Silver **Obv:** Dragon facing left leaning on city arms, date in field at left **Rev:** Crowned imperial eagle, value in orb on breast

Date	Mintage	VG	F	VF	XF	Unc
1616	—	—	—	8,750	13,000	—

KM# 39 THALER

Silver **Obv:** Arms supported by two dragons, date above **Rev:** Crowned double eagle with orb on breast **Note:** Dav. #5952.

Date	Mintage	VG	F	VF	XF	Unc
1614	—	1,750	3,000	5,000	8,500	—

KM# 47 THALER

Silver **Obv. Legend:** ...IMP. CIVIT. VOR: **Note:** Dav. #5954.

Date	Mintage	VG	F	VF	XF	Unc
1616	—	1,900	3,150	5,500	9,500	—

KM# 51 THALER

Silver **Obv:** Lighthouse and seascape **Rev:** Lit candle and book dividing BIB-LIA, date in chronogram **Note:** Dav. #5955.

Date	Mintage	VG	F	VF	XF	Unc
ND(1617)	—	400	750	1,500	3,000	5,000

KM# 52 THALER

Silver **Obv:** Lighthouse and seascape **Rev:** Lit candle and book dividing BIB-LIA, date in chronogram **Note:** Dav. #5955A. Klippe.

Date	Mintage	VG	F	VF	XF	Unc
1617	—	1,000	2,000	4,000	7,000	—

KM# 53 THALER

Silver **Rev:** Without BIB-LIA **Note:** Dav. #5955B.

Date	Mintage	VG	F	VF	XF	Unc
1617	—	900	1,750	3,500	6,000	—

KM# 65 THALER

Silver **Obv:** Crowned imperial eagle **Rev:** Arms, legend, date **Rev. Legend:** MONETA. NOVA. LIB:S.R: IMP:... **Note:** Dav. #5956.

Date	Mintage	VG	F	VF	XF	Unc
16Z0	—	850	1,650	3,250	5,500	—

KM# 73 THALER
Silver **Obv:** Date in legend **Rev:** Arms supported by two dragons **Rev. Legend:** MON. NOV. LIB-IMP... **Note:** Dav. #5958.

Date	Mintage	VG	F	VF	XF	Unc
1622	—	850	1,650	3,250	5,500	—

KM# 77 THALER
Silver **Obv:** Date divided below by imperial eagle **Rev:** Supported arms **Note:** Dav. #5960.

Date	Mintage	VG	F	VF	XF	Unc
1623	—	850	1,650	3,250	5,500	—

KM# 79 THALER
Silver **Obv:** Arms, date above in legend **Rev:** Crowned imperial eagle **Note:** Dav. #5961.

Date	Mintage	VG	F	VF	XF	Unc
16Z4 HIA	—	350	700	1,250	2,500	—

KM# 80 THALER
Silver **Subject:** 100th Anniversary of the Council of Thirteen **Note:** Similar to 2 Thaler, Dav. #LS517. Dav. #LS518.

Date	Mintage	VG	F	VF	XF	Unc
ND(1625)	—	2,000	3,500	6,500	9,500	—

KM# 89 THALER
Silver **Note:** Klippe. Dav. #5962A.

Date	Mintage	VG	F	VF	XF	Unc
1626	—	1,500	2,500	4,500	7,500	—

KM# 88 THALER
Silver **Rev:** More elaborate shield around arms **Note:** Dav. #5962.

Date	Mintage	VG	F	VF	XF	Unc
1626 HIA	—	550	1,000	1,850	3,000	—

KM# 90 THALER
Silver **Obv:** Crowned imperial eagle with orb on breast **Rev:** Arms with elaborate shield, date in legend **Note:** Dav. #5962B.

Date	Mintage	VG	F	VF	XF	Unc
1626	—	2,000	3,500	6,500	9,500	—

KM# 109 THALER
Silver **Rev:** Round shield with date above **Note:** Dav. #5963.

Date	Mintage	VG	F	VF	XF	Unc
1660	—	1,450	2,600	4,200	6,000	—

KM# 126 THALER
Silver **Rev:** Arms in frame, date in legend **Note:** Dav. #5964.

Date	Mintage	VG	F	VF	XF	Unc
1681	—	1,450	2,600	4,200	6,000	—

KM# 41 2 THALER
Silver **Obv:** Crowned imperial eagle with orb on breast **Rev:** Arms supported by two dragons, date above **Note:** Dav. #5951.

Date	Mintage	VG	F	VF	XF	Unc
1614	—	5,000	7,500	11,500	16,500	—

KM# 76 2 THALER
Silver **Obv:** Date in legend left of crown **Note:** Dav. #5957.

Date	Mintage	VG	F	VF	XF	Unc
1622	—	5,000	7,500	11,500	16,500	—

KM# A77 2 THALER
Silver **Note:** Similar to 1 Thaler, Dav. #5960. Dav. #5959.

Date	Mintage	VG	F	VF	XF	Unc
1623	—	5,000	7,500	11,500	16,500	—

KM# 81 2 THALER
Silver, 62 mm. **Subject:** 100th Anniversary of the Council of Thirteen **Obv:** Crowned imperial eagle with arms on breast within 13 shields with initials above each one **Rev:** Supported arms above city view **Note:** Dav. #LS517. Illustration reduced.

Date	Mintage	VG	F	VF	XF	Unc
ND(1625)	—	5,000	7,500	11,500	16,500	—

KM# 48 3 THALER
Silver **Obv:** Crowned imperial eagle with orb on breast **Rev:** Arms supported by two dragons, date below **Note:** Dav. #5953.

Date	Mintage	VG	F	VF	XF	Unc
1616	—	6,000	9,000	13,500	18,500	—

KM# 82 3 THALER
Silver **Subject:** 100th Anniversary of the Council of Thirteen **Note:** Similar to 2 Thaler, Dav. #LS517. Dav. #5953.

Date	Mintage	VG	F	VF	XF	Unc
ND(1625)	—	6,000	9,000	13,500	18,500	—

KM# 83 4 THALER
Silver **Subject:** 100th Anniversary of the Council of Thirteen **Note:** Similar to 2 Thaler, Dav. #LS517. Dav. #LS515.

Date	Mintage	VG	F	VF	XF	Unc
ND(1625)	—	7,500	12,500	17,500	25,000	—

TRADE COINAGE

KM# 42 GOLDGULDEN
3.5000 g., 0.9860 Gold 0.1109 oz. AGW **Rev:** Dragon holding arms at right

Date	Mintage	VG	F	VF	XF	Unc
1614	—	300	475	850	1,800	—
1615	—	300	475	850	1,800	—

KM# 49 GOLDGULDEN
3.5000 g., 0.9860 Gold 0.1109 oz. AGW **Obv:** Dragon holding arms at left **Rev:** Crowned imperial eagle

Date	Mintage	VG	F	VF	XF	Unc
1616	—	300	475	850	1,800	—
1617	—	300	475	850	1,800	—
1618	—	300	475	850	1,800	—
1619	—	300	475	850	1,800	—
1620	—	300	475	850	1,800	—
1621	—	300	475	850	1,800	—
1622	—	300	475	850	1,800	—

KM# 105 DUCAT
3.5000 g., 0.9860 Gold 0.1109 oz. AGW **Obv:** Crowned imperial eagle in inner circle **Rev:** Dragon holding arms in inner circle

Date	Mintage	VG	F	VF	XF	Unc
1651 ET	—	1,750	3,750	7,000	11,500	—
1655 HS	—	1,750	3,750	7,000	11,500	—

KM# 110 DUCAT
3.5000 g., 0.9860 Gold 0.1109 oz. AGW **Obv:** Bust of Johann Philip left in inner circle **Rev:** Capped arms in inner circle, date in legend

Date	Mintage	VG	F	VF	XF	Unc
1663	—	500	1,050	2,400	4,700	—
1664	—	500	1,050	2,400	4,700	—

KM# 116 DUCAT
3.5000 g., 0.9860 Gold 0.1109 oz. AGW **Obv:** Bust of Johann Philip right in inner circle

Date	Mintage	VG	F	VF	XF	Unc
1671	—	500	1,050	2,400	4,700	—

KM# 54 6 DUCAT
21.2800 g., Gold **Obv:** Lighthouse and seascape **Rev:** Lit candle, book dividing BIB-LIA, date in chronogram **Note:** Struck with 1 Thaler dies, Dav. #5955.

Date	Mintage	VG	F	VF	XF	Unc
ND(1617) Rare	—	—	—	—	—	—

KM# 55 8 DUCAT
26.6500 g., Gold **Obv:** Lighthouse and seascape **Rev:** Lit candle and book dividing BIB - LIA, date in chronogram **Note:** Struck with 1 Thaler dies, Dav. #5955, KM#51.

Date	Mintage	VG	F	VF	XF	Unc
ND(1617) Rare	—	—	—	—	—	—

PATTERNS

Including off metal strikes

KM#	Date	Mintage	Identification	Mkt Val
Pn1	1614	—	1/2 Thaler. Gold. KM#40.	—
Pn2	1651 (a)	—	Albus. Gold. KM#100.	—
Pn3	1681	—	Albus. Gold. KM#123.	—
Pn4	1717	—	Ducat. Silver. 1.8200 g. KM#142.	320

WURTTEMBERG

Located in South Germany, between Baden and Bavaria, Württemberg obtained the mint right in 1374. In 1495 the rulers became dukes. In 1802 the duke exchanged some of his land on the Rhine with France for territories nearer his capital city. Napoleon elevated the duke to the status of elector in 1803 and made him a king in 1806. The kingdom joined the German Empire in 1871 and endured until the king abdicated in 1918.

RULERS

Friedrich I, 1593-1608
Johann Friedrich I, 1608-1628
Ludwig Friedrich von Mömpelgart
    Regent and Administrator, 1628-1631
Julius Friedrich von Weiltingen
    Regent and Administrator, 1631-1633
Eberhard III, 1633-1674
Wilhelm Ludwig, 1674-1677
Friedrich Karl, Administrator 1677-1693
Eberhard Ludwig, 1693-1733

MINT MARKS

C, CT - Christophstal Mint
F - Freudenstadt Mint
S - Stuttgart Mint
T - Tübingen Mint

MINT OFFICIALS' INITIALS

Christophstal Mint

Initial	Date	Name
DS	1622-28	David Stein
	1604-05	Andreas Hubner
	1605-08	Wolfgang Ulrich Fischer
	1607-08	Jakob Vischer, warden
	1620-22?	Wolfgang Ulrich Fischer
	1622	Andreas Hubner

Stuttgart Mint

Initial	Date	Name
ICM/M	1669-95	Johann Christoph Müller, die-cutter
IDD	?-1694	Johann David Danielder Altere, die-cutter
IIW/wheel	1681-1702	Johann Jakob Wagner
ILW, LW, W, PHM	1694-1707	Philipp Heinrich Müller, die-cutter
(b)=mask	1620-37	Claude Guichard, die-cutter
Rosette	1610-ca. 1634	Francois Guichard, die-cutter
	1596-1606	Hans Kerber
	1601-34	Hans Pfaffenbruch, die-cutter in Koblenz
	1606-15	Wolf Mayer, warden
	1607	Jakob Wichert
	1608-20	Hans Kerber
	1616-35	Matthias Distler, warden
	1618-19	Caspar Guichard, die-cutter
	1620	Wolfgang Ulrich Fischer

	1622	Andreas Hubner
	1622	Valentin Johann Moser
	1622	Johann Schmidt, superintendant
	1622	Albrecht Vayh, superintendant
	1622	Johann Valentin Vay, superintendant
	1638-50	Kaspar Zur Lahn
	1644-49	Gottfried Kuhorst, warden
	1649-65	Christoph Tauchwitz, warden
	1659-63	Georg Pfrundt, die-cutter
	1660-64	Jeremias Pfaffenhauser (Bopfenhauser)
	1664-77	Johann Christoph Holderer
	1665-77	Jeremias Pfaffenhauser, warden
	1673-81	Johann Mayer
	1677-?	Anstett Ulrich Müller, warden
	1691-94	Johann Christoph Müller, warden
	1694-1707	Johann Christoph Pfaffenhauser, warden

Tübingen Mint

IP	1623-24	Johann Pfister, die-cutter
	1622-23	Franz Kretzmaier, die-cutter
	1622-23	Moritz Salander, die-cutter
	1623	Caspar Zur Lahn, warden

Die-cutters of Various Cities

1579-1616	Francois Briot
1587-1619	Karl Seckler der Jüngere
1597-1609	Josse de Buisson
1602-06	Jean Cassignot
1605-06	Wilhelm Gross
1606-09	Friedrich Daig
1609-10	Johann de Vos of Augsburg
1609-10	Andreas Reichel
1609-10	Andreas Allgewer
1623-66	Paul Zeggin in Munich

ARMS

Württemberg: 3 stag antlers arranged vertically.
Teck (duchy): Field of lozenges (diamond shapes).
Urach: hunting horn with looped hanger
Mömpelgart (principality): 2 fish standing on tails.
Hereditary flag-bearer of the Empire: flag with eagle device

REFERENCES

K&R = Ulrich Klein and Albert Raff, **Die württembergischen Münzen von 1374-1693**, Stuttgart, 1993.
B&E = Christian Binder and Julius Ebner, **Württembergische Münz- und Medaillen-Kunde**, 2 vols., Stuttgart, 1910-12.

REGULAR COINAGE

KM# 22 HELLER

Silver **Ruler:** Johann Friedrich I **Obv:** Hunting horn on which superimposed IHF **Note:** Uniface hohl-type; weight varies 0.19-0.42 grams.

Date	Mintage	VG	F	VF	XF	Unc
ND(1608-1628)	—	65.00	135	275	550	—

KM# 23 HELLER

Silver **Ruler:** Johann Friedrich I **Obv:** Hunting horn, H (=Heller) in center of horn's strap

Date	Mintage	VG	F	VF	XF	Unc
ND(1608-1628)	—	40.00	80.00	160	325	—

KM# 24 HELLER

Silver **Ruler:** Johann Friedrich I **Obv:** Shield of arms, H above **Note:** Uniface schüssel-type.

Date	Mintage	VG	F	VF	XF	Unc
ND(1608-1628)	—	70.00	80.00	160	325	—

KM# 61 HELLER

Copper, 12 mm. **Ruler:** Johann Friedrich I **Obv:** Hunting horn divides date, H in center of horn's strap **Rev:** Value in 3 lines **Rev. Inscription:** CCC / XXX / VI **Note:** Kipper Heller. Weight varies 0.19--0.63 grams.

Date	Mintage	VG	F	VF	XF	Unc
1621	—	16.00	35.00	70.00	145	—
1622	—	16.00	35.00	70.00	145	—

KM# 82 HELLER

Copper **Ruler:** Johann Friedrich I **Obv:** Without H

Date	Mintage	VG	F	VF	XF	Unc
1622	—	20.00	40.00	85.00	170	—

KM# 83 HELLER

Copper **Ruler:** Johann Friedrich I **Obv:** Shield of Württemberg arms, date above **Rev:** Arms of Teck

Date	Mintage	VG	F	VF	XF	Unc
1622	—	20.00	40.00	85.00	170	—
1623	—	20.00	40.00	85.00	170	—

KM# 255 HELLER

0.1200 g., Silver **Ruler:** Eberhard Ludwig **Obv:** Württemberg arms in squarish shield between 2 rosettes, H above **Note:** Uniface.

Date	Mintage	VG	F	VF	XF	Unc
ND(1693-1733)	—	20.00	45.00	90.00	185	—

KM# 25 PFENNIG

Silver, 12 mm. **Ruler:** Johann Friedrich I **Obv:** Hunting horn with IHF superimposed **Note:** Uniface hohl-type. Weight varies 0.31-0.50 grams.

Date	Mintage	VG	F	VF	XF	Unc
ND(1608-1628)	—	15.00	30.00	60.00	120	—

KM# 26 PFENNIG

Silver **Ruler:** Johann Friedrich I **Obv:** Württemberg arms in shield, IFH above **Note:** Uniface schüssel-type.

Date	Mintage	VG	F	VF	XF	Unc
ND(1608-1628)	—	15.00	30.00	60.00	120	—

KM# 175 PFENNIG

Silver **Ruler:** Ludwig Friedrich **Obv:** LFH above arms **Note:** Weight varies 0.31-0.56 grams.

Date	Mintage	VG	F	VF	XF	Unc
ND(1628-1631)	—	15.00	30.00	60.00	120	—

KM# 186 PFENNIG

Silver **Ruler:** Julius Friedrich **Obv:** Hunting horn with IHF **Note:** Uniface, hohl-type. Weight varies 0.38-0.43 grams.

Date	Mintage	VG	F	VF	XF	Unc
ND(1631-1633)	—	15.00	30.00	60.00	120	—

KM# 193 PFENNIG

Silver **Ruler:** Eberhard III **Obv:** Württemberg arms, EH above **Note:** Weight varies 0.26-0.54 grams.

Date	Mintage	VG	F	VF	XF	Unc
ND(1633-1674)	—	15.00	30.00	60.00	120	—

KM# 194 PFENNIG

Silver **Ruler:** Eberhard III **Obv:** Hunting horn divides E-H

Date	Mintage	VG	F	VF	XF	Unc
ND(1633-1674)	—	15.00	30.00	60.00	120	—

KM# 231 PFENNIG

Silver **Ruler:** Wilhelm Ludwig **Obv:** Württemberg arms in shield, WLH above **Note:** Weight varies 0.30-0.36 grams.

Date	Mintage	VG	F	VF	XF	Unc
ND(1674-1677)	—	10.00	25.00	55.00	110	—

KM# 232 PFENNIG

Silver **Ruler:** Friedrich Karl **Obv:** Württemberg arms in oval baroque frame, FCH above **Note:** Weight varies 0.21-0.37 grams.

Date	Mintage	VG	F	VF	XF	Unc
ND(1677-1693)	—	10.00	25.00	55.00	110	—

KM# 233 PFENNIG

Silver **Ruler:** Friedrich Karl **Obv:** Squarish arms

Date	Mintage	VG	F	VF	XF	Unc
ND(1677-1693)	—	10.00	25.00	55.00	110	—

KM# 256 PFENNIG

Silver **Ruler:** Eberhard Ludwig **Obv:** Oval Württemberg arms in baroque frame, ELH above **Note:** Uniface; weight varies 0.24-0.39 grams

Date	Mintage	VG	F	VF	XF	Unc
ND(1693-1733)	—	10.00	25.00	55.00	110	—

KM# 236 1/6 KREUZER

Copper **Ruler:** Friedrich Karl **Obv:** Württemberg arms in oval baroque frame, H above **Rev. Inscription:** VI / EINEN / KREITZER **Note:** Weight varies 0.45-0.70 grams.

Date	Mintage	VG	F	VF	XF	Unc
ND(1680-93)	—	250	500	1,000	2,200	—
ND(1680-93) IIW	—	250	500	1,000	2,200	—

KM# 248 1/6 KREUZER

Copper **Ruler:** Friedrich Karl **Obv:** H at top divides date **Mint:** Stuttgart

Date	Mintage	VG	F	VF	XF	Unc
1687 IIW	—	40.00	82.00	160	325	—

KM# 257 1/6 KREUZER

Copper **Ruler:** Eberhard Ludwig **Obv:** Squarish shield of arms **Note:** Weight varies 0.45-.070 grams

Date	Mintage	VG	F	VF	XF	Unc
ND(1693-1733)	—	—	—	—	—	—

KM# 216 1/2 KREUZER (4 Pfennig)

0.6400 g., Silver **Ruler:** Eberhard III **Obv:** Württemberg arms, value 1/2 in circle above **Rev:** Teck arms, date above

Date	Mintage	VG	F	VF	XF	Unc
1654	—	—	—	—	—	—

KM# 241 1/2 KREUZER (4 Pfennig)

Silver **Ruler:** Friedrich Karl **Obv:** Württemberg arms in oval baroque frame, value 1/2 divides date above **Note:** Uniface; weight varies 0.29-0.53 grams.

Date	Mintage	VG	F	VF	XF	Unc
1680	—	10.00	20.00	40.00	80.00	—
1683	—	10.00	20.00	40.00	80.00	—
1684	—	10.00	20.00	40.00	80.00	—
1689	—	10.00	20.00	40.00	80.00	—
1692	—	10.00	20.00	40.00	80.00	—
1693	—	10.00	20.00	40.00	80.00	—

KM# 270 1/2 KREUZER (4 Pfennig)

Silver **Ruler:** Eberhard Ludwig **Obv:** Round Württemberg arms in baroque frame, value 1/2 divides date above **Note:** Weight varies 0.23-0.50 grams

Date	Mintage	VG	F	VF	XF	Unc
1695	—	10.00	20.00	40.00	80.00	—
1696	—	10.00	20.00	40.00	80.00	—
1697	—	10.00	20.00	40.00	80.00	—
1698	—	10.00	20.00	40.00	80.00	—
1699	—	10.00	20.00	40.00	80.00	—
1700	—	10.00	20.00	40.00	80.00	—

KM# 62 KREUZER

Silver **Ruler:** Johann Friedrich I **Obv:** Bust right **Rev:** Double-cross, arms of Teck in circle in center with value I above, date dividied between ends of cross in upper half **Note:** Weight varies 0.50-0.60 grams.

Date	Mintage	VG	F	VF	XF	Unc
1621	—	24.00	45.00	80.00	160	—

KM# 63 KREUZER

Silver **Ruler:** Johann Friedrich I **Obv:** Württemberg arms in shield, value I above **Rev:** Arms of Teck, date above **Note:** Weight varies 0.50-0.60 grams.

Date	Mintage	VG	F	VF	XF	Unc
1621	—	20.00	40.00	70.00	145	—

KM# 84 KREUZER

Silver **Ruler:** Johann Friedrich I **Obv:** Württemberg arms below value **Rev:** Arms of Teck below date

Date	Mintage	VG	F	VF	XF	Unc
(1)622	—	20.00	40.00	70.00	145	—
1622	—	20.00	40.00	70.00	145	—

KM# 120 KREUZER

Silver **Ruler:** Johann Friedrich I **Obv:** Bust right **Rev:** Württemberg arms divide date, value I above

Date	Mintage	VG	F	VF	XF	Unc
1623	—	24.00	40.00	80.00	160	—

KM# 121 KREUZER

Silver **Ruler:** Johann Friedrich I **Obv:** Württemberg arms in ornamented shield, date above **Rev:** Teck arms in ornamented shield, value I above

Date	Mintage	VG	F	VF	XF	Unc
1623	—	20.00	40.00	70.00	145	—

KM# 122 KREUZER

Silver **Ruler:** Johann Friedrich I **Obv:** Arms divide date

Date	Mintage	VG	F	VF	XF	Unc
1623	—	20.00	40.00	70.00	145	—

KM# 123 KREUZER

Silver **Ruler:** Johann Friedrich I **Obv:** Value above arms **Rev:** Date above arms

Date	Mintage	VG	F	VF	XF	Unc
1623	—	20.00	40.00	70.00	145	—

KM# 152 KREUZER

Silver **Ruler:** Johann Friedrich I **Obv:** Bust right **Rev:** Shield of arms divided between Württemberg and Teck, date above **Mint:** Christophstal

Date	Mintage	VG	F	VF	XF	Unc
1624CT	—	22.00	40.00	75.00	155	—
1624CT	—	22.00	40.00	75.00	155	—
1625CT	—	22.00	40.00	75.00	155	—

KM# 153 KREUZER

Silver **Ruler:** Johann Friedrich I **Rev:** Double-cross, arms of Württemberg in circle in center with value I above, date dividied between ends of cross in upper half

Date	Mintage	VG	F	VF	XF	Unc
1624	—	—	—	—	—	—

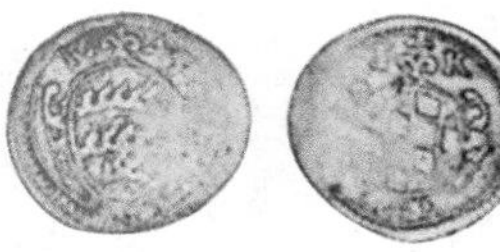

KM# 200 KREUZER

Silver **Ruler:** Eberhard III **Obv:** Oval Württemberg arms in baroque frame, date divided at top **Rev:** Oval arms of Teck in baroque frame, value I-K at top **Note:** Weight varies 0.41-.097 grams.

Date	Mintage	VG	F	VF	XF	Unc
1640	—	11.00	25.00	55.00	110	—
1641	—	11.00	25.00	55.00	110	—
1642	—	11.00	25.00	55.00	110	—
1643	—	11.00	25.00	55.00	110	—
1644	—	11.00	25.00	55.00	110	—
1645	—	11.00	25.00	55.00	110	—
1646	—	11.00	25.00	55.00	110	—

KM# 207 KREUZER

Silver **Ruler:** Eberhard III **Obv:** Arms of Württemberg and Teck divided vertically in shield, date above **Rev:** Imperial banner and arms of Mompelgart divided vertically in shield, I.K above **Note:** Weight varies 0.41-0.97 grams.

Date	Mintage	VG	F	VF	XF	Unc
1648	—	—	—	—	—	—

KM# 249 KREUZER

Silver **Ruler:** Friedrich Karl **Rev:** Titles of Friedrich Karl **Note:** Weight varies 0.29-0.84 grams.

Date	Mintage	VG	F	VF	XF	Unc
1687	—	9.00	20.00	55.00	110	—
1690	—	9.00	20.00	55.00	110	—
1691	—	9.00	20.00	55.00	110	—
1692/1	—	9.00	20.00	55.00	110	—
1692	—	9.00	20.00	55.00	110	—
1693	—	9.00	20.00	55.00	110	—

KM# 258 KREUZER

Silver **Ruler:** Eberhard Ludwig **Obv:** Date above divided arms within shield **Rev:** IK above 2-fold arms on shield within inner circle **Mint:** Stuttgart **Note:** Weight varies 0.43-0.71 grams. Varieties exist.

Date	Mintage	VG	F	VF	XF	Unc
1693	—	9.00	20.00	55.00	110	—
1694	—	9.00	20.00	55.00	110	—
1695	—	9.00	20.00	55.00	110	—
1696	—	9.00	20.00	55.00	110	—
1697	—	9.00	20.00	55.00	110	—
1698	—	9.00	20.00	55.00	110	—
1700	—	9.00	20.00	55.00	110	—

KM# 65 2 KREUZER (Halbbatzen)

Silver **Ruler:** Johann Friedrich I **Obv:** Bust right **Rev:** Württemberg arms in shield, value 2 above, date in legend **Note:** Klippe 2 Kreuzer.

Date	Mintage	VG	F	VF	XF	Unc
1621	—	—	—	—	—	—

KM# 64 2 KREUZER (Halbbatzen)

Silver **Ruler:** Johann Friedrich I **Obv:** Bust right **Rev:** Württemberg arms in shield, value 2 above, date in legend **Note:** Weight varies 0.69-1.43 grams.

Date	Mintage	VG	F	VF	XF	Unc
1621	—	375	750	1,500	—	—

KM# 125 2 KREUZER (Halbbatzen)

Silver **Ruler:** Johann Friedrich I **Obv:** CT above 3 shields **Mint:** Christophstal **Note:** Weight varies 0.69-1.43 grams.

Date	Mintage	VG	F	VF	XF	Unc
1623CT	—	16.00	33.00	75.00	155	—

KM# 124 2 KREUZER (Halbbatzen)

Silver **Ruler:** Johann Friedrich I **Obv:** 3 small shields of arms, 2 above 1, value 2 between 2 shields above, date dividied by shield at bottom **Rev:** Imperial banner, S below **Mint:** Stuttgart

Date	Mintage	VG	F	VF	XF	Unc
1623S	—	16.00	33.00	75.00	155	—
1624/3S	—	16.00	33.00	75.00	155	—
1624S	—	16.00	33.00	75.00	155	—
1625S	—	16.00	33.00	75.00	155	—
1628S	—	16.00	33.00	75.00	155	—

KM# 126 2 KREUZER (Halbbatzen)

Silver **Ruler:** Johann Friedrich I **Obv:** CT in center of 3 shields **Mint:** Christophstal

Date	Mintage	VG	F	VF	XF	Unc
1623CT	—	16.00	33.00	75.00	155	—
1624CT	—	16.00	33.00	75.00	155	—
1624CT	—	16.00	33.00	75.00	155	—
1625 CT/DS	—	—	—	—	—	—
1625/6 CT/DS	—	—	—	—	—	—
1626CT	—	16.00	33.00	75.00	155	—

KM# 185 2 KREUZER (Halbbatzen)

Silver **Ruler:** Ludwig Friedrich **Obv:** 4-fold arms in ornamented shield, date above **Rev:** Imperial orb with 2 **Note:** Weight varies 0.97-1.35 grams.

Date	Mintage	VG	F	VF	XF	Unc
1630	—	60.00	115	200	425	—

KM# 187 2 KREUZER (Halbbatzen)

Silver **Ruler:** Ludwig Friedrich **Obv:** 4-fold arms **Rev:** Imperial orb with 2, cross above divides date **Note:** Weight varies 0.82-1.61 grams.

Date	Mintage	VG	F	VF	XF	Unc
1631	—	60.00	115	200	425	—

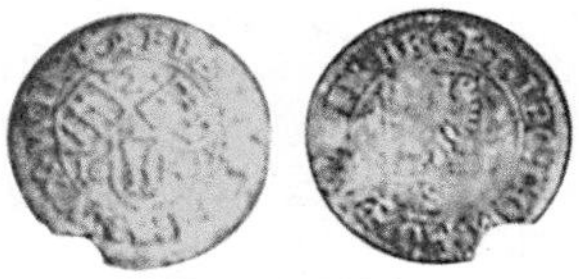

KM# 195 2 KREUZER (Halbbatzen)

Silver **Ruler:** Julius Friedrich **Obv:** 3 small shields of arms, 2 above 1, value 2 between upper shields, date divided by lower shield **Rev:** Imperial banner **Mint:** Stuttgart **Note:** Weight varies 0.82-1.37 grams.

Date	Mintage	VG	F	VF	XF	Unc
1633S	—	13.00	30.00	60.00	120	—
1634S	—	13.00	30.00	60.00	120	—
1639S	—	13.00	30.00	60.00	120	—
1639S	—	13.00	30.00	60.00	120	—
1640S	—	13.00	30.00	60.00	120	—
1641S	—	13.00	30.00	60.00	120	—
1661S	—	13.00	30.00	60.00	120	—
1665S	—	13.00	30.00	60.00	120	—
1668S	—	13.00	30.00	60.00	120	—

KM# 242 2 KREUZER (Halbbatzen)

Silver **Ruler:** Friedrich Karl **Obv:** Titles of Friedrich Karl **Note:** Weight varies 0.99-1.27 grams.

Date	Mintage	VG	F	VF	XF	Unc
1680	—	—	—	—	—	—

KM# 259 2 KREUZER (Halbbatzen)

Silver **Ruler:** Eberhard Ludwig **Obv:** Titles of Eberhard Ludwig **Mint:** Stuttgart **Note:** Weight varies 0.91-1.26 grams.

Date	Mintage	VG	F	VF	XF	Unc
1693	—	13.00	30.00	50.00	90.00	180
1694	—	13.00	30.00	50.00	90.00	180
1694 (wheel)	—	13.00	30.00	50.00	90.00	180
1695	—	13.00	30.00	50.00	90.00	180
1696	—	13.00	30.00	50.00	90.00	180
1697	—	13.00	30.00	50.00	90.00	180

KM# 67 3 KREUZER (Groschen)

Silver **Ruler:** Johann Friedrich I **Obv:** Date in legend

Date	Mintage	VG	F	VF	XF	Unc
1621	—	33.00	65.00	135	275	—

KM# 68 3 KREUZER (Groschen)

Silver **Ruler:** Johann Friedrich I **Rev:** Date in legend

Date	Mintage	VG	F	VF	XF	Unc
1621	—	33.00	65.00	135	275	—
1622	—	33.00	65.00	135	275	—

KM# 66 3 KREUZER (Groschen)

Silver **Ruler:** Johann Friedrich I **Obv:** Bust right **Rev:** Württemberg arms in shield, value 3 above **Note:** Kipper 3 Kreuzer. Weight varies 0.94-1.39 grams.

Date	Mintage	VG	F	VF	XF	Unc
ND(1621/2)	—	33.00	65.00	135	275	—

KM# 260 4 KREUZER (Batzen)

Silver **Ruler:** Eberhard Ludwig **Obv:** Value above 3 shields, date divided by lower shield **Rev:** Crowned arms within baroque frame **Note:** Weight varies 1.62-2.53 grams.

Date	Mintage	VG	F	VF	XF	Unc
1693 (wheel)	—	30.00	65.00	135	275	—
1694	—	30.00	65.00	135	275	—
1694 (wheel)	—	30.00	65.00	135	275	—
1696	—	30.00	65.00	135	275	—
1698	—	30.00	65.00	135	275	—
1700	—	30.00	65.00	135	275	—

KM# 70 6 KREUZER

Silver **Ruler:** Johann Friedrich I **Obv:** Bust right **Rev:** Württemberg arms, value 6 above, date in legend

Date	Mintage	VG	F	VF	XF	Unc
1621	—	20.00	40.00	85.00	—	—

KM# 69 6 KREUZER

Silver **Ruler:** Johann Friedrich I **Obv:** Württemberg arms, value 6 above **Rev:** Arms of Teck, date above **Note:** Weight varies 1.57-2.74 grams Kipper 6 Kreuzer.

Date	Mintage	VG	F	VF	XF	Unc
1621	—	20.00	40.00	85.00	—	—

KM# 85 12 KREUZER (Dreibatzner)

2.4800 g., Silver **Ruler:** Johann Friedrich I **Obv:** Bust right, mint mark C in cartouche below in legend **Rev:** Crowned 4-fold arms, value 12 in oval at bottom, date in legend **Mint:** Christophstal

Date	Mintage	VG	F	VF	XF	Unc
1622C	—	—	—	—	—	—

KM# 192 15 KREUZER (1/4 Gulden)

Silver **Ruler:** Julius Friedrich **Obv:** Bust right **Rev:** Crowned oval 4-fold arms in baroque frame, date in legend, value (15.K) in legend below

Date	Mintage	VG	F	VF	XF	Unc
1632	—	100	200	375	775	—

KM# 191 15 KREUZER (1/4 Gulden)

Silver **Ruler:** Julius Friedrich **Obv:** 1/2-length figure of Julius Friedrich right **Rev:** 3 small oval arms, 2 above 1, large crown above, date divided by lower arms, value (15.K) in legend at bottom **Note:** Weight varies 4.61-5.53 grams.

Date	Mintage	VG	F	VF	XF	Unc
1632	—	115	225	425	875	—

KM# 196 15 KREUZER (1/4 Gulden)
Silver **Ruler:** Eberhard III **Rev:** Date divided at top of arms below crown, value (XV) in legend below **Note:** Weight varies 5.15-5.88 grams.

Date	Mintage	VG	F	VF	XF	Unc
1639	—	90.00	180	360	725	—

KM# 72 24 KREUZER (Sechsbatzner)
Silver **Ruler:** Johann Friedrich I **Rev:** Oval arms

Date	Mintage	VG	F	VF	XF	Unc
ND(1621/2)	—	160	325	650	—	—

KM# 71 24 KREUZER (Sechsbatzner)
Silver **Ruler:** Johann Friedrich I **Obv:** Bust right **Rev:** Crowned 4-fold arms in squarish shield **Note:** Weight varies 3.68-6.15 grams. Kipper 24 Kreuzer.

Date	Mintage	VG	F	VF	XF	Unc
ND(1621/2)	—	160	325	650	—	—

KM# 86 24 KREUZER (Sechsbatzner)
Silver **Ruler:** Johann Friedrich I **Obv:** Bust right, date below **Rev:** Crowned 4-fold arms in squarish shield divide date

Date	Mintage	VG	F	VF	XF	Unc
1622	—	175	350	725	—	—

KM# 87 24 KREUZER (Sechsbatzner)
Silver **Ruler:** Johann Friedrich I **Rev:** Without date

Date	Mintage	VG	F	VF	XF	Unc
1622	—	160	325	650	—	—

KM# 88 24 KREUZER (Sechsbatzner)
Silver **Ruler:** Johann Friedrich I **Rev:** Oval arms in baroque frame, without date

Date	Mintage	VG	F	VF	XF	Unc
1622	—	160	325	650	—	—

KM# 89 24 KREUZER (Sechsbatzner)
Silver **Ruler:** Johann Friedrich I **Obv:** Date in legend

Date	Mintage	VG	F	VF	XF	Unc
1622	—	160	325	650	—	—

KM# 92 24 KREUZER (Sechsbatzner)
18.0100 g., Silver **Ruler:** Johann Friedrich I **Rev:** Date in legend **Mint:** Stuttgart

Date	Mintage	VG	F	VF	XF	Unc
1622S	—	160	325	650	—	—

KM# 95 24 KREUZER (Sechsbatzner)
Silver **Ruler:** Johann Friedrich I **Obv:** Date in legend **Rev:** Squarish arms **Mint:** Christophstal

Date	Mintage	VG	F	VF	XF	Unc
1622CT	—	160	325	650	—	—

KM# 96 24 KREUZER (Sechsbatzner)
Silver **Ruler:** Johann Friedrich I **Rev:** Date divided by arms **Mint:** Christophstal

Date	Mintage	VG	F	VF	XF	Unc
1622CT	—	175	375	750	—	—

KM# 90 24 KREUZER (Sechsbatzner)
18.0100 g., Silver **Ruler:** Johann Friedrich I **Note:** Klippe 24 Kreuzer.

Date	Mintage	VG	F	VF	XF	Unc
1622	—	—	—	—	—	—

KM# 93 24 KREUZER (Sechsbatzner)
5.7900 g., Silver **Ruler:** Johann Friedrich I **Note:** Klippe, 24 Kreuzer.

Date	Mintage	VG	F	VF	XF	Unc
1622	—	—	—	—	—	—

KM# 94 24 KREUZER (Sechsbatzner)
Silver **Ruler:** Johann Friedrich I **Obv:** Mint mark in oval cartouche below bust **Rev:** Oval arms in baroque frame **Note:** Struck at Christophstal and Freudenstadt mints.

Date	Mintage	VG	F	VF	XF	Unc
1622 C	—	135	275	550	—	—
1622 F	—	135	275	550	—	—

KM# 91 24 KREUZER (Sechsbatzner)
Silver **Ruler:** Johann Friedrich I **Obv:** Date in legend **Rev:** Oval arms in baroque frame **Note:** Weight varies 3.68-6.15 grams.

Date	Mintage	VG	F	VF	XF	Unc
(1) 622	—	160	325	650	—	—
1622	—	160	325	650	—	—

KM# 98 30 KREUZER (1/2 Gulden)
Silver **Ruler:** Johann Friedrich I **Obv:** Oval arms in baroque frame

Date	Mintage	VG	F	VF	XF	Unc
1622 (a)	—	165	325	700	1,300	—
1622 T	—	165	325	700	1,300	—
1623 S	—	165	325	700	1,300	—

KM# 97 30 KREUZER (1/2 Gulden)
Silver **Ruler:** Johann Friedrich I **Obv:** Crowned 4-fold arms in squarish shield **Rev:** Stag laying left, value 30 in round cartouche at left, date below **Note:** Kipper, 30 Kreuzer. Weight varies 3.99-5.09 grams.

Date	Mintage	VG	F	VF	XF	Unc
1622 S	—	250	500	1,000	2,000	—
1622 CT	—	250	500	1,000	2,000	—

KM# 127 30 KREUZER (1/2 Gulden)
Silver **Ruler:** Johann Friedrich I **Mint:** Stuttgart **Note:** Klippe 30 Kreuzer.

Date	Mintage	VG	F	VF	XF	Unc
1623S	—	—	—	—	—	—

KM# 129 60 KREUZER (1 Gulden)
Silver **Ruler:** Johann Friedrich I **Obv:** Arms in squarish shield

Date	Mintage	VG	F	VF	XF	Unc
1622	—	135	275	525	1,050	—
1622 C	—	135	275	525	1,050	—
1622 S	—	135	275	525	1,050	—
1623 CT	—	135	275	525	1,050	—
1623 S	—	135	275	525	1,050	—

KM# 130 60 KREUZER (1 Gulden)
Silver **Ruler:** Johann Friedrich I **Obv:** Date in legend **Rev:** Crowned 4-fold arms in oval baroque frame, date above

Date	Mintage	VG	F	VF	XF	Unc
1622	—	200	400	750	1,300	—
(1)622	—	200	400	750	1,300	—

KM# 132 60 KREUZER (1 Gulden)
Silver **Ruler:** Johann Friedrich I **Obv:** Date below bust

Date	Mintage	VG	F	VF	XF	Unc
1622	—	200	400	750	1,500	—

KM# 99 60 KREUZER (1 Gulden)
Silver **Ruler:** Johann Friedrich I **Obv:** Crowned 4-fold arms in oval baroque frame **Rev:** Stag laying left, value 60 in cartouche at left, date below **Note:** Kipper 60 Kreuzer. Weight varies 6.98-10.81 grams.

Date	Mintage	VG	F	VF	XF	Unc
1622	—	165	325	650	1,300	—
1622 (a)	—	165	325	650	1,300	—
1622 C	—	165	325	650	1,300	—
1622 CT	—	165	325	650	1,300	—
1622 (a)	—	165	325	650	1,300	—
1623 CT	—	165	325	650	1,300	—
1623 T	—	165	325	650	1,300	—

KM# 131 60 KREUZER (1 Gulden)
Silver **Ruler:** Johann Friedrich I **Obv:** Date on obverse only **Note:** Weight varies 6.98-10.81 grams.

Date	Mintage	VG	F	VF	XF	Unc
(1)622	—	200	400	750	1,500	—

KM# 128 60 KREUZER (1 Gulden)
16.0500 g., Silver **Ruler:** Johann Friedrich I **Mint:** Christophstal **Note:** Klippe, 60 Kreuzer.

Date	Mintage	VG	F	VF	XF	Unc
1623CT (a)	—	—	—	—	—	—
1623CT	—	—	—	—	—	—

KM# 172 60 KREUZER (1 Gulden)
Silver **Ruler:** Johann Friedrich I **Obv:** Crowned imperial eagle, 60 in orb on breast, date in legend **Rev:** 4-fold arms, 3 ornate helmets above **Mint:** Christophstal **Note:** Reichs, 60 Kreuzer.

Date	Mintage	VG	F	VF	XF	Unc
1626CT	—	—	—	—	—	—

KM# 133 120 KREUZER (2 Gulden)
18.3800 g., Silver **Ruler:** Johann Friedrich I **Obv:** Crowned 4-fold arms in oval baroque frame **Rev:** 2 stags laying facing center, value 120 in cartouche, date below **Note:** Kipper, 120 Kreuzer.

Date	Mintage	VG	F	VF	XF	Unc
1623 T	—	400	750	1,400	2,800	—

KM# 101 7 SCHILLINGE (1/4 Gulden)
Silver **Ruler:** Johann Friedrich I **Obv:** Württemberg arms in ornamented shield **Rev:** Teck arms in ornamented shield, date in legend

Date	Mintage	VG	F	VF	XF	Unc
1622	—	325	600	1,200	2,400	—

KM# 102 7 SCHILLINGE (1/4 Gulden)
Silver **Ruler:** Johann Friedrich I **Obv:** Württemberg arms in baroque frame, date in legend **Rev:** Legend in laurel wreath **Rev. Inscription:** VII / SCHIL- / LINDER / S **Mint:** Stuttgart

Date	Mintage	VG	F	VF	XF	Unc
1622S	—	400	700	1,400	2,750	—

KM# 103 7 SCHILLINGE (1/4 Gulden)
Silver **Ruler:** Johann Friedrich I **Obv:** Small oval Württemberg arms in baroque frame, date in legend **Rev:** Legend in laurel wreath **Rev. Inscription:** VII / SCHIL / LING / ER

Date	Mintage	VG	F	VF	XF	Unc
1622 (a)	—	325	625	1,250	2,500	—

KM# 104 7 SCHILLINGE (1/4 Gulden)
Silver **Ruler:** Johann Friedrich I **Rev. Inscription:** VII / SCHIL / LING

Date	Mintage	VG	F	VF	XF	Unc
1622 (a)	—	325	625	1,250	2,500	—

KM# 100 7 SCHILLINGE (1/4 Gulden)
Silver **Ruler:** Johann Friedrich I **Obv:** Crowned 4-fold arms **Rev:** Stag laying down to left, date below **Note:** Kipper, 7 Schillings.

Date	Mintage	VG	F	VF	XF	Unc
1622	—	325	625	1,250	2,500	—

KM# 105 7 SCHILLINGE (1/4 Gulden)
6.5300 g., Silver **Ruler:** Johann Friedrich I **Note:** Klippe.

Date	Mintage	VG	F	VF	XF	Unc
1622 (a)	—	—	—	—	—	—

KM# 73 1/28 THALER (Schilling)
Silver **Ruler:** Johann Friedrich I **Obv:** Württemberg arms in shield **Rev:** Teck arms in shield, value 28 in legend at top **Note:** Weight varies 0.54-1.49 grams. Kipper 1/28 Thaler.

Date	Mintage	VG	F	VF	XF	Unc
ND(1621/2)	—	135	275	475	950	—

KM# 106 1/28 THALER (Schilling)
Silver **Ruler:** Johann Friedrich I **Rev:** Date in legend, value 28 above Teck arms

Date	Mintage	VG	F	VF	XF	Unc
1622	—	135	275	475	950	—
(1)622	—	135	275	475	950	—

KM# 107 1/28 THALER (Schilling)
Silver **Ruler:** Johann Friedrich I **Obv:** Hunting horn divides date **Rev:** Ornate round arms of Teck, value 28 in legend at top

Date	Mintage	VG	F	VF	XF	Unc
1622	—	135	275	475	950	—

KM# 108 1/28 THALER (Schilling)
Silver **Ruler:** Johann Friedrich I **Obv:** Hunting horn in ornate shield **Rev:** Ornate shield of Teck arms, value (28) in legend at top, date in legend inscription **Note:** Weight varies 0.54-1.49 grams.

Date	Mintage	VG	F	VF	XF	Unc
1622	—	135	275	475	950	—

KM# 75 1/14 THALER (Doppelschilling)
Silver **Ruler:** Johann Friedrich I **Rev:** Date in legend, value 14 at top in legend

Date	Mintage	VG	F	VF	XF	Unc
1621	—	165	325	625	1,250	—
1622	—	165	325	625	1,250	—

KM# 74 1/14 THALER (Doppelschilling)
Silver **Ruler:** Johann Friedrich I **Obv:** Württemberg arms in shield **Rev:** Teck arms in shield, value 14 at top in legend **Note:** Weight varies 0.90-2.41 grams.

Date	Mintage	VG	F	VF	XF	Unc
ND(1621/2)	—	165	325	625	1,250	—

KM# 109 1/14 THALER (Doppelschilling)
Silver **Ruler:** Johann Friedrich I **Rev:** Value 14 above Teck arms

Date	Mintage	VG	F	VF	XF	Unc
1622	—	165	325	625	1,250	—
(16)23	—	165	325	625	1,250	—

KM# 110 1/14 THALER (Doppelschilling)
Silver **Ruler:** Johann Friedrich I **Rev:** Date divided by arms

Date	Mintage	VG	F	VF	XF	Unc
1622	—	165	325	625	1,250	—

KM# 111 1/14 THALER (Doppelschilling)
Silver **Ruler:** Johann Friedrich I **Obv:** Bust right **Rev:** Württemberg arms, value 14 in cartouche in legend at top, date in legend inscription

Date	Mintage	VG	F	VF	XF	Unc
1622	—	165	325	625	1,250	—

KM# 134 1/9 THALER
Silver **Ruler:** Johann Friedrich I **Obv:** Bust right **Rev:** Crowned 4-fold arms, value 1/9 at bottom, date in legend

Date	Mintage	VG	F	VF	XF	Unc
1623	—	75.00	150	300	625	—
1624/3	—	75.00	150	300	625	—

KM# 177 1/9 THALER
3.4800 g., Silver **Ruler:** Johann Friedrich I

Date	Mintage	VG	F	VF	XF	Unc
1626	—	115	220	435	875	—

KM# 135 1/6 THALER
Silver **Ruler:** Johann Friedrich I **Mint:** Stuttgart **Note:** Weight varies 4.74-4.96 grams.

Date	Mintage	VG	F	VF	XF	Unc
1623S	—	135	275	575	1,150	—
1624/3S	—	135	275	575	1,150	—

KM# 178 1/6 THALER
4.7800 g., Silver **Ruler:** Ludwig Friedrich **Rev:** Oval arms in baroque frame

Date	Mintage	VG	F	VF	XF	Unc
1629	—	200	350	700	1,400	—

KM# 205 1/6 THALER
4.8600 g., Silver **Ruler:** Eberhard III **Obv:** 3 ornate helmets, date in legend **Rev:** Crowned oval 4-fold arms in baroque frame, value (1/6) in legend at bottom

Date	Mintage	VG	F	VF	XF	Unc
1647	—	—	—	—	—	—

KM# 12 1/4 THALER
0.8889 Silver Weight varies: 7.20-7.35g. **Ruler:** Friedrich I **Obv:** 4-fold arms, 3 ornate helmets above, date divided near bottom **Rev:** Full-length figure of St. Christopher, child Jesus on shoulder, left arms holding shield with crowned imperial eagle, titles of Rudolf II

Date	Mintage	VG	F	VF	XF	Unc
1606	—	525	900	1,800	—	—

KM# 18 1/4 THALER
Silver **Ruler:** Friedrich I **Obv:** Less ornate helmets above arms **Rev:** St. Christopher walking right on ground

Date	Mintage	VG	F	VF	XF	Unc
1607	—	600	1,100	2,200	—	—

KM# 41 1/4 THALER
6.9600 g., Silver **Ruler:** Johann Friedrich I

Date	Mintage	VG	F	VF	XF	Unc
1611	—	600	1,100	2,200	—	—

KM# 136 1/4 THALER
Silver **Ruler:** Johann Friedrich I **Rev:** Without value **Mint:** Christophstal **Note:** Weight varies 7.03-7.31 grams.

Date	Mintage	VG	F	VF	XF	Unc
1623 CT	—	400	775	1,550	—	—
1624 CT/IP	—	400	775	1,550	—	—

KM# 203 1/4 THALER
Silver **Ruler:** Eberhard III **Obv:** 3 ornate helmets **Rev:** Crowned 4-fold arms in squarish shield, date divided above crown, value (1/4) in legend at bottom **Note:** Weight varies 7.17-7.26 grams.

Date	Mintage	VG	F	VF	XF	Unc
1641 Rare	—	—	—	—	—	—

KM# 208 1/4 THALER
Silver **Ruler:** Eberhard III **Obv:** 3 ornately-shaped shields of arms, 2 above 1, crown above, date divided by lower shield, all in laurel wreath, value (1/4) in legend at bottom **Rev:** Imperial banner in laurel wreath

Date	Mintage	VG	F	VF	XF	Unc
1648 Rare	—	—	—	—	—	—

KM# 225 1/4 THALER
Silver **Ruler:** Eberhard III **Obv:** Bust right **Rev:** Crowned heart-shaped oval, 4-fold arms divide date

Date	Mintage	VG	F	VF	XF	Unc
1668/59	—	—	—	—	—	—

KM# 244 1/4 THALER
Silver **Ruler:** Friedrich Karl **Rev:** Crowned 4-fold arms in laurel wreath, date divided in legend near top **Mint:** Stuttgart **Note:** Weight varies 7.27-7.32 grams.

Date	Mintage	VG	F	VF	XF	Unc
1681	—	800	1,600	3,100	—	—
1681 M	—	800	1,600	3,100	—	—

KM# 261 1/4 THALER
Silver **Ruler:** Eberhard Ludwig **Rev:** Crowned 4-fold arms between 2 palm branches, date divided below **Mint:** Stuttgart **Note:** Weight varies 7.29-7.31 grams.

Date	Mintage	VG	F	VF	XF	Unc
1694 IIW	—	165	325	600	1,300	—
1694 IIW (wheel)	—	165	325	600	1,300	—

KM# 276 1/4 THALER
8.6000 g., Silver **Ruler:** Eberhard Ludwig **Rev:** 4-fold arms, five helmets above, date divided below **Mint:** Stuttgart

Date	Mintage	VG	F	VF	XF	Unc
1699 IIW	—	180	375	750	1,500	—

KM# 179 1/3 THALER
10.0300 g., Silver **Ruler:** Ludwig Friedrich **Note:** Similar to 1/6 Thaler, KM#135, but value: 1/3 bottom reverse.

Date	Mintage	VG	F	VF	XF	Unc
1629	—	550	1,100	2,150	—	—

KM# 13 1/2 THALER
0.8889 Silver Weight varies: 14.12-14.60g. **Ruler:** Friedrich I **Note:** Similar to 1/4 Thaler, KM#12, but date in legend at bottom on reverse.

Date	Mintage	VG	F	VF	XF	Unc
1606	—	1,100	2,000	3,750	—	—

KM# 19 1/2 THALER
6.2000 g., Silver **Ruler:** Friedrich I **Rev:** St. Christopher walking right on ground **Note:** Similar to 1/4 Thaler, KM#12, but less ornate helmets above arms.

Date	Mintage	VG	F	VF	XF	Unc
1607	—	1,100	2,000	3,750	—	—

KM# 29 1/2 THALER
Silver **Ruler:** Johann Friedrich I **Note:** Weight varies 14.27-14.54 grams.

Date	Mintage	VG	F	VF	XF	Unc
1609	—	1,075	2,000	4,000	—	—
1611	—	1,075	2,000	4,000	—	—

KM# 43 1/2 THALER
Silver **Ruler:** Johann Friedrich I **Obv:** Bust right **Rev:** 4-fold arms, three helmets above, date in legend **Note:** Weight varies 14.15-14.73 grams.

Date	Mintage	VG	F	VF	XF	Unc
1612	—	—	—	—	—	—

KM# 46 1/2 THALER
Silver **Ruler:** Johann Friedrich I **Rev:** Crowned 4-fold arms, date in legend

Date	Mintage	VG	F	VF	XF	Unc
1613	—	—	—	—	—	—
1621	—	—	—	—	—	—

KM# 76 1/2 THALER
13.1500 g., Silver **Ruler:** Johann Friedrich I **Note:** Klippe, 1/2 Thaler.

Date	Mintage	VG	F	VF	XF	Unc
1621	—	—	—	—	—	—

KM# 138 1/2 THALER
Silver **Ruler:** Johann Friedrich I **Obv:** Bust right **Rev:** Crowned oval 4-fold arms, date in legend **Mint:** Stuttgart

Date	Mintage	VG	F	VF	XF	Unc
1623 S	—	325	650	1,300	2,600	—
1624/3	—	325	650	1,300	2,600	—
1625	—	325	650	1,300	2,600	—
1626/5	—	325	650	1,300	2,600	—
1626	—	325	650	1,300	2,600	—

KM# 139 1/2 THALER
Silver **Ruler:** Johann Friedrich I **Rev:** Crowned 4-fold arms in heart-shaped shield, date in legend

Date	Mintage	VG	F	VF	XF	Unc
1623	—	325	650	1,300	2,600	—
1624 CT	—	325	650	1,300	2,600	—

KM# 137 1/2 THALER
Silver **Ruler:** Johann Friedrich I **Obv:** Crowned oval 4-fold arms in baroque frame **Rev:** St. Christopher left, with child Jesus on shoulder divides date **Note:** Exists in numerous multiple weight strikes ranging from 19.85 to 55.19 grams.

Date	Mintage	VG	F	VF	XF	Unc
1623	—	—	—	—	—	—

KM# 151 1/2 THALER
Silver **Ruler:** Johann Friedrich I **Mint:** Christophstal **Note:** Klippe 1/2 Thaler.

Date	Mintage	VG	F	VF	XF	Unc
1624CT	—	1,000	1,800	3,500	—	—

KM# 164 1/2 THALER
Silver **Ruler:** Johann Friedrich I **Rev:** Crowned 4-fold arms in oval baroque frame, mermaid at each side **Mint:** Christophstal

Date	Mintage	VG	F	VF	XF	Unc
1625CT (b)	—	400	800	1,600	3,150	—

KM# 180 1/2 THALER
14.3400 g., Silver **Ruler:** Ludwig Friedrich

Date	Mintage	VG	F	VF	XF	Unc
1629	—	525	1,000	2,000	4,000	—

KM# 188 1/2 THALER
14.1700 g., Silver **Ruler:** Julius Friedrich **Obv:** 1/2-length figure of Julius Friedrich right **Rev:** Crowned 4-fold arms, date in legend

Date	Mintage	VG	F	VF	XF	Unc
1631 Rare	—	—	—	—	—	—

KM# 209 1/2 THALER
Silver **Ruler:** Eberhard III **Obv:** Facing bust turned slightly right **Rev:** Crowned 4-fold arms in oval baroque frame, angel's head at top and bottom, date divided above crown **Note:** Weight varies 14.32-14.55 grams.

Date	Mintage	VG	F	VF	XF	Unc
1648 Rare	—	—	—	—	—	—

KM# 217 1/2 THALER
Silver **Ruler:** Eberhard III **Obv:** Bust right **Rev:** Crowned heart-shaped oval 4-fold arms divide date

Date	Mintage	VG	F	VF	XF	Unc
1659 Rare	—	—	—	—	—	—

KM# 245 1/2 THALER
Silver **Ruler:** Friedrich Karl **Rev:** Crowned 4-fold arms in laurel wreath, date divided in legend neart top **Mint:** Stuttgart **Note:** Weight varies 14.53-14.58 grams.

Date	Mintage	VG	F	VF	XF	Unc
1681 M	—	1,200	2,250	4,000	7,250	—
1681 ICM	—	1,200	2,250	4,000	7,250	—

KM# 262 1/2 THALER

Silver **Ruler:** Eberhard Ludwig **Rev:** Crowned 4-fold arms, date divided below **Mint:** Stuttgart **Note:** Weight varies 14.54-14.62 grams.

Date	Mintage	VG	F	VF	XF	Unc
1694 IDD/IIW	—	225	475	900	1,800	—

KM# 263 1/2 THALER

Silver **Ruler:** Eberhard Ludwig **Rev:** Arms between 2 palm branches **Mint:** Stuttgart **Note:** Weight varies 14.56-14.69 grams.

Date	Mintage	VG	F	VF	XF	Unc
1694 *	—	225	475	900	1,800	—
1694 IDD/IIW	—	225	475	900	1,800	—

KM# 271 1/2 THALER

Silver **Ruler:** Eberhard Ludwig **Rev:** R.N. date below arms **Note:** Weight varies 14.53-14.57 grams.

Date	Mintage	VG	F	VF	XF	Unc
MDCXCV (1695)	—	325	625	1,250	2,500	—

KM# 277 1/2 THALER

Silver **Ruler:** Eberhard Ludwig **Rev:** 3 helmets above arms **Mint:** Stuttgart

Date	Mintage	VG	F	VF	XF	Unc
1699 IIW	—	—	—	—	—	—

Note: Reported, not confirmed

KM# 10 THALER

0.8889 Silver **Ruler:** Friedrich I **Obv:** Helmeted arms **Obv. Legend:** FRIDERICVS. D.G. DVX. WIRTEMBERG. **Rev:** St. Christopher with staff and shield, Christ child on shoulder, date in cartouche below **Rev. Legend:** RVDOLPH. II. IMP. AVG. P. F. DECRETO. **Note:** Dav. #7826.

Date	Mintage	VG	F	VF	XF	Unc
1605 Rare	—	—	—	—	—	—

KM# 14 THALER

Silver **Ruler:** Friedrich I **Obv:** Figure changed, shield held higher **Note:** Dav. #7827.

Date	Mintage	VG	F	VF	XF	Unc
1606	—	1,350	2,500	4,500	8,500	16,500

KM# 20 THALER

Silver **Ruler:** Friedrich I **Obv:** Date below St. Christopher, Christ child on left shoulder **Rev:** Date divided by shield below **Note:** Dav. #7828.

Date	Mintage	VG	F	VF	XF	Unc
1607/1607	—	1,500	3,000	5,500	9,500	17,500

KM# 21 THALER

Silver **Ruler:** Friedrich I **Obv:** Without date **Note:** Dav. #7828A.

Date	Mintage	VG	F	VF	XF	Unc
1607	—	2,100	3,850	7,000	—	—

KM# 27 THALER

Silver **Ruler:** Johann Friedrich I **Obv:** Date divided by shield below **Rev:** St. Christopher with cloak flying behind **Note:** Dav. #7829.

Date	Mintage	VG	F	VF	XF	Unc
1608	—	1,900	4,750	7,400	—	—

KM# 28 THALER

Silver **Ruler:** Johann Friedrich I **Obv:** Larger St. Christopher and Christ child **Rev:** Helmeted arms, date in legend **Rev. Legend:** IOHANN: FRID. D.G. DUX... **Note:** Dav. #7831.

Date	Mintage	VG	F	VF	XF	Unc
1608	—	1,450	3,600	5,900	9,000	—
1609	—	1,450	3,600	5,900	9,000	—
1610	—	1,450	3,600	5,900	9,000	—

KM# 30 THALER

Silver **Ruler:** Johann Friedrich I **Rev:** Legend without rosettes **Note:** Dav. #7832.

Date	Mintage	VG	F	VF	XF	Unc
1609	—	1,200	2,400	3,950	—	—

KM# 44 THALER

Silver **Ruler:** Johann Friedrich I **Obv:** Bust right **Rev:** Helmeted arms, date at 5 o'clock **Rev. Legend:** COM: MONT: DOM: IN: HEIDENHE **Note:** Dav. #7834.

Date	Mintage	VG	F	VF	XF	Unc
1612	—	850	1,700	3,150	5,300	—

KM# 47 THALER

Silver **Ruler:** Johann Friedrich I **Rev:** Legend begins at 1 o'clock, date at upper left **Rev. Legend:** COM: ... **Note:** Dav. #7837.

Date	Mintage	VG	F	VF	XF	Unc
1613	—	850	1,700	3,150	5,300	—
1614	—	850	1,700	3,150	5,300	—
1615	—	850	1,700	3,150	5,300	—
1616 Rare	—	—	—	—	—	—

Note: Meister & Sonntag Auction 4, 10-06, VF realized approximately $13,165.

KM# 52 THALER

Silver **Ruler:** Johann Friedrich I **Obv:** Bust right, legend in diamond shape **Rev:** Crowned ams divide date, legend in diamond shape **Note:** Dav. #7838. Klippe Thaler.

Date	Mintage	VG	F	VF	XF	Unc
1617 Rare	—	—	—	—	—	—

KM# 55 THALER

Silver **Ruler:** Johann Friedrich I **Obv. Legend:** IOHANN: FRID: ... **Rev:** Crowned arms, date in legend **Note:** Dav. #7842.

Date	Mintage	VG	F	VF	XF	Unc
1620	—	1,050	2,050	3,750	6,300	—
1621	—	1,050	2,050	3,750	6,300	—
1622	—	1,050	2,050	3,750	6,300	—

KM# 77 THALER

Silver **Ruler:** Johann Friedrich I **Obv. Legend:** IOH:FRI:... **Note:** Dav. #7844.

Date	Mintage	VG	F	VF	XF	Unc
1621	—	1,050	2,050	3,750	6,300	—

KM# 112 THALER

Silver **Ruler:** Johann Friedrich I **Obv. Legend:** IOHANN: FRID: D: G: DUX... **Note:** Dav. #7848.

Date	Mintage	VG	F	VF	XF	Unc
1622	—	1,050	2,050	3,750	6,300	—

KM# 113 THALER

Silver **Ruler:** Johann Friedrich I **Note:** Dav. #7848A. Klippe Thaler.

Date	Mintage	VG	F	VF	XF	Unc
1622 Rare	—	—	—	—	—	—

KM# 140 THALER

Silver **Ruler:** Johann Friedrich I **Obv. Legend:** FRIDER: D: G: DUX. WIRTENB. ET. TEC **Rev:** Crowned oval arms with mermaids at sides, C-T and cherub head below **Note:** Dav. #7850.

Date	Mintage	VG	F	VF	XF	Unc
1623	—	625	1,250	2,750	5,000	—

KM# 141 THALER

Silver **Ruler:** Johann Friedrich I **Obv. Legend:** ... FRID ... WIRTEMB: ET. TECC: **Note:** Dav. #7850A.

Date	Mintage	VG	F	VF	XF	Unc
1623	—	625	1,250	2,750	5,000	—

KM# 143 THALER

Silver **Ruler:** Johann Friedrich I **Obv. Legend:** IOHAN. FRIDERICH... **Note:** Dav. #7850B.

Date	Mintage	VG	F	VF	XF	Unc
1623	—	625	1,250	2,750	5,000	—

KM# 144 THALER

Silver **Ruler:** Johann Friedrich I **Obv:** Without S below bust **Note:** Dav. #7850C.

Date	Mintage	VG	F	VF	XF	Unc
1623	—	625	1,250	2,750	5,000	—

KM# 142 THALER

Silver **Ruler:** Johann Friedrich I **Note:** Dav. #7850D. Klippe Thaler.

Date	Mintage	VG	F	VF	XF	Unc
1623 Rare	—	—	—	—	—	—

KM# 145 THALER

Silver **Ruler:** Johann Friedrich I **Obv:** Bust right, S behind head **Obv. Legend:** IOHANN: FRID...TECC **Rev:** Crowned, unsupported arms in frame **Rev. Legend:** ...HEIDENHEM **Note:** Dav. #7851.

Date	Mintage	VG	F	VF	XF	Unc
1623	—	550	1,150	2,250	3,750	—
1624	—	550	1,150	2,250	3,750	—

KM# 155 THALER

Silver **Ruler:** Johann Friedrich I **Rev:** Mermaid above small oval helmeted arms, C-T below **Note:** Dav. #7853.

Date	Mintage	VG	F	VF	XF	Unc
1624	—	550	1,150	2,250	3,750	—

KM# 156 THALER

Silver **Ruler:** Johann Friedrich I **Obv:** New bust right **Obv. Legend:** IOHANN: FRIDER:...TEC **Rev:** Flat topped shield, C-T at sides **Note:** Dav. #7854.

Date	Mintage	VG	F	VF	XF	Unc
1624	—	500	1,000	2,000	3,500	—

KM# 157 THALER

Silver **Ruler:** Johann Friedrich I **Obv:** Bust right **Obv. Legend:** IOHANN: FRID: ... TECC **Rev:** Crowned oval supported arms, C-T at sides **Note:** Dav. #7855.

Date	Mintage	VG	F	VF	XF	Unc
1624	—	500	1,000	2,000	3,500	—

KM# 158 THALER

Silver **Ruler:** Johann Friedrich I **Obv:** Bust right **Obv. Legend:** ET. TEC **Note:** Dav. #7856.

Date	Mintage	VG	F	VF	XF	Unc
1624	—	600	1,200	2,500	4,000	—
1625	—	600	1,200	2,500	4,000	—

KM# 159 THALER

Silver **Ruler:** Johann Friedrich I **Obv. Legend:** IOHANN.FRIDER: D: G: DUX. WIRTEN: **Rev:** Crowned oval arms with or without C-T **Note:** Dav. #7859.

Date	Mintage	VG	F	VF	XF	Unc
1624	—	500	1,000	2,000	3,500	—
1625	—	500	1,000	2,000	3,500	—

KM# 165 THALER

Silver **Ruler:** Johann Friedrich I **Obv. Legend:** IOHANN: FRID: D: G: DUX. WIRTEMBERG:... **Rev:** Crowned arms with fancy shield **Note:** Dav. #7862.

Date	Mintage	VG	F	VF	XF	Unc
1625	—	500	1,000	2,000	3,500	—
1626/5	—	500	1,000	2,000	3,500	—
1626	—	500	1,000	2,000	3,500	—

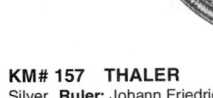

KM# 166 THALER

Silver **Ruler:** Johann Friedrich I **Obv:** Bust right with angel heads in corners **Rev:** St. Christopher wading in water with staff and Christ child, date in Roman numerals below, arms in 4 corners **Note:** Dav. #7864. Klippe Thaler.

Date	Mintage	VG	F	VF	XF	Unc
1625 Rare	—	—	—	—	—	—

KM# 173 THALER

Silver **Ruler:** Johann Friedrich I **Rev:** Crowned supported oval arms **Note:** Dav. #7866.

Date	Mintage	VG	F	VF	XF	Unc
1626	—	1,000	2,000	3,500	—	—
1627	—	1,000	2,000	3,500	—	—
1628 Rare	—	—	—	—	—	—

KM# 176 THALER

Silver **Ruler:** Ludwig Friedrich **Obv:** Bust right **Obv. Legend:** LVDOVIC. FRID: D: G: ... **Rev:** Helmeted arms, date divided below **Rev. Legend:** DO: IN. HAIDEN: DVRAT & ADMINISTRATOR **Note:** Dav. #7867.

Date	Mintage	VG	F	VF	XF	Unc
1628 Rare	—	—	—	—	—	—

KM# 181 THALER

Silver **Ruler:** Ludwig Friedrich **Rev:** Mermaid above helmeted arms, date in legend **Note:** Dav. #7868.

Date	Mintage	VG	F	VF	XF	Unc
1629 Rare	—	—	—	—	—	—

Note: Auktionshaus Meister & Sonntag Auction 4, 10-06, VF-XF realized approximately $15,685

KM# 189 THALER

Silver **Ruler:** Julius Friedrich **Obv:** 1/2 figure right **Obv. Legend:** IVLIVS. FRIDERICVS... **Rev:** Helmeted arms, date **Rev. Legend:** CVRATOR.ET... **Note:** Dav. #7869.

Date	Mintage	VG	F	VF	XF	Unc
1631 Rare	—	—	—	—	—	—

Note: Auktionshaus Meister & Sonntag Auction 4, 10-06, VF-XF realized approximately $15,685

KM# 201 THALER

Silver **Ruler:** Eberhard III **Obv:** Facing bust **Obv. Legend:** EBERHARD... **Rev:** Crowned arms with date divided above **Note:** Dav. #7870.

Date	Mintage	VG	F	VF	XF	Unc
1640 Rare	—	—	—	—	—	—

Note: Auktionshaus Meister & Sonntag Auction 4, 10-06, XF realized approximately $20,705

Date	Mintage	VG	F	VF	XF	Unc
1644 Rare	—	—	—	—	—	—

KM# 204 THALER

Silver **Ruler:** Eberhard III **Obv:** Facing bust with long hair **Rev:** Helmeted arms with date divided in helmets **Note:** Dav. #7871.

Date	Mintage	VG	F	VF	XF	Unc
1645 Rare	—	—	—	—	—	—

KM# 206 THALER

Silver **Ruler:** Eberhard III **Obv:** Larger facing bust with mustache and curly hair **Rev:** Crowned oval arms with date below crown **Note:** Dav. #7872.

Date	Mintage	VG	F	VF	XF	Unc
1647 Rare	—	—	—	—	—	—

KM# 218 THALER

Silver **Ruler:** Eberhard III **Rev:** Crowned arms divide date below, angel heads above and below arms **Note:** Dav. #7873.

Date	Mintage	VG	F	VF	XF	Unc
1659 Rare	—	—	—	—	—	—
1660 Rare	—	—	—	—	—	—

Note: Fritz Rudolf Künker Münzenhandlung Auction 100, 6-05, XF realized approximately $13,955

KM# 226 THALER

Silver **Ruler:** Eberhard III **Obv:** Bust with longer hair right **Rev:** St. Christopher in water with Christ child on right shoulder, shield in front **Note:** Dav. #7874.

Date	Mintage	VG	F	VF	XF	Unc
1669 Rare	—	—	—	—	—	—

KM# 230 THALER

Silver **Ruler:** Eberhard III **Obv:** Bust right **Rev:** Capped arms in wreath **Rev. Legend:** 16. OMNIA. CVM. DEO. 70 **Note:** Dav. #7875.

Date	Mintage	VG	F	VF	XF	Unc
1670 Rare	—	—	—	—	—	—

KM# 234 THALER

Silver **Ruler:** Wilhelm Ludwig **Obv. Legend:** WILH.LUD **Rev:** Capped arms in wreath **Rev. Legend:** 16 IN. DEO. SPES. MEA. 77 **Mint:** Stuttgart **Note:** Dav. #7876.

Date	Mintage	VG	F	VF	XF	Unc
1677 ICM Rare	—	—	—	—	—	—

Note: Auktionshaus Meister & Sonntag Auction 4, 10-06, good XF realized approximately $22,590

KM# 235 THALER

Silver **Ruler:** Wilhelm Ludwig **Subject:** Death of Wilhelm Ludwig **Rev:** 11-line inscription **Mint:** Stuttgart **Note:** Dav. #7877.

Date	Mintage	VG	F	VF	XF	Unc
1677 ICM Rare	—	—	—	—	—	—

Note: Auktionhaus Meistor & Sonntag Auction 8, 10-09, XF realized approximately $14,810

KM# 243 THALER

Silver **Ruler:** Friedrich Karl **Obv. Legend:** FRID: CAROL D: DG... **Rev:** Capped arms in wreath, 1.6. D.P.F. 80 above **Note:** Dav. #7878.

Date	Mintage	VG	F	VF	XF	Unc
1680 Rare	—	—	—	—	—	—

Note: Auktionshaus Meister & Sonntag Auction 4, 10-06, XF realized approximately $18,195

KM# 264 THALER

Silver **Ruler:** Eberhard Ludwig **Obv. Legend:** EBERH. LUD.-D.G... **Rev:** Capped arms, date divided below **Rev. Legend:** CUM \ DEO ET DIE **Mint:** Stuttgart **Note:** Dav. #7880.

Date	Mintage	VG	F	VF	XF	Unc
1694 IDD/IIW	—	750	1,520	3,000	5,000	—

KM# 265 THALER

Silver **Ruler:** Eberhard Ludwig **Rev:** Capped arms in palm sprays **Mint:** Stuttgart **Note:** Dav. #7881.

Date	Mintage	VG	F	VF	XF	Unc
1694 PHM/IIW	—	650	1,350	2,750	4,500	—

KM# 266 THALER

Silver **Ruler:** Eberhard Ludwig **Rev:** Capped flat topped arms with IL-W at sides, date divided below **Mint:** Stuttgart **Note:** Dav. #7882.

Date	Mintage	VG	F	VF	XF	Unc
1694 PHM/IIW	—	675	1,400	2,850	4,750	—

KM# 272 THALER

Silver **Ruler:** Eberhard Ludwig **Rev:** Helmeted arms, date in R.N. divided below **Mint:** Stuttgart **Note:** Dav. #7884.

Date	Mintage	VG	F	VF	XF	Unc
MDCXCVII (1697) IIW	—	500	1,000	2,000	4,000	12,500

KM# 146 1-1/2 THALER

Silver **Ruler:** Johann Friedrich I **Obv:** Crowned oval shield **Obv. Legend:** IOHANN FRID: D: G:... **Rev:** St. Christopher holding Christ child dividing date **Note:** Dav. #7852A.

Date	Mintage	VG	F	VF	XF	Unc
1623 Rare	—	—	—	—	—	—

KM# 11 2 THALER

Silver **Ruler:** Friedrich I **Obv:** St. Christopher with staff and shield, Christ child on shoulder, date in cartouche below **Obv. Legend:** RVDOLPH. II. IMP. AVG ... **Rev:** Helmeted arms **Rev. Legend:** FRIDERICVS. D. G. ... **Note:** Dav. #7825.

Date	Mintage	VG	F	VF	XF	Unc
1605 Rare	—	—	—	—	—	—

KM# 40 2 THALER

Silver **Ruler:** Johann Friedrich I **Obv:** Large St. Christopher and Christ child **Rev:** Helmeted arms, date in legend **Rev. Legend:** IOHANN: FRID. D. G. DUX ... **Note:** Dav. #7830.

Date	Mintage	VG	F	VF	XF	Unc
1610 Rare	—	—	—	—	—	—

KM# 45 2 THALER

Silver **Ruler:** Johann Friedrich I **Obv:** Bust right **Obv. Legend:** IOHANN: FRID: D: G:... **Rev:** Helmeted arms **Rev. Legend:** COM: MONT: DOM:... **Note:** Dav. #7833.

Date	Mintage	VG	F	VF	XF	Unc
1612 Rare	—	—	—	—	—	—

KM# 48 2 THALER

Silver **Ruler:** Johann Friedrich I **Rev:** Legend begins at 1 o'clock, date at upper left **Rev. Legend:** COM: ... **Note:** Dav. #7836. Similar to 1 Thaler, KM#47.

Date	Mintage	VG	F	VF	XF	Unc
1613 Rare	—	—	—	—	—	—
1614 Rare	—	—	—	—	—	—
1615 Rare	—	—	—	—	—	—
1616 Rare	—	—	—	—	—	—

KM# 56 2 THALER

Silver **Ruler:** Johann Friedrich I **Obv. Legend:** IOHANN: FRID: ... **Rev:** Crowned arms, date in legend **Note:** Dav. #7841.

Date	Mintage	VG	F	VF	XF	Unc
1620 Rare	—	—	—	—	—	—
1621 Rare	—	—	—	—	—	—
1622 Rare	—	—	—	—	—	—

KM# 57 2 THALER

Silver **Ruler:** Johann Friedrich I **Note:** Dav. #7841A. Klippe 2 Thaler.

Date	Mintage	VG	F	VF	XF	Unc
1620 Rare	—	—	—	—	—	—

KM# 78 2 THALER

Silver **Ruler:** Johann Friedrich I **Obv:** Bust right **Obv. Legend:** IOH: FRI: D. G:... **Rev:** Crowned shield **Rev. Legend:** COM: MONT: DOM:... **Note:** Dav. #7843.

Date	Mintage	VG	F	VF	XF	Unc
1621 Rare	—	—	—	—	—	—

Note: Auktionhaus Meister & Sonntag Auction 4, 10-06, VF realized approximately $10,030

KM# 114 2 THALER

Silver **Ruler:** Johann Friedrich I **Obv:** Bust right, S below **Obv. Legend:** IOHANN: FRID:...WIRTEMBERG... **Rev:** Crowned arms **Note:** Dav. #7847.

Date	Mintage	VG	F	VF	XF	Unc
1622 Rare	—	—	—	—	—	—
1623 Rare	—	—	—	—	—	—

KM# 115 2 THALER

Silver **Ruler:** Johann Friedrich I **Obv. Legend:** ...WIRTEMB:... **Note:** Dav. #7847A.

Date	Mintage	VG	F	VF	XF	Unc
1622 Rare	—	—	—	—	—	—

KM# 147 2 THALER

Silver **Ruler:** Johann Friedrich I **Obv:** Bust right, date below legend **Obv. Legend:** IOH: FRI: D: G:... **Rev:** Helmeted arms **Rev. Legend:** COMES + MONT: DOM:... **Note:** Dav. #7849.

Date	Mintage	VG	F	VF	XF	Unc
1623 Rare	—	—	—	—	—	—

KM# 149 2 THALER

Silver **Ruler:** Johann Friedrich I **Obv:** Crowned oval shield **Obv. Legend:** IOHANN: FRID:... **Rev:** St. Christopher holding Christ child dividing date **Note:** Dav. #7852.

Date	Mintage	VG	F	VF	XF	Unc
1623 Rare	—	—	—	—	—	—

KM# 148 2 THALER

Silver **Ruler:** Johann Friedrich I **Obv. Legend:** FRIDER: D: G: DUX. WIRTENB. ET. TEC. **Rev:** Crowned oval arms with mermaids at sides, C-T and cherub head below **Note:** Dav. #A7850.

Date	Mintage	VG	F	VF	XF	Unc
1623 Rare	—	—	—	—	—	—

KM# 168 2 THALER

Silver **Ruler:** Johann Friedrich I **Note:** Dav. #7858A. Klippe 2 Thaler.

Date	Mintage	VG	F	VF	XF	Unc
1624 Rare	—	—	—	—	—	—

KM# 169 2 THALER

Silver **Ruler:** Johann Friedrich I **Obv. Legend:** IOHANN: FRID: D: G: DUX. WIRTEMBERG ... **Rev:** Crowned arms with fancy shield **Note:** Dav. #7861.

Date	Mintage	VG	F	VF	XF	Unc
1625 Rare	—	—	—	—	—	—

KM# 170 2 THALER

Silver **Ruler:** Johann Friedrich I **Obv:** Bust right with angel heads in corners **Rev:** St. Christopher wading in water with staff and Christ child, date in R.N. below, arms in 4 corners **Note:** Dav. #7863. Klippe.

Date	Mintage	VG	F	VF	XF	Unc
1625 DS Rare	—	—	—	—	—	—

KM# 167 2 THALER

Silver **Ruler:** Johann Friedrich I **Obv. Legend:** IOHANN. FRIDER: D: G: DUX. WIRTEN: **Rev:** Crowned oval arms with or without C-T **Note:** Dav. #7858.

Date	Mintage	VG	F	VF	XF	Unc
1625 Rare	—	—	—	—	—	—

KM# 174 2 THALER

Silver **Ruler:** Johann Friedrich I **Obv:** Draped bust right **Rev:** Crowned supported oval arms **Note:** Dav. #7865.

Date	Mintage	VG	F	VF	XF	Unc
1626 Rare	—	—	—	—	—	—

KM# 267 2 THALER

Silver **Ruler:** Eberhard Ludwig **Obv:** Bust right, IDD below **Obv. Legend:** EBERH. LUD... **Rev:** Capped arms, date and IIW below **Mint:** Stuttgart **Note:** Dav. #7879.

Date	Mintage	VG	F	VF	XF	Unc
1694 IDD/IIW Rare	—	—	—	—	—	—

KM# 273 2 THALER

Silver **Ruler:** Eberhard Ludwig **Obv:** Bust right **Rev:** Helmeted arms, date in Roman numerals divided below **Mint:** Stuttgart **Note:** Dav. #7883.

Date	Mintage	VG	F	VF	XF	Unc
1697 IIW Rare	—	—	—	—	—	—

KM# 49 3 THALER

Silver **Ruler:** Johann Friedrich I **Obv:** Bust right in inner circle **Rev:** Crowned 4-fold arms, date at upper left **Note:** Dav. #7835.

Date	Mintage	VG	F	VF	XF	Unc
1613 Rare	—	—	—	—	—	—

KM# 58 3 THALER

Silver **Ruler:** Johann Friedrich I **Obv. Legend:** IOHANN: FRID: ... **Rev:** Crowned arms, date in legend **Note:** Dav. #7840.

Date	Mintage	VG	F	VF	XF	Unc
1620 Rare	—	—	—	—	—	—
1621 Rare	—	—	—	—	—	—
1622 Rare	—	—	—	—	—	—

KM# 116 3 THALER

Silver **Ruler:** Johann Friedrich I **Obv:** Bust right, S below **Obv. Legend:** IOHANN: FRID: D: G: DUX. WIRTEMBERG... **Rev:** Crowned arms, date in legend **Note:** Dav. #7846.

Date	Mintage	VG	F	VF	XF	Unc
1622 S Rare	—	—	—	—	—	—
1623 S Rare	—	—	—	—	—	—

KM# 117 3 THALER

Silver **Ruler:** Johann Friedrich I **Obv. Legend:** ...DUX. WIRTEMB: **Note:** Dav. #7846A.

Date	Mintage	VG	F	VF	XF	Unc
1622 Rare	—	—	—	—	—	—

KM# 160 3 THALER

Silver **Ruler:** Johann Friedrich I **Obv:** Draped bust right **Obv. Legend:** IOHANN. FRIDER: D: G: DUX. WIRTEN: **Rev:** Crowned oval arms with or without C-T **Note:** Dav. #7857.

Date	Mintage	VG	F	VF	XF	Unc
1624 Rare	—	—	—	—	—	—

KM# 171 3 THALER

Silver **Ruler:** Johann Friedrich I **Obv:** Draped bust right **Obv. Legend:** IOHANN: FRID: D: G: DUX. WIRTEMBERG: ... **Rev:** Crowned arms with fancy shield **Note:** Dav. #7860.

Date	Mintage	VG	F	VF	XF	Unc
1625 Rare	—	—	—	—	—	—

KM# 59 4 THALER

Silver **Ruler:** Johann Friedrich I **Obv:** Draped bust right in inner circle **Obv. Legend:** IOHANN: FRID: ... **Rev:** Crowned arms, date in legend **Note:** Dav. #7839.

Date	Mintage	VG	F	VF	XF	Unc
1620 Rare	—	—	—	—	—	—
1621 Rare	—	—	—	—	—	—

KM# 79 6 THALER
174.6300 g., Silver **Ruler:** Johann Friedrich I **Obv:** Bust right **Obv. Legend:** IOHANN: FRID: **Rev:** Crowned arms, date in legend

Date	Mintage	VG	F	VF	XF	Unc
1621 Rare	—	—	—	—	—	—

KM# 150 6 THALER
Silver **Ruler:** Johann Friedrich I **Obv:** Bust right, S below **Obv. Legend:** IOHANN: FRID:... **Rev:** Crowned arms, date in legend **Mint:** Stuttgart **Note:** Dav. #7845.

Date	Mintage	VG	F	VF	XF	Unc
1623S Rare	—	—	—	—	—	—

TRADE COINAGE

KM# 15 GOLDGULDEN
3.2470 g., 0.7708 Gold 0.0805 oz. AGW **Ruler:** Friedrich I **Obv:** Armored bust of Friedrich right **Rev:** Arms at center of floriated cross, date in exergue

Date	Mintage	VG	F	VF	XF	Unc
1606	—	1,950	3,600	7,200	21,000	—

KM# 16 GOLDGULDEN
3.5000 g., 0.9860 Gold 0.1109 oz. AGW **Ruler:** Friedrich I **Obv:** Bust right in circle **Rev:** Floriated cross, orb at center, small shield of arms in each angle of cross, date in legend

Date	Mintage	VG	F	VF	XF	Unc
1606	—	2,000	3,850	7,700	14,000	—
1607	—	2,000	3,850	7,700	14,000	—

KM# 31 GOLDGULDEN
3.5000 g., 0.9860 Gold 0.1109 oz. AGW **Ruler:** Johann Friedrich I **Obv:** Bust of Johann Friedrich right **Rev:** Crowned double-headed eagle above arms, date in legend

Date	Mintage	VG	F	VF	XF	Unc
1609 Rare	—	—	—	—	—	—

KM# 51 GOLDGULDEN
3.5000 g., 0.9860 Gold 0.1109 oz. AGW **Ruler:** Johann Friedrich I **Obv:** Armored bust of Johann Friedrich right **Rev:** Cruciform arms with orb at center, date in legend

Date	Mintage	VG	F	VF	XF	Unc
1614 Rare	—	—	—	—	—	—
1620	—	4,400	8,800	16,500	27,500	—
1621	—	4,400	8,800	16,500	27,500	—

KM# 17 2 GOLDGULDEN
6.4940 g., 0.7708 Gold 0.1609 oz. AGW **Ruler:** Friedrich I **Obv:** Armored bust of Friedrich right **Rev:** Arms at center of floriated cross, date in exergue

Date	Mintage	VG	F	VF	XF	Unc
1606 Rare	—	—	—	—	—	—

KM# 60 2 GOLDGULDEN
7.0000 g., 0.9860 Gold 0.2219 oz. AGW **Ruler:** Johann Friedrich I **Obv:** Armored bust of Johann Friedrich right **Rev:** Cruciform arms with orb at center, date in legend **Note:** Thick flan.

Date	Mintage	VG	F	VF	XF	Unc
1620 Rare	—	—	—	—	—	—

KM# 219 1/2 DUCAT
1.7500 g., 0.9860 Gold 0.0555 oz. AGW **Ruler:** Eberhard III

Date	Mintage	VG	F	VF	XF	Unc
ND	—	825	1,650	2,950	4,950	—

KM# 220 1/2 DUCAT
1.7500 g., 0.9860 Gold 0.0555 oz. AGW **Ruler:** Eberhard III **Obv:** Bust right **Rev:** Crowned shield

Date	Mintage	VG	F	VF	XF	Unc
1659	—	1,400	2,950	5,500	9,000	—

KM# 250 1/2 DUCAT
1.7500 g., 0.9860 Gold 0.0555 oz. AGW **Ruler:** Friedrich Karl **Obv:** Head of Friedrich Karl right **Rev:** Crowned arms in palms, date divided at top

Date	Mintage	VG	F	VF	XF	Unc
1688	—	1,250	2,700	4,950	7,900	—

KM# 9 DUCAT
3.5000 g., 0.9860 Gold 0.1109 oz. AGW **Ruler:** Friedrich I **Obv:** Armored 1/2 figure of Friedrich right **Rev:** Crowned double-headed eagle above arms, date in legend

Date	Mintage	VG	F	VF	XF	Unc
1601	—	3,750	7,700	14,000	21,500	—
1603 Rare	—	—	—	—	—	—
1605	—	3,750	7,700	14,000	21,500	—

KM# 80 DUCAT
3.5000 g., 0.9860 Gold 0.1109 oz. AGW **Ruler:** Johann Friedrich I **Obv:** Armored 1/2 figure of Johann Friedrich right

Date	Mintage	VG	F	VF	XF	Unc
1621 Rare	—	—	—	—	—	—

KM# 197 DUCAT
3.5000 g., 0.9860 Gold 0.1109 oz. AGW **Ruler:** Eberhard III **Obv:** Eberhard **Rev:** Crowned arms in cartouche, date divided at top

Date	Mintage	VG	F	VF	XF	Unc
1639	—	1,550	3,100	5,500	9,900	—
1944/39	—	1,550	3,100	5,500	9,900	—
Note: Inverted 6 reads as 9						
1651	—	1,550	3,100	5,500	9,900	—
1659	—	1,550	3,100	5,500	9,900	—
1668	—	1,550	3,100	5,500	9,900	—
1669	—	1,550	3,100	5,500	9,900	—

KM# 246 DUCAT
3.5000 g., 0.9860 Gold 0.1109 oz. AGW **Ruler:** Friedrich Karl **Obv:** Friedrich Karl **Rev:** Crowned arms in branches, date divided at top

Date	Mintage	VG	F	VF	XF	Unc
1681	—	2,300	4,600	8,300	14,500	—
1688	—	2,300	4,600	8,300	14,500	—

KM# 268 DUCAT
3.5000 g., 0.9860 Gold 0.1109 oz. AGW **Ruler:** Eberhard Ludwig **Obv:** Eberhard Ludwig **Rev:** Date in Roman numerals

Date	Mintage	VG	F	VF	XF	Unc
1694	—	750	1,600	3,850	6,400	—
1695	—	750	1,600	3,850	6,400	—
1696	—	750	1,600	3,850	6,400	—

KM# 274 DUCAT
3.5000 g., 0.9860 Gold 0.1109 oz. AGW **Ruler:** Eberhard Ludwig **Rev:** Normal date

Date	Mintage	VG	F	VF	XF	Unc
1697	—	750	1,600	3,850	6,400	—

KM# 190 1-1/4 DUCAT
4.3750 g., 0.9860 Gold 0.1387 oz. AGW **Ruler:** Julius Friedrich **Obv:** Draped bust of Eberhard right in inner circle **Rev:** Crowned oval arms in inner circle, crown divides date at top **Note:** Klippe.

Date	Mintage	VG	F	VF	XF	Unc
1631 Rare	—	—	—	—	—	—

KM# 32 2 DUCAT
7.0000 g., 0.9860 Gold 0.2219 oz. AGW **Ruler:** Johann Friedrich I **Obv:** Armored 1/2 figure of Johann Friedrich right **Rev:** Crowned double-headed eagle above arms, date in legend

Date	Mintage	VG	F	VF	XF	Unc
1609 Rare	—	—	—	—	—	—
1615 Rare	—	—	—	—	—	—

KM# 154 2 DUCAT
7.0000 g., 0.9860 Gold 0.2219 oz. AGW **Ruler:** Johann Friedrich I **Obv:** Johann Friedrich on horseback left **Rev:** Three wreaths

Date	Mintage	VG	F	VF	XF	Unc
1623	—	2,100	4,250	7,300	11,500	—
1624	—	2,100	4,250	7,300	11,500	—

KM# 202 2 DUCAT
7.0000 g., 0.9860 Gold 0.2219 oz. AGW **Ruler:** Eberhard III **Obv:** Armored bust of Eberhard facing in inner circle **Rev:** Crowned oval arms in inner circle, date divided near top of arms

Date	Mintage	VG	F	VF	XF	Unc
1640	—	2,500	5,200	9,400	16,000	—
1644/0	—	2,500	5,200	9,400	16,000	—
1648/4	—	2,500	5,200	9,400	16,000	—
1651	—	2,500	5,200	9,400	16,000	—

KM# 215 2 DUCAT
7.0000 g., 0.9860 Gold 0.2219 oz. AGW **Ruler:** Eberhard III **Obv:** Older armored bust of Eberhard **Rev:** Palm divides 2 birds and date in inner circle

Date	Mintage	VG	F	VF	XF	Unc
1650	—	1,950	3,850	7,200	12,500	—

KM# 247 2 DUCAT
7.0000 g., 0.9860 Gold 0.2219 oz. AGW **Ruler:** Friedrich Karl **Obv:** Armored bust of Friedrich Karl right **Rev:** Crowned arms in branches, date divided at top **Mint:** Stuttgart

Date	Mintage	VG	F	VF	XF	Unc
1681 Rare	—	—	—	—	—	—
1683 ICM Rare	—	—	—	—	—	—

KM# 269 2 DUCAT
7.0000 g., 0.9860 Gold 0.2219 oz. AGW **Ruler:** Eberhard Ludwig **Obv:** Armored bust right **Rev:** Crowned arms in palm branches, date divided at bottom **Mint:** Stuttgart

Date	Mintage	VG	F	VF	XF	Unc
1694 IIW	—	1,650	3,400	8,300	14,000	—

KM# 278 2 DUCAT
7.0000 g., 0.9860 Gold 0.2219 oz. AGW **Ruler:** Eberhard Ludwig **Obv:** Armored draped bust right **Obv. Legend:** EBERH: LUD: D: - G: DUX WURTEMB: **Rev:** Helmeted arms **Rev. Legend:** * CUM DEO ET DIE * **Mint:** Stuttgart

Date	Mintage	VG	F	VF	XF	Unc
1699 IIW	—	1,550	3,050	6,100	11,000	—

KM# 81 2-1/2 DUCAT
8.7500 g., 0.9860 Gold 0.2774 oz. AGW **Ruler:** Johann Friedrich I **Obv:** Armored 1/2 figure of Johann Friedrich right **Rev:** Crowned double-headed eagle above arms, date in legend

Date	Mintage	VG	F	VF	XF	Unc
1621 Rare	—	—	—	—	—	—

KM# 279 3 DUCAT
10.5000 g., 0.9860 Gold 0.3328 oz. AGW **Ruler:** Eberhard Ludwig **Obv:** Armored bust of Eberhard Ludwig right **Rev:** Arms topped by 3 helmets, date divided at bottom **Mint:** Stuttgart

Date	Mintage	VG	F	VF	XF	Unc
1699 IIW Rare	—	—	—	—	—	—

KM# 280 4 DUCAT
14.0000 g., 0.9860 Gold 0.4438 oz. AGW **Ruler:** Eberhard Ludwig **Obv:** Armored bust right **Rev:** Arms topped by 3 helmets, date divided at bottom **Mint:** Stuttgart

Date	Mintage	VG	F	VF	XF	Unc
1699 IIW Rare	—	—	—	—	—	—

KM# 33 5 DUCAT

17.5900 g., 0.9860 Gold 0.5576 oz. AGW **Ruler:** Johann Friedrich I **Obv:** St. Christopher standing facing with child and shield **Rev:** Helmeted arms **Note:** Struck with 1/2 Thaler dies, KM#29.

Date	Mintage	VG	F	VF	XF	Unc
1609 Rare	—	—	—	—	—	—

KM# 42 5 DUCAT

17.5900 g., 0.9860 Gold 0.5576 oz. AGW **Ruler:** Johann Friedrich I **Note:** Similar to 1/4 Thaler, KM#12 but less ornate helmets above arms and St. Christopher walking right.

Date	Mintage	VG	F	VF	XF	Unc
1611 Rare	—	—	—	—	—	—

KM# 50 5 DUCAT

16.7500 g., 0.9860 Gold 0.5310 oz. AGW **Ruler:** Johann Friedrich I **Obv:** Bust right **Rev:** 4-fold arms, 3 helmets above, date in legend

Date	Mintage	VG	F	VF	XF	Unc
1613 Rare	—	—	—	—	—	—

Note: Struck with 1/2 Thaler dies

KM# 210 5 DUCAT

17.3500 g., 0.9860 Gold 0.5500 oz. AGW **Ruler:** Eberhard III **Obv:** Facing bust turned slightly right **Rev:** Crowned 4-fold arms in oval baroque frame, angel's head at top and bottom, date divided above crown **Note:** Struck with 1/2 Thaler dies, KM#209.

Date	Mintage	VG	F	VF	XF	Unc
1648 Rare	—	—	—	—	—	—

KM# 119 10 DUCAT

38.0500 g., 0.9860 Gold 1.2062 oz. AGW **Ruler:** Johann Friedrich I **Obv:** Bust of Johann Friedrich right **Rev:** Crowned arms **Mint:** Stuttgart **Note:** Struck with 2 Thaler dies, KM#114.

Date	Mintage	VG	F	VF	XF	Unc
1622 S Rare	—	—	—	—	—	—

KM# 275 10 DUCAT

34.6200 g., 0.9860 Gold 1.0974 oz. AGW **Ruler:** Eberhard Ludwig **Obv:** Bust of Eberhard Ludwig right **Rev:** Capped arms **Mint:** Stuttgart **Note:** Struck with 1 Thaler dies, KM#272.

Date	Mintage	VG	F	VF	XF	Unc
1697 IIW Rare	—	—	—	—	—	—

KM# 161 20 DUCAT

70.0000 g., 0.9860 Gold 2.2190 oz. AGW **Ruler:** Johann Friedrich I **Obv:** Bust right, S behind head **Obv. Legend:** IOHANN: FRID... TECC **Rev:** Crowned, unsupported arms in frame **Rev. Legend:** HEIDENHEM **Note:** Struck with 1 Thaler dies.

Date	Mintage	VG	F	VF	XF	Unc
1624 S Rare	—	—	—	—	—	—

KM# 162 20 DUCAT

70.0000 g., 0.9860 Gold 2.2190 oz. AGW **Ruler:** Johann Friedrich I **Obv:** Bust of Eberhard Ludwig right **Rev:** Hand from clouds holding imperial banner, legend above **Rev. Legend:** PRO DEO ET IMPERIO

Date	Mintage	VG	F	VF	XF	Unc
ND Rare	—	—	—	—	—	—

KM# 163 30 DUCAT

105.0000 g., 0.9860 Gold 3.3284 oz. AGW **Ruler:** Johann Friedrich I **Obv:** Bust of Eberhard Ludwig right **Rev:** Hand from clouds holding imperial banner, legend above **Rev. Legend:** PRO DEO ET IMPERIO

Date	Mintage	VG	F	VF	XF	Unc
ND Rare	—	—	—	—	—	—

PATTERNS

Including off metal strikes

KM#	Date	Mintage	Identification	Mkt Val
PnA1	ND(ca1501)	—	1/8 Thaler. Copper. Ref. K&R#43a, MB#10.	—
PnA3	ND(1551-56)	—	Kreuzer. Gold. Ref. K&R#115b. MB#78.	—
PnA4	1568 (f)	—	2 Kreuzer. Lead. 4.7600 g. Ref. MB#114.	—
PnA5	1575	—	Goldgulden. Silver. Ref. MB#150. Klippe. Weight varies: 10.09-11.93 g.	—
PnA2	1507//(1587)	—	2 Thaler. Lead. Ref. MB#158.	—
Pn1	1601	—	Ducat. Copper. KM#9.	—
PnAA2	1622	—	60 Kreuzer. Gold. Weight of 4 Ducat.	—
Pn2	1623	—	2 Thaler. Lead. KM#147.	—
Pn3	1631	—	Thaler. Lead. KM#189.	—
Pn4	1688	—	1/2 Ducat. Silver. KM#250.	250
Pn5	ND(1688)	—	1/2 Ducat. Silver. KM#250.	250
Pn6	1688	—	Ducat. Silver. Weight varies 4.49-7.06 grams, KM#246.	—
Pn7	1697	—	Thaler. Lead. KM#272.	—
Pn8	1697	—	Ducat. Silver. 3.3400 g. KM#274.	—
Pn9	1701	—	10 Ducat. Silver. KM#285.	—
Pn10	ND(1701)	—	10 Ducat. Silver. KM#285.	—
Pn11	ND(1701)	—	20 Ducat. Silver. KM#162.	—
Pn12	1706	—	Thaler. Lead. KM#286.	—
Pn13	1706	—	Thaler. Tin. KM#286.	—
Pn14	1716	—	Goldgulden. Silver. KM#301.	100
Pn15	1723	—	Goldgulden. Silver. KM#305.	150
Pn16	1726	—	10 Kreuzer. Lead. KM#310.	—
Pn17	ND(1727)	—	3 Ducat. Silver. KM#311.	375
Pn18	1739	—	Thaler. Pewter. KM#359.	—
Pn19	1740 IT	—	Thaler. Lead. KM#367.	—
Pn20	1740 IT	—	Thaler. Iron. KM#367.	—
Pn21	ND(1740) VS	—	Thaler. Silver. 27.2000 g.	—
Pn22	1741	—	1/2 Kreuzer. Copper. KM#365.	—
Pn23	ND	—	1/2 Gulden. Aluminum.	—
Pn24	1798	—	Thaler. Zinc.	—
Pn25	1798	—	Thaler. Tin.	—
Pn26	1798	—	Thaler. Silver.	—
Pn27	1804 ILW	—	Ducat. Silver. C#136a.	1,200
Pn28	1804 CH	—	Ducat. Silver. C#137.	1,200
Pn29	1808 CH	—	Ducat. Silver. C#155.	1,200
Pn30	1823	—	Gulden. Silver.	2,250
Pn31	1823	—	2 Gulden. Silver.	3,250
Pn32	1824	—	2 Gulden.	—
Pn33	1824	—	10 Gulden. Tin.	—
Pn34	1825	—	10 Gulden. Tin.	—
Pn35	1825 W	—	10 Gulden. Silver. C#200.	1,250
Pn36	1833	—	Thaler. Silver.	6,000
Pn37	1837	—	Gulden. Silver.	—
Pn38	1846	—	2 Thaler. Gold. Marriage of Crown Prince, C#195.	27,500
Pn41	ND(1894)	—	3 Mark. Silver Plated Copper.	—
Pn42	19xxF	—	5 Mark. Copper. Lettered edge.	—
Pn43	1904	—	5 Mark. Silver.	2,500
Pn44	1904F	—	5 Mark. Copper. Y222. Eagle within irregular inner circle, countermarked "N.A.".	—
Pn45	1905	—	5 Mark. Silver.	3,500
Pn46	1905	—	5 Mark. Silver. Beaded rim.	5,500
Pn47	1905F	—	5 Mark. Silver. Lettered edge.	3,500
Pn48	1905F	—	5 Mark. Silver. Reeded edge.	3,500
Pn49	1910F	—	3 Mark. Silver. Irregular "LH" under neck. Y225a.	—
Pn50	1911	—	3 Mark. Silver.	—
Pn53	1911F	—	3 Mark. Silver.	—
Pn51	1911	—	3 Mark. Silver. Busts divide date.	—
Pn52	1911F	—	3 Mark. Aluminum.	—
PnA53	1911F	—	3 Mark. Iron. Aluminum-plated.	—
Pn54	1911F	—	3 Mark. Silver.	—
Pn55	1911F	—	3 Mark. Copper.	—
Pn56	1911F	—	3 Mark. Silver.	—
Pn57	1911F	—	3 Mark. Copper.	—
Pn58	1911F	—	3 Mark. Silver.	3,500
Pn59	1911F	—	3 Mark. Copper.	—
Pn60	1913F	—	2 Mark. Aluminum.	—
Pn61	1913	—	5 Mark. Nickel.	—
Pn62	1916F	—	3 Mark. Aluminum.	6,000
Pn63	1916F	—	3 Mark. Silver.	12,500

WURTTEMBERG-OLS

In 1647, Sylvius Nimrod, the elder son of Duke Julius Friedrich of Württemberg-Weiltingen, married Elisabeth Maria, the only child of the last duke of Münsterberg-Öls in Silesia, Karl Friedrich. The duchy of Öls thus passed to the control of a cadet line of the dukes of Württemberg until nearly the end of the 18th century.

The three surviving sons of Sylvius Nimrod lived under the regency of their mother until 1672, as he had died while they were still young, but then they divided their territory and titles. They established the branches of Württemberg-Öls, Württemberg-Öls-Bernstadt and Württemberg-Öls-Juliusburg. The elder line of Württemberg-Öls became extinct after only one generation and the two younger brothers divided those lands as well. When Bernstadt and Juliusburg died out in 1742 and 1745 respectively, all the Öls territories were reconstituted in the remaining member of the family, Karl Christian Erdmann, nephew of the last Bernstadt duke. He died childless in 1792 and Öls passed to Brunswick-Wolfenbüttel by virtue of his marriage to Friederike, daughter of Friedrich August of that duchy.

RULERS

Sylvius Nimrod, 1647-1664
Sylvius Friedrich, 1664-1697
Christian Ulrich von Bernstadt, 1664-1704
Julius Sigismund von Juliusburg, 1664-1684
Karl von Juliusburg und Bernstadt, 1684-1745

MINT OFFICIALS' INITIALS AND SYMBOLS

Initials	Date	Name
IN	1672-1705	Johann Neidhardt, die-cutter in Öls
(a)= and/or SP	1674-1679	Samuel Pfahler, mintmaster in Öls
FCV	1678-1688	Franz Carl Uhle, warden in Öls
T, IIT	1693-1696 (or 1698)	Johann Justus Tolle, warden
LL	1694-1699	Lukas Laurentius, warden in Öls
CVL	1700-1717	Christian von Loh, warden in Öls

ARMS

Württemberg – refer to that state for pertinent arms.
Silesia – eagle with crescent horizontally on breast.
Öls - eagle.

CROSS REFERENCES

F&S = **Ferdinand Friedensburg and Hans Seger,** *Schlesiens Münzen und Medaillen der neueren Zeit,* **Breslau, 1901.** [reprint Frankfurt/Main, 1976].

J&M = **Norbert Jaschke and Fritz P. Maercker,** *Schlesische Münzen und Medaillen,* **Ihringen, 1985.**

B&E = **Christian Binder and Julius Ebner,** *Württembergische Münz- und Medaillen-Kunde,* **vol. 2, Stuttgart, 1912.**

DUCHY

REGULAR COINAGE

KM# 6 GRöSCHL (3 Pfennig)

0.6500 g., Silver, 16 mm. **Ruler:** Sylvius Friedrich **Obv:** 4-fold arms with central shield of Öls, princely hat above divides date **Rev:** Eagle of Öls in circle **Mint:** Öls **Note:** Ref. F&S#2297, 2304, 2310, 2318, 2326. Varieties exist.

Date	Mintage	VG	F	VF	XF	Unc
1674 SP	—	7.00	15.00	35.00	70.00	—
1675 SP	—	7.00	15.00	35.00	70.00	—
1676 SP	—	7.00	15.00	35.00	70.00	—
1677 SP	—	7.00	15.00	35.00	70.00	—
1678 FCV	—	7.00	15.00	35.00	70.00	—

KM# 35 GRöSCHL (3 Pfennig)

0.7600 g., Silver, 16 mm. **Ruler:** Christian Ulrich **Obv:** Oval 4-fold arms with central shield of Öls in baroque frame supported by mermaid at right, princely hat divides date above **Rev:** Silesian eagle in oval baroque frame, mintmaster's initials below, where present **Mint:** Öls **Note:** Ref. F&S#2363, 2369, 2374, 2377. Varieties exist.

Date	Mintage	VG	F	VF	XF	Unc
1679 FCV	—	7.00	15.00	35.00	70.00	—
1680	—	7.00	15.00	35.00	70.00	—
1681	—	7.00	15.00	35.00	70.00	—
1682	—	7.00	15.00	35.00	70.00	—

KM# 58 GRöSCHL (3 Pfennig)

0.7600 g., Silver, 16 mm. **Ruler:** Christian Ulrich **Obv:** Oval 4-fold arms with central shield of Öls in baroque frame supported by mermaid at right, princely hat divides date above, value '3' in oval at bottom **Rev:** Silesian eagle in oval baroque frame, mintmaster's initials below, where present **Mint:** Öls **Note:** Ref. F&S#2399, 2401, 2403, 2408-09, 2411, 2414-16, 2420, 2424, 2428, 2431-32. Varieties exist.

Date	Mintage	VG	F	VF	XF	Unc
1691	—	5.00	10.00	25.00	55.00	—
1694 LL	—	5.00	10.00	25.00	55.00	—
1695	—	5.00	10.00	25.00	55.00	—
1696	—	5.00	10.00	25.00	55.00	—
1696 LL	—	5.00	10.00	25.00	55.00	—
1697 LL	—	5.00	10.00	25.00	55.00	—
1698 LL	—	5.00	10.00	25.00	55.00	—

Date	Mintage	VG	F	VF	XF	Unc
1698 T	—	5.00	10.00	25.00	55.00	—
1699 LL	—	5.00	10.00	25.00	55.00	—
1700 CVL	—	5.00	10.00	25.00	55.00	—

KM# 59A GRöSCHL (3 Pfennig)

0.6500 g., Silver, 16 mm. **Ruler:** Sylvius Friedrich **Obv:** Oval 4-fold arms with central shield of Öls in baroque frame supported by mermaid at right, princely hat divides date above, value '3' in oval at bottom **Rev:** Silesian eagle in oval baroque frame, mintmaster's initials below **Mint:** Öls **Note:** Ref. F&S#2337, 2343, 2345. Varieties exist.

Date	Mintage	VG	F	VF	XF	Unc
1694 IIT	—	6.00	15.00	30.00	60.00	—
1695 IIT	—	6.00	15.00	30.00	60.00	—
1696 IIT	—	6.00	15.00	30.00	60.00	—

KM# 44 1/2 KREUZER

0.4100 g., Silver, 15 mm. **Ruler:** Christian Ulrich **Obv:** 2 adjacent oval shields of arms, Silesian eagle left, 4-fold arms with central shield of Öls at right, princely hat divides date at top, value 1/2 in cartouche below **Note:** Ref. F&S#2370, 2375, 2378, 2382, 2388. Uniface. Varieties exist.

Date	Mintage	VG	F	VF	XF	Unc
1680	—	7.00	15.00	30.00	50.00	—
1681	—	7.00	15.00	30.00	50.00	—
1682	—	7.00	15.00	30.00	50.00	—
1683	—	7.00	15.00	30.00	50.00	—
1684	—	7.00	15.00	30.00	50.00	—

KM# 36 KREUZER

0.7500 g., Silver, 17 mm. **Ruler:** Christian Ulrich **Obv:** Bust right, value (1) below **Obv. Legend:** CHRI(ST). (V)(U)(L)(R). D.G. D(U)(V)X - W. (T.)(I.) S. O. (&) B. **Rev:** Silesian eagle in oval baroque frame, princely hat divides date above **Rev. Legend:** CO. MON(T). D(O). I. HEI(D). ST(E)(R)(N)(B). (&) M(ED)(ZIB). **Note:** Ref. F&S#2362, 2368, 2376, 2381, 2387, 2390. Varieties exist.

Date	Mintage	VG	F	VF	XF	Unc
1679	—	5.00	10.00	25.00	50.00	—
1680	—	5.00	10.00	25.00	50.00	—
1682	—	5.00	10.00	25.00	50.00	—
1683	—	5.00	10.00	25.00	50.00	—
1684	—	5.00	10.00	25.00	50.00	—
1685	—	5.00	10.00	25.00	50.00	—

KM# 37 KREUZER

Silver **Ruler:** Julius Sigismund **Obv:** Bust right, value (1) below **Obv. Legend:** IULI. SIGM. D G DVX. - W. T. I. S. O. **Rev:** Round shield with Silesian eagle, princely hat divides date above **Rev. Legend:** CO. MONT. DO. I. HEID. STERN & ME. **Note:** Ref. F&S#2441.

Date	Mintage	VG	F	VF	XF	Unc
1679	—	—	—	—	—	—

KM# 66 KREUZER

0.7500 g., Silver, 17 mm. **Ruler:** Christian Ulrich **Obv:** Bust right, value (1) below **Obv. Legend:** D. G. CHRIST. VLR. DUX. - WURT. T. I. S. O. B. **Rev:** Silesian eagle in oval baroque frame, princely hat divides date above **Rev. Legend:** COME(ES). MONTB. DOM. HEIDENH. & M(ED)(ZB). **Note:** Ref. F&S#2407. Varieties exist.

Date	Mintage	VG	F	VF	XF	Unc
1696 LL	—	—	—	—	—	—

KM# 8 3 KREUZER (Groschen)

Silver, 21-22 mm. **Ruler:** Sylvius Friedrich **Obv:** Bust right, value (3) below **Obv. Legend:** SYLVI9 FRID. D. G. - D(V)(U)X. W. T. I. S. O. **Rev:** Silesian eagle in circle, princely hat divides date in margin at top **Rev. Legend:** CO. MON(T). D(O). I. HEID. STER(N). (&)(E.) M(E)(Z)(IB). **Note:** Ref. F&S#2296, 2303, 2309, 2317, 2325. Weight varies: 1.44-1.63 g. Varieties exist.

Date	Mintage	VG	F	VF	XF	Unc
1674 SP	—	6.00	15.00	30.00	60.00	—
1675 SP	—	6.00	15.00	30.00	60.00	—
1676 SP	—	6.00	15.00	30.00	60.00	—
1677 SP	—	6.00	15.00	30.00	60.00	—
1678 FCV	—	6.00	15.00	30.00	60.00	—

KM# 27 3 KREUZER (Groschen)

1.7000 g., Silver, 21 mm. **Ruler:** Christian Ulrich **Obv:** Bust right, value (3) below **Obv. Legend:** CHRISTIAN. VL. D G - DUX. W. T. I. S. O. & B. **Rev:** Silesian eagle in circle, princely hat divides date in margin at top **Rev. Legend:** CO. MONT. DO. I. HEID. STERB. & MEZB. **Note:** Ref. F&S#2353.

Date	Mintage	VG	F	VF	XF	Unc
1678 FCV	—	—	—	—	—	—

KM# 28 3 KREUZER (Groschen)

1.6000 g., Silver, 20 mm. **Ruler:** Julius Sigismund **Obv:** Bust right, value (3) below **Obv. Legend:** IULIUS. SIGISM. D G - DUX. W. T. I. S. O. **Rev:** Silesian eagle in circle, princely hat divides date in margin at top **Rev. Legend:** CO. MONT. DO. I. HEID. STERNB & MEZB. **Note:** Ref. F&S#2437.

Date	Mintage	VG	F	VF	XF	Unc
1678 FCV	—	12.00	25.00	40.00	80.00	—

KM# 59 3 KREUZER (Groschen)

1.4000 g., Silver, 21 mm. **Ruler:** Sylvius Friedrich **Obv:** Bust right, value (3) below **Obv. Legend:** D. G. SYLVI9 FRID. DUX - WURT. TEC. I. S. OLS. **Rev:** Silesian eagle in circle, princely hat divides date in margin at top **Rev. Legend:** COM. MONB. DOM. HEID. STERNB. &. MEDZI(B). **Note:** Ref. F&S#2334, 2342.

Date	Mintage	VG	F	VF	XF	Unc
1693 IIT	—	—	—	—	—	—
1695 IIT	—	—	—	—	—	—

KM# 61 3 KREUZER (Groschen)

1.4500 g., Silver, 21 mm. **Ruler:** Christian Ulrich **Obv:** Bust to right, value (3) below **Obv. Legend:** (D.G.) CHRIST. (U)(V)LR(IC). (—) (D.G.) DUX. (—) W(URT). T. I. S. O. (&) B. **Rev:** Silesian eagle in circle, princely hat divides date in margin at top **Rev. Legend:** COM(ES). MON(T)(B). DOM. I. HEID(ENH). (STE)(R)(N)(B). & M(ED)(ZB). **Note:** Ref. F&S#2402, 2406, 2413, 2423, 2427. Varieties exist. Weight varies 1.45-1.62g.

Date	Mintage	VG	F	VF	XF	Unc
1695 LL	—	10.00	20.00	40.00	80.00	—
1696 LL	—	10.00	20.00	40.00	80.00	—
1698 LL	—	10.00	20.00	40.00	80.00	—

KM# 9 6 KREUZER

Silver, 27 mm. **Ruler:** Sylvius Friedrich **Obv:** Bust right, value (VI) below **Obv. Legend:** SYLVI9 FRID. D.G. DVX. - WIRT. TEC. I. S. OLS. **Rev:** Silesian eagle in circle, princely hat above, date at end of legend **Rev. Legend:** CO. MONT(B). DO. (I.) HEID. STERN. &. ME(D). **Note:** Ref. F&S#2295, 2323. Weight varies: 2.90-3.25 g. Varieties exist.

Date	Mintage	VG	F	VF	XF	Unc
1674 SP	—	8.00	20.00	40.00	85.00	—
1678 SP	—	8.00	20.00	40.00	85.00	—

KM# 29 6 KREUZER

2.8500 g., Silver, 26 mm. **Ruler:** Sylvius Friedrich **Obv:** Bust right, value (VI) below **Obv. Legend:** SYLVI. FRID. D. G. DUX - WURT(EMB). T. I. S. OLS. **Rev:** Silesian eagle in circle, princely hat divides date at top in margin **Rev. Legend:** CO. MONTB. DO(M). I. HEID. STERN(B). & ME(D)ZIBOR. **Note:** Ref. F&S#2324, B&E#56. Varieties exist.

Date	Mintage	VG	F	VF	XF	Unc
1678 FCV	—	—	—	—	—	—
1679 FCV	—	—	—	—	—	—

KM# 30 6 KREUZER

3.3000 g., Silver, 26 mm. **Ruler:** Christian Ulrich **Obv:** Bust right, value (VI) below **Obv. Legend:** CHRISTIAN. UL. D. G. DUX - WURT. T. I. S. OLS. B. **Rev:** Silesian eagle in circle, princely hat divides date at top in margin **Rev. Legend:** CO. MONTB. DO. I. HEID. STERNB. & MEZIBOR. **Note:** Ref. F&S#2352, 2358.

Date	Mintage	VG	F	VF	XF	Unc
1678 FCV	—	—	—	—	—	—
1679 FCV	—	—	—	—	—	—

KM# 31 6 KREUZER

2.6500 g., Silver, 26 mm. **Ruler:** Julius Sigismund **Obv:** Bust right, value (VI) below **Obv. Legend:** IULIUS. SIGISM. D. G. DUX - WURT. T. I. S. OLS. **Rev:** Silesian eagle in circle, princely hat divides date in margin at top **Rev. Legend:** CO. MONTB. DO. I. HEID. STERNB. & MEZ(I)BO(R). **Note:** Ref. F&S#2435-36, 2440. Varieties exist.

Date	Mintage	VG	F	VF	XF	Unc
1678 FCV	—	12.00	25.00	55.00	115	—
1678 SP	—	12.00	25.00	55.00	115	—
1679 FCV	—	12.00	25.00	55.00	115	—

KM# 39 6 KREUZER

3.0000 g., Silver, 26 mm. **Ruler:** Julius Sigismund **Obv:** Bust right, value (VI) below **Obv. Legend:** IULIUS. SIGISM. D. G. DUX - WURT. T. I. S. OLS. **Rev:** Silesian eagle in oval baroque frame, princely hat divides date at top in margin **Rev. Legend:** CO(M). MONTB. DO(M). I. HEID. STERN(B). & ME(D)Z(I)B(R). **Note:** Ref. F&S#2439, 2442. Varieties exist.

Date	Mintage	VG	F	VF	XF	Unc
1679 FCV	—	15.00	35.00	70.00	145	—
1680	—	15.00	35.00	70.00	145	—

KM# 38 6 KREUZER

3.3000 g., Silver, 26 mm. **Ruler:** Christian Ulrich **Obv:** Bust right, value (VI) below **Obv. Legend:** CHRIST(IAN). (V)(U)L(R). D. G. DUX - W(URT). T. I. S. O. & B. **Rev:** Silesian eagle in oval baroque frame, princely hat divides date at top in margin **Rev. Legend:** CO. MONT(B). DO(M). I. HEID. STERN(B). & ME(D)(Z)(IBOR). **Note:** Ref. F&S#2359-61, 2367. Varieties exist.

Date	Mintage	VG	F	VF	XF	Unc
1679	—	12.00	25.00	50.00	100	—
1679 FCV	—	12.00	25.00	50.00	100	—
1680	—	12.00	25.00	50.00	100	—

KM# 10 15 KREUZER

Silver, 30 mm. **Ruler:** Sylvius Friedrich **Obv:** Bust right, value (XV) below **Obv. Legend:** SYLVI9 FRID. D.G. DVX. - WIRT. T. I. S. OLS. **Rev:** Silesian eagle in circle, princely hat above, date at end of legend **Rev. Legend:** CO. MONTB. DO. I. HEID. STERN. &. ME. **Note:** Ref. F&S#2294, 2302. Weight varies: 5.54-6.09g.

Date	Mintage	VG	F	VF	XF	Unc
1674 SP	—	12.00	25.00	55.00	110	—
1675 SP	—	12.00	25.00	55.00	110	—

KM# 14 15 KREUZER

Silver, 30 mm. **Ruler:** Sylvius Friedrich **Obv:** Bust right, value (XV) below **Obv. Legend:** SYLVI9 FRID. D. G. D(V)(U)X. - W(I)(U)RT. T(EC). I. S. OLS. **Rev:** Silesian eagle in circle, princely hat divides date in margin at top **Rev. Legend:** CO(M). MON(T)B. DO(M). (I.) HEID. STERN(B). &. ME(T)(D)(Z)(I)(B)(O)(R). **Note:** B&E#23-30, J&M#162, F&S#2308, 2335. Weight varies: 5.54-6.09 g. Varieties exist.

Date	Mintage	VG	F	VF	XF	Unc
1675 SP	—	12.00	25.00	40.00	85.00	—
1676 SP	—	12.00	25.00	40.00	85.00	—
1676/5 SP	—	12.00	25.00	40.00	85.00	—
1694 IIT	—	12.00	25.00	40.00	85.00	—

KM# 32 15 KREUZER

Silver **Ruler:** Christian Ulrich **Obv:** Bust right, value (XV) below **Obv. Legend:** CHRISTIAN. U. D. G. DUX - WURT. T. I. S. OLS. B. **Rev:** Silesian eagle in circle, princely hat divides date at top in margin **Rev. Legend:** CO. MONTB. DO. I. HEID. STERNB. & MEZIBOR. **Note:** Ref. F&S#2351.

Date	Mintage	VG	F	VF	XF	Unc
1678 FCV	—	12.00	25.00	40.00	85.00	—

KM# 33 15 KREUZER

5.8000 g., Silver, 30 mm. **Ruler:** Julius Sigismund **Obv:** Bust right, value (XV) below **Obv. Legend:** IULIUS. SIGISM. D. G. DUX - WURT. T. I. S. OLS. **Rev:** Silesian eagle in circle, princely hat divides date at top in margin **Rev. Legend:** CO. MONTB. DO. I. HEID. STERNB. & MEZIBOR. **Note:** Ref. F&S#2434.

Date	Mintage	VG	F	VF	XF	Unc
1678 FCV	—	12.00	25.00	40.00	85.00	—

KM# 41 15 KREUZER

5.8000 g., Silver, 30 mm. **Ruler:** Julius Sigismund **Obv:** Bust right, value (XV) below **Obv. Legend:** IULIUS. SIGISM. D. G. DUX - WURT. T. I. S. OLS. **Rev:** Silesian eagle in oval baroque frame, princely hat divides date at top in margin **Rev. Legend:** CO. MONTB. DO. I. HEID. STERNB. & MEZIBOR. **Note:** Ref. F&S#2438.

Date	Mintage	VG	F	VF	XF	Unc
1679 FCV	—	12.00	25.00	40.00	85.00	—

KM# 40 15 KREUZER

Silver **Ruler:** Christian Ulrich **Obv:** Bust right, value (XV) below **Obv. Legend:** CHRIST. VL. D. G. DUX - W. T. I. S. O. & B. **Rev:** Silesian eagle in oval baroque frame, princely hat divides date at top in margin **Rev. Legend:** CO. MONT. DO. I. HEID. STERN. & MEZ. **Note:** Ref. F&S#2357.

Date	Mintage	VG	F	VF	XF	Unc
1679 FCV	—	12.00	25.00	40.00	85.00	—

KM# 60 15 KREUZER

5.7500 g., Silver, 30 mm. **Ruler:** Sylvius Friedrich **Obv:** Bust right, value (XV) below **Obv. Legend:** SYLVI. FRID. D. G. DUX - WURT. TEC. I. S. OLS. **Rev:** Crowned 4-fold arms with central shield of Öls, date divided above **Rev. Legend:** CO. MONB. DOM. HEID. STERNB & MEDZIB. **Note:** Ref. 2336.

Date	Mintage	VG	F	VF	XF	Unc
1694 IIT	—	12.00	250	40.00	85.00	—

KM# 2 1/4 THALER

Silver, 30 mm. **Ruler:** Sylvius Friedrich **Subject:** Shooting Festival in Öls **Obv:** Armored bust to right in circle **Obv. Legend:** SYLVI FRID. D. G. DUX. WIRT. TEC. I. S. OLS. **Rev. Legend:** COM. MONTB. DOM. IN. HEYD. STERNB. METZ. **Rev. Inscription:** SI DEUS / PRO NOBIS / QUIS CONTRA / NOS. IST. KÖ / NIG WORDE / 1662. 5 / IVNY. **Note:** Ref. F&S#2283.

Date	Mintage	VG	F	VF	XF	Unc
1662	—	—	—	—	—	—

KM# 15 1/4 THALER

7.1000 g., Silver, 30 mm. **Ruler:** Sylvius Friedrich **Obv:** Bust right **Obv. Legend:** SYLVI9 FRID. D. G. DUX. WIRT. T. I. S. OLS. **Rev:** 4-fold arms with central shield of Öls in baroque frame, 4 ornate helmets above, date divided among ornaments on top of helmets **Rev. Legend:** CO. MON. DO. I. H - EID. STER. &. ME. **Note:** Ref. F&S#2301.

Date	Mintage	VG	F	VF	XF	Unc
1675 SP-(a)-IN	—	—	—	—	—	—

KM# 22 1/4 THALER

7.1000 g., Silver, 30 mm. **Ruler:** Sylvius Friedrich **Obv:** Bust right **Obv. Legend:** SYLVI9 FRID. D. G. DUX. WIRT. T. I. S. OLS. **Rev:** 4-fold arms with central shield of Öls in baroque frame, 4 ornate helmets above, date divided among ornaments on top of helmets, value '1/4' below arms **Rev. Legend:** CO. MON. DO. I. H - EID. STER. &. ME. **Note:** Ref. F&S#2316.

Date	Mintage	VG	F	VF	XF	Unc
1677 SP (a)	—	—	—	—	—	—

KM# 55 1/4 THALER

6.7500 g., Silver, 31 mm. **Ruler:** Sylvius Friedrich **Subject:** Death of Elizabeth Maria, Widow of Sylvius Nimrod **Obv:** 4-fold arms with central shield, 3 ornate helmets aboe, all in wreath **Obv. Legend:** ELISABET. MARIA. DUCISS. WURTEMBERG. TEC. **Rev:** 8-line inscription with arabesque below, all in wreath **Rev. Legend:** ULTIMA. E. STIRPE. DUC. MONSTERB. OLSN. COM. GLAC. **Rev. Inscription:** NATA. / A 1625 D. XI. MAI. / NUPTA. / 1647. D I. MAII. / DENATA / 1686. D. XVII. MARTII / DULCE. SUI. RELIQ. / MEMORIAM. **Note:** Ref. F&S#2330.

Date	Mintage	VG	F	VF	XF	Unc
1686	—	—	—	—	—	—

KM# 62 1/4 THALER

6.7500 g., Silver, 31 mm. **Ruler:** Sylvius Friedrich **Obv:** Bust right, value [symbol] below, in rhombus with arc at midpoint of each side **Obv. Legend:** D. G. SYLVI' - FRID. DUX. - WURT. TEC. I. S. IL. OLS. **Rev:** Crowned 4-fold arms with central shield of Öls, palm fronts at left and right, all in rhombus with arc at midpoint of each side, date divided at top in margin **Rev. Legend:** COM. MO - NB. DOM. HE - ID. STERNB - &. MEDZIB. **Note:** Ref. F&S#2341.

Date	Mintage	VG	F	VF	XF	Unc
1695 IIT	—	—	—	—	—	—

MB# 23 1/2 THALER

Silver **Ruler:** Sylvius Friedrich **Obv. Legend:** SYLVI9 FRID. D. G. DUX. WIRT. T. I. S. OLS. **Rev:** 4-fold arms with central shield of Öls in baroque frame, 4 ornate helmets above, date divided among ornaments on top of helmets **Rev. Legend:** CO. MON. DO. I. H - EID. STER. &. ME. **Note:** Ref. F&S#2315.

Date	Mintage	VG	F	VF	XF	Unc
1677 SP (a)	—	—	—	—	—	—

KM# 63 1/2 THALER

Silver **Ruler:** Sylvius Friedrich **Obv:** Armored bust to righ **Obv. Legend:** D. G. SYLVI9 FRID. DUX. - WURT. T. I. S. OLS. **Rev:** Crowned 4-fold arms with central shield of Öls between 2 palm branches, date at bottom **Rev. Legend:** COM. MONB. DOM. I. HEID. STERNB. &. MEDZIBOR. **Note:** Ref. F&S#2340.

Date	Mintage	VG	F	VF	XF	Unc
1695 IIT	—	—	—	—	—	—

DAV# 7885 THALER

Silver **Obv:** Bust right **Obv. Legend:** SYLVI FRID. D: G: DUX... **Rev:** Helmeted arms, date divided above, S-P divided below **Rev. Legend:** CO: MON: DO: I. H-EID:...

Date	Mintage	VG	F	VF	XF	Unc
1671 SP Rare	—	—	—	—	—	—

KM# 11 THALER

Silver **Ruler:** Sylvius Friedrich **Obv. Legend:** SYLVIUS. FRIEDERICUS... **Rev. Legend:** CO. MONTB: DOM: I. HE-ID:... **Note:** Dav#7887.

Date	Mintage	VG	F	VF	XF	Unc
1674 SP(a)	—	1,750	3,500	6,500	13,500	—

KM# 16 THALER

Silver **Ruler:** Sylvius Friedrich **Obv:** Without inner circle **Obv. Legend:** SYLVI FRID: D: G: DUX:... **Rev. Legend:** CO: MON: DO.I.H-EID: STER: & ME: **Note:** Dav#7889.

Date	Mintage	VG	F	VF	XF	Unc
1675 SP(a)	—	1,250	2,500	5,000	8,500	—

KM# 17 THALER

Silver **Ruler:** Sylvius Friedrich **Rev:** Changed shield and decoration, larger date **Note:** Dav#7891.

Date	Mintage	VG	F	VF	XF	Unc
1675 SP(a)	—	1,250	2,500	5,000	8,500	—

KM# 20 THALER

Silver **Ruler:** Sylvius Friedrich **Rev:** Date near top **Rev. Legend:** CO: MONT. DO. I. HE-ID. STER & MEZIB: **Note:** Dav#7893.

Date	Mintage	VG	F	VF	XF	Unc
1676 SP(a)	—	1,350	2,700	5,250	8,750	—

KM# 24 THALER

Silver **Ruler:** Sylvius Friedrich **Obv. Legend:** SYLVIUS. FRIDERICUS: D • G. DUX WURT. TEC. IN. SIL: OLS **Rev. Legend:** CO: MONTB. DOM. I. HEIDENH: STERNB: & MEZIBOR **Note:** Dav#7894.

Date	Mintage	VG	F	VF	XF	Unc
1677 SP(a)	—	1,350	2,700	5,250	8,750	—

KM# 25 THALER

Silver **Ruler:** Sylvius Friedrich **Note:** Dav#7894A. 12-sided klippe.

Date	Mintage	VG	F	VF	XF	Unc
1677 SP(a) Rare	—	—	—	—	—	—

KM# 34 THALER

Silver **Ruler:** Sylvius Friedrich **Obv:** Thinner bust right **Rev:** Smaller helmeted arms, date above **Note:** Dav#7895.

Date	Mintage	VG	F	VF	XF	Unc
1678 SP(a) Rare	—	—	—	—	—	—

KM# 42 THALER

Silver **Ruler:** Christian Ulrich **Obv:** Bust right **Obv. Legend:** CHRISTIAN. ULR. D. G. DUX. W. T. I. S. OLS. & B. **Rev:** Helmeted arms, date divided below **Rev. Legend:** DO. I...MEDZIBOR. **Note:** Dav#7900.

Date	Mintage	VG	F	VF	XF	Unc
1679 FCV Rare	—	—	—	—	—	—

Note: Fritz Rudolf Künker Münzenhandlung Auction 131, 10-07, XF realized approximately $21,245

KM# 48 THALER

Silver **Ruler:** Christian Ulrich **Obv:** Bust breaks legend at top **Rev:** Capped arms with date below **Rev. Legend:** ...MEDZIB. **Note:** Dav#7901.

Date	Mintage	VG	F	VF	XF	Unc
1681 Rare	—	—	—	—	—	—

Note: Auktionshaus Meister & Sonntag Auction 2, 9-04, nearly XF realized approximately $17,770; Dr. Busso Peus Nachfolger Auction 379, 4-04, XF-VF realized approximately $10,150

KM# 49 THALER

Silver **Ruler:** Christian Ulrich **Rev:** More scrollwork beside and below shield **Note:** Dav#7901A.

Date	Mintage	VG	F	VF	XF	Unc
1681 Rare	—	—	—	—	—	—

KM# 52 THALER

Silver **Ruler:** Julius Sigismund **Subject:** Death of Julius Sigismund **Rev:** Tree dividing inscription **Note:** Dav#7904.

Date	Mintage	VG	F	VF	XF	Unc
1684	—	1,350	2,750	5,500	10,500	—

KM# 56 THALER

Silver **Ruler:** Sylvius Friedrich **Subject:** Death of Elisabeth Maris, Mother of Sylvius Friedrich **Obv:** Bust left, scrollwork at sides **Rev:** 14-line inscription **Note:** Dav#7896.

Date	Mintage	VG	F	VF	XF	Unc
1686 IN	—	—	—	4,500	8,500	—

Note: Fritz Rudolf Künker Münzenhandlung Auction 135, 1-08, XF-Unc realized approximately $14,795

KM# 57 THALER

Silver **Ruler:** Christian Ulrich **Obv:** Bust right **Obv. Legend:** CHRISTIAN. VLR.-D. G. DUX... **Rev:** Helmeted arms, date above **Rev. Legend:** COM. MONTB. DOM. I. HEID. STERNB. & MEDZIB. **Note:** Dav#7902.

Date	Mintage	VG	F	VF	XF	Unc
1687 Rare	—	—	—	—	—	—

KM# 64 THALER

Silver **Ruler:** Sylvius Friedrich **Obv:** Bust right **Obv. Legend:** D. G. SYLVI FRID. DUX... **Rev:** Crowned arms between palm branches, initials and date below **Note:** Dav#7897.

Date	Mintage	VG	F	VF	XF	Unc
1695 IIT Rare	—	—	—	—	—	—

KM# 65 THALER

Silver **Ruler:** Sylvius Friedrich **Obv:** Bust right without inner circle **Rev:** Helmeted arms, legend, date below **Rev. Legend:** SI DEUS PRO NOBIS AVIS CONTRA NOS **Note:** Dav#7898.

Date	Mintage	VG	F	VF	XF	Unc
1695 IIT Rare	—	—	—	—	—	—

KM# 67 THALER

Silver **Ruler:** Sylvius Friedrich **Subject:** 40th Birthday of Eleonore Charlotte, Wife of Sylvius Friedrich **Obv:** Conjoined busts right **Rev:** DOMINUS-PROVIDEBIT, "Jehovah" in sun above city view, Roman numeral date in exergue **Note:** Dav#7899.

Date	Mintage	VG	F	VF	XF	Unc
1696 IN//IIT Rare	—	—	—	—	—	—

KM# 69 THALER

Silver **Ruler:** Christian Ulrich **Obv:** Bust right **Rev:** Five crowned shields and four monograms with date in center, initials below **Note:** Dav#7903.

Date	Mintage	F	VF	XF	Unc	BU
1697 IN//LL Rare	—	—	—	—	—	—

KM# 12 2 THALER

Silver **Ruler:** Sylvius Friedrich **Note:** Dav#7886. Similar to Thaler, KM#11.

Date	Mintage	VG	F	VF	XF	Unc
1674 SP(a)	—	2,500	4,500	7,500	12,500	—

KM# 18 2 THALER

Silver **Ruler:** Sylvius Friedrich **Note:** Dav#7888. Similar to 1 Thaler, KM#16.

Date	Mintage	VG	F	VF	XF	Unc
1675 SP(a) Rare	—	—	—	—	—	—

KM# 19 2 THALER

Silver **Ruler:** Sylvius Friedrich **Rev:** Larger date, changed shield and decoration **Note:** Dav#7890.

Date	Mintage	VG	F	VF	XF	Unc
1675 Rare	—	—	—	—	—	—

Note: Künker Auction 113, 6-06, XF realized approximately $30,175.

KM# 21 2 THALER

Silver **Rev:** Date higher **Rev. Legend:** CO. MONT...& MEZIB **Note:** Dav#7892.

Date	Mintage	VG	F	VF	XF	Unc
1676 SP(a) Rare	—	—	—	—	—	—

TRADE COINAGE

KM# 53 1/8 DUCAT

0.4375 g., 0.9860 Gold 0.0139 oz. AGW **Ruler:** Christian Ulrich **Obv:** Bust right **Obv. Legend:** CHRIST. VLR. D. G. DUX. W. I. S. O. B. **Rev:** 4-fold arms with central shield of Öls in round baroque frame, date divided by crown at top **Rev. Legend:** CO. MO. D. I. HEID. ST. &. M. **Note:** Ref. J&M#165.

Date	Mintage	VG	F	VF	XF	Unc
1685	—	180	240	325	500	—

KM# 45 1/4 DUCAT

0.8750 g., 0.9860 Gold 0.0277 oz. AGW **Ruler:** Christian Ulrich **Subject:** Death of Anna Elizabeth **Rev:** Bust of Anna Elizabeth right **Note:** Fr#3282.

Date	Mintage	VG	F	VF	XF	Unc
ND(ca.1680)	—	625	1,250	2,200	4,600	—

KM# 54 1/4 DUCAT

0.8750 g., 0.9860 Gold 0.0277 oz. AGW **Ruler:** Christian Ulrich **Obv:** Bust of Christian Ulrich right **Rev:** Crowned arms, crown divides date **Note:** Fr#3279.

Date	Mintage	VG	F	VF	XF	Unc
1685	—	425	875	1,750	3,100	—

KM# 46 1/2 DUCAT

1.7000 g., 0.9860 Gold 0.0539 oz. AGW, 12 mm. **Ruler:** Christian Ulrich **Subject:** Death of Anna Elizabeth von Anhalt-Bernburg, First Wife of Christian Ulrich **Obv:** Bust right **Obv. Legend:** CHRISTIAN. VLR. - D. G. DUX. W. T. I. S. O. B. **Rev:** Bust right **Rev. Legend:** ANNA. ELIS. - DUC. W. T. O. & B. **Note:** Ref. F&S#2365, B&E#74b.

Date	Mintage	VG	F	VF	XF	Unc
ND(1680)	—	—	—	—	—	—

KM# 51 1/2 DUCAT

1.7500 g., 0.9860 Gold 0.0555 oz. AGW **Ruler:** Christian Ulrich **Obv:** Bust of Christian Ulrich right **Rev:** Crowned arms, crown divides date **Note:** Fr#3278.

Date	Mintage	VG	F	VF	XF	Unc
1683	—	550	1,100	2,200	4,050	—

KM# 70 1/2 DUCAT

1.7500 g., 0.9860 Gold 0.0555 oz. AGW **Ruler:** Christian Ulrich **Obv:** Bust of Sybil Marie right **Note:** Klippe. Uniface. Fr#3281.

Date	Mintage	VG	F	VF	XF	Unc
ND	—	975	1,950	3,750	6,600	—

KM# 4 DUCAT

3.5000 g., 0.9860 Gold 0.1109 oz. AGW **Ruler:** Sylvius Friedrich **Subject:** Wedding of Sylvius Friedrich and eleanore Charlotte **Obv:** Bust of Sylvius Friedrich right **Rev:** Bust of Eleanore Charlotte left **Note:** Fr#3275.

Date	Mintage	VG	F	VF	XF	Unc
ND(ca.1672)	—	1,300	2,650	5,300	9,200	—

KM# 13.1 DUCAT

3.5000 g., 0.9860 Gold 0.1109 oz. AGW **Ruler:** Sylvius Friedrich **Obv:** Bust of Sylvius Friedrich right in inner circle **Rev:** Arms topped by four helmets in inner circle, date divided near top **Note:** Fr#3274.1.

Date	Mintage	VG	F	VF	XF	Unc
1674 SP(a)	—	975	1,950	4,050	7,500	—
1675 SP(a)	—	975	1,950	4,050	7,500	—
1676 SP(a)	—	975	1,950	4,050	7,500	—

KM# 13.2 DUCAT

3.5000 g., 0.9860 Gold 0.1109 oz. AGW **Ruler:** Sylvius Friedrich **Obv:** Bust of Sylvius Friedrich right **Rev:** Helmeted arms in inner circle, date divided near toe **Note:** Fr#3274.2.

Date	Mintage	VG	F	VF	XF	Unc
1675 SP(a)	—	975	1,950	4,050	7,500	—

KM# 43 DUCAT

3.5000 g., 0.9860 Gold 0.1109 oz. AGW **Ruler:** Christian Ulrich **Obv:** Bust right in inner circle **Rev:** Arms topped by 4 helmets in inner circle, date divided near top **Note:** Fr#3276.

Date	Mintage	VG	F	VF	XF	Unc
1679	—	1,300	2,600	5,250	9,500	—
1698	—	1,300	2,600	5,250	9,500	—

KM# 47 DUCAT

3.5000 g., 0.9860 Gold 0.1109 oz. AGW, 14 mm. **Ruler:** Christian Ulrich **Subject:** Death of Anna Elisabeth von Anhalt-Bernburg, First Wife of Christian Ulrich **Obv:** Bust right. **Obv. Legend:** CHRIST. VLR. - D. G. DUX. W. T. O. B. **Rev:** Bust right. **Rev. Legend:** ANNA. ELIS. - DUC. W. T. O. & B. **Edge Lettering:** EXTINCTA SUPERSTES. **Note:** Ref. F&S#2364, B&E#74a.

Date	Mintage	VG	F	VF	XF	Unc
ND(1680)	—	—	—	—	—	—

KM# 50 DUCAT

3.5000 g., 0.9860 Gold 0.1109 oz. AGW **Ruler:** Christian Ulrich **Rev:** Crowned arms in inner circle **Note:** Fr#3277.

Date	Mintage	VG	F	VF	XF	Unc
1681	—	1,750	3,500	7,000	11,500	—

KM# 68 DUCAT

3.5000 g., 0.9860 Gold 0.1109 oz. AGW **Ruler:** Christian Ulrich **Rev:** Cruciform arms with shield at center, monograms in angles **Note:** Fr#3280.

Date	Mintage	VG	F	VF	XF	Unc
1696	—	1,400	2,750	5,500	9,600	—

KM# 71 DUCAT

3.5000 g., 0.9860 Gold 0.1109 oz. AGW **Ruler:** Christian Ulrich **Subject:** Wedding of Christian Ulrich and Sophia of Mecklenburg **Obv:** Bust of Christian Ulrich right in inner circle **Rev:** Bust of Sophia left in inner circle **Note:** Fr#3283.

Date	Mintage	VG	F	VF	XF	Unc
ND(ca.1700)	—	1,100	2,300	5,000	9,000	—

KM# 26 2 DUCAT

7.0000 g., 0.9860 Gold 0.2219 oz. AGW **Ruler:** Sylvius Friedrich **Obv:** Bust of Sylvius Friedrich right in inner circle **Rev:** Arms topped by four helmets in inner circle, date divided near top **Note:** Fr#3273.

Date	Mintage	VG	F	VF	XF	Unc
1677 SP(a)	—	3,000	6,000	12,000	20,500	—

PATTERNS

Including off metal strikes

KM#	Date	Mintage	Identification	Mkt Val
Pn1	1662	—	1/4 Thaler. Silver. Ref. B&E#229, KM#2, weight of a 4-3/4 Ducat.	—
Pn3	1679	—	Ducat. Silver. Fr#3276, KM#43.	—
Pn2	ND(1680)	—	Ducat. Silver. Ref. KM#47, B&E#74aa.	—

WURTTEMBERG-WEILTINGEN

Established from the main line of Württemberg dukes in 1608, this branch of the family ruled for about a century. Centered on Weiltingen, about 13 miles (21 km) north-northwest of Nördlingen on the Wörnitz River, the line fell extinct after three generations. The elder son of the first duke married well, however, and inherited the duchy of Öls in Silesia (see Württemberg-Öls). The Weiltingen holdings reverted to Öls upon the death of the last duke in 1705.

RULERS

Julius Friedrich, 1608-1635
Manfred, 1635-1662
Friedrich Ferdinand, 1662-1705

MINT OFFICIALS' INITIALS

Initial	Date	Name
	1622	Joseph Drissler, mintmaster in Brenz (d. 1634)
	1622-23	Johann Georg Kroll, warden in Brenz
P	1622-23	Peter Marcel Pfeiffer, mintmaster
B		Brenz mint

ARMS

Same as Württemberg main line

REFERENCES

K&R = Ulrich Klein and Albert Raff, **Die württembergischen Münzen von 1374-1693**, Stuttgart, 1993.
B&E = Christian Binder and Julius Ebner, **Württembergische Münz- und Medaillen-Kunde**, 2 vols., Stuttgart, 1910-12.

DUCHY

STANDARD COINAGE

KM# 2 1/2 GULDEN
5.2000 g., Silver, 27 mm. **Ruler:** Julius Friedrich **Obv:** Crowned 1/2-length figure of a mermaid **Obv. Legend:** IVLIVS: FRID: D: G. DVX. WIRTE: ET: TEC. **Rev:** Crowned 4-fold arms, 'B' mintmark at left, date at end of legend **Rev. Legend:** COM. MONT: DOM: IN: HEIDEN:. **Mint:** Brenz **Note:** Ref. B&E#5. Kipper coinage.

Date	Mintage	VG	F	VF	XF	Unc
1622 B	—	1,500	2,900	5,600	—	—

KM# 4 30 KREUZER (1/2 Gulden)
Silver, 28-29 mm. **Ruler:** Julius Friedrich **Obv:** Crowned 4-fold arms in baroque frame **Obv. Legend:** IVLIVS. FRID. D. G. DVX. WIR(T). E(T). T. **Rev:** Recumbant stag to left holding in foreleg small round shield of baroque frame with '30' at left, mintmark in field above stag's back, date in exergue **Rev. Legend:** CO. MO. - DO. IN. HEI. **Mint:** Brenz **Note:** Ref. B&E#6-8. Kipper coinage. Weight varies: 4.70-5.20 g. Varieties exist.

Date	Mintage	VG	F	VF	XF	Unc
1622 B	—	675	900	1,400	2,750	—

KM# 5 30 KREUZER (1/2 Gulden)
Silver, 28-29 mm. **Ruler:** Julius Friedrich **Obv:** Crowned 4-fold arms in baroque frame **Obv. Legend:** IVLIVS. FRIDE. D. G. DVX. WIRT. ET. T. **Rev:** Recumbant stag to left holding in foreleg small round shield in baroque frame with '30' at left, mintmark in field above stag's back, date in exergue **Rev. Legend:** CO. MON. D - IN. HAI. **Mint:** Brenz **Note:** Ref. B&E#8a. Kipper coinage. Weight varies: 4.70-5.20 g.

Date	Mintage	VG	F	VF	XF	Unc
1622 B	—	—	—	—	—	—

KM# 7 60 KREUZER (Gulden)
Silver, 33 mm. **Ruler:** Julius Friedrich **Obv:** Crowned 4-fold arms in baroque frame **Obv. Legend:** IVLIVS. FRIDE. D. G. DVX. WIRTEM. ET. TEC. **Rev:** Recumbant stag to left holding in foreleg small round shield in baroque frame with '60' at left, mintmark in field above stag's back, date in exergue **Rev. Legend:** CO. MON. D. - IN. HAI. **Mint:** Brenz **Note:** Ref. B&E#1, 4. Kipper Coinage. Weight varies: 9.00-9.95 g.

Date	Mintage	VG	F	VF	XF	Unc
1622 B	—	—	—	—	—	—

KM# 8 60 KREUZER (Gulden)
Silver, 33 mm. **Ruler:** Julius Friedrich **Obv:** Crowned 4-fold arms in baroque frame **Obv. Legend:** IVLIVS. FRID. D. G. DVX. WIRTEM. ET. TEC. **Rev:** Recumbent stag to left holding in foreleg small round shield in baroque frame with '60' at left, mintmark in field above stag's back, date in exergue **Rev. Legend:** CO. MO. - DO. IN. HEI. **Mint:** Brenz **Note:** Ref. B&E#2-3, 10. Kipper Coinage. Weight varies: 9.00-9.95 g.

Date	Mintage	VG	F	VF	XF	Unc
1622 B	—	275	550	1,100	2,200	—
1623 B-P	—	275	550	1,100	2,200	—

KM# 10 60 KREUZER (Gulden)
Silver, 34 mm. **Ruler:** Julius Friedrich **Obv:** Crowned 4-fold arms in baroque frame **Obv. Legend:** IVLIVS. FRID. D. G. DVX. WIRT. ET. TEC. **Rev:** Recumbent stag to left holding in foreleg small round shield in baroque frame with '60' at left, mintmark in field above stag's back, date in exergue **Rev. Legend:** CO. MO. - DO. IN. HEI. **Mint:** Brenz **Note:** Ref. B&E#10a. Klippe. Kipper coinage.

Date	Mintage	VG	F	VF	XF	Unc
1623 B	—	—	—	—	—	—

KM# 12 120 KREUZER (Doppelgulden)
19.7000 g., Silver, 39 mm. **Ruler:** Julius Friedrich **Obv:** Crowned 4-fold arms in baroque frame **Obv. Legend:** IVLIVS. FRID. D. G. DVX. WIRT. ET. TEC. **Rev:** Value '120' in circle within large baroque frame, stag on each side facing inward, date in exergue divided by (B) **Rev. Legend:** CO. - MO. DO. IN. - HEI. **Mint:** Brenz **Note:** Ref. B&E#9. Kipper coinage.

Date	Mintage	VG	F	VF	XF	Unc
1623 B	—	1,100	2,250	4,500	—	—

WURZBURG

Würzburg is situated on the River Main some 60 miles (100 km) east-southeast of Frankfurt am Main, having been founded during the seventh century. St. Boniface established a bishopric there in 741 and installed the first bishop, St. Burchard. His successors received the right to mint coins in the 11th century. The earliest coins were issued under Bruno von Kärnten (1034-45) and featured a monogram based on his name. This devise usually took the form of a cross with letters attached to the arms. This basic type lasted until the 15th century and was occasionally resurredted after that time. In 1441, the bishop as also invested as the Duke of East Franconia and that title was incorporated into the inscriptions of the episcopal coinage. The bishopric of Würzburg was secularized in 1803 and annexed by Bavaria. Except for the period 1806-14, when it was made into a grand duchy for Archduke Ferdinand of Salzburg and Tuscany, Würzburg remained a part of Bavaria.

RULERS

Julius Echter von Mespelbrunn, 1573-1617
Johann Gottfried I von Aschhausen, 1617-1622
Philipp Adolph von Ehrenberg, 1623-1631
Franz, Graf von Hatzfeld, 1631-1642
Johann Philipp Franz von Schönborn, 1642-1673
Johann Hartmann von Rosenbach, 1673-1675
Peter Philipp von Dernbach, 1675-1683
Konrad Wilhelm von Wertenau, 1683-1684
Johann Gottfried II von Guttenberg, 1684-1698
Johann Philipp II, Frhr. von Greiffenklau-Vollraths, 1699-1719

MINT MARKS

F - Fürth
N - Nürnberg
W - Würzburg

MINT OFFICIALS' INITIALS

Initial	Date	Name
CM	ca. 1610	Christian Maler
CS	1620	Conrad Stutz, mintmaster and die-cutter in Fürth
CS	1632	In Würzburg
CW	1617-19	
IL	ca. 1682	Johann Link
IMW	1693	Johann Michael Wunsch
	1621	Johann Lohrer

MONETARY SYSTEM

3 Drier (Körtling) = 1 Shillinger
7 Shillinger = 15 Kreuzer
28 Shillinger = 1 Guter Gulden
44-4/5 Shillinger = 1 Convention Thaler

REFERENCES

H = Klaus and Rosemarie Helmschrott, **Würzburger Münzen und Medaillen von 1500-1800**, Pfingsten, 1977.
E = Gustave Ewald, **Würzburger Münzen**, Würzburg, 1974.
Sch – Wolfgang Schulten, **Deutsche Münzen aus der Zeit Karls V.**, Frankfurt am Main, 1974.

BISHOPRIC

REGULAR COINAGE

KM# 45 HELLER
Silver **Ruler:** Johann Gottfried **Obv:** Würzburg arms divide date, W above **Note:** Uniface.

Date	Mintage	VG	F	VF	XF	Unc
1622	—	15.00	30.00	65.00	130	—

KM# 46 2 HELLER
Silver **Ruler:** Johann Gottfried **Obv:** Würzburg arms divide date, value II above, W below **Note:** Uniface.

Date	Mintage	VG	F	VF	XF	Unc
1622	—	16.00	33.00	75.00	155	—

KM# 47 3 HELLER
Silver, 17 mm. **Ruler:** Johann Gottfried **Obv:** Würzburg arms in ornamented shield, W divides date above **Rev:** III in wreath of palm branches

Date	Mintage	VG	F	VF	XF	Unc
1622	—	10.00	25.00	55.00	110	—
ND(1622-3)	—	10.00	25.00	55.00	110	—

KM# 53 3 HELLER
Silver **Ruler:** Philipp Adolph **Obv:** Würzburg arms divide date, III above **Note:** Uniface. Varieties exist.

Date	Mintage	VG	F	VF	XF	Unc
16Z3	—	10.00	20.00	40.00	85.00	—
16Z4	—	10.00	20.00	40.00	85.00	—
16Z5	—	10.00	20.00	40.00	85.00	—
16Z9	—	10.00	20.00	40.00	85.00	—

KM# 54 3 HELLER
Silver **Ruler:** Philipp Adolph **Obv:** 2-fold arms of Würzburg behind arms of Ehrenberg

Date	Mintage	VG	F	VF	XF	Unc
ND	—	20.00	40.00	75.00	155	—

KM# A48 3 HELLER
0.4300 g., Silver, 14 mm. **Ruler:** Franz **Obv:** Ornamented shield of Würzburg arms divides date, value 'III' above **Note:** Uniface.

Date	Mintage	VG	F	VF	XF	Unc
1636	—	10.00	20.00	40.00	80.00	—

KM# 166 3 HELLER
Silver **Ruler:** Peter Philipp **Obv:** Three small shields of arms, value III above

Date	Mintage	VG	F	VF	XF	Unc
1676	—	9.00	18.00	35.00	75.00	—
1677	—	9.00	18.00	35.00	75.00	—

KM# 178 3 HELLER
Silver **Ruler:** Konrad Wilhelm **Obv:** Lower arms of Wertenau divide date, III H. above

Date	Mintage	VG	F	VF	XF	Unc
1683	—	7.00	15.00	30.00	60.00	—

KM# 196 3 HELLER
Silver **Ruler:** Johann Gottfried II **Obv:** Lower arms of Guttenberg **Note:** Varieties exist.

Date	Mintage	VG	F	VF	XF	Unc
1685	—	6.00	13.00	30.00	60.00	—
1686	—	6.00	13.00	30.00	60.00	—
1689	—	6.00	13.00	30.00	60.00	—
1693	—	6.00	13.00	30.00	60.00	—
1694	—	6.00	13.00	30.00	60.00	—
1696	—	6.00	13.00	30.00	60.00	—

KM# 211 3 HELLER
Silver **Ruler:** Johann Philipp II **Obv:** Lower arms of Greiffenklau

Date	Mintage	VG	F	VF	XF	Unc
1699	—	—	—	—	—	—

KM# 72 PFENNIG
Silver **Ruler:** Philipp Adolph **Obv:** Shield of 4-fold arms, date **Note:** Uniface.

Date	Mintage	VG	F	VF	XF	Unc
1624	—	—	—	—	—	—

KM# 167 PFENNIG
Silver **Ruler:** Philipp Adolph **Obv:** 2-fold arms divided vertically, Mainz on left, Schonborn on right, A. K. above

Date	Mintage	VG	F	VF	XF	Unc
ND	—	11.00	25.00	55.00	110	—

Note: Compare with Pfennig issues of Mainz, KM#97-99

KM# 168 PFENNIG
Silver **Ruler:** Peter Philipp **Obv:** Small shields of arms, value 1

Date	Mintage	VG	F	VF	XF	Unc
1676	—	11.00	25.00	55.00	110	—
1677	—	11.00	25.00	55.00	110	—

KM# 179 PFENNIG
Silver **Ruler:** Konrad Wilhelm **Obv:** 2-fold arms of Wurzburg behind lower arms of Wertenau which divide date

Date	Mintage	VG	F	VF	XF	Unc
1683	—	—	—	—	—	—

KM# 86 3 PFENNIG (Dreier)
Silver **Ruler:** Philipp Adolph **Subject:** Death of Philipp Adolph **Obv:** Arms of Würzburg and Ehrenberg **Note:** Varieties exist.

Date	Mintage	VG	F	VF	XF	Unc
1631	—	—	—	—	—	—

KM# 33 6 PFENNIG (Sechser)
Silver **Ruler:** Julius Echter **Subject:** Death of Julius Echter **Obv:** Shield of 4-fold arms, 3 ornate helmets above **Rev:** 6-line inscription with dates, imperial orb in shield with 6 divides last two lines **Note:** Varieties exist.

Date	Mintage	VG	F	VF	XF	Unc
1617	—	40.00	75.00	150	300	—

KM# 87 6 PFENNIG (Sechser)
Silver **Ruler:** Philipp Adolph **Subject:** Death of Philipp Adolph **Obv:** Arms of Würzburg and Ehrenberg **Note:** Varieties exist.

Date	Mintage	VG	F	VF	XF	Unc
1631	—	—	—	—	—	—

KM# 55 1/84 GULDEN (Körtling)
Silver **Ruler:** Philipp Adolph **Obv:** Three small shields of arms, two above one, lower shield divides date **Rev:** Imperial orb with 84 in ornamented rhombus

Date	Mintage	VG	F	VF	XF	Unc
1623	—	6.00	15.00	35.00	70.00	—
16Z4	—	6.00	15.00	35.00	70.00	—

KM# 73 1/84 GULDEN (Körtling)
Silver **Ruler:** Philipp Adolph **Obv:** Upper two shields close together, small F above, lower shield divides date **Rev:** Imperial orb with 84 in ornamented rhombus **Mint:** Fürth **Note:** Varieties exist.

Date	Mintage	VG	F	VF	XF	Unc
16Z4	—	6.00	15.00	35.00	70.00	—
16Z5	—	6.00	15.00	35.00	70.00	—
16Z8	—	6.00	15.00	35.00	70.00	—
16Z9	—	6.00	15.00	35.00	70.00	—

KM# 108 1/84 GULDEN (Körtling)
Silver **Ruler:** Franz **Obv:** Arms of Hatzfeld

Date	Mintage	VG	F	VF	XF	Unc
1635	—	—	—	—	—	—
1640	—	—	—	—	—	—

KM# 132 1/84 GULDEN (Körtling)
Silver **Ruler:** Johann Philipp I **Obv:** Upper left arms of Mainz, lower arms of Schonborn, F in center, crown at top **Note:** Varieties exist.

Date	Mintage	VG	F	VF	XF	Unc
1645F	—	6.00	15.00	35.00	70.00	—
1646F	—	6.00	15.00	35.00	70.00	—
1648F	—	6.00	15.00	35.00	70.00	—
1655F	—	6.00	15.00	35.00	70.00	—
1656F	—	6.00	15.00	35.00	70.00	—
1657F	—	6.00	15.00	35.00	70.00	—
1658F	—	6.00	15.00	35.00	70.00	—
1659F	—	6.00	15.00	35.00	70.00	—
1662F	—	6.00	15.00	35.00	70.00	—
1663F	—	6.00	15.00	35.00	70.00	—
1665F	—	6.00	15.00	35.00	70.00	—
1671F	—	6.00	15.00	35.00	70.00	—

KM# 151 1/84 GULDEN (Körtling)
Silver **Ruler:** Johann Hartmann **Obv:** Upper left arms of Wurzburg, lower arms of Rosenbach

Date	Mintage	VG	F	VF	XF	Unc
1673F	—	15.00	35.00	75.00	155	—
1674F	—	15.00	35.00	75.00	155	—

KM# 162 1/84 GULDEN (Körtling)
Silver **Ruler:** Peter Philipp **Obv:** Lower arms of Dernbach **Note:** Varieties exist.

Date	Mintage	VG	F	VF	XF	Unc
1675F	—	13.00	25.00	55.00	110	—
1676F	—	13.00	25.00	55.00	110	—
1677F	—	13.00	25.00	55.00	110	—
1679	—	13.00	25.00	55.00	110	—
NDF	—	13.00	25.00	55.00	110	—

KM# 186 1/84 GULDEN (Körtling)
Silver **Ruler:** Johann Gottfried II **Obv:** Lower arms of Guttenberg **Note:** Varieties exist.

Date	Mintage	VG	F	VF	XF	Unc
1684F	—	6.00	15.00	35.00	70.00	—
1685F	—	6.00	15.00	35.00	70.00	—
1686F	—	6.00	15.00	35.00	70.00	—
1687F	—	6.00	15.00	35.00	70.00	—
1688F	—	6.00	15.00	35.00	70.00	—
1689F	—	6.00	15.00	35.00	70.00	—
1690F	—	6.00	15.00	35.00	70.00	—
1693F	—	6.00	15.00	35.00	70.00	—
1694F	—	6.00	15.00	35.00	70.00	—
1695F	—	6.00	15.00	35.00	70.00	—
1696F	—	6.00	15.00	35.00	70.00	—
1697F	—	6.00	15.00	35.00	70.00	—

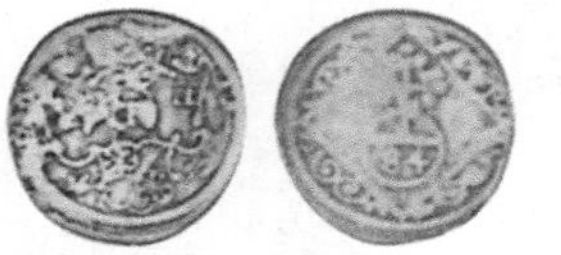

KM# 212 1/84 GULDEN (Körtling)
Silver **Ruler:** Johann Philipp II **Obv:** Lower arms of Greifenklau **Rev:** Value on imperial orb within rhombus **Note:** Varieties exist.

Date	Mintage	VG	F	VF	XF	Unc
1699	—	6.00	15.00	35.00	70.00	—

KM# 139 ALBUS (2 Kreuzer)
Silver **Ruler:** Johann Philipp I **Obv:** 4-fold arms with central shield of Schonborn in laurel wreath **Rev:** I/ALBVS/date in laurel wreath **Note:** Varieties exist.

Date	Mintage	VG	F	VF	XF	Unc
1651	—	6.00	15.00	35.00	70.00	—
1653	—	6.00	15.00	35.00	70.00	—
1654	—	6.00	15.00	35.00	70.00	—
1655	—	6.00	15.00	35.00	70.00	—
1656	—	6.00	15.00	35.00	70.00	—

KM# A133 SCHILLING
Silver **Ruler:** Johann Philipp I **Obv:** Crowned 2-fold arms behind Schonborn arms **Rev:** St. Kilian standing, sword in right hand, staff in left hand **Rev. Legend:** SANCTVS KILIANVS **Note:** Size varies: 20.9-21mm.

Date	Mintage	VG	F	VF	XF	Unc
1644	—	—	—	—	—	—
1645	—	—	—	—	—	—

KM# 56 SCHILLING (8 Pfennig)
Silver **Ruler:** Philipp Adolph **Obv:** 4-fold arms of Würzburg and Ehrenberg in circle, date in legend **Rev:** Full-length facing figure of St. Kilian with sword and crozier

Date	Mintage	VG	F	VF	XF	Unc
1623	—	15.00	30.00	60.00	120	—
16Z4	—	15.00	30.00	60.00	120	—

KM# 77 SCHILLING (8 Pfennig)
Silver **Ruler:** Philipp Adolph **Obv:** Shield of 4-fold arms, pointed at bottom, without inner circle, date at end of legend **Rev:** Standing figure of St. Kilian **Note:** Varieties exist.

Date	Mintage	VG	F	VF	XF	Unc
16Z5	—	15.00	30.00	60.00	120	—
16Z6	—	15.00	30.00	60.00	120	—
16Z8	—	15.00	30.00	60.00	120	—
16Z9	—	15.00	30.00	60.00	120	—

KM# 109 SCHILLING (8 Pfennig)
Silver **Ruler:** Franz **Obv:** Three ornate shields of arms, two above one, lower shield of Hatzfeld divides date **Note:** Varieties exist.

Date	Mintage	VG	F	VF	XF	Unc
1635	—	16.00	35.00	75.00	155	—

KM# 152 SCHILLING (8 Pfennig)
Silver **Ruler:** Johann Philipp I **Obv:** Crowned 4-fold arms of Wurzburg and Rosenbach **Rev:** Standing figure of St. Kilian divides date **Note:** Varieties exist.

Date	Mintage	VG	F	VF	XF	Unc
1650	—	25.00	55.00	110	225	—
1651F	—	25.00	55.00	110	225	—
1656	—	25.00	55.00	110	225	—
1657	—	25.00	55.00	110	225	—
1673	—	25.00	55.00	110	225	—

KM# 163 SCHILLING (8 Pfennig)
Silver **Ruler:** Peter Philipp **Obv:** Central shield of Dernbach arms **Note:** Varieties exist.

Date	Mintage	VG	F	VF	XF	Unc
1675	—	15.00	30.00	60.00	120	—
1676	—	15.00	30.00	60.00	120	—
1677	—	15.00	30.00	60.00	120	—
1678	—	15.00	30.00	60.00	120	—
1679	—	15.00	30.00	60.00	120	—
1680	—	15.00	30.00	60.00	120	—
1681	—	15.00	30.00	60.00	120	—

KM# 180 SCHILLING (8 Pfennig)
Silver **Ruler:** Konrad Wilhelm **Obv:** Lower arms of Wertenau, without value

Date	Mintage	VG	F	VF	XF	Unc
1683	—	16.00	35.00	75.00	155	—

KM# 181 SCHILLING (8 Pfennig)
Silver **Ruler:** Konrad Wilhelm **Obv:** 4-fold arms of Wurzburg and Wertenau

Date	Mintage	VG	F	VF	XF	Unc
1683	—	16.00	30.00	65.00	130	—

KM# 197 SCHILLING (8 Pfennig)
Silver **Ruler:** Johann Gottfried II **Obv:** 4-fold arms of Wurzburg and Guttenberg

Date	Mintage	VG	F	VF	XF	Unc
1685	—	—	—	—	—	—

KM# 198 SCHILLING (8 Pfennig)
Silver **Ruler:** Johann Gottfried II **Obv:** 4-fold arms of Wurzburg and Guttenberg, date divided near bottom **Note:** Varieties exist.

Date	Mintage	VG	F	VF	XF	Unc
1685	—	15.00	30.00	60.00	120	—
1686	—	15.00	30.00	60.00	120	—
1688	—	15.00	30.00	60.00	120	—
1689	—	15.00	30.00	60.00	120	—
1690	—	15.00	30.00	60.00	120	—
1691	—	15.00	30.00	60.00	120	—
1692	—	15.00	30.00	60.00	120	—
1693	—	15.00	30.00	60.00	120	—
1694	—	15.00	30.00	60.00	120	—
(16)95	—	15.00	30.00	60.00	120	—
ND	—	15.00	30.00	60.00	120	—

KM# 207 SCHILLING (8 Pfennig)

Silver **Ruler:** Johann Gottfried II **Obv:** Crowned shield of 2-fold arms of Würzburg, with shield of Guttenberg arms lower down in front **Note:** Varieties exist.

Date	Mintage	VG	F	VF	XF	Unc
1696	—	15.00	30.00	60.00	120	—
1697	—	15.00	30.00	60.00	120	—

KM# 213 SCHILLING (8 Pfennig)

Silver **Ruler:** Johann Philipp II **Obv:** Lower arms of Greifenklau **Rev:** Value on imperial orb within rhombus **Note:** Varieties exist.

Date	Mintage	VG	F	VF	XF	Unc
1699	—	15.00	35.00	75.00	155	—

KM# 48 KREUZER

Copper **Ruler:** Johann Gottfried **Obv:** Ornamented Würzburg arms, W above **Rev:** 4-line inscription with date **Rev. Inscription:** I / KREVT / ZER / (date)

Date	Mintage	VG	F	VF	XF	Unc
1622	—	10.00	25.00	55.00	110	—

KM# 49 KREUZER

Copper **Ruler:** Johann Gottfried **Obv:** Shield of Würzburg arms **Rev:** 4-line inscription with date **Rev. Inscription:** I / KREVTZ / ER / (date)

Date	Mintage	VG	F	VF	XF	Unc
1622	—	10.00	25.00	55.00	110	—

KM# 145 KREUZER

Copper **Ruler:** Johann Philipp I **Obv:** 2-fold arms of Mainz and Schonborn enclosed in laurel wreath **Rev:** Inscription enclosed in laurel wreath **Rev. Inscription:** I / KREVTZ / date

Date	Mintage	VG	F	VF	XF	Unc
1661	—	10.00	25.00	55.00	110	—

Note: Similar to Mainz, KM#115, but without mintmaster's initials.

KM# 32 3 KREUZER (Groschen)

Silver **Ruler:** Julius Echter **Subject:** Death of Julius Echter **Obv:** Ornate shield of 4-fold arms, three ornate helmets above **Rev:** 6-line inscription with dates, imperial orb with 3 in shield divides last 2 lines **Note:** Varieties exist.

Date	Mintage	VG	F	VF	XF	Unc
1617	—	35.00	75.00	150	290	—

KM# 50 3 KREUZER (Groschen)

Silver **Ruler:** Johann Gottfried **Subject:** Death of Gottfried **Obv:** Shield of 4-fold arms with central shield of Aschhausen, 4 ornate helmets above **Rev:** 6-line inscription with date, small imperial orb with W below

Date	Mintage	VG	F	VF	XF	Unc
1622	—	90.00	200	335	675	—

KM# 120 3 KREUZER (Groschen)

Silver **Ruler:** Franz **Subject:** Death of Franz von Hatzfeld **Obv:** Central shield of Hatzfeld

Date	Mintage	VG	F	VF	XF	Unc
1642	—	—	—	—	—	—

KM# 153 3 KREUZER (Groschen)

Silver **Ruler:** Johann Philipp I **Subject:** Death of Johann Philipp I **Obv:** Crowned oval 6-fold arms with central shield of Schonborn **Rev:** 9-line inscription with dates, imperial orb with 3 at bottom, W below **Note:** Varieties exist.

Date	Mintage	VG	F	VF	XF	Unc
1673	—	80.00	160	325	650	—

KM# 164 3 KREUZER (Groschen)

Silver **Ruler:** Johann Hartmann **Subject:** Death of Johann Hartmann **Obv:** Crowned oval 4-fold arms of Wurzburg and Rosenbach **Rev:** 7-line inscription with dates, imperial orb with 3 at bottom

Date	Mintage	VG	F	VF	XF	Unc
1675	—	—	—	—	—	—

KM# 182 3 KREUZER (Groschen)

Silver **Ruler:** Peter Philipp **Subject:** Death of Peter Philipp **Obv:** Crowned round 4-fold arms of Bamburg and Wurzburg with central shield of Dernbach **Rev:** 9-line inscription with dates, imperial orb with 3 at bottom **Note:** Varieties exist.

Date	Mintage	VG	F	VF	XF	Unc
1683	—	35.00	75.00	150	300	—

Note: This was very likely a joint issue for both bishoprics

KM# 187 3 KREUZER (Groschen)

Silver **Ruler:** Konrad Wilhelm **Subject:** Death of Konrad Wilhelm **Obv:** Crowned oval 4-fold arms of Wurzburg and Wertenau **Rev:** 6-line inscription with dates, imperial orb with 3 at bottom **Note:** Varieties exist.

Date	Mintage	VG	F	VF	XF	Unc
1684	—	45.00	90.00	180	360	—

KM# 210 3 KREUZER (Groschen)

Silver **Ruler:** Johann Gottfried II **Subject:** Death of Johann Gottfried II **Obv:** Crowned round 4-fold arms of Wurzburg and Wertenau **Rev:** 6-line inscription with dates, imperial orb with 3 at bottom

Date	Mintage	VG	F	VF	XF	Unc
1698	—	45.00	90.00	180	360	—

KM# 111 4 KREUZER (Batzen)

Silver **Ruler:** Franz **Obv:** Crowned 2-fold arms of Wurzburg behind lower 4-fold arms of Hatzfeld, II - I K above **Rev:** Standing figure of St. Kilian divides date

Date	Mintage	VG	F	VF	XF	Unc
1636	—	35.00	75.00	150	290	—
1637	—	35.00	75.00	150	290	—

KM# 51 12 KREUZER (Schreckenberger)

Silver **Ruler:** Johann Gottfried **Note:** Counterstamp date/W on coin of Brunswick-Wolfenbuttel.

Date	Mintage	VG	F	VF	XF	Unc
16ZZ	—	—	—	—	—	—

Note: Some authorities believe this counterstamp to have been carried out by the Wurzburg city government and not by the bishopric

KM# 5 60 KREUZER (Guldenthaler)

Silver **Ruler:** Julius Echter **Obv:** St. Kilian divides S - K above 4-fold arms in Spanish shield which divides date **Rev:** Crowned imperial eagle, orb on breast, titles of Rudolf II **Note:** Dav. #152.

Date	Mintage	VG	F	VF	XF	Unc
1601	—	700	1,300	2,500	4,800	—

KM# 22 60 KREUZER (Guldenthaler)

Silver **Ruler:** Julius Echter **Obv:** Larger figure and arms **Rev:** Crowned imperial eagle, 60 in orb on breast **Note:** Varieties exist. Dav. #152.

Date	Mintage	VG	F	VF	XF	Unc
1613 CM	—	650	1,250	2,400	4,600	—
1615	—	650	1,250	2,400	4,600	—

KM# 40 60 KREUZER (Guldenthaler)

Silver **Ruler:** Johann Gottfried **Obv:** Crowned ornate oval shield of 4-fold arms with central shield **Rev:** St. Kilian divides date, 60 in oval below **Note:** Dav. #154.

Date	Mintage	VG	F	VF	XF	Unc
1619	—	1,200	2,450	4,500	8,900	—

KM# 6 2 GULDEN

Silver **Ruler:** Julius Echter **Obv:** Crowned imperial eagle, 60 in orb on breast, titles of Rudolf II **Rev:** St. Kilian divides S - K above 4-fold arms in Spanish shield which divides date **Note:** Struck with Gulden dies, KM#5.

Date	Mintage	VG	F	VF	XF	Unc
1601 Rare	—	—	—	—	—	—

KM# 130 1/28 THALER

Silver **Ruler:** Johann Philipp I **Obv:** Crowned 2-fold arms of Wurzburg behind Schonborn arms which divide date, value Z8 below **Rev:** Full-length facing figure of St. Kilian with sword and crozier **Note:** Varieties exist.

Date	Mintage	VG	F	VF	XF	Unc
1643	—	27.00	55.00	110	220	—
1644	—	27.00	55.00	110	220	—
1645	—	27.00	55.00	110	220	—
1646	—	27.00	55.00	110	220	—

KM# 133 1/28 THALER

Silver **Ruler:** Johann Philipp I **Obv:** 4-fold arms of Mainz and Wurzburg with center shield of Schonborn divide date, value Z8 below **Note:** Varieties exist.

Date	Mintage	VG	F	VF	XF	Unc
1648	—	25.00	50.00	100	210	—
1649	—	25.00	50.00	100	210	—
1650	—	25.00	50.00	100	210	—
1651	—	25.00	50.00	100	210	—
1656	—	25.00	50.00	100	210	—
1657	—	25.00	50.00	100	210	—
1658	—	25.00	50.00	100	210	—
1659	—	25.00	50.00	100	210	—
1661	—	25.00	50.00	100	210	—
1668	—	25.00	50.00	100	210	—

KM# 57 1/8 THALER

Silver **Ruler:** Philipp Adolph **Obv:** Shield of 4-fold arms of Würzburg and Ehrenberg divides date **Rev:** Crowned imperial eagle, 1/8 in orb on breast, titles of Ferdinand II

Date	Mintage	VG	F	VF	XF	Unc
1623	—	300	625	1,250	2,500	—

KM# 58 1/4 THALER

Silver **Ruler:** Philipp Adolph **Obv:** Crowned shield of 4-fold arms with central shield divides date **Rev:** Crowned imperial eagle, titles of Ferdinand II **Note:** Varieties exist.

Date	Mintage	VG	F	VF	XF	Unc
1623	—	325	650	1,300	2,600	—

KM# 59 1/4 THALER

Silver **Ruler:** Philipp Adolph **Obv:** Half-length figure of St. Kilian divides date, three small shields below **Rev:** Crowned imperial eagle, orb on breast, titles of Ferdinand II **Note:** Varieties exist.

Date	Mintage	VG	F	VF	XF	Unc
1623	—	250	500	1,000	2,000	—
1624	—	250	500	1,000	2,000	—
1625	—	250	500	1,000	2,000	—

KM# 177 1/4 THALER

Silver **Ruler:** Peter Philipp **Obv:** Bust of Peter Philipp right **Rev:** Crowned 4-fold arms of Bamberg and Wurzburg with center shield of Dernbach in crossed palm fronds, date below

Date	Mintage	VG	F	VF	XF	Unc
1681	—	—	—	—	—	—

Note: This may be a joint issue for both Bamberg and Wurzburg

KM# 208 1/4 THALER

Silver **Ruler:** Johann Gottfried II **Obv:** Bust of Johann Gottfieid II right **Rev:** Crowned round 4-fold arms of Würzburg and Guttenberg, date divided at upper left and right

Date	Mintage	VG	F	VF	XF	Unc
1696	—	150	300	625	1,250	—

KM# 74 1/2 THALER

Silver **Ruler:** Philipp Adolph **Obv:** Facing figure of St. Kilian divides date **Rev:** Crowned imperial eagle, orb on breast

Date	Mintage	VG	F	VF	XF	Unc
16Z4	—	475	1,000	1,900	3,800	—

KM# 85 1/2 THALER

Silver **Ruler:** Philipp Adolph **Obv:** Facing figure of St. Kilian divides date, three shields in front **Rev:** Crowned imperial eagle, value 1/2 in orb on breast

Date	Mintage	VG	F	VF	XF	Unc
1630	—	—	—	—	—	—

KM# 209 1/2 THALER

Silver **Ruler:** Johann Gottfried II **Obv:** Bust of Johann Gottfried II right **Rev:** Three ornate helmets above oval 4-fold arms of Würzburg and Guttenberg, date at top

Date	Mintage	VG	F	VF	XF	Unc
1696	—	225	450	900	1,800	—

KM# 8 THALER

Silver **Ruler:** Julius Echter **Obv:** St. Kilian with sword and scepter behind small oval shield divide date and S-K **Rev:** Crowned imperial eagle, orb on breast **Rev. Legend:** RVDOLPHVS. II... **Note:** Dav. #5965.

Date	Mintage	VG	F	VF	XF	Unc
1601	—	550	1,100	2,200	5,200	9,400

KM# 23 THALER

Silver **Ruler:** Julius Echter **Rev:** Legend, date **Rev. Legend:** MATTHIAS. ROM. IMP. AUG... **Note:** Dav. #5966.

Date	Mintage	VG	F	VF	XF	Unc
1613 CM Rare	—	—	—	—	—	—

KM# 24 THALER

Silver **Ruler:** Julius Echter **Obv:** St. Kilian divides S-K above, shield of 4-fold arms divides date below **Rev:** Crowned imperial eagle, orb on breast, C-M below **Note:** Dav. #5967.

Date	Mintage	VG	F	VF	XF	Unc
1613 CM	—	725	1,400	2,150	3,600	—

KM# 28 THALER

Silver **Ruler:** Julius Echter **Obv:** St. Kilian dividing date and S-K at shoulders **Obv. Legend:** IVILIVS D: G: EPISOPVS-WIRTZBUR: G:... **Note:** Dav. #5968.

Date	Mintage	VG	F	VF	XF	Unc
1615	—	725	1,400	2,150	3,600	—

KM# 29 THALER

Silver **Ruler:** Philipp Adolph **Obv:** Bust right with small shield below **Obv. Legend:** PHILIPPUS. ADOLPHUS. D. G. EPIS. **Rev:** Standing saint **Note:** Dav. #5969.

Date	Mintage	VG	F	VF	XF	Unc
ND Rare	—	—	—	—	—	—

KM# 30 THALER

Silver **Ruler:** Philipp Adolph **Obv:** St. Kilian standing with three shields around **Rev:** Crowned imperial eagle, shield of 2-fold arms on breast **Note:** Dav. #5970.

Date	Mintage	VG	F	VF	XF	Unc
ND	—	1,400	2,250	3,750	6,500	—

KM# 60 THALER

Silver **Ruler:** Philipp Adolph **Obv:** Saint behind shield dividing S-K and date **Obv. Legend:** PHILIP:ADOLP:... **Rev:** Crowned imperial eagle w/orb on breast **Rev. Legend:** FERDINAND: II: D: G:. **Note:** Dav. #5971.

Date	Mintage	VG	F	VF	XF	Unc
1623	—	875	1,650	2,850	4,750	—

KM# 75 THALER

Silver **Ruler:** Philipp Adolph **Obv:** Facing figure of St. Kilian divides date, three shields in front **Obv. Legend:** PHILIPPVS * ADOLPHVS * EPISCO*... **Rev:** Crowned imperial eagle, orb on breast **Rev. Legend:** FERDINANDVS * II * D.G:... **Note:** Dav. #5972.

Date	Mintage	VG	F	VF	XF	Unc
1624	—	700	1,300	2,200	3,600	—
1625	—	700	1,300	2,200	3,600	—

KM# 76 THALER

Silver **Ruler:** Philipp Adolph **Note:** Klippe. Dav. #5972A.

Date	Mintage	VG	F	VF	XF	Unc
16Z4 Rare	—	—	—	—	—	—

KM# 78 THALER

Silver **Ruler:** Philipp Adolph **Obv. Legend:** PHILIP: ADOLPH: D. G: -EPI. WIRCH:... **Note:** Dav. #5973.

Date	Mintage	VG	F	VF	XF	Unc
1626	—	1,350	2,500	4,000	6,750	—
1628	—	1,350	2,500	4,000	6,750	—
1629	—	1,350	2,500	4,000	6,750	—

KM# 110 THALER

Silver **Ruler:** Franz **Obv:** Crowned imperial eagle with Austrian arms on breast, date above **Obv. Legend:** FERDINANDVS. II. D. G... **Rev:** St. Kilian with arms in front **Rev. Legend:** FRANCISC: D: G... **Note:** Dav. #5974.

Date	Mintage	VG	F	VF	XF	Unc
1635 Rare	—	—	—	—	—	—

KM# 112 THALER

Silver **Ruler:** Franz **Obv:** Mitred and helmeted arms **Obv. Legend:** ...EPS: BAM:-ET... **Rev:** Saint standing with date divided above **Note:** Varieties exist. Dav. #5975.

Date	Mintage	VG	F	VF	XF	Unc
1636 CS	—	425	875	1,750	3,250	—
1637	—	425	875	1,750	3,250	—
1638	—	425	875	1,750	3,250	—
1639	—	425	875	1,750	3,250	—

KM# 113 THALER

Silver **Ruler:** Franz **Obv:** St. Kilian standing behind arms dividing S-K above **Rev:** Madonna and child in flaming oval above crowned double eagle with shield on breast, date divided at sides **Note:** Dav. #5976.

Date	Mintage	VG	F	VF	XF	Unc
1637	—	425	875	1,750	3,700	—
1638	—	425	875	1,750	3,700	—
1640	—	425	875	1,750	3,700	—
1641	—	425	875	1,750	3,700	—

KM# 131 THALER

Silver **Ruler:** Johann Philipp I **Obv:** Facing bust with crowned shield below **Obv. Legend:** IOHANN. PHILIPP... **Rev:** Madonna standing with child dividing C-S and date **Rev. Legend:** CLYPEVS OMNIBUS... **Note:** Dav. #5978.

Date	Mintage	VG	F	VF	XF	Unc
1643 CS	—	425	775	1,300	2,250	—

KM# 134 THALER

Silver **Ruler:** Johann Philipp I **Obv. Legend:** IO: PHIL. D: G: S. SED... **Note:** Dav. #5979.

Date	Mintage	VG	F	VF	XF	Unc
1649//1643	—	600	1,200	2,250	3,500	—

KM# 140 THALER

Silver **Ruler:** Johann Philipp I **Obv:** Without inner circle **Rev:** Date divided below **Note:** Dav. #5980.

Date	Mintage	VG	F	VF	XF	Unc
1652	—	350	700	1,450	2,500	3,750
1659	—	350	700	1,450	2,500	3,750

KM# 141 THALER

Silver **Ruler:** Johann Philipp I **Obv:** Bust right, shield below **Obv. Legend:** MOG: A: E: S: R: I:-P: G: A: C: P: E: E:... **Note:** Dav. #5981.

Date	Mintage	VG	F	VF	XF	Unc
ND	—	675	1,350	2,750	5,250	—

KM# 154 THALER

Silver **Ruler:** Johann Hartmann **Obv:** Bust right, shield below **Obv. Legend:** IOAN: HARTMAN:... **Rev:** Madonna standing with child on half moon **Rev. Legend:** CLYPEUS OMNIBUS... **Note:** Dav. #5983.

Date	Mintage	VG	F	VF	XF	Unc
ND	—	1,800	3,000	5,100	7,800	—

KM# 155 THALER

Silver **Ruler:** Johann Hartmann **Obv:** Different bust turned more to right **Rev:** Ornament left of halo **Note:** Dav. #5984.

Date	Mintage	VG	F	VF	XF	Unc
ND	—	650	1,250	2,500	—	—

KM# 156 THALER

Silver **Ruler:** Johann Hartmann **Obv:** Bust right with shield below **Obv. Legend:** PETR. PHILL:... **Note:** Dav. #5985.

Date	Mintage	VG	F	VF	XF	Unc
ND	—	900	1,800	3,250	5,500	—

KM# 157 THALER

Silver **Ruler:** Johann Hartmann **Obv:** Bust with short hair right **Note:** Dav. #5986.

Date	Mintage	VG	F	VF	XF	Unc
ND	—	850	1,650	3,000	5,000	—

KM# 176 THALER

Silver **Ruler:** Peter Philipp **Note:** Dav. #5988.

Date	Mintage	VG	F	VF	XF	Unc
1680	—	1,000	2,000	3,750	6,500	—

KM# 175 THALER

Silver **Ruler:** Peter Philipp **Obv:** Bust divides date **Note:** Cross-reference number Dav. #5987.

Date	Mintage	VG	F	VF	XF	Unc
1680	—	850	1,650	3,000	5,000	—

KM# 174 THALER

Silver **Ruler:** Peter Philipp **Note:** Similar to KM#183 but taller bust with different robes on obverse, and oval arms on reverse, smaller inscriptions with differences on both sides.

Date	Mintage	VG	F	VF	XF	Unc
ND	—	—	—	—	—	—

KM# 183 THALER

Silver **Ruler:** Konrad Wilhelm **Obv:** Bust right **Obv. Legend:** CONRAD. WILH. D: G. EPISC. HERBIP. FRANC. OR. DUX. **Rev:** Helmeted arms **Rev. Legend:** CONSULTE. ET. CONSTANTER. **Note:** Dav. #5989.

Date	Mintage	VG	F	VF	XF	Unc
ND Rare	—	—	—	—	—	—

KM# 188 THALER

Silver **Ruler:** Johann Gottfried II **Obv:** Bust right **Obv. Legend:** IOAN GODEFRID. D. G. EPISC... **Rev:** Helmeted arms **Rev. Legend:** SUPER. OMNIA. GERMANA FIDES **Note:** Dav. #5990.

Date	Mintage	VG	F	VF	XF	Unc
ND(1684-98)	—	350	750	1,800	3,500	5,500

KM# 189 THALER

Silver **Ruler:** Johann Gottfried II **Obv:** Larger bust right, I. L. below **Note:** Dav. #5991.

Date	Mintage	VG	F	VF	XF	Unc
ND IL	—	450	850	1,950	3,750	—

KM# 190 THALER

Silver **Ruler:** Johann Gottfried II **Obv:** Helmeted arms **Obv. Legend:** IOANNES GODEFRID... **Rev:** St. Kilian standing **Note:** Dav. #5992.

Date	Mintage	VG	F	VF	XF	Unc
ND Rare	—	—	—	—	—	—

KM# 205 THALER

Silver **Ruler:** Johann Gottfried II **Obv:** Helmeted arms **Rev:** St. Kilian standing dividing IM-W and date **Note:** Dav. #5993.

Date	Mintage	F	VF	XF	Unc	BU
1693 IMW	—	475	900	2,000	3,500	—

KM# 206 THALER

Silver **Ruler:** Johann Gottfried II **Obv:** Helmeted arms with date divided below **Obv. Legend:** NULLA SALUS BELLO... **Note:** Dav. #5994.

Date	Mintage	F	VF	XF	Unc	BU
1693 IMW	—	500	1,100	2,250	3,750	—

KM# 221 THALER

Silver **Ruler:** Johann Philipp II **Obv:** Legend, date, bust right **Obv. Legend:** IOAN. PHILIP... **Rev:** Helmeted arms **Note:** Dav. #2880

Date	Mintage	VG	F	VF	XF	Unc
1700	—	350	750	1,450	2,800	—

KM# 10 2 THALER

Silver **Ruler:** Julius Echter **Note:** Similar to 1 Thaler, KM#188.

Date	Mintage	VG	F	VF	XF	Unc
ND Rare	—	—	—	—	—	—

KM# 9 2 THALER

Silver **Ruler:** Julius Echter **Note:** Similar to 1 Thaler, KM#8.

Date	Mintage	VG	F	VF	XF	Unc
1601 Rare	—	—	—	—	—	—

TRADE COINAGE

KM# 11 GOLDGULDEN

3.2500 g., 0.7700 Gold 0.0805 oz. AGW **Ruler:** Julius Echter **Obv:** St. Kilian divides S - K above small shield with imperial orb, titles of Rudolf II and date in legend **Rev:** 4-fold arms, three ornate helmets above

Date	Mintage	VG	F	VF	XF	Unc
1601	—	1,100	2,200	3,850	8,300	—

KM# 12 GOLDGULDEN

3.2500 g., 0.7700 Gold 0.0805 oz. AGW **Ruler:** Julius Echter **Obv:** Date also divided by figure of St. Kilian

Date	Mintage	VG	F	VF	XF	Unc
1608	—	1,300	2,650	4,600	8,700	—

KM# 20 GOLDGULDEN

3.2500 g., 0.7700 Gold 0.0805 oz. AGW **Ruler:** Julius Echter **Rev:** Date in legend

Date	Mintage	VG	F	VF	XF	Unc
1611	—	1,300	2,650	4,600	8,700	—

KM# 25 GOLDGULDEN

3.2500 g., 0.7700 Gold 0.0805 oz. AGW **Ruler:** Julius Echter **Obv:** St. Kilian divides S - K, small shield with orb below, Roman numeral date in legend **Rev:** 4-fold arms, three helmets above, titles of Matthias

Date	Mintage	VG	F	VF	XF	Unc
1613	—	850	1,650	3,650	7,700	—

KM# 26 GOLDGULDEN

3.2500 g., 0.7700 Gold 0.0805 oz. AGW **Ruler:** Julius Echter **Rev:** Arabic date in legend

Date	Mintage	VG	F	VF	XF	Unc
1613	—	850	1,650	3,650	7,700	—
1615	—	850	1,650	3,650	7,700	—

KM# 34 GOLDGULDEN

3.2500 g., 0.7700 Gold 0.0805 oz. AGW **Ruler:** Julius Echter **Subject:** Death of Julius Echter **Obv:** Shield of 4-fold arms, 3 ornate helmets above **Rev:** 6-line inscription with dates, orb without value divides last 2 lines

Date	Mintage	VG	F	VF	XF	Unc
1617	—	1,300	2,650	4,600	8,700	—

KM# 35 GOLDGULDEN

3.2500 g., 0.7700 Gold 0.0805 oz. AGW **Ruler:** Johann Gottfried **Obv:** Arms in inner circle **Rev:** Concentric circles with key arms at center, S-P bove Q-W at "corners" **Rev. Legend:** AUGUSTUM PATRIAE...

Date	Mintage	VG	F	VF	XF	Unc
ND(1617)	—	850	1,750	4,250	8,000	—

KM# 36 GOLDGULDEN

3.2500 g., 0.7700 Gold 0.0805 oz. AGW **Ruler:** Johann Gottfried **Rev. Legend:** ORE AURO. CORDE...

Date	Mintage	VG	F	VF	XF	Unc
ND	—	850	1,750	4,250	8,000	—

KM# 37 GOLDGULDEN

3.2500 g., 0.7700 Gold 0.0805 oz. AGW **Ruler:** Johann Gottfried

Date	Mintage	VG	F	VF	XF	Unc
1617 CW	—	1,050	2,300	5,500	10,000	—
1618 CW	—	1,050	2,300	5,500	10,000	—
1619 CW	—	1,050	2,300	5,500	10,000	—

KM# 52 GOLDGULDEN

3.2500 g., 0.7700 Gold 0.0805 oz. AGW **Ruler:** Johann Gottfried **Subject:** Death of Johann Gottfried **Obv:** Arms topped by four helmets **Rev:** 6-line inscription

Date	Mintage	VG	F	VF	XF	Unc
1622	—	1,500	3,100	6,800	13,000	—

KM# 80 GOLDGULDEN

3.2500 g., 0.7700 Gold 0.0805 oz. AGW **Ruler:** Philipp Adolph **Obv:** 4-fold arms topped by three helmets **Rev:** St. Kilian standing half right with crozier dividing S-K

Date	Mintage	VG	F	VF	XF	Unc
ND	—	1,100	2,500	6,200	11,000	—

KM# 79 GOLDGULDEN

3.2500 g., 0.7700 Gold 0.0805 oz. AGW **Ruler:** Philipp Adolph **Obv:** Three helmets above 4-fold arms in circle **Rev:** Half-length bust of St. Kilian slightly to right divides S - K, titles of Ferdinand II

Date	Mintage	VG	F	VF	XF	Unc
1626	—	1,400	2,950	6,400	11,500	—

KM# 92 GOLDGULDEN

3.2500 g., 0.7700 Gold 0.0805 oz. AGW **Ruler:** Philipp Adolph **Rev:** Legend in wreath

Date	Mintage	VG	F	VF	XF	Unc
ND	—	975	2,100	5,300	9,500	—
1631	—	975	2,100	5,300	9,500	—

KM# 91 GOLDGULDEN

3.2500 g., 0.7700 Gold 0.0805 oz. AGW **Ruler:** Philipp Adolph **Subject:** Death of Philipp Adolph **Rev:** 6-line inscription, orb in cartouche at bottom

Date	Mintage	VG	F	VF	XF	Unc
1631	—	1,250	2,650	5,800	11,500	—

KM# 121 GOLDGULDEN
3.2500 g., 0.7700 Gold 0.0805 oz. AGW **Ruler:** Franz **Subject:** Death of Franz von Hatzfeld **Obv:** Four helmets above 4-fold arms with center shield of Hatzfeld **Rev:** 6-line inscription with date, small imperial orb with W below

Date	Mintage	VG	F	VF	XF	Unc
1642	—	1,450	2,900	5,800	11,500	—

KM# 122 GOLDGULDEN
3.2500 g., 0.7700 Gold 0.0805 oz. AGW **Ruler:** Johann Philipp I **Obv:** Bust of Johann Philipp right, crowned arms at bottom **Rev:** Radiant "Jehovah" at top, 4-line inscription in branches, arms at bottom

Date	Mintage	VG	F	VF	XF	Unc
ND(1642)	—	625	1,400	2,900	6,100	—

KM# 123 GOLDGULDEN
3.2500 g., 0.7700 Gold 0.0805 oz. AGW **Ruler:** Johann Philipp I **Obv:** Facing bust of Johann Philipp

Date	Mintage	VG	F	VF	XF	Unc
ND(1642)	—	500	1,000	2,550	5,700	—

KM# 124 GOLDGULDEN
3.2500 g., 0.7700 Gold 0.0805 oz. AGW **Ruler:** Johann Philipp I **Obv:** Arms below mitre **Rev:** Without "Jehovah" at top

Date	Mintage	VG	F	VF	XF	Unc
ND(1642)	—	625	1,400	2,900	6,100	—

KM# 158 GOLDGULDEN
3.2500 g., 0.7700 Gold 0.0805 oz. AGW **Ruler:** Johann Hartmann **Obv:** Bust of Johann Hartman right, crowned arms at bottom

Date	Mintage	VG	F	VF	XF	Unc
ND(1673)	—	1,800	3,650	6,400	13,000	—

KM# 165 GOLDGULDEN
3.2500 g., 0.7700 Gold 0.0805 oz. AGW **Ruler:** Peter Philipp **Obv:** Bust of Peter Philip right

Date	Mintage	VG	F	VF	XF	Unc
ND(1675)	—	1,400	2,750	5,400	11,000	—

KM# 191 GOLDGULDEN
3.2500 g., 0.7700 Gold 0.0805 oz. AGW **Ruler:** Konrad Wilhelm **Obv:** Bust of Konrad Wilhelm right, crowned oval 4-fold arms on shoulder

Date	Mintage	VG	F	VF	XF	Unc
ND(1684) Rare	—	—	—	—	—	—

KM# 193 GOLDGULDEN
3.2500 g., 0.7700 Gold 0.0805 oz. AGW **Ruler:** Johann Gottfried II **Obv:** Arms topped by three helmets **Rev:** Banner in cartouche in inner circle

Date	Mintage	VG	F	VF	XF	Unc
ND(1684)	—	550	1,100	2,750	6,200	—

KM# 199 GOLDGULDEN
3.2500 g., 0.7700 Gold 0.0805 oz. AGW **Ruler:** Johann Gottfried II **Obv:** Bust of Johann Gottfried II

Date	Mintage	VG	F	VF	XF	Unc
ND(1685)	—	1,250	2,500	5,500	11,000	—

KM# 214 GOLDGULDEN
3.2500 g., 0.7700 Gold 0.0805 oz. AGW **Ruler:** Johann Philipp II **Obv:** Oval shield of 4-fold arms in baroque frame, 3 ornate helmets above **Rev:** Round shield of Würzburg key arms in baroque frame

Date	Mintage	VG	F	VF	XF	Unc
ND(1699)	—	650	1,250	2,500	5,500	—

KM# 215 GOLDGULDEN
3.2500 g., 0.7700 Gold 0.0805 oz. AGW **Ruler:** Johann Philipp II **Obv:** Arms with griffin supporters **Rev:** Arms with three saints above on both sides

Date	Mintage	VG	F	VF	XF	Unc
ND(1699)	—	500	1,000	2,250	5,000	—

KM# 13 2 GOLDGULDEN
6.5000 g., 0.7700 Gold 0.1609 oz. AGW **Ruler:** Julius Echter **Obv:** St. Kilian divides S - K and date above small shield with imperial orb, titles of Rudolf II **Rev:** 4-fold arms, three ornate helmets above

Date	Mintage	VG	F	VF	XF	Unc
1608 Rare	—	—	—	—	—	—

KM# 21 2 GOLDGULDEN
6.5000 g., 0.7700 Gold 0.1609 oz. AGW **Ruler:** Julius Echter **Rev:** Date in legend

Date	Mintage	VG	F	VF	XF	Unc
1611 Rare	—	—	—	—	—	—

KM# 27 2 GOLDGULDEN
6.5000 g., 0.7700 Gold 0.1609 oz. AGW **Ruler:** Julius Echter **Obv:** St. Kilian divides S - K, small shield with orb below, Roman numeral date in legend **Rev:** 4-fold arms, three helmets above, titles of Matthias

Date	Mintage	VG	F	VF	XF	Unc
1613 Rare	—	—	—	—	—	—

KM# 38 2 GOLDGULDEN
6.5000 g., 0.7700 Gold 0.1609 oz. AGW **Ruler:** Julius Echter **Subject:** Death of Julius Echter **Obv:** Shield of 4-fold arms, 3 ornate helmets above **Rev:** 6-line inscription with dates, imperial orb divides last 2 lines

Date	Mintage	VG	F	VF	XF	Unc
1617 Rare	—	—	—	—	—	—

KM# 39 2 GOLDGULDEN
6.5000 g., 0.7700 Gold 0.1609 oz. AGW **Ruler:** Johann Gottfried **Obv:** Arms in inner circle **Rev:** Concentric circles with key arms at center and S-P over Q-W at "corners" **Note:** Klippe.

Date	Mintage	VG	F	VF	XF	Unc
ND(1617) Rare	—	—	—	—	—	—

KM# 70 2 GOLDGULDEN
6.5000 g., 0.7700 Gold 0.1609 oz. AGW **Ruler:** Philipp Adolph **Obv:** Arms topped by three helmets **Rev:** St. Kilian standing holding crozier

Date	Mintage	VG	F	VF	XF	Unc
ND(1623) Rare	—	—	—	—	—	—

KM# 71 2 GOLDGULDEN
6.5000 g., 0.7700 Gold 0.1609 oz. AGW **Ruler:** Philipp Adolph **Subject:** New Years Commemorative **Obv:** Three helmets above 4-fold arms, titles of Philipp Adolph around **Rev:** Oval arms of Würzburg (key) in ornate frame divides S - P/Q - W **Rev. Legend:** OBSEQUIUM PATRIAE...

Date	Mintage	VG	F	VF	XF	Unc
ND Rare	—	—	—	—	—	—

KM# 93 2 GOLDGULDEN
6.5000 g., 0.7700 Gold 0.1609 oz. AGW **Ruler:** Philipp Adolph **Subject:** Death of Philipp Adolph **Obv:** Shield of arms, 3 ornate helmets above **Rev:** 6-line inscription, orb in cartouche below

Date	Mintage	VG	F	VF	XF	Unc
1631 Rare	—	—	—	—	—	—

KM# A30 4 GOLDGULDEN
14.0000 g., 0.9860 Gold 0.4438 oz. AGW **Ruler:** Julius Echter **Obv:** St. Kilian above arms **Rev:** Crowned imperial eagle, titles of Matthias

Date	Mintage	VG	F	VF	XF	Unc
1615 Rare	—	—	—	—	—	—

KM# 125 DUCAT
3.5000 g., 0.9860 Gold 0.1109 oz. AGW **Ruler:** Johann Philipp I **Obv:** Bust of Johann Philip right, crowned arms at bottom **Rev:** Three peaks below radiant "Jehovah"

Date	Mintage	VG	F	VF	XF	Unc
ND(1642)	—	875	1,800	3,650	6,500	—

KM# 126 DUCAT
3.5000 g., 0.9860 Gold 0.1109 oz. AGW **Ruler:** Johann Philipp I **Obv:** Facing bust of Johann Philip, crowned arms at bottom

Date	Mintage	VG	F	VF	XF	Unc
ND(1642)	—	1,300	2,650	5,200	8,600	—

KM# 184 DUCAT
3.5000 g., 0.9860 Gold 0.1109 oz. AGW **Ruler:** Konrad Wilhelm **Obv:** Bust of Konrad Wilhelm right **Rev:** Arms

Date	Mintage	VG	F	VF	XF	Unc
ND(1683)	—	1,600	3,050	5,400	9,900	—

KM# 194 DUCAT
3.5000 g., 0.9860 Gold 0.1109 oz. AGW **Ruler:** Johann Gottfried II **Obv:** Bust of Johann Gottfried II right **Rev:** Five ornate helmets above oval 4-fold arms

Date	Mintage	VG	F	VF	XF	Unc
ND	—	1,600	3,050	5,400	9,900	—

KM# 220 DUCAT
3.5000 g., 0.9860 Gold 0.1109 oz. AGW **Ruler:** Johann Philipp II **Obv:** Bust right **Rev:** Arms topped by three helmets

Date	Mintage	VG	F	VF	XF	Unc
1700	—	625	1,450	2,750	4,950	—

KM# 127 1-1/2 DUCAT
5.2500 g., 0.9860 Gold 0.1664 oz. AGW **Ruler:** Johann Philipp I **Obv:** Facing bust of Johann Philipp **Rev:** Three peaks below radiant "Jehovah"

Date	Mintage	VG	F	VF	XF	Unc
ND(1642)	—	925	2,000	3,950	7,300	—

KM# 128 2 DUCAT
7.0000 g., 0.9860 Gold 0.2219 oz. AGW **Ruler:** Johann Philipp I **Obv:** Bust of Johann Philipp right, crowned arms at bottom **Rev:** Three peaks below radiant "Jehovah"

Date	Mintage	VG	F	VF	XF	Unc
ND(1642)	—	1,950	4,000	8,300	15,000	—

KM# 129 2 DUCAT
7.0000 g., 0.9860 Gold 0.2219 oz. AGW **Ruler:** Johann Philipp I **Obv:** Bust of Johann Philipp facing half left

Date	Mintage	VG	F	VF	XF	Unc
ND(1642)	—	1,800	3,600	7,200	13,000	—

KM# 31 4 DUCAT
14.0000 g., 0.9860 Gold 0.4438 oz. AGW **Ruler:** Julius Echter **Obv:** Larger figure of St. Kilian holding sword and scepter divides S - K, date divided by shield below **Rev:** Large crowned imperial eagle, orb on breast, titles of Rudolf II

Date	Mintage	VG	F	VF	XF	Unc
1615 Rare	—	—	—	—	—	—

KM# 142 5 DUCAT
17.5000 g., 0.9860 Gold 0.5547 oz. AGW **Ruler:** Johann Philipp I **Obv:** Bust of Johann Philipp facing **Rev:** Madonna standing facing with child **Note:** Struck with 1 Thaler dies, KM#140.

Date	Mintage	VG	F	VF	XF	Unc
1652 Rare	—	—	—	—	—	—

Note: Hess-Divo Auction 272 10-97 XF realized $10,720

KM# 143 5 DUCAT
17.5000 g., 0.9860 Gold 0.5547 oz. AGW **Ruler:** Johann Philipp I **Obv:** Bust of Johann Philipp, shield below **Obv. Legend:** MOG: A: E: S: R: I: -P: G: A: C: P: E: E:...

Date	Mintage	VG	F	VF	XF	Unc
ND Rare	—	—	—	—	—	—

KM# 159 5 DUCAT
17.5000 g., 0.9860 Gold 0.5547 oz. AGW **Ruler:** Johann Philipp I **Obv:** Bust of Johann Hartmann right **Rev:** Madonna standing facing with child, ornament left of halo

Date	Mintage	VG	F	VF	XF	Unc
ND Rare	—	—	—	—	—	—

KM# 160 5 DUCAT
17.5000 g., 0.9860 Gold 0.5547 oz. AGW **Ruler:** Johann Philipp I **Obv:** Bust right with shield below **Obv. Legend:** PETR. PHILL... **Rev:** Madonna and child, ornament left of halo

Date	Mintage	VG	F	VF	XF	Unc
ND Rare	—	—	—	—	—	—

KM# 161 5 DUCAT
17.5000 g., 0.9860 Gold 0.5547 oz. AGW **Ruler:** Johann Philipp I **Obv:** Bust with short hair right

Date	Mintage	VG	F	VF	XF	Unc
ND Rare	—	—	—	—	—	—

KM# 185 5 DUCAT
17.5000 g., 0.9860 Gold 0.5547 oz. AGW **Ruler:** Konrad Wilhelm **Obv:** Bust right **Obv. Legend:** CONRAD. WILH. D: G: EPISC... **Rev:** Helmeted arms **Rev. Legend:** CONSULTE. ET. CONSTANTER.

Date	Mintage	VG	F	VF	XF	Unc
ND Rare	—	—	—	—	—	—

KM# 195 5 DUCAT
17.5000 g., 0.9860 Gold 0.5547 oz. AGW **Ruler:** Johann Gottfried II **Obv:** Bust of Johann Gottfried right **Rev:** Helmeted arms **Note:** Struck with 1 Thaler dies, KM#188.

Date	Mintage	VG	F	VF	XF	Unc
ND Rare	—	—	—	—	—	—

SWEDISH OCCUPATION COINAGE

KM# 96 4 KREUZER (Batzen)
Silver **Obv:** Crowned shield of 4-fold arms with central shield, IIII K above, titles of Gustavus Adolphus **Rev:** Full-length figure of Christ facing divides date **Note:** Varieties exist.

Date	Mintage	VG	F	VF	XF	Unc
1632	—	33.00	65.00	135	225	—
1634	—	33.00	65.00	135	225	—

KM# 97 1/4 THALER
Silver **Obv:** Half-length figure to right **Rev:** Shield of 4-fold arms with central shield, crown divides date above

Date	Mintage	VG	F	VF	XF	Unc
1632	—	165	350	750	1,500	—

KM# 88 1/2 THALER
Silver **Obv:** Half-length figure to right **Rev:** Shield of 4-fold arms with central shield, crown divides date above

Date	Mintage	VG	F	VF	XF	Unc
1631	—	150	300	600	1,200	—
1632	—	150	300	600	1,200	—

KM# 98 1/2 THALER
Silver **Obv:** Half-length figure to right **Rev:** Shield of 4-fold arms with central shield, crown divides date above

Date	Mintage	VG	F	VF	XF	Unc
1632	—	180	375	750	1,500	—

KM# 89 THALER

Silver **Obv:** Half-length figure with sash **Rev:** Crowned shield, legend divides date **Note:** Dav. #4559.

Date	Mintage	VG	F	VF	XF	Unc
1631	—	175	350	750	2,500	7,000

KM# 90 THALER

Silver **Obv:** Half-length figure to right **Rev:** Shield of 4-fold arms with central shield, crown divides date above **Note:** Dav. #4559A.

Date	Mintage	VG	F	VF	XF	Unc
1631	—	250	450	950	2,850	—

KM# 99 THALER

Silver **Rev:** Top of crown divides date above wreaths **Note:** Dav. #4559B.

Date	Mintage	VG	F	VF	XF	Unc
1632	—	175	350	750	2,500	—

KM# 100 THALER

Silver **Obv:** Half-length portrait without sash **Rev:** Legend divides date **Note:** Dav. #4560.

Date	Mintage	VG	F	VF	XF	Unc
1632	—	175	250	750	2,500	—

KM# 101 THALER

Silver **Rev:** Large date above shield dvided by crown **Note:** Dav. #4560A.

Date	Mintage	VG	F	VF	XF	Unc
1632	—	210	425	925	2,650	—

KM# 102 THALER

Silver **Obv:** Half-length portrait without sash **Rev:** Small date above shield dvided by crown **Note:** Dav. #4560B.

Date	Mintage	VG	F	VF	XF	Unc
1632	—	210	425	925	2,650	—

KM# 103 THALER

Silver **Rev:** Punctuated date **Note:** Dav. #4560C.

Date	Mintage	VG	F	VF	XF	Unc
1632	—	275	550	1,100	3,100	—

KM# 104 THALER

Silver **Rev:** Top of crown divides date **Note:** Dav. #4560D.

Date	Mintage	VG	F	VF	XF	Unc
1632	—	210	425	925	2,650	—

KM# 105 2 THALER

Silver **Note:** Dav. #4558. Similar to 1 Thaler, KM#99.

Date	Mintage	VG	F	VF	XF	Unc
1632 Unique	—	—	—	—	—	—

KM# 94 DUCAT

3.5000 g., 0.9860 Gold 0.1109 oz. AGW **Obv:** Half-length figure to right **Rev:** Shield of 4-fold arms with central shield, crown divides date above

Date	Mintage	VG	F	VF	XF	Unc
1631	—	325	650	1,250	2,500	—
1632	—	325	650	1,250	2,500	—

KM# 106 2 DUCAT

7.0000 g., 0.9860 Gold 0.2219 oz. AGW **Note:** Similar to 1 Ducat, KM#94.

Date	Mintage	VG	F	VF	XF	Unc
1632 Rare	—	—	—	—	—	—

KM# 107 5 DUCAT

17.5000 g., 0.9860 Gold 0.5547 oz. AGW **Note:** Similar to 1 Ducat, KM#94.

Date	Mintage	VG	F	VF	XF	Unc
1632 Rare	—	—	—	—	—	—

KM# 95 10 DUCAT

35.0000 g., 0.9860 Gold 1.1095 oz. AGW **Obv:** Half-length figure with sash, 10 punched in left of bust **Rev:** Crowned shield of arms, legend divides date

Date	Mintage	VG	F	VF	XF	Unc
1631 Rare	—	—	—	—	—	—

PATTERNS

Including off metal strikes

KM#	Date	Mintage	Identification	Mkt Val
Pn1	(15)71	—	60 Kreuzer. Lead. Ref. H#73a, MB#61.	—
Pn3	(15)72	—	120 Kreuzer. Lead. Facing figure of St. Kilian standing behind shield of 4-fold arms, S - K divided at shoulders. FRIDERI. EPS. WIRCBVR. FRANC. ORIENT. DVX.. Crowned imperial eagle, '60' in orb on breast, date at end of legend. MAXIMILI. II. IMP. - AVG. P. F. DECRET.. Ref. H#69a, MB#70.	—
Pn2	1590	—	60 Kreuzer. Lead. 3/4-length facing figure of St. Kilian divides S - K, shield of 4-fold arms divides date below in front. IVLIVS. D. G. (EP)ISCOPVS. WIRTZ. FRA. OR(I). DVX.. Crowned imperial eagle, '60' in orb on breast, date at end of legend. RVDOLPHVS. II. ROM. IMP(ERAT). SEMP. AV(GVST). P. F.. Ref. H#131a, MB#94.	—
Pn4	16Z4	—	Kortling. Gold. KM#55	—
Pn5	16Z5	—	3 Heller. Gold. KM#53	—
Pn7	16Z5	—	Kortling. Gold. KM#73	—
Pn8	16Z5	—	Schilling. Gold. KM#77	—
Pn6	ND	—	3 Heller. Gold. KM#54	—
Pn9	1691	—	Schilling. Gold. Weight of 1 Ducat, KM#198.	—
Pn10	1699	—	Kortling. Gold. KM#212.	—
Pn11	1699	—	Schilling. Gold. KM#213.	—

GREAT BRITAIN

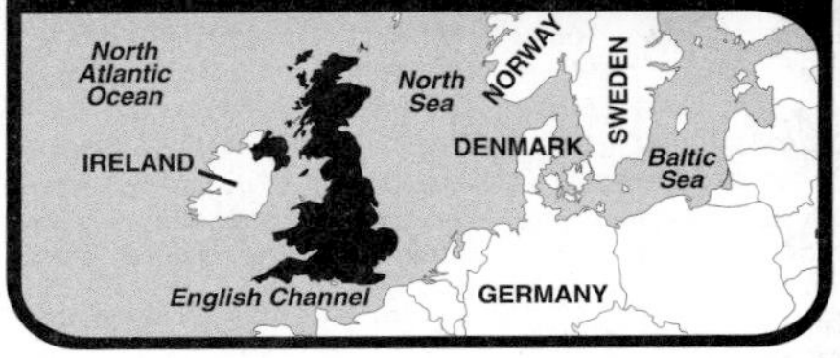

The United Kingdom of Great Britain and Northern Ireland, located off the northwest coast of the European continent, has an area of 94,227 sq. mi. (244,820 sq. km.) and a population of 54 million. Capital: London. The economy is based on industrial activity and trading. Machinery, motor vehicles, chemicals, and textile yarns and fabrics are exported.

After the departure of the Romans, who brought Britain into a more active relationship with Europe, it fell prey to invaders from Scandinavia and the Low Countries who drove the original Britons into Scotland and Wales, and established a profusion of kingdoms that finally united in the 11th century under the Danish King Canute. Norman rule, following the conquest of 1066, stimulated the development of those institutions, which have since distinguished British life. Henry VIII (1509-47) turned Britain from continental adventuring and faced it to the sea - a decision that made Britain a world power during the reign of Elizabeth I (1558-1603). Strengthened by the Industrial Revolution and the defeat of Napoleon, 19th century Britain turned to the remote parts of the world and established a colonial empire of such extent and prosperity that the world has never seen its like. World Wars I and II sealed the fate of the Empire and relegated Britain to a lesser role in world affairs by draining her resources and inaugurating a worldwide movement toward national self-determination in her former colonies.

RULERS

Elizabeth I, 1558-1603
James I, 1603-1625
Charles I, 1625-1649
Commonwealth, 1649-1660
Charles II, 1660-1685
James II, 1685-1688
William and Mary, 1688-1694
William III, 1694-1702

Mint Marks

Under James I, 1603-1625

Mark	Desc.	Date
	Thistle	1603-04
	Lis	1604-05
	Rose	1605-06
	Escallop	1606-07
	Grapes	1607
	Coronet	1607-09
	Key	1609-10
	Bell	1610-11
	Mullet	1611-12
	Tower	1612-13
	Trefoil	1613
	Cinquefoil	1613-15
	Tun	1615-16
	Closed book	161-17
	Crescent	1617-18
	Plain cross	1618-19
	Saltire cross	1619

Mark	Desc.	Date
	Spur rowel	1619-20
	Rose	1620-21
	Thistle	1621-23
	Lis	1623-24
	Trefoil	1624

Under Charles I, 1625-1649

TOWER MINT

Mark	Desc.	Date
	Lis	1625
	Cross Calvary	1625-26
	Negro head	1626-27
	Castle	1627-28
	Anchor	1628-29
	Heart	1629-30
	Plume	1630-31
	Rose	1631-32
	Harp	1632-33
	Portcullis	1633-34
	Bell	1634-35
	Crown	1635-36
	Tun	1636-38
	Anchor	1638-39
	Triangle	1639-40
	Star	1640-41
	Triangle in circle	1641-43

BRIOT'S MINT

Mark	Desc.	Date
	B and flower	1631-32
B	B	1632
	Anchor and B	1638-39
	Anchor and mullet	1638-39

PROVINCIAL MINTS

ABERYSTWYTH MINT

Mark	Desc.	Date
	Open book	1638-42
A	A	1644-46
	Crown	1648-49

BRISTOL MINT

Mark	Desc.	Date
	Cross pattee	1643
	Acorn	1643
	Plume	1643-45
Br	Br	1643-45
	Pellets	1643-45

CHESTER MINT

Mark	Desc.	Date
	Gerb	1644-46

EXETER MINT

Mark	Desc.	Date
	Rose	1643-45
	Castle	1644-46

OXFORD MINT

Mark	Desc.	Date
	Plume	1642-46
	Pellets	1642-46
	Lis	1642-46
	Rosette	1643-45
	Floriated cross	1643-46
	Cross pattee	1644
	Lozenge	1644
	Billet	1644
	Mullet	1644

SALISBURY MINT

Mark	Desc.	Date
	Helmet	1643
	Lis	1643-44
	Bunch of grapes	1643-44
	Bird	1643-44
	Boar's head	1643-44
	Rosette	1643-44

SHREWSBURY MINT

Mark	Desc.	Date
	Plume	1642
	Pellets or pellet	1642

TRURO MINT

Mark	Desc.	Date
	Rose	1642-43

WEYMOUTH MINT

Mark	Desc.	Date
	Castle	1643
	Helmet	1643
	Leopard's head	1643-44
	Two lions	1643-44
	Lis	1643-44
	Bunch of grapes	1643-44
	Bird	1643-44
	Boar's head	1643-44
	Rosette	1643-44

WORCESTER MINT

Mark	Desc.	Date
	Pear	1644-46

YORK MINT

Mark	Desc.	Date
	Lion	1642-44

UNCERTAIN MINT

Mark	Desc.	Date
	Lion rampant	1643-44
	Lis	1644-46
	Plume	1644-46
B	B	1646

Under Parliament

TOWER MINT

Mark	Desc.	Date
(P)	(P)	1643-44
(R)	(R)	1644-45
	Eye	1645
	Sun	1645-46
	Sceptre	1646-48

Commonwealth

Mark	Desc.	Date
	Sun	1649-57
	Anchor	1658-60

Under Charles II

Mark	Desc.	Date
	Crown	1660-62

Under William III

B - Bristol, 1696-1697
C - Chester, 1696-1697
E - Exeter, 1696-1697
N - Norwich, 1696-1697
Y, y - York, 1696-1697

MONETARY SYSTEM

(Until 1970)

4 Farthings = 1 Penny
12 Pence = 1 Shilling
2 Shillings = 1 Florin
5 Shillings = 1 Crown
20 Shillings = 1 Pound (Sovereign)
21 Shillings = 1 Guinea

KINGDOM

PRE-DECIMAL COINAGE

KM# 50 FARTHING

Copper **Ruler:** James I **Obv:** Crown above crossed scepters at center **Rev:** Crowned harp at center **Note:** Normal size. Harrington Issue (1613-14) (Contracted to Lord Harrington.)

Date	Mintage	VG	F	VF	XF	Unc
ND	—	25.00	40.00	100	225	—

KM# 49 FARTHING

Copper **Ruler:** James I **Obv:** Crown above crossed scepters at center **Rev:** Crowned harp at center **Note:** Small size. Harrington Issue (1613-14) (Contracted to Lord Harrington.) At one time called "Half Farthings" because of the small size.

Date	Mintage	VG	F	VF	XF	Unc
ND	—	25.00	40.00	100	225	—

KM# 52 FARTHING

Copper **Ruler:** James I **Note:** Lennox Issue (1614-25). (Contract passed to Duke of Lennox.) Oval shape.

Date	Mintage	VG	F	VF	XF	Unc
ND	—	25.00	55.00	125	250	—

KM# 51 FARTHING

Copper **Ruler:** James I **Note:** Lennox Issue (1614-25). (Contract passed to Duke of Lennox.) Varieties exist.

Date	Mintage	VG	F	VF	XF	Unc
ND	—	15.00	25.00	35.00	100	—

KM# 79 FARTHING

Copper **Ruler:** Charles I **Note:** Richmond Issue (1625-34). (Contract passed to Duchess of Richmond.) Oval shape.

Date	Mintage	VG	F	VF	XF	Unc
ND	—	15.00	30.00	90.00	225	—

KM# 78.1 FARTHING

Copper **Ruler:** Charles I **Obv. Legend:** CARO/IACO **Note:** Richmond Issue (1625-34). (Contract passed to Duchess of Richmond.) Round shape.

Date	Mintage	VG	F	VF	XF	Unc
ND	—	15.00	25.00	60.00	125	—

KM# 78.2 FARTHING

Copper **Ruler:** Charles I **Obv. Legend:** CARA... **Note:** Richmond Issue (1625-34). (Contract passed to Duchess of Richmond.)

Date	Mintage	VG	F	VF	XF	Unc
ND	—	75.00	150	300	500	—

Note: Possibly contemporary counterfeits

KM# 78.3 FARTHING

Copper **Ruler:** Charles I **Obv. Legend:** CARO... **Note:** Richmond Issue (1625-34). (Contract passed to Duchess of Richmond.)

Date	Mintage	VG	F	VF	XF	Unc
ND	—	18.00	30.00	50.00	125	—

KM# 174 FARTHING

Copper **Ruler:** Charles I **Obv:** Crown above crossed scepters in inner circle **Rev:** Crowned harp in inner circle **Note:** Maltravers Issue (1634-36). Contract passed to Lord Maltravers. Oval shape.

Date	Mintage	VG	F	VF	XF	Unc
ND	—	40.00	80.00	150	300	—

KM# 173 FARTHING

Copper **Ruler:** Charles I **Obv:** Crown above crossed scepters in inner circle **Rev:** Crowned harp in inner circle **Note:** Maltravers Issue (1634-36). Contract passed to Lord Maltravers. Round shape.

Date	Mintage	VG	F	VF	XF	Unc
ND	—	18.00	30.00	50.00	125	—

KM# 172 FARTHING

Copper **Ruler:** Charles I **Obv:** Apostrophe punctuation **Rev:** Apostrophe punctuation **Note:** Transitional issue (ca.1634)

Date	Mintage	VG	F	VF	XF	Unc
ND	—	30.00	60.00	125	250	—

KM# 177 FARTHING

Copper **Ruler:** Charles I **Obv:** Crown above crossed scepters in inner circle **Note:** Rose Farthing. Varieties exist.

Date	Mintage	VG	F	VF	XF	Unc
ND	—	20.00	35.00	75.00	150	—

KM# 175 FARTHING

Copper **Ruler:** Charles I **Rev:** Crown above double rose in inner circle **Note:** Rose Farthing. Varieties exist. Many specimens found with a wedge of brass in planchet.

Date	Mintage	VG	F	VF	XF	Unc
ND(1635-44)	—	12.00	20.00	50.00	125	—

KM# 176 FARTHING

Copper **Ruler:** Charles I **Rev:** Crown above single rose in inner circle **Note:** Rose Farthing. Varieties exist.

Date	Mintage	VG	F	VF	XF	Unc
ND 1635	—	12.00	20.00	50.00	125	—

KM# 1 1/2 PENNY

Silver **Ruler:** Elizabeth I **Obv:** Portcullis **Rev:** Long cross with large dots in angles **Note:** Sixth Coinage (1601-02).

Date	Mintage	VG	F	VF	XF	Unc
(160)1	—	25.00	45.00	125	250	—
(160)2	—	25.00	45.00	125	250	—

KM# 8 1/2 PENNY

Silver **Ruler:** James I **Rev:** Long cross with small dots in angles **Note:** First Coinage (1603-04).

Date	Mintage	VG	F	VF	XF	Unc
ND	—	15.00	25.00	65.00	175	—

KM# 22 1/2 PENNY

Silver **Ruler:** James I **Obv:** Double rose **Rev:** Thistle **Note:** Second Coinage (1604-19).

Date	Mintage	VG	F	VF	XF	Unc
ND	—	15.00	25.00	60.00	150	—

KM# 54 1/2 PENNY

Silver **Ruler:** James I **Note:** Third Coinage (1619-25).

Date	Mintage	VG	F	VF	XF	Unc
ND	—	15.00	25.00	50.00	125	—

KM# 178 1/2 PENNY

Silver **Ruler:** Charles I **Obv:** Double rose **Rev:** Double rose **Mint:** Tower

Date	Mintage	VG	F	VF	XF	Unc
ND	—	11.00	22.00	65.00	160	—

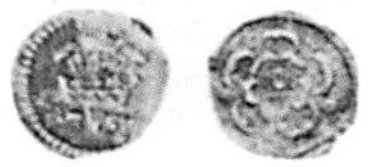

KM# 179 1/2 PENNY

Silver **Ruler:** Charles I **Rev:** Plumes in crown **Mint:** Aberystwyth

Date	Mintage	VG	F	VF	XF	Unc
ND	—	125	250	850	2,000	—

KM# 2 PENNY

Silver **Ruler:** Elizabeth I **Obv:** Crowned bust of Elizabeth I left in inner circle **Rev:** Shield of arms on long cross **Note:** Sixth Coinage (1601-02).

Date	Mintage	VG	F	VF	XF	Unc
(160)1	—	15.00	45.00	125	300	—
(160)2	—	15.00	45.00	125	300	—

KM# 9 PENNY

Silver **Ruler:** James I **Obv:** Crowned bust of James I right with balue behind in inner circle **Rev:** Shield of arms **Note:** First Coinage (1603-04).

Date	Mintage	VG	F	VF	XF	Unc
ND	—	15.00	30.00	100	250	—

KM# 23 PENNY

Silver **Ruler:** James I **Obv:** Rose in inner circle **Rev:** Thistle in inner circle **Note:** Second Coinage (1604-19). Varieties exist.

Date	Mintage	VG	F	VF	XF	Unc
ND	—	14.00	27.00	70.00	150	—

KM# 55 PENNY

Silver **Ruler:** James I **Note:** Third Coinage (1619-25).

Date	Mintage	VG	F	VF	XF	Unc
ND	—	14.00	27.00	65.00	150	—

KM# 56 PENNY

Silver **Ruler:** Charles I **Rev:** Rose in inner circle **Mint:** Tower **Note:** Varieties exist.

Date	Mintage	VG	F	VF	XF	Unc
ND	—	16.00	29.00	70.00	150	—

KM# 80.1 PENNY

Silver **Ruler:** Charles I **Obv:** Crowned bust of Charles I left with value behind in inner circle **Rev:** Oval shield in inner circle **Note:** Varieties exist.

Date	Mintage	VG	F	VF	XF	Unc
ND(1625-49)	—	15.00	35.00	100	250	—

KM# 80.2 PENNY

Silver **Ruler:** Charles I **Rev:** C R at sides of shield **Note:** Varieties exist.

Date	Mintage	VG	F	VF	XF	Unc
ND(1625-49)	—	15.00	25.00	75.00	200	—

KM# 81 PENNY

Silver **Ruler:** Charles I **Obv:** Older bust of Charles I left with value behind in inner circle **Rev:** Shield of arms in inner circle **Mint:** Tower **Note:** Struck (under Parliament).

Date	Mintage	VG	F	VF	XF	Unc
ND(1625-49)	—	17.00	35.00	100	225	—

KM# 155 PENNY

Silver **Ruler:** Charles I **Obv:** Older bust of Charles I left with value behind **Rev:** Shield of arms in inner circle on long cross **Note:** First Milled Briot Issue (1631-32).

Date	Mintage	VG	F	VF	XF	Unc
ND(1631-32)	—	45.00	95.00	225	550	—

KM# 157 PENNY

Silver **Ruler:** Charles I **Rev:** Without inner circle **Mint:** Aberystwyth

Date	Mintage	VG	F	VF	XF	Unc
ND(1631-32)	—	50.00	100	250	550	—

KM# 160 PENNY

Silver **Ruler:** Charles I **Rev:** Large plumes with bands in inner circle **Mint:** Bristol

Date	Mintage	VG	F	VF	XF	Unc
ND(1631-32)	—	250	550	1,300	3,000	—

KM# 156 PENNY

Silver **Ruler:** Charles I **Rev:** Plumes in crown in inner circle **Mint:** Aberystwyth **Note:** Varieties exist.

Date	Mintage	VG	F	VF	XF	Unc
ND(1631-32)	—	45.00	100	250	550	—

KM# 159 PENNY

Silver **Ruler:** Charles I **Obv:** Crowned bust of Charles I left with value behind in inner circle **Rev:** Plumes in crown in inner circle **Mint:** Oxford **Note:** Varieties exist.

Date	Mintage	VG	F	VF	XF	Unc
ND(1631-32)	—	125	250	700	1,600	—

KM# 270 PENNY

Silver **Ruler:** Charles I **Rev:** Declaration

Date	Mintage	VG	F	VF	XF	Unc
1644	—	200	400	1,000	2,500	—

KM# 271 PENNY

Silver **Ruler:** Charles I **Obv:** Crowned thin bust of Charles I left with value behind in inner circle **Rev:** Large rose in inner circle **Mint:** Exeter

Date	Mintage	VG	F	VF	XF	Unc
1644	—	225	500	1,400	3,000	—

KM# 158 PENNY

Silver **Ruler:** Charles I **Rev:** Large plumes in crown in inner circle **Mint:** Aberystwyth - Furnace Mint

Date	Mintage	VG	F	VF	XF	Unc
ND(1648-49)	—	450	850	3,000	—	—

KM# 3 2 PENCE (1/2 Groat)

Silver **Ruler:** Elizabeth I **Obv:** Crowned bust left in inner circle **Rev:** Shield of arms on long cross **Note:** Sixth Coinage.

Date	Mintage	Good	VG	F	VF	XF
(160)1	—	—	17.50	35.00	100	225
(160)2	—	—	17.50	35.00	100	225

KM# 10 2 PENCE (1/2 Groat)

0.8300 g., Silver **Ruler:** James I **Obv:** Crowned bust of James I right with value behind within inner circle **Rev:** Shield of arms **Note:** First Coinage (1603-04).

Date	Mintage	VG	F	VF	XF	Unc
ND(1603-04)	—	22.00	45.00	100	200	—

KM# 24 2 PENCE (1/2 Groat)

Silver **Ruler:** James I **Obv:** Crowned rose in inner circle **Rev:** Crowned thistle in inner circle **Note:** Second Coinage (1604-19). Varieties exist.

Date	Mintage	VG	F	VF	XF	Unc
ND	—	15.00	30.00	75.00	150	—

KM# 57 2 PENCE (1/2 Groat)

Silver **Ruler:** James I **Obv:** Large crowned rose in inner circle **Note:** Third Coinage (1619-25).

Date	Mintage	VG	F	VF	XF	Unc
ND	—	15.00	30.00	70.00	150	—

KM# 58 2 PENCE (1/2 Groat)

Silver **Ruler:** James I **Obv:** Crowned rose in inner circle **Rev:** Crowned rose in inner circle **Mint:** Tower **Note:** Varieties exist.

Date	Mintage	VG	F	VF	XF	Unc
ND(1619-25)	—	15.00	30.00	125	300	—

KM# 82 2 PENCE (1/2 Groat)

Silver **Ruler:** Charles I **Obv:** Crowend bust of Charles I left in ruffled collar and mantle, value behind, in inner circle **Rev:** Oval shield of arms **Note:** Varieties exist.

Date	Mintage	VG	F	VF	XF	Unc
ND(1625-49)	—	15.00	35.00	90.00	225	—

KM# 83 2 PENCE (1/2 Groat)

Silver **Ruler:** Charles I **Obv:** Crowend bust of Charles I left in lace collar, value behind in inner circle **Rev:** Oval arms in inner circle **Note:** Varieties exist.

Date	Mintage	VG	F	VF	XF	Unc
ND(1625-49)	—	15.00	30.00	70.00	150	—

KM# 84 2 PENCE (1/2 Groat)

Silver **Ruler:** Charles I **Rev:** Round arms in inner circle **Note:** Varieties exist.

Date	Mintage	VG	F	VF	XF	Unc
ND(1625-49)	—	15.00	30.00	70.00	150	—

KM# 85 2 PENCE (1/2 Groat)

Silver **Ruler:** Charles I **Obv:** Crowned older bust of Charles I left, value behind in inner circle **Rev:** Oval arms in inner circle **Mint:** Tower **Note:** Struck (under Parliament). Varieties exist.

Date	Mintage	VG	F	VF	XF	Unc
ND(1625-49)	—	15.00	30.00	100	250	—

KM# 161 2 PENCE (1/2 Groat)
Silver **Ruler:** Charles I **Obv:** Briot bust of Charles I left, value behind in inner circle **Rev:** Shield of arms on long cross in inner circle **Note:** First Milled Briot Issue (1631-32)

Date	Mintage	VG	F	VF	XF	Unc
ND(1631-32)	—	45.00	90.00	175	400	—

KM# 162 2 PENCE (1/2 Groat)
Silver **Ruler:** Charles I **Obv:** Crowned bust of Charles I with lace collar left with value behind in inner circle **Rev:** Large plumes in crown in inner circle **Mint:** Aberystwyth **Note:** Varieties exist.

Date	Mintage	VG	F	VF	XF	Unc
ND(1631-32)	—	40.00	75.00	225	600	—

KM# 163.1 2 PENCE (1/2 Groat)
Silver **Ruler:** Charles I **Obv:** Crowned bust of Charles with value behind in inner circle **Mint:** Aberystwyth - Furnace Mint

Date	Mintage	VG	F	VF	XF	Unc
ND(1631)	—	200	450	1,000	2,300	—

KM# 163.2 2 PENCE (1/2 Groat)
Silver **Ruler:** Charles I **Mint:** Oxford

Date	Mintage	VG	F	VF	XF	Unc
ND(1631-32)	—	75.00	150	400	950	—

KM# 272.2 2 PENCE (1/2 Groat)
Silver **Ruler:** Charles I **Rev:** Declaration, BR below **Mint:** Bristol

Date	Mintage	VG	F	VF	XF	Unc
ND(1644)	—	300	550	1,250	3,000	—

KM# 273.1 2 PENCE (1/2 Groat)
Silver **Ruler:** Charles I **Rev:** Oval shield in inner circle **Mint:** Exeter

Date	Mintage	VG	F	VF	XF	Unc
1644	—	150	350	850	2,000	—

KM# 273.2 2 PENCE (1/2 Groat)
Silver **Ruler:** Charles I **Mint:** Worcester

Date	Mintage	VG	F	VF	XF	Unc
ND(1644)	—	350	700	1,700	4,000	—

KM# 274 2 PENCE (1/2 Groat)
Silver **Ruler:** Charles I **Obv:** Large rose in inner circle **Mint:** Exeter

Date	Mintage	VG	F	VF	XF	Unc
1644	—	175	350	900	2,000	—

KM# 163.3 2 PENCE (1/2 Groat)
Silver **Ruler:** Charles I **Rev:** Large plumes divide date **Mint:** Lundy

Date	Mintage	VG	F	VF	XF	Unc
1646	—	225	450	1,100	2,500	—

KM# 86 3 PENCE
Silver **Ruler:** Charles I **Obv:** Crowned bust of Charles I left with value behind in inner circle **Rev:** Crowned arms on log cross with inner circle **Mint:** York

Date	Mintage	VG	F	VF	XF	Unc
ND(1625-49)	—	50.00	100	225	500	—

KM# 88 3 PENCE
Silver **Ruler:** Charles I **Rev:** Crowned and garnished arms in inner circle **Mint:** Aberystwyth - Furnace Mint

Date	Mintage	VG	F	VF	XF	Unc
ND(1625-49)	—	125	250	750	1,800	—

KM# 89 3 PENCE
Silver **Ruler:** Charles I **Obv:** Small bust (Rawlins) of Charles I with value behind in inner circle **Rev:** Crowned oval arms in inner circle **Mint:** Oxford

Date	Mintage	VG	F	VF	XF	Unc
ND(1625-49)	—	75.00	150	400	1,000	—

KM# 87 3 PENCE
Silver **Ruler:** Charles I **Obv:** Plumes before face of Charles I **Mint:** Aberystwyth **Note:** Varieties exist.

Date	Mintage	VG	F	VF	XF	Unc
ND(1625-49)	—	30.00	65.00	175	350	—

KM# 275 3 PENCE
Silver **Ruler:** Charles I **Obv:** Crowned bust (Aberystwyth) of Charles I left, plumes in front, value behind, in inner circle **Rev:** Declaration, date above OX **Mint:** Oxford **Note:** Varieties exist.

Date	Mintage	VG	F	VF	XF	Unc
1644	—	40.00	125	400	1,000	—

KM# 277.1 3 PENCE
Silver **Ruler:** Charles I **Obv:** Crowned bust of Charles I left, plumes in front, value behind, in inner circle **Mint:** Bristol **Note:** Varieties exist.

Date	Mintage	VG	F	VF	XF	Unc
1644	—	125	250	550	1,400	—

KM# 278 3 PENCE
Silver **Ruler:** Charles I **Obv:** Crowned bust of Charles I left with value behind, in inner circle **Rev:** Shield of amrs in inner circle on long cross **Mint:** Exeter

Date	Mintage	VG	F	VF	XF	Unc
1644	—	100	225	500	1,100	—

KM# 279 3 PENCE
Silver **Ruler:** Charles I **Obv:** Crude crowned bust of Charles I left with value behind in inner circle **Rev:** Garnished oval arms in inner circle **Mint:** Worcester

Date	Mintage	VG	F	VF	XF	Unc
ND(1644)	—	250	550	1,000	2,500	—

KM# 280 3 PENCE
Silver **Ruler:** Charles I **Obv:** Crowned bust of Charles I left with value behind, in inner circle **Rev:** Square-topped shield of amrs in inner circle **Mint:** Chester

Date	Mintage	VG	F	VF	XF	Unc
ND(1644)	—	600	1,300	3,500	8,000	—

KM# 277.2 3 PENCE
Silver **Ruler:** Charles I **Mint:** Lundy **Note:** Varieties exist.

Date	Mintage	VG	F	VF	XF	Unc
1645	—	125	250	550	1,300	—
1646	—	60.00	125	400	900	—

KM# 276 3 PENCE
Silver **Ruler:** Charles I **Obv:** Small bust of Charles I left iwth value behind, in inner circle **Rev:** DECLARATION, date below **Mint:** Oxford

Date	Mintage	VG	F	VF	XF	Unc
1646/44	—	65.00	125	400	1,000	—

KM# 91 4 PENCE (Groat)
Silver **Ruler:** Charles I **Rev:** Garnished oval arms with plumes above, in inner circle **Mint:** Aberystwyth - Furnace Mint

Date	Mintage	VG	F	VF	XF	Unc
ND(1625-49)	—	150	300	750	1,400	—

KM# 90 4 PENCE (Groat)
Silver **Ruler:** Charles I **Obv:** Crowned bust of Charles I left, plumes in front, value behind, in inner circle **Rev:** Round arms within wreath in inner circle **Mint:** Aberystwyth **Note:** Varieties exist.

Date	Mintage	VG	F	VF	XF	Unc
ND(1625-49)	—	25.00	50.00	200	650	—

KM# 283.1 4 PENCE (Groat)
Silver **Ruler:** Charles I **Obv:** Bust of Charles I, left **Rev:** Declaration, date and OX below **Mint:** Oxford **Note:** Varieties exist.

Date	Mintage	VG	F	VF	XF	Unc
1644	—	100	200	550	1,300	—

KM# 286.1 4 PENCE (Groat)
Silver **Ruler:** Charles I **Obv:** Crowned bust of Charles I left, value behind in inner circle **Rev:** Declaration, date below **Mint:** Bristol **Note:** Varieties exist.

Date	Mintage	VG	F	VF	XF	Unc
1644	—	350	700	1,900	4,500	—

KM# 286.2 4 PENCE (Groat)
Silver **Ruler:** Charles I **Obv:** Small plume in front of face **Mint:** Bristol **Note:** Varieties exist.

Date	Mintage	VG	F	VF	XF	Unc
1644	—	150	300	800	1,900	—

KM# 283.2 4 PENCE (Groat)
Silver **Ruler:** Charles I **Obv:** Lion's head on shoulder armor decoration **Mint:** Oxford

Date	Mintage	VG	F	VF	XF	Unc
1644	—	85.00	175	550	1,200	—
1645	—	100	225	550	1,300	—

KM# 284 4 PENCE (Groat)
Silver **Ruler:** Charles I **Obv:** Bust reaches to top of coin **Mint:** Oxford

Date	Mintage	VG	F	VF	XF	Unc
1644	—	100	225	550	1,300	—

KM# 285 4 PENCE (Groat)
Silver **Ruler:** Charles I **Obv:** Bust reaches to bottom of coin **Mint:** Oxford

Date	Mintage	VG	F	VF	XF	Unc
1644	—	100	225	550	1,300	—
1645	—	100	225	550	1,300	—

KM# 288 4 PENCE (Groat)
Silver **Ruler:** Charles I **Obv:** Crowned bust of Charles I left, value behind, in nner circle, date in legend **Rev:** Round arms in inner circle **Mint:** Exeter

Date	Mintage	VG	F	VF	XF	Unc
1644	—	85.00	175	400	950	—

KM# 289 4 PENCE (Groat)
Silver **Ruler:** Charles I **Obv:** Bust of Charles I, left **Mint:** Worcester

Date	Mintage	VG	F	VF	XF	Unc
ND(1644)	—	450	1,000	2,300	—	—

KM# 287 4 PENCE (Groat)
Silver **Ruler:** Charles I **Obv:** Crowned bust (Rawlins) of Charles I left with value behind **Rev:** Declaration in cartouche, date below **Mint:** Oxford

Date	Mintage	VG	F	VF	XF	Unc
1645	—	100	200	550	1,300	—
1646	—	100	200	550	1,300	—

KM# 286.3 4 PENCE (Groat)
Silver **Ruler:** Charles I **Obv:** Small plume in front of face **Mint:** Lundy **Note:** Varieties exist.

Date	Mintage	VG	F	VF	XF	Unc
1645 Rare	—	—	—	—	—	—
1646	—	65.00	125	400	900	—

KM# 4 6 PENCE
Silver **Ruler:** Elizabeth I **Obv:** Crowned bust of Elizabeth I left with rose behind head in inner circle **Rev:** Shield of arms **Note:** Sixth Issue, 1601 - 02 with mint marks numerals "1" and "2".

Date	Mintage	Good	VG	F	VF	XF
1601	—	—	35.00	75.00	300	750
1602	—	—	35.00	75.00	300	750

KM# 12 6 PENCE
Silver **Ruler:** James I **Obv:** Second bust of James I

Date	Mintage	VG	F	VF	XF	Unc
1603	—	40.00	80.00	250	600	—
1604	—	40.00	80.00	250	600	—

KM# 11 6 PENCE
Silver **Ruler:** James I **Obv:** First bust of James I right with value behind head, in inner circle **Note:** First Coinage (1603-04).

Date	Mintage	VG	F	VF	XF	Unc
1603	—	40.00	85.00	375	750	—

KM# 25 6 PENCE
Silver **Ruler:** James I **Obv:** Third bust of James I **Note:** Second Coinage (1604-19).

Date	Mintage	VG	F	VF	XF	Unc
1604	—	35.00	70.00	225	500	—
1605	—	35.00	70.00	225	500	—

KM# 48 6 PENCE
Silver **Ruler:** James I **Obv:** Fourth bust of James I

Date	Mintage	VG	F	VF	XF	Unc
1605	—	35.00	70.00	250	550	—
1606	—	35.00	70.00	250	550	—
1607	—	35.00	70.00	250	550	—
1608	—	35.00	70.00	250	550	—
1609	—	35.00	70.00	250	550	—
1610	—	35.00	70.00	250	550	—
1611	—	35.00	70.00	250	550	—
1612	—	35.00	70.00	250	550	—
1613	—	35.00	70.00	250	550	—
1614	—	35.00	70.00	250	550	—
1615	—	35.00	70.00	250	550	—

KM# 53 6 PENCE
Silver **Ruler:** James I **Obv:** Fifth bust of James I

Date	Mintage	VG	F	VF	XF	Unc
1618 Unique	—	—	900	3,000	—	—

KM# 77 6 PENCE
Silver **Ruler:** James I **Obv:** Crowned armored bust of James I (Sixth bust) **Rev:** Shield of arms **Note:** Third Coinage (1619-25).

Date	Mintage	VG	F	VF	XF	Unc
1621	—	50.00	95.00	300	700	—
1622	—	50.00	95.00	300	700	—
1623	—	50.00	95.00	300	700	—
1624	—	50.00	95.00	300	700	—

KM# 93 6 PENCE
Silver **Ruler:** Charles I **Obv:** Second bust of Charles I **Mint:** Tower **Note:** Varieties exist.

Date	Mintage	VG	F	VF	XF	Unc
1625	—	80.00	150	500	1,100	—
1626	—	80.00	150	500	1,100	—
1627	—	80.00	150	500	1,100	—
1628	—	80.00	150	500	1,100	—
1629	—	80.00	150	500	1,100	—
1630	—	100	200	700	1,750	—

KM# 94 6 PENCE
Silver **Ruler:** Charles I **Obv:** Third bust of Charles I **Mint:** Tower **Note:** Varieties exist.

Date	Mintage	VG	F	VF	XF	Unc
ND(1625-49)	—	32.50	105	400	950	—

KM# 95 6 PENCE
Silver **Ruler:** Charles I **Obv:** Fourth bust of Charles I **Mint:** Tower **Note:** Varieties exist.

Date	Mintage	VG	F	VF	XF	Unc
ND(1625-49)	—	30.00	85.00	325	750	—

KM# 96 6 PENCE
Silver **Ruler:** Charles I **Obv:** Fifth bust of Charles I **Mint:** Tower **Note:** Varieties exist.

Date	Mintage	VG	F	VF	XF	Unc
ND(1625-49)	—	30.00	90.00	375	900	—

KM# 97 6 PENCE
Silver **Ruler:** Charles I **Obv:** Sixth bust of Charles I **Mint:** Tower **Note:** Struck (under Parliament).

Date	Mintage	VG	F	VF	XF	Unc
ND(1625-49)	—	45.00	150	500	1,250	—

KM# 98 6 PENCE
Silver **Ruler:** Charles I **Obv:** Seventh bust of Charles I **Mint:** Tower **Note:** Struck (under Parliament).

Date	Mintage	VG	F	VF	XF	Unc
ND(1625-49)	—	50.00	105	325	750	—

KM# 92 6 PENCE
Silver **Ruler:** Charles I **Obv:** First bust of Charles I left with value behind head, in inner circle **Mint:** Tower

Date	Mintage	VG	F	VF	XF	Unc
1625	—	65.00	125	450	1,100	—
1626	—	65.00	125	450	1,100	—

KM# 164 6 PENCE
Silver **Ruler:** Charles I **Obv:** Charles I **Note:** First Milled Briot Issue (1631-32).

Date	Mintage	VG	F	VF	XF	Unc
ND	—	100	200	550	1,300	—

KM# 180 6 PENCE
Silver **Ruler:** Charles I **Obv:** Different lace collar on Charles I **Rev:** Cross inside inner collar **Note:** Second Milled Briot Issue (1638-39).

Date	Mintage	VG	F	VF	XF	Unc
ND	—	55.00	125	350	800	—

KM# 181.1 6 PENCE
Silver **Ruler:** Charles I **Obv:** Crowned bust of Charles I **Rev:** Crowned oval arms with crowned C and R at sides **Mint:** York

Date	Mintage	VG	F	VF	XF	Unc
ND(1638-39)	—	200	400	1,000	2,400	—

KM# 181.2 6 PENCE
Silver **Ruler:** Charles I **Rev:** Withour C R at sides of arms **Mint:** York

Date	Mintage	VG	F	VF	XF	Unc
ND(1638-39)	—	200	400	1,000	2,400	—

KM# 182 6 PENCE
Silver **Ruler:** Charles I **Obv:** Crowned bust of Charles I left, plumes in front, value behind **Rev:** Garnished oval arms with plumes at top **Mint:** Aberystwyth

Date	Mintage	VG	F	VF	XF	Unc
ND(1638-39)	—	225	450	1,300	3,000	—

KM# 185 6 PENCE
Silver **Ruler:** Charles I **Obv:** Crowned bust of Charles I left, plumes in front, value behind, in inner circle **Rev:** Garnished oval arms iwth plumes above in inner circle **Mint:** Aberystwyth - Furnace Mint

Date	Mintage	VG	F	VF	XF	Unc
ND(1638-39) Rare	—	—	—	—	—	—

KM# 183 6 PENCE
Silver **Ruler:** Charles I **Obv:** With inner circle **Rev:** Flat-topped arms in inner circle **Mint:** Aberystwyth **Note:** Varieties exist.

Date	Mintage	VG	F	VF	XF	Unc
ND(1638-39)	—	225	450	1,300	3,000	—

KM# 184 6 PENCE
Silver **Ruler:** Charles I **Obv:** Crown breaks inner circle **Rev:** Large oval arms in inner circle, plumes at top **Mint:** Aberystwyth **Note:** Varieties exist.

Date	Mintage	VG	F	VF	XF	Unc
ND(1638-39)	—	225	450	1,300	3,000	—

KM# 203.1 6 PENCE
Silver **Ruler:** Charles I **Rev:** Declaration with three Oxford plumes above and date below **Mint:** Oxford

Date	Mintage	VG	F	VF	XF	Unc
1642	—	200	400	1,100	2,500	—
1643	—	200	400	1,100	2,500	—

KM# 203.2 6 PENCE
Silver **Ruler:** Charles I **Rev:** Three Shrewsbury plumes above **Mint:** Oxford

Date	Mintage	VG	F	VF	XF	Unc
1643	—	150	350	1,000	2,300	—

KM# 241.1 6 PENCE
Silver **Ruler:** Charles I **Obv:** Crude bust of Charles I left with value behind, in inner circle **Rev:** Declaration with plumes above and date below **Mint:** Bristol

Date	Mintage	VG	F	VF	XF	Unc
1643	—	175	400	1,000	2,500	—

KM# 241.2 6 PENCE
Silver **Ruler:** Charles I **Obv:** Plume added in front of face **Mint:** Bristol

Date	Mintage	VG	F	VF	XF	Unc
1644	—	200	400	950	2,300	—

KM# 342 6 PENCE
Silver **Ruler:** Charles I **Obv:** Garnished round arms in inner circle, date divided by rose in legend **Mint:** Exeter

Date	Mintage	VG	F	VF	XF	Unc
1644	—	225	450	1,100	2,500	—

KM# 203.3 6 PENCE
Silver **Ruler:** Charles I **Rev:** Shrewsbury plumes and three lis above, OX **Mint:** Oxford

Date	Mintage	VG	F	VF	XF	Unc
1644	—	300	750	1,800	4,500	—

KM# 343.1 6 PENCE
Silver **Ruler:** Charles I **Obv:** Crowned bust of Charles I left with small plume in front, value behind in inner circle **Rev:** Declaration with plumes above and date below **Mint:** Lundy

Date	Mintage	VG	F	VF	XF	Unc
1645	—	175	400	1,000	2,500	—

KM# 343.2 6 PENCE
Silver **Ruler:** Charles I **Mint:** Lundy

Date	Mintage	VG	F	VF	XF	Unc
1646	—	75.00	175	400	1,000	—

KM# 367 6 PENCE
Silver **Ruler:** Charles I **Obv:** Crude bust of Charles I left with value behind in inner circle **Rev:** Square-topped shield with paws at sides and top **Mint:** Worcester

Date	Mintage	VG	F	VF	XF	Unc
ND(1646)	—	800	2,000	5,000	—	—

KM# 5 SHILLING
Silver **Ruler:** Elizabeth I **Obv:** Crowned bust left in inner circle **Rev:** Shield of arms **Note:** Sixth Issue (1601-02).

Date	Mintage	Good	VG	F	VF	XF
(160)1	—	—	75.00	175	600	1,500
(160)2	—	—	75.00	175	600	1,500

KM# 14 SHILLING
Silver **Ruler:** James I **Obv:** Second bust (pointed beard resting on chest) of James I

Date	Mintage	VG	F	VF	XF	Unc
ND(1604-19)	—	50.00	100	350	850	—

KM# 27 SHILLING
Silver **Ruler:** James I **Obv:** Fourth bust (plain armor) of James I

Date	Mintage	VG	F	VF	XF	Unc
ND	—	45.00	100	350	850	—

KM# 28 SHILLING
Silver **Ruler:** James I **Obv:** Fifth bust (longer hair) of James I

Date	Mintage	VG	F	VF	XF	Unc
ND	—	50.00	100	350	850	—

KM# 13 SHILLING
Silver **Ruler:** James I **Obv:** First bust (square beard) of James I right with value behind head in inner circle **Rev:** Shield of arms in inner circle **Note:** First Coinage. Mint mark: Thistle.

Date	Mintage	VG	F	VF	XF	Unc
ND(1604-19)	—	50.00	175	600	—	—

KM# 26 SHILLING
Silver **Ruler:** James I **Obv:** Third bust (square beard that stands out) of James I **Note:** Second Coinage.

Date	Mintage	VG	F	VF	XF	Unc
ND(1604-19)	—	50.00	100	350	800	—

KM# 59 SHILLING
Silver **Ruler:** James I **Obv:** Sixth bust (longer and very curly hair) of James I **Note:** Third Coinage.

Date	Mintage	VG	F	VF	XF	Unc
ND(1619-25)	—	55.00	125	400	900	—

KM# 60 SHILLING
Silver **Ruler:** James I **Rev:** Plume above shield

Date	Mintage	VG	F	VF	XF	Unc
ND(1619-25)	—	125	250	1,000	2,100	—

KM# 99 SHILLING
Silver **Ruler:** Charles I **Obv:** First bust (large ruffled collar) of Charles I left in inner circle **Rev:** Square-topped shield of arms on long cross in inner circle **Mint:** Tower

Date	Mintage	VG	F	VF	XF	Unc
ND(1625-49)	—	45.00	200	600	1,350	—

KM# 100 SHILLING
Silver **Ruler:** Charles I **Rev:** Without long cross **Mint:** Tower

Date	Mintage	VG	F	VF	XF	Unc
ND(1625-49)	—	75.00	260	650	1,600	—

KM# 101 SHILLING
Silver **Ruler:** Charles I **Obv:** Second bust (tall and thin with scarf covering armor) of Charles I **Rev:** Square-topped shield of arms in inner circle on long cross **Mint:** Tower

Date	Mintage	VG	F	VF	XF	Unc
ND(1625-49)	—	55.00	175	600	1,350	—

KM# 102 SHILLING
Silver **Ruler:** Charles I **Rev:** Without long cross **Mint:** Tower

Date	Mintage	VG	F	VF	XF	Unc
ND(1625-49)	—	60.00	175	750	1,650	—

KM# 103 SHILLING
Silver **Ruler:** Charles I **Obv:** Third bust (more armor shows around scarf) of Charles I **Rev:** Oval arms with C-R above in inner circle **Mint:** Tower

Date	Mintage	VG	F	VF	XF	Unc
ND(1625-49)	—	40.00	100	400	950	—

KM# 105 SHILLING
Silver **Ruler:** Charles I **Obv:** Fourth bust (with lace collar) of Charles I **Rev:** Oval arms with C-R at sides in inner circle **Mint:** Tower

Date	Mintage	VG	F	VF	XF	Unc
ND(1625-49)	—	27.50	80.00	250	700	—

KM# 106 SHILLING
Silver **Ruler:** Charles I **Rev:** Plume above shield **Mint:** Tower

Date	Mintage	VG	F	VF	XF	Unc
ND(1625-49)	—	300	650	2,000	5,000	—

KM# 107 SHILLING
Silver **Ruler:** Charles I **Obv:** Without inner circle **Rev:** Round arms without C-R or inner circle **Mint:** Tower

Date	Mintage	VG	F	VF	XF	Unc
ND(1625-49)	—	27.50	85.00	250	800	—

KM# 108 SHILLING
Silver **Ruler:** Charles I **Rev:** Plume above shield **Mint:** Tower

Date	Mintage	VG	F	VF	XF	Unc
ND(1625-49)	—	45.00	200	400	1,000	—

KM# 110 SHILLING
Silver **Ruler:** Charles I **Obv:** Sixth bust (very pointed beard) of Charles I **Mint:** Tower

Date	Mintage	VG	F	VF	XF	Unc
ND(1625-49)	—	25.00	70.00	250	700	—

KM# 109 SHILLING
Silver **Ruler:** Charles I **Obv:** Fifth bust (as Aberystwyth) of Charles I **Rev:** Square-topped shield of arms on long cross in inner circle **Mint:** Tower **Note:** Varieties exist.

Date	Mintage	VG	F	VF	XF	Unc
ND(1625-49)	—	35.00	95.00	300	800	—

KM# 165 SHILLING
Silver **Ruler:** Charles I **Obv:** Early Briot bust of Charles I **Note:** First Milled Briot Issue (1631-32).

Date	Mintage	VG	F	VF	XF	Unc
ND(1625-49)	—	250	550	1,100	2,600	—

KM# 186 SHILLING
Silver **Ruler:** Charles I **Obv:** Late Briot bust of Charles I with collar with lace border **Note:** Second Milled Briot Issue (1638-39).

Date	Mintage	VG	F	VF	XF	Unc
ND(1625-49)	—	75.00	375	700	1,750	—

KM# 111 SHILLING
Silver **Ruler:** Charles I **Obv:** Seventh bust (long and narrow, crude) of Charles I **Mint:** Tower **Note:** Struck under Parliament.

Date	Mintage	VG	F	VF	XF	Unc
ND(1643-44)(P)	—	30.00	90.00	300	800	—

KM# 112 SHILLING
Silver **Ruler:** Charles I **Obv:** Eighth bust (shorter and older) of Charles I **Mint:** Tower **Note:** Struck under Parliament.

Date	Mintage	VG	F	VF	XF	Unc
ND(1644-45)(R)	—	35.00	100	450	1,000	—

KM# 104 SHILLING
Silver **Ruler:** Charles I **Rev:** Plume above shield **Mint:** Tower **Note:** Mint marks: Plume, rose.

Date	Mintage	VG	F	VF	XF	Unc
ND(1625-49)	—	90.00	300	1,000	2,500	—

KM# 193 SHILLING
Silver **Ruler:** Charles I **Rev:** Inner circle added **Mint:** Aberystwyth **Note:** Mint mark: Open book.

Date	Mintage	VG	F	VF	XF	Unc
ND(1638-39)	—	250	550	1,700	4,000	—

KM# 187 SHILLING
Silver **Ruler:** Charles I **Obv:** Crude style **Rev:** Crude style **Note:** Briot Hammered Issue.

Date	Mintage	VG	F	VF	XF	Unc
ND(1638-39)	—	250	500	1,400	3,250	—

KM# 188 SHILLING
Silver **Ruler:** Charles I **Obv:** Crowned bust of Charles I left with lace collar and value behind in inner circle **Rev:** Square-topped shield of arms on long cross in inner circle, EBOR... at top **Mint:** York

Date	Mintage	VG	F	VF	XF	Unc
ND(1638-39)	—	100	300	850	2,000	—

KM# 192 SHILLING
Silver **Ruler:** Charles I **Obv:** Crowned bust of Charles I left, plume in front, small value behind **Rev:** Crowned garnished arms **Mint:** Aberystwyth

Date	Mintage	VG	F	VF	XF	Unc
ND(1638-39)	—	300	600	1,700	4,000	—

KM# 194 SHILLING
Silver **Ruler:** Charles I **Obv:** Large value and inner circle added **Mint:** Aberystwyth

Date	Mintage	VG	F	VF	XF	Unc
ND(1638-39)	—	250	550	1,700	3,500	—

KM# 195 SHILLING
Silver **Ruler:** Charles I **Rev:** Different garnish on shield **Mint:** Aberystwyth

Date	Mintage	VG	F	VF	XF	Unc
ND(1638-39)	—	300	600	1,800	4,000	—

KM# 196 SHILLING
Silver **Ruler:** Charles I **Obv:** Crowned bust of Charles I left, plume in front, value behind in inner circle **Rev:** Garnished oval arms in inner circle, plume above **Mint:** Aberystwyth - Furnace Mint

Date	Mintage	VG	F	VF	XF	Unc
ND(1638-39) Rare	—	—	—	—	—	—

KM# 203 SHILLING
Silver **Ruler:** Charles I **Rev:** Declaration, three plumes above, date below in inner circle **Mint:** Shrewsbury

Date	Mintage	VG	F	VF	XF	Unc
1642	—	850	1,700	4,500	9,500	—

KM# 204 SHILLING
Silver **Ruler:** Charles I **Obv:** Cruder bust without plume in front of face **Mint:** Shrewsbury

Date	Mintage	VG	F	VF	XF	Unc
1642	—	850	1,700	4,500	9,500	—

KM# 205 SHILLING
Silver **Ruler:** Charles I **Obv:** Crowned bust (as Shrewsbury) of Charles I **Mint:** Oxford

Date	Mintage	VG	F	VF	XF	Unc
1642	—	300	600	1,600	4,500	—

KM# 206 SHILLING
Silver **Ruler:** Charles I **Obv:** Small new bust of Charles I **Mint:** Oxford

Date	Mintage	VG	F	VF	XF	Unc
1642	—	200	400	1,200	2,800	—
1643	—	200	400	1,100	2,600	—

KM# 242.1 SHILLING
Silver **Ruler:** Charles I **Obv:** Crude bust of Charles I left in inner circle

Date	Mintage	VG	F	VF	XF	Unc
1643	—	80.00	180	550	1,650	—

KM# 189 SHILLING
Silver **Ruler:** Charles I **Obv:** Plain armor, coarse work **Mint:** York

Date	Mintage	VG	F	VF	XF	Unc
ND(1643-1644)	—	90.00	250	750	2,250	—

KM# 190 SHILLING
Silver **Ruler:** Charles I **Rev:** EBOR below oval shield **Mint:** York

Date	Mintage	VG	F	VF	XF	Unc
ND(1643-1644)	—	90.00	265	800	2,400	—

KM# 242.2 SHILLING
Silver **Ruler:** Charles I **Obv:** Crude bust of Charles I left with bent crown in inner circle **Note:** Varieties exist.

Date	Mintage	VG	F	VF	XF	Unc
1643	—	80.00	225	700	2,200	—
1644	—	80.00	225	700	2,200	—

KM# 242.4 SHILLING
Silver **Ruler:** Charles I **Obv:** Crowned bust (Oxford) of Charles I left, value behind in inner circle **Rev:** Declaration with plumes above in inner circle **Mint:** Bristol **Note:** Varieties exist.

Date	Mintage	VG	F	VF	XF	Unc
1643	—	200	450	1,250	3,000	—

KM# 242.5 SHILLING
Silver **Ruler:** Charles I **Obv:** Bust of Charles I left **Mint:** Bristol **Note:** Varieties exist.

Date	Mintage	VG	F	VF	XF	Unc
1643	—	125	300	950	2,800	—
1644	—	125	300	950	2,800	—

KM# 191 SHILLING
Silver **Ruler:** Charles I **Rev:** Crowned oval shield with EBORO below **Mint:** York **Note:** Varieties exist. Mint mark: Lion.

Date	Mintage	VG	F	VF	XF	Unc
ND(1643-44)	—	75.00	200	650	2,000	—

KM# 242.6 SHILLING
Silver **Ruler:** Charles I **Obv:** Crowned bust of Charles I left, plume in front, value behind, in inner circle **Mint:** Bristol **Note:** Varieties exist.

Date	Mintage	VG	F	VF	XF	Unc
1644	—	250	450	1,200	3,000	—
1645	—	250	450	1,200	3,000	—

KM# 242.7 SHILLING
Silver **Ruler:** Charles I **Obv:** Crowned bust of Charles I with square collar to left without plume in front **Mint:** Bristol **Note:** Varieties exist.

Date	Mintage	VG	F	VF	XF	Unc
1644	—	200	400	1,250	3,200	—
1645	—	200	400	1,250	3,200	—

KM# 293 SHILLING
Silver **Ruler:** Charles I **Obv:** Crowned bust (Rawlins) of Charles I **Mint:** Oxford **Note:** Varieties exist.

Date	Mintage	VG	F	VF	XF	Unc
1644	—	200	500	1,300	3,500	—

KM# 292 SHILLING
Silver **Ruler:** Charles I **Obv:** Large, fine style bust of Charles I **Rev:** Declaration, three plumes above in inner circle, OX **Mint:** Oxford

Date	Mintage	VG	F	VF	XF	Unc
1644	—	175	400	1,200	2,900	—
1645	—	175	400	1,200	2,900	—
1646	—	175	400	1,200	2,900	—

KM# 294 SHILLING
Silver **Ruler:** Charles I **Obv:** Small crowned bust of Charles I left with value behind in inner circle **Rev:** Garnished oblong shield of arms in inner circle **Mint:** Truro

Date	Mintage	VG	F	VF	XF	Unc
ND(1644)	—	2,200	4,500	12,500	30,000	—

KM# 295.1 SHILLING
Silver **Ruler:** Charles I **Obv:** Oval arms with scrolls on sides and top in inner circle **Mint:** Truro

Date	Mintage	VG	F	VF	XF	Unc
ND(1644)	—	2,200	4,500	12,500	30,000	—

KM# 295.2 SHILLING
Silver **Ruler:** Charles I **Rev:** Long oval arms with C-R at sides **Mint:** Truro

Date	Mintage	VG	F	VF	XF	Unc
ND(1644)	—	2,200	4,500	12,500	30,000	—

KM# 296 SHILLING
Silver **Ruler:** Charles I **Obv:** Heavier bust of Charles I **Mint:** Truro

Date	Mintage	VG	F	VF	XF	Unc
ND(1644)	—	2,200	4,500	12,500	30,000	—

KM# 297.1 SHILLING
Silver **Ruler:** Charles I **Rev:** Round shield of arms with scrolls on sides and top in inner circle

Date	Mintage	VG	F	VF	XF	Unc
ND(1644)	—	115	350	1,000	3,000	—

KM# 297.2 SHILLING
Silver **Ruler:** Charles I **Rev:** Round arms with scrolls around border in inner circle **Mint:** Exeter

Date	Mintage	VG	F	VF	XF	Unc
1644	—	225	450	1,300	3,200	—
1645	—	225	450	1,300	3,200	—

KM# 297.3 SHILLING
Silver **Ruler:** Charles I **Rev:** Divided date **Mint:** Exeter

Date	Mintage	VG	F	VF	XF	Unc
1644	—	225	450	1,300	3,200	—

KM# 298.1 SHILLING
Silver **Ruler:** Charles I **Rev:** Square-topped shield of arms in inner circle **Mint:** Worcester/Sandsfoot Castle

Date	Mintage	VG	F	VF	XF	Unc
ND(1644)	—	1,200	2,500	5,500	13,000	—

KM# 298.2 SHILLING
Silver **Ruler:** Charles I **Rev:** C-R above shield **Mint:** Worcester/Sandsfoot Castle

Date	Mintage	VG	F	VF	XF	Unc
ND(1644)	—	1,200	2,500	5,500	13,000	—

KM# 299 SHILLING
Silver **Ruler:** Charles I **Rev:** Draped oval arms in inner circle

Date	Mintage	VG	F	VF	XF	Unc
ND(1644)	—	450	850	2,500	7,500	—

KM# 300 SHILLING
Silver **Ruler:** Charles I **Obv:** Crude crowned bust of Charles I **Rev:** Round arms

Date	Mintage	VG	F	VF	XF	Unc
ND(1644)	—	500	1,200	3,500	—	—

KM# 301 SHILLING
Silver **Ruler:** Charles I **Rev:** Square-topped shield of arms with C-R above in inner circle

Date	Mintage	VG	F	VF	XF	Unc
ND(1644)	—	500	1,200	3,500	—	—

KM# 242.12 SHILLING
Silver **Ruler:** Charles I **Rev:** Declaration, plumes above, date below **Mint:** Exeter

Date	Mintage	VG	F	VF	XF	Unc
1645	—	450	1,000	3,000	—	—

KM# 242.8 SHILLING
Silver **Ruler:** Charles I **Mint:** Lundy

Date	Mintage	VG	F	VF	XF	Unc
1645 A	—	300	600	1,800	5,000	—

KM# 242.9 SHILLING
Silver **Ruler:** Charles I **Obv:** Small plume added in front of bust of Charles I **Mint:** Lundy

Date	Mintage	VG	F	VF	XF	Unc
1645 A	—	300	600	1,800	5,000	—

KM# 242.10 SHILLING
Silver **Ruler:** Charles I **Rev:** Scroll above declaration **Mint:** Lundy

Date	Mintage	VG	F	VF	XF	Unc
1646	—	125	300	900	2,700	—

KM# 242.11 SHILLING
Silver **Ruler:** Charles I **Obv:** Bust of Charles I left **Mint:** Lundy

Date	Mintage	VG	F	VF	XF	Unc
1646	—	150	325	1,000	3,000	—

KM# 302.1 SHILLING
Silver **Ruler:** Charles I **Obv:** Crowned bust of Charles I right with value behind in inner circle **Rev:** Crowned and draped oval arms in inner circle

Date	Mintage	VG	F	VF	XF	Unc
ND Unique	—	—	—	—	—	—

KM# 302.2 SHILLING
Silver **Ruler:** Charles I **Rev:** Crowned and draped oval arms divide C-R in inner circle

Date	Mintage	VG	F	VF	XF	Unc
ND	—	450	900	2,700	—	—

KM# 242.3 SHILLING
Silver **Ruler:** Charles I **Rev:** Annulets around and in date

Date	Mintage	VG	F	VF	XF	Unc
1646	—	90.00	250	800	2,400	—

KM# 6 1/2 CROWN
1.4900 g., 0.9250 Silver 0.0443 oz. ASW, 16 mm. **Ruler:** Elizabeth I **Obv:** Crowned bust left **Rev:** Arms on long cross **Note:** Sixth Issue.

Date	Mintage	Good	VG	F	VF	XF
(160)1	—	—	500	1,100	2,900	7,000
(160)2	—	—	2,400	4,500	13,000	30,000

KM# A7 1/2 CROWN
1.1250 g., 0.9170 Gold 0.0332 oz. AGW **Ruler:** Elizabeth I **Obv:** Crowned bust left **Rev:** Crowned arms **Note:** Sixth Issue.

Date	Mintage	VG	F	VF	XF	Unc
(160)1	—	800	1,500	3,750	7,500	—
(160)2	—	800	1,500	3,750	7,500	—

KM# 15 1/2 CROWN
0.9250 Silver **Ruler:** James I **Obv:** King James I on horseback right in inner circle **Rev:** Arms in inner circle **Rev. Legend:** EXURGAT DEUS... **Note:** First Coinage (1603-04).

Date	Mintage	VG	F	VF	XF	Unc
ND	—	750	1,500	4,500	9,500	—

KM# 16 1/2 CROWN
1.1250 g., 0.9170 Gold 0.0332 oz. AGW **Ruler:** James I **Obv:** James I

Date	Mintage	VG	F	VF	XF	Unc
ND(1603-04)	—	650	1,200	2,900	6,000	—

KM# 30 1/2 CROWN
1.1250 g., 0.9170 Gold 0.0332 oz. AGW **Ruler:** James I **Obv:** First crowned bust of James I

Date	Mintage	VG	F	VF	XF	Unc
ND(1604-19)	—	175	300	700	—	—

KM# 31 1/2 CROWN
1.1250 g., 0.9170 Gold 0.0332 oz. AGW **Ruler:** James I **Obv:** Third crowned bust of James I

Date	Mintage	VG	F	VF	XF	Unc
ND(1604-19)	—	175	300	700	—	—

KM# 32 1/2 CROWN
1.1250 g., 0.9170 Gold 0.0332 oz. AGW **Ruler:** James I **Obv:** Fifth crowned bust of James I

Date	Mintage	VG	F	VF	XF	Unc
ND(1604-19)	—	150	300	700	—	—

KM# 29 1/2 CROWN
0.9250 Silver **Ruler:** James I **Obv:** King James I on horseback **Rev:** Arms in inner circle **Rev. Legend:** QUAE DEUS... **Note:** Second Coinage (1604-19).

Date	Mintage	VG	F	VF	XF	Unc
ND	—	750	1,500	4,500	9,500	—

KM# 61 1/2 CROWN
0.9250 Silver **Ruler:** James I **Rev:** Arms in inner circle, bird-headed harp in arms **Note:** Third Coinage (1619-25).

Date	Mintage	VG	F	VF	XF	Unc
ND	—	125	300	1,000	2,400	—

KM# 62 1/2 CROWN
0.9250 Silver **Ruler:** James I **Rev:** Plumes above shield of arms

Date	Mintage	VG	F	VF	XF	Unc
ND	—	250	550	1,500	3,500	—

KM# 113.1 1/2 CROWN
0.9250 Silver **Ruler:** Charles I **Obv:** King Charles I on horseback left with sword uplifted in inner circle, rose on flank cloth, ground line **Rev:** Shield of arms on long cross with inner circle **Mint:** Tower

Date	Mintage	VG	F	VF	XF	Unc
ND(1625-49)	—	100	250	750	—	—

KM# 113.2 1/2 CROWN
0.9250 Silver **Ruler:** Charles I **Obv:** Without rose or ground line **Mint:** Tower

Date	Mintage	VG	F	VF	XF	Unc
ND(1625-49)	—	100	225	750	—	—

KM# 114 1/2 CROWN
0.9250 Silver **Ruler:** Charles I **Rev:** Shield not on cross **Mint:** Tower

Date	Mintage	VG	F	VF	XF	Unc
ND(1625-49)	—	75.00	200	600	—	—

KM# 115.1 1/2 CROWN
0.9250 Silver **Ruler:** Charles I **Rev:** Plume above shield **Mint:** Tower

Date	Mintage	VG	F	VF	XF	Unc
ND(1625-49)	—	300	600	1,300	—	—

KM# 115.2 1/2 CROWN
0.9250 Silver **Ruler:** Charles I **Obv:** Rose on flank cloth **Mint:** Tower

Date	Mintage	VG	F	VF	XF	Unc
ND(1625-49)	—	350	700	1,700	—	—

KM# 116.1 1/2 CROWN
0.9250 Silver **Ruler:** Charles I **Rev:** Arms with C-R at top in inner circle **Mint:** Tower

Date	Mintage	VG	F	VF	XF	Unc
ND(1625-49)	—	75.00	150	450	—	—

KM# 116.2 1/2 CROWN
0.9250 Silver **Ruler:** Charles I **Rev:** C-R divided by plume **Mint:** Tower

Date	Mintage	VG	F	VF	XF	Unc
ND(1625-49)	—	90.00	175	600	—	—

KM# 117 1/2 CROWN
0.9250 Silver **Ruler:** Charles I **Rev:** Arms divide C-R **Mint:** Tower

Date	Mintage	VG	F	VF	XF	Unc
ND(1625-49)	—	75.00	150	400	1,000	—

KM# 118 1/2 CROWN
Silver **Ruler:** Charles I **Rev:** Garnished oval arms with plume above in inner circle **Mint:** Tower

Date	Mintage	VG	F	VF	XF	Unc
ND(1625-49)	—	400	850	2,500	—	—

KM# 119 1/2 CROWN
Silver **Ruler:** Charles I **Obv:** Horse without ornamentation, sword in vertical position **Rev:** Garnished round arms in inner circle **Mint:** Tower

Date	Mintage	VG	F	VF	XF	Unc
ND(1625-49)	—	45.00	95.00	225	650	—

KM# 120.1 1/2 CROWN
Silver **Ruler:** Charles I **Rev:** Plume above shield **Mint:** Tower

Date	Mintage	VG	F	VF	XF	Unc
ND(1625-49)	—	100	200	525	—	—

KM# 120.2 1/2 CROWN
Silver **Ruler:** Charles I **Obv:** Cloak flows from king's shoulder **Mint:** Tower

Date	Mintage	VG	F	VF	XF	Unc
ND(1625-49)	—	45.00	95.00	225	650	—

KM# 120.3 1/2 CROWN
Silver **Ruler:** Charles I **Obv:** Coarse ground below horse **Mint:** Tower

Date	Mintage	VG	F	VF	XF	Unc
ND(1625-49)	—	45.00	95.00	225	650	—

KM# 121 1/2 CROWN
Silver **Ruler:** Charles I **Obv:** Shorter horse, mane flows in front of neck, tail between back legs **Mint:** Tower

Date	Mintage	VG	F	VF	XF	Unc
ND(1625-49)	—	45.00	90.00	225	650	—

KM# 122 1/2 CROWN
Silver **Ruler:** Charles I **Obv:** Coarse style **Mint:** Tower **Note:** Struck under Parliament.

Date	Mintage	VG	F	VF	XF	Unc
ND(1625-49)	—	35.00	75.00	250	700	—

KM# 123 1/2 CROWN
Silver **Ruler:** Charles I **Obv:** Short and awkward horse **Mint:** Tower **Note:** Struck under Parliament.

Date	Mintage	VG	F	VF	XF	Unc
ND(1625-49) Rare	—	—	—	—	—	—

KM# 124 1/2 CROWN
Silver **Ruler:** Charles I **Obv:** Tall horse **Mint:** Tower **Note:** Struck under Parliament.

Date	Mintage	VG	F	VF	XF	Unc
ND(1625-49)	—	35.00	75.00	250	600	—

KM# 166 1/2 CROWN
Silver **Ruler:** Charles I **Obv:** Fine style king on horseback left in inner circle **Rev:** Garnished oval arms with crowned C-R at sides in inner circle **Note:** First Milled Briot Issue.

Date	Mintage	VG	F	VF	XF	Unc
ND(1631-32)	—	300	650	1,900	4,500	—

KM# 197 1/2 CROWN
Silver **Ruler:** Charles I **Rev:** Arms with crowned C-R at sides **Note:** Second Milled Briot Issue.

Date	Mintage	VG	F	VF	XF	Unc
ND(1638-39)	—	225	450	1,100	2,700	—

KM# 198 1/2 CROWN
Silver **Ruler:** Charles I **Obv:** Ground line below horse **Rev:** Garnished square-topped shield in inner circle **Note:** Briot Hammered Issue.

Date	Mintage	VG	F	VF	XF	Unc
ND(1638-39)	—	550	1,100	3,000	7,500	—

KM# 199.1 1/2 CROWN
Silver **Ruler:** Charles I **Obv:** King on horseback with flowing cloak, plume behind, in inner circle **Rev:** Garnished oval arms with large plume above in inner circle **Mint:** Aberystwyth

Date	Mintage	VG	F	VF	XF	Unc
ND(1638-39)	—	550	1,100	4,000	9,000	—

KM# 199.2 1/2 CROWN
Silver **Ruler:** Charles I **Obv:** Ground below horse **Mint:** Aberystwyth

Date	Mintage	VG	F	VF	XF	Unc
ND(1638-39)	—	550	1,100	4,000	9,500	—

KM# 200 1/2 CROWN

Silver **Ruler:** Charles I **Obv:** Lively horse without ground below **Mint:** Aberystwyth

Date	Mintage	VG	F	VF	XF	Unc
ND(1638-39)	—	550	1,100	4,000	9,500	—

KM# 201 1/2 CROWN

Silver **Ruler:** Charles I **Obv:** King on horseback left with plume behind in inner circle **Rev:** Garnished round arms with plume above in inner circle **Mint:** Aberystwyth - Furnace Mint

Date	Mintage	VG	F	VF	XF	Unc
ND(1638-39)	—	1,300	2,800	8,000	—	—

KM# 202 1/2 CROWN

Silver **Ruler:** Charles I **Rev:** Garnished oval arms with plume above in inner circle **Mint:** Shrewsbury

Date	Mintage	VG	F	VF	XF	Unc
ND(1638-39)	—	—	—	—	—	—

KM# 208 1/2 CROWN

Silver **Ruler:** Charles I **Rev:** Declaration, single plume above, date below, in inner circle **Mint:** Shrewsbury

Date	Mintage	VG	F	VF	XF	Unc
1642	—	400	750	2,500	—	—

KM# 209 1/2 CROWN

Silver **Ruler:** Charles I **Obv:** Large plume behind king **Rev:** Three plumes above declaration **Mint:** Shrewsbury

Date	Mintage	VG	F	VF	XF	Unc
1642	—	400	800	2,300	5,500	—

KM# 210 1/2 CROWN

Silver **Ruler:** Charles I **Obv:** Shrewsbury-style horseman **Rev:** One plume above declaration **Mint:** Shrewsbury

Date	Mintage	VG	F	VF	XF	Unc
1642	—	450	850	2,400	5,500	—

KM# 211.1 1/2 CROWN

Silver **Ruler:** Charles I **Rev:** Value 2 and 6 flank plume **Mint:** Shrewsbury

Date	Mintage	VG	F	VF	XF	Unc
1642	—	450	950	2,400	5,500	—

KM# 211.2 1/2 CROWN

Silver **Ruler:** Charles I **Obv:** Ground line below horse **Mint:** Shrewsbury

Date	Mintage	VG	F	VF	XF	Unc
1642	—	450	950	2,400	5,500	—

KM# 212 1/2 CROWN

Silver **Ruler:** Charles I **Rev:** Without value **Mint:** Shrewsbury

Date	Mintage	VG	F	VF	XF	Unc
1642	—	400	850	2,400	5,500	—

KM# 213.1 1/2 CROWN

Silver **Ruler:** Charles I **Rev:** Three thin plumes above declaration **Mint:** Shrewsbury

Date	Mintage	VG	F	VF	XF	Unc
1642	—	350	800	2,200	5,000	—

KM# 213.2 1/2 CROWN

Silver **Ruler:** Charles I **Obv:** Without plume behind king **Mint:** Shrewsbury

Date	Mintage	VG	F	VF	XF	Unc
1642	—	400	750	2,100	5,500	—

KM# 214.1 1/2 CROWN

Silver **Ruler:** Charles I **Obv:** King on horseback left in inner circle **Rev:** Declaration with three plumes above **Mint:** Oxford

Date	Mintage	VG	F	VF	XF	Unc
1642	—	200	400	1,000	2,400	—

KM# 214.3 1/2 CROWN

Silver **Ruler:** Charles I **Obv:** Without ground line **Mint:** Oxford

Date	Mintage	VG	F	VF	XF	Unc
1642	—	200	400	1,000	2,400	—

KM# 214.2 1/2 CROWN

Silver **Ruler:** Charles I **Obv:** Shrewsbury-style horse with ground line **Mint:** Oxford **Note:** Oxford dies.

Date	Mintage	VG	F	VF	XF	Unc
1642	—	125	300	1,000	2,400	—

KM# 215 1/2 CROWN

Silver **Ruler:** Charles I **Mint:** Truro

Date	Mintage	VG	F	VF	XF	Unc
1642	—	850	1,700	4,500	—	—

KM# 216 1/2 CROWN

Silver **Ruler:** Charles I **Obv:** Without weapons below horse **Rev:** Garnished rectangular arms with C-R at sides **Mint:** Truro

Date	Mintage	VG	F	VF	XF	Unc
ND(1642)	—	850	1,700	4,000	—	—

KM# 217 1/2 CROWN

Silver **Ruler:** Charles I **Obv:** New style galloping horse **Mint:** Truro

Date	Mintage	VG	F	VF	XF	Unc
ND(1642)	—	850	1,700	5,500	—	—

KM# 218 1/2 CROWN

Silver **Ruler:** Charles I **Rev:** C-R above arms **Mint:** Truro

Date	Mintage	VG	F	VF	XF	Unc
ND(1642)	—	750	1,600	4,000	—	—

KM# 219 1/2 CROWN

Silver **Ruler:** Charles I **Obv:** Trotting horse **Rev:** C-R divided by arms **Mint:** Truro

Date	Mintage	VG	F	VF	XF	Unc
ND(1642)	—	750	1,400	3,500	8,000	—

KM# 220 1/2 CROWN

Silver **Ruler:** Charles I **Obv:** King on horseback left, sash in bow at back, in inner circle **Rev:** Barrel-like arms divide C-R in inner circle **Mint:** Truro/Exeter

Date	Mintage	VG	F	VF	XF	Unc
ND(1642)	—	275	600	1,500	—	—

KM# 221.1 1/2 CROWN

Silver **Ruler:** Charles I **Rev:** Oval shield with eight scrolls in inner circle **Mint:** Truro/Exeter

Date	Mintage	VG	F	VF	XF	Unc
ND(1642)	—	300	550	1,200	2,900	—

KM# 221.2 1/2 CROWN

Silver **Ruler:** Charles I **Rev:** Oval shield with six scrolls in inner circle **Mint:** Truro/Exeter

Date	Mintage	VG	F	VF	XF	Unc
ND(1642)	—	300	550	1,000	2,300	—

KM# 221.3 1/2 CROWN

Silver **Ruler:** Charles I **Obv:** Sash at king's back flows out to back **Mint:** Truro/Exeter

Date	Mintage	VG	F	VF	XF	Unc
ND(1642)	—	300	550	1,000	2,300	—

KM# 222 1/2 CROWN

Silver **Ruler:** Charles I **Rev:** Garnished barrel-like arms **Mint:** Truro/Exeter

Date	Mintage	VG	F	VF	XF	Unc
ND(1642) Rare	—	—	—	—	—	—

KM# 223.1 1/2 CROWN

Silver **Ruler:** Charles I **Obv:** Briot horseman with ground line below **Rev:** Inverted scrollwork on oval shield **Mint:** Truro/Exeter

Date	Mintage	VG	F	VF	XF	Unc
ND(1642)	—	300	550	1,200	2,900	—

KM# 223.2 1/2 CROWN

Silver **Ruler:** Charles I **Rev:** Upright scrollwork on oval shield **Mint:** Truro/Exeter

Date	Mintage	VG	F	VF	XF	Unc
ND(1642) Rare	—	—	—	—	—	—

KM# 224 1/2 CROWN

Silver **Ruler:** Charles I **Obv:** Briot horseman **Mint:** Truro/Exeter

Date	Mintage	VG	F	VF	XF	Unc
ND(1642)	—	300	550	1,500	—	—

KM# 214.16 1/2 CROWN

Silver **Ruler:** Charles I **Obv:** King on horseback (Oxford), plume behind, in inner circle **Rev:** Declaration, three Bristol plumes above, date below **Mint:** Bristol

Date	Mintage	VG	F	VF	XF	Unc
1643	—	300	550	1,400	3,000	—

KM# 214.17 1/2 CROWN

Silver **Ruler:** Charles I **Rev:** Mint mark: BR. **Mint:** Bristol

Date	Mintage	VG	F	VF	XF	Unc
1643BR.	—	300	550	1,400	3,000	—

KM# 214.18 1/2 CROWN

Silver **Ruler:** Charles I **Obv:** Flat crown on king **Mint:** Bristol

Date	Mintage	VG	F	VF	XF	Unc
1643	—	300	550	1,400	3,000	—

KM# 214.19 1/2 CROWN

Silver **Ruler:** Charles I **Rev:** Mint mark: BR. **Mint:** Bristol

Date	Mintage	VG	F	VF	XF	Unc
1643BR.	—	300	550	1,300	3,000	—
1644BR.	—	300	550	1,300	3,000	—

KM# 214.4 1/2 CROWN

Silver **Ruler:** Charles I **Obv:** Oxford-style horse with ground line **Mint:** Oxford

Date	Mintage	VG	F	VF	XF	Unc
1643	—	175	350	950	2,300	—

KM# 214.5 1/2 CROWN

Silver **Ruler:** Charles I **Obv:** Without ground line **Mint:** Oxford

Date	Mintage	VG	F	VF	XF	Unc
1643	—	150	350	950	2,300	—

KM# 214.6 1/2 CROWN

Silver **Ruler:** Charles I **Obv:** Briot-style horse with grass below in inner circle **Mint:** Oxford

Date	Mintage	VG	F	VF	XF	Unc
1643	—	175	350	1,000	2,300	—

KM# 214.7 1/2 CROWN

Silver **Ruler:** Charles I **Rev:** Large center plume above declaration, OX below date **Mint:** Oxford

Date	Mintage	VG	F	VF	XF	Unc
1643	—	175	350	1,000	2,400	—
1643	—	175	350	1,000	2,400	—
1644	—	175	350	1,000	2,400	—

KM# 214.8 1/2 CROWN

Silver **Ruler:** Charles I **Obv:** Choppy ground beneath horse, OX below date **Mint:** Oxford

Date	Mintage	VG	F	VF	XF	Unc
1643	—	175	350	1,000	2,300	—
1643	—	175	350	1,000	2,300	—

KM# 214.9 1/2 CROWN

Silver **Ruler:** Charles I **Obv:** Plain ground beneath horse, OX below date **Mint:** Oxford

Date	Mintage	VG	F	VF	XF	Unc
1644	—	175	350	1,000	2,100	—
1645	—	175	350	1,000	2,100	—

KM# 214.10 1/2 CROWN

Silver **Ruler:** Charles I **Rev:** Small plumes at sides of date, OX below date **Mint:** Oxford

Date	Mintage	VG	F	VF	XF	Unc
1644	—	200	400	1,000	2,200	—

KM# 214.11 1/2 CROWN

Silver **Ruler:** Charles I **Obv:** Larger horse with plain ground beneath, OX below date **Mint:** Oxford

Date	Mintage	VG	F	VF	XF	Unc
1644	—	175	350	1,000	2,200	—
1645	—	175	350	1,000	2,200	—

KM# 214.12 1/2 CROWN

Silver **Ruler:** Charles I **Obv:** Rocky ground beneath horse, OX below date **Mint:** Oxford

Date	Mintage	VG	F	VF	XF	Unc
1644	—	175	350	1,000	2,200	—
1645	—	175	350	1,000	2,200	—

KM# 306.1 1/2 CROWN

Silver **Ruler:** Charles I **Rev:** Declaration, three plumes above **Mint:** Exeter

Date	Mintage	VG	F	VF	XF	Unc
1644EX	—	800	1,600	5,000	—	—
1645EX	—	800	1,600	5,000	—	—

KM# 306.2 1/2 CROWN

Silver **Ruler:** Charles I **Rev:** EX mint mark also below date **Mint:** Exeter

Date	Mintage	VG	F	VF	XF	Unc
1644	—	700	1,400	4,200	—	—

KM# 307 1/2 CROWN

Silver **Ruler:** Charles I **Obv:** King on horseback left with ground below, in inner circle **Rev:** Square-topped shield of arms divides C-R **Mint:** York

Date	Mintage	VG	F	VF	XF	Unc
ND(1644)	—	175	350	1,100	2,700	—

KM# 308 1/2 CROWN

Silver **Ruler:** Charles I **Rev:** Garnished oval arms in inner circle **Mint:** York

Date	Mintage	VG	F	VF	XF	Unc
ND(1644)	—	200	400	1,200	2,800	—

KM# 310 1/2 CROWN

Silver **Ruler:** Charles I **Obv:** Without ground line **Rev:** Round arms **Mint:** York

Date	Mintage	VG	F	VF	XF	Unc
ND(1644)	—	175	350	1,100	2,600	—

KM# 310a 1/2 CROWN

Base Metal **Ruler:** Charles I **Obv:** EBORO below horse **Mint:** York

Date	Mintage	VG	F	VF	XF	Unc
ND(1644)	—	175	350	1,100	2,600	—

Note: Possibly a contemporary counterfeit

KM# 311 1/2 CROWN

Silver **Ruler:** Charles I **Obv:** Tall horse **Rev:** Crowned square-topped shield divides C-R **Mint:** York

Date	Mintage	VG	F	VF	XF	Unc
ND(1644)	—	175	350	1,000	2,400	—

KM# 312 1/2 CROWN

Silver **Ruler:** Charles I **Obv:** EBORO below horse **Rev:** Crowned oval arms divide crowned C and crowned R **Mint:** York

Date	Mintage	VG	F	VF	XF	Unc
ND(1644)	—	150	350	850	—	—

KM# 313 1/2 CROWN

Silver **Ruler:** Charles I **Obv:** EBORO below horse **Rev:** Crowned oval garnished arms with lion's paws at left and right **Mint:** York

Date	Mintage	VG	F	VF	XF	Unc
ND(1644)	—	150	350	850	—	—

KM# 314 1/2 CROWN

Silver **Ruler:** Charles I **Obv:** King on horseback left with plume behind and CHST below in inner circle **Rev:** Garnished oval arms in inner circle **Mint:** York

Date	Mintage	VG	F	VF	XF	Unc
ND(1644)	—	300	600	1,800	—	—

KM# 315 1/2 CROWN

Silver **Ruler:** Charles I **Obv:** Without plume or CHST **Rev:** Crowned oval arms in inner circle **Mint:** York

Date	Mintage	VG	F	VF	XF	Unc
ND(1644)	—	375	725	2,150	—	—

KM# 316 1/2 CROWN

Silver **Ruler:** Charles I **Rev:** Crowned square-topped shield with crowned C-R at sides **Mint:** York

Date	Mintage	VG	F	VF	XF	Unc
ND(1644)	—	500	1,000	3,000	—	—

KM# 317.1 1/2 CROWN

Silver **Ruler:** Charles I **Rev:** Declaration, three plumes above and date below **Mint:** York

Date	Mintage	VG	F	VF	XF	Unc
1644	—	550	1,000	5,000	—	—

KM# 317.2 1/2 CROWN

Silver **Ruler:** Charles I **Obv:** W below horse **Mint:** Worcester

Date	Mintage	VG	F	VF	XF	Unc
1644	—	550	1,200	—	—	—

KM# 318.1 1/2 CROWN

Silver **Ruler:** Charles I **Rev:** Crowned square-topped shield of arms **Mint:** Worcester

Date	Mintage	VG	F	VF	XF	Unc
ND(1644)	—	450	1,150	—	—	—

KM# 318.2 1/2 CROWN

Silver **Ruler:** Charles I **Obv:** Grass added below horse **Mint:** Worcester

Date	Mintage	VG	F	VF	XF	Unc
ND(1644)	—	500	1,000	3,000	—	—

KM# 319.1 1/2 CROWN

Silver **Ruler:** Charles I **Rev:** Crowned and draped oval arms, LIS in legend **Mint:** Worcester

Date	Mintage	VG	F	VF	XF	Unc
ND(1644)	—	500	1,100	3,200	—	—

KM# 319.2 1/2 CROWN

Silver **Ruler:** Charles I **Rev. Legend:** FLORENT CONCORDIA REGNA. **Mint:** Worcester

Date	Mintage	VG	F	VF	XF	Unc
ND(1644)	—	450	1,000	3,000	—	—

KM# 320 1/2 CROWN

Silver **Ruler:** Charles I **Obv:** Tall king on horseback without W below **Rev:** Roses in legend **Mint:** Worcester

Date	Mintage	VG	F	VF	XF	Unc
ND(1644)	—	450	1,000	3,000	—	—

KM# 321 1/2 CROWN

Silver **Ruler:** Charles I **Rev:** Crowned square-topped shield in inner circle **Mint:** Worcester

Date	Mintage	VG	F	VF	XF	Unc
ND(1644)	—	400	1,000	3,000	—	—

KM# 322.1 1/2 CROWN

Silver **Ruler:** Charles I **Obv:** Briot-style horseman with sword pointing forward, ground line below **Rev:** Crowned and garnished oval arms, roses in legend **Mint:** Worcester

Date	Mintage	VG	F	VF	XF	Unc
ND(1644)	—	450	1,200	3,500	—	—

KM# 322.2 1/2 CROWN

Silver **Ruler:** Charles I **Rev:** C-R added at sides of arms **Mint:** Worcester

Date	Mintage	VG	F	VF	XF	Unc
ND(1644)	—	500	1,200	3,500	—	—

KM# 323 1/2 CROWN

Silver **Ruler:** Charles I **Obv:** Pudgy king on horse of poor style **Rev:** Without C-R at sides of arms **Mint:** Worcester

Date	Mintage	VG	F	VF	XF	Unc
ND(1644)	—	450	1,200	3,500	—	—

KM# 324 1/2 CROWN

Silver **Ruler:** Charles I **Obv:** Thin king and horse **Rev:** Stars in legend **Mint:** Worcester

Date	Mintage	VG	F	VF	XF	Unc
ND(1644)	—	500	1,000	3,000	—	—

KM# 325 1/2 CROWN

Silver **Ruler:** Charles I **Rev:** Arms with H C (Hartlebury Castle) at bottom **Mint:** Worcester

Date	Mintage	VG	F	VF	XF	Unc
ND(1644)	—	600	1,300	3,500	—	—

KM# 327 1/2 CROWN

Silver **Ruler:** Charles I **Rev:** Crowned large round shield with coarse garnish **Mint:** Shrewsbury

Date	Mintage	VG	F	VF	XF	Unc
ND(1644)	—	600	1,250	3,500	—	—

KM# 328 1/2 CROWN

Silver **Ruler:** Charles I **Rev:** Square-topped shield with lion paws at top and sides **Mint:** Shrewsbury

Date	Mintage	VG	F	VF	XF	Unc
ND(1644)	—	600	1,250	3,500	—	—

KM# 329.1 1/2 CROWN

Silver **Ruler:** Charles I **Rev:** Crowned small oval arms in inner circle **Mint:** Shrewsbury

Date	Mintage	VG	F	VF	XF	Unc
ND(1644)	—	600	1,250	3,500	—	—

KM# 329.2 1/2 CROWN

Silver **Ruler:** Charles I **Rev. Legend:** FLORENT CONCORDIA REGNA **Mint:** Shrewsbury

Date	Mintage	VG	F	VF	XF	Unc
ND(1644) Rare	—	—	—	—	—	—

KM# 329.3 1/2 CROWN

Silver **Ruler:** Charles I **Obv:** Grass below horse **Mint:** Shrewsbury

Date	Mintage	VG	F	VF	XF	Unc
ND(1644)	—	600	1,250	3,500	—	—

KM# 329.4 1/2 CROWN

Silver **Ruler:** Charles I **Obv:** Ground below horse **Mint:** Shrewsbury

Date	Mintage	VG	F	VF	XF	Unc
ND(1644)	—	600	1,250	3,500	—	—

KM# 214.20 1/2 CROWN

Silver **Ruler:** Charles I **Obv:** Shrewsbury plume behind king **Rev:** BR in legend above plumes **Mint:** Bristol

Date	Mintage	VG	F	VF	XF	Unc
1644BR.	—	250	500	1,300	3,000	—

KM# 214.23 1/2 CROWN

Silver **Ruler:** Charles I **Rev:** Declaration: RELIG: PRO: **Mint:** Bristol

Date	Mintage	VG	F	VF	XF	Unc
1644	—	250	500	1,300	3,000	—

KM# 214.21 1/2 CROWN

Silver **Ruler:** Charles I **Obv:** BR. mint mark below horse **Rev:** BR. mint mark below date **Mint:** Bristol

Date	Mintage	VG	F	VF	XF	Unc
1644BR.	—	250	500	1,300	3,000	—
1645BR.	—	250	500	1,300	3,000	—

KM# 214.22 1/2 CROWN

Silver **Ruler:** Charles I **Obv:** BR. mint mark also in legend **Mint:** Bristol

Date	Mintage	VG	F	VF	XF	Unc
1644BR.	—	250	500	1,200	3,000	—
1645BR.	—	250	500	1,200	3,000	—

KM# 303.1 1/2 CROWN

Silver **Ruler:** Charles I **Obv:** Crowned king on galloping horse left, weapons below, in inner circle **Rev:** Oval arms with scrollwork in inner circle, date in legend **Mint:** Exeter

Date	Mintage	VG	F	VF	XF	Unc
1644 Rare	—	—	—	—	—	—

KM# 326.1 1/2 CROWN

Silver **Ruler:** Charles I **Obv:** King on horseback with SA (Sopia) below in inner circle **Rev:** Crowned and garnished oval arms in inner circle **Note:** Possibly struck at Sandsfoot Castle.

Date	Mintage	VG	F	VF	XF	Unc
ND(1644) Rare	—	—	—	—	—	—

KM# 326.2 1/2 CROWN

Silver **Ruler:** Charles I **Obv:** Cannon ball (or large pellet) below horse without SA **Note:** Possibly struck at Sandsfoot Castle.

Date	Mintage	VG	F	VF	XF	Unc
ND(1644)	—	900	2,000	—	—	—

KM# 309 1/2 CROWN

Silver **Ruler:** Charles I **Mint:** York **Note:** Klippe. Similar to KM#300.

Date	Mintage	VG	F	VF	XF	Unc
ND(1644) Rare	—	—	—	—	—	—

KM# 305.1 1/2 CROWN

Silver **Ruler:** Charles I **Obv:** Briot-style horse with ground line beneath **Mint:** Exeter

Date	Mintage	VG	F	VF	XF	Unc
1644	—	225	450	1,100	2,600	—

KM# 305.2 1/2 CROWN

Silver **Ruler:** Charles I **Obv:** Flowing king's sash and horse with twisted tail **Mint:** Exeter

Date	Mintage	VG	F	VF	XF	Unc
1644	—	225	450	1,100	2,600	—
1645	—	225	450	1,100	2,600	—

KM# 304 1/2 CROWN

Silver **Ruler:** Charles I **Obv:** Short king on badly proportioned horse - large front, small back, in inner circle **Mint:** Exeter **Note:** Varieties exist.

Date	Mintage	VG	F	VF	XF	Unc
1644	—	350	725	2,100	—	—
16(ROSE)44	—	350	725	2,100	—	—

KM# 305.3 1/2 CROWN

Silver **Ruler:** Charles I **Rev:** Castle mint mark **Mint:** Exeter

Date	Mintage	VG	F	VF	XF	Unc
1645	—	225	500	1,500	—	—

KM# 305.4 1/2 CROWN

Silver **Ruler:** Charles I **Rev:** EX mint mark in legend **Mint:** Exeter

Date	Mintage	VG	F	VF	XF	Unc
1645EX	—	200	500	1,500	—	—

KM# 303.2 1/2 CROWN

Silver **Ruler:** Charles I **Rev:** Castle mint mark **Mint:** Exeter

Date	Mintage	VG	F	VF	XF	Unc
1645 Rare	—	—	—	—	—	—

KM# 329.5 1/2 CROWN

Silver **Ruler:** Charles I **Obv:** Grass below horse **Rev:** Crowned ornate arms flanked by standing crowned lion and unicorn **Mint:** Shrewsbury

Date	Mintage	VG	F	VF	XF	Unc
1645	—	—	—	—	—	—

KM# 214.13 1/2 CROWN

Silver **Ruler:** Charles I **Obv:** Gravelly ground beneath horse, OX **Mint:** Oxford

Date	Mintage	VG	F	VF	XF	Unc
1645	—	175	350	1,000	2,200	—
1646	—	175	350	1,000	2,200	—

KM# 214.14 1/2 CROWN

Silver **Ruler:** Charles I **Rev:** Dots and annulets among and at sides of plumes and date, OX below **Mint:** Oxford

Date	Mintage	VG	F	VF	XF	Unc
1645	—	175	350	1,000	2,200	—
1646	—	175	350	1,000	2,200	—

KM# 214.15 1/2 CROWN

Silver **Ruler:** Charles I **Obv:** Grass beneath horse, OX below date **Mint:** Oxford

Date	Mintage	VG	F	VF	XF	Unc
1645	—	175	350	1,000	2,300	—
1646	—	175	350	1,000	2,300	—

KM# 214.24 1/2 CROWN

Silver **Ruler:** Charles I **Rev:** Scrollwork above declaration **Mint:** Bristol **Note:** Late declaration.

Date	Mintage	VG	F	VF	XF	Unc
1646	—	—	—	—	—	—

KM# B7 CROWN

2.2500 g., 0.9170 Gold 0.0663 oz. AGW **Ruler:** Elizabeth I **Obv:** Crowned bust left **Rev:** Crowned arms **Note:** Sixth Issue.

Date	Mintage	VG	F	VF	XF	Unc
(160)1	—	1,500	3,000	7,500	13,500	—
(160)2	—	1,500	3,000	7,500	13,500	—

KM# 7 CROWN

Silver **Ruler:** Elizabeth I **Obv:** Crowned bust left **Rev:** Arms on long cross **Note:** Sixth Issue. Dav. #3757.

Date	Mintage	VG	F	VF	XF	Unc
(160)1	—	1,300	2,700	6,000	13,000	—
(160)2	—	1,500	2,850	6,000	13,000	—

KM# 17 CROWN

Silver **Ruler:** James I **Obv:** James I on horseback right in inner circle **Rev. Legend:** EXURGAT DEUS... **Note:** First Coinage. Dav. #3758.

Date	Mintage	VG	F	VF	XF	Unc
ND(1603-04)	—	1,050	2,250	5,300	11,500	—

KM# 18 CROWN

2.2500 g., 0.9170 Gold 0.0663 oz. AGW **Ruler:** James I **Obv:** Crowned bust of James I right in inner circle **Rev:** Crowned arms in inner circle

Date	Mintage	VG	F	VF	XF	Unc
ND(1603-04)	—	1,500	3,000	10,500	20,500	—

KM# 34 CROWN

2.2500 g., 0.9170 Gold 0.0663 oz. AGW **Ruler:** James I **Obv:** First crowned bust of James I right in inner circle **Rev:** Crowned square-topped arms **Note:** Britain.

Date	Mintage	VG	F	VF	XF	Unc
ND(1604-19)	—	200	350	800	1,600	—

KM# 33 CROWN

Silver **Ruler:** James I **Obv:** James I on horseback right in inner circle **Rev:** Arms in inner circle **Rev. Legend:** QUAE DEUS... **Note:** Second Coinage Dav. #3759.

Date	Mintage	VG	F	VF	XF	Unc
ND(1604-19)	—	825	1,800	5,300	11,500	—

KM# 35 CROWN

2.2500 g., 0.9170 Gold 0.0663 oz. AGW **Ruler:** James I **Obv:** Third crowned bust of James I right in inner circle **Note:** Britain.

Date	Mintage	VG	F	VF	XF	Unc
ND(1604-19)	—	200	350	800	1,600	—

KM# 36 CROWN

2.2500 g., 0.9170 Gold 0.0663 oz. AGW **Ruler:** James I **Obv:** Fifth crowned bust of James I right in inner circle **Note:** Britain.

Date	Mintage	VG	F	VF	XF	Unc
ND(1604-19)	—	175	300	750	1,500	—

KM# 37 CROWN

2.2500 g., 0.9170 Gold 0.0663 oz. AGW **Ruler:** James I **Obv:** Crowned rose with leaves with I-R at sides **Rev:** Crowned thistle with leaves with I-R at sides **Note:** Thistle.

Date	Mintage	VG	F	VF	XF	Unc
ND(1604-19)	—	200	350	850	1,750	—

KM# 63 CROWN

Silver **Ruler:** James I **Obv:** James I on horseback right in inner circle **Note:** Third Coinage (1619-25). Dav. #3760A.

Date	Mintage	VG	F	VF	XF	Unc
ND(1619-25)	—	600	1,300	3,150	6,800	—

KM# 64 CROWN

Silver **Ruler:** James I **Rev:** Plume above shield of arms **Note:** Dav. #3760.

Date	Mintage	VG	F	VF	XF	Unc
ND(1619-25)	—	825	1,650	4,500	11,500	—

KM# 128 CROWN

Silver **Ruler:** Charles I **Rev:** Plume divides C-R above oval arms without long cross behind **Note:** Dav. #3762.

Date	Mintage	VG	F	VF	XF	Unc
ND(1625-49)	—	750	1,350	3,300	7,500	—

KM# 130 CROWN

Silver **Ruler:** Charles I **Rev:** Garnished oval arms without C-R above or cross behind **Note:** Dav. #3764.

Date	Mintage	VG	F	VF	XF	Unc
ND(1625-49)	—	750	1,300	3,300	7,500	—

KM# 131 CROWN

Silver **Ruler:** Charles I **Rev:** Plume above shield **Note:** Dav. #3764A.

Date	Mintage	VG	F	VF	XF	Unc
ND(1625-49)	—	750	1,300	3,300	7,500	—

KM# 125 CROWN

Silver **Ruler:** Charles I **Obv:** Charles I on horseback left in inner circle **Mint:** Tower **Note:** Struck at Tower Mint. Dav. #3761.

Date	Mintage	VG	F	VF	XF	Unc
ND(1625-49)	—	750	1,450	3,300	7,500	—

KM# 126 CROWN

Silver **Ruler:** Charles I **Rev:** Without cross behind shield, plume above shield

Date	Mintage	VG	F	VF	XF	Unc
ND(1625-49)	—	675	1,350	3,300	—	—

KM# 127 CROWN

Silver **Ruler:** Charles I **Obv:** Small horse with plume on head, king holds sword on shoulder **Rev:** Garnished oval arms on long cross with C-R above in inner circle

Date	Mintage	VG	F	VF	XF	Unc
ND(1625-49)	—	750	1,350	3,150	6,800	—

KM# 129 CROWN

Silver **Ruler:** Charles I **Rev:** Cross added behind oval arms

Date	Mintage	VG	F	VF	XF	Unc
ND(1632-3)	—	750	1,500	3,450	8,300	—

KM# 132 CROWN

Silver **Ruler:** Charles I **Obv:** Briot-style horseman with ground line below **Rev:** Garnished oval arms in inner circle

Date	Mintage	VG	F	VF	XF	Unc
ND(1625-49)	—	1,850	3,650	9,000	—	—

KM# 133 CROWN

Silver **Ruler:** Charles I **Obv:** Small short horse with king holding sword aloft, in inner circle **Rev:** Garnished oval arms in inner circle **Mint:** Tower **Note:** Mint mark: Eye.

Date	Mintage	VG	F	VF	XF	Unc
ND(1625-49)	—	750	1,300	3,150	6,800	—

KM# 134 CROWN

Silver **Ruler:** Charles I **Obv:** Large tall horse **Mint:** Tower **Note:** Mint mark: Sun.

Date	Mintage	VG	F	VF	XF	Unc
ND(1625-49)	—	750	1,450	3,600	8,300	—

KM# 135 CROWN

2.2500 g., 0.9170 Gold 0.0663 oz. AGW **Ruler:** Charles I **Obv:** First crowned bust of Charles I right **Mint:** Tower

Date	Mintage	VG	F	VF	XF	Unc
ND(1625-42)	—	225	350	800	1,600	—

KM# 136 CROWN

2.2500 g., 0.9170 Gold 0.0663 oz. AGW **Ruler:** Charles I **Obv:** Second crowned bust of Charles I left **Mint:** Tower

Date	Mintage	VG	F	VF	XF	Unc
ND(1625-42)	—	200	300	750	1,500	—

KM# 137 CROWN

2.2500 g., 0.9170 Gold 0.0663 oz. AGW **Ruler:** Charles I **Rev:** Crowned oval arms with C-R at sides in inner circle **Mint:** Tower

Date	Mintage	VG	F	VF	XF	Unc
ND(1625-42)	—	200	350	800	1,600	—

KM# 138 CROWN

2.2500 g., 0.9170 Gold 0.0663 oz. AGW **Ruler:** Charles I **Obv:** Third crowned bust of Charles I left in inner circle **Mint:** Tower

Date	Mintage	VG	F	VF	XF	Unc
ND(1625-42)	—	350	600	1,500	3,000	—

KM# 139 CROWN

2.2500 g., 0.9170 Gold 0.0663 oz. AGW **Ruler:** Charles I **Obv:** Fourth crowned bust of Charles I left in inner circle **Mint:** Tower

Date	Mintage	VG	F	VF	XF	Unc
ND(1625-42)	—	225	350	800	1,600	—

KM# 140 CROWN

2.2500 g., 0.9170 Gold 0.0663 oz. AGW **Ruler:** Charles I **Obv:** Fifth crowned bust of Charles I left in inner circle **Mint:** Tower

Date	Mintage	VG	F	VF	XF	Unc
ND(1625-42)	—	350	550	1,200	2,400	—

KM# 141 CROWN

2.2500 g., 0.9170 Gold 0.0663 oz. AGW **Ruler:** Charles I **Obv:** Sixth crowned bust of Charles I left in inner circle **Mint:** Tower

Date	Mintage	VG	F	VF	XF	Unc
ND(1625-42) Unique	—	—	—	—	—	—

KM# 168 CROWN

2.2500 g., 0.9170 Gold 0.0663 oz. AGW **Ruler:** Charles I **Obv:** Finer style crowned bust of Charles I left with value behind head **Rev:** Crowned square-topped arms with C-R at sides **Mint:** Briot **Note:** First milled Briot issue.

Date	Mintage	VG	F	VF	XF	Unc
ND(1631-32)	—	2,400	4,000	9,500	—	—

KM# 167 CROWN

Silver **Ruler:** Charles I **Obv:** Fine style king on horseback with sword pointed aloft, ground below, in inner circle **Rev:** Crowned garnished oval arms divides crowned C and R **Note:** First Milled Briot Issue. Dav. #3763.

Date	Mintage	VG	F	VF	XF	Unc
ND(1631-32)	—	900	1,800	4,500	10,500	—

KM# 225 CROWN

Silver **Ruler:** Charles I **Obv:** King on horseback left with plume behind head, ground line below **Rev:** Declaration with three plumes above and date below **Mint:** Shrewsbury **Note:** Dav. #3767.

Date	Mintage	VG	F	VF	XF	Unc
1642	—	600	1,200	3,300	7,500	—

KM# 226.1 CROWN

Silver **Ruler:** Charles I **Obv:** Shrewsbury-style horseman **Rev:** Declaration with three plumes above and date below **Mint:** Oxford

Date	Mintage	VG	F	VF	XF	Unc
1642	—	900	1,800	3,900	9,000	—
1643	—	900	1,800	3,900	9,000	—

KM# 226.2 CROWN

Silver **Ruler:** Charles I **Obv:** Grass added to ground line **Mint:** Oxford **Note:** Dav. #3770.

Date	Mintage	VG	F	VF	XF	Unc
1643	—	975	1,950	4,500	10,500	—

KM# 243 CROWN

2.2500 g., 0.9170 Gold 0.0663 oz. AGW **Ruler:** Charles I **Obv:** Fourth crowned bust of Charles I left **Mint:** Tower **Note:** Struck under Parliament, 1643-48.

Date	Mintage	VG	F	VF	XF	Unc
ND(1643-48)	—	550	1,000	2,400	5,000	—

KM# 330 CROWN

Silver **Ruler:** Charles I **Obv:** Rawlins-style horsman with city view of Oxford in background **Rev:** Declaration with scrolls above and below, date and OXON at bottom **Mint:** Oxford **Note:** Dav. #3771.

Date	Mintage	VG	F	VF	XF	Unc
1644 Rare	—	—	—	—	—	—

KM# 331 CROWN

Silver **Ruler:** Charles I **Obv:** King on horseback, facing viewer, in inner circle **Rev:** Garnished oval arms in inner circle **Mint:** Truro

Date	Mintage	VG	F	VF	XF	Unc
ND(1644)	—	375	825	2,100	4,500	—

KM# 332 CROWN

Silver **Ruler:** Charles I **Rev:** 12 evenly spaced scrolls around oval arms **Mint:** Truro

Date	Mintage	VG	F	VF	XF	Unc
ND(1644)	—	375	825	2,100	4,500	—

KM# 333 CROWN

Silver **Ruler:** Charles I **Obv:** King in profile **Mint:** Truro

Date	Mintage	VG	F	VF	XF	Unc
ND(1644)	—	375	825	2,100	4,500	—

KM# 334.1 CROWN

Silver **Ruler:** Charles I **Obv:** King on horseback facing viewer **Rev:** Garnished oval arms in inner circle, date in legend divided by mint mark **Mint:** Exeter

Date	Mintage	VG	F	VF	XF	Unc
1644	—	450	900	1,950	4,500	—

KM# 334.2 CROWN

Silver **Ruler:** Charles I **Rev:** Date in legend left of mint mark **Mint:** Exeter

Date	Mintage	VG	F	VF	XF	Unc
1644	—	450	900	1,950	4,500	—

KM# 334.3 CROWN

Silver **Ruler:** Charles I **Rev:** EX added at top of legend as mint mark **Mint:** Exeter **Note:** Dav. #3765A.

Date	Mintage	VG	F	VF	XF	Unc
1645	—	375	900	2,100	4,500	—

KM# 334.4 CROWN

Silver **Ruler:** Charles I **Obv:** King's sash has loose ends instead of bow **Mint:** Exeter **Note:** Varieties exist.

Date	Mintage	VG	F	VF	XF	Unc
1645	—	525	900	1,950	4,500	—

KM# 38 DOUBLE CROWN

4.5000 g., 0.9170 Gold 0.1327 oz. AGW **Ruler:** James I **Obv:** Third crowned bust of James I right **Rev:** Crowned square-topped arms with I-R at sides

Date	Mintage	VG	F	VF	XF	Unc
ND(1604-19)	—	300	600	1,250	2,500	—

KM# 39 DOUBLE CROWN

4.5000 g., 0.9170 Gold 0.1327 oz. AGW **Ruler:** James I **Obv:** Fourth crowned bust of James I right

Date	Mintage	VG	F	VF	XF	Unc
ND(1604-19)	—	300	600	1,250	2,500	—

KM# 40 DOUBLE CROWN

4.5000 g., 0.9170 Gold 0.1327 oz. AGW **Ruler:** James I **Obv:** Fifth crowned bust of James I right

Date	Mintage	VG	F	VF	XF	Unc
ND(1604-19)	—	300	450	1,000	2,200	—

KM# 142 DOUBLE CROWN

4.5000 g., 0.9170 Gold 0.1327 oz. AGW **Ruler:** Charles I **Obv:** First crowned bust of Charles I **Mint:** Tower

Date	Mintage	VG	F	VF	XF	Unc
ND(1625-42)	—	400	700	1,650	3,500	—

KM# 143 DOUBLE CROWN

4.5000 g., 0.9170 Gold 0.1327 oz. AGW **Ruler:** Charles I **Obv:** Second crowned bust of Charles I **Mint:** Tower

Date	Mintage	VG	F	VF	XF	Unc
ND(1625-42)	—	250	450	1,000	2,200	—

KM# 144 DOUBLE CROWN

4.5000 g., 0.9170 Gold 0.1327 oz. AGW **Ruler:** Charles I **Rev:** Crowned oval shield with C-R at sides **Mint:** Tower

Date	Mintage	VG	F	VF	XF	Unc
ND(1625-42)	—	350	600	1,500	3,500	—

KM# 145 DOUBLE CROWN

4.5000 g., 0.9170 Gold 0.1327 oz. AGW **Ruler:** Charles I **Obv:** Third crowned bust of Charles I left, value behind head, in inner circle **Mint:** Tower

Date	Mintage	VG	F	VF	XF	Unc
ND(1625-42)	—	350	600	1,500	3,500	—

KM# 146 DOUBLE CROWN

4.5000 g., 0.9170 Gold 0.1327 oz. AGW **Ruler:** Charles I **Obv:** Fourth crowned bust of Charles I left, value behind head, in inner circle **Mint:** Tower

Date	Mintage	VG	F	VF	XF	Unc
ND(1625-42)	—	300	500	1,250	3,000	—

KM# 147 DOUBLE CROWN

4.5000 g., 0.9170 Gold 0.1327 oz. AGW **Ruler:** Charles I **Obv:** Fifth crowned bust of Charles I left, value behind head, in inner circle **Mint:** Tower

Date	Mintage	VG	F	VF	XF	Unc
ND(1625-42)	—	400	750	1,700	4,000	—

KM# 148 DOUBLE CROWN

4.5000 g., 0.9170 Gold 0.1327 oz. AGW **Ruler:** Charles I **Obv:** Sixth crowned bust of Charles I left, value behind head, in inner circle **Mint:** Tower

Date	Mintage	VG	F	VF	XF	Unc
ND(1625-42)	—	250	550	1,500	3,000	—

KM# 169 DOUBLE CROWN

4.5000 g., 0.9170 Gold 0.1327 oz. AGW **Ruler:** Charles I **Obv:** Bust of Charles I left **Note:** First milled Briot issue.

Date	Mintage	VG	F	VF	XF	Unc
ND(1631-32)	—	1,250	2,500	6,000	1,200	—

KM# 244 DOUBLE CROWN

4.5000 g., 0.9170 Gold 0.1327 oz. AGW **Ruler:** Charles I **Obv:** Fourth crowned bust of Charles I left, value behind head, in inner circle **Mint:** Tower **Note:** Struck under Parliament.

Date	Mintage	VG	F	VF	XF	Unc
ND(1643-48)	—	650	1,200	2,800	5,500	—

KM# 245 DOUBLE CROWN

4.5000 g., 0.9170 Gold 0.1327 oz. AGW **Ruler:** Charles I **Obv:** Fifth crowned bust of Charles I left, value behind head, in inner circle **Mint:** Tower **Note:** Struck under Parliament.

Date	Mintage	VG	F	VF	XF	Unc
ND(1643-48)	—	500	800	1,900	4,000	—

KM# 246 DOUBLE CROWN

4.5000 g., 0.9170 Gold 0.1327 oz. AGW **Ruler:** Charles I **Obv:** Sixth crowned bust of Charles I left, value behind head, in inner circle **Mint:** Tower **Note:** Struck under Parliament.

Date	Mintage	VG	F	VF	XF	Unc
ND(1643-48)	—	400	700	1,800	4,000	—

KM# 247 DOUBLE CROWN

4.5000 g., 0.9170 Gold 0.1327 oz. AGW **Ruler:** Charles I **Obv:** Seventh crowned bust of Charles I left, value behind head, in inner circle **Mint:** Tower **Note:** Struck under Parliament.

Date	Mintage	VG	F	VF	XF	Unc
ND(1643-48)	—	750	1,400	3,000	—	—

KM# C7 1/2 POUND

5.5750 g., 0.9790 Gold 0.1755 oz. AGW **Ruler:** Elizabeth I **Obv:** Crowned bust left **Rev:** Crowned arms **Note:** Sixth Issue.

Date	Mintage	VG	F	VF	XF	Unc
(160)1	—	1,250	2,750	6,500	12,500	—
(160)2	—	1,250	2,750	6,500	12,500	—

KM# 235.5 1/2 POUND

Silver **Ruler:** Charles I **Obv:** Without plume behind or cannon below **Mint:** Shrewsbury **Note:** Dav. #3766.

Date	Mintage	VG	F	VF	XF	Unc
1642	—	1,050	2,100	5,300	13,000	—

KM# 235.1 1/2 POUND

Silver **Ruler:** Charles I **Obv:** King on horseback left with plume behind in inner circle **Rev:** Declaration with three plumes and value above **Mint:** Shrewsbury **Note:** Dav. #3766A.

Date	Mintage	VG	F	VF	XF	Unc
1642	—	1,150	2,250	5,300	13,000	—

KM# 235.2 1/2 POUND

Silver **Ruler:** Charles I **Rev:** Two plumes with value **Mint:** Shrewsbury

Date	Mintage	VG	F	VF	XF	Unc
1642	—	1,200	2,400	5,300	—	—

KM# 235.3 1/2 POUND

Silver **Ruler:** Charles I **Obv:** Ground line below horse **Mint:** Shrewsbury

Date	Mintage	VG	F	VF	XF	Unc
1642	—	1,200	2,250	5,300	13,000	—

KM# 235.4 1/2 POUND

Silver **Ruler:** Charles I **Obv:** Cannon and weapons below horse **Mint:** Shrewsbury

Date	Mintage	VG	F	VF	XF	Unc
1642	—	1,200	2,400	5,300	13,000	—

KM# 235.7 1/2 POUND

Silver **Ruler:** Charles I **Obv:** Oxford dies (plumes with bands) **Mint:** Oxford

Date	Mintage	VG	F	VF	XF	Unc
1642	—	1,050	2,100	4,500	11,500	—
1643	—	1,050	2,100	4,500	11,500	—

KM# 235.6 1/2 POUND

Silver **Ruler:** Charles I **Mint:** Oxford

Date	Mintage	VG	F	VF	XF	Unc
1642	—	1,900	3,400	9,800	19,000	—

KM# 236 1/2 POUND

Silver **Ruler:** Charles I **Obv:** King on horseback left in inner circle **Rev:** Garnished oval arms in inner circle **Mint:** Truro **Note:** Crown dies struck double thick.

Date	Mintage	VG	F	VF	XF	Unc
ND Rare	—	—	—	—	—	—

KM# D7 POUND

11.1500 g., 0.9790 Gold 0.3509 oz. AGW **Ruler:** Elizabeth I **Obv:** Crowned bust left **Rev:** Crowned arms **Note:** Sixth Issue.

Date	Mintage	VG	F	VF	XF	Unc
(160)1	—	1,600	3,500	8,000	15,000	—
(160)2	—	1,600	3,500	8,000	15,000	—

KM# 237.1 POUND

Silver **Ruler:** Charles I **Obv:** King on horseback, plume behind, in inner circle **Rev:** Declaration, three plumes and value above and date below **Mint:** Shrewsbury

Date	Mintage	VG	F	VF	XF	Unc
1642	—	2,250	4,500	12,000	—	—

KM# 237.2 POUND

Silver **Ruler:** Charles I **Obv:** Shrewsbury horseman with weapons below **Mint:** Shrewsbury

Date	Mintage	VG	F	VF	XF	Unc
1642	—	2,250	4,500	11,500	—	—

KM# 237.3 POUND

Silver **Ruler:** Charles I **Rev:** One plume above value **Mint:** Shrewsbury

Date	Mintage	VG	F	VF	XF	Unc
1642	—	2,250	4,500	12,000	—	—

KM# 238.1 POUND

Silver **Ruler:** Charles I **Obv:** Large horseman above armor and weapons **Rev:** Declaration, three Shrewsbury plumes and value above and date below **Mint:** Oxford

Date	Mintage	VG	F	VF	XF	Unc
1642	—	2,250	4,500	13,000	—	—

KM# 239.1 POUND

Silver **Ruler:** Charles I **Obv:** Shrewsbury horseman above weapons and ground line **Mint:** Oxford

Date	Mintage	VG	F	VF	XF	Unc
1642	—	2,250	4,500	11,500	—	—

KM# 239.2 POUND

Silver **Ruler:** Charles I **Obv:** Cannon added to weapons **Mint:** Oxford

Date	Mintage	VG	F	VF	XF	Unc
1642	—	2,250	4,500	11,500	—	—
1643	—	2,250	4,500	11,500	—	—

KM# 240 POUND

Silver **Ruler:** Charles I **Obv:** Exergue space checkered **Mint:** Oxford

Date	Mintage	VG	F	VF	XF	Unc
1642	—	2,250	4,500	12,000	—	—

KM# 258 POUND

Silver **Ruler:** Charles I **Obv:** Briot-style horseman **Mint:** Oxford

Date	Mintage	VG	F	VF	XF	Unc
1643	—	2,250	4,500	13,000	—	—

KM# 238.2 POUND

Silver **Ruler:** Charles I **Rev:** Three Oxford plumes near value **Mint:** Oxford

Date	Mintage	VG	F	VF	XF	Unc
1643	—	2,250	4,500	13,000	—	—

KM# 340 POUND

Silver **Ruler:** Charles I **Mint:** Oxford

Date	Mintage	VG	F	VF	XF	Unc
1644	—	2,500	4,900	13,000	—	—

ANGEL COINAGE

KM# 43 1/2 ANGEL

2.5000 g., 0.9950 Gold 0.0800 oz. AGW **Ruler:** James I **Obv:** St. Michael slaying dragon in inner circle **Rev:** Ship sailing to left with arms

Date	Mintage	VG	F	VF	XF	Unc
ND(1604-19)	—	1,400	3,000	7,500	12,000	—

KM# E7 ANGEL

5.0000 g., 0.9950 Gold 0.1599 oz. AGW **Ruler:** Elizabeth I **Obv:** St. Michael slaying dragon **Rev:** Arms on sailing ship **Note:** Sixth issue.

Date	Mintage	VG	F	VF	XF	Unc
(160)1	—	650	1,250	2,900	6,000	—
(160)2	—	650	1,250	2,900	6,000	—

KM# 44 ANGEL

5.0000 g., 0.9950 Gold 0.1599 oz. AGW **Ruler:** James I

Date	Mintage	VG	F	VF	XF	Unc
ND(1604-19)	—	700	1,400	3,500	6,500	—

KM# 67 ANGEL

5.0000 g., 0.9950 Gold 0.1599 oz. AGW **Ruler:** James I **Rev:** Different ship

Date	Mintage	VG	F	VF	XF	Unc
ND(1619-25)	—	1,000	2,300	8,000	12,000	—

KM# 149.1 ANGEL

5.0000 g., 0.9950 Gold 0.1599 oz. AGW **Ruler:** Charles I **Obv:** St. Michael slaying dragon without mark of value in inner circle **Rev:** Ship sailing to left iwth arms in inner circle **Mint:** Tower

Date	Mintage	VG	F	VF	XF	Unc
ND(1625-42)	—	1,500	3,500	9,000	15,000	—

KM# 149.2 ANGEL

5.0000 g., 0.9950 Gold 0.1599 oz. AGW **Ruler:** Charles I **Obv:** Mark of value in field at left **Mint:** Tower

Date	Mintage	VG	F	VF	XF	Unc
ND(1625-42)	—	1,400	3,500	8,500	13,500	—

KM# 149.3 ANGEL

5.0000 g., 0.9950 Gold 0.1599 oz. AGW **Ruler:** Charles I **Obv:** Mark of value in field at right **Mint:** Tower

Date	Mintage	VG	F	VF	XF	Unc
ND(1625-42)	—	1,300	3,000	8,000	12,000	—

KM# 170 ANGEL
5.0000 g., 0.9950 Gold 0.1599 oz. AGW **Ruler:** Charles I **Mint:** Briot **Note:** Smaller planchet and finer style.

Date	Mintage	VG	F	VF	XF	Unc
ND(1631-32) B	—	3,500	7,000	16,500	—	—

RYAL COINAGE

KM# 41 SPUR RYAL
13.0000 g., 0.9950 Gold 0.4159 oz. AGW **Ruler:** James I

Date	Mintage	VG	F	VF	XF	Unc
ND(1604-19)	—	3,500	7,000	16,500	30,000	—

KM# 65 SPUR RYAL
13.0000 g., 0.9950 Gold 0.4159 oz. AGW **Ruler:** James I

Date	Mintage	VG	F	VF	XF	Unc
ND(1619-25)	—	3,000	6,500	15,000	27,000	—

KM# 42 ROSE RYAL
13.0000 g., 0.9950 Gold 0.4159 oz. AGW **Ruler:** James I

Date	Mintage	VG	F	VF	XF	Unc
ND(1604-19)	—	1,800	3,500	9,000	19,000	—

KM# 66.1 ROSE RYAL
13.0000 g., 0.9950 Gold 0.4159 oz. AGW **Ruler:** James I

Date	Mintage	VG	F	VF	XF	Unc
ND(1619-25)	—	2,100	4,000	9,500	15,000	—

KM# 66.2 ROSE RYAL
13.0000 g., 0.9950 Gold 0.4159 oz. AGW **Ruler:** James I **Obv:** Plain back on throne

Date	Mintage	VG	F	VF	XF	Unc
ND(1619-25)	—	2,100	4,000	9,000	16,000	—

UNITE COINAGE

KM# 227 1/2 UNITE
4.5000 g., 0.9170 Gold 0.1327 oz. AGW **Ruler:** Charles I **Obv:** Crowned bust of Charles I left in inner circle **Rev:** Declaration in three straight lines, plumes above, date below in inner circle **Mint:** Oxford

Date	Mintage	VG	F	VF	XF	Unc
1642	—	1,400	3,000	8,000	15,000	—

KM# 228 1/2 UNITE
4.5000 g., 0.9170 Gold 0.1327 oz. AGW **Ruler:** Charles I **Rev:** Declaration on continuous scroll **Mint:** Oxford

Date	Mintage	VG	F	VF	XF	Unc
1642	—	1,200	2,700	7,500	14,500	—
1643	—	1,200	2,700	7,500	14,500	—

KM# 248.1 1/2 UNITE
4.5000 g., 0.9170 Gold 0.1327 oz. AGW **Ruler:** Charles I **Obv:** Bust of Charles I left **Mint:** Oxford

Date	Mintage	VG	F	VF	XF	Unc
1643	—	850	1,900	5,000	9,000	—

KM# 248.2 1/2 UNITE
4.5000 g., 0.9170 Gold 0.1327 oz. AGW **Ruler:** Charles I **Rev:** OX below date **Mint:** Oxford

Date	Mintage	VG	F	VF	XF	Unc
1644	—	2,400	4,500	8,000	—	—

KM# 344 1/2 UNITE
4.5000 g., 0.9170 Gold 0.1327 oz. AGW **Ruler:** Charles I **Obv:** Crowned bust of Charles I left in inner circle **Rev:** Declaration on continuous scroll, plumes above, date below in inner circle **Mint:** Bristol

Date	Mintage	VG	F	VF	XF	Unc
1645 Rare	—	—	—	—	—	—

KM# 45 UNITE
9.0000 g., 0.9170 Gold 0.2653 oz. AGW **Ruler:** James I **Obv:** Second crowned bust of James I right

Date	Mintage	VG	F	VF	XF	Unc
ND(1604-19)	—	525	1,000	2,050	5,400	—

KM# 46 UNITE
9.0000 g., 0.9170 Gold 0.2653 oz. AGW **Ruler:** James I **Obv:** Fourth crowned bust of James I right

Date	Mintage	VG	F	VF	XF	Unc
ND(1604-19)	—	475	850	1,750	4,950	—

KM# 47 UNITE
9.0000 g., 0.9170 Gold 0.2653 oz. AGW **Ruler:** James I **Obv:** Fifth crowned bust of James I right

Date	Mintage	VG	F	VF	XF	Unc
ND(1604-19)	—	475	850	1,750	4,950	—

KM# 150 UNITE
9.0000 g., 0.9170 Gold 0.2653 oz. AGW **Ruler:** Charles I **Obv:** First crowned bust of Charles I left **Mint:** Tower

Date	Mintage	VG	F	VF	XF	Unc
ND(1625-42)	—	500	1,100	2,650	6,600	—

KM# 151.1 UNITE
9.0000 g., 0.9170 Gold 0.2653 oz. AGW **Ruler:** Charles I **Obv:** Second crowned bust of Charles I left **Mint:** Tower

Date	Mintage	VG	F	VF	XF	Unc
ND(1625-42)	—	500	1,100	2,650	6,600	—

KM# 151.2 UNITE
9.0000 g., 0.9170 Gold 0.2653 oz. AGW **Ruler:** Charles I **Obv:** Anchor below bust **Mint:** Tower

Date	Mintage	VG	F	VF	XF	Unc
ND(1625-42)	—	1,300	2,750	5,500	14,500	—

KM# 152 UNITE

9.0000 g., 0.9170 Gold 0.2653 oz. AGW **Ruler:** Charles I **Obv:** Third crowned bust of Charles I left **Mint:** Tower

Date	Mintage	VG	F	VF	XF	Unc
ND(1625-42)	—	500	1,100	2,650	6,600	—

KM# 153 UNITE

9.0000 g., 0.9170 Gold 0.2653 oz. AGW **Ruler:** Charles I **Obv:** Fourth crowned bust of Charles I left **Mint:** Tower

Date	Mintage	VG	F	VF	XF	Unc
ND(1625-42)	—	500	1,100	2,650	6,600	—

KM# 154.1 UNITE

9.0000 g., 0.9170 Gold 0.2653 oz. AGW **Ruler:** Charles I **Obv:** Sixth crowned bust of Charles I left **Mint:** Tower

Date	Mintage	VG	F	VF	XF	Unc
ND(1625-42)	—	500	1,100	2,650	6,600	—

KM# 154.2 UNITE

9.0000 g., 0.9170 Gold 0.2653 oz. AGW **Ruler:** Charles I **Mint:** Briot **Note:** Mint mark: Anchor.

Date	Mintage	VG	F	VF	XF	Unc
ND(1625-42)	—	3,850	7,400	25,000	—	—

KM# 171 UNITE

9.0000 g., 0.9170 Gold 0.2653 oz. AGW **Ruler:** Charles I **Obv:** Charles I left **Mint:** Briot

Date	Mintage	VG	F	VF	XF	Unc
ND(1631-32)	—	2,050	4,150	9,400	22,000	—

KM# 230 UNITE

9.0000 g., 0.9170 Gold 0.2653 oz. AGW **Ruler:** Charles I **Mint:** Oxford

Date	Mintage	VG	F	VF	XF	Unc
1642	—	1,700	3,700	9,200	19,500	—
1643	—	1,700	3,700	9,200	19,500	—

KM# 229 UNITE

9.0000 g., 0.9170 Gold 0.2653 oz. AGW **Ruler:** Charles I **Obv:** Charles I left **Mint:** Oxford

Date	Mintage	VG	F	VF	XF	Unc
1642	—	1,700	3,700	9,200	19,500	—

KM# 231.1 UNITE

9.0000 g., 0.9170 Gold 0.2653 oz. AGW **Ruler:** Charles I **Rev:** Crowned oval arms with C-R at sides **Mint:** Exeter

Date	Mintage	VG	F	VF	XF	Unc
ND(1642-43)	—	16,500	33,000	112,500	—	—

KM# 231.2 UNITE

9.0000 g., 0.9170 Gold 0.2653 oz. AGW **Ruler:** Charles I **Rev:** Without C-R at sides of arms **Mint:** Exeter

Date	Mintage	VG	F	VF	XF	Unc
ND(1642-43)	—	16,500	33,000	100,000	—	—

KM# 337 UNITE

9.0000 g., 0.9170 Gold 0.2653 oz. AGW **Ruler:** Charles I **Rev:** Crowned oval arms in inner circle **Mint:** Shrewsbury

Date	Mintage	VG	F	VF	XF	Unc
ND(1642) Rare	—	—	—	—	—	—

KM# 253 UNITE

9.0000 g., 0.9170 Gold 0.2653 oz. AGW **Ruler:** Charles I **Obv:** Shorter bust **Mint:** Oxford

Date	Mintage	VG	F	VF	XF	Unc
1643	—	1,700	3,400	8,600	19,500	—
1645	—	1,700	3,400	8,600	19,500	—

KM# 249 UNITE

9.0000 g., 0.9170 Gold 0.2653 oz. AGW **Ruler:** Charles I **Obv:** Fourth crowned bust of Charles I left in inner circle **Rev:** Crowned oval arms **Mint:** Tower **Note:** Struck under Parliament.

Date	Mintage	VG	F	VF	XF	Unc
ND(1643-48)	—	800	1,850	4,600	12,500	—

KM# 250 UNITE

9.0000 g., 0.9170 Gold 0.2653 oz. AGW **Ruler:** Charles I **Obv:** Sixth crowned bust of Charles I left in inner circle **Rev:** Cronwed oval arms **Mint:** Tower **Note:** Struck under Parliament.

Date	Mintage	VG	F	VF	XF	Unc
ND(1643-48)	—	800	1,850	5,300	14,500	—

KM# 251 UNITE

9.0000 g., 0.9170 Gold 0.2653 oz. AGW **Ruler:** Charles I **Obv:** Seventh crowned bust of Charles I left in inner circle, crude style **Rev:** Crowned oval arms **Mint:** Tower **Note:** Struck under Parliament.

Date	Mintage	VG	F	VF	XF	Unc
ND(1643-48)	—	800	1,850	5,300	14,500	—

KM# 252 UNITE

9.0000 g., 0.9170 Gold 0.2653 oz. AGW **Ruler:** Charles I **Mint:** Oxford

Date	Mintage	VG	F	VF	XF	Unc
1643	—	1,700	3,700	9,200	19,500	—

KM# 254 UNITE

9.0000 g., 0.9170 Gold 0.2653 oz. AGW **Ruler:** Charles I **Mint:** Oxford

Date	Mintage	VG	F	VF	XF	Unc
1643	—	1,700	3,600	8,600	19,500	—

KM# 255 UNITE

9.0000 g., 0.9170 Gold 0.2653 oz. AGW **Ruler:** Charles I **Obv:** Crude crowned bust of Charles I left, value behind head in inner circle **Rev:** Crowned oval arms with lion claws at sides **Mint:** Worcester

Date	Mintage	VG	F	VF	XF	Unc
ND(1643-44) Rare	—	—	—	—	—	—

KM# 335 UNITE

9.0000 g., 0.9170 Gold 0.2653 oz. AGW **Ruler:** Charles I **Mint:** Oxford

Date	Mintage	VG	F	VF	XF	Unc
1644	—	1,700	3,950	9,900	22,000	—

KM# 336 UNITE

9.0000 g., 0.9170 Gold 0.2653 oz. AGW **Ruler:** Charles I **Mint:** Oxford

Date	Mintage	VG	F	VF	XF	Unc
1644 Rare	—	—	—	—	—	—

KM# 345 UNITE
9.0000 g., 0.9170 Gold 0.2653 oz. AGW **Ruler:** Charles I **Mint:** Oxford

Date	Mintage	VG	F	VF	XF	Unc
1645	—	1,700	3,950	9,200	19,500	—
1646	—	1,700	3,950	9,200	19,500	—

KM# 346 UNITE
9.0000 g., 0.9170 Gold 0.2653 oz. AGW **Ruler:** Charles I **Rev:** Declaration in three lines on continuous scroll **Mint:** Bristol

Date	Mintage	VG	F	VF	XF	Unc
1645 Rare	—	—	—	—	—	—

KM# 232 TRIPLE UNITE
27.0000 g., 0.9170 Gold 0.7960 oz. AGW **Ruler:** Charles I **Obv:** Crowned half-length figure of Charles I left in inner circle **Rev:** Declaration in two wavy lines, plumes and III above, date below in inner circle **Mint:** Shrewsbury

Date	Mintage	VG	F	VF	XF	Unc
1642 Rare	—	—	—	—	—	—

KM# 233 TRIPLE UNITE
27.0000 g., 0.9170 Gold 0.7960 oz. AGW **Ruler:** Charles I **Rev:** Legend in two lines **Mint:** Oxford

Date	Mintage	VG	F	VF	XF	Unc
1642 Rare	—	—	—	—	—	—

KM# 234 TRIPLE UNITE
27.0000 g., 0.9170 Gold 0.7960 oz. AGW **Ruler:** Charles I **Rev:** Declaration on continuous scroll

Date	Mintage	VG	F	VF	XF	Unc
1642	—	6,100	13,000	33,000	—	—
1643	—	7,700	16,500	38,500	—	—

KM# 256.1 TRIPLE UNITE
27.0000 g., 0.9170 Gold 0.7960 oz. AGW **Ruler:** Charles I **Obv:** Charles I with scarf behind

Date	Mintage	VG	F	VF	XF	Unc
1643	—	6,600	14,000	35,000	—	—

KM# 256.2 TRIPLE UNITE
27.0000 g., 0.9170 Gold 0.7960 oz. AGW **Ruler:** Charles I **Obv:** Charles I without scarf behind

Date	Mintage	VG	F	VF	XF	Unc
1643	—	6,600	14,000	33,000	—	—

KM# 257 TRIPLE UNITE
27.0000 g., 0.9170 Gold 0.7960 oz. AGW **Ruler:** Charles I **Rev:** OXON below date

Date	Mintage	VG	F	VF	XF	Unc
1643	—	11,000	22,000	55,000	—	—

KM# 338 TRIPLE UNITE
27.0000 g., 0.9170 Gold 0.7960 oz. AGW **Ruler:** Charles I

Date	Mintage	VG	F	VF	XF	Unc
1644	—	7,200	15,000	36,000	—	—

KM# 339 TRIPLE UNITE
27.0000 g., 0.9170 Gold 0.7960 oz. AGW **Ruler:** Charles I

Date	Mintage	VG	F	VF	XF	Unc
1644	—	7,700	16,500	38,500	—	—

LAUREL COINAGE

KM# 68 1/4 LAUREL
2.2500 g., 0.9170 Gold 0.0663 oz. AGW **Ruler:** James I **Obv:** Second laureate bust of James I left, value behind head, in inner circle **Rev:** Crowned arms in inner circle

Date	Mintage	VG	F	VF	XF	Unc
ND(1619-25)	—	225	350	900	1,500	—

KM# 69 1/4 LAUREL
2.2500 g., 0.9170 Gold 0.0663 oz. AGW **Ruler:** James I **Obv:** Fourth laureate bust of James I

Date	Mintage	VG	F	VF	XF	Unc
ND(1619-25)	—	225	350	900	1,500	—

KM# 70 1/2 LAUREL
4.5000 g., 0.9170 Gold 0.1327 oz. AGW **Ruler:** James I **Obv:** First laureate bust of James I left, value behind head, in inner circle **Rev:** Crowned arms in inner circle

Date	Mintage	VG	F	VF	XF	Unc
ND(1619-25)	—	450	800	1,900	4,000	—

KM# 71 1/2 LAUREL
4.5000 g., 0.9170 Gold 0.1327 oz. AGW **Ruler:** James I **Obv:** Fourth laureate bust of James I **Note:** Mint mark: Rose.

Date	Mintage	VG	F	VF	XF	Unc
ND(1619-25)	—	350	750	1,500	3,000	—

KM# 72 LAUREL
9.0000 g., 0.9170 Gold 0.2653 oz. AGW **Ruler:** James I **Obv:** First laureate bust of James I left, value behind head, in inner circle **Rev:** Crowned arms in inner circle **Note:** Many minor varieties exist.

Date	Mintage	VG	F	VF	XF	Unc
ND(1619-25)	—	550	1,150	2,650	5,300	—

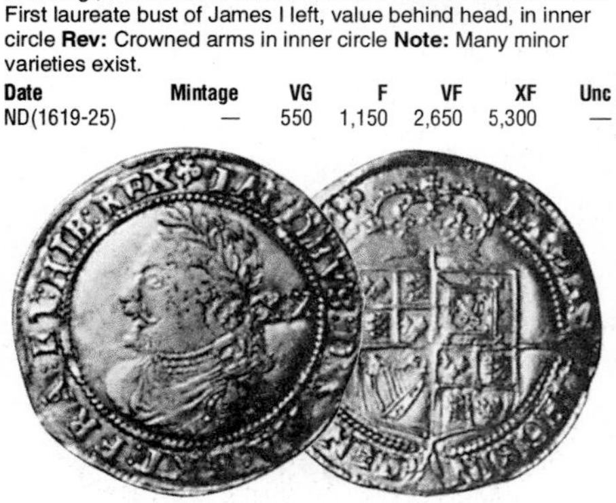

KM# 73 LAUREL
9.0000 g., 0.9170 Gold 0.2653 oz. AGW **Ruler:** James I **Obv:** Second laureate bust of James I left **Note:** Many minor varieties exist.

Date	Mintage	VG	F	VF	XF	Unc
ND(1619-25)	—	550	1,150	2,650	5,300	9,500

KM# 74 LAUREL

9.0000 g., 0.9170 Gold 0.2653 oz. AGW **Ruler:** James I **Obv:** Third laureate bust of James I left **Note:** Many minor varieties exist.

Date	Mintage	VG	F	VF	XF	Unc
ND(1619-25)	—	550	1,150	2,650	5,300	9,500

KM# 75 LAUREL

9.0000 g., 0.9170 Gold 0.2653 oz. AGW **Ruler:** James I **Obv:** Fourth laureate bust of James I left **Note:** Many minor varieties exist.

Date	Mintage	VG	F	VF	XF	Unc
ND(1619-25)	—	550	1,100	2,650	5,300	—

KM# 76 LAUREL

9.0000 g., 0.9170 Gold 0.2653 oz. AGW **Ruler:** James I **Obv:** Fifth laureate bust of James I left **Note:** Many minor varieties exist.

Date	Mintage	VG	F	VF	XF	Unc
ND(1619-25)	—	1,650	3,850	7,200	14,000	—

SOVEREIGN COINAGE

KM# 19 1/2 SOVEREIGN

Gold **Ruler:** James I **Obv:** Crowned bust right **Rev:** Crowned shield, IR flanking

Date	Mintage	VG	F	VF	XF	Unc
ND(1603-04) Rare	—	2,350	5,200	14,000	—	—

KM# 20 SOVEREIGN

11.1500 g., 0.9790 Gold 0.3509 oz. AGW **Ruler:** James I **Obv:** James I in armor

Date	Mintage	VG	F	VF	XF	Unc
ND(1603-04)	—	1,450	2,950	8,800	17,500	—

KM# 21 SOVEREIGN

11.1500 g., 0.9790 Gold 0.3509 oz. AGW **Ruler:** James I **Obv:** James I in ornamented armor

Date	Mintage	VG	F	VF	XF	Unc
ND(1603-04) 1603	—	1,550	3,100	9,600	18,000	—

SIEGE COINAGE

Carlisle

Carlisle is located in the northwest of England at the border of Scotland. The Siege of Carlisle lasted from October 1644 to June 25, 1645. The seige was in the nature of a blockade, and a lack of food ended the siege. Coins were made in two values with two varieties of each.

KM# 347 SHILLING

Silver **Ruler:** Charles I **Obv:** Large crown above C.R/XII in circle **Rev:** Three-line inscription: OBS: /CARL/1645 in circle

Date	Mintage	VG	F	VF	XF	Unc
1645	—	2,300	6,500	15,000	—	—

KM# 348 SHILLING

Silver **Ruler:** Charles I **Rev:** Two-line inscription: OB CARL/1645 in circle

Date	Mintage	VG	F	VF	XF	Unc
1645	—	2,300	6,500	16,000	—	—

KM# 349 3 SHILLING

Silver **Ruler:** Charles I **Obv:** Large crown above C. R/111 in circle **Rev:** Two-line inscription: OB CARL/1645 in circle

Date	Mintage	VG	F	VF	XF	Unc
1645 Rare	—	—	—	—	—	—

KM# 350 3 SHILLING

Silver **Ruler:** Charles I **Rev:** Three-line inscription: OBS: /CARL/1645 in circle

Date	Mintage	VG	F	VF	XF	Unc
1645	—	2,200	10,000	25,000	—	—

Colchester

Colchester was a Royalist center northeast of London. The Seige lasted from June 3 to August 17, 1648. Siege pieces were struck uniface in gold and silver.

KM# 373 NINEPENCE

Silver **Ruler:** Charles I **Note:** Octagonal planchet. Uniface.

Date	Mintage	VG	F	VF	XF	Unc
ND Rare	—	—	—	—	—	—

KM# 372 NINEPENCE

Silver **Ruler:** Charles I **Obv:** Colchester castle with five towers, script legend around top **Note:** Uniface. Round planchet.

Date	Mintage	VG	F	VF	XF	Unc
ND Rare	—	—	—	—	—	—

KM# 375 SHILLING

Silver **Ruler:** Charles I **Obv:** Colchester castle with five towers, script legend around top **Note:** Octagonal planchet. Uniface. Restrikes exist.

Date	Mintage	VG	F	VF	XF	Unc
ND Rare	—	—	—	—	—	—

KM# 374 SHILLING

Silver **Ruler:** Charles I **Obv:** Colchester castle with five towers, script legend around top **Note:** Uniface.

Date	Mintage	VG	F	VF	XF	Unc
ND Rare	—	—	—	—	—	—

KM# 377 10 SHILLING

Gold **Ruler:** Charles I **Obv:** Colchester gateway divides crowned C-R, date in exergue **Note:** Uniface.

Date	Mintage	VG	F	VF	XF	Unc
1648	—	—	—	—	—	—

KM# 376 10 SHILLING

Gold **Ruler:** Charles I **Obv:** Castle with C-R at sides, date and value in exergue **Mint:** Colchester **Note:** Uniface.

Date	Mintage	VG	F	VF	XF	Unc
1648	—	—	—	—	—	—

Lathom House

Lathom House is located in Lancashire. The siege lasted from 1643 into 1644.

KM# 341 10 SHILLING

Gold **Ruler:** Charles I **Obv:** C-R in dotted circle, value in rectangle

Date	Mintage	VG	F	VF	XF	Unc
ND Unique	—	—	—	—	—	—

Newark

Newark-on-Trent in the Midlands was the scene of a number of sieges. The final surrender was May 6, 1646. All pieces are diamond shaped and these pieces are the most available of a generally difficult series.

KM# 368 6 PENCE

Silver **Ruler:** Charles I

Date	Mintage	VG	F	VF	XF	Unc
1646	—	450	950	1,900	4,500	—

KM# 369.1 9 PENCE

Silver **Ruler:** Charles I **Rev. Legend:** OBS: /NEWARK/...

Date	Mintage	VG	F	VF	XF	Unc
1645	—	450	750	1,600	3,500	—
1646	—	450	750	1,600	3,500	—

KM# 369.2 9 PENCE

Silver **Ruler:** Charles I **Rev:** .../NEWARKE/...

Date	Mintage	VG	F	VF	XF	Unc
1645	—	450	750	1,600	3,500	—

KM# 370 SHILLING

Silver **Ruler:** Charles I **Obv:** Flat arched crown divides C-R, value below **Rev. Legend:** OBS/NEWARKE/1645

Date	Mintage	VG	F	VF	XF	Unc
1645	—	500	850	1,800	4,500	—

KM# 370.1 SHILLING

Silver **Ruler:** Charles I **Obv:** Large high-arched crown divides C-R, value below **Rev. Legend:** OBS/NEWARKE/1645

Date	Mintage	VG	F	VF	XF	Unc
1645	—	400	800	1,700	4,000	—

KM# 370.2 SHILLING

Silver **Ruler:** Charles I **Rev:** .../NEWARK/...

Date	Mintage	VG	F	VF	XF	Unc
1645	—	400	800	1,700	4,000	—
1646	—	400	800	1,700	4,000	—

KM# 371 1/2 CROWN

Silver **Ruler:** Charles I

Date	Mintage	VG	F	VF	XF	Unc
1645	—	550	1,100	2,400	6,000	—
1646	—	500	1,000	2,100	5,000	—

Ponterfract

Called by some the - Key to the North, Pontefract (or Pomfret) was the scene of three sieges during this period. The last began in the fall of 1648 and did not end until March 22, 1649, two months after the execution of Charles I. This series comes in two issues: those issued in the name of Charles I and those issued in the name of Charles II.

KM# 381 SHILLING

Silver **Ruler:** Charles I **Note:** First Issue: In the name of Charles I.

Date	Mintage	VG	F	VF	XF	Unc
1648	—	1,700	2,900	6,000	—	—

KM# 379 SHILLING

Silver **Ruler:** Charles I **Note:** First Issue: In the name of Charles I. Diamond-shaped planchet.

Date	Mintage	VG	F	VF	XF	Unc
1648	—	1,700	2,900	6,000	8,500	—

KM# 380 SHILLING

Silver **Ruler:** Charles I **Note:** First Issue: In the name of Charles I. Octagonal planchet.

Date	Mintage	VG	F	VF	XF	Unc
1648	—	1,400	2,300	6,000	8,500	—

KM# 378 SHILLING

Silver **Ruler:** Charles II **Obv:** Castle **Obv. Legend:** CAROLVS: SECVNDVS: **Rev:** Crowned "CR" **Rev. Legend:** DVM: SPIRO: SPERO **Note:** First Issue: In the name of Charles II.

Date	Mintage	VG	F	VF	XF	Unc
1648	—	1,700	2,900	6,000	8,500	—

KM# 383.1 SHILLING

Silver **Obv:** Crown above HANC DE/US DEDIT/1648 in inner circle **Obv. Legend:** Outer legend: CAROL. II. D. G. MAG. B. F. ET. H. REX. **Rev. Legend:** Outer legend: POST. MORTEM: PATRIS: PRO: FILIO **Note:** Second Issue: In the name of Charles II.

Date	Mintage	VG	F	VF	XF	Unc
1648	—	1,800	2,900	6,000	—	—

KM# 383.2 SHILLING

Silver **Rev:** Cannon at right side **Note:** Second Issue: In the name of Charles II.

Date	Mintage	VG	F	VF	XF	Unc
1648 Unique	—	—	—	—	—	—

KM# 382 SHILLING

Silver **Obv:** Castle gateway with OBS at left, PC above and cannon at right **Obv. Legend:** CAROLUS SECUNDUS 1648 **Rev:** Crown above C-R **Rev. Legend:** DUM SPIRO SPERO **Note:** Second Issue: In the name of Charles II. Octagonal planchet.

Date	Mintage	VG	F	VF	XF	Unc
1648	—	1,300	2,800	5,500	6,500	—

KM# 385 UNITE

Gold **Obv:** Crowned C-R in inner circle **Rev:** Castle with banner from tower dividing P-C, date in legend **Note:** Second Issue: In the name of Charles II. Legend varieties exist.

Date	Mintage	VG	F	VF	XF	Unc
1648 Rare	—	—	—	—	—	—
ND Rare	—	—	—	—	—	—

KM# 384 1/2 CROWN

Silver **Ruler:** Charles I **Obv:** Crude crown above C-R in inner circle **Obv. Legend:** DUN: SPIRO: SPERO **Rev:** Castle gateway with OBS at left, PC above, sword at right **Note:** First Issue: In the name of Charles I.

Date	Mintage	VG	F	VF	XF	Unc
1648 Rare	—	—	—	—	—	—

Scarborough

The siege of Scarborough lasted for a year and was concluded on July 22, 1645. The siege pieces are of diverse weights therefore diverse denominations. Shapes are generally rectangular, square or octagonal. All are uniface.

KM# 351 4 PENCE

Silver **Series:** First **Obv:** Castle walls and gateway with value incuse below **Note:** Uniface.

Date	Mintage	VG	F	VF	XF	Unc
ND Rare	—	—	—	—	—	—

KM# 352 6 PENCE

Silver **Series:** First **Obv:** Castle walls and gateway with value incuse below **Note:** Uniface.

Date	Mintage	VG	F	VF	XF	Unc
ND Rare	—	—	—	—	—	—

KM# 259 6 PENCE

Silver **Series:** Second **Obv:** Castle gateway with value below **Note:** Uniface.

Date	Mintage	VG	F	VF	XF	Unc
ND Rare	—	—	—	—	—	—

KM# 260 7 PENCE

Silver **Series:** Second **Obv:** Castle gateway with value below **Note:** Uniface.

Date	Mintage	VG	F	VF	XF	Unc
ND Rare	—	—	—	—	—	—

KM# 261 10 PENCE

Silver **Series:** Second **Obv:** Castle gateway with value below **Note:** Uniface.

Date	Mintage	VG	F	VF	XF	Unc
ND Rare	—	—	—	—	—	—

KM# 262 11 PENCE

Silver **Series:** Second **Obv:** Castle gateway with value below **Note:** Uniface.

Date	Mintage	VG	F	VF	XF	Unc
ND Rare	—	—	—	—	—	—

KM# 353 SHILLING

Silver **Series:** First **Obv:** Castle walls and gateway with value incuse below **Note:** Uniface.

Date	Mintage	VG	F	VF	XF	Unc
ND Rare	—	—	—	—	—	—

KM# 263 SHILLING

Silver **Series:** Second **Obv:** Castle gateway with value below **Note:** Uniface.

Date	Mintage	VG	F	VF	XF	Unc
ND Rare	—	—	—	—	—	—

KM# 361 1/2 CROWN

Silver **Series:** First **Obv:** Castle walls and gateway with value incuse at side (or below) **Note:** Uniface.

Date	Mintage	VG	F	VF	XF	Unc
ND	—	9,500	14,500	26,000	—	—

KM# 365 CROWN (5 Shillings)

Silver **Series:** First **Obv:** Castle walls and gateway with value incuse below **Note:** Uniface.

Date	Mintage	VG	F	VF	XF	Unc
ND Rare	—	—	—	—	—	—

KM# 264 1 SHILLING 1 PENNY

Silver **Series:** Second **Obv:** Castle gateway with value below **Note:** Uniface.

Date	Mintage	VG	F	VF	XF	Unc
ND	—	9,000	14,000	24,000	—	—

KM# 265 1 SHILLING 2 PENCE

Silver **Series:** Second **Obv:** Castle gateway with value below **Note:** Uniface.

Date	Mintage	VG	F	VF	XF	Unc
ND Rare	—	—	—	—	—	—

KM# 354 1 SHILLING 3 PENCE

Silver **Series:** First **Obv:** Castle walls and gateway with value incuse below **Note:** Uniface.

Date	Mintage	VG	F	VF	XF	Unc
ND	—	8,500	14,000	25,000	—	—

KM# 266 1 SHILLING 3 PENCE

Silver **Series:** Second **Obv:** Castle gateway with value below **Note:** Uniface.

Date	Mintage	VG	F	VF	XF	Unc
ND Rare	—	—	—	—	—	—

KM# 355 1 SHILLING 4 PENCE

Silver **Series:** First **Obv:** Castle walls and gateway with value incuse below **Note:** Uniface.

Date	Mintage	VG	F	VF	XF	Unc
ND Rare	—	—	—	—	—	—

KM# 267 1 SHILLING 4 PENCE

Silver **Series:** Second **Obv:** Castle gateway with value below **Note:** Uniface.

Date	Mintage	VG	F	VF	XF	Unc
ND	—	7,500	13,000	24,000	—	—

KM# 356 1 SHILLING 6 PENCE

Silver **Series:** First **Obv:** Castle walls and gateway with value incuse below **Note:** Uniface.

Date	Mintage	VG	F	VF	XF	Unc
ND Rare	—	—	—	—	—	—

KM# 268 1 SHILLING 6 PENCE

Silver **Series:** Second **Obv:** Castle gateway with value below **Note:** Uniface.

Date	Mintage	VG	F	VF	XF	Unc
ND Rare	—	—	—	—	—	—

KM# 357 1 SHILLING 9 PENCE
Silver **Series:** First **Obv:** Castle walls and gateway with value incuse below **Note:** Uniface.

Date	Mintage	VG	F	VF	XF	Unc
ND Rare	—	—	—	—	—	—

KM# 358 2 SHILLING
Silver **Series:** First **Obv:** Castle walls and gateway with value incuse below **Note:** Uniface.

Date	Mintage	VG	F	VF	XF	Unc
ND Rare	—	—	—	—	—	—

KM# 269 2 SHILLING
Silver **Series:** Second **Obv:** Castle gateway with value below **Note:** Uniface.

Date	Mintage	VG	F	VF	XF	Unc
ND Rare	—	—	—	—	—	—

KM# 359 2 SHILLING 2 PENCE
Silver **Series:** First **Obv:** Castle walls and gateway with value incuse below **Note:** Uniface.

Date	Mintage	VG	F	VF	XF	Unc
ND	—	10,000	14,000	25,000	—	—

KM# 360 2 SHILLING 4 PENCE
Silver **Series:** First **Obv:** Castle walls and gateway with value incuse below **Note:** Uniface.

Date	Mintage	VG	F	VF	XF	Unc
ND Rare	—	—	—	—	—	—

KM# 362 2 SHILLING 10 PENCE
Silver **Series:** First **Obv:** Castle walls and gateway with value incuse below **Note:** Uniface.

Date	Mintage	VG	F	VF	XF	Unc
ND	—	12,000	14,000	25,000	—	—

KM# 363 3 SHILLING
Silver **Series:** First **Obv:** Castle walls and gateway with value incuse below **Note:** Uniface.

Date	Mintage	VG	F	VF	XF	Unc
ND Rare	—	—	—	—	—	—

KM# 364 3 SHILLING 4 PENCE
Silver **Series:** First **Obv:** Castle walls and gateway with value incuse below **Note:** Uniface.

Date	Mintage	VG	F	VF	XF	Unc
ND Rare	—	—	—	—	—	—

KM# 366 5 SHILLING 8 PENCE
Silver **Series:** First **Obv:** Castle walls and gateway with value incuse below **Note:** Uniface.

Date	Mintage	VG	F	VF	XF	Unc
ND Rare	—	—	—	—	—	—

COMMONWEALTH

PRE-DECIMAL COINAGE

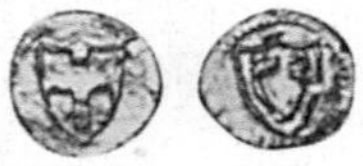

KM# 386 1/2 PENNY
Silver **Obv:** Shield with cross of St. George **Rev:** Shield with Irish harp

Date	Mintage	VG	F	VF	XF	Unc
ND	—	20.00	45.00	125	250	—

KM# 387 PENNY
Silver **Obv:** Shield with St. George's cross in branches **Rev:** Two shields with value above

Date	Mintage	VG	F	VF	XF	Unc
ND	—	20.00	40.00	100	250	—

KM# 388 2 PENCE (1/2 Groat)
Silver

Date	Mintage	VG	F	VF	XF	Unc
ND(1649-60)	—	22.00	45.00	110	250	—

KM# 389.1 6 PENCE
Silver **Note:** Mint mark: Sun.

Date	Mintage	VG	F	VF	XF	Unc
1649	—	110	200	575	1,000	—
1651/49	—	125	300	850	3,000	—
1651	—	95.00	175	450	1,000	—
1652/49	—	125	300	850	3,000	—
1652/1	—	125	300	850	3,000	—
1652	—	85.00	175	450	1,000	—
1653	—	85.00	185	450	1,000	—
1654/3	—	125	300	850	3,000	—
1654	—	125	300	850	3,000	—
1655	—	200	425	1,000	—	—
1656	—	85.00	175	450	1,000	—
1657/6	—	200	425	1,000	—	—

KM# E207 6 PENCE
Silver **Obv:** Bust of Cromwell **Rev:** Crowned arms

Date	Mintage	VG	F	VF	XF	Unc
1658	—	—	—	—	—	—

KM# 389.2 6 PENCE
Silver **Note:** Mint mark: Anchor. Varieties exist.

Date	Mintage	VG	F	VF	XF	Unc
1658/7	—	350	750	1,800	3,500	—
1658	—	350	750	1,800	3,500	—
1659	—	675	1,350	3,500	—	—
1660	—	350	750	1,700	3,500	—

KM# 390.1 SHILLING
Silver **Note:** Mint mark: Sun.

Date	Mintage	VG	F	VF	XF	Unc
1649	—	80.00	300	900	—	—
1651/49	—	85.00	350	950	—	—
1651	—	75.00	250	600	1,900	—
1651	—	125	500	1,400	—	—
Note: "COMONWEALTH" error						
1652/1	—	85.00	300	600	2,000	—
1652	—	75.00	225	600	2,000	—
1652/horizontal 2	—	125	450	1,200	—	—
1652	—	65.00	275	700	3,000	—
Note: "COMMON-WEALTH" error						
1653/2	—	90.00	300	950	—	—
1653	—	75.00	225	600	2,000	—
1653	—	75.00	225	600	2,000	—
Note: "COMMONWEATH" error						
1653	—	150	600	1,600	—	—
Note: "COMMONWEALH" error						
1654/3	—	85.00	250	600	2,000	—
1654	—	75.00	250	600	2,000	—
1655/4	—	150	600	1,600	—	—
1655	—	125	550	1,300	—	—
1656	—	75.00	250	600	2,000	—
1657	—	250	900	2,000	—	—

KM# A207 SHILLING
Silver **Obv:** Bust of Cromwell **Rev:** Crowned arms

Date	Mintage	VG	F	VF	XF	Unc
1658	—	350	850	1,600	3,500	—

KM# 390.2 SHILLING
Silver **Note:** Mint mark: Anchor. Varieties exist.

Date	Mintage	VG	F	VF	XF	Unc
1658/7	—	400	850	2,000	3,500	—
1658	—	400	850	2,000	3,500	—
1659 Rare	—	—	—	—	—	—
1660	—	400	850	2,000	3,500	—

KM# 391.1 1/2 CROWN
Silver **Note:** Mint mark: Sun.

Date	Mintage	VG	F	VF	XF	Unc
1649	—	275	525	1,500	3,500	—
1651	—	195	325	1,200	3,000	—
1652/1	—	195	325	850	2,800	—
1652	—	175	325	850	2,800	—
1653/1	—	175	325	850	2,800	—
1653/2	—	175	325	850	2,800	—
1653	—	150	250	850	2,800	—
1654/3	—	150	300	850	2,800	—
1654	—	150	300	1,000	3,000	—
1655	—	625	1,250	3,500	—	—
1656/5	—	150	300	850	2,600	—
1656	—	150	300	800	2,500	—

KM# B207 1/2 CROWN
Silver **Obv:** Bust of Oliver Cromwell left

Date	Mintage	VG	F	VF	XF	Unc
1656	—	—	—	—	—	—
1658	—	450	1,500	2,900	5,000	—

KM# 391.2 1/2 CROWN
Silver **Note:** Mint mark: Anchor.

Date	Mintage	VG	F	VF	XF	Unc
1658/7	—	750	1,500	3,500	—	—
1658	—	750	1,500	3,500	—	—
1659 Rare	—	1,650	3,250	8,500	—	—
1660	—	750	1,500	3,500	—	—

KM# 393.1 CROWN
2.2500 g., 0.9170 Gold 0.0663 oz. AGW **Note:** Mint mark: Sun.

Date	Mintage	VG	F	VF	XF	Unc
1649	—	550	1,200	3,000	5,500	—
1650	—	550	1,200	2,500	5,500	—
1651	—	550	1,200	3,000	5,500	—
1652	—	550	1,200	2,500	5,000	—
1653	—	550	1,200	2,500	5,000	—
1654	—	550	1,200	3,000	5,500	—
1655	—	700	1,900	3,500	7,000	—
1656	—	650	1,800	3,500	6,500	—
1657	—	650	1,800	3,500	6,500	—

KM# 392 CROWN
Silver **Note:** Mint mark: Sun. Dav. #3772. Varieties exist.

Date	Mintage	VG	F	VF	XF	Unc
1649	—	1,500	2,500	7,500	15,000	—
1651	—	750	1,250	3,250	7,000	—
1652	—	550	1,050	2,300	5,500	—
1652 Large 2	—	550	1,050	2,400	5,500	—
1652/1	—	550	1,050	2,400	5,500	—
1653	—	550	1,100	2,550	6,100	—
1654	—	600	1,200	2,750	6,100	—
1656	—	550	1,050	2,300	5,500	—
1656/4	—	500	1,000	2,300	5,500	—

KM# D207 CROWN

Silver **Obv:** Bust of Oliver Cromwell left **Note:** Dav. #3773.

Date	Mintage	VG	F	VF	XF	Unc
1658	—	1,700	3,000	4,800	6,600	—

KM# 393.2 CROWN

2.2500 g., 0.9170 Gold 0.0663 oz. AGW **Note:** Mint mark: Anchor.

Date	Mintage	VG	F	VF	XF	Unc
1658/7	—	2,100	3,750	10,500	16,500	—
1658	—	2,100	3,700	11,500	15,000	—
1660	—	2,800	5,600	13,500	—	—

KM# 394.1 DOUBLE CROWN

4.5000 g., 0.9170 Gold 0.1327 oz. AGW **Note:** Mint mark: Sun.

Date	Mintage	VG	F	VF	XF	Unc
1649	—	750	1,600	3,500	7,000	—
1650	—	650	1,400	3,500	6,500	—
1651	—	650	1,400	3,000	6,000	—
1652	—	750	1,600	3,500	7,000	—
1653	—	650	1,400	3,000	6,000	—
1654	—	700	1,500	3,500	6,500	—
1655	—	850	1,800	4,000	8,000	—
1656	—	800	1,700	4,000	7,000	—
1657	—	900	1,900	4,500	8,000	—

KM# 394.2 DOUBLE CROWN

4.5000 g., 0.9170 Gold 0.1327 oz. AGW **Note:** Mint mark: Anchor.

Date	Mintage	VG	F	VF	XF	Unc
1660	—	2,800	5,500	12,000	16,000	—

UNITE COINAGE

KM# 395.1 UNITE

9.0000 g., 0.9170 Gold 0.2653 oz. AGW **Note:** Mint mark: Sun.

Date	Mintage	VG	F	VF	XF	Unc
1649	—	1,450	3,000	7,200	18,000	—
1650	—	1,200	2,600	6,000	15,000	—
1651	—	1,150	2,400	5,400	13,500	—
1652	—	1,200	2,600	6,000	15,000	—
1653	—	1,150	2,400	5,400	13,500	—
1654	—	1,200	2,500	5,700	14,500	—
1655	—	1,800	4,200	8,400	20,500	—
1656	—	1,450	3,000	7,200	18,000	—
1657	—	1,300	2,700	6,600	15,000	—

KM# 395.2 UNITE

9.0000 g., 0.9170 Gold 0.2653 oz. AGW **Note:** Mint mark: Anchor.

Date	Mintage	VG	F	VF	XF	Unc
1658	—	6,000	12,000	27,000	—	—
1660	—	3,600	9,000	22,000	—	—

KINGDOM

HAMMERED COINAGE

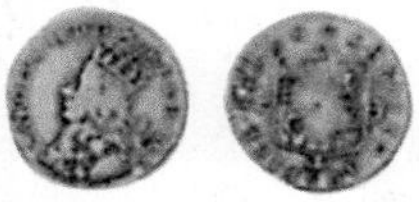

KM# 397 PENNY

Silver **Ruler:** Charles II **Obv:** Value behind head of Charles II **Note:** Second Issue - value added. Varieties exist.

Date	Mintage	VG	F	VF	XF	Unc
ND(1660-62)	—	17.00	35.00	90.00	225	—

KM# 398 PENNY

Silver **Ruler:** Charles II **Obv:** Bust and shield in inner circles **Note:** Third Issue - inner circles added.

Date	Mintage	VG	F	VF	XF	Unc
ND(1660-62)	—	17.50	35.00	125	250	—

KM# 399 2 PENCE (1/2 Groat)

Silver **Ruler:** Charles II **Obv:** Crowned bust of Charles II left **Rev:** Shield of arms on long cross **Note:** First Issue - without inner circles or value.

Date	Mintage	VG	F	VF	XF	Unc
ND(1660-62)	—	20.00	40.00	100	250	—

KM# 400 2 PENCE (1/2 Groat)

Silver **Ruler:** Charles II **Obv:** Value behind head of Charles II **Note:** Second Issue - value added. Varieties exist.

Date	Mintage	VG	F	VF	XF	Unc
ND(1660-62)	—	35.00	75.00	200	500	—

KM# 401 2 PENCE (1/2 Groat)

Silver **Ruler:** Charles II **Rev:** Shield in inner circle **Note:** Third Issue - inner circles added.

Date	Mintage	VG	F	VF	XF	Unc
ND(1660-62)	—	13.00	30.00	95.00	250	—

KM# 281 3 PENCE

Silver **Ruler:** Charles II **Obv:** Crowned bust left of Charles II, value behind head in inner circle **Rev:** Shield in inner circle **Mint:** Chester

Date	Mintage	VG	F	VF	XF	Unc
ND(1660-62)	—	19.00	40.00	100	250	—

KM# 282 3 PENCE

Silver **Ruler:** Charles II **Obv:** Without inner circle, legend begins at bottom-left of bust **Rev:** Without inner circle

Date	Mintage	VG	F	VF	XF	Unc
ND(1660-62)	—	20.00	60.00	150	350	—

KM# 291 4 PENCE (Groat)

Silver **Ruler:** Charles II **Obv:** Without inner circle **Rev:** Without inner circle

Date	Mintage	VG	F	VF	XF	Unc
ND(1660-62)	—	21.00	35.00	95.00	175	—

KM# 290 4 PENCE (Groat)

Silver **Ruler:** Charles II **Obv:** Bust of Charles II and arms in inner circle **Rev:** Square-topped arms in inner circle **Note:** Third Issue.

Date	Mintage	VG	F	VF	XF	Unc
ND(1660-62)	—	18.00	35.00	125	400	—

KM# 402 6 PENCE

Silver **Ruler:** Charles II **Obv:** Charles II, without inner circle or value **Note:** First Issue.

Date	Mintage	VG	F	VF	XF	Unc
ND(1660)	—	100	200	600	1,400	—

KM# 403 6 PENCE

Silver **Ruler:** Charles II **Obv:** Value added behind head of Charles II **Note:** Second Issue. Varieties exist.

Date	Mintage	VG	F	VF	XF	Unc
ND(1660)	—	600	1,200	2,900	—	—

KM# 404 6 PENCE

Silver **Ruler:** Charles II **Obv:** Inner circles added **Note:** Third Issue. Varieties exist.

Date	Mintage	VG	F	VF	XF	Unc
ND(1660)	—	80.00	175	600	1,300	—

KM# 407 SHILLING

Silver **Ruler:** Charles II **Obv:** Inner circles added **Note:** Third Issue. Varieties exist.

Date	Mintage	VG	F	VF	XF	Unc
ND	—	100	225	700	1,500	—

KM# 405 SHILLING

Silver **Ruler:** Charles II **Obv:** Crowned bust of Charles II left, without inner circle or value **Rev:** Shield of arms on long cross **Note:** First Issue. Varieties exist.

Date	Mintage	VG	F	VF	XF	Unc
ND(1660)	—	150	300	800	2,000	—

KM# 406 SHILLING

Silver **Ruler:** Charles II **Obv:** Value added behind head of Charles II **Note:** Second Issue. Varieties exist.

Date	Mintage	VG	F	VF	XF	Unc
ND(1661-62)	—	200	400	1,400	4,500	—

KM# 415 UNITE

9.0000 g., 0.9170 Gold 0.2653 oz. AGW **Ruler:** Charles II **Obv:** Charles II left, without value behind head **Note:** First Issue.

Date	Mintage	VG	F	VF	XF	Unc
ND(1660-62)	—	2,400	5,000	15,000	25,000	—

KM# 416 UNITE

9.0000 g., 0.9170 Gold 0.2653 oz. AGW **Ruler:** Charles II **Obv:** Charles II left, with value behind head

Date	Mintage	VG	F	VF	XF	Unc
ND(1660-62)	—	1,000	2,100	6,000	11,000	—

KM# 408 1/2 CROWN

Silver **Ruler:** Charles II **Obv:** Crowned bust of Charles II left **Rev:** Shield of arms on long cross **Note:** First Issue.

Date	Mintage	VG	F	VF	XF	Unc
ND(1660-85)	—	700	1,350	4,250	7,500	—

KM# 409 1/2 CROWN

Silver **Ruler:** Charles II **Obv:** Value behind head of Charles II **Note:** Second Issue. Varieties exist.

Date	Mintage	VG	F	VF	XF	Unc
ND(1660-62)	—	650	1,250	3,500	—	—

KM# 410 1/2 CROWN

Silver **Ruler:** Charles II **Obv:** Inner circles added **Note:** Third Issue. Varieties exist.

Date	Mintage	VG	F	VF	XF	Unc
ND(1660-62)	—	125	400	1,200	3,500	—

KM# 411 CROWN

Gold **Ruler:** Charles II **Obv:** Bust of Charles II left **Note:** First Issue.

Date	Mintage	VG	F	VF	XF	Unc
ND(1660-62)	—	1,000	1,800	4,600	9,900	—

KM# 412 CROWN

Gold **Ruler:** Charles II **Obv:** Bust of Charles II with value behind head left **Note:** Second Issue.

Date	Mintage	VG	F	VF	XF	Unc
ND(1660-62)	—	1,000	1,800	3,950	9,200	—

KM# 413 DOUBLE CROWN

4.5000 g., 0.9170 Gold 0.1327 oz. AGW **Ruler:** Charles II **Obv:** Bust of Charles II left without value **Note:** First Issue.

Date	Mintage	VG	F	VF	XF	Unc
ND(1660)	—	850	1,850	4,950	10,000	—

KM# 414 DOUBLE CROWN

4.5000 g., 0.9170 Gold 0.1327 oz. AGW **Ruler:** Charles II **Obv:** Bust of Charles II left with value behind head **Note:** Second Issue.

Date	Mintage	VG	F	VF	XF	Unc
ND(1660-62)	—	800	1,600	4,300	9,600	—

PRE-DECIMAL COINAGE

KM# 436.1 FARTHING

Copper **Ruler:** Charles II **Obv:** Bust of Charles II left **Note:** Varieties exist.

Date	Mintage	VG	F	VF	XF	Unc
1672	—	35.00	80.00	300	1,100	—
1673	—	35.00	80.00	300	1,000	—
1674	—	40.00	90.00	325	1,125	—
1675	—	40.00	90.00	325	1,125	—
1679	—	45.00	100	375	1,200	—

KM# 447 FARTHING

Tin with square copper plug **Ruler:** James II **Obv:** Laureate and armored bust of James II right **Rev:** Britannia seated left **Note:** Varieties exist.

Date	Mintage	VG	F	VF	XF	Unc
1684 Rare	—	—	—	—	—	—
1685	—	100	200	750	3,000	—
1686	—	100	225	800	3,000	—
1687 Rare	—	—	—	—	—	—

KM# 436.2 FARTHING

Tin with square copper plug **Ruler:** Charles II **Obv:** Bust of Charles II left **Edge:** Date **Note:** Counterfeits exist.

Date	Mintage	VG	F	VF	XF	Unc
1684	—	75.00	350	1,000	3,600	—
1685 Rare	—	—	—	—	—	—

KM# 461 FARTHING

Tin with square copper plug **Ruler:** William III **Obv:** Draped bust **Note:** Varieties exist.

Date	Mintage	VG	F	VF	XF	Unc
1687	—	70.00	400	1,400	—	—

KM# 466.1 FARTHING

Tin with square copper plug **Ruler:** William and Mary **Obv:** Large armored busts of William and Mary to right **Note:** Varieties exist.

Date	Mintage	VG	F	VF	XF	Unc
1689//90 Rare	—	—	—	—	—	—

Note: 1690 on reverse, 1689 on edge

Date	Mintage	VG	F	VF	XF	Unc
1690	—	75.00	225	850	3,500	—
1691	—	75.00	225	850	3,500	—
1692	—	75.00	225	850	3,500	—

KM# 465 FARTHING

Tin with square copper plug **Ruler:** William and Mary **Obv:** Small draped bust of William and Mary right **Rev:** Date in exergue **Edge:** Date

Date	Mintage	VG	F	VF	XF	Unc
1689	—	650	900	2,250	—	—
1689//90 Rare	—	—	—	—	—	—

Note: 1689 on reverse, 1690 on edge

KM# 465a FARTHING

Copper **Ruler:** William and Mary **Edge:** Plain

Date	Mintage	VG	F	VF	XF	Unc
1689 Proof	—	—	—	—	—	—

KM# 466.1a FARTHING

Copper **Ruler:** William and Mary **Edge:** Plain

Date	Mintage	VG	F	VF	XF	Unc
1690 Proof	—	—	—	—	—	—

KM# 466.2 FARTHING

Copper **Ruler:** William and Mary **Rev:** Date in exergue **Note:** Varieties exist.

Date	Mintage	VG	F	VF	XF	Unc
1693 Rare	—	—	—	—	—	—
1694	—	45.00	100	400	1,200	—

KM# 466.2a FARTHING

Silver **Ruler:** William and Mary **Note:** Varieties exist.

Date	Mintage	VG	F	VF	XF	Unc
1694 Proof	—	—	—	—	—	—

KM# 483.1 FARTHING

Copper **Ruler:** William III **Obv:** Laureate bust of William III right **Rev:** Britannia seated left, date in exergue **Note:** Varieties exist.

Date	Mintage	VG	F	VF	XF	Unc
1695	—	25.00	65.00	250	1,100	—
1696	—	25.00	65.00	250	1,100	—
1697	—	35.00	70.00	300	1,100	—
1698	—	50.00	350	600	1,400	—
1699	—	25.00	65.00	250	1,100	—
1700	—	20.00	55.00	200	1,100	—

KM# 483.1a FARTHING

Silver **Ruler:** William III

Date	Mintage	VG	F	VF	XF	Unc
1695 Proof	—	—	—	—	—	—
1696 Proof	—	—	—	—	—	—
1697 Proof	—	—	—	—	—	—
1700 Proof	—	—	—	—	—	—

KM# 483.2a FARTHING

Silver **Ruler:** William III

Date	Mintage	VG	F	VF	XF	Unc
1698 Proof	—	—	—	—	—	—
1699 Proof	—	—	—	—	—	—

KM# 483.2 FARTHING

Copper **Ruler:** William III **Rev:** Date at end of legend **Note:** Varieties exist.

Date	Mintage	VG	F	VF	XF	Unc
1698	—	18.00	90.00	375	1,250	—
1699	—	18.00	75.00	375	1,250	—

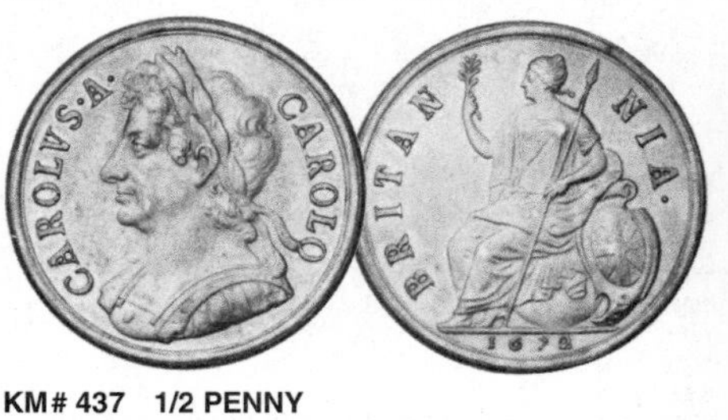

KM# 437 1/2 PENNY

Copper **Ruler:** Charles II **Obv:** Laureate head of Charles II **Rev:** Date in exergue **Note:** Varieties exist.

Date	Mintage	VG	F	VF	XF	Unc
1672	—	45.00	90.00	400	1,700	—
1673	—	45.00	90.00	375	1,500	—
1675	—	45.00	90.00	650	1,750	—

KM# 448 1/2 PENNY
Tin with square copper plug **Ruler:** James II **Obv:** Laureate head of James II right **Edge:** Date **Note:** Varieties exist.

Date	Mintage	VG	F	VF	XF	Unc
1685	—	150	260	1,000	4,500	—
1686	—	165	290	1,025	4,500	—
1687	—	150	275	1,000	4,500	—

KM# 467 1/2 PENNY
Tin **Ruler:** William and Mary **Obv:** Small draped busts of William and Mary right **Edge:** Date **Note:** Varieties exist.

Date	Mintage	VG	F	VF	XF	Unc
1689	—	1,200	1,800	3,000	—	—

KM# 475.1 1/2 PENNY
Tin **Ruler:** William and Mary **Obv:** Large armored busts of William and Mary right **Edge:** Date **Note:** Varieties exist.

Date	Mintage	VG	F	VF	XF	Unc
1690	—	150	300	850	4,000	—

KM# 475.2 1/2 PENNY
Tin **Ruler:** William and Mary **Rev:** Date in exergue **Edge:** Date **Note:** Varieties exist.

Date	Mintage	VG	F	VF	XF	Unc
1691	—	150	300	850	4,000	—
1691//2	—	—	—	—	—	—
Note: 1691 in exergue, 1692 on edge						
1692	—	130	250	775	3,500	—

KM# 475.3 1/2 PENNY
Copper **Ruler:** William and Mary **Rev:** Date in exergue, plain edge **Note:** Varieties exist.

Date	Mintage	VG	F	VF	XF	Unc
1694	—	45.00	85.00	400	1,700	—

KM# A483.1 1/2 PENNY
Copper **Ruler:** William III **Obv:** Laureate head of William III right **Note:** Varieties exist.

Date	Mintage	VG	F	VF	XF	Unc
1695	—	35.00	50.00	225	1,300	—
1696	—	35.00	50.00	200	1,300	—
1697	—	35.00	60.00	200	1,300	—
1698	—	35.00	65.00	250	1,300	—

KM# A483.2 1/2 PENNY
Copper **Ruler:** William III **Rev:** Date in legend **Note:** Varieties exist.

Date	Mintage	VG	F	VF	XF	Unc
1698	—	40.00	70.00	300	1,400	—
1699	—	35.00	55.00	250	1,250	—

KM# 503 1/2 PENNY
Copper **Ruler:** William III **Obv:** Laureate head right **Rev:** Britannia seated left with right hand near knee, date in exergue **Note:** Varieties exist.

Date	Mintage	VG	F	VF	XF	Unc
1699	—	40.00	70.00	250	1,300	—
1700	—	35.00	70.00	250	1,300	—

KM# 396 PENNY
Silver **Ruler:** Charles II **Obv:** Crowned bust of Charles II left **Rev:** Shield of arms on long cross **Note:** First Issue - without inner circles or value. Varieties exist.

Date	Mintage	VG	F	VF	XF	Unc
ND(1660-62)	—	20.00	40.00	100	225	—

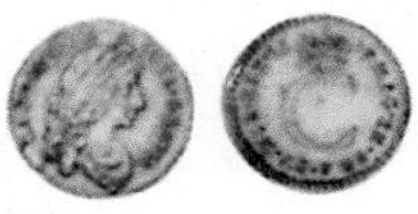

KM# 432 PENNY
Silver **Ruler:** Charles II **Obv:** Laureate bust of Charles II right **Rev:** Crowned C, crown divides date **Note:** Varieties exist.

Date	Mintage	VG	F	VF	XF	Unc
1670	—	15.00	25.00	50.00	200	—
1671	—	15.00	25.00	50.00	200	—
1672/1	—	15.00	25.00	50.00	200	—
1673	—	15.00	25.00	50.00	200	—
1674	—	15.00	25.00	50.00	200	—
1675	—	15.00	25.00	50.00	200	—
1676	—	20.00	35.00	65.00	200	—
1677	—	15.00	25.00	50.00	200	—
1678	—	20.00	35.00	65.00	200	—
1679	—	20.00	35.00	65.00	200	—
1680	—	15.00	25.00	50.00	200	—
1680/79	—	15.00	25.00	50.00	200	—
1681	—	25.00	40.00	75.00	200	—
1681/0	—	25.00	40.00	75.00	200	—
1682/1	—	20.00	35.00	65.00	200	—
1682	—	20.00	35.00	65.00	200	—
1683/1	—	15.00	25.00	50.00	200	—
1683/2	—	15.00	25.00	50.00	200	—
1684/3	—	25.00	40.00	75.00	200	—
1684	—	25.00	40.00	75.00	300	—

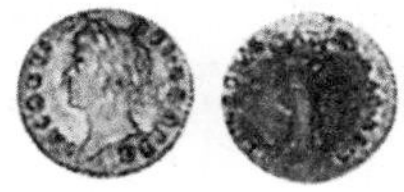

KM# 449 PENNY
Silver **Ruler:** James II **Obv:** Laureate head of James II right **Rev:** Crowned Roman numeral I, crown divides date

Date	Mintage	VG	F	VF	XF	Unc
1685	—	20.00	35.00	70.00	200	—
1685 Prooflike	—	—	—	—	—	—
1686	—	20.00	35.00	70.00	200	—
1687/6	—	20.00	35.00	70.00	200	—
1687/8	—	25.00	40.00	75.00	200	—
1687	—	20.00	35.00	70.00	200	—
1688/7	—	25.00	40.00	75.00	200	—
1688	—	25.00	40.00	75.00	200	—

KM# 468.1 PENNY
Silver **Ruler:** William and Mary **Obv:** Conjoined busts of William and Mary right, continuous legend **Rev:** Crowned Roman numeral I, date above crown **Note:** Varieties exist.

Date	Mintage	VG	F	VF	XF	Unc
1689	—	125	250	800	1,300	—

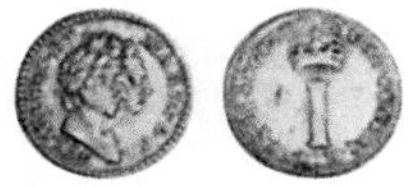

KM# 468.2 PENNY
Silver **Ruler:** William and Mary **Obv:** Legend broken at top **Note:** Varieties exist.

Date	Mintage	VG	F	VF	XF	Unc
1690	—	25.00	40.00	75.00	300	—
1691/0	—	35.00	50.00	95.00	350	—
1691	—	35.00	50.00	95.00	350	—
1692/1	—	35.00	50.00	95.00	400	—
1692	—	35.00	50.00	95.00	350	—
1693	—	35.00	50.00	95.00	300	—
1694	—	30.00	45.00	85.00	250	—

KM# 499 PENNY
Silver **Ruler:** William III **Obv:** Laureate head right **Rev:** Crowned Roman numeral I, crown divides date **Note:** Varieties exist.

Date	Mintage	VG	F	VF	XF	Unc
1698	—	30.00	45.00	85.00	250	—
1699	—	35.00	50.00	95.00	350	—
1700	—	30.00	45.00	85.00	250	—

KM# 429 2 PENCE (1/2 Groat)
Silver **Ruler:** Charles II **Obv:** Laureate bust of Charles II right **Note:** Varieties exist.

Date	Mintage	VG	F	VF	XF	Unc
1668	—	25.00	40.00	75.00	200	—
1668 Prooflike	—	—	—	—	—	—
1670	—	25.00	40.00	75.00	200	—
1671	—	25.00	40.00	75.00	200	—
1672/1	—	25.00	40.00	75.00	200	—
1673	—	25.00	40.00	75.00	200	—
1674	—	25.00	40.00	75.00	200	—
1675	—	25.00	40.00	75.00	200	—
1676	—	25.00	40.00	75.00	200	—
1677	—	25.00	40.00	75.00	200	—
1678/6	—	25.00	40.00	75.00	200	—
1678	—	25.00	40.00	75.00	200	—
1679	—	25.00	40.00	75.00	200	—
1680/79	—	25.00	40.00	75.00	200	—
1680	—	35.00	50.00	85.00	300	—
1681	—	25.00	40.00	75.00	225	—
1681/0	—	35.00	50.00	85.00	300	—
1682/1	—	35.00	50.00	85.00	300	—
1682	—	25.00	40.00	75.00	225	—
1683/2	—	25.00	40.00	75.00	225	—
1683	—	25.00	40.00	75.00	225	—
1684	—	25.00	40.00	75.00	225	—

KM# 454 2 PENCE (1/2 Groat)
Silver **Ruler:** James II **Obv:** Laureate head of James II left **Rev:** Crowned Roman numeral II, crown divides date **Note:** Varieties exist.

Date	Mintage	VG	F	VF	XF	Unc
1686	—	25.00	40.00	75.00	225	—
1687	—	25.00	40.00	75.00	225	—
1688/7	—	25.00	40.00	75.00	225	—
1688	—	25.00	40.00	75.00	225	—

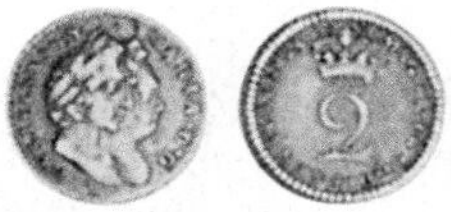

KM# 469 2 PENCE (1/2 Groat)
Silver **Ruler:** William and Mary **Note:** Varieties exist.

Date	Mintage	VG	F	VF	XF	Unc
1689	—	35.00	50.00	95.00	350	—
1691	—	35.00	50.00	95.00	350	—
1692	—	35.00	50.00	95.00	350	—
1693/2	—	30.00	45.00	85.00	250	—
1693	—	30.00	45.00	85.00	250	—
1694/3	—	25.00	40.00	75.00	200	—
1694	—	25.00	40.00	75.00	200	—

KM# 500.1 2 PENCE (1/2 Groat)
Silver **Ruler:** William III **Obv:** Laureate bust right **Rev:** Crowned 2, large crown nearly touches rim

Date	Mintage	VG	F	VF	XF	Unc
1698	—	30.00	45.00	85.00	250	—

KM# 500.2 2 PENCE
Silver **Ruler:** William III **Obv:** Laureate bust right **Rev:** Crown smaller and lower

Date	Mintage	VG	F	VF	XF	Unc
1699	—	30.00	65.00	150	600	—
1700	—	30.00	50.00	95.00	425	—

KM# 433 3 PENCE
Silver **Ruler:** Charles II **Obv:** Bust of Charles II right **Note:** Varieties exist.

Date	Mintage	VG	F	VF	XF	Unc
1670	—	25.00	40.00	75.00	200	—
1671	—	25.00	40.00	75.00	200	—
1672/1	—	25.00	40.00	75.00	200	—
1673	—	25.00	40.00	75.00	200	—
1674	—	25.00	40.00	75.00	200	—
1675	—	25.00	40.00	75.00	200	—
1676/5	—	25.00	40.00	75.00	200	—
1676	—	25.00	40.00	75.00	200	—
1677	—	25.00	40.00	75.00	200	—
1678	—	25.00	40.00	75.00	200	—
1679	—	25.00	40.00	75.00	200	—
1680	—	25.00	40.00	75.00	200	—
1680/79	—	25.00	40.00	75.00	200	—
1681/0	—	25.00	40.00	75.00	200	—
1681	—	25.00	40.00	95.00	225	—
1682/1	—	25.00	40.00	85.00	200	—
1682	—	25.00	40.00	75.00	200	—
1683	—	25.00	40.00	75.00	200	—
1683/2	—	25.00	40.00	95.00	225	—
1684/3	—	25.00	40.00	95.00	225	—
1684	—	25.00	40.00	75.00	200	—

KM# 450 3 PENCE

Silver **Ruler:** James II **Obv:** Bust of James II left **Note:** Varieties exist.

Date	Mintage	VG	F	VF	XF	Unc
1685	—	25.00	40.00	95.00	225	—
1685 Prooflike	—	—	—	—	—	300
1686	—	25.00	40.00	95.00	225	—
1687/6	—	25.00	40.00	95.00	225	—
1687	—	25.00	40.00	95.00	225	—
1688/7	—	25.00	40.00	95.00	225	—
1688	—	25.00	40.00	95.00	225	—

KM# 470.1 3 PENCE

Silver **Ruler:** William and Mary **Obv:** Conjoined busts of William and Mary right without wreath tie **Rev:** Crowned 3, date above crown **Note:** Varieties exist.

Date	Mintage	VG	F	VF	XF	Unc
1689	—	50.00	85.00	150	350	—
1690	—	25.00	40.00	95.00	225	—
1691	—	55.00	95.00	175	400	—

KM# 470.2 3 PENCE

Silver **Ruler:** William and Mary **Obv:** With tie on wreath **Note:** Varieties exist.

Date	Mintage	VG	F	VF	XF	Unc
1691	—	55.00	95.00	175	350	—
1692	—	55.00	95.00	175	350	—
1693	—	40.00	80.00	140	300	—
1694	—	25.00	40.00	95.00	225	—
1695/2	—	30.00	50.00	100	200	—

KM# 501 3 PENCE

Silver **Ruler:** William III **Obv:** Laureate bust right **Rev:** Crowned 3, crown divides date **Note:** Varieties exist.

Date	Mintage	VG	F	VF	XF	Unc
1698	—	30.00	50.00	100	250	—
1699	—	40.00	80.00	140	300	—
1700	—	35.00	55.00	110	250	—

KM# 434 4 PENCE (Groat)

Silver **Ruler:** Charles II **Obv:** Bust of Charles II right **Note:** Varieties exist.

Date	Mintage	VG	F	VF	XF	Unc
1670	—	25.00	40.00	95.00	225	—
1671	—	25.00	40.00	85.00	200	—
1672/1	—	25.00	40.00	95.00	225	—
1673	—	25.00	40.00	95.00	225	—
1674/4	—	25.00	40.00	95.00	225	—
1674/574	—	25.00	40.00	95.00	225	—
1674/64	—	25.00	40.00	95.00	225	—
1674	—	25.00	40.00	95.00	225	—
1675/4	—	25.00	40.00	95.00	225	—
1675	—	25.00	40.00	95.00	225	—
1676/66	—	25.00	40.00	95.00	225	—
1676/5	—	25.00	40.00	95.00	225	—
1676	—	25.00	40.00	95.00	225	—
1677	—	25.00	40.00	85.00	200	—
1678/6	—	25.00	40.00	85.00	200	—
1678/7	—	25.00	40.00	95.00	225	—
1678	—	25.00	40.00	85.00	200	—
1679	—	25.00	40.00	85.00	200	—
1680	—	25.00	40.00	85.00	200	—
1680/79	—	25.00	40.00	95.00	225	—
1681/0	—	25.00	40.00	95.00	225	—
1681	—	25.00	40.00	85.00	200	—
1682/1	—	25.00	40.00	95.00	225	—
1682	—	25.00	40.00	85.00	200	—
1683	—	25.00	40.00	85.00	200	—
1683/2	—	25.00	40.00	95.00	225	—
1684/3	—	25.00	40.00	85.00	200	—
1684	—	25.00	40.00	95.00	225	—

KM# 455.1 4 PENCE (Groat)

Silver **Ruler:** James II **Obv:** Bust of James II left

Date	Mintage	VG	F	VF	XF	Unc
1686	—	25.00	40.00	95.00	225	—
1687/6	—	25.00	40.00	95.00	225	—
1687/77	—	25.00	40.00	95.00	225	—
1687	—	25.00	40.00	95.00	225	—
1688/7	—	25.00	40.00	95.00	225	—
1688/8688	—	25.00	40.00	95.00	225	—
1688	—	25.00	40.00	95.00	225	—

KM# 455.2 4 PENCE (Groat)

Silver **Ruler:** James II **Rev:** Date above crown

Date	Mintage	VG	F	VF	XF	Unc
1686	—	25.00	40.00	95.00	225	—

KM# 471.1 4 PENCE (Groat)

Silver **Ruler:** William and Mary **Obv:** Conjoined busts of William and Mary without wreath tie **Note:** Varieties exist.

Date	Mintage	VG	F	VF	XF	Unc
1689	—	50.00	85.00	150	350	—
1690/1590	—	60.00	95.00	195	450	—
1690	—	35.00	75.00	125	300	—
1691/0	—	60.00	95.00	175	350	—
1691	—	50.00	85.00	185	400	—
1694	—	35.00	75.00	125	300	—

KM# 471.2 4 PENCE (Groat)

Silver **Ruler:** William and Mary **Obv:** Tie on wreath **Note:** Varieties exist.

Date	Mintage	VG	F	VF	XF	Unc
1692/1	—	50.00	85.00	150	350	—
1692	—	50.00	85.00	150	350	—
1693/2	—	35.00	75.00	125	300	—
1693	—	35.00	75.00	125	300	—
1694	—	35.00	75.00	125	300	—

KM# 495 4 PENCE (Groat)

Silver **Ruler:** William III **Obv:** Laureate bust right **Rev:** Crown above value divides date

Date	Mintage	VG	F	VF	XF	Unc
1697 Unique	—	—	—	—	—	—
1697 Prooflike	—	—	—	—	—	—
1698	—	65.00	110	225	500	—
1699	—	75.00	150	300	650	—
1700	—	65.00	110	225	500	—

KM# 441 6 PENCE

Silver **Ruler:** Charles II **Obv:** Bust of Charles II right

Date	Mintage	VG	F	VF	XF	Unc
1674	—	50.00	125	425	1,200	—
1675/4	—	50.00	125	425	1,225	—
1675	—	65.00	130	450	1,300	—
1676/5	—	80.00	175	500	1,400	—
1676	—	80.00	175	500	1,400	—
1677	—	50.00	125	425	1,200	—
1678/7	—	50.00	125	425	1,225	—
1679	—	50.00	125	425	1,225	—
1680	—	100	250	600	1,550	—
1681	—	65.00	150	450	1,225	—
1682/1	—	75.00	200	475	1,350	—
1682	—	75.00	200	475	1,350	—
1683	—	75.00	200	475	1,350	—
1684	—	75.00	200	475	1,350	—

KM# 456.1 6 PENCE

Silver **Ruler:** James II **Obv:** Bust of James II left **Rev:** Cruciform crowned Type I shields (dip in middle of the shield top)

Date	Mintage	VG	F	VF	XF	Unc
1686	—	100	250	625	1,650	—
1687/6	—	100	250	625	1,650	—

KM# 456.2 6 PENCE

Silver **Ruler:** James II **Rev:** Type II shields (rise in the middle of shield top)

Date	Mintage	VG	F	VF	XF	Unc
1687/6	—	100	250	650	1,300	—
1687	—	100	250	600	1,100	—
1688	—	100	250	650	1,250	—

KM# 481 6 PENCE

Silver **Ruler:** William and Mary **Obv:** Conjoined bust of William and Mary right **Rev:** Cruciform crowned arms with WM monograms and date numerals in angles **Note:** Varieties exist.

Date	Mintage	VG	F	VF	XF	Unc
1693	—	125	275	850	1,900	—
1693 Inverted 3	—	125	275	850	1,900	—
1694	—	125	275	850	2,000	—

KM# 484.1 6 PENCE

Silver **Ruler:** William III **Obv:** First bust of William III right **Rev:** Cruciform crowned arms with early harp, date divided by crown **Note:** Varieties exist.

Date	Mintage	VG	F	VF	XF	Unc
1695	—	45.00	85.00	175	600	—
1696/5	—	45.00	85.00	175	600	—
1696	—	45.00	85.00	150	525	—

KM# 484.2 6 PENCE

Silver **Ruler:** William III **Obv:** First bust of William III right; B below bust **Rev:** Cruciform crowned arms with early harp, date divided by crown **Mint:** Bristol **Note:** Varieties exist.

Date	Mintage	VG	F	VF	XF	Unc
1696 B	—	45.00	85.00	175	600	—

KM# 484.7 6 PENCE

Silver **Ruler:** William III **Obv:** First bust of William III right; script Y below bust **Rev:** Cruciform crowned arms iwth early harp, date divided by crown **Mint:** York **Note:** Varieties exist.

Date	Mintage	VG	F	VF	XF	Unc
1696	—	50.00	100	225	700	—

KM# 484.8 6 PENCE

Silver **Ruler:** William III **Obv:** First bust of William III right **Rev:** Late harp, large crowns **Note:** Varieties exist.

Date	Mintage	VG	F	VF	XF	Unc
1696	—	60.00	125	250	675	—

KM# 484.9 6 PENCE

Silver **Ruler:** William III **Obv:** First bust of William III right; B below bust **Rev:** Late harp, large crowns **Mint:** Bristol **Note:** Varieties exist.

Date	Mintage	VG	F	VF	XF	Unc
1696 B	—	75.00	150	350	825	—
1697 B	—	50.00	100	200	650	—

KM# 484.13 6 PENCE

Silver **Ruler:** William III **Obv:** First bust of William III right; B below bust **Rev:** Late harp, small crowns **Mint:** Bristol **Note:** Varieties exist.

Date	Mintage	VG	F	VF	XF	Unc
1696 B	—	50.00	100	250	700	—
1697 B	—	45.00	85.00	175	600	—

KM# 484.14 6 PENCE

Silver **Ruler:** William III **Obv:** First bust of William III right; C below bust **Rev:** Late harp, small crowns **Mint:** Chester **Note:** Varieties exist.

Date	Mintage	VG	F	VF	XF	Unc
1696 C	—	50.00	175	425	900	—
1697 C	—	50.00	100	200	650	—

KM# 489 6 PENCE

Silver **Ruler:** William III **Obv:** Second bust of William III **Note:** Varieties exist.

Date	Mintage	VG	F	VF	XF	Unc
1696	—	150	350	900	1,800	—
1697	—	75.00	200	550	1,700	—

KM# 484.3 6 PENCE

Silver **Ruler:** William III **Obv:** First bust of William III right; C below bust **Rev:** Cruciform crowned arms with early harp, date divided by crown **Mint:** Chester

Date	Mintage	VG	F	VF	XF	Unc
1696 C	—	50.00	100	200	650	—

KM# 484.4 6 PENCE

Silver **Ruler:** William III **Obv:** First bust of William III right; E below bust **Rev:** Cruciform crowned arms iwth early harp, date divided by crown **Mint:** Exeter

Date	Mintage	VG	F	VF	XF	Unc
1696 E	—	60.00	125	250	700	—

KM# 484.5 6 PENCE

Silver **Ruler:** William III **Obv:** First bust of William III right; N below bust **Rev:** Cruciform crowned arms with early harp, date divided by crown **Mint:** Norwich

Date	Mintage	VG	F	VF	XF	Unc
1696 N	—	75.00	140	260	700	—

KM# 484.6 6 PENCE

Silver **Ruler:** William III **Obv:** First bust of William III right; Y below bust **Rev:** Cruciform crowned arms with early harp, date divided by crown **Mint:** York

Date	Mintage	VG	F	VF	XF	Unc
1696 Y	—	85.00	175	400	1,000	—

KM# 484.16 6 PENCE

Silver **Ruler:** William III **Obv:** First bust of William III right; N below bust **Rev:** Late harp, small crowns **Mint:** Norwich

Date	Mintage	VG	F	VF	XF	Unc
1696 N	—	50.00	100	250	650	—
1697 N	—	50.00	100	250	650	—

KM# 496.2 6 PENCE

Silver **Ruler:** William III **Obv:** Third bust of William III right; B below bust **Rev:** Cruciform crowned arms, crown divides date, large crowns **Mint:** Bristol

Date	Mintage	VG	F	VF	XF	Unc
1697 B	—	55.00	110	225	675	—

KM# 496.3 6 PENCE

Silver **Ruler:** William III **Obv:** Third bust of William III right; C below bust **Rev:** Cruciform crowned arms, crown divides date, large crowns **Mint:** Chester

Date	Mintage	VG	F	VF	XF	Unc
1697 C	—	75.00	150	300	800	—

KM# 496.4 6 PENCE

Silver **Ruler:** William III **Obv:** Third bust of William III right; E below bust **Rev:** Cruciform crowned arms, crown divides date, large crowns **Mint:** Exeter

Date	Mintage	VG	F	VF	XF	Unc
1697 E	—	70.00	145	275	775	—

KM# 496.6 6 PENCE

Silver **Ruler:** William III **Obv:** Third bust of William III right; C below bust **Rev:** Cruciform crowned arms, crown divides date, small crowns **Mint:** Chester

Date	Mintage	VG	F	VF	XF	Unc
1697 C	—	75.00	150	300	800	—

KM# 496.7 6 PENCE

Silver **Ruler:** William III **Obv:** Third bust of William III right; E below bust **Rev:** Cruciform crowned arms, crown divides date, small crowns **Mint:** Exeter

Date	Mintage	VG	F	VF	XF	Unc
1697 E	—	70.00	145	275	750	—

KM# 496.8 6 PENCE

Silver **Ruler:** William III **Obv:** Third bust of William III right; Y below bust **Rev:** Cruciform crowned arms, crown divides date, small crowns **Mint:** York

Date	Mintage	VG	F	VF	XF	Unc
1697 Y	—	70.00	145	275	750	—

KM# 484.10 6 PENCE

Silver **Ruler:** William III **Obv:** First bust of William III right; C below bust **Rev:** Late harp, large crowns **Mint:** Chester

Date	Mintage	VG	F	VF	XF	Unc
1697 C	—	65.00	125	250	700	—

KM# 484.11 6 PENCE

Silver **Ruler:** William III **Obv:** First bust of William III right; E below bust **Rev:** Late harp, large crowns **Mint:** Exeter

Date	Mintage	VG	F	VF	XF	Unc
1697 E	—	50.00	100	200	650	—

KM# 496.5 6 PENCE

Silver **Ruler:** William III **Obv:** Third bust of William III right; E below bust **Rev:** Cruciform crowned arms, crown divides date, small crowns **Note:** Varieties exist.

Date	Mintage	VG	F	VF	XF	Unc
1697 E	—	75.00	140	260	725	—

KM# 496.1 6 PENCE

Silver **Ruler:** William III **Obv:** Third bust right **Rev:** Cruciform crowned arms, crown divides date, large crown **Note:** Varieties exist.

Date	Mintage	VG	F	VF	XF	Unc
1697	—	50.00	95.00	150	450	—
1698	—	60.00	110	220	625	—
1699	—	90.00	200	450	1,000	—
1700	—	60.00	110	175	500	—

KM# 484.15 6 PENCE

Silver **Ruler:** William III **Obv:** First bust of William III right; E below bust **Rev:** Late harp, small crowns **Mint:** Exeter **Note:** Varieties exist.

Date	Mintage	VG	F	VF	XF	Unc
1697 E	—	60.00	110	220	625	—

KM# 484.17 6 PENCE

Silver **Ruler:** William III **Obv:** First bust of William III right; script Y below bust **Rev:** Late harp, small crowns **Mint:** York **Note:** Varieties exist.

Date	Mintage	VG	F	VF	XF	Unc
1697 y	—	75.00	150	300	750	—

KM# 484.12 6 PENCE

Silver **Ruler:** William III **Obv:** First bust of William III right **Rev:** Late harp, small crowns **Note:** Varieties exist.

Date	Mintage	VG	F	VF	XF	Unc
1697	—	55.00	95.00	175	450	—

KM# 496.9 6 PENCE

Silver **Ruler:** William III **Obv:** Third bust of William III right **Rev:** Cruciform crowned arms, crown divides date

Date	Mintage	VG	F	VF	XF	Unc
1698	—	65.00	125	300	825	—
1699	—	80.00	185	340	925	—

KM# 496.10 6 PENCE

Silver **Ruler:** William III **Rev:** Roses in angles **Note:** Varieties exist.

Date	Mintage	VG	F	VF	XF	Unc
1699	—	90.00	200	400	1,000	—

KM# 496.11 6 PENCE

Silver **Ruler:** William III **Rev:** Plain fields in angles

Date	Mintage	VG	F	VF	XF	Unc
1700 Rare	—	—	—	—	—	—

KM# 418.2 SHILLING

Silver **Ruler:** Charles II **Obv:** First bust variety of Charles II - one leaf at top of wreath, three curls behind head

Date	Mintage	VG	F	VF	XF	Unc
1663	—	95.00	195	700	2,300	—
1666 Rare	—	—	—	—	—	—
1668	—	250	500	1,500	3,000	—
1669 Rare	—	—	—	—	—	—
1669/6 Rare	—	—	—	—	—	—

KM# 418.1 SHILLING

Silver **Ruler:** Charles II **Obv:** First bust of Charles II right **Rev:** Crowned cruciform arms with linked C's in angles, date divided at top **Note:** Varieties exist.

Date	Mintage	VG	F	VF	XF	Unc
1663	—	95.00	195	700	2,300	—

KM# 427.1 SHILLING

Silver **Ruler:** Charles II **Obv:** Second bust of Charles II **Note:** Varieties exist.

Date	Mintage	VG	F	VF	XF	Unc
1666	—	1,100	2,300	6,500	13,000	—
1668/7	—	125	225	650	1,750	—
1668	—	95.00	195	500	1,500	—
1669 Rare	—	—	—	—	—	—
1670	—	85.00	225	850	2,000	—
1671	—	95.00	250	900	2,200	—
1672	—	85.00	225	850	2,000	—
1673/2	—	125	300	950	2,500	—
1673	—	85.00	225	850	2,000	—
1674/3	—	85.00	225	850	2,000	—
1674	—	95.00	250	900	2,200	—
1675/4	—	115	350	1,700	3,100	—
1675	—	95.00	260	850	1,500	—
1676/5	—	85.00	250	850	2,000	—
1676	—	85.00	225	850	1,850	—
1677	—	85.00	225	850	1,850	—
1678/7	—	150	325	1,150	2,500	—
1678	—	85.00	225	850	2,000	—
1679/7	—	95.00	275	875	2,250	—
1679	—	85.00	225	850	1,850	—
1680 Rare	—	650	950	2,750	6,500	—
1681/0	—	225	475	1,500	2,600	—
1681	—	195	425	1,350	2,550	—
1682/1	—	500	1,050	3,250	—	—
1683 Rare	—	—	—	—	—	—

KM# 418.3 SHILLING

Silver **Ruler:** Charles II **Obv:** First bust variety of Charles II with elephant below

Date	Mintage	VG	F	VF	XF	Unc
1666	—	200	650	2,300	7,500	—

KM# 426 SHILLING

Silver **Ruler:** Charles II **Obv:** GUINEA head of Charles II right with elephant below **Note:** This obverse die was also used to strike the gold guinea, KM#424.2.

Date	Mintage	VG	F	VF	XF	Unc
1666	—	1,250	3,500	7,000	—	—

KM# 485.1 SHILLING

Silver **Ruler:** William III **Obv:** First bust of William III **Rev:** Lion at center **Note:** Varieties exist.

Date	Mintage	VG	F	VF	XF	Unc
1669 Rare; error	—	—	—	—	—	—
1695	—	25.00	60.00	200	925	—
1696/5	—	—	—	—	—	—
1696	—	25.00	60.00	150	650	—
1697	—	25.00	60.00	150	650	—

KM# 427.2 SHILLING
Silver **Ruler:** Charles II **Obv:** Plume added below bust **Rev:** Plume at center of arms

Date	Mintage	VG	F	VF	XF	Unc
1671	—	165	600	1,300	5,000	—
1673	—	150	550	1,350	5,000	—
1674	—	150	575	1,300	5,000	—
1675	—	165	600	1,900	5,500	—
1676	—	165	600	1,350	5,000	—
1679	—	175	625	1,450	5,000	—
1680/79	—	235	700	2,000	6,000	—
1680	—	185	825	2,300	6,000	—

KM# 427.3 SHILLING
Silver **Ruler:** Charles II **Rev:** Plume at center of arms

Date	Mintage	VG	F	VF	XF	Unc
1674	—	200	850	2,200	5,500	—

KM# 442 SHILLING
Silver **Ruler:** Charles II **Obv:** Third (large) bust of Charles II, ties turn down

Date	Mintage	VG	F	VF	XF	Unc
1674	—	150	475	2,000	4,500	—
1675/3	—	250	600	1,800	4,000	—
1675	—	175	600	2,100	5,600	—

KM# 427.4 SHILLING
Silver **Ruler:** Charles II **Obv:** Plume below bust

Date	Mintage	VG	F	VF	XF	Unc
1677	—	350	900	1,900	6,000	—
1679	—	300	800	1,750	5,520	—

KM# 427.5 SHILLING
Silver **Ruler:** Charles II **Obv:** Elephant and castle below bust

Date	Mintage	VG	F	VF	XF	Unc
1681/0	—	1,500	5,000	—	—	—

KM# 446 SHILLING
Silver **Ruler:** Charles II **Obv:** Fourth bust of Charles II, ties turn up

Date	Mintage	VG	F	VF	XF	Unc
1683	—	100	300	975	3,500	—
1684	—	100	240	850	3,000	—

KM# 451.2 SHILLING
Silver **Ruler:** James II **Rev:** Plume at center of arms

Date	Mintage	VG	F	VF	XF	Unc
1685 Rare	—	—	—	—	—	—

KM# 451.1 SHILLING
Silver **Ruler:** James II **Obv:** Bust of James II left **Note:** Varieties exist.

Date	Mintage	VG	F	VF	XF	Unc
1685	—	100	200	700	2,300	—
1686/5	—	100	225	800	2,400	—
1686	—	100	200	800	2,500	—
1687/6	—	100	200	800	2,500	—
1687	—	125	350	800	2,700	—
1688/7	—	125	350	800	2,600	—
1688	—	100	200	800	2,600	—

KM# 480 SHILLING
Silver **Ruler:** William and Mary **Obv:** Conjoined busts of William and Mary right **Rev:** Crowned cruciform arms with WM monograms in angles and numerals of date **Note:** Varieties exist.

Date	Mintage	VG	F	VF	XF	Unc
1692	—	100	250	850	2,900	—
1692 inverted 1	—	125	300	900	3,000	—
1693	—	100	250	825	2,900	—

KM# 497.6 SHILLING
Silver **Ruler:** William III **Obv:** Third bust (short ties) of William III; script y below bust **Mint:** York

Date	Mintage	VG	F	VF	XF	Unc
1696 y Rare	—	—	—	—	—	—
1697 y	—	30.00	70.00	225	850	—

KM# 485.2 SHILLING
Silver **Ruler:** William III **Obv:** First bust of William III; B below bust **Rev:** Lion at center **Mint:** Bristol

Date	Mintage	VG	F	VF	XF	Unc
1696 B	—	30.00	75.00	225	1,000	—
1697 B	—	30.00	75.00	225	1,000	—

KM# 490 SHILLING
Silver **Ruler:** William III **Obv:** Second bust (hair across breast) of William III

Date	Mintage	VG	F	VF	XF	Unc
1696 Unique	—	—	—	—	—	—

KM# 485.3 SHILLING
Silver **Ruler:** William III **Obv:** First bust of William III; C below bust **Rev:** Lion at center **Mint:** Chester **Note:** Varieties exist.

Date	Mintage	VG	F	VF	XF	Unc
1696 C	—	35.00	80.00	225	1,000	—
1697 C	—	35.00	80.00	225	950	—

KM# 485.4 SHILLING
Silver **Ruler:** William III **Obv:** First bust of William III; E below bust **Rev:** Lion at center **Mint:** Exeter **Note:** Varieties exist.

Date	Mintage	VG	F	VF	XF	Unc
1696 E	—	40.00	85.00	250	1,100	—
1697 E	—	40.00	85.00	250	950	—

KM# 485.5 SHILLING
Silver **Ruler:** William III **Obv:** First bust of William III; N below bust **Rev:** Lion at center **Mint:** Norwich **Note:** Varieties exist.

Date	Mintage	VG	F	VF	XF	Unc
1696 N	—	45.00	90.00	250	1,100	—
1697 N	—	45.00	90.00	225	950	—

KM# 485.6 SHILLING
Silver **Ruler:** William III **Obv:** First bust of William III; script Y below bust **Rev:** Lion at center **Mint:** York **Note:** Varieties exist.

Date	Mintage	VG	F	VF	XF	Unc
1696 y	—	40.00	85.00	250	1,000	—
1697 y	—	55.00	110	300	950	—

KM# 485.7 SHILLING
Silver **Ruler:** William III **Obv:** First bust of William III; Y below bust **Rev:** Lion at center **Mint:** York **Note:** Varieties exist.

Date	Mintage	VG	F	VF	XF	Unc
1696 Y	—	30.00	70.00	225	1,100	—
1697 Y	—	30.00	70.00	225	1,075	—

KM# 497.3 SHILLING
Silver **Ruler:** William III **Obv:** Third bust (short ties) of William III; C below bust **Mint:** Chester **Note:** Varieties exist.

Date	Mintage	VG	F	VF	XF	Unc
1696 C	—	45.00	220	725	1,900	—
1697 C	—	35.00	75.00	225	850	—

KM# 497.7 SHILLING
Silver **Ruler:** William III **Obv:** Third bust, long thin ties with y below **Mint:** York **Note:** Varieties exist.

Date	Mintage	VG	F	VF	XF	Unc
1697 y	—	35.00	75.00	200	950	—

KM# 497.9 SHILLING
Silver **Ruler:** William III **Obv:** Third bust (short ties) of William III; C below bust **Mint:** Chester **Note:** Varieties exist.

Date	Mintage	VG	F	VF	XF	Unc
1697 C	—	60.00	180	800	—	—

KM# 497.1 SHILLING
Silver **Ruler:** William III **Obv:** Third bust (short ties) of William III **Note:** Varieties exist.

Date	Mintage	VG	F	VF	XF	Unc
1697	—	30.00	65.00	170	750	—

KM# 497.2 SHILLING
Silver **Ruler:** William III **Obv:** Third bust (short ties) of William III; B below bust **Mint:** Bristol **Note:** Varieties exist.

Date	Mintage	VG	F	VF	XF	Unc
1697 B	—	40.00	85.00	275	1,100	—

KM# 497.4 SHILLING
Silver **Ruler:** William III **Obv:** Third bust (short ties) of William III; E below bust **Mint:** Exeter

Date	Mintage	VG	F	VF	XF	Unc
1697 E	—	35.00	75.00	250	1,100	—

KM# 497.5 SHILLING
Silver **Ruler:** William III **Obv:** Third bust (short ties) of William III; N below bust **Mint:** Norwich

Date	Mintage	VG	F	VF	XF	Unc
1697 N	—	35.00	75.00	250	1,100	—

KM# 497.8 SHILLING
Silver **Ruler:** William III **Obv:** Long, thin ties; B below bust **Mint:** Bristol

Date	Mintage	VG	F	VF	XF	Unc
1697 B	—	40.00	85.00	275	1,150	—

KM# 497.10 SHILLING
Silver **Ruler:** William III **Obv:** Third bust (short ties) of William III **Rev:** Plumes in angles **Mint:** Chester

Date	Mintage	VG	F	VF	XF	Unc
1698	—	125	300	800	2,300	—

KM# 502 SHILLING
Silver **Ruler:** William III **Obv:** Fourth bust (flaming hair) of William III **Note:** Varieties exist.

Date	Mintage	VG	F	VF	XF	Unc
1698	—	75.00	200	700	2,700	—
1699	—	65.00	150	500	1,850	—
1699 Plain edge; Proof	—	—	—	—	—	—

KM# 504.1 SHILLING
Silver **Ruler:** William III **Obv:** Fifth bust (hair high) **Note:** Varieties exist.

Date	Mintage	VG	F	VF	XF	Unc
1699	—	50.00	150	450	1,300	—
1700 Circular 0s	—	30.00	65.00	175	625	—
1700 Oval 0s	—	30.00	65.00	175	625	—

KM# 504.2 SHILLING
Silver **Ruler:** William III **Rev:** Plumes in angles

Date	Mintage	VG	F	VF	XF	Unc
1699	—	75.00	200	650	2,700	—

KM# 504.3 SHILLING
Silver **Ruler:** William III **Obv:** Fifth bust (hair high) of William III **Rev:** Roses in angles

Date	Mintage	VG	F	VF	XF	Unc
1699	—	65.00	175	600	2,300	—

KM# 504.4 SHILLING
Silver **Ruler:** William III **Obv:** Fifth bust (hair high) of William III, plume below bust

Date	Mintage	VG	F	VF	XF	Unc
1700	—	800	3,000	6,000	—	—

KM# 419 1/2 CROWN
Silver **Ruler:** Charles II **Obv:** First bust of Charles II right **Rev:** Crowned cruciform arms with linked C's in angles **Edge:** Regnal year on edge in Roman numerals **Note:** Varieties exist.

Date	Mintage	VG	F	VF	XF	Unc
1663	—	150	250	750	4,000	—

KM# 421 1/2 CROWN
Silver **Ruler:** Charles II **Obv:** Second bust (broader) of Charles II right

Date	Mintage	VG	F	VF	XF	Unc
1664	—	175	300	1,400	5,000	—

KM# 428.1 1/2 CROWN
Silver **Ruler:** Charles II **Obv:** Third bust (smaller) of Charles II right

Date	Mintage	VG	F	VF	XF	Unc
1666/?	—	650	1,800	3,250	—	—

KM# 428.2 1/2 CROWN
Silver **Ruler:** Charles II **Rev:** Different die

Date	Mintage	VG	F	VF	XF	Unc
1666/4	—	650	1,800	3,250	—	—

KM# 428.3 1/2 CROWN
Silver **Ruler:** Charles II **Obv:** Elephant below bust

Date	Mintage	VG	F	VF	XF	Unc
1666	—	600	1,000	3,000	8,000	—

KM# 428.4 1/2 CROWN

Silver **Ruler:** Charles II **Edge:** Regnal year in words **Note:** Varieties exist.

Date	Mintage	VG	F	VF	XF	Unc
1667/4 Rare	—	—	3,500	—	—	—
1668/4	—	200	325	1,250	3,000	—
1669/4	—	200	325	1,300	3,200	—
1669	—	750	1,500	2,400	6,000	—
1670	—	100	200	650	4,000	—

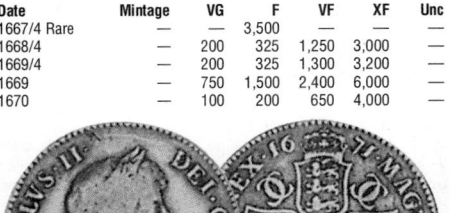

KM# 428.5 1/2 CROWN

Silver **Ruler:** Charles II **Obv:** Variety of the third bust of Charles II **Note:** Varieties exist.

Date	Mintage	VG	F	VF	XF	Unc
1671/0	—	150	300	850	4,500	—
1671	—	90.00	175	550	4,000	—
1672	—	115	250	750	4,000	—

KM# 438.1 1/2 CROWN

Silver **Ruler:** Charles II **Obv:** Fourth bust of Charles II **Note:** Varieties exist.

Date	Mintage	VG	F	VF	XF	Unc
1672	—	115	250	750	4,000	—
1673	—	75.00	150	550	3,750	—
1674/3	—	200	425	1,150	—	—
1674	—	150	300	850	—	—
1675	—	100	200	575	3,500	—
1676	—	75.00	150	525	3,500	—
1677	—	65.00	135	475	3,000	—
1678	—	225	475	1,225	—	—
1679	—	100	200	575	3,500	—
1680	—	150	325	950	—	—
1681/0	—	125	275	800	—	—
1681	—	110	225	675	2,750	—
1682/79	—	150	350	1,400	—	—
1682/1	—	125	275	800	4,500	—
1682	—	110	225	700	5,000	—
1683	—	100	200	600	3,500	—
1684/3	—	200	450	1,200	5,500	—

KM# 438.2 1/2 CROWN

Silver **Ruler:** Charles II **Obv:** Plume below bust

Date	Mintage	VG	F	VF	XF	Unc
1673 Rare	—	—	6,500	15,000	—	—
1683 Rare	—	—	7,500	17,500	—	—

KM# 438.3 1/2 CROWN

Silver **Ruler:** Charles II **Rev:** Plume at center of cruciform arms

Date	Mintage	VG	F	VF	XF	Unc
1673 Rare	—	—	8,500	20,000	—	—

KM# 438.4 1/2 CROWN

Silver **Ruler:** Charles II **Obv:** Elephant and castle below bust **Rev:** Garter star at center of cruciform arms

Date	Mintage	VG	F	VF	XF	Unc
1681 Rare	—	—	3,500	9,000	27,500	—

KM# 452 1/2 CROWN

Silver **Ruler:** James II **Obv:** First bust of James II left **Rev:** Crown above value divides date **Note:** Varieties exist.

Date	Mintage	VG	F	VF	XF	Unc
1685	—	175	350	900	4,000	—
1686/5	—	200	450	1,200	5,000	—
1686	—	185	395	900	4,000	—
1687/6	—	175	400	1,000	4,300	—
1687	—	175	350	950	3,500	—

KM# 462 1/2 CROWN

Silver **Ruler:** James II **Obv:** Second bust of James II left, ties at back of head curve upward

Date	Mintage	VG	F	VF	XF	Unc
1687	—	150	325	850	3,500	—
1688	—	150	325	850	3,500	—

KM# 472.1 1/2 CROWN

Silver **Ruler:** William and Mary **Obv:** First busts of William and Mary **Note:** Varieties exist.

Date	Mintage	VG	F	VF	XF	Unc
1689	—	75.00	150	500	2,200	—

KM# 472.2 1/2 CROWN

Silver **Ruler:** William and Mary **Obv:** First and fourth quarters quartered with arms of France and England **Note:** Varieties exist.

Date	Mintage	VG	F	VF	XF	Unc
1689	—	85.00	175	550	2,200	—
1690	—	150	325	900	3,950	—

KM# 477 1/2 CROWN

Silver **Ruler:** William and Mary **Obv:** Second busts (finer style) of William and Mary right **Rev:** Crowned cruciform arms with WM monograms, date numerals in angles **Note:** Varieties exist.

Date	Mintage	VG	F	VF	XF	Unc
1691	—	115	250	700	3,100	—
1692	—	115	250	700	3,100	—
1693	—	110	225	675	3,100	—
1693 3 over inverted 3	—	115	250	750	3,250	—

KM# 491.1 1/2 CROWN

Silver **Ruler:** William III **Obv:** First bust of William III right **Rev:** Crowned cruciform arms with large shields and early harp **Note:** Varieties exist.

Date	Mintage	VG	F	VF	XF	Unc
1696	—	75.00	150	450	1,100	—

KM# 491.6 1/2 CROWN

Silver **Ruler:** William III **Obv:** First bust of William III right; script y below bust **Rev:** Crowned cruciform arms with large shields and early harp **Mint:** York **Note:** Varieties exist.

Date	Mintage	VG	F	VF	XF	Unc
1696 y	—	150	325	750	2,000	—

KM# 491.7 1/2 CROWN

Silver **Ruler:** William III **Obv:** First bust of William III right **Rev:** Crowned cruciform arms with large shields and ordinary harp **Note:** Varieties exist.

Date	Mintage	VG	F	VF	XF	Unc
1696	—	125	275	700	2,000	—
1697/6	—	—	—	—	—	—
1697	—	75.00	150	450	1,200	—

KM# 491.9 1/2 CROWN

Silver **Ruler:** William III **Obv:** First bust of William III right; C below bust **Rev:** Crowned cruciform arms with large shields and ordinary harp **Mint:** Chester **Note:** Varieties exist.

Date	Mintage	VG	F	VF	XF	Unc
1696 C	—	175	350	800	2,650	—
1697 C	—	85.00	175	550	1,900	—

KM# 491.10 1/2 CROWN

Silver **Ruler:** William III **Obv:** First bust of William III right; E below bust **Rev:** Crowned cruciform arms with large shields and ordinary harp **Mint:** Exeter **Note:** Varieties exist.

Date	Mintage	VG	F	VF	XF	Unc
1696 E	—	175	350	800	2,650	—
1697 E	—	75.00	150	500	1,700	—

KM# 491.11 1/2 CROWN

Silver **Ruler:** William III **Obv:** First bust of William III right; N below bust **Rev:** Crowned cruciform arms with large shields and ordinary harp **Mint:** Norwich **Note:** Varieties exist.

Date	Mintage	VG	F	VF	XF	Unc
1696 N	—	150	300	700	2,300	—
1697 N	—	85.00	175	575	1,900	—

KM# 491.13 1/2 CROWN

Silver **Ruler:** William III **Rev:** Crowned cruciform arms with small shields **Note:** Varieties exist.

Date	Mintage	VG	F	VF	XF	Unc
1696	—	85.00	175	500	1,300	—

KM# 491.2 1/2 CROWN

Silver **Ruler:** William III **Obv:** First bust of William III right; B below bust **Rev:** Crowned cruciform arms with large shields and early harp **Mint:** Bristol

Date	Mintage	VG	F	VF	XF	Unc
1696 B	—	115	250	550	1,600	—

KM# 491.3 1/2 CROWN

Silver **Ruler:** William III **Obv:** First bust of William III right; C below bust **Rev:** Crowned cruciform arms with large shields and early harp **Mint:** Chester

Date	Mintage	VG	F	VF	XF	Unc
1696 C	—	85.00	175	600	1,800	—

KM# 491.4 1/2 CROWN

Silver **Ruler:** William III **Obv:** First bust of William III right; E below bust **Rev:** Crowned cruciform arms with large shields and early harp **Mint:** Exeter

Date	Mintage	VG	F	VF	XF	Unc
1696 E	—	110	225	650	2,100	—

KM# 491.5 1/2 CROWN

Silver **Ruler:** William III **Obv:** First bust of William III right; N below bust **Rev:** Crowned cruciform arms with large shields and early harp **Mint:** Norwich

Date	Mintage	VG	F	VF	XF	Unc
1696 N	—	150	325	800	2,200	—

KM# 491.14 1/2 CROWN

Silver **Ruler:** William III **Obv:** B below bust **Rev:** Crowned cruciform arms with small shields **Mint:** Bristol

Date	Mintage	VG	F	VF	XF	Unc
1696 B	—	75.00	150	500	1,700	—

KM# 491.15 1/2 CROWN
Silver **Ruler:** William III **Obv:** C below bust **Rev:** Crowned cruciform arms with small shields **Mint:** Chester

Date	Mintage	VG	F	VF	XF	Unc
1696 C	—	110	225	650	1,900	—

KM# 491.16 1/2 CROWN
Silver **Ruler:** William III **Obv:** E below bust **Rev:** Crowned cruciform arms with small shields **Mint:** Exeter

Date	Mintage	VG	F	VF	XF	Unc
1696 E	—	150	300	700	1,900	—

KM# 491.17 1/2 CROWN
Silver **Ruler:** William III **Obv:** N below bust **Rev:** Crowned cruciform arms with small shields **Mint:** Norwich

Date	Mintage	VG	F	VF	XF	Unc
1696 N	—	100	200	600	2,100	—

KM# 491.18 1/2 CROWN
Silver **Ruler:** William III **Obv:** Script y below bust **Rev:** Crowned cruciform arms with small shields **Mint:** York

Date	Mintage	VG	F	VF	XF	Unc
1696 y	—	110	225	650	2,200	—

KM# 492.1 1/2 CROWN
Silver **Ruler:** William III **Obv:** Second bust (two curls on breast, without hair below bust) of William III right

Date	Mintage	VG	F	VF	XF	Unc
1696 Unique	—	—	—	—	—	—

KM# 491.12 1/2 CROWN
Silver **Ruler:** William III **Obv:** First bust of William III right; script y below bust **Rev:** Crowned cruciform arms with large shields and ordinary harp **Mint:** York **Note:** Varieties exist.

Date	Mintage	VG	F	VF	XF	Unc
1697 y	—	85.00	175	525	1,700	—

KM# 491.8 1/2 CROWN
Silver **Ruler:** William III **Obv:** First bust of William III right; B below bust **Rev:** Crowned cruciform arms with large shields and ordinary harp **Mint:** Bristol **Note:** Varieties exist.

Date	Mintage	VG	F	VF	XF	Unc
1697 B	—	85.00	175	500	1,800	—

KM# 492.2 1/2 CROWN
Silver **Ruler:** William III **Obv:** Laureate bust right **Rev:** Crowned cruciform arms **Note:** Varieties exist.

Date	Mintage	VG	F	VF	XF	Unc
1698	—	75.00	150	425	1,500	—
1698/7 Rare	—	—	—	—	—	—
1699	—	115	250	550	1,900	—
1700	—	75.00	150	425	1,500	—

KM# 417.1 CROWN
Silver **Ruler:** Charles II **Obv:** First bust of Charles II right **Note:** Dav. #3774.

Date	Mintage	VG	F	VF	XF	Unc
1662	—	200	350	900	4,500	—

KM# 417.2 CROWN
Silver **Ruler:** Charles II **Edge:** Without date

Date	Mintage	VG	F	VF	XF	Unc
1662	—	200	350	900	4,500	—

KM# 417.3 CROWN
Silver **Ruler:** Charles II **Obv:** Without rose below bust **Edge:** Dated **Note:** Dav. #3774A.

Date	Mintage	VG	F	VF	XF	Unc
1662	—	200	350	900	4,500	—

KM# 417.4 CROWN
Silver **Ruler:** Charles II **Edge:** Without date

Date	Mintage	VG	F	VF	XF	Unc
1662	—	200	350	900	4,500	—

KM# 417.5 CROWN
Silver **Ruler:** Charles II **Rev:** Upper and lower shields of arms not quartered **Note:** Dav. #3774B. Varieties exist.

Date	Mintage	VG	F	VF	XF	Unc
1663	—	200	350	900	4,500	—

KM# 422.1 CROWN
Silver **Ruler:** Charles II **Obv:** Second bust (smaller and curved ties on wreath) of Charles II right **Edge:** Regnal year is in Roman numerals **Note:** Dav. #3775. Varieties exist.

Date	Mintage	VG	F	VF	XF	Unc
1664	—	200	350	1,000	5,000	—
1665/4	—	750	1,250	3,250	—	—
1665	—	850	1,350	2,900	—	—
1666	—	185	325	850	5,000	—

KM# 422.2 CROWN
Silver **Ruler:** Charles II **Obv:** Elephant below bust **Note:** Dav. #3775A. Varieties exist.

Date	Mintage	VG	F	VF	XF	Unc
1666	—	400	850	2,250	13,500	—

KM# 422.3 CROWN
Silver **Ruler:** Charles II **Edge:** Regnal year in words **Note:** Dav. #3775B. Varieties exist.

Date	Mintage	VG	F	VF	XF	Unc
1667	—	175	300	750	4,000	—
1668/7	—	175	300	750	4,000	—
1668	—	150	275	675	3,850	—
1669/8	—	300	500	1,300	7,000	—
1669	—	300	500	1,300	7,000	—
1670/69	—	250	450	1,000	5,500	—
1670	—	175	300	750	4,000	—
1671	—	175	300	750	4,000	—

KM# 435 CROWN
Silver **Ruler:** Charles II **Obv:** Third bust (larger and wider) of Charles II right **Note:** Dav. #3776. Varieties exist.

Date	Mintage	VG	F	VF	XF	Unc
1671	—	175	300	750	4,000	—
1672	—	175	300	750	4,000	—
1673/2	—	175	300	750	4,000	—
1673	—	175	300	750	4,000	—
1674 Rare	—	—	—	—	—	—
1675/3	—	450	900	2,200	—	—
1675	—	500	1,000	3,000	—	—
1676	—	175	300	750	4,000	—
1677/6	—	175	300	750	4,000	—
1677	—	175	300	750	4,000	—
1678/7	—	225	450	1,000	6,000	—
1679	—	175	300	750	4,000	—
1680/79	—	200	325	800	4,000	—
1680	—	225	350	850	4,000	—

KM# 445.1 CROWN
Silver **Ruler:** Charles II **Obv:** Fourth bust (larger and older) of Charles II **Note:** Dav. #3776B.

Date	Mintage	VG	F	VF	XF	Unc
1679	—	175	300	750	4,000	—
1680/79	—	200	325	800	4,000	—
1680	—	175	300	750	4,000	—
1681	—	175	300	750	4,000	—
1682/1	—	175	300	750	4,000	—
1682	—	325	550	1,350	5,500	—
1683	—	325	550	1,300	5,500	—
1684	—	225	425	1,000	5,500	—

KM# 445.2 CROWN
Silver **Ruler:** Charles II **Obv:** Elephant and castle below bust **Note:** Dav. #3776A.

Date	Mintage	VG	F	VF	XF	Unc
1681 Rare	—	—	—	—	—	—

KM# 457 CROWN
Silver **Ruler:** James II **Obv:** Laureate first bust of James II left

Rev: Crowned cruciform arms, date divided at top **Note:** Dav. #3778. Varieties exist.

Date	Mintage	VG	F	VF	XF	Unc
1686	—	350	650	1,400	6,000	—

KM# 463 CROWN

Silver **Ruler:** James II **Obv:** Second bust (narrower) of James II left **Note:** Dav. #3779. Varieties exist.

Date	Mintage	VG	F	VF	XF	Unc
1687	—	225	425	950	3,000	—
1688/7	—	225	425	950	3,500	—
1688	—	225	425	950	3,250	—

KM# 478 CROWN

Silver **Ruler:** William and Mary **Obv:** Conjoined busts of William and Mary right **Note:** Dav. #3780. Varieties exist.

Date	Mintage	VG	F	VF	XF	Unc
1691	—	500	725	1,450	4,500	—
1692	—	500	725	1,450	4,500	—

KM# 486 CROWN

Silver **Ruler:** William III **Obv:** First bust of William III right **Rev:** First harp in left shield **Note:** Dav. #3781. Varieties exist.

Date	Mintage	VG	F	VF	XF	Unc
1695	—	150	300	675	1,800	—
1696/5	—	200	350	750	2,000	—
1696	—	135	250	500	1,600	—

KM# 493 CROWN

Silver **Ruler:** William III **Obv:** Second bust (two locks of hair across chest without hair below bust) **Note:** Dav. #3781A. Varieties exist.

Date	Mintage	VG	F	VF	XF	Unc
1696 Unique	—	—	—	—	—	—

KM# 494.1 CROWN

Silver **Ruler:** William III **Obv:** Third bust (straight breastplate on chest) of William III right **Rev:** First harp in left shield **Note:** Dav. #3782. Varieties exist.

Date	Mintage	VG	F	VF	XF	Unc
1696	—	150	275	550	1,700	—

KM# 494.2 CROWN

Silver **Ruler:** William III **Rev:** Second harp in left shield **Note:** Dav. #3782A.

Date	Mintage	VG	F	VF	XF	Unc
1697	—	850	1,350	4,250	15,000	—

KM# 494.3 CROWN

Silver **Ruler:** William III **Rev:** Third harp in left shield **Note:** Dav. #3782B. Varieties exist.

Date	Mintage	VG	F	VF	XF	Unc
1700	—	150	300	675	1,800	—

GUINEA COINAGE

KM# 431 1/2 GUINEA

4.1750 g., 0.9170 Gold 0.1231 oz. AGW **Ruler:** Charles II **Obv:** Charles II with pointed truncation

Date	Mintage	VG	F	VF	XF	Unc
1669	—	400	650	1,600	5,500	—
1670	—	400	650	1,600	5,000	—
1671	—	400	650	1,700	5,500	—
1672	—	400	650	1,700	5,500	—

KM# 439.1 1/2 GUINEA

4.1750 g., 0.9170 Gold 0.1231 oz. AGW **Ruler:** Charles II **Obv:** Rounded truncation

Date	Mintage	VG	F	VF	XF	Unc
1672	—	450	800	1,600	5,500	—
1673	—	450	800	1,700	5,500	—
1674	—	450	800	1,800	6,000	—
1675 Rare	—	—	—	—	—	—
1676	—	450	800	1,600	5,500	—
1677	—	450	800	1,600	5,500	—
1678	—	450	800	1,600	5,500	—
1679	—	450	800	1,600	5,500	—
1680	—	450	800	1,700	5,500	—
1681	—	450	800	1,700	5,500	—
1682	—	450	800	1,700	5,500	—
1683	—	450	800	1,600	5,500	—
1684	—	450	800	1,600	5,500	—

KM# 439.2 1/2 GUINEA

4.1750 g., 0.9170 Gold 0.1231 oz. AGW **Ruler:** Charles II **Obv:** Elephant and castle below bust

Date	Mintage	VG	F	VF	XF	Unc
1676 Rare	—	—	—	—	—	—
1677	—	500	900	2,100	6,000	—
1678/7	—	450	800	2,100	6,000	—
1680 Rare	—	—	—	—	—	—
1682	—	450	800	2,100	6,000	—
1683 Rare	—	—	—	—	—	—
1684	—	500	900	2,100	6,000	—

KM# 458.1 1/2 GUINEA

4.1750 g., 0.9170 Gold 0.1231 oz. AGW **Ruler:** James II **Obv:** Head of James II left

Date	Mintage	VG	F	VF	XF	Unc
1686	—	500	850	1,700	4,500	—
1687	—	500	850	1,900	5,500	—
1688	—	500	850	1,700	5,500	—

KM# 458.2 1/2 GUINEA

4.1750 g., 0.9170 Gold 0.1231 oz. AGW **Ruler:** James II **Obv:** Elephant and castle below bust

Date	Mintage	VG	F	VF	XF	Unc
1686	—	1,200	2,000	5,500	—	—

KM# 473 1/2 GUINEA

4.1750 g., 0.9170 Gold 0.1231 oz. AGW **Ruler:** William and Mary **Obv:** Conjoined heads of William and Mary, right

Date	Mintage	VG	F	VF	XF	Unc
1689	—	400	650	2,100	5,500	—

KM# 476.1 1/2 GUINEA

4.1750 g., 0.9170 Gold 0.1231 oz. AGW **Ruler:** William and Mary **Obv:** Conjoined heads of William and Mary right with hair falling on neck

Date	Mintage	VG	F	VF	XF	Unc
1690	—	450	750	2,100	5,000	—
1691	—	450	750	2,100	5,000	—
1692	—	450	750	2,100	5,000	—
1693/2	—	—	—	—	—	—
1693	—	450	750	2,100	5,000	—
1694	—	450	750	2,100	5,000	—

KM# 476.2 1/2 GUINEA

4.1750 g., 0.9170 Gold 0.1231 oz. AGW **Ruler:** William and Mary **Obv:** Elephant and castle below heads

Date	Mintage	VG	F	VF	XF	Unc
1691	—	450	800	2,200	6,000	—
1692	—	450	800	2,200	6,500	—

KM# 476.3 1/2 GUINEA

4.1750 g., 0.9170 Gold 0.1231 oz. AGW **Ruler:** William and Mary **Obv:** Elephant below heads

Date	Mintage	VG	F	VF	XF	Unc
1692 Rare	—	—	—	—	—	—

KM# 487.1 1/2 GUINEA

4.1750 g., 0.9170 Gold 0.1231 oz. AGW **Ruler:** William III **Obv:** Head of William III right

Date	Mintage	VG	F	VF	XF	Unc
1695	—	350	500	1,000	3,500	—

KM# 487.2 1/2 GUINEA

4.1750 g., 0.9170 Gold 0.1231 oz. AGW **Ruler:** William III **Obv:** Elephant and castle below head

Date	Mintage	VG	F	VF	XF	Unc
1695	—	450	750	1,800	4,000	—
1696	—	450	750	1,800	4,000	—

KM# 487.3 1/2 GUINEA
4.1750 g., 0.9170 Gold 0.1231 oz. AGW **Ruler:** William III **Obv:** Head right **Obv. Legend:** GVLIELMVS • III • DEI • GRA • **Rev:** Crowned shields in cruciform, sceptres at angles **Rev. Legend:** MAG - BR • FRA - ET • HIB • - REX

Date	Mintage	VG	F	VF	XF	Unc
1697	—	350	550	1,400	4,000	—
1698	—	350	500	950	3,000	—
1699 Rare	—	—	—	—	—	—
1700	—	350	500	950	3,000	—

KM# 487.4 1/2 GUINEA
4.1750 g., 0.9170 Gold 0.1231 oz. AGW **Ruler:** William III **Obv:** Elephant and castle below head

Date	Mintage	VG	F	VF	XF	Unc
1698	—	400	750	1,900	5,000	—

KM# 420.1 GUINEA
8.3500 g., 0.9170 Gold 0.2462 oz. AGW **Ruler:** Charles II **Obv:** Laureate bust of Charles II right **Rev:** Crowned cruciform arms with scepters

Date	Mintage	VG	F	VF	XF	Unc
1663	—	1,250	2,750	7,500	27,500	—

KM# 420.2 GUINEA
8.3500 g., 0.9170 Gold 0.2462 oz. AGW **Ruler:** Charles II **Obv:** Laureate bust of Charles II right, elephant

Date	Mintage	VG	F	VF	XF	Unc
1663	—	975	1,750	5,000	17,500	—

KM# 423.1 GUINEA
8.3500 g., 0.9170 Gold 0.2462 oz. AGW **Ruler:** Charles II **Obv:** Laureate bust of Charles II right

Date	Mintage	VG	F	VF	XF	Unc
1664	—	950	1,500	4,250	15,000	—

KM# 423.2 GUINEA
8.3500 g., 0.9170 Gold 0.2462 oz. AGW **Ruler:** Charles II **Obv:** Elephant below bust

Date	Mintage	VG	F	VF	XF	Unc
1664 Rare	—	—	—	—	—	—

KM# 424.1 GUINEA
8.3500 g., 0.9170 Gold 0.2462 oz. AGW **Ruler:** Charles II **Obv:** Laureate bust of Charles II right

Date	Mintage	VG	F	VF	XF	Unc
1664	—	650	1,050	4,000	9,000	—
1665	—	650	1,000	4,000	9,000	—
1666	—	650	1,000	4,000	9,000	—
1667	—	650	1,000	4,000	9,000	—
1668	—	650	1,000	4,000	9,000	—
1669	—	650	1,000	4,000	9,000	—
1670	—	650	1,000	4,000	9,000	—
1671	—	650	1,000	4,000	9,000	—
1672	—	650	1,100	4,000	9,000	—
1673	—	700	1,100	4,000	9,000	—

KM# 424.2 GUINEA
8.3500 g., 0.9170 Gold 0.2462 oz. AGW **Ruler:** Charles II **Obv:** Elephant below bust

Date	Mintage	VG	F	VF	XF	Unc
1664	—	950	1,350	4,500	12,500	—
1665	—	950	1,350	4,500	12,500	—
1668	—	—	—	—	—	—

KM# 440.1 GUINEA
8.3500 g., 0.9170 Gold 0.2462 oz. AGW **Ruler:** Charles II **Obv:** Head of Charles II with rounded truncation

Date	Mintage	VG	F	VF	XF	Unc
1672	—	500	950	3,000	9,000	—
1673	—	500	950	3,000	9,000	—
1674	—	500	950	3,000	9,000	—
1675	—	500	950	3,000	9,000	—
1676	—	500	950	3,000	9,000	—
1677	—	500	950	3,000	9,000	—
1678	—	500	950	3,000	9,000	—
1679	—	500	950	3,000	9,000	—
1680	—	500	950	3,000	9,000	—
1681	—	500	950	3,000	9,000	—
1682	—	500	950	3,000	9,000	—
1683	—	500	950	3,000	9,000	—
1684	—	500	950	3,000	9,000	—

KM# 440.2 GUINEA
8.3500 g., 0.9170 Gold 0.2462 oz. AGW **Ruler:** Charles II **Obv:** Elephant and castle below bust

Date	Mintage	VG	F	VF	XF	Unc
1674	—	900	1,300	4,000	11,000	—
1675	—	850	1,200	3,500	10,000	—
1676	—	850	1,200	3,500	10,000	—
1677	—	850	1,200	3,500	10,000	—
1678	—	850	1,200	3,500	10,000	—
1679	—	850	1,200	3,500	10,000	—
1680	—	900	1,300	4,000	11,000	—
1681	—	850	1,200	3,500	10,000	—
1682	—	850	1,200	3,500	10,000	—
1683	—	900	1,300	4,000	11,000	—
1684	—	850	1,200	3,500	10,000	—

KM# 440.3 GUINEA
8.3500 g., 0.9170 Gold 0.2462 oz. AGW **Ruler:** Charles II **Obv:** Elephant below bust

Date	Mintage	VG	F	VF	XF	Unc
1677 Rare	—	—	—	—	—	—
1677/5	—	—	—	—	—	—
1678 Rare	—	1,750	3,000	8,500	—	—

KM# 453.1 GUINEA
8.3500 g., 0.9170 Gold 0.2462 oz. AGW **Ruler:** James II **Obv:** Head of James II left

Date	Mintage	VG	F	VF	XF	Unc
1685	—	400	900	2,800	7,500	14,000
1686	—	400	900	2,800	7,500	14,000

KM# 453.2 GUINEA
8.3500 g., 0.9170 Gold 0.2462 oz. AGW **Ruler:** James II **Obv:** Elephant and castle below bust

Date	Mintage	VG	F	VF	XF	Unc
1685	—	500	925	3,000	7,500	—
1686 Rare	—	—	1,100	—	—	—

KM# 459.1 GUINEA
8.3500 g., 0.9170 Gold 0.2462 oz. AGW **Ruler:** James II **Obv:** Laureate bust of James II left

Date	Mintage	VG	F	VF	XF	Unc
1686	—	500	950	2,800	6,000	—
1687/6	—	1,000	1,500	2,800	7,000	—
1687	—	500	950	2,800	6,000	—
1688	—	500	950	2,800	6,000	—

KM# 459.2 GUINEA
8.3500 g., 0.9170 Gold 0.2462 oz. AGW **Ruler:** James II **Obv:** Elephant and castle below bust

Date	Mintage	VG	F	VF	XF	Unc
1686	—	600	1,000	3,000	7,500	—
1687	—	500	950	3,000	7,250	—
1688	—	500	950	3,000	7,250	—

KM# 474.1 GUINEA
8.3500 g., 0.9170 Gold 0.2462 oz. AGW **Ruler:** William and Mary **Obv:** Conjoined heads of William and Mary right

Date	Mintage	VG	F	VF	XF	Unc
1689	—	500	925	2,850	7,200	13,000
1690	—	500	925	2,850	7,200	13,000
1691	—	500	925	2,850	7,200	13,000
1692	—	500	925	2,850	7,200	13,000
1693	—	500	925	2,850	7,200	13,000
1694/3	—	500	1,500	3,500	7,500	13,000
1694	—	500	950	2,900	7,500	13,000

KM# 474.2 GUINEA
8.3500 g., 0.9170 Gold 0.2462 oz. AGW **Ruler:** William and Mary **Obv:** Elephant and castle below heads

Date	Mintage	VG	F	VF	XF	Unc
1689	—	600	1,000	3,000	7,500	—
1690	—	600	1,000	3,500	7,700	—
1691	—	600	1,000	3,500	7,500	—
1692	—	600	1,000	3,500	7,500	—
1693	—	600	1,000	3,500	9,500	—
1694	—	600	1,000	3,500	7,500	—

KM# 474.3 GUINEA
8.3500 g., 0.9170 Gold 0.2462 oz. AGW **Ruler:** William and Mary **Obv:** Elephant below heads

Date	Mintage	VG	F	VF	XF	Unc
1692	—	750	1,300	4,500	10,000	—
1693 Rare	—	850	1,400	5,000	11,500	—

KM# 488.1 GUINEA

8.3500 g., 0.9170 Gold 0.2462 oz. AGW **Ruler:** William III **Obv:** Laureate bust of William III right **Rev:** Crowned cruciform arms with scepters in angles, date divided at top

Date	Mintage	VG	F	VF	XF	Unc
1695	—	350	550	1,750	6,000	10,000
1696	—	350	550	1,750	6,000	10,000
1697	—	350	550	1,750	6,000	10,000

KM# 488.2 GUINEA

8.3500 g., 0.9170 Gold 0.2462 oz. AGW **Ruler:** William III **Obv:** Elephant and castle below bust

Date	Mintage	VG	F	VF	XF	Unc
1695 Rare	—	—	900	2,750	10,000	—
1696 Rare	—	—	—	—	—	—

KM# 498.2 GUINEA

8.3500 g., 0.9170 Gold 0.2462 oz. AGW **Ruler:** William III **Obv:** Elephant and castle below bust **Rev:** Crowned shields in cruciform, sceptres at angles **Note:** Struck from gold mined in Guinea, now Ghana.

Date	Mintage	VG	F	VF	XF	Unc
1697	—	550	1,100	5,000	8,500	—
1698	—	550	1,100	4,000	8,500	—
1699 Rare	—	—	—	—	—	—
1700	—	550	1,100	5,000	8,500	—

KM# 498.1 GUINEA

8.3500 g., 0.9170 Gold 0.2462 oz. AGW **Ruler:** William III **Obv:** Laureate head right **Obv. Legend:** GVLIELMVS • - III • DEI • GRA • **Rev:** Crowned shields in cruciform, sceptres at angles **Rev. Legend:** MAG - BR • FRA - ET • HIB - REX •

Date	Mintage	VG	F	VF	XF	Unc
1697	—	400	800	1,800	6,000	9,500
1698	—	400	800	1,800	5,500	9,500
1699	—	400	800	1,800	6,000	9,500
1700	—	400	800	1,800	5,500	9,500

KM# 425.1 2 GUINEAS

16.7000 g., 0.9170 Gold 0.4923 oz. AGW **Ruler:** Charles II **Obv:** Laureate bust of Charles II right, pointed truncation **Rev:** Crowned cruciform arms with scepters in angles, date divided at top

Date	Mintage	VG	F	VF	XF	Unc
1664	—	1,100	2,000	4,000	11,000	—
1665 Rare	—	—	—	—	—	—
1669 Rare	—	—	—	—	—	—
1671	—	1,100	2,000	4,000	11,000	—
1673 Rare	—	—	—	—	—	—

KM# 425.2 2 GUINEAS

16.7000 g., 0.9170 Gold 0.4923 oz. AGW **Ruler:** Charles II **Obv:** Elephant below bust

Date	Mintage	VG	F	VF	XF	Unc
1664	—	1,100	2,000	4,000	11,000	—

KM# 443.1 2 GUINEAS

16.7000 g., 0.9170 Gold 0.4923 oz. AGW **Ruler:** Charles II **Obv:** Rounded truncation

Date	Mintage	VG	F	VF	XF	Unc
1675	—	1,000	1,700	3,250	10,500	—
1676	—	950	1,600	3,000	10,000	—
1677	—	950	1,600	3,000	10,000	—
1678/7	—	900	1,500	3,000	9,600	—
1678	—	950	1,600	3,000	10,000	—
1679	—	950	1,600	3,000	10,000	—
1680	—	1,000	1,700	3,500	11,000	—
1681	—	950	1,600	3,000	10,000	—
1682	—	950	1,600	3,000	10,000	—
1683	—	950	1,600	3,000	10,000	—
1684	—	1,000	1,700	3,250	10,500	—

KM# 443.2 2 GUINEAS

16.7000 g., 0.9170 Gold 0.4923 oz. AGW **Ruler:** Charles II **Obv:** Elephant and castle below bust

Date	Mintage	VG	F	VF	XF	Unc
1676	—	1,100	1,800	4,000	10,000	—
1677 Rare	—	—	—	—	—	—
1678	—	1,100	1,800	4,000	10,000	—
1682	—	1,100	1,800	4,000	10,000	—
1683	—	1,300	2,000	4,500	11,000	—
1684	—	1,200	1,900	4,000	10,000	—

KM# 443.3 2 GUINEAS

16.7000 g., 0.9170 Gold 0.4923 oz. AGW **Ruler:** Charles II **Obv:** Elephant below bust

Date	Mintage	VG	F	VF	XF	Unc
1678 Rare	—	—	—	—	—	—

KM# 464 2 GUINEAS

16.7000 g., 0.9170 Gold 0.4923 oz. AGW **Ruler:** James II **Obv:** Laureate bust of James II left

Date	Mintage	VG	F	VF	XF	Unc
1687	—	1,400	2,200	4,500	13,500	—
1688/7	—	1,500	2,300	5,000	14,000	—

KM# 482.2 2 GUINEAS

16.7000 g., 0.9170 Gold 0.4923 oz. AGW **Ruler:** William and Mary **Obv:** Elephant and castle below heads

Date	Mintage	VG	F	VF	XF	Unc
1691 Rare	—	—	—	—	—	—
1693	—	1,300	2,500	4,500	12,000	—
1694/3	—	1,300	2,500	4,000	10,000	—

KM# 482.1 2 GUINEAS

16.7000 g., 0.9170 Gold 0.4923 oz. AGW **Ruler:** William and Mary **Obv:** Conjoined heads of William and Mary right **Rev:** Crowned arms, crown divides date at top

Date	Mintage	VG	F	VF	XF	Unc
1693	—	1,300	2,500	3,250	8,500	—
1694/3	—	1,300	2,500	3,500	9,000	—

KM# 430.1 5 GUINEAS

41.7500 g., 0.9170 Gold 1.2308 oz. AGW **Ruler:** Charles II **Obv:** Laureate bust of Charles II right, pointed truncation **Rev:** Crowned cruciform arms with scepters in angles, date divided at top

Date	Mintage	VG	F	VF	XF	Unc
1668	—	2,200	2,700	6,000	16,500	—
1669	—	2,200	2,700	6,500	16,500	—
1670	—	2,200	2,700	6,500	16,000	—
1671	—	2,200	2,700	6,500	17,500	—
1672	—	2,200	2,700	6,500	16,500	—
1673	—	2,200	2,700	6,500	16,500	—
1674	—	2,200	2,750	6,500	18,500	—
1675	—	2,200	2,700	6,500	17,000	—
1676	—	2,200	2,700	6,500	16,500	—
1677	—	2,200	2,700	6,500	16,500	—
1678/7	—	2,200	2,700	6,500	16,500	—
1678	—	2,200	2,700	6,500	16,500	—

KM# 430.2 5 GUINEAS

41.7500 g., 0.9170 Gold 1.2308 oz. AGW **Ruler:** Charles II **Obv:** Elephant below bust

Date	Mintage	VG	F	VF	XF	Unc
1668	—	2,500	3,000	6,500	16,000	—
1669	—	2,500	3,000	6,500	18,500	—
1675	—	2,500	3,000	6,500	18,500	—
1677/5 Rare	—	2,500	3,000	6,250	20,000	—

KM# 430.3 5 GUINEAS

41.7500 g., 0.9170 Gold 1.2308 oz. AGW **Ruler:** Charles II **Obv:** Elephant and castle below bust

Date	Mintage	VG	F	VF	XF	Unc
1675	—	2,500	3,000	6,500	27,500	—
1676	—	2,500	3,000	6,000	17,500	—
1677	—	2,500	3,000	6,000	18,500	—
1678/7	—	2,500	3,000	6,000	18,500	—
1678	—	2,500	3,000	6,000	18,500	—

KM# 444.1 5 GUINEAS

41.7500 g., 0.9170 Gold 1.2308 oz. AGW **Ruler:** Charles II **Obv:** Rounded truncation

Date	Mintage	VG	F	VF	XF	Unc
1678	—	2,500	3,000	6,500	17,500	—
1679	—	2,500	3,000	6,500	17,500	—
1680	—	2,500	3,000	6,500	17,500	—
1681	—	2,500	3,000	6,500	17,500	—
1682	—	2,500	3,000	6,500	17,500	—
1683	—	2,500	3,000	6,500	17,500	—
1684	—	2,500	3,000	6,500	17,500	—

KM# 444.2 5 GUINEAS

41.7500 g., 0.9170 Gold 1.2308 oz. AGW **Ruler:** Charles II **Obv:** Elephant and castle below bust

Date	Mintage	VG	F	VF	XF	Unc
1680 Rare	—	2,500	3,000	6,500	20,000	—
1681	—	2,500	3,000	6,500	18,500	—

Date	Mintage	VG	F	VF	XF	Unc
1682	—	2,500	3,000	6,500	17,000	—
1683	—	2,500	3,000	6,500	18,500	—
1684	—	2,500	3,000	6,500	17,000	—

KM# 460.1 5 GUINEAS

41.7500 g., 0.9170 Gold 1.2308 oz. AGW **Ruler:** James II **Obv:** Laureate bust of James II left

Date	Mintage	VG	F	VF	XF	Unc
1686	—	2,500	3,000	6,500	20,000	—
1687	—	2,500	3,000	6,500	17,000	—
1688	—	2,500	3,000	6,500	17,000	—

KM# 460.2 5 GUINEAS

41.7500 g., 0.9170 Gold 1.2308 oz. AGW **Ruler:** James II **Obv:** Elephant and castle below bust

Date	Mintage	VG	F	VF	XF	Unc
1687	—	2,500	3,000	6,500	17,000	—
1688	—	2,500	3,000	6,500	18,500	—

KM# 479.1 5 GUINEAS

41.7500 g., 0.9170 Gold 1.2308 oz. AGW **Ruler:** William and Mary **Obv:** Conjoined heads of William and Mary right

Date	Mintage	VG	F	VF	XF	Unc
1691	—	2,500	3,500	6,500	15,000	—
1692	—	2,500	3,500	6,500	16,000	—
1693	—	2,500	3,500	6,500	15,000	—
1694	—	2,500	3,500	6,500	16,000	—

KM# 479.2 5 GUINEAS

41.7500 g., 0.9170 Gold 1.2308 oz. AGW **Ruler:** William and Mary **Obv:** Elephant and castle below conjoined busts right

Date	Mintage	VG	F	VF	XF	Unc
1691	—	2,500	3,500	6,500	15,000	—
1692	—	2,500	3,500	6,500	15,000	—
1693	—	2,500	3,500	6,500	16,500	—
1694	—	2,500	3,500	6,500	16,500	—

KM# 505.1 5 GUINEAS

41.7500 g., 0.9170 Gold 1.2308 oz. AGW **Ruler:** William III **Obv:** Laureate bust of William III right **Rev:** Crowned cruciform arms with scepters in angles, date divided at top

Date	Mintage	VG	F	VF	XF	Unc
1699	—	2,500	3,000	5,500	16,500	—
1700	—	2,500	3,000	6,000	17,500	—

KM# 505.2 5 GUINEAS

41.7500 g., 0.9170 Gold 1.2308 oz. AGW **Ruler:** William III **Obv:** Elephant and castle below bust

Date	Mintage	VG	F	VF	XF	Unc
1699	—	2,500	3,000	6,500	20,000	—

PATTERNS

Including off metal strikes

KM#	Date	Mintage	Identification	Mkt Val
PnA1	1601	—	Penny. Silver. Crowned bust of Queen Elizabeth I 3/4 face to left. THE PLEDGE OF. Crowned monogram, EAB. A PENNY 1601.	—
Pn1	ND	—	1/4 Angel. Gold. James I	—
Pn2	ND	—	Double Crown. Gold. Charles I	—
Pn3	ND	—	Double Crown. Gold. Charles I	—
Pn4	ND	—	Angel. Gold. Charles I	—
Pn5	ND	—	Unite. Gold. Charles I	—
Pn6	ND	—	Unite. Silver. Charles I	—
Pn7	ND	—	Unite. Gold. Charles I, value behind head.	—
Pn8	ND	—	Unite. Gold. Charles I	—
Pn12	1630	—	Unite. Gold. Charles I, crowned head.	30,000
Pn16	1630	—	Unite. Gold. Charles I, crowned head to bottom	30,000
Pn9	1630	—	Unite. Gold. Charles I	—
Pn10	1630	—	Unite. Gold. Charles I, bare head	—
Pn11	1630	—	Unite. Silver. Charles I	—
Pn13	1630	—	Unite. Silver. Charles I	—
Pn14	1630	—	Unite. Gold. Charles I, bare head to bottom	—
Pn15	1630	—	Unite. Silver. Charles I	—
Pn17	1630	—	Unite. Silver. Charles I	—
PnA18	ND	—	2 Pence. Charles I; by Briot	—
Pn18	1635	—	Unite. Silver. Charles I	—
Pn19	ND	—	Unite. Silver. Charles I	—
Pn20	ND	—	Unite. Gold. Charles I, third bust.	—
Pn22	ND	—	3 Unite. Gold. Charles I, crowned bust.	—
Pn21	ND	—	Unite. Gold. Charles I, fourth bust.	12,500
Pn23	ND	—	5 Unites. Gold. Charles I	—
			Note: Also called the "Juxon Medal."	
Pn26	1656	—	1 Broad. Silver. Cromwell.	—
PnD27	1656	—	1/2 Crown. Silver. Cromwell.	2,200
Pn24	1656	—	50 Shilling. Gold. Cromwell, broad sides, thick, lettered edge	—
			Note: Stacks 50th Anniversary sale 10-85 nearly mint state realized $31,900	
Pn25	1656	—	1 Broad. Gold. Cromwell.	—
			Note: Heritage ANA sale 8-10, AU58 realized $19,000. Ira & Larry Goldberg Auction 59, 5-10, Proof 64 realized $60,000	
PnA26	1656	—	1/2 Broad. Gold. Cromwell.	25,000
			Note: The 1/2 Broad was struck in 1738 from dies made by John Tanner, while other Cromwell patterns were struck from dies made by Thomas Simon contemporary with date	
PnE27	1658	—	6 Pence. Silver. Cromwell Care	—
PnG27	1658	—	Crown. Gold. Cromwell.	—
			Note: Spink London No. 48 Norweb sale part 2 11-85 XF realized $47,850	
PnF27	1658	3	1/2 Crown. Gold. Cromwell.	—
			Note: St. James Auction 11, 5-09, proof realized approximately $102,285.	
Pn27	1660	—	1 Broad. Gold. Charles II.	—
Pn28	1660	—	1 Broad. Silver. Charles II.	—
Pn30	1660	—	1 Broad. Gold. Charles II.	—
Pn31	1660	—	1 Broad. Silver. Charles II.	—
Pn29	1660	—	1 Broad. Copper. Charles II.	—
Pn32	1662	—	1 Broad. Gold. Charles II.	12,500
PnA33	1662	—	Crown. Gold. Charles II.	—
PnE33	1663	—	Crown. Pewter. Lettered in Latin edge. Thomas Simon	8,000
PnF33	1663	—	Crown. Silver. Lettered in English edge. Thomas Simon	—
PnG33	1663	—	Crown. Silver. Lettered in English edge. Thomas Simon	—
PnD33	1663	—	Crown. Silver. Lettered in Latin edge. Thomas Simon	—
			Note: Glendining's Willis sale 10-91 VF realized $14,960	
PnB33	1663	—	Crown. Silver. Thomas Simon Petition, English lettered edge	—
			Note: Stack's sale 12-92 VF realized $34,000	
PnC33	1663	—	Crown. Pewter. Plain edge. Thomas Simon Petition	8,500
PnR33	1665	—	Farthing. Silver. Short hair.	850
PnH33	1665	—	Farthing. Gold. Charles II, short hair.	12,000
PnI33	1665	—	Farthing. Gold. Charles II, long hair.	12,000
PnJ33	1672	—	1/2 Penny. Charles II	—
PnK33	1672	—	1/2 Penny. Silver. KM#437	—
PnL33	1673	—	1/2 Penny. Silver. KM#437	—
PnM33	1694	—	1/2 Penny. William and Mary.	—
PnN33	1694	—	1/2 Penny. Silver. KM# 475.3.	—
PnO33	1696	—	1/2 Penny. Silver. KM# 483.1.	—
PnP33	1699	—	1/2 Penny. Silver. KM# 503.	—

MAUNDY SETS

KM#	Date	Mintage	Identification	Issue Price	Mkt Val
MDS1	ND(1660-62) (4)	—	KM#281, 290, 398, 401	—	1,150
MDS2	ND(1662) (4)	—	KM#282, 291, 397, 400	—	1,350
MDS3	1670 (4)	—	KM#429, 432-434	—	800
MDS4	1671 (4)	—	KM#429, 432-434	—	800
MDS5	1672/1 (4)	—	KM#429, 432-434	—	800
MDS6	1673 (4)	—	KM#429, 432-434	—	800
MDS7	1674 (4)	—	KM#429, 432-434	—	800
MDS8	1675 (4)	—	KM#429, 432-434	—	800
MDS9	1676 (4)	—	KM#429, 432-434	—	800
MDS10	1677 (4)	—	KM#429, 432-434	—	800
MDS11	1678 (4)	—	KM#429, 432-434	—	900
MDS12	1679 (4)	—	KM#429, 432-434	—	800
MDS13	1680/79 (4)	—	KM#429, 432-434	—	850
MDS14	1680 (4)	—	KM#429, 432-434	—	800
MDS15	1681/0 (4)	—	KM#429, 432-434	—	1,000
MDS16	1681 (4)	—	KM#429, 432-434	—	900
MDS17	1682/1 (4)	—	KM#429, 432-434	—	1,000
MDS18	1682 (4)	—	KM#429, 432-434	—	800
MDS19	1683/2 (4)	—	KM#429, 432-434	—	975
MDS20	1683 (4)	—	KM#429, 432-434	—	800
MDS21	1684 (4)	—	KM#429, 432-434	—	800
MDS22	1686 (4)	—	KM#449, 450, 454, 455.1	—	950
MDS23	1687 (4)	—	KM#449, 450, 454, 455.1	—	950
MDS24	1688 (4)	—	KM#449, 450, 454, 455.1	—	950
MDS25	1689 (4)	—	KM#468.1, 469, 470.1, 471.1	—	2,400
MDS26	1691 (4)	—	KM#468.2, 469, 470.1, 471.1	—	1,100
MDS27	1692 (4)	—	KM#468-471	—	1,200
MDS28	1693 (4)	—	KM#468-471	—	1,200
MDS29	1694 (4)	—	KM#468.2, 469, 470.2, 471.1	—	1,000
MDS30	1698 (4)	—	KM#495, 499, 500.1, 501	—	1,000
MDS31	1699 (4)	—	KM#495, 499, 500.1, 501	—	1,000
MDS32	1700 (4)	—	KM#495, 499, 500.2, 501	—	1,000

HUNGARY

Hungary is located in central Europe.

The ancient kingdom of Hungary, founded by the Magyars in the 9th century, achieved its greatest extension in the mid-14th century when its dominions touched the Baltic, Black and Mediterranean Seas. After suffering repeated Turkish invasions, Hungary accepted Habsburg rule to escape Turkish occupation, regaining independence in 1867 with the Emperor of Austria as king of a dual Austro-Hungarian monarchy.

MINT MARKS

A, CA, WI - Vienna (Becs)
B, K, KB - Kremnitz (Kormoczbanya)
BP - Budapest
CH - Pressburg (Pozsony)
CM - Kaschau (Kassa)
(c) - castle - Pressburg
(d) - double trefoil - Pressburg
G, GN, NB - Nagybanya
(g) - GC script monogram - Pressburg
GYF - Karlsburg (Gyulafehervar)
HA - Hall
(L) - ICB monogram - Pressburg
(r) - rampant lion left - Pressburg
S - Schmollnitz (Szomolnok)

MINT OFFICIALS' INITIALS

Nagybanya Mint

Initial	Date	Name
IB	1692-98	J. C. Block
ICB	1698-1728	J. C. block
IS	1677-78	
LM	1673-77, 87, 95	Leopold Mittermayer
PO	1684-99	Peter Osterreicher

Pressburg Mint

Initial	Date	Name
(l)	1684-85	Georg Lippai
	1696-99	Christoph Sigmund Hunger
	1674-76	Georg Cetto

MONETARY SYSTEM

Until 1857

2 Poltura = 3 Krajczar
60 Krajczar = 1 Forint (Gulden)
2 Forint = 1 Convention Thaler

KINGDOM

STANDARD COINAGE

KM# 5.1 OBULUS

Silver **Ruler:** Rudolf II **Obv:** Date above shield of arms **Rev:** Madonna and child divide K-B

Date	Mintage	VG	F	VF	XF	Unc
1601KB	—	9.00	18.00	40.00	85.00	—
1602KB	—	9.00	18.00	40.00	85.00	—
1604KB	—	9.00	18.00	40.00	85.00	—
1606KB	—	9.00	18.00	40.00	85.00	—
1607KB	—	9.00	18.00	40.00	85.00	—
1608KB	—	9.00	18.00	40.00	85.00	—

KM# 5.2 OBULUS

Silver **Ruler:** Rudolf II **Note:** Thick planchet.

Date	Mintage	VG	F	VF	XF	Unc
1601	—	9.00	18.00	40.00	85.00	—
1607	—	9.00	18.00	40.00	85.00	—

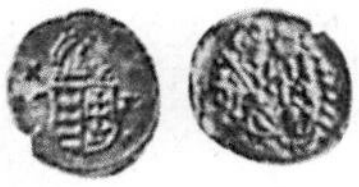

KM# 22 OBULUS

Silver **Ruler:** Rudolf II **Obv:** Crowned arms, crown divides K-B, shield divides date **Rev:** Radiant Madonna and child

Date	Mintage	VG	F	VF	XF	Unc
1608KB	—	9.00	18.00	40.00	85.00	—
1609KB	—	9.00	18.00	40.00	85.00	—
1610KB	—	9.00	18.00	40.00	85.00	—
1611KB	—	9.00	18.00	40.00	85.00	—
1612KB	—	9.00	18.00	40.00	85.00	—
1613	—	9.00	18.00	40.00	85.00	—

KM# 39 OBULUS

Silver **Obv:** Shield of arms divides K-B, date above **Rev:** Without rays **Note:** Varieties exist.

Date	Mintage	VG	F	VF	XF	Unc
1613KB	—	9.00	18.00	40.00	85.00	—
1614KB	—	9.00	18.00	40.00	85.00	—
1615KB	—	9.00	18.00	40.00	85.00	—
1616KB	—	9.00	18.00	40.00	85.00	—
1617KB	—	9.00	18.00	40.00	85.00	—
1618KB	—	9.00	18.00	40.00	85.00	—
1619KB	—	9.00	18.00	40.00	85.00	—
1621KB	—	9.00	18.00	40.00	85.00	—
1622KB	—	9.00	18.00	40.00	85.00	—
1623KB	—	9.00	18.00	40.00	85.00	—
1625KB	—	9.00	18.00	40.00	85.00	—
1626KB	—	9.00	18.00	40.00	85.00	—
1627KB	—	9.00	18.00	40.00	85.00	—
1629KB	—	9.00	18.00	40.00	85.00	—

KM# 62 OBULUS

Silver **Obv:** Shield of arms divides N-B, date above **Rev:** Madonna and child

Date	Mintage	VG	F	VF	XF	Unc
1619NB	—	9.00	18.00	40.00	85.00	—
1631NB	—	9.00	18.00	40.00	85.00	—
1634NB	—	9.00	18.00	40.00	85.00	—
1638NB	—	9.00	18.00	40.00	85.00	—

KM# 105 OBULUS

Silver **Rev:** Madonna and child divide date

Date	Mintage	VG	F	VF	XF	Unc
1634	—	9.00	18.00	40.00	85.00	—
1635	—	9.00	18.00	40.00	85.00	—
1636	—	9.00	18.00	40.00	85.00	—
1637	—	9.00	18.00	40.00	85.00	—
1638	—	9.00	18.00	40.00	85.00	—
1639	—	9.00	18.00	40.00	85.00	—
1640	—	9.00	18.00	40.00	85.00	—
1641	—	9.00	18.00	40.00	85.00	—
1642	—	9.00	18.00	40.00	85.00	—
1645	—	9.00	18.00	40.00	85.00	—
1647	—	9.00	18.00	40.00	85.00	—
1648	—	9.00	18.00	40.00	85.00	—
1649	—	9.00	18.00	40.00	85.00	—
1654	—	9.00	18.00	40.00	85.00	—
1655	—	9.00	18.00	40.00	85.00	—

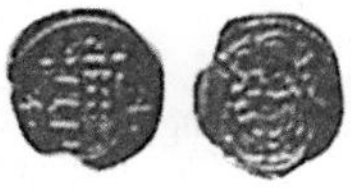

KM# 173 OBULUS

Billon **Ruler:** Leopold I **Obv:** Crowned arms divide K-B **Rev:** Madonna and child divide date **Note:** Varieties exist

Date	Mintage	VG	F	VF	XF	Unc
1662KB	—	9.00	18.00	42.50	90.00	—
1663KB	—	9.00	18.00	42.50	90.00	—
1665KB	—	9.00	18.00	42.50	90.00	—
1674KB	—	9.00	18.00	42.50	90.00	—
1675KB	—	9.00	18.00	42.50	90.00	—
1676KB	—	9.00	18.00	42.50	90.00	—
1679KB	—	9.00	18.00	42.50	90.00	—
1681KB	—	9.00	18.00	42.50	90.00	—
1682KB	—	9.00	18.00	42.50	90.00	—
1684KB	—	9.00	18.00	42.50	90.00	—
1685KB	—	9.00	18.00	42.50	90.00	—
1686KB	—	9.00	18.00	42.50	90.00	—
1687KB	—	9.00	18.00	42.50	90.00	—
1689KB	—	9.00	18.00	42.50	90.00	—
1690KB	—	9.00	18.00	42.50	90.00	—
1691KB	—	9.00	18.00	42.50	90.00	—
1692KB	—	9.00	18.00	42.50	90.00	—
1693KB	—	9.00	18.00	42.50	90.00	—
1695KB	—	9.00	18.00	42.50	90.00	—
1696KB	—	9.00	18.00	42.50	90.00	—
1697KB	—	9.00	18.00	42.50	90.00	—
1699KB	—	9.00	18.00	42.50	90.00	—

KM# 230 DUARIUS

Billon **Obv:** Crowned arms divide C-H in inner circle **Rev:** DVARI/ US/ 1695

Date	Mintage	VG	F	VF	XF	Unc
1695CH	—	12.00	22.50	46.00	95.00	—

KM# 229 DUARIUS

Silver **Obv:** Crowned arms divide K-B in inner circle **Rev:** Madonna and child on right above value and date **Note:** Varities exist

Date	Mintage	VG	F	VF	XF	Unc
1695KB	—	12.00	22.50	46.00	95.00	—
1696KB	—	12.00	22.50	46.00	95.00	—
1697KB	—	12.00	22.50	46.00	95.00	—
1698KB	—	12.00	22.50	46.00	95.00	—
1699KB	—	12.00	22.50	46.00	95.00	—

KM# 243 DUARIUS

Billon **Ruler:** Leopold I **Obv:** Crowned arms divide K-B **Rev:** Madonna and child above value and date

Date	Mintage	VG	F	VF	XF	Unc
1699KB	—	12.00	22.50	46.00	90.00	—
1700KB	—	12.00	22.50	46.00	90.00	—

KM# 244 DUARIUS

Billon

Date	Mintage	VG	F	VF	XF	Unc
1699CH	—	17.00	40.25	80.00	175	—

KM# 7 DENAR

Silver **Obv:** Shield of arms **Rev:** Madonna and child divide N-B, date in legend

Date	Mintage	VG	F	VF	XF	Unc
1601NB	—	9.00	17.00	42.50	85.00	—

MB# 260 DENAR

Silver **Ruler:** Rudolf II **Obv:** 4-fold arms with central shield of Austria **Obv. Legend:** RVD • II • RO • I • S • AV • G • H • B • R • **Rev:** Madonna and child divide mintmarks, date in legend **Rev. Legend:** PATR • (date) HVNG • **Note:** Varieties exist. Known struck on thick flan for years 1581-Z, 1585-6, 1588-94, 1596-7, 1600, 1601 with weights 1.80-6.96g (H-1052).

Date	Mintage	VG	F	VF	XF	Unc
1601KB	—	9.00	17.00	40.00	65.00	—
160ZKB	—	9.00	17.00	40.00	65.00	—

KM# 16 DENAR

Billon **Obv:** Shield of arms in inner circle, small letters in legend **Rev:** Madonna and child divide K-B, date in legend

Date	Mintage	VG	F	VF	XF	Unc
1602KB	—	8.00	17.00	35.00	65.00	—
1603KB	—	8.00	17.00	35.00	65.00	—
1604KB	—	8.00	17.00	35.00	65.00	—
1605KB	—	8.00	17.00	35.00	65.00	—
1606KB	—	8.00	17.00	35.00	65.00	—
1607KB	—	8.00	17.00	35.00	65.00	—
1608KB	—	8.00	17.00	35.00	65.00	—

KM# 23 DENAR

Billon **Obv:** Crowned arms divide K-B in inner circle, date in legend **Rev:** Radiant Madonna and child in inner circle

Date	Mintage	VG	F	VF	XF	Unc
1609KB	—	8.00	17.00	50.00	65.00	—
1610KB	—	8.00	17.00	50.00	65.00	—
1611KB	—	8.00	17.00	50.00	65.00	—

KM# 32 DENAR

Billon **Obv:** Long shield

Date	Mintage	VG	F	VF	XF	Unc
1611	—	8.00	17.00	35.00	65.00	—
1612	—	8.00	17.00	35.00	65.00	—
1613	—	8.00	17.00	35.00	65.00	—

KM# 40.1 DENAR

Billon **Obv:** Shield of arms divides K-B, titles of Matthias **Rev:** Withour rays, date in legend

Date	Mintage	VG	F	VF	XF	Unc
ND	—	6.00	14.00	22.50	48.00	—
1613KB	—	6.00	14.00	22.50	48.00	—
1614KB	—	6.00	14.00	22.50	48.00	—
1615KB	—	6.00	14.00	22.50	48.00	—
1616KB	—	6.00	14.00	22.50	48.00	—
1617KB	—	6.00	14.00	22.50	48.00	—
1618KB	—	6.00	14.00	22.50	48.00	—
1619KB	21,490,000	6.00	14.00	22.50	48.00	—
1620KB	17,315,000	6.00	14.00	22.50	48.00	—

KM# 43.1 DENAR

Silver **Obv:** Shield of arms divides N-B in inner circle, date in legend, titles as king **Rev:** Madonna and child

Date	Mintage	VG	F	VF	XF	Unc
1614NB	—	6.00	14.00	22.50	48.00	—

KM# 40.2 DENAR

Billon **Note:** Thick planchet.

Date	Mintage	VG	F	VF	XF	Unc
1615 Rare	—	—	—	—	—	—
1616 Rare	—	—	—	—	—	—
1619 Rare	—	—	—	—	—	—

KM# 54 DENAR

Silver **Rev:** Madonna and child in inner circle **Note:** Title as emperor. Varieties exist.

Date	Mintage	VG	F	VF	XF	Unc
1615	—	6.00	14.00	22.50	48.00	—
1616	—	6.00	14.00	22.50	48.00	—
1617	—	6.00	14.00	22.50	48.00	—
1618	—	—	—	—	—	—
1619	—	—	—	—	—	—

KM# 63 DENAR

Billon **Obv:** Hungarian arms cover entire inner circle

Date	Mintage	VG	F	VF	XF	Unc
1619	21,490,000	6.00	14.00	22.50	48.00	—
1620	17,315,000	6.00	14.00	22.50	48.00	—
1621	—	6.00	14.00	22.50	48.00	—
1622	—	6.00	14.00	22.50	48.00	—
1623	—	6.00	14.00	22.50	48.00	—
1624	—	6.00	14.00	22.50	48.00	—
1625	—	6.00	14.00	22.50	48.00	—

KM# A63 DENAR

Billon **Note:** Mule. KM#63 and Denar of Transylvania.

Date	Mintage	VG	F	VF	XF	Unc
1621	—	—	—	—	—	—

KM# 80 DENAR

Billon **Obv:** Shield of arms in inner circle **Rev:** Madonna and child, date in legend **Note:** Varieties exist.

Date	Mintage	VG	F	VF	XF	Unc
1623	—	6.00	14.00	22.50	48.00	—
1623 PP	—	6.00	14.00	22.50	48.00	—
1624 PP	—	6.00	14.00	22.50	48.00	—

KM# 88 DENAR

Billon **Obv:** Arms divide K-B, date above, in inner circle

Date	Mintage	VG	F	VF	XF	Unc
1625KB	—	6.00	14.00	22.50	48.00	—
1626KB	—	6.00	14.00	22.50	48.00	—
1627KB	—	6.00	14.00	22.50	48.00	—
1628KB	—	6.00	14.00	22.50	48.00	—
1629KB	—	6.00	14.00	22.50	48.00	—
1630KB	—	6.00	14.00	22.50	48.00	—

KM# 95 DENAR

Billon **Rev:** Date in legend

Date	Mintage	VG	F	VF	XF	Unc
1630	34,049,000	6.00	14.00	22.50	48.00	—
1631	16,165,000	6.00	14.00	22.50	48.00	—
1632	10,980,000	6.00	14.00	22.50	48.00	—
1633	11,360,000	6.00	14.00	22.50	48.00	—
1634	—	6.00	14.00	22.50	48.00	—
1635	8,320,000	6.00	14.00	22.50	48.00	—
1636	—	6.00	14.00	22.50	48.00	—
1637	—	6.00	14.00	22.50	48.00	—

KM# 99 DENAR

Silver **Note:** Titles of Ferdinand II. Varieties exist.

Date	Mintage	VG	F	VF	XF	Unc
1631	—	6.00	12.50	22.50	48.00	—
1632	—	6.00	12.50	22.50	48.00	—
1633	—	6.00	12.50	22.50	48.00	—
1634	—	6.00	12.50	22.50	48.00	—
1635	—	6.00	12.50	22.50	48.00	—

KM# 109 DENAR

Billon **Note:** Posthumous issue.

Date	Mintage	VG	F	VF	XF	Unc
1638	—	—	—	—	—	—

KM# 110 DENAR

Silver **Obv:** Shield of arms in inner circle **Rev:** Madonna and child in inner circle, date in legend

Date	Mintage	VG	F	VF	XF	Unc
1638	12,203,000	7.00	17.00	35.00	65.00	—
1639	11,862,000	7.00	17.00	35.00	65.00	—
1640	8,058,000	7.00	17.00	35.00	65.00	—
1641	6,731,000	7.00	17.00	35.00	65.00	—
1642	4,140,000	7.00	17.00	35.00	65.00	—
1643	3,876,000	7.00	17.00	35.00	65.00	—
1644	—	7.00	17.00	35.00	65.00	—
1645	—	7.00	17.00	35.00	65.00	—
1646	—	7.00	17.00	35.00	65.00	—
1647	—	7.00	17.00	35.00	65.00	—
1648	649,000	7.00	17.00	35.00	65.00	—
1649	1,047,000	7.00	17.00	35.00	65.00	—
1650	1,365,000	7.00	17.00	35.00	65.00	—
1651	1,221,000	7.00	17.00	35.00	65.00	—
1652	—	7.00	17.00	35.00	65.00	—
1653	772,000	7.00	17.00	35.00	65.00	—
1654	613,000	7.00	17.00	35.00	65.00	—
1655	—	7.00	17.00	35.00	65.00	—
1656	72,000	7.00	17.00	35.00	65.00	—
1657	58,000	7.00	17.00	35.00	65.00	—
1658	62,000	7.00	17.00	35.00	65.00	—
1659	—	—	—	—	—	—

KM# 125 DENAR

Silver **Obv:** Crowned oval arms in inner circle **Rev:** Radiant Madonna and child, date in legend

Date	Mintage	VG	F	VF	XF	Unc
1640	—	—	—	—	—	—

KM# 144 DENAR

Silver **Note:** Posthumous issue.

Date	Mintage	VG	F	VF	XF	Unc
1658KB	—	—	—	—	—	—
1659KB	—	—	—	—	—	—

KM# 152 DENAR

Billon **Obv:** Shield divides K-B in inner circle **Rev:** Madonna and child in inner circle, date in legend **Note:** Varieties exist.

Date	Mintage	VG	F	VF	XF	Unc
1659	61,000	7.00	17.00	35.00	65.00	—
1660	—	7.00	17.00	35.00	65.00	—
1661	—	7.00	17.00	35.00	65.00	—
1662	—	7.00	17.00	35.00	65.00	—
1674	—	7.00	17.00	35.00	65.00	—
1675	1,464,000	7.00	17.00	35.00	65.00	—
1676	—	7.00	17.00	35.00	65.00	—
1677	1,520,000	7.00	17.00	35.00	65.00	—
1678	1,459,000	7.00	17.00	35.00	65.00	—
1679	1,647,000	7.00	17.00	35.00	65.00	—
1680	1,652,000	7.00	17.00	35.00	65.00	—
1681	1,650,000	7.00	17.00	35.00	65.00	—
1682	—	7.00	17.00	35.00	65.00	—
1683	—	7.00	17.00	35.00	65.00	—

KM# 174 DENAR

Billon **Obv:** Crown above arms **Rev:** Date in legend

Date	Mintage	VG	F	VF	XF	Unc
1662	—	7.00	17.00	35.00	65.00	—
1663	340,000	7.00	17.00	35.00	65.00	—
1664	313,000	7.00	17.00	35.00	65.00	—
1665	174,000	7.00	17.00	35.00	65.00	—
1666	63,000	7.00	17.00	35.00	65.00	—
1667	81,000	7.00	17.00	35.00	65.00	—
1668	137,000	7.00	17.00	35.00	65.00	—
1670	152,000	7.00	17.00	35.00	65.00	—
1671	125,000	7.00	17.00	35.00	65.00	—
1672	143,000	7.00	17.00	35.00	65.00	—
1673	1,027,000	7.00	17.00	35.00	65.00	—
1683	1,809,000	7.00	17.00	35.00	65.00	—
1684	Inc. above	7.00	17.00	35.00	65.00	—
1685	1,428,000	7.00	17.00	35.00	65.00	—
1686	1,869,000	7.00	17.00	35.00	65.00	—
1687	2,055,000	7.00	17.00	35.00	65.00	—
1688	1,933,000	7.00	17.00	35.00	65.00	—
1689	1,676,000	7.00	17.00	35.00	65.00	—
1690	—	7.00	17.00	35.00	65.00	—
1691	1,733,000	7.00	17.00	35.00	65.00	—
1692	—	7.00	17.00	35.00	65.00	—
1693	2,385,000	7.00	17.00	35.00	65.00	—
1694	1,895,000	7.00	17.00	35.00	65.00	—
1695	1,501,000	7.00	17.00	35.00	65.00	—
1696	956,000	7.00	17.00	35.00	65.00	—

KM# 187 DENAR

Billon **Rev:** Head of Madonna divides date

Date	Mintage	VG	F	VF	XF	Unc
1673	—	7.00	17.00	35.00	65.00	—
1674	—	7.00	17.00	35.00	65.00	—
1675	1,464,000	7.00	17.00	35.00	65.00	—
1676	—	7.00	17.00	35.00	65.00	—
1677	—	7.00	17.00	35.00	65.00	—

KM# 221 DENAR

Silver **Ruler:** Leopold I **Obv:** Crowned arms divid N-B in inner circle **Rev:** Madonna and child in inner circle, date in legend

Date	Mintage	VG	F	VF	XF	Unc
1691NB	—	7.00	17.00	35.00	65.00	—
1693NB	—	7.00	17.00	35.00	65.00	—
1700NB	—	7.00	17.00	35.00	65.00	—

KM# 231 DENAR

Silver **Rev:** Date divided at top

Date	Mintage	VG	F	VF	XF	Unc
1695	—	7.00	17.00	35.00	65.00	—
1698	—	7.00	17.00	35.00	65.00	—
1699	—	7.00	17.00	35.00	65.00	—

MB# 264 GROSCHEN (4 DENAR)

Silver **Ruler:** Rudolf II **Obv:** Madonna and child divide mintmarks **Obv. Legend:** RVDOL • II • D • G • RO • IM • S • AV • GE • HV • BO • R • **Rev:** 4-fold arms with central shield of Austria, date at end of legend **Rev. Legend:** MONETA • NOVA • ANNO • DOMINI • **Note:** H#1048. Varieties exist. Known struck on thick flan for years 1584 and 1589, with weights of 24.75 grams and 10.00 grams (H-1047).

Date	Mintage	VG	F	VF	XF	Unc
160Z	—	22.50	46.00	75.00	115	—
1603	—	22.50	46.00	75.00	115	—
1604	—	22.50	46.00	75.00	115	—
1605	—	22.50	46.00	75.00	115	—
1606	—	22.50	46.00	75.00	115	—
1607	—	22.50	46.00	75.00	115	—

KM# 81 GROSCHEN OF 9 DENARE

Silver **Obv:** Ferdinand II

Date	Mintage	VG	F	VF	XF	Unc
1622	—	—	—	—	—	—
1623	—	17.00	34.50	60.00	110	—

KM# 232 POLTURA

Copper **Ruler:** Leopold I **Obv:** Monogram divides date **Rev:** Crowned value within branches **Note:** Without mint mark. City issue. Varieties exist.

Date	Mintage	VG	F	VF	XF	Unc
1695	1,646,000	9.00	17.00	35.00	70.00	—
1696	1,761,000	9.00	17.00	35.00	70.00	—
1697	2,296,000	7.00	15.00	30.00	65.00	—
1698	2,445,000	7.00	15.00	30.00	65.00	—
1699	2,692,000	7.00	15.00	30.00	65.00	—
1700	1,703,000	7.00	15.00	30.00	65.00	—

KM# 245.1 POLTURA

Silver **Ruler:** Leopold I **Obv:** Laureate bust right in inner circle, initials on truncation **Obv. Legend:** LEOPOLD • D • G • ... **Rev:** Madonna and child above value and date

Date	Mintage	VG	F	VF	XF	Unc
1696	—	12.00	20.00	55.00	85.00	—
1697	—	12.00	20.00	55.00	85.00	—
1699NB ICB	—	12.00	20.00	55.00	85.00	—
1700NB ICB	—	12.00	20.00	55.00	85.00	—
1700NB	—	12.00	20.00	55.00	85.00	—

KM# 256 3 POLTUREN

Copper **Ruler:** Leopold I **Obv:** Crowned L in branches **Rev:** SC monogram divides date **Note:** Schemnitz issue.

Date	Mintage	VG	F	VF	XF	Unc
1695	—	20.00	40.00	80.00	170	—
1696	—	20.00	40.00	80.00	170	—
1697	—	20.00	40.00	80.00	170	—
1699	—	20.00	40.00	80.00	170	—
1700	—	20.00	40.00	80.00	170	—

KM# 227 KRAJCZAR

Silver **Obv:** Small laureate bust of Leopold I right in inner circle, value below **Rev:** Madonna and child divide N-B in inner circle, date divided at top

Date	Mintage	VG	F	VF	XF	Unc
1694NB	—	7.00	14.00	30.00	60.00	—
1695NB	—	7.00	14.00	30.00	60.00	—

KM# 233 KRAJCZAR

Silver **Obv:** Large laureate bust of Leopold I right in inner circle, value below **Rev:** Madonna and child divide C-M in inner circle, date in legend **Note:** Varieties exist.

Date	Mintage	VG	F	VF	XF	Unc
1695CM	—	7.00	14.00	30.00	60.00	—
1697CM	—	7.00	14.00	30.00	60.00	—
1698CM	—	7.00	14.00	30.00	60.00	—
1699CM	—	7.00	14.00	30.00	60.00	—

KM# 234 KRAJCZAR

Silver **Rev:** Date in legend **Note:** Varieties exist.

Date	Mintage	VG	F	VF	XF	Unc
1695NB PO	—	7.00	14.00	30.00	60.00	—
1699NB ICB	—	7.00	14 .00	30.00	60.00	—

KM# 235 KRAJCZAR

Silver **Obv:** Laureate bust of Leopold I right in inner circle, value below **Rev:** Radiant Madonna and child in inner circle, Madonna's head divides date **Note:** Varieties exist.

Date	Mintage	VG	F	VF	XF	Unc
1695CH	—	7.00	14.00	30.00	60.00	—
1698CH	—	7.00	14.00	30.00	60.00	—
1699CH	—	7.00	14.00	30.00	60.00	—
1700CH	—	7.00	14.00	30.00	60.00	—

KM# 241 KRAJCZAR

Silver **Obv:** Large bust **Note:** Varieties exist.

Date	Mintage	VG	F	VF	XF	Unc
1698NB	—	7.00	14.00	30.00	60.00	—
1698NB ICB	—	7.00	14.00	30.00	60.00	—

KM# 188 2 KRAJCZAR

Silver **Obv:** Laureate bust of Leopold I right in inner circle, value below **Rev:** Madonna and child divide K-B in inner circle, date divided at top

Date	Mintage	VG	F	VF	XF	Unc
1673KB	—	12.00	22.50	45.00	80.00	—
1674KB	—	12.00	22.50	45.00	80.00	—

KM# 8 3 KRAJCZAR (Groschen)

Silver **Obv:** Madonna and child diviede N-B in inner circle **Obv. Legend:** RVDOL • II • D • G • RO • IM • S • AV • GE • HVN • B • R • **Rev:** 4-fold arms with central shield of Austria in baroque frame, date at end of legend **Rev. Legend:** MONETA • NOVA • ANNO • DOMINI •

Date	Mintage	VG	F	VF	XF	Unc
1601	—	22.50	46.00	75.00	125	—

KM# 19 3 KRAJCZAR (Groschen)

Silver **Obv:** Retrograde N in mint mark

Date	Mintage	VG	F	VF	XF	Unc
1604NB	—	22.50	45.00	75.00	125	—

KM# 24 3 KRAJCZAR (Groschen)

Silver **Obv:** Crowned arms divide K-B in inner circle **Rev:** Radiant Madonna and child in inner circle, date in legend **Note:** Varieties exist.

Date	Mintage	VG	F	VF	XF	Unc
1609KB	—	20.00	40.00	65.00	110	—
1610KB	—	20.00	40.00	65.00	110	—
1611KB	—	20.00	40.00	65.00	110	—
1612KB	—	20.00	40.00	65.00	110	—
1613KB	—	20.00	40.00	65.00	110	—

KM# 47 3 KRAJCZAR (Groschen)

Silver **Obv:** Without crown above arms **Note:** Varieties exist.

Date	Mintage	VG	F	VF	XF	Unc
1614NB	—	22.50	46.00	75.00	125	—
1615NB	—	22.50	46.00	75.00	125	—
1616NB	—	22.50	46.00	75.00	125	—
1617NB	—	22.50	46.00	75.00	125	—
1618NB	—	22.50	46.00	75.00	125	—
1619NB	—	22.50	46.00	75.00	125	—

KM# 44.1 3 KRAJCZAR (Groschen)

Silver **Obv:** Shield of arms divides K-B in inner circle **Rev:** Madonna and child without rays in inner circle, date in legend

Date	Mintage	VG	F	VF	XF	Unc
1614KB	—	22.50	46.00	75.00	125	—
1615KB	—	22.50	46.00	75.00	125	—

KM# 45 3 KRAJCZAR (Groschen)

Silver **Obv:** Crowned arms divides N-B in inner circle **Rev:** Radiant Madonna and child in inner circle, date in legend

Date	Mintage	VG	F	VF	XF	Unc
1614NB	—	22.50	46.00	75.00	125	—
1615NB	—	22.50	46.00	75.00	125	—

KM# 46 3 KRAJCZAR (Groschen)

Silver **Rev:** Madonna and child without rays in inner circle, date in legend

Date	Mintage	VG	F	VF	XF	Unc
1614	—	22.50	46.00	75.00	125	—

KM# 44.2 3 KRAJCZAR (Groschen)

Silver **Note:** Thick planchet.

Date	Mintage	VG	F	VF	XF	Unc
1615	—	—	—	—	—	—

KM# 82 3 KRAJCZAR (Groschen)

Silver **Obv:** Shield of arms in inner circle **Rev:** Madonna and child in inner circle, date in legend

Date	Mintage	VG	F	VF	XF	Unc
1623CH PP	—	22.50	46.00	75.00	125	—
1624CH PP	—	22.50	46.00	75.00	125	—
1624(d)	—	22.50	46.00	75.00	125	—

KM# 96.1 3 KRAJCZAR (Groschen)

Silver **Obv:** Crowned arms with notched sides divide N-B in inner circle **Rev:** Radiant Madonna and child in inner circle, date in legend

Date	Mintage	VG	F	VF	XF	Unc
1627NB	—	22.50	46.00	75.00	125	—
1630NB	—	22.50	46.00	75.00	125	—

KM# 96.2 3 KRAJCZAR (Groschen)

Silver **Obv:** Crowned arms with straight sides **Note:** Varieties exist.

Date	Mintage	VG	F	VF	XF	Unc
1630	—	22.50	46.00	75.00	125	—
1631	—	22.50	46.00	75.00	125	—

KM# 143 3 KRAJCZAR (Groschen)

Silver **Obv:** Laureate bust of Ferdinand III right in inner circle, value below **Rev:** Crowned double-headed eagle in inner circle, date in legend

Date	Mintage	VG	F	VF	XF	Unc
1657KB	—	22.50	46.00	75.00	125	—

KM# 162 3 KRAJCZAR (Groschen)

Silver **Obv:** Laureate bust of Leopold I right in inner circle, value below **Rev:** Radiant Madonna and child divide K-B in inner circle, date at top **Note:** Varieties exist.

Date	Mintage	VG	F	VF	XF	Unc
1661KB	—	8.00	17.00	35.00	75.00	—
1662KB	—	8.00	17.00	35.00	75.00	—
1663KB	—	8.00	17.00	35.00	75.00	—

KM# 163 3 KRAJCZAR (Groschen)

Silver **Rev:** Date in legend **Note:** Varieties exist.

Date	Mintage	VG	F	VF	XF	Unc
1661KB	—	8.00	17.00	35.00	75.00	—
1665KB	—	8.00	17.00	35.00	75.00	—
1666KB	—	8.00	17.00	35.00	75.00	—
1667KB	—	8.00	17.00	35.00	75.00	—
1668KB	—	8.00	17.00	35.00	75.00	—
1670KB	—	8.00	17.00	35.00	75.00	—
1672KB	—	8.00	17.00	35.00	75.00	—
1673KB	—	8.00	17.00	35.00	75.00	—
1674KB	—	8.00	17.00	35.00	75.00	—
1675KB	—	8.00	17.00	35.00	75.00	—
1676KB	—	8.00	17.00	35.00	75.00	—
1677KB	—	8.00	17.00	35.00	75.00	—
1678KB	—	8.00	17.00	35.00	75.00	—
1679KB	—	8.00	17.00	35.00	75.00	—
1680KB	—	8.00	17.00	35.00	75.00	—
1681KB	—	8.00	17.00	35.00	75.00	—
1682KB	—	8.00	17.00	35.00	75.00	—
1683KB	—	8.00	17.00	35.00	75.00	—
1684KB	—	8.00	17.00	35.00	75.00	—
1685KB	—	8.00	17.00	35.00	75.00	—
1686KB	—	8.00	17.00	35.00	75.00	—
1687KB	—	8.00	17.00	35.00	75.00	—
1688KB	—	8.00	17.00	35.00	75.00	—
1689KB	—	8.00	17.00	35.00	75.00	—
1690KB	—	8.00	17.00	35.00	75.00	—
1691KB	—	8.00	17.00	35.00	75.00	—
1692KB	—	8.00	17.00	35.00	75.00	—
1693KB	—	8.00	17.00	35.00	75.00	—
1694KB	—	8.00	17.00	35.00	75.00	—
1695KB	—	8.00	17.00	35.00	75.00	—
1696KB	—	8.00	17.00	35.00	75.00	—

KM# 194 3 KRAJCZAR (Groschen)

Silver **Ruler:** Leopold I **Obv:** Laureate bust **Rev:** Date divided at top **Note:** Varieties exist.

Date	Mintage	VG	F	VF	XF	Unc
1675CH	—	8.00	17.00	35.00	75.00	—
1695CH	—	8.00	17.00	35.00	75.00	—
1696CH	—	8.00	17.00	35.00	75.00	—
1697CH	—	8.00	17.00	35.00	75.00	—
1698CH	—	8.00	17.00	35.00	75.00	—
1699CH	—	8.00	17.00	35.00	75.00	—

KM# 200 3 KRAJCZAR (Groschen)

Silver **Ruler:** Leopold I **Obv:** Bust right in inner circle **Obv. Legend:** LEOPOLDVS • D • G • ... **Rev:** Radiant Madonna and child divide N-B in inner circle, date in legend **Note:** Varieties exist.

Date	Mintage	VG	F	VF	XF	Unc
1677NB IS	—	8.00	17.00	35.00	75.00	—
1696NB	—	8.00	17.00	35.00	75.00	—
1698NB ICB	—	8.00	17.00	35.00	75.00	—
1699NB ICB	—	8.00	17.00	35.00	75.00	—

KM# 225 3 KRAJCZAR (Groschen)

Silver **Ruler:** Leopold I **Obv:** Bust right in inner circle **Obv. Legend:** LEOPOLD • D • G • R • ... **Rev:** Date divided at top **Note:** Varieties exist.

Date	Mintage	VG	F	VF	XF	Unc
1690NB PO	—	8.00	17.00	35.00	75.00	—
1693NB PO	—	8.00	17.00	35.00	75.00	—
1694NB PO	—	8.00	17.00	35.00	75.00	—
1695NB PO	—	8.00	17.00	35.00	75.00	—
1696NB PO	—	8.00	17.00	35.00	75.00	—
1697NB	—	8.00	17.00	35.00	75.00	—
1698NB PO	—	8.00	17.00	35.00	75.00	—
1699NB PO	—	8.00	17.00	35.00	75.00	—

KM# 236 3 KRAJCZAR (Groschen)

Silver **Ruler:** Leopold I **Obv:** Bust right within inner circle **Obv. Legend:** LEOPOLD • D • G • ... **Rev:** Radiant Madonna and child divides C-M in inner circle, date in legend **Note:** Varieties exist.

Date	Mintage	VG	F	VF	XF	Unc
1695CM	—	8.00	17.00	35.00	75.00	—
1696CM	—	8.00	17.00	35.00	75.00	—
1697CM	—	8.00	17.00	35.00	75.00	—
1698CM	—	8.00	17.00	35.00	75.00	—

KM# A236 3 KRAJCZAR (Groschen)
Silver **Rev:** Madonna with child on right

Date	Mintage	VG	F	VF	XF	Unc
1695NB PO	—	8.00	17.00	34.50	75.00	—
1696NB PO	—	8.00	17.00	34.50	75.00	—
1697NB PO	—	8.00	17.00	34.50	75.00	—
1698NB PO	—	8.00	17.00	34.50	75.00	—

KM# 164 6 KRAJCZAR
Silver **Ruler:** Leopold I **Obv:** Laureate bust right in inner circle, value below **Rev:** Radiant Madonna and child divide K-B in inner circle, date divided at top **Note:** Varieties exist.

Date	Mintage	VG	F	VF	XF	Unc
1661KB	—	9.00	20.00	40.00	80.00	—
1667KB	—	9.00	20.00	40.00	80.00	—
1668KB	—	9.00	20.00	40.00	80.00	—
1669/8KB	—	9.00	20.00	40.00	80.00	—
1669KB	—	9.00	20.00	40.00	80.00	—
1670KB	—	9.00	20.00	40.00	80.00	—
1671KB	—	9.00	20.00	40.00	80.00	—
1672KB	—	9.00	20.00	40.00	80.00	—
1673KB	—	9.00	20.00	40.00	80.00	—
1674KB	—	9.00	20.00	40.00	80.00	—
1681KB	—	9.00	20.00	40.00	80.00	—
1682KB	—	9.00	20.00	40.00	80.00	—

KM# 190 6 KRAJCZAR
Silver **Ruler:** Leopold I **Obv:** Bust right in inner circle **Obv. Legend:** LEOPOLDVS • D • G • R • ... **Rev:** Radiant Madonna and child divide N-B in inner circle **Rev. Legend:** PATRONA • HUNGARIÆ • **Note:** Varieties exist.

Date	Mintage	VG	F	VF	XF	Unc
1674NB LM	—	—	—	—	—	—
1676NB LM	—	9.00	20.00	45.00	85.00	—
1677NB IS	—	9.00	20.00	45.00	85.00	—
1677NB LM	—	9.00	20.00	45.00	85.00	—
1678NB IS	—	9.00	20.00	45.00	85.00	—
1680NB	—	9.00	20.00	45.00	85.00	—
1681NB	—	9.00	20.00	45.00	85.00	—
1684NB	—	9.00	20.00	45.00	85.00	—
1685NB PO/CR	—	9.00	20.00	45.00	85.00	—
1685NB PO	—	9.00	20.00	45.00	85.00	—
1686NB PO	—	9.00	20.00	45.00	85.00	—
1691NB PO	—	9.00	20.00	45.00	85.00	—
1692NB PO	—	9.00	20.00	45.00	85.00	—
1693NB PO	—	9.00	20.00	45.00	85.00	—
1694NB	—	9.00	20.00	45.00	85.00	—
1694NB PO	—	9.00	20.00	45.00	85.00	—

KM# 195 6 KRAJCZAR
Silver **Ruler:** Leopold I **Obv:** Bust laureate right **Note:** Varieties exist.

Date	Mintage	VG	F	VF	XF	Unc
1675(g)	—	9.00	20.00	40.00	80.00	—
1676(g)	—	9.00	20.00	40.00	80.00	—
1684(r)	—	9.00	20.00	40.00	80.00	—
1685(r)	—	9.00	20.00	40.00	80.00	—

KM# 165 15 KRAJCZAR
Silver **Ruler:** Leopold I **Obv:** Young laureate bust right in inner circle, value below **Rev:** Radiant Madonna and child above K-B in inner circle, date in legned

Date	Mintage	VG	F	VF	XF	Unc
1661KB	—	12.00	22.50	46.00	95.00	—

KM# 166 15 KRAJCZAR
Silver **Ruler:** Leopold I **Rev:** Madonna's head divides K-B

Date	Mintage	VG	F	VF	XF	Unc
1661KB	—	14.00	30.00	55.00	110	—

KM# 167 15 KRAJCZAR
Silver **Ruler:** Leopold I **Rev:** Date at top

Date	Mintage	VG	F	VF	XF	Unc
1661	—	12.00	22.50	46.00	95.00	—

KM# 175 15 KRAJCZAR
Silver **Ruler:** Leopold I **Obv:** Bust laureate right, legends on scroll **Rev:** Radiant Madonna and child, legends on scroll **Note:** Varieties exist.

Date	Mintage	VG	F	VF	XF	Unc
1661KB	—	12.00	22.50	46.00	95.00	—
1662KB	—	12.00	22.50	46.00	95.00	—
1663KB	—	12.00	22.50	46.00	95.00	—
1664KB	—	12.00	22.50	46.00	95.00	—
1665KB	—	12.00	22.50	46.00	95.00	—
1667KB	—	12.00	22.50	46.00	95.00	—
1674KB	—	12.00	22.50	46.00	95.00	—
1675/4KB	—	12.00	22.50	46.00	95.00	—
1675KB	—	12.00	22.50	46.00	95.00	—
1676KB	—	12.00	22.50	46.00	95.00	—
1677KB	—	12.00	22.50	46.00	95.00	—
1678KB	—	12.00	22.50	46.00	95.00	—
1679KB	—	12.00	22.50	46.00	95.00	—
1680KB	—	12.00	22.50	46.00	95.00	—
1681KB	—	12.00	22.50	46.00	95.00	—
1682KB	—	12.00	22.50	46.00	95.00	—
1683KB	—	12.00	22.50	46.00	95.00	—
1684KB	—	12.00	22.50	46.00	95.00	—
1685KB	—	12.00	22.50	46.00	95.00	—
1686/5KB	—	12.00	22.50	46.00	95.00	—
1686KB	—	12.00	22.50	46.00	95.00	—

KM# 179 15 KRAJCZAR
Silver **Ruler:** Leopold I **Note:** Klippe.

Date	Mintage	VG	F	VF	XF	Unc
1664	—	—	—	—	—	—

KM# 181 15 KRAJCZAR
Silver **Ruler:** Leopold I **Rev:** Madonna's head divides date, solid inner circles

Date	Mintage	VG	F	VF	XF	Unc
1669	—	—	—	—	—	—
1696	—	—	—	—	—	—

KM# 191 15 KRAJCZAR
Silver **Ruler:** Leopold I **Obv:** Bust laureate right **Rev:** Radiant Madonna with child held on left

Date	Mintage	VG	F	VF	XF	Unc
1674NB LM	—	12.00	22.50	46.00	95.00	—
1675NB LM	—	12.00	22.50	46.00	95.00	—
1676NB LM	—	12.00	22.50	46.00	95.00	—
1677NB LM	—	12.00	22.50	46.00	95.00	—
1677NB IS	—	12.00	22.50	46.00	95.00	—
1678NB IS	—	12.00	22.50	46.00	95.00	—
1679NB	—	12.00	22.50	46.00	95.00	—
1680NB	—	12.00	22.50	46.00	95.00	—
1682NB	—	12.00	22.50	46.00	95.00	—
1683NB PO	—	12.00	22.50	46.00	95.00	—
1683NB	—	12.00	22.50	46.00	95.00	—
1684NB PO	—	12.00	22.50	46.00	95.00	—
1684NB	—	12.00	22.50	46.00	95.00	—
1685NB PO	—	12.00	22.50	46.00	95.00	—
1686NB PO	—	12.00	22.50	46.00	95.00	—
1687NB PO	—	12.00	22.50	46.00	95.00	—
1688NB PO	—	12.00	22.50	46.00	95.00	—
1689NB PO	—	12.00	22.50	46.00	95.00	—
1690NB PO	—	12.00	22.50	46.00	95.00	—
1691NB PO	—	12.00	22.50	46.00	95.00	—
1694NB PO	—	12.00	22.50	46.00	95.00	—
1695NB PO	—	12.00	22.50	46.00	95.00	—

KM# 192 15 KRAJCZAR
Silver **Ruler:** Leopold I **Obv:** Bust laureate right **Rev:** Radiant Madonna with child **Note:** Varieties exist.

Date	Mintage	VG	F	VF	XF	Unc
1674(g)	—	12.00	22.50	46.00	95.00	—
1675(g)	—	12.00	22.50	46.00	95.00	—
1676(g)	—	12.00	22.50	46.00	95.00	—
1695CH	—	12.00	22.50	46.00	95.00	—
1696CH CHS	—	12.00	22.50	46.00	95.00	—
1696CH	—	12.00	22.50	46.00	95.00	—

KM# 208 15 KRAJCZAR
Silver **Ruler:** Leopold I **Obv:** Bust laureate right, legend in scroll **Rev:** Radiant Madonna and child, legend in scroll **Note:** Varieties exist.

Date	Mintage	VG	F	VF	XF	Unc
1685KB	—	12.00	22.50	46.00	95.00	—
1686KB	—	12.00	22.50	46.00	95.00	—
1687KB	—	12.00	22.50	46.00	95.00	—
1688KB	—	12.00	22.50	46.00	95.00	—
1689KB	—	12.00	22.50	46.00	95.00	—
1690KB	—	12.00	22.50	46.00	95.00	—

KM# 209 15 KRAJCZAR
Silver **Ruler:** Leopold I **Obv:** Bust laureate right, solid inner circle **Rev:** Radiant Madonna and child, solid inner circle, date in legend **Note:** Varieties exist.

Date	Mintage	VG	F	VF	XF	Unc
1685	—	12.00	22.50	46.00	95.00	—
1690	—	12.00	22.50	46.00	95.00	—
1691	—	12.00	22.50	46.00	95.00	—
1692	—	12.00	22.50	46.00	95.00	—
1693	—	12.00	22.50	46.00	95.00	—
1694	—	12.00	22.50	46.00	95.00	—
1695/4	—	12.00	22.50	46.00	95.00	—
1695	—	12.00	22.50	46.00	95.00	—
1696	—	12.00	22.50	46.00	95.00	—

KM# 237 15 KRAJCZAR
Silver **Ruler:** Leopold I **Obv:** Laureate bust right in inner circle, value below **Rev:** Radiant Madonna and child divides C-M in inner circle, date in legend **Note:** Varieties exist.

Date	Mintage	VG	F	VF	XF	Unc
1695CM	—	—	—	—	—	—
1696CM	—	—	—	—	—	—

KM# A192 15 KRAJCZAR
Silver **Ruler:** Leopold I **Obv:** Bust laureate right **Rev:** Madonna with child on right **Note:** Varieties exist.

Date	Mintage	VG	F	VF	XF	Unc
1696NB PO	—	12.00	22.50	46.00	95.00	—
1696NB	—	12.00	22.50	46.00	95.00	—
1697NB PO	—	12.00	22.50	46.00	95.00	—
1698NB PO	—	12.00	22.50	46.00	95.00	—
1699NB ICB	—	12.00	22.50	46.00	95.00	—

MB# 266 1/4 THALER (18 KREUZER)

Silver **Ruler:** Rudolf II **Obv:** Armored bust right, small 4-fold arms and small Madonna and child divide legend **Obv. Legend:** + RVDOL • II • - D • G • RO • IM • S • AV • GER • HV - BO • REX • **Rev:** Crowned imperial eagle holding sword and scepter, imperial orb on breast, date at end of legend **Rev. Legend:** ARC • DVX • AVS • DVX • BVR • MAR • MO • **Note:** H#1046. Varieties exist.

Date	Mintage	VG	F	VF	XF	Unc
1601KB	—	60.00	115	230	400	—
160ZKB	—	60.00	115	230	400	—
1603KB	—	60.00	115	230	400	—
1604KB	—	60.00	115	230	400	—
1607KB	—	60.00	115	230	400	—
1608KB	—	60.00	115	230	400	—

KM# 25 1/4 THALER

Silver **Ruler:** Matthias **Obv:** Crowned bust right in inner circle, designatus legend **Rev:** Crowned arms divide K-B in Order collar and inner circle, date in legend

Date	Mintage	VG	F	VF	XF	Unc
1609KB	—	60.00	115	230	400	—
1610KB	—	60.00	115	230	400	—
1611KB	—	60.00	115	230	400	—

KM# 33.1 1/4 THALER

Silver **Ruler:** Matthias **Obv:** Crowned bust right **Note:** Legend as King of Hungary and Bohemia

Date	Mintage	VG	F	VF	XF	Unc
1611KB	—	60.00	115	230	400	—
1612KB	—	60.00	115	230	400	—
1613KB	—	60.00	115	230	400	—

KM# 33.2 1/4 THALER

Silver **Ruler:** Matthias **Note:** Thick planchet.

Date	Mintage	VG	F	VF	XF	Unc
1612	—	—	—	—	—	—

KM# 48 1/4 THALER

Silver **Ruler:** Matthias **Obv:** Laureate bust right in inner circle **Rev:** Crowned imperial eagle in inner circle, date in legend **Note:** Varieties exist.

Date	Mintage	VG	F	VF	XF	Unc
1614KB	—	46.00	100	190	350	—
1616KB	—	46.00	100	190	350	—
1617KB	—	46.00	100	190	350	—
1618KB	—	46.00	100	190	350	—
1619KB	—	46.00	100	190	350	—

KM# 71 1/4 THALER

Silver **Ruler:** Ferdinand II **Obv:** Laureate bust right

Date	Mintage	VG	F	VF	XF	Unc
1620KB	—	50.00	105	200	350	—
1622KB	—	50.00	105	200	350	—
1630KB	—	50.00	105	200	350	—
1631KB	—	50.00	105	200	350	—
1632KB	—	50.00	105	200	350	—
1633KB	—	50.00	105	200	350	—
1634KB	—	50.00	105	200	350	—
1635KB	—	50.00	105	200	350	—
1636KB	—	50.00	105	200	350	—
1637KB	—	50.00	105	200	350	—

KM# 70 1/4 THALER

Silver **Ruler:** Matthias **Obv:** Bust laureate right **Note:** Posthumous issue.

Date	Mintage	VG	F	VF	XF	Unc
1620	—	75.00	145	260	450	—

KM# 103 1/4 THALER

Silver **Ruler:** Ferdinand II **Obv:** Modified laureate bust right in inner circle

Date	Mintage	VG	F	VF	XF	Unc
1633	—	—	—	—	—	—
1634	—	—	—	—	—	—

KM# 116 1/4 THALER

Silver **Ruler:** Ferdinand III **Obv:** Laureate bust right **Note:** Varieties exist.

Date	Mintage	VG	F	VF	XF	Unc
1639	—	46.00	90.00	175	300	—
1640	—	46.00	90.00	175	300	—
1641	—	46.00	90.00	175	300	—
1642	—	46.00	90.00	175	300	—
1643	—	46.00	90.00	175	300	—
1644	—	46.00	90.00	175	300	—
1645	—	46.00	90.00	175	300	—
1647	—	46.00	90.00	175	300	—
1648	—	46.00	90.00	175	300	—
1649	—	46.00	90.00	175	300	—
1650	—	46.00	90.00	175	300	—
1651	—	46.00	90.00	175	300	—
1652	—	46.00	90.00	175	300	—
1653	—	46.00	90.00	175	300	—
1654	—	46.00	90.00	175	300	—
1655	—	46.00	90.00	175	300	—
1656	—	46.00	90.00	175	300	—
1657	—	46.00	90.00	175	300	—

KM# 130 1/4 THALER

Silver **Ruler:** Ferdinand III **Obv:** Laureate bust right in inner circle **Rev:** Crowned imperial eagle with N-B divided at bottom in inner circle, date in legend

Date	Mintage	VG	F	VF	XF	Unc
1643NB	—	—	—	—	—	—

KM# 145 1/4 THALER

Silver **Ruler:** Ferdinand III **Obv:** Laureate bust right **Note:** Posthumous issue.

Date	Mintage	VG	F	VF	XF	Unc
1658KB	—	22.50	46.00	90.00	180	—
1659KB	—	22.50	46.00	90.00	180	—

KM# 153 1/4 THALER

Silver **Ruler:** Leopold I **Obv:** Young laureate bust right in inner circle **Rev:** Crowned imperial eagle in inner circle, date in legend **Note:** Varieties exist.

Date	Mintage	VG	F	VF	XF	Unc
1659	—	22.50	46.00	90.00	180	—
1660	—	22.50	46.00	90.00	180	—
1661	—	22.50	46.00	90.00	180	—

KM# 176 1/4 THALER

Silver **Ruler:** Leopold I **Obv:** Laureate bust right, date below, legend on scroll **Rev:** Legend on scroll

Date	Mintage	VG	F	VF	XF	Unc
1662	—	22.50	46.00	90.00	180	—
1664	—	22.50	46.00	90.00	180	—
1665	—	22.50	46.00	90.00	180	—
1677	—	22.50	46.00	90.00	180	—
1687	—	22.50	46.00	90.00	180	—

KM# 213 1/4 THALER

Silver **Ruler:** Leopold I **Obv:** Laureate bust right **Rev:** Imperial eagle, crown divides date **Note:** Varieties exist.

Date	Mintage	VG	F	VF	XF	Unc
1688KB	—	22.50	46.00	90.00	180	—
1693KB	—	22.50	46.00	90.00	180	—

KM# 228 1/4 THALER

Silver **Ruler:** Leopold I **Obv:** Laureate bust right flanked by arms and Madonna, value below, all in rhombus **Obv. Legend:** LEOPOLD • - D: G: ... **Rev:** Crowned imperial eagle in diamond, date in legend **Rev. Legend:** ARCHID • - AVST • DVX • ... **Note:** Varieties exist.

Date	Mintage	VG	F	VF	XF	Unc
1694KB	—	14.00	30.00	60.00	125	—
1695KB	—	14.00	30.00	60.00	125	—
1696KB	—	14.00	30.00	60.00	125	—
1698KB	—	14.00	30.00	60.00	125	—
1699KB	—	14.00	30.00	60.00	125	—
1700KB	—	14.00	30.00	60.00	125	—

KM# 238 1/4 THALER

Silver **Ruler:** Leopold I **Rev:** Radiant Madonna and child divided N-B in diamond, date in legend

Date	Mintage	VG	F	VF	XF	Unc
1695NB PO	—	14.00	30.00	60.00	120	—

KM# 250 1/4 THALER

Silver **Ruler:** Leopold I **Obv:** Crowned arms and Madonna and child added at sides of bust **Rev:** Crowned imperial eagle divides N-B in rhombus, date divided at top **Note:** Varieties exist.

Date	Mintage	VG	F	VF	XF	Unc
1700NB	—	14.00	30.00	60.00	125	—

MB# 268 1/2 THALER (36 KREUZER)

Silver **Ruler:** Rudolf II **Obv:** Armored bust right, small 4-fold arms and small Madonna and child divide legend **Obv. Legend:** + RVDOL • II • - D • G • RO • IM • S • AV • GER • HV - BO • REX • **Rev:** Crowned imperial eagle holding sword and scepter, imperial orb on breast, date at end of legend **Rev. Legend:** ARCHI • DVX • AVS • DVX • BVRG • MAR • MORA • **Note:** H#1043. Varieties exist.

Date	Mintage	VG	F	VF	XF	Unc
1601KB	—	75.00	145	260	425	—
1602KB	—	75.00	145	260	425	—
1603KB	—	75.00	145	260	425	—
1604KB	—	75.00	145	260	425	—
1605KB	—	75.00	145	260	425	—
1607KB	—	75.00	145	260	425	—
1608KB	—	75.00	145	260	425	—

KM# 29 1/2 THALER

Silver **Ruler:** Matthias **Note:** Klippe

Date	Mintage	VG	F	VF	XF	Unc
1608NB	—	85.00	175	290	500	—

KM# 26 1/2 THALER
Silver **Ruler:** Matthias **Obv:** Crowned bust right in inner circle, designatus legend **Rev:** Crowned arms divide K-B in Order collar and inner circle, date in legend

Date	Mintage	VG	F	VF	XF	Unc
1609KB	—	75.00	145	260	425	—
1610KB	—	75.00	145	260	425	—
1611	—	75.00	145	260	425	—

KM# 38 1/2 THALER
Silver **Ruler:** Matthias **Obv:** Crowned bust right **Note:** Legend as King of Hungary and Bohemia.

Date	Mintage	VG	F	VF	XF	Unc
161ZKB	—	115	200	375	575	—
1613KB	—	115	200	375	575	—

KM# 49 1/2 THALER
Silver **Ruler:** Matthias **Obv:** Laureate bust right **Rev:** Crowned double-headed eagle **Note:** Varieties exist.

Date	Mintage	VG	F	VF	XF	Unc
1614	—	50.00	100	200	400	—
1615	—	50.00	100	200	400	—
1616	—	50.00	100	200	400	—
1617	—	50.00	100	200	400	—
1618	—	50.00	100	200	400	—
1619	—	50.00	100	200	400	—

KM# 58 1/2 THALER
Silver **Ruler:** Matthias **Rev:** Crowned arms in cartouche divide N-B in inner circle, date in legend

Date	Mintage	VG	F	VF	XF	Unc
1617NB	—	—	—	—	—	—

KM# 72 1/2 THALER
Silver **Ruler:** Matthias **Obv:** Laureate bust right **Note:** Posthumous issue.

Date	Mintage	VG	F	VF	XF	Unc
1620KB	—	85.00	175	325	525	—
1622KB	—	85.00	175	325	525	—

KM# 73 1/2 THALER
Silver **Ruler:** Ferdinand II **Obv:** Laureate bust right in inner circle **Rev:** Crowned imperial eagle in inner circle, date in legend **Note:** Varieties exist.

Date	Mintage	VG	F	VF	XF	Unc
1620	—	46.00	90.00	185	375	—
1622	—	46.00	90.00	185	375	—
1623	—	46.00	90.00	185	375	—
1625	—	46.00	90.00	185	375	—
1630	—	46.00	90.00	185	375	—
1631	—	46.00	90.00	185	375	—
1632	—	46.00	90.00	185	375	—
1633	—	46.00	90.00	185	375	—
1634	—	46.00	90.00	185	375	—
1635	—	46.00	90.00	185	375	—
1636	—	46.00	90.00	185	375	—
1637	—	46.00	90.00	185	375	—

KM# 86.1 1/2 THALER
Silver **Ruler:** Ferdinand II **Obv:** Laureate bust right in inner circle

Date	Mintage	VG	F	VF	XF	Unc
1624CH	—	70.00	140	290	450	—

KM# 86.2 1/2 THALER
Silver **Ruler:** Ferdinand II

Date	Mintage	VG	F	VF	XF	Unc
1630NB	—	60.00	115	230	375	—
1633NB	—	60.00	115	230	375	—
1635NB	—	60.00	115	230	375	—

KM# 111 1/2 THALER
Silver **Ruler:** Ferdinand III **Obv:** Laureate bust right in inner circle **Rev:** Crowned imperial eagle with N-B divided at bottom inner circle, date in legend

Date	Mintage	VG	F	VF	XF	Unc
1638NB	—	—	—	—	—	—

KM# 117 1/2 THALER
13.7300 g., Silver **Ruler:** Ferdinand III **Obv:** Laureate armored bust right within inner circle **Obv. Legend:** BOH REX FERDINAND III DG ROIS... **Rev:** Crowned imperial eagle holding shield of arms **Note:** Varieties exist.

Date	Mintage	VG	F	VF	XF	Unc
1639KB	—	46.00	90.00	185	375	—
1640KB	—	46.00	90.00	185	375	—
1641KB	—	46.00	90.00	185	375	—
1642KB	—	46.00	90.00	185	375	—
1643KB	—	46.00	90.00	185	375	—
1644KB	—	46.00	90.00	185	375	—
1645KB	—	46.00	90.00	185	375	—
1646KB	—	46.00	90.00	185	375	—
1647KB	—	46.00	90.00	185	375	—
1648KB	—	46.00	90.00	185	375	—
1649KB	—	46.00	90.00	185	375	—
1650KB	—	46.00	90.00	185	375	—
1651KB	—	46.00	90.00	185	375	—
1652KB	—	46.00	90.00	185	375	—
1653KB	—	46.00	90.00	185	375	—
1654KB	—	46.00	90.00	185	375	—
1655KB	—	46.00	90.00	185	375	—
1656KB	—	46.00	90.00	185	375	—
1657KB	—	46.00	90.00	185	375	—

KM# A146 1/2 THALER
Silver **Ruler:** Ferdinand III **Obv:** • I • K • / • E • M • / date and ornaments **Rev:** Crowned imperial eagle

Date	Mintage	VG	F	VF	XF	Unc
1655	—	—	—	—	—	—

KM# 146 1/2 THALER
Silver **Ruler:** Ferdinand III **Note:** Posthumous issue.

Date	Mintage	VG	F	VF	XF	Unc
1658KB	—	46.00	90.00	185	375	—
1659KB	—	46.00	90.00	185	375	—

KM# 154 1/2 THALER
Silver **Ruler:** Leopold I **Obv:** Young laureate bust right in inner circle **Rev:** Crowned imperial eagle in inner circle, date in legend **Note:** Varieties exist.

Date	Mintage	VG	F	VF	XF	Unc
1659KB	—	46.00	90.00	185	375	—
1660KB	—	46.00	90.00	185	375	—
1661KB	—	46.00	90.00	185	375	—

KM# 168 1/2 THALER
Silver **Ruler:** Leopold I **Obv:** Young laureate bust right in inner circle

Date	Mintage	VG	F	VF	XF	Unc
1661NB	—	46.00	90.00	185	375	—

KM# 169 1/2 THALER
Silver **Ruler:** Leopold I **Note:** Klippe. Varieties exist.

Date	Mintage	VG	F	VF	XF	Unc
1661	—	—	—	—	—	—

KM# 177 1/2 THALER
Silver **Ruler:** Leopold I **Obv:** Laureate bust right, date below, legend on scroll **Rev:** Legend on scroll **Note:** Varieties exist.

Date	Mintage	VG	F	VF	XF	Unc
1662KB	—	40.00	80.00	175	375	—
1663KB	—	40.00	80.00	175	375	—
1665KB	—	40.00	80.00	175	375	—

KM# 185 1/2 THALER
Silver **Ruler:** Leopold I **Obv:** Long haired armored bust to right breaks circle at top, date below shoulder, legend divided by 2 small shields of arms at lower left and right. **Obv. Legend:**

LEOPOLD - D.G. R. I. S. AV. GE - HV. B. REX. **Rev:** Crowned imperial eagle, crowned shield of 4-fold arms with central shield of Hungary on breast **Rev. Legend:** ARCHID. AV. DV. BV. MAR. MOR. CO. TYR. **Note:** Solid inner circle on both sides. Varieties exist.

Date	Mintage	VG	F	VF	XF	Unc
1670 KB	—	40.00	80.00	175	375	—
1682 KB	—	40.00	80.00	175	375	—
1688 KB	—	40.00	80.00	175	375	—

KM# 220 1/2 THALER

Silver **Ruler:** Leopold I **Obv:** Laureate bust right **Note:** Varieties exist.

Date	Mintage	VG	F	VF	XF	Unc
1690KB	—	35.00	75.00	150	285	—
1691/0KB	—	35.00	75.00	150	285	—
1691KB	—	35.00	75.00	150	285	—
1692KB	—	35.00	75.00	150	285	—
1693KB	—	35.00	75.00	150	285	—
1694KB	—	35.00	75.00	150	285	—
1695KB	—	35.00	75.00	150	285	—
1696KB	—	35.00	75.00	150	285	—
1697KB	—	35.00	75.00	150	285	—
1698KB	—	35.00	75.00	150	285	—
1699KB	—	35.00	75.00	150	285	—

KM# 251 1/2 THALER

Silver **Ruler:** Leopold I **Obv:** Armored bust right **Obv. Legend:** LEOPOLD:- D: G: R: I: S: A: GER: - HV: BO: REX: **Rev:** Crowned arms within Order chain on eagle's breast **Rev. Legend:** ARCHID: AV: DVX: BV: MAR: MOR: ... **Note:** Varieties exist.

Date	Mintage	VG	F	VF	XF	Unc
1700KB	—	34.50	70.00	150	285	—

KM# 12 THALER

Silver **Ruler:** Rudolf II **Obv:** Crowned half figure right holding sceptre **Note:** Dav. #3014.

Date	Mintage	VG	F	VF	XF	Unc
1601NB	—	275	550	1,150	2,250	3,500
160ZNB	—	275	550	1,150	2,250	3,500
1603NB	—	275	550	1,150	2,250	3,500
1604NB	—	275	550	1,150	2,250	3,500

KM# 18 THALER

Silver **Ruler:** Rudolf II **Obv:** Armored bust in ruffled collar right in inner circle **Note:** Dav. #3015.

Date	Mintage	VG	F	VF	XF	Unc
1603	—	375	750	1,200	2,100	—
1604	—	375	750	1,200	2,100	—
1605	—	375	750	1,200	2,100	—
1607	—	375	750	1,200	2,100	—
1608	—	375	750	1,200	2,100	—

KM# 4 THALER

Silver **Ruler:** Rudolf II **Note:** Klippe. Dav. #3014A.

Date	Mintage	VG	F	VF	XF	Unc
1604 Rare	—	—	—	—	—	—

KM# 20 THALER

Silver **Ruler:** Rudolf II **Note:** Klippe. Dav. #3015A.

Date	Mintage	VG	F	VF	XF	Unc
1604 Rare	—	—	—	—	—	—
1608 Rare	—	—	—	—	—	—

KM# 27 THALER

Silver **Obv:** Crowned bust of Matthias right in inner circle, designatus legend **Rev:** Crowned arms divide K-B in Order collar and inner circle, date in legend **Note:** Dav. #3051.

Date	Mintage	VG	F	VF	XF	Unc
1609KB	22,000	210	450	750	1,250	—
1610KB	35,000	210	450	750	1,250	—
1611KB	72,000	210	450	750	1,250	—
1612KB	43,000	210	450	750	1,250	—

KM# 34 THALER

Silver **Obv:** Legend as King of Hungary and Bohemia **Note:** Dav. #3053.

Date	Mintage	VG	F	VF	XF	Unc
1611	Inc. above	265	550	950	1,550	—
1612	Inc. above	265	550	950	1,550	—
1613	48,000	265	550	950	1,550	—

KM# 41 THALER

Silver **Obv:** Laureate bust of Matthias right, titles of Holy Roman Emperor **Rev:** Crowned imperial eagle holding sword and sceptre **Note:** Varieties exist. Dav. #3054.

Date	Mintage	VG	F	VF	XF	Unc
1613KB	Inc. above	725	1,300	2,400	4,000	—
1614KB	—	725	1,300	2,400	4,000	—
1615/14KB	—	1,300	2,400	4,000	6,000	—
1615KB	—	725	1,300	2,400	4,000	—
1616KB	—	725	1,300	2,400	4,000	—
1617KB	—	725	1,300	2,400	4,000	—

KM# 59 THALER

Silver **Rev:** Small arms **Note:** Dav. #3056.

Date	Mintage	VG	F	VF	XF	Unc
1617KB	—	145	285	500	1,150	3,500
1618KB	—	145	285	500	1,150	3,500
1619KB	37,000	145	285	500	1,150	3,500
1620KB posthumous	—	145	285	500	1,150	3,500

KM# 75 THALER

Silver **Note:** Varieties exist. Dav. #3129.

Date	Mintage	VG	F	VF	XF	Unc
1620KB	67,000	130	250	400	650	—
1622KB	—	130	250	400	650	—
1623KB	—	130	250	400	650	—
1630KB	130,000	130	250	400	650	—
1631KB	255,000	130	250	400	650	—
1631KB Without mint mark	Inc. above	130	250	400	650	—
1632KB	181,000	130	250	400	650	—
1633KB	80,000	130	250	400	650	—
1634KB	—	130	250	400	650	—
1635KB	78,000	130	250	400	650	—
1636KB	—	130	250	400	650	—
1637KB	—	130	250	400	650	—

KM# 93 THALER

Silver **Obv:** Bust of Ferdinand II right **Rev:** Bust of Eleonora left **Note:** Show thaler

Date	Mintage	VG	F	VF	XF	Unc
1627	—	210	450	750	1,250	—

KM# 97.1 THALER

Silver **Obv:** Large bust **Note:** Dav. #3130.

Date	Mintage	VG	F	VF	XF	Unc
1630NB	—	235	500	875	1,450	—

KM# 97.2 THALER

Silver **Obv:** Smaller bust **Note:** Varieties exist. Dav. #3131.

Date	Mintage	VG	F	VF	XF	Unc
1630NB	—	190	375	650	1,150	—
1631NB	—	190	375	650	1,150	—
1632NB	—	190	375	650	1,150	—
1633NB	—	190	375	650	1,150	—
1634NB	—	190	375	650	1,150	—
1635NB	—	190	375	650	1,150	—

KM# 106.1 THALER

Silver **Obv:** Laureate armored bust of Ferdinand II to right breaks top of inner circle **Note:** Dav. #A3132.

Date	Mintage	VG	F	VF	XF	Unc
1636NB	—	295	600	1,100	1,800	—

KM# 106.2 THALER

Silver **Obv:** Cloaked bust to right breaks top of inner circle **Note:** Varieties exist. Dav. #3132.

Date	Mintage	VG	F	VF	XF	Unc
1637	—	235	500	875	1,450	—

KM# 107 THALER

Silver **Note:** Dav. #3198.

Date	Mintage	VG	F	VF	XF	Unc
1637KB	—	130	250	400	650	—
1638KB	22,000	130	250	400	650	—
1639KB	13,000	130	250	400	650	—
1640KB	24,000	130	250	400	650	—
1641KB	59,000	130	250	400	650	—
1642KB	29,000	130	250	400	650	—
1643KB	30,000	130	250	400	650	—
1644KB	—	130	250	400	650	—
1645KB	—	130	250	400	650	—
1646KB	—	130	250	400	650	—
1647KB	—	130	250	400	650	—
1648KB	140,000	130	250	400	650	—
1649KB	261,000	130	250	400	650	—
1650KB	281,000	130	250	400	650	—
1651KB	305,000	130	250	400	650	—
1652KB	—	130	250	400	650	—
1653KB	367,000	130	250	400	650	—
1654KB	385,000	130	250	400	650	—
1655KB	—	130	250	400	650	—
1656KB	390,000	130	250	400	650	—
1657KB	365,000	130	250	400	650	—
1658KB posthumous	—	130	250	400	650	—
1659KB posthumous	—	130	250	400	650	—
1661KB posthumous	—	130	250	400	650	—

KM# 108 THALER

Silver **Obv:** Facing bust of Ferdinand III in inner circle **Note:** Dav. #3200.

Date	Mintage	VG	F	VF	XF	Unc
1637NB	—	265	550	950	1,550	—

KM# 112 THALER

Silver **Obv:** Laureate bust of Ferdinand III in ruffled collar right in inner circle **Note:** Dav. #3201.

Date	Mintage	VG	F	VF	XF	Unc
1638NB	—	875	1,600	2,850	4,750	—

KM# 113.1 THALER

Silver **Obv:** Laureate bust of Ferdinand III in lace collar right in inner circle **Note:** Dav. #3202.

Date	Mintage	VG	F	VF	XF	Unc
1638NB Rare	—	—	—	—	—	—

KM# 113.2 THALER

Silver **Note:** Varieties exist. Dav. #3203.

Date	Mintage	VG	F	VF	XF	Unc
1639NB	—	825	1,450	2,400	4,250	—
1640NB	—	825	1,450	2,400	4,250	—
1641NB	—	825	1,450	2,400	4,250	—
1642NB	—	825	1,450	2,400	4,250	—
1643NB	—	825	1,450	2,400	4,250	—
1644NB	—	825	1,450	2,400	4,250	—
1658NB	—	825	1,450	2,400	4,250	—
1659NB	—	825	1,450	2,400	4,250	—
1661NB	—	825	1,450	2,400	4,250	—

KM# 131 THALER

Silver **Note:** Klippe. Dav. #3203A.

Date	Mintage	VG	F	VF	XF	Unc
1643NB Rare	—	—	—	—	—	—

KM# 140 THALER

Silver **Note:** Klippe. Dav. #3198A.

Date	Mintage	VG	F	VF	XF	Unc
1650KB Rare	—	—	—	—	—	—

KM# 147 THALER

Silver **Subject:** Funeral of Johann Kewiczky, recorder at city of Kaschau **Note:** Struck on the request of the widow, Elisabeth Madarassy. Dav. #3199.

Date	Mintage	VG	F	VF	XF	Unc
1655KB	—	1,050	1,900	3,400	5,700	—

KM# 148 THALER
Silver **Obv:** Leopold I **Note:** Varieties exist. Dav. #3254.

Date	Mintage	VG	F	VF	XF	Unc
1658KB	337,000	—	—	—	—	—
Note: Reported, not confirmed						
1659KB	278,000	75.00	160	400	750	—
1660KB	282,000	75.00	160	400	750	—
1661KB	—	75.00	160	400	750	—

KM# 161.1 THALER
Silver **Note:** Klippe. Dav. #3266A.

Date	Mintage	VG	F	VF	XF	Unc
1660NB Rare	—	—	—	—	—	—

KM# 160.1 THALER
Silver **Note:** Dav. #3266.

Date	Mintage	VG	F	VF	XF	Unc
1660NB	—	325	575	1,000	1,800	—
1661NB	—	325	575	1,000	1,800	—

KM# 160.2 THALER
Silver **Note:** Dav. #3267.

Date	Mintage	VG	F	VF	XF	Unc
1660NB	—	350	650	1,100	1,850	—
1662NB	—	350	650	1,100	1,850	—

KM# 170.1 THALER
Silver **Note:** Dav. #3255.

Date	Mintage	VG	F	VF	XF	Unc
1661KB	—	200	500	1,200	2,250	3,750

KM# 178.1 THALER
Silver **Obv:** Bust with lion face on shoulder **Note:** Dav. #3256.

Date	Mintage	VG	F	VF	XF	Unc
1662KB	—	700	1,350	2,750	4,750	—
1663KB	28,000	700	1,350	2,750	4,750	—

KM# 178.2 THALER
Silver **Obv:** Bust without lion face on shoulder **Note:** Dav. #3257.

Date	Mintage	VG	F	VF	XF	Unc
1662KB	—	500	1,000	2,000	3,500	—
1663KB	—	500	1,000	2,000	3,500	—

KM# 161.2 THALER
Silver **Note:** Dav. #3267A.

Date	Mintage	VG	F	VF	XF	Unc
1662NB Rare	—	105	220	375	625	—

KM# 160.3 THALER
Silver **Note:** Dav. #3268.

Date	Mintage	VG	F	VF	XF	Unc
1663NB	—	400	800	1,500	2,500	—
1664NB	—	400	800	1,500	2,500	—

KM# 161.3 THALER
Silver **Note:** Dav. #3268A.

Date	Mintage	VG	F	VF	XF	Unc
1663NB Rare	—	—	—	—	—	—

KM# 170.2 THALER
Silver **Note:** Varieties exist. Dav. #3258.

Date	Mintage	VG	F	VF	XF	Unc
1664KB	—	285	575	975	1,750	—
1665KB	20,000	285	575	975	1,750	—
1667KB	22,000	285	575	975	1,750	—
1668KB	—	285	575	975	1,750	—
1671KB	1,774	350	725	1,200	2,150	—
1673KB	1,822	350	725	1,200	2,150	—

KM# 161.4 THALER
Silver **Note:** Varieties exist. Dav. #3269A.

Date	Mintage	VG	F	VF	XF	Unc
1665NB Rare	—	—	—	—	—	—

KM# 160.4 THALER
Silver **Note:** Dav. #3269.

Date	Mintage	VG	F	VF	XF	Unc
1665NB	—	650	1,150	1,900	3,400	6,000

KM# 160.5 THALER
Silver **Note:** Dav. #3270.

Date	Mintage	VG	F	VF	XF	Unc
1666NB	—	650	1,150	1,900	3,400	6,000

KM# 160.6 THALER
Silver **Note:** Dav. #3271.

Date	Mintage	VG	F	VF	XF	Unc
1667NB	—	650	1,150	1,900	3,400	—
1668NB	—	650	1,150	1,900	3,400	—
1669NB	—	650	1,150	1,900	3,400	—

KM# 180.1 THALER
Silver **Note:** Octagonal klippe. Dav. #3271A.

Date	Mintage	VG	F	VF	XF	Unc
1668NB Rare	—	—	—	—	—	—

KM# 160.7 THALER
Silver **Note:** Dav. #3272.

Date	Mintage	VG	F	VF	XF	Unc
1670NB	—	450	950	1,750	3,250	—
1671NB	—	450	950	1,750	3,250	—

KM# 180.2 THALER
Silver **Note:** Dav. #3272A.

Date	Mintage	VG	F	VF	XF	Unc
1670NB Rare	—	—	—	—	—	—

KM# 160.8 THALER
Silver **Note:** Varieties exist. Dav. #3273.

Date	Mintage	VG	F	VF	XF	Unc
1671NB	—	650	1,200	2,750	3,750	—
1672NB	—	650	1,200	2,750	3,750	—
1673NB	—	650	1,200	2,750	3,750	—
1679NB	—	650	1,200	2,750	3,750	—

KM# 196 THALER
Silver **Note:** Dav. #3275.

Date	Mintage	VG	F	VF	XF	Unc
1674NB LM	—	1,000	2,000	4,000	7,000	—
1675NB LM	—	1,000	2,000	4,000	7,000	—
1687NB-PO	—	1,000	2,000	4,000	7,000	—
Note: WAG Auction 49, 2-09, Unc realize approximately $16,065.						
1688NB-PO	—	—	—	—	—	—
1695NB	—	1,000	2,000	4,000	7,000	—

KM# 205 THALER
Silver **Note:** Dav. #3259.

Date	Mintage	VG	F	VF	XF	Unc
1681KB	—	175	350	700	1,200	—
1682KB	—	175	350	700	1,200	—

KM# 214.1 THALER
Silver **Obv:** Laureate bust of Leopold I right in inner circle **Rev:** Crown of imperial eagle divides date **Note:** Dav. #3260.

Date	Mintage	VG	F	VF	XF	Unc
1687KB	19,000	125	275	550	950	—
1688KB	25,000	125	275	550	950	—
1689KB	43,000	125	275	550	950	—
1690KB	—	125	275	550	950	—
1691KB	779,000	125	275	550	950	—

KM# 214.2 THALER
Silver **Note:** Dav. #3261.

Date	Mintage	VG	F	VF	XF	Unc
1691KB	Inc. above	100	200	450	750	—

KM# 214.3 THALER

Silver **Note:** Dav. #3262.

Date	Mintage	VG	F	VF	XF	Unc
1692KB	512,000	75.00	150	250	475	—

KM# 214.4 THALER

Silver **Obv:** With four loops in bow knot **Note:** Dav. #3262A.

Date	Mintage	VG	F	VF	XF	Unc
1692KB	Inc. above	75.00	150	250	475	—

KM# 214.5 THALER

Silver **Obv:** Smaller bust **Note:** Dav. #3262B.

Date	Mintage	VG	F	VF	XF	Unc
1692KB	Inc. above	75.00	150	250	475	—

KM# 214.6 THALER

Silver **Note:** Dav. #3263.

Date	Mintage	VG	F	VF	XF	Unc
1692KB	Inc. above	75.00	150	250	475	—
1693KB	358,000	75.00	150	250	475	—

KM# 214.7 THALER

Silver **Obv:** Smaller bust **Note:** Dav. #3263A.

Date	Mintage	VG	F	VF	XF	Unc
1693KB	Inc. above	75.00	150	250	475	—

KM# 214.8 THALER

Silver **Note:** Dav. #3264.

Date	Mintage	VG	F	VF	XF	Unc
1693KB	—	75.00	150	250	475	—
1694KB	82,000	75.00	150	250	475	—
1695KB	443,000	75.00	150	250	475	—
1696KB	324,000	75.00	150	250	475	—
1697KB	214,000	75.00	150	250	475	—
1698KB	364,000	75.00	150	250	475	—
1699KB	440,000	75.00	150	250	475	—

KM# 226 THALER

Silver **Note:** Klippe. Dav. #3264B.

Date	Mintage	VG	F	VF	XF	Unc
1693KB Rare	—	—	—	—	—	—

KM# 240 THALER

Silver **Obv:** Laureate bust of Leopold I right in inner circle **Rev:** Crowned imperial eagle in inner circle, date divided at top **Note:** Dav. #3276.

Date	Mintage	VG	F	VF	XF	Unc
1697CH Rare	—	—	—	—	—	—

KM# 214.9 THALER

Silver **Ruler:** Leopold I **Obv:** Laureate bust right **Obv. Legend:** LEOPOLDUS - D: G: ROM: IMP: S: A: - CE: HV: BO: R: **Rev:** Crown divides date at top **Rev. Legend:** ARCHIDVX • AVS: DVX... **Note:** Dav. #3265.

Date	Mintage	VG	F	VF	XF	Unc
1700KB	337,000	150	280	550	1,150	—

MB# 254 THALER (72 Kreuzer)

Silver **Ruler:** Rudolf II **Obv:** Armored bust right, small 4-fold arms and small Madonna and child divide legend **Obv. Legend:** + RVDOL. II. - D.G. RO. IM. S. AV. GER. HVN - BOE. REX. **Rev:** Crowned imperial eagle holding sword and scepter, imperial orb on breast, date at end of legend **Rev. Legend:** ARCHI. DVX. AVS. DVX. BVRG. MAR. MORA. **Note:** Dav. #8066 (ref. H#1030). Varieties exist.

Date	Mintage	VG	F	VF	XF	Unc
1601KB	—	110	220	375	625	—
160ZKB	—	110	220	375	625	—
1603KB	—	110	220	375	625	—
1604KB	—	110	220	375	625	—
1605KB	—	110	220	375	625	—
1607KB	—	110	220	375	625	—
1608KB	—	110	220	375	625	—

KM# 13 1-1/2 THALER

Silver **Ruler:** Rudolf II **Obv:** Young armored bust of Rudolph II in ruffled collar right in inner circle **Rev:** Crowned imperial eagle with sword and sceptre divide K-B in inner circle, date in legend **Note:** Dav. #3012.

Date	Mintage	VG	F	VF	XF	Unc
1601KB	—	—	—	—	—	—

KM# 141 1-1/2 THALER

Silver **Obv:** Laureate bust of Ferdinand III right in inner circle **Rev:** Crowned imperial eagle in inner circle, date in legend

Date	Mintage	VG	F	VF	XF	Unc
1650	—	—	—	—	—	—

KM# 14.1 2 THALER

Silver **Obv:** Young armored bust of Rudolph II in ruffled collar right in inner circle **Rev:** Crowned imperial eagle with sword and sceptre divide K-B in inner circle, date in legend **Note:** Dav. #3011.

Date	Mintage	VG	F	VF	XF	Unc
1601KB	—	575	950	1,650	2,850	—
1604KB	—	575	950	1,650	2,850	—

KM# 14.2 2 THALER

Silver **Note:** Thicker planchet.

Date	Mintage	VG	F	VF	XF	Unc
1603	—	575	950	1,650	2,850	—

KM# 21 2 THALER

Silver **Note:** Two strikings of Thaler dies on rectangular bar.

Date	Mintage	VG	F	VF	XF	Unc
1608NB	—	575	950	1,650	2,850	—

KM# 28 2 THALER

Silver **Obv:** Crowned bust of Matthias right in inner circle, designatus legend **Rev:** Crowned arms divide K-B in Order collar and inner circle, date in legend **Note:** Dav. #A3050.

Date	Mintage	VG	F	VF	XF	Unc
1609KB	—	1,000	1,700	2,850	5,000	—

KM# 35 2 THALER

Silver **Note:** Legend as King of Hungary and Bohemia. Dav. #A3052.

Date	Mintage	VG	F	VF	XF	Unc
1611KB	—	1,000	1,700	2,850	5,000	—
1612KB	—	1,000	1,700	2,850	5,000	—

KM# 50 2 THALER

Silver **Obv:** Laureate bust of Mathias right in inner circle, titles of Holy Roman Emperor **Rev:** Crowned imperial eagle holding sword and sceptre in inner circle, date in legend **Note:** Varieties exist. Dav. #B3055.

Date	Mintage	VG	F	VF	XF	Unc
1614	—	1,000	1,700	2,850	5,000	—
1616	—	1,000	1,700	2,850	5,000	—

KM# 77 2 THALER

Silver **Obv:** Laureate bust of Ferdinand II right in inner circle **Rev:** Crowned imperial eagle in inner circle, date in legend **Note:** Dav. #3128.

Date	Mintage	VG	F	VF	XF	Unc
1622KB	—	450	825	1,250	2,250	—
1633KB	—	450	825	1,250	2,250	—
1636KB	—	450	825	1,250	2,250	—

KM# 83 2 THALER

Silver **Note:** Dav. #3133.

Date	Mintage	VG	F	VF	XF	Unc
1623 BZ Rare	—	—	—	—	—	—

KM# 132 2 THALER

Silver **Obv:** Portrait and titles of Ferdinand III **Note:** Varieties exist. Dav. #3197.

Date	Mintage	VG	F	VF	XF	Unc
1640KB	—	575	950	1,650	2,850	—
1641KB	—	575	950	1,650	2,850	—
1644KB	—	575	950	1,650	2,850	—
1650KB	—	575	950	1,650	2,850	—
1651KB	—	575	950	1,650	2,850	—
1652KB	—	575	950	1,650	2,850	—
1653KB	—	575	950	1,650	2,850	—
1655KB	—	575	950	1,650	2,850	—

KM# 149 2 THALER

Silver **Note:** Posthumous issue.

Date	Mintage	VG	F	VF	XF	Unc
1658	—	575	950	1,650	2,850	—

KM# 155 2 THALER

Silver **Obv:** Young laureate bust of Leopold I right **Rev:** Crowned imperial eagle **Note:** Dav. #A3254.

Date	Mintage	VG	F	VF	XF	Unc
1659KB Rare	—	—	—	—	—	—

KM# 212 2 THALER

Silver **Obv:** Laureate bust of Leopold I right in inner circle **Rev:** Radiant Madonna and child divide N-B in inner circle, date in legend **Note:** Dav. #3274.

Date	Mintage	VG	F	VF	XF	Unc
1687NB LM Rare	—	—	—	—	—	—
1695NB PO	—	—	—	—	—	—
1695NB LM Rare	—	—	—	—	—	—

KM# 222.1 2 THALER

Silver **Obv:** Older laureate bust of Leopold I **Rev:** Crown divides date **Note:** Dav. #A3261.

Date	Mintage	VG	F	VF	XF	Unc
1691KB Rare	—	—	—	—	—	—

KM# 222.2 2 THALER

Silver **Note:** Varieties exist. Dav. #A3262.

Date	Mintage	VG	F	VF	XF	Unc
1692KB Rare	—	—	—	—	—	—

KM# 15.1 3 THALER

Silver **Obv:** Young armored bust of Rudolph II in ruffled collar right in inner circle **Rev:** Crowned imperial eagle with sword and sceptre divide K-B in inner circle, date in legend **Note:** Dav. #A3011.

Date	Mintage	VG	F	VF	XF	Unc
1601KB	—	1,250	2,500	4,000	7,000	—

KM# 15.2 3 THALER

Silver **Note:** Thicker planchet. Dav. #A3011.

Date	Mintage	VG	F	VF	XF	Unc
1603KB	—	1,250	2,500	4,000	7,000	—

KM# 36 3 THALER

Silver **Obv:** Crowned bust of Matthias right in inner circle, legend as King of Hungary and Bohemia **Rev:** Crowned arms divide K-B in Order collar and inner circle, date in legend **Note:** Dav. #3052.

Date	Mintage	VG	F	VF	XF	Unc
1611KB Rare	—	—	—	—	—	—

KM# 84 3 THALER

Silver **Note:** Thick planchet, 85.20-85.73 grams. Dav. #3127.

Date	Mintage	VG	F	VF	XF	Unc
1623KB Rare	—	—	—	—	—	—
1637KB Rare	—	—	—	—	—	—

KM# 126 3 THALER

Silver **Obv:** Portrait and titles of Ferdinand III **Note:** Varieties exist. Dav. #3196.

Date	Mintage	VG	F	VF	XF	Unc
1641KB	—	1,250	2,500	4,000	7,000	—
1644KB	—	1,250	2,500	4,000	7,000	—
1645KB	—	1,250	2,500	4,000	7,000	—
1647KB	—	1,250	2,500	4,000	7,000	—
1653KB	—	1,250	2,500	4,000	7,000	—
1655KB	—	1,250	2,500	4,000	7,000	—

KM# 30 4 THALER

Silver **Obv:** Crowned bust of Matthias right in inner circle, designatus legend **Rev:** Crowned arms divide K-B in Order collar and inner circle, date in legend **Note:** Dav. #B3050.

Date	Mintage	VG	F	VF	XF	Unc
1610KB Rare	—	—	—	—	—	—

KM# 57 4 THALER

Silver **Obv:** Laureate bust of Matthias right in inner circle **Rev:** Crowned imperial eagle holding sword and sceptre in inner circle, date in legend **Note:** Dav. #A3055.

Date	Mintage	VG	F	VF	XF	Unc
1616KB Rare	—	—	—	—	—	—

KM# 85 4 THALER

Silver **Obv:** Laureate bust of Ferdinand II right in inner circle **Rev:** Crowned imperial eagle in inner circle, date in legend **Note:** Dav. #3126.

Date	Mintage	VG	F	VF	XF	Unc
1623KB Rare	—	—	—	—	—	—
1631KB Rare	—	—	—	—	—	—

KM# 127 4 THALER

Silver **Obv:** Portrait and titles of Ferdinand III **Note:** Dav. #3195.

Date	Mintage	VG	F	VF	XF	Unc
1641KB Rare	—	—	—	—	—	—
1648KB Rare	—	—	—	—	—	—
1651KB Rare	—	—	—	—	—	—
1658KB Rare, posthumous	—	—	—	—	—	—

KM# 31 5 THALER

Silver **Obv:** Crowned bust of Matthias right in inner circle, designatus legend **Rev:** Crowned arms divide K-B in Order collar and inner circle, date in legend

Date	Mintage	VG	F	VF	XF	Unc
1610KB Rare	—	—	—	—	—	—

KM# 142 5 THALER

Silver **Obv:** Laureate bust of Ferdinand III right in inner circle **Rev:** Crowned imperial eagle in inner circle, date in legend **Note:** Varieties exist. Dav. #A3195.

Date	Mintage	VG	F	VF	XF	Unc
1651KB Rare	—	—	—	—	—	—
1654KB Rare	—	—	—	—	—	—

TRADE COINAGE

MB# 258 GOLDGULDEN

3.5000 g., 0.9860 Gold 0.1109 oz. AGW **Ruler:** Rudolf II **Obv:** Madonna and Child on crescent, small shield of Austria arms at bottom **Obv. Legend:** RVDOL. II. D.G. RO. — I. S. AV. GE. HV. B. R. **Rev:** Crowned and armored full-length figure of St. Ladislaus, holding halbert, divides mintmarks, legend ends with date **Rev. Legend:** S. LADISLAVS. — REX. **Note:** Varieties exist; FR#63; (ref. H-1002).

Date	Mintage	VG	F	VF	XF	Unc
1601KB	—	185	300	500	850	1,350
160ZKB	—	185	300	500	850	1,350
1603KB	—	185	300	500	850	1,350
1604KB	—	185	300	500	850	1,350

MB# 304 GOLDGULDEN

3.5000 g., 0.9860 Gold 0.1109 oz. AGW **Ruler:** Rudolf II **Obv:** Crowned and armored full-length figure of St. Ladislaus, holding halbert, divides mintmarks **Obv. Legend:** RVDOL. II. D.G. ROM — IM. S. A. G. H. B. R. **Rev:** Madonna and Child, date at end of legend **Rev. Legend:** PATRONA. HVNGARIÆ. **Note:** Varieties exist; FR#68; (ref. H-1007).

Date	Mintage	VG	F	VF	XF	Unc
160ZNB	—	185	325	575	950	—
1603NB	—	185	325	575	950	—
1604NB	—	185	325	575	950	—
1607NB	—	185	325	575	950	—
1608NB	—	185	325	575	950	—

KM# B29 3 GOLDGULDEN

10.5000 g., 0.9860 Gold 0.3328 oz. AGW **Ruler:** Rudolf II **Note:** Struck on thick flan from Goldgulden dies, KM#A29; FR#69; (ref. H-1000).

Date	Mintage	VG	F	VF	XF	Unc
1605CB (cg)	—	2,500	4,750	9,000	16,000	—

KM# 189 1/6 DUCAT
0.5833 g., 0.9860 Gold 0.0185 oz. AGW **Obv:** Leopold I **Rev:** Radiant Madonna and child above arms

Date	Mintage	VG	F	VF	XF	Unc
1673NB LM	—	130	195	350	575	900
1674NB LM	—	130	195	350	575	900
1679NB	—	130	195	350	575	900
1682NB	—	130	195	350	575	900
1685NB	—	130	195	350	575	900
1686NB	—	130	195	350	575	900
1689NB	—	130	195	350	575	900
1690NB	—	130	195	350	575	900
1692NB	—	130	195	350	575	900
1695NB PO	—	130	195	350	575	900
1696NB	—	130	195	350	575	900
1697NB PO	—	130	195	350	575	900
1698NB IB	—	130	195	350	575	900

KM# A16 1/4 DUCAT
0.8750 g., 0.9860 Gold 0.0277 oz. AGW **Obv:** Shield of arms **Rev:** Madonna and child divide N-B, date in legend **Note:** Struck with 1 Denar dies, KM#7.

Date	Mintage	VG	F	VF	XF	Unc
1601NB	—	425	800	1,500	2,600	—
1604NB	—	425	800	1,500	2,600	—

KM# 67 1/4 DUCAT
0.8750 g., 0.9860 Gold 0.0277 oz. AGW **Note:** Similar to 1 Ducat, KM#3.

Date	Mintage	VG	F	VF	XF	Unc
1608	—	375	775	1,400	2,350	—

KM# A50 1/4 DUCAT
0.8750 g., 0.9860 Gold 0.0277 oz. AGW **Obv:** Shield of arms divides N-B, date in legend, titles as king **Rev:** Madonna and child **Note:** Struck with 1 Denar dies, KM#43.

Date	Mintage	VG	F	VF	XF	Unc
1614NB	—	425	850	1,550	2,750	—

KM# 55.1 1/4 DUCAT
0.8750 g., 0.9860 Gold 0.0277 oz. AGW **Obv:** Matthias standing right in inner circle **Rev:** Madonna and child above arms in inner circle

Date	Mintage	VG	F	VF	XF	Unc
1615	—	300	600	1,200	2,200	—

KM# 55.2 1/4 DUCAT
0.8750 g., 0.9860 Gold 0.0277 oz. AGW **Obv:** Without mint mark

Date	Mintage	VG	F	VF	XF	Unc
1615	—	300	600	1,200	2,200	—

KM# A100 1/4 DUCAT
0.8750 g., 0.9860 Gold 0.0277 oz. AGW **Obv:** Ferdinand II **Note:** Struck with 1 Thaler dies, KM#71.

Date	Mintage	VG	F	VF	XF	Unc
1632	—	425	850	1,550	2,750	—

KM# A104 1/4 DUCAT
0.8750 g., 0.9860 Gold 0.0277 oz. AGW **Note:** Titles of Ferdinand II. Struck with 1 Denar dies, KM#99.

Date	Mintage	VG	F	VF	XF	Unc
1635	—	425	850	1,550	2,750	—

KM# A131 1/4 DUCAT
0.8750 g., 0.9860 Gold 0.0277 oz. AGW **Obv:** Shield of arms in inner circle **Rev:** Madonna and child in inner circle, date in legend **Note:** Struck with 1 Denar dies, KM#110.

Date	Mintage	VG	F	VF	XF	Unc
1639	—	425	850	1,550	2,750	—
1642	—	425	850	1,550	2,750	—

KM# A134 1/4 DUCAT
0.8750 g., 0.9860 Gold 0.0277 oz. AGW **Obv:** Crowned oval arms in inner circle **Rev:** Raidiant Madonna and child, date in legend **Note:** Struck with 1 Denar dies, KM#125.

Date	Mintage	VG	F	VF	XF	Unc
1640	—	—	—	375	775	—
1643	—	—	—	375	775	—

KM# 201 1/4 DUCAT
0.8750 g., 0.9860 Gold 0.0277 oz. AGW **Obv:** Laureate bust of Leopold right in inner circle, value at shoulder **Rev:** Radiant Madonna standing with child above arms, date above

Date	Mintage	VG	F	VF	XF	Unc
1679NB	—	155	230	375	700	—

KM# 207 1/4 DUCAT
0.8750 g., 0.9860 Gold 0.0277 oz. AGW **Rev:** Seated Madonna and child divide mint mark in inner circle, arms below

Date	Mintage	VG	F	VF	XF	Unc
1684	—	115	195	350	600	1,150
1685	—	115	195	350	600	1,150
1696	—	115	195	350	600	1,150

KM# 242 1/4 DUCAT
0.8750 g., 0.9860 Gold 0.0277 oz. AGW **Obv:** Laureate bust of Leopold without value at shoulder **Rev:** Date divided at top

Date	Mintage	VG	F	VF	XF	Unc
1698 ICB	—	155	230	375	700	—

KM# 246 1/4 DUCAT
0.8750 g., 0.9860 Gold 0.0277 oz. AGW **Obv:** Value at shoulder **Rev:** Date at upper left

Date	Mintage	VG	F	VF	XF	Unc
1699 ICB	—	155	230	375	700	—

KM# 156 1/3 DUCAT
1.1666 g., 0.9860 Gold 0.0370 oz. AGW **Obv:** 6-line inscription

Date	Mintage	VG	F	VF	XF	Unc
1655	—	425	850	1,550	2,700	—

KM# 197 1/3 DUCAT
1.1666 g., 0.9860 Gold 0.0370 oz. AGW **Obv:** Leopold I **Rev:** Radiant Madonna and child above arms

Date	Mintage	VG	F	VF	XF	Unc
1675CH (g)	—	230	375	775	1,400	—

KM# A5 1/2 DUCAT
1.7500 g., 0.9860 Gold 0.0555 oz. AGW **Obv:** Shield of arms **Rev:** Madonna and child divide N-B, date in legend **Note:** Struck with 1 Denar dies, KM#7.

Date	Mintage	VG	F	VF	XF	Unc
1604N-B	—	270	425	925	1,550	—

KM# A120 1/2 DUCAT
1.7500 g., 0.9860 Gold 0.0555 oz. AGW **Obv:** 4-line inscription **Rev:** Scale divides date

Date	Mintage	VG	F	VF	XF	Unc
1625	—	270	425	925	1,550	—

KM# A130 1/2 DUCAT
1.7500 g., 0.9860 Gold 0.0555 oz. AGW **Obv:** Shield of arms in inner circle **Rev:** Madonna and child in inner circle, date in legend **Note:** Struck with 1 Denar dies, KM#110.

Date	Mintage	VG	F	VF	XF	Unc
1642K-B	—	300	550	1,050	1,950	—

KM# C180 1/2 DUCAT
1.7500 g., 0.9860 Gold 0.0555 oz. AGW **Obv:** Crown above arms **Rev:** Date in legend **Note:** Struck with 1 Denar dies, KM#174.

Date	Mintage	VG	F	VF	XF	Unc
1667	—	300	550	1,150	2,050	—

KM# 1.1 DUCAT
3.5000 g., 0.9860 Gold 0.1109 oz. AGW **Obv:** Legend around Madonna and child **Obv. Legend:** RVDOL. II. D.G... **Rev:** St. Ladislaus

Date	Mintage	VG	F	VF	XF	Unc
1601K-B	—	195	265	500	800	—
1602K-B	—	195	265	500	800	—
1603K-B	—	195	265	500	800	—
1604K-B	—	195	265	500	800	—

KM# 1.2 DUCAT
3.5000 g., 0.9860 Gold 0.1109 oz. AGW **Obv:** Roses added to Madonna and child

Date	Mintage	VG	F	VF	XF	Unc
1604K-B	—	195	265	500	800	—
1605K-B	—	195	265	500	800	—
1606K-B	—	195	265	500	800	—
1607K-B	—	195	265	500	800	—
1608K-B	—	195	265	500	800	—

KM# A29 DUCAT
3.5000 g., 0.9860 Gold 0.1109 oz. AGW **Rev:** Crowned imperial eagle **Note:** Klausenberg mint mark: C-B/Castle. Previously KM#29.

Date	Mintage	VG	F	VF	XF	Unc
1604	—	625	1,200	2,200	3,750	—
1605	—	625	1,200	2,200	3,750	—

KM# 37 DUCAT
3.5000 g., 0.9860 Gold 0.1109 oz. AGW **Obv:** Matthias **Rev:** Radiant Madonna and child

Date	Mintage	VG	F	VF	XF	Unc
1609K-B	—	195	375	700	1,100	1,750
1610K-B	—	195	375	700	1,100	1,750
1611K-B	—	195	375	700	1,100	1,750
161ZKB	—	195	375	700	1,100	1,750
1613K-B	—	195	375	700	1,100	1,750

KM# 42 DUCAT
3.5000 g., 0.9860 Gold 0.1109 oz. AGW **Rev:** Arms added below Madonna and child

Date	Mintage	VG	F	VF	XF	Unc
1613KB	—	195	375	700	1,100	1,750
1614KB	—	195	375	700	1,100	1,750
1615KB	—	195	375	700	1,100	1,750
1616KB	—	195	375	700	1,100	1,750
1617KB	—	195	375	700	1,100	1,750
1618KB	—	195	375	700	1,100	1,750
1619KB	32,000	195	375	700	1,100	1,750
1620KB	44,000	195	375	700	1,100	1,750

KM# 51 DUCAT
3.5000 g., 0.9860 Gold 0.1109 oz. AGW

Date	Mintage	VG	F	VF	XF	Unc
1614NB	—	245	475	950	1,750	—

KM# 52 DUCAT
3.5000 g., 0.9860 Gold 0.1109 oz. AGW **Rev:** Madonna with child at left in inner circle

Date	Mintage	VG	F	VF	XF	Unc
1614	—	245	475	950	1,750	—

KM# 56 DUCAT
3.5000 g., 0.9860 Gold 0.1109 oz. AGW **Rev:** Madonna with ornate gown

Date	Mintage	VG	F	VF	XF	Unc
1615	—	245	425	950	1,750	—
1616	—	245	425	950	1,750	—
1619	—	245	425	950	1,750	—

KM# 60 DUCAT
3.5000 g., 0.9860 Gold 0.1109 oz. AGW **Obv:** Matthias standing facing divides mint mark in inner circle **Rev:** Madonna with child at right in inner circle, crowned arms below

Date	Mintage	VG	F	VF	XF	Unc
1617	—	245	425	950	1,750	—

KM# 61 DUCAT

3.5000 g., 0.9860 Gold 0.1109 oz. AGW **Rev:** Madonna with child at left

Date	Mintage	VG	F	VF	XF	Unc
1617	—	245	425	950	1,750	—
1618	—	245	425	950	1,750	—
1619	—	245	425	950	1,750	—

KM# 76 DUCAT

3.5000 g., 0.9860 Gold 0.1109 oz. AGW **Obv:** Ferdinand II standing right divides mint mark in inner circle **Rev:** Madonna and child in inner circle, crowned arms below

Date	Mintage	VG	F	VF	XF	Unc
1620K-B	—	195	375	700	1,200	—

KM# 78 DUCAT

3.5000 g., 0.9860 Gold 0.1109 oz. AGW **Rev:** Radiant Madonna and child

Date	Mintage	VG	F	VF	XF	Unc
1622KB	—	195	350	575	1,000	1,650
1623KB	—	195	350	575	1,000	1,650
1624KB	—	195	350	575	1,000	1,650
1625KB	—	195	350	575	1,000	1,650
1626KB	—	195	350	575	1,000	1,650
1627KB	—	195	350	575	1,000	1,650
1628KB	—	195	350	575	1,000	1,650
1629KB	—	195	350	575	1,000	1,650
1630KB	—	195	350	575	1,000	1,650
1631KB	—	195	350	575	1,000	1,650
1632KB	—	195	350	575	1,000	1,650
1633KB	—	195	350	575	1,000	1,650
1634KB	—	195	350	575	1,000	1,650
1635KB	—	195	350	575	1,000	1,650
1636KB	—	195	350	575	1,000	1,650
1637KB	—	195	350	575	1,000	1,650

KM# 98 DUCAT

3.5000 g., 0.9860 Gold 0.1109 oz. AGW **Rev:** Madonna and child in inner circle, crowned arms below

Date	Mintage	VG	F	VF	XF	Unc
1630N-B	—	245	500	975	1,800	—
1631N-B	—	245	500	975	1,800	—
1632N-B	—	245	500	975	1,800	—
1633N-B	—	245	500	975	1,800	—
1634N-B	—	245	500	975	1,800	—
1635N-B	—	245	500	975	1,800	—
1636N-B	—	245	500	975	1,800	—
1637N-B	—	245	500	975	1,800	—

KM# 100 DUCAT

3.5000 g., 0.9860 Gold 0.1109 oz. AGW **Rev:** Crescent below Madonna

Date	Mintage	VG	F	VF	XF	Unc
1632K-B	—	195	375	700	1,200	—

KM# 101 DUCAT

3.5000 g., 0.9860 Gold 0.1109 oz. AGW **Rev:** Cushion beneath Madonna

Date	Mintage	VG	F	VF	XF	Unc
1632N-B	—	280	575	1,150	2,050	—

KM# 104 DUCAT

3.5000 g., 0.9860 Gold 0.1109 oz. AGW **Rev:** Madonna with child at right

Date	Mintage	VG	F	VF	XF	Unc
1633	—	210	425	750	1,300	—

KM# 114 DUCAT

3.5000 g., 0.9860 Gold 0.1109 oz. AGW **Obv:** Ferdinand III **Rev:** Radiant Madonna and child

Date	Mintage	VG	F	VF	XF	Unc
1638K-B	—	195	350	575	1,000	1,650
1639K-B	—	195	350	575	1,000	1,650
1640K-B	—	195	350	575	1,000	1,650
1641K-B	—	195	350	575	1,000	1,650
1642K-B	—	195	350	575	1,000	1,650
1643K-B	—	195	350	575	1,000	1,650
1644K-B	—	195	350	575	1,000	1,650
1645K-B	—	195	350	575	1,000	1,650
1646K-B	—	195	350	575	1,000	1,650
1647K-B	—	195	350	575	1,000	1,650
1648K-B	—	195	350	575	1,000	1,650
1649K-B	—	195	350	575	1,000	1,650
1650K-B	—	195	350	575	1,000	1,650
1651K-B	—	195	350	575	1,000	1,650
1652K-B	—	195	350	575	1,000	1,650
1653K-B	—	195	350	575	1,000	1,650
1654K-B	—	195	350	575	1,000	1,650
1655K-B	—	195	350	575	1,000	1,650
1656K-B	—	195	350	575	1,000	1,650
1657K-B	—	195	350	575	1,000	1,650
1658K-B posthumous	—	195	350	575	1,000	1,650
1659K-B posthumous	—	195	350	575	1,000	1,650

KM# 115 DUCAT

3.5000 g., 0.9860 Gold 0.1109 oz. AGW **Rev:** Madonna with ornate gown and child in inner circle, crowned arm below

Date	Mintage	VG	F	VF	XF	Unc
1638NB	—	280	575	1,150	2,200	—

KM# 118 DUCAT

3.5000 g., 0.9860 Gold 0.1109 oz. AGW **Rev:** Madonna with plain gown

Date	Mintage	VG	F	VF	XF	Unc
1639	—	280	575	1,150	2,200	—

KM# 119 DUCAT

3.5000 g., 0.9860 Gold 0.1109 oz. AGW **Rev:** Rays surround Madonna and child

Date	Mintage	VG	F	VF	XF	Unc
1639	—	280	575	1,150	2,200	—
1642	—	280	575	1,150	2,200	—
1643	—	280	575	1,150	2,200	—
1644	—	280	575	1,150	2,200	—

KM# 120 DUCAT

3.5000 g., 0.9860 Gold 0.1109 oz. AGW **Obv:** Ferdinand III standing facing

Date	Mintage	VG	F	VF	XF	Unc
1639	—	280	575	1,150	2,200	—
1641	—	280	575	1,150	2,200	—

KM# 129 DUCAT

3.5000 g., 0.9860 Gold 0.1109 oz. AGW **Rev:** Madonna with child at right

Date	Mintage	VG	F	VF	XF	Unc
1642	—	280	575	1,150	2,200	—

KM# B130 DUCAT

3.5000 g., 0.9860 Gold 0.1109 oz. AGW **Note:** Struck with 1 Dinar dies, KM#26.

Date	Mintage	VG	F	VF	XF	Unc
1642K-B	—	450	950	1,750	2,850	—

KM# 133 DUCAT

3.5000 g., 0.9860 Gold 0.1109 oz. AGW **Rev:** Madonna with ornate gown holds child at left, without rays

Date	Mintage	VG	F	VF	XF	Unc
1644NB	—	280	575	1,150	2,200	—

KM# 134 DUCAT

3.5000 g., 0.9860 Gold 0.1109 oz. AGW **Rev:** Madonna with child at right

Date	Mintage	VG	F	VF	XF	Unc
1644	—	280	525	1,100	2,150	—

KM# 151 DUCAT

3.5000 g., 0.9860 Gold 0.1109 oz. AGW **Ruler:** Leopold I **Obv:** Leopold standing right divides mint mark in inner circle **Obv. Legend:** LEOPOLD: D: G: R - S: A: G: H: B: R E X **Rev:** Madonna with child at right **Rev. Legend:** • AR • AV • DV • BV • M • - MOCO • TY • date

Date	Mintage	VG	F	VF	XF	Unc
1658K-B	—	195	350	550	850	1,550
1659K-B	—	195	350	550	850	1,550
1660K-B	—	195	350	550	850	1,550
1661K-B	—	195	350	550	850	1,550
1662K-B	—	195	350	550	850	1,550
1663K-B	—	195	350	550	850	1,550
1664K-B	—	195	350	550	850	1,550
1665K-B	—	195	350	550	850	1,550
1666K-B	—	195	350	550	850	1,550
1667K-B	—	195	350	550	850	1,550
1668K-B	—	195	350	550	850	1,550
1669K-B	—	195	350	550	850	1,550
1670K-B	—	195	350	550	850	1,550
1671K-B	—	195	350	550	850	1,550
1672K-B	—	195	350	550	850	1,550
1673K-B	—	195	350	550	850	1,550
1674K-B	—	195	350	550	850	1,550
1675K-B	—	195	350	550	850	1,550
1676K-B	—	195	350	550	850	1,550
1677K-B	—	195	350	550	850	1,550
1678K-B	—	195	350	550	850	1,550
1679K-B	—	195	350	550	850	1,550
1680K-B	—	195	350	550	850	1,550
1681K-B	—	195	350	550	850	1,550
1682K-B	—	195	350	550	850	1,550
1683K-B	—	195	350	550	850	1,550
1684K-B	—	195	350	550	850	1,550
1685K-B	—	195	350	550	850	1,550
1686K-B	—	195	350	550	850	1,550
1687K-B	64,000	195	350	550	850	1,550
1688K-B	55,000	195	350	550	850	1,550
1689K-B	55,000	195	350	550	850	1,550
1690K-B	70,000	195	350	550	850	1,550
1691K-B	108,000	195	350	550	850	1,550
1692K-B	—	195	350	550	850	1,550
1693K-B	83,000	195	350	550	850	1,550
1694K-B	87,000	195	350	550	850	1,550
1695K-B	—	195	350	550	850	1,550
1696K-B	—	195	350	550	850	1,550
1697K-B	—	195	350	550	850	1,550
1698K-B	—	195	350	550	850	1,550
1699K-B	—	195	350	550	850	1,550
1700K-B	—	195	350	550	850	1,550

KM# 171 DUCAT

3.5000 g., 0.9860 Gold 0.1109 oz. AGW **Rev:** Radiant Madonna and child in inner circle, crowned arms below

Date	Mintage	VG	F	VF	XF	Unc
1661/0N-B	—	280	525	1,100	2,200	—
1667N-B	—	280	525	1,100	2,200	—
1671N-B	—	280	525	1,100	2,200	—

KM# 186 DUCAT

3.5000 g., 0.9860 Gold 0.1109 oz. AGW **Obv:** Madonna with child at right in inner circle **Rev:** Radiant Madonna with child at left in inner circle, crowned arms below **Note:** Without mint mark.

Date	Mintage	VG	F	VF	XF	Unc
1671	—	195	350	550	850	1,450

KM# 193 DUCAT

3.5000 g., 0.9860 Gold 0.1109 oz. AGW **Obv:** Laureate bust of Leopold right in inner circle **Rev:** Radiant Madonna and child divides mint mark in inner circle, crowned arms below

Date	Mintage	VG	F	VF	XF	Unc
1674 LM	—	350	850	1,800	3,500	—
1676 LM	—	350	850	1,800	3,500	—
1677 IS	—	350	850	1,800	3,500	—
1677 LM	—	350	850	1,800	3,500	—
1678 IS	—	350	850	1,800	3,500	—

KM# 198 DUCAT

3.5000 g., 0.9860 Gold 0.1109 oz. AGW **Rev:** Radiant Madonna and child in inner circle, 3 shields below

Date	Mintage	VG	F	VF	XF	Unc
1675	—	350	850	1,800	3,500	—

KM# 206 DUCAT

3.5000 g., 0.9860 Gold 0.1109 oz. AGW **Obv:** Leopold standing in finer style

Date	Mintage	VG	F	VF	XF	Unc
1683N-B	—	210	425	775	1,300	—
1687N-B	—	210	425	775	1,300	—
1691N-B	—	210	425	775	1,300	—
1692N-B	—	210	425	775	1,300	—
1694N-B	—	210	425	775	1,300	—
1695N-B	—	210	425	775	1,300	—
1696N-B	—	210	425	775	1,300	—
1697N-B	—	210	425	775	1,300	—
1698N-B	—	210	425	775	1,300	—

KM# 210 DUCAT

3.5000 g., 0.9860 Gold 0.1109 oz. AGW **Rev:** Madonna and child

Date	Mintage	VG	F	VF	XF	Unc
1685K-B	—	195	350	550	850	1,450

KM# 211 DUCAT

3.5000 g., 0.9860 Gold 0.1109 oz. AGW **Obv:** Leopold standing divides mint mark, moneyers initials

Date	Mintage	VG	F	VF	XF	Unc
1685N-B	—	195	300	475	775	1,400
1687N-B	—	195	300	475	775	1,400
1689N-B	—	195	300	475	775	1,400

KM# A214.1 DUCAT

3.5000 g., 0.9860 Gold 0.1109 oz. AGW **Obv:** Leupold standing divides mint mark, moneyer's initials **Note:** Prev. KM#214.1.

Date	Mintage	VG	F	VF	XF	Unc
1689	—	195	300	475	775	1,400

KM# 223 DUCAT

3.5000 g., 0.9860 Gold 0.1109 oz. AGW **Note:** Octagonal klippe.

Date	Mintage	VG	F	VF	XF	Unc
1691	—	700	1,400	2,800	4,250	—

KM# 224 DUCAT

3.5000 g., 0.9860 Gold 0.1109 oz. AGW **Rev:** Madonna and child divides moneyers initials

Date	Mintage	VG	F	VF	XF	Unc
1691 PO	—	195	300	550	925	1,500
1695 PO	—	195	300	550	925	1,500
1696 PO	—	195	300	550	925	1,500
1697 PO	—	195	300	550	925	1,500
1698 PO	—	195	300	550	925	1,500

KM# 239 DUCAT

3.5000 g., 0.9860 Gold 0.1109 oz. AGW **Obv:** Leopold standing right divides mint mark in inner circle

Date	Mintage	VG	F	VF	XF	Unc
1695CH	—	450	900	1,700	2,800	—
1696CH	—	450	900	1,700	2,800	—
1699CH	—	450	900	1,700	2,800	—

KM# A238 DUCAT

3.5000 g., 0.9860 Gold 0.1109 oz. AGW **Obv:** Bust Leopold facing right in inner circle **Rev:** Madonna and child divide date at top

Date	Mintage	VG	F	VF	XF	Unc
1695 C-H Rare	—	—	—	—	—	—

KM# 247 DUCAT

3.5000 g., 0.9860 Gold 0.1109 oz. AGW **Ruler:** Leopold I **Obv:** Initials below Leopold standing

Date	Mintage	VG	F	VF	XF	Unc
1699NB	—	280	550	1,100	2,000	—
1700NB	—	280	550	1,100	2,000	—

KM# 2 2 DUCAT

7.0000 g., 0.9860 Gold 0.2219 oz. AGW **Obv:** Legend around Madonna and child **Obv. Legend:** RVDOL \ II \ D.G... **Rev:** St. Ladislaus

Date	Mintage	VG	F	VF	XF	Unc
1601K-B	—	1,000	2,200	4,000	7,000	—

KM# 53 2 DUCAT

7.0000 g., 0.9860 Gold 0.2219 oz. AGW **Obv:** Matthias standing right divides mint mark in inner circle **Obv. Legend:** RVDOL • II • D.G... **Rev:** Radiant Madonna and child in inner circle, crowned arms below

Date	Mintage	VG	F	VF	XF	Unc
1614	—	475	925	1,950	3,850	—
1616	—	475	925	1,950	3,850	—
1618	—	475	925	1,950	3,850	—

KM# 79 2 DUCAT

7.0000 g., 0.9860 Gold 0.2219 oz. AGW **Obv:** Ferdinand II standing right in inner circle **Note:** Without mint mark

Date	Mintage	VG	F	VF	XF	Unc
1616	—	475	925	1,950	3,850	—
1622	—	475	925	1,950	3,850	—
1624	—	475	925	1,950	3,850	—

KM# 89 2 DUCAT

7.0000 g., 0.9860 Gold 0.2219 oz. AGW

Date	Mintage	VG	F	VF	XF	Unc
1617NB	—	475	925	1,950	3,850	—

KM# 87 2 DUCAT

7.0000 g., 0.9860 Gold 0.2219 oz. AGW **Obv:** Ferdinand II standing divides mint mark

Date	Mintage	VG	F	VF	XF	Unc
1624K-B	—	375	775	1,550	3,100	—
1625K-B	—	375	775	1,550	3,100	—
1626K-B	—	375	775	1,550	3,100	—
1627K-B	—	375	775	1,550	3,100	—
1628K-B	—	375	775	1,550	3,100	—
1629K-B	—	375	775	1,550	3,100	—
1630K-B	—	375	775	1,550	3,100	—
1631K-B	—	375	775	1,550	3,100	—
1632K-B	—	375	775	1,550	3,100	—
1633K-B	—	375	775	1,550	3,100	—
1634K-B	—	375	775	1,550	3,100	—
1635K-B	—	375	775	1,550	3,100	—
1636K-B	—	375	775	1,550	3,100	—
1637K-B	—	375	775	1,550	3,100	—

KM# 94 2 DUCAT

7.0000 g., 0.9860 Gold 0.2219 oz. AGW

Date	Mintage	VG	F	VF	XF	Unc
1630	—	375	775	1,550	3,100	—

KM# 128 2 DUCAT

7.0000 g., 0.9860 Gold 0.2219 oz. AGW **Obv:** Ferdinand II standing right divides mint mark in inner circle

Date	Mintage	VG	F	VF	XF	Unc
1641KB	—	375	700	1,500	2,850	—
1644KB	—	375	700	1,500	2,850	—
1645KB	—	375	700	1,500	2,850	—
1646KB	—	375	700	1,500	2,850	—
1647KB	—	375	700	1,500	2,850	—
1648KB	—	375	700	1,500	2,850	—
1649KB	—	375	700	1,500	2,850	—
1650KB	—	375	700	1,500	2,850	—
1651KB	—	375	700	1,500	2,850	—
1654KB	—	375	700	1,500	2,850	—

KM# 172 2 DUCAT

7.0000 g., 0.9860 Gold 0.2219 oz. AGW **Obv:** Leopold standing right divides mint mark in inner circle

Date	Mintage	VG	F	VF	XF	Unc
1661	—	550	1,050	2,300	4,250	—
1667	—	550	1,050	2,300	4,250	—

KM# B16 3 DUCAT

10.5000 g., 0.9860 Gold 0.3328 oz. AGW **Obv:** Armored 1/2 figure of Rudolph II **Note:** Struck with 1/2 Thaler dies, KM#10.

Date	Mintage	VG	F	VF	XF	Unc
1601KB Rare	—	—	—	—	—	—

KM# A211 3 DUCAT

10.5000 g., 0.9860 Gold 0.3328 oz. AGW **Note:** Leopold I

Date	Mintage	F	VF	XF	Unc	BU
1687	—	—	—	6,500	10,000	—

KM# A240 3 DUCAT

10.5000 g., 0.9860 Gold 0.3328 oz. AGW **Obv:** Laureate bust of Leopold I right in inner circle **Rev:** Crowned imperial eagle in inner circle, date in legend **Note:** Struck with 1/2 Thaler dies, KM#220.

Date	Mintage	VG	F	VF	XF	Unc
1695KB	—	—	—	6,500	10,000	—

KM# A102 4 DUCAT

14.0000 g., 0.9860 Gold 0.4438 oz. AGW **Obv:** Laureate bust of Ferdinand right **Rev:** Crowned imperial eagle **Note:** Struck with 1/2 Thaler dies, KM#75. Klippe.

Date	Mintage	VG	F	VF	XF	Unc
1622K-B Rare	—	—	—	—	—	—

KM# B211 4 DUCAT

14.0000 g., 0.9860 Gold 0.4438 oz. AGW **Note:** Leopold I

Date	Mintage	VG	F	VF	XF	Unc
1687NB LM	—	—	4,500	7,500	12,500	—

KM# C211 4 DUCAT

14.0000 g., 0.9860 Gold 0.4438 oz. AGW **Note:** Struck with 1/2 Thaler dies, KM#220.

Date	Mintage	VG	F	VF	XF	Unc
1695 PO	—	—	4,500	7,500	12,500	—

KM# B1 5 DUCAT

17.5000 g., 0.9860 Gold 0.5547 oz. AGW

Date	Mintage	VG	F	VF	XF	Unc
1601NB Rare	—	—	—	—	—	—

KM# C16 5 DUCAT

17.5000 g., 0.9860 Gold 0.5547 oz. AGW **Obv:** Armored 1/2 figure Rudolph II right **Rev:** Crowned imperial eagle divides mint mark NB **Note:** Struck with 1 Thaler dies, KM#10.

Date	Mintage	VG	F	VF	XF	Unc
1601NB Rare	—	—	—	—	—	—

KM# A53 5 DUCAT

17.5000 g., 0.9860 Gold 0.5547 oz. AGW **Obv:** Standing figure right **Rev:** Madonna and child

Date	Mintage	VG	F	VF	XF	Unc
1614KB	—	—	3,850	7,000	12,500	—
1617KB	—	—	3,850	7,000	12,500	—

KM# A90 5 DUCAT

17.5000 g., 0.9860 Gold 0.5547 oz. AGW **Rev:** Crowned arms in cartouche divide N-B in inner circle, date in legend **Note:** Struck with 1/2 Thaler dies, KM#58.

Date	Mintage	VG	F	VF	XF	Unc
1617NB Rare	—	—	—	—	—	—

KM# 102 5 DUCAT

17.5000 g., 0.9860 Gold 0.5547 oz. AGW **Obv:** Ferdinand II

Date	Mintage	VG	F	VF	XF	Unc
1622KB	—	—	4,200	7,500	13,500	—
1632KB	—	—	4,200	7,500	13,500	—

KM# A95 5 DUCAT

17.5000 g., 0.9860 Gold 0.5547 oz. AGW **Obv:** Different laureate bust of Ferdinand II right in inner circle **Note:** Struck with 1/4 Thaler dies, KM#103.

Date	Mintage	VG	F	VF	XF	Unc
1631 Rare	—	—	—	—	—	—

KM# A105 5 DUCAT

17.5000 g., 0.9860 Gold 0.5547 oz. AGW **Obv:** Laureate bust of Ferdinand II right in inner circle **Rev:** Crowned imperial eagle in inner circle, date in legend **Note:** Struck with 1/2 Thaler dies, KM#73.

Date	Mintage	VG	F	VF	XF	Unc
1634KB Rare	—	—	—	—	—	—
1637KB	—	—	5,600	9,500	16,500	—

KM# A180 5 DUCAT

17.5000 g., 0.9860 Gold 0.5547 oz. AGW **Obv:** Laureate bust of Leopold in inner circle **Note:** Struck with 1 Thaler dies, KM#170.2.

Date	Mintage	VG	F	VF	XF	Unc
1665	—	—	4,200	7,500	13,500	—

KM# 182 5 DUCAT

17.5000 g., 0.9860 Gold 0.5547 oz. AGW **Obv:** Leopold standing **Rev:** Madonna and child

Date	Mintage	VG	F	VF	XF	Unc
1669	—	—	4,000	7,000	12,500	—
1674	—	—	4,000	7,000	12,500	—

KM# A186 5 DUCAT

17.5000 g., 0.9860 Gold 0.5547 oz. AGW **Ruler:** Leopold I **Obv:** Long haired armored bust to right breaks circle at top, date below shoulder, legend divided by 2 small shields of arms at lower left and right. **Obv. Legend:** LEOPOLD - D.G. R. I. S. AV. GE - HV. B. REX. **Rev:** Crowned imperial eagle, crowned shield of 4-fold arms with central shield of Hungary on breast **Rev. Legend:** ARCHID. AV. DV. BV. MAR. MOR. CO. TYR. **Note:** Struck with 1/2 Thaler dies, KM#185.

Date	Mintage	VG	F	VF	XF	Unc
1670 KB	—	—	—	—	—	—

Note: Künker auction, 3-09, XF realized approximately $31,000.

KM# 199 5 DUCAT

17.5000 g., 0.9860 Gold 0.5547 oz. AGW **Obv:** Leopold

Date	Mintage	VG	F	VF	XF	Unc
1675(g)	—	—	5,750	9,750	18,000	—

KM# B240 5 DUCAT

17.5000 g., 0.9860 Gold 0.5547 oz. AGW **Obv:** Laureate bust of Leopold I right in inner circle **Rev:** Radiant Madonna and child divide N-B in inner circle, date in legend **Note:** Struck with 2 Thaler dies, KM#212.

Date	Mintage	VG	F	VF	XF	Unc
1695NB-PO	—	—	5,750	9,750	18,000	—

KM# C1 10 DUCAT

35.0000 g., 0.9860 Gold 1.1095 oz. AGW **Obv:** Armored 1/2 figure of Rudolph II **Note:** Struck with 1 Thaler dies, KM#12.

Date	Mintage	VG	F	VF	XF	Unc
1601NB Rare	—	—	—	—	—	—

KM# B53 10 DUCAT

35.0000 g., 0.9860 Gold 1.1095 oz. AGW **Obv:** Legend as King of Hungary and Bohemia **Note:** Struck with 1 Thaler dies, KM#34.

Date	Mintage	VG	F	VF	XF	Unc
1612KB Rare	—	—	—	—	—	—

KM# A98 10 DUCAT

35.0000 g., 0.9860 Gold 1.1095 oz. AGW **Obv:** Bust righrt **Rev:** Heraldic double eagle

Date	Mintage	VG	F	VF	XF	Unc
1631NB Rare	—	—	—	—	—	—
1632NB Rare	—	—	—	—	—	—
1635NB Rare	—	—	—	—	—	—

KM# A78 10 DUCAT

35.0000 g., 0.9860 Gold 1.1095 oz. AGW **Obv:** Bust righrt **Rev:** Madonna and child

Date	Mintage	VG	F	VF	XF	Unc
1637KB Rare	—	—	—	—	—	—

KM# 121 10 DUCAT

35.0000 g., 0.9860 Gold 1.1095 oz. AGW **Obv:** Laureate bust of Ferdinand III right **Rev:** Crowned imperial eagle **Note:** Struck with 1 Thaler dies, KM#113.2.

Date	Mintage	VG	F	VF	XF	Unc
1639NB Rare	—	—	—	—	—	—

KM# 123 10 DUCAT

35.0000 g., 0.9860 Gold 1.1095 oz. AGW **Obv:** Laureate bust of Leopold I right **Rev:** Crowned imperial eagle **Note:** Struck with 1 Thaler dies, KM#155.

Date	Mintage	VG	F	VF	XF	Unc
1659KB Rare	—	—	—	—	—	—

KM# B180 10 DUCAT

35.0000 g., 0.9860 Gold 1.1095 oz. AGW **Obv:** Laureate bust of Leopold right 9 **Rev:** Crowned imperial eagle **Note:** Struck with 1 Thaler dies, KM#170.2.

Date	Mintage	VG	F	VF	XF	Unc
1666KB Rare	—	—	—	—	—	—
1668KB Rare	—	—	—	—	—	—

KM# C215 10 DUCAT

35.0000 g., 0.9860 Gold 1.1095 oz. AGW **Obv:** Laureate bust of Leopold right **Rev:** Madonna and child divide NB in flaming oval **Note:** Struck with 1 Thaler dies, KM#196.

Date	Mintage	VG	F	VF	XF	Unc
1687NB Rare	—	—	—	—	—	—

KM# C240 10 DUCAT

35.0000 g., 0.9860 Gold 1.1095 oz. AGW **Note:** Struck with 1 Thaler dies, KM#214.8.

Date	Mintage	VG	F	VF	XF	Unc
1695KB Rare	—	—	—	—	—	—

KM# B78 12 DUCAT

35.0000 g., 0.9860 Gold 1.1095 oz. AGW **Obv:** Bust right **Rev:** Heraldic double eagle **Note:** Struck with 1 Thaler dies, KM#75.

Date	Mintage	VG	F	VF	XF	Unc
1626KB Rare	—	—	—	—	—	—

PATTERNS

Including off metal strikes

KM#	Date	Mintage	Identification	Mkt Val
PnA1	ND(1500-02)	—	Obol. Gold. MB#3. (Fr.36).	—
PnB1	ND(1526-40)	—	Obol. Gold. MB#100, H#877a.	—
PnI1	15Z7	—	Denar. Gold. MB#114. H#875.	—
PnC1	ND(1527-64)	—	Obol. Gold. 1.2500 g. KM#102, H#906.	—
PnJ1	1530	—	Denar. Gold. MB#114. H#876.	—
PnD1	154ZKB	—	Obol. Gold. 0.8800 g. MB#145, H#907.	—
	1558KB	—	Goldgulden. Lead. MB#124.	—
PnE1	1559KB	—	Obol. Gold. 0.8800 g. MB#145. H#907.	—
PnK1	1577KB	—	Denar. Gold. H#975. MB#237.	—
PnL1	1579KB	—	Denar. Gold. 1.7500 g. MB#247. H#1012.	—
PnQ1	158ZNB	—	Denar. Gold. MB#289, 0.94g (Fr. 73 - 1/4 Goldgulden). H#1015.	—
PnM1	1588KB	—	Denar. Gold. MB#260, 1.77-1.81g (Fr.71). H#1013.	—
PnN1	1590KB	—	Denar. Gold. MB#260, 1.77-1.81g (Fr.71).	—
PnO1	1591KB	—	Denar. Gold. MB#260, 1.77-1.81g (Fr.71).	—
PnF1	1594KB	—	Obol. Gold. MB#245 (Fr.74 - 1/4 Goldgulden). H#1017.	—
PnP1	1599KB	—	Denar. Gold. MB#260, 1.77-1.81g (Fr.71).	—
PnG1	1600KB	—	Obol. Gold. MB#245 (Fr.74 - 1/4 Goldgulden).	—
Pn3	1607	—	Denar. Gold. KM#7	—
PnA5	1608	—	Denar. Gold.	—
Pn4	1608KB	—	Denar. Gold. KM#16.1	—
PnB5	1609KB	—	Denar. Gold. 3.4000 g.	—
Pn5	1610	—	Obol. Gold. KM#22	—
PnA7	1615KB	—	Denar. Gold. 1.1000 g.	—
PnB7	1615NB	—	1/4 Ducat. Silver.	—
PnA8	1620KB	—	Denar. Gold. Weight of 1/4 Ducat.	—
Pn8	1625	—	Denar. Silver. KM#88	—
Pn9	1625	—	Denar. Gold. KM#88	—
Pn10	1626	—	Thaler. Gold. KM#75. Weight of 12 Ducat.	—
Pn11	1630	—	Denar. Silver. KM#88	—
Pn12	1630	—	Denar. Gold. KM#88	—
Pn14	1633	—	Denar. Gold. KM#95.1	—
Pn15	1634	—	Denar. Silver. KM#95.1	—
Pn19	1639	—	Denar. Gold. KM#125. Weight of 1/4 Ducat.	—
Pn20	1640	—	Denar. Gold. KM#110.1	—
Pn22	1641	—	Denar. Gold. KM#110.1	—
Pn23	1642	—	Obol. Gold. KM#105	—
Pn27	1643	—	Denar. Gold. KM#110.1	—
Pn29	1644	—	Denar. Gold. KM#110.1	—
Pn30	1646	—	Obol. Gold. KM#105	—
Pn31	1646	—	Denar. Gold. KM#110.1	—
Pn32	1650	—	Denar. Gold. KM#110.1	—
Pn33	1652	—	Obol. Gold. KM#105	—
Pn34	1655	—	Denar. Gold. KM#110.1	—
Pn35	1659K-B	—	Denar. Gold. KM#174	—
Pn36	1660K-B	—	Obol. Gold. KM#173	—
Pn37	1660K-B	—	Denar. Gold. KM#174	—
Pn38	1661K-B	—	15 Krajczar. Gold. KM#165	—
Pn39	1662K-B	—	Obol. Gold. KM#173	—
Pn40	1662K-B	—	Denar. Gold. KM#174	—
Pn41	1665K-B	—	Obol. Gold. KM#173	—
Pn42	1665KB	—	2 Ducat. Silver. KM#172	175
Pn43	1666K-B	—	Denar. Gold. KM#174	—
Pn45	1674K-B	—	Denar. Gold. KM#174	—
Pn46	1675K-B	—	Obol. Gold. KM#173	—
Pn47	1677K-B	—	Denar. Gold. KM#174	—
Pn48	1678K-B	—	Denar. Gold. KM#174	—
Pn49	1679K-B	—	Denar. Gold. KM#174	—
Pn50	1680K-B	—	Obol. Gold. KM#173	—
Pn51	1681	—	15 Krajczar. Copper. KM#175	—
Pn52	1682K-B	—	Obol. Gold. KM#173	—
Pn53	1682K-B	—	Denar. Gold. KM#174	—
Pn54	1683	—	Denar. Gold. KM#174	—
Pn55	1683	—	Ducat. Copper. KM#151	150
Pn56	1684	—	Denar. Gold. KM#174	—
Pn57	1684K-B	—	6 Krajczar. Gold. KM#164	—
Pn58	1685	—	Denar. Gold. KM#174	—
Pn59	1685	—	Ducat. Silver. KM#151	175
Pn60	1686K-B	—	Denar. Gold. KM#174	—
Pn61	1689K-B	—	Obol. Gold. KM#173	—
Pn62	1689K-B	—	Denar. Gold. KM#174	—
Pn63	1692K-B	—	Denar. Gold. KM#174	—
Pn64	1694K-B	—	Denar. Gold. KM#174	—
Pn65	1695K-B	—	Denar. Gold. KM#174	—
Pn67	1696K-B	—	Denar. Gold. KM#174	—
Pn68	1696K-B	—	Denar. Gold. KM#231	—
Pn69	1698K-B	—	Denar. Gold. KM#174	—
Pn70	1698K-B	—	Denar. Gold. KM#231	—
Pn72	1699 ICB/N-B	—	Krajczar. Gold. KM#234	—
Pn71	1699K-B	—	Denar. Gold. KM#231	—

PIEFORTS

KM#	Date	Mintage	Identification	Mkt Val
P1	1601	—	Denar. KM#6	—
P2	1607	—	Denar. KM#16	—
P3	1609	—	Denar. KM#23	—
P4	1612	—	Denar. KM#32	—
P5	1615	—	Denar. KM#40	—
P6	1616	—	Denar. KM#40	—
P7	1619	—	Denar. KM#40	—
P8	1625	—	Denar. KM#63	—
P9	1634	—	Denar. KM#95	—
P10	1649	—	Denar. KM#110	—
P11	1650	—	Denar. KM#110	—
P12	1655	—	Denar. KM#110	—
P13	1659	—	Denar. KM#144	—

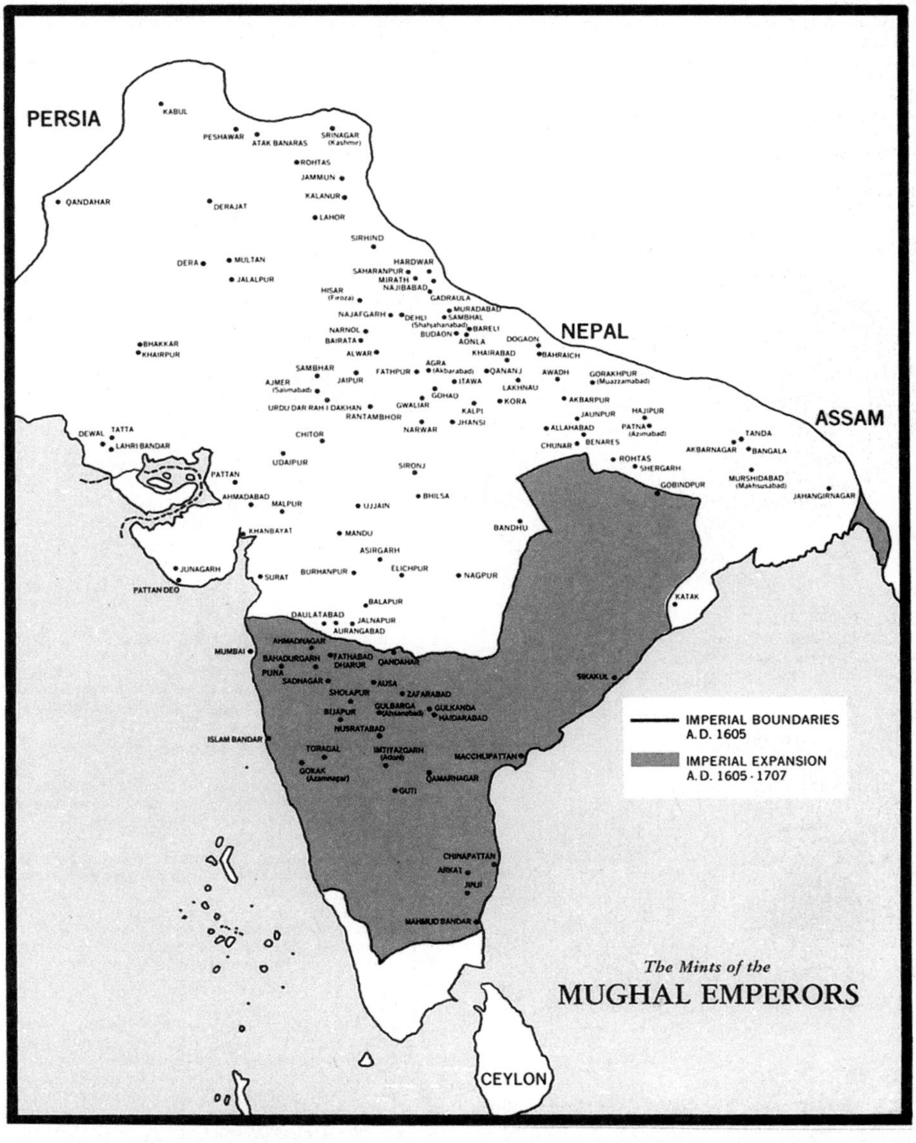

The Mints of the
MUGHAL EMPERORS

The Lodi Sultanate of Delhi was conquered by Zahir-ud-din Muhammad Babur, a Chagatai Turk descended from Tamerlane, in 1525AD. His son, Nasir-ud-din Muham-mad Humayun, lost the new empire in a series of battles with the Bihari Afghan Sher Shah, who founded the short-lived Suri dynasty. Humayun, with the assistance of the Emperor of Persia, recovered his kingdom from Sher Shah's successors in 1555AD. He did not long enjoy the fruits of victory for his fatal fall down his library steps brought his teenage son Jalal-ud-din Muhammad Akbar to the throne in the following year. During Akbar's long reign of a half century, the Mughal Empire was firmly established throughout much of North India. Under Akbar's son and grandson, the emperors Nur-ud-din Muhammad Jahangir and Shihab-ud-din Muhammad Shah Jahan, the state reached its apogee and art, culture and commerce flourished.

One of the major achievements of the Mughal government was the establishment of a universal silver currency, based on the rupee, a coin of 11.6 grams and as close to pure silver content as the metallurgy of the time was capable of attaining. Supplementary coins were the copper dam and gold mohur. The values of these coin denominations were nominally fixed at 40 dams to 1 rupee, and 8 rupees to 1 mohur; however, market forces determined actual exchange rates.

The maximum expansion of the geographical area under direct Mughal rule was achieved during the reign of Aurangzeb Alamgir. By his death in 1707AD, the whole peninsula, with minor exceptions, the whole subcontinent of India owed fealty to the Mughal emperor.

Aurangzeb's wars, lasting decades, upset the stability and prosperity of the kingdom. The internal dissension and rebellion which resulted brought the eclipse of the empire in succeeding reigns. The Mughal monetary system, especially the silver rupee, supplanted most local currencies throughout India. The number of Mughal mints rose sharply and direct central control declined, so that by the time of the emperor Shah Alam II, many nominally Mughal mints served independent states. The common element in all these coinage issues was the presence of the Mughal emperor's name and titles on the obverse. In the following listings no attempt has been made to solve the problem of separating Mughal from Princely State coins by historical criteria: all Mughal-style coins are considered products of the Mughal empire until the death of Muhammad Shah in 1784AD; thereafter all coins are considered Princely State issues unless there is evidence of the mint being under ever-diminishing Imperial control.

EMPERORS

Akbar, Jalal-ud-din Muhammad

جلال الدين محمد اكبر

AH963-1014/1556-1605AD

Copper Coinage

Persian Word Dates

The copper coins of Akbar issued from AH963 until 1014 were often dated with written Persian words rather than (or in addition to) Arabic numerals. These dates are obviously bulky and crowd one whole face of the flan often with much of the date cut. The pattern of the worded dates follows; with patience the date can be reconstructed even if numerals are missing. The legends read right to left, bottom to top.

Examples:

Two	دو
Seventy and	هفتاد و
Nine hundred and	نهصد و
Year	سنه
AH972	٩٧٢
Ninety	نود
Nine hundred and	نهصد و
Year	سنه
AH990	٩٩٠

Persian Numbers:

يك or يک one	شصت sixty
دو two	هفتاد seventy
سـ or سه three	هشتاد eighty
چهار or چهار four	نود ninety
پنج five	نهصد نهصد nine hundred
شش six	يك هزار one thousand
هفت seven	
هشت eight	سنـ or سنه year
نـ or نه nine	و and

Silver Coinage

The standard for the Mughal rupee was 11.444 g of .984 Silver with an actual silver weight (ASW) of .362 ounce.

Type 88

In the second half of Akbar's reign the pattern of the silver coinage was changed drastically. The Kalima, the Muslim profession of faith, was dropped from the obverse and the expression *Allahu Akbar Jalla Jalalahu*. "God is great, bright is His glory" (thought to have been meant as a punning reference to the emperor's name) was substituted. Akbar's name and titles were deleted from the reverse, and the mintname with Ilahi year and Persian month placed in center flan.

Type 97

During the last decade of Akbar's reign, his son Salim grew increasingly restive in the desire to assume supreme power. He rebelled outright several times, and, as governor of Allahabad Province, refused to recognize Akbar's suzereignty. The silver coins struck at Allahabad of this period were issued anonymously without following the imperial style, but with a Persian poetic couplet giving mintname and date.

Rebellion Coinage

Akbar's was a conquest state, the major provinces of which were independent kingdoms before incorporation in the Empire. On several occasions coinage was issued by displaced local kings during attempts to re-conquer their kingdoms from Akbar. These issues, coming after the initiation of Mughal-style coinage in their provinces,are listed here.

Gold Coinage

First general issue in gold, the mohur with Hejira dating. All mohurs during Akbar's first thirty years (and some thereafter) carried the Kalima on the obverse and his name and titles on the reverse. They maintained the same weight standard, around 11 grams. Planchets were regularly round except for the rare lozenge-shaped "mehrabi" and some square types after AH987. There was much variety in borders and ornamentation, and some in royal titulature. Representative varieties of various mints are illustrated below.

Heavy "Mohur" Gold Coinage

Between AH986 and 988 gold mohurs were struck at some of the main Mughal mints on square planchets and on a "heavy" weight standard of about 12 grams. This was repeated in the millennial year AH1000 at the travelling camp mint Urdu Zafar Qarin with the striking of heavy mohurs and fractions. A few heavy mohurs on round planchets and with special designs were also struck in the Ilahi dating system, as illustrated.

INDIA, MUGHAL EMPIRE

Jahangir, Nur-ud-din Muhammad,

نور الدين محمد جهانگير

AH1014-1037/1605-1627AD

Copper Coinage

The copper coinage of Jahangir is scarce in comparison with the profuse issues of Akbar. No comprehensive type listing is possible given the few specimens available for study.

Silver Coinage

Type 149

Obv. and rev. form a poetic couplet. Each mint has a distinctive couplet. A typical word from the central portion of the rev. legend is given as identifier for each sub-type in this section.

Type 158

Obv. and rev. form a poetic couplet. Each mint has a distinctive couplet. A typical word from the rev. legend is given as identifier for each sub-type in this section.

Nisar

The nisar was a specially struck coin for ceremonial largesse. Unusual denominations struck by Jahangir were the *Nur Afshan* or "light scattering", and the *Khair-i-qabul* or "acceptable".

Gold Coinage

Type 176

The standard issue mohurs of Jahangir show much variation in execution. Illustrated is a Burhanpur mohur, typical of the average size and design. For comparison sake, two of the very handsomely executed mohurs of Agra are also shown. The design of the Agra mohur tended to be altered frequently, with much variation in border design and calligraphy.

Type 186

Poetic couplets based on Ilahi month names. From the year 1019, at a few mints, a specially composed poetic couplet was employed on the coin for each month. The decorative borders and calligraphy varied monthly. Only a sample illustration is included.

5 Mohurs

Jahangir's treasury stockpiled gold and silver in the form of stamped ingots which were in effect giant coins. 5, 10, 20, 50, 100 and higher mohur denominations are recorded by contemporary observers. In some instances these multiple mohurs were presented to ambassadors, and probably others, and so not all passed away with the Mughal treasury in later reigns. We have illustrated just one such coin.

Dawar Bakhsh, in Lahore

داور بخش

AH1037/1627AD

Shah Jahan, Shihab-ud-din Muhammad,

شهاب الدين محمد شاه جهان

AH1037-1068/1628-1658AD

Copper Coinage

Like the copper coinage of his predecessor Jahangir, Shah Jahan's copper has not survived in sufficient quantities to permit a comprehensive typology. What is listed is a tentative listing.

Silver Coinage

Nazarana

Certain of the previous coin-types of Shah Jahan were specially struck on wide planchets to produce "nazarana" or presentation coins. These are recognizable by the full die impression appearing on wider-than-normal flans.

Murad Bakhsh, Murawwij-ud-din Muhammad, in Gujarat,

محمد مراد بخش

AH1068/1658AD

Shah Shuja, in Bengal,

شاه شجاع

AH1068-1070/1657-1660AD

Aurangzeb Alamgir, Muhayyi-ud-din

اورنگ زيب عالمگير

AH1068-1118/1658-1707AD

Silver Coinage

The standard for the Mughal Rupee was 11.444 g of .984 Silver with an actual silver weight (ASW) of .362 ounce.

Legal Dirham

The "legal dirham" was an exotic coin struck in order to satisfy the strictest interpretations of the Quran in regard to dowry, capitation tax and charity giving. The weight of the coin, at 2.97 g, was intended to equal the dirham of the early Caliphs. The coins are rare, and probably not more than a token number were struck to satisfy the emperor's whim.

MINT NAMES

Adoni (Imtiyazgarh)	ادوني
Advani	ادواني
Agra (Akbarabad)	اگره
Ahmadabad	احمداباد
Ahmadnagar	احمدنگر
Ahsanabad (Gulbarga)	احسن اباد
Ajmer (Salimabad)	اجمير
Ajmer Salimabad	اجمير سليم اباد
Akbarabad (Agra)	اكبراباد
Akbarnagar	اكبرنگر
Akbarpur (Tanda)	اكبرپور
Akbarpur Tanda	اكبرپور تانده

Akhtarnagar (Awadh)	اخترنگر
Alamgirpur (Bhilsa)	عالم گيرپور
Alamgirnagar	عالمگيرنگر
Alinagar (Kalkatta)	علي نگر
Allahabad (Ilahabad)	الله اباد
Alwar	الوار
Anhirwala Pattan	انحيروالا پتن
Anwala (Anola)	انوله
Arkat	اركات
Asadnagar (Aklooj)	
Asafabad (Bareli)	اصف اباد
Asafabad Bareli	اصف اباد بريلي
Asir	اسير
Atak	اتك
Atak Banaras	اتك بنارس
Aurangabad (Khujista Bunyad)	اورنگ اباد
Aurangnagar	اورنگ نگر
Ausa	اوسا
Awadh, Oudh (Khitta)	اوده
Azamnagar (Gokak)	اعظم نگر
Azamnagar Gokak	اعظم نگر گوكاك
Azimabad (Patna)	عظيم اباد
Badakhshan	بدخشان
Bahadarqarh	بهادرگره
Bahraich	بهرايچ بهريچ
Bairata	بيراتة
Bakkar (Bhakkar)	بهكّر بهكهر
Balapur	بالاپور
Balkh	بلخ

Balwantnagar (Jhansi)	بلونت نگر
Bandar Shahi	بندرشاهي
Bandhu (Qila)	بندحو
Bangala	بنگالة
Bankapur	بنكپ بنكاپور
Baramati	بارامتي برامتي
Bareli (Asafabad)	بريلي
Bairata	بيراتة
Berar	برار
Bhakkar	بهكّر بهكهر
Bhalki (?)	
Bharoch (Baroch)	بهروچ
Bhilsa (Alamgirpur)	بهيلسة
Bijapur	بيجاپور
Bikanir	بيكانير
Budaon	بداون
Burhanabad	برهان اباد
Burhanpur	برهانپور
Chinapattan	چيناپتن
Chitor (Akbarpur)	چيتور
Chunar	چنار
Daulatabad (Deogir)	دولت اباد دولتاباد
Dehli (Shahjahanabad)	دهلي
Deogir (Daulatabad)	ديوگير
Derajat	ديرجات
Dewal Bandar	ديول بندر
Dicholi	ديچولي
Dilshadabad	دلشاداباد
Dogaon	دوگاون
Elichpur	ايلچپور
Farkhanda Bunyad (Haidarabad)	فرخنده بنياد

Farrukhabad (Ahmadnagar)	فرخ اباد
Fathabad Dharur	فبح اباد دهرور
Fathnagar	فتحنگر
Fathpur	فتحپور
Firozgarh (Yadgir)	فيروزگره
Firoznagar	فيروزنگر
Gadraula	گدرولة
Gajjikota	گنجيكوت
Garha (Known from rupees of Akbar)	گارحة
Gobindpur	گوبندپور
Gohad	گوهد
Gokak (Azamnagar)	گوكاك
Gokulgarh	گوكل گره
Goraghat	
Gorakhpur (Muazzamabad)	گوركپور
Gulbarga (Ahsanabad)	گلبرگة
Gulkanda (Golkonda)	گلكندة
Gulshanabad (Nasik)	گلشن اباد
Guti	گوتي
Gwalior	گواليار
Hafizabad	هافظاباد
Haidarabad (Farkhanda Bunyad)	حيدراباد
Hajipur	حجيپور
Hardwar (Haridwar) (Tirath)	هاردوار
Hathras	هاتهرس
Hisar (Firoza)	حصر
Hisar Firoza	حصار فيروزة
Hukeri	هوكري
Imtiyazgarh (Adoni)	امتيازگره
Islamabad (Mathura)	اسلام اباد
Islam Bandar (Rajapur)	اسلام بندر

Islamnagar	اسلام نگر
Ismailgahr	اسمعیل گره
Itawa	اتاوه اتاوا
Jahangirnagar (Dacca)	جهانگیرنگر
Jaipur (Sawai)	جي پور
Jalalnagar	جلال نگر
Jalalpur	جلالپور
Jalesar	جليسار
Jallandar	جالندر جلّندر
Jalnapur (Jalna)	جالنة پور
Jaunpur	جونپور
Jinji (Nusratgarh)	جنجي
Jodhpur	جودهپور
Junagarh	جونة گره
Kabul	كابل
Kalanur	كالانور
Kalkatta (Alinagar)	كلكته
Kalpi	كلپي
Kanauj (Qanauj)	قنوج
Kanbayat (Khambayat)	كمبايت
Kanji (Kanchipuram)	كنجي
Kankurti	كانكرتي
Kararabad (Karad)	كراراباد
Karimabad	كريم اباد
Karnatak	كرناتك
Karpa	كرپا
Kashmir (Srinagar)	كشمير
Katak	كتك
Katak Banaras	كتك بنارس
Khairabad	خيراباد
Khairnagar	خيرنگر
Khairpur	خيرپور
Khambayat (Kanbayat)	كمنبايت
Kherawar (?)	
Khujista Bunyad (Aurangabad)	خجسته بنياد
Kishtwar	كشتوار
Koilkunda	كويلكونده
Kolapur	كولاپور كلاپور
Kora	كورا
Lahore	لاهور
Lahri Bandar	لهري بندر
Lakhnau	
Machhlipattan	مچهلي پتن
Madankot	مدنكوت
Mahindurpur (Mahe Indrapur)	مهه اندرپور
Mahmud Bandar	محمودبندر
Mailapur	ميلاپور
Makhsusabad (Murshidabad)	مخصوص اباد
Maliknagar	ملك نگر
Malpur	مالپور
Mandu	مندو
Mangarh (Manghar)	مانگره
Manikpur	مانكپور
Mathura (Islamabad)	متهره
Mirath (Mirtha)	ميرتا ميرتة
Muazzamabad (Gorakhpur)	معظم اباد
Muhammadabad (Udaipur)	محمداباد
Muhammadabad Banaras	محمداباد بنارس
Mulher (Aurangnagar)	ملهر
Multan	ملتان
Mumbai (Bombay)	منبي
Mungir	مهنگير
Muradabad	مراداباد
Murshidabad (Makhsusabad)	مرشداباد
Murtazabad	مرتضاباد
Muzaffargarh	مظفرگره
Nagor	ناگور
Najibabad	نجيباباد
Narnol	نارنول
Narwar	نرور
Nasirabad (Dharwar)	نصيراباد
Nusratabad (Nasratabad) (Fathpur)	نصرت اباد
Nusratgarh (Jinji)	نصرت گره
Orissa	اوريسة
Patna (Azimabad)	پتنة
Pattan (Anhirwala)	پتن
Pattan Deo (Somnath)	پتن ديو
Peshawar	پشاور
Phonda	پهونده
Punamali	پونامالي
Punch	پونچ
Pune (Muhiabad Poona)	پونه
Purbandar	پوربندر
Purenda	پرينده
Qamarnagar (Qarnool)	قمرنگر
Qanauj (Shahgarh Qanauj)	قنوج
Qandahar	قندهار
Rajapur (Islam Bandar)	راجاپور
Ranthambhor	رنتهبور
Ranthor	رنتهور
Rohtas (Rohtak)	رحتاس رهتاس
Saharanpur	سهارنپور
Sahrind (Sarhind)	سرهند سهرند
Saimur	سيمور
Salimabad (Ajmer)	سليم اباد

Sambhal	سنبل
Sambhar	سانبهر
Sangamner	سنگمنر
Sarangpur	سارنگپور
Sarhind (Sahrind)	سرهند سهرند
Satara	ستارا
Shahabad Qanauj	شاه اباد قنوج
Shahgarh Qanauj	شاه گره قنوج
Shahjahanabad (Dehli)	شاه جهان اباد
Shergarh	شيرگره
Sherkot	شيركوت
Sherpur	شيرپور
Sholapur	شولاپور
Sikakul	سيكاكل
Sikandarah	سكندره
Sind	سند
Sironj	سرونج
Sitapur	سيتاپور
Srinagar (Kashmir)	سرينگر
Surat	سورت
Tanda (Akbarpur)	تانده
Tarapatri	تراپتري
Tatta	تته
Tibet-i-Kalan	
Toragal	تورگل توراگال
Trichanapally	
Udaipur (Muhammadabad)	اوديپور اديپور
Udgir	ادگير
Ujjain	اجين
Ujjainpur	اجين پور
Umarkot (in Sind)	امركوت
Urdu	اردو
Urdu Dar Rahi-i-Dakkin	اردو دار راه دكين
Urdu Zafar Qarin	اردو ظفر قرين
Zafarabad	ظفراباد
Zafarnagar	ظفرنگر
Zafarpur	ظفرپور
Zain-ul-bilad (Zinat-ul-Bilad), (Ahmadabad)	زين البلاد

MINT EPITHETS

Mughal mintnames were often accompanied by honorific epithets. Quite often the epithet is visible on the flan when the mintname is absent or cut; in such cases the epithet is the best identification for the coin's mint of issue.

I. Geographical Terms:

بلدات
Baldat
City - Agra, Allahabad, Burhanpur, Bikanir, Patna, Sirhind, Ujjain

بندر
Bandar
Port - Dewal, Lahri, Surat, Machhlipattan

داخل
Dakhil
Breach (in Fort) - Chitor

خطة
Khitta
District - Awadh, Kalpi, Kashmir, Lakhnau

قصبة
Qasba
Town - Panipat, Sherkot

قلعة قلع
Qila
Fort - Agra, Alwar, Bandhu, Gwalior, Punch

قلعة مقام
Qila Muqam
Fort Residence - Gwalior

قطة
Qita
District - Bareli

سركار
Sarkar
County – Lakhnau, Torgal

شهر
Shahr
City - Anhirwala Pattan

سوبة
Suba
Province - Awadh

ترتة
Tirtha
Shrine - Hardwar

II. Poetic Allusion:

اشراف البلاد
Ashraf al-Bilad
Most Noble of Cities - Qandahar/Ahmadshahi

بلدات فخيرة
Baldat-i-Fakhira
Splendid City - Burhanpur

بندر مبارك
Bandar-i-Mubarak
Blessed Port - Surat

دار الامان
Dar-ul-Aman
Seat of Safety - Agra, Jammun, Multan, Sirhind

دار البركات
Dar-ul-Barakat
Seat of Blessings - Nagor

دار الفتح
Dar-ul-Fath
Seat of Conquest - Ujjain

دار الاسلام
Dar-ul-Islam
Seat of Islam - Dogaon, Mandisor

دار الجهاد
Dar-ul-Jihad
Seat of Holy War - Haidarabad

دار الخير
Dar-ul-Khair
Seat of Welfare - Ajmer

دار الخلافة
Dar-ul-Khilafa
Capital (Seat of Caliphate) - Agra, Ahmadabad, Akbarabad, Akbarpur Tanda, Awadh, Bahraich, Daulatabad, Dogaon, Gorakhpur, Gwalior, Jaunpur, Lahore, Lakhnau, Malpur, Shahgarh Qanauj, Shahjahanabad

دار المنصور
Dar-ul-Mansur
Seat of the Victorious - Ajmer, Jodhpur

دار الملك
Dar-ul-Mulk
Capital (Seat of the Kingdom) - Dehli, Fathpur, Kabul

دار السلام
Dar-us-Salam
Seat of Peace – Dogaon, Mandsor

دار السرور
Dar-us-Sarur
Seat of Delight - Burhanpur, Saharanpur

دار السلطنة
Dar-us-Sultanat
Seat of Sovereignty - Ahmadabad, Burhanpur, Fathpur, Kora, Lahore

دار الظفر
Dar-uz-Zafar
Seat of Victory - Advani, Bijapur

دار الضرب
Dar-uz-Zarb
Seat of the Mint - Jaunpur, Kalpi, Patna

فرخنده بنياد
Farkhanda Bunyad
Of Auspicious Foundation - Haidarabad

حضرت
Hazrat
Venerable - Dehli

خجستة بنياد
Khujista Bunyad
Of Fortunate Foundation - Aurangabad

مستقر الخلافة
Mustaqir-ul-Khilafat
Abode of the Caliphate - Akbarabad, Ajmer

مستقر الملك
Mustaqir-ul-Mulk
Abode of the Kingdom - Akbarabad, Azimabad

سواي
Sawai
1-1/4 (A Notch Better) - Jaipur

زين البلاد
Zain-ul-Bilad
Beauty of Cities - Ahmadabad

DATING

The Mughal coins were dated both in the Hejira era and in the regnal era of each emperor. The four-digit Hejira year usually was shown on the obverse, with the one or two-digit regnal (jalus) year on the reverse. Since the regnal and calendar years did not coincide, it was common for two different regnal years to appear on the coins produced during any calendar year. The first jalus year of each reign was usually written as a word, *ahd,* rather than as a numeral.

An exception to the foregoing is that the date on certain coins struck in the Islamic millenial year AH1000 is sometimes represented by the Arabic word *Alf,* meaning,"one thousand". This device was especially used by the Urdu Zafar Qarin Mint.

THE ILAHI ERA

In his 29th regnal year Akbar determined to use a regnal era based on solar years in his administration, instead of the Hejira or Era of the Hegira based on lunar years. The new dating system appeared on the coins the same year, and continued until Akbar's death in Year 50. Mints gradually changed their usage from AH to Ilahi, although some did not convert. During the Ilahi period, many of the mints included the Persian month names as well as year of issue. Use of Ilahi dates continued into the reign of Shah Jahan.

Synchronization of Ilahi, Hejira and AD Eras:

Ilahi	Hejira	AD
Ilahi 30	AH993/4	1585/6
Ilahi 31	AH994/5	1586/7
Ilahi 32	AH995/6	1587/8
Ilahi 33	AH996/7	1588/9
Ilahi 34	AH997/8	1589/90
Ilahi 35	AH998/9	1590/1
Ilahi 36	AH999/1000	1591/2
Ilahi 37	AH1000	1592/3
Ilahi 38	AH1001/2	1593/4
Ilahi 39	AH1002/3	1594/5
Ilahi 40	AH1003/4	1595/6
Ilahi 41	1004/5	1596/7
Ilahi 42	1005/6	1597/8
Ilahi 43	1006/7	1598/9
Ilahi 44	1007/8	1599/1600
Ilahi 45	1008/9	1600/1
Ilahi 46	1009/10	1601/2
Ilahi 47	1010/11	1602/3
Ilahi 48	1011/12	1603/4
Ilahi 49	1012/13	1604/5
Ilahi 50	1013/14	1605/6
Ilahi 51	1014/15	1606/7

Ilahi months:

(1) Farwardin	فروردي فروردين
(2) Ardibihisht	ارديبهشت
(3) Khurdad	خرداد
(4) Tir	تير
(5) Amardad	امرداد
(6) Shahrewar	شهريور
(7) Mihr	مهر
(8) Aban	آبان
(9) Azar	آذر
(10) Di	دي
(11) Bahman	بهمن
(12) Isfandarmuz	اسفندارمز

Standard Coin Pattern

The Mughal Rupees and Mohurs from the time of Aurangzeb (d.1707AD), generally followed a standard pattern of layout.

OBVERSE

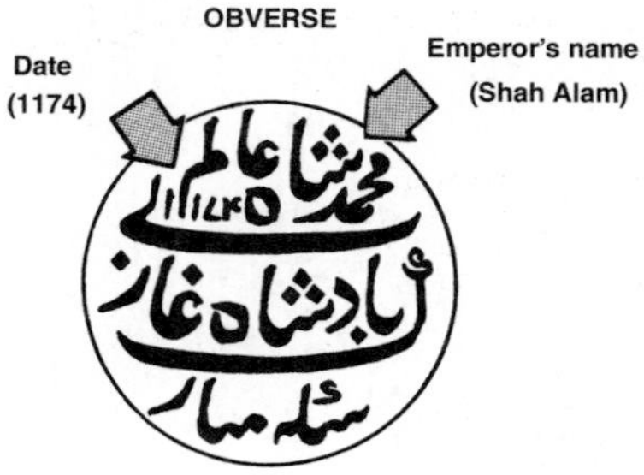

Legend, (read right to left, bottom to top) 'Auspicious coin of the fighter of infidels, the emperor of Shah Alam'.

REVERSE

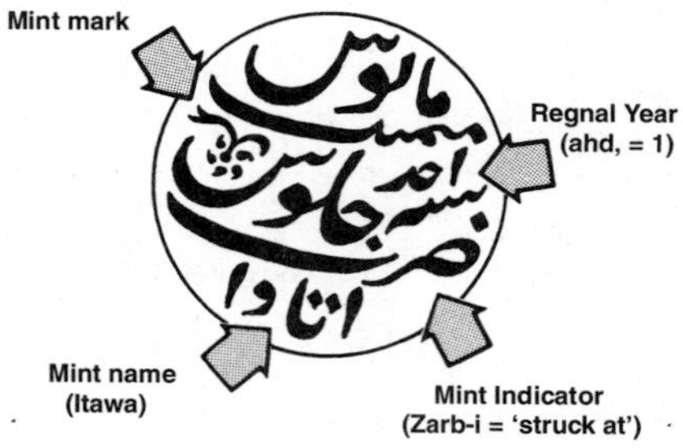

Legend, (read right to left, bottom to top) 'Struck in Itawa in the Year One of the accession associated with prosperity'.

There are many variations of this layout, especially as to the poetic couplet comtaining the king's name on the obverse. In general however the provincial mints and th independent state mints used the simple standard pattern.

LARGESSE COINAGE

نسار

Nisar

The nisar, literally scattering coins, were lightweight silver and gold coins minted especially as largesse money to be scattered amongst the crowd during festival processions and such-like state occasions. The coins were struck to 1/32 rupee, 1/16 rupee, 1/8 rupee, 1/4 rupee and 1/2 rupee weights. To better to economize, they were very thin with wide flans, appearing more generous than was the case. All coins bore the name nisar, and the different weights should not be considered separate denominations, since this was ceremonial and not circulating currrency. The 1/4 rupee weight is encountered more frequently while specimens struck in the other weights remain quite rare.

TABLE OF PERSO-ARABIC WORDS

Obverse and reverse form a poetic couplet. Each mint has a distinctive couplet. A typical word from the central portion of the reverse legend is given as identifier for each sub-type in this section. These are found on the 1 Rupee, KM#149 series.

Yaft	يافت
Muzaiyan	مزين
Kishwar	كشور
Inayat	عنايات
Firoz	فروز
Fath	فتح
Gardun	گردون
Hamisha	هميشه
Din panah	دين پناه
Sakhat Nurani	ساخت نوراني
Khusro	خسرو
Mihr	مهر
Ruy	روي
Bada bar	بادابر
Ta falak	تا فلك
Ba-sharq wa gharb	بشرق و غرب

EMPIRE

Muhammad Akbar

AH963-1014 / 1556-1605AD

HAMMERED COINAGE

Delhi

KM# 11.2 DAMRI (Type 11)

Copper **Obv:** Akbar Shahi **Note:** Weight varies 2.48 - 2.58 grams.

Date	Mintage	Good	VG	F	VF	XF
IE47 (1602-03)	—	10.00	25.00	65.00	100	—
IE48 (1603-04)	—	10.00	25.00	65.00	100	—

Without Mint Name

KM# 11.5 DAMRI (Type 11)

Copper **Obv. Inscription:** "One-sixteenth part of a Tanka" **Note:** Weight varies 2.48 - 2.58 grams.

Date	Mintage	Good	VG	F	VF	XF
IE46 (1601-02)	—	10.00	25.00	50.00	80.00	—
IE47 (1602-03)	—	10.00	25.00	50.00	80.00	—
IE49 (1604-05)	—	10.00	25.00	50.00	80.00	—
IE50 (1605-06)	—	10.00	25.00	50.00	80.00	—

Urdu Zafar Qarin

KM# 13.1 DAMRI (Type 13)

Copper **Obv:** Mint name **Note:** Weight varies 2.00-2.40 grams.

Date	Mintage	Good	VG	F	VF	XF
ND(1556-1605)	—	5.00	12.00	25.00	40.00	—

Kabul

KM# 14.1 DAMRI (Type 14)

Copper **Note:** Weight varies 2.48 - 2.58 grams.

Date	Mintage	Good	VG	F	VF	XF
IE46 (1601-02)	—	10.00	25.00	50.00	80.00	—

Atak Banaras

KM# 23.21 NISFI (Type 23)

Copper **Obv:** Mint name **Rev:** Ilahi date, Persian month

Date	Mintage	Good	VG	F	VF	XF
IE48	—	20.00	50.00	100	160	—

Bairata

KM# 23.10 NISFI (Type 23)

Copper **Obv:** Mint name **Rev:** Ilahi date, Persian month **Note:** Weight varies: 9.95-10.35 grams.

Date	Mintage	Good	VG	F	VF	XF
IE46 (1601-03)	—	13.00	32.50	65.00	100	—
IE48 (1603-04)	—	13.00	32.50	65.00	100	—

Balapur

KM# 23.11 NISFI (Type 23)

Copper **Obv:** Mint name **Rev:** Ilahi date, Persian month **Note:** Weight varies: 9.95-10.35 grams.

Date	Mintage	Good	VG	F	VF	XF
IE46 (1601-02)	—	12.00	30.00	60.00	95.00	—
IE47 (1602-03)	—	12.00	30.00	60.00	95.00	—

Berar

KM# 23.12 NISFI (Type 23)

Copper **Obv:** Mint name **Rev:** Ilahi date, Persian month **Note:** Weight varies: 9.95-10.35 grams.

Date	Mintage	Good	VG	F	VF	XF
IE46 (1601-02)	—	8.00	20.00	40.00	65.00	—
IE48 (1603-04)	—	8.00	20.00	40.00	65.00	—

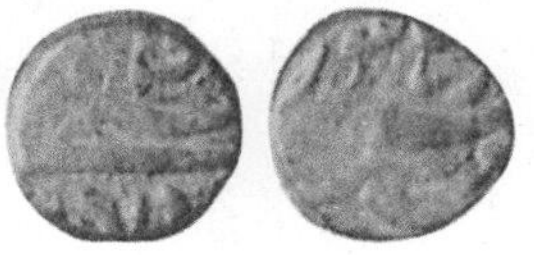

Burhanpur

KM# 23.13 NISFI (Type 23)

Copper **Obv:** Mint name **Rev:** Ilahi date, Persian month **Note:** Weight varies: 9.95-10.35 grams.

Date	Mintage	Good	VG	F	VF	XF
IE46 (1601-02)	—	10.00	25.00	50.00	80.00	—
IE47 (1602-03)	—	10.00	25.00	50.00	80.00	—

Gorakhpur

KM# 23.3 NISFI (Type 23)

Copper **Obv:** Mint name **Rev:** Ilahi date, Persian month **Note:** Weight varies: 9.95-10.35 grams.

Date	Mintage	Good	VG	F	VF	XF
IE50 (1605-06)	—	10.00	25.00	50.00	80.00	—

Without Mint Name

KM# 23.7 NISFI (Type 23)

Copper **Obv. Inscription:** "Fourth part of a tanka; Akbar Shahi" **Note:** Weight varies: 9.95-10.35 grams.

Date	Mintage	Good	VG	F	VF	XF
IE46 (1601-02)	—	9.00	22.50	45.00	72.00	—
IE48 (1603-04)	—	9.00	22.50	45.00	72.00	—

Without Mint Name

KM# 25.1 NISFI (Type 25)

Copper **Obv:** Border of dots, AH date **Obv. Inscription:** nisfi **Rev:** Geometric designs **Note:** Without mint name. Weight varies 9.90-10.00 grams. Type 25.

Date	Mintage	Good	VG	F	VF	XF
AH1013	—	10.00	25.00	50.00	80.00	—
AH1031 (sic)	—	10.00	25.00	50.00	80.00	—

Dogaon

KM# 28.19 DAM (Type 28)

Copper **Rev. Inscription:** "Dar-us-Salam" **Note:** Weight varies 19.40-20.80 grams.

Date	Mintage	Good	VG	F	VF	XF
AH1011	—	2.50	6.00	12.00	20.00	—
AH1012	—	2.50	6.00	12.00	20.00	—
AH1013	—	2.50	6.00	12.00	20.00	—

Bairata

KM# 30.1 DAM (Type 30)

Copper **Obv:** Mint and date **Rev. Inscription:** rawani **Note:** Weight varies: 19.9 - 20.7 grams; Type 30.

Date	Mintage	Good	VG	F	VF	XF
AH1010	—	15.00	37.50	75.00	120	—

Agra

KM# 32.1 DAM (Type 32)

Copper **Obv:** Mint name; Border of dots **Rev:** Ilahi date, Persian month; Border of dots **Note:** Weight varies 19.40-20.85 grams.

Date	Mintage	Good	VG	F	VF	XF
IE46 (1601-02)	—	6.00	15.00	30.00	50.00	—
IE47 (1602-03)	—	6.00	15.00	30.00	50.00	—
IE48 (1603-04)	—	6.00	15.00	30.00	50.00	—

Ahmadabad

KM# 32.2 DAM (Type 32)

Copper **Obv. Legend:** TANKA (sic); AKBAR SHAHI **Obv. Inscription:** "Tanka (sic); Akbar Shahi" **Note:** Weight varies: 19.9 - 20.7 grams.

Date	Mintage	Good	VG	F	VF	XF
IE46 (1601-02)	—	4.00	10.00	20.00	32.50	—
IE47 (1602-03)	—	4.00	10.00	20.00	32.50	—
IE48 (1603-04)	—	4.00	10.00	20.00	32.50	—
IE49 (1604-05)	—	4.00	10.00	20.00	32.50	—
IE50 (1605-06)	—	4.00	10.00	20.00	32.50	—

Atak Banaras

KM# 32.4 DAM (Type 32)

Copper **Note:** Weight varies: 19.9 - 20.7 grams.

Date	Mintage	Good	VG	F	VF	XF
IE48 (1603-04)	—	9.00	22.50	45.00	70.00	—

Bairata

KM# 32.5 DAM (Type 32)

Copper **Obv. Legend:** HALF TANKA; AKBAR SHAHI **Note:** Weight varies: 19.9 - 20.7 grams.

Date	Mintage	Good	VG	F	VF	XF
IE46 (1601-02)	—	4.00	10.00	20.00	32.50	—
IE47 (1602-03)	—	4.00	10.00	20.00	32.50	—
IE48 (1603-04)	—	4.00	10.00	20.00	32.50	—
IE49 (1604-05)	—	4.00	10.00	20.00	32.50	—

Balapur

KM# 32.32 DAM (Type 32)

Copper **Note:** Weight varies: 19.9 - 20.7 grams.

Date	Mintage	Good	VG	F	VF	XF
IE46 (1601-02)	—	7.00	17.50	35.00	55.00	—
IE47 (1602-03)	—	7.00	17.50	35.00	55.00	—

Berar

KM# 32.34 DAM (Type 32)

Copper **Note:** Weight varies: 19.9 - 20.7 grams.

Date	Mintage	Good	VG	F	VF	XF
IE46 (1601-02)	—	4.00	10.00	20.00	32.50	—
IE47 (1602-03)	—	4.00	10.00	20.00	32.50	—

Burhanpur

KM# 32.7 DAM (Type 32)

Copper **Note:** Weight varies 19.40-20.85 grams.

Date	Mintage	Good	VG	F	VF	XF
IE46 (1601-02)	—	6.00	15.00	30.00	50.00	—
IE49 (1604-05)	—	6.00	15.00	30.00	50.00	—
IE50 (1605-06)	—	6.00	15.00	30.00	50.00	—

Delhi

KM# 32.9 DAM (Type 32)

Copper **Obv:** Without denomination **Note:** Weight varies: 19.9 - 20.7 grams.

Date	Mintage	Good	VG	F	VF	XF
IE46 (1601-02)	—	4.00	10.00	20.00	32.50	—
IE47 (1602-03)	—	4.00	10.00	20.00	32.50	—

Delhi

KM# 32.10 DAM (Type 32)

Copper **Obv. Legend:** HALF TANKA; AKBAR SHAHI **Note:** Weight varies: 19.9 - 20.7 grams.

Date	Mintage	Good	VG	F	VF	XF
IE46 (1601-02)	—	7.00	17.50	35.00	55.00	—
IE47 (1602-03)	—	7.00	17.50	35.00	55.00	—
IE50 (1605-06)	—	7.00	17.50	35.00	55.00	—

Gobindpur

KM# 32.12 DAM (Type 32)

Copper **Obv. Legend:** TANKA (sic); AKBAR SHAHI **Note:** Weight varies: 19.9 - 20.7 grams.

Date	Mintage	Good	VG	F	VF	XF
IE46 (1601-02)	—	4.00	10.00	20.00	32.50	—
IE47 (1602-03)	—	4.00	10.00	20.00	32.50	—
IE48 (1603-04)	—	4.00	10.00	20.00	32.50	—

Gorakhpur

KM# 32.13 DAM (Type 32)

Copper **Note:** Weight varies 19.9 - 20.7 grams.

Date	Mintage	Good	VG	F	VF	XF
IE50 (1605-06)	—	9.00	22.50	45.00	70.00	—
IE51 (1606-07)	—	9.00	22.50	45.00	70.00	—

Hisar

KM# 32.15 DAM (Type 32)

Copper **Note:** Weight varies: 19.9 - 20.7 grams.

Date	Mintage	Good	VG	F	VF	XF
IE47 (1602-03)	—	8.00	20.00	40.00	65.00	—
IE48 (1603-04)	—	8.00	20.00	40.00	65.00	—

Lahore

KM# 32.17 DAM (Type 32)

Copper **Obv:** Without denomination **Note:** Weight varies: 19.40-20.85 grams.

Date	Mintage	Good	VG	F	VF	XF
IE46 (1601-02)	—	4.00	10.00	20.00	32.50	—
IE47 (1602-03)	—	4.00	10.00	20.00	32.50	—
IE49 (1604-05)	—	4.00	10.00	20.00	32.50	—
IE50 (1605-06)	—	4.00	10.00	20.00	32.50	—

Lahore

KM# 32.18 DAM (Type 32)

Copper **Obv. Legend:** "Half Tanka", Akbar Shahi" **Note:** Weight varies: 19.40-20.85 grams.

Date	Mintage	Good	VG	F	VF	XF
IE46 (1601-02)	—	8.00	20.00	40.00	65.00	—
IE49 (1604-05)	—	8.00	20.00	40.00	65.00	—

Mangarh

KM# 32.19 DAM (Type 32)

Copper **Note:** Weight varies: 19.40-20.85 grams.

Date	Mintage	Good	VG	F	VF	XF
IE47 (1602-03)	—	10.00	25.00	50.00	80.00	—

Narnol

KM# 32.21 DAM (Type 32)

Copper **Obv. Legend:** "Half Tanka" and "Akbar Shahi" **Note:** Weight varies: 19.40-20.85 grams.

Date	Mintage	Good	VG	F	VF	XF
IE47 (1602-03)	—	6.00	15.00	30.00	50.00	—
IE48 (1603-04)	—	6.00	15.00	30.00	50.00	—
IE50 (1605-06)	—	6.00	15.00	30.00	50.00	—

Srinagar

KM# 32.26 DAM (Type 32)

Copper **Note:** Weight varies: 19.40-20.85 grams.

Date	Mintage	Good	VG	F	VF	XF
IE47 (1602-03)	—	8.00	20.00	40.00	65.00	—

Ujjainpur

KM# 32.28 DAM (Type 32)

Copper **Obv. Legend:** "Akbar Shahi" **Note:** Weight varies: 19.40-20.85 grams.

Date	Mintage	Good	VG	F	VF	XF
IE47 (1602-03)	—	8.00	20.00	40.00	65.00	—
IE5x (1605-06)	—	8.00	20.00	40.00	65.00	—

Urdu Zafar Qarin

KM# 32.29 DAM (Type 32)

Copper **Note:** Weight varies: 19.40-20.85 grams.

Date	Mintage	Good	VG	F	VF	XF
IE47 (1602-03)	—	5.00	12.50	25.00	40.00	—
IE48 (1603-04)	—	5.00	12.50	25.00	40.00	—
IE50(1605-06)	—	5.00	12.50	25.00	40.00	—

Ahmadabad

KM# 38.2 TANKA (Type 38)

Copper **Obv:** Border of dots **Obv. Inscription:** "Tanka, Akbar Shahi" **Rev:** Border of dots **Note:** Weight varies: 39.80-41.40 grams.

Date	Mintage	Good	VG	F	VF	XF
IE46 (1601-02)	—	15.00	37.50	75.00	120	—

Bairata

KM# 38.3 TANKA (Type 38)

Copper **Note:** Weight varies: 39.80-41.40 grams.

Date	Mintage	Good	VG	F	VF	XF
IE48 (1603-04)	—	9.00	22.50	45.00	70.00	—
IE50 (1605-06)	—	9.00	22.50	45.00	70.00	—

Gobindpur

KM# 38.5 TANKA (Type 38)

Copper **Note:** Weight varies: 39.80-41.40 grams.

Date	Mintage	Good	VG	F	VF	XF
IE46 (1601-02)	—	10.00	25.00	50.00	80.00	—
IE47 (1602-03)	—	10.00	25.00	50.00	80.00	—

Agra

KM# 40.1 TANKI (Type 40)

Copper **Obv. Inscription:** "Yak Tnaki", Akbar Shahi" **Rev:** Mint name and Ilahi date, Persian month **Note:** Weight varies: 3.75-3.90 grams.

Date	Mintage	Good	VG	F	VF	XF
IE47 (1602-03)	—	9.00	22.50	45.00	70.00	—

Kabul

KM# 40.2 TANKI (Type 40)

Copper **Note:** Weight varies: 3.75-3.90 grams.

Date	Mintage	Good	VG	F	VF	XF
IE47 (1602-03)	—	6.00	15.00	30.00	50.00	—
IE50 (1605-06)	—	6.00	15.00	30.00	50.00	—

Lahore

KM# 40.3 TANKI (Type 40)

Copper **Note:** Weight varies: 3.75-3.90 grams.

Date	Mintage	Good	VG	F	VF	XF
IE46 (1601-02)	—	10.00	22.50	45.00	70.00	—

Agra

KM# 41.1 2 TANKI (Type 41)

Copper **Obv:** "Do (2) Tanki" and "Akbar Shahi" **Rev:** Mint name, Ilahi date, Persian month **Note:** Weight varies: 6.80-7.90 grams.

Date	Mintage	Good	VG	F	VF	XF
IE46 (1601-02)	—	8.00	20.00	40.00	65.00	—
IE47 (1602-03)	—	8.00	20.00	40.00	65.00	—
IE48 (1603-04)	—	8.00	20.00	40.00	65.00	—
IE50 (1605-06)	—	8.00	20.00	40.00	65.00	—

Ahmadabad

KM# 41.4 2 TANKI (Type 41)

Copper **Note:** Weight varies: 6.80-7.90 grams.

Date	Mintage	Good	VG	F	VF	XF
IE46 (1601-02)	—	9.00	22.50	45.00	70.00	—
IE47 (1602-03)	—	9.00	22.50	45.00	70.00	—
IE49 (1604-05)	—	9.00	22.50	45.00	70.00	—

Kabul

KM# 41.2 2 TANKI (Type 41)

Copper **Note:** Weight varies: 6.80-7.90 grams.

Date	Mintage	Good	VG	F	VF	XF
IE47 (1602-03)	—	9.00	22.50	45.00	70.00	—

Agra

KM# 42.1 4 TANKI (Type 42)

Copper **Obv:** "Jo (4) Tanki", and "Akbar Shahi" **Rev:** Mint name, Ilahi date, Persian month **Note:** Weight varies: 14.90-15.75 grams.

Date	Mintage	Good	VG	F	VF	XF
IE46 (1601-02)	—	10.00	25.00	50.00	80.00	—

Ahmadabad

KM# 42.2 4 TANKI (Type 42)

Copper **Note:** Weight varies: 14.90-15.75 grams.

Date	Mintage	Good	VG	F	VF	XF
IE46 (1601-02)	—	10.00	25.00	50.00	80.00	—
IE47 (1602-03)	—	10.00	25.00	50.00	80.00	—
IE48 (1603-04)	—	10.00	25.00	50.00	80.00	—
IE49 (1604-05)	—	10.00	25.00	50.00	80.00	—
IE50 (1605-06)	—	10.00	25.00	50.00	80.00	—

Kabul

KM# 42.3 4 TANKI (Type 42)

Copper **Note:** Weight varies: 14.90-15.75 grams.

Date	Mintage	Good	VG	F	VF	XF
IE47 (1602-03)	—	13.00	37.50	65.00	105	—
IE48 (1603-04)	—	13.00	37.50	65.00	105	—

Lahore

KM# 42.4 4 TANKI (Type 42)

Copper **Note:** Weight varies: 14.90-15.75 grams.

Date	Mintage	Good	VG	F	VF	XF
IE46 (1601-02)	—	13.00	37.50	65.00	105	—
IE47 (1602-03)	—	13.00	37.50	65.00	105	—

Ujjainpur

KM# 47.1 TANKA (Type 47)

Copper **Shape:** Square **Note:** Weight varies: 6.35-6.70 grams.

Date	Mintage	Good	VG	F	VF	XF
IE47 (1602-03)	—	8.00	20.00	40.00	65.00	—

Lahore

KM# 58.2 1/4 RUPEE (Type 58)

2.8610 g., Silver **Obv:** Similar to 1 Rupee, Type 93 **Rev:** Similar to 1 Rupee, Type 93

Date	Mintage	VG	F	VF	XF	Unc
IE46 (1601-02)	—	20.00	35.00	60.00	90.00	—
IE47 (1602-03)	—	20.00	35.00	60.00	90.00	—
IE48 (1603-04)	—	20.00	35.00	60.00	90.00	—
IE49 (1604-05)	—	20.00	35.00	60.00	90.00	—
IE50 (1605-06)	—	20.00	35.00	60.00	90.00	—

Ahmadabad

KM# 66.1 1/2 RUPEE (Type 66)

Silver **Note:** Weight varies: 5.50-5.80 grams.

Date	Mintage	VG	F	VF	XF	Unc
IE47 (1602-03)	—	18.00	30.00	50.00	75.00	—

Burhanpur

KM# 66.6 1/2 RUPEE (Type 66)

Silver **Note:** Weight varies: 5.50-5.80 grams.

Date	Mintage	VG	F	VF	XF	Unc
IE48 (1603-04)	—	20.00	35.00	60.00	90.00	—

Kabul

KM# 66.2 1/2 RUPEE (Type 66)

Silver **Note:** Weight varies: 5.50-5.80 grams.

Date	Mintage	VG	F	VF	XF	Unc
IE46 (1601-02)	—	20.00	32.50	55.00	80.00	—
IE47 (1602-03)	—	20.00	32.50	55.00	80.00	—
IE48 (1603-04)	—	20.00	32.50	55.00	80.00	—
IE49 (1604-05)	—	20.00	32.50	55.00	80.00	—
IE50 (1605-06)	—	20.00	32.50	55.00	80.00	—

Lahore

KM# 66.3 1/2 RUPEE (Type 66)

Silver **Note:** Weight varies: 5.50-5.80 grams.

Date	Mintage	VG	F	VF	XF	Unc
IE46 (1601-02)	—	15.00	27.50	45.00	65.00	—
IE47 (1602-03)	—	15.00	27.50	45.00	65.00	—
IE48 (1603-04)	—	15.00	27.50	45.00	65.00	—
IE49 (1604-05)	—	15.00	27.50	45.00	65.00	—

Patna

KM# 66.4 1/2 RUPEE (Type 66)

Silver **Note:** Weight varies: 5.50-5.80 grams.

Date	Mintage	VG	F	VF	XF	Unc
IE47 (1602-03)	—	20.00	35.00	60.00	90.00	—
IE48 (1603-04)	—	20.00	35.00	60.00	90.00	—

Agra

KM# 67.A1 1/2 RUPEE (Type 67)

Silver **Obv:** Similar to Rupee, Type 94 **Rev:** Similar to Rupee, Type 94 **Note:** Weight varies: 5.50-5.80 grams.

Date	Mintage	VG	F	VF	XF	Unc
IE47 (1602-03) with "Darb"	—	60.00	100	175	260	—

Agra

KM# 67.B1 1/2 RUPEE (Type 67)

Silver **Note:** Weight varies: 5.50-5.80 grams. Similar to 1 Mohur, KM# 115.1.

Date	Mintage	VG	F	VF	XF	Unc
IE50 (1605-06)	—	70.00	120	200	300	—

Ahmedabad

KM# 67.2 1/2 RUPEE (Type 67)

Note: Weight varies: 5.50-5.80 grams

Date	Mintage	VG	F	VF	XF	Unc
IE47(1602-03)	—	30.00	50.00	85.00	130	—

Lahore

KM# 67.1 1/2 RUPEE (Type 67)

Silver **Note:** Weight varies: 5.50-5.80 grams.

Date	Mintage	VG	F	VF	XF	Unc
IE48 (1603-04)	—	20.00	30.00	55.00	80.00	—
IE49 (1604-05)	—	20.00	30.00	55.00	80.00	—
IE50 (1605-06)	—	20.00	30.00	55.00	80.00	—

Ujjain

KM# 84.2 RUPEE (Type 84)

Silver **Shape:** Square **Note:** Weight varies: 11.20-11.60 grams. Ilahi date.

Date	Mintage	VG	F	VF	XF	Unc
IE46 (1601-02)	—	16.00	27.50	45.00	70.00	—

Bangala

KM# 86.1 RUPEE (Type 86)
Silver **Rev:** Poetic couplet, AH date **Shape:** Square **Note:** Weight varies: 11.20-11.60 grams.

Date	Mintage	VG	F	VF	XF	Unc
AH1010	—	30.00	50.00	80.00	120	—
AH1011	—	30.00	50.00	80.00	120	—
AH1018 Posthumous	—	30.00	50.00	80.00	120	—

Tatta

KM# 88.7 RUPEE (Type 88)
11.4440 g., Silver **Obv. Inscription:** "... Jalalahu" **Rev:** Mint name, Ilahi date and Persian month **Shape:** Square **Note:** Weight varies: 11.20-11.60 grams.

Date	Mintage	VG	F	VF	XF	Unc
IE48 (1603-04)	—	15.00	22.50	35.00	55.00	—
IE49 (1604-05)	—	15.00	22.50	35.00	55.00	—
IE50 (1605-06)	—	15.00	22.50	35.00	55.00	—

Tatta

KM# 89.2 RUPEE (Type 89)
Silver **Rev:** Ilahi date, without Persian month **Shape:** Square **Note:** Weight varies: 11.20-11.60 grams.

Date	Mintage	VG	F	VF	XF	Unc
IE46 (1601-02)	—	22.50	36.00	60.00	90.00	—
IE48 (1603-04)	—	22.50	36.00	60.00	90.00	—

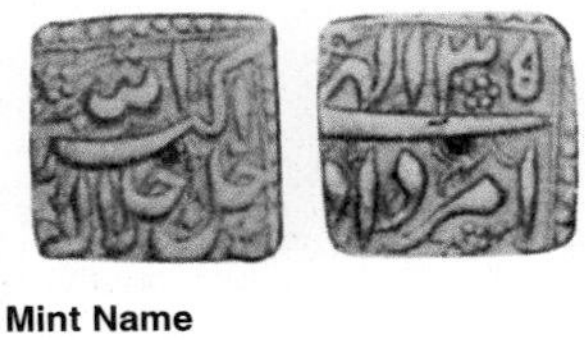

Without Mint Name

KM# 90.1 RUPEE (Type 90)
Silver **Rev:** Ilahi date, Persian month **Shape:** Square **Note:** Weight varies: 11.20-11.60 grams.

Date	Mintage	VG	F	VF	XF	Unc
IE47 (1602-03)	—	20.00	36.00	55.00	82.50	—
IE48 (1603-04)	—	20.00	36.00	55.00	82.50	—

Agra

KM# 93.1 RUPEE (Type 93)
Silver **Obv. Legend:** "...Jalalahu" **Rev:** Ilahi date and Persian month **Note:** Weight varies: 11.20-11.60 grams.

Date	Mintage	VG	F	VF	XF	Unc
IE46 (1601-02)	—	25.00	40.00	70.00	110	—
IE47 (1602-03)	—	25.00	40.00	70.00	110	—

Agra

KM# 93.1A RUPEE (Type 93)
Silver **Obv. Legend:** "...Jalalahu" **Rev:** Ilahi date and Persian month **Note:** Weight varies: 11.20-11.60 grams. Large thin planchet.

Date	Mintage	VG	F	VF	XF	Unc
IE47 (1602-03)	—	270	450	750	1,125	—

Ahmadabad

KM# 93.2 RUPEE (Type 93)
Silver **Obv. Inscription:** "...Jalalahu" **Rev:** Ilahi date and Persian month **Note:** Weight varies: 11.20-11.60 grams.

Date	Mintage	VG	F	VF	XF	Unc
IE46 (1601-02)	—	16.00	27.50	45.00	70.00	—
IE47 (1602-03)	—	16.00	27.50	45.00	70.00	—
IE48 (1603-04)	—	16.00	27.50	45.00	70.00	—
IE49 (1604-05)	—	16.00	27.50	45.00	70.00	—
IE50 (1605-06)	—	16.00	27.50	45.00	70.00	—

Ahmadanagar

KM# 93.3 RUPEE (Type 93)
Silver **Obv. Inscription:** "...Jalalahu" **Rev:** Ilahi date and Persian month **Note:** Weight varies: 11.20-11.60 grams.

Date	Mintage	VG	F	VF	XF	Unc
IE46 (1601-02) 0	—	90.00	150	250	375	—
IE50 (1605-06) 0	—	90.00	150	250	375	—

Akbarnagar

KM# 93.4 RUPEE (Type 93)
Silver **Obv. Inscription:** "...Jalalahu" **Rev:** Ilahi date and Persian month **Note:** Weight varies: 11.20-11.60 grams.

Date	Mintage	VG	F	VF	XF	Unc
IE50 (1605-06)	—	90.00	150	250	375	—

Bairata

KM# 93.20 RUPEE (Type 93)
Silver **Obv. Inscription:** "...Jalalahu" **Rev:** Ilahi date and Persian month **Note:** Weight varies: 11.20-11.60 grams.

Date	Mintage	VG	F	VF	XF	Unc
IE49 (1604-05)	—	90.00	150	250	375	—

Berar

KM# 93.6 RUPEE (Type 93)
Silver **Obv. Inscription:** "...Jalalahu" **Rev:** Ilahi date and Persian month **Note:** Weight varies: 11.20-11.60 grams.

Date	Mintage	Good	VG	F	VF	XF
IE46 (1601-02)	—	7.00	9.00	13.00	20.00	30.00
IE47 (1602-03)	—	7.00	9.00	13.00	20.00	30.00
IE48 (1603-04)	—	7.00	9.00	13.00	20.00	30.00
IE49 (1604-05)	—	7.00	9.00	13.00	20.00	30.00
IE50 (1605-06)	—	7.00	9.00	13.00	20.00	30.00

Burhanpur

KM# 93.7 RUPEE (Type 93)
Silver **Obv. Inscription:** "...Jalalahu" **Rev:** Ilahi date and Persian month **Note:** Weight varies: 11.20-11.60 grams.

Date	Mintage	VG	F	VF	XF	Unc
IE46 (1601-02)	—	18.00	30.00	50.00	75.00	—
IE47 (1602-03)	—	18.00	30.00	50.00	75.00	—
IE48 (1603-04)	—	18.00	30.00	50.00	75.00	—
IE49 (1604-05)	—	18.00	30.00	50.00	75.00	—
IE50 (1605-06)	—	18.00	30.00	50.00	75.00	—

Delhi

KM# 93.8 RUPEE (Type 93)
Silver **Obv. Inscription:** "...Jalalahu" **Rev:** Ilahi date and Persian month **Note:** Weight varies: 11.20-11.60 grams.

Date	Mintage	VG	F	VF	XF	Unc
IE47 (1602-03)	—	16.00	27.00	45.00	70.00	—
IE49 (1604-05)	—	16.00	27.00	45.00	70.00	—
IE50 (1605-06)	—	16.00	27.00	45.00	70.00	—

Elichpur

KM# 93.10 RUPEE (Type 93)
Silver **Obv. Inscription:** "...Jalalahu" **Rev:** Ilahi date and Persian month **Note:** Weight varies: 11.20-11.60 grams.

Date	Mintage	VG	F	VF	XF	Unc
IE48 (1603-04)	—	90.00	150	250	375	—
IE50 (1605-06)	—	90.00	150	250	375	—

Lahore

KM# 93.11 RUPEE (Type 93)
Silver **Obv. Inscription:** "...Jalalahu" **Rev:** Ilahi date and Persian month **Note:** Weight varies: 11.20-11.60 grams.

Date	Mintage	VG	F	VF	XF	Unc
IE46 (1601-02)	—	16.00	27.00	45.00	70.00	—
IE47 (1602-03)	—	16.00	27.00	45.00	70.00	—
IE48 (1603-04)	—	16.00	27.00	45.00	70.00	—
IE49 (1604-05)	—	16.00	27.00	45.00	70.00	—

Patna

KM# 93.14 RUPEE (Type 93)
Silver **Obv. Inscription:** "...Jalalahu" **Rev:** Ilahi date and Persian month **Note:** Weight varies: 11.20-11.60 grams.

Date	Mintage	VG	F	VF	XF	Unc
IE47 (1602-03)	—	18.00	30.00	50.00	75.00	—
IE48 (1603-04)	—	18.00	30.00	50.00	75.00	—
IE49 (1604-05)	—	18.00	30.00	50.00	75.00	—
IE50 (1605-06)	—	18.00	30.00	50.00	75.00	—

Saimur

KM# 93.21 RUPEE (Type 93)
Silver **Obv. Inscription:** "...Jalalahu" **Rev:** Ilahi date and Persian month **Note:** Weight varies: 11.20-11.60 grams.

Date	Mintage	VG	F	VF	XF	Unc
IE47 (1602-03)	—	—	—	—	—	—

Sitapur

KM# 93.18 RUPEE (Type 93)
Silver **Obv. Inscription:** "...Jalalahu" **Rev:** Ilahi date and Persian month **Note:** Weight varies: 11.20-11.60 grams.

Date	Mintage	VG	F	VF	XF	Unc
IE49 (1604-05)	—	27.00	45.00	75.00	115	—

Srinagar

KM# 93.15 RUPEE (Type 93)
Silver **Obv. Inscription:** "...Jalalahu" **Rev:** Ilahi date and Persian month **Note:** Weight varies: 11.20-11.60 grams.

Date	Mintage	VG	F	VF	XF	Unc
IE46 (1601-02)	—	30.00	50.00	85.00	130	—
IE47 (1602-03)	—	30.00	50.00	85.00	130	—
IE48 (1603-04)	—	30.00	50.00	85.00	130	—
IE49 (1604-05)	—	30.00	50.00	85.00	130	—
IE50 (1605-06)	—	30.00	50.00	85.00	130	—

Ujjain

KM# 93.16 RUPEE (Type 93)
Silver **Obv. Inscription:** "...Jalalahu" **Rev:** Ilahi date and Persian month **Note:** Weight varies: 11.20-11.60 grams.

Date	Mintage	VG	F	VF	XF	Unc
IE46 (1601-02)	—	60.00	100	175	260	—
IE47 (1602-03)	—	60.00	100	175	260	—
IE48 (1603-04)	—	60.00	100	175	260	—

Delhi

KM# 93A.1 RUPEE (Type 93A)
Silver **Obv. Inscription:** "...Jalalahu" **Rev:** Ilahi date and Persian month **Note:** Weight varies: 11.20-11.60 grams.

Date	Mintage	VG	F	VF	XF	Unc
IE50 (1605-06)	—	110	180	300	450	—

Agra

KM# 94.1 RUPEE (Type 94)

Silver **Obv:** Quatrefoil borders **Obv. Inscription:** "...Jalalahu" **Rev:** Octagonal borders, mint name, Ilahi date and Persian month **Note:** Weight varies: 11.20-11.60 grams. Rare specimens of the Agra rupee bear the word "Rupiya" also.

Date	Mintage	VG	F	VF	XF	Unc
IE47 (1602-03)	—	42.50	70.00	120	180	—
IE48 (1603-04)	—	42.50	70.00	120	180	—
IE49 (1604-05)	—	42.50	70.00	120	180	—
IE50 (1605-06)	—	42.50	70.00	120	180	—

Agra

KM# 94.6 RUPEE (Type 94)

11.4440 g., Silver **Note:** With only "Rupiya".

Date	Mintage	VG	F	VF	XF	Unc
IE47	—	275	450	750	1,125	—

Ahmadabad

KM# 94.2 RUPEE (Type 94)

Silver **Obv:** Quatrefoil borders **Obv. Inscription:** "...Jalalahu" **Rev:** Octagonal borders, mint name, Ilahi date and Persian month **Note:** Weight varies: 11.20-11.60 grams.

Date	Mintage	VG	F	VF	XF	Unc
IE47 (1602-03)	—	32.50	55.00	90.00	135	—

Lahore

KM# 94.3 RUPEE (Type 94)

Silver **Obv:** Quatrefoil borders **Obv. Inscription:** "...Jalalahu" **Rev:** Octagonal borders, mint name, Ilahi date and Persian month **Note:** Weight varies: 11.20-11.60 grams.

Date	Mintage	VG	F	VF	XF	Unc
IE47 (1602-03)	—	27.50	45.00	75.00	115	—
IE48 (1603-04)	—	27.50	45.00	75.00	115	—
IE49 (1604-05)	—	27.50	45.00	75.00	115	—
IE50 (1605-06)	—	27.50	45.00	75.00	115	—

Saimur

KM# 94.5 RUPEE (Type 94)

Silver **Obv:** Quatrefoil borders **Obv. Inscription:** "...Jalalahu" **Rev:** Octagonal borders, mint name, Ilahi date and Persian month **Note:** Weight varies: 11.20-11.60 grams.

Date	Mintage	VG	F	VF	XF	Unc
IE47 (1602-03)	—	125	210	350	525	—
IE48 (1603-04)	—	125	210	350	525	—

Sitapur

KM# 94.4 RUPEE (Type 94)

Silver **Obv:** Quatrefoil borders **Obv. Inscription:** "...Jalalahu" **Rev:** Octagonal borders, mint name, Ilahi date and Persian month **Note:** Weight varies: 11.20-11.60 grams.

Date	Mintage	VG	F	VF	XF	Unc
IE47 (1602-03)	—	55.00	90.00	150	225	—
IE48 (1603-04)	—	55.00	90.00	150	225	—
IE49 (1604-05)	—	55.00	90.00	150	225	—

Agra

KM# 95.1 RUPEE (Type 95)

11.3400 g., Silver **Obv:** Eight-pointed double star **Rev:** Eight-pointed double star

Date	Mintage	VG	F	VF	XF	Unc
IE50 (1605-06)	—	—	—	1,500	2,500	—

Agra

KM# 103.1 1/2 MOHUR (Type 103)

Gold **Note:** Weight varies: 4.80-5.40 grams.

Date	Mintage	VG	F	VF	XF	Unc
IE48 (1603-04) Rare	—	—	—	—	—	—
IE50 (1605-06) Rare	—	—	—	—	—	—

Lahore

KM# 103.2 1/2 MOHUR (Type 103)

Gold **Note:** Weight varies: 4.80-5.40 grams.

Date	Mintage	VG	F	VF	XF	Unc
IE48 (1603-04) Rare	—	—	—	—	—	—

Lahore

KM# 104.1 1/2 MOHUR (Type 104)

Gold **Obv:** Sita and Rama **Rev:** Ilahi date and Persian month **Note:** Weight varies: 4.80-5.40 grams.

Date	Mintage	VG	F	VF	XF	Unc
IE50 (1605-06) Rare	—	—	—	—	—	—

Agra

KM# 114.1 MOHUR (Type 114)

Gold **Obv:** Within dotted circles **Obv. Legend:** "...Jalalahu" **Rev:** Mint name and date, within dotted circles **Shape:** Square **Note:** Weight varies: 10.70-11.00 grams.

Date	Mintage	VG	F	VF	XF	Unc
IE48 (1603-04)	—	—	1,500	2,250	3,500	—
IE49 (1604-05)	—	—	1,500	2,250	3,500	—

Agra

KM# 114.3 MOHUR (Type 114)

Gold **Shape:** Oblong **Note:** Mehrabi. Weight varies: 10.80-11.00 grams.

Date	Mintage	Good	VG	F	VF	XF
IE49 (1604-05) Rare	—	—	—	—	—	—

Agra

KM# 114.2 MOHUR (Type 114)

Gold **Obv:** Within 8-pointed doubled star **Obv. Legend:** "...Jalalahu" **Rev:** Mint name and date, within 8-pointed doubled star **Shape:** Square **Note:** Weight varies: 10.70-11.00 grams.

Date	Mintage	VG	F	VF	XF	Unc
IE50 (1605-06) Rare	—	—	—	—	—	—

Burhanpur

KM# 114.5 MOHUR (Type 114)

Gold **Obv:** Within dotted circle **Obv. Legend:** "...Jalalahu" **Rev:** Mint name and date, within dotted circle **Shape:** Oblong **Note:** Weight varies: 10.80-11.00 grams.

Date	Mintage	VG	F	VF	XF	Unc
IE48 (1603-04)	—	—	1,000	1,300	1,800	—
IE49 (1604-05)	—	—	1,000	1,300	1,800	—

Lahore

KM# 114.6 MOHUR (Type 114)

Gold **Obv:** Within dotted circle **Obv. Legend:** "...Jalalahu" **Rev:** Mint name and date, within dotted circle **Shape:** Oblong **Note:** Weight varies: 10.80-11.00 grams.

Date	Mintage	VG	F	VF	XF	Unc
IE47 (1602-03)	—	—	900	1,100	1,600	—
IE48 (1603-04)	—	—	900	1,100	1,600	—
IE49 (1604-05)	—	—	900	1,100	1,600	—
IE50 (1605-06)	—	—	900	1,100	1,600	—

Sitapur

KM# 114.7 MOHUR (Type 114)

Gold **Obv:** Within dotted circle **Obv. Legend:** "...Jalalahu" **Rev:** Mint name and date, within dotted circle **Shape:** Oblong **Note:** Weight varies: 10.80-11.00 grams.

Date	Mintage	VG	F	VF	XF	Unc
IE47 (1602-03)	—	—	1,500	2,250	3,500	—

Agra

KM# 115.1 MOHUR (Type 115)

Gold **Obv:** Long Persian couplet **Rev:** Long Persian couplet **Note:** Weight varies: 10.70-11.00 grams.

Date	Mintage	F	VF	XF	Unc	BU
IE49 (1604-05) Rare	—	—	—	—	—	—
IE50 (1605-06) Rare	—	—	—	—	—	—

Agra

KM# 115.2 MOHUR (Type 115)

Gold **Obv:** Short Persian couplet **Rev:** Short Persian couplet **Note:** Weight varies: 10.70-11.00 grams.

Date	Mintage	Good	VG	F	VF	XF
IE50 (1605-06) Rare	—	—	—	—	—	—
IE51 (1606-07) Rare	—	—	—	—	—	—

Agra

KM# 115.3 MOHUR (Type 115)

Gold **Obv:** "Dinar-i Jalali" **Note:** Weight varies: 10.70-11.00 grams.

Date	Mintage	Good	VG	F	VF	XF
IE50 (1605-06) Rare	—	—	—	—	—	—

Agra

KM# 118.2 HEAVY 1/2 MOHUR (Type 118)

5.9600 g., Gold **Obv:** Ilahi date, Persian month **Rev:** Hawk to right **Shape:** Square

Date	Mintage	Good	VG	F	VF	XF
IE50 (1605-06) Rare	—	—	—	—	—	—

Agra

KM# 119C.3 HEAVY MOHUR (Type 119)

Gold **Obv:** Hawk left, ornamented field **Rev:** Legend, mint, and date **Rev. Legend:** "Allahu Akbar" **Note:** Weight varies: 11.80-12.20 grams.

Date	Mintage	VG	F	VF	XF	Unc
IE47 (1602-03) Rare	—	—	—	—	—	—

Agra

KM# 119C.2 HEAVY MOHUR (Type 119)

12.2000 g., Gold **Obv:** Duck, ornamented field

Date	Mintage	VG	F	VF	XF	Unc
IE50 (1605-06) Rare	—	—	—	—	—	—

REBELLION COINAGE

Allahabad

KM# 97.1 RUPEE (Type 97)

Silver **Obv:** "Riwaj Sikka Akbar" **Rev:** Mint name **Note:** Weight varies: 11.20-11.60 grams.

Date	Mintage	VG	F	VF	XF	Unc
IE46 (1601-02)	—	30.00	50.00	85.00	130	—
IE47 (1602-03)	—	30.00	50.00	85.00	130	—
IE48 (1603-04)	—	30.00	50.00	85.00	130	—
IE49 (1604-05)	—	30.00	50.00	85.00	130	—

Muhammad Jahangir
AH1014-1037 / 1605-1627AD
HAMMERED COINAGE

Delhi

KM# 120.1 1/8 DAM (Type 120)
Copper **Note:** Weight varies: 2.30-2.60 grams.

Date	Mintage	Good	VG	F	VF	XF
AH1021//7	—	15.00	37.50	75.00	120	—
AH1023//x	—	15.00	37.50	75.00	120	—
AH102x//11	—	15.00	37.50	75.00	120	—
AH1029//1x	—	15.00	37.50	75.00	120	—

Agra

KM# 122.1 1/4 DAM (Type 122)
Copper **Note:** Weight varies: 4.80-5.20 grams. Varieties exist.

Date	Mintage	Good	VG	F	VF	XF
AH1014//1	—	15.00	37.50	75.00	120	—
AH1017//4	—	15.00	37.50	75.00	120	—
AH1018//4	—	15.00	37.50	75.00	120	—
AH1019//5	—	15.00	37.50	75.00	120	—
AH1020//5(sic)	—	15.00	37.50	75.00	120	—
AH1020//6	—	15.00	37.50	75.00	120	—
AH1021//6(sic)	—	15.00	37.50	75.00	120	—
AH1021//7	—	15.00	37.50	75.00	120	—

Ahmadabad

KM# 122.4 1/4 DAM (Type 122)
Copper **Note:** Weight varies: 4.80-5.20 grams.

Date	Mintage	Good	VG	F	VF	XF
AH1018//5	—	20.00	30.00	100	160	—

Ahmadanagar

KM# 122.5 1/4 DAM (Type 122)
Copper **Note:** Weight varies: 4.80-5.20 grams.

Date	Mintage	Good	VG	F	VF	XF
ND	—	18.00	30.00	60.00	95.00	—

Burhanpur

KM# 122.3 1/4 DAM (Type 122)
Copper **Note:** Weight varies: 4.80-5.20 grams.

Date	Mintage	Good	VG	F	VF	XF
ND	—	18.00	30.00	60.00	95.00	—

Delhi

KM# 122.2 1/4 DAM (Type 122)
Copper **Note:** Weight varies: 4.80-5.20 grams.

Date	Mintage	Good	VG	F	VF	XF
AHxxxx//6 Rare	—	—	—	—	—	—

Agra

KM# 124.5 1/2 DAM (Type 124)
Copper **Note:** Weight varies: 9.80-10.50 grams.

Date	Mintage	Good	VG	F	VF	XF
AH1023	—	18.00	30.00	60.00	95.00	—

Ahmadabad

KM# 124.3 1/2 DAM (Type 124)
Copper **Note:** Weight varies: 9.80-10.50 grams.

Date	Mintage	Good	VG	F	VF	XF
AH10xx	—	10.00	25.00	50.00	80.00	—

Ahmadanagar

KM# 124.4 1/2 DAM (Type 124)
Copper **Note:** Weight varies: 9.80-10.50 grams.

Date	Mintage	Good	VG	F	VF	XF
ND Rare	—	—	—	—	—	—

Ajmer

KM# 124.1 1/2 DAM (Type 124)
Copper **Note:** Weight varies: 9.80-10.50 grams.

Date	Mintage	Good	VG	F	VF	XF
AH1023//9 Rare	—	—	—	—	—	—
AH1024//9(sic) Rare	—	—	—	—	—	—

Bairata

KM# 124.6 1/2 DAM (Type 124)
Copper **Note:** Weight varies: 9.80-10.50 grams.

Date	Mintage	Good	VG	F	VF	XF
ND	—	14.00	35.00	70.00	110	—
AH1025//11	—	14.00	35.00	70.00	110	—

Burhanpur

KM# 124.7 1/2 DAM (Type 124)
Copper **Note:** Weight varies: 9.80-10.50 grams.

Date	Mintage	Good	VG	F	VF	XF
ND Azar	—	10.00	25.00	50.00	80.00	—
ND(1605) Di	—	10.00	25.00	50.00	80.00	—
ND//3 Di	—	10.00	25.00	50.00	80.00	—

Qandahar

KM# 124.2 1/2 DAM (Type 124)
Copper **Note:** Weight varies: 9.80-10.50 grams.

Date	Mintage	Good	VG	F	VF	XF
AH1019//5	—	30.00	75.00	150	250	—
AH1026	—	30.00	75.00	150	250	—

Agra

KM# 126.1 DAM (Type 126)
Copper **Note:** Weight varies: 20.20-20.90 grams.

Date	Mintage	Good	VG	F	VF	XF
AH1020//6	—	10.00	25.00	50.00	80.00	—
AH1020//7	—	10.00	25.00	50.00	80.00	—
AH1021//7	—	10.00	25.00	50.00	80.00	—
AH1022//8	—	10.00	25.00	50.00	80.00	—
AH1022//9	—	10.00	25.00	50.00	80.00	—
AH1023//8	—	10.00	25.00	50.00	80.00	—
AH1023//9	—	10.00	25.00	50.00	80.00	—
AH1023//10	—	10.00	25.00	50.00	80.00	—
AH1024//x	—	10.00	25.00	50.00	80.00	—
AH1026//12	—	10.00	25.00	50.00	80.00	—
AH1029//xx	—	10.00	25.00	50.00	80.00	—

Agra

KM# 126.1B DAM (Type 126)
Copper **Obv:** "Jahangiri" and regnal year **Rev:** Mint and date

Date	Mintage	Good	VG	F	VF	XF
AH1022//8	—	8.00	15.00	28.00	50.00	—
AH1023//9	—	8.00	15.00	28.00	50.00	—
AH1024//11	—	8.00	15.00	28.00	50.00	—
AH1030//15	—	8.00	15.00	28.00	50.00	—

Ahmadabad

KM# 126.2 DAM (Type 126)
Copper **Obv:** "Jahangiri" and date **Rev:** Mint and Persian month **Note:** Weight varies: 20.20-20.90 grams.

Date	Mintage	Good	VG	F	VF	XF
AH1016//6(sic)	—	12.00	30.00	60.00	95.00	—
AH1018//4	—	12.00	30.00	60.00	95.00	—
AH10xx//6	—	12.00	30.00	60.00	95.00	—
AH1025	—	15.00	37.50	75.00	120	—
AH1026//11	—	15.00	37.50	75.00	120	—
AH1026//11(sic)	—	15.00	37.50	75.00	120	—
AH1028//31 Error for 13	—	15.00	37.50	75.00	120	—

Ajmer

KM# 126.8 DAM (Type 126)
Copper **Note:** Weight varies: 20.20-20.90 grams.

Date	Mintage	Good	VG	F	VF	XF
AH1024//10	—	12.00	30.00	60.00	95.00	—
AH1024//11	—	12.00	30.00	60.00	95.00	—
AH1025//11	—	12.00	30.00	60.00	95.00	—

Bairata

KM# 126.3 DAM (Type 126)
Copper **Note:** Weight varies: 20.20-20.90 grams.

Date	Mintage	Good	VG	F	VF	XF
AH1015//2	—	6.00	15.00	30.00	50.00	—
AH1016//3	—	6.00	15.00	30.00	50.00	—
AH1017//4	—	6.00	15.00	30.00	50.00	—
AH1018//4	—	6.00	15.00	30.00	50.00	—
AH1018//5	—	6.00	15.00	30.00	50.00	—
AH1019//6	—	6.00	15.00	30.00	50.00	—
AH1019/5	—	6.00	15.00	30.00	50.00	—
AH1020//6	—	6.00	15.00	30.00	50.00	—
AH1021//7	—	6.00	15.00	30.00	50.00	—
AH1022//8	—	6.00	15.00	30.00	50.00	—
AH102x//13	—	6.00	15.00	30.00	50.00	—
AH1028//14	—	6.00	15.00	30.00	50.00	—
AH1030//61(sic) Error for 16	—	6.00	15.00	30.00	50.00	—
AH103x//16	—	6.00	15.00	30.00	50.00	—
AH1034//19(sic)	—	6.00	15.00	30.00	50.00	—
AH1034//20	—	6.00	15.00	30.00	50.00	—
AH1036//18(sic)	—	6.00	15.00	30.00	50.00	—

Burhanpur

KM# 126.10 DAM (Type 126)
Copper **Note:** Weight varies: 20.20-20.90 grams.

Date	Mintage	Good	VG	F	VF	XF
AH1017 Azar	—	15.00	37.50	75.00	120	—

Delhi

KM# 126.4 DAM (Type 126)
Copper **Note:** Weight varies: 20.20-20.90 grams.

Date	Mintage	Good	VG	F	VF	XF
AH103x//21	—	15.00	37.50	75.00	120	—

Gobindpur

KM# 126.9 DAM (Type 126)
Copper **Note:** Weight varies: 20.20-20.90 grams.

Date	Mintage	Good	VG	F	VF	XF
AH1029//15	—	12.00	30.00	60.00	95.00	—

Kabul

KM# 126.5 DAM (Type 126)
Copper **Note:** Weight varies: 20.20-20.90 grams.

Date	Mintage	Good	VG	F	VF	XF
AH102x//6	—	20.00	50.00	100	160	—
AH1028//14	—	20.00	50.00	100	160	—

Narnol

KM# 126.6 DAM (Type 126)
Copper **Note:** Weight varies: 20.20-20.90 grams.

Date	Mintage	Good	VG	F	VF	XF
AH102x//7	—	12.00	30.00	60.00	95.00	—

Srinagar

KM# 126.11 DAM (Type 126)
Copper **Note:** Weight varies: 20.20-20.90 grams.

Date	Mintage	Good	VG	F	VF	XF
AH1022//8	—	20.00	50.00	100	160	—

Udaipur

KM# 126.7 DAM (Type 126)
Copper **Note:** Weight varies: 20.20-20.90 grams.

Date	Mintage	Good	VG	F	VF	XF
AH1020//5	—	20.00	50.00	100	160	—

Ajmir

KM# A127.1 TANKA (Type A127)
40.0000 g., Copper

Date	Mintage	VG	F	VF	XF	Unc
AH1024//10	—	40.00	100	200	320	—
ND(1605-27)	—	30.00	75.00	150	275	—

Ujjain

KM# 127.1 1/2 FALUS (Type 127)
Copper **Obv:** Emperor's name **Rev:** Mint name **Shape:** Square

Date	Mintage	Good	VG	F	VF	XF
ND	—	7.00	17.50	35.00	55.00	—

Ujjain

KM# 128.1 FALUS (Type 128)
Copper **Obv:** Without Emperors name **Shape:** Square

Date	Mintage	Good	VG	F	VF	XF
ND	—	5.00	12.50	25.00	40.00	—
AH102x//14	—	5.00	12.50	25.00	40.00	—
AH102x//15	—	5.00	12.50	25.00	40.00	—
AH1019//14	—	5.00	12.50	25.00	40.00	—

Ahmadabad

KM# 131.3 1/8 RUPEE (Type 131)
1.4300 g., Silver

Date	Mintage	VG	F	VF	XF	Unc
AH-	—	55.00	90.00	150	225	—

Ahmadanagar

KM# 131.4 1/8 RUPEE (Type 131)
1.4300 g., Silver

Date	Mintage	VG	F	VF	XF	Unc
AH-	—	55.00	90.00	150	225	—

Ajmer

KM# 131.1 1/8 RUPEE (Type 131)
1.4300 g., Silver

Date	Mintage	VG	F	VF	XF	Unc
AH1031//18	—	55.00	90.00	150	225	—

Burhanpur

KM# 131.5 1/8 RUPEE (Type 131)
1.4300 g., Silver

Date	Mintage	VG	F	VF	XF	Unc
AH1014	—	55.00	90.00	150	225	—
AH1033	—	55.00	90.00	150	225	—

Lahore

KM# 131.2 1/8 RUPEE (Type 131)
1.4300 g., Silver

Date	Mintage	VG	F	VF	XF	Unc
AH1029//15	—	55.00	90.00	150	225	—
AH1031//17	—	55.00	90.00	150	225	—

Burhanpur

KM# A131.3 1/8 RUPEE (Type A131)
1.4300 g., Silver **Shape:** Square

Date	Mintage	VG	F	VF	XF	Unc
AH-	—	45.00	75.00	125	200	—

Jahangirnagar

KM# A131.1 1/8 RUPEE (Type A131)
1.4300 g., Silver **Shape:** Square

Date	Mintage	VG	F	VF	XF	Unc
AH-	—	60.00	100	175	280	—

Kabul

KM# A131.2 1/8 RUPEE (Type A131)
1.4300 g., Silver **Shape:** Square

Date	Mintage	VG	F	VF	XF	Unc
AHxxxx//7	—	80.00	135	225	360	—

Agra

KM# 132.1 1/4 RUPEE (Type 132)
3.1750 g., Silver **Rev. Inscription:** "Sakhat Nurani" **Note:** Similar to KM#155.1.

Date	Mintage	VG	F	VF	XF	Unc
AH1014//1	—	120	200	320	—	—

Ahmadanagar

KM# 132.3 1/4 RUPEE (Type 132)
3.1750 g., Silver

Date	Mintage	VG	F	VF	XF	Unc
AH-	—	35.00	60.00	100	160	—

Fathnagar

KM# 132.4 1/4 RUPEE (Type 132)
3.1750 g., Silver

Date	Mintage	VG	F	VF	XF	Unc
AH-	—	55.00	90.00	150	240	—

Jahangirnagar

KM# 132.5 1/4 RUPEE (Type 132)
3.1750 g., Silver

Date	Mintage	VG	F	VF	XF	Unc
AHxxxx//17	—	60.00	100	175	280	—

Patna

KM# 132.2 1/4 RUPEE (Type 132)
3.1750 g., Silver **Note:** Similar to 1 Rupee, KM# 145.12.

Date	Mintage	VG	F	VF	XF	Unc
AH1027//13	—	70.00	120	200	320	—
AH1034//20	—	70.00	120	200	320	—

Ahmedabad

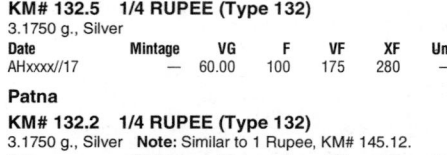

KM# 133.2 1/2 RUPEE (Type 133)
5.7220 g., Silver **Obv:** Pre-accession name, "Selim Shah", mint name **Note:** Jahangir Regnal year.

Date	Mintage	VG	F	VF	XF	Unc
AH101x//2	—	110	180	300	480	—

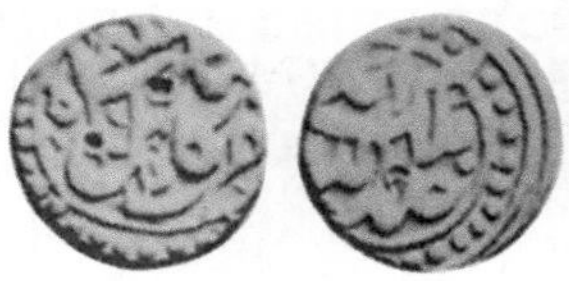

Kabul

KM# 133.1 1/2 RUPEE (Type 133)
5.7220 g., Silver **Obv:** Pre-accession name "Selim Shah", mint name, and AH date **Rev:** Benediction

Date	Mintage	Good	VG	F	VF	XF
AH1014	—	—	215	360	600	950

Kabul

KM# 133.3 1/2 RUPEE (Type 133)
5.7220 g., Silver **Obv:** Pre-accession name "Selim Shah" with "Hamisha" couplet

Date	Mintage	Good	VG	F	VF	XF
AH1014	—	—	215	360	600	950

Ahmadanagar

KM# 134.1 1/2 RUPEE (Type 134)
5.7220 g., Silver **Obv:** Kalima

Date	Mintage	Good	VG	F	VF	XF
AH-	—	10.00	20.00	45.00	75.00	120

Elichpur

KM# 134.6 1/2 RUPEE (Type 134)
5.7220 g., Silver **Obv:** Kalima

Date	Mintage	VG	F	VF	XF	Unc
AH1015	—	35.00	60.00	100	160	—

Fathnagar

KM# 134.3 1/2 RUPEE (Type 134)
5.7220 g., Silver **Obv:** Kalima

Date	Mintage	VG	F	VF	XF	Unc
AH-	—	55.00	90.00	150	240	—

Lahore

KM# 134.2 1/2 RUPEE (Type 134)
5.7220 g., Silver **Obv:** Kalima

Date	Mintage	VG	F	VF	XF	Unc
AH1015//1 Rare	—	55.00	90.00	150	240	—

Zafarnagar

KM# 134.4 1/2 RUPEE (Type 134)
5.7220 g., Silver **Obv:** Kalima

Date	Mintage	VG	F	VF	XF	Unc
AH-	—	140	240	400	640	—

Kashmir

KM# 135.3 1/2 RUPEE (Type 135)
5.7220 g., Silver **Obv:** Names of "Jahangir" and "Akbar" **Rev:** AH date

Date	Mintage	VG	F	VF	XF	Unc
AH1031//17	—	110	180	300	480	—

Lahore

KM# 135.1 1/2 RUPEE (Type 135)
5.7220 g., Silver **Obv:** Names of "Jahangir" and "Akbar" **Rev:** AH date

Date	Mintage	Good	VG	F	VF	XF
AH1035//20	—	—	160	270	450	720

Qandahar

KM# 135.2 1/2 RUPEE (Type 135)
5.7220 g., Silver **Obv:** Names of "Jahangir" and "Akbar" **Rev:** AH date

Date	Mintage	VG	F	VF	XF	Unc
AH1026//12	—	60.00	110	175	260	—
AH1027//13	—	60.00	110	175	260	—
AH1028//14	—	60.00	110	175	260	—
AH103x//xx	—	60.00	110	175	260	—

Ahmadabad

KM# 136.6 1/2 RUPEE (Type 136)
5.7220 g., Silver

Date	Mintage	VG	F	VF	XF	Unc
AHxxxx	—	60.00	110	175	260	—

Akbarnagar

KM# 136.3 1/2 RUPEE (Type 136)

5.7220 g., Silver

Date	Mintage	VG	F	VF	XF	Unc
AH101x//6	—	70.00	120	200	300	—

Burhanpur

KM# 136.5 1/2 RUPEE (Type 136)

5.7220 g., Silver **Rev:** AH date and Ilahi month

Date	Mintage	VG	F	VF	XF	Unc
AH-	—	70.00	120	200	300	—

Patna

KM# 136.1 1/2 RUPEE (Type 136)

5.7220 g., Silver **Rev:** AH date and Ilahi month

Date	Mintage	VG	F	VF	XF	Unc
AH1027//13 Rare	—	—	—	—	—	—

Qandahar

KM# 136.4 1/2 RUPEE (Type 136)

5.7220 g., Silver **Rev:** AH date and Ilahi month

Date	Mintage	VG	F	VF	XF	Unc
AH1024//11	—	180	300	500	750	—

Tatta

KM# 136.2 1/2 RUPEE (Type 136)

5.7220 g., Silver **Rev:** AH date and Ilahi month

Date	Mintage	VG	F	VF	XF	Unc
AH10xx//15	—	110	180	300	450	—

Ahmadabad

KM# 137.1 1/2 RUPEE (Type 137)

5.7220 g., Silver **Obv. Legend:** Poetic couplet **Rev. Legend:** Poetic couplet

Date	Mintage	VG	F	VF	XF	Unc
AH1022//xx	—	60.00	110	175	260	—
AH1023//xx	—	60.00	110	175	260	—
AH1025//xx	—	60.00	110	175	260	—

Kabul

KM# 137.3 1/2 RUPEE (Type 137)

5.7220 g., Silver **Rev:** AH date and Ilahi month **Note:** Similar to 1 Rupee, KM#149.12.

Date	Mintage	VG	F	VF	XF	Unc
ND	—	160	270	450	675	—

Ahmadabad

KM# 138.1 1/2 RUPEE (Type 138)

5.7220 g., Silver **Obv:** Taurus (bull)

Date	Mintage	Good	VG	F	VF	XF
AH1027//13 Rare	—	—	—	—	—	—

Ahmadabad

KM# 138.2 1/2 RUPEE (Type 138)

5.7220 g., Silver **Obv:** Leo (lion) **Note:** Zodiac 1/2 Rupees of Agra Mint have been reported, but are believed to be counterfeit.

Date	Mintage	VG	F	VF	XF	Unc
AH1027//13 Rare	—	—	—	—	—	—

Ahmadabad

KM# A139.1 1/2 RUPEE (Type A139)

7.1000 g., Silver **Series:** "Sawai" **Obv:** "Jahangir" and "Akbar" **Rev:** "inayat couplet"

Date	Mintage	VG	F	VF	XF	Unc
AHxxxx//3 Rare	—	—	—	—	—	—
AHxxxx//6 Rare	—	—	—	—	—	—

Agra

KM# 139.2 SULTANI (Type 139 - Heavier weight standard)

Silver **Obv:** Kalima **Note:** Weight varies: 6.70-6.85 grams.

Date	Mintage	VG	F	VF	XF	Unc
AH101x//4	—	280	480	800	1,200	—

Ahmadabad

KM# 139.3 SULTANI (Type 139 - Heavier weight standard)

Silver **Obv:** Kalima **Note:** Weight varies: 6.70-6.85 grams.

Date	Mintage	VG	F	VF	XF	Unc
AH1016	—	280	480	800	1,200	—

Kabul

KM# 139.1 SULTANI (Type 139 - Heavier weight standard)

Silver **Obv:** Kalima **Note:** Weight varies: 6.70-6.85 grams.

Date	Mintage	VG	F	VF	XF	Unc
AH1014//1	—	125	210	350	525	—
AH1015//1	—	125	210	350	525	—
AH1016//x	—	125	210	350	525	—

Ahmadabad

KM# 140.1 RUPEE (Type 140)

11.4440 g., Silver **Obv:** Pre-accession name, "Selim Shah" in couplet, date **Rev:** Mint name; regnal year of Akbar, Ilahi month **Note:** Months of Azar to Isfandarmuz only associated with the regnal year 50 of this type.

Date	Mintage	VG	F	VF	XF	Unc
ND(Il 50 of Akbar)	—	40.00	70.00	110	160	—

Ahmadabad

KM# 140.2 RUPEE (Type 140)

11.4440 g., Silver **Obv:** Pre-accession name "Selim Shah" in couplet **Rev:** Regnall year of Jahangir, Ilahi month **Note:** Months of Farwardin to Tir only associated with regnal year 2 of this type.

Date	Mintage	VG	F	VF	XF	Unc
AHxxxx//2	—	26.00	55.00	100	150	—

Ahmadabad

KM# A141.1 RUPEE (Type A141)

11.4440 g., Silver **Obv:** Kalima **Obv. Inscription:** "Jahangir..."

Date	Mintage	Good	VG	F	VF	XF
AH1015//2	—	—	—	—	—	—

Ahmadanagar

KM# 141.1 RUPEE (Type 141)

11.4440 g., Silver **Obv:** Kalima **Rev:** AH date **Rev. Inscription:** "Nur-ud-din Muhammad Jahangir"

Date	Mintage	VG	F	VF	XF	Unc
AH1014	—	28.00	50.00	80.00	120	—
AH1020	—	28.00	50.00	80.00	120	—
AH1027	—	28.00	50.00	80.00	120	—

Akbarnagar

KM# 141.2 RUPEE (Type 141)

11.4440 g., Silver **Obv:** Kalima **Rev:** AH date **Rev. Inscription:** "Nur-ud-din Muhammad Jahangir"

Date	Mintage	VG	F	VF	XF	Unc
AH1014	—	28.00	50.00	80.00	120	—

Berar

KM# 141.3 RUPEE (Type 141)

11.4440 g., Silver **Obv:** Kalima **Rev:** AH date, bird **Rev. Inscription:** "Nur-ud-din Muhammad Jahangir"

Date	Mintage	VG	F	VF	XF	Unc
AH1014	—	55.00	90.00	150	225	—

Burhanpur

KM# 141.4 RUPEE (Type 141)

11.4440 g., Silver **Obv:** Kalima **Rev:** AH date **Rev. Inscription:** "Nur-ud-din Muhammad Jahangir"

Date	Mintage	VG	F	VF	XF	Unc
AH1015//2	—	55.00	90.00	150	225	—

Elichpur

KM# 141.5 RUPEE (Type 141)

11.4440 g., Silver **Obv:** Kalima **Rev:** AH date **Rev. Inscription:** "Nur-ud-din Muhammad Jahangir"

Date	Mintage	VG	F	VF	XF	Unc
AH1014//x	—	35.00	60.00	100	150	—
AH1015	—	35.00	60.00	100	150	—
AH1015 bird//bird	—	35.00	60.00	100	150	—
AH1015 Erichpur Error	—	35.00	60.00	100	150	—
AH1016//x	—	35.00	60.00	100	150	—
AH1017//4	—	35.00	60.00	100	150	—

Fathnagar

KM# 141.8 RUPEE (Type 141)

11.4440 g., Silver **Obv:** Kalima **Rev:** AH date **Rev. Inscription:** "Nur-ud-din Muhammad Jahangir"

Date	Mintage	VG	F	VF	XF	Unc
ND	—	35.00	60.00	100	150	—

Jalnapur

KM# 141.6 RUPEE (Type 141)

11.4440 g., Silver **Obv:** Kalima **Rev:** AH date **Rev. Inscription:** "Nur-ud-din Muhammad Jahangir"

Date	Mintage	VG	F	VF	XF	Unc
AH1014	—	30.00	50.00	80.00	120	—
AH1015//3 (sic)	—	30.00	50.00	80.00	120	—
AH1017//x	—	30.00	50.00	80.00	120	—

Tatta

KM# 141.9 RUPEE (Type 141)

11.4440 g., Silver **Obv:** Kalima **Rev:** AH date **Rev. Inscription:** "Nur-ud-din Muhammad Jahangir"

Date	Mintage	VG	F	VF	XF	Unc
AH1015//2	—	30.00	50.00	80.00	120	—
AH1016//2	—	30.00	50.00	80.00	120	—
AH1016//3	—	30.00	50.00	80.00	120	—
AH1017//3	—	30.00	50.00	80.00	120	—
AH1017//4	—	30.00	50.00	80.00	120	—
AH1018//5	—	30.00	50.00	80.00	120	—
AH1019//5	—	30.00	50.00	80.00	120	—
AH1020//6	—	30.00	50.00	80.00	120	—

Zafarnagar

KM# 141.7 RUPEE (Type 141)

11.4440 g., Silver **Obv:** Kalima **Rev:** AH date **Rev. Inscription:** "Nur-ud-din Muhammad Jahangir"

Date	Mintage	VG	F	VF	XF	Unc
ND	—	55.00	90.00	150	225	—

Ahmadnagar

KM# 142.1 RUPEE (Type 142)

11.4440 g., Silver **Obv:** Names of "Jahangir" and "Akbar" **Rev:** AH date

Date	Mintage	VG	F	VF	XF	Unc
AH1032	—	35.00	80.00	100	150	—
AH1035	—	35.00	80.00	100	150	—
AH1036//xx	—	35.00	80.00	100	150	—
AH1037	—	35.00	80.00	100	150	—

Qandahar

KM# 142.2 RUPEE (Type 142)

11.4440 g., Silver **Obv:** Names of "Jahangir" and "Akbar" **Rev:** AH date

Date	Mintage	VG	F	VF	XF	Unc
AH1025//11	—	14.00	22.00	35.00	50.00	—
AH1025//12	—	14.00	22.00	35.00	50.00	—
AH1026//12	—	14.00	22.00	35.00	50.00	—
AH1026//13	—	14.00	22.00	35.00	50.00	—
AH1027//13	—	14.00	22.00	35.00	50.00	—
AH1027//14	—	14.00	22.00	35.00	50.00	—
AH1028//14	—	14.00	22.00	35.00	50.00	—
AH1028//15	—	14.00	22.00	35.00	50.00	—
AH1029//15	—	14.00	22.00	35.00	50.00	—
AH1029//16	—	14.00	22.00	35.00	50.00	—
AH1030//16	—	14.00	22.00	35.00	50.00	—
AH1030//17	—	14.00	22.00	35.00	50.00	—
AH1031/16	—	14.00	22.00	35.00	50.00	—
AH1031//17	—	14.00	22.00	35.00	50.00	—

Agra

KM# 143.1 RUPEE (Type 143)

11.4440 g., Silver **Obv. Inscription:** ...Sakhat Nurani... **Rev:** "Jahangir..."

Date	Mintage	VG	F	VF	XF	Unc
AH1016	—	220	360	600	900	—

Burhanpur

KM# 143.3 RUPEE (Type 143)
11.4440 g., Silver **Obv. Inscription:** "...Sakhatnurani..."

Date	Mintage	VG	F	VF	XF	Unc
AH1014	—	220	360	600	900	—

Qandahar

KM# 143.2 RUPEE (Type 143)
11.4440 g., Silver **Shape:** Square

Date	Mintage	VG	F	VF	XF	Unc
AH1026//11	—	360	600	1,000	1,500	—

Agra

KM# A144.1 RUPEE (Type A144)
11.4440 g., Silver **Shape:** Round **Note:** With Persian Solar months.

Date	Mintage	VG	F	VF	XF	Unc
AH1020//6 Khúrdád	—	220	360	600	900	—
AH1020//6 Mihr	—	220	360	600	900	—
AH1020//6 Azar	—	220	360	600	900	—
AH1020//6 Bahman	—	220	360	600	900	—
AH1020//6 Amardád	—	220	360	600	900	—
AH1021//7 Khúrdád	—	220	360	600	900	—
AH1021//7 Mihr	—	220	360	600	900	—
AH1021//7 Amardád	—	220	360	600	900	—
AH1021//7 Farwardín	—	220	360	600	900	—
AH1021//7 Bahman	—	220	360	600	900	—

Agra

KM# 144.1 RUPEE (Type 144)
11.4440 g., Silver **Shape:** Square **Note:** With Persian Solar months.

Date	Mintage	VG	F	VF	XF	Unc
AH1020//6 Di	—	250	420	700	1,050	—
AH1020//6 Shahrewar	—	250	420	700	1,050	—
AH1020//6 Aban	—	250	420	700	1,050	—
AH1020//6 Tir	—	250	420	700	1,050	—
AH1020//6 (Ardíbihisht?)	—	250	420	700	1,050	—
AH1021//6(sic) Isfandármuz	—	250	420	700	1,050	—
AH1021//7 Aban	—	250	420	700	1,050	—
AH1021//7 Ardíbihisht	—	250	420	700	1,050	—
AH1021//7 Shahrewar	—	250	420	700	1,050	—
AH1021//7 Tir	—	250	420	700	1,050	—

Agra

KM# 145.1 RUPEE (Type 145)
11.4440 g., Silver **Obv:** "Nur al-Din Jahangir" and "Akbar" **Rev:** AH date and/or regnal year

Date	Mintage	VG	F	VF	XF	Unc
AH1020//6	—	100	200	325	450	—
AH1020//7	—	100	200	325	450	—
AH1021//7	—	100	200	325	450	—
AH1021//8	—	40.00	65.00	110	200	—
AH1022//8	—	40.00	65.00	110	200	—
AH1022//9	—	40.00	65.00	110	200	—
AH1023//9	—	40.00	65.00	110	200	—
AH1023//10	—	40.00	65.00	110	200	—
AH1024/10	—	40.00	65.00	110	200	—
AH1024//11	—	40.00	65.00	110	200	—
AH1025//11	—	40.00	65.00	110	200	—
AH1025//12	—	40.00	65.00	110	200	—
AH1026//12	—	40.00	65.00	110	200	—
AH1026//13	—	40.00	65.00	110	200	—
AH1027//13	—	40.00	65.00	110	200	—
AH1028//13(sic)	—	40.00	65.00	110	200	—

Ahmadabad

KM# 145.2 RUPEE (Type 145)
11.4440 g., Silver **Obv:** "Nur al-Din Jahangir" and "Akbar" **Rev:** AH date and/or regnal year

Date	Mintage	VG	F	VF	XF	Unc
AH1020//6	—	18.00	30.00	50.00	75.00	—
AH1020//7	—	18.00	30.00	50.00	75.00	—
AH1021//7	—	18.00	30.00	50.00	75.00	—
AH1021//8	—	18.00	30.00	50.00	75.00	—
AH1022//x	—	18.00	30.00	50.00	75.00	—
AH1022//8	—	18.00	30.00	50.00	75.00	—

Ahmadnagar

KM# 145.19 RUPEE (Type 145)
11.4440 g., Silver **Obv:** "Nur al-Din Jahangir" and "Akbar" **Rev:** AH date and/or regnal year

Date	Mintage	VG	F	VF	XF	Unc
AH1037	—	110	180	300	450	—

Note: Mint name appears as "Ahmadanagar"

Akbarnagar

KM# 145.4 RUPEE (Type 145)
11.4440 g., Silver **Obv:** "Nur al-Din Jahangir" and "Akbar" **Rev:** AH date and/or regnal year

Date	Mintage	VG	F	VF	XF	Unc
AH1017//x	—	22.00	36.00	60.00	90.00	—
AH1021//7	—	22.00	36.00	60.00	90.00	—
AH1021//8	—	22.00	36.00	60.00	90.00	—
AH1022//8	—	22.00	36.00	60.00	90.00	—
AH1022//9	—	22.00	36.00	60.00	90.00	—
AH1023//9	—	22.00	36.00	60.00	90.00	—
AH1023//10	—	22.00	36.00	60.00	90.00	—
AH1024//10	—	22.00	36.00	60.00	90.00	—
AH1024//11	—	22.00	36.00	60.00	90.00	—
AH1025//xx	—	22.00	36.00	60.00	90.00	—
AH10xx//13	—	22.00	36.00	60.00	90.00	—
AH10xx//15	—	22.00	36.00	60.00	90.00	—
AH10xx//17	—	22.00	36.00	60.00	90.00	—
AH10xx//18	—	22.00	36.00	60.00	90.00	—
AH10xx//19	—	22.00	36.00	60.00	90.00	—
AH10xx//20	—	22.00	36.00	60.00	90.00	—
AH10xx//21	—	22.00	36.00	60.00	90.00	—
AH10xx//22	—	22.00	36.00	60.00	90.00	—

Burhanpur

KM# 145.5 RUPEE (Type 145)
11.4440 g., Silver **Obv:** "Nur al-Din Jahangir" and "Akbar" **Rev:** AH date and/or regnal year

Date	Mintage	VG	F	VF	XF	Unc
AH1019//x	—	16.00	27.00	45.00	70.00	—
AH1020//6	—	16.00	27.00	45.00	70.00	—
AH1020//7	—	16.00	27.00	45.00	70.00	—
AH1021//7	—	16.00	27.00	45.00	70.00	—
AH1021//8	—	16.00	27.00	45.00	70.00	—
AH102x//9	—	16.00	27.00	45.00	70.00	—
AH102x//11	—	16.00	27.00	45.00	70.00	—
AH102x//14	—	16.00	27.00	45.00	70.00	—
AH10xx//15	—	16.00	27.00	45.00	70.00	—
AH103x//16	—	16.00	27.00	45.00	70.00	—
AH103x//17	—	16.00	27.00	45.00	70.00	—
AH103x//18	—	16.00	27.00	45.00	70.00	—
AH103x//19	—	16.00	27.00	45.00	70.00	—
AH103x//20	—	16.00	27.00	45.00	70.00	—
AH1035//21	—	16.00	27.00	45.00	70.00	—
AH1037//22(sic)	—	16.00	27.00	45.00	70.00	—

Delhi

KM# 145.6 RUPEE (Type 145)
11.4440 g., Silver **Obv:** "Nur al-Din Jahangir" and "Akbar" **Rev:** AH date and/or regnal year

Date	Mintage	VG	F	VF	XF	Unc
AH1018//4	—	22.00	36.00	60.00	90.00	—
AH1020//6	—	22.00	36.00	60.00	90.00	—
AH1020//7	—	22.00	36.00	60.00	90.00	—
AH1021//7	—	22.00	36.00	60.00	90.00	—
AH1021//8	—	22.00	36.00	60.00	90.00	—
AH1022//8	—	22.00	36.00	60.00	90.00	—
AH1022//9	—	22.00	36.00	60.00	90.00	—
AH1023//9	—	22.00	36.00	60.00	90.00	—
AH1023//10	—	22.00	36.00	60.00	90.00	—
AH1024//10	—	22.00	36.00	60.00	90.00	—
AH1024//11	—	22.00	36.00	60.00	90.00	—
AH1025//11	—	22.00	36.00	60.00	90.00	—
AH1025//12	—	22.00	36.00	60.00	90.00	—
AH1026//12	—	22.00	36.00	60.00	90.00	—
AH1027//14	—	22.00	36.00	60.00	90.00	—
AH1026//13	—	22.00	36.00	60.00	90.00	—

Date	Mintage	VG	F	VF	XF	Unc
AH1027//13	—	22.00	36.00	60.00	90.00	—
AH1028//14	—	22.00	36.00	60.00	90.00	—
AH1028//15	—	22.00	36.00	60.00	90.00	—
AH1029//15	—	22.00	36.00	60.00	90.00	—
AH1029//16	—	22.00	36.00	60.00	90.00	—
AH1030//16	—	22.00	36.00	60.00	90.00	—
AH1030//17	—	22.00	36.00	60.00	90.00	—
AH1031//17	—	22.00	36.00	60.00	90.00	—
AH1032//xx	—	22.00	36.00	60.00	90.00	—
AH1033//19	—	22.00	36.00	60.00	90.00	—
AH1037//23	—	22.00	36.00	60.00	90.00	—

Jahangirnagar

KM# 145.7 RUPEE (Type 145)
11.4440 g., Silver **Obv:** "Nur al-Din Jahangir" and "Akbar" **Rev:** AH date and/or regnal year **Note:** Some dates exist with a decorative border.

Date	Mintage	VG	F	VF	XF	Unc
ND//7	—	42.50	70.00	120	180	—
ND//9	—	42.50	70.00	120	180	—
ND//10	—	42.50	70.00	120	180	—
ND//11	—	42.50	70.00	120	180	—
ND//12	—	42.50	70.00	120	180	—
ND//13	—	42.50	70.00	120	180	—
ND//14	—	42.50	70.00	120	180	—
ND//15	—	42.50	70.00	120	180	—
ND//16	—	42.50	70.00	120	180	—
ND//17	—	42.50	70.00	120	180	—
ND//18	—	42.50	70.00	120	180	—
ND//19	—	42.50	70.00	120	180	—
ND//20	—	42.50	70.00	120	180	—

Jalesar

KM# 145.8 RUPEE (Type 145)
11.4440 g., Silver **Obv:** "Nur al-Din Jahangir" and "Akbar" **Rev:** AH date and/or regnal year

Date	Mintage	VG	F	VF	XF	Unc
AH1031	—	220	360	600	900	—

Kabul

KM# 145.9 RUPEE (Type 145)
11.4440 g., Silver **Obv:** "Nur al-Din Jahangir" and "Akbar" **Rev:** AH date and/or regnal year

Date	Mintage	VG	F	VF	XF	Unc
AH1016//3	—	40.00	65.00	110	165	—
AH1022//8	—	40.00	65.00	110	165	—
AH1023//9	—	40.00	65.00	110	165	—
AH1025//11	—	40.00	65.00	110	165	—
AH1026//11(sic)	—	40.00	65.00	110	165	—
AH1026//12	—	40.00	65.00	110	165	—
AH1027//12(sic)	—	40.00	65.00	110	165	—
AH1027//13	—	40.00	65.00	110	165	—
AH1028//13(sic)	—	40.00	65.00	110	165	—
AH1028//14	—	40.00	65.00	110	165	—
AH1029//14(sic)	—	40.00	65.00	110	165	—
AH103x//21	—	40.00	65.00	110	165	—

Kashmir

KM# 145.10 RUPEE (Type 145)
11.4440 g., Silver **Obv:** "Nur al-Din Jahangir" and "Akbar" **Rev:** AH date and/or regnal year

Date	Mintage	VG	F	VF	XF	Unc
AH1021//7	—	45.00	75.00	125	190	—
AH1022//8	—	45.00	75.00	125	190	—
AH1022//9	—	45.00	75.00	125	190	—
AH1023//9	—	45.00	75.00	125	190	—
AH1023//10	—	45.00	75.00	125	190	—
AH1024//10	—	45.00	75.00	125	190	—
AH1024//11	—	45.00	75.00	125	190	—
AH1025//11	—	45.00	75.00	125	190	—
AH1025//12	—	45.00	75.00	125	190	—
AH1026//12	—	45.00	75.00	125	190	—
AH1026//13	—	45.00	75.00	125	190	—

Date	Mintage	VG	F	VF	XF	Unc
AH1027//13	—	45.00	75.00	125	190	—
AH1027//14	—	45.00	75.00	125	190	—
AH1028//14	—	45.00	75.00	125	190	—
AH1028//15	—	45.00	75.00	125	190	—
AH1029//15	—	45.00	75.00	125	190	—
AH1031//17	—	45.00	5.00	125	190	—

Katak

KM# 145.18 RUPEE (Type 145)
11.4440 g., Silver **Obv:** "Nur al-Din Jahangir" and "Akbar" **Rev:** AH date and/or regnal year

Date	Mintage	VG	F	VF	XF	Unc
AH1027	—	180	300	500	750	—

Kishtwar

KM# 145.20 RUPEE (Type 145)
11.4440 g., Silver **Obv:** "Nur al-Din Jahangir" and "Akbar" **Rev:** AH date and/or regnal year

Date	Mintage	VG	F	VF	XF	Unc
AH1024//10	—	360	600	1,000	1,500	—

Lahore

KM# 145.11 RUPEE (Type 145)
11.4440 g., Silver **Obv:** "Nur al-Din Jahangir" and "Akbar" **Rev:** AH date and/or regnal year

Date	Mintage	VG	F	VF	XF	Unc
ND//5	—	27.00	45.00	75.00	115	—
ND//6	—	27.00	45.00	75.00	115	—
ND//7	—	27.00	45.00	75.00	115	—
ND//8	—	27.00	45.00	75.00	115	—
ND//9	—	27.00	45.00	75.00	115	—
ND//10	—	27.00	45.00	75.00	115	—
ND//11	—	27.00	45.00	75.00	115	—

Patna

KM# 145.12 RUPEE (Type 145)
11.4440 g., Silver **Obv:** "Nur al-Din Jahangir" and "Akbar" **Rev:** AH date and/or regnal year

Date	Mintage	VG	F	VF	XF	Unc
AH1020//6	—	18.00	30.00	50.00	75.00	—
AH1021//7	—	18.00	30.00	50.00	75.00	—
AH1021//7	—	18.00	30.00	50.00	75.00	—
AH1021//8	—	18.00	30.00	50.00	75.00	—
AH1022//8	—	18.00	30.00	50.00	75.00	—
AH1022//9	—	18.00	30.00	50.00	75.00	—
AH1023//9	—	18.00	30.00	50.00	75.00	—
AH1023//10	—	18.00	30.00	50.00	75.00	—
AH1024//10	—	18.00	30.00	50.00	75.00	—
AH1024//11	—	18.00	30.00	50.00	75.00	—
AH1025//11	—	18.00	30.00	50.00	75.00	—
AH1025//12	—	18.00	30.00	50.00	75.00	—
AH1026//12	—	18.00	30.00	50.00	75.00	—
AH1026//13	—	18.00	30.00	50.00	75.00	—
AH1027//13	—	18.00	30.00	50.00	75.00	—
AH1027//14	—	18.00	30.00	50.00	75.00	—
AH1028//14	—	18.00	30.00	50.00	75.00	—
AH1028//15	—	18.00	30.00	50.00	75.00	—
AH1029//15	—	18.00	30.00	50.00	75.00	—
AH1029//16	—	18.00	30.00	50.00	75.00	—
AH1030//16	—	18.00	30.00	50.00	75.00	—
AH1030//17	—	18.00	30.00	50.00	75.00	—
AH1031//16	—	18.00	30.00	50.00	75.00	—
AH1031//17	—	18.00	30.00	50.00	75.00	—
AH1031//18	—	18.00	30.00	50.00	75.00	—
AH1032//18	—	18.00	30.00	50.00	75.00	—
AH1032//19	—	18.00	30.00	50.00	75.00	—
AH1033//19	—	18.00	30.00	50.00	75.00	—
AH1033//20	—	18.00	30.00	50.00	75.00	—
AH1034//20	—	18.00	30.00	50.00	75.00	—
AH1034//21	—	18.00	30.00	50.00	75.00	—
AH1035//21	—	18.00	30.00	50.00	75.00	—
AH1035//22	—	18.00	30.00	50.00	75.00	—
AH1036//21	—	18.00	30.00	50.00	75.00	—
AH1036//22	—	18.00	30.00	50.00	75.00	—
AH1037//22(sic)	—	18.00	30.00	50.00	75.00	—

Qandahar

KM# 145.13 RUPEE (Type 145)
11.4440 g., Silver **Obv:** "Nur al-Din Jahangir" and "Akbar" **Rev:** AH date and/or regnal year

Date	Mintage	VG	F	VF	XF	Unc
AH1020//x	—	18.00	30.00	50.00	75.00	—
AH1022//8	—	18.00	30.00	50.00	75.00	—
AH1023//9	—	18.00	30.00	50.00	75.00	—
AH1024//10	—	18.00	30.00	50.00	75.00	—
AH1025//11	—	18.00	30.00	50.00	75.00	—
AH1029//15	—	18.00	30.00	50.00	75.00	—

Rohtas

KM# 145.14 RUPEE (Type 145)
11.4440 g., Silver **Obv:** "Nur al-Din Jahangir" and "Akbar" **Rev:** AH date and/or regnal year

Date	Mintage	VG	F	VF	XF	Unc
AH1034//19	—	220	360	600	900	—
ND//20	—	220	360	600	900	—

Surat

KM# 145.15 RUPEE (Type 145)
11.4440 g., Silver **Obv:** "Nur al-Din Jahangir" and "Akbar" **Rev:** AH date and/or regnal year

Date	Mintage	VG	F	VF	XF	Unc
AH1029//15	—	70.00	120	200	300	—
AH103x//17	—	70.00	120	200	300	—
AH1035//20	—	70.00	120	200	300	—

Tatta

KM# 145.17 RUPEE (Type 145)
11.4440 g., Silver **Obv:** "Nur al-Din Jahangir" and "Akbar" **Rev:** AH date and/or regnal year

Date	Mintage	VG	F	VF	XF	Unc
AH10xx//3	—	16.00	27.00	45.00	65.00	—
AH1020//6	—	16.00	27.00	45.00	65.00	—
AH1020//7	—	16.00	27.00	45.00	65.00	—
AH1021//7	—	16.00	27.00	45.00	65.00	—
AH1021//8	—	16.00	27.00	45.00	65.00	—
AH1022//8	—	16.00	27.00	45.00	65.00	—
AH1022//9	—	16.00	27.00	45.00	65.00	—
AH1023//9	—	16.00	27.00	45.00	65.00	—
AH1023//10	—	16.00	27.00	45.00	65.00	—
AH1024//10	—	16.00	27.00	45.00	65.00	—
AH1024//11	—	16.00	27.00	45.00	65.00	—
AH1025//11	—	16.00	27.00	45.00	65.00	—
AH1025//12	—	16.00	27.00	45.00	65.00	—
AH1026//12	—	16.00	27.00	45.00	65.00	—
AH1026//13	—	16.00	27.00	45.00	65.00	—
AH1027//13	—	16.00	27.00	45.00	65.00	—
AH1027//14	—	16.00	27.00	45.00	65.00	—
AH1028//14	—	16.00	27.00	45.00	65.00	—
AH1028//15	—	16.00	27.00	45.00	65.00	—
AH1029//15	—	16.00	27.00	45.00	65.00	—
AH1029//16	—	16.00	27.00	45.00	65.00	—
AH10xx//17	—	16.00	27.00	45.00	65.00	—
AH10xx//18	—	16.00	27.00	45.00	65.00	—
AH10xx//19	—	16.00	27.00	45.00	65.00	—
AH10xx//20	—	16.00	27.00	45.00	65.00	—
AH1035//21	—	16.00	27.00	45.00	65.00	—
AH1037//22	—	16.00	27.00	45.00	65.00	—

Ujjain

KM# 145.16 RUPEE (Type 145)
11.4440 g., Silver **Obv:** "Nur al-Din Jahangir" and "Akbar" **Rev:** AH date and/or regnal year

Date	Mintage	VG	F	VF	XF	Unc
AH10xx//15	—	145	240	400	600	—

Agra

KM# 147.1 RUPEE (Type 147)
Silver **Obv:** Fancy hexafoil boarder **Rev:** Fancy hexafoil boarder **Shape:** Square **Note:** Weight varies: 11.20-11.50 grams.

Date	Mintage	VG	F	VF	XF	Unc
AH1020//6	—	200	480	800	1,200	—
AH1020//7	—	200	480	800	1,200	—
AH1021//7	—	200	480	800	1,200	—

Agra

KM# 147.2 RUPEE (Type 147)
Obv: Plain dotted square boarder **Rev:** Plain dotted square boarder **Note:** Weight varies: 11.20-11.50 grams.

Date	Mintage	VG	F	VF	XF	Unc
AH1021//8	—	140	280	450	675	—
AH1022//8	—	140	280	450	675	—
AH1023//9	—	140	280	450	675	—
AH1023//10	—	140	280	450	675	—
AH1024//9	—	140	280	450	675	—
AH1024//10	—	140	280	450	675	—
AH1024//11	—	140	280	450	675	—
AH1025//11	—	140	280	450	675	—
AH1025//12	—	140	280	450	675	—
AH1026//12	—	140	280	450	675	—
AH1026//13	—	140	280	450	675	—
AH1027//13	—	140	280	450	675	—
AH1028//1x	—	140	280	450	675	—

Surat

KM# 148.1 RUPEE (Type 148)
11.4440 g., Silver

Date	Mintage	VG	F	VF	XF	Unc
AH102x//8	—	30.00	50.00	85.00	140	—
AH1023//9	—	30.00	50.00	85.00	140	—
AH103x//15	—	30.00	50.00	85.00	140	—
AH1030//16	—	30.00	50.00	85.00	140	—
AH1030//17	—	30.00	50.00	85.00	140	—
AH1031//17	—	30.00	50.00	85.00	140	—
AH1031//18	—	30.00	50.00	85.00	140	—
AH1032//18	—	30.00	50.00	85.00	140	—
AH1032//19	—	30.00	50.00	85.00	140	—
AH1033//18(sic)	—	30.00	50.00	85.00	140	—

Agra

KM# 149.1 RUPEE (Type 149)
11.4440 g., Silver **Rev:** "Yaft"

Date	Mintage	VG	F	VF	XF	Unc
AH1030//16	—	28.00	50.00	80.00	140	—
AH1031//17	—	28.00	50.00	80.00	140	—
AH1031//18	—	28.00	50.00	80.00	140	—
AH1032//18	—	28.00	50.00	80.00	140	—
AH103x//19	—	28.00	50.00	80.00	140	—
AH1034//20	—	28.00	50.00	80.00	140	—
AH1034//21	—	28.00	50.00	80.00	140	—
AH1035//21	—	28.00	50.00	80.00	140	—
AH1036//2x	—	28.00	50.00	80.00	140	—

Ahmadabad

KM# 149.4 RUPEE (Type 149)
11.4440 g., Silver **Rev. Inscription:** "Inayat"

Date	Mintage	VG	F	VF	XF	Unc
AH1016//3	—	15.00	22.00	35.00	75.00	—
AHxxxx//6	—	15.00	22.00	35.00	75.00	—
AH1022//8	—	15.00	22.00	35.00	75.00	—
AH1027//13	—	15.00	22.00	35.00	75.00	—

Date	Mintage	VG	F	VF	XF	Unc
AH1027//14	—	15.00	22.00	35.00	75.00	—
AH1028//14	—	15.00	22.00	35.00	75.00	—
AH1028//15	—	15.00	22.00	35.00	75.00	—
AH1029//15	—	15.00	22.00	35.00	75.00	—
AH1029//16	—	15.00	22.00	35.00	75.00	—
AH1030//15	—	15.00	22.00	35.00	75.00	—
AH1030//16	—	15.00	22.00	35.00	75.00	—
AH1030//17	—	15.00	22.00	35.00	75.00	—
AH1031//61(error for 16)	—	15.00	22.00	35.00	75.00	—
AH1031//16	—	15.00	22.00	35.00	75.00	—
AH1031//17	—	15.00	22.00	35.00	75.00	—
AH1032//18	—	15.00	22.00	35.00	75.00	—
AH1032//19	—	15.00	22.00	35.00	75.00	—
AH1033//19	—	15.00	22.00	35.00	75.00	—

Ahmadabad

KM# 149.2 RUPEE (Type 149)
11.4440 g., Silver **Rev. Inscription:** "Muzaiyan"

Date	Mintage	VG	F	VF	XF	Unc
AH1022//8	—	16.00	25.00	40.00	80.00	—
AH1022//9	—	16.00	25.00	40.00	80.00	—
AH1023//9	—	16.00	25.00	40.00	80.00	—
AH1023//10	—	16.00	25.00	40.00	80.00	—
AH1024//10	—	16.00	25.00	40.00	80.00	—
AH1024//11	—	16.00	25.00	40.00	80.00	—
AH1025//11	—	16.00	25.00	40.00	80.00	—
AH1025//12	—	16.00	25.00	40.00	80.00	—
AH1026//12	—	16.00	25.00	40.00	80.00	—

Ahmadabad

KM# 149.2A RUPEE (Type 149)
11.4440 g., Silver **Note:** "Hamisha" couplet.

Date	Mintage	VG	F	VF	XF	Unc
AH1027//12	—	36.00	60.00	100	200	—

Ahmadabad

KM# 149.3 RUPEE (Type 149)
11.4440 g., Silver **Rev:** "Kishwar" **Note:** Struck from gold mohur dies.

Date	Mintage	VG	F	VF	XF	Unc
AH1027//12(sic)	—	36.00	60.00	100	200	—
AH1029//14(sic)	—	36.00	60.00	100	200	—

Ajmer

KM# 149.5 RUPEE (Type 149)
11.4440 g., Silver **Rev. Inscription:** "Firoz"

Date	Mintage	VG	F	VF	XF	Unc
AH1023//9	—	75.00	120	200	300	—
AH1023//10	—	75.00	120	200	300	—
AH1024//10	—	75.00	120	200	300	—
AH1025//11	—	75.00	120	200	300	—

Ajmer

KM# 149.6 RUPEE (Type 149)
11.4440 g., Silver **Rev:** "Fath"

Date	Mintage	VG	F	VF	XF	Unc
AH1024//10	—	75.00	120	200	300	—

Akbarnagar

KM# 149.7 RUPEE (Type 149)
11.4440 g., Silver **Rev:** "Gardun"

Date	Mintage	VG	F	VF	XF	Unc
AH1019//x	—	55.00	90.00	150	225	—
AH1020//x	—	55.00	90.00	150	225	—

Allahabad

KM# 149.8 RUPEE (Type 149)
11.4440 g., Silver **Rev:** "Hamisha"

Date	Mintage	VG	F	VF	XF	Unc
AH10xx//15	—	32.00	55.00	90.00	145	—
AH1032//1x	—	32.00	55.00	90.00	145	—
AH1034//19(sic)	—	32.00	55.00	90.00	145	—
AH1035//21	—	32.00	55.00	90.00	145	—
AH1037//22(sic)	—	32.00	55.00	90.00	145	—

Burhanpur

KM# 149.10 RUPEE (Type 149)
11.4440 g., Silver **Rev. Inscription:** "Din Panah"

Date	Mintage	VG	F	VF	XF	Unc
AH1014//(1)	—	18.00	30.00	50.00	75.00	—
AH1017//3	—	18.00	30.00	50.00	75.00	—
AH101x//4	—	18.00	30.00	50.00	75.00	—
AH101x//5	—	18.00	30.00	50.00	75.00	—

Jalnapur

KM# 149.11 RUPEE (Type 149)
11.4440 g., Silver **Rev:** "Sakhat Nurani"

Date	Mintage	VG	F	VF	XF	Unc
ND	—	270	450	750	1,125	—

Kabul

KM# 149.12 RUPEE (Type 149)
11.4440 g., Silver

Date	Mintage	VG	F	VF	XF	Unc
AH1023//9	—	80.00	135	225	340	—
AH1024//10	—	80.00	135	225	340	—
AH103x//17	—	80.00	135	225	340	—
AH103x//18	—	80.00	135	225	340	—
AH1033//19	—	80.00	135	225	340	—
AH1034//19(sic)	—	80.00	135	225	340	—
AH1034//20	—	80.00	135	225	340	—
AH1036//21(sic)	—	80.00	135	225	340	—

Kabul

KM# 149.13 RUPEE (Type 149)
11.4440 g., Silver **Rev:** "Khusro"

Date	Mintage	VG	F	VF	XF	Unc
AH1024//9(sic)	—	45.00	75.00	125	180	—
AH1034//19(sic)	—	45.00	75.00	125	180	—

Kabul

KM# 149.12A RUPEE (Type 149)
11.4440 g., Silver **Obv:** "Ilhahi" and month "Tir" in loop of "Kabul"

Date	Mintage	VG	F	VF	XF	Unc
AHxxxx//16	—	80.00	135	225	340	—

Kabul

KM# 149.12B RUPEE (Type 149)
11.4440 g., Silver **Note:** "Inayat" couplet.

Date	Mintage	VG	F	VF	XF	Unc
AH103x//21	—	60.00	100	175	260	—

Katak

KM# 149.18 RUPEE (Type 149)
11.4440 g., Silver **Note:** Couplet and month "Tir".

Date	Mintage	VG	F	VF	XF	Unc
AH1035	—	125	210	350	525	—

Lahore

KM# 149.14 RUPEE (Type 149)
11.4440 g., Silver **Rev:** "Hamisha" at top

Date	Mintage	VG	F	VF	XF	Unc
AH1025//11	—	18.00	30.00	50.00	110	—
AH1025//12	—	18.00	30.00	50.00	110	—
AH1026//12	—	18.00	30.00	50.00	110	—
AH1026//13	—	18.00	30.00	50.00	110	—
AH1027//12	—	18.00	30.00	50.00	110	—
AH1027//13	—	18.00	30.00	50.00	110	—
AH1027//14	—	18.00	30.00	50.00	110	—
AH1028//13	—	18.00	30.00	50.00	110	—
AH1028//14	—	18.00	30.00	50.00	110	—
AH1029//14	—	18.00	30.00	50.00	110	—
AH1028//15	—	18.00	30.00	50.00	110	—

Lahore

KM# 149.16 RUPEE (Type 149)
11.4440 g., Silver **Rev:** "Bada bar"

Date	Mintage	VG	F	VF	XF	Unc
AH1029//15	—	18.00	30.00	50.00	110	—
AH1029//16	—	18.00	30.00	50.00	110	—
AH1030//16	—	18.00	30.00	50.00	110	—
AH1030//17	—	18.00	30.00	50.00	110	—
AH1031//16	—	18.00	30.00	50.00	110	—
AH1031//17	—	18.00	30.00	50.00	110	—
AH1031//18	—	18.00	30.00	50.00	110	—
AH1032//17	—	18.00	30.00	50.00	110	—
AH1032//18	—	18.00	30.00	50.00	110	—
AH1032//19	—	18.00	30.00	50.00	110	—
AH1033//19	—	18.00	30.00	50.00	110	—
AH1033//20	—	18.00	30.00	50.00	110	—
AH1034//20	—	18.00	30.00	50.00	110	—
AH1034//21	—	18.00	30.00	50.00	110	—
AH1035//21	—	18.00	30.00	50.00	110	—
AH1035//22	—	18.00	30.00	50.00	110	—
AH1036//22	—	18.00	30.00	50.00	110	—
AH1036//23	—	18.00	30.00	50.00	110	—
AH1037//22	—	18.00	30.00	50.00	110	—

Lahore

KM# 149.15 RUPEE (Type 149)
11.4440 g., Silver **Rev:** "Ruy"

Date	Mintage	VG	F	VF	XF	Unc
AH1029//14(sic)	—	27.00	45.00	75.00	115	—
AH1029//15	—	27.00	45.00	75.00	115	—

Mandu

KM# 149.19A RUPEE (Type 149)
11.4440 g., Silver **Note:** "Z nam--jahangir" couplet.

Date	Mintage	VG	F	VF	XF	Unc
AH1026//12	—	270	450	750	1,150	—

Mandu

KM# 149.19 RUPEE (Type 149)
11.4440 g., Silver **Note:** "Fath-i-dakkam" couplet.

Date	Mintage	VG	F	VF	XF	Unc
AH1026//12	—	270	450	750	1,150	—

Orissa

KM# 149.20 RUPEE (Type 149)
11.4440 g., Silver

Date	Mintage	VG	F	VF	XF	Unc
AH1023//9	—	325	540	900	1,350	—

Urdu Dar Rah-i-Dakhan

KM# 149.17 RUPEE (Type 149)
11.4440 g., Silver

Date	Mintage	VG	F	VF	XF	Unc
AH1025//11	—	360	600	1,000	1,500	—

Agra

KM# 150.9 ZODIAC RUPEE (Type 150)
11.4440 g., Silver **Obv:** Cancer (crab) **Rev:** Names of "Jahangir" and "Akbar"

Date	Mintage	VG	F	VF	XF	Unc
AH1027//13	—	450	750	1,250	1,875	—
AH1029//15	—	450	750	1,250	1,875	—

Agra

KM# 150.4 ZODIAC RUPEE (Type 150)
11.4440 g., Silver **Obv:** Taurus (bull) to right **Rev:** Names of "Jahangir" and "Akbar" **Note:** Struck from gold mohur dies.

Date	Mintage	VG	F	VF	XF	Unc
AH1028//13(sic)	—	360	600	1,000	1,500	—
AH1029//15	—	360	600	1,000	1,500	—
AH1029//16	—	360	600	1,000	1,500	—
AH1030//16	—	360	600	1,000	1,500	—

Agra

KM# 150.6 ZODIAC RUPEE (Type 150)
11.4440 g., Silver **Obv:** Gemini (twins) **Rev:** Names of "Jahangir" and "Akbar" **Note:** Struck from gold mohur dies.

Date	Mintage	VG	F	VF	XF	Unc
AH1028//14	—	650	1,150	1,750	2,800	—
AH1029//15	—	650	1,150	1,750	2,800	—
AH1033//19	—	650	1,150	1,750	2,800	—

Agra

KM# 150.12 ZODIAC RUPEE (Type 150)
11.4440 g., Silver **Obv:** Capricorn (goat) to left **Rev:** Names of "Jahangir" and "Akbar" **Note:** Struck from gold mohur dies.

Date	Mintage	VG	F	VF	XF	Unc
AH1029//14(sic)	—	750	1,250	2,000	3,000	—

Agra

KM# 150.1 ZODIAC RUPEE (Type 150)
11.4440 g., Silver **Obv:** Aries (ram) to left **Rev:** Names of "Jahangir" and "Akbar" **Note:** Struck from gold mohur dies.

Date	Mintage	VG	F	VF	XF	Unc
AH1030//16	—	450	750	1,250	2,000	—

Ahmadabad

KM# 150.10 ZODIAC RUPEE (Type 150)
11.4440 g., Silver **Obv:** Cancer (crab) **Rev:** Names of "Jahangir" and "Akbar"

Date	Mintage	VG	F	VF	XF	Unc
AH1027//13	—	450	750	1,250	2,000	—

Ahmadabad

KM# 150.11 ZODIAC RUPEE (Type 150)
11.4440 g., Silver **Obv:** Leo (lion) to left **Rev:** Names of "Jahangir" and "Akbar"

Date	Mintage	VG	F	VF	XF	Unc
AH1027//13	—	375	600	1,100	1,750	—

Ahmadabad

KM# 150.2 ZODIAC RUPEE (Type 150)
11.4440 g., Silver **Obv:** Aries (ram) to left **Rev:** Names of "Jahangir" and "Akbar"

Date	Mintage	VG	F	VF	XF	Unc
AH1027//13	—	450	750	1,250	2,000	—

Ahmadabad

KM# 150.5 ZODIAC RUPEE (Type 150)
11.4440 g., Silver **Obv:** Taurus (bull) to right **Rev:** Names of "Jahangir" and "Akbar"

Date	Mintage	VG	F	VF	XF	Unc
AH1027//13	—	275	600	1,100	1,750	—

Ahmadabad

KM# 150.7 ZODIAC RUPEE (Type 150)
11.4440 g., Silver **Obv:** Gemini (twins) **Rev:** Names of "Jahangir" and "Akbar"

Date	Mintage	VG	F	VF	XF	Unc
AH1027//13	—	750	1,250	2,000	3,000	—

Fathpur

KM# 150.3 ZODIAC RUPEE (Type 150)
11.4440 g., Silver **Obv:** Aries (ram) to left **Rev:** Names of "Jahangir" and "Akbar" **Note:** Weight varies 13.4 - 13.7 grams; Struck from gold mohur dies.

Date	Mintage	Good	VG	F	VF	XF
AH1028//14 Rare	—	—	—	—	—	—

Fathpur

KM# 150.13 ZODIAC RUPEE (Type 150)
11.4440 g., Silver **Obv:** Capricorn (goat) to left **Rev:** Names of "Jahangir" and "Akbar" **Note:** Weight varies 13.4 - 13.7 grams; Struck from gold mohur dies.

Date	Mintage	Good	VG	F	VF	XF
AH1028//14 Rare	—	—	—	—	—	—

Kashmir

KM# 150.8 ZODIAC RUPEE (Type 150)
11.4440 g., Silver **Obv:** Gemini (twins) **Rev:** Names of "Jahangir" and "Akbar" **Note:** Weight varies 13.4 - 13.7 grams.

Date	Mintage	Good	VG	F	VF	XF
AH10xx//15 Rare	—	—	—	—	—	—

Agra

KM# 152.1 JAHANGIRI RUPEE (Type 152)
Silver **Obv:** Kalima, AH date **Rev. Legend:** "Nur-ud'din Muhammad Jahangir" **Note:** First Issue: 20 percent overweight. Weight varies: 13.40-13.70 grams.

Date	Mintage	VG	F	VF	XF	Unc
AH1014//1	—	70.00	120	200	300	—
AH1015//1	—	70.00	120	200	300	—
AH1015//2	—	70.00	120	200	300	—
AH1016//x	—	70.00	120	200	300	—

Ahmadabad

KM# 152.2 JAHANGIRI RUPEE (Type 152)
Silver **Obv:** Kalima, AH date **Rev. Legend:** "Nur-ud'din Muhammad Jahangir" **Note:** Weight varies: 13.40-13.70 grams.

Date	Mintage	VG	F	VF	XF	Unc
AH1014//1	—	65.00	110	180	270	—
AH1015//1	—	65.00	110	180	270	—
AH1016//2	—	65.00	110	180	270	—
AH1016//3	—	65.00	110	180	270	—
AH1017//3	—	65.00	110	180	270	—

Burhanpur

KM# 152.3 JAHANGIRI RUPEE (Type 152)
Silver **Obv:** Kalima, AH date **Rev. Legend:** "Nur-ud'din Muhammad Jahangir" **Note:** Weight varies: 13.40-13.70 grams.

Date	Mintage	VG	F	VF	XF	Unc
AHxxxx//2	—	90.00	150	250	375	—

Delhi

KM# 152.8 JAHANGIRI RUPEE (Type 152)
Silver **Obv:** Kalima, AH date **Rev. Legend:** "Nur-ud'din Muhammad Jahangir" **Note:** Weight varies: 13.40-13.70 grams.

Date	Mintage	VG	F	VF	XF	Unc
AH1016//2	—	270	450	750	1,125	—

Jalnapur

KM# 152.9 JAHANGIRI RUPEE (Type 152)
Silver **Obv:** Kalima, AH date **Rev. Legend:** "Nur-ud'din Muhammad Jahangir" **Note:** Weight varies: 13.40-13.70 grams.

Date	Mintage	VG	F	VF	XF	Unc
ND	—	450	750	1,250	1,875	—

Lahore

KM# 152.4 JAHANGIRI RUPEE (Type 152)
Silver **Obv:** Kalima, AH date **Rev. Legend:** "Nur-ud'din Muhammad Jahangir" **Note:** Weight varies: 13.40-13.70 grams.

Date	Mintage	VG	F	VF	XF	Unc
AH1015//1	—	70.00	120	200	300	—
AH1019//5	—	70.00	120	200	300	—

Patna

KM# 152.5 JAHANGIRI RUPEE (Type 152)
Silver **Obv:** Kalima, AH date **Rev. Legend:** "Nur-ud'din Muhammad Jahangir" **Note:** Weight varies: 13.40-13.70 grams.

Date	Mintage	VG	F	VF	XF	Unc
AH1014//1	—	70.00	120	200	300	—
AH1015//1	—	70.00	120	200	300	—
AH1015//2	—	70.00	120	200	300	—
AH1016//2	—	70.00	120	200	300	—
AH1016//3	—	70.00	120	200	300	—
AH1017//3	—	70.00	120	200	300	—
AH1018//5	—	70.00	120	200	300	—
AH1019//5	—	70.00	120	200	300	—

Qandahar

KM# 152.6 JAHANGIRI RUPEE (Type 152)
Silver **Obv:** Kalima, AH date **Rev. Legend:** "Nur-ud'din Muhammad Jahangir" **Note:** Weight varies: 13.40-13.70 grams.

Date	Mintage	VG	F	VF	XF	Unc
AH1020//6	—	100	165	275	415	—
AH1021//7	—	100	165	275	415	—

Tatta

KM# 152.7 JAHANGIRI RUPEE (Type 152)
Silver **Obv:** Kalima, AH date **Rev. Legend:** "Nur-ud'din Muhammad Jahangir" **Note:** Weight varies: 13.40-13.70 grams.

Date	Mintage	VG	F	VF	XF	Unc
AH1015//2	—	80.00	135	225	340	—
AH1016//2	—	80.00	135	225	340	—

Date	Mintage	VG	F	VF	XF	Unc
AH1016//3	—	80.00	135	225	340	—
AH1017//3	—	80.00	135	225	340	—
AH1017//4	—	80.00	135	225	340	—
AH1018//4	—	80.00	135	225	340	—
AH1018//5	—	80.00	135	225	340	—
AH1019//5	—	80.00	135	225	340	—
AH1019//6	—	80.00	135	225	340	—
AH1020//6	—	80.00	135	225	340	—

Lahore

KM# 154.1 JAHANGIRI RUPEE (Type 154)

13.6200 g., Silver **Obv:** Kalima and mint name **Shape:** Square **Note:** First Issue: 20 percent overweight. Weight varies: 13.40-13.70 grams.

Date	Mintage	VG	F	VF	XF	Unc
AH1015//2	—	360	600	1,000	1,500	—
AH1016//2	—	360	600	1,000	1,500	—
AH1016//3	—	360	600	1,000	1,500	—

Agra

KM# A155.1 JAHANGIRI RUPEE (Type A155)

Silver **Obv:** Similar to Mohur KM#186 **Rev:** Similar to Mohur KM#186 **Note:** Weight varies 13.4 - 13.8 grams; "Azar" couplet.

Date	Mintage	VG	F	VF	XF	Unc
AH1019//5	—	540	900	1,500	2,250	—

Agra

KM# 155.1 JAHANGIRI RUPEE (Type 155)

Silver **Rev:** "Sakhat Nurani" **Note:** Weight varies: 13.40-13.70 grams. Obverse and reverse form a poetic couplet, distinguished by certain words in the reverse legend.

Date	Mintage	VG	F	VF	XF	Unc
AH1014//1	—	60.00	110	175	260	—
AH1015//1	—	60.00	110	175	260	—
AH1015//2	—	60.00	110	175	260	—

Agra

KM# 155.1A JAHANGIRI RUPEE (Type 155)

Silver **Note:** Weight varies 13.4 - 13.8 grams; "Khursu" couplet.

Date	Mintage	VG	F	VF	XF	Unc
AH1018//4	—	220	360	600	900	—

Akbarnagar

KM# 155.2A JAHANGIRI RUPEE (Type 155)

Silver **Note:** Weight varies 13.4 - 13.8 grams; "Gardun" couplet.

Date	Mintage	VG	F	VF	XF	Unc
AHxxxx	—	450	750	1,250	1,875	—

Akbarnagar

KM# 155.2 JAHANGIRI RUPEE (Type 155)

Silver **Rev:** "Sakhat Nurani" **Note:** Weight varies: 13.40-13.70 grams. Obverse and reverse form a poetic couplet, distinguished by certain words in the reverse legend.

Date	Mintage	VG	F	VF	XF	Unc
AH1014//x	—	145	240	400	600	—
AH1015//x	—	145	240	400	600	—
AH1016//x	—	145	240	400	600	—

Delhi

KM# 155.7 JAHANGIRI RUPEE (Type 155)

Silver **Rev:** "Ta falak" **Note:** Weight varies: 13.40-13.70 grams. Obverse and reverse form a poetic couplet, distinguished by certain words in the reverse legend.

Date	Mintage	VG	F	VF	XF	Unc
AH1014//x	—	110	180	300	450	—

Kashmir

KM# 155.3 JAHANGIRI RUPEE (Type 155)

Silver **Rev:** "Sakhat Nurani" **Note:** Weight varies: 13.40-13.70 grams. Obverse and reverse form a poetic couplet, distinguished by certain words in the reverse legend.

Date	Mintage	VG	F	VF	XF	Unc
AH1017//x	—	90.00	150	250	375	—
AH1018//x	—	90.00	150	250	375	—
AH1019//x	—	90.00	150	250	375	—
AH1020//x	—	90.00	150	250	375	—

Lahore

KM# 155.4 JAHANGIRI RUPEE (Type 155)

Silver **Rev:** "Sakhat Nurani" **Note:** Weight varies: 13.40-13.70 grams. Obverse and reverse form a poetic couplet, distinguished by certain words in the reverse legend.

Date	Mintage	VG	F	VF	XF	Unc
AH1014//1	—	55.00	90.00	150	225	—
AH1015//1	—	55.00	90.00	150	225	—

Lahore

KM# 155.6 JAHANGIRI RUPEE (Type 155)

Silver **Rev:** "Ta falak" **Note:** Weight varies: 13.40-13.70 grams. Obverse and reverse form a poetic couplet, distinguished by certain words in the reverse legend.

Date	Mintage	VG	F	VF	XF	Unc
AH1017//3	—	55.00	90.00	150	225	—
AH1017//4	—	55.00	90.00	150	225	—
AH1018//4	—	55.00	90.00	150	225	—
AH1018//5	—	55.00	90.00	150	225	—
AH1019//5	—	55.00	90.00	150	225	—

Qandahar

KM# 155.5 JAHANGIRI RUPEE (Type 155)

Silver **Rev:** "Sakhat Nurani" **Note:** Weight varies: 13.40-13.70 grams. Obverse and reverse form a poetic couplet, distinguished by certain words in the reverse legend.

Date	Mintage	VG	F	VF	XF	Unc
AH1020//6	—	70.00	110	200	300	—
AH1021//7	—	70.00	110	200	300	—
AH1021//8	—	70.00	110	200	300	—
AH1022//8	—	70.00	110	200	300	—

Lahore

KM# 156.1 JAHANGIRI RUPEE (Type 156)

Silver **Note:** Weight varies: 13.40-13.70 grams. Obverse and reverse form a poetic couplet incorporating the Ilahi month name. Couplet changed monthly.

Date	Mintage	VG	F	VF	XF	Unc
AH1019//5	—	140	240	400	600	—

Lahore

KM# A157.1 JAHANGIRI RUPEE (Type A157)

Silver **Note:** Weight varies 13.4 - 13.8 grams.

Date	Mintage	VG	F	VF	XF	Unc
AH1020//6 Farwardin	—	360	600	1,000	1,500	—

Lahore

KM# B157.1 JAHANGIRI RUPEE (Type B157)

Silver **Obv:** Inscription in octagonal star **Rev:** Inscription in octagonal star **Note:** Weight varies 13.4 - 13.8 grams; square.

Date	Mintage	VG	F	VF	XF	Unc
AH1020//6 Ardibihisht	—	360	600	1,000	1,500	—

Lahore

KM# 157.1 JAHANGIRI RUPEE (Type 157)

Silver **Rev:** "Sakhat Nurani" **Shape:** Square **Note:** Weight varies: 13.40-13.70 grams. Obverse and reverse form a poetic couplet.

Date	Mintage	VG	F	VF	XF	Unc
AH1015//2	—	360	600	1,000	1,500	—
AH1016//2	—	360	600	1,000	1,500	—
AH1016//3	—	360	600	1,000	1,500	—
AH1017//3	—	360	600	1,000	1,500	—

Agra

KM# 158.1 SAWAI RUPEE (Type 158)

13.9000 g., Silver **Obv:** "Jahangir" and "Akbar" **Rev:** "Khusru" **Note:** Second Issue: 25 percent overweight. Weight varies: 14.00-14.40 grams. Obverse and reverse form a poetic couplet. Each mint has a distinctive couplet. A typical word from the reverse legend is given as identifier for er each sub-type in this section.

Date	Mintage	VG	F	VF	XF	Unc
AH1017//3	—	65.00	110	180	270	—
AH1017//4	—	65.00	110	180	270	—
AH1018//4	—	65.00	110	180	270	—
AH1018//5	—	65.00	110	180	270	—
AH1019//5	—	65.00	110	180	270	—

Ahmadabad

KM# 158.3 SAWAI RUPEE (Type 158)

Silver **Obv:** Names of "Jahangir" and "Akbar" **Rev:** "Inayat" couplet **Note:** Weight varies: 14.00-14.40 grams. Obverse and reverse form a poetic couplet. Each mint has a distinctive couplet. A typical word from the reverse legend is given as identifier for er each sub-type in this section.

Date	Mintage	VG	F	VF	XF	Unc
AH1016//3	—	60.00	110	175	265	—
AH1017//3	—	60.00	110	175	265	—
AH1017//4	—	60.00	110	175	265	—
AH1018//4	—	60.00	110	175	265	—
AH1018//5	—	60.00	110	175	265	—
AH1019//5	—	60.00	110	175	265	—
AH1019//6	—	60.00	110	175	265	—

Burhanpur

KM# 158.4 SAWAI RUPEE (Type 158)

Silver **Obv:** "Jahangir" and "Akbar" **Rev:** "Din panah" **Note:** Weight varies: 14.00-14.40 grams. Obverse and reverse form a poetic couplet. Each mint has a distinctive couplet. A typical word from the reverse legend is given as identifier for er each sub-type in this section.

Date	Mintage	VG	F	VF	XF	Unc
AH1019	—	125	200	350	525	—

Kabul

KM# 158.2 SAWAI RUPEE (Type 158)

Silver **Obv:** Names of "Jahangir" and "Akbar" **Rev:** "Khusru" **Note:** Weight varies: 14.00-14.40 grams. Obverse and reverse form a poetic couplet. Each mint has a distinctive couplet. A typical word from the reverse legend is given as identifier for er each sub-type in this section.

Date	Mintage	VG	F	VF	XF	Unc
AH1017//3	—	90.00	150	250	375	—
AH1018//4	—	90.00	150	250	375	—
AH1020//6	—	90.00	150	250	375	—

Lahore

KM# 158.5 SAWAI RUPEE (Type 158)

Silver **Obv:** "Jahangir" and "Akbar" **Rev:** "Ta falak" **Note:** Weight varies: 14.00-14.40 grams. Obverse and reverse form a poetic couplet. Each mint has a distinctive couplet. A typical word from the reverse legend is given as identifier for er each sub-type in this section.

Date	Mintage	VG	F	VF	XF	Unc
AH1017//3	—	55.00	90.00	150	225	—
AH1017//4	—	55.00	90.00	150	225	—
AH1018//4	—	55.00	90.00	150	225	—
AH1018//5	—	55.00	90.00	150	225	—
AH1019//5	—	55.00	90.00	150	225	—

Patna

KM# 158.6 SAWAI RUPEE (Type 158)

Silver **Obv:** "Jahangir" and "Akbar" **Rev:** "Khusru" **Note:** Weight varies: 14.00-14.40 grams. Obverse and reverse form a poetic couplet. Each mint has a distinctive couplet. A typical word from the reverse legend is given as identifier for er each sub-type in this section.

Date	Mintage	Good	VG	F	VF	XF
AH1017//3	—	30.00	80.00	135	225	304

Date	Mintage	Good	VG	F	VF	XF
AH1019//6	—	30.00	80.00	135	225	340
AH1020//6	—	30.00	80.00	135	225	340

Akbarnagar

KM# A159.1 SAWAI RUPEE (Type A159)
Silver **Note:** "Gardun" couplet; weight varies 14.0 - 14.4 grams.

Date	Mintage	VG	F	VF	XF	Unc
AH1017//4	—	360	600	1,000	1,500	—

Agra

KM# 159.2 SAWAI RUPEE (Type 159)
Silver **Note:** Obverse and reverse form a poetic couplet incorporating the Ilahi month. Couplet changed monthly; Weight varies 14.0 - 14.4 grams.

Date	Mintage	VG	F	VF	XF	Unc
AH1019//5	—	540	900	1,500	2,250	—

Lahore

KM# 159.1 SAWAI RUPEE (Type 159)
Silver **Note:** Obverse and reverse form a poetic couplet incorporating the Ilahi month. Couplet changed monthly; Weight varies 14.0 - 14.4 grams.

Date	Mintage	VG	F	VF	XF	Unc
AH1019//5	—	180	300	500	750	—
AH1019//6	—	180	300	500	750	—
AH1020//6	—	180	300	500	750	—

Agra

KM# 160.1 SAWAI RUPEE (Type 160)
Silver **Shape:** Square **Note:** Weight varies: 14.00-14.40 grams.The circlular and square rupees were struck at Agra in alternate months.

Date	Mintage	VG	F	VF	XF	Unc
AH1019//5	—	360	600	1,000	1,500	—
AH1020//6	—	360	600	1,000	1,500	—

Lahore

KM# 160.2 SAWAI RUPEE (Type 160)
Silver **Shape:** Square **Note:** Weight varies: 14.00-14.40 grams.

Date	Mintage	VG	F	VF	XF	Unc
AH1019//5 Isfandármuz	—	325	540	900	1,350	—
AH1020//6 Ardíbihisht	—	325	540	900	1,350	—
AHxxxx//6 Tír	—	325	540	900	1,350	—

Patna

KM# A167.1 1/4 RUPEE (Type A167)
2.8610 g., Silver **Obv. Inscription:** "...Jahangir" **Rev. Inscription:** "...Nur Jahan"

Date	Mintage	VG	F	VF	XF	Unc
AH1037//23	—	145	240	400	600	—

Agra

KM# 167.4 1/2 RUPEE (Type 167)
5.7220 g., Silver **Obv. Inscription:** "...Jahangir" **Rev. Inscription:** "...Nur Jahan"

Date	Mintage	VG	F	VF	XF	Unc
AH1036//2x	—	145	240	400	600	—

Ahmadabad

KM# 167.3 1/2 RUPEE (Type 167)
5.7220 g., Silver **Obv. Inscription:** "...Jahangir" **Rev. Inscription:** "...Nur Jahan"

Date	Mintage	VG	F	VF	XF	Unc
AH1034//x	—	145	240	400	600	—

Patna

KM# 167.1 1/2 RUPEE (Type 167)
5.7220 g., Silver **Obv. Inscription:** "...Jahangir" **Rev. Inscription:** "...Nur Jahan"

Date	Mintage	VG	F	VF	XF	Unc
AH1037//22(sic)	—	110	180	300	450	—

Surat

KM# 167.2 1/2 RUPEE (Type 167)
5.7220 g., Silver **Obv. Inscription:** "...Jahangir" **Rev. Inscription:** "...Nur Jahan"

Date	Mintage	VG	F	VF	XF	Unc
AH1034//2x	—	110	180	300	450	—
AH1035//x	—	110	180	300	450	—
AH1036//x	—	110	180	300	450	—

Agra

KM# 168.1 RUPEE (Type 168)
11.4440 g., Silver **Obv. Inscription:** "...Jahangir" **Rev. Inscription:** "...Nur Jahan"

Date	Mintage	VG	F	VF	XF	Unc
AH1034//19(sic)	—	40.00	70.00	115	175	—
AH1034//20	—	40.00	70.00	115	175	—
AH1034//21	—	40.00	70.00	115	175	—
AH1035//21	—	40.00	70.00	115	175	—
AH1035//22	—	40.00	70.00	115	175	—
AH1036//22	—	40.00	70.00	115	175	—
AH1037//22(sic)	—	40.00	70.00	115	175	—

Ahmadabad

KM# 168.2 RUPEE (Type 168)
11.4440 g., Silver **Obv. Inscription:** "...Jahangir" **Rev. Inscription:** "...Nur Jahan"

Date	Mintage	VG	F	VF	XF	Unc
AH1033//19	—	36.00	60.00	100	150	—
AH1034//xx	—	36.00	60.00	100	150	—
AH1036//21(sic)	—	36.00	60.00	100	150	—
AH1036//22	—	36.00	60.00	100	150	—
AH1036//23	—	36.00	60.00	100	150	—
AH1037//2x	—	36.00	60.00	100	150	—

Akbarnagar

KM# 168.3 RUPEE (Type 168)
11.4440 g., Silver **Obv. Inscription:** "...Jahangir" **Rev. Inscription:** "...Nur Jahan"

Date	Mintage	VG	F	VF	XF	Unc
AH1037//22(sic)	—	110	180	300	450	—

Allahabad

KM# 168.7 RUPEE (Type 168)
11.4440 g., Silver **Obv. Inscription:** "...Jahangir" **Rev. Inscription:** "...Nur Jahan"

Date	Mintage	VG	F	VF	XF	Unc
AH1037//22(sic)	—	220	360	600	900	—

Lahore

KM# 168.4 RUPEE (Type 168)
11.4440 g., Silver **Obv. Inscription:** "...Jahangir" **Rev. Inscription:** "...Nur Jahan"

Date	Mintage	VG	F	VF	XF	Unc
AH1034//19(sic)	—	55.00	90.00	150	225	—
AH1034//20	—	55.00	90.00	150	225	—
AH1035//20	—	55.00	90.00	150	225	—

Patna

KM# 168.5 RUPEE (Type 168)
11.4440 g., Silver **Obv. Inscription:** "...Jahangir" **Rev. Inscription:** "...Nur Jahan"

Date	Mintage	VG	F	VF	XF	Unc
AH1037//22(sic)	—	55.00	90.00	150	225	—

Surat

KM# 168.6 RUPEE (Type 168)
11.4440 g., Silver **Obv. Inscription:** "...Jahangir" **Rev. Inscription:** "...Nur Jahan"

Date	Mintage	VG	F	VF	XF	Unc
AH1033//19	—	36.00	60.00	100	150	—
AH1033//91 Error for 19	—	36.00	60.00	100	150	—
AH1034//20	—	36.00	60.00	100	150	—
AH1035//20	—	36.00	60.00	100	150	—
AH1035//21	—	36.00	60.00	100	150	—
AH1036//21	—	36.00	60.00	100	150	—
AH1036//22	—	36.00	60.00	100	150	—
AH1037//22(sic)	—	36.00	60.00	100	150	—

Lahore

KM# 169.1 RUPEE (Type 169)
11.4440 g., Silver **Rev:** Couplet with inscription **Rev. Inscription:** "Fazudah nur Jahan"

Date	Mintage	VG	F	VF	XF	Unc
AH1035//21	—	220	360	600	900	—

Fathpur

KM# 170.1 1/30 MOHUR (Type 170)
0.3600 g., Gold

Date	Mintage	Good	VG	F	VF	XF
AH10xx//xx Rare	—	—	—	—	—	—

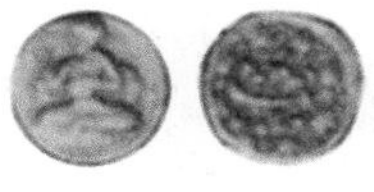

Without Mint Name

KM# 172.1 1/4 MOHUR (Type 172)
2.7000 g., Gold **Note:** "Shahi". Without mint name, probably Ajmer.

Date	Mintage	Good	VG	F	VF	XF
AH102x//x Rare	—	—	—	—	—	—

Ajmer

KM# 172.2 1/4 MOHUR (Type 172)
2.7000 g., Gold **Obv:** Date **Rev:** "Ya'Muinu" and regnal year

Date	Mintage	VG	F	VF	XF	Unc
AH1024//10 Rare	—	—	—	—	—	—

Mandu

KM# 172.3 1/4 MOHUR (Type 172)
2.7000 g., Gold **Obv:** "Jahangir" and regnal year **Rev:** Mint name, AH date

Date	Mintage	VG	F	VF	XF	Unc
AH1026/12 Rare	—	—	—	—	—	—

Shikargarh

KM# 172.4 1/4 MOHUR (Type 172)
2.7000 g., Gold **Obv:** "Jahangir" and regnal year **Rev:** Mint name, AH date

Date	Mintage	Good	VG	F	VF	XF
AH1026//20 Rare	—	—	—	—	—	—

Agra

KM# A173.1 HEAVY 1/4 MOHUR (Type A173)
3.2000 g., Gold **Obv. Legend:** ...Sakhat nurani **Note:** Previous KM#173.1.

Date	Mintage	Good	VG	F	VF	XF
AH1014//1 Rare	—	—	—	—	—	—

Agra

KM# 173.1 1/2 MOHUR (Type 173)
5.3800 g., Gold **Note:** Previous KM#A173.1.

Date	Mintage	Good	VG	F	VF	XF
AH102x//8 Rare	—	—	—	—	—	—

Agra

KM# 174.1 MOHUR (Type 174)
Gold **Obv:** Kalima, mint name, date **Rev:** Jahangir's full name **Note:** Weight varies: 10.80-10.90 grams.

Date	Mintage	VG	F	VF	XF	Unc
AH1014//1	—	—	2,520	4,200	6,000	—
AH1015//1	—	—	2,520	4,200	6,000	—
AH1015//2	—	—	2,520	4,200	6,000	—

Agra

KM# 175.1 MOHUR (Type 175)
Gold **Obv:** Names of "Jahangir" and "Akbar" **Rev:** AH date and mint name **Note:** Weight varies: 10.80-10.90 grams.

Date	Mintage	VG	F	VF	XF	Unc
AH1020//6	—	—	2,500	3,500	5,000	—

Agra

KM# 176.1 MOHUR (Type 176)
Gold **Obv:** Names of "Jahangir" and "Akbar" **Rev:** Mint name, AH date, Ilahi month **Note:** Weight varies: 10.60-10.90 grams.

Date	Mintage	VG	F	VF	XF	Unc
AH1020/6	—	—	1,500	2,100	3,000	—
AH1020/7	—	—	1,500	2,100	3,000	—
Note: Ilahi month Ardibihisht (2)						
AH1021/7	—	—	1,500	2,100	3,000	—
AH1021/8	—	—	1,500	2,100	3,000	—
AH1022/8	—	—	1,500	2,100	3,000	—
AH1023/8	—	—	1,500	2,100	3,000	—
AH1022//9	—	—	1,500	2,100	3,000	—
AH1023//9	—	—	1,500	2,100	3,000	—
AH1023//10	—	—	1,500	2,100	3,000	—
AH1024//10	—	—	1,500	2,100	3,000	—
AH1024//11	—	—	1,500	2,100	3,000	—
AH1025//11	—	—	1,500	2,100	3,000	—
AH1025//12	—	—	1,500	2,100	3,000	—
AH1026//12	—	—	1,500	2,100	3,000	—
AH1026//13	—	—	1,500	2,100	3,000	—
AH1027//13	—	—	1,500	2,100	3,000	—
Note: Ilahi month Azar (9)						
AH1031//17	—	—	1,500	2,100	3,000	—

Ahmadanagar

KM# 176.2 MOHUR (Type 176)
Gold **Obv:** Names of "Jahangir" and "Akbar" **Rev:** Mint name, AH date, Ilahi month **Note:** Weight varies: 10.60-10.90 grams.

Date	Mintage	VG	F	VF	XF	Unc
AH-	—	—	1,500	2,100	3,000	—

Burhanpur

KM# 176.3 MOHUR (Type 176)
Gold **Obv:** Names of "Jahangir" and "Akbar" **Rev:** Mint name, AH date, Ilahi month **Note:** Weight varies: 10.60-10.90 grams.

Date	Mintage	VG	F	VF	XF	Unc
AH1023//8(sic)	—	—	735	1,050	1,500	—
AH102x//12	—	—	735	1,050	1,500	—
AHxxxx//14	—	—	735	1,050	1,500	—
AH10xx//15	—	—	735	1,050	1,500	—
AH103x//16	—	—	735	1,050	1,500	—
AH103x//17	—	—	735	1,050	1,500	—
Note: Ilahi month Farwardin						
AH103x//18	—	—	735	1,050	1,500	—
AH1037//22(sic)	—	—	735	1,050	1,500	—

Jahangirnagar

KM# 176.4 MOHUR (Type 176)
Gold **Obv:** Names of "Jahangir" and "Akbar" **Rev:** Mint name, AH date, Ilahi month **Note:** Weight varies: 10.60-10.90 grams.

Date	Mintage	VG	F	VF	XF	Unc
ND//19	—	—	1,700	2,450	3,500	—

Patna

KM# 176.5 MOHUR (Type 176)
Gold **Obv:** Names of "Jahangir" and "Akbar" **Rev:** Mint name, AH date, Ilahi month **Note:** Weight varies: 10.60-10.90 grams.

Date	Mintage	VG	F	VF	XF	Unc
AH1027//13	—	—	1,225	1,750	2,500	—
AH1035//20(sic)	—	—	1,225	1,750	2,500	—

Tatta

KM# 176.6 MOHUR (Type 176)
Gold **Obv:** Names of "Jahangir" and "Akbar" **Rev:** Mint name, AH date, Ilahi month **Note:** Weight varies: 10.60-10.90 grams.

Date	Mintage	VG	F	VF	XF	Unc
AH1027//13 0	—	—	2,000	2,800	4,000	—
AH1031//16(sic) 0	—	—	2,000	2,800	4,000	—
AH1031//17 0	—	—	2,000	2,800	4,000	—
AH1032//18 0	—	—	2,000	2,800	4,000	—
AH1036//22 0	—	—	2,000	2,800	4,000	—

Agra

KM# 177.1 MOHUR (Type 177)
Gold **Obv:** Legend in cartouche within square **Rev:** Legend in cartouche within square **Shape:** Square **Note:** Weight varies: 10.60-10.90 grams. Similar to 1 Rupee, KM#160.1.

Date	Mintage	VG	F	VF	XF	Unc
AH1019//5	—	—	3,000	4,200	6,000	—
AH1019//6	—	—	3,000	4,200	6,000	—
AH1020//6	—	—	3,000	4,200	6,000	—
AH1022//x	—	—	3,000	4,200	6,000	—
AH102x//12	—	—	3,000	4,200	6,000	—

Agra

KM# 178.9 MOHUR (Type 178)
Gold **Rev:** "Sakhat Nurani" **Note:** Weight varies: 10.60-10.90 grams.

Date	Mintage	VG	F	VF	XF	Unc
AH1014//1	—	—	—	2,450	3,500	5,000

Agra

KM# 178.1 MOHUR (Type 178)
Gold **Rev:** "Yaft" **Note:** Weight varies: 10.60-10.90 grams. Obverse and reverse form a poetic couplet, wording individual to mints.

Date	Mintage	VG	F	VF	XF	Unc
AH1035//21	—	—	2,450	3,500	5,000	—

Ahmadabad

KM# 178.2 MOHUR (Type 178)
Gold **Rev:** "Ba-sharq wa gharb" **Note:** Weight varies: 10.60-10.90 grams. Obverse and reverse form a poetic couplet, wording individual to mints.

Date	Mintage	VG	F	VF	XF	Unc
AH1028//14	—	—	2,000	2,800	4,000	—
AH1028//15	—	—	2,000	2,800	4,000	—
AH1029//15	—	—	2,000	2,800	4,000	—
AH1030//15(sic)	—	—	2,000	2,800	4,000	—
AH1033//18(sic)	—	—	2,000	2,800	4,000	—

Ajmir

KM# 178.3 MOHUR (Type 178)
Gold **Rev:** "Din panah" **Note:** Weight varies: 10.60-10.90 grams. Obverse and reverse form a poetic couplet, wording individual to mints.

Date	Mintage	VG	F	VF	XF	Unc
AH1023//9	—	—	1,725	2,450	3,500	—
AH1023//10	—	—	1,725	2,450	3,500	—
AH1024//10	—	—	1,725	2,450	3,500	—
AH1025//11	—	—	1,725	2,450	3,500	—

Delhi

KM# 178.4 MOHUR (Type 178)
Gold **Rev:** "Fazl" **Note:** Weight varies: 10.60-10.90 grams. Obverse and reverse form a poetic couplet, wording individual to mints.

Date	Mintage	VG	F	VF	XF	Unc
AH1035//21	—	—	1,725	2,450	3,500	—

Kabul

KM# 178.8 MOHUR (Type 178)
Gold **Note:** Weight varies: 10.60-10.90 grams. Obverse and reverse form a poetic couplet, wording individual to mints. Similar to 1 rupee, KM#149.12; Previous KM#178.1.

Date	Mintage	VG	F	VF	XF	Unc
ND	—	—	2,450	3,500	5,000	—

Lahore

KM# 178.7 MOHUR (Type 178)
Gold **Note:** Weight varies: 10.60-10.90 grams. Obverse and reverse form a poetic couplet, wording individual to mints.

Date	Mintage	VG	F	VF	XF	Unc
AH1032//17(sic)	—	—	1,500	2,100	3,000	—

Lahore

KM# 178.5 MOHUR (Type 178)
Gold **Rev:** "Bada bar" **Note:** Weight varies: 10.60-10.90 grams. Obverse and reverse form a poetic couplet, wording individual to mints.

Date	Mintage	Good	VG	F	VF	XF
AH1036//22	—	—	—	2,200	3,150	4,500

Mandu

KM# 178.6 MOHUR (Type 178)
Gold **Rev:** "Bada bar" **Note:** Weight varies: 10.60-10.90 grams. Obverse and reverse form a poetic couplet, wording individual to mints.

Date	Mintage	VG	F	VF	XF	Unc
AH1026//12	—	—	2,940	4,200	6,000	—

Without Mint Name

KM# 179.1 MOHUR (Type 179)
Gold **Obv:** Jahangir left, hand on book **Rev:** Lion left **Note:** Weight varies: 10.80-10.90 grams.

Date	Mintage	VG	F	VF	XF	Unc
AH1020//6	—	—	12,250	17,500	25,000	—

Note: High quality gold electrotypes were made by the British Museum in the late 19th and early 20th centuries. Worth $2,000-$2,500. Modern fabrications also exist.

Without Mint Name

KM# 179.3 MOHUR (Type 179)

Gold **Obv:** Jahangir left, holding fruit **Rev:** Lion right **Note:** Weight varies: 10.80-10.90 grams.

Date	Mintage	VG	F	VF	XF	Unc
AH1020//6	—	12,250	17,500	25,000	—	—

Note: High quality gold electrotypes were made by the British Museum in the late 19th and early 20th centuries. Worth $2,000-$2,500. Modern fabrications also exist.

Without Mint Name

KM# 179.2 MOHUR (Type 179)

Gold **Obv:** Jahangir left, hand on book **Rev:** Lion right **Note:** Weight varies: 10.80-10.90 grams.

Date	Mintage	VG	F	VF	XF	Unc
AH1020//6	—	—	12,250	17,500	25,000	—

Note: High quality gold electrotypes were made by the British Museum in the late 19th and early 20th centuries. Worth $2,000-$2,500. Modern fabrications also exist.

Without Mint Name

KM# 179.4 MOHUR (Type 179)

Gold **Obv:** Jahangir left, holding goblet **Rev:** Lion right **Note:** Weight varies: 10.80-10.90 grams.

Date	Mintage	VG	F	VF	XF	Unc
AH1020//6	—	—	12,250	17,500	25,000	—

Note: High quality gold electrotypes were made by the British Museum in the late 19th and early 20th centuries. Worth $2,000-$2,500. Modern fabrications also exist.

Ajmer

KM# 179.5 MOHUR (Type 179)

Gold **Obv:** Jahangir seated left, holding goblet with legend around **Rev:** Lion right with legend around **Note:** Weight varies: 10.80-10.90 grams.

Date	Mintage	VG	F	VF	XF	Unc
AH1023//8(sic)	—	—	19,600	28,000	40,000	—

Note: High quality gold electrotypes were made by the British Museum in the late 19th and early 20th centuries. Worth $2,000-$2,500. Modern fabrications also exist.

Ajmer

KM# 179.6 MOHUR (Type 179)

Gold **Obv:** Jahangir seated left, holding goblet **Rev:** Sun, legend around **Note:** Weight varies: 10.80-10.90 grams.

Date	Mintage	VG	F	VF	XF	Unc
AH1023//9	—	—	9,600	17,500	25,000	—

Note: High quality gold electrotypes were made by the British Museum in the late 19th and early 20th centuries. Worth $2,000-$2,500. Modern fabrications also exist.

Agra

KM# 180.9 ZODIAC MOHUR (Type 180)

Gold **Obv:** Leo (lion) right **Note:** Weight varies: 10.80-10.90 grams.

Date	Mintage	Good	VG	F	VF	XF
AH1028//14	—	—	900	1,500	2,750	5,000
AH1028//15	—	—	900	1,500	2,750	5,000
AH1029//15	—	—	900	1,500	2,750	5,000
AH1031//17	—	—	900	1,500	2,750	5,000
AH1033//18(sic)	—	—	900	1,500	2,750	5,000

Agra

KM# 180.1 ZODIAC MOHUR (Type 180)

Gold **Obv:** Aries (ram) left **Note:** Weight varies: 10.70-10.90 grams.

Date	Mintage	VG	F	VF	XF	Unc
AH1028//14	—	—	9,800	14,000	20,000	—
AH1028//15	—	—	9,800	14,000	20,000	—
AH1029//15	—	—	9,800	14,000	20,000	—
AH1029//16	—	—	9,800	14,000	20,000	—
AH1030//16	—	—	9,800	14,000	20,000	—
AH1032//18	—	—	9,800	14,000	20,000	—

Agra

KM# 180.4 ZODIAC MOHUR (Type 180)

Gold **Obv:** Taurus (bull) left **Note:** Weight varies: 10.70-10.90 grams.

Date	Mintage	VG	F	VF	XF	Unc
AH1028//14	—	—	9,800	14,000	20,000	—
AH1028//15	—	—	9,800	14,000	20,000	—
AH1029//15	—	—	9,800	14,000	20,000	—
AH1033//19	—	—	9,800	14,000	20,000	—

Agra

KM# 180.6 ZODIAC MOHUR (Type 180)

Gold **Obv:** Gemini (twins) left leg raised **Note:** Weight varies: 10.80-10.90 grams.

Date	Mintage	VG	F	VF	XF	Unc
AH1028//1x	—	—	12,250	17,500	25,000	—
AH1029//15	—	—	12,250	17,500	25,000	—
AH1029//16	—	—	12,250	17,500	25,000	—
AH1030//16	—	—	12,250	17,500	25,000	—
AH1030//17	—	—	12,250	17,500	25,000	—
AH1031//17	—	—	12,250	17,500	25,000	—
AH1031//18	—	—	12,250	17,500	25,000	—
AH1032//18	—	—	12,250	17,500	25,000	—
AH1032//19	—	—	12,250	17,500	25,000	—
AH1033//19	—	—	12,250	17,500	25,000	—

Agra

KM# 180.8 ZODIAC MOHUR (Type 180)

Gold **Obv:** Cancer (crab) **Note:** Weight varies: 10.80-10.90 grams.

Date	Mintage	VG	F	VF	XF	Unc
AH1027//13	—	—	14,700	21,000	30,000	—
AH1028//14	—	—	14,700	21,000	30,000	—
AH1028//15	—	—	14,700	21,000	30,000	—
AH1029//15	—	—	14,700	21,000	30,000	—
AH1029//16	—	—	14,700	21,000	30,000	—
AH1030//16	—	—	14,700	21,000	30,000	—
AH1030//17	—	—	14,700	21,000	30,000	—
AH1031//17	—	—	14,700	21,000	30,000	—
AH1033//19	—	—	14,700	21,000	30,000	—

Agra

KM# 180.11 ZODIAC MOHUR (Type 180)

Gold **Obv:** Virgo (maiden) left **Note:** Weight varies: 10.80-10.90 grams.

Date	Mintage	VG	F	VF	XF	Unc
AH1028//14	—	—	14,700	21,000	30,000	—
AH1028//15	—	—	14,700	21,000	30,000	—
AH1029//15	—	—	14,700	21,000	30,000	—
AH1031//16(sic)	—	—	14,700	21,000	30,000	—
AH1031//17	—	—	14,700	21,000	30,000	—
AH1033//19	—	—	14,700	21,000	30,000	—

Note: Other depictions exist, of crude workmanship and possibly spurious

Agra

KM# 180.13 ZODIAC MOHUR (Type 180)

Gold **Obv:** Libra (scales) **Note:** Weight varies: 10.80-10.90 grams.

Date	Mintage	VG	F	VF	XF	Unc
AH1028//14	—	—	12,250	17,500	25,000	—
AH1029//14	—	—	12,250	17,500	25,000	—
AH1029//15	—	—	12,250	17,500	25,000	—
AH1030//16	—	—	12,250	17,500	25,000	—
AH1030//17	—	—	12,250	17,500	25,000	—
AH1031//17	—	—	12,250	17,500	25,000	—
AH1031//18	—	—	12,250	17,500	25,000	—
AH1032//18	—	—	12,250	17,500	25,000	—
AH1032//19	—	—	12,250	17,500	25,000	—
AH1033//19	—	—	12,250	17,500	25,000	—
AH1034//19(sic)	—	—	12,250	17,500	25,000	—

Agra

KM# 180.19 ZODIAC MOHUR (Type 180)

Gold **Obv:** Capricornus (goat) left **Rev:** Poetic couplet **Note:** Weight varies: 10.80-10.90 grams.

Date	Mintage	VG	F	VF	XF	Unc
AH1028//14	—	—	12,250	17,500	25,000	—
AH1028//15	—	—	12,250	17,500	25,000	—
AH1029//15	—	—	12,250	17,500	25,000	—
AH1029//16	—	—	12,250	17,500	25,000	—
AH1030//16	—	—	12,250	17,500	25,000	—
AH1030//17	—	—	12,250	17,500	25,000	—
AH1031//17	—	—	12,250	17,500	25,000	—
AH1031//18	—	—	12,250	17,500	25,000	—
AH1032//18	—	—	12,250	17,500	25,000	—
AH1032//19	—	—	12,250	17,500	25,000	—
AH1033//19	—	—	12,250	17,500	25,000	—
AH1034//29(sic)	—	—	12,250	17,500	25,000	—

Agra

KM# 180.20 ZODIAC MOHUR (Type 180)

Gold **Obv:** Pisces (fish) **Rev:** Poetic couplet **Note:** Weight varies: 10.80-10.90 grams.

Date	Mintage	VG	F	VF	XF	Unc
AH1028//13(sic)	—	—	12,250	17,500	25,000	—
AH1031//17	—	—	12,250	17,500	25,000	—
AH1031//18	—	—	12,250	17,500	25,000	—
AH1032//18	—	—	12,250	17,500	25,000	—
AH1033//18(sic)	—	—	12,250	17,500	25,000	—

Agra

KM# 180.17 ZODIAC MOHUR (Type 180)
Gold **Obv:** Sagittarius (archer) **Note:** Weight varies: 10.80-10.90 grams.

Date	Mintage	VG	F	VF	XF	Unc
AH1029//14(sic)	—	—	14,700	21,000	30,000	—
AH1029//15	—	—	14,700	21,000	30,000	—
AH1029//16	—	—	14,700	21,000	30,000	—
AH1030//16	—	—	14,700	21,000	30,000	—
AH1030//17	—	—	14,700	21,000	30,000	—
AH1031//17	—	—	14,700	21,000	30,000	—
AH1031//18	—	—	14,700	21,000	30,000	—
AH1032//18	—	—	14,700	21,000	30,000	—
AH1032//19	—	—	14,700	21,000	30,000	—
AH1033//19	—	—	14,700	21,000	30,000	—
AH1033//20	—	—	14,700	21,000	30,000	—
AH1034//20	—	—	14,700	21,000	30,000	—
AH1034//29(sic)	—	—	14,700	21,000	30,000	—

Agra

KM# 180.14 ZODIAC MOHUR (Type 180)
Gold **Obv:** Scorpio (scorpion) left **Note:** Weight varies: 10.80-10.90 grams.

Date	Mintage	VG	F	VF	XF	Unc
AH1028//15	—	—	14,700	21,000	30,000	—
AH1029//15	—	—	14,700	21,000	30,000	—
AH1029//16	—	—	14,700	21,000	30,000	—
AH1030//16	—	—	14,700	21,000	30,000	—
AH1030//17	—	—	14,700	21,000	30,000	—
AH1031//17	—	—	14,700	21,000	30,000	—
AH1033//18(sic)	—	—	14,700	21,000	30,000	—

Agra

KM# 180.15 ZODIAC MOHUR (Type 180)
Gold **Obv:** Scorpio (scorpion) right **Note:** Weight varies: 10.80-10.90 grams.

Date	Mintage	VG	F	VF	XF	Unc
AH1031//16(sic)	—	—	14,700	21,000	30,000	—
AH1031//17	—	—	14,700	21,000	30,000	—
AH1031//18	—	—	14,700	21,000	30,000	—
AH1032//17(sic)	—	—	14,700	21,000	30,000	—

Agra

KM# 180.5 ZODIAC MOHUR (Type 180)
Gold **Obv:** Taurus (bull) right **Note:** Weight varies: 10.70-10.90 grams.

Date	Mintage	VG	F	VF	XF	Unc
AH1030//16	—	—	9,800	14,000	20,000	—
AH1031//16(sic)	—	—	9,800	14,000	20,000	—
AH1031//17	—	—	9,800	14,000	20,000	—
AH1031//18	—	—	9,800	14,000	20,000	—
AH1032//18	—	—	9,800	14,000	20,000	—

Agra

KM# 180.10 ZODIAC MOHUR (Type 180)
Gold **Obv:** Leo (lion) left **Note:** Weight varies: 10.80-10.90 grams.

Date	Mintage	VG	F	VF	XF	Unc
AH1031//17	—	—	9,800	14,000	20,000	—

Ajmer

KM# 180.21 ZODIAC MOHUR (Type 180)
Gold **Obv:** Aquarius (water bearer) **Rev:** Poetic couplet **Note:** Weight varies: 10.80-10.90 grams.

Date	Mintage	Good	VG	F	VF	XF
AH1032//18 Rare	—	—	—	—	—	—

Ajmer

KM# 180.7 ZODIAC MOHUR (Type 180)
Gold **Obv:** Gemini (twins) right leg raised **Note:** Weight varies: 10.80-10.90 grams.

Date	Mintage	VG	F	VF	XF	Unc
AH1033//18 Rare	—	—	—	—	—	—

Fathpur

KM# 180.2 ZODIAC MOHUR (Type 180)
Gold **Obv:** Aries (ram) left **Note:** Weight varies: 10.70-10.90 grams.

Date	Mintage	Good	VG	F	VF	XF
AH1028//13 Rare	—	—	—	—	—	—

Lahore

KM# 180.12 ZODIAC MOHUR (Type 180)
Gold **Note:** Different portrayal of Virgo. Weight varies: 10.80-10.90 grams.

Date	Mintage	Good	VG	F	VF	XF
AH1032//17(sic) Rare	—	—	—	—	—	—

Lahore

KM# 180.16 ZODIAC MOHUR (Type 180)
Gold **Obv:** Scorpio (scorpion) right **Note:** Weight varies: 10.80-10.90 grams.

Date	Mintage	Good	VG	F	VF	XF
AH1032//17(sic) Rare	—	—	—	—	—	—

Lahore

KM# 180.18 ZODIAC MOHUR (Type 180)
Gold **Obv:** Smaller Sagittarius (archer) **Rev:** Poetic couplet **Note:** Weight varies: 10.80-10.90 grams.

Date	Mintage	Good	VG	F	VF	XF
AH1035//20	—	—	—	—	—	—
AH1036//21(sic) Rare	—	—	—	—	—	—

Urdu

KM# 180.3 ZODIAC MOHUR (Type 180)
Gold **Obv:** Aries (ram) right **Note:** Weight varies: 10.70-10.90 grams.

Date	Mintage	VG	F	VF	XF	Unc
AH1036//22 Rare	—	—	—	—	—	—

Burhanpur

KM# 182.1 HEAVY MOHUR (Type 182)
Gold **Subject:** "Nur Jahani" **Obv:** Kalima **Note:** First Issue: 20 percent overweight. Weight varies: 12.80-1300 grams.

Date	Mintage	VG	F	VF	XF	Unc
AH1014(1)	—	980	1,400	2,000	3,000	—

Lahore

KM# 182.2 HEAVY MOHUR (Type 182)
Gold **Obv:** Kalima **Note:** Weight varies: 12.80-1300 grams.

Date	Mintage	VG	F	VF	XF	Unc
AH1015//1	—	980	1,400	2,000	3,000	—

Agra

KM# 183.1 HEAVY MOHUR (Type 183)
Gold **Rev:** "Sakhat Nurani" **Note:** Poetic couplets on obverse and reverse. Weight varies: 12.80-13.00 grams.

Date	Mintage	VG	F	VF	XF	Unc
AH1014//1	—	1,470	2,100	3,000	4,500	—
AH1015//1	—	1,470	2,100	3,000	4,500	—
AH1015//2	—	1,470	2,100	3,000	4,500	—

Lahore

KM# 183.2 HEAVY MOHUR (Type 183)
Gold **Rev:** "Sakhat Nurani" **Note:** Poetic couplets on obverse and reverse. Weight varies: 12.80-13.00 grams.

Date	Mintage	VG	F	VF	XF	Unc
AH1014(1)	—	980	1,400	2,000	3,000	—
AH1015//1	—	980	1,400	2,000	3,000	—

Lahore

KM# 183.3 HEAVY MOHUR (Type 183)
13.0300 g., Gold **Rev:** "Khusru" **Note:** Weight varies: 12.95-13.10 grams.

Date	Mintage	VG	F	VF	XF	Unc
AH1017//3	—	980	1,400	2,000	3,000	—
AH1017//4	—	980	1,400	2,000	3,000	—
AH1018//4	—	980	1,400	2,000	3,000	—

Lahore

KM# 184.1 HEAVY MOHUR (Type 184)
Gold **Rev:** "Sakhat Nurani" **Shape:** Square **Note:** Poetic couplets on obverse and reverse. Weight varies: 12.90-13.00 grams.

Date	Mintage	VG	F	VF	XF	Unc
AH1015//1	—	2,200	3,150	4,500	6,750	—
AH1015//2	—	2,200	3,150	4,500	6,750	—
AH1016//2	—	2,200	3,150	4,500	6,750	—
AH1016//3	—	2,200	3,150	4,500	6,750	—

Agra

KM# 185.1 HEAVY MOHUR (Type 185)

Gold **Rev:** "Khusru" **Note:** Second Issue: 25 percent overweight. Poetic couplets on obverse and reverse. Weight varies: 13.55-13.70 grams.

Date	Mintage	VG	F	VF	XF	Unc
AH1017//3	—	1,470	2,100	3,000	4,500	—
AH1017//4	—	1,470	2,100	3,000	4,500	—
AH1018//4	—	1,470	2,100	3,000	4,500	—
AH1018//5	—	1,470	2,100	3,000	4,500	—

Agra

KM# 186.1 HEAVY MOHUR (Type 186)

Gold **Note:** Poetic couplets based on Ilahi month names. From the year 1019, at a few mints, a specially composed poetic couplet was employed on the coin for each month. The decorative borders and calligraphy varied monthly. Only a sample illustration is included here. Weight varies: 13.55-13.70 grams.

Date	Mintage	VG	F	VF	XF	Unc
AH1019//5 Mihr	—	2,950	4,200	6,000	9,000	—
AH1019//5 Azar	—	2,950	4,200	6,000	9,000	—
AH1019//6	—	2,950	4,200	6,000	9,000	—
AH1020//6	—	2,950	4,200	6,000	9,000	—

Note: Some specimens of the type dated AH1020/6 are reported to be of normal weight

Agra

KM# 187.1 HEAVY MOHUR (Type 187)

Gold **Shape:** Square **Note:** Weight varies: 13.55-13.70 grams.

Date	Mintage	VG	F	VF	XF	Unc
AH1017//3	—	3,950	5,600	8,000	12,000	—
AH1019//5	—	3,950	5,600	8,000	12,000	—

Agra

KM# 188.1 5 MOHURS (Type 188)

54.6300 g., Gold

Date	Mintage	Good	VG	F	VF	XF
AH1028//14 Rare	—	—	—	—	—	—

Note: Many counterfeits known.

Ahmadabad

KM# 190.1 MOHUR (Type 190)

Gold **Obv. Inscription:** "...Jahangir" **Rev. Inscription:** "...Nur Jahan" **Note:** Weight varies: 10.80-10.90 grams.

Date	Mintage	VG	F	VF	XF	Unc
AH1034//19(sic)	—	735	1,050	1,500	2,250	—
AH1037//2x	—	735	1,050	1,500	2,250	—

Surat

KM# 190.2 MOHUR (Type 190)

Gold **Obv. Inscription:** "...Jahangir" **Rev. Inscription:** "...Nur Jahan" **Note:** Weight varies: 10.80-10.90 grams.

Date	Mintage	VG	F	VF	XF	Unc
AH1036//2x	—	650	840	1,200	1,800	—

Kashmir

KM# 192.1 ZODIAC MOHUR (Type 192)

Gold **Obv:** Cancer (crab) **Rev. Inscription:** "Jahangir...Nur Jahan" **Note:** Weight varies: 10.80-10.90 grams.

Date	Mintage	Good	VG	F	VF	XF
AH1034//20 Rare	—	—	—	—	—	—

Lahore

KM# 192.2 ZODIAC MOHUR (Type 192)

Gold **Obv:** Sagittarius (archer) **Rev. Inscription:** "Jahangir...Nur Jahan" **Note:** Weight varies: 10.80-10.90 grams.

Date	Mintage	Good	VG	F	VF	XF
AH1035//20(sic) Rare	—	—	—	—	—	—

Lahore

KM# 192.3 ZODIAC MOHUR (Type 192)

Gold **Obv:** Capricorn (goat) **Rev. Inscription:** "Jahangir...Nur Jahan" **Note:** Weight varies: 10.80-10.90 grams.

Date	Mintage	Good	VG	F	VF	XF
AH1036//21(sic) Rare	—	—	—	—	—	—

Lahore

KM# 192.4 ZODIAC MOHUR (Type 192)

Gold **Obv:** Pisces (fish) **Rev. Inscription:** "Jahangir...Nur Jahan" **Note:** Weight varies: 10.80-10.90 grams.

Date	Mintage	Good	VG	F	VF	XF
AH1036//21(sic) Rare	—	—	—	—	—	—

Agra

KM# 189.1 NAZARANA 1000 MOHURS

11935.7998 g., Gold, 210 mm. **Obv. Inscription:** "...Jahangir" **Rev. Inscription:** Dar-ul-Kalifa

Date	Mintage	Good	VG	F	VF	XF
AH1022//8 Unique	—	—	—	—	—	—

LARGESSE COINAGE

Agra

KM# A161.1 NISAR (Type A161)

0.6000 g., Silver **Obv. Inscription:** "Jahangir Padshah"

Date	Mintage	VG	F	VF	XF	Unc
AH1033//19	—	125	210	350	550	—
AH1034//19	—	125	210	350	550	—

Patna

KM# B161.1 NISAR (Type B161)

0.9000 g., Silver **Obv. Inscription:** "Nisar Jahangir"

Date	Mintage	VG	F	VF	XF	Unc
AH1034	—	145	240	400	650	—

Agra

KM# C161.1 NISAR (Type C161)

1.2000 g., Silver **Obv. Inscription:** "Nisar Jahangir"

Date	Mintage	VG	F	VF	XF	Unc
AHxxxx//3	—	125	210	350	550	—

Agra

KM# D161.1 NISAR (Type D161)

1.7000 g., Silver **Obv. Inscription:** "Nisar Jahangir" **Rev. Inscription:** "Dar al-Khilafa"

Date	Mintage	VG	F	VF	XF	Unc
AH1032//18	—	—	125	210	350	550

Agra

KM# E161.1 NISAR (Type E161)

1.4000 g., Silver **Obv. Inscription:** "Jahangir Padshah Ghazi"

Date	Mintage	VG	F	VF	XF	Unc
AH1033	—	135	210	350	550	—

Ajmir

KM# E161.2 NISAR (Type E161)

1.5000 g., Silver **Obv. Inscription:** "Jahangir Padshah Ghazi"

Date	Mintage	VG	F	VF	XF	Unc
AH1032//18	—	220	360	600	950	—

Burhanpur

KM# F161.1 NISAR (Type F161)

1.4000 g., Silver **Obv. Inscription:** "Nisar Jahangir" **Shape:** Square

Date	Mintage	VG	F	VF	XF	Unc
AHxxxx//x Azar	—	180	300	500	800	—
AHxxxx//x Di	—	180	300	500	800	—

Kabul

KM# G161.1 NISAR (Type G161)

1.4000 g., Silver **Obv. Inscription:** "Jahangir Shahi"

Date	Mintage	VG	F	VF	XF	Unc
AHxxxx//8(?)	—	360	600	1,000	1,700	—

Lahore

KM# H161.1 NISAR (Type H161)

Silver **Obv. Inscription:** "Jahangir Padshah" **Note:** Weight varies 1.0 - 1.2 grams.

Date	Mintage	VG	F	VF	XF	Unc
AH1033//18 (sic)	—	135	210	350	550	—
AH1034//19	—	135	210	350	550	—
AH1036//21	—	135	210	350	550	—

Kashmir

KM# J161.1 NISAR (Type J161)

2.7000 g., Silver **Obv. Inscription:** "Jahangir Shah"

Date	Mintage	VG	F	VF	XF	Unc
AH1032//19	—	220	360	600	950	—

Lahore

KM# K161.1 NISAR (Type K161)

5.7000 g., Silver **Obv. Inscription:** "Jahangir Shah Akbar Shah"

Date	Mintage	VG	F	VF	XF	Unc
AH1031//17	—	280	475	800	1,250	—

Lahore

KM# K161.2 NISAR (Type K161)

5.7000 g., Silver **Obv. Inscription:** "Jahangir Shah Akbar Shah"

Date	Mintage	VG	F	VF	XF	Unc
AH1033//18	—	280	475	800	1,250	—

Ajmer

KM# 161.1 NISAR (Type 161)

0.9000 g., Silver **Note:** 1/12 rupee weight varies .80 - .90 grams.

Date	Mintage	VG	F	VF	XF	Unc
AH1014	—	180	300	500	750	—
AH1024//10	—	180	300	500	750	—

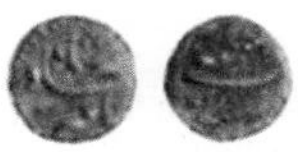

Kashmir

KM# 161.2 NISAR (Type 161)

Silver **Obv. Inscription:** "Jahangir Shah Akbar Shah" **Note:** Weight varies 1.0 - 1.7 grams.

Date	Mintage	VG	F	VF	XF	BU
AH1037//22(sic)	—	220	360	600	900	—

Kashmir

KM# 162.1 NISAR (Type 162)

1.1300 g., Silver **Shape:** Square **Note:** 1/8 rupee weight.

Date	Mintage	VG	F	VF	XF	Unc
AH1023//10	—	220	360	600	900	—

Agra

KM# 163.1 NISAR (Type 163)

2.7000 g., Silver **Obv. Inscription:** "Nisar Jahangiri" **Rev. Inscription:** Epithet: "Dar al-Khilafa" **Note:** Weight varies: 2.46-2.80 grams, (1/4 rupee weight).

Date	Mintage	VG	F	VF	XF	Unc
AH1028//14	—	145	240	400	600	—
AH1029//14 (sic)	—	145	240	400	600	—

Agra

KM# 163.9 NISAR (Type 163)
Silver **Obv. Legend:** "Jalus Nisar Jahangiri" **Note:** Weight varies 2.5 - 2.9 grams.

Date	Mintage	VG	F	VF	XF	Unc
AH1037//18	—	145	240	400	600	—

Ahmadabad

KM# 163.2 NISAR (Type 163)
Silver **Obv. Inscription:** "Nisar Jahangir" **Note:** Weight varies: 2.46-2.80 grams, (1/4 rupee weight). Large flan.

Date	Mintage	VG	F	VF	XF	Unc
AH1027//12	—	160	270	450	675	—
AH1027//13	—	160	270	450	675	—

Ahmadabad

KM# 163.4 NISAR (Type 163)
Silver **Obv. Inscription:** "Nisar Jahangir" **Note:** Weight varies: 2.5-2.90 grams, (1/4 rupee weight). Small flan.

Date	Mintage	VG	F	VF	XF	Unc
AH1034//19(sic)	—	160	270	450	675	—

Akbarnagar

KM# 163.7 NISAR (Type 163)
Silver **Rev. Inscription:** "Jahangir Shah" **Note:** Weight varies: 2.50-2.90 grams.

Date	Mintage	VG	F	VF	XF	Unc
AH1033//19	—	180	300	500	750	—

Burhanpur

KM# 163.6 NISAR (Type 163)
Silver **Obv. Inscription:** "Nisar Jahangiri" **Note:** Weight varies: 2.50-2.80 grams.

Date	Mintage	VG	F	VF	XF	Unc
AH102x//6	—	160	270	450	675	—
AH(10)31//21 (error for 16)	—	160	270	450	675	—

Burhanpur

KM# 163.3 NISAR (Type 163)
Silver **Obv. Inscription:** "Nisar Jahangiri" **Note:** Weight varies: 2.50-2.80 grams. Large flan.

Date	Mintage	VG	F	VF	XF	Unc
AH1031//16(sic)	—	160	270	450	675	—

Lahore

KM# 163.8 NISAR (Type 163)
2.5000 g., Silver **Obv. Inscription:** "Jalus Nisar Jahangiri"

Date	Mintage	VG	F	VF	XF	Unc
AH1029//14	—	160	270	450	675	—

Lahore

KM# 163.5 NISAR (Type 163)
2.7000 g., Silver **Obv. Inscription:** "Nisar Jahangiri" **Note:** Weight varies: 2.50-2.80 grams.

Date	Mintage	VG	F	VF	XF	Unc
AH1029//14(sic)	—	160	270	450	675	—
AH1029//15	—	160	270	450	675	—

Ahmadabad

KM# A164.1 NISAR (Type A164)
0.7000 g., Silver **Rev. Inscription:** "Khair-i-qabul"

Date	Mintage	VG	F	VF	XF	Unc
AH1033//19	—	125	210	350	525	—

Without Mint Name

KM# B164.1 NISAR (Type B164)
Silver **Obv. Inscription:** "Jahangir Padshah Ghazi" **Rev. Inscription:** "Khair-i-qabul" **Note:** Weight varies 1.3 - 1.4 grams.

Date	Mintage	VG	F	VF	XF	Unc
AH1014	—	125	210	350	525	—
AH1015//2	—	125	210	350	525	—
AH1016//3	—	125	210	350	525	—
AH1020	—	125	210	350	525	—

Lahore

KM# 164.1 NISAR (Type 164)
Silver **Obv. Inscription:** "Jahangir Shah Akbar Shah" **Rev. Inscription:** "Khair-i-qabaul" **Note:** Weight varies: 1.30-1.40 grams.

Date	Mintage	VG	F	VF	XF	Unc
AH1029//15	—	145	240	400	600	—
AHxxxx//29	—	145	240	400	600	—

Agra

KM# 165.1 NISAR (Type 165)
Silver **Rev. Inscription:** "Nur Afshan" **Note:** Weight varies: 0.58-0.65 grams, 1/12 rupee weight.

Date	Mintage	VG	F	VF	XF	Unc
AH1019//5	—	145	240	400	600	—
AH1025//11	—	145	240	400	600	—
AH1031//16 (sic)	—	145	240	400	600	—

Lahore

KM# 165.2 NISAR (Type 165)
0.6000 g., Silver **Note:** Weight varies: 0.58-0.65 grams, 1/12 rupee weight.

Date	Mintage	VG	F	VF	XF	Unc
AH1033//18(sic)	—	145	240	400	600	—
AH103x//20	—	145	240	400	600	—

Ajmir

KM# 166.1 NISAR (Type 166)
1.1000 g., Gold **Obv. Inscription:** "Nisar Jahangir Shahi"

Date	Mintage	VG	F	VF	XF	Unc
AHxxxx//7	—	—	350	500	750	—

Dawar Bakhsh

In Lahore, AH1037 / 1627AD

HAMMERED COINAGE

Lahore

KM# 195.1 RUPEE (Type 195)
10.9500 g., Silver

Date	Mintage	VG	F	VF	XF	Unc
AH1037//1	—	2,150	3,600	6,000	9,000	—

Muhammad Shah Jahan

AH1037-1068 / 1628-1658AD

HAMMERED COINAGE

Kabul

KM# 197.2 RUPEE (Type 197)
11.4440 g., Silver **Obv:** Pre-accession name of "Khurram"

Date	Mintage	VG	F	VF	XF	Unc
ND	—	280	480	800	1,200	—

Lahore

KM# 197.1 RUPEE (Type 197)
11.4440 g., Silver **Obv:** Pre-accession name of "Khurram" **Note:** In pre-accession name: "Khurram". Weight varies: 11.00-11.15 grams; Previous KM#220.1.

Date	Mintage	VG	F	VF	XF	Unc
AH1037//1	—	180	300	500	750	—

Lahore

KM# 198 NISAR (Type 198)
2.9000 g., Silver **Obv:** Pre-accession name of "Khurram" **Note:** Pre-Accession Largesse

Date	Mintage	VG	F	VF	XF	Unc
AH1037//(I) Ahad	—	725	1,200	2,000	3,000	—

Without Mint Name

KM# 199.1 1/16 DAM (Type 199)
Copper **Note:** Without mint name or mint name off flan; weight varies 1.2 - 1.3 grams.

Date	Mintage	Good	VG	F	VF	XF
ND	—	—	—	—	—	—

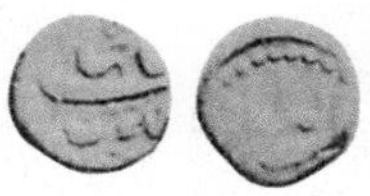

Akbarabad

KM# 200.1 1/8 DAM (Type 200)
Copper **Note:** Weight varies: 2.00-2.40 grams.

Date	Mintage	Good	VG	F	VF	XF
AH1044//7	—	5.00	12.50	25.00	40.00	—
AH104x//8	—	5.00	12.50	25.00	40.00	—
AH105x//14	—	5.00	12.50	25.00	40.00	—
AH105x//15	—	5.00	12.50	25.00	40.00	—
AH105x//19	—	5.00	12.50	25.00	40.00	—

Allahabad

KM# 200.5 1/8 DAM (Type 200)
Copper **Note:** Weight varies 4.8 - 5.1 grams.

Date	Mintage	Good	VG	F	VF	XF
AH1044//7	—	7.00	17.50	35.00	55.00	—

Bairata

KM# 200.2 1/8 DAM (Type 200)
Copper **Note:** Weight varies: 2.00-2.40 grams.

Date	Mintage	Good	VG	F	VF	XF
AH104x//7	—	6.00	15.00	30.00	50.00	—
AH1045//x	—	6.00	15.00	30.00	50.00	—

Delhi

KM# 200.3 1/8 DAM (Type 200)
Copper **Note:** Weight varies: 2.00-2.40 grams.

Date	Mintage	Good	VG	F	VF	XF
AH104x//7	—	6.00	15.00	30.00	50.00	—
AH104x//9	—	6.00	15.00	30.00	50.00	—
AH104x//12	—	6.00	15.00	30.00	50.00	—
AH1051//1x	—	6.00	15.00	30.00	50.00	—
AH10xx//16	—	6.00	15.00	30.00	50.00	—

Narnol

KM# 200.4 1/8 DAM (Type 200)
Copper **Note:** Weight varies: 2.00-2.40 grams.

Date	Mintage	Good	VG	F	VF	XF
AH10xx//1x	—	10.00	25.00	50.00	80.00	—

Ujjain

KM# 201.1 1/2 FALUS (Type 201)
Copper **Obv:** Emperor's name **Rev:** Mint **Shape:** Square **Note:** Weight varies 3.0 - 3.4 grams.

Date	Mintage	Good	VG	F	VF	XF
ND(1628-58)	—	3.00	7.50	15.00	25.00	—

Ahmadabad

KM# 202.2 1/4 DAM (Type 202)
Copper **Note:** Weight varies: 4.80-5.10 grams.

Date	Mintage	Good	VG	F	VF	XF
ND	—	6.00	15.00	30.00	50.00	—
AH104x//4	—	6.00	15.00	30.00	50.00	—

Ahmadanagar

KM# 202.3 1/4 DAM (Type 202)
Copper **Note:** Weight varies 4.8 - 5.1 grams.

Date	Mintage	Good	VG	F	VF	XF
ND	—	8.00	20.00	40.00	65.00	—

Surat

KM# 202.1 1/4 DAM (Type 202)
Copper **Note:** Weight varies: 4.80-5.10 grams.

Date	Mintage	Good	VG	F	VF	XF
AH106x//29	—	8.00	20.00	40.00	65.00	—

Ujjain

KM# 203.1 FALUS (Type 203)

6.7000 g., Copper **Series:** Malwa **Shape:** Square

Date	Mintage	Good	VG	F	VF	XF
ND	—	3.00	7.50	15.00	28.00	—

Ahmadabad

KM# 204.1 1/2 DAM (Type 204)

Copper **Note:** Weight varies: 9.80-10.40 grams.

Date	Mintage	Good	VG	F	VF	XF
AH104x//6	—	5.00	12.50	25.00	40.00	—
AH1044//7	—	5.00	12.50	25.00	40.00	—
AH1044//8	—	5.00	12.50	25.00	40.00	—
AH1046//9	—	5.00	12.50	25.00	40.00	—
AH1046//10	—	5.00	12.50	25.00	40.00	—

Bairata

KM# 204.3 1/2 DAM (Type 204)

Copper **Note:** Weight varies: 9.80-10.40 grams.

Date	Mintage	Good	VG	F	VF	XF
AH1048//1x	—	7.00	17.50	35.00	50.00	—

Lakhnau

KM# 204.2 1/2 DAM (Type 204)

Copper **Note:** Weight varies: 9.80-10.40 grams.

Date	Mintage	Good	VG	F	VF	XF
AH1049//1x	—	10.00	25.00	50.00	75.00	—

Patna

KM# 204.5 1/2 DAM (Type 204)

Copper **Note:** Weight varies: 9.80-10.40 grams.

Date	Mintage	Good	VG	F	VF	XF
ND	—	8.00	20.00	40.00	60.00	—

Qandahar

KM# 204.6 1/2 DAM (Type 204)

Copper **Note:** Weight varies: 9.80-10.40 grams.

Date	Mintage	Good	VG	F	VF	XF
AH1051//15	—	10.00	25.00	50.00	75.00	—

Surat

KM# 204.4 1/2 DAM (Type 204)

Copper **Note:** Weight varies: 9.80-10.40 grams.

Date	Mintage	Good	VG	F	VF	XF
AH106x//29	—	6.00	15.00	30.00	45.00	—

Akbarabad

KM# 205.1 1/2 DAM (Type 205)

Copper **Note:** Weight varies: 9.80-10.40 grams.

Date	Mintage	Good	VG	F	VF	XF
AH1041//4	—	10.00	25.00	50.00	75.00	—

Narnol

KM# A206.1 2 FALUS (Type A206)

13.7000 g., Copper

Date	Mintage	Good	VG	F	VF	XF
ND	—	12.00	30.00	60.00	90.00	—

Agra

KM# 206.13 DAM (Type 206)

Copper **Note:** Weight varies: 19.00-20.80 grams.

Date	Mintage	Good	VG	F	VF	XF
AH104x//8	—	6.00	15.00	30.00	45.00	—

Ahmadabad

KM# 206.9 DAM (Type 206)

Copper **Obv:** Emperor's name, regnal year **Rev:** Mint and date **Note:** Weight varies: 19.00-20.80 grams.

Date	Mintage	Good	VG	F	VF	XF
AH1044//7	—	6.00	15.00	30.00	45.00	—
AH1044//8	—	6.00	15.00	30.00	45.00	—
AH1045//8	—	6.00	15.00	30.00	45.00	—
AH1046	—	6.00	15.00	30.00	45.00	—
AH1051//13(sic)	—	6.00	15.00	30.00	45.00	—
AH1051//15	—	6.00	15.00	30.00	45.00	—

Akbarabad

KM# 206.1 DAM (Type 206)

Copper **Note:** Mint epithet: "Dar-ul-Khilafat". Weight varies: 19.00-20.80 grams.

Date	Mintage	Good	VG	F	VF	XF
AH1041//4	—	5.00	12.50	25.00	37.50	—
AH1044//7	—	5.00	12.50	25.00	37.50	—
AH1045//8	—	5.00	12.50	25.00	37.50	—
AH1045//9	—	5.00	12.50	25.00	37.50	—
AH1046//9	—	5.00	12.50	25.00	37.50	—
AH1046//10	—	5.00	12.50	25.00	37.50	—
AH1050//13	—	5.00	12.50	25.00	37.50	—
AH1052//16	—	5.00	12.50	25.00	37.50	—
AH1053/16	—	5.00	12.50	25.00	37.50	—
AH1055//1x	—	5.00	12.50	25.00	37.50	—

Akbarnagar

KM# A206.8 DAM (Type 206)

21.6100 g., Copper

Date	Mintage	Good	VG	F	VF	XF
AH1067//31	—	8.00	20.00	40.00	60.00	—

Allahabad

KM# 206.8 DAM (Type 206)

Copper **Note:** Weight varies: 19.00-20.80 grams.

Date	Mintage	Good	VG	F	VF	XF
AH1051//15	—	9.00	22.50	45.00	67.50	—
AH1052	—	9.00	22.50	45.00	67.50	—

Bairata

KM# 206.2 DAM (Type 206)

Copper **Note:** Weight varies: 19.00-20.80 grams.

Date	Mintage	Good	VG	F	VF	XF
AH1037//(1) Ahad	—	6.00	15.00	30.00	45.00	—
AH1038//2	—	6.00	15.00	30.00	45.00	—
AH1039//x	—	6.00	15.00	30.00	45.00	—
AH1040//x	—	6.00	15.00	30.00	45.00	—
AH1042//x	—	6.00	15.00	30.00	45.00	—
AH1044//x	—	6.00	15.00	30.00	45.00	—
AH1045//x	—	6.00	15.00	30.00	45.00	—
AH1048//1x	—	6.00	15.00	30.00	45.00	—
AH1065//29	—	6.00	15.00	30.00	45.00	—

Daulatabad

KM# 206.14 DAM (Type 206)

Copper **Note:** Weight varies: 19.00-20.80 grams.

Date	Mintage	Good	VG	F	VF	XF
ND	—	10.00	25.00	50.00	75.00	—

Dogaon

KM# 206.3 DAM (Type 206)

Copper **Note:** Weight varies: 19.00-20.80 grams.

Date	Mintage	Good	VG	F	VF	XF
AH104x//10	—	10.00	25.00	50.00	75.00	—
AH105x//15	—	10.00	25.00	50.00	75.00	—

Kashmir

KM# 206.10 DAM (Type 206)

Copper **Note:** Weight varies: 19.00-20.80 grams.

Date	Mintage	Good	VG	F	VF	XF
AH1043//x	—	10.00	25.00	50.00	75.00	—
AHxxxx//29	—	10.00	25.00	50.00	75.00	—

Lakhnau

KM# 206.4 DAM (Type 206)

Copper **Note:** Weight varies: 19.00-20.80 grams.

Date	Mintage	Good	VG	F	VF	XF
AH1041//7	—	8.00	20.00	40.00	60.00	—

Multan

KM# 206.15 DAM (Type 206)

Copper **Note:** Weight varies: 19.00-20.80 grams.

Date	Mintage	Good	VG	F	VF	XF
AH104x//4	—	8.00	20.00	40.00	60.00	—

Narnol

KM# 206.12 DAM (Type 206)

Copper **Note:** Weight varies: 19.00-20.80 grams.

Date	Mintage	Good	VG	F	VF	XF
ND	—	6.00	15.00	30.00	45.00	—
AH106x//31	—	6.00	15.00	30.00	45.00	—

Patna

KM# 206.11 DAM (Type 206)

Copper **Note:** Weight varies: 19.00-20.80 grams.

Date	Mintage	Good	VG	F	VF	XF
AH10xx//x	—	6.00	15.00	30.00	45.00	—

Shahjahanabad

KM# 206.5 DAM (Type 206)

Copper **Note:** Weight varies: 19.00-20.80 grams.

Date	Mintage	Good	VG	F	VF	XF
ND	—	4.00	10.00	20.00	40.00	—

Surat

KM# 206.6 DAM (Type 206)

Copper **Note:** Weight varies: 19.00-20.80 grams.

Date	Mintage	Good	VG	F	VF	XF
AH104x//7	—	3.50	9.00	18.00	27.50	—
AH104x/9	—	3.50	9.00	18.00	27.50	—
AH106x//29	—	3.50	9.00	18.00	27.50	—
AH1067//30	—	3.50	9.00	18.00	27.50	—
AH106x//32	—	3.35	9.00	18.00	27.50	—

Udaipur

KM# 206.7 DAM (Type 206)

Copper **Note:** Weight varies: 19.00-20.80 grams.

Date	Mintage	Good	VG	F	VF	XF
AH10xx//3	—	10.00	25.00	50.00	75.00	—

Lakhnau

KM# 208.1 2 DAMS (Type 208)
Copper **Note:** Weight varies: 40.00-41.50 grams.

Date	Mintage	Good	VG	F	VF	XF
AH104x//5	—	20.00	50.00	100	150	—

Akbarabad

KM# 210.1 1/16 RUPEE (Type 210)
0.7150 g., Silver

Date	Mintage	Good	VG	F	VF	XF
AH1039//2	—	—	70.00	135	225	325

Aurangnagar

KM# 210.2 1/16 RUPEE (Type 210)
0.7150 g., Silver

Date	Mintage	VG	F	VF	XF	Unc
ND	—	90.00	150	250	375	—

Burhanpur

KM# 210.3 1/16 RUPEE (Type 210)
0.7150 g., Silver

Date	Mintage	VG	F	VF	XF	Unc
AHxxxx	—	90.00	150	250	375	—

Kabul

KM# 210.4 1/16 RUPEE (Type 210)
0.7150 g., Silver

Date	Mintage	VG	F	VF	XF	Unc
AHxxxx	—	70.00	120	200	300	—

Akbarabad

KM# 211.2 1/8 RUPEE (Type 211)
1.4300 g., Silver

Date	Mintage	VG	F	VF	XF	Unc
AH1064//2x	—	70.00	120	200	300	—

Burhanpur

KM# 211.3 1/8 RUPEE (Type 211)
1.4300 g., Silver **Obv:** Inscription in square outlined with dots

Date	Mintage	Good	VG	F	VF	XF
AH1058	—	—	90.00	150	250	375

Patna

KM# 211.4 1/8 RUPEE (Type 211)
1.4300 g., Silver **Obv:** Inscription in outlined square

Date	Mintage	VG	F	VF	XF	Unc
AHxxxx//25	—	70.00	120	200	300	—

Without Mint Name

KM# 211.1 1/8 RUPEE (Type 211)
1.4300 g., Silver

Date	Mintage	Good	VG	F	VF	XF
AH104x//5	—	—	45.00	85.00	140	200

Ujjain

KM# A212.1 1/8 RUPEE (Type A212)
1.4300 g., Silver **Shape:** Square

Date	Mintage	VG	F	VF	XF	Unc
ND	—	75.00	120	200	300	—

Burhanpur

KM# 212.4 1/4 RUPEE (Type 212)
2.8610 g., Silver

Date	Mintage	VG	F	VF	XF	Unc
AHxxxx//(1) Ahad	—	60.00	100	175	265	—

Daulatabad

KM# 212.3 1/4 RUPEE (Type 212)
2.8610 g., Silver **Obv:** Central legend within quatrefoil **Rev:** Central legend within quatrefoil **Note:** Similar to 1/2 Rupee, KM#213.

Date	Mintage	VG	F	VF	XF	Unc
AH104x//5	—	70.00	120	200	300	—

Golkonda

KM# 212.5 1/4 RUPEE (Type 212)
2.8610 g., Silver **Note:** Similar to Rupee KM#223.

Date	Mintage	VG	F	VF	XF	Unc
ND	—	60.00	100	175	265	—

Surat

KM# 212.6 1/4 RUPEE (Type 212)
2.8610 g., Silver

Date	Mintage	VG	F	VF	XF	Unc
AHxxxx	—	35.00	60.00	100	150	—

Without Mint Name

KM# 212.2 1/4 RUPEE (Type 212)
2.8610 g., Silver **Obv:** Central inscription within square **Rev:** Central inscription within square

Date	Mintage	Good	VG	F	VF	XF
AH1040//x	—	15.00	37.50	75.00	125	175
AH1065//29	—	15.00	37.50	75.00	125	175
AH1069//32	—	15.00	37.50	75.00	125	175

Without Mint Name

KM# 212.1 1/4 RUPEE (Type 212)
2.8610 g., Silver **Obv:** Central inscription within quatrefoil **Rev:** Central inscription within quatrefoil

Date	Mintage	Good	VG	F	VF	XF
AH1053//1x	—	—	37.50	75.00	125	175

Ahmadabad

KM# B213.1 1/4 RUPEE (Type B213)
2.8610 g., Silver **Obv:** Inscription in square area

Date	Mintage	VG	F	VF	XF	Unc
AHxxxx	—	55.00	90.00	150	225	—

Burhanpur

KM# B213.2 1/4 RUPEE (Type B213)
2.8610 g., Silver **Obv:** Inscription in square outlined with dots

Date	Mintage	VG	F	VF	XF	Unc
AH1063	—	55.00	90.00	150	225	—
AH1068	—	55.00	90.00	150	225	—

Patna

KM# B213.3 1/4 RUPEE (Type B213)
2.8610 g., Silver **Obv:** Inscription in square area

Date	Mintage	VG	F	VF	XF	Unc
AH1044//7	—	55.00	90.00	150	225	—
AHxxxx//16	—	55.00	90.00	150	225	—
AHxxxx//19	—	55.00	90.00	150	225	—

Surat

KM# B213.4 1/4 RUPEE (Type B213)
2.8610 g., Silver **Obv:** Inscription in square area

Date	Mintage	VG	F	VF	XF	Unc
AHxxxx	—	27.00	45.00	75.00	110	—

Ujjain

KM# B213.5 1/4 RUPEE (Type B213)
2.8610 g., Silver **Obv:** Inscription in square area

Date	Mintage	VG	F	VF	XF	Unc
AHxxxx	—	55.00	90.00	150	225	—

Allahabad

KM# C213.1 1/4 RUPEE (Type C213)
2.8610 g., Silver **Obv:** Inscription in square area **Obv. Inscription:** "Shah Jahan Padshah Ghazi" **Rev:** Inscription in square area with mint name and AH date

Date	Mintage	VG	F	VF	XF	Unc
AH1045//8	—	70.00	120	200	300	—

Surat

KM# D213.1 1/2 RUPEE (Type D213)
5.7220 g., Silver **Note:** Similar to Rupee KM#221.1.

Date	Mintage	VG	F	VF	XF	Unc
AHxxxx	—	55.00	90.00	150	225	—

Ahmadabad

KM# 213.1 1/2 RUPEE (Type 213)
5.7220 g., Silver **Obv:** AH date

Date	Mintage	Good	VG	F	VF	XF
AH1037//(1) Ahad	—	—	37.50	75.00	125	175

Akbarabad

KM# 213.5 1/2 RUPEE (Type 213)
5.7220 g., Silver

Date	Mintage	VG	F	VF	XF	Unc
AHxxxx//2	—	45.00	75.00	125	190	—
AH1039//3	—	45.00	75.00	125	190	—

Akbarnagar

KM# 213.6 1/2 RUPEE (Type 213)
5.7220 g., Silver

Date	Mintage	VG	F	VF	XF	Unc
AHxxxx//5	—	60.00	100	175	265	—
AH1044//7	—	60.00	100	175	265	—

Bhakkar

KM# 213.7 1/2 RUPEE (Type 213)
5.7220 g., Silver

Date	Mintage	VG	F	VF	XF	Unc
AHxxxx	—	90.00	120	200	300	—

Burhanpur

KM# 213.8 1/2 RUPEE (Type 213)
5.7220 g., Silver

Date	Mintage	VG	F	VF	XF	Unc
AHxxxx	—	55.00	90.00	150	225	—

Daulatabad

KM# 213.9 1/2 RUPEE (Type 213)
5.7220 g., Silver

Date	Mintage	VG	F	VF	XF	Unc
AH1037//(1)	—	60.00	100	175	265	—

Goraghat

KM# 213.10 1/2 RUPEE (Type 213)
5.7220 g., Silver

Date	Mintage	VG	F	VF	XF	Unc
ND	—	125	2,120	350	525	—

Patna

KM# 213.3 1/2 RUPEE (Type 213)
5.7220 g., Silver **Obv:** AH date

Date	Mintage	VG	F	VF	XF	Unc
AH1038//2	—	37.50	75.00	125	175	—
AH1039//2	—	37.50	75.00	125	175	—
AH1039//3	—	37.50	75.00	125	175	—
AH1040//4	—	37.50	75.00	125	175	—
AH1042//5	—	37.50	75.00	125	175	—

Surat

KM# 213.2 1/2 RUPEE (Type 213)
5.7220 g., Silver **Obv:** AH date

Date	Mintage	VG	F	VF	XF	Unc
AH1037//(1) Ahad	—	16.00	27.00	45.00	67.50	—
AH1038//(1) Ahad	—	16.00	27.00	45.00	67.50	—
AH1040//3	—	16.00	27.00	45.00	67.50	—
AH1042	—	16.00	27.00	45.00	67.50	—

Ujjain

KM# 213.4 1/2 RUPEE (Type 213)
5.7220 g., Silver **Obv:** AH date

Date	Mintage	VG	F	VF	XF	Unc
AH104x//4	—	35.00	60.00	100	150	—

Akbarabad

KM# A214.1 1/2 RUPEE (Type A214)
5.7220 g., Silver **Note:** Similar to Rupee, KM#227.10.

Date	Mintage	VG	F	VF	XF	Unc
ND	—	55.00	90.00	150	225	—

Gulkanda

KM# 214.1 1/2 RUPEE (Type 214)
5.7220 g., Silver **Note:** Crude calligraphy.

Date	Mintage	VG	F	VF	XF	Unc
AH104x//5	—	27.50	45.00	75.00	115	—

Ahmadnagar

KM# 215.1 1/2 RUPEE (Type 215)
5.7220 g., Silver **Obv:** Ilahi month **Rev:** AH date

Date	Mintage	VG	F	VF	XF	Unc
AH1042//x	—	45.00	75.00	125	190	—

Patna

KM# 215.2 1/2 RUPEE (Type 215)

5.7220 g., Silver **Obv:** Ilahi month **Rev:** AH date **Note:** Struck on large planchet.

Date	Mintage	VG	F	VF	XF	Unc
AH1038//2	—	55.00	90.00	150	225	—

Surat

KM# 216.1 1/2 RUPEE (Type 216)

5.7220 g., Silver **Obv:** Central legend within circle **Rev:** Central legend within circle

Date	Mintage	VG	F	VF	XF	Unc
AH1067//31	—	28.50	50.00	85.00	125	—

Surat

KM# 217.1 1/2 RUPEE (Type 217)

5.7220 g., Silver **Obv:** Inscription within quatrefoil **Rev:** Inscription within quatrefoil

Date	Mintage	VG	F	VF	XF	Unc
AH1057//20	—	28.50	50.00	85.00	125	—
AH1057//21	—	28.50	50.00	85.00	125	—

Ahmadabad

KM# 218.1 1/2 RUPEE (Type 218)

5.7220 g., Silver **Obv:** Inscription within square **Rev:** Inscription within square **Note:** Similar to Rupee, Type 235.

Date	Mintage	VG	F	VF	XF	Unc
AH1044//8	—	28.00	50.00	80.00	120	—
AH104x//12	—	28.00	50.00	80.00	120	—
AH105x//17	—	28.00	50.00	80.00	120	—

Akbarabad

KM# 218.2 1/2 RUPEE (Type 218)

5.7220 g., Silver **Obv:** Inscription within square **Rev:** Inscription within square

Date	Mintage	VG	F	VF	XF	Unc
AH1042//5	—	36.00	60.00	100	150	—

Akbarnagar

KM# 218.3 1/2 RUPEE (Type 218)

5.7220 g., Silver **Obv:** Inscription within square **Rev:** Inscription within square

Date	Mintage	VG	F	VF	XF	Unc
AH1045//8	—	45.00	75.00	125	190	—

Daulatabad

KM# 218.4 1/2 RUPEE (Type 218)

5.7220 g., Silver **Obv:** Inscription within square **Rev:** Inscription within square

Date	Mintage	VG	F	VF	XF	Unc
AH1043//x	—	36.00	60.00	100	150	—
AH1044//x	—	36.00	60.00	100	150	—
AH1061//24	—	36.00	60.00	100	150	—

Junagadh

KM# 218.15 1/2 RUPEE (Type 218)

5.7220 g., Silver **Obv:** Inscription within square **Rev:** Inscription within square

Date	Mintage	VG	F	VF	XF	Unc
AH1049//13	—	55.00	90.00	150	225	—
AH1053//xx	—	55.00	90.00	150	225	—
AH1057//xx	—	55.00	90.00	150	225	—

Kabul

KM# 218.5 1/2 RUPEE (Type 218)

5.7220 g., Silver **Obv:** Inscription within square **Rev:** Inscription within square

Date	Mintage	VG	F	VF	XF	Unc
AH1053//17	—	70.00	120	200	300	—

Khambayat

KM# 218.13 1/2 RUPEE (Type 218)

5.7220 g., Silver **Obv:** Inscription within square **Rev:** Inscription within square

Date	Mintage	VG	F	VF	XF	Unc
ND	—	30.00	50.00	85.00	130	—

Lahore

KM# 218.6 1/2 RUPEE (Type 218)

5.7220 g., Silver **Obv:** Inscription within square **Rev:** Inscription within square

Date	Mintage	VG	F	VF	XF	Unc
AH1054//1x	—	45.00	75.00	125	190	—

Patna

KM# 218.14 1/2 RUPEE (Type 218)

5.7220 g., Silver **Obv:** Inscription within square **Rev:** Inscription within square **Shape:** Square

Date	Mintage	VG	F	VF	XF	Unc
AH10xx//3	—	—	—	—	—	—

Patna

KM# 218.7 1/2 RUPEE (Type 218)

5.7220 g., Silver **Obv:** Inscription within square **Rev:** Inscription within square

Date	Mintage	VG	F	VF	XF	Unc
AH1044//7	—	30.00	50.00	85.00	130	—
AH1045//8	—	30.00	50.00	85.00	130	—
AH104x//10	—	30.00	50.00	85.00	130	—
AH104x//12	—	30.00	50.00	85.00	130	—
AH1054//18	—	30.00	50.00	85.00	130	—
AH105x//20	—	30.00	50.00	85.00	130	—

Pattan Deo

KM# 218.11 1/2 RUPEE (Type 218)

5.7220 g., Silver **Obv:** Inscription within square **Rev:** Inscription within square

Date	Mintage	VG	F	VF	XF	Unc
AH1047//10	—	100	180	300	450	—

Surat

KM# 218.8 1/2 RUPEE (Type 218)

5.7220 g., Silver **Obv:** Inscription within square **Rev:** Inscription within square

Date	Mintage	Good	VG	F	VF	XF
AH1044//7	—	5.50	13.50	20.00	35.00	50.00
AH1044//8	—	5.50	13.50	20.00	35.00	50.00
AH1045//8	—	5.50	13.50	20.00	35.00	50.00
AH104x//10	—	5.50	13.50	20.00	35.00	50.00
AH1047//9(sic)	—	5.50	13.50	20.00	35.00	50.00
AH1048//12	—	5.50	13.50	20.00	35.00	50.00
AH1049//12	—	5.50	13.50	20.00	35.00	50.00
AH105x//15	—	5.50	13.50	20.00	35.00	50.00
AH105x//16	—	5.50	13.50	20.00	35.00	50.00
AH1055//18	—	5.50	13.50	20.00	35.00	50.00
AH1055//19	—	5.50	13.50	20.00	35.00	50.00
AH105x//21	—	5.50	13.50	20.00	35.00	50.00
AH105x//22	—	5.50	13.50	20.00	35.00	50.00
AH10xx//23	—	9.00	13.50	20.00	35.00	50.00
AH106x//24	—	5.50	13.50	20.00	35.00	50.00
AH106x//25	—	5.50	13.50	20.00	35.00	50.00
AH106x//27	—	5.50	13.50	20.00	35.00	50.00
AH1065//28	—	5.50	13.50	20.00	35.00	50.00
AH1065//29	—	5.50	13.50	20.00	35.00	50.00
AH1067//30	—	5.50	13.50	20.00	35.00	50.00
AH106x//31	—	5.50	13.50	20.00	35.00	50.00

Ujjain

KM# 218.9 1/2 RUPEE (Type 218)

5.7220 g., Silver **Obv:** Inscription within square **Rev:** Inscription within square

Date	Mintage	VG	F	VF	XF	Unc
ND	—	36.00	60.00	100	150	—

Zafarnagar

KM# 218.12 1/2 RUPEE (Type 218)

5.7220 g., Silver **Obv:** Inscription within square **Rev:** Inscription within square

Date	Mintage	VG	F	VF	XF	Unc
AH1043//x	—	55.00	90.00	150	225	—

Daulatabad

KM# 219.1 1/2 RUPEE (Type 219)

5.7220 g., Silver **Obv:** Inscription within foliated eightfoil **Rev:** Inscription within foliated eightfoil **Note:** Similar to 1 Rupee, KM#232.1.

Date	Mintage	VG	F	VF	XF	Unc
AH1068//31	—	28.00	50.00	80.00	120	—

Burhanpur

KM# A220 1/2 RUPEE (Type A220)

5.7220 g., Silver **Obv:** Inscription in square outlined with dots

Date	Mintage	VG	F	VF	XF	Unc
AH1052	—	45.00	75.00	125	190	—

Balkh

KM# 220.1 SHAHRUKHI (Type 220)

4.3000 g., Silver **Obv:** Inscription in square

Date	Mintage	VG	F	VF	XF	Unc
ND	—	35.00	70.00	120	—	—

Note: 30-50% flat strike

Surat

KM# 221.1 RUPEE (Type 221)

11.4440 g., Silver **Obv:** Date **Rev:** "Shah Jahan" with "raij" at top **Note:** Legend varieties exist.

Date	Mintage	Good	VG	F	VF	XF
AH1037//(1) Ahad	—	10.00	25.00	45.00	75.00	120

Surat

KM# 221.2 RUPEE (Type 221)

Silver **Obv:** Date **Rev:** With "Shah Jahan" at top of legend **Note:** Weight varies: 11.00-11.15 grams.

Date	Mintage	Good	VG	F	VF	XF
AH1037//(1) Ahad	—	14.00	35.00	65.00	100	150

Agra

KM# 222.1 RUPEE (Type 222)

11.4440 g., Silver **Obv:** AH date **Note:** Mint epithet: "Dar-ul-Khilafat".

Date	Mintage	Good	VG	F	VF	XF
AH1037//(1) Ahad	—	8.00	12.00	20.00	32.00	50.00
AH1038//(1) Ahad	—	8.00	12.00	20.00	32.00	50.00
AH1038//2	—	8.00	12.00	20.00	32.00	50.00

Ahmadabad

KM# 222.2 RUPEE (Type 222)

11.4440 g., Silver **Obv:** AH date

Date	Mintage	VG	F	VF	XF	Unc
AH1037//(1) Ahad	—	12.00	20.00	32.00	50.00	—
AH1038//(1) Ahad	—	12.00	20.00	32.00	50.00	—
AH1038//2	—	12.00	20.00	32.00	50.00	—

Akbarnagar

KM# 222.3 RUPEE (Type 222)
11.4440 g., Silver **Obv:** AH date

Date	Mintage	VG	F	VF	XF	Unc
AH1037//(1) Ahad	—	16.00	24.00	40.00	60.00	—
AH1038//(1) Ahad	—	16.00	24.00	40.00	60.00	—
AH1038//2	—	16.00	24.00	40.00	60.00	—

Allahabad

KM# 222.4 RUPEE (Type 222)
11.4440 g., Silver **Obv:** AH date

Date	Mintage	VG	F	VF	XF	Unc
AH1038//(1) Ahad	—	18.00	30.00	50.00	75.00	—
AH1038//2	—	18.00	30.00	50.00	75.00	—

Burhanpur

KM# 222.5 RUPEE (Type 222)
11.4440 g., Silver **Obv:** AH date

Date	Mintage	VG	F	VF	XF	Unc
AH1037//(1) Ahad	—	16.00	24.00	35.00	50.00	—
AH1038//(1) Ahad	—	16.00	24.00	35.00	50.00	—
AH1038//2	—	16.00	24.00	35.00	50.00	—

Darur

KM# 222.17 RUPEE (Type 222)
11.4440 g., Silver **Obv:** AH date **Note:** Mint epithet: Fathabad.

Date	Mintage	VG	F	VF	XF	Unc
AH1041//4	—	180	300	500	750	—

Daulatabad

KM# 222.6 RUPEE (Type 222)
11.4440 g., Silver **Obv:** AH date

Date	Mintage	VG	F	VF	XF	Unc
AH1037//(1) Ahad	—	18.00	30.00	50.00	75.00	—

Delhi

KM# 222.7 RUPEE (Type 222)
11.4440 g., Silver **Obv:** AH date

Date	Mintage	VG	F	VF	XF	Unc
AH1037//(1) Ahad	—	18.00	30.00	50.00	75.00	—
AH1038//(1) Ahad	—	18.00	30.00	50.00	75.00	—
AH1038//2	—	18.00	30.00	50.00	75.00	—

Fathpur

KM# 222.8 RUPEE (Type 222)
11.4440 g., Silver **Obv:** AH date **Note:** Mint epithet: "Dar-us-Sultanat".

Date	Mintage	VG	F	VF	XF	Unc
AH1038//(1) Ahad	—	36.00	60.00	100	150	—

Goraghat

KM# 222.20 RUPEE (Type 222)
11.4440 g., Silver

Date	Mintage	VG	F	VF	XF	Unc
AH1037//(1) Ahad	—	125	210	350	525	—

Kabul

KM# 222.9 RUPEE (Type 222)
11.4440 g., Silver **Obv:** AH date

Date	Mintage	Good	VG	F	VF	XF
AH1040//x	—	8.00	12.00	20.00	32.00	50.00
AH1041//4	—	8.00	12.00	20.00	32.00	50.00
AH1041//5	—	8.00	12.00	20.00	32.00	50.00
AH104x//6	—	8.00	12.00	20.00	32.00	50.00
AH105x//16	—	8.00	12.00	20.00	32.00	50.00
AH105x19	—	8.00	12.00	20.00	32.00	50.00

Lahore

KM# 222.10 RUPEE (Type 222)
11.4440 g., Silver **Obv:** AH date **Note:** Mint epithet: "Dar-us-Sultanat".

Date	Mintage	VG	F	VF	XF	Unc
AH1037//(1) Ahad	—	16.00	24.00	40.00	60.00	—
AH1038//(1) Ahad	—	16.00	24.00	40.00	60.00	—
AH1038//2	—	161	24.00	40.00	60.00	—

Multan

KM# 222.11 RUPEE (Type 222)
11.4440 g., Silver **Obv:** AH date

Date	Mintage	VG	F	VF	XF	Unc
AH1037//(1) Ahad	—	16.00	27.00	45.00	67.50	—
AH1038//(1) Ahad	—	16.00	27.00	45.00	67.50	—
AH1038//2	—	16.00	27.00	45.00	67.50	—
AH1039//2	—	16.00	24.00	40.00	60.00	—

Patna

KM# 222.12 RUPEE (Type 222)
11.4440 g., Silver **Obv:** AH date

Date	Mintage	VG	F	VF	XF	Unc
AH1037/(/1) Ahad	—	16.00	24.00	40.00	60.00	—
AH1037//2(sic)	—	16.00	24.00	40.00	60.00	—
AH1038//x	—	16.00	24.00	40.00	60.00	—

Surat

KM# 222.13 RUPEE (Type 222)
11.4440 g., Silver **Obv:** AH date

Date	Mintage	VG	F	VF	XF	Unc
AH1037//(1) Ahad	—	12.00	20.00	32.00	50.00	—
AH1038//(1) Ahad	—	12.00	20.00	32.00	50.00	—
AH1038//2	—	12.00	20.00	32.00	50.00	—
AH1040//x	—	12.00	20.00	32.00	50.00	—
AH1041//x	—	12.00	20.00	32.00	50.00	—
AH1042//x	—	12.00	20.00	32.00	50.00	—
AH1043//x	—	12.00	20.00	32.00	50.00	—
AH1046//x	—	12.00	20.00	32.00	50.00	—

Tatta

KM# 222.14 RUPEE (Type 222)
11.4440 g., Silver **Obv:** AH date **Rev:** Regnal year expressed as numeral "1"

Date	Mintage	VG	F	VF	XF	Unc
AH1038//(1) Ahad	—	20.00	33.00	55.00	82.50	—

Ujjain

KM# 222.15 RUPEE (Type 222)
11.4440 g., Silver **Obv:** Mint epithet Baldat

Date	Mintage	VG	F	VF	XF	Unc
AH1039//2	—	30.00	50.00	85.00	130	—

Ujjain

KM# 222.16 RUPEE (Type 222)
11.4440 g., Silver **Obv:** Without mint epithet

Date	Mintage	VG	F	VF	XF	Unc
AH1040//4	—	28.00	50.00	80.00	120	—
AH1041//5	—	28.00	50.00	80.00	120	—

Urdu Zafar Qarin

KM# 222.21 RUPEE (Type 222)
11.4440 g., Silver

Date	Mintage	VG	F	VF	XF	Unc
AH1038//(1) Ahad	—	145	240	400	600	—

Zafarnagar

KM# 222.18 RUPEE (Type 222)
11.4440 g., Silver

Date	Mintage	VG	F	VF	XF	Unc
AH1038//(1) Ahad	—	90.00	150	250	375	—
AH1039//x	—	90.00	150	250	375	—

Gulkanda

KM# 223.1 RUPEE (Type 223)
11.4440 g., Silver **Obv:** Inscription in crude calligraphy **Rev:** Inscription in crude calligraphy

Date	Mintage	VG	F	VF	XF	Unc
ND	—	16.00	24.00	40.00	60.00	—

Akbarabad

KM# A224.1 RUPEE (Type A224)
11.4440 g., Silver **Obv:** Mint name in circle **Obv. Inscription:** "Kalima" **Rev:** Inscription with titles similar to Rupee, KM#224 series

Date	Mintage	VG	F	VF	XF	Unc
AH1040//4	—	—	—	—	—	—

Agra

KM# 224.20 RUPEE (Type 224)
11.4440 g., Silver

Date	Mintage	VG	F	VF	XF	Unc
AH1038//2	—	55.00	90.00	150	225	—

Ahmadabad

KM# 224.1 RUPEE (Type 224)
11.4440 g., Silver

Date	Mintage	VG	F	VF	XF	Unc
AH1038//1	—	16.00	27.00	45.00	65.00	—
AH1039//2	—	16.00	27.00	45.00	65.00	—
AH1040//3	—	16.00	27.00	45.00	65.00	—
AH1040//4	—	16.00	27.00	45.00	65.00	—
AH1041//4	—	16.00	27.00	45.00	65.00	—
AH1041//5	—	16.00	27.00	45.00	65.00	—
AH1042//5	—	16.00	27.00	45.00	65.00	—

Ahmadnagar

KM# 224.2 RUPEE (Type 224)
11.4440 g., Silver

Date	Mintage	VG	F	VF	XF	Unc
AH1038//2	—	18.00	30.00	50.00	75.00	—
AH1039//3	—	18.00	30.00	50.00	75.00	—
AH1041//x	—	18.00	30.00	50.00	75.00	—
AH1042//x	—	18.00	30.00	50.00	75.00	—

Ajmer

KM# 224.3 RUPEE (Type 224)
11.4440 g., Silver

Date	Mintage	VG	F	VF	XF	Unc
AH1041//x	—	90.00	150	250	375	—

Akbarabad

KM# 224.4 RUPEE (Type 224)
11.4440 g., Silver **Note:** Mint epithet: "Dar-ul-Khilatat".

Date	Mintage	VG	F	VF	XF	Unc
AH1038//(1) Ahad	—	18.00	30.00	50.00	75.00	—
AH1038//2	—	18.00	30.00	50.00	75.00	—
AH1039//2	—	18.00	30.00	50.00	75.00	—
AH1041//4	—	18.00	30.00	50.00	75.00	—
AH10xx//5	—	18.00	30.00	50.00	75.00	—

Akbarnagar

KM# 224.5 RUPEE (Type 224)
11.4440 g., Silver

Date	Mintage	VG	F	VF	XF	Unc
AH1038//2	—	24.00	40.00	65.00	100	—
AH1039//2	—	24.00	40.00	65.00	100	—
AH1039//3	—	24.00	40.00	65.00	100	—
AH1040//4	—	24.00	40.00	65.00	100	—
AH1042//5	—	24.00	40.00	65.00	100	—
AH1042//6	—	24.00	40.00	65.00	100	—
AH1043//6	—	24.00	40.00	65.00	100	—
AH1043//7	—	24.00	40.00	65.00	100	—
AH1044//7	—	24.00	40.00	65.00	100	—

Allahabad

KM# 224.6 RUPEE (Type 224)
11.4440 g., Silver

Date	Mintage	VG	F	VF	XF	Unc
AH1038//2	—	22.00	36.00	60.00	90.00	—
AH1039//2	—	22.00	36.00	60.00	90.00	—
AH1039//3	—	22.00	36.00	60.00	90.00	—
AH1040//3	—	22.00	36.00	60.00	90.00	—
AH1040//4	—	22.00	36.00	60.00	90.00	—
AH1041//4	—	22.00	36.00	60.00	90.00	—
AH1041//5	—	22.00	36.00	60.00	90.00	—

Bhakkar

KM# 224.7 RUPEE (Type 224)
11.4440 g., Silver **Note:** Mint name spelled Bakkar and often miss read as Nagar.

Date	Mintage	VG	F	VF	XF	Unc
AH1040//3	—	22.00	36.00	60.00	90.00	—
AH1040//4	—	22.00	36.00	60.00	90.00	—
AH1041//4	—	22.00	36.00	60.00	90.00	—
AH1041//5	—	22.00	36.00	60.00	90.00	—
AH1042//5	—	22.00	36.00	60.00	90.00	—
AH1043//5(sic)	—	22.00	36.00	60.00	90.00	—

Burhanpur

KM# 224.8 RUPEE (Type 224)
11.4440 g., Silver

Date	Mintage	VG	F	VF	XF	Unc
AH103x//(1) Ahad	—	18.00	30.00	50.00	75.00	—
AH1038//2	—	18.00	30.00	50.00	75.00	—
AH1039//2	—	18.00	30.00	50.00	75.00	—
AH1039//3	—	18.00	30.00	50.00	75.00	—
AH1040//3	—	18.00	30.00	50.00	75.00	—

Delhi

KM# 224.9 RUPEE (Type 224)
11.4440 g., Silver

Date	Mintage	VG	F	VF	XF	Unc
AH103x//(1) Ahad	—	16.00	21.00	35.00	50.00	—
AH1038//2	—	16.00	21.00	35.00	50.00	—
AH1039//2	—	16.00	21.00	35.00	50.00	—
AH1039//3	—	16.00	21.00	35.00	50.00	—
AH1040//3	—	16.00	21.00	35.00	50.00	—
AH1040//4	—	16.00	21.00	35.00	50.00	—

Jahangirnagar

KM# 224.10 RUPEE (Type 224)
11.4440 g., Silver **Obv:** Emperor's name and titles, date **Rev:** Kalima, mint and regnal year

Date	Mintage	VG	F	VF	XF	Unc
AH103x//(1) Ahad	—	16.00	27.00	45.00	65.00	—
AH1038//2	—	16.00	27.00	45.00	65.00	—
AH1039//2	—	16.00	27.00	45.00	65.00	—
AH1039//3	—	16.00	27.00	45.00	65.00	—
AH1040//3	—	16.00	27.00	45.00	65.00	—
AH1040//4	—	16.00	27.00	45.00	65.00	—
AH1041//4	—	16.00	27.00	45.00	65.00	—
AH1041//5	—	16.00	27.00	45.00	65.00	—
AH1042//5	—	16.00	27.00	45.00	65.00	—
AH1042//6	—	16.00	27.00	45.00	65.00	—
AH1043//6	—	16.00	27.00	45.00	65.00	—
AH1043//7	—	16.00	27.00	45.00	65.00	—

Kabul

KM# 224.11 RUPEE (Type 224)
11.4440 g., Silver

Date	Mintage	VG	F	VF	XF	Unc
AH1038//2	—	30.00	50.00	85.00	130	—
AH104x//6	—	30.00	50.00	85.00	130	—
AH104x//8	—	30.00	50.00	85.00	130	—
AH1047//10	—	30.00	50.00	85.00	130	—
AH105x//17	—	30.00	50.00	85.00	130	—

Kashmir

KM# 224.12 RUPEE (Type 224)
11.4440 g., Silver **Obv:** Ilahi month and regnal year **Rev:** AH date

Date	Mintage	VG	F	VF	XF	Unc
AH1040//4	—	36.00	60.00	100	150	—
AH1041//5	—	36.00	60.00	100	150	—
AH1042//x	—	36.00	60.00	100	150	—

Katak

KM# 224.13 RUPEE (Type 224)
11.4440 g., Silver **Obv:** Ilahi month and regnal year **Rev:** AH date

Date	Mintage	VG	F	VF	XF	Unc
AH1037//(1) Ahad	—	30.00	50.00	80.00	120	—
AH10xx//3	—	30.00	50.00	80.00	120	—
AH104x//5	—	30.00	50.00	80.00	120	—
AH104x//8	—	30.00	50.00	80.00	120	—

Lahore

KM# 224.14 RUPEE (Type 224)
11.4440 g., Silver **Obv:** Ilahi month and regnal year **Rev:** AH date

Date	Mintage	VG	F	VF	XF	Unc
AH1038//2	—	25.00	40.00	70.00	110	—
AH1039//2	—	25.00	40.00	70.00	110	—

Multan

KM# 224.15 RUPEE (Type 224)
11.4440 g., Silver **Obv:** Ilahi month and regnal year **Rev:** AH date

Date	Mintage	VG	F	VF	XF	Unc
AH1038//2	—	21.00	36.00	60.00	90.00	—
AH1039//2	—	21.00	36.00	60.00	90.00	—
AH1039//3	—	21.00	36.00	60.00	90.00	—

Patna

KM# 224.16 RUPEE (Type 224)
11.4440 g., Silver **Obv:** Ilahi month and regnal year **Rev:** AH date

Date	Mintage	VG	F	VF	XF	Unc
AH1037//2(sic)	—	16.00	21.00	35.00	50.00	—
AH1038//2	—	16.00	21.00	35.00	50.00	—
AH1039//2	—	16.00	21.00	35.00	50.00	—
AH1039//3	—	16.00	21.00	35.00	50.00	—
AH1040//3	—	16.00	21.00	35.00	50.00	—
AH1040//4	—	16.00	21.00	35.00	50.00	—
AH1041//4	—	16.00	21.00	35.00	50.00	—
AH1041//5	—	16.00	21.00	35.00	50.00	—
AH1042//5	—	16.00	21.00	35.00	50.00	—

Qandahar

KM# 224.17 RUPEE (Type 224)
11.4440 g., Silver **Obv:** Ilahi month and regnal year **Rev:** AH date

Date	Mintage	VG	F	VF	XF	Unc
AH104x//5	—	100	180	300	450	—
AH104x//11	—	100	180	300	450	—

Tatta

KM# 224.18 RUPEE (Type 224)
11.4440 g., Silver **Obv:** Ilahi month and regnal year **Rev:** AH date

Date	Mintage	VG	F	VF	XF	Unc
AH1038//(1) Ahad	—	16.00	20.00	30.00	45.00	—
AH1038//2	—	16.00	20.00	30.00	45.00	—
AH1039//2	—	16.00	20.00	30.00	45.00	—
AH1039//3	—	16.00	20.00	30.00	45.00	—
AH1040//3	—	16.00	20.00	30.00	45.00	—
AH1040//4	—	16.00	20.00	30.00	45.00	—
AH1041//4	—	16.00	20.00	30.00	45.00	—
AH1041//5	—	16.00	20.00	30.00	45.00	—
AH1042//5	—	16.00	20.00	30.00	45.00	—
AH1042//6	—	16.00	20.00	30.00	45.00	—
AH1043//6	—	16.00	20.00	30.00	45.00	—
AH1043//7	—	16.00	20.00	30.00	45.00	—
AH1044//7	—	16.00	20.00	30.00	45.00	—
AH1044//8	—	16.00	20.00	30.00	45.00	—
AH1045//8	—	16.00	20.00	30.00	45.00	—
AH1045//9	—	16.00	20.00	30.00	45.00	—
AH1046//9	—	16.00	20.00	30.00	45.00	—
AH1046//10	—	16.00	20.00	30.00	45.00	—
AH1047//10	—	16.00	20.00	30.00	45.00	—
AH1047//11	—	16.00	20.00	30.00	45.00	—
AH1048//11	—	16.00	20.00	30.00	45.00	—
AH1048//12	—	16.00	20.00	30.00	45.00	—
AH1049//12	—	16.00	20.00	30.00	45.00	—
AH1049//13	—	16.00	20.00	30.00	45.00	—
AH1050//13	—	16.00	20.00	30.00	45.00	—
AH1050//14	—	16.00	20.00	30.00	45.00	—
AH1051//14	—	16.00	20.00	30.00	45.00	—
AH1051//15	—	16.00	20.00	30.00	45.00	—
AH1052//15	—	16.00	20.00	30.00	45.00	—
AH1052//16	—	16.00	20.00	30.00	45.00	—
AH1053//16	—	16.00	20.00	30.00	45.00	—
AH1053//17	—	16.00	20.00	30.00	45.00	—
AH1054//17	—	16.00	20.00	30.00	45.00	—
AH1054//18	—	16.00	20.00	30.00	45.00	—
AH1055//18	—	16.00	20.00	30.00	45.00	—

Date	Mintage	VG	F	VF	XF	Unc
AH1055//19	—	16.00	20.00	30.00	45.00	—
AH1056//19	—	16.00	20.00	30.00	45.00	—
AH1056//20	—	16.00	20.00	30.00	45.00	—
AH1057//20	—	61.00	20.00	30.00	45.00	—
AH1057//21	—	16.00	20.00	30.00	45.00	—
AH1058//21	—	16.00	20.00	30.00	45.00	—
AH1058//22	—	16.00	20.00	30.00	45.00	—
AH1059//22	—	16.00	20.00	30.00	45.00	—
AH1059//23	—	16.00	20.00	30.00	45.00	—
AH1060//23	—	16.00	20.00	30.00	45.00	—
AH1060//24	—	16.00	20.00	30.00	45.00	—
AH1061//24	—	16.00	20.00	30.00	45.00	—
AH1061//25	—	16.00	20.00	30.00	45.00	—
AH1062//25	—	16.00	20.00	30.00	45.00	—
AH1062//26	—	16.00	20.00	30.00	45.00	—
AH1063//26	—	16.00	20.00	30.00	45.00	—
AH1063//27	—	16.00	20.00	30.00	45.00	—
AH1064//27	—	16.00	20.00	30.00	45.00	—
AH1064//28	—	16.00	20.00	30.00	45.00	—
AH1065//28	—	16.00	20.00	30.00	45.00	—
AH1065//29	—	16.00	20.00	30.00	45.00	—
AH1066//29	—	16.00	20.00	30.00	45.00	—
AH1066//30	—	16.00	20.00	30.00	45.00	—
AH1067//30	—	16.00	20.00	30.00	45.00	—
AH1067//31	—	16.00	20.00	30.00	45.00	—
AH1068//31	—	16.00	20.00	30.00	45.00	—
AH1068//32	—	16.00	20.00	30.00	45.00	—
AH1069//32	—	16.00	20.00	30.00	45.00	—
AH1069//33	—	16.00	20.00	30.00	45.00	—

Ujjain

KM# 224.22 RUPEE (Type 224)

11.4440 g., Silver **Obv:** Ilahi month and regnal year **Rev:** AH date

Date	Mintage	VG	F	VF	XF	Unc
AH104x//4	—	18.00	30.00	50.00	75.00	—
AH1040//5	—	18.00	30.00	50.00	75.00	—

Zafarnagar

KM# 224.19 RUPEE (Type 224)

11.4440 g., Silver **Obv:** Ilahi month and regnal year **Rev:** AH date

Date	Mintage	VG	F	VF	XF	Unc
AH10xx//3	—	25.00	42.00	70.00	110	—
AH1041//4	—	25.00	42.00	70.00	110	—
AH1041//5	—	25.00	42.00	70.00	110	—
AH1042//5	—	25.00	42.00	70.00	110	—
AH104x//6	—	25.00	42.00	70.00	110	—
AH1046//x	—	25.00	42.00	70.00	110	—

Akbarabad

KM# 225.1 RUPEE (Type 225)

11.4440 g., Silver **Shape:** Square

Date	Mintage	VG	F	VF	XF	Unc
AH1038//2	—	200	400	700	1,000	—

Akbarabad

KM# 226.1 RUPEE (Type 226)

11.4440 g., Silver **Obv:** Names of four Caliphs above Kalima

Date	Mintage	VG	F	VF	XF	Unc
AH1039//2	—	18.00	30.00	50.00	75.00	—
AH1039//3	—	18.00	30.00	50.00	75.00	—
AH1040//3	—	18.00	30.00	50.00	75.00	—
AH1040//4	—	18.00	30.00	50.00	75.00	—
AH1041//4	—	18.00	30.00	50.00	75.00	—
AH1041//5	—	18.00	30.00	50.00	75.00	—
AH1042//x	—	18.00	30.00	50.00	75.00	—

Bhilsa

KM# 226.3 RUPEE (Type 226)

11.4440 g., Silver **Obv:** Names of four Caliphs above Kalima

Date	Mintage	VG	F	VF	XF	Unc
AH1042//6	—	70.00	120	200	300	—

Burhanpur

KM# 226.2 RUPEE (Type 226)

11.4440 g., Silver **Obv:** Names of four Caliphs above Kalima

Date	Mintage	VG	F	VF	XF	Unc
AH//2	—	16.00	24.00	40.00	60.00	—
AH1040//3	—	16.00	24.00	40.00	60.00	—
AH1040//4	—	16.00	24.00	40.00	60.00	—
AH1041//4	—	16.00	24.00	40.00	60.00	—
AH1041//5	—	16.00	24.00	40.00	60.00	—
AH1042//5	—	16.00	24.00	40.00	60.00	—
AH1044//x	—	16.00	24.00	40.00	60.00	—

Akbarabad

KM# A227 RUPEE (Type A227)

Silver **Obv:** Kalima within circle **Rev:** Emperor's full name and title in square

Date	Mintage	VG	F	VF	XF	Unc
AH1042/5	—	30.00	50.00	85.00	130	—

Ahmadnagar

KM# 227.1 RUPEE (Type 227)

11.4440 g., Silver **Obv:** Kalima within circle **Rev:** Emperor's fullname and title in legend, layouts vary

Date	Mintage	VG	F	VF	XF	Unc
AH10xx//3	—	25.00	42.00	70.00	110	—
AH1044//8	—	25.00	42.00	70.00	110	—

Akbarabad

KM# 227.2 RUPEE (Type 227)

11.4440 g., Silver **Obv:** Kalima within circle **Rev:** Emperor's full name and title in legend, layouts vary

Date	Mintage	VG	F	VF	XF	Unc
AH1039//2	—	16.00	27.00	45.00	65.00	—
AH1039//3	—	16.00	27.00	45.00	65.00	—
AH1040//3	—	16.00	27.00	45.00	65.00	—
AH1040//4	—	16.00	27.00	45.00	65.00	—
AH1041//4	—	16.00	27.00	45.00	65.00	—
AH1041//5	—	16.00	27.00	45.00	65.00	—
AH1042//5	—	16.00	27.00	45.00	65.00	—
AH1042//6	—	16.00	27.00	45.00	65.00	—
AH1043//6	—	16.00	27.00	45.00	65.00	—
AH1045//8	—	16.00	27.00	45.00	65.00	—

Akbarabad

KM# 227.9 RUPEE (Type 227)

11.4440 g., Silver **Obv:** KM#235.3 **Rev:** KM#227.2 **Note:** Mule.

Date	Mintage	VG	F	VF	XF	Unc
AH1041//5	—	—	—	—	—	—
AH1042//5	—	—	—	—	—	—

Akbarabad

KM# 227.10 RUPEE (Type 227)

11.4440 g., Silver **Obv:** KM#227.2 **Rev:** KM#235.3 **Note:** Mule.

Date	Mintage	Good	VG	F	VF	XF
AH1042//x	—	—	—	—	—	—

Allahabad

KM# 227.3 RUPEE (Type 227)

11.4440 g., Silver **Obv:** Kalima within circle **Rev:** Emperor's full name and title in legend; layouts vary

Date	Mintage	VG	F	VF	XF	Unc
AH1040//3	—	21.00	36.00	60.00	90.00	—

Bhakkar

KM# 227.4 RUPEE (Type 227)

11.4440 g., Silver **Obv:** Kalima within circle **Rev:** Emperor's full name and title in legend; layouts vary

Date	Mintage	VG	F	VF	XF	Unc
AH1040//3	—	27.00	45.00	75.00	110	—
AH1042//5	—	27.00	45.00	75.00	110	—
AH1042//6	—	27.00	45.00	75.00	110	—

Burhanpur

KM# 227.5 RUPEE (Type 227)

11.4440 g., Silver **Obv:** Kalima within circle **Rev:** Emperor's full name and title in legend; layouts vary

Date	Mintage	VG	F	VF	XF	Unc
AH1040//3	—	21.00	36.00	60.00	90.00	—
AH1042//x	—	21.00	36.00	60.00	90.00	—

Delhi

KM# 227.6 RUPEE (Type 227)

11.4440 g., Silver **Obv:** Kalima within circle **Rev:** Emperor's full name and title in legend; layouts vary

Date	Mintage	VG	F	VF	XF	Unc
AH1040//4	—	20.00	33.00	55.00	80.00	—
AH1041//4	—	20.00	33.00	55.00	80.00	—
AH1041//5	—	20.00	33.00	55.00	80.00	—
AH1042//5	—	20.00	33.00	55.00	80.00	—
AH1042//6	—	20.00	33.00	55.00	80.00	—
AH1043//6	—	20.00	3.00	55.00	80.00	—
AH1043//7	—	20.00	33.00	55.00	80.00	—
AH1044//7	—	20.00	33.00	55.00	80.00	—
AH1044//8	—	20.00	33.00	55.00	80.00	—
AH1045//8	—	20.00	33.00	55.00	80.00	—
AH1048//1x	—	20.00	33.00	55.00	80.00	—
AH1049//12	—	20.00	33.00	55.00	80.00	—
AH1051//15	—	20.00	33.00	55.00	80.00	—
AH105X//16	—	20.00	33.00	55.00	80.00	—
AH1054//17	—	20.00	33.00	55.00	80.00	—
AH1055//18	—	20.00	33.00	55.00	80.00	—
AH1056//xx	—	20.00	33.00	55.00	80.00	—
AH1058//2x	—	20.00	33.00	55.00	80.00	—

Note: For later issues see Shahjahanabad.

Lahore

KM# 227.7 RUPEE (Type 227)

11.4440 g., Silver **Obv:** Kalima within circle **Rev:** Emperor's full name and title in legend; layouts vary

Date	Mintage	VG	F	VF	XF	Unc
AH1039//3	—	16.00	22.00	32.00	48.00	—
AH1040//3	—	16.00	22.00	32.00	48.00	—
AH1040//4	—	16.00	22.00	32.00	48.00	—
AH1041//4	—	16.00	22.00	32.00	48.00	—
AH1041//5	—	16.00	22.00	32.00	48.00	—
AH1042//5	—	16.00	22.00	32.00	48.00	—

Multan

KM# 227.8 RUPEE (Type 227)

11.4440 g., Silver **Obv:** Kalima within circle **Rev:** Emperor's full name and title in legend; layouts vary

Date	Mintage	VG	F	VF	XF	Unc
AH1039//3	—	16.00	22.00	32.00	48.00	—
AH1040//3	—	16.00	22.00	32.00	48.00	—
AH1041//4	—	16.00	22.00	32.00	48.00	—
AH1041//5	—	16.00	22.00	32.00	48.00	—
AH1042//5	—	16.00	22.00	32.00	48.00	—
AH1043//6	—	16.00	22.00	32.00	48.00	—

Akbarabad

KM# 228.1 RUPEE (Type 228)
11.4440 g., Silver **Obv:** Central inscription within circle **Rev:** Central inscription within circle

Date	Mintage	VG	F	VF	XF	Unc
AH1047//10	—	27.00	45.00	75.00	110	—

Bhakkar

KM# 228.2 RUPEE (Type 228)
11.4440 g., Silver **Obv:** Central inscription within circle **Rev:** Central inscription within circle **Note:** Mint name spelled Bakkar.

Date	Mintage	VG	F	VF	XF	Unc
AH1042//5	—	36.00	60.00	100	150	—
AH1042//6	—	36.00	60.00	100	150	—
AH1043//6	—	36.00	60.00	100	150	—

Qandahar

KM# 228.3 RUPEE (Type 228)
11.4440 g., Silver **Obv:** Central inscription within circle **Rev:** Central inscription within circle

Date	Mintage	VG	F	VF	XF	Unc
AH1048//11	—	90.00	150	250	375	—
AH1048//12	—	90.00	150	250	375	—

Shahjahanabad

KM# 228.4 RUPEE (Type 228)
11.4440 g., Silver **Obv:** Central inscription within circle **Rev:** Central inscription within circle **Note:** For earlier issues see Dehli.

Date	Mintage	VG	F	VF	XF	Unc
AH1058//22	—	27.00	45.00	75.00	110	—
AH1060//24	—	27.00	45.00	75.00	110	—
AH106x//25	—	27.00	45.00	75.00	110	—
AH1062//2x	—	27.00	45.00	75.00	110	—
AH106x//27	—	27.00	45.00	75.00	110	—
AH1065//28	—	27.00	45.00	75.00	110	—
AH1065//29	—	27.00	45.00	75.00	110	—
AH1066//29	—	27.00	45.00	75.00	110	—
AH1066//30	—	27.00	45.00	75.00	110	—
AH106x//31	—	27.00	45.00	75.00	110	—

Surat

KM# 228.5 RUPEE (Type 228)
11.4440 g., Silver **Obv:** Central inscription within circle **Rev:** Central inscription within circle

Date	Mintage	VG	F	VF	XF	Unc
AH1067//31	—	27.00	45.00	75.00	110	—
AH1068//31	—	27.00	45.00	75.00	110	—

Akbarabad

KM# 229.1 RUPEE (Type 229)
11.4440 g., Silver **Obv:** Central inscription within foliated quatrefoil

Date	Mintage	VG	F	VF	XF	Unc
AH104x//4	—	16.00	27.00	45.00	65.00	—
AH1041//5	—	16.00	27.00	45.00	65.00	—
AH1042//5	—	16.00	27.00	45.00	65.00	—
AH1042//6	—	16.00	27.00	45.00	65.00	—

Burhanpur

KM# 229.2 RUPEE (Type 229)
11.4440 g., Silver **Obv:** Central inscription within foliated quatrefoil

Date	Mintage	VG	F	VF	XF	Unc
AH103x//2	—	18.00	30.00	50.00	75.00	—
AH1040//3	—	18.00	30.00	50.00	75.00	—
AH104x//4	—	18.00	30.00	50.00	75.00	—

Shahjahanabad

KM# 229.3 RUPEE (Type 229)
11.4440 g., Silver **Obv:** Central inscription within foliated quatrefoil **Rev:** Central inscription within circle

Date	Mintage	VG	F	VF	XF	Unc
AH1060//24	—	70.00	120	200	300	—
AH1061//24	—	70.00	120	200	300	—

Akbarabad

KM# 230.1 RUPEE (Type 230)
11.4440 g., Silver **Obv:** Central inscription within foliated quatrefoil **Rev:** Central inscription within foliated quatrefoil

Date	Mintage	VG	F	VF	XF	Unc
AH1043//6	—	21.00	36.00	60.00	90.00	—
AH104x//7	—	21.00	36.00	60.00	90.00	—

Shahjahanabad

KM# 230.2 RUPEE (Type 230)
11.4440 g., Silver **Obv:** Central inscription within foliated quatrefoil **Rev:** Central inscription within foliated quatrefoil **Note:** For earlier issues see Dehli.

Date	Mintage	VG	F	VF	XF	Unc
AH1058//22	—	21.00	36.00	60.00	90.00	—
AH1059//22	—	21.00	36.00	60.00	90.00	—

Surat

KM# 230.3 RUPEE (Type 230)
11.4440 g., Silver **Obv:** Central inscription within foliated quatrefoil **Rev:** Central inscription within foliated quatrefoil

Date	Mintage	VG	F	VF	XF	Unc
AH1051//1x	—	18.00	30.00	50.00	75.00	—
AH1054//1x	—	18.00	30.00	50.00	75.00	—
AH1057//20	—	18.00	30.00	50.00	75.00	—
AH1057//21	—	18.00	30.00	50.00	75.00	—
AH1057//22 (sic)	—	18.00	30.00	50.00	75.00	—

Akbarabad

KM# 231.1 RUPEE (Type 231)
11.4440 g., Silver **Obv:** Central inscription within sixfoil

Date	Mintage	VG	F	VF	XF	Unc
AH1040//3	—	21.00	36.00	60.00	90.00	—
AH1040//4	—	21.00	36.00	60.00	90.00	—
AH1041//4	—	21.00	36.00	60.00	90.00	—
AH1041//5	—	21.00	36.00	60.00	90.00	—

Burhanpur

KM# 231.2 RUPEE (Type 231)
11.4440 g., Silver **Obv:** Central within sixfoil

Date	Mintage	VG	F	VF	XF	Unc
AH1040//3	—	28.00	48.00	80.00	120	—

Ahmadabad

KM# 232.3 RUPEE (Type 232)
11.4440 g., Silver **Obv:** Central inscription within foliated eightfoil **Rev:** Central inscription within foliated eightfoil

Date	Mintage	VG	F	VF	XF	Unc
AH1067//31	—	16.00	27.00	45.00	65.00	—
AH1068//31	—	16.00	27.00	45.00	65.00	—

Akbarabad

KM# 232.4 RUPEE (Type 232)
11.4440 g., Silver **Obv:** Central inscription within foliated eightfoil **Rev:** Central inscription within foliated eightfoil **Note:** Mint epithet: "Dar-ul Khilafat"

Date	Mintage	VG	F	VF	XF	Unc
AH1068//31	—	16.00	25.00	40.00	60.00	—
AH1068//32	—	16.00	25.00	40.00	60.00	—
AH1069//32	—	16.00	25.00	40.00	60.00	—

Daulatabad

KM# 232.1 RUPEE (Type 232)
11.4440 g., Silver **Obv:** Central inscription within foliated eightfoil **Rev:** Central inscription within foliated eightfoil

Date	Mintage	VG	F	VF	XF	Unc
AH1067//31	—	21.00	36.00	60.00	90.00	—
AH1068//31	—	21.00	36.00	60.00	90.00	—
AH1068//32	—	21.00	36.00	60.00	90.00	—

Shahjahanabad

KM# 232.2 RUPEE (Type 232)
11.4440 g., Silver **Obv:** Central inscription within foliated eightfoil **Rev:** Central inscription within foliated eightfoil

Date	Mintage	VG	F	VF	XF	Unc
AH1065//29	—	18.00	30.00	50.00	75.00	—
AH1067//31	—	18.00	30.00	50.00	75.00	—
AH1068//31	—	18.00	30.00	50.00	75.00	—
AH1069//32	—	18.00	30.00	50.00	75.00	—

Akbarabad

KM# 233.1 RUPEE (Type 233)
11.4440 g., Silver **Obv:** Central inscription within foliated lozenge

Date	Mintage	VG	F	VF	XF	Unc
AH1039//2	—	23.00	40.00	65.00	95.00	—
AH1041//4	—	23.00	40.00	65.00	95.00	—
AH1041//5	—	23.00	40.00	65.00	95.00	—
AH1042//2 (sic)	—	23.00	40.00	65.00	95.00	—
AH1042//5	—	23.00	40.00	65.00	95.00	—
AH1042//6	—	23.00	40.00	65.00	95.00	—
AH1043//6	—	23.00	40.00	65.00	95.00	—

Akbarabad

KM# 234.1 RUPEE (Type 234)
11.4440 g., Silver **Obv:** Central inscription within lozenge **Rev:** Central inscription within lozenge

Date	Mintage	VG	F	VF	XF	Unc
AH1042//6	—	28.00	48.00	80.00	120	—
AH1043//6	—	28.00	48.00	80.00	120	—
AH1043//7	—	28.00	48.00	80.00	120	—

Ahmadabad

KM# 235.1 RUPEE (Type 235)
11.4440 g., Silver **Obv:** Central inscription within square, knots at corners **Rev:** Central inscription within square, knots at corners

Date	Mintage	VG	F	VF	XF	Unc
AH1043//6	—	—	16.00	25.00	40.00	—
AH1043//7	—	—	16.00	25.00	40.00	—
AH1044//7	—	—	16.00	25.00	40.00	—
AH1044//8	—	—	16.00	25.00	40.00	—
AH1045//8	—	—	16.00	25.00	40.00	—
AH1045//9	—	—	16.00	25.00	40.00	—
AH1046//9	—	—	16.00	25.00	40.00	—
AH1046//10	—	—	16.00	25.00	40.00	—
AH1047//10	—	—	16.00	25.00	40.00	—
AH1047//11	—	—	16.00	25.00	40.00	—
AH1048//11	—	—	16.00	25.00	40.00	—
AH1048//12	—	—	16.00	25.00	40.00	—
AH1049//12	—	—	16.00	25.00	40.00	—
AH1049//13	—	—	16.00	25.00	40.00	—
AH1050//13	—	—	16.00	25.00	40.00	—
AH1050//14	—	—	16.00	25.00	40.00	—

Date	Mintage	VG	F	VF	XF	Unc
AH1053//16	—	—	16.00	25.00	40.00	—
AH1053//17	—	—	16.00	25.00	40.00	—
AH1054//17	—	—	16.00	25.00	40.00	—
AH1054//18	—	—	16.00	25.00	40.00	—
AH1055//18	—	—	16.00	25.00	40.00	—
AH1055//19	—	—	16.00	25.00	40.00	—
AH1056//19	—	—	16.00	25.00	40.00	—
AH1056//20	—	—	16.00	25.00	40.00	—
AH1057//20	—	—	16.00	25.00	40.00	—
AH1057//21	—	—	16.00	25.00	40.00	—
AH1058//21	—	—	16.00	25.00	40.00	—
AH1061//24	—	—	16.00	25.00	40.00	—
AH1063//27	—	—	16.00	25.00	40.00	—
AH1065//29	—	—	16.00	25.00	40.00	—
AH1066//29	—	—	6.00	25.00	40.00	—
AH1067//3x	—	—	16.00	25.00	40.00	—
AH1069//32	—	—	16.00	25.00	40.00	—
AH106x//33	—	—	16.00	25.00	40.00	—

Ahmadnagar

KM# 235.2 RUPEE (Type 235)

11.4440 g., Silver **Obv:** Central inscription within square, knots at corners **Rev:** Central inscription within square, knots at corners

Date	Mintage	VG	F	VF	XF	Unc
AH1043//x	—	16.00	24.00	40.00	60.00	—
AH1044//7	—	16.00	24.00	40.00	60.00	—
AH1053//xx	—	16.00	24.00	40.00	60.00	—
AH1055//1x	—	16.00	24.00	40.00	60.00	—
AH1058//21	—	16.00	24.00	40.00	60.00	—
AH105x//22	—	16.00	24.00	40.00	60.00	—
AH1061//24	—	16.00	24.00	40.00	60.00	—
AH1061//25	—	16.00	24.00	40.00	60.00	—
AH1062//25	—	16.00	24.00	40.00	60.00	—
AH1062//26	—	16.00	24.00	40.00	60.00	—
AH1063//26	—	16.00	24.00	40.00	60.00	—
AH1063//27	—	16.00	24.00	40.00	60.00	—
AH1066//29	—	16.00	24.00	40.00	60.00	—
AH1067//30	—	16.00	24.00	40.00	60.00	—
AH1067//31	—	16.00	24.00	40.00	60.00	—
AH1068//31	—	16.00	24.00	40.00	60.00	—
AH1068//32	—	16.00	24.00	40.00	60.00	—
AH1069//32	—	16.00	24.00	40.00	60.00	—
AH1069//33	—	16.00	24.00	40.00	60.00	—

Akbarabad

KM# 235.3 RUPEE (Type 235)

11.4440 g., Silver **Obv:** Central inscription within square, knots at corners **Rev:** Central inscription within square, knots at corners

Date	Mintage	VG	F	VF	XF	Unc
AH1041//4	—	16.00	22.00	30.00	45.00	—
AH1041//5	—	16.00	22.00	30.00	45.00	—
AH1042//5	—	16.00	2.00	30.00	45.00	—
AH1042//6	—	16.00	22.00	30.00	45.00	—
AH1043//6	—	16.00	22.00	30.00	45.00	—
AH1043//7	—	16.00	22.00	30.00	45.00	—
AH1044//7	—	16.00	22.00	30.00	45.00	—
AH1044//8	—	16.00	22.00	30.00	45.00	—
AH1045//8	—	16.00	22.00	30.00	45.00	—
AH1045//9	—	16.00	22.00	30.00	45.00	—
AH1046//9	—	16.00	22.00	30.00	45.00	—
AH1046//10	—	16.00	22.00	30.00	45.00	—
AH1047//10	—	16.00	22.00	30.00	45.00	—
AH1047//11	—	16.00	22.00	30.00	45.00	—
AH1048//11	—	16.00	22.00	30.00	45.00	—
AH1048//12	—	16.00	22.00	30.00	45.00	—
AH1049//12	—	16.00	22.00	30.00	45.00	—
AH1049//13	—	16.00	22.00	30.00	45.00	—
AH1050//13	—	16.00	22.00	30.00	45.00	—
AH1050//14	—	16.00	22.00	30.00	45.00	—
AH1051//14	—	16.00	22.00	30.00	45.00	—
AH1051//15	—	16.00	22.00	30.00	45.00	—
AH1052//15	—	16.00	22.00	30.00	45.00	—
AH1052//16	—	16.00	22.00	30.00	45.00	—
AH1053//17	—	16.00	22.00	30.00	45.00	—
AH1054//17	—	16.00	22.00	30.00	45.00	—
AH1054//18	—	16.00	22.00	30.00	45.00	—
AH1055//18	—	16.00	22.00	30.00	45.00	—
AH1055//19	—	16.00	22.00	30.00	45.00	—
AH1056//19	—	16.00	22.00	30.00	45.00	—
AH1056//20	—	16.00	22.00	30.00	45.00	—
AH1057//20	—	16.00	22.00	30.00	45.00	—
AH1057//21	—	16.00	22.00	30.00	45.00	—
AH1058//21	—	16.00	22.00	30.00	45.00	—
AH1058//22	—	16.00	22.00	30.00	45.00	—
AH1059//22	—	16.00	22.00	30.00	45.00	—
AH1059//23	—	16.00	22.00	30.00	45.00	—
AH1060//23	—	16.00	22.00	30.00	45.00	—
AH1061//24	—	16.00	22.00	30.00	45.00	—
AH1060//24	—	16.00	22.00	30.00	45.00	—
AH1061//25	—	16.00	22.00	30.00	45.00	—
AH1062//25	—	16.00	22.00	30.00	45.00	—
AH1062//26	—	16.00	22.00	30.00	45.00	—
AH1063//26	—	16.00	22.00	30.00	45.00	—
AH1063//27	—	16.00	22.00	30.00	45.00	—
AH1064//27	—	16.00	22.00	30.00	45.00	—
AH1064//28	—	16.00	22.00	30.00	45.00	—
AH1065//29	—	16.00	22.00	30.00	45.00	—

Akbarnagar

KM# 235.4 RUPEE (Type 235)

11.4440 g., Silver **Obv:** Central inscription within square, knots at corners **Rev:** Central inscription within square, knots at corners

Date	Mintage	VG	F	VF	XF	Unc
AH1044//7	—	16.00	22.00	35.00	52.50	—
AH1044//8	—	16.00	22.00	35.00	52.50	—
AH1045//8	—	16.00	22.00	35.00	52.50	—
AH1045//9	—	16.00	22.00	35.00	52.50	—
AH1046//9	—	16.00	22.00	35.00	52.50	—
AH1046//10	—	16.00	22.00	35.00	52.50	—
AH1047//10	—	16.00	22.00	35.00	52.50	—
AH1047//11	—	16.00	22.00	35.00	52.50	—
AH1048//11	—	16.00	22.00	35.00	52.50	—
AH1048//12	—	16.00	22.00	35.00	52.50	—
AH1049//12	—	16.00	22.00	35.00	52.50	—
AH1049//13	—	16.00	22.00	35.00	52.50	—
AH1050//13	—	16.00	22.00	35.00	52.50	—
AH1050//14	—	16.00	22.00	35.00	52.50	—
AH1051//14	—	16.00	22.00	35.00	52.50	—
AH1051//15	—	16.00	22.00	35.00	52.50	—
AH1052//15	—	16.00	22.00	35.00	52.50	—
AH1052//16	—	16.00	22.00	35.00	52.50	—
AH1055//19	—	16.00	22.00	35.00	52.50	—
AH1056//19	—	16.00	22.00	35.00	52.50	—
AH1056//20	—	16.00	22.00	35.00	52.50	—
AH1057//20	—	16.00	22.00	35.00	52.50	—
AH1057//21	—	16.00	22.00	35.00	52.50	—
AH1058//21	—	16.00	22.00	35.00	52.50	—
AH1058//22	—	16.00	22.00	35.00	52.50	—
AH1059//22	—	16.00	22.00	35.00	52.50	—
AH1059//23	—	16.00	22.00	35.00	52.50	—
AH1060//23	—	16.00	22.00	35.00	52.50	—
AH1060//24	—	16.00	22.00	35.00	52.50	—
AH1062//26	—	16.00	22.00	35.00	52.50	—
AH1063//26	—	16.00	22.00	35.00	52.50	—
AH1063//27	—	16.00	22.00	35.00	52.50	—
AH1064//27	—	16.00	22.00	35.00	52.50	—
AH1064//28	—	16.00	22.00	35.00	52.50	—
AH1065//28	—	16.00	22.00	35.00	52.50	—
AH1065//29	—	16.00	22.00	35.00	52.50	—
AH1066//29	—	16.00	22.00	35.00	52.50	—
AH1066//30	—	16.00	22.00	35.00	52.50	—
AH1067//30	—	16.00	22.00	35.00	52.50	—
AH1067//31	—	16.00	22.00	35.00	52.50	—
AH1068//31	—	16.00	22.00	35.00	52.50	—
AH1068//32	—	16.00	22.00	35.00	52.50	—

Allahabad

KM# 235.5 RUPEE (Type 235)

11.4440 g., Silver **Obv:** Central inscription within square, knots at corners **Rev:** Central inscription within square, knots at corners

Date	Mintage	VG	F	VF	XF	Unc
AH1042//6	—	16.00	22.00	35.00	52.50	—
AH1043//6	—	16.00	22.00	35.00	52.50	—
AH1043//7	—	16.00	22.00	35.00	52.50	—
AH1044//7	—	16.00	22.00	35.00	52.50	—
AH1045//8	—	16.00	22.00	35.00	52.50	—
AH1045//9	—	16.00	22.00	35.00	52.50	—
AH1046//10	—	16.00	22.00	35.00	52.50	—
AH1047//10	—	16.00	22.00	35.00	52.50	—
AH1048//12	—	16.00	22.00	35.00	52.50	—
AH1049//12	—	16.00	22.00	35.00	52.50	—
AH1050//14	—	16.00	22.00	35.00	52.50	—
AH0151//14(error for 1051)	—	16.00	22.00	35.00	52.50	—
AH1051//14	—	16.00	22.00	35.00	52.50	—
AH1051//15	—	16.00	22.00	35.00	52.50	—
AH1052//15	—	16.00	22.00	35.00	52.50	—
AH1052//16	—	16.00	22.00	35.00	52.50	—
AH1054//17	—	16.00	22.00	35.00	52.50	—
AH1054//18	—	16.00	22.00	35.00	52.50	—
AH1057//20	—	16.00	22.00	35.00	52.50	—
AH1062//26	—	16.00	22.00	35.00	52.50	—

Aurangabad

KM# 235.6 RUPEE (Type 235)

11.4440 g., Silver **Obv:** Central inscription within square, knots at corners **Rev:** Central inscription within square, knots at corners

Date	Mintage	VG	F	VF	XF	Unc
AH104x//12	—	110	180	300	450	—

Aurangnagar

KM# 235.30 RUPEE (Type 235)

11.4440 g., Silver **Obv:** Central inscription within square, knots at corners **Rev:** Central inscription within square, knots at corners

Date	Mintage	VG	F	VF	XF	Unc
AH1048//xx	—	110	180	300	450	—

Ausa

KM# 235.31 RUPEE (Type 235)

11.4440 g., Silver **Obv:** Central inscription within square, knots at corners **Rev:** Central inscription within square, knots at corners

Date	Mintage	VG	F	VF	XF	Unc
AHxxxx//11	—	125	210	350	460	—

Balkh

KM# 235.29 RUPEE (Type 235)

11.4440 g., Silver **Obv:** Central inscription within square, knots at corners **Rev:** Central inscription within square, knots in corners **Shape:** Square

Date	Mintage	VG	F	VF	XF	Unc
ND(ca.1056-57)	—	270	450	750	1,125	—

Bhakkar

KM# 235.7 RUPEE (Type 235)

11.4440 g., Silver **Obv:** Central inscription within square, knots at corners **Rev:** Central inscription within square, knots at corners

Date	Mintage	VG	F	VF	XF	Unc
AH1043//7	—	16.00	24.00	40.00	60.00	—
AH1044//7	—	16.00	24.00	40.00	60.00	—
AH1044//8	—	16.00	24.00	40.00	60.00	—
AH1045//9	—	16.00	24.00	40.00	60.00	—
AH1046//9	—	16.00	24.00	40.00	60.00	—
AH104x//10	—	16.00	24.00	40.00	60.00	—
AH1047//11	—	16.00	24.00	40.00	60.00	—
AH1048//12	—	16.00	24.00	40.00	60.00	—
AH10xx//13	—	16.00	24.00	40.00	60.00	—
AH1050//14	—	16.00	24.00	40.00	60.00	—
AH1052//15	—	16.00	24.00	40.00	60.00	—
AH1052//16	—	16.00	24.00	40.00	60.00	—
AH1053//17	—	16.00	24.00	40.00	60.00	—
AH1054//17	—	16.00	4.00	40.00	60.00	—
AH105x//18	—	16.00	24.00	40.00	60.00	—
AH1056//20	—	16.00	24.00	40.00	60.00	—
AH1057//20	—	16.00	24.00	40.00	60.00	—
AH1057//21	—	16.00	24.00	40.00	60.00	—
AH1058//21	—	16.00	24.00	40.00	60.00	—
AH1058//22	—	16.00	24.00	40.00	60.00	—
AH1059/22	—	16.00	24.00	40.00	60.00	—
AH1059//23	—	16.00	24.00	40.00	60.00	—
AH1060//24	—	16.00	24.00	40.00	60.00	—
AH1061//25	—	16.00	24.00	40.00	60.00	—
AH1062//25	—	16.00	24.00	40.00	60.00	—
AH1062//26	—	16.00	24.00	40.00	60.00	—
AH1063//26	—	16.00	24.00	40.00	60.00	—
AH1065//29	—	16.00	24.00	40.00	60.00	—
AH1066//29	—	16.00	24.00	40.00	60.00	—
AH1066//30	—	16.00	24.00	40.00	60.00	—
AH1067//30	—	16.00	24.00	40.00	60.00	—
AH1067//31	—	16.00	24.00	40.00	60.00	—
AH1068//31	—	16.00	24.00	40.00	60.00	—
AH1068//32	—	16.00	24.00	40.00	60.00	—

Bhilsa

KM# 235.8 RUPEE (Type 235)

11.4440 g., Silver **Obv:** Central inscription within square, knots at corners **Rev:** Central inscription within square, knots at corners

Date	Mintage	VG	F	VF	XF	Unc
AH104x//12	—	16.00	24.00	45.00	62.50	—
AH1049//13	—	16.00	24.00	45.00	62.50	—
AH1049//14(sic)	—	16.00	24.00	45.00	62.50	—
AH1051//14	—	16.00	24.00	45.00	62.50	—
AH1051//15	—	16.00	24.00	45.00	62.50	—
AH1052//15	—	16.00	24.00	45.00	62.50	—
AH105x//16	—	16.00	24.00	45.00	62.50	—
AH1054//xx	—	16.00	24.00	45.00	62.50	—
AH105x//18	—	16.00	24.00	45.00	62.50	—
AH1055//19	—	16.00	24.00	45.00	62.50	—
AH1056//19	—	16.00	24.00	45.00	62.50	—
AH1056/20	—	16.00	24.00	45.00	62.50	—
AH1057//20	—	16.00	24.00	45.00	62.50	—
AH1057//21	—	16.00	24.00	45.00	62.50	—
AH1058//21	—	16.00	24.00	45.00	62.50	—
AH1058//22	—	16.00	24.00	45.00	62.50	—
AH1059//22	—	16.00	24.00	45.00	62.50	—

Date	Mintage	VG	F	VF	XF	Unc
AH1059//23	—	16.00	24.00	45.00	62.50	—
AH1060//23	—	16.00	24.00	45.00	62.50	—
AH1061//25	—	16.00	24.00	45.00	62.50	—
AH1062//26	—	16.00	24.00	45.00	62.50	—
AH1063//26	—	16.00	24.00	45.00	62.50	—
AH1063//27	—	16.00	24.00	45.00	62.50	—
AH1064//27	—	16.00	24.00	45.00	62.50	—
AH1064//28	—	16.00	24.00	45.00	62.50	—
AH1065//28	—	16.00	24.00	45.00	62.50	—
AH1065//29	—	16.00	24.00	45.00	62.50	—
AH1066//29	—	16.00	24.00	45.00	62.50	—

Burhanpur

KM# 235.33 RUPEE (Type 235)

11.4440 g., Silver **Obv:** Central inscription within square **Obv. Legend:** Khallada Allah Mulkahu **Rev:** Central inscription within square

Date	Mintage	VG	F	VF	XF	Unc
AH1040//3	—	18.00	30.00	50.00	75.00	—
AH1040//4	—	18.00	30.00	50.00	75.00	—
AH1042//5	—	18.00	30.00	50.00	75.00	—
AH10xx//5	—	18.00	30.00	50.00	75.00	—

Burhanpur

KM# 235.36 RUPEE (Type 235)

11.4440 g., Silver **Obv:** Legend at left **Obv. Legend:** "May God preserve the kingdom"

Date	Mintage	Good	VG	F	VF	XF
AH1040//3	—	—	—	—	—	—
AH1040//4	—	—	—	—	—	—
AH1042//5	—	—	—	—	—	—

Burhanpur

KM# 235.9 RUPEE (Type 235)

11.4440 g., Silver **Obv:** Central inscription within square, knots at corners **Rev:** Central inscription within square, knots at corners

Date	Mintage	VG	F	VF	XF	Unc
AH1042//5	—	16.00	20.00	25.00	37.50	—
AH1043//6	—	16.00	20.00	25.00	37.50	—
AH1043//7	—	16.00	20.00	25.00	37.50	—
AH1044//7	—	16.00	20.00	25.00	37.50	—
AH1044//8	—	16.00	20.00	25.00	37.50	—
AH1045//8	—	16.00	20.00	25.00	37.50	—
AH1045//9	—	16.00	20.00	25.00	37.50	—
AH1046//9	—	16.00	20.00	25.00	37.50	—
AH1046//10	—	16.00	20.00	25.00	37.50	—
AH1047//10	—	16.00	20.00	25.00	37.50	—
AH1047//11	—	16.00	20.00	25.00	37.50	—
AH1648//11	—	16.00	20.00	25.00	37.50	—
AH1048//12	—	16.00	20.00	25.00	37.50	—
AH1049//1x	—	16.00	20.00	25.00	37.50	—
AH1051//1x	—	16.00	20.00	25.00	37.50	—
AH1052//1x	—	16.00	20.00	25.00	37.50	—
AH1053//xx	—	16.00	20.00	25.00	37.50	—
AH1054//1x	—	16.00	20.00	25.00	37.50	—
AH1055//xx	—	16.00	20.00	25.00	37.50	—
AH1056//xx	—	16.00	20.00	25.00	37.50	—
AH1060//24	—	16.00	20.00	25.00	37.50	—
AH1061//24	—	16.00	20.00	25.00	37.50	—
AH1061//25	—	16.00	20.00	25.00	37.50	—
AH1064//2x	—	16.00	20.00	25.00	37.50	—
AH1068//31	—	16.00	20.00	25.00	37.50	—
AH1068//32	—	16.00	20.00	25.00	37.50	—

Daulatabad

KM# 235.10 RUPEE (Type 235)

11.4440 g., Silver **Obv:** Central inscription within square, knots at corners **Rev:** Central inscription within square, knots at corners

Date	Mintage	VG	F	VF	XF	Unc
AH1043//x	—	16.00	22.00	30.00	45.00	—
AH1045//x	—	16.00	22.00	30.00	45.00	—
AH1047//x	—	16.00	22.00	30.00	45.00	—
AH1050//14	—	16.00	22.00	30.00	45.00	—
AH1053//1x	—	16.00	22.00	30.00	45.00	—
AH1054//17	—	16.00	22.00	30.00	45.00	—
AH1054//18	—	16.00	22.00	30.00	45.00	—
AH1055//18	—	16.00	22.00	30.00	45.00	—
AH1055//19	—	16.00	22.00	30.00	45.00	—
AH1056//19	—	16.00	22.00	30.00	45.00	—
AH1056//20	—	16.00	22.00	30.00	45.00	—

Date	Mintage	VG	F	VF	XF	Unc
AH1057//20	—	16.00	22.00	30.00	45.00	—
AH1057//21	—	16.00	22.00	30.00	45.00	—
AH1058//21	—	16.00	22.00	30.00	45.00	—
AH1058//22	—	16.00	22.00	30.00	45.00	—
AH1059//22	—	16.00	22.00	30.00	45.00	—
AH1059//23	—	16.00	22.00	30.00	45.00	—
AH1060//23	—	16.00	22.00	30.00	45.00	—
AH1060//24	—	16.00	22.00	30.00	45.00	—
AH1061//24	—	16.00	22.00	30.00	45.00	—
AH1061//25	—	16.00	22.00	30.00	45.00	—
AH1062//25	—	16.00	22.00	30.00	45.00	—
AH1062//26	—	16.00	22.00	30.00	45.00	—
AH1063//27	—	16.00	22.00	30.00	45.00	—
AH1064//27	—	16.00	22.00	30.00	45.00	—
AH1064//28	—	16.00	22.00	30.00	45.00	—
AH1065//28	—	16.00	22.00	30.00	45.00	—
AH1065//29	—	16.00	22.00	30.00	45.00	—
AH1066//29	—	16.00	22.00	30.00	45.00	—
AH1066//30	—	16.00	22.00	30.00	45.00	—
AH1067//30	—	16.00	22.00	30.00	45.00	—
AH1067//31	—	16.00	22.00	30.00	45.00	—

Golkonda

KM# 235.34 RUPEE (Type 235)

11.4440 g., Silver **Obv:** Central inscription within square, knots at corners **Rev:** Central inscription within square, knots at corners

Date	Mintage	VG	F	VF	XF	Unc
AH1045//9	—	125	210	350	525	—

Jahangirnagar

KM# 235.11 RUPEE (Type 235)

11.4440 g., Silver **Obv:** Central inscription within square, knots at corners **Rev:** Central inscription within square, knots at corners

Date	Mintage	VG	F	VF	XF	Unc
AH1043//7	—	18.00	30.00	50.00	75.00	—
AH1044//7	—	18.00	30.00	50.00	75.00	—
AH1044//8	—	18.00	30.00	50.00	75.00	—
AH1045//9	—	18.00	30.00	50.00	75.00	—
AH1046//9	—	18.00	30.00	50.00	75.00	—
AH1046//10	—	18.00	30.00	50.00	75.00	—
AH1047//10	—	18.00	30.00	50.00	75.00	—
AH1047//11	—	18.00	30.00	50.00	75.00	—
AH1048//11	—	18.00	30.00	50.00	75.00	—
AH1048//12	—	18.00	30.00	50.00	75.00	—
AH1049//12	—	18.00	30.00	50.00	75.00	—
AH1049//13	—	18.00	30.00	50.00	75.00	—
AH1051//14	—	18.00	30.00	50.00	75.00	—
AH1051//15	—	18.00	30.00	50.00	75.00	—
AH1052//15	—	18.00	30.00	50.00	75.00	—
AH1052//16	—	18.00	30.00	50.00	75.00	—
AH1054//1x	—	18.00	30.00	50.00	75.00	—
AH106x//31	—	18.00	30.00	50.00	75.00	—

Junagadh

KM# 235.12 RUPEE (Type 235)

11.4440 g., Silver **Obv:** Central inscription within square, knots at corners **Rev:** Central inscription within square, knots at corners

Date	Mintage	VG	F	VF	XF	Unc
AH1045//8	—	16.00	25.00	40.00	60.00	—
AH1047//1x	—	16.00	25.00	40.00	60.00	—
AH1049//12	—	16.00	25.00	40.00	60.00	—
AH1049//13	—	16.00	25.00	40.00	60.00	—
AH1050//14	—	16.00	25.00	40.00	60.00	—
AH1051//14	—	16.00	25.00	40.00	60.00	—
AH1051//15	—	16.00	25.00	40.00	60.00	—
AH1052//15	—	16.00	25.00	40.00	60.00	—
AH1052//16	—	16.00	25.00	40.00	60.00	—
AH1053//16	—	16.00	25.00	40.00	60.00	—
AH1053//17	—	16.00	25.00	40.00	60.00	—
AH1054//17	—	16.00	25.00	40.00	60.00	—
AH1054//18	—	16.00	25.00	40.00	60.00	—
AH1055//18	—	16.00	25.00	40.00	60.00	—
AH1055//19	—	16.00	25.00	40.00	60.00	—
AH1056//19	—	16.00	25.00	40.00	60.00	—
AH1056//20	—	16.00	25.00	40.00	60.00	—
AH1057//2x	—	16.00	25.00	40.00	60.00	—
AH1059//2x	—	16.00	25.00	40.00	60.00	—
AH1060//23	—	16.00	25.00	40.00	60.00	—
AH1060//24	—	16.00	25.00	40.00	60.00	—
AH1061//24	—	16.00	25.00	40.00	60.00	—
AH1061//25	—	16.00	25.00	40.00	60.00	—
AH1062//25	—	16.00	25.00	40.00	60.00	—
AH1062//26	—	16.00	25.00	40.00	60.00	—
AH1063//26	—	16.00	25.00	40.00	60.00	—
AH1063//27	—	16.00	25.00	40.00	60.00	—
AH1064//27	—	16.00	25.00	40.00	60.00	—
AH1064//28	—	16.00	25.00	40.00	60.00	—
AH1065//28	—	16.00	25.00	40.00	60.00	—
AH1065//29	—	16.00	25.00	40.00	60.00	—
AH1066//29	—	16.00	25.00	40.00	60.00	—

Date	Mintage	VG	F	VF	XF	Unc
AH1066//30	—	16.00	25.00	40.00	60.00	—
AH1067//30	—	16.00	25.00	40.00	60.00	—
AH1067//31	—	16.00	25.00	40.00	60.00	—
AH1068//31	—	16.00	25.00	40.00	60.00	—
AH1068//32	—	16.00	25.00	40.00	60.00	—
AH1069//3x	—	16.00	25.00	40.00	60.00	—

Kabul

KM# 235.13 RUPEE (Type 235)

11.4440 g., Silver **Obv:** Central inscription within square, knots at corners **Rev:** Central inscription within square, knots at corners

Date	Mintage	VG	F	VF	XF	Unc
AH1047//10	—	27.00	45.00	75.00	115	—
AH1047//11	—	27.00	45.00	75.00	115	—
AH1048//11	—	27.00	45.00	75.00	115	—
AH10xx//14	—	27.00	45.00	75.00	115	—
AH1052//16	—	27.00	45.00	75.00	115	—
AH1053//16	—	27.00	45.00	75.00	115	—
AH1053//17	—	27.00	45.00	75.00	115	—
AH1054//17	—	27.00	45.00	75.00	115	—
AH1062//25	—	27.00	45.00	75.00	115	—
AH1065//28	—	27.00	45.00	75.00	115	—
AH1067//30	—	27.00	45.00	75.00	115	—

Kalpi

KM# 235.35 RUPEE (Type 235)

11.4440 g., Silver **Obv:** Central inscription in square, knots at corners **Rev:** Central inscription in square, knots at corners

Date	Mintage	VG	F	VF	XF	Unc
AHxxxx//27	—	110	180	300	450	—

Kashmir

KM# 235.14 RUPEE (Type 235)

11.4440 g., Silver **Obv:** Central inscription within square, knots at corners **Rev:** Central inscription within square, knots at corners

Date	Mintage	VG	F	VF	XF	Unc
AH104x//12	—	29.00	48.00	80.00	120	—
AH1051//14	—	29.00	48.00	80.00	120	—
AH1052//15	—	29.00	48.00	80.00	120	—
AH1052//16	—	29.00	48.00	80.00	120	—
AH1053//16	—	29.00	48.00	80.00	120	—
AH105x//17	—	29.00	48.00	80.00	120	—
AH1055//18	—	29.00	48.00	80.00	120	—
AH1057//21	—	29.00	48.00	80.00	120	—
AH1059//2x	—	29.00	48.00	80.00	120	—
AH1065//2x	—	29.00	48.00	80.00	120	—

Katak

KM# 235.15 RUPEE (Type 235)

11.4440 g., Silver **Obv:** Central inscription within square, knots at corners **Rev:** Central inscription within square, knots at corners

Date	Mintage	VG	F	VF	XF	Unc
AH10xx//13	—	18.00	30.00	50.00	75.00	—
AH105x//14	—	18.00	30.00	50.00	75.00	—
AH1052//1x	—	18.00	30.00	50.00	75.00	—
AH1054//18	—	18.00	30.00	50.00	75.00	—
AH105x//81(sic)	—	18.00	30.00	50.00	75.00	—
AH10xx//22	—	18.00	30.00	50.00	75.00	—
AH10xx//23	—	18.00	30.00	50.00	75.00	—
AH1062//26	—	18.00	30.00	50.00	75.00	—
AH1064//27	—	18.00	30.00	50.00	75.00	—
AH1064//28	—	18.00	30.00	50.00	75.00	—
AH1065//28	—	18.00	30.00	50.00	75.00	—
AH1065//29	—	18.00	30.00	50.00	75.00	—
AH1066//29	—	18.00	30.00	50.00	75.00	—
AH1066//30	—	18.00	30.00	50.00	75.00	—
AH1067//30	—	18.00	30.00	50.00	75.00	—
AH1067//31	—	18.00	30.00	50.00	75.00	—
AH1068//31	—	18.00	30.00	50.00	75.00	—
AH1068//32	—	18.00	30.00	50.00	75.00	—
AH1069//32	—	18.00	30.00	50.00	75.00	—

Khambayat

KM# 235.16 RUPEE (Type 235)

11.4440 g., Silver **Obv:** Central inscription within square, knots at corners **Rev:** Central inscription within square, knots at corners

Date	Mintage	VG	F	VF	XF	Unc
AH104x//8	—	16.00	22.00	30.00	45.00	—
AH1046/10	—	16.00	22.00	30.00	45.00	—
AH1057//20	—	16.00	22.00	30.00	45.00	—
AH1057//12(sic)	—	16.00	22.00	30.00	45.00	—
AH1058//20	—	16.00	22.00	30.00	45.00	—
AH105x//21	—	16.00	22.00	30.00	45.00	—
AH10xx//23	—	16.00	22.00	30.00	45.00	—
AH1060//2x	—	16.00	22.00	30.00	45.00	—
AH1061//24	—	16.00	22.00	30.00	45.00	—
AH1061//25	—	16.00	22.00	30.00	45.00	—
AH1062//25	—	16.00	22.00	30.00	45.00	—
AH1062//26	—	16.00	22.00	30.00	45.00	—
AH1063//26	—	16.00	22.00	30.00	45.00	—
AH1063//27	—	16.00	22.00	30.00	45.00	—
AH1064//27	—	16.00	22.00	30.00	45.00	—
AH1064//28	—	16.00	22.00	30.00	45.00	—
AH1065//28	—	16.00	22.00	30.00	45.00	—
AH1065//29	—	16.00	22.00	30.00	45.00	—
AH1067//3x	—	16.00	22.00	30.00	45.00	—
AH1068//31	—	16.00	22.00	30.00	45.00	—
AH1068//32	—	16.00	22.00	30.00	45.00	—
AH1069//32	—	16.00	22.00	30.00	45.00	—

Lahore

KM# 235.17 RUPEE (Type 235)

11.4440 g., Silver **Obv:** Central inscription within square, knots at corners **Rev:** Central inscription within square, knots at corners

Date	Mintage	VG	F	VF	XF	Unc
AH1042//6	—	16.00	22.00	30.00	45.00	—
AH1043//6	—	16.00	22.00	30.00	45.00	—
AH1043//7	—	16.00	22.00	30.00	45.00	—
AH1044//7	—	16.00	22.00	30.00	45.00	—
AH1044//8	—	16.00	22.00	30.00	45.00	—
AH1045//8	—	16.00	22.00	30.00	45.00	—
AH1045//9	—	16.00	22.00	30.00	45.00	—
AH1046//9	—	16.00	22.00	30.00	45.00	—
AH1046//10	—	16.00	22.00	30.00	45.00	—
AH1047//10	—	16.00	22.00	30.00	45.00	—
AH1047//11	—	16.00	22.00	30.00	45.00	—
AH1048//11	—	16.00	22.00	30.00	45.00	—
AH1048//12	—	16.00	22.00	30.00	45.00	—
AH1049//12	—	16.00	22.00	30.00	45.00	—
AH1049//13	—	16.00	22.00	30.00	45.00	—
AH1050//13	—	16.00	22.00	30.00	45.00	—
AH1050//14	—	16.00	22.00	30.00	45.00	—
AH1051//14	—	16.00	22.00	30.00	45.00	—
AH1051//15	—	16.00	22.00	30.00	45.00	—
AH1052//15	—	16.00	22.00	30.00	45.00	—
AH1052//16	—	16.00	22.00	30.00	45.00	—
AH1053//16	—	16.00	22.00	30.00	45.00	—
AH1053//17	—	16.00	22.00	30.00	45.00	—
AH1054//17	—	16.00	22.00	30.00	45.00	—
AH1054//18	—	16.00	22.00	30.00	45.00	—
AH1055//18	—	16.00	22.00	30.00	45.00	—
AH1055//19	—	16.00	22.00	30.00	45.00	—
AH1056//19	—	16.00	22.00	30.00	45.00	—
AH1056//20	—	16.00	22.00	30.00	45.00	—
AH1057//20	—	16.00	22.00	30.00	45.00	—
AH1057//21	—	16.00	22.00	30.00	45.00	—
AH1058//21	—	16.00	22.00	30.00	45.00	—
AH1058//22	—	16.00	22.00	30.00	45.00	—
AH1059//22	—	16.00	22.00	30.00	45.00	—
AH1059//23	—	16.00	22.00	30.00	45.00	—
AH1060//23	—	16.00	22.00	30.00	45.00	—
AH1060//24	—	16.00	22.00	30.00	45.00	—
AH1061//24	—	16.00	22.00	30.00	45.00	—
AH1061//25	—	16.00	22.00	30.00	45.00	—
AH1062//25	—	16.00	22.00	30.00	45.00	—
AH1062//26	—	16.00	22.00	30.00	45.00	—
AH1063//26	—	16.00	22.00	30.00	45.00	—
AH1063//27	—	16.00	22.00	30.00	45.00	—
AH1064//27	—	16.00	22.00	30.00	45.00	—
AH1064//28	—	16.00	22.00	30.00	45.00	—
AH1065//28	—	16.00	22.00	30.00	45.00	—
AH1065//29	—	16.00	22.00	30.00	45.00	—
AH1066//29	—	16.00	22.00	30.00	45.00	—
AH1066//30	—	16.00	22.00	30.00	45.00	—
AH1067//30	—	16.00	22.00	30.00	45.00	—
AH1067//31	—	16.00	22.00	30.00	45.00	—
AH1068//31	—	16.00	22.00	30.00	45.00	—
AH1068//32	—	16.00	22.00	30.00	45.00	—
AH1069//32	—	16.00	22.00	30.00	45.00	—
AH1069//33	—	16.00	22.00	30.00	45.00	—

Lakhnau

KM# 235.18 RUPEE (Type 235)

11.4440 g., Silver **Obv:** Central inscription within square, knots at corners **Rev:** Central inscription within square, knots at corners

Date	Mintage	VG	F	VF	XF	Unc
AH1045//x	—	21.00	36.00	60.00	90.00	—
AH1049//11(sic)	—	21.00	36.00	60.00	90.00	—
AH10xx//13	—	21.00	36.00	60.00	90.00	—
AH1050//14	—	21.00	36.00	60.00	90.00	—
AH1055//19	—	21.00	36.00	60.00	90.00	—
AH1056//19	—	21.00	36.00	60.00	90.00	—
AH1065//29	—	21.00	36.00	60.00	90.00	—
AH1068//31	—	21.00	36.00	60.00	90.00	—

Multan

KM# 235.19 RUPEE (Type 235)

11.4440 g., Silver **Obv:** Central inscription within square, knots at corners **Rev:** Central inscription within square, knots at corners

Date	Mintage	VG	F	VF	XF	Unc
AH1042//5	—	16.00	18.00	22.00	33.00	—
AH1042//6	—	16.00	18.00	22.00	33.00	—
AH1043//6	—	16.00	18.00	22.00	33.00	—
AH1043//7	—	16.00	18.00	22.00	33.00	—
AH1044//7	—	16.00	18.00	22.00	33.00	—
AH1044//8	—	16.00	18.00	22.00	33.00	—
AH1045//8	—	16.00	18.00	22.00	33.00	—
AH1045//9	—	16.00	18.00	22.00	33.00	—
AH1046//9	—	16.00	18.00	22.00	33.00	—
AH1046//10	—	16.00	18.00	22.00	33.00	—
AH1047//10	—	16.00	18.00	22.00	33.00	—
AH1047//11	—	16.00	18.00	22.00	33.00	—
AH1048//11	—	16.00	18.00	22.00	33.00	—
AH1048//12	—	16.00	18.00	22.00	33.00	—
AH1049//12	—	16.00	18.00	22.00	33.00	—
AH1049//13	—	16.00	18.00	22.00	33.00	—
AH1050//13	—	16.00	18.00	22.00	33.00	—
AH1050//14	—	16.00	18.00	22.00	33.00	—
AH1051//14	—	16.00	18.00	22.00	33.00	—
AH1051//15	—	16.00	18.00	22.00	33.00	—
AH1052//15	—	16.00	18.00	22.00	33.00	—
AH1052//16	—	16.00	18.00	22.00	33.00	—
AH1653//16	—	16.00	18.00	22.00	33.00	—
AH1053//17	—	16.00	18.00	22.00	33.00	—
AH1054//17	—	16.00	18.00	22.00	33.00	—
AH1054//18	—	16.00	18.00	22.00	33.00	—
AH1055//18	—	16.00	18.00	22.00	33.00	—
AH1055//19	—	16.00	18.00	22.00	33.00	—
AH1056//19	—	16.00	18.00	22.00	33.00	—
AH1056//20	—	16.00	18.00	22.00	33.00	—
AH1057//20	—	16.00	18.00	22.00	33.00	—
AH1057//21	—	16.00	18.00	22.00	33.00	—
AH1058//21	—	16.00	18.00	22.00	33.00	—
AH1058//22	—	16.00	18.00	22.00	33.00	—
AH1059//22	—	16.00	18.00	22.00	33.00	—
AH1059//23	—	16.00	18.00	22.00	33.00	—
AH1060//23	—	16.00	18.00	22.00	33.00	—
AH1060//24	—	16.00	18.00	22.00	33.00	—
AH1061//24	—	16.00	18.00	22.00	33.00	—
AH1061//25	—	16.00	18.00	22.00	33.00	—
AH1062//25	—	16.00	18.00	22.00	33.00	—
AH1062//26	—	16.00	18.00	22.00	33.00	—
AH1063//26	—	16.00	18.00	22.00	33.00	—
AH1063//27	—	16.00	18.00	22.00	33.00	—
AH1064//27	—	16.00	18.00	22.00	33.00	—
AH1064//28	—	16.00	18.00	22.00	33.00	—
AH1065//28	—	16.00	18.00	22.00	33.00	—
AH1065//29	—	16.00	18.00	22.00	33.00	—
AH1066//29	—	16.00	18.00	22.00	33.00	—
AH1066//30	—	16.00	18.00	22.00	33.00	—
AH1067//30	—	16.00	18.00	22.00	33.00	—
AH1067//31	—	16.00	18.00	22.00	33.00	—
AH1068//31	—	16.00	18.00	22.00	33.00	—
AH1068//32	—	16.00	18.00	22.00	33.00	—
AH1069//32	—	16.00	18.00	22.00	33.00	—
AH1069//33	—	16.00	18.00	22.00	33.00	—

Patna

KM# 235.20 RUPEE (Type 235)

11.4440 g., Silver **Obv:** Central inscription within square, knots at corners **Rev:** Central inscription within square, knots at corners

Date	Mintage	VG	F	VF	XF	Unc
AH1042//5	—	16.00	20.00	25.00	37.50	—
AH1042//6	—	16.00	20.00	25.00	37.50	—
AH1043//6	—	16.00	20.00	25.00	37.50	—
AH1043//7	—	16.00	20.00	25.00	37.50	—
AH1044//7	—	16.00	20.00	25.00	37.50	—
AH1044//8	—	16.00	20.00	25.00	37.50	—
AH1045//8	—	16.00	20.00	25.00	37.50	—
AH1045//9	—	16.00	20.00	25.00	37.50	—
AH1046//9	—	16.00	20.00	25.00	37.50	—
AH1046//10	—	16.00	20.00	25.00	37.50	—
AH1047//10	—	16.00	20.00	25.00	37.50	—
AH1047//11	—	16.00	20.00	25.00	37.50	—
AH1048//11	—	16.00	20.00	25.00	37.50	—
AH1048//12	—	16.00	20.00	25.00	37.50	—
AH1049//12	—	16.00	20.00	25.00	37.50	—
AH1049//13	—	16.00	20.00	25.00	37.50	—
AH1050//13	—	16.00	20.00	25.00	37.50	—
AH1050//14	—	16.00	20.00	25.00	37.50	—
AH1051//14	—	16.00	20.00	25.00	37.50	—
AH105x//15	—	16.00	20.00	25.00	37.50	—
AH1053//16	—	16.00	20.00	25.00	37.50	—
AH105x//17	—	16.00	20.00	25.00	37.50	—
AH1055//18	—	16.00	20.00	25.00	37.50	—
AH105x//19	—	16.00	20.00	25.00	37.50	—
AH105x//20	—	16.00	20.00	25.00	37.50	—
AH105x//21	—	16.00	20.00	25.00	37.50	—
AH105x//22	—	16.00	20.00	25.00	37.50	—
AH10xx//23	—	16.00	20.00	25.00	37.50	—
AH1061//24	—	16.00	20.00	25.00	37.50	—
AH106x//25	—	16.00	20.00	25.00	37.50	—
AH106x//26	—	16.00	20.00	25.00	37.50	—
AH1063//27	—	16.00	20.00	25.00	37.50	—
AH1064//27	—	16.00	20.00	25.00	37.50	—
AH1064//28	—	16.00	20.00	25.00	37.50	—
AH1065//29	—	16.00	20.00	25.00	37.50	—
AH1066//29	—	16.00	20.00	25.00	37.50	—
AH1066//30	—	16.00	20.00	25.00	37.50	—
AH1067//30	—	16.00	20.00	25.00	37.50	—
AH1067//31	—	16.00	20.00	25.00	37.50	—
AH1068//31	—	16.00	20.00	25.00	37.50	—
AH1068//32	—	16.00	20.00	25.00	37.50	—
AH1069//32	—	16.00	20.00	25.00	37.50	—
AH1069//33	—	16.00	20.00	25.00	37.50	—

Pattan Deo

KM# 235.21 RUPEE (Type 235)

11.4440 g., Silver **Obv:** Central inscription within square, knots at corners **Rev:** Central inscription within square, knots at corners

Date	Mintage	VG	F	VF	XF	Unc
AH1047//10	—	90.00	150	250	375	—

Qandahar

KM# 235.22 RUPEE (Type 235)

11.4440 g., Silver **Obv:** Central inscription within square, knots at corners **Rev:** Central inscription within square, knots at corners

Date	Mintage	VG	F	VF	XF	Unc
AH1042//5	—	24.00	40.00	65.00	100	—
AH1044//5	—	24.00	40.00	65.00	100	—
AH1044//8	—	24.00	40.00	65.00	100	—
AH1048//12	—	24.00	40.00	65.00	100	—
AH1049//12	—	24.00	40.00	65.00	100	—
AH1049//13	—	24.00	40.00	65.00	100	—
AH1050//13	—	24.00	40.00	65.00	100	—
AH1050//14	—	24.00	40.00	65.00	100	—
AH1051//14	—	24.00	40.00	65.00	100	—
AH1051//15	—	24.00	40.00	65.00	100	—
AH1052//16	—	24.00	40.00	65.00	100	—
AH1053//16	—	24.00	40.00	65.00	100	—
AH1053//17	—	24.00	40.00	65.00	100	—
AH1054//17	—	24.00	40.00	65.00	100	—
AH1054//18	—	24.00	40.00	65.00	100	—
AH1055//18	—	24.00	40.00	65.00	100	—
AH1055//19	—	24.00	40.00	65.00	100	—
AH1056//19	—	24.00	40.00	65.00	100	—
AH1056//20	—	24.00	40.00	65.00	100	—
AH1056//21 (sic)	—	24.00	40.00	65.00	100	—
AH1057//16 (sic)	—	24.00	40.00	65.00	100	—
AH1057//21	—	24.00	40.00	65.00	100	—
AH1058//21	—	24.00	40.00	65.00	100	—
ND(1628)	—	24.00	40.00	65.00	100	—

Sironj

KM# 235.27 RUPEE (Type 235)
11.4440 g., Silver **Obv:** Central inscription within square, knots at corners **Rev:** Central inscription within square, knots at corners

Date	Mintage	VG	F	VF	XF	Unc
AH1065//2x	—	100	180	300	450	—
AH106x//31	—	100	180	300	450	—

Surat

KM# 235.23 RUPEE (Type 235)
11.4440 g., Silver **Obv:** Central inscription within square, knots at corners **Rev:** Central inscription within square, knots at corners

Date	Mintage	VG	F	VF	XF	Unc
AH1042//6	—	16.00	19.00	22.00	33.00	—
AH1043//6	—	16.00	19.00	22.00	33.00	—
AH1043//7	—	16.00	19.00	22.00	33.00	—
AH1044//7	—	16.00	19.00	22.00	33.00	—
AH1044//8	—	16.00	19.00	22.00	33.00	—
AH1045//8	—	16.00	19.00	22.00	33.00	—
AH1045//9	—	16.00	19.00	22.00	33.00	—
AH1046//9	—	16.00	19.00	22.00	33.00	—
AH1046//10	—	16.00	19.00	22.00	33.00	—
AH1047//10	—	16.00	19.00	22.00	33.00	—
AH1047//11	—	16.00	19.00	22.00	33.00	—
AH1048//11	—	16.00	19.00	22.00	33.00	—
AH1048//12	—	16.00	19.00	22.00	33.00	—
AH1049//12	—	16.00	19.00	22.00	33.00	—
AH1049//13	—	16.00	19.00	22.00	33.00	—
AH1050//13	—	16.00	19.00	22.00	33.00	—
AH1050//14	—	16.00	19.00	22.00	33.00	—
AH1051//14	—	16.00	19.00	22.00	33.00	—
AH1051//15	—	16.00	19.00	22.00	33.00	—
AH1052//15	—	16.00	19.00	22.00	33.00	—
AH1052//16	—	16.00	19.00	22.00	33.00	—
AH1053//16	—	16.00	19.00	22.00	33.00	—
AH1053//17	—	16.00	19.00	22.00	33.00	—
AH1054//17	—	16.00	19.00	22.00	33.00	—
AH1054//18	—	16.00	19.00	22.00	33.00	—
AH1055//18	—	16.00	19.00	22.00	33.00	—
AH1055//19	—	16.00	19.00	22.00	33.00	—
AH1056//19	—	16.00	19.00	22.00	33.00	—
AH1056//20	—	16.00	19.00	22.00	33.00	—
AH1057//20	—	16.00	19.00	22.00	33.00	—
AH1057//21	—	16.00	19.00	22.00	33.00	—
AH1058//21	—	16.00	19.00	22.00	33.00	—
AH1058//12 (error for 22)	—	16.00	19.00	22.00	33.00	—
AH1058//22	—	16.00	19.00	22.00	33.00	—
AH1059//22	—	16.00	19.00	22.00	33.00	—
AH1059//23	—	16.00	19.00	22.00	33.00	—
AH1006//23 (error for 1060)	—	16.00	19.00	22.00	33.00	—
AH1060//23	—	16.00	19.00	22.00	33.00	—
AH1060//24	—	16.00	19.00	22.00	33.00	—
AH1061//24	—	16.00	19.00	22.00	33.00	—
AH1061//25	—	16.00	19.00	22.00	33.00	—
AH1062//25	—	16.00	19.00	22.00	33.00	—
AH1062/26	—	16.00	19.00	22.00	33.00	—
AH1063//26	—	16.00	19.00	22.00	33.00	—
AH1063//27	—	16.00	19.00	22.00	33.00	—
AH1064//27	—	16.00	19.00	22.00	33.00	—
AH1064//28	—	16.00	19.00	22.00	33.00	—
AH1065//28	—	16.00	19.00	22.00	33.00	—
AH1065//29	—	16.00	19.00	22.00	33.00	—
AH1066//29	—	16.00	19.00	22.00	33.00	—
AH1066//30	—	16.00	19.00	22.00	33.00	—
AH1067//30	—	16.00	19.00	22.00	33.00	—
AH1067//31	—	16.00	19.00	22.00	33.00	—
AH1068//31	—	16.00	19.00	22.00	33.00	—
AH1068//32	—	16.00	19.00	22.00	33.00	—
AH1069//32	—	16.00	19.00	22.00	33.00	—

Ujjain

KM# 235.24 RUPEE (Type 235)
11.4440 g., Silver **Obv:** Central inscription within square, knots at corners **Rev:** Central inscription within square, knots at corners

Date	Mintage	VG	F	VF	XF	Unc
AH10xx//3	—	24.00	40.00	65.00	100	—
AH104x//5	—	24.00	40.00	65.00	100	—
AH1013//6 error for 1043	—	27.00	45.00	75.00	110	—
AH1046//x	—	24.00	40.00	65.00	100	—
AH10xx//13	—	24.00	40.00	65.00	100	—

Date	Mintage	VG	F	VF	XF	Unc
AH105x//14	—	24.00	40.00	65.00	100	—
AH1054//18	—	24.00	40.00	65.00	100	—
AH106x//31	—	24.00	40.00	65.00	100	—

Zafarabad

KM# 235.25 RUPEE (Type 235)
11.4440 g., Silver **Obv:** Central inscription within square, knots at corners **Rev:** Central inscription within square, knots at corners

Date	Mintage	VG	F	VF	XF	Unc
AH1067//31	—	29.00	50.00	80.00	120	—
AH1068//31	—	29.00	50.00	80.00	120	—
AH1068//32	—	29.00	50.00	80.00	120	—
AH1069//32	—	29.00	50.00	80.00	120	—

Zafarnagar

KM# 235.26 RUPEE (Type 235)
11.4440 g., Silver **Obv:** Central inscription within square, knots at corners **Rev:** Central inscription within square, knots at corners

Date	Mintage	VG	F	VF	XF	Unc
AH1043//x	—	36.00	60.00	100	150	—
AH1044//x	—	36.00	60.00	100	150	—
AH104x//12	—	36.00	60.00	100	150	—

Ahmadabad

KM# 236.1 RUPEE (Type 236)
Silver **Shape:** Square **Note:** Weight varies: 10.80-11.20 grams.

Date	Mintage	VG	F	VF	XF	Unc
AH104x//6	—	45.00	95.00	150	250	—

Lahore

KM# 236.4 RUPEE (Type 236)
Silver **Shape:** Square **Note:** Weight varies: 10.80-11.20 grams.

Date	Mintage	Good	VG	F	VF	XF
AH1040//4	—	—	45.00	95.00	150	250

Multan

KM# 236.2 RUPEE (Type 236)
Silver **Shape:** Square **Note:** Weight varies: 10.80-11.20 grams.

Date	Mintage	VG	F	VF	XF	Unc
AH1042//6	—	45.00	95.00	150	250	—
AH1047	—	45.00	95.00	150	250	—

Surat

KM# 236.3 RUPEE (Type 236)
11.4440 g., Silver **Shape:** Square

Date	Mintage	VG	F	VF	XF	Unc
AHxxxx//x	—	45.00	95.00	150	240	—

Akbarabad

KM# 249.1 NAZARANA RUPEE (Type 249)
Silver **Note:** Weight varies: 10.15-10.40 grams.

Date	Mintage	VG	F	VF	XF	Unc
AH1054//18	—	—	—	2,500	3,500	—

Agra

KM# 252.1 1/4 MOHUR (Type 252)
Gold **Note:** Weight varies: 2.60-2.75 grams.

Date	Mintage	VG	F	VF	XF	Unc
AH1037//(1) Ahad	—	—	1,050	1,625	2,500	—

Tatta

KM# 253.1 1/2 MOHUR (Type 253)
Gold **Note:** Similar to 1 Rupee, KM#224.18; Weight varies 5.4 - 5.5 grams.

Date	Mintage	VG	F	VF	XF	Unc
AH1039//2	—	—	1,175	1,950	3,000	—

Agra

KM# 254.1 MOHUR (Type 254)
Gold **Obv:** Within dotted borders; Kalima, mint name, AH date **Rev:** Within dotted borders; Emperor's full name and titles **Note:** Weight varies: 10.80-11.00 grams. Mint epithet: "Dar-ul-Khilafat".

Date	Mintage	F	VF	XF	Unc	BU
AH1037//(1) Ahad	—	750	1,000	1,250	—	—
AH1038//(1) Ahad	—	750	1,000	1,250	—	—

Burhanpur

KM# 254.2 MOHUR (Type 254)
Gold **Obv:** Within dotted borders; Kalima, mint name, AH dates **Rev:** Within dotted borders; Emperor's full name and titles **Note:** Weight varies: 10.80-11.00 grams.

Date	Mintage	VG	F	VF	XF	Unc
AH1037//(1) Ahad	—	—	650	720	800	—
AH1038//(1) Ahad	—	—	650	720	800	—
AH1038//2	—	—	650	720	800	—

Gulkanda

KM# 254.3 MOHUR (Type 254)
Gold **Obv:** Within dotted borders; Kalima, mint name, AH dates **Rev:** Within dotted borders; Emperor's full name and titles **Note:** Weight varies: 10.80-11.00 grams.

Date	Mintage	VG	F	VF	XF	Unc
ND	—	—	650	720	800	—

Kabul

KM# 254.4 MOHUR (Type 254)
Gold **Obv:** Within dotted borders; Kalima, mint name, AH dates **Rev:** Within dotted borders; Emperor's full name and titles **Note:** Weight varies: 10.80-11.00 grams.

Date	Mintage	VG	F	VF	XF	Unc
AH1039//3	—	—	700	850	1,000	—
AH1040//4	—	—	700	850	1,000	—

Kashmir

KM# 254.7 MOHUR (Type 254)
Gold **Obv:** Kalima, AH date and mint name within dotted border **Rev:** Emperor's full name and titles within dotted border **Note:** Weight varies 10.8 - 11 grams.

Date	Mintage	VG	F	VF	XF	Unc
ND	—	—	700	850	1,000	—

Lahore

KM# 254.5 MOHUR (Type 254)
Gold **Obv:** Within dotted borders; Kalima, mint name, AH dates **Rev:** Within dotted borders; Emperor's full name and titles **Note:** Weight varies: 10.80-11.00 grams.

Date	Mintage	VG	F	VF	XF	Unc
AH1037//(1) Ahad	—	—	650	720	800	—

Surat

KM# 254.6 MOHUR (Type 254)
Gold **Obv:** Within dotted borders; Kalima, mint name, AH date **Rev:** Within dotted borders; Emperor's full name and titles **Note:** Weight varies: 10.80-11.00 grams.

Date	Mintage	VG	F	VF	XF	Unc
AH1037//(1) Ahad	—	—	700	800	900	—
AH1038//(1) Ahad	—	—	700	800	900	—

Ahmadabad

KM# 255.1 MOHUR (Type 255)
Gold **Obv:** Kalima, mint name, Ilahi month **Rev:** AH date **Note:** Weight varies: 10.80-11.00 grams.

Date	Mintage	VG	F	VF	XF	Unc
AH1038//2	—	—	650	720	800	—
AH1039//2	—	—	650	720	800	—
AH1039//3	—	—	650	720	800	—
AH1040//4	—	—	650	720	800	—
AH1041//4	—	—	650	720	800	—
AH1041//5	—	—	650	720	800	—
AH1042//x	—	—	650	720	800	—

Akbarabad

KM# 255.8 MOHUR (Type 255)
Gold **Obv:** Kalima, mint name, Ilahi month **Rev:** AH date **Note:** Weight varies: 10.80-11.00 grams. Mint epithet: "Dar-ul-Khilafat".

Date	Mintage	VG	F	VF	XF	Unc
AH1037//(1) Ahad	—	—	650	720	800	—
AH1038//(1) Ahad	—	—	650	720	800	—
AH1038//2	—	—	650	720	800	—

Burhanpur

KM# 255.2 MOHUR (Type 255)
Gold **Obv:** Kalima, mint name, Ilahi month **Rev:** AH date **Note:** Weight varies: 10.80-11.00 grams.

Date	Mintage	VG	F	VF	XF	Unc
AH1038//2	—	—	650	720	800	—

Jahangirnagar

KM# 255.3 MOHUR (Type 255)
Gold **Obv:** Kalima, mint name, Ilahi month **Rev:** AH date **Note:** Struck at Jahangirnagar. Weight varies: 10.80-11.00 grams.

Date	Mintage	VG	F	VF	XF	Unc
AH1042//6	—	—	750	850	1,000	—

Katak

KM# 255.9 MOHUR (Type 255)
Gold **Obv:** Kalima, mint name, Ilahi month **Rev:** AH date **Note:** Weight varies: 10.80-11.00 grams.

Date	Mintage	VG	F	VF	XF	Unc
AH1046 "Aban"	—	—	950	1,250	1,500	—
AH1049 "Shawwal"	—	—	950	1,250	15,000	—

Lahore

KM# 255.4 MOHUR (Type 255)
Gold **Obv:** Kalima, mint name, Ilahi month **Rev:** AH date **Note:** Weight varies: 10.80-11.00 grams.

Date	Mintage	VG	F	VF	XF	Unc
AH1039//2	—	—	675	750	850	—

Patna

KM# 255.5 MOHUR (Type 255)
Gold **Obv:** Kalima, mint name, Ilahi month **Rev:** AH date **Note:** Weight varies: 10.80-11.00 grams.

Date	Mintage	VG	F	VF	XF	Unc
AH1039//2	—	—	70.00	800	900	—
AH1041//5	—	—	700	800	900	—

Surat

KM# 255.6 MOHUR (Type 255)
Gold **Obv:** Regnal years only **Rev:** AH date **Note:** Weight varies: 10.80-11.00 grams.

Date	Mintage	VG	F	VF	XF	Unc
AHxxxx//2	—	—	650	700	800	—
AH104x//4	—	—	650	700	800	—
AH104x//5	—	—	650	700	800	—

Tatta

KM# 255.7 MOHUR (Type 255)
Gold **Obv:** Regnal years only **Rev:** AH date **Note:** Weight varies: 10.80-11.00 grams.

Date	Mintage	VG	F	VF	XF	Unc
AH1047//10	—	—	700	850	1,000	—
AH1066//30	—	—	700	850	1,000	—

Burhanpur

KM# A256.1 MOHUR (Type A256)
Gold **Obv:** Inscription without quatrefoil **Obv. Inscription:** "Kalima" **Rev:** Emperor's full name and titles, AH date **Note:** Weight varies 10.8 - 11 grams

Date	Mintage	VG	F	VF	XF	Unc
AH1040//3	—	—	750	1,000	1,250	—

Akbarabad

KM# 256.1 MOHUR (Type 256)
Gold **Obv:** Within dotted borders; Kalima within quatrefoil **Rev:** Within dotted border; Emperor's full name and titles, date **Note:** Weight varies: 10.80-11.00 grams.

Date	Mintage	VG	F	VF	XF	Unc
AH1041//4	—	—	700	800	900	—
AH1042//5	—	—	700	800	900	—
AH1042//6	—	—	700	800	900	—
AH1043//6	—	—	700	800	900	—

Burhanpur

KM# 256.2 MOHUR (Type 256)
Gold **Obv:** Within dotted borders; Kalima within quatrefoil **Rev:** Within dotted border; Emperor's full name and titles, date **Note:** Weight varies: 10.80-11.00 grams.

Date	Mintage	VG	F	VF	XF	Unc
AH1040//3	—	—	700	850	1,000	—

Burhanpur

KM# 257.2 MOHUR (Type 257)
Gold **Obv:** Kalima within small circle **Note:** Weight varies: 10.80-11.00 grams.

Date	Mintage	VG	F	VF	XF	Unc
AH1039//2	—	—	700	850	1,000	—

Lahore

KM# 257.1 MOHUR (Type 257)
Gold **Obv:** Kalima within duofoil, AH date **Note:** Weight varies: 10.80-11.00 grams.

Date	Mintage	VG	F	VF	XF	Unc
AH1042//5	—	—	700	850	1,000	—

Akbarabad

KM# 258.1 MOHUR (Type 258)
Gold **Obv:** Kalima within quatrefoil **Rev:** "Shah Jahan Padshah Ghazi" within quatrefoil, AH date **Note:** Weight varies: 10.80-11.00 grams.

Date	Mintage	VG	F	VF	XF	Unc
AH1043//6	—	—	650	720	800	—
AH1044//7	—	—	650	720	800	—
AH1044//8	—	—	650	720	800	—
AH1045//8	—	—	650	720	800	—
AH1045//9	—	—	650	720	800	—
AH1046//9	—	—	650	720	800	—
AH1047//10	—	—	650	720	800	—
AH1047//11	—	—	650	720	800	—
AH1048//11	—	—	650	720	800	—
AH1048//12	—	—	650	720	800	—
AH1049//13	—	—	650	720	800	—
AH1050//13	—	—	650	720	800	—
AH1051//15	—	—	650	720	800	—
AH1052//16	—	—	650	720	800	—
AH1053//16	—	—	650	720	800	—
AH1053//17	—	—	650	720	800	—
AH1054//17	—	—	650	720	800	—
AH1054//18	—	—	650	720	800	—
AH1055//18	—	—	650	720	800	—
AH1057//20	—	—	650	720	800	—
AH1057//21	—	—	650	720	800	—
AH1059//22	—	—	650	720	800	—
AH1059//23	—	—	650	720	800	—
AH1060//23	—	—	650	720	800	—
AH1061//25	—	—	650	720	800	—
AH1060//24	—	—	650	720	800	—
AH1062//26	—	—	650	720	800	—
AH1062//27 (sic)	—	—	650	720	800	—
AH1064//28	—	—	650	720	800	—

Akbarabad

KM# 258.2 MOHUR (Type 258)
Gold **Obv:** Kalima within quatrefoil, date **Rev:** "Shah Jahan Badshah Ghazi" within quatrefoil, AH date **Note:** Weight varies: 10.80-11.00 grams.

Date	Mintage	VG	F	VF	XF	Unc
AH1051//15	—	—	700	800	900	—
AH1062//26	—	—	700	800	900	—
AH1064//28	—	—	700	800	900	—

Daulatabad

KM# 258.3 MOHUR (Type 258)
Gold **Obv:** Kalima within quatrefoil, date **Rev:** "Shah Jahan Bad Shah Ghazi" within quatrefoil, AH date **Note:** Weight varies: 10.80-11.00 grams.

Date	Mintage	VG	F	VF	XF	Unc
AH1050//1x	—	—	700	800	900	—
AH1051//14	—	—	700	800	900	—
AH1052//15	—	—	700	800	900	—
AH1061//24	—	—	700	800	900	—
AH1062//25	—	—	700	800	900	—
AH1063//27	—	—	700	800	900	—
AH1064//27	—	—	700	800	900	—
AH1065//29	—	—	700	800	900	—
AH1066//30	—	—	700	800	900	—
AH1067//30	—	—	700	800	900	—
AH1067//31	—	—	700	800	900	—

Akbarabad

KM# A259.1 MOHUR (Type A259)
Gold **Obv:** Inscription within eightfoil **Rev:** Inscription within eightfoil, AH date **Note:** Weight varies 10.8 - 11 grams.

Date	Mintage	VG	F	VF	XF	Unc
AH1043//1x	—	—	950	1,250	1,500	—

Daulatabad

KM# A259.2 MOHUR (Type A259)
Gold **Obv:** Inscription within eightfoil **Rev:** Inscription within eightfoil, AH date **Note:** Weight varies 10.8 - 11 grams.

Date	Mintage	Good	VG	F	VF	XF
AH103x//2 Rare	—	—	—	—	—	—

Akbarabad

KM# 259.5 MOHUR (Type 259)
11.4440 g., Gold **Obv:** Inscription within lozenge **Rev:** Inscription within lozenge

Date	Mintage	VG	F	VF	XF	Unc
AH1043	—	—	750	1,000	1,250	—

Akbarabad

KM# 259.1 MOHUR (Type 259)
Gold **Obv:** Inscription within eightfoil **Rev:** AH date, inscription within eightfoil **Note:** Weight varies: 10.80-11.00 grams.

Date	Mintage	Good	VG	F	VF	XF
AH10xx//31	—	350	410	525	650	900
AH1068//32	—	350	410	525	650	900
AH1069//32	—	350	410	525	650	900

Daulatabad

KM# 259.2 MOHUR (Type 259)
Gold **Obv:** Inscription within eightfoil, AH date **Rev:** Inscription within eightfoil **Note:** Weight varies: 10.80-11.00 grams.

Date	Mintage	VG	F	VF	XF	Unc
AH1068//31	—	—	750	1,000	1,250	—
AH1068//32	—	—	750	1,000	1,250	—
AH1069//32	—	—	750	1,000	1,250	—

Kabul

KM# 259.3 MOHUR (Type 259)
Gold **Obv:** Inscription within eightfoil, AH date **Rev:** Inscription within eightfoil **Note:** Weight varies: 10.80-11.00 grams.

Date	Mintage	VG	F	VF	XF	Unc
AH1067//31	—	—	1,150	1,450	1,750	—

Shahjahanabad

KM# 259.4 MOHUR (Type 259)
Gold **Obv:** Inscription within eightfoil, AH date **Rev:** Inscription within eightfoil **Rev. Inscription:** "dar al-khilafa" **Note:** Weight varies 10.8 - 11 grams.

Date	Mintage	VG	F	VF	XF	Unc
AH1069	—	—	950	1,250	1,500	—

Ahmadabad

KM# 260.1 MOHUR (Type 260)
Gold **Obv:** Inscription within square, with knots at corners; Kalima, AH date **Rev:** Inscription within square, with knots at corners;"Shah Jahan Padshah Ghazi" **Note:** Weight varies: 10.80-11.00 grams.

Date	Mintage	VG	F	VF	XF	Unc
AH1044//8	—	—	650	720	800	—
AH1045//8	—	—	650	720	800	—
AH1046//9	—	—	650	720	800	—
AH1052//16	—	—	650	720	800	—
AH1067//30	—	—	650	720	800	—

Akbarabad

KM# 260.24 MOHUR (Type 260)

Gold, 27.5 mm. **Obv:** Inscription within square, with knots at corners; Kalima, AH date **Rev:** Mint epithet: "May God preserve the kingdom" in right margin **Note:** Weight varies: 10.80-11.00 grams.

Date	Mintage	VG	F	VF	XF	Unc
AH1038//2	—	—	—	—	—	—

Akbarabad

KM# 260.2 MOHUR (Type 260)

Gold **Obv:** Inscription within square, with knots at corners; Kalima, AH date **Rev:** Inscription within square, with knots at corners;"Shah Jahan Padshah Ghazi" **Note:** Weight varies: 10.80-11.00 grams.

Date	Mintage	VG	F	VF	XF	Unc
AH1046//9	—	—	725	925	1,150	—
AH1056//19	—	—	725	925	1,150	—

Allahabad

KM# 260.3 MOHUR (Type 260)

Gold **Obv:** Legend within square, with knots at corners; Kalima, AH date **Rev:** Legend within square, with knots at corners; "Shah Jahan Padshah Ghazi" **Note:** Weight varies: 10.80-11.00 grams.

Date	Mintage	VG	F	VF	XF	Unc
AH1045//9	—	—	700	800	900	—
AH1046//9	—	—	700	800	900	—
AH1046//10	—	—	700	800	900	—
AH1052//15	—	—	700	800	900	—
AH1055//18	—	—	700	800	900	—
AH1057//21	—	—	700	800	900	—
AH1058//21	—	—	700	800	900	—

Aurangabad

KM# 260.4 MOHUR (Type 260)

Gold **Obv:** Legend within square, with knots at corners; Kalima, AH date **Rev:** Legend within square, with knots at corners; "Shah Jahan Padshah Ghazi" **Note:** Weight varies: 10.80-11.00 grams.

Date	Mintage	VG	F	VF	XF	Unc
AH1049//13	—	—	700	850	1,000	—

Aurangnagar

KM# 260.23 MOHUR (Type 260)

Gold **Obv:** Legend within square, with knots at corners; Kalima, AH date **Rev:** Legend within square, with knots at corners; "Shah Jahan Padshah Ghazi" **Note:** Weight varies: 10.80-11.00 grams.

Date	Mintage	VG	F	VF	XF	Unc
AH1048//11	—	—	1,150	1,450	1,750	—

Balkh

KM# 260.16 MOHUR (Type 260)

Gold **Obv:** Legend within square, with knots at corners; Kalima, AH date **Rev:** Legend within square, with knots at corners; "Shah Jahan Padshah Ghazi" **Note:** Weight varies: 10.80-11.00 grams.

Date	Mintage	VG	F	VF	XF	Unc
AH1056//20	—	—	950	1,250	1,500	—
AH1056//1057	—	—	950	1,250	1,500	—
AH1057//20	—	—	950	1,250	1,500	—

Bhilsa

KM# 260.5 MOHUR (Type 260)

Gold **Obv:** Legend within square, with knots at corners; Kalima, AH date **Rev:** Legend within square, with knots at corners; "Shah Jahan Padshah Ghazi" **Note:** Weight varies: 10.80-11.00 grams.

Date	Mintage	VG	F	VF	XF	Unc
AH1059//2x	—	—	750	1,000	1,250	—
AH106x//24	—	—	750	1,000	1,250	—
AH1065//29	—	—	750	1,000	1,250	—

Burhanpur

KM# 260.6 MOHUR (Type 260)

Gold **Obv:** Inscription within square, with knots at corners; Kalima, AH date **Rev:** Inscription within square, with knots at corners; "Shah Jahan Padshah Ghazi" **Note:** Weight varies: 10.80-11.00 grams. Inscription within linear square or square of dots

Date	Mintage	VG	F	VF	XF	Unc
AH1040//4	—	—	650	720	800	—
AH1041//4	—	—	650	720	800	—
AH1042//x	—	—	650	720	800	—
AH1043//6	—	—	650	720	800	—
AH1043//7	—	—	650	720	800	—
AH1047//xx	—	—	650	720	800	—
AH1048//xx	—	—	650	720	800	—
AH1049//12	—	—	650	720	800	—
AH1050//xx	—	—	650	720	800	—
AH1051//15	—	—	650	720	800	—
AH1052//15	—	—	650	720	800	—
AH1052//16	—	—	650	720	800	—
AH1053//16	—	—	650	720	800	—
AH1053//17	—	—	650	720	800	—
AH1054//17	—	—	650	720	800	—
AH1054//18	—	—	650	720	800	—
AH1055//18	—	—	650	720	800	—
AH1055//19	—	—	650	720	800	—
AH1056//19	—	—	650	720	800	—
AH1056//20	—	—	650	720	800	—
AH1057//20	—	—	650	720	800	—
AH1057//21	—	—	650	720	800	—
AH1058//21	—	—	650	720	800	—
AH1058//22	—	—	650	720	800	—
AH1059//22	—	—	650	720	800	—
AH1059//23	—	—	650	720	800	—
AH1060//23	—	—	650	720	800	—
AH1060//24	—	—	650	720	800	—
AH1061//24	—	—	650	720	800	—
AH1061//25	—	—	650	720	800	—
AH1063//26	—	—	650	720	800	—
AH1063//27	—	—	650	720	800	—
AH1068//32	—	—	650	720	800	—

Burhanpur

KM# 260.26 MOHUR (Type 260)

Gold **Obv:** Inscription within square, with knots at corners; Kalima, AH date **Rev:** Inscription within square, with knots at corners; mint epithet: "May God preserve the kingdom" in right margin **Rev. Inscription:** "Shah Jahan Padshah Ghazi" **Note:** Weight varies: 10.80-11.00 grams.

Date	Mintage	VG	F	VF	XF	Unc
AH1040//4	—	—	—	—	—	—
AH1041//4	—	—	—	—	—	—
AH1041//5	—	—	—	—	—	—

Daulatabad

KM# 260.21 MOHUR (Type 260)

Gold **Obv:** Inscription within square, with knots at corners; Kalima, AH date **Rev:** Inscription within square, with knots at corners **Rev. Inscription:** "Shah Jahan Padshah Ghazi" **Note:** Weight varies: 10.80-11.00 grams.

Date	Mintage	VG	F	VF	XF	Unc
AH1043//x	—	—	700	900	1,100	—
AH1049//x	—	—	700	900	1,100	—
AH1061//23(sic)	—	—	700	900	1,100	—

Gulkanda

KM# 260.17 MOHUR (Type 260)

Gold **Obv:** Inscription within square, with knots at corners; Kalima, AH date **Rev:** Inscription within square, with knots at corners **Rev. Inscription:** "Shah Jahan Padshah Ghazi" **Note:** Weight varies: 10.80-11.00 grams.

Date	Mintage	VG	F	VF	XF	Unc
AH1045//9	—	—	700	850	1,000	—

Junagarh

KM# 260.7 MOHUR (Type 260)

Gold **Obv:** Inscription within square, with knots at corners; Kalima, AH date **Rev:** Inscription within square, with knots at corners **Rev. Inscription:** "Shah Jahan Padshah Ghazi" **Note:** Weight varies: 10.80-11.00 grams.

Date	Mintage	VG	F	VF	XF	Unc
AH1044//7	—	—	750	1,000	1,250	—

Kabul

KM# 260.8 MOHUR (Type 260)

Gold **Obv:** Inscription within square, with knots at corners; Kalima, AH date **Rev:** Inscription within square, with knots at corners **Rev. Inscription:** "Shah Jahan Padshah Ghazi" **Note:** Weight varies: 10.80-11.00 grams.

Date	Mintage	VG	F	VF	XF	Unc
AH1048//11	—	—	700	850	1,000	—
AH106x//25	—	—	700	850	1,000	—

Kashmir

KM# 260.9 MOHUR (Type 260)

Gold **Obv:** Inscription within square, with knots at corners; Kalima, AH date **Rev:** Inscription within square, with knots at corners **Rev. Inscription:** "Shah Jahan Padshah Ghazi" **Note:** Weight varies: 10.80-11.00 grams.

Date	Mintage	VG	F	VF	XF	Unc
AH105x//19	—	—	700	850	1,000	—
AH105x//22	—	—	700	850	1,000	—
AH1065//2x	—	—	700	850	1,000	—
AH1068//31	—	—	700	850	1,000	—

Katak

KM# 260.22 MOHUR (Type 260)

Gold **Obv:** Inscription within square, with knots at corners; Kalima, AH date **Rev:** Inscription within square, with knots at corners **Rev. Inscription:** "Shah Jahan Padshah Ghazi" **Note:** Weight varies: 10.80-11.00 grams.

Date	Mintage	VG	F	VF	XF	Unc
AH1054//1x	—	—	725	950	1,200	—

Khambayat

KM# 260.10 MOHUR (Type 260)

Gold **Obv:** Inscription within square, with knots at corners; Kalima, AH date **Rev:** Inscription within square, with knots at corners; "Shah Jahan Badshah Ghazi" **Rev. Inscription:** "Shah Jahan Padshah Ghazi" **Note:** Weight varies: 10.80-11.00 grams.

Date	Mintage	VG	F	VF	XF	Unc
AH1060//24	—	—	700	850	1,000	—
AH1064//27	—	—	700	850	1,000	—
AH1067//30	—	—	700	850	1,000	—

Lahore

KM# 260.11 MOHUR (Type 260)

Gold **Obv:** Inscription within square, with knots at corners; Kalima, AH date **Rev:** Inscription within square, with knots at corners **Rev. Inscription:** "Shah Jahan Padshah Ghazi" **Note:** Weight varies: 10.80-11.00 grams.

Date	Mintage	VG	F	VF	XF	Unc
AH1046//9	—	—	675	750	850	—
AH1047//10	—	—	675	750	850	—
AH1048//12	—	—	675	750	850	—
AH1052//16	—	—	675	750	850	—
AH1053//17	—	—	675	750	850	—
AH1057//21	—	—	675	750	850	—
AH1058//22	—	—	675	750	850	—
AH1062//25	—	—	675	750	850	—
AH1062//26	—	—	675	750	850	—

Lakhnau

KM# 260.12 MOHUR (Type 260)

Gold **Obv:** Inscription within square, with knots at corners; Kalima, AH date **Rev:** Inscription within square, with knots at corners; "Shah Jahan Padshah Ghazi" **Note:** Struck at Lakhnau. Weight varies: 10.80-11.00 grams.

Date	Mintage	VG	F	VF	XF	Unc
AH1051//15	—	—	750	1,000	1,250	—

Multan

KM# 260.13 MOHUR (Type 260)

Gold **Obv:** Inscription within square, with knots at corners; Kalima, AH date **Rev:** Inscription within square, with knots at corners **Rev. Inscription:** "Shah Jahan Padshah Ghazi" **Note:** Weight varies: 10.80-11.00 grams.

Date	Mintage	VG	F	VF	XF	Unc
AH1043//6	—	—	650	720	800	—
AH1044//7	—	—	650	720	800	—
AH1059//22	—	—	650	720	800	—
AH1064//28	—	—	650	720	800	—
AH1066//29	—	—	650	720	800	—
AH1066//30	—	—	650	720	800	—
AH1068//31	—	—	650	720	800	—
AH1068//32	—	—	650	720	800	—
AH1069//33	—	—	650	720	800	—

Patna

KM# 260.14 MOHUR (Type 260)

Gold **Obv:** Inscription within square, with knots at corners; Kalima, AH date **Rev:** Inscription within square, with knots at corners **Rev. Inscription:** "Shah Jahan Padshah Ghazi" **Note:** Weight varies: 10.80-11.00 grams.

Date	Mintage	VG	F	VF	XF	Unc
AH1042//6	—	—	650	720	800	—
AH1045//8	—	—	650	720	800	—
AH1047//11	—	—	650	720	800	—
AH10xx//13	—	—	650	720	800	—
AH105x//15	—	—	650	720	800	—
AH105x//16	—	—	650	720	800	—
AH105x//17	—	—	650	720	800	—
AH105x//21	—	—	650	720	800	—
AH106x//25	—	—	650	720	800	—

Pattan Deo

KM# 260.19 MOHUR (Type 260)

Gold **Obv:** Inscription within square, with knots at corners; Kalima, AH date **Rev:** Inscription within square, with knots at corners **Rev. Inscription:** "Shah Jahan Padshah Ghazi" **Note:** Weight varies: 10.80-11.00 grams.

Date	Mintage	VG	F	VF	XF	Unc
AH1047//1x	—	—	950	1,250	1,500	—

Qandahar

KM# 260.18 MOHUR (Type 260)

Gold **Obv:** Inscription within square, with knots at corners; Kalima, AH date **Rev:** Inscription within square, with knots at corners **Rev. Inscription:** "Shah Jahan Padshah Ghazi" **Note:** Weight varies: 10.80-11.00 grams.

Date	Mintage	VG	F	VF	XF	Unc
AH105x//18	—	—	950	1,250	1,500	—

Surat

KM# 260.15 MOHUR (Type 260)

Gold **Obv:** Inscription within square, with knots at corners; Kalima, AH date **Rev:** Inscription within square, with knots at corners **Rev. Inscription:** "Shah Jahan Padshah Ghazi" **Note:** Weight varies: 10.80-11.00 grams.

Date	Mintage	VG	F	VF	XF	Unc
AH1043//6	—	—	650	720	800	—
AH1045//8	—	—	650	720	800	—
AH1045//9	—	—	650	720	800	—
AH1046//9	—	—	650	720	800	—
AH1047//11	—	—	650	720	800	—
AH1048//11	—	—	650	720	800	—
AH1069//32	—	—	650	720	800	—

Ujjain

KM# 260.20 MOHUR (Type 260)

Gold **Obv:** Inscription within square, with knots at corners; Kalima, AH date **Rev:** Inscription within square, with knots at corners **Rev. Inscription:** "Shah Jahan Padshah Ghazi" **Note:** Weight varies: 10.80-11.00 grams.

Date	Mintage	VG	F	VF	XF	Unc
AH106x//25	—	—	725	950	1,200	—

Delhi

KM# 261.2 MOHUR (Type 261)

Gold **Obv:** Inscription, Kalima in circle, date **Rev:** Ruler's name and titles, mint name **Note:** Weight varies: 10.80-11.00 grams.

Date	Mintage	VG	F	VF	XF	Unc
AH1047//1x	—	—	750	1,000	1,250	—
AH1054//17	—	—	750	1,000	1,250	—

Shahjahanabad

KM# 262.1 MOHUR (Type 262)

Gold **Obv:** Within dotted borders; Kalima within circle, AH date **Rev:** Within dotted borders; inscription within circle **Rev. Inscription:** "Shah Jahan Padshah Ghazi" **Note:** Weight varies: 10.80-11.00 grams.

Date	Mintage	VG	F	VF	XF	Unc
AH10xx//25	—	—	750	1,000	1,250	—
AH106x//26	—	—	750	1,000	1,250	—
AH1065//29	—	—	750	1,000	1,250	—
AH1066//xx	—	—	750	1,000	1,250	—
AH1067//30	—	—	750	1,000	1,250	—

Surat

KM# 262.2 MOHUR (Type 262)

Gold **Obv:** Within dotted borders; Kalima within circle, AH date **Rev:** Within dotted borders; inscription within circle **Rev. Inscription:** "Shah Jahan Padshah Ghazi" **Note:** Weight varies: 10.80-11.00 grams.

Date	Mintage	VG	F	VF	XF	Unc
AH1068//31	—	—	700	900	1,100	—

Without Mint Name

KM# 264.2 MOHUR (Type 263)

Gold **Obv:** Kalima within square **Rev:** Inscription within square, AH date **Rev. Inscription:** "Shah Jahan Padshah Ghazi" **Shape:** Square **Note:** Weight varies: 10.80-11.00 grams.

Date	Mintage	VG	F	VF	XF	Unc
AH104x//6	—	—	—	—	—	—

Akbarabad

KM# 264.1 MOHUR (Type 263)

Gold **Obv:** inscription, Kalima within square **Rev:** Inscription within square, AH date **Rev. Inscription:** "Shah Jahan Padshah Ghazi" **Shape:** Square **Note:** Weight varies: 10.80-11.00 grams.

Date	Mintage	VG	F	VF	XF	Unc
AH1057//21	—	—	—	—	—	—

Gulkanda

KM# 263.1 MOHUR (Type 263)

Gold **Note:** Weight varies: 10.80-11.00 grams. Crude calligraphy.

Date	Mintage	VG	F	VF	XF	Unc
ND	—	—	675	750	850	—

Akbarabad

KM# A264.1 MOHUR (Type A264)

Gold **Obv:** Inscription with names of four caliphs above Kalima **Rev:** Ruler's name, mint name **Note:** Weight varies 10.8 - 11 grams; similar to Rupee, KM#226.1.

Date	Mintage	Good	VG	F	VF	XF
AH1039//2	—	—	—	—	—	—

Akbarabad

KM# B264.2 MOHUR (Type B264)

Gold **Obv:** Inscription in wavy pentagon **Obv. Inscription:** "Kalima" **Rev:** Ruler's titles in oblong outline **Note:** Weight varies 10.8 - 11 grams.

Date	Mintage	Good	VG	F	VF	XF
AH1040//4	—	—	—	—	—	—

Without Mint Name

KM# 266.1 HEAVY MOHUR (Type 266)

Gold **Obv:** Inscription within square with knots at corners **Rev:** Inscription within square with knots at corners **Shape:** Square **Note:** Weight varies: 12.00-12.20 grams.

Date	Mintage	Good	VG	F	VF	XF
ND	—	—	—	1,500	2,000	2,500

Shahjahanabad

KM# 268.1 NAZARANA 200 MOHURS (Type 268)

2177.0000 g., Gold, 102 mm.

Date	Mintage	Good	VG	F	VF	XF
AH1064//28 Unique	—	—	—	—	—	—

Lahore

KM# A268.1 NAZARANA 100 MOHURS

1094.5000 g., Gold **Rev. Inscription:** Dar-us-Sultana. **Note:** Illustration reduced, actual size 94mm.

Date	Mintage	Good	VG	F	VF	XF
AH1048//12 Unique	—	—	—	—	—	—

LARGESSE COINAGE

Lahore

KM# 237.1 NISAR (Type 237)

2.8500 g., Silver

Date	Mintage	VG	F	VF	XF	Unc
AH1037	—	90.00	150	250	375	—

Lahore

KM# 238.1 NISAR (Type 238)

5.7000 g., Silver **Obv. Inscription:** "Z nam Shah Jahan Bad Shah" **Rev. Inscription:** "Sahib-i-qiran sani" **Note:** 1/2 Rupee weight.

Date	Mintage	VG	F	VF	XF	Unc
AH1037//(1) Ahad	—	145	240	400	600	—
AH1039//3	—	145	240	400	600	—

Ahmadabad

KM# A239.1 NISAR (Type A239)

0.7000 g., Silver **Obv. Inscription:** "Nizar Shah Jahan"

Date	Mintage	VG	F	VF	XF	Unc
1063//27	—	70.00	120	200	300	—

Akbarabad

KM# A239.2 NISAR (Type A239)

Silver **Obv:** Inscription **Rev:** Inscription **Note:** Weight varies .6 - .7 grams.

Date	Mintage	VG	F	VF	XF	Unc
AH1039//2	—	70.00	120	200	300	—

Burhanpur

KM# A239.3 NISAR (Type A239)

Silver **Obv. Inscription:** "Shah Jahan Padshah" **Note:** Weight varies .6 - .7 grams

Date	Mintage	VG	F	VF	XF	Unc
AH1040	—	90.00	150	250	375	—

Shahjahanabad

KM# B239.1 NISAR (Type B239)

1.4000 g., Silver **Obv. Inscription:** "Shah Jahan Padshah Ghazi" **Note:** Square.

Date	Mintage	VG	F	VF	XF	Unc
AH1059//23	—	90.00	150	250	375	—

Agra

KM# 239.2 NISAR (Type 239)

1.4000 g., Silver **Obv. Inscription:** "Shah Jahan Padshah Ghazi"

Date	Mintage	VG	F	VF	XF	Unc
AHxxxx	—	90.00	150	250	375	—

Ahmadabad

KM# 239.3 NISAR (Type 239)

Silver **Obv. Inscription:** "Nisar Shah Jahan Padshah" **Note:** Weight varies 1.2 - 1.4 grams.

Date	Mintage	VG	F	VF	XF	Unc
AH1052//15	—	90.00	150	250	375	—
AH1062	—	90.00	150	250	375	—
AH1063//27	—	90.00	150	250	375	—

Akbarabad

KM# 239.4 NISAR (Type 239)

Silver **Obv. Inscription:** "Nisar Shah Jahan Padshah Ghazi" **Note:** Weight varies 1.1 - 1.3 grams.

Date	Mintage	VG	F	VF	XF	Unc
AH1043//6	—	90.00	150	250	375	—
AH1049//13	—	90.00	150	250	375	—
AH1052//16	—	90.00	150	250	375	—

Akbarnagar

KM# 239.5 NISAR (Type 239)

1.4000 g., Silver **Obv. Inscription:** "Nisar Shah Jahani"

Date	Mintage	VG	F	VF	XF	Unc
AH1056	—	90.00	150	250	375	—

Allahabad

KM# 239.6 NISAR (Type 239)

1.4000 g., Silver **Obv. Inscription:** "Shah Jahan Padshah Ghazi"

Date	Mintage	VG	F	VF	XF	Unc
AH1045//8	—	90.00	150	250	375	—

Bhilsa

KM# 239.7 NISAR (Type 239)

1.5000 g., Silver **Obv. Inscription:** "(Shah Jahan) Padshah Ghazi"

Date	Mintage	VG	F	VF	XF	Unc
AHxxxx	—	125	200	350	525	—

Burhanpur

KM# 239.8 NISAR (Type 239)

1.5000 g., Silver **Obv. Inscription:** "Nisar Shah Jahan Padshah Ghazi"

Date	Mintage	VG	F	VF	XF	Unc
AH1040//3	—	90.00	150	250	375	—

Daulatabad

KM# 239.9 NISAR (Type 239)

1.4000 g., Silver **Obv. Inscription:** "Nisar Shah Jahan Padshah Ghazi"

Date	Mintage	VG	F	VF	XF	Unc
AH1045	—	125	210	350	525	—
AH1047	—	125	210	350	525	—

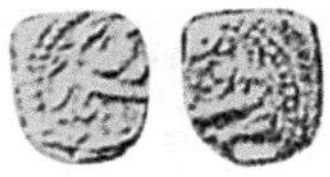

Ujjain

KM# 239.1 NISAR (Type 239)
1.3000 g., Silver **Obv:** Inscription **Rev:** Inscription **Note:** 1/8 Rupee weight.

Date	Mintage	VG	F	VF	XF	Unc
ND	—	180	300	500	750	—

Agra

KM# 240.1 NISAR (Type 240)
Silver **Obv. Inscription:** "Nisar Shah Jahan Bad Shah Ghazi" **Note:** 1/4 Rupee weight varies 2.65 - 2.9 grams; Mint epithet: "Dar-ul-Khilafat". For later issues see Akbarabad.

Date	Mintage	Good	VG	F	VF	XF
AH1037//(1) Ahad	—	—	110	185	250	360
AH1038//(1) Ahad	—	—	110	185	250	360
AH1038//2	—	—	110	185	250	360

Ahmadabad

KM# 240.6 NISAR (Type 240)
2.8000 g., Silver **Obv. Inscription:** "Nisar Shah Jahan" **Note:** 1/4 Rupee weight.

Date	Mintage	Good	VG	F	VF	XF
AH1054//1x	—	35.00	85.00	125	190	275
AH1069//33	—	35.00	85.00	125	190	275

Akbarabad

KM# 240.2 NISAR (Type 240)
Silver **Obv. Inscription:** "Nisar Shah Jahan Padshah Ghazi" **Rev. Inscription:** "dar al-khilafa" **Note:** 1/4 Rupee weight. Weight varies: 2.65-2.90 grams. Mint epithet: "Dar-ul-Khilafat".

Date	Mintage	Good	VG	F	VF	XF
AH1039//2	—	45.00	110	175	250	360
AH1041//5	—	45.00	110	175	250	360
AH1042//5	—	45.00	110	175	250	360
AH1042//6	—	45.00	110	175	250	360
AH1043//6	—	45.00	110	175	250	360
AH1043//7	—	45.00	110	175	250	360
AH1044//7	—	45.00	110	175	250	360
AH1044//8	—	45.00	110	175	250	360
AH1045//8	—	45.00	110	175	250	360
AH1045//9	—	45.00	110	175	250	360
AH1046//9	—	45.00	110	175	250	360
AH1046//10	—	45.00	110	175	250	360
AH1047//10	—	45.00	110	175	250	360
AH1047//11	—	45.00	110	175	250	360
AH1048//11	—	45.00	110	175	250	360
AH1052//16	—	45.00	110	175	250	360
AH1054//17	—	45.00	110	175	250	360
AH1054//18	—	45.00	110	175	250	360
AH1056//20	—	45.00	110	175	250	360
AH1060//24	—	45.00	110	175	250	360
AH1064//28	—	45.00	110	175	250	360

Akbarabad

KM# 240.7 NISAR (Type 240)
2.8000 g., Silver **Obv. Inscription:** "Shah Jahan Padshah Ghazi"

Date	Mintage	VG	F	VF	XF	Unc
AH1049//13	—	90.00	150	250	375	—

Akbarnagar

KM# 240.8 NISAR (Type 240)
2.8000 g., Silver **Obv. Inscription:** "Nisar Shah Jahani"

Date	Mintage	VG	F	VF	XF	Unc
AH1056//20	—	110	180	300	450	—
AH1061//25	—	110	180	300	450	—

Burhanpur

KM# 240.9 NISAR (Type 240)
Silver **Obv. Inscription:** "Nisar Shah Jahan Padshah Ghazi" **Note:** Weight varies 2.6 - 2.9 grams.

Date	Mintage	VG	F	VF	XF	Unc
AH1040//3	—	90.00	150	250	375	—
AH1041//5	—	90.00	150	250	375	—

Daulatabad

KM# 240.10 NISAR (Type 240)
2.7000 g., Silver **Obv. Inscription:** "Nisar Shah Jahan Padshah Ghazi"

Date	Mintage	VG	F	VF	XF	Unc
AH1045//9	—	110	180	300	450	—

Jahangirnagar

KM# 240.11 NISAR (Type 240)
2.8000 g., Silver **Obv. Inscription:** "Nisar Shah Jahani"

Date	Mintage	VG	F	VF	XF	Unc
AHxxxx//22	—	160	270	450	675	—

Kabul

KM# 240.12 NISAR (Type 240)
2.8000 g., Silver **Obv. Inscription:** "Nisar Shah Jahan Padshah Ghazi"

Date	Mintage	VG	F	VF	XF	Unc
AH1059 (?)	—	215	360	600	900	—

Kashmir

KM# 240.3 NISAR (Type 240)
Silver **Obv. Inscription:** "Nisar Shah Jahan Padshah Ghazi" **Note:** 1/4 Rupee weight. Weight varies: 2.65-2.90 grams.

Date	Mintage	VG	F	VF	XF	Unc
AHxxxx//13	—	180	300	500	750	—

Lahore

KM# 240.5 NISAR (Type 240)
Silver **Obv. Legend:** "Nisar Shah Jahan Padshah Ghazi" **Note:** 1/4 Rupee weight. Weight varies: 2.65-2.90 grams. Without epithet.

Date	Mintage	VG	F	VF	XF	Unc
AH1044//7	—	90.00	150	250	375	—

Lahore

KM# 240.13 NISAR (Type 240)
Silver **Obv. Inscription:** "Nisar Shah Jahan Padshah Ghazi" **Rev. Inscription:** "dar al-Zarb" **Note:** Weight varies 2.1 - 2.9 grams.

Date	Mintage	VG	F	VF	XF	Unc
AH1047//11	—	90.00	150	250	375	—

Lahore

KM# 240.4 NISAR (Type 240)
Silver **Obv. Inscription:** "Shah Jahan" **Rev. Inscription:** "Dar-al-Sultana" **Note:** 1/4 Rupee weight. Weight varies: 2.65-2.90 grams.

Date	Mintage	VG	F	VF	XF	Unc
AH1048//12	—	70.00	120	200	300	—
AH1049//12	—	70.00	120	200	300	—
AH1049//13	—	70.00	120	200	300	—
AH1050//13	—	70.00	120	200	300	—
AH1050//14	—	70.00	120	200	300	—
AH1051//14	—	70.00	120	200	300	—
AH1051//15	—	70.00	120	200	300	—
AH1052//15	—	70.00	120	200	300	—
AH1053//17	—	70.00	120	200	300	—
AH106x//30	—	70.00	120	200	300	—
AH1068//32	—	70.00	120	200	300	—

Urdu Zafar Qarin

KM# 240.14 NISAR (Type 240)
Silver **Note:** Weight varies 2.1 - 2.9 grams.

Date	Mintage	VG	F	VF	XF	Unc
ND	—	270	450	750	1,125	—

Kashmir

KM# 241.1 NISAR (Type 241)
Silver **Obv. Legend:** "Shah Jahan" **Note:** Weight varies: 5.60-5.80 g (1/2 Rupee weight).

Date	Mintage	VG	F	VF	XF	Unc
AH1048//13	—	215	360	600	900	—

Shahjahanabad

KM# 242.1 NISAR (Type 242)
Silver **Obv. Legend:** "Nisar Sahib Qiran Sani Shah Jahan Padshah Ghazi" **Note:** 1/2 Rupee weight. Weight varies: 5.60-5.80 grams. Mint epithet: Dar-ul-Khilafat".

Date	Mintage	VG	F	VF	XF	Unc
AH1060//24	—	90.00	150	250	375	—
AH1063//26	—	90.00	150	250	375	—

Akbarabad

KM# 243.1 NISAR (Type 243)
Silver **Obv. Legend:** "Sahib Qiran" **Note:** 1/16 Rupee weight. Weight varies: 0.55-0.75 grams.

Date	Mintage	VG	F	VF	XF	Unc
AH1047//11	—	70.00	120	200	300	—

Akbarabad

KM# 244.3 NISAR (Type 244)
1.1000 g., Silver **Obv. Legend:** "Nisar Sahib Qiran Sani" **Note:** 1/8 Rupee weight.

Date	Mintage	VG	F	VF	XF	Unc
AH1064//2x	—	70.00	120	200	300	—
AH106x//29	—	70.00	120	200	300	—

Akbarnagar

KM# 244.4 NISAR (Type 244)
Silver **Obv. Inscription:** "Sahib Qiran Sani" **Note:** Weight varies 1.1 - 1.4 grams.

Date	Mintage	VG	F	VF	XF	Unc
AH1055//19	—	100	180	300	450	—

Akbarnagar

KM# 244.1 NISAR (Type 244)
Silver **Obv. Inscription:** "Nisar Sahib Qiran Sani" **Note:** 1/8 Rupee weight. Weight varies: 1.30-1.45 grams.

Date	Mintage	VG	F	VF	XF	Unc
AH1064//28	—	100	180	300	450	—
AH1068//32	—	100	180	300	450	—

Shahjahanabad

KM# 244.2 NISAR (Type 244)
Silver **Obv. Inscription:** "Nisar Sahib Qiran Sani" **Rev. Inscription:** "dar al-khilafa" **Note:** 1/8 Rupee weight. Weight varies: 1.30-1.45 grams.

Date	Mintage	VG	F	VF	XF	Unc
AH1067//3x	—	80.00	135	225	340	—
AH106x//32 (sic)	—	80.00	135	225	340	—

Akbarabad

KM# A246.1 NISAR (Type A246)
Silver **Note:** Weight varies 2.55 - 2.9 grams; without epithet.

Date	Mintage	VG	F	VF	XF	Unc
AH1047//11	—	100	165	275	415	—

Akbarabad

KM# 246.7 NISAR (Type 246)
2.8000 g., Silver **Obv. Inscription:** "Sahib Qiran Sani"

Date	Mintage	VG	F	VF	XF	Unc
AH1047//10	—	100	165	275	415	—

Akbarabad

KM# 246.1 NISAR (Type 246)
Silver **Obv. Inscription:** "Nisar Sahib Qiran sani" **Rev. Inscription:** "dar al-khilafa" **Note:** Weight varies: 2.55-2.90 grams. 1/4 Rupee weight. For earlier issues see Agra.

Date	Mintage	VG	F	VF	XF	Unc
AH1048//11	—	80.00	135	225	340	—
AH1053//17	—	80.00	135	225	340	—
AH1054//17	—	80.00	135	225	340	—
AH1058//21	—	80.00	135	225	340	—
AH1060//23	—	80.00	135	225	340	—
AH1060//24	—	80.00	135	225	340	—
AH1064//28	—	80.00	135	225	340	—
AH1068//31	—	80.00	135	225	340	—
AH1069//33	—	80.00	135	225	340	—

Akbarnagar

KM# 246.2 NISAR (Type 246)
Silver **Obv. Inscription:** "Nisar Sahib Qiran Sani" **Note:** Weight varies: 2.55-2.90 grams. 1/4 Rupee weight.

Date	Mintage	VG	F	VF	XF	Unc
AH1065//29	—	100	180	300	450	—
AH1066//29	—	100	180	300	450	—
AH1068//32	—	100	180	300	450	—

Kabul

KM# 246.3 NISAR (Type 246)
Silver **Obv. Inscription:** "Sahib Qiran" **Note:** Weight varies: 2.55-2.90 grams. 1/4 Rupee weight.

Date	Mintage	VG	F	VF	XF	Unc
AH1049//9 (sic)	—	240	400	350	925	—
AH1049//12	—	240	400	350	925	—

Kashmir

KM# 246.4 NISAR (Type 246)
Silver **Obv. Inscription:** "Nisar Sahib Qiran Sani" **Note:** Weight varies: 2.55-2.90 grams. 1/4 Rupee weight.

Date	Mintage	VG	F	VF	XF	Unc
AH1050//13	—	215	360	600	925	—
AH1061//25	—	215	360	600	925	—
AH1064//27	—	215	360	600	925	—

Lahore

KM# 246.5 NISAR (Type 246)
Silver **Obv. Inscription:** "Nisar Sahib Qiran Sani" **Rev. Inscription:** "dar al-Saltana" **Note:** Weight varies: 2.55-2.90 grams. 1/4 Rupee weight.

Date	Mintage	VG	F	VF	XF	Unc
AH1052//15	—	100	180	300	450	—
AH1055//18	—	100	180	300	450	—
AH105x//19	—	100	180	300	450	—
AH1056//20	—	100	180	300	450	—
AH1057//20	—	100	180	300	450	—
AH1058//2x	—	100	180	300	450	—
AH1061//24	—	100	180	300	450	—
AH1062//2x	—	100	180	300	450	—
AH1062//26	—	100	180	300	450	—
AH1063//26	—	100	180	300	450	—

Shahjahanabad

KM# 246.6 NISAR (Type 246)
Silver **Obv. Inscription:** "Nisar Sahib Qiran Sani" **Note:** Weight varies: 2.55-2.90 grams. 1/4 Rupee weight. For earlier issues see Dehli.

Date	Mintage	VG	F	VF	XF	Unc
AH1060//24	—	90.00	150	250	375	—
AH1061//24	—	90.00	150	250	375	—
AH1061//25	—	90.00	150	250	375	—
AH1062//25	—	90.00	150	250	375	—
AH1062//26	—	90.00	150	250	375	—
AH1063//26	—	90.00	150	250	375	—
AH1063//27	—	90.00	150	250	375	—
AH1066//29	—	90.00	150	250	375	—
AH1066//30	—	90.00	150	250	375	—
AH1067//30	—	90.00	150	250	375	—
AH1067//31	—	90.00	150	250	375	—

Akbarabad

KM# 247.3 NISAR (Type 247)
Silver **Obv. Inscription:** "Jalus Nisar Sahib Qiran Sani" **Rev. Inscription:** "dar al-khilafa" **Note:** Weight varies: 5.50-5.80 grams. 1/2 Rupee weight.

Date	Mintage	VG	F	VF	XF	Unc
AH1046//10	—	90.00	150	250	375	—
AH1046//9	—	90.00	150	250	375	—
AH1054//(18)	—	90.00	150	250	375	—

Akbarabad

KM# 247.4 NISAR (Type 247)
5.5000 g., Silver **Obv. Inscription:** "Sahib Qiran Sani Shah Jahan Bad Shah Ghazi" **Rev. Inscription:** "dar al-Khilafa"

Date	Mintage	VG	F	VF	XF	Unc
AH1047	—	125	260	350	525	—

Akbarabad

KM# 247.5 NISAR (Type 247)
5.3000 g., Silver **Obv. Inscription:** "Nisar Shah Qiran Sani Shah Jahan Bad Shah Ghazi" **Rev. Inscription:** "dar al-Khilafa"

Date	Mintage	VG	F	VF	XF	Unc
AH1054//18	—	100	180	300	450	—

Akbarabad

KM# 247.6 NISAR (Type 247)
Silver **Obv. Inscription:** "Nisar Sahib Qiran Sani" **Rev. Inscription:** "dar al-Khilafa" **Note:** Weight varies 5.4 - 5.7 grams.

Date	Mintage	VG	F	VF	XF	Unc
AH1069//33 (sic)	—	110	180	300	450	—

Daulatabad

KM# 247.7 NISAR (Type 247)
5.6000 g., Silver **Obv. Inscription:** "Nisar Sahib Qiran Sani"

Date	Mintage	VG	F	VF	XF	Unc
AH1045//8	—	145	240	400	600	—

Lahore

KM# 247.1 NISAR (Type 247)
Silver **Obv. Inscription:** "Sahib Qiran Sani" **Note:** Weight varies: 5.50-5.80 grams. 1/2 Rupee weight. Mint epithet: "Dar-us-Sultanat".

Date	Mintage	VG	F	VF	XF	Unc
AH1048//13	—	130	210	300	420	—
AH1051//15	—	130	210	300	420	—
AH1055//19	—	130	210	300	420	—

Shahjahanabad

KM# 247.2 NISAR (Type 247)
Silver **Obv. Inscription:** "Nisar Sahib Qiran Sani" **Rev. Inscription:** "dar al-khilafa" **Note:** Weight varies: 5.50-5.80 grams. 1/2 Rupee weight. For earlier issues see Dehli.

Date	Mintage	VG	F	VF	XF	Unc
AH1047//11	—	145	240	400	600	—
AH1066//29	—	145	240	400	600	—

Akbarabad

KM# 248.1 NISAR (Type 248)
Gold **Obv. Legend:** "Sahib Qiran" **Note:** Prev. KM#A267.1; Weight varies: 2.50-2.85 grams.

Date	Mintage	VG	F	VF	XF	Unc
AH1068//31	—	—	150	200	320	—

Shahjahanabad

KM# 248.2 NISAR (Type 248)
Gold **Obv. Legend:** "Sahib Qiran" **Note:** Prev. KM#A267.2; Weight varies: 2.50-2.85 grams.

Date	Mintage	Good	VG	F	VF	XF
AH1069//3x	—	—	—	175	250	375

Agra

KM# A249.1 NISAR (Type A249)
Gold **Obv. Legend:** "Shah Jahan" **Note:** Prev. KM#267.1; Weight varies: 2.50-2.85 grams.

Date	Mintage	Good	VG	F	VF	XF
AH1037//1	—	—	—	275	450	675

Akbarabad

KM# A249.2 NISAR (Type A249)
Gold **Obv. Legend:** "Shah Jahan" **Note:** Prev. KM#267.2; Weight varies: 2.50-2.85 grams.

Date	Mintage	Good	VG	F	VF	XF
AH1042//5	—	—	—	175	250	375
AH1047//1x	—	—	—	175	250	375
AH1048//11	—	—	—	175	250	375

Akbarabad

KM# 267.1 NISAR (Type 267)
Gold **Obv. Legend:** Shah Jahan **Note:** Weight varies 2.5-2.85 grams (1/4 Mohur weight).

Date	Mintage	Good	VG	F	VF	XF
AH1037//(1) Ahad	—	—	—	250	400	625

Akbarabad

KM# 267.2 NISAR (Type 267)
Gold **Obv. Legend:** Shah Jahan **Note:** Weight varies 2.5-2.85 grams (1/4 Mohur weight).

Date	Mintage	Good	VG	F	VF	XF
AH1042//5	—	—	—	200	300	475
AH1047//11	—	—	—	200	300	475
AH1048//11	—	—	—	200	300	475

Akbarabad

KM# A267.1 NISAR (Type A267)
Gold **Obv. Legend:** Sahib Qiran **Note:** Weight varies 2.5-2.85 grams (1/4 Mohur weight).

Date	Mintage	Good	VG	F	VF	XF
AH1068//31	—	—	—	225	350	550

Shahjahanabad

KM# A267.2 NISAR (Type A267)
Gold **Obv. Legend:** Sahib Qiran **Note:** Weight varies 2.5-2.85 grams (1/4 Mohur weight).

Date	Mintage	Good	VG	F	VF	XF
AH1069	—	—	—	225	350	550

Shah Shuja, in Bengal

AH1068-1070 / 1657-1660AD

HAMMERED COINAGE

Akbarnagar

KM# A274.1 1/2 RUPEE (Type A274)
5.7220 g., Silver **Note:** Similar to Rupee, KM#275.1.

Date	Mintage	VG	F	VF	XF	Unc
AHxxxx//(1) Ahad	—	1,450	2,400	4,000	6,000	—

Akbarnagar

KM# 274.1 1/2 RUPEE (Type 274)
5.7220 g., Silver **Note:** Similar to Rupee, KM#276.1.

Date	Mintage	VG	F	VF	XF	Unc
AH1068//(1) Ahad	—	1,450	2,400	4,000	6,000	—

Akbarnagar

KM# 275.1 RUPEE (Type 275)
11.4440 g., Silver **Obv:** Inscription in outlined square **Obv. Inscription:** "Kalima" **Rev:** Ruler's name and titles in 4-line inscription

Date	Mintage	VG	F	VF	XF	Unc
AH1068//(1) Ahad	—	1,100	1,800	3,000	4,500	—

Patna

KM# 276.1 RUPEE (Type 276)
11.4440 g., Silver **Obv:** Inscription in outlined square **Obv. Inscription:** "Kalima" **Rev:** Inscription with ruler's name in lower part of outlined square

Date	Mintage	VG	F	VF	XF	Unc
AH1068//(1) Ahad	—	1,450	240	4,000	6,000	—

Akbarnagar

KM# 277.1 RUPEE (Type 277)
11.4440 g., Silver **Obv:** Inscription in outlined square **Obv. Inscription:** "Kalima" **Rev:** Inscription with ruler's name in upper part of Outlined square

Date	Mintage	VG	F	VF	XF	Unc
AH1068//(1) Ahad	—	1,800	3,000	5,000	7,500	—

Katak

KM# 277.2 RUPEE (Type 277)
11.4440 g., Silver

Date	Mintage	VG	F	VF	XF	Unc
AH1068//(1) Ahad	—	1,450	2,400	4,000	6,000	—

LARGESSE COINAGE

Akbarnagar

KM# A278.1 NISAR (Type A278)
2.7000 g., Silver **Note:** Similar to Nisar, KM#278.1.

Date	Mintage	VG	F	VF	XF	Unc
AH1068//(1) Ahad	—	1,100	1,800	3,000	4,500	—

Akbarnagar

KM# 278 NISAR (Type 278)
5.7200 g., Silver

Date	Mintage	VG	F	VF	XF	Unc
AH1068//(1)	—	1,100	1,800	3,000	4,500	—

Akbarnagar

KM# 278.1 NISAR (Type 278)
5.7200 g., Silver **Note:** Type 278.

Date	Mintage	VG	F	VF	XF	Unc
AH1068	—	1,100	1,800	3,000	4,500	—

Muhammad Murad Bakhsh

In Gujarat; AH 1068 / 1658AD

HAMMERED COINAGE

Surat

KM# A269.1 1/2 DAM (Type A269)
Copper **Note:** Weight varies 10.2 - 10.8 grams.

Date	Mintage	Good	VG	F	VF	XF
AH(1068)//(1) Ahad	—	37.50	75.00	150	240	—

Surat

KM# 269.1 DAM (Type 269)
Copper **Note:** Weight varies: 20.40-21.60 grams.

Date	Mintage	Good	VG	F	VF	XF
AH(1068)//(1) Ahad Rare	—	80.00	150	225	300	—

Ahmadabad

KM# A270.1 1/4 RUPEE (Type A270)
2.8610 g., Silver **Obv:** Central inscription within square **Rev:** Central inscription within square

Date	Mintage	VG	F	VF	XF	Unc
AH1068//(1) Ahad	—	300	480	800	1,200	—

Surat

KM# A270.2 1/4 RUPEE (Type A270)
2.8610 g., Silver **Obv:** Central inscription within square **Rev:** Central inscription within square

Date	Mintage	VG	F	VF	XF	Unc
AH1068//(1) Ahad	—	300	480	800	1,200	—

Ahmadabad

KM# 270.1 1/2 RUPEE (Type 270)
5.7220 g., Silver **Obv:** Central inscription within square **Rev:** Central inscription within square

Date	Mintage	VG	F	VF	XF	Unc
AH1068//(1) Ahad	—	180	300	500	750	—

Khambayat

KM# 270.3 1/2 RUPEE (Type 270)
5.7220 g., Silver **Obv:** Central inscription within square **Rev:** Central inscription within square

Date	Mintage	VG	F	VF	XF	Unc
AHxxxx	—	180	300	500	750	—

Surat

KM# 270.2 1/2 RUPEE (Type 270)
5.7220 g., Silver **Obv:** Central inscription within square **Rev:** Central inscription within square

Date	Mintage	VG	F	VF	XF	Unc
AH1068//(1) Ahad	—	145	240	400	600	—

Surat

KM# A271.1 1/2 RUPEE (Type A271)
5.7220 g., Silver **Note:** Similar to Rupee, KM#271.1.

Date	Mintage	VG	F	VF	XF	Unc
AHxxxx//(1)	—	145	240	400	600	—

Surat

KM# 271.1 RUPEE (Type 271)
11.4440 g., Silver

Date	Mintage	VG	F	VF	XF	Unc
AH1068//(1) Ahad	—	180	330	550	825	—

Khambayat

KM# A272.2 RUPEE (Type A272)
11.4440 g., Silver **Obv:** Central inscription within squares; ruler's name excludes "Muhammad" **Rev:** Central inscription within squares **Note:** Previous KM#272.2; Varieties exist.

Date	Mintage	VG	F	VF	XF	Unc
AH1068//(1) Ahad	—	80.00	135	225	340	—

Ahmadabad

KM# 272.1 RUPEE (Type 272)
11.4440 g., Silver **Obv:** Central inscription within squares, ruler's name includes "Muhammad" **Rev:** Central inscription within squares

Date	Mintage	VG	F	VF	XF	Unc
AH1068//(1) Ahad	—	55.00	90.00	150	225	—

Surat

KM# 272.3 RUPEE (Type 272)
11.4440 g., Silver **Obv:** Central inscription within squares **Rev:** Central inscription within squares

Date	Mintage	VG	F	VF	XF	Unc
AH1068//(1) Ahad	—	36.00	60.00	100	150	—

Ahmadabad

KM# 273.1 MOHUR (Type 273)
Gold **Note:** Weight varies 10.8 - 11 grams.

Date	Mintage	VG	F	VF	XF	Unc
AH1068//(1) Ahad	—	1,200	2,000	3,250	5,000	—

Khambayat

KM# 273.2 MOHUR (Type 273)
Gold **Note:** Weight varies 10.8 - 11 grams.

Date	Mintage	Good	VG	F	VF	XF
AH1068//(1) Ahad	—	—	1,200	2,000	3,250	5,000

Surat

KM# 273.3 MOHUR (Type 273)
Gold Weight varies: 10.8-11.0 grams. **Obv:** Name and titles in square, mint in left segment **Rev:** Kalima in square, date

Date	Mintage	VG	F	VF	XF	Unc
AH1068/(1) Ahad	—	500	850	1,400	2,100	—

Aurangzeb Alamgir

AH1068-1118 / 1658-1707AD

HAMMERED COINAGE

Lahore

KM# 280.1 1/8 PAISA (Type 280)
Copper **Note:** Type 280. Weight varies 1.90-2.20 grams.

Date	Mintage	Good	VG	F	VF	XF
AH1075	—	9.00	15.00	30.00	48.00	—

Narnol

KM# 280.2 1/8 PAISA (Type 280)
Copper **Note:** Weight varies 1.9 - 2.2 grams.

Date	Mintage	Good	VG	F	VF	XF
ND(1658-1707)	—	5.00	12.50	25.00	40.00	—

Haidarabad

KM# 281.3 1/4 PAISA (Type 281)
Copper **Note:** Weight varies 3.90-4.05 grams.

Date	Mintage	Good	VG	F	VF	XF
ND(1658-1707)	—	5.00	12.50	25.00	40.00	—

Multan

KM# 282.1 1/4 PAISA (Type 282)
Copper **Note:** Weight varies 3.90-4.05 grams.

Date	Mintage	Good	VG	F	VF	XF
AH1073//x	—	9.00	15.00	30.00	48.00	—

Surat

KM# 282.2 1/4 PAISA (Type 282)
Copper **Note:** Weight varies 3.90-4.05 grams.

Date	Mintage	Good	VG	F	VF	XF
ND(1658-1707)	—	4.00	10.00	20.00	32.00	—

Bijapur

KM# 283.7 1/2 PAISA (Type 283)
Copper **Note:** Weight varies 6.15-7.05 grams.

Date	Mintage	Good	VG	F	VF	XF
AHxxxx//x	—	4.00	10.00	20.00	32.00	—

Burhanpur

KM# 283.6 1/2 PAISA (Type 283)
Copper **Note:** Weight varies 6.15-7.05 grams.

Date	Mintage	Good	VG	F	VF	XF
AHxxxx//19	—	10.00	25.00	50.00	80.00	—
AHxxxx//21	—	10.00	25.00	50.00	80.00	—
AHXXXX//31	—	10.00	25.00	50.00	80.00	—
No date	—	10.00	25.00	50.00	80.00	—

Haidarabad (Farkhanda Bunyad)

KM# 283.1 1/2 PAISA (Type 283)
Copper **Note:** Weight varies 6.15-7.05 grams.

Date	Mintage	Good	VG	F	VF	XF
AH1xxx//32	—	5.00	12.50	25.00	40.00	—
AH1103//35	—	5.00	12.50	25.00	40.00	—
AH1104//xx	—	5.00	12.50	25.00	40.00	—
AH1106//38	—	5.00	12.50	25.00	40.00	—
AH1108//4x	—	5.00	12.50	25.00	40.00	—
AH1109//41	—	5.00	12.50	25.00	40.00	—
AH1112//45	—	5.00	12.50	25.00	40.00	—

Kabul

KM# 283.10 1/2 PAISA (Type 283)
Copper **Note:** Weight varies 6.15 - 7.05 grams.

Date	Mintage	Good	VG	F	VF	XF
AH1074	—	15.00	37.50	75.00	120	—

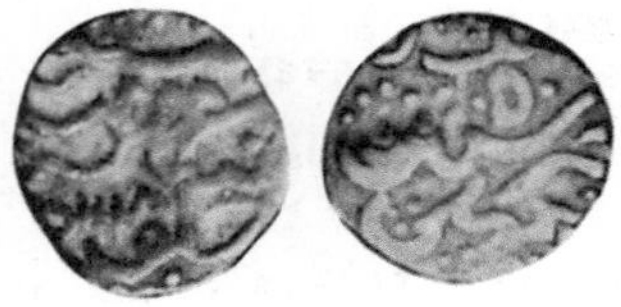

Macchlipattan

KM# 283.2 1/2 PAISA (Type 283)
Copper **Obv. Inscription:** "Mubarak julus sanah" **Rev. Inscription:** "Zarb bandar machhlipatan sanah" **Note:** Weight varies 6.15-7.05 grams.

Date	Mintage	Good	VG	F	VF	XF
AH1110//42	—	5.50	11.00	25.00	40.00	—
AH1111//43	—	6.00	12.00	30.00	50.00	—
AH1111//44	—	5.50	11.00	25.00	40.00	—
AH1112//45	—	6.00	12.00	30.00	50.00	—

Shahjahanabad

KM# 283.3 1/2 PAISA (Type 283)
Copper **Note:** Weight varies 6.15-7.05 grams.

Date	Mintage	Good	VG	F	VF	XF
AH1074//6	—	5.00	12.50	25.00	40.00	—

Sholapur

KM# 283.4 1/2 PAISA (Type 283)
Copper **Note:** Weight varies 6.15-7.05 grams.

Date	Mintage	Good	VG	F	VF	XF
ND(1658-1707)	—	10.00	25.00	50.00	80.00	—

Surat

KM# 283.8 1/2 PAISA (Type 283)
Copper **Note:** Weight varies 6.15 - 7.05 grams.

Date	Mintage	Good	VG	F	VF	XF
AH1093	—	4.00	10.00	20.00	32.00	—

Surat

KM# 284.1 1/2 DAM (Type 284)
Copper **Obv. Inscription:** "Julus sanah mubarak" **Note:** Weight varies 9.50-10.30 grams.

Date	Mintage	Good	VG	F	VF	XF
year 1	—	4.00	10.00	20.00	32.00	—
AH107x//3	—	4.00	10.00	20.00	32.00	—
AH1073//5	—	4.00	10.00	20.00	32.00	—
AH107x//7	—	4.00	10.00	20.00	32.00	—
AH177x//11	—	4.00	10.00	20.00	32.00	—
AH108x//13	—	4.00	10.00	20.00	32.00	—
AH1082//1x	—	4.00	10.00	20.00	32.00	—
AH1083//15	—	4.00	10.00	20.00	32.00	—
AH1086//1x	—	4.00	10.00	20.00	32.00	—
AH1088//2x	—	4.00	10.00	20.00	32.00	—

Ahmadabad

KM# 285.12 PAISA (Type 285)
Copper **Note:** Weight varies 12.30-14.10 grams.

Date	Mintage	Good	VG	F	VF	XF
AH1100//xx	—	7.00	17.50	35.00	55.00	—

Ahmadanagar

KM# 285.18 PAISA (Type 285)
Copper **Note:** Weight varies 12.3 - 14.1 grams.

Date	Mintage	Good	VG	F	VF	XF
AH109x//26	—	10.00	25.00	50.00	80.00	—

Akbarabad

KM# 285.1 PAISA (Type 285)
Copper **Note:** Weight varies 12.3 - 14.1 grams.

Date	Mintage	Good	VG	F	VF	XF
AH1074//7	—	9.00	15.00	30.00	50.00	—
AH1075//8	—	9.00	15.00	30.00	50.00	—

Azamnagar

KM# 285.19 PAISA (Type 285)
Copper **Note:** Weight varies 12.3 - 14.1 grams.

Date	Mintage	Good	VG	F	VF	XF
AH1099//32	—	15.00	37.50	75.00	120	—
AH110x//33	—	15.00	37.50	75.00	120	—

Azimabad

KM# 285.20 PAISA (Type 285)
Copper **Note:** Weight varies 12.3 - 14.1 grams.

Date	Mintage	Good	VG	F	VF	XF
AH1110//xx	—	12.00	30.00	60.00	100	—

Bairata

KM# 285.2 PAISA (Type 285)
Copper **Note:** Weight varies 12.3 - 14.1 grams.

Date	Mintage	Good	VG	F	VF	XF
ND(1658-1707)	—	10.00	25.00	50.00	80.00	—

Banaras

KM# 285.25 PAISA (Type 285)
Copper **Note:** Weight varies 12.30-14.10 grams.

Date	Mintage	Good	VG	F	VF	XF
ND(1658-1707)	—	10.00	25.00	50.00	80.00	—

Bijapur

KM# 285.21 PAISA (Type 285)
Copper **Note:** Weight varies 12.3 - 14.1 grams.

Date	Mintage	Good	VG	F	VF	XF
ND(1658-1707)	—	10.00	25.00	50.00	80.00	—

Burhanpur

KM# 285.22 PAISA (Type 285)
Copper **Note:** Weight varies 12.3 - 14.1 grams.

Date	Mintage	Good	VG	F	VF	XF
AH108x//21	—	10.00	25.00	50.00	80.00	—

Chinapattan

KM# 285.23 PAISA (Type 285)
Copper **Note:** Weight varies 12.3 - 14.1 grams.

Date	Mintage	Good	VG	F	VF	XF
ND(1658-1707)	—	20.00	50.00	100	160	—

Haidarabad (Farkhanda Bunyad)

KM# 285.3 PAISA (Type 285)
Copper **Note:** Weight varies 12.3 - 14.1 grams.

Date	Mintage	Good	VG	F	VF	XF
AH1xxx//32	—	4.00	10.00	20.00	32.00	—
AH1102//3x	—	4.00	10.00	20.00	32.00	—
AH1103//3x	—	4.00	10.00	20.00	32.00	—
AH1106//38	—	4.00	10.00	20.00	32.00	—
AH1106//39	—	4.00	10.00	20.00	32.00	—
AH1107//39	—	4.00	10.00	20.00	32.00	—
AH1107//40	—	4.00	10.00	20.00	32.00	—
AH1108//4x	—	4.00	10.00	20.00	32.00	—
AH1109//41	—	4.00	10.00	20.00	32.00	—
AH1111//43	—	4.00	10.00	20.00	32.00	—
AH1111//44	—	4.00	10.00	20.00	32.00	—
AH1112//44	—	4.00	10.00	20.00	32.00	—
AH1112//45	—	4.00	10.00	20.00	32.00	—

Kabul

KM# 285.13 PAISA (Type 285)
Copper **Note:** Weight varies 12.3 - 14.1 grams.

Date	Mintage	Good	VG	F	VF	XF
ND(1658-1707)	—	13.00	32.50	65.00	100	—

Katak

KM# 285.4 PAISA (Type 285)
Copper **Note:** Weight varies 12.3 - 14.1 grams.

Date	Mintage	Good	VG	F	VF	XF
AH108x//16	—	10.00	25.00	50.00	80.00	—

Lahore

KM# 285.5 PAISA (Type 285)
Copper **Note:** Weight varies 12.30-14.10 grams.

Date	Mintage	Good	VG	F	VF	XF
AH1074//7	—	9.00	22.50	45.00	75.00	—
AH1075//x	—	9.00	22.50	45.00	75.00	—
AH1079//11	—	9.00	22.50	45.00	75.00	—
AH1084//16	—	9.00	22.50	45.00	75.00	—
AH108x//17	—	9.00	22.50	45.00	75.00	—
AHxxxx//18	—	9.00	22.50	45.00	75.00	—
AH1092//24	—	9.00	22.50	45.00	75.00	—
AH110x//39	—	9.00	22.50	45.00	75.00	—

Lakhnau

KM# 285.14 PAISA (Type 285)
Copper **Note:** Weight varies 12.3 - 14.1 grams.

Date	Mintage	Good	VG	F	VF	XF
AH1095//2x	—	5.00	12.50	25.00	40.00	—

Macchlipattan

KM# 285.6 PAISA (Type 285)
Copper **Obv. Inscription:** "Mubarak julus sanah" **Rev. Inscription:** "Zarb bandar machhlipatan sanah" **Note:** Weight varies 12.30-14.10 grams.

Date	Mintage	Good	VG	F	VF	XF
AH1079//11	—	2.25	5.00	12.00	25.00	—
AH1087//18	—	2.25	5.00	12.00	25.00	—
AH1110//-	—	2.25	5.00	12.00	25.00	—
AH110x//34	—	2.25	5.00	12.00	25.00	—
AH110x//41	—	2.25	5.00	12.00	25.00	—
AH1110//42	—	2.25	5.00	12.00	25.00	—
AH1111//43	—	2.25	5.00	12.00	25.00	—
AH1111//44	—	2.25	5.00	12.00	25.00	—
AH1112//44	—	2.25	5.00	12.00	25.00	—
AH1112//45	—	2.25	5.00	12.00	25.00	—

Muazzamabad

KM# 285.15 PAISA (Type 285)
Copper **Note:** Struck at Mu'azzamabad Mint.

Date	Mintage	Good	VG	F	VF	XF
AH10xx//12	—	20.00	50.00	100	160	—

Multan

KM# 285.7 PAISA (Type 285)

Copper **Obv:** Emperor's name and titles, date **Rev:** Mint and regnal year **Note:** Weight varies 12.3 - 14.1 grams.

Date	Mintage	Good	VG	F	VF	XF
AH1107//39	—	9.00	22.50	45.00	75.00	—
AH1107//40	—	9.00	22.50	45.00	75.00	—
AH1108//40	—	9.00	22.50	45.00	75.00	—

Narnol

KM# 285.8 PAISA (Type 285)

Copper **Obv:** Emperor's name **Rev:** Mint **Note:** Weight varies 12.3 - 14.1 grams.

Date	Mintage	Good	VG	F	VF	XF
AH1075//7	—	8.00	20.00	40.00	65.00	—
AH107x//8	—	8.00	20.00	40.00	65.00	—
AH109x//xx	—	8.00	20.00	40.00	65.00	—
ND(1658-1707)	—	8.00	20.00	40.00	65.00	—

Nusratabad

KM# 285.29 PAISA (Type 285)

Copper **Note:** Weight varies 12.3 - 14.1 grams.

Date	Mintage	Good	VG	F	VF	XF
AH1101//33	—	15.00	37.50	75.00	120	—

Patna

KM# 285.28 PAISA (Type 285)

Copper **Note:** Weight varies 12.3 - 14.1 grams.

Date	Mintage	Good	VG	F	VF	XF
AHxxxx//x	—	12.00	30.00	60.00	95.00	—

Sakkhar

KM# 285.26 PAISA (Type 285)

Copper **Note:** Weight varies 12.3 - 14.1 grams.

Date	Mintage	Good	VG	F	VF	XF
AHxxxx//x	—	30.00	75.00	150	240	—

Shahjahanabad

KM# 285.9 PAISA (Type 285)

Copper **Note:** Weight varies 12.3 - 14.1 grams.

Date	Mintage	Good	VG	F	VF	XF
AH1068//(1) Ahad	—	7.00	17.50	35.00	55.00	—
AH1069//2	—	7.00	17.50	35.00	55.00	—
AH1069//3	—	7.00	17.50	35.00	55.00	—
AHxxxx//4	—	7.00	17.50	35.00	55.00	—
AH1072//5	—	7.00	17.50	35.00	55.00	—
AH1074//6	—	7.00	17.50	35.00	55.00	—
AH1075//7	—	7.00	17.50	35.00	55.00	—
AH1075//8	—	7.00	17.50	35.00	55.00	—
AH1076//8	—	7.00	17.50	35.00	55.00	—
AH10xx//9	—	7.00	17.50	35.00	55.00	—
AH1078//10	—	7.00	17.50	35.00	55.00	—
AH1079//11	—	7.00	17.50	35.00	55.00	—
AH1080//12	—	7.00	17.50	35.00	55.00	—
AH1081//14	—	7.00	17.50	35.00	55.00	—
AH1084//16	—	7.00	17.50	35.00	55.00	—
AHxxxx//18	—	7.00	17.50	35.00	55.00	—

Sholapur

KM# 285.10 PAISA (Type 285)

Copper **Note:** Weight varies 12.3 - 14.1 grams.

Date	Mintage	Good	VG	F	VF	XF
AHxxxx//4	—	10.00	25.00	50.00	80.00	—
AHxxxx//30	—	10.00	25.00	50.00	80.00	—
AHxxxx//32	—	10.00	25.00	50.00	80.00	—
AHxxxx//34	—	10.00	25.00	50.00	80.00	—

Surat

KM# 285.11 PAISA (Type 285)

Copper **Obv:** Emperor's name **Rev:** Mint and date **Note:** Weight varies 12.30-14.10 grams.

Date	Mintage	Good	VG	F	VF	XF
AH1079//12	—	4.00	10.00	20.00	32.00	—
AH1080//13	—	4.00	10.00	20.00	32.00	—
AH1082//14	—	4.00	10.00	20.00	32.00	—
AH1083//15	—	4.00	10.00	20.00	32.00	—
AH1088//22	—	4.00	10.00	20.00	32.00	—
AH1089//22	—	4.00	10.00	20.00	32.00	—
AH1091	—	4.00	10.00	20.00	32.00	—
AH109x//24	—	4.00	10.00	20.00	32.00	—
AH1095//27	—	4.00	10.00	20.00	32.00	—
AH109x//26	—	4.00	10.00	20.00	32.00	—
AH1098//3x	—	4.00	10.00	20.00	32.00	—
AH1105//3x	—	4.00	10.00	20.00	32.00	—
AH11xx//42	—	4.00	10.00	20.00	32.00	—
AH1111//44	—	4.00	10.00	20.00	32.00	—
AH1115//4x	—	4.00	10.00	20.00	32.00	—

Zafarabad

KM# 285.24 PAISA (Type 285)

11.4000 g., Copper **Note:** Weight varies 12.3 - 14.1 grams.

Date	Mintage	Good	VG	F	VF	XF
ND(1658-1707)	—	12.00	30.00	60.00	100	—

Bairata

KM# 286.6 DAM (Type 286)

Copper **Note:** Weight varies 17.00-18.60 grams.

Date	Mintage	Good	VG	F	VF	XF
AH110x//xx	—	8.00	20.00	40.00	65.00	—

Elichpur

KM# 286.1 DAM (Type 286)

Copper **Note:** Weight varies 19.7 - 20.2 grams.

Date	Mintage	Good	VG	F	VF	XF
AH1078//1x	—	6.00	15.00	30.00	48.00	—

Lakhnau

KM# 286.7 DAM (Type 286)

19.9500 g., Copper **Note:** Weight varies 19.50-20.20 grams.

Date	Mintage	Good	VG	F	VF	XF
AH1085//9	—	8.00	20.00	40.00	65.00	—
AH1095//19	—	8.00	20.00	40.00	65.00	—

Narnol

KM# 286.2 DAM (Type 286)

Copper **Note:** Weight varies 19.7 - 20.2 grams.

Date	Mintage	Good	VG	F	VF	XF
AH108x//21	—	8.00	20.00	40.00	65.00	—

Shahjahanabad

KM# 286.3 DAM (Type 286)

Copper **Note:** Weight varies 19.7 - 20.2 grams.

Date	Mintage	Good	VG	F	VF	XF
AH1069//(1) Ahad	—	5.00	12.50	25.00	40.00	—
AH1069//2	—	5.00	12.50	25.00	40.00	—
AH107x//3	—	5.00	12.50	25.00	40.00	—
AH1071//4	—	5.00	12.50	25.00	40.00	—

Surat

KM# 286.4 DAM (Type 286)

Copper, 20.8 mm. **Note:** Weight varies 19.7 - 20.2 grams.

Date	Mintage	Good	VG	F	VF	XF
AH106x//(1) Ahad	—	5.00	12.50	25.00	40.00	—
AH107x//3	—	5.00	12.50	25.00	40.00	—
AH107x//4	—	5.00	12.50	25.00	40.00	—
AH107x//5	—	5.00	12.50	25.00	40.00	—
AH1075//7	—	5.00	12.50	25.00	40.00	—
AH1075//8	—	5.00	12.50	25.00	40.00	—
AH107x//9	—	5.00	12.50	25.00	40.00	—
AH107x//10	—	5.00	12.50	25.00	40.00	—
AH107x//11	—	5.00	12.50	25.00	40.00	—
AH108x//13	—	5.00	12.50	25.00	40.00	—
AH1083//15	—	5.00	12.50	25.00	40.00	—
AH//29	—	5.00	12.50	25.00	40.00	—
ND	—	5.00	12.50	25.00	40.00	—

Zafarabad

KM# 286.5 DAM (Type 286)

Copper **Note:** Weight varies 19.7 - 20.2 grams.

Date	Mintage	Good	VG	F	VF	XF
ND	—	15.00	37.50	75.00	120	—

Patna

KM# 288.1 2 DAM (Type 288)

43.4000 g., Copper **Obv. Legend:** FALUS ALAMGIR SHAHI **Note:** Weight varies 42.90-43.41 grams.

Date	Mintage	Good	VG	F	VF	XF
AH107x//6	—	30.00	75.00	150	240	—
AH107x//9	—	30.00	75.00	150	240	—

Lahore

KM# 289.1 1/32 RUPEE (Type 289)

0.3580 g., Silver **Obv:** Legend is a poetic couplet

Date	Mintage	VG	F	VF	XF	Unc
AH1105//3x	—	36.00	60.00	100	150	—
AH1109//42	—	36.00	60.00	100	150	—

Ujjain

KM# 289.2 1/32 RUPEE (Type 289)

0.3580 g., Silver

Date	Mintage	VG	F	VF	XF	Unc
AH108x//21	—	70.00	120	200	300	—

Akbarnagar

KM# 290.3 1/16 RUPEE (Type 290)

0.7150 g., Silver **Obv:** Legend is a poetic couplet

Date	Mintage	Good	VG	F	VF	XF
AH1081//1x	—	—	55.00	90.00	150	225

Gulkanda

KM# 290.1 1/16 RUPEE (Type 290)

0.7150 g., Silver

Date	Mintage	VG	F	VF	XF	Unc
AH1076//1x	—	30.00	48.00	80.00	120	—
AH108x//15	—	30.00	48.00	80.00	120	—

Sholapur

KM# 290.4 1/16 RUPEE (Type 290)
0.7150 g., Silver

Date	Mintage	VG	F	VF	XF	Unc
AHxxxx//x	—	72.00	120	200	300	—

Surat

KM# 290.5 1/16 RUPEE (Type 290)
0.7150 g., Silver

Date	Mintage	VG	F	VF	XF	Unc
AHxxxx//x	—	72.00	120	200	300	—

Ujjain

KM# 290.6 1/16 RUPEE (Type 290)
0.7150 g., Silver **Rev:** Inscription and mint name **Rev. Inscription:** "dar al-Fath"

Date	Mintage	VG	F	VF	XF	Unc
AH1084//17	—	72.00	120	200	300	—
AH1109	—	72.00	120	200	300	—

Zafarabad

KM# 290.2 1/16 RUPEE (Type 290)
0.7150 g., Silver **Obv:** Mihr

Date	Mintage	VG	F	VF	XF	Unc
AH1079//12	—	72.00	120	200	300	—

Jahangirnagar

KM# 291.1 1/16 RUPEE (Type 291)
0.7150 g., Silver **Obv. Legend:** SIKKA ALAMGIR SHAHI

Date	Mintage	VG	F	VF	XF	Unc
AH1071//x	—	60.00	105	175	260	—

Burhanpur

KM# A292.1 1/8 RUPEE (Type A292)
1.4300 g., Silver **Obv:** Couplet legend. **Shape:** Square.

Date	Mintage	VG	F	VF	XF	Unc
ND	—	36.00	60.00	100	160	—

Ujjain

KM# A292.2 1/8 RUPEE (Type A292)
1.4305 g., Silver **Shape:** Square

Date	Mintage	VG	F	VF	XF	Unc
AH1079//10	—	30.00	48.00	80.00	120	—
AH1084//17	—	30.00	48.00	80.00	120	—
AH1086//18	—	30.00	48.00	80.00	120	—

Ahmadnagar

KM# 292.9 1/8 RUPEE (Type 292)
Silver

Date	Mintage	VG	F	VF	XF	Unc
AH107x	—	72.00	120	200	300	—

Akbarnagar

KM# 292.3 1/8 RUPEE (Type 292)
1.4300 g., Silver **Obv:** Legend is a couplet

Date	Mintage	VG	F	VF	XF	Unc
AH108x//16	—	63.00	110	175	260	—

Burhanpur

KM# 292.4 1/8 RUPEE (Type 292)
Silver **Obv:** Inscription **Rev:** Inscription **Note:** Weight varies 1.38-1.45 grams.

Date	Mintage	VG	F	VF	XF	Unc
ND	—	55.00	90.00	150	225	—

Gulkanda

KM# 292.1 1/8 RUPEE (Type 292)
Silver **Note:** Weight varies 1.38-1.45 grams.

Date	Mintage	VG	F	VF	XF	Unc
AH1076//20 (sic)	—	27.00	45.00	75.00	115	—

Sholapur

KM# 292.6 1/8 RUPEE (Type 292)
1.4305 g., Silver

Date	Mintage	VG	F	VF	XF	Unc
AH1071	—	70.00	120	200	300	—

Surat

KM# 292.7 1/8 RUPEE (Type 292)
1.4305 g., Silver

Date	Mintage	VG	F	VF	XF	Unc
AHxxxx//35	—	55.00	90.00	150	225	—

Ujjain

KM# 292.5 1/8 RUPEE (Type 292)
1.4300 g., Silver **Obv:** Inscription **Rev:** Inscription **Shape:** Round **Note:** Weight varies 1.38-1.45 grams.

Date	Mintage	VG	F	VF	XF	Unc
ND	—	55.00	90.00	150	225	—

Zafarabad

KM# 292.8 1/8 RUPEE (Type 292)
1.4305 g., Silver

Date	Mintage	VG	F	VF	XF	Unc
AH1079//12	—	90.00	150	250	375	—

Burhanpur

KM# A293.1 1/4 RUPEE (Type A293)
2.8610 g., Silver **Obv:** Inscription **Rev:** Inscription **Shape:** Square **Note:** Weight varies: 2.75-2.90 grams.

Date	Mintage	VG	F	VF	XF	Unc
ND	—	—	—	—	—	—

Ujjain

KM# A293.2 1/4 RUPEE (Type A293)
2.8610 g., Silver **Rev:** Inscription and mint name **Rev. Inscription:** "dar al-Fath" **Note:** Square.

Date	Mintage	Good	VG	F	VF	XF
AH1082//15	—	—	—	—	—	—
AH1109	—	—	—	—	—	—

Burhanpur

KM# B293.1 1/4 RUPEE (Type B293)
2.8610 g., Silver **Obv. Inscription:** "...Muhi al-Din"

Date	Mintage	VG	F	VF	XF	Unc
AHxxxx//(1) Ahad	—	125	210	350	525	—

Patna

KM# B293.2 1/4 RUPEE (Type B293)
2.8610 g., Silver **Obv. Inscription:** "...Muhi al-Din"

Date	Mintage	Good	VG	F	VF	XF
AHxxxx//(1) Ahad	—	—	125	210	350	525

Gulkanda

KM# C293.1 1/4 RUPEE (Type C293)
Silver **Note:** Similar to Rupee, KM#299.1.

Date	Mintage	Good	VG	F	VF	XF
AH1069//(1) Ahad	—	—	90.00	150	250	375

Ajmir

KM# 293.11 1/4 RUPEE (Type 293)
2.8610 g., Silver

Date	Mintage	VG	F	VF	XF	Unc
AH1111	—	125	210	350	525	—

Akbarabad

KM# 293.2 1/4 RUPEE (Type 293)
2.8610 g., Silver

Date	Mintage	VG	F	VF	XF	Unc
AH1079//1x	—	55.00	90.00	150	225	—
AH1107//xx	—	55.00	90.00	150	225	—
AH111x//45	—	55.00	90.00	150	225	—

Akbarnagar

KM# 293.6 1/4 RUPEE (Type 293)
2.8610 g., Silver

Date	Mintage	VG	F	VF	XF	Unc
AHxxxx//5	—	55.00	90.00	150	225	—
AH108x//14	—	55.00	90.00	150	225	—
AH109x//24	—	55.00	90.00	150	225	—

Aurangabad

KM# 293.12 1/4 RUPEE (Type 293)
2.8610 g., Silver **Rev:** Inscription with mint name at top

Date	Mintage	Good	VG	F	VF	XF
AH1081	—	—	70.00	120	200	300

Aurangabad

KM# 293.13 1/4 RUPEE (Type 293)
2.8610 g., Silver **Rev:** Inscription with mint name at bottom

Date	Mintage	VG	F	VF	XF	Unc
AH1092	—	70.00	120	200	300	—
AH1093	—	70.00	120	200	300	—

Bijapur

KM# 293.14 1/4 RUPEE (Type 293)
2.8610 g., Silver **Rev:** Inscription and mint name **Rev. Inscription:** "dar al-Zafar"

Date	Mintage	VG	F	VF	XF	Unc
AHxxxx//x	—	90.00	150	250	375	—

Burhanpur

KM# 293.3 1/4 RUPEE (Type 293)
2.8610 g., Silver

Date	Mintage	VG	F	VF	XF	Unc
AH107x//3	—	55.00	90.00	150	225	—
AH1072	—	55.00	90.00	150	225	—
AHxxxx//25	—	55.00	90.00	150	225	—

Gulkanda

KM# 293.1 1/4 RUPEE (Type 293)
2.8610 g., Silver

Date	Mintage	VG	F	VF	XF	Unc
AH107x//5	—	15.00	35.00	75.00	125	—
AH1076//8	—	15.00	35.00	75.00	125	—
AHxxxx//11	—	15.00	35.00	75.00	125	—
AHxxxx//13	—	15.00	35.00	75.00	125	—
AH108x//20	—	15.00	35.00	75.00	125	—
AHxxxx//21	—	15.00	35.00	75.00	125	—
AHxxxx//23	—	15.00	35.00	75.00	125	—
AH1076//27 (sic)	—	15.00	35.00	75.00	125	—
AH109x//27	—	15.00	35.00	75.00	125	—

Kabul

KM# 293.8 1/4 RUPEE (Type 293)
2.8610 g., Silver

Date	Mintage	VG	F	VF	XF	Unc
AH107x//5	—	110	180	300	450	—

Kabul

KM# 293.15 1/4 RUPEE (Type 293)
2.8610 g., Silver **Rev. Inscription:** "dar al-Mulk"

Date	Mintage	VG	F	VF	XF	Unc
AH1096	—	110	180	300	450	—

Khambayat

KM# 293.7 1/4 RUPEE (Type 293)
2.8610 g., Silver

Date	Mintage	VG	F	VF	XF	Unc
AH1090//22	—	32.50	55.00	90.00	135	—

Khujista Bunyad

KM# 293.9 1/4 RUPEE (Type 293)
Silver **Note:** Weight varies 2.75-2.90 grams.

Date	Mintage	VG	F	VF	XF	Unc
AH1112//4x	—	70.00	120	200	300	—

Sholapur

KM# 293.16 1/4 RUPEE (Type 293)
2.8610 g., Silver

Date	Mintage	VG	F	VF	XF	Unc
AH1095//2x	—	62.50	110	175	265	—

Surat

KM# 293.17 1/4 RUPEE (Type 293)
2.8610 g., Silver **Note:** Weight varies 2.75-2.90 grams.

Date	Mintage	VG	F	VF	XF	Unc
AH1098	—	62.50	110	175	265	—

Ujjain

KM# 293.5 1/4 RUPEE (Type 293)
Silver **Obv:** Inscription **Rev. Inscription:** Dar-ul Fath **Note:** Weight varies 2.60-2.90 grams

Date	Mintage	VG	F	VF	XF	Unc
AH1088//21	—	70.00	120	200	300	—

Aurangabad

KM# A294.1 1/2 RUPEE (Type A294)
5.7220 g., Silver **Obv. Inscription:** "Muhi al-Din"

Date	Mintage	Good	VG	F	VF	XF
AH1071//3	—	—	—	—	—	—

Kabul

KM# A294.2 1/2 RUPEE (Type A294)
5.7220 g., Silver **Obv:** Short inscription **Obv. Legend:** "Muhi al-Din"

Date	Mintage	Good	VG	F	VF	XF
AH1072//5	—	—	—	—	—	—

Patna

KM# A294.3 1/2 RUPEE (Type A294)
5.7220 g., Silver **Obv. Inscription:** "Muhi al-Din"

Date	Mintage	Good	VG	F	VF	XF
AH1071//(1) (sic) Ahad	—	—	—	—	—	—
AHxxxx//3	—	—	—	—	—	—
AH1072//4	—	—	—	—	—	—

Ahmadabad

KM# 294.1 1/2 RUPEE (Type 294)
Silver **Note:** Weight varies: 5.50-5.80 grams.

Date	Mintage	VG	F	VF	XF	Unc
AH1075//7	—	40.00	65.00	110	165	—
AH1079//12	—	40.00	65.00	110	165	—
AH10xx//18	—	40.00	65.00	110	165	—
AH109x//23	—	40.00	65.00	110	165	—
AH1091//23	—	40.00	65.00	110	165	—
AH1103//3x	—	40.00	65.00	110	165	—
AH1109	—	40.00	65.00	110	165	—

Ajmir

KM# 294.35 1/2 RUPEE (Type 294)
Silver

Date	Mintage	VG	F	VF	XF	Unc
AH1094//26	—	90.00	150	250	375	—

Akbarnagar

KM# 294.24 1/2 RUPEE (Type 294)
5.7220 g., Silver

Date	Mintage	VG	F	VF	XF	Unc
AHxxxx//11	—	110	180	300	450	—
AH10xx//15	—	110	180	300	450	—
AH1096//29	—	110	180	300	450	—

Allahabad

KM# 294.14 1/2 RUPEE (Type 294)
5.7220 g., Silver

Date	Mintage	VG	F	VF	XF	Unc
AH1080//13	—	110	180	300	450	—
AH1081//13	—	110	180	300	450	—

Aurangabad

KM# 294.25 1/2 RUPEE (Type 294)
5.7220 g., Silver **Rev:** Inscription with mint name at top

Date	Mintage	VG	F	VF	XF	Unc
AH1086//19	—	70.00	120	200	300	—

Bijapur

KM# 294.2 1/2 RUPEE (Type 294)
5.7220 g., Silver

Date	Mintage	VG	F	VF	XF	Unc
AH1089//22	—	65.00	110	175	265	—
AH1091//23	—	65.00	110	175	265	—
AH1091//26 (sic)	—	65.00	110	175	265	—
AH109x//31	—	65.00	110	175	265	—

Burhanpur

KM# 294.15 1/2 RUPEE (Type 294)
5.7220 g., Silver

Date	Mintage	VG	F	VF	XF	Unc
AH1098	—	55.00	90.00	150	225	—
AH111x//42	—	55.00	90.00	150	225	—
AH1111//4x	—	55.00	90.00	150	225	—

Gulbarga

KM# 294.26 1/2 RUPEE (Type 294)
5.7220 g., Silver

Date	Mintage	VG	F	VF	XF	Unc
AH1102//3x	—	50.00	90.00	150	225	—
AH1110//42	—	50.00	90.00	150	225	—
AH111x//43	—	50.00	90.00	150	225	—

Gulkanda

KM# 294.27 1/2 RUPEE (Type 294)
5.7220 g., Silver **Note:** Similar to Rupee, KM#299.1.

Date	Mintage	VG	F	VF	XF	Unc
AH1069//(1) Ahad	—	90.00	150	250	375	—

Gulkanda

KM# 294.3 1/2 RUPEE (Type 294)
5.7220 g., Silver

Date	Mintage	Good	VG	F	VF	XF
AHxxxx//4	—	6.00	15.00	35.00	75.00	125
AHxxxx//5	—	6.00	15.00	35.00	75.00	125
AHxxxx//6	—	6.00	15.00	35.00	75.00	125
AH107x//7	—	6.00	15.00	35.00	75.00	125
AH1076//9	—	6.00	15.00	35.00	75.00	125
AH107x//11	—	6.00	15.00	35.00	75.00	125
AH10xx//12	—	6.00	15.00	35.00	75.00	125
AH108x//13	—	6.00	15.00	35.00	75.00	125
AHxxxx//17	—	6.00	15.00	35.00	75.00	125
AHxxxx//18	—	6.00	15.00	35.00	75.00	125
AH108x//20	—	6.00	15.00	35.00	75.00	125
AH108x//21	—	6.00	15.00	35.00	75.00	125
AH10xx//22	—	6.00	15.00	35.00	75.00	125
AHxxxx//24	—	6.00	15.00	35.00	75.00	125
AH109x//25	—	6.00	15.00	35.00	75.00	125
AHxxxx//25	—	6.00	15.00	35.00	75.00	125
AH1076//28	—	6.00	15.00	35.00	75.00	125
AH10xx//30	—	6.00	15.00	35.00	75.00	125

Haidarabad

KM# 294.28 1/2 RUPEE (Type 294)
5.7220 g., Silver

Date	Mintage	VG	F	VF	XF	Unc
AHxxxx//32	—	65.00	110	175	260	—

Hukeri

KM# 294.10 1/2 RUPEE (Type 294)
5.7220 g., Silver

Date	Mintage	VG	F	VF	XF	Unc
AH1110//4x	—	90.00	150	250	375	—

Islamnagar

KM# 294.29 1/2 RUPEE (Type 294)
5.7220 g., Silver

Date	Mintage	VG	F	VF	XF	Unc
AHxxxx//x	—	160	270	450	675	—

Itawa

KM# 294.30 1/2 RUPEE (Type 294)
5.7220 g., Silver

Date	Mintage	VG	F	VF	XF	Unc
AH1108//40	—	145	240	400	600	—

Kabul

KM# 294.31 1/2 RUPEE (Type 294)
5.7220 g., Silver

Date	Mintage	Good	VG	F	VF	XF
AHxxxx//8	—	—	145	240	400	600

Katak

KM# 294.13 1/2 RUPEE (Type 294)
5.7220 g., Silver

Date	Mintage	VG	F	VF	XF	Unc
AH1080//1x	—	75.00	120	200	300	—

Khambayat

KM# 294.4 1/2 RUPEE (Type 294)
5.7220 g., Silver

Date	Mintage	VG	F	VF	XF	Unc
AH108x//15	—	36.00	60.00	100	150	—
AH1085//18	—	36.00	60.00	100	150	—
AH1086	—	36.00	60.00	100	150	—
AH1087//19	—	36.00	60.00	100	150	—
AH1087//2x	—	36.00	60.00	100	150	—
AH1089//2x	—	36.00	60.00	100	150	—
AH1091//24	—	36.00	60.00	100	150	—
AH1095//27	—	36.00	60.00	100	150	—
AH1095//28	—	36.00	60.00	100	150	—
AH1098//30	—	36.00	60.00	100	150	—
AH1100//3x	—	36.00	60.00	100	150	—
AH1102//34	—	36.00	60.00	100	150	—
AH1104//3x	—	36.00	60.00	100	150	—

Macchlipattan

KM# 294.32 1/2 RUPEE (Type 294)
5.7220 g., Silver

Date	Mintage	Good	VG	F	VF	XF
AH1100	—	—	180	300	500	750

Patna

KM# 294.11 1/2 RUPEE (Type 294)
5.7220 g., Silver

Date	Mintage	VG	F	VF	XF	Unc
AH1070//(1) Ahad	—	55.00	90.00	150	225	—
AH107x//3	—	55.00	90.00	150	225	—
AH108x//16	—	55.00	90.00	150	225	—
AH1089//22	—	55.00	90.00	150	225	—

Sangamner

KM# 294.22 1/2 RUPEE (Type 294)
Silver **Note:** Struck at Sangamner Mint.

Date	Mintage	VG	F	VF	XF	Unc
AHxxxx//x	—	215	360	600	900	—

Sholapur

KM# 294.21 1/2 RUPEE (Type 294)
5.7220 g., Silver

Date	Mintage	VG	F	VF	XF	Unc
AH1087	—	65.00	100	175	260	—
AH1093//25	—	65.00	100	175	260	—
AH1095//28	—	65.00	100	175	260	—
AH1097	—	65.00	100	175	260	—

Surat

KM# 294.6 1/2 RUPEE (Type 294)
Silver **Rev:** Without mint epithet **Note:** Weight varies 5.50-5.80 grams.

Date	Mintage	VG	F	VF	XF	Unc
AH107x//3	—	16.00	20.00	28.00	42.50	—
AH1072//x	—	16.00	20.00	28.00	42.50	—
AHxxxx//7	—	16.00	20.00	28.00	42.50	—
AH1075//8	—	16.00	20.00	28.00	42.50	—
AH1078//1x	—	16.00	20.00	28.00	42.50	—
AH1079//11	—	16.00	20.00	28.00	42.50	—
AH1079//12	—	16.00	20.00	28.00	42.50	—
AH1080//12	—	16.00	20.00	28.00	42.50	—
AH108x//13	—	16.00	20.00	28.00	42.50	—
AH108x//18	—	16.00	20.00	28.00	42.50	—
AH1089//21	—	16.00	20.00	28.00	42.50	—
AH1089//22	—	16.00	20.00	28.00	42.50	—
AH1090//22	—	16.00	20.00	28.00	42.50	—
AH1090//23	—	16.00	20.00	28.00	42.50	—
AH1091//23	—	16.00	20.00	28.00	42.50	—
AH1091//24	—	16.00	20.00	28.00	42.50	—
AH1092//24	—	16.00	20.00	28.00	42.50	—
AH1092//25	—	16.00	20.00	28.00	42.50	—
AH1093//25	—	16.00	20.00	28.00	42.50	—
AH1093//26	—	16.00	20.00	28.00	42.50	—
AH1094//26	—	16.00	20.00	28.00	42.50	—
AH1094//27	—	16.00	20.00	28.00	42.50	—
AH1095//27	—	16.00	20.00	28.00	42.50	—
AH1095//28	—	16.00	20.00	28.00	42.50	—
AH1096//28	—	16.00	20.00	28.00	42.50	—
AH1096//29	—	16.00	20.00	28.00	42.50	—
AH1097//29	—	16.00	20.00	28.00	42.50	—
AH109x//30	—	16.00	20.00	28.00	42.50	—
AH109x//31	—	16.00	20.00	28.00	42.50	—
AH10xx//32	—	16.00	20.00	28.00	42.50	—
AH1102//34	—	16.00	20.00	28.00	42.50	—
AH1102//35	—	16.00	20.00	28.00	42.50	—
AH1103//35	—	16.00	20.00	28.00	42.50	—
AH1103//36	—	16.00	20.00	28.00	42.50	—
AH1104//36	—	16.00	20.00	28.00	42.50	—
AH1104//37	—	16.00	20.00	28.00	42.50	—
AH1105//37	—	16.00	20.00	28.00	42.50	—
AH1105//38	—	16.00	20.00	28.00	42.50	—
AH1106//38	—	16.00	20.00	28.00	42.50	—
AH1106//39	—	16.00	20.00	28.00	42.50	—
AH1107//39	—	16.00	20.00	28.00	42.50	—
AH1108//40	—	16.00	20.00	28.00	42.50	—
AH1109//41	—	16.00	20.00	28.00	42.50	—
AH1110//42	—	16.00	20.00	28.00	42.50	—
AH1110//4x	—	16.00	20.00	28.00	42.50	—
AH1111//43	—	16.00	20.00	28.00	42.50	—
AH1111//44	—	16.00	20.00	28.00	42.50	—
AH1112//44	—	16.00	20.00	28.00	42.50	—

Surat

KM# 294.5 1/2 RUPEE (Type 294)
5.7220 g., Silver **Note:** Mint epithet: "Bandar-i-Mubarak".

Date	Mintage	Good	VG	F	VF	XF
AH1070//1 sic	—	18.00	30.00	60.00	125	200

Tatta

KM# 294.16 1/2 RUPEE (Type 294)
5.7220 g., Silver

Date	Mintage	VG	F	VF	XF	Unc
AHxxxx//20	—	90.00	150	250	375	—

Ujjain

KM# 294.33 1/2 RUPEE (Type 294)
5.7220 g., Silver **Rev:** Inscription with mint name at bottom

Date	Mintage	VG	F	VF	XF	Unc
AHxxxx//3	—	90.00	150	250	375	—

Ujjain

KM# 294.34 1/2 RUPEE (Type 294)
5.7220 g., Silver **Rev:** Inscription with mint name at top **Rev. Inscription:** "dar al-Fath"

Date	Mintage	VG	F	VF	XF	Unc
AH1078//11	—	90.00	150	250	375	—
AH1084//17	—	90.00	150	250	375	—

Jahangirnagar

KM# 295.2 1/2 RUPEE (Type 295)
5.7220 g., Silver **Obv:** Central inscription in square **Rev:** Central inscription in square

Date	Mintage	VG	F	VF	XF	Unc
AH1082//15	—	160	270	450	675	—

Junagarh

KM# 295.1 1/2 RUPEE (Type 295)
5.7220 g., Silver **Obv:** Central inscription within square **Rev:** Central inscription within square

Date	Mintage	VG	F	VF	XF	Unc
AH1074	—	70.00	120	200	300	—
AH1077	—	70.00	120	200	300	—
AH1095//28	—	70.00	120	200	300	—

Ahmadanagar

KM# 297.1 RUPEE (Type 297)
11.4440 g., Silver **Obv:** Ruler's full name and titles

Date	Mintage	VG	F	VF	XF	Unc
AH1070//(1) Ahad	—	36.00	60.00	100	150	—
AH1072	—	36.00	60.00	100	150	—
AH1074//x	—	36.00	60.00	100	150	—
AH1075//7	—	36.00	60.00	100	150	—
AH1075//8	—	36.00	60.00	100	150	—
AH1079//12	—	36.00	60.00	100	150	—
AH1086//18	—	36.00	60.00	100	150	—
AH1087//18 (sic)	—	36.00	60.00	100	150	—
AH10xx//21	—	36.00	60.00	100	150	—

Akbarabad

KM# 297.11 RUPEE (Type 297)
11.4440 g., Silver **Obv:** Ruler's full name and titles

Date	Mintage	VG	F	VF	XF	Unc
AH1069//(1) Ahad	—	110	180	300	450	—

Akbarnagar

KM# 297.12 RUPEE (Type 297)
11.4440 g., Silver

Date	Mintage	VG	F	VF	XF	Unc
AH10xx//(1) Ahad	—	110	180	300	450	—

Aurangabad

KM# 297.2 RUPEE (Type 297)
11.4440 g., Silver **Obv:** Ruler's full name and titles

Date	Mintage	VG	F	VF	XF	Unc
AH1071//3	—	72.00	120	200	300	—

Burhanpur

KM# 297.3 RUPEE (Type 297)
11.4440 g., Silver **Obv:** Ruler's full name and titles

Date	Mintage	VG	F	VF	XF	Unc
AHxxxx//(1) Ahad	—	72.00	120	200	300	—

Kabul

KM# 297.4 RUPEE (Type 297)
11.4440 g., Silver **Obv:** Ruler's full name and titles

Date	Mintage	VG	F	VF	XF	Unc
AH1069//(1) Ahad	—	55.00	90.00	150	225	—
AH1070//x	—	55.00	90.00	150	225	—
AH107x//3	—	55.00	90.00	150	225	—
AH107x//4	—	55.00	90.00	150	225	—
AH107x//5	—	55.00	90.00	150	225	—
AH107x//6	—	55.00	90.00	150	225	—
AH1078//11	—	55.00	90.00	150	225	—

Multan

KM# 297.5 RUPEE (Type 297)
11.4440 g., Silver **Obv:** Ruler's full name and titles

Date	Mintage	VG	F	VF	XF	Unc
AH1069//(1) Ahad	—	90.00	150	250	375	—

Patna

KM# 297.6 RUPEE (Type 297)
11.4440 g., Silver **Obv:** Ruler's full name and titles

Date	Mintage	VG	F	VF	XF	Unc
AH1070//(1) Ahad	—	65.00	110	175	260	—
AH1070//2	—	65.00	110	175	260	—
AH1070//3	—	65.00	110	175	260	—
AH1071//3	—	65.00	110	175	260	—
AH1071//4	—	65.00	110	175	260	—
AH1072//4	—	65.00	110	175	260	—

Shahjahanabad

KM# 297.7 RUPEE (Type 297)
11.4440 g., Silver **Obv:** Ruler's full name and titles

Date	Mintage	VG	F	VF	XF	Unc
AH1069//(1) Ahad	—	55.00	90.00	150	225	—
AH1071//4	—	55.00	90.00	150	225	—

Tatta

KM# 297.8 RUPEE (Type 297)
11.4440 g., Silver **Obv:** Ruler's full name and titles

Date	Mintage	VG	F	VF	XF	Unc
AH1069//(1) Ahad	—	55.00	90.00	150	225	—
AH1070//(1) Ahad	—	55.00	90.00	150	225	—
AH1070//3	—	55.00	90.00	150	225	—
AH1071//3	—	55.00	90.00	150	225	—
AH1071//4	—	55.00	90.00	150	225	—
AH1072//4	—	55.00	90.00	150	225	—

Ujjain

KM# 297.9 RUPEE (Type 297)
11.4440 g., Silver **Obv:** Ruler's full name and titles

Date	Mintage	VG	F	VF	XF	Unc
AH1070	—	70.00	120	200	300	—
AH1072//4	—	70.00	120	200	300	—

Zafarabad

KM# 297.10 RUPEE (Type 297)
11.4440 g., Silver **Obv:** Ruler's full name and titles

Date	Mintage	VG	F	VF	XF	Unc
AH1069//(1) Ahad	—	90.00	150	250	375	—
AH1069//2	—	90.00	150	250	375	—
AH1070//3	—	90.00	150	250	375	—
AH1070//2	—	90.00	150	250	375	—
AH1071//3	—	90.00	150	250	375	—
AH1071//4	—	90.00	150	250	375	—

Akbarabad

KM# 298.1 RUPEE (Type 298)
11.4440 g., Silver **Obv:** Ruler's full name and titles, central inscription within square **Rev:** Mint name within square

Date	Mintage	VG	F	VF	XF	Unc
AH1069//(1) Ahad	—	16.00	27.00	45.00	67.50	—
AH1070//1	—	16.00	27.00	45.00	67.50	—
AH1070//3	—	16.00	27.00	45.00	67.50	—
AH1071//3	—	16.00	27.00	45.00	67.50	—
AH1071//4	—	16.00	27.00	45.00	67.50	—
AH1072//4	—	16.00	27.00	45.00	67.50	—
AH1072//5	—	16.00	27.00	45.00	67.50	—
AH1073//5	—	16.00	27.00	45.00	67.50	—
AH1073//6	—	16.00	27.00	45.00	67.50	—
AH1074//6	—	16.00	27.00	45.00	67.50	—
AH1074//7	—	16.00	27.00	45.00	67.50	—
AH1075//7	—	16.00	27.00	45.00	67.50	—
AH1075//8	—	16.00	27.00	45.00	67.50	—
AH1076//8	—	16.00	27.00	45.00	67.50	—
AH1076//9	—	16.00	27.00	45.00	67.50	—
AH1077//9	—	16.00	27.00	45.00	67.50	—
AH1077//10	—	16.00	27.00	45.00	67.50	—
AH1078//10	—	16.00	27.00	45.00	67.50	—
AH1080//xx	—	16.00	27.00	45.00	67.50	—
AH1081//13	—	16.00	27.00	45.00	67.50	—
AH1081//14	—	16.00	27.00	45.00	67.50	—
AH1082//14	—	16.00	27.00	45.00	67.50	—
AH1082//15	—	16.00	27.00	45.00	67.50	—
AH1083//15	—	16.00	27.00	45.00	67.50	—
AH1083//16	—	16.00	27.00	45.00	67.50	—
AH1084//16	—	16.00	27.00	45.00	67.50	—
AH1084//17	—	16.00	27.00	45.00	67.50	—
AH1085//17	—	16.00	27.00	45.00	67.50	—
AH1085//18	—	16.00	27.00	45.00	67.50	—
AH1086//18	—	16.00	27.00	45.00	67.50	—
AH1086//19	—	16.00	27.00	45.00	67.50	—
AH1087//19	—	16.00	27.00	45.00	67.50	—
AH1087//20	—	16.00	27.00	45.00	67.50	—
AH1088//20	—	16.00	27.00	45.00	67.50	—
AH1088//21	—	16.00	27.00	45.00	67.50	—
AH1089//21	—	16.00	27.00	45.00	67.50	—
AH1089//22	—	16.00	27.00	45.00	67.50	—
AH1090//22	—	16.00	27.00	45.00	67.50	—
AH1090//23	—	16.00	27.00	45.00	67.50	—
AH1091//23	—	16.00	27.00	45.00	67.50	—
AH1091//24	—	16.00	27.00	45.00	67.50	—
AH1092//24	—	16.00	27.00	45.00	67.50	—
AH1092//25	—	16.00	27.00	45.00	67.50	—
AH1094//26	—	16.00	27.00	45.00	67.50	—
AH1094//27	—	16.00	27.00	45.00	67.50	—
AH1095//27	—	16.00	27.00	45.00	67.50	—
AH1095//28	—	16.00	27.00	45.00	67.50	—
AH1096//28	—	16.00	27.00	45.00	67.50	—
AH1096//29	—	16.00	27.00	45.00	67.50	—
AH1097//29	—	16.00	27.00	45.00	67.50	—

Shahjahanabad

KM# 298.2 RUPEE (Type 298)
11.4440 g., Silver **Obv:** Ruler's full name and titles, central inscription within square **Rev:** Mint name in square **Rev. Inscription:** "dar al-Khilafa"

Date	Mintage	VG	F	VF	XF	Unc
AH1070//(1) Ahad	—	270	450	750	1,125	—

Gulkanda

KM# 299.1 RUPEE (Type 299)
11.4440 g., Silver **Obv:** Legend is crude, clumsy, idiosyncratic execution **Rev:** Legend is crude, clumsy, idosyncratic execution

Date	Mintage	VG	F	VF	XF	Unc
AH1069//(1) Ahad	—	14.00	26.00	45.00	70.00	—

Advani

KM# 300.1 RUPEE (Type 300)
Silver **Obv. Inscription:** Poetic couplet **Note:** Weight varies 11.00-11.60 grams.

Date	Mintage	VG	F	VF	XF	Unc
AHxxxx//30	—	110	180	300	450	—

Ahmadabad

KM# 300.2 RUPEE (Type 300)
Silver **Obv:** Poetic couplet **Rev:** Inscription **Note:** Weight varies 11.00-11.60 grams.

Date	Mintage	VG	F	VF	XF	Unc
AH1069//(1) Ahad	—	15.00	18.00	25.00	40.00	—
AH1070//2	—	15.00	18.00	25.00	40.00	—
AH1070//3	—	15.00	18.00	25.00	40.00	—
AH1071//3	—	15.00	18.00	25.00	40.00	—
AH1071//4	—	15.00	18.00	25.00	40.00	—
AH1072//4	—	15.00	18.00	25.00	40.00	—
AH1072//5	—	15.00	18.00	25.00	40.00	—
AH1073//5	—	15.00	18.00	25.00	40.00	—
AH1073//6	—	15.00	18.00	25.00	40.00	—
AH1074//6	—	15.00	18.00	25.00	40.00	—
AH1074//7	—	15.00	18.00	25.00	40.00	—
AH1075//7	—	15.00	18.00	25.00	40.00	—
AH1075//8	—	15.00	18.00	25.00	40.00	—
AH1076//8	—	15.00	18.00	25.00	40.00	—
AH1076//9	—	15.00	18.00	25.00	40.00	—
AH1077//9	—	15.00	18.00	25.00	40.00	—
AH1079//11	—	15.00	18.00	25.00	40.00	—
AH1079//12	—	15.00	18.00	25.00	40.00	—
AH1080//12	—	15.00	18.00	25.00	40.00	—
AH108x//15	—	15.00	18.00	25.00	40.00	—
AH1085//17	—	15.00	18.00	25.00	40.00	—
AH1085//18	—	15.00	18.00	25.00	40.00	—
AH1086//18	—	15.00	18.00	25.00	40.00	—
AH1086//19	—	15.00	18.00	25.00	40.00	—
AH1087//19	—	15.00	18.00	25.00	40.00	—
AH1087//20	—	15.00	18.00	25.00	40.00	—
AH1090//23	—	15.00	18.00	25.00	40.00	—
AH1091//23	—	15.00	18.00	25.00	40.00	—
AH1095//27	—	15.00	18.00	25.00	40.00	—

Date	Mintage	VG	F	VF	XF	Unc
AH1095//28	—	15.00	18.00	25.00	40.00	—
AH1096//28	—	15.00	18.00	25.00	40.00	—
AH1096//29	—	15.00	18.00	25.00	40.00	—
AH1097//29	—	15.00	18.00	25.00	40.00	—
AH1099//30	—	15.00	18.00	25.00	40.00	—
AH1099//31	—	15.00	18.00	25.00	40.00	—
AH1101//34	—	15.00	18.00	25.00	40.00	—
AH1102//34	—	15.00	18.00	25.00	40.00	—
AH1105//38	—	15.00	18.00	25.00	40.00	—
AH1108//40	—	15.00	18.00	25.00	40.00	—
AH1108//41	—	15.00	18.00	25.00	40.00	—
AH1109//41	—	15.00	18.00	25.00	40.00	—
AH1111//43	—	15.00	18.00	25.00	40.00	—
AH1111//44	—	15.00	18.00	25.00	40.00	—
AH1112//4x	—	15.00	18.00	25.00	40.00	—

Ahmadanagar

KM# 300.3 RUPEE (Type 300)

Silver **Note:** Weight varies 11.00-11.60 grams.

Date	Mintage	VG	F	VF	XF	Unc
AH1072//8	—	15.00	20.00	30.00	48.00	—
AH1074//6	—	15.00	20.00	30.00	48.00	—
AH1079//12	—	15.00	20.00	30.00	48.00	—
AH108x//19	—	15.00	20.00	30.00	48.00	—
AH1090//22	—	15.00	20.00	30.00	48.00	—
AH1091//23	—	15.00	20.00	30.00	48.00	—
AH109x//27	—	15.00	20.00	30.00	48.00	—
AH1095//28	—	15.00	20.00	30.00	48.00	—
AH1096//28	—	15.00	20.00	30.00	48.00	—
AH1096//29	—	15.00	20.00	30.00	48.00	—
AH1097//29	—	15.00	20.00	30.00	48.00	—
AH1097//30	—	15.00	20.00	30.00	48.00	—
AH1098//30	—	15.00	20.00	30.00	48.00	—
AH1098//31	—	15.00	20.00	30.00	48.00	—
AH1099//31	—	15.00	20.00	30.00	48.00	—
AH1099//32	—	15.00	20.00	30.00	48.00	—
AH1100//32	—	15.00	20.00	30.00	48.00	—
AH1100//33	—	15.00	20.00	30.00	48.00	—
AH1101//32	—	15.00	20.00	30.00	48.00	—
AH1108//40	—	15.00	20.00	30.00	48.00	—
AH1108//41	—	15.00	20.00	30.00	48.00	—

Ahsanabad

KM# 300.4 RUPEE (Type 300)

Silver **Note:** Weight varies 11.00-11.60 grams.

Date	Mintage	VG	F	VF	XF	Unc
AH1112//45	—	55.00	90.00	150	240	—

Ajmer

KM# 300.5 RUPEE (Type 300)

Silver **Obv:** Inscription, date **Rev. Inscription:** Dar-ul-Khair **Note:** Weight varies 11.00-11.60 grams.

Date	Mintage	VG	F	VF	XF	Unc
AH1097//29	—	15.00	20.00	30.00	48.00	—
AH1098//30	—	15.00	20.00	30.00	48.00	—
AH1098//31	—	15.00	20.00	30.00	48.00	—
AH1100//32	—	15.00	20.00	30.00	48.00	—
AH1101//33	—	15.00	20.00	30.00	48.00	—
AH1101//34	—	15.00	20.00	30.00	48.00	—
AH1103//35	—	15.00	20.00	30.00	48.00	—
AH1104//36	—	15.00	20.00	30.00	48.00	—
AH1104//37	—	15.00	20.00	30.00	48.00	—
AH1105//37	—	15.00	20.00	30.00	48.00	—
AH1105//38	—	15.00	20.00	30.00	48.00	—
AH1106//38	—	15.00	20.00	30.00	48.00	—
AH1106//39	—	15.00	20.00	30.00	48.00	—
AH1107//39	—	15.00	20.00	30.00	48.00	—
AH1107//40	—	15.00	20.00	30.00	48.00	—
AH1108//40	—	15.00	20.00	30.00	48.00	—

Date	Mintage	VG	F	VF	XF	Unc
AH1108//41	—	15.00	20.00	30.00	48.00	—
AH1109//41	—	15.00	20.00	30.00	48.00	—
AH1109//42	—	15.00	20.00	30.00	48.00	—
AH1110//42	—	15.00	20.00	30.00	48.00	—
AH1110//43	—	15.00	20.00	30.00	48.00	—
AH1111//43	—	15.00	20.00	30.00	48.00	—
AH1111//44	—	15.00	20.00	30.00	48.00	—
AH1112//44	—	15.00	20.00	30.00	48.00	—
AH1112//45	—	15.00	20.00	30.00	48.00	—

Akbarabad

KM# 300.6 RUPEE (Type 300)

Silver **Obv:** Mustagir-ul-Khirafa **Rev. Inscription:** Inscription **Note:** Weight varies 11.00-11.60 grams.

Date	Mintage	VG	F	VF	XF	Unc
AH109x//28	—	15.00	20.00	28.00	45.00	—
AH1096//29	—	15.00	20.00	28.00	45.00	—
AH1097//29	—	15.00	20.00	28.00	45.00	—
AH1097//30	—	15.00	20.00	28.00	45.00	—
AH1098//30	—	15.00	20.00	28.00	45.00	—
AH1098//31	—	15.00	20.00	28.00	45.00	—
AH1099//31	—	15.00	20.00	28.00	45.00	—
AH1099//32	—	15.00	20.00	28.00	45.00	—
AH1101//33	—	15.00	20.00	28.00	45.00	—
AH1101//34 (sic)	—	15.00	20.00	28.00	45.00	—
AH1102//34	—	15.00	20.00	28.00	45.00	—
AH1102//35	—	15.00	20.00	28.00	45.00	—
AH1103//35	—	15.00	20.00	28.00	45.00	—
AH1103//36	—	15.00	20.00	28.00	45.00	—
AH1104//36	—	15.00	20.00	28.00	45.00	—
AH110x//38	—	15.00	20.00	28.00	45.00	—
AH1106//39	—	15.00	20.00	28.00	45.00	—
AH1107//39	—	15.00	20.00	28.00	45.00	—
AH1108//40	—	15.00	20.00	28.00	45.00	—
AH1108//41	—	15.00	20.00	28.00	45.00	—
AH1109//41	—	15.00	20.00	28.00	45.00	—
AH1109//42	—	15.00	20.00	28.00	45.00	—
AH1110//42	—	15.00	20.00	28.00	45.00	—
AH1110//43	—	15.00	20.00	28.00	45.00	—
AH1111//43	—	15.00	20.00	28.00	45.00	—
AH1111//44	—	15.00	20.00	28.00	45.00	—
AH1112//44	—	15.00	20.00	28.00	45.00	—
AH1112//45	—	15.00	20.00	28.00	45.00	—

Akbarnagar

KM# 300.7 RUPEE (Type 300)

Silver **Note:** "Mihr" couplet; Weight varies 11.00-11.60 grams.

Date	Mintage	VG	F	VF	XF	Unc
AH1070//3	—	15.00	22.00	30.00	48.00	—
AH1071//3	—	15.00	22.00	30.00	48.00	—
AH1071//4	—	15.00	22.00	30.00	48.00	—
AH1072//4	—	15.00	22.00	30.00	48.00	—
AH1072//5	—	15.00	22.00	30.00	48.00	—
AH1073//5	—	15.00	22.00	30.00	48.00	—
AH1073//6	—	15.00	22.00	30.00	48.00	—
AH1074//6	—	15.00	22.00	30.00	48.00	—
AH1074//7	—	15.00	22.00	30.00	48.00	—
AH1075//7	—	15.00	22.00	30.00	48.00	—
AH1075//8	—	15.00	22.00	30.00	48.00	—
AH1076//8	—	15.00	22.00	30.00	48.00	—
AH1076//9	—	15.00	22.00	30.00	48.00	—
AH1078//10	—	15.00	22.00	30.00	48.00	—
AH1078//11	—	15.00	22.00	30.00	48.00	—
AH1079//11	—	15.00	22.00	30.00	48.00	—
AH1079//12	—	15.00	22.00	30.00	8.00	—
AH1080//13(sic)	—	15.00	22.00	30.00	48.00	—
AH1081//12	—	15.00	22.00	30.00	48.00	—
AH1081//13	—	15.00	22.00	30.00	48.00	—
AH1081//14	—	15.00	22.00	30.00	48.00	—
AH1082//14	—	15.00	22.00	30.00	48.00	—
AH1082//15	—	15.00	22.00	30.00	48.00	—
AH1083//15	—	15.00	22.00	30.00	48.00	—
AH1083//16	—	15.00	22.00	30.00	48.00	—
AH108x//18	—	15.00	22.00	30.00	48.00	—
AH108x//20	—	15.00	22.00	30.00	48.00	—
AH108x//21	—	15.00	22.00	30.00	48.00	—
AH1090//22	—	15.00	22.00	30.00	48.00	—
AH1090//23	—	15.00	22.00	30.00	48.00	—
AH1091//23	—	15.00	22.00	30.00	48.00	—
AH1091//24	—	15.00	22.00	30.00	48.00	—

Date	Mintage	VG	F	VF	XF	Unc
AH1092//24	—	15.00	2.00	30.00	48.00	—
AH1092//25	—	15.00	22.00	30.00	48.00	—
AH1093//25	—	15.00	22.00	30.00	48.00	—
AH1094//26	—	15.00	22.00	30.00	48.00	—
AH1093//26	—	15.00	22.00	30.00	48.00	—
AH1094//27	—	15.00	22.00	30.00	48.00	—
AH1095//27	—	15.00	22.00	30.00	48.00	—
AH1095//28	—	15.00	22.00	30.00	48.00	—
AH1096//28	—	15.00	22.00	30.00	48.00	—
AH1096//29	—	15.00	22.00	30.00	48.00	—
AH1097//29	—	15.00	22.00	30.00	48.00	—
AH1097//30	—	15.00	22.00	30.00	48.00	—
AH1098//30	—	15.00	22.00	30.00	48.00	—
AH1098//31	—	15.00	22.00	30.00	48.00	—
AH1099//31	—	15.00	22.00	30.00	48.00	—
AH1099//32	—	15.00	22.00	30.00	48.00	—
AH1100//32	—	15.00	22.00	30.00	48.00	—
AH1100//33	—	15.00	22.00	30.00	48.00	—
AH1101//33	—	15.00	22.00	30.00	48.00	—
AH1101//34	—	15.00	22.00	30.00	48.00	—
AH1102//34	—	15.00	22.00	30.00	48.00	—
AH1102//35	—	15.00	22.00	30.00	48.00	—
AH1103//35	—	15.00	22.00	30.00	48.00	—
AH1103//36	—	15.00	22.00	30.00	48.00	—
AH1104//36	—	15.00	22.00	30.00	48.00	—
AH1104//37	—	15.00	22.00	30.00	48.00	—
AH1105//37	—	15.00	22.00	30.00	48.00	—
AH1105//38	—	15.00	22.00	30.00	48.00	—
AH1106//38	—	15.00	22.00	30.00	48.00	—
AH1107//39	—	15.00	22.00	30.00	48.00	—
AH1108//40	—	15.00	22.00	30.00	48.00	—
AH1108//41	—	15.00	22.00	30.00	48.00	—
AHxxxx//43	—	15.00	22.00	30.00	48.00	—
AH1112//45	—	15.00	22.00	30.00	48.00	—

Akbarnagar

KM# 300.100 RUPEE (Type 300)

11.4440 g., Silver **Note:** "Badr" couplet

Date	Mintage	VG	F	VF	XF	Unc
AH1109//42	—	16.00	22.00	30.00	48.00	—
AH1110//42	—	16.00	22.00	30.00	48.00	—
AH1111//43	—	16.00	22.00	30.00	48.00	—
AH1111//44	—	16.00	22.00	30.00	48.00	—
AH1112//45	—	16.00	22.00	30.00	48.00	—

Alamgirpur

KM# 300.8 RUPEE (Type 300)

Silver **Obv:** Mint name at right **Note:** Struck at Alamgirpur Mint.

Date	Mintage	VG	F	VF	XF	Unc
AH1071//3	—	45.00	75.00	125	200	—

Alamgirpur

KM# 300.9 RUPEE (Type 300)

11.4440 g., Silver **Rev:** Mint name at top

Date	Mintage	VG	F	VF	XF	Unc
AH1072//x	—	16.00	27.00	45.00	72.00	—
AH1073//5	—	16.00	27.00	45.00	72.00	—
AH1073//6	—	16.00	27.00	45.00	72.00	—
AH1074//6	—	16.00	27.00	45.00	72.00	—
AH1074//7	—	16.00	27.00	45.00	72.00	—
AH1075//7	—	16.00	27.00	45.00	72.00	—
AH1075//8	—	16.00	27.00	45.00	72.00	—
AH1076//8	—	16.00	27.00	45.00	72.00	—
AH1076//9	—	16.00	27.00	45.00	72.00	—
AH1077//9	—	16.00	27.00	45.00	72.00	—
AH1077//10	—	16.00	27.00	45.00	72.00	—
AH1078//10	—	16.00	27.00	45.00	72.00	—
AH1078//11	—	16.00	27.00	45.00	72.00	—
AH1079//11	—	16.00	27.00	45.00	72.00	—
AH1079//12	—	16.00	27.00	45.00	72.00	—
AH1081//14	—	16.00	27.00	45.00	72.00	—
AH1082//14	—	16.00	27.00	45.00	72.00	—
AH1082//15	—	16.00	27.00	45.00	72.00	—
AH1083//15	—	16.00	27.00	45.00	72.00	—
AH1083//16	—	16.00	27.00	45.00	72.00	—
AH1084//16	—	16.00	27.00	45.00	72.00	—
AH1084//17	—	16.00	27.00	45.00	72.00	—
AH1085//17	—	16.00	27.00	45.00	72.00	—
AH1085//18	—	16.00	27.00	45.00	72.00	—
AH1086//18	—	16.00	27.00	45.00	72.00	—
AH1086//19	—	16.00	27.00	45.00	72.00	—
AH1087//19	—	16.00	27.00	45.00	72.00	—
AH1087//20	—	16.00	27.00	45.00	72.00	—
AH1088//20	—	16.00	27.00	45.00	72.00	—
AH1088//21	—	16.00	27.00	45.00	72.00	—
AH1090//23	—	16.00	27.00	45.00	72.00	—
AH1095//27	—	16.00	27.00	45.00	72.00	—
AH1096//xx	—	16.00	27.00	45.00	72.00	—
AH1105//4x	—	16.00	27.00	45.00	72.00	—

Alamgirpur

KM# 300.10 RUPEE (Type 300)

Silver **Rev:** Mint name at bottom **Note:** Weight varies 11.00-11.60 grams.

Date	Mintage	VG	F	VF	XF	Unc
AH1089//xx	—	16.00	27.00	45.00	72.00	—
AH1090//22	—	16.00	27.00	45.00	72.00	—
AH1090//23	—	16.00	27.00	45.00	72.00	—
AH1091//23	—	16.00	27.00	45.00	72.00	—
AH1091//24	—	16.00	27.00	45.00	72.00	—
AH1092//24	—	16.00	27.00	45.00	72.00	—
AH1093//25	—	16.00	27.00	45.00	72.00	—
AH1092//25	—	16.00	27.00	45.00	72.00	—
AH1094//26	—	16.00	27.00	45.00	72.00	—
AH1093//26	—	16.00	27.00	45.00	72.00	—
AH1094//27	—	16.00	27.00	45.00	72.00	—
AH1095//27	—	16.00	27.00	45.00	72.00	—
AH1095//28	—	16.00	27.00	45.00	72.00	—
AH1096//28	—	16.00	27.00	45.00	72.00	—
AH1096//29	—	16.00	27.00	45.00	72.00	—
AH1097//29	—	16.00	27.00	45.00	72.00	—
AH1098//30	—	16.00	27.00	45.00	72.00	—
AH1098//31	—	16.00	27.00	45.00	72.00	—
AH1099//31	—	16.00	27.00	45.00	72.00	—
AH1099//32	—	16.00	27.00	45.00	72.00	—
AH1100//32	—	16.00	27.00	45.00	72.00	—
AH1100//33	—	16.00	27.00	45.00	72.00	—
AH1101//33	—	16.00	27.00	45.00	72.00	—
AH1101//34	—	16.00	27.00	45.00	72.00	—
AH1102//34	—	16.00	27.00	45.00	72.00	—
AH1102//35	—	16.00	27.00	45.00	72.00	—
AH1103//35	—	16.00	27.00	45.00	72.00	—
AH1103//36	—	16.00	27.00	45.00	72.00	—
AH1104//36	—	16.00	27.00	45.00	72.00	—
AH1104//37	—	16.00	27.00	45.00	72.00	—
AH1105//37	—	16.00	27.00	45.00	72.00	—
AH1105//38	—	16.00	27.00	45.00	72.00	—
AH1106//38	—	16.00	27.00	45.00	72.00	—
AH110x//39	—	16.00	27.00	45.00	72.00	—
AH1107//4x	—	16.00	27.00	45.00	72.00	—
AHxxxx//41	—	16.00	27.00	45.00	72.00	—
AH1109//42	—	16.00	27.00	45.00	72.00	—
AH1111//44	—	16.00	27.00	45.00	72.00	—
AH1112//45	—	16.00	27.00	45.00	72.00	—

Allahabad

KM# 300.11 RUPEE (Type 300)
Silver **Rev:** Epithet Balda + "mihr" couplet, and mint name at top **Note:** Weight varies: 11.00-11.60 grams.

Date	Mintage	VG	F	VF	XF	Unc
AH1070//(1) Ahad	—	24.00	39.00	65.00	100	—
AH1070//3	—	24.00	39.00	65.00	100	—
AH1071//3	—	24.00	39.00	65.00	100	—
AH1071//4	—	24.00	39.00	65.00	100	—
AH1072//4	—	24.00	39.00	65.00	100	—
AH1086//xx	—	24.00	39.00	65.00	100	—

Allahabad

KM# 300.102 RUPEE (Type 300)
11.4440 g., Silver **Rev:** Mint name at bottom **Note:** "Mihr" couplet.

Date	Mintage	VG	F	VF	XF	Unc
AH1073//6	—	24.00	39.00	65.00	100	—

Allahabad

KM# 300.12 RUPEE (Type 300)
Silver **Obv:** Inscription **Rev:** "badr" couplets, mint name at bottom **Note:** Weight varies 11.00-11.60 grams.

Date	Mintage	VG	F	VF	XF	Unc
AH1074//6	—	16.00	22.00	35.00	55.00	—
AH1074//7	—	16.00	22.00	35.00	55.00	—
AH1075//7	—	16.00	22.00	35.00	55.00	—
AH1075//8	—	16.00	22.00	35.00	55.00	—
AH1076//8	—	16.00	22.00	35.00	55.00	—
AH1076//9	—	16.00	22.00	35.00	55.00	—
AH1077//9	—	16.00	22.00	35.00	55.00	—
AH1077//10	—	16.00	22.00	35.00	55.00	—
AH1078//10	—	16.00	22.00	35.00	55.00	—
AH10xx//12	—	16.00	22.00	5.00	55.00	—
AH1085//18	—	16.00	22.00	5.00	55.00	—
AH1087//19	—	16.00	22.00	35.00	55.00	—
AH1091//24	—	16.00	22.00	35.00	55.00	—
AH1094//27	—	16.00	22.00	35.00	55.00	—
AH1095//27	—	16.00	2.00	35.00	55.00	—
AH1095//28	—	16.00	22.00	35.00	55.00	—
AH1098//30	—	16.00	22.00	35.00	55.00	—
AH1098//31	—	16.00	22.00	35.00	55.00	—
AH1099//31	—	16.00	22.00	35.00	55.00	—
AH1099//32	—	16.00	22.00	35.00	55.00	—
AH1103//35	—	16.00	22.00	35.00	55.00	—
AH1105//38	—	16.00	22.00	35.00	55.00	—
AH1106//38	—	16.00	22.00	35.00	55.00	—
AH1106//39	—	16.00	22.00	35.00	55.00	—
AH1107//39	—	16.00	22.00	35.00	55.00	—
AH1107//40	—	16.00	22.00	35.00	55.00	—
AH1109//41	—	16.00	22.00	35.00	55.00	—
AH1111//43	—	16.00	22.00	35.00	55.00	—
AH1111//44	—	16.00	22.00	35.00	55.00	—
AH1112//44	—	16.00	22.00	35.00	55.00	—
AH111x//45	—	16.00	22.00	35.00	55.00	—

Atak

KM# 300.103 RUPEE (Type 300)
Silver **Note:** Weight varies 11.00-11.60 grams.

Date	Mintage	VG	F	VF	XF	Unc
AH1108//xx	—	90.00	150	250	400	—

Aurangabad

KM# 300.13 RUPEE (Type 300)
Silver **Rev:** Mint name at top **Note:** Weight varies: 11.00-11.60 grams.

Date	Mintage	VG	F	VF	XF	Unc
AH1071//3	—	16.00	22.00	28.00	45.00	—
AH1071//4	—	16.00	22.00	28.00	45.00	—
AH1072//4	—	16.00	22.00	28.00	45.00	—
AH1072//5	—	16.00	22.00	28.00	45.00	—
AH1073//5	—	16.00	22.00	28.00	45.00	—
AH1073//6	—	16.00	22.00	28.00	45.00	—
AH1074//6	—	16.00	22.00	28.00	45.00	—
AH1074//7	—	16.00	22.00	28.00	45.00	—
AH1075//7	—	16.00	22.00	28.00	45.00	—
AH1075//8	—	16.00	22.00	28.00	45.00	—
AH1076//8	—	16.00	22.00	28.00	45.00	—
AH1076//9	—	16.00	22.00	28.00	45.00	—
AH1077//9	—	16.00	22.00	28.00	45.00	—
AH1077//10	—	16.00	22.00	28.00	45.00	—
AH1079//12	—	16.00	22.00	28.00	45.00	—
AH1080//13	—	16.00	22.00	28.00	45.00	—
AH1081//13	—	16.00	22.00	28.00	45.00	—
AH1081//14	—	16.00	22.00	8.00	45.00	—
AH1082//14	—	16.00	22.00	28.00	45.00	—
AH1082//15	—	16.00	22.00	28.00	45.00	—
AH1083//15	—	16.00	22.00	28.00	45.00	—
AH1083//16	—	16.00	22.00	8.00	45.00	—
AH1084//16	—	16.00	22.00	28.00	45.00	—
AH1086//18	—	16.00	22.00	28.00	45.00	—
AH1086//19	—	16.00	22.00	28.00	45.00	—
AH1087//19	—	16.00	22.00	28.00	45.00	—
AH1087//20	—	16.00	22.00	28.00	45.00	—
AH1088//20	—	16.00	22.00	28.00	45.00	—
AH1090//xx	—	16.00	22.00	28.00	45.00	—
AH1092//25	—	16.00	22.00	28.00	45.00	—
AH1093//26	—	16.00	22.00	28.00	45.00	—
AH1099//30	—	16.00	22.00	28.00	45.00	—

Aurangabad

KM# 300.14 RUPEE (Type 300)
Silver **Rev:** Mint name at bottom **Note:** Weight varies: 11.00-11.60 grams. For later issues see Khujista Bunyad.

Date	Mintage	VG	F	VF	XF	Unc
AH1091//24	—	16.00	22.00	28.00	45.00	—
AH1093//25	—	16.00	22.00	28.00	45.00	—
AH1094//27	—	16.00	22.00	28.00	45.00	—
AH1093//26	—	16.00	22.00	28.00	45.00	—
AH1096//xx	—	16.00	22.00	28.00	45.00	—
AH1097//30	—	16.00	22.00	28.00	45.00	—
AH1098//30	—	16.00	22.00	28.00	45.00	—
AH1098//31	—	16.00	22.00	28.00	45.00	—
AH1099//31	—	16.00	22.00	28.00	45.00	—

Azamnagar

KM# 300.15 RUPEE (Type 300)
Silver **Note:** Weight varies 11.00-11.60 grams.

Date	Mintage	VG	F	VF	XF	Unc
AH1110//48 8 struck as dot	—	18.00	30.00	50.00	80.00	—
AH1110//4x	—	18.00	30.00	50.00	80.00	—

Bankapur

KM# 300.18 RUPEE (Type 300)
Silver **Note:** Weight varies 11.00-11.60 grams.

Date	Mintage	VG	F	VF	XF	Unc
AHxxxx//44	—	25.00	42.00	75.00	115	—

Bareli

KM# 300.19 RUPEE (Type 300)
Silver **Obv:** Inscription, date **Rev:** Inscription **Note:** Weight varies 11.00-11.60 grams.

Date	Mintage	VG	F	VF	XF	Unc
AH1097//29	—	16.00	20.00	25.00	40.00	—
AH1097//30	—	16.00	20.00	25.00	40.00	—
AH1098//30	—	16.00	20.00	25.00	40.00	—
AH1098//31	—	16.00	20.00	25.00	40.00	—
AH1099//31	—	16.00	20.00	25.00	40.00	—
AH1099//32	—	16.00	20.00	25.00	40.00	—
AH1100//32	—	16.00	20.00	25.00	40.00	—
AH1100//33	—	16.00	20.00	25.00	40.00	—
AH1101//33	—	16.00	20.00	25.00	40.00	—
AH1101//34	—	16.00	20.00	25.00	40.00	—
AH1102//34	—	16.00	20.00	25.00	40.00	—
AH1102//35	—	16.00	20.00	25.00	40.00	—
AH1103//35	—	16.00	20.00	25.00	40.00	—
AH1103//36	—	16.00	20.00	25.00	40.00	—
AH1107//39	—	16.00	20.00	25.00	40.00	—
AH1107//40	—	16.00	20.00	25.00	40.00	—
AH1108//40	—	16.00	20.00	25.00	40.00	—
AH1108//41	—	16.00	20.00	25.00	40.00	—
AH1109//41	—	16.00	20.00	25.00	40.00	—
AH1109//42	—	16.00	20.00	25.00	40.00	—
AH1110//42	—	16.00	20.00	25.00	40.00	—
AH1110//43	—	16.00	20.00	25.00	40.00	—
AH1111//43	—	16.00	20.00	25.00	40.00	—
AH1111//44	—	16.00	20.00	25.00	40.00	—
AH1112//44	—	16.00	20.00	25.00	40.00	—
AH1112//45	—	16.00	20.00	25.00	40.00	—

Bhakkar

KM# 300.20 RUPEE (Type 300)
Silver **Note:** Weight varies 11.00-11.60 grams.

Date	Mintage	VG	F	VF	XF	Unc
AH1081//13	—	18.00	30.00	50.00	75.00	—
AH1083//15	—	18.00	30.00	50.00	75.00	—
AH1083//16	—	18.00	30.00	50.00	75.00	—
AH1088//21	—	18.00	30.00	50.00	75.00	—
AH1091//24	—	18.00	30.00	50.00	75.00	—
AH1094//27	—	18.00	30.00	50.00	75.00	—
AH1095//27	—	18.00	30.00	50.00	75.00	—
AH1097//30	—	18.00	30.00	50.00	75.00	—
AH1108//41	—	18.00	30.00	50.00	75.00	—

Bhakkar

KM# 300.104 RUPEE (Type 300)
11.4440 g., Silver **Rev:** Inscription and mint name **Rev. Inscription:** "wala julus"

Date	Mintage	VG	F	VF	XF	Unc
AH1083//15	—	18.00	30.00	50.00	75.00	—
AH1086//18	—	18.00	30.00	50.00	75.00	—

Bhilsa

KM# 300.21 RUPEE (Type 300)
Silver **Rev:** Mint name at bottom **Note:** Weight varies: 11.00-11.60 grams; "Mihr" couplet. For later issues see Alamgirpur.

Date	Mintage	VG	F	VF	XF	Unc
AH1069//(1) Ahad	—	45.00	75.00	125	200	—
AHxxxx//3	—	45.00	75.00	125	200	—

Bijapur

KM# 300.22 RUPEE (Type 300)
Silver **Rev:** Without mint epithet **Note:** Weight varies: 11.00-11.60 grams.

Date	Mintage	VG	F	VF	XF	Unc
AH1091//23	—	16.00	22.00	35.00	55.00	—
AH1091//24	—	16.00	22.00	35.00	55.00	—
AH1092//2x	—	16.00	22.00	35.00	55.00	—
AH109x//26	—	16.00	22.00	35.00	55.00	—
AH1100//32	—	16.00	22.00	35.00	55.00	—
AH1106//38	—	16.00	22.00	35.00	55.00	—
AH1107//40	—	16.00	22.00	35.00	55.00	—
AH1108//41	—	16.00	22.00	35.00	55.00	—
AH1109//42	—	16.00	22.00	35.00	55.00	—
AH1111//43	—	16.00	22.00	35.00	55.00	—
AH1112//44	—	16.00	22.00	35.00	55.00	—
AH1112//45	—	16.00	22.00	35.00	55.00	—

Bijapur

KM# 300.23 RUPEE (Type 300)

Silver **Obv:** Inscription **Rev. Inscription:** Dar-uz-Zafar **Note:** Weight varies 11.00-11.60 grams. Mint name exist in various arrangements.

Date	Mintage	VG	F	VF	XF	Unc
AH1097//30	—	16.00	22.00	28.00	45.00	—
AH1098//30	—	16.00	22.00	28.00	45.00	—
AH1098//31	—	16.00	22.00	28.00	45.00	—
AH1099//31	—	16.00	22.00	28.00	45.00	—
AH1099//32	—	16.00	22.00	28.00	45.00	—
AH1100//32	—	16.00	22.00	28.00	45.00	—
AH1100//33	—	16.00	22.00	28.00	45.00	—
AH1101//33	—	16.00	22.00	28.00	45.00	—
AH1101//34	—	16.00	22.00	28.00	45.00	—
AH1102//34	—	16.00	22.00	28.00	45.00	—
AH1102//35	—	16.00	22.00	28.00	45.00	—
AH1103//35	—	16.00	22.00	28.00	45.00	—
AH1103//36	—	16.00	22.00	28.00	45.00	—
AH1104//36	—	16.00	22.00	28.00	45.00	—
AH1104//37	—	16.00	22.00	28.00	45.00	—
AH1105//37	—	16.00	22.00	28.00	45.00	—
AH1105//38	—	16.00	22.00	28.00	45.00	—
AH1106//38	—	16.00	22.00	28.00	45.00	—
AH1106//39	—	16.00	22.00	28.00	45.00	—
AH1107//39	—	16.00	22.00	28.00	45.00	—
AH1107//40	—	16.00	22.00	28.00	45.00	—
AH1108//40	—	16.00	22.00	28.00	45.00	—
AH1108//41	—	16.00	22.00	28.00	45.00	—
AH1109//42	—	16.00	22.00	28.00	45.00	—
AH1110//43	—	16.00	22.00	28.00	45.00	—
AH1111//43	—	16.00	22.00	28.00	45.00	—
AH1111//44	—	16.00	22.00	28.00	45.00	—
AH1112//44	—	16.00	22.00	28.00	45.00	—
AH1112//45	—	16.00	22.00	28.00	45.00	—

Burhanpur

KM# 300.24 RUPEE (Type 300)

Silver **Note:** "Badr" couplet; Weight varies 11.00-11.60 grams.

Date	Mintage	VG	F	VF	XF	Unc
AH107x//3	—	16.00	20.00	25.00	40.00	—
AH107x//7	—	16.00	20.00	25.00	40.00	—
AH1078//10	—	16.00	20.00	25.00	40.00	—
AH108x//15	—	16.00	20.00	25.00	40.00	—
AH1085//18	—	16.00	20.00	25.00	40.00	—
AH1086//18	—	16.00	20.00	25.00	40.00	—
AH1086//19	—	16.00	20.00	25.00	40.00	—
AH1087//19	—	16.00	20.00	25.00	40.00	—
AH1087//20	—	16.00	20.00	25.00	40.00	—
AH1088//20	—	16.00	20.00	25.00	40.00	—
AH1088//21	—	16.00	20.00	25.00	40.00	—
AH1089//21	—	16.00	20.00	25.00	40.00	—
AH1089//22	—	16.00	20.00	25.00	40.00	—
AH1090//22	—	16.00	20.00	25.00	40.00	—
AH1090//23	—	16.00	20.00	25.00	40.00	—
AH1091//23	—	16.00	20.00	25.00	40.00	—
AH1091//24	—	16.00	20.00	25.00	40.00	—
AH1092//24	—	16.00	20.00	25.00	40.00	—
AH1092//25	—	16.00	20.00	25.00	40.00	—
AH1093//25	—	16.00	20.00	25.00	40.00	—
AH1096//29	—	16.00	20.00	25.00	40.00	—
AH1093//28	—	16.00	20.00	25.00	40.00	—
AH1097//29	—	16.00	20.00	25.00	40.00	—
AH1097//30	—	16.00	20.00	25.00	40.00	—
AH1098//30	—	16.00	20.00	25.00	40.00	—
AH1098//31	—	16.00	20.00	25.00	40.00	—
AH1099//31	—	16.00	20.00	25.00	40.00	—
AH1099//32	—	16.00	20.00	25.00	40.00	—
AH1100//32	—	16.00	20.00	25.00	40.00	—
AH1100//33	—	16.00	20.00	25.00	40.00	—
AH1101//33	—	16.00	20.00	25.00	40.00	—
AH1101//34	—	16.00	20.00	25.00	40.00	—
AH1102//34	—	16.00	20.00	25.00	40.00	—
AH1102//35	—	16.00	20.00	25.00	40.00	—
AH1103//36	—	16.00	20.00	25.00	40.00	—
AH110x//38	—	16.00	20.00	25.00	40.00	—
AH1107//39	—	16.00	20.00	25.00	40.00	—
AH1107//40	—	16.00	20.00	25.00	40.00	—
AH1108//40	—	16.00	20.00	25.00	40.00	—
AH1108//41	—	16.00	20.00	25.00	40.00	—
AH1109//41	—	16.00	20.00	25.00	40.00	—

Date	Mintage	VG	F	VF	XF	Unc
AH1109//42	—	16.00	20.00	25.00	40.00	—
AH1110//42	—	16.00	20.00	25.00	40.00	—
AH1110//43	—	16.00	20.00	25.00	40.00	—
AH1111//43	—	16.00	20.00	25.00	40.00	—
AH1111//44	—	16.00	20.00	25.00	40.00	—
AH1112//44	—	16.00	20.00	25.00	40.00	—

Burhanpur

KM# 300.105 RUPEE (Type 300)

11.4440 g., Silver **Note:** "Mihr" couplet.

Date	Mintage	VG	F	VF	XF	Unc
AH1086//xx	—	16.00	20.00	25.00	40.00	—
AH1088//xx	—	16.00	20.00	25.00	40.00	—
AHxxxx//31	—	16.00	20.00	25.00	40.00	—
AHxxxx//34	—	16.00	20.00	25.00	40.00	—
AHxxxx//39	—	16.00	20.00	25.00	40.00	—

Dicholi

KM# 300.106 RUPEE (Type 300)

Silver **Note:** Weight varies 11.00-11.60 grams.

Date	Mintage	VG	F	VF	XF	Unc
AHxxxx//35	—	36.00	60.00	100	160	—
AHxxxx//41	—	36.00	60.00	100	160	—

Gulbarga

KM# 300.27 RUPEE (Type 300)

Silver **Note:** Weight varies: 11.00-11.60 grams. For later issues see Ahsanabad.

Date	Mintage	VG	F	VF	XF	Unc
AH1096//xx	—	16.00	24.00	40.00	65.00	—
AH1097//30	—	16.00	24.00	40.00	65.00	—
AH1098//30	—	16.00	24.00	40.00	65.00	—
AH1098//31	—	16.00	24.00	40.00	65.00	—
AH1099//31	—	16.00	24.00	40.00	65.00	—
AH1099//32	—	16.00	24.00	40.00	65.00	—
AH1101//33	—	16.00	24.00	40.00	65.00	—
AH1101//34	—	16.00	24.00	40.00	65.00	—
AH1102//34	—	16.00	24.00	40.00	65.00	—
AH1102//35	—	16.00	24.00	40.00	65.00	—
AH1103//35	—	16.00	24.00	40.00	65.00	—
AH1103//36	—	16.00	24.00	40.00	65.00	—
AH1104//36(sic)	—	16.00	24.00	40.00	65.00	—
AH1104//38	—	16.00	24.00	40.00	65.00	—
AH1104//37	—	16.00	24.00	40.00	65.00	—
AH1105//37	—	16.00	24.00	40.00	65.00	—
AH1105//38	—	16.00	24.00	40.00	65.00	—
AH1106//38	—	16.00	24.00	40.00	65.00	—
AH1106//39	—	16.00	24.00	40.00	65.00	—
AH1107//39	—	16.00	24.00	40.00	65.00	—
AH110x//40	—	16.00	24.00	40.00	65.00	—

Gulkanda

KM# 300.28 RUPEE (Type 300)

Silver **Note:** Weight varies: 11.00-11.60 grams.

Date	Mintage	VG	F	VF	XF	Unc
AH107x//3	—	16.00	24.00	40.00	65.00	—
AH1071//4	—	16.00	24.00	40.00	65.00	—
AH107x//5	—	16.00	24.00	40.00	65.00	—
AH107x//6	—	16.00	24.00	40.00	65.00	—
AH107x//7	—	16.00	24.00	40.00	65.00	—
AH1076//8	—	16.00	24.00	40.00	65.00	—
AH1076//11	—	16.00	24.00	40.00	65.00	—
AHxxxx//12	—	16.00	24.00	40.00	65.00	—
AHxxxx//13	—	16.00	24.00	40.00	65.00	—
AH1072//14(sic)	—	16.00	24.00	40.00	65.00	—
AH1076//14	—	16.00	24.00	40.00	65.00	—
AH1076//15	—	16.00	24.00	40.00	65.00	—
AH1072//16(sic)	—	16.00	24.00	40.00	65.00	—
AH1084//16	—	16.00	24.00	40.00	65.00	—
AH1072//18(sic)	—	16.00	24.00	40.00	65.00	—
AHxxxx//19	—	16.00	24.00	40.00	65.00	—
AH1076//20	—	16.00	24.00	40.00	65.00	—
AHxxxx//22	—	16.00	24.00	40.00	65.00	—
AH1076//23(sic)	—	16.00	24.00	40.00	65.00	—
AH1094//25	—	16.00	24.00	40.00	65.00	—
AHxxxx//26	—	—	—	—	—	—
AHxxxx//27	—	16.00	24.00	40.00	65.00	—
AHxxxx//28	—	16.00	24.00	40.00	65.00	—
AH1097//29	—	16.00	24.00	40.00	65.00	—
AH1076//30(sic)	—	16.00	24.00	40.00	65.00	—
AH1096//30(sic)	—	16.00	24.00	40.00	65.00	—
AH1098//30	—	16.00	24.00	40.00	65.00	—
AH1098//31	—	16.00	24.00	40.00	65.00	—

Guti

KM# 300.29 RUPEE (Type 300)

Silver **Note:** Weight varies: 11.00-11.60 grams.

Date	Mintage	VG	F	VF	XF	Unc
AH1107//41(sic)	—	110	180	300	480	—

Gwalior

KM# 300.30 RUPEE (Type 300)

Silver **Note:** Weight varies: 11.00-11.60 grams.

Date	Mintage	VG	F	VF	XF	Unc
AH1096//29	—	16.00	22.00	35.00	55.00	—
AH1097//29	—	16.00	22.00	35.00	55.00	—
AH1097//30	—	16.00	22.00	35.00	55.00	—
AH1098//30	—	16.00	22.00	35.00	55.00	—
AH1098//31	—	16.00	22.00	35.00	55.00	—
AH1099//31	—	16.00	22.00	35.00	55.00	—
AH1099//32	—	16.00	22.00	35.00	55.00	—
AH1100//32	—	16.00	22.00	35.00	55.00	—
AH1100//33	—	16.00	22.00	35.00	55.00	—
AH1101//33	—	16.00	22.00	35.00	55.00	—
AH1011//33 (Error for 1101)	—	16.00	22.00	35.00	55.00	—

Haidarabad

KM# 300.31 RUPEE (Type 300)

Silver **Obv:** Inscription **Rev. Inscription:** Dar-ul-Jihad **Note:** Weight varies 11.00-11.60 grams.

Date	Mintage	VG	F	VF	XF	Unc
AH1098//xx	—	16.00	20.00	28.00	45.00	—
AH1099//31	—	16.00	20.00	28.00	45.00	—
AH1099//32	—	16.00	20.00	28.00	45.00	—
AH1100//32	—	16.00	20.00	28.00	45.00	—
AH1100//33	—	16.00	20.00	28.00	45.00	—
AH1105//38	—	16.00	20.00	28.00	45.00	—
AH1106//38	—	16.00	20.00	28.00	45.00	—
AH1106//39	—	16.00	20.00	28.00	45.00	—
AH1107//39	—	16.00	20.00	28.00	45.00	—
AH1111//43	—	16.00	20.00	28.00	45.00	—
AH1111//44	—	16.00	20.00	28.00	45.00	—
AH1112//44	—	16.00	20.00	28.00	45.00	—
AH1112//45	—	16.00	20.00	28.00	45.00	—

Hukeri

KM# 300.33 RUPEE (Type 300)

Silver **Note:** Weight varies 11.00-11.60 grams.

Date	Mintage	VG	F	VF	XF	Unc
AH1110//49	—	45.00	75.00	125	200	—

Imtiyazgarh

KM# 300.34 RUPEE (Type 300)

Silver **Rev:** Without mint epithet **Note:** Weight varies: 11.00-11.60 grams.

Date	Mintage	VG	F	VF	XF	Unc
AH111x//43	—	65.00	110	175	280	—

Islam Bandar

KM# 300.37 RUPEE (Type 300)

Silver

Date	Mintage	VG	F	VF	XF	Unc
AHxxxx//4x	—	110	180	300	480	—

Islamabad

KM# 300.35 RUPEE (Type 300)

Silver **Rev:** Mint name at top **Note:** Weight varies: 11.00-11.60 grams.

Date	Mintage	VG	F	VF	XF	Unc
AH107x//3	—	24.00	40.00	65.00	105	—
AH1072//4	—	24.00	40.00	65.00	105	—
AH1074//7	—	24.00	40.00	65.00	105	—
AH1076//8	—	24.00	40.00	65.00	105	—
AH1076//9	—	24.00	40.00	65.00	105	—
AH1077//x	—	24.00	40.00	65.00	105	—
AH1078	—	24.00	40.00	65.00	105	—
AH1079//12	—	24.00	40.00	65.00	105	—

Islamabad

KM# 300.36 RUPEE (Type 300)

Silver **Rev:** Mint name at bottom **Note:** Weight varies: 11.00-11.60 grams.

Date	Mintage	VG	F	VF	XF	Unc
AH1094//27	—	18.00	30.00	50.00	80.00	—
AH1098//30	—	18.00	30.00	50.00	80.00	—
AH1098//3x	—	18.00	30.00	50.00	80.00	—
AH1099//3x	—	18.00	30.00	50.00	80.00	—
AH1103//35	—	18.00	30.00	50.00	80.00	—
AH1106//38	—	18.00	30.00	50.00	80.00	—
AH1106//39	—	18.00	30.00	50.00	80.00	—
AH1107//40	—	18.00	30.00	50.00	80.00	—
AH1108//40	—	18.00	30.00	50.00	80.00	—
AH1109//41	—	18.00	30.00	50.00	80.00	—
AH1111//xx	—	18.00	30.00	50.00	80.00	—
AH1112//44	—	18.00	30.00	50.00	80.00	—
AH1112//45	—	18.00	30.00	50.00	80.00	—

Islamnagar

KM# 300.38 RUPEE (Type 300)

Silver **Note:** Weight varies 11.00-11.60 grams.

Date	Mintage	VG	F	VF	XF	Unc
AH1077//10	—	125	210	350	560	—
AH1078//11	—	125	210	350	560	—
AH107x//12	—	125	210	350	560	—
AH1080//12	—	125	210	350	560	—

Itawa

KM# 300.39 RUPEE (Type 300)

Silver **Obv:** Inscription **Rev:** Inscription **Note:** Weight varies 11.00-11.60 grams.

Date	Mintage	VG	F	VF	XF	Unc
AH1096//29	—	16.00	20.00	25.00	40.00	—
AH1097//29	—	16.00	20.00	25.00	40.00	—
AH1098//30	—	16.00	20.00	25.00	40.00	—
AH1098//31	—	16.00	20.00	25.00	40.00	—
AH1099//31	—	16.00	20.00	25.00	40.00	—
AH1099//32	—	16.00	20.00	25.00	40.00	—
AH1100//32	—	16.00	20.00	25.00	40.00	—
AH1100//33	—	16.00	20.00	25.00	40.00	—
AH1101//33	—	16.00	20.00	25.00	40.00	—
AH1101//34	—	16.00	20.00	25.00	40.00	—
AH1102//34	—	16.00	20.00	25.00	40.00	—
AH1102//35	—	16.00	20.00	25.00	40.00	—
AH1103//35	—	16.00	20.00	25.00	40.00	—
AH1103//36	—	16.00	20.00	25.00	40.00	—
AH1104//36	—	16.00	20.00	25.00	40.00	—
AH1104//37	—	16.00	20.00	25.00	40.00	—
AH1105//37	—	16.00	20.00	25.00	40.00	—
AH1105//38	—	16.00	20.00	25.00	40.00	—
AH1106//38	—	16.00	20.00	25.00	40.00	—
AH1106//39	—	16.00	20.00	25.00	40.00	—
AH1107//39	—	16.00	20.00	25.00	40.00	—
AH1107//40	—	16.00	20.00	25.00	40.00	—
AH1108//40	—	16.00	20.00	25.00	40.00	—
AH1108//41	—	16.00	20.00	25.00	40.00	—
AH1109//41	—	16.00	20.00	25.00	40.00	—
AH1110//42	—	16.00	20.00	25.00	40.00	—
AH1111//43	—	16.00	20.00	25.00	40.00	—
AH1111//44	—	16.00	20.00	25.00	40.00	—
AH1112//44	—	16.00	20.00	25.00	40.00	—
AH1112//45	—	16.00	20.00	25.00	40.00	—

Jahangirnagar

KM# 300.107 RUPEE (Type 300)

11.4440 g., Silver **Rev:** Mint name at top **Note:** "Mihr" couplet.

Date	Mintage	VG	F	VF	XF	Unc
AH1070//3	—	16.00	24.00	40.00	65.00	—
AH1071//3	—	16.00	24.00	40.00	65.00	—
AHxxxx//4	—	16.00	24.00	40.00	65.00	—

Jahangirnagar

KM# 300.108 RUPEE (Type 300)

11.4440 g., Silver **Rev:** Mint name at bottom **Note:** "Mihr" couplet.

Date	Mintage	VG	F	VF	XF	Unc
AHxxxx//5	—	16.00	24.00	40.00	65.00	—
AH1073//6	—	16.00	24.00	40.00	65.00	—
AH1102//35	—	16.00	24.00	40.00	65.00	—

Jahangirnagar

KM# 300.40 RUPEE (Type 300)

Silver **Obv:** Inscription **Rev:** Inscription **Note:** Weight varies 11.00-11.60 grams.

Date	Mintage	VG	F	VF	XF	Unc
AH107x//10	—	16.00	20.00	32.00	52.50	—
AH108x//20	—	16.00	20.00	32.00	52.50	—
AH1092//24	—	16.00	20.00	32.00	52.50	—
AH1092//25	—	16.00	20.00	32.00	52.50	—
AH1093//25	—	16.00	20.00	32.00	52.50	—
AH1094//26	—	16.00	20.00	32.00	52.50	—
AH1093//26	—	16.00	20.00	32.00	52.50	—
AH1094//27	—	16.00	20.00	32.00	52.50	—
AH1095//27	—	16.00	20.00	32.00	52.50	—
AH1095//28	—	16.00	20.00	32.00	52.50	—
AH1096//28	—	16.00	20.00	32.00	52.50	—
AH109x//30	—	16.00	20.00	32.00	52.50	—
AH109x//31	—	16.00	20.00	32.00	52.50	—
AH1099//32	—	16.00	20.00	32.00	52.50	—
AH1100//32	—	16.00	20.00	32.00	52.50	—
AH1100//33	—	16.00	20.00	32.00	52.50	—
AH1101//33	—	16.00	20.00	32.00	52.50	—
AH1101//34	—	16.00	20.00	32.00	52.50	—
AH1102//34	—	16.00	20.00	32.00	52.50	—
AH1102//35	—	16.00	20.00	32.00	52.50	—
AH1103//35	—	16.00	20.00	32.00	52.50	—
AH1103//36	—	16.00	20.00	32.00	52.50	—
AH1104//36	—	16.00	20.00	32.00	52.50	—
AH1104//37	—	16.00	20.00	32.00	52.50	—
AH1105//37	—	16.00	20.00	32.00	52.50	—
AH1105//38	—	16.00	20.00	32.00	52.50	—
AH1106//38	—	16.00	20.00	32.00	52.50	—
AH1106//39	—	16.00	20.00	32.00	52.50	—
AH1107//39	—	16.00	20.00	32.00	52.50	—
AH1107//40	—	16.00	20.00	32.00	52.50	—
AH1108//40	—	16.00	20.00	32.00	52.50	—
AH1108//41	—	16.00	20.00	32.00	52.50	—
AH1109//41	—	16.00	20.00	32.00	52.50	—
AH1109//42	—	16.00	20.00	32.00	52.50	—
AH1110//42	—	16.00	20.00	32.00	52.50	—
AH1110//43	—	16.00	20.00	32.00	52.50	—
AH1111//43	—	16.00	20.00	32.00	52.50	—
AH1111//44	—	16.00	20.00	32.00	52.50	—
AH1112//45	—	16.00	20.00	32.00	52.50	—

Jaunpur

KM# 300.41 RUPEE (Type 300)

Silver **Note:** Weight varies: 11.00-11.60 grams.

Date	Mintage	VG	F	VF	XF	Unc
AH1097//30	—	22.00	36.00	60.00	95.00	—
AH1099//31	—	22.00	36.00	60.00	95.00	—
AH1099//32	—	22.00	36.00	60.00	95.00	—
AH1101//3x	—	22.00	36.00	60.00	95.00	—

Jinji

KM# 300.42 RUPEE (Type 300)

Silver **Note:** Weight varies: 11.00-11.60 grams.

Date	Mintage	VG	F	VF	XF	Unc
AH1106//42	—	70.00	120	200	320	—
AH1109//xx	—	70.00	120	200	320	—

Junagadh

KM# 300.43 RUPEE (Type 300)

Silver **Note:** Weight varies 11.00-11.60 grams.

Date	Mintage	VG	F	VF	XF	Unc
AH1099//31	—	16.00	27.00	45.00	67.50	—
AH1099//32	—	16.00	27.00	45.00	67.50	—
AH1100//32	—	16.00	27.00	45.00	67.50	—
AH1100//33	—	16.00	27.00	45.00	67.50	—
AH1101//33	—	16.00	27.00	45.00	67.50	—
AH1101//34	—	16.00	27.00	45.00	67.50	—
AH1102//34	—	16.00	27.00	45.00	67.50	—
AH1102//35	—	16.00	27.00	45.00	67.50	—
AH1103//35	—	16.00	27.00	45.00	67.50	—
AH1103//36	—	16.00	27.00	45.00	67.50	—
AH1104//36	—	16.00	27.00	45.00	67.50	—
AH1104//37	—	16.00	27.00	45.00	67.50	—
AH1105//37	—	16.00	27.00	45.00	67.50	—
AH1105//38	—	16.00	27.00	45.00	67.50	—
AH1106//38	—	16.00	27.00	45.00	67.50	—
AH1108//40	—	16.00	27.00	45.00	67.50	—
AH1108//41	—	16.00	27.00	45.00	67.50	—
AH1109//41	—	16.00	27.00	45.00	67.50	—
AH1109//42	—	16.00	27.00	45.00	67.50	—
AH1110//42	—	16.00	27.00	45.00	67.50	—
AH1110//43	—	16.00	27.00	45.00	67.50	—
AH1111//43	—	16.00	27.00	45.00	67.50	—

Kabul

KM# 300.109 RUPEE (Type 300)

11.4440 g., Silver **Rev:** Without mint epithet **Note:** "Mihr" couplet.

Date	Mintage	VG	F	VF	XF	Unc
AH1082//15	—	25.00	42.50	70.00	105	—
AH1083//16	—	25.00	42.50	70.00	105	—
AH1085//18	—	25.00	42.50	70.00	105	—
AH1088//21	—	25.00	42.50	70.00	105	—

Kabul

KM# 300.44 RUPEE (Type 300)

Silver **Rev:** Without mint epithet **Note:** "Badr" couplet; Weight varies: 11.00-11.60 grams.

Date	Mintage	VG	F	VF	XF	Unc
AH1082//14	—	25.00	42.50	70.00	105	—
AH1082//15	—	25.00	42.50	70.00	105	—
AH1083//15	—	25.00	42.50	70.00	105	—
AH1086//18	—	25.00	42.50	70.00	105	—
AH108x//20	—	25.00	42.50	70.00	105	—
AH1089//xx	—	25.00	42.50	70.00	105	—
AH1092//24	—	25.00	42.50	70.00	105	—
AH109x//27	—	25.00	42.50	70.00	105	—
AH1101//34	—	25.00	42.50	70.00	105	—

Kabul

KM# 300.45 RUPEE (Type 300)

Silver **Obv:** Inscription **Rev. Inscription:** Dar-ul-Mulk and mint name **Note:** Weight varies 11.00-11.60 grams.

Date	Mintage	VG	F	VF	XF	Unc
AH1094//27	—	21.00	36.00	60.00	90.00	—
AH1096//29	—	21.00	36.00	60.00	90.00	—
AH1098//30	—	21.00	36.00	60.00	90.00	—
AH1098//31	—	21.00	36.00	60.00	90.00	—
AH1099//31	—	21.00	36.00	60.00	90.00	—
AH1099//32	—	21.00	36.00	60.00	90.00	—
AH1100//32	—	21.00	36.00	60.00	90.00	—
AH110x//33	—	21.00	36.00	60.00	90.00	—
AH1101//XX	—	21.00	36.00	60.00	90.00	—
AH1102//34	—	21.00	36.00	60.00	90.00	—
AH1102//35	—	21.00	36.00	60.00	90.00	—
AH1104//36	—	21.00	36.00	60.00	90.00	—
AH110X//37	—	21.00	36.00	60.00	90.00	—
AH1105//xx	—	21.00	36.00	60.00	90.00	—
AH1106//38	—	21.00	36.00	60.00	90.00	—
AH1106//39	—	21.00	36.00	60.00	90.00	—
AH1107//39	—	21.00	36.00	60.00	90.00	—
AH1107//40	—	21.00	36.00	60.00	90.00	—
AH1110//42	—	21.00	36.00	60.00	90.00	—
AH1111//43	—	21.00	36.00	60.00	90.00	—
AH1111//44	—	21.00	36.00	60.00	90.00	—
AH1112//44	—	21.00	36.00	60.00	90.00	—

Kanji

KM# 300.46 RUPEE (Type 300)

Silver **Note:** Weight varies: 11.00-11.60 grams.

Date	Mintage	VG	F	VF	XF	Unc
AH1xxx//32	—	65.00	105	175	265	—
AH1105	—	65.00	105	175	265	—
AH1106//38	—	65.00	105	175	265	—
AH1106//39	—	65.00	105	175	265	—
AH1106//40(sic)	—	65.00	105	175	265	—
AH1106//41(sic)	—	65.00	105	175	265	—
AH1106//42(sic)	—	65.00	105	175	265	—
AH11xx//45	—	65.00	105	175	265	—

Karappa

KM# 300.97 RUPEE (Type 300)

Silver **Note:** Weight varies: 11.00-11.60 grams.

Date	Mintage	VG	F	VF	XF	Unc
AHxxxx//32	—	120	200	325	525	—
AH11xx//34	—	120	200	325	525	—
AH11xx//37	—	120	200	325	525	—

Karnatak

KM# 300.47 RUPEE (Type 300)

Silver **Note:** Weight varies: 11.00-11.60 grams.

Date	Mintage	VG	F	VF	XF	Unc
AH1xxx//32	—	125	210	350	525	—

Karnatik

KM# 300.110 RUPEE (Type 300)
11.4440 g., Silver **Rev. Inscription:** "dar al-Zafar Bijapur"

Date	Mintage	VG	F	VF	XF	Unc
AH1110//43	—	160	270	450	675	—

Kashmir

KM# 300.48 RUPEE (Type 300)
Silver **Obv:** Couplet in three lines **Note:** Weight varies 11.00-11.60 grams.

Date	Mintage	VG	F	VF	XF	Unc
AH107x//4	—	21.00	36.00	60.00	90.00	—
AHxxxx//9	—	21.00	36.00	60.00	90.00	—
AH107x//10	—	21.00	36.00	60.00	90.00	—
AH1089//21	—	21.00	36.00	60.00	90.00	—
AH1096//xx	—	21.00	36.00	60.00	90.00	—
AH109x//30	—	21.00	36.00	60.00	90.00	—
AH1xxx//32	—	21.00	36.00	60.00	90.00	—
AH1105//3x	—	21.00	36.00	60.00	90.00	—
AH1106//39	—	21.00	36.00	60.00	90.00	—
AH1108//40	—	21.00	36.00	60.00	90.00	—
AH1108//41	—	21.00	36.00	60.00	90.00	—
AH1109//41	—	21.00	36.00	60.00	90.00	—
AH1109//42	—	21.00	36.00	60.00	90.00	—
AH1110//42	—	21.00	36.00	60.00	90.00	—
AH111x//43	—	21.00	36.00	60.00	90.00	—
AH111x//44	—	21.00	36.00	60.00	90.00	—
AH111x//45	—	21.00	36.00	60.00	90.00	—

Katak

KM# 300.50 RUPEE (Type 300)
Silver **Obv:** Inscription **Rev:** Mint name at bottom **Note:** "Badr" couplet; Weight varies 11.00-11.60 grams.

Date	Mintage	VG	F	VF	XF	Unc
AHxxxx//2	—	16.00	21.00	35.00	52.50	—
AH107x//3	—	16.00	21.00	35.00	52.50	—
AH1072//4	—	16.00	21.00	35.00	52.50	—
AH1073//5	—	16.00	21.00	35.00	52.50	—
AH107x//7	—	16.00	21.00	35.00	52.50	—
AH107x//9	—	16.00	21.00	35.00	52.50	—
AH1082//15	—	16.00	21.00	35.00	52.50	—
AH1085//18	—	16.00	21.00	35.00	52.50	—
AH108x//19	—	16.00	21.00	35.00	52.50	—
AH108x//20	—	16.00	21.00	35.00	52.50	—
AH1088//21	—	16.00	21.00	35.00	52.50	—
AH1089//22	—	16.00	21.00	35.00	52.50	—
AH109x//23	—	16.00	21.00	35.00	52.50	—
AH1092//25	—	16.00	21.00	35.00	52.50	—
AH1094//26	—	16.00	21.00	35.00	52.50	—
AH1094//27	—	16.00	21.00	35.00	52.50	—
AH1095//27	—	16.00	21.00	35.00	52.50	—
AH1095//28	—	16.00	21.00	35.00	52.50	—
AH1097//30	—	16.00	21.00	35.00	52.50	—
AH1099//31	—	16.00	21.00	35.00	52.50	—
AH1099//32	—	16.00	21.00	35.00	52.50	—
AH1100//32	—	16.00	21.00	35.00	52.50	—
AH110x//33	—	16.00	21.00	35.00	52.50	—
AH1102//35	—	16.00	21.00	35.00	52.50	—
AH1103//35	—	16.00	21.00	35.00	52.50	—
AH1103//36	—	16.00	21.00	35.00	52.50	—
AH1104//36	—	16.00	21.00	35.00	52.50	—
AH1104//37	—	16.00	21.00	35.00	52.50	—
AH1105//37	—	16.00	21.00	35.00	52.50	—
AH1105//38	—	16.00	21.00	35.00	52.50	—
AH1106//38	—	16.00	21.00	35.00	52.50	—
AH1106//39	—	16.00	21.00	35.00	52.50	—
AH1107//39	—	16.00	21.00	35.00	52.50	—
AH1107//40	—	16.00	21.00	35.00	52.50	—
AH1108//40	—	16.00	21.00	35.00	52.50	—
AH1108//41	—	16.00	21.00	35.00	52.50	—
AH1109//41	—	16.00	21.00	35.00	52.50	—
AH1109//42	—	16.00	21.00	35.00	52.50	—
AH1110//42	—	16.00	21.00	35.00	52.50	—
AH1110//43	—	16.00	21.00	35.00	52.50	—
AH1112//44	—	16.00	21.00	35.00	52.50	—
AH1112//45	—	16.00	21.00	35.00	52.50	—

Katak

KM# 300.49 RUPEE (Type 300)
Silver **Rev:** Mint name at top **Note:** "Mihr" couplet; Weight varies: 11.00-11.60 grams.

Date	Mintage	VG	F	VF	XF	Unc
AH1070//(1) Ahad	—	16.00	21.00	35.00	52.50	—
AH1071//3	—	16.00	21.00	35.00	52.50	—
AHxxxx//4	—	16.00	21.00	35.00	52.50	—
AH1072//5	—	16.00	21.00	35.00	52.50	—
AH1073//5	—	16.00	21.00	35.00	52.50	—
AHxxxx//18	—	16.00	21.00	35.00	52.50	—
AHxxxx//25	—	16.00	21.00	35.00	52.50	—
AHxxxx//33	—	16.00	21.00	35.00	52.50	—
AHxxxx//36	—	16.00	21.00	35.00	52.50	—
AHxxxx//43	—	16.00	21.00	35.00	52.50	—

Khambayat

KM# 300.51 RUPEE (Type 300)
Silver **Obv:** Inscription **Rev:** Mint name at bottom **Note:** "Badr" couplet; Weight varies 11.00-11.60 grams.

Date	Mintage	VG	F	VF	XF	Unc
AH1070//(1) Ahad	—	16.00	20.00	25.00	37.50	—
AH1072//4	—	16.00	20.00	25.00	37.50	—
AH1072//5	—	16.00	20.00	25.00	37.50	—
AH1073//5	—	16.00	20.00	25.00	37.50	—
AH1073//6	—	16.00	20.00	25.00	37.50	—
AH1074//6	—	16.00	20.00	25.00	37.50	—
AH1074//7	—	16.00	20.00	25.00	37.50	—
AH1075//7	—	16.00	20.00	25.00	37.50	—
AH1075//8	—	16.00	20.00	25.00	37.50	—
AH1076//8	—	16.00	20.00	25.00	37.50	—
AH1076//7	—	16.00	20.00	25.00	37.50	—
AH1077//x	—	16.00	20.00	25.00	37.50	—
AH1078//10	—	16.00	20.00	25.00	37.50	—
AH1078//11	—	16.00	20.00	25.00	37.50	—
AH1079//11	—	16.00	20.00	25.00	37.50	—
AH1079//12	—	16.00	20.00	25.00	37.50	—
AH1080//12	—	16.00	20.00	25.00	37.50	—
AH1080//13	—	16.00	20.00	25.00	37.50	—
AH1081//13	—	16.00	20.00	25.00	37.50	—
AH1081//14	—	16.00	20.00	25.00	37.50	—
AH1082//14	—	16.00	20.00	25.00	37.50	—
AH1082//15	—	16.00	20.00	25.00	37.50	—
AH1083//15	—	16.00	20.00	25.00	37.50	—
AH1083//16	—	16.00	20.00	25.00	37.50	—
AH1084//16	—	16.00	20.00	25.00	37.50	—
AH1084//17	—	16.00	20.00	25.00	37.50	—
AH1085//17	—	16.00	20.00	25.00	37.50	—
AH1085//18	—	16.00	20.00	25.00	37.50	—
AH1086//18	—	16.00	20.00	25.00	37.50	—
AH1086//19	—	16.00	20.00	25.00	37.50	—
AH1087//19	—	16.00	20.00	25.00	37.50	—
AH1087//20	—	16.00	20.00	25.00	37.50	—
AH1088//20	—	16.00	20.00	25.00	37.50	—
AH1088//21	—	16.00	20.00	25.00	37.50	—
AH1089//21	—	16.00	20.00	25.00	37.50	—
AH1089//22	—	16.00	20.00	25.00	37.50	—
AH1090//22	—	16.00	20.00	25.00	37.50	—
AH1090//23	—	16.00	20.00	25.00	37.50	—
AH1091//23	—	16.00	20.00	25.00	37.50	—
AH1091//24	—	16.00	20.00	25.00	37.50	—
AH1092//24	—	16.00	20.00	25.00	37.50	—
AH1092//25	—	16.00	20.00	25.00	37.50	—
AH1093//25	—	16.00	20.00	25.00	37.50	—
AH1094//26	—	16.00	20.00	25.00	37.50	—
AH1093//26	—	16.00	20.00	25.00	37.50	—
AH1094//27	—	16.00	20.00	25.00	37.50	—
AH1095//27	—	16.00	20.00	25.00	37.50	—
AH1095//28	—	16.00	20.00	25.00	37.50	—
AH1096//28	—	16.00	20.00	25.00	37.50	—
AH1096//29	—	16.00	20.00	25.00	37.50	—
AH1097//29	—	16.00	20.00	25.00	37.50	—
AH1097//30	—	16.00	20.00	25.00	37.50	—
AH1098//30	—	16.00	20.00	25.00	37.50	—
AH1098//31	—	16.00	20.00	25.00	37.50	—
AH1099//31	—	16.00	20.00	25.00	37.50	—
AH1099//32	—	16.00	20.00	25.00	37.50	—
AH1100//32	—	16.00	20.00	25.00	37.50	—
AH1100//33	—	16.00	20.00	25.00	37.50	—
AH1101//33	—	16.00	20.00	25.00	37.50	—
AH1101//34	—	16.00	20.00	25.00	37.50	—
AH1102//34	—	16.00	20.00	25.00	37.50	—
AH1102//35	—	16.00	20.00	25.00	37.50	—
AH1103//35	—	16.00	20.00	25.00	37.50	—
AH1104//36	—	16.00	20.00	25.00	37.50	—
AH1105//37	—	16.00	20.00	25.00	37.50	—
AH1106//38	—	16.00	20.00	25.00	37.50	—
AH1107//39	—	16.00	20.00	25.00	37.50	—
AH1107//40	—	16.00	20.00	25.00	37.50	—
AH1109//41	—	16.00	20.00	25.00	37.50	—
AH1109//43 (sic)	—	16.00	20.00	25.00	37.50	—
AH1110//42	—	16.00	20.00	25.00	37.50	—
AH1111//43	—	16.00	20.00	25.00	37.50	—
AH1112//44	—	16.00	20.00	25.00	37.50	—

Khambayat

KM# 300.95 RUPEE (Type 300)
Silver **Rev:** Mint name at top **Note:** Weight varies: 11.00-11.60 grams.

Date	Mintage	VG	F	VF	XF	Unc
AH1070//(1) Ahad	—	55.00	90.00	150	225	—

Khambayat

KM# 300.111 RUPEE (Type 300)
11.4440 g., Silver **Rev:** Mint name at bottom **Note:** "Mihr" couplet.

Date	Mintage	VG	F	VF	XF	Unc
AH1109//41	—	16.00	20.00	25.00	37.50	—

Khujista Bunyad

KM# 300.52 RUPEE (Type 300)
Silver **Obv:** Inscription **Rev:** Inscription **Note:** Weight varies 11.00-11.60 grams.

Date	Mintage	VG	F	VF	XF	Unc
AH1107//(1) ahd error for 1070	—	16.00	28.00	40.00	65.00	—
AH1091//23	—	16.00	20.00	28.00	42.50	—
AH1091//24	—	16.00	20.00	28.00	42.50	—
AH1094//26	—	16.00	20.00	28.00	42.50	—
AH1096//28	—	16.00	20.00	28.00	42.50	—
AH1100//32	—	16.00	20.00	28.00	42.50	—
AH1100//33	—	16.00	20.00	28.00	42.50	—
AH1101//33	—	16.00	20.00	28.00	42.50	—
AH1101//34	—	16.00	20.00	28.00	42.50	—
AH1102//34	—	16.00	20.00	28.00	42.50	—
AH1102//35	—	16.00	20.00	28.00	42.50	—
AH1103//35	—	16.00	20.00	28.00	42.50	—
AH1106//38	—	16.00	20.00	28.00	42.50	—
AH1106//39	—	16.00	20.00	28.00	42.50	—
AH1107//39	—	16.00	20.00	28.00	42.50	—
AH1107//40	—	16.00	20.00	28.00	42.50	—
AH1108//40	—	16.00	20.00	28.00	42.50	—
AH1108//41	—	16.00	20.00	28.00	42.50	—
AH1109//41	—	16.00	20.00	28.00	42.50	—
AH1109//42	—	16.00	20.00	28.00	42.50	—
AH1110//42	—	16.00	20.00	28.00	42.50	—
AH1110//43	—	16.00	20.00	28.00	42.50	—
AH1111//43	—	16.00	20.00	28.00	42.50	—
AH1111//44	—	16.00	20.00	28.00	42.50	—
AH1112//44	—	16.00	20.00	28.00	42.50	—

Lahore

KM# 300.112 RUPEE (Type 300)
11.4440 g., Silver **Rev. Inscription:** "dar al-Sultanat" **Note:** "Mihr" couplet.

Date	Mintage	VG	F	VF	XF	Unc
AH1069//(1) Ahad	—	16.00	21.00	35.00	52.50	—
AH1070//(1) Ahad	—	16.00	21.00	35.00	52.50	—
AH1070//2	—	16.00	21.00	35.00	52.50	—
AH1071//3	—	16.00	21.00	35.00	52.50	—
AH1071//4	—	16.00	21.00	35.00	52.50	—
AH1072//4	—	16.00	21.00	35.00	52.00	—
AHxxxx//5	—	16.00	21.00	35.00	52.50	—
AHxxxx//6	—	16.00	21.00	35.00	52.50	—
AH1085//18	—	16.00	21.00	35.00	52.50	—
AH1109//42	—	16.00	21.00	35.00	52.50	—

Lahore

KM# 300.53 RUPEE (Type 300)
Silver **Obv:** Inscription **Rev. Inscription:** "Dar-us-Sultanat", mint name **Note:** "Badr couplet"; Weight varies 11.00-11.60 grams.

Date	Mintage	VG	F	VF	XF	Unc
AH1072//5	—	16.00	19.00	22.00	33.00	—
AH1073//5	—	16.00	19.00	22.00	33.00	—
AH1074//6	—	16.00	19.00	22.00	33.00	—
AH1076//8	—	16.00	19.00	22.00	33.00	—
AH1076//9	—	16.00	19.00	22.00	33.00	—
AH1077//9	—	16.00	19.00	22.00	33.00	—
AH1077//10	—	16.00	19.00	22.00	33.00	—
AH1078//10	—	16.00	19.00	22.00	33.00	—
AH1078//11	—	16.00	19.00	22.00	33.00	—
AH1079//11	—	16.00	19.00	22.00	33.00	—
AH1079//12	—	16.00	19.00	22.00	33.00	—
AH1080//12	—	16.00	19.00	22.00	33.00	—
AH1080//13	—	16.00	19.00	22.00	33.00	—
AH1081//13	—	16.00	19.00	22.00	33.00	—
AH1081//14	—	16.00	19.00	22.00	33.00	—
AH1083//16	—	16.00	19.00	22.00	33.00	—
AH1085//17	—	16.00	19.00	22.00	33.00	—
AH1087//19	—	16.00	19.00	22.00	33.00	—
AH1088//20	—	16.00	19.00	22.00	33.00	—
AH1089//21	—	16.00	19.00	22.00	33.00	—
AH1090//22	—	16.00	19.00	22.00	33.00	—
AH1090//23	—	16.00	19.00	22.00	33.00	—
AH1091//23	—	16.00	19.00	22.00	33.00	—
AH1092//24	—	16.00	19.00	22.00	33.00	—

Date	Mintage	VG	F	VF	XF	Unc
AH1093//25	—	16.00	19.00	22.00	33.00	—
AH1094//26	—	16.00	19.00	22.00	33.00	—
AH1094//27	—	16.00	19.00	22.00	33.00	—
AH1095//28	—	16.00	19.00	22.00	33.00	—
AH1096//29	—	16.00	19.00	22.00	33.00	—
AH1097//29	—	16.00	19.00	22.00	33.00	—
AH1097//30	—	16.00	19.00	22.00	33.00	—
AH1098//30	—	16.00	19.00	22.00	33.00	—
AH1098//31	—	16.00	19.00	22.00	33.00	—
AH1099//31	—	16.00	19.00	22.00	33.00	—
AH1099//32	—	16.00	19.00	22.00	33.00	—
AH1100//32	—	16.00	19.00	22.00	33.00	—
AH1100//33	—	16.00	19.00	22.00	33.00	—
AH1101//33	—	16.00	19.00	22.00	33.00	—
AH1101//34	—	16.00	19.00	22.00	33.00	—
AH1102//34	—	16.00	19.00	22.00	33.00	—
AH1103//35	—	16.00	19.00	22.00	33.00	—
AH1103//36	—	16.00	19.00	22.00	33.00	—
AH1104//36	—	16.00	19.00	22.00	33.00	—
AH1104//37	—	16.00	19.00	22.00	33.00	—
AH1105//37	—	16.00	19.00	22.00	27.50	—
AH1105//38	—	16.00	19.00	22.00	33.00	—
AH1106//38	—	16.00	19.00	22.00	33.00	—
AH1106//39	—	16.00	19.00	22.00	33.00	—
AH1107//39	—	16.00	19.00	22.00	33.00	—
AH1107//40	—	16.00	19.00	22.00	33.00	—
AH1108//40	—	16.00	19.00	22.00	33.00	—
AH1108//41	—	16.00	19.00	22.00	33.00	—
AH1109//41	—	16.00	19.00	22.00	33.00	—
AH1109//42	—	16.00	19.00	22.00	33.00	—
AH1110//42	—	16.00	19.00	22.00	33.00	—
AH1110//43	—	16.00	19.00	22.00	33.00	—
AH1111//43	—	16.00	19.00	22.00	33.00	—
AH1111//44	—	16.00	19.00	22.00	33.00	—
AH1112//44	—	16.00	19.00	22.00	33.00	—
AH1112//45	—	16.00	19.00	22.00	33.00	—

Lakhnau

KM# 300.54 RUPEE (Type 300)

Silver **Obv:** Inscription **Rev:** Inscription **Note:** Weight varies 11.00-11.60 grams.

Date	Mintage	VG	F	VF	XF	Unc
AH1081//14	—	16.00	22.00	28.00	42.50	—
AH1084//16	—	16.00	22.00	28.00	42.50	—
AH1084//17	—	16.00	22.00	28.00	42.50	—
AH1085//17	—	16.00	22.00	28.00	42.50	—
AH1085//18	—	16.00	22.00	28.00	42.50	—
AH1087//19	—	16.00	22.00	28.00	42.50	—
AH1087//20	—	16.00	22.00	28.00	42.50	—
AH1088//20	—	16.00	22.00	28.00	42.50	—
AH1088//21	—	16.00	22.00	28.00	42.50	—
AH1089//21	—	16.00	22.00	28.00	42.50	—
AH1091//23	—	16.00	22.00	28.00	42.50	—
AH11xx//25	—	16.00	22.00	28.00	42.50	—
AH1095//27	—	16.00	22.00	28.00	42.50	—
AH1095//28	—	16.00	22.00	28.00	42.50	—
AH1097//29	—	16.00	22.00	28.00	42.50	—
AH1098//30	—	16.00	22.00	28.00	42.50	—
AH1098//31	—	16.00	22.00	28.00	42.50	—
AH1099//32	—	16.00	22.00	28.00	42.50	—
AH1100//32	—	16.00	22.00	28.00	42.50	—
AH1101//33	—	16.00	22.00	28.00	42.50	—
AH1102//34	—	16.00	22.00	28.00	42.50	—
AH1103//35	—	16.00	22.00	28.00	42.50	—
AH110x//36	—	16.00	22.00	28.00	42.50	—
AH11xx//38	—	16.00	22.00	28.00	42.50	—
AH11xx//39	—	16.00	22.00	28.00	42.50	—
AH11xx//40	—	16.00	22.00	28.00	42.50	—
AH11xx//41	—	16.00	22.00	28.00	42.50	—
AH11xx//42	—	16.00	22.00	28.00	42.50	—
AH1110//43	—	16.00	22.00	28.00	42.50	—
AH11xx//44	—	16.00	22.00	28.00	42.50	—
AH11xx//45	—	16.00	22.00	28.00	42.50	—
AH1113//46	—	16.00	22.00	28.00	42.50	—

Macchlipattan

KM# 300.55 RUPEE (Type 300)

Silver **Note:** Weight varies 11.00-11.60 grams.

Date	Mintage	VG	F	VF	XF	Unc
AH1099//31	—	40.00	70.00	120	180	—
AH1099//32	—	40.00	70.00	120	180	—
AH10100//32(sic)	—	40.00	70.00	120	180	—
AH1100//32	—	40.00	70.00	120	180	—
AH1100//33	—	40.00	70.00	120	180	—
AH1111//43	—	40.00	70.00	120	180	—
AH1111//44	—	40.00	70.00	120	180	—
AH1112//44	—	40.00	70.00	120	180	—
AH1112//45	—	40.00	70.00	120	180	—

Makhsusabad

KM# 300.58 RUPEE (Type 300)

Silver **Obv:** Inscription, date **Rev:** Inscription **Note:** Weight varies 11.00-11.60 grams. For later isues see Murshidabad, KM#300.65.

Date	Mintage	VG	F	VF	XF	Unc
AH1111//44	—	50.00	85.00	140	210	—

Muazzamabad

KM# 300.60 RUPEE (Type 300)

Silver **Note:** Weight varies: 11.00-11.60 grams.

Date	Mintage	VG	F	VF	XF	Unc
AH1096//29	—	36.00	60.00	100	150	—
AH1097//29	—	36.00	60.00	100	150	—
AH1097//30	—	36.00	60.00	100	150	—
AH1098//30	—	36.00	60.00	100	150	—
AH1098//31	—	36.00	60.00	100	150	—
AH1099//31	—	36.00	60.00	100	150	—
AH1099//32	—	36.00	60.00	100	150	—
AH1100//32	—	36.00	60.00	100	150	—
AH1100//33	—	36.00	60.00	100	150	—
AH110x//34	—	36.00	60.00	100	150	—

Muhammadabad

KM# 300.61 RUPEE (Type 300)

Silver **Note:** Weight varies: 11.00-11.60 grams.

Date	Mintage	VG	F	VF	XF	Unc
AHxxxx//28	—	90.00	150	250	375	—
AH1096//29	—	90.00	150	250	375	—
AH1099//31	—	90.00	150	250	375	—
AH1102//34	—	90.00	150	250	375	—

Mulher

KM# 300.59 RUPEE (Type 300)

Silver **Note:** Weight varies: 11.00-11.60 grams.

Date	Mintage	VG	F	VF	XF	Unc
AH1095//28	—	90.00	150	250	375	—
AH1098//30	—	90.00	150	250	375	—

Multan

KM# 300.62 RUPEE (Type 300)

Silver **Rev:** "Dar-ul-Aman" with mint name at top **Note:** "Mihr" couplet; Weight varies: 11.00-11.60 grams.

Date	Mintage	VG	F	VF	XF	Unc
AH1070//(1) Ahad	—	16.00	20.00	25.00	37.50	—
AH1070//2	—	16.00	20.00	25.00	37.50	—
AH1070//3	—	16.00	20.00	25.00	37.50	—
AH1071//3	—	16.00	20.00	25.00	37.50	—
AH1071//4	—	16.00	20.00	25.00	37.50	—
AH1072//4	—	16.00	20.00	25.00	37.50	—
AH1072//5	—	16.00	20.00	25.00	37.50	—
AH1073//5	—	16.00	20.00	25.00	37.50	—

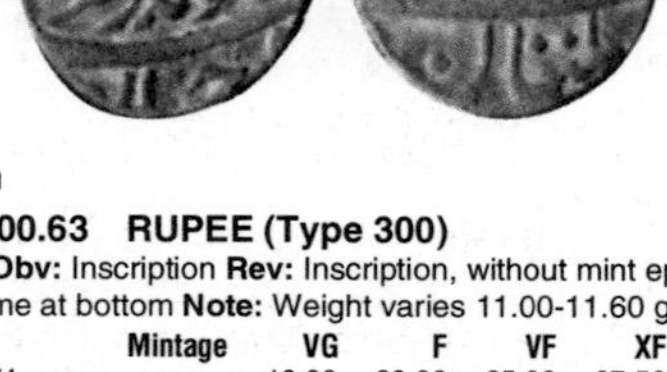

Multan

KM# 300.63 RUPEE (Type 300)

Silver **Obv:** Inscription **Rev:** Inscription, without mint epithet, mint name at bottom **Note:** Weight varies 11.00-11.60 grams.

Date	Mintage	VG	F	VF	XF	Unc
AH1072//4	—	16.00	20.00	25.00	37.50	—
AH1072//5	—	16.00	20.00	25.00	37.50	—
AH1073//5	—	16.00	20.00	25.00	37.50	—
AH1074//6	—	16.00	20.00	25.00	37.50	—
AH1074//7	—	16.00	20.00	25.00	37.50	—
AH1075//7	—	16.00	20.00	25.00	37.50	—
AH1075//8	—	16.00	20.00	25.00	37.50	—
AH1076//8	—	16.00	20.00	25.00	37.50	—
AH1076//9	—	16.00	20.00	25.00	37.50	—
AH1077//9	—	16.00	20.00	25.00	37.50	—
AH1077//10	—	16.00	20.00	25.00	37.50	—
AH1078//10	—	16.00	20.00	25.00	37.50	—
AH1078//11	—	16.00	20.00	25.00	37.50	—
AH1079//11	—	16.00	20.00	25.00	37.50	—
AH1079//12	—	16.00	20.00	25.00	37.50	—
AH1080//12	—	16.00	20.00	25.00	37.50	—
AH1080//13	—	16.00	20.00	25.00	37.50	—
AH1081//13	—	16.00	20.00	25.00	37.50	—
AH1081//14	—	16.00	20.00	25.00	37.50	—
AH1082//14	—	16.00	20.00	25.00	37.50	—
AH1082//15	—	16.00	20.00	25.00	37.50	—
AH1083//15	—	16.00	20.00	25.00	37.50	—
AH1083//16	—	16.00	20.00	25.00	37.50	—
AH1084//16	—	16.00	20.00	25.00	37.50	—
AH1084//17	—	16.00	20.00	25.00	37.50	—
AH1085//17	—	16.00	20.00	25.00	37.50	—
AH1085//18	—	16.00	20.00	25.00	37.50	—
AH1086//19	—	16.00	20.00	25.00	37.50	—
AH1087//20	—	16.00	20.00	25.00	37.50	—
AH1088//20	—	16.00	20.00	25.00	37.50	—
AH1088//21	—	16.00	20.00	25.00	37.50	—
AH1089//21	—	16.00	20.00	25.00	37.50	—
AH1089//22	—	16.00	20.00	25.00	37.50	—
AH1090//22	—	16.00	20.00	25.00	37.50	—
AH1090//23	—	16.00	20.00	25.00	37.50	—
AH1091//23	—	16.00	20.00	25.00	37.50	—
AH1091//24	—	16.00	20.00	25.00	37.50	—
AH1092//24	—	16.00	20.00	25.00	37.50	—
AH1092//25	—	16.00	20.00	25.00	37.50	—
AH1093//25	—	16.00	20.00	25.00	37.50	—
AH1093//26	—	16.00	20.00	25.00	37.50	—
AH1094//26	—	16.00	20.00	25.00	37.50	—
AH1094//27	—	16.00	20.00	25.00	37.50	—
AH1095//27	—	16.00	20.00	25.00	37.50	—
AH1095//28	—	16.00	20.00	25.00	37.50	—
AH1096//28	—	16.00	20.00	25.00	37.50	—
AH1096//29	—	16.00	20.00	25.00	37.50	—
AH1097//29	—	16.00	20.00	25.00	37.50	—
AH1097//30	—	16.00	20.00	25.00	37.50	—
AH1098//30	—	16.00	20.00	25.00	37.50	—
AH1098//31	—	16.00	20.00	25.00	37.50	—
AH1099//31	—	16.00	20.00	25.00	37.50	—
AH1099//32	—	16.00	20.00	25.00	37.50	—
AH1100//32	—	16.00	20.00	25.00	37.50	—
AH1100//33	—	16.00	20.00	25.00	37.50	—
AH1101//33	—	16.00	20.00	25.00	37.50	—
AH1101//34	—	16.00	20.00	25.00	37.50	—
AH1102//34	—	16.00	20.00	25.00	37.50	—
AH1102//35	—	16.00	20.00	25.00	37.50	—
AH1103//35	—	16.00	20.00	25.00	37.50	—
AH1103//36	—	16.00	20.00	25.00	37.50	—
AH1104//36	—	16.00	20.00	25.00	37.50	—
AH1104//37	—	16.00	20.00	25.00	37.50	—
AH1105//37	—	16.00	20.00	25.00	37.50	—
AH1105//38	—	16.00	20.00	25.00	37.50	—
AH1106//38	—	16.00	20.00	25.00	37.50	—
AH1106//39	—	16.00	20.00	25.00	37.50	—
AH1107//39	—	16.00	20.00	25.00	37.50	—
AH1107//40	—	16.00	20.00	25.00	37.50	—
AH1108//40	—	16.00	20.00	25.00	37.50	—
AH1108//41	—	16.00	20.00	25.00	37.50	—
AH1109//41	—	16.00	20.00	25.00	37.50	—
AH1109//42	—	16.00	20.00	25.00	37.50	—
AH1110//42	—	16.00	20.00	25.00	37.50	—
AH1110//43	—	16.00	20.00	25.00	37.50	—
AH1111//43	—	16.00	20.00	25.00	37.50	—
AH1111//44	—	16.00	20.00	25.00	37.50	—
AH1112//44	—	16.00	20.00	25.00	37.50	—

Muradabad

KM# 300.64 RUPEE (Type 300)

Silver **Rev:** Without mint epithet; mint name at bottom **Note:** Weight varies: 11.00-11.60 grams.

Date	Mintage	VG	F	VF	XF	Unc
AH1097//29	—	120	180	300	450	—

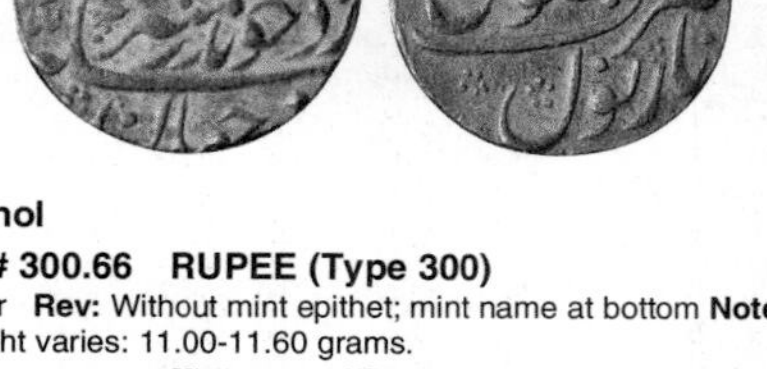

Narnol

KM# 300.66 RUPEE (Type 300)

Silver **Rev:** Without mint epithet; mint name at bottom **Note:** Weight varies: 11.00-11.60 grams.

Date	Mintage	VG	F	VF	XF	Unc
AH1098//30	—	27.00	45.00	75.00	115	—
AH1098//31	—	27.00	45.00	75.00	115	—
AH1099//31	—	27.00	45.00	75.00	115	—

Date	Mintage	VG	F	VF	XF	Unc
AH1099//32	—	27.00	45.00	75.00	115	—
AH1100//32	—	27.00	45.00	75.00	115	—
AH1100//33	—	27.00	45.00	75.00	115	—
AH1101//33	—	27.00	45.00	75.00	115	—
AH1101//34	—	27.00	45.00	75.00	115	—
AH1102//34	—	27.00	45.00	75.00	115	—

Nasirabad

KM# 300.67 RUPEE (Type 300)

Silver **Rev:** Without mint epithet; mint name at bottom **Note:** Weight varies: 11.00-11.60 grams.

Date	Mintage	VG	F	VF	XF	Unc
AH1101//3x	—	90.00	150	250	375	—
AH1102//34	—	90.00	150	250	375	—
AH1102//35	—	90.00	150	250	375	—
AH1102//36 (sic)	—	90.00	150	250	375	—
AH1109//4x	—	90.00	150	250	375	—
AH1110//32(sic)	—	90.00	150	250	375	—
AH1110//35(sic)	—	90.00	150	250	375	—
AH1112//4x	—	90.00	150	250	375	—

Nusratabad

KM# 300.68 RUPEE (Type 300)

Silver **Note:** Weight varies 11.00-11.60 grams.

Date	Mintage	VG	F	VF	XF	Unc
AH1xxx//32	—	40.00	66.00	110	165	—
AH1101//33	—	40.00	66.00	110	165	—
AH1106//38	—	40.00	66.00	110	165	—
AHxxxx//40	—	40.00	66.00	110	165	—
AH1109//41	—	40.00	66.00	110	165	—
AH1112//44	—	40.00	66.00	110	165	—

Nusratgarh

KM# 300.69 RUPEE (Type 300)

Silver **Rev:** Without mint epithet; mint name at bottom **Note:** Weight varies: 11.00-11.60 grams.

Date	Mintage	VG	F	VF	XF	Unc
AH1110//42	—	65.00	105	175	265	—
AH1110//43	—	65.00	105	175	265	—
AH1111//43	—	65.00	105	175	265	—
AH111x//44	—	65.00	105	175	265	—

Patna

KM# 300.71 RUPEE (Type 300)

Silver **Note:** Weight varies 11.00-11.60 grams. For later issues see Azimabad, KM#300.16.

Date	Mintage	VG	F	VF	XF	Unc
AH1069//(1) Ahad	—	16.00	21.00	28.00	42.50	—
AH1070//1	—	16.00	21.00	28.00	42.50	—
AH1070//3	—	16.00	21.00	28.00	42.50	—
AH107x//4	—	16.00	21.00	28.00	42.50	—
AH107x//5	—	16.00	21.00	28.00	42.50	—
AH1074//6	—	16.00	21.00	28.00	42.50	—
AH107x//7	—	16.00	21.00	28.00	42.50	—
AH107x//9	—	16.00	21.00	28.00	42.50	—
AH10xx//12	—	16.00	21.00	28.00	42.50	—
AH1080//13	—	16.00	21.00	28.00	42.50	—
AH1081//13	—	16.00	21.00	28.00	42.50	—
AH1081//14	—	16.00	21.00	28.00	42.50	—
AH108x//15	—	16.00	21.00	28.00	42.50	—
AHxxxx//17	—	16.00	21.00	28.00	42.50	—
AH108x//18	—	16.00	21.00	28.00	42.50	—
AH108x//21	—	16.00	21.00	28.00	42.50	—
AH1089//22	—	16.00	21.00	28.00	42.50	—
AH1090//22	—	16.00	21.00	28.00	42.50	—
AH1090//23	—	16.00	21.00	28.00	42.50	—
AH1091//23	—	16.00	21.00	28.00	42.50	—
AH1091//24	—	16.00	21.00	28.00	42.50	—
AH1092//24	—	16.00	21.00	28.00	42.50	—
AH1092//25	—	16.00	21.00	28.00	42.50	—
AH1093//25	—	16.00	21.00	28.00	42.50	—
AH1093//26	—	16.00	21.00	28.00	42.50	—
AH1094//26	—	16.00	21.00	28.00	42.50	—
AH1094//27	—	16.00	21.00	28.00	42.50	—
AH1095//27	—	16.00	21.00	28.00	42.50	—
AH1095//28	—	16.00	21.00	28.00	42.50	—
AH1096//28	—	16.00	21.00	28.00	42.50	—
AH1096//29	—	16.00	21.00	28.00	42.50	—
AH1097//29	—	16.00	21.00	28.00	42.50	—
AH1097//30	—	16.00	21.00	28.00	42.50	—
AH1098//30	—	16.00	21.00	28.00	42.50	—
AH1098//31	—	16.00	21.00	28.00	42.50	—
AH1099//31	—	16.00	21.00	28.00	42.50	—
AH1099//32	—	16.00	21.00	28.00	42.50	—
AH1100//32	—	16.00	21.00	28.00	42.50	—
AH1100//33	—	16.00	21.00	28.00	42.50	—
AH1101//33	—	16.00	21.00	28.00	42.50	—
AH1101//34	—	16.00	21.00	28.00	42.50	—
AH1102//34	—	16.00	21.00	28.00	42.50	—
AH1102//35	—	16.00	21.00	28.00	42.50	—
AH1103//35	—	16.00	21.00	28.00	42.50	—
AH1103//36	—	16.00	21.00	28.00	42.50	—
AH1104//36	—	16.00	21.00	28.00	42.50	—
AH1104//37	—	16.00	21.00	28.00	42.50	—
AH1105//37	—	16.00	21.00	28.00	42.50	—
AH1105//38	—	16.00	21.00	28.00	42.50	—
AH1106//38	—	16.00	21.00	28.00	42.50	—
AH1106//39	—	16.00	21.00	28.00	42.50	—
AH1107//40	—	16.00	21.00	28.00	42.50	—
AH1108//41	—	16.00	21.00	28.00	42.50	—
AH1109//41	—	16.00	21.00	28.00	42.50	—
AH1109//42	—	16.00	21.00	28.00	42.50	—
AH1110//42	—	16.00	21.00	28.00	42.50	—
AH1110//43	—	16.00	21.00	28.00	42.50	—
AH1111//43	—	16.00	21.00	28.00	42.50	—
AH1111//44	—	16.00	21.00	28.00	42.50	—
AH1112//44	—	16.00	21.00	28.00	42.50	—

Phonda

KM# 300.72 RUPEE (Type 300)

Silver **Rev:** Without mint epithet; mint name at bottom **Note:** Weight varies: 11.00-11.60 grams.

Date	Mintage	VG	F	VF	XF	Unc
AHxxxx//43	—	160	270	450	675	—

Punamali

KM# 300.73 RUPEE (Type 300)

Silver **Rev:** Without mint epithet; mint name at bottom **Note:** Weight varies: 11.00-11.60 grams.

Date	Mintage	VG	F	VF	XF	Unc
AH1111//45 (sic)	—	125	210	350	525	—
AH1112//44	—	125	210	350	525	—

Pune

KM# 300.74 RUPEE (Type 300)

Silver **Rev:** Without mint epithet; mint name at bottom **Note:** Weight varies: 11.00-11.60 grams.

Date	Mintage	VG	F	VF	XF	Unc
AH1111/4x	—	110	180	300	450	—
AH111x/45	—	100	180	300	450	—

Qamarnagar

KM# 300.75 RUPEE (Type 300)

Silver **Rev:** Without mint epithet; mint name at bottom **Note:** Weight varies: 11.00-11.60 grams.

Date	Mintage	VG	F	VF	XF	Unc
AHxxxx//4x	—	50.00	85.00	140	210	—

Ranthambhor

KM# 300.76 RUPEE (Type 300)

Silver **Rev:** Without mint epithet; mint name at bottom **Note:** Weight varies: 11.00-11.60 grams.

Date	Mintage	VG	F	VF	XF	Unc
AH1097//30	—	110	180	300	450	—
AH1098//30	—	110	180	300	450	—
AH1098//31	—	110	180	300	450	—
AH1099//31	—	110	180	300	450	—
AH1099//32	—	110	180	300	450	—
AH1100//32	—	110	180	300	450	—

Saharanpur

KM# 300.77 RUPEE (Type 300)

Silver **Rev:** Without mint epithet; mint name at bottom **Note:** Struck at Saharanpur. Weight varies: 11.00-11.60 grams.

Date	Mintage	VG	F	VF	XF	Unc
AH109x//28	—	90.00	150	250	375	—
AH1097//30	—	90.00	150	250	375	—

Sahrind

KM# 300.78 RUPEE (Type 300)

Silver **Obv:** Inscription, date **Rev:** Inscription **Note:** Weight varies 11.00-11.60 grams.

Date	Mintage	VG	F	VF	XF	Unc
AH1098//30	—	16.00	27.00	45.00	67.50	—
AH1098//31	—	16.00	27.00	45.00	67.50	—
AH1099//31	—	16.00	27.00	45.00	67.50	—
AH1099//32	—	16.00	27.00	45.00	67.50	—
AH1100//32	—	16.00	27.00	45.00	67.50	—
AH1100//33	—	16.00	27.00	45.00	67.50	—
AH1101//33	—	16.00	27.00	45.00	67.50	—
AH1101//34	—	16.00	27.00	45.00	67.50	—
AH1102//34	—	16.00	27.00	45.00	67.50	—
AH1102//35	—	16.00	27.00	45.00	67.50	—
AH1103//35	—	16.00	27.00	45.00	67.50	—
AH1103//36	—	16.00	27.00	45.00	67.50	—
AH1104//36	—	16.00	27.00	45.00	67.50	—
AH1104//37	—	16.00	27.00	45.00	67.50	—
AH1105//37	—	16.00	27.00	45.00	67.50	—
AH1105//38	—	16.00	27.00	45.00	67.50	—
AH1106//38	—	16.00	27.00	45.00	67.50	—
AH1106//39	—	16.00	27.00	45.00	67.50	—
AH1107//39	—	16.00	27.00	45.00	67.50	—
AH1107//40	—	16.00	27.00	45.00	67.50	—
AH1108//40	—	16.00	27.00	45.00	67.50	—
AH1108//41	—	16.00	27.00	45.00	67.50	—
AH1109//41	—	16.00	27.00	45.00	67.50	—
AH1109//42	—	16.00	27.00	45.00	67.50	—
AH1110//42	—	16.00	27.00	45.00	67.50	—
AH1110//43	—	16.00	27.00	45.00	67.50	—
AH1111//43	—	16.00	27.00	45.00	67.50	—
AH1111//44	—	16.00	27.00	45.00	67.50	—
AH1112//44	—	16.00	27.00	45.00	67.50	—

Sambhar

KM# 300.79 RUPEE (Type 300)

Silver **Rev:** Without mint epithet; mint name at bottom **Note:** Weight varies: 11.00-11.60 grams.

Date	Mintage	VG	F	VF	XF	Unc
AH1098//31	—	90.00	150	250	375	—
AH1099//31	—	90.00	150	250	375	—
AH1099//32	—	90.00	150	250	375	—
AH1100//32	—	90.00	150	250	375	—
AH1101//33	—	90.00	150	250	375	—

Sarangpur

KM# 300.98 RUPEE (Type 300)

Silver **Rev:** Without mint epithet; mint name at bottom **Note:** Weight varies: 11.00-11.60 grams.

Date	Mintage	VG	F	VF	XF	Unc
AHxxxx//x	—	145	240	400	600	—

Shahjahanabad

KM# 300.113 RUPEE (Type 300)

11.4440 g., Silver **Rev:** Inscription and mint name **Rev. Inscription:** "Dar al-Khilafa" **Note:** "Mihr" couplet.

Date	Mintage	VG	F	VF	XF	Unc
AH1069//(1) Ahad	—	55.00	90.00	150	225	—

Shahjahanabad

KM# 300.81 RUPEE (Type 300)

Silver **Obv:** Inscription **Rev. Inscription:** Dar-ul-Khilafat and mint name **Note:** "Badr" couplet; Weight varies 11.00-11.60 grams.

Date	Mintage	VG	F	VF	XF	Unc
AH1069//2	—	16.00	18.00	22.00	33.00	—
AH1070//2	—	16.00	18.00	22.00	33.00	—
AH1070//3	—	16.00	18.00	22.00	33.00	—
AH1071//3	—	16.00	18.00	22.00	33.00	—
AH1071//4	—	16.00	18.00	22.00	33.00	—
AH1072//4	—	16.00	18.00	22.00	33.00	—
AH1072//5	—	16.00	18.00	22.00	33.00	—
AH1073//5	—	16.00	18.00	22.00	33.00	—
AH1073//6	—	16.00	18.00	22.00	33.00	—
AH1074//6	—	16.00	18.00	22.00	33.00	—
AH1074//7	—	16.00	18.00	22.00	33.00	—
AH1075//7	—	16.00	18.00	22.00	33.00	—
AH1075//8	—	16.00	18.00	22.00	33.00	—
AH1076//8	—	16.00	18.00	22.00	33.00	—
AH1076//9	—	16.00	18.00	22.00	33.00	—
AH1077//9	—	16.00	18.00	22.00	33.00	—
AH1077//10	—	16.00	18.00	22.00	33.00	—
AH1078//10	—	16.00	18.00	22.00	33.00	—
AH1078//11	—	16.00	18.00	22.00	33.00	—
AH1079//11	—	16.00	18.00	22.00	33.00	—
AH1079//12	—	16.00	18.00	22.00	33.00	—
AH1080//12	—	16.00	18.00	22.00	33.00	—
AH1080//13	—	16.00	18.00	22.00	33.00	—
AH1081//13	—	16.00	18.00	22.00	33.00	—
AH1081//14	—	16.00	18.00	22.00	33.00	—
AH1082//14	—	16.00	18.00	22.00	33.00	—
AH1082//15	—	16.00	18.00	22.00	33.00	—
AH1083//15	—	16.00	18.00	22.00	33.00	—
AH1083//16	—	16.00	18.00	22.00	33.00	—
AH1084//16	—	16.00	18.00	22.00	33.00	—
AH1084//17	—	16.00	18.00	22.00	33.00	—
AH1085//17	—	16.00	18.00	22.00	33.00	—
AH1085//18	—	16.00	18.00	22.00	33.00	—
AH1086//18	—	16.00	18.00	22.00	33.00	—
AH1086//19	—	16.00	18.00	22.00	33.00	—
AH1087//19	—	16.00	18.00	22.00	33.00	—
AH1087//20	—	16.00	18.00	22.00	33.00	—
AH1088//20	—	16.00	18.00	22.00	33.00	—
AH1088//21	—	16.00	18.00	22.00	33.00	—
AH1089//21	—	16.00	18.00	22.00	33.00	—
AH1089//22	—	16.00	18.00	22.00	33.00	—
AH1090//22	—	16.00	18.00	22.00	33.00	—
AH1090//23	—	16.00	18.00	22.00	33.00	—
AH1091//23	—	16.00	18.00	22.00	33.00	—
AH1091//24	—	16.00	18.00	22.00	33.00	—

Date	Mintage	VG	F	VF	XF	Unc
AH1092//24	—	16.00	18.00	22.00	33.00	—
AH1092//25	—	16.00	18.00	22.00	33.00	—
AH1093//25	—	16.00	18.00	22.00	33.00	—
AH1094//26	—	16.00	18.00	22.00	33.00	—
AH1093//26	—	16.00	18.00	22.00	33.00	—
AH1094//27	—	16.00	18.00	22.00	33.00	—
AH1095//27	—	16.00	18.00	22.00	33.00	—
AH1095//28	—	16.00	18.00	22.00	33.00	—
AH1096//28	—	16.00	18.00	22.00	33.00	—
AH1096//29	—	16.00	18.00	22.00	33.00	—
AH1097//29	—	16.00	18.00	22.00	33.00	—
AH1097//30	—	16.00	18.00	22.00	33.00	—
AH1098//30	—	16.00	18.00	22.00	33.00	—
AH1098//31	—	16.00	18.00	22.00	33.00	—
AH1099//31	—	16.00	18.00	22.00	33.00	—
AH1099//32	—	16.00	18.00	22.00	33.00	—
AH1100//32	—	16.00	18.00	22.00	33.00	—
AH1100//33	—	16.00	18.00	22.00	33.00	—
AH1101//33	—	16.00	18.00	22.00	33.00	—
AH1101//34	—	16.00	18.00	22.00	33.00	—
AH1102//34	—	16.00	18.00	22.00	33.00	—
AH1102//35	—	16.00	18.00	22.00	33.00	—
AH1103//35	—	16.00	18.00	22.00	33.00	—
AH1103//36	—	16.00	18.00	22.00	33.00	—
AH1104//36	—	16.00	18.00	22.00	33.00	—
AH1104//37	—	16.00	18.00	22.00	33.00	—
AH1105//37	—	16.00	18.00	22.00	33.00	—
AH1105//38	—	16.00	18.00	22.00	33.00	—
AH1106//38	—	16.00	18.00	22.00	33.00	—
AH1106//39	—	16.00	18.00	22.00	33.00	—
AH1107//39	—	16.00	18.00	22.00	33.00	—
AH1107//40	—	16.00	18.00	22.00	33.00	—
AH1108//40	—	16.00	18.00	22.00	33.00	—
AH1108//41	—	16.00	18.00	22.00	33.00	—
AH1109//41	—	16.00	18.00	22.00	33.00	—
AH1109//42	—	16.00	18.00	22.00	33.00	—
AH1110//42	—	16.00	18.00	22.00	33.00	—
AH1110//43	—	16.00	18.00	22.00	33.00	—
AH1111//43	—	16.00	18.00	22.00	33.00	—
AH1111//44	—	16.00	18.00	22.00	33.00	—
AH1112//44	—	16.00	18.00	22.00	33.00	—

Sholapur

KM# 300.99 RUPEE (Type 300)

Silver **Rev:** Mint name in middle **Note:** Weight varies: 11.00-11.60 grams.

Date	Mintage	VG	F	VF	XF	Unc
AH1079//13(sic)	—	45.00	75.00	125	190	—
AH1089//21	—	45.00	75.00	125	190	—
AH1090//23	—	45.00	75.00	125	190	—
AH1096//29	—	45.00	75.00	125	190	—

Sholapur

KM# 300.82 RUPEE (Type 300)

Silver **Rev:** Mint name at bottom **Note:** Weight varies 11.00-11.60 grams.

Date	Mintage	VG	F	VF	XF	Unc
AH1085//18	—	16.00	24.00	40.00	60.00	—
AH1087//20	—	16.00	24.00	40.00	60.00	—
AH1089//21	—	16.00	24.00	40.00	60.00	—
AH1089//22	—	16.00	24.00	40.00	60.00	—
AH1090//22	—	16.00	24.00	40.00	60.00	—
AH1090//23	—	16.00	24.00	40.00	60.00	—
AH1091//23	—	16.00	24.00	40.00	60.00	—
AH1091//24	—	16.00	24.00	40.00	60.00	—
AH1092//24	—	16.00	24.00	40.00	60.00	—
AH1092//25	—	16.00	24.00	40.00	60.00	—
AH1093//25	—	16.00	24.00	40.00	60.00	—
AH1094//26	—	16.00	24.00	40.00	60.00	—
AH1093//26	—	16.00	24.00	40.00	60.00	—
AH1094//27	—	16.00	24.00	40.00	60.00	—
AH1095//27	—	16.00	24.00	40.00	60.00	—
AH1095//28	—	16.00	24.00	40.00	60.00	—
AH1096//28	—	16.00	24.00	40.00	60.00	—
AH1096//29	—	16.00	24.00	40.00	60.00	—
AH1097//29	—	16.00	24.00	40.00	60.00	—
AH1097//30	—	16.00	24.00	40.00	60.00	—
AH1098//30	—	16.00	24.00	40.00	60.00	—
AH1098//31	—	16.00	24.00	40.00	60.00	—
AH1100//32	—	16.00	24.00	40.00	60.00	—
AH1100//33	—	16.00	24.00	40.00	60.00	—
AH1101//3x	—	16.00	24.00	40.00	60.00	—
AH1108//41	—	16.00	24.00	40.00	60.00	—
AH1100//42	—	16.00	24.00	40.00	60.00	—
AH1111//4x	—	16.00	24.00	40.00	60.00	—

Sikakul

KM# 300.83 RUPEE (Type 300)

Silver **Rev:** Mint name in middle **Note:** Weight varies: 11.00-11.60 grams.

Date	Mintage	VG	F	VF	XF	Unc
AH109x//23	—	36.00	60.00	100	150	—
AH1100//32	—	36.00	60.00	100	150	—
AH110x//36	—	36.00	60.00	100	150	—

Sikandarah

KM# 300.84 RUPEE (Type 300)

Silver **Rev:** Mint name in middle **Note:** Weight varies: 11.00-11.60 grams.

Date	Mintage	VG	F	VF	XF	Unc
AH1xxx//32	—	145	240	400	600	—

Surat

KM# 300.85 RUPEE (Type 300)

Silver **Rev:** "Bandar-i-Mubarak" and mint name **Note:** Weight varies: 11.00-11.60 grams.

Date	Mintage	VG	F	VF	XF	Unc
AH1069//(1) Ahad	—	36.00	60.00	100	150	—
AH1070//(1) Ahad	—	36.00	60.00	100	150	—
AH1070//2	—	36.00	60.00	100	150	—
AH1071//x	—	36.00	60.00	100	150	—
AH1090//22	—	36.00	60.00	100	150	—
AH1093//25	—	36.00	60.00	100	150	—
AH1094//26	—	36.00	60.00	100	150	—

Surat

KM# 300.86 RUPEE (Type 300)

Silver **Obv:** Inscription **Rev:** Inscription, without mint epithet **Note:** Weight varies 11.00-11.60 grams.

Date	Mintage	VG	F	VF	XF	Unc
AH1070//2	—	14.00	16.00	20.00	30.00	—
AH1070//3	—	14.00	16.00	20.00	30.00	—
AH1071//3	—	14.00	16.00	20.00	30.00	—
AH1071//4	—	14.00	16.00	20.00	30.00	—
AH1072//4	—	14.00	16.00	20.00	30.00	—
AH1072//5	—	14.00	16.00	20.00	30.00	—
AH1073//5	—	14.00	16.00	20.00	30.00	—
AH1073//6	—	14.00	16.00	20.00	30.00	—
AH1074//6	—	14.00	16.00	20.00	30.00	—
AH1074//7	—	14.00	16.00	20.00	30.00	—
AH1075//7	—	14.00	16.00	20.00	30.00	—
AH1075//8	—	14.00	16.00	20.00	30.00	—
AH1076//8	—	14.00	16.00	20.00	30.00	—
AH1076//9	—	14.00	16.00	20.00	30.00	—
AH1077//9	—	14.00	16.00	20.00	30.00	—
AH1077//10	—	14.00	16.00	20.00	30.00	—
AH1078//10	—	14.00	16.00	20.00	30.00	—
AH1078//11	—	14.00	16.00	20.00	30.00	—
AH1079//11	—	14.00	16.00	20.00	30.00	—
AH1079//12	—	14.00	16.00	20.00	30.00	—
AH1080//12	—	14.00	16.00	20.00	30.00	—
AH1080//13	—	14.00	16.00	20.00	30.00	—
AH1081//13	—	14.00	16.00	20.00	30.00	—
AH1081//14	—	14.00	16.00	20.00	30.00	—
AH1082//14	—	14.00	16.00	20.00	30.00	—
AH1082//15	—	14.00	16.00	20.00	30.00	—
AH1083//15	—	14.00	16.00	20.00	30.00	—
AH1083//16	—	14.00	16.00	20.00	30.00	—
AH1084//16	—	14.00	16.00	20.00	30.00	—
AH1084//17	—	14.00	16.00	20.00	30.00	—
AH1085//17	—	14.00	16.00	20.00	30.00	—
AH1085//18	—	14.00	16.00	20.00	30.00	—
AH1086//18	—	14.00	16.00	20.00	30.00	—
AH1086//19	—	14.00	16.00	20.00	30.00	—
AH1087//19	—	14.00	16.00	20.00	30.00	—
AH1087//20	—	14.00	16.00	20.00	30.00	—
AH1088//20	—	14.00	16.00	20.00	30.00	—
AH1088//21	—	14.00	16.00	20.00	30.00	—
AH1089//21	—	14.00	16.00	20.00	30.00	—
AH1089//22	—	14.00	16.00	20.00	30.00	—
AH1090//22	—	14.00	16.00	20.00	30.00	—
AH1090//23	—	14.00	16.00	20.00	30.00	—
AH1091//23	—	14.00	16.00	20.00	30.00	—
AH1091//24	—	14.00	16.00	20.00	30.00	—
AH1092//24	—	14.00	16.00	20.00	30.00	—
AH1092//25	—	14.00	16.00	20.00	30.00	—
AH1093//25	—	14.00	16.00	20.00	30.00	—
AH1094//26	—	14.00	16.00	20.00	30.00	—
AH1093//26	—	14.00	16.00	20.00	30.00	—
AH1094//27	—	14.00	16.00	20.00	30.00	—
AH1095//27	—	14.00	16.00	20.00	30.00	—
AH1095//28	—	14.00	16.00	20.00	30.00	—
AH1096//28	—	14.00	16.00	20.00	30.00	—
AH1096//29	—	14.00	16.00	20.00	30.00	—
AH1097//28	—	14.00	16.00	20.00	30.00	—
AH1097//29	—	14.00	16.00	20.00	30.00	—
AH1097//30	—	14.00	16.00	20.00	30.00	—
AH1098//30	—	14.00	16.00	20.00	30.00	—
AH1098//31	—	14.00	16.00	20.00	30.00	—
AH1099//31	—	14.00	16.00	20.00	30.00	—
AH1099//32	—	14.00	16.00	20.00	30.00	—
AH1100//32	—	14.00	16.00	20.00	30.00	—
AH1100//33	—	14.00	16.00	20.00	30.00	—
AH1101//33	—	14.00	16.00	20.00	30.00	—
AH1101//34	—	14.00	16.00	20.00	30.00	—
AH1102//34	—	14.00	16.00	20.00	30.00	—
AH1102//35	—	14.00	16.00	20.00	30.00	—
AH1103//35	—	14.00	16.00	20.00	30.00	—
AH1103//36	—	14.00	16.00	20.00	30.00	—
AH1104//36	—	14.00	16.00	20.00	30.00	—
AH1104//37	—	14.00	16.00	20.00	30.00	—
AH1105//37	—	14.00	16.00	20.00	30.00	—
AH1105//38	—	14.00	16.00	20.00	30.00	—
AH1106//38	—	14.00	16.00	20.00	30.00	—
AH1106//39	—	14.00	16.00	20.00	30.00	—
AH1107//39	—	14.00	16.00	20.00	30.00	—
AH1107//40	—	14.00	16.00	20.00	30.00	—
AH1108//40	—	14.00	16.00	20.00	30.00	—
AH1108//41	—	14.00	16.00	20.00	30.00	—
AH1109//41	—	14.00	16.00	20.00	30.00	—
AH1109//42	—	14.00	16.00	20.00	30.00	—
AH1110//42	—	14.00	16.00	20.00	30.00	—
AH1110//43	—	14.00	16.00	20.00	30.00	—
AH1111//43	—	14.00	16.00	20.00	30.00	—
AH1111//44	—	14.00	16.00	20.00	30.00	—
AH1112//44	—	14.00	16.00	20.00	30.00	—
AH1112//45	—	14.00	16.00	20.00	30.00	—

Tatta

KM# 300.87 RUPEE (Type 300)

Silver **Note:** "Badr" couplet; Weight varies 11.00-11.60 grams.

Date	Mintage	VG	F	VF	XF	Unc
AH1072//4	—	16.00	22.00	28.00	42.00	—
AH1072//5	—	16.00	22.00	28.00	42.00	—
AH1073//5	—	16.00	22.00	28.00	42.00	—
AH1073//6	—	16.00	22.00	28.00	42.00	—
AH1074//6	—	16.00	22.00	28.00	42.00	—
AH107x//7	—	16.00	22.00	28.00	42.00	—
AH1076//8	—	16.00	22.00	28.00	42.00	—
AH107x//9	—	16.00	22.00	28.00	42.00	—
AH107x//10	—	16.00	22.00	28.00	42.00	—
AH1079//11	—	16.00	22.00	28.00	42.00	—
AH1079//12	—	16.00	22.00	28.00	42.00	—
AH1080//12	—	16.00	22.00	28.00	42.00	—
AH1080//13	—	16.00	22.00	28.00	42.00	—
AH1081//13	—	16.00	22.00	28.00	42.00	—
AH1081//14	—	16.00	22.00	28.00	42.00	—
AH1082//14	—	16.00	22.00	28.00	42.00	—
AH1083//16	—	16.00	22.00	28.00	42.00	—
AH1084//16	—	16.00	22.00	28.00	42.00	—
AH1084//17	—	16.00	22.00	28.00	42.00	—
AH1085//17	—	16.00	22.00	28.00	42.00	—
AH1085//18	—	16.00	22.00	28.00	42.00	—
AH1086//18	—	16.00	22.00	28.00	42.00	—
AH1086//19	—	16.00	22.00	28.00	42.00	—
AH1087//19	—	16.00	22.00	28.00	42.00	—
AH1087//20	—	16.00	22.00	28.00	42.00	—
AH1088//20	—	16.00	22.00	28.00	42.00	—
AH1088//21	—	16.00	22.00	28.00	42.00	—
AH1089//21	—	16.00	22.00	28.00	42.00	—
AH1089//22	—	16.00	22.00	28.00	42.00	—
AH1090//22	—	16.00	22.00	28.00	42.00	—
AH1090//23	—	16.00	22.00	28.00	42.00	—
AH1091//23	—	16.00	22.00	28.00	42.00	—
AH1091//24	—	16.00	22.00	28.00	42.00	—
AH1092//24	—	16.00	22.00	28.00	42.00	—
AH1092//25	—	16.00	22.00	28.00	42.00	—
AH1093//25	—	16.00	22.00	28.00	42.00	—
AH1094//26	—	16.00	22.00	28.00	42.00	—
AH1093//26	—	16.00	22.00	28.00	42.00	—
AH1094//27	—	16.00	22.00	28.00	42.00	—
AH1095//27	—	16.00	22.00	28.00	42.00	—
AH1095//28	—	16.00	22.00	28.00	42.00	—
AH1097//29	—	16.00	22.00	28.00	42.00	—
AH1098//30	—	16.00	22.00	28.00	42.00	—
AH1098//31	—	16.00	22.00	28.00	42.00	—
AH1099//31	—	16.00	22.00	28.00	42.00	—
AH1100//32	—	16.00	22.00	28.00	42.00	—
AH1100//33	—	16.00	22.00	28.00	42.00	—
AH1101//34	—	16.00	22.00	28.00	42.00	—
AH1102//34	—	16.00	22.00	28.00	42.00	—
AH1103//35	—	16.00	22.00	28.00	42.00	—
AH1104//36	—	16.00	22.00	28.00	42.00	—
AH1105//37	—	16.00	22.00	28.00	42.00	—
AH1105//38	—	16.00	22.00	28.00	42.00	—
AH1106//38	—	16.00	22.00	28.00	42.00	—
AH1107//40	—	16.00	22.00	28.00	42.00	—
AH1108//40	—	16.00	22.00	28.00	42.00	—
AH1108//41	—	16.00	22.00	28.00	42.00	—
AH1109//xx	—	16.00	22.00	28.00	42.00	—
AH1110//42	—	16.00	22.00	28.00	42.00	—
AH1110//43	—	16.00	22.00	28.00	42.00	—
AH1111//4x	—	16.00	22.00	28.00	42.00	—
AH1112//44	—	16.00	22.00	28.00	42.00	—

Tatta

KM# 300.114 RUPEE (Type 300)

11.4440 g., Silver **Note:** "Mihr" couplet.

Date	Mintage	VG	F	VF	XF	Unc
AHxxxx//8	—	16.00	22.00	28.00	42.00	—
AHxxxx//10	—	16.00	22.00	28.00	42.00	—
AHxxxx//11	—	16.00	22.00	28.00	42.00	—
AH1086//18	—	16.00	22.00	28.00	42.00	—
AHxxxx//19	—	16.00	22.00	28.00	42.00	—

Trichanapally

KM# 300.115 RUPEE (Type 300)

11.4440 g., Silver

Date	Mintage	VG	F	VF	XF	Unc
AH1106//39	—	125	210	350	525	—

Udgir

KM# 300.89 RUPEE (Type 300)

Silver **Note:** "Dar-uz-Zafar Qila". Weight varies: 11.00-11.60 grams.

Date	Mintage	VG	F	VF	XF	Unc
AH1098//xx	—	90.00	150	250	375	—

Ujjain

KM# 300.90 RUPEE (Type 300)

Silver **Rev:** "Dar al-Fath" and mint name at top **Note:** "Dar-ul-Fath". Weight varies: 11.00-11.60 grams.

Date	Mintage	VG	F	VF	XF	Unc
AH1070//(1) Ahad	—	18.00	30.00	50.00	75.00	—
AHxxxx//3	—	18.00	30.00	50.00	75.00	—
AH1072	—	18.00	30.00	50.00	75.00	—
AH1073//5	—	18.00	30.00	50.00	75.00	—
AH1075	—	18.00	30.00	50.00	75.00	—
AH1077//x	—	18.00	30.00	50.00	75.00	—
AH1082//14	—	18.00	30.00	50.00	75.00	—
AH1087//19	—	18.00	30.00	50.00	75.00	—

Ujjain

KM# 300.91 RUPEE (Type 300)

Silver **Rev:** "Dar al-Fath" and mint name at bottom **Note:** Weight varies 11.00-11.60 grams.

Date	Mintage	VG	F	VF	XF	Unc
AH1072//4	—	18.00	30.00	50.00	75.00	—
AH1072//5	—	18.00	30.00	50.00	75.00	—
AH1073//5	—	18.00	30.00	50.00	75.00	—
AH1078//11	—	18.00	30.00	50.00	75.00	—
AH1082//15	—	18.00	30.00	50.00	75.00	—
AH1088//21	—	18.00	30.00	50.00	75.00	—
AH1099//xx	—	18.00	30.00	50.00	75.00	—
AH1100//32	—	18.00	30.00	50.00	75.00	—
AH1103//35	—	18.00	30.00	50.00	75.00	—
AH110x//40	—	18.00	30.00	50.00	75.00	—
AH1108//41	—	18.00	30.00	50.00	75.00	—
AH1109//41	—	18.00	30.00	50.00	75.00	—
AH110x//44	—	18.00	30.00	50.00	75.00	—
AH1111//44	—	18.00	30.00	50.00	75.00	—
AH1112//45	—	18.00	30.00	50.00	75.00	—

Ujjain

KM# 300.92 RUPEE (Type 300)

Silver **Obv:** Without mint epithet **Note:** Weight varies: 11.00-11.60 grams.

Date	Mintage	VG	F	VF	XF	Unc
AH1095	—	18.00	30.00	50.00	75.00	—
AH1097//29	—	18.00	30.00	50.00	75.00	—
AH1101//xx	—	18.00	30.00	50.00	75.00	—

Zafarabad

KM# 300.93 RUPEE (Type 300)

Silver **Obv:** Inscription **Rev:** Inscription **Note:** "Badr" couplet; Weight varies 11.00-11.60 grams.

Date	Mintage	VG	F	VF	XF	Unc
AHxxxx//(1) Ahad	—	21.00	36.00	60.00	90.00	—
AH107x//3	—	21.00	36.00	60.00	90.00	—
AH1074//6	—	21.00	36.00	60.00	90.00	—
AH1074//7	—	21.00	36.00	60.00	90.00	—
AH1075//7	—	21.00	36.00	60.00	90.00	—
AH1075//8	—	21.00	36.00	60.00	90.00	—
AH1075//9(sic)	—	21.00	36.00	60.00	90.00	—
AH1078//11	—	21.00	36.00	60.00	90.00	—
AH1079//11	—	21.00	36.00	60.00	90.00	—
AH1079//12	—	21.00	36.00	60.00	90.00	—
AH1080//12	—	21.00	36.00	60.00	90.00	—
AH1080//13	—	21.00	36.00	60.00	90.00	—
AH108x//14	—	21.00	36.00	60.00	90.00	—
AH108x//18	—	21.00	36.00	60.00	90.00	—
AH108x//19	—	21.00	36.00	60.00	90.00	—
AH108x//21	—	21.00	36.00	60.00	90.00	—
AH10xx//22	—	21.00	36.00	60.00	90.00	—
AH1093//25	—	21.00	36.00	60.00	90.00	—
AH1093//26	—	21.00	36.00	60.00	90.00	—
AH1094//26	—	21.00	36.00	60.00	90.00	—
AH1094//27	—	21.00	36.00	60.00	90.00	—
AH109x//28	—	21.00	36.00	60.00	90.00	—
AH1098//30	—	21.00	36.00	60.00	90.00	—
AH1098//31	—	21.00	36.00	60.00	90.00	—
AH1099//31	—	21.00	36.00	60.00	90.00	—
AH1099//32	—	21.00	36.00	60.00	90.00	—
AH1100//32	—	21.00	36.00	60.00	90.00	—
AH1100//33	—	21.00	36.00	60.00	90.00	—
AH110x//35	—	21.00	36.00	60.00	90.00	—
AH1104//37	—	21.00	36.00	60.00	90.00	—
AH1106//39	—	21.00	36.00	60.00	90.00	—
AH1108//40	—	21.00	36.00	60.00	90.00	—
AH1108//41	—	21.00	36.00	60.00	90.00	—
AH1112//45	—	21.00	36.00	60.00	90.00	—

Zafarabad

KM# 300.116 RUPEE (Type 300)

11.4440 g., Silver **Note:** "Mihr" couplet.

Date	Mintage	Good	VG	F	VF	XF
AH1074//6	—	8.00	12.00	20.00	32.00	50.00
AH1075//8	—	8.00	12.00	20.00	32.00	50.00
AH1079//12	—	8.00	12.00	20.00	32.00	50.00
AH1080//12	—	8.00	12.00	20.00	32.00	50.00
AHxxxx//17	—	8.00	12.00	20.00	32.00	50.00
AHxxxx//22	—	8.00	12.00	20.00	32.00	50.00
AH1099//31	—	8.00	12.00	20.00	32.00	50.00

Zafarpur

KM# 300.94 RUPEE (Type 300)

Silver **Note:** Weight varies: 11.00-11.60 grams.

Date	Mintage	VG	F	VF	XF	Unc
AH109x//28	—	27.00	45.00	75.00	115	—
AH1097//30	—	27.00	45.00	75.00	115	—
AH1098//30	—	27.00	45.00	75.00	115	—
AH1098//31	—	27.00	45.00	75.00	115	—
AH1099//31	—	27.00	45.00	75.00	115	—
AH1099//32	—	27.00	45.00	75.00	115	—
AH1100//32	—	27.00	45.00	75.00	115	—
AH1100//33	—	27.00	45.00	75.00	115	—
AH1101//33	—	27.00	45.00	75.00	115	—
AH1101//34	—	27.00	45.00	75.00	115	—
AH1102//34	—	27.00	45.00	75.00	115	—

Jahangirnagar

KM# 301.1 RUPEE (Type 301)

Silver **Obv:** Couplet with ruler's name within square **Rev:** Inscription within square **Rev. Inscription:** "Jalus (maimanat manus)" **Note:** Weight varies: 11.00-11.60 grams.

Date	Mintage	VG	F	VF	XF	Unc
AH1081//14	—	155	255	425	640	—
AH1087//20	—	155	255	425	640	—

Junagadh

KM# 301.2 RUPEE (Type 301)

Silver **Obv:** Couplet with ruler's name within square **Rev:** Inscription within square **Rev. Legend:** "Jalus (maimamat manus)" **Note:** Two obverse varieties exist; Weight varies: 11.00-11.60 grams.

Date	Mintage	VG	F	VF	XF	Unc
AH1071//3	—	16.00	20.00	30.00	45.00	—
AH1071//4	—	16.00	20.00	30.00	45.00	—
AH1072//4	—	16.00	20.00	30.00	45.00	—
AH107x//5	—	16.00	20.00	30.00	45.00	—
AH1075//x	—	16.00	20.00	30.00	45.00	—
AH107x//8	—	16.00	20.00	30.00	45.00	—
AH107x//9	—	16.00	20.00	30.00	45.00	—
AH1077//x	—	16.00	20.00	30.00	45.00	—
AH1078//10	—	16.00	20.00	30.00	45.00	—
AH1078//11	—	16.00	20.00	30.00	45.00	—
AH1079//11	—	16.00	20.00	30.00	45.00	—
AH1079//12	—	16.00	20.00	30.00	45.00	—
AH1080//12	—	16.00	20.00	30.00	45.00	—
AH1080//13	—	16.00	20.00	30.00	45.00	—
AH1081//13	—	16.00	20.00	30.00	45.00	—
AH1081//14	—	16.00	20.00	30.00	45.00	—
AH1082//14	—	16.00	20.00	30.00	45.00	—
AH1082//15	—	16.00	20.00	30.00	45.00	—
AH1083//15	—	16.00	20.00	30.00	45.00	—
AHxxxx//17	—	16.00	20.00	30.00	45.00	—
AH108x//18	—	16.00	20.00	30.00	45.00	—
AH1087//1086	—	16.00	20.00	30.00	45.00	—
AH109x//23	—	16.00	20.00	30.00	45.00	—
AH109x//24	—	16.00	20.00	30.00	45.00	—
AH1093//xx	—	16.00	20.00	30.00	45.00	—
AH1094//27	—	16.00	20.00	30.00	45.00	—
AH1094//26	—	16.00	20.00	30.00	45.00	—
AH1095//27	—	16.00	20.00	30.00	45.00	—
AH1095//28	—	16.00	20.00	30.00	45.00	—
AH1096//28	—	16.00	20.00	30.00	45.00	—
AH1096//29	—	16.00	20.00	30.00	45.00	—
AH1097//29	—	16.00	20.00	30.00	45.00	—
AH109x//31	—	16.00	20.00	30.00	45.00	—
AH1108//41	—	16.00	20.00	30.00	45.00	—

Bhakkar

KM# 302.1 RUPEE (Type 302)

Silver **Obv:** Poetic couplet **Rev:** Poetic couplet **Note:** Weight varies: 11.00-11.60 grams.

Date	Mintage	VG	F	VF	XF	Unc
AH1071//3	—	28.00	48.00	80.00	120	—
AH1071//4	—	28.00	48.00	80.00	120	—
AH1072//4	—	28.00	48.00	80.00	120	—
AH1072//5	—	28.00	48.00	80.00	120	—
AH1073//5	—	28.00	48.00	80.00	120	—
AH1075//7	—	28.00	48.00	80.00	120	—
AH1075//8	—	28.00	48.00	80.00	120	—
AH1076//8	—	28.00	48.00	80.00	120	—
AH1076//9	—	28.00	48.00	80.00	120	—
AH1077//9	—	28.00	48.00	80.00	120	—
AH1077//10	—	28.00	48.00	80.00	120	—
AH1078//10	—	28.00	48.00	80.00	120	—

Bhakkar

KM# 302.2 RUPEE (Type 302)

11.4440 g., Silver **Obv. Inscription:** "Alanagir Shah Aurangzeb" **Rev:** Mint name, date formula

Date	Mintage	VG	F	VF	XF	Unc
AH1084//16	—	90.00	150	250	375	—
AH1086//18	—	90.00	150	250	375	—

Shahjahanabad

KM# 304.1 200 RUPEES (Type 304)

2275.0000 g., Silver **Obv:** Ruler's name and titles within square, poetic couplet around **Note:** " Dar-ul-Khilafat"

Date	Mintage	Good	VG	F	VF	XF
AH1083//15 Unique	—	—	—	—	—	—

Akbarabad

KM# 307.1 LEGAL DIRHAM (Type 307)

Silver **Note:** Square. Weight varies: 2.80-3.25 grams.

Date	Mintage	VG	F	VF	XF	Unc
AH1091//24	—	160	270	450	675	—

Allahabad

KM# 307.2 LEGAL DIRHAM (Type 307)

Silver **Note:** Square. Weight varies: 2.80-3.25 grams.

Date	Mintage	VG	F	VF	XF	Unc
AH1092//24	—	180	300	500	750	—
AH1105//37	—	180	300	500	750	—

Katak

KM# 307.3 LEGAL DIRHAM (Type 307)

Silver **Note:** Square. Weight varies: 2.80-3.25 grams.

Date	Mintage	VG	F	VF	XF	Unc
AHxxxx//29	—	180	300	500	750	—
AHxxxx//30	—	180	300	500	750	—

Lahore

KM# 307.4 LEGAL DIRHAM (Type 307)

Silver **Note:** Square. Weight varies: 2.80-3.25 grams.

Date	Mintage	VG	F	VF	XF	Unc
AH1091//23	—	160	270	450	675	—
AH1092//24	—	160	270	450	675	—

Multan

KM# 307.5 LEGAL DIRHAM (Type 307)
Silver **Note:** Square. Weight varies: 2.80-3.25 grams.

Date	Mintage	VG	F	VF	XF	Unc
AH1091//xx	—	160	270	450	675	—
AH1093//xx	—	160	270	450	675	—
AH1094//xx	—	160	270	450	675	—

Patna

KM# 307.6 LEGAL DIRHAM (Type 307)
Silver **Note:** Square. Weight varies: 2.80-3.25 grams.

Date	Mintage	VG	F	VF	XF	Unc
AHxxxx//24	—	160	270	450	675	—

Shahjahanabad

KM# 307.7 LEGAL DIRHAM (Type 307)
Silver **Note:** Square. Weight varies: 2.80-3.25 grams.

Date	Mintage	VG	F	VF	XF	Unc
ND	—	160	270	450	675	—

Akbarabad

KM# 308.1 LEGAL DIRHAM (Type 308)
2.9700 g., Silver

Date	Mintage	VG	F	VF	XF	Unc
AH1093//26	—	145	240	400	600	—
AH1106	—	145	240	400	600	—
AH111x//x	—	145	240	400	600	—

Shahjahanabad

KM# 308.2 LEGAL DIRHAM (Type 308)
2.9700 g., Silver

Date	Mintage	VG	F	VF	XF	Unc
AH109x//25	—	160	270	450	675	—

Bijapur

KM# 309.1 1/4 MOHUR (Type 309)
Gold **Note:** "Dar-ul Zafar". Weight varies: 2.70-2.75 grams.

Date	Mintage	VG	F	VF	XF	Unc
AHxxxx//9	—	—	2,400	4,000	6,000	—

Surat

KM# 309A 1/2 MOHUR (Type 309A)
Gold

Date	Mintage	VG	F	VF	XF	Unc
AHxxxx//17	—	—	2,400	4,000	6,000	—

Akbarnagar

KM# 310.1 MOHUR (Type 310)
Gold **Obv:** Ruler's titles **Note:** Weight varies: 10.80-11.00 grams.

Date	Mintage	VG	F	VF	XF	Unc
AH1074//6	—	—	1,150	1,400	1,750	—
AHxxxx//13	—	—	1,150	1,400	1,750	—
AHxxxx//14	—	—	1,150	1,400	1,750	—
AH1082//15	—	—	1,150	1,400	1,750	—
AH1090//22	—	—	1,150	1,400	1,750	—
AH1090//23	—	—	1,150	1,400	1,750	—
AHxxxx//27	—	—	1,150	1,400	1,750	—
AHxxxx//28	—	—	1,150	1,400	1,750	—
AH11xx//33	—	—	1,150	1,400	1,750	—

Kabul

KM# 314.1 MOHUR (Type 314)
Gold **Note:** Weight varies: 10.80-11.00 grams.

Date	Mintage	VG	F	VF	XF	Unc
AHxxxx//3	—	—	1,350	1,750	2,000	—
AHxxxx//4	—	—	1,350	1,750	2,000	—
AHxxxx//5	—	—	1,350	1,750	2,000	—
AHxxxx//6	—	—	1,350	1,750	2,000	—
AH1074//7	—	—	1,350	1,750	2,000	—
AHxxxx//7	—	—	1,350	1,750	2,000	—
AHxxxx//8	—	—	1,350	1,750	2,000	—

Patna

KM# 314.2 MOHUR (Type 314)
Gold **Note:** Weight varies 10.8 - 11 grams.

Date	Mintage	VG	F	VF	XF	Unc
AH1070//3(?)	—	—	1,000	1,300	1,500	—

Ahmadabad

KM# 315.1 MOHUR (Type 315)
Gold **Note:** Weight varies: 10.80-11.00 grams.

Date	Mintage	VG	F	VF	XF	Unc
AH1073//5	—	—	650	720	800	—
AH1074//7	—	—	650	720	800	—
AH1075//7	—	—	650	720	800	—
AH1075//8	—	—	650	720	800	—
AH1076//8	—	—	650	720	800	—
AH1076//9	—	—	650	720	800	—
AH1077//9	—	—	650	720	800	—
AH1077//10	—	—	650	720	800	—
AH1078//10	—	—	650	720	800	—
AH1078//11	—	—	650	720	800	—
AH1079//11	—	—	650	720	800	—
AH1079//12	—	—	650	720	800	—
AH1080//12	—	—	650	720	800	—
AH1080//13	—	—	650	720	800	—
AH1081//13	—	—	650	720	800	—
AH1081//14	—	—	650	720	800	—
AH1082//14	—	—	650	720	800	—
AH1082//15	—	—	650	720	800	—
AH1083//15	—	—	650	720	800	—
AH1083//16	—	—	650	720	800	—
AH1084//16	—	—	650	720	800	—
AH1084//17	—	—	650	720	800	—
AH1085//17	—	—	650	720	800	—
AH1085//18	—	—	650	720	800	—
AH1086//18	—	—	650	720	800	—
AH1086//19	—	—	650	720	800	—
AH1087//19	—	—	650	720	800	—
AH1087//20	—	—	650	720	800	—
AH1088//20	—	—	650	720	800	—
AH1088//21	—	—	650	720	800	—
AH1089//21	—	—	650	720	800	—
AH1089//22	—	—	650	720	800	—
AH1090//22	—	—	650	720	800	—
AH1090//23	—	—	650	720	800	—
AH1091//23	—	—	650	720	800	—
AH1091//24	—	—	650	720	800	—
AH1092//24	—	—	650	720	800	—
AH1092//25	—	—	650	720	800	—
AH1093//25	—	—	650	720	800	—
AH1093//26	—	—	650	720	800	—
AH1094//26	—	—	650	720	800	—
AH1094//27	—	—	650	720	800	—
AH1095//27	—	—	650	720	800	—
AH1095//28	—	—	650	720	800	—
AH1096//28	—	—	650	720	800	—
AH1096//29	—	—	650	720	800	—
AH1097//29	—	—	650	720	800	—
AH1097//30	—	—	650	720	800	—
AH1098//30	—	—	650	720	800	—
AH1098//31	—	—	650	720	800	—
AH1099//31	—	—	650	720	800	—
AH1092//32	—	—	650	720	800	—
AH1100//32	—	—	650	720	800	—
AH1100//33	—	—	650	720	800	—
AH1101//33	—	—	650	720	800	—
AH1101//34	—	—	650	720	800	—
AH1102//34	—	—	650	720	800	—
AH1102//35	—	—	650	720	800	—
AH1103//35	—	—	650	720	800	—
AH1103//36	—	—	650	720	800	—
AH1104//36	—	—	650	720	800	—
AH1104//37	—	—	650	720	800	—
AH1105//37	—	—	650	720	800	—
AH1105//38	—	—	650	720	800	—
AH1106//38	—	—	650	720	800	—
AH1106//39	—	—	650	720	800	—
AH1107//39	—	—	650	720	800	—
AH1107//40	—	—	650	720	800	—
AH1108//40	—	—	650	720	800	—
AH1108//41	—	—	650	720	800	—
AH1109//41	—	—	650	720	800	—
AH1109//42	—	—	650	720	800	—
AH1110//42	—	—	650	720	800	—
AH1110//43	—	—	650	720	800	—
AH1111//43	—	—	650	720	800	—
AH1111//44	—	—	650	720	800	—
AH1112//44	—	—	650	720	800	—

Ahmadanagar

KM# 315.2 MOHUR (Type 315)
Gold **Note:** Weight varies 10.80-11.00 grams.

Date	Mintage	VG	F	VF	XF	Unc
AH1080//13	—	—	1,000	1,250	1,400	—
AHxxxx//14	—	—	1,000	1,250	1,400	—
AH1097//29	—	—	1,000	1,250	1,400	—
AH1098//30	—	—	1,000	1,250	1,400	—
AH1099//31	—	—	1,000	1,250	1,400	—
AH1100//32	—	—	1,000	1,250	1,400	—
AH1112//44	—	—	1,000	1,250	1,400	—

Ajmir

KM# 315.4 MOHUR (Type 315)
Gold **Note:** Weight varies: 10.80-11.00 grams.

Date	Mintage	VG	F	VF	XF	Unc
AH1109//42	—	—	1,750	2,000	2,250	—

Akbarabad

KM# 315.5 MOHUR (Type 315)
Gold **Note:** Without mint epithet. Weight varies: 10.80-11.00 grams.

Date	Mintage	VG	F	VF	XF	Unc
AH1070//(1) Ahad	—	—	650	720	800	—
AH1070//2	—	—	650	720	800	—
AH1071//4	—	—	650	720	800	—
AH1072//4	—	—	650	720	800	—
AH1075//7	—	—	650	720	800	—
AH1078//11	—	—	650	720	800	—
AH1080//13	—	—	650	720	800	—
AH1084//16	—	—	650	720	800	—
AH1086//18	—	—	650	720	800	—
AH1086//19	—	—	650	720	800	—
AH1087//19	—	—	650	720	800	—
AH1089//21	—	—	650	720	800	—
AH1089//22	—	—	650	720	800	—
AH1090//23	—	—	650	720	800	—
AH1091//23	—	—	650	720	800	—
AH1091//24	—	—	605	720	800	—
AH1099//31	—	—	650	720	800	—

Akbarabad

KM# 315.6 MOHUR (Type 315)
Gold **Obv:** Inscription **Rev. Inscription:** Mustaqir-ul-Mulk **Note:** Weight varies 10.80-11.00 grams.

Date	Mintage	VG	F	VF	XF	Unc
AH1096//29	—	—	650	720	800	—
AH1097//29	—	—	650	720	800	—
AH1097//30	—	—	650	720	800	—
AH1098//30	—	—	650	720	800	—
AH1098//31	—	—	650	720	800	—
AH1099//31	—	—	650	720	800	—
AH1099//32	—	—	650	720	800	—
AH1100//32	—	—	650	720	800	—
AH1103//3x	—	—	650	720	800	—
AH1105//37	—	—	650	720	800	—
AH1105//38	—	—	650	720	800	—
AH1107//39	—	—	650	720	800	—
AH1109//41	—	—	650	720	800	—
AH1109//42	—	—	650	720	800	—

Alamgirpur

KM# 315.7 MOHUR (Type 315)
Gold **Rev:** Mint name at top **Note:** Weight varies: 10.80-11.00 grams.

Date	Mintage	VG	F	VF	XF	Unc
AH1071//2	—	—	650	765	850	—
AH1071//4	—	—	650	765	850	—
AH1077//10	—	—	650	765	850	—
AH1082//xx	—	—	650	765	850	—

Date	Mintage	VG	F	VF	XF	Unc
AH1084//17	—	—	650	765	850	—
AH1085//18	—	—	650	765	850	—
AH111x//43	—	—	650	765	850	—

Alamgirpur

KM# 315.66 MOHUR (Type 315)

Gold **Rev:** Mint name at bottom **Note:** Weight varies 10.8 - 11 grams.

Date	Mintage	VG	F	VF	XF	Unc
AH1106//3x	—	—	650	765	850	—

Allahabad

KM# 315.9 MOHUR (Type 315)

Gold **Obv:** Inscription **Rev:** Inscription, mint name below **Note:** Weight varies 10.80-11.00 grams.

Date	Mintage	VG	F	VF	XF	Unc
AH1072//4	—	—	725	810	900	—
AH1074//7	—	—	725	810	900	—
AH1076//8	—	—	725	810	900	—
AH1076//9	—	—	725	810	900	—
AH1078//11	—	—	725	810	900	—
AH1079//12	—	—	725	810	900	—
AH1080//13	—	—	725	810	900	—
AH1081//13	—	—	725	810	900	—
AH1084//17	—	—	725	810	900	—
AH1085//18	—	—	725	810	900	—
AH1088//21	—	—	725	810	900	—
AH1099//31	—	—	725	810	900	—
AH1099//32	—	—	725	810	900	—
AH1110//xx	—	—	725	810	900	—
AH1104//36	—	—	725	810	900	—
AH1108//40	—	—	725	810	900	—
AH1109//42	—	—	725	810	900	—
AH1111//4x	—	—	725	810	900	—
AH1112//45	—	—	725	810	900	—

Aurangabad

KM# 315.10 MOHUR (Type 315)

Gold **Note:** Mint name above. Weight varies: 10.80-11.00 grams.

Date	Mintage	VG	F	VF	XF	Unc
AH1070//3	—	—	650	720	800	—
AH1073//5	—	—	650	720	800	—
AH1073//6	—	—	650	720	800	—
AH1074//6	—	—	650	720	800	—
AH1074//7	—	—	650	720	800	—
AH1075//7	—	—	650	720	800	—
AH1075//8	—	—	650	720	800	—
AH1076//8	—	—	650	720	800	—
AH1077//9	—	—	650	720	800	—
AH1077//10	—	—	650	720	800	—
AH1078//10	—	—	650	720	800	—
AH1078//11	—	—	650	720	800	—
AH1079//11	—	—	650	720	800	—
AH1079//12	—	—	650	720	800	—
AH1080//12	—	—	650	720	800	—
AH1081//14	—	—	650	720	850	—
AH1082//14	—	—	650	720	850	—
AH1082//15	—	—	650	720	850	—
AH1084//16	—	—	650	720	850	—
AH1084//17	—	—	650	720	850	—
AH1085//xx	—	—	650	720	850	—
AH1086//18	—	—	650	720	850	—
AH1086//19	—	—	650	720	850	—
AH1087//19	—	—	650	720	850	—
AH1087//20	—	—	650	720	850	—
AH1088//20	—	—	650	720	850	—
AH1088//21	—	—	650	720	850	—
AH1089//21	—	—	650	720	850	—
AH1093	—	—	650	720	850	—
AH1098//30	—	—	650	720	850	—
AH1098//31	—	—	650	720	850	—
AH1099	—	—	650	720	850	—
AH1100//32	—	—	650	720	850	—

Aurangabad

KM# 315.11 MOHUR (Type 315)

Gold **Obv:** Emperor's name and titles, date **Rev:** Mint and regnal year **Note:** Mint name below. Weight varies: 10.80-11.00 grams.

Date	Mintage	VG	F	VF	XF	Unc
AH1089//22	—	—	650	720	800	—
AH1091//23	—	—	650	720	800	—
AH1091//24	—	—	650	720	800	—
AH1092//24	—	—	650	720	800	—
AH1092//25	—	—	650	720	800	—
AH1093//27	—	—	650	720	800	—
AH1095//28	—	—	650	720	800	—
AH1096//28	—	—	650	720	800	—
AH1096//29	—	—	650	720	800	—
AH1097//29	—	—	650	720	800	—

Bhakkar

KM# 315.14 MOHUR (Type 315)

Gold

Date	Mintage	VG	F	VF	XF	Unc
AH1112//44	—	—	1,000	1,250	1,400	—

Bijapur

KM# 315.15 MOHUR (Type 315)

Gold **Obv:** Inscription **Rev. Inscription:** Dar-uz-Zafar **Note:** Arrangement of the mint name varies. Weight varies 10.80-11.00 grams.

Date	Mintage	VG	F	VF	XF	Unc
AH1101//33	—	—	650	765	850	—
AH1102//34	—	—	650	765	850	—
AH1103//35	—	—	650	765	850	—
AH1103//36	—	—	650	765	850	—
AH1104//36	—	—	650	765	850	—
AH1105//37	—	—	650	765	850	—
AH1106//38	—	—	650	765	850	—
AH1107//39	—	—	650	765	850	—
AH1106//39	—	—	650	765	850	—
AH1107//40	—	—	650	765	850	—
AH1108//40	—	—	650	765	850	—
AH1108//41	—	—	650	765	850	—
AH1109//41	—	—	650	765	850	—
AH1109//42	—	—	650	765	850	—
AH1110//42	—	—	650	765	850	—
AH1110//43	—	—	650	765	850	—
AH1111//43	—	—	650	765	850	—
AH1111//44	—	—	650	765	850	—
AH1112//44	—	—	650	765	850	—
AH1112//45	—	—	650	765	850	—

Burhanpur

KM# 315.16 MOHUR (Type 315)

Gold **Note:** Weight varies 10.80-11 grams.

Date	Mintage	VG	F	VF	XF	Unc
AH1069//2	—	—	650	765	850	—
AH1077//10	—	—	650	765	850	—
AH1085//18	—	—	650	765	850	—
AH1089//21	—	—	650	765	850	—
AH1089//22	—	—	650	765	850	—
AH1092//23	—	—	650	765	850	—
AH109x//24	—	—	650	765	850	—
AH109x//25	—	—	650	765	850	—
AH109x//28	—	—	650	765	850	—
AH109x//29	—	—	650	765	850	—
AH1098//30	—	—	650	765	850	—
AH1xxx//32	—	—	650	765	850	—
AH1100//3x	—	—	650	765	850	—
AH1103//36	—	—	650	765	850	—
AHxxxx//37	—	—	650	765	850	—
AH1105//38	—	—	650	765	850	—
AH1109//41	—	—	650	765	850	—
AH1110//42	—	—	650	765	850	—

Date	Mintage	VG	F	VF	XF	Unc
AH1111//43	—	—	650	765	850	—
AH1111//44	—	—	650	765	850	—
AH1112//44	—	—	650	765	850	—

Burhanpur

KM# 315.57 MOHUR (Type 315)

Gold **Rev. Inscription:** "Baldat-i-Fakhira" **Note:** Weight varies 10.8 - 11 grams.

Date	Mintage	VG	F	VF	XF	Unc
AHxxxx//3	—	—	1,200	1,350	1,500	—

Golkonda

KM# 315.18 MOHUR (Type 315)

Gold **Note:** Weight varies: 10.80-11.00 grams.

Date	Mintage	VG	F	VF	XF	Unc
AH1086//19	—	—	725	800	900	—
AH1086//20(sic)	—	—	725	800	900	—
AH1086//22(sic)	—	—	725	800	900	—
AH1086//23 (sic)	—	—	725	800	900	—
AH1086//25 (sic)	—	—	725	800	900	—
AH1086//30(sic)	—	—	725	800	900	—
AH1086//31(sic)	—	—	725	800	900	—

Gulbarga

KM# 315.19 MOHUR (Type 315)

Gold **Note:** Weight varies: 10.80-11.00 grams.

Date	Mintage	VG	F	VF	XF	Unc
AH1096//2x	—	—	750	850	950	—
AH1097//30	—	—	750	850	950	—
AH1098//30	—	—	750	850	950	—
AH1098//31	—	—	750	850	950	—
AH1099//32	—	—	750	850	950	—
AH1100//33	—	—	750	850	950	—
AH1101//33	—	—	750	850	950	—
AH1104//3x	—	—	750	850	950	—
AH1105//39	—	—	750	850	950	—
AH1106//40 (sic)	—	—	750	850	950	—
AH1107//xx	—	—	750	850	950	—
AH1108//41 (sic)	—	—	750	850	950	—
AH1109//42	—	—	750	850	950	—
AH1110//42	—	—	750	850	950	—
AH1110//43	—	—	750	850	950	—

Gwalior

KM# 315.59 MOHUR (Type 315)

Gold **Note:** Weight varies 10.8 - 11 grams.

Date	Mintage	VG	F	VF	XF	Unc
AH1100//33	—	—	900	1,000	1,100	—

Haidarabad

KM# 315.20 MOHUR (Type 315)

Gold **Obv:** Inscription **Rev. Inscription:** Dar-ul-Jihad, mint name **Note:** Weight varies 10.80-11.00 grams.

Date	Mintage	VG	F	VF	XF	Unc
AH1099//32	—	—	700	800	900	—
AH1100//3x	—	—	700	800	900	—
AH110x//34	—	—	700	800	900	—
AH1102//35	—	—	700	800	900	—
AH1105//38	—	—	700	800	900	—
AH1106//38	—	—	700	800	900	—
AH1107//39	—	—	700	800	900	—
AH1108//41	—	—	700	800	900	—
AH1110//43	—	—	700	800	900	—
AH1111//43	—	—	700	800	900	—
AH1111//44	—	—	700	800	900	—
AH1112//44	—	—	700	800	900	—
AH1112//45	—	—	700	800	900	—

Islamabad

KM# 315.21 MOHUR (Type 315)

Gold **Note:** Weight varies: 10.80-11.00 grams.

Date	Mintage	VG	F	VF	XF	Unc
AH1079//11	—	—	700	775	850	—
AH1098//30	—	—	700	775	850	—
AH1102//3x	—	—	700	775	850	—
AH110x//38	—	—	700	775	850	—
AH1112//44	—	—	700	775	850	—

Itawa

KM# 315.22 MOHUR (Type 315)
Gold **Note:** Weight varies 10.80-11.00 grams.

Date	Mintage	VG	F	VF	XF	Unc
AH1106//38	—	—	700	800	900	—
AH1106//39	—	—	700	800	900	—
AH1107//39	—	—	700	800	900	—
AH1109//41	—	—	700	800	900	—
AH1109//42	—	—	700	800	900	—
AH1111//43	—	—	700	800	900	—
AH1111//44	—	—	700	800	900	—
AH1112//44	—	—	700	800	900	—

Jahangirnagar

KM# 315.23 MOHUR (Type 315)
Gold **Note:** Weight varies: 10.80-11.00 grams.

Date	Mintage	VG	F	VF	XF	Unc
AH1107//40	—	—	800	900	1,000	—
AH1111//44	—	—	800	900	1,000	—
AH1112//45	—	—	800	900	1,000	—

Kabul

KM# 315.24 MOHUR (Type 315)
Gold **Note:** Without mint epithet. Weight varies: 10.80-11.00 grams.

Date	Mintage	VG	F	VF	XF	Unc
AH1071//3	—	—	700	800	900	—
AH10xx//4	—	—	700	800	900	—
AH108x//15	—	—	700	800	900	—
AH(10)85//17	—	—	700	800	900	—
AH1085//17	—	—	700	800	900	—
AH109x//23	—	—	700	800	900	—
AH109x//26	—	—	700	800	900	—

Kabul

KM# 315.61 MOHUR (Type 315)
Gold **Rev:** Mint name **Rev. Inscription:** "Dar al-Mulk" **Note:** "Badr" couplet; Weight varies 10.8 - 11 grams.

Date	Mintage	VG	F	VF	XF	Unc
AH1110//xx	—	—	700	800	900	—

Kabul

KM# 315.25 MOHUR (Type 315)
Gold **Obv:** Inscription **Rev. Inscription:** Dar-ul-Mulk, mint name **Note:** "Mihr" couplet; Weight varies 10.8 - 11 grams.

Date	Mintage	VG	F	VF	XF	Unc
AHxxxx//32	—	—	700	800	900	—
AH1104//36	—	—	700	800	900	—
AHxxxx//38	—	—	700	800	900	—
AH1106//39	—	—	700	800	900	—
AH1107//40	—	—	700	800	900	—
AH1108//40	—	—	700	800	900	—
AH1110//42	—	—	700	800	900	—
AH1111//43	—	—	700	800	900	—
AH1111//44	—	—	700	800	900	—

Kanbayat

KM# 315.27 MOHUR (Type 315)
Gold **Note:** Mint name below. Weight varies: 10.80-11.00 grams.

Date	Mintage	VG	F	VF	XF	Unc
AH1072//4	—	—	650	750	850	—
AH1074//7	—	—	650	750	850	—
AH1077//9	—	—	650	750	850	—
AH1082//14	—	—	650	750	850	—
AH1084//16	—	—	650	750	850	—
AH1086//1x	—	—	650	750	850	—
AH1090//xx	—	—	650	750	850	—
AH1091//xx	—	—	650	750	850	—
AH1092//24	—	—	650	750	850	—
AH1100//33	—	—	650	750	850	—
AH1106//38	—	—	650	750	850	—
AH1109//41	—	—	650	750	850	—
AH1112//xx	—	—	650	750	850	—

Kashmir

KM# 315.28 MOHUR (Type 315)
Gold **Note:** Weight varies: 10.80-11.00 grams.

Date	Mintage	VG	F	VF	XF	Unc
AHxxxx//2	—	—	960	1,200	1,500	—
AHxxxx//15	—	—	960	1,200	1,500	—
AHxxxx//32	—	—	960	1,200	1,500	—

Katak

KM# 315.29 MOHUR (Type 315)
Gold **Obv:** Ruler's name and titles, date **Rev:** Mint and regnal year **Note:** Weight varies: 10.80-11.00 grams.

Date	Mintage	VG	F	VF	XF	Unc
AH10xx//31	—	—	725	950	1,300	—
AH1099//32	—	—	725	950	1,300	—
AH11xx//33	—	—	725	950	1,300	—
AHxxxx//39	—	—	725	950	1,300	—
AHxxxx//44	—	—	725	950	1,300	—

Khambayat

KM# 315.26 MOHUR (Type 315)
Gold **Note:** Mint name above. Weight varies: 10.80-11.00 grams.

Date	Mintage	VG	F	VF	XF	Unc
AH1069//(1) Ahad	—	—	900	1,100	1,400	—

Khujista Bunyad

KM# 315.30 MOHUR (Type 315)
Gold **Note:** Weight varies 10.80-11.00 grams.

Date	Mintage	VG	F	VF	XF	Unc
AH1xxx//32	—	—	650	750	850	—
AH1101//33	—	—	650	750	850	—
AH1102//34	—	—	650	750	850	—
AH1102//35	—	—	650	750	850	—
AH1104//36	—	—	650	750	850	—
AH110x//37	—	—	650	750	850	—
AH1106//38	—	—	650	750	850	—
AH1107//39	—	—	650	750	850	—
AH1108//40	—	—	650	750	850	—
AH1108//41	—	—	650	750	850	—
AH1109//41	—	—	650	750	850	—
AH1109//42	—	—	650	750	850	—
AH1110//42	—	—	650	750	850	—
AH1110//43	—	—	650	750	850	—
AH1111//44	—	—	650	750	850	—
AH1112//43	—	—	650	750	850	—
AH1112//44	—	—	650	750	850	—
AH1112//45	—	—	650	750	850	—

Lahore

KM# 315.31 MOHUR (Type 315)
Gold **Obv:** Inscription **Rev. Inscription:** Dar-us-Sultanat **Note:** Weight varies 10.80-11.00 grams.

Date	Mintage	VG	F	VF	XF	Unc
AH1097//29	—	—	650	720	800	—
AH1105//37	—	—	650	720	800	—
AH1106//38	—	—	650	720	800	—
AH1106//39	—	—	650	720	800	—
AH1107//39	—	—	650	720	800	—
AH1108//41	—	—	650	720	800	—
AH1108//40	—	—	650	720	800	—
AH1109//41	—	—	650	720	800	—
AH1110//43	—	—	650	720	800	—
AH1112//44	—	—	650	720	800	—
AH1112//45	—	—	650	720	800	—

Lakhnau

KM# 315.32 MOHUR (Type 315)
Gold **Obv:** Emperor's name and titles, date **Rev:** Mint and regnal year **Note:** Weight varies: 10.80-11.00 grams.

Date	Mintage	VG	F	VF	XF	Unc
AH1082//14	—	—	675	850	1,000	—
AH1084//16	—	—	675	850	1,000	—
AH1084//61 (error for 16)	—	—	675	850	1,000	—
AH1090//2x	—	—	675	850	1,000	—
AH1097//29	—	—	675	850	1,000	—

Macchlipattan

KM# 315.62 MOHUR (Type 315)
Gold **Note:** Weight varies 10.8 - 11 grams.

Date	Mintage	VG	F	VF	XF	Unc
AH1105//37	—	—	1,900	2,400	3,000	—

Muazzamabad

KM# 315.33 MOHUR (Type 315)
Gold **Note:** Weight varies: 10.80-11.00 grams.

Date	Mintage	VG	F	VF	XF	Unc
AHxxxx//39	—	—	900	1,100	1,400	—

Muhammadabad

KM# 315.34 MOHUR (Type 315)
Gold **Note:** Weight varies: 10.80-11.00 grams.

Date	Mintage	VG	F	VF	XF	Unc
AH1099//31	—	—	1,300	1,600	2,000	—
AH1100//32	—	—	1,300	1,600	2,000	—

Multan

KM# 315.35 MOHUR (Type 315)
Gold **Note:** Mint epithet: "Dar-ul-Aman". Weight varies: 10.80-11.00 grams.

Date	Mintage	VG	F	VF	XF	Unc
AH1069//2	—	—	700	800	900	—
AH1070//3	—	—	700	800	900	—
AH1071//3	—	—	700	800	900	—
AH1072//4	—	—	700	800	900	—
AH1073//x	—	—	700	800	900	—
AH1080//12	—	—	700	800	900	—
AH1091//24	—	—	700	800	900	—
AH1096//29	—	—	700	800	900	—

Multan

KM# 315.53 MOHUR (Type 315)
Gold **Obv:** Four-line couplet **Rev:** Date and Regnal Year **Note:** Mint epithet: "Dar-ul-Aman". Weight varies: 10.80-11.00 grams; Previous KM#315.35A.

Date	Mintage	VG	F	VF	XF	Unc
AH1069//(1) Ahad	—	—	1,100	1,400	1,750	—

Multan

KM# 315.36 MOHUR (Type 315)
Gold **Obv:** Inscription **Rev:** Inscription, without mint epithet, mint name at bottom **Note:** Weight varies 10.80 - 11.00 grams.

Date	Mintage	VG	F	VF	XF	Unc
AH1072//4	—	—	700	800	900	—
AH1072//5	—	—	700	800	900	—
AH1073//5	—	—	700	800	900	—
AH1073//6	—	—	700	800	900	—
AH1074//6	—	—	700	800	900	—
AH1074//7	—	—	700	800	900	—
AH1075//7	—	—	700	800	900	—
AH1075//8	—	—	700	800	900	—
AH1076//8	—	—	700	800	900	—

Date	Mintage	VG	F	VF	XF	Unc
AH1076//9	—	—	700	800	900	—
AH1077//9	—	—	700	800	900	—
AH1077//10	—	—	700	800	900	—
AH1078//10	—	—	700	800	900	—
AH1078//11	—	—	700	800	900	—
AH1079//11	—	—	700	800	900	—
AH1079//12	—	—	700	800	900	—
AH1081//13	—	—	700	800	900	—
AH1081//14	—	—	700	800	900	—
AH1082//14	—	—	700	800	900	—
AH1082//15	—	—	700	800	900	—
AH1083//15	—	—	700	800	900	—
AH1083//16	—	—	700	800	900	—
AH1084//17	—	—	700	800	900	—
AH1086//18	—	—	700	800	900	—
AH1087//19	—	—	700	800	900	—
AH1087//20	—	—	700	800	900	—
AH1088//20	—	—	700	800	900	—
AH1094//26	—	—	700	800	900	—
AH1100//32	—	—	700	800	900	—
AH1112//44	—	—	700	800	900	—

Narnol

KM# 315.38 MOHUR (Type 315)

Gold **Obv:** Four-line couplet **Rev:** Date and Regnal Year **Note:** Weight varies: 10.80-11.00 grams.

Date	Mintage	VG	F	VF	XF	Unc
AH1102//3x	—	—	1,150	1,400	1,750	—

Nusratabad

KM# 315.39 MOHUR (Type 315)

Gold **Note:** Weight varies 10.80 - 11.00 grams.

Date	Mintage	VG	F	VF	XF	Unc
AH1101//34	—	—	800	1,000	1,250	—
AHxxxx//38	—	—	800	1,000	1,250	—
AH11xx//42	—	—	800	1,000	1,250	—

Patna

KM# 315.40 MOHUR (Type 315)

Gold **Note:** Weight varies: 10.80-11.00 grams.

Date	Mintage	VG	F	VF	XF	Unc
AH107x//8	—	—	700	800	900	—
AHxxxx//18	—	—	700	800	900	—
AH1090//22	—	—	700	800	900	—
AH1102//3x	—	—	700	800	900	—
AH1103//36	—	—	700	800	900	—
AH1104//36	—	—	700	800	900	—
AH1105//37	—	—	700	800	900	—
AH1105//38	—	—	700	800	900	—
AH1106//38	—	—	700	800	900	—
AH1109//41	—	—	700	800	900	—
AH1109//42	—	—	700	800	900	—
AH1110//43	—	—	700	800	900	—

Shahjahanabad

KM# 315.42 MOHUR (Type 315)

Gold **Obv:** Inscription **Rev. Inscription:** Dar-ul-Khilafat, mint name **Note:** "Badr" couplet; Weight varies 10.80 - 11.00 grams.

Date	Mintage	VG	F	VF	XF	Unc
AH1069//(1) Ahad	—	—	650	720	800	—
AH1070//3	—	—	650	720	800	—
AH1071//3	—	—	650	720	800	—
AH107x//4	—	—	650	720	800	—
AH1072//5	—	—	650	720	800	—
AH1073//5	—	—	650	720	800	—
AH1073//6	—	—	650	720	800	—
AH1074//6	—	—	650	720	800	—
AH1075//7	—	—	650	720	800	—
AH1076//8	—	—	650	720	800	—
AH1080//12	—	—	650	720	800	—
AH1082//14	—	—	650	720	800	—
AH1082//15	—	—	650	720	800	—
AH1083//15	—	—	650	720	800	—
AH1083//16	—	—	650	720	800	—
AH1084//16	—	—	650	720	800	—
AH1084//17	—	—	650	720	800	—
AH1086//19	—	—	650	720	800	—
AH1087//19	—	—	650	720	800	—
AH1088//xx	—	—	650	720	800	—
AH1089//21	—	—	650	720	800	—
AH1090//22	—	—	650	720	800	—
AH1090//23	—	—	650	720	800	—
AH1091//23	—	—	650	720	800	—
AH1091//24	—	—	650	720	800	—
AH1093//25	—	—	650	720	800	—
AH1094//26	—	—	650	720	800	—
AH1094//27	—	—	650	720	800	—
AH1095//27	—	—	650	720	800	—
AH1096//28	—	—	650	720	800	—
AH1096//29	—	—	650	720	800	—
AH1097//29	—	—	650	720	800	—
AH1097//30	—	—	650	720	800	—
AH1098//31	—	—	650	720	800	—
AH1099//31	—	—	650	720	800	—
AH1099//32	—	—	650	720	800	—
AH1100//32	—	—	650	720	800	—
AH1100//33	—	—	650	720	800	—
AH1101//33	—	—	650	720	800	—
AH1101//34	—	—	650	720	800	—
AH1102//34	—	—	650	720	800	—
AH1103//35	—	—	650	720	800	—
AH1104//37	—	—	650	720	800	—
AH1105//37	—	—	650	720	800	—
AH1106//38	—	—	650	720	800	—
AH1106//39	—	—	650	720	800	—
AH1107//39	—	—	650	720	800	—
AH1107//40	—	—	650	720	800	—
AH1108//40	—	—	650	720	800	—
AH1108//41	—	—	650	720	800	—
AH1109//41	—	—	650	720	800	—
AH1109//42	—	—	650	720	800	—
AH1110//42	—	—	650	720	800	—
AH1110//43	—	—	650	720	800	—
AH1111//42	—	—	650	720	800	—
AH1112//44	—	—	650	720	800	—
AH1112//45	—	—	650	720	800	—

Shahjahanabad

KM# 315.55 MOHUR (Type 315)

Gold **Note:** Weight varies: 10.80-11.00 grams.

Date	Mintage	VG	F	VF	XF	Unc
AH1069//(1) Ahad	—	—	—	—	—	—

Shahjahanabad

KM# 315.63 MOHUR (Type 315)

Gold **Rev:** Mint name **Rev. Inscription:** "Dar al-Khilafat" **Note:** "Badr" couplet; Weight varies 10.8 - 11 grams.

Date	Mintage	VG	F	VF	XF	Unc
AHxxxx//12	—	—	650	750	800	—

Sholapur

KM# 315.43 MOHUR (Type 315)

Gold **Note:** Weight varies: 10.80-11.00 grams.

Date	Mintage	VG	F	VF	XF	Unc
AH1080//12	—	—	700	800	900	—
AH1080//13	—	—	700	800	900	—
AH1081//13	—	—	700	800	900	—
AH1081//14	—	—	700	800	900	—
AH1082//14	—	—	700	800	900	—
AH1082//15	—	—	700	800	900	—
AH1083//15	—	—	700	800	900	—
AH1085//18	—	—	700	800	900	—
AH1087//19	—	—	700	800	900	—
AH1087//20	—	—	700	800	900	—
AH1094//27	—	—	700	800	900	—
AH1097//29	—	—	700	800	900	—

Surat

KM# 315.44 MOHUR (Type 315)

Gold **Rev:** Inscription and mint name **Rev. Inscription:** "Bandar-i-Mubarak". **Note:** "Badr" couplet; Weight varies: 10.80-11.00 grams.

Date	Mintage	VG	F	VF	XF	Unc
AH1070//(1) Ahad	—	—	725	900	1,150	—

Surat

KM# 315.45 MOHUR (Type 315)

Gold **Note:** Without mint epithet. Weight varies: 10.80-11.00 grams.

Date	Mintage	VG	F	VF	XF	Unc
AH1071//3	—	—	650	725	800	—
AH1073//5	—	—	650	725	800	—
AH1073//6	—	—	650	725	800	—
AH1074//6	—	—	650	725	800	—
AH1074//7	—	—	650	725	800	—
AH1075//7	—	—	650	725	800	—
AH1075//8	—	—	650	725	800	—
AH1077//x	—	—	650	725	800	—
AH1079//11	—	—	650	725	800	—
AH1079//12	—	—	650	725	800	—
AH1080//12	—	—	650	725	800	—
AH1082//14	—	—	650	725	800	—
AH1083//15	—	—	650	725	800	—
AH1083//16	—	—	650	725	800	—
AH1084//16	—	—	650	725	800	—
AH1084//17	—	—	650	725	800	—
AH1085//17	—	—	650	725	800	—
AHxxxx//18	—	—	650	725	800	—
AH1089//22	—	—	650	725	800	—
AH1090//23	—	—	650	725	800	—
AH1091//23	—	—	650	725	800	—
AH1091//24	—	—	650	725	800	—
AH1092//24	—	—	650	725	800	—
AH1092//25	—	—	650	725	800	—
AH1093//25	—	—	650	725	800	—
AH1094//26	—	—	650	725	800	—
AH1094//27	—	—	650	725	800	—
AH1093//26	—	—	650	725	800	—
AH1095//27	—	—	650	725	800	—
AH1095//28	—	—	650	725	800	—
AH1096//28	—	—	650	725	800	—
AH1096//29	—	—	650	725	800	—
AH1097//29	—	—	650	725	800	—
AH1097//30	—	—	650	725	800	—
AH1098//30	—	—	650	725	800	—
AH1098//31	—	—	650	725	800	—
AH1099//xx	—	—	650	725	800	—
AH1xxx//32	—	—	650	725	800	—
AH1101//3x	—	—	650	725	800	—
AH1102//35	—	—	650	725	800	—
AH1104//36	—	—	650	725	800	—
AH1104//37	—	—	650	725	800	—
AH1105//37	—	—	650	725	800	—
AH1105//38	—	—	650	725	800	—
AH1106//38	—	—	650	725	800	—
AH1107//39	—	—	650	725	800	—
AH1107//40	—	—	650	725	800	—
AH1109//41	—	—	650	725	800	—
AH1109//42	—	—	650	725	800	—
AH1110//42	—	—	650	725	800	—
AH1110//43	—	—	650	725	800	—
AH1111//43	—	—	650	725	800	—
AH1111//44	—	—	650	725	800	—
AH1112//44	—	—	650	725	800	—
AH1112//45	—	—	650	725	800	—

Tatta

KM# 315.46 MOHUR (Type 315)

Gold **Obv:** Inscription **Rev:** Inscription **Note:** "Mihr" couplet; Weight varies 10.80 to 11.00 grams.

Date	Mintage	VG	F	VF	XF	Unc
AH1071//4	—	—	800	900	1,000	—
AH1072//5	—	—	800	900	1,000	—
AH107x//6	—	—	800	900	1,000	—
AH1075//8	—	—	800	900	1,000	—
AH107x//9	—	—	800	900	1,000	—
AHxxxx//17	—	—	800	900	1,000	—
AH1088//21	—	—	800	900	1,000	—
AH1102//35	—	—	800	900	1,000	—
AH1112//45	—	—	800	900	1,000	—

Tatta

KM# 315.64 MOHUR (Type 315)

Gold **Note:** "Badr" couplet; Weight varies 10.8 - 11 grams.

Date	Mintage	VG	F	VF	XF	Unc
AH1073//5	—	—	800	900	1,000	—

Tibet-i-Kalan

KM# 315.65 MOHUR (Type 315)

Gold **Note:** Weight varies 10.8 - 11 grams.

Date	Mintage	VG	F	VF	XF	Unc
AH1076//8	—	—	—	—	—	—

Toragal

KM# 315.47 MOHUR (Type 315)

Gold **Note:** Weight varies: 10.80-11.00 grams.

Date	Mintage	Good	VG	F	VF	XF
AH1110//xx	—	—	—	950	1,200	1,500
AH111x//50	—	—	—	950	1,200	1,500

Ujjain

KM# 315.48 MOHUR (Type 315)

Gold **Obv:** Inscription **Rev. Inscription:** Dar-ul-Fath **Note:** Weight varies 10.80 - 11.00 grams.

Date	Mintage	VG	F	VF	XF	Unc
AH1073//x	—	—	700	800	900	—
AH1105//37	—	—	700	800	900	—
AH1105//38	—	—	700	800	900	—
AH1106//39	—	—	700	800	900	—
AH1112//xx	—	—	700	800	900	—

Zafarabad

KM# 315.49 MOHUR (Type 315)
Gold **Note:** Weight varies 10.80 - 11.00 grams.

Date	Mintage	VG	F	VF	XF	Unc
AH1074//6	—	—	750	850	950	—
AH1075//8	—	—	750	850	950	—
AH1080//13	—	—	750	850	950	—
AH108x//14	—	—	750	850	950	—
AH108x//17	—	—	750	850	950	—
AH108x//18	—	—	750	850	950	—
AH10xx//22	—	—	750	850	950	—
AH1097//29	—	—	750	850	950	—
AH1097//30	—	—	750	850	950	—
AH1098//30	—	—	750	850	950	—
AH1098//31	—	—	750	850	950	—
AH1099//31	—	—	750	850	950	—
AH1101//33	—	—	750	850	950	—

Zafarpur

KM# 315.50 MOHUR (Type 315)
Gold **Note:** Weight varies: 10.80-11.00 grams.

Date	Mintage	VG	F	VF	XF	Unc
AH1098//31	—	1,150	1,400	1,750	—	—

Akbarnagar

KM# 320.1 MOHUR (Type 320)
Gold **Obv:** Central inscription with ruler's name and titles in outlined square **Rev:** Mint name appears on top or bottom of inscription within outlined square **Note:** Weight varies: 10.80-11.00 grams.

Date	Mintage	VG	F	VF	XF	Unc
AH1070//3	—	—	960	1,200	1,500	—
AH1073//5	—	—	960	1,200	1,500	—
AH1074//6	—	—	960	1,200	1,500	—
AH10xx//12	—	—	960	1,200	1,500	—

Patna

KM# 320.3 MOHUR (Type 320)
Gold **Obv:** Central inscription with ruler's name and titles in outlined square **Rev:** Central inscription in outlined square **Note:** Weight varies: 10.80-11.00 grams.

Date	Mintage	VG	F	VF	XF	Unc
AH1070//3	—	—	1,300	1,600	2,000	—

Jahangirnagar

KM# 323.1 MOHUR (Type 323)
Gold **Obv:** Central inscription with ruler's name and titles in outlined square, couplet **Rev:** Central inscription outlined in square **Note:** Weight varies: 10.80-11.00 grams.

Date	Mintage	VG	F	VF	XF	Unc
AH1082//14	—	—	1,300	1,600	2,000	—
AH108x//15	—	—	1,300	1,600	2,000	—
AH1085//18	—	—	1,300	1,600	2,000	—

Junagadh

KM# 323.2 MOHUR (Type 323)
Gold **Note:** Weight varies: 10.80-11.00 grams; previous KM#320.2.

Date	Mintage	Good	VG	F	VF	XF
AHxxxx//x	—	—	—	1,100	1,400	1,750

Balapur

KM# 324.1 FANAM (Type 324)
0.3700 g., Gold, 6-6.5 mm. **Obv:** Ruler's name and titles **Rev:** Mintname

Date	Mintage	VG	F	VF	XF	Unc
ND(1658-1707)	—	60.00	80.00	100	125	—

Nasirabad

KM# 325.1 1/2 PAGODA (Type 325)
1.7000 g., Gold

Date	Mintage	VG	F	VF	XF	Unc
AH1102	—	—	—	—	—	—

Chinapattan

KM# 326.1 NISAR OR PAGODA (Type 326)
2.9800 g., Gold **Note:** Weight varies 3 - 3.3 grams.

Date	Mintage	VG	F	VF	XF	Unc
AH1103//35	—	—	1,600	2,000	2,500	—
AH1111//4x	—	—	1,600	2,000	2,500	—

Nasirabad

KM# 326.2 NISAR OR PAGODA (Type 326)
Gold **Note:** Weight varies 3 - 3.3 grams.

Date	Mintage	Good	VG	F	VF	XF
AH1100//33	—	250	350	500	700	1,000

LARGESSE COINAGE

Akbarabad

KM# A306.1 NISAR (Type A306)
Silver **Obv. Inscription:** "Nisar Alamgir" **Note:** Weight varies .30 - .40 grams.

Date	Mintage	VG	F	VF	XF	Unc
AHxxxx//x	—	60.00	100	175	260	—

Lahore

KM# A306.2 NISAR (Type A306)
Silver **Obv. Inscription:** "Alamgir" **Note:** Weight varies .30 - .40 grams.

Date	Mintage	VG	F	VF	XF	Unc
AH1109//42	—	75.00	120	200	300	—

Ahmadabad

KM# B306.1 NISAR (Type B306)
Silver **Obv. Inscription:** "Almagir" **Note:** Weight varies .60 - .70 grams.

Date	Mintage	VG	F	VF	XF	Unc
AHxxxx//14	—	75.00	120	200	300	—

Akbarabad

KM# B306.3 NISAR (Type B306)
Silver **Obv. Inscription:** "Nisar Bad Shah 'Alamgir" **Rev:** Inscription and mint name **Rev. Inscription:** "Mustagir al-Khilafa" **Note:** Weight varies .60 - .70 grams.

Date	Mintage	Good	VG	F	VF	XF
AHxxxx//x	—	—	—	—	—	—

Akbarabad

KM# B306.2 NISAR (Type B306)
Silver **Obv. Inscription:** "Nisar 'Alamgiri" **Note:** Weight varies .60 - .70 grams.

Date	Mintage	VG	F	VF	XF	Unc
AH1089//22	—	60.00	100	175	260	—

Jahangirnagar

KM# B306.6 NISAR (Type B306)
Silver **Obv. Inscription:** "Sikka 'Alamgir Shah" **Note:** Weight varies .60 - .70 grams.

Date	Mintage	VG	F	VF	XF	Unc
AH1071	—	70.00	120	200	300	—

Lahore

KM# B306.7 NISAR (Type B306)
Silver **Obv. Inscription:** "Alamgir Bad Shah" **Note:** Weight varies .60 - .70 grams.

Date	Mintage	VG	F	VF	XF	Unc
AHxxxx//26	—	70.00	120	200	300	—

Shahjahanabad

KM# B306.8 NISAR (Type B306)
Silver **Obv. Inscription:** "Nisar 'Alamgir Bad Shah" **Rev:** Mint **Rev. Inscription:** "dar al-Khilafa" **Note:** Weight varies 0.60-0.70 grams.

Date	Mintage	VG	F	VF	XF	Unc
AHxxxx//x	—	55.00	90.00	150	225	—

Akbarabad

KM# C306.1 NISAR (Type C306)
Silver **Obv. Inscription:** "Alamgir Bad Shah Ghazi" **Note:** Weight varies 1.1 - 1.5 grams.

Date	Mintage	VG	F	VF	XF	Unc
AH1071	—	60.00	100	175	260	—
AH1074	—	60.00	100	175	260	—

Akbarabad

KM# C306.2 NISAR (Type C306)
Silver **Obv. Inscription:** "Nisar 'Alamgir" **Note:** Weight varies 1.1 - 1.5 grams.

Date	Mintage	VG	F	VF	XF	Unc
AH1081//14	—	60.00	100	175	260	—

Akbarnagar

KM# C306.3 NISAR (Type C306)
Silver **Obv. Inscription:** "Nisar Bad Shah" **Rev:** Mint name **Rev. Inscription:** "Alamgir Shah" **Note:** Weight varies 1.1 - 1.5 grams.

Date	Mintage	VG	F	VF	XF	Unc
AHxxxx//3	—	90.00	150	250	375	—

Allahabad

KM# C306.4 NISAR (Type C306)
Silver **Obv. Inscription:** "Nisar 'Alamgir Bad Shah Ghazi" **Note:** Weight varies 1.1 - 1.5 grams.

Date	Mintage	VG	F	VF	XF	Unc
AH1070	—	90.00	150	250	375	—
AH1173/6	—	90.00	150	250	375	—

Bijapur

KM# C306.5 NISAR (Type C306)
Silver **Obv. Inscription:** "Alamgir..." **Note:** Weight varies 1.1 - 1.5 grams.

Date	Mintage	VG	F	VF	XF	Unc
AHxxxx//x	—	90.00	150	250	375	—

Lahore

KM# C306.6 NISAR (Type C306)
Silver **Obv. Inscription:** "Alamgir Bad Shah" **Note:** Weight varies 1.1 - 1.5 grams.

Date	Mintage	VG	F	VF	XF	Unc
AH1086//19	—	70.00	120	200	300	—
AH1112//45	—	70.00	120	200	300	—

Lahore

KM# C306.7 NISAR (Type C306)
Silver **Obv. Inscription:** "Nisar 'Alamgir Bad Shah" **Note:** Weight varies 1.1 - 1.5 grams.

Date	Mintage	VG	F	VF	XF	Unc
AHxxxx//35	—	70.00	120	200	300	—

Macchlipattan

KM# C306.8 NISAR (Type C306)
Silver **Obv. Inscription:** "Alamgir Bad Shah Sanah" **Note:** Weight varies 1.1 - 1.5 grams.

Date	Mintage	VG	F	VF	XF	Unc
AH1113//42	—	180	300	500	750	—

Shahjahanabad

KM# C306.9 NISAR (Type C306)
Silver **Obv. Inscription:** "Nisar 'Alamgir Bad Shah Ghazi" **Note:** Weight varies 1.1 - 1.5 grams.

Date	Mintage	VG	F	VF	XF	Unc
AH1089	—	55.00	90.00	150	225	—

Ahmadabad

KM# D306.1 NISAR (Type D306)
Silver **Obv. Inscription:** "Aurangzeb Bad Shah Ghazi" **Note:** Weight varies 2.5 - 2.9 grams.

Date	Mintage	VG	F	VF	XF	Unc
AHxxxx//(1) Ahad	—	70.00	120	200	300	—

Akbarabad

KM# D306.3 NISAR (Type D306)
Silver **Obv. Inscription:** "Nisar 'Alamgir Bad Shah Ghazi" **Rev:** Mint name **Rev. Inscription:** "Jalus Maimanat Manus" **Note:** Weight varies 2.5 - 2.9 grams.

Date	Mintage	VG	F	VF	XF	Unc
AHxxxx//x	—	60.00	150	175	260	—

Akbarabad

KM# D306.4 NISAR (Type D306)
Silver **Obv. Inscription:** "Nisar 'Alamgir Bad Shah Ghazi" **Rev:** With mint name in inscription, but without "jalus...." **Note:** Weight varies 2.5 - 2.9 grams.

Date	Mintage	VG	F	VF	XF	Unc
AH1071//4	—	55.00	90.00	150	225	—
AH1073//6	—	55.00	90.00	150	225	—
AH1076//8	—	55.00	90.00	150	225	—
AH1076//9	—	55.00	90.00	150	225	—
AH1077	—	55.00	90.00	150	225	—
AH1080//12	—	55.00	90.00	150	225	—
AH1081//14	—	55.00	90.00	150	225	—
AH1089//22	—	55.00	90.00	150	225	—
AH1092//25	—	55.00	90.00	150	225	—

Akbarabad

KM# D306.5 NISAR (Type D306)
Silver **Rev. Inscription:** "dar al-Khilafa" **Note:** Weight varies 2.5 - 2.9 grams.

Date	Mintage	VG	F	VF	XF	Unc
AH1098//31	—	60.00	100	175	260	—
AH1101//3x	—	60.00	100	175	260	—

Akbarnagar

KM# D306.6 NISAR (Type D306)
Silver **Note:** Weight varies 2.5 - 2.9 grams.

Date	Mintage	VG	F	VF	XF	Unc
AHxxxx//15	—	70.00	120	200	300	—
AHxxxx//32	—	70.00	120	200	300	—

Alamgirpur

KM# D306.7 NISAR (Type D306)
Silver **Obv. Inscription:** "Nisar Bad Shah 'Alamgir" **Note:** Weight varies 2.5 - 2.9 grams.

Date	Mintage	VG	F	VF	XF	Unc
AH1089//21	—	100	165	275	410	—

Alamgirpur

KM# D306.8 NISAR (Type D306)

Silver **Obv. Inscription:** "Nisar Aurangzeb 'Alamgir" **Note:** Weight varies 2.5 - 2.9 grams.

Date	Mintage	VG	F	VF	XF	Unc
AH1102	—	100	165	275	410	—

Itawa

KM# D306.9 NISAR (Type D306)

Silver **Note:** Weight varies 2.5-2.9 grams.

Date	Mintage	VG	F	VF	XF	Unc
AH1097//29	—	90.00	150	250	375	—

Jahangirnagar

KM# D306.10 NISAR (Type D306)

Silver **Obv. Inscription:** "Nisar Bad Shah 'Alamgir" **Note:** Weight varies 2.5 - 2.9 grams.

Date	Mintage	VG	F	VF	XF	Unc
AHxxxx//19	—	110	180	300	450	—
AH1090	—	110	180	300	450	—

Shahjahanabad

KM# D306.11 NISAR (Type D306)

Silver **Obv. Inscription:** "Nisar 'Alamgir Bad Shah Ghazi **Rev:** Mint name **Rev. Inscription:** "dar al-Khilafa" **Note:** Weight varies 2.5 - 2.9 grams.

Date	Mintage	VG	F	VF	XF	Unc
AH1070//3	—	55.00	90.00	150	225	—
AH1071//4	—	55.00	90.00	150	225	—
AH1074//7	—	55.00	90.00	150	225	—
AH1076//8	—	55.00	90.00	150	225	—
AH1077//10	—	55.00	90.00	150	225	—
AH1078//10	—	55.00	90.00	150	225	—
AHxxxx//11	—	55.00	90.00	150	225	—
AH1080//12	—	55.00	90.00	150	225	—
AH1082//14	—	55.00	90.00	150	225	—
AH1083//16	—	55.00	90.00	150	225	—
AH1102//3x	—	55.00	90.00	150	225	—
AH1103//36	—	55.00	90.00	150	225	—

Akbarabad

KM# 306.1 NISAR (Type 306)

Silver **Obv. Inscription:** "Nisar 'Alamgir Bad Shah Ghazi" **Rev:** Mint name and AH date in inscription **Note:** Weight varies: 5.6 - 5.8 grams.

Date	Mintage	VG	F	VF	XF	Unc
AH1077//9	—	90.00	150	250	375	—
AH1078//11	—	90.00	150	250	375	—
AH1080//12	—	90.00	150	250	375	—
AH1080//13	—	90.00	150	250	375	—
AH1081//13	—	90.00	150	250	375	—

Akbarabad

KM# 306.2 NISAR (Type 306)

Silver **Rev:** Mint epithet: "Mustaqir-ul-Khilafat" **Note:** Weight varies: 0.35-2.90 grams.

Date	Mintage	VG	F	VF	XF	Unc
AH1098//31	—	90.00	150	250	375	—

Akbarnagar

KM# 306.4 NISAR (Type 306)

Silver **Note:** Weight varies: 0.35-2.90 grams.

Date	Mintage	VG	F	VF	XF	Unc
AH1073//6	—	110	180	300	450	—
AHxxxx//15	—	110	180	300	450	—
AHxxxx//32	—	110	180	300	450	—

Alamgirpur

KM# 306.8 NISAR (Type 306)

Silver **Note:** Weight varies: 0.35-2.90 grams.

Date	Mintage	VG	F	VF	XF	Unc
AH1102//xx	—	110	180	300	450	—

Allahabad

KM# 306.10 NISAR (Type 306)

Silver **Obv. Inscription:** "Nisar 'Alamgir Bad Shah Ghazi" **Note:** Weight varies 5.60 - 5.80 grams.

Date	Mintage	VG	F	VF	XF	Unc
AH1082//14	—	110	180	300	450	—

Itawa

KM# 306.9 NISAR (Type 306)

Silver **Note:** Weight varies: 0.35-2.90 grams.

Date	Mintage	VG	F	VF	XF	Unc
AH1112//4x	—	110	180	300	450	—

Jahangirnagar

KM# 306.5 NISAR (Type 306)

Silver **Note:** Weight varies: 0.35-2.90 grams.

Date	Mintage	VG	F	VF	XF	Unc
AHxxxx//19	—	110	180	300	450	—

Lahore

KM# 306.6 NISAR (Type 306)

Silver **Note:** Weight varies: 5.60-5.80 grams (1/2 Rupee weight).

Date	Mintage	VG	F	VF	XF	Unc
AHxxxx//26	—	90.00	150	250	325	—
AHxxxx//35	—	90.00	150	250	325	—
AH1112//45	—	90.00	150	250	325	—

Shahjahanabad

KM# 306.7 NISAR (Type 306)

Silver **Note:** Mint epithet: "Dar-ul- Khalifat". Weight varies: 5.60-5.80 grams (1/2 Rupee weight).

Date	Mintage	VG	F	VF	XF	Unc
AH1070//3	—	90.00	150	250	325	—
AH1071//4	—	90.00	150	250	325	—
AH1074//7	—	90.00	150	250	325	—
AH1076//8	—	90.00	150	250	325	—
AH1077//10	—	90.00	150	250	325	—
AH1078//10	—	90.00	150	250	325	—
AH1078//11	—	90.00	150	250	325	—
AH1079//11	—	90.00	150	250	325	—
AH1079//12	—	90.00	150	250	325	—
AH1080//12	—	90.00	150	250	325	—
AH1082//14	—	90.00	150	250	325	—
AH1083//1x	—	90.00	150	250	325	—
AH108x//17	—	90.00	150	250	325	—

Shahjahanabad

KM# A307.1 NISAR (A307)

2.7200 g., Gold

Date	Mintage	VG	F	VF	XF	Unc
AH1072//5	—	720	1,200	2,000	3,000	—

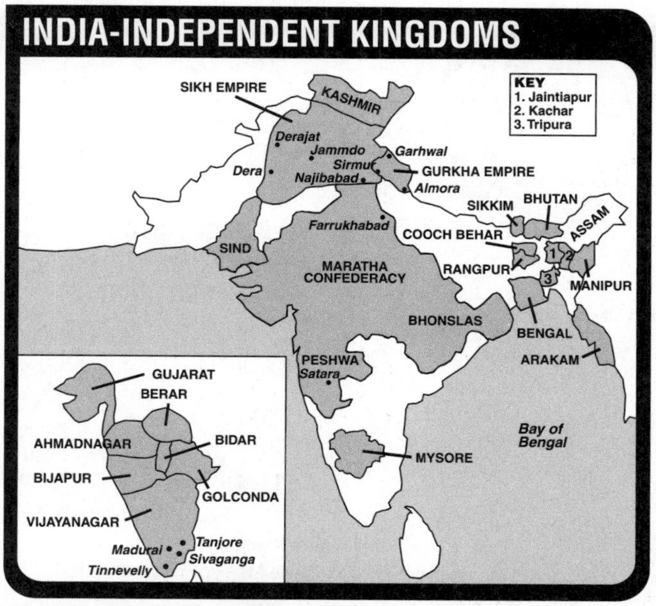

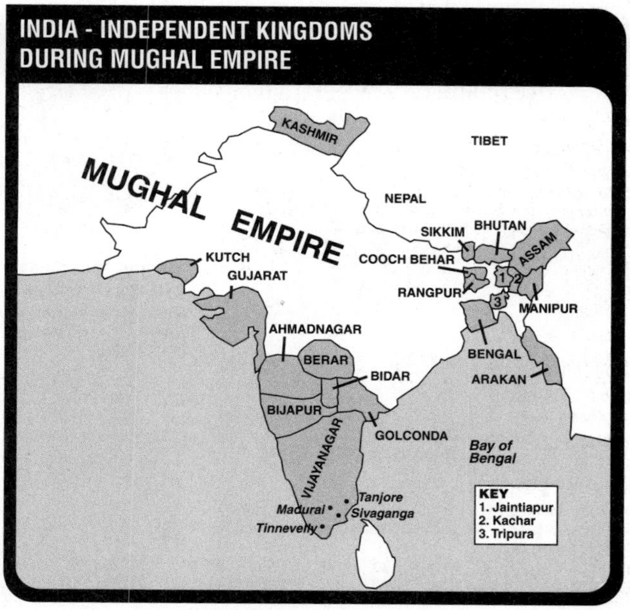

ARAKAN

A coastal region of Burma on the Bay of Bengal. The Buddhist Arakanese trace their history back 4500 years.

Arakan surrendered to the Burmese King Bodawpaya in 1784 and coins were issued by the king's governor in Arakan, bearing the following inscription: Amarapura, Kingdom of the Lord of Many White Elephants.

RULERS

Min Raza Gyi, Naradibbati,
BE955-974/1593-1612AD
Min Khamaung, Waradhamma Raza,
Hussein Shah, BE974-984/1612-1622AD
Thirithudhamma,
BE984-1000/1622-1638AD
Narabadigyi, BE1000-1007/1638-1645AD
Thado, BE1007-1014/1645-1652AD
Sanda Thudhamma, BE1014-1047/
1652-1685AD
Waradhamma Raza, BE1047-1059/
1685-1697AD
Kalamandat, BE1059-1072/1697-1710AD

KINGDOM

Min Raza Gyu, Naradibbati
BE955-974/1593-1612AD
HAMMERED COINAGE

Without Mint Name

KM# 6.1 TANKAH

Silver **Rev. Inscription:** Selim Shah... **Note:** Weight varies: 10.00-10.30 grams.

Date	Mintage	Good	VG	F	VF	XF
BE963 (1601)	—	100	200	350	500	—

Min Khamaung, Waradhamma Raza, Hussein Shah
BE974-984/1612-22AD
HAMMERED COINAGE

Without Mint Name

KM# 7 TANKAH

Silver **Rev. Inscription:** Hussein Shah... **Note:** Weight varies: 9.98-10.06 grams. Varieties exist.

Date	Mintage	Good	VG	F	VF	XF
BE974 (1612)	—	125	225	375	500	—

Thirithudhamma
BE984-1000/1622-38AD
HAMMERED COINAGE

Without Mint Name

KM# 8.1 TANKAH

Silver **Note:** Weight varies: 9.95-10.15 grams. Varieties exist.

Date	Mintage	Good	VG	F	VF	XF
BE984 (1622)	—	42.00	85.00	140	200	—

Without Mint Name

KM# 8.2 TANKAH

Silver **Obv:** Legend within dotted border **Note:** Weight varies: 9.95-10.15 grams.

Date	Mintage	Good	VG	F	VF	XF
BE98x (1626)	—	45.00	90.00	175	300	—

Without Mint Name

KM# 9 TANKAH

Silver **Subject:** Coronation **Note:** Weight varies: 9.95-10.15 grams.

Date	Mintage	Good	VG	F	VF	XF
BE996 (1634)	—	75.00	125	275	500	—

Narabadigyi
BE1000-07/1638-45AD
HAMMERED COINAGE

Without Mint Name

KM# 10 TANKAH

Silver **Note:** Weight varies: 10.12-10.30 grams.

Date	Mintage	Good	VG	F	VF	XF
BE1000 (1638)	—	30.00	60.00	110	170	—

Thado
BE1007-14/1645-52AD
HAMMERED COINAGE

Without Mint Name

KM# 11 TANKAH

Silver **Note:** Weight varies: 9.37-10.33 grams.

Date	Mintage	Good	VG	F	VF	XF
BE1005/7 (1645)	—	40.00	70.00	115	180	—

Without Mint Name

KM# 12.1 TANKAH

Silver **Note:** Weight varies: 9.37-10.33 grams.

Date	Mintage	Good	VG	F	VF	XF
BE1007 (1645)	—	20.00	35.00	55.00	85.00	—

Without Mint Name

KM# 12.2 TANKAH

Silver **Note:** Weight varies: 9.37-10.33 grams. Broad flan.

Date	Mintage	Good	VG	F	VF	XF
BE1007 (1645)	—	30.00	60.00	110	175	—

Sanda Thudhamma
BE1014-47/1652-85AD
HAMMERED COINAGE

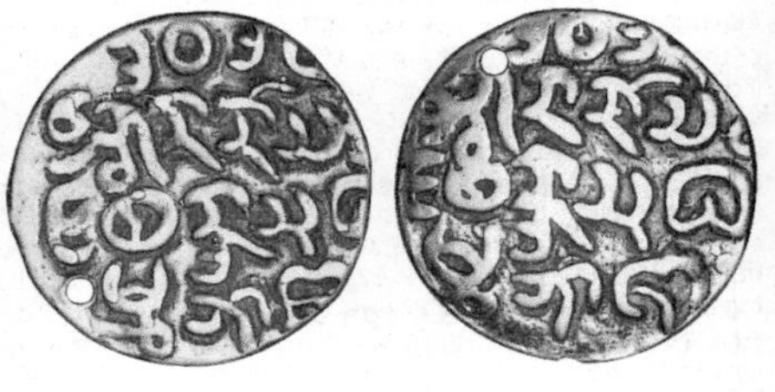

Without Mint Name

KM# 13 TANKAH

Silver **Note:** Weight varies: 8.84-10.32 grams.

Date	Mintage	Good	VG	F	VF	XF
BE1014 (1652)	—	18.00	336	62.00	90.00	—

Without Mint Name

KM# 14 TANKAH

Silver **Rev:** Legend divided **Note:** Weight varies: 8.84-10.32 grams.

Date	Mintage	Good	VG	F	VF	XF
BE1014 (1652)	—	25.00	40.00	65.00	100	—

Waradhamma Raza
BE1047-59/1685-97AD
HAMMERED COINAGE

Without Mint Name

KM# 15 TANKAH

Silver **Note:** Weight varies: 8.84-10.32 grams.

Date	Mintage	Good	VG	F	VF	XF
BE1047 (1685)	—	35.00	75.00	140	200	—

Kalamandat
BE1059-72/1697-1710AD
HAMMERED COINAGE

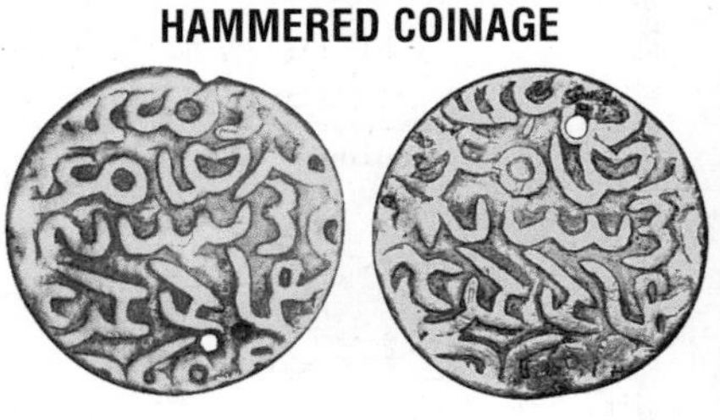

Without Mint Name

KM# 16 TANKAH

Silver **Note:** Weight varies: 9.84-10.04 grams. Varieties exist.

Date	Mintage	Good	VG	F	VF	XF
BE1059 (1697)	—	50.00	100	175	250	—

ASSAM

It was in the 13th century that a tribal leader called Sukapha, with about 9,000 followers, left their traditional home in the Shan States of Northern Burma, and carved out the Ahom Kingdom in upper Assam.

The Ahom Kingdom gradually increased in power and extent over the following centuries, particularly during the reign of King Suhungmung (1497-1539). This king also took on a Hindu title,

Svarga Narayan, which shows the increasing influence of the Brahmins over the court. Although several of the other Hindu states in north-east India started a silver coinage during the 16th century, it was not until the mid-17th century that the Ahoms first struck coin.

From the time of Kusain Shah's invasion of Cooch Behar in 1494AD the Muslims had cast acquisitive eyes towards the valley of the Brahmaputra, but the Ahoms managed to preserve their independence. In 1661 Aurangzeb's governor in Bengal, Mir Jumla, made a determined effort to bring Assam under Mughal rule. Cooch Behar was annexed without difficulty, and in March 1662 Mir Jumla occupied Gargaon, the Ahom capital, without opposition. However, during the rainy season the Muslim forces suffered severely from disease, lack of food and from the occasional attacks from the Ahom forces, who had tactically withdrawn from the capital together with the king. After the end of the monsoon a supply line was opened with Bengal again, but morale in the Muslim army was low, so Mir Jumla was forced to agree to peace terms somewhat less onerous than the Mughals liked to impose on subjugated states. The Ahoms agreed to pay tribute, but the Ahom kingdom remained entirely independent of Mughal control, and never again did a Muslim army venture into upper Assam.

RULERS

Ruler's names, where present on the coins, usually appear on the obverse (dated) side, starting either at the end of the first line, after <I>Shri, </I>or in the second line. Most of the Ahom rulers after the adoption of Hinduism in about 1500AD had both an Ahom and a Hindu name.

HINDU NAME	AHOM NAME	Dates
Khora Raja	Sukhampa	SE1474-1525/1552-1603AD
Pratap Singh or Burha Raja	Susengpha	SE1525-1563/1603-1641AD
Jayaditya or Bhaga Raja	Surampha	SE1563-1566/1641-1644AD
Nariya Raja	Sutyinpha	SE1566-1570/1644-1648AD
Jayadhvaja Simha or Surga Narayana	Sutamla	SE1570-1585/1648-1663AD
Chakradhvaja Simha	Supungmung	SE1585-1592/1663-1670AD
Udayaditya	Sunyatpha	SE1592-1594/1670-1672AD
Ramadhvaja Simha	Suklampha	SE1594-1596/1672-1675AD
Chamaguriya Raja	Suhung	SE1596-7/1675AD
Gobar Raja		SE1597/1675AD
Dihingia Raja II	Suhung	SE1597-1599/1675-1677AD
Parvatia Raja	Sudaipha	SE1599-1601/1677-1679AD
Ratnadhvaja Simha	Sulikpha	SE1601-1603/1679-1681AD
Gadadhara Simha	Supatpha	SE1603-1618/1681-1696AD
Rudra Simha	Sukhrungpha	SE1618-1636/1696-1714/AD

COINAGE

It is frequently stated that coins were first struck in Assam during the reign of King Suklenmung (1539-1552), but this is merely due to a misreading of the Ahom legend on the coins of King Supungmung (1663-70). The earliest Ahom coins known, therefore, were struck during the reign of King Jayadhvaja Simha (1648-1663). Although the inscription and general design of these first coins of the Ahom Kingdom were copied from the coins of Cooch Behar, the octagonal shape was entirely Ahom, and according to tradition was chosen because of the belief that the Ahom country was eight sided. Apart from the unique shape, the coins were of similar fabric and weight standard to the Moghul rupee.

The earliest coins had inscriptions in Sanskrit using the Bengali script, but the retreat of the Moghul army under Mir Jumla in 1663 seems to have led to a revival of Ahom nationalism that may account for the fact that most of the coins struck between 1663 and 1696 had inscriptions in the old Ahom script, with invocations to Ahom deities.

Up to this time all the coins, following normal practice in Northeast India, were merely dated to the coronation year of the ruler, but Rudra Simha (1696-1714) insti-tuted the practice of dating coins to the year of issue. This ruler was a fervent Hindu, and reinstated Sanskrit inscriptions on the coins. After this the Ahom script was used on a few rare ceremonial issues.

The majority of coins issued were of silver, with binary subdivions down to a fraction of 1/32nd rupee. Cowrie shells were used for small change. Gold coins were struck throughout the period, often using the same dies as were used for the silver coins. A few copper coins were struck during the reign of Brajanatha Simha (1818-19), but these are very rare.

NUMERALS

The early coinage is usually dated in the Saka era using Bengali numerals while later issues use modified numerals called Assamese.

MINT NAMES

گرگاو

Gargaon

رنگپور

Rangpur

REGNAL YEARS

Some of the earliest dated coins have the regnal years in written characters. These listings will have the numerical regnal years in parenthesis in the following listings.

Written	Numeric	Symbol
RAITYEO	13	
PLEKNGI	15	
KAPSAN	21	
KHUCHNGI for KHUTNGI	27	
RAISAN	33	
KATKEU	36	
RAISINGA	43	

KINGDOM

Jayadhvaja Simha (Sutamla)
SE1570-1585 / 1648-1663AD

HAMMERED COINAGE

Without Mint Name

KM# 1 RUPEE

Silver

Date	Mintage	Good	VG	F	VF	XF
SE1570	—	60.00	150	250	350	500

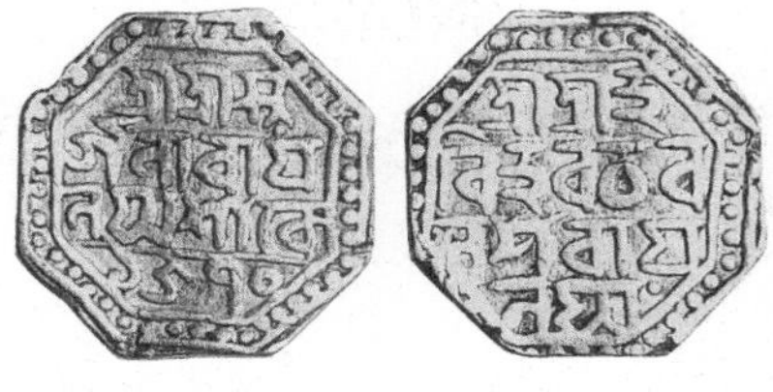

Without Mint Name

KM# 2 RUPEE

Silver **Obv. Inscription:** "Deva" included

Date	Mintage	Good	VG	F	VF	XF
SE1570	—	60.00	150	250	350	500

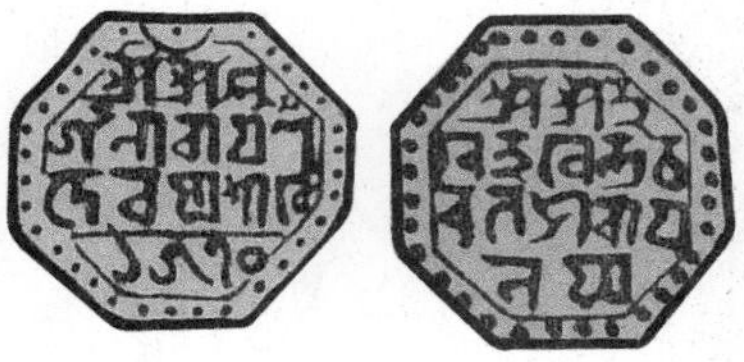

Without Mint Name

KM# 3 RUPEE

Silver **Rev. Inscription:** Different style

Date	Mintage	Good	VG	F	VF	XF
SE1570	—	60.00	150	250	350	500

Without Mint Name

KM# 4 RUPEE

Silver **Rev. Inscription:** Chinese "Ysang Pao"

Date	Mintage	Good	VG	F	VF	XF
SE1570	—	120	300	600	750	1,250

Note: The Chinese inscription may be translated as "Tibetan Coin", so this coin may have been intended as a trade coin for use in Tibet

Without Mint Name

KM# 5 MOHUR

11.2000 g., Gold **Shape:** Octagonal **Note:** Similar to KM#1, Rupee.

Date	Mintage	Good	VG	F	VF	XF
SE1570 (1648)	—	—	—	1,200	2,000	3,500

Without Mint Name

KM# A6 MOHUR

11.2000 g., Gold **Note:** Similar to KM#2, Rupee.

Date	Mintage	Good	VG	F	VF	XF
SE1570 (1648)	—	—	—	1,200	2,000	3,500

Chakradhvaja Simha (Supungmung)
SE1585-1592 / 1663-1670AD

HAMMERED COINAGE

Without Mint Name

KM# 8 RUPEE

Silver **Obv:** Sanskrit legend **Rev:** Sanskrit legend

Date	Mintage	Good	VG	F	VF	XF
SE1585	—	30.00	60.00	120	200	300

Without Mint Name

KM# 9 RUPEE

Silver **Obv. Inscription:** Ahomese **Rev. Inscription:** Ahomese

Date	Mintage	Good	VG	F	VF	XF
ND//(15)	—	32.00	80.00	160	250	360

Without Mint Name

KM# 10 RUPEE

Silver **Obv:** Without lion

Date	Mintage	Good	VG	F	VF	XF
ND//(15)	—	25.00	55.00	110	175	270

Without Mint Name

KM# 11 RUPEE

Silver **Obv:** Lion at left

Date	Mintage	Good	VG	F	VF	XF
ND//(15)	—	25.00	55.00	110	175	270

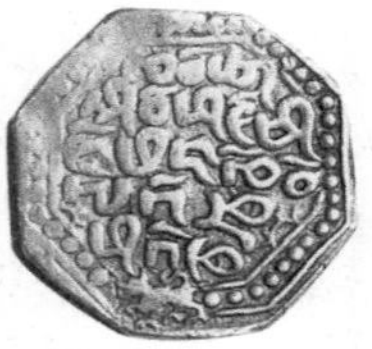

Without Mint Name

KM# 12 RUPEE

Silver **Obv:** Lion at bottom

Date	Mintage	Good	VG	F	VF	XF
ND//(15)	—	25.00	55.00	110	175	270

Without Mint Name

KM# 13 RUPEE

Silver **Rev:** Crescents in border

Date	Mintage	Good	VG	F	VF	XF
ND//(15)	—	25.00	55.00	110	175	270

Without Mint Name

KM# 16 MOHUR

Gold **Obv:** Without lion **Note:** Similar to Rupee, KM#10.

Date	Mintage	Good	VG	F	VF	XF
ND//(15)	—	700	1,000	1,400	2,000	3,000

Without Mint Name

KM# 18 MOHUR

Gold **Obv:** Lion at bottom **Note:** Similar to Rupee, KM#12.

Date	Mintage	Good	VG	F	VF	XF
ND//(15)	—	700	1,000	1,400	2,000	3,000

Without Mint Name

KM# 19 MOHUR

Gold **Rev:** Crescents in border **Note:** Similar to Rupee, KM#13.

Date	Mintage	Good	VG	F	VF	XF
ND//(15)	—	700	1,000	1,400	2,000	3,000

Udayaditya (Sunyatpha)
SE1592-1594 / 1670-1672AD
HAMMERED COINAGE

Without Mint Name

KM# 21 RUPEE

Silver

Date	Mintage	Good	VG	F	VF	XF
ND//(21)	—	64.00	160	320	500	720

Without Mint Name

KM# 23 MOHUR

Gold **Obv:** Bird at bottom

Date	Mintage	Good	VG	F	VF	XF
ND//(21)	—	—	—	2,200	3,000	4,200

Dihingia Raja
SE1597-1599 / 1675-1677AD
HAMMERED COINAGE

Without Mint Name

KM# 25 RUPEE

Silver

Date	Mintage	Good	VG	F	VF	XF
ND//(27)	—	65.00	165	330	550	775

Without Mint Name

KM# 26 RUPEE

Silver

Date	Mintage	Good	VG	F	VF	XF
ND//(27)	—	65.00	165	330	550	775

Gadadhara Simha (Supatpha)
SE1603-1618 / 1681-1696AD
HAMMERED COINAGE

Without Mint Name

KM# 28 RUPEE

Silver **Obv:** Without animals **Rev:** Without animals

Date	Mintage	Good	VG	F	VF	XF
ND//(33)	—	12.00	26.00	55.00	90.00	140

Without Mint Name

KM# 29 RUPEE

Silver **Rev:** Lion

Date	Mintage	Good	VG	F	VF	XF
ND//(33)	—	12.00	26.00	55.00	90.00	140

Without Mint Name

KM# 30 RUPEE

Silver **Rev:** Lion and bird

Date	Mintage	Good	VG	F	VF	XF
ND//(33)	—	12.00	26.00	55.00	90.00	140

Without Mint Name

KM# 31 RUPEE

Silver **Rev:** Lion and two birds

Date	Mintage	Good	VG	F	VF	XF
ND//(33)	—	12.00	26.00	55.00	90.00	140

Without Mint Name

KM# 32 RUPEE

Silver **Obv:** Lion **Rev:** Bird preening itself

Date	Mintage	Good	VG	F	VF	XF
ND//(33)	—	12.00	26.00	55.00	90.00	140

Without Mint Name

KM# 33 RUPEE

Silver **Rev:** Bird preening itself facing right

Date	Mintage	Good	VG	F	VF	XF
ND//(33)	—	12.00	26.00	55.00	90.00	140

Without Mint Name

KM# 34 RUPEE

Silver **Rev:** Bird at top

Date	Mintage	Good	VG	F	VF	XF
ND//(33)	—	13.00	32.00	65.00	100	160

Rudra Simha (Sukhrungpha)
SE1618-1636 / 1696-1714AD
HAMMERED COINAGE

Without Mint Name

KM# 36 1/4 RUPEE

Silver **Note:** Weight varies 2.67 - 2.9 grams.

Date	Mintage	Good	VG	F	VF	XF
SE1619	—	32.00	80.00	160	250	360

Without Mint Name

KM# 38 1/2 RUPEE

Silver **Note:** Weight varies 5.35 - 5.8 grams.

Date	Mintage	Good	VG	F	VF	XF
ND(1696-1714)	—	20.00	45.00	95.00	150	240

Without Mint Name

KM# 40 RUPEE

Silver **Obv:** Inscription **Rev:** Inscription **Note:** Weight varies: 10.70-11.60 grams.

Date	Mintage	Good	VG	F	VF	XF
SE1618	—	—	16.00	28.00	40.00	55.00
SE1620	—	—	16.00	28.00	40.00	55.00
SE1621	—	—	16.00	28.00	40.00	55.00
SE1622	—	—	16.00	28.00	40.00	55.00

Without Mint Name

KM# 41 RUPEE

Silver **Note:** Weight varies: 10.70-11.60 grams.

Date	Mintage	Good	VG	F	VF	XF
SE1619	—	13.00	65.00	130	200	320

Without Mint Name

KM# 43 1/4 MOHUR

Gold **Note:** Weight varies 2.67 - 2.9 grams.

Date	Mintage	Good	VG	F	VF	XF
SE1619	—	—	—	550	750	1,000

Without Mint Name

KM# 44 1/2 MOHUR

Gold **Note:** Weight varies 5.35 - 5.7 grams.

Date	Mintage	Good	VG	F	VF	XF
ND(1696-1714)	—	—	—	530	700	900

Without Mint Name

KM# 45 MOHUR

Gold **Obv:** Inscription **Rev:** Inscription **Note:** Weight varies: 10.70-11.40 grams.

Date	Mintage	Good	VG	F	VF	XF
SE1620	—	—	—	700	1,100	1,600

BAGLANA

KINGDOM

HAMMERED COINAGE

Mulher

KM# 1 1/2 MAHMUDI

Silver Weight varies 2.70-2.80g. **Obv:** Akbar's name and titles, date **Rev:** Kalima in square **Note:** In name of Mughal Akbar, continued into 19th c. with posthumous dates. Previous India-Mughal Empire, KM# 71.1.

Date	Mintage	Good	VG	F	VF	XF
AH1025	—	—	27.00	45.00	75.00	115
ND(1578-1810)	—	—	15.00	25.00	40.00	60.00

Mulher

KM# 2 MAHMUDI

Silver Weight varies, 5.40-5.60g **Obv:** Akbar's name and titles, date **Rev:** Kalima in square **Note:** In name of Mughal Akbar, continued into 19th c. with posthumous dates. Previous India-Mughal Empire, KM# 72.1.

Date	Mintage	Good	VG	F	VF	XF
AH1009	—	—	12.00	20.00	35.00	60.00
AH1010	—	—	12.00	20.00	35.00	60.00
AH1011	—	—	12.00	20.00	35.00	60.00
AH1012	—	—	12.00	20.00	35.00	60.00
AH1013	—	—	12.00	20.00	35.00	60.00
AH1014	—	—	12.00	20.00	35.00	60.00
AH1015	—	—	12.00	20.00	35.00	60.00
AH1016	—	—	12.00	20.00	35.00	60.00
AH1017	—	—	12.00	20.00	35.00	60.00
AH1018	—	—	12.00	20.00	35.00	60.00
AH1019	—	—	12.00	20.00	35.00	60.00
AH1020	—	—	12.00	20.00	35.00	60.00
AH1021	—	—	12.00	20.00	35.00	60.00
AH1022	—	—	12.00	20.00	35.00	60.00
AH1023	—	—	12.00	20.00	35.00	60.00
AH1024	—	—	12.00	20.00	35.00	60.00
AH1025	—	—	12.00	20.00	35.00	60.00
AH1026	—	—	12.00	20.00	35.00	60.00
AH1027	—	—	12.00	20.00	35.00	60.00
AH1028	—	—	12.00	20.00	35.00	60.00
AH1029	—	—	12.00	20.00	35.00	60.00
ND	—	—	6.00	10.00	17.00	25.00

COOCH BEHAR

During the 15th century, the area that was to become Cooch Behar was ruled by the powerful Hindu kings of Kamata, who were defeated by Sultan Ala al din Husain, Shah of Bengal in 1494AD. In 1511AD the kingdom of Cooch Behar was established by Chandan, a chieftain of the Koch tribe.

Chandan was succeeded about 1522 by Visvasimha, who consolidated the kingdom, and set up his capital at the present town of Cooch Behar. It was he who laid the foundations of the prosperity of the area by developing the Tibetan trade routes through Bhutan. Visvasimha is said to have abdicated about 1555AD to become an ascetic, and was succeeded by his son Nara Narayan, under whose reign the state reached the zenith of its power.

From the solid basis set up by his father, Nara Narayan set out, assisted by his brother Sukladhvaja, to extend the borders of his kingdom. Over the next quarter century he proceeded to subdue part of the Assam Valley, Kachar, Manipur, the Khasi and Jaintia Hills and part of Tripura and Sylhet. Nara Narayan was the first king of Cooch Behar to strike coins, and the varied style may indicate that he set up several mints over his empire. The style of one piece is very similar to that of later pieces struck by the Rajas of Jaintiapur, which suggests Jaintiapur as the mint for this variety, but no other varieties have been assigned to specific mints.

After the death of Sukladhvaja, who was a great general, the military strength of the kingdom waned. Nara Narayan quarrelled with Sukladhvaja's son Raghu Deva, and the latter set himself up as ruler of the eastern part of the kingdom in 1581, initially under the suzerainty of his uncle, but after Nara Narayan's death, as full independent ruler.

Nara Narayan's son, Lakshmi Narayan inherited the western part of the kingdom, but no attempt was made to consolidate the conquests made by his father, and Kachar, Tripura and other states reverted to their former fully independent state. Lakshmi Narayan was a weak, peace loving king who preferred to declare himself a vassal of the Mughal Emperor in 1596, rather than make any attempt to preserve his independence. In accepting any attempt to preserve his independence. In accepting Mughal suzerainty, he gravely offended his subjects, who rose in revolt. The Mughals assisted Lakshmi Narayan quell the rebellion, and in 1603 a treaty was signed under which Lakshmi Narayan agreed never again to strike full rupees and to abandon certain other royal prerogatives. The Eastern Kingdom under Raghu Deva and his son Parikshit refused to bow to Mughal domination in the same way, and in 1612 the Mughals invaded and destroyed their kingdom.

After Lakshmi Narayan's death in 1627, the new ruler Vira Narayan exhibited a certain degree of independence by striking full rupees and retaking the former Eastern Cooch Behar Kingdom from the Mughals. By this time, however, a powerful leader had emerged in Bhutan, and trade was disrupted by wars between Bhutan and Tibet, causing a reduction in the number of coins struck.

The Mughals soon recaptured the eastern territories, but the next ruler, Prana Narayan, was able to reopen trade links with Tibet through Bhutan. In 1661 Prana Narayan was expelled from his capital by the Mughal governor of Bengal, Mir Jumia, and sought refuge in Bhutan. At this time, Mir Jumia struck coins in Cooch Behar in the name of the Mughal Emperor Aurangzeb, but while Mir Jumia was stuck in Assam during the monsoon of 1663, Prana Narayan managed to regain control of his kingdom paying tribute to the Mughal Emperor.

For the next century Cooch Behar was relatively peaceful until there was a dispute over the succession in 1772. After a confusing period during which the Bhutanese installed their own nominated ruler and captured Dhairyendra Narandra, the Chief Minister appealed to the British for assistance. With an eye on the potentially lucrative Tibetan trade, which had increased somewhat in volume since Prithvi Narayan's rise to power in Nepal, the British agreed to support Darendra Narayan, so long as British suzerainty was acknowledged.

RULERS

Lakshmi Narayan, CB77-117/
SE1509-1549/1587-1627AD

Raghu Deva, CB71-93/
SE1503-1525/1581-1603AD

Parikshit Narayan, C93-102/
SE1525-1534/1603-1612AD

Vira Narayan, CB117-123/
SE1549-1555/1627-1633AD

Prana Narayan, CB123-156/
SE1555-1588/1633-1666AD

Aurangzeb, during Mughal occupation,
CB151-153/SE1583-1585/1661-1663AD

Mada narayan, CB156-171/
SE1588-1603/1666-1681AD

Vasudeva Narayan, CB171-173/
SE1603-1605/1681-1683AD

Mahendra Narayan, CB173-185/
SE1605-1617/1683-1695AD

Rupa Narayan, CB185-205/
SE1617-1637/1695-1715AD

DATING

The coins are dated in either the Saka era (Saka yr. + 78 = AD year) or the Cooch Behar era (CB yr. + 1510 = AD year) calculated from the year of the founding of the kingdom by Chandan in 1511AD. Some coins have dates in both eras, but as the Saka always refers back to the accession year, and the Cooch Behar year seems to show the actual date of striking, the two years seems to show the actual date of striking, the two years do not necessarily correspond to the same AD year.

Unfortunately the dies for the half rupees were usually rather broader than the flans, so the year is only rarely visible.

KINGDOM

Parikshit Narayan

SE1525-1534 / 1603-1612AD

STANDARD COINAGE

KM# 59 RUPEE

Silver

Date	Mintage	Good	VG	F	VF	XF
SE1525 (1603)	—	32.00	80.00	160	250	360

Vira Narayan

SE1549-1555 / 1627-1633AD

STANDARD COINAGE

KM# 64 1/2 RUPEE

4.9000 g., Silver

Date	Mintage	Good	VG	F	VF	XF
SE1548 CB117 (1627)	—	40.00	90.00	180	360	—

KM# 66 RUPEE

10.2000 g., Silver

Date	Mintage	Good	VG	F	VF	XF
SE1548 CB117 (1627)	—	60.00	150	250	350	500

Prana Narayan
SE1555-1588 / 1633-1666AD
STANDARD COINAGE

KM# 72 1/2 RUPEE
4.7000 g., Silver **Note:** Several varieties of ornamentation exist. The date is rarely visible. Prices given are for invisible or incomplete dates - pieces with clear dates are worth slightly more. Some pieces may exist with a date in the Saka era, but no clear specimens have been noted.

Date	Mintage	VG	F	VF	XF	Unc
CB129 (1639)	—	30.00	48.00	80.00	—	—
CB131 (1641)	—	30.00	48.00	80.00	—	—
CB141 (1651)	—	30.00	48.00	80.00	—	—
CB151 (1661)	—	30.00	48.00	80.00	—	—
CB152 (1662)	—	30.00	48.00	80.00	—	—
ND	—	12.00	18.00	30.00	—	—

KM# 74 RUPEE
9.4000 g., Silver

Date	Mintage	VG	F	VF	XF	Unc
SE1554 (1632)	—	—	—	—	—	—
SE1555 (1633)	—	32.50	55.00	90.00	120	—

BRITISH PROTECTORATE

Prana Narayan
SE1555-1588 / 1633-1666AD
STANDARD COINAGE

KM# 75 RUPEE
9.4000 g., Silver

Date	Mintage	Good	VG	F	VF	XF
CB130 (1640)	—	32.00	80.00	160	250	360
CB140 (1650)	—	32.00	80.00	160	250	360

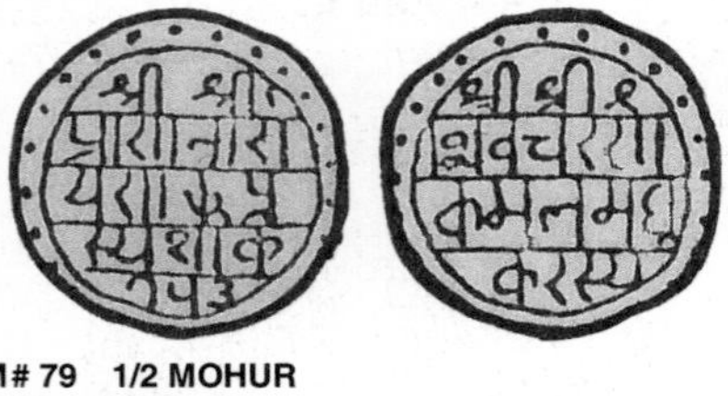

KM# 79 1/2 MOHUR
6.9000 g., Gold

Date	Mintage	Good	VG	F	VF	XF
NS753 (1633)	—	1,100	1,500	2,200	3,000	4,200

Aurangzeb
Mughal Occupation, SE1583-1585 / 1661-1663AD
STANDARD COINAGE

KM# 85 1/2 RUPEE
Silver **Note:** See Mughal Empire, KM#296.1.

Date	Mintage	VG	F	VF	XF	Unc
ND(1661-63)	—	250	420	700	—	—

Note: Struck during the Mughal occupation between 1661 and 1663AD

Mada Narayan
SE1588-1603 / 1666-1681AD
STANDARD COINAGE

KM# 91 1/2 RUPEE
Silver **Note:** The dates are very rarely legible. Some pieces may be dated with SE dates, but no clear pieces have been noted.

Date	Mintage	VG	F	VF	XF	Unc
CB16x (1670-79)	—	12.50	22.00	35.00	—	—
CB170 (1680)	—	16.00	27.00	45.00	—	—
CB171 (1681)	—	16.00	27.00	45.00	—	—
ND	—	7.50	12.00	20.00	—	—

Vasudeva Narayan
SE1603-1605 / 1681-1683AD
STANDARD COINAGE

KM# 97 1/2 RUPEE
Silver

Date	Mintage	Good	VG	F	VF	XF
ND(1681-83)	—	10.00	20.00	45.00	65.00	—

Rupa Narayan
SE1617-1637 / 1695-1715AD
STANDARD COINAGE

KM# 109 1/2 RUPEE
Silver

Date	Mintage	VG	F	VF	XF	Unc
ND(1695-1715)	—	7.50	12.00	20.00	—	—

DECCAN SULTANATES

In 1347 an officer in the service of Muhammad bin Tughluq, the Dehli sultan, occupied the fortress of Daulatabad in the Western Deccan and declared his independence of the Dehli Sultanate. It was from such small beginnings that the sprawling Bahmani kingdom of the Deccan arose. A hundred years later the Bahmanis also began to disintegrate under the disastrous leadership of Sultan Mahmud Shah (1482-1518). In their place five regional kingdoms arose, each founded by an officer or provincial governor in the service of Mahmud. The comparative vigor of these individual sultanates may to some extent be measured by the size and quality of their coinage. The Adil Shah dynasty of Bijapur, the Nizam Shahs of Ahmadnagar, and the Qutb Shahs of Golkonda (Hyderabad) all minted fairly prolifically although mostly in copper. Coins of the Barid Shahs of Bidar are few and far between, and no coins of the Imad Shahs of Berar are known. The Barid Shahs were absorbed by Bijapur, the Imad Shahs by Ahmadnagar, and the others were all annexed by the Mughals between 1596 and1687.

Further details on the coins of the Nizam Shahi dynasty of Ahmadnagar, the Barid Shahi dynasty of Bidar, the Adil Shahi dynasty of Bijapur, and the Qutb Shahi dynasty of Golkonda may be found in the *Standard Catalogue of Sultanate Coins of India*, by Dilip Rajgor, Bombay, India 1991.

AHMADNAGAR

Nizam Shahs

The Nizam Shahi dynasty owed its origin as an independent kingdom to Malik Ahmad, the Bahmani governor of Junnar. In 1490, Malik Ahmad revolted against his superiors by defeating Mahmud Bahmani's army. He then assumed the name of Ahmad Nizam Shah, from which name the dynasty itself became known.About 1574 Ahmadnagar annexed Berar and the short-lived Imad Shahi dynasty came to an end. Ahmadnagar came under increasing Mughal pressure after 1596 and was annexed by Shah Jahan in 1637.

RULERS
(after 1556AD)
Murtaza II as Mughal vassal, AH1009-1019/1600-1610AD
Burhan III, as Mughal vassal, AH1019-1041/1610-1631AD
Hosayn III, AH1041-1043/1631-1633AD
Murtaza III, AH1043-1046/1633-1636AD
(conquest, annexation by Mughal Emperor Aurangzeb)

MINTS
Ahmadnagar
Burhanabad
Parenda

INDEPENDENT KINGDOM

Murtaza II as Mughal Vassal
AH1009-1019/1600-1610AD
HAMMERED COINAGE

Ahmadnagar

KM# 10.1 1/2 FALUS
Copper **Obv:** King's name, mint name **Note:** Fine style. Weight varies: 9.00-10.00 grams. Size varies: 15-17 millimeters. Prev. KM # 11.3.

Date	Mintage	Good	VG	F	VF	XF
AH1011 (1602)	—	3.00	7.50	15.00	25.00	—
AH1013 (1604)	—	3.00	7.50	15.00	25.00	—
AH1017 (1608)	—	3.00	7.50	15.00	25.00	—
AH1018 (1609)	—	3.00	7.50	15.00	25.00	—

Ahmadnagar

KM# 12.3 2/3 FALUS
Copper

Date	Mintage	Good	VG	F	VF	XF
AH1014	—	4.00	10.00	20.00	30.00	—
AH1017	—	4.00	10.00	20.00	30.00	—

Ahmadnagar

KM# 12.1 FALUS
Copper **Note:** Weight varies: 14.00-15.00 grams. Prev. KM#11.4.

Date	Mintage	Good	VG	F	VF	XF
AH1011 (1602)	—	4.00	10.00	20.00	30.00	—
AH1013 (1604)	—	4.00	10.00	20.00	30.00	—
AH1017 (1608)	—	4.00	10.00	20.00	30.00	—

Burhan III as Mughal Vassal
AH1019-1041/1610-1631AD
HAMMERED COINAGE

Ahmadnagar

KM# 15.2 1/2 FALUS
Copper

Date	Mintage	Good	VG	F	VF	XF
AH1029	—	5.00	12.50	25.00	40.00	—
AH1032	—	5.00	12.50	25.00	40.00	—

Daulatabad

KM# 10.2 1/2 FALUS
Copper **Note:** Weight varies: 6.80-7.20grams. Prev. KM #11.2.

Date	Mintage	Good	VG	F	VF	XF
AH1012 (1603)	—	5.00	12.50	25.00	40.00	—

Daulatabad

KM# 10.4 1/2 FALUS
Copper

Date	Mintage	VG	F	VF	XF	Unc
AH1037	—	6.00	14.00	30.00	65.00	—

Parenda

KM# 13.3 1/2 FALUS
Copper **Note:** Fine style. Weight varies: 7.00-8.00 grams. Prev. KM # 15.2.

Date	Mintage	Good	VG	F	VF	XF
AH1027 (1618)	—	10.00	22.50	45.00	70.00	—

Daulatabad

KM# 15.3 2/3 FALUS

9.3300 g., Copper **Obv:** King's name **Rev:** Mint name **Note:** Fine style. Weight varies: 9.20-9.60 grams. Size varies: 17-18 mm.

Date	Mintage	Good	VG	F	VF	XF
AH1031 (1622)	—	3.50	7.00	14.00	22.00	—
AH1037 (1627)	—	3.50	7.00	14.00	22.00	—

Daulatabad

KM# 15.4 FALUS

Copper **Note:** Fine style. Weight varies: 13.70-14.50 grams. Size varies: 18-20 mm.

Date	Mintage	Good	VG	F	VF	XF
AH1037 (1628)	—	4.00	9.00	18.00	28.00	—

BIDAR

Barid Shahs

For all practical purposes the Barid Shahi sultans established their kingdom at Bidar about 1492 when Qasim Barid, minister of Mahmud Bahmani, asserted his independence. Beyond a few majestic buildings at Bidar, the capital, and an impressive fortress, the dynasty left little impression on the Deccan. About 1619 the kingdom was absorbed by Bijapur.

RULERS

(after 1556AD)

Mirza 'Ali III, AH1009-c.1018/1601-c.1609AD
Amir III, AH1018-1028/c.1609-1618AD
Kingdom annexed by Adil Shahs of Bijapur, AH1028/1619AD

FALUS

The Barid Shahs of Bidar based on the traditional *gani* weighing around 15 grams, maintained a copper coinage on a weight standard different from that of the neighboring Adil Shahs of Bijapur who eventually absorbed their principality. Their coins are generally scarce or rare, and are without mintname although struck at Bidar.

DECCAN SULTANATE

Amir III
c.AH1018-1028/1609-1618AD

HAMMERED COINAGE

Without Mint Name

KM# 14 2/3 GANI

Copper **Note:** Weight varies: 10.00-12.00 grams. Size varies: 18-19 milimeters. Prev. KM#14.2.

Date	Mintage	Good	VG	F	VF	XF
ND(1609-18)	—	20.00	50.00	100	175	—

Without Mint Name

KM# 15 GANI

Copper **Note:** Weight varies: 15.00-18.00 grams. Size varies: 20-22 milimeters. Prev. KM#14.3.

Date	Mintage	Good	VG	F	VF	XF
ND(1609-18)	—	10.00	24.00	48.00	80.00	—
AH1018	—	24.00	60.00	120	200	—

BIJAPUR

Adil Shahs

The Adil Shahi dynasty of Bijapur was named after its founder, Yusuf Adil Khan, the Bahmani governor of the region. In 1489, reacting to Bahmani weakness and to the outrageous leadership of Mahmud Shah, Yusuf Adil Khan asserted his independence. If the records can be trusted, Yusuf was a scion of the Turkish royal house who had fled to India only to be sold as a slave in Bidar to a minister of the Bahmani ruler. Remarkably, he worked his way up from so unpromising a situation to the position of a regional governor, and then sultan, over what was destined to become the most prominent of the five Muslim sultanates of the Deccan. Bijapur became famed as a center of Sufism, a form of Muslim mysticism and sensitivity, and was renowned for the elegance of its city and its architecture. Even its coinage had a distinctive quality. In the copper series some of the calligraphy is conspicuously superior to that of Bijapur's neighbors and its silver larins are almost unique. The dynasty flourished for almost two centuries until, in 1686, the city of Bijapur and its surrounding areas were annexed by the Mughal emperor Aurangzeb.

RULERS

(after 1556AD)

Ibrahim II, AH988-1037/1580-1627AD
Muhammad, AH1037-1068/1627-1657AD
'Ali II, AH1068-1083/1657-1672AD
Sultan Sikander, AH1083-1097/1672-1686AD
Conquered and annexed by Mughal
Emperor Aurangzeb Alamgir, AH1097/1686AD

MINT

Daboli

FALUS

Many Islamic copper coins were known as "falus" irrespective of weight. The Adil Shahi copper coinage appears to have been based on a unit of around 12 grams - the normal tola weight - with fractional units.

DECCAN SULTANATE

Ibrahim II
AH988-1037/1580-1627AD

HAMMERED COINAGE

Without Mint Name

KM# 16 HEAVY 1/2 FALUS

Copper **Shape:** square **Note:** Weight varies: 7.5 - 7.6 grams. Prev. KM#A5.

Date	Mintage	Good	VG	F	VF	XF
AH1022	—	36.00	90.00	180	300	—

Without Mint Name

KM# 17 HEAVY FALUS

Copper **Note:** Type 5. Weight varies: 15.00-15.20 grams. Size varies: 17-18 millimeters. Square. Prev. KM#5.1.

Date	Mintage	Good	VG	F	VF	XF
AH1022 (1613)	—	45.00	110	210	350	—

Muhammad
AH1037-1068/1627-1657AD

HAMMERED COINAGE

Without Mint Name

KM# 18 1/3 FALUS

Copper **Rev:** Couplet including King's name, large letters **Note:** Type 6. Weight varies: 3.40-4.00 grams. Size varies: 13-15 millimeters. Prev. KM#6.1.

Date	Mintage	Good	VG	F	VF	XF
ND(1627-57)	—	4.80	12.00	24.00	40.00	—

Without Mint Name

KM# 22 1/3 FALUS

Copper **Obv:** Couplet including king's name, smaller letters and finer style; circle of dots and rosette **Rev:** Circle of dots and rosette **Note:** Type 7. Weight varies: 3.60-4.00 grams. Size varies: 13-15 millimeters. Prev. KM#7.1.

Date	Mintage	Good	VG	F	VF	XF
ND(1627-57)	—	6.80	17.00	34.00	85.00	—

Without Mint Name

KM# 25 1/3 FALUS

Copper **Obv:** Dotted leaf, legend around within solid circle **Rev:** Dotted leaf, legend around within solid circle **Note:** Type 8. Weight varies: 3.50-4.00 grams. Size varies: 13-15 millimeters. Prev. KM#8.1.

Date	Mintage	Good	VG	F	VF	XF
ND(1627-57)	—	3.60	9.00	18.00	30.00	—

Without Mint Name

KM# 19 2/3 FALUS

Copper **Rev:** Couplet including King's name, large letters **Note:** Type 6. Weight varies: 7.60-8.00grams. Size varies: 15-17 millimeters. Prev. KM#6.2.

Date	Mintage	Good	VG	F	VF	XF
ND(1627-57)	—	4.80	12.00	24.00	40.00	—

Without Mint Name

KM# 23 2/3 FALUS

Copper **Obv:** Couplet including king's name, smaller letters and finer style; circle of dots and rosette **Rev:** Circle of dots and rosette **Note:** Type 7. Weight varies: 7.60-8.00 grams. Size varies: 15-17 millimeters. Prev. KM#7.2.

Date	Mintage	Good	VG	F	VF	XF
ND(1627-57)	—	10.00	25.00	50.00	85.00	—

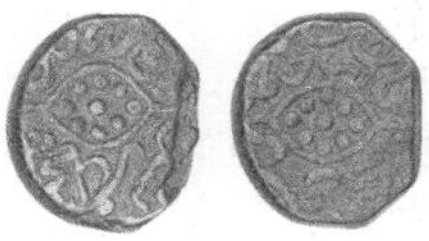

Without Mint Name

KM# 26 2/3 FALUS

Copper **Obv:** Dotted leaf, legend around within solid circle **Rev:** Dotted leaf, legend around within solid circle **Note:** Type 8. Weight varies: 7.40-8.00 grams. Size varies: 16-18 millimeters. Prev. KM#8.2.

Date	Mintage	Good	VG	F	VF	XF
ND(1627-57)	—	6.00	15.00	30.00	50.00	—

Without Mint Name

KM# 20 FALUS

Copper **Rev:** Couplet including King's name, large script **Note:** Type 6. Weight varies: 11.20-12.00 grams. Size varies: 18-20 millimeters. Prev. KM#6.3.

Date	Mintage	Good	VG	F	VF	XF
ND(1627-57)	—	6.00	15.00	30.00	50.00	—

Without Mint Name

KM# 24 FALUS

Copper **Obv:** Couplet including king's name, smaller script and finer style; circle of dots and rosette **Rev:** Circle of dots and rosette **Note:** Type 7. Weight varies: 11.20-12.00 grams. Size varies: 18-20 millimeters. Prev. KM#7.3.

Date	Mintage	Good	VG	F	VF	XF
ND(1627-57)	—	8.00	20.00	40.00	70.00	—

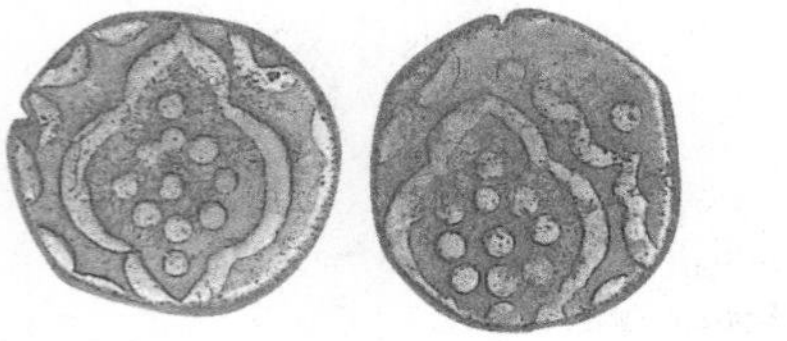

Without Mint Name

KM# 27 FALUS

Copper **Obv:** Dotted leaf, legend around within solid circle **Rev:** Dotted leaf, legend around within solid circle **Note:** Type 8. Weight varies: 11.20-12.00 grams. Size varies: 18-20 millimeters. Crude issues are believed to be later imitations. Prev. KM#8.3.

Date	Mintage	Good	VG	F	VF	XF
ND(1627-57)	—	—	6.00	12.00	25.00	—

Dabul

KM# 33 LARIN

Silver **Obv. Inscription:** Sultan Muhammad 'Adil Shah **Note:** Type 9. Weight varies: 4.20-4.90 grams. Size varies: 50-60 millimeters long. Prev. KM#9.1.

Date	Mintage	Good	VG	F	VF	XF
ND(1627-57)	—	8.00	20.00	40.00	65.00	—
Note: Date off flan						
AH1037	—	18.00	45.00	90.00	150	—

Dabul

KM# 30 PAGODA

3.4000 g., Gold **Obv:** Persian couplet **Rev:** Persian couplet **Note:** Prev. KM#9A.1

Date	Mintage	Good	VG	F	VF	XF
ND(1627-57)	—	—	—	300	500	700

'Ali 'Adil Shah II

AH1068-1083/1657-1672AD

HAMMERED COINAGE

Without Mint Name

KM# 36 1/3 FALUS

Copper **Obv:** Dotted circular border **Rev:** King's name, dotted circular border **Note:** Type 10. Weight varies: 3.80-4.20 grams. Size varies: 13-14 millimeters. Prev. KM#10.1

Date	Mintage	Good	VG	F	VF	XF
ND(1657-72)	—	3.60	9.00	18.00	30.00	—

Without Mint Name

KM# 37 2/3 FALUS

Copper **Obv:** King's name; dotted circular border **Rev:** Dotted circular border **Note:** Type 10. Weight varies: 7.50-8.00 grams. Size varies: 15-16 millimeters. Prev. KM#10.2.

Date	Mintage	Good	VG	F	VF	XF
ND(1657-72)	—	3.60	9.00	18.00	30.00	—

Without Mint Name

KM# 38 FALUS

Copper **Obv:** King's name; dotted circular border **Rev:** Dotted circular border **Note:** Type 10. Weight varies: 11.20-12.00 grams. Size varies: 17-18 millimeters. Prev. KM#10.3.

Date	Mintage	Good	VG	F	VF	XF
ND(1657-72)	—	3.00	7.50	15.00	25.00	—

Dabul

KM# 40 LARIN

Silver **Obv. Inscription:** 'Ali 'Adil Shah **Note:** Weight varies: 4.50-4.90 grams. Size varies: 40-45 millimeters long. Prev. KM#11.1

Date	Mintage	Good	VG	F	VF	XF
AH1066	—	9.00	22.50	45.00	75.00	—
Note: error for 1077						
ND(1657-72)	—	5.50	13.50	27.00	45.00	—
Note: Date off flan						
AH1067	—	9.00	22.50	45.00	75.00	—
AH1069	—	9.00	22.50	45.00	75.00	—
AH1071	—	9.00	22.50	45.00	75.00	—
AH1072	—	9.00	22.50	45.00	75.00	—
AH1075	—	9.00	22.50	45.00	75.00	—
AH1077	—	9.00	22.50	45.00	75.00	—
AH1082	—	9.00	22.50	45.00	75.00	—

Sultan Sikander

AH1083-1097/1672-1686AD

HAMMERED COINAGE

Without Mint Name

KM# 42 1/3 FALUS

Copper **Obv:** King's name **Note:** Type 12. Weight varies: 3.60-4.00 grams. Size varies: 13-15 millimeters. Prev. KM#12.1

Date	Mintage	Good	VG	F	VF	XF
ND(1672-86)	—	6.00	12.00	25.00	40.00	—

Without Mint Name

KM# 44 FALUS

Copper **Obv:** King's name **Rev. Inscription:** Khusro giti **Note:** Type 12. Weight varies: 11.20-1200 grams. Size varies: 18-20 millimeters. Fine style. Prev. KM#12.3.

Date	Mintage	Good	VG	F	VF	XF
AH1086 (1675)	—	3.00	7.50	15.00	25.00	—
AH1087 (1676)	—	3.00	7.50	15.00	25.00	—

Without Mint Name

KM# 48 FANAM

0.3800 g., Gold, 5 mm. **Obv:** Sultan's name **Rev:** Date **Note:** Type 13. Prev. KM#13.

Date	Mintage	Good	VG	F	VF	XF
AH1087 (1676)	—	—	—	140	200	260

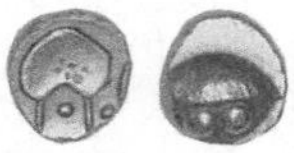

Without Mint Name

KM# 46 1/2 PAGODA

1.7000 g., Gold, 10 mm. **Note:** With Arabic "S" on top of shaft. Prev. KM#14.

Date	Mintage	Good	VG	F	VF	XF
ND(1672-86)	—	—	—	100	175	225

Without Mint Name

KM# 47 PAGODA

3.4000 g., Gold, 18 mm. **Note:** With Arabic "S" on top of shaft. Prev. KM#15.

Date	Mintage	Good	VG	F	VF	XF
ND(1672-86)	—	—	—	150	225	300

ANONYMOUS COINAGE

Without Mint Name

KM# 49 1/2 PAGODA

1.7000 g., Gold **Note:** Similar to 1/2 Pagoda, KM# 46 but without Arabic "S" on top of shaft.

Date	Mintage	Good	VG	F	VF	XF
ND(1686-1750)	—	—	—	150	180	230

Without Mint Name

KM# 50 PAGODA

3.4000 g., Gold **Note:** Similar to Pagoda, KM#47 but without Arabic "S" on top of shaft.

Date	Mintage	Good	VG	F	VF	XF
ND(1686-1750)	—	—	—	160	200	250

GOLKONDA

Qutb Shahs

The Qutb Shahi kingdom of Golkonda was the last of the five Deccani sultanates to break free of the Bahmanis and the last to fall to the Mughal army. The dynasty was founded in 1518 by an officer who came to be known as Quli Qutb Shah, whose long and prosperous reign laid a solid foundation for his successors. Early in his reign he moved his capital to Golkonda from Warangal, once capital of the old Hindu Kakatiya kingdom which had fallen to the Tughluqs of Delhi. Here at Golkonda the Qutb Shahs built a powerful fortress seven miles in circumference, and from here they governed the area until increasing Mughal pressures led to its annexation by Aurangzeb in 1687. Within fifty years, in the twilight of Mughal fortunes, regionalism again asserted itself and Golkonda became the citadel of Nizam-ul Mulk, the founder of Hyderabad State.

RULERS

(after 1556AD)

Muhammad Quli, AH988-1020/1580-1612AD
Sultan Muhammad, AH1020-1035/1612-1626AD
Abdullah, AH1035-1083/1626-1672AD
Abu'l Hasan, AH1083-1098/1672-1686AD
Conquered and annexed by Mughal
Emperor Aurangzeb Alamgir, AH1098/1686AD

NOTE: The only known coins of the Qutb Shahs are copper. While weight systems vary between rulers, and even within a single reign, the coins in any one system clearly comprise a basic unit and its fractions - two thirds, one-half and one-third - by weight. Further details may be found in QUTUB SHAHI COINS IN THE ANDHRA PRADESH GOVERNMENT MUSEUM, by Muhammad Abdul Wali Khan, Hyderabad, India, 1961.

COPPER COINAGE

Around 1604AD copper coins began to be struck in the name of Muhammad Quli on a heavier weight standard (17-18 grams) from a new mint, Hyderabad. All are on round planchets and most carry the apparently frozen date AH1012.

Sultan Muhammad continued his predecessor's copper coinage type from Hyderabad, with the apparently frozen date AH1025 (1585AD). Fractions are extremely rare.

The decline of the Qutb Shahi kingdom can be seen in the changes in Abdullah's copper coinage which began with coins bearing his name and titles on a relatively heavy weight standard, declining into lighter, cruder coins and ending in anonymous issues bearing a pathetic, fatalistic verse.

DECCAN SULTANATE

Muhammad Quli

AH988-1020/1580-1612AD

HAMMERED COINAGE

Hyderabad

KM# 8.1 1/3 FALUS

Copper **Obv:** King's name **Rev:** Mint name, date **Note:** Size varies: 16-18 mm. Weight varies: 5.60-6.00 grams.

Date	Mintage	Good	VG	F	VF	XF
AH1012 (1603)	—	9.00	22.50	45.00	75.00	—

Hyderabad

KM# 8.2 1/2 FALUS

Copper **Note:** Size varies: 18-20 millimeters. Weight varies: 8.50-9.00 grams.

Date	Mintage	Good	VG	F	VF	XF
AH1012 (1603)	—	6.00	15.00	30.00	50.00	—

Hyderabad

KM# 8.3 3/4 FALUS

Copper **Note:** Size varies: 19-22 millimeters. Weight varies: 11.00-12.00 grams.

Date	Mintage	Good	VG	F	VF	XF
AH1012 (1603)	—	7.20	18.00	36.00	60.00	—

Hyderabad

KM# 8.4 FALUS

Copper **Note:** Weight varies: 17.00-18.00 grams. Size varies: 20-24 millimeters.

Date	Mintage	Good	VG	F	VF	XF
AH1012 (1603)	—	12.00	30.00	62.00	90.00	—

Sultan Muhammad

AH1020-1035/1612-1626AD

HAMMERED COINAGE

Hyderabad Shahr

KM# 10.1 1/3 FALUS

6.0000 g., Copper, 16 mm. **Obv:** King's name **Rev:** Mint name, date **Rev. Inscription:** "Dar-us-Sultanat"

Date	Mintage	Good	VG	F	VF	XF
AH1025 (1616)	—	18.00	45.00	90.00	150	—

Hyderabad Shahr

KM# 10.3 FALUS

Copper **Rev. Inscription:** "Dar-us-Sultanat" **Note:** Weight varies: 17.50-18.00 grams. Size varies: 20-24 millimeters.

Date	Mintage	Good	VG	F	VF	XF
AH1025 (1616)	—	30.00	75.00	150	250	—

Abdullah

AH1035-1083/1626-1672AD

NAMED COINAGE

Hyderabad

KM# 12.1 1/2 FALUS

6.5000 g., Copper, 16 mm. **Obv:** King's name, "Sultan Badshah Ghazi"; eight-foil lozenge in center **Rev:** Mint name, eight-foil lozenge in center **Rev. Inscription:** "Dar-us-Sultanat"

Date	Mintage	Good	VG	F	VF	XF
ND(1626-72)	—	6.00	15.00	30.00	50.00	—

Hyderabad

KM# 12.2 2/3 FALUS

Copper **Rev. Inscription:** "Dar-us-Sultanat" **Note:** Weight varies: 8.40-9.20 grams. Size varies: 16-18 milimeters.

Date	Mintage	Good	VG	F	VF	XF
ND(1626-72)	—	6.00	15.00	30.00	50.00	—

Hyderabad

KM# 14.2 2/3 FALUS

Copper **Obv:** King's name, "Sultan Badshah Ghazi" **Rev. Inscription:** "Dar-us-Sultanat" **Note:** Weight varies: 7.00-8.00 grams. Size varies: 16-18 milimeters.

Date	Mintage	Good	VG	F	VF	XF
ND(1626-72)	—	3.60	9.00	18.00	30.00	—

Hyderabad

KM# 12.3 FALUS

Copper **Rev. Inscription:** "Dar-us-Sultanat" **Note:** Weight varies: 12.80-13.60 grams. Size varies: 20-22 milimeters.

Date	Mintage	Good	VG	F	VF	XF
ND(1626-72)	—	5.20	13.50	27.00	45.00	—

Hyderabad

KM# 14.3 FALUS

Copper, 18-20 mm. **Rev. Inscription:** "Dar-us-Sultanat" **Note:** Weight varies: 11.00-12.00 grams.

Date	Mintage	Good	VG	F	VF	XF
ND(1626-72)	—	2.40	6.00	12.00	20.00	—

Hyderabad

KM# 12.4 DOUBLE FALUS

24.0000 g., Copper, 26 mm. **Rev. Inscription:** "Dar-us-Sultanat"

Date	Mintage	Good	VG	F	VF	XF
ND(1626-72)	—	30.00	75.00	150	250	—

ANONYMOUS COINAGE

Hyderabad

KM# 16.1 1/3 FALUS

3.0000 g., Copper, 15 mm. **Obv:** Persian legend **Obv. Inscription:** "It has ended peacefully and auspiciously" **Rev:** Mint name

Date	Mintage	Good	VG	F	VF	XF
ND(1626-72)	—	9.00	22.50	45.00	75.00	—

Hyderabad

KM# 16.2 2/3 FALUS

Copper **Note:** Weight varies: 7.40-8.20 grams. Size varies: 16-18 milimeters.

Date	Mintage	Good	VG	F	VF	XF
ND(1626-72)	—	6.00	15.00	30.00	50.00	—

Hyderabad

KM# 18.3 2/3 FALUS

Copper **Note:** Struck at Hyderabad. Weight varies: 6.00-7.40 grams. Size varies: 16-19 milimeters.

Date	Mintage	Good	VG	F	VF	XF
AH1068 (1657)	—	1.80	4.50	9.00	15.00	—

Hyderabad

KM# 16.3 FALUS

Copper **Note:** Weight varies: 11.00-12.20 grams. Size varies: 18-21 milimeters.

Date	Mintage	Good	VG	F	VF	XF
ND(1626-72)	—	4.80	12.00	24.00	40.00	—

Hyderabad

KM# 18.4 FALUS

Copper **Note:** Weight varies: 10.30-11.00 grams. Size varies: 19-22 milimeters.

Date	Mintage	Good	VG	F	VF	XF
AH1068	—	1.50	3.75	7.50	12.50	—
AH1028 Error	—	3.00	7.50	15.00	25.00	—

Muhammadnagar

KM# 20.1 FALUS

Copper, 21 mm. **Obv:** "Sultan Abdullah Badshah" **Rev:** Mint name **Note:** Weight varies: 10.60-10.70 grams.

Date	Mintage	Good	VG	F	VF	XF
ND(1626-72)	—	12.00	30.00	60.00	100	—

Abu'l Hasan

AH1083-1098/1672-1686AD

ANONYMOUS COINAGE

Hyderabad

KM# 22.2 2/3 FALUS

Copper **Obv:** Date, Persian legend **Obv. Legend:** "It has ended peacefully and auspiciously" **Rev:** Mint name **Rev. Inscription:** "Dar-us-Sultanat" **Note:** Weight varies: 6.70-7.00 grams. Size varies: 15-18 milimeters.

Date	Mintage	Good	VG	F	VF	XF
AH1095 (1683)	—	4.00	10.00	20.00	35.00	—

Hyderabad

KM# 22.3 FALUS

Copper **Rev. Inscription:** "Dar-us-Sultanat" **Note:** Weight varies: 10.00-11.00 grams. Size varies: 18-22 milimeters.

Date	Mintage	Good	VG	F	VF	XF
AH1095 (1683)	—	3.60	9.00	18.00	30.00	—

JAINTIAPUR

The territory ruled over by the Jaintia Rajas consisted of the Jaintia Hills, and a section of the adjoining plains to the north of Sylhet.

In the Cooch Behar chronicle it is recorded that when Nara Narayan defeated the Jaintia Raja about 1564AD, one of the conditions imposed on the defeated monarch was that he should never put his own name on his coins, but only that of his capital city. Whether this is the true reason is open to debate, but virtually all the coins of Jaintiapur are anonymous, and merely bear the accession year of the ruler during whose reign they were issued.

The earliest known coins of Jaintiapur are dated 1633AD, and are clearly copied in general design and weight standard from the coins of Cooch Behar. During the 18th century the right to strike coins was sold by the Raja to the highest bidder, and this resulted in a serious debasement of the coinage, which therefore never circulated outside the confines of the State.

Independence was retained until 1835AD, when the administration was finally taken over by the British.

RULERS

Local traditions have preserved the names of the Jaintia Kings since the kingdom was founded, but few reliable dated are known for the early Kings.

Dhan Manik, c1602
Jasa Manik, c1606/18
Sundar Ray, or
Chota Parbat Ray, SE1555-1569/1633-1647AD
Jasamanta Ray, SE1569-1582/1647-1660AD
Ban Simha, SE1582-1591/1660-1669AD
Pratap Simha, SE1591-1592/1669-1670AD
Lakshmi Narayan, SE1592-1625/1670-1703AD

KINGDOM

Sundar Ray or Chota Parbat Ray

SE1555-1569 / 1633-1647AD

HAMMERED COINAGE

Anonymous

Without Mint Name

KM# 100 RUPEE

9.2000 g., Silver

Date	Mintage	Good	VG	F	VF	XF
SE1555	—	65.00	165	330	550	775

Ban Simha

SE1582-1591 / 1660-1669 AD

HAMMERED COINAGE

Anonymous

Without Mint Name

KM# 120 RUPEE

9.2000 g., Silver

Date	Mintage	Good	VG	F	VF	XF
SE1582	—	65.00	165	330	550	775

Pratap Simha

SE1591-1592 / 1669-1670 AD

HAMMERED COINAGE

Anonymous

Without Mint Name

KM# 130 RUPEE

9.2000 g., Silver

Date	Mintage	Good	VG	F	VF	XF
SE1591	—	80.00	200	400	650	925

Lakshmi Narayan

SE1592-1625 / 1670-1703AD

HAMMERED COINAGE

Anonymous

Without Mint Name

KM# 140 RUPEE

9.2000 g., Silver

Date	Mintage	Good	VG	F	VF	XF
SE1592	—	32.00	80.00	160	250	360

KACHAR

The Kacharis are probably the original inhabitants of the Assam Valley, and in the 13th century ruled much of the south bank of the Brahmaputra from their capital at Dimapur.

Around 1530 the Ahoms inflicted several crushing defeats on the Kacharis, Dimapur was sacked, and the Kacharis were forced to retreat further south and set up a new capital at Maibong.

Very little is known about this obscure state, and the only time that coins were struck in any quantity was during the late 16th and early 17th centuries. One coin, indeed, proudly announces the conquest of Sylhet, but the military prowess seems to have been short lived, and the small kingdom was only saved from Muslim domination by its isolation and lack of economic worth.

A few coins were struck during the 18th and 19th centuries, but this was probably merely as a demonstration of independence, rather than for any economic reason.

In 1819, the last Kachari ruler, Govind Chandra was ousted by the Manipuri ruler Chaurajit Simha, and during the Burmese occupation of Manipur and Assam, the Manipuris remained in control of Kachar. In 1824, Govind Chandra was restored to his throne by the British, and ruled under British suzerainty. By all accounts his administration was not a success, and in 1832, soon after Govind Chandra had been murdered, the British took over the administration of the State in "compliance with the frequent and earnestly expressed wishes of the people.

The earliest coins of Kachar were clearly copied from the contemporary coins of Cooch Behar, with weight standard also copied from the Bengali standard. The flans are, however, even broader than those of the Cooch Behar coins, making the coins very distinctive.

A number of spectacular gold and silver coins, purporting to come from Kachar, appeared in Calcutta during the 1960's, but as their authenticity has been doubted, they have been omitted from this listing.

RULERS

A list of the Kings of Kachar has been preserved in local traditions, but is rather unreliable. The following list has been compiled from this traditional list, together with names and dates obtained from other sources, but may not be completely accurate.

Yaso Narayan, SE1505-1523/1583-1601AD
Pratap Narayan, SE1523-1533/1601-after 1611AD
Nar Narayan, SEc.1537/c.1615AD
Bhim Darpa, SEc.1540/c.1618AD
Indra Ballabh, SEc.1550/c.1628AD
Bir Darpa, SEc.1566-1603/c.1644-1681AD
Garur Dhvaja, SE1603-1617/1681-1695AD
Makar Dhvaja, SE1617-/1695-AD
Udayaditya, SEc.1622/c.1700AD
Tamradhvaja, SEc.1622-1630/c.1700-1708AD

KINGDOM

Pratap Narayan

SE1523-1533 / 1601-1611AD

HAMMERED COINAGE

Without Mint Name

KM# 114 1/4 RUPEE

Silver **Note:** Varieties exist.

Date	Mintage	Good	VG	F	VF	XF
ND(1601-11) (1601)	—	100	250	500	800	1,150

Without Mint Name

KM# 116 RUPEE

Silver

Date	Mintage	Good	VG	F	VF	XF
SE1523 (1601)	—	180	450	900	1,500	2,100

Without Mint Name

KM# 117 RUPEE

Silver **Subject:** Victory over Sylhet

Date	Mintage	Good	VG	F	VF	XF
SE1524 (1602)	—	120	300	600	1,000	1,450

Without Mint Name

KM# 122 MOHUR

Gold **Note:** Similar to 1 Rupee, KM#117.

Date	Mintage	Good	VG	F	VF	XF
SE1524 (1602)	—	—	—	—	—	—

Note: Reported, not confirmed

Bir Darpa

SE1566-1603 / 1644-1681AD

HAMMERED COINAGE

Without Mint Name

KM# 127 1/4 RUPEE

Silver

Date	Mintage	Good	VG	F	VF	XF
ND(1644-81) (1644)	—	100	250	500	850	1,200

Without Mint Name

KM# 130 MOHUR

Gold

Date	Mintage	Good	VG	F	VF	XF
SE1565 (1644)	—	—	—	2,400	3,500	5,000

Tamradhvaja

SE c.1622-1630 / c.1700-1708AD

HAMMERED COINAGE

Without Mint Name

KM# 132 1/4 RUPEE

Silver **Obv:** Inscription within circle **Rev:** Inscription within circle

Date	Mintage	Good	VG	F	VF	XF
ND(ca.1700-08)	—	120	300	600	1,000	1,450

KUTCH

State located in northwest India, consisting of a peninsula north of the Gulf of Kutch.

The rulers of Kutch were Jareja Rajputs who, coming from Tatta in Sind, conquered Kutch in the 14th or 15th centuries. The capital city of Bhuj is thought to date from the mid-16th century. In 1617, after Akbar's conquest of Gujerat and the fall of the Gujerat sultans, the Kutch ruler, Rao Bharmal I (1586-1632) visited Jahangir and established a relationship which was sufficiently warm as to leave Kutch virtually independent throughout the Mughal period. Early in the 19th century internal disorder and the existence of rival claimants to the throne resulted in British intrusion into the state's affairs. Rao Bharmalji II was deposed in favor of Rao Desalji II who proved much more amenable to the Government of India's wishes. He and his successors continued to rule in a manner considered by the British to be most enlightened and, as a result, Maharao Khengarji III was created a Knight Grand Commander of the Indian Empire. In view of its geographical isolation Kutch came under the direct control of the Central Government at India's independence.

First coinage was struck in 1617AD.

RULERS

राउ श्री भारमलजी

Raos
Bharmalji I, 1586-1632AD

राउ श्री भाराजी

Ra-o Sri Bha-ra-jl
Bhorajji, 1632-1645AD

राउ श्री षंगार जी

Ra-o Sri Bho-j-ji
Khengarji II, 1645-1654AD

राउ श्री तमाची जी

Ra-o Sri Shen-ga-r-ji
Tamachiji

राउ श्री राय धणजी

Ra-o Sri T(a)-ma-chi-ji
Rayadhanji I, 1666-1698AD

राउ श्री प्रागजी

Ra-o Sri Ra-y(a)-dh(a)-n-ji
Pragmalji I, 1698-1715AD

MINT

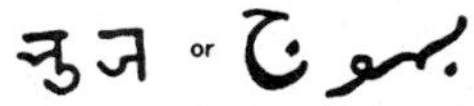

Bhuj (Devanagari) (Persian)

MONETARY SYSTEM

1/2 Trambiyo = 1 Babukiya
2 Tramiyo = 1 Dokda
3 Trambiyo = 1 Dhinglo
2 Dhinglo = 1 Dhabu
2 Dhabu = 1 Payalo
2 Payalo = 1 Adlinao
2 Adlina = 1 Kori

NOTE: All coins through Bharmalji II bear a common type, derived from the Gujarati coinage of Muzaffar III (late 16th century AD), and bear a stylized form of the date AH978 (1570AD). The silver issues of Bharmalji II also have the fictitious date AH1165. The rulers name appears in the Devanagri script on the obverse.

NOTE: Br#'s are in reference to *Coinage of Kutch* by Richard K. Bright.

KINGDOM

Bhorajji (Bhojraji)
AH1042-1055 / 1632-1645AD

HAMMERED COINAGE

Without Mint Name

KM# 9 DOKDO
Copper **Note:** Br.#7.

Date	Mintage	Good	VG	F	VF	XF
ND(1632-45)	—	—	25.00	35.00	50.00	70.00

Without Mint Name

KM# 10 DHINGLO
12.0000 g., Copper **Rev:** Inscription in Nagari below **Rev. Inscription:** "Rao Sri Bharaji" **Note:** Br.#8.

Date	Mintage	Good	VG	F	VF	XF
ND(1632-45)	—	4.80	12.00	24.00	40.00	—

Without Mint Name

KM# 11 1/2 KORI
2.5000 g., Silver **Obv:** Katar **Rev:** Trident, inscription in Nagari **Rev. Inscription:** "Rao Sri Bhojji" **Note:** Br.#9.

Date	Mintage	Good	VG	F	VF	XF
ND(1632-45)	—	3.60	12.00	27.00	54.00	90.00

Without Mint Name

KM# 12 KORI
4.5500 g., Silver **Note:** Br.#10.

Date	Mintage	Good	VG	F	VF	XF
AH978 Frozen date	—	3.00	7.20	18.00	36.00	60.00

Khengarji II
AH1055-1065 / 1645-1654AD

HAMMERED COINAGE

Without Mint Name

KM# 14 1/2 TRAMBIYO
1.1000 g., Copper **Obv:** Katar **Rev:** Trident, inscription in Nagari **Rev. Inscription:** "Rao Sri Shengarji" **Note:** Br.#A11. Size varies: 8-9 millimeters.

Date	Mintage	Good	VG	F	VF	XF
ND(1645-54)	—	2.40	8.00	20.00	40.00	—

Without Mint Name

KM# 16 DOKDO
9.2000 g., Copper **Note:** Br.#12.

Date	Mintage	Good	VG	F	VF	XF
ND(1645-54)	—	2.75	9.00	22.50	45.00	—

Without Mint Name

KM# 18 1/4 KORI
1.1000 g., Silver **Obv:** Katar **Rev:** Trident, inscription in Nagari **Rev. Inscription:** "Rao Sri Shengarji" **Note:** Br.#A14. Size varies: 8-10 millimeters.

Date	Mintage	Good	VG	F	VF	XF
ND(1645-54)	—	12.00	30.00	75.00	150	250

Without Mint Name

KM# 19 1/2 KORI
2.5000 g., Silver, 12.7 mm. **Obv:** Katar **Rev:** Trident, "Rao Sri Shengarji" in Nagari **Note:** Br.#14.

Date	Mintage	Good	VG	F	VF	XF
ND(1645-54)	—	4.50	15.00	37.50	75.00	125

Without Mint Name

KM# 20 KORI
4.5500 g., Silver **Note:** Br.#15.

Date	Mintage	Good	VG	F	VF	XF
AH(9)78 Frozen date	—	3.00	9.00	22.50	45.00	75.00

Tamachiji
AH1066-1077 / 1655-1666AD

HAMMERED COINAGE

Without Mint Name

KM# 24 DOKDO
8.6000 g., Copper **Note:** Br.#17.

Date	Mintage	Good	VG	F	VF	XF
ND(1655-66)	—	3.00	10.00	25.00	50.00	—

Without Mint Name

KM# 26 1/4 KORI
1.2000 g., Silver **Obv:** Katar **Rev:** Inscription in Nagari **Rev. Inscription:** "Rao Sri Tmachiji" **Note:** Br.#A19. Size varies: 8-10 millimeters.

Date	Mintage	Good	VG	F	VF	XF
ND(1655-66)	—	6.00	20.00	50.00	100	165

Without Mint Name

KM# 27 1/2 KORI
2.1300 g., Silver, 11.9 mm. **Obv:** Katar **Rev:** Inscription in Nagari **Rev. Inscription:** "Rao Sri Tmachiji" **Note:** Br.#19.

Date	Mintage	Good	VG	F	VF	XF
ND(1655-66)	—	4.50	14.50	36.00	72.00	120

Without Mint Name

KM# 28 KORI
4.4000 g., Silver **Note:** Br.#20.

Date	Mintage	Good	VG	F	VF	XF
AH(9)78 Frozen date	—	3.00	10.00	25.00	50.00	85.00

Rayadhanji I
AH1077-1110 / 1666-98AD

HAMMERED COINAGE

Without Mint Name

KM# 31 TRAMBIYO
4.2000 g., Copper, 14 mm. **Obv:** Katar **Rev:** Inscription in Nagari **Rev. Inscription:** "Rao Sri Raydhnji" **Note:** Br.#21.

Date	Mintage	Good	VG	F	VF	XF
ND(1666-98)	—	3.60	9.00	18.00	30.00	—

Without Mint Name

KM# 32 DOKDO
8.0000 g., Copper **Note:** Br.#22.

Date	Mintage	Good	VG	F	VF	XF
ND(1666-98)	—	3.60	9.00	18.00	30.00	—

Without Mint Name

KM# 33 DHINGLO
Copper, 22 mm. **Obv:** Katar **Rev:** Inscription in Nagari **Rev. Inscription:** "Rao Sri Raydhnji" **Note:** Br.#23. Weight varies: 12.00-12.50 grams.

Date	Mintage	Good	VG	F	VF	XF
ND(1666-98)	—	2.40	6.00	12.00	20.00	—

Without Mint Name

KM# 35 1/2 KORI
2.2000 g., Silver **Note:** Br.#24.

Date	Mintage	Good	VG	F	VF	XF
ND(1666-98)	—	3.60	12.00	30.00	60.00	100

Without Mint Name

KM# 36 KORI
4.5500 g., Silver, 15 mm. **Obv:** Katar **Rev:** Inscription in Nagari **Rev. Inscription:** "Rao Sri Raydhnji" **Note:** Br.#25.

Date	Mintage	Good	VG	F	VF	XF
AH(9)78 Frozen date	—	3.00	6.00	15.00	30.00	50.00

Pragmalji I
AH1110-1127 / 1698-1715AD

HAMMERED COINAGE

Without Mint Name

KM# 39 DOKDO
Copper **Obv:** Inscription, date **Rev:** Inscription **Note:** Br.#27.

Date	Mintage	Good	VG	F	VF	XF
ND(1698-1715)	—	1.20	4.00	10.00	20.00	—

Without Mint Name

KM# 40 DHINGLO
11.8000 g., Copper **Obv:** Inscription **Rev:** Inscription, scissors **Note:** Br.#28.

Date	Mintage	Good	VG	F	VF	XF
ND(1698-1715)	—	1.50	5.00	12.50	25.00	—

Without Mint Name

KM# 43 KORI
4.5000 g., Silver **Obv:** Inscription, date **Rev:** Inscription **Note:** Br.#30.

Date	Mintage	Good	VG	F	VF	XF
AH(9)78 Frozen	—	3.00	8.00	20.00	40.00	65.00

Gohadaji I
AH1127-1132 / 1715-1719AD

HAMMERED COINAGE

Without Mint Name

KM# 45 KORI
4.5000 g., Silver, 15 mm. **Obv:** Inscription, trident **Rev. Inscription:** Rao Sri Gohodji (Nagari in small characters) **Note:** Br.#35.

Date	Mintage	Good	VG	F	VF	XF
AH978 Frozen; Rare	—	—	—	—	—	—

MADURAI

Nayakas

Located in South India approximately 180 miles north of the southernmost tip. It is noted for its great temple with colonnades and nine massive gate towers (gopuras) adorned with elaborate carvings and enclosing a quadrangle, the "Tank of the Golden Lilies". It was the capital of the Pandya dynasty from 5th century B.C. to the end of the 11th century A.D. It came under Vijayanagar control in the 14th century A.D.; and then under the Nayak dynasty from about the middle of the 16th century to 1735AD when it was taken by the Nawab of the Carnatic. Later, in 1801, it came under the rule of the British East India Company.

KINGDOM

HAMMERED COINAGE

Without Mint Name

KM# 2 KASU

Copper **Obv:** Inscription in two lines **Obv. Inscription:** "Tiru Vengala" **Rev:** Inscription in two lines **Rev. Inscription:** "Mudu Krishna" **Note:** Struck in the name of Muttu Krishnappa Nayaka.

Date	Mintage	Good	VG	F	VF	XF
ND(1601-09)	—	0.75	2.50	6.00	12.00	—

Without Mint Name

KM# 1 KASU

Copper **Obv:** Venkatesvara standing, altar at left, banner to right **Rev. Inscription:** "Vemkatapa" **Note:** Struck in the name of Venkata(pati)raya (Vi jayanagar).

Date	Mintage	Good	VG	F	VF	XF
ND(1630-41)	—	0.75	2.50	6.00	12.00	—

MARATHA CONFEDERACY

INDEPENDENT KINGDOM

Aurangzeb Alamgir

AH1068-1119 / 1658-1707AD

HAMMERED COINAGE

Nipani

KM# 200 1/4 RUPEE

Silver **Obv. Inscription:** Aurangzeb Alamgir **Note:** Weight varies: 2.68-2.90 grams.

Date	Mintage	VG	F	VF	XF	Unc
ND(1658-1707)	—	22.50	37.50	75.00	120	—

Chikodi

KM# 95 1/2 RUPEE

Silver **Obv. Inscription:** Mughal Emperor Aurangzeb **Note:** Weight varies 5.35-5.80 grams.

Date	Mintage	VG	F	VF	XF	Unc
ND(1658-1707)	—	16.50	27.50	45.00	75.00	—

Nipani

KM# 201 1/2 RUPEE

Silver, 17-18 mm. **Obv. Inscription:** Aurangzeb Alamgir **Note:** Size varies. Weight varies: 5.35-5.80 grams.

Date	Mintage	VG	F	VF	XF	Unc
ND(1658-1707)	—	22.50	37.50	75.00	120	—

Chikodi

KM# 96 RUPEE

Silver **Obv. Inscription:** Mughal Emperor Aurangzeb **Note:** Weight varies: 10.70-11.60 grams.

Date	Mintage	VG	F	VF	XF	Unc
ND(1658-1707)	—	23.50	40.00	65.00	110	—

Nipani

KM# 202 RUPEE

Silver, 23-24 mm. **Obv. Inscription:** Aurangzeb Alamgir **Note:** Size varies. Weight varies: 10.70-11.60 grams.

Date	Mintage	VG	F	VF	XF	Unc
ND(1658-1707)	—	28.00	50.00	80.00	130	—

TRIPURA

Hill Tipperah

Tripura was a Hindu Kingdom consisting of a strip of the fertile plains east of Bengal, and a large tract of hill territory beyond, which had a reputation for providing wild elephants.

At times when Bengal was weak, Tripura rose to prominence and extended its rule into the plains, but when Bengal was strong the kingdom consisted purely of the hill area, which was virtually impregnable and not of enough economic worth to encourage the Muslims to conquer it. In this way Tripura was able to maintain its full independence until the 19th century.

The origins of the Kingdom are veiled in legend, but the first coins were struck during the reign of Ratna Manikya (1464-89) and copied the weight and fabric of the contemporary issues of the Sultans of Bengal. He also copied the lion design that had appeared on certain rare tangkas of Nasir-ud-din Mahmud Shah I dated AH849 (1445AD). In other respects the designs were purely Hindu, and the lion was retained on most of the later issues as a national emblem.

Tripura rose to a political zenith during the 16th century, while Muslim rule in Bengal was weak, and several coins were struck to commemorate successful military campaigns from Chittagong in the south to Sylhetin the north. These conquests were not sustained, and in the early 17th century the Mughal army was able to inflict severe defeats on Tripura, which was forced to pay tribute.

In about 1733AD all the territory in the plains was annexed by the Mughals, and the Raja merely managed his estate there as a zemindar, although he still retained control as independent King of his hill territory.

The situation remained unchanged when the British took over the administration of Bengal in 1765, and it was only in 1871 that the British appointed an agent in the hills, and began to assist the Maharaja in the administration of his hill territory, which became known as the State of Hill Tipperah.

After the middle of the 18th century, coins were not struck for monetary reasons, but merely for ceremonial use at coronations and other ceremonies, and to keep up the treasured right of coinage.

The coins of Tripura are unusual in that the majority have the name of the King together with that of his Queen, and is the only coinage in the world where this was done consistently.

In common with most other Hindu coinages of northeast India, the coins bear fixed dates. Usually the date used was that of the coronation ceremony, but during the 16th century, coins which were struck with a design commemorating a particular event, bore the date of that event, which can be useful as a historical source, where other written evidence is virtually non-existent.

All modern Tripura coins were presentation pieces, more medallic than monetary in nature. They were struck in very limited numbers and although not intended for local circulation as money, they are often encountered in worn condition.

RULERS

Yaso Manikya

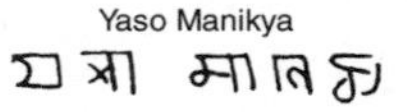

Sec1521-22, c1522-48/
C1599-1600, c1600-26AD
Queens of Yaso Manikya
Queen Lakshmi
Queen Gauri

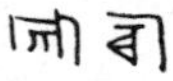

Isvara Manikya
Sec1522/c1600AD

Kalyana Manikya
Sec1548-82/c1626-60AD
Queen of Kalyana Manikya
Queen Kalavati

Govinda Manikya

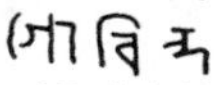

Queen of Govinda Manikya
Queen Gunavati

Chattra Manikya
Sec1583-89/c1661-67AD

Rama Manikya

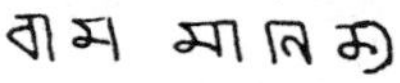

Sec1598-1603/c1676-81AD
Queen of Rama Manikya
Queen Ratnavati

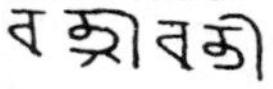

Ratna Manikya II

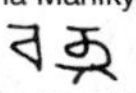

Sec1607-15, c1617-34/
1685-93, c1695-1712AD
Queens of Ratna Manikya II
Queen Satyavati
Queen Bhagavati

Narendra Manikya
Sec1615-1617/c1693-1695AD

DATING

While the early coinage is dated in the Saka Era (SE) the later issues are dated in the Tripurabda era (TE). To convert, TE date plus 590 = AD date. The dates appear to be accession years.

KINGDOM

Dharma Manikya with Selim

SE1523 / 1601AD

HAMMERED COINAGE

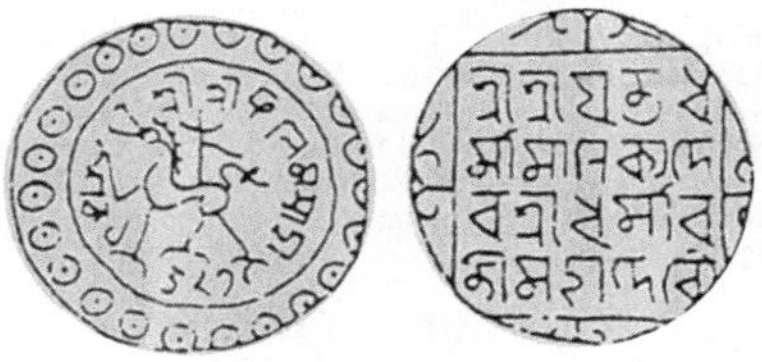

Without Mint Name

KM# 118 TANKA

Silver

Date	Mintage	VG	F	VF	XF	Unc
SEca1523 (1601)	—	300	500	850	1,400	—

Kalyana Manikya

SEc.1548-1582 / c.1626-1660AD

HAMMERED COINAGE

Without Mint Name

KM# 122 1/4 RUPEE

2.6000 g., Silver

Date	Mintage	VG	F	VF	XF	Unc
SE1548 (1626)	—	100	200	400	650	—

Without Mint Name

KM# 123 1/2 RUPEE

5.2000 g., Silver

Date	Mintage	VG	F	VF	XF	Unc
SE1548 (1626)	—	100	200	400	650	—

Without Mint Name

KM# 124 RUPEE

10.5000 g., Silver

Date	Mintage	VG	F	VF	XF	Unc
SE1548 (1626)	—	110	180	300	500	—

Without Mint Name

KM# 127 MOHUR

Gold

Date	Mintage	VG	F	VF	XF	Unc
SE1548 (1626) Rare	—	—	—	—	—	—

Govinda Manikya

SE c.1582, 1589-1598 / c.1660, 1667-1676AD

HAMMERED COINAGE

Without Mint Name

KM# 130 1/16 RUPEE
Silver **Obv:** Lion left

Date	Mintage	VG	F	VF	XF	Unc
ND(1660) (1660)	—	150	250	400	650	—

Without Mint Name

KM# 131 1/8 RUPEE
1.3000 g., Silver **Obv:** Lion left

Date	Mintage	VG	F	VF	XF	Unc
ND (1660)	—	50.00	85.00	140	220	—

Without Mint Name

KM# 132 1/8 RUPEE
1.3000 g., Silver **Obv:** Lion left

Date	Mintage	VG	F	VF	XF	Unc
ND (1660)	—	45.00	75.00	120	200	—

Without Mint Name

KM# 133 1/4 RUPEE
2.6000 g., Silver

Date	Mintage	VG	F	VF	XF	Unc
SE1582 (1660)	—	45.00	75.00	120	200	—

Without Mint Name

KM# 135 RUPEE
10.5000 g., Silver **Rev. Legend:** "Queen Gunavati..."

Date	Mintage	VG	F	VF	XF	Unc
SE1582 (1660)	—	220	360	600	1,000	—

Chattra Manikya

SEc1583-1589 / c 1661-1667AD

HAMMERED COINAGE

Without Mint Name

KM# 143 1/4 RUPEE
2.6000 g., Silver

Date	Mintage	VG	F	VF	XF	Unc
SE1583 (1661)	—	180	300	500	800	—

Without Mint Name

KM# 145 RUPEE
10.5000 g., Silver **Rev:** Inscription without Queen's name

Date	Mintage	VG	F	VF	XF	Unc
SE1583 (1661)	—	220	360	600	1,000	—

Rama Manikya

SEc.1598-1603 / c.1676-1681AD

HAMMERED COINAGE

Without Mint Name

KM# 153 1/4 RUPEE
2.6000 g., Silver

Date	Mintage	VG	F	VF	XF	Unc
SE1598 (1676)	—	70.00	120	200	320	—

Without Mint Name

KM# 155 RUPEE
10.5000 g., Silver **Rev. Inscription:** *Srimati Ratnavati Maha Devi*

Date	Mintage	VG	F	VF	XF	Unc
SE1598 (1676)	—	130	220	360	600	—

Without Mint Name

KM# 158 MOHUR
10.5000 g., Gold

Date	Mintage	VG	F	VF	XF	Unc
SE1598 (1676)	—	—	3,200	5,000	7,500	—

Ratna Manikya II

SE1607-1615 / c.1695-1712AD

HAMMERED COINAGE

Without Mint Name

KM# 161 1/16 RUPEE
0.6500 g., Silver

Date	Mintage	VG	F	VF	XF	Unc
ND (1681)	—	75.00	120	200	350	—

Without Mint Name

KM# 164 1/4 RUPEE
2.6000 g., Silver

Date	Mintage	VG	F	VF	XF	Unc
SE1607 (1685)	—	75.00	120	200	350	—

Without Mint Name

KM# 166 RUPEE
10.5000 g., Silver **Rev:** Inscription without Queen's name

Date	Mintage	VG	F	VF	XF	Unc
SE1607 (1685)	—	110	180	300	500	—

Without Mint Name

KM# 167 RUPEE
10.5000 g., Silver **Rev. Legend:** "Queen Satyavati..."

Date	Mintage	VG	F	VF	XF	Unc
SE1607 (1685)	—	150	240	400	600	—

Without Mint Name

KM# 168 RUPEE
10.5000 g., Silver **Rev. Legend:** "Queen Bhagyavati..."

Date	Mintage	VG	F	VF	XF	Unc
SE1607 (1685)	—	360	600	1,000	1,700	—

Without Mint Name

KM# 162 1/16 MOHUR
0.6500 g., Gold

Date	Mintage	VG	F	VF	XF	Unc
ND (1685)	—	—	1,000	1,600	2,500	—

Narendra Manikya

SEc.1615-1617 / c.1693-1695AD

HAMMERED COINAGE

Without Mint Name

KM# 175 1/8 RUPEE
Silver

Date	Mintage	VG	F	VF	XF	Unc
(1692)	—	270	450	750	1,200	—

Without Mint Name

KM# 178 RUPEE
10.5000 g., Silver

Date	Mintage	VG	F	VF	XF	Unc
SE1615 (1693)	—	325	550	900	1,500	—

Without Mint Name

KM# 180 MOHUR
10.0000 g., Gold

Date	Mintage	VG	F	VF	XF	Unc
SE1615 (1693)	—	—	3,200	5,000	7,500	—

VIJAYANAGAR

The Vijayanagar kingdom was founded by two brothers, Harihari and Bukka, from the Telangana region of present day Andhra Pradesh in East Central India. They had previously served the raja of Warangal until they were captured and transported to Delhi where they were reputed to have become converts to Islam. They then revolted and, returning to the Hindu fold, in 1336 founded the kingdom as a bulwark against further Muslim inroads into the South. Vijayanagar (literally, City of Victory) grew into the most remarkable of all the medieval Hindu kingdoms. Some 19 square miles in area, Vijayanage itself - the capital after which the empire was named – sat on the southern bank of the Kristna river, not far from modern Hospet in Mysore State. Contemporary observers compared the city both in size and stature to ancient Rome.

Even to this day, the ruins of this remarkable capital are among the most impressive anywhere in India. Resplendent with intricate stone carving, fine temples and broad public ways, it was a city whose wealth knew no equal in South or Central India. Its sovereignty extended over virtually the whole of South India. The rulers, or rayas, of Vijayanagar were patrons of the arts and under their authority art, architecture and literature flourished. Its Hinduism was eclectic, Vaishnavite in sentiment and vibrant in expression. It was a wealthy city, whose vices were the vices of the rich. Its coinage was predominantly in gold and, like its culture, distinctly South Indian in style.

After the period of the 2 chiefs Harihari (1336-1354) and Bukka (1354-1377), Vijayanagar history fell into 4 periods, viz., the Sangama dynasty (1377-1485), the Saluva dynasty (1486-ca.1503), the Tuluva dynasty(ca. 1503-1570), and the Aravidu (or Karnata) dynasty (1570-ca. 1646). For over 2 centuries the Vijayanagar kingdom was more or less in a constant state of war against the Bahmanis and their successor sultanates in the Deccan. And for those two hundred years Vijayanagar effectively halted Muslim attempts to encroach southwards. This was the empire's golden age as Vijayanagar grew to be the one real center in India for Hindu self-expression within a context of political self-determination. Vassal to none, Vijayanagar held the south of India as a constant rebuke to Muslim expansionism.

Then, in 1565, disaster struck. The sultanates of Ahmadnagar, Bijapur, Bidar and Golkonda combined forces to bring about the destruction of Vijayanagar. Vijayanagar was well equipped for this confrontation, putting perhaps as many as a million men on the field. But, by one of those quirks in the fortunes of war, the Vijayanagar commander, Ramaraja (who was also the regent and controlling noble of the kingdom), was cut off from his troops, dragged down from his elephant, and at once beheaded. His army immediately panicked and their strategy fell apart. This battle, remembered as the battle of Talikota, was followed by a complete rout of the forces of Vijayanagar and by the plunder and destruction of their capital city.

The nominal king, in whose place Ramaraja had ruled, fled to Penukonda. There on this rocky hill further south he re-established the dynasty. Five years later he was overthrown by Tirumala, his brother, and the Karnata dynasty was inaugurated. A few years later the capital was shifted to Chandragiri, under Venkata I. Here, for a while, the truncated kingdom seemed to regain some of its lost vigor. But after Venkata's death even this dynasty disintegrated and the remnants of this once-proud empire were reduced to the status of local chiefs. Yet, in spite of Muslim encroachment into the Deccan, first by the Adil Shahis of Bijapur and the Qutb Shahis of Golkonda, and by the Mughal armies under Aurangzeb, these chieftains continued to exercise a considerable degree of local independence.

But Vijayanagar was gone, and in its passing the brightest star of Hindu art, architecture, philosophy and culture was extinguished. Never again would there rise a Hindu kingdom comparable to Vijayanagar, and never again until Indian Independence, would South India be so free of foreign domination.

RULERS

Aravidu Dynasty

वेंकटराय

Venkata(pati)raya II,
1586-1614AD

रगराय

Rama Devaraya II,
1614-1630AD

वेंकटराय

Venkata(pati)raya III,
1630-1641AD

Rama Deva Raya III,
1642-1649; 1679AD

KINGDOM

ANONYMOUS HAMMERED COINAGE

1642-1757AD

Without Mint Name

KM# 8 PAGODA

3.4000 g., Gold **Obv:** Venkatesvara kneeling **Note:** Uniface.

Date	Mintage	VG	F	VF	XF	Unc
ND	—	—	—	—	240	265

Without Mint Name

KM# 9 PAGODA

3.4000 g., Gold **Obv:** Sri-devi Venkatesvara and Bhu-devi standing

Date	Mintage	VG	F	VF	XF	Unc
ND	—	—	—	—	240	265

Rama Devaraya II

HAMMERED COINAGE

Without Mint Name

KM# 5 DAM

3.5000 g., Copper **Obv:** Elephant left **Rev:** Inscription in three lines **Rev. Inscription:** "Sri Chalama Rama"

Date	Mintage	Good	VG	F	VF	XF
ND(1614-30)	—	6.00	15.00	30.00	50.00	—

Venkata(pati)raya III

HAMMERED COINAGE

Without Mint Name

KM# 6 DAM

3.5000 g., Copper **Obv:** Two animals **Rev:** Inscription in two lines **Rev. Inscription:** "Chalama Venkata"

Date	Mintage	Good	VG	F	VF	XF
ND(1630-41)	—	7.20	18.00	36.00	60.00	—

Without Mint Name

KM# 7 1/2 PAGODA

1.7000 g., Gold **Obv:** Venkatesvara standing in archway **Rev:** Inscription in three lines **Rev. Inscription:** "Sri Venkatesvara Yanamah"

Date	Mintage	Good	VG	F	VF	XF
ND(1630-41)	—	—	—	100	125	200

INDIA - BRITISH

The civilization of India, which began about 2500 B.C., flourished under a succession of empires - notably those of the Mauryas, the Kushans, the Guptas, the Delhi Sultans and the Mughals – until undermined in the 18th and 19th centuries by European colonial powers.

The Portuguese were the first to arrive, off Calicut in May 1498. It wasn't until 1612, after the Portuguese and Spanish power had begun to wane, that the British East India Company established its initial settlement at Surat. Britain could not have chosen a more propitious time as the central girdle of petty states, and the southern Vijayanagar Empire were crumbling and ripe for foreign exploitation. By the end of the century, English traders were firmly established in Bombay, Madras, Calcutta and lesser places elsewhere, and Britain was implementing its announced policy to create such civil and military institutions as may be the foundation of secure English domination for all time'. By 1757, following the successful conclusion of a war of colonial rivalry with France during which the military victories of Robert Clive, a young officer with the British East India Company, made him a powerful man in India, the British were firmly settled in India not only as traders but as conquerors. During the next 60 years, the British East India Company acquired dominion over most of India by bribery and force, and governed it directly or through puppet princelings.

BOMBAY PRESIDENCY

Following a naval victory over the Portuguese on December 24, 1612 negotiations were started that developed into the opening of the first East India Company factory in Surat in 1613. Silver coins for the New World as well as various other foreign coins were used in early trade. Within the decade the Mughal mint at Surat was melting all of these foreign coins and re-minting them as various denominations of Mughal coinage.

Bombay became an English holding as part of the dowry of Catherine of Braganza, Princess of Portugal when she was betrothed to Charles II of England. Also included in the dowry was Tangier and $500,000. With this acquisition the trading center of the Indian West Coast moved from Surat to Bombay.

Possession of Bombay Island took place on February 8, 1665 and by 1672 the East India Company had a mint in Bombay to serve their trading interests. European designed coins were struck here until 1717. Experimental issues of Mughal style rupees with regnal years pertaining to the reigns of James II and William and Mary were made in 1693-94.

MINTS

احمداباد

Ahmadabad

منبي

Bombay (Mumbai)

سورت

Surat

تلجري تالچري

Tellicherry

MONETARY SYSTEM

3 Pies = 1 Pice (Paisa)
11 Tinnys (Bujruk) = 1 Copperoon (Pice)
48 Copperoons = 1 Anglina (Rupee)

BRITISH COLONY

CAST COINAGE

KM# 130 TINNY (Bujruk)

1.5600 g., Tin **Obv:** U.E.I.Co. bale mark **Rev:** 1/72 (first issue) **Mint:** Without Mint Name **Note:** P227.

Date	Mintage	Good	VG	F	VF	XF
(16)72	—	10.00	18.50	28.50	45.00	—

KM# 138 TINNY (Bujruk)

2.7100 g., Tin **Obv:** U.E.I.Co. arms **Rev:** 2/75 (second issue) **Mint:** Without Mint Name **Note:** P228.

Date	Mintage	Good	VG	F	VF	XF
(16)75	—	30.00	45.00	75.00	115	—

KM# 131 PICE

13.0000 g., Copper **Obv:** Honorable English Co. of the East Indies arms **Obv. Legend:** HON: SOC: ANG: IND: ORI **Rev:** Inscription, legend in outer circle **Rev. Legend:** A: DEO: PAX: & INCREMENTUM: **Rev. Inscription:** MON: BOMBAYA ANGLIC REGINS Ao7o **Mint:** Bombay **Note:** P78.

Date	Mintage	Good	VG	F	VF	XF
ND(1672)/7	—	30.00	45.00	65.00	95.00	—
Note: Ao7o = 1672						
ND(1673)/8	—	30.00	45.00	65.00	95.00	—
Note: Ao8o = 1673						
ND(1674)/9	—	30.00	45.00	65.00	95.00	—
Note: Ao9o = 1674						

KM# 133 PICE

13.0000 g., Copper **Rev:** Inscription: MON. BOMBAY ANGLIC REGIMS Ao7o **Mint:** Bombay

Date	Mintage	Good	VG	F	VF	XF
ND(1672)/7 (1672)	—	20.00	30.00	50.00	85.00	—

KM# 132 PICE

13.0000 g., Copper **Rev. Legend:** MON: BMBAYA ANGLIC REGIMS Ao7o **Mint:** Bombay **Note:** P80.

Date	Mintage	Good	VG	F	VF	XF
ND(1672)/7 (1672)	—	30.00	45.00	65.00	95.00	—

KM# 136 PICE

13.0000 g., Copper **Rev. Legend:** A DEO PAX & INCREMENTVM 74 **Mint:** Bombay **Note:** P81.

Date	Mintage	Good	VG	F	VF	XF
(16)73/8	—	—	—	—	—	—
Note: Ao8o appears as Ao&o with the & inverted						
(16)74/9	—	30.00	45.00	65.00	95.00	—

KM# A143 PICE

13.0000 g., Copper **Rev:** Date: Ao9o **Mint:** Bombay

Date	Mintage	Good	VG	F	VF	XF
(16)74	—	30.00	45.00	65.00	95.00	—

KM# 141 PICE

13.0000 g., Copper **Rev:** Inscription: MONETA BOMBAYES ANGLICI REGIMs ANDOR **Rev. Legend:** A DEO PAX ET INCREMENTVM 78 **Mint:** Bombay **Note:** P87.

Date	Mintage	Good	VG	F	VF	XF
(16)78	—	30.00	45.00	65.00	95.00	—

KM# 142 PICE

13.0000 g., Copper **Rev:** Inscription: MONETA BOMBAYES ANGLICI REGIMS ANoDo **Mint:** Bombay **Note:** P89.

Date	Mintage	Good	VG	F	VF	XF
(16)78	—	30.00	45.00	65.00	95.00	—

KM# 145 PICE

13.0000 g., Copper **Rev:** Inscription: MOET BOMBAY ANGLIC REGIMs AoD9(Arabic)2 **Rev. Legend:** HON SOC ANG IND ORI **Mint:** Bombay **Note:** P90.

Date	Mintage	Good	VG	F	VF	XF
(16)92	—	30.00	45.00	65.00	95.00	—

KM# 146 PICE

13.0000 g., Copper **Rev:** 5-line inscription with date in Persian numerals **Rev. Inscription:** MONET/BONBAY/ANGLIC/ REGIMs/ AoD92 **Mint:** Bombay **Note:** P93.

Date	Mintage	Good	VG	F	VF	XF
(16)92	—	30.00	45.00	65.00	95.00	—

HAMMERED COINAGE

KM# 134 1/2 RUPEE

5.7500 g., Silver **Obv:** Honorable English Co. of the East Indies arms **Obv. Legend:** HON: SOC: ANG: IND: ORI **Rev:** Inscription: MON: BOMBAYr ANGELIC REGIMs Ao7o **Rev. Legend:** A: DEO: PAX: SS: INCREMENTVM in outer circle **Mint:** Bombay **Note:** P13; The authenticity of KM#134 is questionable.

Date	Mintage	VG	F	VF	XF	Unc
ND(1672)7	—	—	—	—	—	—

Note: The authenticity of KM#134 is questionable.

KM# 139 1/2 RUPEE

5.7500 g., Silver **Obv:** Honorable English Co. of the East Indies arms **Rev. Legend:** MONETA BOMBAIENSIS **Rev. Inscription:** PAX / DEO **Mint:** Bombay **Note:** P18; The authenticity of KM#139 is questionable.

Date	Mintage	VG	F	VF	XF	Unc
ND(1676)	—	—	—	—	—	—

KM# 147 1/2 RUPEE

5.7500 g., Silver **Obv:** Persian inscription: "Coin struck during the reign of King William and Queen Mary" **Rev:** Persian inscription: In their 5th regnal year; Coin of the English Company **Mint:** Bombay **Note:** P29.

Date	Mintage	VG	F	VF	XF	Unc
1693/5 (1693) Rare	—	—	—	—	—	—

KM# 135 RUPEE (Anglina)

11.4800 g., Silver **Obv:** Honorable English Co. of the East Indies arms **Obv. Legend:** HON: SOC: ANG: IND: ORI **Rev:** Inscription: MON: BOMBAYr ANGLIC REGIMs Ao7o **Rev. Legend:** A: DEO: PAX: SS: INCREMENTVM: **Mint:** Bombay **Note:** P12.

Date	Mintage	VG	F	VF	XF	Unc
ND(1672)7	—	1,000	2,200	4,500	7,500	—

Note: Ao7o = 1672

KM# 137 RUPEE (Anglina)

11.6200 g., Silver **Obv. Legend:** HON: SOC: ANG: IND: ORI **Rev:** Crowned, linked C's **Rev. Legend:** A: DEO: PAX: ET: INCREMENTVM: **Mint:** Bombay **Note:** P14.

Date	Mintage	VG	F	VF	XF	Unc
1674 (1675)	—	1,000	2,200	4,500	7,500	—

KM# 140 RUPEE (Anglina)

11.7500 g., Silver **Obv:** Honorable English Co. of the East Indies arms **Rev. Legend:** MONETA • BOMBAIENSIS **Rev. Inscription:** PAX / DEO **Mint:** Bombay **Note:** P16.

Date	Mintage	VG	F	VF	XF	Unc
ND(1676)	—	700	1,500	3,500	6,000	—

KM# 143 RUPEE (Anglina)

11.7500 g., Silver **Obv:** Rosettes in H.E. Co. arms, between ships **Mint:** Bombay **Note:** Varieties exist.

Date	Mintage	VG	F	VF	XF	Unc
1687	—	—	—	—	—	—

KM# 144 RUPEE (Anglina)

Silver **Obv:** Persian inscription: Struck in the name of King James II **Rev:** Persian inscription: "Regnal year 4..." **Mint:** Bombay **Note:** P10; Weight varies: 10.70-11.60 grams.

Date	Mintage	VG	F	VF	XF	Unc
ND(1687)/4 Rare	—	—	—	—	—	—

KM# 148.1 RUPEE (Anglina)

Silver **Obv:** Persian inscription: "Coin struck during the reign of King William and Queen Mary" **Rev:** Persian inscription: "in their 4-6 regnal year" **Mint:** Bombay **Note:** Weight varies: 10.70-11.60 grams.

Date	Mintage	VG	F	VF	XF	Unc
ND(1692)/4	—	850	1,650	3,750	6,500	—

KM# 148.2 RUPEE (Anglina)

Silver **Obv:** Inscription: Finer style **Rev:** Inscription: Finer style **Mint:** Bombay **Note:** P27; Weight varies: 10.70-11.60 grams.

Date	Mintage	VG	F	VF	XF	Unc
ND(1693)/5	—	500	1,000	2,000	3,500	—
ND(1694)/6	—	500	1,000	2,000	3,500	—

PATTERNS

Including off metal strikes

KM#	Date	Mintage	Identification	Mkt Val
Pn1	1677	—	Rupee. Silver. Pr19; English manufacture.	—
Pn2	1678	—	Rupee. Silver. Pr20; English manufacture.	—
Pn3	1678	—	Rupee. Pewter. Pr22; English manufacture.	—
Pn4	1678	—	Rupee. Silver. Pr25.	—

MADRAS PRESIDENCY

English trade was begun on the east coast of India in 1611. The first factory was at Mazulipatam and was maintained intermittently until modern times.

Madras was founded in 1639 and Fort St. George was made the chief factory on the east coast in 1641. A mint was established at Fort St. George where coins of the style of Vijayanagar were struck.

The Madras mint began minting copper coins after the renovation. In 1689 silver fanams were authorized to be struck by the new Board of Directors.

In 1692 the Mughal Emperor Aurangzeb gave permission for Mughal type rupees to be struck at Madras. These circulated locally and were also sent to Bengal. The chief competition for the Madras coins were the Arcot rupees. Some of the bulk coins from Madras were sent to the Nawabs mint to be made into Arcot rupees.

MONETARY SYSTEM

36 Fanam = 1 Pagoda (1688-1802)

MINT

چيناپتن

Chinapatton

مچهلي پتن

Masulipatnam (Machilipatnam)

BRITISH COLONY

HAMMERED COINAGE

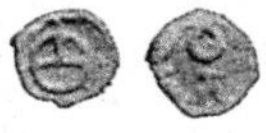

KM# 281 CASH

0.5300 g., Copper **Obv:** Bale mark **Rev:** Inscription: Telugu in two lines **Mint:** Without Mint Name **Note:** P89; Size varies: 6.50-7.00mm.

Date	Mintage	Good	VG	F	VF	XF
ND(1660-78)	—	9.00	15.00	25.00	50.00	—

KM# 282 CASH

Copper **Obv:** Bull walking left **Rev:** "65" in beaded circle **Mint:** Without Mint Name **Note:** P1.

Date	Mintage	Good	VG	F	VF	XF
(16)65	—	15.00	28.00	50.00	100	—

KM# 286 CASH

0.5900 g., Copper, 7.50 mm. **Obv:** Bale mark in dotted circle **Mint:** Without Mint Name **Note:** P91.

Date	Mintage	Good	VG	F	VF	XF
1678	—	9.00	15.00	25.00	50.00	—

KM# 287 CASH

0.8800 g., Copper, 8.0 mm. **Obv:** Bale markwith date "78" in bottom half in beaded circle **Mint:** Without Mint Name **Note:** P92.

Date	Mintage	Good	VG	F	VF	XF
(16)78	—	9.00	15.00	25.00	50.00	—

KM# 292 CASH

0.8800 g., Copper, 8.0 mm. **Obv:** Date in two lines in beaded circle **Rev:** Inscription, Telugu in two lines in beaded circle **Mint:** Without Mint Name **Note:** P93.

Date	Mintage	Good	VG	F	VF	XF
1698	—	9.00	15.00	25.00	50.00	—

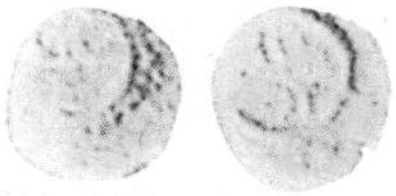

KM# 290 1/2 DUDU (5 Cash)

4.4300 g., Copper **Obv:** Bale mark with CC/E or GC/E **Rev:** Date in 2 lines **Mint:** Without Mint Name

Date	Mintage	Good	VG	F	VF	XF
1691	—	7.00	11.00	22.00	35.00	—

KM# 300 1/2 DUDU (5 Cash)

4.4300 g., Copper **Obv:** Bale mark with CC/E or GC/E **Rev:** Date with wavy lines above and below **Mint:** Without Mint Name **Note:** Type of Dudu; weight of 1/2 Dudu.

Date	Mintage	Good	VG	F	VF	XF
1700	—	10.00	20.00	35.00	55.00	—

KM# 291 DUDU (10 Cash)

Copper, 16.9 mm. **Obv:** Bale mark with CC/E or GC/E **Rev:** Date with wavy lines above and below **Mint:** Without Mint Name **Note:** Weight varies 8.21-8.35 grams.

Date	Mintage	Good	VG	F	VF	XF
1693	—	3.50	9.00	18.00	30.00	—
1695	—	3.50	9.00	18.00	30.00	—
1700	—	3.50	9.00	18.00	30.00	—

KM# 297 1/2 FANAM

0.5100 g., Silver **Obv:** Large deity Vishnu **Rev:** Bead at left and right of interlocked C's **Mint:** Without Mint Name **Note:** P17.

Date	Mintage	Good	VG	F	VF	XF
ND(1690-1763)	—	12.00	30.00	60.00	100	165

KM# 293 FANAM

1.2300 g., Silver **Obv:** Small Vishnu ideity **Rev:** 1 before interlocked C's **Mint:** Without Mint Name

Date	Mintage	Good	VG	F	VF	XF
ND(1689)	—	5.50	18.00	45.00	90.00	150

KM# 298 FANAM

1.0300 g., Silver **Obv:** Large deity Vishnu **Rev:** Bead at left and right of interlocked C's **Mint:** Without Mint Name **Note:** P16.

Date	Mintage	Good	VG	F	VF	XF
ND(1690-1763)	—	4.50	15.00	37.50	75.00	125

KM# 296 2 FANAM

2.4600 g., Silver **Obv:** Large deity Vishnu **Rev:** Bead at left and right of interlocked C's **Mint:** Without Mint Name

Date	Mintage	Good	VG	F	VF	XF
ND(1690-1763)	—	3.50	12.00	30.00	60.00	100

KM# A289 RUPEE

11.5900 g., Silver **Obv:** Inscription in Persian **Obv. Inscription:** "Aurangzeb Alamgir..." **Rev:** Inscription in Persian **Mint:** Chinapattan **Note:** It has been determined that the AH date is lacking for all but AH1103//38. Prev. KM#300.25.

Date	Mintage	Good	VG	F	VF	XF
AH1103//38	—	24.00	60.00	120	200	300
AH-//38	—	10.00	18.00	35.00	75.00	125
AH-//39	—	10.00	18.00	35.00	75.00	125

Date	Mintage	Good	VG	F	VF	XF
AH-//40	—	10.00	18.00	35.00	75.00	125
AH-//41	—	10.00	18.00	35.00	75.00	125
AH-//42	—	10.00	18.00	35.00	75.00	125
AH-//43	—	10.00	18.00	35.00	75.00	125
AH-//44	—	10.00	18.00	35.00	75.00	125
AH-//45	—	10.00	18.00	35.00	75.00	125

HAMMERED COINAGE

Pagoda Series

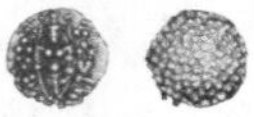

KM# A288 1/4 PAGODA

0.8370 g., Gold **Obv:** Single standing deity Vishnu **Rev:** Granulated **Mint:** Madras **Note:** Single swami type. Fr. #1574.

Date	Mintage	Good	VG	F	VF	XF
ND(c.1678-1740)	—	—	60.00	125	200	300

KM# B280 1/2 PAGODA

1.7250 g., Gold, 9.3 mm. **Obv:** 3 full swami **Rev:** Granulated **Mint:** Fort St. George **Note:** P. #4. Fr. #1573.

Date	Mintage	Good	VG	F	VF	XF
ND(1691-1740)	—	—	100	200	300	425

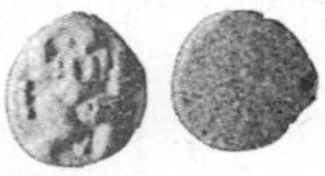

KM# 280 PAGODA

3.4500 g., Gold, 13 mm. **Obv:** Large crude deity Vishnu **Mint:** Fort St. George **Note:** P. #1. Fr. #1572.

Date	Mintage	Good	VG	F	VF	XF
ND(c.1643-77)	—	—	200	300	400	—

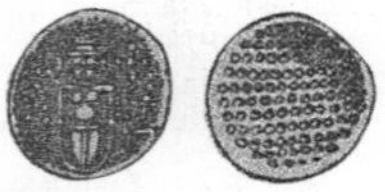

KM# 288 PAGODA

3.4300 g., Gold **Obv:** Single standing deity Vishnu **Rev:** Granulated **Mint:** Fort St. George **Note:** Struck at Madras Mint. P. #2. Fr. #1572.

Date	Mintage	Good	VG	F	VF	XF
ND(c.1678-1740)	—	—	BV	200	300	400

KM# 289 PAGODA

3.4000 g., Gold **Obv:** 3 full length dieties **Rev:** Granulated **Mint:** Fort St. George **Note:** Struck at Madras Mint. P3A.

Date	Mintage	Good	VG	F	VF	XF
ND(c.1691-1740)	—	BV	BV	200	300	400

INDIA-DANISH TRANQUEBAR

Danish India or Tranquebar is a town and former Danish colony on the southeast coast of India. In Danish times, 1620-1845, it was a factory site and seaport operated by the Danish Asiatic Company. Tranquebar and the other Danish settlements in India were sold to the British East India Company in 1845.

RULER

Danish, until 1845

ADMINISTRATION OF TRANQUEBAR

Danish East India Company (DOC)
1620-(1650)
Danish Crown
ca.1630-1670
Christian IV, 1588-1648
Danish East India Company (DOC)
1670-1729

MONETARY SYSTEM

80 Kas (Cash) = Royaliner (Fano or
8 Royaliner = 1 Rupee
18 Royaliner = 1 Speciesdaler

Danish East India Co.

Lead Cash (Kas)

The lead cash (Kas) of Danish India were struck in many varieties. The following listings are representative only.

DANISH COLONY

HAMMERED COINAGE

Lead

KM# 48 1/2 CASH

Lead **Ruler:** Christian IV **Mint:** Without Mint Name **Note:** Weight about 2.0 grams.

Date	Mintage	Good	VG	F	VF	XF
ND	—	10.00	20.00	40.00	80.00	—

KM# 33 CASH

Lead **Ruler:** Christian IV **Rev:** D/CAS/1644 in three lines **Mint:** Without Mint Name

Date	Mintage	Good	VG	F	VF	XF
1644	—	20.00	40.00	100	200	—

KM# 34 CASH

Lead **Ruler:** Christian IV **Rev:** CH/CAS (S retrograd)/1645 **Mint:** Without Mint Name

Date	Mintage	Good	VG	F	VF	XF
1645	—	20.00	40.00	100	200	—

KM# 35 CASH

Lead **Ruler:** Christian IV **Obv:** Similar to KM#34 **Rev:** TR/CAS/1645 in three lines **Mint:** Without Mint Name

Date	Mintage	Good	VG	F	VF	XF
1645	—	30.00	60.00	120	250	—

KM# 36 CASH

Lead **Ruler:** Christian IV **Rev:** St/MICA/EL in three lines **Mint:** Without Mint Name

Date	Mintage	Good	VG	F	VF	XF
ND	—	20.00	40.00	100	200	—

KM# 37 CASH

Lead **Ruler:** Christian IV **Rev:** PE/JT in two lines **Mint:** Without Mint Name

Date	Mintage	Good	VG	F	VF	XF
ND	—	15.00	30.00	80.00	200	—

KM# 38 CASH

Lead **Ruler:** Christian IV **Rev:** DAN/MAR/CK in three lines **Mint:** Without Mint Name

Date	Mintage	Good	VG	F	VF	XF
ND	—	15.00	30.00	100	200	—

KM# 39 CASH

Lead **Ruler:** Christian IV **Rev:** IHS/date in two lines **Mint:** Without Mint Name

Date	Mintage	Good	VG	F	VF	XF
1646	—	30.00	60.00	140	250	—

KM# 40 CASH

Lead **Ruler:** Christian IV **Rev:** SPSP/1646DB (4 and D retrograde) **Mint:** Without Mint Name

Date	Mintage	Good	VG	F	VF	XF
1646	—	25.00	60.00	140	250	—

KM# 41 CASH

Lead **Ruler:** Christian IV **Rev:** IeHO/VS/Dan=/1647 in four lines **Mint:** Without Mint Name

Date	Mintage	Good	VG	F	VF	XF
1647	—	20.00	50.00	120	200	—

KM# 42 CASH

Lead **Ruler:** Christian IV **Obv:** Similar to KM#41 **Rev:** WB/1647 **Mint:** Without Mint Name

Date	Mintage	Good	VG	F	VF	XF
1647	—	20.00	40.00	100	200	—

KM# 43 CASH

Lead **Ruler:** Christian IV **Obv:** Crowned C4 **Rev:** DB/1648 in two lines **Mint:** Without Mint Name

Date	Mintage	Good	VG	F	VF	XF
1648	—	20.00	50.00	100	250	—

KM# 44 CASH

Lead **Ruler:** Christian IV **Obv:** Crowned C4 (4 retrograde) **Mint:** Without Mint Name

Date	Mintage	Good	VG	F	VF	XF
1648	—	15.00	25.00	70.00	160	—

KM# 45 CASH

Lead **Ruler:** Christian IV **Rev:** DBS with • + • above S **Mint:** Without Mint Name

Date	Mintage	Good	VG	F	VF	XF
1648	—	15.00	30.00	80.00	170	—

KM# 47.1 CASH

Lead **Ruler:** Christian IV **Mint:** Without Mint Name **Note:** Weight about 4.0 grams.

Date	Mintage	Good	VG	F	VF	XF
ND	—	20.00	35.00	100	200	—

KM# 47.2 CASH

Lead **Ruler:** Christian IV **Mint:** Without Mint Name **Note:** Weight about 8.0 grams.

Date	Mintage	Good	VG	F	VF	XF
ND Rare	—	—	—	—	—	—

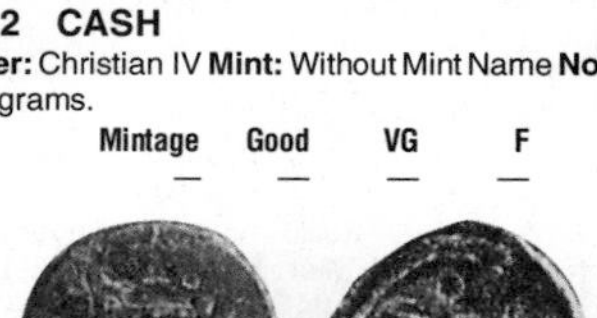

KM# 49 CASH

Lead **Ruler:** Frederik III **Obv:** Crowned F **Rev:** 3RD **Mint:** Without Mint Name

Date	Mintage	Good	VG	F	VF	XF
ND	—	35.00	50.00	140	300	—

KM# 50 CASH

Lead **Ruler:** Frederik III **Obv:** Crowned F3 monogram **Rev:** DB/1650 **Mint:** Without Mint Name **Note:** Weight about 2.0 grams.

Date	Mintage	Good	VG	F	VF	XF
1650	—	20.00	40.00	80.00	160	—

KM# 51 CASH
Lead **Ruler:** Frederik III **Obv:** Similar to KM#50 **Rev:** CH/1650 **Mint:** Without Mint Name

Date	Mintage	Good	VG	F	VF	XF
1650	—	20.00	40.00	80.00	180	—

KM# 52 CASH
Lead **Ruler:** Frederik III **Obv:** Similar to KM#50 **Rev:** S/PP/50 **Mint:** Without Mint Name

Date	Mintage	Good	VG	F	VF	XF
1650	—	20.00	40.00	80.00	160	—

KM# 53 CASH
Lead **Ruler:** Frederik III **Obv:** Similar to KM#50 **Rev:** D:B. **Mint:** Without Mint Name

Date	Mintage	Good	VG	F	VF	XF
ND	—	20.00	40.00	80.00	160	—

KM# 54 CASH
Lead **Ruler:** Frederik III **Obv:** Similar to KM#50 **Rev:** HAAB (Danish for hope) **Mint:** Without Mint Name

Date	Mintage	Good	VG	F	VF	XF
ND	—	20.00	40.00	80.00	160	—

KM# 55 CASH
Lead **Ruler:** Frederik III **Obv:** Similar to KM#50 **Rev:** Cross in circle **Mint:** Without Mint Name

Date	Mintage	Good	VG	F	VF	XF
ND	—	20.00	30.00	70.00	160	—

KM# 56 CASH
Lead **Ruler:** Frederik III **Obv:** Similar to KM#50 **Rev:** NOR **Mint:** Without Mint Name

Date	Mintage	Good	VG	F	VF	XF
ND	—	20.00	30.00	70.00	160	—

KM# 57 CASH
Lead **Ruler:** Frederik III **Obv:** Similar to KM#50 **Rev:** S/PP/50 **Mint:** Without Mint Name

Date	Mintage	Good	VG	F	VF	XF
1650	—	25.00	40.00	80.00	200	—

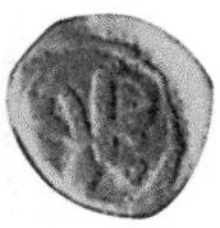

KM# 58 CASH
Lead **Ruler:** Frederik III **Obv:** Similar to KM#50 **Rev:** NOR **Mint:** Without Mint Name

Date	Mintage	Good	VG	F	VF	XF
ND Rare	—	—	—	—	—	—

KM# 59 CASH
Lead **Ruler:** Frederik III **Obv:** Similar to KM#50 **Rev:** DB/1652 **Mint:** Without Mint Name

Date	Mintage	Good	VG	F	VF	XF
1652	—	20.00	30.00	80.00	160	—

KM# 60 CASH
Lead **Ruler:** Frederik III **Obv:** Crowned F3 monogram **Rev:** PAX **Mint:** Without Mint Name

Date	Mintage	Good	VG	F	VF	XF
ND	—	35.00	50.00	100	250	—

KM# 69 CASH
Lead **Ruler:** Frederik III **Obv:** Similar to KM#61 **Rev:** Norse lion right **Mint:** Without Mint Name

Date	Mintage	Good	VG	F	VF	XF
ND	—	20.00	50.00	100	200	—

KM# 65 CASH
Lead **Ruler:** Frederik III **Obv:** Crowned F3 **Rev:** Horseman above C **Mint:** Without Mint Name

Date	Mintage	Good	VG	F	VF	XF
ND	—	15.00	25.00	70.00	160	—

KM# 61 CASH
Lead **Ruler:** Frederik III **Obv:** Crowned F3 monogram **Rev:** CAS **Mint:** Without Mint Name

Date	Mintage	Good	VG	F	VF	XF
ND	—	35.00	50.00	150	300	—

KM# 62 CASH
Lead **Ruler:** Frederik III **Obv:** Similar to KM#61 **Rev:** Crown **Mint:** Without Mint Name

Date	Mintage	Good	VG	F	VF	XF
ND	—	20.00	30.00	80.00	180	—

KM# 63 CASH
Lead **Ruler:** Frederik III **Obv:** Similar to KM#61 **Rev:** Three crowns **Mint:** Without Mint Name

Date	Mintage	Good	VG	F	VF	XF
ND	—	20.00	30.00	80.00	180	—

KM# 64 CASH
Lead **Ruler:** Frederik III **Obv:** Similar to KM#61 **Rev:** Horse **Mint:** Without Mint Name

Date	Mintage	Good	VG	F	VF	XF
ND	—	25.00	40.00	90.00	230	—

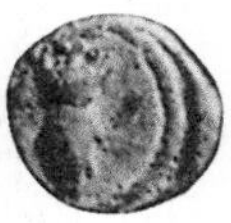

KM# 66 CASH
Lead **Ruler:** Frederik III **Obv:** Similar to KM#61 **Rev:** Crowned codfish **Mint:** Without Mint Name

Date	Mintage	Good	VG	F	VF	XF
ND	—	25.00	50.00	100	220	—

KM# 67 CASH
Lead **Ruler:** Frederik III **Rev:** Crowned codfish, A **Mint:** Without Mint Name

Date	Mintage	Good	VG	F	VF	XF
ND	—	15.00	25.00	70.00	160	—

KM# 68 CASH
Lead **Ruler:** Frederik III **Rev:** Crowned codfish, N **Mint:** Without Mint Name

Date	Mintage	Good	VG	F	VF	XF
ND	—	20.00	40.00	100	200	—

KM# 70 CASH
Lead **Ruler:** Frederik III **Obv:** Similar to KM#61 **Rev:** Nettle leaf **Mint:** Without Mint Name

Date	Mintage	Good	VG	F	VF	XF
ND	—	20.00	50.00	100	200	—

KM# 71 CASH
Lead **Ruler:** Frederik III **Rev:** Nettle leaf, O **Mint:** Without Mint Name

Date	Mintage	Good	VG	F	VF	XF
ND	—	20.00	30.00	80.00	180	—

KM# 72 CASH
Lead **Ruler:** Frederik III **Rev:** Lamb right **Mint:** Without Mint Name

Date	Mintage	Good	VG	F	VF	XF
ND	—	20.00	30.00	70.00	180	—

KM# 73 CASH
Lead **Ruler:** Frederik III **Obv:** Similar to KM#65 **Rev:** Lamb left, b **Mint:** Without Mint Name

Date	Mintage	Good	VG	F	VF	XF
ND	—	10.00	20.00	60.00	120	—

KM# 74 CASH
Lead **Ruler:** Frederik III **Rev:** Lamb left, F **Mint:** Without Mint Name

Date	Mintage	Good	VG	F	VF	XF
ND	—	20.00	30.00	80.00	160	—

KM# 75 CASH

Lead **Ruler:** Frederik III **Rev:** The Wendish Wyvern (crowned swan) right **Mint:** Without Mint Name

Date	Mintage	Good	VG	F	VF	XF
ND	—	20.00	30.00	80.00	180	—

KM# 76 CASH

Lead **Ruler:** Frederik III **Obv:** Similar to KM#75 **Rev:** Cross **Mint:** Without Mint Name

Date	Mintage	Good	VG	F	VF	XF
ND	—	20.00	30.00	80.00	180	—

KM# 77 CASH

Lead **Ruler:** Frederik III **Rev:** Cross, 'e' in lower left quadrant **Mint:** Without Mint Name

Date	Mintage	Good	VG	F	VF	XF
ND	—	20.00	30.00	80.00	180	—

KM# 78 CASH

Lead **Ruler:** Frederik III **Obv:** Similar to KM#74 **Rev:** Cross divides JO **Mint:** Without Mint Name

Date	Mintage	Good	VG	F	VF	XF
ND	—	35.00	60.00	100	200	—

KM# 79 CASH

Lead **Ruler:** Frederik III **Obv:** Crowned F3 **Rev:** Elephant left **Mint:** Without Mint Name

Date	Mintage	Good	VG	F	VF	XF
ND	—	15.00	25.00	70.00	160	—

KM# 80 CASH

Lead **Ruler:** Frederik III **Obv:** F3 Crowned **Rev:** Norse lion left **Mint:** Without Mint Name

Date	Mintage	Good	VG	F	VF	XF
ND	—	20.00	35.00	80.00	180	—

KM# 81 CASH

Lead **Ruler:** Frederik III **Rev:** Norse lion left, E **Mint:** Without Mint Name

Date	Mintage	Good	VG	F	VF	XF
ND	—	15.00	25.00	70.00	180	—

KM# 82 CASH

Lead **Ruler:** Frederik III **Rev:** Norse lion left, DC **Mint:** Without Mint Name

Date	Mintage	Good	VG	F	VF	XF
ND	—	20.00	40.00	80.00	180	—

KM# 83 CASH

Lead **Ruler:** Frederik III **Obv:** Similar to KM#82 **Rev:** Norse lion left above I **Mint:** Without Mint Name

Date	Mintage	Good	VG	F	VF	XF
ND	—	30.00	60.00	110	220	—

KM# 84 CASH

Lead **Ruler:** Frederik III **Rev:** Slesvig lion right above I **Mint:** Without Mint Name

Date	Mintage	Good	VG	F	VF	XF
ND	—	20.00	40.00	80.00	180	—

KM# 85 CASH

Lead **Ruler:** Frederik III **Rev:** Gothic lion left, nine hearts **Mint:** Without Mint Name

Date	Mintage	Good	VG	F	VF	XF
ND	—	15.00	25.00	70.00	160	—

KM# 86 CASH

Lead **Ruler:** Frederik III **Obv:** Similar to KM#81 **Rev:** Nine hearts **Mint:** Without Mint Name

Date	Mintage	Good	VG	F	VF	XF
ND	—	15.00	25.00	70.00	160	—

KM# 87 CASH

Lead **Ruler:** Frederik III **Rev:** Flower **Mint:** Without Mint Name

Date	Mintage	Good	VG	F	VF	XF
ND	—	20.00	40.00	80.00	180	—

KM# 88 CASH

Lead **Ruler:** Frederik III **Rev:** Flower above 76 **Mint:** Without Mint Name

Date	Mintage	Good	VG	F	VF	XF
ND	—	20.00	40.00	80.00	180	—

KM# 89 CASH

Lead **Ruler:** Frederik III **Rev:** Swan right, S **Mint:** Without Mint Name

Date	Mintage	Good	VG	F	VF	XF
ND	—	20.00	40.00	80.00	180	—

KM# 90 CASH

Lead **Ruler:** Christian V **Obv:** C5 monogram **Rev:** DC **Mint:** Without Mint Name **Note:** Weight about 2.3 grams.

Date	Mintage	Good	VG	F	VF	XF
ND	—	6.00	15.00	40.00	80.00	—

KM# 91 CASH

Lead **Ruler:** Christian V **Obv:** Crowned C5 monogram **Mint:** Without Mint Name

Date	Mintage	Good	VG	F	VF	XF
ND	—	8.00	20.00	50.00	100	—

KM# 92 CASH

Lead **Ruler:** Christian V **Obv:** Crowned DOC **Mint:** Without Mint Name **Note:** Varieties exist.

Date	Mintage	Good	VG	F	VF	XF
ND	—	7.00	15.00	40.00	80.00	—

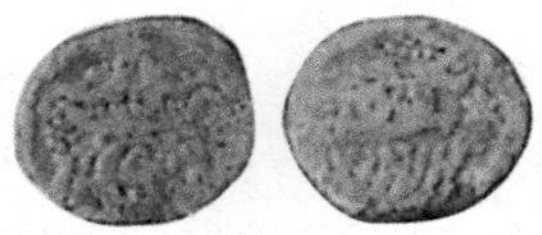

KM# 100 CASH

Lead **Ruler:** Christian V **Obv:** Similar to KM#99 **Rev:** Crowned *DOC* above WHVK **Mint:** Without Mint Name

Date	Mintage	Good	VG	F	VF	XF
1688	—	15.00	25.00	60.00	150	—

Note: "K" and "WHVK" = W.H. von Kalnien.

KM# 46 2 CASH

Lead **Ruler:** Christian IV **Obv:** C4 **Rev:** Outlined castle gate with three turrets **Mint:** Without Mint Name **Note:** Weight about 8.0 grams.

Date	Mintage	Good	VG	F	VF	XF
ND	—	35.00	70.00	150	300	—

KM# 93.1 2 CASH

Lead **Ruler:** Christian V **Obv:** Crowned C5 monogram **Rev:** Crowned DOC, small letters **Mint:** Without Mint Name **Note:** Weight about 4.6 grams.

Date	Mintage	Good	VG	F	VF	XF
ND	—	10.00	20.00	40.00	100	—

KM# 93.2 2 CASH

Lead **Ruler:** Christian V **Obv:** Crowned C5 monogram **Rev:** Crowned DOC, large letters **Mint:** Without Mint Name **Note:** Varieties exist.

Date	Mintage	Good	VG	F	VF	XF
ND	—	12.00	20.00	45.00	110	—

KM# 95.1 2 CASH

Lead **Ruler:** Christian V **Rev:** Crowned DOC above K, small letters **Mint:** Without Mint Name

Date	Mintage	Good	VG	F	VF	XF
ND	—	20.00	30.00	80.00	160	—

Note: "K" and "WHVK" = W.H. von Kalnien.

KM# 95.2 2 CASH

Lead **Ruler:** Christian V **Obv:** Similar to KM#95 **Rev:** Crowned DOC above K, large letters **Mint:** Without Mint Name

Date	Mintage	Good	VG	F	VF	XF
ND	—	15.00	25.00	60.00	140	—

Note: "K" and "WHVK" = W.H. von Kalnien.

KM# 97 2 CASH

Lead **Ruler:** Christian V **Obv:** Crowned C5 divides date **Rev:** Crowned DOC above WHVK **Mint:** Without Mint Name

Date	Mintage	Good	VG	F	VF	XF
1687	—	20.00	35.00	80.00	200	—

Note: "K" and "WHVK" = W.H. von Kalnien.

KM# 98 2 CASH

Lead **Ruler:** Christian V **Obv:** Similar to KM#97, with rosettes **Mint:** Without Mint Name **Note:** Previously KM#98.1

Date	Mintage	Good	VG	F	VF	XF
1687	—	30.00	50.00	130	240	—

KM# 99 2 CASH

Lead **Ruler:** Christian V **Mint:** Without Mint Name **Note:** Previously KM#98.2

Date	Mintage	Good	VG	F	VF	XF
1688	—	12.00	20.00	50.00	120	—

HAMMERED COINAGE

Copper

KM# 119 CASH

1.0000 g., Copper **Ruler:** Christian V **Obv:** Crowned double C5 monogram divides last two digits of date **Rev:** Crowned DOC monogram divides W H, VK below **Mint:** Without Mint Name

Date	Mintage	Good	VG	F	VF	XF
(16)89	—	5.00	10.00	20.00	60.00	—
(16)90	—	5.00	10.00	30.00	70.00	—
(16)91	—	7.00	15.00	40.00	80.00	—

KM# 120 CASH

1.0000 g., Copper **Ruler:** Christian V **Obv:** Crowned double C5 monogram **Rev:** Crowned DOC monogram divides 1 6, two digits below **Mint:** Without Mint Name **Note:** Monogram varieties exist.

Date	Mintage	Good	VG	F	VF	XF
1692	—	5.00	10.00	30.00	80.00	—
1694	—	5.00	10.00	20.00	60.00	—
1697	—	5.00	10.00	25.00	70.00	—

Note: Varieties exist

KM# 117 CASH
1.0000 g., Copper **Ruler:** Christian V **Obv:** Crowned C5 monogram. **Mint:** Without Mint Name **Note:** Uniface. Previously KM#A122.

Date	Mintage	Good	VG	F	VF	XF
ND	—	10.00	20.00	40.00	80.00	—

KM# 124 CASH
Copper **Ruler:** Frederik IV **Issuer:** Danish East India Company **Obv:** Crowned F4 monogram **Rev:** Crowned DOC monogram **Mint:** Without Mint Name

Date	Mintage	Good	VG	F	VF	XF
ND1700	—	10.00	20.00	40.00	100	—

Note: Posthumous issue, struck in 1700 and after.

KM# 121 CASH
Copper **Ruler:** Frederik IV **Issuer:** Danish East India Company **Obv:** Crowned double F4 monogram **Rev:** Crowned DOC monogram **Mint:** Without Mint Name **Note:** Previously KM#122.

Date	Mintage	Good	VG	F	VF	XF
ND1700	—	10.00	20.00	40.00	100	—

Note: Posthumous issue, struck in 1700 and after.

KM# 122 CASH
Copper **Ruler:** Frederik IV **Issuer:** Danish East India Company **Obv:** Crowned F4 monogram using one vertical for both **Rev:** Crowned DOC monogram **Mint:** Without Mint Name **Note:** Previously KM#123.1. Weight varies: 0.40-1.65 grams.

Date	Mintage	Good	VG	F	VF	XF
ND1700	—	5.00	8.00	20.00	40.00	—

Note: Posthumous issue, struck in 1700 and after.

KM# 123 CASH
Copper **Ruler:** Frederik IV **Issuer:** Danish East India Company **Rev:** Inverted DOC monogram **Mint:** Without Mint Name **Note:** Previously KM#123.2.

Date	Mintage	Good	VG	F	VF	XF
	—	30.00	60.00	120	250	—

Note: Posthumous issue, struck in 1700 and after.

KM# 111 2 CASH
2.3000 g., Copper **Ruler:** Frederik III **Obv:** Crowned F3 monogram in half circle, ANO 1667 below **Rev:** Norse lion on battle axe to left in beaded circle **Mint:** Without Mint Name **Note:** Previously KM#125.

Date	Mintage	Good	VG	F	VF	XF
1667	—	25.00	50.00	100	200	—

KM# A135 2 CASH
1.6000 g., Copper **Ruler:** Frederik IV **Issuer:** Danish East India Company **Obv:** Crowned double F4 monogram **Rev:** DOC monogram, 2 KAS below **Mint:** Without Mint Name

Date	Mintage	Good	VG	F	VF	XF
ND	—	15.00	30.00	60.00	120	—

Note: Posthumous issue, struck in 1700 and after.

KM# 126.1 4 CASH
4.8000 g., Copper **Ruler:** Frederik IV **Issuer:** Danish East India Company **Obv:** Crowned double F4 monogram **Rev:** DOC monogram, 4 KAS below **Mint:** Without Mint Name

Date	Mintage	Good	VG	F	VF	XF
ND	—	100	200	500	1,000	—

Note: Posthumous issue, struck in 1700 and after.

KM# 126.2 4 CASH
4.8000 g., Copper **Ruler:** Frederik IV **Issuer:** Danish East India Company **Rev:** 4 CAS below monogram **Mint:** Without Mint Name

Date	Mintage	Good	VG	F	VF	XF
ND Rare	—	—	—	—	—	—

Note: Posthumous issue, struck in 1700 and after.

KM# 127 10 CASH
10.0000 g., Copper **Ruler:** Frederik IV **Issuer:** Danish East India Company **Obv:** Crowned double F4 monogram **Rev:** Crowned DAC monogram, 10 and Kass below **Mint:** Without Mint Name

Date	Mintage	Good	VG	F	VF	XF
ND1700	—	300	700	1,500	3,000	—

Note: Posthumous issue, struck in 1700 and after.

INDIA-DUTCH

The Netherlands, operating as the United East India Company of the Netherlands, were the real successors to the Portuguese in India. They maintained a number of thriving establishments on the subcontinent until 1795, when Robert Clive, founder of the empire of British India, completed Britain's conquest of Bengal. Thereafter the Dutch holdings were gradually ceded to Britain, the most important to numismatics being Cochin, ceded in 1814; Negapatnam, ceded in 1784; Pulicat, ceded in 1824; and Tuticorin, ceded in 1795.

MINT MARK

NOTE: On Princely style coins the Dutch East India Company often used the mint mark: Lazy J (possibly a Kris: Malay knife).

COLONY

HAMMERED COINAGE

KM# 2 BAZARUK
Tin **Obv:** VOC monogram **Rev:** Cauri shell **Mint:** Cochin

Date	Mintage	Good	VG	F	VF	XF
ND(1663-1724)	—	—	—	—	—	—

KM# 4 1/2 RASI
Copper **Mint:** Cochin **Note:** Struck for trade with Muscat. Weight varies 5.42-5.89 grams. Similar to 1 Rasi, KM#5.

Date	Mintage	Good	VG	F	VF	XF
ND(1663-1724)	—	20.00	35.00	75.00	150	—

KM# 5 RASI
Copper **Mint:** Cochin **Note:** Weight varies 10.84-11.79 grams. Struck for trade with Muscat.

Date	Mintage	Good	VG	F	VF	XF
	—	5.00	10.00	20.00	40.00	—

KM# 40 FANAM
Gold **Obv:** Degenerated Kali **Rev:** Similar to 1 Cash, KM#35; Arabic legend **Rev. Legend:** "In the name of Sultan Abd'allah" **Mint:** Pulicat

Date	Mintage	VG	F	VF	XF	Unc
ND(1646-1781)	—	75.00	125	200	—	—

KM# 6 FANAM
Gold **Rev:** Lazy "J" above OC/three rows of four dots each **Mint:** Cochin

Date	Mintage	VG	F	VF	XF	Unc
ND(1663-1724)	—	25.00	35.00	50.00	90.00	—

KM# 10 PAGODA
Gold **Obv:** Facing figures of three gods with two pointed crowns **Rev:** Granular dots **Mint:** Masulipatnam

Date	Mintage	VG	F	VF	XF	Unc
ND(1646-1747)	—	120	200	350	—	—

Note: Copied by the British (Madras KM#3a) and the Nawab of Arcot (KM#13)

KM# 41 PAGODA
Gold **Obv:** Facing figure of God Ganesh **Rev:** Three-line Nagari inscription **Mint:** Pulicat

Date	Mintage	VG	F	VF	XF	Unc
ND(1646-1781) Unique	—	—	160	275	450	—

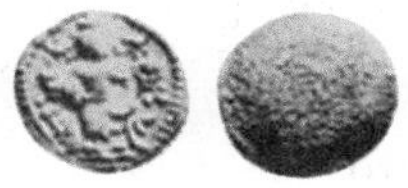

KM# 21 PAGODA
Gold **Obv:** Facing god, lazy "J" at right **Rev:** Granulated **Mint:** Negapatnam

Date	Mintage	VG	F	VF	XF	Unc
ND(1662-1749)	—	—	175	300	500	—

CAST COINAGE

KM# 14.1 CASH
Lead **Obv:** N/VOC monogram **Rev:** Legend in two lines **Rev. Legend:** Tamil "Nakapattanam" **Mint:** Negapatnam

Date	Mintage	Good	VG	F	VF	XF
ND	—	20.00	30.00	42.50	65.00	—

KM# 14.2 CASH
Lead **Obv:** Retrograde N **Mint:** Negapatnam

Date	Mintage	Good	VG	F	VF	XF
ND	—	—	—	—	—	—

HAMMERED COINAGE

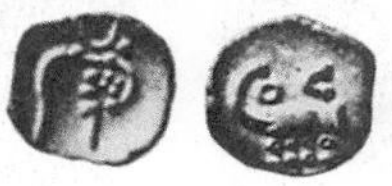

KM# 30 FANAM
Silver **Obv:** Degenerated Kali **Rev:** "OC" above lazy "J" above three rows of four dots each **Mint:** Negapatnam **Note:** This series for circulation in Ceylon.

Date	Mintage	VG	F	VF	XF	Unc
ND(ca.1675)	—	12.00	20.00	30.00	50.00	—

KM# 31 FANAM
Gold **Obv:** Degenerated Kali **Rev:** "OC" above lazy "J" above three rows of four dots each **Mint:** Negapatnam **Note:** This series for circulation in Ceylon. Weight varies: 0.33-0.37 grams.

Date	Mintage	VG	F	VF	XF	Unc
ND(ca.1675)	—	20.00	35.00	75.00	125	—

KM# 13 CASH
Copper **Obv:** N above VOC monogram **Rev:** Nagari legend in two lines **Mint:** Negapatnam

Date	Mintage	Good	VG	F	VF	XF
ND(1662-74)	—	—	—	—	—	—

KM# 15.1 CASH
Copper **Mint:** Negapatnam

Date	Mintage	Good	VG	F	VF	XF
ND	—	15.00	22.50	32.50	50.00	—

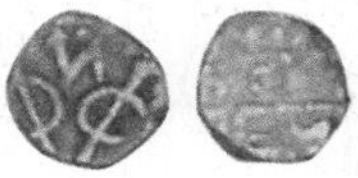

KM# 15.2 CASH
Copper **Obv:** Retrograde "N"/VOC monogram **Mint:** Negapatnam

Date	Mintage	Good	VG	F	VF	XF
ND	—	50.00	70.00	100	—	—

KM# 16.1 2 CASH
Copper **Rev:** Legend in three lines **Rev. Inscription:** Tamil "Nakapattanam" **Mint:** Negapatnam

Date	Mintage	Good	VG	F	VF	XF
ND	—	10.00	15.00	20.00	35.00	—

KM# 16.2 2 CASH
Copper **Obv:** Retrograde N/VOC monogram **Mint:** Negapatnam

Date	Mintage	Good	VG	F	VF	XF
ND	—	—	—	—	—	—

KM# 18 4 CASH
Copper **Obv:** N/VOC monogram/IV **Mint:** Negapatnam

Date	Mintage	Good	VG	F	VF	XF
ND 1 known	—	—	—	—	—	—

KM# 17 4 CASH
Copper **Obv:** N/VOC monogram/4 **Rev:** Inscription in two lines **Rev. Inscription:** Tamil "Nakapattanam" **Mint:** Negapatnam

Date	Mintage	Good	VG	F	VF	XF
ND	—	17.50	25.00	45.00	75.00	—

KM# 19 10 CASH
Copper **Obv:** N/VOC monogram/10 **Rev. Inscription:** Tamil "Nakapattanam" **Mint:** Negapatnam

Date	Mintage	Good	VG	F	VF	XF
ND Rare	—	—	—	—	—	—

KM# 20 15 CASH

Copper **Obv:** N/VOC monogram/15 **Rev. Inscription:** Tamil "Nakapattanam" **Mint:** Negapatnam

Date	Mintage	Good	VG	F	VF	XF
ND Rare	—	—	—	—	—	—

KM# 25 1/2 DUIT

Copper **Obv:** Facing figure of God Kali **Rev. Inscription:** Tamil "Nakapattanam" **Mint:** Negapatnam **Note:** This series for circulation in Ceylon. Weight varies: 1.60-1.80 grams.

Date	Mintage	Good	VG	F	VF	XF
ND(1695)	—	40.00	55.00	90.00	—	—

KM# 26 DUIT

Copper **Obv:** Facing figure of God Kali **Rev:** Inscription in two lines **Rev. Inscription:** Tamil "Nakapattanam" **Mint:** Negapatnam **Note:** This series for circulation in Ceylon. Weight varies: 2.60-3.60 grams.

Date	Mintage	Good	VG	F	VF	XF
ND(1695)	—	20.00	30.00	40.00	60.00	—

KM# 27 STUIVER

Copper **Obv:** 1 ST in sprays **Rev:** 1 ST in sprays **Mint:** Negapatnam **Note:** This series for circulation in Ceylon. Also struck in Ceylon but with different sprays.

Date	Mintage	Good	VG	F	VF	XF
ND(1675)	—	5.00	10.00	18.00	30.00	—

KM# 28 STUIVER

Copper **Obv:** Facing figure of God Kali **Rev:** Inscription in two lines **Rev. Inscription:** Tamil "Nakapattanam" **Mint:** Negapatnam **Note:** This series for circulation in Ceylon. Weight varies: 25.70-28.20 grams.

Date	Mintage	Good	VG	F	VF	XF
ND	—	27.50	40.00	60.00	100	—

KM# 29 2 STUIVERS

Copper **Obv:** Facing figure of God Kali **Rev:** Inscription in two lines **Rev. Inscription:** Tamil "Nakapattanam" **Mint:** Negapatnam **Note:** This series for circulation in Ceylon. Weight varies: 53.60-57.10 grams.

Date	Mintage	Good	VG	F	VF	XF
ND(1695)	—	65.00	100	150	225	—

HAMMERED COINAGE

First Series

KM# 34 CASH

Copper **Obv:** P/VOC monogram **Rev:** Two-line Nandi-Nagara inscription **Mint:** Pulicat

Date	Mintage	Good	VG	F	VF	XF
ND(1615-46)	—	20.00	35.00	60.00	100	—

KM# 35.1 CASH

Copper **Rev:** Arabic inscription "in the name of Sultan Abd'allah" **Mint:** Pulicat

Date	Mintage	Good	VG	F	VF	XF
ND(1646-)	—	7.50	15.00	25.00	45.00	—

KM# 35.2 CASH

Copper **Obv:** Retrograde P **Mint:** Pulicat

Date	Mintage	Good	VG	F	VF	XF
ND(1646-)	—	15.00	25.00	45.00	75.00	—

KM# 36.1 2 CASH

Copper **Obv:** VOC monogram with P above **Rev:** Two-line Nandi-Nagara inscription **Mint:** Pulicat

Date	Mintage	Good	VG	F	VF	XF
ND(1615-46) Rare	—	—	—	—	—	—

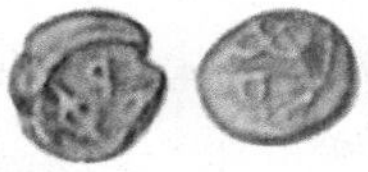

KM# 36.2 2 CASH

Copper **Obv:** P/VOC monogram **Rev:** Arabic inscription "in the name of Sultan Abd'allah" **Mint:** Pulicat

Date	Mintage	Good	VG	F	VF	XF
ND(1646-)	—	15.00	30.00	60.00	120	—

KM# 37 2 CASH

Copper **Obv:** II/VOC monogram **Rev:** Similar to 1 Cash, KM#35 **Mint:** Pulicat

Date	Mintage	Good	VG	F	VF	XF
ND(1646-)	—	15.00	30.00	65.00	125	—

KM# 38 4 CASH

Copper **Obv. Inscription:** PAL/IIII/VOC **Rev:** Similar to 1 Cash, KM#35 **Mint:** Pulicat

Date	Mintage	Good	VG	F	VF	XF
ND(1646-)	—	35.00	75.00	165	275	—

KM# 39 8 CASH

Copper **Obv. Inscription:** PAL/VIII/VOC **Rev:** Similar to 1 Cash, KM#35 **Mint:** Pulicat

Date	Mintage	Good	VG	F	VF	XF
ND(1646-)	—	50.00	100	200	350	—

HAMMERED COINAGE

Second Series

KM# 42 5 CASH

Copper **Obv:** V/VOC monogram **Rev:** Similar to 1 Cash, KM#35 **Mint:** Pulicat **Note:** Struck for circulation in Ceylon.

Date	Mintage	VG	F	VF	XF	Unc
ND(1646-74)	—	65.00	125	225	375	—

KM# 43 10 CASH

Copper **Obv:** X/VOC monogram **Rev:** Similar to 1 Cash, KM#35 **Mint:** Pulicat **Note:** Struck for circulation in Ceylon.

Date	Mintage	VG	F	VF	XF	Unc
ND(1646-74)	—	30.00	60.00	120	200	—

PONDICHERY

HAMMERED COINAGE

KM# 23 CASH

Bronze **Obv:** Deity Kali **Mint:** Without Mint Name **Note:** Prev. India-French KM#32.

Date	Mintage	Good	VG	F	VF	XF
ND(1693-98)	—	15.00	30.00	60.00	100	—

INDIA-FRENCH

It was not until 1664, during the reign of Louis XIV, that the Compagnie des Indes Orientales was formed for the purpose of obtaining holdings on the subcontinent of India. Between 1666 and 1721, French settlements were established at Arcot, Mahe, Surat, Pondichery, Masulipatam, Karikal, Yanam, Murshidabad, Chandernagore, Balasore and Calicut. War with Britain reduced the French holdings to Chandernagore, Pondichery, Karikal, Yanam and Mahe. Chandernagore voted in 1949 to join India and became part of the Republic of India in 1950. Pondichery, Karikal, Yanam and Mahe formed the Pondichery union territory and joined the republic of India in 1954.

RULER

French, until 1954

MINTS

پهلچري

Pondichery

A city south of Madras on the southeast coast which became the site of the French Mint from 1700-1841. Pondichery was settled by the French in 1683. It became their main Indian possession even though it was occupied by the Dutch in 1693-98 and several times by the British from 1761-1816.

سورت

Surat

MONETARY SYSTEM

Cache Kas or Cash
Doudou = 4 Caches
Biche = 1 Pice
2 Royalins = 1 Fanon Pondichery
5 Heavy Fanons = 1 Rupee Mahe
64 Biches = 1 Rupee

PONDICHERY

HAMMERED COINAGE

KM# 40 FANON

0.9480 Silver **Obv:** Lis **Obv. Legend:** PONDICHERY **Rev:** Lis in center of outlined cross **Note:** Weight varies 2.50-2.70 grams. Size varies 13-15 mm.

Date	Mintage	VG	F	VF	XF	Unc
1700	—	200	300	550	850	—

INDIA-PORTUGUESE

Vasco da Gama, the Portuguese explorer, first visited India in 1498. Portugal seized control of a number of islands and small enclaves on the west coast of India, and for the next hundred years enjoyed a monopoly on trade. With the arrival of powerful Dutch and English fleets in the first half of the 17th century, Portuguese power in the area declined until virtually all of India that remained under Portuguese control were the west coast enclaves of Goa, Damao and Diu. They were forcibly annexed by India in 1962.

RULER

Portuguese, until 1961

DENOMINATION

The denomination of most copper coins appears in numerals on the reverse, though 30 Reis is often given as "1/2 T", and 60 Reis as "T" (T = Tanga). The silver coins have the denomination in words, usually on the obverse until 1850, then on the reverse.

BACAIM

(Bessein)

Located less than 30 miles north of Bombay on the Gulf of Cambay. In 1611 the Portuguese opened a mint at Bacaim. The greatest minting activity was between 1678 and 1697. Many issues for Bacaim were in conjunction with other Portuguese settlements. The British took Bacaim in 1780.

MINT MARK

B - Bacain

MONETARY SYSTEM

375 Bazarucos = 1 Pardao
2 Pardaos = 1 Rupia

COLONY

HAMMERED COINAGE

KM# 1 XERAFIM

10.4800 g., Silver **Subject:** Alfonso VI **Obv:** Crowned arms divide FB in inner circle **Rev:** Numerals of date in angles of cross

Date	Mintage	Good	VG	F	VF	XF
1661	—	225	425	700	1,350	—
1662	—	225	425	700	1,350	—
1663	—	225	425	700	1,350	—
1664	—	225	425	700	1,350	—

BACAIM & CHAUL

These two Portuguese settlements flanked the city of Bombay and minted coins as a joint venture in the 1650's after minting permission was granted in 1646. These coins are identified by the coat of arms being flanked by B-C or C-B.

COLONY

HAMMERED COINAGE

KM# 4 4 BAZARUCOS

4.2200 g., Copper **Subject:** John IV **Obv:** Crowned arms flanked by C & B **Rev:** Numerals in angles of cross; all in dotted circles

Date	Mintage	Good	VG	F	VF	XF
1654	—	80.00	160	300	600	—

KM# 2 TANGA

2.1000 g., Silver **Subject:** John IV **Obv:** Crowned arms flanked by C and B **Rev:** St. John standing left divides S and T; date divided at bottom

Date	Mintage	Good	VG	F	VF	XF
1653	—	120	250	450	900	—

KM# 6 TANGA

1.3000 g., Silver **Obv:** Crowned arms divide C and B **Rev:** Gridiron of St. Lawrence divides date which is placed as 5-4 above 1-6

Date	Mintage	Good	VG	F	VF	XF
1654	—	—	—	—	—	—

KM# 1 2 TANGAS

4.2000 g., Silver **Subject:** John IV **Obv:** Crowned arms divide B and C in dotted circle **Rev:** Gridiron of St. Lawrence divides date in dotted circle

Date	Mintage	Good	VG	F	VF	XF
1645	—	125	250	500	1,100	—

Note: Exists overstruck on Goa 2 Tanga, KM#68.

KM# 3 2 TANGAS

4.2400 g., Silver **Obv:** Crowned arms divide C and B in dotted circle **Rev:** St. John standing left divides S and T; date divided at bottom

Date	Mintage	Good	VG	F	VF	XF
1653	—	100	200	450	1,000	—

KM# 5 2 TANGAS

3.8900 g., Silver **Subject:** Effigy of St. John **Obv:** Crowned arms divide C and B **Rev:** St. John standing left divides S and I, date placement is 1-6 above 5-3

Date	Mintage	Good	VG	F	VF	XF
1653	—	—	—	—	—	—

COCHIN

(Cochim)

Cochim was the first European settlement in India. Vasco da Gama founded a trading factory for the Portuguese at this location in 1502. Alfonso d'Albuquerque (who was to be the second governor of Portuguese settlements in India, 1509-1515) built a fort here in 1503. This location was an important Portuguese center until the British withdrew when the Dutch attacked in 1663. The town was retaken by the British in 1795.

COLONY

HAMMERED COINAGE

KM# 15 XERAFIM

10.2300 g., Silver **Obv:** Crowned arms divides CO in inner circle **Rev:** Numerals of date in angles of cross

Date	Mintage	Good	VG	F	VF	XF
1661	—	450	850	1,500	2,750	—

DAMAO

(Daman)

A city located 100 miles north of Bombay. It was captured by the Portuguese in 1559. A mint was opened in Damao in 1611. This mint continued in operation until 1854. While important to early Portuguese trade, Damao dwindled as time passed. It was annexed to India in 1962.

MONETARY SYSTEM

375 Bazacucos = 300 Reis
300 Reis = 1 Pardao
60 Reis = 1 Tanga
2 Pardao (Xerafins) = 1 Rupia

COLONY

HAMMERED COINAGE

KM# 6 5 BAZARUCOS

14.6000 g., Copper **Subject:** Philip II **Obv:** Crowned arms in inner circle divide VB; legend in outer circle **Rev:** Cross with stars in angles in inner circle; legend in outer circle

Date	Mintage	Good	VG	F	VF	XF
1611	—	120	240	425	825	—

DIU

A district in Western India formerly belonging to Portugal. It is 170 miles northwest of Bombay on the Kathiawar peninsula. The Portuguese settled here and built a fort in 1535. A mint was opened in 1685 and was closed in 1859. As with Damao, the importance of Diu diminished with the passage of time. It was annexed to India in 1962.

MONETARY SYSTEM

750 Bazarucos = 600 Reis
40 Atia = 10 Tanga = 1 Rupia

COLONY

HAMMERED COINAGE

KM# 1 1/2 BAZARUCO

2.8000 g., Copper **Obv:** Crowned arms divide DO **Rev:** Numerals of date in angles of cross potent

Date	Mintage	Good	VG	F	VF	XF
1686	—	10.00	20.00	35.00	65.00	—
1698	—	10.00	20.00	35.00	65.00	—

KM# 2 BAZARUCO

4.5700 g., Copper **Subject:** Peter, as Prince Regent **Obv:** Crowned arms divide DO **Rev:** Numerals of date in angles of cross potent

Date	Mintage	Good	VG	F	VF	XF
1668	—	15.00	30.00	50.00	95.00	—
1670	—	8.50	17.50	27.50	48.00	—
1670 Retrograde 7	—	15.00	25.00	40.00	70.00	—
1678	—	8.50	17.50	27.50	48.00	—
1678	—	10.00	20.00	35.00	60.00	—
1680 Large 8	—	8.50	17.50	30.00	55.00	—
1680 Small 8	—	10.00	20.00	35.00	60.00	—
1682	—	10.00	20.00	35.00	60.00	—

KM# 6 BAZARUCO

7.5000 g., Copper **Subject:** Peter II **Obv:** Crowned medium arms divide DO **Rev:** Numerals of date in angles of cross potent

Date	Mintage	Good	VG	F	VF	XF
1686	—	8.50	17.50	27.50	48.00	—
1688	—	10.00	20.00	35.00	60.00	—
1689	—	8.50	17.50	27.50	48.00	—
1697	—	8.50	17.50	30.00	55.00	—
1698	—	8.50	17.50	30.00	55.00	—

KM# 10 BAZARUCO

6.9700 g., Copper **Obv:** Crowned small arms **Rev:** Numerals of date in angles of cross

Date	Mintage	Good	VG	F	VF	XF
1699	—	10.00	20.00	35.00	65.00	—

KM# 11 BAZARUCO

7.5000 g., Copper **Obv:** Crowned large arms divide D (retrograde), O in beaded circle **Rev:** Numerals of date in angles of cross potent

Date	Mintage	Good	VG	F	VF	XF
1700	—	10.00	20.00	35.00	65.00	—

KM# 3 2 BAZARUCOS

6.2000 g., Copper **Subject:** Peter, as Prince Regent **Obv:** Crowned small arms divide DO in inner circle **Rev:** Numerals of date in angles of cross potent

Date	Mintage	Good	VG	F	VF	XF
1679	—	27.50	70.00	120	245	—

KM# 7 2 BAZARUCOS
6.8000 g., Copper **Subject:** Peter II **Obv:** Crowned small arms divide DO in plain circle **Rev:** Numerals of date in angles of cross potent

Date	Mintage	Good	VG	F	VF	XF
1686	—	20.00	40.00	70.00	150	—

KM# 12 2 BAZARUCOS
8.2000 g., Copper **Obv:** Crowned large arms divide DO in plain circle **Rev:** Numerals of date in angles of cross potent

Date	Mintage	Good	VG	F	VF	XF
1700	—	17.00	35.00	65.00	140	—

KM# 4 1/2 XERAFIM
5.8900 g., Silver **Ruler:** Peter II **Obv:** Crude crowned arms in branches **Rev:** Voided floreated cross

Date	Mintage	Good	VG	F	VF	XF
ND(1683-1706)	—	80.00	160	285	475	—

KM# A4 1/2 XERAFIM
5.0000 g., Silver **Subject:** Peter II **Obv:** Crowned arms divide DO in circle **Rev:** Numerals of date in angles of cross in circle

Date	Mintage	Good	VG	F	VF	XF
1684	—	175	325	575	1,000	—
1690	—	175	325	575	1,000	—
1691	—	175	325	575	1,000	—
1692	—	175	325	575	1,000	—
1694	—	175	325	575	1,000	—
1697	—	175	325	575	1,000	—

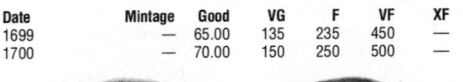

KM# 5 XERAFIM
11.4700 g., Silver **Ruler:** Peter II **Obv:** Crowned arms in branches **Rev:** Voided floreated cross

Date	Mintage	Good	VG	F	VF	XF
ND(1683-1706)	—	65.00	125	225	375	—

KM# 8 XERAFIM
10.6300 g., Silver **Ruler:** Peter II **Obv:** Crowned arms divide DO within circle **Rev:** Numerals of date in angles of cross within circle

Date	Mintage	Good	VG	F	VF	XF
1684	—	70.00	150	250	500	—
1686	—	70.00	150	250	500	—
1688	—	70.00	150	250	500	—
1690	—	65.00	135	235	450	—
1691	—	70.00	150	250	500	—
1692	—	70.00	150	250	500	—
1693	—	70.00	150	250	500	—
1694	—	70.00	150	250	500	—
1695	—	70.00	150	250	500	—
1696	—	65.00	135	235	450	—
1697	—	65.00	135	235	450	—
1698	—	70.00	150	250	500	—
1699	—	65.00	135	235	450	—
1700	—	70.00	150	250	500	—

KM# 9 2 XERAFINS
21.3600 g., Silver **Subject:** Peter II **Obv:** Crowned arms divide OD (retrograde) in plain circle **Rev:** Numerals of date in angles of cross in plain circle

Date	Mintage	Good	VG	F	VF	XF
1688	—	250	450	750	1,450	—

GOA

Goa was the capitol of Portuguese India and is located 250 miles south of Bombay on the west coast of India. It was taken by Albuquerque in 1510. A mint was established immediately and operated until closed by the British in 1869. Later coins were struck at Calcutta and Bombay. Goa was annexed by India in 1962.

MONETARY SYSTEM
375 Bazarucos = 300 Reis
240 Reis = 1 Pardao
2 Xerafim = 1 Rupia

NOTE: The silver Xerafim was equal to the silver Pardao, but the gold Xerafim varied according to fluctuations in the gold/silver ratio.

COLONY

HAMMERED COINAGE

KM# 58 1/2 TANGA (30 Reis)
1.0200 g., Silver **Subject:** Philip III **Obv:** Crowned arms divide GA in circle **Rev:** Standing figure of St. Philip with cross at left, F at right

Date	Mintage	Good	VG	F	VF	XF
ND	—	120	240	400	650	—

KM# 59 1/2 TANGA (30 Reis)
0.9800 g., Silver **Rev:** MTA monogram in circle

Date	Mintage	Good	VG	F	VF	XF
ND	—	60.00	120	240	425	—

KM# 64 1/2 TANGA (30 Reis)
0.9000 g., Silver **Subject:** John IV **Obv:** Crowned arms divide AD in circle **Rev:** MTA monogram in circle

Date	Mintage	Good	VG	F	VF	XF
ND	—	150	300	475	875	—

KM# 69 1/2 TANGA (30 Reis)
1.0400 g., Silver **Obv:** Standing figure of St. John divides SI and date

Date	Mintage	Good	VG	F	VF	XF
ND	—	85.00	165	325	—	—

KM# 75 1/2 TANGA (30 Reis)
0.9000 g., Silver **Subject:** Peter as Prince Regent **Obv:** Crowned arms divide GA in circle **Rev:** Numerals of date in angles of cross

Date	Mintage	Good	VG	F	VF	XF
1678	—	180	350	600	1,000	—

KM# 79 1/2 TANGA (30 Reis)
0.9400 g., Silver **Subject:** Peter II **Rev:** Numerals of date in angles of cross in circle

Date	Mintage	Good	VG	F	VF	XF
1691	—	120	240	425	775	—

KM# 63 TANGA (60 Reis)
2.1700 g., Silver **Subject:** Philip III **Obv:** Crowned arms divide GA in circle **Rev:** Standing figure of St. Philip divides date and SF

Date	Mintage	Good	VG	F	VF	XF
1634	—	85.00	175	325	550	—
1640	—	50.00	100	200	375	—
1641	—	50.00	100	200	375	—

KM# 65 TANGA (60 Reis)
2.2000 g., Silver **Obv:** Crowned arms divide GA **Rev:** Gridiron of St. Lawrence divides date; crown below

Date	Mintage	Good	VG	F	VF	XF
1640	—	40.00	85.00	175	325	—

KM# 70 TANGA (60 Reis)
1.5500 g., Silver **Subject:** John IV **Obv:** Crowned arms divide GA in circle **Rev:** Standing figure of St. John divides SI and date

Date	Mintage	Good	VG	F	VF	XF
1644	—	70.00	145	265	450	—

KM# 71 TANGA (60 Reis)
1.9400 g., Silver **Rev:** Numerals of date in angles of cross in circle

Date	Mintage	Good	VG	F	VF	XF
1650	—	40.00	80.00	150	275	—
1654	—	60.00	120	225	425	—
1655	—	60.00	120	225	425	—

KM# 74 TANGA (60 Reis)
1.9800 g., Silver **Subject:** Alfonso VI

Date	Mintage	Good	VG	F	VF	XF
1661	—	100	200	350	650	—
1662	—	100	200	350	600	—
1663	—	100	200	350	650	—
1664	—	100	200	350	650	—
1676	—	40.00	80.00	135	270	—
1677	—	40.00	80.00	135	270	—
1681	—	40.00	80.00	135	270	—
1682	—	40.00	80.00	135	270	—
1683	—	45.00	90.00	155	300	—
1684	—	35.00	70.00	120	250	—
1686	—	35.00	70.00	120	250	—
1687	—	30.00	60.00	100	220	—
1691	—	30.00	60.00	100	220	—
1692	—	30.00	60.00	100	220	—
1698	—	35.00	70.00	120	250	—

KM# 66 2 TANGAS
4.2500 g., Silver **Subject:** John IV **Obv:** Crowned arms divide GA in circle **Rev:** Standing figure of St. Philip divides SF and date

Date	Mintage	Good	VG	F	VF	XF
1640	—	75.00	135	225	375	—
1641	—	65.00	125	200	350	—

KM# 68 2 TANGAS

4.4000 g., Silver **Rev:** Standing figure of St. John divides SI and date

Date	Mintage	Good	VG	F	VF	XF
1642	—	45.00	90.00	165	300	—
1643	—	45.00	90.00	165	300	—
1649	—	50.00	100	180	325	—
1650	—	30.00	65.00	120	220	—
1651	—	35.00	75.00	135	250	—
1652	—	25.00	55.00	110	205	—
1653	—	50.00	100	120	325	—
1655	—	50.00	100	120	325	—
1656	—	50.00	100	120	325	—

KM# A68 2 TANGAS

4.4000 g., Silver **Rev:** Gridiron of St. Lawrence divides date, crown below

Date	Mintage	Good	VG	F	VF	XF
1645	—	60.00	120	240	400	—

KM# 72 1/2 XERAFIM (150 Reis)

5.3400 g., Silver **Subject:** John IV **Obv:** Crowned arms divide GA in circle **Rev:** Numerals of date in angles of cross in circle

Date	Mintage	Good	VG	F	VF	XF
1650	—	50.00	100	200	375	—
1665	—	200	400	750	1,400	—
1666	—	250	525	950	1,700	—
1668	—	250	525	950	1,700	—
1672	—	50.00	100	200	375	—
1673	—	35.00	65.00	135	275	—
1680	—	35.00	65.00	135	275	—
1681	—	30.00	60.00	120	220	—
1682	—	30.00	60.00	120	220	—
1683	—	30.00	60.00	120	220	—
1684	—	30.00	60.00	120	220	—
1685	—	20.00	40.00	85.00	180	—
1686	—	22.50	45.00	100	205	—
1688	—	20.00	40.00	85.00	180	—
1690	—	20.00	40.00	85.00	180	—
1693	—	20.00	40.00	85.00	180	—
1694	—	20.00	40.00	85.00	180	—
1697	—	20.00	40.00	85.00	180	—
1699	—	20.00	40.00	85.00	180	—
1700	—	25.00	50.00	110	220	—

KM# 67 XERAFIM

11.0000 g., Silver **Subject:** John IV **Obv:** Crowned arms divide GA in inner circle **Rev:** Standing figure of St. Philip left divides SF and date

Date	Mintage	Good	VG	F	VF	XF
ND	—	200	400	750	1,400	—
1641	—	300	650	1,150	1,950	—
1642	—	125	275	525	1,000	—
1643	—	200	400	750	1,400	—
1644	—	200	400	750	1,400	—
1649	—	125	275	525	1,000	—

KM# 73 XERAFIM

10.4400 g., Silver **Obv:** Crowned arms divide GA in inner circle **Rev:** Numerals of date in angles of cross in circle

Date	Mintage	Good	VG	F	VF	XF
1650	—	60.00	125	300	550	—
1651	—	60.00	125	300	550	—
1652	—	75.00	150	325	600	—
1653	—	65.00	135	310	575	—
1654	—	50.00	110	275	525	—
1655	—	50.00	110	275	525	—
1656	—	50.00	110	275	525	—
1657	—	50.00	110	275	525	—
1659	—	250	450	750	1,400	—
1664	—	250	450	750	1,400	—
1668	—	250	450	750	1,400	—
1669	—	45.00	90.00	200	375	—
1671	—	35.00	75.00	150	300	—
1672	—	35.00	75.00	150	300	—
1673	—	35.00	75.00	150	300	—
1675	—	35.00	75.00	150	300	—
1676	—	35.00	75.00	150	300	—
1678	—	35.00	75.00	150	300	—
1681	—	30.00	65.00	125	275	—
1682	—	30.00	65.00	125	275	—
1683	—	30.00	65.00	125	275	—

KM# 76 XERAFIM

0.6800 g., Gold **Subject:** Alfonso VI **Obv:** Crowned arms divide GA in inner circle **Rev:** Numerals of date in angles of cross in inner circle

Date	Mintage	Good	VG	F	VF	XF
1678	—	700	1,200	2,200	4,250	—
1679	—	700	1,200	2,200	4,250	—
1680	—	700	1,200	2,200	4,250	—

KM# 77 XERAFIM

10.5700 g., Silver **Subject:** Peter II

Date	Mintage	Good	VG	F	VF	XF
1683	—	45.00	90.00	165	325	—
1684	—	32.50	75.00	125	250	—
1685	—	32.50	75.00	125	250	—
1686	—	30.00	60.00	60.00	220	—
1687	—	30.00	60.00	60.00	220	—
1688	—	30.00	60.00	60.00	220	—
1689	—	30.00	60.00	60.00	220	—
1690	—	30.00	60.00	60.00	220	—
1691	—	30.00	60.00	60.00	220	—
1700	—	40.00	85.00	85.00	290	—

KM# 60 1/2 PATACAO

8.6300 g., Silver **Subject:** Philip III **Obv:** Crowned arms divide GA in inner circle **Rev:** Cross fleury in inner circle

Date	Mintage	Good	VG	F	VF	XF
1630 Rare	—	—	—	—	—	—

KM# 61 PATACAO

17.2900 g., Silver **Subject:** Philip III **Obv:** Crowned arms divide GA in inner circle, date below **Rev:** Cross fleury in inner circle

Date	Mintage	Good	VG	F	VF	XF
1630 Rare	—	—	—	—	—	—
1631 Rare	—	—	—	—	—	—

KM# 78 2 XERAFINS

21.0000 g., Silver **Subject:** Peter II **Obv:** Crowned arms divide GA in circle **Rev:** Numerals of date in angles of cross in circle **Note:** This issue is often encountered with various local countermarks.

Date	Mintage	Good	VG	F	VF	XF
1685	—	85.00	175	325	600	—
1686	—	85.00	175	325	600	—
1694	—	85.00	175	325	600	—
1700	—	100	200	350	650	—

KM# 57 5 XERAFINS

3.4600 g., Gold **Subject:** Philip II **Obv:** Crowned arms divide GA in inner circle; legend around border **Rev:** Standing figure of St. Thomas left in inner circle; legend around border

Date	Mintage	Good	VG	F	VF	XF
1616 Rare	—	—	—	—	—	—

Note: Hess-Divo Romanones Auction 269 10-96 GVF realized $19,055

KM# 62 5 XERAFINS

3.6000 g., Gold **Subject:** Philip III

Date	Mintage	Good	VG	F	VF	XF
1632	—	1,000	2,500	5,500	9,500	—
1633	—	1,000	2,500	5,500	9,500	—
1634	—	1,000	2,500	5,500	9,500	—
1635	—	1,000	2,500	5,500	9,500	—
1650 Rare	—	—	—	—	—	—
1651 Rare	—	—	—	—	—	—

Note: Hess-Divo Romanones Auction 269 10-96 VF realized $13,255

Date	Mintage	Good	VG	F	VF	XF
1660 Rare	—	—	—	—	—	—
1670 Rare	—	—	—	—	—	—
1677 Rare	—	—	—	—	—	—
1678 Rare	—	—	—	—	—	—
1680 Rare	—	—	—	—	—	—
1681 Rare	—	—	—	—	—	—
1682 Rare	—	—	—	—	—	—
	—	950	2,250	4,500	9,000	—

TOKEN COINAGE

KM# Tn1 BAZARUCO

7.2900 g., Copper **Obv:** Crowned arms between symbols, date below **Rev:** Cross in inner circle; legend around border **Note:** Antonio Telles de Menezes, issuer of this token was captain of

Diu and later Governor of all Portuguese India (1639-1640). Many varieties exist in the legends and shield.

Date	Mintage	Good	VG	F	VF	XF
1626	—	25.00	50.00	100	185	—
1627	—	25.00	50.00	100	185	—
1628	—	25.00	50.00	100	185	—

IRAN

Iran (historically known as Persia until 1931AD) is one of the world's most ancient and resilient nations. Strategically astride the lower land gate to Asia, it has been conqueror and conquered, sovereign nation and vassal state, ever emerging from its periods of glory or travail with its culture and political individuality intact. Iran (Persia) was a powerful empire under Cyrus the Great (600-529 B.C.), its borders extending from the Indus to the Nile. It has also been conquered by the predatory empires of antique and recent times - Assyrian, Medean, Macedonian, Seljuq, Turk, Mongol - and more recently been coveted by Russia, the Third Reich and Great Britain. Revolts against the absolute power of the Persian shahs resulted in the establishment of a constitutional monarchy in1906.

RULERS

Abbas I, AH997-1039/1588-1629AD
Safi I, AH1038-52/1629-42AD
Abbas II, AH1052-77/1642-66AD
Safi II, AH1077-79/1666-68AD
Sulayman I, AH1079-1105/1668-94AD
Husayn I, AH1105-35/1694-1722AD

MINT NAMES

Abu Shahr (Bushire) ابو سهر

Ardanush اردنوش

Ardebil (Ardabil) اردبيل

Astarabad (Iran) استراباد

Baghdad (Iraq) بغداد

Bandar Abbas بندر عباس

Bandar Abu Shahr بندر ابو شهر

Basra (al-Basrah, Iraq) البصرة

Behbahan (Bihbihan) بهبهان

Bahkar (Afghanistan) بكهر بكّر

Borujerd بروجرد

Dadiyan داديان

Darband دربند

Dawraq دورق

Dehdasht دهدشت

Dezful دزفول

Eravan (Iravan, Armenia) ايروان

Farahabad فرح اباد

Fuman فومان

Ganjeh (Ganja, Azerbaijan) گنجه

Gilan گنلان

Hamadan همدان

Herat, (Afghanistan) هراة هرات

Huwayza حويزة

Iravan (Yeravan, Armenia) ايروان

Isfahan (Esfahan) اصفهان

Jelou (Army Mint) جلو

Kashan كاشان

Kirman (Kerman) كرمان

Kirmanshahan (Kermanshah) كرمانساهان

Khoy (Khoi, Khuy) خوي

Lahijan لاهيجان

Lahore (Afghanistan) لاهور

Maragheh مراغة

Mashhad (Meshad Iman Rida) مشهد امام رضى

Mazandaran مازندران

Nahawand نهاوند

Nakhjawan (Azerbaijan) نخجوان

Naseri ناصري

Nimruz نمرز نيمروز

Nukhwi نخوي

Panahabad (Azerbaijan) پناه اباد

Peshawar (Afghanistan) پشاور

Qandahar (Kandahar, Afghanistan) قندهار

Qazvin قزوين

Qomm (Kumm, Qumm) قم

Ra'nash (Ramhurmuz) رعنش

Rasht رشت

Rekab (Rikab) ركاب

Reza'iyeh (Army Mint) رضائية

Sarakhs سرخس

Sari ساري

Sawuj Balagh ساوج بلاق

Shamakha (Shemakhi, Shimakhi, Azerbaijan) شماخي شماخه

Shiraz شيراز

Shirwan (Azerbaijan) شيروان شروان

Shushtar شوستر

Simnan (Semnan) سمنان

Sind (Afghanistan) سند

Sultanabad سلطاناباد

Tabaristan (Tabarestan, region N.W. of Iran) طبرستان

Tabriz	تبريز
Tehran	طهران
Tiflis (Georgia)	تفليس
Tuyserkan	توي سركان
Urumi (Reza'iyeh)	ارمية
Yazd	يزد
Zanjan	زنجان
Zegam	زگام

MONETARY SYSTEM

The Shahi was a fixed unit, first coined in AD1501, equal to 50 Dinars. The Toman, introduced as a unit of account about AH1240 (1824AD) was always fixed at 10,000 Dinars. The value of the Rupee for this period is not known with certainty.

SILVER and GOLD COINAGE

The precious metal monetary system of Qajar Persia prior to the reforms of 1878 was the direct descendant of the Mongol system introduced by Ghazan Mahmud in 1297AD, and was the last example of a medieval Islamic coinage. It is not a modern system, and cannot be understood as such. It is not possible to list types, dates, and mints as for other countries, both because of the nature of the coinage, and because very little research has been done on the series. The following comments should help elucidate its nature.

DENOMINATIONS

In addition to the primary denominations, noted in the last paragraph, fractional pieces were coined, valued at one-eighth, one-fourth, and one-half the primary denomination, usually in much smaller quantities. These were ordinarily struck from the same dies as the larger pieces, sometimes on broad, thin flans, sometimes on thick, dumpy flans. On the smaller coins, the denomination can best be determined only by weighing the coin. The denomination is almost never expressed on the coin!

NOTE: This is a sampling of what dates and types exist. For pricing other examples use same mint and judge by strike and grade.

NOTE: Grade and clarity of strike are both important in pricing Iranian coins. Prices listed here are for average strikes. Fully struck and well centered can can command a premium up to two times what is appropriate. For examples of an excellent strike see KM209; common strike see KM 241; poor strike see KM 195.

KINGDOM

Anonymous

HAMMERED COINAGE

Ardabil

KM# 150 FALUS

10.8200 g., Copper **Obv:** Fish in sprays **Rev:** Inscription with value, mint name and date

Date	Mintage	Good	VG	F	VF	XF
AH1052	—	12.00	30.00	50.00	—	—

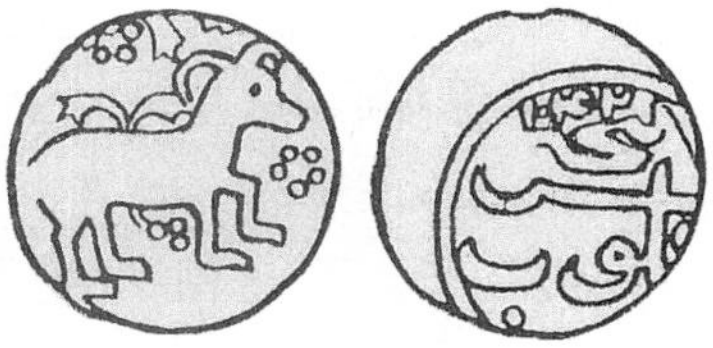

Ganjah

KM# 126 FALUS

8.9100 g., Copper **Obv:** Goat right, branches behind **Rev:** Inscription with value, mint name and date

Date	Mintage	Good	VG	F	VF	XF
AH1042	—	12.00	30.00	50.00	—	—

KM# A208 FALUS

8.1400 g., Copper **Obv:** Lion (?) left, branches above **Rev:** Inscription with value, mint name and AH date

Date	Mintage	Good	VG	F	VF	XF
AH1081	—	10.00	25.00	40.00	—	—

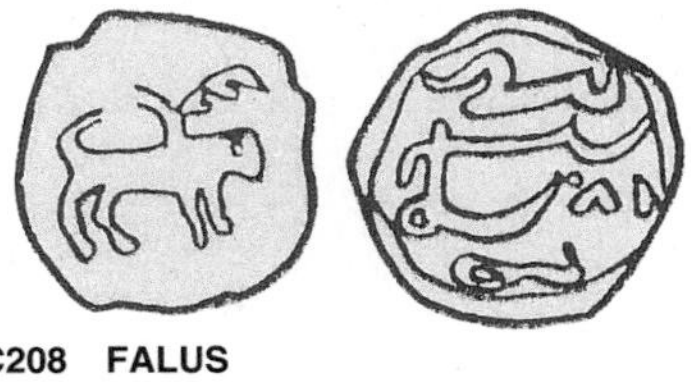

KM# C208 FALUS

7.7000 g., Copper **Obv:** Lion (?) right, branches above **Rev:** Inscription with mint name and AH date

Date	Mintage	Good	VG	F	VF	XF
AH1088	—	10.00	25.00	40.00	—	—

KM# 241 FALUS

10.6000 g., Copper **Obv:** Lion left **Rev:** Inscription with mint name and AH date

Date	Mintage	Good	VG	F	VF	XF
AH1106	—	10.00	25.00	40.00	—	—

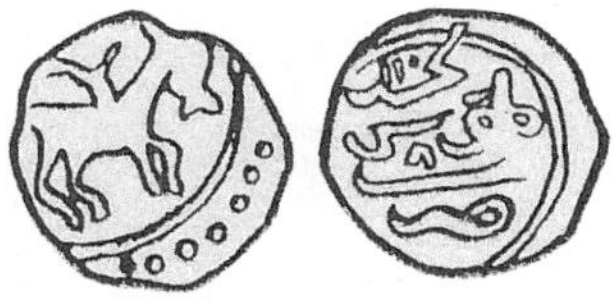

KM# 244 FALUS

4.4600 g., Copper **Obv:** Stag right **Rev:** Inscription with value, mint name and AH date

Date	Mintage	Good	VG	F	VF	XF
AH1108	—	10.00	25.00	40.00	—	—

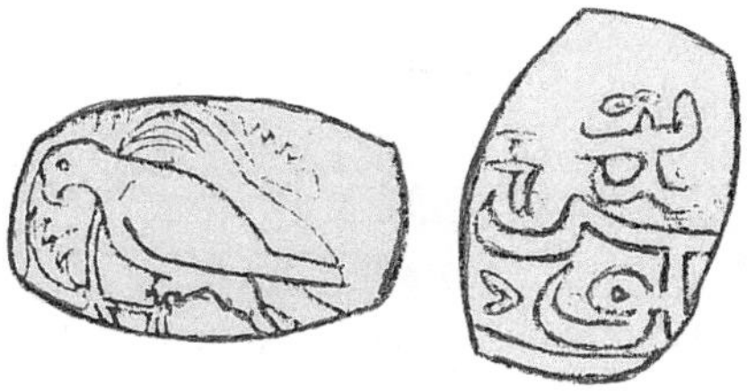

Hamadan

KM# 128 FALUS

10.7400 g., Copper **Obv:** Bird perched at left, branches behind **Rev:** Inscription with value, mint name and date

Date	Mintage	Good	VG	F	VF	XF
AH1048	—	15.00	35.00	60.00	—	—

KM# C209 FALUS

15.8100 g., Copper **Obv:** Lion left, rayed sunface behind **Rev:** Inscription with value, mint name and AH date

Date	Mintage	Good	VG	F	VF	XF
AH1098	—	11.50	27.50	45.00	—	—

KM# D209 FALUS

10.5200 g., Copper **Obv:** Brahma bull left **Rev:** Inscription with value, mint name and AH date

Date	Mintage	Good	VG	F	VF	XF
AH1099	—	10.00	25.00	40.00	—	—

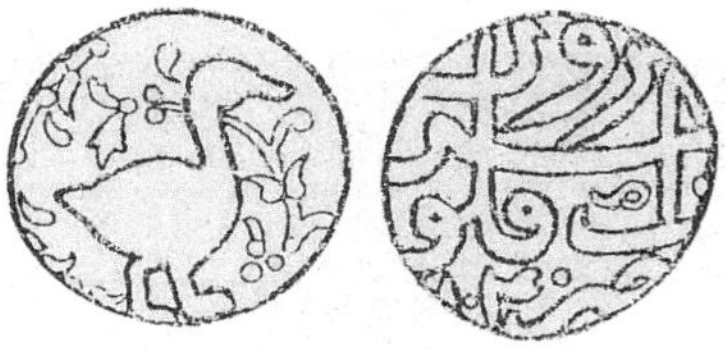

Iravan (Yerevan)

KM# 124 FALUS

11.1900 g., Copper **Obv:** Duck right, branches behind **Rev:** Inscription with value, mint name and date

Date	Mintage	Good	VG	F	VF	XF
AH1040	—	10.00	25.00	45.00	—	—

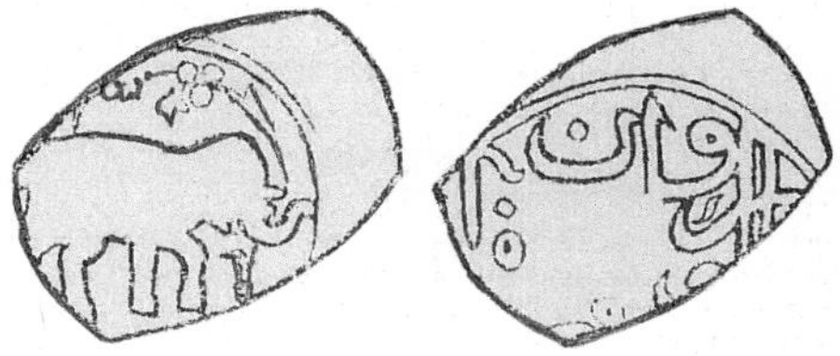

KM# 152 FALUS

10.4200 g., Copper **Obv:** Elephant right, branch behind **Rev:** Inscription with value, mint name and AH date

Date	Mintage	Good	VG	F	VF	XF
AH1057	—	10.00	25.00	45.00	—	—

KM# 154 FALUS

10.5900 g., Copper **Obv:** Lion right, facing **Rev:** Inscription with value, mint name and AH date

Date	Mintage	Good	VG	F	VF	XF
AH1060	—	10.00	25.00	45.00	—	—

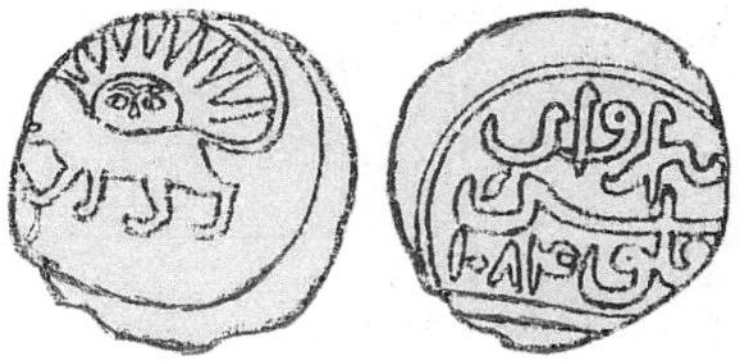

KM# B208 FALUS

7.9700 g., Copper **Obv:** Lion left, rayed sunface behind **Rev:** Inscription with value, mint name and AH date

Date	Mintage	Good	VG	F	VF	XF
AH1084	—	10.00	25.00	45.00	—	—

KM# 208 FALUS

8.1300 g., Copper **Obv:** Sheep resting amongst bushes **Rev:** Inscription with value, mint name and AH date

Date	Mintage	Good	VG	F	VF	XF
AH1095	—	14.00	35.00	50.00	—	—

For coins without mint listed see coin above.

KM# 209 FALUS
9.8500 g., Copper **Obv:** Bird left in bushes **Rev:** Inscription with value, mint name and AH date

Date	Mintage	Good	VG	F	VF	XF
AH1104	—	15.00	35.00	60.00	—	—

KM# 245 FALUS
8.5400 g., Copper **Obv:** Peacock left **Rev:** Inscription with value, mint name and AH date

Date	Mintage	Good	VG	F	VF	XF
AH1108	—	12.00	30.00	50.00	—	—

Isfahan

KM# 195 FALUS
7.7100 g., Copper **Obv:** Stag left, branches above **Rev:** Inscription with value, mint name and AH date

Date	Mintage	Good	VG	F	VF	XF
AH1078	—	8.00	20.00	30.00	—	—

Qandahar

KM# 81 FALUS
Copper **Obv:** Sun over lion walking left

Date	Mintage	Good	VG	F	VF	XF
AH1058	—	15.00	25.00	45.00	80.00	—

KM# 82 FALUS
Copper **Obv:** Lion left seizing stag right **Note:** Type 82.

Date	Mintage	Good	VG	F	VF	XF
AH1059	—	20.00	30.00	45.00	85.00	—

KM# 83 FALUS
Copper **Obv:** Sun over lion walking left **Note:** Type 83.

Date	Mintage	Good	VG	F	VF	XF
AH107x	—	12.00	20.00	35.00	60.00	—
AH1085	—	12.00	20.00	35.00	60.00	—
AH1086	—	12.00	20.00	35.00	60.00	—

KM# 84 FALUS
Copper **Obv:** Horse galloping right **Note:** Type 84.

Date	Mintage	Good	VG	F	VF	XF
AH1080	—	20.00	30.00	50.00	90.00	—

KM# 85 FALUS
Copper **Obv:** Horse galloping left **Note:** Type 85.

Date	Mintage	Good	VG	F	VF	XF
AH1080	—	20.00	30.00	50.00	90.00	—

KM# 86 FALUS
Copper **Obv:** Camel left **Note:** Type 86.

Date	Mintage	Good	VG	F	VF	XF
AH1082	—	20.00	30.00	50.00	90.00	—

KM# 87 FALUS
Copper **Obv:** Camel right **Note:** Type 87.

Date	Mintage	Good	VG	F	VF	XF
AH1082	—	20.00	30.00	50.00	90.00	—
AH1083	—	20.00	30.00	50.00	90.00	—

KM# 88 FALUS
Copper **Obv:** Flowers at left, two-bladed sabre at center **Note:** Type 88.

Date	Mintage	Good	VG	F	VF	XF
AH1097	—	15.00	25.00	40.00	75.00	—
ND Date effaced	—	9.00	15.00	25.00	45.00	—

KM# 89 FALUS
Copper **Obv:** Sun over lion walking right **Note:** Type 89.

Date	Mintage	Good	VG	F	VF	XF
AH1107	—	15.00	25.00	40.00	70.00	—

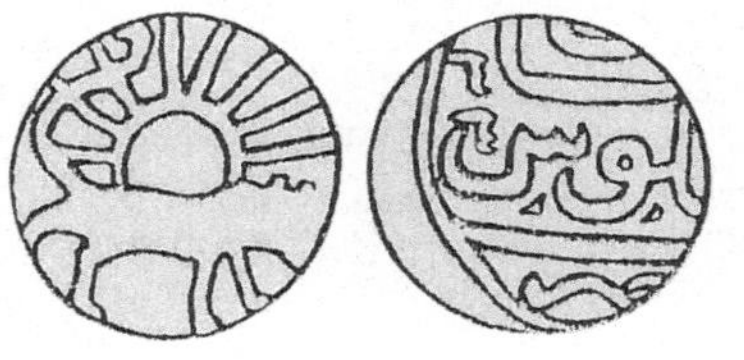

Ra'nash

KM# A112 FALUS
8.6500 g., Copper **Obv:** Rayed sun behind lion at right **Rev:** Inscription with value, mint name and date

Date	Mintage	Good	VG	F	VF	XF
AH1033	—	20.00	50.00	80.00	—	—

Rasht

KM# 151 FALUS
10.7300 g., Copper **Obv:** Peacock right **Rev:** Inscription with value, mint name and AH date

Date	Mintage	Good	VG	F	VF	XF
AH1054	—	15.00	35.00	55.00	—	—

Shamakha

KM# 158 FALUS
10.3900 g., Copper **Obv:** Bird standing left, branches behind **Rev:** Value, mint name

Date	Mintage	Good	VG	F	VF	XF
AH1076	—	15.00	35.00	60.00	—	—

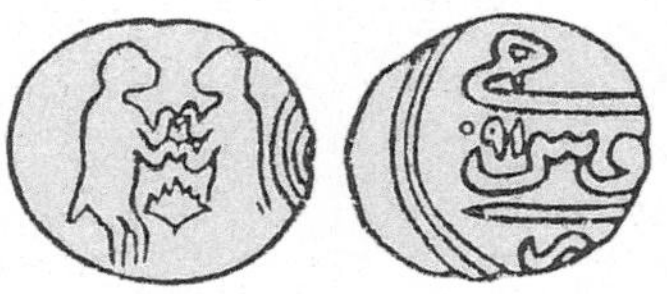

KM# D208 FALUS
5.6600 g., Copper **Obv:** Two upright animals facing each other **Rev:** Inscription with value, mint name and AH date

Date	Mintage	Good	VG	F	VF	XF
AH1091	—	20.00	45.00	75.00	—	—

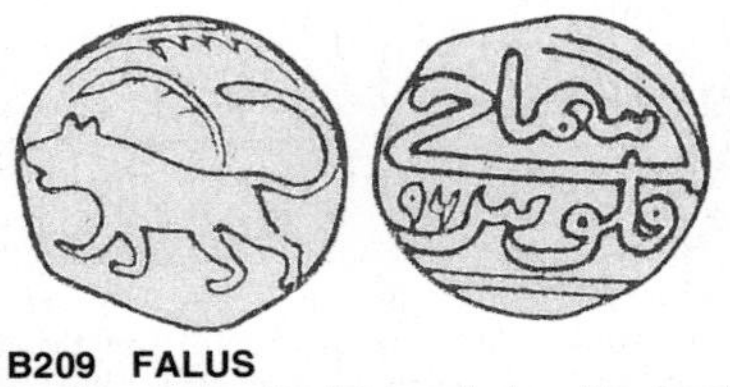

KM# B209 FALUS
8.4500 g., Copper **Obv:** Lion left, branch above **Rev:** Inscription with value, mint name and AH date

Date	Mintage	Good	VG	F	VF	XF
AH1096	—	10.00	25.00	40.00	—	—

KM# 247 FALUS
10.2100 g., Copper **Obv:** Peacock left **Rev:** Inscription with value, mint name and AH date

Date	Mintage	Good	VG	F	VF	XF
AH1110	—	12.00	30.00	50.00	—	—

Tabriz

KM# 127 FALUS
10.9500 g., Copper **Obv:** Peacock right, branches behind **Rev:** Inscription with value, mint name and date

Date	Mintage	Good	VG	F	VF	XF
AH1048	—	15.00	30.00	50.00	—	—

KM# 129 FALUS
10.5700 g., Copper **Obv:** Elephant right, branches behind **Rev:** Inscription with value, mint name and date

Date	Mintage	Good	VG	F	VF	XF
AH1051	—	10.00	25.00	40.00	—	—

KM# 101 FALUS

Copper **Obv:** Elephant right **Note:** Type 101.

Date	Mintage	Good	VG	F	VF	XF
AH1051	—	18.00	30.00	50.00	90.00	—

KM# 155 FALUS

9.5500 g., Copper **Obv:** Bird attacking animal right **Rev:** Inscription with value, mint name and AH date

Date	Mintage	Good	VG	F	VF	XF
AH1062	—	10.00	20.00	35.00	—	—

KM# 156 FALUS

9.8100 g., Copper **Obv:** Peacock right **Rev:** Inscription with value, mint name and AH date

Date	Mintage	Good	VG	F	VF	XF
AH1069	—	10.00	20.00	35.00	—	—

KM# 157 FALUS

9.7800 g., Copper **Obv:** Bramabull right **Rev:** Value, mint name

Date	Mintage	Good	VG	F	VF	XF
AH1072	—	8.00	18.00	30.00	—	—

KM# 102 FALUS

Copper **Obv:** Peacock left **Note:** Type 102.

Date	Mintage	Good	VG	F	VF	XF
AH1081	—	12.00	20.00	40.00	65.00	—

KM# 103 FALUS

Copper **Obv:** Lion left and sun **Note:** Type 103.

Date	Mintage	Good	VG	F	VF	XF
AH(10)85	—	10.00	18.00	30.00	50.00	—

KM# 104 FALUS

Copper **Obv:** Brahma bull right, branch below in wreath border **Note:** Type 104.

Date	Mintage	Good	VG	F	VF	XF
AH1095	—	10.00	18.00	30.00	50.00	—

KM# A209 FALUS

10.8700 g., Copper **Obv:** Brama bull right **Rev:** Inscription with value, mint name and AH date

Date	Mintage	Good	VG	F	VF	XF
AH1095	—	10.00	25.00	40.00	—	—

KM# 246 FALUS

10.4700 g., Copper **Obv:** Large animal right, palm tree behind **Rev:** Inscription with value, mint name and AH date

Date	Mintage	Good	VG	F	VF	XF
AH1108	—	8.00	20.00	35.00	—	—

KM# 105 FALUS

Copper **Obv:** Brahma bull right, fish below **Note:** Type 105.

Date	Mintage	Good	VG	F	VF	XF
AH1112	—	15.00	25.00	40.00	70.00	—

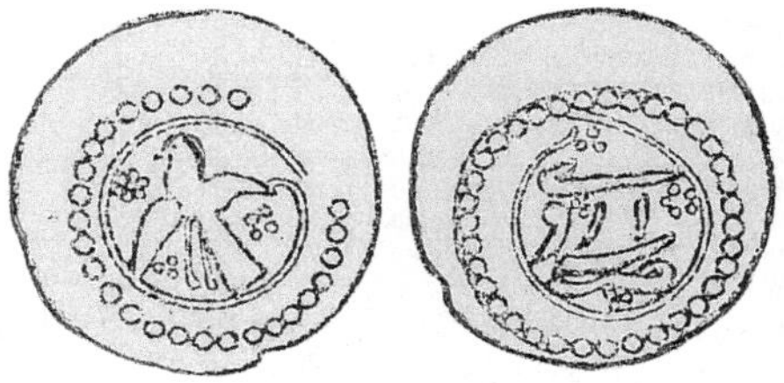

Urumi

KM# 153 FALUS

8.3200 g., Copper **Obv:** Dove in flight **Rev:** Mint name

Date	Mintage	Good	VG	F	VF	XF
AH1058	—	15.00	30.00	50.00	—	—

Abbas I

AH996-1038 / 1588-1629AD

HAMMERED COINAGE

Ardabil

KM# 112.1 SHAHI (50 Dinars)

1.9200 g., Silver

Date	Mintage	VG	F	VF	XF	Unc
AH1025	—	25.00	65.00	100	145	—

Farahabad

KM# 112.2 SHAHI (50 Dinars)

1.9200 g., Silver

Date	Mintage	VG	F	VF	XF	Unc
ND	—	30.00	70.00	125	165	—

Herat

KM# 112.4 SHAHI (50 Dinars)

1.9200 g., Silver

Date	Mintage	VG	F	VF	XF	Unc
ND	—	30.00	70.00	125	165	—

Iravan (Yerevan)

KM# 112.3 SHAHI (50 Dinars)

1.9200 g., Silver

Date	Mintage	VG	F	VF	XF	Unc
AH1024	—	20.00	50.00	75.00	110	—

Isfahan

KM# 112.5 SHAHI (50 Dinars)

1.9200 g., Silver

Date	Mintage	VG	F	VF	XF	Unc
AH1011	—	15.00	35.00	60.00	100	—
AH1022	—	15.00	35.00	60.00	100	—
AH1033	—	15.00	35.00	60.00	100	—
AH1034	—	15.00	35.00	60.00	100	—

Rasht

KM# 112.6 SHAHI (50 Dinars)

1.9200 g., Silver

Date	Mintage	VG	F	VF	XF	Unc
AH1022	—	12.00	40.00	70.00	115	—
AH1024	—	12.00	40.00	70.00	115	—
AH1030	—	12.00	40.00	70.00	115	—

Tabriz

KM# 112.7 SHAHI (50 Dinars)

1.9200 g., Silver

Date	Mintage	VG	F	VF	XF	Unc
AH1028	—	15.00	35.00	60.00	100	—

Urdu

KM# 112.8 SHAHI (50 Dinars)

1.9200 g., Silver

Date	Mintage	VG	F	VF	XF	Unc
ND	—	25.00	60.00	100	135	—

Baghdad

KM# 113.1 2 SHAHI (Mahmudi)

3.8400 g., Silver

Date	Mintage	VG	F	VF	XF	Unc
ND	—	35.00	95.00	125	170	—

Behbehán

KM# 113.2 2 SHAHI (Mahmudi)

3.8400 g., Silver

Date	Mintage	VG	F	VF	XF	Unc
AH1018	—	25.00	60.00	100	145	—
AH1029	—	25.00	60.00	100	145	—

Dawraq

KM# 113.3 2 SHAHI (Mahmudi)

3.8400 g., Silver

Date	Mintage	VG	F	VF	XF	Unc
AH1015	—	10.00	25.00	40.00	75.00	—
ND	—	5.00	12.00	20.00	35.00	—

Isfahan

KM# 113.4 2 SHAHI (Mahmudi)

3.8400 g., Silver

Date	Mintage	VG	F	VF	XF	Unc
AH1023	—	8.00	20.00	40.00	65.00	—
AH1034	—	8.00	20.00	40.00	65.00	—

Mashhad

KM# 113.5 2 SHAHI (Mahmudi)

3.8400 g., Silver

Date	Mintage	VG	F	VF	XF	Unc
AH10(2)7	—	30.00	70.00	100	150	—

Ramhurmuz

KM# 113.6 2 SHAHI (Mahmudi)

3.8400 g., Silver

Date	Mintage	VG	F	VF	XF	Unc
AH1031	—	40.00	95.00	150	220	—

Tabriz

KM# 127.7 2 SHAHI (Mahmudi)

3.8400 g., Silver

Date	Mintage	VG	F	VF	XF	Unc
AH1035	—	15.00	35.00	60.00	85.00	—

Ardabil

KM# 114.1 ABBASI

7.6800 g., Silver

Date	Mintage	VG	F	VF	XF	Unc
AH1017	—	20.00	45.00	75.00	135	—
AH1028	—	8.00	20.00	35.00	60.00	—
AH1029	—	8.00	20.00	35.00	60.00	—
AH1030	—	8.00	20.00	35.00	60.00	—
AH1032	—	8.00	20.00	35.00	60.00	—
AH1035	—	8.00	20.00	35.00	60.00	—
AH1036	—	8.00	20.00	35.00	60.00	—
AH1037	—	8.00	20.00	35.00	60.00	—
AH1038	—	8.00	20.00	35.00	60.00	—

Astarabad

KM# 114.2 ABBASI

7.6800 g., Silver

Date	Mintage	VG	F	VF	XF	Unc
ND	—	20.00	50.00	75.00	110	—

Baghdad

KM# 114.3 ABBASI

7.6800 g., Silver

Date	Mintage	VG	F	VF	XF	Unc
AH1031	—	35.00	95.00	125	180	—
AH1032	—	35.00	95.00	125	180	—
AH1033	—	35.00	95.00	125	180	—
AH1035	—	35.00	95.00	125	180	—

Behbehán

KM# 114.4 ABBASI

7.6800 g., Silver

Date	Mintage	VG	F	VF	XF	Unc
AH1029	—	20.00	65.00	100	125	—
AH1031	—	20.00	65.00	100	125	—

For coins without mint listed see coin above.

Dawraq

KM# 114.5 ABBASI
7.6800 g., Silver

Date	Mintage	VG	F	VF	XF	Unc
AH1032	—	20.00	30.00	50.00	75.00	—
AH1038	—	20.00	30.00	50.00	75.00	—

Dezful

KM# 114.6 ABBASI
7.6800 g., Silver

Date	Mintage	VG	F	VF	XF	Unc
AH1031	—	25.00	60.00	100	155	—

Farahabad

KM# 114.8 ABBASI
7.6800 g., Silver

Date	Mintage	VG	F	VF	XF	Unc
ND	—	25.00	60.00	100	140	—
AH1027	—	40.00	90.00	150	210	—

KM# 114.9 ABBASI
7.6800 g., Silver

Date	Mintage	VG	F	VF	XF	Unc
AH1019	—	15.00	40.00	60.00	90.00	—
AH1020	—	15.00	40.00	60.00	90.00	—
AH1029	—	8.00	20.00	30.00	50.00	—
AH1031	—	8.00	20.00	30.00	50.00	—
AH1032	—	8.00	20.00	30.00	50.00	—
AH1036	—	8.00	20.00	30.00	50.00	—

Hamadan

KM# 114.22 ABBASI
7.6800 g., Silver

Date	Mintage	VG	F	VF	XF	Unc
AH1019	—	25.00	60.00	100	140	—

Iravan (Yerevan)

KM# 114.7 ABBASI
7.6800 g., Silver

Date	Mintage	VG	F	VF	XF	Unc
AH1021	—	15.00	35.00	50.00	75.00	—
AH1024	—	15.00	35.00	50.00	75.00	—
AH1026	—	7.00	17.00	25.00	45.00	—
AH1027	—	7.00	17.00	25.00	45.00	—
AH1030	—	7.00	17.00	25.00	45.00	—
AH1031	—	7.00	17.00	25.00	45.00	—
AH1032	—	7.00	17.00	25.00	45.00	—
AH1033	—	7.00	17.00	25.00	45.00	—
AH1034	—	7.00	17.00	25.00	45.00	—
AH1035	—	7.00	17.00	25.00	45.00	—
AH1036	—	7.00	17.00	25.00	45.00	—
AH1037	—	7.00	17.00	25.00	45.00	—

Isfahan

KM# 114.10 ABBASI
7.6800 g., Silver

Date	Mintage	VG	F	VF	XF	Unc
AH1017	—	12.00	30.00	45.00	70.00	—
AH1018	—	12.00	30.00	45.00	70.00	—
AH1022	—	12.00	30.00	45.00	70.00	—
AH1024	—	12.00	30.00	45.00	70.00	—
AH1025	—	12.00	30.00	45.00	70.00	—
AH1028	—	8.00	18.00	30.00	45.00	—
AH1030	—	8.00	18.00	30.00	45.00	—
AH1033	—	8.00	18.00	30.00	45.00	—

Qazvin

KM# 114.11 ABBASI
7.6800 g., Silver

Date	Mintage	VG	F	VF	XF	Unc
AH1014(?)	—	18.00	40.00	60.00	95.00	—
AH1025	—	18.00	40.00	60.00	95.00	—
AH1027	—	10.00	25.00	35.00	60.00	—
AH1028	—	10.00	25.00	35.00	60.00	—
AH1030	—	10.00	25.00	35.00	60.00	—
AH1037	—	10.00	25.00	35.00	60.00	—

Ramhurmuz

KM# 114.12 ABBASI
7.6800 g., Silver

Date	Mintage	VG	F	VF	XF	Unc
AH1021	—	25.00	60.00	100	145	—

Rasht

KM# 114.13 ABBASI
7.6800 g., Silver

Date	Mintage	VG	F	VF	XF	Unc
AH1027	—	20.00	50.00	80.00	130	—
AH1031	—	20.00	50.00	80.00	130	—

Shamakha

KM# 114.21 ABBASI
7.6800 g., Silver

Date	Mintage	VG	F	VF	XF	Unc
AH1015	—	15.00	40.00	75.00	110	—

Shushtar

KM# 114.15 ABBASI
7.6800 g., Silver

Date	Mintage	VG	F	VF	XF	Unc
AH1031	—	9.00	22.00	35.00	60.00	—
AH1034	—	9.00	22.00	35.00	60.00	—

Tabriz

KM# 114.16 ABBASI
7.6800 g., Silver

Date	Mintage	VG	F	VF	XF	Unc
AH1017	—	12.00	30.00	45.00	70.00	—
AH1019	—	12.00	30.00	45.00	70.00	—
AH1021	—	12.00	30.00	45.00	70.00	—
AH1022	—	12.00	30.00	45.00	70.00	—
AH1024	—	12.00	30.00	45.00	70.00	—
AH1026	—	5.00	12.00	18.00	35.00	—
AH1027	—	5.00	12.00	18.00	35.00	—
AH1028	—	5.00	12.00	18.00	35.00	—
AH1030	—	5.00	12.00	18.00	35.00	—
AH1031	—	5.00	12.00	18.00	35.00	—
AH1032	—	5.00	12.00	18.00	35.00	—
AH1033//1032	—	8.00	20.00	30.00	60.00	—
AH1035	—	5.00	12.00	18.00	35.00	—
AH1036	—	5.00	12.00	18.00	35.00	—
AH1037	—	5.00	12.00	18.00	35.00	—
AH1038	—	5.00	12.00	18.00	35.00	—

Tehran

KM# 114.17 ABBASI
7.6800 g., Silver

Date	Mintage	VG	F	VF	XF	Unc
AH1011	—	60.00	90.00	150	200	—

Tiflis

KM# 114.18 ABBASI
7.6800 g., Silver

Date	Mintage	VG	F	VF	XF	Unc
AH1028	—	12.00	30.00	42.00	65.00	—
AH1038	—	12.00	30.00	42.00	65.00	—

Urdu

KM# 114.19 ABBASI
7.6800 g., Silver

Date	Mintage	VG	F	VF	XF	Unc
AH1014	—	20.00	50.00	75.00	115	—
AH1020	—	20.00	50.00	75.00	115	—
AH1023	—	20.00	50.00	75.00	115	—
AH1032	—	8.00	35.00	60.00	95.00	—
AH1035	—	8.00	35.00	60.00	95.00	—

Zegam

KM# 114.20 ABBASI
7.6800 g., Silver

Date	Mintage	VG	F	VF	XF	Unc
ND	—	35.00	90.00	125	175	—

KM# 118.2 ABBASI (type 118)
7.6800 g., Silver **Note:** Without mint name.

Date	Mintage	VG	F	VF	XF	Unc
AH1033	—	12.00	30.00	45.00	80.00	—

Mazandaran

KM# 118.1 ABBASI (type 118)
7.6800 g., Silver

Date	Mintage	VG	F	VF	XF	Unc
AH1037	—	15.00	40.00	65.00	120	—
ND Undated	—	8.00	20.00	35.00	65.00	—

Mashhad

KM# 108 ASHRAFI (Heavy Standard)
3.9000 g., Gold **Rev:** Mintname and epithet in central cartouche

Date	Mintage	VG	F	VF	XF	Unc
AH1014	—	—	BV	250	325	—

Qazvín

KM# B116 ASHRAFI (Heavy Standard)
3.9000 g., Gold

Date	Mintage	VG	F	VF	XF	Unc
AH1019	—	275	300	450	550	—

Safi I

AH1038-1052 / 1629-1642AD

HAMMERED COINAGE

Ardabil

KM# 132.1 SHAHI (50 Dinars)
1.9200 g., Silver **Note:** Type B.

Date	Mintage	VG	F	VF	XF	Unc
AH1045	—	30.00	75.00	125	200	—
AH1046	—	30.00	75.00	125	200	—

Farahabad

KM# 132.2 SHAHI (50 Dinars)
1.9200 g., Silver **Note:** Type B.

Date	Mintage	VG	F	VF	XF	Unc
AH1049	—	40.00	100	150	220	—

Ganjah

KM# 132.3 SHAHI (50 Dinars)
1.9200 g., Silver **Note:** Type B.

Date	Mintage	VG	F	VF	XF	Unc
AH1040	—	20.00	50.00	80.00	125	—

Hamadan

KM# 132.4 SHAHI (50 Dinars)
1.9200 g., Silver **Note:** Type B.

Date	Mintage	VG	F	VF	XF	Unc
AH1039	—	25.00	60.00	100	160	—

Isfahan

KM# 132.5 SHAHI (50 Dinars)
1.9200 g., Silver **Note:** Type B.

Date	Mintage	VG	F	VF	XF	Unc
AH1040	—	15.00	35.00	60.00	85.00	—
AH1042	—	15.00	35.00	60.00	85.00	—

Rasht

KM# 132.6 SHAHI (50 Dinars)
1.9200 g., Silver **Note:** Type B.

Date	Mintage	VG	F	VF	XF	Unc
AHxxxx	—	20.00	30.00	75.00	115	—

Shiraz

KM# 132.7 SHAHI (50 Dinars)
1.9200 g., Silver **Note:** Type B.

Date	Mintage	VG	F	VF	XF	Unc
AHxxxx	—	20.00	65.00	100	150	—

Tabriz

KM# 132.8 SHAHI (50 Dinars)
1.9200 g., Silver **Note:** Type B.

Date	Mintage	VG	F	VF	XF	Unc
AH1044	—	15.00	35.00	60.00	95.00	—

Shamakha

KM# 140.1 SHAHI (50 Dinars - type 140)
1.9200 g., Silver **Note:** Type C.

Date	Mintage	VG	F	VF	XF	Unc
ND	—	25.00	65.00	100	140	—

Tiflis

KM# 140.2 SHAHI (50 Dinars - type 140)
1.9200 g., Silver **Note:** Type C.

Date	Mintage	VG	F	VF	XF	Unc
AH1052	—	30.00	70.00	125	180	—

Ardabil

KM# 133.1 2 SHAHI (Mahmudi)
3.8400 g., Silver **Note:** Type B.

Date	Mintage	VG	F	VF	XF	Unc
AH1045	—	18.00	65.00	100	135	—

Baghdad

KM# 133.2 2 SHAHI (Mahmudi)
3.8400 g., Silver **Note:** Type B.

Date	Mintage	VG	F	VF	XF	Unc
AH1038	—	40.00	100	150	220	—
AH1042	—	40.00	100	150	220	—
AH1047	—	40.00	100	150	220	—

Dawraq

KM# 133.3 2 SHAHI (Mahmudi)
3.8400 g., Silver **Note:** Type B.

Date	Mintage	VG	F	VF	XF	Unc
AH1047	—	20.00	50.00	80.00	110	—

Dehdasht

KM# 133.4 2 SHAHI (Mahmudi)
3.8400 g., Silver **Note:** Type B.

Date	Mintage	VG	F	VF	XF	Unc
AH1044	—	30.00	80.00	125	190	—

KM# 133.5 2 SHAHI (Mahmudi)
3.8400 g., Silver **Note:** Type B.

Date	Mintage	VG	F	VF	XF	Unc
AH1041	—	25.00	60.00	80.00	100	—

Isfahan

KM# 133.6 2 SHAHI (Mahmudi)
3.8400 g., Silver **Note:** Type B.

Date	Mintage	VG	F	VF	XF	Unc
AH1038	—	12.00	35.00	50.00	70.00	—
AH1042	—	12.00	35.00	50.00	70.00	—

Kashan

KM# 133.7 2 SHAHI (Mahmudi)
3.8400 g., Silver **Note:** Type B.

Date	Mintage	VG	F	VF	XF	Unc
AH1038	—	20.00	50.00	75.00	100	—

Nimruz

KM# 133.8 2 SHAHI (Mahmudi)
3.8400 g., Silver **Note:** Type B.

Date	Mintage	VG	F	VF	XF	Unc
AH1038	—	45.00	115	175	250	—

Rasht

KM# 133.9 2 SHAHI (Mahmudi)
3.8400 g., Silver **Note:** Type B.

Date	Mintage	VG	F	VF	XF	Unc
AH1038	—	20.00	60.00	75.00	110	—
AH1040	—	20.00	60.00	75.00	110	—

Tehran

KM# 133.10 2 SHAHI (Mahmudi)
3.8400 g., Silver **Note:** Type B.

Date	Mintage	VG	F	VF	XF	Unc
ND	—	35.00	85.00	125	165	—

Tiflis

KM# 141 2 SHAHI (Mahmudi - type 141)
3.8400 g., Silver **Note:** Type C.

Date	Mintage	VG	F	VF	XF	Unc
AH1052	—	30.00	70.00	100	160	—

Ardabil

KM# 142.1 ABBASI (Heavy Standard - type 142)
7.6800 g., Silver **Note:** Type C.

Date	Mintage	VG	F	VF	XF	Unc
AH1052	—	18.00	45.00	80.00	120	—

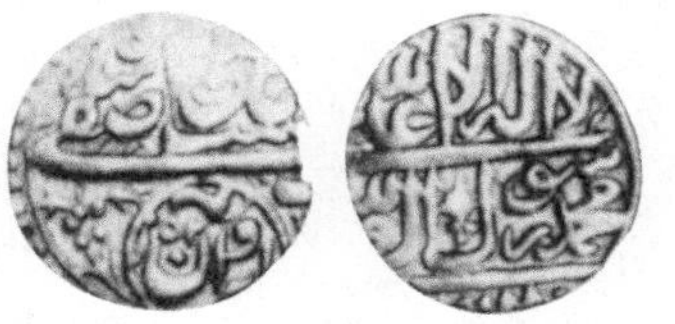

Ganjah

KM# 142.3 ABBASI (Heavy Standard - type 142)
7.6800 g., Silver **Note:** Type C.

Date	Mintage	VG	F	VF	XF	Unc
AH1050	—	12.00	27.00	40.00	62.00	—
AH1052	—	12.00	27.00	40.00	62.00	—

Hamadan

KM# 142.10 ABBASI (Heavy Standard - type 142)
7.6800 g., Silver **Note:** Type C.

Date	Mintage	VG	F	VF	XF	Unc
AH1050	—	20.00	45.00	75.00	110	—

Iravan (Yerevan)

KM# 142.2 ABBASI (Heavy Standard - type 142)
7.6800 g., Silver **Note:** Type C.

Date	Mintage	VG	F	VF	XF	Unc
AH1050	—	10.00	25.00	40.00	60.00	—
AH1051	—	10.00	25.00	40.00	60.00	—
AH1052	—	10.00	25.00	40.00	60.00	—

Isfahan

KM# 142.7 ABBASI (Heavy Standard - type 142)
7.6800 g., Silver **Note:** Type C.

Date	Mintage	VG	F	VF	XF	Unc
AH1051	—	15.00	35.00	60.00	95.00	—
AH1052	—	15.00	35.00	60.00	95.00	—

Rasht

KM# 142.9 ABBASI (Heavy Standard - type 142)
7.6800 g., Silver **Note:** Type C.

Date	Mintage	VG	F	VF	XF	Unc
AH1050	—	15.00	35.00	60.00	95.00	—
AH1051	—	15.00	35.00	60.00	95.00	—

Shamakha

KM# 142.8 ABBASI (Heavy Standard - type 142)
7.6800 g., Silver **Note:** Type C.

Date	Mintage	VG	F	VF	XF	Unc
ND	—	15.00	35.00	60.00	90.00	—

Tabriz

KM# 142.4 ABBASI (Heavy Standard - type 142)
7.6800 g., Silver **Note:** Type C.

Date	Mintage	VG	F	VF	XF	Unc
AH1050	—	15.00	35.00	50.00	75.00	—
AH1051	—	15.00	35.00	50.00	75.00	—
AH1052	—	15.00	35.00	50.00	75.00	—

Tiflis

KM# 142.5 ABBASI (Heavy Standard - type 142)
7.6800 g., Silver **Note:** Type C.

Date	Mintage	VG	F	VF	XF	Unc
AH1051	—	16.00	40.00	60.00	90.00	—
AH1052	—	16.00	40.00	60.00	90.00	—

Zegam

KM# 142.6 ABBASI (Heavy Standard - type 142)
7.6800 g., Silver **Note:** Type C.

Date	Mintage	VG	F	VF	XF	Unc
ND	—	30.00	80.00	150	220	—

Ardabil

KM# 134.1 ABBASI
7.6800 g., Silver **Note:** Type B.

Date	Mintage	VG	F	VF	XF	Unc
AH1039	—	10.00	25.00	40.00	60.00	—
AH1040	—	10.00	25.00	40.00	60.00	—
AH1041	—	10.00	25.00	40.00	60.00	—
AH1042	—	10.00	25.00	40.00	60.00	—
AH1045	—	10.00	25.00	40.00	60.00	—
AH1046	—	10.00	25.00	40.00	60.00	—

Ardanush

KM# 134.2 ABBASI
7.6800 g., Silver **Note:** Type B.

Date	Mintage	VG	F	VF	XF	Unc
AH1043	—	80.00	140	200	315	—

Baghdad

KM# 130.1 ABBASI
7.6800 g., Silver **Note:** Type A.

Date	Mintage	VG	F	VF	XF	Unc
AH1038	—	35.00	90.00	150	210	—

KM# 134.3 ABBASI
7.6800 g., Silver **Note:** Type B.

Date	Mintage	VG	F	VF	XF	Unc
AH1038	—	40.00	100	39.00	60.00	—
AH1040	—	40.00	100	39.00	60.00	—
AH1044	—	40.00	100	39.00	60.00	—
AH1045	—	40.00	100	39.00	60.00	—
AH1046	—	40.00	100	39.00	60.00	—
AH1047	—	40.00	100	39.00	60.00	—

Dehdasht

KM# 134.4 ABBASI
7.6800 g., Silver **Note:** Type B.

Date	Mintage	VG	F	VF	XF	Unc
AH1044	—	55.00	90.00	150	225	—

Ganjah

KM# 130.2 ABBASI
7.6800 g., Silver **Note:** Type A.

Date	Mintage	VG	F	VF	XF	Unc
AH1038	—	25.00	60.00	100	140	—

KM# 134.6 ABBASI
7.6800 g., Silver **Note:** Type B.

Date	Mintage	VG	F	VF	XF	Unc
AH1038	—	6.00	15.00	25.00	40.00	—
AH1039	—	6.00	15.00	25.00	40.00	—
AH1040	—	6.00	15.00	25.00	40.00	—
AH1041	—	6.00	15.00	25.00	40.00	—
AH1042	—	6.00	15.00	25.00	40.00	—
AH1044	—	6.00	15.00	25.00	40.00	—
AH1045	—	6.00	15.00	25.00	40.00	—
AH1047	—	6.00	15.00	25.00	40.00	—
AH1048	—	6.00	15.00	25.00	40.00	—

Hamadan

KM# 134.7 ABBASI
7.6800 g., Silver **Note:** Type B.

Date	Mintage	VG	F	VF	XF	Unc
AH1038	—	10.00	25.00	40.00	60.00	—
AH1039	—	10.00	25.00	40.00	60.00	—
AH1049	—	10.00	25.00	40.00	60.00	—
AH1050	—	10.00	25.00	40.00	60.00	—

Herat

KM# 134.8 ABBASI
7.6800 g., Silver **Note:** Type B.

Date	Mintage	VG	F	VF	XF	Unc
ND	—	60.00	100	150	250	—

Iravan (Yerevan)

KM# 134.5 ABBASI
7.6800 g., Silver **Note:** Type B.

Date	Mintage	VG	F	VF	XF	Unc
AH1038	—	6.00	15.00	25.00	40.00	—
AH1039	—	6.00	15.00	25.00	40.00	—
AH1040	—	6.00	15.00	25.00	40.00	—
AH1041	—	6.00	15.00	25.00	40.00	—
AH1042	—	6.00	15.00	25.00	40.00	—
AH1043	—	6.00	15.00	25.00	40.00	—
AH1044	—	6.00	15.00	25.00	40.00	—
AH1045	—	6.00	15.00	25.00	40.00	—
AH1046	—	6.00	15.00	25.00	40.00	—
AH1047	—	6.00	15.00	25.00	40.00	—
AH1048	—	6.00	15.00	25.00	40.00	—
AH1049	—	6.00	15.00	25.00	40.00	—

KM# 130.3 ABBASI
7.6800 g., Silver **Note:** Type A.

Date	Mintage	VG	F	VF	XF	Unc
AH1038	—	15.00	35.00	60.00	95.00	—

Isfahan

KM# 130.4 ABBASI
7.6800 g., Silver **Note:** Type A.

Date	Mintage	VG	F	VF	XF	Unc
AH1038	—	15.00	35.00	60.00	85.00	—

KM# 134.9 ABBASI
7.6800 g., Silver **Note:** Type B.

Date	Mintage	VG	F	VF	XF	Unc
AH1038	—	6.00	13.00	20.00	35.00	—
AH1039	—	6.00	13.00	20.00	35.00	—
AH1040	—	6.00	13.00	20.00	35.00	—
AH1041	—	6.00	13.00	20.00	35.00	—
AH1042	—	6.00	13.00	20.00	35.00	—
AH1044	—	6.00	13.00	20.00	35.00	—
AH1048	—	6.00	13.00	20.00	35.00	—

Kashan

KM# 134.10 ABBASI
7.6800 g., Silver **Note:** Type B.

Date	Mintage	VG	F	VF	XF	Unc
AH1038	—	10.00	23.00	35.00	45.00	—
AH1040	—	10.00	23.00	35.00	45.00	—

Nakhchawan

KM# 134.11 ABBASI
7.6800 g., Silver **Note:** Type B.

Date	Mintage	VG	F	VF	XF	Unc
ND	—	25.00	60.00	100	160	—

Nimruz

KM# 134.22 ABBASI
7.6800 g., Silver **Note:** Type B.

Date	Mintage	VG	F	VF	XF	Unc
ND	—	30.00	75.00	125	190	—

Qazvín

KM# 134.12 ABBASI
7.6800 g., Silver **Note:** Type B.

Date	Mintage	VG	F	VF	XF	Unc
AH1038	—	6.00	15.00	22.50	37.50	—
AH1039	—	6.00	15.00	22.50	37.50	—
AH1040	—	6.00	15.00	22.50	37.50	—
AH1042	—	6.00	15.00	22.50	37.50	—
AH1045	—	6.00	15.00	22.50	37.50	—
AH1046	—	6.00	15.00	22.50	37.50	—
AH1047	—	6.00	15.00	22.50	37.50	—

Rasht

KM# 134.13 ABBASI
7.6800 g., Silver **Note:** Type B.

Date	Mintage	VG	F	VF	XF	Unc
AH1038	—	12.00	30.00	50.00	75.00	—
AH1039	—	12.00	30.00	50.00	75.00	—
AH1049	—	12.00	30.00	50.00	75.00	—

Shamakha

KM# 134.14 ABBASI
7.6800 g., Silver **Note:** Type B.

Date	Mintage	VG	F	VF	XF	Unc
AH1038	—	12.00	30.00	45.00	65.00	—
AH1040	—	12.00	30.00	45.00	65.00	—
AH1041	—	12.00	30.00	45.00	65.00	—
AH1042	—	12.00	30.00	45.00	65.00	—
AH1043	—	12.00	30.00	45.00	65.00	—
AH1050	—	12.00	30.00	45.00	65.00	—

Shiraz

KM# 134.21 ABBASI
7.8600 g., Silver **Note:** Type B.

Date	Mintage	VG	F	VF	XF	Unc
AH103x	—	10.00	25.00	40.00	60.00	—
AH1041	—	25.00	60.00	100	160	—

For coins without mint listed see coin above.

Shushtar

KM# 134.15 ABBASI
7.6800 g., Silver **Note:** Type B.

Date	Mintage	VG	F	VF	XF	Unc
AH1042	—	15.00	35.00	60.00	80.00	—

Tabriz

KM# 130.5 ABBASI
7.6800 g., Silver **Note:** Type A.

Date	Mintage	VG	F	VF	XF	Unc
AH1038	—	12.00	30.00	50.00	75.00	—

KM# 134.16 ABBASI
7.6800 g., Silver **Note:** Type B.

Date	Mintage	VG	F	VF	XF	Unc
AH1038	—	5.00	13.00	18.00	30.00	—
AH1039	—	5.00	13.00	18.00	30.00	—
AH1040	—	5.00	13.00	18.00	30.00	—
AH1041	—	5.00	13.00	18.00	30.00	—
AH1042	—	5.00	13.00	18.00	30.00	—
AH1043	—	5.00	13.00	18.00	30.00	—
AH1044	—	5.00	13.00	18.00	30.00	—
AH1045	—	5.00	13.00	18.00	30.00	—
AH1046	—	5.00	13.00	18.00	30.00	—
AH1047	—	5.00	13.00	18.00	30.00	—
AH1048	—	5.00	13.00	18.00	30.00	—
AH1049	—	5.00	13.00	18.00	30.00	—
AH1050	—	5.00	13.00	18.00	30.00	—

Tehran

KM# 134.17 ABBASI
7.6800 g., Silver **Note:** Type B.

Date	Mintage	VG	F	VF	XF	Unc
AH1041	—	27.00	70.00	100	145	—

Tiflis

KM# 130.6 ABBASI
7.6800 g., Silver **Note:** Type A.

Date	Mintage	VG	F	VF	XF	Unc
AH1039	—	15.00	35.00	60.00	95.00	—

KM# 134.18 ABBASI
7.6800 g., Silver **Note:** Type B.

Date	Mintage	VG	F	VF	XF	Unc
AH1039	—	12.00	30.00	50.00	80.00	—
AH1040	—	12.00	30.00	50.00	80.00	—
AH1041	—	12.00	30.00	50.00	80.00	—
AH1043	—	12.00	30.00	50.00	80.00	—
AH1045	—	12.00	30.00	50.00	80.00	—
AH1046	—	12.00	30.00	50.00	80.00	—

Urdu

KM# 134.19 ABBASI
7.6800 g., Silver **Note:** Type B.

Date	Mintage	VG	F	VF	XF	Unc
AH1045	—	20.00	50.00	80.00	115	—

Yazd

KM# 134.20 ABBASI
7.6800 g., Silver **Note:** Type B.

Date	Mintage	VG	F	VF	XF	Unc
AH1039	—	15.00	40.00	70.00	90.00	—
AH1040	—	15.00	40.00	70.00	90.00	—

Zegam

KM# 134.23 ABBASI
7.6800 g., Silver **Note:** Type B.

Date	Mintage	VG	F	VF	XF	Unc
AH1045	—	35.00	90.00	150	225	—

HAMMERED COINAGE

Local Type of Khuzistan

Dawraq

KM# 147.1 2 SHAHI (Mahmudi)
Silver **Note:** 3.84 grams or less.

Date	Mintage	VG	F	VF	XF	Unc
ND	—	7.00	17.00	35.00	50.00	—

Huwayza

KM# 147.2 2 SHAHI (Mahmudi)
Silver **Note:** 3.84 grams or less.

Date	Mintage	VG	F	VF	XF	Unc
ND	—	8.00	18.00	25.00	40.00	—

Abbas II

AH1052-1077 / 1642-1666AD

HAMMERED COINAGE

Tabriz

KM# 166 1/2 SHAHI (25 Dinars)
0.9600 g., Silver **Note:** Type B2.

Date	Mintage	VG	F	VF	XF	Unc
AH1064	—	10.00	22.50	80.00	110	—
ND Date and mint off flan.	—	10.00	17.50	30.00	40.00	—

Isfahan

KM# 161 SHAHI (50 Dinars)
1.9200 g., Silver **Note:** Type A.

Date	Mintage	VG	F	VF	XF	Unc
AH1053	—	35.00	90.00	125	180	—

Ganjah

KM# 167.21 SHAHI (50 Dinars - type 167)
1.8400 g., Silver **Note:** Type B2.

Date	Mintage	VG	F	VF	XF	Unc
AH1064	—	20.00	50.00	80.00	115	—

Isfahan

KM# 167.11 SHAHI (50 Dinars - type 167)
1.8400 g., Silver **Note:** Type B1.

Date	Mintage	VG	F	VF	XF	Unc
AH1057	—	15.00	40.00	50.00	75.00	—

Mashhad

KM# 167.12 SHAHI (50 Dinars - type 167)
1.8400 g., Silver **Note:** Type B1.

Date	Mintage	VG	F	VF	XF	Unc
AH1060	—	30.00	75.00	100	145	—

Rasht

KM# 167.13 SHAHI (50 Dinars - type 167)
1.8400 g., Silver **Note:** Type B1.

Date	Mintage	VG	F	VF	XF	Unc
AHxxxx	—	13.00	35.00	50.00	70.00	—

Shamakha

KM# 167.14 SHAHI (50 Dinars - type 167)
1.8400 g., Silver **Note:** Type B1.

Date	Mintage	VG	F	VF	XF	Unc
AH1061	—	30.00	75.00	100	145	—

Tabriz

KM# 167.15 SHAHI (50 Dinars - type 167)
1.8400 g., Silver **Note:** Type B1.

Date	Mintage	VG	F	VF	XF	Unc
AH1057	—	18.00	45.00	60.00	85.00	—
AH1059	—	18.00	45.00	60.00	85.00	—

Tiflis

KM# 167.22 SHAHI (50 Dinars - type 167)
1.8400 g., Silver **Note:** Type B2.

Date	Mintage	VG	F	VF	XF	Unc
AH1064	—	35.00	90.00	150	220	—

Unknown

KM# 174 SHAHI (50 Dinars - type 174)
1.8400 g., Silver **Note:** Type C1 or C2.

Date	Mintage	VG	F	VF	XF	Unc
AHxxxx	—	8.00	20.00	35.00	50.00	—

Isfahan

KM# 162.1 2 SHAHI (Mahmudi)
3.8400 g., Silver **Note:** Type A.

Date	Mintage	VG	F	VF	XF	Unc
AH1053	—	20.00	50.00	75.00	110	—

Tiflis

KM# 162.2 2 SHAHI (Mahmudi)
3.8400 g., Silver **Note:** Type A.

Date	Mintage	VG	F	VF	XF	Unc
AH1052	—	20.00	55.00	90.00	145	—

Ardabil

KM# 168.11 2 SHAHI (Mahmudi - type 168)
3.6900 g., Silver **Note:** Type B1.

Date	Mintage	VG	F	VF	XF	Unc
AH1059	—	25.00	55.00	80.00	105	—
AH1064	—	25.00	55.00	80.00	105	—

Iravan (Yerevan)

KM# 168.12 2 SHAHI (Mahmudi - type 168)
3.6900 g., Silver **Note:** Type B1.

Date	Mintage	VG	F	VF	XF	Unc
AH1058	—	12.50	35.00	50.00	70.00	—

Kashan

KM# 168.13 2 SHAHI (Mahmudi - type 168)
3.6900 g., Silver **Note:** Type B1.

Date	Mintage	VG	F	VF	XF	Unc
AH1056	—	15.00	40.00	60.00	90.00	—

Mashhad

KM# 168.14 2 SHAHI (Mahmudi - type 168)
3.6900 g., Silver **Note:** Type B1.

Date	Mintage	VG	F	VF	XF	Unc
AH1061	—	25.00	65.00	100	145	—

Qazvín

KM# 168.21 2 SHAHI (Mahmudi - type 168)
3.6900 g., Silver **Note:** Type B2.

Date	Mintage	VG	F	VF	XF	Unc
AH1065	—	25.00	55.00	80.00	115	—

Shamakha

KM# 168.22 2 SHAHI (Mahmudi - type 168)
3.6900 g., Silver **Note:** Type B2.

Date	Mintage	VG	F	VF	XF	Unc
AH1065	—	15.00	40.00	60.00	85.00	—

Shushtar

KM# 168.15 2 SHAHI (Mahmudi - type 168)
3.6900 g., Silver **Note:** Type B1.

Date	Mintage	VG	F	VF	XF	Unc
AHxxxx	—	10.00	30.00	50.00	70.00	—
AH1056	—	10.00	30.00	50.00	70.00	—
AH1063	—	10.00	30.00	50.00	70.00	—

Tiflis

KM# 168.16 2 SHAHI (Mahmudi - type 168)
3.6900 g., Silver **Note:** Type B1.

Date	Mintage	VG	F	VF	XF	Unc
AH1054	—	15.00	40.00	60.00	85.00	—
AH1061	—	15.00	40.00	60.00	85.00	—

Ardabil

KM# 163.1 ABBASI
7.6800 g., Silver **Note:** Type A.

Date	Mintage	VG	F	VF	XF	Unc
AH1052	—	20.00	50.00	90.00	140	—
AH1053	—	20.00	50.00	90.00	140	—

Dadiyan

KM# 163.13 ABBASI
7.6800 g., Silver **Note:** Type A.

Date	Mintage	VG	F	VF	XF	Unc
AH1053	—	25.00	60.00	100	160	—

Ganjah

KM# 163.3 ABBASI
7.6800 g., Silver **Note:** Type A.

Date	Mintage	VG	F	VF	XF	Unc
AH1052	—	20.00	45.00	75.00	110	—
AH1053	—	20.00	45.00	75.00	110	—
AH1054	—	20.00	45.00	75.00	110	—

Hamadan

KM# 163.10 ABBASI
7.6800 g., Silver **Note:** Type A.

Date	Mintage	VG	F	VF	XF	Unc
AH1053	—	25.00	60.00	100	160	—

Iravan (Yerevan)

KM# 163.2 ABBASI
7.6800 g., Silver **Note:** Type A.

Date	Mintage	VG	F	VF	XF	Unc
AH1052	—	15.00	35.00	60.00	85.00	—
AH1053	—	15.00	35.00	60.00	85.00	—

Isfahan

KM# 163.4 ABBASI
7.6800 g., Silver **Note:** Type A.

Date	Mintage	VG	F	VF	XF	Unc
AH1052	—	12.00	30.00	50.00	70.00	—
AH1053	—	12.00	30.00	50.00	70.00	—

Mashhad

KM# 163.11 ABBASI
7.6800 g., Silver **Note:** Type A.

Date	Mintage	VG	F	VF	XF	Unc
AH1052	—	20.00	45.00	75.00	110	—
AH1054	—	20.00	45.00	75.00	110	—

Nimruz

KM# 163.5 ABBASI

7.6800 g., Silver **Note:** Type A.

Date	Mintage	VG	F	VF	XF	Unc
AH1054 (sic)	—	40.00	95.00	150	220	—

Qazvin

KM# 163.12 ABBASI

7.6800 g., Silver **Note:** Type A.

Date	Mintage	VG	F	VF	XF	Unc
AH1052	—	20.00	45.00	75.00	110	—
AH1053	—	20.00	45.00	75.00	110	—

Rasht

KM# 163.6 ABBASI

7.6800 g., Silver **Note:** Type A.

Date	Mintage	VG	F	VF	XF	Unc
AH1052	—	17.00	40.00	60.00	85.00	—
AH1054	—	17.00	40.00	60.00	85.00	—

Shamakha

KM# 163.7 ABBASI

7.6800 g., Silver **Note:** Type A.

Date	Mintage	VG	F	VF	XF	Unc
AH1052	—	20.00	45.00	75.00	110	—
AH1053	—	20.00	45.00	75.00	110	—

Tabriz

KM# 163.8 ABBASI

7.6800 g., Silver **Note:** Type A.

Date	Mintage	VG	F	VF	XF	Unc
AH1052	—	10.00	27.00	45.00	65.00	—
AH1053	—	10.00	27.00	45.00	65.00	—
	—	10.00	27.00	45.00	65.00	—

Tiflis

KM# 163.9 ABBASI

7.6800 g., Silver **Note:** Type A.

Date	Mintage	VG	F	VF	XF	Unc
AH1052	—	15.00	40.00	55.00	85.00	—
AH1053	—	15.00	40.00	55.00	85.00	—
AH1054	—	15.00	40.00	55.00	85.00	—

Ardabil

KM# 169.1 ABBASI (type 169)

7.3900 g., Silver **Note:** Type B1.

Date	Mintage	VG	F	VF	XF	Unc
AH1054	—	8.00	20.00	30.00	50.00	—
AH1055	—	8.00	20.00	30.00	50.00	—
AH1056	—	8.00	20.00	30.00	50.00	—
AH1057	—	8.00	20.00	30.00	50.00	—
AH1059	—	8.00	20.00	30.00	50.00	—
AH1059/8	—	8.00	20.00	30.00	50.00	—
AH1063	—	8.00	20.00	30.00	50.00	—
AH1064	—	8.00	20.00	30.00	50.00	—

KM# 169.21 ABBASI (type 169)

7.3900 g., Silver **Note:** Type B2.

Date	Mintage	VG	F	VF	XF	Unc
AH1067	—	9.00	22.50	35.00	50.00	—

Dadiyan

KM# 169.2 ABBASI (type 169)

7.3900 g., Silver **Note:** Type B1.

Date	Mintage	VG	F	VF	XF	Unc
ND	—	50.00	115	150	200	—

Dawraq

KM# 169.22 ABBASI (type 169)

7.3900 g., Silver **Note:** Type B2.

Date	Mintage	VG	F	VF	XF	Unc
AH1063	—	20.00	50.00	75.00	100	—

Ganjah

KM# 169.4 ABBASI (type 169)

7.3900 g., Silver **Note:** Type B1.

Date	Mintage	VG	F	VF	XF	Unc
AH1054	—	5.00	15.00	22.50	35.00	—
AH1055	—	5.00	15.00	22.50	35.00	—
AH1056	—	5.00	15.00	22.50	35.00	—
AH1057	—	5.00	15.00	22.50	35.00	—
AH1058	—	5.00	15.00	22.50	35.00	—
AH1059	—	5.00	15.00	22.50	35.00	—
AH1060	—	5.00	15.00	22.50	35.00	—
AH1061	—	5.00	15.00	22.50	35.00	—
AH1062	—	5.00	15.00	22.50	35.00	—
AH1063	—	5.00	15.00	22.50	35.00	—

KM# 169.24 ABBASI (type 169)

7.3900 g., Silver **Note:** Type B2.

Date	Mintage	VG	F	VF	XF	Unc
AH1064	—	6.00	15.00	25.00	40.00	—
AH1066	—	6.00	15.00	25.00	40.00	—
AH1067	—	6.00	15.00	25.00	40.00	—
AH1068	—	6.00	15.00	25.00	40.00	—

Hamadan

KM# 169.5 ABBASI (type 169)

7.3900 g., Silver **Note:** Type B1.

Date	Mintage	VG	F	VF	XF	Unc
AH1054	—	10.00	25.00	40.00	55.00	—
AH1056	—	10.00	25.00	40.00	55.00	—
AH1061	—	10.00	25.00	40.00	55.00	—

KM# 169.25 ABBASI (type 169)

7.3900 g., Silver **Note:** Type B2.

Date	Mintage	VG	F	VF	XF	Unc
AH1066	—	15.00	35.00	50.00	70.00	—

Herat

KM# 169.17 ABBASI (type 169)

7.3900 g., Silver **Note:** Type B1.

Date	Mintage	VG	F	VF	XF	Unc
AH1060	—	25.00	60.00	100	160	—

Iravan (Yerevan)

KM# 169.3 ABBASI (type 169)

7.3900 g., Silver **Note:** Type B1.

Date	Mintage	VG	F	VF	XF	Unc
AH1054	—	5.00	15.00	22.50	35.00	—
AH1055	—	5.00	15.00	22.50	35.00	—
AH1056	—	5.00	15.00	22.50	35.00	—
AH1057	—	5.00	15.00	22.50	35.00	—
AH1058	—	5.00	15.00	22.50	35.00	—
AH1059	—	5.00	15.00	22.50	35.00	—
AH1060	—	5.00	15.00	22.50	35.00	—
AH1061	—	5.00	15.00	22.00	35.00	—
AH1062	—	5.00	15.00	22.50	35.00	—
AH1063	—	5.00	15.00	22.50	35.00	—
AH1064	—	5.00	15.00	22.50	35.00	—

KM# 169.23 ABBASI (type 169)

7.3900 g., Silver **Note:** Type B2.

Date	Mintage	VG	F	VF	XF	Unc
AH1064	—	6.00	15.00	25.00	40.00	—
AH1065	—	6.00	15.00	25.00	40.00	—
AH1066	—	6.00	15.00	25.00	40.00	—
AH1067	—	6.00	15.00	25.00	40.00	—
AH1068	—	6.00	15.00	25.00	40.00	—

Isfahan

KM# 169.6 ABBASI (type 169)

7.3900 g., Silver **Note:** Type B1.

Date	Mintage	VG	F	VF	XF	Unc
AH1054	—	5.00	12.00	18.00	30.00	—
AH1055	—	5.00	12.00	18.00	30.00	—
AH1057	—	5.00	12.00	18.00	30.00	—
AH1058	—	5.00	12.00	18.00	30.00	—
AH1063	—	5.00	12.00	18.00	30.00	—
AH1025	—	5.00	12.00	18.00	30.00	—

Note: Error for 1065 with retrograde 6

Kashan

KM# 169.7 ABBASI (type 169)

7.3900 g., Silver **Note:** Type B1.

Date	Mintage	VG	F	VF	XF	Unc
AH1054	—	8.00	20.00	30.00	45.00	—
AH1055	—	8.00	20.00	30.00	45.00	—
AH1056	—	8.00	20.00	30.00	45.00	—
AH1060	—	8.00	20.00	30.00	45.00	—
AH1063	—	8.00	20.00	30.00	45.00	—
AH1064	—	8.00	20.00	30.00	45.00	—

Mashhad

KM# 169.8 ABBASI (type 169)

7.3900 g., Silver **Note:** Type B1.

Date	Mintage	VG	F	VF	XF	Unc
AH1054	—	12.00	30.00	45.00	60.00	—
AH1056	—	12.00	30.00	45.00	60.00	—
AH1058	—	12.00	30.00	45.00	60.00	—
AH1059	—	12.00	30.00	45.00	60.00	—
AH1061	—	12.00	30.00	45.00	60.00	—

Qandahar

KM# 169.16 ABBASI (type 169)

7.3900 g., Silver **Note:** Type B1.

Date	Mintage	VG	F	VF	XF	Unc
AH1059	—	50.00	120	200	320	—

Qazvin

KM# 169.14 ABBASI (type 169)

7.3900 g., Silver **Note:** Type B1.

Date	Mintage	VG	F	VF	XF	Unc
AH1055	—	6.00	15.00	25.00	40.00	—
AH1056	—	6.00	15.00	25.00	40.00	—
AH1060	—	6.00	15.00	25.00	40.00	—

KM# 169.31 ABBASI (type 169)

7.3900 g., Silver **Note:** Type B2.

Date	Mintage	VG	F	VF	XF	Unc
AH1063	—	10.00	25.00	40.00	65.00	—
AH1065	—	10.00	25.00	40.00	65.00	—

Rasht

KM# 169.9 ABBASI (type 169)

7.3900 g., Silver **Note:** Type B1.

Date	Mintage	VG	F	VF	XF	Unc
AH1056	—	12.00	28.00	40.00	52.00	—
AH1057	—	12.00	28.00	40.00	52.00	—

Shamakha

KM# 169.10 ABBASI (type 169)

7.3900 g., Silver **Note:** Type B1.

Date	Mintage	VG	F	VF	XF	Unc
AH1054	—	10.00	25.00	40.00	65.00	—
AH1055	—	10.00	25.00	40.00	65.00	—
AH1057	—	10.00	25.00	40.00	65.00	—
AH1061	—	10.00	25.00	40.00	65.00	—
AH1062	—	10.00	25.00	40.00	65.00	—

KM# 169.26 ABBASI (type 169)

7.3900 g., Silver **Note:** Type B2.

Date	Mintage	VG	F	VF	XF	Unc
AH1065	—	12.00	28.00	45.00	65.00	—

Shushtar

KM# 169.11 ABBASI (type 169)

7.3900 g., Silver **Note:** Type B1.

Date	Mintage	VG	F	VF	XF	Unc
AH1056	—	12.00	32.50	50.00	75.00	—

KM# 169.27 ABBASI (type 169)

7.3900 g., Silver **Note:** Type B2.

Date	Mintage	VG	F	VF	XF	Unc
AH1063	—	14.00	35.00	50.00	65.00	—

Tabriz

KM# 169.12 ABBASI (type 169)

7.3900 g., Silver **Note:** Type B1.

Date	Mintage	VG	F	VF	XF	Unc
AH1054	—	5.00	12.00	18.00	28.00	—
AH1055	—	5.00	12.00	18.00	28.00	—
AH1056	—	5.00	12.00	18.00	28.00	—
AH1057	—	5.00	12.00	18.00	28.00	—
AH1058	—	5.00	12.00	18.00	28.00	—
AH1059	—	5.00	12.00	18.00	28.00	—
AH1059/6	—	5.00	12.00	18.00	28.00	—
AH1060	—	5.00	12.00	18.00	28.00	—
AH1061	—	5.00	12.00	18.00	28.00	—
AH1062	—	5.00	12.00	18.00	28.00	—
AH1063	—	5.00	12.00	18.00	28.00	—
AH1064	—	5.00	12.00	18.00	28.00	—

KM# 169.28 ABBASI (type 169)

7.3900 g., Silver **Note:** Type B2.

Date	Mintage	VG	F	VF	XF	Unc
AH1063	—	5.00	14.00	20.00	32.00	—
AH1064	—	5.00	14.00	20.00	32.00	—
AH1065	—	5.00	14.00	20.00	32.00	—
AH1066	—	5.00	14.00	20.00	32.00	—
AH1067	—	5.00	14.00	20.00	32.00	—
AH1068	—	5.00	14.00	20.00	32.00	—

Tiflis

KM# 169.13 ABBASI (type 169)

7.3900 g., Silver **Note:** Type B1.

Date	Mintage	VG	F	VF	XF	Unc
AH1054	—	8.00	20.00	30.00	40.00	—
AH1055	—	8.00	20.00	30.00	40.00	—
AH1056	—	8.00	20.00	30.00	40.00	—
AH1058	—	8.00	20.00	30.00	40.00	—
AH1059	—	8.00	20.00	30.00	40.00	—
AH1060	—	8.00	20.00	30.00	40.00	—
AH1061	—	8.00	20.00	30.00	40.00	—
AH1062	—	8.00	20.00	30.00	40.00	—
AH1063	—	8.00	20.00	30.00	40.00	—
AH1064	—	8.00	20.00	30.00	40.00	—

KM# 169.29 ABBASI (type 169)

7.3900 g., Silver **Note:** Type B2.

Date	Mintage	VG	F	VF	XF	Unc
AH1063	—	8.00	20.00	35.00	60.00	—
AH1064	—	8.00	20.00	35.00	60.00	—
AH1065	—	8.00	20.00	35.00	60.00	—
AH1065//1064	—	12.00	30.00	45.00	65.00	—
AH1066	—	8.00	20.00	35.00	60.00	—
AH1067	—	8.00	20.00	35.00	60.00	—

Urdu

KM# 169.15 ABBASI (type 169)

7.3900 g., Silver **Note:** Type B1.

Date	Mintage	VG	F	VF	XF	Unc
AH1058	—	30.00	75.00	125	200	—
AH1059	—	30.00	75.00	125	200	—

For coins without mint listed see coin above.

Zegam

KM# 169.18 ABBASI (type 169)
7.3900 g., Silver **Note:** Type B1.

Date	Mintage	VG	F	VF	XF	Unc
ND	—	40.00	105	175	280	—

Ardabil

KM# 176.1 5 SHAHI
9.2400 g., Silver **Note:** Type C1.

Date	Mintage	VG	F	VF	XF	Unc
AH1067	—	12.00	30.00	45.00	70.00	—
AH1068	—	12.00	30.00	45.00	70.00	—
AH1070	—	12.00	30.00	45.00	70.00	—

KM# 176.31 5 SHAHI
9.2400 g., Silver **Note:** Type C1.

Date	Mintage	VG	F	VF	XF	Unc
AH1075	—	11.00	27.50	45.00	65.00	—

Ganjah

KM# 176.3 5 SHAHI
9.2400 g., Silver **Note:** Type C2.

Date	Mintage	VG	F	VF	XF	Unc
AH1067	—	13.00	35.00	50.00	75.00	—
AH1069	—	13.00	35.00	50.00	75.00	—

KM# 176.33 5 SHAHI
9.2400 g., Silver **Note:** Type C2.

Date	Mintage	VG	F	VF	XF	Unc
AH1071	—	10.00	25.00	40.00	60.00	—
AH1074	—	10.00	25.00	40.00	60.00	—
AH1075	—	10.00	25.00	40.00	60.00	—

Iravan (Yerevan)

KM# 176.2 5 SHAHI
9.2400 g., Silver **Note:** Type C1.

Date	Mintage	VG	F	VF	XF	Unc
AH1067	—	13.00	35.00	50.00	75.00	—
AH1068	—	13.00	35.00	50.00	75.00	—

KM# 176.32 5 SHAHI
9.2400 g., Silver **Note:** Type C2.

Date	Mintage	VG	F	VF	XF	Unc
AH1069	—	10.00	25.00	35.00	55.00	—
AH1070	—	10.00	25.00	35.00	55.00	—
AH1071	—	10.00	25.00	35.00	55.00	—
AH1072	—	10.00	25.00	35.00	55.00	—
AH1073	—	10.00	25.00	35.00	55.00	—
AH1074	—	10.00	25.00	35.00	55.00	—
AH1076	—	10.00	25.00	35.00	55.00	—
AH1077	—	10.00	25.00	35.00	55.00	—

Isfahan

KM# 176.34 5 SHAHI
9.2400 g., Silver **Note:** Type C2.

Date	Mintage	VG	F	VF	XF	Unc
AH1067	—	10.00	25.00	40.00	60.00	—
AH1071	—	10.00	25.00	40.00	60.00	—

Kashan

KM# 176.35 5 SHAHI
9.2400 g., Silver **Note:** Type C2.

Date	Mintage	VG	F	VF	XF	Unc
AH1073	—	15.00	35.00	50.00	75.00	—

Mashhad

KM# 176.36 5 SHAHI
9.2400 g., Silver **Note:** Type C2.

Date	Mintage	VG	F	VF	XF	Unc
ND	—	15.00	35.00	60.00	95.00	—

Qazvín

KM# 176.37 5 SHAHI
9.2400 g., Silver **Note:** Type C2.

Date	Mintage	VG	F	VF	XF	Unc
AH1072	—	14.00	36.00	50.00	70.00	—

Shamakha

KM# 176.38 5 SHAHI
9.2400 g., Silver **Note:** Type C2.

Date	Mintage	VG	F	VF	XF	Unc
AH1069	—	12.00	30.00	45.00	80.00	—
AH1071	—	12.00	30.00	45.00	80.00	—
AH1072	—	12.00	30.00	45.00	80.00	—
AH1073	—	12.00	30.00	45.00	80.00	—
AH1074	—	12.00	30.00	45.00	80.00	—
AH1075	—	12.00	30.00	45.00	80.00	—
AH1076	—	12.00	30.00	45.00	80.00	—

Shushtar

KM# 176.39 5 SHAHI
9.2400 g., Silver **Note:** Type C2.

Date	Mintage	VG	F	VF	XF	Unc
AH1068	—	10.00	28.00	45.00	75.00	—
AHxxxx	—	10.00	28.00	45.00	75.00	—

Tabriz

KM# 176.4 5 SHAHI
9.2400 g., Silver **Note:** Type C1.

Date	Mintage	VG	F	VF	XF	Unc
AH1067	—	10.00	25.00	40.00	75.00	—

KM# 176.21 5 SHAHI
9.2400 g., Silver **Note:** Type C - Special. Central cartouche on Royal Side.

Date	Mintage	VG	F	VF	XF	Unc
AH1068	—	30.00	80.00	125	225	—
AH1069	—	30.00	80.00	125	225	—

KM# 176.40 5 SHAHI
9.2400 g., Silver **Note:** Type C2.

Date	Mintage	VG	F	VF	XF	Unc
AH1069	—	8.00	20.00	28.00	45.00	—
AH1070	—	8.00	20.00	28.00	45.00	—
AH1071	—	8.00	20.00	28.00	45.00	—
AH1072	—	8.00	20.00	28.00	45.00	—
AH1073	—	8.00	20.00	28.00	45.00	—
AH1076	—	8.00	20.00	28.00	45.00	—

Tiflis

KM# 176.41 5 SHAHI
9.2400 g., Silver **Note:** Type C2.

Date	Mintage	VG	F	VF	XF	Unc
AH1069	—	8.00	20.00	30.00	50.00	—
AH1070	—	8.00	20.00	30.00	50.00	—
AH1071	—	8.00	20.00	30.00	50.00	—
AH1072	—	8.00	20.00	30.00	50.00	—
AH1073	—	8.00	20.00	30.00	50.00	—
AH1074	—	8.00	20.00	30.00	50.00	—
AH1075	—	8.00	20.00	30.00	50.00	—
AH1076	—	8.00	20.00	30.00	50.00	—

Urdu

KM# 180 2-1/2 ABBASI (10 Shahi)
18.4800 g., Silver **Note:** Type D (Kalb).

Date	Mintage	VG	F	VF	XF	Unc
AHxxxx Rare	—	—	—	—	—	—

Kashan

KM# 178 5 ABBASI (20 Shahi)
36.9600 g., Silver **Note:** Type C1.

Date	Mintage	VG	F	VF	XF	Unc
AH1068 Rare	—	—	—	—	—	—

Urdu

KM# 181 5 ABBASI (20 Shahi - type 181)
36.9600 g., Silver **Note:** Type D (Kalb).

Date	Mintage	VG	F	VF	XF	Unc
AHxxxx Rare	—	—	—	—	—	—

Ardabil

KM# 184 1/2 ASHRAFI
1.7500 g., Gold **Obv:** Date above second line **Note:** Type R1.

Date	Mintage	VG	F	VF	XF	Unc
AH1072 Rare	—	—	—	—	—	—

Isfahan

KM# 185 ASHRAFI
3.5000 g., Gold **Obv:** Date in third line **Note:** Type R2.

Date	Mintage	VG	F	VF	XF	Unc
AH1081 Rare	—	—	—	—	—	—

Note: Error for 1071?

HAMMERED COINAGE

Local Type of Khuzistan

Dawraq

KM# 187.1 MAHMUDI
3.5000 g., Silver **Note:** Type HA.

Date	Mintage	VG	F	VF	XF	Unc
ND	—	8.00	20.00	35.00	50.00	—

Dezful

KM# 187.2 MAHMUDI
3.5000 g., Silver **Note:** Type HA.

Date	Mintage	VG	F	VF	XF	Unc
ND	—	10.00	25.00	40.00	60.00	—

Huwayza

KM# 187.3 MAHMUDI
3.5000 g., Silver **Note:** Type HA.

Date	Mintage	VG	F	VF	XF	Unc
AH1053	—	10.00	30.00	40.00	65.00	—
AH1054	—	10.00	30.00	40.00	65.00	—
AH1055	—	10.00	30.00	40.00	65.00	—
ND	—	3.50	8.00	20.00	55.00	—

Dawraq

KM# 188.1 MAHMUDI (type 188)
3.5000 g., Silver **Note:** Type HB.

Date	Mintage	VG	F	VF	XF	Unc
AH1061	—	12.00	30.00	50.00	70.00	—

Huwayza

KM# 188.2 MAHMUDI (type 188)
3.5000 g., Silver **Note:** Type HB.

Date	Mintage	VG	F	VF	XF	Unc
AH1063	—	8.00	20.00	30.00	45.00	—
AH1064	—	8.00	20.00	30.00	45.00	—
AH1066	—	8.00	20.00	30.00	45.00	—
AH1067	—	8.00	20.00	30.00	45.00	—
AH1072	—	8.00	20.00	30.00	45.00	—
AH1076	—	8.00	20.00	30.00	45.00	—
AH1077	—	8.00	20.00	30.00	45.00	—
ND	—	4.00	10.00	15.00	25.00	—

Ramhurmuz

KM# 188.3 MAHMUDI (type 188)
3.5000 g., Silver **Note:** Type HB.

Date	Mintage	VG	F	VF	XF	Unc
AH1056	—	30.00	70.00	100	150	—

Safi II

AH1077-1079 / 1666-1668AD

HAMMERED COINAGE

Dawraq

KM# 207.1 MAHMUDI
Silver **Note:** Type H; About 3.60 grams.

Date	Mintage	VG	F	VF	XF	Unc
ND	—	50.00	130	175	250	—

Huwayza

KM# 207.2 MAHMUDI
Silver **Note:** Type H; About 3.60 grams.

Date	Mintage	VG	F	VF	XF	Unc
ND	—	25.00	60.00	80.00	120	—

Isfahan

KM# 201.1 SHAHI (50 Dinars)
1.8400 g., Silver **Note:** Type A.

Date	Mintage	VG	F	VF	XF	Unc
AH1078	—	40.00	90.00	140	240	—

Tabriz

KM# 201.2 SHAHI (50 Dinars)
1.8400 g., Silver **Note:** Type A.

Date	Mintage	VG	F	VF	XF	Unc
AH1078	—	40.00	90.00	140	240	—

Iravan (Yerevan)

KM# 202.1 2 SHAHI (Mahmudi)
3.6900 g., Silver

Date	Mintage	VG	F	VF	XF	Unc
AH1078	—	40.00	105	175	280	—

Unknown

KM# 202.2 2 SHAHI (Mahmudi)
3.6900 g., Silver

Date	Mintage	VG	F	VF	XF	Unc
AHxxxx	—	15.00	35.00	60.00	95.00	—

Iravan (Yerevan)

KM# 203.1 ABBASI
7.3900 g., Silver **Note:** Type A.

Date	Mintage	VG	F	VF	XF	Unc
AH1079	—	40.00	90.00	140	230	—

Tabriz

KM# 203.2 ABBASI
7.3900 g., Silver **Note:** Type A.

Date	Mintage	VG	F	VF	XF	Unc
AH1077	—	45.00	105	160	245	—

Tiflis

KM# 203.3 ABBASI
7.3900 g., Silver **Note:** Type A.

Date	Mintage	VG	F	VF	XF	Unc
AH1078	—	50.00	120	200	315	—
AH1079	—	50.00	120	200	315	—

Isfahan

KM# 205 5 ABBASI (20 Shahi)
36.9500 g., Silver **Note:** Type B.

Date	Mintage	VG	F	VF	XF	Unc
AH1078	—	—	1,100	1,500	2,850	—

Note: Most pieces are ex-mount. These values are for attractive pieces.

Sulayman I

AH1079-1105 / 1668-1694AD

HAMMERED COINAGE

Qazvín

KM# 210 1/2 SHAHI (25 Dinars)
0.9600 g., Silver **Note:** Type A.

Date	Mintage	VG	F	VF	XF	Unc
AHxxxx	—	20.00	75.00	100	135	—

Unknown

KM# 211 SHAHI (50 Dinars)
1.8400 g., Silver **Note:** Type A.

Date	Mintage	VG	F	VF	XF	Unc
AHxxxx	—	15.00	40.00	60.00	80.00	—

Ardabil

KM# 218.1 SHAHI (50 Dinars - type 218)
1.8400 g., Silver **Note:** Type B.

Date	Mintage	VG	F	VF	XF	Unc
AH1088	—	30.00	70.00	100	140	—

Iravan (Yerevan)

KM# 218.2 SHAHI (50 Dinars - type 218)
1.8400 g., Silver **Note:** Type B.

Date	Mintage	VG	F	VF	XF	Unc
AH1083	—	20.00	50.00	70.00	100	—

Mashhad

KM# 218.5 SHAHI (50 Dinars - type 218)
Silver **Note:** Type C.

Date	Mintage	Good	VG	F	VF	XF
AH1084	—	—	25.00	60.00	80.00	115

Tabriz

KM# 218.3 SHAHI (50 Dinars - type 218)
1.8400 g., Silver **Note:** Type B.

Date	Mintage	VG	F	VF	XF	Unc
AH1082	—	20.00	50.00	70.00	100	—

Tiflis

KM# 218.4 SHAHI (50 Dinars - type 218)
1.8400 g., Silver **Note:** Type B.

Date	Mintage	VG	F	VF	XF	Unc
AH1094	—	35.00	85.00	120	170	—

Ardabil

KM# 224.1 SHAHI (50 Dinars - type 224)
1.8400 g., Silver **Note:** Type C.

Date	Mintage	VG	F	VF	XF	Unc
AH1104	—	35.00	85.00	125	170	—

Ganjah

KM# 224.3 SHAHI (50 Dinars - type 224)
1.8400 g., Silver **Note:** Type C.

Date	Mintage	VG	F	VF	XF	Unc
AH1102	—	30.00	70.00	100	130	—
AH1103	—	30.00	70.00	100	130	—
AH1104	—	30.00	70.00	100	130	—

Iravan (Yerevan)

KM# 224.2 SHAHI (50 Dinars - type 224)
1.8400 g., Silver **Note:** Type C.

Date	Mintage	VG	F	VF	XF	Unc
AH1103	—	22.00	55.00	80.00	110	—
AH1105	—	22.00	55.00	80.00	110	—

Isfahan

KM# 224.4 SHAHI (50 Dinars - type 224)
1.8400 g., Silver **Note:** Type C.

Date	Mintage	VG	F	VF	XF	Unc
AH1095	—	15.00	35.00	50.00	70.00	—
AH1096	—	15.00	35.00	50.00	70.00	—
AH1098	—	15.00	35.00	50.00	70.00	—
AH1099	—	15.00	35.00	50.00	70.00	—
AH1100	—	15.00	35.00	50.00	70.00	—
AH1104	—	15.00	35.00	50.00	70.00	—
AH1105	—	15.00	35.00	50.00	70.00	—

Nakhchawan

KM# 224.5 SHAHI (50 Dinars - type 224)
1.8400 g., Silver **Note:** Type C.

Date	Mintage	VG	F	VF	XF	Unc
AH1096	—	20.00	55.00	80.00	115	—
AH1097	—	20.00	55.00	80.00	115	—
AH1099	—	20.00	55.00	80.00	115	—
AH1102	—	20.00	55.00	80.00	115	—

Rasht

KM# 224.6 SHAHI (50 Dinars - type 224)
1.8400 g., Silver **Note:** Type C.

Date	Mintage	VG	F	VF	XF	Unc
AH1097	—	25.00	60.00	80.00	110	—
AH1098	—	25.00	60.00	80.00	110	—
AH1100	—	25.00	60.00	80.00	110	—

Tabriz

KM# 224.7 SHAHI (50 Dinars - type 224)
1.8400 g., Silver **Note:** Type C.

Date	Mintage	VG	F	VF	XF	Unc
AH1098	—	20.00	55.00	80.00	115	—
AH1099	—	20.00	55.00	80.00	115	—
AH1101	—	20.00	55.00	80.00	115	—

Isfahan

KM# 212 2 SHAHI (Mahmudi)
3.6900 g., Silver **Note:** Type A.

Date	Mintage	VG	F	VF	XF	Unc
AH1079	—	65.00	140	175	275	—

Ganjah

KM# 219.4 2 SHAHI (Mahmudi - type 219)
3.6900 g., Silver **Note:** Type B.

Date	Mintage	VG	F	VF	XF	Unc
AH1091	—	25.00	60.00	100	150	—

Iravan (Yerevan)

KM# 219.1 2 SHAHI (Mahmudi - type 219)
3.6900 g., Silver **Note:** Type B.

Date	Mintage	VG	F	VF	XF	Unc
AH1083	—	30.00	70.00	100	140	—

Tabriz

KM# 219.2 2 SHAHI (Mahmudi - type 219)
3.6900 g., Silver **Note:** Type B.

Date	Mintage	VG	F	VF	XF	Unc
AH1081	—	15.00	40.00	60.00	80.00	—

Tiflis

KM# 219.3 2 SHAHI (Mahmudi - type 219)
3.6900 g., Silver **Note:** Type B.

Date	Mintage	VG	F	VF	XF	Unc
AH1086	—	20.00	65.00	100	135	—

Ganjah

KM# 225.2 2 SHAHI (Mahmudi - type 225)
3.6900 g., Silver **Note:** Type C.

Date	Mintage	VG	F	VF	XF	Unc
AH1103	—	24.00	60.00	85.00	110	—
AH1105	—	24.00	60.00	85.00	110	—

Hamadan

KM# 225.3 2 SHAHI (Mahmudi - type 225)
3.6900 g., Silver **Note:** Type C.

Date	Mintage	VG	F	VF	XF	Unc
AH1097	—	35.00	90.00	120	160	—

Iravan (Yerevan)

KM# 225.1 2 SHAHI (Mahmudi - type 225)
3.6900 g., Silver **Note:** Type C.

Date	Mintage	VG	F	VF	XF	Unc
AH1104	—	22.50	55.00	75.00	100	—
AH1105	—	22.50	55.00	75.00	100	—

Isfahan

KM# 225.4 2 SHAHI (Mahmudi - type 225)
3.6900 g., Silver **Note:** Type C.

Date	Mintage	VG	F	VF	XF	Unc
AH1095	—	12.00	30.00	50.00	70.00	—
AH1096	—	12.00	30.00	50.00	70.00	—
AH1099	—	12.00	30.00	50.00	70.00	—

Mashhad

KM# 225.9 2 SHAHI (Mahmudi - type 225)
3.6900 g., Silver **Note:** Type C.

Date	Mintage	VG	F	VF	XF	Unc
AH1099	—	30.00	75.00	125	185	—

Nakhchawan

KM# 225.5 2 SHAHI (Mahmudi - type 225)
3.6900 g., Silver **Note:** Type C.

Date	Mintage	VG	F	VF	XF	Unc
AH1097	—	20.00	50.00	80.00	110	—
AH1101	—	20.00	50.00	80.00	110	—

Qazvín

KM# 225.6 2 SHAHI (Mahmudi - type 225)
3.6900 g., Silver **Note:** Type C.

Date	Mintage	VG	F	VF	XF	Unc
AH1097	—	25.00	60.00	80.00	110	—

Rasht

KM# 225.7 2 SHAHI (Mahmudi - type 225)
3.6900 g., Silver **Note:** Type C.

Date	Mintage	VG	F	VF	XF	Unc
AH1097	—	20.00	50.00	70.00	90.00	—
AH1098	—	20.00	50.00	70.00	90.00	—

Tabriz

KM# 225.8 2 SHAHI (Mahmudi - type 225)
3.6900 g., Silver **Note:** Type C.

Date	Mintage	VG	F	VF	XF	Unc
AH1098	—	15.00	40.00	60.00	80.00	—

Ardabil

KM# 213.1 ABBASI
7.3900 g., Silver **Note:** Type A.

Date	Mintage	VG	F	VF	XF	Unc
AH1081	—	40.00	110	150	215	—

Ganjah

KM# 213.2 ABBASI
7.3900 g., Silver **Note:** Type A.

Date	Mintage	VG	F	VF	XF	Unc
AH1080	—	20.00	70.00	100	140	—

Qazvín

KM# 213.3 ABBASI
7.3900 g., Silver **Note:** Type A.

Date	Mintage	VG	F	VF	XF	Unc
AH1080	—	20.00	70.00	100	140	—

Shamakha

KM# 213.4 ABBASI
7.3900 g., Silver **Note:** Type A.

Date	Mintage	VG	F	VF	XF	Unc
ND	—	40.00	110	150	215	—

Tiflis

KM# 213.5 ABBASI
7.3900 g., Silver **Note:** Type A.

Date	Mintage	VG	F	VF	XF	Unc
AH1080	—	35.00	90.00	125	180	—

Ardabil

KM# 220.1 ABBASI (type 220)
7.3900 g., Silver **Note:** Type B.

Date	Mintage	VG	F	VF	XF	Unc
AH1082	—	20.00	55.00	80.00	130	—
AH1089	—	20.00	55.00	80.00	130	—

Ganjah

KM# 220.3 ABBASI (type 220)
7.3900 g., Silver **Note:** Type B.

Date	Mintage	VG	F	VF	XF	Unc
AH1081	—	25.00	60.00	80.00	110	—
AH1090	—	25.00	60.00	80.00	110	—

Iravan (Yerevan)

KM# 220.2 ABBASI (type 220)
7.3900 g., Silver **Note:** Type B.

Date	Mintage	VG	F	VF	XF	Unc
AH1082	—	15.00	40.00	60.00	95.00	—
AH1083	—	15.00	40.00	60.00	95.00	—
AH1084	—	15.00	40.00	60.00	95.00	—
AH1086	—	15.00	40.00	60.00	95.00	—
AH1087	—	15.00	40.00	60.00	95.00	—
AH1088	—	15.00	40.00	60.00	95.00	—

Mashhad

KM# 220.4 ABBASI (type 220)
7.3900 g., Silver **Note:** Type B.

Date	Mintage	VG	F	VF	XF	Unc
AH1082	—	30.00	70.00	100	135	—

Qazvín

KM# 220.5 ABBASI (type 220)
7.3900 g., Silver **Note:** Type B.

Date	Mintage	VG	F	VF	XF	Unc
AH108x	—	20.00	55.00	80.00	130	—

Shamakha

KM# 220.6 ABBASI (type 220)
7.3900 g., Silver **Note:** Type B.

Date	Mintage	VG	F	VF	XF	Unc
AH1087	—	30.00	80.00	120	185	—

For coins without mint listed see coin above.

Tabriz

KM# 220.7 ABBASI (type 220)
7.3900 g., Silver **Note:** Type B.

Date	Mintage	VG	F	VF	XF	Unc
AH1081	—	17.50	65.00	100	160	—
AH1082	—	17.50	65.00	100	160	—
AH1087	—	17.50	65.00	100	160	—

Tiflis

KM# 220.8 ABBASI (type 220)
7.3900 g., Silver **Note:** Type B.

Date	Mintage	VG	F	VF	XF	Unc
AH1085	—	5.00	20.00	65.00	100	—
AH1086	—	5.00	20.00	65.00	100	—
AH1087	—	5.00	20.00	65.00	100	—
AH1088	—	5.00	20.00	65.00	100	—
AH1090	—	5.00	20.00	65.00	100	—
AH1091	—	5.00	20.00	65.00	100	—
AH1092	—	5.00	20.00	65.00	100	—

Ardabil

KM# 226.1 ABBASI (type 226)
7.3900 g., Silver **Note:** Type C.

Date	Mintage	VG	F	VF	XF	Unc
AH1104	—	20.00	50.00	75.00	115	—

Ganjah

KM# 226.3 ABBASI (type 226)
7.3900 g., Silver **Note:** Type C.

Date	Mintage	VG	F	VF	XF	Unc
AH1103	—	10.00	20.00	30.00	60.00	—
AH1104	—	10.00	20.00	30.00	60.00	—
AH1105	—	10.00	20.00	30.00	60.00	—

Hamadan

KM# 226.4 ABBASI (type 226)
7.3900 g., Silver **Note:** Type C.

Date	Mintage	VG	F	VF	XF	Unc
AH1096	—	18.00	45.00	60.00	100	—

Iravan (Yerevan)

KM# 226.2 ABBASI (type 226)
7.3900 g., Silver **Note:** Type C.

Date	Mintage	VG	F	VF	XF	Unc
AH1103	—	BV	20.00	30.00	60.00	—
AH1104	—	BV	20.00	30.00	60.00	—
AH1105	—	BV	20.00	30.00	60.00	—

Isfahan

KM# 226.5 ABBASI (type 226)
7.3900 g., Silver **Note:** Type C.

Date	Mintage	VG	F	VF	XF	Unc
AH1095	—	15.00	35.00	50.00	85.00	—
AH1096	—	BV	13.00	20.00	40.00	—
AH1097	—	BV	12.00	20.00	45.00	—
AH1098	—	BV	12.00	20.00	45.00	—
AH1099	—	BV	12.00	20.00	45.00	—
AH1100	—	BV	12.00	20.00	45.00	—
AH1102	—	BV	12.00	20.00	45.00	—
AH1103	—	BV	12.00	20.00	45.00	—
AH1104	—	BV	12.00	20.00	45.00	—
AH1105	—	BV	12.00	20.00	45.00	—

Kashan

KM# 226.6 ABBASI (type 226)
7.3900 g., Silver **Note:** Type C.

Date	Mintage	VG	F	VF	XF	Unc
AH1096	—	12.00	30.00	40.00	65.00	—
AH1097	—	12.00	30.00	40.00	65.00	—

Mashhad

KM# 226.7 ABBASI (type 226)
7.3900 g., Silver **Note:** Type C.

Date	Mintage	VG	F	VF	XF	Unc
AH1095	—	20.00	50.00	75.00	110	—
AH1096	—	15.00	35.00	45.00	75.00	—
AH1098	—	15.00	35.00	45.00	75.00	—
AH(110)4	—	15.00	35.00	45.00	75.00	—

Note: Only final digit engraved

Nakhchawan

KM# 226.8 ABBASI (type 226)
7.3900 g., Silver **Note:** Type C.

Date	Mintage	VG	F	VF	XF	Unc
AH1096	—	8.00	15.00	25.00	50.00	—
AH1097	—	8.00	15.00	25.00	50.00	—
AH1098	—	8.00	15.00	25.00	50.00	—
AH1099	—	8.00	15.00	25.00	50.00	—
AH1100	—	8.00	15.00	25.00	50.00	—
AH1101	—	8.00	15.00	25.00	50.00	—
AH1102	—	8.00	15.00	25.00	50.00	—
AH1103	—	8.00	15.00	25.00	50.00	—
AH1104	—	8.00	15.00	25.00	50.00	—
AH1105	—	8.00	15.00	25.00	50.00	—

Qazvín

KM# 226.9 ABBASI (type 226)
7.3900 g., Silver **Note:** Type C.

Date	Mintage	VG	F	VF	XF	Unc
AH1096	—	8.00	20.00	30.00	50.00	—
AH1097	—	8.00	20.00	30.00	50.00	—
AH1099	—	8.00	20.00	30.00	50.00	—
AH1105	—	8.00	20.00	30.00	50.00	—

Rasht

KM# 226.10 ABBASI (type 226)
7.3900 g., Silver **Note:** Type C.

Date	Mintage	VG	F	VF	XF	Unc
AH1095	—	12.00	30.00	50.00	70.00	—
AH1097	—	10.00	22.00	30.00	55.00	—
AH1098	—	10.00	22.00	30.00	55.00	—
AH1100	—	10.00	22.00	30.00	55.00	—
AH1105	—	10.00	22.00	30.00	55.00	—

Shamakha

KM# 226.11 ABBASI (type 226)
7.3900 g., Silver **Note:** Type C.

Date	Mintage	VG	F	VF	XF	Unc
AH1104	—	13.00	33.00	50.00	75.00	—

Tabriz

KM# 226.12 ABBASI (type 226)
7.3900 g., Silver **Note:** Type C.

Date	Mintage	VG	F	VF	XF	Unc
AH1096	—	BV	10.00	18.00	35.00	—
AH1097	—	BV	10.00	18.00	35.00	—
AH1098	—	BV	10.00	18.00	35.00	—
AH1099	—	BV	10.00	18.00	35.00	—
AH1100	—	BV	10.00	18.00	35.00	—
AH1101	—	BV	10.00	18.00	35.00	—
AH1102	—	BV	10.00	18.00	35.00	—
AH1103	—	BV	10.00	18.00	35.00	—
AH1104	—	BV	10.00	18.00	35.00	—
AH1105	—	BV	10.00	18.00	35.00	—

Tiflis

KM# 226.13 ABBASI (type 226)
7.3900 g., Silver **Note:** Type C.

Date	Mintage	VG	F	VF	XF	Unc
AH1103	—	18.00	45.00	75.00	115	—
AH1104	—	18.00	45.00	75.00	115	—
AH1105	—	18.00	45.00	75.00	115	—

Isfahan

KM# 214 2-1/2 ABBASI (10 Shahi)
18.4800 g., Silver **Note:** Type A.

Date	Mintage	VG	F	VF	XF	Unc
AH1079	—	200	500	800	1,500	—
AH1081	—	200	500	800	1,500	—
AH1082	—	200	500	800	1,500	—
AH1087	—	200	500	800	1,500	—
AH1090	—	200	500	800	1,500	—
AH1093	—	200	500	800	1,500	—
AH1094	—	200	500	800	1,500	—

Note: This type is almost always found with mounting. These prices are for attractive examples.

Isfahan

KM# 227 2-1/2 ABBASI (10 Shahi - type 227)
18.4800 g., Silver

Date	Mintage	VG	F	VF	XF	Unc
AH1094	—	150	375	700	1,400	—
AH1096	—	150	375	700	1,400	—

Isfahan

KM# 215.1 5 ABBASI (20 Shahi)
36.9500 g., Silver

Date	Mintage	VG	F	VF	XF	Unc
AH1083	—	425	680	1,000	2,200	—
AH1084	—	425	680	1,000	2,200	—
AH1090	—	425	680	1,000	2,200	—
AH1091	—	425	680	1,000	2,200	—

Qazvín

KM# 215.2 5 ABBASI (20 Shahi)
36.9500 g., Silver **Note:** Struck at Qazvín.

Date	Mintage	VG	F	VF	XF	Unc
AH1085 Rare	—	—	—	—	—	—

Isfahan

KM# 228 5 ABBASI (20 Shahi - type 228)
36.9500 g., Silver **Rev:** Without border inscription

Date	Mintage	VG	F	VF	XF	Unc
AH1096	—	460	760	1,200	3,000	—

Isfahan

KM# 229 5 ABBASI (20 Shahi - type 229)
36.9500 g., Silver **Rev:** With border inscription

Date	Mintage	VG	F	VF	XF	Unc
AH1099	—	420	700	1,100	2,800	—

Isfahan

KM# 230.1 7 1/2 ABBASI
56.3700 g., Gold **Obv. Inscription:** "Shi'a Kalima"

Date	Mintage	VG	F	VF	XF	Unc
AH1096 Rare	—	—	—	—	—	—

Ganjah

KM# 231 1/4 ASHRAFI
0.8800 g., Gold **Note:** Type C.

Date	Mintage	VG	F	VF	XF	Unc
AHxxxx Rare	—	—	—	—	—	—

Isfahan

KM# 232 ASHRAFI
3.5000 g., Gold

Date	Mintage	VG	F	VF	XF	Unc
AH1095 Rare	—	—	—	—	—	—

Isfahan

KM# 233 16 ASHRAFI
57.0000 g., Gold **Note:** Struck with dies of KM#228.

Date	Mintage	F	VF	XF	Unc	BU
AH1096 Rare	—	—	—	—	—	—

HAMMERED COINAGE
Local Type of Khuzistan

Huwayza

KM# 235 MAHMUDI
Silver **Note:** Type H; Weight varies: 3.00-3.50 grams. Sometimes debased.

Date	Mintage	VG	F	VF	XF	Unc
ND	—	BV	10.00	25.00	70.00	—
Note: Symbol in place of date.						
AH1084	—	7.00	15.00	40.00	100	—
AH1085	—	7.00	15.00	40.00	100	—
AH1086	—	7.00	15.00	40.00	100	—
AH1087	—	7.00	15.00	40.00	100	—
AH1088	—	7.00	15.00	40.00	100	—
AH1089	—	7.00	15.00	40.00	100	—
AH1090	—	7.00	15.00	40.00	100	—
AH1091	—	7.00	15.00	40.00	100	—
AH1092	—	7.00	15.00	40.00	100	—

Husayn I
AH1105-1135 / 1694-1722AD
HAMMERED COINAGE

Isfahan

KM# 255 1/2 SHAHI (25 Dinars)
0.9200 g., Silver **Note:** Type B.

Date	Mintage	VG	F	VF	XF	Unc
AH111x	—	30.00	60.00	75.00	150	—

Ganjah

KM# 256.2 SHAHI (50 Dinars)
1.8400 g., Silver **Note:** Type B.

Date	Mintage	VG	F	VF	XF	Unc
AH1110	—	30.00	70.00	100	140	—

Iravan (Yerevan)

KM# 256.1 SHAHI (50 Dinars)
1.8400 g., Silver **Note:** Type B.

Date	Mintage	VG	F	VF	XF	Unc
AH1108	—	30.00	70.00	100	140	—

Isfahan

KM# 251 SHAHI (50 Dinars)
1.8400 g., Silver **Note:** Type A.

Date	Mintage	VG	F	VF	XF	Unc
AH1106	—	25.00	65.00	85.00	110	—

KM# 256.3 SHAHI (50 Dinars)
1.8400 g., Silver **Note:** Type B.

Date	Mintage	VG	F	VF	XF	Unc
AH1109	—	18.00	45.00	65.00	85.00	—
AH1110	—	18.00	45.00	65.00	85.00	—
AH1112	—	18.00	45.00	65.00	85.00	—

Iravan (Yerevan)

KM# 252 2 SHAHI (Mahmudi)
3.6900 g., Silver **Note:** Type A.

Date	Mintage	VG	F	VF	XF	Unc
AH1106	—	35.00	90.00	125	155	—

KM# 257.3 2 SHAHI (Mahmudi)
3.6900 g., Silver **Note:** Type B.

Date	Mintage	VG	F	VF	XF	Unc
1107	—	40.00	75.00	100	130	—

Isfahan

KM# 257.1 2 SHAHI (Mahmudi)
3.6900 g., Silver **Note:** Type B.

Date	Mintage	VG	F	VF	XF	Unc
AH1112	—	35.00	50.00	65.00	80.00	—

Tiflis

KM# 257.2 2 SHAHI (Mahmudi)
3.6900 g., Silver **Note:** Type B.

Date	Mintage	VG	F	VF	XF	Unc
AH1107	—	20.00	70.00	100	125	—

Ganjah

KM# 253.2 ABBASI
9.2400 g., Silver **Note:** Type A.

Date	Mintage	VG	F	VF	XF	Unc
AH1105	—	25.00	60.00	85.00	115	—

Iravan (Yerevan)

KM# 253.1 ABBASI
9.2400 g., Silver **Note:** Type A.

Date	Mintage	VG	F	VF	XF	Unc
AH1106	—	20.00	50.00	65.00	90.00	—
AH1107	—	20.00	50.00	65.00	90.00	—

Isfahan

KM# 253.3 ABBASI
9.2400 g., Silver **Note:** Type A.

Date	Mintage	VG	F	VF	XF	Unc
AH1106	—	12.00	30.00	50.00	70.00	—
AH1107	—	12.00	30.00	50.00	70.00	—

Nakhchawan

KM# 253.4 ABBASI
9.2400 g., Silver **Note:** Type A.

Date	Mintage	VG	F	VF	XF	Unc
AH1106	—	18.00	45.00	75.00	110	—
AH1107	—	18.00	45.00	75.00	110	—

Qazvín

KM# 253.5 ABBASI
9.2400 g., Silver **Note:** Type A.

Date	Mintage	VG	F	VF	XF	Unc
AH1105	—	20.00	50.00	75.00	110	—

Rasht

KM# 253.6 ABBASI
9.2400 g., Silver **Note:** Type A.

Date	Mintage	VG	F	VF	XF	Unc
AH1105	—	15.00	40.00	60.00	80.00	—

Tabriz

KM# 253.7 ABBASI
9.2400 g., Silver **Note:** Type A.

Date	Mintage	VG	F	VF	XF	Unc
AH1106	—	12.00	30.00	50.00	70.00	—
AH1107	—	12.00	30.00	50.00	70.00	—

Tiflis

KM# 253.8 ABBASI
9.2400 g., Silver **Note:** Type A.

Date	Mintage	VG	F	VF	XF	Unc
AH1106	—	18.00	45.00	75.00	110	—
AH1107	—	18.00	45.00	75.00	110	—

Ganjah

KM# 258.2 ABBASI (type 258)
7.3900 g., Silver **Note:** Type B.

Date	Mintage	VG	F	VF	XF	Unc
AH1107	—	18.00	45.00	60.00	100	—
AH1108	—	18.00	45.00	60.00	100	—
AH1110	—	18.00	45.00	60.00	100	—
AH1111	—	18.00	45.00	60.00	100	—
AH1112	—	18.00	45.00	60.00	100	—

Iravan (Yerevan)

KM# 258.1 ABBASI (type 258)
7.3900 g., Silver **Note:** Type B.

Date	Mintage	VG	F	VF	XF	Unc
AH1108	—	12.00	30.00	50.00	80.00	—
AH1109	—	12.00	30.00	50.00	80.00	—
AH1110	—	12.00	30.00	50.00	80.00	—
AH1111	—	12.00	30.00	50.00	80.00	—
AH1112	—	12.00	30.00	50.00	80.00	—

Isfahan

KM# 258.4 ABBASI (type 258)
7.3900 g., Silver **Note:** Type B.

Date	Mintage	VG	F	VF	XF	Unc
AH1107	—	10.00	25.00	35.00	60.00	—
AH1108	—	10.00	25.00	35.00	60.00	—
AH1109	—	10.00	25.00	35.00	60.00	—
AH1111	—	10.00	25.00	35.00	60.00	—
AH1112	—	10.00	25.00	35.00	60.00	—

Nakhchawan

KM# 258.5 ABBASI (type 258)
7.3900 g., Silver **Note:** Type B.

Date	Mintage	VG	F	VF	XF	Unc
AH1107	—	18.00	45.00	75.00	110	—
AH1108	—	18.00	45.00	75.00	110	—
AH1110	—	18.00	45.00	75.00	110	—
AH1111	—	18.00	45.00	75.00	110	—

Rasht

KM# 258.6 ABBASI (type 258)
7.3900 g., Silver **Note:** Type B.

Date	Mintage	VG	F	VF	XF	Unc
AH1109	—	18.00	45.00	75.00	110	—

Tabriz

KM# 258.7 ABBASI (type 258)
7.3900 g., Silver **Note:** Type B.

Date	Mintage	VG	F	VF	XF	Unc
AH1108	—	15.00	35.00	50.00	85.00	—
AH1110	—	15.00	35.00	50.00	85.00	—

Tiflis

KM# 258.8 ABBASI (type 258)
7.3900 g., Silver **Note:** Type B.

Date	Mintage	VG	F	VF	XF	Unc
AH1107	—	20.00	50.00	75.00	125	—
AH1108	—	20.00	50.00	75.00	125	—
AH1109	—	20.00	50.00	75.00	125	—
AH1110	—	20.00	50.00	75.00	125	—
AH1111	—	20.00	50.00	75.00	125	—
AH1112	—	20.00	50.00	75.00	125	—

Ganjah

KM# 259.2 5 SHAHI
9.2400 g., Silver **Note:** Type B.

Date	Mintage	VG	F	VF	XF	Unc
AH1107	—	40.00	100	175	250	—
AH1108	—	40.00	100	175	250	—

Iravan (Yerevan)

KM# 259.1 5 SHAHI
9.2400 g., Silver **Note:** Type B.

Date	Mintage	VG	F	VF	XF	Unc
AH1108	—	45.00	110	175	235	—

Isfahan

KM# 259.3 5 SHAHI
9.2400 g., Silver **Note:** Type B.

Date	Mintage	VG	F	VF	XF	Unc
AH1107	—	35.00	90.00	150	215	—

Tabriz

KM# 259.4 5 SHAHI
9.2400 g., Silver **Note:** Type B.

Date	Mintage	VG	F	VF	XF	Unc
AH1107	—	35.00	90.00	150	215	—

Isfahan

KM# 261 5 ABBASI (20 Shahi)
36.9600 g., Silver **Note:** Type B.

Date	Mintage	VG	F	VF	XF	Unc
AH1109 Rare	—	—	—	—	—	—

HAMMERED COINAGE
Local Type of Khuzistan

Huwayza

KM# 295 2 SHAHI (Mahmudi)
Silver **Note:** Type H. About 3.00 grams.

Date	Mintage	VG	F	VF	XF	Unc
AH1108	—	50.00	150	200	265	—
ND	—	18.50	55.00	75.00	100	—

Note: Most examples known with either date or mint missing. Prices here are for examples with date and mint.

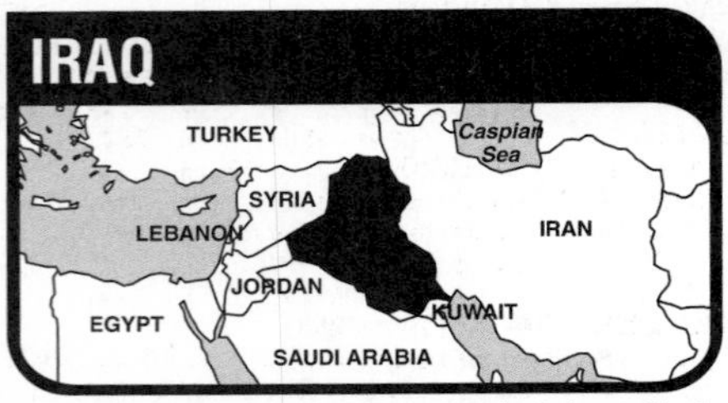

Iraq, historically known as Mesopotamia, is located in the Near East and is bordered by Kuwait, Iran, Turkey, Syria, Jordan and Saudi Arabia. Mesopotamia was the site of a number of flourishing civilizations of antiquity - Sumeria, Assyria, Babylonia, Parthia, Persia and the Biblical cities of Ur, Nineveh and Babylon. Desired because of its favored location, which embraced the fertile alluvial plains of the Tigris and Euphrates Rivers, Mesopotamia - 'land between the rivers'- was conquered by Cyrus the Great of Persia, Alexander of Macedonia and by Arabs who made the legendary city of Baghdad the capital of the ruling caliphate. Suleiman the Magnificent conquered Mesopotamia for Turkey in 1534, and it formed part of the Ottoman Empire until 1623, and from 1638 to 1917

RULER
Ottoman, until 1917

MESOPOTAMIA
Ottoman Empire

MONETARY SYSTEM
40 Para = 1 Piastre (Kurus)

MINT NAMES

بغداد
Baghdad

البصرة
al-Basrah (Basra)

الحلة
al-Hille

Ahmed I
AH1012-1026 / 1603-1617AD
HAMMERED COINAGE

KM# 8 DIRHEM (Shahi)
Silver **Obv:** 5-line inscription **Note:** Weight varies 4.07 - 4.82 grams.

Date	Mintage	VG	F	VF	XF	Unc
AH1012	—	100	200	300	—	—

KM# 9 SULTANI
3.3500 g., Gold

Date	Mintage	VG	F	VF	XF	Unc
AH1012	—	—	800	1,500	2,000	—

Mustafa I
AH1026-1027/1617-1618AD
HAMMERED COINAGE

KM# 10 MANGIR
1.0400 g., Copper, 14 mm. **Obv:** Toughra **Rev:** Mint name in ornament

Date	Mintage	VG	F	VF	XF	Unc
ND	—	250	400	550	—	—

Osman II
AH1027-1031 / 1618-1622AD
HAMMERED COINAGE

KM# 12 DIRHEM (Shahi)
Silver **Obv:** 5-line inscription **Note:** Weight varies 4.26 - 4.70 grams.

Date	Mintage	VG	F	VF	XF	Unc
AHxxxx Rare	—	—	—	—	—	—

For coins without mint listed see coin above.

Murad IV
AH1032-1049 / 1623-1640AD
HAMMERED COINAGE

KM# 15 DIRHEM (Shahi)
Silver **Obv:** Toughra **Rev:** 5-line inscription **Note:** Weight Varies: 2.8 to 3.0 g.

Date	Mintage	VG	F	VF	XF	Unc
AH1048	—	65.00	100	135	200	—
AH1049	—	50.00	75.00	100	200	—
ND	—	30.00	50.00	80.00	150	—

KM# 17 SULTANI
Gold

Date	Mintage	Good	VG	F	VF	XF
AH1043 Rare	—	—	—	—	—	—

Ibrahim
AH1049-1058 / 1640-1648AD
HAMMERED COINAGE

KM# 19 MANGIR
1.8200 g., Copper **Obv:** Bird **Note:** Previous KM#24.

Date	Mintage	VG	F	VF	XF	Unc
AH1049	—	50.00	90.00	150	—	—

KM# A20 MANGIR
1.6500 g., Copper **Obv:** Seal of Solomon

Date	Mintage	VG	F	VF	XF	Unc
AH105x	—	50.00	90.00	150	—	—

KM# 23 DIRHEM (Shahi)
Silver **Obv:** Toughra **Note:** Five varieties exist. Weight Varies: 2.8 to 3.0 g.

Date	Mintage	VG	F	VF	XF	Unc
AH1049	—	35.00	60.00	100	—	—
Note: Five varieties exist						
ND Date Missing	—	18.00	35.00	65.00	—	—

KM# 18 SULTANI
3.4500 g., Gold

Date	Mintage	VG	F	VF	XF	Unc
AH1049 Rare	—	—	—	—	—	—

Mehmed IV
AH1058-1099 / 1648-1687AD
HAMMERED COINAGE

KM# 25 MANGIR
0.9000 g., Copper, 15 mm. **Obv:** Ornament **Rev:** Mint name

Date	Mintage	VG	F	VF	XF	Unc
AH1058	—	150	200	—	—	—

KM# 26 DIRHEM (Shahi)
Silver **Obv:** 4-line inscription **Rev:** 5-line inscription **Note:** Weight varies: 2.59-2.90 grams.

Date	Mintage	VG	F	VF	XF	Unc
AH1058	—	30.00	45.00	60.00	90.00	—

KM# 27 DIRHEM (Shahi)
Silver **Obv:** Toughra **Rev:** 5-line inscription **Note:** Weight varies: 2.77-2.90 grams.

Date	Mintage	VG	F	VF	XF	Unc
AH1058	—	30.00	45.00	60.00	90.00	—

KM# 28 DIRHEM (Shahi)
Silver **Rev. Legend:** Around inner circle with mintname **Note:** Weight varies: 2.77-2.90 grams.

Date	Mintage	VG	F	VF	XF	Unc
AH1058	—	40.00	60.00	90.00	130	—

KM# 29 DIRHEM (Shahi)
Silver **Obv:** 3-line inscription **Rev:** 3-line inscripton **Note:** Weight varies: 2.77-2.90 grams.

Date	Mintage	VG	F	VF	XF	Unc
AH1059	—	45.00	75.00	90.00	165	—

KM# 30 DIRHEM (Shahi)
Silver **Rev:** 4-line inscripton **Note:** Weight varies: 2.77-2.90 grams.

Date	Mintage	VG	F	VF	XF	Unc
AH1061	—	40.00	60.00	100	150	—
AH1062	—	50.00	75.00	125	190	—

KM# 32 SULTANI
3.1000 g., Gold

Date	Mintage	VG	F	VF	XF	Unc
AH1058 Rare	—	—	—	—	—	—

Suleyman II
AH1099-1102 / 1687-1691AD
HAMMERED COINAGE

KM# 34 MANGIR
0.8000 g., Copper **Obv:** Floral Ornament **Rev:** Mint name and date

Date	Mintage	VG	F	VF	XF	Unc
AH(1)099	—	150	200	—	—	—

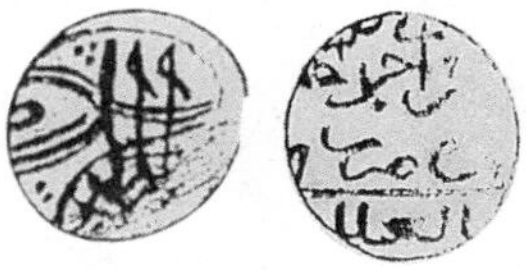

KM# 36 DIRHEM (Shahi)
2.8500 g., Silver **Obv:** Toughra **Rev:** 4-line inscription

Date	Mintage	VG	F	VF	XF	Unc
AH1099 Rare	—	—	—	—	—	—

KM# 37 LARIN
Silver

Date	Mintage	VG	F	VF	XF	Unc
ND Rare	—	—	—	—	—	—

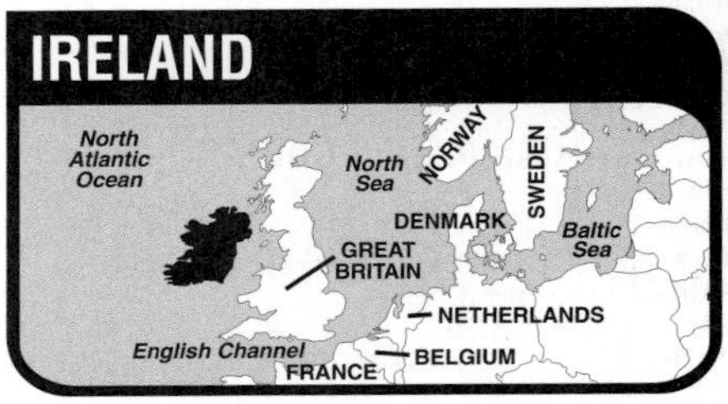

Ireland, the island located in the Atlantic Ocean west of Great Britain, was settled by a race of tall, red-haired Celts from Gaul about 400 BC. They assimilated the native Erainn and Picts and established a Gaelic civilization. After the arrival of St. Patrick in 432 AD, Ireland evolved into a center of Latin learning, which sent missionaries to Europe and possibly North America. In 1154, Pope Adrian IV gave all of Ireland to English King Henry II to administer as a Papal fief. Because of the enactment of anti-Catholic laws and the awarding of vast tracts of Irish land to Protestant absentee landowners, English control did not become reasonably absolute until 1800 when England and Ireland became the "United Kingdom of Great Britain and Ireland". Religious freedom was restored to the Irish in 1829, but agitation for political autonomy continued until the Irish Free State was established as a Dominion on Dec. 6, 1921 while Northern Ireland remained under the British rule.

RULER
British to 1921

MONETARY SYSTEM
4 Farthings = 1 Penny
12 Pence = 1 Shilling
5 Shillings = 1 Crown

UNITED KINGDOM
STANDARD COINAGE

KM# 20.1 FARTHING
Tin Plated Copper **Obv:** Crown on crossed sceptres, titles of James I **Rev:** Crowned harp **Note:** Small "Harrington" Issue. No mintmark.

Date	Mintage	VG	F	VF	XF	Unc
ND(1613)	—	40.00	9.00	375	750	—

KM# 20.2 FARTHING
Tin Plated Copper **Obv:** Crown on crossed sceptres, titles of James I **Rev:** Crowned harp **Note:** Small "Harrington" Issue; mintmark: A.

Date	Mintage	VG	F	VF	XF	Unc
ND(1613)	—	40.00	90.00	375	750	—

KM# 20.3 FARTHING
Tin Plated Copper **Obv:** Crown on crossed sceptres, titles of James I **Rev:** Crowned harp **Note:** Small "Harrington" Issue; mintmark: B.

Date	Mintage	VG	F	VF	XF	Unc
ND(1613)	—	40.00	90.00	375	750	—

KM# 20.4 FARTHING
Tin Plated Copper **Obv:** Crown on crossed sceptres, titles of James I **Rev:** Crowned harp **Note:** Small "Harrington" Issue; mintmark: C.

Date	Mintage	VG	F	VF	XF	Unc
ND(1613)	—	40.00	90.00	375	750	—

KM# 20.5 FARTHING

Tin Plated Copper **Obv:** Crown on crossed sceptres, titles of James I **Rev:** Crowned harp **Note:** Small "Harrington" Issue; mintmark: D.

Date	Mintage	VG	F	VF	XF	Unc
ND(1613)	—	40.00	90.00	375	750	—

KM# 20.6 FARTHING

Tin Plated Copper **Obv:** Crown on crossed sceptres, titles of James I **Rev:** Crowned harp **Note:** Small "Harrington" Issue; mintmark: F.

Date	Mintage	VG	F	VF	XF	Unc
ND(1613)	—	40.00	90.00	375	750	—

KM# 20.7 FARTHING

Tin Plated Copper **Obv:** Crown on crossed sceptres, titles of James I **Rev:** Crowned harp **Note:** Small "Harrington" Issue; mintmark: L.

Date	Mintage	VG	F	VF	XF	Unc
ND(1613)	—	40.00	90.00	375	750	—

KM# 20.8 FARTHING

Tin Plated Copper **Obv:** Crown on crossed sceptres, titles of James I **Rev:** Crowned harp **Note:** Small "Harrington" Issue; mintmark: Crescent.

Date	Mintage	VG	F	VF	XF	Unc
ND(1613)	—	40.00	90.00	375	750	—

KM# 20.9 FARTHING

Tin Plated Copper **Obv:** Crown on crossed sceptres, titles of James I **Rev:** Crowned harp **Note:** Small "Harrington" Issue; mintmark: Ermine.

Date	Mintage	VG	F	VF	XF	Unc
ND(1613)	—	40.00	90.00	375	750	—

KM# 20.10 FARTHING

Tin Plated Copper **Obv:** Crown on crossed sceptres, titles of James I **Rev:** Crowned harp **Note:** Small "Harrington" Issue; mintmark: Millrind.

Date	Mintage	VG	F	VF	XF	Unc
ND(1613)	—	40.00	90.00	375	750	—

KM# 20.11 FARTHING

Tin Plated Copper **Obv:** Crown on crossed sceptres, titles of James I **Rev:** Crowned harp **Note:** Small "Harrington" Issue; mintmark: Mullet.

Date	Mintage	VG	F	VF	XF	Unc
ND(1613)	—	40.00	90.00	375	750	—

KM# 20.12 FARTHING

Tin Plated Copper **Obv:** Crown on crossed sceptres, titles of James I **Rev:** Crowned harp **Note:** Small "Harrington" Issue; mintmark: Pellet.

Date	Mintage	VG	F	VF	XF	Unc
ND(1613)	—	40.00	90.00	375	750	—

KM# 20.13 FARTHING

Tin Plated Copper **Obv:** Crown on crossed sceptres, titles of James I **Rev:** Crowned harp **Note:** Small "Harrington" Issue; mintmark: Trefoil.

Date	Mintage	VG	F	VF	XF	Unc
ND(1613)	—	40.00	90.00	375	750	—

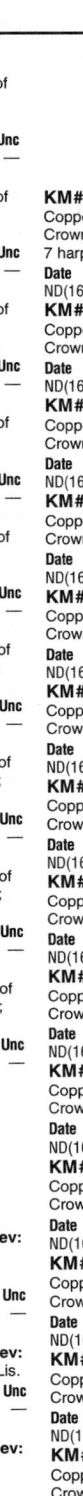

KM# 21.1 FARTHING

Copper **Obv:** Crown on crossed sceptres, titles of James I **Rev:** Crowned harp **Note:** Normal "Harrington" Issue; mintmark: Cinquefoil.

Date	Mintage	VG	F	VF	XF	Unc
ND(1613)	—	18.00	37.50	95.00	190	—

KM# 21.2 FARTHING

Copper **Obv:** Crown on crossed sceptres, titles of James I **Rev:** Crowned harp **Note:** Normal "Harrington" Issue; mintmark: Lis.

Date	Mintage	VG	F	VF	XF	Unc
ND(1613)	—	18.00	37.50	95.00	190	—

KM# 21.3 FARTHING

Copper **Obv:** Crown on crossed sceptres, titles of James I **Rev:** Crowned harp **Note:** Normal "Harrington" Issue; mintmark: Martlet.

Date	Mintage	VG	F	VF	XF	Unc
ND(1613)	—	18.00	37.50	95.00	190	—

KM# 21.4 FARTHING

Copper **Obv:** Crown on crossed sceptres, titles of James I **Rev:** Crowned harp **Note:** Normal "Harrington" Issue; mintmark: Mullet.

Date	Mintage	VG	F	VF	XF	Unc
ND(1613)	—	18.00	37.50	95.00	190	—

KM# 21.5 FARTHING

Copper **Obv:** Crown on crossed sceptres, titles of James I **Rev:** Crowned harp **Note:** Normal "Harrington" Issue; mintmark: Saltire.

Date	Mintage	VG	F	VF	XF	Unc
ND(1613)	—	18.00	37.50	959	190	—

KM# 21.6 FARTHING

Copper **Obv:** Crown on crossed sceptres, titles of James I **Rev:** Crowned harp **Note:** Normal "Harrington" Issue; mintmark: Trefoil.

Date	Mintage	VG	F	VF	XF	Unc
ND(1613)	—	18.00	37.50	95.00	190	—

KM# 22.1 FARTHING

Copper **Obv:** Crown on crossed sceptres, titles of James I **Rev:** Crowned harp **Note:** Lennox Issue; Mint mark: Annulet with 6 or 7 harp strings.

Date	Mintage	VG	F	VF	XF	Unc
ND(1613)	—	7.50	18.00	37.50	75.00	—

KM# 22.2 FARTHING

Copper **Obv:** Crown on crossed sceptres, titles of James I **Rev:** Crowned harp **Note:** Lennox Issue; Mint mark: Ball.

Date	Mintage	VG	F	VF	XF	Unc
ND(1613)	—	7.50	18.00	37.50	75.00	—

KM# 22.3 FARTHING

Copper **Obv:** Crown on crossed sceptres, titles of James I **Rev:** Crowned harp **Note:** Lennox Issue; Mint mark: Bell.

Date	Mintage	VG	F	VF	XF	Unc
ND(1613)	—	7.50	18.00	37.50	75.00	—

KM# 22.4 FARTHING

Copper **Obv:** Crown on crossed sceptres, titles of James I **Rev:** Crowned harp **Note:** Lennox Issue; Mint mark: Coronet.

Date	Mintage	VG	F	VF	XF	Unc
ND(1613)	—	7.50	18.00	37.50	75.00	—

KM# 22.5 FARTHING

Copper **Obv:** Crown on crossed sceptres, titles of James I **Rev:** Crowned harp **Note:** Lennox Issue; Mint mark: Crescent.

Date	Mintage	VG	F	VF	XF	Unc
ND(1613)	—	7.50	18.00	37.50	75.00	—

KM# 22.6 FARTHING

Copper **Obv:** Crown on crossed sceptres, titles of James I **Rev:** Crowned harp **Note:** Lennox Issue; Mint mark: Cross.

Date	Mintage	VG	F	VF	XF	Unc
ND(1613)	—	7.50	18.00	37.50	75.00	—

KM# 22.7 FARTHING

Copper **Obv:** Crown on crossed sceptres, titles of James I **Rev:** Crowned harp **Note:** Lennox Issue; Mint mark: Dagger.

Date	Mintage	VG	F	VF	XF	Unc
ND(1613)	—	7.50	18.00	37.50	75.00	—

KM# 22.8 FARTHING

Copper **Obv:** Crown on crossed sceptres, titles of James I **Rev:** Crowned harp **Note:** Lennox Issue; Mint mark: Double rose.

Date	Mintage	VG	F	VF	XF	Unc
ND(1613)	—	7.50	18.00	37.50	75.00	—

KM# 22.9 FARTHING

Copper **Obv:** Crown on crossed sceptres, titles of James I **Rev:** Crowned harp **Note:** Lennox Issue; Mint mark: Eagle's head.

Date	Mintage	VG	F	VF	XF	Unc
ND(1613)	—	7.50	18.00	37.50	75.00	—

KM# 22.10 FARTHING

Copper **Obv:** Crown on crossed sceptres, titles of James I **Rev:** Crowned harp **Note:** Lennox Issue; Mint mark: Flower.

Date	Mintage	VG	F	VF	XF	Unc
ND(1613)	—	7.50	18.00	37.50	75.00	—

KM# 22.11 FARTHING

Copper **Obv:** Crown on crossed sceptres, titles of James I **Rev:** Crowned harp **Note:** Lennox Issue; Mint mark: Grapes.

Date	Mintage	VG	F	VF	XF	Unc
ND(1613)	—	7.50	18.00	37.50	75.00	—

KM# 22.12 FARTHING

Copper **Obv:** Crown on crossed sceptres, titles of James I **Rev:** Crowned harp **Note:** Lennox Issue; Mint mark: Keg.

Date	Mintage	VG	F	VF	XF	Unc
ND(1613)	—	7.50	18.00	37.50	75.00	—

KM# 22.13 FARTHING

Copper **Obv:** Crown on crossed sceptres, titles of James I **Rev:** Crowned harp **Note:** Lennox Issue; Mint mark: Key.

Date	Mintage	VG	F	VF	XF	Unc
ND(1613)	—	7.50	18.00	37.50	75.00	—

KM# 22.14 FARTHING

Copper **Obv:** Crown on crossed sceptres, titles of James I **Rev:** Crowned harp **Note:** Lennox Issue; Mint mark: Lion.

Date	Mintage	VG	F	VF	XF	Unc
ND(1613)	—	7.50	18.00	37.50	75.00	—

KM# 22.15 FARTHING

Copper **Obv:** Crown on crossed sceptres, titles of James I **Rev:** Crowned harp **Note:** Lennox Issue; Mint mark: 3 Lis.

Date	Mintage	VG	F	VF	XF	Unc
ND(1613)	—	7.50	18.00	37.50	75.00	—

KM# 22.16 FARTHING

Copper **Obv:** Crown on crossed sceptres, titles of James I **Rev:** Crowned harp **Note:** Lennox Issue; Mint mark: Lombardic A.

Date	Mintage	VG	F	VF	XF	Unc
ND(1613)	—	7.50	18.00	37.50	75.00	—

KM# 22.17 FARTHING

Copper **Obv:** Crown on crossed sceptres, titles of James I **Rev:** Crowned harp **Note:** Lennox Issue; Mint mark: Mascle.

Date	Mintage	VG	F	VF	XF	Unc
ND(1613)	—	7.50	18.00	37.50	75.00	—

KM# 22.18 FARTHING

Copper **Obv:** Crown on crossed sceptres, titles of James I **Rev:** Crowned harp **Note:** Lennox Issue; Mint mark: Mussel.

Date	Mintage	VG	F	VF	XF	Unc
ND(1613)	—	7.50	18.00	37.50	75.00	—

KM# 22.19 FARTHING

Copper **Obv:** Crown on crossed sceptres, titles of James I **Rev:** Crowned harp **Note:** Lennox Issue; Mint mark: Quatrefoil.

Date	Mintage	VG	F	VF	XF	Unc
ND(1613)	—	7.50	18.00	37.50	75.00	—

KM# 22.20 FARTHING

Copper **Obv:** Crown on crossed sceptres, titles of James I **Rev:** Crowned harp **Note:** Lennox Issue; Mint mark: Rose.

Date	Mintage	VG	F	VF	XF	Unc
ND(1613)	—	7.50	18.00	37.50	75.00	—

KM# 22.21 FARTHING

Copper **Obv:** Crown on crossed sceptres, titles of James I **Rev:** Crowned harp **Note:** Lennox Issue; Mint mark: Star.

Date	Mintage	VG	F	VF	XF	Unc
ND(1613)	—	7.50	18.00	37.50	75.00	—

KM# 22.22 FARTHING

Copper **Obv:** Crown on crossed sceptres, titles of James I **Rev:** Crowned harp **Note:** Lennox Issue; Mint mark: Stirrup.

Date	Mintage	VG	F	VF	XF	Unc
ND(1613)	—	7.50	18.00	37.50	75.00	—

KM# 22.23 FARTHING

Copper **Obv:** Crown on crossed sceptres, titles of James I **Rev:** Crowned harp **Note:** Lennox Issue; Mint mark: Thistle.

Date	Mintage	VG	F	VF	XF	Unc
ND(1613)	—	7.50	18.00	37.50	75.00	—

KM# 22.24 FARTHING

Copper **Obv:** Crown on crossed sceptres, titles of James I **Rev:** Crowned harp **Note:** Lennox Issue; Mint mark: Trefoil.

Date	Mintage	VG	F	VF	XF	Unc
ND(1613)	—	7.50	18.00	37.50	75.00	—

KM# 22.25 FARTHING

Copper **Obv:** Crown on crossed sceptres, titles of James I **Rev:** Crowned harp **Note:** Lennox Issue; Mint mark: Triangle.

Date	Mintage	VG	F	VF	XF	Unc
ND(1613)	—	7.50	18.00	37.50	75.00	—

KM# 23 FARTHING

Copper **Obv:** Crown on crossed sceptres, legend begins at lower left. **Rev:** Crowned harp **Note:** Oval planchet; Mint mark: Cross.

Date	Mintage	VG	F	VF	XF	Unc
ND(1613)	—	18.00	37.50	115	225	—

KM# 25.1 FARTHING

Copper **Obv:** Single arched crown on crossed sceptres, titles of Charles I. **Rev:** Crowned harp **Note:** Richmond Issue. Mint Mark: A.

Date	Mintage	VG	F	VF	XF	Unc
ND(1625-44)	—	7.50	18.00	37.50	75.00	—

KM# 25.2 FARTHING

Copper **Obv:** Single arched crown on crossed sceptres, titles of Charles I. **Rev:** Crowned harp **Note:** Richmond Issue; Mint mark: Annulet.

Date	Mintage	VG	F	VF	XF	Unc
ND(1625-44)	—	7.50	18.00	37.50	75.00	—

KM# 25.3 FARTHING

Copper **Obv:** Single arched crown on crossed sceptres, titles of Charles I. **Rev:** Crowned harp **Note:** Richmond Issue; Mint mark: Bell.

Date	Mintage	VG	F	VF	XF	Unc
ND(1625-44)	—	7.50	18.00	37.50	75.00	—

KM# 25.4 FARTHING

Copper **Obv:** Single arched crown on crossed sceptres, titles of Charles I. **Rev:** Crowned harp **Note:** Richmond Issue; Mint mark: Book.

Date	Mintage	VG	F	VF	XF	Unc
ND(1625-44)	—	7.50	18.00	37.50	75.00	—

KM# 25.5 FARTHING

Copper **Obv:** Single arched crown on crossed sceptres, titles of Charles I. **Rev:** Crowned harp **Note:** Richmond Issue; Mint mark: Cinquefoil.

Date	Mintage	VG	F	VF	XF	Unc
ND(1625-44)	—	7.50	18.00	37.50	75.00	—

KM# 25.6 FARTHING

Copper **Obv:** Single arched crown on crossed sceptres, titles of Charles I. **Rev:** Crowned harp **Note:** Richmond Issue; Mint mark: Coronet.

Date	Mintage	VG	F	VF	XF	Unc
ND(1625-44)	—	7.50	18.00	37.50	75.00	—

KM# 25.7 FARTHING

Copper **Obv:** Single arched crown on crossed sceptres, titles of Charles I. **Rev:** Crowned harp **Note:** Richmond Issue; Mint mark: Crescent.

Date	Mintage	VG	F	VF	XF	Unc
ND(1625-44)	—	7.50	18.00	37.50	75.00	—

KM# 25.8 FARTHING

Copper **Obv:** Single arched crown on crossed sceptres, titles of Charles I. **Rev:** Crowned harp **Note:** Richmond Issue; Mint mark: Cross with pellets

Date	Mintage	VG	F	VF	XF	Unc
ND(1625-44)	—	7.50	18.00	37.50	75.00	—

KM# 25.9 FARTHING

Copper **Obv:** Single arched crown on crossed sceptres, titles of Charles I. **Rev:** Crowned harp **Note:** Richmond Issue; Mint mark: Dagger.

Date	Mintage	VG	F	VF	XF	Unc
ND(1625-44)	—	7.50	18.00	37.50	75.00	—

KM# 25.10 FARTHING

Copper **Obv:** Single arched crown on crossed sceptres, titles of Charles I. **Rev:** Crowned harp **Note:** Richmond Issue; Mint mark: Ermine.

Date	Mintage	VG	F	VF	XF	Unc
ND(1625-44)	—	7.50	18.00	37.50	75.00	—

KM# 25.11 FARTHING

Copper **Obv:** Single arched crown on crossed sceptres, titles of Charles I. **Rev:** Crowned harp **Note:** Richmond Issue; Mint mark: Eye.

Date	Mintage	VG	F	VF	XF	Unc
ND(1625-44)	—	7.50	18.00	37.50	75.00	—

KM# 25.12 FARTHING

Copper **Obv:** Single arched crown on crossed sceptres, titles of Charles I. **Rev:** Crowned harp **Note:** Richmond Issue; Mint mark: Fish-hook.

Date	Mintage	VG	F	VF	XF	Unc
ND(1625-44)	—	7.50	18.00	37.50	75.00	—

KM# 25.13 FARTHING

Copper **Obv:** Single arched crown on crossed sceptres, titles of Charles I. **Rev:** Crowned harp **Note:** Richmond Issue; Mint mark: Fleece.

Date	Mintage	VG	F	VF	XF	Unc
ND(1625-44)	—	7.50	18.00	37.50	75.00	—

KM# 25.14 FARTHING

Copper **Obv:** Single arched crown on crossed sceptres, titles of Charles I. **Rev:** Crowned harp **Note:** Richmond Issue; Mint mark: Gauntlet.

Date	Mintage	VG	F	VF	XF	Unc
ND(1625-44)	—	7.50	18.00	37.50	75.00	—

KM# 25.15 FARTHING

Copper **Obv:** Single arched crown on crossed sceptres, titles of Charles I. **Rev:** Crowned harp **Note:** Richmond Issue; Mint mark: Grapes.

Date	Mintage	VG	F	VF	XF	Unc
ND(1625-44)	—	7.50	18.00	37.50	75.00	—

KM# 25.16 FARTHING

Copper **Obv:** Single arched crown on crossed sceptres, titles of Charles I. **Rev:** Crowned harp **Note:** Richmond Issue; Mint mark: Halberd.

Date	Mintage	VG	F	VF	XF	Unc
ND(1625-44)	—	7.50	18.00	37.50	75.00	—

KM# 25.17 FARTHING

Copper **Obv:** Single arched crown on crossed sceptres, titles of Charles I. **Rev:** Crowned harp **Note:** Richmond Issue; Mint mark: Harp.

Date	Mintage	VG	F	VF	XF	Unc
ND(1625-44)	—	7.50	18.00	37.50	75.00	—

KM# 25.18 FARTHING

Copper **Obv:** Single arched crown on crossed sceptres, titles of Charles I. **Rev:** Crowned harp **Note:** Richmond Issue; Mint mark: Heart.

Date	Mintage	VG	F	VF	XF	Unc
ND(1625-44)	—	7.50	18.00	37.50	75.00	—

KM# 25.19 FARTHING

Copper **Obv:** Single arched crown on crossed sceptres, titles of Charles I. **Rev:** Crowned harp **Note:** Richmond Issue; Mint mark: Horse shoe.

Date	Mintage	VG	F	VF	XF	Unc
ND(1625-44)	—	7.50	18.00	37.50	75.00	—

KM# 25.20 FARTHING

Copper **Obv:** Single arched crown on crossed sceptres, titles of Charles I. **Rev:** Crowned harp **Note:** Richmond Issue; Mint mark: Key.

Date	Mintage	VG	F	VF	XF	Unc
ND(1625-44)	—	7.50	18.00	37.50	75.00	—

KM# 25.21 FARTHING

Copper **Obv:** Single arched crown on crossed sceptres, titles of Charles I. **Rev:** Crowned harp **Note:** Richmond Issue; Mint mark: Leaf.

Date	Mintage	VG	F	VF	XF	Unc
ND(1625-44)	—	7.50	18.00	37.50	75.00	—

KM# 25.22 FARTHING

Copper **Obv:** Single arched crown on crossed sceptres, titles of Charles I. **Rev:** Crowned harp **Note:** Richmond Issue; Mint mark: Lion.

Date	Mintage	VG	F	VF	XF	Unc
ND(1625-44)	—	7.50	18.00	37.50	75.00	—

KM# 25.23 FARTHING

Copper **Obv:** Single arched crown on crossed sceptres, titles of Charles I. **Rev:** Crowned harp **Note:** Richmond Issue; Mint mark: Lis.

Date	Mintage	VG	F	VF	XF	Unc
ND(1625-44)	—	7.50	18.00	37.50	75.00	—

KM# 25.24 FARTHING

Copper **Obv:** Single arched crown on crossed sceptres, titles of Charles I. **Rev:** Crowned harp **Note:** Richmond Issue; Mint mark: Demi-lis.

Date	Mintage	VG	F	VF	XF	Unc
ND(1624-44)	—	7.50	18.00	37.50	75.00	—

KM# 25.25 FARTHING

Copper **Obv:** Single arched crown on crossed sceptres, titles of Charles I. **Rev:** Crowned harp **Note:** Richmond Issue; Mint mark: 3 Lis.

Date	Mintage	VG	F	VF	XF	Unc
ND(1625-44)	—	7.50	18.00	37.50	75.00	—

KM# 25.26 FARTHING

Copper **Obv:** Single arched crown on crossed sceptres, titles of Charles I. **Rev:** Crowned harp **Note:** Richmond Issue; Mint mark: Martlet.

Date	Mintage	VG	F	VF	XF	Unc
ND(1625-44)	—	7.50	18.00	37.50	75.00	—

KM# 25.27 FARTHING

Copper **Obv:** Single arched crown on crossed sceptres, titles of Charles I. **Rev:** Crowned harp **Note:** Richmond Issue; Mint mark: Mascle.

Date	Mintage	VG	F	VF	XF	Unc
ND(1625-44)	—	7.50	18.00	37.50	75.00	—

KM# 25.28 FARTHING

Copper **Obv:** Single arched crown on crossed sceptres, titles of Charles I. **Rev:** Crowned harp **Note:** Richmond Issue; Mint mark: Musket.

Date	Mintage	VG	F	VF	XF	Unc
ND(1625-44)	—	7.50	18.00	37.50	75.00	—

KM# 25.29 FARTHING

Copper **Obv:** Single arched crown on crossed sceptres, titles of Charles I. **Rev:** Crowned harp **Note:** Richmond Issue; Mint mark: 2 Muskets.

Date	Mintage	VG	F	VF	XF	Unc
ND(1625-44)	—	7.50	18.00	37.50	75.00	—

KM# 25.30 FARTHING

Copper **Obv:** Single arched crown on crossed sceptres, titles of Charles I. **Rev:** Crowned harp **Note:** Richmond Issue; Mint mark: Nautilus.

Date	Mintage	VG	F	VF	XF	Unc
ND(1625-44)	—	7.50	18.00	37.50	75.00	—

KM# 25.31 FARTHING

Copper **Obv:** Single arched crown on crossed sceptres, titles of Charles I. **Rev:** Crowned harp **Note:** Richmond Issue; Mint mark: Rose.

Date	Mintage	VG	F	VF	XF	Unc
ND(1625-44)	—	7.50	18.00	37.50	75.00	—

KM# 25.32 FARTHING

Copper **Obv:** Single arched crown on crossed sceptres, titles of Charles I. **Rev:** Crowned harp **Note:** Richmond Issue; Mint mark: Shield.

Date	Mintage	VG	F	VF	XF	Unc
ND(1625-44)	—	7.50	18.00	37.50	75.00	—

KM# 25.33 FARTHING

Copper **Obv:** Single arched crown on crossed sceptres, titles of Charles I. **Rev:** Crowned harp **Note:** Richmond Issue; Mint mark: Spearhead.

Date	Mintage	VG	F	VF	XF	Unc
ND(1625-44)	—	7.50	18.00	37.50	75.00	—

KM# 25.34 FARTHING

Copper **Obv:** Single arched crown on crossed sceptres, titles of Charles I. **Rev:** Crowned harp **Note:** Richmond Issue; Mint mark: Tower.

Date	Mintage	VG	F	VF	XF	Unc
ND(1625-44)	—	7.50	18.00	37.50	75.00	—

KM# 25.35 FARTHING

Copper **Obv:** Single arched crown on crossed sceptres, titles of Charles I. **Rev:** Crowned harp **Note:** Richard Issue; Mint mark: Trefoil.

Date	Mintage	VG	F	VF	XF	Unc
ND(1625-44)	—	7.50	18.00	37.50	75.00	—

Note: Varieties exist

KM# 25.36 FARTHING

Copper **Obv:** Single arched crown on crossed sceptres, titles of Charles I **Rev:** Crowned harp **Note:** Richmond Issue. Mint mark: Woolpack.

Date	Mintage	VG	F	VF	XF	Unc
ND(1625-44)	—	7.50	18.00	37.50	75.00	—

KM# 26.1 FARTHING

Copper **Obv:** Double-arched crown **Note:** Transitional Issue; Mint mark: Harp.

Date	Mintage	VG	F	VF	XF	Unc
ND(1625-44)	—	18.00	37.50	115	225	—

KM# 26.2 FARTHING

Copper **Obv:** Double-arched crown **Note:** Transitional Issue; Mint mark: Quatrefoil.

Date	Mintage	VG	F	VF	XF	Unc
ND(1625-44)	—	18.00	37.50	115	225	—

KM# 27.1 FARTHING

Copper **Obv:** Crown on crossed sceptres within inner circle **Rev:** Crowned harp within inner circle **Note:** "Maltravers" Issue; Mint mark: Bell with 5 or 6 harp strings.

Date	Mintage	VG	F	VF	XF	Unc
ND(1625-44)	—	7.50	18.00	37.50	75.00	—

KM# 27.2 FARTHING

Copper **Obv:** Crown on crossed sceptres within inner circle **Rev:** Crowned harp within inner circle **Note:** "Maltravers" Issue; Mint mark: Billet.

Date	Mintage	VG	F	VF	XF	Unc
ND(1625-44)	—	7.50	18.00	37.50	75.00	—

KM# 27.3 FARTHING

Copper **Obv:** Crown on crossed sceptres within inner circle **Rev:** Crowned harp within inner circle **Note:** "Maltravers" Issue; Mint mark: Cross.

Date	Mintage	VG	F	VF	XF	Unc
ND(1625-44)	—	7.50	18.00	37.50	75.00	—

KM# 27.4 FARTHING

Copper **Obv:** Crown on crossed sceptres within inner circle **Rev:** Crowned harp within inner circle **Note:** "Maltravers" Issue; Mint mark: Harp.

Date	Mintage	VG	F	VF	XF	Unc
ND(1625-44)	—	7.50	18.00	37.50	75.00	—

KM# 27.5 FARTHING

Copper **Obv:** Crown on crossed sceptres within inner circle **Rev:** Crowned harp within inner circle **Note:** "Maltravers" Issue; Mint mark: Lis.

Date	Mintage	VG	F	VF	XF	Unc
ND(1625-44)	—	7.50	18.00	37.50	75.00	—

KM# 27.6 FARTHING

Copper **Obv:** Crown on crossed sceptres within inner circle **Rev:** Crowned harp within inner circle **Note:** "Maltravers" Issue; Mint mark: Martlet.

Date	Mintage	VG	F	VF	XF	Unc
ND(1625-44)	—	7.50	18.00	37.50	75.00	—

KM# 27.7 FARTHING

Copper **Obv:** Crown on crossed sceptres within inner circle **Rev:** Crowned harp within inner circle **Note:** "Maltravers" Issue; Mint mark: Portcullis.

Date	Mintage	VG	F	VF	XF	Unc
ND(1625-44)	—	7.50	18.00	37.50	75.00	—

KM# 27.8 FARTHING

Copper **Obv:** Crown on crossed sceptres within inner circle **Rev:** Crowned harp within inner circle **Note:** "Maltravers" Issue; Mint mark: Rose.

Date	Mintage	VG	F	VF	XF	Unc
ND(1625-44)	—	7.50	18.00	37.50	75.00	—

Note: Varieties exist

KM# 28.1 FARTHING

Copper **Note:** "Maltravers" Issue; Mint mark: Crescent; oval planchet.

Date	Mintage	VG	F	VF	XF	Unc
ND(1625-44)	—	18.00	35.00	110	220	—

KM# 27.9 FARTHING

Copper **Obv:** Crown on crossed sceptres within inner circle **Rev:** Crowned harp within inner circle **Note:** "Maltravers" Issue; mint mark: Woolpack.

Date	Mintage	VG	F	VF	XF	Unc
ND(1625-44)	—	7.50	18.00	37.50	75.00	—

KM# 28.2 FARTHING

Copper **Note:** "Maltravers" Issue; Mint mark: Cross; oval planchet.

Date	Mintage	VG	F	VF	XF	Unc
ND(1625-44)	—	18.00	35.00	110	220	—

KM# 28.3 FARTHING

Copper **Note:** "Maltravers" Issue; Mint mark: Demi-lis; oval planchet.

Date	Mintage	VG	F	VF	XF	Unc
ND(1625-44)	—	18.00	35.00	110	220	—

KM# 28.4 FARTHING

Copper **Note:** "Maltravers" Issue; Mint mark: Martlet; oval planchet.

Date	Mintage	VG	F	VF	XF	Unc
ND(1625-44)	—	18.00	35.00	110	220	—

KM# 28.5 FARTHING

Copper **Note:** "Maltravers" Issue; Mint mark: Rose; oval planchet.

Date	Mintage	VG	F	VF	XF	Unc
ND(1625-44)	—	18.00	35.00	110	220	—

KM# 28.6 FARTHING

Copper **Note:** "Maltravers" Issue; Mint mark: Scroll; oval planchet.

Date	Mintage	VG	F	VF	XF	Unc
ND(1625-44)	—	18.00	35.00	110	220	—

KM# 28.7 FARTHING

Copper **Note:** "Maltravers" Issue; Mint mark: 9; oval planchet.

Date	Mintage	VG	F	VF	XF	Unc
ND(1625-44)	—	18.00	35.00	110	220	—

Note: Varieties exist

KM# 29 FARTHING

Copper **Obv:** Double-arched crown **Note:** "Maltravers" Issue; Mint mark: Lis; oval planchet.

Date	Mintage	VG	F	VF	XF	Unc
ND(1625-44)	—	25.00	47.00	145	300	—

KM# 30.1 FARTHING

Copper **Rev:** Crowned rose **Note:** "Rose" Issue; Mint mark: Crescent.

Date	Mintage	VG	F	VF	XF	Unc
ND(1625-44)	—	7.50	18.00	37.50	75.00	—

KM# 30.2 FARTHING

Copper **Rev:** Crowned rose **Note:** "Rose" Issue; Mint mark: Cross.

Date	Mintage	VG	F	VF	XF	Unc
ND(1625-44)	—	7.50	18.00	37.50	75.00	—

KM# 30.3 FARTHING

Copper **Rev:** Crowned rose **Note:** "Rose" Issue; Mint mark: Lis.

Date	Mintage	VG	F	VF	XF	Unc
ND(1625-44)	—	7.50	18.00	37.50	75.00	—

KM# 30.4 FARTHING

Copper **Rev:** Crowned rose **Note:** "Rose" Issue; Mint mark: Martlet.

Date	Mintage	VG	F	VF	XF	Unc
ND(1625-44)	—	7.50	18.00	37.50	75.00	—

KM# 30.5 FARTHING

Copper **Rev:** Crowned rose **Note:** "Rose" Issue; Mint mark: Mullet.

Date	Mintage	VG	F	VF	XF	Unc
ND(1625-44)	—	7.50	18.00	37.50	75.00	—

Note: Varieties exist

KM# 31.1 FARTHING

Copper **Obv:** Single-arched crown **Note:** "Rose" Issue; Mint mark: Crescent.

Date	Mintage	VG	F	VF	XF	Unc
ND(1625-44)	—	7.50	18.00	37.50	75.00	—

KM# 31.2 FARTHING

Copper **Obv:** Single-arched crown **Note:** "Rose" Issue; Mint mark: Mullet.

Date	Mintage	VG	F	VF	XF	Unc
ND(1625-44)	—	7.50	18.00	37.50	75.00	—

Note: Varieties exist

KM# 32 FARTHING

Copper **Obv:** Sceptres below crown **Note:** "Rose" Issue; Mint mark: Mullet.

Date	Mintage	VG	F	VF	XF	Unc
ND(1625-44)	—	13.00	22.50	70.00	140	—

KM# 85 FARTHING

Copper **Obv:** Crown over crossed sceptres, titles of Charles II **Rev:** Crowned harp **Note:** Armstrong Issue; Mint mark: Plumes.

Date	Mintage	VG	F	VF	XF	Unc
ND(1660-1)	—	37.50	75.00	190	400	—

KM# 86.1 FARTHING

Copper **Obv:** St. Patrick with cross driving out snakes, church at right **Rev:** Crown above King David playing harp **Note:** St. Patrick's Issue; Mint mark: Annulet

Date	Mintage	VG	F	VF	XF	Unc
ND(ca. 1678)	—	100	300	900	2,000	—

KM# 86.2 FARTHING

Copper **Obv:** St. Patrick with cross driving out snakes, church at right **Rev:** Crown above King David playing harp **Note:** St. Patrick's Issue; Mint mark: Martlet.

Date	Mintage	VG	F	VF	XF	Unc
ND	—	150	400	1,000	2,500	—

Note: Varieties exist

KM# 86.2a FARTHING

Silver **Obv:** St. Patrick with cross driving out snakes, church at right **Rev:** Crown above King David playing harp **Note:** St. Patrick's Issue.

Date	Mintage	VG	F	VF	XF	Unc
ND Rare	—	—	—	3,800	—	—

KM# 86.2b FARTHING

Gold **Obv:** St. Patrick with cross driving out snakes, church at right **Rev:** Crown above King David playing harp **Note:** St. Patrick's Issue.

Date	Mintage	VG	F	VF	XF	Unc
ND Rare	—	—	—	—	—	—

KM# 86.3 FARTHING

Copper **Obv:** St. Patrick with cross driving out snakes, church at right **Rev:** Crown above King David playing harp **Note:** St. Patrick's Issue. At least 180 die varieties.

Date	Mintage	VG	F	VF	XF	Unc
ND	—	150	400	1,000	3,000	—

KM# 5.1 1/2 PENNY

Copper **Obv:** Shield of arms in inner circle, titles of Elizabeth I **Rev:** Crowned harp divides date in inner circle **Note:** Mint mark: Star.

Date	Mintage	VG	F	VF	XF	Unc
1601	—	27.50	65.00	160	320	—

KM# 5.2 1/2 PENNY

Copper **Obv:** Shield of arms in inner circle, titles of Elizabeth I **Rev:** Crowned harp divides date in inner circle **Note:** Mint mark: Trefoil.

Date	Mintage	VG	F	VF	XF	Unc
1601	—	27.50	65.00	160	320	—

KM# 5.3 1/2 PENNY

Copper **Obv:** Shield of arms in inner circle, titles of Elizabeth I **Rev:** Crowned harp divides date in inner circle **Note:** Mint mark: Martlet.

Date	Mintage	VG	F	VF	XF	Unc
1602	—	27.50	65.00	185	375	—

KM# 87 1/2 PENNY

Copper **Obv:** St. Patrick holding cross and crozier preaching to multitude, arms of Dublin at right **Rev:** King David playing harp, crown above **Note:** St. Patrick issue. Varieties, including off-metal strikes in silver and gold exist.

Date	Mintage	VG	F	VF	XF	Unc
ND(ca. 1678)	—	350	850	2,000	—	—

KM# 90.1 1/2 PENNY

Copper **Obv:** Laureate and draped bust right, large letters **Rev:** Crowned harp, large letters **Note:** Armstrong and Legg issue.

Date	Mintage	VG	F	VF	XF	Unc
1680	—	13.00	25.00	100	250	—
1681	—	8.00	19.00	75.00	190	—
1682 Rare	—	—	—	—	—	—

KM# 90.1a 1/2 PENNY

Silver **Obv:** Large letters **Rev:** Large letters **Note:** Armstrong and Legg issue.

Date	Mintage	VG	F	VF	XF	Unc
1680 Proof, Rare	—	—	—	—	—	—

KM# 90.2 1/2 PENNY

Copper **Obv:** I in circle on King's shoulder **Rev:** Large letters **Note:** Armstrong and Legg issue.

Date	Mintage	VG	F	VF	XF	Unc
1680 Rare	—	—	—	—	—	—

KM# 91 1/2 PENNY

Copper **Obv:** Laureate and draped bust right, small letters **Rev:** Crowned harp, small letters **Note:** Armstrong and Legg issue.

Date	Mintage	VG	F	VF	XF	Unc
1681 Unique	—	—	—	—	—	—
1682	—	8.00	19.00	75.00	190	—
1683	—	13.00	25.00	100	220	—
1684	—	50.00	120	280	600	—

KM# 91a 1/2 PENNY

Silver **Obv:** Small letters **Rev:** Small letters **Note:** Armstrong and Legg issue.

Date	Mintage	VG	F	VF	XF	Unc
1681 Proof, Rare	—	—	—	—	—	—

KM# 92 1/2 PENNY

Copper **Obv:** Laureate and draped bust of James II right **Rev:** Crowned harp divides date

Date	Mintage	VG	F	VF	XF	Unc
1685	—	15.00	37.50	150	350	—
1686	—	13.00	25.00	115	280	—
1687 Rare	—	—	—	—	—	—
1688	—	19.00	37.50	190	450	—

KM# 92a 1/2 PENNY

Silver **Obv:** Laureate and draped bust of James II right **Rev:** Crowned harp divides date

Date	Mintage	VG	F	VF	XF	Unc
1686	—	—	—	—	—	—

KM# 109 1/2 PENNY

Copper **Obv:** Conjoined busts of William and Mary right **Rev:** Crowned harp divides date

Date	Mintage	VG	F	VF	XF	Unc
1692	—	9.00	19.00	95.00	250	—
1693	—	8.00	16.00	75.00	220	—
1694	—	9.00	19.00	95.00	250	—

KM# 109a 1/2 PENNY

Silver **Obv:** Conjoined busts of William and Mary right **Rev:** Crowned harp divides date

Date	Mintage	VG	F	VF	XF	Unc
1693 Proof, rare	—	—	—	—	—	—

KM# 110 1/2 PENNY

Copper **Obv:** Laureate and draped bust of William III **Rev:** Crowned harp divides date

Date	Mintage	VG	F	VF	XF	Unc
1696	—	25.00	47.00	220	750	—

Note: Reverse legend varieties exist

KM# 110a 1/2 PENNY

Silver **Obv:** Laureate and draped bust of William III **Rev:** Crowned harp divides date

Date	Mintage	VG	F	VF	XF	Unc
1696 Proof, Rare	—	—	—	—	—	—

KM# 110b 1/2 PENNY

Silver Gilt **Obv:** Laureate and draped bust of William III **Rev:** Crowned harp divides date

Date	Mintage	VG	F	VF	XF	Unc
1696 Proof, 3 known	—	—	—	—	—	—

KM# 111 1/2 PENNY

Copper **Obv:** Crude undraped bust **Rev:** Crowned harp divides date

Date	Mintage	VG	F	VF	XF	Unc
1696	—	75.00	155	650	1,400	—

KM# 6.1 PENNY

Copper **Obv:** Shield of arms in inner circle, titles of Elizabeth I **Rev:** Crowned harp divides date in inner circle **Note:** Mint mark: Star.

Date	Mintage	VG	F	VF	XF	Unc
1601	—	25.00	50.00	95.00	190	—
ND Rare	—	—	—	—	—	—

KM# 6.2 PENNY

Copper **Obv:** Shield of arms in inner circle, titles of Elizabeth I **Rev:** Crowned harp divides date in inner circle **Note:** Mint mark: Trefoil.

Date	Mintage	VG	F	VF	XF	Unc
1601	—	25.00	50.00	95.00	190	—

KM# 6.3 PENNY

Copper **Obv:** Shield of arms in inner circle, titles of Elizabeth I **Rev:** Crowned harp divides date in inner circle **Note:** Mint mark: Martlet.

Date	Mintage	VG	F	VF	XF	Unc
1602	—	25.00	50.00	105	220	—

KM# 7.1 3 PENCE
Billon **Obv:** Shield of arms in inner circle, titles of Elizabeth I **Rev:** Crowned harp divides date in inner circle **Note:** Mint mark: Martlet.

Date	Mintage	VG	F	VF	XF	Unc
ND(1601-02)	—	125	325	625	1,400	—

KM# 7.2 3 PENCE
Billon **Obv:** Shield of arms in inner circle, titles of Elizabeth I **Rev:** Crowned harp divides date in inner circle **Note:** Mint mark: Star

Date	Mintage	VG	F	VF	XF	Unc
ND	—	125	325	625	1,400	—

KM# 7.3 3 PENCE
Billon **Obv:** Shield of arms in inner circle, titles of Elizabeth I **Rev:** Crowned harp divides date in inner circle **Note:** Mint mark: Trefoil.

Date	Mintage	VG	F	VF	XF	Unc
ND	—	125	325	625	1,400	—

KM# 8.1 6 PENCE
Billon **Obv:** Shield of arms in inner circle, titles of Elizabeth I **Rev:** Crowned harp divides date in inner circle **Note:** Mint mark: Martlet.

Date	Mintage	VG	F	VF	XF	Unc
ND(1601-02)	—	43.75	125	375	825	—

KM# 8.2 6 PENCE
Billon **Obv:** Shield of arms in inner circle, titles of Elizabeth I **Rev:** Crowned harp divides date in inner circle **Note:** Mint mark: Star.

Date	Mintage	VG	F	VF	XF	Unc
ND	—	43.75	125	375	825	—

KM# 8.3 6 PENCE
Billon **Obv:** Shield of arms in inner circle, titles of Elizabeth I **Rev:** Crowned harp divides date in inner circle **Note:** Mint mark: Trefoil.

Date	Mintage	VG	F	VF	XF	Unc
ND	—	43.75	125	375	825	—

KM# 10.1 6 PENCE
Silver **Obv:** Crowned first bust of James I right in inner circle **Obv. Legend:** IACOBVS. D. G. Ang... **Rev:** Crowned harp in inner circle **Rev. Legend:** TVEATVR... **Note:** Mint mark: bell.

Date	Mintage	VG	F	VF	XF	Unc
ND(1603-04)	—	37.50	100	250	525	—

KM# 10.2 6 PENCE
Silver **Obv:** Crowned first bust of James I right in inner circle **Obv. Legend:** IACOBVS. D. G. Ang... **Rev:** Crowned harp in inner circle **Rev. Legend:** TUEATUR... **Note:** Mint mark: Martlet.

Date	Mintage	VG	F	VF	XF	Unc
ND	—	30.00	80.00	200	425	—

KM# 11.1 6 PENCE
Silver **Obv:** Crowned first bust of James I right in inner circle **Obv. Legend:** MAG BRIT... **Rev:** Crowned harp in inner circle **Rev. Legend:** TVEATVR... **Note:** Mint mark: Martlet.

Date	Mintage	VG	F	VF	XF	Unc
ND(1603-4)	—	37.50	100	280	600	—

KM# 11.2 6 PENCE
Silver **Obv:** Crowned first bust of James I right in inner circle **Obv. Legend:** MAG BRIT... **Rev:** Crowned harp in inner circle **Rev. Legend:** TVEATVR... **Note:** Mint mark: Rose.

Date	Mintage	VG	F	VF	XF	Unc
ND(1604-7)	—	37.50	100	280	600	—

KM# 11.3 6 PENCE
Silver **Obv:** Crowned first bust of James I right in inner circle **Obv. Legend:** MAG BRIT... **Rev:** Crowned harp in inner circle **Rev. Legend:** TVEATVR... **Note:** Mint mark: Scallop shell.

Date	Mintage	VG	F	VF	XF	Unc
ND	—	43.75	100	325	625	—

KM# 9.1 SHILLING
Billon **Note:** Mint mark: Martlet.

Date	Mintage	VG	F	VF	XF	Unc
ND(1601-02)	—	65.00	125	475	875	—

KM# 9.2 SHILLING
Billon **Note:** Mint mark: Star.

Date	Mintage	VG	F	VF	XF	Unc
ND	—	65.00	125	475	875	—

KM# 9.3 SHILLING
Billon **Note:** Mint mark: Trefoil.

Date	Mintage	VG	F	VF	XF	Unc
ND	—	65.00	125	475	875	—

KM# 12 SHILLING
Silver **Obv:** Crowned first bust of James I, short square-cut beard **Obv. Legend:** IACOBVS. D.G. Ang. SCO... **Note:** Mint mark: Bell.

Date	Mintage	VG	F	VF	XF	Unc
ND(1603-4)	—	37.50	100	280	600	—

KM# 13 SHILLING
Silver **Obv:** Second bust - pointed beard **Note:** Mint mark: Martlet.

Date	Mintage	VG	F	VF	XF	Unc
ND	—	37.50	105	375	750	—

KM# 14.1 SHILLING
Silver **Obv:** Third bust - longer square-cut beard **Obv. Legend:** IACOBVS. D. G. MAG. BRIT. FRA... **Note:** Mint mark: Martlet

Date	Mintage	VG	F	VF	XF	Unc
ND	—	37.50	100	280	600	—

KM# 14.2 SHILLING
Silver **Obv:** Third bust - longer square-cut beard **Obv. Legend:** IACOBVS. D. G. MAG. BRIT. FRA... **Note:** Mint mark: Rose.

Date	Mintage	VG	F	VF	XF	Unc
ND rose/martlet	—	37.50	100	280	600	—
ND	—	37.50	100	280	600	—

KM# 14.3 SHILLING
Silver **Obv:** Third bust - longer square-cut beard **Obv. Legend:** IACOBVS. D. G. MAG. BRIT. FRA... **Note:** Mint mark: Scallop shell.

Date	Mintage	VG	F	VF	XF	Unc
ND	—	37.50	100	280	600	—

KM# 15.1 SHILLING
Silver **Obv:** Fourth bust - long beard **Note:** Mint mark: Scallop shell

Date	Mintage	VG	F	VF	XF	Unc
ND	—	65.00	125	475	1,000	—

KM# 15.2 SHILLING
Silver **Obv:** Fourth bust - long beard **Note:** Mint mark: Rose.

Date	Mintage	VG	F	VF	XF	Unc
ND	—	50.00	100	375	800	—

GREAT REBELLION

Public dissension had been accumulating through the early part of the 17th century until rebellion broke out in Ireland in October, 1641. During the next 8 years various issues of coins were produced. They fall into 3 basic categories: Issues of the Lords Justices (representing the Crown), Issues of the Catholic Confederacy (representing the people) and Local Issues of the Cities of Refuge.

LORDS JUSTICES COINAGE

Inchiquin Money

These pieces are struck from cut pieces of flattened plate.

KM# 35 GROAT
1.9400 g., Silver **Obv:** Weight in double circle **Rev:** Weight in double circle

Date	Mintage	VG	F	VF	XF	Unc
ND(1642) Rare	—	—	—	—	—	—

KM# 36 6 PENCE
2.9800 g., Silver **Obv:** Weight in double circle **Rev:** Weight in double circle

Date	Mintage	VG	F	VF	XF	Unc
ND(1642) Rare	—	—	—	—	—	—

KM# 37 9 PENCE
4.4100 g., Silver **Obv:** Weight in triple circle, outer circle beaded **Rev:** Weight in triple circle, outer circle beaded

Date	Mintage	VG	F	VF	XF	Unc
ND(1642)	—	5,000	7,500	—	—	—

KM# 38 SHILLING
6.0300 g., Silver **Obv:** Weight in triple beaded circle **Rev:** Weight in triple beaded circle

Date	Mintage	VG	F	VF	XF	Unc
ND(1642)	—	2,250	4,500	8,500	—	—

KM# 40 1/2 CROWN
15.0300 g., Silver **Obv:** Weight in double circle **Rev:** Weight in double circle

Date	Mintage	VG	F	VF	XF	Unc
ND(1642)	—	1,650	3,250	5,750	—	—

KM# 41 CROWN
30.0700 g., Silver **Obv:** Weight in double circle, outer circle beaded **Rev:** Weight in double circle, outer circle beaded **Note:** Dav. #3790.

Date	Mintage	VG	F	VF	XF	Unc
ND(1642)	—	1,250	2,500	5,000	—	—

LORDS JUSTICES COINAGE
Annulets Coinage

KM# 43 3 PENCE
1.4900 g., Silver **Obv:** Weight in circle **Rev:** 3 annulets in double circle

Date	Mintage	VG	F	VF	XF	Unc
ND(1642) 4 known	—	5,000	8,000	12,000	—	—

KM# 44 4 PENCE (Groat)
1.9400 g., Silver **Obv:** Weight in double circle **Rev:** 4 annulets in double circle

Date	Mintage	VG	F	VF	XF	Unc
ND(1642)	—	5,500	8,500	12,500	—	—

KM# 45 6 PENCE
2.9800 g., Silver **Obv:** Weight in double circle **Rev:** 6 annulets in double circle

Date	Mintage	VG	F	VF	XF	Unc
ND(1642) Rare	—	2,750	4,500	7,500	—	—

KM# 46 9 PENCE
4.4100 g., Silver **Obv:** Weight in double circle **Rev:** 9 annulets in double circle

Date	Mintage	VG	F	VF	XF	Unc
ND(1642) Rare	—	—	—	—	—	—

LORDS JUSTICES COINAGE
"Dublin" Money

KM# 53 1/2 CROWN
Silver **Obv:** Value in circle **Rev:** Value in circle

Date	Mintage	VG	F	VF	XF	Unc
ND(1643)	—	1,750	3,500	6,000	—	—

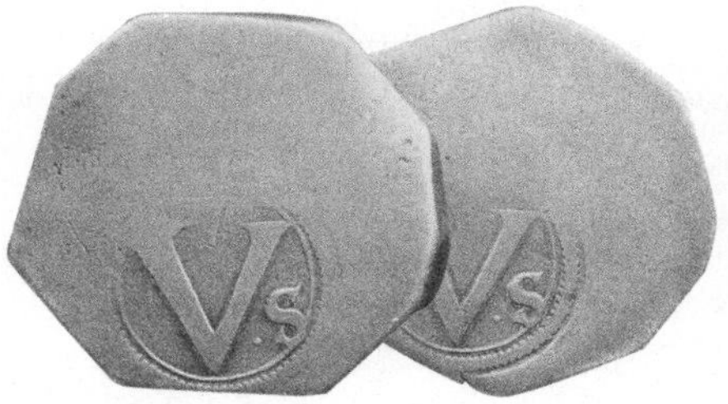

KM# 54 CROWN
30.0000 g., Silver **Obv:** Value in circle **Rev:** Value in circle **Note:** Dav. #3791.

Date	Mintage	VG	F	VF	XF	Unc
ND(1643)	—	2,250	4,250	8,500	—	—

KM# 55 CROWN
30.0000 g., Silver **Obv:** Value in circle **Rev:** Value in circle **Note:** Smaller dies. Dav. #3791.

Date	Mintage	VG	F	VF	XF	Unc
ND(1643)	—	2,500	5,000	9,000	—	—

Note: 19th century copies exist of some of the preceeding silver siege issues.

LORDS JUSTICES COINAGE
"Ormonde" Money

The Earl of Ormonde was Lieutenant of Ireland from 1643 to 1649.

KM# 56 2 PENCE (1/2 Groat)
0.9100 g., Silver **Obv:** Crown above C-R **Rev:** Value in circle

Date	Mintage	VG	F	VF	XF	Unc
ND(1643-44)	—	300	600	1,200	2,000	—

Note: Varieties exist

KM# 57 3 PENCE
1.4300 g., Silver **Obv:** Crown above C-R **Rev:** Value in circle

Date	Mintage	VG	F	VF	XF	Unc
ND(1643-44)	—	250	500	1,000	1,750	—

Note: Varieties exist

KM# 58 4 PENCE (Groat)
1.9400 g., Silver **Obv:** Crown above C-R **Rev:** Value in circle

Date	Mintage	VG	F	VF	XF	Unc
ND(1643-44)	—	150	300	500	900	—

Note: Varieties exist

KM# 59 6 PENCE
2.9800 g., Silver **Obv:** Crown above C-R **Rev:** Value in circle

Date	Mintage	VG	F	VF	XF	Unc
ND(1643-44)	—	115	225	450	850	—

Note: Varieties exist

KM# 60 SHILLING
Silver **Obv:** Crown above C-R **Rev:** Value in circle

Date	Mintage	VG	F	VF	XF	Unc
ND(1643-44)	—	150	300	650	1,150	—

Note: Varieties exist

KM# 61 1/2 CROWN
14.7100 g., Silver **Obv:** Crown above C-R **Rev:** Value in circle

Date	Mintage	VG	F	VF	XF	Unc
ND(1643-44)	—	250	500	900	1,600	—

Note: Varieties exist

KM# 63 CROWN
Silver **Obv:** Crown above C-R **Rev:** Value in circle with ornamental S

Date	Mintage	VG	F	VF	XF	Unc
ND(1643-44)	—	400	750	1,250	3,000	—

Note: Varieties exist

KM# 64 CROWN
Silver **Obv:** Crown above C-R **Rev:** Value in circle with plain S **Note:** Dav. #3792

Date	Mintage	VG	F	VF	XF	Unc
ND(1643-44)	—	350	700	1,150	2,750	—

Note: Varieties exist. Contemporary copies, in silver with copper cores, exist for the crown and half crown and has been suggested as an an attempt to conserve silver by the official mint. Copies made in the last century are easily distinguishable by their neatness of strike

KM# 67 PISTOLE
6.6100 g., Gold **Obv:** 4 DWTT. 7 GR. in circle **Rev:** 4 DWTT. 7 GR. in circle

Date	Mintage	VG	F	VF	XF	Unc
ND(1646) Rare	10	—	—	—	—	—

Note: Whyte's Millennial collection sale 4-2000, VF realized $135,650

KM# A68 2 PISTOLE
13.2200 g., Gold **Obv:** 8 DWTT. 14 GR. in circle **Rev:** 8 DWTT. 14 GR. in circle

Date	Mintage	VG	F	VF	XF	Unc
ND(1646) Rare	2	—	—	—	—	—

LORDS JUSTICES COINAGE
Charles II Issue

Issued upon the execution of Charles I in 1649 by the royalist Marquis of Ormond to proclaim Charles II as King of Ireland.

KM# 83 1/2 CROWN
14.7100 g., Silver **Obv:** Crown in inner circle **Rev:** Value in inner circle

Date	Mintage	VG	F	VF	XF	Unc
ND(1649) Rare	—	—	—	—	—	—

Note: Dix-Noonan-Webb Auction 78, 6-2008, about VF realized approximately $16,030.

KM# 84 CROWN
Silver **Obv:** Crown in inner circle **Rev:** Value in inner circle **Note:** Dav. #3794.

Date	Mintage	VG	F	VF	XF	Unc
ND(1649)	5	—	—	—	—	—

Note: Dix-Noonan-Webb Auction 78, 6-2008, about VF realized approximately $10,165.

CATHOLIC CONFEDERACY COINAGE
Kilkenny Issues

KM# 47 FARTHING
2.2000 g., Bronze **Obv:** Crown on crossed scepters without inner circle **Rev:** Crowned harp

Date	Mintage	VG	F	VF	XF	Unc
ND(1642-43)	—	350	950	1,850	—	—

KM# 48 FARTHING
2.2000 g., Bronze **Obv:** KILKENNY stamped in long rectangle on blank plachet **Note:** Uniface.

Date	Mintage	VG	F	VF	XF	Unc
ND Rare	—	—	—	—	—	—

KM# 49 1/2 PENNY
4.8600 g., Bronze **Obv:** Crown on crossed sceptres in inner circle **Rev:** Crowned harp divides C-R in inner circle

Date	Mintage	VG	F	VF	XF	Unc
ND(1642-43)	—	250	700	1,450	—	—

Note: Contemporary counterfeits of the 1/2 penny are often encountered

KM# 51.1 1/2 CROWN
14.3900 g., Silver **Obv:** Similar to KM#51.2 but with cross on flank cloth

Date	Mintage	VG	F	VF	XF	Unc
ND	—	385	750	1,650	2,800	—

KM# 51.2 1/2 CROWN
14.3900 g., Silver **Obv:** Without cross on flank cloth

Date	Mintage	VG	F	VF	XF	Unc
ND	—	500	1,200	2,400	4,000	—

CATHOLIC CONFEDERACY COINAGE
Rebel Money

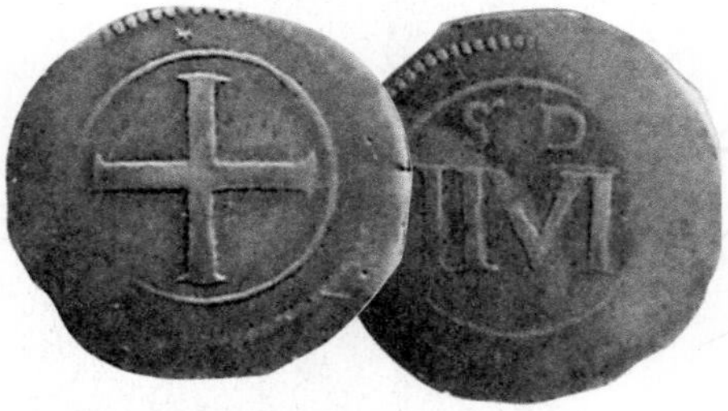

KM# 65 1/2 CROWN
12.1800 g., Silver **Obv:** Cross in inner circle, star in outer circle **Rev:** Value in inner circle

Date	Mintage	VG	F	VF	XF	Unc
ND(1643-44)	—	1,750	3,250	7,000	—	—

KM# 66 CROWN
24.3600 g., Silver **Obv:** Cross in inner circle **Rev:** Value VS in inner circle **Note:** Dav. #3793.

Date	Mintage	VG	F	VF	XF	Unc
ND(1643-44)	—	1,500	3,000	6,500	—	—

LOCAL COINAGE
Bandon

KM# 68 FARTHING
1.9400 g., Copper **Issuer:** Bandon **Obv:** BB in circle (BB = Bandon Bridge) **Rev:** 3 castles, 1 above 2 in circle

Date	Mintage	VG	F	VF	XF	Unc
ND Rare	2	—	—	—	—	—

KM# 69 FARTHING
1.9400 g., Copper **Issuer:** Bandon **Obv:** BB i **Rev:** BB (or EE) back to back

Date	Mintage	VG	F	VF	XF	Unc
ND	—	—	—	—	—	—

LOCAL COINAGE
Cork

KM# 70 FARTHING
2.2700 g., Copper **Issuer:** Cork **Obv:** CORK (or CORKE) in dotted circle **Rev:** Castle in dotted circle

Date	Mintage	VG	F	VF	XF	Unc
ND	—	1,000	2,000	4,000	7,500	—

KM# 72 FARTHING
2.2700 g., Copper **Issuer:** Cork **Note:** CORK (or CORKE) countermarked on foreign copper coins.

Date	Mintage	VG	F	VF	XF	Unc
ND	—	525	875	2,100	—	—

KM# 73 1/2 PENNY
5.4400 g., Copper **Issuer:** Cork **Obv:** CORK in circle **Rev:** Castle

Date	Mintage	VG	F	VF	XF	Unc
ND	—	3,000	6,000	10,000	—	—

KM# 80 6 PENCE
2.2000 g., Silver **Issuer:** Cork **Obv:** CORK/1647 in circle **Rev:** Value in circle

Date	Mintage	VG	F	VF	XF	Unc
1647	—	1,200	2,500	4,500	—	—

KM# 81 SHILLING

4.4100 g., Silver **Issuer:** Cork **Obv:** CORK/1647 in circle **Rev:** Value in circle

Date	Mintage	VG	F	VF	XF	Unc
1647	—	—	6,000	12,500	—	—

Note: There are modern cast counterfeits of these silver coins

KM# 82 SHILLING

4.4100 g., Silver **Issuer:** Cork **Note:** CORKE (or CORK) countermarked on Elizabethan Shillings.

Date	Mintage	VG	F	VF	XF	Unc
ND	—	—	—	—	—	—

LOCAL COINAGE

Kinsale

KM# 74 FARTHING

2.2700 g., Copper **Issuer:** Kinsale **Obv:** K-S in circle **Rev:** Checkered shield of arms

Date	Mintage	VG	F	VF	XF	Unc
ND	—	400	800	1,600	—	—

KM# 75 SHILLING

Copper **Issuer:** Kilkenny **Note:** Castle with K below countermarked on Charles I Kilkenny 1/2 Penny.

Date	Mintage	VG	F	VF	XF	Unc
ND	—	850	1,750	3,250	—	—

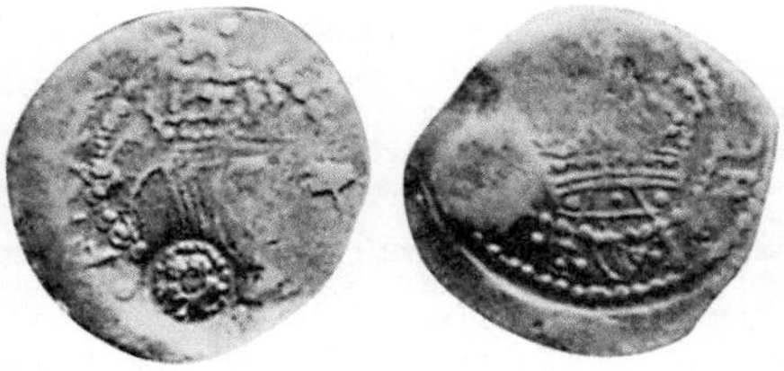

KM# 76 SHILLING

Copper **Issuer:** Kilkenny **Note:** 5 castles in rosette form countermarked on Charles I Kilkenny 1/2 Penny

Date	Mintage	VG	F	VF	XF	Unc
ND	—	1,200	2,500	4,500	—	—

LOCAL COINAGE

Youghal

KM# 78 FARTHING

0.9700 g., Copper **Issuer:** Youghal **Obv:** Bird above Y.T/1646 in circle **Rev:** Ship in circle

Date	Mintage	VG	F	VF	XF	Unc
1646	—	1,750	3,500	7,000	—	—

KM# 79 FARTHING

0.5800 g., Copper **Issuer:** Youghal **Obv:** Y. T in circle **Rev:** Fish in circle

Date	Mintage	VG	F	VF	XF	Unc
ND Rare	—	—	—	—	—	—

CIVIL WAR

After leaving the throne of England James II gathered popular support in Ireland. He landed in Ireland in March, 1689 and proceeded to raise an army. Adequate funds were not available to him so a plan was devised whereby base metal coins could be exchanged for silver following the war. Metal for the new coinage came from church bells, cannon (hence gun money) and any other compatible metal.

A unique feature of these coins is that they are dated by month as well as year. England was still on the Julian calendar and the new year began on March 25. Therefore March, 1689 and March, 1690 are the same month and December and January follow each other in 1689.

"Gun Money" comes in 2 issues: The first authorized in June, 1689 and consisting of 6 pence, shillings and 1/2 crowns. The second issue was authorized in April and June of 1690 and the crown denomination was added. The original values were reduced in size and many pieces of the second issue were struck over those of the first issue.

NOTE: Varieties of spelling, punctuation and placement of design elements exist. Not all have been listed.

GUN MONEY COINAGE

Pewter Money

KM# 96 1/2 PENNY

Pewter **Obv:** Head of James II left

Date	Mintage	VG	F	VF	XF	Unc
1689	—	190	375	825	1,900	—
1690	—	95.00	190	450	1,000	—

KM# 96a 1/2 PENNY

Silver **Obv:** Head of James II left **Edge:** Reeded

Date	Mintage	VG	F	VF	XF	Unc
1690 Proof	—	—	—	—	—	—

KM# 96b 1/2 PENNY

Silver **Obv:** Head of James II left **Edge:** Plain

Date	Mintage	VG	F	VF	XF	Unc
1690 Proof	—	—	—	—	—	—

KM# 104 1/2 PENNY

Pewter **Obv:** Small laureate head, leaf below **Note:** Brass plug through planchet.

Date	Mintage	VG	F	VF	XF	Unc
1690	—	65.00	150	375	825	—

KM# 97 PENNY

Pewter **Obv:** Laureate head of James II left **Rev:** Crowned harp, date at top

Date	Mintage	VG	F	VF	XF	Unc
1689	—	—	—	—	—	—
1690	—	250	500	1,250	2,800	—

KM# 105 PENNY

Pewter **Obv:** Small laureate head of James II left, value behind **Rev:** Crowned harp divides date

Date	Mintage	VG	F	VF	XF	Unc
1690	—	190	400	1,000	2,000	—

KM# 98 4 PENCE (Groat)

Pewter **Obv:** Laureate bust of James II left **Rev:** Crowned harp divides value, date at top

Date	Mintage	VG	F	VF	XF	Unc
1689 Rare	—	—	—	—	—	—

KM# A106 1/2 CROWN

Pewter **Obv:** Laureate head of James II left **Rev:** Crowned divides ornate JR

Date	Mintage	VG	F	VF	XF	Unc
1690 Rare	—	—	—	—	—	—

Note: Struck with dies of 1/2 Crown, KM#95

KM# 106.1 CROWN

Pewter With Brass **Edge:** Lettered **Note:** Plug pressed in planchet.

Date	Mintage	VG	F	VF	XF	Unc
1690	—	575	1,150	2,250	5,000	—
1690 Proof, Rare	—	—	—	—	—	—

KM# 106.2 CROWN

Pewter With Brass **Edge:** Plain **Note:** Plug pressed in planchet.

Date	Mintage	VG	F	VF	XF	Unc
1690	—	—	—	—	—	—
1690 Proof, Rare	—	—	—	—	—	—

GUN MONEY COINAGE

A unique feature of these coins is that they are dated by month as well as year. England was still on the Julian calendar and the new year began on March 25. Therefore March, 1689 and March 1690 are the same month and December and January follow each other in 1689.

KM# 93a SIXPENCE

Silver **Obv:** Head of James II left

Date	Mintage	VG	F	VF	XF	Unc
1689 July Proof	—	—	—	—	—	—
1689 Aug Proof	—	—	—	—	—	—
1689 Sepr Proof	—	—	—	—	—	—
1689 Jan Proof, Rare	—	—	—	—	—	—
1689 Feb Proof	—	Value: 2,000				

KM# 93 SIXPENCE

Brass **Obv:** Head of James II left

Date	Mintage	VG	F	VF	XF	Unc
1689 June	—	19.00	31.25	65.00	105	—
1689 Jvne	—	19.00	31.25	65.00	105	—
1689 July	—	19.00	31.25	65.00	105	—
1689 Aug	—	19.00	31.25	65.00	105	—
1689 Augt	—	19.00	31.25	65.00	105	—
1689 Sep	—	19.00	31.25	65.00	105	—
1689 Sepr	—	19.00	31.25	65.00	105	—
1689 7ber	—	37.50	75.00	200	400	—
1689 Oct	—	—	—	—	—	—
1689 Nov	—	19.00	31.25	65.00	105	—
1689 Dec	—	19.00	31.25	65.00	105	—
1689 Jan	—	19.00	31.25	65.00	105	—
1689 Feb	—	19.00	31.25	65.00	105	—
1689 Mar	—	19.00	31.25	65.00	105	—
1690 Mar	—	19.00	31.25	65.00	105	—
1690 April	—	19.00	31.25	65.00	105	—
1690 May	—	19.00	31.25	65.00	105	—

KM# 93b SIXPENCE

Gold **Obv:** Head of James II left

Date	Mintage	VG	F	VF	XF	Unc
1689 Feb Proof, Rare	—	—	—	—	—	—

Note: Gold strikings not contemporary

KM# 94 SHILLING

Brass **Obv:** Head of James II left **Note:** Large size.

Date	Mintage	VG	F	VF	XF	Unc
1689 July	—	19.00	31.25	65.00	100	—
1689 Aug	—	19.00	31.25	65.00	100	—
1689 Augt	—	19.00	31.25	65.00	100	—
1689 Sep	—	19.00	31.25	65.00	100	—
1689 Sepr	—	19.00	31.25	65.00	100	—
1689 Sept	—	19.00	31.25	65.00	100	—
1689 Septr	—	19.00	31.25	65.00	100	450
1689 Oct	—	19.00	31.25	65.00	100	—
1689 OCT	—	19.00	31.25	65.00	100	—
1689 OCTR	—	19.00	31.25	65.00	100	—
1689 OCTr	—	19.00	31.25	65.00	100	—
1689 8BER	—	19.00	34.50	90.00	190	—
1689 8Ber	—	19.00	34.50	90.00	190	—
1689 8BR	—	19.00	34.50	90.00	190	—
1689 8br	—	19.00	34.50	90.00	190	—

Date	Mintage	VG	F	VF	XF	Unc
1689 Nov	—	19.00	31.25	65.00	100	—
1689 novr	—	19.00	31.25	65.00	100	—
1689 9	—	19.00	34.50	90.00	190	—
1689 9r	—	19.00	31.25	65.00	100	—
1689 Dec	—	19.00	31.25	65.00	100	—
1689 Decr	—	19.00	31.25	65.00	100	—
1689 10r	—	19.00	31.25	65.00	100	—
1689 Jan	—	19.00	31.25	65.00	100	—
1689 Feb	—	19.00	31.25	65.00	100	375
1689 Mar	—	19.00	31.25	65.00	100	—
1690 Mar	—	19.00	31.25	65.00	100	—
1690 Apr	—	19.00	31.25	65.00	100	—

KM# 94a SHILLING

Silver **Obv:** Head of James II left **Note:** Large size.

Date	Mintage	VG	F	VF	XF	Unc
1689 July Proof, Rare	—	—	—	—	—	—
1689 Aug Proof, Rare	—	—	—	—	—	—
1689 Augt Proof, Rare	—	—	—	—	—	—
1689 Sepr Proof, Rare	—	—	—	—	—	—
1689 Sept Proof, Rare	—	—	—	—	—	—
1689 Septr Proof, Rare	—	—	—	—	—	—
1689 Jan Proof, Rare	—	—	—	—	—	—
1689 Feb Proof, Rare	—	—	—	—	—	—
1689 Mar Proof, Rare	—	—	—	—	—	—
1690 Mar Proof, Rare	—	—	—	—	—	—
1690 Apr Proof, Rare	—	—	—	—	—	—

KM# 100 SHILLING

Brass **Obv:** Head of James II left **Note:** Small size.

Date	Mintage	VG	F	VF	XF	Unc
1690 Apr	—	19.00	31.25	65.00	125	—
1690 May	—	19.00	31.25	65.00	100	375
1690 MAY	—	19.00	31.25	65.00	100	—
1690 June	—	19.00	31.25	65.00	100	—
1690 Sep	—	31.25	65.00	125	250	—

KM# 100a SHILLING

Silver **Obv:** Head of James II left **Note:** Small size.

Date	Mintage	VG	F	VF	XF	Unc
1690 May Proof	—	Value: 2,250				
1690 June Proof, Rare	—	—	—	—	—	—

KM# 100b SHILLING

Gold **Obv:** Head of James II left **Note:** Small size.

Date	Mintage	VG	F	VF	XF	Unc
1690 June Proof, Rare	—	—	—	—	—	—

Note: Gold strikings not contemporary

KM# 95a 1/2 CROWN

Silver **Obv:** Head of James II left

Date	Mintage	VG	F	VF	XF	Unc
1689 jan Proof, Rare	—	—	—	—	—	—
1689 Jan Proof, Rare	—	—	—	—	—	—
1689 Feb Proof, Rare	—	—	—	—	—	—
1689 Mar Proof, Rare	—	—	—	—	—	—
1689 Aug Proof, Rare	—	—	—	—	—	—
1689 Augt Proof,f Rare	—	—	—	—	—	—
1689 Sepr Proof, Rare	—	—	—	—	—	—
1689 Sept Proof, Rare	—	—	—	—	—	—
1689 Septr Proof, Rare	—	—	—	—	—	—
1689 Nov Proof, Rare	—	—	—	—	—	—
1689 Novr Proof, Rare	—	—	—	—	—	—
1690 Mar Proof, Rare	—	—	—	—	—	—
1690 Apr Proof, Rare	—	—	—	—	—	—

KM# 95 1/2 CROWN

Brass **Obv:** Head of James II left

Date	Mintage	VG	F	VF	XF	Unc
1689 July	—	19.00	37.50	105	170	—
1689 Aug	—	19.00	31.25	65.00	125	—
1689 Augt	—	19.00	31.25	65.00	125	—
1689 Sep	—	—	—	—	—	—
1689 Sepr	—	19.00	31.25	70.00	150	—
1689 Sept	—	19.00	31.25	70.00	150	—
1689 Septr	—	19.00	31.25	70.00	150	—
1689 Oct	—	19.00	31.25	70.00	150	—
1689 OCTR	—	19.00	31.25	65.00	125	—
1689 Octr	—	19.00	31.25	65.00	125	—
1689 OCT	—	19.00	31.25	65.00	125	—
1689 8r	—	50.00	100	250	525	—
1689 8BER	—	50.00	100	250	525	—
1689 Nov	—	19.00	31.25	65.00	125	—
1689 Novr	—	19.00	31.25	65.00	125	—
1689 Dec	—	19.00	31.25	65.00	125	—
1689 Decr	—	19.00	31.25	65.00	125	—
1689 10r	—	65.00	125	280	625	—
1689 Jan	—	19.00	31.25	65.00	125	—
1689 jan	—	19.00	31.25	65.00	125	—
1689 Feb	—	19.00	31.25	65.00	125	—
1689 Mar	—	19.00	31.25	70.00	150	—
1690 Mar	—	19.00	31.25	70.00	150	—
1690 Apr	—	19.00	31.25	65.00	125	575
1690 May	—	19.00	37.50	105	230	—

KM# 101a 1/2 CROWN

Silver **Obv:** Head of James II left **Note:** Small size.

Date	Mintage	VG	F	VF	XF	Unc
1690 May Proof, Rare	—	—	—	—	—	—

KM# 101b 1/2 CROWN

Gold **Obv:** Head of James II left **Note:** Small size.

Date	Mintage	VG	F	VF	XF	Unc
1690 May Proof, Rare	—	—	—	—	—	—

KM# 101 1/2 CROWN

Brass **Obv:** Head of James II left **Note:** Small size.

Date	Mintage	VG	F	VF	XF	Unc
1690 Apr Rare	—	—	—	—	—	—
1690 May	—	19.00	31.25	65.00	100	750
1690 May	—	19.00	31.25	65.00	100	—
1690 Jun	—	19.00	31.25	65.00	120	—
1690 June	—	19.00	31.25	65.00	120	950
1690 Jnue (error)	—	25.00	50.00	120	250	—
1690 July	—	19.00	31.25	65.00	150	—
1690 Aug	—	25.00	50.00	125	280	—
1690 Oct Rare	—	—	—	—	—	—

KM# 95b 1/2 CROWN

Gold **Obv:** Head of James II left

Date	Mintage	VG	F	VF	XF	Unc
1690 Apr Proof, Rare	—	—	—	—	—	—

KM# 102 CROWN

Brass **Obv:** Sword points to E in REX **Note:** Overstruck on large size 1/2 Crown.

Date	Mintage	VG	F	VF	XF	Unc
1690	—	100	750	800	1,600	—

KM# 103.1a CROWN

Silver **Note:** Overstruck on large size 1/2 Crown.

Date	Mintage	VG	F	VF	XF	Unc
1690 Proof, Rare	—	—	—	—	—	—

KM# 103.1b CROWN

Gold **Note:** Overstruck on large size 1/2 Crown.

Date	Mintage	VG	F	VF	XF	Unc
1690 Proof, Rare	—	—	—	—	—	—

KM# 103.2 CROWN

Brass **Rev. Legend:** ...VICTO/ RE... **Note:** Overstruck on large size 1/2 Crown.

Date	Mintage	VG	F	VF	XF	Unc
1690	—	25.00	35.00	400	800	—

KM# 103.3 CROWN

Brass **Rev. Legend:** ...RIX... **Note:** Overstruck on large size 1/2 Crown.

Date	Mintage	VG	F	VF	XF	Unc
1690	—	25.00	75.00	400	800	—

KM# 103.1 CROWN

Brass **Obv:** Sword points between REX and IAC **Note:** Overstruck on large size 1/2 Crown. Many varieies exist.

Date	Mintage	VG	F	VF	XF	Unc
1690	—	25.00	75.00	400	800	1,800

Note: Legend varieties exist

SIEGE COINAGE

Siege of Limerick

KM# 107.1 FARTHING

Brass **Obv:** Laureate bust of James II left. **Rev:** Hibernia seated left, harp at right, retrograde N in HIBERNIA **Note:** Struck over small "Gun Money" Shillings.

Date	Mintage	VG	F	VF	XF	Unc
1691	—	31.25	65.00	105	250	—

KM# 107.2 FARTHING

Brass **Obv:** Laureate bust of James II left. **Rev:** Hibernia seated left, harp at right, normal N in HIBERNIA **Note:** Struck over small "Gun Money" Shillings.

Date	Mintage	VG	F	VF	XF	Unc
1691	—	55.00	125	190	450	—

KM# 108 1/2 PENNY

Brass **Obv:** Laureate bust of James II left. **Rev:** Hibernia seated left, harp at right, retrogradel N in HIBERNIA **Note:** Struck over large "Gun Money" Shillings.

Date	Mintage	VG	F	VF	XF	Unc
1691	—	19.00	37.50	95.00	190	—

PATTERNS

Including off metal strikes

KM#	Date	Mintage	Identification	Mkt Val
Pn1	1689	—	1/2 Penny. Copper. Lion on crown above harp. KM96. 2 examples are known, one at the National Museum of Ireland and the other in private hands.	—
Pn2	1689	—	Penny. Pewter. 8.4200 g. KM97. Unique example is in the National Museum of Ireland.	600
Pn3	1689	—	4 Pence. Pewter. 3.3700 g. KM98.	1,200
Pn4	1690	—	1/2 Penny. Silver. Milled edge. KM96.	1,000
Pn5	1690	—	1/2 Penny. Silver. Plain edge. KM96.	—
Pn6	1690	—	1/2 Penny. Pewter. Plugged, KM104.	—
Pn7	1690	—	Penny. Pewter. 8.4200 g. KM105.	600
Pn8	1690	—	Crown. White Metal. 18.3400 g. KM106.	—
Pn9	1690	—	Crown. White Metal. 18.3400 g. With brass plug, KM106.	—
Pn10	1690	—	Crown. Tin. Plain edge. KM106.	—
Pn11	1690	—	Crown. Silver. Lettered edge. KM106.	6,000
Pn12	1690	—	Crown. Silver. Gun money, small legends, KM103.	—
Pn13	1690	—	Crown. Silver. Gun money, large legends, KM103.	—
Pn14	1690	—	Crown. Gold. Gun money, small legends, KM103.	—
Pn15	1690	—	Crown. Gold. Gun money, large legends, KM103.	—
Pn16	1690	—	Crown. Gold. Lettered edge. KM103.	—
Pn17	ND	—	Farthing. Bath Metal. Bust. Seated woman holding orb, leaning on shield.	—

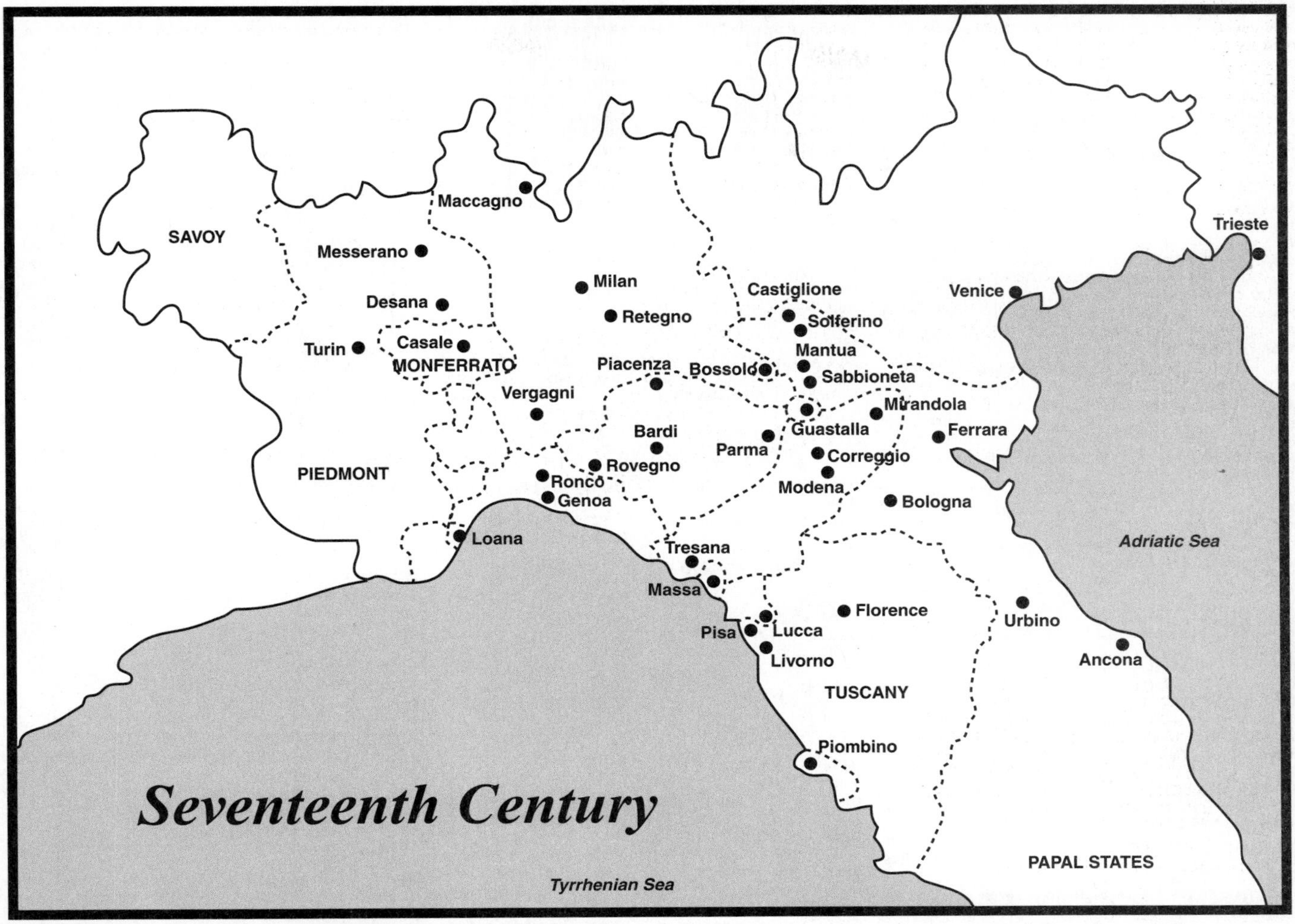

ALBERA

A feudal fief in Piedmont with an unauthorized coinage in 1678 at the Genoa Mint by a member of the Vescova family.

RULER
Carlo Settola, 1653--

FEUDAL FIEF

HAMMERED COINAGE

KM# 1 27 MILANESE SOLDI
7.3900 g., Silver, 33 mm. **Obv:** Arms supported by angels **Rev:** Saint offering a blessing

Date	Mintage	VG	F	VF	XF	Unc
ND Rare	—	—	—	—	—	—

KM# 2 54 MILANESE SOLDI
13.7600 g., Silver, 34 mm. **Obv:** Arms supported by angels **Rev:** Saint offering a blessing

Date	Mintage	VG	F	VF	XF	Unc
ND Rare	—	—	—	—	—	—

ARQUATA

RULERS
Filippo Spinola, 1641-1667
Guilio Spinola, Marquis 1661-1691
Gerardo Spinola, 1682-1694

STATE

STANDARD COINAGE

KM# A2 LUIGINO
Silver **Ruler:** Filippo Spinola **Obv:** Female bust right **Obv. Legend:** PVLCRAA. VERT. IMAGO. DOM **Rev:** Crowned shield of 3 lis **Rev. Legend:** DEVS. MEVS. ET. OMNIA. IN. SECV. SE.

Date	Mintage	VG	F	VF	XF	Unc
1666	—	—	—	375	—	—

KM# 2 LUIGINO
Billon **Note:** Weight varies: 2.14-2.41 grams. Anonymous for the Levant

Date	Mintage	VG	F	VF	XF	Unc
1668	—	42.00	90.00	200	325	—
1669	—	42.00	90.00	200	325	—

KM# 6 LUIGINO
2.5100 g., Silver **Ruler:** Gerardo Spinola **Obv:** Bust of Gerardo left **Rev:** Double eagle with supported arms, date in legend

Date	Mintage	VG	F	VF	XF	Unc
1682	—	175	350	625	1,050	—

KM# 7 1/8 SCUDO
5.1200 g., Silver **Ruler:** Gerardo Spinola **Obv:** Bust of Gerardo left **Rev:** Crowned arms in branches, date in legend

Date	Mintage	VG	F	VF	XF	Unc
ND	—	210	375	700	1,200	—

KM# 1 1/4 SCUDO
7.7000 g., Silver **Ruler:** Filippo Spinola **Obv:** Bust of Filippo right **Rev:** Crowned eagle with arms

Date	Mintage	VG	F	VF	XF	Unc
1644 Rare	—	—	—	—	—	—

KM# 3 1/4 SCUDO
7.7000 g., Silver **Ruler:** Guilio Spinola **Obv:** Bust of Guilio left **Rev:** Crowned Spinola arms in branches

Date	Mintage	VG	F	VF	XF	Unc
1681 Rare	—	—	—	—	—	—

Note: Künker Auction 188, 6-11, VF-XF realized approximately $15,740

KM# 4 1/4 SCUDO
7.7000 g., Silver **Ruler:** Gerardo Spinola **Obv:** Bust of Gerardo left

Date	Mintage	VG	F	VF	XF	Unc
ND Rare	—	—	—	—	—	—

KM# 5 1/2 DOPPIA
3.5000 g., 0.9860 Gold 0.1109 oz. AGW **Ruler:** Guilio Spinola **Obv:** Bust of Guilio left in inner circle **Rev:** Crowned Spinola arms, date in legend

Date	Mintage	VG	F	VF	XF	Unc
1681	—	2,250	4,500	9,000	15,000	—

KM# 8 DOPPIA
7.0000 g., 0.9860 Gold 0.2219 oz. AGW **Ruler:** Gerardo Spinola **Obv:** Bust of Gerardo left **Rev:** Crowned arms in branches, date in legend

Date	Mintage	VG	F	VF	XF	Unc
1682	—	3,000	6,000	12,000	22,500	—

BOZZOLO

Bozzolo is located a little west of Mantua. Charles V granted the mint right in 1497. Bozzolo was given to the Gonzaga family by the Emperor Rudolph in 1593, and Guilio Cesare was created prince of Bozzolo. Guilio was succeeded by his 13-year-old nephew, Scipione who ruled under the regency of his mother Isabella until 1613. Scipione became duke of Sabbioneta in 1636. The mint was closed at his death in 1670.

RULERS
Guilio Cesare Gonzaga, 1593-1609
Scipione Gonzaga, 1609-1670

Reference:
V = Alberto Varesi, ***Monete Italiane Regionali: Lombardia, Zecche Minori. Pavia***, 1995.

PRINCIPALITY

STANDARD COINAGE

KM# 5 SESINO
Billon **Obv:** Head right, PRINCEPS **Rev:** Sun **Note:** Weight varies: 0.75-1.25 grams.

Date	Mintage	Good	VG	F	VF	XF
ND	—	18.00	36.00	80.00	155	260

KM# 6 SESINO
Billon **Obv:** Head right, I.C. PRIN **Rev:** St. Peter **Note:** Weight varies: 0.75-1.25 grams.

Date	Mintage	Good	VG	F	VF	XF
ND	—	8.00	18.00	39.00	85.00	165

KM# 7 SESINO
Billon **Obv:** Head right, PRINCEPS **Note:** Weight varies: 0.75-1.25 grams.

Date	Mintage	Good	VG	F	VF	XF
ND	—	8.00	18.00	39.00	85.00	165

KM# 8 SESINO
Billon **Obv:** Head right, IVLI **Rev:** St. Andrew **Note:** Weight varies: 0.75-1.25 grams.

Date	Mintage	Good	VG	F	VF	XF
ND	—	12.00	25.00	50.00	110	230

KM# 9 SESINO
Billon **Obv:** Cross with four eagles **Rev:** Large crowned F **Note:** Weight varies: 0.75-1.25 grams.

Date	Mintage	Good	VG	F	VF	XF
ND	—	7.00	17.00	36.50	70.00	130

KM# 10 SESINO
Billon **Obv:** Eagle, SCIP **Rev:** St. Peter **Note:** Weight varies: 0.75-1.25 grams.

Date	Mintage	Good	VG	F	VF	XF
ND	—	11.00	22.50	45.50	100	195

KM# 72 SESINO
Billon **Obv:** Cross with three stars **Rev:** Madonna and child **Note:** Weight varies: 0.75-1.25 grams.

Date	Mintage	Good	VG	F	VF	XF
1660	—	7.00	17.00	36.50	70.00	130

KM# 73 SESINO
Billon **Obv:** Madonna and child **Rev:** Cross, BOZ **Note:** Weight varies: 0.75-1.25 grams.

Date	Mintage	Good	VG	F	VF	XF
ND	—	22.50	42.00	90.00	175	325

KM# 74 SESINO
Billon **Rev:** Ornate cross **Note:** Weight varies: 0.75-1.25 grams.

Date	Mintage	Good	VG	F	VF	XF
ND	—	7.00	17.00	36.50	70.00	130

KM# 75 SESINO
Billon **Obv:** Flame **Rev:** Large L **Note:** Weight varies: 0.75-1.25 grams.

Date	Mintage	Good	VG	F	VF	XF
ND	—	11.00	22.50	45.50	100	195

KM# 76 SESINO
Billon **Obv:** Bust right **Rev:** Large star with 16 points **Note:** Weight varies: 0.75-1.25 grams.

Date	Mintage	Good	VG	F	VF	XF
ND	—	7.00	17.00	36.50	70.00	130

KM# 77 SESINO
Billon **Obv:** Crowned arms **Rev:** John the Baptist **Note:** Weight varies: 0.75-1.25 grams.

Date	Mintage	Good	VG	F	VF	XF
ND	—	8.00	18.00	39.00	85.00	165

KM# 78 SESINO
Billon **Obv:** Bust right, SCIP **Rev:** Crowned arms, MAR **Note:** Weight varies: 0.75-1.25 grams.

Date	Mintage	Good	VG	F	VF	XF
ND	—	7.00	17.00	36.50	80.00	145

KM# 79 SESINO
Billon **Rev:** Crowned arms, SCIP **Note:** Weight varies: 0.75-1.25 grams.

Date	Mintage	Good	VG	F	VF	XF
ND	—	7.00	17.00	36.50	80.00	145

KM# 80 SESINO
Billon **Obv:** Head left **Rev:** Crowned eagle, SAC **Note:** Weight varies: 0.75-1.25 grams.

Date	Mintage	Good	VG	F	VF	XF
ND	—	7.00	17.00	36.50	80.00	145

KM# 81 SESINO
Billon **Obv:** Head right **Rev:** Crowned eagle, BOZ **Note:** Weight varies: 0.75-1.25 grams.

Date	Mintage	Good	VG	F	VF	XF
ND	—	7.00	17.00	36.50	80.00	145

KM# 82 SESINO
Billon **Rev:** Crowned eagle, SABL **Note:** Weight varies: 0.75-1.25 grams.

Date	Mintage	Good	VG	F	VF	XF
ND	—	7.00	17.00	36.50	80.00	145

KM# 83 SESINO
Billon **Obv:** Crowned eagle **Rev:** Bust left **Note:** Weight varies: 0.75-1.25 grams.

Date	Mintage	Good	VG	F	VF	XF
ND	—	7.00	17.00	36.50	80.00	145

KM# 84 SESINO
Billon **Obv:** Cross on shield with three stars **Rev:** Madonna in nimbus **Note:** Weight varies: 0.75-1.25 grams.

Date	Mintage	Good	VG	F	VF	XF
ND	—	8.00	18.00	39.00	85.00	165

KM# 85 SESINO
Billon **Obv:** Head right **Rev:** Cross with eagle and lion **Note:** Weight varies: 0.75-1.25 grams.

Date	Mintage	Good	VG	F	VF	XF
ND	—	8.00	18.00	39.00	85.00	165

KM# 86 SESINO
Billon **Obv:** Crowned arms **Rev:** Madonna and child **Note:** Weight varies: 0.75-1.25 grams.

Date	Mintage	Good	VG	F	VF	XF
ND	—	8.00	18.00	39.00	85.00	165

KM# 11 BAGATTINO
Billon **Obv:** Head right **Rev:** Eagle, value **Note:** Weight varies: 0.40-0.80 grams.

Date	Mintage	Good	VG	F	VF	XF
ND	—	12.00	25.00	50.00	100	195

KM# 12 BAGATTINO
Billon **Obv:** Medici arms **Rev:** John the Baptist **Note:** Weight varies: 0.40-0.80 grams.

Date	Mintage	Good	VG	F	VF	XF
ND	—	18.00	36.00	65.00	115	240

KM# 38 QUATTRINO
Billon **Obv:** Mountain, FIDES **Rev:** Foliate cross **Note:** Weight varies: 0.46-1.11 grams.

Date	Mintage	Good	VG	F	VF	XF
1605	—	22.50	42.00	100	165	295

KM# 39 QUATTRINO
Billon **Obv:** Head right, IVL **Rev:** Crowned arms with large star **Note:** Weight varies: 0.46-1.11 grams.

Date	Mintage	Good	VG	F	VF	XF
ND	—	12.00	25.00	45.50	85.00	165

KM# 40 QUATTRINO
Billon **Obv:** Head right, PRINCEPS **Rev:** Crowned arms with star, ME. DVCAT. **Note:** Weight varies: 0.46-1.11 grams.

Date	Mintage	Good	VG	F	VF	XF
ND	—	12.00	25.00	45.50	85.00	165

KM# 41 QUATTRINO
Billon **Obv:** Head left **Rev:** Crowned arms with star **Note:** Weight varies: 0.46-1.11 grams.

Date	Mintage	Good	VG	F	VF	XF
ND	—	12.00	25.00	45.50	85.00	165

KM# 42 QUATTRINO
Billon **Obv:** Crowned arms **Rev:** Madonna and child, ESTO **Note:** Weight varies: 0.46-1.11 grams.

Date	Mintage	Good	VG	F	VF	XF
ND	—	12.00	25.00	45.50	85.00	165

KM# 43 QUATTRINO
Billon **Obv:** Head right **Rev:** Large star **Note:** Weight varies: 0.46-1.11 grams.

Date	Mintage	Good	VG	F	VF	XF
ND	—	12.00	25.00	45.50	85.00	165

KM# 70 QUATTRINO
Billon **Obv:** BOZALI/ PRI/ NCEPS/ date **Rev:** Rampant lion **Note:** Weight varies: 0.46-1.11 grams.

Date	Mintage	Good	VG	F	VF	XF
1657	—	8.00	18.00	39.00	65.00	115
1665	—	8.00	18.00	39.00	65.00	115
1667	—	8.00	18.00	39.00	65.00	115

KM# 13 PARPAGLIOLA
1.7800 g., Billon **Obv:** Crowned arms **Rev:** Woman with vase

Date	Mintage	Good	VG	F	VF	XF
ND	—	18.00	36.00	80.00	130	260

KM# 14 CAVALOTTO
Billon **Obv:** Pegasus **Rev:** St. Catharine standing **Note:** Weight varies: 1.70-2.50 grams.

Date	Mintage	Good	VG	F	VF	XF
ND	—	25.00	48.00	105	195	325

KM# 15 FIORINO
4.6700 g., Billon

Date	Mintage	Good	VG	F	VF	XF
ND	—	150	250	550	1,000	1,750

KM# 16 SOLDO
1.6500 g., Billon **Obv:** Crowned arms **Rev:** Cross in ornate frame

Date	Mintage	Good	VG	F	VF	XF
ND	—	12.00	25.00	39.00	85.00	165

KM# 17 3 SOLDI
Billon **Obv:** Bust right, 3 below, SCIP **Rev:** Crowned quartered arms **Note:** Weight varies: 1.14-1.75 grams.

Date	Mintage	Good	VG	F	VF	XF
ND	—	22.50	42.00	100	210	375

KM# 18 3 SOLDI
Billon **Obv:** Crowned quartered arms **Rev:** Crowned double eagle, 3 below **Note:** Weight varies: 1.14-1.75 grams.

Date	Mintage	Good	VG	F	VF	XF
ND	—	12.00	25.00	39.00	85.00	165

KM# 19 3 SOLDI
Billon **Obv:** Bust right, 3 below, SCI **Rev:** Three shields in triangle **Note:** Weight varies: 1.14-1.75 grams.

Date	Mintage	Good	VG	F	VF	XF
ND	—	12.00	25.00	39.00	85.00	165

KM# 20 3 SOLDI
Billon **Obv:** Crowned double eagle, 3 below, SVBPEN **Note:** Weight varies: 1.14-1.75 grams.

Date	Mintage	Good	VG	F	VF	XF
ND	—	22.50	42.00	100	210	375

KM# 21 3 SOLDI
Billon **Obv:** Bust left **Rev:** Crowned double eagle, 3 below **Note:** Weight varies: 1.14-1.75 grams.

Date	Mintage	Good	VG	F	VF	XF
ND	—	18.00	36.00	80.00	165	295

KM# 22 3 SOLDI
Billon **Rev:** Crowned double eagle, 3 below cross **Note:** Weight varies: 1.14-1.75 grams.

Date	Mintage	Good	VG	F	VF	XF
ND	—	18.00	36.00	80.00	165	295

KM# 23 3 SOLDI
Billon **Rev:** Without 3 **Note:** Weight varies: 1.14-1.75 grams.

Date	Mintage	Good	VG	F	VF	XF
ND	—	12.00	25.00	50.00	100	195

KM# 24 3 SOLDI
Billon **Obv:** Crowned arms **Rev:** Pisside **Note:** Weight varies: 1.14-1.75 grams.

Date	Mintage	Good	VG	F	VF	XF
ND	—	12.00	25.00	45.50	85.00	165

KM# 25 5 SOLDI
Billon **Obv:** Bust right **Rev:** St. Nicholas standing **Note:** Weight varies: 1.79-2.49 grams.

Date	Mintage	Good	VG	F	VF	XF
ND	—	25.00	48.00	110	215	400

KM# 26 8 SOLDI
3.7500 g., Billon **Obv:** Crowned arms in cartouche **Rev:** St. Peter with keys

Date	Mintage	Good	VG	F	VF	XF
ND	—	42.00	70.00	130	260	450

KM# 64 8 SOLDI
3.7500 g., Billon **Obv:** Draped bust left **Rev:** Crowned quartered arms

Date	Mintage	Good	VG	F	VF	XF
ND Rare	—	—	—	—	—	—

KM# 65 8 SOLDI
3.7500 g., Billon **Obv:** Armored bust, date before, VIII below **Rev:** Crowned oval arms

Date	Mintage	Good	VG	F	VF	XF
1641	—	48.00	90.00	165	285	500

KM# 66 8 SOLDI
3.7500 g., Billon **Obv:** *80*SCIPION in six lines **Rev:** Sun with rays

Date	Mintage	Good	VG	F	VF	XF
ND	—	25.00	48.00	100	165	325

KM# 27 10 SOLDI
2.7100 g., Billon **Obv:** Bust right **Rev:** Five-line inscription

Date	Mintage	Good	VG	F	VF	XF
ND	—	30.00	60.00	130	230	400

KM# 28 10 SOLDI
2.7100 g., Billon **Obv:** Cross with four stars **Rev:** Madonna and child

Date	Mintage	Good	VG	F	VF	XF
ND	—	18.00	36.00	65.00	130	260

KM# 29 15-1/2 SOLDI
4.0300 g., Billon **Obv:** Bust right **Rev:** Crowned double eagle with quartered arms

Date	Mintage	Good	VG	F	VF	XF
ND Rare	—	—	—	—	—	—

KM# 30 30 SOLDI
5.3500 g., Billon **Obv:** Bust right **Rev:** St. Catharine with palms, XX* below

Date	Mintage	Good	VG	F	VF	XF
ND Rare	—	—	—	—	—	—

KM# 49 LIRA
Silver **Obv:** Bust right **Rev:** Figure of Hope **Note:** Weight varies: 4.00-6.75 grams.

Date	Mintage	Good	VG	F	VF	XF
1614	—	300	450	900	1,350	3,000

KM# 50 LIRA
Silver **Obv:** Bust left **Note:** Weight varies: 4.00-6.75 grams.

Date	Mintage	Good	VG	F	VF	XF
1618	—	375	600	1,150	1,900	3,550

KM# 51 LIRA
Silver **Obv:** Crowned quartered arms **Rev:** St. Peter with keys **Note:** Weight varies: 4.00-6.75 grams.

Date	Mintage	Good	VG	F	VF	XF
ND	—	125	275	450	—	—

KM# 31 TESTONE
Silver **Obv:** Bust right **Rev:** St. Peter kneeling left **Note:** Weight varies: 8.50-8.70 grams.

Date	Mintage	Good	VG	F	VF	XF
ND Rare	—	—	—	—	—	—

KM# 32 1/4 TALLERO
Silver **Obv:** Half figure right **Rev:** Crowned double eagle **Note:** Weight varies: 6.46-6.85 grams.

Date	Mintage	Good	VG	F	VF	XF
ND Rare	—	—	—	—	—	—

KM# 33 TALLERO
Silver **Obv:** Armed half figure right **Rev:** Four arms in frame **Note:** Weight varies: 21.00-27.00 grams. Dav. #3849.

Date	Mintage	Good	VG	F	VF	XF
ND Rare	—	—	—	—	—	—

KM# 44 TALLERO

Silver **Obv:** Confronted busts **Rev:** Rampant lion **Note:** Weight varies: 21.00-27.00 grams. Dav. #3850.

Date	Mintage	Good	VG	F	VF	XF
1613 Rare	—	—	—	—	—	—

KM# 45 TALLERO

Silver **Obv:** Armed half figure right **Rev:** Two shields of Gonzaga arms **Note:** Weight varies: 21.00-27.00 grams. Dav. #3853.

Date	Mintage	Good	VG	F	VF	XF
ND Rare	—	—	—	—	—	—

KM# 46 TALLERO

Silver **Obv:** Half figure right, 80 below **Rev:** Crowned double eagle with arms **Note:** Weight varies: 21.00-27.00 grams. Dav. #3854.

Date	Mintage	Good	VG	F	VF	XF
ND	—	1,050	1,750	3,500	6,100	10,500

KM# 47 TALLERO

Silver **Obv:** Bust right, C.80.C below **Rev:** Crowned quartered arms **Note:** Weight varies: 21.00-27.00 grams. Dav. #3855.

Date	Mintage	Good	VG	F	VF	XF
ND	—	1,050	1,750	3,500	6,100	—

KM# 55 TALLERO

Silver **Obv:** Warrior behind shield **Rev:** Rampant lion **Note:** Weight varies: 21.00-27.00 grams. Dav. #3856.

Date	Mintage	Good	VG	F	VF	XF
1638	—	220	450	800	1,650	—
1659	—	220	450	800	1,650	—

KM# 88 TALLERO

Silver **Obv:** Warrior behind shield **Obv. Legend:** SCIP. G. DVX... **Rev:** Rampant lion **Rev. Legend:** VICIT. LEO. DETRIBV... **Note:** Weight varies: 21.00-27.00 grams. Dav. #3858.

Date	Mintage	Good	VG	F	VF	XF
1659 Rare	—	—	—	—	—	—

KM# 34 1/2 DUCATONE

13.1600 g., Silver **Obv:** Laureate head right **Rev:** Ornate cross

Date	Mintage	Good	VG	F	VF	XF
ND Rare	—	—	—	—	—	—

KM# 35 DUCATONE

Silver **Obv:** Bust of Giulio right **Rev:** Crowned quartered arms in Order chain **Note:** Weight varies: 31.00-32.00 grams. Dav. #3848.

Date	Mintage	Good	VG	F	VF	XF
ND Rare	—	—	—	—	—	—

KM# 48.1 DUCATONE

Silver **Obv:** Bust left, GASP below **Rev:** Christ giving keys to St. Peter **Note:** Weight varies: 31.00-32.00 grams. Dav. #3851.

Date	Mintage	Good	VG	F	VF	XF
1613	—	800	1,500	2,900	5,300	8,800

KM# 48.2 DUCATONE

Silver **Obv:** Bust left, G. MOLO **Note:** Weight varies: 31.00-32.00 grams. Dav. #3852.

Date	Mintage	Good	VG	F	VF	XF
1617	—	800	1,500	2,900	5,300	8,800

KM# 48.3 DUCATONE

Silver **Obv. Legend:** SCIP: D: G: DVX: SABL:... **Rev. Legend:** TV ES PETRVS:-PRAESIDIVM... **Note:** Weight varies: 31.00-32.00 grams. Dav. #3857.

Date	Mintage	Good	VG	F	VF	XF
1639	—	300	525	975	1,750	3,500

KM# 48.4 DUCATONE

Silver **Obv:** Different bust **Rev:** Legend without space after PETRVS: **Note:** Weight varies: 31.00-32.00 grams. Dav. #3859.

Date	Mintage	Good	VG	F	VF	XF
1665	—	300	525	975	1,750	3,500
1666	—	300	525	975	1,750	3,500

KM# 57 DUCATONE

Silver **Rev:** Crowned quartered arms **Note:** Weight varies: 31.00-32.00 grams. Dav. #3860.

Date	Mintage	Good	VG	F	VF	XF
ND Rare	—	1,300	2,200	4,400	7,900	13,000

KM# 58 DUCATONE

Silver **Rev:** Star with 16 points **Note:** Weight varies: 31.00-32.00 grams. Dav. #3861.

Date	Mintage	Good	VG	F	VF	XF
ND Rare	—	1,050	1,750	3,500	6,100	11,500

KM# 87 2 DUCATONE

63.8000 g., Silver **Obv:** Bust left **Rev:** Christ giving keys to St. Peter **Note:** Dav. #A3859.

Date	Mintage	Good	VG	F	VF	XF
1666 Rare	—	—	—	—	—	—

KM# 52 DOPPIA

7.0000 g., 0.9860 Gold 0.2219 oz. AGW **Obv:** Crowned arms in inner circle **Rev:** Figure of crowned female

Date	Mintage	VG	F	VF	XF	Unc
1618	—	4,000	7,500	15,000	25,000	—

KM# 53 DOPPIA

7.0000 g., 0.9860 Gold 0.2219 oz. AGW **Obv:** Bust of Scipio left in inner circle **Rev:** Two shields in inner circle

Date	Mintage	VG	F	VF	XF	Unc
ND Rare	—	—	—	—	—	—

KM# 54 DOPPIA

7.0000 g., 0.9860 Gold 0.2219 oz. AGW **Rev:** Crowned arms in inner circle

Date	Mintage	VG	F	VF	XF	Unc
ND Rare	—	—	—	—	—	—

KM# 59 4 DOPPIE

26.0700 g., Gold **Obv:** Bust left **Rev:** Christ giving keys to St. Peter

Date	Mintage	VG	F	VF	XF	Unc
1639 Rare	—	—	—	—	—	—

KM# 60 6 DOPPIE

Gold **Obv:** Bust left **Rev:** Christ giving keys to St. Peter **Note:** Weight varies: 39.11-39.36 grams.

Date	Mintage	VG	F	VF	XF	Unc
1639 Rare	—	—	—	—	—	—

KM# 61 6 DOPPIE

Gold **Rev:** Crowned quartered arms **Note:** Weight varies: 39.11-39.36 grams.

Date	Mintage	VG	F	VF	XF	Unc
ND Rare	—	—	—	—	—	—

KM# 37 DUCAT

3.5000 g., 0.9860 Gold 0.1109 oz. AGW **Obv:** Soldier standing **Rev:** Four-line inscription in tablet

Date	Mintage	VG	F	VF	XF	Unc
ND	—	2,000	3,000	6,000	15,000	—

CAGLIARI

The ancient city of Calaris, founded by the Phoenicians about 540 BC on the south coast of Sardinia, was devastated by the Muslims during the period of their conquests. In 1323, Jaime II of Aragon (1291-1327) reconquered the island and began a long period of Spanish rule. Cagliari passed to the control of Savoy in 1720.

RULERS

Filippo III, King of Spain, 1598-1621
Filippo IV, King of Spain, 1621-1665
Carlo II, King of Spain, 1665-1700
Filippo V, King of Spain, 1700-1719

Reference:

V = Alberto Varesi, ***Monete Italiane Regionali: Piemonte, Sardegna, Liguria, Isola di Corsica.*** Pavia, 1996

CITY

STANDARD COINAGE

KM# 1 CAGLIARESE (2 Denari)

Billon Weight varies: 0.60-1.26g., 12 mm. **Ruler:** Filippo IV **Obv:** Crowned bust to left **Obv. Legend:** PHILIPPVS. REX. **Rev:** Cross in circle, annulet in each angle **Rev. Legend:** INI. EIVS. IND. CON. **Note:** Ref. V#77.

Date	Mintage	F	VF	XF	Unc	BU
ND(1621-65)	—	65.00	110	250	450	—

KM# 2 CAGLIARESE (2 Denari)

Billon Weight varies: 0.60-1.26g., 12 mm. **Ruler:** Filippo IV **Obv:** Bare head to left **Obv. Legend:** PHILIPPVS. REX. **Rev:** Cross in circle, annulet in each angle **Rev. Legend:** INI. EIVS. IND. CON. **Note:** Ref. V#78.

Date	Mintage	F	VF	XF	Unc	BU
ND(1621-65)	—	75.00	138	250	525	—

KM# 17 CAGLIARESE (2 Denari)

Copper Weight varies: 2.36-4.13g., 21 mm. **Ruler:** Carlo II **Obv:** Bust to right **Obv. Legend:** CAROLVS. II. D. G. R. **Rev:** Floriated cross, small head to left in each angle, date at end of legend **Rev. Legend:** ARAM. ET. SAE. **Note:** Ref. V#92. Varieties exist.

Date	Mintage	F	VF	XF	Unc	BU
1668	—	15.00	28.00	75.00	145	—
1669	—	15.00	28.00	75.00	145	—
1670	—	25.00	45.00	95.00	185	—
1672	—	35.00	72.00	115	235	—
1688	—	35.00	72.00	115	235	—
1691	—	30.00	55.00	100	200	—
1695	—	35.00	72.00	115	235	—

KM# 3 2 CAGLIARESI (4 Denari)

1.0100 g., Billon, 14-15 mm. **Ruler:** Filippo IV **Obv:** Crowned bust to left, 2 small pellets behind head **Obv. Legend:** PHILLIPVS. REX. **Rev:** Floriated cross in circle, 'Q' in each angle **Rev. Legend:** INI. EIVS. IND. CONF. **Note:** Ref. V#76.

Date	Mintage	F	VF	XF	Unc	BU
ND(1621-65)	—	70.00	138	350	600	—

KM# 4 3 CAGLIARESE (6 Denari)

Billon Weight varies: 1.10-2.35g., 17 mm. **Ruler:** Filippo IV **Obv:** Crowned bust to left in circle, 3 small pellets behind head **Obv. Legend:** REX. PHILIPPVS. **Rev:** Cross with lily ends in circle, figure '6' in each angle **Rev. Legend:** MONETA. SARDINIAE. REGNI. **Note:** Ref. V#75.

Date	Mintage	F	VF	XF	Unc	BU
ND(1621-65)	—	30.00	55.00	165	325	—

KM# 19 3 CAGLIARESE (6 Denari)

Copper Weight varies: 9.20-15.50g., 26 mm. **Ruler:** Carlo II **Obv:** Crowned bust to right divides 3 - C **Obv. Legend:** CAROLVS. II. D. G. R. **Rev:** Floriated cross, small head to left in each angle, date at end of legend **Rev. Legend:** ARAM. ET. SAE. **Note:** Ref. V#91. Varieties exist.

Date	Mintage	F	VF	XF	Unc	BU
1668	—	25.00	45.00	95.00	185	—
1669	—	18.00	35.00	85.00	170	—
1670	—	18.00	35.00	85.00	170	—
1671	—	25.00	45.00	95.00	185	—
1673	—	30.00	55.00	100	200	—
1678	—	18.00	35.00	85.00	170	—
1680	—	30.00	55.00	100	200	—
1685	—	18.00	35.00	85.00	170	—
1689	—	18.00	35.00	85.00	170	—
1695	—	30.00	55.00	100	200	—

KM# 18 3 CAGLIARESE (6 Denari)

Copper Weight varies: 10.50-17.29g., 26 mm. **Ruler:** Carlo II **Obv:** Bust to right divides 3 - C. **Obv. Legend:** CAROLVS. II. D. G. R. **Rev:** Floriated cross, small head to left in each angle, date at end of legend **Rev. Legend:** ARAM. ET. SAE. **Note:** Ref. V#90.

Date	Mintage	F	VF	XF	Unc	BU
1668	—	25.00	45.00	100	200	—

KM# 11 1/2 REALE (Mezzo Reale)

Silver Weight varies: 0.80-1.36g., 15-16 mm. **Ruler:** Carlo II **Obv:** Head to right in circle **Obv. Legend:** CARLVS. II. R. SPN. **Rev:** Cross with lily ends in quatrefoil **Rev. Legend:** INIMICOS. EIVS. DESTRVAT. **Note:** Ref. V#89.

Date	Mintage	F	VF	XF	Unc	BU
ND(1665-1700)	—	100	180	350	600	—

KM# 5 SOLDO

Billon Weight varies 2.16-3.94g., 22 mm. **Ruler:** Filippo IV **Obv:** Crowned head to left in circle **Obv. Legend:** REX. PHILIPPVS. **Rev:** Cross with lily ends in circle, small head to left in each angle **Rev. Legend:** MONETA. SARDINIAE. REGNI. **Note:** Ref. V#74.

Date	Mintage	F	VF	XF	Unc	BU
ND(1621-65)	—	20.00	40.00	120	195	—

KM# 10 REALE

2.3600 g., Silver, 20 mm. **Ruler:** Filippo IV **Obv:** Crowned bust to left in circle, date below and behind head **Obv. Legend:** PHI. R. A. E. S. **Rev:** Cross in circle **Rev. Legend:** INI. EIVS. IND. CON. **Note:** Ref. V#73.

Date	Mintage	F	VF	XF	Unc	BU
1652 Rare	—	—	—	—	—	—

KM# 12 REALE

Silver Weight varies: 2.15-2.25g., 22-23 mm. **Ruler:** Carlo II **Obv:** Large bust to right in circle, C/I behind head **Obv. Legend:** CAROLVS. II. R. SPARVM. **Rev:** Cross with lily ends in quatrefoil, date at end of legend **Rev. Legend:** INIMICOS. EIVS. DESTRVAT. **Note:** Ref. V#87. Varieties exist.

Date	Mintage	F	VF	XF	Unc	BU
ND(1665-1700)	—	85.00	155	375	600	—
1671	—	70.00	120	275	450	—
1673	—	85.00	155	375	600	—
1676	—	49.50	90.00	220	350	—
1677	—	49.50	90.00	220	350	—

KM# 24 REALE

Silver Weight varies: 2.15-2.25g., 22-23 mm. **Ruler:** Carlo II **Obv:** Small bust to right divides C/I and star, in circle **Obv. Legend:** CAROLVS. II. R. SPARVM **Rev:** Cross with lily ends in quatrefoil, date at end of legend **Rev. Legend:** INIMICOS. EIVS. DESTRVAT. **Note:** Ref. V#88. Varieties exist.

Date	Mintage	F	VF	XF	Unc	BU
1689	—	27.50	49.50	95.00	170	—
1690	—	20.00	38.50	85.00	130	—
1691	—	38.50	70.00	155	250	—
1692	—	27.50	49.50	95.00	170	—
1694	—	20.00	38.50	85.00	130	—
1695	—	33.00	60.00	140	200	—
1696	—	20.00	38.50	85.00	130	—
1699	—	20.00	38.50	85.00	130	—
1700	—	20.00	38.50	85.00	130	—

KM# 6 2-1/2 REALI (12 Soldi, 6 Denari)

6.5000 g., Silver, 26-27 mm. **Ruler:** Filippo IV **Obv:** Crowned head to right in circle divides 12 - 6 **Obv. Legend:** PHILIP. R. ARA. ET. SARDINIE. **Rev:** Foliated cross in circle **Rev. Legend:** INIMICOS. EIVS. INDVAM. CONFVSIO. **Note:** Rev. V#72. Irregular flan.

Date	Mintage	F	VF	XF	Unc	BU
ND(1621-65) Rare	—	—	—	—	—	—

KM# 13 2-1/2 REALI (12 Soldi, 6 Denari)

6.4400 g., Silver, 27-29 mm. **Ruler:** Carlo II **Obv:** Crowned head to right in circle divides 12 - 6, date below, where present **Obv. Legend:** CAROLVS. II. HISPAM. SARD. REX. **Rev:** Foliated cross in circle, pellet in each angle **Rev. Legend:** INIMICOS. IEVS. INDVAM. CONFVSIONE. **Note:** Ref. V#85. Irregular flan.

Date	Mintage	F	VF	XF	Unc	BU
ND(1665-1700)	—	300	550	1,100	1,800	—
1666	—	300	550	1,100	1,800	—

KM# 16 2-1/2 REALI (12 Soldi, 6 Denari)

6.4400 g., Silver, 27-29 mm. **Ruler:** Carlo II **Obv:** Crowned head to right in circle divides 12 - 6, date below **Obv. Legend:** CAROLVS. II. D. G. R. A. E. SARDIN. **Rev:** Foliated cross in circle, pellet in each angle **Rev. Legend:** INIMICOS. EIVS. INDVAM. CONFVSIONE. **Note:** Ref. V#84. Irregular flan.

Date	Mintage	F	VF	XF	Unc	BU
1666	—	325	600	1,200	2,000	—

KM# 25 2-1/2 REALI (12 Soldi, 6 Denari)

Silver Weight varies 5.73-6.25g., 22-24 mm. **Ruler:** Carlo II **Obv:** Crowned bust to right in circle divides 12 - 6, date below **Obv. Legend:** CAROL. II. HISPAN. ET. SARD. REX. **Rev:** Cross with scroll ends, star in each angle **Rev. Legend:** INIMIC. EIVS. INDVAM. CONFVS. **Note:** Ref. V#86. Varieties exist.

Date	Mintage	F	VF	XF	Unc	BU
1694	—	36.00	65.00	155	235	—
1695	—	36.00	65.00	155	235	—
1696	—	55.00	90.00	210	300	—
1699	—	65.00	115	240	350	—
1700	—	48.00	80.00	190	265	—

KM# 7 5 REALI
Silver Weight varies: 12.93-13.58g., 36-38.5 mm. **Ruler:** Filippo IV **Obv:** Crowned bust to right divides C - V, date below **Obv. Legend:** PHILIP. R. ARA. ET. SARDINIE. **Rev:** Floriated cross in circle, pellet in each angle **Rev. Legend:** INIMICOS. IEVS. INDVAM. CONFVSIONE. **Note:** Ref. V#70. Irregular flan.

Date	Mintage	F	VF	XF	Unc	BU
1641	—	36.00	65.00	205	325	—
1642	—	36.00	65.00	205	325	—
1643	—	36.00	65.00	205	325	—
1644	—	36.00	65.00	205	325	—

KM# 20 5 REALI
Silver Weight varies: 12.93-13.58g., 36-38.5 mm. **Ruler:** Filippo IV **Obv:** Crowned bust to right divides C/V - A, date below **Obv. Legend:** PHILIP. R. ARA. ET. SARDINIE. **Rev:** Floriated cross in circle, small head to left in each angle **Rev. Legend:** INIMICOS. IEVS. INDVAM. CONFVSIONE. **Note:** Ref. V#71. Irregular flan.

Date	Mintage	F	VF	XF	Unc	BU
1666	—	—	—	—	—	—

Note: Numismatica Ars Classica Auction 53, XF realized approximately $11,900

KM# 21 5 REALI
Silver Weight varies: 12.33-12.50g., 32 mm. **Ruler:** Carlo II **Obv:** Crowned bust to right divides C/V - R, date below **Obv. Legend:** CAROLVS. II. HISP. ET. SARDIE. REX. **Rev:** Foliated cross, star in each angle **Rev. Legend:** INIMICOS. EIVS. INDVAM. CONFVS. **Note:** Ref. V#82.

Date	Mintage	F	VF	XF	Unc	BU
1671	—	375	600	1,300	1,800	—
1672	—	375	600	1,300	1,800	—

KM# 22 5 REALI
Silver Weight varies: 12.10-12.80g., 32 mm. **Ruler:** Carlo II **Obv:** Crowned bust to right divides C/V - R, date below **Obv. Legend:** CAROLVS. II. ARAG. ET. SARDIE. REX. **Rev:** Foliated cross, rosette in each angle **Rev. Legend:** INIMICOS. EIVS. INDVAM. CONFVS. **Note:** Ref. V#83.

Date	Mintage	F	VF	XF	Unc	BU
1674	—	400	600	1,400	1,800	—
1685	—	350	525	1,300	1,700	—

KM# 8 10 REALI
Silver Weight varies: 25.36-27.80g., 39-40 mm. **Ruler:** Filippo IV **Obv:** Crowned bust to right in circle divides C/X - A, date below **Obv. Legend:** PHILIP. REX. ARA. ET. SARDINE. **Rev:** Floriated cross in circle, pellet in each angle **Rev. Legend:** INIMICO. ICO. SEIVS. INDVAM. CONFVSIONE. **Note:** Ref. V#68; Dav. 4147. Varieties exist. Irregular flan. Prev. listed under Sardinia.

Date	Mintage	F	VF	XF	Unc	BU
1641	—	36.00	65.00	220	325	—
1642	—	36.00	65.00	220	325	—
1643	—	36.00	65.00	220	325	—
1644	—	90.00	170	475	800	—
1646	—	90.00	170	475	800	—
1647	—	90.00	170	475	800	—

KM# 9 10 REALI
Silver Weight varies: 24.20-27.60g., 39-40 mm. **Ruler:** Filippo IV **Obv:** Crowned bust to right in circle divides C/X - R, date below **Obv. Legend:** PHILIP. REX. ARA. ET. SARDINE. **Rev:** Floriated cross in circle, small head to left in each angle **Rev. Legend:** INIMICO. ICO. SEIVS. INDVAM. CONFVSIONE. **Note:** Ref. V#69; Dav. 4147. Varieties exist. Irregular flan. Prev. listed under Sardinia.

Date	Mintage	F	VF	XF	Unc	BU
1643	—	70.00	130	350	550	—
1650	—	70.00	130	350	550	—
1652	—	70.00	130	350	550	—
1653	—	70.00	130	350	550	—
1664	—	70.00	130	350	550	—

KM# 15 10 REALI
Silver Weight varies: 25.44-26.67g., 38-40 mm. **Ruler:** Carlo II **Obv:** Crowned bust to right divides C/X - R, date below **Obv. Legend:** CAROLVS. II. HISP. E(T). SARDIE. REX. **Rev:** Cross with lily ends, rosette in each angle **Rev. Legend:** INIMICOS. EIVS. INDVAM. CONFVS. **Note:** Ref. V#80; Dav. 4148. Varieties exist. Prev. listed under Sardinia.

Date	Mintage	F	VF	XF	Unc	BU
ND(1665-1700)	—	650	1,000	2,300	4,500	—
1671	—	600	875	2,200	4,200	—
1672	—	600	875	2,200	4,200	—
1674	—	600	875	2,200	4,200	—

KM# 14 10 REALI
Silver Weight varies: 25.36-26.29g., 33-35 mm. **Ruler:** Carlo II **Obv:** Crowned bust to right in circle divides C/X - R **Obv. Legend:** CARLVS. II. HISPANIAR. ET. SARDI. REX. **Rev:** Floriated cross in circle, small head to left in each angle **Rev. Legend:** INIMICOS. EIVS. INDVAM. CONFVSIONE. **Note:** Ref. V#79. Irregular flan.

Date	Mintage	F	VF	XF	Unc	BU
ND(1665-1700)	—	3,600	5,500	15,000	—	—

KM# 23 10 REALI
Silver Weight varies: 24.45-25.47g., 38-40 mm. **Ruler:** Carlo II **Obv:** Crowned bust to right divides C/X - R, date below **Obv. Legend:** CAROLVS. II. ARA(G). E(T). SARDIE. REX. **Rev:** Cross with lily ends, pellet in each angle **Rev. Legend:** INIMICOS. EIVS. INDVAM. CONFVS. **Note:** Ref. V#81; Dav. 4149. Varieties exist. Prev. listed under Sardinia.

Date	Mintage	F	VF	XF	Unc	BU
1674	—	600	875	2,200	4,200	—
1675	—	850	1,300	2,900	5,700	—
1677	—	600	875	2,200	4,200	—
1678	—	650	1,000	2,300	4,500	—
1683	—	650	1,000	2,300	4,500	—
1684	—	600	875	2,200	4,200	—
1685	—	700	1,100	2,400	4,950	—
1689	—	700	1,100	2,400	4,950	—

CAMPI

An ancient feudal enclave in the Valle di Trebbia ruled by the Scotti dynasty. Emperor Ferdinand III conveyed the right to strike coinage on the rulers in 1654.

RULERS
Carlo Centurioni Scotti, 1654-1663
Giovanni Battista Centurioni Scotti, 1663-1715
Giulia Maria Serra, 1663-?

Reference:
V = Alberto Varesi, ***Monete Italiane Regionali: Piemonte, Sardegna, Liguria, Isola di Corsica.*** Pavia, 1996.

LORDSHIP

STANDARD COINAGE

KM# 3.1 LUIGINO
Billon Weight varies: 1.50-2.70g., 20-21 mm. **Ruler:** Giovanni Battista Centurioni Scotti **Obv:** Bust of princess to right **Obv. Legend:** IVLIA. M. PRINCIP. CAMP(I). **Rev:** Crowned shield of French arms (3 lilies) divides date **Rev. Legend:** C(-)E(-)NTVPLV(M). GERMIN(-)(A). (-) B (-)(V). **Note:** Ref. Varesi 116. Struck in the name of Princess Giulia Maria Serra for the Levant. Varieties exist.

Date	Mintage	VG	F	VF	XF	Unc
1668	—	55.00	115	275	475	—

KM# 3.2 LUIGINO
1.8000 g., Billon, 20-21 mm. **Ruler:** Giovanni Battista Centurioni Scotti **Obv:** Bust of princess to right **Obv. Legend:** IVLIA. M. PRINCIP. CAMPI. **Rev:** Crowned shield of French arms (3 lilies) divides date **Rev. Legend:** PVLCRA. GERMINAT. BON. **Note:** Ref. Varesi 117. Struck in the name of Princess Giulia Maria Serra for the Levant.

Date	Mintage	VG	F	VF	XF	Unc
1669	—	65.00	140	275	500	—

KM# 7 LUIGINO
Billon, 20-21 mm. **Ruler:** Giovanni Battista Centurioni Scotti **Obv:** Bust of princess to right **Obv. Legend:** IVL. M. S. R. I. PRINC. SOW. DOM. **Rev:** Crowned shield of French arms (3 lilies) divides date **Rev. Legend:** MELLIBAT. EXLILLIIS. **Note:** Ref. Varesi 118. Struck in the name of Princess Giulia Maria Serra for the Levant.

Date	Mintage	VG	F	VF	XF	Unc
1669	—	80.00	175	350	625	—

KM# 2 TESTONE
7.9800 g., Silver, 29-30 mm. **Ruler:** Carlo Centurioni Scotti **Obv:** Armored long-haired bust to right **Obv. Legend:** CAROLVS. CENTVR. MAR. CAMPI. **Rev:** Crowned shield of family arms superimposed on imperial eagle, date at end of legend **Rev. Legend:** ET. SAC. ROM. IMP. PRINCEPS. **Note:** Ref. Varesi 112.

Date	Mintage	VG	F	VF	XF	Unc
1662 Rare	—	—	—	—	—	—

KM# 4 TESTONE
7.9600 g., Silver, 31-32 mm. **Ruler:** Giovanni Battista Centurioni Scotti **Obv:** Accolated busts of Giovanni Battista and Giulia Maria to right **Obv. Legend:** IO. BAPT. CENTVRIO. ET. IVL. M. MAR. CAM. **Rev:** Crowned shield of family arms superimposed on crowned imperial eagle, date at end of legend **Rev. Legend:** ET. SAC. ROM. IMP. PRINCEPES. **Note:** Ref. Varesi 115.

Date	Mintage	VG	F	VF	XF	Unc
1672 Rare	—	—	—	—	—	—

TRADE COINAGE

KM# 5 1/2 DOPPIA (Mezza Doppia)
3.2300 g., Gold, 21 mm. **Ruler:** Giovanni Battista Centurioni Scotti **Obv:** Bust to right **Obv. Legend:** IO. BAP. CENTVR. MAR. CAMPI. **Rev:** Shield of family arms superimposed on crowned imperial eagle, date at end of legend **Rev. Legend:** ET. SAC. ROM. IMP. PRIN. AN. **Note:** Ref. Varesi 113; Fr. 152.

Date	Mintage	VG	F	VF	XF	Unc
1668 Rare	—	—	—	—	—	—

KM# 1 DOPPIA
6.5300 g., Gold, 29-30 mm. **Ruler:** Carlo Centurioni Scotti **Obv:** Armored long-haired bust to right **Obv. Legend:** CAROLVS. CENTVR. MAR. CAMPI. **Rev:** Crowned shield of family arms superimposed on imperial eagle, date at end of legend **Rev. Legend:** ET. SAC. ROM. IMP. PRINCEPS. **Note:** Ref. Varesi 111; Fr. 151.

Date	Mintage	VG	F	VF	XF	Unc
1661 Rare	—	—	—	—	—	—
1662 Rare	—	—	—	—	—	—

KM# 6 DOPPIA
6.5300 g., Gold, 31-32 mm. **Ruler:** Giovanni Battista Centurioni Scotti **Obv:** Accolated busts of Giovanni Battista and Giulia Maria to right **Obv. Legend:** IO. BAPT. CENTVRIO. ET. IVL. M. MAR. CAM. **Rev:** Crowned shield of family arms superimposed on crowned imperial eagle, date at end of legend. **Rev. Legend:** ET. SAC. ROM. IMP. PRINCEPES. **Note:** Ref. Varesi 114; Fr. 153.

Date	Mintage	VG	F	VF	XF	Unc
1668 Rare	—	—	—	—	—	—

Note: Superior Pipito sale 12-87 VF realized $30,250

CASALE

Marquisate and Duchy

Of very ancient origin, the city of Casale, 40 miles (67 kilometers) southwest of Milan, became the capital of Monferrat, a marquisate erected in 967 by Emperor Otto I (936-73). The first ruling dynasty of the Aleramidi died out in 1305 and Casale passed to the Paleologi, which in turn became extinct in the male line in 1533. The marchese was raised to the rank of Prince of the Empire in 1464. Emperor Carlo V (1516-56) assigned the succession of Casale to the Gonzaga Duke of Mantua (which see), who married the daughter of the last Paleologo marchese. Austrian and Spanish forces besieged the French defenders in the city from 1628 to 1630, resulting in several issues of obsidional coinage. When a later Gonzaga ruler was accused of a felony in 1703, Emperor Leopold I (1658-1705) transferred Casale to Savoy, an act which was finalized as a part of the Treaty of Utrecht in 1713.

RULERS
Vincenzo I Gonzaga, 1587-1612
Francesco IV Gonzaga, 1612 (Feb-Dec)
Ferdinando Gonzaga, 1612-1626
Vincenzo II Gonzaga, 1627 (May-Dec)
Carlo I Gonzaga, 1627-1637
Carlo II Gonzaga, 1637-1665
Maria, regent 1637-1647
Ferdinando Carlo Gonzaga, 1669-1707

MINT OFFICIAL'S INITIALS

Initial	Date	Name
GC	ca. 1617-1622	Giulio Campo, die-cutter

ARMS
2-fold, divided horizontally, upper half shaded (early type)

Reference:
V = Alberto Varesi, ***Monete Italiane Regionali: Piemonte, Sardegna, Liguria, Isola di Corsica***. Pavia, 1996.

DUCHY

STANDARD COINAGE

KM# 9A 1/2 QUATTRINO (Mezzo Quattrino)
0.4500 g., Billon, 13 mm. **Ruler:** Ferdinando **Obv:** Large 'F' **Rev:** Large cross with small cross in each angle **Note:** Ref. V-346.

Date	Mintage	VG	F	VF	XF	Unc
ND(1612-26)	—	40.00	80.00	165	265	—

KM# 8 QUATTRINO
Billon Weight varies: 0.34-0.86g., 15 mm. **Ruler:** Vincenzo I **Obv:** Bust to right in circle **Obv. Legend:** VIN. D. G. DVX. MA. IIII. ET. M. F. II. **Rev:** Standing figure of St. Catherine, date at end of legend **Rev. Legend:** SAN - CATARINA. **Note:** Ref. V-311. Varieties exist.

Date	Mintage	VG	F	VF	XF	Unc
1602	—	20.00	35.00	75.00	180	—
1603	—	20.00	35.00	75.00	180	—
1604	—	20.00	35.00	75.00	180	—
1605	—	20.00	35.00	75.00	180	—
1606	—	20.00	35.00	75.00	180	—
1608	—	20.00	35.00	75.00	180	—
1609	—	20.00	35.00	75.00	180	—

KM# 9.1 QUATTRINO
Billon Weight varies: 0.52-1.22g., 14-15 mm. **Ruler:** Vincenzo I **Obv:** Crescent moon enclosing 'SIC' **Obv. Legend:** VIN. D. G. DVX. MAN. IIII. **Rev:** Double letter 'C,' one reversed, back-to-back **Rev. Legend:** ET. MONTIS. FERRA(TI). II. **Note:** Ref. V-312. Prev. KM#9.

Date	Mintage	VG	F	VF	XF	Unc
ND(1587-1612)	—	20.00	35.00	75.00	180	—

KM# 9.2 QUATTRINO
Billon Weight varies: 0.74-1.02g., 14 mm. **Ruler:** Vincenzo I **Obv:** Crescent moon enclosing 'SIC' **Obv. Legend:** VIN. D. G. DVX. MANT. IIII. **Rev:** Double letter 'C,' one reverse, in monogram **Rev. Legend:** ET. MONTIS. FERRATIS. **Note:** Ref. V-313.

Date	Mintage	VG	F	VF	XF	Unc
ND(1587-1612)	—	—	—	—	—	—

KM# 10 QUATTRINO

Billon Weight varies: 1.30-1.64g., 14 mm. **Ruler:** Ferdinando **Obv:** Displayed eagle **Obv. Legend:** FER. D. G. DVX. MA. VI. ET. M. F. IIII. **Rev:** Radiant sun in circle **Rev. Legend:** NON. MVTVATA. LVCE. **Note:** Ref. V-343.

Date	Mintage	VG	F	VF	XF	Unc
ND(1612-26)	—	20.00	35.00	75.00	180	—

KM# 11 QUATTRINO

Billon Weight varies: 0.68-1.29g., 14 mm. **Ruler:** Ferdinando **Obv:** Letters in 3 lines F / D - M / M **Rev:** Large cross with small cross in each angle, no legend **Note:** Ref. V-344.

Date	Mintage	VG	F	VF	XF	Unc
ND(1612-26)	—	20.00	35.00	75.00	180	—

KM# 66 SOLDO

Billon Weight varies: 1.28-1.88g., 17-18 mm. **Ruler:** Carlo II **Obv:** Bust to left **Obv. Legend:** CAR. II. D. G. DVX. MANT. **Rev:** Radiant sunface, date at end of legend **Rev. Legend:** ET. MONTIS. FERRATI. ETC. **Note:** Ref. V-361.

Date	Mintage	VG	F	VF	XF	Unc
1661	—	15.00	25.00	60.00	120	—

KM# 33 2 SOLDI

0.6100 g., Billon, 14 mm. **Ruler:** Ferdinando **Obv:** Crowned shield of manifold arms **Obv. Legend:** FER. D. G. DVX. M. VI. ET. M. F. IV. **Rev:** Radiant sun in circle **Rev. Legend:** NON. MVTVATA. LVCE. **Note:** Ref. V-342.

Date	Mintage	VG	F	VF	XF	Unc
ND(1612-26)	—	20.00	35.00	85.00	200	—

KM# 32.1 1/2 BIANCO (Mezzo Bianco)

0.7000 g., Billon, 13 mm. **Ruler:** Ferdinando **Obv:** Radiant sun **Obv. Legend:** NON. MVTVATA. LVCE. **Rev:** Large cross with small cross in each angle, no legend **Note:** Ref. V-339. Prev. KM#32.

Date	Mintage	VG	F	VF	XF	Unc
ND(1612-26)	—	30.00	60.00	135	240	—

KM# 32.2 1/2 BIANCO (Mezzo Bianco)

1.3700 g., Billon, 16 mm. **Ruler:** Ferdinando **Obv:** Mt. Olympus, crown over 'FIDES' above **Obv. Legend:** +FERDINAN. D. G. DVX. MAN. VI. **Rev:** Large cross with small cross in each angle **Rev. Legend:** ET. MONTIS. FERRATI. IV. **Note:** Ref. V-340.

Date	Mintage	VG	F	VF	XF	Unc
ND(1612-26)	—	25.00	55.00	120	200	—

KM# 32.3 1/2 BIANCO (Mezzo Bianco)

1.0700 g., Billon, 13 mm. **Ruler:** Ferdinando **Obv:** Mt. Olympus, crown over 'FIDES' above **Obv. Legend:** FERD. D. G. DVX. MANT. VI. **Rev:** Crowned shield of manifold arms **Rev. Legend:** ET. MONTIS. FERRATI. IV. **Note:** Ref. V-341.

Date	Mintage	VG	F	VF	XF	Unc
ND(1612-26)	—	25.00	55.00	120	200	—

KM# 23 SESINO

0.8100 g., Billon, 15-16 mm. **Ruler:** Ferdinando **Obv:** Crown over 'FIDES' above Mt. Olympus, all in oval frame **Obv. Legend:** FERD. D. G. DVX. MAN. V. MO. FE. IIII. **Rev:** Ornate floriated cross, date divided in angles, no legend **Note:** Ref. V-345.

Date	Mintage	VG	F	VF	XF	Unc
1614	—	75.00	140	225	400	—

KM# 61 QUARTO

Billon Weight varies: 0.95-1.37g., 17 mm. **Ruler:** Carlo I **Obv:** Mt. Olympus, crown over 'FIDES' above **Obv. Legend:** CAROLVS. I. DVX. MANT. VIII. **Obv. Inscription:** FIDES on mountain **Rev:** Large cross in circle, small cross in each angle **Rev. Legend:** ET. MONTIS. FERRATI. VI. **Note:** Ref. V-353.

Date	Mintage	VG	F	VF	XF	Unc
ND(1627-37)	—	50.00	110	215	400	—

KM# 70 QUARTO

Billon Weight varies: 1.81-2.02g., 14-15 mm. **Ruler:** Ferdinando Carlo **Obv:** Displayed crowned eagle in circle **Obv. Legend:** FER. CAR. D. G. DVX. MANT. M. FE. **Rev:** Radiant sun in circle **Rev. Legend:** NON. MVTVATA. LVCE. **Note:** Ref. V-364.

Date	Mintage	VG	F	VF	XF	Unc
ND(1669-1708)	—	12.00	28.00	60.00	95.00	—

KM# 5 PARPAGLIOLA (2-1/2 Soldi)

Billon Weight varies: 1.58-2.79g., 20 mm. **Ruler:** Vincenzo I **Obv:** Displayed eagle **Obv. Legend:** +VIN. D. G. DVX. MAN. IIII. E. MO. FE. II. **Rev:** Kneeling St. Francis receiving the stigmata, date in exergue **Rev. Legend:** SANCTVS. FRANCISCVS. **Note:** Ref. V-307. Varieties exist.

Date	Mintage	VG	F	VF	XF	Unc
1601	—	15.00	25.00	60.00	120	—
1602	—	15.00	25.00	60.00	120	—
1605	—	15.00	25.00	60.00	120	—
1608	—	15.00	25.00	60.00	120	—
1609	—	15.00	25.00	60.00	120	—

KM# 20 PARPAGLIOLA (2-1/2 Soldi)

Billon Weight varies: 0.94-2.17g., 19-20 mm. **Ruler:** Francesco IV **Obv:** Crowned displayed eagle **Obv. Legend:** FRAN. IIII. DVX. MAN. V. ET. M. F. III. **Rev:** Kneeling St. Francis receiving the stigmata, date in exergue **Rev. Legend:** SANCT. - FRANCISCVS. **Note:** Ref. V-317.

Date	Mintage	VG	F	VF	XF	Unc
1612	—	20.00	35.00	75.00	180	—
1613	—	20.00	35.00	75.00	180	—

KM# 24 PARPAGLIOLA (2-1/2 Soldi)

Billon Weight varies: 1.44-2.36g., 19-20 mm. **Ruler:** Ferdinando **Obv:** Crowned displayed eagle **Obv. Legend:** FERD. D. G. DVX. MAN. VI. ET. M. F. IIII. **Rev:** Kneeling St. Francis receiving the stigmata, date in exergue **Rev. Legend:** SANC. FRANCISCVS. **Note:** Ref. V-336.

Date	Mintage	VG	F	VF	XF	Unc
1613	—	15.00	25.00	60.00	120	—
1614	—	15.00	25.00	60.00	120	—
1615	—	15.00	25.00	60.00	120	—
1616	—	15.00	25.00	60.00	120	—
1617	—	15.00	25.00	60.00	120	—
1618	—	15.00	25.00	60.00	120	—
1619	—	15.00	25.00	60.00	120	—
1620	—	15.00	25.00	60.00	120	—
1623	—	15.00	25.00	60.00	120	—
1624	—	15.00	25.00	60.00	120	—

KM# 51 PARPAGLIOLA (2-1/2 Soldi)

Billon Weight varies: 2.43-2.86g., 20 mm. **Ruler:** Carlo I **Obv:** Crowned displayed eagle **Obv. Legend:** CAR. D. G. DVX. MAN. ET. M. FER. ET. C. **Rev:** Facing bust of St. Evasius, date in exergue **Rev. Legend:** SANCT. EVASIVS. PRO. **Note:** Ref. V-351.

Date	Mintage	VG	F	VF	XF	Unc
1629	—	20.00	35.00	75.00	180	—
1632	—	20.00	35.00	75.00	180	—

KM# 65 PARPAGLIOLA (2-1/2 Soldi)

Billon Weight varies: 1.22-2.50g., 19-20 mm. **Ruler:** Carlo II **Obv:** Crowned displayed eagle **Obv. Legend:** CAR. II. D. G. DVX. MAN. ET. M. FER. C. **Rev:** Facing bust of St. Evasius, date in exergue **Rev. Legend:** SANCT. EVASIVS. PRO. **Note:** Ref. V-360.

Date	Mintage	VG	F	VF	XF	Unc
1661	—	15.00	25.00	60.00	120	—

KM# 80 PARPAGLIOLA (2-1/2 Soldi)

Billon Weight varies: 1.80-2.22g., 18-19 mm. **Ruler:** Ferdinando Carlo **Obv:** Crowned displayed eagle **Obv. Legend:** FER. CAR. D. G. DVX. MAN. ET. M. FER. **Rev:** Facing bust of St. Evasius, date in exergue **Rev. Legend:** SANCT. EVASIVS. PRO. **Note:** Ref. V-362.

Date	Mintage	VG	F	VF	XF	Unc
1684	—	15.00	25.00	60.00	120	—
1693	—	15.00	25.00	60.00	120	—

KM# 15 GROSSO

Billon Weight varies: 0.90-1.21g., 18-19 mm. **Ruler:** Vincenzo I **Obv:** Mt. Olympus, crown over 'FIDES' above, all in oval shield **Obv. Legend:** +VIN. D. G. DVX. MAN. IIII. ET. MO. FE. II. **Rev:** Ornate floriated cross, date divided in angles, no legend **Note:** Ref. V-308. Varieties exist.

Date	Mintage	VG	F	VF	XF	Unc
1604	—	15.00	25.00	55.00	100	—
1607	—	15.00	25.00	55.00	100	—
1608	—	15.00	25.00	55.00	100	—
1609	—	15.00	25.00	55.00	100	—
1610	—	15.00	25.00	55.00	100	—
1611	—	15.00	25.00	55.00	100	—

KM# 17 GROSSO

Billon Weight varies: 0.94-1.03g., 17 mm. **Ruler:** Francesco IV **Obv:** Mt. Olympus, crown over 'FIDES' above, all in oval shield **Obv. Legend:** FRAN. IIII. D. G. DVX. MA. V. ET. M. F. III. **Rev:** Ornate floriated cross, date divided in angles, no legend **Note:** Ref. V-318.

Date	Mintage	VG	F	VF	XF	Unc
1612	—	20.00	40.00	110	300	—
1613	—	20.00	40.00	110	300	—

KM# 19 GROSSO

Billon Weight varies: 0.70-1.30g., 16 mm. **Ruler:** Ferdinando **Obv:** Mt. Olympus, crown over 'FIDES' above, all in oval shield **Obv. Legend:** FERD. VI. D. G. DVX. MA. VI. ET. M. F. IIII. **Rev:** Ornate floriated cross, date divided in angles, no legend **Note:** Ref. V-337. Varieties exist. Prev. listed as 1-1/2 Reali.

Date	Mintage	VG	F	VF	XF	Unc
1612	—	18.00	30.00	65.00	150	—
1613	—	18.00	30.00	65.00	150	—
1615	—	18.00	30.00	65.00	150	—
1619	—	18.00	30.00	65.00	150	—
1620	—	18.00	30.00	65.00	150	—
1623	—	18.00	30.00	65.00	150	—

KM# 29 GROSSO

Billon Weight varies: 1.64-2.17g., 18 mm. **Ruler:** Ferdinando **Obv:** 4-line inscription within wreath **Obv. Inscription:** FER. / DVX. / MAN. / ET M. F. **Rev:** Large cross with small cross in each angle, all in wreath **Note:** Ref. V-338. Prev. listed as 1-1/2 Reali.

Date	Mintage	VG	F	VF	XF	Unc
ND(1612-26)	—	18.00	30.00	65.00	150	—

KM# 47 GROSSO

Billon Weight varies: 1.23-1.44g., 19-20 mm. **Ruler:** Carlo I **Obv:** 4-line inscription within wreath **Obv. Inscription:** CAR. / DVX. / MAN. / ET. M. F. **Rev:** Large cross with small cross in each angle, all in wreath **Note:** Ref. V-352.

Date	Mintage	VG	F	VF	XF	Unc
ND(1627-37)	—	20.00	35.00	75.00	180	—

KM# 69 GROSSO

Billon, 19 mm. **Ruler:** Ferdinando Carlo **Obv:** Mt. Olympus, crown over 'FIDES' above **Obv. Legend:** FERD. CAR. D. G. DVX. MANT. X. **Rev:** Large cross with small cross in each angle **Rev. Legend:** ET. MONTIS. FERRATI. VIII. **Note:** Ref. V-363.

Date	Mintage	VG	F	VF	XF	Unc
ND(1669-1708)	—	18.00	32.00	70.00	160	—

KM# 34 3 GROSSI

Billon Weight varies: 2.12-2.70g., 21 mm. **Ruler:** Ferdinando **Obv:** Mt. Olympus, crown over 'FIDES' above, all in shield dividing G - 3 **Obv. Legend:** +FERDINAN. D. G. DVX. MANT. VI. **Rev:** Crowned shield of 4-fold arms of Mantua divides date, where present **Rev. Legend:** ET. MONTIS. FERRATI. IV. **Note:** Ref. V-334. Varieties exist.

Date	Mintage	VG	F	VF	XF	Unc
1621	—	25.00	40.00	95.00	210	—
1622	—	25.00	40.00	95.00	210	—
1626	—	25.00	40.00	95.00	210	—
ND	—	25.00	40.00	95.00	210	—

KM# 35 3 GROSSI

1.1500 g., Billon, 17 mm. **Ruler:** Ferdinando **Obv:** Crowned displayed eagle in circle **Obv. Legend:** +FERD. D. G. DVX. MANTVÆ. VI. **Rev:** Cartouche with CAS/ALE divides G - 3 **Rev. Legend:** ET. MONTIS. FERRATI. IIII. **Note:** Ref. V-335.

Date	Mintage	VG	F	VF	XF	Unc
ND(1612-26)	—	40.00	95.00	200	400	—

KM# 31 7 SOLDI

Billon Weight varies: 1.54-1.95g., 20-21 mm. **Ruler:** Ferdinando **Obv:** Crowned shield of manifold arms **Obv. Legend:** FERD. D. G. DVX. MAN. VI. ET. M. F. IV. **Rev:** Radiant sunface in circle, value '7' below in margin **Rev. Legend:** NON. MVTVATA. LVCE. **Note:** Ref. V-333.

Date	Mintage	VG	F	VF	XF	Unc
ND(1612-26)	—	25.00	50.00	100	200	—

KM# 75 7 SOLDI

1.7300 g., Billon, 19-20 mm. **Ruler:** Vincenzo II **Obv:** Crowned shield of 9-fold arms **Obv. Legend:** VINC. II. D. G. DVX. MAN. VII. ET. M. F. V. **Rev:** Radiant sunface in circle, value '7' below in margin **Rev. Legend:** NON. MVTVATA. LVCE. **Note:** Ref. V-349.

Date	Mintage	VG	F	VF	XF	Unc
ND(1626-27) Rare	—	—	—	—	—	—

KM# 30 6 GROSSI

Billon Weight varies: 1.78-2.24g., 22-23 mm. **Ruler:** Ferdinando **Obv:** Cartouche with 5-line inscription, cherub's head and wings above, all within wreath, '6' in margin at bottom **Obv. Inscription:** FERDIN. / D. G. DVX. / MANT. VI / ET. MON. F. / IIII. **Rev:** Madonna and Child in circle, 'CASALE' in exergue **Rev. Legend:** DIVÆ. VIRGINIS. CRETÆ. **Note:** Ref. V-332.

Date	Mintage	VG	F	VF	XF	Unc
ND(1612-26)	—	36.00	70.00	145	240	—

KM# 36 1-1/2 REALI (18 Grossi)

Billon Weight varies: 3.52-3.87g., 23-24 mm. **Ruler:** Ferdinando **Obv:** Crown over ornate frame with 6-line inscription, which divides G - 18, all in wreath **Obv. Inscription:** FERDIN / D. G. DVX / MAN. VI / ET. MONT. / FER. / IV. **Rev:** Stag leaping to left, small shield of arms in exergue divides 'CAS-ALE' and date in 2 lines **Rev. Legend:** ITA. ANIMA. MEA. AD. ET. DEVS. **Note:** Ref. V-331.

Date	Mintage	VG	F	VF	XF	Unc
1621	—	80.00	145	240	450	—
1622	—	80.00	145	240	450	—

KM# 67 2 REALI

Billon Weight varies: 3.55-4.63g., 25-26 mm. **Ruler:** Carlo II **Obv:** Crowned ornamented shield with 6-line inscription, all in wreath **Obv. Inscription:** CARO. II. / D.G. DVX / MANT / ET. MON / FERA / E. C. **Rev:** Madonna and Child in wreath, 'CAS-ALE' and date in exergue divided by small shield of arms **Rev. Legend:** DIVÆ. VIRGINIS. CRETÆNS. **Note:** Ref. V-359.

Date	Mintage	VG	F	VF	XF	Unc
1662	—	90.00	180	325	550	—

KM# 41 4 REALI

Billon Weight varies: 6.67-7.42g., 28-29 mm. **Ruler:** Ferdinando **Obv:** Crown over ornate frame with 6-line inscription, which divides R - 4, all in wreath **Obv. Inscription:** FERDIN / D. G. DVX / MAN. VI / ET. MONT. / FER. / IV. **Rev:** Stag leaping to left, small shield of arms in exergue divides 'CAS-ALE' and date in 2 lines **Rev. Legend:** ITA. ANIMA. MEA. AD. ET. DEVS. **Note:** Ref. V-330.

Date	Mintage	VG	F	VF	XF	Unc
1623	—	120	240	350	650	—
1626	—	120	240	350	650	—

KM# 68 4 REALI

Billon Weight varies: 7.37-7.52g., 27-29 mm. **Ruler:** Carlo II **Obv:** Crowned ornamented shield with 6-line inscription, all i wreath **Obv. Inscription:** CARO. II / D. GRA / DVX / MANT / ET. MON / FER. **Rev:** Stag leaping to left, 'CAS-ALE' and date divided by small shield of arms in exergue **Rev. Legend:** ITA. ANIMA. AD. ET. DEVS. **Note:** Ref. V-358.

Date	Mintage	VG	F	VF	XF	Unc
1662	—	120	240	425	700	—

KM# 72 1/4 DUCATONE

Silver Weight varies: 6.40-7.77g., 30-31 mm. **Ruler:** Ferdinando **Obv:** Ornate frame with 5-line inscription, all in wreath **Obv. Inscription:** FERDIN / D. G. DVX / MANT. VI / ET. MONT. / IIII. **Rev:** St. George on horseback to right slaying dragon below, 'CASALE' in exergue **Rev. Legend:** PROTECTOR. NOSTER .ASPICE. **Note:** Ref. V-329.

Date	Mintage	VG	F	VF	XF	Unc
ND(1612-26)	—	1,000	1,700	4,200	6,000	—

KM# 37 1/4 DUCATONE

Silver Weight varies: 6.40-7.77g., 30-31 mm. **Ruler:** Ferdinando **Obv:** Armored bust wearing high collar to right, date below shoulder **Obv. Legend:** FERDIN. D. G. DVX. MAN. VI. ET. M. F. IIII. **Rev:** St. George on horseback to right slaying dragon below, 'CASALE' in exergue **Rev. Legend:** PROTECTOR. NOSTER. ASPICE. **Note:** Ref. V-328.

Date	Mintage	VG	F	VF	XF	Unc
1621 GC	—	900	1,300	3,600	5,400	—

KM# 45 1/2 TALLERO (8 Bianchi)

Silver Weight varies: 10.73-11.28g., 30-31 mm. **Ruler:** Ferdinando **Obv:** Crowned shield of Mantua arms, with central shield of manifold Monferrat arms, chain of order around **Obv. Legend:** FERDINANDVS - D. G. DVX. MAT. VI. **Rev:** Short cross with cross in angles **Rev. Legend:** ET. MONTIS. FERRATI. IV. **Note:** Ref. V-327.

Date	Mintage	VG	F	VF	XF	Unc
ND(1612-26)	—	775	1,200	2,400	3,950	—

KM# 38 1/2 DUCATONE

15.4000 g., Silver, 34-35 mm. **Ruler:** Ferdinando **Obv:** Armored bust with high collar to right, date below shoulder **Obv. Legend:** FERD. D. G. DVX. MANT. VI. ET. MO. F. IIII. **Rev:** St. George on horseback to right, slaying dragon below with lance, 'CASALE' in exergue **Rev. Legend:** PROTECTOR. NOSTER. ASPICE. **Note:** Ref. V-326.

Date	Mintage	VG	F	VF	XF	Unc
1621 GC	—	900	1,300	3,600	5,400	—

KM# 71 TALLERO (16 Bianchi)

21.9000 g., Silver, 39-40 mm. **Ruler:** Ferdinando **Obv:** Crowned shield of Mantua arms, with central shield of manifold Monferrat arms, chain of order around **Obv. Legend:** FERDINANDVS. D. G. DVX. MAN. VI. **Rev:** Large cross in circle, small cross in each angle **Rev. Legend:** ET. MONTIS. FERRATI. IV. **Note:** Ref. V-325; Dav. 3870.

Date	Mintage	VG	F	VF	XF	Unc
ND(1612-26)	—	1,000	1,650	3,700	5,500	—

KM# 76 TALLERO (16 Bianchi)

22.3200 g., Silver, 42 mm. **Ruler:** Vincenzo II **Obv:** Crowned shield of Mantua arms, with central shield of manifold Monferrat arms, chain of order around **Obv. Legend:** VINCENTIVS. II. - D. G. DVX. MAN. VII. **Rev:** Large cross in circle, small cross in each angle **Rev. Legend:** ET. MONTIS - FERRATI. V. **Note:** Ref. V-348.

Date	Mintage	VG	F	VF	XF	Unc
ND(1627) Rare	—	—	—	—	—	—

KM# 6 DUCATONE

Silver Weight varies: 31.30-31.89g., 40-41 mm. **Ruler:** Vincenzo I **Obv:** Large bust with high collar to right **Obv. Legend:** VINC. D. G. DVX. MAN. IIII. ET. MON. FER. II. **Rev:** St. George on horseback to right, slaying dragon below with lance, 'CASAL' in margin below, date at end of legend **Rev. Legend:** PROTECTOR. NOSTER. ASPICE. **Note:** Ref. V-292/1; Dav. 3862.

Date	Mintage	VG	F	VF	XF	Unc
1601	—	400	825	1,850	3,300	—

KM# 12 DUCATONE

Silver Weight varies: 31.30-31.89g., 40-41 mm. **Ruler:** Vincenzo I **Obv:** Large bust with high collar to right **Obv. Legend:** VINC. D. G. DVX. MAN. IIII. ET. MON. FER. II. **Rev:** St. George on horseback to right, slaying dragon below with lance, date below horse, 'CASAL' in margin at bottom **Rev. Legend:** PROTECTOR. NOSTER. ASPICE. **Note:** Ref. V-292/2; Dav. 3863.

Date	Mintage	VG	F	VF	XF	Unc
1603	—	400	825	1,800	3,300	—

KM# 13 DUCATONE

30.7600 g., Silver, 43 mm. **Ruler:** Vincenzo I **Obv:** Bust to left, date below shoulder **Obv. Legend:** VINC. D. G. DVX. MAN. II. ET. MON. FER. II. **Rev:** St. George on horseback to right, slaying dragon below with lance, 'CASAL' in exergue **Rev. Legend:** PROTECTOR. NOSTER. ASPICE. **Note:** Ref. V-294; Dav. 3864.

Date	Mintage	VG	F	VF	XF	Unc
1603	—	500	900	1,850	3,000	—

KM# 14 DUCATONE

Silver Weight varies: 30.38-31.35g., 42 mm. **Ruler:** Vincenzo I **Obv:** Bust to left **Obv. Legend:** VINC. D. G. DVX. MAN. IIII. ET. MON. FER. II. **Rev:** St. George on horseback to right, slaying dragon below with lance, date below horse, 'CASAL' in exergue **Rev. Legend:** PROTECTOR. NOSTER. ASPICE. **Note:** Ref. V-293/1; Dav. 3865.

Date	Mintage	VG	F	VF	XF	Unc
1603	—	900	1,650	4,000	6,600	—

KM# 16 DUCATONE

Silver Weight varies: 30-38-31.35g., 42 mm. **Ruler:** Vincenzo I **Obv:** Bust to left, date below shoulder **Obv. Legend:** VINC. D. G. DVX. MAN. IIII. ET. MON. FER. II. **Rev:** St. George on horseback to right, slaying dragon below with lance, date beneath horse, 'CASAL' in exergue **Rev. Legend:** PROTECTOR. NOSTER. ASPICE. **Note:** Ref. V-293/2,3; Dav. 3866.

Date	Mintage	VG	F	VF	XF	Unc
1604//1604	—	900	1,650	4,000	6,600	—
1606//1606	—	900	1,650	4,000	6,600	—

KM# 25 DUCATONE

Silver Weight varies: 38-80-31.75g., 42-43 mm. **Ruler:** Ferdinando **Obv:** Armored bust with high collar to right, date below shoulder **Obv. Legend:** FERDIN. D. G. DVX. MANT. VI. ET. MON. FER. IIII. **Rev:** St. George on horseback to right, slaying dragon below, 'CASALE' in exergue **Rev. Legend:** PROTECTOR. NOSTER. ASPICE. **Note:** Ref. V-323; Dav. 3868.

Date	Mintage	VG	F	VF	XF	Unc
1617 CG	—	850	1,400	3,250	5,000	—
1622 CG	—	850	1,400	3,250	2,500	—

KM# 26 DUCATONE

31.7500 g., Silver, 42-43 mm. **Ruler:** Ferdinando **Obv:** Armored bust to left with high collar, date below shoulder **Obv. Legend:** FERDIN. D. G. DVX. MANT. ET. M. FER. IV. **Rev:** St. George on horseback to right, slaying dragon below, 'CASALE' in exergue **Rev. Legend:** PROTECTOR. NOSTER. ASPICE. **Note:** Ref. V-324; Dav. 3869.

Date	Mintage	VG	F	VF	XF	Unc
1617 CG	—	700	1,000	2,750	3,900	—

TRADE COINAGE

KM# 5a DOPPIA

6.6700 g., Gold, 22 mm. **Ruler:** Vincenzo I **Obv:** Displayed eagle **Obv. Legend:** +VIN. D. G. DVX. MAN. IIII. ET. MO. F. II. **Rev:** Kneeling St. Francis receiving the stigmata, date in exergue **Rev. Legend:** SANCT - FRANCISCVS. **Note:** Ref. V-287. Possibly a gold strike of a Parpagliola.

Date	Mintage	VG	F	VF	XF	Unc
1608 Rare	—	—	—	—	—	—

KM# 21 DOPPIA

6.1000 g., Gold, 27-29 mm. **Ruler:** Francesco IV **Obv:** Busts of Francesco and Margherita facing each other, inscription with date in exergue **Obv. Legend:** FRANCISCVS. ET. MARGARITA. **Obv. Inscription:** DVCES / (date) **Rev:** Large daisy bloom in circle **Rev. Legend:** MANTVÆ. ET. MONTIS. FERRATI. **Note:** Ref. V-315; Fr. 185.

Date	Mintage	VG	F	VF	XF	Unc
1612 Rare	—	—	—	—	—	—

KM# 21A DOPPIA

Gold, 27-28 mm. **Ruler:** Francesco IV **Obv:** Large cross with small cross in each angle, all in circle **Obv. Legend:** FRANCISCVS. IIII. D. G. DVX. MANT. V. **Rev:** Crowned shield of 9-fold arms divides date **Rev. Legend:** ET. MONTIS. - FERRATI. III. **Note:** Ref. V-316; Fr. 186. Prev. KM#22.

Date	Mintage	VG	F	VF	XF	Unc
1612 Rare	—	—	—	—	—	—

KM# 27 DOPPIA

Gold Weight varies: 6.42-6.56g., 28-29 mm. **Ruler:** Ferdinando **Obv:** Armored bust to left wearing high collar **Obv. Legend:** FERDIN. D. G. DVX. MANTVÆ. VI. **Rev:** Crowned shield of Mantua arms, with central shield of manifold Monferrat arms, chain of order around, crown divides date **Rev. Legend:** ET. MONTIS. - FERRATI. IV. **Note:** Ref. V-322; Fr. 188.

Date	Mintage	VG	F	VF	XF	Unc
1617 GC	—	1,250	2,500	5,000	7,500	—
ND GC	—	1,250	2,500	4,400	6,900	—

KM# 46 DOPPIA

6.4100 g., Gold, 30 mm. **Ruler:** Vincenzo II **Obv:** Armored bust to left wearing high collar, date below shoulder **Obv. Legend:** VINCEN. II. D. G. DVX. MANT. VII. **Rev:** Crowned shield of Mantua arms, with central shield of manifold Monferrat arms, chain of order around **Rev. Legend:** ET. MONTIS. - FERRAT. V. **Note:** Ref. V-347; Fr. 191.

Date	Mintage	VG	F	VF	XF	Unc
1627	—	1,500	2,500	6,000	9,000	—

MB# 225 2 DOPPIE

Gold Weight varies: 11.71-13.10g., 36-37 mm. **Ruler:** Vincenzo I **Obv:** Mature bust to right **Obv. Legend:**

VINCENTIVS. D. G. DVX. MANT. IIII. **Rev:** Crowned shield of arms of Mantua, with central shield of manifold Casale arms, all in ornate frame, date divided at lower left and right **Rev. Legend:** ET. MONTIS - FERRATI. II. **Note:** Ref. V-286; Fr. 182. Prev. KM#7.

Date	Mintage	VG	F	VF	XF	Unc
1601	—	1,300	2,500	10,000	15,000	—

KM# 22 2 DOPPIE

12.8900 g., Gold, 27-28 mm. **Ruler:** Francesco IV **Obv:** Large cross with small cross in each angle, all in circle **Obv. Legend:** FRANCISCVS. IIII. D. G. DVX. MANT. V. **Rev:** Crowned shield of 9-fold arms divides date **Rev. Legend:** ET. MONTIS. - FERRATI. III. **Note:** Ref. V-314.

Date	Mintage	VG	F	VF	XF	Unc
1612 Rare	—	—	—	—	—	—

KM# 28 2 DOPPIE

Gold Weight varies: 12.95-13.06g., 28-29 mm. **Ruler:** Ferdinando **Obv:** Armored bust to left wearing high collar **Obv. Legend:** FERDIN. D. G. DVX. MANTVÆ. VI. **Rev:** Crowned shield of Mantua arms, with central shield of manifold Monferrat arms, chain of order around, crown divides date **Rev. Legend:** ET. MONTIS. - FERRATI. IV. **Note:** Ref. V-320; Fr. 187.

Date	Mintage	VG	F	VF	XF	Unc
1617 GC	—	1,000	2,000	5,600	10,000	—

KM# 39 2 DOPPIE

Gold Weight varies: 12.95-13.06g., 28-29 mm. **Ruler:** Ferdinando **Obv:** Armored bust to right wearing high collar, date below shoulder **Obv. Legend:** FERDIN. D. G. DVX. MAN. VI. ET. M. F. IIII. **Rev:** Crowned shield of Mantua arms, with central shield of manifold Monferrat arms, chain of order around **Rev. Legend:** ET. MONTIS. FERRATI. VI. ET. C. **Note:** Ref. V-321; Fr. 187.

Date	Mintage	VG	F	VF	XF	Unc
1621	—	1,000	2,000	5,600	10,000	—

KM# 74 5 DOPPIE

Gold, 43-44 mm. **Ruler:** Ferdinando **Obv:** Armored bust to right, wearing high collar **Obv. Legend:** FERDIN. D. G. DVX. MANT. VI. ET. M. F. IV. **Rev:** Recumbent stag to left, right leg resting on crowned shield of manifold arms **Rev. Legend:** ITA ANIMA MEA ADTE DEVS. **Note:** Ref. V-319; Fr. 189.

Date	Mintage	VG	F	VF	XF	Unc
ND(1612-26) Rare	—	—	—	—	—	—

SIEGE COINAGE

KM# 55 3 GROSSI (Fiorino)

Copper Weight varies: 1.90-2.87g., 15-16 mm. **Obv:** Crowned shield with 3 lilies, date at end of legend **Obv. Legend:** HIS. FAVENTIBVS. **Rev:** Two palm branches in cartouche, crown above, 'C' below, 'G - 3' to left and right **Rev. Legend:** OPPRESSA. BIS. EXALTOR.

Date	Mintage	VG	F	VF	XF	Unc
1630	—	550	1,100	3,000	5,000	—

KM# 56 5 FIORINI

Copper Weight varies: 3.81-5.81g., 25 mm. **Obv:** Crowned shield with 3 lilies divides F - 5 **Obv. Legend:** VOS. CANDIDI. ME. PVRA. **Rev:** Trophies and siren in circle, 'CASALE' in exergue, date at bottom in margin **Rev. Legend:** NEC. VI. NEC. FRAVDE. **Note:** Ref. V-356.

Date	Mintage	VG	F	VF	XF	Unc
1630	—	1,000	2,000	4,500	7,000	—

KM# 57.1 10 FIORINI

Copper Weight varies: 10.50-11.81g., 30 mm. **Obv:** Crowned shield with 3 lilies divides F - X **Obv. Legend:** HORVM. AVXILIO. NON. OPPRIMAR. **Rev:** Seated figure holding palm branch in double hexagonal frame, 'CASALE' in margin at bottom **Rev. Legend:** TENTATA. SED. INCORVPTA. **Note:** Ref. V-355. Prev. KM#57.

Date	Mintage	VG	F	VF	XF	Unc
ND(1630)	—	450	900	2,250	4,000	—

KM# 57.2 10 FIORINI

Copper Weight varies: 10.50-11.81g., 30 mm. **Obv:** Crowned shield with 3 lilies divides F - X **Obv. Legend:** HORVM. AVXILIO. NON. OPPRIMAR. **Rev:** Seated figure holding palm branch in double hexagonal frame, 'CASALE' with date above in margin at bottom **Rev. Legend:** TENTATA. SED. INCORVPTA. **Note:** Ref. V-355/1.

Date	Mintage	VG	F	VF	XF	Unc
1630	—	400	825	1,700	2,500	—

KM# 58.1 20 FIORINI

Copper Weight varies: 19.27-21.40g., 38-39 mm. **Obv:** Crowned shield with 3 lilies divides F - XX, 'CASALE' in exergue **Obv. Legend:** INSTAR. HORVM - FLORESCAM. **Rev:** Two full-length allegorical figures of Justice and Strength, 2-line inscription in exergue **Rev. Legend:** HIS. DVBICIVS. OMNIA. DOMANTVR. **Rev. Inscription:** TOIRACE. CLI / PEO. **Note:** Ref. V-354/1.

Date	Mintage	VG	F	VF	XF	Unc
ND(1630)	—	600	1,200	2,700	3,700	—

KM# 58.2 20 FIORINI

Copper Weight varies: 19.27-21.40g., 38-39 mm. **Obv:** Crowned shield with 3 lilies divides F - XX, 'CASALE' in exergue **Obv. Legend:** INSTAR. HORVM - FLORESCAM. **Rev:** Two full-length allegorical figures of Justice and Strength, 2-line inscription in exergue, date at bottom in margin **Rev. Legend:** HIS. DVBICIVS. OMNIA. DOMANTVR. **Rev. Inscription:** TOIRACE. CLI / PEO. **Note:** Ref. V-354. Prev. KM#58.

Date	Mintage	VG	F	VF	XF	Unc
1630	—	550	1,100	2,500	3,500	—

KM# 50.1 DUCATONE (12 Reali)

Silver Weight varies: 23.44-28.37g., 39-40 mm. **Ruler:** Carlo I **Obv:** Elongated octagonal tablet in ornamented frame containing 4-line inscription with date, value 'R - XII' divided above **Obv. Legend:** CAROLVS. D. G. DVX. MANTVÆ. VIII. **Obv. Inscription:** CASALIS / IN OBSIDE / INIVSTA / (date) **Rev:** Crowned shield of Mantua arms, with central shield of manifold Monferrat arms, chain of order around **Rev. Legend:** ET. MONTIS. - FERRATI. VI. **Note:** Ref. V-350; Dav. 3871. Prev. KM#50.

Date	Mintage	VG	F	VF	XF	Unc
1628	—	2,500	5,000	8,800	14,000	—

KM# 50.2 DUCATONE (12 Reali)

Silver Weight varies: 23.44-28.37g., 39-40 mm. **Ruler:** Carlo I **Obv:** elongated octagonal tablet in ornamented frame containing 4-line inscription with date, value 'R - VI' (error) divided above **Obv. Legend:** CAROLVS. D. G. DVX. MANTVÆ. VIII. **Obv. Inscription:** CASALIS / IN OBSIDE / INIVTA / (date) **Rev:** Crowned shield of Mantua arms, with central shield of manifold Monferrat arms, chain of order around **Rev. Legend:** ET. MONTIS. - FERRATI. VI. **Note:** Ref. V-350/1; Dav. 3871A.

Date	Mintage	VG	F	VF	XF	Unc
1628	—	3,000	6,000	10,000	16,000	—

KM# 50.3 DUCATONE (12 Reali)

Silver Weight varies: 23.44-28.37g., 39-40 mm. **Ruler:** Carlo I **Obv:** Elongated octagonal tablet in ornamented frame containing 4-line inscription with date, no indication of value **Obv. Legend:** CAROLVS. D. G. DVX. MANTVÆ. VIII. **Rev:** Crowned shield of Mantua arms, with central shield of manifold Monferrat arms, chain of order around **Rev. Legend:** ET. MONTIS. - FERRATI. VI. **Note:** Ref. V-350/2; Dav. 3871B.

Date	Mintage	VG	F	VF	XF	Unc
1628	—	3,000	6,000	10,000	16,000	—

CASTIGLIONE DELLE STIVIERE

Marquisate and Principality

This large, fortified town in the province of Brescia, just south of the Lago di Garda and about one-third of the way between Brescia and Mantua, came into the hands of the powerful Gonzaga family of Mantua in 1404. A branch of the Gonzagas ruled in Castiglione, first as marchesi, into the early 18th century, at which time coin production ceased. In 1609, the ruling marchese was raised to the rank of prince. Castiglione was taken by the Spanish and eventually became an imperial possession in 1772. The dispossessed princely line became extinct in the early 19th century.

RULERS

Ferrante Gonzaga, 1580-1586
Rodolfo Gonzaga, 1586-1593
Francesco Gonzaga, 1593-1616, Prince 1609
Ferdinand I Gonzaga, 1616-1678
Carlo Gonzaga, 1678-1680
Ferdinando II Gonzaga, 1680-1723
Luigi I Gonzaga, 1723-1768
Luigi II Gonzaga, 1768-1819

Reference:

V = Alberto Varesi, ***Monete Italiane Regionali: Lombardia, Zecche Minori***, Pavia, 1995.

PRINCIPALITY

STANDARD COINAGE

KM# 1 1/2 SOLDO (Mezzo Soldo)

Copper Weight varies: 0.78-0.87g., 17 mm. **Ruler:** Francesco **Obv:** Crowned FG (F retrograde) monogram in circle **Obv. Legend:** PRINC. CASTILLIONIS. EC. **Rev:** Dog rampant to left in circle **Rev. Legend:** FIDES. INCORRVPTA. **Note:** Ref. V-194. Prev. KM#41.

Date	Mintage	VG	F	VF	XF	Unc
ND(1609-16)	—	18.00	36.00	80.00	135	180

KM# 2 SOLDO

Copper Weight varies: 1.15-1.65g., 18 mm. **Ruler:** Francesco **Obv:** Crowned FG (F retrograde) monogram in circle **Obv. Legend:** PRINC. CASTILLIONIS. EC. **Rev:** Dog rampant to left in circle **Rev. Legend:** FIDES. INCORRVPTA. **Note:** Ref. V-193. Prev. KM#57.

Date	Mintage	VG	F	VF	XF	Unc
ND(1609-16)	—	11.00	22.50	50.00	80.00	115

KM# 14 SOLDO

Billon Weight varies: 1.27-2.10g., 21 mm. **Ruler:** Ferdinando I **Obv:** Crowned shield of 4-fold arms, with central shield **Obv. Legend:** FER. D. G. S. R. I. ET. CAS. PRIN. **Rev:** Pyx in circle **Rev. Legend:** QVOS. PRETIOSO. SANG. REDEMISTI. **Note:** Ref. V-221/1. Prev. KM#30. Prev. listed as a Muraiola.

Date	Mintage	VG	F	VF	XF	Unc
ND(1616-78)	—	36.00	80.00	160	270	—

KM# 15 SOLDO

Billon Weight varies: 1.27-2.10g., 21 mm. **Ruler:** Ferdinando I **Obv:** Crowned shield of 4-fold arms, with central shield **Obv. Legend:** FER. D. G. S. R. I. ET. CAS. PRIN. **Rev:** Pyx in circle **Rev. Legend:** TVRRIS. FORTITVDINIS. **Note:** Ref. V-221/2. Prev. KM#31.

Date	Mintage	VG	F	VF	XF	Unc
ND(1616-78)	—	36.00	80.00	160	270	—

KM# 16 SOLDO

1.1000 g., Billon, 16 mm. **Ruler:** Ferdinando I **Obv:** Crowned shield of Savoy arms (plain cross) in circle **Obv. Legend:** FER. D. G. PRIN. CASTI. **Rev:** St. Maurice cross with double-C monograms in angles, one C in each pair is retrograde **Rev. Legend:** IN. TE. DOMINE. CONF. **Note:** Ref. V-222. Prev. KM#32. Prev. listed as a Muraiola.

Date	Mintage	VG	F	VF	XF	Unc
ND(1616-78)	—	36.00	80.00	160	270	—

KM# 17 SOLDO

Billon Weight varies: 0.90-1.04g., 15 mm. **Ruler:** Ferdinando I **Obv:** Spade-shaped shield with cross and small star at left, top and right **Obv. Legend:** FERD. D. G. CAST. PRIN. **Rev:** Madonna and Child, 2 small stars in exergue **Rev. Legend:** REGINA. COELI. **Note:** Ref. V-223. Prev. KM#34. Prev. listed as a Muraiola.

Date	Mintage	VG	F	VF	XF	Unc
ND(1616-78)	—	36.00	80.00	160	270	—

KM# 13 SOLDO

Billon Weight varies: 1.40-2.05g., 21 mm. **Ruler:** Ferdinando I **Obv:** Crowned shield of 4-fold arms, with central shield **Obv. Legend:** FERDI. D. G. S. R. I. ET. CASTI. PR. **Rev:** Full-length facing nimbate figure of St. Nazario holding palm frond **Rev. Legend:** S. NAZARIVS. PATR. CASTI. **Note:** Ref. V-220. Prev. KM#27. Prev. listed as a Parpagliola.

Date	Mintage	VG	F	VF	XF	Unc
ND(1616-78)	—	10.00	22.00	45.00	65.00	110

KM# 18 SOLDO

0.8500 g., Billon, 18 mm. **Ruler:** Ferdinando I **Obv:** Crowned displayed eagle **Obv. Legend:** FERDINANDVS. D. G. PRINC. CAST. **Rev:** Facing crowned head of steer **Rev. Legend:** MARCHIO. MEDVLARVM. **Note:** Ref. V-224.

Date	Mintage	VG	F	VF	XF	Unc
ND(1616-78)	—	45.00	100	180	295	450

KM# 62 SOLDO

1.6500 g., Billon, 20-21 mm. **Ruler:** Ferdinando I **Obv:** Crowned displayed eagle **Obv. Legend:** FERDI. D. G. PRIN. CASTI. **Rev:** St. Louis kneeling to left, date below **Rev. Legend:** BEATVS. ALVVIGI. **Note:** Ref. V-218. Prev. KM#44.

Date	Mintage	VG	F	VF	XF	Unc
1657	—	80.00	160	325	550	—

KM# 64 SOLDO

Billon Weight varies: 1.33-1.80g., 20-21 mm. **Ruler:** Ferdinando I **Obv:** Crowned snake in circle, date at end of legend **Obv. Legend:** FERD. D. G. CAST. PRIN. **Rev:** St. Peter standing with keys **Rev. Legend:** IANITOR. - COELI. **Note:** Ref. V-219. Prev. KM#43.

Date	Mintage	VG	F	VF	XF	Unc
1666	—	35.00	75.00	200	350	—

KM# 67 SOLDO

Copper Weight varies: 1.07-1.10g., 20 mm. **Ruler:** Carlo **Obv:** Crowned CG (C retrograde) monogram in cartouche **Obv. Legend:** PRINC. CASTILLIONIS. **Rev:** Dog rampant to left in beaded circle **Rev. Legend:** FIDES. INCORRVPTA. **Note:** Ref. V-249. Prev. KM#87.

Date	Mintage	VG	F	VF	XF	Unc
ND(1678-80)	—	55.00	110	205	350	—

KM# 68 SOLDO

Copper, 20 mm. **Ruler:** Carlo **Obv:** Shield of 6-fold arms **Obv. Legend:** CAR. D. G. S. R. I. P. CASTI. PRI. **Rev:** Standing figure of St. Hilary **Rev. Legend:** S. HILARIVS. PATR. CAST. **Note:** Ref. V-250. Prev. KM#88.

Date	Mintage	VG	F	VF	XF	Unc
ND(1678-80)	—	160	350	575	1,150	—

KM# 70 SOLDO

Billon Weight varies: 1.63-2.24g., 18 mm. **Ruler:** Ferdinando II **Obv:** Crowned displayed eagle **Obv. Legend:** FER. II. D. G. PRIN. CASTIL. **Rev:** Nimbate figure of St. Aloysius kneeling to left **Rev. Legend:** B. ALOYSIVS. GON. PAT. NOSTER. **Note:** Ref. V-255.

Date	Mintage	VG	F	VF	XF	Unc
ND(1680-1723)	—	45.00	100	160	250	450

KM# 71 SOLDO

Billon Weight varies: 1.63-2.24g., 18 mm. **Ruler:** Ferdinando II **Obv:** Crowned displayed eagle **Obv. Legend:** FER. II. D. G. PRIN. CASTIL. **Rev:** Nimbate figure of St. Aloysius kneeling to left **Rev. Legend:** BEATVS. ALVYSI. **Note:** Ref. 255/1.

Date	Mintage	VG	F	VF	XF	Unc
ND(1680-1723)	—	70.00	145	245	350	575

KM# 84 SOLDO

Billon Weight varies: 1.02-1.30. Prev. listed as a Sesino. **Ruler:** Ferdinando II **Obv:** Armored bust to left **Obv. Legend:** FER. II. PRIN. CASTI. **Rev:** Radiant sun, date at end of legend **Rev. Legend:** MARC. MANTVE. ET. MED. S. D. EC. **Note:** Ref. V-256. Prev. KM#92.

Date	Mintage	VG	F	VF	XF	Unc
1683	—	70.00	145	245	350	575

KM# 19 SESINO

Billon Weight varies: 0.66-1.06g., 17 mm. **Ruler:** Ferdinando I **Obv:** Crowned shield of 4-fold arms, with central shield, in baroque frame **Obv. Legend:** FER. GON. PRI. **Rev:** 3-line inscription, rosette above and below **Rev. Inscription:** SESIN / V.S / CASTI **Note:** Ref. V-226. Prev. KM#5.

Date	Mintage	VG	F	VF	XF	Unc
ND(1616-78)	—	32.50	65.00	125	225	—

KM# 20 SESINO

0.7000 g., Billon, 17 mm. **Ruler:** Ferdinando I **Obv:** Crowned displayed eagle in circle, no legend **Rev:** Standing facing figure of St. Nazar holding palm frond **Rev. Legend:** S. NAZARIVS. P. C. **Note:** Ref. V-225. Prev. KM#6.

Date	Mintage	VG	F	VF	XF	Unc
ND(1616-78)	—	32.50	65.00	125	225	—

KM# 21 SESINO

0.7200 g., Billon, 17 mm. **Ruler:** Ferdinando I **Obv:** Crowned oval shield of Medici arms (six balls in circle) **Obv. Legend:** FER. D. G. CAST. PRIN. **Rev:** Standing figure of St. John the Baptist **Rev. Legend:** S. IOANES. BAPTIST. **Note:** Ref. V-227.

Date	Mintage	VG	F	VF	XF	Unc
ND(1616-78)	—	22.50	50.00	90.00	135	225

KM# 22 SESINO

Billon Weight varies: 0.57-0.84g., 15 mm. **Ruler:** Ferdinando I **Obv:** Head to right **Obv. Legend:** FERDI. D. G. PRIN. CAST. **Rev:** Crowned displayed eagle **Rev. Legend:** MARCHIO. MEDVL. **Note:** Ref. V-228.

Date	Mintage	VG	F	VF	XF	Unc
ND(1616-78)	—	22.50	50.00	90.00	135	225

KM# 72 SESINO

Billon Weight varies: 0.68-1.05g., 18 mm. **Ruler:** Ferdinando II **Obv:** Armored bust to right **Obv. Legend:** FER. II. PRIN. CAS. **Rev:** 3-line inscription **Rev. Inscription:** SESIN / VS / CASTI **Note:** Ref. V-257/1. Prev. KM#93.

Date	Mintage	VG	F	VF	XF	Unc
ND(1680-1723)	—	32.50	65.00	125	225	—

KM# 73 SESINO

Billon Weight varies: 0.58-0.86g., 16-17 mm. **Ruler:** Ferdinando II **Obv:** 3-line inscription **Obv. Inscription:** FER / II / S R I **Rev:** 3-line inscription **Rev. Inscription:** PRI / CAST / ETC **Note:** Ref. V-258. Prev. KM#95.

Date	Mintage	VG	F	VF	XF	Unc
ND(1680-1723)	—	45.00	80.00	145	270	—

KM# 74 SESINO

Billon Weight varies: 0.71-1.01g., 17 mm. **Ruler:** Ferdinando II **Obv:** Armored bust to right **Obv. Legend:** FER. II. PRIN. CAS. **Rev:** 3-line inscription in wreath **Rev. Inscription:** MEDV / MAR / ETC **Note:** Ref. V-259. Prev. KM#96.

Date	Mintage	VG	F	VF	XF	Unc
ND(1680-1723)	—	45.00	80.00	145	270	—

KM# 75 SESINO

Billon Weight varies: 0.71-1.01g., 17 mm. **Ruler:** Ferdinando II **Obv:** Armored bust to right **Obv. Legend:** FER. II. PRIN. CAS. **Rev:** 3-line inscription in wreath **Rev. Inscription:** MAR / MEDV / ETC **Note:** Ref. V-259/1. Prev. KM#97.

Date	Mintage	VG	F	VF	XF	Unc
ND(1680-1723)	—	45.00	80.00	145	270	—

KM# 76 SESINO

1.2500 g., Billon, 17 mm. **Ruler:** Ferdinando II **Obv:** Crowned oval shield of Medici arms (6 small balls in circle) **Obv. Legend:** FERD. II. D. G. P. CAST. **Rev:** Standing facing figure of St. John the Baptist holding cross on long staff **Rev. Legend:** S. IOANNES. BAPTIS. **Note:** Ref. V-261. Prev. KM#98.

Date	Mintage	VG	F	VF	XF	Unc
ND(1680-1723)	—	45.00	70.00	145	270	—

KM# 77 SESINO

1.4800 g., Billon, 18 mm. **Ruler:** Ferdinando II **Obv:** Bust to right **Obv. Legend:** FER. II. PRIN. CAS. **Rev:** Ornate cross **Rev. Legend:** CAST. C... **Note:** Ref. V-260.

Date	Mintage	VG	F	VF	XF	Unc
ND(1680-1723)	—	90.00	180	270	375	575

KM# 85 SESINO

Billon Weight varies: 0.68-1.05g., 18 mm. **Ruler:** Ferdinando II **Obv:** Armored bust to right, date below **Obv. Legend:** FER. II. PRIN. CAS. **Rev:** 3-line inscription **Rev. Inscription:** PRI / CAST / ETC **Note:** Ref. V-257/2. Prev. KM#94.

Date	Mintage	VG	F	VF	XF	Unc
1688	—	45.00	80.00	145	270	—

KM# 23 QUATTRINO

0.7000 g., Copper, 16 mm. **Ruler:** Ferdinando I **Obv:** Head to left **Obv. Legend:** FERDIN. GONZ. M. CA. **Rev:** Facing standing figure of St. Peter **Rev. Legend:** S. PETRVS. D. CAS. **Note:** Ref. V-230. Prev. KM#7.

Date	Mintage	VG	F	VF	XF	Unc
ND1616-78)	—	45.00	70.00	145	280	—

KM# 24 QUATTRINO

Copper Weight varies: 0.50-0.65g., 15-16 mm. **Ruler:** Ferdinando I **Obv:** Crowned shield of 4-fold arms **Obv. Legend:** FERDI. GONZ. **Rev:** Facing standing figure of St. Peter holding keys **Rev. Legend:** S. PETRVS. D. CAS. **Note:** Ref. V-231. Prev. KM#8.

Date	Mintage	VG	F	VF	XF	Unc
ND(1616-78)	—	22.50	45.00	90.00	180	—

KM# 25 QUATTRINO

0.4100 g., Copper, 16 mm. **Ruler:** Ferdinando I **Obv:** Shield of 4-fold arms **Obv. Legend:** F. R. D. GON. **Rev:** Figure of St. Serus standing **Rev. Legend:** S. SIRVS. CASTIV. **Note:** Ref. V-232. Prev. KM#9.

Date	Mintage	VG	F	VF	XF	Unc
ND(1616-78)	—	90.00	180	400	800	—

KM# 26 QUATTRINO

1.0500 g., Copper, 15 mm. **Ruler:** Ferdinando I **Obv:** Crowned shield of 4-fold arms in baroque frame **Obv. Legend:** FER. D. G. S. R. I. E. C. P. **Rev:** Bust of St. Ignatius to right **Rev. Legend:** SANCTVS. IGNATIVS. **Note:** Ref. V-229.

Date	Mintage	VG	F	VF	XF	Unc
ND(1616-78)	—	36.00	80.00	125	180	250

KM# 27 QUATTRINO

Copper Weight varies: 0.60-0.90g., 16-17 mm. **Ruler:** Ferdinando I **Obv:** Large 'F' in circle **Obv. Legend:** FERD. D. G. S. R. IMPE. **Rev:** Flame in circle **Rev. Legend:** ET. CAST. PRIN. **Note:** Ref. V-233. Prev. KM#10.

Date	Mintage	VG	F	VF	XF	Unc
ND(1616-78)	—	22.50	45.00	90.00	180	—

KM# 28 QUATTRINO

Copper Weight varies: 0.47-1.61g., 18 mm. **Ruler:** Ferdinando I **Obv:** Crowned shield of 4-fold arms in baroque frame **Obv. Legend:** FERDI. D. G. PRIN. CASTI. **Rev:** Standing facing figure of St. John the Baptist holding cross **Rev. Legend:** S. IONNES. BAPTISTA. **Note:** Ref. V-234. Prev. KM#11.

Date	Mintage	VG	F	VF	XF	Unc
ND(1616-78)	—	22.50	45.00	90.00	180	—

KM# 29 QUATTRINO

Copper Weight varies: 0.62-0.90g., 16 mm. **Ruler:** Ferdinando I **Obv:** Shield of Medici arms (6 balls in 3 rows) **Obv. Legend:** FER. D. G. CAST. PRIN. **Rev:** Facing figure of St. John the Baptist holding cross **Rev. Legend:** S. IONES. BAPTISTA. **Note:** Ref. V-235. Prev. KM#12.

Date	Mintage	VG	F	VF	XF	Unc
ND(1616-78)	—	22.50	45.00	90.00	180	—

KM# 30 QUATTRINO

Copper Weight varies: 0.39-0.80g., 15 mm. **Ruler:** Ferdinando I **Obv:** Displayed eagle in crowned ornamented shield **Obv. Legend:** FE - RD. GO - N. **Rev:** Standing figure of St. Peter holding keys **Rev. Legend:** S. PETRVS - CASTIV. **Note:** Ref. V-237. Prev. KM#14.

Date	Mintage	VG	F	VF	XF	Unc
ND(1616-78)	—	45.00	70.00	145	280	—

KM# 31 QUATTRINO

0.5000 g., Copper, 15 mm. **Ruler:** Ferdinando I **Obv:** Oval shield with rampant lion to left, crossed keys above **Obv. Legend:** FER. - GON. **Rev:** Bust of St. Paternian to left holding crozier **Rev. Legend:** S. PATERNIANVS. **Note:** Ref. V-238. Prev. KM#15.

Date	Mintage	VG	F	VF	XF	Unc
ND(1616-78)	—	55.00	115	225	450	—

KM# 32 QUATTRINO

Copper Weight varies: 0.64-0.67g., 16-17 mm. **Ruler:** Ferdinando I **Obv:** Oval shield with rampant lion to left, crossed keys above **Obv. Legend:** FER. - GON. **Rev:** Full-length facing figure of St. Cyriac holding cross **Rev. Legend:** S. CVRIA - CVS. CAS. **Note:** Ref. V-239. Prev. KM#16.

Date	Mintage	VG	F	VF	XF	Unc
ND(1616-78)	—	22.50	45.00	90.00	180	—

KM# 33 QUATTRINO

0.8900 g., Copper, 16-17 mm. **Ruler:** Ferdinando I **Obv:** Crowed displayed eagle in circle **Obv. Legend:** FERDI. D. G. P. ET. CAST. PRIN. **Rev:** Crowned snake in circle **Rev. Legend:** MARCHIO. MEDVLARVM. **Note:** Ref. V-240. Prev. KM#17.

Date	Mintage	VG	F	VF	XF	Unc
ND(1616-78)	—	45.00	70.00	145	280	—

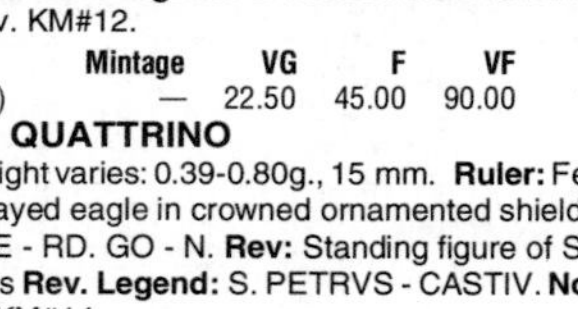

KM# 34 QUATTRINO

Copper Weight varies: 1.18-1.47g., 18 mm. **Ruler:** Ferdinando I **Obv:** High-collared bust to right **Obv. Legend:** FER. D. G. S. R. IIII. ET. C. P. **Rev:** Crowned snake **Rev. Legend:** MARCHIO. MEDOLANI. **Note:** Ref. V-241. Prev. KM#18.

Date	Mintage	VG	F	VF	XF	Unc
ND(1616-78)	—	27.50	55.00	115	225	—

KM# 35 QUATTRINO

Copper Weight varies: 0.83-1.15g., 14 mm. **Ruler:** Ferdinando I **Obv:** Bust to right **Obv. Legend:** FER. D. G. ... **Rev:** 4-fold arms with central shield **Rev. Legend:** MEDVLARV. **Note:** Ref. V-242. Prev. KM#19.

Date	Mintage	VG	F	VF	XF	Unc
ND(1616-78)	—	22.50	45.00	90.00	180	—

KM# 36 QUATTRINO

Copper Weight varies: 0.83-1.15g., 14 mm. **Ruler:** Ferdinando I **Obv:** High-collared bust to right **Obv. Legend:** FER. D. G. .... **Rev:** 4-fold arms with central shield **Rev. Legend:** MARCHIO. MEDVLARV. **Note:** Ref. V-242/1.

Date	Mintage	VG	F	VF	XF	Unc
ND(1616-78)	—	27.50	60.00	100	145	245

KM# 37 QUATTRINO

Copper Weight varies: 0.54-0.85g., 14-15 mm. **Ruler:** Ferdinando I **Obv:** Large crowned 'F' **Obv. Legend:** FERD. D. G. S. R. I. E. CAS. PRI. **Rev:** 4-fold arms **Rev. Legend:** MARCHIO. MEDVLAR. **Note:** Ref. V-243. Prev. KM#20.

Date	Mintage	VG	F	VF	XF	Unc
ND(1616-78)	—	45.00	70.00	145	280	—

KM# 63 QUATTRINO

Copper Weight varies: 0.64-1.04g., 15-16 mm. **Ruler:** Ferdinando I **Obv:** Large ornate 'L' with partial date divided by vertical part of letter **Obv. Legend:** FER. D. G. CAS. PRINC. **Rev:** Facing crowned bust of St. Vultus, turned slightly to left **Rev. Legend:** SANCTVS. VVLTVS. **Note:** Ref. V-236. Prev. KM#13.

Date	Mintage	VG	F	VF	XF	Unc
(16)65	—	22.50	45.00	90.00	180	—

KM# 38 MURAIOLA

Billon Weight varies: 0.82-1.36g., 20-21 mm. **Ruler:** Ferdinando I **Obv:** Bust of St. Peter to right as the first pope **Obv. Legend:** S. PETRVS. PONTI. MAX. **Rev:** Full-length facing figure of St. Anthony holding crozier **Rev. Legend:** S. ANTONIVS. PROT. CAST. **Note:** Ref. V-217. Prev. KM#28.

Date	Mintage	VG	F	VF	XF	Unc
ND(1616-78)	—	32.00	65.00	130	175	240

KM# 39 MURAIOLA

Billon Weight varies: 0.82-1.36g., 20-21 mm. **Ruler:** Ferdinando I **Obv:** Bust of St. Peter to right as first pope **Obv. Legend:** S. PETRVS. PONTI. MAX. **Rev:** Full-length facing figure of St. Martin **Rev. Legend:** S. MARTIN. CAST. PROT. **Note:** Ref. V-217/2. Prev. KM#29.

Date	Mintage	VG	F	VF	XF	Unc
ND(1616-78)	—	40.00	90.00	185	265	350

KM# 40 PARPAGLIOLA

Billon Weight varies: 1.45-2.02g., 18 mm. **Ruler:** Ferdinando I **Obv:** Crowned shield of 4-fold arms **Obv. Legend:** FER. D. G. S. R. I. ET. CAST. PRI. **Rev:** Female facing figure holding stick **Rev. Legend:** PRVDE - NTIA. **Note:** Ref. V-216. Prev. KM#25.

Date	Mintage	VG	F	VF	XF	Unc
ND(1616-78)	—	48.00	105	175	265	350

KM# 41 PARPAGLIOLA

Billon Weight varies: 1.45-2.02g., 18 mm. **Ruler:** Ferdinando I **Obv:** Crowned shield of 4-fold arms **Obv. Legend:** FER. D. G. S. R. I. ET. CAST. PRI. **Rev:** Female facing figure holding stick **Rev. Legend:** FORTI - TVDO. **Note:** Ref. V-216/1. Prev. KM#26.

Date	Mintage	VG	F	VF	XF	Unc
ND(1616-78)	—	45.00	80.00	135	200	—

KM# 78 PARPAGLIOLA

Billon Weight varies: 1.40-2.20g., 22 mm. **Ruler:** Carlo **Obv:** Crowned CG monogram (C retrograde) in cartouche **Obv. Legend:** PRINC. CASTILLIONIS. ETC. **Rev:** Full-length facing figure of St. Aloysius **Rev. Legend:** B. ALOYSIVS. GON. PATR. CAST. **Note:** Ref. V-248.

Date	Mintage	VG	F	VF	XF	Unc
ND	—	19.00	44.75	90.00	130	215

KM# 42 GIORGINO

Billon Weight varies: 1.30-2.05g., 21-22 mm. **Ruler:** Ferdinando I **Obv:** Bust to right **Obv. Legend:** FERD. D. G. CAST. PRINC. **Rev:** Kneeling saint **Rev. Legend:** PROTECTOR - NOSTER. **Note:** Ref. V-212/1. Prev. KM#36.

Date	Mintage	VG	F	VF	XF	Unc
ND(1616-78)	—	48.00	105	200	325	525

KM# 43 GIORGINO

Billon Weight varies: 1.30-2.05g., 21-22 mm. **Ruler:** Ferdinando I **Obv:** Bust to right **Obv. Legend:** FERD. D. G. CAST. PRINC. **Rev:** Kneeling figure of St. Nicolas **Rev. Legend:** S. NICOL. - PROTE. **Note:** Ref. V-212/2. Prev. KM#37.

Date	Mintage	VG	F	VF	XF	Unc
ND(1616-78)	—	65.00	135	255	400	600

KM# 44 GIORGINO

Billon Weight varies: 1.30-2.05g., 21-22 mm. **Ruler:** Ferdinando I **Obv:** Bust to right **Obv. Legend:** FERD. D. G. CAST. PRINC. **Rev:** Kneeling figure of St. Martin **Rev. Legend:** S. MARTINVS. - PATR. **Note:** Ref. V-212/3. Prev. KM#38.

Date	Mintage	VG	F	VF	XF	Unc
ND(1616-78)	—	105	225	350	525	725

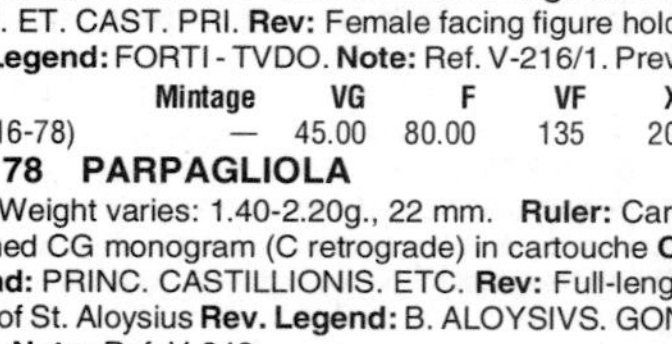

KM# 45 4 SOLDI

Billon Weight varies: 1.31-2.28g., 21 mm. **Ruler:** Ferdinando I

Obv: Crowned shield of 4-fold arms, with central shield **Obv. Legend:** FERDI. D. G. P. CAST. **Rev:** Full-length facing female figure **Rev. Legend:** MALVIT. MORI. QVAM. FĐDARI. **Note:** Ref. V-215. Prev. KM#77.

Date	Mintage	VG	F	VF	XF	Unc
ND(1616-78)	—	32.00	70.00	150	240	375

KM# 65 4 SOLDI

Billon Weight varies: 1.63-2.25g. **Ruler:** Ferdinando I **Obv:** Bust to left **Obv. Legend:** FERD. D. G. CAST. PRINC. **Rev:** Crowned shield of 4-fold arms in baroque frame, date below **Rev. Legend:** MARCHIO. - MEDVL. ETC. **Note:** Ref. V-214. Prev. KM#76.

Date	Mintage	VG	F	VF	XF	Unc
1666	—	90.00	160	300	475	725

KM# 46 5 SOLDI

Billon Weight varies: 1.41-2.05g., 20 mm. **Ruler:** Ferdinando I **Obv:** Crowned shield of manifold arms in baroque frame **Obv. Legend:** FER. D. G. S. R. I. ET. CAS. PRIN. **Rev:** Half-length facing figure of the Virgin, value 'V' in exergue **Rev. Legend:** ITER. PARA. TVTVM. **Note:** Ref. V-213. Prev. KM#78.

Date	Mintage	VG	F	VF	XF	Unc
ND(1616-78)	—	32.00	70.00	160	265	450

KM# 69 1/2 LIRA

Billon Weight varies: 1.62-2.40g., 25 mm. **Ruler:** Carlo **Obv:** Large crown above shield of 6-fold arms in baroque frame **Obv. Legend:** CAROLVS. DG. CAST. PRINC. **Rev:** Half-length facing figure of St. Nicolas, wearing miter and holding crozier **Rev. Legend:** S. NICOLAVS. SOLE. PROT. **Note:** Ref. V-247. Prev. KM#85.

Date	Mintage	VG	F	VF	XF	Unc
1678	—	110	175	375	550	800
1679	—	110	175	375	550	800

KM# 47 8 SOLDI

Billon Weight varies: 1.45-2.25g., 23 mm. **Ruler:** Ferdinando I **Obv:** Value '8' between 2 rosettes above 6-line inscription **Obv. Inscription:** FERDI(N) / D. G. S. R. I. / E. CAST(IL). (P) / (PRIN). ET / MARCH / M(*)E. **Rev:** Radiant sun in circle **Rev. Legend:** VBIQVE. FVLGET. **Note:** Ref. V-211. Varieties exist. Prev. KM#80.

Date	Mintage	VG	F	VF	XF	Unc
ND(1616-78)	—	40.00	90.00	185	265	400

KM# 66 8 SOLDI

Billon Weight varies: 2.56-2.75g., 27 mm. **Ruler:** Ferdinando I **Obv:** Bust to left in partial circle **Obv. Legend:** FERD. D. G. CAST. PRIN. **Rev:** Crowned displayed eagle at left, crowned snake at right, all in circle, date below in margin **Rev. Legend:** BENE. CONVENIVT. **Note:** Ref. V-210. Prev. KM#79.

Date	Mintage	VG	F	VF	XF	Unc
1666	—	130	230	550	875	1,300

KM# 49 12 SOLDI

2.3000 g., Billon Weight varies: 2.30-2.35g., 25 mm. **Ruler:** Ferdinando I **Obv:** Crowned Spanish shield of 6-fold arms in circle **Obv. Legend:** + MONETA. NOVA. ARGENTIA. CH. **Rev:** Crowned imperial eagle, 12 in orb on breast **Rev. Legend:** SVB. VMBRA. ALARVM. TVARVM. **Note:** Ref. V-245, 246. Varieties exist. Prev. KM#125.

Date	Mintage	VG	F	VF	XF	Unc
ND(1616-78) Rare	—	—	—	—	—	—

KM# 48 12 SOLDI

2.3000 g., Billon, 25 mm. **Ruler:** Ferdinando I **Obv:** Spanish shield of 4-fold arms, ornate crowned helmet above with eagle crest **Obv. Legend:** MONETA. NOVA. ARGENTIA. CH. **Rev:** Crowned imperial eagle, 12 in circle on breast **Rev. Legend:** + INITIVM. SAPIENTIAE. TIMOR. DOMINI **Note:** Ref. V-244. Prev. KM#124.

Date	Mintage	VG	F	VF	XF	Unc
ND(1616-78) Rare	—	—	—	—	—	—

KM# 3 GROSSETTO

Silver Weight varies: 0.76-1.01g., 17 mm. **Ruler:** Francesco **Obv:** Crowned displayed eagle in circle **Obv. Legend:** FRANCISCVS. D. G. PRIN. CAST. **Rev:** Crowned facing head of steer in circle **Rev. Legend:** CASTIONI. MARCH. M. ETC. **Note:** Ref. V-187. Prev. KM#56.

Date	Mintage	VG	F	VF	XF	Unc
ND(1609-16)	—	48.00	95.00	175	350	450

KM# 4 GROSSETTO

Silver Weight varies: 0.76-1.01g., 17 mm. **Ruler:** Francesco **Obv:** Crowned displayed eagle in circle **Obv. Legend:** FRANCISCVS. D. G. PRIN. CAST. **Rev:** Crowned facing head of steer in circle **Rev. Legend:** MARCHIO. MEDVLARVM. ET. C. **Note:** Ref. V-187/1. Prev. KM#58.

Date	Mintage	VG	F	VF	XF	Unc
ND(1609-16)	—	48.00	95.00	175	350	450

KM# 5 GROSSETTO

0.8900 g., Silver, 17 mm. **Ruler:** Francesco **Obv:** Crowned displayed eagle in circle **Obv. Legend:** FRANCISCVS. D. G. PRINC. CAST. **Rev:** Six-pointed star **Rev. Legend:** MARCHIO. MEDVLARVM. ET. C. **Note:** Ref. V-188. Prev. KM#59.

Date	Mintage	VG	F	VF	XF	Unc
ND(1609-16)	—	65.00	130	265	450	650

KM# 50 BIANCO (10 Soldi)

3.9000 g., Billon, 26 mm. **Ruler:** Ferdinando I **Obv:** Crowned shield of 4-fold arms, with central shield, in baroque frame **Obv. Legend:** FERD. GON. MARCH. CAS. **Rev:** Floriated cross with lily in each angle **Rev. Legend:** A STIV. SAC. ROMA. IMPER. PRIN. **Note:** Ref. V-209. Prev. KM#45.

Date	Mintage	VG	F	VF	XF	Unc
ND(1616-78)	—	350	550	850	1,600	—

KM# 79 25 SOLDI

Silver Weight varies: 4.32-5.15g., 30-31 mm. **Ruler:** Ferdinando II **Obv:** Armored bust to right, value (XXV) below shoulder **Obv. Legend:** FERD. II. S. RO. IMPERII. ET. CAST. PRIN. **Rev:** Crowned imperial eagle, Oval shield of 4-fold arms with central shield on breast **Rev. Legend:** MAN. ET. MED. M. S. D. HISP. MAG. ETC. **Note:** Ref. V-254. Prev. KM#91.

Date	Mintage	VG	F	VF	XF	Unc
ND(1680-1732)	—	55.00	110	220	450	650

KM# 83 25 SOLDI

4.4900 g., Silver, 30-31 mm. **Ruler:** Ferdinando II **Obv:** Armored bust to right in beaded circle, value (XXV) below in margin **Obv. Legend:** FERDI. II. S. R. IMPE. - ET. CAST. PRINC. **Rev:** Ornate shield of manifold arms in beaded circle, crown above divides date **Rev. Legend:** MANT. MED. M. S. D. ET. HISP. MAG. ETC. **Note:** Ref. V-253a. Prev. KM#90.

Date	Mintage	VG	F	VF	XF	Unc
1682	—	190	350	625	1,050	1,700
1685	—	190	350	625	1,050	1,700

KM# 55 FIORINO

Silver, 31 mm. **Ruler:** Ferdinando I **Obv:** Crowned shield of 4-fold arms, date at end of legend **Obv. Legend:** MONETA. NOVA. MARC. CHA. ST. **Rev:** Crowned imperial eagle in circle **Rev. Legend:** INITIVM. SAPIENTIE. TIMOR. DOMINE. **Note:** Ref. V-206. Prev. KM#126.

Date	Mintage	VG	F	VF	XF	Unc
1617	—	950	1,400	3,750	5,300	—

KM# 56 FIORINO

Silver, 31 mm. **Ruler:** Ferdinando I **Obv:** Crowned shield of 4-fold arms, date at end of legend **Obv. Legend:** MONETA. NOVA. ARGENT. EACHA. **Rev:** Crowned imperial eagle in circle **Rev. Legend:** SIT. NOMEN. DOMINI. BENEDICTVM. **Note:** Ref. V-206/1. Prev. KM#127.

Date	Mintage	VG	F	VF	XF	Unc
1617	—	950	1,400	3,750	5,300	—

KM# 11 LIRA (Mezzo Testone)

Silver Weight varies: 4.79-4.90g., 25-26 mm. **Ruler:** Francesco **Obv:** Bust to right, date below **Obv. Legend:** FRANC. D. G. PRINCEPS. CASTILIONI. **Rev:** Crowned shield of 4-fold arms, with central shield, Order of Golden Fleece around **Rev. Legend:** MARCHI. MEDVLARVM. ETC. **Note:** Ref. V-181. Prev. KM#46.

Date	Mintage	VG	F	VF	XF	Unc
1614	—	220	450	825	1,400	2,050

KM# 51 LIRA (Mezzo Testone)

Silver Weight varies: 4.08-4.78g., 28-29 mm. **Ruler:** Ferdinando I **Obv:** Crowned shield of 4-fold arms, with central shield, in baroque frame **Obv. Legend:** FERDINANDVS. D. G. PRIN. CASTI. **Rev:** Full-length facing figure of St. Aloysius **Rev. Legend:** B. ALOYSIVS. GO. - PATRONVS. CAS. **Note:** Ref. V-207. Varieties exist. Prev. KM#60.

Date	Mintage	VG	F	VF	XF	Unc
ND(1616-78)	—	350	575	1,150	1,750	—

KM# 52 LIRA (Mezzo Testone)

Silver Weight varies: 3.98-4.66g., 28 mm. **Ruler:** Ferdinando I **Obv:** Crowned shield of 4-fold arms, with central shield, in baroque frame **Obv. Legend:** FERDINANDVS. D. G. PRIN. CAST. **Rev:** Full-length facing figure of St. Paul **Rev. Legend:** TV. ES. VAS. E - LECTIONIS. **Note:** Ref. V-208.

Date	Mintage	VG	F	VF	XF	Unc
ND(1616-78)	—	220	400	1,000	1,400	—

KM# 80 1/3 TALLERO

7.3400 g., Silver, 34 mm. **Ruler:** Ferdinando II **Obv:** Draped bust to right **Obv. Legend:** FERDINANDVS. II. SAC. RO. IMPER. **Rev:** Three small shields of arms, 1 above 2, with crown over upper shield, small tower below, all in circle **Rev. Legend:** ET. CAST. PRIN. MED. MAR. SOL. DOM. ETC. **Note:** Ref. V-253. Prev. KM#61.

Date	Mintage	VG	F	VF	XF	Unc
ND(1680-1723)	—	1,250	2,050	4,750	8,300	—

KM# 81 2/3 TALLERO

Silver Weight varies: 16.97-17.27g., 38 mm. **Ruler:** Ferdinando II **Obv:** Draped bust to right, value (2/3) in oval below shoulder **Obv. Legend:** FERD. II. S. R. IMPE. ET. AS. P. MED. M. SOL. D. ETC. **Rev:** Crowned displayed eagle in circle **Rev. Legend:** SPLENDOREM SECTATA SVVM. **Note:** Ref. V-251. Prev. KM#62.

Date	Mintage	VG	F	VF	XF	Unc
ND(1680-1723)	—	1,450	2,400	6,000	10,500	—

KM# 82 2/3 TALLERO

Silver Weight varies: 15.51-16.31g., 37 mm. **Ruler:** Ferdinando II **Obv:** Draped bust to right in circle **Obv. Legend:** FERDINANDVS. II. SAC. RO. IMPER. **Rev:** Three small shields of arms, 1 above 2, with crown over upper shield, small tower below, all in circle **Rev. Legend:** ET. CAST. PRIN. MED. MAR. SOL. DOM. ETC. **Note:** Ref V-252. Prev. KM#63.

Date	Mintage	VG	F	VF	XF	Unc
ND(1680-1723)	—	1,200	1,950	4,500	6,900	—

KM# 86 2/3 TALLERO

Silver, 35 mm. **Ruler:** Ferdinando II **Obv:** Draped bust to right **Obv. Legend:** FERD. II. PRINC. DE. DOMO. MAN. T. **Rev:** Crowned imperial eagle, shield of 4-fold arms with central shield on breast, date at end of legend **Rev. Legend:** IMPERII. ET. CASTL. ETC. **Note:** Ref. V-251a. Prev. KM#99. Existence of this coin is questionable.

Date	Mintage	VG	F	VF	XF	Unc
1689 Rare	—	—	—	—	—	—

KM# 6 SCUDO (Piastra)

Silver Weight varies: 26.37-27.60g., 38-39 mm. **Ruler:** Francesco **Obv:** Half-length armored figure to right **Obv. Legend:** +F. D. G. SAC. ROMAN. - IMP. PRIN. M. C. ET. M. **Rev:** Crowned displayed eagle with shield of 4-fold arms on breast **Rev. Legend:** +SAC. CE. MA. A. CON. CAM. ET. AP. S. P. OR. **Note:** Ref. V-178; Dav. 3872.Prev. KM#A49.

Date	Mintage	VG	F	VF	XF	Unc
ND(1609-16)	—	1,950	3,300	5,500	8,300	—

KM# 7 SCUDO (5 Lira)

Silver Weight varies: 26.25-26.65g., 39-40 mm. **Ruler:** Francesco **Obv:** Half-length armored figure to right, value '5' below **Obv. Legend:** FRANCISCVS. D. G. PR - INCEPS. CASTILIONI. **Rev:** Crowned shield of 4-fold arms, with central shield of 6-fold arms, Order of Golden Fleece around **Rev. Legend:** MARCHIO. ME - DVLARVM. ET. C. **Note:** Ref. V-179; Dav. 3874. Prev. KM#50.

Date	Mintage	VG	F	VF	XF	Unc
ND(1609-16) Rare	—	—	—	—	—	—

KM# 8 DUCATONE (Tallero)

31.6700 g., Silver, 43 mm. **Ruler:** Francesco **Obv:** Armored bust to right **Obv. Legend:** FRAN. GON. PRINC. CAS. ET. SA. RO. IMP. **Rev:** Full-length armored female figure holding lance and shield, surrounded by arms and trophies **Rev. Legend:** IN PECTORE TROIA **Note:** Ref. V-177; Dav. 3873. Prev. KM#51.

Date	Mintage	VG	F	VF	XF	Unc
ND(1609-16) Rare	—	—	—	—	—	—

KM# 12 5 DOPPIE (10 Ducati)

35.0000 g., 0.9860 Gold 1.1095 oz. AGW, 40 mm. **Ruler:** Francesco **Obv:** Half-length armored figure to right, date below **Obv. Legend:** FRANCISCVS. D. G. PR - INCEPS. CASTILIONI. **Rev:** Crowned shield of 4-fold arms, with central shield of 6-fold arms, Order of Golden Fleece around **Rev. Legend:** MARCHIO. ME - DVLARVM. ET. C. **Note:** Ref. V-174; Fr. 199. Prev. KM#55.

Date	Mintage	VG	F	VF	XF	Unc
1614 Rare	—	—	—	—	—	—

TRADE COINAGE

KM# 9 1/4 DUCATO (1/8 Doppia)

0.8750 g., 0.9860 Gold Weight varies: 0.75-0.82g. 0.0277 oz. AGW, 15 mm. **Ruler:** Francesco **Obv:** Crowned lion rampant to left in circle **Obv. Legend:** FRAN. D. G. PRINC. CASTIL. **Rev:** Crowned facing head of steer in circle **Rev. Legend:** MARCH. MEDVLAR. ET. C. **Note:** Ref. V-176; Fr. 201. Prev. KM#52.

Date	Mintage	VG	F	VF	XF	Unc
ND(1609-16) Rare	—	—	—	—	—	—

KM# 10 DUCATO (1/2 Doppia)

3.5000 g., 0.9860 Gold Weight varies: 3.11-3.23g. 0.1109 oz. AGW, 19-20 mm. **Ruler:** Francesco **Obv:** Bust to right **Obv. Legend:** FRAN. D. G. PRINC. CASTILIONI. **Rev:** Crowned shield of 4-fold arms, with central shield, Order of Golden Fleece around **Rev. Legend:** MARCHIO. MEDVLAR. E. C. **Note:** Ref. V-175; Fr. 200. Prev. KM#53.

Date	Mintage	VG	F	VF	XF	Unc
ND(1609-16)	—	1,250	2,500	6,000	12,000	—

KM# 53 FIORINO

3.5000 g., 0.9860 Gold 0.1109 oz. AGW, 23-24 mm. **Ruler:** Ferdinando I **Obv:** Madonna and Child divide value L - 10 in circle **Obv. Legend:** SANCT. MARTA. ORA PRONCRES. **Rev:** 5-line inscription in ornamented square **Rev. Inscription:** DVCAT / VS. NOV / VS. NC / CASTN / .... **Note:** Ref. V-204; Fr. 205. Prev. KM#68. The stated value of the coin is 10 Lira.

Date	Mintage	VG	F	VF	XF	Unc
ND(1616-78) Rare	—	—	—	—	—	—

KM# 54 FIORINO
3.5000 g., 0.9860 Gold 0.1109 oz. AGW, 23-24 mm. **Ruler:** Ferdinando I **Obv:** Rampant lion to left holding small shield of arms in paws, no legend **Rev:** 6-line inscription in ornamented square **Rev. Inscription:** FLORI / NVS. AV / RE. AV / REVS. L / IB. XI. S / OL. VIII. **Note:** Ref. V-205; Fr. 206. Prev. KM#69. The stated value of the coin is 11 Lira, 8 Soldi.

Date	Mintage	VG	F	VF	XF	Unc
ND(1616-78) Rare	—	—	—	—	—	—

KM# 57 FIORINO
3.3300 g., Gold, 23-24 mm. **Ruler:** Ferdinando I **Obv:** Full-length armored figure wearing sword, head turned to right, date at end of legend **Obv. Legend:** SANCTVS. FERD - I - NANDVS. **Rev:** Crowned displayed eagle in circle **Rev. Legend:** FLOREN. AVR. PRIN. CAST. VAL. LIB. DECEM. **Note:** Ref. V-201; Fr. 202. Prev. KM#65. The value stated on the coin is 10 Lira.

Date	Mintage	VG	F	VF	XF	Unc
1639 Rare	—	—	—	—	—	—

KM# 58 FIORINO
3.3400 g., Gold, 23 mm. **Ruler:** Ferdinando I **Obv:** Full-length armored figure of St. Nazario, wearing sword, head turned to right, date at end of legend **Obv. Legend:** S. NAZARIVS. M. PR - OT. CAST. **Rev:** 5-line inscription in ornamented square **Rev. Inscription:** FLORI / NVS. AV / REVS. L / IB. IX. S / OL. VIII. **Note:** Ref. V-202; Fr. 202a. Prev. KM#66. The value stated on the coin is 9 Lira 8 Soldi.

Date	Mintage	VG	F	VF	XF	Unc
1639 Rare	—	—	—	—	—	—

KM# 59 FIORINO
3.5000 g., 0.9860 Gold 0.1109 oz. AGW, 23-24 mm. **Ruler:** Ferdinando I **Obv:** Full-length armored figure wearing sword, head turned to right, date at end of legend **Obv. Legend:** SANTVS. FERD - I - NANDVS. IO. **Rev:** 5-line inscription in ornamented square **Rev. Inscription:** DVCAT / VS. NOV / VS. NC / FRITI / CASNILLIONI. **Note:** Ref. V-202/2; Fr. 204. Prev. KM#67.

Date	Mintage	VG	F	VF	XF	Unc
1639 Rare	—	—	—	—	—	—

KM# 60 FIORINO
Gold, 23-24 mm. **Ruler:** Ferdinando I **Obv:** Full-length armored figure, holding sword over shoulder and lantern in other hand, value '10' at left, date at end of legend **Obv. Legend:** SANCTVS. - FERDINANDVS. **Rev:** 5-line inscription in ornamented square **Rev. Inscription:** LONDI / NVS AVI / REVS. L / IB. IX. S / OL. LII. **Note:** Ref. V-203. The stated value of this coin is 10 Lira on obverse, but 9 Lira, 52 Soldi on reverse.

Date	Mintage	VG	F	VF	XF	Unc
1639 Rare	—	—	—	—	—	—

KM# 61 FIORINO
3.5000 g., 0.9860 Gold 0.1109 oz. AGW **Ruler:** Ferdinando I **Obv:** Full-length armored figure holding sword and bundle of arrows, head turned to right, divides date **Obv. Legend:** FERDINAN. D - G - S. R. I. E. CASTI. P. **Rev:** 5-line inscription in ornamented square **Rev. Inscription:** DVCATV / S. AVRE. / .. PRIN / CAST. L / .... **Note:** Prev. KM#70.

Date	Mintage	VG	F	VF	XF	Unc
1655	—	1,500	3,000	6,000	10,000	—

CISTERNA

Principality

An ancient feudatory centered on Alessandria, to the southwest of Milan. Emperor Henry III (1039-56) assigned Cisterna to Vescovo d'Asti in 1041. In the 15th century, it passed from the Garretti family to Domenico and Antonio Paletta, who ceded their rights in Cisterna to Antonio della Rovere, the nephew of Pope Sixtus IV (1471-84). Finally, Cisterna was sold in 1665 to Giacomo Dal Pozzo, the Marchese di Voghera (near Pavia). The place already having received the mint right in 1660, Cisterna was erected into a principality by imperial decree in 1670.

RULER
Giacomo Dal Pozzo, 1665-1696

Reference
V = Alberto Varesi, ***Monete Italiane Regionali: Piemonte, Sardegna, Liguria, Isola di Corsica***. Pavia, 1996.

PRINCIPALITY

STANDARD COINAGE

KM# 1 SOLDINO
1.7200 g., Copper, 17 mm. **Ruler:** Giacomo Dal Pozzo **Obv:** Bust to right, date below **Obv. Legend:** I. AP... E. EC. **Rev:** Ornate cross with lily ends **Rev. Legend:** CIST. ET. BELG. PRINC. **Note:** Ref. V-408.

Date	Mintage	F	VF	XF	Unc	BU
1675	—	1,650	2,500	3,750	6,000	—

KM# 2 1/2 SCUDO (Mezzo Scudo)
13.0000 g., Silver, 31-33 mm. **Ruler:** Giacomo Dal Pozzo **Obv:** Draped bust to right **Obv. Legend:** I. A. PVT. CIST. ET. BELG. PRIN. **Rev:** Crowned shield of 4-fold arms with central shield, date at end of legend **Rev. Legend:** qVI. BIBET. SITIET. ITERVM. **Note:** Ref. V-407.

Date	Mintage	VG	F	VF	XF	Unc
1677	—	2,500	3,300	4,800	6,500	8,800

KM# 3 SCUDO
Silver, 40-41 mm. **Ruler:** Giacomo Dal Pozzo **Obv:** Bust to right, date at top in legend **Obv. Legend:** IA. A. PVT. PRIN. (date) CIS. ET. B. D. **Rev:** Two ornate crossed keys with small oval shield of family arms in center, small crowned shield of arms in each angle **Rev. Legend:** A. DNO - FACT - EST - ISTVD. **Note:** Ref. V-406; Dav. 3875.

Date	Mintage	VG	F	VF	XF	Unc
1677 Rare	—	—	—	—	—	—

TRADE COINAGE

KM# 4 2 DOPPIE
Gold, 32-33 mm. **Ruler:** Giacomo Dal Pozzo **Obv:** Draped bust to right **Obv. Legend:** I. A. PVT. CIST. ET. BELG. PRIN. **Rev:** Crowned shield of 4-fold arms with central shield, date at end of legend **Rev. Legend:** qVI. BIBET. SITIET. ITERVM. **Note:** Ref. V-405; Fr. 213.

Date	Mintage	VG	F	VF	XF	Unc
1677 Rare	—	—	—	—	—	—

KM# 5 10 SCUDI D'ORO
32.9780 g., Gold, 40-41 mm. **Ruler:** Giacomo Dal Pozzo **Obv:** Bust to right, date at top in legend **Obv. Legend:** IA. A. PVT. PRIN. (date) CIS. ET. B. D. **Rev:** Two ornate crossed keys with small oval shield of family arms in center, small crowned shield of arms in each angle **Rev. Legend:** A. DNO - FACT - EST - ISTVD. **Note:** Ref. V-404; Fr. 212.

Date	Mintage	VG	F	VF	XF	Unc
1677 Rare	—	—	—	—	—	—

COMPIANO

Principality

A commune in the province of Parma approximately eight miles N.W. of Emilia ruled by the Landi Family until 1862. The Landi's also held the commune de Bardi and the principality of Borgotaro. During the hundreds of years that the Landi Family ruled, Compiano developed as a progressive center with a public school system and eventually coinage. Granted the mintage right in 1551, the Landi Family did not strike coins until the rule of Frederico Landi, 1590-1630, after which the mint was closed.

RULER
Federico Landi, 1590-1630

MINT OFFICIALS INITIALS

Initial	Date	Name
G	ca.1622	Gandusio
GF	1622	Gandusio or Gaspare (Fecit – made)
NG	1622	Nicola Gandusio
OG	1622	?

Reference:
Alberto Varesi, ***Monete Italiane Regionali: Emilia***. Pavia, 1998.

PRINCIPALITY

STANDARD COINAGE

KM# 16 LIRA (20 Soldi)
5.9000 g., Silver, 28-29 mm. **Ruler:** Federico Landi **Obv:** High-collared armored bust to right **Obv. Legend:** D. FED. LAN. S. R. I. AC. VAL. TARI. PRIN. IV. ET. C. **Rev:** Full-length facing figure of St. John the Baptist, date in exergue **Rev. Legend:** S. IO. BAPTIS - T. - PROTEC. NOST. **Note:** Ref. Varesi 89/2. Prev. KM#9.

Date	Mintage	VG	F	VF	XF	Unc
1622 Rare	—	—	—	—	—	—

KM# 17 DUCATONE
Silver Weight varies: 30.65-31.47g., 42 mm. **Ruler:** Federico Landi **Obv:** High-collared armored bust to right, mint official's initials below **Obv. Legend:** D. FED. LAN. S. R. I. AC. VALL. TARI. PRIN. IV. ET C. **Rev:** St. Francis kneeling to left, receiving the stigmata, Roman numeral date in exergue, mint official's initials below. **Rev. Legend:** S. FRANCIS. - PROTECT. NOSTER. **Note:** Ref. Varesi 88; Dav. 3847. Prev. KM#11.

Date	Mintage	VG	F	VF	XF	Unc
MDCXXII (1622) OG//NG	—	2,000	3,000	7,000	12,000	—

TRADE COINAGE

KM# 19 DOPPIA
Gold Weight varies: 6.40-6.46g., 25-26 mm. **Ruler:** Federico Landi **Obv:** High-collared armored bust to right, mint official's initial below **Obv. Legend:** D. FED. LAN. - S. R. I. AC. VALL. **Rev:** Crowned imperial eagle, shield of manifold arms on breast, Order of Golden Fleece around **Rev. Legend:** TAR. ET. CEN. PRIN. - IIII. BAR. M. C. C. P. D. **Note:** Ref. Varesi 85; Fr. 73. Prev. KM#12.

Date	Mintage	VG	F	VF	XF	Unc
ND(ca. 1622) G Rare	—	—	—	—	—	—

Note: 4 examples known.

KM# 20 DOPPIA
6.5700 g., Gold, 24-25 mm. **Ruler:** Federico Landi **Obv:** High-collared armored bust to right, mint official's initials below **Obv. Legend:** D. FED. L. S. R. I. - AC. V. T. P. IV. ET. C. **Rev:** Facing half-legnth figure of St. Theresa, Roman numeral date below **Rev. Legend:** S. MATER. TERESIA. CVS. MEA. **Note:** Ref. Varesi 86; Fr. 74.

Date	Mintage	VG	F	VF	XF	Unc
MDCXXII (1622) GF Unique	—	—	—	—	—	—

KM# 22 2 DOPPIE
12.9500 g., Gold, 29 mm. **Ruler:** Federico Landi **Obv:** High-collared armored but to right, mint official's initial below **Obv. Legend:** D. FEDERICVS. LAND. - S. R. I. AC. VALL. **Rev:** Imperial eagle in shield, arms on breast, large crown above, Order of Golden Fleece around **Rev. Legend:** TAR. ET. CEN. PRIN. IIII. BAR. M. C. C. P. D. **Note:** Ref. Varesi 84; Fr. 72. Prev. KM#14.

Date	Mintage	VG	F	VF	XF	Unc
ND(ca. 1622) G	—	—	—	—	—	—

Note: 8 examples known. Numismatica Ars Classica Auction 60, 6-11, VF realized approximately $42,355

KM# 26 2 DOPPIE
13.0500 g., Gold, 30 mm. **Ruler:** Federico Landi **Obv:** High-collared armored bust to right **Obv. Legend:** D. FED. LAN. S. R. I. AC. VAL. TARI. PRIN. IV. ET. C. **Rev:** Full-length facing figure of St. John the Baptist, date in exergue **Rev. Legend:** S. IO. BAPTIS - T. - PROTEC. NOST. **Note:** Ref. Varesi 83; Fr. 71. Prev. KM#13.

Date	Mintage	VG	F	VF	XF	Unc
1623 Rare	—	—	—	—	—	—

Note: 2 examples known.

KM# 24 5 DOPPIE
32.0000 g., Gold, 42 mm. **Ruler:** Federico Landi **Obv:** High-collared armored bust to right, mint official's initials below **Obv. Legend:** D. FED. LAN. S. R. I. AC. VALL. TARI. PRIN. IV. ET C. **Rev:** St. Francis kneeling to left, receiving the stigmata, Roman numeral date in exergue and mint official's initials below **Rev. Legend:** S. FRANCIS. - PROTECT. NOSTER. **Note:** Ref. Varesi 82; Fr. 70. Prev. KM#15. Struck from Ducatone dies, KM#17.

Date	Mintage	VG	F	VF	XF	Unc
MDCXXII (1622) OG//NG Rare	—	—	—	—	—	—

Note: Existence of this coin is questionable.

CORREGGIO

Countship and Principality

First mentioned in the 10th century, the town of Correggio is located about 8 miles (14 kilometers) northeast of Reggio nell' Emilia and a like distance northwest of Modena. The local lords of the place trace back to a certain Frogerio and his descendants were raised to the rank of count in 1452, reconfirmed by Emperor Carlo V in 1520. The title of Prince of the Empire was bestowed on the count by Emperor Mattia (Mathias) in 1616. However, cordial relations with the imperial court did not last, as the prince abused his right to strike coins. After years of issuing substandard coinage in spite of warnings and investigations, the prince was deposed in 1631 and the principality was sold to Modena in 1635. The last territorial prince died impoverished in 1645 at the age of 70, although the line itself did not become extinct until 1711.

RULERS
Camillo, 1597-1605 (Camillo d'Austria)
Giovanni Siro, 1597-1631, Prince in 1616

Reference:
V = Alberto Varesi, ***Monete Italiane Regionali: Emelia***. Pavia, 1998.

COUNTSHIP

STANDARD COINAGE

KM# 2 SESINO
0.9200 g., Billon, 18 mm. **Ruler:** Giovanni Siro **Obv:** Bust to left **Obv. Legend:** SIRVS. AVS. CORR. C. **Rev:** Crowned displayed eagle **Rev. Legend:** SVB VMBRA ALARVM. TVAR. **Note:** Ref. V-163.

Date	Mintage	VG	F	VF	XF	Unc
ND(1605-16) Rare	—	—	—	—	—	—

KM# 4 SOLDO
Copper Weight varies: 2.88-4.44g., 22-23 mm. **Ruler:** Giovanni Siro **Obv:** Bare head to right **Obv. Legend:** SYRVS. AVSTRIAC. CORR. DNS. **Rev:** Heart pierced by 4 arrows, small head above **Rev. Legend:** SIGNAT. GRATIOSA. NOM. **Note:** Ref. V-164.

Date	Mintage	VG	F	VF	XF	Unc
ND(1605-16)	—	35.00	75.00	150	375	—

KM# 6 3 SOLDI
Billon Weight varies: 1.25-1.86g., 21-22 mm. **Ruler:** Giovanni Siro **Obv:** Armored bust to right **Obv. Legend:** SIRVS. AVSTRIAC, COR. CO. **Rev:** Crowned shield of 4-fold arms with central shield **Rev. Legend:** ORIG. INCL. SIG. INSIG. **Note:** Ref. V-161.

Date	Mintage	VG	F	VF	XF	Unc
ND(1605-16)	—	130	275	550	1,350	—

KM# 7 3 SOLDI
Billon Weight varies: 1.54-1.95g., 21-22 mm. **Ruler:** Giovanni Siro **Obv:** Bare head to right **Obv. Legend:** SIRVS. AVSTRIACVS. CORR. COMES. **Rev:** Crowned shield of 4-fold arms surmounted on 2 crossed scepters **Rev. Legend:** ORIG. INCLIT. SIGN. INSIG. **Note:** Ref. V-162.

Date	Mintage	VG	F	VF	XF	Unc
ND(1605-16)	—	130	275	550	1,350	—

MB# 46 TALLERO (70 Soldi)

Silver Weight varies: 25.29-27.10g., 41-44 mm. **Ruler:** Camillo **Obv:** Half-length armored figure behind shield of arms with rampant lion to left below, date at bottom right **Obv. Legend:** MO. NO. CAM. - AVS. CO(M). CO. **Rev:** Rampant lion to left in circle **Rev. Legend:** CONFIDENS. DNO. NON. MOVENTVR. **Note:** Ref. V-147; Dav. 3876. Varieties exist. Design in imitation of Holland Daalder, KM#11.

Date	Mintage	VG	F	VF	XF	Unc
1603	—	400	800	1,400	3,000	—

TRADE COINAGE

KM# 10 ONGARO

3.3800 g., Gold, 22-23 mm. **Ruler:** Giovanni Siro **Obv:** Full-length armored figure of count, holding sword over shoulder and group of arrows in other hand, divides date, head turned to right **Obv. Legend:** CONCORDIA. RESPAR. CRES. TRA. **Rev:** 5-line inscription in ornamented square tablet **Rev. Inscription:** MO. NOVA / CIVITAT / COR. SAC / RO. ROMA / N. IMPERI. **Note:** Ref. V-160; Fr. 224.

Date	Mintage	VG	F	VF	XF	Unc
1609 Rare	—	—	—	—	—	—

PRINCIPALITY

STANDARD COINAGE

KM# 12 SESINO

Billon Weight varies: 0.63-1.06g., 16-17 mm. **Ruler:** Giovanni Siro **Obv:** Bust to right **Obv. Legend:** SIRVS. AVSTR. CORR. PRIN. **Rev:** Crowned displayed eagle **Rev. Legend:** SVB. VMBRA. ALARVM. TVARVM. **Note:** Ref. V-205.

Date	Mintage	VG	F	VF	XF	Unc
ND(1616-31)	—	30.00	60.00	110	300	—

KM# 13 SESINO

Billon Weight varies: 0.63-0.76g., 16-17 mm. **Ruler:** Giovanni Siro **Obv:** Head to left **Obv. Legend:** SIRVS. AVSTRIACVS. CORIGGI. PRIN. **Rev:** Crowned displayed eagle **Rev. Legend:** SVB. VMBRA. ALARVM. TVARVM. **Note:** Ref. V-206.

Date	Mintage	VG	F	VF	XF	Unc
ND(1616-31)	—	70.00	150	300	—	—

KM# 14 SESINO

Silver, 18 mm. **Ruler:** Giovanni Siro **Obv:** Bust to left **Obv. Legend:** SIRVS. AVSTRIACVS. SACR. ROMAN. **Rev:** Crowned displayed eagle in circle **Rev. Legend:** SVB. VMBRA. ALARVM. TVARVM. **Note:** Ref. V-204.

Date	Mintage	VG	F	VF	XF	Unc
ND(1616-31) Rare	—	—	—	—	—	—

Note: Only one example known.

KM# 63 SOLDO (12 Denari)

1.2700 g., Billon, 24 mm. **Ruler:** Giovanni Siro **Obv:** Standing figure with long club divides date in circle **Obv. Legend:** SYRVS. AVSTRIÆ. PRIN. COR. **Rev:** Crowned imperial eagle, '1Z' on breast **Rev. Legend:** MONETA. NOVA. ARGE. CIVI. C. **Note:** Ref. V-203.

Date	Mintage	VG	F	VF	XF	Unc
1622 Rare	—	—	—	—	—	—

KM# 16 2 SOLDI (24 Denari)

Silver Plated Copper Weight varies: 3.15-3.50g., 27 mm. **Ruler:** Giovanni Siro **Obv:** Armored bust to right in clrcle **Obv. Legend:** SYRVS. AVSTRIA. PRIN. COR. **Rev:** Displayed eagle, 'Z4' in orb on breast **Rev. Legend:** MONETA. NOVA. ARGENTE. CIVI. C. **Note:** Ref. V-202.

Date	Mintage	VG	F	VF	XF	Unc
ND(1616-31) Rare	—	—	—	—	—	—

KM# 18 3 SOLDI

Billon Weight varies: 1.20-2.06g., 18 mm. **Ruler:** Giovanni Siro **Obv:** Armored bust to right in circle **Obv. Legend:** SYRVS. AVSTRIAC. SACR. ROMAN. **Rev:** Crowned shield of manifold arms **Rev. Legend:** IMP. ET. CORRIGGI. PRIN. ET. C. **Note:** Ref. V-201.

Date	Mintage	VG	F	VF	XF	Unc
ND(1616-31)	—	40.00	80.00	175	450	—

KM# 59 3 SOLDI

Silver Weight varies: 1.45-2.21g., 20-21 mm. **Ruler:** Giovanni Siro **Obv:** Imperial eagle, '3' in orb on breast **Obv. Legend:** SYRS. AVSTRIAC. CORR. **Rev:** Spanish shield of family arms, date above **Rev. Legend:** SI. PRONOBIS. QVIS. CON. NOS. **Note:** Ref. V-198.

Date	Mintage	VG	F	VF	XF	Unc
1617	—	100	200	385	750	—

KM# 20 12 QUATTRINI

Billon Weight varies: 2.33-2.55g., 26-27 mm. **Ruler:** Giovanni Siro **Obv:** Crowned Spanish shield of 4-fold arms **Obv. Legend:** SYRVS. AVSTRIA. PRIN. COR. **Rev:** Crowned imperial eagle, 'IZ' in orb on breast **Rev. Legend:** MONETA. NOVA. ARGENTE. CIVI. C. **Note:** Ref. V-199.

Date	Mintage	VG	F	VF	XF	Unc
ND(1616-31)	—	40.00	80.00	165	325	—

KM# 21 12 QUATTRINI

Billon Weight varies: 2.68-2.76g., 26-27 mm. **Ruler:** Giovanni Siro **Obv:** Crowned Spanish shield of 2-fold arms divided diagonally from lower left to upper right **Obv. Legend:** SIRVS. ASTRIAR. RIN. CC. **Rev:** Imperial eagle with '12' in circle on breast **Rev. Legend:** MONETA. NOVA. ACENTEI. VIC. **Note:** Ref. V-200.

Date	Mintage	VG	F	VF	XF	Unc
ND(1616-31)	—	60.00	125	275	600	—

KM# 23 4 SOLDI

Billon Weight varies: 1.63-2.08g., 23-24 mm. **Ruler:** Giovanni Siro **Obv:** Crowned shield of manifold arms **Obv. Legend:** SYRVS. AVST. CORR. PRIN. **Rev:** Figure of St. John the Austere seated to left, value 'IIII' in exergue **Rev. Legend:** S. IO. AVST. DE. CORR. AB. **Note:** Ref. V-196.

Date	Mintage	VG	F	VF	XF	Unc
ND(1616-31)	—	40.00	80.00	165	325	—

KM# 24 4 SOLDI

Billon Weight varies: 1.63-2.08g., 23-24 mm. **Ruler:** Giovanni Siro **Obv:** Crowned shield of manifold arms **Obv. Legend:** SYRVS. AVST. CORR. PRIN. **Rev:** Figure of St. John the Austere seated to left, no mark of value in exergue **Rev. Legend:** S. IO. AVST. DE. CORR. AB. **Note:** Ref. V-196/1.

Date	Mintage	VG	F	VF	XF	Unc
ND(1616-31)	—	40.00	80.00	165	325	—

KM# 65 4 SOLDI

Billon Weight varies: 1.63-2.08g., 23-24 mm. **Ruler:** Giovanni Siro **Obv:** Crowned shield of 4-fold arms with central shield **Obv. Legend:** SYRVS. AVST. CORR. PRIN. **Rev:** Figure of St. John the Austere to the left, date in exergue **Rev. Legend:** S. IO. AVST. DE. CORR. AB. **Note:** Ref. V-195.

Date	Mintage	VG	F	VF	XF	Unc
1628 Rare	—	—	—	—	—	—

KM# 25 4 SOLDI (48 Denari)

Silver Plated Copper Weight varies: 7.15-8.18g., 33 mm. **Ruler:** Giovanni Siro **Obv:** Crowned imperial eagle, '48' in orb on breast **Obv. Legend:** SYR. AVSTRIA. PRIN. P. C. ET. DE. S. R. IMP. C. P. **Rev:** Crowned round shield of manifold arms, chain of order around **Rev. Legend:** MONET. NOVA. ARGENTEA. CIVI. COR. **Note:** Ref. V-197. Design in imitation of various Austrian issues.

Date	Mintage	VG	F	VF	XF	Unc
ND(1616-31)	—	100	200	385	750	—

KM# 67 6 SOLDI

Silver Weight varies: 1.97-2.35g., 20 mm. **Ruler:** Giovanni Siro **Obv:** Ruffed-collared bust to right **Obv. Legend:** SYRVS. AVSTR. S. R. I. AC. C. P. **Rev:** Small displayed eagle divides date above 3-line inscription **Rev. Inscription:** FABR. ROSS. / AC. CAMP. / COM. **Note:** Ref. V-194. Design in imitation of Poland 3 Grozy, KM#31.

Date	Mintage	VG	F	VF	XF	Unc
1628 Rare	—	—	—	—	—	—

KM# 27 1/2 GIULIO (7 Soldi)

1.8200 g., Silver **Ruler:** Giovanni Siro **Obv:** Crowned shield of 4-fold arms with central shield **Obv. Legend:** SYRVS. AVSTRIACVS. CORR. PRIN. **Rev:** The Annunciation scene **Rev. Legend:** AVE. MARIA. GR. PLE. **Note:** Ref. V-193.

Date	Mintage	VG	F	VF	XF	Unc
ND(1616-31) Rare	—	—	—	—	—	—

KM# 29 8 SOLDI

Billon Weight varies: 3.40-3.83g., 27-28 mm. **Ruler:** Giovanni Siro **Obv:** Armored bust to right **Obv. Legend:** SYRVS. AVSTR. S. R. IMP. ET. CO. P. **Rev:** Crowned Spanish shield of 5-fold arms with central shield **Rev. Legend:** ANTIQVISS. FAM. INSIGNIA. **Note:** Ref. V-191.

Date	Mintage	VG	F	VF	XF	Unc
ND(1616-31)	—	200	400	825	2,000	—

KM# 30 8 SOLDI

Billon Weight varies: 2.88-3.77g., 24-25 mm. **Ruler:** Giovanni Siro **Obv:** Armored bust to right **Obv. Legend:** SYRVS. AVSTR. CORR. PRIN. **Rev:** Seated Madonna with Child, value '8' in exergue **Rev. Legend:** VBERV. TVOR. MEMORES. **Note:** Ref. V-192.

Date	Mintage	VG	F	VF	XF	Unc
ND(1616-31)	—	225	450	950	1,750	—

KM# 32 FIORINO

Silver Weight varies: 4.84-5.00g., 29 mm. **Ruler:** Giovanni Siro **Obv:** Crowned Spanish shield of manifold arms, with central shield of family arms **Obv. Legend:** SYR. AVST. S. R. I. COR. PRIN. COM. FAB. **Rev:** Crowned imperial eagle in circle **Rev. Legend:** SI. PRONOBIS. QVIS. CONTRA. NOS. **Note:** Ref. V-184.

Date	Mintage	VG	F	VF	XF	Unc
ND(1616-31)	—	150	325	660	1,150	—

KM# 33 FIORINO

Silver Weight varies: 4.46-4.50g., 29-30 mm. **Ruler:** Giovanni Siro **Obv:** Crowned Spanish shield of manifold arms, with central shield of family arms **Obv. Legend:** MO. NO. SYRVS. AVSTR. COR. PRIN. **Rev:** Crowned imperial eagle in circle **Rev. Legend:** SI. PRONOBIS. QVIS. CONTRA. NOS. **Note:** Ref. V-185.

Date	Mintage	VG	F	VF	XF	Unc
ND(1616-31)	—	200	450	825	1,750	—

KM# 34 FIORINO

Silver Weight varies: 3.87-4.72g., 29-30 mm. **Ruler:** Giovanni Siro **Obv:** Crowned Spanish shield of manifold arms, with central shield of family arms **Obv. Legend:** MO. NOV. SYRI. AVSTRI. COR. PRI. **Rev:** Crowned imperial eagle in circle **Rev. Legend:** SVB. VMBRA. ALARVM. TVARVM. **Note:** Ref. V-186.

Date	Mintage	VG	F	VF	XF	Unc
ND(1616-31)	—	150	300	550	1,000	—

KM# 35 FIORINO

Billon Weight varies: 4.20-4.74g., 28-29 mm. **Ruler:** Giovanni Siro **Obv:** Crowned imperial eagle in circle **Obv. Legend:** SYRI. AVSTRI. SA. RO. IM. PRIN. ET. C. **Rev:** Crowned Spanish shield of 6-fold arms in circle **Rev. Legend:** MON - ETA. NO - VA. CI - VITAS. - CO. **Note:** Ref. V-187.

Date	Mintage	VG	F	VF	XF	Unc
ND(1616-31)	—	150	300	550	1,000	—

KM# 36 FIORINO

Billon Weight varies: 3.33-4.69g., 29-30 mm. **Ruler:** Giovanni Siro **Obv:** Crowned imperial eagle, orb on breast, in circle **Obv. Legend:** SYRI. AVSTRI. SA. RO. IM. PRIN. ET. C. **Rev:** Crowned Spanish shield of 4-fold arms, superimposed on 2 crossed scepters, in circle **Rev. Legend:** MO - NETA. NO - VA. CI - VITATI. - CO. **Note:** Ref. V-188.

Date	Mintage	VG	F	VF	XF	Unc
ND(1616-31)	—	150	300	550	1,000	—

KM# 37 FIORINO

Billon Weight varies: 3.24-4.22g., 28 mm. **Ruler:** Giovanni Siro **Obv:** Crowned imperial eagle, orb on breast, in circle **Obv. Legend:** SYRI. AVSTRI. SA. RO. IM. PRIN. ET. C. **Rev:** Crowned Spanish shield of 4-fold arms in circle **Rev. Legend:** MONETA. NOVA. CIVITATI. CO. **Note:** Ref. V-189.

Date	Mintage	VG	F	VF	XF	Unc
ND(1616-31)	—	150	300	550	1,000	—

KM# 38 FIORINO

Billon Weight varies: 3.05-4.10g., 28 mm. **Ruler:** Giovanni Siro **Obv:** Crowned Spanish shield of 4-fold arms **Obv. Legend:** SYRVS. AVSTRI. S. R. I. P. ET. C. **Rev:** Crowned imperial eagle in circle **Rev. Legend:** DOMINE. AVDIE. NOS. **Note:** Ref. V-190.

Date	Mintage	VG	F	VF	XF	Unc
ND(1616-31)	—	275	575	1,100	2,150	—

KM# 40 GROSSO (20 Soldi)

Silver Weight varies: 4.75-8.14g., 28 mm. **Ruler:** Giovanni Siro **Obv:** Imperial eagle in circle **Obv. Legend:** MON. NOVA. SYR. AVSTRIA. COR. PRIN. **Rev:** Rampant lion at left of castle, all in circle **Rev. Legend:** LAQVEVS. CONTRITVS. EST. **Note:** Ref. V-183.

Date	Mintage	VG	F	VF	XF	Unc
ND(1616-31)	—	700	1,350	2,750	4,750	—

KM# 44 TESTONE (24 Soldi)

Silver, 29 mm. **Ruler:** Giovanni Siro **Obv:** Imperial eagle in circle, small shield of family arms below **Obv. Legend:** MONETA. NOV. - CORRIGIENS. **Rev:** Half-length figure of St. Quirinus to right with crozier and palm branch **Rev. Legend:** SANCT. QVIRIN. EPS. **Note:** Ref. V-180.

Date	Mintage	VG	F	VF	XF	Unc
ND(1616-31) Rare	—	—	—	—	—	—

KM# 42 TESTONE (24 Soldi)

8.2000 g., Silver, 29 mm. **Ruler:** Giovanni Siro **Obv:** Half-length armored figure to right, small shield of family arms at bottom **Obv. Legend:** MO. NOV(A). ARG. SYR. AVST. C. PRI. **Rev:** Imperial eagle in circle **Rev. Legend:** SVB. VMBRA. ALARVM. TVARVM. **Note:** Ref. V-178.

Date	Mintage	VG	F	VF	XF	Unc
ND(1616-31) Rare	—	—	—	—	—	—

KM# 43 TESTONE (24 Soldi)

Silver, 29 mm. **Ruler:** Giovanni Siro **Obv:** Half-length armored figure to right, small shield of family arms at bottom **Obv. Legend:** MO. NOVA. ARG. SYR. AVST. C. PRI. **Rev:** Imperial eagle in circle, small shield of family arms below **Rev. Legend:** MONETA. NOV. - CORRIGIENS. **Note:** Ref. V-179. Existence of this coin not certain.

Date	Mintage	VG	F	VF	XF	Unc
ND(1616-31) Rare	—	—	—	—	—	—

KM# 45 TESTONE (24 Soldi)

Silver Weight varies: 4.82-8.08g., 30 mm. **Ruler:** Giovanni Siro **Obv:** Shield of 5-fold arms, with central shield, in circle **Obv. Legend:** SYRVS. AVSTRIA. SAC. ROM. IMP. PRIN. C. **Rev:** Bare-headed and bearded bust of St. Quirinus to right in circle **Rev. Legend:** DIVVS. QVIRINVS. EPS. PROTECTOR. COR. **Note:** Ref. V-181.

Date	Mintage	VG	F	VF	XF	Unc
ND(1616-31)	—	1,250	2,500	5,000	8,500	—

KM# 46 TESTONE (24 Soldi)

Silver Weight varies: 5.70-7.79g., 30-31 mm. **Ruler:** Giovanni Siro **Obv:** Ornately-shaped shield of family arms in circle **Obv. Legend:** MON. NO. ARGENT. SYR. AVSTRIÆ. P. CO. **Rev:** Large lily in circle **Rev. Legend:** GLORIA. IN. EXCELSIS. DEO. **Note:** Ref. V-182.

Date	Mintage	VG	F	VF	XF	Unc
ND(1616-31)	—	2,000	4,000	6,500	11,500	—

KM# 61 TESTONE (24 Soldi)

Silver Weight varies: 7.50-8.25g., 29 mm. **Ruler:** Giovanni Siro **Obv:** Imperial eagle, small shield of family arms below **Obv. Legend:** SYR. AVSTR. S. R. IMP. PR. **Rev:** Nimbate bust of St. Quirinus to right holding cross, date at end of legend **Rev. Legend:** SANCT. QVIR. PRO. COR. **Note:** Ref. V-177.

Date	Mintage	VG	F	VF	XF	Unc
1617	—	1,250	2,500	5,000	3,200	—

KM# 69 1/2 DUCATONE (Mezzo Ducatone)

14.1000 g., Silver, 35 mm. **Ruler:** Giovanni Siro **Obv:** High-collared armored bust to right **Obv. Legend:** SYRVS. AVSTRIA. S. R. IMPERI. AC. P. CO. **Rev:** Crowned Spanish shield of manifold arms in baroque frame, date at end of legend **Rev. Legend:** ANTIQVISS. FAM. INSIGNIA. **Note:** Ref. V-175.

Date	Mintage	VG	F	VF	XF	Unc
1628 Rare	—	—	—	—	—	—

KM# 74 1/2 DUCATONE (Mezzo Ducatone)

17.2500 g., Silver, 39 mm. **Ruler:** Giovanni Siro **Obv:** Crowned imperial eagle, shield of family arms on breast **Obv. Legend:** SVB. VMBRA. ALARVM. TVARVM. **Rev:** Crowned ornate Spanish shield of 9-fold arms in baroque frame, date at end of legend **Note:** Ref. V-176.

Date	Mintage	VG	F	VF	XF	Unc
1629 Rare	—	—	—	—	—	—

KM# 48 TALLERO (70 Soldi)

20.0000 g., Silver, 40 mm. **Ruler:** Giovanni Siro **Obv:** Crowned Spanish shield of 4-fold arms witih central shield **Obv. Legend:** MONETA. NOVA. CIVITATI. C. **Rev:** Rampant lion to left in circle **Rev. Legend:** CONFIDENS. DNO. NON. MOVETVR. **Note:** Ref. V-174; Dav. 3880. Rev. in imitation of generic Netherlands Daalder.

Date	Mintage	VG	F	VF	XF	Unc
ND(1616-31) Rare	—	—	—	—	—	—

KM# 50 DUCATONE

Silver Weight varies: 21.74-23.39g., 39 mm. **Ruler:** Giovanni Siro **Obv:** Armored bust to left **Obv. Legend:** SYRI. AVST. SACR. R. IMP. PRIN. ET. C - ORRIGII. **Rev:** Crowned Spanish shield of 4-fold arms formed by cross, small shield in center **Rev. Legend:** MONETA. - NOVA. - CIVITA - TI. CO(R). **Note:** Ref. V-170; Dav. 3885. Varieties exist.

Date	Mintage	VG	F	VF	XF	Unc
ND(1616-31)	—	2,500	5,500	17,000	22,000	—

KM# 51 DUCATONE

Silver Weight varies: 26.45-26.92g., 40-41 mm. **Ruler:** Giovanni Siro **Obv:** Armored bust to right **Obv. Legend:** SYRVS. AVSTRI. S. R. IMP. PRIN. ET. CO. FAB. COM. **Rev:** Crowned Spanish shield of complex 4-fold arms, with small 4-fold arms in third quadrant, small central shield, chain of order around **Rev. Legend:** ANTIQVISS. FAM. AVS. INSIGN. **Note:** Ref. V-171; Dav. 3886.

Date	Mintage	VG	F	VF	XF	Unc
ND(1616-31)	—	1,350	2,750	8,000	13,800	—

KM# 52 DUCATONE

Silver Weight varies: 25.42-27.95g., 40-41 mm. **Ruler:** Giovanni Siro **Obv:** Armored bust to right **Obv. Legend:** SYRVS. AVSTRI. S. R. IMP. PRIN. ET. CO. FAB. COM. **Rev:** Crowned Spanish shield of complex 4-fold arms, with small 4-fold arms in both first and third quadrants, small central shield, chain of order around **Rev. Legend:** ANTIQVISS. FAM. AVS. INSIGN. **Note:** Ref. V-172; Dav. 3886a.

Date	Mintage	VG	F	VF	XF	Unc
ND(1616-31)	—	900	1,650	5,500	8,300	—

KM# 64 DUCATONE

Silver Weight varies: 28.33-28.59g., 40 mm. **Ruler:** Giovanni Siro **Obv:** Armored and draped bust to right **Obv. Legend:** SYRVS. AVSTRIA. S. R. IMPER. ET. CO. P. **Rev:** Crowned Spanish shield of 5-fold arms with central shield, date at end of legend **Rev. Legend:** ANTIQVISS. FAM. INSIGNIA. **Note:** Ref. V-167; Dav. 3882.

Date	Mintage	VG	F	VF	XF	Unc
1627 Rare	—	—	—	—	—	—

KM# 71 DUCATONE

Silver Weight varies: 28.83-29.40g., 41 mm. **Ruler:** Giovanni Siro **Obv:** Armored and draped bust to right **Obv. Legend:** SYRVS. AVSTRIA. S. R. IMPER. ET. CO. P. **Rev:** Crowned Spanish shield of manifold arms in baroque frame, date at end of legend **Rev. Legend:** ANTIQVISS. FAM. - INSIGNIA. **Note:** Ref. V-168; Dav. 3883.

Date	Mintage	VG	F	VF	XF	Unc
1628	—	2,300	4,500	16,500	22,000	—

Note: Numismatica Ars Classica Auction 32, 1-06, nearly XF realized approximately $16,670

Date	Mintage	VG	F	VF	XF	Unc
1629 Rare	—	—	—	—	—	—

KM# 72 DUCATONE

26.8800 g., Silver, 40 mm. **Ruler:** Giovanni Siro **Obv:** Armored and draped bust to right, date below **Obv. Legend:** SYRVS. AVSTRI. S. R. IMP. PRIN. ET. CO. FAB. COM. **Rev:** Crowned Spanish shield of complex 4-fold arms, with central shield, chain of order around **Rev. Legend:** ANTIQVISS. FAM. AVS. INSIGN. **Note:** Ref. V-169; Dav. 3884.

Date	Mintage	VG	F	VF	XF	Unc
1628 Rare	—	—	—	—	—	—

KM# 54 SCUDO (140 Soldi)

Silver Weight varies: 30.49-31.60g., 41 mm. **Ruler:** Giovanni Siro **Obv:** Floriated cross incircle, 'SCP' in exergue (=Syrus Corrigii Princeps) **Obv. Legend:** SI. PRO. NOBIS. QVIS. CONTRA. NOS. **Rev:** Shield with lion of St. Mark, value '140' in exergue **Rev. Legend:** SANCTVS. MARCVS. EVANG. **Note:** Ref. V-173; Dav. 3887. Design in imitation of a contemporary Scudo of Venice.

Date	Mintage	VG	F	VF	XF	Unc
ND(1616-31) Rare	—	—	—	—	—	—

DAV# 3881 SCUDO (140 Soldi)

Silver **Obv:** Bust of Siro right, 1620 below **Rev:** Crowned arms **Rev. Legend:** ANTIQVISS. FAM. AVS. INSIGN

Date	Mintage	Good	VG	F	VF	XF
1620 Rare	—	—	—	—	—	—

TRADE COINAGE

KM# 56 1/2 SCUDO D'ORO

1.5000 g., Gold, 22 mm. **Ruler:** Giovanni Siro **Obv:** Crowned imperial eagle, orb on breast **Obv. Legend:** SVB. VMBRA. ALAR. TVAR. **Rev:** Full-length facing figure of St. Quirinus holding crozier, small shield of 4-fold arms below **Rev. Legend:** S. QVIR. EPS. - PROT. COR. **Note:** Ref. V-165.

Date	Mintage	VG	F	VF	XF	Unc
ND(1616-31) Rare	—	—	—	—	—	—

KM# 57 1/2 SCUDO D'ORO

1.5000 g., Gold, 22 mm. **Ruler:** Giovanni Siro **Obv:** Small shield of family arms in ornamented hexalobe **Obv. Legend:** MON. AVREA. - CIVITAT. C. **Rev:** Youthful full-length figure of St. Quirinus walking left holding palm branch **Rev. Legend:** DIVS. QVI. - EPS. PROT. C. **Note:** Ref. V-166.

Date	Mintage	VG	F	VF	XF	Unc
ND(1616-31) Rare	—	—	—	—	—	—

CUNEO

Town

The commune of Cuneo was founded near the end of the 12th century and was acquired by the counts of Savoy in 1382. Located near the mountainous border with France in northwestern Italy, the town was besieged by the French a number of times. Only during the siege of 1641 was obsidional coinage struck, at the order of the Savoyard governor, Count Vivalda.

REFERENCE

Cud = Sergio Cudazzo, **Monete Italiane Regionali: Casa Savoia**, Pavia: Numismatica Varesi, 2005.

TOWN

SIEGE COINAGE

KM# 1 LIRA

Silver Weight varies: 10.72-11.90g., 34 mm. **Obv:** Ornate shield of manifold arms with central shield of Savoy, superimposed on 2 crossed palm branches **Obv. Legend:** +CI - VITAS. CVNEI. S: OBSES - SA. **Rev:** Crossed column and flag on staff in circle, date below **Rev. Legend:** FIDE. ET + FERRO. **Note:** Ref. Cud. 775.

Date	Mintage	VG	F	VF	XF	Unc
1641 Rare	—	3,250	5,400	8,400	13,000	—

Note: Fritz Rudolf Künker Münzenhandlung Auction 116, 9-06, VF realized approximately $20,335

KM# 2 DOPPIA
Gold Weight varies: 6.35-6.65g., 30 mm. **Obv:** Spanish shield with concave sides of manifold arms with central shield of Savoy, superimposed on 2 crossed palm branches, FER - EN - DO at left, above and right of arms **Obv. Legend:** +C - IVITAS. CVNEI. S: OBSESS - A. **Rev:** Crossed column and flag on staff in circle, date below **Rev. Legend:** FIDE. ET + FERRO. **Note:** Ref. Cud. 774; Fr. 228.

Date	Mintage	VG	F	VF	XF	Unc
1641 Rare	—	—	—	—	—	—

KM# 3 5 DOPPIE
Gold Weight varies: 33.14-33.20g., 34 mm. **Obv:** Ornate shield of manifold arms with central shield of Savoy, superimposed on 2 crossed palm branches **Obv. Legend:** +CI - VITAS. CVNEI. S: OBSES - SA. **Rev:** Crossed column and flag on staff in circle, date below **Rev. Legend:** FIDE. ET + FERRO. **Note:** Ref. Cud. 773; Fr. 227. Varieties exist.

Date	Mintage	VG	F	VF	XF	Unc
1641 Rare	—	—	—	—	—	—

DESANA

Countship

The town of Desana in Piedmont, less than five miles (7.5 kilometers) southwest of Vercelli, was under the control of the bishop of that city from 1003. Teodosio II of Montferrat was proclaimed lord of the town in 1411 and persuaded the town council to cede power to Ludovico (I) Tizzone. Ludovico II received the mint right in 1482 and was raised to the rank of count in 1510. Because the count had sided with Emperor Carlo V, King Francis II of France took the feudal lordship away from the Tizzone family and conferred it upon François de Mareuil in 1515. The latter then ceded the rights over Desana to Pierre de Beraud the next year, who in turn sold half of the countship to Filippo Tornielli. The count then sold Desana to Duke Carlo III of Savoy, who restored it to the Tizzone family in 1529. The widow of the last count sold the countship to Duke Vittorio Amadeo II of Savoy in 1693.

RULERS
Antonio Maria II Tizzone, 1598-1641
Carlo Giuseppe Francesco Tizzone, 1641-1676

Arms:
5 diagonal firebrands (Italian = tizzone)

Reference:
Alberto Varesi, ***Monete Italiane Regionali: Piemonte, Sardegna, Liguria, Isola di Corsica***. *Pavia, 1996.*

COUNTSHIP

STANDARD COINAGE

KM# 2 TRILLINA
1.0000 g., Billon, 16 mm. **Ruler:** Antonio Maria II **Obv:** Crowned "T.11" in circle **Obv. Legend:** MONETA. CAESARI. **Rev:** Floriated cross in circle **Rev. Legend:** CRVX. SANTA. ET. BEN. **Note:** Ref. V-585.

Date	Mintage	VG	F	VF	XF	Unc
ND(1618-30)	—	75.00	140	300	500	—

KM# 75 TRILLINA
Billon Weight varies: 1.08-1.20g., 14-15 mm. **Ruler:** Carlo **Obv:** Oval shield of four-fold arms **Obv. Legend:** CAR. IOS. TICO. D. **Rev:** Crown above 'PHI' **Rev. Legend:** CIAN. SAC. RO. IMP. **Note:** Ref. V-600. Prev. KM# 15.

Date	Mintage	VG	F	VF	XF	Unc
ND(1641-76)	—	40.00	80.00	170	275	—

KM# 76 TRILLINA
Billon, 14-15 mm. **Ruler:** Carlo **Obv:** Crown over 'PTI' **Obv. Legend:** ...EX. A...E. **Rev:** Nimbate facing bust divides S - A **Rev. Legend:** ME... NIDX. **Note:** Ref. V-601.

Date	Mintage	VG	F	VF	XF	Unc
ND(1641-76)	—	80.00	165	325	550	—

KM# 82 SOLDINO
Billon Weight varies: 1.27-1.40g., 16-17 mm. **Ruler:** Carlo **Obv:** Bust to right, date below, where present **Obv. Legend:** CAROLVS. - IO. COM. **Rev:** Floriated cross **Rev. Legend:** VIC. PERP. S. R. IMP. **Note:** Ref. V-598. Prev. KM# 95.

Date	Mintage	VG	F	VF	XF	Unc
1672	—	55.00	110	225	350	—
ND	—	55.00	110	225	350	—

KM# 85 SOLDINO
Billon Weight varies: 1.58-1.88g., 16-17 mm. **Ruler:** Carlo **Obv:** Bust to right, date below **Obv. Legend:** CAROL. - TI. C. D. SA. **Rev:** Floriated cross **Rev. Legend:** MARC. MEDIOL. **Note:** Ref. V-599. Prev. KM# 96.

Date	Mintage	VG	F	VF	XF	Unc
1676	—	55.00	110	225	350	—

KM# 5 QUATTRINO
Billon Weight varies: 0.50-0.65g., 14 mm. **Ruler:** Antonio Maria II **Obv:** Armored bust to right **Obv. Legend:** ANT. MAR. TIT. BL. COM. **Rev:** Ornate shield of crowned arms **Rev. Legend:** DECIAN. VIC. IMP. PER. **Note:** Ref. V-586.

Date	Mintage	VG	F	VF	XF	Unc
ND(1618-30)	—	40.00	80.00	200	330	—

KM# 6 QUATTRINO
0.5100 g., Billon, 16 mm. **Ruler:** Antonio Maria II **Obv:** Head to left **Obv. Legend:** ANT. MAR. TIT. BL. COM. DEC. V. IMP. **Rev:** Ornate cross in circle **Rev. Legend:** IN. HOC. SIGNO. CONFIDO. **Note:** Ref. V-587.

Date	Mintage	VG	F	VF	XF	Unc
ND(1618-30)	—	40.00	80.00	200	330	—

KM# 7 QUATTRINO
Billon Weight varies: 0.59-0.61g., 14 mm. **Ruler:** Antonio Maria II **Obv:** Head to left **Obv. Legend:** ANT. MAR. TIT. BL. COM. DEC. V. IMP. **Rev:** Bear walking to left **Rev. Legend:** AB. INVIDIS. ERIPE. ME. D. **Note:** Ref. V-588.

Date	Mintage	VG	F	VF	XF	Unc
ND(1618-30)	—	40.00	80.00	200	330	—

KM# 8 QUATTRINO
Billon Weight varies: 0.42-0.52g., 15 mm. **Ruler:** Antonio Maria II **Obv:** Crowned 'MA' monogram superimposed on two crossed palm branches **Obv. Legend:** TIT. BLA. COMES. **Rev:** Crowned arms **Rev. Legend:** COMES. DECIANE. **Note:** Ref. V-589.

Date	Mintage	VG	F	VF	XF	Unc
ND(1618-30)	—	40.00	80.00	200	330	—

KM# 9 QUATTRINO
Billon Weight varies: 0.50-0.62g., 15 mm. **Ruler:** Antonio Maria II **Obv:** Crowned 'MA' monogram superimposed on two crossed palm branches **Obv. Legend:** TIT. BLA. COM. DEC. **Rev:** Cross with lily ends **Rev. Legend:** IN. HOC. SIGNO. CONFIDO. **Note:** Ref. V-590.

Date	Mintage	VG	F	VF	XF	Unc
ND(1618-30)	—	40.00	80.00	200	330	—

KM# 10 QUATTRINO
0.4300 g., Billon, 14 mm. **Ruler:** Antonio Maria II **Obv:** Crowned 'MA' monogram superimposed on two crossed palm branches **Obv. Legend:** TIT. BLA. COM. DEC. **Rev:** Bear walking to left **Rev. Legend:** AB. INVID. VT. AB. VRSO. ERIP. N. D. **Note:** Ref. V-591.

Date	Mintage	VG	F	VF	XF	Unc
ND(1618-30)	—	75.00	140	325	550	—

KM# 77 QUATTRINO
Copper Weight varies: 1.32-2.47g., 15-16 mm. **Ruler:** Carlo **Obv:** High-collared bust to right **Obv. Legend:** CAR. GIOS. TICONE. CONT. **Rev:** Round four-fold arms **Rev. Legend:** DESANA. VIC. IMP. PERPETVO. **Note:** Ref. V-602. Prev. KM# 85.

Date	Mintage	VG	F	VF	XF	Unc
ND(1641-76)	—	55.00	110	225	350	—

KM# 83 KREUZER
Billon Weight varies: 1.48-1.49g., 18 mm. **Ruler:** Carlo **Obv:** Shield of 2-fold arms, displayed eagle above **Obv. Legend:** CARLO. GIOS. TIZ. B. A. **Rev:** Cross in circle, date at end of legend **Rev. Legend:** S. THEODOLVS. **Note:** Ref. V-597, where date is incorrectly read as 1628. Prev. KM#79.

Date	Mintage	VG	F	VF	XF	Unc
1673	—	80.00	165	325	550	—

KM# 11 2 KREUZER
0.8800 g., Billon, 19 mm. **Ruler:** Antonio Maria II **Obv:** Crowned shield of 4-fold arms with central shield **Obv. Legend:** ANT. MAR. TIT. BLAN. COM. DEC. **Rev:** Crowned imperial eagle, '2' in orb on breast **Rev. Legend:** SAC. ROM. IMP. VIC. PERPE. **Note:** Ref. V-579. Prev. KM#77.

Date	Mintage	VG	F	VF	XF	Unc
ND(1618-30)	—	200	385	875	1,500	—

KM# 12 3 KREUZER
1.3600 g., Billon, 19 mm. **Ruler:** Antonio Maria II **Obv:** Shield of 4-fold arms **Obv. Legend:** ANT. MAR. TITIO. COM. DEC. **Rev:** Crowned imperial eagle, '3' in circle on breast **Rev. Legend:** SAC. ROM. IMP. VICA. PERPE. **Note:** Ref. V-578. Prev. KM#76.

Date	Mintage	VG	F	VF	XF	Unc
ND(1618-30)	—	150	275	550	900	—

KM# 53 SOLDO
Billon Weight varies: 0.93-1.04, 18-19 mm. **Ruler:** Antonio Maria II **Obv:** Small shield of 2-fold arms divides L - V, small imperial eagle above, all in quatrefoil **Obv. Legend:** MONETA. DECIEN. **Rev:** 3/4-length facing figure of St. Ludger **Rev. Legend:** SANCT - LVDIGA. **Note:** Ref. V-582. Prev. KM#11.

Date	Mintage	VG	F	VF	XF	Unc
ND(1630-41)	—	150	275	650	1,000	—

KM# 54 SOLDO
Billon Weight varies: 0.63-1.29g., 18-19 mm. **Ruler:** Antonio Maria II **Obv:** Crowned imperial eagle over small shield of arms **Obv. Legend:** MON. NOV. COM. DEC. **Rev:** Facing bust of St. Leonard **Rev. Legend:** SANCTVS. LEONAR. **Note:** Ref. V-583. Prev. KM#12. Design in imitation of Luzern (Switz.) Schilling, KM#25.

Date	Mintage	VG	F	VF	XF	Unc
ND(1630-41)	—	80.00	165	325	550	—

KM# 55 SOLDO
Billon Weight varies: 0.63-1.29g., 18-19 mm. **Ruler:** Antonio Maria II **Obv:** Crowned imperial eagle over small shield of arms **Obv. Legend:** MONETA. DECIAN. **Rev:** Facing bust of St. Leonard **Rev. Legend:** SANCTVS. LEONAR. **Note:** Ref. V-583/1. Prev. KM#13. Design in imitation of Luzern (Switz.) Schilling, KM#25.

Date	Mintage	VG	F	VF	XF	Unc
ND(1630-41)	—	90.00	195	425	700	—

KM# 56 SOLDO
Billon, 18 mm. **Ruler:** Antonio Maria II **Obv:** Crowned imperial eagle over small shield of arms **Obv. Legend:** MONETA - DECIAN. **Rev:** Full-length facing figure of St. Martin **Rev. Legend:** SANCTV - MARINV. **Note:** Ref. V-584. Prev. KM#14.

Date	Mintage	VG	F	VF	XF	Unc
ND(1630-41) Rare	—	—	—	—	—	—

KM# 13 PARPAGLIOLA
2.3000 g., Silver Plated Copper, 20 mm. **Ruler:** Antonio Maria II **Obv:** Crowned shield of 4-fold arms, quartered with eagle and head of dolphin **Obv. Legend:** MEDIO - ANT. D. **Rev:** Standing allegorical figure of Providence **Rev. Legend:** PROVIDENTIA. **Note:** Ref. V-580.

Date	Mintage	VG	F	VF	XF	Unc
ND(1618-30)	—	125	220	475	750	—

KM# 14 PARPAGLIOLA
1.3600 g., Silver Plated Copper, 19 mm. **Ruler:** Antonio Maria II **Obv:** Crowned shield of 4-fold arms, quartered with firebrands and coiled adder **Obv. Legend:** MEDD - LANI. D. **Rev:** Standing figure of Providence **Rev. Legend:** PROVIDENTIA. **Note:** Ref. V-581.

Date	Mintage	VG	F	VF	XF	Unc
ND(1618-30)	—	125	220	475	700	—

KM# 49 30 KREUZER
3.2500 g., Billon, 24-25 mm. **Ruler:** Antonio Maria II **Obv:** Arms of Bern in baroque frame, date at end of legend **Obv. Legend:** MONE. NOV. T. B. DESANENSIS. **Rev:** Imperial eagle in circle **Rev. Legend:** +BERTH. D. TERR. IM. FVNDATOR. **Note:** Ref. V-577. Prev. KM#75. Design in imitation of Bern (Switz.) 1/2 Dicken, KM#A20.

Date	Mintage	VG	F	VF	XF	Unc
16ZZ Rare	—	—	—	—	—	—

KM# 15 4 GROSSI
Billon Weight varies: 3.55-3.74g., 23-24 mm. **Ruler:** Antonio Maria II **Obv:** Two adjacent shields of arms, crown above, value 'IIII' below, all in circle **Obv. Legend:** ANT. MAR. TIT. BLAN. COM. D. V. IM. P. **Rev:** Bust of St. Ladislaus right in circle **Rev. Legend:** SANCTVS. LADISLAVS. REX. **Note:** Ref. V-576. Prev. KM#74. Design in imitation of an issue of Lithuania.

Date	Mintage	VG	F	VF	XF	Unc
ND(1618-30)	—	275	440	950	1,400	—

KM# 50 FIORINO (12 Grossi)
5.5900 g., Billon, 24 mm. **Ruler:** Antonio Maria II **Obv:** Oval 2-fold arms in baroque frame, value 'XII.G.' in exergue **Obv. Legend:** MONETA. NOVA. M. T. B. COMES. D. **Rev:** Bust of St. Stephen to left, date in exergue **Rev. Legend:** S. STEPHANVS. PROTHOM. **Note:** Ref. V-565. Prev. KM#65. Design in imitation of Metz 12 Groschen, KM#2.

Date	Mintage	VG	F	VF	XF	Unc
1622	—	550	825	1,600	2,750	—

KM# 16 FIORINO
5.5500 g., Billon, 29 mm. **Ruler:** Antonio Maria II **Obv:** Lion rampant to left in circle **Obv. Legend:** MONETA. NOVA. ARGENTEA. D. T. D. **Rev:** Full-length facing figure of Madonna and Child, crescent below, rays around **Rev. Legend:** SANCTA. MAR - IA. VIRGO. **Note:** Ref. V-566. Prev. KM#66.

Date	Mintage	VG	F	VF	XF	Unc
ND(1618-30) Rare	—	—	—	—	—	—

KM# 17 FIORINO
6.5900 g., Billon, 27-28 mm. **Ruler:** Antonio Maria II **Obv:** Shield of 4-fold arms with central shield, all in circle **Obv. Legend:** ANT. MAR. TIT. BLA. COM. DEC. VIC. I. P. **Rev:** Bust of St. Leonard to right in circle **Rev. Legend:** DIVVS. LEONARDVS. EPISC. PROTEC. **Note:** Ref. V-567. Prev. KM#67. Design in imitation of Teston of Hanau-Lichtenberg, KM#30.

Date	Mintage	VG	F	VF	XF	Unc
ND(1618-30)	—	775	1,100	2,750	4,500	—

KM# 18 FIORINO
Billon Weight varies: 3.55-4.61g., 28 mm. **Ruler:** Antonio Maria II **Obv:** Crowned shield of 4-fold arms in circle **Obv. Legend:** ANT. MAR. TIT. BLA. COM. DEC. VIC. IMP. P. **Rev:** Crowned imperial eagle in circle **Rev. Legend:** SVB. VMBRA. ALAR. TVAR. PROTEGOR. **Note:** Ref. V-570. Prev. KM#69. Design in imitation of Campen 6 Stuivers, KM#7ff.

Date	Mintage	VG	F	VF	XF	Unc
ND(1618-30)	—	275	500	1,000	1,650	—

KM# 19 FIORINO

Billon, 28 mm. **Ruler:** Antonio Maria II **Obv:** Large five-petaled rose in circle **Obv. Legend:** ANT. MAR. TIT. BL. COM. DEC. VIC. IMP. P. **Rev:** Crowned imperial eagle, '12' in circle on breast **Rev. Legend:** SVB. VMBRA. ALAR. TVAR. PROTEC. **Note:** Ref. V-571. Prev. KM#70. Design in imitation of Hagenau 12 Kreuzer, KM#37.

Date	Mintage	VG	F	VF	XF	Unc
ND(1618-30) Rare	—	—	—	—	—	—

KM# 20 FIORINO

4.4300 g., Billon, 26-27 mm. **Ruler:** Antonio Maria II **Obv:** Large lily in circle **Obv. Legend:** MON. ARGENTEA. COM. D. VIC. IM. P. **Rev:** Cross with floriated ends in circle **Rev. Legend:** IN HOC. SIGNO VINCES. **Note:** Ref. V-572. Prev. KM#71. Design in imitation of Strassburg (city) 12 Kreuzer MB#144.

Date	Mintage	VG	F	VF	XF	Unc
ND(1618-30)	—	1,150	2,250	4,250	7,000	—

KM# 21 FIORINO

Billon, 26-27 mm. **Ruler:** Antonio Maria II **Obv:** Large lily in circle, value (XII) at top in margin **Obv. Legend:** MONE. NOVA. ARGENT. CO. DEC. **Rev:** Cross with floriated ends in circle **Rev. Legend:** GLORIA. IN EXCELSIS. DE. **Note:** Ref. V-573. Prev. KM#72. Design in imitation of Strassburg (city) 12 Kreuzer MB#144.

Date	Mintage	VG	F	VF	XF	Unc
ND(1618-30) Rare	—	—	—	—	—	—

KM# 22 FIORINO

Billon, 26-27 mm. **Ruler:** Antonio Maria II **Obv:** Large lily in circle **Obv. Legend:** SICVT. LILIVM. INTER. SPINAS. **Rev:** Cross with floriated ends in circle **Rev. Legend:** MON. ARG. COM. DEC. VIC. IMP. PER. **Note:** Ref. V-574. Prev. KM#73. Design in imitation of Strassburg (city) 12 Kreuzer MB#150.

Date	Mintage	VG	F	VF	XF	Unc
ND(1618-30) Rare	—	—	—	—	—	—

KM# 47 FIORINO

Billon, 31 mm. **Ruler:** Antonio Maria II **Obv:** Crowned imperial eagle in circle **Obv. Legend:** ANT. MAR. TIT. BL. COM. DEC. VI. IMP. P. P. **Rev:** Half-length figure of St. Charles Borromeo to right divides date **Rev. Legend:** S. CAROL. BOROM. AR. ME. P. M. **Note:** Ref. V-568. Prev. KM#60.

Date	Mintage	VG	F	VF	XF	Unc
1619 Rare	—	—	—	—	—	—

KM# 48 FIORINO

4.2700 g., Billon, 27 mm. **Ruler:** Antonio Maria II **Obv:** Crowned shield of 4-fold arms in circle **Obv. Legend:** ANT. MAR. TIT. BLA. COM. DE. VIC. IMP. P. **Rev:** Crowned imperial eagle, '12' in circle on breast **Rev. Legend:** SVB. VMBRA. ALAR. TVAR. PROTEG. **Note:** Ref. V-569. Prev. KM#68.

Date	Mintage	VG	F	VF	XF	Unc
1621	—	1,000	2,000	3,500	6,000	—
ND	—	1,000	2,000	3,500	6,000	—

KM# 57 FIORINO

3.7600 g., Billon, 28-29 mm. **Ruler:** Antonio Maria II **Obv:** Shield with crowned displayed eagle, ornate crowned helmet above **Obv. Legend:** ANT. MAR. TIT. COM. DEC. VI. IMP. P. **Rev:** Crowned imperial eagle with shield of Austrian arms on breast **Rev. Legend:** SVB. VMBRA. ALAR. TVAR. PROTEGOR. **Note:** Ref. V-575. Prev. KM#78.

Date	Mintage	VG	F	VF	XF	Unc
ND(1630-41)	—	1,000	1,650	3,300	5,000	—

KM# 23 3 BIANCHI

Silver Weight varies: 7.95-8.07g., 29 mm. **Ruler:** Antonio Maria II **Obv:** Imperial eagle above small shield of Tizzone arms **Obv. Legend:** MON. NOV. COM. DECI. **Rev:** Bust of St. Leonard to right **Rev. Legend:** SANCTVS - LEONARDVS. **Note:** Ref. V-563. Prev. KM#22. Design in imitation of Luzern (Switz.) Dicken, KM#16.

Date	Mintage	VG	F	VF	XF	Unc
ND(1618-30)	—	750	1,200	2,750	4,500	—

KM# 58 3 BIANCHI

7.1400 g., Silver, 30 mm. **Ruler:** Antonio Maria II **Obv:** Imperial eagle in circle **Obv. Legend:** MONETA. COM. DEC. VICARII. IMP. PE. **Rev:** Lion emerging to left from castle tower at right **Rev. Legend:** IN. FORTITVDINE. MEA. **Note:** Ref. V-564. Prev. KM#21.

Date	Mintage	VG	F	VF	XF	Unc
ND(1630-41)	—	850	1,350	3,250	5,250	—

KM# 81 1/4 TALLERO (15 Quattrini)

7.2500 g., Silver, 29 mm. **Ruler:** Carlo **Obv:** Armored bust to right, value (XV) below **Obv. Legend:** CAROLVS. TIT. D. G. COM. DECIANÆ. **Rev:** Imperial eagle with shield of Tizzone arms on breast, large crown above divides date **Rev. Legend:** MONETA. NOVA. ARGENTEA. **Note:** Ref. V-595. Prev. KM#91.

Date	Mintage	VG	F	VF	XF	Unc
1669 Rare	—	—	—	—	—	—

KM# 24 TESTONE

Silver Weight varies: 5.09-5.65g., 28-29 mm. **Ruler:** Antonio Maria II **Obv:** Bust to right in circle **Obv. Legend:** ANT. MAR. TIT. BLA. COM. DEC. VIC. IMPE. **Rev:** Full-length facing female figure, right hand resting on column **Rev. Legend:** FORTITV. ILLIVS. DEXT. EIVS. **Note:** Ref. V-558. Prev. KM#16.

Date	Mintage	VG	F	VF	XF	Unc
ND(1618-30)	—	650	1,000	2,500	3,850	—

KM# 25 TESTONE

Silver Weight varies: 5.30-6.24g., 28 mm. **Ruler:** Antonio Maria II **Obv:** Bust with high collar to right **Obv. Legend:** ANT. MAR. TIT. COM. DEC. PRO. IMP. **Rev:** Crowned shield of 4-fold arms, with oval central shield of Tizzone arms, in baroque frame **Rev. Legend:** SACRIQVE. ROM. IMP. VICARIVS. PERP. **Note:** Ref. V-559. Prev. KM#17.

Date	Mintage	VG	F	VF	XF	Unc
ND(1618-30) Rare	—	—	—	—	—	—

KM# 26 TESTONE

Silver Weight varies: 5.82-6.67g., 29 mm. **Ruler:** Antonio Maria II **Obv:** Half-length armored figure to right in circle **Obv. Legend:** ANT. MAR. TIT. COM. DEC. VIC. IMP. PERP. **Rev:** Crowned imperial eagle with oval shield of Austrian arms on breast **Rev. Legend:** VIRTVTE. CAESAREA. DVCE. **Note:** Ref. V-560. Prev. KM#18.

Date	Mintage	VG	F	VF	XF	Unc
ND(1618-30)	—	300	550	1,400	2,200	—

KM# 27 TESTONE

Billon Weight varies: 4.49-5.04g., 28 mm. **Ruler:** Antonio Maria II **Subject:** To the memory of Antonio Maria II's father, Delfino **Obv:** Half-length armored figure to right in circle **Obv. Legend:** DELPHINVS. PAT. ANT. MAR. TIT. BL. CO. DE. **Rev:** Crowned imperial eagle with oval shield of Austrian arms on breast **Rev. Legend:** ET. SACRI. ROMANI. IMPER. VICARII. PE. **Note:** Ref. V-561. Prev. KM#19.

Date	Mintage	VG	F	VF	XF	Unc
ND(1618-30)	—	300	550	1,400	2,200	—

KM# 59 TESTONE

7.2400 g., Silver, 28-29 mm. **Ruler:** Antonio Maria II **Obv:** High-collared bust to right **Obv. Legend:** ANT. MAR. TIT. COM. DEC. PRO. IMP. **Rev:** Crowned displayed eagle **Rev. Legend:** SVM. (sic) VMBRA. ALAR. TVAR. PROTEGOR. **Note:** Ref. V-562. Prev. KM#20.

Date	Mintage	VG	F	VF	XF	Unc
ND(1630-41)	—	900	1,650	3,800	5,500	—

KM# 80 TESTONE

Silver Weight varies: 7.54-7.82g., 30-31 mm. **Ruler:** Carlo **Obv:** Draped bust to right in circle, date at end of legend **Obv. Legend:** FRAN. TIT. M. ROD. C. DE. CS. R. I. VI. **Rev:** Virgin Mary at right in adoration of baby Jesus at left **Rev. Legend:** QVÆ. SOLA. VIRGO. PARTVRIT. **Note:** Ref. V-596. Prev. KM#90.

Date	Mintage	VG	F	VF	XF	Unc
1667	—	750	1,100	2,850	4,500	—

KM# 28 TALLERO

Silver (Debased) Weight varies: 27.20-28.97g., 39-40 mm. **Ruler:** Antonio Maria II **Subject:** In memory of Antonio Maria II's father, Delfino **Obv:** High-collared bust of Delfino to right **Obv. Legend:** DELPHINVS. PATER. ANTO. MAR. TIT. BL. COM. D. **Rev:** Crowned shield of manifold arms, with central shield of displayed eagle, garland around. **Rev. Legend:** SACRIQVE. ROM. IMPER. VICARIVS. PERPET. **Note:** Ref. V-547; Dav. 3888. Prev. KM#23.

Date	Mintage	VG	F	VF	XF	Unc
ND(1618-30)	—	900	1,650	4,000	6,600	—

KM# 29 TALLERO

Silver (Debased) Weight varies: 17.90-19.04g., 39 mm. **Ruler:** Antonio Maria II **Subject:** In memory of Antonio Maria II's father, Delfino **Obv:** Half-length armored figure of Delfino to right **Obv. Legend:** DELPHINVS. PAT. ANT. MAR. TIT. BL. COM. DEC. **Rev:** Crowned imperial eagle, shield of Austrian arms on breast **Rev. Legend:** ET. SACRI. ROMANI. IMPER. VICARII. PERPE. **Note:** Ref. V-548. Prev. KM#24.

Date	Mintage	VG	F	VF	XF	Unc
ND(1618-30)	—	750	1,350	3,000	6,000	—

KM# 30 TALLERO

26.1700 g., Silver, 40 mm. **Ruler:** Antonio Maria II **Obv:** Half-length armored figure to right **Obv. Legend:** ANT. MAR. TIT. COM. DEC. PRO. IMP. **Rev:** Crowned imperial eagle, shield of Tizzone arms on breast **Rev. Legend:** SACRIQVE. ROM. IM. VICARIVS. PERPETVVS. **Note:** Ref. V-549; Dav. 3889. Prev. KM#24a.

Date	Mintage	VG	F	VF	XF	Unc
ND(1618-30)	—	2,000	3,500	6,500	10,000	—

KM# 31 TALLERO

Silver, 41 mm. **Ruler:** Antonio Maria II **Obv:** Half-length armored figure to right, holding scepter over right shoulder **Obv. Legend:** ANTONIVS. MARIA. TITIO. COMES. DECIANE. **Rev:** Crowned imperial eagle, small shield of arms on breast **Rev. Legend:** SACRIQVE. ROM. IMP. VICARIVS. PERPETVVS. **Note:** Ref. V-550; Dav. 3890. Prev. KM#26.

Date	Mintage	VG	F	VF	XF	Unc
ND(1618-30) Rare	—	—	—	—	—	—

KM# 32 TALLERO

28.7500 g., Silver, 40 mm. **Ruler:** Antonio Maria II **Obv:** Crowned oval 3-fold arms in baroque frame **Obv. Legend:** ANT. MAR. TIT. BLANC. COM. DEC. VIC. IMP. P. **Rev:** Seated facing figure of St. Ubertus on throne **Rev. Legend:** SANCTVS. VBERTVS. EPISC. PROTECTOR. **Note:** Ref. V-551; Dav. 3891. Prev. KM#27. Design in imitation of Salzburg Thaler, KM# 38ff.

Date	Mintage	VG	F	VF	XF	Unc
ND(1618-30) Rare	—	—	—	—	—	—

Note: WAG Auction 36, 2-06, VF realized approximately $26,800

KM# 33 TALLERO

Silver, 40 mm. **Ruler:** Antonio Maria II **Obv:** Crowned oval 3-fold arms in baroque frame **Obv. Legend:** ANT. MAR. TIT. BLAN. COM. DEC. VIC. IMP. P. **Rev:** St. George on horseback to right slaying dragon below **Rev. Legend:** SANCTVS. GEORGIVS. PROTECT. DECIA. **Note:** Ref. V-552; Dav. 3892. Prev. KM#29. Mule of KM#32 obv. and KM#34 rev.

Date	Mintage	VG	F	VF	XF	Unc
ND(1618-30) Rare	—	—	—	—	—	—

KM# 34 TALLERO

26.6700 g., Silver, 40 mm. **Ruler:** Antonio Maria II **Obv:** Shield of 4-fold arms, 2 ornate helmets above, 'AM / 97' at top **Obv. Legend:** ANT. MAR. TIT. BLA. COM. DEC. V. IMP. P. **Rev:** St. George on horseback to right slaying dragon below **Rev. Legend:** SANCTVS. GEORGIVS. PROTECT. DECIA. **Note:** Ref. V-553; Dav. 3893. Prev. KM#28. Design in imitation of Mansfeld-Friedeburg Thaler, MB#52.

Date	Mintage	VG	F	VF	XF	Unc
ND(1618-30)	—	900	1,650	4,000	6,600	—

KM# 35 TALLERO

25.8000 g., Silver, 38-39 mm. **Ruler:** Antonio Maria II **Obv:** Crowned 4-fold arms, with central shield of Tizzone, in baroque frame **Obv. Legend:** CESARIE. MAIESTATIS. ROMANOROM. IMPERIO. **Rev:** St. George on horseback to right slaying dragon below **Rev. Legend:** SANCTVS. GEORGIVS. PROTECT. DECIA. **Note:** Ref. V-555; Dav. 3894. Prev. KM#31. Mule of two rev. dies-KM# 60 and KM# 34.

Date	Mintage	VG	F	VF	XF	Unc
ND(1618-30)	—	1,250	2,200	4,500	6,600	—

KM# 60 TALLERO

23.9100 g., Silver, 39-40 mm. **Ruler:** Antonio Maria II **Obv:** Half-length armored figure to right **Obv. Legend:** MONETA. NOVA. ANT. MAR. TI. COM. DEC. PRO. VI. **Rev:** Crowned 4-fold arms, with central shield of Tizzone, in baroque frame **Rev. Legend:** CESARIE. MAIESTATIS. ROMANOROM. IMPERIO. **Note:** Ref. V-554; Dav. 3895. Prev. KM#32.

Date	Mintage	VG	F	VF	XF	Unc
ND(1630-41) Rare	—	—	—	—	—	—

KM# 61 TALLERO

Silver, 40 mm. **Ruler:** Antonio Maria II **Obv:** Half-length armored figure to right **Obv. Legend:** ANT. MAR. TIT. COM. DEC. PRO. IMPE. **Rev:** Crowned 4-fold arms, with central shield of Tizzone, in baroque frame **Rev. Legend:** CESARIE. MAIESTATIS. ROMANOROM. IMPERIO. **Note:** Ref. V554/1; Dav. 3896. Prev. KM#34.

Date	Mintage	VG	F	VF	XF	Unc
ND(1630-41)	—	2,000	3,500	6,500	10,000	—

KM# 62 TALLERO
Silver, 40-41 mm. **Ruler:** Antonio Maria II **Obv:** Large half-length armored figure to right **Obv. Legend:** MONETA. NOVA. ANT. MAR. TI. COM. DEC. PRO. VI. **Rev:** Crowned imperial eagle, shield of Tizzone arms on breast, 'R XI III' in margin at bottom **Rev. Legend:** SACRO. ROM. IMP. - VICAR. PERPET. **Note:** Ref. V-556; Dav. 3897. Prev. KM#33.

Date	Mintage	VG	F	VF	XF	Unc
ND(1630-41) Rare	—	—	—	—	—	—

KM# 63 TALLERO
27.9600 g., Silver, 39-40 mm. **Ruler:** Antonio Maria II **Obv:** Displayed eagle with shield of Tizzone arms on breast **Obv. Legend:** NVMVS. ARG. IMP. COMITIS. DECIANE. **Rev:** Crowned half-length armored figure to left, holding scepter over left shoulder **Rev. Legend:** FERDI. D.G. RO. VNG. BOE. DAL. CR. REX. **Note:** Ref. V-557; Dav. 3898. Prev. KM#35.

Date	Mintage	VG	F	VF	XF	Unc
ND(1630-41) Rare	—	—	—	—	—	—

TRADE COINAGE

KM# 36 FIORINO
Gold, 21-22 mm. **Ruler:** Antonio Maria II **Obv:** Half-length facing armored figure turned slightly to right, holding scepter over right shoulder **Obv. Legend:** ANT. MAR. TIT. BL. COM. DEC. VIC. IM. PER. **Rev:** Crowned imperial eagle, round shield of Austrian arms on breast **Rev. Legend:** SVB. VMBRA. AL - TVAR. PROTEG. **Note:** Ref. V-534; Fr. 244. Prev. KM#45.

Date	Mintage	VG	F	VF	XF	Unc
ND(1618-30) Rare	—	—	—	—	—	—

KM# 37 FIORINO
2.5900 g., Gold, 20 mm. **Ruler:** Antonio Maria II **Obv:** Half-length facing armored figure turned slightly to right, holding scepter over right shoulder **Obv. Legend:** ANT. MAR. TIT. BL. COM. DEC. VIC. IM. PER. **Rev:** Crowned shield of manifold arms, with central shield, in circle **Rev. Legend:** LVX. MEA. LVCEM. AB. ALIA. NON. MVTVAT. **Note:** Ref. V-535; Fr. 244a. Prev. KM#46.

Date	Mintage	VG	F	VF	XF	Unc
ND(1618-30)	—	1,200	2,300	4,600	6,600	—

KM# 38 FIORINO
Gold, 21-22 mm. **Ruler:** Antonio Maria II **Obv:** Crowned shield of manifold arms, with central shield, in circle **Obv. Legend:** LVX. MEA. LVCEM. AB. ALIA. NON. MVTVAT. **Rev:** Facing figure of St. Peter standing behind shield of arms below **Rev. Legend:** SANT. PETRVS. - PROP. DECIA. **Note:** Ref. V-536; Fr. 245. Prev. KM#47.

Date	Mintage	VG	F	VF	XF	Unc
ND(1618-30) Rare	—	—	—	—	—	—

KM# 39 FIORINO
3.1500 g., Gold, 21 mm. **Ruler:** Antonio Maria II **Obv:** Crowned imperial eagle in circle **Obv. Legend:** MONETA. NOVA. AVREA. **Rev:** Small shield of arms, ornate helmet above **Rev. Legend:** NON. EST. CONS. ADVERS. DNM. **Note:** Ref. V-537; Fr. 246. Prev. KM#48.

Date	Mintage	VG	F	VF	XF	Unc
ND(1618-30)	—	1,200	2,300	4,600	6,600	—

KM# 40 SCUDO D'ORO
3.0200 g., Gold, 22 mm. **Ruler:** Antonio Maria II **Obv:** Crowned shield of 4-fold arms with central shield of Tizzone family arms **Obv. Legend:** MONE. AVREA. FI. DECI. CVSSA. **Rev:** Cross with lily ends in circle **Rev. Legend:** IN. HOC. SIGNO VINCES. **Note:** Ref. V-540; Fr. 248. Prev. KM#36.

Date	Mintage	VG	F	VF	XF	Unc
ND(1618-30)	—	1,500	2,650	5,400	7,900	—

KM# 64 SCUDO D'ORO
3.0200 g., Gold, 20 mm. **Ruler:** Antonio Maria II **Obv:** Crowned shield of 4-fold arms with central shield of Tizzone family arms **Obv. Legend:** ANT. MAR. TITI. COM. DEC. V. I. P. **Rev:** Crowned imperial eagle, shield of Austrian arms on breast **Rev. Legend:** VIRTVTE. CAESAREA. DVCE. **Note:** Ref. V-541. Prev. KM#37.

Date	Mintage	VG	F	VF	XF	Unc
ND(1630-41)	—	1,600	2,650	6,000	9,200	—

KM# 65 SCUDO D'ORO
Gold, 21-22 mm. **Ruler:** Antonio Maria II **Obv:** Crowned shield of 4-fold arms with central shield of Tizzone family arms **Obv. Legend:** ANT. MAR. TITI. COM. DEC. V. I. P. **Rev:** Seated facing figure of St. Catherine holding palm frond and wheel **Rev. Legend:** SANCTA - CATERINA. **Note:** Ref. V-542; Fr. 251. Prev. KM#52.

Date	Mintage	VG	F	VF	XF	Unc
ND(1630-41) Rare	—	—	—	—	—	—

KM# 66 SCUDO D'ORO
Gold, 22 mm. **Ruler:** Antonio Maria II **Obv:** Displayed eagle in circle **Obv. Legend:** +MONETA. NOVA. AVREA. **Rev:** Full-length figure of St. Lawrence, turned slightly to right, holding grill and book **Rev. Legend:** SANCTVS - LAVRENTIVS. **Note:** Ref. V-543; Fr. 252. Prev. KM#53.

Date	Mintage	VG	F	VF	XF	Unc
ND(1630-41) Rare	—	—	—	—	—	—

KM# 67 SCUDO D'ORO
Gold, 21-22 mm. **Ruler:** Antonio Maria II **Obv:** Imperial eagle in circle **Obv. Legend:** +SVB. VMBRA. ALARVM. TVARVM. **Rev:** Full-length facing figure of St. Louis **Rev. Legend:** SANCTVS - LVDOVICVS. **Note:** Ref. V-544; Fr. 253. Prev. KM#54.

Date	Mintage	VG	F	VF	XF	Unc
ND(1630-41) Rare	—	—	—	—	—	—

KM# 68 SCUDO D'ORO
3.0700 g., Gold, 22 mm. **Ruler:** Antonio Maria II **Obv:** Crowned imperial eagle, orb on breast **Obv. Legend:** MONETA. NOVA. AVREA. **Rev:** Small shield of arms with displayed eagle, ornate helmet above **Rev. Legend:** SIT. NOMEN. DOMINI. BENEDI. **Note:** Ref. V-545. Prev. KM#49.

Date	Mintage	VG	F	VF	XF	Unc
ND(1630-41)	—	950	1,850	3,500	—	—

KM# 1 DUCATO
Gold, 22 mm. **Ruler:** Antonio Maria II **Obv:** Full-length armored figure of count, holdling sword over right shoulder, divides date **Obv. Legend:** DOM. ANT. MA. TIT. COM. DECI. **Rev:** Square tablet in ornamented frame with 5-line inscription **Rev. Inscription:** MO. NOV. / AV. DO. AN. / MAR. TIT. / COM. DEC. / PRO. IMP. **Note:** Ref. V-538; Fr. 249. Prev. KM#50.

Date	Mintage	VG	F	VF	XF	Unc
1603 Rare	—	—	—	—	—	—

KM# 69 DUCATO
3.4200 g., Gold, 23 mm. **Ruler:** Antonio Maria II **Obv:** Crowned shield of 4-fold arms with central shield of Tizzone family arms **Obv. Legend:** CONCORDIA. PAR. RES. CRESCV. **Rev:** Crowned imperial eagle in circle **Rev. Legend:** SVB. VMBRA. ALARVM. TVARVM. **Note:** Ref. V-546; Fr. 247. Prev. KM#38.

Date	Mintage	VG	F	VF	XF	Unc
ND(1630-41) Rare	—	—	—	—	—	—

KM# 70 DUCATO
Gold, 21-22 mm. **Ruler:** Antonio Maria II **Obv:** Full-length armored figure of count turned slightly to right, 2 small crowned shields of arms at left and right **Obv. Legend:** ANT. MAR. TITI. COM. DEC. VI. **Rev:** Square tablet in ornamented frame with 5-line inscription **Rev. Inscription:** LVX. ET I / AM. IN TE / NEBRIS / POSITA / LVCET. **Note:** Ref. V-539; Fr. 250.

Date	Mintage	VG	F	VF	XF	Unc
ND(1630-41) Rare	—	—	—	—	—	—

KM# 71 DUCATO
Gold, 21-22 mm. **Ruler:** Antonio Maria II **Obv:** Full-length armored figure turned slightly to right **Obv. Legend:** ANT. MAR. TITI. COM. DEC. VI. **Rev:** Square tablet in ornamented frame with 5-line inscription **Rev. Inscription:** LVX. ET I / AM. IN TE / NEBRIS / POSITA / LVCET. **Note:** Ref. V-539/1. Prev. KM#51.

Date	Mintage	VG	F	VF	XF	Unc
ND(1630-41)	—	1,200	2,300	4,500	6,600	—

KM# 78 DUCATO
Gold, 22-23 mm. **Ruler:** Carlo **Obv:** Full-length armored figure of count to right holding sword with point down **Obv. Legend:** VIRTVS. VNIT - A. - FORTIOR. EST. **Rev:** Square tablet in ornamented frame witih 5-line inscription **Rev. Inscription:** LEOPOL. / I. IMP. FI. / FERD. CO. / DEC. FEL. / PERPET. **Note:** Ref. V-592; Fr. 254. Prev. KM#86.

Date	Mintage	VG	F	VF	XF	Unc
ND(1641-76) Rare	—	—	—	—	—	—

KM# 79 DUCATO
Gold Weight varies: 3.01-3.16g., 22-23 mm. **Ruler:** Carlo **Obv:** Full-length armored figure of count to right holding sword with point down **Obv. Legend:** VIRTVS. VNIT - A. - FORTIOR. EST. **Rev:** Square tablet in ornamented frame with 5-line inscription **Rev. Inscription:** NON. TIM / EBO. MAL / A. QVIAT / V. DOM. M / ECVM. ES. **Note:** Ref. V-593-4; Fr. 255. Prev. KM#87.

Date	Mintage	VG	F	VF	XF	Unc
ND(1641-76)	—	1,200	2,300	4,200	6,000	—

KM# 41 DOPPIA
Gold Weight varies: 6.52-6.57g., 28 mm. **Ruler:** Antonio Maria II **Obv:** High-collared armored bust to right **Obv. Legend:** ANT. MAR. TIT. COM. DEC. PRO. IMP. **Rev:** Crowned shield of 4-fold arms with central shield of Tizzone family arms **Rev. Legend:** SOLI. DEO. HONOR. ET. GLORIA. **Note:** Ref. V-531; Fr. 238. Prev. KM#39.

Date	Mintage	VG	F	VF	XF	Unc
ND(1618-30)	—	1,850	3,300	7,500	12,000	—

KM# 42 DOPPIA
6.4000 g., Gold, 27 mm. **Ruler:** Antonio Maria II **Obv:** High-collared armored bust to right. **Obv. Legend:** ANT. MARIA. TIT. BLA. COM. **Rev:** Crowned shield of manifold arms in baroque frame, FLOR. AVR in exergue **Rev. Legend:** DECI. VIC. - IMP. PER. **Note:** Ref. V-532. Prev. KM#40.

Date	Mintage	VG	F	VF	XF	Unc
ND(1618-30) Rare	—	—	—	—	—	—

Note: Numismatica Ars Classica Auction 35, 12-06, VF realized approximately $11,995

KM# 43 DOPPIA
Gold Weight varies: 6.48-6.56g., 25 mm. **Ruler:** Antonio Maria II **Obv:** Head to right **Obv. Legend:** ANT. MAR. TIT. BL. COM. DEC. VIC. IMP. P. **Rev:** Standing figure of St. Dorothea holding flower **Rev. Legend:** SANCTA. - DOROTHEA. **Note:** Ref. V-533; Fr. 243. Prev. KM#41.

Date	Mintage	VG	F	VF	XF	Unc
ND(1618-30)	—	2,250	4,200	8,500	13,800	—

KM# 72 DOPPIA
Gold, 28 mm. **Ruler:** Antonio Maria II **Obv:** High-collared bearded bust to right **Obv. Legend:** ANT. MAR. TIT. COM. DEC. PRO. IMP. **Rev:** Crowned shield of 4-fold arms with central shield of Tizzone family arms **Rev. Legend:** SOLI. DEO. HONOR. ET. GLORIA. **Note:** Ref. V-531/1; Fr. 241.

Date	Mintage	VG	F	VF	XF	Unc
ND(1630-41) Rare	—	—	—	—	—	—

KM# 44 2 DOPPIE
Gold Weight varies: 13.00-13.05g., 28-29 mm. **Ruler:** Antonio Maria II **Obv:** High-collared armored bust to right **Obv. Legend:** ANT. MAR. TIT. COM. DEC. PRO. IMP. **Rev:** Crowned shield of 4-fold arms with central shield of Tizzone family arms **Rev. Legend:** SACRIQVE. ROM. IMP. VICARIVS. PERP. **Note:** Ref. V-529; Fr. 237. Prev. KM#42.

Date	Mintage	VG	F	VF	XF	Unc
ND(1618-30)	—	2,500	4,500	8,500	16,000	—

KM# 45 2 DOPPIE
Gold, 31 mm. **Ruler:** Antonio Maria II **Obv:** Head to right **Obv. Legend:** ANT. MAR. TIT. BLA. COM. DEC. VIC. IMP. PE. **Rev:** Standing female figure resting right hand on column **Rev. Legend:** FORTITV. ILLUS. DEXT. EIVS. **Note:** Ref. V-530; Fr. 242. Prev. KM#44.

Date	Mintage	VG	F	VF	XF	Unc
ND(1618-30) Rare	—	—	—	—	—	—

KM# 73 2 DOPPIE
Gold Weight varies: 13.00-13.05g., 31 mm. **Ruler:** Antonio Maria II **Obv:** High-collared bearded bust to right **Obv. Legend:** ANT. MAR. TIT. COMES. DEC. PRO. IMP. **Rev:** Crowned shield of 4-fold arms with central shield of Tizzone family arms **Rev. Legend:** SACRIQVE. ROM. IMP. VICARIVS. PERP. **Note:** Ref. V-529/1; Fr. 240. Prev. KM#43.

Date	Mintage	VG	F	VF	XF	Unc
ND(1630-41) Rare	—	—	—	—	—	—

GAZOLDO

Town and Countship

A small town located only 10 miles (17 kilometers) west-northwest of Mantua, Gazoldo came into the possession of the illustrious Ippoliti family of Mantua by the end of the 13th century. They eventually became counts of Gazoldo and had their own coinage struck beginning the late 16th century. Although the Ippoliti continued to rule in Gazoldo well into the 18th century, the last coinage was produced about the mid-17th century.

RULERS
Paolo, Mattia, Ercole and Francesco degli Ippoliti, ca. 1590-1615
Francesco degli Ippoliti, 1616-1632
Annibale degli Ippoliti, 1632-1666
Francesco degli Ippoliti, 1666-?

Reference:
V = Alberto Varesi, ***Monete Italiane Regionali: Lombardia, Zecche Minori***. Pavia, 1995.
G = E. Gnecchi, Catalog - ***Sammlung des Cav. e. Gnecchi in Mailand***, 3 parts, Frankfurt am Main, 1901-2.

COUNTSHIP

STANDARD COINAGE

KM# 7 SESINO
1.2600 g., Billon, 17-18 mm. **Ruler:** Francesco **Obv:** Head to left **Obv. Legend:** FRAN. D. HI. CO. G. SA. RO. IMP. **Rev:** Standing facing figure of St. Nicholas **Rev. Legend:** SANCTVS. NICOLAVS. **Note:** Ref. V-321.

Date	Mintage	VG	F	VF	XF	Unc
ND(1616-32)	—	175	350	775	1,700	—

KM# 11 1/2 TALLERO
Silver Weight varies: 12.85-15.33g., 34 mm. **Ruler:** Francesco **Obv:** Draped bust to left, date below **Obv. Legend:** ANIBAL. DE. HIPPO. MAR. S. R. I. CO. GAZOLDI. **Rev:** Phoenix rising from flames below rayed sunface **Rev. Legend:** HINC. VITA. PERENNIS. **Note:** Ref. V-323.

Date	Mintage	VG	F	VF	XF	Unc
1663	—	400	825	1,650	3,500	—

TRADE COINAGE

KM# 10 2 DOPPIE

Gold Weight varies: 12.92-13.05g., 29 mm. **Ruler:** Francesco **Obv:** Draped bust to left **Obv. Legend:** ANNIBAL. DE. HIPPO. MAR. S. R. I. CO. GAZOLD. **Rev:** Facing standing figure St. Hippolitus, holding sword and palm branch, in circle, date at end of legend **Rev. Legend:** SANCTVS. HIPPOLITVS. PROTECTOR. NOST. **Note:** Ref. V-322; Fr. 350.

Date	Mintage	VG	F	VF	XF	Unc
1662	—	3,500	7,000	14,000	25,000	—
1663	—	3,500	7,000	14,000	25,000	—

GENOA

A seaport in Liguria, Genoa was a dominant republic and colonial power in the Middle Ages. In 1798 Napoleon remodeled it into the Ligurian Republic, and in 1805 it was incorporated in the Kingdom of Napoleon. Following a brief restoration of the republic, it was absorbed by the Kingdom of Sardinia in 1815.

RULER

Conrad II, 1554-1637

MINT MARKS

During the occupation by the French forces regular French coins, 1/2, 1, 2, 5, 20 and 40 Francs were struck between 1813 and 1814 with the mint mark C.L.

After Sardinia absorbed Genoa in 1815, regular Sardinian coins were struck until 1860 with a fouled anchor mint mark.

MINT OFFICIALS' INITIALS

Initials	Date	Name
HP	1607	Hieronimus Palvis
MC	1610	Michael Cavus
IZ	1615	Joseph Zinus
(IB) DN	1618	John Baptist Damian Novarius
GF	1619	Georgius de Franchis
(IB) SVS	1634	John Benedictus Seminus
IBN	1647	John Baptist Nascius
IAB	1652	Johannes Anthonius Buronus
AB	1661	Augustinus Boniventus
ISS	1668	Johannes Stephanus Spinola
GSS	1668	Giovanni Stefano Spinola
(GBT) IBT	1672	Iohn Baptista Turris
(GLM) ILM	1674	Johannes Lucas Maiolus
ITC	1687	Io. Thomas Caminata

MONETARY SYSTEM

12 Denari = 1 Soldo
20 Soldi = 10 Parpagliola =
5 Cavallotti = 1 Lira (Madonnina)

REPUBLIC

STANDARD COINAGE

KM# 9 MINUTO

Copper **Obv:** Castle **Rev:** Cross

Date	Mintage	Good	VG	F	VF	XF
ND(1607-09) HP	—	8.00	18.00	37.50	75.00	—
ND(1615-18) IZ	—	8.00	18.00	37.50	75.00	—
ND(1619-21) GF	—	8.00	18.00	37.50	75.00	—

KM# 77 MINUTO

Copper **Obv:** Bust of Madonna and child **Obv. Legend:** E R E **Rev:** Cross **Rev. Legend:** D G R G

Date	Mintage	Good	VG	F	VF	XF
ND(1638-1752)	—	10.00	19.00	42.00	85.00	—
1643	—	10.00	19.00	42.00	85.00	—
1671	—	10.00	19.00	42.00	85.00	—

KM# 141 3 DENARI

3.8000 g., Billon **Obv:** Oval shield **Rev:** Legend

Date	Mintage	Good	VG	F	VF	XF
1671 ISS	—	25.00	36.00	75.00	150	—

KM# 20 4 DENARI

Billon **Ruler:** Conrad II **Obv:** Castle in shield **Obv. Legend:** DVX GBV RP GENV **Rev:** Cross with date in angles **Rev. Legend:** CONRA II RO REX

Date	Mintage	Good	VG	F	VF	XF
1601 IV	—	6.00	12.00	30.00	70.00	—
1602 IV	—	6.00	12.00	30.00	70.00	—
1603 IV	—	6.00	12.00	30.00	70.00	—
1605 IV	—	6.00	12.00	30.00	70.00	—
1606 IV	—	6.00	12.00	30.00	70.00	—
1607 HP	—	6.00	12.00	30.00	70.00	—
1608	—	6.00	12.00	30.00	70.00	—
1608 IA	—	6.00	12.00	30.00	70.00	—
1609 HP	—	6.00	12.00	30.00	70.00	—
1610 MC	—	6.00	12.00	30.00	70.00	—
1611 MC	—	6.00	12.00	30.00	70.00	—
1612 MC	—	6.00	12.00	30.00	70.00	—
1613 MC	—	6.00	12.00	30.00	70.00	—
1615 IZ	—	6.00	12.00	30.00	70.00	—
1616 IZ	—	6.00	12.00	30.00	70.00	—
1617 IZ	—	6.00	12.00	30.00	70.00	—
1618	—	6.00	12.00	30.00	70.00	—
1619	—	6.00	12.00	30.00	70.00	—
1621	—	6.00	12.00	30.00	70.00	—
1625	—	6.00	12.00	30.00	70.00	—
1626	—	6.00	12.00	30.00	70.00	—

KM# 161 4 DENARI

Billon **Obv:** Bust of Madonna and child **Rev:** Cross

Date	Mintage	Good	VG	F	VF	XF
1700 OM	—	—	—	—	—	—

KM# 142 6 DENARI

4.5000 g., Copper **Obv:** Oval shield **Rev:** Legend

Date	Mintage	Good	VG	F	VF	XF
1671 SS	—	30.00	42.00	90.00	180	—

KM# 42.1 8 DENARI

Billon **Ruler:** Conrad II **Obv:** Castle **Obv. Legend:** DVX GVB REIP GENV **Rev:** Stars flank shield **Rev. Legend:** CONRA II RO REX **Note:** Weight varies: 0.70-0.90 grams.

Date	Mintage	Good	VG	F	VF	XF
1619	—	8.00	18.00	37.50	85.00	—
1625	—	8.00	18.00	37.50	85.00	—
1626	—	8.00	18.00	37.50	85.00	—
1627	—	8.00	18.00	37.50	85.00	—

KM# 42.2 8 DENARI

Billon **Rev:** Three stars surround shield **Note:** Weight varies: 0.70-0.90 grams.

Date	Mintage	Good	VG	F	VF	XF
1626	—	8.00	18.00	37.50	85.00	—
1627	—	8.00	18.00	37.50	85.00	—
1628	—	8.00	18.00	37.50	85.00	—
1629	—	8.00	18.00	37.50	85.00	—
1630	—	8.00	18.00	37.50	85.00	—
1631	—	8.00	18.00	37.50	85.00	—
1633	—	8.00	18.00	37.50	85.00	—

KM# 115 8 DENARI

3.1000 g., Billon **Obv:** Three stars surround shield **Rev:** Bust of Madonna and child

Date	Mintage	Good	VG	F	VF	XF
1653	—	8.00	18.00	37.50	85.00	—
1654	—	8.00	18.00	37.50	85.00	—
1656	—	8.00	18.00	37.50	85.00	—
1699 OM	—	8.00	18.00	37.50	85.00	—
1700 OM	—	8.00	18.00	37.50	85.00	—

KM# 140 12 DENARI (Soldo)

9.2500 g., Copper **Obv:** Crowned shield **Obv. Legend:** DVX ET GVBERNATORES **Rev:** Date, denomination **Rev. Legend:** REIPVBLICE GENV

Date	Mintage	Good	VG	F	VF	XF
1670 ISS	—	36.00	60.00	115	225	—
1671 ISS	—	36.00	60.00	115	225	—

KM# 71 20 DENARI (Soldo)

2.9600 g., Billon **Ruler:** Conrad II **Obv:** Castle, date and 20 below **Obv. Legend:** DVX ET GVB REIP GEN **Rev:** Oval shield **Rev. Legend:** CONRADVS II RO RX

Date	Mintage	Good	VG	F	VF	XF
1631	—	14.00	25.00	55.00	100	—
1632	—	14.00	25.00	55.00	100	—
1633	—	14.00	25.00	55.00	100	—
1634	—	14.00	25.00	55.00	100	—
1635 IBS	—	14.00	25.00	55.00	100	—
1635	—	14.00	25.00	55.00	100	—

KM# 109 20 DENARI (Soldo)

2.9600 g., Billon **Obv:** Crowned oval shield **Obv. Legend:** DVX ET GVB REIP GEN **Rev:** Madonna and child, date and 20 below **Rev. Legend:** ET REGE EOS

Date	Mintage	Good	VG	F	VF	XF
1643	—	11.00	22.50	45.00	90.00	—
1644	—	11.00	22.50	45.00	90.00	—
1645	—	11.00	22.50	45.00	90.00	—

KM# 143 30 DENARI

Silver **Obv:** Oval shield **Rev. Legend:** DENARI TRENTA

Date	Mintage	VG	F	VF	XF	Unc
1671	—	42.00	65.00	130	265	—

KM# 22 SOLDINO

Billon **Obv:** Castle in arches **Obv. Legend:** DVX ET GBV RIED GENV **Rev:** Cross in arches **Rev. Legend:** CONRADVS II RO REX

Date	Mintage	Good	VG	F	VF	XF
1601 IV	—	18.00	30.00	60.00	105	—
1602 IV	—	18.00	30.00	60.00	105	—
1605 IV	—	18.00	30.00	60.00	105	—
1611 MC	—	18.00	30.00	60.00	105	—
1612 MC	—	18.00	30.00	60.00	105	—
1615 IZ	—	18.00	30.00	60.00	105	—
1616 IZ	—	18.00	30.00	60.00	105	—
1618 IZ	—	18.00	30.00	60.00	105	—

KM# 144 2-1/2 SOLIDI

0.5500 g., Silver **Obv:** Oval shield **Rev:** Legend

Date	Mintage	Good	VG	F	VF	XF
1671	—	48.00	70.00	135	280	—

KM# 88 5 SOLDI

Billon **Obv:** Crowned oval shield **Obv. Legend:** DVX ET GVB REIP GEN **Rev:** Bust of Madonna, V below **Rev. Legend:** ET REG EOS

Date	Mintage	Good	VG	F	VF	XF
1639 IBS	—	8.00	18.00	42.00	75.00	—
1641	—	8.00	18.00	42.00	75.00	—
1642 CS	—	8.00	18.00	42.00	75.00	—
1648 IBN	—	8.00	18.00	42.00	75.00	—

KM# 120 5 SOLDI

Billon **Obv:** Crowned shield **Rev:** Shield with LIBERT on band across **Rev. Legend:** IN AETERNUM VIVET

Date	Mintage	Good	VG	F	VF	XF
1663 AB	—	18.00	36.00	75.00	135	—

KM# 145 5 SOLDI

Billon **Rev:** St. John

Date	Mintage	Good	VG	F	VF	XF
1671	—	8.00	18.00	42.00	75.00	—
1672	—	8.00	18.00	42.00	75.00	—
1673	—	8.00	18.00	42.00	75.00	—
1674	—	8.00	18.00	42.00	75.00	—
1675	—	8.00	18.00	42.00	75.00	—

KM# 117 8 SOLDI

2.2000 g., Silver **Obv:** Cross with four stars **Rev:** Madonna and child, VIII below

Date	Mintage	VG	F	VF	XF	Unc
1653 IAB	—	12.00	24.00	49.50	90.00	—
1654 IAB	—	12.00	24.00	49.50	90.00	—
1655 IAB	—	12.00	24.00	49.50	90.00	—
1656 IAB	—	12.00	24.00	49.50	90.00	—

KM# 89 10 SOLDI (1/2 Lire)

Billon **Obv:** Crowned oval shield **Obv. Legend:** DVX ET GVB GVB REIP **Rev:** Bust of the Madonna, X below **Rev. Legend:** ET REGE EOS

Date	Mintage	Good	VG	F	VF	XF
1639 IBS	—	15.00	30.00	60.00	105	—
1640 IBS	—	15.00	30.00	60.00	105	—
1641 CS	—	15.00	30.00	60.00	105	—
1642 CS	—	15.00	30.00	60.00	105	—
1643 CS	—	15.00	30.00	60.00	105	—
1644 CS	—	15.00	30.00	60.00	105	—
1649 IBN	—	15.00	30.00	60.00	105	—

KM# 146 10 SOLDI (1/2 Lire)

Billon **Rev:** St. John

Date	Mintage	VG	F	VF	XF	Unc
1671	—	15.00	30.00	60.00	105	—
1672	—	15.00	30.00	60.00	105	—
1673	—	15.00	30.00	60.00	105	—
1674	—	15.00	30.00	60.00	105	—
1675	—	15.00	30.00	60.00	105	—
1679	—	15.00	30.00	60.00	105	—

KM# 103 20 SOLDI (Lira)

6.3000 g., Silver **Obv:** Crowned shield **Rev:** Madonna and child, 20 below

Date	Mintage	VG	F	VF	XF	Unc
1641 CS	—	27.50	55.00	115	240	—
1643 CS	—	27.50	55.00	115	240	—
1648 CS	—	27.50	55.00	115	240	—

KM# 147 20 SOLDI (Lira)

6.3000 g., 0.8590 Silver 0.1740 oz. ASW **Obv:** Crowned shield **Rev:** St. John, 20 below

Date	Mintage	VG	F	VF	XF	Unc
1671 ISS	—	24.00	48.00	105	225	—
1672	—	24.00	48.00	105	225	—
1673	—	24.00	48.00	105	225	—
1675	—	24.00	48.00	105	225	—
1679	—	24.00	48.00	105	225	—
1687	—	24.00	48.00	105	225	—

KM# 70 CAVALOTTO

Silver **Ruler:** Conrad II **Obv:** Castle in three arches **Obv. Legend:** DVX ET GVBER REIP GENV **Rev:** St. Bernard standing **Rev. Legend:** NON OBLIVISCAR TVI **Note:** Weight varies: 2.76-3.00 grams.

Date	Mintage	VG	F	VF	XF	Unc
1630	—	45.00	85.00	150	270	—

KM# 132 CAVALOTTO

2.8500 g., Billon **Obv:** Castle **Obv. Legend:** REIPVBLICAE GEN **Rev:** Shield **Rev. Legend:** DVX ET GVBERNATORES

Date	Mintage	VG	F	VF	XF	Unc
1669 ISS	—	37.50	70.00	130	250	—
1670 ISS	—	37.50	70.00	130	250	—

KM# 148 2 LIRE

10.0000 g., 0.8890 Silver 0.2858 oz. ASW **Obv:** Griffins support crowned shield **Rev:** St. John

Date	Mintage	VG	F	VF	XF	Unc
1671 ISS	—	50.00	75.00	150	280	—
1672 ISS	—	50.00	75.00	150	280	—
1675 GLM	—	50.00	75.00	150	280	—
1676 GLM	—	50.00	75.00	150	280	—
1677 GLM	—	50.00	75.00	150	280	—
1679 GLM	—	50.00	75.00	150	280	—
1684 PBM	—	50.00	75.00	150	280	—
1685 PBM	—	50.00	75.00	150	280	—
1687 ILM	—	50.00	75.00	150	280	—

KM# 150 2 LIRE

10.0000 g., 0.8890 Silver 0.2858 oz. ASW **Obv:** Griffins support crowned arms **Obv. Legend:** DVX ET GVBER REIPV GENVEN **Rev:** St. John **Rev. Legend:** NON SVRREXIT MAIOR

Date	Mintage	VG	F	VF	XF	Unc
1672 ISS	—	55.00	100	225	375	—
1673 GBT	—	55.00	100	225	375	—
1675 ILM	—	55.00	100	225	375	—
1676 GLM	—	55.00	100	225	375	—
1678 GLM	—	55.00	100	225	375	—
1679 GLM	—	55.00	100	225	375	—

KM# 121 REAL

Silver **Obv:** Palm fronds flank crowned shield with LIBERTAS in banner across **Obv. Legend:** DVX ET GVB REIP GENV **Rev:** St. George slaying dragon

Date	Mintage	VG	F	VF	XF	Unc
1666	—	600	1,150	2,100	3,600	—

KM# 122 2 REALI

Silver **Obv:** Crowned shield **Rev:** St. George slaying dragon

Date	Mintage	VG	F	VF	XF	Unc
1666	—	900	1,800	3,300	5,400	—

KM# 123 4 REALI
Silver **Obv:** Palm fronds flank crowned shield with LIBERTAS in banner across **Obv. Legend:** DVX ET VB REIP GENV **Rev:** St. George slaying dragon **Note:** Weight varies: 12.30-12.50 grams.

Date	Mintage	VG	F	VF	XF	Unc
1666	—	1,500	3,000	5,400	9,000	—

KM# 124 8 REALI
Silver **Obv:** Palm fronds flank crowned shield with LIBERTAS in banner across **Obv. Legend:** DVX ET VB REIP GENV **Rev:** St. George slaying dragon

Date	Mintage	VG	F	VF	XF	Unc
1666 Rare	—	—	—	—	—	—

KM# 23 1/2 DUCATONE
15.8000 g., Silver **Obv:** Doge kneeling before Christ **Obv. Legend:** DVX ET GVB REIP GENVEN **Rev:** Griffins support crowned shield **Rev. Legend:** CONRADVS II RO REX

Date	Mintage	VG	F	VF	XF	Unc
1601 IV	—	1,800	3,350	5,400	9,000	—
1605 IV	—	1,800	3,350	5,400	9,000	—
1615 IZ	—	1,800	3,350	5,400	9,000	—

KM# 24 DUCATONE
32.2500 g., Silver **Obv:** Savior blessing kneeling Doge and attendants **Obv. Legend:** DVX ET GVB REIP GEN **Rev:** Crowned and supported city arms **Rev. Legend:** CONRADVS II RO REX **Note:** Dav. #3899.

Date	Mintage	VG	F	VF	XF	Unc
1601 IV	—	2,400	4,800	7,800	11,500	—
1607 HP	—	2,400	4,800	7,800	11,500	—

KM# 50 1/8 SCUDO
4.5000 g., Silver **Ruler:** Conrad II **Obv:** Stars flank castle, cross above **Obv. Legend:** DVX ET GVB REIP GEN **Rev:** Oval shield **Rev. Legend:** CONRADVS II RO REX

Date	Mintage	VG	F	VF	XF	Unc
1621 GF	—	37.50	70.00	125	250	—

KM# 54 1/8 SCUDO
4.5000 g., Silver **Rev:** Cross with stars in angles

Date	Mintage	VG	F	VF	XF	Unc
1622 GF	—	30.00	55.00	100	205	—
1623 GF	—	30.00	55.00	100	205	—
1624 GF	—	30.00	55.00	100	205	—
1625	—	30.00	55.00	100	205	—
1626	—	30.00	55.00	100	205	—
1627	—	30.00	55.00	100	205	—
1628	—	30.00	55.00	100	205	—
1630	—	30.00	55.00	100	205	—
1633	—	30.00	55.00	100	205	—

KM# 57 1/8 SCUDO
4.5000 g., Silver **Rev:** Cross with stars in angles **Rev. Legend:** IN HOC SALVS MUNDI

Date	Mintage	VG	F	VF	XF	Unc
1624	—	33.00	60.00	105	225	—

KM# 75 1/8 SCUDO (Stretto)
4.5000 g., Silver **Rev:** Cross with stars in angles **Rev. Legend:** IN HOC SALVS MUNDI

Date	Mintage	VG	F	VF	XF	Unc
1635	—	33.00	60.00	105	225	—

KM# 104 1/8 SCUDO (Stretto)
4.5000 g., Silver **Obv:** Cross **Rev:** Madonna and child

Date	Mintage	VG	F	VF	XF	Unc
1641 IBS	—	21.00	42.00	85.00	150	—
1650 IBN	—	21.00	42.00	85.00	150	—
1653 IAB	—	21.00	42.00	85.00	150	—
1654 IAB	—	21.00	42.00	85.00	150	—
1655 IAB	—	21.00	42.00	85.00	150	—
1658 IBN	—	21.00	42.00	85.00	150	—
1661 AB	—	21.00	42.00	85.00	150	—
1662 AB	—	21.00	42.00	85.00	150	—
1664 AB	—	21.00	42.00	85.00	150	—
1665 AB	—	21.00	42.00	85.00	150	—
1668 ISS	—	21.00	42.00	85.00	150	—
1670 ISS	—	21.00	42.00	85.00	150	—

KM# 119 1/8 SCUDO (Largo)
4.5000 g., Silver **Obv:** Cross **Rev:** Madonna and child

Date	Mintage	VG	F	VF	XF	Unc
1661 AB	—	22.50	45.00	90.00	165	—
1664 AB	—	22.50	45.00	90.00	165	—
1668 AB	—	22.50	45.00	90.00	165	—
1693 ITC	—	22.50	45.00	90.00	165	—

KM# 29 1/4 SCUDO
Silver **Ruler:** Conrad II **Obv:** Stars flank crowned castle, date below **Rev:** Cross with stars in angles **Note:** Weight varies: 8.70-9.50 grams.

Date	Mintage	VG	F	VF	XF	Unc
1604 IV	—	65.00	130	255	425	—
1610 MC	—	65.00	130	255	425	—
1611 MC	—	65.00	130	255	425	—
1612 MC	—	65.00	130	255	425	—
1613 MC	—	65.00	130	255	425	—
1614 MC	—	65.00	130	255	425	—
1615 IZ	—	65.00	130	255	425	—
1616 IZ	—	65.00	130	255	425	—
1617 IZ	—	65.00	130	255	425	—
1618 DN	—	65.00	130	255	425	—
1622 GF	—	65.00	130	255	425	—
1623 GF	—	65.00	130	255	425	—
1624 GF	—	65.00	130	255	425	—
1625	—	65.00	130	255	425	—
1626	—	65.00	130	255	425	—
1627	—	65.00	130	255	425	—
1628	—	65.00	130	255	425	—
1630	—	65.00	130	255	425	—
1633	—	65.00	130	255	425	—
1634 IBS	—	65.00	130	255	425	—
1635 IBS	—	65.00	130	255	425	—
1636	—	65.00	130	255	425	—

KM# 80 1/4 SCUDO (Stretto)
0.8890 Silver **Obv:** Cross **Rev:** Madonna and child **Note:** Weight varies: 8.70-9.50 grams.

Date	Mintage	VG	F	VF	XF	Unc
1638 IBS	—	60.00	115	245	425	—
1639 IBS	—	60.00	115	245	425	—
1640 IBS	—	60.00	115	245	425	—
1648 IBN	—	60.00	115	245	425	—
1649 IBN	—	60.00	115	245	425	—
1651 IBN	—	60.00	115	245	425	—
1653 IAB	—	60.00	115	245	425	—
1654 IAB	—	60.00	115	245	425	—
1655 IAB	—	60.00	115	245	425	—
1658 IBN	—	60.00	115	245	425	—
1661 AB	—	60.00	115	245	425	—
1663 AB	—	60.00	115	245	425	—
1664 AB	—	60.00	115	245	425	—
1665 AB	—	60.00	115	245	425	—
1666 AB	—	60.00	115	245	425	—
1667 AB	—	60.00	115	245	425	—
1668 AB	—	60.00	115	245	425	—
1668 ISS	—	60.00	115	245	425	—
1670 ISS	—	60.00	115	245	425	—
1672 IBT	—	60.00	115	245	425	—
1673 IBT	—	60.00	115	245	425	—
1676 ILM	—	60.00	115	245	425	—
1677 ILM	—	60.00	115	245	425	—
1680 SM	—	60.00	115	245	425	—
1682 SM	—	60.00	115	245	425	—
1684 SM	—	60.00	115	245	425	—
1685 ILM	—	60.00	115	245	425	—
1687 GLM	—	60.00	115	245	425	—
1689 ILM	—	100	195	425	650	—
1691 ITC	—	60.00	115	245	425	—
1692 ITC	—	60.00	115	245	425	—
1694 ITC	—	60.00	115	245	425	—
1698 ITC	—	60.00	115	245	425	—
1699 IBM	—	60.00	115	245	425	—

KM# 108 1/4 SCUDO (Largo)
Silver **Obv:** Cross **Rev:** Madonna and child **Note:** Weight varies: 8.70-9.50 grams.

Date	Mintage	VG	F	VF	XF	Unc
1642 CS	—	70.00	145	270	475	—
1650 IBN	—	70.00	145	270	475	—
1651 IBN	—	70.00	145	270	475	—
1652 IAB	—	70.00	145	270	475	—
1653 IAB	—	70.00	145	270	475	—
1654 IAB	—	70.00	145	270	475	—
1661 AB	—	70.00	145	270	475	—
1664 AB	—	70.00	145	270	475	—
1665 AB	—	70.00	145	270	475	—
1666 AB	—	70.00	145	270	475	—
1670 ISS	—	70.00	145	270	475	—
1673 IBT	—	70.00	145	270	475	—
1680 SM	—	70.00	145	270	475	—
1682 SM	—	70.00	145	270	475	—
1691 ITC	—	70.00	145	270	475	—
1692 ITC	—	70.00	145	270	475	—
1693 ITC	—	70.00	145	270	475	—

KM# 26 1/2 SCUDO
Silver **Ruler:** Conrad II **Obv:** Stars flank castle, II below **Obv. Legend:** DVX ET GVB REIP GENV **Rev:** Cross with stars in angles **Rev. Legend:** CONRADVS II **Note:** Weight varies: 18.40-18.60 grams.

Date	Mintage	VG	F	VF	XF	Unc
1603 IV	—	80.00	155	325	575	—
1604 IV	—	80.00	155	325	575	—
1607 HP	—	80.00	155	325	575	—
1608 HP	—	80.00	155	325	575	—
1609 HP	—	80.00	155	325	575	—
1610 MC	—	80.00	155	325	575	—
1611 MC	—	80.00	155	325	575	—
1613 MC	—	80.00	155	325	575	—
1614 MC	—	80.00	155	325	575	—
1615 IZ	—	80.00	155	325	575	—
1618 DN	—	80.00	155	325	575	—
1622 GF	—	80.00	155	325	575	—
1623 GF	—	80.00	155	325	575	—
1624 GF	—	80.00	155	325	575	—
1625	—	80.00	155	325	575	—
1626	—	80.00	155	325	575	—
1627	—	80.00	155	325	575	—
1628	—	80.00	155	325	575	—
1629	—	80.00	155	325	575	—
1630	—	80.00	155	325	575	—
1633	—	80.00	155	325	575	—
1634 IBS	—	80.00	155	325	575	—
1635 IBS	—	80.00	155	325	575	—
1636	—	80.00	155	325	575	—

KM# 81.1 1/2 SCUDO (Stretto)
0.8890 Silver **Obv:** Cross **Rev:** Madonna and child **Note:** Weight varies: 18.4-18.6 grams.

Date	Mintage	VG	F	VF	XF	Unc
1638 IBS	—	55.00	110	200	385	—
1639 IBS	—	55.00	110	200	385	—
1642 CS	—	55.00	110	200	385	—
1643 CS	—	55.00	110	200	385	—
1646 CS	—	55.00	110	200	385	—
1649 IBN	—	55.00	110	200	385	—
1651 IBN	—	55.00	110	200	385	—
1653 IAB	—	55.00	110	200	385	—
1654 IAB	—	55.00	110	200	385	—
1656 IAB	—	55.00	110	200	385	—
1661 AB	—	55.00	110	200	385	—
1664 AB	—	55.00	110	200	385	—
1665 AB	—	55.00	110	200	385	—
1666 AB	—	55.00	110	200	385	—
1667 AB	—	55.00	110	200	385	—
1668 AB	—	55.00	110	200	385	—
1668 ISS	—	55.00	110	200	385	—
1670 ISS	—	55.00	110	200	385	—
1671 ISS	—	55.00	110	200	385	—
1672 IBT	—	55.00	110	200	385	—
1672 ISS	—	55.00	110	200	385	—
1673 IBT	—	55.00	110	200	385	—
1674 ILM	—	55.00	110	200	385	—
1675 ILM	—	55.00	110	200	385	—
1676 ILM	—	55.00	110	200	385	—
1677 ILM	—	55.00	110	200	385	—
1679 ILM	—	55.00	110	200	385	—
1679 SM	—	55.00	110	200	385	—
1680 SM	—	55.00	110	200	385	—
1681 SM	—	55.00	110	200	385	—
1682 SM	—	55.00	110	200	385	—
1683 SM	—	55.00	110	200	385	—
1685 ILM	—	55.00	110	200	385	—
1686 ILM	—	55.00	110	200	385	—
1687 ILM	—	55.00	110	200	385	—
1689 ILM	—	55.00	110	200	385	—
1690 ILM	—	55.00	110	200	385	—
1691 ITC	—	55.00	110	200	385	—
1692 ITC	—	55.00	110	200	385	—
1693 ITC	—	55.00	110	200	385	—
1694 ITC	—	55.00	110	200	385	—
1695 ITC	—	55.00	110	200	385	—
1696 ITC	—	55.00	110	200	385	—
1697 ITC	—	55.00	110	200	385	—
1698 IBM	—	55.00	110	200	385	—
1699 IBM	—	55.00	110	200	385	—
1700 IBM	—	55.00	110	200	385	—

KM# 81.2 1/2 SCUDO (Largo)
0.8890 Silver **Note:** Weight varies: 18.4-18.6 grams.

Date	Mintage	VG	F	VF	XF	Unc
1642 CS	—	60.00	120	220	400	—
1648 IBN	—	60.00	120	220	400	—
1649 IBN	—	60.00	120	220	400	—
1650 IBN	—	60.00	120	220	400	—
1651 IBN	—	60.00	120	220	400	—
1652 IAB	—	60.00	120	220	400	—
1653 IAB	—	60.00	120	220	400	—
1654 IAB	—	60.00	120	220	400	—
1655 IAB	—	60.00	120	220	400	—
1662 AB	—	60.00	120	220	400	—
1664 AB	—	60.00	120	220	400	—
1665 AB	—	60.00	120	220	400	—
1666 AB	—	60.00	120	220	400	—
1668 AB	—	60.00	120	220	400	—
1670 ISS	—	60.00	120	220	400	—
1671 ISS	—	60.00	120	220	400	—
1672 IBT	—	60.00	120	220	400	—
1673 IBT	—	60.00	120	220	400	—
1679 SM	—	60.00	120	220	400	—
1680 SM	—	60.00	120	220	400	—
1682 SM	—	60.00	120	220	400	—
1683 SM	—	60.00	120	220	400	—
1691 ITC	—	60.00	120	220	400	—
1692 ITC	—	60.00	120	220	400	—
1693 ITC	—	60.00	120	220	400	—
1694 ITC	—	60.00	120	220	400	—
1695 ITC	—	60.00	120	220	400	—
1698 IBM	—	60.00	120	220	400	—
1699 IBM	—	60.00	120	220	400	—

KM# 25 SCUDO (Stretto)

Silver **Obv:** Crowned porta, crosses at sides, date below **Rev:** Cross with stars in angles **Note:** Weight varies: 35.0-38.0 grams. Dav. #3900.

Date	Mintage	VG	F	VF	XF	Unc
1602 IV	—	85.00	175	325	650	—
1603 IV	—	85.00	175	325	650	—
1604 IV	—	85.00	175	325	650	—
1607 HP	—	85.00	175	325	650	—
1608 HP	—	85.00	175	325	650	—
1609 HP	—	85.00	175	325	650	—
1610 MC	—	85.00	175	325	650	—
1611 MC	—	85.00	175	325	650	—
1612 MC	—	85.00	175	325	650	—
1613 MC	—	85.00	175	325	650	—
1614 MC	—	85.00	175	325	650	—
1615 IZ	—	85.00	175	325	650	—
1616 IZ	—	85.00	175	325	650	—
1618 DN	—	85.00	175	325	650	—
1622 GF	—	85.00	175	325	650	—
1623 GF	—	85.00	175	325	650	—
1624 GF	—	85.00	175	325	650	—
1625	—	85.00	175	325	650	—
1626	—	85.00	175	325	650	—
1627	—	85.00	175	325	650	—
1628	—	85.00	175	325	650	—
1629	—	85.00	175	325	650	—
1630	—	85.00	175	325	650	—
1631	—	85.00	175	325	650	—
1632	—	85.00	175	325	650	—
1633	—	85.00	175	325	650	—
1634 IBS	—	85.00	175	325	650	—
1635 IBS	—	85.00	175	325	650	—
1636 IBS	—	85.00	175	325	650	—
1637 IBS	—	85.00	175	325	650	—

KM# 56 SCUDO (Stretto)

Silver **Ruler:** Conrad II **Obv:** Stars flank crowned castle **Obv. Legend:** DVX ET GVB REIP GEN **Rev:** Cross with stars in angles **Rev. Legend:** IN HOC SALVS MUNDI **Note:** Weight varies: 35.0-38.0 grams.

Date	Mintage	VG	F	VF	XF	Unc
1624	—	90.00	170	350	700	—

KM# 79 SCUDO (Stretto)

19.0000 g., 0.8890 Silver 0.5430 oz. ASW **Obv:** Cross with four stars in angles **Rev:** Virgin and child on cloud **Note:** Dav. #3901. Illustration reduced.

Date	Mintage	VG	F	VF	XF	Unc
1637 IBS	—	75.00	140	275	600	—
1638 IBS	—	75.00	140	275	600	—
1639 IBS	—	75.00	140	275	600	—
1640 IBS	—	75.00	140	275	600	—
1641 IBS	—	75.00	140	275	600	—
1642 CS	—	75.00	140	275	600	—
1644 CS	—	75.00	140	275	600	—
1646 CS	—	75.00	140	275	600	—
1647 IBN	—	75.00	140	275	600	—
1648 IBN	—	75.00	140	275	600	—
1649 IBN	—	75.00	140	275	600	—
1650 IBN	—	75.00	140	275	600	—
1651 IBN	—	75.00	140	275	600	—
1652 IAB	—	75.00	140	275	600	—
1653 IAB	—	75.00	140	275	600	—
1654 IAB	—	75.00	140	275	600	—
1655 IAB	—	75.00	140	275	600	—
1656 IAB	—	75.00	140	275	600	—
1661 AB	—	75.00	140	275	600	—
1662 AB	—	75.00	140	275	600	—
1664 AB	—	75.00	140	275	600	—
1665 AB	—	75.00	140	275	600	—
1666 AB	—	75.00	140	275	600	—
1667 AB	—	75.00	140	275	600	—
1668 AB	—	75.00	140	275	600	—
1668 ISS	—	75.00	140	275	600	—
1668 GSS	—	75.00	140	275	600	—
1669 ISS	—	75.00	140	275	600	—
1670 ISS	—	75.00	14.00	275	600	—
1671 ISS	—	75.00	140	275	600	—
1672 ISS	—	75.00	140	275	600	—
1672 IBT	—	75.00	140	275	600	—
1673 IBT	—	75.00	140	275	600	—
1674 ILM	—	75.00	140	275	600	—
1675 ILM	—	75.00	140	275	600	—
1676 ILM	—	75.00	140	275	600	—
1679 ILM	—	75.00	140	275	600	—
1679 SM	—	75.00	140	275	600	—

Note: Ira & Larry Goldberg Coins & Collectibles Auction 46 - The Millennia Collection, 5-08, MS-64 realized $7,250

Date	Mintage	VG	F	VF	XF	Unc
1680 SM	—	75.00	140	275	600	—
1681 SM	—	75.00	140	275	600	—
1682 SM	—	75.00	140	275	600	—
1683 PBM	—	75.00	140	275	600	—
1683 SM	—	75.00	140	275	600	—
1684 SM	—	75.00	140	275	600	—
1684 PBM	—	75.00	140	275	600	—
1685 ILM	—	65.00	140	275	600	—
1687 ILM	—	75.00	140	275	600	—
1688 ILM	—	75.00	140	275	600	—
1689 ILM	—	75.00	140	275	600	—
1690 ILM	—	75.00	140	275	600	—
1690 ITC	—	75.00	140	275	600	—
1691 ITC	—	75.00	140	275	600	—
1692 ITC	—	75.00	140	275	600	—
1693 ITC	—	75.00	140	275	600	—
1694 ITC	—	75.00	140	275	600	—
1695 ITC	—	75.00	140	275	600	—
1696 ITC	—	75.00	140	275	600	—
1697 ITC	—	75.00	140	275	600	—
1698 ITC	—	75.00	140	275	600	—
1698 IBM	—	75.00	140	275	600	—
1699 IBM	—	75.00	140	275	600	—
1700 IBM	—	75.00	140	275	600	—

KM# 113 SCUDO (Largo)

38.0000 g., Silver **Obv:** Ornate cross with cherub heads and wings in angles **Obv. Legend:** GVBERNATORES * REIP * GENV + DVX * ET * **Rev:** Madonna and child on cloud, two cherubs above **Rev. Legend:** * ET * REGE *.... **Note:** Dav. #LS555. Illustration reduced.

Date	Mintage	VG	F	VF	XF	Unc
1649 IBN	—	550	1,150	2,250	4,500	—
1650 IBN	—	550	1,150	2,250	4,500	—
1652 IAB	—	550	1,150	2,250	4,500	—
1653 IAB	—	550	1,150	2,250	4,500	—
1656 IAB	—	550	1,150	2,250	4,500	—
1664 AB	—	550	1,150	2,250	4,500	—
1666 AB	—	550	1,150	2,250	4,500	—
1670 ISS	—	550	1,150	2,250	4,500	—
1676 ILM	—	550	1,150	2,250	4,500	—
1680 SM	—	550	1,150	2,250	4,500	—
1681 SM	—	550	1,150	2,250	4,500	—
1682 SM	—	550	1,150	2,250	4,500	—
1683 SM	—	550	1,150	2,250	4,500	—
1684 PBM	—	550	1,150	2,250	4,500	—
1689 GLM	—	550	1,150	2,250	4,500	—
1691 ITC	—	550	1,150	2,250	4,500	—
1692 ITC	—	550	1,150	2,250	4,500	—
1693 ITC	—	550	1,150	2,250	4,500	—
1694 ITC	—	550	1,150	2,250	4,500	—
1698 IBM	—	550	1,150	2,250	4,500	—
1699 IBM	—	550	1,150	2,250	4,500	—
1700 IBM	—	550	1,150	2,250	4,500	—

KM# 74 1-1/2 SCUDI

47.0000 g., Silver **Note:** Similar to 2 Scudos, Dav. #1364. Dav. #LS554.

Date	Mintage	VG	F	VF	XF	Unc
1634 IBS	—	650	1,250	2,500	5,000	—
1641	—	650	1,250	2,500	5,000	—

KM# 31 2 SCUDI

76.0000 g., Silver **Obv:** Ring above cipher supported by two griffins, cherub winged head below **Rev:** Cross with winged cherub heads in angles **Note:** Dav. #LS542.

Date	Mintage	VG	F	VF	XF	Unc
1607 HP Rare	—	—	—	—	—	—
1608 HP Rare	—	—	—	—	—	—
1610 MC Rare	—	—	—	—	—	—
1611 MC Rare	—	—	—	—	—	—
1612 MC Rare	—	—	—	—	—	—
1613 MC Rare	—	—	—	—	—	—
1614 MC Rare	—	—	—	—	—	—

KM# 40 2 SCUDI

76.0000 g., Silver **Obv:** Cross above crown breaks legend **Note:** Dav. #LS545. Illustration reduced.

Date	Mintage	VG	F	VF	XF	Unc
1615 IZ Rare	—	—	—	—	—	—
1623 GF Rare	—	—	—	—	—	—
1625 Rare	—	—	—	—	—	—
1626 Rare	—	—	—	—	—	—

KM# 59 2 SCUDI

76.0000 g., Silver **Obv:** Crown breaks legend, griffins with spread wings **Note:** Dav. #LS547. Illustration reduced.

Date	Mintage	VG	F	VF	XF	Unc
1627	—	1,150	2,200	3,400	5,300	—
1628	—	1,150	2,200	3,400	5,300	—
1629	—	1,150	2,200	3,400	5,300	—
1630	—	1,150	2,200	3,400	5,300	—
1631	—	1,150	2,200	3,400	5,300	—
1633	—	1,150	2,200	3,400	5,300	—
1634 IBS	—	1,150	2,200	3,400	5,300	—
1635 IBS	—	1,150	2,200	3,400	5,300	—
1636 IBS	—	1,150	2,200	3,400	5,300	—
1637 IBS	—	1,150	2,200	3,400	5,300	—

KM# 82 2 SCUDI

76.0000 g., 0.8890 Silver 2.1721 oz. ASW **Obv:** Ornate cross with cherub heads and wings in angles **Rev:** Madonna and child on cloud, two cherubs above **Note:** Dav. #LS553. Illustration reduced.

Date	Mintage	VG	F	VF	XF	Unc
1638 IBS	—	500	800	1,500	2,500	—
1640 CS	—	500	800	1,500	2,500	—
1642 CS	—	500	800	1,500	2,500	—
1645 IBS	—	500	800	1,500	2,500	—
1649 IBN	—	500	800	1,500	2,500	—
1650 IBN	—	500	800	1,500	2,500	—
1652 IAB	—	500	800	1,500	2,500	—
1653 IAB	—	500	800	1,500	2,500	—
1664 AB	—	500	800	1,500	2,500	—
1666 AB	—	500	800	1,500	2,500	—
1670 ISS	—	500	800	1,500	2,500	—
1676 ILM	—	500	800	1,500	2,500	—
1680 SM	—	500	800	1,500	2,500	—
1681 SM	—	500	800	1,500	2,500	—
1682 SM	—	500	800	1,500	2,500	—
1684 PBM	—	2,250	4,000	6,500	—	—
1685 GLM	—	500	800	1,500	2,500	—
1687 GLM	—	500	800	1,500	2,500	—
1687 GLM	—	500	800	1,500	2,500	—
1689 GLM	—	500	800	1,500	2,500	—
1691 ITC	—	500	800	1,500	2,500	—
1692 ITC	—	500	800	1,500	2,500	—
1693 ITC	—	500	800	1,500	2,500	—
1694 ITC	—	500	800	1,500	2,500	—
1695 ITC	—	500	800	1,500	2,500	—
1697 ITC	—	500	800	1,500	2,500	—
1698 ITC	—	500	800	1,500	2,500	—
1698 IBM	—	500	800	1,500	2,500	—
1699 IBM	—	500	800	1,500	2,500	—
1700 IBM	—	500	800	1,500	2,500	—

KM# 83 3 SCUDI

114.0000 g., 0.8890 Silver 3.2582 oz. ASW **Note:** Similar to 2 Scudi, Dav. #1364. Dav. #1363, #LS552.

Date	Mintage	VG	F	VF	XF	Unc
1638 IBS	—	975	1,900	3,000	4,900	—
1652 IAB	—	975	1,900	3,000	4,900	—
1666 AB	—	975	1,900	3,000	4,900	—
1670 ISS	—	975	1,900	3,000	4,900	—
1680 SM	—	975	1,900	3,000	4,900	—
1682 SM	—	975	1,900	3,000	4,900	—
1684 PBM	—	975	1,900	3,000	4,900	—
1692 ITC	—	975	1,900	3,000	4,900	—
1693 ITC	—	975	1,900	3,000	4,900	—

KM# 58 4 SCUDI

Silver **Note:** Similar to 2 Scudi, Dav. #LS545. Dav. #LS544.

Date	Mintage	VG	F	VF	XF	Unc
1625 Rare	—	—	—	—	—	—

KM# 60 4 SCUDI

Silver **Note:** Similar to 2 Scudi, Dav. #LS547. Dav. #LS546.

Date	Mintage	VG	F	VF	XF	Unc
1628 Rare	—	—	—	—	—	—
1632 Rare	—	—	—	—	—	—
1633 Rare	—	—	—	—	—	—
1634 IBS Rare	—	—	—	—	—	—
1635 IBS Rare	—	—	—	—	—	—
1636 IBS Rare	—	—	—	—	—	—
1637 IBS Rare	—	—	—	—	—	—

KM# 84 4 SCUDI

152.0000 g., Silver **Note:** Similar to 2 Scudi, Dav. #1364. Dav. #1362, #LS551. Illustration reduced.

Date	Mintage	VG	F	VF	XF	Unc
1638 IBS	—	1,500	3,000	5,300	9,000	—
1649 IBN	—	1,500	3,000	5,300	9,000	—
1652 IAB	—	1,500	3,000	5,300	9,000	—
1664 AB	—	1,500	3,000	5,300	9,000	—
1670 ISS	—	1,500	3,000	5,300	9,000	—
1680 SM	—	1,500	3,000	5,300	9,000	—
1681 SM	—	1,500	3,000	5,300	9,000	—
1682 SM	—	1,500	3,000	5,300	9,000	—
1684 PBM	—	1,500	3,000	5,300	9,000	—
1685 GLM	—	1,500	3,000	5,300	9,000	—
1689 GLM	—	1,500	3,000	5,300	9,000	—
1692 ITC	—	1,500	3,000	5,300	9,000	—
1694 ITC	—	1,500	3,000	5,300	9,000	—
1697 ITC	—	1,500	3,000	5,300	9,000	—

KM# 157 5 SCUDI

190.0000 g., Silver **Note:** Similar to 2 Scudi, Dav. #1360. Dav. #LS550.

Date	Mintage	VG	F	VF	XF	Unc
1693 ITC Rare	—	—	—	—	—	—

KM# 158 6 SCUDI

230.0000 g., Silver **Note:** Similar to 2 Scudi, Dav. #1364. Dav. #1361, #LS549.

Date	Mintage	VG	F	VF	XF	Unc
1695 ITC Rare	—	—	—	—	—	—
1697 ITC Rare	—	—	—	—	—	—
1700 IBM Rare	—	—	—	—	—	—

KM# 51 1/8 DOPPIA

0.8750 g., 0.9860 Gold 0.0277 oz. AGW **Obv:** Symbolic castle, date below **Rev:** Ornate cross

Date	Mintage	VG	F	VF	XF	Unc
1621 GF Rare	—	—	—	—	—	—
1623 GF Rare	—	—	—	—	—	—
1624 GF Rare	—	—	—	—	—	—

KM# 105 1/8 DOPPIA

0.8750 g., 0.9860 Gold 0.0277 oz. AGW **Obv:** Madonna and child on cloud in stars, date in legend

Date	Mintage	VG	F	VF	XF	Unc
1641 Rare	—	—	—	—	—	—

KM# 53 1/4 DOPPIA

1.7500 g., 0.9860 Gold 0.0555 oz. AGW **Obv:** Symbolic castle, date below in inner circle **Rev:** Ornate cross

Date	Mintage	VG	F	VF	XF	Unc
1621 GF Rare	—	—	—	—	—	—
1623 GF Rare	—	—	—	—	—	—
1629 Rare	—	—	—	—	—	—
1636 Rare	—	—	—	—	—	—

KM# 106 1/4 DOPPIA

1.7500 g., 0.9860 Gold 0.0555 oz. AGW **Obv:** Madonna and child on cloud in stars, date in legend **Rev:** Ornate cross

Date	Mintage	VG	F	VF	XF	Unc
1641 Rare	—	—	—	—	—	—

KM# 30 1/2 DOPPIA

3.5000 g., 0.9860 Gold 0.1109 oz. AGW **Ruler:** Conrad II **Obv:** Ornate cross in inner circle **Rev:** Symbolic castle, date below in inner circle

Date	Mintage	VG	F	VF	XF	Unc
1604 IV	—	375	700	1,250	2,650	—
1605 IV	—	375	700	1,250	2,650	—
1613 MC	—	375	700	1,250	2,650	—
1617 IZ	—	375	700	1,250	2,650	—
1618 DN	—	375	700	1,250	2,650	—
1619 DN	—	375	700	1,250	2,650	—
1620 GF	—	375	700	1,250	2,650	—
1623 GF	—	375	700	1,250	2,650	—
1624 GF	—	375	700	1,250	2,650	—
1625	—	375	700	1,250	2,650	—
1626	—	375	700	1,250	2,650	—
1627	—	375	700	1,250	2,650	—
1632	—	375	700	1,250	2,650	—
1637	—	375	700	1,250	2,650	—

KM# 90 1/2 DOPPIA

3.5000 g., 0.9860 Gold 0.1109 oz. AGW **Obv:** Madonna and child on cloud in stars, date in legend **Rev:** Ornate cross in inner circle

Date	Mintage	VG	F	VF	XF	Unc
1639 IBS	—	425	600	1,800	4,000	—
1640 IBS	—	425	600	1,800	4,000	—
1641 IBS	—	425	600	1,800	4,000	—
1648 IBS	—	425	600	1,800	4,000	—
1652 IAB	—	425	600	1,800	4,000	—
1655 IAB	—	425	600	1,800	4,000	—
1656 IAB	—	425	600	1,800	4,000	—
1658 IBN	—	425	600	1,800	4,000	—
1664 AB	—	425	600	1,800	4,000	—
1675 ILM	—	425	600	1,800	4,000	—
1690 GLM	—	425	600	1,800	4,000	—
1691 ITC	—	425	600	1,800	4,000	—
1692 ITC	—	425	600	1,800	4,000	—
1697 ITC	—	425	600	1,800	4,000	—

KM# 14.1 DOPPIA (2 Scudi)

7.0000 g., 0.9860 Gold 0.2219 oz. AGW **Obv:** Cross **Obv. Legend:** CONRADVS II RO REX **Rev:** Castle **Rev. Legend:** DVX ET GVB REIP GENV

Date	Mintage	VG	F	VF	XF	Unc
1601 IV	—	450	650	1,250	3,000	—
1602 IV	—	450	650	1,250	3,000	—
1602 PP	—	450	650	1,250	3,000	—
1603 IV	—	450	650	1,250	3,000	—
1604 IV	—	450	650	1,250	3,000	—
1607 HP	—	450	650	1,250	3,000	—
1609 HP	—	450	650	1,250	3,000	—
1613 MC	—	450	650	1,250	3,000	—
1616 IZ	—	450	650	1,250	3,000	—
1617 IZ	—	450	650	1,250	3,000	—
1619 DN	—	450	650	1,250	3,000	—
1621 GF	—	450	650	1,250	3,000	—
1624 GF	—	450	650	1,250	3,000	—
1625	—	450	650	1,250	3,000	—
1626	—	450	650	1,250	3,000	—
1627	—	450	650	1,250	3,000	—
1628	—	450	650	1,250	3,000	—
1629	—	450	650	1,250	3,000	—
1633	—	450	650	1,250	3,000	—
1637	—	450	650	1,250	3,000	—

KM# 14.2 DOPPIA (2 Scudi)

7.0000 g., 0.9860 Gold 0.2219 oz. AGW **Rev:** Ornate cross **Rev. Legend:** IN HOC SALVS MVNDI

Date	Mintage	VG	F	VF	XF	Unc
1624	—	475	700	1,500	2,800	—

KM# 99 DOPPIA (2 Scudi)

7.0000 g., 0.9860 Gold 0.2219 oz. AGW **Rev:** Madonna and child on cloud

Date	Mintage	VG	F	VF	XF	Unc
1640 IBS	—	700	1,500	3,000	6,000	—
1641 IBS	—	700	1,500	3,000	6,000	—
1653 IAB	—	700	1,500	3,000	6,000	—
1654 IAB	—	700	1,500	3,000	6,000	—
1656 IAB	—	700	1,500	3,000	6,000	—
1658 IBN	—	700	1,500	3,000	6,000	—
1670 ISS	—	700	1,500	3,000	6,000	—
1676 ILM	—	700	1,500	3,000	6,000	—
1694 ITC	—	700	1,500	3,000	6,000	—

KM# 28 2 DOPPIE

14.0000 g., 0.9860 Gold 0.4438 oz. AGW **Obv:** Symbolic castle, date below in inner circle **Rev:** Ornate cross in inner circle

Date	Mintage	VG	F	VF	XF	Unc
1603 IV	—	950	1,850	4,000	6,500	—
1608 HP	—	950	1,850	4,000	6,500	—
1609 HP	—	950	1,850	4,000	6,500	—
1612 MC	—	950	1,850	4,000	6,500	—
1617 IZ	—	950	1,850	4,000	6,500	—
1618 IZ	—	950	1,850	4,000	6,500	—
1619 DN	—	950	1,850	4,000	6,500	—
1621 GF	—	950	1,850	4,000	6,500	—
1623 GF	—	950	1,850	4,000	6,500	—
1624 GF	—	950	1,850	4,000	6,500	—
1625 GF	—	950	1,850	4,000	6,500	—
1627	—	950	1,850	4,000	6,500	—
1628	—	950	1,850	4,000	6,500	—
1629	—	950	1,850	4,000	6,500	—
1630	—	950	1,850	4,000	6,500	—
1632	—	950	1,850	4,000	6,500	—
1637 IBS	—	950	1,850	4,000	6,500	—

KM# 85 2 DOPPIE

14.0000 g., 0.9860 Gold 0.4438 oz. AGW **Rev:** Madonna and child on cloud

Date	Mintage	VG	F	VF	XF	Unc
1638 IBS	—	1,500	3,000	7,000	14,000	—
1639 IBS	—	1,500	3,000	7,000	14,000	—
1640 IBS	—	1,500	3,000	7,000	14,000	—
1641 IBS	—	1,500	3,000	7,000	14,000	—
1650 IBN	—	1,500	3,000	7,000	14,000	—
1651 IAB	—	1,500	3,000	7,000	14,000	—
1653 IAB	—	1,500	3,000	7,000	14,000	—
1654 IAB	—	1,500	3,000	7,000	14,000	—
1655 IAB	—	1,500	3,000	7,000	14,000	—
1658 IAB	—	1,500	3,000	7,000	14,000	—
1659	—	1,500	3,000	7,000	14,000	—
1661 AB	—	1,500	3,000	7,000	14,000	—
1662 AB	—	1,500	3,000	7,000	14,000	—
1668 ISS	—	1,500	3,000	7,000	14,000	—
1669 ISS	—	1,500	3,000	7,000	14,000	—
1670 ISS	—	1,500	3,000	7,000	14,000	—
1671 ISS	—	1,500	3,000	7,000	14,000	—
1675 ILM	—	1,500	3,000	7,000	14,000	—
1698 ITC	—	1,500	3,000	7,000	14,000	—

KM# 152 2-1/2 DOPPIE

17.5000 g., 0.9860 Gold 0.5547 oz. AGW **Obv:** Ornate cross in inner circle **Rev:** Madonna and child on cloud in stars, date in legend

Date	Mintage	VG	F	VF	XF	Unc
1675 ILM	—	—	—	8,000	16,000	—
1676 ILM	—	—	—	8,000	16,000	—
1697 ITC	—	—	—	8,000	16,000	—

KM# 39 4 DOPPIE (Quadrupia)

28.0000 g., 0.9860 Gold 0.8876 oz. AGW **Ruler:** Conrad II **Obv:** Cross **Obv. Legend:** CONRADVS II RO REX **Rev:** Castle **Rev. Legend:** DVX ET GVB REIP GEN

Date	Mintage	VG	F	VF	XF	Unc
1613 MC	—	—	—	—	—	—
1614 MC	—	—	—	—	—	—
1615 IZ	—	—	—	—	—	—
1616 IZ	—	—	—	—	—	—

KM# 16 5 DOPPIE

35.0000 g., 0.9860 Gold 1.1095 oz. AGW **Ruler:** Conrad II

Date	Mintage	VG	F	VF	XF	Unc
1613 MC Rare	—	—	—	—	—	—
1615 IZ Rare	—	—	—	—	—	—
1616 IZ Rare	—	—	—	—	—	—
1620 GF Rare	—	—	—	—	—	—
1623 GF Rare	—	—	—	—	—	—
1633 Rare	—	—	—	—	—	—

KM# 100 5 DOPPIE

35.0000 g., 0.9860 Gold 1.1095 oz. AGW **Rev:** Madonna and child on cloud

Date	Mintage	VG	F	VF	XF	Unc
1640 IBS	—	2,500	5,000	10,000	22,000	—
1641 IBS	—	2,500	5,000	10,000	22,000	—
1642 CS	—	2,500	5,000	10,000	22,000	—
1643 CS	—	2,500	5,000	10,000	22,000	—
1644 CS	—	2,500	5,000	10,000	22,000	—
1645 CS	—	2,500	5,000	10,000	22,000	—
1646 CS	—	2,500	5,000	10,000	22,000	—
1647 IBN	—	2,500	5,000	10,000	22,000	—
1649 IBN	—	2,500	5,000	10,000	22,000	—
1650 IBN	—	2,500	5,000	10,000	22,000	—
1651 IBN	—	2,500	5,000	10,000	22,000	—
1652 IAB	—	2,500	5,000	10,000	22,000	—
1653 IAB	—	2,500	5,000	10,000	22,000	—
1655 IAB	—	2,500	5,000	10,000	22,000	—
1673 IBT	—	2,500	5,000	10,000	22,000	—
1675 ILM	—	2,500	5,000	10,000	22,000	—
1679 ILM	—	2,500	5,000	10,000	22,000	—
1685 GLM	—	2,500	5,000	10,000	22,000	—
1691 ITC	—	2,500	5,000	10,000	22,000	—
1692 ITC	—	2,500	5,000	10,000	22,000	—
1697 ITC	—	2,500	5,000	10,000	22,000	—

KM# 107 10 DOPPIE

70.0000 g., 0.9860 Gold 2.2190 oz. AGW **Obv:** Ornate cross in inner circle **Rev:** Madonna and child on cloud in stars, date in legend

Date	Mintage	VG	F	VF	XF	Unc
1641 IBS Rare	—	—	—	—	—	—
1649 IBN Rare	—	—	—	—	—	—
1650 IBN Rare	—	—	—	—	—	—
1666 AB Rare	—	—	—	—	—	—
1670 ISS Rare	—	—	—	—	—	—
1694 ITC Rare	—	—	—	—	—	—

KM# 72 12-1/2 DOPPIE

0.9860 Gold **Obv:** Symbolic castle, date below in inner circle **Rev:** Ornate cross in inner circle **Note:** Weight varies: 82.0-85.0 grams. Actual gold weight varies: 2.6000-2.6960 ounces.

Date	Mintage	VG	F	VF	XF	Unc
1632 Rare	—	—	—	—	—	—
1634 Rare	—	—	—	—	—	—
1636 IBS Rare	—	—	—	—	—	—
1637 IBS Rare	—	—	—	—	—	—

KM# 86 12-1/2 DOPPIE

0.9860 Gold **Obv:** Cherubs between ends of cross within circle **Rev:** Madonna and child on cloud in stars, date in legend **Note:** 82-85 grams.

Date	Mintage	VG	F	VF	XF	Unc
1638 IBS Rare	—	—	—	—	—	—
1641 IBS Rare	—	—	—	—	—	—
Note: Stack's International sale 3-88 near XF realized $38,500						
1649 IBN Rare	—	—	—	—	—	—
1650 IBN Rare	—	—	—	—	—	—
1653 IAB Rare	—	—	—	—	—	—
1656 IAB Rare	—	—	—	—	—	—
1680 SM Rare	—	—	—	—	—	—
1694 ITC Rare	—	—	—	—	—	—
1698 ITC Rare	—	—	—	—	—	—

KM# 110 20 DOPPIE

132.0000 g., 0.9860 Gold 4.1843 oz. AGW **Obv:** Ornate cross in inner circle **Rev:** Madonna and child on cloud in stars, date in legend

Date	Mintage	VG	F	VF	XF	Unc
1645 CS Rare	—	—	—	—	—	—

KM# 76 25 DOPPIE

175.0000 g., 0.9860 Gold 5.5474 oz. AGW **Ruler:** Conrad II **Obv:** Symbolic castle, date below in inner circle **Rev:** Ornate cross in inner circle

Date	Mintage	VG	F	VF	XF	Unc
1636 IBS Rare	—	—	—	—	—	—

KM# 87 25 DOPPIE

175.0000 g., 0.9860 Gold 5.5474 oz. AGW **Obv:** Madonna and child on cloud

Date	Mintage	VG	F	VF	XF	Unc
1638 IBS Rare	—	—	—	—	—	—
1642 CS Rare	—	—	—	—	—	—
1653 Rare	—	—	—	—	—	—
1670 Rare	—	—	—	—	—	—
1694 Rare	—	—	—	—	—	—
1697 Rare	—	—	—	—	—	—

TRADE COINAGE

(for Levante)

KM# 125 LIGURINO

Billon **Obv:** Crowned shield with griffin supporters, LIBERTAS on shield **Rev:** Bust of female and Arabic legend

Date	Mintage	VG	F	VF	XF	Unc
1668	—	350	750	1,250	—	—
1669	—	350	750	1,250	—	—

KM# 126 GIUSTINO

2.0000 g., Billon **Obv:** Crowned shield with griffin supporters, LIBERTAS on shield **Rev:** Female seated

Date	Mintage	VG	F	VF	XF	Unc
1668	—	350	500	1,000	—	—
1669	—	350	500	1,000	—	—

KM# 127 GIANUINO

2.2000 g., Billon **Obv:** Crowned shield **Rev:** Janiform head of male and female

Date	Mintage	VG	F	VF	XF	Unc
1668	—	200	400	750	1,250	—

KM# 128 GIORGINO

1.7500 g., Silver **Obv:** Griffin supporting crowned arms, LIBERTAS on shield **Obv. Legend:** DVX ET GVB REIP GENV **Rev:** St. George slaying dragon **Rev. Legend:** S. GEOR PROT BONVIN VII

Date	Mintage	VG	F	VF	XF	Unc
1668	—	850	1,650	3,250	5,500	—

KM# 154 SCUDO

27.2500 g., Silver **Obv:** Crowned shield in palm **Obv. Legend:** DVX ET GVBER REIP GENV **Rev:** Griffin holding shield with Arabic text **Note:** Dav. #3903.

Date	Mintage	VG	F	VF	XF	Unc
1677 ILM Rare	—	—	—	—	—	—

PATTERNS

Including off metal strikes

KM#	Date	Mintage	Identification	Mkt Val
Pn1	1681	—	5 Doppie. Gold.	—

GUASTALLA

Town, Countship and Duchy

Located on the south side of the River Po, some 16 miles (26 kilometers) south-southwest of Mantua, Guastalla was controlled by the Visconti and then the Torelli families during the late Middle Ages. The town and environs were ceded to the Gonzagas of Mantua in 1539, who were then invested as counts by Emperor Carlo V (1519-56). In 1557, the count received the mint right and later was raised to the rank of duke in 1621. At the death of Ferrante III in 1678, the Gonzaga duke of Mantua took possession of Guastalla until it was restored to the branch line of the family in 1692. Upon the death of the last of the line in 1746, Emperor Francesco I transferred Guastalla to the duke of Parma. The duchy was annexed to the Kingdom of Italy during the Napoleonic Era. In 1847, it passed to Modena and became part of modern Italy in 1859.

RULERS

Ferrante II Gonzaga, 1575-1630, Duke in 1622
Cesare II Gonzaga, 1630-1632
Ferrante III Gonzaga, 1632-1678
Ferdinando Carlo Gonzaga of Mantua, 1678-1692
Vincenzo Gonzaga, 1692-1702

Note: The given name, Ferrante, is rendered as Ferdinando on the coins.

MINT OFFICIALS

GMF/G. MOLO/GASP. MOLO = Gaspare Molo (Fecit=made), ca. 1613-1614
IO = ? ca. 1615
LC = Luca Xell, ca. 1619-1620
GGF = Giovanni Gualtieri (Fecit), ca. 1664

Reference:

Alberto Varesi, ***Monete Italiane Regionali:*** Emilia. Pavia, 1998.

COUNTSHIP

STANDARD COINAGE

KM# 50 SOLDO

Copper Weight varies: 2.20-2.53g., 17 mm. **Ruler:** Ferrante II **Obv:** Head to left in circle **Obv. Legend:** FERD. GON. MELF. P. G. COM. **Rev:** Lion rampant to left in circle, date at end of legend **Rev. Legend:** INSIG. COMVNIT. GVAST. **Note:** Varesi 401.

Date	Mintage	Good	VG	F	VF	XF
1621	—	25.00	50.00	100	200	325

KM# 35 3 SOLDI

Silver Weight varies: 1.06-1.48g., 18-19 mm. **Ruler:** Ferrante II **Obv:** Crowned shield of 4-fold arms with central shield, Order of Golden Fleece around **Obv. Legend:** MO. NO. GVASTALLÆ. **Rev:** Crowned imperial eagle, '3' in orb on breast, date at end of legend **Rev. Legend:** BONIS. AVIBVS. **Note:** Varesi 397.

Date	Mintage	Good	VG	F	VF	XF
1618	—	25.00	50.00	110	185	350
1619	—	25.00	50.00	110	185	350

KM# 29 4 SOLDI

1.4700 g., Silver, 19-20 mm. **Ruler:** Ferrante II **Obv:** Head to right, 'IIII' below, all in circle **Obv. Legend:** IMAGO. PATRIS. GLORIA. FILII. **Rev:** Standing figure of St. Catherine holding palm frond and wheel, date in exergue **Rev. Legend:** SANCTA. CATERINA. **Note:** Varesi 395.

Date	Mintage	Good	VG	F	VF	XF
1617 Rare	—	—	—	—	—	—

KM# 37 LIRA

Silver Weight varies: 4.00-4.59g., 29 mm. **Ruler:** Ferrante II **Obv:** Crowned imperial eagle in circle **Obv. Legend:** FERD. GONZAGA. MELFI. PRINC. GVASTALLÆ. DNS. **Rev:** Crowned shield of manifold arms divides date in circle **Rev. Legend:** ANTIQVA. E. - MATERNA - INSIGNA. **Note:** Varesi 386.

Date	Mintage	Good	VG	F	VF	XF
1618	—	—	1,650	3,000	5,000	—
1619	—	—	1,650	3,000	5,000	—

KM# 39 LIRA

Silver Weight varies: 4.10-4.85g., 25-26 mm. **Ruler:** Ferrante II **Obv:** Crowned imperial eagle, date in exergue **Obv. Legend:** FERD. GON. ME. - PRI. GVASTA. D. **Rev:** Crowned shield of manifold arms **Rev. Legend:** ANTIQVA - ET. MAT. - INSIGN. **Note:** Varesi 387.

Date	Mintage	Good	VG	F	VF	XF
1619	—	—	1,650	3,000	5,000	—

KM# 16 LIRA (20 Soldi)

Silver Weight varies: 4.54-4.84g., 28-29 mm. **Ruler:** Ferrante II **Obv:** Armored bust to right, mint official's name (G. MOLO) below **Obv. Legend:** FERD. GON. MELFICTI. PRINC. **Rev:** Mariner's compass with needle pointing to top, value (XX) at bottom **Rev. Legend:** NEC. SPE. - NEC. METV. **Note:** Varesi 384/1.

Date	Mintage	Good	VG	F	VF	XF
ND(1613-14)	—	—	1,350	2,750	5,250	—

KM# 31 LIRA (20 Soldi)

Silver Weight varies: 4.54-4.84g., 28-29 mm. **Ruler:** Ferrante II **Obv:** Armored bust to right, date below **Obv. Legend:** FERD. GON. MELFICTI. PRINC. **Rev:** Mariner's compass with needle pointing to top, value (XX) at bottom **Rev. Legend:** NEX. SPE. - NEC. METV. **Note:** Varesi 384/2.

Date	Mintage	Good	VG	F	VF	XF
1617	—	—	1,350	2,750	5,250	—

KM# 40 PAOLO (22 Soldi)

Silver Weight varies: 4.97-5.65g., 30 mm. **Ruler:** Ferrante II **Obv:** Crowned shield of 4-fold arms with central shield, Order of Golden Fleece around **Obv. Legend:** FERDI. GON. MEL. - PRI. ET. GVASTAL. D. **Rev:** Facing full-length figure of St. Paul with sword and book, 'L. ZZ. X' in exergue **Rev. Legend:** SANCT. PAVLVS. - DOCT. GENTIVM. **Note:** Varesi 382.

Date	Mintage	Good	VG	F	VF	XF
ND(1619-20) LX	—	—	400	825	1,700	2,500

KM# 27 TESTONE

Silver Weight varies: 7.26-8.10g., 28 mm. **Ruler:** Ferrante II **Obv:** Crowned imperial eagle in circle **Obv. Legend:** FERD. GON(Z). MELFI. PRINC. GVASTAL. D. **Rev:** 1/2-length figure of St. Charles Borromeo to right, wearing miter and holding crozier, divides date, legend begins at upper right **Rev. Legend:** S. CAROL. BORO(M). - AR. MEDIOL. **Note:** Varesi 378. Varieties exist.

Date	Mintage	Good	VG	F	VF	XF
1615	—	—	750	1,400	2,300	4,250
1618	—	—	750	1,400	2,300	4,250
1619 LX	—	—	750	1,400	2,300	4,250

KM# 41 TESTONE

Silver Weight varies: 6.08-7.97g., 28-29 mm. **Ruler:** Ferrante II **Obv:** Armored bust to right **Obv. Legend:** FERD. GON. MELF(I). PRINC. GVASTAL(L)Æ. D. **Rev:** Crowned 4-fold arms with central shield divides date, where present **Rev. Legend:** ANTIQVA. ET. - MATER(NA). INSIG. **Note:** Varesi 379. Varieties exist.

Date	Mintage	Good	VG	F	VF	XF
1619 LX	—	—	900	1,650	3,250	6,750
1620 LX	—	—	900	1,650	3,250	6,750
ND(ca1619-20) LX	—	—	900	1,650	3,250	6,750

KM# 56 TESTONE

Silver Weight varies: 5.75-7.89g., 28-29 mm. **Ruler:** Ferrante II **Obv:** Armored bust to right divides date **Obv. Legend:** FERD. GONZ. MELFIC. PRINC. GVAST. DS. **Rev:** Crowned 4-fold arms with central shield **Rev. Legend:** ANTIQVA. ET. MATERNA. INSIG. **Note:** Varesi 380.

Date	Mintage	Good	VG	F	VF	XF
1622	—	—	750	1,400	2,300	4,250

KM# 57 TESTONE

Silver Weight varies: 7.30-8.05g., 29 mm. **Ruler:** Ferrante II **Obv:** Crowned imperial eagle in circle **Obv. Legend:** FERD. GONZ. MELFI. PRINC. GVASTALÆ. D. **Rev:** Half-length figure of St. Charles Borromeo to right, wearing miter and holding crozier, date in exergue, legend begins at lower left **Rev. Legend:** S. CAROL. - BOR. AR. MED.

Date	Mintage	Good	VG	F	VF	XF
16ZZ	—	—	850	1,600	2,650	5,000

KM# 18 50 SOLDI

Silver Weight varies: 10.50-11.20g., 29 mm. **Ruler:** Ferrante II **Obv:** High-collared armored bust to right, value '50' in exergue **Obv. Legend:** FERD. GON. MELFICTI. PRINC. **Rev:** Figure of Ferrante I trampling on a satyr and stabbing it with lance, Roman numeral date in exergue, mint official's initials on base **Rev. Legend:** SIMVLACRVM AVITÆ VIRTVTIS. **Note:** Varesi 376.

Date	Mintage	Good	VG	F	VF	XF
MDCXIII(1613) Rare	—	—	—	—	—	—

KM# 33 1/2 SCUDO (70 Soldi)

Silver Weight varies: 13.50-14.00g., 31 mm. **Ruler:** Ferrante II **Obv:** High-collared armored bust to right, date with value '70' in exergue **Obv. Legend:** FERD. GON. MELFICTI. PRI. **Rev:** Crowned shield of 4-fold arms with central shield, Order of Golden Fleece around **Rev. Legend:** CÆSARIS. FILIVS. **Note:** Varesi 375.

Date	Mintage	Good	VG	F	VF	XF
1617 Rare	—	—	—	—	—	—

Note: Existence of this coin uncertain.

KM# 2 TALLERO

Silver Weight varies: 27.65-28.45g., 44 mm. **Ruler:** Ferrante II **Obv:** Half-length armored figure to right, date below, where present **Obv. Legend:** FERDINANDVS. GONZAGA. CÆSARIS. FILIVS. **Rev:** Crowned shield of 4-fold arms with central shield, Order of Golden Fleece around **Rev. Legend:** MELFICTI. PRIN(C). - ET. GVASTALLÆ. DNS. **Note:** Varesi 369; Dav. 3905. Varieties exist.

Date	Mintage	VG	F	VF	XF	Unc
1601	—	1,250	2,200	6,850	12,000	—
1602	—	1,250	2,200	6,850	12,000	—
1603	—	1,250	2,200	6,850	12,000	—
ND(1600-4)	—	1,250	2,200	6,850	12,000	—

KM# 44 TALLERO

Silver Weight varies: 27.71-29.60g., 41-42 mm. **Ruler:** Ferrante II **Obv:** High-collared armored bust to right divides date, where present, mint official's monogram below **Obv. Legend:**

FERDINANDVS. (-) GON. (-ZAGA.) CAESARIS. FILIVS. **Rev:** Crowned shield of 4-fold arms with central shield, Order of Golden Fleece around **Rev. Legend:** MELFICTI. PRINC(EPS). (ET.) - GVASTAL(L)Æ. COM. **Note:** Varesi 371; Dav. 3913. Varieties exist.

Date	Mintage	VG	F	VF	XF	Unc
1619 LX	—	750	1,400	3,250	5,500	—
1620 LX	—	600	1,100	2,650	4,500	—
ND(ca1619-20) LX	—	950	1,900	4,250	7,250	—

KM# 43 TALLERO

28.4300 g., Silver, 41-42 mm. **Ruler:** Ferrante II **Obv:** High-collared armored bust to right, date divided by 'LX' below **Obv. Legend:** FERDINANDVS. GONZAGA. **Rev:** Crowned shield of 4-fold arms with central shield, Order of Golden Fleece around **Rev. Legend:** MELFICTI. PRINCEPS. - GVASTALÆ. COM. **Note:** Varesi 370; Dav. 3912.

Date	Mintage	VG	F	VF	XF	Unc
1619 LX Rare	—	—	—	—	—	—

KM# 45 TALLERO

Silver Weight varies: 28.00-29.00g., 40 mm. **Ruler:** Ferrante II **Obv:** High-collared armored bust to right divides date, mint official's monogram below **Obv. Legend:** FERDINANDVS. GONZAGA. CÆSARIS. FIL **Rev:** Crowned shield of 4-fold arms with central shield, Order of Golden Fleece around **Rev. Legend:** MELFICTI. PRINCEPS. GVASTALLÆ. COMES. **Note:** Dav. 3910.

Date	Mintage	VG	F	VF	XF	Unc
1619 LX	—	600	1,100	2,650	4,500	—

KM# 46 TALLERO

Silver Weight varies: 28.00-29.00g., 40 mm. **Ruler:** Ferrante II **Obv:** High-collared armored bust to right divides date, mint official's monogram below **Obv. Legend:** FERDINANDVS: GONZ: - CÆSARIS. FILIVS. **Rev:** Crowned shield of 4-fold arms with central shield, Order of Golden Fleece around **Rev. Legend:** MELFI: PRINC*: - GVA: COMES: **Note:** Dav. 3911.

Date	Mintage	VG	F	VF	XF	Unc
1619	—	600	1,100	2,650	4,500	—

KM# 48 TALLERO

Silver Weight varies: 26.51-28.62g., 40 mm. **Ruler:** Ferrante II **Obv:** High-collared armored bust to right divides date, mint official's monogram below **Obv. Legend:** FERDINANDVS. G - ONZA(GA). CAESAR. FILIVS. **Rev:** Crowned shield of 4-fold arms with central shield **Rev. Legend:** MELFICTI. PRINCEPS. GVASTALLA. COM. **Note:** Varesi 372; Dav. 3914. Varieties exist.

Date	Mintage	VG	F	VF	XF	Unc
1620 LX	—	600	1,100	2,650	4,500	—

KM# 9 DUCATONE

31.8700 g., Silver, 41-43 mm. **Ruler:** Ferrante II **Obv:** Draped and armored bust to right **Obv. Legend:** FERDIN. GON.- MELF. P. ET. G. D. **Rev:** The Annunciation scene, date in exergue **Rev. Legend:** ECCE. ANCI. - DOMINI. FIAT. - MICHI. **Note:** Varesi 365; Dav. 3907.

Date	Mintage	VG	F	VF	XF	Unc
1610 Rare	—	—	—	—	—	—

KM# 20 DUCATONE

30.8900 g., Silver, 41 mm. **Ruler:** Ferrante II **Obv:** Armored bust to right, in small letters below shoulder 'GASP. MOLO F.' **Obv. Legend:** FERDINANDVS. GON. MELFICTI. PRINC. **Rev:** Full-length figure of Ferrante I trampling a satyr and stabbing it with lance, Roman numeral date in exergue **Rev. Legend:** SIMVLACRVM - AVI - TÆ VIRTVTIS. **Note:** Varesi 366.

Date	Mintage	VG	F	VF	XF	Unc
MDCXIII (1613) Rare	—	—	—	—	—	—

Note: Numismatica Ars Classica Auction 44, 11-07 VF realized approximately $16,280

KM# 24 DUCATONE

Silver, 41 mm. **Ruler:** Ferrante II **Obv:** Armored bust to right, date below **Obv. Legend:** FERDINANDVS. GON. MELFICTI. PRINC. **Rev:** Full-length figure of Ferrante I trampling a satyr and stabbing it with lance **Rev. Legend:** SIMVLACRVM - AVI - TÆ VIRTVTIS. **Note:** Varesi 367; Dav. 3909.

Date	Mintage	VG	F	VF	XF	Unc
1614	—	4,500	7,500	15,000	25,000	—

KM# 4 2 TALLERI

Silver Weight varies: 55.75-56.60g., 45 mm. **Ruler:** Ferrante II **Obv:** Half-length armored figure to right, date below **Obv. Legend:** FERDINANDVS. GONZAGA. CÆSARIS. FILIVS. **Rev:** Crowned shield of 4-fold arms with central shield, Order of Golden Fleece around **Rev. Legend:** MELFICTI. PRIN(C). - ET. GVASTALLÆ. DNS. **Note:** Varesi 364; Dav. 8286, 3904.

Date	Mintage	VG	F	VF	XF	Unc
1601 Rare	—	—	—	—	—	—
1603 Rare	—	—	—	—	—	—

Note: Reported, not confirmed

KM# 11 2 DUCATONI

63.5400 g., Silver, 41-43 mm. **Ruler:** Ferrante II **Obv:** Draped and armored bust to right **Obv. Legend:** FERDIN. GON. - MELF. P. ET. G. D. **Rev:** The Annunciation scene, date in exergue **Rev. Legend:** ECCE. ANCI. - DOMINI. FIAT. - MICHI. **Note:** Varesi 362; Dav. 3906. Struck on thick flan from Ducatone dies, KM#9.

Date	Mintage	VG	F	VF	XF	Unc
1610 Rare	—	—	—	—	—	—

KM# 25 2 DUCATONI

62.6600 g., Silver, 41 mm. **Ruler:** Ferrante II **Obv:** Armored bust to right, date below **Obv. Legend:** FERDINANDVS. GON. MELFICTI. PRINC. **Rev:** Full-length figure of Ferrante I trampling a satyr and stabbing it with lance **Rev. Legend:** SIMVLACRVM - AVI - TÆ VIRTVTIS. **Note:** Varesi 363; Dav. 3908. Struck on thick flan from Ducatone dies, KM#24.

Date	Mintage	VG	F	VF	XF	Unc
1614 Rare	—	—	—	—	—	—

Note: 2 examples known.

TRADE COINAGE

KM# 6 2 DOPPIE

13.2800 g., Gold, 28 mm. **Ruler:** Ferrante II **Obv:** High-collared armored bust to right in circle **Obv. Legend:** FERD. GON. II. MELFICTI. PRIN. ET. GVAST. - DNS. **Rev:** The Annunciation scene, date in exergue **Rev. Legend:** ECCE. ANCILLA. A. DOMINI. **Note:** Varesi 354a.

Date	Mintage	VG	F	VF	XF	Unc
1604 Rare	—	—	—	—	—	—

KM# 22 2 DOPPIE

13.1400 g., Gold, 30 mm. **Ruler:** Ferrante II **Obv:** High-collared armored bust to right, 'G. MOLO' in small letters below **Obv. Legend:** FERD. GON. MELFICTI. PRINC. **Rev:** Full-length figure of Ferrante I trampling a satyr and stabbing it with lance, Roman numeral date in exergue **Rev. Legend:** SIMVLACRVM - AVITÆ VIRTVTIS. **Note:** Varesi 355.

Date	Mintage	VG	F	VF	XF	Unc
MDCXIII (1613) Rare	—	—	—	—	—	—

KM# 7 4 DOPPIE

26.3000 g., Gold, 28 mm. **Ruler:** Ferrante II **Obv:** High-collared armored bust to right in circle **Obv. Legend:** FERD. GON. II. MELFICTI. PRIN. ET. GVAST. - DNS. **Rev:** The Annunciation scene, date in exergue **Rev. Legend:** ECCE. ANCILLA. A. DOMINI. **Note:** Varesi 354; Fr. A459. Struck on thick flan from 2 Doppie dies, KM#6.

Date	Mintage	VG	F	VF	XF	Unc
1604 Rare	—	—	—	—	—	—

KM# 13 10 DOPPIE

Gold Weight varies: 66.10-66.41g., 43 mm. **Ruler:** Ferrante II **Obv:** Draped and armored bust to right **Obv. Legend:** FERDIN. GON. - MELF. P. ET. G. D. **Rev:** The Annunciation scene, date in exergue **Rev. Legend:** ECCE. ANCI. - DOMINI. FIAT. - MICHI. **Note:** Varesi 353; Fr. 458. Struck from Ducatone dies, KM#9.

Date	Mintage	VG	F	VF	XF	Unc
1610 Rare	—	—	—	—	—	—

KM# 14 11 DOPPIE

72.2600 g., Gold, 43 mm. **Ruler:** Ferrante II **Obv:** Draped and armored bust to right **Obv. Legend:** FERDIN. GON. - MELF. P. ET. G. D. **Rev:** The Annunciation scene, date in exergue **Rev. Legend:** ECCE. ANCI. - DOMINI. FIAT. - MICHI. **Note:** Varesi 352. Struck from Ducatone dies, KM#9.

Date	Mintage	VG	F	VF	XF	Unc
1610 Rare	—	—	—	—	—	—

DUCHY

STANDARD COINAGE

KM# 62 SESINO

Billon Weight varies: 0.60-1.19g., 16-17 mm. **Ruler:** Ferrante III **Obv:** Lion rampant to left **Obv. Legend:** FERDINANDVS. GONZAGA. **Rev:** Crowned monogram **Rev. Legend:** DVX. III. GVASTALLÆ. **Note:** Varesi 423.

Date	Mintage	Good	VG	F	VF	XF
ND(1632-78)	—	9.00	18.00	35.00	75.00	150

KM# 63 SESINO

Billon Weight varies: 0.71-1.47g., 16 mm. **Ruler:** Ferrante III **Obv:** Standing figure of St. Catherine **Obv. Legend:** S. CATARINA. PROTECTRIX. **Rev:** 3-line inscription **Rev. Inscription:** SESINO / DI GVAS / TALLA **Note:** Varesi 424.

Date	Mintage	Good	VG	F	VF	XF
ND(1632-78)	—	9.00	18.00	35.00	75.00	150

KM# 52 2 SOLDI (Gazzetta)

Billon Weight varies: 1.15-1.18g., 20-21 mm. **Ruler:** Ferrante II **Obv:** Crowned shield of 4-fold arms with central shield **Obv. Legend:** FERDINANDVS. - GON. GVAS. DVX. **Rev:** St. Mary, supported by angels to left and right, being crowned by 2 angels above, denomination at end of legend **Rev. Legend:** AVE. REGI. ANGEL. SOL. 2. **Note:** Varesi 410.

Date	Mintage	Good	VG	F	VF	XF
ND(1622-30)	—	7.00	15.00	35.00	75.00	125

KM# 60 4 SOLDI

Silver Weight varies: 1.40-1.62g., 19-20 mm. **Ruler:** Ferrante II **Obv:** Crowned shield of 4-fold arms with central shield, Order of Golden Fleece around **Obv. Legend:** FERDINAND. GON. GVA. DVX. **Rev:** Standing figure of St. Catherine holding palm frond and wheel, value 'IIII' in exergue, date at end of legend **Rev. Legend:** SANCTA. CATERINA. **Note:** Varesi 409.

Date	Mintage	Good	VG	F	VF	XF
16Z3	—	10.00	20.00	45.00	75.00	145

KM# 65 4 SOLDI

1.6200 g., Silver, 20 mm. **Ruler:** Ferrante III **Obv:** Crowned shield of 4-fold arms with central shield **Obv. Legend:** FERD. D. G. GVAST. LVZ. REG. DVX. III. **Rev:** Standing figure of nimbate St. Catherine holding palm frond and wheel **Rev. Legend:** S. CATARINA. PROTECTRIX. **Note:** Varesi 422.

Date	Mintage	Good	VG	F	VF	XF
ND(1632-78)	—	60.00	125	275	500	850

KM# 67 5 SOLDI

Billon Weight varies: 1.13-2.36g., 19-20 mm. **Ruler:** Ferrante III **Obv:** Crowned shield of 4-fold arms with central shield **Obv. Legend:** FERD. D.G. GVAST. - LVX. REG. DVX. III. **Rev:** Standing figure of crowned St. Catherine holding wheel and palm frond **Rev. Legend:** S. CATARINA. PROTECTRIX. **Note:** Varesi 421.

Date	Mintage	Good	VG	F	VF	XF
ND(1632-78)	—	20.00	40.00	80.00	125	200

KM# 73 10 SOLDI (1/2 Lira)

Silver Weight varies: 2.06-3.35g., 23-24 mm. **Ruler:** Ferrante III **Obv:** Crowned shield of 4-fold arms with central shield **Obv. Legend:** FERD. D.G. GVAST. - LVZ. REG. DVX. III. **Rev:** The Annunciation scene, date in exergue **Rev. Legend:** ECCE. ANCILLA. DOMINI. **Note:** Varesi 420.

Date	Mintage	Good	VG	F	VF	XF
1664	—	—	125	275	500	850
1673	—	—	125	275	500	850
1674 Rare	—	—	—	—	—	—

KM# 69 LIRA (20 Soldi)

4.3300 g., Silver, 25-26 mm. **Ruler:** Ferrante III **Obv:** Crowned shield of 4-fold arms with central shield, in baroque frame **Obv. Legend:** FERDIN. GONZAGA. DVX. III. **Rev:** Crowned facing figure of St. Mary in robe **Rev. Legend:** REFVGIVM. GVASTALLEN. **Note:** Varesi 419.

Date	Mintage	Good	VG	F	VF	XF
ND(1632-78) Rare	—	—	—	—	—	—

Note: 2 examples known.

KM# 54 PAOLO

Silver Weight varies: 3.90-5.17g., 27-28 mm. **Ruler:** Ferrante II **Obv:** Crowned shield of 4-fold arms with central shield, Order of Golden Fleece around **Obv. Legend:** FERD. GONZ. GV - AS. DVX. ET. MEL. P. **Rev:** Facing full-length figure of St. Paul with sword and book **Rev. Legend:** SAN. PAVLVS. - DOCT. GENTIVM. **Note:** Varesi 408.

Date	Mintage	Good	VG	F	VF	XF
ND(1622-30)	—	—	150	275	575	950

KM# 84 2 LIRE

Silver Weight varies: 7.37-7.70g., 30-31 mm. **Ruler:** Ferrante III **Obv:** Crowned shield of 4-fold arms with central shield in ornamented frame **Obv. Legend:** FERD. D.G. GVAST. LVZ. REG. DVX. III. **Rev:** The Annunciation scene, date in exergue **Rev. Legend:** ECCE. ANCILLA. DOMINI. **Note:** Varesi 417.

Date	Mintage	Good	VG	F	VF	XF
1674	—	—	500	950	1,800	2,750
1675	—	—	500	950	1,800	2,750

KM# 71 2 LIRE (40 Soldi)

8.6000 g., Silver, 29-30 mm. **Ruler:** Ferrante III **Obv:** Crowned shield of 4-fold arms with central shield in ornamented frame **Obv. Legend:** FERDINANDVS. GONZAGA. DVX. III. **Rev:** St. Francis kneeling towards left, receiving the stigmata. **Rev. Legend:** S. FRANCISCVS. PROTECT GVASTALLÆ. **Note:** Varesi 418.

Date	Mintage	Good	VG	F	VF	XF
ND(1632-78) Rare	—	—	—	—	—	—

Note: 2 examples known.

KM# 75 1/2 SCUDO

9.2600 g., Silver, 34 mm. **Ruler:** Ferrante III **Obv:** Armored bust to right, date in exergue **Obv. Legend:** FERD. D.G. GVAST. LVZ. REG. DVX. III. **Rev:** Full-length figure of Ferrante I trampling on satyr and stabbing it with lance **Rev. Legend:** SIMVLACRVM. AVITÆ. VIRTVTIS. **Note:** Varesi 416.

Date	Mintage	Good	VG	F	VF	XF
1664	—	—	1,000	1,900	4,850	7,700

KM# 81 1/2 SCUDO (80 Soldi = 4 Lire)

Silver Weight varies: 10.89-11.32g., 33 mm. **Ruler:** Ferrante III **Obv:** Armored bust to right, value '80' in exergue **Obv. Legend:** FER. D.G. GVAS. LVZ. REG. DVX. III. **Rev:** Crowned shield of 4-fold arms with central shield in ornamented frame, date at end of legend **Rev. Legend:** INTER. PLVRA. COGNITA. **Note:** Varesi 415.

Date	Mintage	Good	VG	F	VF	XF
1673 Rare	—	—	—	—	—	—

Note: Astarte S.A. Auction XIX, 5-06, VF realized approximately $17,965

KM# 77 SCUDO (7 Lire)

19.0000 g., Silver Weight varies: 15.90-19.46g., 42 mm. **Ruler:** Ferrante III **Obv:** Armored bust to right, date and mint official's initials below **Obv. Legend:** FERD. D.G. GVAST. LVZ. REG. DVX. III. **Rev:** Full-length figure of Ferrante I trampling satyr and stabbing it with lance **Rev. Legend:** SIMVLACRVM - AVI - TÆ. VIRTVTIS. **Note:** Varesi 414; Dav. 3917A.

Date	Mintage	VG	F	VF	XF	Unc
1664 GGF	—	900	1,650	5,000	—	—

KM# 82 SCUDO (8 Lire = 160 Soldi)

19.1700 g., Silver, 42 mm. **Ruler:** Ferrante III **Obv:** Armored bust to right, value '160' below **Obv. Legend:** FERD. D.G. GVAST. LVZ. REG. DVX. III. **Rev:** Mariner's compass with needle pointing to top, date in margin at bottom **Rev. Legend:** NEC. SPE - NEC. METV. **Note:** Varesi 413; Dav. 3918.

Date	Mintage	VG	F	VF	XF	Unc
1673 Rare	—	—	—	—	—	—

KM# 58 DUCATONE

Silver Weight varies: 31.67-31.75g., 41 mm. **Ruler:** Ferrante II **Obv:** Draped and armored bust to right, mint official's initials in exergue **Obv. Legend:** FERD. GONZ. GVAST. DVX. ET. MELF. PRI. **Rev:** Full-length figure of Ferrante I trampling a satyr and stabbing it with lance, Roman numeral date in exergue **Rev. Legend:** SIMVLACRVM. AVI - TAE. - VIRTVTIS. **Note:** Varesi 407; Dav. 3915.

Date	Mintage	VG	F	VF	XF	Unc
MDCXXII (1622) LX Rare	—	—	—	—	—	—

Note: Numismatica Ars Classica Auction 30, 6-05, XF realized approximately $15,970

KM# 79 2 SCUDI

40.5700 g., Silver, 42 mm. **Ruler:** Ferrante III **Obv:** Armored bust to right, date and mint official's initials below **Obv. Legend:** FERD. D.G. GVAST. LVZ. REG. DVX. III. **Rev:** Full-length figure of Ferrante I trampling a satyr and stabbing it with lance **Rev. Legend:** SIMVLACRVM - AVI - TÆ. VIRTVTIS. **Note:** Varesi 412; Dav. 3917. Struck on thick flan from Scudo dies, KM#77.

Date	Mintage	VG	F	VF	XF	Unc
1664 GGF Rare	—	—	—	—	—	—

LIVORNO

Livorno (Leghorn), a city on the Tyrrhenian Sea in western Tuscany, had a mint at which the Medici dukes struck coins with the mark LIBVRNI.

RULERS

Ferdinand II Medici, 1621-1670
Cosimo III Medici, 1670-1723

CITY

STANDARD COINAGE

KM# 8 LUIGINO

2.2200 g., Silver **Obv:** Head of Ferdinand right **Rev:** Crowned French shield

Date	Mintage	VG	F	VF	XF	Unc
1657	—	100	200	350	600	—
1659	—	100	200	350	600	—
1660	—	100	200	350	600	—
1661	—	100	200	350	600	—
1662	—	100	200	350	600	—
1663	—	100	200	350	600	—
1664	—	100	200	350	600	—
1665	—	100	200	350	600	—

KM# 20 LUIGINO

2.2200 g., Silver **Obv:** Bust of Cosimo right **Rev:** Crowned French shield

Date	Mintage	VG	F	VF	XF	Unc
1675	—	180	300	475	875	—
ND	—	180	300	475	875	—

KM# 10 1/4 PEZZA

Silver **Obv:** Crowned oval arms, FERDINANDO **Rev:** Rosebush **Note:** Weight varies: 6.00-6.40 grams.

Date	Mintage	VG	F	VF	XF	Unc
1665	—	250	425	675	1,100	—

KM# 30 1/4 PEZZA

Silver **Obv:** Crowned arms of Medici, COSMVS **Note:** Weight varies: 6.00-6.40 grams.

Date	Mintage	VG	F	VF	XF	Unc
1697	—	350	650	1,250	—	—
1699	—	350	650	1,250	—	—

KM# 11 1/2 PEZZA

13.0000 g., Silver **Obv:** Crowned oval arms, FERDINANDO **Rev:** Rosebush

Date	Mintage	VG	F	VF	XF	Unc
1665	—	425	650	1,100	1,800	—

KM# 31 1/2 PEZZA

13.0000 g., Silver **Obv:** Crowned oval arms of Medici, COSMVS

Date	Mintage	VG	F	VF	XF	Unc
1697	—	325	600	1,100	1,900	—

KM# 12 PEZZA DELLA ROSA

Silver **Obv:** Crowned arms of Medici, FERDINAND **Rev:** Rosebush **Note:** Dav. #4208.

Date	Mintage	VG	F	VF	XF	Unc
1665	—	1,650	3,250	5,500	9,000	—

KM# 15.1 PEZZA DELLA ROSA

Silver **Obv:** Crowned arms of Medici, unbroken legend **Obv. Legend:** COSMVS III... **Note:** Dav. #4216A.

Date	Mintage	VG	F	VF	XF	Unc
1670	—	350	650	1,100	1,900	—
1684	—	350	650	1,100	1,900	—

Note: Varieties exist for 1684

KM# 15.2 PEZZA DELLA ROSA

Silver **Obv:** Crown breaks legend **Note:** Dav. #4216.

Date	Mintage	VG	F	VF	XF	Unc
1684	—	215	425	775	1,450	—
1697	—	270	550	850	1,550	—
1698	—	270	550	850	1,550	—
1699	—	270	550	850	1,550	—
1700	—	270	550	850	1,550	—

KM# 25 1/4 TOLLERO

6.1500 g., Silver **Obv:** Crowned head right **Rev:** Fortress of Livorno, date below

Date	Mintage	VG	F	VF	XF	Unc
1683	—	450	850	1,500	—	—

KM# 26 1/2 TOLLERO

13.0000 g., Silver **Obv:** Crowned bust right **Rev:** Ship, LIBVRNI below

Date	Mintage	VG	F	VF	XF	Unc
1683	—	225	450	775	1,850	—

KM# 7.1 TOLLERO

27.0000 g., Silver **Obv:** Head of Ferdinand right, curved crown points **Rev:** Port of Livorno **Note:** Dav. #4204.

Date	Mintage	VG	F	VF	XF	Unc
1656 Rare	—	—	—	—	—	—

KM# 7.2 TOLLERO

27.0000 g., Silver **Obv:** Straight crown points **Note:** Dav. #4206.

Date	Mintage	VG	F	VF	XF	Unc
1659	—	600	1,150	2,250	—	—
1666	—	750	1,450	2,800	—	—
1669 Rare	—	—	—	—	—	—

KM# 16.1 TOLLERO

27.0000 g., Silver **Obv:** Crowned bust of Cosmus III right **Note:** Dav. #A4214.

Date	Mintage	VG	F	VF	XF	Unc
1670	—	775	1,550	2,950	5,500	—
1675	—	775	1,550	2,950	5,500	—

KM# 16.2 TOLLERO

27.0000 g., Silver **Obv. Legend:** D. G. MAG. DVX... **Note:** Dav. #4214.

Date	Mintage	VG	F	VF	XF	Unc
1680	—	30.00	30.00	30.00	30.00	—

KM# 16.3 TOLLERO

27.0000 g., Silver **Obv:** Without border around wide bust **Obv. Legend:** ...ETRVR. VI. **Note:** Dav. #4215A.

Date	Mintage	VG	F	VF	XF	Unc
1681	—	300	600	1,200	2,500	—

KM# 16.4 TOLLERO

27.0000 g., Silver **Obv:** Narrow bust **Note:** Dav. #4215.

Date	Mintage	VG	F	VF	XF	Unc
1683	—	150	325	525	975	1,750
1685	—	150	325	525	975	1,750
1687	—	150	325	525	975	1,750
1688	—	150	325	525	975	1,750
1692	—	150	325	525	975	1,750
1694	—	150	325	525	975	1,750
1695	—	150	325	525	975	1,750
1697	—	150	325	525	975	1,750
1698	—	150	325	525	975	1,750
1699	—	150	325	525	975	1,750
1700	—	150	325	525	975	1,750

KM# 5 ONGARO

2.3500 g., Gold **Obv:** Head of Ferdinand right **Rev:** Fortress, DIVERSIS

Date	Mintage	VG	F	VF	XF	Unc
1655 Rare	—	—	—	—	—	—

KM# 6 ONGARO

2.3500 g., Gold **Rev:** Harbor, ET PAVET

Date	Mintage	VG	F	VF	XF	Unc
ND Rare	—	—	—	—	—	—

KM# 17 ONGARO

2.3500 g., Gold **Obv:** Head of Cosimo right

Date	Mintage	VG	F	VF	XF	Unc
ND Rare	—	—	—	—	—	—

Note: Superior Pipito sale 12-87 choice XF realized $42,900

KM# 18 ONGARO

2.3500 g., Gold **Obv:** Grand Duke standing **Rev:** Six-line inscription in cartouche

Date	Mintage	VG	F	VF	XF	Unc
1674	—	400	600	2,500	4,500	—
1675	—	400	600	2,500	4,500	—
1676	—	400	600	2,500	4,500	—
1678	—	400	600	2,500	4,500	—
1691	—	400	600	2,500	4,500	—
ND	—	400	600	2,500	4,500	—

KM# 19 ONGARO

2.3500 g., Gold **Obv:** Grand Duke standing **Rev:** Fame on clouds with stars and rays

Date	Mintage	VG	F	VF	XF	Unc
ND	—	3,000	6,000	9,000	18,000	—

LOANO

Loana, a county in Liguria on the Tyrrhenian Sea, was acquired by Oberti Doria in 1263, but sold by the family in 1505 to Gian Luigi Fieschi. Thru marriage, however, it came back to Giovanni Andrea Doria, who restored the castle and built walls. The mint privilege had been conferred in 1547.

RULERS
Giovanni Andrea Dorea I, 1560-1606
Giovanni Andrea Doria II, 1622-1640
Giovanni Andrea Doria III, 1654-1737

COUNTY

STANDARD COINAGE

KM# 16 LUIGINO

Billon **Rev:** Crowned baroque arms **Rev. Legend:** SPES... **Note:** Weight varies: 1.80-2.45 grams.

Date	Mintage	VG	F	VF	XF	Unc
1665	—	100	200	325	650	1,250
1666	—	100	200	450	1,000	3,000

KM# 17 LUIGINO

Billon **Rev:** Crowned arms divide date **Rev. Legend:** DEVS... **Note:** Weight varies: 1.80-2.45 grams.

Date	Mintage	VG	F	VF	XF	Unc
1665	—	75.00	150	325	650	1,250
1666	—	100	200	450	1,000	3,000

KM# 18 LUIGINO

Billon **Rev:** Crowned arms, date above **Rev. Legend:** DEVS... **Note:** Weight varies: 1.80-2.45 grams.

Date	Mintage	VG	F	VF	XF	Unc
1665	—	130	290	575	1,100	1,900
1666	—	130	290	575	1,100	1,900

KM# 15 LUIGINO

Silver **Rev:** Crowned arms divide date **Rev. Legend:** SPES... **Note:** Weight varies: 1.74-2.22 grams.

Date	Mintage	VG	F	VF	XF	Unc
1665	—	170	350	700	1,350	—
1666	—	170	350	700	1,350	—

KM# 23 LUIGINO

Billon **Obv:** Bust right **Obv. Legend:** VIOLANTE... **Rev:** Crowned French arms divide date **Rev. Legend:** DEVS... **Note:** Weight varies: 1.80-2.45 grams.

Date	Mintage	VG	F	VF	XF	Unc
1665	—	75.00	150	400	950	—
1666	—	100	200	450	1,000	—

KM# 15a LUIGINO

Billon **Note:** Weight varies: 1.80-2.45 grams.

Date	Mintage	VG	F	VF	XF	Unc
1666	—	—	—	—	—	—

KM# 22 LUIGINO

Billon **Obv:** Bust of Volante Lomellini, widow of Andrea III right **Obv. Legend:** GRATIOR... **Rev:** Crowned French arms divide date (one lis above two) **Rev. Legend:** SANCTE **Note:** Weight varies: 1.80-2.45 grams.

Date	Mintage	VG	F	VF	XF	Unc
1666	—	42.00	90.00	220	400	—
1667	—	42.00	90.00	220	400	—
1668	—	42.00	90.00	220	400	—

KM# 24 LUIGINO

Billon **Obv:** Bust right **Obv. Legend:** GRATIOR... **Rev:** Crowned French arms divide date (two lis above one) **Note:** Weight varies: 1.80-2.45 grams.

Date	Mintage	VG	F	VF	XF	Unc
1667	—	42.00	90.00	220	400	—
1668	—	42.00	90.00	220	400	—
1669	—	42.00	90.00	220	400	—

KM# 25 LUIGINO

Billon **Obv:** Bust right **Obv. Legend:** PVLCRA... **Rev:** Crowned French arms **Rev. Legend:** BONITAS... **Note:** Weight varies: 1.80-2.45 grams.

Date	Mintage	VG	F	VF	XF	Unc
1668	—	42.00	90.00	220	400	—
1669	—	42.00	90.00	220	400	—

KM# 26 LUIGINO

Billon **Rev:** Crowned arms divide date **Rev. Legend:** SIT NOMEN... **Note:** Weight varies: 1.80-2.45 grams.

Date	Mintage	VG	F	VF	XF	Unc
1669	—	150	300	575	1,050	—

KM# 27 LUIGINO

Billon **Obv:** Bust right **Obv. Legend:** PVLCRA... **Rev:** Crowned French arms divide date **Rev. Legend:** *TRES **Note:** Weight varies: 1.80-2.45 grams.

Date	Mintage	VG	F	VF	XF	Unc
1669	—	75.00	180	375	725	—

KM# 19 REALE

4.5000 g., Silver **Obv:** Bust of Gio right **Rev:** Crowned arms divide date

Date	Mintage	VG	F	VF	XF	Unc
1665 Rare	—	—	—	—	—	—

KM# 6 SCUDO

Silver **Obv:** Bust left **Rev:** Caduceus and cornucopia **Note:** Weight varies: 31.00-38.00 grams. Dav. #3920.

Date	Mintage	VG	F	VF	XF	Unc
1601 Rare	—	—	—	—	—	—

KM# 30 SCUDO

Silver **Obv:** Bust right, date below **Rev:** Crowned eagle arms **Note:** Weight varies: 31.00-38.00 grams. Dav. #3922.

Date	Mintage	VG	F	VF	XF	Unc
1670 Rare	—	—	—	—	—	—

KM# 7 DUCATONE

42.0400 g., Silver **Obv:** Bust left **Rev:** Crowned eagle arms, date below **Note:** Dav. #3921.

Date	Mintage	VG	F	VF	XF	Unc
1606 Rare	—	—	—	—	—	—

KM# 10 DOPPIA

7.0000 g., 0.9860 Gold 0.2219 oz. AGW **Obv:** Bust of Giovanni Andrea Doria II right in inner circle **Rev:** Crowned eagle arms in inner circle

Date	Mintage	VG	F	VF	XF	Unc
1639 Rare	—	—	—	—	—	—

KM# 20 DOPPIA

7.0000 g., 0.9860 Gold 0.2219 oz. AGW **Obv:** Bust of Giovanni Andrea Doria III to right **Rev:** Crowned arms on St. Andrew's cross, date at top

Date	Mintage	VG	F	VF	XF	Unc
1665 Rare	—	—	—	—	—	—

KM# 21 DOPPIA

7.0000 g., 0.9860 Gold 0.2219 oz. AGW **Rev:** Arms divide date

Date	Mintage	VG	F	VF	XF	Unc
1665 Rare	—	—	—	—	—	—

KM# 11 2 DOPPIE

14.0000 g., 0.9860 Gold 0.4438 oz. AGW **Obv:** Bust of Giovanni Andrea Doria II right in inner circle **Rev:** Crowned eagle arms in inner circle

Date	Mintage	VG	F	VF	XF	Unc
1639 Rare	—	—	—	—	—	—

TRADE COINAGE

KM# 8 DUCAT

3.5000 g., 0.9860 Gold 0.1109 oz. AGW **Obv:** Madonna and child **Rev:** Four-line inscription in tablet

Date	Mintage	VG	F	VF	XF	Unc
ND	—	2,500	4,000	7,500	12,500	—

LUCCA

Luca, Lucensis

Lucca and Piombino

A town in Tuscany and the residence of a marquis, was nominally a fief but managed to maintain a *de facto* independence until awarded by Napoleon to his sister Elisa in 1805. In 1814 it was occupied by the Neapolitans, from 1817 to 1847 it was a duchy of the queen of Etruria, after which it became a division of Tuscany.

Republic, 1369-1799

MONETARY SYSTEM
2 Quattrini = 1 Duetto
3 Quattrini = 1 Soldo
12 Soldi = 6 Bolognini = 2 Grossi = 1 Barbone
25 Soldi = 1 Santa Croce
2 Scudi D'oro = 1 Doppia

REPUBLIC

STANDARD COINAGE

KM# 5 QUATTRINO

0.7500 g., Copper **Obv:** Large L divides date **Rev:** Head of St. Vultus

Date	Mintage	VG	F	VF	XF	Unc
1601	—	10.00	20.00	40.00	75.00	—
1602	—	10.00	20.00	40.00	75.00	—
1607	—	10.00	20.00	40.00	75.00	—
1610	—	10.00	20.00	40.00	75.00	—
1611	—	10.00	20.00	40.00	75.00	—
1613	—	10.00	20.00	40.00	75.00	—
1614	—	10.00	20.00	40.00	75.00	—
1615	—	10.00	20.00	40.00	75.00	—
1616	—	10.00	20.00	40.00	75.00	—
1620	—	10.00	20.00	40.00	75.00	—
1621	—	10.00	20.00	40.00	75.00	—
1623	—	10.00	20.00	40.00	75.00	—
1625	—	10.00	20.00	40.00	75.00	—
1626	—	10.00	20.00	40.00	75.00	—
1627	—	10.00	20.00	40.00	75.00	—
1628	—	10.00	20.00	40.00	75.00	—
1629	—	10.00	20.00	40.00	75.00	—
1630	—	10.00	20.00	40.00	75.00	—
1631	—	10.00	20.00	40.00	75.00	—
1636	—	10.00	20.00	40.00	75.00	—
1637	—	10.00	20.00	40.00	75.00	—
1638	—	10.00	20.00	40.00	75.00	—
1639	—	10.00	20.00	40.00	75.00	—
1640	—	10.00	20.00	40.00	75.00	—
(16)64	—	10.00	20.00	40.00	75.00	—
1674	—	10.00	20.00	40.00	75.00	—

KM# 42 PANTERINO

Copper **Obv:** Oval republic arms **Rev:** City arms **Note:** Weight varies: 0.60-1.00 grams.

Date	Mintage	VG	F	VF	XF	Unc
1682	—	8.00	16.00	30.00	55.00	—
1683	—	8.00	16.00	30.00	55.00	—
1684	—	8.00	16.00	30.00	55.00	—
1691	—	8.00	16.00	30.00	55.00	—
1692	—	8.00	16.00	30.00	55.00	—

KM# 9 GROSSETTO

Billon **Obv:** L-V-C-A around center rosette **Rev:** Bust of St. Vultus **Note:** Weight varies: 0.80-1.52 grams.

Date	Mintage	VG	F	VF	XF	Unc
1602	—	75.00	160	325	525	—

KM# 20 GROSSETTO

Billon **Obv:** LIBERTAS in field **Obv. Legend:** CAROLVS **Rev:** St. Peter standing **Note:** Weight varies: 0.80-1.52 grams.

Date	Mintage	VG	F	VF	XF	Unc
1645	—	25.00	55.00	100	180	—

KM# 30 GROSSETTO

Billon **Obv:** Arms in cartouche **Obv. Legend:** OTTO **Rev:** St. Peter **Note:** Weight varies: 0.80-1.52 grams.

Date	Mintage	VG	F	VF	XF	Unc
1661	—	11.00	18.00	35.00	65.00	—
1662	—	11.00	18.00	35.00	65.00	—
1675	—	11.00	18.00	35.00	65.00	—

KM# 32 GROSSETTO

Billon **Obv:** L-V-C-A around a rose **Obv. Legend:** OTTO **Note:** Weight varies: 0.80-1.52 grams.

Date	Mintage	VG	F	VF	XF	Unc
1666	—	14.00	25.00	55.00	95.00	—

KM# 40 DUETTO (2 Quattrino)

1.5000 g., Billon **Obv:** LVCA cruciform around center rosette, date at bottom **Obv. Legend:** CARLO L.O.D.I.D. ... **Rev:** St. Peter standing

Date	Mintage	VG	F	VF	XF	Unc
1681	—	11.00	18.00	32.00	60.00	—
1682	—	11.00	18.00	32.00	60.00	—
1683	—	11.00	18.00	32.00	60.00	—
1686	—	11.00	18.00	32.00	60.00	—
1691	—	11.00	18.00	32.00	60.00	—
1692	—	11.00	18.00	32.00	60.00	—

KM# 26 SOLDO

Copper **Obv:** Crowned shield **Obv. Legend:** OTTO **Rev:** St. Paul **Note:** Weight varies: 1.81-2.07 grams.

Date	Mintage	VG	F	VF	XF	Unc
1658	—	12.00	22.50	45.00	90.00	—
1681	—	12.00	22.50	45.00	90.00	—

KM# 41 SOLDO

Copper **Obv:** Crowned shield **Obv. Legend:** RESPVBLICA **Note:** Weight varies: 1.81-2.07 grams.

Date	Mintage	VG	F	VF	XF	Unc
1681	—	11.00	18.00	35.00	65.00	—
1682	—	11.00	18.00	35.00	65.00	—
1691	—	11.00	18.00	35.00	65.00	—
1692	—	11.00	18.00	35.00	65.00	—

KM# 33 LUIGINO

Silver **Rev:** Crowned French arms **Note:** Weight varies: 1.50-1.60 grams. Struck for the Levant

Date	Mintage	VG	F	VF	XF	Unc
1668	—	125	250	450	—	—

KM# 10 MEZZO (1/2) GROSSO

Billon **Obv:** L-V-C-A around center rosette **Rev:** St. Peter **Note:** Weight varies: 0.96-1.58 grams.

Date	Mintage	VG	F	VF	XF	Unc
1602	—	—	—	—	—	—
1658	—	—	—	—	—	—

KM# 6 GROSSO

Silver **Obv:** L-V-C-A around center rosette **Rev:** St. Vultus **Note:** Weight varies: 3.40-3.50 grams.

Date	Mintage	VG	F	VF	XF	Unc
1601	—	30.00	55.00	150	285	—
1602	—	30.00	55.00	150	285	—
1607	—	30.00	55.00	150	285	—

KM# 11 GROSSO

Silver **Obv:** Crowned arms **Note:** Weight varies: 3.40-3.50 grams.

Date	Mintage	VG	F	VF	XF	Unc
1603	—	30.00	55.00	150	285	—
1605	—	30.00	55.00	150	285	—
1606	—	30.00	55.00	150	285	—

KM# 13 GROSSO

Silver **Obv:** L-V-C-A in Gothic letters **Note:** Weight varies: 3.40-3.50 grams.

Date	Mintage	VG	F	VF	XF	Unc
1609	—	30.00	55.00	150	285	—
1610	—	30.00	55.00	150	285	—
1624	—	30.00	55.00	150	285	—

KM# 25 GROSSO

Silver **Obv:** Oval arms **Rev. Legend:** SANCTVS. VULTVS. DE LVCA. **Note:** Weight varies: 3.40-3.50 grams.

Date	Mintage	VG	F	VF	XF	Unc
1651	—	22.50	45.00	125	250	—

KM# 31 GROSSO

Silver **Obv:** L-V-C-A in garland **Note:** Weight varies: 3.40-3.50 grams.

Date	Mintage	VG	F	VF	XF	Unc
1661	—	22.50	45.00	125	250	—

KM# 34 BARBONE (Grosso - 12 Soldi)

Silver **Obv:** Crowned arms with supporters **Rev:** Justice seated **Note:** Weight varies: 2.94-3.11 grams.

Date	Mintage	VG	F	VF	XF	Unc
1668	—	37.50	75.00	185	350	—
1669	—	37.50	75.00	185	350	—
1682	—	37.50	75.00	185	350	—
1686	—	37.50	75.00	185	350	—
1691	—	37.50	75.00	185	350	—

KM# 16 SANTACROCE (25 Soldi)

8.6400 g., 0.8950 Silver 0.2486 oz. ASW **Obv:** Crowned republic arms, date below **Obv. Legend:** LUCENSIS • RESPUBLICA **Rev:** St. Vultus on cross **Rev. Legend:** ...VULTUS •

Date	Mintage	VG	F	VF	XF	Unc
1615	—	60.00	120	225	450	—
1619	—	60.00	120	225	450	—
1622	—	60.00	120	225	450	—
1625	—	60.00	120	225	450	—
1668	—	60.00	120	225	450	—
1682	—	60.00	120	225	450	—

KM# 12 1/4 SCUDO (San Martino - 15 Soldi)

6.1100 g., Silver **Obv:** Oval shield **Rev:** St. Martin on horseback

Date	Mintage	VG	F	VF	XF	Unc
1603	—	48.00	95.00	185	350	—
1604	—	48.00	95.00	185	350	—
1605	—	48.00	95.00	185	350	—
1607	—	48.00	95.00	185	350	—
1610	—	48.00	95.00	185	350	—
1613	—	48.00	95.00	185	350	—
1615	—	48.00	95.00	185	350	—
1623	—	48.00	95.00	185	350	—
1625	—	48.00	95.00	185	350	—

KM# 35 1/4 SCUDO (San Martino - 15 Soldi)

6.1100 g., Silver **Obv:** Crowned arms

Date	Mintage	VG	F	VF	XF	Unc
1668	—	145	265	575	975	—

KM# 15 1/3 SCUDO (San Martino - 25 Soldi)

10.8400 g., Silver **Obv:** Oval arms **Rev:** St. Martin on horseback

Date	Mintage	VG	F	VF	XF	Unc
1613	—	500	800	1,500	—	—

KM# 7 1/2 SCUDO

15.5000 g., Silver **Obv:** Crowned shield **Rev:** St. Martin on horseback

Date	Mintage	VG	F	VF	XF	Unc
1601	—	—	—	—	—	—
1603	—	—	—	—	—	—
1615	—	—	—	—	—	—

KM# 8 SCUDO

Silver **Obv:** Oval arms, LV-CA below **Rev:** St. Martin and beggar **Note:** Dav. #3923.

Date	Mintage	VG	F	VF	XF	Unc
1601	—	1,500	2,750	5,000	—	—
1604	—	1,500	2,750	5,000	—	—
1605	—	1,500	2,750	5,000	—	—
1607	—	1,500	2,750	5,000	—	—

KM# 17 SCUDO

Silver **Obv:** Crowned elongated shield **Note:** Dav. #3924.

Date	Mintage	VG	F	VF	XF	Unc
1615	—	1,000	2,000	3,500	—	—
1616	—	1,000	2,000	3,500	—	—
1617	—	1,000	2,000	3,500	—	—

MACCAGNO

This county in the province of Como south of Lake Lucerne had been in possession of the Mandelli family since 960. The short coinage ceased with the death of Giovanni Francesco in 1668.

RULERS
Giacomo III Mandelli, 1618-1645
Giovanni Francesco Mandelli, 1645-1668

COUNTY

STANDARD COINAGE

KM# 5 SESINO

Billon **Obv:** Bust right **Rev:** Foliate cross **Note:** Weight varies: 0.70-1.30 grams.

Date	Mintage	VG	F	VF	XF	Unc
ND	—	90.00	180	375	—	—

KM# 6 SESINO

Billon **Obv:** Head right in ruffled collar **Rev:** Plain cross **Note:** Weight varies: 0.70-1.30 grams.

Date	Mintage	VG	F	VF	XF	Unc
ND	—	60.00	125	250	—	—

KM# 24 SOLDO

1.1500 g., Silver **Obv:** Crowned double eagle, date below **Rev:** Bust of St. Aloyius

Date	Mintage	VG	F	VF	XF	Unc
1623	—	475	850	1,800	—	—

KM# 7 QUATTRINO

Copper **Obv:** Bust right **Obv. Legend:** IACO **Rev:** Eagle and lion arms **Note:** Weight varies: 1.34-2.29 grams.

Date	Mintage	VG	F	VF	XF	Unc
ND	—	70.00	150	350	—	—

KM# 35 QUATTRINO

Copper **Obv:** Head right, IOA **Rev:** Cross **Note:** Weight varies: 1.34-2.29 grams.

Date	Mintage	VG	F	VF	XF	Unc
ND	—	115	225	400	—	—

KM# 36 QUATTRINO

Copper **Obv:** Head right, IOAN **Note:** Weight varies: 1.34-2.29 grams.

Date	Mintage	VG	F	VF	XF	Unc
ND	—	115	225	400	—	—

KM# 25 DICKEN

6.7100 g., Billon **Obv:** Double eagle, date below **Rev:** St. Aloysius

Date	Mintage	VG	F	VF	XF	Unc
1623	—	—	—	—	—	—

KM# 8 1/2 DUCATONE

15.4300 g., Silver **Obv:** Bust right **Rev:** Crowned multiple arms

Date	Mintage	VG	F	VF	XF	Unc
ND Rare	—	—	—	—	—	—

KM# 9 TALLERO

24.7400 g., Silver **Obv:** Bust right **Rev:** Crowned double eagle **Note:** Dav. #3930.

Date	Mintage	VG	F	VF	XF	Unc
ND Rare	—	—	—	—	—	—

KM# 15 DUCATONE

Silver **Obv:** Warrior behind shield **Obv. Legend:** ...MAN. L. D. MAC*. **Rev:** Rampant lion **Note:** Weight varies: 31.00-32.00 grams. Dav. #3925.

Date	Mintage	VG	F	VF	XF	Unc
1621 Rare	—	—	—	—	—	—
1622 Rare	—	—	—	—	—	—

KM# 16 DUCATONE

Silver **Obv. Legend:** ...M. G. I. V. P*. **Note:** Weight varies: 31.00-32.00 grams. Dav. #3926.

Date	Mintage	VG	F	VF	XF	Unc
1622 Rare	—	—	—	—	—	—

KM# 30 DUCATONE

Silver **Obv:** Armored bust right **Rev:** Crowned arms, date below **Note:** Weight varies: 31.00-32.00 grams. Dav. #3927.

Date	Mintage	VG	F	VF	XF	Unc
1626 Rare	—	—	—	—	—	—

KM# 31 DUCATONE

Silver **Obv:** Bust right **Rev:** Crowned arms, SACRIQ **Note:** Weight varies: 31.00-32.00 grams. Dav. #3928.

Date	Mintage	VG	F	VF	XF	Unc
ND Rare	—	—	—	—	—	—

KM# 32 DUCATONE

Silver **Rev:** Crowned double eagle with Mandelli arms **Note:** Weight varies: 31.00-32.00 grams. Dav. #3929.

Date	Mintage	VG	F	VF	XF	Unc
ND Rare	—	—	—	—	—	—

KM# 10 DOPPIA

7.0000 g., 0.9860 Gold 0.2219 oz. AGW **Obv:** Giacomo standing facing in inner circle **Rev:** Crowned arms in inner circle

Date	Mintage	VG	F	VF	XF	Unc
ND Rare	—	—	—	—	—	—

KM# 29.1 DOPPIA

7.0000 g., 0.9860 Gold 0.2219 oz. AGW **Obv:** Bust of Giacomo right **Obv. Legend:** IACOBVS MANDELLVS... **Rev:** Crowned arms

Date	Mintage	VG	F	VF	XF	Unc
1625 Rare	—	—	—	—	—	—

KM# 29.2 DOPPIA

7.0000 g., 0.9860 Gold 0.2219 oz. AGW **Obv. Legend:** MON. NO. AV...

Date	Mintage	VG	F	VF	XF	Unc
ND Rare	—	—	—	—	—	—

KM# 11 ZECCHINO

3.5000 g., 0.9860 Gold 0.1109 oz. AGW **Obv:** Giacomo

Date	Mintage	VG	F	VF	XF	Unc
ND	—	1,750	3,500	6,500	10,000	—

KM# 22 ZECCHINO

3.5000 g., 0.9860 Gold 0.1109 oz. AGW **Rev:** Crowned arms in inner circle

Date	Mintage	VG	F	VF	XF	Unc
1622	—	750	1,500	3,000	5,500	—
1623	—	750	1,500	3,000	5,500	—

KM# 12 ZECCHINO

3.5000 g., 0.9860 Gold 0.1109 oz. AGW **Rev:** Orb in inner circle

Date	Mintage	VG	F	VF	XF	Unc
ND	—	1,750	3,500	6,500	10,000	—

KM# 17.1 ZECCHINO

3.5000 g., 0.9860 Gold 0.1109 oz. AGW **Obv:** St. Stephen kneeling in inner circle **Rev:** Crowned eagle in inner circle

Date	Mintage	VG	F	VF	XF	Unc
1622	—	750	1,500	3,000	5,500	—

KM# 17.2 ZECCHINO

3.5000 g., 0.9860 Gold 0.1109 oz. AGW **Rev:** Crowned arms in inner circle

Date	Mintage	VG	F	VF	XF	Unc
1622	—	750	1,500	3,000	5,500	—

KM# 18 ZECCHINO

3.5000 g., 0.9860 Gold 0.1109 oz. AGW **Obv:** Helmeted arms in inner circle, date in legend **Rev:** Crowned imperial eagle in inner circle

Date	Mintage	VG	F	VF	XF	Unc
1622	—	750	1,500	3,000	5,500	—
ND	—	750	1,500	3,000	5,500	—

KM# 19 ZECCHINO

3.5000 g., 0.9860 Gold 0.1109 oz. AGW **Rev:** Orb in inner circle

Date	Mintage	VG	F	VF	XF	Unc
1622	—	750	1,500	3,000	5,500	—

KM# 20 ZECCHINO

3.5000 g., 0.9860 Gold 0.1109 oz. AGW **Obv:** Giacomo standing facing in inner circle **Rev:** Crowned arms in inner circle, date above crown

Date	Mintage	VG	F	VF	XF	Unc
1622	—	800	1,800	3,750	6,500	—
ND	—	800	1,800	3,750	6,500	—

KM# 21 ZECCHINO

3.5000 g., 0.9860 Gold 0.1109 oz. AGW **Rev:** Crowned double-headed eagle in inner circle

Date	Mintage	VG	F	VF	XF	Unc
ND	—	800	1,800	3,750	6,500	—

KM# 23 ZECCHINO

3.5000 g., 0.9860 Gold 0.1109 oz. AGW

Date	Mintage	VG	F	VF	XF	Unc
1622	—	1,200	2,400	5,000	9,000	—

KM# 26 ZECCHINO

3.5000 g., 0.9860 Gold 0.1109 oz. AGW **Rev:** Four-line inscription in tablet

Date	Mintage	VG	F	VF	XF	Unc
1623	—	750	1,500	3,000	5,500	—
ND	—	750	1,500	3,000	5,500	—

KM# 27 ZECCHINO

3.5000 g., 0.9860 Gold 0.1109 oz. AGW, 22 mm. **Ruler:** Giacomo III **Obv:** Madonna with child

Date	Mintage	VG	F	VF	XF	Unc
ND	—	825	1,650	3,250	5,750	—

KM# 28 ZECCHINO

3.5000 g., 0.9860 Gold 0.1109 oz. AGW **Obv:** Bishop **Rev:** Crowned imperial eagle in inner circle

Date	Mintage	VG	F	VF	XF	Unc
ND	—	900	1,750	3,500	6,250	—

MANTUA

Mantova

Marquisate and Duchy

Originally of Etruscan foundation, Mantua is situated about 22 miles (37 kilometers) south-southwest of Verona and 36 miles (60 kilometers) east of Cremona. The city was famous in antiquity as the birthplace of Virgil and was made part of the kingdom of the Lombards in 601. Charlemagne made Mantua the seat of a countship, which was combined with the office of the local bishop by the later 9th century. Secular counts ruled Mantua again until the hereditary line died out in 1115 and Mantua became a republic. Elected administrators continually fell under imperial influence and the city was contested by the rival factions of Guelfs and Ghibellines. The family of Bonaccolsi controlled affairs in Mantua for about half a century before they were dispossessed by Luigi Gonzaga in 1328. He founded the dynasty that would rule Mantua and its considerable territory until the early 18th century.

At first, the Gonzagas were content with the title of captain, but the head of the family was named Vicar of the Empire in 1365. Mantua was raised to the status of Marquisate in 1432, but in 1530 the marchese was made duke. The city was sacked by imperial forces in 1630 and during the War of the Spanish Succession. The last duke was forced to allow French troops to occupy Mantua in 1703. The French left Italy in 1707 and the emperor declared the action by the duke to have allowed them entrance earlier as a felony. Invoking his right after the death of the last duke in 1708, the emperor claimed the fief reverted to the crown. It remained an imperial possession until Napoleon besieged and captured the city in 1797. It was returned to Austria in 1814 and became part of united Italy in 1866.

The Gonzagas followed the unusual practice of giving themselves numbers as the first, second, third, etc. marchese, then duke. The numbers are found on most of their coins in the form of Roman numerals and begin over again at 'I' when the marchese became the first duke.

RULERS

Francesco II, 1484-1519
Federico II, 1519-1540
Francesco III, 1540-1550
Guglielmo, 1550-1587
Vincenzo I, 1587-1612
Eleonora de'Medici, 1584-1611
Francesco IV, 1612, (Feb.–Dec.)
Ferdinando, 1612-1626
Vincenzo II, 1626-1627
Carlo I, 1627-1637
Carlo II Gonzaga-Nevers, 1637-1665
w/his mother Maria as regent, 1637-1647
Ferdinando Carlo Gonzaga-Nevers, 1665-1707
w/his mother Isabella Clara, as regent, 1665-1669

MONETARY SYSTEM

6 Denari = 1 Sesino
2 Sesini = 1 Soldo
20 Soldi = 1 Lira
12 Lire = 1 Tallero

MINT

Mantua

MINTMASTERS' INITIALS

CT - Carol Torre
GM, GMF - Gaspare Molo

Reference:
V = Alberto Varesi, ***Monete Italiane Regionali: Lombareia, Zecche Minori***. Pavia, 1995.

DUCHY

STANDARD COINAGE

KM# 217 QUATTRINO

Billon Weight varies: 0.68-0.75g., 15 mm. **Ruler:** Ferdinando Carlo **Obv:** Crowned FC monogram between 2 rosettes, no legend **Rev:** Large Mt. Olympus, FIDES in ribbon band above, no legend **Note:** Ref. V-751. Prev. KM#183.

Date	Mintage	VG	F	VF	XF	Unc
ND(1669-1707)	—	12.00	28.00	65.00	125	—

KM# 64 SOLDO

2.3500 g., Copper, 20-21 mm. **Ruler:** Ferdinando **Obv:** Crowned baroque frame with 4-line inscription **Obv. Inscription:** FERDIN / D G. DVX / MANTVÆ / ETC. **Rev:** Radiant sunface in circle, date in margin below **Rev. Legend:** NON MVTVATA LVCE. **Note:** Ref. V-618.

Date	Mintage	VG	F	VF	XF	Unc
1615	—	80.00	165	335	550	—

KM# 85 SOLDO

Copper Weight varies: 3.17-4.07g., 24 mm. **Ruler:** Vincenzo II **Obv:** Two large pyxes in partial circle **Obv. Legend:** NIHIL. ISTO. TRISTE. RECEPTO. **Rev:** Elephant to left in circle **Rev. Legend:** ACCENSVS. SANGVINE. IN. HOSTES. **Note:** Ref. V-636. Prev. KM#158.

Date	Mintage	VG	F	VF	XF	Unc
ND(1626-27)	—	80.00	165	360	600	—

KM# 86 SOLDO

2.6900 g., Copper, 21 mm. **Ruler:** Vincenzo II **Obv:** 6-line inscription in wreath **Obv. Inscription:** .VIN. / II. D. G. / DVX. MAN / VII. ET. / .M.F. / .V. **Rev:** 3-masted ship sailing to left **Rev. Legend:** HAC. MONSTRANTE. VIAM. **Note:** Ref. V-637. Prev. KM#161.

Date	Mintage	VG	F	VF	XF	Unc
ND(1626-27)	—	125	275	600	900	—

KM# 87 SOLDO

1.5000 g., Copper, 19-20 mm. **Ruler:** Vincenzo II **Obv:** Crown above 4-line inscription in wreath **Obv. Inscription:** IVSTITIA / ET. PAX / OSCVLATÆ / SVNT **Rev:** Crossed sword and olive branch, no legend **Note:** Ref. V-638. Prev. KM#163.

Date	Mintage	VG	F	VF	XF	Unc
ND(1626-27)	—	70.00	140	315	500	—

KM# 107 SOLDO

Copper Weight varies: 2.14-4.46g., 20-21 mm. **Ruler:** Carlo I **Obv:** 5-line inscription in circle **Obv. Inscription:** CAROL / I. D. G. DVX / MANTVÆ / MON. FER / ET. C. **Rev:** Laureate bust of Virgil to left in circle **Rev. Legend:** VIRGILIV(S). MAR. MANT. **Note:** Ref. V-658. Prev. KM#186.

Date	Mintage	VG	F	VF	XF	Unc
ND(1627-37)	—	40.00	80.00	150	275	—

KM# 154 SOLDO

Billon Weight varies: 1.07-2.41g., 20 mm. **Ruler:** Carlo II under regency of Maria **Obv:** Crowned shield of 4-fold arms, with central shield of 9-fold arms **Obv. Legend:** MAR. M. CAR. II. D. M. ET. M. FE. **Rev:** Large pyx in plain field **Rev. Legend:** TAB. SANG - CHRIST. IES. **Note:** Ref. V-684.

Date	Mintage	VG	F	VF	XF	Unc
ND(1637-47)	—	8.00	16.00	35.00	75.00	—

KM# 167 SOLDO

Copper, 22 mm. **Ruler:** Carlo II **Obv:** Crowned shield of 4-fold arms, with central shield of 9-fold arms, FIDES above **Obv. Legend:** CAR. II. DVX. MAN. ET. M. F. ET. C. **Rev:** Large pyx in plain field **Rev. Legend:** TAB. SANG. + CHRIST. IESV. **Note:** Ref. V-709a. Prev. KM#272.

Date	Mintage	VG	F	VF	XF	Unc
ND(1647-65) Rare	—	—	—	—	—	—

KM# 218 SOLDO

Copper Weight varies: 1.18-3.44g., 20 mm. **Ruler:** Ferdinando Carlo **Obv:** 3-line inscription in wreath **Obv. Inscription:** FER / CAR / D. C. D. **Rev:** 3-line inscription in wreath **Rev. Inscription:** MAN / E. M. F / C. V. G. **Note:** Ref. V-749.

Date	Mintage	VG	F	VF	XF	Unc
ND(1669-1707)	—	10.00	22.00	35.00	75.00	—

KM# 108 SESINO

Billon Weight varies: 1.00-1.26g., 16-17 mm. **Ruler:** Carlo I **Obv:** Ornate cross with trefoil ends **Obv. Legend:** CAR. I. D. G. D. MAN. MON. ET. C. **Rev:** Laureate bust of Virgil to right **Rev. Legend:** VIRGILIVS. MARO. **Note:** Ref. V-659. Prev. KM#192.

Date	Mintage	VG	F	VF	XF	Unc
ND(1627-37)	—	22.00	45.00	80.00	160	—

KM# 168 SESINO

Copper Weight varies: 0.85-0.87g., 15-16 mm. **Ruler:** Carlo II **Obv:** Head to left **Obv. Legend:** CAROLVS. II. D. G. DVX. **Rev:** 3-line inscription in wreath, no legend **Rev. Inscription:** MAN / TV / A. **Note:** Ref. V-710. Prev. KM#305.

Date	Mintage	VG	F	VF	XF	Unc
ND(1647-65)	—	30.00	65.00	140	250	—

KM# 219 SESINO

Copper Weight varies: 0.80-1.55g., 18 mm. **Ruler:** Ferdinando Carlo **Obv:** Crowned ornate script double, mirror-image FC monogram between 2 palm branches, no legend **Rev:** 4-line inscription with date, where present, in ornamented cartouche **Rev. Inscription:** SESINO / DI. MAN / TOVA / (date) **Note:** Ref. V-750.

Date	Mintage	VG	F	VF	XF	Unc
ND(1669-1707)	—	20.00	40.00	85.00	165	—

KM# 16 4 SOLDI

0.9900 g., Billon, 19 mm. **Ruler:** Ferdinando **Obv:** Crowned shield of 4-fold arms, with central shield of 9-fold arms **Obv. Legend:** FERD. D. G. DVX. MANT. VI. ET. MA. F. IV. **Rev:** Radiant sunface in circle, value '4' in margin at top **Rev. Legend:** NON. MVTVATA. LVCE. **Note:** Ref. V-615.

Date	Mintage	VG	F	VF	XF	Unc
ND(1612-26)	—	150	325	700	1,000	—

KM# 44 4 SOLDI

Billon Weight varies: 0.62-1.40g., 19 mm. **Ruler:** Ferdinando **Obv:** Displayed eagle in wreath, date at end of legend **Obv. Legend:** FER. S. R. E. D. CA. D. G. DVX. MA. VI. ET. M. F. IIII. **Rev:** Radiant sunface, value '4' below **Rev. Legend:** NON MVTVATA LVCE. **Note:** Ref. V-614a.

Date	Mintage	VG	F	VF	XF	Unc
1613	—	80.00	165	350	550	—

KM# 57 4 SOLDI

Billon Weight varies: 0.62-1.40g., 19 mm. **Ruler:** Ferdinando **Obv:** Displayed eagle in wreath, value '4' below **Obv. Legend:** FER. S. R. E. D. CA. D. G. DVX. MA. VI. ET. M. F. IIII. **Rev:** Radiant sunface, date below in cartouche **Rev. Legend:** NON MVTVATA LVCE. **Note:** Ref. V-614b.

Date	Mintage	VG	F	VF	XF	Unc
1614	—	80.00	165	350	550	—

MB# 212 BARBARINA

Billon Weight varies: 1.40-2.24g., 21-22 mm. **Ruler:** Vincenzo I **Obv:** Full-length facing figure of St. Barbara **Obv. Legend:** SANCTA - BARBARA. **Rev:** Sunflower growing towards sun at upper left **Rev. Legend:** IAM (-) N(-)VLLA (-) FVGA **Note:** Ref. V-553. Varieties exist. Prev. KM#45.

Date	Mintage	VG	F	VF	XF	Unc
1605	—	6.00	12.00	35.00	75.00	—

KM# 3 BARBARINA

1.9400 g., Silver, 21 mm. **Ruler:** Francesco IV **Obv:** Shield of 4-fold arms, with central shield of 9-fold arms, crown with FIDES above, Order of The Redeemer around **Obv. Legend:** FRAN. IIII. D.G. DVX. MAN. V. ET. M. F. III. **Rev:** Full-length standing figure of St. Barbara holding palm branch, small tower to left **Rev. Legend:** SANCTA - BARBARA. **Note:** Ref. V-569. Prev. KM#55.

Date	Mintage	VG	F	VF	XF	Unc
ND(1612)	—	40.00	80.00	150	275	—

KM# 109 PARPAGLIOLA

Billon Weight varies: 1.39-1.53g., 20 mm. **Ruler:** Carlo I **Obv:** Large Mt. Olympus with FIDES above **Obv. Legend:** CAR. I. D. G. DVX. MAN. ETC. **Rev:** St. Charles kneeling before cross **Rev. Legend:** SANCTVS. CAROLVS. **Note:** Ref. V-656. Prev. KM#185.

Date	Mintage	VG	F	VF	XF	Unc
ND(1627-37)	—	65.00	100	175	300	—

KM# 147 PARPAGLIOLA

Billon Weight varies: 1.85-3.24g., 21-22 mm. **Ruler:** Carlo I **Obv:** Shield of 4-fold arms, with central shield of 9-fold arms, crown and small Mt. Olympus above **Obv. Legend:** CAROL. I. DVX. MAN. ET. MON. FE. **Rev:** Full-length standing figure of St. Patrick, date in exergue **Rev. Legend:** SANCTVS - PATRITIVS. **Note:** Ref. V-655.

Date	Mintage	VG	F	VF	XF	Unc
1633	—	22.00	45.00	80.00	160	—
1635	—	22.00	45.00	80.00	160	—

KM# 155 PARPAGLIOLA

Billon Weight varies: 1.31-2.00g., 20 mm. **Ruler:** Carlo II under regency of Maria **Obv:** Two angels holding large pyx between them, MANTVA in exergue **Obv. Legend:** TABER. SAN - G. XPI. IESV. **Rev:** Madonna and Child in circle **Rev. Legend:** MARIA. MATER. GRATIÆ. **Note:** Ref. V-683. Prev. KM#190.

Date	Mintage	VG	F	VF	XF	Unc
ND(1637-47)	—	15.00	28.00	55.00	100	—

KM# 169 PARPAGLIOLA

Billon Weight varies: 1.76-2.00g., 22 mm. **Ruler:** Carlo II **Obv:** Shield of 4-fold arms, with central shield of 9-fold arms, crown with FIDES and small Mt. Olympus above **Obv. Legend:** CAR. II. D. G. DVX. MANT. ET. M. F. **Rev:** Facing figure of St. Barbara standing and resting on a small tower **Rev. Legend:** SANCTA. - BARBARA. **Note:** Ref. V-709. Prev. KM#307.

Date	Mintage	VG	F	VF	XF	Unc
ND(1647-65)	—	20.00	40.00	85.00	170	—

KM# 192 PARPAGLIOLA

Billon Weight varies: 2.20-2.86g., 23 mm. **Ruler:** Carlo II **Obv:** Crowned shield of 4-fold arms, with central shield of 9-fold arms **Obv. Legend:** CAR. II. DVX. MAN. ET. MON. ET.C. **Rev:** Figure of St. Patrick kneeling to left, date in exergue **Rev. Legend:** SANCTVS. - PATRITIVS. **Note:** Ref. V-708. Prev. KM#353.

Date	Mintage	VG	F	VF	XF	Unc
1661	—	30.00	65.00	140	250	—

KM# 72 1/2 GROSSETTO

Silver Weight varies: 0.39-0.75g., 13 mm. **Ruler:** Vincenzo II **Obv:** Crown above large V between 2 small I's, no legend **Rev:** Crucible within flames, no legend **Note:** Ref. V-634. Prev. KM#169.

Date	Mintage	VG	F	VF	XF	Unc
ND(1626-27)	—	40.00	80.00	175	285	—

KM# 73 1/2 GROSSETTO

Billon Weight varies: 1.20-1.51g., 17-18 mm. **Ruler:** Vincenzo II **Obv:** 4-line legend in crowned baroque frame **Obv. Inscription:** VINC / II. DVX / MANT / VII **Rev:** Crucible within flames **Rev. Legend:** DOMINE. - PROBASTI. **Note:** Ref. V-635. Prev. KM#171.

Date	Mintage	VG	F	VF	XF	Unc
ND(1626-27)	—	30.00	65.00	115	200	—

KM# 110 1/2 GROSSETTO

Billon Weight varies: 1.33-1.37g., 18 mm. **Ruler:** Carlo I **Obv:** 5-line legend in baroque frame **Obv. Inscription:** CAR. I. D. / G. MAN / M. F. NI / MAY. R. / DVX. **Rev:** Crucible within flames **Rev. Legend:** DOMINE. - PROBASTI. **Note:** Ref. V-657. Prev. KM#187 and 195.

Date	Mintage	VG	F	VF	XF	Unc
ND(1627-37)	—	25.00	55.00	115	200	—

KM# 17 GROSSETTO
Billon Weight varies: 0.97-1.14g., 16-17 mm. **Ruler:** Ferdinando **Obv:** 5-line inscription in wreath **Obv. Inscription:** FER / D. G. / DVX / MAN / VI. **Rev:** Crowned displayed eagle in circle, no legend **Note:** Ref. V-616.

Date	Mintage	VG	F	VF	XF	Unc
ND(1612-26)	—	12.00	28.00	55.00	100	—

KM# 18 GROSSETTO
0.8400 g., Billon, 20-21 mm. **Ruler:** Ferdinando **Obv:** 4-line inscription in wreath **Obv. Inscription:** FERD / D. G. DVX. / MAN. VI. / ET M. F. IIII. **Rev:** Large pyx in plain field **Rev. Legend:** NIHIL. ISTO. TRISTE. RECEPTO. **Note:** Ref. V-617.

Date	Mintage	VG	F	VF	XF	Unc
ND(1612-26)	—	20.00	45.00	100	180	—

KM# 88 GROSSETTO
1.0500 g., Silver, 16 mm. **Ruler:** Vincenzo II **Obv:** Shield of 4-fold arms, with central shield of 9-fold arms, crown and small Mt. Olympus above, Order of The Redeemer around **Obv. Legend:** VIN. II. D. G. DVX. - MAN. VII. ET. M. F. V. **Rev:** Crossed sword and olive branch, 4 I's around, no legend **Note:** Ref. V-633. Prev. KM#173.

Date	Mintage	VG	F	VF	XF	Unc
ND(1626-27)	—	75.00	140	275	475	—

KM# 58 7 SOLDI
2.2200 g., Billon, 20-21 mm. **Ruler:** Ferdinando **Obv:** Crowned shield of 9-fold arms **Obv. Legend:** FERD. D. G. DVX. MAN. VI. ET. M. F. IV. **Rev:** Radiant sunface in circle, value '7' below in margin **Rev. Legend:** NON. MVTVATA. LVCE. **Note:** Ref. V-613. Prev. KM#115.

Date	Mintage	VG	F	VF	XF	Unc
ND(1614)	—	30.00	65.00	150	250	—

KM# A89 7 SOLDI
Billon **Ruler:** Vincenzo II **Obv:** Crowned shield **Obv. Legend:** VINS DG DVX MAN VI M F V **Rev:** Radiant sunface, 7 below **Rev. Legend:** MONETA LVCE **Note:** Prev. KM#A187. Not in Varesi, existence doubtful.

Date	Mintage	VG	F	VF	XF	Unc
ND(1627)	—	15.00	30.00	60.00	125	—

Note: Reported, not confirmed.

KM# 222 1/16 SCUDO
Silver Weight varies: 1.10-1.36g., 19 mm. **Ruler:** Ferdinando Carlo **Obv:** Spanish shield of 2-fold arms, Austria at left, complex Mantua arms at right, crown and small Mt. Olympus above, value '12 - 1/2' divided at top **Obv. Legend:** FERDINANDVS. CAROLVS. D. G. DVX. **Rev:** Cross with trefoil ends, heraldic symbols in each angle, all in square with arc in each side, date above **Rev. Legend:** MANTVÆ. MONTISFER. CAROLI. VIL. ET. C. **Note:** Ref. V-746.

Date	Mintage	VG	F	VF	XF	Unc
1675	—	20.00	40.00	85.00	165	—
1676	—	20.00	40.00	85.00	165	—

KM# 89 GROSSO
1.5600 g., Silver, 21 mm. **Ruler:** Vincenzo II **Obv:** 6-line inscription within wreath **Obv. Inscription:** .VIN. / II. D. G. / DVX. MAN / VII. ET. / .M. F. / .V. **Rev:** 3-masted ship sailing to left **Rev. Legend:** HAC. MONSTRANTE. VIAM. **Note:** Ref. V-631. Prev. KM#22.

Date	Mintage	VG	F	VF	XF	Unc
ND(1626-27) Rare	—	—	—	—	—	—

KM# 90 GROSSO
Silver Weight varies: 1.50-1.65g., 19-20 mm. **Ruler:** Vincenzo II **Obv:** Crown above 4-line inscription in wreath **Obv. Inscription:** IVSTITIA / ET. PAX / OSCVLATÆ / SVNT **Rev:** Crossed sword and olive branch, no legend **Note:** Ref. V-632. Prev. KM#175.

Date	Mintage	VG	F	VF	XF	Unc
ND(1626-27)	—	265	425	725	1,150	—

KM# 91 2 GROSSI (Doppio Grosso)
2.7700 g., Silver, 24 mm. **Ruler:** Vincenzo II **Obv:** Two large pyxes in partial circle **Obv. Legend:** NIHIL. ISTO. TRISTE. RECEPTO. **Rev:** Elephant to left in circle **Rev. Legend:** ACCENSVS. SANGVINE. IN. HOSTES. **Note:** Ref. V-630. Prev. KM#177.

Date	Mintage	VG	F	VF	XF	Unc
ND(1626-27) Rare	—	—	—	—	—	—

KM# 190 LUIGINO
2.4200 g., Silver, 22 mm. **Ruler:** Carlo II **Obv:** Armored bust to left **Obv. Legend:** CAR. II. D. G. DVX. - MANT. M. F. ET C. **Rev:** Crowned shield with 3 lilies, 2 above 1, small Mt. Olympus at top, date at end of legend **Rev. Legend:** AVORVM. LILIIS. FLORET. OLYMPVS. **Note:** Ref. V-703. Prev. KM#351.

Date	Mintage	VG	F	VF	XF	Unc
1660 Rare	—	—	—	—	—	—

MB# 217 GIULIO
Silver Weight varies: 2.69-3.64g., 25-26 mm. **Ruler:** Vincenzo I **Obv:** Pyx divides date, where present, in circle **Obv. Legend:** CHRISTI. IESV. TABER(N). SANGVINI(S). **Rev:** St. Francis receiving the stigmata **Rev. Legend:** + SVB (+) TV(V)M + PRA(E)SIDIVM. **Note:** Ref. V-551. Varieties exist. Prev. KM#24 and 47.

Date	Mintage	VG	F	VF	XF	Unc
1601	—	25.00	45.00	125	225	—
1605	—	25.00	45.00	125	225	—

KM# 19 8 SOLDI
Billon Weight varies: 1.91-2.68g., 24 mm. **Ruler:** Ferdinando **Obv:** 6-line inscription in circle beginning with value **Obv. Inscription:** 8 / .FERDIN. / .D.G. DVX. / .MANT. VI. / .ET. MONT. / .F. IIII. **Rev:** Radiant sunface in circle **Rev. Legend:** NON. MVTVATA. LVCE. **Note:** Ref. V-612. Prev. KM#56.

Date	Mintage	VG	F	VF	XF	Unc
ND(1612-26)	—	20.00	45.00	90.00	175	—

KM# 59 8 SOLDI
3.0000 g., Billon, 23 mm. **Ruler:** Ferdinando **Obv:** Displayed eagle in wreath, value '8' below in margin **Obv. Legend:** FER. CAR. D. G. DVX. M. VI. ET. M. F. IIII. **Rev:** Radiant sunface in circle, date below in cartouche **Rev. Legend:** NON MVTVATA LVCE. **Note:** Ref. V-611. Prev. KM#117.

Date	Mintage	VG	F	VF	XF	Unc
1614	—	125	275	725	1,150	—

KM# 111 8 SOLDI
Silver Weight varies: 1.83-2.16g., 19 mm. **Ruler:** Carlo I **Obv:** Crowned shield of 4-fold arms, with central shield of 9-fold arms **Obv. Legend:** CAROLVS. I. D. G. DVX. MA. ET. M. F. ETC. **Rev:** Madonna standing on upturned crescent moon, surrounded by stars **Rev. Legend:** MARIA. MATER - MISERICORDIE. **Note:** Ref. V-653.

Date	Mintage	VG	F	VF	XF	Unc
ND(1627-37) Rare	—	—	—	—	—	—

KM# 112 8 SOLDI
Silver Weight varies: 1.52-1.62g., 20 mm. **Ruler:** Carlo I **Obv:** Shield of 4-fold arms, with central shield of 9-fold arms, crown and small Mt. Olympus above **Obv. Legend:** CA. I. D. G. D. M. ET. M. F. ET. **Rev:** Full-length facing figure of St. Lucia holding cup **Rev. Legend:** SANCTA. - LVCIA. **Note:** Ref. V-654. Prev. KM#264, as 1/2 Giulio.

Date	Mintage	VG	F	VF	XF	Unc
ND(1627-37)	—	225	375	800	1,500	—

KM# 170 8 SOLDI
Billon Weight varies: 1.81-2.41g., 21-22 mm. **Ruler:** Carlo II **Obv:** 6-line inscription with value in top line **Obv. Inscription:** +8+ / .CAROLVS. / .D.G. DVX. / MANT. VIIII. / .E. MONT. / F. VII. **Rev:** Radiant sunface in circle **Rev. Legend:** NON. MVTVATA. LVCE. **Note:** Ref. V-707. Prev. KM#309.

Date	Mintage	VG	F	VF	XF	Unc
ND(1647-65)	—	15.00	28.00	55.00	100	—

KM# 20 1/2 LIRA (Mezza Lira)
3.7800 g., Silver, 20 mm. **Ruler:** Ferdinando **Obv:** St. Andrew holding cross, consigning pyx to kneeling duke at right, .IIII. in exergue **Obv. Legend:** FER. D. G. DVX. - MAN. VI. ET. M. F. **Rev:** Madonna standing on upturned crescent moon in Venetian style ellipse **Rev. Legend:** PRÆSIDIVM. - NOSTRVM. **Note:** Ref. V-609.

Date	Mintage	VG	F	VF	XF	Unc
ND(1612-26) Rare	—	—	—	—	—	—

KM# 21 1/2 LIRA (Mezza Lira)
2.7000 g., Silver, 21 mm. **Ruler:** Ferdinando **Obv:** 5-line inscription in shield within wreath **Obv. Inscription:** FERDIN / D. G. DVX / MAN. VI / ET. MONF / IIII. **Rev:** Full-length standing figure of St. Longinus with lance, turned to left **Rev. Legend:** AB. OMNI. - MALO - D - EFENDE. NOS. **Note:** Ref. V-610. Prev. KM#67.

Date	Mintage	VG	F	VF	XF	Unc
ND(1612-26)	—	125	275	725	1,150	—

KM# 148 1/2 LIRA (Mezza Lira)
2.0000 g., Silver, 24 mm. **Ruler:** Carlo I **Obv:** Shield of 4-fold arms, with central shield of 9-fold arms, crown and small Mt. Olympus above **Obv. Legend:** CAR. I. D. G. DVX. MAN. ET. M. F. **Rev:** Full-length facing figure of St. Lucia, holding palm branch, divides date **Rev. Legend:** SANCTA - LVCIA. **Note:** Ref. V-652. Prev. KM#197.

Date	Mintage	VG	F	VF	XF	Unc
1633 Rare	—	—	—	—	—	—

KM# 226 1/8 SCUDO
Silver Weight varies: 2.37-2.65g., 23 mm. **Ruler:** Ferdinando Carlo **Obv:** Shield of 2-fold arms, Austria at left, complex Mantua arms at right, crown and small Mt. Olympus above **Obv. Legend:** FERDINANDVS. CAROLVS. D. G. DVX. **Rev:** Cross with trefoil ends, heraldic symbols in each angle, all in square with arc in each side, date above **Rev. Legend:** MANTVÆ. MONTISFER. CAROLI. VIL. ET. C. **Note:** Ref. V-742.

Date	Mintage	VG	F	VF	XF	Unc
1676	—	30.00	55.00	115	200	—

KM# 4 10 SOLDI
1.2800 g., Silver, 21 mm. **Ruler:** Francesco IV **Obv:** Crowned shield with cross, small shield of Gonzaga arms superimposed on upper arm **Obv. Legend:** FRAN. IIII. D. G. DVX. MAN. V. ET. M. F. III. **Rev:** Crucible within flames, date in exergue **Rev. Legend:** DOMINE - PROBASTI. **Note:** Ref. V-568.

Date	Mintage	VG	F	VF	XF	Unc
1612	—	50.00	110	275	485	—

KM# 172 15 SOLDI
2.8800 g., Billon, 24 mm. **Ruler:** Carlo II **Obv:** Armored bust to left, star below **Obv. Legend:** CAROLVS. II. D. G. DVX. MANTVE. **Rev:** Large Mt. Olympus, FIDES in ribbon band above, nothing in exergue **Rev. Legend:** ET. MON. FER. NEVER. RET. VMENE. ET. C. **Note:** Ref. V-705.

Date	Mintage	VG	F	VF	XF	Unc
ND(1647-65) Rare	—	—	—	—	—	—

KM# 173 15 SOLDI
3.4500 g., Billon, 26-27 mm. **Ruler:** Carlo II **Obv:** Large armored bust to left, value '15' behind shoulder at lower right **Obv. Legend:** CAROLVS. II. D. G. DVX. MANT. **Rev:** Crowned shield of 4-fold arms, Order of The Redeemer around, FIDES at top **Rev. Legend:** ET. MONT. - FERATI. ET. C. **Note:** Ref. V-704.

Date	Mintage	VG	F	VF	XF	Unc
ND(1647-65) Rare	—	—	—	—	—	—

KM# 200 15 SOLDI
Billon Weight varies: 3.22-3.57g., 25 mm. **Ruler:** Ferdinando Carlo under regency of Isabella Clara **Obv:** Two accolated busts to right, date below **Obv. Legend:** ISABELLA. CLARA. FERD. CAR. D. G. D. MAN. - M. F. ET. C. **Rev:** Radiant sunface above sea and below clouds in circle, value 'SOL:15' in margin at bottom **Rev. Legend:** ALTA. A. LONGE. COGNOSCIT. **Note:** Ref. V-726. Prev. KM#365.

Date	Mintage	VG	F	VF	XF	Unc
1666	—	40.00	80.00	185	300	—

KM# 197 1/8 DUCATONE
Silver Weight varies: 2.82-2.99g., 27 mm. **Ruler:** Carlo II **Obv:** Crowned shield of 4-fold arms, with central shield of 9-fold arms, in oval baroque frame, Order of The Redeemer suspended from sides and below **Obv. Legend:** CAR. II. D. G. DVX - MAN. M. F. ET. C. **Rev:** St. George on horse to right with lance, slaying dragon below, date in exergue **Rev. Legend:** PROTECTOR. NOSTER. ASPICE. **Note:** Ref. V-702.

Date	Mintage	VG	F	VF	XF	Unc
1664	—	700	1,000	1,600	2,500	—

KM# 22 1/4 TALLERO
Silver Weight varies: 5.54-6.25g., 30 mm. **Ruler:** Ferdinando **Obv:** Shield of 4-fold arms, with central shield of 9-fold arms, crown with FIDES and small Mt. Olympus above, Order of The Redeemer around **Obv. Legend:** FERD. D. G. DVX. - MAN. VI. ET. M. F. IV. **Rev:** St. Andrew holding cross and pyx **Rev. Legend:** NIHIL. ISTO. TRISTE. RECEPTO. **Note:** Ref. V-606. Prev. KM#57, as 30 Soldi.

Date	Mintage	VG	F	VF	XF	Unc
ND(1612-26)	—	325	660	1,250	2,250	—

KM# 5 LIRA
Silver Weight varies: 5.54-6.00g., 30 mm. **Ruler:** Francesco IV **Obv:** Crowned shield of 4-fold arms, with central shield of 9-fold arms, crown with FIDES over small Mt. Olympus above **Obv. Legend:** FRAN. IIII. D. G. DVX. MAN. V. ET. M. F. III. **Rev:** Full-length facing figure of St. Anselm holding crozier, value '20' in exergue **Rev. Legend:** SANCTVS - ANSELMVS. EPS. **Note:** Ref. V-567. Prev. KM#69. 20 Soldi.

Date	Mintage	VG	F	VF	XF	Unc
1612	—	75.00	140	325	600	—
ND(1612)	—	75.00	140	325	600	—

KM# 23 LIRA
Silver Weight varies: 5.23-5.52g., 29 mm. **Ruler:** Ferdinando **Obv:** Crowned shield of 4-fold arms, with central shield of 9-fold arms, cardinal's hat above **Obv. Legend:** FER. CAR. D. G. DV - X. MAN. VI. ET. M. F. IIII. **Rev:** Full-length facing figure of St. Anselm holding crozier, value '20' in exergue **Rev. Legend:** SANCTVS - A - NSELM. EP. **Note:** Ref. V-607. 20 Soldi.

Date	Mintage	VG	F	VF	XF	Unc
ND(1612-26)	—	175	360	675	1,250	—

KM# 24 LIRA
Silver Weight varies: 5.14-6.23g., 30 mm. **Ruler:** Ferdinando **Obv:** Shield of 4-fold arms, with central shield of 9-fold arms, in baroque frame, crown with FID-ES and small Mt. Olympus above **Obv. Legend:** FERD. D. G. DVX. - MAN. VI. ET. M. F. IV. **Rev:** Full-length facing figure of St. Anselm holding crozier, value '20'

in exergue **Rev. Legend:** SANCTVS - A - NSELM. EP. **Note:** Ref. V-608. 20 Soldi.

Date	Mintage	VG	F	VF	XF	Unc
ND(1612-26)	—	75.00	140	325	600	—

KM# 113 LIRA

2.7700 g., Silver, 25-26 mm. **Ruler:** Carlo I **Obv:** Ornate cross with trefoil ends, rosette in each angle, value '20' below in margin **Obv. Legend:** CAROLVS. I. D. G. DVX. MANTVÆ. **Rev:** Shield of 4-fold arms, with central shield of 9-fold arms, crown and small Mt. Olympus above, Order of The Redeemer around **Rev. Legend:** ET. MON. - FER. ETC. **Note:** Ref. V-651. Prev. KM#189. 20 Soldi.

Date	Mintage	VG	F	VF	XF	Unc
ND(1627-37) Rare	—	—	—	—	—	—

KM# 149 LIRA

Silver Weight varies: 3.99-4.72g., 27 mm. **Ruler:** Carlo I **Obv:** Shield of 4-fold arms, with central shield of 9-fold arms, crown, small Mt. Olympus and FIDES above **Obv. Legend:** CAR. I. D.G. D. M. ET. M. F. ET. **Rev:** Full-length standing figure of St. Lucia to left, holding cup, divides date **Rev. Legend:** SANCTA - LVCIA. **Note:** Ref. V-650. Prev. KM#266.

Date	Mintage	VG	F	VF	XF	Unc
1633	—	30.00	65.00	115	200	—

KM# 194 LIRA

4.0800 g., Silver, 27 mm. **Ruler:** Carlo II **Obv:** Shield of 4-fold arms, with central shield of 9-fold arms, in baroque frame, crown with FIDES above **Obv. Legend:** CAR. II. D.G. D. M. ET. M. F. ET.C. **Rev:** Standing figure of St. Lucy to left, holding pyx, divides date **Rev. Legend:** SANCTA - LVCIA. **Note:** Ref. V-701. Prev. KM#357.

Date	Mintage	VG	F	VF	XF	Unc
1663	—	75.00	140	325	600	—

KM# 231 LIRA

Billon Weight varies: 3.50-4.82g., 27-28 mm. **Ruler:** Ferdinando Carlo **Obv:** Bust to right **Obv. Legend:** FERDINAN. - CAR. D. G. DVX. **Rev:** Large Mt. Olympus, FIDES above, date below in margin **Rev. Legend:** MANTVÆ. MON. FER. CAR. VIL. GVAS. EC. **Note:** Ref. V-740. Prev. KM#419. 5 Soldi.

Date	Mintage	VG	F	VF	XF	Unc
1689	—	65.00	110	315	575	—

KM# 232 LIRA

Billon Weight varies: 7.61-7.93g., 31 mm. **Ruler:** Ferdinando Carlo **Obv:** Bust to right **Obv. Legend:** FERDI. CAR. D. G. DVX. MANTVÆ. MON. FER. CAR. VIL. GVAS. ET.C. **Rev:** Allegorical figure of Abundance standing among fruites, city in left distance, eagle above with 2 tablets in claws, DE/COR in left, FIDES in right. Roman numeral date in exergue **Rev. Legend:** NON OMNIBVS - OMNIA. **Note:** Ref. V-738. Prev. KM#426. 40 Sesini.

Date	Mintage	VG	F	VF	XF	Unc
MDCXC (1690)	—	300	550	1,250	2,250	—

KM# 174 30 SOLDI (1/4 Scudo)

Billon Weight varies: 6.58-7.03g., 30 mm. **Ruler:** Carlo II **Obv:** Armored bust to left, value 'XXX' below **Obv. Legend:** CAROLVS. II. D. G. DVX. MANT. **Rev:** Shield of 4-fold arms in baroque frame, crown and small Mt. Olympus above, Order of The Redeemer around **Rev. Legend:** ET. MONT. - FERATI. ET. C. **Note:** Ref. V-699. Prev. KM#311.

Date	Mintage	VG	F	VF	XF	Unc
ND(1647-65)	—	70.00	140	300	600	—

KM# 175 30 SOLDI (1/4 Scudo)

5.8800 g., Billon, 30 mm. **Ruler:** Carlo II **Obv:** Armored bust to left, star below **Obv. Legend:** CAROLVS. II. D. G. DVX. MANTVE. **Rev:** Large Mt. Olympus, FIDES in ribbon band above, value 'XXX' in exergue **Rev. Legend:** ET. MON. FER. NEVER. RET. VMENE. ET. C. **Note:** Ref. V-700. Prev. KM#313.

Date	Mintage	VG	F	VF	XF	Unc
ND(1647-65)	—	550	750	1,250	2,250	—

KM# 201 30 SOLDI (1/4 Scudo)

Billon Weight varies: 6.38-6.82g., 30 mm. **Ruler:** Ferdinando Carlo under regency of Isabella Clara **Obv:** Two accolated busts to right, date below **Obv. Legend:** ISABELLA. CLARA. FERD. CAR. D. G. D. MAN. - ET. M. F. ET. C. **Rev:** Radiant sunface between clouds above and sea below, all in circle, value 'SOL:30' in margin at bottom **Rev. Legend:** ALTA. A. LONGE. COGNOSCIT. **Note:** Ref. V-725. Prev. KM#367.

Date	Mintage	VG	F	VF	XF	Unc
1666	—	55.00	100	225	425	—

KM# 6 40 SOLDI

7.7200 g., Silver, 29 mm. **Ruler:** Francesco IV **Obv:** Two high-collared busts facing each other, DVCES over date in exergue **Obv. Legend:** FRANCISCVS. ET. MARGARITA. **Rev:** Crucible within flames, value '40' below **Rev. Legend:** DOMINE. - PROBASTI. **Note:** Ref. V-566. Prev. KM#61.

Date	Mintage	VG	F	VF	XF	Unc
1612 Rare	—	—	—	—	—	—

KM# 176 40 SOLDI

Silver Weight varies: 5.35-6.83g., 33 mm. **Ruler:** Carlo II **Obv:** Shield of 4-fold arms, with central shield of 9-fold arms, in baroque frame, crown and small Mt. Olympus above, Order of The Redeemer around **Obv. Legend:** CAROLVS. II. D. G. - DVX. MANT. ET. M. F. **Rev:** Full-length facing figure of St. Barbara, looking to left, holding palm branch and leaning on small tower, value '40' in exergue **Rev. Legend:** SANCTA. BARBA - RA. PROTECTRIX. **Note:** Ref. V-698. Prev. KM#315.

Date	Mintage	VG	F	VF	XF	Unc
ND(1647-65)	—	225	400	1,100	1,850	—

KM# 25 1/4 DUCATONE

Silver Weight varies: 7.58-7.88g., 29 mm. **Ruler:** Ferdinando **Obv:** Bust to left wearing cardinal's robes and biretta **Obv. Legend:** FER. CAR. D. G. DVX. M. VI. ET. M. F. IIII. **Rev:** Radiant sunface in circle **Rev. Legend:** NON. MVTVATA. LVCE. **Note:** Ref. V-604.

Date	Mintage	VG	F	VF	XF	Unc
ND(1612-26) Rare	—	—	—	—	—	—

KM# 26 1/4 DUCATONE

Silver Weight varies: 7.74-8.40g., 32 mm. **Ruler:** Ferdinando **Obv:** Large Mt. Olympus, FIDES in ribbon band above, value '40' in exergue **Obv. Legend:** FERD. D. G. DVX. MANT. VI. ET. M. F. IV. **Rev:** Full-length standing figure of St. Barbara holding palm branch and resting on small tower, MANTVAE in exergue **Rev. Legend:** SANCTA. BARBA - RA. PROTECTRIX. **Note:** Ref. V-605. Prev. KM#59. 40 Soldi.

Date	Mintage	VG	F	VF	XF	Unc
ND(1612-26)	—	125	275	600	1,000	—

KM# 92 1/4 DUCATONE

Silver Weight varies: 7.35-7.38g., 32 mm. **Ruler:** Vincenzo II **Obv:** Shield of 4-fold arms, with central shield of 9-fold arms, crown with FID-ES and small Mt. Olympus above, Order of The Redeemer around **Obv. Legend:** VINC. II. D.G. DVX. - MANT. VII. ET. M. F. V. **Rev:** Alois Gonzaga kneeling to left, looking at angel in upper left, value '40' in exergue **Rev. Legend:** B. ALOIIS - GONZ. PROT. MAN. **Note:** Ref. V-629. Prev. KM#164, as 2 Lire. 40 Soldi.

Date	Mintage	VG	F	VF	XF	Unc
ND(1626-27)	—	100	225	725	1,350	—

KM# 114 1/4 DUCATONE

Silver Weight varies: 6.99-7.54g., 31 mm. **Ruler:** Carlo I **Obv:** Crowned shield of 4-fold arms, with central shield of 9-fold arms, FID-ES and small Mt. Olympus at top, Order of The Redeemer around **Obv. Legend:** CAROL. I. D. G. MAN. M. F. - NIV. MAY. RET. DVX. ETC. **Rev:** Alois Gonzaga kneeling to left, looking at angel at upper left, value '40' in exergue **Rev. Legend:** B: ALOIIS - GONZ. PROT: MAN. **Note:** Ref. V-648. Prev. KM#167, as 2 Lire. 40 Soldi.

Date	Mintage	VG	F	VF	XF	Unc
ND(1627-37)	—	200	325	775	1,500	—

KM# 102 1/4 DUCATONE

Silver Weight varies: 6.67-7.75g., 30-31 mm. **Ruler:** Vincenzo II **Obv:** Armored high-collared bust to left, Roman numeral date below **Obv. Legend:** VINC. II. D. G. DVX. MAN. VII. ET. M. F. V. **Rev:** Dog standing to left in circle **Rev. Legend:** FERIS. TANTVM. INFENSVS. **Note:** Ref. V-628. Prev. KM#165, as 2 Lire.

Date	Mintage	VG	F	VF	XF	Unc
MDCXXVII (1627)	—	400	700	1,300	2,750	—

KM# 132 1/4 DUCATONE

6.8600 g., Billon, 28 mm. **Ruler:** Carlo I **Obv:** Armored bust to right in circle, date in exergue **Obv. Legend:** CAROLVS. D. G. DVX. MANTVÆ. VIII. **Rev:** Shield of 4-fold arms, with central shield of 9-fold arms, in baroque frame, crown and small Mt. Olympus above **Rev. Legend:** ET. MONTIS. FERRATI. VI. ET. C. **Note:** Ref. V-649.

Date	Mintage	VG	F	VF	XF	Unc
1629	—	600	825	2,250	4,250	—

KM# 198 1/4 DUCATONE

Silver Weight varies: 8.61-8.82g., 31-32 mm. **Ruler:** Carlo II **Obv:** Crowned shield of 4-fold arms, with central shield of 9-fold arms, in oval baroque frame, Order of The Redeemer suspended from sides and bottom **Obv. Legend:** CAR. II. D.G. - DVX. MAN. ET. M. FE. ET. C. **Rev:** St. George on horse to right, with lance, slaying dragon below, date in exergue **Rev. Legend:** PROTECTOR. NOSTER. ASPICE. **Note:** Ref. V-697. Prev. KM#301, 361. 40 Soldi.

Date	Mintage	VG	F	VF	XF	Unc
1664	—	225	400	1,000	2,000	—

KM# 202 1/4 SCUDO

5.2200 g., Silver, 29 mm. **Ruler:** Ferdinando Carlo under regency of Isabella Clara **Obv:** Shield of 2-fold arms, Austria at left, complex arms of Mantua at right, large crown and small Mt. Olympus above **Obv. Legend:** ISABELLA. CLARA. FERD. CAROL. D. G. DV. **Rev:** Cross with trefoil ends, heraldic device in each angle, all in quatrefoil with pointed sides, date at top in margin **Rev. Legend:** MANT. MONF. CARLO. VIL. RETH. ET. C. **Note:** Ref. V-724. Prev. KM#371.

Date	Mintage	VG	F	VF	XF	Unc
1666 Rare	—	—	—	—	—	—

KM# 223 1/4 SCUDO

Silver Weight varies: 4.86-5.26g., 29-30 mm. **Ruler:** Ferdinando Carlo **Obv:** Shield of 2-fold arms, Austria at left, complex Mantua arms at right, crown and small Mt. Olympus above **Obv. Legend:** FERDINANDVS. CAROLVS. D. G. DVX. **Rev:** Cross with trefoil ends, heraldic symbols in each angle, all in modified square with arc in each side, date above **Rev. Legend:** MANTVÆ. MONTISFER. CAROLI. VIL. ET. C. **Note:** Ref. V-737.

Date	Mintage	VG	F	VF	XF	Unc
1675	—	85.00	165	325	650	—

KM# 7 TESTONE

8.8400 g., Silver, 31-32 mm. **Ruler:** Francesco IV **Obv:** Crowned shield of 4-fold arms, with central shield of 9-fold arms, Order of The Redeemer around **Obv. Legend:** FRANC. IIII. DVX - MANT. V. ET. MO. FE. III. **Rev:** Facing bust of radiant Madonna in circle, date in legend **Rev. Legend:** HAC. MOSTRANTE. VIAM. (date) IIII. **Note:** Ref. V-565. Prev. KM#71.

Date	Mintage	VG	F	VF	XF	Unc
1612 Rare	—	—	—	—	—	—

KM# 46 1/2 TALLERO

13.3100 g., Silver, 35-36 mm. **Ruler:** Ferdinando **Obv:** Shield of 4-fold arms, with central shield of 9-fold arms, crown and small Mt. Olympus above, cardinal's hat at top, Order of The Redeemer around **Obv. Legend:** FER. S. R. C. D. CAR. D. G. - DVX. MAN. VI. ET. M. F. IIII. **Rev:** St. Andrew at left with cross, date below feet, consigning pyx to St. Longinus at right, value '60' in exergue **Rev. Legend:** NIHIL - ISTO - TRISTE - RECEPTO. **Note:** Ref. V-602. Prev. KM#103. 60 Soldi.

Date	Mintage	VG	F	VF	XF	Unc
1613 Rare	—	—	—	—	—	—

KM# 66 1/2 TALLERO

13.1000 g., Silver, 35 mm. **Ruler:** Ferdinando **Obv:** Armored high-collared bust to right, MANT and date below **Obv. Legend:** FERDINANDVS. D. G. DVX. MAN. VI. **Rev:** Shield of 4-fold arms, with central shield of 9-fold arms, crown and small Mt. Olympus above, Order of The Redeemer around, value 'SOLDI - 55' in exergue **Rev. Legend:** ET. MONTIS - FERRATI. IV. **Note:** Ref. V-603. Prev. KM#125. 55 Soldi.

Date	Mintage	VG	F	VF	XF	Unc
1616 Rare	—	—	—	—	—	—

KM# 177 1/2 SCUDO (60 Soldi)

Silver Weight varies: 10.65-11.93g., 33 mm. **Ruler:** Carlo II **Obv:** Armored bust to left, star below **Obv. Legend:** CAROLVS. II. D. G. DVX. MANTVE. **Rev:** Large Mt. Olympus, FIDES in ribbon band above, value '60' in exergue **Rev. Legend:** ET. MON. FER. NEVER. RET. VMENE. ET. C. **Note:** Ref. V-696. Prev. KM#317.

Date	Mintage	VG	F	VF	XF	Unc
ND(1647-65)	—	850	1,400	3,750	6,250	—

KM# 203 1/2 SCUDO (60 Soldi)

10.7200 g., Silver, 36 mm. **Ruler:** Ferdinando Carlo under regency of Isabella Clara **Obv:** Shield of 2-fold arms, Austria at left, complex arms of Mantua at right, large crown and small Mt. Olympus above **Obv. Legend:** ISABELLA. CLARA. FERD. CAROL. D. G. SV. **Rev:** Cross with trefoil ends, heraldic device in each angle, all in quatrefoil with pointed sides, date at top in margin **Rev. Legend:** MANT. MONF. CARLO. VIL. RETH. ET. C. **Note:** Ref. V-722.

Date	Mintage	VG	F	VF	XF	Unc
1666 Rare	—	—	—	—	—	—

KM# 195 60 SOLDI

Silver Weight varies: 8.10-8.45g., 34 mm. **Ruler:** Carlo II **Obv:** Armored bust to left, value '60' below, date at end of legend **Obv. Legend:** CAR. II. D. G. DVX. MAN. ET. M. F. ET. C. **Rev:** Radiant sun in zodiac band with other symbols, stars around, clouds, and earth below **Rev. Legend:** NEC. RETROGRADIOR. NEC. DEVIO. **Note:** Ref. V-695. Prev. KM#355, as 2 Lire.

Date	Mintage	VG	F	VF	XF	Unc
1663	—	1,200	1,900	4,500	7,500	—

KM# 204 60 SOLDI

Billon Weight varies: 13.75-14.18g., 32-33 mm. **Ruler:** Ferdinando Carlo under regency of Isabella Clara **Obv:** Two accolated busts to right, date below **Obv. Legend:** ISABELLA. CLARA. FERD. CAR. D.G. D. MAN. ET. M. F. ET. C. **Rev:** Radiant sunface between clouds above and sea below, in circle, value 'SOL:60' in margin at bottom **Rev. Legend:** ALTA. A. LONGE. COGNOSCIT. **Note:** Ref. V-723. Prev. KM#369.

Date	Mintage	VG	F	VF	XF	Unc
1666	—	60.00	110	225	475	—

KM# 178 80 SOLDI

Silver Weight varies: 9.97-15.80g., 35-36 mm. **Ruler:** Carlo II **Obv:** Shield of 4-fold arms, with central shield of 9-fold arms, in baroque frame, small Mt. Olympus and large crown above, FIDES at top, Order of The Redeemer around **Obv. Legend:** CAROLVS. II. D. G. - DVX. MANT. ET. M. F. **Rev:** Full-length standing figure of St. Barbara looking to left, holding palm branch and leaning on small tower, value '80' in exergue **Rev. Legend:** SANCTA. BARBA - RA. PROTECTRIX. **Note:** Ref. V-694. Prev. KM#318.

Date	Mintage	VG	F	VF	XF	Unc
ND(1647-65)	—	1,800	2,750	8,000	12,500	—

KM# 224 1/2 SCUDO

Silver Weight varies: 10.54-10.68g., 34 mm. **Ruler:** Ferdinando Carlo **Obv:** Shield of 2-fold arms, Austria at left, complex Mantua arms at right, crown and small Mt. Olympus above **Obv. Legend:** FERDINANDVS. CAROLVS. D. G. DVX. **Rev:** Cross with trefoil ends, heraldic symbols in each angle, all in modified square with arc in each side, date above **Rev. Legend:** MANTVÆ. MONTISFERRATI. CAROLI. VIL. ET. C. **Note:** Ref. V-732. Prev. KM#417.

Date	Mintage	VG	F	VF	XF	Unc
1675	—	200	375	950	1,750	—
1680	—	200	375	950	1,750	—

KM# 227 1/2 SCUDO

10.0000 g., Silver, 36-37 mm. **Ruler:** Ferdinando Carlo **Obv:** Bust to right **Obv. Legend:** FERD. CAR. D. G. DVX. MANTVÆ. MON. FER. ET. C. **Rev:** Radiant sun rising over horizon, clouds and eagle in flight above, date in margin at bottom **Rev. Legend:** QVAE - MAIOR - ORIGO. **Note:** Ref. V-733.

Date	Mintage	VG	F	VF	XF	Unc
1676 Rare	—	—	—	—	—	—

KM# 233 1/2 SCUDO

Silver Weight varies: 17.46-18.04g., 34 mm. **Ruler:** Ferdinando Carlo **Obv:** Armored bust to right **Obv. Legend:** FERDINAN - CAR. D. G. DVX. **Rev:** Crowned ornate shield of 4-fold arms, with central shield of 9-fold arms, in baroque frame, Order of The Redeemer around, date in margin at bottom **Rev. Legend:** MANTVÆ. MON. - FER. CAR. VIL. G. **Note:** Ref. V-734. Prev. KM#428.

Date	Mintage	VG	F	VF	XF	Unc
1691	—	400	650	1,500	2,750	—

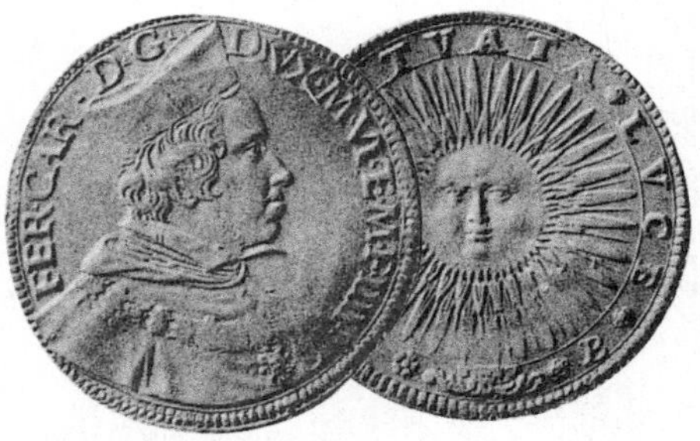

KM# 27 1/2 DUCATONE

Silver Weight varies: 15.34-15.72g., 34 mm. **Ruler:** Ferdinando **Obv:** Bust to right wearing cardinal's robes and biretta **Obv. Legend:** FER. CAR. - D. G. - DVX. M. VI. ET. M. F. IIII. **Rev:** Radiant sunface in circle **Rev. Legend:** NON. MVTVATA. LVCE. **Note:** Ref. V-599. Prev. KM#198.

Date	Mintage	VG	F	VF	XF	Unc
ND(1612-26)	—	900	1,650	4,250	7,500	—

KM# 28 1/2 DUCATONE

Silver Weight varies: 15.34-15.95g., 35 mm. **Ruler:** Ferdinando **Obv:** Armored bust to right **Obv. Legend:** FER. D. G. DVX. - MAN. VI. ET. M. F. IIII. **Rev:** Radiant sunface in circle **Rev. Legend:** NON. MVTVATA. LVCE. **Note:** Ref. V-600.

Date	Mintage	VG	F	VF	XF	Unc
ND(1612-26)	—	900	1,650	4,250	7,500	—

KM# 103 1/2 DUCATONE

Silver Weight varies: 15.00-15.82g., 37 mm. **Ruler:** Vincenzo II **Obv:** Armored high-collared bust to left, Roman numeral date below **Obv. Legend:** VINC. II. D. G. DVX. MAN. VII. ET. M. F. V. **Rev:** Dog standing to left in circle **Rev. Legend:** FERIS. TANTVM. INFENSVS. **Note:** Ref. V-626. Prev. KM#199.

Date	Mintage	VG	F	VF	XF	Unc
MDCXXVII (1627)	—	700	1,100	3,500	6,500	—
MDCXXVIII (1628)	—	—	—	—	—	—

Note: Reported, not confirmed.

KM# 137 1/2 DUCATONE

Silver Weight varies: 15.57-16.09g., 35 mm. **Ruler:** Carlo I **Obv:** Armored high-collared bust to right, date below **Obv. Legend:** CAROLVS. I. D. G. DVX. M. ET. M. F. **Rev:** Radiant sunface in Zodiac band with other symbols, stars around, earth below **Rev. Legend:** NEC. RETROGRADIOR. NEC. DEVIO. **Note:** Ref. V-646. Prev. KM#241.

Date	Mintage	VG	F	VF	XF	Unc
1629	—	1,250	1,900	6,000	9,000	—
1631	—	1,250	1,900	6,000	9,000	—

KM# 156 1/2 DUCATONE

Silver Weight varies: 15.82-15.92g., 37 mm. **Ruler:** Carlo II under regency of Maria **Obv:** Two accolated busts to left **Obv. Legend:** MARIA ET CAR II DGC MAN ET MON FETC **Rev:** Madonna and Child, MANTVAE in exergue **Rev. Legend:** MARIA MATER GRACIAE PROTECTRIX NOSTRA MANTVAE **Note:** Ref. V-682. Prev. KM#274.

Date	Mintage	VG	F	VF	XF	Unc
ND(1637-47)	—	1,000	1,550	5,800	9,000	—

KM# 188 1/2 DUCATONE

Silver Weight varies: 13.37-13.54g., 33 mm. **Ruler:** Carlo II **Obv:** Armored bust to right **Obv. Legend:** CAROL. II. D. G. - DVX. MAN. ET. M. **Rev:** Crowned shield with 3 lilies, 2 above 1, date at end of legend **Rev. Legend:** SIT. NOMEN. DOMINI. - BENEDICTVM. **Note:** Ref. V-692. Prev. KM#340, 342.

Date	Mintage	VG	F	VF	XF	Unc
1653 Rare	—	—	—	—	—	—

KM# 205 1/2 DUCATONE

15.9000 g., Silver, 38 mm. **Ruler:** Ferdinando Carlo under regency of Isabella Clara **Obv:** Two accolated busts to right, date below **Obv. Legend:** ISABELLA. CLARA. FERD. CAR. D. G. D. MAN. - ET. M. F. ET. C. **Rev:** Radiant sunface between clouds above and sea below, in circle **Rev. Legend:** ALTA. A. LONGE. COGNOSCIT. **Note:** Ref. V-721. Prev. KM#375.

Date	Mintage	VG	F	VF	XF	Unc
1666	—	750	1,350	2,250	4,500	—

KM# 47 1/2 DUCATONE (80 Soldi)

Silver, 34 mm. **Ruler:** Ferdinando **Obv:** Displayed eagle in laurel wreath, date in margin at top **Obv. Legend:** FERDINAND. CAR. D. G. DVX. MANTVE. ET. MON. F. **Rev:** Crown above Maltese cross, lower arm divides value '80,' cardinal's hat at top **Rev. Legend:** MANVS. DOMINI. FECIT. OMNIA. **Note:** Prev. KM#99.

Date	Mintage	VG	F	VF	XF	Unc
1613 Unique	—	—	—	—	—	—

KM# 83 1/2 DUCATONE (80 Soldi)

15.6200 g., Silver, 38 mm. **Ruler:** Ferdinando **Obv:** Large Mt. Olympus, FIDES in ribbon band above, all in circle, date in exergue **Obv. Legend:** FERD. D.G. DVX. MANT. VI. ET. MON. F. IV. **Rev:** Full-length standing figure of St. Barbara looking to left, holding palm branch and resting on small tower, value '80' in exergue **Rev. Legend:** SANCTA. BARBA - RA. PAROTECTRIX. **Note:** Ref. V-601. Prev. KM#154, as 1/2 Scudo (60 Soldi).

Date	Mintage	VG	F	VF	XF	Unc
1622	—	700	1,100	3,200	5,800	—
1624	—	700	1,100	3,200	5,800	—

KM# 93 1/2 DUCATONE (80 Soldi)

Silver Weight varies: 15.02-15.20g., 37 mm. **Ruler:** Vincenzo II **Obv:** Shield of 4-fold arms, with central shield of 9-fold arms, crown with FIDES and small Mt. Olympus above, Order of The Redeemer around **Obv. Legend:** VINCEN. II. D. G. DVX. - MANT. VII. ET. MON. F. V. **Rev:** Alois Gonzaga kneeling to left, looking at angel in upper left, value '80' in exergue **Rev. Legend:** B. ALOIIS - GONZ. PROT. MAN. **Note:** Ref. V-627. Prev. KM#179, as 1/2 Scudo (60 Soldi).

Date	Mintage	VG	F	VF	XF	Unc
ND(1626-27)	—	175	275	750	1,400	—

KM# 115 1/2 DUCATONE (80 Soldi)

Silver Weight varies: 14.89-15.18g., 38 mm. **Ruler:** Carlo I **Obv:** Shield of 4-fold arms, with central shield of 9-fold arms, crown with OLYMPOS above, FID-ES divided at top, Order of The Redeemer around **Obv. Legend:** CAROL. I. D. G. DVX. MAN. ET. MON. FER. **Rev:** Alois Gonzaga kneeling to left, looking at angel at upper left, value '80' in exergue **Rev. Legend:** B: ALOIIS - GONZ: PROT: MAN. **Note:** Ref. V-647. Prev. KM#193.1.

Date	Mintage	VG	F	VF	XF	Unc
ND(1627-37)	—	250	450	750	1,100	—

KM# 116 1/2 DUCATONE (80 Soldi)

Silver Weight varies: 14.89-15.18g., 38 mm. **Ruler:** Carlo I **Obv:** Shield of 4-fold arms, with central shield of 9-fold arms, crown with OLYMPOS above, FID-ES divided at top, Order of The Redeemer around **Obv. Legend:** CAROLVS. I. D. G. MAN. MON. - F. NIV. MAY. RET. DVX. ET.C. **Rev:** Alois Gonzaga kneeling to left, looking at angel at upper left, value '80' in exergue **Rev. Legend:** B: ALOIIS - GONZ: PROT: MAN. **Note:** Ref. V-647/1. Prev. KM#193.2.

Date	Mintage	VG	F	VF	XF	Unc
ND(1627-37)	—	250	450	750	1,100	—

KM# 196 1/2 DUCATONE (120 Soldi)

17.7600 g., Silver, 38 mm. **Ruler:** Carlo II **Obv:** Armored bust to left, value '120' and date below shoulder **Obv. Legend:** CAR. II. D. G. DVX. MAN. ET. M. F. ET. C. **Rev:** Radiant sunface in Zodiac band with other symbols, stars around, clouds and earth below **Rev. Legend:** NEC. RETROGRADIOR. NEC. DEVIO. **Note:** Ref. V-693. Prev. KM#359.

Date	Mintage	VG	F	VF	XF	Unc
1663	—	1,800	2,750	6,000	9,000	—

KM# 206 SCUDO

Silver Weight varies: 19.50-22.08g., 39 mm. **Ruler:** Ferdinando Carlo under regency of Isabella Clara **Obv:** Shield of 2-fold arms, Austria at left, complex arms of Mantua at right, large crown and small Mt. Olympus above **Obv. Legend:** ISABELLA. CLARA. FERD. CAROL. D. G. DVC. **Rev:** Cross with trefoil ends, heraldic device in each angle, all in quatrefoil with pointed sides, date at top in margin **Rev. Legend:** MANT. MONF. CARLO. VIL. RETH. ET. C. **Note:** Ref. V-720; Dav. 3968. Prev. KM#373.

Date	Mintage	VG	F	VF	XF	Unc
1666	—	575	875	1,450	2,150	—

KM# 225 SCUDO

Silver Weight varies: 21.30-21.94g., 40 mm. **Ruler:** Ferdinando Carlo **Obv:** Shield of 2-fold arms, Austria at left, complex Mantua arms at right, crown and small Mt. Olympus above **Obv. Legend:** FERDINANDVS. CAROLVS. D. G. DVX. **Rev:** Cross with trefoil ends, heraldic symbol in each angle, all in modified square with arc in each side, date above **Rev. Legend:** MANTVÆ MONTISFERRATI. CAROLI. VIL. ET. C. **Note:** Ref. V-729; Dav. 3969. Prev. KM#406.

Date	Mintage	VG	F	VF	XF	Unc
1675	—	325	575	1,300	1,750	—
1678/7	—	260	450	975	1,250	—
1678	—	195	350	775	825	—
1680	—	195	350	775	825	—

KM# 228 SCUDO

31.9500 g., Silver, 42-43 mm. **Ruler:** Ferdinando Carlo **Obv:** Armored bust to right **Obv. Legend:** FERDINANDVS. CAR. D. G. DVX. MANTVÆ. MON. FER. ET. C. **Rev:** Radiant sun rising over horizon, clouds and eagle in flight above, date in margin at bottom **Rev. Legend:** QVAE - MAIOR - ORIGO. **Note:** Ref. V-730; Dav. 3970. Prev. KM#408.

Date	Mintage	VG	F	VF	XF	Unc
1676 Rare	—	—	—	—	—	—

KM# 30 TALLERO

Silver Weight varies: 25.95-30.96g., 41-42 mm. **Ruler:** Ferdinando **Obv:** Shield of 4-fold arms, with central shield of 9-fold arms, crown with FID-ES and small Mt. Olympus above, Order of The Redeemer around **Obv. Legend:** FERDINAN. DG. DVX. - MANT. VI. ET. MONF. IV. **Rev:** St. Andrew at left with cross, consigning pyx to St. Longinus at right, date below feet, where present **Rev. Legend:** NIHIL - ISTO - TRISTE - RECEPTO. **Note:** Ref. V-598; Dav. 3935. Prev. KM#101.

Date	Mintage	VG	F	VF	XF	Unc
ND(1612-26)	—	1,350	2,000	5,100	7,000	—
1613	—	1,350	2,000	5,100	7,000	—

KM# 29 TALLERO

Silver Weight varies: 25.90-26.32g., 42-43 mm. **Ruler:** Ferdinando **Obv:** Shield of 4-fold arms, with central shield of 9-fold arms, crown with FID-ES and small Mt. Olympus above, cardinal's hat at top, Order of The Redeemer around **Obv. Legend:** FER. S. R. E. D. CAR. D. G. - DVX. MAN. VI. ET. M. F. IIII. **Rev:** St. Andrewat left with cross, date below feet, consigning pyx to St. Longinus at right, value '120' in exergue **Rev. Legend:** NIHIL - ISTO - TRISTE - RECEPTO. **Note:** Ref. V-597/1; Dav. 3933. Prev. KM#65.1. 120 Soldi.

Date	Mintage	VG	F	VF	XF	Unc
1612	—	1,350	2,000	5,100	7,000	—

KM# 49 TALLERO

Silver Weight varies: 25.90-26.32g., 42 mm. **Ruler:** Ferdinando **Obv:** Shield of 4-fold arms, with central shield of 9-fold arms, crown with FID-ES and small Mt. Olympus above, cardinal's hat at top, Order of The Redeemer around **Obv. Legend:** FER. S. R. E. D. CAR. D. G. - DVX. MAN. VI. ET. M. F. IIII. **Rev:** St. Andrew at left with cross, date below feet, consigning pyx to St. Longinus at right, arabesque in exergue instead of value **Rev. Legend:** NIHIL - ISTO - TRISTE - RECEPTO. **Note:** Ref. V-597/2,3; Dav. 3934. Prev. KM#65.2.

Date	Mintage	VG	F	VF	XF	Unc
1613	—	1,350	2,000	5,100	7,000	—
1615	—	1,350	2,000	5,100	7,000	—

KM# 48 TALLERO

Silver Weight varies: 25.90-26.32g., 42-43 mm. **Ruler:** Ferdinando **Obv:** Shield of 4-fold arms, with central shield of 9-fold arms, crown with FID-ES and small Mt. Olympus above, cardinal's hat at top, Order of The Redeemer around **Obv. Legend:** FER. S. R. E. D. CAR. D. G. - DVX. MAN. VI. ET. M. F. IIII. **Rev:** St. Andrew at left with cross, date below feet, consigning pyx to St. Longinus at right, value '6' in exergue **Rev. Legend:** NIHIL - ISTO - TRISTE - RECEPTO. **Note:** Ref. V-597/2; Dav. 3933. Prev. KM#65.1. 6 Lire.

Date	Mintage	VG	F	VF	XF	Unc
1613	—	1,350	2,000	5,100	7,000	—

KM# 80 TALLERO

21.3400 g., Silver, 44-45 mm. **Ruler:** Ferdinando **Obv:** 4-fold arms, eagle in each quarter, in quatrefoil with pointed and indented sides, date in margin at top **Obv. Legend:** FERDINANDVS. D. G. DVX. MANT. VI. **Rev:** Shield of 9-fold arms, crown with FID-ES and small Mt. Olympus above, Order of The Redeemer around **Rev. Legend:** ET. MONTIS - FERRATI. IV. **Note:** Ref. V-596; Dav. 3946. Prev. KM#146.

Date	Mintage	VG	F	VF	XF	Unc
1620	—	2,000	3,400	6,800	9,900	—
1622	—	2,000	3,400	6,800	9,900	—

KM# 78 TALLERO

Silver Weight varies: 27.99-28.42g., 41 mm. **Ruler:** Ferdinando **Obv:** Half-length armored figure to right, holding scepter over right shoulder, divides date **Obv. Legend:** FERDIN. D.G. DVX. MAN(T). VI. ET. MONT(I). F. IV. **Rev:** Shield of 4-fold arms, with central shield of 9-fold arms, crown with FID-ES and small Mt. Olympus above, Order of The Redeemer around **Rev. Legend:** DOMINE. - PROBASTI. **Note:** Ref. V-593; Dav. 3943. Prev. KM#142.

Date	Mintage	VG	F	VF	XF	Unc
1620	—	3,000	6,500	10,000	—	—

KM# 79 TALLERO

28.1800 g., Silver, 41 mm. **Ruler:** Ferdinando **Obv:** Half-length armored figure to right, holding scepter over right shoulder, divides date **Obv. Legend:** FERDIN. D. G. DVX. MAN. VI. ET. MONT. F. IV. **Rev:** Shield of 9-fold arms, crown with FID-ES and small Mt. Olympus above, Order of The Redeemer around **Rev. Legend:** DOMINE. - PROBASTI. **Note:** Ref. V-594; Dav. 3944. Prev. KM#144.

Date	Mintage	VG	F	VF	XF	Unc
1620 Rare	—	—	—	—	—	—

KM# 82 TALLERO

Silver Weight varies: 25.25-26.47g., 42-43 mm. **Ruler:** Ferdinando **Obv:** Armored high-collared bust to right, Roman numeral date below **Obv. Legend:** FERDINANDVS. DG. DVX. MANT. VI. **Rev:** Ornate shield of 4-fold arms, with central shield of 9-fold arms, crown with FID-ES and small Mt. Olympus above, Order of The Redeemer around **Rev. Legend:** ET. MONTIS - FERRATI. IV. **Note:** Ref. V-595/4,5; Dav. 3945. Prev. KM#150.

Date	Mintage	VG	F	VF	XF	Unc
MDCXXI (1621)	—	1,550	2,500	6,600	9,900	—
MDCXXII (1622)	—	1,550	2,500	6,600	9,900	—

KM# 150 TALLERO

25.4600 g., Silver, 40-41 mm. **Ruler:** Carlo I **Obv:** Crowned shield of 4-fold arms, with central shield of 9-fold arms, FIDES at top **Obv. Legend:** CAROLVS. I. D. G. D. MAN. MON. FER. **Rev:** Cross with trefoil ends, armorial devices in each angle, al in pointed and indented quatrefoil, date at top in margin **Rev. Legend:** NIVER. MAIEN. RETHEL. DVX. ET. C. **Note:** Ref. V-645; Dav. 3955. Prev. KM#268.

Date	Mintage	VG	F	VF	XF	Unc
1633 Rare	—	—	—	—	—	—

KM# 67 TALLERO (110 Soldi)

Silver Weight varies: 25.15-26.47g., 41 mm. **Ruler:** Ferdinando **Obv:** Armored high-collared bust to right, MANTVÆ and date below **Obv. Legend:** FERDINAND(VS). D.G. DVX. MAN(T)(V). VI. **Rev:** Ornate shield of 4-fold arms, with central shield of 9-fold arms, crown with FID-ES and small Mt. Olympus above, Order of The Redeemer around, value 'SOLDI - 110' in exergue **Rev. Legend:** ET. MONTIS - FERRATI. IV. **Note:** Ref. V-595/1,3; Dav. 3939. Prev. KM#127.

Date	Mintage	VG	F	VF	XF	Unc
1616	—	1,450	2,000	5,400	9,000	—
1618	—	1,450	2,000	5,400	9,000	—

KM# 74 TALLERO (110 Soldi)

Silver Weight varies: 25.25-26.47g., 41 mm. **Ruler:** Ferdinando **Obv:** Armored high-collared bust to right, MANT. and date below **Obv. Legend:** FERDINANDVS. D. G. DVX. MAN. VI. **Rev:** Ornate shield of 4-fold arms, with central shield of 9-fold arms, crown with FID-ES and small Mt. Olympus above, Order of The Redeemer around, value 'SOLDI - 110' in exergue **Rev. Legend:** ET. MONTIS - FERRATI. IV. **Note:** Ref. V-595/2; Dav. 3941. Prev. KM#49.

Date	Mintage	VG	F	VF	XF	Unc
1617	—	1,500	2,050	5,600	8,300	—
1617	—	3,050	6,000	12,000	—	—
Note: Error: 100 in reverse exergue						
1607 error for 1617	—	2,200	3,700	8,300	—	—
1618	—	1,500	2,050	5,600	8,300	—

KM# 9 DUCATONE

Silver Weight varies: 30.94-31.74g., 44 mm. **Ruler:** Francesco IV **Obv:** Armored high-collared bust to right, date below **Obv. Legend:** FRAN. IIII. D. G. DVX. MANT. V. ET. M. F. III. **Rev:** St. Francis kneeling toward the left, embracing cross, church in distance at left **Rev. Legend:** PROTECTOR FACTVS EST MIHI. **Note:** Ref. V-563; Dav. 3931. Prev. KM#73.

Date	Mintage	VG	F	VF	XF	Unc
1612	—	1,050	1,650	4,200	6,000	—

KM# 10 DUCATONE

Silver Weight varies: 26.74-26.79g., 41-42 mm. **Ruler:** Francesco IV **Obv:** Shield of 4-fold arms, with central shield of 9-fold arms, crown with FIDES above, Order of The Redeemer around **Obv. Legend:** FRAN. IIII. D.G. DVX. - MAN. V. ET. MON. III. **Rev:** St. Andrew with cross at left, date below feet, consigning pyx to kneeling St. Longinus at right, value '120' in exergue **Rev. Legend:** NIHIL - ISTO - TRI - STE. RECEPTO. **Note:** Ref. V-564; Dav. 3932. Prev. KM#63. 120 Soldi.

Date	Mintage	VG	F	VF	XF	Unc
1612 Rare	—	—	—	—	—	—

KM# 31 DUCATONE

Silver Weight varies: 31.39-31.97g., 42-43 mm. **Ruler:** Ferdinando **Obv:** Large armored high-collared bust to right **Obv. Legend:** FERD. D. G. DVX. MAN. VI. ET. M. F. IIII. **Rev:** Radiant sunface in circle **Rev. Legend:** NON. MVTVATA. LVCE. **Note:** Ref. V-591/1; Dav. 3947. Prev. KM#105.3.

Date	Mintage	VG	F	VF	XF	Unc
ND(1612-26)	—	750	1,200	2,850	5,000	—

KM# 32 DUCATONE

Silver Weight varies: 31.39-31.97g., 42-43 mm. **Ruler:** Ferdinando **Obv:** Small armored high-collared bust to right **Obv. Legend:** FERD. D. G. DVX. MAN. ET. M. F. IIII. **Rev:** Radiant sunface in circle **Rev. Legend:** NON. MVTVATA. LVCE. **Note:** Ref. V-591/1; Dav. 3947A. Prev. KM#105.4.

Date	Mintage	VG	F	VF	XF	Unc
ND(1612-26)	—	750	1,200	2,850	5,000	—

KM# 33 DUCATONE

Silver Weight varies: 31.36-31.79g., 41-42 mm. **Ruler:** Ferdinando **Obv:** Large Mt. Olympus FIDES in ribbon band above, all in circle, value '160' in exergue **Obv. Legend:** FERD. D. G. DVX. MANT. VI. ET. MONT. F. IV. **Rev:** Full-length figure of St. Barbara, looking to left, holding palm branch, leaning on small tower, MANTVÆ in exergue **Rev. Legend:** SANCTA. BARBA(-)RA. PROTECTRIX. **Note:** Ref. V-592; Dav. 3948. Prev. KM#75, 230. 160 Soldi.

Date	Mintage	VG	F	VF	XF	Unc
ND(1612-26)	—	550	950	2,650	5,000	—

KM# 50 DUCATONE

Silver Weight varies: 31.32-31.63g., 41-42 mm. **Ruler:** Ferdinando **Obv:** Bust to right, wearing cardinal's robes and biretta, Arabic or Roman numeral date below **Obv. Legend:** FERD. CARD. D. G. DVX. MAN. VI. ET. M. F. IIII. **Rev:** Radiant sunface in circle **Rev. Legend:** NON. MVTVATA. LVCE. **Note:** Ref. V-590; Dav. 3937. Prev. KM#105.1.

Date	Mintage	VG	F	VF	XF	Unc
1613	—	950	1,750	4,500	7,000	—
MDCXIIII (1614)	—	950	1,750	4,500	7,000	—
MDCXV (1615)	—	950	1,750	4,500	7,000	—

KM# 75 DUCATONE

Silver Weight varies: 31.39-31.97g., 43-44 mm. **Ruler:** Ferdinando **Obv:** Armored high-collared bust to right, date below **Obv. Legend:** FERD. DG. DVX. MANT. VI. ET. MONFER. IV. **Rev:** Radiant sunface in circle **Rev. Legend:** NON. MVTVATA. LVCE. **Note:** Ref. V-591/2; Dav. 3940. Prev. KM#105.2.

Date	Mintage	VG	F	VF	XF	Unc
1617	—	750	1,500	4,000	6,750	—

KM# 94 DUCATONE

Silver Weight varies: 29.00-31.80g., 42-43 mm. **Ruler:** Vincenzo II **Obv:** Large armored high-collared bust to left, date below, where present **Obv. Legend:** VINCEN. II. D. G. DVX. MANT. VII. ET. M. F. V. **Rev:** Dog standing to left in circle **Rev. Legend:** FERIS. TANTVM. INFENSVS. **Note:** Ref. V-623; Dav. 3951. Prev. KM#203.1.

Date	Mintage	VG	F	VF	XF	Unc
ND(1626-27)	—	1,000	1,850	4,750	7,500	—
1627	—	1,000	1,850	4,750	7,500	—

KM# 95 DUCATONE

Silver Weight varies: 29.00-31.80g., 42-43 mm. **Ruler:** Vincenzo II **Obv:** Large armored high-collared bust to left, angel at shoulder **Obv. Legend:** VINCEN. II. D. G. DVX. MANT. VII. ET. M. F. V. **Rev:** Dog standing to left, in circle **Rev. Legend:** FERIS. TANTVM. INFENSVS. **Note:** Ref. Dav. 3951A. Prev. KM#203.2.

Date	Mintage	VG	F	VF	XF	Unc
ND(1626-27)	—	850	1,250	2,500	4,500	—

KM# 96 DUCATONE

Silver Weight varies: 31.20-31.42g., 48-49 mm. **Ruler:** Vincenzo II **Obv:** 6-line inscription in wreath **Obv. Inscription:** VINCENTI. / II: D: G: DVX / MANTVÆ: VII / ET: MONTIS / FERRATI / V. **Rev:** Galley with oars sailing to left **Rev. Legend:** HAC MONSTRANTI VIAM. **Note:** Ref. V-624; Dav. 3953. Prev. KM#207.

Date	Mintage	VG	F	VF	XF	Unc
ND(1626-27) Rare	—	—	—	—	—	—

KM# 97 DUCATONE

39.1000 g., Silver, 42-43 mm. **Ruler:** Vincenzo II **Obv:** Armored bust to right **Obv. Legend:** D: PRINC: VINCENTIVS: GONZA. **Rev:** Armillary sphere in circle **Rev. Legend:** IMMOBILIS IN MOTV **Note:** Ref. V-625; Dav. 3952. Prev. KM#201.

Date	Mintage	VG	F	VF	XF	Unc
ND(1626-27) Rare	—	—	—	—	—	—

KM# 104 DUCATONE

Silver Weight varies: 31.25-31.80g., 43 mm. **Ruler:** Vincenzo II **Obv:** Armored high-collared bust to right **Obv. Legend:** VINCEN II D G DVX MANT VII ET M F V. **Rev:** Dog standing to left, Roman numeral date below, all in circle **Rev. Legend:** FERIS. TANTVM. INFENSVS. **Note:** Ref. V-622; Dav. 3950. Prev. KM#205.

Date	Mintage	VG	F	VF	XF	Unc
MDCXXVII (1627)	—	1,200	2,250	5,500	8,500	—

KM# 120 DUCATONE

Silver Weight varies: 30.60-32.03g., 43 mm. **Ruler:** Carlo I **Obv:** Armored high-collared bust to right, date below **Obv. Legend:** CAROLVS. I. D. G. DVX. MAN. ET. M. F. ETC. **Rev:** Radiant sunface in Zodiac band with other symbols, stars around, clouds and earth below **Rev. Legend:** NEC. RETROGRADIOR. NEC. DEVIO. **Note:** Ref. V-644; Dav. 3954. Prev. KM#213.

Date	Mintage	VG	F	VF	XF	Unc
1628 Rare	—	—	—	—	—	—
Note: Peus Auction 403, 4-11, VF-XF realized approximately $13,530						
1631 Rare	—	—	—	—	—	—
Note: Numismatica Ars Classica Auction 32, 1-06, XF realized approximately $12,465						
1632 Rare	—	—	—	—	—	—
1633 Rare	—	—	—	—	—	—
1636 Rare	—	—	—	—	—	—

KM# 157 DUCATONE
Silver Weight varies: 30.80-32.30g., 42-43 mm. **Ruler:** Carlo II under regency of Maria **Obv:** Two accolated busts to left **Obv. Legend:** MARIA. ET. CAR. II. D. G. D. MAN. ET. MON. F. ET. C. **Rev:** Madonna and Child, MANTVAE in exergue **Rev. Legend:** MARIA. MATER. GRATIÆ. PROTETRIX. NOSTRA. **Note:** Ref. V-681; Dav. 3961. Prev. KM#276.

Date	Mintage	VG	F	VF	XF	Unc
ND(1637-47)	—	1,200	2,750	6,500	9,500	—

KM# 179 DUCATONE
31.2000 g., Silver, 41 mm. **Ruler:** Carlo II **Obv:** Armored high-collared bust to right **Obv. Legend:** CAROLVS. D. G. DVX. MANT. IX. **Rev:** Shield of 4-fold arms, with central shield of 9-fold arms, in baroque frame, crown with FID-ES and small Mt. Olympus above, Order of The Redeemer around **Rev. Legend:** ET. MONTIS. - FERRATI. VII. **Note:** Ref. V-690; Dav. 3963. Prev. KM#319.

Date	Mintage	VG	F	VF	XF	Unc
ND(1647-65) Rare	—	—	—	—	—	—

KM# 180 DUCATONE
31.0000 g., Silver, 42 mm. **Ruler:** Carlo II **Obv:** Large armored bust to left **Obv. Legend:** CAROLVS. II. D. G. DVX. MAN. ET. M. F. ET. C. **Rev:** Madonna and Child, MANTVAE in exergue **Rev. Legend:** MARIA. MATER. GRATIÆ. PROTETRIX. NOSTRA. **Note:** Ref. V-691; Dav. 3964. Prev. KM#321.

Date	Mintage	VG	F	VF	XF	Unc
ND(1647-65) Rare	—	—	—	—	—	—

KM# 184 DUCATONE
Silver Weight varies: 31.17-32.26g., 45 mm. **Ruler:** Carlo II **Obv:** Large armored bust to left **Obv. Legend:** CAROLVS. II. D. G. DVX. MAN. ET. M.F. ET. C. **Rev:** Radiant sun above clouds, which are pouring rain below, all in oval baroque frame, date divided below **Rev. Legend:** TV. AVTEM. PERMANES. **Note:** Rev. V-689; Dav. 3962. Prev. KM#327.

Date	Mintage	VG	F	VF	XF	Unc
1649 Rare	—	—	—	—	—	—

KM# 207 DUCATONE
Silver Weight varies: 31.79-32.02g., 44 mm. **Ruler:** Ferdinando Carlo under regency of Isabella Clara **Obv:** Two accolated busts to right, date below **Obv. Legend:** ISABELLA. CLARA. FERD. CAR. D. G. MAN. - ET. M. F. ET. C. **Rev:** Radiant sunface between clouds above and sea below, in circle **Rev. Legend:** ALTA. A. LONGE. COGNOSCIT. **Note:** Ref. V-718; Dav. 3966. Prev. KM#377.

Date	Mintage	VG	F	VF	XF	Unc
1666	—	650	1,200	2,500	4,750	—

KM# 208 DUCATONE
33.3800 g., Silver, 42-43 mm. **Ruler:** Ferdinando Carlo under regency of Isabella Clara **Obv:** Two accolated busts to right, date below **Obv. Legend:** ISABELLA. CLARA. FERD. CAR. D. G. D. MAN. - ET. M. F. ET. C. **Rev:** Madonna and Child, MANTVAE in exergue **Rev. Legend:** MARIA. MATER. GRATIÆ. PROTETRIX. NOSTRA. **Note:** Ref. V-719; Dav. 3967. Prev. KM#379.

Date	Mintage	VG	F	VF	XF	Unc
1666	—	800	1,650	3,200	6,750	—

KM# 51 2 DUCATONI
63.2300 g., Silver, 42 mm. **Ruler:** Ferdinando **Obv:** Bust to right, wearing cardinal's robes and biretta, Arabic or Roman numeral date below **Obv. Legend:** FERD. CARD. D. G. DVX. MAN. VI. ET. M. F. IIII. **Rev:** Radiant sunface in circle **Rev. Legend:** NON. MVTVATA. LVCE. **Note:** Ref. V-589; Dav. 3936.

Date	Mintage	VG	F	VF	XF	Unc
1613 Rare	—	—	—	—	—	—

KM# 158 2 DUCATONI
63.5600 g., Silver, 42-43 mm. **Ruler:** Carlo II under regency of Maria **Obv:** Two accolated busts to left **Obv. Legend:** MARIA. ET. CAR. II. D. G. D. MAN. ET. MON. F. ET. C. **Rev:** Madonna and Child, MANTVAE in exergue **Rev. Legend:** MARIA. MATER. GRATIÆ. PROTETRIX. NOSTRA. **Note:** Ref. V-680; Dav. 3960. Prev. KM#278.

Date	Mintage	VG	F	VF	XF	Unc
ND(1637-47) Rare	—	—	—	—	—	—

KM# 209 2 DUCATONI
Silver Weight varies: 63.62-63.95g., 44 mm. **Ruler:** Ferdinando Carlo under regency of Isabella Clara **Obv:** Two accolated busts to right, date below **Obv. Legend:** ISABELLA. CLARA. FERD. CAR. D. G. D. MAN. - ET. M. F. ET. C. **Rev:** Radiant sunface between clouds above and sea below, in circle **Rev. Legend:** ALTA. A. LONGE. COGNOSCIT. **Note:** Ref. V-717; Dav. 3965. Prev. KM#A379.

Date	Mintage	VG	F	VF	XF	Unc
1666 Rare	—	—	—	—	—	—

KM# 60 3 DUCATONI
94.9000 g., Silver, 45 mm. **Ruler:** Ferdinando **Obv:** Bust to right wearing cardinal's robes and biretta, holding scepter over right shoulder, Roman numeral date below **Obv. Legend:** FERDINANDVS. - S. R. E. D. CARD. D. G. DVX. **Rev:** Madonna seated with Child between 2 vine branches growing from bottom **Rev. Legend:** TIT. S. M. IN. PORTICV. S. R. E. DIAC. CARD. **Note:** Ref. V-588; Dav. 3938.

Date	Mintage	VG	F	VF	XF	Unc
MDCXIIII (1614) Rare	—	—	—	—	—	—

KM# 159 3 DUCATONI
96.4300 g., Silver, 42-43 mm. **Ruler:** Ferdinando Carlo under regency of Isabella Clara **Obv:** Two accolated busts to left **Obv. Legend:** MARIA. ET. CAR. II. D. G. D. MAN. ET. MON. F. ET. C. **Rev:** Madonna and Child, MANTVAE in exergue **Rev. Legend:** MARIA. MATER. GRATIÆ. PROTETRIX. NOSTRA. **Note:** Ref. V-679; Dav. 3959. Prev. KM#280.

Date	Mintage	VG	F	VF	XF	Unc
ND(1637-47) Rare	—	—	—	—	—	—

TRADE COINAGE

KM# 34 1/2 ZECCHINO
Gold Weight varies: 1.60-1.65g., 16.5 mm. **Ruler:** Ferdinando **Obv:** Armored high-collared bust to right **Obv. Legend:** FERDINAND. D. G. DVX. MANT. VI. **Rev:** Crowned shield of 4-fold arms, with central shield of 9-fold arms, Order of The Redeemer around **Rev. Legend:** ET. MONTIS - FERRATI. IV. **Note:** Ref. V-587; Fr. 562. Prev. KM#79.

Date	Mintage	VG	F	VF	XF	Unc
ND(1612-26) Rare	—	—	—	—	—	—

KM# 35 DUCATO (Zecchino)
3.4400 g., Gold, 20 mm. **Ruler:** Ferdinando **Obv:** Full-length standing figure of duke to left **Obv. Legend:** FER. D. G. DVX. MAN. - VI. ET. MON. F. IIII.. **Rev:** Seated Madonna with Child between 2 vine branches growing from bottom **Rev. Legend:** TIT. S. M. IN. PORTICV. S. R. E. D. CAR. **Note:** Ref. V-585; Fr. 565. Prev. KM#77.

Date	Mintage	VG	F	VF	XF	Unc
ND(1612-26) Rare	—	—	—	—	—	—

KM# 36 DUCATO (Zecchino)
Gold Weight varies: 3.35-3.37g., 21-22 mm. **Ruler:** Ferdinando **Obv:** Large rose in circle **Obv. Legend:** FERDIN. D. G. DVX. MANT. VI. ET. MON. FER. IIII. **Rev:** Seated Madonna with Child, rays around, in circle **Rev. Legend:** TV. GLORIA. IERVSALEM. **Note:** Ref. V-586; Fr. 566. Prev. KM#83, as Doppia.

Date	Mintage	VG	F	VF	XF	Unc
ND(1612-26)	—	950	1,400	3,300	4,150	—

KM# 98 DUCATO (Zecchino)
2.5300 g., Gold, 21 mm. **Ruler:** Vincenzo II **Obv:** 6-line inscription in wreath **Obv. Inscription:** .VIN. / II. D. G. /DVX. MAN / VII. ET. / .M. F. / .V. **Rev:** 3-masted ship sailing to left **Rev. Legend:** HAC. MONSTRANTE. VIAM. **Note:** Ref. V-621; Fr. 568. Prev. KM#181.

Date	Mintage	VG	F	VF	XF	Unc
ND(1626-27) Rare	—	—	—	—	—	—

KM# 37 DOPPIA (2 Ducati)
Gold Weight varies: 6.42-6.47g., 25-26 mm. **Ruler:** Ferdinando **Obv:** Bust to left wearing cardinal's robes and biretta **Obv. Legend:** FER. CAR. DG. DVX. M. VI. ET. M. F. IIII. **Rev:** St. Andrew at left holding cross, date below feet, where present, consigning pyx to St. Longinus kneeling at right **Rev. Legend:** NIHIL - ISTO - TRISTE - RECEPTO. **Note:** Ref. V-582; Fr. 555. Prev. KM#107.

Date	Mintage	VG	F	VF	XF	Unc
ND(1612-26) Rare	—	—	—	—	—	—
1613 Rare	—	—	—	—	—	—

KM# 12 DOPPIA (2 Ducati)
Gold Weight varies: 6.35-6.54g., 26 mm. **Ruler:** Francesco IV **Obv:** Armored high-collared bust to right, date below shoulder **Obv. Legend:** FRAN. IIII. D. G. DVX. MANT. V. **Rev:** Shield of 4-fold arms, with central shield of 9-fold arms, crown with FI-DES and small Mt. Olympus above **Rev. Legend:** ET. MONTI - FERRA. III. **Note:** Ref. V-562; Fr. 549. Prev. KM#85.

Date	Mintage	VG	F	VF	XF	Unc
1612	—	600	1,900	5,000	6,000	—

KM# 38 DOPPIA (2 Ducati)
Gold Weight varies: 6.18-6.45g., 26-27 mm. **Ruler:** Ferdinando **Obv:** Armored high-collared bust to left **Obv. Legend:** FERDINAN. D. G. DVX. MANT. VI. **Rev:** Shield of 4-fold arms, with central shield of 9-fold arms, crown with FID-ES and small Mt. Olympus above, Order of The Redeemer around **Rev. Legend:** ET. MONTIS. FERRATI. IV. **Note:** Ref. V-584; Fr. 556a. Prev. KM#81, 104.

Date	Mintage	VG	F	VF	XF	Unc
ND(1612-26)	—	1,000	1,650	4,000	7,000	—

KM# 52 DOPPIA (2 Ducati)
Gold Weight varies: 6.49-6.54g., 25-26 mm. **Ruler:** Ferdinando **Obv:** Bust to left wearing cardinal's robes and biretta **Obv. Legend:** FER. CAR. D. G. DVX. M. VI. ET. M. F. IIII. **Rev:** Two angels holding up large pyx, Arabic or Roman numeral date in exergue **Rev. Legend:** NIHIL ISTO TRISTE RECEPTO. **Note:** Ref. V-581; Fr. 554. Prev. KM#119.

Date	Mintage	VG	F	VF	XF	Unc
1613	—	2,000	2,750	6,800	10,000	—
MDCXIIII (1614)	—	2,000	2,750	6,800	10,000	—
MDCXVI (1616)	—	2,000	2,750	6,800	10,000	—

KM# 68 DOPPIA (2 Ducati)
Gold Weight varies: 6.30-6.52g., 27 mm. **Ruler:** Ferdinando **Obv:** Armored high-collared bust to left **Obv. Legend:** FERD: DG: DVX: MAN: VI • ET: M: F: IIII. **Rev:** Full-length figure of St. Longinus to left holding pyx and lance, Roman numeral date in exergue **Rev. Legend:** AB. OMNI. MALO. DEFENDE. NOS. **Note:** Ref. V-583; Fr. 556. Prev. KM#129.

Date	Mintage	VG	F	VF	XF	Unc
MDCXVI (1616)	—	1,500	2,200	5,700	8,800	—

KM# 99 DOPPIA (2 Ducati)

Gold, 26 mm. **Ruler:** Vincenzo II **Obv:** Armored high-collared bust to left **Obv. Legend:** VINCEN. II. D. G. DVX. MANT. VII. **Rev:** Shield of 4-fold arms, with central shield of 9-fold arms, crown with FID-ES and small Mt. Olympus above, Order of The Redeemer around **Rev. Legend:** ET. MONTIS. - FERRATI. V. **Note:** Ref. Fr. 567a. Prev. KM#209.

Date	Mintage	VG	F	VF	XF	Unc
ND(1626-27	—	1,900	3,750	7,500	13,500	—
1627	—	1,900	3,750	7,500	13,500	—

KM# 118 DOPPIA (2 Ducati)

6.5800 g., Gold, 27-28 mm. **Ruler:** Carlo I **Obv:** Armored high-collared bust to right **Obv. Legend:** CAROLVS. I. D. G. DVX. MANT. **Rev:** Shield of 4-fold arms, with central shield of 9-fold arms, crown and small Mt. Olympus dividing FID - ES above, Order of The Redeemer around **Rev. Legend:** ET. MONTIS - FERRATI. ETC. **Note:** Ref. V-643; Fr. 573. Prev. KM#262.

Date	Mintage	VG	F	VF	XF	Unc
ND(1627-37)	—	1,900	3,750	7,500	13,500	—

KM# 160 DOPPIA (2 Ducati)

6.5000 g., Gold, 28 mm. **Ruler:** Carlo II under regency of Maria **Obv:** Two accolated busts to left **Obv. Legend:** MARIA. ET. CAR. II. D. G. D. MAN. ET. M. F. ET. C. **Rev:** Crowned shield of 4-fold arms, with central shield of 9-fold arms, in baroque frame **Rev. Legend:** ET. MONTIS. FERRATI. **Note:** Ref. V-678c. Prev. KM#282.

Date	Mintage	VG	F	VF	XF	Unc
ND(1637-47) Rare	—	—	—	—	—	—

KM# 181 DOPPIA (2 Ducati)

6.4400 g., Gold, 28-29 mm. **Ruler:** Carlo II **Obv:** Armored bust to left **Obv. Legend:** CAROLVS. II. D. G. DVX. MAN. **Rev:** Shield of 4-fold arms, with central shield of 9-fold arms, in baroque frame, crown with FIDES and small Mt. Olympus above, Order of The Redeemer around **Rev. Legend:** ET. MONTIS. - FERRATI. ET. C. **Note:** Ref. V-688; Fr. 583. Prev. KM#323.

Date	Mintage	VG	F	VF	XF	Unc
ND(1647-65) Rare	—	—	—	—	—	—

KM# 13 2 DOPPIE (4 Ducati)

Gold Weight varies: 12.88-13.08g., 30 mm. **Ruler:** Francesco IV **Obv:** Armored high-collared bust to right, date below shoulder **Obv. Legend:** FRAN. IIII. D. G. DVX. MANTVA. V. **Rev:** Shield of 4-fold arms, with central shield of 9-fold arms, crown with FI-DES and small Mt. Olympus above **Rev. Legend:** ET. MONTIS - FERRAT. III. **Note:** Ref. V-561; Fr. 548. Prev. KM#87.

Date	Mintage	VG	F	VF	XF	Unc
1612	—	2,650	5,300	13,500	24,000	—

KM# 39 2 DOPPIE (4 Ducati)

Gold, 26-27 mm. **Ruler:** Ferdinando **Obv:** Armored high-collared bust to left **Obv. Legend:** FERDINAN. D. G. DVX. MANT. VI. **Rev:** Shield of 4-fold arms, with central shield of 9-fold arms, crown with FID-ES and small Mt. Olympus above, Order of The Redeemer around **Rev. Legend:** ET. MONTIS. - FERRATI. IV. **Note:** Ref. Fr. 560. Prev. KM#93.

Date	Mintage	VG	F	VF	XF	Unc
ND(1612-26) CT	—	1,550	3,250	7,500	13,000	—

KM# 40 2 DOPPIE (4 Ducati)

Gold Weight varies: 13.00-13.03g., 29-30 mm. **Ruler:** Ferdinando **Obv:** Armored high-collared bust to right **Obv. Legend:** FERD. D. G. DVX. MAN. VI. ET. M. F. IIII. **Rev:** Full-length facing figure of St. Longinus holding pyx and lance **Rev. Legend:** AB. OMNI. MALO. D - EFENDE. NOS. **Note:** Ref. V-579. Prev. KM#89.

Date	Mintage	VG	F	VF	XF	Unc
ND(1612-26)	—	3,250	4,400	10,000	14,000	—

KM# 41 2 DOPPIE (4 Ducati)

Gold Weight varies: 13.00-13.07g., 30-31 mm. **Ruler:** Ferdinando **Obv:** Armored high-collared bust to right **Obv. Legend:** FERDIN. DG - DVX. MANT. VI. **Rev:** Shield of 4-fold arms, with central shield of 9-fold arms, in baroque frame, crown with FID-ES and small Mt. Olympus above, Order of The Redeemer around **Rev. Legend:** ET. MONTIS - FERRATI. IV. **Note:** Ref. V-580; Fr. 560. Prev. KM#91.

Date	Mintage	VG	F	VF	XF	Unc
ND(1612-26)	—	1,250	1,900	4,800	6,600	—

KM# 53 2 DOPPIE (4 Ducati)

Gold Weight varies: 12.60-13.12g., 29-30 mm. **Ruler:** Ferdinando **Obv:** Bust to left wearing cardinal's robes and biretta, GASP M F below **Obv. Legend:** FER. CAR. D. G. DVX. M. VI. ET. M. F. IIII. **Rev:** Two angels holding up large pyx, Roman numeral date in exergue **Rev. Legend:** NIHIL ISTO TRISTE RECEPTIO. **Note:** Ref. V-577; Fr. 553. Prev. KM#109.

Date	Mintage	VG	F	VF	XF	Unc
MDXCIII (1613)	—	2,000	4,800	6,800	14,500	—
MDCXIIII (1614)	—	1,750	4,400	6,400	13,500	—
MDCXV (1615)	—	1,750	4,400	6,400	13,500	—
MDCXIIIII (1615)	—	1,750	4,400	6,400	13,500	—

KM# 54 2 DOPPIE (4 Ducati)

10.9000 g., Gold, 30-31 mm. **Ruler:** Ferdinando **Obv:** Shield of 4-fold arms, with central shield of 9-fold arms, crown with FID-ES and small Mt. Olympus above, Order of The Redeemer around **Obv. Legend:** FERD. D. G. DVX. MAN. VI. ET. MON. FER. IIII. **Rev:** St. Andrew at left with cross, date below feet, consigning pyx to St. Longinus kneeling at right, arabesque in exergue **Rev. Legend:** NIHIL - ISTO - TRISTE - RECEPTO. **Note:** Ref. V-578; Fr. 563. Prev. KM#111.

Date	Mintage	VG	F	VF	XF	Unc
1613 Rare	—	—	—	—	—	—

KM# 100 2 DOPPIE (4 Ducati)

Gold Weight varies: 13.00-13.05g., 29 mm. **Ruler:** Vincenzo II **Obv:** Armored high-collared bust to left, date below, where present **Obv. Legend:** VINCEN. II. D. G. DVX. MANT. VII. **Rev:** Shield of 4-fold arms, with central shield of 9-fold arms, in baroque frame, crown with FID-ES and small Mt. Olympus above, Order of The Redeemer around **Rev. Legend:** ET. MONTIS - FERRATI. V. **Note:** Ref. V-620; Fr. 567. Prev. KM#211.

Date	Mintage	VG	F	VF	XF	Unc
ND(1626-27)	—	4,250	6,600	14,500	21,000	—
1627	—	4,400	7,900	12,000	30,000	—

KM# 146 2 DOPPIE (4 Ducati)

Gold Weight varies: 12.96-13.06g., 31 mm. **Ruler:** Carlo I **Obv:** Armored high-collared bust to right, date below **Obv. Legend:** CAROLVS. I. D. G. DVX. MANT. **Rev:** Shield of 4-fold arms, with central shield of 9-fold arms, in baroque frame, crown with FID-ES and small Mt. Olympus above, Order of The Redeemer around **Rev. Legend:** ET. MONTIS - FERRATI. ETC. **Note:** Ref. V-642; Fr. 572. Prev. KM#251.

Date	Mintage	VG	F	VF	XF	Unc
1629	—	3,800	5,500	11,000	16,500	—
1631	—	3,800	5,500	11,000	16,500	—
1636	—	2,650	6,100	9,800	15,000	—

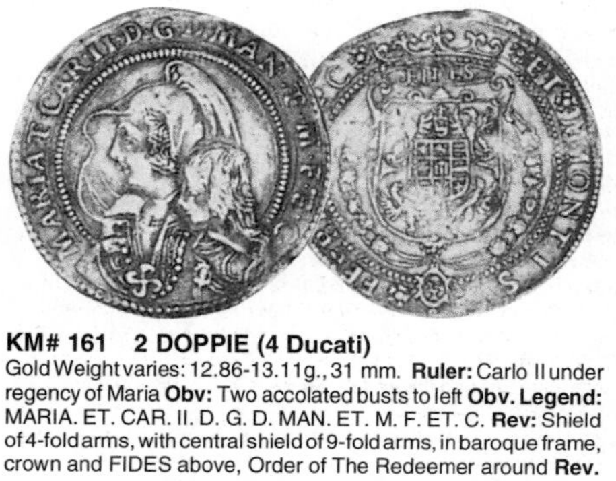

KM# 161 2 DOPPIE (4 Ducati)

Gold Weight varies: 12.86-13.11g., 31 mm. **Ruler:** Carlo II under regency of Maria **Obv:** Two accolated busts to left **Obv. Legend:** MARIA. ET. CAR. II. D. G. D. MAN. ET. M. F. ET. C. **Rev:** Shield of 4-fold arms, with central shield of 9-fold arms, in baroque frame, crown and FIDES above, Order of The Redeemer around **Rev. Legend:** ET. MONTIS - FERRATI. ET. C. **Note:** Ref. V-678a; Fr. 578. Prev. KM#284.

Date	Mintage	VG	F	VF	XF	Unc
ND(1637-47)	—	2,200	5,700	12,000	18,000	—

KM# 182 2 DOPPIE (4 Ducati)

13.1000 g., Gold, 32 mm. **Ruler:** Carlo II **Obv:** Armored bust to left **Obv. Legend:** CAROLVS. II. D. G. DVX. MANTVE. **Rev:** Shield of 4-fold arms, with central shield of 9-fold arms, in baroque frame, crown with FIDES and small Mt. Olympus above, Order of The Redeemer around **Rev. Legend:** ET. MONTIS. - FERRATI. ET. C. **Note:** Ref. V-687; Fr. 582. Prev. KM#363.

Date	Mintage	VG	F	VF	XF	Unc
ND(1647-65) Rare	—	—	—	—	—	—

KM# 210 2 DOPPIE (4 Ducati)

13.0700 g., Gold, 30 mm. **Ruler:** Ferdinando Carlo under regency of Isabella Clara **Obv:** Two accolated busts to right, date below **Obv. Legend:** ISABELLA. CLARA. FERD. CAR. D. G. D. MAN. - ET. M. F. ET. C. **Rev:** Radiant sunface between clouds above and sea below, in circle **Rev. Legend:** ALTA. A. LONGE. COGNOSCIT. **Note:** Ref. V-716; Fr. 588. Prev. KM#381.

Date	Mintage	VG	F	VF	XF	Unc
1666 Rare	—	—	—	—	—	—

KM# 220 2 DOPPIE (4 Ducati)

Gold Weight varies: 13.03-13.12g., 33 mm. **Ruler:** Ferdinando Carlo **Obv:** Draped and armored bust to right **Obv. Legend:** FERDIN. CAR. D. G. DVX. MANTVÆ. **Rev:** Shield of 4-fold arms, with central shield of 9-fold arms, in baroque frame, crown and small Mt. Olympus above, Order of The Redeemer around **Rev. Legend:** M. FER. CAR. VIL. - GVASTALÆ. ET. C. **Note:** Ref. V-728; Fr. 591. Prev. KM#393.

Date	Mintage	VG	F	VF	XF	Unc
ND(1669-1707) Rare	—	—	—	—	—	—

KM# 42 4 DOPPIE (8 Ducati)

Gold Weight varies: 26.10-26.20g., 34 mm. **Ruler:** Ferdinando **Obv:** Bust to right wearing cardinal's robes and biretta **Obv. Legend:** FERD. CARD. D. G. DVX. MAN. VI. ET. M. F. IIII. **Rev:** Radiant sunface in circle **Rev. Legend:** NON. MATVATA. LVCE. **Note:** Ref. V-576; Fr. 552. Prev. KM#95.

Date	Mintage	VG	F	VF	XF	Unc
ND(1612-26)	—	6,000	8,300	22,500	33,000	—

KM# 162 4 DOPPIE (8 Ducati)

26.0500 g., Gold, 42-43 mm. **Ruler:** Carlo II under regency of Maria **Obv:** Two accolated busts to left **Obv. Legend:** MARIA. ET. CAR. II. D. G. D. MAN. ET. MON. F. ET. C. **Rev:** Madonna and Child, MANTVAE in exergue **Rev. Legend:** MARIA. MATER. GRATIÆ. PROTETRIX. NOSTRA. **Note:** Ref. V-678; Fr. 577. Prev. KM#286.

Date	Mintage	VG	F	VF	XF	Unc
ND(1637-47)	—	6,000	8,300	22,500	33,000	—

KM# 211 4 DOPPIE (8 Ducati)

26.0900 g., Gold, 38 mm. **Ruler:** Ferdinando Carlo under regency of Isabella Clara **Obv:** Two accolated busts to right, date below **Obv. Legend:** ISABELLA. CLARA. FERD. CAR. D. G. D. MAN. - ET. M. F. ET. C. **Rev:** Radiant sunface between clouds above and sea below, in circle **Rev. Legend:** ALTA. A. LONGE. COGNOSCIT. **Note:** Ref. V-715; Fr. 587. Prev. KM#383.

Date	Mintage	VG	F	VF	XF	Unc
1666 Rare	—	—	—	—	—	—

Note: Bowers and Merena Guia sale 3-88 AU realized $20,900

KM# 14 5 DOPPIE (10 Ducati)

32.7100 g., Gold, 41-42 mm. **Ruler:** Francesco IV **Obv:** Shield of 4-fold arms, with central shield of 9-fold arms, crown with FI-DES and small Mt. Olympus above, Order of The Redeemer around **Obv. Legend:** FRAN. IIII. D. G. DVX. - MAN. V. ET. MON. III. **Rev:** St. Andrew at left with cross, date below feet, consigning pyx to kneeling St. Longinus at right, value '5' in exergue **Rev. Legend:** NIHIL - ISTO - TRI - STE RECEPTO. **Note:** Ref. V-560; Fr. 547. Prev. KM#97.

Date	Mintage	VG	F	VF	XF	Unc
1612 Rare	—	—	—	—	—	—

KM# 153 5 DOPPIE (10 Ducati)
32.7000 g., Gold, 42-43 mm. **Ruler:** Carlo I **Obv:** Armored high-collared bust to right, date below **Obv. Legend:** CAROLVS. I. D. G. DVX. MAN. ET. M. F. **Rev:** Radiant sunface in Zodiac band with other symbols, stars around, clouds and earth below **Rev. Legend:** NEC. RETROGRADIOR. NEC. DEVIO. **Note:** Ref. V-641; Fr. 571. Prev. KM#270.

Date	Mintage	VG	F	VF	XF	Unc
1636 Rare	—	—	—	—	—	—

KM# 163 5 DOPPIE (10 Ducati)
32.7000 g., Gold, 42-43 mm. **Ruler:** Carlo II under regency of Maria **Obv:** Two accolated busts to left **Obv. Legend:** MARIA. ET. CAR. II. D. G. D. MAN. ET. MON. F. ET. C. **Rev:** Madonna and Child, MANTVAE in exergue **Rev. Legend:** MARIA. MATER. GRATIÆ. PROTETRIX. NOSTRA. **Note:** Ref. V-677; Fr. 576. Prev. KM#285.

Date	Mintage	VG	F	VF	XF	Unc
ND(1637-47) Rare	—	—	—	—	—	—

KM# 186 5 DOPPIE (10 Ducati)
33.0000 g., Gold, 45 mm. **Ruler:** Carlo II **Obv:** Large armored bust to left **Obv. Legend:** CAROLVS. II. D. G. DVX. MAN. ET. M. F. ET. C. **Rev:** Radiant sun above clouds, which are pouring rain below, all in oval baroque frame, date divided below **Rev. Legend:** TV. AVTEM. PERMANES. **Note:** Ref. V-686. Prev. KM#329.

Date	Mintage	VG	F	VF	XF	Unc
1649 Rare	—	—	—	—	—	—

KM# 214 5 DOPPIE (10 Ducati)
32.1000 g., Gold, 42-43 mm. **Ruler:** Ferdinando Carlo under regency of Isabella Clara **Obv:** Two accolated busts to right, date below **Obv. Legend:** ISABELLA. CLARA. FERD. CAR. D. G. D. MAN. - ET. M. F. ET. C. **Rev:** Radiant sunface between clouds above and sea below, in circle **Rev. Legend:** ALTA. A. LONGE. COGNOSCIT. **Note:** Ref. V-714; Fr. 586. Prev. KM#385.

Date	Mintage	VG	F	VF	XF	Unc
1666 Rare	—	—	—	—	—	—

KM# 55 6 DOPPIE (12 Ducati)
Gold Weight varies: 38.82-39.33g., 42-43 mm. **Ruler:** Ferdinando **Obv:** Bust to right wearing cardinal's robes and biretta, Arabic or Roman numeral date below **Obv. Legend:** FERD. CARD. D. G. DVX. MAN. VI. ET. M. F. IIII. **Rev:** Radiant sunface in circle **Rev. Legend:** NON. MVTVATA. LVCE. **Note:** Ref. V-571; Fr. 551. Prev. KM#113.

Date	Mintage	VG	F	VF	XF	Unc
1613 Rare	—	—	—	—	—	—
MDCXIV (1614) Rare	—	—	—	—	—	—
MDCXV (1615) Rare	—	—	—	—	—	—

KM# 61 6 DOPPIE (12 Ducati)
39.1300 g., Gold, 43 mm. **Ruler:** Ferdinando **Obv:** Bust to right wearing cardinal's robes and biretta, holding scepter over right shoulder, Roman numeral date below **Obv. Legend:** FERDINANDVS. - S. R. E. D. CARD. D. G. DVX. **Rev:** Seated Madonna with Child between 2 vine branches growing from bottom **Rev. Legend:** TIT. S. M. IN PORTICV. S. R. E. DIAC. CARD. **Note:** Ref. V-572; Fr. 558. Prev. KM#572.

Date	Mintage	VG	F	VF	XF	Unc
MDCXIIII (1614) Rare	—	—	—	—	—	—

KM# 70 6 DOPPIE (12 Ducati)
39.2600 g., Gold, 42-43 mm. **Ruler:** Ferdinando **Obv:** Armored high-collared bust to right, MANTVÆ and date below **Obv. Legend:** FERDINANDVS. D. G. DVX. MAN. VI. **Rev:** Shield of 4-fold arms, with central shield of 9-fold arms, in baroque frame, crown with FID-ES and small Mt. Olympus above, Order of The Redeemer around **Rev. Legend:** ET. MONTIS - FERRATI. IV. **Note:** Ref. V-573; Fr. 559. Prev. KM#131.

Date	Mintage	VG	F	VF	XF	Unc
1616 Rare	—	—	—	—	—	—

KM# 81 6 DOPPIE (12 Ducati)
39.7100 g., Gold, 40 mm. **Ruler:** Ferdinando **Obv:** 4-fold arms, eagle in each quarter, in quatrefoil with pointed and indented sides, date in margin at top **Obv. Legend:** FERDINANDVS. D. G. DVX. MANT. VI. **Rev:** Shield of 9-fold arms, crown with FID-ES and small Mt. Olympus above, Order of The Redeemer around **Rev. Legend:** ET. MONTIS - FERRATI. IV. **Note:** Ref. V-575; Fr. 564. Prev. KM#148.

Date	Mintage	VG	F	VF	XF	Unc
1620 Rare	—	—	—	—	—	—

KM# 105 6 DOPPIE (12 Ducati)
39.2000 g., Gold, 42 mm. **Ruler:** Vincenzo II **Obv:** Armored high-collared bust to left, date below **Obv. Legend:** VINCEN. II. D. G. DVX. MANT. VII. ET. M. F. V. **Rev:** Dog standing to left in circle **Rev. Legend:** FERIS. TANTVM. INFENSVS. **Note:** Ref. V-619; Fr. 566a.

Date	Mintage	VG	F	VF	XF	Unc
1627 Rare	—	—	—	—	—	—

KM# 121 6 DOPPIE (12 Ducati)
38.2400 g., Gold, 42-43 mm. **Ruler:** Carlo I **Obv:** Armored high-collared bust to right, date below **Obv. Legend:** CAROLVS. I. D.G. DVX. MAN. ET. M. F. ET. C. **Rev:** Radiant sunface in Zodiac band with other symbols, stars around, clouds and earth below **Rev. Legend:** NEC. RETROGRADIOR. NEC. DEVIO. **Note:** Ref. V-640; Fr. 570. Prev. KM#215.

Date	Mintage	VG	F	VF	XF	Unc
1628 Rare	—	—	—	—	—	—
1632 Rare	—	—	—	—	—	—

KM# 164 6 DOPPIE (12 Ducati)
Gold Weight varies: 39.00-39.20g., 41-42 mm. **Ruler:** Carlo II under regency of Maria **Obv:** Two accolated busts to left **Obv. Legend:** MARIA ET CAR II D G D MAN ET MON F ETC **Rev:** Madonna and Child, MANTVAE in exergue **Rev. Legend:** MARIA MATER GRATIAE PROTECTRIX NOSTRA MANTVAE **Note:** Ref. V-676. Prev. KM#290.

Date	Mintage	VG	F	VF	XF	Unc
ND(1637-47) Rare	—	—	—	—	—	—

KM# 185 6 DOPPIE (12 Ducati)
Gold Weight varies: 39.10-39.25g., 45 mm. **Ruler:** Carlo II **Obv:** Large armored bust to left **Obv. Legend:** CAROLVS. II. D. G. DVX. MAN. ET. M. F. ET. C. **Rev:** Radiant sun above clouds, which are pouring rain below, all in oval baroque frame, date divided below **Rev. Legend:** TV. AVTEM. PERMANES. **Note:** Ref. V-685; Fr. 581. Prev. KM#331.

Date	Mintage	VG	F	VF	XF	Unc
1649 Rare	—	—	—	—	—	—
1669 Error; rare	—	—	—	—	—	—

KM# 212 6 DOPPIE (12 Ducati)
39.3200 g., Gold, 42-43 mm. **Ruler:** Ferdinando Carlo under regency of Isabella Clara **Obv:** Two accolated busts to right, date below **Obv. Legend:** ISABELLA. CLARA. FERD. CAR. D. G. D. MAN. ET. M. F. ET. C. **Rev:** Radiant sunface between clouds above and sea below, in circle **Rev. Legend:** ALTA. A. LONGE. COGNOSCIT. **Note:** Ref. V-713; Fr. 585. Prev. KM#389.

Date	Mintage	VG	F	VF	XF	Unc
1666 Rare	—	—	—	—	—	—

KM# 213 6 DOPPIE (12 Ducati)
39.2300 g., Gold, 42 mm. **Ruler:** Ferdinando Carlo under regency of Isabella Clara **Obv:** Two accolated busts to right, date below **Obv. Legend:** ISABELLA. CLARA. FERD. CAR. D. G. D. MAN. - ET. M. F. ET. C. **Rev:** Madonna and Child, MANTVAE in exergue **Rev. Legend:** MARIA. MATER. GRATIÆ. PROTETRIX. NOSTRA. **Note:** Ref. V-712; Fr. 589. Prev. KM#387.

Date	Mintage	VG	F	VF	XF	Unc
1666 Rare	—	—	—	—	—	—

KM# 122 8 DOPPIE (16 Ducati)
52.4300 g., Gold, 42-43 mm. **Ruler:** Carlo I **Obv:** Armored high-collared bust to right, date below **Obv. Legend:** CAROLVS. I. G. D. DVX. MAN. ET. M. F. ET. C. **Rev:** Radiant sunface in Zodiac band with other symbols, stars around, clouds and earth below **Rev. Legend:** NEC. RETROGRADIOR. NEC. DEVIO. **Note:** Ref. V-639; Fr. 569. Prev. KM#217.

Date	Mintage	VG	F	VF	XF	Unc
1628 Rare	—	—	—	—	—	—

KM# 165 8 DOPPIE (16 Ducati)
52.2400 g., Gold, 42-43 mm. **Ruler:** Carlo II under regency of Maria **Obv:** Two accolated busts to left **Obv. Legend:** MARIA. ET. CAR. II. D. G. D. MAN. ET. MON. F. ET. C. **Rev:** Madonna and Child, MANTVAE in exergue **Rev. Legend:** MARIA. MATER. GRATIÆ. PROTETRIX. NOSTRA. **Note:** Ref. V-675; Fr. 575. Prev. KM#292.

Date	Mintage	VG	F	VF	XF	Unc
ND(1637-47) Rare	—	—	—	—	—	—

KM# 229 8 DOPPIE (16 Ducati)
52.4200 g., Gold, 42-43 mm. **Ruler:** Ferdinando Carlo **Obv:** Bust to right **Obv. Legend:** FERDINANDVS. CAR. D. G. DVX. MANTVÆ. MON. FER. ET. C. **Rev:** Radiant sun rising over horizon, clouds and eagle in flight above, date in margin at bottom **Rev. Legend:** QVAE - MAIOR - ORIGO. **Note:** Ref. V-727; Fr. 590. Prev. KM#410.

Date	Mintage	VG	F	VF	XF	Unc
1676 Rare	—	—	—	—	—	—

KM# 76 10 DOPPIE (20 Ducati)
65.1600 g., Gold, 43 mm. **Ruler:** Ferdinando **Obv:** Armored high-collared bust to right, date below **Obv. Legend:** FERD. D. G. DVX. MANT. VI. ET. MONFER. IV. **Rev:** Radiant sunface in circle **Rev. Legend:** NON. MVTVATA. LVCE. **Note:** Ref. V-574; Fr. 550. Prev. KM#133.

Date	Mintage	VG	F	VF	XF	Unc
1617 CT Rare	—	—	—	—	—	—

KM# 62 12 DOPPIE (24 Ducati)
78.8700 g., Gold, 43 mm. **Ruler:** Ferdinando **Obv:** Bust to right wearing cardinal's robes and biretta, holding scepter over right shoulder, Roman numeral date below **Obv. Legend:** FERDINANDVS. - S. R. E. D. CARD. D. G. DVX. **Rev:** Seated Madonna with Child between 2 vine branches growing from bottom **Rev. Legend:** TIT. S. M. IN PORTICV. S. R. E. DIAC. CARD. **Note:** Ref. V-570; Fr. 557. Prev. KM#123.

Date	Mintage	VG	F	VF	XF	Unc
MDCXIIII (1614) Rare	—	—	—	—	—	—

KM# 215 12 DOPPIE (24 Ducati)
71.9000 g., Gold, 42-43 mm. **Ruler:** Ferdinando Carlo under regency of Isabella Clara **Obv:** Two accolated busts to right, date below **Obv. Legend:** ISABELLA. CLARA. FERD. CAR. D. G. D. MAN. - ET. M. F. ET. C. **Rev:** Radiant sunface between clouds above and sea below, in circle **Rev. Legend:** ALTA. A. LONGE. COGNOSCIT. **Note:** Ref. V-711; Fr. 584. Prev. KM#391.

Date	Mintage	VG	F	VF	XF	Unc
1666 Rare	—	—	—	—	—	—

SIEGE COINAGE

1629-1630

Besieged by Austrian and Spanish Forces

KM# 124 2 SOLDI (Soldone)
Copper Or Billon Weight varies: 1.52-2.13g., 17-18 mm. **Obv:** Pyx in partial circle **Obv. Legend:** TABER. SA - NG. CRIS. **Rev:** Value 'II' in wreath **Note:** Ref. V-674. Prev. KM#223.

Date	Mintage	VG	F	VF	XF	Unc
ND(1629-30)	—	25.00	55.00	115	200	—

KM# 125 4 SOLDI
Billon Weight varies: 1.54-2.26g., 20-21 mm. **Obv:** Shield of 4-fold arms, crown and small Mt. Olympus above, date at end of legend, where present **Obv. Legend:** MANT. ANNO. SALVTIS. **Rev:** Intertwined reversed C and normal G monogram, value 'IIII' below, all in wreath, no legend **Note:** Ref. V-672. Prev. KM#219, as a Cinquinta.

Date	Mintage	VG	F	VF	XF	Unc
ND(1629-30)	—	22.00	45.00	95.00	200	—
1629	—	65.00	130	250	400	—

KM# 126 4 SOLDI
Copper Weight varies: 2.86-3.90g., 21-22 mm. **Obv:** Large pyx in partial circle **Obv. Legend:** TABER. SA - NG. CHRIS. **Rev:** Value 'II.II' in wreath, no legend **Note:** Ref. V-673. Prev. KM#221, as a Cinquinta.

Date	Mintage	VG	F	VF	XF	Unc
ND(1629-30)	—	18.00	35.00	65.00	125	—

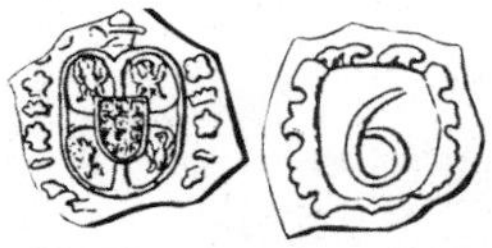

KM# 127 6 SOLDI
2.1000 g., Lead, 17 mm. **Obv:** Shield of 4-fold arms, with central shield of 9-fold arms, crown and small Mt. Olympus above, Order of The Redeemer around, no legend **Rev:** Value '6' in oval baroque frame, no legend **Note:** Ref. V-670. Prev. KM#225.

Date	Mintage	VG	F	VF	XF	Unc
ND(1629-30)	—	60.00	110	225	375	—

KM# 128 6 SOLDI
2.2900 g., Lead, 20 mm. **Obv:** Crowned shield of 4-fold arms, with central shield of 9-fold arms **Obv. Legend:** OBSE - PEOS. **Rev:** Value '6' in rectangular baroque frame with rounded corners, no legend **Note:** Ref. V-671.

Date	Mintage	VG	F	VF	XF	Unc
ND(1629-30)	—	50.00	100	200	375	—

KM# 129 7 SOLDI
Lead Weight varies: 4.96-6.91g., 22 mm. **Obv:** Crowned M in partial multilobe with 5 double arches, value '7' in exergue, no legend **Rev:** Seated figure of St. Anselm facing left, holding crozier **Rev. Legend:** SANCTVS - ANSELMVS. **Note:** Ref. V-668. Prev. KM#227.

Date	Mintage	VG	F	VF	XF	Unc
ND(1629-30)	—	50.00	100	200	375	—

KM# 130 7 SOLDI
2.3400 g., Lead, 17 mm. **Obv:** Value '7' in oval baroque frame, no legend **Rev:** Seated figure of St. Anselm facing left, holding crozier **Rev. Legend:** SANCTVS. - ANSELMVS. **Note:** Ref. V-669.

Date	Mintage	VG	F	VF	XF	Unc
ND(1629-30)	—	50.00	100	200	375	—

KM# 133 1/4 SCUDO
Silver Weight varies: 6.49-7.48g., 31 mm. **Obv:** Crowned shield of 4-fold arms in baroque frame, date at end of legend **Obv. Legend:** MANTVÆ. ANNO. SALVTIS. **Rev:** Sunflower bending toward sun in upper left, all in circle, all in wreath, value '40' in margin at bottom, no legend **Note:** Ref. V-667. Prev. KM#233. 40 Soldi.

Date	Mintage	VG	F	VF	XF	Unc
1629	—	750	1,000	2,500	3,500	—

KM# 135 1/2 SCUDO (80 Soldi)
Billon Weight varies: 9.77-9.97g., 31 mm. **Obv:** Full-length facing figure of St. Andrew holding cross and pyx, MAN. OBSES. in exergue **Obv. Legend:** NIHIL. ISTO - T - R - ISTE RECEPTO. **Rev:** Crucible within flames, in circle **Rev. Legend:** DOMINE. PROBASTI. ME. ET. COGNOVISTI. ME. **Note:** Ref. V-665. Prev. KM#237, as 60 Soldi.

Date	Mintage	VG	F	VF	XF	Unc
ND(1629-30)	—	200	325	400	750	—
1630	—	375	550	1,100	1,850	—

KM# 134 1/2 SCUDO (80 Soldi)
Silver Or Billon Weight varies: 11.94-13.01g., 33 mm. **Obv:** Full-length facing figure of St. Andrew holding cross and pyx, MANTVÆ in exergue **Obv. Legend:** NIHIL(.) ISTO - T(-)R(-)ISTE RECEPTO. **Rev:** Crucible within flames, in circle **Rev. Legend:** DOMINE. PROBASTI. ME. ET. COGNOVISTI. ME. **Note:** Ref. V-664. Prev. KM#235, as 60 Soldi. Varieties exist.

Date	Mintage	VG	F	VF	XF	Unc
ND(1629-30)	—	200	325	400	750	—

KM# 136 1/2 SCUDO (80 Soldi)
Silver Or Billon Weight varies: 14.77-15.00g., 35-36 mm. **Obv:** Crowned shield of 4-fold arms in baroque frame, date at end of legend **Obv. Legend:** MANTVÆ. ANNO. SALVTIS. **Rev:** Sunflower bending toward sun in upper left, in beaded circle within wreath, value '80' in margin at bottom, no legend **Note:** Ref. V-666. Prev. KM#229, 237a.

Date	Mintage	VG	F	VF	XF	Unc
1629	—	450	675	1,650	2,750	—

KM# 138 SCUDO
Silver Weight varies: 21.87-26.46g., 40 mm. **Obv:** Full-length facing figure of St. Andrew, date below feet, where present, holding cross and pyx, MANT(VÆ) in exergue **Obv. Legend:** NIHIL - ISTO - T - R - ISTE RECEPTO. **Rev:** Crucible within flames, in circle **Rev. Legend:** DOMINE. PROBASTI. ME. ET. COGNOVISTI. ME. **Note:** Ref. V-660; Dav. 3956. Prev. KM#239.

Date	Mintage	VG	F	VF	XF	Unc
ND(1629-30)	—	600	900	2,250	3,250	—
1629	—	2,000	4,000	6,500	11,000	—

KM# 139 SCUDO
Billon Weight varies: 17.52-21.29g., 41 mm. **Obv:** Full-length facing figure of St. Andrew holding cross and pyx, date below feet, where present, MAN • OBSES. in exergue **Obv. Legend:** NIHIL. ISTO - T - R - ISTE RECEPTO. **Rev:** Crucible within flames, in circle **Rev. Legend:** DOMINE. PROBASTI. ME. ET. COGNOVISTI. ME. **Note:** Ref. V-661; Dav. 3957. Prev. KM#260.

Date	Mintage	VG	F	VF	XF	Unc
ND(1629-30)	—	600	900	2,250	3,250	—
1630	—	750	1,000	2,500	3,500	—

KM# 140 SCUDO (160 Soldi)
Silver Or Billon Weight varies: 28,49-29.42g., 41-42 mm. **Obv:** Crowned shield of 4-fold arms in baroque frame, date at end of legend **Obv. Legend:** MANTVÆ. ANNO. SALVTIS. **Rev:** Sunflower bending toward sun in upper left, all in circle within wreath, value '160' in margin at bottom, no legend **Note:** Ref. V-662; Dav. 3958. Prev. KM#231.

Date	Mintage	VG	F	VF	XF	Unc
1629	—	500	700	1,650	2,750	—

Note: Ira & Larry Goldberg Coins & Collectibles Auction 46 - The Millennia Collection, 5-08, AU-55 realized $9,500

KM# 141 SCUDO (160 Soldi)
Silver Weight varies: 28.40-29.42g., 41-42 mm. **Obv:** Crowned shield of 4-fold arms in baroque frame, IN BELLO in small letters inside curve of crown, date at end of legend **Obv. Legend:** MANTVÆ. ANNO. SALVTIS. **Rev:** Sunflower bending toward sun in upper left, all in circle within wreath, value '160' in margin at bottom, no legend **Note:** Ref. V-662/1.

Date	Mintage	VG	F	VF	XF	Unc
1629	—	800	1,100	2,750	4,250	—

KM# 142 SCUDO D'ORO
2.5000 g., Gold **Obv:** St. Andrew holding pyx **Obv. Legend:** NIHL ISTO TRISTE RECEPTO **Note:** Prev. KM#243.

Date	Mintage	VG	F	VF	XF	Unc
ND(1629) Rare	—	—	—	—	—	—

KM# 143 SCUDO D'ORO
2.5000 g., Gold **Rev:** Crucible within flames **Rev. Legend:** DOMINE. PROBASTI. ME. ET. COGNOVISTI. ME. **Note:** Prev. KM#245.

Date	Mintage	VG	F	VF	XF	Unc
ND(1629) Rare	—	—	—	—	—	—

KM# 144 SCUDO D'ORO
2.5000 g., Gold **Obv:** Crowned shield of 4-fold arms, IN BELLO in small letters within curve of crown **Obv. Legend:** MANTVÆ. ANNO. SALTIS. **Note:** Prev. KM#247.

Date	Mintage	VG	F	VF	XF	Unc
1629 Rare	—	—	—	—	—	—

PATTERNS

Including off metal strikes

KM#	Date	Mintage	Identification	Mkt Val
Pn1	MDCXIIII (1614)	—	Ducatone. Copper. KM#50.	—

MASEGRA

The castle of Masegra was located in the vicinity of Sondrio, north of Bergamo, in the foothills of the Alps. The place was a fief of the Beccaria, a family of possible Germanic origins. They struck a few small copper coins during the 17th century.

Reference: V = Alberto Varesi, ***Monete Italiane Regionali: Lombardia, Zecche Minori***, Pavia, 1995.

FORTRESS

STANDARD COINAGE

KM# 1 1/2 QUATTRINO (Mezzo Quattrino)
0.4000 g., Copper, 9.5 mm. **Obv:** 2-line inscription **Obv. Inscription:** 1/2 / QVATR. **Rev:** 3-line inscription **Rev. Inscription:** DI / BECCA / RIA. **Note:** Ref. V-778.

Date	Mintage	VG	F	VF	XF	Unc
ND(17th c.)	—	150	275	575	825	—

KM# 2 QUATTRINO
Copper Weight varies: 0.56-0.67g., 11 mm. **Obv:** 3-line inscription **Obv. Inscription:** 1 / QVATRI / NO **Rev:** 3-line inscription **Rev. Inscription:** DI / BECCA / RIA **Note:** Ref. V-777.

Date	Mintage	VG	F	VF	XF	Unc
ND(17th c.)	—	150	275	575	825	—

MASSA DI LUNIGIANO

Massa was a city north of Pisa and Lucca. In 1559 Ferdinand I had given the mint right to Prince Alberico I Cybo Malaspina, who subsequently inherited the marquisate of Massa thru his mother. Father, son and grandson coined until 1667.

RULERS
Alberico I Cybo Malaspina, prince of Massa, 1568-1623
Carlo I Cybo Malaspina, 1623-1662
Alberico II Cybo Malaspina, 1662-1690

MARQUISATE

STANDARD COINAGE

KM# 7 QUATTRINO
0.5600 g., Copper **Obv:** Cybo arms **Rev:** Pyramid

Date	Mintage	VG	F	VF	XF	Unc
1616	—	30.00	60.00	120	—	—
1617	—	30.00	60.00	120	—	—
ND	—	30.00	60.00	120	—	—

KM# 8 QUATTRINO
0.5600 g., Copper **Rev:** Thornbush

Date	Mintage	VG	F	VF	XF	Unc
ND	—	30.00	60.00	120	—	—

KM# 9 CRAZIA
0.7300 g., Silver **Obv:** Cybo arms **Rev:** .S./.R.I.ET./MASS./.P.I.

Date	Mintage	VG	F	VF	XF	Unc
ND	—	—	—	—	—	—

KM# 10 DUETTO
Copper **Obv:** Cybo arms **Rev:** Thornbush

Date	Mintage	VG	F	VF	XF	Unc
1616	—	35.00	75.00	150	—	—

KM# 11 DUETTO
Copper **Rev:** St. Peter **Note:** Weight varies: 1.09-1.50 grams.

Date	Mintage	VG	F	VF	XF	Unc
ND	—	35.00	75.00	150	—	—

KM# 12 1/2 BOLOGNINO
0.3500 g., Silver **Obv:** Cybo arms **Rev:** Cross

Date	Mintage	VG	F	VF	XF	Unc
ND	—	—	—	—	—	—

KM# 13 BOLOGNINO (2 Soldi)
Silver **Obv:** Cybo arms **Rev:** Cross in cartouche **Note:** Weight varies: 0.60-0.95 grams.

Date	Mintage	VG	F	VF	XF	Unc
ND	—	175	350	600	—	—

KM# 40 7 BOLOGNINI
2.1300 g., Silver **Obv:** Bust right, VII or 7 below **Rev:** Crowned Cybo arms

Date	Mintage	VG	F	VF	XF	Unc
1666	—	—	—	—	—	—
1667	—	350	900	2,250	4,500	—

KM# 41 7 BOLOGNINI
2.1300 g., Silver **Obv:** Facing head

Date	Mintage	VG	F	VF	XF	Unc
1666 Rare	—	—	—	—	—	—

KM# 35 8 BOLOGNINI
2.2700 g., Silver **Obv:** Bust right **Rev:** Peacock

Date	Mintage	VG	F	VF	XF	Unc
1662	—	—	—	—	—	—

KM# 36 8 BOLOGNINI
2.2700 g., Silver

Date	Mintage	VG	F	VF	XF	Unc
1662	—	45.00	100	275	450	—
1663	—	45.00	100	275	450	—

KM# 38 8 BOLOGNINI
2.2700 g., Silver **Obv:** 8 below bust

Date	Mintage	VG	F	VF	XF	Unc
1664	—	35.00	90.00	225	400	—
1665	—	35.00	90.00	225	400	—

KM# 39 8 BOLOGNINI
2.2700 g., Silver **Obv:** Bust right **Obv. Legend:** ...DVX...

Date	Mintage	VG	F	VF	XF	Unc
1664	—	45.00	100	275	450	—
1665	—	45.00	100	275	450	—
1666	—	45.00	100	275	450	—

KM# 37 16 BOLOGNINI
4.8900 g., Silver **Obv:** Bust right, 16 below **Rev:** Similar to 8 Bolognini, KM#36

Date	Mintage	VG	F	VF	XF	Unc
1663	—	100	200	400	650	—
1664	—	100	200	400	650	—

KM# 25 CERVIA
2.3100 g., Silver **Obv:** Bust right **Rev:** Stag left

Date	Mintage	VG	F	VF	XF	Unc
1617 Rare	—	—	—	—	—	—
1618 Rare	—	—	—	—	—	—

KM# 26 4 CERVIA
5.3400 g., Silver **Obv:** Bust right, date below **Rev:** St. Peter standing

Date	Mintage	VG	F	VF	XF	Unc
1618	—	—	—	—	—	—

KM# 14 PAOLA
2.5400 g., Silver **Obv:** Arms **Rev:** St. Peter

Date	Mintage	VG	F	VF	XF	Unc
ND	—	700	1,200	2,250	—	—

KM# 15 PAOLA
2.5400 g., Silver **Obv:** Cybo arms **Rev:** Crowned double eagle

Date	Mintage	VG	F	VF	XF	Unc
ND	—	500	900	1,850	—	—

KM# 16 1/4 LIRA
Silver **Obv:** Cybo arms **Rev:** Cross in circle **Note:** Weight varies: 2.70-3.21 grams.

Date	Mintage	VG	F	VF	XF	Unc
ND	—	850	1,400	2,500	—	—

KM# 17 TESTONE (2 Lire - 20 Bolognini)
9.4000 g., Silver **Obv:** Bust right **Rev:** Legend, burning barrel **Rev. Legend:** VON. GVETTEN: IN . PESSER.

Date	Mintage	VG	F	VF	XF	Unc
ND Rare	—	—	—	—	—	—

KM# 18 80 SOLDI (Tallero)
Billon **Obv:** Knight behind shield **Rev:** Rampant lion **Rev. Legend:** ...SOL * LXXX **Note:** Dav. #A3973.

Date	Mintage	Good	VG	F	VF	XF
ND	—	575	1,200	2,700	4,500	—

KM# 19 80 SOLDI (Tallero)
Billon **Rev:** Rampant lion **Rev. Legend:** ...SOLD. 80 **Note:** Dav. #B3973.

Date	Mintage	Good	VG	F	VF	XF
ND	—	625	1,250	2,800	4,700	—

KM# 5 DUCATONE
32.1600 g., Silver **Obv:** Bust right **Rev:** Crowned double eagle with arms **Note:** Dav. #3971.

Date	Mintage	Good	VG	F	VF	XF
1601 Rare	—	—	—	—	—	—

Note: Numismatica Ars Classica Auction 35, XF, 12-06 realized approximately $37,310

KM# 6 DUCATONE
32.1600 g., Silver **Obv:** Bust of Alberico right **Rev:** Three stags swimming left **Note:** Dav. #3972.

Date	Mintage	Good	VG	F	VF	XF
ND Rare	—	—	—	—	—	—

KM# 30 DUCATONE
32.1600 g., Silver **Obv:** Bust of Carlo right **Rev:** Crowned Cybo arms **Note:** Dav. #3973.

Date	Mintage	Good	VG	F	VF	XF
ND Rare	—	—	—	—	—	—

KM# 20 1/2 SCUDO D'ORO
1.6800 g., Gold **Obv:** Cybo arms **Rev:** Pyramid with sun above

Date	Mintage	VG	F	VF	XF	Unc
ND	—	1,150	2,250	4,700	7,500	—

KM# 21 SCUDO D'ORO (1/2 Doppia)
3.3100 g., Gold **Obv:** Oval arms **Rev:** Ornate cross

Date	Mintage	VG	F	VF	XF	Unc
ND	—	2,250	4,400	8,800	14,000	—

KM# 22 SCUDO D'ORO (1/2 Doppia)
3.3100 g., Gold **Obv:** Cybo arms **Rev. Legend:** DVRABO

Date	Mintage	VG	F	VF	XF	Unc
ND	—	2,250	4,400	8,800	14,000	—

KM# 23 DOPPIA
6.8300 g., Gold **Obv:** Cybo arms **Obv. Legend:** ALB... **Rev:** Crowned double eagle

Date	Mintage	VG	F	VF	XF	Unc
ND	—	2,500	5,000	10,000	16,500	—

KM# 24 2 DOPPIE
13.9000 g., Gold **Obv:** Bust right **Obv. Legend:** ALBERICVS... **Rev:** Crowned double eagle with Cybo arms

Date	Mintage	VG	F	VF	XF	Unc
ND	—	3,150	5,600	11,500	19,000	—

KM# 31 5 DOPPIE
Gold **Obv:** Bust of Carlo right **Rev:** Crowned Cybo arms

Date	Mintage	VG	F	VF	XF	Unc
ND Rare	—	—	—	—	—	—

MESSERANO

(Masserano)
(Lordship, Countship, Marquisate, Principality)

The small village of Messerano, situated in Piedmont about 9 miles (15 kilometers) east of Biella, came under the control of the bishop of Vercelli in the 9th century. The bishop in turn sold the lordship of Messerano to the town of Vercelli in 1240, but it eventually passed to the Fieschi family in 1381, who also acquired nearby Crevacuore (which see) in 1394. The Fieschi became counts of Messerano in 1508 and the countship passed by inheritance to the Ferrero dynasty in 1532. The feudal domain was raised by Pope Paolo III to a marquisate in 1547 and Crevacuore was sold to Savoy in 1554. Pope Clement VIII made Messerano a principality in 1598. After the production of an extensive coinage spanning much of the 16th and 17th centuries, the mint of Messerano was closed in 1690. Prince Vittorio Filippo sold the sovereignty of Messerano to Savoy in 1767 and the Ferrero dynasty became extinct in 1833.

RULERS

Ferrero Dynasty
Francesco Filiberto, 1584-1629
Paolo Besso, 1629-1667
Francesco Ludovico, 1667-1685
Maria Cristina Simiana, wife of Francesco Ludovico
Carlo Besso, 1685-1720

Reference: Alberto Varesi, ***Monete Italiane Regionali: Piemonte, Sardegna, Liguria, Isola di Corsica.*** Pavia, 1996.

PRINCIPALITY

STANDARD COINAGE

KM# 5 QUATTRINO
Billon Weight varies: 1.37-1.98g., 15 mm. **Ruler:** Paolo Besso **Obv:** Bust to right **Obv. Legend:** P. FE. FL. II. P. MEN. M. **Rev:** Shield of 4-fold arms **Rev. Legend:** MARCHI. CREP. ET. C. **Note:** Ref. Varesi 828. Prev. KM#50.

Date	Mintage	VG	F	VF	XF	Unc
ND(1629-67)	—	30.00	65.00	135	195	—

KM# 4 QUATTRINO
Copper Weight varies: 1.81-1.82g., 18 mm. **Ruler:** Paolo Besso **Obv:** High collared bust to right **Obv. Legend:** P. FE. FL. II. P. MEN. M. **Rev:** Crowned serpent **Rev. Legend:** MARCHI. CREP. ET. C. **Note:** Ref. Varesi 827. Prev. KM#51.

Date	Mintage	VG	F	VF	XF	Unc
ND(1629-67)	—	60.00	110	225	330	—

KM# 38 QUATTRINO
Billon, 15 mm. **Ruler:** Francesco Ludovico **Obv:** Head to right **Obv. Legend:** ... RIN. MESSE. **Rev:** Cross with trefoil ends in circle **Rev. Legend:** MARCH(IO) ... **Note:** Ref. Varesi 836. Prev. KM#80.

Date	Mintage	VG	F	VF	XF	Unc
ND(1667-85)	—	40.00	80.00	170	250	—

KM# 39 QUATTRINO
Billon Weight varies: 1.77-2.45g., 16 mm. **Ruler:** Francesco Ludovico **Obv:** Head to right **Obv. Legend:** FRAN. LVD. FER... PR. M. **Rev:** Crowned serpent **Rev. Legend:** MARC. CR. COM. LAVA. **Note:** Ref. Varesi 837. Prev. KM#81.

Date	Mintage	VG	F	VF	XF	Unc
ND(1667-85)	—	40.00	80.00	170	250	—

KM# 50 QUATTRINO
Copper, 18 mm. **Ruler:** Carlo Besso **Obv:** Bust to right **Obv. Legend:** CAR. BESS. PRIN. MESSERA. **Rev:** Crowned shield of 4-fold arms with central shield, date at top **Rev. Legend:** MARCHIO. CREP. COM. LAVA. **Note:** Ref. Varesi 843. Prev. KM#100.

Date	Mintage	VG	F	VF	XF	Unc
1689	—	90.00	195	375	550	—

KM# 52 QUATTRINO
0.6600 g., Copper, 14 mm. **Obv:** Standing figure of St. Teonesto facing left **Obv. Legend:** S. THEONESTVS. PRO. NOBIS. **Rev:** Lion of St. Mark in circle **Rev. Legend:** NON. NOBIS. D....O. **Note:** Ref. Varesi 844. Prev. KM#101.

Date	Mintage	VG	F	VF	XF	Unc
ND(1690)	—	50.00	100	150	225	—

KM# 53 QUATTRINO
Copper Weight varies: 0.96-1.16g., 18 mm. **Obv:** Winged lion holding sword and scales of justice **Obv. Legend:** FACTVS. MAIOR. VEHITVR. **Rev:** Lion of St. Mark walking to left **Rev. Legend:** DILIGITE. IVSTITIAM. **Note:** Ref. Varesi 845. Prev. KM#102.

Date	Mintage	VG	F	VF	XF	Unc
ND(1690)	—	50.00	100	150	210	—

KM# 6 TRILLINA
Billon **Ruler:** Paolo Besso **Obv:** Crown over 'PBF' **Obv. Legend:** P. MESS. ... **Rev:** Crowned oval shield of arms **Rev. Legend:** ... CREP. ET. C.... **Note:** Ref. Varesi 826. Prev. KM#59.

Date	Mintage	VG	F	VF	XF	Unc
ND(1629-67)	—	115	225	450	700	—

KM# 7 1/2 SOLDO
1.3500 g., Billon, 18 mm. **Ruler:** Paolo Besso **Obv:** Crowned shield of 4-fold arms with central shield, collar of order around **Obv. Legend:** P. FER. FLIS. PRIN. MESS. **Rev:** Ornate floriated cross **Rev. Legend:** SALVS. MONDO. **Note:** Ref. Varesi 825. Prev. KM#10.

Date	Mintage	VG	F	VF	XF	Unc
ND(1629-67)	—	50.00	110	200	300	—

KM# 40 1/2 SOLDO
Billon, 15-16 mm. **Ruler:** Francesco Ludovico **Obv:** Head to right **Obv. Legend:** FRAN. LVD. ... . **Rev:** Cross with lily ends **Rev. Legend:** MAR. CREP. ET. COM. LAV. **Note:** Ref. Varesi 835. Prev. KM#82.

Date	Mintage	VG	F	VF	XF	Unc
ND(1667-85)	—	55.00	110	225	330	—

KM# 8 SOLDO
Billon Weight varies: 1.50-1.85g., 20 mm. **Ruler:** Paolo Besso **Obv:** Crowned shield of 4-fold arms in baroque frame with central shield of rampant lion left **Obv. Legend:** P. B. F. ... PRI. MESSE. **Rev:** Cross with trefoil ends in baroque frame **Rev. Legend:** ADM. ... GLORIA. **Note:** Ref. Varesi 824. Prev. KM#11.

Date	Mintage	VG	F	VF	XF	Unc
ND(1629-67)	—	80.00	165	300	500	—

KM# 41 SOLDO
Billon, 20 mm. **Ruler:** Francesco Ludovico **Obv:** Crowned shield of 4-fold arms **Obv. Legend:** MONETA ... . **Rev:** Ornate cross **Rev. Legend:** ... (M)ESSERANO.... **Note:** Ref. Varesi 834. Prev. KM#90.2.

Date	Mintage	VG	F	VF	XF	Unc
ND(1667-85)	—	100	195	325	550	—

KM# 43 SOLDO
1.7900 g., Billon, 19 mm. **Ruler:** Francesco Ludovico **Obv:** Bust to right, date below **Obv. Legend:** FRA. LVD. F. F. PRIN. MES. **Rev:** Cross in circle **Rev. Legend:** COME. LAVA. MARC. CREP. **Note:** Ref. Varesi 833. Prev. KM#90.1.

Date	Mintage	VG	F	VF	XF	Unc
1672	—	115	220	550	900	—

KM# 1 3 KREUZER
1.4700 g., Billon, 19 mm. **Ruler:** Francesco Filiberto **Obv:** Shield of 3-fold arms, date above **Obv. Legend:** MONETA. NOVA. PRINC. MESSE. **Rev:** Crowned imperial eagle, 3 in orb on breast **Rev. Legend:** DOMINE. SALVA. NOS. SPES. **Note:** Ref. Varesi 795. Prev. KM#30 (3 Grossi).

Date	Mintage	VG	F	VF	XF	Unc
1603	—	100	195	325	550	—

KM# 9 4 SOLDI
Billon Weight varies: 4.27-4.97g., 25-26 mm. **Ruler:** Paolo Besso **Obv:** Crowned shield of 4-fold arms with central shield **Obv. Legend:** PAVLVS. FERRERIVS. P. MA. **Rev:** Cross with trefoil ends, rosette in each angle, value at end of legend **Rev. Legend:** + MONETA. NOVA. DA. SOL. 4. **Note:** Ref. Varesi 822. Prev. KM#13.

Date	Mintage	VG	F	VF	XF	Unc
ND(1629-67)	—	225	415	775	1,100	—

KM# 10 4-1/2 SOLDI
Billon Weight varies: 2.93-3.66g., 28 mm. **Ruler:** Paolo Besso **Obv:** Crowned shield of 4-fold arms in baroque frame with central shield **Obv. Legend:** P. FER. FLISC. PRINC. MES. **Rev:** Full-length standing figure of St. Paul, 'G' between feet **Rev. Legend:** PROTECTOR - NOSTER. **Note:** Ref. Varesi 821. Prev. KM#14.

Date	Mintage	VG	F	VF	XF	Unc
ND(1629-67)	—	200	360	675	1,000	—

KM# 11 5 SOLDI
Billon Weight varies: 3.87-5.55g., 28-29 mm. **Ruler:** Paolo Besso **Obv:** Crowned oval shield of manifold arms in baroque frame **Obv. Legend:** P. BES. FER. FLIS. PRIN. MESS. II. **Rev:** Full-length standing figure of Blessed Andreas holding shield with B./AN/DRE/AS **Rev. Legend:** NON. NOB. DOM. SE - D. NOM. TVO. DA. GLO. **Note:** Ref. Varesi 820. Prev. KM#15.

Date	Mintage	VG	F	VF	XF	Unc
ND(1629-67)	—	135	275	550	900	—

KM# 37 1/17 SCUDO
2.0400 g., Silver, 16-17 mm. **Ruler:** Paolo Besso **Obv:** Cross with star in each angle **Obv. Legend:** PRNI. MES. MAR. CREP. CO. L. **Rev:** Madonna and Child in circle, date at end of legend **Rev. Legend:** PROTECT. NOSTRA. **Note:** Ref. Varesi 823. Prev. KM#38.

Date	Mintage	VG	F	VF	XF	Unc
1662	—	100	200	325	500	—

KM# 44 LUIGINO
Silver, 21 mm. **Ruler:** Maria Cristina Simiana **Obv:** Bust to right **Obv. Legend:** MARIA. CRISTINA. SIMIANA. **Rev:** Crowned shield of arms, date above **Rev. Legend:** PRINCIPESA. MESSERANI. **Note:** Ref. Varesi 838. Prev. KM#91.

Date	Mintage	VG	F	VF	XF	Unc
1672	—	125	250	450	775	—

KM# 48 TESTONE
Silver, 31-32 mm. **Ruler:** Carlo Besso **Obv:** Bust to right **Obv. Legend:** CAR. BESS. PRIN. MESSERANI. **Rev:** Crowned shield of 4-fold arms with central shield, date at top **Rev. Legend:** MARCHIO. CREP. COM. LAVAN. **Note:** Ref. Varesi 841. Prev. KM#103.

Date	Mintage	VG	F	VF	XF	Unc
1686 Rare	—	—	—	—	—	—

KM# 54 LIRA
5.6700 g., Silver, 28 mm. **Ruler:** Carlo Besso **Obv:** Bust to right **Obv. Legend:** CAR. BESS. PRIN. MESSERANI. **Rev:** Crowned shield of 4-fold arms with central shield, date at top **Rev. Legend:** MARCHIO. CREP. COM. LAVAN. **Note:** Ref. Varesi 842. Prev. KM#110.

Date	Mintage	VG	F	VF	XF	Unc
1690	—	750	1,100	2,300	3,500	—

KM# 45 1/2 SCUDO
12.8600 g., Silver, 32 mm. **Ruler:** Francesco Ludovico **Obv:** Bust to right **Obv. Legend:** FRA. LVD. F.F. PRIN. MESSERANI. **Rev:** Crowned shield of 4-fold arms with central shield, date at top in margin **Rev. Legend:** MARCHIO. CREP. COM. LAVANIÆ. **Note:** Ref. Varesi 832. Prev. KM#94.

Date	Mintage	VG	F	VF	XF	Unc
1672 Rare	—	—	—	—	—	—
1673 Rare	—	—	—	—	—	—

KM# 12 1/2 TALLERO (12 Soldi)
15.8000 g., Silver, 35 mm. **Ruler:** Paolo Besso **Obv:** Bust wearing high collar to right, value at end of legend **Obv. Legend:** P. FER. MES. P. ET. MAR. CREP. III. S. XII. **Rev:** St. George on horseback to right, slaying dragon below, in exergue S. G. CASNIL **Rev. Legend:** PROTECTOR. NOSTER. ASPICE. **Note:** Ref. Varesi 818. Prev. KM#52.

Date	Mintage	VG	F	VF	XF	Unc
ND(1629-67)	—	1,250	2,200	4,250	6,500	—

KM# 13 1/2 TALLERO (12 Soldi)
15.8500 g., Silver, 37-38 mm. **Ruler:** Paolo Besso **Obv:** Bust wearing high collar to right, value at end of legend **Obv. Legend:** P. FER. MES. P. ET. MAR. CREP. III. S. XII. **Rev:** Sun with stars around in Zodiac, clouds and earth below **Rev. Legend:** NVN. QVAM. RETRO. CVRSVM. VERTO. **Note:** Ref. Varesi 819. Prev. KM#53.

Date	Mintage	VG	F	VF	XF	Unc
ND(1629-67)	—	1,250	2,200	4,250	6,500	—

KM# 46 SCUDO
Silver, 40-41 mm. **Ruler:** Francesco Ludovico **Obv:** Draped bust to right **Obv. Legend:** FRA. LVD. F. F. PRIN. MESSERANI. **Rev:** Four small shields of arms in cruciform around small shield of arms in central circle, lily in each angle, date divided to outer edge above crowns of arms **Rev. Legend:** MARC - CREP - COME - LAVA. **Note:** Ref. Varesi 831; Dav. 3994. Prev. KM#92.

Date	Mintage	VG	F	VF	XF	Unc
1672 Rare	—	—	—	—	—	—

KM# 49 SCUDO
Silver, 43 mm. **Ruler:** Carlo Besso **Obv:** Draped bust to right **Obv. Legend:** CAR. BESS. PRIN. MESSERANI. **Rev:** Crowned shield of 4-fold arms with central shield, date in margin at top **Rev. Legend:** MARCHIO. CREP. COM. LAVAN. **Note:** Ref. Varesi 840; Dav. 3995. Prev. KM#104.

Date	Mintage	VG	F	VF	XF	Unc
1686 Rare	—	—	—	—	—	—

KM# 2 TALLERO
Silver Weight varies: 26.77-27.39g., 42 mm. **Ruler:** Francesco Filiberto **Obv:** Half-length armored figure to right **Obv. Legend:** FRANC. FIL. FER(R). FLI. PRINCE. MESSERA. **Rev:** Crowned imperial eagle, oval shield of 2-fold arms on breast, date divided to lower left and right, where present, 'F. VIII' in cartouche at bottom **Rev. Legend:** CAROLI. QVINTI. - IMPERATOR. GRA(TIA). **Note:** Ref. Varesi 762; Dav. 3974. Varieties exist. Prev. KM#40.

Date	Mintage	VG	F	VF	XF	Unc
1612	—	300	600	1,750	3,400	—
1613	—	300	600	1,750	3,400	—
ND	—	300	600	1,750	3,400	—

KM# 3 TALLERO
Silver, 40-42 mm. **Ruler:** Francesco Filiberto **Obv:** Half-length armored figure to right **Obv. Legend:** FRAN. PRINCEPS. PRIMVS. M. ET. M. **Rev:** Crowned imperial eagle, shield of arms on breast, crown divides date **Rev. Legend:** STABILITAS. ALTA. PETIT. F. S. 9. **Note:** Ref. Varesi 767; Dav. 3975. Prev. KM#45.1.

Date	Mintage	VG	F	VF	XF	Unc
1621	—	20.00	20.00	20.00	20.00	—

KM# 20 TALLERO
Silver Weight varies: 28.55-32.83g., 42-43 mm. **Ruler:** Paolo Besso **Obv:** Bust with high collar to right, 'L.1.' below shoulder, Roman numeral date at end of legend **Obv. Legend:** P. FER. MES. P. ET. MAR. CREP. III. **Rev:** St. George on horseback to right, slaying dragon below, in exergue S. G. C(A)S(NI)L **Rev. Legend:** PROTECTOR. NOSTER. ASPICE. **Note:** Ref. Varesi 811/1; Dav. 3983. Prev. KM#66.1.

Date	Mintage	VG	F	VF	XF	Unc
MDCXXXIII(1633)	—	900	1,650	3,500	6,500	—

KM# 21 TALLERO
Silver Weight varies: 30.58-31.29g., 44 mm. **Ruler:** Paolo Besso **Obv:** Bust with high collar to right, 'L.1.' below shoulder, Roman numeral date at end of legend **Obv. Legend:** P. FER. MES. P. ET. MAR. CREP. III. **Rev:** Sun with stars around in Zodiac, clouds and earth below **Rev. Legend:** NVN. QVAM. RETRO. CVRSVM. VERTO. L. 1. **Note:** Ref. Varesi 813; Dav. 3984. Prev. KM#67.1.

Date	Mintage	VG	F	VF	XF	Unc
MDCXXXIII(1633)	—	1,350	2,750	5,500	9,000	—

KM# 22 TALLERO
Silver Weight varies: 28.25-30.78g., 44 mm. **Ruler:** Paolo Besso **Obv:** Bust with high collar to right, L.1. below shoulder, Roman numeral date at end of legend **Obv. Legend:** P. FER. MES. P. ET. MAR. CREP. III. **Rev:** Sunface with rays around in circle, 'B' between 2 scrollwork ornaments at bottom **Rev. Legend:** NON. MVTABO. LVCEM. L. 1. **Note:** Ref. Varesi 816/1; Dav. 3985. Prev. KM#68.1.

Date	Mintage	VG	F	VF	XF	Unc
MDCXXXIII(1633)	—	1,350	2,750	5,500	9,000	—

KM# 23 TALLERO
Silver, 45 mm. **Ruler:** Paolo Besso **Obv:** Sun with stars around in Zodiac, clouds and earth below **Obv. Legend:** NVN. QVAM. RETRO. CVRSVM. VERTO. L. I. **Rev:** Sunface with rays around in circle, B between two scrollwork ornaments **Rev. Legend:** NON. MVTABO. LVCEM. L. I. **Note:** Ref. Varesi 817. Prev. KM#67.4. Mule of reverse die of KM #21 and reverse die of KM #22.

Date	Mintage	VG	F	VF	XF	Unc
ND(1633-38) Rare	—	—	—	—	—	—

KM# 24 TALLERO
Silver Weight varies: 28.55-32.83g., 42-43 mm. **Ruler:** Paolo Besso **Obv:** Bust with high collar to right **Obv. Legend:** P. FER. MA. P. ET. MAR. CRE. III **Rev:** St. George on horseback to right, slaying dragon below, in exergue S. G. CA. SNI. L, Roman numeral date at end of legend **Rev. Legend:** PROTECTOR. NOSTER. ASPICE. **Note:** Ref. Varesi 811/3; Dav. 3986. Prev. KM#66.2.

Date	Mintage	VG	F	VF	XF	Unc
MDCXXXV(1635)	—	900	1,650	3,500	6,500	—

KM# 25 TALLERO
Silver Weight varies: 28.55-32.83g., 43-44 mm. **Ruler:** Paolo Besso **Obv:** Bust with high collar to right, Roman numeral date at end of legend **Obv. Legend:** P. FER. MA. P. ET. MAR. CREP. **Rev:** St. George on horseback to right, slaying dragon below, in exergue S. G. CA. SNI. L, Roman numeral date at end of legend **Rev. Legend:** PROTECTOR. NOSTER. ASPICE. **Note:** Ref. Varesi 811/4; Dav. 3987. Prev. KM#66.3.

Date	Mintage	VG	F	VF	XF	Unc
MDCXXXV(1635)	—	900	1,650	3,500	6,500	—

KM# 26 TALLERO
Silver, 43-44 mm. **Ruler:** Paolo Besso **Obv:** Bust with high collar to right, Roman numeral date at end of legend **Obv. Legend:** P. FER. MA. P. ET. MAR. CREP. **Rev:** St. George on horseback to right, slaying dragon below, in exergue S. G. CA. SNI. L **Rev. Legend:** ROTECTOR. NOSTER. ASPICE. **Note:** Ref. Dav. 3987A. Prev. KM#66.5.

Date	Mintage	VG	F	VF	XF	Unc
MDCXXXV(1635)	—	900	1,650	3,500	6,500	—

KM# 27 TALLERO
Silver, 42-43 mm. **Ruler:** Paolo Besso **Obv:** Bust with high collar to right, Roman numeral date at end of legend **Obv. Legend:** P. FER. MES. P. ET. MAR. CREP. **Rev:** St. George on horseback to right, slaying dragon below, in exergue S. G. CA. SNI. L **Rev. Legend:** PROTECTOR. NOSTER. ASPICE. **Note:** Ref. Varesi 811/2; Dav. 3987B. Prev. KM#66.6.

Date	Mintage	VG	F	VF	XF	Unc
MDCXXXV(1635)	—	900	1,650	3,500	6,500	—

KM# 28 TALLERO
Silver, 42-43 mm. **Ruler:** Paolo Besso **Obv:** Bust wearing high collar to right, Roman numeral date at end of legend **Obv. Legend:** FER. MA. P. ET. MAR. CRE. III. P. **Rev:** St. George on horseback to right, slaying dragon below, in exergue S. G. CA. SNI. L **Rev. Legend:** PROTECTOR. NOSTER. ASPICE. **Note:** Ref. Dav. 3987C. Prev. KM#66.7.

Date	Mintage	VG	F	VF	XF	Unc
MDCXXXV(1635)	—	900	1,650	3,500	6,500	—

KM# 29 TALLERO
Silver, 44 mm. **Ruler:** Paolo Besso **Obv:** Armored and mantled bust to right, 'LI' below shoulder, Roman numeral date in legend **Obv. Legend:** CAROLVS. I. MDCVX[XX]. MA. P. E. MAR. CRE. **Rev:** Sun with stars around in Zodiac, clouds and earth below **Rev. Legend:** NVN. QVAM. RETRO. CVRSVM. VERTO. L. I. **Note:** Ref. Varesi 814; Dav. 3988. Prev. KM#67.2.

Date	Mintage	VG	F	VF	XF	Unc
MDCX[XX]V (1635) Rare	—	—	—	—	—	—

KM# 30 TALLERO
Silver, 43 mm. **Ruler:** Paolo Besso **Obv:** Armored and mantled bust to right, 'LI' below shoulder, Roman numeral date in legend **Obv. Legend:** CAROLVS. I. M.DCVX[XX]. MA. P. E. MAR. CRE. **Rev:** Sunface with rays around in circle, 'B' in margin below between two scrollwork ornaments **Rev. Legend:** NON. MVTABO. LVCEM. L. I. **Note:** Ref. Varesi 815; Dav. 3989. Prev. KM#68.2.

Date	Mintage	VG	F	VF	XF	Unc
MDCX[XX]V Rare	—	—	—	—	—	—

KM# 31 TALLERO
Silver Weight varies: 28.25-30.78g., 43 mm. **Ruler:** Paolo Besso **Obv:** Bust with high collar to right, Roman numeral date at end of legend **Obv. Legend:** P. FER. MA. P. ET. MAR. CREP. **Rev:** Sunface with rays around in circle, 'B' in margin below between two scrollwork ornaments **Rev. Legend:** nON. MVTABO. LVCEM. L. I. **Note:** Ref. Varesi 816/2; Dav. 3990. Prev. KM#70.1.

Date	Mintage	VG	F	VF	XF	Unc
MDCXXXV(1635)	—	1,350	2,750	5,500	9,000	—

KM# 32 TALLERO
Silver, 44 mm. **Ruler:** Paolo Besso **Obv:** Bust with high collar to right, 'L.1.' below shoulder, Roman numeral date at end of legend **Obv. Legend:** P. FER. MES. P. ET. MAR. CREP. **Rev:** Sunface with rays around in circle, 'B' between two scrollwork ornaments at bottom **Rev. Legend:** NON. MVTABO. LVCEM. L. I. **Note:** Ref. Dav. 3991. Prev. KM#70.2.

Date	Mintage	VG	F	VF	XF	Unc
MDCXXXV(1635) Rare	—	—	—	—	—	—

KM# 33 TALLERO
Silver Weight varies: 28.55-32.83g., 43-44 mm. **Ruler:** Paolo Besso **Obv:** Bust with high collar to right **Obv. Legend:** FER. MA. P. ET. MAR. CRE. III. P. **Rev:** St. George on horseback to right, slaying dragon below, in exergue S. G. CASL., Roman numeral date at end of legend **Rev. Legend:** PROTECTOR. NOSTER. ASPICE. **Note:** Ref. Varesi 811/5; Dav. 3992. Prev. KM#66.4.

Date	Mintage	VG	F	VF	XF	Unc
MDCVXIII(1638)	—	900	1,650	3,500	6,500	—

KM# 34 TALLERO
Silver, 44 mm. **Ruler:** Paolo Besso **Obv:** Bust wearing high collar to right, Roman numeral date in legend **Obv. Legend:** P. FER. MA. CRE. EC. D. S. P. B. F. (date) P. **Rev:** Sun with stars around in Zodiac, clouds and earth below **Rev. Legend:** NVNQVAM RETRORSVM. VERTO. **Note:** Ref. Varesi 812; Dav. 3993. Prev. KM#67.3.

Date	Mintage	VG	F	VF	XF	Unc
MDCVXVIII(163 8) Rare	—	—	—	—	—	—

TRADE COINAGE

KM# 14 DUCATO (Ongaro)
Gold, 23 mm. **Ruler:** Paolo Besso **Obv:** Full-length figure of armored prince turned slightly to right, holding sword with point down **Obv. Legend:** P. FER. MES. PRIN. M. - CREP. MO. AVR. D. IIII. **Rev:** 5-line inscription in ornamented square tablet **Rev. Inscription:** PAV. FER / MES. PRI / MAR. CR / P. MON. AVR / DA. IIII. **Note:** Ref. Varesi 806; Fr. 625. Prev. KM#55.2.

Date	Mintage	VG	F	VF	XF	Unc
ND(1629-67)	—	600	1,300	2,200	3,300	—

KM# 15 DUCATO (Ongaro)
Gold Weight varies: 3.30-3.47g., 22.5 mm. **Ruler:** Paolo Besso **Obv:** Full-length figure of armored prince turned slightly to right, holding sword with point down **Obv. Legend:** F. FER. MES. PRIN. M. CREP. MO. AVR. DA. VII. **Rev:** 5-line inscription in ornamented square tablet **Rev. Inscription:** MONE / TA / NOVA / AVREA / CO. LAV. **Note:** Ref. Varesi 808; Fr. 625. Prev. KM#56.

Date	Mintage	VG	F	VF	XF	Unc
ND(1629-67)	—	1,000	1,800	3,850	5,500	—

KM# 16 DUCATO (Ongaro)
3.2400 g., Gold, 21-21.5 mm. **Ruler:** Paolo Besso **Obv:** Full-length figure of armored prince turned slightly to right, holding sword with point down **Obv. Legend:** P. FER. MES. PRIN. M. CREP. MO. AVR. DA. L. III. **Rev:** 5-line inscription in ornamented square tablet **Rev. Inscription:** P. FER. MES / PRIN. M / CREP. MO / AVR. DA. L. III / F. **Note:** Ref. Varesi 809; Fr. 625. Prev. KM#57.

Date	Mintage	VG	F	VF	XF	Unc
ND(1629-67)	—	1,000	1,800	3,850	5,500	—

KM# 17 DUCATO (Ongaro)
Gold, 23.5 mm. **Ruler:** Paolo Besso **Obv:** 5-line inscription in ornamented square tablet **Obv. Inscription:** MONE / TA / NOVA / AVREA / CO. LA. **Rev:** Crowned imperial eagle, shield of arms on breast **Rev. Legend:** SVB. VMBRA. ALARVM. TVARVM. **Note:** Ref. Varesi 810; Fr. 626. Prev. KM#58.

Date	Mintage	VG	F	VF	XF	Unc
ND(1629-67)	—	600	1,300	2,200	3,300	—

KM# 19 DUCATO (Ongaro)
Gold, 23 mm. **Ruler:** Paolo Besso **Obv:** Full-length figure of armored prince, head turned to right, holding sword over right shoulder and bundle of arrows in left hand, divides date **Obv. Legend:** DE. PVGNABO - SIC. PROFII. **Rev:** 5-line inscription in ornamented square tablet **Rev. Inscription:** P. B. FER. / D. MA. A. / C. R. EF / MO. DO / DA. SOL. X. **Note:** Ref. Varesi 807. Prev. KM#55.1.

Date	Mintage	VG	F	VF	XF	Unc
1632	—	600	1,300	2,200	3,300	—

KM# 36 SCUDO D'ORO
3.2000 g., Gold, 22 mm. **Ruler:** Paolo Besso **Obv:** High-collared bust to right, Roman numeral date at end of legend **Obv. Legend:** P. FER. MA. D. ET. MAR. CREP. **Rev:** Crowned shield of 4-fold arms with central shield, all within chain of order **Rev. Legend:** MON. NOR. D. O. RA. SO. LVI. D. FLOR. **Note:** Ref. Varesi 805; Fr. 624. Prev. KM#75.

Date	Mintage	VG	F	VF	XF	Unc
MDCXL(1640)	—	10.00	10.00	10.00	10.00	—

KM# 42 DOPPIA
Gold, 25 mm. **Ruler:** Francesco Ludovico **Obv:** Draped bust to right **Obv. Legend:** FRANN. LVD. FER. FL. PRI. MESS. **Rev:** Crowned shield of 4-fold arms with central shield, date above crown **Rev. Legend:** MARH. CREP. - COM. LAVA. **Note:** Ref. Varesi 830; Fr. 627. Prev. KM#88.

Date	Mintage	VG	F	VF	XF	Unc
1667 Rare	—	—	—	—	—	—

KM# 51 DOPPIA
Gold, 26 mm. **Ruler:** Carlo Besso **Obv:** Bust to right **Obv. Legend:** CAR. BESS. PRIN. MESSERA. **Rev:** Crowned shield of 4-fold arms with central shield, date above crown **Rev. Legend:** MARCHIO. CREP. COM. LAVA. **Note:** Ref. Varesi 839; Fr. 629. Prev. KM#105.

Date	Mintage	VG	F	VF	XF	Unc
1689 Rare	—	—	—	—	—	—

KM# 18 2 DOPPIE
12.6000 g., Gold, 32 mm. **Ruler:** Paolo Besso **Obv:** High-collared armored bust to right **Obv. Legend:** P. FER. MA. L. DVX. A. C. S. R. E. F. E. V. **Rev:** Crowned shield of 4-fold arms, with central shield, within chain of order **Rev. Legend:** AV. MO. D. V. FLOR. **Note:** Ref. Varesi 804; Fr. 623a. Prev. KM#54.

Date	Mintage	VG	F	VF	XF	Unc
ND(1629-67) Rare	—	—	—	—	—	—

KM# 35 5 DOPPIE
Gold, 43 mm. **Ruler:** Paolo Besso **Obv:** Mantled bust to left, date behind shoulder in margin **Obv. Legend:** PAVLVS. BESSVS. FERRERIVS. FLISCVS. **Rev:** Crowned shield of 4-fold arms, with central shield, in baroque frame **Rev. Legend:** PRINC. MESSERANI. MARCHIO. CREPAC. LAV. C. **Note:** Ref. Varesi 803; Fr. 623. Prev. KM#71.

Date	Mintage	VG	F	VF	XF	Unc
1638 Rare	—	—	—	—	—	—

KM# 47 5 DOPPIE
Gold, 40-41 mm. **Ruler:** Francesco Ludovico **Obv:** Draped bust to right **Obv. Legend:** FRA. LVD. F. F. PRIN. MESSERANI. **Rev:** Four small crowned shields of arms in cruciform around small shield of arms in central circle, lily in each angle, date divided to outer edge above crowns of arms **Rev. Legend:** MARC - CREP - COME - LAVA. **Note:** Ref. Varesi 829; Fr. 628. Prev. KM#93.

Date	Mintage	VG	F	VF	XF	Unc
1672 Rare	—	—	—	—	—	—

PATTERNS

Including off metal strikes

KM#	Date	Mintage	Identification	Mkt Val
Pn1	1686	—	Scudo. Copper. 43 mm. KM#49.	—

MILAN

(Milano)

The principal city in northern Italy and the second largest city of the modern republic, Milan is located in Lombardy, south of the foothills of the Alps. It is of ancient Gaulic tribal foundation, conquered by Rome in 222 BC and named Mediolanum. Sacked by Attila in 452 and destroyed by the Goths in 539, the city belonged to the Kingdom of the Lombards after being rebuilt and later, belonged to the Germanic Empire. Various families ruled the city in the later Middle Ages and it was also a republic for periods in the 13th, 14th and 15th centuries. The Visconti family became Lords of Milan in the early 14th century and the form of government was changed from elective to hereditary, the lord being raised to the rank of duke in 1395. In 1450, Francesco I Sforza inherited the duchy through marriage to the Visconti heiress and the Sforza's began to enhance the power and prestige of Milan. The city became a pawn in the power struggles between France and the Habsburgs, passing to the control of Spain in 1535, then to Austria in 1740. Conquered by France in 1796, Milan formed part of the Cisalpine Republic (see) from 1797, then the Italian Republic in 1802 and of the Kingdom of Italy from 1805 until 1814. In the latter year, Milan was ceded to Austria and became part of Lombardy-Venetia. In 1859, the city and territory was annexed to Sardinia, becoming part of united Italy.

RULER
Filippo III, King of Spain 1598-1621
Filippo IV, King of Spain 1621-1665
Carlo II, King of Spain 1665-1700

ARMS
Snake, coiled wavelike vertically, sometimes with crown
Dragon, in various forms

REFERENCE
N&V = Raffaele Negrini and Alberto Varesi, ***La Monetazione di Milano (dal 756 al 1802).*** Milan, 1991.

DUCHY

REGULAR COINAGE

KM# 1 QUATTRINO
Copper Weight varies: 1.66-2.75g., 18 mm. **Ruler:** Filippo III **Obv:** High-collared bust to right, date below **Obv. Legend:** PHIL. - REX. HIS. **Rev:** Round 4-fold arms **Rev. Legend:** MEDIOLANI. DVX. **Note:** N&V 376. Varieties exist.

Date	Mintage	VG	F	VF	XF	Unc
1601	—	115	210	375	585	—
1602	—	115	210	375	585	—
1603	—	6.00	10.00	20.00	60.00	—
1606	—	60.00	125	250	425	—
1614	—	115	210	375	585	—

KM# 31 QUATTRINO
Copper Weight varies: 1.70-2.93g., 15-16 mm. **Ruler:** Filippo IV **Obv:** High-collared bust to right. **Obv. Legend:** PHI. III. REX. H. **Rev:** Round 4-fold arms. **Rev. Legend:** MEDIO. DVX. ET. **Note:** N&V 393.

Date	Mintage	VG	F	VF	XF	Unc
ND(1621-65)	—	8.00	15.00	35.00	80.00	—

KM# 32 QUATTRINO
Copper Weight varies: 1.30-2.72g., 16-17 mm. **Ruler:** Filippo IV **Obv:** High-collared bust to right **Obv. Legend:** PHILIPP. IIII. REX. H. **Rev:** Crowned snake arms of Milan **Rev. Legend:** MEDIOL. - DVX. ET. **Note:** N&V 394.

Date	Mintage	VG	F	VF	XF	Unc
ND(1621-65)	—	8.00	15.00	35.00	80.00	—

KM# 67 QUATTRINO
Copper Weight varies: 1.51-2.07g., 18-19 mm. **Ruler:** Carlo II **Obv:** Bust to right **Obv. Legend:** CAROLVS. II. REX. H. **Rev:** Crowned snake arms of Milan **Rev. Legend:** MEDIOLANI. DVX. ET. C. **Note:** N&V 410.

Date	Mintage	VG	F	VF	XF	Unc
ND(1665-1700)	—	7.00	12.00	20.00	65.00	—

KM# 68 QUATTRINO

Copper Weight varies: 1.15-2.36g. **Ruler:** Carlo II **Obv:** Bust to right **Obv. Legend:** CAROLVS. II. REX. H. **Rev:** Crowned 2-line inscription in wreath **Rev. Inscription:** MLNI/DVX **Note:** N&V 411.

Date	Mintage	VG	F	VF	XF	Unc
ND(1665-1700)	—	4.00	8.00	15.00	55.00	—

KM# 34 SESINO

Billon Weight varies: 1.09-1.49g., 13-14 mm. **Ruler:** Filippo IV **Obv:** High-collared bust to right **Obv. Legend:** PHILIPP. IIII. REX. H. **Rev:** Floriated cross **Rev. Legend:** MEDIOLANI. DVX. 7C **Note:** N&V 391.

Date	Mintage	Good	VG	F	VF	XF
ND(1621-65)	—	—	8.00	15.00	30.00	85.00

KM# 35 SESINO

Billon Weight varies: 1.06-1.67g., 15-16 mm. **Ruler:** Filippo IV **Obv:** Crowned "PHI." **Obv. Legend:** IIII. REX. - HISP. **Rev:** Crowned shield of oval 4-fold arms **Rev. Legend:** MEDIO - LANI. D. **Note:** N&V 392.

Date	Mintage	Good	VG	F	VF	XF
ND(1621-65)	—	—	7.00	15.00	30.00	80.00

KM# 70 SOLDINO

Billon Weight varies: 1.67-2.61g., 18 mm. **Ruler:** Carlo II **Obv:** Youthful bust to right **Obv. Legend:** CAROLVS. II. REX. HISP. **Rev:** Ornate cross **Rev. Legend:** MEDIOLANI. DVX. ET. C. **Note:** N&V 401.

Date	Mintage	Good	VG	F	VF	XF
ND(1665-1700)	—	—	8.00	15.00	30.00	65.00

KM# 82 SOLDINO

2.0200 g., Billon, 17-18 mm. **Ruler:** Carlo II **Obv:** Youthful bust to right, date below **Obv. Legend:** CAROLVS. II. REX. H. **Rev:** Crowned shield of 4-fold arms **Rev. Legend:** MEDIO - LANI. DVX. **Note:** N&V 400.

Date	Mintage	VG	F	VF	XF	Unc
1672 Rare	—	—	—	—	—	—

KM# 83 SOLDINO

Billon Weight varies: 1.67-2.61g., 18 mm. **Ruler:** Carlo II **Obv:** Youthful bust to right, date below **Obv. Legend:** CAROLVS. II. REX. HISP. **Rev:** Ornate cross **Rev. Legend:** MEDIOLANI. DVX. ET. C. **Note:** N&V 402.

Date	Mintage	VG	F	VF	XF	Unc
1672	—	8.00	15.00	30.00	65.00	—

KM# 2 PARPAGLIOLA

Billon Weight varies: 1.17-2.67g., 23 mm. **Ruler:** Filippo III **Obv:** Crowned shield of 4-fold arms **Obv. Legend:** MEDIO - LANI. D. **Rev:** Standing figure of Providence, date in exergue **Rev. Legend:** PROVIDENTIA. **Note:** N&V 371. Varieties exist.

Date	Mintage	VG	F	VF	XF	Unc
1602	—	50.00	110	225	500	—
1603	—	30.00	65.00	110	285	—
1608	—	8.00	15.00	30.00	125	—

KM# 37 PARPAGLIOLA

Billon Weight varies: 2.12-2.13g., 17-18 mm. **Ruler:** Filippo IV **Obv:** High-collared bust to right **Obv. Legend:** PHILIPP. IIII. REX. H. **Rev:** Crowned 'PHI.' **Rev. Legend:** MEDIOLANI. DVX. ET. C. **Note:** N&V 390.

Date	Mintage	VG	F	VF	XF	Unc
ND(1621-65)	—	40.00	85.00	175	415	—

KM# 15 4 SOLDI

Billon Weight varies: 2.45-3.08g., 23-24 mm. **Ruler:** Filippo III **Obv:** Crown above 2-line inscription, date in exergue **Obv. Legend:** HISPAN. - REX. ETC. **Obv. Inscription:** PHI/III. **Rev:** Crown with 2 branches above ornate shield of 4-fold arms, '4' in exergue **Rev. Legend:** MLI - DVX. **Note:** N&V 370.

Date	Mintage	VG	F	VF	XF	Unc
1608	—	18.00	35.00	80.00	225	—

KM# 7 5 SOLDI

Billon Weight varies: 1.94-3.18g., 23 mm. **Ruler:** Filippo III **Obv:** Armored bust to right, '5' under shoulder, date below **Obv. Legend:** PHILIPP. III. REX. HISP. **Rev:** Crowned shield of manifold arms **Rev. Legend:** MEDIOLANI. DVX. ETC. **Note:** N&V 369. Varieties exist.

Date	Mintage	VG	F	VF	XF	Unc
1604	—	20.00	40.00	100	275	—
1605	—	50.00	100	225	500	—
1606 Rare	—	—	—	—	—	—

KM# 9 10 SOLDI

Silver Weight varies: 3.02-3.40g., 25 mm. **Ruler:** Filippo III **Obv:** High-collared bust to right, date under shoulder **Obv. Legend:** PHILIPP. III. REX. HISP. **Rev:** Crowned shield of manifold arms, '10' in exergue **Rev. Legend:** MEDIOLA - DVX. ETC. **Note:** N&V 367.

Date	Mintage	VG	F	VF	XF	Unc
1604	—	50.00	100	225	500	—

KM# 25 10 SOLDI

Silver Weight varies: 2.36-2.78g., 23-24 mm. **Ruler:** Filippo III **Obv:** High-collared bust to right, date under shoulder **Obv. Legend:** PHILIPPVS. III. REX. HISPAN. **Rev:** St. Ambrose on horse galloping to right, '10' in exergue **Rev. Legend:** DE. CAELO - FORTITVDO. **Note:** N&V 368.

Date	Mintage	VG	F	VF	XF	Unc
1611 Rare	—	—	—	—	—	—
1614	—	350	750	1,200	2,500	—

KM# 72 1/8 FILIPPO

Silver Weight varies: 3.10-3.35g., 24-25 mm. **Ruler:** Carlo II **Obv:** Accolated busts of Carlo II and his mother to right, date below **Obv. Legend:** CAROLVS. II. H. REX. ET. MARIA. ANNA. T. ET. G. **Rev:** Crowned shield of manifold arms **Rev. Legend:** MEDIOLANI. - DVX. ET. C. **Note:** N&V 399.

Date	Mintage	VG	F	VF	XF	Unc
1666	—	200	375	650	1,625	—

KM# 85 1/8 FILIPPO

Silver Weight varies: 3.20-3.45g., 25 mm. **Ruler:** Carlo II **Obv:** Bust to right, date below **Obv. Legend:** CAROLVS. II. REX. HISPANIARV. **Rev:** Crowned shield of manifold arms **Rev. Legend:** MEDIOLANI. - DVX. ET. C. **Note:** N&V 409. Varieties exist.

Date	Mintage	VG	F	VF	XF	Unc
1676	—	80.00	165	325	1,000	—
1694	—	120	250	500	1,250	—

KM# 17 20 SOLDI

Silver Weight varies: 5.33-5.48g., 27-28 mm. **Ruler:** Filippo III **Obv:** High-collared bust to right, date below **Obv. Legend:** PHILIPPVS. III. REX. HIS(I)P(AN). **Rev:** Crown with 2 branches over 5-line inscription, all in ornate frame **Rev. Inscription:** MEDIO/LANI/DVX/ET. C/Z0. **Note:** N&V 366. Varieties exist.

Date	Mintage	VG	F	VF	XF	Unc
1608	—	350	650	1,150	2,500	—

KM# 57 20 SOLDI

Silver Weight varies: 4.76-4.90g., 26-27 mm. **Ruler:** Filippo IV **Obv:** High-collared bust to right, date below **Obv. Legend:** PHILIPPVS. IIII. REX. HIS. **Rev:** Crown with 2 branches over 5-line inscription, all in ornate frame **Rev. Inscription:** MEDIO/LANI/DVX/ET. C/Z0. **Note:** N&V 389.

Date	Mintage	VG	F	VF	XF	Unc
1655	—	375	700	1,500	3,250	—

KM# 65 1/4 FILIPPO

Silver Weight varies: 6.02-6.88g., 29-30 mm. **Ruler:** Filippo IV **Obv:** High-collared bust to right, date below **Obv. Legend:** PHILIPPVS. IIII. REX. HISP. **Rev:** Crowned shield of manifold arms **Rev. Legend:** MEDIOLA - NI. DVX. ET. C. **Note:** N&V 388.

Date	Mintage	VG	F	VF	XF	Unc
1658	—	200	375	850	2,000	—

KM# 74 1/4 FILIPPO

Silver Weight varies: 6.60-6.95g., 28-29 mm. **Ruler:** Carlo II **Obv:** Accolated busts of Carlo II and his mother to right, date below **Obv. Legend:** CAROLVS. II. HIS. REX. ET. MARIA. ANNA. TVT. E. G. **Rev:** Crowned shield of manifold arms **Rev. Legend:** MEDIOLANI - DVX. ET. C. **Note:** N&V 398.

Date	Mintage	VG	F	VF	XF	Unc
1666	—	300	650	1,250	3,750	—

KM# 87 1/4 FILIPPO

Silver Weight varies: 6.34-6.90g., 30 mm. **Ruler:** Carlo II **Obv:** Bust to right, date below **Obv. Legend:** CAROLVS. II. REX. HISPANIAR. **Rev:** Crowned shield of manifold arms **Rev. Legend:** MEDIOLANI - DVX. ET. C. **Note:** N&V 408. Varieties exist.

Date	Mintage	VG	F	VF	XF	Unc
1676	—	150	285	625	1,650	—
1694	—	200	375	1,000	2,850	—

KM# 53 1/4 DUCATONE

Silver Weight varies: 7.70-7.95g., 27 mm. **Ruler:** Filippo IV **Obv:** Crowned high-collared bust to right, date below **Obv. Legend:** PHILIPPVS - IIII. REX. HISP. **Rev:** Crowned shield of 4-fold arms in baroque frame **Rev. Legend:** MEDIOLA - NI. DVX. ET. **Note:** N&V 387.

Date	Mintage	VG	F	VF	XF	Unc
1644	—	450	825	1,500	3,250	—

KM# 19 40 SOLDI

Silver Weight varies: 10.85-11.04g., 31 mm. **Ruler:** Filippo III **Obv:** High-collared bust to right, date below **Obv. Legend:** PHILIPPVS. III. REX. HISPAN. **Rev:** Crown with 2 branches above 5-line inscription, all in ornate frame **Rev. Inscription:** MEDIO/LANI/DVX/ET. C/40. **Note:** N&V 365.

Date	Mintage	VG	F	VF	XF	Unc
1608	—	3,000	5,000	8,500	13,500	—

KM# 59 40 SOLDI

Silver Weight varies: 9.0-9.85g., 29-30 mm. **Ruler:** Filippo IV **Obv:** High-collared bust to right, date below **Obv. Legend:** PHILIPPVS. IIII. REX. HIS'(AN). **Rev:** Crown with 2 branches above 5-line inscription, all in ornate frame **Note:** N&V 386. Varieties exist.

Date	Mintage	VG	F	VF	XF	Unc
1655	—	450	825	1,650	3,750	—

KM# 11 50 SOLDI

Silver Weight varies: 12.10-13.78g., 35 mm. **Ruler:** Filippo III **Obv:** High-collared bust to right, date under shoulder **Obv. Legend:** PHILIPPVS. III. REX. HISPA. **Rev:** Crowned shield of manifold arms, value '50' in exergue **Rev. Legend:** MEDIOLANI - DVX. ET. C. **Note:** N&V 364.

Date	Mintage	VG	F	VF	XF	Unc
1604	—	400	750	1,325	2,850	—
1605	—	1,200	2,500	4,150	8,000	—

KM# 54 1/2 FILIPPO
Silver Weight varies: 13.25-13.47g., 37 mm. **Ruler:** Filippo IV **Subject:** Marriage of Filippo IV and Maria Anna of Austria **Obv:** Crowned high-collared bust of Fillippo IV to right, 2-line inscription in exergue **Obv. Legend:** PHILIPP. IIII. HISP. RE. ET. ME(D). DVC. **Obv. Inscription:** CARACENA/GVBERN(AN). **Rev:** Crowned bust of Maria Anna to left, date below **Rev. Legend:** MARIÆ. ANNÆ. PHILIP(P). IIII. HISP. ETC. REG. VX. **Note:** Varieties exist.

Date	Mintage	VG	F	VF	XF	Unc
1649 Rare	—	—	—	—	—	—

Note: Numismatica Ars Classica, Jan. 2006 realized $33,336.

KM# 63 1/2 FILIPPO
Silver Weight varies: 13.39-13.80g., 33 mm. **Ruler:** Filippo IV **Obv:** High-collared bust to right, date below **Obv. Legend:** PHILIPPVS. IIII. REX. HISPANIAR. **Rev:** Crowned shield of manifold arms in baroque frame **Rev. Legend:** MEDIOLANI. - DVX. ET. C. **Note:** N&V 385.

Date	Mintage	VG	F	VF	XF	Unc
1657	—	400	825	1,650	3,750	—

KM# 76 1/2 FILIPPO
Silver Weight varies: 13.40-13.85g., 32-33 mm. **Ruler:** Carlo II **Obv:** Accolated busts of Carlo II and his mother to right, date below **Obv. Legend:** CAROLVS. II. HISP. REX. ET. MARIA. ANNA. TVT. ET. G. **Rev:** Crowned shield of manifold arms **Rev. Legend:** MEDIOLANI. - DVX. ET. C. **Note:** N&V 397.

Date	Mintage	VG	F	VF	XF	Unc
1666	—	200	415	1,000	3,750	—
1675	—	650	1,250	2,800	5,000	—

KM# 90 1/2 FILIPPO
Silver Weight varies: 13.27-13.60g., 41 mm. **Ruler:** Carlo II **Obv:** Bust to right, date below **Obv. Legend:** CAROLVS. II. REX. HISPANIARVM. **Rev:** Crowned shield of manifold arms **Rev. Legend:** MEDIOLANI. - DVX. ET. C. **Note:** N&V 406. Struck on thin flan from full Filippo dies, KM#92.

Date	Mintage	VG	F	VF	XF	Unc
1676	—	850	1,650	3,250	6,600	—
1694	—	1,250	2,100	3,750	8,250	—

KM# 89 1/2 FILIPPO
Silver Weight varies: 13.20-14.97g., 35-36 mm. **Ruler:** Carlo II **Obv:** Bust to right, date below **Obv. Legend:** CAROLVS. II. REX. HISPANIARVM. **Rev:** Crowned shield of manifold arms **Rev. Legend:** MEDIOLANI. - DVX. ET. C. **Note:** N&V 407. Varieties exist.

Date	Mintage	VG	F	VF	XF	Unc
1676	—	150	285	625	1,650	—
1694	—	200	375	825	2,000	—

KM# 27 1/2 DUCATONE
Silver Weight varies: 15.27-16g., 33 mm. **Ruler:** Filippo III **Obv:** Crowned high-collared bust to right, date below **Obv. Legend:** PHILIPPVS. III. REX. HISPANIA. **Rev:** Crowned ornate shield of 4-fold arms **Rev. Legend:** MEDIOLA. - DVX. ET. C. **Note:** N&V 363.

Date	Mintage	VG	F	VF	XF	Unc
1611	—	600	1,000	1,650	3,750	—

KM# 45 1/2 DUCATONE
Silver Weight varies: 15.79-16.06g., 40 mm. **Ruler:** Filippo IV **Obv:** Crowned high-collared but to right, date below shoulder **Obv. Legend:** PHILIPPVS. IIII. REX. HISPAN. **Rev:** Crowned ornate shield of 4-fold arms **Rev. Legend:** MEDIOLAN - DVX. ET. C. **Note:** N&V 384.

Date	Mintage	VG	F	VF	XF	Unc
1630	—	1,200	2,150	4,250	7,500	—
1641	—	1,200	2,150	4,250	7,500	—

KM# 21 80 SOLDI
Silver Weight varies: 21.96-22.15g., 35 mm. **Ruler:** Filippo III **Obv:** High-collared bust to right, date below **Obv. Legend:** PHILIPPVS. III. REX. HISPAN. **Rev:** Crown with 2 branches above 5-line inscription, all in ornate frame **Rev. Inscription:** MEDIO/LANI/DVX/ET. C./80. **Note:** N&V 361.

Date	Mintage	VG	F	VF	XF	Unc
1608	—	2,500	5,800	10,000	17,500	—

KM# 61 80 SOLDI
Silver Weight varies: 17.72-20.70g., 35-38 mm. **Ruler:** Filippo IV **Obv:** High-collared bust to right, date below **Obv. Legend:** PHILIPPVS. IIII. REX. HISPAN. **Rev:** Crown with 2 branches above 5-line inscription, all in ornate frame **Rev. Inscription:** MEDIO/LANI/DVX/ET. C./80. **Note:** N&V 383.

Date	Mintage	VG	F	VF	XF	Unc
1655	—	1,300	2,500	4,500	8,250	—

KM# 13 100 SOLDI
Silver Weight varies: 26.0-28.22g., 40-42 mm. **Ruler:** Filippo III **Obv:** High-collared bust to right, date below **Obv. Legend:** PHILIPPVS. III. REX. HIS(P)(A). **Rev:** Crowned shield of manifold arms in baroque frame, '100' in exergue **Rev. Legend:** MEDIOLAN(I) - DVX. ET. C. **Note:** N&V 359. Dav.#3998. Varieties exist.

Date	Mintage	VG	F	VF	XF	Unc
1604	—	800	1,650	2,850	5,000	—
1605	—	275	575	1,150	2,150	—
1606	—	800	1,650	2,850	5,000	—
1607	—	600	1,250	2,300	4,250	—

KM# 55 FILIPPO
Silver Weight varies: 26.87-27.96g., 42-43 mm. **Ruler:** Filippo IV **Obv:** High-collared bust to right, date below shoulder **Obv. Legend:** PHILIPPVS. IIII. REX. HISPANI(A)(R)(V)(M). **Rev:** Crowned shield of manifold arms in baroque frame **Rev. Legend:** MEDIOLANI. - DVX. ET. C. **Note:** N&V 382. Dav.#4003. Varieties exist.

Date	Mintage	VG	F	VF	XF	Unc
1652	—	170	325	650	1,200	—
1657	—	175	325	575	1,500	—

KM# 78 FILIPPO
Silver Weight varies: 27.27-27.82g., 41-42 mm. **Ruler:** Carlo II **Obv:** Accolated busts of Carlo II and his mother to right, date below **Obv. Legend:** CAROLVS. II. HISP. REX. ET. MARIA. ANNA. TVT. ET. G. **Rev:** Crowned shield of manifold arms in baroque frame **Rev. Legend:** MEDIOLANI. - DVX. ET. C. **Note:** N&V 396. Dav.#4004.

Date	Mintage	VG	F	VF	XF	Unc
1666	—	200	415	1,000	2,650	—

KM# 92 FILIPPO
Silver Weight varies: 25.58-27.85g., 46-47 mm. **Ruler:** Carlo II **Obv:** Bust to right, date below **Obv. Legend:** CAROLVS. II. REX. HISPANIARVM. **Rev:** Crowned shield of manifold arms in baroque frame **Rev. Legend:** MEDIOLANI. - DVX. ET. C. **Note:** N&V 405. Dav.#4005, 4007. Varieties exist.

Date	Mintage	VG	F	VF	XF	Unc
1676	—	100	210	375	875	—
1694	—	100	210	375	875	—

KM# 3.1 DUCATONE

Silver Weight varies: 31,0-32.2g., 40-41 mm. **Ruler:** Filippo III **Obv:** Crowned high-collared bust to right, date below shoulder **Obv. Legend:** PHILIPP(VS). III. REX. HISPAN(IA)(R). **Rev:** Crowned shield of 4-fold arms in baroque frame **Rev. Legend:** DVX. MEDIO - LANI. ET(.)C. **Note:** N&V 358. Dav.#3997.

Date	Mintage	VG	F	VF	XF	Unc
1602	—	800	1,650	2,850	5,800	—
1603	—	800	1,650	2,850	5,800	—
1605	—	—	—	—	—	—
Note: Reported, not confirmed.						
1606	—	—	—	—	—	—
Note: Reported, not confirmed.						
1608	—	200	375	575	1,650	—

KM# 3.2 DUCATONE

Silver Weight varies: 31.0-32.2g., 40-41 mm. **Ruler:** Filippo III **Obv:** Crowned high-collared but to right, date below shoulder **Obv. Legend:** PHILIPP. III. REX. HISPANIA. **Rev:** Crowned shield of 4-fold arms in baroque frame **Rev. Legend:** MEDIOLANI - DVX. ET. C. **Note:** N&V 358 variety; Dav.#3997 variety.

Date	Mintage	VG	F	VF	XF	Unc
1608	—	200	375	575	1,650	—

KM# 43 DUCATONE

Silver Weight varies: 29.54-32.20g., 42 mm. **Ruler:** Filippo IV **Obv:** Crowned high-collared bust to right, date below shoulder **Obv. Legend:** PHILIPP(V)S. IIII. REX. HISP(A)(N). **Rev:** Crowned shield of 4-fold arms in baroque frame **Rev. Legend:** MEDIOLANI - DVX. ET. C. **Note:** N&V 381. Dav.#4001. Varieties exist.

Date	Mintage	VG	F	VF	XF	Unc
1622	—	200	375	650	2,100	—
1625	—	—	—	—	—	—
Note: Reported, not confirmed.						
1630	—	400	825	1,500	3,250	—
ND	—	—	—	—	—	—
Note: Reported, not confirmed.						

KM# 96 2 FILIPPI

Silver Weight varies: 51.0-55.5g., 41 mm. **Ruler:** Carlo II **Obv:** Bust to right, date below **Obv. Legend:** CAROLVS. II. REX. HISPANIARVM. **Rev:** Crowned shield of manifold arms in baroque frame **Rev. Legend:** MEDIOLANI. - DVX. ET. C. **Note:** Dav.#4006. Struck on thick flan from Filippo dies, KM#92.

Date	Mintage	VG	F	VF	XF	Unc
1694 Rare	—	—	—	—	—	—

KM# 5 2 DUCATONE

Silver, 40-41 mm. **Ruler:** Filippo III **Obv:** Crowned high-collared bust to right, date below shoulder **Obv. Legend:** PHILIPPVS. III. REX. HISPANIAR. **Rev:** Crowned shield of 4-fold arms in baroque frame **Rev. Legend:** DVX. MEDIO - LANI. ET. C. **Note:** Dav. #3996.

Date	Mintage	VG	F	VF	XF	Unc
1603 Rare	—	—	—	—	—	—

KM# 44 2 DUCATONE

Silver Weight varies: 60-65g., 42 mm. **Ruler:** Filippo IV **Obv:** Crowned high-collared bust to right, date below shoulder. **Obv. Legend:** PHILIPP(V)S. IIII. REX. HISP(A)(N). **Rev:** Crowned shield of 4-fold arms in baroque frame **Rev. Legend:** MEDIOLANI - DVX. ET. C. **Note:** Dav.#4000. Struck on thick flan with Ducatone dies, KM#43.

Date	Mintage	VG	F	VF	XF	Unc
1622 Rare	—	—	—	—	—	—
1630 Rare	—	—	—	—	—	—

KM# 51 2 DUCATONE

Silver Weight varies: 60-64g., 49 mm. **Ruler:** Filippo IV **Obv:** Crowned high-collared bust to right, date below **Obv. Legend:** PHILIPPVS. IIII. REX. HISPANIA(R) **Rev:** Ornately shaped shield of 4-fold arms in baroque frame, large crown above **Rev. Legend:** MEDIOLANI. - DVX. ET. C. **Note:** Dav.#4002. Varieties exist.

Date	Mintage	VG	F	VF	XF	Unc
1641 Rare	—	—	—	—	—	—
1643 Rare	—	—	—	—	—	—

KM# 46 3 DUCATONE

Silver Weight varies: 89-97g., 42 mm. **Ruler:** Filippo IV **Obv:** Crowned high-collared bust to right, date below shoulder **Obv. Legend:** PHILIPPVS. IIII. REX. HISPAN. **Rev:** Crowned shield of 4-fold arms in baroque frame **Rev. Legend:** MEDIOLANI - DVX. ET. C. **Note:** Dav.#3999. Struck on thick flan from Ducatone dies, KM#43.

Date	Mintage	VG	F	VF	XF	Unc
1630 Rare	—	—	—	—	—	—

TRADE COINAGE

KM# 29 DOPPIA

Gold Weight varies: 6.25-6.50g., 25-26 mm. **Ruler:** Filippo III **Obv:** Crowned high-collared bust to right, date below **Obv. Legend:** PHILIPPVS. III. REX. HISP. **Rev:** Crowned shield of 4-fold arms in baroque frame **Rev. Legend:** MEDIOLANI. - DVX. ET. C. **Note:** N&V 357; Fr.#721.

Date	Mintage	VG	F	VF	XF	Unc
1617	—	1,800	3,325	6,750	12,500	—

KM# 39 DOPPIA

Gold Weight varies: 6.45-6.70g., 25 mm. **Ruler:** Filippo IV **Obv:** Crowned high-collared bust to right **Obv. Legend:** PHILIPP. IIII. REX. HISP. **Rev:** Crowned ornate shield of 4-fold arms **Rev. Legend:** MEDIOLANI. - DVX. ET. C. **Note:** N&V 379; Fr.#725.

Date	Mintage	VG	F	VF	XF	Unc
ND(1621-65)	—	1,750	3,300	5,500	9,500	—

KM# 47 DOPPIA

Gold Weight varies: 6.45-6.70g., 25 mm. **Ruler:** Filippo IV **Obv:** Crowned high-collared bust to right, date below **Obv. Legend:** PHILIPP. IIII. REX. HISP. **Rev:** Crowned ornate shield of 4-fold arms **Rev. Legend:** MEDIOLANI. - DVX. ET. C. **Note:** N&V 380; Fr.#A725.

Date	Mintage	VG	F	VF	XF	Unc
1630	—	2,250	4,250	6,750	12,000	—

KM# 94 DOPPIA

Gold Weight varies: 6.30-6.61g., 25-26 mm. **Ruler:** Carlo II **Obv:** Crowned high-collared youthful bust to right **Obv. Legend:** CAROLVS. II. REX. HISPANIAR. **Rev:** Crowned ornate shield of 4-fold arms **Rev. Legend:** MEDIOLANI. - DVX. ET. C. **Note:** N&V 403; Fr.#727.

Date	Mintage	VG	F	VF	XF	Unc
1676	—	7,500	12,500	18,000	26,500	—

KM# 98 DOPPIA

Gold Weight varies: 6.30-6.61g., 25-26 mm. **Ruler:** Carlo II **Obv:** Mature, full crowned bust to right, date below **Obv. Legend:** CAROLVS. II. REX. HISPANIAR. **Rev:** Crowned ornate shield of 4-fold arms **Rev. Legend:** MEDIOLANI. - DVX. ET. C. **Note:** N&V 404; Fr.#728.

Date	Mintage	VG	F	VF	XF	Unc
1698	—	7,500	12,500	19,000	28,500	—
Note: Bowers and Merena Guia sale 3-88 choice VF realized $26,400						

KM# 23 2 DOPPIE

Gold Weight varies: 12.84-13.27g., 30 mm. **Ruler:** Filippo III **Obv:** Crowned high-collared bust to right, date below **Obv. Legend:** PHILIPPVS. III. REX. HISPANI. **Rev:** Crowned shield of 4-fold arms in baroque frame **Rev. Legend:** MEDIOLAN - I. DVX. ET. C. **Note:** N&V 355; Fr.#720.

Date	Mintage	VG	F	VF	XF	Unc
1610	—	3,000	5,000	7,500	11,500	—
1617	—	1,250	2,250	3,500	7,000	—

KM# 41 2 DOPPIE

Gold Weight varies: 12.79-13.50g., 28-29 mm. **Ruler:** Filippo IV **Obv:** Crowned high-collared bust to right **Obv. Legend:** PHILIPPVS. IIII. REX. HIS(P). **Rev:** Crowned shield of 4-fold arms in baroque frame **Rev. Legend:** MEDIOLANI - DVX. ET. C. **Note:** N&V 377; Fr.#724.

Date	Mintage	VG	F	VF	XF	Unc
ND(1621-65)	—	1,250	2,250	3,500	7,000	—

KM# 49 2 DOPPIE

Gold Weight varies: 12.79-13.50g., 28-29 mm. **Ruler:** Filippo IV **Obv:** Crowned high-collared bust to right, date below **Obv. Legend:** PHILIPP(VS). IIII. REX. H(I)(S)(P)(A)(N)(I). **Rev:** Crowned shield of 4-fold arms in baroque frame **Rev. Legend:** MEDIOLANI - DVX. ET. C. **Note:** N&V 378; Fr.#724. Varieties exist.

Date	Mintage	VG	F	VF	XF	Unc
1630	—	850	1,500	2,750	5,500	—

KM# 80 2 DOPPIE

Gold Weight varies: 12.95-13.85g., 29 mm. **Ruler:** Carlo II **Obv:** Accolated busts of Carlo II and his mother to right, date below **Obv. Legend:** CAROLVS. II. HIS. REX. ET. MARIA. ANNA. T. ET. G. **Rev:** Crowned shield of 4-fold arms in baroque frame **Rev. Legend:** MEDIOLANI. - DVX. ET. C. **Note:** N&V 395; Fr.#726.

Date	Mintage	VG	F	VF	XF	Unc
1666	—	4,500	9,000	18,500	33,000	—
1675	—	4,500	9,000	18,500	33,000	—

KM# 50 4 DOPPIE

0.9860 Gold Weight varies: 25-27g., 28-29 mm. **Ruler:** Filippo IV **Obv:** Crowned high-collared bust to right, date below **Obv. Legend:** PHILIPPVS. IIII. REX. HISPANI. **Rev:** City view of Milan in circle **Note:** Fr.#722.

Date	Mintage	VG	F	VF	XF	Unc
1630 Rare	—	—	—	—	—	—

KM# 52 20 ZECCHINI

65.6000 g., 0.9100 Gold 1.9192 oz. AGW **Ruler:** Filippo IV **Obv:** Crowned high-collared bust to right, date below **Obv. Legend:** PHILIPPVS. IIII. REX. HISPANIA. **Rev:** Ornately shaped 4-fold arms in baroque frame, large crown with 2 branches above **Rev. Legend:** MEDIOLANI - DVX. ET. C. **Note:** Fr.#723. Struck from 2 Ducatone dies, KM#51.

Date	Mintage	VG	F	VF	XF	Unc
1643 Rare	—	—	—	—	—	—

Note: Bowers and Merena Guia sale 3-88 XF realized $82,500

MIRANDOLA

Mirandola, a duchy in Modena, was originally associated with an abbey. It belonged to several families before coming into possession of the Pico. Minting rights were granted in 1515. The scudo coinage is confined to the two dukes of the 17th century. It was sold to the Estes in Modena sometime after 1708.

RULERS

Alessandro I Pico, 1602-1637
Alessandro II Pico, 1637-1691

DUCHY

STANDARD COINAGE

DAV# 4008 SCUDO

Silver **Obv:** Bust left, date below **Obv. Legend:** ALEXANDER. DVX. MIRANDVLAE **Rev:** Crowned arms in Order chain **Rev. Legend:** CONCORDIAE**MARCHIO*III

Date	Mintage	VG	F	VF	XF	Unc
1613 Rare	—	—	—	—	—	—

DAV# 4010 SCUDO

Silver **Obv:** Bust left, date below **Obv. Legend:** ALEXAN* PICVS* MIRANDVLAE* DVX* I **Rev:** Figure standing on globe, spray in hand **Rev. Legend:** ...NVNC* PEDE... CERTO

Date	Mintage	VG	F	VF	XF	Unc
1617 Rare	—	—	—	—	—	—

Note: Numismatica Ars Classica Auction 44, 11-07, VF realized approximately $34,130

DAV# 4011 SCUDO

Silver **Obv. Legend:** ALEXAN*MIRANDVLA(E)*DUX. I.

Date	Mintage	VG	F	VF	XF	Unc
1618 Rare	—	—	—	—	—	—

DAV# 4012 SCUDO

Silver **Obv:** Bust left dividing date **Obv. Legend:** ALEXANDER. DUX MIRANDVLAE. **Rev:** Crowned arms in Order chain **Rev. Legend:** CONCORDIAE*MARCHIO*III

Date	Mintage	VG	F	VF	XF	Unc
1618	—	1,850	3,250	6,500	—	—

DAV# 4013 SCUDO

Silver **Obv:** Bust right, date below legend **Obv. Legend:** ALEX. DUX. MIR... **Rev. Legend:** INSIGNA ANTIQUI-SSIMA ET MATERNO

Date	Mintage	VG	F	VF	XF	Unc
1622	—	1,800	3,000	6,000	—	—

DAV# 4014 SCUDO

Silver **Obv. Legend:** ALEXANDER. PICVS. DVS. MIR **Rev:** Crowned arms **Rev. Legend:** CONCORDIAE. MARCHIO. III.

Date	Mintage	VG	F	VF	XF	Unc
1633 Rare	—	—	—	—	—	—

DAV# 4019 SCUDO

Silver **Obv. Legend:** ALEX. PICVS. DVX. MIRA: I: E. C. **Rev:** Crowned arms **Rev. Legend:** S. ALEX. MON. -DA. BOL. TREN.

Date	Mintage	VG	F	VF	XF	Unc
ND Rare	—	—	—	—	—	—

DAV# 4009 2 SCUDI

Silver **Obv:** Bust left, date below **Rev:** Figure standing on globe, spray in hand

Date	Mintage	VG	F	VF	XF	Unc
1617 Rare	—	—	—	—	—	—

DAV# 4015 TALLERO

Silver **Obv:** Half figure of knight behind shield **Obv. Legend:** MO. NOV. DEL. DVC... **Rev:** Lion, legend, date **Rev. Legend:** VICIT. LEO. DE. TRIBV. IVDA.

Date	Mintage	VG	F	VF	XF	Unc
1636	—	850	1,650	3,200	6,500	—

DAV# 4016 TALLERO

Silver **Obv. Legend:** MO. NO. DA. SESIN.-LXX. DEL. DVX. MI.

Date	Mintage	VG	F	VF	XF	Unc
1637	—	950	1,750	3,250	6,750	—

DAV# 4017 TALLERO

Silver **Obv:** Bust right **Obv. Legend:** ALEX* DEI* GRA* AC* SACRI* ROM* IMP* DVX* M* I* **Rev:** Crowned arms in Order chain **Rev. Legend:** CONCOR* MAR* III *-* SAN* MART* BARO

Date	Mintage	VG	F	VF	XF	Unc
ND Rare	—	—	—	—	—	—

Note: Numismatica Ars Classica Auction 32, 1-06, VF realized approximately $25,400

DAV# 4018 TALLERO

Silver **Obv. Legend:** ALEX. DVX. MIR. I. CON. MAR. III. S. MART. IN. SPI. DOM. **Rev. Legend:** ANTIQVISSIMAE FA-MI...

Date	Mintage	VG	F	VF	XF	Unc
ND Rare	—	—	—	—	—	—

Note: Numismatica Ars Classica Auction 35, 12-06, XF realized approximately $27,980

DAV# 4020 DUCATONE

Silver **Obv:** Bust of Alessandro II right **Rev:** Phoenix rising from flames

Date	Mintage	VG	F	VF	XF	Unc
ND Rare	—	—	—	—	—	—

Note: Numismatica Ars Classica Auction 32, 1-06, XF realized approximately $75,400

KM# 25 24 SCUDI D'ORO

78.7800 g., Gold **Obv:** Armored bust of Alexander I left in inner circle, date below **Rev:** Crowned arms in Order collar in inner circle

Date	Mintage	VG	F	VF	XF	Unc
1618 Rare	—	—	—	—	—	—

KM# 27 2 DOPPIE

13.0900 g., Gold **Obv:** Bust of Alexander II right **Rev:** St. Savinus kneeling 3/4 facing left

Date	Mintage	VG	F	VF	XF	Unc
ND Unique	—	—	—	—	—	—

MODENA

Mutina

The ancient Mutina is a territorial division of Italy fronting on the Adriatic Sea between Venetia and Marches which became Roman in 215-212 B.C. Ravaged by Attila and Lombard attacks, it was rebuilt in the 9th century. Obizzo d'Este became its lord in 1288 and it was constituted a duchy in favor of Borso d'Este in 1452. Modena was included in the Napoleonic complex from 1796 to 1813, after which it was governed by the House of Austria-Este. Modena began coining in the 13th century and ceased in 1796.

RULERS

Cesare d'Este, 1598-1628
Francesco I d'Este, 1629-1658
Alfonso IV d'Este, 1658-1662
Francesco II d'Este, 1662-1694
Rinaldo D'Este, 1694-1737

DUCHY

STANDARD COINAGE

DAV# 4027 4 LIRE (Levant)

Silver **Obv:** Half-figure left **Obv. Legend:** CAESAR. DVX. MVT. REG. E. C. **Rev:** Crowned arms in Order chain, L4 below **Rev. Legend:** NOBILITAS.-ESTENSIS

Date	Mintage	VG	F	VF	XF	Unc
ND Rare	—	—	—	—	—	—

DAV# 4026 SCUDO

Silver **Obv:** Bust left **Obv. Legend:** CASEAR. DUX. MVT. REG. E. C. **Rev:** Crowned arms in Order chain **Rev. Legend:** NOBILITAS. ESTENSIS

Date	Mintage	VG	F	VF	XF	Unc
1613 Rare	—	—	—	—	—	—

Note: Rauch Auction 85, 11-09, XF realized approximately $37,640

DAV# 4039 SCUDO

26.4400 g., 0.9100 Silver 0.7735 oz. ASW, 42.6 mm. **Obv:** Bust right, 103 below **Obv. Legend:** FR(A) (N). (I). MV (T)... **Rev:** Crowned arms in frame **Rev. Legend:** LIBRAT. AFFERT. ET. EFERT. **Note:** Varieties exist.

Date	Mintage	VG	F	VF	XF	Unc
ND	—	1,650	3,250	5,500	9,500	—

DAV# 4038 2 SCUDI

Silver **Obv:** Bust right, 103 below **Obv. Legend:** FR(A) (N). (I). MV (T)... **Rev:** Crowned arms in frame **Rev. Legend:** LIBRAT. AFFERT. ET. EFERT.

Date	Mintage	VG	F	VF	XF	Unc
ND Rare	—	—	—	—	—	—

DAV# 4021 TALLERO (Levant)

25.8100 g., 0.9100 Silver 0.7551 oz. ASW **Obv:** Bust right, date below **Obv. Legend:** CAESAR. DVX.-MVT. REG. E. C. **Rev:** Crowned arms in frame **Rev. Legend:** NOBILITAS.-ESTENSIS

Date	Mintage	VG	F	VF	XF	Unc
1601 Rare	—	—	—	—	—	—
1602 Rare	—	—	—	—	—	—

DAV# 4022 MEZZO (1/2) DUCATONE

Silver **Obv:** Bust right **Obv. Legend:** CAESAR. DVX.-MVTINAE... **Rev:** Abundance with cornucopia **Rev. Legend:** FIRMISSIMAE...

Date	Mintage	VG	F	VF	XF	Unc
1603	—	1,750	3,400	6,400	—	—
1605	—	1,750	3,400	6,400	—	—

DAV# 4025 DUCATONE

Silver **Obv:** Bust right with LS below **Obv. Legend:** CAESAR. DVX. MVT. REG. EC. . **Rev:** Abundance with cornucopia **Rev. Legend:** FIRMISSIMAE. SPEI.

Date	Mintage	VG	F	VF	XF	Unc
1610	—	2,000	3,750	7,100	—	—
1611	—	2,000	3,750	7,100	—	—
1612	—	2,000	3,750	7,100	—	—

DAV# 4036 DUCATONE

Silver **Obv. Legend:** FR(AN) (CISCVS). I. MV(T)*R(EG)-E(T). C. DV(X). VIII.

Date	Mintage	VG	F	VF	XF	Unc
ND	—	2,150	4,000	7,500	—	—

DAV# 4036A DUCATONE

Silver **Obv:** Large draped bust

Date	Mintage	VG	F	VF	XF	Unc
ND	—	2,150	4,000	7,500	—	—

DAV# 4037 DUCATONE

Silver **Obv:** Bust right **Rev:** FRANCISCVS. I. MVT. RE(G) E(VS). C. DVX. VIII.

Date	Mintage	VG	F	VF	XF	Unc
ND Rare	—	—	—	—	—	—

Note: Künker Auction 180, 1-11, VF realized approximately $14,380

DAV# 4031 DUCATONE

Silver **Obv:** Bust right with date below **Obv. Legend:** FRANCISCVS. I. MVT. REG. ET. C. DVX. VIII **Rev:** Ship with stars above, legend, date below **Rev. Legend:** NON. ALIO. SIDERE

Date	Mintage	VG	F	VF	XF	Unc
1631	—	2,500	5,000	9,400	—	—
1632	—	2,500	5,000	9,400	—	—
1633	—	2,500	5,000	9,400	—	—
1634	—	2,500	5,000	9,400	—	—
1637	—	2,500	5,000	9,400	—	—
ND	—	2,500	5,000	9,400	—	—

DAV# 4031A DUCATONE

Silver **Obv:** Bust right **Rev:** Date below

Date	Mintage	VG	F	VF	XF	Unc
1633	—	2,500	5,000	9,400	—	—
1634	—	2,500	5,000	9,400	—	—
1637	—	2,500	5,000	9,400	—	—

DAV# 4032 DUCATONE

Silver **Obv:** Bust left **Obv. Legend:** FRAN*I*... **Rev:** Date in legend

Date	Mintage	VG	F	VF	XF	Unc
1639	—	2,150	4,000	7,500	—	—

DAV# 4034 DUCATONE

Silver **Obv:** Bust left breaking legend at top **Obv. Legend:** FR*I*MVT*RE-E*C...

Date	Mintage	VG	F	VF	XF	Unc
1640	—	2,150	4,000	7,500	—	—
1646	—	2,150	4,000	7,500	—	—
1649	—	2,150	4,000	7,500	—	—
ND	—	2,150	4,000	7,500	—	—

DAV# 4040 DUCATONE

Silver **Obv:** Bust right with date and ET below **Obv. Legend:** ALPH. IV. MV. RE. E. C. DVX. IX. **Rev:** Sword in spray circle **Rev. Legend:** ALTERVTRVM...

Date	Mintage	VG	F	VF	XF	Unc
1659 Rare	—	—	—	—	—	—

Note: Numismatica Ars Classica Auction 32, 1-06, XF realized approximately $39,685

DAV# 4024 2 DUCATONE

Silver **Obv:** Bust right with LS below **Obv. Legend:** CAESAR... **Rev:** Abundance with cornucopia, date below **Rev. Legend:** FIRMISSIMAE. SPEI.

Date	Mintage	VG	F	VF	XF	Unc
1612 Rare	—	—	—	—	—	—

DAV# 4028 2 DUCATONE

Silver **Obv:** Bust right with date and BS below **Obv. Legend:** FR*I*MV*R*-E*C*DV*VIII

Date	Mintage	VG	F	VF	XF	Unc
1630 Rare	—	—	—	—	—	—

DAV# 4030 2 DUCATONE

Silver **Obv:** Bust right with date bwlow **Obv. Legend:** FRANCISCVS. I… **Rev:** Ship with stars above **Rev. Legend:** NON. ALIO. SIDERE.

Date	Mintage	VG	F	VF	XF	Unc
1631	—	6,000	12,000	20,000	—	—
1632	—	6,000	12,000	20,000	—	—
1633 Rare	—	—	—	—	—	—

Note: Künker Auction 159, 9-09, VF realized approximately $19,825; Rauch Auction 75, 5-05, VF without exerge, realized approximately $40,120

Date	Mintage	VG	F	VF	XF	Unc
1634 Rare	—	—	—	—	—	—
1637 Rare	—	—	—	—	—	—
1640 Rare	—	—	—	—	—	—

DAV# 4030A 2 DUCATONE

Silver **Obv:** Bust right **Rev:** Date below

Date	Mintage	VG	F	VF	XF	Unc
1633 Rare	—	—	—	—	—	—
1634 Rare	—	—	—	—	—	—
1637 Rare	—	—	—	—	—	—

DAV# 4033 2 DUCATONE

Silver **Obv:** Bust left **Obv. Legend:** FR(AN) (CISCVS)…

Date	Mintage	VG	F	VF	XF	Unc
1649 Rare	—	—	—	—	—	—
ND Rare	—	—	—	—	—	—

DAV# 4035 2 DUCATONE

Silver **Obv:** Without initials below bust **Rev:** Without initials in exergue

Date	Mintage	VG	F	VF	XF	Unc
ND Rare	—	—	—	—	—	—

Note: Numismatica Ars Classica Auction 32, 1-06, VF/XF realized approximately $18,255

DAV# 4035A 2 DUCATONE

Silver **Obv:** Large draped bust **Obv. Legend:** FR*I*MV*R*…

Date	Mintage	VG	F	VF	XF	Unc
ND Rare	—	—	—	—	—	—

DAV# 4029 3 DUCATONE

Silver **Obv:** Bust right, legend, date below **Obv. Legend:** FRANCISCVS... **Rev:** Ship with stars above and initials in exergue

Date	Mintage	VG	F	VF	XF	Unc
1633 Rare	—	—	—	—	—	—

FR# 791 1/3 SCUDO D'ORO (103 Soldi)

0.7800 g., 0.9860 Gold 0.0247 oz. AGW **Obv:** Shield **Rev:** Displayed eagle

Date	Mintage	VG	F	VF	XF	Unc
ND	—	175	325	550	900	—

FR# 785 1/2 SCUDO D'ORO

1.7500 g., 0.9860 Gold 0.0555 oz. AGW **Obv:** Bust of Francesco I right **Rev:** Displayed eagle

Date	Mintage	VG	F	VF	XF	Unc
ND Rare	—	—	—	—	—	—

FR# A784 SCUDO D'ORO

3.5000 g., 0.9860 Gold 0.1109 oz. AGW **Obv:** Bust of Francesco I right in inner circle **Rev:** Crowned arms in inner circle

Date	Mintage	VG	F	VF	XF	Unc
1651	—	775	1,400	2,100	4,200	—

FR# 784 SCUDO D'ORO

3.5000 g., 0.9860 Gold 0.1109 oz. AGW **Obv:** Bust of Francesco I right **Rev:** Displayed eagle

Date	Mintage	VG	F	VF	XF	Unc
ND Rare	—	—	—	—	—	—

FR# 779 2 SCUDI D'ORO

7.0000 g., 0.9860 Gold 0.2219 oz. AGW **Obv:** Bust of Francesco I right in inner circle **Rev:** Madonna facing child in inner circle

Date	Mintage	VG	F	VF	XF	Unc
1631	—	800	2,000	3,750	7,500	—
ND	—	800	2,000	3,750	7,500	—

FR# 783 2 SCUDI D'ORO

7.0000 g., 0.9860 Gold 0.2219 oz. AGW **Rev:** Displayed eagle

Date	Mintage	VG	F	VF	XF	Unc
ND	—	5,300	8,300	13,500	—	—

FR# A783 2 SCUDI D'ORO

7.0000 g., 0.9860 Gold 0.2219 oz. AGW **Obv:** Bust of Alfonso right **Rev:** Crowned arms on eagle

Date	Mintage	VG	F	VF	XF	Unc
1660 Rare	—	—	—	—	—	—
ND Rare	—	—	—	—	—	—

FR# 778.2 4 SCUDI D'ORO

14.0000 g., 0.9860 Gold 0.4438 oz. AGW **Obv:** Bust of Francesco I right with ruffled collar **Rev:** Madonna facing child in inner circle **Note:** Varieties exist.

Date	Mintage	VG	F	VF	XF	Unc
ND(1629-58) IT	—	2,400	4,200	6,000	11,500	—

FR# 778.1 4 SCUDI D'ORO

14.0000 g., 0.9860 Gold 0.4438 oz. AGW **Obv:** Bust of Francesco I right **Rev:** Madonna with child

Date	Mintage	VG	F	VF	XF	Unc
1632	—	775	1,500	2,400	5,500	—
1634	—	775	1,500	2,400	5,500	—
ND GFM	—	775	1,500	2,400	5,500	—

FR# 782 4 SCUDI D'ORO

14.0000 g., 0.9860 Gold 0.4438 oz. AGW **Rev:** Displayed eagle

Date	Mintage	VG	F	VF	XF	Unc
ND Rare	—	—	—	—	—	—

FR# A782 4 SCUDI D'ORO

14.0000 g., 0.9860 Gold 0.4438 oz. AGW **Obv:** Bust of Alfonso right **Rev:** Crowned arms on eagle

Date	Mintage	VG	F	VF	XF	Unc
1660 Rare	—	—	—	—	—	—

FR# 776 6 SCUDI D'ORO

21.0000 g., 0.9860 Gold 0.6657 oz. AGW **Obv:** Bust of Francesco I left **Rev:** Sailing ship

Date	Mintage	VG	F	VF	XF	Unc
ND	—	3,500	7,000	13,000	22,500	—

FR# 775 8 SCUDI D'ORO

28.0000 g., 0.9860 Gold 0.8876 oz. AGW **Obv:** Bust of Francesco I left **Rev:** Sailing ship

Date	Mintage	VG	F	VF	XF	Unc
1631 Rare	—	—	—	—	—	—
1633 Rare	—	—	—	—	—	—
ND Rare	—	—	—	—	—	—

Note: Stack's International sale 3-88 VF realized $14,300

FR# 777 8 SCUDI D'ORO

28.0000 g., 0.9860 Gold 0.8876 oz. AGW **Obv:** Bust of Francesco I left **Rev:** Madonna with child

Date	Mintage	VG	F	VF	XF	Unc
1631 Rare	—	—	—	—	—	—

FR# 773 12 SCUDI D'ORO

42.0000 g., 0.9860 Gold 1.3314 oz. AGW **Obv:** Bust of Francesco I right **Rev:** Madonna with child

Date	Mintage	VG	F	VF	XF	Unc
1633 Rare	—	—	—	—	—	—

Note: Stack's International sale 3-88 XF realized $28,600

FR# 770 24 SCUDI D'ORO

84.0000 g., 0.9860 Gold 2.6627 oz. AGW **Obv:** Bust of Francesco I left **Rev:** Sailing ship

Date	Mintage	VG	F	VF	XF	Unc
1631 Rare	—	—	—	—	—	—
ND Rare	—	—	—	—	—	—

Note: Bowers and Merena Guia sale 3-88 choice VF realized $48,400

FR# 765 DOPPIA

7.0000 g., 0.9860 Gold 0.2219 oz. AGW **Obv:** Cesare **Rev:** Patience

Date	Mintage	VG	F	VF	XF	Unc
1605	—	1,800	3,750	7,500	14,500	—
1606	—	1,800	3,750	7,500	14,500	—
1608	—	1,800	3,750	7,500	14,500	—
1609	—	1,800	3,750	7,500	14,500	—

FR# 787 DOPPIA

7.0000 g., 0.9860 Gold 0.2219 oz. AGW **Obv:** Francesco I standing right divides date **Rev:** Double-headed eagle

Date	Mintage	VG	F	VF	XF	Unc
1639 Rare	—	—	—	—	—	—

FR# 780 DOPPIA

3.5000 g., 0.9860 Gold 0.1109 oz. AGW **Obv:** Bust of Francesco I right in inner circle **Rev:** Crowned arms in inner circle

Date	Mintage	VG	F	VF	XF	Unc
1651 Rare	—	—	—	—	—	—

FR# 766 2 DOPPIE

14.0000 g., 0.9860 Gold 0.4438 oz. AGW **Obv:** Bust of Cesare right in inner circle **Rev:** Woman standing

Date	Mintage	VG	F	VF	XF	Unc
1608 Rare	—	—	—	—	—	—

FR# 767 4 DOPPIE

28.0000 g., 0.9860 Gold 0.8876 oz. AGW **Obv:** Bust of Cesare right in inner circle **Rev:** Soldier seated left in inner circle

Date	Mintage	VG	F	VF	XF	Unc
1612 Rare	—	—	—	—	—	—

FR# 768 4 DOPPIE

28.0000 g., 0.9860 Gold 0.8876 oz. AGW **Obv:** Bust of Cesare left in inner circle **Rev:** Crowned displayed eagle wtih head left

Date	Mintage	VG	F	VF	XF	Unc
ND Rare	—	—	—	—	—	—

TRADE COINAGE

FR# 764 1/4 DUCAT

0.8750 g., 0.9860 Gold 0.0277 oz. AGW **Obv:** Cesare standing right **Rev:** Crowned arms

Date	Mintage	VG	F	VF	XF	Unc
ND Rare	—	—	—	—	—	—

FR# 786 DUCAT

3.5000 g., 0.9860 Gold 0.1109 oz. AGW **Obv:** Francesco I standing right **Rev:** Value and date in tablet

Date	Mintage	VG	F	VF	XF	Unc
1649	—	425	825	1,450	2,550	—

FR# 788 DUCAT

3.5000 g., 0.9860 Gold 0.1109 oz. AGW **Obv:** Francesco I standing divides date **Rev:** Double-headed eagle

Date	Mintage	VG	F	VF	XF	Unc
1649	—	450	875	1,550	3,200	—

FR# 789 DUCAT

3.5000 g., 0.9860 Gold 0.1109 oz. AGW **Rev:** Displayed eagle with shield of arms on breast

Date	Mintage	VG	F	VF	XF	Unc
1649	—	425	825	1,450	3,000	—

KM# A789 DUCAT

3.5000 g., 0.9860 Gold 0.1109 oz. AGW **Ruler:** Francesco I d'Este **Obv:** Francesco I standing, divides date **Obv. Legend:** FRA(retro N)C • I • MV • & • E • C • DV : X • VIII **Rev:** Crowned shield, small eagle at top of shield **Rev. Legend:** NOBILITAS ESTENSIS

Date	Mintage	VG	F	VF	XF	Unc
1649 Rare	—	—	—	—	—	—

Note: Auktionshaus H. D. Rauch GmbH Auction 82, 4-08, VF+ realized approximately $12,700; Baldwin's Auctions Ltd. Auction 48, 9-06, VF+ realized approximately $6,825

FR# 795 DUCAT

3.5000 g., 0.9860 Gold 0.1109 oz. AGW **Ruler:** Francesco II d'Este

Date	Mintage	VG	F	VF	XF	Unc
ND	—	800	1,200	3,000	6,000	—

NAPLES & SICILY

Two Sicilies

Consisting of Sicily and the south of Italy, Naples & Sicily came into being in 1130. It passed under Spanish control in 1502; Naples was conquered by Austria in 1707. In 1733 Don Carlos of Spain was recognized as king. From then until becoming part of the United Kingdom of Italy, Naples and Sicily, together and separately, were contested for by Spain, Austria, France, and the republican and monarchial factions of Italy.

RULERS

Spanish

Philip IV, 1621-1665
Charles II, 1665-1700

MINT OFFICIALS' INITIALS

Initial	Date	Name
AC	1676, 78-83	Antonio Caputo
AG	1683-1714	Andrea Giovane
B, FB	1622-25	Fabrizio Biblia
DC	1648-?	Domenico Caropreso
GAC	1636-48	Giovanni Andrea Cavo
GM	1647-48	Giuseppe Maffei
MC	1621-26	Michele Cavo
O	1635-36	Orazio Calentano
OC	1677	Ottavio Caropreso
P	1625-31	Pietro Palomera
S	1631-35	Lorenzo Salomone

ASSAYERS' INITIALS

A	1676, 78-83	F. Antonio Ariani
C	1621-30	Constantino Di Costanzo
C	1631-35	Antonio Di Costanzo
C	1635	G. Antonio Consolo
N	1642-47, 48	Germano De Novellis
P	1647	Geronimo Pontecorvo

ENGRAVERS' INITIALS

Usually found on the obverse below the portrait.

AH	1674	Arina Amerani
IM	1688	Giovanni Montemein
NG	1621	Nicola Galoti at the Torre Annunziata Mint

KINGDOM

Spanish Rule

STANDARD COINAGE

KM# 1 CAVALLO

0.7100 g., Copper, 18 mm. **Ruler:** Filippo III **Obv:** Cornucopia divides date **Obv. Legend:** +PHILIPP. III. (DG.) REX. ARA. VT. **Rev:** Flint stone with 4 flames and 4 steel strikers around, no legend **Note:** Ref. F-286.

Date	Mintage	VG	F	VF	XF	Unc
1606 Rare	—	—	—	—	—	—
1607	—	45.00	90.00	325	500	—
1609 Rare	—	—	—	—	—	—

KM# 32 CAVALLO

0.8900 g., Copper, 15 mm. **Ruler:** Filippo IV **Obv:** Crowned and armored bust to right **Obv. Legend:** PHILIPP. IIII. D. G. R. **Rev:** Horse walking to left **Rev. Legend:** EQVITAS - REGNI. **Note:** Ref. F-280.

Date	Mintage	VG	F	VF	XF	Unc
ND(1621-23) MC Rare	—	—	—	—	—	—
ND(1626-30) M/C	—	140	300	700	1,150	—

KM# 33 2 CAVALLI

1.7800 g., Copper, 20 mm. **Ruler:** Filippo IV **Obv:** Crowned youthful head to left **Obv. Legend:** PHILIPPVS. IIII. REX. **Rev:** Crown with 2 crossed scepters placed through it **Rev. Legend:** ARAGO. VTR. SICILIE. **Note:** Ref. F-277. Irregular flan.

Date	Mintage	VG	F	VF	XF	Unc
ND(1621-23)	—	55.00	115	475	725	—
ND(1623-25) B	—	20.00	45.00	225	365	—

KM# 43 2 CAVALLI

1.7800 g., Copper, 19 mm. **Ruler:** Filippo IV **Obv:** Armored bust to right, date at end of legend **Obv. Legend:** PHILIPP. IIII. R. **Rev:** Two cornucopias crossed at lower ends **Rev. Legend:** PBVLICA. COMMODITAS. **Note:** Ref. F-279.

Date	Mintage	VG	F	VF	XF	Unc
1622 M/C	—	—	—	—	—	—

Note: Reported, not confirmed.

Date	Mintage	VG	F	VF	XF	Unc
1632 S	—	100	220	550	900	—

KM# 59 2 CAVALLI

1.7800 g., Copper, 20 mm. **Ruler:** Filippo IV **Obv:** Youthful head to right **Obv. Legend:** PHILIPPVS. IIII. D. **Rev:** Royal crown in plain field **Rev. Legend:** DEVS. CVSTODIAT. **Note:** Ref. F-278. Irregular flan.

Date	Mintage	VG	F	VF	XF	Unc
ND(1630-34) S/C	—	70.00	145	450	775	—

KM# 62 2 CAVALLI

1.7800 g., Copper, 20 mm. **Ruler:** Filippo IV **Obv:** Youthful head to left **Obv. Legend:** PHILIPPVS. IIII. D. **Rev:** Royal crown in plain field **Rev. Legend:** DEVS. CVSTODIAT. **Note:** Ref. F-278/1.

Date	Mintage	VG	F	VF	XF	Unc
1632 S/C Rare	—	—	—	—	—	—

KM# 63 2 CAVALLI

1.7800 g., Copper, 20 mm. **Ruler:** Filippo IV **Obv:** Youthful head to left **Obv. Legend:** PHILIPPVS. IIII. D. **Rev:** Royal crown in plain field **Rev. Legend:** ARAG. VTRIV. SICIL. **Note:** Ref. F-278/3.

Date	Mintage	VG	F	VF	XF	Unc
1632 Rare	—	—	—	—	—	—

KM# 67 2 CAVALLI

1.7800 g., Copper, 20 mm. **Ruler:** Filippo IV **Obv:** Crowned head to right **Obv. Legend:** PHILIPPVS. IIII. D. **Rev:** Royal crown in plain field **Rev. Legend:** DEVS. CVSTODIAT. **Note:** Ref. F-278/4.

Date	Mintage	VG	F	VF	XF	Unc
1636 O/C	—	70.00	145	450	775	—

KM# 68 2 CAVALLI

1.7800 g., Copper, 20 mm. **Ruler:** Filippo IV **Obv:** Crowned head to right **Obv. Legend:** PHILIPPVS. IIII. D. G. REX. **Rev:** Royal crown within wreath, no legend **Note:** Ref. F-278/5.

Date	Mintage	VG	F	VF	XF	Unc
1636 GA/C Rare	—	—	—	—	—	—

KM# 34 3 CAVALLI

2.0000 g., Copper, 16-20 mm. **Ruler:** Filippo IV **Obv:** Crowned young head to right, date at end of legend **Obv. Legend:** PHILIPP(VS). (IIII) D G. **Rev:** Jerusalem cross with small cross in each angle, all within wreath, no legend **Note:** Ref. F-272. Varieties exist.

Date	Mintage	VG	F	VF	XF	Unc
1621 MC Rare	—	—	—	—	—	—
1622 MC	—	55.00	115	400	700	—

KM# 54 3 CAVALLI

1.8900 g., Copper, 20 mm. **Ruler:** Filippo IV **Obv:** Crowned young head to right, date below **Obv. Legend:** PHILIPPVS. IIII. REX. **Rev:** Jerusalem cross with flame in each angle **Rev. Legend:** IN. HOC. SIGNO. VINCES. **Note:** Ref. F-273.

Date	Mintage	VG	F	VF	XF	Unc
1625	—	20.00	45.00	200	350	—
1625 B	—	15.00	30.00	175	300	—
1628 B Rare	—	—	—	—	—	—

KM# 56 3 CAVALLI

2.6700 g., Copper, 20 mm. **Ruler:** Filippo IV **Obv:** Crowned and armored bust to right **Obv. Legend:** PHILIPP. IIII. D. G. R. **Rev:** Steel striker above flint stones and flames, date at bottom in margin **Rev. Legend:** ANTE. FERIT. **Note:** Ref. F-274.

Date	Mintage	VG	F	VF	XF	Unc
1626 M/C	—	20.00	45.00	215	365	—
1627 M/C	—	140	290	750	1,150	—
1629 M/C	—	140	290	750	1,150	—

KM# 61 3 CAVALLI

2.6700 g., Copper, 20 mm. **Ruler:** Filippo IV **Obv:** Crowned and armored bust to left, date at end of legend, where present **Obv. Legend:** PHILIPP. IIII (D.G.) R. (S). **Rev:** Foliated cross, flame in each angle **Rev. Legend:** IN. HOC. SIGNO. VINCES. **Note:** Ref. F-275.

Date	Mintage	VG	F	VF	XF	Unc
1631	—	35.00	75.00	300	575	—
1631 S	—	22.00	45.00	250	450	—
1632 S	—	60.00	130	475	725	—
1636 O/C	—	115	225	800	1,300	—
1636 GA/C	—	115	225	800	1,300	—
ND(1636) O/C Rare	—	—	—	—	—	—
1638 GA/C	—	115	225	800	1,300	—

KM# 69 3 CAVALLI

2.0000 g., Copper, 20 mm. **Ruler:** Filippo IV **Obv:** Crowned bust to left **Obv. Legend:** PHILIPPVS. IIII. D. G. R. SI. **Rev:** Jerusalem cross with small cross in each angle, all within wreath, no legend **Note:** Ref. F-272/4.

Date	Mintage	VG	F	VF	XF	Unc
1636 GA/C	—	55.00	115	400	650	—

KM# 70 3 CAVALLI

2.6700 g., Copper, 20 mm. **Ruler:** Filippo IV **Obv:** Crowned and armored bust to right, date at end of legend **Obv. Legend:** PHILIPP. IIII. D. G. R. **Rev:** Foliated cross, flame in each angle **Rev. Legend:** IN. HOC. SIGNO. VINCES. **Note:** Ref. F-275/7.

Date	Mintage	VG	F	VF	XF	Unc
1636 O/C	—	60.00	130	475	725	—

KM# 81 3 CAVALLI

2.6700 g., Copper, 19 mm. **Ruler:** Filippo IV **Obv:** Bare head to right, date below **Obv. Legend:** PHILIPP. IIII. D. G. REX. **Rev:** Foliated cross, flame in each angle **Rev. Legend:** IN. HOC. SIGNO. VINCES. **Note:** Ref. F-276.

Date	Mintage	VG	F	VF	XF	Unc
(16)46 GA/C	—	85.00	175	700	1,150	—
1647 GA/C Rare	—	—	—	—	—	—

KM# 2 TORNESE

5.2500 g., Copper, 25 mm. **Ruler:** Filippo III **Obv:** Four flint stones alternating with 4 flames around steel striker in center **Obv. Legend:** +PHILIPP. III. D G. REX. ARA. VTR. **Rev:** Cornucopia divides date within laurel wreath, no legend **Note:** Ref. F-222/10, 11.

Date	Mintage	VG	F	VF	XF	Unc
1606 Rare	—	—	—	—	—	—
1607 Rare	—	—	—	—	—	—

KM# 4 TORNESE

5.2500 g., Copper, 25 mm. **Ruler:** Filippo III **Obv:** Four flint stones alternating with 4 flames around steel striker in center **Obv. Legend:** +PHILIPP. III. D G. REX. ARA. VTR. **Rev:** Cornucopia divides date within oak wreath, no legend **Note:** Ref. F-222. An example of the 1607 date, weighting 21.42g, is probably a die trial.

Date	Mintage	VG	F	VF	XF	Unc
1607	—	8.00	15.00	90.00	145	—
1609	—	20.00	45.00	220	365	—
1610	—	10.00	22.00	110	175	—
1611	—	10.00	22.00	110	175	—
1613	—	30.00	60.00	325	500	—
1614	—	15.00	30.00	110	220	—
1615	—	8.00	15.00	90.00	145	—
1616	—	8.00	15.00	90.00	145	—
1617	—	30.00	60.00	325	500	—

KM# 10 TORNESE

5.2500 g., Copper, 24 mm. **Ruler:** Filippo III **Obv:** Cornucopia divides date **Obv. Legend:** +PHILIPP. III. D. G. REX. **Rev:** Lion lying on altar **Rev. Legend:** *VIGILAT. ET. CVSTODIT. **Note:** Ref. F-225. Numerous varieties with different letters and symbols beneath the altar on the reverse exist. An example dated 1618, weighing 24.02g is considered to be a die trial.

Date	Mintage	VG	F	VF	XF	Unc
ND(1610-20)	—	55.00	115	235	365	—
1610	—	55.00	115	235	365	—
1616	—	55.00	115	235	365	—
1617	—	10.00	22.00	100	175	—
1618	—	10.00	22.00	100	175	—
1619	—	8.00	15.00	85.00	145	—
1620	—	15.00	30.00	115	220	—

KM# 12 TORNESE

5.2500 g., Copper, 25 mm. **Ruler:** Filippo III **Obv:** Four steel strikers alternating with 4 flames around flint stone in center **Obv. Legend:** +PHILIPP. III. D G. REX. ARA. VTR. **Rev:** Cornucopia divides date within wreath, no legend **Note:** Ref. F-224.

Date	Mintage	VG	F	VF	XF	Unc
1611	—	22.00	45.00	175	290	—
1613	—	22.00	45.00	175	290	—
1615	—	22.00	45.00	175	290	—

KM# 21 TORNESE

5.2500 g., Copper, 25 mm. **Ruler:** Filippo III **Obv:** Steel striker superimposed on 2 crossed clubs, 2 flint stones alternating with 2 flames in angles **Obv. Legend:** +PHILIPP. III. D G. REX. ARA. VT. **Rev:** Large cornucopia divides date in wreath **Note:** Ref. F-223.

Date	Mintage	VG	F	VF	XF	Unc
1613	—	70.00	145	500	800	—
1616	—	30.00	60.00	225	375	—

KM# 26 TORNESE

5.2500 g., Copper, 29 mm. **Ruler:** Filippo III **Obv:** Crowned high-collared armored bust to right, date below **Obv. Legend:** PHILIP. III. D G. REX. **Rev:** Sheaves fo wheat bound together **Rev. Legend:** POPVLORVM. QVIES. **Note:** Ref. F-227.

Date	Mintage	VG	F	VF	XF	Unc
1618 FC/GC	—	125	225	1,000	1,450	—

KM# 28 TORNESE

5.2500 g., Copper, 23 mm. **Ruler:** Filippo III **Obv:** Cornucopia divides date **Obv. Legend:** +PHILIPP. III. D. G. REX. **Rev:** Lion lying on altar **Rev. Legend:** VIGILAT ET CVSTODIT. **Note:** Ref. F-226.

Date	Mintage	VG	F	VF	XF	Unc
1620	—	20.00	45.00	225	365	—
1621	—	35.00	75.00	300	450	—

KM# 35 TORNESE

3.8000 g., Copper, 23 mm. **Ruler:** Filippo IV **Obv:** Large cornucopia divides date **Obv. Legend:** PHILIPP. IIII. D. G. REX. **Rev:** Lion lying to right on altar with straight sides **Rev. Legend:** VIGILAT. ET. CVSTODIT. **Note:** Ref. F-264. Various letters appear below the altar. A very rare variety was reportedly machine-struck.

Date	Mintage	VG	F	VF	XF	Unc
1621	—	20.00	45.00	285	450	—

KM# 36 TORNESE

3.8000 g., Copper, 23 mm. **Ruler:** Filippo IV **Obv:** Large cornucopia divides date **Obv. Legend:** PHILIPP. IIII. D. G. REX. **Rev:** Lion lying to right on altar with curved sides **Rev. Legend:** VIGILAT. ET. CVSTODIT. **Note:** Ref. F-264/2. Various letters appear below altar.

Date	Mintage	VG	F	VF	XF	Unc
1621	—	50.00	115	500	750	—

KM# 37 TORNESE

3.8000 g., Copper, 28 mm. **Ruler:** Filippo IV **Obv:** Crowned head to left **Obv. Legend:** PHILIPPVS. IIII. D. G. **Rev:** Large cornucopia divides date, in circle **Rev. Legend:** PHILIP. IIII D. G. REX. **Note:** Ref. F-265.

Date	Mintage	VG	F	VF	XF	Unc
1621 MC	—	125	250	900	1,450	—

KM# 45 TORNESE

3.8000 g., Copper, 23 mm. **Ruler:** Filippo IV **Obv:** Crowned head to left, date at end of legend **Obv. Legend:** PHILIPP. IIII. D. G. **Rev:** Large cornucopia, date at end of legend, where present **Rev. Legend:** PHILIPPVS. IIII. D. G. **Note:** Ref. F-267.

Date	Mintage	VG	F	VF	XF	Unc
1622//1622 MC Rare	—	—	—	—	—	—
1622	—	125	250	750	1,150	—
1622 MC	—	55.00	115	325	575	—
1625	—	125	250	750	1,150	—

KM# 44 TORNESE

3.8000 g., Copper, 28 mm. **Ruler:** Filippo IV **Obv:** Crowned head to left, date at end of legend **Obv. Legend:** PHILIPPVS. IIII. D. G. **Rev:** Large cornucopia divides date, in circle **Rev. Legend:** PHILIP. IIII. D. G. REX. **Note:** Ref. F-265/2, 3.

Date	Mintage	VG	F	VF	XF	Unc
1622//1621 M/C	—	125	250	900	1,450	—

KM# 46 TORNESE

3.8000 g., Copper, 23 mm. **Ruler:** Filippo IV **Obv:** Crowned head to right, date at end of legend **Obv. Legend:** PHILIPP. IIII. D. G. **Rev:** Large cornucopia **Rev. Legend:** PHILIPPVS. IIII. D. G. **Note:** Ref. F-267/4.

Date	Mintage	VG	F	VF	XF	Unc
1622 Rare	—	—	—	—	—	—

KM# 55 TORNESE

3.8000 g., Copper, 23 mm. **Ruler:** Filippo IV **Obv:** Crowned head to right, date below, where present **Obv. Legend:** PHILIPPVS. IIII. REX. HISPA. **Rev:** Large cornucopia **Rev. Legend:** PVBLICE. COMMODITATI. **Note:** Ref. F-266.

Date	Mintage	VG	F	VF	XF	Unc
1625 B Rare	—	—	—	—	—	—
ND(1626-30) MC Rare	—	—	—	—	—	—

KM# 60 TORNESE

5.3000 g., Copper, 22 mm. **Ruler:** Filippo IV **Obv:** Crowned bust to left, date at end of legend, where present **Obv. Legend:** PHILIPP. IIII. D. G. R. **Rev:** Golden Fleece suspended to left in laurel wreath, no legend **Note:** Ref. F-268. Many varieties exist with letters and symbols of die-cutters.

Date	Mintage	VG	F	VF	XF	Unc
1630 GA/C	—	115	220	800	1,150	—
1631 S	—	55.00	115	425	650	—
1632 S	—	15.00	30.00	185	290	—
1633 S	—	22.00	45.00	300	450	—
1635 O/C	—	115	220	750	1,150	—
1636 O/C	—	15.00	30.00	185	290	—
1636 GA/C	—	15.00	30.00	185	290	—
ND(1636-49) GA/C	—	15.00	30.00	185	290	—
1637 O/C	—	115	220	750	1,150	—
1637 GA/C	—	55.00	115	425	750	—
1638 GA/C	—	15.00	30.00	200	375	—

KM# 71 TORNESE

5.3000 g., Copper, 24 mm. **Ruler:** Filippo IV **Obv:** Crowned and armored bust to right, date below **Obv. Legend:** PHILIPP. IIII. D. G. REX. **Rev:** Golden Fleece suspended to left in laurel wreath, no legend **Note:** Ref. F-269.

Date	Mintage	VG	F	VF	XF	Unc
1636 O/C	—	35.00	75.00	350	575	—
1637 GA/C	—	140	300	1,000	1,600	—

KM# 77 TORNESE

4.4500 g., Copper, 23 mm. **Ruler:** Filippo IV **Obv:** Bare head to left, date below, where present **Obv. Legend:** PHILIPP. IIII. D. G. R. **Rev:** Golden Fleece suspended to left, divides date, in laurel wreath, no legend **Note:** Ref. F-271.

Date	Mintage	VG	F	VF	XF	Unc
(16)42 GA/C	—	35.00	75.00	300	500	—
(16)46//(16)46 GA/C	—	15.00	30.00	150	220	—
(16)46//(16)47 GA/C	—	35.00	75.00	300	500	—
(16)47//(16)47 GA/C	—	15.00	30.00	150	220	—
(16)48//(16)47 GA/C	—	35.00	75.00	300	500	—
(16)48//(16)48 GA/C	—	15.00	30.00	165	290	—

KM# 76 TORNESE

5.3000 g., Copper, 23 mm. **Ruler:** Filippo IV **Obv:** Crowned and armored bust to left, date below, where present **Obv. Legend:** PHILIPP. IIII. D. G. R. **Rev:** Golden Fleece suspended to left, divides date, in laurel wreath, no legend **Note:** Ref. F-270.

Date	Mintage	VG	F	VF	XF	Unc
(16)42 GA/C	—	40.00	90.00	325	500	—
1642//(16)42 GA/C	—	55.00	115	425	725	—
1638//(16)42 GA/C error (1638)	—	35.00	75.00	400	700	—
1638//(16)42 GA/N error (1638)	—	35.00	75.00	400	700	—

KM# 57 9 CAVALLI

7.2100 g., Copper, 31 mm. **Ruler:** Filippo IV **Obv:** Armored bust to left **Obv. Legend:** PHILIPPVS. IIII. D. G. R. **Rev:** Castle with 3 towers divides date, lion rampant to left above, holding up sword **Rev. Legend:** FIDEI. CATHOLICE. CVLTOR. **Note:** Ref. F-263. There are many varieties of isolated letters and symbols of die-cutters. An example of 1627, 35mm, 27.63g. is likely a die trial strike.

Date	Mintage	VG	F	VF	XF	Unc
ND(1626-30) M/C	—	55.00	115	425	725	—
1626 M/C	—	35.00	75.00	300	450	—
1627 M/C	—	35.00	75.00	300	450	—
1628 M/C	—	115	220	900	1,450	—
1629 M/C	—	35.00	75.00	300	450	—
1630 M/C	—	22.00	45.00	185	290	—

KM# 3 GRANO

10.0100 g., Copper, 28 mm. **Ruler:** Filippo III **Obv:** Flint stone superimposed on 2 crossed clubs, 2 steel strikers and 2 flames alternating in angles, all in circle **Obv. Legend:** +PHILIPP. III. D G. REX. AR. VT. SI. E. T. IERV. **Rev:** Heart-shaped shield, with horizontal band, in crowned baroque frame, divides date, all in oak wreath, no legend **Note:** Ref. F-218.

Date	Mintage	VG	F	VF	XF	Unc
1606 Rare	—	—	—	—	—	—

KM# 22 GRANO

9.9000 g., Copper, 28 mm. **Ruler:** Filippo III **Obv:** Crowned high-collared bust to right **Obv. Legend:** +PHILIPP. III. D G. REX. **Rev:** Radiant sunface **Rev. Legend:** CLARITAS. VNIVERSA. **Note:** Ref. F-219.

Date	Mintage	VG	F	VF	XF	Unc
ND(1616-21) GC Rare	—	—	—	—	—	—

KM# 38 GRANO

7.6100 g., Copper, 28-31 mm. **Ruler:** Filippo IV **Obv:** Crowned bust to right **Obv. Legend:** PHILIPPVS. IIII. D. G. **Rev:** Jerusalem cross with small cross in each angle **Rev. Legend:** NEAPOLIS. REX. **Note:** Ref. F-258/9.

Date	Mintage	VG	F	VF	XF	Unc
ND(1621-23) Rare	—	—	—	—	—	—

KM# 47 GRANO

7.6100 g., Copper, 28-31 mm. **Ruler:** Filippo IV **Obv:** Crowned bust to left, date at end of legend **Obv. Legend:** PHILIPPVS. IIII. D. G. **Rev:** Jerusalem cross with small cross in each angle, date at end of legend, where present **Rev. Legend:** NEAPOLIS. REX. **Note:** Ref. F-258. A very rare example dated 1621 is machine-struck.

Date	Mintage	VG	F	VF	XF	Unc
1622//1622	—	30.00	60.00	300	475	—
1622//1622 MC	—	30.00	60.00	300	475	—
1622//1622 MC/P	—	100	220	1,000	1,600	—
1622 MC	—	15.00	30.00	185	295	—
1623//1623 MC	—	22.00	45.00	225	375	—
1623//1622 MC Rare	—	—	—	—	—	—
-//1624 M Rare	—	—	—	—	—	—

KM# 64 GRANO

10.6900 g., Copper, 32 mm. **Ruler:** Filippo IV **Obv:** Crowned and armored bust to left, date at end of legend **Obv. Legend:** PHILIPPVS. IIII. R. **Rev:** Crowned ornately-shaped shield of 2-fold arms, 4-fold arms formed by a St. Andrew's cross on left, Jerusalem cross on right **Rev. Legend:** SICILI. ET - HIERVSALEM. **Note:** Ref. F-259.

Date	Mintage	VG	F	VF	XF	Unc
1633 S	—	30.00	60.00	300	475	—
1633 O/C	—	80.00	175	450	750	—
1635 O/C	—	30.00	60.00	300	475	—
1636 O/C	—	80.00	175	450	750	—

KM# 72 GRANO

10.6900 g., Copper, 29 mm. **Ruler:** Filippo IV **Obv:** Crowned and armored bust to right, date below, where present **Obv. Legend:** PHILIPPVS. IIII. D G. R. **Rev:** Crowned Spanish shield of 2-fold arms, 4-fold arms formed by a St. Andrew's cross on left, Jerusalem cross on right, divides date **Rev. Legend:** +SICILIÆ. ET. HIERVSALEM. **Note:** Ref. F-260.

Date	Mintage	VG	F	VF	XF	Unc
-//1636 GA/C	—	185	290	800	1,250	—
1636//1636 GA/C	—	100	220	600	900	—
-//1637	—	185	290	800	1,250	—
1637//1637 GA/C	—	100	220	600	900	—
1638//1638 GA/C	—	35.00	75.00	425	675	—

KM# 73 GRANO

10.6900 g., Copper, 29 mm. **Ruler:** Filippo IV **Obv:** Crowned and armored bust to left, date below **Obv. Legend:** PHILIPPVS. IIII. D. G. R(EX). **Rev:** Crowned ornately-shaped shield of 2-fold arms, 4-fold arms formed by a St. Andrew's cross on left, Jerusalem cross on right, divides date **Rev. Legend:** +SICILIÆ. ET. HIERVSALEM. **Note:** Ref. F-261. Many varieties of die-cutters letters and symbols.

Date	Mintage	VG	F	VF	XF	Unc
1636//1636 O/C	—	22.00	45.00	350	575	—
1637//1637 GA/C	—	22.00	45.00	350	575	—
1638//1637 GA/C	—	55.00	115	600	900	—
1638//1638 GA/C	—	35.00	75.00	425	675	—
1639//1639 GA/C	—	55.00	115	600	900	—
1642//1638 GA/C	—	55.00	115	600	900	—
1642//1642 GA/C	—	55.00	115	600	900	—

KM# 78 GRANO

10.6900 g., Copper, 29 mm. **Ruler:** Filippo IV **Obv:** Bare head to left, date below **Obv. Legend:** PHILIPP. IIII. D. G. REX. **Rev:** Crowned Spanish shield of 2-fold arms, 4-fold arms formed by a St. Andrew's cross on left, Jerusalem cross on right, divides date **Rev. Legend:** SICILIÆ. ET. HIERVSALEM. **Note:** Ref. F-262. Many varieties of die-cutters letters and symbols.

Date	Mintage	VG	F	VF	XF	Unc
(16)42//1642 GA/C	—	30.00	60.00	350	575	—
1638//(16)44 GA/C	—	70.00	145	575	875	—
1644//(16)44 GA/C	—	35.00	75.00	425	650	—
1646//(16)46 GA/C	—	15.00	30.00	185	290	—
1647//(16)46 GA/C	—	35.00	75.00	375	500	—
1647//(16)47 GA/C	—	15.00	30.00	185	290	—
1647//(16)47 GAC/M	—	55.00	115	475	725	—
1648//(16)47 GA/C Rare	—	—	—	—	—	—
1648//(16)48 GA/C	—	35.00	75.00	375	500	—

KM# 48 2 GRANA

15.2200 g., Copper, 30 mm. **Ruler:** Filippo IV **Obv:** Crowned and armored bust to left **Obv. Legend:** PHILIPPVS. IIII. D. G. **Rev:** Wheat stalks tied together in bundle **Rev. Legend:** POPVLORVM. QVIES. **Note:** Ref. F-256.

Date	Mintage	VG	F	VF	XF	Unc
ND(1622-23)	—	350	575	1,500	2,500	—
ND(1622-23) MC	—	350	575	1,500	2,500	—
1622 MC	—	350	575	1,500	2,500	—

KM# 49 PUBBLICA (3 Tornesi)

Copper Weight varies: 14.32-15.22g., 30 mm. **Ruler:** Filippo IV **Obv:** Crowned and draped bust to left, date at end of legend **Obv. Legend:** PHILIPPVS. IIII. D. G. **Rev:** 4-line inscription in wreath **Rev. Inscription:** PVBLI / CA / COMMO / DITAS **Note:** Ref. F-257.

Date	Mintage	VG	F	VF	XF	Unc
1622 MC	—	22.00	45.00	225	375	—
1622 MC//P	—	80.00	175	600	900	—
1623 MC	—	35.00	75.00	350	500	—

KM# 74 CINQUINA

0.7500 g., Silver, 15 mm. **Ruler:** Filippo IV **Obv:** Crowned head to right in circle, date below **Obv. Legend:** PHILIPP. IIII. REX. **Rev:** Jerusalem cross in laurel wreath, no legend **Note:** Ref. F-255.

Date	Mintage	VG	F	VF	XF	Unc
1639 Rare	—	—	—	—	—	—

KM# 5 1/2 CARLINO

1.2500 g., Silver, 15 mm. **Ruler:** Filippo III **Obv:** Crowned and draped bust to right **Obv. Legend:** PHILIPP. III. D. G. REX. ARA. **Rev:** Two steel strikeers alternating with 2 flames around central pellet, all in wreath, no legend **Note:** Ref. F-217.

Date	Mintage	VG	F	VF	XF	Unc
ND(1609-11) IAF/G	—	30.00	60.00	125	220	—
ND(1611-21) GF/GI	—	30.00	60.00	125	220	—
ND(1611-21) G/GF	—	30.00	60.00	125	220	—

KM# 6 1/2 CARLINO

1.2500 g., Silver, 15 mm. **Ruler:** Filippo III **Obv:** Crowned head to left **Obv. Legend:** PHILIPP. III. D. G. RE. **Rev:** Two steel strikeers alternating with 2 flames around central pellet, all in wreath, no legend **Note:** Ref. F-217/3, 4.

Date	Mintage	VG	F	VF	XF	Unc
ND(1609-11) IAF/G	—	55.00	115	300	475	—

KM# 13 1/2 CARLINO

1.2500 g., Silver, 15 mm. **Ruler:** Filippo III **Obv:** Crowned head to left **Obv. Legend:** +PHILIPP. III. REX. ARA. VTRI. **Rev:** Suspended Golden Fleece facing left **Rev. Legend:** SICILIAE. ET. HIERVSA. **Note:** Ref. F-214.

Date	Mintage	VG	F	VF	XF	Unc
ND(1611-21) GF/GF	—	30.00	60.00	125	220	—
ND(1611-21) CF/CF	—	45.00	90.00	180	290	—
ND(1620) P	—	55.00	115	300	475	—

KM# 14 1/2 CARLINO

1.2500 g., Silver, 15 mm. **Ruler:** Filippo III **Obv:** Crowned youthful bust to right in circle **Obv. Legend:** +PHILIPP. III. D. G. REX. ARA. VTR. S. **Rev:** Suspended Golden Fleece facing left in circle **Rev. Legend:** +SICILIAE. ET HIERVSAL. **Note:** Ref. F-214/7.

Date	Mintage	VG	F	VF	XF	Unc
ND(1611-21)	—	55.00	115	300	475	—

KM# 15 1/2 CARLINO

1.2500 g., Silver, 19 mm. **Ruler:** Filippo III **Obv:** Crowned and draped bust to right **Obv. Legend:** +PHILIPP. III. D G. REX. ARA. VT. **Rev:** Suspended Golden Fleece facing right in laurel wreath, no legend **Note:** Ref. F-215.

Date	Mintage	VG	F	VF	XF	Unc
ND(1611-21) GF/GF	—	30.00	60.00	125	220	—
ND(1611-21) GF/GI	—	30.00	60.00	125	220	—

KM# 16 1/2 CARLINO

1.2500 Silver, 15 mm. **Ruler:** Filippo III **Obv:** Crowned and draped bust to right **Obv. Legend:** +PHILIPP. III. D G. REX. ARA. VT. SI. **Rev:** Suspended Golden Fleece facing left in laurel wreath, no legend **Note:** Ref. F-216. Zanetta.

Date	Mintage	VG	F	VF	XF	Unc
1611 IAF/G	—	55.00	115	300	475	—
ND(1611-21) GF/GI	—	15.00	30.00	95.00	175	—
ND(1611-21) GI/GF	—	15.00	30.00	95.00	175	—
ND(1611-21) GF/G	—	15.00	30.00	95.00	175	—
ND(1611-21) GF	—	15.00	30.00	95.00	175	—
ND(1611-21) GF/GF	—	45.00	90.00	180	290	—
ND(1611-21) FC/G	—	30.00	60.00	125	220	—

KM# 17 1/2 CARLINO

1.2500 g., Silver, 15 mm. **Ruler:** Filippo III **Obv:** Crowned head to left **Obv. Legend:** +PHILIPP. III. D G. REX. ARA. VT. SI. **Rev:** Suspended Golden Fleece to left in laurel wreath, no legend **Note:** Ref. F-216/8, 9.

Date	Mintage	VG	F	VF	XF	Unc
ND(1611-12)	—	30.00	60.00	125	220	—
ND(1611-21) GF/GI	—	20.00	45.00	110	220	—

KM# 18 3 CINQUINE

2.0700 g., Silver, 20 mm. **Ruler:** Filippo III **Obv:** 3-line inscription in laurel wreath **Obv. Inscription:** PHIL / III. D G. R. / HISP. **Rev:** Vertical crowned scepter divides 2-line inscription in laurel wreath **Rev. Inscription:** PAX - ET / VBER - TAS **Note:** Ref. F-212.

Date	Mintage	VG	F	VF	XF	Unc
ND(1611-21)	—	50.00	100	175	290	—
ND(1611-21) C/FC	—	20.00	45.00	150	220	—

KM# 19 3 CINQUINE

2.0700 g., Silver, 20 mm. **Ruler:** Filippo III **Obv:** Crowned high-collared bust to right **Obv. Legend:** PHILIPP. III. REX. HIS. **Rev:** Jerusalem cross with pellet in each angle **Rev. Legend:** PAC. ET. IVST. CVLTO. **Note:** Ref. F-213.

Date	Mintage	VG	F	VF	XF	Unc
ND(1611-21) FC/C	—	60.00	115	350	500	—

KM# 82 3 CINQUINE

2.3500 g., Silver, 20 mm. **Ruler:** Filippo IV **Obv:** Crowned and armored bust to right, date below **Obv. Legend:** PHILIPP. IIII. D. G. REX. **Rev:** Jerusalem cross **Rev. Legend:** IN. HOC. SIGNO. VINCES. **Note:** Ref. F-254.

Date	Mintage	VG	F	VF	XF	Unc
1647 GAC/N	—	30.00	60.00	300	475	—
1648 GAC/N	—	115	220	850	1,350	—

KM# 7 CARLINO

2.9900 g., Silver, 22 mm. **Ruler:** Filippo III **Obv:** Crowned and armored bust to right **Obv. Legend:** PHILIPP. III. D G. REX. ARA. **Rev:** 3-line inscription in wreath **Rev. Inscription:** FIDEI / DEFEN / SOR. **Note:** Ref. F-210.

Date	Mintage	VG	F	VF	XF	Unc
ND(1609-11) IAF/G	—	55.00	115	325	500	—
ND(1609-11) IAF/C	—	150	290	800	1,250	—

KM# 20 CARLINO

2.9900 g., Silver, 23 mm. **Ruler:** Filippo III **Obv:** Crowned and armored bust to right **Obv. Legend:** PHILIPP. III. D. G. REX. ARA. VT. **Rev:** Eagle perched to left **Rev. Legend:** EGO. IN. FIDE. **Note:** Ref. F-209.

Date	Mintage	VG	F	VF	XF	Unc
ND(1611-21) CF	—	100	220	850	1,350	—
ND(1611-21) CF/G	—	450	725	1,850	2,900	—

KM# 30 CARLINO

2.9600 g., Silver, 20 mm. **Ruler:** Filippo IV **Obv:** Crowned and armored high-collared bust to right **Obv. Legend:** PHILIP(P). - IIII. REX. **Rev:** Jerusalem cross, date below **Rev. Legend:** IN. HOC. SIGNO. VINCES. **Note:** Ref. F-249.

Date	Mintage	VG	F	VF	XF	Unc
1620 (error) MC/C Rare	—	—	—	—	—	—
1621 MC/C	—	30.00	60.00	185	290	—

KM# 29 CARLINO

2.4900 g., Silver, 21 mm. **Ruler:** Filippo III **Obv:** Crowned high-collared and armored bust to right **Obv. Legend:** PHILIPP. - III. REX. **Rev:** Jerusalem cross, date below **Rev. Legend:** IN HOC. SIGNO. VINCES. **Note:** Ref. F-211.

Date	Mintage	VG	F	VF	XF	Unc
16Z0	—	150	290	800	1,250	—
16Z0 FC/C	—	20.00	45.00	150	250	—
16Z1	—	150	290	800	1,250	—
16Z1 FC/C	—	20.00	45.00	150	250	—

KM# 52 CARLINO

2.9600 g., Silver, 22 mm. **Ruler:** Filippo IV **Obv:** Armored high-collared bust to right within 2 linear circles, each divided equidistantly by 'C.1' or 'G.10' in outer circle, 'G.V' in inner circle **Obv. Legend:** PHILIPPVS. IIII. REX. **Rev:** Crowned Spanish shield of manifold arms **Rev. Legend:** HISPAN(IAR). VTR. SICILIÆ. **Note:** Ref. H-250. The value indicators in the obverse circles are C.1 (Carlino 1), G.10 (Grana 10) and G.V (Grana 5), as an attempt to discourage clipping. If the outer ring could be seen, the coin would have full value. If only the inner ring was visitble, the coin would be worth only half its value.

Date	Mintage	VG	F	VF	XF	Unc
ND(1623-25) B-C	—	55.00	115	500	800	—
ND(1623-25) F/B-C	—	80.00	175	750	1,150	—
1624 F/B-C	—	185	290	1,000	1,650	—
ND(1625-26) P-C	—	55.00	115	500	800	—

MB# 53 CARLINO

3.5800 g., Silver, 25 mm. **Ruler:** Carlo V **Obv:** Large crowned bust to right **Obv. Legend:** CAROLVS. V. IM. RO. **Rev:** 4-line inscripton **Rev. Inscription:** REX. / .ARAGO. / .VTRIVS / .SI. ET. **Note:** Ref. F-147.

Date	Mintage	VG	F	VF	XF	Unc
ND(1628-46) R	—	80.00	175	475	750	—

KM# 65 CARLINO

2.9600 g., Silver, 21 mm. **Ruler:** Filippo IV **Obv:** Bare-headed armored bust to right, date below **Obv. Legend:** PHILIPPVS. IIII. R. **Rev:** Crowned Spanish shield of manifold arms **Rev. Legend:** HISPANI(AR). VTR. SICILI. **Note:** Ref. F-251.

Date	Mintage	VG	F	VF	XF	Unc
1633 S/C-P/C	—	115	220	800	1,250	—

KM# 66 CARLINO

2.9600 g., Silver, 22 mm. **Ruler:** Filippo IV **Obv:** Bare-headed armored bust to right, date at end of legend **Obv. Legend:** PHILIPPVS. IIII. R. **Rev:** Crowned ornately-shaped shield of manifold arms **Rev. Legend:** HISPANIA. V. SICILIÆ. **Note:** Ref. F-252.

Date	Mintage	VG	F	VF	XF	Unc
1634 O	—	185	290	1,500	2,200	—
1634 S	—	185	290	1,500	2,200	—
1634 S/C	—	35.00	75.00	300	475	—

KM# 83 CARLINO

2.9800 g., Silver, 19 mm. **Ruler:** Filippo IV **Obv:** Crowned and armored bust to right in beaded and linear circles **Obv. Legend:** PHILIPP. IIII. D. G. REX. **Rev:** Jerusalem cross in beaded and linear circles, date at end of legend **Rev. Legend:** IN. HOC. SIGNO. VINCES. **Note:** Ref. F-253.

Date	Mintage	VG	F	VF	XF	Unc
1647 GM/P-N Rare	—	—	—	—	—	—

KM# 27 15 GRANA

3.7400 g., Silver, 24 mm. **Ruler:** Filippo III **Obv:** Armored high-collared bust to left **Obv. Legend:** PHILIP. III. REX. HI. **Rev:** Castle with 3 towers, each of which is surmounted by an heraldic animal, date in exergue, where present **Rev. Legend:** SVFFICIT. OMNIB. **Note:** Ref. F-208.

Date	Mintage	VG	F	VF	XF	Unc
1618 FC/C	—	35.00	75.00	300	475	—
1619 FC/C	—	35.00	75.00	300	475	—
ND(1619-21) FC/C	—	100	220	800	1,250	—

KM# 84 15 GRANA

4.9900 g., Silver, 24 mm. **Ruler:** Filippo IV **Obv:** Crowned and armored bust to right in beaded circle, date in margin below **Obv. Legend:** PHILIPP. IIII. D. G. REX. **Rev:** Jerusalem cross, flame in each angle, all in beaded circle **Rev. Legend:** IN. HOC. SIGNO. VINCES. **Note:** Ref. F-248.

Date	Mintage	VG	F	VF	XF	Unc
1647 GAC/N	—	55.00	115	500	800	—
1647 GAC/M	—	100	220	775	1,350	—
1648 GAC/N	—	55.00	115	500	800	—

KM# 8 TARI

5.9800 g., Silver, 28 mm. **Ruler:** Filippo III **Obv:** Crowned and armored bust to right **Obv. Legend:** PHILIPP. III. D G. REX. AR(A). **Rev:** Heart-shaped shield of manifold arms in crowned baroque frame **Rev. Legend:** SICILIAE. - HIERVSALE. **Note:** Ref. F-206.

Date	Mintage	VG	F	VF	XF	Unc
ND(1609-11) IAF/G	—	55.00	115	600	900	—
ND(1609-11) G/G	—	140	290	1,000	1,650	—

KM# 31 TARI

5.9800 g., Silver, 26 mm. **Ruler:** Filippo III **Obv:** Armored high-collared bust to right **Obv. Legend:** PHILIPPVS. III. REX. HISP. **Rev:** Radiant sunface in circle, date in margin at bottom **Rev. Legend:** OMNES. AB. IPSO. **Note:** Ref. F-207.

Date	Mintage	VG	F	VF	XF	Unc
1620 FC/C-NGF	—	1,000	1,450	5,500	8,750	—

KM# 41 TARI

5.9800 g., Silver, 27-28 mm. **Ruler:** Filippo IV **Obv:** Crowned and draped high-collared bust to right, date at end of legend, where present **Obv. Legend:** PHILIPP. IIII. D. G. **Rev:** Heart-shaped shield of manifold arms in crowned baroque frame **Rev. Legend:** HISP. VTRIV. SICILIE. REX. **Note:** Ref. F-245.

Date	Mintage	VG	F	VF	XF	Unc
ND(1621-23) MC/C	—	55.00	115	325	575	—
1622	—	55.00	115	325	575	—
1622 M/C	—	70.00	145	650	1,000	—
1622 MC/C	—	30.00	60.00	225	365	—
1622 BC	—	55.00	115	350	575	—
1622 BC/C	—	115	220	1,000	1,500	—
1623 MC/C	—	80.00	145	675	1,000	—
1623 B/C	—	55.00	115	350	575	—
1625 P/C	—	450	725	2,200	3,600	—
1626 MC/C	—	450	725	2,200	3,600	—

KM# 39 TARI

5.9800 g., Silver, 27 mm. **Ruler:** Filippo IV **Obv:** Young crowned and draped bust to left **Obv. Legend:** PHILIPP. IIII. D. G. REX. HISP. **Rev:** Crowned Spanish shield of manifold arms, Order of Golden Fleece suspended around **Rev. Legend:** HISP. VTR - SICIL. REX. **Note:** Ref. F-244.

Date	Mintage	VG	F	VF	XF	Unc
ND(1621) NG Rare	—	—	—	—	—	—

KM# 40 TARI

5.9800 g., Silver, 27 mm. **Ruler:** Filippo IV **Obv:** Young crowned and draped bust to left **Obv. Legend:** PHILIPP. IIII. D. G. REX. HISP. **Rev:** Crowned Spanish shield of manifold arms **Rev. Legend:** VTRIVSQUE - SICILIÆ. **Note:** Ref. F-244/1, 2.

Date	Mintage	VG	F	VF	XF	Unc
ND(1621-23) MC Rare	—	—	—	—	—	—

KM# 53 TARI

5.9800 g., Silver, 27 mm. **Ruler:** Filippo IV **Obv:** Armored high-collared bust to right within 2 linear circles, each divided equidistantly by 'C.II' in outer circle, 'C.I' in inner circle **Obv. Legend:** PHILIP - IIII. REX. **Rev:** Crowned ornately-shaped shield of manifold arms in double circle **Rev. Legend:** HISPANIAR. - VTRIV. SICILIÆ. **Note:** Ref. F-247. The value indicators in the obverse circles are C.II (Carlini 2) and C.I (Carlino I), as an attempt to discourage clipping. If the outer ring could be seen, the coin would have full value. If only the inner ring was visitble, the coin would be worth only half its value.

Date	Mintage	VG	F	VF	XF	Unc
ND(1623-25) Rare	—	—	—	—	—	—

KM# 79 TARI

5.9800 g., Silver, 26 mm. **Ruler:** Filippo IV **Obv:** Bare-headed bust to left, date below **Obv. Legend:** +PHILIPPVS + IIII + D + G + REX + **Rev:** Oval shield of manifold arms in crowned baroque frame **Rev. Legend:** +SICILIAE+ - +HIERVSAL+ **Note:** Ref. F-246.

Date	Mintage	VG	F	VF	XF	Unc
1642 GAC/N	—	1,500	2,200	7,500	11,500	—

KM# 85 3 CARLINI

10.0000 g., Silver, 29 mm. **Ruler:** Filippo IV **Obv:** Draped bust to right in circle, date in margin at bottom **Obv. Legend:** PHILIPP. IIII. DEI. GRA. **Rev:** Large crown in circle, within laurel wreath, no legend **Note:** Ref. F-242.

Date	Mintage	VG	F	VF	XF	Unc
1647 GM/P	—	600	875	2,350	3,800	—

KM# 23 1/3 SCUDO

11.3400 g., Silver, 31 mm. **Ruler:** Filippo III **Obv:** Armored high-collared bust to left **Obv. Legend:** PHILIPP III. D G REX HIS. **Rev:** Jerusalem cross, date below **Rev. Legend:** + IN. HOC. **Note:** Ref. F-203.

Date	Mintage	VG	F	VF	XF	Unc
1617 IC/C	—	450	725	1,200	1,850	—
1618 IC/C	—	800	1,150	1,800	2,750	—

KM# 9 1/2 DUCATO

14.9500 g., Silver, 38 mm. **Ruler:** Filippo III **Obv:** Crowned and armored bust to left **Obv. Legend:** PHILIPP. III. D G. REX. ARAG. VT(RI). **Rev:** Heart-shaped shield of manifold arms in crowned baroque frame **Rev. Legend:** + SICILIAE. ET - HIERVSALE + **Note:** Ref. F-202.

Date	Mintage	VG	F	VF	XF	Unc
ND(1609-11) IAF/G	—	150	290	1,100	1,850	—
1609 IAF/G	—	75.00	145	600	900	—
1609 IAF	—	150	290	1,100	1,850	—
1609 G	—	275	450	1,850	2,750	—
1610 IAF/G	—	150	290	1,100	1,850	—

KM# 50 1/2 DUCATO

14.8200 g., Silver, 37 mm. **Ruler:** Filippo IV **Obv:** Crowned and armored bust to right, date at end of legend **Obv. Legend:** PHILIPPVS. IIII. D. G. **Rev:** Heart-shaped shield of man arms in crowned baroque frame **Rev. Legend:** HISP. VTRIVS. SICILIE. REX. **Note:** Ref. F-240.

Date	Mintage	VG	F	VF	XF	Unc
1622 MC/C	—	1,500	2,750	8,000	11,500	—

KM# 90 1/2 DUCATO

14.8200 g., Silver, 37 mm. **Ruler:** Filippo IV **Obv:** Crowned and armored high-collared bust to right, date below, where present **Obv. Legend:** PHILIPPVS. IIII. DEI. GRA. REX. **Rev:** Heart-shaped shield of manifold arms in large crowned baroque frame, no legend **Note:** Ref. F-241.

Date	Mintage	VG	F	VF	XF	Unc
1648 DC/N	—	1,500	2,750	8,000	11,500	—
1648 GP/N Rare	—	—	—	—	—	—
ND(1648)	—	1,000	1,450	5,500	8,750	—
ND(1648) P Rare	—	—	—	—	—	—

KM# 24 1/2 SCUDO

16.5700 g., Silver, 37 mm. **Ruler:** Filippo III **Obv:** Crowned and armored high-collared bust to right, date below **Obv. Legend:** PHILIPP. III. D. G. REX. HIS. **Rev:** Crowned displayed eagle in circle **Rev. Legend:** + Q - VOD + VIS + **Note:** Ref. F-201.

Date	Mintage	VG	F	VF	XF	Unc
1617 IC	—	800	1,150	3,800	5,250	—
1617 IC/C	—	800	1,150	3,800	5,250	—

KM# 51 DUCATO

29.6400 g., Silver, 44 mm. **Ruler:** Filippo IV **Obv:** Crowned and armored bust to right, in circle, date below in margin **Obv. Legend:** PHILIPPVS. IIII. D(EI). G(RA). **Rev:** Heart-shaped shield of manifold arms in crowned baroque frame **Rev. Legend:** HISP. VTRIVSQ. SICILIE. REX. **Note:** Ref. F-239; Dav. 4043.

Date	Mintage	VG	F	VF	XF	Unc
1622 MC/C Rare	—	—	—	—	—	—

Note: Numismatica Ars Classica Auction 32, 1-06, XF realized approximately $29,600

KM# 25 SCUDO

33.1400 g., Silver, 43 mm. **Ruler:** Filippo III **Obv:** Crowned and armored high-collared bust to right, date below shoulder **Obv. Legend:** PHILIPP III: D G: REX: HI. **Rev:** Crowned displayed eagle in circle **Rev. Legend:** + Q - VOD + VI - S + **Note:** Ref. F-200; Dav. 4042.

Date	Mintage	VG	F	VF	XF	Unc
1617 IC Rare	—	—	—	—	—	—
1617 IC/C Rare	—	—	—	—	—	—

Note: Numismatica Ars Classica Auction 35, 12-06, VF realized approximately $17,340

TRADE COINAGE

KM# 42 SCUDO D'ORO

3.3800 g., Gold, 21 mm. **Ruler:** Filippo IV **Obv:** Youthful bare head to right, date below **Obv. Legend:** PHILIPP. IIII. HISPA. RE(X). **Rev:** Heart-shaped shield of manifold arms in crowned baroque frame **Rev. Legend:** SICILIAE. HIERVSAL. **Note:** Ref. F-237; Fr. 840.

Date	Mintage	VG	F	VF	XF	Unc
1621 B/C Rare	—	—	—	—	—	—
ND(1621-23) MC/C Rare	—	—	—	—	—	—
ND(1621-25) Rare	—	—	—	—	—	—
1622 MC/C	—	2,000	2,900	10,000	14,500	—
ND(1623-25) B/C Rare	—	—	—	—	—	—
1623 B/C	—	600	875	1,850	3,000	—
1623 P/C Rare	—	—	—	—	—	—
1624 BC	—	800	1,150	2,350	3,750	—
1625 P/C	—	1,000	1,450	8,000	11,500	—
ND(1625-26) P/C Rare	—	—	—	—	—	—
1625 Rare	—	—	—	—	—	—
1626 MC/C	—	600	875	1,850	3,000	—
1627 MC/C	—	600	875	1,850	3,000	—
1628 MC/C	—	900	1,300	7,500	11,500	—

KM# 80 SCUDO D'ORO

3.3800 g., Gold, 23 mm. **Ruler:** Filippo IV **Obv:** Bare-headed bust to left, date below shoulder **Obv. Legend:** PHILIPPVS. IIII. D. G. REX. **Rev:** Heart-shaped shield of manifold arms in crowned baroque frame **Rev. Legend:** +SICILIAE+ - +HIERVSAL+ **Note:** Ref. F-238; Fr. 841.

Date	Mintage	VG	F	VF	XF	Unc
1642 GAC/N	—	1,600	2,900	7,500	11,500	—
1647 GAC/N	—	1,700	2,500	6,000	10,000	—
1649 GAC/N	—	1,600	2,900	7,500	11,500	—

NEAPOLITAN REPUBLIC

STANDARD COINAGE

KM# 86 TORNESE

2.3500 g., Copper, 21 mm. **Obv:** Crowned squarish shield with rounded bottom, SPQN in band across center **Obv. Legend:** HEN. DE. LOR. DVX. REIP. N. **Rev:** Bunch of grapes in circle, date at end of legend **Rev. Legend:** LETIFICAT. **Note:** Ref. F-284.

Date	Mintage	VG	F	VF	XF	Unc
1648 GA/C	—	30.00	60.00	275	450	—

KM# 87 GRANO

4.9700 g., Copper, 24 mm. **Obv:** Crowned squarish shield with rounded bottom, SPQN in horizontal band across center **Obv. Legend:** HEN. DE. LOR. DVX. REIP. N. **Rev:** Basket containing fruits and grains, date below **Rev. Legend:** HINC. LIBERTAS. **Note:** Ref. F-283.

Date	Mintage	VG	F	VF	XF	Unc
1648 GA/C	—	22.00	45.00	275	450	—

KM# 88 PUBBLICA (3 Tornesi)

Copper Weight varies: 7.05-7.72g., 29-31 mm. **Obv:** Crowned ornate shield with SPQN in horizontal band across center **Obv. Legend:** HEN. DE. LOR. DVX. REI. N. **Rev:** Three wheat stalks and olive branch tied together, date above **Rev. Legend:** PAX. ET. VBERTAS. **Note:** Ref. F-282.

Date	Mintage	VG	F	VF	XF	Unc
1648 GA/C	—	30.00	60.00	375	575	—

KM# 89 15 GRANA

4.7200 g., Silver, 28 mm. **Obv:** Crowned ornate shield with SPQN in horizontal band across center **Obv. Legend:** HENR. DE. LOREN. DVX. REI. NEAP. **Rev:** Half-length facing figure of St. Januarius holding crozier **Rev. Legend:** S. I. REGE. ET. PROTE. NOS. **Note:** Ref. F-281.

Date	Mintage	VG	F	VF	XF	Unc
1648 GAC/M	—	300	450	2,750	4,500	—
1648 GAC/S	—	350	500	3,750	5,800	—

KINGDOM
Spanish Rule
STANDARD COINAGE

KM# 100 3 CAVALLI
2.1500 g., Copper, 22 mm. **Ruler:** Carlo II **Obv:** Bare head to right, date below **Obv. Legend:** CAROLVS. II. D. G. REX. **Rev:** Cross with trefoil ends, flame in each angle **Rev. Legend:** IN. HOC. SIGNO. VIN. **Note:** Ref. F-309. Machine-struck copper coinage began in 1680, with both hammered and machine-struck being produced that year.

Date	Mintage	VG	F	VF	XF	Unc
(16)77 Rare	—	—	—	—	—	—
(16)77 OC/A Rare	—	—	—	—	—	—
(16)78 AC/A	—	8.00	15.00	100	175	—
(16)79 AC/A	—	8.00	15.00	100	175	—
(16)80 AC/A	—	8.00	15.00	100	175	—
(16)82 AC/A	—	30.00	60.00	225	365	—
(16)82 AG/A	—	30.00	60.00	225	365	—
(16)83 AG/A	—	30.00	60.00	225	365	—

KM# 101 TORNESE
4.2000 g., Copper, 26 mm. **Ruler:** Carlo II **Obv:** Bare-headed draped bust to right, date below **Obv. Legend:** CAROLVS. II. D. G. REX. **Rev:** Golden Fleece suspended to left in laurel wreath, no legend **Note:** Ref. F-308. Machine-struck copper coinage began in 1680, both hammered and machine-struck issues were produced that year.

Date	Mintage	VG	F	VF	XF	Unc
(16)77 OC/A	—	8.00	15.00	150	220	—
(16)78 AC/A	—	8.00	15.00	100	175	—
(16)79 Rare	—	—	—	—	—	—
(16)79 AC/A	—	8.00	15.00	100	175	—
(16)80 AC/A	—	8.00	15.00	100	175	—
(16)81 AC/A	—	8.00	15.00	100	175	—
(16)82 AC/A	—	8.00	15.00	100	175	—
(16)82 AG/A	—	8.00	15.00	100	175	—
(16)83 AG/A	—	8.00	15.00	100	175	—

KM# 105 9 CAVALLI
6.1000 g., Copper, 27 mm. **Ruler:** Carlo II **Obv:** Long-haired draped bust to right in circle, date below in margin **Obv. Legend:** CAROLVS. II. D. G. REX. **Rev:** Cross with trefoil ends, leaf in each angle, in circle within wreath, no legend **Note:** Ref. F-309.

Date	Mintage	VG	F	VF	XF	Unc
1683 AG/A Rare	—	—	—	—	—	—

KM# 102 GRANO
9.0000 g., Copper, 30 mm. **Ruler:** Carlo II **Obv:** Long-haired armored bust to right, date below **Obv. Legend:** CAROLVS. II. D. G. REX. **Rev:** Crowned heart-shaped shield of 2-fold arms **Rev. Legend:** SICILIÆ. ET. HIERVSA. **Note:** Ref. F-306.

Date	Mintage	VG	F	VF	XF	Unc
(16)77 OC/A	—	8.00	15.00	225	365	—
(16)78 AC/A	—	8.00	15.00	150	220	—
(16)79 AC/A	—	8.00	15.00	150	220	—
(16)80 AC/A	—	8.00	15.00	150	220	—
(16)81 AC/A	—	8.00	15.00	150	220	—
(16)82 AC/A	—	8.00	15.00	150	220	—
(16)82 AG/A	—	8.00	15.00	175	290	—
(16)83 AG/A	—	8.00	15.00	150	220	—

KM# 118 GRANO
9.0000 g., Copper, 30 mm. **Ruler:** Carlo II **Obv:** Long-haired armored bust to right, date below **Obv. Legend:** CAROLVS. II. D. G. REX. **Rev:** Crowned heart-shaped shield of 2-fold arms **Rev. Legend:** HIERVSA - ET - SICILIA. **Note:** Ref. F-306/10.

Date	Mintage	VG	F	VF	XF	Unc
(16)92 Rare	—	—	—	—	—	—

KM# 106 3 TORNESI
10.3300 g., Copper, 30 mm. **Ruler:** Carlo II **Obv:** Long-haired draped bust to right, date at end of legend **Obv. Legend:** CAROLVS. II. D. G. REX. **Rev:** Large crown above 2-line inscription within wreath **Rev. Inscription:** TORNES / TRE **Note:** Ref. F-305.

Date	Mintage	VG	F	VF	XF	Unc
(16)83 AG/A Rare	—	—	—	—	—	—

KM# 112 8 GRANA
2.0000 g., Silver, 20 mm. **Ruler:** Carlo II **Obv:** Armored bust to right **Obv. Legend:** CAROLVS. II. D. G. REX. HISP. **Rev:** Cross with double-scrolled ends, rays streaming from center, date at end of legend **Rev. Legend:** IN. HOC. SIGNO. VINCES. G. VIII. **Note:** Ref. F-304.

Date	Mintage	VG	F	VF	XF	Unc
1688 AG/A-IM	—	22.00	45.00	150	220	—
1689 AG/A-IM	—	22.00	45.00	150	220	—
1690 AG/A-IM	—	22.00	45.00	150	220	—

KM# 93 CARLINO
2.6500 g., Silver, 20 mm. **Ruler:** Carlo II and regent Maria Anna **Obv:** Crowned and armored bust to left **Obv. Legend:** CAROLVS. II. HISP. REX. **Rev:** Crowned shield of manifold arms, date at end of legend **Rev. Legend:** ET. VTRIV. SICI. **Note:** Ref. F-290.

Date	Mintage	VG	F	VF	XF	Unc
1665 Rare	—	—	—	—	—	—
1666	—	2,000	2,900	9,500	14,500	—

KM# 92 CARLINO
2.6500 g., Silver, 20 mm. **Ruler:** Carlo II and regent Maria Anna **Obv:** Crowned bust to left **Obv. Legend:** CAROLVS. II. HISPANIA. REX. **Rev:** Crowned shield of manifold arms, date at end of legend **Rev. Legend:** ET. VTRIVSQ - SICILIE. **Note:** Ref. F-289.

Date	Mintage	VG	F	VF	XF	Unc
1665 Rare	—	—	—	—	—	—

KM# 107 CARLINO
2.9000 g., Silver, 23 mm. **Ruler:** Carlo II **Obv:** Armored bust to right **Obv. Legend:** CAROLVS. II. D. G. REX. HIS. ET. NÆ. **Rev:** Lion lying to left, looking at crown and scepter on table, legend in ribbon band above, date in exergue **Rev. Legend:** MAIESTATE. SECVRVS. **Note:** Ref. F-301.

Date	Mintage	VG	F	VF	XF	Unc
1683 AG/A	—	22.00	45.00	150	220	—
1684 AG/A	—	15.00	30.00	100	175	—
1684 AG/A-IM	—	15.00	30.00	100	175	—
1685 AG/A-IM	—	15.00	30.00	100	175	—
1685 IM	—	15.00	30.00	100	175	—
1686 AG/A-IM	—	15.00	30.00	100	175	—
1687 AG/A-IM	—	15.00	30.00	100	175	—

KM# 111 CARLINO
2.5000 g., Silver, 22 mm. **Ruler:** Carlo II **Obv:** Armored bust to right **Obv. Legend:** CAROLVS. (-) II. (-) D. G. REX. HISP. **Rev:** Crowned ornate shield of 4-fold arms, with central shield, date below **Rev. Legend:** VTRIVS. SIC. - HIERVS. G. X. **Note:** Ref. F-302. Varieties exist. 10 Grana.

Date	Mintage	VG	F	VF	XF	Unc
1687 AG/A-IM	—	22.00	45.00	185	290	—
1688 AG/A	—	15.00	30.00	120	220	—
1688 AG/A-IM	—	15.00	30.00	120	220	—
1689 AG/A-IM	—	15.00	30.00	120	220	—
1690 AG/A-IM	—	15.00	30.00	120	220	—

KM# 116 CARLINO
2.1000 g., Silver, 21 mm. **Ruler:** Carlo II **Obv:** Crowned and draped bust to right **Obv. Legend:** CAR. II. D. G. REX. - HISP. ET. NEAP. **Rev:** Suspended Golden Fleece divides date and value 'G - X' in baroque frame, no legend **Note:** Ref. F-303, 303/1, 2. 10 Grana.

Date	Mintage	VG	F	VF	XF	Unc
1691 IM/AG-A	—	15.00	30.00	120	220	—
1692 IM/AG-A	—	15.00	30.00	120	220	—
1693 IM/AG-A	—	15.00	30.00	120	220	—

KM# 119 CARLINO
2.1000 g., Silver, 21 mm. **Ruler:** Carlo II **Obv:** Crowned and draped bust to right **Obv. Legend:** CAR. II. D. G. REX. - HISP. ET. NEAP. **Rev:** Suspended Golden Fleece divides date, value '.G.X.' below, all in baroque frame, no legend **Note:** Ref. F-303/3-9. 10 Grana.

Date	Mintage	VG	F	VF	XF	Unc
1693 IM//AG-A	—	15.00	30.00	120	220	—
1694 IM//AG-A	—	15.00	30.00	120	220	—
1695 IM//AG-A	—	15.00	30.00	120	220	—
1696 IM//AG-A	—	15.00	30.00	120	220	—
1697 IM//AG-A Rare	—	—	—	—	—	—
1699 IM//AG-A	—	15.00	30.00	120	220	—
1700 IM//AG-A	—	15.00	30.00	120	220	—

KM# 96 TARI
5.2500 g., Silver, 27 mm. **Ruler:** Carlo II and regent Maria Anna **Obv:** Two accolated busts to right in circle, date in exergue **Obv. Legend:** CAROLVS. II. D. G. HISPANIAR. ET. NEAP. ET. C. REX. **Rev:** Crowned shield of manifold arms in baroque frame **Rev. Legend:** ET. MARIAN. EIVS. - MATER. REGN(I). GVB. **Note:** Ref. F-288.

Date	Mintage	VG	F	VF	XF	Unc
1674 AH Rare	—	—	—	—	—	—

KM# 104 TARI
Silver Weight varies: 5.60-5.64g., 27 mm. **Ruler:** Carlo II **Obv:** Crowned shield of manifold arms, Order of Golden Fleece around **Obv. Legend:** CAROLVS. II. D. G. - HISP. NEAP. REX. **Rev:** Globe with date in either relief or incuse in lower edge, crowne over crossed fasces and cornucopia above **Rev. Legend:** HIS. VICI. - ET. REGNO. **Note:** Ref. F-209. Varieties exist.

Date	Mintage	VG	F	VF	XF	Unc
ND(1682-87) AG/A	—	70.00	145	500	725	—
1683 AG-A Rare	—	—	—	—	—	—
1684 AG-A	—	22.00	45.00	150	220	—
1685 AG-A	—	22.00	45.00	150	220	—
1686 AG-A	—	22.00	45.00	150	220	—
1687 AG-A	—	22.00	45.00	150	220	—

KM# 113 TARI
5.1000 g., Silver, 25 mm. **Ruler:** Carlo II **Obv:** Armored bust to right **Obv. Legend:** CAROLVS. (-) II. D. G. REX. HISP. **Rev:** Crowned shield of manifold arms, suspended Golden Fleece divides date below, value 'G.XX' at end of legend **Rev. Legend:** VTRIVS. SIC. - HIERVS. G. XX. **Note:** Ref. F-299. Varieties exist. 20 Grana.

Date	Mintage	VG	F	VF	XF	Unc
1688 AG/A	—	55.00	115	300	450	—
1689 AG/A	—	22.00	45.00	150	220	—

KM# 117 TARI
4.5000 g., Silver, 25 mm. **Ruler:** Carlo II **Obv:** Crowned and draped bust to right. **Obv. Legend:** CAR. II. D G. REX. - HISP. ET. NEAP. **Rev:** Suspended Golden Fleece divides date, value 'GXX' below, all in baroque frame, no legend **Note:** Ref. F-300. 20 Grana.

Date	Mintage	VG	F	VF	XF	Unc
1691 IM//AG-A	—	30.00	60.00	185	290	—
1692 IM//AG-A	—	30.00	60.00	185	290	—
1693 IM//AG-A	—	30.00	60.00	185	290	—
1694 IM//AG-A	—	30.00	60.00	185	290	—
1695 IM//AG-A	—	30.00	60.00	185	290	—
1696 IM//AG-A	—	30.00	60.00	185	290	—
1697 IM//AG-A	—	30.00	60.00	185	290	—
1698 IM//AG-A	—	30.00	60.00	225	365	—
1699 IM//AG-A	—	30.00	60.00	185	290	—
1700 IM//AG-A	—	35.00	75.00	300	450	—

KM# 97 1/2 DUCATO
13.4000 g., Silver, 34 mm. **Ruler:** Carlo II and regent Maria Anna **Obv:** Two accolated busts to right in circle, date in exergue **Obv. Legend:** CAROLVS. II. D. G. HISPANIAR. ET. NEAP. ET. C. REX. **Rev:** Large crowned manifold arms in baroque frame, Golden Fleece suspended below **Rev. Legend:** ET. MARIAN. EIVS. - MATER. REGN(I). GVB. **Note:** Ref. F-287.

Date	Mintage	VG	F	VF	XF	Unc
1674 AH Rare	—	—	—	—	—	—

KM# 108 1/2 DUCATO

14.0000 g., Silver, 35 mm. **Ruler:** Carlo II **Obv:** Draped and armored bust to right **Obv. Legend:** CAROLVS. II. D. G. HISP. ET. VTR. SICIL. REX. **Rev:** Victory seated on globe, looking to right and holding out palmbranch, and oval shield at left with 2-fold arms, date at end of legend **Rev. Legend:** RELIGIONE. ET. GLADIO. **Note:** Ref. F-295.

Date	Mintage	VG	F	VF	XF	Unc
1683 AG/A	—	125	250	1,500	2,250	—
1684 AG/A	—	115	220	1,150	1,850	—
1684 AG/A-IM	—	275	450	2,000	3,200	—

KM# 114 1/2 DUCATO

12.6700 g., Silver, 35 mm. **Ruler:** Carlo II **Obv:** Crowned and draped armored bust to right **Obv. Legend:** CAROLVS. II. - D. G. REX. HISP. **Rev:** Crowned ornate shield of manifold arms with central shield, suspended Golden Fleece divides date below, value 'G.50' at end of legend **Rev. Legend:** VTRIVS. SICI. - HIERVS. G. 50. **Note:** Ref. F-296. 50 Grana.

Date	Mintage	VG	F	VF	XF	Unc
1689 AG/A-IM	—	125	250	1,250	2,250	—

KM# 120 1/2 DUCATO

Silver Weight varies: 10.70-11.00g., 32 mm. **Ruler:** Carlo II **Obv:** Crowned and draped armored bust to right **Obv. Legend:** CAR. II. D. G. REX. - HISP. ET. NEAP. **Rev:** Suspended Golden Fleece divides date near top, value 'G.50' below, all in baroque frame, no legend **Note:** Ref. F-297. 50 Grana.

Date	Mintage	VG	F	VF	XF	Unc
1693 IM//AG/A	—	70.00	145	425	700	—
1694 IM//AG/A	—	100	220	625	900	—

KM# 98 DUCATO

26.8900 g., Silver, 44 mm. **Ruler:** Carlo II and regent Maria Anna **Obv:** Two accolated busts to right in circle, date in exergue **Obv. Legend:** CAROLVS. II. D. G. HISPANIAR. ET. NEAP. ET. C. REX. **Rev:** Large crowned shield of manifold arms in baroque frame, Golden Fleece suspended below **Rev. Legend:** ET. MARIAN EIVS. - MATER. REGN(I). GVB. **Note:** Ref. F-286; Dav. 4044.

Date	Mintage	VG	F	VF	XF	Unc
1674 AH Rare	—	—	—	—	—	—

KM# 109 DUCATO

28.0000 g., Silver, 42 mm. **Ruler:** Carlo II **Obv:** Draped and armored bust to right **Obv. Legend:** CAROLVS. II. D. G. HISPANIAR. ET. NEAP. REX. **Rev:** Crowned scepter between 2 globes of eastern and western hemispheres, date divided at bottom end of scepter, ribbon band above with legend **Rev. Legend:** VNVS. NON. SVFFICIT. **Note:** Ref. F-291.

Date	Mintage	VG	F	VF	XF	Unc
1683 GH Rare	—	—	—	—	—	—

KM# 110 DUCATO

28.0000 g., Silver, 42 mm. **Ruler:** Carlo II **Obv:** Draped and armored bust to right **Obv. Legend:** CAROLVS. II. D. G. HISP(A)NIAR. ET. NEAP. REX. **Rev:** Crowned scepter between 2 globes of eastern and western hemispheres, mintmark to left and date to right of bottom of scepter, ribbon band above with legend **Rev. Legend:** VNVS. NON. SVFFICIT. **Note:** Ref. F-292; Dav. 4045.

Date	Mintage	VG	F	VF	XF	Unc
1684 IM//AG/A	—	325	500	2,850	4,500	—

KM# 115 DUCATO

25.2000 g., Silver, 41 mm. **Ruler:** Carlo II **Obv:** Crowned and armored bust to right **Obv. Legend:** CAROLVS. II. - D. G. REX. HISP. **Rev:** Crowned ornate shield of manifold arms, with central shield, date divided by suspended Golden Fleece at bottom, value 'G.100' at end of legend **Rev. Legend:** VTRIVS. SICI. - HIERVS. **Note:** Ref. F-293; Dav. 4046. 100 Grana.

Date	Mintage	VG	F	VF	XF	Unc
1689 IM Rare	—	—	—	—	—	—
1689 AG/A	—	175	300	1,000	1,750	3,500

KM# 121 DUCATO

Silver Weight varies: 21.78-22.00g., 39 mm. **Ruler:** Carlo II **Obv:** Small crowned and draped armored bust to right **Obv. Legend:** CAR. II. D. G. REX. - HISP. ET. NEAP. **Rev:** Suspended Golden Fleece divides date, value 'G.100' below, all in baroque frame, no legend **Note:** Ref. F-294; Dav. 4047. 100 Grana.

Date	Mintage	VG	F	VF	XF	Unc
1693 IM//AG/A	—	100	175	750	1,500	—

TRADE COINAGE

KM# 94 DUCATO

3.5000 g., 0.9860 Gold 0.1109 oz. AGW, 21 mm. **Ruler:** Carlo II and regent Maria Anna **Obv:** Crowned and armored bust to right, date below in margin **Obv. Legend:** CAROLVS. II. HISPA. REX. **Rev:** Crowned shield of manifold arms, Order of Golden Fleece around **Rev. Legend:** ET. VTRI. SICILIE. **Note:** Ref. F-285; Fr. 842.

Date	Mintage	VG	F	VF	XF	Unc
1665 Rare	—	—	—	—	—	—

NOVELLARA

Countship

The small town and surrounding area of Novellara, 20 miles (34 kilometers) south of Mantua and 16 miles (27 kilometers) northwest of Modena, was of ancient origin. It was long ruled by a branch of the Gonzagas of Mantua, from at least the mid-14th century. Giampietro Gonzaga of Novellara was raised to the rank of count by Emperor Massimiliano I (1493-1519) in 1501. Several generations of Giampietro's successors ruled jointly and received the mint right from Emperor Carlo V (1519-56), reconfirmed by Emperor Ferdinando I (1556-64) in 1559. The counts issued anonymous coins until 1650, when Alfonso II began striking coins in his own name. The line of counts died out in 1728 and Novellara passed to the Este family of Modena in 1737.

RULERS

Anonymous, 1560-1650
Camillo II Gonzaga, 1595-1640
Alessandro III Gonzaga, 1640-1644
Camillo II, 2nd time 1644-1650
Alfonso II Gonzaga, 1650-1678
Camillo III Gonzaga, 1678-1727

REFERENCE:

Alberto Varesi, ***Monete Italiane Regionali: Emilia.*** Pavia, 1998.

COUNTSHIP

STANDARD COINAGE

KM# 18 QUATTRINO

Copper Weight varies: 0.55-0.86g., 15-16 mm. **Ruler:** Alfonso II Gonzaga **Obv:** Large 'L' divides date **Obv. Legend:** LAVS. E. PROT. NOV. **Rev:** Facing crowned head of St. Vultus **Rev. Legend:** VVLTVS. SANCTVS. **Note:** Varesi 886. Varieties exist.

Date	Mintage	Good	VG	F	VF	XF
(16)61	—	—	25.00	55.00	120	200
(16)62	—	—	25.00	55.00	120	200
(16)63	—	—	25.00	55.00	120	200
(16)67	—	—	25.00	55.00	120	200

KM# 19 QUATTRINO

Copper Weight varies: 0.38-0.70g., 15 mm. **Ruler:** Alfonso II Gonzaga **Obv:** Large 'L' divides date **Obv. Legend:** LAVS. E. PROT. NOV. **Rev:** Facing crowned head of St. Vultus **Rev. Legend:** DEFEND. NOV. IN. PRE. **Note:** Varesi 887. Varieties exist.

Date	Mintage	Good	VG	F	VF	XF
(16)61	—	—	25.00	55.00	120	200
(16)63	—	—	25.00	55.00	120	200
(16)66	—	—	25.00	55.00	120	200

KM# 21 QUATTRINO

Copper Weight varies: 0.51-1.10g., 16 mm. **Ruler:** Alfonso II Gonzaga **Obv:** Large 'L' divides date **Obv. Legend:** ET. PROT. NOVEL. **Rev:** Facing crowned head of St. Vultus **Rev. Legend:** VNICA. SPES. ET. SALVS. **Note:** Varesi 889. Varieties exist.

Date	Mintage	Good	VG	F	VF	XF
(16)61	—	—	25.00	55.00	120	200
(16)63	—	—	25.00	55.00	120	200
(16)64	—	—	25.00	55.00	120	200
(16)65	—	—	25.00	55.00	120	200

KM# 16 QUATTRINO

Copper Weight varies: 0.47-0.88g., 15 mm. **Ruler:** Alfonso II Gonzaga **Obv:** Large 'L' divides date **Obv. Legend:** COMIT. IMPERAT. **Rev:** Facing crowned head of St. Vultus **Rev. Legend:** VVLTVS. SANCTVS. NP. **Note:** Varesi 884.

Date	Mintage	Good	VG	F	VF	XF
(16)61	—	—	25.00	55.00	120	200

KM# 17 QUATTRINO

Copper Weight varies: 0.51-0.93g., 15 mm. **Ruler:** Alfonso II Gonzaga **Obv:** Large 'L' divides date **Obv. Legend:** FIDES. IMPERAT. **Rev:** Facing crowned head of St. Vultus. **Rev. Legend:** VVLTVS. SANCTVS. NP. **Note:** Varesi 885.

Date	Mintage	Good	VG	F	VF	XF
(16)61	—	—	25.00	55.00	120	200

KM# 20 QUATTRINO

0.9000 g., Copper, 17 mm. **Ruler:** Alfonso II Gonzaga **Obv:** Large 'L' divides date **Obv. Legend:** LAVS. E. PROT. NOVI. **Rev:** Facing crowned head of St. Vultus **Rev. Legend:** DEFEND. NOV. IN. PRE. **Note:** Varesi 888.

Date	Mintage	Good	VG	F	VF	XF
(16)61	—	—	75.00	140	300	500

KM# 22 QUATTRINO

0.5000 g., Copper, 16 mm. **Ruler:** Alfonso II Gonzaga **Obv:** Large 'L' divides date **Obv. Legend:** PROTECT. NOVEL. **Rev:** Facing crowned head of St. Vultus **Rev. Legend:** VNICA. SPES. ET. SALVS. **Note:** Varesi 890.

Date	Mintage	Good	VG	F	VF	XF
(16)61	—	—	25.00	55.00	120	200

KM# 23 QUATTRINO

0.5200 g., Copper, 16 mm. **Ruler:** Alfonso II Gonzaga **Obv:** Large 'L' divides date **Obv. Legend:** LAVS. ONOR. E. GLOR. **Rev:** Facing crowned head of St. Vultus **Rev. Legend:** SALV. MON. D. E. P. NOV. **Note:** Varesi 891.

Date	Mintage	Good	VG	F	VF	XF
(16)61	—	—	25.00	55.00	120	200

KM# 24 QUATTRINO

0.8800 g., Copper, 16 mm. **Ruler:** Alfonso II Gonzaga **Obv:** Large 'L' divides date **Obv. Legend:** LAVS. ONOR. E. GLOR. **Rev:** Facing crowned head of St. Vultus **Rev. Legend:** DEFENDE. NOS. IN. PRE. **Note:** Varesi 892.

Date	Mintage	Good	VG	F	VF	XF
(16)61	—	—	25.00	55.00	120	200

KM# 26 QUATTRINO

Copper Weight varies: 0.96-1.46g., 20 mm. **Ruler:** Alfonso II Gonzaga **Obv:** 4-line inscription with date **Obv. Inscription:** BA NO / VEL / CO. ET / (date) **Rev:** Lion rampant to left holding pennant, no legend **Note:** Varesi 895.

Date	Mintage	Good	VG	F	VF	XF
1664	—	—	40.00	80.00	175	300

KM# 28 QUATTRINO

0.6800 g., Copper, 16 mm. **Ruler:** Alfonso II Gonzaga **Obv:** Large 'L' divides date **Obv. Legend:** E. PROT. NOVEL. **Rev:** Facing crowned head of St. Vultus **Rev. Legend:** DEFENDE. NOS. IN. PRE. **Note:** Varesi 893.

Date	Mintage	Good	VG	F	VF	XF
(16)66	—	—	75.00	140	300	440

KM# 29 QUATTRINO

0.6300 g., Copper, 16 mm. **Ruler:** Alfonso II Gonzaga **Obv:** Large 'L' divides date **Obv. Legend:** E. PROT. NOVELLVS. **Rev:** Facing crowned head of St. Vultus **Rev. Legend:** VVLTVS. SANCTVS. **Note:** Varesi 894.

Date	Mintage	Good	VG	F	VF	XF
(16)67	—	—	25.00	55.00	120	200

KM# 1 SESINO

Billon Weight varies: 0.62-1.18g., 17-18 mm. **Ruler:** Alfonso II Gonzaga **Obv:** Crowned shield of 4-fold arms with central shield **Obv. Legend:** ALPH. II. GON. N. C. **Rev:** 3-line inscription **Rev. Inscription:** SESINO/DI. NOV/LLARA. **Note:** Varesi 881.

Date	Mintage	Good	VG	F	VF	XF
ND(1650-78)	—	—	25.00	55.00	135	250

KM# 2 SESINO

Billon Weight varies: 0.61-0.95g., 16 mm. **Ruler:** Alfonso II Gonzaga **Obv:** Head with long hair to right **Obv. Legend:** ALPH. II. GON. **Rev:** Displayed crowned eagle **Rev. Legend:** NO. ET. BA. CO. **Note:** Varesi 882.

Date	Mintage	Good	VG	F	VF	XF
ND(1650-78)	—	—	25.00	55.00	135	250

KM# 3 SESINO

Billon Weight varies: 0.45-0.75g., 16 mm. **Ruler:** Alfonso II Gonzaga **Obv:** Head with short hair to right **Obv. Legend:** ALPH. II. GON. **Rev:** Displayed crowned eagle **Rev. Legend:** NOBILITAS. ET. INSIG. **Note:** Varesi 883.

Date	Mintage	Good	VG	F	VF	XF
ND(1650-78)	—	—	25.00	55.00	135	250

KM# 5 5 SOLDI

Billon Weight varies: 1.29-2.85g., 19 mm. **Ruler:** Alfonso II Gonzaga **Obv:** Head with long hair to right **Obv. Legend:** ALPHONSVS. II. GONZAGA. **Rev:** Crowned shield of 4-fold arms with central shield **Rev. Legend:** NOVEL. ET. BAGN. CO. **Note:** Varesi 880.

Date	Mintage	Good	VG	F	VF	XF
ND(1650-78)	—	—	80.00	165	400	700

KM# 7 6 SOLDI (Cavallotto)

Billon Weight varies: 1.23-1.75g., 19 mm. **Ruler:** Alfonso II Gonzaga **Obv:** Crowned shield of 4-fold arms with central shield in baroque frame **Obv. Legend:** ALPH. II. GON. NOVEL. CO. **Rev:** Horse walking to left, value '6' below, no legend **Note:** Varesi 878.

Date	Mintage	Good	VG	F	VF	XF
ND(1650-78)	—	—	115	220	675	1,250

KM# 8 CAVALLOTTO

1.4200 g., Billon, 20 mm. **Ruler:** Alfonso II Gonzaga **Obv:** Crowned shield of 4-fold arms with central shield **Obv. Legend:** ALPH. II. GONZAGA. **Rev:** Pyx in circle **Rev. Legend:** NOVEL. ET. BAG. COMES. E. C. **Note:** Varesi 879.

Date	Mintage	Good	VG	F	VF	XF
ND(1650-78)	—	—	115	220	675	1,250

KM# 10 10 SOLDI

Billon Weight varies: 3.56-6.71g., 28-29 mm. **Ruler:** Alfonso II Gonzaga **Obv:** Armored bust to left, value '10' below **Obv. Legend:** ALPHONSVS. II. GONZAGA. **Rev:** Crowned shield of 4-fold arms with central shield in baroque frame **Rev. Legend:** NOVEL. ET. BAGNOLI. COMES. ET. C. **Note:** Varesi 877.

Date	Mintage	Good	VG	F	VF	XF
ND(1650-78)	—	—	175	330	975	1,650

KM# 12 30 SOLDI

Billon, 29 mm. **Ruler:** Alfonso II Gonzaga **Obv:** Armored bust to left, value 'XXX' below **Obv. Legend:** ALPHONSVS. II. GONZAGA. **Rev:** Crowned shield of 4-fold arms with central shield in baroque frame, chain of order around **Rev. Legend:** NOVEL. BA. - CO. ET. R. AE. **Note:** Varesi 876.

Date	Mintage	Good	VG	F	VF	XF
ND(1650-78)	—	—	325	660	1,450	2,500

KM# 14 2 LIRE

2.8500 g., Silver, 27-28 mm. **Ruler:** Alfonso II Gonzaga **Obv:** Crowned shield of 4-fold arms with central shield in baroque frame **Obv. Legend:** ALPH. II. GON. NO. ET. BA. CO. **Rev:** Madonna seated with Child in circle **Rev. Legend:** VIRGO. TVA. GLORIA. PARTVS. **Note:** Varesi 875.

Date	Mintage	Good	VG	F	VF	XF
ND(1650-78)	—	—	250	550	1,400	2,500

PAPAL STATES

During many centuries prior to the formation of the unified Kingdom of Italy, when Italy was divided into numerous independent papal and ducal states, the Popes held temporal sovereignty over an area in central Italy comprising some 17,000 sq. mi. (44,030 sq. km.) including the city of Rome. At the time of the general unification of Italy under the Kingdom of Sardinia, 1861, the papal dominions beyond Rome were acquired by that kingdom diminishing the Pope's sovereignty to Rome and its environs. In 1870, while France's opposition to papal dispossession was neutralized by its war with Prussia, the Italian army seized weakly defended Rome and made it the capital of Italy, thereby abrogating the last vestige of papal temporal power. In 1871, the Italian Parliament enacted the Law of Guarantees, which guaranteed a special status for the Vatican area, and spiritual freedom and a generous income for the Pope. Pope Pius IX and his successors adamantly refused to acknowledge the validity of these laws and voluntarily "imprisoned" themselves in the Vatican. The impasse between State and Church lasted until the signing of the Lateran Treaty, Feb. 11, 1929, by which Italy recognized the sovereignty and independence of the new Vatican City state.

PONTIFFS

Clement VIII, 1592-1605
Sede Vacante, (March 5 - April 1) 1605
Leo XI, (April 1 - April 28) 1605
Sede Vacante, (April 28 - May 16) 1605
Paul V, 1605-1621
Sede Vacante, 1621
Gregory XV, 1621-1623
Sede Vacante, 1623
Urban VIII, 1623-1644
Sede Vacante, 1644
Innocent X, 1644-1655
Sede Vacante, 1655
Alexander VII, 1655-1667
Sede Vacante, 1667
Clement IX, 1667-1669
Sede Vacante, 1669-1670
Clement X, 1670-1676
Sede Vacante, 1676
Innocent XI, 1676-1689
Sede Vacante, 1689
Alexander VIII, 1689-1691
Sede Vacante, 1691
Innocent XII, 1691-1700
Sede Vacante, 1700
Clement XI, 1700-1721

MINT MARKS

B - Bologna
R – Rome

MONETARY SYSTEM

(Until 1860)

5 Quattrini = 1 Baiocco
5 Baiocchi = 1 Grosso
6 Grossi = 4 Carlini = 3 Giulio =
3 Paoli = 1 Testone.
14 Carlini = 1 Piastre
100 Baiocchi = 1 Scudo
10 Testone = Doppia

PAPACY

STANDARD COINAGE

KM# 19 QUATTRINO

Copper **Ruler:** Clement VIII **Obv:** Arms **Rev:** Veronica's veil

Date	Mintage	Good	VG	F	VF	XF
1602 Unique	—	—	—	—	—	—

KM# 21 QUATTRINO

Copper **Ruler:** Paul V **Rev:** St. Paul standing holding sword downward left, book right

Date	Mintage	Good	VG	F	VF	XF
ND(1605)-I Rare	—	—	—	—	—	—
ND(1606)-II	—	10.00	20.00	35.00	60.00	—
ND	—	10.00	20.00	35.00	60.00	—

KM# 22 QUATTRINO

Copper **Ruler:** Paul V **Rev:** St. Paul standing holding hand downward

Date	Mintage	Good	VG	F	VF	XF
ND(1605)-I	—	10.00	20.00	35.00	60.00	—

KM# 35 QUATTRINO

Copper **Ruler:** Paul V **Rev:** St. Paul standing holding book at left and sword upward at right

Date	Mintage	Good	VG	F	VF	XF
ND(1606)-II	—	10.00	20.00	35.00	60.00	—
ND(1607)-III	—	10.00	20.00	35.00	60.00	—
ND(1608)-IIII	—	10.00	20.00	35.00	60.00	—
ND(1609)-V	—	10.00	20.00	35.00	60.00	—
ND(1610)-VI	—	10.00	20.00	35.00	60.00	—
ND(1611)-VII	—	10.00	20.00	35.00	60.00	—
ND(1612)-VIII	—	10.00	20.00	35.00	60.00	—
ND(1613)-VIIII	—	10.00	20.00	35.00	60.00	—
ND	—	10.00	20.00	35.00	60.00	—

KM# 64 QUATTRINO

Copper **Ruler:** Paul V **Rev:** St. Paul standing both hands holding sword

Date	Mintage	Good	VG	F	VF	XF
ND(1611)-VII	—	10.00	20.00	35.00	60.00	—
ND(1612)-VIII	—	10.00	20.00	35.00	60.00	—

KM# 72 QUATTRINO

Copper **Ruler:** Paul V **Rev:** St. Paul standing, book left, sword downward at right

Date	Mintage	Good	VG	F	VF	XF
ND(1615)-XI	—	10.00	20.00	35.00	60.00	—
ND(1616)XII	—	10.00	20.00	35.00	60.00	—
ND	—	10.00	20.00	35.00	60.00	—

KM# 90 QUATTRINO

Copper **Ruler:** Paul V **Obv:** Arms

Date	Mintage	Good	VG	F	VF	XF
ND(1621)	—	15.00	30.00	55.00	90.00	—

KM# 101 QUATTRINO

Copper **Ruler:** Gregory XV **Obv:** Bust of Gregory XV right **Rev:** Radiant Virgin Mary standing on crescent

Date	Mintage	Good	VG	F	VF	XF
ND(1622)-II	—	30.00	50.00	85.00	145	—

KM# 106 QUATTRINO

Copper **Obv:** Arms of Cardinal Ippolito Aldobrandini **Rev:** Christ standing in rays **Note:** Sede Vacante issue.

Date	Mintage	Good	VG	F	VF	XF
1623	—	50.00	100	175	320	—

KM# 128 QUATTRINO

Copper **Ruler:** Urban VIII **Obv:** Arms **Rev:** Holy Door with Veronica's veil **Rev. Legend:** ...TVVM **Note:** Holy year issue.

Date	Mintage	Good	VG	F	VF	XF
1625-I	—	10.00	22.00	40.00	70.00	—
1625-II	—	10.00	22.00	40.00	70.00	—

KM# 129 QUATTRINO

Copper **Ruler:** Urban VIII **Rev:** Holy Door with Veronica's veil **Rev. Legend:** ...MACVLA **Note:** Holy year issue.

Date	Mintage	Good	VG	F	VF	XF
ND(1625)	—	10.00	22.00	40.00	70.00	—

KM# 130 QUATTRINO

Copper **Ruler:** Urban VIII **Rev:** Holy Door with Veronica's veil, date at sides **Note:** Holy year issue.

Date	Mintage	Good	VG	F	VF	XF
1625-II	—	12.00	25.00	45.00	80.00	—

KM# 131 QUATTRINO

Copper **Ruler:** Urban VIII **Rev:** Holy Door, ROMA at sides within wreath **Note:** Holy year issue.

Date	Mintage	Good	VG	F	VF	XF
ND(1625)-I	—	10.00	22.00	40.00	70.00	—
ND(1625)-II	—	10.00	22.00	40.00	70.00	—

KM# 132 QUATTRINO

Copper **Ruler:** Urban VIII **Rev:** Radiant Virgin Mary standing on crescent

Date	Mintage	Good	VG	F	VF	XF
ND(1625) Rare	—	—	—	—	—	—

KM# 150 QUATTRINO

Copper **Ruler:** Urban VIII **Note:** Busts of SS. Peter and Paul. An error legend exists with PETERVS repeated.

Date	Mintage	Good	VG	F	VF	XF
ND(1626)-II	—	10.00	20.00	35.00	65.00	—
ND(1627)-III	—	10.00	20.00	35.00	65.00	—
ND(1628)-IIII	—	10.00	20.00	35.00	65.00	—

KM# 155 QUATTRINO

Copper **Ruler:** Urban VIII **Rev:** Bust of St. Peter left

Date	Mintage	Good	VG	F	VF	XF
ND(1628)-IIII	—	12.00	25.00	45.00	80.00	—

KM# 186 QUATTRINO

Copper **Ruler:** Urban VIII **Obv:** Bust right **Rev:** St. Michael the Archangel expelling Lucifer

Date	Mintage	Good	VG	F	VF	XF
ND(1636)-XIII	—	10.00	22.00	40.00	70.00	—
ND(1637)-XIIII	—	10.00	22.00	40.00	70.00	—

KM# 187 QUATTRINO

Copper **Ruler:** Urban VIII **Obv:** Arms

Date	Mintage	Good	VG	F	VF	XF
ND(1636)-XIII	—	10.00	20.00	35.00	60.00	—
ND(1637)-XIIII	—	10.00	20.00	35.00	60.00	—

KM# 200 QUATTRINO

Copper **Ruler:** Urban VIII **Obv:** Bust right **Rev:** Papal arms in wreath

Date	Mintage	Good	VG	F	VF	XF
ND(1641)-XVIII	—	10.00	20.00	40.00	70.00	—

KM# 206 QUATTRINO

Copper **Ruler:** Innocent X **Obv:** Arms **Rev:** Bust of St. Paul **Rev. Legend:** ...APOS ALMA

Date	Mintage	Good	VG	F	VF	XF
ND(1644)-I	—	10.00	22.00	40.00	70.00	—

KM# 207 QUATTRINO

Copper **Ruler:** Innocent X **Rev:** Bust of St. Paul **Rev. Legend:** ...ALMA

Date	Mintage	Good	VG	F	VF	XF
ND(1644)-I	—	10.00	22.00	40.00	70.00	—
ND(1645)-II	—	10.00	22.00	40.00	70.00	—

KM# 224 QUATTRINO

Copper **Ruler:** Innocent X **Rev:** Bust of St. Paul in wreath **Rev. Legend:** ...APOS • ALMA

Date	Mintage	Good	VG	F	VF	XF
ND(1645)-II	—	15.00	30.00	45.00	80.00	—

KM# 225 QUATTRINO

Copper **Ruler:** Innocent X **Rev:** St. Paul standing in wreath **Rev. Legend:** ...SANCT PAVLVS

Date	Mintage	Good	VG	F	VF	XF
ND(1645)-II	—	10.00	22.00	35.00	65.00	—

KM# 226 QUATTRINO

Copper **Ruler:** Innocent X **Rev:** St. Paul standing in wreath **Rev. Legend:** S. PAVLVS APOS.

Date	Mintage	Good	VG	F	VF	XF
ND(1645)-II	—	12.00	25.00	40.00	75.00	—

KM# 20 MEZZO (1/2) BAIOCCO

Copper **Obv:** Arms divide RO-MA **Rev:** Facing bust of St. Paul wearing tiara

Date	Mintage	Good	VG	F	VF	XF
1602 Rare	—	—	—	—	—	—

KM# 65 MEZZO (1/2) BAIOCCO

Copper **Ruler:** Paul V **Obv:** Arms **Rev:** Value: MEZO/BAIOCCO

Date	Mintage	Good	VG	F	VF	XF
ND(1611)-VI	—	12.00	22.00	45.00	70.00	—
MDCXI (1611)-VI	—	12.00	22.00	45.00	70.00	—
ND(1617)-XII	—	12.00	22.00	45.00	70.00	—
1617-XII	—	12.00	22.00	45.00	70.00	—
1619-XII	—	12.00	22.00	45.00	70.00	—

KM# 133 MEZZO (1/2) BAIOCCO

Copper **Ruler:** Urban VIII **Rev:** Holy Door with Veronica's veil **Note:** Holy year issue.

Date	Mintage	Good	VG	F	VF	XF
MDCXXV (1625)-II	—	10.00	20.00	40.00	65.00	—

KM# 23 1/2 GROSSO

Silver **Obv:** Arms **Rev:** Bust of St. Peter **Rev. Legend:** ...ALMA ROM

Date	Mintage	Good	VG	F	VF	XF
ND(1605-21)	—	12.00	22.00	45.00	75.00	—

KM# 24 1/2 GROSSO

Silver **Rev:** Bust of St. Peter **Rev. Legend:** ...ROMA

Date	Mintage	Good	VG	F	VF	XF
ND(1605-21)	—	12.00	22.00	45.00	75.00	—

KM# 36 1/2 GROSSO

Silver **Ruler:** Paul V **Rev:** Bust of Christ left

Date	Mintage	Good	VG	F	VF	XF
ND(1606)-II	—	12.00	25.00	50.00	90.00	—
ND	—	12.00	25.00	50.00	90.00	—

KM# 37 1/2 GROSSO

Silver **Ruler:** Paul V **Rev:** Bust of St. Paul right

Date	Mintage	Good	VG	F	VF	XF
ND(1606)-II	—	12.00	22.00	45.00	75.00	—
ND(1607)-III	—	12.00	22.00	45.00	75.00	—
ND(1608)-IIII	—	12.00	22.00	45.00	75.00	—
ND(1609)-V	—	12.00	22.00	45.00	75.00	—
ND(1610)-VI	—	12.00	22.00	45.00	75.00	—
ND(1611)-VII	—	12.00	22.00	45.00	75.00	—
ND(1612)-VIII	—	12.00	22.00	45.00	75.00	—
ND(1613)-VIIII	—	12.00	22.00	45.00	75.00	—
ND(1614)-X	—	12.00	22.00	45.00	75.00	—
ND(1615)-XI	—	12.00	22.00	45.00	75.00	—

KM# 38 1/2 GROSSO

Silver **Ruler:** Paul V **Rev:** Bust of St. Paul left

Date	Mintage	Good	VG	F	VF	XF
ND(1606)-II	—	12.00	22.00	45.00	75.00	—
ND(1607)-III	—	12.00	22.00	45.00	75.00	—
ND(1608)-IIII	—	12.00	22.00	45.00	75.00	—
ND(1609)-V	—	12.00	22.00	45.00	75.00	—
ND(1610)-VI	—	12.00	22.00	45.00	75.00	—
ND(1611)-VII	—	12.00	22.00	45.00	75.00	—
ND(1612)-VIII	—	12.00	22.00	45.00	75.00	—
ND(1613)-VIIII	—	12.00	22.00	45.00	75.00	—
ND(1614)-X	—	12.00	22.00	45.00	75.00	—
ND(1615)-XI	—	12.00	22.00	45.00	75.00	—

KM# 77 1/2 GROSSO

Silver **Ruler:** Paul V **Rev:** St. Paul standing

Date	Mintage	Good	VG	F	VF	XF
ND(1616)-XII	—	12.00	22.00	45.00	75.00	—
ND	—	12.00	22.00	45.00	75.00	—

KM# 78 1/2 GROSSO

Silver **Ruler:** Paul V **Obv:** Bust right

Date	Mintage	Good	VG	F	VF	XF
ND(1616)-XII	—	20.00	40.00	80.00	135	—
ND(1617)-XIII	—	20.00	40.00	80.00	135	—
ND(1618)-XIIII	—	20.00	40.00	80.00	135	—

KM# 91 1/2 GROSSO

Silver **Ruler:** Gregory XV **Obv:** Arms **Rev:** St. Paul standing

Date	Mintage	Good	VG	F	VF	XF
ND(1621-23)	—	20.00	40.00	80.00	135	—

KM# 92 1/2 GROSSO

Silver **Ruler:** Gregory XV **Rev:** Radiant Virgin Mary standing on crescent

Date	Mintage	Good	VG	F	VF	XF
ND(1621-23)	—	20.00	40.00	80.00	135	—

KM# 102 1/2 GROSSO

Silver **Ruler:** Gregory XV **Obv:** Bust right

Date	Mintage	Good	VG	F	VF	XF
ND(1622)-II	—	30.00	60.00	120	185	—
ND(1623)-III	—	30.00	60.00	120	185	—
ND	—	30.00	60.00	120	185	—

KM# 108 1/2 GROSSO

Silver **Obv:** Bust right **Rev:** Busts of SS. Peter and Paul

Date	Mintage	Good	VG	F	VF	XF
ND(1623-44)	—	20.00	40.00	80.00	135	—

KM# 109 1/2 GROSSO

Silver **Obv:** Arms **Rev:** Radiant Virgin Mary standing on crescent

Date	Mintage	Good	VG	F	VF	XF
ND(1623-44)	—	20.00	40.00	80.00	135	—

KM# 107 1/2 GROSSO

Silver **Obv:** Arms of Cardinal Ippolito Aldobrandini **Rev:** Christ standing with banner **Note:** Sede Vacante issue.

Date	Mintage	Good	VG	F	VF	XF
1623	—	65.00	125	225	350	—

KM# 123 1/2 GROSSO

Silver **Ruler:** Urban VIII **Obv:** Arms

Date	Mintage	Good	VG	F	VF	XF
ND(1624)-II	—	18.00	35.00	55.00	95.00	—
ND(1625)-III	—	18.00	35.00	55.00	95.00	—
ND(1626)-IIII	—	18.00	35.00	55.00	95.00	—
ND(1627)-V	—	18.00	35.00	55.00	95.00	—
ND(1628)-VI	—	18.00	35.00	55.00	95.00	—
ND	—	18.00	35.00	55.00	95.00	—

KM# 134 1/2 GROSSO

Silver **Ruler:** Urban VIII **Rev:** Bust of Madonna right

Date	Mintage	Good	VG	F	VF	XF
ND(1625)-III	—	18.00	35.00	55.00	95.00	—
ND(1626)-V	—	18.00	35.00	55.00	95.00	—
ND(1627)-VI	—	18.00	35.00	55.00	95.00	—

KM# 135 1/2 GROSSO

Silver **Ruler:** Urban VIII **Rev:** Holy Door **Note:** Holy year issue.

Date	Mintage	Good	VG	F	VF	XF
1625-III	—	20.00	40.00	65.00	110	—
ND	—	20.00	40.00	65.00	110	—

KM# 136 1/2 GROSSO

Silver **Ruler:** Urban VIII **Rev:** Holy Door, 1625 and ROMA at sides within wreath **Note:** Holy year issue.

Date	Mintage	Good	VG	F	VF	XF
1625	—	18.00	35.00	55.00	95.00	—

KM# 137 1/2 GROSSO

Silver **Ruler:** Urban VIII **Rev:** Holy Door inscribed 1625 in wreath **Note:** Holy year issue.

Date	Mintage	Good	VG	F	VF	XF
1625	—	18.00	35.00	55.00	95.00	—

KM# 138 1/2 GROSSO

Silver **Ruler:** Urban VIII **Rev:** Holy Door, 1625 at sides in wreath **Note:** Holy year issue.

Date	Mintage	Good	VG	F	VF	XF
1625	—	20.00	40.00	65.00	110	—

KM# 179 1/2 GROSSO

Silver **Ruler:** Urban VIII **Obv:** Bust left **Rev:** St. Peter standing

Date	Mintage	Good	VG	F	VF	XF
ND(1634)-X	—	20.00	40.00	80.00	135	—

KM# 180 1/2 GROSSO

Silver **Ruler:** Urban VIII **Obv:** Arms

Date	Mintage	Good	VG	F	VF	XF
ND(1634)-X	—	18.00	35.00	55.00	95.00	—

KM# 204 1/2 GROSSO

Silver **Ruler:** Urban VIII **Rev:** Bust of Madonna right

Date	Mintage	Good	VG	F	VF	XF
1643-XX	—	18.00	35.00	55.00	95.00	—
1644-XXI	—	18.00	35.00	55.00	95.00	—
ND	—	18.00	35.00	55.00	95.00	—

KM# 208 1/2 GROSSO

Silver **Ruler:** Innocent X **Rev:** Radiant Virgin Mary standing on crescent

Date	Mintage	Good	VG	F	VF	XF
ND(1644)-I	—	12.00	22.00	45.00	80.00	—

KM# 209 1/2 GROSSO

Silver **Ruler:** Innocent X **Subject:** Immaculate Conception **Rev:** Half-length figure of Madonna with child

Date	Mintage	Good	VG	F	VF	XF
ND(1644)-I	—	12.00	22.00	45.00	80.00	—
ND(1645)-II	—	12.00	22.00	45.00	80.00	—
ND(1646)-III	—	12.00	22.00	45.00	80.00	—
ND(1647)-IIII	—	12.00	22.00	45.00	80.00	—
ND(1648)-V	—	12.00	22.00	45.00	80.00	—

KM# 210 1/2 GROSSO

Silver **Ruler:** Innocent X **Rev:** Bust of Madonna right

Date	Mintage	Good	VG	F	VF	XF
ND(1644)-I	—	12.00	22.00	45.00	80.00	—
ND(1645)-II	—	12.00	22.00	45.00	80.00	—

KM# 250 1/2 GROSSO

Silver **Ruler:** Innocent X **Rev:** Holy Door, 1650 in exergue **Note:** Holy year issue.

Date	Mintage	Good	VG	F	VF	XF
1650-VI	—	12.00	25.00	50.00	90.00	—
1650-VII	—	12.00	25.00	50.00	90.00	—

KM# 255 1/2 GROSSO

Silver **Ruler:** Innocent X **Rev:** Holy Door with cross, 1651 in exergue **Note:** Holy year issue.

Date	Mintage	Good	VG	F	VF	XF
1651-VII	—	12.00	25.00	50.00	90.00	—
1651-VIII	—	12.00	25.00	50.00	90.00	—

KM# 258 1/2 GROSSO

Silver **Ruler:** Innocent X **Rev:** Bust of St. Paul left

Date	Mintage	Good	VG	F	VF	XF
ND(1652)-IX	—	12.00	22.00	45.00	80.00	—
ND(1653)-X	—	12.00	22.00	45.00	80.00	—

KM# 265 1/2 GROSSO

Silver **Ruler:** Alexander VII **Obv:** Arms **Rev:** Legend on ornate shield **Rev. Legend:** TEMPE/RATO/SPLEN/DEAT/VSV

Date	Mintage	Good	VG	F	VF	XF
ND(1655-67)	—	9.00	18.00	35.00	60.00	—

KM# 266 1/2 GROSSO

Silver **Ruler:** Alexander VII **Rev:** Inscription on simple shield

Date	Mintage	Good	VG	F	VF	XF
ND(1655-67)	—	9.00	18.00	35.00	60.00	—

KM# 267 1/2 GROSSO

Silver **Ruler:** Alexander VII **Subject:** Immaculate Conception **Rev:** Radiant Virgin Mary standing on crescent

Date	Mintage	Good	VG	F	VF	XF
ND(1655-67)	—	10.00	20.00	40.00	65.00	—

KM# 264 1/2 GROSSO

Silver **Obv:** Arms of Cardinal Antonio Barberini **Rev:** Radiant dove **Note:** Sede Vacante issue.

Date	Mintage	Good	VG	F	VF	XF
ND(1655)	—	30.00	60.00	125	220	—

KM# 301 1/2 GROSSO

Silver **Ruler:** Clement IX **Rev:** SACROS / BASILIC / LATERAN / POSSESS in round cartouche **Note:** Lateran issue.

Date	Mintage	Good	VG	F	VF	XF
1667	—	16.00	32.00	65.00	110	—

KM# 300 1/2 GROSSO

Silver **Ruler:** Clement IX **Rev:** Head of St. Peter right

Date	Mintage	Good	VG	F	VF	XF
ND(1667-69)	—	10.00	20.00	40.00	65.00	—

KM# 315 1/2 GROSSO

Silver **Obv:** Arms of Cardinal Antonio Barberini **Rev:** Radiant dove **Note:** Sede Vacante issue.

Date	Mintage	Good	VG	F	VF	XF
MDCLXIX (1669)	—	12.00	25.00	45.00	80.00	—

KM# 330 1/2 GROSSO

Silver **Ruler:** Clement X **Obv:** Arms **Rev:** SACROSAN / BASILIC / LATERAN / POSSESS in round cartouche **Note:** Lateran issue.

Date	Mintage	Good	VG	F	VF	XF
MDCLXX (1670)	—	9.00	18.00	35.00	60.00	—

KM# 331 1/2 GROSSO

Silver **Ruler:** Clement X **Obv:** Capped bust left **Rev:** Papal arms within wreath

Date	Mintage	Good	VG	F	VF	XF
ND(1670)	—	20.00	40.00	80.00	125	—

KM# 332 1/2 GROSSO

Silver **Ruler:** Clement X **Obv:** Capped bust right

Date	Mintage	Good	VG	F	VF	XF
ND(1670)	—	10.00	20.00	40.00	70.00	—

KM# 333 1/2 GROSSO

Silver **Ruler:** Clement X **Obv:** Arms **Rev:** St. Peter standing

Date	Mintage	Good	VG	F	VF	XF
ND(1670)	—	8.00	16.00	32.00	55.00	—

KM# 334 1/2 GROSSO

Silver **Ruler:** Clement X **Rev:** CVMME / LAVDARENT / SIMVL ASTRA / MATVTINA within wreath

Date	Mintage	Good	VG	F	VF	XF
ND(1670)	—	8.00	16.00	32.00	55.00	—

KM# 357 1/2 GROSSO

Silver **Ruler:** Clement X **Rev:** Holy Door open **Note:** Holy year issue.

Date	Mintage	Good	VG	F	VF	XF
1675	—	9.00	18.00	35.00	60.00	—

KM# 358 1/2 GROSSO

Silver **Ruler:** Clement X **Rev:** Holy Door closed **Note:** Holy year issue.

Date	Mintage	Good	VG	F	VF	XF
1675	—	9.00	18.00	35.00	60.00	—

KM# 383 1/2 GROSSO

Silver **Ruler:** Innocent XI **Rev:** Inscription: SACROSAN / BASILIC / LATERAN / POSSESS **Note:** Lateran issue.

Date	Mintage	Good	VG	F	VF	XF
MDCLXXVI (1676)	—	5.00	12.00	22.00	40.00	—

KM# 378 1/2 GROSSO

Silver **Obv:** Arms of Cardinal Paluzzo Paluzzi-Altieri **Rev:** Radiant dove **Note:** Sede Vacante issue.

Date	Mintage	Good	VG	F	VF	XF
MDCLXXVI (1676)	—	18.00	35.00	55.00	95.00	—

KM# 379 1/2 GROSSO

Silver **Ruler:** Innocent XI **Obv:** Arms **Rev:** Bust of St. Paul right **Rev. Legend:** SAN PALVS

Date	Mintage	Good	VG	F	VF	XF
ND(1676-89)	—	5.00	10.00	20.00	35.00	—

KM# 380 1/2 GROSSO

Silver **Ruler:** Innocent XI **Rev:** Bust of St. Paul right **Rev. Legend:** SANC PAVLVS. AP.

Date	Mintage	Good	VG	F	VF	XF
ND(1676-89)	—	5.00	10.00	20.00	35.00	—

KM# 381 1/2 GROSSO

Silver **Ruler:** Innocent XI **Rev:** Bust of St. Paul right with halo

Date	Mintage	Good	VG	F	VF	XF
ND(1676-89)	—	5.00	10.00	20.00	35.00	—

KM# 382 1/2 GROSSO

Silver **Ruler:** Innocent XI **Rev:** Bust of St. Paul left

Date	Mintage	Good	VG	F	VF	XF
ND(1676-89)	—	5.00	10.00	20.00	35.00	—

KM# 459 1/2 GROSSO

Silver **Ruler:** Innocent XI **Rev:** Inscription in cartouche **Rev. Inscription:** QVID / PRODEST / STVLTO

Date	Mintage	Good	VG	F	VF	XF
ND(1685-88)	—	4.00	8.00	18.00	30.00	—

KM# 460 1/2 GROSSO

Silver **Ruler:** Innocent XI **Rev:** Inscription on palm wreath

Date	Mintage	Good	VG	F	VF	XF
ND(1685-88)	—	4.00	8.00	18.00	30.00	—

KM# 461 1/2 GROSSO

Silver **Ruler:** Innocent XI **Rev:** Inscription in laurel wreath

Date	Mintage	Good	VG	F	VF	XF
ND(1685-88)	—	4.00	8.00	18.00	30.00	—

KM# 462 1/2 GROSSO

Silver **Ruler:** Innocent XI **Rev:** Inscription in cartouche **Rev. Inscription:** NOCET / MINVS

Date	Mintage	Good	VG	F	VF	XF
1685	—	3.00	7.00	15.00	25.00	—
1686	—	3.00	7.00	15.00	25.00	—
1687	—	3.00	7.00	15.00	25.00	—
1688	—	3.00	7.00	15.00	25.00	—
ND	—	3.00	7.00	15.00	25.00	—

KM# 463 1/2 GROSSO

Silver **Ruler:** Innocent XI **Rev:** Inscription in palm wreath

Date	Mintage	Good	VG	F	VF	XF
1685	—	3.00	7.00	15.00	25.00	—

KM# 464 1/2 GROSSO

Silver **Ruler:** Innocent XI **Rev:** Inscription in laurel wreath

Date	Mintage	Good	VG	F	VF	XF
1685	—	3.00	7.00	15.00	25.00	—
ND	—	3.00	7.00	15.00	25.00	—

KM# 482 1/2 GROSSO

Silver **Ruler:** Alexander VII **Obv:** Arms **Rev:** Bust of St. Peter right

Date	Mintage	Good	VG	F	VF	XF
1689	—	8.00	16.00	32.00	55.00	—

KM# 481 1/2 GROSSO

Silver **Obv:** Arms of Cardinal Paluzzo Paluzzi-Altieri **Rev:** Radiant dove **Note:** Sede Vacante issue.

Date	Mintage	Good	VG	F	VF	XF
MDCLXXXIX (1689)	—	10.00	20.00	40.00	65.00	—

KM# 483 1/2 GROSSO

Silver **Ruler:** Alexander VII **Rev:** Inscription in cartouche **Rev. Inscription:** SACROS / BASILIC / LATERAN / POSSESS **Note:** Lateran issue.

Date	Mintage	Good	VG	F	VF	XF
1689	—	10.00	20.00	40.00	65.00	—

KM# 521 1/2 GROSSO

Silver **Obv:** Arms of Cardinal Paluzzo Paluzzi-Altieri **Rev:** Radiant dove ascending **Note:** Sede Vacante issue.

Date	Mintage	Good	VG	F	VF	XF
MDCLXXXXI (1690)	—	10.00	20.00	45.00	70.00	—

KM# 531 1/2 GROSSO

Silver **Obv:** Arms of Cardinal Paluzzo Paluzzi-Altieri **Rev:** Radiant dove flying left **Note:** Sede Vacante issue.

Date	Mintage	Good	VG	F	VF	XF
MDCLXXXXI (1690)	—	10.00	20.00	45.00	70.00	—
1690	—	—	2,000	4,000	7,000	11,500

KM# 532 1/2 GROSSO

Silver **Ruler:** Innocent XII **Obv:** Arms **Rev:** Head of St. Peter, halo behind

Date	Mintage	Good	VG	F	VF	XF
1691	—	6.00	12.00	25.00	45.00	—

KM# 543 1/2 GROSSO

Silver **Ruler:** Innocent XII **Rev:** Head of St. Peter, halo above

Date	Mintage	Good	VG	F	VF	XF
1692	—	6.00	12.00	25.00	45.00	—

KM# 544 1/2 GROSSO

Silver **Ruler:** Innocent XII **Rev. Inscription:** SACRO ISAN / BASILIC / LATERAN / POSSESS **Note:** Lateran issue.

Date	Mintage	Good	VG	F	VF	XF
MDCXCII (1692)	—	6.00	12.00	25.00	45.00	—

KM# 548 1/2 GROSSO

Silver **Ruler:** Innocent XII **Rev:** Inscription in cartouche **Rev. Inscription:** FAC / VT / IVVET

Date	Mintage	Good	VG	F	VF	XF
1692	—	6.00	12.00	25.00	45.00	—

KM# 560 1/2 GROSSO

Silver **Ruler:** Innocent XII **Rev:** St. Paul's head right

Date	Mintage	Good	VG	F	VF	XF
ND(1693)-III	—	6.00	12.00	25.00	45.00	—

KM# 564 1/2 GROSSO

Silver **Ruler:** Innocent XII **Rev:** Bust of St. Peter left

Date	Mintage	Good	VG	F	VF	XF
ND(1693)-III	—	6.00	12.00	25.00	45.00	—

KM# 570 1/2 GROSSO

Silver **Ruler:** Innocent XII **Rev:** Inscription in palm wreath **Rev. Inscription:** VT/OCTVR

Date	Mintage	Good	VG	F	VF	XF
1694	—	5.00	10.00	22.00	35.00	—

KM# 571 1/2 GROSSO

Silver **Ruler:** Innocent XII **Rev:** Inscription in laurel wreath

Date	Mintage	Good	VG	F	VF	XF
1694	—	5.00	10.00	22.00	35.00	—

KM# 581 1/2 GROSSO

Silver **Ruler:** Innocent XII **Rev:** Inscription in olive or laurel wreath **Rev. Inscription:** DA / PAVPERI

Date	Mintage	Good	VG	F	VF	XF
1695-V	—	5.00	10.00	22.00	35.00	—

KM# 582 1/2 GROSSO

Silver **Ruler:** Innocent XII **Rev:** Inscription in carotuche ornamented by vases

Date	Mintage	Good	VG	F	VF	XF
1695	—	5.00	10.00	22.00	35.00	—

KM# 589 1/2 GROSSO

Silver **Ruler:** Innocent XII **Rev:** Inscription curved in carotuche

Date	Mintage	Good	VG	F	VF	XF
1696	—	5.00	10.00	22.00	35.00	—

KM# 604 1/2 GROSSO

Silver **Ruler:** Innocent XII **Rev:** Inscription between foliage

Date	Mintage	Good	VG	F	VF	XF
1698	—	5.00	10.00	22.00	35.00	—

KM# 50 GROSSO

Silver **Ruler:** Paul V **Obv:** Arms **Obv. Legend:** ...P.M. **Rev:** St. Paul standing holding sword and book at right

Date	Mintage	Good	VG	F	VF	XF
ND(1608)-IIII	—	14.00	28.00	55.00	95.00	—
ND	—	14.00	28.00	55.00	95.00	—

KM# 73 GROSSO

Silver **Ruler:** Paul V **Obv:** Arms **Obv. Legend:** ...PONT•MAXIM

Date	Mintage	Good	VG	F	VF	XF
1615-XI	—	12.00	25.00	50.00	90.00	—
1615-XII	—	12.00	25.00	50.00	90.00	—

KM# 74 GROSSO

Silver **Ruler:** Paul V **Obv:** Bust right

Date	Mintage	Good	VG	F	VF	XF
1615-XI	—	20.00	40.00	75.00	135	—
1615-XII	—	20.00	40.00	75.00	135	—

KM# 75 GROSSO

Silver **Ruler:** Paul V **Rev:** St. Paul standing, sword at right, book at left

Date	Mintage	Good	VG	F	VF	XF
ND(1615)-XI Unique	—	—	—	—	—	—

KM# 93 GROSSO

Silver **Ruler:** Gregory XV **Rev:** St. Paul standing

Date	Mintage	Good	VG	F	VF	XF
ND(1621-23)	—	25.00	50.00	95.00	175	—

KM# 94 GROSSO

Silver **Ruler:** Gregory XV **Rev:** Radiant Virgin Mary standing on crescent

Date	Mintage	Good	VG	F	VF	XF
ND(1621-23)	—	22.00	45.00	90.00	170	—

KM# 111 GROSSO

Silver **Obv:** Arms **Rev:** ROMA below

Date	Mintage	Good	VG	F	VF	XF
ND(1623-44)	—	15.00	30.00	60.00	110	—

KM# 110 GROSSO

Silver **Obv:** Arms of Cardinal Ippolito Aldobrandini **Rev:** Christ standing in rays **Note:** Sede Vacante issue.

Date	Mintage	Good	VG	F	VF	XF
1623	—	85.00	165	325	600	—

KM# 139 GROSSO

Silver **Ruler:** Urban VIII **Rev:** Holy Door with Veronica's veil, 1625 at sides **Note:** Holy year issue.

Date	Mintage	Good	VG	F	VF	XF
1625-II	—	15.00	30.00	60.00	110	—

KM# 140 GROSSO

Silver **Ruler:** Urban VIII **Rev:** Date in exergue **Note:** Holy year issue.

Date	Mintage	Good	VG	F	VF	XF
1625-II	—	15.00	30.00	60.00	110	—

KM# 151 GROSSO

Silver **Ruler:** Urban VIII **Rev:** St. Paul standing **Rev. Legend:** ...ALMA ROMA

Date	Mintage	Good	VG	F	VF	XF
ND(1627)-VI	—	15.00	30.00	60.00	110	—
ND	—	15.00	30.00	60.00	110	—

KM# 152 GROSSO

Silver **Ruler:** Urban VIII **Rev:** Radiant Virgin Mary standing on crescent

Date	Mintage	Good	VG	F	VF	XF
ND(1627)-VI	—	15.00	30.00	60.00	110	—
ND(1628)-VII	—	15.00	30.00	60.00	110	—
ND	—	15.00	30.00	60.00	110	—

KM# 156 GROSSO

Silver **Ruler:** Urban VIII **Rev:** Bust of Christ left

Date	Mintage	Good	VG	F	VF	XF
ND(1628)-VII	—	15.00	30.00	60.00	110	—
ND(1630)-XVIII	—	15.00	30.00	60.00	110	—
ND	—	15.00	30.00	60.00	110	—

KM# 192 GROSSO

Silver **Ruler:** Urban VIII **Rev:** St. Paul standing **Rev. Legend:** ...ALMA ROMA

Date	Mintage	Good	VG	F	VF	XF
ND(1639)-XVIII	—	15.00	30.00	60.00	110	—
ND(1641)-XX	—	15.00	30.00	60.00	110	—
1642-XX	—	15.00	30.00	60.00	110	—
ND(1644)-XXI	—	15.00	30.00	60.00	110	—

KM# 213 GROSSO

Silver **Ruler:** Innocent X **Rev:** Bust of St. Paul, ROMA in exergue

Date	Mintage	Good	VG	F	VF	XF
ND(1644)-I	—	20.00	40.00	85.00	150	—
ND(1645)-II	—	20.00	40.00	85.00	150	—
ND(1652)-IX	—	20.00	40.00	85.00	150	—
ND(1653)-X	—	20.00	40.00	85.00	150	—

KM# 214 GROSSO

Silver **Ruler:** Innocent X **Subject:** Immaculate Conception **Rev:** Radiant Virgin Mary standing on crescent

Date	Mintage	Good	VG	F	VF	XF
ND(1644)-I	—	18.00	35.00	70.00	125	—
ND(1645)-II	—	18.00	35.00	70.00	125	—

KM# 211 GROSSO

Silver **Ruler:** Urban VIII **Rev:** St. Paul standing **Rev. Legend:** ...APOSTOL

Date	Mintage	Good	VG	F	VF	XF
ND(1644)-XXI	—	15.00	30.00	60.00	110	—

KM# 212 GROSSO

Silver **Ruler:** Urban VIII **Rev:** Head of St. Peter left

Date	Mintage	Good	VG	F	VF	XF
ND(1644)-XXI	—	18.00	35.00	70.00	125	—

KM# 215 GROSSO

Silver **Ruler:** Innocent X **Rev:** St. Paul standing **Rev. Legend:** ...ALMA ROMA

Date	Mintage	Good	VG	F	VF	XF
ND(1644)-I	—	20.00	40.00	85.00	150	—

KM# 227 GROSSO

Silver **Ruler:** Innocent X **Rev. Legend:** ...AP

Date	Mintage	Good	VG	F	VF	XF
ND(1645)-II	—	18.00	35.00	70.00	125	—

KM# 229 GROSSO

Silver **Ruler:** Innocent X **Rev. Legend:** ...ALMA ROMA

Date	Mintage	Good	VG	F	VF	XF
ND(1645)-II	—	18.00	35.00	70.00	125	—
ND(1648)-V	—	18.00	35.00	70.00	125	—

KM# 228 GROSSO

Silver **Ruler:** Innocent X **Rev. Legend:** ...AP ROMA

Date	Mintage	Good	VG	F	VF	XF
ND(1645)-II	—	18.00	35.00	70.00	125	—

KM# 251 GROSSO

Silver **Ruler:** Innocent X **Rev:** Holy Door **Note:** Holy year issue.

Date	Mintage	Good	VG	F	VF	XF
1650-VI	—	20.00	40.00	85.00	150	—
MDCL (1650)-VI	—	20.00	40.00	85.00	150	—
1650-VII	—	20.00	40.00	85.00	150	—

KM# 289 GROSSO

Silver **Ruler:** Innocent X **Rev. Legend:** ...APOSTOLVS

Date	Mintage	Good	VG	F	VF	XF
ND(1653)-X	—	20.00	40.00	85.00	160	—

KM# 268 GROSSO

Silver **Obv:** Arms of Cardinal Antonio Barberini **Rev:** Radiant dove **Note:** Sede Vacante issue.

Date	Mintage	Good	VG	F	VF	XF
ND(1655)	—	80.00	165	300	500	—

KM# 269 GROSSO

Silver **Ruler:** Alexander VII **Obv:** Arms **Rev:** Inscription on shield **Rev. Inscription:** HILAREM / DATOREM / DILIGIT / DEVS

Date	Mintage	VG	F	VF	XF	Unc
ND(1655-67)	—	22.00	45.00	85.00	160	—

KM# 270 GROSSO

Silver **Ruler:** Alexander VII **Rev:** Inscription on simple shield

Date	Mintage	VG	F	VF	XF	Unc
ND(1655-67)	—	22.00	45.00	85.00	160	—

KM# 271 GROSSO

Silver **Ruler:** Alexander VII **Rev:** Inscription without shield

Date	Mintage	VG	F	VF	XF	Unc
ND(1655-67)	—	22.00	45.00	85.00	160	—

KM# 272 GROSSO

Silver **Ruler:** Alexander VII **Subject:** Immaculate Conception **Rev:** Radiant Virgin Mary standing on crescent

Date	Mintage	VG	F	VF	XF	Unc
ND(1655-67)	—	28.00	55.00	100	175	—

KM# 302 GROSSO

Silver **Ruler:** Clement IX **Rev:** Bust of St. Peter

Date	Mintage	VG	F	VF	XF	Unc
1667 Rare	—	—	—	—	—	—
ND Rare	—	—	—	—	—	—

KM# 304 GROSSO

Silver **Ruler:** Clement IX **Rev:** Inscription in round cartouche

Date	Mintage	VG	F	VF	XF	Unc
1667	—	28.00	55.00	100	175	—

KM# 303 GROSSO

Silver **Ruler:** Clement IX **Rev. Inscription:** SACROS / BASILIC / LATERAN / POSSESS **Note:** Lateran issue.

Date	Mintage	VG	F	VF	XF	Unc
1667	—	28.00	55.00	100	175	—

KM# 316 GROSSO

Silver **Obv:** Arms of Cardinal Antonio Barberini **Rev:** Radiant dove **Note:** Sede Vacante issue.

Date	Mintage	VG	F	VF	XF	Unc
MDCLXIX (1669)	—	35.00	70.00	125	200	—

KM# 335 GROSSO

Silver **Ruler:** Clement X **Obv:** Capped bust right **Rev:** St. Peter crowned by angel

Date	Mintage	VG	F	VF	XF	Unc
MDCLXX (1670)	—	28.00	55.00	100	175	—

KM# 336 GROSSO

Silver **Ruler:** Clement X **Obv:** Arms **Rev. Inscription:** SACROS / BASILIC / LATERAN / POSSESS **Note:** Lateran issue.

Date	Mintage	VG	F	VF	XF	Unc
MDCLXX (1670)	—	20.00	40.00	75.00	125	—

KM# 337 GROSSO

Silver **Ruler:** Clement X **Obv:** Capped bust right **Rev:** Half-figure of Madonna and child

Date	Mintage	VG	F	VF	XF	Unc
ND(1670-76)	—	25.00	50.00	90.00	165	—

KM# 338 GROSSO

Silver **Ruler:** Clement X **Rev:** St. Paul standing

Date	Mintage	VG	F	VF	XF	Unc
ND(1670-76)	—	22.00	45.00	80.00	140	—

KM# 339 GROSSO

Silver **Ruler:** Clement X **Rev:** Papal arms

Date	Mintage	VG	F	VF	XF	Unc
ND(1670-76)	—	22.00	45.00	85.00	150	—

KM# 359 GROSSO

Silver **Ruler:** Clement X **Rev:** Holy Door closed **Note:** Holy year issue.

Date	Mintage	VG	F	VF	XF	Unc
1675	—	22.00	45.00	80.00	140	—

KM# 360 GROSSO

Silver **Ruler:** Clement X **Rev:** Holy Door open **Note:** Holy year issue.

Date	Mintage	VG	F	VF	XF	Unc
1675	—	22.00	45.00	80.00	140	—

KM# 384 GROSSO

Silver **Obv:** Arms of Cardinal Paluzzo Paluzzi-Altieri **Rev:** Radiant dove **Note:** Sede Vacante issue.

Date	Mintage	VG	F	VF	XF	Unc
MDCLXXVI (1676)	—	35.00	70.00	125	200	—

KM# 385 GROSSO

Silver **Ruler:** Innocent XI **Obv:** Arms **Rev. Inscription:** SACROSAN / BASILIC / LATERAN / POSSESS **Note:** Lateran issue.

Date	Mintage	VG	F	VF	XF	Unc
MDCLXXVI (1676)	—	12.00	25.00	45.00	80.00	—

KM# 386 GROSSO

Silver **Ruler:** Innocent XI **Rev:** Bust of St. Peter

Date	Mintage	VG	F	VF	XF	Unc
ND(1676-85)	—	12.00	22.00	40.00	70.00	—

KM# 465 GROSSO

Silver **Ruler:** Innocent XI **Rev:** Inscription in ornate cartouche **Rev. Inscription:** NOCET / MINVS

Date	Mintage	VG	F	VF	XF	Unc
1685	—	10.00	20.00	35.00	65.00	—

KM# 468 GROSSO

Silver **Ruler:** Innocent XI **Rev:** Inscription on palm wreath

Date	Mintage	VG	F	VF	XF	Unc
1685	—	10.00	20.00	35.00	65.00	—
ND	—	10.00	20.00	35.00	65.00	—

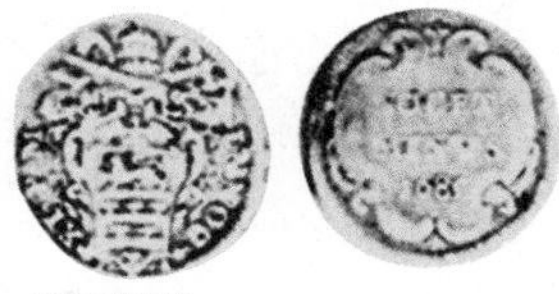

KM# 466 GROSSO

Silver **Ruler:** Innocent XI **Rev:** Inscription in plain cartouche

Date	Mintage	VG	F	VF	XF	Unc
1685	—	10.00	20.00	35.00	65.00	—

KM# 467 GROSSO

Silver **Ruler:** Innocent XI **Rev:** Inscription in cartouche turned inward at top

Date	Mintage	VG	F	VF	XF	Unc
ND(1685-88)	—	10.00	20.00	35.00	65.00	—

KM# 476 GROSSO

Silver **Ruler:** Innocent XI **Rev:** St. Peter's head left

Date	Mintage	VG	F	VF	XF	Unc
1686	—	22.00	45.00	85.00	150	—

KM# 480 GROSSO

Silver **Ruler:** Innocent XI **Rev:** Inscription in ornate cartouche

Date	Mintage	VG	F	VF	XF	Unc
1688	—	10.00	20.00	35.00	65.00	—

KM# 487 GROSSO

Silver **Ruler:** Alexander VIII **Rev:** St. Peter standing

Date	Mintage	VG	F	VF	XF	Unc
1689	—	22.00	45.00	85.00	150	—

KM# 484 GROSSO

Silver **Obv:** Arms of Cardinal Paluzzo Paluzzi-Altieri **Rev:** Radiant dove **Note:** Sede Vacante issue.

Date	Mintage	VG	F	VF	XF	Unc
MDCLXXXIX (1689)	—	28.00	55.00	100	175	—

KM# 485 GROSSO

Silver **Ruler:** Alexander VIII **Obv:** Arms **Rev:** Inscription in cartouche **Rev. Inscription:** SACROS / BASILIC / LATERAN / POSSESS / 1689 **Note:** Lateran issue.

Date	Mintage	VG	F	VF	XF	Unc
1689	—	25.00	50.00	90.00	165	—

KM# 486 GROSSO

Silver **Ruler:** Alexander VIII **Rev:** Inscription in palm wreath **Note:** Lateran issue.

Date	Mintage	VG	F	VF	XF	Unc
1689	—	28.00	55.00	100	175	—

KM# 533 GROSSO

Silver **Obv:** Arms of Cardinal Paluzzo Paluzzi-Altieri **Rev:** Radiant dove ascending **Note:** Sede Vacante issue.

Date	Mintage	VG	F	VF	XF	Unc
MDCLXXXXI (1691)	—	25.00	50.00	90.00	165	—

KM# 547 GROSSO

Silver **Rev:** St. Peter's head 3/4 left, upwards

Date	Mintage	VG	F	VF	XF	Unc
ND(1691-1700)	—	14.00	28.00	55.00	95.00	—

KM# 534 GROSSO

Silver **Rev:** Dove flying left

Date	Mintage	VG	F	VF	XF	Unc
MDCLXXXXI (1691)	—	25.00	50.00	90.00	165	—

KM# 546 GROSSO

Silver **Rev:** St. Peter's head left

Date	Mintage	VG	F	VF	XF	Unc
1691	—	14.00	28.00	55.00	95.00	—

KM# A548 GROSSO

Silver **Ruler:** Innocent XII **Obv:** Arms **Rev. Inscription:** SACRO / SAN BASILIC / LATERAN / POSSESS **Note:** Lateran issue.

Date	Mintage	VG	F	VF	XF	Unc
MDCXCII (1692)	—	14.00	28.00	55.00	95.00	—

KM# 549 GROSSO

Silver **Ruler:** Innocent XII **Rev. Inscription:** PECCATA / REDIME

Date	Mintage	VG	F	VF	XF	Unc
1692	—	14.00	28.00	50.00	90.00	—

KM# 565 GROSSO

Silver **Ruler:** Innocent XII **Rev:** St. Paul's head right

Date	Mintage	VG	F	VF	XF	Unc
ND(1693)-III	—	14.00	28.00	55.00	95.00	—

KM# 572 GROSSO

Silver **Ruler:** Innocent XII **Rev:** Inscription in laurel wreath **Rev. Inscription:** CVM / EGENIS

Date	Mintage	VG	F	VF	XF	Unc
1694	—	14.00	28.00	55.00	95.00	—

KM# 573 GROSSO

Silver **Ruler:** Innocent XII **Rev:** Inscription in palm wreath

Date	Mintage	VG	F	VF	XF	Unc
1694	—	14.00	28.00	55.00	95.00	—

KM# 583 GROSSO

Silver **Ruler:** Innocent XII **Rev:** Inscription in polygonal cartouche **Rev. Inscription:** EGENIO / SPEIS

Date	Mintage	VG	F	VF	XF	Unc
1695	—	12.00	25.00	48.00	85.00	—

KM# 584 GROSSO

Silver **Ruler:** Innocent XII **Rev:** Inscription in oval cartouche

Date	Mintage	VG	F	VF	XF	Unc
1695	—	12.00	25.00	48.00	85.00	—

KM# 590 GROSSO

Silver **Ruler:** Innocent XII **Rev:** Inscription in floral wreath, seraph above

Date	Mintage	VG	F	VF	XF	Unc
1696	—	12.00	25.00	48.00	85.00	—

KM# 591 GROSSO

Silver **Ruler:** Innocent XII **Rev:** Inscription in floral wreath without seraph

Date	Mintage	VG	F	VF	XF	Unc
1696	—	12.00	25.00	48.00	85.00	—
1697	—	12.00	25.00	48.00	85.00	—

KM# 592 GROSSO

Silver **Ruler:** Innocent XII **Rev:** Inscription in palm wreath

Date	Mintage	VG	F	VF	XF	Unc
1696	—	12.00	25.00	48.00	85.00	—
1697	—	12.00	25.00	48.00	85.00	—

KM# 600 GROSSO

Silver **Ruler:** Innocent XII **Rev:** Inscription in cartouche with dot above

Date	Mintage	VG	F	VF	XF	Unc
1697	—	12.00	25.00	48.00	85.00	—

KM# 605 GROSSO

Silver **Ruler:** Innocent XII **Rev:** Inscription in olive wreath

Date	Mintage	VG	F	VF	XF	Unc
1698	—	12.00	25.00	48.00	85.00	—

KM# 609 GROSSO

Silver **Ruler:** Innocent XII **Rev:** Holy Door **Rev. Legend:** PORTA AVREA **Note:** Holy year issue.

Date	Mintage	VG	F	VF	XF	Unc
1699	—	14.00	28.00	50.00	90.00	—

KM# 610 GROSSO

Silver **Ruler:** Innocent XII **Rev:** Holy Door **Rev. Legend:** PORTA COELI **Note:** Holy year issue.

Date	Mintage	VG	F	VF	XF	Unc
1699	—	15.00	30.00	55.00	95.00	—

KM# 611 GROSSO

Silver **Ruler:** Innocent XII **Rev:** Holy Door **Rev. Legend:** PORTA PARADISI **Note:** Holy year issue.

Date	Mintage	VG	F	VF	XF	Unc
1699	—	15.00	30.00	55.00	95.00	—

KM# 635 GROSSO

Silver **Ruler:** Clement XI **Obv:** Papal arms **Rev:** Inscription in cartouche **Rev. Inscription:** DEDIT / PAVPE / RIBVS

Date	Mintage	VG	F	VF	XF	Unc
ND(1700-21)	—	10.00	22.00	38.00	60.00	100

KM# 636 GROSSO

Silver **Ruler:** Clement XI **Obv:** Papal arms **Rev:** Inscription in cartouche **Rev. Inscription:** ESVRI / ENTEM / NE / DESPRE / XERIS

Date	Mintage	VG	F	VF	XF	Unc
ND(1700-21)	—	10.00	22.00	38.00	60.00	100

KM# 637 GROSSO

Silver **Ruler:** Clement XI **Obv:** Papal arms **Rev:** Inscription without cartouche

Date	Mintage	VG	F	VF	XF	Unc
ND(1700-21)	—	10.00	22.00	38.00	60.00	100

KM# 714 GROSSO

Silver **Ruler:** Clement XI **Obv:** Papal arms **Rev:** Inscription in cartouche **Rev. Inscription:** DEDIT / PAVPE / RIBVS

Date	Mintage	VG	F	VF	XF	Unc
ND(1700-21)	—	10.00	22.00	38.00	60.00	100

KM# 26 GIULIO

Silver **Ruler:** Paul V **Obv:** Arms **Rev:** St. Paul standing with sword and book

Date	Mintage	Good	VG	F	VF	XF
ND(1605)-I	—	20.00	40.00	85.00	160	—
ND(1606)-II	—	20.00	40.00	85.00	160	—
ND(1607)-III	—	20.00	40.00	85.00	160	—
ND(1608)-IIII	—	20.00	40.00	85.00	160	—
ND(1609)-V	—	20.00	40.00	85.00	160	—
ND(1610)-VI	—	20.00	40.00	85.00	160	—
ND(1611)-VII	—	20.00	40.00	85.00	160	—
ND(1612)-VIII	—	20.00	40.00	85.00	160	—
ND(1613)-VIIII	—	20.00	40.00	85.00	160	—
ND(1614)-X	—	20.00	40.00	85.00	160	—
ND(1615)-XI	—	20.00	40.00	85.00	160	—
ND	—	20.00	40.00	85.00	160	—

KM# 27 GIULIO

Silver **Ruler:** Paul V **Rev:** St. Paul seated left

Date	Mintage	Good	VG	F	VF	XF
ND(1605)-I Rare	—	—	—	—	—	—
ND(1606)-II	—	28.00	50.00	85.00	160	—
ND(1607)-III	—	28.00	50.00	85.00	160	—

KM# 25 GIULIO

Silver **Obv:** Arms of Cardinal Pietro Aldobrandini **Rev:** St. Paul standing **Note:** Sede Vacante issue.

Date	Mintage	Good	VG	F	VF	XF
MDCV (1605)	—	100	200	325	500	—

KM# 39 GIULIO

Silver **Ruler:** Paul V **Rev:** St. Paul standing right

Date	Mintage	Good	VG	F	VF	XF
ND(1606)-II	—	28.00	50.00	85.00	160	—
ND(1607)-III	—	28.00	50.00	85.00	160	—

KM# 40 GIULIO

Silver **Ruler:** Paul V **Rev:** St. Paul standing with hand raised

Date	Mintage	Good	VG	F	VF	XF
ND(1606)-II	—	35.00	60.00	100	165	—
ND(1607)-III	—	35.00	60.00	100	165	—
ND(1608)-IIII	—	35.00	60.00	100	165	—
ND(1609)-V	—	35.00	60.00	100	165	—
ND(1610)-VI	—	35.00	60.00	100	165	—

Date	Mintage	Good	VG	F	VF	XF
ND(1611)-VII	—	35.00	60.00	100	165	—
ND(1612)-VIII	—	35.00	60.00	100	165	—
ND(1613)-VIIII	—	35.00	60.00	100	165	—
ND(1614)-X	—	35.00	60.00	100	165	—

KM# 60 GIULIO

Silver **Ruler:** Paul V **Obv:** Bust left

Date	Mintage	Good	VG	F	VF	XF
ND(1610)-VI	—	35.00	60.00	100	165	—
ND(1611)-VII	—	35.00	60.00	100	165	—

KM# 96 GIULIO

Silver **Ruler:** Gregory XV **Obv:** Arms **Rev:** Radiant Virgin Mary standing on crescent

Date	Mintage	Good	VG	F	VF	XF
ND(1621-23)	—	40.00	70.00	115	185	—

KM# 95 GIULIO

Silver **Obv:** Arms of Cardinal Pietro Aldobrandini **Rev:** Faith standing **Note:** Sede Vacante issue.

Date	Mintage	Good	VG	F	VF	XF
1621	—	65.00	120	200	300	—

KM# 112 GIULIO

Silver **Ruler:** Alexander VIII **Obv:** Arms of Cardinal Ippolito Aldobrandini **Rev:** Radiant Christ standing **Note:** Sede Vacante issue.

Date	Mintage	Good	VG	F	VF	XF
1623	—	140	250	425	650	—

KM# 113 GIULIO

Silver **Ruler:** Urban VIII **Obv:** Arms **Rev:** SS. Peter and Paul, dove above

Date	Mintage	Good	VG	F	VF	XF
ND(1623) (i)(P)	—	22.00	40.00	70.00	120	—
ND(1624)-II	—	22.00	40.00	70.00	120	—
ND(1625)-III	—	22.00	40.00	70.00	120	—
ND(1626)-IIII	—	22.00	40.00	70.00	120	—
ND(1627)-V	—	22.00	40.00	70.00	120	—
ND(1628)-VI	—	22.00	40.00	70.00	120	—
ND(1629)-VII	—	22.00	40.00	70.00	120	—
ND(1630)-VIII	—	22.00	40.00	70.00	120	—

KM# 141 GIULIO

Silver **Ruler:** Urban VIII **Rev:** Holy Door with Veronica's veil **Rev. Legend:** QVI DILIGVNT NOMEN TVVM **Note:** Holy year issue.

Date	Mintage	Good	VG	F	VF	XF
ND(1625)	—	22.00	40.00	70.00	120	—

KM# 142 GIULIO

Silver **Ruler:** Urban VIII **Rev:** Date in exergue **Rev. Legend:** QVI INGREDITVR SINE MACVLA **Note:** Holy year issue.

Date	Mintage	Good	VG	F	VF	XF
MDCXX (1620) Error	—	22.00	40.00	70.00	120	—
MDCXXV(1625)	—	22.00	40.00	70.00	120	—

KM# 143 GIULIO

Silver **Ruler:** Urban VIII **Rev:** Holy Door with Veronica's veil, date below veil **Note:** Holy year issue.

Date	Mintage	Good	VG	F	VF	XF
MDCXXV (1625)-II	—	22.00	40.00	70.00	120	—
MDCXXV (1625)-III	—	22.00	40.00	70.00	120	—

KM# 144 GIULIO

Silver **Ruler:** Urban VIII **Rev:** Date divided by Holy Door **Note:** Holy year issue.

Date	Mintage	Good	VG	F	VF	XF
MDCXXV (1625)-II	—	22.00	40.00	70.00	120	—
MDCXXV (1625)-III	—	22.00	40.00	70.00	120	—

KM# 161 GIULIO

Silver **Ruler:** Urban VIII **Rev:** Half-figure of Madonna with child

Date	Mintage	Good	VG	F	VF	XF
ND(1629)-VII	—	22.00	40.00	70.00	120	—
ND(1630)-VIII	—	22.00	40.00	70.00	120	—
ND(1631)-VIIII	—	22.00	40.00	70.00	120	—
ND(1632)-X	—	22.00	40.00	70.00	120	—
ND(1633)-XI	—	22.00	40.00	70.00	120	—
ND(1634)-XII	—	22.00	40.00	70.00	120	—
ND(1635)-XIII	—	22.00	40.00	70.00	120	—
ND(1636)-XIIII	—	22.00	40.00	70.00	120	—
ND(1637)-XV	—	22.00	40.00	70.00	120	—
ND(1638)-XVI	—	22.00	40.00	70.00	120	—
ND(1639)-XVII	—	22.00	40.00	70.00	120	—
ND(1640)-XVIII	—	22.00	40.00	70.00	120	—
ND(1641)-XVIIII	—	22.00	40.00	70.00	120	—
ND(1642)-XX	—	22.00	40.00	70.00	120	—

KM# 170 GIULIO

Silver **Ruler:** Urban VIII **Rev:** Pope kneeling left, before St. Michael the Archangel in clouds

Date	Mintage	Good	VG	F	VF	XF
ND(1630)-VIII	—	40.00	80.00	125	200	—
ND(1631)-VIIII	—	40.00	80.00	125	200	—

KM# 177 GIULIO

Silver **Ruler:** Urban VIII **Rev:** Without door

Date	Mintage	Good	VG	F	VF	XF
1633	—	22.00	40.00	70.00	120	—

KM# 201 GIULIO

Silver **Ruler:** Urban VIII **Rev:** Radiant Virgin Mary standing on crescent

Date	Mintage	Good	VG	F	VF	XF
ND(1642)-XX	—	22.00	40.00	70.00	120	—
ND(1643)-XXI	—	22.00	40.00	70.00	120	—
ND	—	22.00	40.00	70.00	120	—

KM# 216 GIULIO

Silver **Ruler:** Innocent X **Rev:** St. Paul standing with sword right **Rev. Legend:** S • PAVLVS ALMA ROMA

Date	Mintage	Good	VG	F	VF	XF
ND(1644)-I	—	35.00	60.00	100	165	—
ND(1645)-II	—	35.00	60.00	100	165	—
ND(1652)-VIIII	—	35.00	60.00	100	165	—
ND(1653)-X	—	35.00	60.00	100	165	—

KM# 217 GIULIO

Silver **Ruler:** Innocent X **Rev. Legend:** S PAVLVS AP ALMA ROMA

Date	Mintage	Good	VG	F	VF	XF
ND(1644)-I	—	35.00	60.00	100	165	—

KM# 230 GIULIO

Silver **Ruler:** Innocent X **Subject:** Immaculate Conception **Rev:** Radiant Virgin Mary standing on crescent

Date	Mintage	Good	VG	F	VF	XF
ND(1644)-I	—	35.00	60.00	100	165	—
ND(1645)-II	—	35.00	60.00	100	165	—

KM# 231 GIULIO

Silver **Ruler:** Innocent X **Rev:** St. Paul standing with sword left **Rev. Legend:** S PAVLVS ALMA ROMA

Date	Mintage	Good	VG	F	VF	XF
ND(1645)-II	—	35.00	60.00	100	165	—
ND(1646)-III	—	35.00	60.00	100	165	—

KM# 245 GIULIO

Silver **Ruler:** Innocent X **Rev:** Confronted busts of SS. Peter and Paul

Date	Mintage	Good	VG	F	VF	XF
ND(1646)-II	—	40.00	70.00	115	185	—

KM# 252 GIULIO

Silver **Ruler:** Innocent X **Rev:** Holy Door with Veronica's veil **Note:** Holy year issue.

Date	Mintage	Good	VG	F	VF	XF
ND(1650)-VII	—	40.00	70.00	115	185	—

KM# 273 GIULIO

Silver **Obv:** Arms of Cardinal Antonio Barberini **Rev:** Radiant dove **Note:** Sede Vacante issue.

Date	Mintage	Good	VG	F	VF	XF
MDCLV (1655)	—	100	200	325	500	—

KM# 274 GIULIO

Silver **Ruler:** Alexander VII **Obv:** Arms **Rev:** Table with coins

Date	Mintage	VG	F	VF	XF	Unc
ND(1655-67)	—	40.00	85.00	150	250	—

KM# 275 GIULIO

Silver **Ruler:** Alexander VII **Obv:** Simple arms

Date	Mintage	VG	F	VF	XF	Unc
ND(1655-67)	—	40.00	85.00	150	250	—

KM# 276 GIULIO

Silver **Ruler:** Alexander VII **Subject:** Immaculate Conception **Obv:** Arms **Rev:** Radiant Virgin Mary standing on crescent

Date	Mintage	VG	F	VF	XF	Unc
ND(1655-56)	—	35.00	75.00	135	225	—

KM# 305 GIULIO

Silver **Obv:** Arms of Cardinal Antonio Barberini **Rev:** Radiant dove **Note:** Sede Vacante issue.

Date	Mintage	VG	F	VF	XF	Unc
MDCLXVII (1667)	—	55.00	110	200	325	—

KM# 306 GIULIO

Silver **Ruler:** Clement IX **Rev:** St. Peter walking right

Date	Mintage	VG	F	VF	XF	Unc
ND(1667-69)	—	40.00	85.00	150	250	—

KM# 307 GIULIO

Silver **Ruler:** Clement IX **Rev:** Inscription in cartouche, wreath below **Rev. Inscription:** SACROSAN / BASILIC / LATERAN / POSSESS **Note:** Lateran issue.

Date	Mintage	VG	F	VF	XF	Unc
MDCLXVII (1667)	—	50.00	95.00	175	285	—

KM# 317 GIULIO

Silver **Obv:** Arms of Cardinal Antonio Barberini **Rev:** Radiant dove **Note:** Sede Vacante issue.

Date	Mintage	VG	F	VF	XF	Unc
MDCLXIX (1669)	—	50.00	95.00	175	285	—

KM# 340 GIULIO

Silver **Obv:** Bust of Clement X right **Rev:** St. Peter standing crowned by angel

Date	Mintage	VG	F	VF	XF	Unc
MDCLXX (1670)-I	—	70.00	140	250	400	—

KM# 341 GIULIO

Silver **Subject:** Immaculate Conception **Obv:** Arms **Rev:** Radiant Virgin Mary standing on crescent

Date	Mintage	VG	F	VF	XF	Unc
ND(1670-76)	—	55.00	110	200	325	—

KM# 348 GIULIO

Silver **Rev:** Inscription in round cartouche **Rev. Inscription:** SACROSAN / BASILIC / LATERAN / POSSESS **Note:** Lateran issue.

Date	Mintage	VG	F	VF	XF	Unc
MDCLXX (1670)	—	60.00	125	225	375	—

KM# 352 GIULIO

Silver **Obv:** Capped bust right **Rev:** Inscription in wreath **Rev. Inscription:** DA PACEM / DOMINE / IN DIEBVS / NOSTRIS

Date	Mintage	VG	F	VF	XF	Unc
MDCLXXII (1672)-III	—	50.00	100	185	300	—

KM# 354 GIULIO

Silver **Rev:** St. Venantius standing

Date	Mintage	VG	F	VF	XF	Unc
MDCLXXIII (1673)-IIII	—	120	225	400	650	—

KM# 361 GIULIO

Silver **Obv:** Arms **Rev:** Holy Door open **Note:** Holy year issue.

Date	Mintage	VG	F	VF	XF	Unc
1675	—	55.00	110	200	325	—

KM# 362 GIULIO

Silver **Rev:** Holy Door closed **Note:** Holy year issue.

Date	Mintage	VG	F	VF	XF	Unc
1675	—	55.00	110	200	325	—

KM# 387 GIULIO

Silver **Obv:** Arms of Cardinal Paluzzo Paluzzi-Altieri **Rev:** Radiant dove **Note:** Sede Vacante issue.

Date	Mintage	VG	F	VF	XF	Unc
MDCLXXVI (1676)	—	55.00	110	200	325	—

KM# 388 GIULIO

Silver **Ruler:** Innocent XI **Obv:** Arms **Rev:** Inscription in cartouche **Rev. Inscription:** DELECTA BOR / IN / MVLTTVDINE / PACIS

Date	Mintage	VG	F	VF	XF	Unc
ND(1676-89)	—	22.00	45.00	85.00	160	—

KM# 409 GIULIO

Silver **Ruler:** Innocent XI **Rev:** Inscription in cartouche **Rev. Inscription:** SACROSAN / BASILIC / LATERAN / POSSESS **Note:** Lateran issue.

Date	Mintage	VG	F	VF	XF	Unc
MDCLXXVI (1676)	—	28.00	55.00	100	170	—

KM# 396 GIULIO

Silver **Ruler:** Innocent XI **Rev:** Bust of Innocent XI right

Date	Mintage	VG	F	VF	XF	Unc
1677-II	—	28.00	55.00	100	175	—
ND-III	—	28.00	55.00	100	175	—

KM# 405 GIULIO

Silver **Ruler:** Innocent XI **Rev:** Inscription on drapery **Rev. Inscription:** MODICVM / IVSTO

Date	Mintage	VG	F	VF	XF	Unc
ND(1679)-IIII	—	28.00	55.00	100	170	—

KM# 420 GIULIO

Silver **Ruler:** Innocent XI **Rev:** Cartouche replaces drapery

Date	Mintage	VG	F	VF	XF	Unc
ND(1680)-V	—	28.00	55.00	100	160	—

KM# 423 GIULIO

Silver **Ruler:** Innocent XI **Rev:** Inscription within laurel wreath **Rev. Inscription:** QVID / PRODEST / HOMINI

Date	Mintage	VG	F	VF	XF	Unc
ND(1681)-VI	—	28.00	55.00	100	160	—

KM# 535 GIULIO

Silver **Obv:** Arms of Cardinal Paluzzo Paluzzi-Altieri **Rev:** Radiant dove **Note:** Sede Vacante issue.

Date	Mintage	VG	F	VF	XF	Unc
MDCLXXXI (1681)	—	28.00	55.00	100	185	—

KM# 432 GIULIO

Silver **Ruler:** Innocent XI **Rev:** Inscription in cartouche **Rev. Inscription:** QVI DAT / PAVPERI / NON / TNDIGEBIT

Date	Mintage	VG	F	VF	XF	Unc
1684-VIII	—	22.00	45.00	80.00	140	—
1685-X	—	22.00	45.00	80.00	140	—
1686-XI	—	22.00	45.00	80.00	140	—
1688-XIII	—	22.00	45.00	80.00	140	—
ND	—	22.00	45.00	80.00	140	—

KM# 477 GIULIO

Silver **Ruler:** Innocent XI **Rev:** Inscription in palm wreath

Date	Mintage	VG	F	VF	XF	Unc
1686-XI	—	22.00	45.00	80.00	140	—

KM# 478 GIULIO

Silver **Ruler:** Innocent XI **Rev:** Inscription in ornamental wreath

Date	Mintage	VG	F	VF	XF	Unc
1686-XI	—	22.00	45.00	80.00	140	—

KM# 489 GIULIO

Silver **Ruler:** Alexander VIII **Obv:** Arms **Rev:** St. Paul standing

Date	Mintage	VG	F	VF	XF	Unc
1689-I	—	28.00	55.00	100	175	—
1690-II	—	28.00	55.00	100	175	—

KM# 488 GIULIO

Silver **Obv:** Arms of Cardinal Paluzzo Paluzzi-Altieri **Rev:** Radiant dove **Note:** Sede Vacante issue.

Date	Mintage	VG	F	VF	XF	Unc
MDCLXXXIX (1689)	—	35.00	70.00	125	200	—

KM# 490 GIULIO

Silver **Ruler:** Alexander VIII **Rev. Inscription:** SACROS / BASLIC / LATERAN / POSSESS **Note:** Lateran issue.

Date	Mintage	VG	F	VF	XF	Unc
1689	—	28.00	55.00	100	185	—

KM# 491 GIULIO

Silver **Ruler:** Alexander VIII **Rev:** St. Bruno kneeling right

Date	Mintage	VG	F	VF	XF	Unc
1689	—	35.00	65.00	120	200	—

KM# 553 GIULIO

Silver **Ruler:** Innocent XII **Obv:** Arms **Rev:** Inscription in cartouche **Rev. Inscription:** QVI / VIDET TE / REDDET / TIBI

Date	Mintage	VG	F	VF	XF	Unc
ND(1692)-II	—	35.00	65.00	110	200	—

KM# 536 GIULIO

Silver **Ruler:** Innocent XII **Obv:** Arms **Rev:** Legend in cartouche **Rev. Inscription:** SACRO • SAN / BASILIC / LATERAN / POSSESS **Note:** Lateran issue.

Date	Mintage	VG	F	VF	XF	Unc
MDCXCII (1692)	—	25.00	55.00	100	185	—

KM# 566 GIULIO

Silver **Ruler:** Innocent XII **Rev:** Inscription in cartouche **Rev. Inscription:** NE / OBLIVISCARIS / PAAVPERVM

Date	Mintage	VG	F	VF	XF	Unc
1693	—	25.00	55.00	100	185	—

KM# 523 GIULIO

Silver **Ruler:** Innocent XII **Rev:** St. Paul standing

Date	Mintage	VG	F	VF	XF	Unc
1694	—	28.00	55.00	100	185	—

KM# 574 GIULIO

Silver **Ruler:** Innocent XII **Rev:** Cannon firing right, artillery man standing left

Date	Mintage	VG	F	VF	XF	Unc
(16)94-IIII	—	40.00	85.00	150	250	—

KM# 585 GIULIO

Silver **Ruler:** Innocent XII **Rev:** Inscription in cartouche **Rev. Inscription:** ELEVAT / PAVPEREM

Date	Mintage	VG	F	VF	XF	Unc
1695-V	—	28.00	55.00	100	185	—

KM# 586 GIULIO

Silver **Ruler:** Innocent XII **Rev:** Three vases above cartouche

Date	Mintage	VG	F	VF	XF	Unc
1695-V	—	25.00	55.00	100	185	—

KM# 587 GIULIO

Silver **Ruler:** Innocent XII **Rev:** Inscription on drapery without vases

Date	Mintage	VG	F	VF	XF	Unc
1695-V	—	25.00	55.00	100	185	—

KM# 593 GIULIO

Silver **Ruler:** Innocent XII **Rev:** Inscription curved upward or downward in cartouche

Date	Mintage	VG	F	VF	XF	Unc
1696-V	—	28.00	60.00	100	185	—
1697-VII	—	28.00	60.00	100	185	—

KM# 612 GIULIO

Silver **Ruler:** Innocent XII **Rev:** Inscription in cartouche **Rev. Inscription:** PECCATA / ELEEMOSYNIS / REDIME

Date	Mintage	VG	F	VF	XF	Unc
1699	—	25.00	50.00	90.00	150	—

KM# 639 GIULIO

Silver **Ruler:** Innocent XII **Rev:** Holy Door with four columns **Note:** Holy Year issue.

Date	Mintage	VG	F	VF	XF	Unc
MDCC (1700)-IX	—	35.00	70.00	125	200	—

KM# 640 GIULIO

Silver **Ruler:** Innocent XII **Rev:** Holy Door with two columns **Note:** Holy Year issue.

Date	Mintage	VG	F	VF	XF	Unc
MDCC (1700)-IX	—	35.00	70.00	125	200	—

KM# 643 GIULIO

Silver **Ruler:** Clement XI **Obv:** Arms **Rev:** Holy Door, triangular or curved top **Note:** Holy Year issue.

Date	Mintage	VG	F	VF	XF	Unc
MDCC (1700)-I	—	30.00	60.00	110	200	—

KM# 642 GIULIO

Silver **Ruler:** Innocent XII **Obv:** Arms of Cardinal Giovanni Spinola **Rev:** Radiant dove upwards **Note:** Sede Vacante issue.

Date	Mintage	VG	F	VF	XF	Unc
MDCC (1700)	—	50.00	95.00	175	285	—

KM# 641 GIULIO

Silver **Obv:** Arms of Cardinal Giovanni Spinola **Rev:** Radiant dove upwards **Note:** Sede Vacante issue.

Date	Mintage	VG	F	VF	XF	Unc
MDCC (1700)	—	50.00	95.00	175	285	—

KM# 31 TESTONE (30 Baiocchi)

9.5960 g., 0.9160 Silver 0.2826 oz. ASW **Ruler:** Paul V **Obv:** Arms **Rev:** Miracle of the Snakes

Date	Mintage	Good	VG	F	VF	XF
ND(1605)-I	—	35.00	70.00	135	225	—
ND(1606)-II	—	35.00	70.00	135	225	—
ND(1607)-III	—	35.00	70.00	135	225	—

KM# 32 TESTONE (30 Baiocchi)

9.5960 g., 0.9160 Silver 0.2826 oz. ASW **Ruler:** Paul V **Obv:** Bust left **Rev:** Bust of St. Paul left

Date	Mintage	Good	VG	F	VF	XF
ND(1605-21)	—	35.00	70.00	125	200	—

KM# 33 TESTONE (30 Baiocchi)

9.5960 g., 0.9160 Silver 0.2826 oz. ASW **Ruler:** Paul V **Obv:** Papal arms supported by two angels **Rev:** Madonna and child seated on altar, SS. Peter and Paul at sides

Date	Mintage	Good	VG	F	VF	XF
ND(1605-21)	—	320	525	875	1,400	—

KM# 28 TESTONE (30 Baiocchi)

9.5960 g., 0.9160 Silver 0.2826 oz. ASW **Obv:** Arms of Cardinal Pietro Aldobrandini **Rev:** St. Peter standing **Note:** Sede Vacante issue.

Date	Mintage	Good	VG	F	VF	XF
ND(1605)	—	150	300	475	750	—

KM# 29 TESTONE (30 Baiocchi)

9.5960 g., 0.9160 Silver 0.2826 oz. ASW **Obv:** Arms of Cardinal

Pietro Aldobrandini **Rev:** Confronted busts of SS. Peter and Paul **Note:** Sede Vacante issue.

Date	Mintage	Good	VG	F	VF	XF
ND(1605)	—	200	400	650	1,000	—

KM# 30 TESTONE (30 Baiocchi)

9.5960 g., 0.9160 Silver 0.2826 oz. ASW **Obv:** Arms of Cardinal Pietro Aldobrandini **Rev:** SS. Peter and Paul standing **Note:** Sede Vacante issue.

Date	Mintage	Good	VG	F	VF	XF
MDCV (1605)	—	200	400	650	1,000	—

KM# 41 TESTONE (30 Baiocchi)

9.5960 g., 0.9160 Silver 0.2826 oz. ASW **Ruler:** Paul V **Rev:** SS. Peter and Paul standing

Date	Mintage	Good	VG	F	VF	XF
ND(1606)-II	—	28.00	55.00	100	185	—
ND(1607)-III	—	28.00	55.00	100	185	—
ND(1608)-IIII	—	28.00	55.00	100	185	—

KM# 46 TESTONE (30 Baiocchi)

9.5960 g., 0.9160 Silver 0.2826 oz. ASW **Ruler:** Paul V **Obv:** Bust left

Date	Mintage	Good	VG	F	VF	XF
ND(1607)-III	—	60.00	120	200	300	—

KM# 47 TESTONE (30 Baiocchi)

9.5960 g., 0.9160 Silver 0.2826 oz. ASW **Ruler:** Paul V **Obv:** Bust left

Date	Mintage	Good	VG	F	VF	XF
ND(1607)-III	—	45.00	90.00	145	225	—

KM# 51 TESTONE (30 Baiocchi)

9.5960 g., 0.9160 Silver 0.2826 oz. ASW **Ruler:** Paul V **Obv:** Arms **Rev:** St. Paul standing with sword left, book right

Date	Mintage	Good	VG	F	VF	XF
ND(1608)-IIII	—	28.00	55.00	100	185	—
ND(1609)-IIIII	—	28.00	55.00	100	185	—
ND(1610)-VI	—	28.00	55.00	100	185	—
ND(1611)-VII	—	28.00	55.00	100	185	—

KM# 52 TESTONE (30 Baiocchi)

9.5960 g., 0.9160 Silver 0.2826 oz. ASW **Ruler:** Paul V **Obv:** Bust left **Rev:** St. Paul standing holding sword and book

Date	Mintage	Good	VG	F	VF	XF
ND(1608)-IIII	—	45.00	90.00	145	245	—
ND(1609)-IIIII	—	45.00	90.00	145	245	—

KM# 61 TESTONE (30 Baiocchi)

9.5960 g., 0.9160 Silver 0.2826 oz. ASW **Ruler:** Paul V **Rev:** St. Paul seated with sword

Date	Mintage	Good	VG	F	VF	XF
ND(1610)-VI	—	28.00	55.00	100	185	—
1610	—	28.00	55.00	100	185	—
ND(1611)-VII	—	28.00	55.00	100	185	—
1611	—	28.00	55.00	100	185	—
MDCII (1602) error for 1612	—	28.00	55.00	100	185	—
ND(1612)-VIII	—	28.00	55.00	100	185	—
ND	—	28.00	55.00	100	185	—

KM# 62 TESTONE (30 Baiocchi)

9.5960 g., 0.9160 Silver 0.2826 oz. ASW **Ruler:** Paul V **Rev:** St. Paul seated without sword

Date	Mintage	Good	VG	F	VF	XF
ND(1610)-VI	—	28.00	55.00	100	185	—
ND(1611)-VII	—	28.00	55.00	100	185	—
ND(1612)-VIII	—	28.00	55.00	100	185	—
ND(1613)-VIIII	—	28.00	55.00	100	185	—
ND(1614)-X	—	28.00	55.00	100	185	—
ND(1615)-XI	—	28.00	55.00	100	185	—

KM# 66 TESTONE (30 Baiocchi)

9.5960 g., 0.9160 Silver 0.2826 oz. ASW **Ruler:** Paul V **Rev:** St. Paul seated with sword right and book left

Date	Mintage	Good	VG	F	VF	XF
ND(1611)-VII	—	28.00	55.00	100	175	—
1612-VIII	—	28.00	55.00	100	175	—
1613-VIIII	—	28.00	55.00	100	175	—
1614-X	—	28.00	55.00	100	175	—
1615-XI	—	28.00	55.00	100	175	—
1616-XII	—	28.00	55.00	100	175	—
1617-XIII	—	28.00	55.00	100	175	—
ND	—	28.00	55.00	100	175	—

KM# 63 TESTONE (30 Baiocchi)

9.5960 g., 0.9160 Silver 0.2826 oz. ASW **Ruler:** Paul V **Obv:** Papal arms supported by two angels, no legend **Rev:** St. Paul seated with sword and book

Date	Mintage	Good	VG	F	VF	XF
ND	—	300	500	800	1,250	—

KM# 68 TESTONE (30 Baiocchi)

9.5960 g., 0.9160 Silver 0.2826 oz. ASW **Ruler:** Paul V **Rev:** St. Paul seated without sword

Date	Mintage	Good	VG	F	VF	XF
1612	—	300	500	800	1,250	—

KM# 69 TESTONE (30 Baiocchi)

9.5960 g., 0.9160 Silver 0.2826 oz. ASW **Ruler:** Paul V **Obv:** Bust of Paul V left **Obv. Legend:** PAVLVS • V • P • M • **Rev:** Papal arms supported by two angels

Date	Mintage	Good	VG	F	VF	XF
ND(1612)-VIII	—	50.00	100	165	265	—
ND(1613)-VIIII	—	50.00	100	165	265	—
1613	—	50.00	100	165	265	—

KM# 70 TESTONE (30 Baiocchi)

9.5960 g., 0.9160 Silver 0.2826 oz. ASW **Ruler:** Paul V **Obv:** Arms

Date	Mintage	Good	VG	F	VF	XF
ND(1612)-VIII	—	100	200	325	500	—
ND(1615)-XI	—	100	200	325	500	—

KM# 71 TESTONE (30 Baiocchi)

9.5960 g., 0.9160 Silver 0.2826 oz. ASW **Ruler:** Paul V **Obv. Legend:** PAVLVS V PONT OPT MAX

Date	Mintage	Good	VG	F	VF	XF
ND(1614)-IX	—	50.00	100	165	285	—
MDCXIV (1614)	—	50.00	100	165	285	—

KM# 76 TESTONE (30 Baiocchi)

9.5960 g., 0.9160 Silver 0.2826 oz. ASW **Ruler:** Paul V **Obv:** Arms **Rev:** Madonna and child seated on altar, SS. Peter and Paul at sides

Date	Mintage	Good	VG	F	VF	XF
ND(1615)-XI	—	300	500	800	1,250	—
ND(1616)-XII	—	300	500	800	1,250	—
ND	—	300	500	800	1,250	—

KM# 79 TESTONE (30 Baiocchi)

9.5960 g., 0.9160 Silver 0.2826 oz. ASW **Ruler:** Paul V **Obv:** Bust right **Rev:** Conversion of St. Paul

Date	Mintage	Good	VG	F	VF	XF
ND(1616)-XII	—	200	400	650	1,000	—

KM# 98 TESTONE (30 Baiocchi)

9.5960 g., 0.9160 Silver 0.2826 oz. ASW **Ruler:** Gregory XV **Obv:** Arms **Rev:** St. Paul standing

Date	Mintage	Good	VG	F	VF	XF
ND(1621-23)	—	70.00	135	225	350	—

KM# 100 TESTONE (30 Baiocchi)

9.5960 g., 0.9160 Silver 0.2826 oz. ASW **Ruler:** Gregory XV **Rev:** Radiant Virgin Mary standing on crescent

Date	Mintage	Good	VG	F	VF	XF
ND(1621-23)	—	40.00	80.00	150	275	—

KM# 97 TESTONE (30 Baiocchi)

9.5960 g., 0.9160 Silver 0.2826 oz. ASW **Obv:** Arms of Cardinal Pietro Aldobrandini **Rev:** Faith standing **Note:** Sede Vacante issue.

Date	Mintage	Good	VG	F	VF	XF
1621	—	115	225	400	600	—

KM# 99 TESTONE (30 Baiocchi)

9.5960 g., 0.9160 Silver 0.2826 oz. ASW **Ruler:** Gregory XV **Rev:** Madonna and child seated on altar, SS. Peter and Paul at sides **Note:** Legend varieties exist.

Date	Mintage	Good	VG	F	VF	XF
ND(1621-33)	—	50.00	100	185	280	—

KM# 114 TESTONE (30 Baiocchi)

9.5960 g., 0.9160 Silver 0.2826 oz. ASW **Obv:** Arms of Cardinal Ippolito Aldobrandini **Rev:** Christ standing with banner **Note:** Sede Vacante issue.

Date	Mintage	Good	VG	F	VF	XF
1623	—	175	350	575	900	—

KM# 115 TESTONE (30 Baiocchi)
9.5960 g., 0.9160 Silver 0.2826 oz. ASW **Obv:** Arms of Cardinal Ippolito Aldobrandini **Rev:** Radiant Christ standing with banner **Note:** Sede Vacante issue.

Date	Mintage	Good	VG	F	VF	XF
1623	—	250	450	775	1,200	—

KM# 116 TESTONE (30 Baiocchi)
9.5960 g., 0.9160 Silver 0.2826 oz. ASW **Ruler:** Urban VIII **Obv:** Arms **Rev:** SS. Peter and Paul standing, keys to left

Date	Mintage	Good	VG	F	VF	XF
ND(1623)-I	—	28.00	60.00	100	185	—
ND(1624)-II	—	28.00	60.00	100	185	—
ND(1625)-III	—	28.00	60.00	100	185	—
ND(1626)-IIII	—	28.00	60.00	100	185	—
ND(1627)-V	—	28.00	60.00	100	185	—
ND(1628)-VI	—	28.00	60.00	100	185	—
ND(1629)-VII	—	28.00	60.00	100	185	—
ND	—	28.00	60.00	100	185	—

KM# 124 TESTONE (30 Baiocchi)
9.5960 g., 0.9160 Silver 0.2826 oz. ASW **Ruler:** Urban VIII **Rev:** SS. Peter and Paul standing, keys at right

Date	Mintage	Good	VG	F	VF	XF
ND(1624)-II	—	30.00	60.00	110	195	—
ND(1625)-III	—	30.00	60.00	110	195	—
ND(1626)-IIII	—	30.00	60.00	110	195	—
ND(1627)-V	—	30.00	60.00	110	195	—
ND(1628)-VII	—	30.00	60.00	110	195	—
ND(1629)-VIII	—	30.00	60.00	110	195	—
ND	—	30.00	60.00	110	195	—

KM# 145 TESTONE (30 Baiocchi)
9.5960 g., 0.9160 Silver 0.2826 oz. ASW **Ruler:** Urban VIII **Rev:** Holy Door with Veronica's veil, dove above **Note:** Holy Year issue.

Date	Mintage	Good	VG	F	VF	XF
1625-II	—	30.00	60.00	110	195	—

KM# 147 TESTONE (30 Baiocchi)
9.5960 g., 0.9160 Silver 0.2826 oz. ASW **Ruler:** Urban VIII **Rev:** Holy Door with Veronica's veil **Note:** Holy Year issue.

Date	Mintage	Good	VG	F	VF	XF
1625-II	—	35.00	70.00	115	200	—

KM# 146 TESTONE (30 Baiocchi)
9.5960 g., 0.9160 Silver 0.2826 oz. ASW **Ruler:** Urban VIII **Rev:** Holy Door with Veronica's veil, Madonna above **Note:** Holy Year issue.

Date	Mintage	Good	VG	F	VF	XF
1625-II	—	28.00	55.00	100	185	—
1625-III	—	28.00	55.00	100	185	—

KM# 157 TESTONE (30 Baiocchi)
9.5960 g., 0.9160 Silver 0.2826 oz. ASW **Ruler:** Urban VIII **Obv:** Bust right **Rev:** SS. Peter and Paul standing, dove above

Date	Mintage	Good	VG	F	VF	XF
ND(1628)-V	—	40.00	80.00	125	200	—
ND(1628)-VI	—	40.00	80.00	125	200	—
1628	—	40.00	80.00	125	200	—

KM# 172 TESTONE (30 Baiocchi)
9.5960 g., 0.9160 Silver 0.2826 oz. ASW **Ruler:** Urban VIII **Rev:** Roma seated right

Date	Mintage	Good	VG	F	VF	XF
ND(1631)-VIII	—	50.00	100	165	250	—

KM# 173 TESTONE (30 Baiocchi)
9.5960 g., 0.9160 Silver 0.2826 oz. ASW **Ruler:** Urban VIII **Obv:** Arms

Date	Mintage	Good	VG	F	VF	XF
ND(1631)-VIII	—	30.00	60.00	125	200	—
ND(1632)-VIIII	—	30.00	60.00	125	200	—

KM# 175 TESTONE (30 Baiocchi)
9.5960 g., 0.9160 Silver 0.2826 oz. ASW **Ruler:** Urban VIII **Obv:** Bust left

Date	Mintage	Good	VG	F	VF	XF
1632-VIIII	—	45.00	90.00	150	250	—

KM# 176 TESTONE (30 Baiocchi)
9.5960 g., 0.9160 Silver 0.2826 oz. ASW **Ruler:** Urban VIII **Obv:** Arms

Date	Mintage	Good	VG	F	VF	XF
ND(1632)-VIII	—	30.00	60.00	115	190	—
1632	—	30.00	60.00	115	190	—
1633	—	30.00	60.00	115	190	—
ND	—	30.00	60.00	115	190	—

KM# 174 TESTONE (30 Baiocchi)
9.5960 g., 0.9160 Silver 0.2826 oz. ASW **Ruler:** Urban VIII **Obv:** Bust right **Rev:** St. Peter seated

Date	Mintage	Good	VG	F	VF	XF
1632-VIII	—	45.00	90.00	150	250	—
1632-VIIII	—	45.00	90.00	150	250	—

KM# 191 TESTONE (30 Baiocchi)
9.5960 g., 0.9160 Silver 0.2826 oz. ASW **Ruler:** Urban VIII **Obv:** Bust right **Rev:** Radiant Virgin Mary standing on crescent

Date	Mintage	Good	VG	F	VF	XF
ND(1636)-XII	—	50.00	100	165	265	—
ND(1637)-XIII	—	50.00	100	165	265	—
ND(1638)-XIIII	—	50.00	100	165	265	—
ND(1639)-XV	—	50.00	100	165	265	—
ND(1640)-XVI	—	50.00	100	165	265	—
ND(1641)-XVII	—	50.00	100	165	265	—
ND(1642)-XVIII	—	50.00	100	165	265	—
1642	—	50.00	100	165	265	—
ND(1643)-XVIIII	—	50.00	100	165	265	—
ND(1644)-XX	—	50.00	100	165	265	—

KM# 193 TESTONE (30 Baiocchi)
9.5960 g., 0.9160 Silver 0.2826 oz. ASW **Ruler:** Urban VIII **Rev:** St. Michael defeating Lucifer

Date	Mintage	Good	VG	F	VF	XF
ND(1638)-XIV	—	70.00	135	225	350	—
1643	—	70.00	135	225	350	—
ND(1644)-XX	—	70.00	135	225	350	—

KM# 218 TESTONE (30 Baiocchi)
9.5960 g., 0.9160 Silver 0.2826 oz. ASW **Ruler:** Urban VIII **Obv:** Arms **Note:** Varieties in placement of rays exist.

Date	Mintage	Good	VG	F	VF	XF
1642	—	30.00	60.00	125	200	—
ND(1644)-XX	—	30.00	60.00	125	200	—
ND(1645)-XXI	—	30.00	60.00	125	200	—

KM# 219 TESTONE (30 Baiocchi)
9.5960 g., 0.9160 Silver 0.2826 oz. ASW **Ruler:** Urban VIII **Obv:** Arms

Date	Mintage	Good	VG	F	VF	XF
ND(1644)-XX	—	35.00	70.00	130	220	—

KM# 221 TESTONE (30 Baiocchi)
9.5960 g., 0.9160 Silver 0.2826 oz. ASW **Ruler:** Innocent X **Obv:** Arms **Rev:** Justice seated right in legend

Date	Mintage	Good	VG	F	VF	XF
ND(1644)-I	—	35.00	70.00	115	190	—
ND(1645)-II	—	35.00	70.00	115	190	—
ND(1653)-X	—	35.00	70.00	115	190	—

KM# 222 TESTONE (30 Baiocchi)
9.5960 g., 0.9160 Silver 0.2826 oz. ASW **Ruler:** Innocent X **Rev:** Justice seated right in wreath

Date	Mintage	Good	VG	F	VF	XF
ND(1644)-I	—	35.00	70.00	115	190	—
ND(1645)-II	—	35.00	70.00	115	190	—
ND(1652)-IX	—	35.00	70.00	115	190	—
ND(1653)-X	—	35.00	70.00	115	190	—

KM# 220 TESTONE (30 Baiocchi)
9.5960 g., 0.9160 Silver 0.2826 oz. ASW **Obv:** Arms of Cardinal Antonio Barberini **Rev:** Half figure of Madonna and child **Note:** Sede Vacante issue.

Date	Mintage	Good	VG	F	VF	XF
1644	—	600	1,000	1,650	2,500	—
ND	—	600	1,000	1,650	2,500	—

KM# 237 TESTONE (30 Baiocchi)
9.5960 g., 0.9160 Silver 0.2826 oz. ASW **Ruler:** Innocent X **Obv:** Arms **Note:** Varieties exist with angel in exergue.

Date	Mintage	Good	VG	F	VF	XF
ND(1645)-II	—	40.00	80.00	125	200	—

KM# 232 TESTONE (30 Baiocchi)
9.5960 g., 0.9160 Silver 0.2826 oz. ASW **Ruler:** Innocent X **Obv:** Bust right **Rev:** Justice seated right in legend

Date	Mintage	Good	VG	F	VF	XF
ND(1645)-II	—	185	375	625	950	—

KM# 233 TESTONE (30 Baiocchi)
9.5960 g., 0.9160 Silver 0.2826 oz. ASW **Ruler:** Innocent X **Obv:** Arms **Rev:** St. Paul standing

Date	Mintage	Good	VG	F	VF	XF
ND(1645)-II	—	35.00	70.00	115	190	—

KM# 234 TESTONE (30 Baiocchi)
9.5960 g., 0.9160 Silver 0.2826 oz. ASW **Ruler:** Innocent X **Obv:** Bust right **Rev:** St. Paul seated right

Date	Mintage	Good	VG	F	VF	XF
1645-II	—	70.00	135	225	365	—

KM# 235 TESTONE (30 Baiocchi)
9.5960 g., 0.9160 Silver 0.2826 oz. ASW **Ruler:** Innocent X **Obv:** Arms

Date	Mintage	Good	VG	F	VF	XF
ND(1645)-II	—	35.00	70.00	115	190	—

KM# 236 TESTONE (30 Baiocchi)
9.5960 g., 0.9160 Silver 0.2826 oz. ASW **Ruler:** Innocent X **Obv:** Bust right **Rev:** St. Paul seated left

Date	Mintage	Good	VG	F	VF	XF
ND(1645)-II Rare	—	—	—	—	—	—

KM# 238 TESTONE (30 Baiocchi)
9.5960 g., 0.9160 Silver 0.2826 oz. ASW **Ruler:** Innocent X **Rev:** Virgin Mary standing on crescent, angels at sides

Date	Mintage	Good	VG	F	VF	XF
ND(1645)-II	—	115	225	400	625	—

KM# 239 TESTONE (30 Baiocchi)
9.5960 g., 0.9160 Silver 0.2826 oz. ASW **Ruler:** Innocent X **Rev:** Without angels at sides

Date	Mintage	Good	VG	F	VF	XF
ND(1645)-II Unique	—	—	—	—	—	—

KM# 240 TESTONE (30 Baiocchi)
9.5960 g., 0.9160 Silver 0.2826 oz. ASW **Ruler:** Innocent X **Subject:** Immaculate Conception **Rev:** Radiant Virgin Mary standing on crescent

Date	Mintage	Good	VG	F	VF	XF
ND(1645)-II	—	40.00	80.00	125	200	—

KM# 253 TESTONE (30 Baiocchi)
9.5960 g., 0.9160 Silver 0.2826 oz. ASW **Ruler:** Innocent X **Rev:** Holy Door with Veronica's veil **Note:** Holy Year issue.

Date	Mintage	Good	VG	F	VF	XF
MDCL (1650)-VI	—	100	200	325	500	—

KM# 277 TESTONE (30 Baiocchi)
9.5960 g., 0.9160 Silver 0.2826 oz. ASW **Obv:** Arms of Cardinal Antonio Barberini **Rev:** Radiant dove **Note:** Sede Vacante issue.

Date	Mintage	VG	F	VF	XF	Unc
MDCLV (1655)	—	250	450	775	1,250	—

KM# 278.1 TESTONE (30 Baiocchi)
9.5960 g., 0.9160 Silver 0.2826 oz. ASW **Ruler:** Alexander VII **Obv:** Arms **Rev:** Hand of God holding scale

Date	Mintage	VG	F	VF	XF	Unc
ND(1655-67)	—	65.00	130	235	450	—

KM# 278.2 TESTONE (30 Baiocchi)
9.5960 g., 0.9160 Silver 0.2826 oz. ASW **Ruler:** Alexander VII **Obv:** Baroque shield

Date	Mintage	VG	F	VF	XF	Unc
ND(1655-67)	—	65.00	130	235	450	—

KM# 309 TESTONE (30 Baiocchi)
9.5960 g., 0.9160 Silver 0.2826 oz. ASW **Ruler:** Clement IX **Obv:** Arms **Rev:** St. Peter seated

Date	Mintage	VG	F	VF	XF	Unc
ND(1667-69)	—	60.00	125	225	400	—

KM# 308 TESTONE (30 Baiocchi)
9.5960 g., 0.9160 Silver 0.2826 oz. ASW **Obv:** Arms of Cardinal Antonio Barberini **Rev:** Radiant dove **Note:** Sede Vacante issue.

Date	Mintage	VG	F	VF	XF	Unc
MDCLXVII (1667)	—	70.00	140	250	475	—

KM# 318 TESTONE (30 Baiocchi)
9.5960 g., 0.9160 Silver 0.2826 oz. ASW **Obv:** Arms of Cardinal Antonio Barberini **Rev:** Radiant dove **Note:** Sede Vacante issue.

Date	Mintage	VG	F	VF	XF	Unc
MDCLXIX (1669)	—	70.00	140	250	475	—

KM# 342 TESTONE (30 Baiocchi)
9.5960 g., 0.9160 Silver 0.2826 oz. ASW **Ruler:** Clement X **Obv:** Arms **Rev:** Half-length figure of Christ holding orb

Date	Mintage	VG	F	VF	XF	Unc
ND(1670-76)	—	300	550	900	1,600	—

KM# 343 TESTONE (30 Baiocchi)
9.5960 g., 0.9160 Silver 0.2826 oz. ASW **Rev:** Tiara in front of Pope kneeling left

Date	Mintage	VG	F	VF	XF	Unc
ND(1670-76)	—	85.00	165	300	550	—

KM# 349 TESTONE (30 Baiocchi)
9.5960 g., 0.9160 Silver 0.2826 oz. ASW **Obv:** Capped bust of Clement X right **Rev:** Standing St. Peter being crowned by angel

Date	Mintage	VG	F	VF	XF	Unc
MDCLXX (1670)-I	—	85.00	165	300	550	—
MDCLXXI (1671)-II	—	85.00	165	300	550	—

KM# 350 TESTONE (30 Baiocchi)
9.5960 g., 0.9160 Silver 0.2826 oz. ASW **Obv:** Arms **Rev:** King David seated playing harp

Date	Mintage	VG	F	VF	XF	Unc
ND	—	85.00	165	300	550	—

KM# 363 TESTONE (30 Baiocchi)
9.5960 g., 0.9160 Silver 0.2826 oz. ASW **Obv:** Capped bust right **Rev:** Holy Door open with pilgrims **Note:** Holy Year issue.

Date	Mintage	VG	F	VF	XF	Unc
1675	—	100	200	350	600	—

KM# 364 TESTONE (30 Baiocchi)
9.5960 g., 0.9160 Silver 0.2826 oz. ASW **Obv:** Arms **Rev:** Holy Door open with pilgrims **Note:** Holy Year issue.

Date	Mintage	VG	F	VF	XF	Unc
1675	—	45.00	90.00	175	325	—

KM# 365 TESTONE (30 Baiocchi)
9.5960 g., 0.9160 Silver 0.2826 oz. ASW **Obv:** Capped bust right **Rev:** Closed Holy Door **Note:** Holy Year issue.

Date	Mintage	VG	F	VF	XF	Unc
1675	—	100	200	350	600	—

KM# 366 TESTONE (30 Baiocchi)
9.5960 g., 0.9160 Silver 0.2826 oz. ASW **Obv:** Arms **Note:** Holy Year issue.

Date	Mintage	VG	F	VF	XF	Unc
1675	—	45.00	100	200	350	—

KM# 389 TESTONE (30 Baiocchi)
9.5960 g., 0.9160 Silver 0.2826 oz. ASW **Obv:** Arms of Cardinal Paluzzo Paluzzi-Altieri **Rev:** Radiant dove **Note:** Sede Vacante issue.

Date	Mintage	VG	F	VF	XF	Unc
MDCLXXVI (1676)	—	65.00	125	235	400	—

KM# 390 TESTONE (30 Baiocchi)
9.5960 g., 0.9160 Silver 0.2826 oz. ASW **Ruler:** Innocent XI **Obv:** Arms **Rev:** Madonna and child seated

Date	Mintage	VG	F	VF	XF	Unc
ND(1676)-I	—	50.00	100	200	350	—

KM# 397 TESTONE (30 Baiocchi)
9.5960 g., 0.9160 Silver 0.2826 oz. ASW **Ruler:** Innocent XI **Rev:** St. Peter helping invalid

Date	Mintage	VG	F	VF	XF	Unc
1677-II	—	70.00	135	250	475	—
ND(1680)-V	—	70.00	135	250	475	—

KM# 401 TESTONE (30 Baiocchi)
9.5960 g., 0.9160 Silver 0.2826 oz. ASW **Ruler:** Innocent XI
Rev: Inscription in palm wreath **Rev. Inscription:** NOLITE / COR / APPONERE

Date	Mintage	VG	F	VF	XF	Unc
ND(1678)-III	—	28.00	60.00	100	185	—

KM# 402 TESTONE (30 Baiocchi)
9.5960 g., 0.9160 Silver 0.2826 oz. ASW **Ruler:** Innocent XI
Rev: Inscription in cartouche **Rev. Inscription:** NOLT / ANXIVS / ESSE

Date	Mintage	VG	F	VF	XF	Unc
ND(1678)-III	—	25.00	50.00	100	185	—
ND(1679)-IIII	—	25.00	50.00	100	185	—
ND(1680)-V	—	25.00	50.00	100	185	—

KM# 424 TESTONE (30 Baiocchi)
9.5960 g., 0.9160 Silver 0.2826 oz. ASW **Ruler:** Innocent XI
Rev: Inscription in cartouche

Date	Mintage	VG	F	VF	XF	Unc
ND(1681)-VI	—	28.00	60.00	100	185	—

KM# 434 TESTONE (30 Baiocchi)
9.5960 g., 0.9160 Silver 0.2826 oz. ASW **Ruler:** Innocent XI
Rev: Cartouche with pellets at top and bottom of frame

Date	Mintage	VG	F	VF	XF	Unc
1684-VIII	—	25.00	50.00	100	185	—

KM# 435 TESTONE (30 Baiocchi)
9.5960 g., 0.9160 Silver 0.2826 oz. ASW **Ruler:** Innocent XI
Rev: Cartouche without pellet ornamentation

Date	Mintage	VG	F	VF	XF	Unc
1684-VIII	—	28.00	60.00	100	185	—

KM# 436 TESTONE (30 Baiocchi)
9.5960 g., 0.9160 Silver 0.2826 oz. ASW **Ruler:** Innocent XI
Rev: Cartouche ends left, pellets and flora around

Date	Mintage	VG	F	VF	XF	Unc
1684-VIII	—	28.00	60.00	100	185	—

KM# 437 TESTONE (30 Baiocchi)
9.5960 g., 0.9160 Silver 0.2826 oz. ASW **Ruler:** Innocent XI

Date	Mintage	VG	F	VF	XF	Unc
1684	—	30.00	60.00	120	200	—

KM# 438 TESTONE (30 Baiocchi)
9.5960 g., 0.9160 Silver 0.2826 oz. ASW **Ruler:** Innocent XI

Date	Mintage	VG	F	VF	XF	Unc
1684	—	28.00	60.00	100	185	—

KM# 439 TESTONE (30 Baiocchi)
9.5960 g., 0.9160 Silver 0.2826 oz. ASW **Ruler:** Innocent XI
Rev: Laurel and branch ornamentation

Date	Mintage	VG	F	VF	XF	Unc
1684	—	28.00	60.00	100	185	—

KM# 440 TESTONE (30 Baiocchi)
9.5960 g., 0.9160 Silver 0.2826 oz. ASW **Ruler:** Innocent XI
Rev: Floral leaves

Date	Mintage	VG	F	VF	XF	Unc
1684	—	28.00	60.00	100	185	—

KM# 441 TESTONE (30 Baiocchi)
9.5960 g., 0.9160 Silver 0.2826 oz. ASW **Ruler:** Innocent XI

Date	Mintage	VG	F	VF	XF	Unc
ND(1684-86)	—	28.00	85.00	110	190	—

KM# 442 TESTONE (30 Baiocchi)
9.5960 g., 0.9160 Silver 0.2826 oz. ASW **Ruler:** Innocent XI

Date	Mintage	VG	F	VF	XF	Unc
ND(1684-86)	—	28.00	60.00	110	190	—

KM# 443 TESTONE (30 Baiocchi)
9.5960 g., 0.9160 Silver 0.2826 oz. ASW **Ruler:** Innocent XI

Date	Mintage	VG	F	VF	XF	Unc
ND(1684-86)	—	30.00	60.00	120	200	—

KM# 444 TESTONE (30 Baiocchi)
9.5960 g., 0.9160 Silver 0.2826 oz. ASW **Ruler:** Innocent XI

Date	Mintage	VG	F	VF	XF	Unc
ND(1684-86)	—	28.00	60.00	110	190	—

KM# 445 TESTONE (30 Baiocchi)
9.5960 g., 0.9160 Silver 0.2826 oz. ASW **Ruler:** Innocent XI

Date	Mintage	VG	F	VF	XF	Unc
ND(1684-86)	—	28.00	60.00	110	190	—

KM# 446 TESTONE (30 Baiocchi)
9.5960 g., 0.9160 Silver 0.2826 oz. ASW **Ruler:** Innocent XI
Rev: Inscription in flora, shield below

Date	Mintage	VG	F	VF	XF	Unc
ND(1684-86)	—	28.00	60.00	100	190	—

KM# 447 TESTONE (30 Baiocchi)

9.5960 g., 0.9160 Silver 0.2826 oz. ASW **Ruler:** Innocent XI
Rev: Legend in frame

Date	Mintage	VG	F	VF	XF	Unc
ND(1684-86)	—	28.00	60.00	100	185	—

KM# 448 TESTONE (30 Baiocchi)

9.5960 g., 0.9160 Silver 0.2826 oz. ASW **Ruler:** Innocent XI
Rev: Legend in cartouche

Date	Mintage	VG	F	VF	XF	Unc
ND(1684-86)-VII	—	28.00	60.00	100	185	—

KM# 449 TESTONE (30 Baiocchi)

9.5960 g., 0.9160 Silver 0.2826 oz. ASW **Ruler:** Innocent XI

Date	Mintage	VG	F	VF	XF	Unc
1684	—	28.00	60.00	100	185	—

KM# 450 TESTONE (30 Baiocchi)

9.5960 g., 0.9160 Silver 0.2826 oz. ASW **Ruler:** Innocent XI
Rev: Legend in plaque, wreath behind

Date	Mintage	VG	F	VF	XF	Unc
1684	—	28.00	60.00	100	185	—

KM# 433 TESTONE (30 Baiocchi)

9.5960 g., 0.9160 Silver 0.2826 oz. ASW **Ruler:** Innocent XI
Rev: Cartouche with seraphim above, bottom tip curls left **Note:** Reform weight.

Date	Mintage	VG	F	VF	XF	Unc
1684	—	30.00	60.00	120	200	—

KM# 469 TESTONE (30 Baiocchi)

9.5960 g., 0.9160 Silver 0.2826 oz. ASW **Ruler:** Innocent XI
Rev: Cartouche with two laurel sprigs, top curves outwards

Date	Mintage	VG	F	VF	XF	Unc
1685-IX	—	28.00	60.00	100	185	—

KM# 470 TESTONE (30 Baiocchi)

9.5960 g., 0.9160 Silver 0.2826 oz. ASW **Ruler:** Innocent XI
Rev: Cartouche with two laurel sprigs, top curves inwards

Date	Mintage	VG	F	VF	XF	Unc
1685-IX	—	30.00	60.00	120	200	—

KM# 471 TESTONE (30 Baiocchi)

9.5960 g., 0.9160 Silver 0.2826 oz. ASW **Ruler:** Innocent XI
Rev: Bands with pellets at top and sides

Date	Mintage	VG	F	VF	XF	Unc
1685-IX	—	28.00	60.00	100	185	—

KM# 472 TESTONE (30 Baiocchi)

9.5960 g., 0.9160 Silver 0.2826 oz. ASW **Ruler:** Innocent XI

Date	Mintage	VG	F	VF	XF	Unc
1685-IX	—	28.00	60.00	100	185	—

KM# 473 TESTONE (30 Baiocchi)

9.5960 g., 0.9160 Silver 0.2826 oz. ASW **Ruler:** Innocent XI

Date	Mintage	VG	F	VF	XF	Unc
1685-XI	—	28.00	60.00	100	185	—

KM# 474 TESTONE (30 Baiocchi)

9.5960 g., 0.9160 Silver 0.2826 oz. ASW **Ruler:** Innocent XI
Rev: Rectangular shield in leaves

Date	Mintage	VG	F	VF	XF	Unc
1685-XI	—	28.00	60.00	100	185	—

KM# 492 TESTONE (30 Baiocchi)

9.5960 g., 0.9160 Silver 0.2826 oz. ASW **Ruler:** Innocent XI

Date	Mintage	VG	F	VF	XF	Unc
1686-X	—	28.00	60.00	100	185	—

KM# 493 TESTONE (30 Baiocchi)

9.5960 g., 0.9160 Silver 0.2826 oz. ASW **Ruler:** Innocent XI

Date	Mintage	VG	F	VF	XF	Unc
1686-X	—	30.00	60.00	120	200	—

KM# 494 TESTONE (30 Baiocchi)

9.5960 g., 0.9160 Silver 0.2826 oz. ASW **Ruler:** Innocent XI

Date	Mintage	VG	F	VF	XF	Unc
1686-X	—	30.00	60.00	120	200	—

KM# 507 TESTONE (30 Baiocchi)

9.5960 g., 0.9160 Silver 0.2826 oz. ASW **Ruler:** Innocent XI

Date	Mintage	VG	F	VF	XF	Unc
1686-X	—	30.00	60.00	120	200	—

KM# 495 TESTONE (30 Baiocchi)

9.5960 g., 0.9160 Silver 0.2826 oz. ASW **Ruler:** Innocent XI

Date	Mintage	VG	F	VF	XF	Unc
1687-XI	—	28.00	60.00	110	190	—

KM# 505 TESTONE (30 Baiocchi)

9.5960 g., 0.9160 Silver 0.2826 oz. ASW **Rev:** SS. Peter and Paul standing, dove above

Date	Mintage	VG	F	VF	XF	Unc
1689-I	—	165	300	550	900	—

KM# 506 TESTONE (30 Baiocchi)

9.5960 g., 0.9160 Silver 0.2826 oz. ASW **Obv:** Capped bust right **Rev:** St. Bruno kneeling right

Date	Mintage	VG	F	VF	XF	Unc
1689-I	—	50.00	100	200	350	—

KM# 522 TESTONE (30 Baiocchi)
9.5960 g., 0.9160 Silver 0.2826 oz. ASW **Ruler:** Alexander VIII **Obv:** Arms

Date	Mintage	VG	F	VF	XF	Unc
1689	—	50.00	100	185	325	—
1690-I	—	50.00	100	185	325	—
1690	—	50.00	100	185	325	—

KM# A495 TESTONE (30 Baiocchi)
9.5960 g., 0.9160 Silver 0.2826 oz. ASW **Ruler:** Innocent XI **Obv:** Papal Arms **Rev:** Legend within palm wreath **Rev. Inscription:** MELIVS / EST • DARE / QVAM / ACCIPERE /(date)

Date	Mintage	VG	F	VF	XF	Unc
1689-XIII	—	—	—	—	—	—

KM# 496 TESTONE (30 Baiocchi)
9.5960 g., 0.9160 Silver 0.2826 oz. ASW **Obv:** Arms of Cardinal Paluzzo Paluzzi-Altieri **Rev:** Radiant dove **Note:** Sede Vacante issue.

Date	Mintage	VG	F	VF	XF	Unc
MDCLXXXIX (1689)	—	28.00	60.00	100	185	—

KM# A523 TESTONE (30 Baiocchi)
9.5960 g., 0.9160 Silver 0.2826 oz. ASW **Ruler:** Alexander VIII **Rev:** SS. Magnus and Bruno standing

Date	Mintage	VG	F	VF	XF	Unc
ND(1690)-II	—	50.00	100	200	350	—
1690-II	—	50.00	100	200	350	—

KM# 524 TESTONE (30 Baiocchi)
9.5960 g., 0.9160 Silver 0.2826 oz. ASW **Ruler:** Alexander VIII **Obv:** Capped bust right **Rev:** Two oxen right

Date	Mintage	VG	F	VF	XF	Unc
MDCXC (1690)-I	—	70.00	145	275	450	—

KM# 538 TESTONE (30 Baiocchi)
9.5960 g., 0.9160 Silver 0.2826 oz. ASW **Rev:** Radiant dove flying upwards

Date	Mintage	VG	F	VF	XF	Unc
MDCLXXXXI (1691)	—	50.00	100	200	350	—

KM# 539 TESTONE (30 Baiocchi)
9.5960 g., 0.9160 Silver 0.2826 oz. ASW **Rev:** Radiant dove flying downwards

Date	Mintage	VG	F	VF	XF	Unc
MDCLXXXXI (1691)	—	50.00	100	200	350	—

KM# 540 TESTONE (30 Baiocchi)
9.5960 g., 0.9160 Silver 0.2826 oz. ASW **Ruler:** Innocent XII **Obv:** Arms **Rev:** Inscription in cartouche **Rev. Inscription:** NOLI / AMARE / NE / PERDAS

Date	Mintage	VG	F	VF	XF	Unc
ND(1691)-I	—	28.00	60.00	100	185	—

KM# 541 TESTONE (30 Baiocchi)
9.5960 g., 0.9160 Silver 0.2826 oz. ASW **Ruler:** Innocent XII **Rev:** Inscription in cartouche **Rev. Inscription:** TANQVAM / LVTVM / AESTIMABITVR

Date	Mintage	VG	F	VF	XF	Unc
ND(1691)-I	—	28.00	60.00	100	175	—

KM# 537 TESTONE (30 Baiocchi)
9.5960 g., 0.9160 Silver 0.2826 oz. ASW **Obv:** Arms of Cardinal Paluzzo Paluzzi-Altieri **Rev:** Radiant dove flying right **Note:** Sede vacante issue.

Date	Mintage	VG	F	VF	XF	Unc
MDCLXXXXI (1691)	—	50.00	100	200	350	—

KM# 552 TESTONE (30 Baiocchi)
9.5960 g., 0.9160 Silver 0.2826 oz. ASW **Ruler:** Innocent XII **Rev:** Inscription in cartouche **Rev. Inscription:** NON SIT/TECVM IN/ PERDIT/ONEM

Date	Mintage	VG	F	VF	XF	Unc
(1692)-II	—	28.00	60.00	100	185	—

KM# A553 TESTONE (30 Baiocchi)
9.5960 g., 0.9160 Silver 0.2826 oz. ASW **Ruler:** Innocent XII **Rev:** Inscription in cartouche

Date	Mintage	VG	F	VF	XF	Unc
1692-II	—	28.00	60.00	100	185	—
1693-III	—	28.00	60.00	100	185	—

KM# 567 TESTONE (30 Baiocchi)
9.5960 g., 0.9160 Silver 0.2826 oz. ASW **Ruler:** Innocent XII **Rev:** Eagle with two eaglets

Date	Mintage	VG	F	VF	XF	Unc
1693-III	—	65.00	135	250	450	—

KM# 575 TESTONE (30 Baiocchi)
9.5960 g., 0.9160 Silver 0.2826 oz. ASW **Ruler:** Innocent XII **Rev:** Abundance standing

Date	Mintage	VG	F	VF	XF	Unc
1694-III	—	50.00	100	175	325	—

KM# 588 TESTONE (30 Baiocchi)
9.5960 g., 0.9160 Silver 0.2826 oz. ASW **Ruler:** Innocent XII **Rev:** Pope listening to peace exhortation

Date	Mintage	VG	F	VF	XF	Unc
1695-V	—	60.00	125	225	400	—

KM# 595 TESTONE (30 Baiocchi)
9.5960 g., 0.9160 Silver 0.2826 oz. ASW **Ruler:** Innocent XII **Rev:** Straight inscription in cartouche

Date	Mintage	VG	F	VF	XF	Unc
1696-VI	—	25.00	50.00	100	185	—

KM# 594 TESTONE (30 Baiocchi)
9.5960 g., 0.9160 Silver 0.2826 oz. ASW **Ruler:** Innocent XII **Rev:** Inscription in arched cartouche **Rev. Inscription:** ROGATE EA / QVAE AD PACEM / SVNT

Date	Mintage	VG	F	VF	XF	Unc
1696-V	—	28.00	60.00	100	185	—
1696-VI	—	28.00	60.00	100	185	—

KM# 606 TESTONE (30 Baiocchi)
9.5960 g., 0.9160 Silver 0.2826 oz. ASW **Ruler:** Innocent XII **Rev:** Christ standing with orb

Date	Mintage	VG	F	VF	XF	Unc
1698-VII	—	50.00	100	185	325	—

KM# 648 TESTONE (30 Baiocchi)
9.5960 g., 0.9160 Silver 0.2826 oz. ASW **Obv:** Rounded bottom shield **Note:** Holy Year Issue.

Date	Mintage	VG	F	VF	XF	Unc
ND (1700)	—	165	300	500	850	—

KM# 645 TESTONE (30 Baiocchi)
9.5960 g., 0.9160 Silver 0.2826 oz. ASW **Obv:** Arms of Cardinal Giovanni Spinola **Rev:** Radiant dove flying upwards **Note:** Sede Vacante issue.

Date	Mintage	VG	F	VF	XF	Unc
MDCC (1700)	—	165	300	550	900	—

KM# 646 TESTONE (30 Baiocchi)
9.5960 g., 0.9160 Silver 0.2826 oz. ASW **Rev:** Radiant dove flying left **Note:** Sede Vacante issue.

Date	Mintage	VG	F	VF	XF	Unc
MDCC (1700)	—	165	300	550	900	—

KM# 644 TESTONE (30 Baiocchi)
9.5960 g., 0.9160 Silver 0.2826 oz. ASW **Ruler:** Innocent XII **Rev:** Holy Door **Note:** Holy Year issue.

Date	Mintage	VG	F	VF	XF	Unc
1700-IX	—	45.00	95.00	185	300	—

KM# 647 TESTONE (30 Baiocchi)
9.5960 g., 0.9160 Silver 0.2826 oz. ASW **Ruler:** Clement XI **Obv:** Arms **Rev:** Holy Door **Note:** Holy Year issue.

Date	Mintage	VG	F	VF	XF	Unc
1700-I	—	75.00	150	285	475	—

KM# A18 1/2 PIASTRA
Silver **Ruler:** Clement VIII **Obv:** Bust of Clement VIII left **Rev:** Holy Door **Note:** Holy Year issue.

Date	Mintage	VG	F	VF	XF	Unc
ND(1601)-X Rare	—	—	—	—	—	—

KM# 429 1/2 PIASTRA
Silver **Ruler:** Innocent XI **Obv:** Arms **Rev:** In cartouche **Rev. Inscription:** AVARVS / NON / IMPLEBITVR

Date	Mintage	VG	F	VF	XF	Unc
ND(1683)-VII	—	50.00	100	200	350	—
ND	—	50.00	100	200	350	—

KM# 430 1/2 PIASTRA
Silver **Ruler:** Innocent XI **Rev:** Seraphin above and below, lion's head at sides

Date	Mintage	VG	F	VF	XF	Unc
ND(1683)-VII	—	50.00	100	200	350	—

KM# 431 1/2 PIASTRA
Silver **Ruler:** Innocent XI **Rev:** Inscription in palm wreath

Date	Mintage	VG	F	VF	XF	Unc
ND(1683)-VII	—	50.00	100	200	350	—

KM# 554 1/2 PIASTRA
Silver **Ruler:** Innocent XII **Obv:** Capped bust right **Rev:** The Church seated in clouds

Date	Mintage	VG	F	VF	XF	Unc
ND(1692)-II	—	100	200	325	575	—

KM# 555 1/2 PIASTRA
Silver **Ruler:** Innocent XII **Obv:** Arms **Rev:** Pelican right feeding young

Date	Mintage	VG	F	VF	XF	Unc
1692-II	—	80.00	175	285	500	—

KM# 556 1/2 PIASTRA
Silver **Ruler:** Innocent XII **Obv:** Capped bust right **Rev:** Peace standing

Date	Mintage	VG	F	VF	XF	Unc
1692-II	—	85.00	185	300	525	—

KM# 568 1/2 PIASTRA
Silver **Ruler:** Innocent XII **Obv:** Arms **Rev:** Pelican feeding young

Date	Mintage	VG	F	VF	XF	Unc
1693-III	—	80.00	175	285	500	—

KM# 596 1/2 PIASTRA
Silver **Ruler:** Innocent XII **Rev:** Pope kneeling right in prayer

Date	Mintage	VG	F	VF	XF	Unc
1696-V Rare	—	—	—	—	—	—

KM# 597 1/2 PIASTRA
Silver **Ruler:** Innocent XII **Obv:** Capped bust right **Rev:** Pope kneeling left in prayer

Date	Mintage	VG	F	VF	XF	Unc
1696-V	—	85.00	185	300	525	—

KM# 601 1/2 PIASTRA
Silver **Ruler:** Innocent XII **Obv:** Arms

Date	Mintage	VG	F	VF	XF	Unc
ND(1697)-VI	—	75.00	150	265	450	—
ND(1698)-VII	—	75.00	150	265	450	—

KM# 607 1/2 PIASTRA
Silver **Ruler:** Innocent XII **Subject:** Signing of the Peace of Ryswick **Obv:** Bust right **Rev:** Noah's Ark

Date	Mintage	VG	F	VF	XF	Unc
ND(1698)-VII	—	150	350	600	1,000	—

KM# 613 1/2 PIASTRA
Silver **Ruler:** Innocent XII **Obv:** Capped bust right **Rev:** St. John the Baptist preaching to crowd

Date	Mintage	VG	F	VF	XF	Unc
1699-IX	—	85.00	185	300	525	—

KM# 650 1/2 PIASTRA
Silver **Ruler:** Innocent XII **Rev:** Holy Door **Note:** Holy Year issue.

Date	Mintage	VG	F	VF	XF	Unc
MDCC (1700)-IX	—	100	200	350	600	—

KM# 178 PIASTRA (Scudo of 80 Bolognini)
Silver **Ruler:** Urban VIII **Obv:** Bust right, ANXI in legend **Rev:** St. Michael the Archangel fighting four demons **Note:** Dav. #4055. Pope's collar in floral or St. Peter design.

Date	Mintage	VG	F	VF	XF	Unc
ND(1633)-XI	—	250	450	800	2,250	7,500

KM# 181 PIASTRA (Scudo of 80 Bolognini)
Silver **Ruler:** Urban VIII **Obv:** Bust right, ANXII below **Note:** Dav. #4056. Pope's collar in floral or St. Peter design.

Date	Mintage	VG	F	VF	XF	Unc
ND(1634)-XII	—	250	450	800	2,250	—

KM# 184 PIASTRA (Scudo of 80 Bolognini)
Silver **Ruler:** Urban VIII **Rev:** Radiant Virgin Mary standing on crescent **Note:** Dav. #4057.

Date	Mintage	VG	F	VF	XF	Unc
ND(1634)-XII	—	300	550	1,000	2,750	—
ND(1643)-XX	—	300	550	1,000	2,750	—

KM# 182 PIASTRA (Scudo of 80 Bolognini)
Silver **Ruler:** Urban VIII **Rev:** St. Michael the Archangel fighting one demon, arms in exergue **Note:** Dav. #4058.

Date	Mintage	VG	F	VF	XF	Unc
ND(1634)-XII	—	275	525	900	2,500	—

KM# 183 PIASTRA (Scudo of 80 Bolognini)
Silver **Ruler:** Urban VIII **Rev:** Pope kneeling left before St. Michael the Archangel in clouds left **Note:** Dav. #4060.

Date	Mintage	VG	F	VF	XF	Unc
ND(1634)-XII	—	400	700	1,350	2,750	—
1643-XII GM	—	350	650	1,150	2,000	—

KM# 190 PIASTRA (Scudo of 80 Bolognini)
Silver **Ruler:** Urban VIII **Rev:** St. Michael the Archangel fighting one demon, mint mark (arms) in left field **Note:** Dav. #4059.

Date	Mintage	VG	F	VF	XF	Unc
ND(1637)-XV	—	250	450	900	1,650	—
1643-XX	—	250	450	900	1,650	—

KM# 205 PIASTRA (Scudo of 80 Bolognini)
Silver **Ruler:** Urban VIII **Rev:** Busts of SS. Peter and Paul, radiant dove above **Note:** Dav. #4061.

Date	Mintage	VG	F	VF	XF	Unc
1643-XXI GM	—	300	500	950	1,850	—

KM# 241 PIASTRA (Scudo of 80 Bolognini)
Silver **Ruler:** Urban VIII **Obv:** Bust of Innocent X right **Rev:** Jesus standing, blessing St. Peter kneeling right **Note:** Dav. #4064. Varieties exist in ornamentation of collar.

Date	Mintage	VG	F	VF	XF	Unc
ND(1645)-II	—	450	750	1,350	2,750	—
ND(1646)-III	—	450	750	1,350	2,750	—
ND(1647)-IV	—	450	750	1,350	2,750	—

KM# 254 PIASTRA (Scudo of 80 Bolognini)
Silver **Ruler:** Urban VIII **Obv:** Bust wearing tiara right **Rev:** Holy Door with Veronica's veil **Note:** Dav. #4065. Holy Year issue.

Date	Mintage	VG	F	VF	XF	Unc
MDCL (1650)-VII	—	750	1,250	2,500	5,000	—

KM# 279 PIASTRA (Scudo of 80 Bolognini)
Silver **Ruler:** Urban VIII **Rev:** Jesus standing, blessing St. Peter kneeling right **Note:** Dav. #4066.

Date	Mintage	VG	F	VF	XF	Unc
ND(1653)-IX Rare	—	—	—	—	—	—
ND(1654)-X Rare	—	—	—	—	—	—

Note: Numismatica Ars Classica Auction 30, 6-05, XF realized approximately $19,640

KM# 280 PIASTRA (Scudo of 80 Bolognini)
Silver **Obv:** Arms of Cardinal Antonio Barberini **Rev:** Radiant dove **Note:** Dav. #4069. Sede Vacante issue.

Date	Mintage	VG	F	VF	XF	Unc
MDCLV (1655)	—	250	450	900	1,650	—

KM# 290 PIASTRA (Scudo of 80 Bolognini)
Silver **Ruler:** Alexander VII **Obv:** Arms, St. Peter reclining above **Rev:** St. Thomas of Villanova giving alms to beggar **Note:** Dav. #4070.

Date	Mintage	VG	F	VF	XF	Unc
ND(1658)	—	250	400	850	1,750	—

KM# 310 PIASTRA (Scudo of 80 Bolognini)
Silver **Obv:** Arms of Cardinal Antonio Barberini **Rev:** Radiant dove **Note:** Dav. #4071. Sede Vacante issue.

Date	Mintage	VG	F	VF	XF	Unc
MDCLXVII (1667)	—	250	400	700	1,100	2,000

KM# 311 PIASTRA (Scudo of 80 Bolognini)
Silver **Ruler:** Clement IX **Obv:** Arms **Rev:** Chair of St. Peter between four seraphim **Note:** Dav. #4072.

Date	Mintage	VG	F	VF	XF	Unc
ND(1667-69)	—	250	400	700	1,750	—

KM# 319 PIASTRA (Scudo of 80 Bolognini)
Silver **Ruler:** Clement X **Obv:** Arms of Cardinal Antonio Barberini **Rev:** Radiant dove **Note:** Dav. #4073. Sede Vacante issue.

Date	Mintage	VG	F	VF	XF	Unc
MDCLXIX (1669)	—	250	400	700	1,750	—

KM# 351 PIASTRA (Scudo of 80 Bolognini)
Silver **Obv:** Capped bust of Clement X right **Rev:** Clemency and Abundance standing **Note:** Dav. #4074.

Date	Mintage	VG	F	VF	XF	Unc
MDCLXXI (1671)-II	—	275	525	950	1,750	—
MDCLXXII (1672)-II	—	275	525	950	1,750	—

KM# 353 PIASTRA (Scudo of 80 Bolognini)
Silver **Obv:** Arms **Rev:** Port of Civitavecchia **Note:** Dav. #4075.

Date	Mintage	VG	F	VF	XF	Unc
MDCLXXII (1672)	—	400	600	1,100	2,000	—

KM# 355 PIASTRA (Scudo of 80 Bolognini)
Silver **Subject:** Beautification of Pius V **Obv:** Capped bust right **Rev:** St. Pius kneeling right by altar, angel holding Battle of Lepanto shround **Note:** Dav. #4076.

Date	Mintage	VG	F	VF	XF	Unc
MDCLXXIII (1673)-IIII	—	400	600	1,100	2,000	—

KM# 367 PIASTRA (Scudo of 80 Bolognini)
Silver **Rev:** Portico of St. Peter with pilgrims **Note:** Dav. #4077.

Date	Mintage	VG	F	VF	XF	Unc
MDCLXXV (1675-IV)	—	225	350	650	1,150	—

KM# 368 PIASTRA (Scudo of 80 Bolognini)
Silver **Obv:** Arms **Note:** Dav. #4078.

Date	Mintage	VG	F	VF	XF	Unc
MDCLXXV (1675)	—	225	350	650	1,150	—

KM# 369 PIASTRA (Scudo of 80 Bolognini)
Silver **Obv:** Capped bust right **Rev:** Holy Door closed **Rev. Legend:** CIAVSIS FORBVS... **Note:** Dav. #4079.

Date	Mintage	VG	F	VF	XF	Unc
MDCLXXV (1675)	—	250	400	700	1,350	—

KM# 371 PIASTRA (Scudo of 80 Bolognini)
Silver **Rev:** Holy Door closed **Rev. Legend:** DABIT FRVCTVM... **Note:** Dav. #4081. Holy Year issue.

Date	Mintage	VG	F	VF	XF	Unc
MDCLXXV (1675)	—	250	400	675	1,250	—

KM# 370 PIASTRA (Scudo of 80 Bolognini)
Silver **Obv:** Arms **Note:** Holy Year issue. Dav.#4080.

Date	Mintage	VG	F	VF	XF	Unc
MDCLXXV (1675)	—	250	400	675	1,250	—

KM# 391 PIASTRA (Scudo of 80 Bolognini)
Silver **Obv:** Arms of Cardinal Paluzzo Paluzzi-Altieri **Rev:** Radiant dove **Note:** Sede Vacante issue. Dav.#4084.

Date	Mintage	VG	F	VF	XF	Unc
MDCLXXVI (1676)	—	250	400	675	1,250	—

KM# 392 PIASTRA (Scudo of 80 Bolognini)
Silver **Ruler:** Innocent XI **Obv:** Capped bust right **Rev:** St. Mathew standing on chair, angel left **Note:** Dav. #4085.

Date	Mintage	VG	F	VF	XF	Unc
ND(1676)-I	—	225	350	650	1,150	—

KM# 393 PIASTRA (Scudo of 80 Bolognini)
Silver **Ruler:** Innocent XI **Rev:** St. Matthew standing on cloud, angel left **Note:** Dav. #4086.

Date	Mintage	VG	F	VF	XF	Unc
ND(1676)-I	—	225	350	650	1,150	—

KM# 408 PIASTRA (Scudo of 80 Bolognini)
Silver **Ruler:** Innocent XI **Rev:** Inscription within palm wreath **Note:** Dav. #4095.

Date	Mintage	VG	F	VF	XF	Unc
ND(1676-89)	—	200	300	600	1,000	—

KM# 407 PIASTRA (Scudo of 80 Bolognini)
Silver **Ruler:** Innocent XI **Obv:** Arms **Rev:** Inscription in wreath **Rev. Inscription:** NON / TRODERVNT / IN DIE / VLTIONIS **Note:** Dav. #4096.

Date	Mintage	VG	F	VF	XF	Unc
ND(1676-89)	—	200	300	600	1,000	—

KM# 398 PIASTRA (Scudo of 80 Bolognini)
Silver **Ruler:** Innocent XI **Obv:** Capped bust right **Rev:** Façade of St. Peter's Basilica **Note:** Dav. #4087.

Date	Mintage	VG	F	VF	XF	Unc
ND(1677)-II	—	250	450	800	1,500	—

KM# 399 PIASTRA (Scudo of 80 Bolognini)
Silver **Ruler:** Innocent XI **Obv:** Arms **Rev:** Façade of St. Peter's **Note:** Dav. #4088.

Date	Mintage	VG	F	VF	XF	Unc
ND(1677)-II	—	250	450	825	1,600	—

KM# 403 PIASTRA (Scudo of 80 Bolognini)
Silver **Ruler:** Innocent XI **Obv:** Capped bust right **Rev:** Christ on boat with apostles, calming the storm **Note:** Dav. #4089.

Date	Mintage	VG	F	VF	XF	Unc
ND(1678)-III	—	265	475	850	1,650	—

KM# 421.1 PIASTRA (Scudo of 80 Bolognini)
Silver **Ruler:** Innocent XI **Obv:** Pointed arms **Rev:** St. Peter enthroned **Note:** Dav. #4090.

Date	Mintage	VG	F	VF	XF	Unc
1680	—	225	350	650	1,150	—
1681	—	225	350	650	1,150	—

KM# 421.2 PIASTRA (Scudo of 80 Bolognini)
Silver **Ruler:** Innocent XI **Obv:** Curved arms

Date	Mintage	VG	F	VF	XF	Unc
1680	—	225	350	650	1,150	—
1681	—	225	350	650	1,150	—

KM# 426 PIASTRA (Scudo of 80 Bolognini)
Silver **Ruler:** Innocent XI **Rev:** Inscription in cartouche with seraph at top **Rev. Inscription:** NON / PRODERVNT / IN DIE / VLTIONIS **Note:** Dav. #4091.

Date	Mintage	VG	F	VF	XF	Unc
ND(1682)-VII	—	200	350	550	1,000	—

KM# 427 PIASTRA (Scudo of 80 Bolognini)
Silver **Ruler:** Innocent XI **Rev:** Without seraph at top **Note:** Dav. #4092.

Date	Mintage	VG	F	VF	XF	Unc
ND(1682)-VII	—	200	350	550	1,000	—

KM# 452.1 PIASTRA (Scudo of 80 Bolognini)
Silver **Ruler:** Innocent XI **Rev:** Inscription and date in palm wreath **Note:** Dav. #4094.

Date	Mintage	VG	F	VF	XF	Unc
1684-IX	—	200	350	550	1,000	2,000

KM# 451.1 PIASTRA (Scudo of 80 Bolognini)
Silver **Ruler:** Innocent XI **Obv:** Capped bust right **Rev:** Inscription in palm sprays, date below **Rev. Inscription:** DEXTERA / TVA DOMINE / PERCVSSIT / INIMICVM **Note:** Dav. #4093.

Date	Mintage	VG	F	VF	XF	Unc
1684-VIII	—	200	350	550	1,000	2,000

KM# 451.2 PIASTRA (Scudo of 80 Bolognini)
Silver **Ruler:** Innocent XI **Rev:** Date in palm sprays **Note:** Dav. #4093A.

Date	Mintage	VG	F	VF	XF	Unc
1684-VIII	—	200	350	550	1,000	2,000

KM# 451.3 PIASTRA (Scudo of 80 Bolognini)
Silver **Ruler:** Innocent XI **Rev:** Without date **Note:** Dav. #4093B.

Date	Mintage	VG	F	VF	XF	Unc
ND(1684)-VIII	—	200	350	550	1,000	2,000

KM# 451.4 PIASTRA (Scudo of 80 Bolognini)
Silver **Ruler:** Innocent XI **Rev:** Inscription in palm wreath **Note:** Dav. #4093C.

Date	Mintage	VG	F	VF	XF	Unc
1684-VIII	—	200	350	550	1,000	2,000
1684-IX	—	200	350	550	1,000	2,000

KM# 452.2 PIASTRA (Scudo of 80 Bolognini)
Silver **Ruler:** Innocent XI **Rev:** Date below palm wreath **Note:** Dav. #4094A.

Date	Mintage	VG	F	VF	XF	Unc
1684-IX	—	200	350	550	1,000	2,000

KM# 497 PIASTRA (Scudo of 80 Bolognini)
Silver **Obv:** Arms of Cardinal Paluzzo Paluzzi-Altieri **Rev:** Radiant dove **Note:** Dav. #4098. Sede Vacante issue.

Date	Mintage	VG	F	VF	XF	Unc
MDCLXXXIX (1689)	—	200	350	650	1,150	—

KM# 498.1 PIASTRA (Scudo of 80 Bolognini)
Silver **Ruler:** Alexander VIII **Rev:** SS. Peter and Paul standing, radiant dove above **Note:** Dav. #4099.

Date	Mintage	VG	F	VF	XF	Unc
ND(1689)-I	—	750	1,250	2,750	5,000	—

KM# 498.2 PIASTRA (Scudo of 80 Bolognini)
Silver **Ruler:** Alexander VIII **Rev. Legend:** S. PAVLVS. **Note:** Dav. #4099A.

Date	Mintage	VG	F	VF	XF	Unc
ND(1689)-I	—	—	—	—	—	—

KM# 528 PIASTRA (Scudo of 80 Bolognini)
Silver **Ruler:** Alexander VIII **Obv:** Capped bust right **Rev:** Church standing left, holding church and standard **Note:** Dav. #4100.

Date	Mintage	VG	F	VF	XF	Unc
MDCXC (1690)-I	—	300	575	950	1,550	—
MDCXCI (1691)-II	—	300	575	950	1,550	—

KM# 557 PIASTRA (Scudo of 80 Bolognini)
Silver **Ruler:** Innocent XII **Obv:** Capped bust right **Rev:** St. Michael defeating Lucifer **Note:** Dav. #4102.

Date	Mintage	VG	F	VF	XF	Unc
1692-II	—	200	350	550	1,000	2,000
1693-II	—	200	350	550	1,000	2,000

KM# 558 PIASTRA (Scudo of 80 Bolognini)
Silver **Ruler:** Innocent XII **Rev:** Radiant throne of St. Peter, supported by angels **Note:** Dav. #4101.

Date	Mintage	VG	F	VF	XF	Unc
ND(1692)-II	—	400	700	1,250	2,000	—

KM# 569 PIASTRA (Scudo of 80 Bolognini)
Silver **Ruler:** Innocent XII **Rev:** Charity seated right, nursing infant **Note:** Dav. #4103.

Date	Mintage	VG	F	VF	XF	Unc
1693-III	—	225	425	600	1,250	—

KM# 576 PIASTRA (Scudo of 80 Bolognini)
Silver **Ruler:** Innocent XII **Rev:** Woman seated left, leaning on altar **Note:** Dav. #4104.

Date	Mintage	VG	F	VF	XF	Unc
1694-IIII	—	225	425	600	1,250	—

KM# 598 PIASTRA (Scudo of 80 Bolognini)
Silver **Ruler:** Innocent XII **Rev:** Enthroned Pope facing Consistory **Rev. Legend:** LOQVETVR PAC... **Note:** Dav. #4106.

Date	Mintage	VG	F	VF	XF	Unc
1696-V	—	225	425	600	1,250	2,500
1696-VI	—	225	425	600	1,250	2,500

KM# 599 PIASTRA (Scudo of 80 Bolognini)
Silver **Ruler:** Innocent XII **Rev:** Enthroned Pope right in Consistory **Rev. Legend:** PACEM LOQVETUR... **Note:** Dav. #4105.

Date	Mintage	VG	F	VF	XF	Unc
ND(1696)-V	—	225	425	675	1,350	—
ND(1696)-VI	—	225	425	675	1,350	—

KM# 608 PIASTRA (Scudo of 80 Bolognini)
Silver **Ruler:** Innocent XII **Subject:** First Anniversary - Peace of Ryswick **Rev:** St. Peter blessing reclining crowd **Note:** Dav. #4107.

Date	Mintage	VG	F	VF	XF	Unc
1698-VIII	—	265	475	800	1,650	—

KM# 614 PIASTRA (Scudo of 80 Bolognini)
Silver **Ruler:** Innocent XII **Subject:** Reduction of Tax on Wheat Flour **Rev:** Israelites gathering manna **Note:** Dav. #4108.

Date	Mintage	VG	F	VF	XF	Unc
MDCIC (1699)-VIII	—	275	550	1,150	2,500	6,000

KM# 615 PIASTRA (Scudo of 80 Bolognini)
Silver **Ruler:** Innocent XII **Subject:** Restoration of the Port of Anzio **Rev:** Port of Anzio **Note:** Dav. #4109.

Date	Mintage	VG	F	VF	XF	Unc
MDCXCIX (1699)-VIII	—	450	950	1,850	4,500	—

KM# 649 PIASTRA (Scudo of 80 Bolognini)
Silver **Ruler:** Innocent XII **Rev:** Holy Door flanked by standing angels **Note:** Dav. #4110. Holy Year issue.

Date	Mintage	VG	F	VF	XF	Unc
MDCC (1700)-IX	—	265	475	850	1,650	—

KM# 651 PIASTRA (Scudo of 80 Bolognini)
Silver **Obv:** Arms of Cardinal Giovanni Spinola, pointed bottom shield **Rev:** Radiant dove **Note:** Dav. #4112. Sede Vacante issue.

Date	Mintage	VG	F	VF	XF	Unc
MDCC (1700)	—	275	550	1,150	2,500	—

KM# 652 PIASTRA (Scudo of 80 Bolognini)
Silver **Obv:** Arms of Cardinal Giovanni Spinola, rounded bottom shield **Note:** Dav. #4113. Sede Vacante issue.

Date	Mintage	VG	F	VF	XF	Unc
MDCC (1700)	—	265	475	1,000	1,850	—

KM# 653 PIASTRA (Scudo of 80 Bolognini)
Silver **Ruler:** Clement XI **Rev:** Holy Door **Note:** Holy Year issue. Dav.#1428.

Date	Mintage	VG	F	VF	XF	Unc
MDCC (1700)-I	—	265	475	1,000	1,850	—

KM# 577 1/2 SCUDO D'ORO
Gold **Ruler:** Innocent XII **Obv:** Papal arms **Rev:** Bust of St. Peter left

Date	Mintage	VG	F	VF	XF	Unc
ND(1694)-III	—	725	1,400	3,000	5,000	—

KM# 578 1/2 SCUDO D'ORO
Silver **Ruler:** Innocent XII **Rev:** Holy Door

Date	Mintage	VG	F	VF	XF	Unc
ND(1694)-III	—	725	1,400	3,000	5,000	—

KM# 34 SCUDO D'ORO
3.5000 g., 0.9860 Gold 0.1109 oz. AGW **Obv:** Arms of Cardinal Pietro Aldobrandini **Note:** Sede Vacante issue.

Date	Mintage	VG	F	VF	XF	Unc
MDCV (1605) Rare	—	—	—	—	—	—

KM# 42 SCUDO D'ORO
3.5000 g., 0.9860 Gold 0.1109 oz. AGW, 23 mm. **Ruler:** Paul V **Obv:** Papal arms of Paul V **Rev:** St. Paul seated left

Date	Mintage	VG	F	VF	XF	Unc
ND(1606)-II	—	725	1,400	3,000	4,500	—

KM# 43 SCUDO D'ORO
3.5000 g., 0.9860 Gold 0.1109 oz. AGW **Ruler:** Paul V **Rev:** Year in exergue

Date	Mintage	VG	F	VF	XF	Unc
ND(1606)-III	—	725	1,400	3,000	4,500	—

KM# 48 SCUDO D'ORO
3.5000 g., 0.9860 Gold 0.1109 oz. AGW, 19 mm. **Ruler:** Paul V **Rev:** St. Paul bust right

Date	Mintage	VG	F	VF	XF	Unc
ND(1607)-III	—	725	1,400	3,000	4,500	—
ND(1612)-VIII	—	725	1,400	3,000	4,500	—
ND(1615)-XI	—	725	1,400	3,000	4,500	—
ND(1616)-XII	—	725	1,400	3,000	4,500	—

KM# 53 SCUDO D'ORO
3.5000 g., 0.9860 Gold 0.1109 oz. AGW **Ruler:** Paul V **Rev:** Conjoined busts of SS. Peter and Paul left

Date	Mintage	VG	F	VF	XF	Unc
ND(1608)-IV	—	900	1,800	3,600	7,500	—

KM# 80 SCUDO D'ORO
3.5000 g., 0.9860 Gold 0.1109 oz. AGW **Ruler:** Paul V **Obv:** Bust right **Rev:** St. Paul standing

Date	Mintage	VG	F	VF	XF	Unc
ND(1617)-XIII	—	900	1,800	3,600	7,500	—

KM# 103 SCUDO D'ORO
3.5000 g., 0.9860 Gold 0.1109 oz. AGW **Ruler:** Gregory XV **Rev:** Santa Maria Maggiore church façade

Date	Mintage	VG	F	VF	XF	Unc
ND(1622)-II	—	1,000	3,000	4,500	9,000	—

KM# 104 SCUDO D'ORO
3.5000 g., 0.9860 Gold 0.1109 oz. AGW **Ruler:** Paul V **Rev:** Radiant Madonna standing

Date	Mintage	VG	F	VF	XF	Unc
ND(1622)-II	—	900	1,800	3,600	7,500	—

KM# 105 SCUDO D'ORO
3.5000 g., 0.9860 Gold 0.1109 oz. AGW **Ruler:** Paul V **Obv:** Papal arms **Rev:** Facing busts of SS. Peter and Paul

Date	Mintage	VG	F	VF	XF	Unc
ND Rare	—	—	—	—	—	—

KM# 148 SCUDO D'ORO
3.5000 g., 0.9860 Gold 0.1109 oz. AGW **Ruler:** Urban VIII **Obv:** Bust right **Rev:** Holy Door divides date **Note:** Holy Year issue.

Date	Mintage	VG	F	VF	XF	Unc
1625	—	750	1,500	3,000	4,500	—

KM# 149 SCUDO D'ORO
3.5000 g., 0.9860 Gold 0.1109 oz. AGW **Ruler:** Urban VIII **Rev:** Holy Door, date in exergue **Note:** Holy Year issue.

Date	Mintage	VG	F	VF	XF	Unc
1625-II Rare	—	—	—	—	—	—

KM# A149 SCUDO D'ORO
3.5000 g., 0.9860 Gold 0.1109 oz. AGW **Ruler:** Urban VIII **Obv:** Papal arms **Rev:** Holy Door with Veronica's veil, date flanking, ROMA in exergue **Note:** Holy Year issue.

Date	Mintage	VG	F	VF	XF	Unc
1625 Rare	—	—	—	—	—	—

KM# 154 SCUDO D'ORO
3.5000 g., 0.9860 Gold 0.1109 oz. AGW **Ruler:** Urban VIII **Rev:** Madonna standing

Date	Mintage	VG	F	VF	XF	Unc
ND(1627)-IIII	—	1,500	3,000	4,500	9,000	—
ND(1636)-XIII	—	1,500	3,000	4,500	9,000	—
ND(1638)-XV	—	1,500	3,000	4,500	9,000	—
ND	—	1,500	3,000	4,500	9,000	—

KM# 153 SCUDO D'ORO
3.5000 g., 0.9860 Gold 0.1109 oz. AGW **Ruler:** Urban VIII **Obv:** Papal arms **Rev:** Bust of St. Paul right

Date	Mintage	VG	F	VF	XF	Unc
ND(1627)-IIII	—	900	1,800	3,600	4,500	—

KM# 159 SCUDO D'ORO
3.5000 g., 0.9860 Gold 0.1109 oz. AGW **Ruler:** Urban VIII **Rev:** St. Michael slaying the devil

Date	Mintage	VG	F	VF	XF	Unc
ND(1629)-VI	—	900	1,800	3,600	4,500	—

KM# 171 SCUDO D'ORO

3.5000 g., 0.9860 Gold 0.1109 oz. AGW **Ruler:** Urban VIII **Rev:** Bust of Christ

Date	Mintage	VG	F	VF	XF	Unc
ND(1630)-VII	—	900	1,800	3,600	4,500	—

KM# 202 SCUDO D'ORO

3.5000 g., 0.9860 Gold 0.1109 oz. AGW **Ruler:** Urban VIII **Obv:** Papal arms **Rev:** Radiant Madonna standing

Date	Mintage	VG	F	VF	XF	Unc
1642-XX	—	725	1,400	3,000	4,500	—
1643-XXI	—	725	1,400	3,000	4,500	—
ND	—	725	1,400	3,000	4,500	—

KM# 203 SCUDO D'ORO

3.5000 g., 0.9860 Gold 0.1109 oz. AGW **Ruler:** Urban VIII **Rev:** St. Michael slaying the devil

Date	Mintage	VG	F	VF	XF	Unc
1642-XX	—	900	1,800	3,600	4,500	—
ND(1643)-XXI	—	900	1,800	3,600	4,500	—

KM# 243 SCUDO D'ORO

3.5000 g., 0.9860 Gold 0.1109 oz. AGW **Ruler:** Innocent X **Subject:** Immaculate Conception **Rev:** Radiant Madonna standing

Date	Mintage	VG	F	VF	XF	Unc
ND(1645)-II Unique	—	—	—	—	—	—

KM# 242 SCUDO D'ORO

3.5000 g., 0.9860 Gold 0.1109 oz. AGW, 20 mm. **Ruler:** Innocent X **Rev:** St. Peter holding keys

Date	Mintage	VG	F	VF	XF	Unc
1644-I	—	1,800	3,300	6,000	9,600	—

KM# 244 SCUDO D'ORO

3.5000 g., 0.9860 Gold 0.1109 oz. AGW **Ruler:** Innocent X **Rev:** Madonna standing in inner circle, date below

Date	Mintage	VG	F	VF	XF	Unc
ND(1645)-II	—	1,800	3,300	6,000	9,600	—
1652-VIII	—	1,800	3,300	6,000	9,600	—
ND(1653)-VIIII	—	1,800	3,300	6,000	9,600	—

KM# 248 SCUDO D'ORO

3.5000 g., 0.9860 Gold 0.1109 oz. AGW **Ruler:** Innocent X **Rev:** Without date

Date	Mintage	VG	F	VF	XF	Unc
ND(1653)-IX	—	1,800	3,300	6,000	9,600	—

KM# 261 SCUDO D'ORO

3.5000 g., 0.9860 Gold 0.1109 oz. AGW **Ruler:** Alexander VII **Rev:** Inscription in cartouche **Rev. Inscription:** DEVS / DAT OMNI / BVS...NON IMPRO / PERAT

Date	Mintage	VG	F	VF	XF	Unc
ND	—	725	2,200	4,200	7,200	—

KM# 262 SCUDO D'ORO

3.5000 g., 0.9860 Gold 0.1109 oz. AGW **Ruler:** Alexander VII **Rev:** Simple Papal arms

Date	Mintage	VG	F	VF	XF	Unc
ND	—	725	2,200	4,200	7,200	—

KM# 263 SCUDO D'ORO

3.5000 g., 0.9860 Gold 0.1109 oz. AGW, 19 mm. **Ruler:** Alexander VII

Date	Mintage	VG	F	VF	XF	Unc
ND	—	875	2,750	4,800	7,800	—

KM# 312 SCUDO D'ORO

3.5000 g., 0.9860 Gold 0.1109 oz. AGW **Obv:** Arms of Cardinal Antonio Barberini **Note:** Sede Vacante issue.

Date	Mintage	VG	F	VF	XF	Unc
MDCLXVII (1667)	—	1,800	3,300	6,000	9,600	—

KM# 313 SCUDO D'ORO

3.5000 g., 0.9860 Gold 0.1109 oz. AGW **Ruler:** Clement IX **Obv:** Papal arms **Rev:** Madonna standing in inner circle

Date	Mintage	VG	F	VF	XF	Unc
ND	—	725	2,200	4,200	7,200	—

KM# 320 SCUDO D'ORO

3.5000 g., 0.9860 Gold 0.1109 oz. AGW **Obv:** Arms of Cardinal Antonio Barberini **Rev:** Radiant and flaming dove **Note:** Sede Vacante issue.

Date	Mintage	VG	F	VF	XF	Unc
MDCLXIX (1669)	—	875	2,750	4,800	7,800	—

KM# 321 SCUDO D'ORO

3.5000 g., 0.9860 Gold 0.1109 oz. AGW **Ruler:** Clement IX **Obv:** Papal arms **Rev:** St. Peter standing facing

Date	Mintage	VG	F	VF	XF	Unc
ND	—	725	2,200	4,200	7,200	—

KM# 322 SCUDO D'ORO

3.5000 g., 0.9860 Gold 0.1109 oz. AGW, 21 mm. **Ruler:** Clement X **Rev:** Madonna and child on clouds

Date	Mintage	VG	F	VF	XF	Unc
ND Rare	—	—	—	—	—	—

KM# 372 SCUDO D'ORO

3.5000 g., 0.9860 Gold 0.1109 oz. AGW **Ruler:** Clement X **Rev:** Closed Holy Door **Note:** Holy Year issue.

Date	Mintage	VG	F	VF	XF	Unc
1675	—	725	2,200	4,200	7,200	—

KM# 373 SCUDO D'ORO

3.5000 g., 0.9860 Gold 0.1109 oz. AGW **Ruler:** Clement X **Rev:** Open Holy Door **Note:** Holy Year issue.

Date	Mintage	VG	F	VF	XF	Unc
1675	—	550	1,100	2,400	3,900	—

KM# 374 SCUDO D'ORO

3.5000 g., 0.9860 Gold 0.1109 oz. AGW **Ruler:** Innocent XI **Rev:** Head of St. Peter right

Date	Mintage	VG	F	VF	XF	Unc
ND	—	550	1,100	2,400	3,900	—

KM# 375 SCUDO D'ORO

3.5000 g., 0.9860 Gold 0.1109 oz. AGW **Ruler:** Innocent XI **Subject:** Immaculate Conception **Rev:** Radiant Madonna standing

Date	Mintage	VG	F	VF	XF	Unc
ND	—	550	1,100	2,400	3,900	—

KM# 376 SCUDO D'ORO

3.5000 g., 0.9860 Gold 0.1109 oz. AGW **Ruler:** Innocent XI **Rev:** Madonna and child in clouds

Date	Mintage	VG	F	VF	XF	Unc
ND	—	550	1,100	2,400	3,900	—

KM# 377 SCUDO D'ORO

3.5000 g., 0.9860 Gold 0.1109 oz. AGW **Ruler:** Innocent XI **Rev:** Inscription in wreath **Rev. Inscription:** NEQVE / DIVITIAS

Date	Mintage	VG	F	VF	XF	Unc
ND	—	500	1,100	2,400	3,900	—

KM# 453 SCUDO D'ORO

3.5000 g., 0.9860 Gold 0.1109 oz. AGW **Ruler:** Innocent XI **Rev:** Date below inscription in cartouche **Rev. Inscription:** POSSIDE / SAPIENTIAM

Date	Mintage	VG	F	VF	XF	Unc
1684	—	550	1,100	2,400	3,900	—
1685 Unique	—	—	—	—	—	—

KM# 454 SCUDO D'ORO

3.5000 g., 0.9860 Gold 0.1109 oz. AGW **Ruler:** Innocent XI **Rev:** Inscription in wreath **Rev. Inscription:** POSSIDE / SAPIENTIAM

Date	Mintage	VG	F	VF	XF	Unc
ND	—	550	1,100	2,400	3,900	—

KM# 455 SCUDO D'ORO

3.5000 g., 0.9860 Gold 0.1109 oz. AGW **Ruler:** Innocent XI **Rev:** Inscription in cartouche, small shield at bottom **Rev. Inscription:** PRO / PRETIO / ANIMAE

Date	Mintage	VG	F	VF	XF	Unc
ND	—	550	1,100	2,400	3,900	—

KM# 456 SCUDO D'ORO

3.5000 g., 0.9860 Gold 0.1109 oz. AGW **Ruler:** Innocent XI **Rev:** Different small shield at bottom

Date	Mintage	VG	F	VF	XF	Unc
ND	—	550	1,100	2,400	3,900	—

KM# 499 SCUDO D'ORO

3.5000 g., 0.9860 Gold 0.1109 oz. AGW **Ruler:** Alexander VIII **Rev:** St. Peter standing facing, date in exergue

Date	Mintage	VG	F	VF	XF	Unc
1689-I	—	725	1,450	2,650	4,200	—

KM# 529 SCUDO D'ORO

3.5000 g., 0.9860 Gold 0.1109 oz. AGW **Ruler:** Alexander VIII **Rev:** Conjoined busts of SS. Peter and Paul right, date in exergue

Date	Mintage	VG	F	VF	XF	Unc
MDCXC (1690)-I	—	550	1,100	2,400	3,900	—

KM# A544 SCUDO D'ORO

3.5000 g., 0.9860 Gold 0.1109 oz. AGW **Ruler:** Innocent XII **Rev:** Head of St. Peter right

Date	Mintage	VG	F	VF	XF	Unc
ND(1691)-I	—	725	1,450	2,650	4,200	—

KM# 559 SCUDO D'ORO

3.5000 g., 0.9860 Gold 0.1109 oz. AGW **Ruler:** Innocent XII **Rev:** Head of St. Peter with halo right, date below

Date	Mintage	VG	F	VF	XF	Unc
1692-II	—	550	1,100	2,400	3,900	—

KM# 579 SCUDO D'ORO

3.5000 g., 0.9860 Gold 0.1109 oz. AGW **Ruler:** Innocent XII **Rev:** Sunflower on stalk with sun at upper left, date at lower right

Date	Mintage	VG	F	VF	XF	Unc
1694-III	—	1,250	2,400	4,800	8,100	—

KM# 602 SCUDO D'ORO

3.5000 g., 0.9860 Gold 0.1109 oz. AGW **Ruler:** Innocent XII **Rev:** Sheaf of grain, date in exergue

Date	Mintage	VG	F	VF	XF	Unc
1697-VII	—	550	1,100	2,400	3,900	—

KM# 654 SCUDO D'ORO

3.5000 g., 0.9860 Gold 0.1109 oz. AGW **Ruler:** Innocent XII **Rev:** Holy Door, date in exergue **Note:** Holy Year issue.

Date	Mintage	VG	F	VF	XF	Unc
MDCC (1700)	—	550	1,100	2,400	3,900	—

KM# 655 SCUDO D'ORO

3.5000 g., 0.9860 Gold 0.1109 oz. AGW **Obv:** Arms of Cardinal Giovanni Spinola, date in legend **Rev:** Radiant dove **Note:** Sede Vacante issue.

Date	Mintage	VG	F	VF	XF	Unc
1700	—	1,100	2,200	4,200	7,200	—

KM# 117 DOPPIA (2) SCUDO D'ORO

7.0000 g., 0.9860 Gold 0.2219 oz. AGW **Ruler:** Paul V **Rev:** St. Paul

Date	Mintage	VG	F	VF	XF	Unc
ND	—	875	1,750	3,900	6,600	—

KM# 118 DOPPIA (2) SCUDO D'ORO

7.0000 g., 0.9860 Gold 0.2219 oz. AGW **Ruler:** Paul V **Rev:** Radiant Madonna with wide rays in inner circle

Date	Mintage	VG	F	VF	XF	Unc
ND	—	1,800	3,600	7,200	11,000	—

KM# 119 DOPPIA (2) SCUDO D'ORO

7.0000 g., 0.9860 Gold 0.2219 oz. AGW **Ruler:** Paul V **Rev:** Short rays

Date	Mintage	VG	F	VF	XF	Unc
ND	—	1,800	3,600	7,200	11,000	—

KM# 120 DOPPIA (2) SCUDO D'ORO

7.0000 g., 0.9860 Gold 0.2219 oz. AGW **Ruler:** Paul V **Rev:** St. Paul standing

Date	Mintage	VG	F	VF	XF	Unc
ND Unique	—	—	—	—	—	—

KM# 121 DOPPIA (2) SCUDO D'ORO

7.0000 g., 0.9860 Gold 0.2219 oz. AGW **Obv:** Arms of Cardinal Ippolito Aldobrandini **Rev:** Christ standing with banner **Note:** Sede Vacante issue.

Date	Mintage	VG	F	VF	XF	Unc
1623 Rare	—	—	—	—	—	—

KM# 125 DOPPIA (2) SCUDO D'ORO

7.0000 g., 0.9860 Gold 0.2219 oz. AGW **Ruler:** Urban VIII **Rev:** Madonna standing

Date	Mintage	VG	F	VF	XF	Unc
ND(1624)-I	—	650	1,300	2,400	4,200	—

KM# 126 DOPPIA (2) SCUDO D'ORO

7.0000 g., 0.9860 Gold 0.2219 oz. AGW **Ruler:** Urban VIII **Obv:** Bust **Rev:** Facing busts of SS. Peter and Paul

Date	Mintage	VG	F	VF	XF	Unc
1624-I Rare	—	—	—	—	—	—

KM# 127 DOPPIA (2) SCUDO D'ORO

7.0000 g., 0.9860 Gold 0.2219 oz. AGW **Ruler:** Urban VIII **Obv:** Papal arms

Date	Mintage	VG	F	VF	XF	Unc
1624-I	—	2,200	4,400	8,400	12,500	—

KM# 256 DOPPIA (2) SCUDO D'ORO

7.0000 g., 0.9860 Gold 0.2219 oz. AGW **Ruler:** Innocent X **Rev:** Holy Door divides RO-MA, date in exergue

Date	Mintage	VG	F	VF	XF	Unc
MDCLI (1651)-VII Unique	—	—	—	—	—	—

KM# 257 DOPPIA (2) SCUDO D'ORO

7.0000 g., 0.9860 Gold 0.2219 oz. AGW **Ruler:** Innocent X **Rev:** Holy Door divides date, ROMA in exergue

Date	Mintage	VG	F	VF	XF	Unc
1651-VII Rare	—	—	—	—	—	—

KM# 259 DOPPIA (2) SCUDO D'ORO

7.0000 g., 0.9860 Gold 0.2219 oz. AGW **Ruler:** Innocent X **Rev:** Bust of St. Peter in inner circle, date below

Date	Mintage	VG	F	VF	XF	Unc
1652-VIII Rare	—	—	—	—	—	—

KM# 281 DOPPIA (2) SCUDO D'ORO

7.0000 g., 0.9860 Gold 0.2219 oz. AGW **Obv:** Arms of Cardinal Antonio Barberini, date in legend **Rev:** Radiant and flaming dove, ROMA in exergue **Note:** Sede Vacante issue.

Date	Mintage	VG	F	VF	XF	Unc
MDCLV (1655)	—	2,750	5,500	11,000	16,500	—

KM# 282 DOPPIA (2) SCUDO D'ORO

7.0000 g., 0.9860 Gold 0.2219 oz. AGW **Ruler:** Alexander VII **Obv:** Quartered Papal arms **Rev. Inscription:** NON EX / TRISTITIA / AVT EX / NECESSITA / TE

Date	Mintage	VG	F	VF	XF	Unc
ND Rare	—	—	—	—	—	—

KM# 283 DOPPIA (2) SCUDO D'ORO

7.0000 g., 0.9860 Gold 0.2219 oz. AGW **Ruler:** Alexander VII **Obv:** Simple Papal arms

Date	Mintage	VG	F	VF	XF	Unc
ND Rare	—	—	—	—	—	—

KM# 284 DOPPIA (2) SCUDO D'ORO

7.0000 g., 0.9860 Gold 0.2219 oz. AGW **Ruler:** Clement IX **Rev:** Madonna standing

Date	Mintage	VG	F	VF	XF	Unc
ND	—	1,800	3,250	6,500	10,000	—

KM# 323 DOPPIA (2) SCUDO D'ORO

7.0000 g., 0.9860 Gold 0.2219 oz. AGW **Obv:** Arms of Cardinal Antonio Barberini **Note:** Sede Vacante issue.

Date	Mintage	VG	F	VF	XF	Unc
MDCLXIX (1669)	—	2,400	4,700	9,000	15,000	—

KM# 344 DOPPIA (2) SCUDO D'ORO

7.0000 g., 0.9860 Gold 0.2219 oz. AGW **Ruler:** Clement X **Obv:** Bust right **Rev:** St. Peter standing being crowned by an angel, date in exergue

Date	Mintage	VG	F	VF	XF	Unc
MDCLXX (1670)-I Rare	—	—	—	—	—	—

KM# 345 DOPPIA (2) SCUDO D'ORO

7.0000 g., 0.9860 Gold 0.2219 oz. AGW **Ruler:** Clement X **Rev:** St. Venantius standing holding banner

Date	Mintage	VG	F	VF	XF	Unc
ND	—	1,250	2,400	4,800	7,800	—

KM# 346 DOPPIA (2) SCUDO D'ORO

7.0000 g., 0.9860 Gold 0.2219 oz. AGW **Ruler:** Clement X **Rev:** SS. Peter and Paul standing, RO-MA in exergue

Date	Mintage	VG	F	VF	XF	Unc
ND	—	1,250	2,400	4,800	7,800	—

KM# 400 DOPPIA (2) SCUDO D'ORO

7.0000 g., 0.9860 Gold 0.2219 oz. AGW **Ruler:** Innocent XI **Rev:** Inscription in cartouche **Rev. Inscription:** MVLTOS / PERDIDIT / AVRVM

Date	Mintage	VG	F	VF	XF	Unc
ND(1677)-II	—	1,350	2,750	5,000	8,500	—
ND(1681)-VI	—	1,350	2,750	5,000	8,500	—

KM# 406 DOPPIA (2) SCUDO D'ORO

7.0000 g., 0.9860 Gold 0.2219 oz. AGW **Ruler:** Innocent XI **Rev:** Inscription in cartouche **Rev. Inscription:** NIHIL AVARO / SCELESTIVS

Date	Mintage	VG	F	VF	XF	Unc
ND(1679)-IIII	—	1,500	3,050	6,000	9,600	—

KM# 422 DOPPIA (2) SCUDO D'ORO

7.0000 g., 0.9860 Gold 0.2219 oz. AGW **Ruler:** Innocent XI **Rev:** Different cartouche for motto

Date	Mintage	VG	F	VF	XF	Unc
ND(1680)-V	—	1,500	3,050	6,000	9,600	—

KM# 457 DOPPIA (2) SCUDO D'ORO

7.0000 g., 0.9860 Gold 0.2219 oz. AGW **Ruler:** Innocent XI **Rev:** Date in cartouche **Rev. Inscription:** QVI / CONFIDIT / IN.DIVITIIS / CORRVET

Date	Mintage	VG	F	VF	XF	Unc
1684-IX	—	1,500	3,050	6,000	9,600	—

KM# 458 DOPPIA (2) SCUDO D'ORO

7.0000 g., 0.9860 Gold 0.2219 oz. AGW **Ruler:** Innocent XI **Rev:** Different cartouche for motto

Date	Mintage	VG	F	VF	XF	Unc
1684-XI	—	1,500	3,050	6,000	9,600	—

KM# 475 DOPPIA (2) SCUDO D'ORO

7.0000 g., 0.9860 Gold 0.2219 oz. AGW **Ruler:** Innocent XI **Rev:** Different Papal arms

Date	Mintage	VG	F	VF	XF	Unc
1685-IX	—	1,500	3,050	6,000	9,600	—

KM# 500 DOPPIA (2) SCUDO D'ORO

7.0000 g., 0.9860 Gold 0.2219 oz. AGW **Ruler:** Innocent XI **Obv:** Papal arms **Rev:** Date in cartouche **Rev. Inscription:** DIVES / IN / HUMILITATE

Date	Mintage	VG	F	VF	XF	Unc
1687-XII Rare	—	—	—	—	—	—

KM# 501 DOPPIA (2) SCUDO D'ORO

7.0000 g., 0.9860 Gold 0.2219 oz. AGW **Obv:** Arms of Cardinal Paluzzo Paluzzi-Altieri **Rev:** Radiant and flaming dove, RO-MA divided below **Note:** Sede Vacante issue.

Date	Mintage	VG	F	VF	XF	Unc
MDCLXXXIX (1689) Unique	—	—	—	—	—	—

KM# 502 DOPPIA (2) SCUDO D'ORO

7.0000 g., 0.9860 Gold 0.2219 oz. AGW **Ruler:** Alexander VIII **Obv:** Papal arms **Rev:** St. Bruno in clouds, date divided at bottom

Date	Mintage	VG	F	VF	XF	Unc
1689-I	—	1,100	2,200	4,300	7,200	—
ND(1689)-I	—	1,100	2,200	4,300	7,200	—

KM# 530 DOPPIA (2) SCUDO D'ORO

7.0000 g., 0.9860 Gold 0.2219 oz. AGW **Ruler:** Alexander VIII **Rev:** Altar with garlands, date in exergue

Date	Mintage	VG	F	VF	XF	Unc
MDCXC (1690)	—	1,250	2,400	4,800	7,800	—

KM# 545 DOPPIA (2) SCUDO D'ORO

7.0000 g., 0.9860 Gold 0.2219 oz. AGW **Obv:** Arms of Cardinal Paluzzi-Altieri **Rev:** Radiant dove, RO-MA divided below **Note:** Sede Vacante issue.

Date	Mintage	VG	F	VF	XF	Unc
MDCXCI (1691) Rare	—	—	—	—	—	—

KM# 562 DOPPIA (2) SCUDO D'ORO

7.0000 g., 0.9860 Gold 0.2219 oz. AGW **Ruler:** Innocent XII **Obv:** Papal arms **Rev:** St. Paul standing holding sword, date in exergue

Date	Mintage	VG	F	VF	XF	Unc
1692	—	1,500	3,050	6,000	9,600	—

KM# 603 DOPPIA (2) SCUDO D'ORO

7.0000 g., 0.9860 Gold 0.2219 oz. AGW **Ruler:** Innocent XII **Obv:** Bust right **Rev:** Noah's ark with dove in flight with olive branch

Date	Mintage	VG	F	VF	XF	Unc
ND(1697)-VI	—	1,800	3,600	8,000	15,000	—

Note: Superior Pipito sale 12-87 about XF realized $10,120

KM# 616 DOPPIA (2) SCUDO D'ORO

7.0000 g., 0.9860 Gold 0.2219 oz. AGW **Ruler:** Innocent XII **Obv:** Papal arms **Rev:** Holy Door, date in exergue

Date	Mintage	VG	F	VF	XF	Unc
1699-IX	—	1,800	3,600	7,200	13,000	—

KM# 656 DOPPIA (2) SCUDO D'ORO

7.0000 g., 0.9860 Gold 0.2219 oz. AGW **Ruler:** Clement XI **Obv:** Bust right **Rev:** Closed Holy Door **Note:** Holy Year issue.

Date	Mintage	VG	F	VF	XF	Unc
ND(1700)-I	—	875	1,800	3,600	6,000	—

KM# 44 QUADRUPLA (4) SCUDO D'ORO

14.0000 g., 0.9860 Gold 0.4438 oz. AGW **Ruler:** Paul V **Obv:** Bust left **Rev:** St. Paul reclining holding sword vertically

Date	Mintage	VG	F	VF	XF	Unc
ND(1606)-II	—	2,200	4,400	10,000	20,000	—

KM# 45 QUADRUPLA (4) SCUDO D'ORO
14.0000 g., 0.9860 Gold 0.4438 oz. AGW **Ruler:** Paul V **Obv:** Bust left **Rev:** St. Paul seated holding sword at an angle

Date	Mintage	VG	F	VF	XF	Unc
ND(1606)-II	—	2,200	4,400	10,000	18,000	—

KM# 49 QUADRUPLA (4) SCUDO D'ORO
14.0000 g., 0.9860 Gold 0.4438 oz. AGW **Ruler:** Paul V **Obv:** Bust left **Rev:** St. Paul seated holding sword at an angle

Date	Mintage	VG	F	VF	XF	Unc
ND(1607)-III	—	2,200	4,400	10,000	18,000	—

KM# 55 QUADRUPLA (4) SCUDO D'ORO
14.0000 g., 0.9860 Gold 0.4438 oz. AGW **Ruler:** Paul V **Obv:** Papal arms **Rev:** Bust of St. Paul left in inner circle, date in exergue

Date	Mintage	VG	F	VF	XF	Unc
MDCVIII (1608)-IV	—	1,250	2,500	5,400	9,000	—
MDCIX (1609)-IV	—	1,250	2,500	5,400	9,000	—
MDCIX (1609)-V	—	1,250	2,500	5,400	9,000	—

KM# 54 QUADRUPLA (4) SCUDO D'ORO
14.0000 g., 0.9860 Gold 0.4438 oz. AGW **Ruler:** Paul V **Rev:** St. Paul standing in inner circle

Date	Mintage	VG	F	VF	XF	Unc
ND(1608)-III	—	2,200	4,400	8,400	14,000	—

KM# 67 QUADRUPLA (4) SCUDO D'ORO
14.0000 g., 0.9860 Gold 0.4438 oz. AGW **Ruler:** Paul V **Obv:** Papal arms **Rev:** St. Paul seated right, date in exergue

Date	Mintage	VG	F	VF	XF	Unc
1611-VI	—	1,100	2,200	5,500	9,500	—

KM# 81 QUADRUPLA (4) SCUDO D'ORO
14.0000 g., 0.9860 Gold 0.4438 oz. AGW **Ruler:** Paul V **Obv:** Bust right **Rev:** St. Paul seated right, without date in exergue

Date	Mintage	VG	F	VF	XF	Unc
ND(1617)-XIII	—	1,100	2,200	5,500	9,500	—

KM# 82 QUADRUPLA (4) SCUDO D'ORO
14.0000 g., 0.9860 Gold 0.4438 oz. AGW **Ruler:** Paul V **Obv:** Bust of Paul V right in inner circle, ROMA below

Date	Mintage	VG	F	VF	XF	Unc
ND	—	1,100	2,200	5,500	9,500	—

KM# 83 QUADRUPLA (4) SCUDO D'ORO
14.0000 g., 0.9860 Gold 0.4438 oz. AGW **Ruler:** Gregory XV **Obv:** Papal arms **Rev:** Radiant Madonna standing **Note:** Varieties exist in shield shape.

Date	Mintage	VG	F	VF	XF	Unc
ND	—	2,500	4,950	12,000	18,000	—

KM# 122 QUADRUPLA (4) SCUDO D'ORO
14.0000 g., 0.9860 Gold 0.4438 oz. AGW **Obv:** Arms of Cardinal Ippolito Aldobrandini **Rev:** Christ standing holding banner **Note:** Sede Vacante issue.

Date	Mintage	VG	F	VF	XF	Unc
1623 Rare	—	—	—	—	—	—

KM# 185 QUADRUPLA (4) SCUDO D'ORO
14.0000 g., 0.9860 Gold 0.4438 oz. AGW **Ruler:** Urban VIII **Obv:** Bust right in inner circle **Rev:** St. Michael slaying the devil, date in exergue

Date	Mintage	VG	F	VF	XF	Unc
1634-XII	—	3,300	6,600	11,500	17,500	—

KM# 189 QUADRUPLA (4) SCUDO D'ORO
14.0000 g., 0.9860 Gold 0.4438 oz. AGW **Ruler:** Urban VIII **Obv:** Bust right **Rev:** Madonna standing, RO-MA in exergue

Date	Mintage	VG	F	VF	XF	Unc
1636-XIV	—	3,300	6,600	11,500	17,500	—

KM# 246 QUADRUPLA (4) SCUDO D'ORO
14.0000 g., 0.9860 Gold 0.4438 oz. AGW **Ruler:** Innocent X **Obv:** Bust right in inner circle, date below **Rev:** Papal arms

Date	Mintage	VG	F	VF	XF	Unc
1647-III Rare	—	—	—	—	—	—

KM# 285 QUADRUPLA (4) SCUDO D'ORO
14.0000 g., 0.9860 Gold 0.4438 oz. AGW **Obv:** Arms of Cardinal Antonio Barberini **Rev:** Radiant and flaming dove in inner circle, ROMA in exergue **Note:** Sede Vacante issue.

Date	Mintage	VG	F	VF	XF	Unc
MDCLV (1655) Rare	—	—	—	—	—	—

KM# 286 QUADRUPLA (4) SCUDO D'ORO
14.0000 g., 0.9860 Gold 0.4438 oz. AGW **Obv:** Arms of Cardinal Antonio Barberini **Rev:** Radiant and flaming dove in inner circle, Without ROMA in exergue **Note:** Roman numeral date. Sede Vacante issue.

Date	Mintage	VG	F	VF	XF	Unc
MDCLV (1655) Rare	—	—	—	—	—	—

Note: Superior Pipito sale 12-87 XF realized $34,100

KM# 287 QUADRUPLA (4) SCUDO D'ORO
14.0000 g., 0.9860 Gold 0.4438 oz. AGW **Ruler:** Alexander VII **Obv:** Papal arms **Rev:** Chest with bags of coins inside

Date	Mintage	VG	F	VF	XF	Unc
ND Rare	—	—	—	—	—	—

KM# 288 QUADRUPLA (4) SCUDO D'ORO
14.0000 g., 0.9860 Gold 0.4438 oz. AGW **Ruler:** Clement IX **Obv:** Papal arms **Rev:** Madonna standing in inner circle

Date	Mintage	VG	F	VF	XF	Unc
ND Rare	—	—	—	—	—	—

KM# 324 QUADRUPLA (4) SCUDO D'ORO
14.0000 g., 0.9860 Gold 0.4438 oz. AGW **Obv:** Arms of Cardinal Antonio Barberini **Rev:** Radiant and flaming dove in inner circle, ROMA in exergue **Note:** Sede Vacante issue.

Date	Mintage	VG	F	VF	XF	Unc
MDCLXIX (1669) Rare	—	—	—	—	—	—

KM# 347 QUADRUPLA (4) SCUDO D'ORO
14.0000 g., 0.9860 Gold 0.4438 oz. AGW **Ruler:** Clement X **Obv:** Papal arms

Date	Mintage	VG	F	VF	XF	Unc
ND(1670-76) Rare	—	—	—	—	—	—

KM# 356 QUADRUPLA (4) SCUDO D'ORO
14.0000 g., 0.9860 Gold 0.4438 oz. AGW **Ruler:** Clement X **Obv:** Bust right **Rev:** King David seated right, playing harp

Date	Mintage	VG	F	VF	XF	Unc
MDCLXXIII (1673)-IIII Rare	—	—	—	—	—	—

KM# 394 QUADRUPLA (4) SCUDO D'ORO
14.0000 g., 0.9860 Gold 0.4438 oz. AGW **Ruler:** Innocent XI **Rev:** Madonna seated with child on throne

Date	Mintage	VG	F	VF	XF	Unc
ND(1676)-I Rare	—	—	—	—	—	—

KM# 395 QUADRUPLA (4) SCUDO D'ORO
14.0000 g., 0.9860 Gold 0.4438 oz. AGW **Ruler:** Innocent XI **Obv:** Bust of Innocent XI right **Rev:** Enthroned Madonna and child with SS. Lawrence and Augustine at left and SS. Stephen and Francis of Asisis at right

Date	Mintage	VG	F	VF	XF	Unc
ND(1676)-I Rare	—	—	—	—	—	—
ND(1677)-II Rare	—	—	—	—	—	—

KM# 404 QUADRUPLA (4) SCUDO D'ORO
14.0000 g., 0.9860 Gold 0.4438 oz. AGW **Ruler:** Innocent XI **Subject:** Immaculate Conception **Rev:** Radiant Madonna on clouds above rainbow

Date	Mintage	VG	F	VF	XF	Unc
ND(1678)-III Rare	—	—	—	—	—	—

KM# 425 QUADRUPLA (4) SCUDO D'ORO
14.0000 g., 0.9860 Gold 0.4438 oz. AGW **Ruler:** Innocent XI **Rev:** Inscription in cartouche **Rev. Inscription:** VBI / THESAVRVS / IBI COR

Date	Mintage	VG	F	VF	XF	Unc
ND(1681)-VI Rare	—	—	—	—	—	—

KM# 428 QUADRUPLA (4) SCUDO D'ORO
14.0000 g., 0.9860 Gold 0.4438 oz. AGW **Ruler:** Innocent XI **Rev:** Inscription and date in wreath

Date	Mintage	VG	F	VF	XF	Unc
ND(1682)-VII Rare	—	—	—	—	—	—
1685-X Rare	—	—	—	—	—	—

Note: Superior Pipito sale 12-87 AU realized $17,050

KM# 479 QUADRUPLA (4) SCUDO D'ORO
14.0000 g., 0.9860 Gold 0.4438 oz. AGW **Ruler:** Innocent XI **Obv:** Papal arms **Rev:** Date in cartouche

Date	Mintage	VG	F	VF	XF	Unc
1687-XII Rare	—	—	—	—	—	—

KM# 504 QUADRUPLA (4) SCUDO D'ORO
14.0000 g., 0.9860 Gold 0.4438 oz. AGW **Ruler:** Alexander VIII **Obv:** Bust right **Rev:** SS. Peter and Paul standing below radiant dove, date in exergue

Date	Mintage	VG	F	VF	XF	Unc
1689-I	—	2,200	4,400	8,400	14,000	—

KM# 503 QUADRUPLA (4) SCUDO D'ORO
14.0000 g., 0.9860 Gold 0.4438 oz. AGW **Obv:** Arms of Cardinal Paluzzo Paluzzi-Altieri **Rev:** Radiant and flaming dove, RO-MA divided below **Note:** Sede Vacante issue.

Date	Mintage	VG	F	VF	XF	Unc
MDCLXXXIX (1689) Rare	—	—	—	—	—	—

KM# A531 QUADRUPLA (4) SCUDO D'ORO
14.0000 g., 0.9860 Gold 0.4438 oz. AGW **Ruler:** Alexander VIII **Rev:** SS. Magnus and Bruno standing facing, date in exergue

Date	Mintage	VG	F	VF	XF	Unc
1690-II	—	2,200	4,400	8,400	14,000	—

KM# A532 QUADRUPLA (4) SCUDO D'ORO
14.0000 g., 0.9860 Gold 0.4438 oz. AGW **Ruler:** Innocent XII **Rev:** Two oxen right

Date	Mintage	VG	F	VF	XF	Unc
MDCXC (1690)-I	—	1,550	3,100	6,000	10,000	—

KM# A533 QUADRUPLA (4) SCUDO D'ORO
14.0000 g., 0.9860 Gold 0.4438 oz. AGW **Ruler:** Alexander VIII **Rev:** St. Bruno in clouds

Date	Mintage	VG	F	VF	XF	Unc
ND(1690)-I Rare	—	—	—	—	—	—

KM# 580 QUADRUPLA (4) SCUDO D'ORO
14.0000 g., 0.9860 Gold 0.4438 oz. AGW **Ruler:** Alexander VIII **Subject:** Papal aid to Venice **Obv:** Bust right **Rev:** Church standing with building and standard

Date	Mintage	VG	F	VF	XF	Unc
(MD)CXC (1690)-I Rare	—	—	—	—	—	—

KM# 617 QUADRUPLA (4) SCUDO D'ORO
14.0000 g., 0.9860 Gold 0.4438 oz. AGW **Ruler:** Innocent XII **Obv:** Bust right **Rev:** Fountain of Sancta Maria in Trastevere, divided date in exergue

Date	Mintage	VG	F	VF	XF	Unc
1694-IIII	—	2,400	4,700	9,000	15,000	—

PATTERNS

Including off metal strikes

KM#	Date	Mintage	Identification	Mkt Val
Pn1	NDYr. III	—	Baiocco. Bi-Metallic. Arms. Veronica's veil.	—

PAPAL CITY STATES

The 21 Papal City States spanned the Papal states from one end to the other. Most of the cities had been the holy see for hundreds of years. Many of them housed religious architecture and relics that were a veritable history of the church. Many had strong local families that helped administrate the city and occasionally opposed the Papal authority. Most of these cities stayed in the Papal states until 1860 when Papal territories began to crumble due to the move for unification of all Italy.

MINTS

17 of the mints functioned only during the Napoleonic period.

1. Ancona
2. Ascoli
3. Bologna
4. Civitavecchia
5. Fano
6. Fermo
7. Ferrara
8. Foligno
9. Gubbio
10. Macerata
11. Matelica
12. Montaito
13. Pergola
14. Perugia
15. Ravenna
16. Ronciglione
17. San Severino
18. Spoleto
19. Terni
20. Tivoli
21. Viterbo

EXTRINSIC MINT

Avignon (Southern France)

PONTIFFS

Refer to Papal States.

MONETARY SYSTEM

6 Quattrini = 1 Bolognino or Baiocco
5 Baiocchi = 1 Grossi
2 Grossi = 1 Giuli = 1 Paoli
3 Giulio = 3 Paoli = 1 Testone
10 Giulio = 10 Paoli = 1 Scudo
3 Scudi = 1 Doppia

PAPAL STATES-AVIGNON

A commercial and manufacturing city located in southeastern France, near the confluence of the Rhone and Durance rivers. Leading industries are chemicals, leather products and soap. It is the sight of an ancient cathedral and papal palace.

Founded as Phocaean colony; later conquered by the Romans, Goths, Burgundians, Ostrogoths, and finally the Franks. Part of kingdom of Arles it became a republic in 1135-46. Later as part of Venaissin it was sold by Joanna I of Naples to Pope Clement VI 1348. It became the seat of the papacy from 1309-77 and of the Avignonese popes during Western Schism from 1378-1417; remaining in the possession of the popes until finally being annexed to France in 1791.

RULER

Papal, until 1791

CITY

STANDARD COINAGE

KM# 1 PATARD
Billon **Subject:** Clement VIII **Obv:** Crossed keys **Rev:** Cross in quadrilobe **Rev. Legend:** S • PETRVS • ET • PAVLVS • AVEN:

Date	Mintage	Good	VG	F	VF	XF
1601	—	15.00	25.00	40.00	65.00	—
1602	—	15.00	25.00	40.00	65.00	—
1603	—	15.00	25.00	40.00	65.00	—
ND	—	15.00	25.00	40.00	65.00	—

KM# 21 PATARD
Billon **Subject:** Paul V **Obv:** Crossed keys **Rev:** Cross in quadrilobe

Date	Mintage	Good	VG	F	VF	XF
1614	—	15.00	25.00	40.00	65.00	—
ND	—	15.00	25.00	40.00	65.00	—

KM# 30 PATARD
Billon **Subject:** Gregory XV **Obv:** Crossed keys **Rev:** Cross in quadrilobe

Date	Mintage	Good	VG	F	VF	XF
1621	—	20.00	32.00	50.00	80.00	—
1622	—	20.00	32.00	50.00	80.00	—

KM# 41 PATARD
Billon **Subject:** Urban VIII **Obv:** Crossed keys **Rev:** Cross in quadrilobe

Date	Mintage	Good	VG	F	VF	XF
ND	—	15.00	25.00	40.00	65.00	—

KM# 67 PATARD
Billon **Subject:** Innocent X **Obv:** Crossed keys, fleur-de-lis above **Rev:** Cross in quadrilobe

Date	Mintage	Good	VG	F	VF	XF
ND	—	15.00	25.00	40.00	65.00	—

KM# 73 PATARD
Billon **Obv:** Crossed keys without fleur-de-lis

Date	Mintage	Good	VG	F	VF	XF
ND Rare	—	—	—	—	—	—

KM# 86 PATARD
Billon **Subject:** Alexander VII **Obv:** Crossed keys **Rev:** Cross in quadrilobe

Date	Mintage	Good	VG	F	VF	XF
ND	—	15.00	25.00	40.00	65.00	—

KM# 53 DOUBLE TOURNOIS
Copper **Obv:** Bust of Urban VIII right **Rev:** Three bees

Date	Mintage	Good	VG	F	VF	XF
1635	—	10.00	20.00	30.00	50.00	—
1636	—	10.00	20.00	30.00	50.00	—
1637	—	10.00	20.00	30.00	50.00	—
1638	—	10.00	20.00	30.00	50.00	—
1639	—	10.00	20.00	30.00	50.00	—
1640	—	10.00	20.00	30.00	50.00	—
ND	—	10.00	20.00	30.00	50.00	—

KM# 42 LIARD
Billon **Subject:** Urban VIII **Obv:** Tiara above V among three bees **Rev:** Maltese cross

Date	Mintage	Good	VG	F	VF	XF
ND	—	6.00	12.00	22.00	40.00	—

KM# 43 LIARD
Billon **Obv:** Tiara above M among three bees

Date	Mintage	Good	VG	F	VF	XF
ND	—	6.00	12.00	22.00	40.00	—

KM# 2 DOUZAIN
Billon **Subject:** Clement VIII **Obv:** Cross surmounted by tiara, A at sides **Rev:** Cross with eagles in angles

Date	Mintage	Good	VG	F	VF	XF
1601	—	27.50	45.00	75.00	125	—
1602	—	27.50	45.00	75.00	125	—
1603	—	27.50	45.00	75.00	125	—
ND	—	27.50	45.00	75.00	125	—

KM# 3 DOUZAIN
Billon **Note:** Similar to KM#2 but without A at sides.

Date	Mintage	Good	VG	F	VF	XF
1601 Rare	—	—	—	—	—	—
1602 Rare	—	—	—	—	—	—
1603 Rare	—	—	—	—	—	—
ND Rare	—	—	—	—	—	—

KM# 11 DOUZAIN
Billon **Subject:** Paul V **Obv:** Arms surmounted by tiara, A's flanking **Rev:** Cross, eagles, and dragons in angles **Rev. Legend:** SCIPIO BURGHESIVS CARD LEG AVEN

Date	Mintage	Good	VG	F	VF	XF
1609 Rare	—	—	—	—	—	—
1610 Rare	—	—	—	—	—	—
1611 Rare	—	—	—	—	—	—
1612 Rare	—	—	—	—	—	—
ND Rare	—	—	—	—	—	—

KM# 22 DOUZAIN

Billon **Obv:** Arms surmounted by tiara **Rev:** Cross, eagles, and oaks in angles **Rev. Legend:** PHI • S • R • E • CARD • PHILONARDVS • P • LEG • AVEN

Date	Mintage	Good	VG	F	VF	XF
1614 Rare	—	—	—	—	—	—

KM# 45 DOUZAIN

Billon **Subject:** Urban VIII **Obv:** Shield surmounted by tiara **Rev:** Floral cross, bee in angle **Rev. Legend:** FRANC • CARD...

Date	Mintage	Good	VG	F	VF	XF
1624 Rare	—	—	—	—	—	—
1625 Rare	—	—	—	—	—	—

KM# 51 DOUZAIN

Billon **Obv:** A's flanking shield

Date	Mintage	Good	VG	F	VF	XF
1632 Rare	—	—	—	—	—	—
1633 Rare	—	—	—	—	—	—

KM# 54 DOUZAIN

Billon **Obv:** Shield surmounted by tiara **Rev:** Floral cross **Rev. Legend:** ANTONIV. S CAR...

Date	Mintage	Good	VG	F	VF	XF
1635 Rare	—	—	—	—	—	—

KM# 44 JULES (Barberino)

Silver **Subject:** Uban VIII **Obv:** Arms **Rev:** Half-length figure of St. Peter

Date	Mintage	Good	VG	F	VF	XF
1623	—	20.00	40.00	65.00	100	—
1624	—	20.00	40.00	65.00	100	—
1625	—	20.00	40.00	65.00	100	—
1626	—	20.00	40.00	65.00	100	—
1627	—	20.00	40.00	65.00	100	—
1628	—	20.00	40.00	65.00	100	—
1629	—	20.00	40.00	65.00	100	—
1630	—	20.00	40.00	65.00	100	—
1631	—	20.00	40.00	65.00	100	—
1632	—	20.00	40.00	65.00	100	—
1633	—	20.00	40.00	65.00	100	—
1634	—	20.00	40.00	65.00	100	—
1635	—	20.00	40.00	65.00	100	—
1636	—	20.00	40.00	65.00	100	—
1637	—	20.00	40.00	65.00	100	—

KM# 4 1/3 FRANC (1/8 Piastre)

Silver **Obv:** Bust of Clement VIII right **Rev:** Shield

Date	Mintage	Good	VG	F	VF	XF
1601 Unique	—	—	—	—	—	—

KM# 88 LUIGINO

Silver **Obv:** Bust of Alexander VII right **Rev:** Shield **Rev. Legend:** FLAVIVS CARD GHISIVS LEGATVS

Date	Mintage	VG	F	VF	XF	Unc
1658	—	105	210	500	800	—

KM# 91 LUIGINO

Silver **Obv:** Bust right with different shield on shoulder

Date	Mintage	VG	F	VF	XF	Unc
1659	—	105	210	500	800	—
1660	—	105	210	500	800	—

KM# 92 LUIGINO

Silver **Rev:** Crowned shield **Rev. Legend:** PAX • ORIETVR • EX • MONTIBVS

Date	Mintage	VG	F	VF	XF	Unc
1660	—	105	210	500	800	—
1661	—	105	210	500	800	—
1662	—	105	210	500	800	—
1663	—	105	210	500	800	—
1664	—	105	210	500	800	—
1665	—	105	210	500	800	—
1666	—	105	210	500	800	—

KM# 94 LUIGINO

Silver **Rev:** Shield as octalobe **Rev. Legend:** EXUMONTIBVS PAX ORIETVR

Date	Mintage	VG	F	VF	XF	Unc
1662	—	75.00	150	350	725	—
1663	—	75.00	150	350	725	—
1664	—	75.00	150	350	725	—
1665	—	75.00	150	350	725	—

KM# 96 LUIGINO

Silver **Obv:** Bust right with different shield on shoulder

Date	Mintage	VG	F	VF	XF	Unc
1666	—	85.00	170	350	550	—

KM# 99 LUIGINO

Silver **Obv:** Bust of Cardinal Chigi **Obv. Legend:** FLAVIVS • CAR • GHISIVS • LE • A • **Rev:** Crowned shield **Rev. Legend:** AB • STELLA • LVX • ORITVR •

Date	Mintage	VG	F	VF	XF	Unc
1666	—	85.00	170	350	550	—
1667	—	85.00	170	350	550	—

KM# 100 LUIGINO

Silver **Rev:** Crowned shield **Rev. Legend:** PAX • MONTIBVS • EX • MONTIBVS

Date	Mintage	VG	F	VF	XF	Unc
1666 Rare	—	—	—	—	—	—

KM# 14 1/4 FRANC

Silver **Obv:** Bust of Paul V right **Rev:** Floral cross **Rev. Legend:** SCIPIO • BVRGHESIVS • CARD • LEG • AVEN

Date	Mintage	Good	VG	F	VF	XF
1611	—	180	300	650	1,000	—
161Z	—	180	300	650	1,000	—
1613	—	180	300	650	1,000	—

KM# 56 1/4 FRANC

Silver **Obv:** Bust of Urban VIII right **Rev:** Floral cross

Date	Mintage	Good	VG	F	VF	XF
1636 Rare	—	—	—	—	—	—

KM# 8 1/2 FRANC

Silver **Obv:** Bust of Paul V right **Rev:** Shield of cardinal **Rev. Legend:** SCIPIO • BVRGHESIVS • CARD • LEG • AVEN

Date	Mintage	Good	VG	F	VF	XF
1608	—	100	180	400	750	—
1609	—	100	180	400	750	—
1610	—	100	180	400	750	—
1611	—	100	180	400	750	—
1612	—	100	180	400	750	—
1613	—	100	180	400	750	—

KM# 12 1/2 FRANC

Silver **Obv:** Bust of Paul V right **Rev:** Floral cross

Date	Mintage	Good	VG	F	VF	XF
1609	—	100	180	400	750	—
1617/XIII	—	100	180	400	750	—
1618/XIII	—	100	180	400	750	—
ND(1618)/XIII	—	100	180	400	750	—

KM# 16 1/2 FRANC

Silver **Obv:** Bust of Paul V left **Rev:** Floral cross **Rev. Legend:** PHILIP • PHILONARD • CARD • P.LEG • AVEN

Date	Mintage	Good	VG	F	VF	XF
1612 Rare	—	—	—	—	—	—

KM# 31 1/2 FRANC

Silver **Obv:** Bust of Gregory XV right **Rev:** Floral cross

Date	Mintage	Good	VG	F	VF	XF
1621 Rare	—	—	—	—	—	—

KM# 57 1/2 FRANC

Silver **Obv:** Bust of Urban VIII right **Rev:** Floral cross

Date	Mintage	Good	VG	F	VF	XF
1636	—	125	300	800	2,000	—
1637	—	125	300	800	2,000	—
1638	—	125	300	800	2,000	—
1639	—	125	300	800	2,000	—
1640	—	125	300	800	2,000	—

KM# 61 1/2 FRANC

Silver **Obv:** Bust of Urban VIII right **Rev:** Floral cross, V at center

Date	Mintage	Good	VG	F	VF	XF
1641 Rare	—	—	—	—	—	—
1642 Rare	—	—	—	—	—	—

KM# 87 CARLIN

Silver **Subject:** Alexander VII **Obv:** Arms **Rev:** Half-length figure of St. Peter above arms

Date	Mintage	Good	VG	F	VF	XF
1656	—	25.00	45.00	75.00	125	—
1657	—	25.00	45.00	75.00	125	—
1658	—	25.00	45.00	75.00	125	—
1659	—	25.00	45.00	75.00	125	—
1660	—	25.00	45.00	75.00	125	—
1661	—	25.00	45.00	75.00	125	—
1662	—	25.00	45.00	75.00	125	—

KM# 5 TESTONE

Silver **Obv:** Bust of Clement VIII right **Rev:** Shield

Date	Mintage	Good	VG	F	VF	XF
1601	—	190	325	500	825	—

KM# 9 TESTONE

Silver **Obv:** Bust of Paul V right, arms below **Rev:** Arms

Date	Mintage	Good	VG	F	VF	XF
1608	—	350	650	1,100	1,700	—

KM# 13 TESTONE

Silver **Rev:** Floral cross, different from mintmark below

Date	Mintage	Good	VG	F	VF	XF
1610	—	400	750	1,250	2,000	—

KM# 17 TESTONE

Silver **Rev:** View of Avignon **Rev. Legend:** AVENIO 1612

Date	Mintage	Good	VG	F	VF	XF
1612 Rare	—	—	—	—	—	—

KM# 18 TESTONE
Silver **Rev. Legend:** PHILIP PHILONARD CARD P. LEG AVEN.

Date	Mintage	Good	VG	F	VF	XF
1612 Rare	—	—	—	—	—	—
1613 Rare	—	—	—	—	—	—

KM# 20 TESTONE
Silver **Rev. Legend:** PHI • S • R • E • CARD • PHILONARDVS P. LEG AVEN 1613

Date	Mintage	Good	VG	F	VF	XF
1613 Unique	—	—	—	—	—	—

KM# 24 TESTONE
Silver **Rev. Legend:** SCIPIO • BVRGHESIVS • CARD • LEG • AVEN

Date	Mintage	Good	VG	F	VF	XF
1617 Rare	—	—	—	—	—	—
1618 Rare	—	—	—	—	—	—
ND(1618)/XIII Rare	—	—	—	—	—	—

KM# 48 TESTONE
Silver **Obv:** Bust of Urban VIII right **Rev:** Shield

Date	Mintage	VG	F	VF	XF	Unc
1629	—	105	205	375	625	—
1630	—	105	205	375	625	—
1631	—	105	205	375	625	—
1632	—	105	205	375	625	—
1633	—	105	205	375	625	—
1634	—	105	205	375	625	—

KM# 49 TESTONE
Silver **Obv:** Bust of Urban VIII right **Rev:** Shield

Date	Mintage	VG	F	VF	XF	Unc
1631	—	120	225	400	650	—

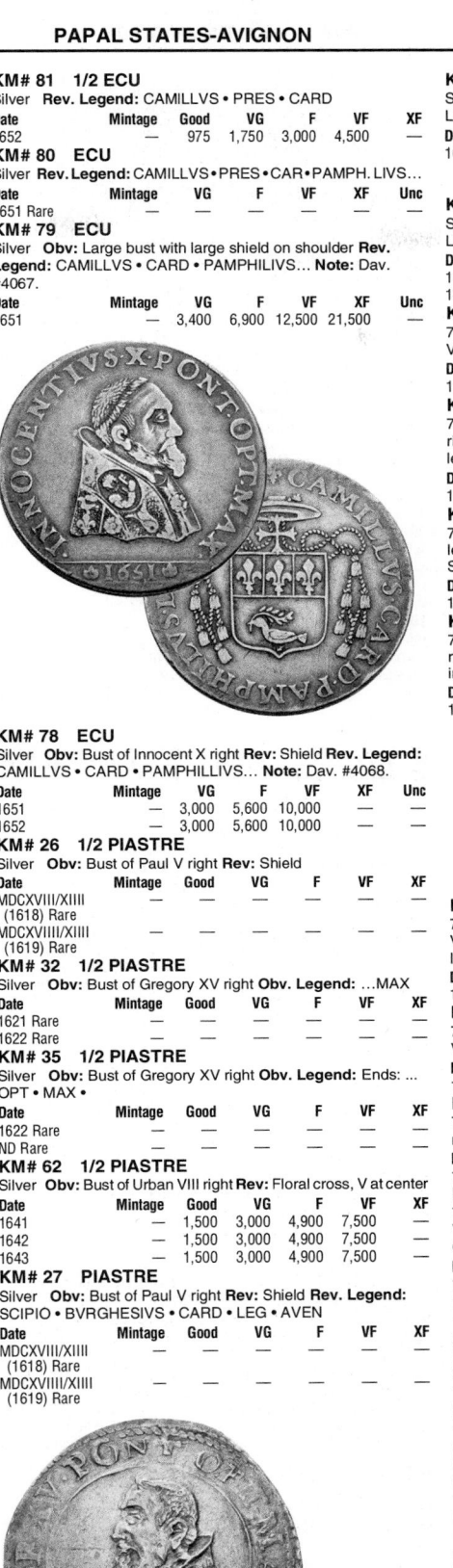

KM# 105 1/12 ECU
Silver **Obv:** Bust of Innocent XII capped right with shield on shoulder **Rev:** Shield **Rev. Legend:** PETRVS • CARD • OTTHOBONVS • LEGAT

Date	Mintage	VG	F	VF	XF	Unc
1692/II	—	75.00	150	350	575	—
1693/II	—	75.00	150	350	575	—

KM# 106 1/12 ECU
Silver **Obv:** Bust of Innocent XII capped right with shield on shoulder **Rev:** Mirrored PCL monogram

Date	Mintage	VG	F	VF	XF	Unc
1692/II C	—	70.00	140	250	400	—

KM# 107 1/12 ECU
Silver **Obv:** Bust of Innocent XII capped right with shield on shoulder **Rev:** Papal arms

Date	Mintage	VG	F	VF	XF	Unc
1693/II	—	60.00	120	200	325	—

KM# 68 1/2 ECU
Silver **Obv:** Bust of Innocent X right **Rev:** Floral cross

Date	Mintage	Good	VG	F	VF	XF
1645 Rare	—	—	—	—	—	—

Note: Numismatica Ars Classica Auction 44, 11-07, XF realized approximately $28,195

Date	Mintage	Good	VG	F	VF	XF
1646 Rare	—	—	—	—	—	—
1647 Rare	—	—	—	—	—	—

KM# 77 1/2 ECU
Silver **Obv:** Bust right with different shield at shoulder **Rev. Legend:** CAMILLVS • CARD...

Date	Mintage	Good	VG	F	VF	XF
1651	—	700	1,200	2,050	3,050	—

KM# 81 1/2 ECU
Silver **Rev. Legend:** CAMILLVS • PRES • CARD

Date	Mintage	Good	VG	F	VF	XF
1652	—	975	1,750	3,000	4,500	—

KM# 80 ECU
Silver **Rev. Legend:** CAMILLVS•PRES•CAR•PAMPH. LIVS...

Date	Mintage	VG	F	VF	XF	Unc
1651 Rare	—	—	—	—	—	—

KM# 79 ECU
Silver **Obv:** Large bust with large shield on shoulder **Rev. Legend:** CAMILLVS • CARD • PAMPHILIVS... **Note:** Dav. #4067.

Date	Mintage	VG	F	VF	XF	Unc
1651	—	3,400	6,900	12,500	21,500	—

KM# 78 ECU
Silver **Obv:** Bust of Innocent X right **Rev:** Shield **Rev. Legend:** CAMILLVS • CARD • PAMPHILLIVS... **Note:** Dav. #4068.

Date	Mintage	VG	F	VF	XF	Unc
1651	—	3,000	5,600	10,000	—	—
1652	—	3,000	5,600	10,000	—	—

KM# 26 1/2 PIASTRE
Silver **Obv:** Bust of Paul V right **Rev:** Shield

Date	Mintage	Good	VG	F	VF	XF
MDCXVIII/XIIII (1618) Rare	—	—	—	—	—	—
MDCXVIIII/XIIII (1619) Rare	—	—	—	—	—	—

KM# 32 1/2 PIASTRE
Silver **Obv:** Bust of Gregory XV right **Obv. Legend:** ...MAX

Date	Mintage	Good	VG	F	VF	XF
1621 Rare	—	—	—	—	—	—
1622 Rare	—	—	—	—	—	—

KM# 35 1/2 PIASTRE
Silver **Obv:** Bust of Gregory XV right **Obv. Legend:** Ends: ... OPT • MAX •

Date	Mintage	Good	VG	F	VF	XF
1622 Rare	—	—	—	—	—	—
ND Rare	—	—	—	—	—	—

KM# 62 1/2 PIASTRE
Silver **Obv:** Bust of Urban VIII right **Rev:** Floral cross, V at center

Date	Mintage	Good	VG	F	VF	XF
1641	—	1,500	3,000	4,900	7,500	—
1642	—	1,500	3,000	4,900	7,500	—
1643	—	1,500	3,000	4,900	7,500	—

KM# 27 PIASTRE
Silver **Obv:** Bust of Paul V right **Rev:** Shield **Rev. Legend:** SCIPIO • BVRGHESIVS • CARD • LEG • AVEN

Date	Mintage	Good	VG	F	VF	XF
MDCXVIII/XIIII (1618) Rare	—	—	—	—	—	—
MDCXVIIII/XIIII (1619) Rare	—	—	—	—	—	—

KM# 33 PIASTRE
Silver **Obv:** Bust of Gregory XV left **Rev. Legend:** LVD CARD LVDOVISIVS LEGATVS AVEN **Note:** Dav. #4052.

Date	Mintage	Good	VG	F	VF	XF
1621 Unique	—	—	—	—	—	—

Note: Numismatica Ars Classica Auction 44, 11-07, near XF realized approximately $54,905

KM# 34 PIASTRE
Silver **Obv:** Bust of Gregory XV right **Rev. Legend:** ...CAMER. LEG. AVEN. **Note:** Dav. #4053.

Date	Mintage	Good	VG	F	VF	XF
1621 Rare	—	—	—	—	—	—
1622 Rare	—	—	—	—	—	—

KM# 6 DOPPIA
7.0000 g., 0.9860 Gold 0.2219 oz. AGW **Obv:** Bust of Clement VIII right **Rev:** Shield

Date	Mintage	VG	F	VF	XF	Unc
1602	—	2,200	3,600	9,000	12,000	—

KM# 10 DOPPIA
7.0000 g., 0.9860 Gold 0.2219 oz. AGW **Obv:** Bust of Paul V right in inner circle, date in legend **Rev:** Arms, legend of Papal legate, Scipio Borghese

Date	Mintage	VG	F	VF	XF	Unc
1608	—	1,000	1,900	6,000	9,000	—

KM# 23 DOPPIA
7.0000 g., 0.9860 Gold 0.2219 oz. AGW **Obv:** Bust of Paul V left in inner circle, date in legend **Rev:** Legend of Papal legate, Scipio Borghese

Date	Mintage	VG	F	VF	XF	Unc
1614 Rare	—	—	—	—	—	—

KM# 25 DOPPIA
7.0000 g., 0.9860 Gold 0.2219 oz. AGW **Obv:** Bust of Paul V right, shield in inner circle, date below **Rev:** Floreate cross in inner circle

Date	Mintage	VG	F	VF	XF	Unc
1617/XIII Rare	—	—	—	—	—	—

KM# 59 DOPPIA
7.0000 g., 0.9860 Gold 0.2219 oz. AGW **Obv:** Bust of Urban VIII right in inner circle, date in legend **Rev:** Arms, legend of Papal legate, Antonio Barberini

Date	Mintage	VG	F	VF	XF	Unc
1639	—	1,600	3,100	5,700	9,500	—

KM# 60 DOPPIA
7.0000 g., 0.9860 Gold 0.2219 oz. AGW **Obv:** Bust of Urban VIII right in inner circle, date below

Date	Mintage	VG	F	VF	XF	Unc
1640 Rare	—	—	—	—	—	—

KM# 69 DOPPIA
7.0000 g., 0.9860 Gold 0.2219 oz. AGW **Obv:** Bust of Innocent X right in inner circle **Rev:** Arms, legend of Papal legate, Lorenzo Corsi

Date	Mintage	VG	F	VF	XF	Unc
1644	—	4,000	7,000	12,000	20,000	—

KM# 70 DOPPIA
7.0000 g., 0.9860 Gold 0.2219 oz. AGW **Obv:** Bust of Alexander VII right in inner circle **Rev:** Arms, legend of Papal legate, Fabio Chigi

Date	Mintage	VG	F	VF	XF	Unc
1664	—	1,000	2,000	3,700	6,000	—

KM# 15 QUADRUPLA
14.0000 g., 0.9860 Gold 0.4438 oz. AGW **Obv:** Bust of Paul V right in inner circle, date in legend **Rev:** Arms, legend of Papal legate, Scipio Borghese

Date	Mintage	VG	F	VF	XF	Unc
1611 Unique	—	—	—	—	—	—

KM# 19 QUADRUPLA
14.0000 g., 0.9860 Gold 0.4438 oz. AGW **Obv:** Bust of Paul V right, date below **Rev:** Arms, legend of Papal legate, Philip Filonardi

Date	Mintage	VG	F	VF	XF	Unc
1612 Rare	—	—	—	—	—	—

KM# 28 QUADRUPLA
14.0000 g., 0.9860 Gold 0.4438 oz. AGW **Rev:** Floriate cross in inner circle

Date	Mintage	VG	F	VF	XF	Unc
1618/XIII	—	2,250	4,500	7,000	11,500	—

KM# 46 QUADRUPLA
14.0000 g., 0.9860 Gold 0.4438 oz. AGW **Obv:** Bust of Urban VIII right in inner circle, date in legend **Rev:** Arms, legend of Papal legate, Francis Barberini

Date	Mintage	VG	F	VF	XF	Unc
1624	—	2,250	4,500	7,000	11,500	—
1628	—	2,250	4,500	7,000	11,500	—
1629	—	2,250	4,500	7,000	11,500	—
1631	—	2,250	4,500	7,000	11,500	—
1632	—	2,250	4,500	7,000	11,500	—

KM# 47 QUADRUPLA
14.0000 g., 0.9860 Gold 0.4438 oz. AGW **Rev:** Arms, legend of Papal legate, Cosimo Bardi

Date	Mintage	VG	F	VF	XF	Unc
1626 Rare	—	—	—	—	—	—

KM# 50 QUADRUPLA

14.0000 g., 0.9860 Gold 0.4438 oz. AGW **Obv:** Bust of Urban VIII right **Rev. Legend:** FRANCIVCVS CAR. BARBERINVS...

Date	Mintage	VG	F	VF	XF	Unc
1631 Rare	—	—	—	—	—	—
1632 Rare	—	—	—	—	—	—

KM# 52 QUADRUPLA

14.0000 g., 0.9860 Gold 0.4438 oz. AGW **Obv:** Bust of Urban VIII right in inner circle, date in exergue **Rev:** Arms, legend of Papal legate, Antonio Barberini

Date	Mintage	VG	F	VF	XF	Unc
1634 Unique	—	—	—	—	—	—

KM# 55 QUADRUPLA

14.0000 g., 0.9860 Gold 0.4438 oz. AGW **Obv:** Bust of Urban VIII right in inner circle, date in legend

Date	Mintage	VG	F	VF	XF	Unc
1635 Rare	—	—	—	—	—	—
1636 Rare	—	—	—	—	—	—

KM# 58 QUADRUPLA

14.0000 g., 0.9860 Gold 0.4438 oz. AGW **Obv:** Different shield on bust

Date	Mintage	VG	F	VF	XF	Unc
1637	—	1,750	3,250	5,000	8,000	—
1638	—	1,750	3,250	5,000	8,000	—
1639	—	1,750	3,250	5,000	8,000	—
1640	—	1,750	3,250	5,000	8,000	—
1641	—	1,750	3,250	5,000	8,000	—
1642	—	1,750	3,250	5,000	8,000	—
1643	—	1,750	3,250	5,000	8,000	—
1644	—	1,750	3,250	5,000	8,000	—

KM# 71 QUADRUPLA

14.0000 g., 0.9860 Gold 0.4438 oz. AGW **Obv:** Bust of Innocent X right in inner circle, date in legend **Rev:** Legend of Papal legate, Antonio Barberini

Date	Mintage	VG	F	VF	XF	Unc
1644	—	1,500	2,500	4,400	7,500	—

KM# 72 QUADRUPLA

14.0000 g., 0.9860 Gold 0.4438 oz. AGW **Obv:** Tall bust of Innocent X right in inner circle, date in legend **Rev:** Arms, legend of Papal legate, Camillo Pamphilj

Date	Mintage	VG	F	VF	XF	Unc
1644	—	1,500	2,500	4,400	7,500	—

KM# 74 QUADRUPLA

14.0000 g., 0.9860 Gold 0.4438 oz. AGW **Obv:** Different shield on shoulder

Date	Mintage	VG	F	VF	XF	Unc
1645 Rare	—	—	—	—	—	—
1646 Rare	—	—	—	—	—	—
1647 Rare	—	—	—	—	—	—

KM# 75 QUADRUPLA

14.0000 g., 0.9860 Gold 0.4438 oz. AGW **Rev:** Shield on Maltese cross

Date	Mintage	VG	F	VF	XF	Unc
1645 Rare	—	—	—	—	—	—
1646 Rare	—	—	—	—	—	—

KM# 76 QUADRUPLA

14.0000 g., 0.9860 Gold 0.4438 oz. AGW **Obv:** Large bust of Innocent X right in inner circle, date in legend **Rev:** Arms, legend of Papal legate, Lorenzo Corsi

Date	Mintage	VG	F	VF	XF	Unc
1647 Unique	—	—	—	—	—	—

KM# 89 QUADRUPLA

14.0000 g., 0.9860 Gold 0.4438 oz. AGW **Rev:** Papal arms **Rev. Legend:** PONTIFICATVS-SVI-ANNO. II. 1657.

Date	Mintage	VG	F	VF	XF	Unc
1657 Rare	—	—	—	—	—	—

KM# 90 QUADRUPLA

14.0000 g., 0.9860 Gold 0.4438 oz. AGW **Obv:** Bust of Alexander VII right in inner circle **Rev:** Arms, legend of Papal legate, Fabio Chigi

Date	Mintage	VG	F	VF	XF	Unc
1658	—	2,050	3,750	6,000	10,000	—
1659 Rare	—	—	—	—	—	—
1662	—	2,050	3,750	6,000	10,000	—

KM# 95 QUADRUPLA

14.0000 g., 0.9860 Gold 0.4438 oz. AGW **Obv:** Different shield on shoulder

Date	Mintage	VG	F	VF	XF	Unc
1665 Rare	—	—	—	—	—	—

KM# 36 OCTUPLE

28.0000 g., 0.9860 Gold 0.8876 oz. AGW **Obv:** Bust of Gregory XV **Rev. Legend:** LVD. CARD. LVDOVISIVS...

Date	Mintage	VG	F	VF	XF	Unc
1622 Rare	—	—	—	—	—	—

PAPAL STATES-BOLOGNA

(Bolonia)

A city in Emilia, began as an independent commune, and after serving under various masters became a papal possession in 1506. Except for the Napoleonic period (1797-1815) and the revolutions of 1821 and 1831, it remained a papal state until 1860.

MINT OFFICIALS' INITIALS

Initial	Date	Name
BP	1644-76	Bartolomeo Provagli
CF	1700-21	Carlo Falconi
GB	1700-21	Girolamo Bevilacqua
GCG	1691-1700	Giovan Carlo Gualchierl
LS	1623-44	Ludovico Salvatici

MINT MARK

B – Bologna

MONETARY SYSTEM

(Until 1777)

6 Quattrini = 1 Bolognino
12 Bolognini = 1 Giulio = 1 Bianco
80 to 108 Bolognini = 1 Scudo

CITY

STANDARD COINAGE

KM# 5 QUATTRINO

Copper **Subject:** Clement VIII **Obv:** Crowned lion ramant left with banner **Rev:** BONO/NIA/DOCET

Date	Mintage	Good	VG	F	VF	XF
1604	—	16.00	25.00	40.00	75.00	—

KM# 13 QUATTRINO

Copper **Subject:** Paul V **Obv:** Lion rampant left with banner **Rev:** BONO INIA/DOCET

Date	Mintage	Good	VG	F	VF	XF
1607	—	8.00	12.50	22.00	40.00	—
1608	—	8.00	12.50	22.00	40.00	—
1609	—	8.00	12.50	22.00	40.00	—
1610	—	8.00	12.50	22.00	40.00	—
1611	—	8.00	12.50	22.00	40.00	—
1612	—	8.00	12.50	22.00	40.00	—
1613	—	8.00	12.50	22.00	40.00	—
1614	—	8.00	12.50	22.00	40.00	—
1615	—	8.00	12.50	22.00	40.00	—
1616	—	8.00	12.50	22.00	40.00	—
1617	—	8.00	12.50	22.00	40.00	—
1618	—	8.00	12.50	22.00	40.00	—
1619	—	8.00	12.50	22.00	40.00	—
1620	—	8.00	12.50	22.00	40.00	—

KM# 30 QUATTRINO

Copper **Subject:** Gregory XV **Obv:** Lion rampant left with banner **Rev:** BONO/NIA/DOCET

Date	Mintage	Good	VG	F	VF	XF
1621	—	10.00	16.50	25.00	45.00	—
1622	—	10.00	16.50	25.00	45.00	—

KM# 32 QUATTRINO

Copper **Subject:** Urban VII **Obv:** Lion rampant left with banner **Rev:** BONO/NIA/DOCET

Date	Mintage	Good	VG	F	VF	XF
1624	—	8.00	12.50	22.00	40.00	—
1625	—	8.00	12.50	22.00	40.00	—
1626	—	8.00	12.50	22.00	40.00	—
1627	—	8.00	12.50	22.00	40.00	—
1628	—	8.00	12.50	22.00	40.00	—
1629	—	8.00	12.50	22.00	40.00	—
1630	—	8.00	12.50	22.00	40.00	—
1631	—	8.00	12.50	22.00	40.00	—
1632	—	8.00	12.50	22.00	40.00	—
1633	—	8.00	12.50	22.00	40.00	—
1634	—	8.00	12.50	22.00	40.00	—
1635	—	8.00	12.50	22.00	40.00	—
1636	—	8.00	12.50	22.00	40.00	—
1637	—	8.00	12.50	22.00	40.00	—
1638	—	8.00	12.50	22.00	40.00	—
1639	—	8.00	12.50	22.00	40.00	—
1640	—	8.00	12.50	22.00	40.00	—
1641	—	8.00	12.50	22.00	40.00	—
1642	—	8.00	12.50	22.00	40.00	—

KM# 40 QUATTRINO

Copper **Subject:** Innocent X **Obv:** Lion rampant left with banner **Rev. Inscription:** BONO / NIA / DOCET

Date	Mintage	Good	VG	F	VF	XF
1646	—	6.00	17.50	22.00	40.00	—
1647	—	6.00	17.50	22.00	40.00	—
1648	—	6.00	17.50	22.00	40.00	—
1649	—	6.00	17.50	22.00	40.00	—

KM# 67 QUATTRINO

Copper **Subject:** Alexander VII **Obv:** Lion rampant left with banner **Rev. Inscription:** BONO / NIA / DOCET

Date	Mintage	VG	F	VF	XF	Unc
1663	—	10.00	18.00	32.00	60.00	—
1664	—	10.00	18.00	32.00	60.00	—
1665	—	10.00	18.00	32.00	60.00	—
1666	—	10.00	18.00	32.00	60.00	—
1667	—	10.00	18.00	32.00	60.00	—

KM# 75 QUATTRINO

Copper **Subject:** Clement IX **Obv:** Lion rampant left with banner **Rev. Inscription:** BONO / NIA / DOCET

Date	Mintage	VG	F	VF	XF	Unc
1668	—	12.00	20.00	35.00	65.00	—
1669	—	12.00	20.00	35.00	65.00	—

KM# 88 QUATTRINO

Copper **Subject:** Clement X **Obv:** Lion rampant left with banner **Rev. Inscription:** BONO / NIA / DOCET

Date	Mintage	VG	F	VF	XF	Unc
1676	—	10.00	18.00	32.00	60.00	—

KM# 90 QUATTRINO

Copper **Subject:** Innocent XI **Obv:** Lion rampant left with banner **Rev. Inscription:** BONO / NIA / DOCET

Date	Mintage	VG	F	VF	XF	Unc
1677	—	10.00	18.00	32.00	65.00	—
1678	—	10.00	18.00	32.00	65.00	—
1679	—	10.00	18.00	32.00	65.00	—
1680	—	10.00	18.00	32.00	65.00	—
1681	—	10.00	18.00	32.00	65.00	—
1682	—	10.00	18.00	32.00	65.00	—
1683	—	10.00	18.00	32.00	65.00	—
1684	—	10.00	18.00	32.00	65.00	—
1685	—	10.00	18.00	32.00	65.00	—
1686	—	10.00	18.00	32.00	65.00	—
1687	—	10.00	18.00	32.00	65.00	—
1688	—	10.00	18.00	32.00	65.00	—
1689	—	10.00	18.00	32.00	65.00	—

KM# 110 QUATTRINO

Copper **Subject:** Alexander VIII **Obv:** Lion rampant left with banner **Rev. Inscription:** BONO / NIA / DOCET

Date	Mintage	VG	F	VF	XF	Unc
1690	—	9.00	16.00	27.50	50.00	—

KM# 114 QUATTRINO

Copper **Subject:** Innocent XII **Obv:** Lion rampant left with banner showing cross **Rev. Inscription:** BONO / NIA / DOCET

Date	Mintage	VG	F	VF	XF	Unc
1691	—	9.00	16.00	27.50	50.00	—
1692	—	9.00	16.00	27.50	50.00	—
1693	—	9.00	16.00	27.50	50.00	—
1694	—	9.00	16.00	27.50	50.00	—
1695	—	9.00	16.00	27.50	50.00	—
1696	—	9.00	16.00	27.50	50.00	—
1697	—	9.00	16.00	27.50	50.00	—
1698	—	9.00	16.00	27.50	50.00	—
1699	—	9.00	16.00	27.50	50.00	—
1700	—	9.00	16.00	27.50	50.00	—

KM# 120 QUATTRINO

Copper **Obv:** Lion rampant left with banner showing LIBER

Date	Mintage	VG	F	VF	XF	Unc
1692	—	9.00	16.00	27.50	50.00	—
1693	—	9.00	16.00	27.50	50.00	—
1694	—	9.00	16.00	27.50	50.00	—
1695	—	9.00	16.00	27.50	50.00	—
1696	—	9.00	16.00	27.50	50.00	—
1697	—	9.00	16.00	27.50	50.00	—
1698	—	9.00	16.00	27.50	50.00	—
1699	—	9.00	16.00	27.50	50.00	—
1700	—	9.00	16.00	27.50	50.00	—

KM# 130 QUATTRINO

Copper **Obv:** Shield below canopy and keys **Rev. Inscription:** LI / BER / TAS **Note:** Sede Vacante issue.

Date	Mintage	VG	F	VF	XF	Unc
ND(1700)	—	40.00	75.00	140	195	—

KM# 20 1/2 BOLOGNINO

Copper **Subject:** Paul V **Obv:** Shield **Obv. Legend:** BONONIA DOCET **Rev:** Half lion rampant left above legend in cartouche **Rev. Legend:** MEZO BOLOGNINO

Date	Mintage	Good	VG	F	VF	XF
MDCXII (1612)	—	12.50	20.00	32.00	60.00	—
MDCXIII (1613)	—	12.50	20.00	32.00	60.00	—
MDCIIII (1614)	—	12.50	20.00	32.00	60.00	—
MDCXV (1615)	—	12.50	20.00	32.00	60.00	—
MDCXVI (1616)	—	12.50	20.00	32.00	60.00	—
MDCXVII (1617)	—	12.50	20.00	32.00	60.00	—
MDCXVIII (1618)	—	12.50	20.00	32.00	60.00	—
MDCXVIIII (1619)	—	12.50	20.00	32.00	60.00	—
MDCXX (1620)	—	12.50	20.00	32.00	60.00	—

KM# 31 1/2 BOLOGNINO

Copper **Subject:** Gregory XV **Obv:** Shield **Obv. Legend:** BONONIA DOCET **Rev:** Half lion rampant left **Rev. Legend:** MEZO BOLOGNINO

Date	Mintage	Good	VG	F	VF	XF
MDCXXI (1621)	—	20.00	32.00	50.00	80.00	—
MDCXXII (1622)	—	20.00	32.00	50.00	80.00	—

KM# 33 1/2 BOLOGNINO

Copper **Subject:** Urban VIII **Obv:** Shield, BONONIA DOCET **Rev:** MEZO BOLOGNINO, half lion rampant left

Date	Mintage	Good	VG	F	VF	XF
1624	—	10.00	18.00	32.00	65.00	—
1625	—	10.00	18.00	32.00	65.00	—
1626	—	10.00	18.00	32.00	65.00	—
1627	—	10.00	18.00	32.00	65.00	—
1628	—	10.00	18.00	32.00	65.00	—
1629	—	10.00	18.00	32.00	65.00	—
1630	—	10.00	18.00	32.00	65.00	—
1631	—	10.00	18.00	32.00	65.00	—

KM# 41 1/2 BOLOGNINO

Copper **Subject:** Innocent X **Obv:** Shield, BONONIA DOCET **Rev:** MEZO BOLOGNINO, half lion rampant left

Date	Mintage	Good	VG	F	VF	XF
1647	—	9.00	16.00	27.50	55.00	—
1648	—	9.00	16.00	27.50	55.00	—
1649	—	9.00	16.00	27.50	55.00	—

KM# 95 1/2 BOLOGNINO

Copper **Subject:** Innocent XI **Obv:** BONONIA DOCET, shield **Rev:** MEZO BOLOGNINO, half lion rampant left

Date	Mintage	VG	F	VF	XF	Unc
1680	—	14.00	25.00	40.00	70.00	—
1681	—	14.00	25.00	40.00	70.00	—
1682	—	14.00	25.00	40.00	70.00	—
1683	—	14.00	25.00	40.00	70.00	—
1684	—	14.00	25.00	40.00	70.00	—
1685	—	14.00	25.00	40.00	70.00	—
1686	—	14.00	25.00	40.00	70.00	—
1687	—	14.00	25.00	40.00	70.00	—
1688	—	14.00	25.00	40.00	70.00	—
1689	—	14.00	25.00	40.00	70.00	—

KM# 111 1/2 BOLOGNINO

Copper **Subject:** Alexander VIII **Obv:** BONONIA DOCET and shield **Rev:** MEZO BOLOGNINO, half lion rampant left

Date	Mintage	VG	F	VF	XF	Unc
1690	—	14.00	25.00	40.00	70.00	—
ND	—	14.00	25.00	40.00	70.00	—

KM# 115 1/2 BOLOGNINO

Copper **Subject:** Innocent XII **Obv:** Shield, BONONIA DOCET **Rev:** MEZO BOLOGNINO, half lion rampant left

Date	Mintage	VG	F	VF	XF	Unc
1691	—	14.00	25.00	40.00	70.00	—
1692	—	14.00	25.00	40.00	70.00	—
1693	—	14.00	25.00	40.00	70.00	—
1694	—	14.00	25.00	40.00	70.00	—
1695	—	14.00	25.00	40.00	70.00	—
1696	—	14.00	25.00	40.00	70.00	—
1697	—	14.00	25.00	40.00	70.00	—
1698	—	14.00	25.00	40.00	70.00	—
1699	—	14.00	25.00	40.00	70.00	—

KM# 121 1/2 BOLOGNINO

Copper **Obv:** Different shield

Date	Mintage	VG	F	VF	XF	Unc
1692	—	16.50	30.00	50.00	80.00	—

KM# 127 1/2 BOLOGNINO

Copper **Obv:** SENAT • POP • QVE • BONONIE, shield below canopy and keys **Rev:** LI/BER/TAS **Note:** Sede Vacante issue.

Date	Mintage	VG	F	VF	XF	Unc
ND	—	50.00	85.00	165	250	—

KM# 132 BOLOGNINO

Billon **Subject:** Clement XI **Obv:** BONONIA MATER, lion rampant left with banner **Rev:** STVDIORVM, crossed keys

Date	Mintage	VG	F	VF	XF	Unc
ND	—	10.00	20.00	40.00	70.00	—

KM# 131 BOLOGNINO

Billon **Obv:** SENAT • POP • QVE • BONONIE, shield below canopy and keys **Rev:** LI/BER/TAS **Note:** Sede Vacante issue.

Date	Mintage	VG	F	VF	XF	Unc
ND(1700)	—	35.00	60.00	120	210	—

KM# 42 2 BOLOGNINI

Billon **Obv:** Bust of Innocent X right **Rev:** St. Petronius standing

Date	Mintage	Good	VG	F	VF	XF
1647	—	14.00	28.00	45.00	75.00	—
1648	—	14.00	28.00	45.00	75.00	—
1649	—	14.00	28.00	45.00	75.00	—

KM# 49 2 BOLOGNINI

Billon **Obv:** Bust of Alexander VII right

Date	Mintage	Good	VG	F	VF	XF
ND	—	7.00	15.00	25.00	45.00	—

KM# 71 2 BOLOGNINI

Billon **Obv:** Capped bust of Clement IX right

Date	Mintage	Good	VG	F	VF	XF
ND(1667-69)	—	30.00	60.00	120	180	—

KM# 80 2 BOLOGNINI

Billon **Obv:** Bust of Clement X right

Date	Mintage	Good	VG	F	VF	XF
ND(1670-76)	—	12.00	25.00	42.00	75.00	—

KM# 89 2 BOLOGNINI

Billon **Obv:** Bust of Innocent XI right

Date	Mintage	VG	F	VF	XF	Unc
ND(1676-89)	—	10.00	20.00	36.00	70.00	—

KM# 104 2 BOLOGNINI

Billon **Obv:** Bust of Alexander VIII right

Date	Mintage	VG	F	VF	XF	Unc
ND(1689-91)	—	10.00	22.00	45.00	80.00	—

KM# 117 2 BOLOGNINI

Billon **Obv:** Bust of Innocent XII right

Date	Mintage	VG	F	VF	XF	Unc
ND(1691-1700)	—	12.00	25.00	60.00	120	—

KM# 116 2 BOLOGNINI

Billon **Obv:** Two shields below canopy and keys **Note:** Sede Vacante issue.

Date	Mintage	VG	F	VF	XF	Unc
ND(1691)	—	15.00	30.00	75.00	150	—

KM# 133 2 BOLOGNINI

Billon **Obv:** Two shields below canopy and keys **Note:** Sede Vacante issue.

Date	Mintage	VG	F	VF	XF	Unc
1700	—	20.00	35.00	65.00	120	—

KM# 6 2-1/2 BOLOGNIA (1/2 Carlino)

Billon **Subject:** Paul V **Obv:** Arms **Rev:** BONO/NIA/DOCET within wreath

Date	Mintage	Good	VG	F	VF	XF
ND	—	28.00	50.00	85.00	140	—

KM# 7 2-1/2 BOLOGNIA (1/2 Carlino)

Billon **Obv:** Bust of St. Petronius **Rev:** BONO / NIA / DOCET

Date	Mintage	Good	VG	F	VF	XF
ND	—	22.00	40.00	70.00	120	—

KM# 8 5 BOLOGNINI (Carlino)

Silver **Subject:** Paul V **Obv:** Arms **Rev:** Madonna with child **Rev. Legend:** PRAE SIDIVM ET DECVS

Date	Mintage	Good	VG	F	VF	XF
ND	—	35.00	70.00	120	185	—

KM# 9 5 BOLOGNINI (Carlino)

Silver **Obv:** Shield **Obv. Legend:** BONONIA DOCET

Date	Mintage	Good	VG	F	VF	XF
ND	—	27.00	50.00	85.00	140	—

KM# 10 5 BOLOGNINI (Carlino)

Silver **Obv:** Shield **Obv. Legend:** BONONIA • DOCET **Rev:** Bust of Madonna with child

Date	Mintage	Good	VG	F	VF	XF
ND	—	18.00	35.00	55.00	110	—

KM# 81 5 BOLOGNINI (Carlino)

Silver **Subject:** Clement X **Rev:** Half-length figure of Madonna with child

Date	Mintage	Good	VG	F	VF	XF
1671	—	16.50	32.50	55.00	110	—
1672	—	16.50	32.50	55.00	110	—
1673	—	16.50	32.50	55.00	110	—
1674	—	16.50	32.50	55.00	110	—
1675	—	16.50	32.50	55.00	110	—
1676	—	16.50	32.50	55.00	110	—

KM# 91 5 BOLOGNINI (Carlino)

Silver **Subject:** Innocent XI

Date	Mintage	Good	VG	F	VF	XF
1677	—	16.50	32.50	55.00	110	—
1678	—	16.50	32.50	55.00	110	—
1679	—	16.50	32.50	55.00	110	—
1680	—	16.50	32.50	55.00	110	—
1681	—	16.50	32.50	55.00	110	—
1682	—	16.50	32.50	55.00	110	—
1683	—	16.50	32.50	55.00	110	—
1684	—	16.50	32.50	55.00	110	—
1685	—	16.50	32.50	55.00	110	—
1686	—	16.50	32.50	55.00	110	—
1687	—	16.50	32.50	55.00	110	—
1688	—	16.50	32.50	55.00	110	—
1689	—	16.50	32.50	55.00	110	—

KM# 112 5 BOLOGNINI (Carlino)

Silver **Subject:** Alexander VII

Date	Mintage	Good	VG	F	VF	XF
1690	—	18.00	35.00	55.00	110	—

KM# 122 5 BOLOGNINI (Carlino)

Silver **Subject:** Innocent XII

Date	Mintage	Good	VG	F	VF	XF
1692	—	18.00	35.00	55.00	110	—

KM# 11 8 BOLOGNINI (Giulio)

Silver **Obv:** Bust of Paul V left **Rev:** Shield **Rev. Legend:** BONONIA DOCET

Date	Mintage	Good	VG	F	VF	XF
ND	—	50.00	85.00	160	295	—

KM# 12 8 BOLOGNINI (Giulio)

Silver **Obv:** Inscription in quadrilobe **Obv. Inscription:** BO/NONIA/DO/CET **Rev:** St. Petronius enthroned

Date	Mintage	Good	VG	F	VF	XF
ND Rare	—	—	—	—	—	—

KM# 22 10 BOLOGNINI (Bianca)

Silver **Obv:** Bust of Paul V left **Rev:** Lion rampant left, holding banner, Paul on shield

Date	Mintage	Good	VG	F	VF	XF
1615	—	65.00	120	220	400	—
1616	—	65.00	120	220	400	—
1617	—	65.00	120	220	400	—
1618	—	65.00	120	220	400	—
1619	—	65.00	120	220	400	—

KM# 23 10 BOLOGNINI (Bianca)

Silver **Obv:** Bust of St. Petronius

Date	Mintage	Good	VG	F	VF	XF
1615	—	40.00	70.00	125	230	—

KM# 24 10 BOLOGNINI (Bianca)

Silver **Obv:** Half-length figure of St. Petronius **Rev:** Lion rampant left, holding banner

Date	Mintage	Good	VG	F	VF	XF
ND	—	40.00	70.00	125	230	—

KM# 35 10 BOLOGNINI (Bianca)

Silver **Obv:** Bust of Urban VIII right **Rev:** Shield **Rev. Legend:** BONONIA DOCET

Date	Mintage	Good	VG	F	VF	XF
MDCXXV (1625)	—	45.00	85.00	160	295	—

KM# 50 10 BOLOGNINI (Bianca)

Silver **Subject:** Alexander VII **Obv:** Arms **Rev:** Bust of Madonna with child, shields at side

Date	Mintage	Good	VG	F	VF	XF
ND	—	55.00	100	180	325	—

KM# 51 10 BOLOGNINI (Bianca)

Silver **Rev:** Different shields

Date	Mintage	Good	VG	F	VF	XF
ND	—	55.00	100	180	325	—

KM# 98 10 BOLOGNINI (Bianca)

Silver **Obv:** Bust of Innocent XI right **Rev:** Lion rampant left with banner **Rev. Legend:** BONONIA DOCET MATER STVD

Date	Mintage	Good	VG	F	VF	XF
1686	—	45.00	75.00	140	260	—

KM# 99 10 BOLOGNINI (Bianca)

Silver **Obv:** Capped bust right

Date	Mintage	Good	VG	F	VF	XF
1686	—	45.00	75.00	140	260	—

KM# 21 20 BOLOGNINI (Lira)

Silver **Subject:** Paul V **Obv:** Felsina standing with pennant **Rev:** St. Petronius enthroned

Date	Mintage	Good	VG	F	VF	XF
MDCXIIII (1614)	—	55.00	100	180	325	—
MDCXV (1615)	—	55.00	100	180	325	—

KM# 25 20 BOLOGNINI (Lira)

Silver **Obv:** Arms, BOL/XX

Date	Mintage	Good	VG	F	VF	XF
MDCXV (1615)	—	45.00	85.00	160	295	—
MDCXIX (1619)	—	45.00	85.00	160	295	—

KM# 45 20 BOLOGNINI (Lira)

Silver **Subject:** Innocent X **Obv:** St. Petronius enthroned **Rev:** Lion rampant left

Date	Mintage	Good	VG	F	VF	XF
1650 Rare	—	—	—	—	—	—

KM# 52 20 BOLOGNINI (Lira)

Silver **Subject:** Alexander VII **Obv:** Arms **Rev:** Lion rampant left, two shields **Rev. Legend:** BONONIA DOCET

Date	Mintage	Good	VG	F	VF	XF
1655	—	60.00	115	200	300	—
1656	—	60.00	115	200	300	—
1657	—	60.00	115	200	300	—
1658	—	60.00	115	200	300	—

KM# 56 20 BOLOGNINI (Lira)

Silver **Rev:** Different shields

Date	Mintage	Good	VG	F	VF	XF
1658	—	60.00	115	200	300	—
1659	—	60.00	115	200	300	—
1660	—	60.00	115	200	300	—
1661	—	60.00	115	200	300	—

KM# 65 20 BOLOGNINI (Lira)

Silver **Rev:** Different shields

Date	Mintage	Good	VG	F	VF	XF
1662	—	60.00	115	200	300	—
1663	—	60.00	115	200	300	—
1664	—	60.00	115	200	300	—
1665	—	60.00	115	200	300	—

KM# 68 20 BOLOGNINI (Lira)

Silver **Rev:** Different shields

Date	Mintage	Good	VG	F	VF	XF
1665	—	60.00	115	200	300	—
1666	—	60.00	115	200	300	—

KM# 73 20 BOLOGNINI (Lira)

Silver **Subject:** Clement IX **Obv:** Arms **Rev:** St. Petronius standing

Date	Mintage	Good	VG	F	VF	XF
1667 Rare	—	—	—	—	—	—

KM# 72 20 BOLOGNINI (Lira)

Silver **Obv:** Two shields below canopy and keys **Rev:** St. Petronius kneeling left, XX in exergue **Note:** Sede Vacante issue.

Date	Mintage	Good	VG	F	VF	XF
1667	—	80.00	145	270	500	—

KM# 82 20 BOLOGNINI (Lira)

Silver **Subject:** Clement X **Obv:** Arms, shields at sides **Rev:** Lion rampant left with banner

Date	Mintage	VG	F	VF	XF	Unc
1671	—	60.00	120	220	425	—
1672	—	60.00	120	220	425	—
1673	—	60.00	120	220	425	—

KM# 84 20 BOLOGNINI (Lira)

Silver **Obv:** Different shields

Date	Mintage	VG	F	VF	XF	Unc
1673	—	60.00	120	220	425	—
1674	—	60.00	120	220	425	—

KM# 96 20 BOLOGNINI (Lira)

Silver **Subject:** Innocent XI **Obv:** Arms with shields at sides **Rev:** Rampant lion with banner left **Rev. Legend:** BONONIA DOCET

Date	Mintage	VG	F	VF	XF	Unc
1682	—	60.00	120	220	425	—
1683	—	60.00	120	220	425	—

KM# 100 20 BOLOGNINI (Lira)

Silver **Obv:** Arms with different shields at sides

Date	Mintage	VG	F	VF	XF	Unc
1686	—	60.00	120	220	425	—
1687	—	60.00	120	220	425	—

KM# 105 20 BOLOGNINI (Lira)

Silver **Obv:** Arms with different shields at sides

Date	Mintage	VG	F	VF	XF	Unc
1689	—	85.00	150	275	550	—

KM# 106 20 BOLOGNINI (Lira)

Silver **Subject:** Alexander VIII **Obv:** Arms, shields at sides **Rev:** Rampant lion with banner left

Date	Mintage	VG	F	VF	XF	Unc
1689	—	75.00	135	250	500	—
1690	—	75.00	135	250	500	—

KM# 118 20 BOLOGNINI (Lira)

Silver **Obv:** Two shields below canopy and keys **Rev:** St. Petronius kneeling left

Date	Mintage	VG	F	VF	XF	Unc
1691	—	75.00	135	250	500	—

KM# 123 20 BOLOGNINI (Lira)

Silver **Subject:** Innocent XII **Obv:** Arms, two shields at sides **Rev:** Rampant lion wtih banner left

Date	Mintage	VG	F	VF	XF	Unc
1692	—	60.00	120	220	425	—
ND	—	60.00	120	220	425	—

KM# 124 20 BOLOGNINI (Lira)

Silver **Obv:** Arms, two different shields at sides

Date	Mintage	VG	F	VF	XF	Unc
ND	—	60.00	120	220	425	—

KM# 134 20 BOLOGNINI (Lira)

Silver **Obv:** Two shields below canopy and keys **Rev:** St. Petronius kneeling left **Note:** Sede Vacante issue.

Date	Mintage	VG	F	VF	XF	Unc
1700 Unique	—	—	—	—	—	—

KM# 101 24 BOLOGNINI

Silver **Subject:** Innocent XI **Obv:** Arms, shields at sides **Rev:** St. Petronius enthroned

Date	Mintage	VG	F	VF	XF	Unc
1686	—	50.00	100	195	375	—
1687	—	50.00	100	195	375	—

KM# 107 24 BOLOGNINI

Silver **Obv:** Arms, three different shields at sides

Date	Mintage	VG	F	VF	XF	Unc
1689	—	65.00	125	250	500	—

KM# 34 26 BOLOGNINI (Gabellone)

12.0560 g., Silver **Obv:** Bust of Urban VIII right **Rev:** Shield **Rev. Legend:** BONONIA DOCET

Date	Mintage	Good	VG	F	VF	XF
1624	—	220	350	750	1,500	—
1625	—	220	350	750	1,500	—

KM# 26 30 BOLOGNINI (Testone)

Silver **Obv:** Bust of Paul V left **Rev:** Shield **Rev. Legend:** BONONIA DOCET

Date	Mintage	Good	VG	F	VF	XF
MDCXV (1615)	—	200	325	700	1,350	—

KM# 97 30 BOLOGNINI (Testone)

Silver **Obv:** Bust of Innocent XI right **Rev:** Radiant cross, shields **Rev. Legend:** BONONIA DOCET

Date	Mintage	VG	F	VF	XF	Unc
1683	—	50.00	100	220	425	—

KM# 102 30 BOLOGNINI (Testone)

Silver **Obv:** Capped bust of Paul V right

Date	Mintage	VG	F	VF	XF	Unc
1686	—	60.00	120	250	500	—

KM# 119 30 BOLOGNINI (Testone)

Silver **Obv:** Capped bust of Innocent XII right **Rev:** Shield **Rev. Legend:** BONONIA DOCET

Date	Mintage	VG	F	VF	XF	Unc
ND	—	60.00	120	250	500	—

KM# 85 40 BOLOGNINI (1/2 Scudo - 2 Lire)

Silver **Subject:** Clement X **Obv:** Arms **Rev:** Floral cross, two shields **Rev. Legend:** BONONIA DOCET

Date	Mintage	VG	F	VF	XF	Unc
1673	—	205	375	625	1,250	—

KM# 86 40 BOLOGNINI (1/2 Scudo - 2 Lire)

Silver **Rev:** Different shields

Date	Mintage	VG	F	VF	XF	Unc
1673	—	205	375	625	1,250	—
1674	—	205	375	625	1,250	—
1675	—	205	375	625	1,250	—

KM# 113 40 BOLOGNINI (1/2 Scudo - 2 Lire)
Silver **Subject:** Alexander VIII **Rev:** Floral cross, two shields **Rev. Legend:** BONONIA DOCET

Date	Mintage	VG	F	VF	XF	Unc
1690 Rare	—	—	—	—	—	—

KM# 125 40 BOLOGNINI (1/2 Scudo - 2 Lire)
Silver **Subject:** Innocent XII

Date	Mintage	VG	F	VF	XF	Unc
1692 Rare	—	—	—	—	—	—

KM# 83 80 BOLOGNIA (4 Lire - Scudo)
Silver **Subject:** Clement X **Obv:** Arms **Rev:** Floral cross, shields **Rev. Legend:** BONONIA DOCET **Note:** Dav. #4082.

Date	Mintage	VG	F	VF	XF	Unc
1671	—	2,000	4,000	7,000	—	—
1672	—	2,000	4,000	7,000	—	—
1673	—	2,000	4,000	7,000	—	—

KM# 87 80 BOLOGNIA (4 Lire - Scudo)
Silver **Rev:** Different shields **Note:** Dav. #4083.

Date	Mintage	VG	F	VF	XF	Unc
1673	—	2,000	4,000	7,000	—	—
1674	—	2,000	4,000	7,000	—	—

KM# 103 80 BOLOGNIA (4 Lire - Scudo)
Silver **Subject:** Innocent XI **Rev:** Radiant cross **Rev. Legend:** BONONIA DOCET **Note:** Dav. #4097.

Date	Mintage	VG	F	VF	XF	Unc
1687	—	—	—	—	—	—
ND Rare	—	—	—	—	—	—

KM# 126 80 BOLOGNIA (4 Lire - Scudo)
Silver **Subject:** Innocent XII **Rev:** Floral cross, two shields **Rev. Legend:** BONONIA DOCET **Note:** Dav. #4111.

Date	Mintage	VG	F	VF	XF	Unc
1692 Rare	—	—	—	—	—	—

KM# 46 SCUDO D'ORO
3.5000 g., 0.9860 Gold 0.1109 oz. AGW **Subject:** Innocent X **Obv:** Papal arms divide date **Rev:** Floriate cross with two small shields at bottom

Date	Mintage	VG	F	VF	XF	Unc
1654 Rare	—	—	—	—	—	—

KM# 53 SCUDO D'ORO
3.5000 g., 0.9860 Gold 0.1109 oz. AGW **Obv:** Papal arms **Rev:** Floriate cross divides date, two small shields at bottom

Date	Mintage	VG	F	VF	XF	Unc
1655	—	1,100	2,200	4,200	7,200	—
1656	—	1,100	2,200	4,200	7,200	—
1657	—	1,100	2,200	4,200	7,200	—
1658	—	1,100	2,200	4,200	7,200	—

KM# 57 SCUDO D'ORO
3.5000 g., 0.9860 Gold 0.1109 oz. AGW **Rev:** Different shields

Date	Mintage	VG	F	VF	XF	Unc
1658	—	1,100	2,200	4,200	7,200	—
1659	—	1,100	2,200	4,200	7,200	—
1660	—	1,100	2,200	4,200	7,200	—
1661	—	1,100	2,200	4,200	7,200	—
1662	—	1,100	2,200	4,200	7,200	—

KM# 66 SCUDO D'ORO
3.5000 g., 0.9860 Gold 0.1109 oz. AGW **Rev:** Different shields

Date	Mintage	VG	F	VF	XF	Unc
1662	—	1,100	2,200	4,200	7,200	—
1663	—	1,100	2,200	4,200	7,200	—
1664	—	1,100	2,200	4,200	7,200	—

KM# 70 SCUDO D'ORO
3.5000 g., 0.9860 Gold 0.1109 oz. AGW **Rev:** Different shields **Note:** Varieties exist.

Date	Mintage	VG	F	VF	XF	Unc
1666	—	1,100	2,200	4,200	7,200	—

KM# 47 DOPPIA D'ORO
7.0000 g., 0.9860 Gold 0.2219 oz. AGW **Subject:** Innocent X **Obv:** Papal arms **Rev:** Floriate cross with two small shields at bottom

Date	Mintage	VG	F	VF	XF	Unc
1654 Rare	—	—	—	—	—	—

KM# 54 DOPPIA D'ORO
7.0000 g., 0.9860 Gold 0.2219 oz. AGW **Subject:** Alexander VII **Obv:** Papal arms **Rev:** Floriate arms divide date, two small shields at bottom

Date	Mintage	VG	F	VF	XF	Unc
1655	—	1,100	2,200	4,200	7,200	—
1656	—	1,100	2,200	4,200	7,200	—
1657	—	1,100	2,200	4,200	7,200	—
1658	—	1,100	2,200	4,200	7,200	—

KM# 58 DOPPIA D'ORO
7.0000 g., 0.9860 Gold 0.2219 oz. AGW **Rev:** Different shields

Date	Mintage	VG	F	VF	XF	Unc
1658	—	1,100	2,200	4,200	7,200	—
1659	—	1,100	2,200	4,200	7,200	—
1660	—	1,100	2,200	4,200	7,200	—
1661	—	1,100	2,200	4,200	7,200	—

KM# 69 DOPPIA D'ORO
7.0000 g., 0.9860 Gold 0.2219 oz. AGW

Date	Mintage	VG	F	VF	XF	Unc
1665	—	1,100	2,200	4,200	7,200	—
1666	—	1,100	2,200	4,200	7,200	—

KM# 48 4 DOPPIE D'ORO (Quadrupla)
14.0000 g., 0.9860 Gold 0.4438 oz. AGW **Subject:** Innocent X **Obv:** Papal arms divide date **Rev:** Floriate cross, two small shields at bottom

Date	Mintage	VG	F	VF	XF	Unc
1654 Rare	—	—	—	—	—	—

KM# 55 QUADRUPLA (4 Scudi D'oro)
14.0000 g., 0.9860 Gold 0.4438 oz. AGW **Subject:** Alexander VII **Obv:** Papal arms in inner circle **Rev:** Floriate cross divides date, two small shields at bottom **Note:** Varieties exist.

Date	Mintage	VG	F	VF	XF	Unc
1655	—	2,000	5,000	7,500	15,000	—
1656	—	2,000	5,000	7,500	15,000	—
1657	—	2,000	5,000	7,500	15,000	—

KM# 59 QUADRUPLA (4 Scudi D'oro)
14.0000 g., 0.9860 Gold 0.4438 oz. AGW **Rev:** Two different small shields at bottom

Date	Mintage	VG	F	VF	XF	Unc
1659	—	2,000	5,000	7,500	15,000	—
1660	—	2,000	5,000	7,500	15,000	—
1661	—	2,000	5,000	7,500	15,000	—

KM# 74 QUADRUPLA (4 Scudi D'oro)
14.0000 g., 0.9860 Gold 0.4438 oz. AGW **Subject:** Clement IX **Obv:** Papal arms in inner circle **Rev:** Floriate cross divides arms, two small shields at bottom

Date	Mintage	VG	F	VF	XF	Unc
1667 Rare	—	—	—	—	—	—

PAPAL STATES-FERRARA

A city located in northeastern Italy in Emalia. With the Papacy 1598-1859.

MINT OFFICIALS' INITIALS

Initial	Date	Name
FR	1605-21	Nicolo Franchini and Agostino Rivarola
NF	1621-23	Nicolo Franchini
TA, TAB, (TA)B	1621-44	Tommaso and Agostino Bellegrandi

CITY

STANDARD COINAGE

KM# 5 QUATTRINO
Copper **Subject:** Paul V **Obv:** Arms **Rev:** FERRARI

Date	Mintage	Good	VG	F	VF	XF
ND	—	13.50	22.50	40.00	80.00	—

KM# 6 QUATTRINO
Copper **Rev:** FER / RARI / Æ

Date	Mintage	Good	VG	F	VF	XF
ND	—	13.50	22.50	40.00	80.00	—

KM# 7 QUATTRINO
Copper **Obv:** Capped bust of Pual V left, PP in legend **Rev:** St. George slaying dragon **Rev. Legend:** FERRARIAE • PROTECTOR

Date	Mintage	Good	VG	F	VF	XF
ND	—	15.00	25.00	38.00	70.00	—
VIII/1614	—	15.00	25.00	30.00	70.00	—

KM# 15 QUATTRINO
Copper **Obv:** Legend without • PP •

Date	Mintage	Good	VG	F	VF	XF
1612	—	15.00	25.00	38.00	70.00	—
1613	—	15.00	25.00	38.00	70.00	—

KM# 16 QUATTRINO
Copper **Rev. Legend:** • PROTECTCTOR • FERRARIAE

Date	Mintage	Good	VG	F	VF	XF
1613	—	15.00	25.00	38.00	70.00	—
ND	—	15.00	25.00	38.00	70.00	—

KM# 17 QUATTRINO
Copper **Rev. Legend:** S • GEOR • PROT • FERRARIAE

Date	Mintage	Good	VG	F	VF	XF
1613	—	15.00	25.00	38.00	70.00	—

KM# 18 QUATTRINO
Copper **Obv:** Legend without • PP •

Date	Mintage	Good	VG	F	VF	XF
1613	—	15.00	26.00	40.00	75.00	—

KM# 40 QUATTRINO
Copper **Subject:** Gregory XV **Obv:** Arms **Rev. Inscription:** FER / RARI / 1622

Date	Mintage	Good	VG	F	VF	XF
1622	—	15.00	26.00	40.00	75.00	—

KM# 42 QUATTRINO
Copper **Obv:** Bust right **Rev:** FER/RARI/date

Date	Mintage	Good	VG	F	VF	XF
1622	—	35.00	55.00	85.00	135	—
1623	—	35.00	55.00	85.00	135	—

KM# 41 QUATTRINO
Copper **Rev:** FER/RARI within wreath

Date	Mintage	Good	VG	F	VF	XF
ND	—	15.00	26.00	40.00	75.00	—

KM# 46 QUATTRINO
Copper **Obv:** Arms of Cardinal **Rev:** CIVITAS • FERRARIAE • 1623 **Note:** Sede Vacante Issue.

Date	Mintage	Good	VG	F	VF	XF
1623	—	70.00	115	175	275	—

KM# 47 QUATTRINO
Copper **Obv:** Capped bust of Urban VIII right **Rev:** St. George slaying dragon

Date	Mintage	Good	VG	F	VF	XF
1623	—	13.50	22.50	35.00	65.00	—

KM# 60 QUATTRINO
Copper **Obv:** Arms **Rev:** Within wreath **Rev. Inscription:** FER / RARI / Æ

Date	Mintage	Good	VG	F	VF	XF
1636	—	9.00	15.00	22.00	50.00	100
ND	—	9.00	15.00	22.00	50.00	100

KM# 65 QUATTRINO

Copper **Subject:** Innocent X **Obv:** Arms, A • X **Rev. Inscription:** FER / RARI

Date	Mintage	Good	VG	F	VF	XF
ND	—	10.00	16.50	25.00	55.00	—

KM# 78 QUATTRINO

Copper **Rev:** Fer/RARIAE/date within wreath

Date	Mintage	Good	VG	F	VF	XF
1655	—	6.50	13.50	25.00	50.00	—
1656	—	6.50	13.50	25.00	50.00	—

KM# 79 QUATTRINO

Copper **Rev:** St. George slaying dragon

Date	Mintage	Good	VG	F	VF	XF
1655	—	6.50	13.50	25.00	50.00	—

KM# 76 QUATTRINO

Copper **Obv:** Arms of Cardinal **Rev:** FER/RARI within wreath **Note:** Sede Vacante Issue.

Date	Mintage	Good	VG	F	VF	XF
1655	—	60.00	100	150	250	—

KM# 77 QUATTRINO

Copper **Subject:** Alexander VII **Obv:** Arms

Date	Mintage	VG	F	VF	XF	Unc
ND Unique	—	—	—	—	—	—

KM# 91 QUATTRINO

Copper **Subject:** Clement X **Rev:** FER/RARI

Date	Mintage	Good	VG	F	VF	XF
1675	—	6.50	13.50	25.00	45.00	—
1676	—	6.50	13.50	25.00	45.00	—

KM# 92 QUATTRINO

Copper **Rev:** FER/RARI within wreath

Date	Mintage	Good	VG	F	VF	XF
1675	—	6.50	13.50	25.00	45.00	—

KM# 93 QUATTRINO

Copper **Rev:** Wreath

Date	Mintage	Good	VG	F	VF	XF
1675	—	6.50	13.50	25.00	45.00	—
1676	—	6.50	13.50	25.00	45.00	—

KM# 95 QUATTRINO

Copper **Obv:** Arms of Cardinal **Rev:** FER/RARI/1676 **Note:** Sede Vacante Issue.

Date	Mintage	Good	VG	F	VF	XF
1676	—	13.50	27.50	50.00	90.00	—

KM# 98 QUATTRINO

Copper **Obv:** FER/RARI/1677 **Rev:** St. George slaying dragon

Date	Mintage	Good	VG	F	VF	XF
1677	—	6.50	13.50	25.00	50.00	—

KM# 33 1/2 BAIOCCO

Copper **Subject:** Gregory XV **Obv:** Arms **Rev:** FER/RARI/1621 within wreath

Date	Mintage	Good	VG	F	VF	XF
1621	—	22.50	40.00	60.00	95.00	—

KM# 43 1/2 BAIOCCO

Copper **Rev:** FER/RARI/date without wreath

Date	Mintage	Good	VG	F	VF	XF
1622	—	22.50	40.00	60.00	100	—
1623	—	22.50	40.00	60.00	100	—

KM# 49 1/2 BAIOCCO

Copper **Subject:** Urban VIII **Obv:** Arms **Rev:** FER/RARI/1623

Date	Mintage	Good	VG	F	VF	XF
1623	—	8.00	16.00	30.00	55.00	—

KM# 48 1/2 BAIOCCO

Copper **Obv:** Arms of Cardinal **Rev:** CIVITAS FERRARIAE 1623 **Note:** Sede Vacante issue.

Date	Mintage	VG	F	VF	XF	Unc
1623 Rare	—	—	—	—	—	—

KM# 70 1/2 BAIOCCO

Copper **Subject:** Innocent X **Rev:** FER/RARI

Date	Mintage	Good	VG	F	VF	XF
1654(sic)	—	12.00	25.00	45.00	85.00	—

KM# 90 1/2 BAIOCCO

Copper **Subject:** Clement X **Note:** Varieties exist.

Date	Mintage	Good	VG	F	VF	XF
1674	—	8.00	16.00	32.00	70.00	175
1675	—	8.00	16.00	32.00	70.00	175
1676	—	8.00	16.00	32.00	70.00	175
ND	—	8.00	16.00	32.00	70.00	175

KM# 94 1/2 BAIOCCO

Copper **Rev:** St. George slaying dragon

Date	Mintage	Good	VG	F	VF	XF
1675	—	8.00	16.00	30.00	65.00	175
1676	—	8.00	16.00	30.00	65.00	175

KM# 96 1/2 BAIOCCO

Copper **Obv:** Arms of Cardinal **Rev:** FER/RARI/1676 **Note:** Sede Vacante issue.

Date	Mintage	Good	VG	F	VF	XF
1676	—	20.00	40.00	70.00	135	—

KM# 97 1/2 BAIOCCO

Copper **Obv:** Arms of Cardinal **Rev:** FER/RARI/date **Note:** Sede Vacante issue.

Date	Mintage	Good	VG	F	VF	XF
1676	—	7.00	14.00	25.00	50.00	—
1677	—	7.00	14.00	25.00	50.00	—

KM# 8 1/2 GROSSO

Silver **Obv:** Bust right **Rev:** FER/RARI in wreath

Date	Mintage	Good	VG	F	VF	XF
ND	—	35.00	60.00	100	180	—

KM# 9 1/2 GROSSO

Silver **Rev:** FER/RARI in arabesque border

Date	Mintage	Good	VG	F	VF	XF
ND	—	35.00	60.00	100	180	—

KM# 34 1/2 GROSSO

Silver **Obv:** Bust of Gregory XV right **Rev:** FER/RARI within wreath

Date	Mintage	Good	VG	F	VF	XF
1621	—	40.00	70.00	115	210	—
1622	—	40.00	70.00	115	210	—
1623	—	40.00	70.00	115	210	—

KM# 35 1/2 GROSSO

Silver **Obv:** Bust of Gregory XV right **Rev:** FER/RARI in arabesque border

Date	Mintage	Good	VG	F	VF	XF
1621	—	40.00	70.00	115	210	—
1622	—	40.00	70.00	115	210	—
1623	—	40.00	70.00	115	210	—

KM# 71 1/2 GROSSO

Silver **Subject:** Innocent X **Obv:** Arms **Rev:** Within wreath **Rev. Inscription:** FER / RARI

Date	Mintage	Good	VG	F	VF	XF
1654/X	—	20.00	40.00	65.00	120	—
1655/X	—	20.00	40.00	65.00	120	—
ND	—	20.00	40.00	65.00	120	—

KM# 72 1/2 GROSSO

Silver **Subject:** Alexander VII **Rev. Inscription:** FER / RARI / 1654

Date	Mintage	Good	VG	F	VF	XF
1654	—	18.00	35.00	60.00	100	—

KM# 10 GROSSO

Silver **Subject:** Paul V **Obv:** Arms **Rev:** St. George slaying dragon

Date	Mintage	Good	VG	F	VF	XF
ND	—	25.00	50.00	80.00	150	250

KM# 36 GROSSO

Silver **Subject:** Gregory XV

Date	Mintage	Good	VG	F	VF	XF
1621 NF	—	40.00	80.00	130	240	—
1622 TAB	—	40.00	80.00	130	240	—
1623 TAB	—	40.00	80.00	130	240	—
1624(sic) TAB	—	40.00	80.00	130	240	—

KM# 50 GROSSO

Silver **Obv:** Arms of Cardinal **Rev:** CIVITAS FERRARIAE 1623 **Note:** Sede Vacante issue.

Date	Mintage	Good	VG	F	VF	XF
1623	—	70.00	135	225	425	—

KM# 52 GROSSO

Silver **Subject:** Urban VIII **Obv:** Arms **Obv. Legend:** PONT MAX **Rev:** St. George slaying dragon

Date	Mintage	Good	VG	F	VF	XF
1624 TAB	—	35.00	60.00	100	180	—

KM# 53 GROSSO

Silver **Obv:** Arms **Obv. Legend:** PM

Date	Mintage	Good	VG	F	VF	XF
1624	—	35.00	60.00	100	180	—

KM# 73 GROSSO

Silver **Subject:** Innocent X **Obv:** Arms

Date	Mintage	Good	VG	F	VF	XF
1654	—	35.00	60.00	100	180	—

KM# 81 GROSSO

Silver **Subject:** Alexander VII **Obv:** Arms **Rev:** St. George slaying dragon

Date	Mintage	Good	VG	F	VF	XF
1655	—	35.00	60.00	100	180	—
1656	—	35.00	60.00	100	180	—
ND	—	35.00	60.00	100	180	—

KM# 80 GROSSO

Silver **Obv:** Arms of Cardinal **Rev:** Shield and CIVITAS FERRARIAE 1655 **Note:** Sede Vacante issue.

Date	Mintage	Good	VG	F	VF	XF
1655	—	90.00	175	300	550	—

KM# 20 GIULIO

Silver **Subject:** Paul V **Obv:** Arms **Rev:** St. George slaying dragon

Date	Mintage	Good	VG	F	VF	XF
1619	—	40.00	70.00	125	225	—
1620	—	40.00	70.00	125	225	—
1621	—	40.00	70.00	125	225	—

KM# 37 GIULIO

Silver **Obv:** Arms of Cardinal **Rev:** CIVITAS FERRARIAE 1621 **Note:** Sede Vacante issue.

Date	Mintage	Good	VG	F	VF	XF
1621	—	80.00	160	290	525	—

KM# 44 GIULIO

Silver **Subject:** Gregory XV **Obv:** Arms **Rev:** St. George slaying dragon

Date	Mintage	Good	VG	F	VF	XF
1622 TAB	—	70.00	135	250	450	—

KM# 51 GIULIO

Silver **Obv:** Arms of Cardinal **Rev:** CIVITAS FERRARIAE 1623 **Note:** Sede Vacante issue.

Date	Mintage	Good	VG	F	VF	XF
1623	—	250	500	1,000	1,850	—

KM# 74 GIULIO

Silver **Subject:** Innocent X **Obv:** Arms **Rev:** St. George slaying dragon

Date	Mintage	Good	VG	F	VF	XF
1654	—	40.00	80.00	145	260	—

KM# 83 GIULIO

Silver **Subject:** Alexander VII **Obv:** Arms **Rev:** St. George slaying dragon

Date	Mintage	Good	VG	F	VF	XF
1655	—	30.00	60.00	110	180	—
1656	—	30.00	60.00	110	180	—

KM# 82 GIULIO

Silver **Obv:** Arms of Cardinal **Rev:** Shield and CIVITAS FERRARIE 1655 **Note:** Sede Vacante issue.

Date	Mintage	Good	VG	F	VF	XF
1655	—	100	200	350	650	—

KM# 21 TESTONE

Silver **Obv:** Capped bust of Paul V right **Rev:** St. George slaying dragon

Date	Mintage	Good	VG	F	VF	XF
1619	—	100	200	475	—	—
1620	—	100	200	475	—	—

KM# 38 TESTONE

Silver **Obv:** Arms of Cardinal **Rev:** CIVITAS FERRARIAE 1621 **Note:** Sede Vacante issue.

Date	Mintage	Good	VG	F	VF	XF
1621	—	200	350	600	1,000	—

KM# 45 TESTONE

Silver **Obv:** Capped bust of Gregory XV right **Rev:** St. George slaying dragon

Date	Mintage	Good	VG	F	VF	XF
1622 TAB	—	100	200	400	800	—

KM# 75 TESTONE

Silver **Subject:** Innocent X

Date	Mintage	Good	VG	F	VF	XF
1654	—	75.00	135	270	550	—

KM# 85 TESTONE

Silver **Subject:** Alexander VII **Obv:** Arms **Rev:** St. George slaying dragon

Date	Mintage	Good	VG	F	VF	XF
1655	—	50.00	100	200	400	—

KM# 86 TESTONE

Silver **Obv:** Different arms

Date	Mintage	Good	VG	F	VF	XF
1655	—	50.00	100	200	400	—

KM# 84 TESTONE

Silver **Obv:** Arms of Cardinal **Rev:** CIVITAS FERRARIAE 1655 and shield **Note:** Sede Vacante issue.

Date	Mintage	Good	VG	F	VF	XF
1655	—	200	350	650	1,000	—

KM# 87 TESTONE

Silver **Obv:** Bust of Alexander VII right

Date	Mintage	Good	VG	F	VF	XF
1656	—	50.00	100	200	400	—

KM# 19 PIASTRA

Silver **Obv:** Capped bust of Paul V right **Rev:** Arms of Cardinal Borghese **Note:** Dav. #4048.

Date	Mintage	VG	F	VF	XF	Unc
MDCXVIII/XIIII (1618)	—	900	1,750	3,500	9,500	—
MDCXVIII (1618)	—	900	1,750	3,500	9,500	—

KM# 22 PIASTRA

Silver **Obv:** Capped bust right, legend starts at lower left **Rev:** St. George slaying dragon, exergue line **Note:** Dav. #4049.

Date	Mintage	VG	F	VF	XF	Unc
1619	—	950	1,750	3,500	9,500	—

KM# 23 PIASTRA

Silver **Rev:** St. George slaying dragon without exergue line below **Note:** Dav. #4050.

Date	Mintage	VG	F	VF	XF	Unc
1619	—	900	1,750	3,500	9,500	—

KM# 30 PIASTRA

Silver **Obv:** Capped bust right, legend starts above bust **Rev:** St. George slaying dragon with exergue line below **Note:** Dav. #4051.

Date	Mintage	VG	F	VF	XF	Unc
1620	—	950	1,750	3,500	9,500	—

KM# 39 PIASTRA

Silver **Obv:** Capped bust of Gregory XV right **Note:** Dav. #4054.

Date	Mintage	VG	F	VF	XF	Unc
1621 NF	—	3,000	6,000	10,000	16,500	—
1622 TAB	—	3,000	6,000	10,000	16,500	—
1623 TAB	—	3,000	6,000	10,000	16,500	—

KM# 54 PIASTRA

Silver **Obv:** Capped bust of Urban VIII right **Note:** Dav. #4062.

Date	Mintage	VG	F	VF	XF	Unc
1624	—	4,500	7,500	11,500	—	—

KM# 55 PIASTRA

Silver **Rev:** Without exergue line **Note:** Dav. #4063.

Date	Mintage	VG	F	VF	XF	Unc
1624	—	4,500	7,500	11,500	—	—

KM# 31 DOPPIA

Gold **Obv:** Capped bust of Paul V right **Rev:** St. George slaying dragon **Note:** Withdrawn issue.

Date	Mintage	VG	F	VF	XF	Unc
1620 Rare	—	—	—	—	—	—

KM# 32 QUADRUPLA

14.0000 g., 0.9860 Gold 0.4438 oz. AGW **Obv:** Bust of Paul V right in inner circle, date in legend **Rev:** St. George and St. Maurelius facing standing **Note:** Withdrawn issue.

Date	Mintage	VG	F	VF	XF	Unc
1620 Rare	—	—	—	—	—	—

PAPAL STATES-GUBBIO

A city in Umbria, was part of the donation of Charlemagne to the pope in 774. It became a consul-governed republic in 1151, came under the dukes of Urbino in 1387, and was ceded to the pope in 1624.

NOTE: For later issues see Roman Republic-Gubbio.

CITY

STANDARD COINAGE

KM# 5 QUATTRINO

Copper, 19.8 mm. **Subject:** Innocent X **Obv:** Arms **Rev:** St. Paul standing **Rev. Legend:** SANCTVS PAVIVS. AP.

Date	Mintage	VG	F	VF	XF	Unc
II (1645)	—	15.00	28.00	55.00	85.00	—
III (1646)	—	15.00	28.00	55.00	85.00	—
IIII (1647)	—	15.00	28.00	55.00	85.00	—
V (1648)	—	15.00	28.00	55.00	85.00	—
VI (1649)	—	15.00	28.00	55.00	85.00	—
VII (1650)	—	15.00	28.00	55.00	85.00	—
VIII (1651)	—	15.00	28.00	55.00	85.00	—
VIIII (1652)	—	15.00	28.00	55.00	85.00	—
X (1653)	—	15.00	28.00	55.00	85.00	—

KM# 6 QUATTRINO

Copper **Rev:** Without AP at end of legend

Date	Mintage	VG	F	VF	XF	Unc
III (1646)	—	15.00	28.00	55.00	85.00	—
IIII (1647)	—	15.00	28.00	55.00	85.00	—
IX (1652)	—	15.00	28.00	55.00	85.00	—

KM# 10 QUATTRINO

Copper **Obv:** Arms, FG at sides **Rev:** Holy Door open **Note:** Holy Year Issue.

Date	Mintage	VG	F	VF	XF	Unc
VI (1650)	—	16.50	30.00	60.00	90.00	—

KM# 11 QUATTRINO

Copper **Rev:** Holy door closed **Note:** Holy Year Issue.

Date	Mintage	VG	F	VF	XF	Unc
VI (1650)	—	16.50	30.00	60.00	90.00	—

KM# 12 QUATTRINO

Copper **Subject:** Alexander VII **Obv:** Arms **Rev:** St. Paul standing

Date	Mintage	VG	F	VF	XF	Unc
I (1655)	—	16.50	30.00	60.00	90.00	—

KM# 13 QUATTRINO

Copper **Rev:** Without AP in legend

Date	Mintage	VG	F	VF	XF	Unc
I (1655)	—	16.50	30.00	60.00	90.00	—

KM# 14 QUATTRINO

Copper **Obv:** Simple arms

Date	Mintage	VG	F	VF	XF	Unc
I (1655)	—	15.00	28.00	55.00	85.00	—

KM# 15 QUATTRINO

Copper **Rev:** Virgin Mary standing on crescent

Date	Mintage	VG	F	VF	XF	Unc
I (1655)	—	16.50	30.00	60.00	90.00	—

KM# 25 QUATTRINO

Copper **Subject:** Clement IX **Obv:** Arms **Rev:** St. Paul standing

Date	Mintage	VG	F	VF	XF	Unc
I (1667)	—	22.00	40.00	70.00	110	—
ND	—	22.00	40.00	70.00	110	—

KM# 32 QUATTRINO

Copper **Rev:** Holy Door open

Date	Mintage	VG	F	VF	XF	Unc
ND	—	20.00	35.00	65.00	100	—

KM# 31 QUATTRINO

Copper **Subject:** Clement X **Rev:** Closed Holy Door **Note:** Holy Year Issue.

Date	Mintage	VG	F	VF	XF	Unc
ND	—	20.00	35.00	65.00	100	—

KM# 33 QUATTRINO

Copper **Rev:** Bust of St. Paul left, ROMA in exergue **Note:** Varieties in quality of engraving.

Date	Mintage	VG	F	VF	XF	Unc
ND	—	16.50	30.00	60.00	90.00	—

KM# 34 QUATTRINO

Copper **Rev:** Bust of SS. Peter and Paul

Date	Mintage	VG	F	VF	XF	Unc
ND	—	16.50	30.00	60.00	90.00	—

KM# 35 QUATTRINO

Copper **Subject:** Innocent XI **Rev:** St. Paul standing, sword right

Date	Mintage	VG	F	VF	XF	Unc
I (1676)	—	12.00	22.00	45.00	70.00	—

KM# 36 QUATTRINO

Copper **Rev:** St. Peter standing

Date	Mintage	VG	F	VF	XF	Unc
II (1677)	—	12.00	22.00	45.00	70.00	—
III (1678)	—	12.00	22.00	45.00	70.00	—

KM# 38 QUATTRINO

Copper **Rev:** Half-length figure of Madonna and child **Rev. Legend:** MONSTRA • TE • ESSEIMATR

Date	Mintage	VG	F	VF	XF	Unc
III (1678)	—	12.00	22.00	45.00	70.00	—

KM# 40 QUATTRINO

Copper **Rev:** St. Paul standing, sword left

Date	Mintage	VG	F	VF	XF	Unc
V (1680)	—	12.00	22.00	45.00	70.00	—

KM# 41 QUATTRINO
Copper **Rev:** Half-length figure of Madonna and child **Rev. Legend:** SVB • TVVM PRAESIDIVM

Date	Mintage	VG	F	VF	XF	Unc
V (1680)	—	14.00	27.00	50.00	80.00	—

KM# 43 QUATTRINO
Copper **Obv:** Inscription on cartouche **Obv. Inscription:** INNOCE / NTVS / XIPM / (year) **Rev:** Papal arms

Date	Mintage	VG	F	VF	XF	Unc
VII (1682)	—	14.00	27.00	50.00	80.00	—
VIII (1683)	—	14.00	27.00	50.00	80.00	—
VIIII (1684)	—	14.00	27.00	50.00	80.00	—
X (1685)	—	14.00	27.00	50.00	80.00	—
XI (1686)	—	14.00	27.00	50.00	80.00	—
XII (1687)	—	14.00	27.00	50.00	80.00	—

KM# 44 QUATTRINO
Copper **Subject:** Alexander VIII **Obv:** Arms **Rev:** St. Paul standing

Date	Mintage	VG	F	VF	XF	Unc
ND	—	13.50	25.00	45.00	70.00	—

KM# 51 QUATTRINO
Copper **Rev:** AP at end of legend

Date	Mintage	VG	F	VF	XF	Unc
ND	—	13.50	25.00	45.00	70.00	—

KM# 52 QUATTRINO
Copper **Obv:** Arms, without legend

Date	Mintage	VG	F	VF	XF	Unc
ND	—	13.50	25.00	45.00	70.00	—

KM# 50 QUATTRINO
Copper **Rev:** St. Paul standing without AP at end of legend

Date	Mintage	VG	F	VF	XF	Unc
II (1690)	—	13.50	25.00	45.00	70.00	—

KM# 54 QUATTRINO
Copper **Subject:** Innocent XII **Obv:** Within wreath **Rev:** Papal arms **Rev. Inscription:** INNOC / XII / PONT • M / AI

Date	Mintage	VG	F	VF	XF	Unc
I (1691)	—	14.00	27.00	50.00	75.00	—

KM# 55 QUATTRINO
Copper **Obv:** Arms **Rev:** St. Paul standing

Date	Mintage	VG	F	VF	XF	Unc
II (1692)	—	10.00	20.00	40.00	65.00	—

KM# 56 QUATTRINO
Copper **Rev:** St. Paul standing

Date	Mintage	VG	F	VF	XF	Unc
II (1692)	—	10.00	20.00	40.00	65.00	—

KM# 57 QUATTRINO
Copper **Rev:** St. Paul standing, sword right

Date	Mintage	VG	F	VF	XF	Unc
III (1693)	—	4.00	10.00	22.00	40.00	—
IIII (1694)	—	4.00	10.00	22.00	40.00	—
V (1695)	—	4.00	10.00	22.00	40.00	—
VI (1696)	—	4.00	10.00	22.00	40.00	—
VII (1697)	—	4.00	10.00	22.00	40.00	—
VIII (1698)	—	4.00	10.00	22.00	40.00	—
IX (1699)	—	4.00	10.00	22.00	40.00	—
10 (1700)	—	4.00	10.00	22.00	40.00	—

KM# 58 QUATTRINO
Copper **Rev:** St. Paul seated right

Date	Mintage	VG	F	VF	XF	Unc
III (1693)	—	4.00	10.00	22.00	40.00	—

KM# 59 QUATTRINO
Copper **Rev:** St. Paul standing facing, holding keys right

Date	Mintage	VG	F	VF	XF	Unc
III (1693)	—	4.00	10.00	22.00	40.00	—

KM# 60 QUATTRINO
Copper **Rev:** St. Paul standing right, keys right

Date	Mintage	VG	F	VF	XF	Unc
III (1693)	—	4.00	10.00	22.00	40.00	—

KM# 61 QUATTRINO
Copper **Rev:** St. Paul standing facing, keys left, book right

Date	Mintage	VG	F	VF	XF	Unc
III (1693)	—	4.00	10.00	22.00	40.00	—

KM# 62 QUATTRINO
Copper **Rev:** St. Paul standing facing without keys or book

Date	Mintage	VG	F	VF	XF	Unc
III (1693)	—	4.00	10.00	22.00	40.00	—

KM# 63 QUATTRINO
Copper **Rev:** St. Paul standing, keys lower left, book right

Date	Mintage	VG	F	VF	XF	Unc
IIII (1694)	—	4.00	10.00	22.00	40.00	—
V (1695)	—	4.00	10.00	22.00	40.00	—
VI (1696)	—	4.00	10.00	22.00	40.00	—
VII (1697)	—	4.00	10.00	22.00	40.00	—
VIII (1698)	—	4.00	10.00	22.00	40.00	—
VIIII (1699)	—	4.00	10.00	22.00	40.00	—
10 (1700)	—	4.00	10.00	22.00	40.00	—

KM# 64 QUATTRINO
Copper **Rev:** St. Paul standing, keys upper left, book right

Date	Mintage	VG	F	VF	XF	Unc
IIII (1694)	—	10.00	20.00	40.00	70.00	—
V (1695)	—	10.00	20.00	40.00	70.00	—
VI (1696)	—	10.00	20.00	40.00	70.00	—
VII (1697)	—	10.00	20.00	40.00	70.00	—
VIII (1698)	—	10.00	20.00	40.00	70.00	—
IX (1699)	—	10.00	20.00	40.00	70.00	—
10 (1700)	—	10.00	20.00	40.00	70.00	—

KM# 65 QUATTRINO
Copper **Rev:** St. Paul standing, both hands on sword

Date	Mintage	VG	F	VF	XF	Unc
IIII (1694)	—	10.00	20.00	40.00	65.00	—

KM# 67 QUATTRINO
Copper **Rev:** St. Paul standing, sword left

Date	Mintage	VG	F	VF	XF	Unc
VII (1697)	—	10.00	20.00	40.00	65.00	—

KM# 68 QUATTRINO
Copper **Rev:** St. Paul seated, sword left

Date	Mintage	VG	F	VF	XF	Unc
IX (1699)	—	10.00	20.00	40.00	65.00	—
10 (1700)	—	10.00	20.00	40.00	65.00	—

KM# 75 QUATTRINO
Copper **Rev:** St. Paul seated, EVG in exergue

Date	Mintage	VG	F	VF	XF	Unc
10 (1700)	—	10.00	20.00	40.00	65.00	—

KM# 76 QUATTRINO
Copper **Rev:** St. Paul seated, with sword left, EVG in exergue

Date	Mintage	VG	F	VF	XF	Unc
10 (1700)	—	10.00	20.00	40.00	65.00	—

KM# 7 1/2 BAIOCCO
Copper **Subject:** Innocent X **Obv:** Arms **Rev:** Inscription within wreath **Rev. Inscription:** MEZZO / BAIOC / CO

Date	Mintage	VG	F	VF	XF	Unc
V (1648)	—	10.00	20.00	40.00	65.00	—
VI (1649)	—	10.00	20.00	40.00	65.00	—
VII (1650)	—	10.00	20.00	40.00	65.00	—
VIII (1651)	—	10.00	20.00	40.00	65.00	—
VIIII (1652)	—	10.00	20.00	40.00	65.00	—
X (1653)	—	10.00	20.00	40.00	65.00	—

KM# 16 1/2 BAIOCCO
Copper **Subject:** Alexander VII **Rev:** In laurel wreath **Rev. Inscription:** MEZO / BAIOC / CO

Date	Mintage	VG	F	VF	XF	Unc
ND	—	10.00	20.00	40.00	65.00	—

KM# 17 1/2 BAIOCCO
Copper **Obv:** Simple arms

Date	Mintage	VG	F	VF	XF	Unc
ND	—	12.00	22.00	45.00	70.00	—

KM# 18 1/2 BAIOCCO
Copper **Obv:** Arms **Rev:** Legend in oak wreath

Date	Mintage	VG	F	VF	XF	Unc
ND	—	10.00	20.00	40.00	65.00	—

KM# 19 1/2 BAIOCCO
Copper **Obv:** Simple arms

Date	Mintage	VG	F	VF	XF	Unc
ND	—	12.00	22.00	45.00	70.00	—

KM# 26 1/2 BAIOCCO
Copper **Subject:** Clement IX **Obv:** Arms **Rev:** Inscription within laurel wreath **Rev. Inscription:** MEZZO / BAIOC / CO **Note:** Varieties exist.

Date	Mintage	VG	F	VF	XF	Unc
ND	—	15.00	30.00	60.00	90.00	—

KM# 27 1/2 BAIOCCO
Copper **Rev:** Inscription within oak wreath **Rev. Inscription:** MEZZO / BAIOC / CO

Date	Mintage	VG	F	VF	XF	Unc
ND	—	15.00	30.00	60.00	90.00	—

KM# 30 1/2 BAIOCCO
Copper **Subject:** Clement X **Rev:** Inscription within laurel wreath **Rev. Inscription:** MEZZO / BAIOC / CO

Date	Mintage	VG	F	VF	XF	Unc
ND	—	9.00	18.00	35.00	55.00	—

KM# 37 1/2 BAIOCCO
Copper **Subject:** Innocent XI **Rev:** Inscription in cartouche, symbol above and/or below **Rev. Inscription:** MEZZO / BAIOC / CO

Date	Mintage	VG	F	VF	XF	Unc
II (1677)	—	8.00	15.00	28.00	50.00	—
III (1678)	—	8.00	15.00	28.00	50.00	—
IIII (1679)	—	8.00	15.00	28.00	50.00	—
V (1680)	—	8.00	15.00	28.00	50.00	—
VI (1681)	—	8.00	15.00	28.00	50.00	—
VII (1682)	—	8.00	15.00	28.00	50.00	—
VIII (1683)	—	8.00	15.00	28.00	50.00	—
IX (1684)	—	8.00	15.00	28.00	50.00	—
ND	—	8.00	15.00	28.00	50.00	—

KM# 42 1/2 BAIOCCO
Copper **Rev:** Legend within laurel wreath

Date	Mintage	VG	F	VF	XF	Unc
V (1680)	—	8.00	15.00	28.00	50.00	—
VI (1681)	—	8.00	15.00	28.00	50.00	—
VII (1682)	—	8.00	15.00	28.00	50.00	—
VIII (1683)	—	8.00	15.00	28.00	50.00	—
IX (1684)	—	8.00	15.00	28.00	50.00	—
X (1685)	—	8.00	15.00	28.00	50.00	—
XI (1686)	—	8.00	15.00	28.00	50.00	—

KM# 45 1/2 BAIOCCO
Copper **Subject:** Alexander VIII **Rev:** Inscription in laurel wreath **Rev. Inscription:** MEZZO / BAIOC / CO

Date	Mintage	VG	F	VF	XF	Unc
I (1689)	—	9.00	18.00	35.00	55.00	—

KM# 53 1/2 BAIOCCO
Copper **Subject:** Innocent XII

Date	Mintage	VG	F	VF	XF	Unc
II (1690)	—	8.00	15.00	28.00	50.00	—
III (1691)	—	8.00	15.00	28.00	50.00	—
IIII (1692)	—	8.00	15.00	28.00	50.00	—
V (1693)	—	8.00	15.00	28.00	50.00	—
VI (1694)	—	8.00	15.00	28.00	50.00	—
VII (1695)	—	8.00	15.00	28.00	50.00	—
1696	—	8.00	15.00	28.00	50.00	—
ND	—	8.00	15.00	28.00	50.00	—

KM# 66 1/2 BAIOCCO
Copper **Rev:** Inscription in palm wreath **Rev. Inscription:** MEZZO / BAIOC / CO

Date	Mintage	VG	F	VF	XF	Unc
VI (1694)	—	8.00	15.00	28.00	50.00	—
1696	—	8.00	15.00	28.00	50.00	—
ND	—	8.00	15.00	28.00	50.00	—

PARMA

A town in Emilia, which was a papal possession from 1512 to 1545, was seized by France in 1796, and was attached to the Napoleonic Empire in 1808. In 1814, Parma was assigned to Marie Louise, empress of Napoleon I. It was annexed to Sardinia in 1860.

RULERS
Ranuccio Farnese I, 1592-1622
Odardo Farnese, 1622-1646
Ranuccio Farnese II, 1646-1694
Francesco Farnese I, 1694-1727

DUCHY

STANDARD COINAGE

DAV# 4120 SCUDO
Silver **Ruler:** Odardo Farnese **Obv:** Bust right, date below **Obv. Legend:** ODOARDVS. FAR. PAR. ET. PLA. DVX. V **Rev:** Half figure right, SCVDO below **Rev. Legend:** S. VITALIS. PARME. PROTECTOR.

Date	Mintage	VG	F	VF	XF	Unc
1626	—	300	650	1,350	3,750	—
1627	—	300	650	1,350	3,750	—
1628	—	300	650	1,350	3,750	—
1629	—	300	650	1,350	3,750	—
ND	—	300	650	1,350	3,750	—

DAV# 4125 SCUDO
Silver **Ruler:** Ranuccio Farnese II **Obv. Legend:** RAN. FAR. PAR. ET. PLA. DVX. VI. **Rev. Legend:** S. VITALIS. PARMAE. PROT.

Date	Mintage	VG	F	VF	XF	Unc
ND	—	350	700	1,450	4,000	—

DAV# 4117 TALLERO (10 Guillie)
Silver **Ruler:** Odardo Farnese **Obv:** Crowned arms in Order chain **Rev:** Half-length figure of saint right

Date	Mintage	VG	F	VF	XF	Unc
ND	—	1,200	2,200	4,500	—	—

DAV# 4115 DUCATON
25.7040 g., 0.9020 Silver 0.7454 oz. ASW **Ruler:** Ranuccio Farnese I **Obv. Legend:** RAIN. FA(R) (N). PAR. ET. PLAC. DVX. IIII or IV **Rev:** Pallas and Mars holding crown above trees

Date	Mintage	VG	F	VF	XF	Unc
1603	—	1,000	2,000	4,000	—	—
1604	—	1,000	2,000	4,000	—	—
1605	—	1,000	2,000	4,000	—	—
1606	—	1,000	2,000	4,000	10,000	—
1607	—	1,000	2,000	4,000	—	—
1614	—	750	1,500	3,000	5,500	—
1615	—	750	1,500	3,000	5,500	—
1616	—	750	1,500	3,000	5,500	—
1617	—	750	1,500	3,000	5,500	—
1624	—	750	1,500	3,000	5,500	—

DAV# 4116 DUCATON
25.7040 g., 0.9020 Silver 0.7454 oz. ASW **Ruler:** Ranuccio Farnese I **Obv:** Different bust left **Rev:** Ship with date below **Rev. Legend:** ADVERSIS. PROVECTA. NOTIS.

Date	Mintage	VG	F	VF	XF	Unc
1621 Rare	—	—	—	—	—	—

DAV# 4118 DUCATON
25.7040 g., 0.9020 Silver 0.7454 oz. ASW **Ruler:** Odardo Farnese **Obv:** Bust right with or without border **Obv. Legend:** ODOARDVS... **Rev:** Cherubs above Madonna and child **Rev. Legend:** MILLE. CLYPEI-PENDENT*

Date	Mintage	VG	F	VF	XF	Unc
1623	—	1,250	2,500	6,500	—	—
1624	—	1,250	2,500	6,500	—	—
1625	—	1,000	2,250	6,000	—	—
1626	—	1,000	2,250	6,000	—	—
1629	—	1,500	3,000	7,000	—	—
ND	—	1,000	2,000	5,000	—	—

DAV# 4121 DUCATON
25.7040 g., 0.9020 Silver 0.7454 oz. ASW **Ruler:** Odardo Farnese **Obv:** A flanking date in exergue **Rev:** PARME below legend **Rev. Legend:** MILE...

Date	Mintage	VG	F	VF	XF	Unc
1629	—	1,250	2,500	6,500	—	—
1638	—	1,250	2,500	6,500	—	—

DAV# 4123 DUCATON
25.7040 g., 0.9020 Silver 0.7454 oz. ASW **Ruler:** Ranuccio Farnese II **Obv:** Bust of Ranuccio II left **Obv. Legend:** RAN(V). II. FAR. PAR. ET. PLA. DVX. W. **Rev:** Roman numerals below Pallas and Mars **Rev. Legend:** QVESITAM. **. MERITAS.

Date	Mintage	VG	F	VF	XF	Unc
1660	—	1,650	2,750	5,500	—	—
1673	—	1,250	2,200	4,750	—	—
1674	—	1,250	2,200	4,750	—	—
1676	—	1,250	2,200	4,750	—	—
1677	—	1,250	2,200	4,750	—	—

DAV# 4124 DUCATON
25.7040 g., 0.9020 Silver 0.7454 oz. ASW **Ruler:** Ranuccio Farnese II **Obv:** Bust of Ranuccio II left **Obv. Inscription:** Roman numeral date below bust **Rev:** Fleur-de-lis below Pallas and Mars

Date	Mintage	VG	F	VF	XF	Unc
1692	—	1,400	2,500	5,000	—	—

DAV# 4114 2 DUCATONE
Silver **Ruler:** Ranuccio Farnese I **Obv:** Bust of Ranuccio II left

Date	Mintage	VG	F	VF	XF	Unc
1604	—	2,000	4,000	7,000	13,000	—
1614	—	2,000	4,000	7,000	13,000	—
1615	—	2,000	4,000	7,000	13,000	—
1616	—	2,000	4,000	7,000	13,000	—
1617	—	2,000	4,000	7,000	13,000	—

DAV# 4119 2 DUCATONE

14.2820 g., Silver **Ruler:** Odardo Farnese **Obv:** Bust of Odoardo left **Rev:** Madonna seated and child under crown held by two cherubs

Date	Mintage	VG	F	VF	XF	Unc
1626	—	3,000	5,600	9,000	16,000	—
ND	—	3,000	5,600	9,000	16,000	—

DAV# 4122 2 DUCATONE

14.2820 g., Silver **Ruler:** Ranuccio Farnese II **Note:** Similar to 1 Ducatone, Dav. #4123.

Date	Mintage	VG	F	VF	XF	Unc
1660	—	7,000	15,000	25,000	—	—

FR# 912 DOPPIA

7.1410 g., 0.8910 Gold 0.2046 oz. AGW **Ruler:** Odardo Farnese **Obv:** Bust of Odoardo right in inner circle **Rev:** Madonna and child under crown held by two cherubs

Date	Mintage	VG	F	VF	XF	Unc
ND	—	1,000	2,500	6,000	12,000	—

FR# 920 DOPPIA

7.1410 g., 0.8910 Gold 0.2046 oz. AGW **Ruler:** Ranuccio Farnese II **Obv:** Bust of Ranuccio II left **Rev:** Saint Viyae standing, date below

Date	Mintage	VG	F	VF	XF	Unc
1687	—	2,400	5,000	10,000	—	—

FR# 921 DOPPIA

7.1410 g., 0.8910 Gold 0.2046 oz. AGW **Ruler:** Ranuccio Farnese II **Obv:** Bust of Ranuccio II left, date below **Rev:** Head of wind blowing from right to left into clouds

Date	Mintage	VG	F	VF	XF	Unc
1692 GG	—	3,000	5,400	11,000	—	—

FR# 925 DOPPIA

7.1410 g., 0.8910 Gold 0.2046 oz. AGW **Ruler:** Francesco Farnese I **Obv:** Bust of Francesco right **Rev:** Crowned arms

Date	Mintage	VG	F	VF	XF	Unc
1695 GG	—	3,600	6,000	12,000	—	—

FR# 911.1 2 DOPPIE

0.8910 Gold **Ruler:** Odardo Farnese **Obv:** Large bust of Odoardo **Rev:** Madonna and child under crown held by two cherubs

Date	Mintage	VG	F	VF	XF	Unc
1625 AA	—	1,200	2,000	4,500	8,750	—
1639 VC	—	1,200	2,000	4,500	8,750	—

FR# 911.2 2 DOPPIE

0.8910 Gold **Ruler:** Odardo Farnese **Obv:** Small bust of Odoardo right

Date	Mintage	VG	F	VF	XF	Unc
ND	—	1,200	2,000	3,750	6,750	—

FR# 919 2 DOPPIE

0.8910 Gold **Ruler:** Ranuccio Farnese II **Obv:** Bust of Ranuccio II left, date below

Date	Mintage	VG	F	VF	XF	Unc
1658 Rare	—	—	—	—	—	—
ND Rare	—	—	—	—	—	—

FR# 914 3 DOPPIE

21.4230 g., 0.8910 Gold 0.6137 oz. AGW **Ruler:** Odardo Farnese **Obv:** Bust of Odoardo right in inner circle **Rev:** Three nude graces standing, date 1574 above in legend

Date	Mintage	VG	F	VF	XF	Unc
1633 AC Rare	—	—	—	—	—	—

Note: First 3 retrograde

FR# 901 DUCAT

3.5000 g., 0.9860 Gold 0.1109 oz. AGW **Ruler:** Ranuccio Farnese I **Obv:** Ranuccio I standing left **Rev:** Crowned arms in Order collar

Date	Mintage	VG	F	VF	XF	Unc
1602 LS Rare	—	—	—	—	—	—
1603 LS Rare	—	—	—	—	—	—

FR# 902 DUCAT

3.5000 g., 0.9860 Gold 0.1109 oz. AGW **Ruler:** Ranuccio Farnese I **Rev:** Madonna and child facing

Date	Mintage	VG	F	VF	XF	Unc
ND	—	800	1,200	2,500	3,750	—

FR# 910 6 DUCAT

0.9860 Gold **Ruler:** Odardo Farnese **Obv:** Youthful, ruffled and armored bust right **Rev:** Crown supported by two cherubs above Madonna and child

Date	Mintage	VG	F	VF	XF	Unc
ND(1622-46) Rare	—	—	—	—	—	—

PIACENZA

Placentia
Placentia

The city of Piacenza located in northern Italy some 35 miles (60 kilometers) southeast of Milan and about halfway between the latter and Parma, is the present0day capital of the province of the same name. The site of Piacenza was a former Etruscan town at which the Romans founded, along with Cremona, a colony in May 218 BC. The Latin name of the place is Placentia, meaning "pleasant abode." The city faced many hardships over the centuries of Roman rule, the period of late antiquity and the early Middle Ages. During the High Middle Ages, Piacenza became an important center on the trade routes of northern Italy. From 1126, the city was a free commune and an important member of the Lombard League. Several powerful families, the Scotti and Pallaricini among them, contended for power during the late 13th and early 14th centuries until the capture of the city by by the Visconti of Milan in 1313. They held the city until 1447, when it became a possession of the Sforza dukes until 1499. From then until 1512, Piacenza was ruled by France, then briefly as part of the Papal States under Leo X (1513-21). In 1545, Piacenza and its territory formed part of the new duchy of Parma and Piacenza, ruled by the Farnese family. When the capital of the duchy was transferred to Parma in the late 16th century, Piacenza underwent a long period of decline and devastation. It passed to Parma in 1731, to the Habsburgs in 1735, briefly to Sardinia-Piedmont in 1744-45, then again to Parma under the Borbone dynasty to 1848. When Napoleon conquered much of Italy, Piacenza was annexed to his empire in 1802. By a plebiscite held in 1848, Piacenza voted overwhelmingly to join Sardinia-Piedmont and was henceforth known as the "First-born of the Unification of Italy." Note that some issues in the name of Alessandro were struck for years after his death in 1592.

RULERS

Pierluigi Farnese, 1545-1547
Ottavio Farnese, 1547-1586
Ottavio and his son, Alessandro, 1565-1586
Alessandro Farnese, 1586-1592
Ranuccio I Farnese, 1592-1622
Odoardo Farnese, 1622-1646
Ranuccio II Farnese, 1646-1694
Francesco Farnese, 1694-1727

MINT OFFICIALS' INITIALS

Initials	Date	Name
AC	1574-75, 1580-82, 1589-92	Andrea Casalino
AP	1595-98	Alessandro Pindemonte
LF	1631-36, 1649	Ludovico Fermi
LX	1626-29, 1633	Luca Xell
GC	1684-85	Unknown
GR	1676	Guido Riviera
PC	1574, 1583-87	Paolo Campi
PG	1586	Unknown
PP	1599-1620	Paolo Pindemonte
RER	1673	Unknown
SA	1598-99	Unknown
VR	1592-95	Vincenzo Rivalta

REFERENCES

Var = Alberto Varesi, ***Monete Italiane Regionali: Emilia***. Pavia, 1998.

Cud = Sergio Cudazzo, **Monete Italiane Regionali: Casa Savoia**, Pavia: Numismatica Varesi, 2005.

DUCHY

STANDARD COINAGE

MB# 26 QUATTRINO

Billon Weight varies: 0.49-0.86g., 16 mm. **Ruler:** Alessandro **Obv:** Crowned 'A' superimposed on palm and olive branches **Obv. Legend:** FARNESIVS. DVX. III. **Rev:** Wolf facing left, lily above, mintmaster's initials below, where present, date in exergue **Rev. Legend:** PLAT. PAR. ET. C. **Note:** Ref. Var 1148. Struck for many years after ruler's death.

Date	Mintage	Good	VG	F	VF	XF
1610	—	10.00	18.00	35.00	55.00	120
1611	—	10.00	18.00	35.00	55.00	120
1612	—	10.00	18.00	35.00	55.00	120
1613	—	10.00	18.00	35.00	55.00	120
1620	—	10.00	18.00	35.00	55.00	120
ND	—	10.00	18.00	35.00	55.00	120

KM# 4 SESINO

Copper Weight varies: 2.60-3.85g., 19-20 mm. **Ruler:** Odoardo **Obv:** Crowned shield of manifold arms **Obv. Legend:** ODO. FA. - DVX. V. **Rev:** Foliated cross in circle **Rev. Legend:** SALVS. - MVNDI. **Note:** Ref. Var 1170.

Date	Mintage	Good	VG	F	VF	XF
ND(1622-46)	—	7.00	15.00	28.00	55.00	80.00

KM# 5 SESINO

Copper Weight varies: 2.60-3.85g., 20 mm. **Ruler:** Odoardo **Obv:** Crowned shield of manifold arms **Obv. Legend:** ODO. FAR. PLA. E. PAR. DVX. V. **Rev:** Foliated cross in circle **Rev. Legend:** SALVS. - MVNDI. **Note:** Ref. Var 1171.

Date	Mintage	Good	VG	F	VF	XF
ND(1622-46)	—	7.00	15.00	28.00	55.00	80.00

KM# 19 SESINO

Copper Weight varies: 0.68-1.08g., 14 mm. **Ruler:** Ranuccio II **Obv:** Crowned shield of manifold arms **Obv. Legend:** RAN. F. DVX. VI. **Rev:** St. Antoninus on horseback to left **Rev. Legend:** S. ANT. M. - PRO. PL. **Note:** Rev. Var 1179.

Date	Mintage	Good	VG	F	VF	XF
ND(1646-94)	—	7.00	15.00	28.00	55.00	80.00

KM# 27 SESINO
Copper Weight varies: 1.00-1.90g., 17 mm. **Ruler:** Francesco **Obv:** Crowned shield of manifold arms **Obv. Legend:** FRAN. I. F. P. P. DVX. VI. **Rev:** Floriated cross in circle **Rev. Legend:** SALVS. - MVNDI. **Note:** Ref. Var 1184.

Date	Mintage	Good	VG	F	VF	XF
ND(1694-1727)	—	7.00	15.00	28.00	55.00	80.00

KM# 20 2 SESINI
Copper Weight varies: 1.55-2.79g., 17-18 mm. **Ruler:** Ranuccio II **Obv:** Crowned ornate shield of arms **Obv. Legend:** RAN. F. P. P. DVX. VI. **Rev:** Foliated cross **Rev. Legend:** SALVS. - MVNDI. **Note:** Ref. Var 1178.

Date	Mintage	Good	VG	F	VF	XF
ND(1646-94)	—	8.00	15.00	28.00	55.00	80.00

KM# 8 SOLDO
Copper Weight varies: 7.30-7.92g., 27-28 mm. **Ruler:** Odoardo **Obv:** Crowned ornate shield of manifold arms **Obv. Legend:** ODOAR. F. PL. P. DVX. V. **Rev:** St. Antoninus on horseback to left, holding pennant, date in exergue **Rev. Legend:** PLACENTIAE - COMVNITAS. **Note:** Ref. Var 1168/1-2.

Date	Mintage	Good	VG	F	VF	XF
1623	—	15.00	30.00	65.00	135	220
ND	—	15.00	30.00	65.00	135	220

KM# 9 SOLDO
Copper Weight varies: 7.30-7.92g., 27-28 mm. **Ruler:** Odoardo **Obv:** Small crowned shield of ornate arms **Obv. Legend:** ODOAR. F. PL. P. DVX. V. **Rev:** St. Antoninus on horseback to left, holding pennant, date in exergue **Rev. Legend:** PLACENTIAE - COMVNITAS. **Note:** Ref. Var 1168/3.

Date	Mintage	Good	VG	F	VF	XF
1623	—	40.00	85.00	165	315	550

KM# 11 SOLDO
Copper, 26 mm. **Ruler:** Odoardo **Obv:** Armored bust to right wearing high collar, mintmaster's initials below **Obv. Legend:** ODOARDVS. FAR. PLAC. ET. PAR. DVX. V. **Rev:** St. Antoninus on horseback to right, holding pennant, Roman numeral date in exergue **Rev. Legend:** S. ANTON. - MART: PROT. PLAC. **Note:** Ref. Var 1169.

Date	Mintage	Good	VG	F	VF	XF
MDCXXVI (1626) Rare	—	—	—	—	—	—

KM# 6 5 SOLDI
1.5800 g., Billon, 19 mm. **Ruler:** Odoardo **Obv:** Crowned shield of manifold arms **Obv. Legend:** ODOA. FAR. PLA. E. PAR. DVX. V. **Rev:** St. Antoninus on horseback to left, holding pennant **Rev. Legend:** S. ANTONINO. M. PROT. PLA. **Note:** Ref. Var 1166.

Date	Mintage	VG	F	VF	XF	Unc
ND(1622-46)	—	25.00	50.00	90.00	140	—

KM# 18 5 SOLDI
2.4200 g., Billon, 19 mm. **Ruler:** Odoardo **Obv:** Crowned shield of manifold arms **Obv. Legend:** ODO. FAR. PLA. E. PAR. DVX. V. **Rev:** Full-length facing figure of St. Justine, date in exergue, where present **Rev. Legend:** S. IVSTINA. - PLA. PROTE. **Note:** Ref. Var 1167.

Date	Mintage	VG	F	VF	XF	Unc
1640	—	20.00	45.00	80.00	120	—
ND	—	20.00	45.00	80.00	120	—

KM# 21 5 SOLDI
Billon Weight varies: 1.73-2.30g., 20 mm. **Ruler:** Ranuccio II **Obv:** Crowned shield of manifold arms **Obv. Legend:** RAN. FAR. PLA. E. PAR. DVX. VI. **Rev:** Full-length facing figure of St. Justine, holding crozier **Rev. Legend:** S. IVSTINA - PLA. PROTE. **Note:** Ref. Var 1177.

Date	Mintage	VG	F	VF	XF	Unc
ND(1646-94)	—	25.00	55.00	100	165	—

KM# 7 10 SOLDI
Billon Weight varies: 4.73-5.47g., 22-23 mm. **Ruler:** Odoardo **Obv:** Crowned ornate shield of arms **Obv. Legend:** ODOA. FAR. PLA. E. PAR. DVX. V. **Rev:** St. Antoninus on horseback to left, holding pennant, SOLD. X in exergue **Rev. Legend:** S. ANTONINVS. M. PROT. PLA. **Note:** Ref. Var 1165.

Date	Mintage	Good	VG	F	VF	XF
ND(1622-46)	—	8.00	20.00	40.00	75.00	110

KM# 22 10 SOLDI
Billon Weight varies: 4.43-4.59g., 23 mm. **Ruler:** Ranuccio II **Obv:** Crowned shield of manifold arms **Obv. Legend:** RAN. FAR. PLA. E. PAR. DVX. VI. **Rev:** St. Antoninus on horseback to left, holding pennant, SOLDI X in exergue **Rev. Legend:** S. ANTONINVS. M. PROT. PLA. **Note:** Ref. Var 1176.

Date	Mintage	Good	VG	F	VF	XF
ND(1646-94)	—	10.00	25.00	55.00	95.00	165

KM# 28 10 SOLDI
Billon Weight varies: 2.28-4.11g., 23 mm. **Ruler:** Francesco **Obv:** Crowned shield of manifold arms **Obv. Legend:** FRAN. I. FAR. PLA. ET. PAR. DVX. VII. **Rev:** St. Antoninus on horseback to left, holding pennant, SOLDI X in exergue **Rev. Legend:** S. ANTONINVS. M. PROT. PLA. **Note:** Ref. Var 1182.

Date	Mintage	VG	F	VF	XF	Unc
ND(1694-1727)	—	12.00	28.00	45.00	80.00	—

KM# 29 10 SOLDI
Billon, 23 mm. **Ruler:** Francesco **Obv:** Crowned shield of manifold arms **Obv. Legend:** FRAN. FAR. PLA. ET. PAR. DVX. VII. **Rev:** Standing figure of St. Justine holding palm frond **Rev. Legend:** S. IVSTINA - PLA. PROTE. **Note:** Ref. Var 1183. Existence of this coin uncertain.

Date	Mintage	VG	F	VF	XF	Unc
ND(1694-1727)	—	—	—	—	—	—

MB# 10 PARPAGLIOLA
Billon Weight varies: 1.02-2.96g., 21 mm. **Ruler:** Ottavio and Alessandro **Obv:** Accolated busts of Ottavio and Alessandro to left **Obv. Legend:** OCT. P. ET. ALE. F. PP. **Rev:** Seated allegorical figure of the city, in guise of Minerva, to left, resting left arm on shield, holding flower plant in right hand, date in exergue **Rev. Legend:** FEL. SVB. HIS. PLAC. **Note:** Ref. Var 1135. Varieties exist.

Date	Mintage	Good	VG	F	VF	XF
1601	—	20.00	40.00	80.00	165	220
1602	—	20.00	40.00	80.00	165	220
1604	—	20.00	40.00	80.00	165	220
1605	—	20.00	40.00	80.00	165	220
1607	—	20.00	40.00	80.00	165	220
1609	—	20.00	40.00	80.00	165	220
ND	—	20.00	40.00	80.00	165	220

KM# 30 20 SOLDI (Lira)
Silver Weight varies: 2.28-2.85g., 22-23 mm. **Ruler:** Francesco **Obv:** Draped bust to right **Obv. Legend:** FRANCISCVS. I. FARNESIVS. PLACENTIÆ. ET. PARMÆ. DV. VII. **Rev:** Full-length standing figure of St. Francis Xaverius holding up crucifix **Rev. Legend:** S. FRANCISCVS. SAVERIVS. PLACENTIÆ. COM. PROTETOR. **Note:** Ref. Var 1180.

Date	Mintage	VG	F	VF	XF	Unc
ND(1694-1727) Rare	—	—	—	—	—	—

KM# 31 20 SOLDI (Lira)
Silver Weight varies: 2.28-2.85g., 22-23 mm. **Ruler:** Francesco **Obv:** Draped bust to right **Obv. Legend:** FRAN. I. FAR. PLA. ET. PAR. DVX. VII. **Rev:** Full-length standing figure of St. Francis Xaverius, holding up crucifix, S. XX in exergue **Rev. Legend:** S. F. XAVERIVS. PLA. COM. PROT. **Note:** Ref. Var 1181.

Date	Mintage	VG	F	VF	XF	Unc
ND(1694-1727)	—	70.00	150	325	450	—

KM# 23 40 SOLDI (Quarentano)
Silver Weight varies: 7.11-10.19g., 29 mm. **Ruler:** Ranuccio II **Obv:** Crowned shield of manifold arms in baroque frame **Obv. Legend:** RANVT. FAR. PLA. E. PAR. DVX. VI. C. P. **Rev:** Standing Madonna with Child, date at end of legend, SOLDI. XXXX and mintmaster's initials in exergue **Rev. Legend:** MONSTRA. TE. ESSE. MATREM. **Note:** Ref. Var 1175.

Date	Mintage	VG	F	VF	XF	Unc
1649 LF	—	35.00	80.00	145	250	—
1673 RER	—	100	215	350	550	—

MB# 22 TESTONE
Silver Weight varies: 7.45-7.91g., 31 mm. **Ruler:** Alessandro **Obv:** Draped bust to left **Obv. Legend:** ALEXANDER. FAR. DVX. III. **Rev:** Crowned shield of manifold arms in baroque frame, date in exergue **Rev. Legend:** PLACENTIÆ. - ET. PARMÆ. ET C. **Note:** Ref. Var 1146. Known dated 1590 struck on thick flan weighing 12.87g.

Date	Mintage	VG	F	VF	XF	Unc
1613 PP	—	425	650	1,800	3,200	—

KM# 26 TESTONE
Silver Weight varies: 8.05-9.71g., 30 mm. **Ruler:** Ranuccio II **Obv:** Large armored and draped bust to left **Obv. Legend:** RAN(V). FAR. PLA. ET. PAR. DVX. VI. **Rev:** St. Antoninus on horseback to left, holding pennant, date in oval below **Rev. Legend:** S. ANTONINVS - MART. PROT. PLA(C). **Note:** Ref. Var 1174. Varieties exist.

Date	Mintage	VG	F	VF	XF	Unc
1684 GC	—	600	1,000	2,000	3,500	—
1685 GC	—	600	1,000	2,000	3,500	—
1687	—	600	1,000	2,000	3,500	—

MB# 23 SCUDO
Silver Weight varies: 29.55-31.94g., 40 mm. **Ruler:** Alessandro **Obv:** Armored bust to right **Obv. Legend:** ALEX. FAR. - DVX. III. PLA. P. ET C. **Rev:** Allegorical figure of city, holding lily and cornucopia, allegorical figure of River Po at lower left, wolf seated at lower right, date divides mintmaster's initials in exergue **Rev. Legend:** PLAC. ROMAN. COLON. **Note:** Ref. Var 1144; Dav. 8358, 4126. Varieties exist.

Date	Mintage	VG	F	VF	XF	Unc
1601 PP	—	325	475	1,150	2,500	—
1602 PP	—	325	475	1,150	2,500	—
1603 PP	—	325	475	1,150	2,500	—
1604 PP	—	325	475	1,150	2,500	—
1605 PP	—	325	475	1,150	2,500	—
1609 PP	—	325	475	1,150	2,500	—
1620 PP	—	325	475	1,150	2,500	—

MB# 36 SCUDO
Silver Weight varies: 26.39-31.68g., 42-43 mm. **Ruler:** Alessandro **Obv:** Armored bust to right **Obv. Legend:** ALEX.

FAR. - DVX. III. PL. P. ET C. **Rev:** Allegorical figure of city, holding lily and cornucopia, allegorical figure of River Po at lower left, date divides mintmaster's initials in exergue **Rev. Legend:** PLAC. ROMAN. COLON. **Note:** Ref. Var 1145; Dav. 8364.

Date	Mintage	VG	F	VF	XF	Unc
1603	—	475	750	1,600	2,750	—
1604	—	475	750	1,600	2,750	—
1604 Retrograde 4	—	475	750	1,600	2,750	—

KM# 12.1 SCUDO

Silver Weight varies: 31.40-31.84g., 44-48 mm. **Ruler:** Odoardo **Obv:** Armored bust with high collar to right, mintmaster's initials below **Obv. Legend:** ODOARDVS. FAR: PLAC: ET: PAR: DVX. V. **Rev:** St. Antoninus on horseback to right, holding pennant, Roman numeral date in exergue **Rev. Legend:** S: ANTON: - :MART: PROT: PLAC. **Note:** Ref. Var 1163/1; Dav. 4127.

Date	Mintage	VG	F	VF	XF	Unc
MDCXXVI (1626) LX	—	425	650	1,450	2,500	—

KM# 16 SCUDO

Silver Weight varies: 26.17-31.60g., 41-46 mm. **Ruler:** Odoardo **Obv:** Armored bust with high collar to right **Obv. Legend:** ODOARDVS. FAR: PL: ET. PAR: DVX. V. **Rev:** Full-length standing figure of St. Antoninus holding pennant, date divides mintmaster's initials in exergue **Rev. Legend:** S: ANTONINVS. - M(ART): PROT: PLAC(C). **Note:** Ref. Var 1164; Dav. 4128. Varieties exist.

Date	Mintage	VG	F	VF	XF	Unc
1628 LX	—	225	350	750	1,450	—
1629 LX	—	225	350	750	1,450	—
1630 LX	—	225	350	750	1,450	—
1631 LF	—	225	350	750	1,450	—
1632 LF	—	225	350	750	1,450	—
1636 LF	—	225	350	750	1,450	—

KM# 12.2 SCUDO

Silver Weight varies: 31.40-31.60g., 43 mm. **Ruler:** Odoardo **Obv:** Armored bust with high collar to right **Obv. Legend:** ODOARDVS. FAR: PLAC: ET: PAR: DVX. V. **Rev:** St. Antoninus on horseback to right, holding pennant, part-Roman numeral and part-Arabic date divides mintmaster's initials in exergue **Rev. Legend:** S. ANTO - NINs. - M: P: PL: **Note:** Ref. Var 1163/2; Dav. 4129.

Date	Mintage	VG	F	VF	XF	Unc
16XXX3 (1633) LX	—	425	750	1,650	2,750	—

KM# 24 SCUDO

Silver Weight varies: 31.75-32.02g., 44 mm. **Ruler:** Ranuccio II **Obv:** Large armored and draped bust to left **Obv. Legend:** RANV. FAR. PLA. ET. PAR. DVX. VI. **Rev:** St. Antoninus on horseback to right, holding pennant, Roman numeral date in exergue **Rev. Legend:** S. ANTON. - .MART. PROT. PLAC. **Note:** Ref. Var 1173; Dav. 4130.

Date	Mintage	VG	F	VF	XF	Unc
MDCLXXVI (1676) GR	—	1,450	2,200	5,500	9,500	—

TRADE COINAGE

KM# 1 ONGARO

Gold Weight varies: 3.25-3.45g., 22 mm. **Ruler:** Ranuccio I **Obv:** 5-line inscription in ornamented square **Obv. Inscription:** RAN. FAR / PLA. PAR / DVX. IVS / ROE. CON / FAL. PER. **Rev:** Full-length armored figure of duke, holding sword over shoulder and lily, divides date **Rev. Legend:** MON. NOVA. AV - R - EA. CIV. PL. R. C. **Note:** Ref. Var 1155; Fr. 908. This coin imitates the Netherlands ducat of the period.

Date	Mintage	VG	F	VF	XF	Unc
1601 Rare	—	—	—	—	—	—

MB# 37 DOPPIA

6.6200 g., Gold, 27 mm. **Ruler:** Ranuccio I **Obv:** Armored bust to left **Obv. Legend:** RANVT. FAR. PLA. P. DVX. IV. S. R. E. CONF. P. **Rev:** Clouds expelling wind, date divides mintmaster's initials in margin at bottom **Rev. Legend:** PELLIT. ET. ATRHAIT. **Note:** Ref. Var 1154; Fr. 906.

Date	Mintage	VG	F	VF	XF	Unc
1612 PP Rare	—	—	—	—	—	—
ND Rare	—	—	—	—	—	—

KM# 13 DOPPIA

6.5000 g., Gold, 27 mm. **Ruler:** Odoardo **Obv:** Armored bust with high collar to right, mintmaster's initials below **Obv. Legend:** ODOAR. F. PLA. - ET. PAR. DVX. V. **Rev:** Wolf facing left, crowned 3-stemmed plant in background, date in exergue **Rev. Legend:** PLAC - ENTIA - FLORET. **Note:** Ref. Var 1162; Fr 918.

Date	Mintage	VG	F	VF	XF	Unc
1626 LX Rare	—	—	—	—	—	—

MB# 35 2 DOPPIE

Gold Weight varies: 12.05-13.37g., 29-30 mm. **Ruler:** Ranuccio I **Obv:** Armored bust to left **Obv. Legend:** RANVT. FAR. PLA. P. DVX. IV. S. R. E. CONF. PER. **Rev:** Wolf facing left, crowned 3-stemmed plant in background, mintmaster's initials and date below **Rev. Legend:** PLACENTI - A. FLORET. **Note:** Ref. Var 1152; Fr. 907. Varieties exist.

Date	Mintage	VG	F	VF	XF	Unc
1601 PP	—	600	1,000	3,000	6,000	—
1602 PP	—	600	1,000	3,000	6,000	—
1604 PP	—	600	1,000	3,000	6,000	—
1607 PP	—	600	1,000	3,000	6,000	—
1608 PP	—	600	1,000	3,000	6,000	—
1609 PP	—	600	1,000	3,000	6,000	—
1610 PP	—	600	1,000	3,000	6,000	—
1611 PP	—	600	1,000	3,000	6,000	—
1613 PP	—	600	1,000	3,000	6,000	—
1614 PP	—	600	1,000	3,000	6,000	—
1615 PP	—	600	1,000	3,000	6,000	—
1616 PP	—	600	1,000	3,000	6,000	—
1617 PP	—	600	1,000	3,000	6,000	—
1618 PP	—	600	1,000	3,000	6,000	—
1619 PP	—	600	1,000	3,000	6,000	—
1622	—	600	1,000	3,000	6,000	—

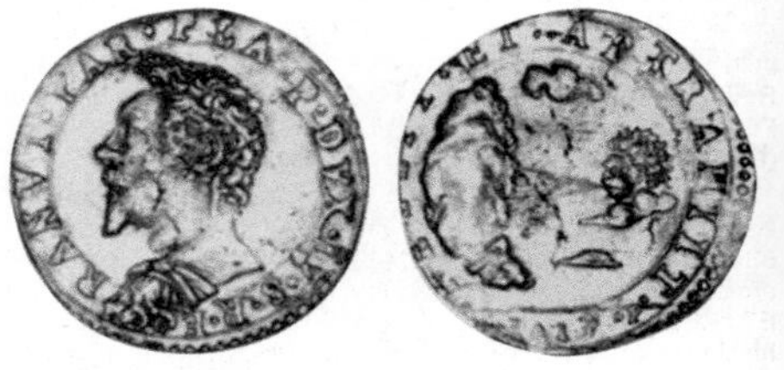

MB# 39 2 DOPPIE

Gold Weight varies: 12.94-13.48g., 27 mm. **Ruler:** Ranuccio I **Obv:** Armored bust to left **Obv. Legend:** RANVT. FAR. PLA. P. DVX. IV. S. R. E. CONF. PER. **Rev:** Clouds expelling wind, date divides mintmaster's initials in exergue **Rev. Legend:** PELLIT. ET. ATRAHIT. **Note:** Ref. Var 1151; Fr. 905. Varieties exist.

Date	Mintage	VG	F	VF	XF	Unc
1612 PP	—	2,200	3,850	9,500	16,500	—
1613 PP	—	2,200	3,850	9,500	16,500	—

KM# 3 2 DOPPIE

Gold, 31 mm. **Ruler:** Ranuccio I **Obv:** Armored bust to right, mintmaster's initials below **Obv. Legend:** RANVAR. PAR. PLA. P. DVX. IV. S. R. E. CONF. **Rev:** Wolf facing left, crowned 3-stemmed plant in background, mintmaster's initials and date below **Rev. Legend:** PLACENT - A - I. - FLORET. **Note:** Ref. Var 1153.

Date	Mintage	VG	F	VF	XF	Unc
1619 PP//PP Rare	—	—	—	—	—	—

KM# 10 2 DOPPIE

Gold Weight varies: 13.06-13.13g., 31 mm. **Ruler:** Odoardo **Obv:** Armored bust with high collar to left **Obv. Legend:** ODOARD. FARN. PLA. ET. PAR. DVX. V. **Rev:** Large flowering plant, date in margin at bottom **Rev. Legend:** FLOREBIT. E - T - GERMINABIT. **Note:** Ref. Var 1160; Fr. 915.

Date	Mintage	VG	F	VF	XF	Unc
1623	—	7,500	11,000	20,000	27,500	—
1624	—	7,500	11,000	20,000	27,500	—

KM# 14 2 DOPPIE
Gold Weight varies: 12.90-13.15g., 31 mm. **Ruler:** Odoardo **Obv:** Armored bust with high collar to right **Obv. Legend:** ODOAR: FAR: PL. - ET. PAR: DVX. V. **Rev:** Wolf facing left, crowned 3-stemmed plant in background, Roman numeral or Arabic date and mintmaster's initials in exergue **Rev. Legend:** PLAC - EN - TIA. FLORET. **Note:** Ref. Var 1161; Fr. 917.

Date	Mintage	VG	F	VF	XF	Unc
MDCXXVI (1626) LX	—	750	1,200	3,300	4,800	—
1626 LX	—	750	1,200	3,300	4,800	—
1631 LX	—	750	1,200	3,300	4,800	—

KM# 2 4 DOPPIE
26.8500 g., Gold, 35 mm. **Ruler:** Ranuccio I **Obv:** Armored bust to left in circle **Obv. Legend:** RANVT. FAR. PLA. P. DVX. IV. S. R. E. CONF. PER. **Rev:** Clouds expelling wind in circle, date divides mintmaster's initials in exergue **Rev. Legend:** PELLIT. ET. ATTRAHIT. **Note:** Ref. Var 1149; Fr. 904.

Date	Mintage	VG	F	VF	XF	Unc
1601 PP Rare	—	—	—	—	—	—

KM# 15 6 DOPPIE
39.5100 g., Gold, 43 mm. **Ruler:** Odoardo **Obv:** Armored bust with high collar to right, mintmaster's initials below **Obv. Legend:** ODOARDVS. FAR: PLAC: ET; PAR: DVX. V. **Rev:** St. Antoninus on horseback to right, holding pennant, Roman numeral date in exergue **Rev. Legend:** S: ANTN: - :MART: PROT: PLAC. **Note:** Ref. Var 1159; Fr. 916.

Date	Mintage	VG	F	VF	XF	Unc
MDCXXVI (1626) LX Rare	—	—	—	—	—	—

KM# 17 8 DOPPIE
52.6200 g., Gold, 43 mm. **Ruler:** Odoardo **Obv:** Armored bust with high collar, to right **Obv. Legend:** ODOARDVS. FAR: PL: ET. PAR: DVX. V. **Rev:** St. Antoninus on horseback to right, holding pennant, date divides mintmaster's initials in exergue **Rev. Legend:** S. ANTO - NIN: - .M: P: PL: **Note:** Ref. Var 1158; Fr. 915a.

Date	Mintage	VG	F	VF	XF	Unc
1629 LX Rare	—	—	—	—	—	—

KM# 25 10 DOPPIE
66.3100 g., Gold, 44 mm. **Ruler:** Ranuccio II **Obv:** Large armored and draped bust to left **Obv. Legend:** RANV. FAR. PLA. ET. PAR. DVX. VI. **Rev:** St. Antoninus on horseback to right, holding pennant, Roman numeral date in exergue **Rev. Legend:** S. ANTON. - .MART. PROT. PLAC. **Note:** Ref. Var 1172; Fr. 924.

Date	Mintage	VG	F	VF	XF	Unc
MDCLXXVI (1676) GR Rare	—	—	—	—	—	—

PIOMBINO

Piombino, a seaport near Leghorn in Tuscany opposite Elba, was variously owned and occupied but under general Pisan jurisdiction. A mint was opened in 1509. When Pisa was ceded to the Visconti, the Appiani family kept Piombino and Elba, and it was made an independent princedom in 1594 by Rudolph II. It passed to the Ludovici family, and finally thru marriage to the Boncompagni family. Its last coinage occurred in the Ludovici period by a father and son.

RULERS
Niccolo Ludovici, 1634-1665
Giovanni Baptiste Ludovisi, 1665-1699

PRINCIPALITY

STANDARD COINAGE

KM# 15 CRAZIA
Billon **Obv:** Crowned Ludovici arms, ASTRIS **Rev:** Madonna standing **Note:** Weight varies: 0.77-0.85 grams.

Date	Mintage	VG	F	VF	XF	Unc
1651	—	45.00	90.00	180	375	—
1652	—	45.00	90.00	180	375	—
ND	—	37.50	75.00	155	325	—

KM# 21 CRAZIA
Billon **Obv:** Ludovici arms **Rev:** St. Anastasia **Note:** Weight varies: 0.77-0.85 grams.

Date	Mintage	VG	F	VF	XF	Unc
1668	—	—	—	—	—	—

KM# 28 CRAZIA
Billon **Obv:** Crowned Ludovici arms D. IO. BAT. **Rev:** Madonna and child **Note:** Weight varies: 0.77-0.85 grams.

Date	Mintage	VG	F	VF	XF	Unc
1694	—	30.00	55.00	125	300	—
1695	—	30.00	55.00	125	300	—
1696	—	30.00	55.00	125	300	—

KM# 16 QUATTRINO
Copper **Obv:** Bust left, NICOL **Rev:** Crowned Ludovici arms **Note:** Weight varies: 0.90-1.20 grams.

Date	Mintage	VG	F	VF	XF	Unc
1651	—	60.00	105	215	400	—
1654	—	60.00	105	215	400	—
ND	—	55.00	90.00	180	350	—

KM# 25 QUATTRINO
Copper **Obv:** Crowned Ludovici arms **Rev:** PRINC./PLVMB./date **Note:** Weight varies: 0.90-1.20 grams.

Date	Mintage	VG	F	VF	XF	Unc
1692	—	37.50	60.00	135	325	—
1693	—	37.50	60.00	135	325	—
1694	—	37.50	60.00	135	325	—

KM# 26 QUATTRINO
Copper **Obv:** Bust of Gio left, IO:BAT **Rev:** Crowned Ludovici arms, ASTRIS **Note:** Weight varies: 0.90-1.20 grams.

Date	Mintage	VG	F	VF	XF	Unc
ND	—	30.00	55.00	125	300	—

KM# 29 DUETTA (2 Quattrino)
Copper **Obv:** Crowned Ludovici arms **Rev:** 1694 in circle **Note:** Weight varies: 0.98-1.16 grams.

Date	Mintage	VG	F	VF	XF	Unc
1694	—	55.00	90.00	180	375	—

KM# 27 SOLDO (3 Quattrino)
1.8700 g., Copper **Obv:** Crowned Ludovici arms **Rev:** PRINC./PLVMB./date

Date	Mintage	VG	F	VF	XF	Unc
1693	—	60.00	105	80.00	400	—
1694	—	60.00	105	80.00	400	—
1695	—	60.00	105	80.00	400	—

KM# 8 1/2 PAOLA
1.4700 g., Silver **Obv:** Bust left **Obv. Legend:** NICOL. **Rev:** Crowned Ludovici arms

Date	Mintage	VG	F	VF	XF	Unc
1642	—	—	—	—	—	—
1643	—	—	—	—	—	—

KM# 9 1/2 PAOLA
1.4700 g., Silver **Obv:** Crowned multiple arms **Rev:** MA monogram

Date	Mintage	VG	F	VF	XF	Unc
ND	—	—	—	—	—	—

KM# 10 1/2 PAOLA
1.4700 g., Silver **Obv:** Crowned Ludovici arms **Rev:** B in cartouche

Date	Mintage	VG	F	VF	XF	Unc
ND	—	—	—	—	—	—

KM# 20 PAOLA
Silver **Obv:** Bust of Gio right **Rev:** Crowned multiple arms **Note:** Weight varies: 2.05-2.75 grams.

Date	Mintage	VG	F	VF	XF	Unc
ND(1665)	—	—	—	—	—	—

KM# 7 TESTONE
8.9000 g., Silver **Obv:** Bust left **Rev:** Crowned multiple arms

Date	Mintage	VG	F	VF	XF	Unc
1641	—	—	—	—	—	—
1651	—	—	—	—	—	—

KM# 30 TESTONE
8.9000 g., Silver **Obv:** Bust right **Obv. Legend:** PRINCEPS. **Rev:** Crowned Ludovici arms

Date	Mintage	VG	F	VF	XF	Unc
1695	—	—	—	—	—	—
ND	—	—	—	—	—	—

KM# 35 1/2 PIASTRE
13.1100 g., Silver **Obv:** Crowned multiple arms **Rev:** Sea with two fortresses

Date	Mintage	VG	F	VF	XF	Unc
1697 Rare	—	—	—	—	—	—

KM# 31 PIASTRE
25.6100 g., Silver **Obv:** Bust right **Rev:** Harbor and city view **Note:** Dav. #4133.

Date	Mintage	VG	F	VF	XF	Unc
1695 Rare	—	—	—	—	—	—

KM# 5 1/2 SCUDO
15.9000 g., Silver **Obv:** Bust right **Rev:** Crowned Ludovici arms

Date	Mintage	VG	F	VF	XF	Unc
1640 Rare	—	—	—	—	—	—

KM# 6 SCUDO
32.0000 g., Silver **Obv:** Bust left, date below **Rev:** Crowned multiple arms **Note:** Dav. #4131.

Date	Mintage	VG	F	VF	XF	Unc
1640 Rare	—	—	—	—	—	—

KM# 18 SCUDO
32.0000 g., Silver **Obv:** Bust right **Rev:** Crowned multiple arms divide date **Note:** Dav. #4132.

Date	Mintage	VG	F	VF	XF	Unc
1654 Rare	—	—	—	—	—	—

KM# 32 ZECCHINO
3.3800 g., 0.9860 Gold 0.1071 oz. AGW **Obv:** Head of Giovanni Baptiste right, date below **Rev:** Crowned arms

Date	Mintage	VG	F	VF	XF	Unc
1695 Rare	—	—	—	—	—	—

KM# 33 ZECCHINO
3.3800 g., 0.9860 Gold 0.1071 oz. AGW **Obv:** Head of Giovanni Baptiste right **Rev:** Crowned and mantled arms, date divided at top

Date	Mintage	VG	F	VF	XF	Unc
1696 Rare	—	—	—	—	—	—

KM# 11 DOPPIA
7.0000 g., 0.9860 Gold 0.2219 oz. AGW **Obv:** Crowned Ludovici arms **Rev:** Madonna standing

Date	Mintage	VG	F	VF	XF	Unc
1644 Rare	—	—	—	—	—	—

KM# 34 DOPPIA
7.0000 g., 0.9860 Gold 0.2219 oz. AGW **Obv:** Bust of Giovanni Baptiste right, date below **Rev:** Crowned arms in Order collar

Date	Mintage	VG	F	VF	XF	Unc
1695 Rare	—	—	—	—	—	—

KM# 17 2 DOPPIE
13.2700 g., Gold **Obv:** Crowned arms **Rev:** Madonna standing

Date	Mintage	VG	F	VF	XF	Unc
1651 Rare	—	—	—	—	—	—

PISA

A city located on the Arno River in western Tuscany on the Tyrrhenian Sea, site of the famous leaning tower and mint. Rebelled against Florentine rule 1494-1509 and was under the Medici lineage of the Tuscan Grand Dukes, except for the French occupation between 1807-14. It joined the Kingdom of Italy in 1860.

GRAND DUKES
Ferdinand I de'Medici, 1595-1608
Cosimo II de'Medici, 1608-1620
Ferdinand II de'Medici, 1620-1670
Cosimo III de'Medici, 1670-1723

MINT NAME
Pisa

CITY

STANDARD COINAGE

KM# 5 CRAZIA
Billon **Obv:** Medici arms **Rev:** Pisan cross **Note:** Weight varies: 0.62-1.06 grams.

Date	Mintage	VG	F	VF	XF	Unc
ND	—	—	—	—	—	—

KM# 6 2 QUATTRINI (1 Duetto)
Billon **Obv:** Pisan cross **Rev:** QVAT/TRI/NI/II **Note:** Weight varies: 0.65-1.18 grams.

Date	Mintage	VG	F	VF	XF	Unc
ND	—	—	—	—	—	—

KM# 35 2 QUATTRINI (1 Duetto)
Copper **Ruler:** Fian Gastone **Obv:** Medici arms **Obv. Legend:** QVAT TRIN. II. **Rev:** Pisan cross, date **Note:** Weight varies: 1.06-1.40 grams.

Date	Mintage	VG	F	VF	XF	Unc
1679	—	12.00	22.00	45.00	80.00	—
1680	—	12.00	22.00	45.00	80.00	—
1681	—	12.00	22.00	45.00	80.00	—
1682	—	12.00	22.00	45.00	80.00	—
1687	—	12.00	22.00	45.00	80.00	—
1689	—	12.00	22.00	45.00	80.00	—

KM# 7 3 QUATTRINI (1 Soldo)
Billon **Obv:** Pisan cross **Rev. Inscription:** QVATTRI / NI / III **Note:** Weight varies: 1.14-1.18 grams.

Date	Mintage	VG	F	VF	XF	Unc
ND	—	—	—	—	—	—

KM# 36 3 QUATTRINI (1 Soldo)
Billon **Ruler:** Fian Gastone **Obv:** Medici arms **Obv. Legend:** QVAT TRINI. III **Rev:** Pisan cross **Note:** Weight varies: 1.14-1.18 grams.

Date	Mintage	VG	F	VF	XF	Unc
1679	—	15.00	25.00	50.00	90.00	—
1680	—	15.00	25.00	50.00	90.00	—
1681	—	15.00	25.00	50.00	90.00	—
1687	—	15.00	25.00	50.00	90.00	—

KM# 8 4 QUATTRINI
Billon **Obv:** Pisan cross **Rev:** QUATTRI/NI/IIII **Note:** Weight varies: 1.07-1.10 grams.

Date	Mintage	VG	F	VF	XF	Unc
ND	—	—	—	—	—	—

KM# 9 10 SOLDI
2.5100 g., Silver **Obv:** Crowned Medici arms **Rev:** Arms of Florence **Note:** Struck for the Levant.

Date	Mintage	VG	F	VF	XF	Unc
ND	—	—	—	—	—	—

KM# 10 10 SOLDI
2.5100 g., Silver **Rev:** Grand Duke standing, three figures kneeling

Date	Mintage	VG	F	VF	XF	Unc
ND	—	—	—	—	—	—

KM# 15 TALLERO

Silver **Ruler:** Ferdinand I de'Medici **Note:** Weight varies: 25.38-28.72 grams. Dav. #4186.

Date	Mintage	VG	F	VF	XF	Unc
1601	—	150	300	600	1,000	2,500
1603	—	150	300	600	1,000	2,500
1604	—	150	300	600	1,000	2,500
1605	—	150	300	600	1,000	2,500
1606	—	150	300	600	1,000	2,500
1607	—	150	300	600	1,000	2,500
1608	—	150	300	600	1,000	2,500

KM# 16.1 TALLERO

Silver **Obv:** Half figure right, 1609 below **Obv. Legend:** COSMVS. MED. MAGN. ETR. DVX. IIII. **Rev. Legend:** PISA. INVETVSTAE. MAIESTATIS. MEMORIAM. **Note:** Weight varies: 23.98-29.50 grams. Dav. #4193.

Date	Mintage	VG	F	VF	XF	Unc
1609	—	250	500	1,000	1,750	—

KM# 16.2 TALLERO

Silver **Obv:** Larger bust **Note:** Weight varies: 23.98-29.50 grams. Dav. #4194.

Date	Mintage	VG	F	VF	XF	Unc
1611	—	250	500	1,000	1,750	—
1612	—	250	500	1,000	1,750	—

KM# 16.3 TALLERO

Silver **Note:** Weight varies: 23.98-29.50 grams. Dav. #4195.

Date	Mintage	VG	F	VF	XF	Unc
1614	—	85.00	175	350	750	—
1615	—	85.00	175	350	750	—
1616	—	85.00	175	350	750	—
1618	—	85.00	175	350	750	—
1619	—	85.00	175	350	750	—
1620	—	85.00	175	350	750	—

KM# 20 TALLERO

Silver **Obv:** Bust of Ferdinand II right **Rev:** Crowned Medici arms **Note:** Weight varies: 27.95-28.31 grams. Dav. #4197.

Date	Mintage	VG	F	VF	XF	Unc
1621	—	100	200	500	1,000	3,500
1623	—	100	200	500	1,000	3,500
1629	—	100	200	500	1,000	3,500

KM# 16.4 TALLERO

Silver **Note:** Varieties exist. Certain dies were re-engraved, sometimes leaving the earlier ruler's name quite discernable.Weight varies: 23.98-29.50 grams. Dav. #4196.

Date	Mintage	VG	F	VF	XF	Unc
1621	—	85.00	175	350	750	—
ND	—	85.00	175	350	750	—

KM# 29 TALLERO

Silver **Obv:** Mature bust **Note:** Weight varies: 27.95-28.31 grams. Dav. #4203.

Date	Mintage	VG	F	VF	XF	Unc
1648	—	85.00	175	350	750	—
1654	—	85.00	175	350	750	—

KM# 25 1/2 DOPPIA

Gold **Obv:** Pisan cross **Rev:** Ascension of the Virgin Mary **Note:** Weight varies: 3.06-3.25 grams.

Date	Mintage	VG	F	VF	XF	Unc
1643	—	550	850	1,750	3,250	—
ND	—	550	850	1,750	3,250	—

KM# 26 DOPPIA

6.5300 g., Gold **Obv:** Pisan cross **Rev:** Ascension of the Virgin Mary

Date	Mintage	VG	F	VF	XF	Unc
1641	—	550	875	1,750	5,500	—
1644	—	550	875	1,750	5,500	—
1647	—	550	875	1,750	5,500	—
1655	—	550	875	1,750	5,500	—
ND	—	550	875	1,750	5,500	—

KM# 27 DOPPIA

6.5300 g., Gold **Obv:** Plain cross **Obv. Legend:** COSMVS

Date	Mintage	VG	F	VF	XF	Unc
ND	—	3,000	5,400	7,800	12,000	—

KM# 28 2 DOPPIE

13.2000 g., Gold **Obv:** Pisan cross **Rev:** Ascension of the Virgin Mary

Date	Mintage	VG	F	VF	XF	Unc
ND Rare	—	—	—	—	—	—

RETEGNO

(Trivulzio)

A commune in the province of Milan, it was made a barony in 1654 by Ferdinand II. The mint right was given to Cardinal Gian Giacomo Teodoro Trivulzio. The family held the county of Misox in Switzerland.

RULERS

Hercules Teodoro Trivulzio, 1656-1664
Antonio Teodoro Trivulzio, 1676-1678
Antonio Gaetano Trivulzio-Gallio, 1679-1705

BARONY

STANDARD COINAGE

KM# 5 1/4 FILIPPO

6.9500 g., Silver **Obv:** Bust of Hercules Teodoro right **Obv. Legend:** THEO. **Rev:** Crowned arms

Date	Mintage	VG	F	VF	XF	Unc
ND(1656)	—	700	1,350	3,000	—	—

KM# 10 1/4 FILIPPO

Silver **Obv:** Bust of Antonio Teodor right **Obv. Legend:** THEODORVS. **Rev:** Arms in cartouche, VNICA/MENS at sides **Note:** Weight varies: 5.89-6.70 grams.

Date	Mintage	VG	F	VF	XF	Unc
1676	—	350	700	1,850	—	—

KM# 25 1/4 FILIPPO

Silver **Obv:** Bust of Antonio Gaetano right **Obv. Legend:** ANT. **Rev:** Crowned arms above two shields, date in legend **Note:** Weight varies: 6.75-6.90 grams.

Date	Mintage	VG	F	VF	XF	Unc
1686	—	350	750	1,950	—	—

KM# 6 1/2 FILIPPO
13.9000 g., Silver, 43 mm. **Obv:** Bust of Hercules Teodoro right **Obv. Legend:** THEO. **Rev:** Crowned arms

Date	Mintage	VG	F	VF	XF	Unc
ND(1656)	—	650	1,250	3,000	—	—

KM# 11 1/2 FILIPPO
13.5000 g., Silver **Obv:** Bust of Antonio Teodoro right **Obv. Legend:** THEOD(O).

Date	Mintage	VG	F	VF	XF	Unc
1676	—	250	600	1,850	—	—

KM# 12 1/2 FILIPPO
Silver, 43 mm. **Ruler:** Antonio Teodoro Trivulzio **Note:** Weight varies: 13.32-13.85 grams.

Date	Mintage	VG	F	VF	XF	Unc
1676	—	200	500	1,500	2,500	—

KM# 26 1/2 FILIPPO
13.5000 g., Silver **Obv:** Bust of Antonio Gaetano right **Obv. Legend:** ANT. **Rev:** Crowned arms above two shields, date in legend

Date	Mintage	VG	F	VF	XF	Unc
1686	—	350	650	1,650	2,750	—

KM# 13 FILIPPO (Largo)
Silver, 51 mm. **Obv. Legend:** THEODORVS... **Note:** Weight varies: 27.28-27.50 grams. Similar to KM#14. Dav. #4136.

Date	Mintage	VG	F	VF	XF	Unc
1676	—	300	600	1,150	2,250	—

KM# 14 FILIPPO (Stretto)
Silver, 40 mm. **Obv. Legend:** THEOD(O). **Note:** Weight varies: 27.28-27.50 grams. Dav. #4137.

Date	Mintage	VG	F	VF	XF	Unc
1676	—	300	550	1,000	1,850	—

KM# 28 FILIPPO (Stretto)
28.5000 g., Silver, 43 mm. **Obv:** Bust of Antonio right, .130. below **Note:** Dav. #4141.

Date	Mintage	VG	F	VF	XF	Unc
1686	—	300	600	1,450	2,750	—

KM# 27 FILIPPO (Stretto)
28.5000 g., Silver **Note:** Similar to KM#28. Dav. #4140.

Date	Mintage	VG	F	VF	XF	Unc
1686	—	300	600	1,400	2,700	—

KM# 15.1 2 FILIPPI (Largo)
Silver, 50 mm. **Obv:** Bust of Antonio Teodoro right **Obv. Legend:** THEON(ORVS). **Note:** Weight varies: 55.34-55.50 grams. Dav. #4135.

Date	Mintage	VG	F	VF	XF	Unc
1676	—	350	650	1,350	2,500	—

KM# 15.2 2 FILIPPI (Stretto)
Silver, 50 mm. **Note:** Weight varies: 55.34-55.50 grams. Dav. #4138.

Date	Mintage	VG	F	VF	XF	Unc
1677 Rare	—	—	—	—	—	—

KM# 15.3 2 FILIPPI (Stretto)
Silver, 50 mm. **Note:** Weight varies: 55.34-55.50 grams. Dav. #4138A.

Date	Mintage	VG	F	VF	XF	Unc
1677 Rare; restrike	—	—	—	—	—	—

KM# 16 3 FILIPPI
Silver **Obv:** Bust of Antonio Teodaro right **Obv. Legend:** THEODORVS **Rev:** Supported arms **Note:** Weight varies: 82.20-83.20 grams. Dav. #4134.

Date	Mintage	VG	F	VF	XF	Unc
1676	—	1,200	2,500	4,500	7,500	—

KM# 29 3 FILIPPI

83.2500 g., Silver, 48 mm. **Obv:** Bust of Antonio Gaetano right **Obv. Legend:** ANT. **Rev:** Crowned arms above two shields, date in legend **Note:** Dav. #4139.

Date	Mintage	VG	F	VF	XF	Unc
1686	—	1,500	3,000	5,500	9,000	—

KM# 17 4 FILIPPI

Silver, 53.5 mm. **Obv:** Bust of Antonio Teodoro right **Obv. Legend:** THEODORVS. **Rev:** Supported arms

Date	Mintage	VG	F	VF	XF	Unc
1676 Rare	—	—	—	—	—	—

Note: Numismatica Ars Classica Auction 32, 1-06, VF realized approximately $16,270

KM# 30 2 DOPPIE

7.0000 g., 0.9860 Gold 0.2219 oz. AGW **Obv:** Soldier standing right in circle with 12 rays, three Volti with imperial crown **Rev:** Seven-line inscription

Date	Mintage	VG	F	VF	XF	Unc
1686 Rare	—	—	—	—	—	—

KM# 18 ZECCHINO

3.5000 g., 0.9860 Gold 0.1109 oz. AGW **Obv:** Equestrian figure of Antonio Teodoro right **Rev:** Tied bundle of corn ears

Date	Mintage	VG	F	VF	XF	Unc
1676	—	1,650	3,250	5,500	8,500	—

KM# 19 10 ZECCHINI

35.0000 g., 0.9860 Gold 1.1095 oz. AGW **Obv:** Teodoro

Date	Mintage	VG	F	VF	XF	Unc
1677	—	—	—	25,000	35,000	—

Note: Stack's International sale 3-88 VF realized $20,900

KM# 31 10 ZECCHINI

35.0000 g., 0.9860 Gold 1.1095 oz. AGW **Obv:** Bust of Antonio Gaetano **Rev:** Elaborately crested helmet above arms, date in legend

Date	Mintage	VG	F	VF	XF	Unc
1686	—	—	—	20,000	30,000	—

Note: Bowers and Merena Guia sale 3-88 Unc. realized $17,600

TRADE COINAGE

KM# 20 DUCAT

3.5000 g., 0.9860 Gold 0.1109 oz. AGW **Obv:** Soldier standing right in inner circle **Rev:** 6-line inscription in tablet **Note:** Fr. #988.

Date	Mintage	VG	F	VF	XF	Unc
1677	—	2,000	3,500	6,500	10,000	—

KM# 32 DUCAT

3.5000 g., 0.9860 Gold 0.1109 oz. AGW **Ruler:** Antonio GaetanoTrivulzio-Gallio **Obv:** Soldier standing right divides date **Rev:** 6-line inscription in tablet **Note:** Fr. #992.

Date	Mintage	VG	F	VF	XF	Unc
ND(1686)	—	900	2,000	5,000	9,000	—
1686	—	900	2,000	5,000	9,000	—

KM# 21 2 DUCAT

7.0000 g., 0.9860 Gold 0.2219 oz. AGW **Obv:** Soldier standing right in inner circle **Rev:** 6-line inscription in tablet **Note:** Fr. #987.

Date	Mintage	VG	F	VF	XF	Unc
1677	—	2,500	4,000	7,500	12,500	—

KM# 33 2 DUCAT

7.0000 g., 0.9860 Gold 0.2219 oz. AGW **Ruler:** Antonio GaetanoTrivulzio-Gallio **Obv:** Soldier standing right divdies date **Rev:** 6-line inscription in tablet **Note:** Fr. #991.

Date	Mintage	VG	F	VF	XF	Unc
ND(1686)	—	1,500	3,000	6,000	10,000	—
1686	—	1,500	3,000	6,000	10,000	—

RONCO

This county in Liguria north of Genoa belonged to a branch of the Spinola family. Mint privileges were obtained from Ferdinand III. Napoleon and his grandson, who were also marquises of Roccaforte were the only members of the family to strike coins. The mint was closed in 1699.

RULERS

Napoleone Spinola, 1647-1672
Carlo Spinola, 1699-1720

COUNTY

STANDARD COINAGE

KM# 10 LUIGINO

Silver **Obv:** Bust right, VS8 below **Rev:** Crowned double eagle, shield divides date **Note:** Weight varies: 1.90-2.22 grams.

Date	Mintage	VG	F	VF	XF	Unc
1668	—	225	450	950	1,750	3,500
1669	—	225	450	950	1,750	3,500

KM# 11 LUIGINO

Silver **Obv:** Crowned double eagle **Rev:** Crowned double eagle **Note:** Weight varies: 1.90-2.22 grams.

Date	Mintage	VG	F	VF	XF	Unc
1668	—	125	250	400	750	—

KM# 12 LUIGINO

Silver **Obv:** Bust right, date below **Rev:** Crowned double eagle **Note:** Weight varies: 1.90-2.22 grams.

Date	Mintage	VG	F	VF	XF	Unc
1668	—	235	475	1,000	1,850	—

KM# 5 1/4 SCUDO

Silver **Obv:** Bust left, date below **Rev:** Crowned double eagle with shield **Note:** Weight varies: 5.45-7.75 grams.

Date	Mintage	VG	F	VF	XF	Unc
1647	—	1,000	2,000	5,000	—	—

Note: Numismatica Ars Classical Auction 60, 6-11, XF realized approximately $18,260

KM# 14 1/4 SCUDO

Silver **Obv:** Bust right **Rev:** Crowned double eagle with shield, date in legend **Note:** Weight varies: 5.45-7.75 grams.

Date	Mintage	VG	F	VF	XF	Unc
1669	—	1,250	2,500	6,000	—	—

KM# 20 1/4 SCUDO

Silver **Obv:** Bust of Carlo right **Note:** Weight varies: 5.45-7.75 grams.

Date	Mintage	VG	F	VF	XF	Unc
1699	—	1,750	3,500	8,000	—	—

KM# 21 1/2 SCUDO

19.2200 g., Silver **Obv:** Bust right, *B:VII:12 below **Rev:** Crowned double eagle with shield

Date	Mintage	VG	F	VF	XF	Unc
1699 Rare	—	—	—	—	—	—

KM# 15 SCUDO

Silver **Obv:** Napoleone standing **Rev:** Crowned double eagle with shield **Note:** Dav. #4142. Weight varies: 28.90-37.50 grams.

Date	Mintage	VG	F	VF	XF	Unc
1669 Rare	—	—	—	—	—	—

Note: Künker Auction 180, 1-11, XF-Unc realized approximately $136,930. Numismatica Ars Classica, Auction 60, 6-11, XF realized approximately $46,740. Numismatica Ars Classica Auction 32, planchet flaw, otherwise XF/near Unc realized approximately $24,605

KM# 16 SCUDO

Silver **Obv:** Bust of Napoleone right **Note:** Dav. #4143. Weight varies: 28.90-37.50 grams.

Date	Mintage	VG	F	VF	XF	Unc
1669	—	3,500	7,500	15,000	—	—

Note: Numismatica Ars Classica Auction 60, 6-11, XF realized approximately $30,670

KM# 22 SCUDO

Silver **Obv:** Bust of Carlo right **Note:** Dav. #4144. Weight varies: 28.90-37.50 grams.

Date	Mintage	VG	F	VF	XF	Unc
1699 Rare	—	—	—	—	—	—

KM# 23 DOPPIA

7.0000 g., 0.9860 Gold 0.2219 oz. AGW **Obv:** Bust of Carlo right **Rev:** Crowned arms on crowned imperial eagle

Date	Mintage	VG	F	VF	XF	Unc
ND(1699) Rare	—	—	—	—	—	—

KM# 6 2 DOPPIE

12.2800 g., Gold **Obv:** Bust of Napoleone left **Rev:** Crowned double eagle with Spinola arms

Date	Mintage	VG	F	VF	XF	Unc
1647 Rare	—	—	—	—	—	—

TRADE COINAGE

KM# 13 DUCAT

3.5000 g., 0.9860 Gold 0.1109 oz. AGW **Obv:** Bust of Napoleone right **Rev:** Crowned imperial eagle with crowned arms on chest

Date	Mintage	VG	F	VF	XF	Unc
1668 Rare	—	—	—	—	—	—

KM# 7 4 DUCAT

14.0000 g., 0.9860 Gold 0.4438 oz. AGW **Obv:** Bust of Napoleone left, date below **Rev:** Crowned imperial eagle with crowned arms on breast

Date	Mintage	VG	F	VF	XF	Unc
1647 Rare	—	—	—	—	—	—

ROVEGNO

A small territory in the province of Pavia in Lombardy. It was in the possession of the Doria of Genoa. The young prince, who was also Count of Loana, struck a piece in imitation of the Dutch lion dollar.

RULER

Giovanni Andrea III Doria, 1654-1700

PRINCIPALITY

STANDARD COINAGE

KM# 1 TALLERO

Silver **Obv:** Knight behind shield **Rev:** Rampant lion **Note:** Dav. #4145

Date	Mintage	VG	F	VF	XF	Unc
1669 Rare	—	—	—	—	—	—

SABBIONETA

Provincial Town

The village of Sabbioneta was founded in ancient times and was ceded by the Venetians to Duke Gianfrancesco II Gonzaga of Mantua in 1426. His grandson, Gianfrancesco the Younger, established a cadet line of the Gonzagas in Sabbioneta and died in 1496. The ruling captain in 1565 was raised to the rank of marchese, then to prince in 1574 and finally to duke in 1577. The line of Gonzagas died out in 1637, but the titles were inherited through marriage to a Spaniard, Ramiro de Guzmán. His son died without heirs and the coinage came to an end. In 1748, Sabbioneta was acquired by the Duke of Parma.

RULERS

Isabella, 1591-1637
 Luigi Carafa de Stigliano, 1591-1638
Anna, 1638-1644
 Ramiro de Guzmán, Duke of Medinas les Torres, 1644-1668
Nicolò Ramirez de Guzmán, 1644-1684

Reference:

V = Alberto Varesi, ***Monete Italiane Regionali: Lombardia, Zecche Minori***. Pavia, 1995.

PROVINCIAL TOWN

STANDARD COINAGE

KM# 1 DUCATO

21.4000 g., Billon, 39 mm. **Ruler:** Luigi Carafa and Isabella **Obv:** Crowned shield of 2-fold arms divided horizontally, imperial eagle in upper half, LIBERTAS in diagonal band in lower half, chain of Order of the Golden Fleece suspended around **Obv. Legend:** ALOY. CARRAF. ET. ISABEL. - GONZ. SABLONET. DVCS. **Rev:** Madonna standing on upturned crescent moon, holding Child, rays and flames around, date divided in margin below **Rev. Legend:** LVNA. SVB. PE - DIBVS. EIVS. **Note:** Ref. V-941. Prev. KM#15.

Date	Mintage	VG	F	VF	XF	Unc
1605 Rare	—	—	—	—	—	—

KM# 3 TALLERO

Billon Weight varies: 25.35-26.87g., 42-43 mm. **Ruler:** Luigi Carafa **Obv:** Armored knight turned to right, shield of arms with rampant lion to left below in front **Obv. Legend:** MO. ARG. PRO. D. AL. - CARAF. D. SABL. **Rev:** Rampant lion to left in circle, date at end of legend **Rev. Legend:** CONFIDENS. DNO. NON. MOVETVR. **Note:** Ref. V-950. Prev. KM#20.

Date	Mintage	VG	F	VF	XF	Unc
1637 Rare	—	—	—	—	—	—

KM# 4 TALLERO

Billon Weight varies: 25.35-26.87g., 42-43 mm. **Ruler:** Luigi Carafa **Obv:** Armored knight turned to right, shield of arms with rampant lion left below in front **Obv. Legend:** MO x NO x ALOY x - CARF x DVX x SAB. **Rev:** Rampant lion in circle **Rev. Legend:** CONFIDENS x DNO x NON x MOVETVR. **Note:** Ref. V-950. Imitation of lion daalder of Holland. Prev. KM#12.

Date	Mintage	VG	F	VF	XF	Unc
ND(1637-38)	—	3,000	6,000	9,000	13,500	—

KM# 6 DUCATONE

Silver Weight varies: 31.20-31.65g., 45-46 mm. **Ruler:** Nicolò Ramirez **Obv:** Crowned ornate shield of 4-fold arms with central shield, chain of Order of the Golden Fleece suspended around **Obv. Legend:** • NICOLAVS • D • G • SABLONET – DVX • ET • OBSTIL • PRIN • ET • C • **Rev:** Madonna standing on upturned crescent moon, holding Child, flames and rays around, date in margin below **Rev. Legend:** • - LVNA • SVB • PE • – • DIBVS • EIVS • ❊ • **Note:** Ref. V-951; Dav. 4146. Prev. KM#25.

Date	Mintage	VG	F	VF	XF	Unc
1666 Rare	—	—	—	—	—	—

Note: Numismatica Ars Classica Auction 32, 1-06, XF realized approximately $24,605; Astarte S.A. Auction XIX, 5-06, VF realized approximately $17,510

SAN MARTINO

A commune in the province of Mantua was a fief given to the Gonzaga family who were also lords of Bozzolo.

RULER

Scipione Gonzaga, prince of Bozzolo

COMMUNE

STANDARD COINAGE

KM# 5 QUATTRINO

Copper **Obv:** Head right **Rev:** SANTO/MARTIN in cartouche **Note:** Weight varies: 0.46-0.70 grams.

Date	Mintage	VG	F	VF	XF	Unc
ND	—	160	300	550	—	—

KM# 6 2 QUATTRINI

1.4700 g., Billon **Obv:** Head right **Rev:** SANTO/MARTIN in cartouche

Date	Mintage	VG	F	VF	XF	Unc
ND	—	240	500	900	—	—

SAVOY

(Savoia)

The territory of Savoy encompassed the northwestern corner of Italy and parts of southeastern France, although the extent of its borders fluctuated over the centuries. Savoy was part of the Kingdom of Arles until 1032, when a son of a count of Bellay gained a measure of independence with the title Count of Aosta-Maurienne. His son, Oddone (1056-60), is recognized as the first ruler of the House of Savoy, but it was not until 1125 that the title became Count of the Empire. During the next few centuries, Savoy expanded to include most of the territory south of Lake Geneva (now in Switzerland) and gained Piedmont, with its capital of Torino (Turin). The count was raised to the rank of Prince of the Empire in 1310 and became Duke of Savoy in 1416.

Savoy was almost constantly caught up in conflicts between the various powers of Europe - the Empire, France and Spain. During 1533 to 1536, Savoy lost consecutively Vaud, Geneva, Valais, Chablais and Gex, then suffered French occupation until 1559. Montferrat was partly acquired in 1631, with the rest following in 1708. The Countship of Desana (see) also became part of the duchy in 1676. During the war year of 1713, Savoy conquered a number of fortresses along the French frontier and was given Sicily in reward. That island was exchanged with Austria for Sardinia in 1720 and all the holdings of the House of Savoy became the Kingdom of Sardinia (see), also called Sardinia-Piedmont.

RULERS

Carlo Emanuele I il Grande, 1580-1630
Vittorio Amedeo I il Leone di Susa, 1630-1637
Francesco Giacinto, Fior di Paradiso, 1637-1638
 under regency of his mother, Maria Cristina di Borbone
Carlo Emanuele II, 1638-1675
 under regency of his mother, Maria Cristina, 1638-1648
 under supposed regency of his uncles, Tommaso and Maurizio, 1639-1641
Vittorio Amedeo II, 1675-1730
 under regency of his mother, Maria Giovanna Battista di Savoia-Namours, 1675-
 1680
 alone as Duke, 1680-1720

MINT MARKS AND OFFICIALS' INITIALS

Aosta Mint

Initial	Date	Name
A or rosette	ca. 1553-1630	Aosta mint

Asti Mint

5-pointed star	1559-1630	Asti mint

Bourg Mint

BD, D	ca. 1580-1630	Emanuele or Filiberto Diano
B	ca. 1580-1630	Bourg mint

Chambéry Mint

Small 5-pointed star	ca. 1580-1630	Chambéry mint
CI	ca. 1580-1630	Caspare Cornaglia (?)
HG	ca. 1580-1630	Heredes Grobert
P	1640-42	Pietro Perrinet

Gex Mint

G	ca. 1580-1630	Gex mint
I, IG	ca. 1580-1630	Claudio Janin

Leipzig Mint

L		Leipzig mint

Nizza Mint

N	ca. 1504-1630	Nizza (Nice) mint

Torino Mint

RG, G	ca. 1553-80 (perhaps to 1630)	Rolando Gastaldo (Cornuato)
T or bull's head	ca. 1580-1630	Torino mint
G + 6-pointed star	ca. 1580-1630	Chiaffredo Grobert
MT	ca. 1580-1630	Mario d'Alvigi
TAV	ca. 1648	Unknown

Vercelli Mint

V	ca. 1504-1630	Vercelli mint
BS	ca. 1580-1630	Unknown

Unknown Mint

C	ca. 1580-1630	Unknown (Aosta?
HA	ca. 1580-1630	Unknown
ST	ca. 1580-1630	Unknown
V	ca. 1580-1630	Cesari Valgrandi

Other mints without known mint officials' initials or symbols: Biella, Cuneo, Ivrea, Moncalieri, Santhia'

ARMS

Plain cross with equal length arms

REFERENCE

Cud = Sergio Cudazzo, **Monete Italiane Regionali: Casa Savoia**, Pavia: Numismatica Varesi, 2005.

DUCHY

STANDARD COINAGE

KM# 180 QUARTO (1/4 Soldo)

0.9100 g., Copper, 17 mm. **Ruler:** Carlo Emanuele II under regency **Obv:** Monogram of 2 intertwined letter C's, one reversed, crown above **Obv. Legend:** CAROLVS. EMANVEL. **Rev:** Crowned shield of Savoy arms, date at end of legend **Rev. Legend:** D. G. DVX. SAB. **Note:** Ref. Cud. 772.

Date	Mintage	Good	VG	F	VF	XF
1641 Rare	—	—	—	—	—	—

KM# 224 QUARTO (1/4 Soldo)

Billon Weight varies: 1.03-1.50g., 17 mm. **Ruler:** Carlo Emanuele II alone **Obv:** Large knot, crown above, rosette below **Obv. Legend:** CAR. EM. D. G. DVX. SAB. **Rev:** Plain cross in circle **Rev. Legend:** PRIN. PEDEMON. REX. CY. **Note:** Ref. Cud. 830.

Date	Mintage	Good	VG	F	VF	XF
ND(1648-75)	—	18.00	35.00	70.00	225	—

KM# 261 QUARTO (1/4 Soldo)

1.0600 g., Billon, 15.5 mm. **Ruler:** Carlo Emanuele II alone **Obv:** Crowned 'CE' monogram, date below **Obv. Legend:** CAR. EM. D. G. DVX. SAB. **Rev:** Plain cross in circle **Rev. Legend:** PRIN. PEDEMON. REX. CY. **Note:** Ref. Cud. 831. Mint uncertain.

Date	Mintage	Good	VG	F	VF	XF
1657 Rare	—	—	—	—	—	—

KM# 320 QUARTO (1/4 Soldo)

Copper Weight varies: 3.80-3.95g., 22 mm. **Ruler:** Vittorio Amedeo II alone **Obv:** Plain cross, lily in each angle **Obv. Legend:** VIC. AM. II. D. G. DVX. SAB. **Rev:** 'VA' monogram divides date, large crown above **Rev. Legend:** PRIN. PEDE. REX. CYP. **Note:** Ref. Cud. 875.

Date	Mintage	Good	VG	F	VF	XF
1688	256,000	20.00	40.00	70.00	185	—

KM# 273 2 DENARI
Copper Weight varies: 2.04-2.48g., 20 mm. **Ruler:** Carlo Emanuele II alone **Obv:** Bust to right **Obv. Legend:** CAR. EM. II. D. G. DVX. SAB. P. P. R. C. **Rev:** Large crown and 2 rosettes above knot, date below, no legend **Note:** Ref. Cud. 829.

Date	Mintage	Good	VG	F	VF	XF
1664	—	25.00	50.00	95.00	215	—
1666 Rare	—	—	—	—	—	—

KM# 300 2 DENARI
Copper Weight varies: 1.74-2.15g., 19 mm. **Ruler:** Vittorio Amedeo II under regency **Obv:** Plain cross in circle **Obv. Legend:** M. I. BAP. VIC. AM. DVX. SAB. P. P. REG. CYPRI. **Rev:** Large crown above knot, date below, no legend **Note:** Ref. Cud. 841.

Date	Mintage	Good	VG	F	VF	XF
1676	—	40.00	85.00	175	350	—
1677	—	40.00	85.00	175	350	—
1679	—	40.00	85.00	175	350	—

KM# 299 2 DENARI
Copper Weight varies: 2.05-2.20g., 19 mm. **Ruler:** Vittorio Amedeo II under regency **Obv:** Cross with trefoil ends **Obv. Legend:** M. I. BAP. VIC. AM. DVX. SAB. P. P. REG. CYP. **Rev:** Large crown above knot, date below, no legend **Note:** Ref. Cud. 840.

Date	Mintage	Good	VG	F	VF	XF
1676	—	115	225	475	1,000	—

KM# 304 2 DENARI
Copper Weight varies: 2.05-2.18g., 19 mm. **Ruler:** Vittorio Amedeo II alone **Obv:** Plain cross **Obv. Legend:** VIC. AM II. D. G. D. SAB. P. PED. REX. CYP. **Rev:** Large crown above knot, date below, no legend **Note:** Ref. Cud. 876.

Date	Mintage	Good	VG	F	VF	XF
1680 Rare	—	—	—	—	—	—
1681 Rare	—	—	—	—	—	—

KM# 331 2 DENARI
Copper Weight varies: 2.15-2.16g., 18 mm. **Ruler:** Vittorio Amedeo II alone **Obv:** Plain cross **Obv. Legend:** VIC. AM. II. D. G. D. SAB. P. P(ED). R(EX). CYP. **Rev:** Large crown and 2 rosettes above knot, date below, no legend **Note:** Ref. Cud. 877. Varieties exist.

Date	Mintage	Good	VG	F	VF	XF
1691 Rare	—	—	—	—	—	—
1694	—	40.00	80.00	175	450	—
1695 Rare	—	—	—	—	—	—
1696 Rare	—	—	—	—	—	—

MB# 338.3 1/2 GROSSO (Mezzo Grosso)
Billon Weight varies: 0.61-0.95g., 16 mm. **Ruler:** Carlo Emanuele I **Obv:** Winged crest above shield of Savoy arms **Obv. Legend:** C. EM. - DVX. - SAB. **Rev:** Cross with trefoil ends in circle, date and mintmarks at end of legend **Rev. Legend:** +TIBI. SOLI. ADERERE. **Note:** Ref. Cud. 674b,e-j. Varieties exist.

Date	Mintage	Good	VG	F	VF	XF
1603 T	—	10.00	20.00	35.00	85.00	—

KM# 338.5 1/2 GROSSO (Mezzo Grosso)
Billon Weight varies: 0.61-0.95g., 16 mm. **Ruler:** Carlo Emanuele I **Obv:** Winged crest above shield of Savoy arms **Obv. Legend:** C. EM. - DVX. - SAB. **Rev:** Cross with trefoil ends in center, date at end of legend **Rev. Legend:** +TIBI. SOLI. ADERERE. **Note:** Ref. Cud. 674k,l,m. Varieties exist.

Date	Mintage	Good	VG	F	VF	XF
1607	—	10.00	20.00	35.00	85.00	—
1608	—	10.00	20.00	35.00	85.00	—
1610	—	10.00	20.00	35.00	85.00	—

KM# 156 3 DENARI
Billon Weight varies: 0.95-1.45g., 18 mm. **Ruler:** Vittorio Amedeo I **Obv:** Shield of Savoy arms divides date, where present, winged crest above **Obv. Legend:** V. AMED. D - G DVX. SAB. **Rev:** Cross with trefoil ends in wreath **Rev. Legend:** PRIN. PED. REX. CYPRI. **Note:** Ref. Cud. 723.

Date	Mintage	Good	VG	F	VF	XF
1635	—	16.00	35.00	65.00	175	—
1636	—	16.00	35.00	65.00	175	—
ND	—	16.00	35.00	65.00	175	—

KM# 3 1/2 SOLDO (Mezzo Soldo)
Billon Weight varies: 0.85-1.40g., 19 mm. **Ruler:** Carlo Emanuele I **Obv:** Double C monogram (one C reversed), small crown above, star below **Obv. Legend:** +CAROLVS. EMANVEL. **Rev:** Small shield of Savoy arms, winged crest above, date and mintmark at end of legend, where present **Rev. Legend:** D. G. DVX - SAB. **Note:** Ref. Cud. 665. Varieties exist.

Date	Mintage	Good	VG	F	VF	XF
1606	—	15.00	35.00	70.00	165	—
1610	—	15.00	35.00	70.00	165	—
1621	—	15.00	35.00	70.00	165	—
1626	—	15.00	35.00	70.00	165	—
1628	—	15.00	35.00	70.00	165	—

KM# 120 1/2 SOLDO (Mezzo Soldo)
Billon Weight varies: 1.30-1.60g., 21 mm. **Ruler:** Vittorio Amedeo I **Obv:** Crowned VACC complex monogram between two palm fronds **Obv. Legend:** V. AMED. D. G. DVX. SAB. P. PED. **Rev:** Ornate cross composed of knots, with rosette in enter, F - E - R - T in angles, date at end of legend **Rev. Legend:** IN. TE. DOMINE. CONFIDO. **Note:** Ref. Cud. 720.

Date	Mintage	Good	VG	F	VF	XF
1631	—	60.00	125	265	575	—
1632	—	40.00	85.00	180	420	—
1634	—	80.00	150	300	635	—

KM# 121 1/2 SOLDO (Mezzo Soldo)
Billon Weight varies: 1.51-1.59g., 20 mm. **Ruler:** Vittorio Amedeo I **Obv:** Crowned VACC monogram in circle **Obv. Legend:** V. AMED. D. G. DVX. SAB. P. P. **Rev:** Ornate cross composed of knots, with rosette in center, F - E - R - T in angles, date at end of legend **Rev. Legend:** IN. TE. DOMINE. CONFIDO. **Note:** Ref. Cud. 721.

Date	Mintage	Good	VG	F	VF	XF
1631	—	275	600	950	1,400	—
1632	—	275	600	950	1,400	—

KM# 181 1/2 SOLDO (Mezzo Soldo)
Billon Weight varies: 1.13-1.83g., 19 mm. **Ruler:** Carlo Emanuele II under regency **Obv:** Large knot, crown above, date below **Obv. Legend:** CH. F. C. EM. DG. D. SAB. P. P. REG. CYP. **Rev:** Cross with trefoil ends **Rev. Legend:** IN. TE. DOMINE. CONFIDO. **Note:** Ref. Cud. 768.

Date	Mintage	Good	VG	F	VF	XF
1641 Rare	—	—	—	—	—	—
1647	—	25.00	50.00	95.00	215	—

KM# 206 1/2 SOLDO (Mezzo Soldo)
1.1200 g., Billon, 18 mm. **Ruler:** Carlo Emanuele II under regency **Obv:** Crowned shield of Savoy arms divides date **Obv. Legend:** CH. FRAN. CAR. EMANVEL. D. SAB. **Rev:** Cross with trefoil ends superimposed on Maltese cross **Rev. Legend:** REGES. CIPRI. P. P. PED. **Note:** Ref. Cud. 769.

Date	Mintage	Good	VG	F	VF	XF
1642 Rare	—	—	—	—	—	—

KM# 207 1/2 SOLDO (Mezzo Soldo)
2.0200 g., Billon, 19 mm. **Ruler:** Carlo Emanuele II under regency **Obv:** Crowned shield of Savoy arms divides date **Obv. Legend:** CHR. FR. C. EMAN. DVCES. SAB. **Rev:** Cross with trefoil ends superimposed on Maltese cross **Rev. Legend:** REGES. CIPRI. P. P. PEDEMON. **Note:** Ref. Cud. 770.

Date	Mintage	Good	VG	F	VF	XF
1642 Rare	—	—	—	—	—	—

KM# 219 1/2 SOLDO (Mezzo Soldo)
1.3400 g., Billon, 19 mm. **Ruler:** Carlo Emanuele II under regency **Obv:** Large knot, crown above, date below **Obv. Legend:** P. PEDEMONT. REG. CIPRI. **Rev:** Cross with trefoil ends **Rev. Legend:** IN. TE. DOMINE. CONFIDO. **Note:** Ref. Cud. 771.

Date	Mintage	Good	VG	F	VF	XF
1646 Rare	—	—	—	—	—	—

KM# 225 1/2 SOLDO (Mezzo Soldo)
Billon Weight varies: 0.99-1.80g., 19 mm. **Ruler:** Carlo Emanuele II alone **Obv:** Youthful bust to right **Obv. Legend:** CAR. EMAN. II. D. G. DVX. SAB. **Rev:** Cross with trefoil ends, date at end of legend **Rev. Legend:** +PRIN. PEDEMON. REX. CYPRI. **Note:** Ref. Cud. 827.

Date	Mintage	Good	VG	F	VF	XF
1648	—	40.00	80.00	150	350	—
1649	—	40.00	80.00	150	350	—
1650	—	40.00	80.00	150	350	—

KM# 228 1/2 SOLDO (Mezzo Soldo)
Billon Weight varies: 0.85-1.28g., 17 mm. **Ruler:** Carlo Emanuele II alone **Obv:** Young head to right **Obv. Legend:** CAROLVS. EMANVEL. **Rev:** Cross with trefoil ends in circle, date at end of legend **Rev. Legend:** +II. D. G. DVX. SABAVD. **Note:** Ref. Cud 826.

Date	Mintage	Good	VG	F	VF	XF
1649	—	125	275	475	1,200	—
1650	—	125	275	475	1,200	—

KM# 245 1/2 SOLDO (Mezzo Soldo)
Billon Weight varies: 0.99-1.80g., 19 mm. **Ruler:** Carlo Emanuele II alone **Obv:** Youthful bust to right **Obv. Legend:** CAR. EM. II. D. G. DVX. S. **Rev:** Cross with trefoil ends **Rev. Legend:** +PRIN. PEDEMON. REX. CYP. **Note:** Ref. Cud. 828.

Date	Mintage	Good	VG	F	VF	XF
ND(ca1650)	—	15.00	30.00	60.00	145	—

KM# 321 1/2 SOLDO (Mezzo Soldo)
Billon Weight varies: 0.85-0.87g., 16 mm. **Ruler:** Vittorio Amedeo II alone **Obv:** Head to right, date below **Obv. Legend:** VIC. AM. II. - D. G. D. SAB. **Rev:** Cross with trefoil ends **Rev. Legend:** PRIN. PEDE. REX. CYPRI. **Note:** Ref. Cud. 874.

Date	Mintage	Good	VG	F	VF	XF
1688	—	125	275	475	1,000	—
1691 Rare	—	—	—	—	—	—

KM# 72 GROSSETTO
Billon Weight varies: 1.85-2.12g., 18 mm. **Ruler:** Carlo Emanuele I **Obv:** Shield of Savoy arms, letters F - E - R - T around, alternating with 4 rosettes **Obv. Legend:** CAR. EM. DVX. SAB. **Rev:** Cross with trefoil ends, date at end of legend **Rev. Legend:** MIHI. ABSIT. GLORIARI. **Note:** Ref. Cud. 671.

Date	Mintage	Good	VG	F	VF	XF
1621	—	22.00	45.00	75.00	185	—
1623	—	22.00	45.00	75.00	185	—
1625	—	22.00	45.00	75.00	185	—
1629	—	22.00	45.00	75.00	185	—

KM# 82 GROSSETTO
Billon Weight varies: 0.95-1.55g., 18 mm. **Ruler:** Carlo Emanuele I **Obv:** High-collared bust to right **Obv. Legend:** +CAR. EM. D. G. DVX. SAB. P. P. **Rev:** Cross with trefoil ends, date at end of legend **Rev. Legend:** MIHI. ABSIT. GLORIARI. **Note:** Ref. Cud. 673a-c,e,f.

Date	Mintage	Good	VG	F	VF	XF
1622	—	12.00	25.00	45.00	95.00	—
1624	—	12.00	25.00	45.00	95.00	—
1627	—	12.00	25.00	45.00	95.00	—
1628	—	12.00	25.00	45.00	95.00	—
1629	—	12.00	25.00	45.00	95.00	—

KM# 85 GROSSETTO
Billon Weight varies: 1.85-2.12g., 19 mm. **Ruler:** Carlo Emanuele I **Obv:** Shield of Savoy arms, letters F - E - R - T around **Obv. Legend:** CAR. EM. DVX. SAB. **Rev:** Cross with trefoil ends, date at end of legend **Rev. Legend:** MIHI. ABSIT. GLORIARI. **Note:** Ref. Cud. 672.

Date	Mintage	Good	VG	F	VF	XF
1625	—	25.00	50.00	85.00	225	—

KM# 98 GROSSETTO
Billon Weight varies: 0.95-1.55g., 18 mm. **Ruler:** Carlo Emanuele I **Obv:** High-collared bust to right **Obv. Legend:** +CAR. EM. D. G. DVX. SAB. P. P. **Rev:** Cross with trefoil ends, date at end of legend **Rev. Legend:** MIHI. ABSIT. GLORIARI. **Note:** Ref. Cud. 673d.

Date	Mintage	Good	VG	F	VF	XF
1628	—	12.00	25.00	45.00	95.00	—

KM# 113 GROSSETTO
Billon Weight varies: 0.94-1.60g., 17 mm. **Ruler:** Vittorio Amedeo I **Obv:** High-collared bust to right **Obv. Legend:** VICT. AM. D. G. DVX. SAB. **Rev:** Cross with trefoil ends in circle, date at end of legend **Rev. Legend:** MIHI. ABSIT. GLORIARI. **Note:** Ref. Cud. 722.

Date	Mintage	Good	VG	F	VF	XF
1630 Rare	—	—	—	—	—	—
1631	—	60.00	125	240	525	—
1632	—	70.00	145	265	675	—

KM# 122 SOLDO
Billon Weight varies: 1.42-2.35g., 25 mm. **Ruler:** Vittorio Amedeo I **Obv:** Crowned shield of 4-fold arms with central shield of Savoy **Obv. Legend:** V. AMED. D. G. DVX. SAB(AV). P(R). P(ED). **Rev:** Cross with trefoil ends, small angel's head in each angle, date at end of legend **Rev. Legend:** IN. TE. DOMINE. CONFIDO. **Note:** Ref. Cud. 719. Varieties exist.

Date	Mintage	Good	VG	F	VF	XF
1631	—	25.00	50.00	95.00	225	—
1632	—	25.00	50.00	95.00	225	—
1633	—	25.00	50.00	95.00	225	—
1634	—	28.00	60.00	120	300	—
1635	—	28.00	60.00	120	300	—
1636	—	40.00	75.00	145	350	—

KM# 127 SOLDO
Billon, 23 mm. **Ruler:** Vittorio Amedeo I **Obv:** Crowned shield of 4-fold arms, with central shield of Savoy, mintmark below, where present **Obv. Legend:** V. AMED. D. G. DVX. SABAV. P. P. **Rev:** Cross with trefoil ends in quatrefoil, date at end of legend **Rev. Legend:** +IN. TE. DOMINE. CONFIDO. **Note:** Ref. Cud. 718.

Date	Mintage	Good	VG	F	VF	XF
1632 Rare	—	—	—	—	—	—
163x V Rare	—	—	—	—	—	—

KM# 174 SOLDO
Billon Weight varies: 1.24-1.30g., 21 mm. **Ruler:** Carlo Emanuele II under regency **Obv:** Crowned shield of manifold arms with central shield of Savoy **Obv. Legend:** +C. EMANVEL. II. D. G. DVX. SAB. **Rev:** Cross with trefoil ends, date and mintmark at end of legend **Rev. Legend:** IN. TE. DOMINE. CONFIDO. **Note:** Ref. Cud. 765.

Date	Mintage	Good	VG	F	VF	XF
1640 P	—	45.00	100	180	400	—
1641 P	—	45.00	100	180	400	—
1642 P	—	45.00	100	180	400	—
1643 P Rare	—	—	—	—	—	—

KM# 182 SOLDO
Billon Weight varies: 1.64-1.69g., 23 mm. **Ruler:** Carlo Emanuele II under regency **Obv:** Crowned shield of Savoy arms divides date **Obv. Legend:** CHR. FR. CAR. EM. DVC. SAB. P. P. P. REX. CYPRI. **Rev:** Cross with trefoil ends, double C monogram in each angle, date at end of legend **Rev. Legend:** IN. TE. DOMINI. CONFIDO. **Note:** Ref. Cud. 766.

Date	Mintage	Good	VG	F	VF	XF
1641//1641	—	200	375	650	1,050	—

KM# 183 SOLDO
Billon Weight varies: 1.65-1.75g., 23 mm. **Ruler:** Carlo Emanuele II under regency **Obv:** Crowned shield of Savoy arms divides date **Obv. Legend:** CHR. FR. CAR. EM. DVC, SAB. P. P. P. R. CYPRI. **Rev:** Cross with trefoil ends, double C monogram in each angle **Rev. Legend:** IN. TE. DOMINI. CONFIDO. **Note:** Ref. Cud. 767.

Date	Mintage	Good	VG	F	VF	XF
1641	—	30.00	65.00	125	350	—

KM# 229 SOLDO
1.8500 g., Billon, 21 mm. **Ruler:** Carlo Emanuele II alone **Obv:** Crowned shield of Savoy arms **Obv. Legend:** C. EM. II. DVX. SABA. REX. CYP. **Rev:** Cross with trefoil ends, 'CE' monogram in each angle, date at end of legend **Rev. Legend:** IN. TE. DOMINE. CONFIDO. **Note:** Ref. Cud. 825.

Date	Mintage	Good	VG	F	VF	XF
1649 Rare	—	—	—	—	—	—

MB# 319.2 SOLDO (4 Denari)
Billon Weight varies: 1.40-1.95g., 23 mm. **Ruler:** Carlo Emanuele I **Obv:** Crowned shield of 4-fold arms, with central shield of Savoy, mintmark below **Obv. Legend:** C. EMANVEL. D. G. DVX. SABAV. **Rev:** Cross with trefoil ends in quatrefoil, mintmark at end of legend, date divided in outer angles of quatrefoil **Rev. Legend:** +IN. TE. DOMINE. CONFIDO. **Note:** Ref. Cud. 661a,c,f,i,l,p,r,u,w,x. Varieties exist.

Date	Mintage	Good	VG	F	VF	XF
1628 (star)//-	—	10.00	18.00	30.00	120	—

KM# 332 2 1/2 SOLDI

Billon Weight varies: 3.31-3.48g., 23 mm. **Ruler:** Vittorio Amedeo II alone **Obv:** Cross with trefoil ends superimposed on Maltese cross, all in wreath **Obv. Legend:** VICTOR. AM. II. D. G. DVX. SAB. **Rev:** Crowned shield of manifold arms with central shield of Savoy, divides date, where present **Rev. Legend:** PRIN. PEDE. REX. CYPRI. **Note:** Ref. Cud. 872. Varieties exist.

Date	Mintage	Good	VG	F	VF	XF
1691	—	12.00	30.00	60.00	145	—
1693	—	20.00	40.00	75.00	195	—
ND Rare	—	—	—	—	—	—

KM# 220 2.6 SOLDI

2.5300 g., Copper, 27 mm. **Ruler:** Carlo Emanuele II under regency **Obv:** Accolated busts to right of Carlo Emanuele and his mother, value 'SOL 2.6' below **Obv. Legend:** CHR. FRAN. CAR. EM. DVCES. SAB. **Rev:** Crowned shield of Savoy arms divide date **Rev. Legend:** P. P. PEDEMON. REGES. CYPRI. **Note:** Ref. Cud. 764.

Date	Mintage	Good	VG	F	VF	XF
1647	—	225	400	725	1,650	—

KM# 1 GROSSO

Billon Weight varies: 0.93-1.80g., 19 mm. **Ruler:** Carlo Emanuele I **Obv:** Seated lion holding shield of Savoy arms at left **Obv. Legend:** +CAR. EM. D. G. DVX. SAB. P. (P)(ED). **Rev:** Cross with trefoil ends, date at end of legend **Rev. Legend:** +MIHI. ABSIT. GLORIARI. **Note:** Ref. Cud. 670e,f,h,i,k,l,m.

Date	Mintage	Good	VG	F	VF	XF
1610	—	10.00	25.00	50.00	140	—
1611	—	10.00	25.00	50.00	140	—
1622	—	10.00	25.00	50.00	140	—
1623	—	10.00	25.00	50.00	140	—
1624	—	10.00	25.00	50.00	140	—

KM# 36 GROSSO

Billon Weight varies: 0.93-1.80g., 19 mm. **Ruler:** Carlo Emanuele I **Obv:** Seated lion holding shield of Savoy arms at left, date at end of legend **Obv. Legend:** +CAR. EM. D. G. DVX. SAB. P. PED. **Rev:** Cross with trefoil ends, date at end of legend **Rev. Legend:** +MIHI. ABSIT. GLORIARI. **Note:** Ref. Cud. 670g.

Date	Mintage	Good	VG	F	VF	XF
1610//1610	—	10.00	25.00	50.00	140	—

MB# 339.3 GROSSO

Billon Weight varies: 0.93-1.80g., 19 mm. **Ruler:** Carlo Emanuele I **Obv:** Seated lion holding shield of Savoy arms at left, mintmark at beginning of legend, where present **Obv. Legend:** +CAR. EM. D. G. DVX. SAB. P. (PED.). **Rev:** Cross with trefoil ends, date and mintmark at end of legend, where present **Rev. Legend:** +MIHI. ABSIT. GLORIARI. **Note:** Ref. Cud. 670c,j.

Date	Mintage	Good	VG	F	VF	XF
1613 (star)	—	10.00	25.00	50.00	140	—

KM# 28 CAVALLOTTO (3 Grossi)

Billon Weight varies: 1.83-2.12g., 24 mm. **Ruler:** Carlo Emanuele I **Obv:** Horse prancing to right, looking back to left, mintmark below, date in exergue **Obv. Legend:** CAR. EM. D. G. DVX. SAB. P. P. **Rev:** Crowned shield of Savoy arms **Rev. Legend:** PATRIÆ. LIBERTATE. SERVATA. **Note:** Ref. Cud. 657.

Date	Mintage	Good	VG	F	VF	XF
1608 V	—	55.00	115	240	525	850
1610 V	—	55.00	115	240	525	850
1610 V//BS	—	55.00	115	240	525	850
1619 V	—	55.00	115	240	525	850

KM# 49.1 CAVALLOTTO (3 Grossi)

Billon Weight varies: 1.41-2.90g., 24 mm. **Ruler:** Carlo Emanuele I **Obv:** Horse prancing to right, looking back to left, date in exergue **Obv. Legend:** CAR. EM. D. G. DVX. SAB. P. P. **Rev:** Crowned shield of Savoy arms, knot at left and right **Rev. Legend:** PATRIÆ. LIBERTATE. SERVATA. **Note:** Ref. Cud. 658a-h,j,l. Varieties exist.

Date	Mintage	Good	VG	F	VF	XF
1611	—	15.00	30.00	60.00	165	300
1612	—	15.00	30.00	60.00	165	300
1613	—	15.00	30.00	60.00	165	300
1614	—	15.00	30.00	60.00	165	300
1615	—	15.00	30.00	60.00	165	300
1616	—	15.00	30.00	60.00	165	300
1619	—	15.00	30.00	60.00	165	300
1620	—	15.00	30.00	60.00	165	300
1628	—	15.00	30.00	60.00	165	300
ND	—	15.00	30.00	60.00	165	300

KM# 56.1 CAVALLOTTO (3 Grossi)

Billon Weight varies: 1.94-2.35g., 23 mm. **Ruler:** Carlo Emanuele I **Obv:** Horse prancing to right, looking back to left, date in exergue **Obv. Legend:** CAR. EM. D. G. DVX. SAB. P. P. **Rev:** Crowned shield of Savoy arms, rosette at left and right **Rev. Legend:** PATRIÆ. LIBERTATE. SERVATA. **Note:** Ref. Cud. 659a,c.

Date	Mintage	Good	VG	F	VF	XF
1618	—	35.00	70.00	145	350	625
1619 Rare	—	—	—	—	—	—

KM# 56.2 CAVALLOTTO (3 Grossi)

Billon Weight varies: 1.94-2.35g., 23 mm. **Ruler:** Carlo Emanuele I **Obv:** Horse prancing to right, looking back to left, mintmark below, date in exergue **Obv. Legend:** CAR. EM. D. G. DVX. SAB. P. P. **Rev:** Crowned shield of Savoy arms, rosette at left and right **Rev. Legend:** PATRIÆ. LIBERTATE. SERVATA. **Note:** Ref. Cud. 659b.

Date	Mintage	Good	VG	F	VF	XF
1618 V Rare	—	—	—	—	—	—

KM# 49.2 CAVALLOTTO (3 Grossi)

Billon Weight varies: 1.41-2.90g., 24 mm. **Ruler:** Carlo Emanuele I **Obv:** Horse prancing to right, looking back to left, mintmark below, date in exergue **Obv. Legend:** CAR. EM. D. G. DVX. SAB. P. P. **Rev:** Crowned shield of Savoy arms, knot at left and right **Rev. Legend:** PATRIÆ. LIBERTATE. SERVATA. **Note:** Ref. Cud. 658i.

Date	Mintage	Good	VG	F	VF	XF
1628 V	—	15.00	30.00	60.00	165	300

KM# 49.3 CAVALLOTTO (3 Grossi)

Billon Weight varies: 1.41-2.90g., 24 mm. **Ruler:** Carlo Emanuele I **Obv:** Horse prancing to right, looking back to left, mintmark in exergue **Obv. Legend:** CAR. EM. D. G. DVX. SAB. P. P. **Rev:** Crowned shield of Savoy arms, knot at left and right **Rev. Legend:** PATRIÆ. LIBERTATE. SERVATA. **Note:** Ref. Cud. 658k.

Date	Mintage	Good	VG	F	VF	XF
ND(ca1628) VERCEL	—	15.00	30.00	60.00	165	300

KM# 175 4 SOLDI

Billon Weight varies: 4.55-5.95g., 25 mm. **Ruler:** Carlo Emanuele II under regency **Obv:** Crowned shield of manifold arms, with central shield of Savoy, divides FE - RT **Obv. Legend:** +C. EMANVEL. II. D. G. DVX. SAB. P. PED. **Rev:** Cross with trefoil ends in quatrefoil, date and mintmark at end of legend **Rev. Legend:** IN. TE. DOMINE. CONFIDO. **Note:** Ref. Cud. 763.

Date	Mintage	Good	VG	F	VF	XF
1640 P	—	175	400	725	1,200	—
1641 P	—	175	400	725	1,200	—
1642 P	—	175	400	725	1,200	—
1643 P	—	175	400	725	1,200	—

KM# 50 4 GROSSI

Billon Weight varies: 2.25-3.20g., 27 mm. **Ruler:** Carlo Emanuele I **Obv:** Crowned ornately-shaped shield of Savoy arms divides FE - RT **Obv. Legend:** CAR. EM. D. G. DVX. SAB. P. P. **Rev:** Large cross with trefoil ends, date at end of legend **Rev. Legend:** IN. TE. DOMINE. CONFIDO. **Note:** Ref. Cud. 655.

Date	Mintage	VG	F	VF	XF	Unc
1611 Rare	—	—	—	—	—	—
1618 Rare	—	—	—	—	—	—

KM# 128 5 SOLDI

Billon Weight varies: 5.07-6.55g., 30 mm. **Ruler:** Vittorio Amedeo I **Obv:** Crowned shield of 4-fold arms, with central shield of Savoy, in baroque frame, chain of order around, date at end of legend **Obv. Legend:** V. AMED. D. G. DVX - SABAV(DIE). P. PED. **Rev:** Full-length figure of the Blessed Amedeo, holding oval shield with 6-line inscription, value 'S.5' in exergue **Rev. Legend:** BENEDIC - HER - EDITATI TVE. **Rev. Inscription:** F. / IVDI / TE. IVS / D. PAV / TE. DO / D. P. **Note:** Ref. Cud. 715.

Date	Mintage	Good	VG	F	VF	XF
1632	—	90.00	200	375	850	—
ND	—	100	225	475	950	—

KM# 129 5 SOLDI

Billon Weight varies: 5.07-6.55g., 30 mm. **Ruler:** Vittorio Amedeo I **Obv:** Crowned shield of 4-fold arms, with central shield of Savoy, in baroque frame, chain of order around, date at end of legend **Obv. Legend:** V. AMED. D. G. DVX - SABAV. P. PED. **Rev:** Full-length figure of the Blessed Amedeo, holding oval shield with 6-line inscription, value 'S.5' in exergue **Rev. Legend:** BENEDIC - HER - EDITATI TVÆ. **Rev. Inscription:** F. / IVDI / TE. IVS / D. PAV / TE. DO / D. P. **Note:** Ref. Cud. 716.

Date	Mintage	Good	VG	F	VF	XF
1632	—	175	400	825	1,400	—

KM# 130 5 SOLDI

Billon Weight varies: 5.50-6.05g., 30 mm. **Ruler:** Vittorio Amedeo I **Obv:** Crowned shield of 4-fold arms, with central shield of Savoy, in baroque frame, chain of order around **Obv. Legend:** V. AM. D. G. DVX. SAB. - P. PE. REX. CYPRI. **Rev:** Full-length figure of the Blessed Amedeo, holding oval shield with 6-line inscription, value 'S.5' in exergue **Rev. Legend:** BENEDIC. HÆR - EDITATI TVÆ. **Rev. Inscription:** F. / IVDI / TE. IVS / D. PAV / TE. DO / D. P. **Note:** Ref. Cud. 717.

Date	Mintage	Good	VG	F	VF	XF
ND(ca1632)	—	75.00	160	315	825	—

KM# 222 5 SOLDI

Billon Weight varies: 4.35-4.95g., 28 mm. **Ruler:** Carlo Emanuele II under regency **Obv:** Accolated busts of Carol Emanuele and his mother to right, value 'SOL 5' below **Obv. Legend:** CHR. FR. CAR. EM. DVCES. SAB. **Rev:** Crowned shield of Savoy arms divides date **Rev. Legend:** P. P. PEDEMON. REGES. CYPRI. **Note:** Ref. Cud. 762.

Date	Mintage	Good	VG	F	VF	XF
1647	—	30.00	65.00	125	350	—
1648	—	30.00	65.00	125	350	—

KM# 274 5 SOLDI

Billon Weight varies: 4.78-6.72g., 29 mm. **Ruler:** Carlo Emanuele II alone **Obv:** Bust to right **Obv. Legend:** CAR. EM. II. D. G. DVX. SAB. **Rev:** Crowned shield of Savoy arms, date at end of legend **Rev. Legend:** PRIN. PEDE. REX. CYP. **Note:** Ref. Cud. 823.

Date	Mintage	Good	VG	F	VF	XF
1664	—	35.00	80.00	150	500	—
1665	—	35.00	80.00	150	500	—

KM# 275 5 SOLDI

Billon Weight varies: 4.33-5.50g., 29 mm. **Ruler:** Carlo Emanuele II alone **Obv:** Bust to right **Obv. Legend:** CAR. EM. II. D. - G. DVX. SAB. **Rev:** Crowned shield of Savoy arms, date at end of legend **Rev. Legend:** PRINCEP. PEDE(MON). REX. CYP. **Note:** Ref. Cud. 824. Varieties exist.

Date	Mintage	Good	VG	F	VF	XF
1667	—	90.00	200	325	950	—
1668	—	35.00	80.00	150	450	—
1669	—	35.00	80.00	150	450	—

KM# 333 5 SOLDI

Billon Weight varies: 3.54-5.25g., 28 mm. **Ruler:** Vittorio Amedeo II alone **Obv:** Draped bust to right divides FE - RT **Obv. Legend:** VICTOR. AM. II. D. G. DVX. SAB. **Rev:** Crowned shield of Savoy arms divides date, value 'S . 5' below in margin **Rev. Legend:** PRIN. PEDE - REX. CYPRI. **Note:** Ref. Cud. 869. Varieties exist.

Date	Mintage	Good	VG	F	VF	XF
1691	—	175	400	725	2,000	—
1695 Rare	—	—	—	—	—	—
1696	—	30.00	65.00	125	350	—
1697	—	30.00	65.00	125	350	—

KM# 343 5 SOLDI

Billon Weight varies: 4.84-5.10g., 27-28 mm. **Ruler:** Vittorio Amedeo II alone **Obv:** Draped bust to right, date below **Obv. Legend:** VIC. AM. II. D. - G. DVX. SAB. **Rev:** Crowned shield of Savoy arms divides FE - RT, value '5. S' below in margin **Note:** Ref. Cud. 871.

Date	Mintage	Good	VG	F	VF	XF
1700	—	45.00	100	200	575	—

KM# 99 6 SOLDI

Billon Weight varies: 4.90-6.15g., 30 mm. **Ruler:** Carlo Emanuele I **Obv:** Crowned shield of Savoy arms, knot at left and right, mintmark below, date at end of legend **Obv. Legend:** CAR(OLVS). EMANVEL. DEI. GRA(TIA). **Rev:** FE . RT across center, large knot above and below, value in exergue 'VI. S.' **Rev. Legend:** DVX. SABAVDIE. PED. PR. ET. C. **Note:** Ref. Cud. 643. Varieties exist.

Date	Mintage	Good	VG	F	VF	XF
1628 (star)	—	50.00	110	215	450	—
1629 (star)	—	50.00	110	215	450	—
ND (star)	—	50.00	110	215	450	—

KM# 230 1/24 DUCATONE

1.3800 g., Silver, 17 mm. **Ruler:** Carlo Emanuele II alone **Obv:** Bust to right, 6 pellets in line below **Obv. Legend:** CAROLVS. EMANVEL. **Rev:** Cross with trefoil ends in circle, date at end of legend **Rev. Legend:** II. D. G. DVX. SABAVD. **Note:** Ref. Cud. 821.

Date	Mintage	VG	F	VF	XF	Unc
1649	—	1,500	3,600	7,200	11,000	—

KM# 231 1/24 DUCATONE

1.4300 g., Silver, 18 mm. **Ruler:** Carlo Emanuele II alone **Obv:** Bust to right, 6 pellets in line below **Obv. Legend:** CAROLVS. EMANVEL. **Rev:** Crowned shield of Savoy arms in baroque frame, date at end of legend **Rev. Legend:** II. D. G. DVX. SAB. **Note:** Ref. Cud. 822.

Date	Mintage	VG	F	VF	XF	Unc
1649 Rare	—	—	—	—	—	—

KM# 263 1/12 SCUDO

Silver Weight varies: 1.57-2.23g., 20 mm. **Ruler:** Carlo Emanuele II alone **Obv:** Head to right **Obv. Legend:** CAR. EM. II. D. G. DVX. SAB. **Rev:** Crowned shield of Savoy arms, chain of order around, date at end of legend **Rev. Legend:** PRIN. PEDEM - REX. CIPRI. **Note:** Ref. Cud. 820.

Date	Mintage	VG	F	VF	XF	Unc
1659	—	650	1,000	2,400	6,000	—
1660 Rare	—	—	—	—	—	—

KM# 32 FIORINO

Silver Weight varies: 2.93-4.45g., 25 mm. **Ruler:** Carlo Emanuele I **Obv:** High-collared armored bust to right **Obv. Legend:** CAR. EM. D. G. - DV - X. SAB. P. P. **Rev:** Shield of Savoy arms, in ornate decorated frame, divides date, crown above **Rev. Legend:** EXPECTA. DM - VIRILIT. RAGE. **Note:** Ref. Cud. 652a.

Date	Mintage	VG	F	VF	XF	Unc
1609	—	60.00	125	350	650	—

KM# 38 FIORINO

3.1500 g., Silver, 26 mm. **Ruler:** Carlo Emanuele I **Obv:** High-collared armored bust to right **Obv. Legend:** CAR. EM. D. G. DV - X. SAB. P. P. **Rev:** Crowned shield of Savoy arms superimposed on cross with trefoil ends, date at end of legend **Rev. Legend:** IN. HOC. EGO. SPERABO. **Note:** Ref. Cud. 651.

Date	Mintage	VG	F	VF	XF	Unc
1610	—	375	725	1,300	1,850	—
1611	—	375	725	1,300	1,850	—

KM# 83 FIORINO

Silver Weight varies: 2.93-4.45g., 25 mm. **Ruler:** Carlo Emanuele I **Obv:** High-collared armored bust to right, mintmark below, where present **Obv. Legend:** CAR. EM. D. G. - DV - X. SAB. P. P. **Rev:** Shield of Savoy arms, in ornate decorated frame, divides date, crown above **Rev. Legend:** EXPECTA. DM - VIRILIT. RAGE. **Note:** Ref. Cud. 652b,c,d,f,g,i. Varieties exist.

Date	Mintage	VG	F	VF	XF	Unc
1623 Rare	—	—	—	—	—	—
1625 V Rare	—	—	—	—	—	—
1626 Rare	—	—	—	—	—	—
1629 V	—	60.00	125	350	650	—
1630 V	—	60.00	125	350	650	—

KM# 105 FIORINO

Silver Weight varies: 2.93-4.45g., 25 mm. **Ruler:** Carlo Emanuele I **Obv:** High-collared armored bust to right **Obv. Legend:** CAR. EM. D. G. - DV - X. SAB. P. P. **Rev:** Shield of Savoy arms, in ornate decorated frame, divides date, crown above **Rev. Legend:** EXPECTA. DM - VIRILIT. RAGE. **Note:** Ref. Cud. 652e,h.

Date	Mintage	VG	F	VF	XF	Unc
1629	—	60.00	125	350	650	—
1630	—	60.00	125	350	650	—

KM# 106.1 FIORINO

Silver Weight varies: 3.05-3.80g., 25 mm. **Ruler:** Carlo Emanuele I **Obv:** Small high-collared armored bust to right, mint mark below **Obv. Legend:** CAR. EM. D. G. - DV - X. SAB. P. P. **Rev:** Crowned shield of Savoy arms, in ornate decorated frame, date above **Rev. Legend:** EXPECTA. DM - VIRILIT. RAGE. **Note:** Cud. 653a.

Date	Mintage	VG	F	VF	XF	Unc
1629 V	—	75.00	145	350	525	—

KM# 106.2 FIORINO

Silver Weight varies: 3.05-3.80g., 25 mm. **Ruler:** Carlo Emanuele I **Obv:** Small high-collared armored bust to right **Obv. Legend:** CAR. EM. D. G. - DV - X. SAB. P. P. **Rev:** Crowned shield of Savoy arms, in ornate decorated frame, date above **Rev. Legend:** EXPECTA. DM - VIRILIT. RAGE. **Note:** Ref. Cud. 653b.

Date	Mintage	VG	F	VF	XF	Unc
1629	—	75.00	145	350	525	—

KM# 107 FIORINO

Silver **Ruler:** Carlo Emanuele I **Obv:** Large high-collared armored bust to right **Obv. Legend:** CAR. EM. D. G. DVX. SAB. P. P. **Rev:** Crowned shield of Savoy arms, in ornate decorated frame, date above **Rev. Legend:** EXPECTA. DM - VIRILIT. RAGE. **Note:** Ref. Cud. 654.

Date	Mintage	VG	F	VF	XF	Unc
1629 Rare	—	—	—	—	—	—

KM# 168 1/2 LIRA (10 Soldi)

Silver Weight varies: 6.74-8.00g., 33 mm. **Ruler:** Carlo Emanuele II under regency **Obv:** Accolated busts of Carlo Emanuele and his mother to right, date at end of legend **Obv. Legend:** CHR. FRAN. CAR. EMAN. DVCES. SAB. **Rev:** Crowned shield of manifold arms, with central shield of Savoy, in baroque frame, value 'S.X' in exergue **Rev. Legend:** P. P. PEDEMON. REGES. CYPRI. **Note:** Ref. Cud. 754.

Date	Mintage	VG	F	VF	XF	Unc
1639	—	125	300	725	1,100	—
1643	—	125	300	725	1,100	—

KM# 169 1/2 LIRA (10 Soldi)

Silver Weight varies: 6.74-8.00g., 33 mm. **Ruler:** Carlo Emanuele II under regency **Obv:** Accolated busts of Carlo Emanuele and his mother to right, date at end of legend **Obv. Legend:** CHR. FRAN. CAR. EMAN. DVCES. SAB. **Rev:** Crowned shield of manifold arms, with central shield of Savoy, in baroque frame, no value showing **Rev. Legend:** P. P. PEDEMON. REGES. CYPRI. **Note:** Ref. Cud. 755.

Date	Mintage	VG	F	VF	XF	Unc
1639 Rare	—	—	—	—	—	—

KM# 170 1/2 LIRA (10 Soldi)

Silver Weight varies: 7.55-7.78g., 33 mm. **Ruler:** Carlo Emanuele II under regency **Obv:** Accolated busts of Carlo Emanuele and his mother to the right, date at end of legend **Obv. Legend:** CHR. FRAN. CAR. EMAN. DVCES. SAB. **Rev:** Crowned shield of manifold arms, with central shield, in baroque frame, divides value S - X. **Rev. Legend:** P. P. PEDEMON. REGES. CYPRI. **Note:** Ref. Cud. 756.

Date	Mintage	VG	F	VF	XF	Unc
1639	—	400	725	1,650	2,300	—

KM# 176 1/2 LIRA (10 Soldi)

Silver Weight varies: 6.15-6.97g., 33 mm. **Ruler:** Carlo Emanuele II under regency **Obv:** Accolated busts of Carlo Emanuele and his mother to right, value 'S.X' in exergue **Obv. Legend:** CHR. FRAN. CAR. EMAN. DVCES. SAB. **Rev:** Crowned shield of manifold arms, with central shield of Savoy, in baroque frame, value 'S.X' in exergue **Rev. Legend:** P. P. PEDEMON. REGES. CYPRI. **Note:** Ref. Cud. 761.

Date	Mintage	VG	F	VF	XF	Unc
ND(1640-2)	—	250	500	1,200	2,000	—

KM# 185 1/2 LIRA (10 Soldi)

Silver Weight varies: 7.23-8.05g., 33 mm. **Ruler:** Carlo Emanuele II under regency **Obv:** Accolated busts of Carlo Emanuele and his mother to the right, date at end of legend **Obv. Legend:** CHR. FRAN. CAR. EMAN. DVCES. SAB. **Rev:** Crowned shield of manifold arms, with central shield of Savoy, in baroque frame, value 'S.X' in exergue **Rev. Legend:** P. P. PEDEMON. REGES. CYPRI. **Note:** Ref. Cud. 758.

Date	Mintage	VG	F	VF	XF	Unc
1641	—	70.00	145	650	1,000	—
1642	—	70.00	145	650	1,000	—

KM# 184 1/2 LIRA (10 Soldi)

7.7200 g., Silver, 33 mm. **Ruler:** Carlo Emanuele II under regency **Obv:** Accolated busts of Carlo Emanuele and his mother to the right, date in exergue **Obv. Legend:** CHR. FRAN. CAR. EMAN. DVCES. SAB. **Rev:** Crowned shield of manifold arms, with central shield of Savoy, in baroque frame, no value shown **Rev. Legend:** P. P. PEDEMON. REGES. CYPRI. **Note:** Ref. Cud. 757.

Date	Mintage	VG	F	VF	XF	Unc
1641 Rare	—	—	—	—	—	—

KM# 209 1/2 LIRA (10 Soldi)

Silver Weight varies: 7.23-8.05g., 33 mm. **Ruler:** Carlo Emanuele II under regency **Obv:** Accolated busts of Carlo Emanuele and his mother to right, date at end of leged **Obv. Legend:** CHR. FRAN. CAR. EMAN. DVCES. DAB. **Rev:** Crowned shield of manifold arms, with central shield of Savoy, in baroque frame, date in exergue **Rev. Legend:** P. P. PEDEMON. REGES. CYPRI. **Note:** Ref. Cud. 759.

Date	Mintage	VG	F	VF	XF	Unc
1642//1642	—	225	475	1,000	1,650	—

KM# 210 1/2 LIRA (10 Soldi)

Silver Weight varies: 9.15-10.79g., 33 mm. **Ruler:** Carlo Emanuele II under regency **Obv:** Accolated busts of Carlo Emanuele and his mother to right, date below in margin **Obv. Legend:** CHR. FRAN. CAR. EMAN. DVCES. SAB. **Rev:** Crowned shield of manifold arms, with central shield of Savoy, in baroque frame, value (X) in margin at bottom **Rev. Legend:** P. P. PEDEMON. REGES. CYPRI. **Note:** Ref. Cud. 760.

Date	Mintage	VG	F	VF	XF	Unc
1642	—	275	525	1,400	2,150	—

KM# 232 1/2 LIRA (10 Soldi)

Silver Weight varies: 6.17-8.15g., 33 mm. **Ruler:** Carlo Emanuele II alone **Obv:** Bust to right, date in exergue **Obv. Legend:** CAR. EMAN. II. D. G. DVX. SABAVDIE. **Rev:** Crowned oval shield of manifold arms, with central shield of Savoy, in baroque frame, value 'S.X' in exergue **Rev. Legend:** PRIN. PEDEMON. REX. CYPRI. ET. C. **Note:** Ref. Cud. 817.

Date	Mintage	VG	F	VF	XF	Unc
1649 Rare	—	—	—	—	—	—
1652	—	400	725	1,400	2,250	—

KM# 249 1/2 LIRA (10 Soldi)

Silver Weight varies: 6.17-8.15g., 33 mm. **Ruler:** Carlo Emanuele II alone **Obv:** Bust to right, date in exergue **Obv. Legend:** CAR. EMAN. II. D. G. DVX. SABAVDIE. **Rev:** Crowned oval shield of manifold arms, with central shield of Savoy, in baroque frame, date in exergue **Rev. Legend:** PRIN. PEDEMON. REX. CYPRI. ET. C. **Note:** Ref. Cud. 818.

Date	Mintage	VG	F	VF	XF	Unc
1652//1652 Rare	—	—	—	—	—	—

KM# 250 1/2 LIRA (10 Soldi)

Silver Weight varies: 6.40-8.11g., 31 mm. **Ruler:** Carlo Emanuele II alone **Obv:** Bust to right, value 'S.X' in exergue **Obv. Legend:** CAROL. EM. II. D. G. DVX. SAB. **Rev:** Crowed shield of manifold arms, with central shield of Savoy, in baroque frame, date at end of legend **Rev. Legend:** PRIN. PEDE. REX. CYP. **Note:** Ref. Cud. 819.

Date	Mintage	VG	F	VF	XF	Unc
1653	—	475	825	1,800	2,500	—
1654 Rare	—	—	—	—	—	—

KM# 289 1/2 LIRA (10 Soldi)

Silver Weight varies: 2.83-3.06g., 22 mm. **Ruler:** Vittorio Amedeo II under regency **Obv:** Accolated busts of Vittorio Amedeo and his mother to right **Obv. Legend:** MAR. IO. BAP. VIC. AM. II. D. G. DVC. SAB. **Rev:** Crowned shield of manifold arms, with central shield of Savoy, date divided at top, value 'S.10' at bottom **Rev. Legend:** PRIN. PEDEM - REGES. CYPRI. **Note:** Ref. Cud. 839.

Date	Mintage	VG	F	VF	XF	Unc
1675 Rare	—	—	—	—	—	—
1676	—	90.00	200	385	900	—
1677	—	80.00	180	350	825	—
1678	—	80.00	180	350	825	—
1679	—	90.00	200	385	900	—
1680	—	135	300	600	1,250	—

KM# 316 1/2 LIRA (10 Soldi)

Silver Weight varies: 2.85-3.00g., 22 mm. **Ruler:** Vittorio Amedeo II alone **Obv:** Draped bust to right **Obv. Legend:** VIC. AM. II. - D. G. DVX. SAB. **Rev:** Crowned shield of manifold arms, with central shield of Savoy, date divided at top, value 'S.10' at bottom **Rev. Legend:** PRIN. PEDE - REX. CYPRI. **Note:** Ref. Cud. 867.

Date	Mintage	VG	F	VF	XF	Unc
1681	—	150	325	600	1,000	—
1682	—	175	350	725	1,250	—

KM# 337 15 SOLDI

Billon Weight varies: 6.02-7.50g., 29 mm. **Ruler:** Vittorio Amedeo II alone **Obv:** Four crowned VA monograms in cruciform, rosette in center **Obv. Legend:** VIC. - AM. II. - D. G. D. - SAB. **Rev:** Crowned shield of Savoy arms, chain of order around, date divided at top, value 'S . 15' in exergue **Rev. Legend:** PRIN. PEDE - REX. CYPRI. **Note:** Ref. Cud. 866.

Date	Mintage	VG	F	VF	XF	Unc
1692	—	40.00	85.00	225	575	—
1693	—	40.00	85.00	225	575	—
1694	—	40.00	85.00	225	575	—

KM# 21 2 FIORINI

Silver Weight varies: 5.70-7.20g., 30 mm. **Ruler:** Carlo Emanuele I **Obv:** High-collared armored bust to right, date below **Obv. Legend:** CAR. EM. D. G. DVX. SAB. P. P. **Rev:** Crowned shield of Savoy arms superimposed on cross with trefoil ends, date at end of legend **Rev. Legend:** IN. HOC. EGO. SPERABO. **Note:** Ref. Cud. 646.

Date	Mintage	VG	F	VF	XF	Unc
1607//1611 Rare	—	—	—	—	—	—

KM# 39 2 FIORINI

Silver Weight varies: 5.70-7.20g., 30 mm. **Ruler:** Carlo Emanuele I **Obv:** High-collared armored bust to right, mintmark below, where present **Obv. Legend:** CAR. EM. D.G. DVX. SAB. P. P(ED). (ET.C). **Rev:** Crowned shield of Savoy arms superimposed on cross with trefoil ends, date at end of legend **Rev. Legend:** IN. HOC. EGO. SPERABO. **Note:** Cud. 645. Varieties exist.

Date	Mintage	VG	F	VF	XF	Unc
1610	—	135	250	525	875	—
1611	—	135	250	525	875	—
1611 T	—	135	250	525	875	—
1612	—	135	250	525	875	—
1613	—	135	250	525	875	—
1613 T	—	135	250	525	875	—
1614 T	—	135	250	525	875	—
1615 T	—	135	250	525	875	—
1616	—	135	250	525	875	—
1617	—	135	250	525	875	—
1618	—	135	250	525	875	—
1620	—	135	250	525	875	—

KM# 73.1 2 FIORINI

Silver Weight varies: 5.70-7.20g., 30 mm. **Ruler:** Carlo Emanuele I **Obv:** High-collared armored bust to right, mintmark below **Obv. Legend:** CAR. EM. D. G. DVX. SAB. P. PED. ET. C. **Rev:** Crowned shield of Savoy arms superimposed on cross with trefoil ends, date above crown **Rev. Legend:** IN. HOC. EGO. SPERABO. **Note:** Ref. Cud. 647a,d. Varieties exist.

Date	Mintage	VG	F	VF	XF	Unc
1621 V	—	90.00	200	425	875	—
1625 V	—	90.00	200	425	875	—

KM# 73.2 2 FIORINI

Silver Weight varies: 5.70-7.20g., 30 mm. **Ruler:** Carlo Emanuele I **Obv:** High-collared armored bust to right **Obv. Legend:** CAR. EM. D. G. DVX. SAB. P. PED. ET. C. **Rev:** Crowned shield of Savoy arms superimposed on cross with trefoil ends, date above crown **Rev. Legend:** IN. HOC. EGO. SPERABO. **Note:** Ref. Cud. 647b,c,e,g.

Date	Mintage	VG	F	VF	XF	Unc
1624	—	90.00	200	425	875	—
1625	—	90.00	200	425	875	—
1626	—	90.00	200	425	875	—
ND	—	90.00	200	425	875	—

KM# 87 2 FIORINI

Silver Weight varies: 6.10-6.75g., 30 mm. **Ruler:** Carlo Emanuele I **Obv:** High-collared armored bust to right, mintmark and date below **Obv. Legend:** CAR. EM. D. G. DVX. SAB. P. PED. ET. C. **Rev:** Crowned shield of Savoy arms superimposed on cross with trefoil ends **Rev. Legend:** IN. HOC. EGO. SPERABO. **Note:** Ref. Cud. 648.

Date	Mintage	VG	F	VF	XF	Unc
1626 V	—	110	250	700	1,100	—
1629 V	—	110	250	700	1,100	—

KM# 73.3 2 FIORINI

Silver Weight varies: 5.70-7.20g., 30 mm. **Ruler:** Carlo Emanuele I **Obv:** High-collared armored bust to right **Obv. Legend:** CAR. EM. D. G. DVX. SAB. P. PED. ET. C. **Rev:** Crowned shield of Savoy arms superimposed on cross with trefoil ends, date at end of legend **Rev. Legend:** IN. HOC. EGO. SPERABO. **Note:** Ref. Cud. 647f.

Date	Mintage	VG	F	VF	XF	Unc
1626	—	90.00	200	425	875	—

KM# 88 2 FIORINI

Silver Weight varies: 6.10-6.75g., 30 mm. **Ruler:** Carlo Emanuele I **Obv:** High-collared armored bust to right, date divided by mintmark in exergue **Obv. Legend:** CAR. EM. D. G. DVX. SAB. P. PED. ET. C. **Rev:** Crowned shield of Savoy arms superimposed on cross with trefoil ends **Rev. Legend:** IN. HOC. EGO. SPERABO. **Note:** Ref. Cud. 649.

Date	Mintage	VG	F	VF	XF	Unc
1626 V	—	175	385	725	1,150	—

KM# 111 2 FIORINI

4.4500 g., Silver, 27 mm. **Ruler:** Carlo Emanuele I **Obv:** High-collared armored bust to right **Obv. Legend:** CAR. EM. D. G. DVX. SAB. P. PED. ET. C. **Rev:** Crowned shield of Savoy arms superimposed on cross with trefoil ends, date at top in margin **Rev. Legend:** IN. HOC. EGO. SPRABO. **Note:** Ref. Cud. 650. Mint uncertain.

Date	Mintage	VG	F	VF	XF	Unc
162x Rare	—	—	—	—	—	—

KM# 65 3 FIORINI

Silver Weight varies: 6.95-7.92g., 33 mm. **Ruler:** Carlo Emanuele I **Obv:** High-collared armored bust to right in circle, mintmark and Roman numeral date below shoulder **Obv. Legend:** CAROLVS. EM. D. G. DVX. SAB. ET. C. **Rev:** Full-length facing figure of the Blessed Amadeus, head turned to right, holding large oval shield at right with 6-line inscription, value 'ff.3' in exergue **Rev. Legend:** BENEDIC. HÆR - EDITATI. TVÆ. **Rev.**

Inscription: F. / IVD / ET. IVS / DIL. / PAV / ET. C. **Note:** Ref. Cud. 640.

Date	Mintage	VG	F	VF	XF	Unc
MDCXX (1620) V	—	2,000	4,200	10,000	17,500	—

KM# 276 1/4 SCUDO BIANCO

Silver Weight varies: 6.75-6.78g., 29 mm. **Ruler:** Carlo Emanuele II alone **Obv:** Bust to right **Obv. Legend:** CAR. EM. I. D. - G. DVX. SAB. **Rev:** Crowned shield of Savoy arms supported by 2 lions, date in exergue **Rev. Legend:** PRIN. PEDE. REX. CYPRI. **Note:** Ref. Cud. 815.

Date	Mintage	VG	F	VF	XF	Unc
1667 Rare	—	—	—	—	—	—

KM# 74 1/4 DUCATONE

Silver Weight varies: 7.94-8.15g., 33 mm. **Ruler:** Carlo Emanuele I **Obv:** High-collared armored bust to right, mintmark and date below **Obv. Legend:** CAROLVS. EM. D. G. DVX. SABAVDIÆ. **Rev:** Crowned shield of 4-fold arms, with central shield of Savoy, in baroque frame, divides FE - RT **Rev. Legend:** DEVENTRE. MATRIS. DEVS. PROTECTOR. MEVS. **Note:** Ref. Cud. 627.

Date	Mintage	VG	F	VF	XF	Unc
1621 T Rare	—	—	—	—	—	—
1622 T Rare	—	—	—	—	—	—

KM# 211.1 1/4 DUCATONE

7.9300 g., Silver, 31 mm. **Ruler:** Carlo Emanuele II under regency **Obv:** Accolated busts of Carlo Emanuele and his mother to right, 2-line inscription of value below **Obv. Legend:** CHR. FRAN. CAR. EMAN. DVCES. SAB. **Obv. Inscription:** QVARTI. DI. / D. **Rev:** Crowned shield of manifold arms, with central shield of Savoy, in baroque frame, date at end of legend **Rev. Legend:** PRINCIPES. PEDEM. REGES. CYPRI. **Note:** Ref. Cud. 651a.

Date	Mintage	VG	F	VF	XF	Unc
1642 Rare	—	—	—	—	—	—

KM# 211.2 1/4 DUCATONE

7.9300 g., Silver, 31 mm. **Ruler:** Carlo Emanuele II under regency **Obv:** Accolated busts of Carlo Emanuele and his mother to right, 2-line inscription of value below **Obv. Legend:** CHR. FRAN. CAR. EMAN. DVCES. SAB. **Obv. Inscription:** QVARTI. DI. / D. **Rev:** Crowned shield of manifold arms, with central shield of Savoy, in baroque frame **Rev. Legend:** REGES. CYPRI - P. P. PEDEMON. **Note:** Ref. Cud. 751b.

Date	Mintage	VG	F	VF	XF	Unc
ND(ca1642) Rare	—	—	—	—	—	—

KM# 233 1/4 DUCATONE

7.9400 g., Silver, 35 mm. **Ruler:** Carlo Emanuele II alone **Obv:** Youthful armored bust to right, 2-line inscription below with value and date **Obv. Legend:** CAR. EMAN. II. D. G. DVX. SABAVDIE. **Obv. Inscription:** QVART. DV / (date) **Rev:** Crowned shield of manifold arms, with central shield of Savoy, in baroque frame, chain of order around **Rev. Legend:** PRIN. PEDEMON. - REX. CYPRI. ETC. **Note:** Ref. Cud. 811.

Date	Mintage	VG	F	VF	XF	Unc
1649 Rare	—	—	—	—	—	—

KM# 14 TESTONE

Silver Weight varies: 7.20-7.95g., 30 mm. **Ruler:** Carlo Emanuele I **Obv:** Armored bust to right, mintmark below shoulder **Obv. Legend:** CAR. EM. D. G. DVX. SAB. P. PED. **Rev:** Large shield of Savoy arms divides date, knot above **Rev. Legend:** NIL. DEEST. TIMENTIBVS. DEVM. **Note:** Ref. Cud. 636.

Date	Mintage	VG	F	VF	XF	Unc
1604 T	—	5,000	10,500	16,500	28,000	—

KM# 15 TESTONE

9.3600 g., Silver, 30 mm. **Ruler:** Carlo Emanuele I **Obv:** Armored bust to right, mintmark below shoulder **Obv. Legend:** CAR. EM. D. G. DVX. SAB. P. PED. **Rev:** Crowned shield of 4-fold arms, with central shield of Savoy, in baroque frame, date at end of legend **Rev. Legend:** AVXILIVM. MEVM. A DOMINO. **Note:** Ref. Cud. 637.

Date	Mintage	VG	F	VF	XF	Unc
1604 Rare	—	—	—	—	—	—

KM# 20 TESTONE

Silver Weight varies: 7.20-7.95g., 30 mm. **Ruler:** Carlo Emanuele I **Obv:** High-collared bust to right **Obv. Legend:** CAR. EM. D. G. DVX. SAB. P. P. **Rev:** Large shield of Savoy arms divides date, knot above **Rev. Legend:** NIL. DEEST. TIMENTIBVS. DEVM. **Note:** Ref. Cud. 638a.

Date	Mintage	VG	F	VF	XF	Unc
1606	—	5,000	10,500	16,500	28,000	—

KM# 22 TESTONE

Silver Weight varies: 7.20-7.95g., 30 mm. **Ruler:** Carlo Emanuele I **Obv:** High-collared bust to right, date below **Obv. Legend:** CAR. EM. D. G. DVX. SAB. P. P. **Rev:** Large shield of Savoy arms divides date, knot above **Rev. Legend:** NIL. DEST. TIMENTIBVS. DEVM. **Note:** Ref. Cud. 638b.

Date	Mintage	VG	F	VF	XF	Unc
1607//1606	—	5,000	10,500	16,500	28,000	—

KM# 187 TESTONE

9.5600 g., Silver, 30 mm. **Ruler:** Carlo Emanuele II under regency **Obv:** Accolated busts of Carlo Emanuele and his mother to right **Obv. Legend:** +CAR. EM. CHR. FRAN. D. G. DD. SAB. PP. PED. RR. CYPR. **Rev:** Crowned shield of manifold arms, with central shield of Savoy, divides crowned 'C - E,' mintmark at end of legend, date below in margin **Rev. Legend:** AVXILIVM. NOS - A. DOMINO. **Note:** Ref. Cud. 752.

Date	Mintage	VG	F	VF	XF	Unc
1641 Rare	—	—	—	—	—	—

KM# 188 LIRA

Silver, 38 mm. **Ruler:** Carlo Emanuele II under regency **Obv:** Accolated busts of Carlo Emanuele II and his mother to right, date at lower left, below shoulder, legend begins with double-C monogram **Obv. Legend:** CHR. FR. CAR. EM. DVCES. SAB. P. P. PDEM. R. R. CYPRI. **Rev:** Madonna and Child in laurel wreath, legend begins with double-C monogram **Rev. Legend:** IVSTVM - DEDVXIT - PER - VIAS - RECTAS. **Note:** Ref. Cud. 753.

Date	Mintage	VG	F	VF	XF	Unc
1641 Rare	—	—	—	—	—	—

KM# 123 LIRA (20 Soldi)

Silver Weight varies: 9.72-13.48g., 37 mm. **Ruler:** Vittorio Amedeo I **Obv:** Crowned shield of 4-fold arms, with central shield of Savoy, in baroque frame **Obv. Legend:** V. AMEDEVS. D. G. DVX. SABAVD. P. P. **Rev:** 3 flags on staffs protruding through large crown, date, mintmark and value 'S.20' in exergue **Rev. Legend:** NEC - NVMINA - DESVNT. **Note:** Ref. Cud. 708.

Date	Mintage	VG	F	VF	XF	Unc
1631 T Rare	—	—	—	—	—	—
1631 TAVR Rare	—	—	—	—	—	—
1632 Rare	—	—	—	—	—	—

KM# 125 LIRA (20 Soldi)

Silver Weight varies: 13.35-13.60g., 37 mm. **Ruler:** Vittorio Amedeo I **Obv:** Mantled bust to right **Obv. Legend:** V. AMEDEVS. D. G. DVX. SAB. P. PED. **Rev:** 3 flags on staffs protruding through large crown, date, mintmark and value 'S.20' in exergue **Rev. Legend:** NEC - NVMINA - DESVNT. **Note:** Ref. Cud. 710a,c.

Date	Mintage	VG	F	VF	XF	Unc
1631 T	—	4,000	8,500	16,500	28,000	—
1633	—	4,000	8,500	16,500	28,000	—

KM# 126 LIRA (20 Soldi)

Silver Weight varies: 13.35-13.60g., 37 mm. **Ruler:** Vittorio Amedeo I **Obv:** Mantled bust to right **Obv. Legend:** V. AMEDEVS. D. G. DVX. SAB. P. PED. **Rev:** 3 flags on staffs protruding through large crown, value 'S.20' and date in exergue **Rev. Legend:** NEC - NVMINA - DESVNT. **Note:** Ref. Cud. 711a,c. Mint uncertain.

Date	Mintage	VG	F	VF	XF	Unc
1632	—	4,000	8,500	16,500	28,000	—
1634 Rare	—	—	—	—	—	—

KM# 124 LIRA (20 Soldi)

Silver Weight varies: 13.35-13.60g., 37 mm. **Ruler:** Vittorio Amedeo I **Obv:** Mantled bust to right, date below **Obv. Legend:** V. AMEDEVS. D. G. SVX. SABAVDIÆ. **Rev:** 3 flags on saffs protruding through large crown, date mintmark and value 'S.20' in exergue **Rev. Legend:** NEC - NVMINA - DESVNT. **Note:** Ref. Cud. 709.

Date	Mintage	VG	F	VF	XF	Unc
1632//1631 T	—	4,500	9,500	17,500	30,000	—

KM# 137 LIRA (20 Soldi)

Silver Weight varies: 13.35-13.60g., 37 mm. **Ruler:** Vittorio Amedeo I **Obv:** Mantled bust to right, date below **Obv. Legend:** V. AMEDEVS. D. G. DVX. SAB. P. PED. **Rev:** 3 flags on staffs protruding through large crown, value 'SOLDI 20' in exergue **Rev. Legend:** NEC - NVMINA - DESVNT. **Note:** Ref. Cud. 710b.

Date	Mintage	VG	F	VF	XF	Unc
1633	—	4,000	8,500	16,500	28,000	—

KM# 138 LIRA (20 Soldi)

Silver Weight varies: 13.35-13.60g., 37 mm. **Ruler:** Vittorio Amedeo I **Obv:** Mantled bust to right, date below **Obv. Legend:** V. AMEDEVS. D. G. DVX. SAB. P. PED. **Rev:** 3 flags with staffs protruding through large crown, value 'S*20' and date in exergue **Rev. Legend:** NEC - NVMINA - DESVNT. **Note:** Ref. Cud. 711b. Mint uncertain.

Date	Mintage	VG	F	VF	XF	Unc
1633//1633 Rare	—	—	—	—	—	—

KM# 139 LIRA (20 Soldi)

13.3500 g., Silver, 37 mm. **Ruler:** Vittorio Amedeo I **Obv:** Mantled bust to right **Obv. Legend:** V. AMEDEVS. D. G. DVX. SAB. P. PED. **Rev:** 3 flags on staffs protruding through large crown, value 'SCVDI.4' and date in 2 lines in exergue **Rev. Legend:** NEC - NVMINA - DESVNT. **Note:** Ref. Cud. 714. Struck from 4 Scudi dies, KM#141.

Date	Mintage	VG	F	VF	XF	Unc
1633 Rare	—	—	—	—	—	—

KM# 148 LIRA (20 Soldi)

Silver Weight varies: 12.66-13.25g., 38 mm. **Ruler:** Vittorio Amedeo I **Obv:** Mantled bust to right, date below **Obv. Legend:** V. AMEDEVS. D. G. DVX. SAB. P. PED. **Rev:** 3 flags on staffs protruding through large crown, value 'S.20' in exergue **Rev. Legend:** NEC - NVMINA - DESVNT. **Note:** Ref. Cud. 712. Varieties exist.

Date	Mintage	VG	F	VF	XF	Unc
1634	—	5,850	8,400	14,500	20,000	—

KM# 149 LIRA (20 Soldi)

Silver Weight varies: 12.66-13.25g., 38 mm. **Ruler:** Vittorio Amedeo I **Obv:** Mantled bust to right, date below **Obv. Legend:** V. AMEDEVS. D. G. DVX. SAB. P. PED. **Rev:** 3 flags on staffs protruding through large crown, value 'S.20' in exergue **Rev. Legend:** NEC - NVMINA - DESVNT. **Note:** Ref. Cud. 713.

Date	Mintage	VG	F	VF	XF	Unc
1634 Rare	—	—	—	—	—	—

KM# 291 LIRA (20 Soldi)

Silver Weight varies: 5.48-6.11g., 29 mm. **Ruler:** Vittorio Amedeo II under regency **Obv:** Accolated busts of Vittorio Amedeo II and his mother to right **Obv. Legend:** MARI. IO. BAP. VIC. AM. II. D. G. DVC. SAB. **Rev:** Crowned shield of manifold arms with central shield of Savoy, date divided at top, value 'S. 20' below **Rev. Legend:** PRIN. PEDEM - REGES. CYPRI. **Note:** Ref. Cud. 838.

Date	Mintage	VG	F	VF	XF	Unc
1675 Rare	—	—	—	—	—	—
1676	—	120	250	525	950	—
1677	—	85.00	180	350	775	—
1678	—	85.00	180	350	775	—
1679	—	120	250	525	950	—
1680	—	120	250	525	950	—
ND Rare	—	—	—	—	—	—

KM# 306 LIRA (20 Soldi)

Silver Weight varies: 5.80-6.60g., 29 mm. **Ruler:** Vittorio Amedeo II alone **Obv:** Armored bust to right **Obv. Legend:** VIC AM. II. (-) D. (-) G. DVX SAB. **Rev:** Crowned shield of manifold arms with central shield of Savoy, date divided at top, value 'S. 20' at bottom **Rev. Legend:** PRIN. PEDE - REX. CYPRI. **Note:** Ref. Cud. 862. Varieties exist.

Date	Mintage	VG	F	VF	XF	Unc
1680	—	200	475	950	1,300	—
1681	—	225	500	1,050	1,500	—
1682	—	160	350	825	1,150	—
1683	—	160	350	825	1,150	—
1684 Rare	—	—	—	—	—	—
1687 Rare	—	—	—	—	—	—

KM# 323 LIRA (20 Soldi)

Silver Weight varies: 5.80-5.99g., 29 mm. **Ruler:** Vittorio Amedeo II alone **Obv:** Draped bust to right **Obv. Legend:** VICTOR. AM. II. - D. G. DVX. SAB. **Rev:** Crowned shield of manifold arms with central shield of Savoy, date divided at top, value 'S. 20' below **Rev. Legend:** PRIN. PEDE - REX. CYPRI. **Note:** Ref. Cud. 863.

Date	Mintage	VG	F	VF	XF	Unc
1690	—	95.00	215	575	1,000	—
1691	—	95.00	215	575	1,000	—
1692 Rare	—	—	—	—	—	—
1694 Rare	—	—	—	—	—	—

KM# 344 LIRA (20 Soldi)

Silver Weight varies: 5.83-6.05g., 29 mm. **Ruler:** Vittorio Amedeo II alone **Obv:** Draped and armored bust to right **Obv. Legend:** VIC. AM. II. D. - G. DVX. SAB. **Rev:** Crowned shield of manifold arms, with central shield of Savoy, in baroque frame, date divided at top, value 'S. 20' in margin at bottom **Rev. Legend:** PRIN. PEDE - REX. CYPRI. **Note:** Ref. Cud. 864, 865.

Date	Mintage	VG	F	VF	XF	Unc
1700 Rare	—	—	—	—	—	—

KM# 290 LIRA NUOVA (20 Soldi)

Silver Weight varies: 5.15-6.13g., 29 mm. **Ruler:** Carlo Emanuele II alone **Obv:** Bust to right, date below **Obv. Legend:** CAR. EM. II. D. - G. DVX. SAB. **Rev:** Crowned shield of manifold arms, with central shield of Savoy, value 'S.20' in margin below **Rev. Legend:** PRIN. PEDE - REX. CYPRI. **Note:** Ref. Cud. 816.

Date	Mintage	VG	F	VF	XF	Unc
1675	—	175	350	825	2,100	—

KM# 324 1 1/2 LIRE (30 Soldi)
Silver Weight varies: 8.90-9.02g., 32 mm. **Ruler:** Vittorio Amedeo II alone **Obv:** Armored bust to right **Obv. Legend:** VICTOR. AM. II. D. G. DVX. SAB. **Rev:** Crowned shield of manifold arms with central shield of Savoy, date divided above, value 'S. 30' below in margin **Rev. Legend:** PRIN. PEDE - REX. CYPRI. **Note:** Ref. Cud. 861.

Date	Mintage	VG	F	VF	XF	Unc
1690 Rare	—	—	—	—	—	—

KM# 335 2 LIRE (40 Soldi)
Silver Weight varies: 12.02-12.08g., 32 mm. **Ruler:** Vittorio Amedeo II alone **Obv:** Draped bust to right **Obv. Legend:** VICTOR. AM. II. D. G. DVX. SAB. **Rev:** Crowned shield of manifold arms with central shield of Savoy, date divided above, value 'S. 40' below in margin **Rev. Legend:** PRIN. PEDE - REX. CYPRI. **Note:** Ref. Cud. 859.

Date	Mintage	VG	F	VF	XF	Unc
1691	—	400	825	1,800	3,500	—
ND	—	800	1,600	3,350	6,500	—

KM# 277 1/2 SCUDO BIANCO
Silver Weight varies: 13.42-13.45g., 35 mm. **Ruler:** Carlo Emanuele II alone **Obv:** Bust to right **Obv. Legend:** CAR. EM. II. - D. G. DVX. SAB. **Rev:** Crowned shield of Savoy arms supported by 2 lions, date in exergue **Rev. Legend:** PRIN. PEDE. - REX. CYPRI. **Note:** Ref. Cud. 814.

Date	Mintage	VG	F	VF	XF	Unc
1667	—	4,650	9,000	15,000	32,000	—

KM# 307 1/2 SCUDO BIANCO
Silver Weight varies: 13.17-13.45g., 35 mm. **Ruler:** Vittorio Amedeo II alone **Obv:** Draped bust to right **Obv. Legend:** VIC. AM. II. - D. G. DVX. SAB. **Rev:** Crowned shield of Savoy arms supported by 2 lions, date in exergue **Rev. Legend:** PRIN. PEDE. - REX. CYPRI. **Note:** Ref. Cud. 856.

Date	Mintage	VG	F	VF	XF	Unc
1680	—	800	1,800	4,200	9,000	—
1681	—	950	2,000	4,500	10,500	—
1682 Rare	—	—	—	—	—	—

KM# 325 1/2 SCUDO BIANCO
Silver Weight varies: 13.35-13.48g., 35 mm. **Ruler:** Vittorio Amedeo II alone **Obv:** Draped bust to right **Obv. Legend:** VICTOR. AM. II. - D. G. DVX. SAB. **Rev:** Crowned shield of Savoy arms supported by 2 lions, date in exergue **Rev. Legend:** PRIN. PEDE. REX. CYPRI. **Note:** Ref. Cud. 857.

Date	Mintage	VG	F	VF	XF	Unc
1690 Rare	—	—	—	—	—	—
1695 Rare	—	—	—	—	—	—

KM# 60 6 FIORINI
15.4700 g., Silver, 37 mm. **Ruler:** Carlo Emanuele I **Obv:** High-collared armored bust to right, Roman numeral date and mintmark below **Obv. Legend:** CAROLVS. EM. D. G. DVX. SABAVDIÆ. **Rev:** Crowned shield of 4-fold arms, with central shield of Savoy, in baroque frame, chain of order suspended under lower half, value 'ff-6' in cartouche at bottom **Rev. Legend:** IN. TE. DOM. - CONFIDO. **Note:** Ref. Cud. 626.

Date	Mintage	VG	F	VF	XF	Unc
MDCXIX (1619) V Rare	—	—	—	—	—	—

KM# 5 1/2 DUCATONE
Silver Weight varies: 15.60-15.91g., 37 mm. **Ruler:** Carlo Emanuele I **Obv:** Armored bust to right, mintmark below **Obv. Legend:** CAR. EM D. G. DVX. SAB. P. PED. **Rev:** Crowned shield of 4-fold arms, with central shield of Savoy, in baroque frame, divides date **Rev. Legend:** NIL. DEEST. TIMENTIBVS. DEVM. **Note:** Ref. Cud. 623. Varieties exist.

Date	Mintage	VG	F	VF	XF	Unc
1601 T Rare	—	—	—	—	—	—
1604 T	—	6,500	12,000	18,000	32,500	—
1606 T	—	6,500	12,000	18,000	32,500	—
1607 T Rare	—	—	—	—	—	—

KM# 23 1/2 DUCATONE
Silver Weight varies: 15.60-15.91g., 37 mm. **Ruler:** Carlo Emanuele I **Obv:** Large high-collared armored bust to right, date below **Obv. Legend:** CAR. EM. D. G. DVX. SAB. P. PED. **Rev:** Crowned shield of 4-fold arms, with central shield of Savoy, in baroque frame, divides date **Rev. Legend:** NIL. DEEST. TIMENTIBVS. DEVM. **Note:** Ref. Cud. 624. Mint uncertain.

Date	Mintage	VG	F	VF	XF	Unc
1607//1606	—	6,500	12,000	18,000	32,500	—

KM# 76 1/2 DUCATONE
Silver Weight varies: 15.80-15.97g., 37 mm. **Ruler:** Carlo Emanuele I **Obv:** Large high-collared armored bust to right, date below **Obv. Legend:** CAROLVS. EM. D.G. DVX. SABAVDIÆ. **Rev:** Crowned shield of 4-fold arms with central shield of Savoy, in baroque frame, divides FE - RT. **Rev. Legend:** DEVENTRE. MATRIS. DEVS. PROTECTOR. MEVS. **Note:** Ref. Cud. 625. Mint uncertain.

Date	Mintage	VG	F	VF	XF	Unc
1621	—	6,800	11,500	17,500	25,000	—

KM# 132 1/2 DUCATONE
Silver Weight varies: 15.82-15.95g., 38 mm. **Ruler:** Vittorio Amedeo I **Obv:** Armored bust to right, date below **Obv. Legend:** V. AMEDEVS. D. G. DVX. SAB(AVDIÆ). (P. PED). **Rev:** Crowned shield of 4-fold arms, with central shield of Savoy, in baroque frame, chain of order around **Rev. Legend:** ET - PRINCEPS - PEDEMONTIVM. **Note:** Ref. Cud. 707. Varieties exist.

Date	Mintage	VG	F	VF	XF	Unc
1632	—	3,250	6,000	18,500	35,000	—
1633 Rare	—	—	—	—	—	—

KM# 213 1/2 DUCATONE
Silver Weight varies: 15.89-16.65g., 37 mm. **Ruler:** Carlo Emanuele II under regency **Obv:** Accolated busts of Carlo Emanuele II and his mother to right, 2-line inscription with value and date below **Obv. Legend:** CHR. FRAN. CAR. EMAN. DVCES. SABAV. **Obv. Inscription:** MEZZI DVCAT / (date) **Rev:** Crowned shield of manifold arms, with central shield of Savoy, in baroque frame **Rev. Legend:** PRINCIPES. PEDEMON. REGES. CYPRI. **Note:** Ref. Cud. 750.

Date	Mintage	VG	F	VF	XF	Unc
1642 Rare	—	—	—	—	—	—

KM# 234 1/2 DUCATONE
15.8700 g., Silver, 40 mm. **Ruler:** Carlo Emanuele II alone **Obv:** Draped bust to right, 2-line inscription below with value and date **Obv. Legend:** CAR. EMAN. II. D. G. DVX. SABAVDIAE. **Rev:** Crowned shield of manifold arms, with central shield of Savoy, in baroque frame, chain of order around **Rev. Legend:** PRIN. PEDEMON - REX. CYPRI. ETC. **Note:** Ref. Cud. 810.

Date	Mintage	VG	F	VF	XF	Unc
1649 Rare	—	—	—	—	—	—

KM# 326 3 LIRE (60 Soldi)
Silver Weight varies: 17.98-18.05g., 37 mm. **Ruler:** Vittorio Amedeo II alone **Obv:** Draped and armored bust to right **Obv. Legend:** VICTOR. AM. II. - D. G. DVX. SAB. **Rev:** Crowned shield of manifold arms with central shield of Savoy, date divided above, value 'S. 60' below in margin **Rev. Legend:** PRIN. PEDE - REX. CYPRI. **Note:** Ref. Cud. 858.

Date	Mintage	VG	F	VF	XF	Unc
1690	—	3,500	7,200	10,500	18,000	—

KM# 33.1 9 FIORINI
Silver Weight varies: 21.50-23.50g., 43 mm. **Ruler:** Carlo Emanuele I **Obv:** High-collared bust to right, mintmark and date below **Obv. Legend:** CAROLVS. EM. D. G. DVX. SAB. **Rev:** Full-length figure of Blessed Amadeus, head turned to left, value **ff*9* in exergue **Rev. Legend:** BENEDIC - HÆREDITATI - TVÆ. **Note:** Ref. Cud. 613a-d,g,h; Dav. 4155.

Date	Mintage	VG	F	VF	XF	Unc
1609 T	—	700	1,450	3,500	6,500	—
1610 T	—	700	1,450	3,500	6,500	—
1619 T	—	550	1,250	3,250	6,500	—
1620 T	—	550	1,250	3,250	6,500	—
1628 T	—	650	1,450	3,500	6,500	—
1629 T	—	650	1,450	3,500	6,500	—

KM# 52 9 FIORINI
Silver Weight varies: 26.38-26.80g., 43 mm. **Ruler:** Carlo Emanuele I **Obv:** Large high-collared armored bust to right, date below **Obv. Legend:** CAROLVS. EM. D. G. DVX. SAB. **Rev:** Full-length facing figure of Blessed Amadeus, B. AMEDEVS in exergue **Rev. Legend:** BENEDIC - HEREDITATI - TVAE. **Note:** Ref. Cud. 614; Dav. 4156.

Date	Mintage	VG	F	VF	XF	Unc
1614	—	6,000	10,500	19,000	36,000	—
1616	—	6,000	10,500	19,000	36,000	—
1618	—	6,000	10,500	19,000	36,000	—

KM# 53 9 FIORINI
Silver Weight varies: 23.60-26.71g., 45 mm. **Ruler:** Carlo Emanuele I **Obv:** High-collared armored bust to right, date below **Obv. Legend:** CAROLVS. EM. D. G. DVX. SAB. **Rev:** Full-length standing figure of St. Charles, turned to right, holding cross, S • CAROLVS in exergue **Rev. Legend:** DISCERNE - CAVSAM - MEAM. **Note:** Ref. Cud. 617; Dav. 4157.

Date	Mintage	VG	F	VF	XF	Unc
1614	—	2,400	4,500	7,500	13,000	—
1615	—	2,400	4,500	7,500	13,000	—
1618	—	2,400	4,500	7,500	13,000	—

KM# 61 9 FIORINI
Silver Weight varies: 20.55-23.45g., 45 mm. **Ruler:** Carlo Emanuele I **Obv:** High-collared bust to right, mintmark and date below **Obv. Legend:** CAROLVS. EM. D. G. DVX. SAB. ET. C. **Rev:** Full-length figure of Blessed Amedeus, head to right, holding large oval shield in baroque frame with 8-line inscription, value .ff.9. in exergue **Rev. Legend:** BENEDIC - HÆR - EDITATI - TVÆ. **Rev. Inscription:** FAC. / IVDITIVM / ET. IVSTIT. / DILIG. PAVP / ET. DOM. DAB / P. IN. FINI / /VEST. / B. A. **Note:** Ref. Cud. 615; Dav. 4159.

Date	Mintage	VG	F	VF	XF	Unc
1619 VER	—	1,650	3,500	7,200	13,500	—
1620 VER	—	1,650	3,500	7,200	13,500	—

KM# 33.2 9 FIORINI
Silver Weight varies: 21.50-23.50g., 43 mm. **Ruler:** Carlo Emanuele I **Obv:** High-collared bust to right, date below **Obv. Legend:** CAROLVS. EM. D. G. DVX. SAB. **Rev:** Full-length figure of Blessed Amadeus, head turned to left, value **ff*9* in exergue **Rev. Legend:** BENEDIC - HÆREDITATI - TVÆ. **Note:** Ref. Cud. 613e,f; Dav. 4155.

Date	Mintage	VG	F	VF	XF	Unc
1620	—	700	1,450	3,500	6,500	—
1624	—	700	1,450	3,500	6,500	—

KM# 109 9 FIORINI
Silver Weight varies: 22.90-23.60g., 45 mm. **Ruler:** Carlo Emanuele I **Obv:** Large high-collared armored bust to right **Obv. Legend:** CAROLVS. EM. D:G - DVX. SAB. P. P. ET. C. **Rev:** Full-length figure of Blessed Amadeus, head to right, holding large oval shield in baroque frame with 7-line inscription, value .ff.9. divides date in exergue **Rev. Legend:** BENEDIC. HÆR - EDITATI. TVÆ. **Note:** Ref. Cud. 616; Dav. 4160.

Date	Mintage	VG	F	VF	XF	Unc
1629	—	3,000	6,000	12,000	—	—

Note: Numismatica Ars Classica Auction 32, 1-06, XF realized approximately $23,020

KM# 54 SCUDO

Silver Weight varies: 25.58-26.58g., 43 mm. **Ruler:** Carlo Emanuele I **Obv:** High-collared armored bust to right, date below **Obv. Legend:** CAROLVS. EM. D. G. DVX. SAB. **Rev:** Full-length figure of St. Maurice, turned slightly to left, holding staff with pennant and breast plate, S. MAVR. PROT. in exergue **Rev. Legend:** PRÆLIA. DOMINE. PRÆMIA. **Note:** Ref. Cud. 618; Dav. 4158.

Date	Mintage	VG	F	VF	XF	Unc
1616 Rare	—	—	—	—	—	—
1618 Rare	—	—	—	—	—	—

KM# 67 SCUDO

Silver Weight varies: 23.96-25.40g., 43 mm. **Ruler:** Carlo Emanuele I **Obv:** High-collared armored bust to right **Obv. Legend:** CAROLVS. EM. D. G. - DVX. SAB. P. P. ET. C. **Rev:** Mailed arm from clouds at right holding sword with blade pointing up, ornate cartouche at bottom **Rev. Legend:** OMNIA. DAT. QVI. IVSTA. NEGAT. **Note:** Ref. Cud. 619; Dav. 4164, 4164A.

Date	Mintage	VG	F	VF	XF	Unc
ND(ca1620)	—	1,850	3,500	8,000	15,000	—

KM# 68 SCUDO

Silver Weight varies: 25.30-25.40g., 43 mm. **Ruler:** Carlo Emanuele I **Obv:** High-collared armored bust to right **Obv. Legend:** CAROLVS. EM. D. G. - DVX. SAB. P. P. ET. C. **Rev:** Mailed arm from clouds at right holding sword with blade pointing up, blank exergue **Rev. Legend:** OMNIA. DAT. QVI. IVSTA. NEGAT. **Note:** Ref. Cud. 620; Dav. 4164B.

Date	Mintage	VG	F	VF	XF	Unc
ND(ca1620)	—	2,500	5,600	10,500	18,000	—

KM# 265 SCUDO BIANCO

27.1000 g., Silver, 42 mm. **Ruler:** Carlo Emanuele II alone **Obv:** Armored bust to right **Obv. Legend:** CAR. EMAN. II. D. G. DVX. SABAVDIE. **Rev:** Crowned shield of Savoy arms, chain of order around, date divided in margin at top **Rev. Legend:** PRIN. PEDEMO - N. REX. CIPRI. **Note:** Ref. Cud. 812; Dav. 4169.

Date	Mintage	VG	F	VF	XF	Unc
1659 Rare	—	—	—	—	—	—

KM# 278 SCUDO BIANCO

27.1000 g., Silver, 42 mm. **Ruler:** Carlo Emanuele II alone **Obv:** Bust to right **Obv. Legend:** CAR. EM. II. D. - G. DVX. SAB. **Rev:** Crowned shield of Savoy arms supported by 2 lions, date in exergue **Rev. Legend:** PRIN. PEDE - REX. CYPRI. **Note:** Ref. Cud. 813; Dav. 4170.

Date	Mintage	VG	F	VF	XF	Unc
1667	—	4,500	9,500	16,500	28,000	—

KM# 292 SCUDO BIANCO

Silver Weight varies: 26.82-27.00g., 44 mm. **Ruler:** Vittorio Amedeo II under regency **Obv:** Accolated busts of Vittorio Amedeo II and his mother to right **Obv. Legend:** MAR. IO. BAP. VIC. AM. II. D. G. DVC. SAB. **Rev:** Crowned shield of Savoy arms supported by 2 lions, date in exergue **Rev. Legend:** PRINCI. PEDEM. REGES. CYP. **Note:** Ref. Cud. 837; Dav. 4171.

Date	Mintage	VG	F	VF	XF	Unc
1675 Rare	—	—	—	—	—	—
1680	—	1,350	3,000	6,500	11,000	—

KM# 308 SCUDO BIANCO

Silver Weight varies: 26.80-27.62g., 42 mm. **Ruler:** Vittorio Amedeo II alone **Obv:** Draped and armored bust to right **Obv. Legend:** VIC(TOR). AM. II. D. (-) G. DVX. SAB. **Rev:** Crowned shield of Savoy arms supported by 2 lions, date in exergue **Rev. Legend:** PRIN(C). PEDEM. REX. CYPRI. **Note:** Ref. Cud. 853. Varieties exist.

Date	Mintage	VG	F	VF	XF	Unc
1680	—	3,500	4,800	9,250	14,500	—
1681 Rare	—	—	—	—	—	—
1682 Rare	—	—	—	—	—	—

KM# 327 SCUDO BIANCO

Silver Weight varies: 26.85-26.92g., 42 mm. **Ruler:** Vittorio Amedeo II alone **Obv:** Draped bust to right **Obv. Legend:** VICTOR. AM. II. - D. G. DVX. SAB. **Rev:** Crowned shield of Savoy arms supported by 2 lions, date in exergue **Rev. Legend:** PRIN. PEDE. REX. CYPRI. **Note:** Ref. Cud. 854; Dav. 4173.

Date	Mintage	VG	F	VF	XF	Unc
1690	—	2,800	4,800	9,250	14,500	—
1695 Rare	—	—	—	—	—	—

KM# 6 DUCATONE

Silver Weight varies: 29.20-31.80g., 43 mm. **Ruler:** Carlo Emanuele I **Obv:** Armored bust to right, date and mintmark below **Obv. Legend:** CAROLVS. EM. D. G. DVX. SABAVDIA. **Rev:** Crowned shield of 4-fold arms, with central shield of Savoy, in baroque frame, divides FE - RT **Rev. Legend:** +DEVENTRE. MATRIS. DEVS. PROTECTOR. MEVS. **Note:** Ref. Cud. 605; Dav. 4150.

Date	Mintage	VG	F	VF	XF	Unc
1601 T Rare	—	—	—	—	—	—
1603 T Rare	—	—	—	—	—	—

KM# 12 DUCATONE

Silver Weight varies: 29.20-31.80g., 43 mm. **Ruler:** Carlo Emanuele I **Obv:** Armored bust to right, mintmark and date below **Obv. Legend:** CAROLVS. EM. D. G. DVX. SABAVDIÆ. **Rev:** Crowned shield of 4-fold arms, with central shield of Savoy, in baroque frame, divides FE - RT **Rev. Legend:** +DEVENTRE. MATRIS. DEVS. PROTECTOR. MEVS. **Note:** Ref. Cud. 606; Dav. 4150.

Date	Mintage	VG	F	VF	XF	Unc
1603 T Rare	—	—	—	—	—	—
1604 T	—	3,250	7,000	10,500	18,000	—
1608 T Rare	—	—	—	—	—	—

KM# 25 DUCATONE

31.6500 g., Silver, 44 mm. **Ruler:** Carlo Emanuele I **Obv:** High-collared armored bust to right, mintmark and date below **Obv. Legend:** CAROLVS. EM. D. G. DVX. SABAVDIÆ. **Rev:** Crowned shield of 4-fold arms, with central shield of Savoy arms, in baroque frame, divides FE - RT **Rev. Legend:** *DEVENTRE. MATRIS. DEVS. PROTECTOR. MEVS. **Note:** Ref. Cud. 607; Dav. 4151.

Date	Mintage	VG	F	VF	XF	Unc
1607 T Rare	—	—	—	—	—	—

KM# 30 DUCATONE

Silver, 45 mm. **Ruler:** Carlo Emanuele I **Obv:** High-collared armored bust to right, mintmark and date below **Obv. Legend:** CAROLVS. EM. DVX. SABAVDIÆ. **Rev:** Crowned shield of 4-fold arms, with central shield of Savoy, in baroque frame **Rev. Legend:** *DEVENTRE. MATRIS. DEVS. PROTECTOR. MEVS. **Note:** Ref. Cud. 608; Dav. 4152.

Date	Mintage	VG	F	VF	XF	Unc
1608 T Rare	—	—	—	—	—	—

KM# 34 DUCATONE

Silver Weight varies: 31.68-31.75g., 45 mm. **Ruler:** Carlo Emanuele I **Obv:** High-collared armored bust to right, mintmark, where present, and date below **Obv. Legend:** CAROLVS. EM. D. G. DVX. SABAVDIÆ. **Rev:** Crowned shield of 4-fold arms, with central shield of Savoy, in baroque frame, divides FE - RT **Rev. Legend:** *DEVENTRE. MATRIS. DEVS. PROTECTOR. DEVS. **Note:** Ref. Cud. 609; Dav. 4153.

Date	Mintage	VG	F	VF	XF	Unc
1609 T	—	6,500	14,000	24,000	36,000	—
1610	—	6,500	14,000	24,000	36,000	—
1611	—	6,500	14,000	24,000	36,000	—

KM# 70 DUCATONE
Silver Weight varies: 31.20-31.97g., 45 mm. **Ruler:** Carlo Emanuele I **Obv:** Large high-collared armored bust to right, date and mintmark (where present) below **Obv. Legend:** CAR(OLVS). EM. D. G. DVX. SABAVD(IÆ). (P. P ED). **Rev:** Crowned shield of 4-fold arms, with central shield of Savoy, in baroque frame, divides FE - RT **Rev. Legend:** *DEVENTRE. MATRIS. DEVS. PROTECTOR. MEVS. **Note:** Ref. Cud. 610; Dav. 4154. Varieties exist.

Date	Mintage	VG	F	VF	XF	Unc
1620 T	—	1,650	3,000	4,800	8,500	—
1621	—	1,650	3,000	4,800	8,500	—
1622	—	1,650	3,000	4,800	8,500	—

KM# 78 DUCATONE
Silver Weight varies: 31.72-31.85g., 44 mm. **Ruler:** Carlo Emanuele I **Obv:** Large high-collared bust to right, date below **Obv. Legend:** CAROLVS. EM. D. G. DVX. SABAVDIÆ. **Rev:** Large drawing compass in circle **Rev. Legend:** DVM - PRÆMOR - AMPLIOR. **Note:** Ref. Cud. 612a; Dav. 4161.

Date	Mintage	VG	F	VF	XF	Unc
1621 Rare	—	—	—	—	—	—

KM# 90.1 DUCATONE
Silver Weight varies: 30.40-31.97g., 45 mm. **Ruler:** Carlo Emanuele I **Obv:** Large high-collared armored bust to right, mintmark (where present) and date below **Obv. Legend:** CAR. EM. D. G. DVX. SAB. P. PED. ET. C. **Rev:** Crowned shield of 4-fold arms, with central shield of Savoy, in baroque frame, divides FE - RT **Rev. Legend:** DEVENTRE. MATRIS. DEVS. PROTECTOR. MEVS. **Note:** Ref. Cud. 611a,b; Dav. 4154.

Date	Mintage	VG	F	VF	XF	Unc
1627 T	—	4,000	7,500	10,500	18,500	—
1627	—	4,000	7,500	10,500	18,500	—

KM# 91 DUCATONE
Silver Weight varies: 31.72-31.85g., 44 mm. **Ruler:** Carlo Emanuele I **Obv:** Large high-collared armored bust to right, date below **Obv. Legend:** CAR. EM. D. G. DVX. SAB. P. PED. ET. C. **Rev:** Large drawing compass in circle **Rev. Legend:** *DVM - PRÆMOR - AMPLIOR. **Note:** Ref. Cud. 612b; Dav. 4161.

Date	Mintage	VG	F	VF	XF	Unc
1627 Rare	—	—	—	—	—	—

Note: Numismatica Ars Classica Auction 32, 1-06, XF realized approximately $66,675

KM# 90.2 DUCATONE
Silver Weight varies: 30.40-31.97g., 45 mm. **Ruler:** Carlo Emanuele I **Obv:** High-collared armored bust to right, mintmark and date below **Obv. Legend:** CAROLVS. EM. D: G: DVX. SABAVDIE P. P. **Rev:** Crowned shield of 4-fold arms, with central shield of Savoy, in baroque frame, divides FE - RT **Rev. Legend:** DEVENTRE. MATRIS. DEVS. PROTECTOR. MEVS. **Note:** Ref. Cud. 611c; Dav. 4163.

Date	Mintage	VG	F	VF	XF	Unc
1628 V	—	6,500	12,500	—	—	—

Note: Numismatica Arts Classica Auction 32, 1-06, Fine realized approximately $11,115

KM# 133 DUCATONE
Silver Weight varies: 31.25-32.20g., 45 mm. **Ruler:** Vittorio Amedeo I **Obv:** Armored bust to right, date below **Obv. Legend:** V. AMEDEVS. D: G. DVX. SABAVDIÆ. **Rev:** Crowned shield of 4-fold arms, with central shield of Savoy, in baroque frame, chain of order around **Rev. Legend:** ET PRINCEPS - PEDEMONTIVM. **Note:** Ref. Cud. 706; Dav. 4165. Varieties exist.

Date	Mintage	VG	F	VF	XF	Unc
1632	—	1,700	3,250	6,000	11,000	—
1633 Rare	—	—	—	—	—	—

KM# 190 DUCATONE
Silver Weight varies: 31.42-31.90g., 45 mm. **Ruler:** Carlo Emanuele II under regency **Obv:** Accolated busts of Carlo Emanuele II and his mother to right, date below in cartouche **Obv. Legend:** CHR. FRAN. CAR. EMAN. DVCES. SAB. **Rev:** Crowned shield of manifold arms, with central shield of Savoy, in baroque frame **Rev. Legend:** PRINCIPES. PEDEMON. REGES. CYPRI. **Note:** Ref. Cud. 749; Dav. 4167.

Date	Mintage	VG	F	VF	XF	Unc
1641	—	3,750	5,400	8,400	14,400	—
1642	—	3,750	5,400	8,400	14,400	—

Note: Numismatica Ars Classica Auction 32, 1-06, XF/Unc realized approximately $28,575

Date	Mintage	VG	F	VF	XF	Unc
1643 Rare	—	—	—	—	—	—
1644 Rare	—	—	—	—	—	—

KM# 235 DUCATONE
Silver Weight varies: 31.83-31.90g., 46 mm. **Ruler:** Carlo Emanuele II alone **Obv:** Draped bust to right, date below in margin **Obv. Legend:** CAR. EMAN. II. D. G. DVX. SABAVDIÆ. **Rev:** Crowned shield of manifold arms, with central shield of Savoy, in baroque frame, chain of order around **Rev. Legend:** PRIN. PEDEMON - REX. CYPRI. ET. C. **Note:** Ref. Cud. 809; Dav. 4168.

Date	Mintage	VG	F	VF	XF	Unc
1649 Rare	—	—	—	—	—	—
1650 Rare	—	—	—	—	—	—

KM# 100 2 DUCATONE (Doppio Ducatone)
Silver Weight varies: 63.75-63.80g., 45 mm. **Ruler:** Carlo Emanuele I **Obv:** Large high-collared bust to right, mintmark and date below **Obv. Legend:** CAROLVS. EM. D. G. DVX. SABAVDE. P. P. **Rev:** Crowned shield of 4-fold arms, with central shield of Savoy, in baroque frame, divides FE - RT **Rev. Legend:** DEVENTRE. MATRIS. DEVS. PROTEC. MEVS. **Note:** Ref. Cud. 595; Dav. 4162.

Date	Mintage	VG	F	VF	XF	Unc
1628 V Rare	—	—	—	—	—	—

KM# 215 2 DUCATONE (Doppio Ducatone)
64.0100 g., Silver, 48 mm. **Ruler:** Carlo Emanuele II under regency **Obv:** Accolated busts of Carlo Emanuele II and his mother to right, date in exergue **Obv. Legend:** CHR. FRAN. CAR. EMAN. DVCES. SABAV. **Rev:** Crowned shield of manifold arms, with central shield of Savoy, in baroque frame **Rev. Legend:** PRINCIPES - PEDEMON - REGES - CYPRI. **Note:** Ref. Cud. 748; Dav. 4166.

Date	Mintage	VG	F	VF	XF	Unc
1642 Rare	—	—	—	—	—	—

TRADE COINAGE

KM# 41 1/2 SCUDO D'ORO
1.8000 g., Gold, 18 mm. **Ruler:** Carlo Emanuele I **Obv:** Small shield of Savoy arms with winged crest above **Obv. Legend:** C. EM. DVX. - SAB. **Rev:** Cross with trefoil ends in circle, date at end of legend **Rev. Legend:** TIBI. SOLI. ADERERE. **Note:** Ref. Cud. 593. Previous KM#8.

Date	Mintage	VG	F	VF	XF	Unc
1610 Rare	—	—	—	—	—	—

KM# 93 1/2 SCUDO D'ORO
1.7600 g., Gold, 17 mm. **Ruler:** Carlo Emanuele I **Obv:** Armored bust to right, mintmark below **Obv. Legend:** CAR. EM. D.G. DVX. SAB. P. P. **Rev:** Cross of St. Maurice in inner circle, date at end of legend **Rev. Legend:** +MIHI. ABSIT. GLORIARI. **Note:** Cud. 594; Fr. 1051.

Date	Mintage	VG	F	VF	XF	Unc
1627 T Rare	—	—	—	—	—	—

KM# 165 1/2 SCUDO D'ORO
1.6900 g., Gold, 19 mm. **Ruler:** Carlo Emanuele II under regency **Obv:** Four interlocking C's, small crown above each **Obv. Legend:** CHR - FRA - CAR - EMA. **Rev:** Accolated busts of Carlo Emanuele II and his mother to right **Rev. Legend:** DVCES. SAB. PP. PEDE. RR. CYPRY. **Note:** Cud. 747; Fr. 1076.

Date	Mintage	VG	F	VF	XF	Unc
ND(1638-48) P	—	2,500	4,500	8,000	14,000	—

KM# 237 1/2 SCUDO D'ORO
1.6500 g., Gold, 18 mm. **Ruler:** Carlo Emanuele II alone **Obv:** Youthful bust to right, 6 pellets in a row below **Obv. Legend:** CAROLVS. EMANVEL. **Rev:** Crowned shield of Savoy arms, date at end of legend **Rev. Legend:** II. D.G. DVX. SAB. **Note:** Cud. 808; Fr. 1085.

Date	Mintage	VG	F	VF	XF	Unc
1649 Rare	—	—	—	—	—	—

KM# 94 SCUDO D'ORO
3.2800 g., Gold, 19 mm. **Ruler:** Carlo Emanuele I **Obv:** Small high-collared bust to right **Obv. Legend:** CAR. EM. D.G. DVX. SAB. P. P. **Rev:** Cross with trefoil ends in circle, date at end of legend **Rev. Legend:** +MIHI. ABSIT. GLORIARI. **Note:** Cud. 592; Fr. 1050.

Date	Mintage	VG	F	VF	XF	Unc
1627 Rare	—	—	—	—	—	—

KM# 115 SCUDO D'ORO
3.1900 g., 0.9860 Gold 0.1011 oz. AGW, 22 mm. **Ruler:** Carlo Emanuele I **Subject:** Death of Carlo Emanuele I **Obv:** Large high-collared armored bust to right **Obv. Legend:** CAR. EM. D.G. DVX. SAB. P. P. ETC. **Rev:** 5-line inscription in circle, Roman numeral date and age in legend **Rev. Legend:** AN. SAL. M. DC. XXX. ÆT. LXIX. **Rev. Inscription:** BENE- / DICES / CORONÆ / ANNI / +. **Note:** Cud. 591; Fr. 1052A.

Date	Mintage	VG	F	VF	XF	Unc
MDCXXX (1630) Rare	—	—	—	—	—	—

KM# 166 SCUDO D'ORO
Gold Weight varies: 3.15-3.28g., 24 mm. **Ruler:** Carlo Emanuele II under regency **Obv:** Crowned shield of manifold arms with central shield of Savoy **Obv. Legend:** CHR. FRAN. CAR. EM. DVCES. SAB. **Rev:** Four interlocking letter C's, small letter F - E - R - T in each 'C,' small crown above **Rev. Legend:** PRIN - PEDEM - REGES - CYPRI. **Note:** Cud 746; Fr. 1075.

Date	Mintage	VG	F	VF	XF	Unc
ND(1638-48)	—	3,000	5,000	7,500	12,000	—

KM# 238 SCUDO D'ORO
3.3300 g., 0.9860 Gold 0.1056 oz. AGW, 19 mm. **Ruler:** Carlo Emanuele II alone **Obv:** Youthful bust to right **Obv. Legend:** CAR. EM. II. D.G. DVX. SA. **Rev:** Cross with trefoil ends **Rev. Legend:** +PRIN. PEDEMON. REX. CYP. **Note:** Cud. 806; Fr. 1088.

Date	Mintage	VG	F	VF	XF	Unc
ND(ca1649) Rare	—	—	—	—	—	—

KM# 283 SCUDO D'ORO
3.2700 g., 0.9860 Gold 0.1037 oz. AGW, 21 mm. **Ruler:** Carlo Emanuele II alone **Obv:** Bust to right, date below **Obv. Legend:** CAR. EM. II. - D.G. DVX. SAB. **Rev:** Four double-C monograms in cruciform, crown between each pair, rosette in center **Rev. Legend:** PRIN. - PEDE. - REX. - CYP. **Note:** Cud. 807; Fr. 1086.

Date	Mintage	VG	F	VF	XF	Unc
1670 Rare	—	—	—	—	—	—

KM# 7 DUCATO
Gold Weight varies: 3.10-3.48g., 23 mm. **Ruler:** Carlo Emanuele I **Obv:** Crowned shield of 4-fold arms with central shield of Savoy, Order Collar of the Annunziata around, date divided in margin at bottom **Obv. Legend:** C. EMANVEL. D.G. DVX. SAB. **Rev:** Seated Madonna and Child **Rev. Legend:** PAX. IN. VI - RT. TVA. **Note:** Cud. 587; Fr. 1056. Varieties exist.

Date	Mintage	VG	F	VF	XF	Unc
1601	—	250	475	900	1,650	—
1602	—	250	475	900	1,650	—
1603	—	250	475	900	1,650	—

KM# 293 1/2 DOPPIA

Gold Weight varies: 3.27-3.32g., 22 mm. **Ruler:** Vittorio Amedeo II under regency **Obv:** Accolated busts of Vittorio Amedeo II and his mother to right **Obv. Legend:** MAR. IO. BAP. VIC. AM. II. D.G. DVC. SAB. **Rev:** Crowned shield of manifold arms with central shield of Savoy, Order collar of the Annunziata around, date at end of legend **Rev. Legend:** PRINCI. PEDEM - REGES. CYP. **Note:** Cud. 836; Fr. 1091.

Date	Mintage	VG	F	VF	XF	Unc
1675 Rare	—	—	—	—	—	—
1676	—	625	1,250	2,300	4,250	—
1677	—	625	1,250	2,300	4,250	—
1678 Rare	—	—	—	—	—	—
1679 Rare	—	—	—	—	—	—

KM# 302 1/2 DOPPIA

Gold Weight varies: 3.21-3.32g., 22 mm. **Ruler:** Vittorio Amedeo II alone **Obv:** Youthful draped bust to right **Obv. Legend:** VICTOR. AM. II. - D.G. DVX. SAB. **Rev:** Crowned shield of manifold arms with central shield of Savoy, Order collar of the Annunziata around, date at end of legend **Rev. Legend:** PRINCI. PEDEM. - REGES. CYP. **Note:** Cud. 849; Fr. 1098.

Date	Mintage	VG	F	VF	XF	Unc
1679	—	650	1,350	2,500	4,750	—

KM# 310 1/2 DOPPIA

3.2900 g., 0.9860 Gold 0.1043 oz. AGW, 22 mm. **Ruler:** Vittorio Amedeo II alone **Obv:** Youthful draped bust to right **Obv. Legend:** VICTOR. AM. II. - D.G. DVX. SAB. **Rev:** Crowned shield of manifold arms with central shield of Savoy, chain of order around, date at end of legend **Rev. Legend:** PRINC. PEDEM. - REX. CYP. **Note:** Cud. 850; Fr. A1098.

Date	Mintage	VG	F	VF	XF	Unc
1680 Rare	—	—	—	—	—	—
1681 Rare	—	—	—	—	—	—

KM# 339 1/2 DOPPIA

3.2900 g., 0.9860 Gold 0.1043 oz. AGW, 22 mm. **Ruler:** Vittorio Amedeo II alone **Obv:** Draped and armored bust to right **Obv. Legend:** VICTOR. AM. - II. D.G. D. SAB. **Rev:** Crowned shield of manifold arms with central shield of Savoy, Order collar of the Annunziata around, date at end of legend **Rev. Legend:** PRINC. PEDE - REX. CYP. **Note:** Cud. 851; Fr. 1100.

Date	Mintage	Good	VG	F	VF	XF
1692 Rare	—	—	—	—	—	—

MB# 335.2 DOPPIA

Gold Weight varies: 6.41-6.65g., 29 mm. **Ruler:** Carlo Emanuele I **Obv:** Large high-collared armored bust to right **Obv. Legend:** CAR. EM. D.G. DVX. SAB. P. PED. **Rev:** Crowned shield of 4-fold arms with central shield of Savoy in baroque frame, date and mintmark at end of legend **Rev. Legend:** IN. TE. DOMINE. CONFIDO. **Note:** Cud. 580b, 581a,c,d; Fr. 1049. Varieties exist.

Date	Mintage	VG	F	VF	XF	Unc
1601	—	1,600	2,750	5,500	8,500	—

KM# 8 DOPPIA

Gold Weight varies: 6.67-6.70g., 28 mm. **Ruler:** Carlo Emanuele I **Obv:** Armored bust to right **Obv. Legend:** CAR. EM. D.G. DVX. SAB. P. PED. **Rev:** Crowned shield of 4-fold arms with central shield of Savoy, collar of order around, date at end of legend **Rev. Legend:** IN. TE. DOMINE - CONFIDO. **Note:** Cud. 583a,b; Fr. 1049.1.

Date	Mintage	VG	F	VF	XF	Unc
1601	—	950	1,900	4,200	7,200	—
1604	—	950	1,900	4,200	7,200	—

KM# 17.1 DOPPIA

Gold Weight varies: 6.56-6.70g., 28 mm. **Ruler:** Carlo Emanuele I **Obv:** High-collared armored bust to right **Obv. Legend:** CAR. EM. D.G. DVX. SAB. P. P. **Rev:** Crowned shield of 4-fold arms with central shield of Savoy in baroque frame, date at end of legend **Rev. Legend:** AVXILIVM. MEVM. ADOMINO. **Note:** Cud. 584a.

Date	Mintage	VG	F	VF	XF	Unc
1605	—	8,500	12,000	19,000	27,500	—

KM# 17.2 DOPPIA

Gold Weight varies: 6.56-6.70g., 28 mm. **Ruler:** Carlo Emanuele I **Obv:** High-collared armored bust to right, date in exergue **Obv. Legend:** CAR. EM. - D.G. DVX. S. **Rev:** Crowned shield of 4-fold arms with central shield of Savoy in baroque frame **Rev. Legend:** AVXILIVM. MEVM. ADOMINO. **Note:** Cud. 584d; Fr. 1049.3.

Date	Mintage	VG	F	VF	XF	Unc
ND(ca1605) T	—	8,500	12,000	19,000	27,500	—

KM# 17.3 DOPPIA

Gold Weight varies: 6.56-6.70g., 28 mm. **Ruler:** Carlo Emanuele I **Obv:** High-collared armored bust to right, 5-pointed star below **Obv. Legend:** CAR. EM. D.G. DVX. SAB. P. P. **Rev:** Crowned shield of 4-fold arms with central shield of Savoy in baroque frame, date at end of legend **Rev. Legend:** AVXILIVM. MEVM. ADOMINO. **Note:** Cud. 584c.

Date	Mintage	VG	F	VF	XF	Unc
ND(ca1605)	—	8,500	12,000	19,000	27,500	—

KM# 43 DOPPIA

6.5500 g., 0.9860 Gold 0.2076 oz. AGW, 28 mm. **Ruler:** Carlo Emanuele I **Obv:** High-collared armored bust to right, 5-pointed star below **Obv. Legend:** CAR. EM. D.G. DVX. SAB. P. P. **Rev:** Crowned shield of Savoy arms superimposed on cross with trefoil ends, date at end of legend **Rev. Legend:** IN. HOC. EGO. SPERABO. **Note:** Cud. 585a,b; Fr. 1049.2.

Date	Mintage	VG	F	VF	XF	Unc
1610	—	950	1,900	4,200	7,200	—
1611	—	950	1,900	4,200	7,200	—

KM# 63 DOPPIA

4.5800 g., Gold, 24 mm. **Ruler:** Carlo Emanuele I **Obv:** Horse prancing to right, looking back to left, date in exergue **Obv. Legend:** CAR. EM. D.G. DVX. SAB. P. P. **Rev:** Crowned shield of Savoy arms, rosette at left and right **Rev. Legend:** CAR. EM. D.G. DVX. SAB. P. P. **Note:** Cud. 586.

Date	Mintage	VG	F	VF	XF	Unc
1619 Rare	—	—	—	—	—	—

KM# 116 DOPPIA

Gold Weight varies: 6.47-6.58g., 28 mm. **Ruler:** Vittorio Amedeo I **Obv:** Mantled bust to right **Obv. Legend:** V. AMEDEVS. D.G. DVX. SABAVDIÆ. **Rev:** Crowned shield of 4-fold arms with central shield of Savoy in baroque frame **Rev. Legend:** PRIN. PEDEMON. REX. CYPRI. ET. C. **Note:** Cud. 705; Fr. 1064.

Date	Mintage	VG	F	VF	XF	Unc
ND(1630-37) Rare	—	—	—	—	—	—

KM# 178 DOPPIA

Gold Weight varies: 6.62-6.65g., 29 mm. **Ruler:** Carlo Emanuele II under regency **Obv:** Accolated busts of Carlo Emanuele II and his mother to left, date below in margin **Obv. Legend:** CAROLV. EMANV. - CHRIS. FRAN. **Rev:** Crowned shield of manifold arms, with central shield of Savoy, in baroque frame **Rev. Legend:** DVCES. SAB. PP. PED. RR. CYPRY. **Note:** Cud. 744; Fr. 1072.1.

Date	Mintage	VG	F	VF	XF	Unc
1640	—	1,800	3,300	6,000	11,000	—

KM# 192 DOPPIA

Gold Weight varies: 6.55-6.70g., 30 mm. **Ruler:** Carlo Emanuele II under regency **Obv:** Accolated busts of Carlo Emanuele II and his mother to right, legend begins with double-C monogram **Obv. Legend:** CHR. FRAN. CAR. EMAN. DVCES. SABAV. **Rev:** Crowned shield of manifold arms, with central shield of Savoy, in baroque frame, date at end of legend **Rev. Legend:** P. P. PEDEMON. REGES. CYPRI. **Note:** Cud. 745; Fr. 1072.2.

Date	Mintage	VG	F	VF	XF	Unc
1641 Rare	—	—	—	—	—	—

KM# 247 DOPPIA

Gold Weight varies: 6.57-6.65g., 28 mm. **Ruler:** Carlo Emanuele II alone **Obv:** Armored youthful bust to right, date below **Obv. Legend:** CAR. EMAN. II. D.G. DVX. SABAVDIE. **Rev:** Crowned shield of manifold arms with central shield of Savoy, in baroque frame, Order collar of the Annunziata around **Rev. Legend:** PRIN. PEDEM - REX. CYPRI. ETC. **Note:** Cud. 802; Fr. 1084.1.

Date	Mintage	VG	F	VF	XF	Unc
1650 Rare	—	—	—	—	—	—

KM# 252 DOPPIA

Gold Weight varies: 6.53-6.67g., 25 mm. **Ruler:** Carlo Emanuele II alone **Obv:** Draped bust to right **Obv. Legend:** CAROL. EM. II. D.G. DVX. SAB. **Rev:** Crowned shield of manifold arms with central shield of Savoy, date at end of legend **Rev. Legend:** PRIN. PEDE. REX. CYP. **Note:** Cud. 803; Fr. 1084.2.

Date	Mintage	VG	F	VF	XF	Unc
1653 Rare	—	—	—	—	—	—
1654	—	2,250	5,750	6,500	12,000	—
1655 Rare	—	—	—	—	—	—

KM# 284 DOPPIA

6.3500 g., 0.9860 Gold 0.2013 oz. AGW, 24 mm. **Ruler:** Carlo Emanuele II alone **Obv:** Bust to right, date below **Obv. Legend:** CAR. EM. II. - D.G. DVX. SAB. **Rev:** Four double-C monograms in cruciform, crown between each pair, rosette in center **Rev. Legend:** PRIN. - PEDE. - REX. - CYP. **Note:** Cud. 804; Fr. 1085a.

Date	Mintage	VG	F	VF	XF	Unc
1670 Rare	—	—	—	—	—	—

KM# 295 DOPPIA

Gold Weight varies: 6.64-6.66g., 27 mm. **Ruler:** Carlo Emanuele II alone **Obv:** Bust to right, date below **Obv. Legend:** CAR. EM. II. - D.G. DVX. SAB. **Rev:** Crowned shield of manifold arms with central shield of Savoy, Order collar of the Annunziata around **Rev. Legend:** PRIN. PEDE - REX. CYPRI. **Note:** Cud. 805; Fr. 1087.

Date	Mintage	VG	F	VF	XF	Unc
1675	—	1,800	3,500	6,000	9,500	—

KM# 296 DOPPIA

Gold Weight varies: 6.60-6.66g., 25 mm. **Ruler:** Vittorio Amedeo II under regency **Obv:** Accolated busts of Vittorio Amedeo II and his mother to right **Obv. Legend:** MAR. IO. BAP. VIC. AM. II. D.G. DVC. SAB. **Rev:** Crowned shield of manifold arms with central shield of Savoy, chain of order around, date at end of legend **Rev. Legend:** PRINCI. PEDEM - REGES. CYP. **Note:** Cud. 835; Fr. 1090.

Date	Mintage	VG	F	VF	XF	Unc
1675 Rare	—	—	—	—	—	—
1676	—	800	1,200	2,500	5,500	—
1677 Rare	—	—	—	—	—	—
1678	—	800	1,200	2,500	5,500	—
1679	10,000	800	1,200	2,500	5,500	—
1680 Rare	—	—	—	—	—	—

KM# 311 DOPPIA

Gold Weight varies: 6.59-6.62g., 27 mm. **Ruler:** Vittorio Amedeo II alone **Obv:** Bust to right, date below **Obv. Legend:** VIC. AM. II. - D.G. DVX. SAB. **Rev:** Crowned shield of manifold arms with central shield of Savoy, chain of order around **Rev. Legend:** PRIN. PEDE - REX. CYPRI. **Note:** Cud. 846; Fr. 1097.

Date	Mintage	VG	F	VF	XF	Unc
1680	—	3,200	5,000	7,800	13,000	—
1681	—	3,500	5,500	9,500	15,000	—
1682	—	3,000	4,800	7,500	12,500	—

KM# 329 DOPPIA

Gold Weight varies: 6.55-6.60g., 27 mm. **Ruler:** Vittorio Amedeo II alone **Obv:** Bust to right, date below **Obv. Legend:** VICTOR. AM. II. - D.G. DVX. SAB. **Rev:** Crowned shield of manifold arms with central shield of Savoy, chain of order around **Rev. Legend:** PRIN. PEDE - REX. CYPRI. **Note:** Cud. 847; Fr. A1099.

Date	Mintage	VG	F	VF	XF	Unc
1690 Rare	—	—	—	—	—	—
1691 Rare	800	—	—	—	—	—

KM# 10.3 QUADRUPLA

Gold Weight varies: 12.02-13.30g., 30 mm. **Ruler:** Carlo Emanuele I **Obv:** High-collared armored bust to right **Obv. Legend:** CAR. EM. D.G. DVX. SAB. P. P. **Rev:** Crowned shield of 4-fold arms with central shield of Savoy in baroque frame, mintmark below **Rev. Legend:** AVXILIVM. MEVM. ADOMINO. **Note:** Cud. 575e; Fr. 1049. Previous KM#77.

Date	Mintage	VG	F	VF	XF	Unc
ND(ca1600-10) (star)	—	10,000	14,500	21,500	—	—

KM# 10.1 QUADRUPLA

Gold Weight varies: 12.02-13.30g., 30 mm. **Ruler:** Carlo Emanuele I **Obv:** Small high-collared armored bust to right **Obv. Legend:** CAR. EM. D.G. DVX. SAB. P. P. **Rev:** Crowned shield of 4-fold arms with central shield of Savoy in baroque frame, date at end of legend **Rev. Legend:** AVXILIVM. MEVM. ADOMINO. **Note:** Cud. 575a,b; Fr. 1048. Previous KM#75.

Date	Mintage	VG	F	VF	XF	Unc
1601 Rare	—	10,000	14,500	21,500	—	—
1605 Rare	—	10,000	14,500	21,500	—	—

KM# 18 QUADRUPLA

Gold Weight varies: 12.02-13.30g., 30 mm. **Ruler:** Carlo Emanuele I **Obv:** Small high-collared armored bust to right, mintmark below **Obv. Legend:** CAR. EM. D.G. DVX. SAB. P. P. **Rev:** Crowned shield of 4-fold arms with central shield of Savoy in baroque frame **Rev. Legend:** AVXILIVM. MEVM. ADOMINO. **Note:** Cud. 576; Fr. 1048.

Date	Mintage	VG	F	VF	XF	Unc
ND(ca1605) T	—	10,000	14,500	21,500	—	—
ND(ca1605)	—	10,000	14,500	21,500	—	—

KM# 10.2 QUADRUPLA

Gold Weight varies: 12.02-13.30g., 30 mm. **Ruler:** Carlo Emanuele I **Obv:** Small high-collared armored bust to right, date below **Obv. Legend:** CAR. EM. D.G. DVX. SAB. P. P. **Rev:** Crowned shield of 4-fold arms with central shield of Savoy in baroque frame, date at end of legend **Rev. Legend:** AVXILIVM. MEVM. ADOMINO. **Note:** Cud. 575c,d; Fr. 1048. Previous KM#75.

Date	Mintage	VG	F	VF	XF	Unc
1607//1605	—	10,000	14,500	21,500	—	—
1610//1605	—	10,000	14,500	21,500	—	—

Note: The 1610 date is inverted.

KM# 44 QUADRUPLA

13.3500 g., Gold, 36 mm. **Ruler:** Carlo Emanuele I **Obv:** Large high-collared armored bust to right **Obv. Legend:** CAR. EM. D.G. DVX. SAB. P. PED. **Rev:** Crowned ornate shield of 4-fold arms with central shield of Savoy, chain of order around **Rev. Legend:** AVXILIVM. MEVM. ADOMINO. **Note:** Cud. 577.

Date	Mintage	VG	F	VF	XF	Unc
ND(1610-30) Rare	—	—	—	—	—	—

KM# 297 QUADRUPLA

Gold Weight varies: 13.25-13.30g., 31 mm. **Ruler:** Vittorio Amedeo II under regency **Obv:** Accolated busts of Vittorio Amedeo II and his mother to right **Obv. Legend:** MAR. IO. BAP. VIC. AM. II. D.G. DVX. SAB. PRIN. PEDE. REG. CYP. **Rev:** Seated Madonna facing, Child standing at right holding orb, date in exergue **Rev. Legend:** PVPILLVM. ET. VIDVAM. SVSPICIET. **Note:** Cud. 834; Fr. 1092.

Date	Mintage	VG	F	VF	XF	Unc
1675 Rare	—	—	—	—	—	—
1676 Rare	—	—	—	—	—	—
1677	—	3,500	6,000	10,000	22,000	—

KM# 312 QUADRUPLA

13.2900 g., 0.9860 Gold 0.4213 oz. AGW, 29 mm. **Ruler:** Vittorio Amedeo II alone **Obv:** Armored bust to right **Obv. Legend:** VIC. AM. II. D. - G. DVX. SAB. **Rev:** Crowned shield of manifold arms, with central shield of Savoy, divides date, Order collar of the Annunziata around **Rev. Legend:** PRIN. PEDE - REX. CYPRI. **Note:** Cud. 845; Fr. 1096.

Date	Mintage	VG	F	VF	XF	Unc
1680 Rare	—	—	—	—	—	—

KM# 336.2 QUADRUPLA

Gold Weight varies: 12.74-12.85g., 33 mm. **Ruler:** Carlo Emanuele I **Obv:** High-collared bust to right **Obv. Legend:** CAR. EM. D.G. DVX. SABAVDIE. P. P. **Rev:** Crowned shield of 4-fold arms with central shield of Savoy, date and mintmark at end of legend **Rev. Legend:** IN. TE. DOMINE. CONFIDO. **Note:** Cud. 573; Fr. 1047.

Date	Mintage	VG	F	VF	XF	Unc
1686 Rare	—	—	—	—	—	—

KM# 141 4 SCUDI D'ORO

13.2100 g., 0.9860 Gold 0.4187 oz. AGW, 38 mm. **Ruler:** Vittorio Amedeo I **Obv:** Mantled bust to right, date below left **Obv. Legend:** V. AMEDEVS. D.G. DVX. SAB. P. PED. **Rev:** Three flags on staffs protruding through large crown, value "SCVDI. 4" in exergue **Rev. Legend:** NEC - NVMINA - DESVNT. **Note:** Cud. 701; Fr. 1058.

Date	Mintage	VG	F	VF	XF	Unc
1633 Rare	—	—	—	—	—	—

KM# 142 4 SCUDI D'ORO

13.3500 g., 0.9860 Gold 0.4232 oz. AGW, 38 mm. **Ruler:** Vittorio Amedeo I **Obv:** Mantled bust to right, date below **Obv. Legend:** V. AMEDEVS. D.G. DVX. SABAVDIÆ. **Rev:** Three flags on staffs protruding through large crown, value "SCVDI. 4" in exergue **Rev. Legend:** NEC - NVMINA - DESVNT. **Note:** Cud. 702; Fr. 1058A.

Date	Mintage	VG	F	VF	XF	Unc
1633 Rare	—	—	—	—	—	—
1634 Rare	—	—	—	—	—	—

KM# 151 4 SCUDI D'ORO

Gold Weight varies: 13.21-13.30g., 38 mm. **Ruler:** Vittorio Amedeo I **Obv:** Mantled bust to right, date below **Obv. Legend:** V. AMEDEVS. D.G. DVX. SABAVDIÆ. **Rev:** Crowned shield of 4-fold arms with central shield of Savoy, Order collar of the Annunziata around **Rev. Legend:** PRIN. PEDEM - REX. CYPRI. ET. C. **Note:** Cud. 703; Fr. 1063.

Date	Mintage	VG	F	VF	XF	Unc
1634 Rare	—	—	—	—	—	—
ND(ca1635) Rare	—	—	—	—	—	—

KM# 152 4 SCUDI D'ORO

Gold Weight varies: 13.21-13.30g., 38 mm. **Ruler:** Vittorio Amedeo I **Obv:** Mantled bust to right, date below **Obv. Legend:** V. AMEDEVS. D.G. DVX. SAB. P. PED. **Rev:** Crowned shield of 4-fold arms with central shield of Savoy, chain of order around **Rev. Legend:** PRIN. PEDEM - REX. CYPRI. ET. C. **Note:** Cud. 704; Fr. 1063.

Date	Mintage	VG	F	VF	XF	Unc
1634 Rare	—	—	—	—	—	—

KM# 162 4 SCUDI D'ORO

Gold Weight varlies: 12.33-13.32g., 37 mm. **Ruler:** Francesco Giacinto **Obv:** Accolated busts of Francesco Giacinto and his mother to right right **Obv. Legend:** +CHR. FR. FR. HYAC. DVCES. SABAV. P. P. PED. R. R. CYPRI. **Rev:** Seated Madonna with Child in laurel wreath **Rev. Legend:** DEDVCET. NOS. MIRABILITER. DEXTERA. TVA. **Note:** Cud. 725; Fr. 1067.

Date	Mintage	VG	F	VF	XF	Unc
ND(1637-8)	—	5,000	8,000	14,500	24,000	—

KM# 163 4 SCUDI D'ORO

Gold Weight varies: 11.55-11.60g., 37 mm. **Ruler:** Francesco Giacinto **Obv:** Large accolated busts of Francesco Giacinto and his mother to right **Obv. Legend:** +CHR. FR. FR. HYAC. DVCES. SABAV. P. P. PED. R. R. CYPRI. **Rev:** Large seated Madonna with Child in laurel wreath **Rev. Legend:** DEDVCET. NOS. MIRABILITER. DEXTERA. TVA. **Note:** Cud. 726; Fr. 1067.

Date	Mintage	VG	F	VF	XF	Unc
ND(1637-8) Rare	—	—	—	—	—	—

KM# 172.1 4 SCUDI D'ORO

Gold Weight varies: 13.22-13.35g., 34 mm. **Ruler:** Carlo Emanuele II under regency **Obv:** Accolated busts of Carlo Emanuele II and his mother to right, date below in cartouche **Obv. Legend:** CHR. FRAN. CAR. EMAN. DVCES. SAB. **Rev:** Crowned shield of manifold arms, with central shield of Savoy, in baroque frame **Rev. Legend:** P. P. PEDEMON. REGES. CYPRI. **Note:** Cud. 738a-c; Fr. 1071.1.

Date	Mintage	VG	F	VF	XF	Unc
1639	—	1,650	2,400	4,100	7,200	—
1640	—	1,400	2,150	3,600	6,000	—
1641	—	1,400	2,150	3,600	6,000	—
1644 I (sic)	—	700	1,500	3,000	5,000	—

KM# 193 4 SCUDI D'ORO

Gold Weight varies: 12.89-13.25g., 34 mm. **Ruler:** Carlo Emanuele II under regency **Obv:** Accolated busts of Carlo Emanuele II and his mother to right, date below in cartouche **Obv. Legend:** CHR. FRAN. CAR. EMAN. DVCES. SAB. **Rev:** Large crowned shield of manifold arms, with central shield of Savoy, in baroque frame **Rev. Legend:** P. P. PEDEMON. REGES. CYPRI. **Note:** Cud. 739a-d; Fr. 1071.1.

Date	Mintage	VG	F	VF	XF	Unc
1641	—	1,800	2,650	4,200	7,500	—
1643	—	1,800	2,650	4,200	7,500	—
1644	—	1,800	2,650	4,200	7,500	—
1648	—	1,800	2,650	4,200	7,500	—

KM# 194 4 SCUDI D'ORO

Gold Weight varies: 12.89-13.25g., 34 mm. **Ruler:** Carlo Emanuele II under regency **Obv:** Accolated busts of Carlo Emanuele II and his mother to right, date below in cartouche **Obv. Legend:** CHR. FRAN. CAR. EMAN. DVCES. SAB. **Rev:** Crowned shield of manifold arms with central shield of Savoy in baroque frame, date at end of legend **Rev. Legend:** PRINCEPS. PEDEM. REGES. CYPRI. **Note:** Cud. 740; Fr. 1071.2.

Date	Mintage	VG	F	VF	XF	Unc
1641//1642	—	1,750	3,000	6,000	10,000	—
1643//1642	—	1,750	3,000	6,000	10,000	—

KM# 195 4 SCUDI D'ORO

13.1800 g., Gold, 34 mm. **Ruler:** Carlo Emanuele II under regency **Obv:** Accolated busts of Carlo Emanuele II and his mother to right, date below in cartouche **Obv. Legend:** CHR. FRAN. CAR. EMAN. DVCES. SAB. **Rev:** Crowned shield of manifold arms with central shield of Savoy in baroque frame, date in exergue **Rev. Legend:** P. P. PEDEMON. REGES. CYPRI. **Note:** Cud. 741; Fr. 1071.3.

Date	Mintage	VG	F	VF	XF	Unc
1641//1641 Rare	—	—	—	—	—	—
1641//1642 Rare	—	—	—	—	—	—
1642//1641 Rare	—	—	—	—	—	—

KM# 196 4 SCUDI D'ORO

Gold Weight varies: 13.10-13.30g., 30 mm. **Ruler:** Carlo Emanuele II under regency **Obv:** Accolated busts of Carlo Emanuele II and his mother to right, date and mintmark at end of legend **Obv. Legend:** +CARO. EMANVEL. CHRIS. FRAN. **Rev:** Large crown over small shield of manifold arms, with central shield of Savoy, in baroque frame **Rev. Legend:** DVCES. SAB. PP. PEDE. RR. CYPRY. **Note:** Cud. 742; Fr. 1071.4.

Date	Mintage	VG	F	VF	XF	Unc
1641 P	—	9,000	13,000	19,000	26,000	—
1642 P	—	9,000	13,000	19,000	26,000	—
1643 P Rare	—	—	—	—	—	—

KM# 217 4 SCUDI D'ORO

13.2000 g., 0.9860 Gold 0.4184 oz. AGW, 30 mm. **Ruler:** Carlo Emanuele II under regency **Obv:** Accolated busts of Carlo Emanuele II and his mother to right, date in exergue **Obv. Legend:** CHR. FRAN. CAR. EMAN. DVCES. SA. **Rev:** Crowned oval shield of manifold arms, with central shield of Savoy, in baroque frame, value 'S. X' in exergue **Rev. Legend:** P. P. PEDEMON + REGES. CYPRI. **Note:** Cud. 743; Fr. 1073. Struck from dies of an intended 1/2 Lira which apparently was not issued.

Date	Mintage	VG	F	VF	XF	Unc
1642 Rare	—	—	—	—	—	—

KM# 172.2 4 SCUDI D'ORO

Gold Weight varies: 13.22-13.35g., 34 mm. **Ruler:** Carlo Emanuele II under regency **Obv:** Accolated busts of Carlo Emanuele II and his mother to right **Obv. Legend:** CHR. FRAN. CAR. EMAN. DVCES. SAB. **Rev:** Crowned shield of manifold arms, with central shield of Savoy, in baroque frame, date at end of legend **Rev. Legend:** PRINCPS. PEDEM. REGES. CYPRI. **Note:** Cud. 738d; Fr. 1071.1.

Date	Mintage	VG	F	VF	XF	Unc
1642 Rare	—	—	—	—	—	—

KM# 240 4 SCUDI D'ORO

Gold Weight varies: 13.21-16.25g., 31 mm. **Ruler:** Carlo Emanuele II alone **Obv:** Youthful armored bust to right, date below shoulder **Obv. Legend:** CAR + EMAN + II + D + G + DVX + SABAVDI(E)(Æ). **Rev:** Crowned shield of manifold arms with central shield of Savoy, Order collar of the Annunziata around **Rev. Legend:** PRIN + PEDEM + - REX + CYPTRI + EC. **Note:** Cud. 800; Fr. 1083.

Date	Mintage	VG	F	VF	XF	Unc
1649 Rare	—	—	—	—	—	—
1650 Rare	—	—	—	—	—	—
1652 Rare	—	—	—	—	—	—

KM# 254 4 SCUDI D'ORO

13.2500 g., 0.9860 Gold 0.4200 oz. AGW, 30 mm. **Ruler:** Carlo Emanuele II alone **Obv:** Draped bust to right **Obv. Legend:** CAROL. EM. II. D.G. DVX. SAB. **Rev:** Crowned shield of manifold arms with central shield of Savoy, chain of order around, date at end of legend **Rev. Legend:** PRIN. PEDE - REX. CYP. **Note:** Cud. 801; Fr. A1083.

Date	Mintage	VG	F	VF	XF	Unc
1654 Rare	—	—	—	—	—	—

KM# 1070 8 SCUDI D'ORO

Gold Weight varies: 25.70-26.60g., 38 mm. **Ruler:** Carlo Emanuele II under regency **Obv:** Accolated busts of Carlo Emanuele II and his mother to right, date at lower left below shoulder, legend begins with double-C monogram **Obv. Legend:** CHR. FR. CAR. EM. DVCES. DAB. P. P. PEDEM. R. R. CYPRI. **Rev:** Madonna and Child in laurel wreath **Rev. Legend:** IVSTVM - DEDVXIT - PER - VIAS - RECTAS. **Note:** Cud. 736a; Fr. 1070.

Date	Mintage	VG	F	VF	XF	Unc
1641	—	8,000	11,000	18,000	31,000	—

KM# 200 8 SCUDI D'ORO

Gold Weight varies: 25.70-26.60g., 38 mm. **Ruler:** Carlo Emanuele II under regency **Obv:** Accolated busts of Carlo Emanuele II and his mother to right, date at lower left below shoulder, legend begins with double-C monogram **Obv. Legend:** CHR. FR. CAR. EM. DVCES. SABAV. P. P. PE. REGES. CYPRI. **Rev:** Madonna and Child in laurel wreath **Rev. Legend:** IVSTVM - DEDVXIT - PER - VIAS - RECTAS. **Note:** Cud. 737; Fr. 1070.

Date	Mintage	VG	F	VF	XF	Unc
1641	—	10,000	15,000	24,000	40,000	—

KM# 199 8 SCUDI D'ORO
Gold Weight varies: 25.70-26.60g., 38 mm. **Ruler:** Carlo Emanuele II under regency **Obv:** Accolated busts of Carlo Emanuele II and his mother to right, legend begins with double-C monogram **Obv. Legend:** CHR. FR. CAR. EMAN. DVCES. SAB. P. P. PE. R. R. CYP. **Rev:** Madonna and Child in laurel wreath **Rev. Legend:** IVSTVM - DEDVXIT - PER - VIAS - RECTAS. **Note:** Cud. 736b; Fr. 1070.

Date	Mintage	VG	F	VF	XF	Unc
ND(ca1641)	—	8,000	11,000	18,000	31,000	—

KM# 27 10 SCUDI D'ORO
33.1700 g., 0.9860 Gold 1.0515 oz. AGW, 45 mm. **Ruler:** Carlo Emanuele I **Obv:** High-collared armored bust to right, mintmark and date below **Obv. Legend:** CAROLVS. EM. D.G. DVX. SABAVDIÆ. **Rev:** Crowned shield of 4-fold arms with central shield of Savoy, Order collar of the Annunziata around **Rev. Legend:** DVENTRE. MATRIS. DEVS. PROTECTOR. MEVS. **Note:** Cud. 567; Fr. 1046.

Date	Mintage	VG	F	VF	XF	Unc
1607 T Rare	—	—	—	—	—	—

KM# 46 10 SCUDI D'ORO
Gold Weight varies: 33.20-33.37g., 45 mm. **Ruler:** Carlo Emanuele I **Obv:** Large high-collared armored bust to left, wide date below **Obv. Legend:** CAROLVS. EM. D. G. DVX. SABAVDIÆ. **Rev:** Crowned shield of 4-fold arms, with central shield of Savoy, in baroque frame, divide FE - RT **Rev. Legend:** DEVENTRE. MATRIS. DEVS. PROTECTOR. MEVS. **Note:** Cud. 568; Fr. A1046. Struck from Ducatone dies, KM#34.

Date	Mintage	VG	F	VF	XF	Unc
1610 Rare	—	—	—	—	—	—

KM# 58 10 SCUDI D'ORO
Gold Weight varies: 32.33-33.50g., 45 mm. **Ruler:** Carlo Emanuele I **Obv:** Large high-collared armored bust to right, mintmark and date below **Obv. Legend:** CAROLVS. EM. D. G. - DVX. SABAVDIÆ. **Rev:** Crowned shield of 4-fold arms, with central shield of Savoy, in baroque frame, divides FE - RT **Rev. Legend:** DEVENTRE. MATRIS. DEVS. PROTECTOR. MEVS. **Note:** Cud. 569; Fr. B1046.

Date	Mintage	VG	F	VF	XF	Unc
1618 HA Rare	—	—	—	—	—	—
1619 HA Rare	—	—	—	—	—	—
1619 Rare	—	—	—	—	—	—

KM# 80 10 SCUDI D'ORO
Gold Weight varies: 33.33-33.50g., 45 mm. **Ruler:** Carlo Emanuele I **Obv:** Large high-collared armored bust to right, date below **Obv. Legend:** CAR(OLVS). EM. D. G. DVX. SABAVD(IÆ). P. PED. **Rev:** Crowned shield of 4-fold arms, with central shield of Savoy, in baroque frame, divides FE - RT **Rev. Legend:** DEVENTRE. MATRIS DEVS. PROTECTOR. MEVS. **Note:** Cud. 570a,b; Fr. B1046. Struck from Ducatone dies, KM#70.

Date	Mintage	VG	F	VF	XF	Unc
1621 Rare	—	—	—	—	—	—

KM# 96 10 SCUDI D'ORO
Gold Weight varies: 33.33-33.50g., 45 mm. **Ruler:** Carlo Emanuele I **Obv:** Large high-collared armored bust to right, mintmark and date below **Obv. Legend:** CAR. EM. D.G. DVX. SAB. P. PED. ET. C. **Rev:** Crowned shield of 4-fold arms, with central shield of Savoy, in baroque frame, divides FE - RT **Rev. Legend:** DEVENTRE. MATRIS. DEVS. PROTECTOR. MEVS. **Note:** Cud. 570c,d; Fr. B1046. Struck from Ducatone dies, KM#90.1.

Date	Mintage	VG	F	VF	XF	Unc
1627 Rare	—	—	—	—	—	—
1627 T Rare	—	—	—	—	—	—

KM# 102 10 SCUDI D'ORO
Gold Weight varies: 33.33-33.50g., 45 mm. **Ruler:** Carlo Emanuele I **Obv:** Large high-collared armored bust to right, mintmark and date below **Obv. Legend:** CAROLVS. EM. D.G. DVX. SABAVDIE. P. P. **Rev:** Crowned shield of 4-fold arms, with central shield of Savoy, in baroque frame, divides FE - RT **Rev. Legend:** DEVENTRE + MATRIS + DEVS + PROTEC + MEVS. **Note:** Cud. 570e; Fr. C1046. Struck from Ducatone dies, KM#90.2.

Date	Mintage	VG	F	VF	XF	Unc
1628 V Rare	—	—	—	—	—	—

KM# 103.1 10 SCUDI D'ORO
33.3200 g., 0.9860 Gold 1.0562 oz. AGW, 45 mm. **Ruler:** Carlo Emanuele I **Obv:** Large high-collared armored bust to right, date below **Obv. Legend:** CAROLVS. EM. D. G. DVX. SABAVDIÆ. **Rev:** Large drawing compass **Rev. Legend:** DVM - PREMOR - AMPLIOR. **Note:** Cud. 571a; Fr. 1053. Assignment to this mint is not certain; decade of date not engraved, but implied.

Date	Mintage	VG	F	VF	XF	Unc
16[2]8 Rare	—	—	—	—	—	—

KM# 118 10 SCUDI D'ORO
Gold Weight varies: 33.33-33.50g., 45 mm. **Ruler:** Carlo Emanuele I **Obv:** Large high-collared armored bust to right, date below **Obv. Legend:** CAROLVS. EM. D.G. DVX. SAB. P. P. ET. c. **Rev:** Crowned shield of 4-fold arms, with central shield of Savoy, in baroque frame, divides FE - RT **Rev. Legend:** DEVENTRE. MATRIS. DEVS. PROTECTOR. MEVS. **Note:** Cud. 570f; Fr. A1053.

Date	Mintage	VG	F	VF	XF	Unc
1630 Rare	—	—	—	—	—	—

KM# 103.2 10 SCUDI D'ORO
33.3200 g., Gold, 45 mm. **Ruler:** Carlo Emanuele I **Obv:** Large high-collared armored bust to right, date below **Obv. Legend:** CAROLVS. EM. D.G. - DVX. SAB. P. P. ET. C. **Rev:** Large drawing compass **Rev. Legend:** DVM - PREMOR - AMPLIOR. **Note:** Ref. Cud. 571b; Fr. 1053.

Date	Mintage	VG	F	VF	XF	Unc
1630 Rare	—	—	—	—	—	—

KM# 135 10 SCUDI D'ORO
Gold Weight varies: 32.77-33.30g., 46 mm. **Ruler:** Vittorio Amedeo I **Obv:** Mantled and armored bust to right, date below **Obv. Legend:** V. AMEDEVS. D.G. DVX. SABAVDIÆ. **Rev:** Three flags on staffs protruding through large crown, ornamental device below **Rev. Legend:** NEC - NVMINA - DESVNT. **Note:** Cud. 699; Fr. 1062.

Date	Mintage	VG	F	VF	XF	Unc
1632 Rare	—	—	—	—	—	—
1633 Rare	—	—	—	—	—	—

KM# 144 10 SCUDI D'ORO
33.1500 g., 0.9860 Gold 1.0508 oz. AGW, 45 mm. **Ruler:** Vittorio Amedeo I **Obv:** Armored bust to right, date below **Obv. Legend:** V. AMEDEVS. - D.G. DVX. SABAVDIÆ. **Rev:** Crowned shield of manifold arms, with central shield of Savoy, chain of order around **Rev. Legend:** ET PRINCEPTS - PEDEMONTIVM. **Note:** Cud. 695; Fr. 1057.

Date	Mintage	VG	F	VF	XF	Unc
1633 Rare	—	—	—	—	—	—

KM# 145 10 SCUDI D'ORO
Gold Weight varies: 32.70-33.15g., 47 mm. **Ruler:** Vittorio Amedeo I **Obv:** Mantled bust to right, date below **Obv. Legend:** V. AMEDEVS. - D.G. DVX. SABAVDIÆ. **Rev:** Crowned large shield of manifold arms, with central shield of Savoy, Order collar of the Annunziata around **Rev. Legend:** PRIN., - PEDEMON - REX. CYPRI. ET. C. **Note:** Cud. 696; Fr. 1062.

Date	Mintage	VG	F	VF	XF	Unc
1633 Rare	—	—	—	—	—	—
1634	—	22,000	30,000	42,000	78,000	—

KM# 146 10 SCUDI D'ORO
Gold Weight varies: 32.70-33.15g., 47 mm. **Ruler:** Vittorio Amedeo I **Obv:** Large mantles bust to right, date below **Obv. Legend:** V. AMEDEVS. - D.G. DVX. SABAVDIÆ. **Rev:** Crowned large shield of manifold arms with central shield of Savoy, chain of order around **Rev. Legend:** PRIN. - PEDEMON - REX. CYPRI. ET. C. **Note:** Cud. 697; Fr. 1062. Varieties exist.

Date	Mintage	VG	F	VF	XF	Unc
1633 Rare	—	—	—	—	—	—
1635	—	22,000	30,000	42,000	78,000	—
1636 Rare	—	—	—	—	—	—

KM# 154 10 SCUDI D'ORO
Gold Weight varies: 32.70-33.15g., 47 mm. **Ruler:** Vittorio Amedeo I **Obv:** Large mantled bust to right, date below **Obv. Legend:** V. AMEDEVS. - D.G. DVX. SABAVDIÆ. **Rev:** Very large crown above shield of manifold arms with central shield of Savoy, chain of order around **Rev. Legend:** PRIN. - PEDEMON - REX. CYPRI. ET. C. **Note:** Cud. 698; Fr. 1062.

Date	Mintage	VG	F	VF	XF	Unc
1634 Rare	—	—	—	—	—	—

KM# 158 10 SCUDI D'ORO
32.9600 g., Gold, 48 mm. **Ruler:** Vittorio Amedeo I **Obv:** Armored bust to right, date below **Obv. Legend:** V. AMEDEVS. D.G. DVX. SABAVDIÆ. **Rev:** Cross made of 4 large knots, small shield of Savoy arms in center, narrow band around with legend, outer margin of knots and branches **Rev. Legend:** FOEDERE - ET - RELIGIONE - TENEMVR. **Note:** Cud. 700; Fr. 1065.

Date	Mintage	VG	F	VF	XF	Unc
1635 Rare	—	—	—	—	—	—

KM# 202 10 SCUDI D'ORO
Gold Weight varies: 33.02-33.94g., 46 mm. **Ruler:** Carlo Emanuele II under regency **Obv:** Accolated busts of Carlo Emanuele II and his mother to right, date in cartouche below **Obv. Legend:** CHR + FRAN + CAR + EMAN + DVCES + DVCES + SAB. **Rev:** Large crowned shield of manifold arms, with central shield of Savoy, in baroque frame **Rev. Legend:** PRINCIPES. PEDEMON. REGES. CYPRI. ET. C. **Note:** Cud. 735a; Fr. 1069.

Date	Mintage	VG	F	VF	XF	Unc
1641	—	14,000	20,000	36,000	60,000	—

KM# 227 10 SCUDI D'ORO
Gold Weight varies: 33.02-33.94g., 46 mm. **Ruler:** Carlo Emanuele II under regency **Obv:** Accolated busts of Carlo Emanuele II and his mother to right, mintmark and date in cartouche below **Obv. Legend:** CHR + FRAN + CAR + EMAN + DVCES + SAB. **Rev:** Large crowned shield of manifold arms, with central shield of Savoy, in baroque frame **Rev. Legend:** PRINCIPES. PEDEMON. REGES. CYPRI. ET. C. **Note:** Cud. 735b; Fr. A1069.

Date	Mintage	VG	F	VF	XF	Unc
1648 TAV Rare	—	—	—	—	—	—

KM# 242 10 SCUDI D'ORO
Gold Weight varies: 32.71-33.15g., 46 mm. **Ruler:** Carlo Emanuele II alone **Obv:** Draped bust to right, date below in margin **Obv. Legend:** CAR. EMAN. II. D.G. DVX. SABAVDIÆ. **Rev:** Crowned shield of manifold arms, with central shield of Savoy, in baroque frame, Order collar of the Annunziata around **Rev. Legend:** PRIN. PEDEMON - REX. CYPRI. ET. C. **Note:** Cud. 792; Fr. 1082.

Date	Mintage	VG	F	VF	XF	Unc
1649 Rare	—	—	—	—	—	—
1650 Rare	—	—	—	—	—	—
1654 Rare	—	—	—	—	—	—

KM# 256 10 SCUDI D'ORO
Gold Weight varies: 32.25-33.10g., 45 mm. **Ruler:** Carlo Emanuele II alone **Obv:** Youthful armored bust to right, large date below **Obv. Legend:** CAR. EMAN. II. D.G. DVX. SABAVDIE. **Rev:** Crowned shield of manifold arms, with central shield of Savoy, in baroque frame, chain of order around **Rev. Legend:** PRIN. PEDEMON - REX. CYPRI. ET. C. **Note:** Cud. 793; Fr. 1082.

Date	Mintage	VG	F	VF	XF	Unc
1656 Rare	—	—	—	—	—	—
1658 Rare	—	—	—	—	—	—

KM# 267 10 SCUDI D'ORO
Gold Weight varies: 32.25-33.32g., 45 mm. **Ruler:** Carlo Emanuele II alone **Obv:** Armored and draped bust to right, small date below **Obv. Legend:** CAR. EMAN. II. D.G. DVX. SABAVDIE. **Rev:** Crowned shield of manifold arms, with central shield of Savoy, in baroque frame, chain of order around **Rev. Legend:** PRIN. PEDEMON - REX. CYPRI. ET. C. **Note:** Cud. 794; Fr. 1082.

Date	Mintage	VG	F	VF	XF	Unc
1660 Rare	—	—	—	—	—	—
1661 Rare	—	—	—	—	—	—

KM# 270.1 10 SCUDI D'ORO
Gold Weight varies: 33.08-33.28g., 45 mm. **Ruler:** Carlo Emanuele II alone **Obv:** Large draped bust to right, date at end of legend **Obv. Legend:** CAR. EM. II. D.G. DVX. SAB. **Rev:** Crowned shield of manifold arms, with central shield of Savoy, in baroque frame, chain of order around **Rev. Legend:** PRINCIP. PEDE - MON. REX. CYP. **Note:** Cud. 795a,d,e; Fr. B1082. Varieties exist. Illustration reduced.

Date	Mintage	VG	F	VF	XF	Unc
1663	—	48,000	60,000	84,000	—	—
1667 Rare	—	—	—	—	—	—

KM# 270.2 10 SCUDI D'ORO
Gold Weight varies: 33.08-33.28g., 45 mm. **Ruler:** Carlo Emanuele II alone **Obv:** Large draped bust to right, date below **Obv. Legend:** CAR. EMAN. II. D.G. DVX. SABAVD. **Rev:** Crowned shield of manifold arms, with central shield of Savoy, in baroque frame, chain of order around **Rev. Legend:** PRIN. PEDEMON - REX. CYP. EC. **Note:** Cud. 795b; Fr. C1082.

Date	Mintage	VG	F	VF	XF	Unc
1663 Rare	—	—	—	—	—	—

KM# 270.3 10 SCUDI D'ORO
Gold Weight varies: 33.08-33.28g., 45 mm. **Ruler:** Carlo Emanuele II alone **Obv:** Large draped bust to right, date at beginning of legend **Obv. Legend:** CARO. EMAN. II. D.G. DVX. SAB. **Rev:** Crowned shield of manifold arms, with central shield of Savoy, in baroque frame, chain of order around **Rev. Legend:** PRINCIP. PEDE - MON. REX. CYP. **Note:** Cud. 795c; Fr. C1082.

Date	Mintage	VG	F	VF	XF	Unc
1663 Rare	—	—	—	—	—	—

KM# 271 10 SCUDI D'ORO
Gold Weight varies: 33.08-33.28g., 45 mm. **Ruler:** Carlo Emanuele II alone **Obv:** Large draped bust to right, date at beginnig of legend **Obv. Legend:** CARO. FRANC. EM. D.G. DVX. SAB. **Rev:** Crowned shield of manifold arms, with central shield of Savoy, collar of order around **Rev. Legend:** PRIN. PEDEMON - REX. CYPRI. ET. C. **Note:** Cud. 796; Fr. 1082.

Date	Mintage	VG	F	VF	XF	Unc
1663 Rare	—	—	—	—	—	—

KM# 281 10 SCUDI D'ORO
Gold Weight varies: 33.05-33.15g., 45 mm. **Ruler:** Carlo Emanuele II alone **Obv:** Large draped bust to right, **Obv. Legend:** CAR. EM. II. D. - G. DVX. SAB. **Rev:** Crowned shield of manifold arms, with central shield of Savoy, collar of order around, date at end of legend **Rev. Legend:** +PRINCEIP. PEDE - REX. CYP. **Note:** Cud. 797; Fr. D1082.

Date	Mintage	VG	F	VF	XF	Unc
1668 Rare	—	—	—	—	—	—

KM# 286 10 SCUDI D'ORO
Gold Weight varies: 33.12-33.20g., 42 mm. **Ruler:** Carlo Emanuele II alone **Obv:** Draped bust to right **Obv. Legend:** CAR. EM. II. - D.G. DVX. SAB. **Rev:** Crowned shield of manifold arms with central shield of Savoy, supported by 2 lions, date divided in exergue **Rev. Legend:** PRIN. PEDE + REX. CYPRI. **Note:** Cud. 798; Fr. E1082.

Date	Mintage	VG	F	VF	XF	Unc
1670 Rare	—	—	—	—	—	—
1671 Rare	—	—	—	—	—	—

KM# 287 10 SCUDI D'ORO
33.2500 g., 0.9860 Gold 1.0540 oz. AGW, 43 mm. **Ruler:** Carlo Emanuele II alone **Obv:** Bust to right **Obv. Legend:** CAR. EMAN. II. D.G. DVX. SABAVDIE. **Rev:** Crowned shield of manifold arms, with central shield of Savoy, in baroque frame, chain of order around **Rev. Legend:** PRIN. PEDEMON - REX. CYPRI. ET. C. **Note:** Cud. 799; Fr. A1082.

Date	Mintage	VG	F	VF	XF	Unc
ND(ca1670) Rare	—	—	—	—	—	—

KM# 314 10 SCUDI D'ORO
33.6000 g., 0.9860 Gold 1.0651 oz. AGW, 43 mm. **Ruler:** Vittorio Amedeo II alone **Obv:** Draped and armored bust to right **Obv. Legend:** VICTOR. AM. II. D.G. DVX. SAB. **Rev:** Crowned shield of manifold arms with central shield of Savoy, supported by 2 lions, date divided in exergue **Rev. Legend:** PRIN. PEDE - REX. CYPRI. **Note:** Cud. 843; Fr. 1094.

Date	Mintage	VG	F	VF	XF	Unc
1680 Rare	—	—	—	—	—	—
1684 Rare	—	—	—	—	—	—

KM# 298 5 DOPPIE
Gold Weight varies: 33.13-33.30g., 43 mm. **Ruler:** Vittorio Amedeo II under regency **Obv:** Accolated busts of Vittorio Amedeo II and his mother to right **Obv. Legend:** MAR. IO. BAP. VIC. AM. II. D.G. DVC. SAB. **Rev:** Crowned shield of manifold arms, with central shield of Savoy, in baroque frame, date at end of legend **Rev. Legend:** PRINI. PEDEM. REGES. CYPRI. **Note:** Cud. 833; Fr. 1089.

Date	Mintage	VG	F	VF	XF	Unc
1675 Rare	—	—	—	—	—	—
1678 Rare	—	—	—	—	—	—

KM# 341 5 DOPPIE
33.5000 g., 0.9860 Gold 1.0619 oz. AGW, 42 mm. **Ruler:** Vittorio Amedeo II alone **Obv:** Armored figure of duke on horse rearing to left, date in exergue **Obv. Legend:** VIC. AM. II. D.G. DVX. SAB. PRI. PED. REX. CYP. **Rev:** Justice seated facing on cloud, holding sword and scales **Rev. Legend:** FIDEM - SERVANDO. - PATRIAM - TVENDO. **Note:** Cud. 844; Fr. 1095.

Date	Mintage	VG	F	VF	XF	Unc
1694 Rare	—	—	—	—	—	—

KM# 47 20 SCUDI D'ORO
66.5000 g., 0.9860 Gold 2.1080 oz. AGW, 45 mm. **Ruler:** Carlo Emanuele I **Obv:** High-collared armored bust to right, date below **Obv. Legend:** CAROLVS. EM. D.G. DVX. SABAVDIÆ. **Rev:** Crowned shield of 4-fold arms, with central shield of Savoy, in baroque frame, divides FE - RT **Rev. Legend:** DEVENTRE. MATRIS. DEVS. PROTECTOR. MEVS. **Note:** Cud. 566. Previous KM#140. Struck from Ducatone dies, KM#34.

Date	Mintage	VG	F	VF	XF	Unc
1610 Rare	—	—	—	—	—	—

KM# 159 20 SCUDI D'ORO
Gold, 47 mm. **Ruler:** Vittorio Amedeo I **Obv:** Mantled bust to right, date below **Obv. Legend:** V. AMEDEVS. D.G. DVX. SABAVDIÆ. **Rev:** Crowned shield of 4-fold arms, with central shield of Savoy, in baroque frame, Order collar of the Annunziata around **Rev. Legend:** PRIN. PEDEMON - REX. CYPRI. ET. C. **Note:** Cud. 694; Fr. 1061.

Date	Mintage	VG	F	VF	XF	Unc
1635 Rare	—	—	—	—	—	—

KM# 204 20 SCUDI D'ORO
66.3100 g., Gold, 45 mm. **Ruler:** Carlo Emanuele II under regency **Obv:** Accolated busts of Carlo Emanuele II and his mother to right, date in exergue **Obv. Legend:** CHR. FRAN. CAR. EMAN. DVCES. SABAV. **Rev:** Large crowned shield of manifold arms, with central shield of Savoy, in baroque frame **Rev. Legend:** PRINCIPES. PEDEMON. REGES. CYPRI. ET. C. **Note:** Cud. 734a,b; Fr. 1068.

Date	Mintage	VG	F	VF	XF	Unc
1641 Rare	—	—	—	—	—	—
1642 Rare	—	—	—	—	—	—

KM# 243 20 SCUDI D'ORO
66.3700 g., 0.9860 Gold 2.1039 oz. AGW, 47 mm. **Ruler:** Carlo Emanuele II alone **Obv:** Draped bust to right, date below in margin **Obv. Legend:** CAR. EMAN. II. D.G. DVX. SABAVDIÆ. **Rev:** Crowned shield of manifold arms, with central shield of Savoy, in baroque frame, Order collar of the Annunziata around **Rev. Legend:** PRIN. PEDEMON - REX. CYPRI. ET. C. **Note:** Cud. 787; Fr. 1081.

Date	Mintage	VG	F	VF	XF	Unc
1649 Rare	—	—	—	—	—	—

KM# 257 20 SCUDI D'ORO
66.3500 g., 0.9860 Gold 2.1032 oz. AGW, 45 mm. **Ruler:** Carlo Emanuele II alone **Obv:** Youthful armored bust to right, large date below **Obv. Legend:** CAR. EMAN. II. D.G. DVX. SABAVDIE. **Rev:** Crowned shield of manifold arms, with central shield of Savoy, in baroque frame, chain of order around **Rev. Legend:** PRIN. PEDEMON - REX. CYPRI. ET. C. **Note:** Cud. 788; Fr. A1081.

Date	Mintage	VG	F	VF	XF	Unc
1656 Rare	—	—	—	—	—	—
1657 Rare	—	—	—	—	—	—

KM# 268 20 SCUDI D'ORO
Gold Weight varies: 66.50-66.55g., 48 mm. **Ruler:** Carlo Emanuele II alone **Obv:** Armored and draped bust to right, small date below **Obv. Legend:** CAR. EMAN. II. D.G. DVX. SABAVDIE. **Rev:** Crowned shield of manifold arms, with central shield of Savoy, in baroque frame, chain of order around **Rev. Legend:** PRIN. PEDEMON - REX. CYPRI. ETC. **Note:** Cud. 789; Fr. B1081.

Date	Mintage	VG	F	VF	XF	Unc
1660 Rare	—	—	—	—	—	—

KM# 280 20 SCUDI D'ORO
66.3200 g., Gold, 48 mm. **Ruler:** Carlo Emanuele II alone **Obv:** Bust to right, date below **Obv. Legend:** CAR. EMAN. II. D.G. DVX. SABAVDIÆ. **Rev:** Crowned shield of manifold arms, with central shield of Savoy, in baroque frame, chain of order around **Rev. Legend:** PRIN. PEDEMON - REX. CYPRI. ETC. **Note:** Cud. 790; Fr. B1081.

Date	Mintage	VG	F	VF	XF	Unc
1667 Rare	—	—	—	—	—	—

KM# 288 20 SCUDI D'ORO
Gold Weight varies: 66.38-66.46g., 42 mm. **Ruler:** Carlo Emanuele II alone **Obv:** Mature armored bust to right **Obv. Legend:** CAR. EM. II. D. - G. DVX. SAB. **Rev:** Crowned shield of manifold arms, with central shield of Savoy, supported by 2 lions, date divided in exergue **Rev. Legend:** PRIN. PEDE + REX. CYPRI. **Note:** Cud. 791; Fr. C1081.

Date	Mintage	VG	F	VF	XF	Unc
1671 Rare	—	—	—	—	—	—

KM# 318 20 SCUDI D'ORO
67.2000 g., 0.9860 Gold 2.1302 oz. AGW, 43 mm. **Ruler:** Vittorio Amedeo II alone **Obv:** Youthful draped and armored bust to right **Obv. Legend:** VICTOR. AM. II. D.G. DVX. SAB. **Rev:** Crowned shield of manifold arms, with central shield of Savoy, supported by 2 lions, date divided in exergue **Rev. Legend:** PRIN. PEDE - REX. CYPRI. **Note:** Cud. 842; Fr. 1093.

Date	Mintage	VG	F	VF	XF	Unc
1684 Rare	—	—	—	—	—	—

KM# 160 30 SCUDI D'ORO
99.5000 g., Gold, 47 mm. **Ruler:** Vittorio Amedeo I **Obv:** Mantled and armored bust to right, date below **Obv. Legend:** V. AMEDEVS. D. G. DVX - SABAVDIÆ **Rev:** Crowned shield of manifold arms, with central shield of Savoy, in baroque frame, Order collar of the Annunziata around **Rev. Legend:** PRIN. PEDEMON - REX. CYPRI. ET. C. **Note:** Cud. 693; Fr. 1060.

Date	Mintage	VG	F	VF	XF	Unc
1635 Rare	—	—	—	—	—	—

KM# 258 30 SCUDI D'ORO
99.0000 g., Gold, 48 mm. **Ruler:** Carlo Emanuele II alone **Obv:** Youthful armored bust to right, large date below **Obv. Legend:** CAR. EMAN. II. D.G. DVX. SABAVDIE. **Rev:** Crowned shield of manifold arms, with central shield of Savoy, in baroque frame, chain of order around **Rev. Legend:** PRIN. PEDEMON - REX. CYPRI. ET. C. **Note:** Cud. 786; Fr. 1080.

Date	Mintage	VG	F	VF	XF	Unc
1656 Rare	—	—	—	—	—	—

KM# 259 40 SCUDI D'ORO
132.0000 g., Gold, 48 mm. **Ruler:** Carlo Emanuele II alone **Obv:** Youthful armored bust to right, large date below **Obv. Legend:** CAR. EMAN. II. D.G. DVX. SABAVDIE. **Rev:** Crowned shield of manifold arms, with central shield of Savoy, in baroque frame, Order collar of the Annunziata around **Rev. Legend:** PRIN. PEDEMON - REX. CYPRI. ET. C. **Note:** Cud. 785; Fr. 1079.

Date	Mintage	VG	F	VF	XF	Unc
1656 Rare	—	—	—	—	—	—

PATTERNS

Including off metal strikes

KM#	Date	Mintage	Identification	Mkt Val
Pn5	1629	—	Fiorino. Copper. KM#106.2. Ref. Cud. 653c.	—

SEBORGA

Seborga, a commune in the province of Porto Maurizio, was a fief of the Benedictine Monastery of Lerino. The abbot coined luigini without authorization.

COMMUNE

STANDARD COINAGE

KM# 5 LUIGINI
Silver **Obv:** Bust right **Rev:** Crowned arms, date above **Rev. Legend:** SVBVMBAR **Note:** Weight varies: 2.09-3.05 grams.

Date	Mintage	VG	F	VF	XF	Unc
1667	—	200	375	850	1,750	—
1668	—	200	375	850	1,750	—

KM# 6 LUIGINI
Silver **Rev:** Crowned arms in sprays **Rev. Legend:** MONAST. **Note:** Weight varies: 2.09-3.05 grams.

Date	Mintage	VG	F	VF	XF	Unc
1668	—	200	375	850	1,750	—

KM# 7 LUIGINI
Silver **Obv:** Bust right **Obv. Legend:** DECVS **Rev:** Crowned arms divide date **Note:** Weight varies: 2.09-3.05 grams.

Date	Mintage	VG	F	VF	XF	Unc
1669	—	250	450	950	2,000	—
1671	—	150	325	750	1,600	—

SICILY

Sicily lies off the southwestern tip of mainland Italy and is the largest island in the Mediterranean Sea. It has been inhabited for millennia, early on by tribal peoples form various places around the Mediterranean in prehistoric times, followed by Elymians from the Aegean Sea and Phoenicians in the early historical period. Greek colonists began settling in Sicily around 750 BC and their most important urban center was Syracuse. Carthage also founded colonies in the western part of the island and clashe between those enclaves and the Greek area led to the series o conflicts known as the Punic Wars. The Roman Republic even tually intervened and upon defeating Carthage, annexed Sicily a the first Roman province outside of mainland Italy. The history o the island followed that of the Roman Republic and subsequer Empire, falling victim to barbarian invasions as the latter dis integrated. As the Byzantine Empire succeeded the Roman, Sicily came under a new threat in the rise of Islam in North Africa. The Muslim conquest of Sicily extended over more than a century a one town or city after another fell during the 9th and 10th centuries This lasted until the second half of the 11th century, when Nor mans from northern Europe, who had gained a foothold in south ern Italy, eventually conquered the island, culminating in the cap ture of Palermo in 1072. The Normans established the Kingdon of Sicilly and the island was ruled from that time on by a suc cession of European dynasties. The Spanish gained control of the island and the southern half of Italy by the 15th century and in the 18th century, a branch of the Bourbon dynasty ruled in both Sicily and Naples (see), usually as separate entities. After the Napo leonic Wars, Sicily and Naples were permanently united in the Kingdom of the Two Sicilies from 1816 until 1860. It was annexe by Sardinia-Piedmont in the latter year and became part of unite Italy in 1861.

Coinage produced solely in Naples for use there are liste under that name.

RULERS

Spanish

Filippo III, 1598-1621
Filippo IV, 1621-1665
Carlo II, 1665-1700

MINT MASTERS' INITIALS

Messina Mint

Initials	Date	Name
DC	1608-11	Decio Cirino
DFA	1612-13	Don Francesco Abate
DFF	1642-44	Francesco Foti
DGV	1655-66	Don Gregorio Vigevi
DI-BV	1667-74	Don Giovanni Battista Vigevi
ILV, DLV, DLLV	?-1652	Giovanni Lorenzo Vigeri
IP	1611-38	Giovanni del Pozzo
IP-MP	1643-51	Giovanni del Pozzo & Mario Parisi
IP-PP	1650-54	Giovanni del Pozzo & Principe del Parc
RC	1678-	Regia Corte

Palermo Mint

Initials	Date	Name
OG	?-1635	Orazio Giancardo

MONETARY SYSTEM

6 Piccioli = 1 Grano
5 Cinquina = 1 Tari
15 Tari = 1 Scudo
2 Scudi = 1 Oncia

ARMS

Displayed eagle, often crowned, sometimes with various shields of arms on breast

REFERENCES

V = Alberto Varesi, **Monete Italiane Regionali: Sicilia**. Pavia:Numismatica Varesi, 2001.

Sp = Rodolfo Spahr, Le Monete Siciliane dagli Aragonesi ai Bo boni (1282-1836). Graz, 1982.

KINGDOM

Spanish Rule

STANDARD COINAGE

KM# 6 PICCIOLO
Copper Weight varies: 0.45-0.50g., 11 mm. **Ruler:** Filippo III **Obv:** Crowned displayed eagle, head to left **Obv. Legend:** +PHIL. III. D. G. **Rev:** Foliated cross, date at end of legend **Rev. Legend:** +REX. SICI. **Note:** Ref. V-354; Sp. 129, 130.

Date	Mintage	VG	F	VF	XF	Un
1609	—	10.00	20.00	45.00	65.00	—
1609 DC	—	10.00	20.00	45.00	65.00	—

KM# 19 PICCIOLO
0.4400 g., Copper, 10 mm. **Ruler:** Filippo IV **Obv:** Crowned displayed eagle, head to right **Obv. Legend:** PHIL. IIII. D. G. **Rev:** Foliated cross **Rev. Legend:** REX. SICILIE. **Note:** Ref. V-363; Sp. 177.

Date	Mintage	VG	F	VF	XF	Un
ND(1621-65)	—	25.00	55.00	115	165	—

KM# 3 3 PICCIOLI
Copper Weight varies: 2.15-2.25g., 14 mm. **Ruler:** Filippo III **Obv:** Crowned displayed eagle, head to left **Obv. Legend:** +PHIL(IP). III. D(E). G. **Rev:** Large '3' in plain field, date at end of legend **Rev. Legend:** REX. SICI(LI). **Note:** Ref. V-353; Sp. 124-127. Varieties exist.

Date	Mintage	VG	F	VF	XF	Un
1608 DC	—	8.00	15.00	35.00	50.00	—
1609 DC	—	8.00	15.00	35.00	50.00	—
1610 DC	—	8.00	15.00	35.00	50.00	—
1611 DC	—	8.00	15.00	35.00	50.00	—
1611 IP	—	8.00	15.00	35.00	50.00	—
1611 DFA	—	8.00	15.00	35.00	50.00	—

KM# 2 3 PICCIOLI

2.2400 g., Copper, 14 mm. **Ruler:** Filippo III **Obv:** Crowned displayed eagle, head to right **Obv. Legend:** +PHIL(I). III. D(E). G(R). **Rev:** Large '3' in plain field, date at end of legend **Rev. Legend:** +REX. SI(CILIAE). **Note:** Ref. V-352; Sp. 123, 128. Varieties exist.

Date	Mintage	VG	F	VF	XF	Unc
1608 DC	—	12.00	28.00	55.00	80.00	—

KM# 26 3 PICCIOLI

Copper Weight varies: 1.00-1.25g., 14 mm. **Ruler:** Filippo IV **Obv:** Crowned displayed eagle, head to right, in circle **Obv. Legend:** +PHILIPP. IIII. D. G. **Rev:** Large '3' divides mintmaster's initials in circle, date at end of legend **Rev. Legend:** +REX. SICILIAE. **Note:** Ref. V-362; Sp. 168-176.

Date	Mintage	VG	F	VF	XF	Unc
1629 IP	—	6.00	12.00	20.00	35.00	—
1630 IP	—	6.00	12.00	20.00	35.00	—
1631 IP	—	6.00	12.00	20.00	35.00	—
1634 IP	—	6.00	12.00	20.00	35.00	—
1643 IP-MP	—	6.00	12.00	20.00	35.00	—
1644 IP-MP	—	6.00	12.00	20.00	35.00	—
1644 DF-F	—	6.00	12.00	20.00	35.00	—
1646 IP-MP	—	6.00	12.00	20.00	35.00	—
1647 IP-MP	—	6.00	12.00	20.00	35.00	—

KM# 35 3 PICCIOLI

Copper Weight varies: 1.08-1.60g., 15 mm. **Ruler:** Carlo II **Obv:** Crowned displayed eagle, head to left, in circle **Obv. Legend:** +CAROLVS. II. D. G. **Rev:** Large '3' divides mintmaster's initials in circle, date at end of legend **Rev. Legend:** +REX. SICILI. **Note:** Ref. V-370; Sp. 25.

Date	Mintage	VG	F	VF	XF	Unc
1670 DI-BV	—	12.00	28.00	55.00	80.00	—

KM# 48 3 PICCIOLI

2.1800 g., Copper, 16 mm. **Ruler:** Carlo II **Obv:** Crowned displayed eagle, head to right, in circle **Obv. Legend:** CAROLVS. II. D. G. **Rev:** Large '3' divides date in circle **Rev. Legend:** REX. SICILIAE. **Note:** Ref. V-488; Sp. 60-60A.

Date	Mintage	VG	F	VF	XF	Unc
1686	—	6.00	12.00	20.00	35.00	—
1687	—	6.00	12.00	20.00	35.00	—

KM# 69 3 PICCIOLI

, 16 mm. **Ruler:** Carlo II **Obv:** Crowned displayed eagle, head to left **Obv. Legend:** CA - ROLVS. II. DEI. GRA - TIA. **Rev:** '3' in baroque frame, date at end of legend **Rev. Legend:** +TRINACREA(E). - REX. **Note:** Weight varies: 2.35-2.75g.

Date	Mintage	VG	F	VF	XF	Unc
1698 RC	—	6.00	12.00	20.00	35.00	—
1699 RC	—	6.00	12.00	20.00	35.00	—
1700 RC	—	6.00	12.00	20.00	35.00	—

KM# 4 GRANO

Copper Weight varies: 2.75-3.85g., 17 mm. **Ruler:** Filippo III **Obv:** Large crowned displayed eagle, head to left **Obv. Legend:** +PHILI(P). III. DE. GR. **Rev:** 3-line inscription, date at end of legend **Rev. Legend:** +REX. SICI(LI). **Rev. Inscription:** VT / COMMO / DIVS. **Note:** Ref. V-351; Sp. 116-121. Varieties exist.

Date	Mintage	VG	F	VF	XF	Unc
1608 DC	—	8.00	15.00	40.00	65.00	—
1609 DC	—	8.00	15.00	40.00	65.00	—
1610 DC	—	8.00	15.00	40.00	65.00	—
1611 DC	—	8.00	15.00	40.00	65.00	—
1611 IP	—	8.00	15.00	40.00	65.00	—
1612 IP	—	8.00	15.00	40.00	65.00	—
1612 DFA	—	8.00	15.00	40.00	65.00	—
1613 DFA	—	8.00	15.00	40.00	65.00	—
1614 DFA	—	8.00	15.00	40.00	65.00	—

KM# 23 GRANO

Copper Weight varies: 3.05-3.90g., 20 mm. **Ruler:** Filippo IV **Obv:** Large crowned displayed eagle, head to right **Obv. Legend:** PHILIPP. - IIII. D. G. **Rev:** 3-line inscription, date at end of legend **Rev. Legend:** REX. SICILIAE. **Rev. Inscription:** VT / COMMO / DIVS. **Note:** Ref. V-360; Sp. 159.

Date	Mintage	VG	F	VF	XF	Unc
1622 IP	—	7.00	15.00	35.00	50.00	—

KM# 25 GRANO

Copper Weight varies: 3.05-3.90g., 20 mm. **Ruler:** Filippo IV **Obv:** Large crowned displayed eagle, head to left **Obv. Legend:** +PHILIP - IIII. D. G. **Rev:** 3-line inscription, date at end of legend **Rev. Legend:** REX. SICILIAE. **Note:** Ref. V-361; Sp. 160-167.

Date	Mintage	VG	F	VF	XF	Unc
1623 IP	—	6.00	12.00	20.00	35.00	—
1629 IP	—	6.00	12.00	20.00	35.00	—
1630 IP	—	6.00	12.00	20.00	35.00	—
1638 IP-MP	—	6.00	12.00	20.00	35.00	—
1640 IP-MP	—	6.00	12.00	20.00	35.00	—
1641 IP-MP	—	6.00	12.00	20.00	35.00	—
1643 DF-F	—	6.00	12.00	20.00	35.00	—
1644 IP-MP	—	6.00	12.00	20.00	35.00	—
1647 IP-MP	—	6.00	12.00	20.00	35.00	—
1652 IL-V	—	6.00	12.00	20.00	35.00	—

KM# 36 GRANO

Copper Weight varies: 3.10-4.50g., 20 mm. **Ruler:** Carlo II **Obv:** Large crowned displayed eagle, head to left, in circle **Obv. Legend:** +CAROLVS. II. D. G. **Rev:** 3-line inscription in circle, date at end of legend **Rev. Legend:** +REX. SICILIAE. **Rev. Inscription:** VT / COMMO / DIVS. **Note:** Ref. V-369; Sp. 24.

Date	Mintage	VG	F	VF	XF	Unc
1670 DI-BV	—	12.00	28.00	55.00	80.00	—

KM# 47 GRANO

Copper Weight varies: 4.20-5.05g., 23 mm. **Ruler:** Carlo II **Obv:** Crowned displayed eagle, head to left, in beaded circle **Obv. Legend:** +CAROLVS. II. D(EI). G(RATIA). **Rev:** 4-line inscription with date in beaded circle **Rev. Legend:** +REX. SICILIAE. **Rev. Inscription:** VT / COMMO / DIVS / (date) **Note:** Ref. V-487; Sp. 56-59. Varieties exist.

Date	Mintage	VG	F	VF	XF	Unc
1685 RC	—	12.00	25.00	45.00	65.00	—
1686 RC	—	6.00	12.00	20.00	35.00	—
1687 RC	—	8.00	15.00	35.00	50.00	—

KM# 62 GRANO

5.0000 g., Copper, 21 mm. **Ruler:** Carlo II **Obv:** Crowned displayed eagle, head to right, in beaded circle **Obv. Legend:** +CAROLVS. II. D. G. **Rev:** 3-line inscription in beaded circle, date at end of legend **Rev. Legend:** +REX. SICILIAE. **Rev. Inscription:** VT / COMMO / DIVS. **Note:** Ref. V-495; Sp. 80.

Date	Mintage	VG	F	VF	XF	Unc
1697 RC Rare	—	—	—	—	—	—

KM# 71 GRANO

Copper Weight varies: 4.50-5.00g., 23 mm. **Ruler:** Carlo II **Obv:** Large crowned displayed eagle, head to left **Obv. Legend:** CAROLVS. II. DEI. GRA - TIA. **Rev:** 4-line inscription with date in baroque frame **Rev. Legend:** + - REX - . - SI - CILIÆ. **Rev. Inscription:** FE / LICI / TAS / (date) **Note:** Ref. V-497; Sp. 82-84A.

Date	Mintage	VG	F	VF	XF	Unc
1698 RC	—	8.00	15.00	35.00	50.00	—
1699 RC	—	8.00	15.00	35.00	50.00	—
1700 RC	—	8.00	15.00	35.00	50.00	—

KM# 70 GRANO

4.6000 g., Copper, 23 mm. **Ruler:** Carlo II **Obv:** Large crowned displayed eagle, head to left **Obv. Legend:** CAROLVS. II. DEI. GRATIA. **Rev:** 4-line inscription with date **Rev. Legend:** +REX. SICILIAE. **Rev. Inscription:** FE / LICI / TAS / (date) **Note:** Ref. V-496; Sp. 81.

Date	Mintage	VG	F	VF	XF	Unc
1698 RC Rare	—	—	—	—	—	—

KM# 13 CINQUINA

0.5600 g., Silver, 12 mm. **Ruler:** Filippo III **Obv:** Crowned 'P' **Obv. Legend:** +PHILI. III. D. G. **Rev:** Cross in circle, date at end of legend **Rev. Legend:** +REX. SICI. **Note:** Ref. V-350; Sp. 114, 115.

Date	Mintage	VG	F	VF	XF	Unc
1610	—	22.00	45.00	95.00	140	—

KM# 7 1/2 TARI (Mezzo Tari)

Silver Weight varies: 1.15-1.24g., 15 mm. **Ruler:** Filippo III **Obv:** Crowned bust to right **Obv. Legend:** +PHIL(I)(P)(P). III. D. G. **Rev:** Crowned displayed eagle, head to left, date at end of legend **Rev. Legend:** +REX. SICI(LI). **Note:** Ref. V-349; Sp. 105-113. Varieties exist.

Date	Mintage	VG	F	VF	XF	Unc
1609	—	18.00	35.00	75.00	110	—
1610	—	18.00	35.00	75.00	110	—
1611	—	18.00	35.00	75.00	110	—
1615	—	18.00	35.00	75.00	110	—
1616 IP	—	18.00	35.00	75.00	110	—
1618 IP	—	18.00	35.00	75.00	110	—
1619	—	18.00	35.00	75.00	110	—
1621	—	18.00	35.00	75.00	110	—

KM# 24 1/2 TARI (Mezzo Tari)

Silver Weight varies: 1.14-1.26g., 14 mm. **Ruler:** Filippo IV **Obv:** Crowned and armored bust to right **Obv. Legend:** PHILI(P) - IIII. D. G. **Rev:** Crowned displayed eagle, head to left, date at end of legend **Rev. Legend:** REX. SICILI. **Note:** Ref. V-359; Sp. 138-150, 154-158.

Date	Mintage	VG	F	VF	XF	Unc
1622	—	15.00	28.00	65.00	110	—
1623	—	15.00	28.00	65.00	110	—
1624	—	15.00	28.00	65.00	110	—
1625	—	15.00	28.00	65.00	110	—
1627	—	15.00	28.00	65.00	110	—
1632	—	15.00	28.00	65.00	110	—
1636	—	15.00	28.00	65.00	110	—
1639	—	15.00	28.00	65.00	110	—
1640	—	15.00	28.00	65.00	110	—
1644	—	15.00	28.00	65.00	110	—
1645	—	15.00	28.00	65.00	110	—
1646	—	15.00	28.00	65.00	110	—
1647	—	15.00	28.00	65.00	110	—
1648	—	15.00	28.00	65.00	110	—
1649	—	15.00	28.00	65.00	110	—
1650	—	15.00	28.00	65.00	110	—
1651	—	15.00	28.00	65.00	110	—
1652	—	15.00	28.00	65.00	110	—
1655	—	15.00	28.00	65.00	110	—
1663	—	15.00	28.00	65.00	110	—
1664	—	15.00	28.00	65.00	110	—

KM# 30 1/2 TARI (Mezzo Tari)

Silver Weight varies: 1.18-1.20g., 14 mm. **Ruler:** Carlo II **Obv:** Youthful crowned bust to right **Obv. Legend:** CARO. - II. D. G. **Rev:** Crowned displayed eagle, head to left, date at end of legend **Rev. Legend:** REX. SICILI. **Note:** Ref. V-368; Sp. 22-23.

Date	Mintage	VG	F	VF	XF	Unc
1665	—	30.00	65.00	185	275	—
1672	—	30.00	65.00	185	275	—

KM# 49 1/2 TARI (Mezzo Tari)

Silver **Ruler:** Carlo II **Obv:** Youthful crowned bust to left **Rev:** Crowned displayed eagle **Note:** Ref. V-485; Sp. 54. Date uncertain.

Date	Mintage	VG	F	VF	XF	Unc
1686 Rare	—	—	—	—	—	—

KM# 57 1/2 TARI (Mezzo Tari)

1.1400 g., Silver, 14 mm. **Ruler:** Carlo II **Obv:** Youthful crowned bust to left **Obv. Legend:** CAROLVS. II. D. G. **Rev:** Crowned displayed eagle, head to left, date at end of legend **Rev. Legend:** REX. SICILIAE. **Note:** Ref. V-486; Sp. 55.

Date	Mintage	VG	F	VF	XF	Unc
1693 RC	—	50.00	110	275	450	—

KM# 63 1/2 TARI (Mezzo Tari)

1.2500 g., Silver, 14 mm. **Ruler:** Carlo II **Obv:** Crowned bust to right **Obv. Legend:** CAROLVS. - II. D. G. **Rev:** Crowned displayed eagle, head to right, in circle, date at end of legend **Rev. Legend:** REX. SICILIA(-)E. **Note:** Ref. V-494; Sp. 77-79.

Date	Mintage	VG	F	VF	XF	Unc
1697 RC	—	40.00	80.00	210	325	—

KM# 8 TARI

Silver Weight varies: 2.43-2.48g., 18 mm. **Ruler:** Filippo III **Obv:** Armored high-collared bust to left **Obv. Legend:** +PHILI(P) (-) III. D(E). G(R). **Rev:** Crowned displayed eagle, head to right, date at end of legend **Rev. Legend:** +REX. SICIL(I). **Note:** Ref. V-348; Sp. 81-104. Varieties exist.

Date	Mintage	VG	F	VF	XF	Unc
1609 DC	—	22.00	45.00	130	200	—
1610 DC	—	22.00	45.00	130	200	—
1611 IP	—	22.00	45.00	130	200	—
1611	—	22.00	45.00	130	200	—
1612 IP	—	22.00	45.00	130	200	—
1612 DFA	—	22.00	45.00	130	200	—
1613 DFA	—	22.00	45.00	130	200	—
1613 IP	—	22.00	45.00	130	200	—
1615 IP	—	22.00	45.00	130	200	—
1616 IP	—	22.00	45.00	130	200	—
1617 IP	—	22.00	45.00	130	200	—
1618 IP	—	22.00	45.00	130	200	—
1619 IP	—	22.00	45.00	130	200	—
1620 IP	—	22.00	45.00	130	200	—
1621 IP	—	22.00	45.00	130	200	—

KM# 20 TARI

Silver Weight varies: 2.39-2.54g., 18 mm. **Ruler:** Filippo IV **Obv:** Armored high-collared bust to left, annulet below **Obv. Legend:** +PHILI(P)(P). - IIII. D. G. **Rev:** Crowned displayed eagle, head to right, in circle, date at end of legend **Rev. Legend:** +REX. SICILI(AE). **Note:** Ref. V-358; Sp. 111-137. Varieties exist.

Date	Mintage	VG	F	VF	XF	Unc
1621 IP	—	22.00	45.00	130	200	—
1622 IP	—	22.00	45.00	130	200	—
1623 IP	—	22.00	45.00	130	200	—
1624 IP	—	22.00	45.00	130	200	—
1626 IP	—	22.00	45.00	130	200	—
1630 IP	—	22.00	45.00	130	200	—
1632 IP	—	22.00	45.00	130	200	—
1642 IP-MP	—	22.00	45.00	130	200	—
1644 IP-MP	—	22.00	45.00	130	200	—
1645 IP-MP	—	22.00	45.00	130	200	—
1646 IP-MP	—	22.00	45.00	130	200	—
1647 IP-MP	—	22.00	45.00	130	200	—
1648 IP-MP	—	22.00	45.00	130	200	—
1649 IP-MP	—	22.00	45.00	130	200	—
1650	—	22.00	45.00	130	200	—
1651 IP-PP	—	22.00	45.00	130	200	—
1652 DG-V	—	22.00	45.00	130	200	—
1653 IP-PP	—	22.00	45.00	130	200	—
1654 IP-PP	—	22.00	45.00	130	200	—
1655 DG-V	—	22.00	45.00	130	200	—
1659 DG-V	—	22.00	45.00	130	200	—
1661 DG-V	—	22.00	45.00	130	200	—
1662 DG-V	—	22.00	45.00	130	200	—
1663 DG-V	—	22.00	45.00	130	200	—
1664 DG-V	—	22.00	45.00	130	200	—
1665 DG-V	—	22.00	45.00	130	200	—

KM# 31 TARI

Silver Weight varies: 2.38-2.57g., 15 mm. **Ruler:** Carlo II **Obv:** Youthful armored bust to right in circle **Obv. Legend:** +CAROLVS. II. D. G(RA). **Rev:** Crowned displayed eagle, head to left, in circle, date at end of legend **Rev. Legend:** +REX. SICILI(AE). **Note:** Ref. V-367; Sp. 19-21. Varieties exist.

Date	Mintage	VG	F	VF	XF	Unc
1665 DG-V	—	50.00	110	325	550	—
1666 DG-V	—	50.00	110	325	550	—
1674 DI-BV	—	50.00	110	325	550	—

KM# 40 TARI

2.3300 g., Silver, 17 mm. **Ruler:** Carlo II **Obv:** Youthful armored bust to right in circle **Obv. Legend:** +CAROLVS. II. DEI. GRA. **Rev:** Crowned displayed eagle, head to left, in circle, date at end of legend **Rev. Legend:** +REX. SICILIAE. **Note:** Ref. V-470; Sp. 32.

Date	Mintage	VG	F	VF	XF	Unc
1678 RC	—	40.00	80.00	200	325	—

KM# 64 TARI

2.6000 g., Silver, 18 mm. **Ruler:** Carlo II **Obv:** Crowned bust to right **Obv. Legend:** CAROLVS. (-) II. D. G. **Rev:** Crowned displayed eagle, head to right, in circle, date at end of legend **Rev. Legend:** REX. SICILIAE. **Note:** Ref. V-493; Sp. 69-76. Varieties exist.

Date	Mintage	VG	F	VF	XF	Unc
1697 RC	—	40.00	80.00	200	325	—

KM# 9 2 TARI

Silver Weight varies: 4.75-5.22g., 23 mm. **Ruler:** Filippo III **Obv:** Crowned high-collared bust to right, 2 annulets below **Obv. Legend:** +PHILI(P)(P). (-) III. D(E). G(R). **Rev:** Crowned displayed eagle, head to left, date at end of legend **Rev. Legend:** +REX. SICILIAE. **Note:** Ref. V-347; Sp. 63-80. Varieties exist.

Date	Mintage	VG	F	VF	XF	Unc
1609 DC	—	25.00	55.00	160	225	—
1610 DC	—	25.00	55.00	160	225	—
1611 DC	—	25.00	55.00	160	225	—
1611 IP	—	25.00	55.00	160	225	—
1611 DFA	—	25.00	55.00	160	225	—
1612 DFA	—	25.00	55.00	160	225	—
1612 IP	—	25.00	55.00	160	225	—
1613 DFA	—	25.00	55.00	160	225	—
1614 IP	—	25.00	55.00	160	225	—
1615 IP	—	25.00	55.00	160	225	—
1616 IP	—	25.00	55.00	160	225	—
1617 IP	—	25.00	55.00	160	225	—
1618 IP	—	25.00	55.00	160	225	—
1619 IP	—	25.00	55.00	160	225	—
1620 IP	—	25.00	55.00	160	225	—

KM# 17 2 TARI

Silver Weight varies: 4.90-5.21g., 22 mm. **Ruler:** Filippo IV **Obv:** Crowned high-collared bust to right, 2 annulets below **Obv. Legend:** +PHILI(PP). - IIII. D. G. **Rev:** Crowned displayed eagle, head to left, date at end of legend **Rev. Legend:** +REX. SICILIAE. **Note:** Ref. V-357; Sp. 80-110.

Date	Mintage	VG	F	VF	XF	Unc
1620 IP	—	25.00	60.00	180	275	—
1621 IP	—	25.00	60.00	180	275	—
1622 IP	—	25.00	60.00	180	275	—
1623 IP	—	25.00	60.00	180	275	—
1624 IP	—	25.00	60.00	180	275	—
1625 IP	—	25.00	60.00	180	275	—
1626 IP	—	25.00	60.00	180	275	—
1627 IP	—	25.00	60.00	180	275	—
1628 IP	—	25.00	60.00	180	275	—
1636 IP	—	25.00	60.00	180	275	—
1637 IP	—	25.00	60.00	180	275	—
1638 IP	—	25.00	60.00	180	275	—
1640 IP-MP	—	25.00	60.00	180	275	—
1642 IP-MP	—	25.00	60.00	180	275	—
1644 DF-F	—	25.00	60.00	180	275	—
1645 IP-MP	—	25.00	60.00	180	275	—
1646 IP-MP	—	25.00	60.00	180	275	—
1647 IP-MP	—	25.00	60.00	180	275	—
1648 IP-MP	—	25.00	60.00	180	275	—
1649 IP-MP	—	25.00	60.00	180	275	—
1650 IP-MP	—	25.00	60.00	180	275	—
1651 IP-MP	—	25.00	60.00	180	275	—
1652 IL-V	—	25.00	60.00	180	275	—
1654 IL-V	—	25.00	60.00	180	275	—
1655 DG-V	—	25.00	60.00	180	275	—
1656 DG-V	—	25.00	60.00	180	275	—
1659 DG-V	—	25.00	60.00	180	275	—
1661 DG-V	—	25.00	60.00	180	275	—
1663 DG-V	—	25.00	60.00	180	275	—
1664 DG-V	—	25.00	60.00	180	275	—
1665 DG-V	—	25.00	60.00	180	275	—

KM# 32 2 TARI

Silver Weight varies: 5.03-5.10g., 24 mm. **Ruler:** Carlo II **Obv:** Youthful crowned bust to right **Obv. Legend:** +CAROLVS. - II. - DEI. G(RA). **Rev:** Crowned displayed eagle, head to left, in circle, date at end of legend **Rev. Legend:** (+) REX. SICILI(AE)(Æ). **Note:** Ref. V-366; Sp. 16-18. Varieties exist.

Date	Mintage	VG	F	VF	XF	Unc
1665 DG-V	—	70.00	140	475	750	—
1666 DG-V	—	70.00	140	475	750	—
1674 DI-BV	—	70.00	140	475	750	—

KM# 38 2 TARI

Silver, 23-24 mm. **Ruler:** Carlo II **Obv:** Youthful bust to left **Obv. Legend:** +CAROLVS. II. D. G. **Rev:** Crowned displayed eagle, head to left, in circle, date at end of legend **Rev. Legend:** +REX. SICILIAE. **Note:** Ref. V-483; Sp. 52.

Date	Mintage	VG	F	VF	XF	Unc
1677 RC Rare	—	—	—	—	—	—

KM# 41 2 TARI

5.1200 g., Silver, 22 mm. **Ruler:** Carlo II **Obv:** Youthful crowned bust to right **Obv. Legend:** +CAROLVS. II. DEI. GRATIA. **Rev:** Crowned displayed eagle, head to left, in circle, date at end of legend **Rev. Legend:** +REX. SICILIAE. **Note:** Ref. V-469; Sp. 31.

Date	Mintage	VG	F	VF	XF	Unc
1678 RC	—	75.00	140	525	825	—

KM# 50 2 TARI

5.2600 g., Silver, 24 mm. **Ruler:** Carlo II **Obv:** Crowned bust to left **Obv. Legend:** CAROLV - II. D. G. **Rev:** Crowned displayed eagle, head to left, in circle, date at end of legend **Rev. Legend:** +REX. SICILIAE. **Note:** Ref. V-484; Sp. 53.

Date	Mintage	VG	F	VF	XF	Unc
1686 RC	—	135	275	850	1,400	—

KM# 65 2 TARI

5.2400 g., Silver, 22 mm. **Ruler:** Carlo II **Obv:** Crowned bust to right **Obv. Legend:** CAROLVS. - II. D(EI). G. **Rev:** Crowned displayed eagle, head to right, in circle, date at end of legend **Rev. Legend:** REX. SICILIAE. **Note:** Ref. V-492; Sp. 67, 68.

Date	Mintage	VG	F	VF	XF	Unc
1697 RC	—	135	275	850	1,400	—

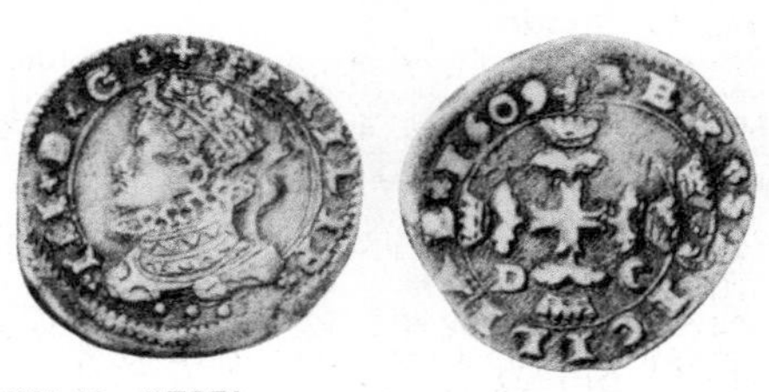

KM# 10 3 TARI

Silver Weight varies: 7.52-7.84g., 27 mm. **Ruler:** Filippo III **Obv:** Crowned and armored bust, with high collar, to left, 3 annulets below **Obv. Legend:** +PHIL(I)(P)(P) - III. D. G. **Rev:** Cross with flame and small crown at each end, date at end of legend **Rev. Legend:** +REX. SICILI(A)E. **Note:** Ref. V-346; Sp. 42-62. Varieties exist.

Date	Mintage	VG	F	VF	XF	Unc
1609 DC	—	35.00	70.00	185	275	—
1610 DC	—	35.00	70.00	185	275	—
1610 IP	—	35.00	70.00	185	275	—
1611 IP	—	35.00	70.00	185	275	—
1612 DFA	—	35.00	70.00	185	275	—
1613 DFA	—	35.00	70.00	185	275	—
1613 IP	—	35.00	70.00	185	275	—
1614 IP	—	35.00	70.00	185	275	—
1615 IP	—	35.00	70.00	185	275	—
1616 IP	—	35.00	70.00	185	275	—
1617 IP	—	35.00	70.00	185	275	—
1618 IP	—	35.00	70.00	185	275	—
1619 IP	—	35.00	70.00	185	275	—
1620 IP	—	35.00	70.00	185	275	—

KM# 18 3 TARI

Silver Weight varies: 7.55-7.80g., 25 mm. **Ruler:** Filippo IV **Obv:** Crowned and armored bust, with high collar, to left, 3 annulets below **Obv. Legend:** +PHIL(I)PP - IIII. D. G. **Rev:** Cross with flame and small crown at each end, date at end of legend **Rev. Legend:** +REX. SICILIAE. **Note:** Ref. V-356; Sp. 45-79.

Date	Mintage	VG	F	VF	XF	Unc
1620 IP	—	35.00	70.00	185	275	—
1622 IP	—	35.00	70.00	185	275	—
1623 IP	—	35.00	70.00	185	275	—
1624 IP	—	35.00	70.00	185	275	—
1625 IP	—	35.00	70.00	185	275	—
1626 IP	—	35.00	70.00	185	275	—
1627 IP	—	35.00	70.00	185	275	—
1628 IP	—	35.00	70.00	185	275	—
1631 IP	—	35.00	70.00	185	275	—
1632 IP	—	35.00	70.00	185	275	—
1636 IP	—	35.00	70.00	185	275	—
1638 IP	—	35.00	70.00	185	275	—
1640 IP-MP	—	35.00	70.00	185	275	—
1642 DF-F	—	35.00	70.00	185	275	—
1643 IP-MP	—	35.00	70.00	185	275	—
1644 DF-F	—	35.00	70.00	185	275	—
1644 IP-MP	—	35.00	70.00	185	275	—
1645 IP-MP	—	35.00	70.00	185	275	—
1646 IP-MP	—	35.00	70.00	185	275	—
1647 IP-MP	—	35.00	70.00	185	275	—
1648 IP-MP	—	35.00	70.00	185	275	—
1649 IP-MP	—	35.00	70.00	185	275	—
1650 IP-MP	—	35.00	70.00	185	275	—
1651 IP-PP	—	35.00	70.00	185	275	—
1652 IL-V	—	35.00	70.00	185	275	—
1653 IP-PP	—	35.00	70.00	185	275	—
1653 DP-DV	—	35.00	70.00	185	275	—
1654 IP-PP	—	35.00	70.00	185	275	—
1655 DG-V	—	35.00	70.00	185	275	—
1659 DG-V	—	35.00	70.00	185	275	—
1661 IP-P	—	35.00	70.00	185	275	—
1661 DG-V	—	35.00	70.00	185	275	—
1663 DG-V	—	35.00	70.00	185	275	—
1664 DG-V	—	35.00	70.00	185	275	—
1665 DG-V	—	35.00	70.00	185	275	—

KM# 33 3 TARI

Silver Weight varies: 7.69-7.82g., 27 mm. **Ruler:** Carlo II **Obv:** Youthful crowned bust to left **Obv. Legend:** +CAROLVS. II. - D(EI). GRA(TIA). **Rev:** Cross with flame and small crown at each end, date at end of legend **Rev. Legend:** +REX. SICILI(AE)(Æ). **Note:** Ref. V-365; Sp. 7-15. Varieties exist.

Date	Mintage	VG	F	VF	XF	Unc
1665 DG-V	—	100	200	700	1,000	—
1666 DG-V	—	100	200	700	1,000	—
1667 DI-BV	—	125	250	850	1,325	—
1670 DI-BV	—	125	250	850	1,325	—
1672 DI-BV	—	125	250	850	1,325	—
1674 DI-BV	—	100	200	700	1,000	—
1675 DI-BV	—	125	250	850	1,325	—

KM# 39 3 TARI

7.4300 g., Silver, 26 mm. **Ruler:** Carlo II **Obv:** Youthful bust to left in circle **Obv. Legend:** +CAROLVS. II. D. G. **Rev:** Cross with flame and small crown at each end, date at end of legend **Rev. Legend:** +REX. SICILIAE. **Note:** Ref. V-477; Sp. 45.

Date	Mintage	VG	F	VF	XF	Unc
1677 RC	—	210	415	1,500	2,100	—

KM# 42 3 TARI

7.8300 g., Silver, 26 mm. **Ruler:** Carlo II **Obv:** Youthful crowned bust to left **Obv. Legend:** +CAROLVS. II. DEI. GRATIA. **Rev:** Cross with flame and small crown at each end, date at end of legend **Rev. Legend:** +REX. SICILIAE. **Note:** Ref. V-468; Sp. 30.

Date	Mintage	VG	F	VF	XF	Unc
1678 RC	—	115	225	850	1,400	—

KM# 45 3 TARI

7.5400 g., Silver, 27 mm. **Ruler:** Carlo II **Obv:** Crowned and armored bust to right **Obv. Legend:** +CAROLVS. II. DEI. GRATIA. **Rev:** Cross with flame and small crown at each end, date at end of legend **Rev. Legend:** +REX. SICILIAE. **Note:** Ref. V-478; Sp. 46.

Date	Mintage	VG	F	VF	XF	Unc
1683 RC	—	210	415	1,500	2,100	—

KM# 51 3 TARI

7.5500 g., Silver, 27 mm. **Ruler:** Carlo II **Obv:** Crowned and armored bust to left **Obv. Legend:** +CAROLVS. II. DEI. GRATIA. **Rev:** Cross with flame and small crown at each end, date at end of legend **Rev. Legend:** +REX. SICILIAE. **Note:** Ref. V-479; Sp. 47, 48.

Date	Mintage	VG	F	VF	XF	Unc
1686 RC	—	125	250	875	1,400	—

KM# 52 3 TARI

7.8500 g., Silver, 27 mm. **Ruler:** Carlo II **Obv:** Small crowned and armored bust to left **Obv. Legend:** +CAROLVS. II. DEI. GRATIA. **Rev:** Cross with flame and small crown at each end, date at end of legend **Rev. Legend:** +REX. SICILIAE. **Note:** Ref. V-480; Sp. 49.

Date	Mintage	VG	F	VF	XF	Unc
1686 RC	—	125	250	875	1,400	—

KM# 58 3 TARI

7.5500 g., Silver, 27 mm. **Ruler:** Carlo II **Obv:** Large crowned bust to right **Obv. Legend:** CAROLVS. II. DEI. GRATIA. **Rev:** Cross with flame and small crown at each end, date at end of legend **Rev. Legend:** +REX. SICILIAE. **Note:** Ref. V-481; Sp. 50.

Date	Mintage	VG	F	VF	XF	Unc
1693 RC	—	220	425	1,600	2,200	—

KM# 59 3 TARI

7.5000 g., Silver, 27 mm. **Ruler:** Carlo II **Obv:** Small crowned bust to right **Obv. Legend:** CAROLVS. II. DEI. GRATIA. **Rev:** Cross with flame and small crown at each end, date at end of legend **Rev. Legend:** +REX. SICILIAE. **Note:** Ref. V-482; Sp. 51.

Date	Mintage	VG	F	VF	XF	Unc
1693 RC	—	220	425	1,600	2,200	—

KM# 66 3 TARI

7.9000 g., Silver, 27 mm. **Ruler:** Carlo II **Obv:** Crowned bust to left **Obv. Legend:** CAROLVS - II. D. G. **Rev:** Cross with flame and small crown at each end, date at end of legend **Rev. Legend:** REX. SICILIÆ. **Note:** Ref. V-491; Sp. 66.

Date	Mintage	VG	F	VF	XF	Unc
1697 RC	—	210	415	1,500	2,100	—

KM# 11 4 TARI

Silver Weight varies: 10.30-10.54g., 30 mm. **Ruler:** Filippo III **Obv:** Armored high-collared bust to right, 4 annulets below **Obv. Legend:** +PHILIP(P) - III. D. G. **Rev:** Crowned displayed eagle, head to left, in circle, date at end of legend **Rev. Legend:** (+)REX. SICILIAE. **Note:** Ref. V-345; Sp. 20-41. Varieties exist.

Date	Mintage	VG	F	VF	XF	Unc
1609 DC	—	40.00	85.00	185	275	—
1610 DC	—	40.00	85.00	185	275	—
1610 IP	—	40.00	85.00	185	275	—
1611 DC	—	40.00	85.00	185	275	—
1611 IP	—	40.00	85.00	185	275	—
1612 IP	—	40.00	85.00	185	275	—
1612 DFA	—	40.00	85.00	185	275	—
1613 DFA	—	40.00	85.00	185	275	—
1613 IP	—	40.00	85.00	185	275	—
1614 IP	—	40.00	85.00	185	275	—
1615 IP	—	40.00	85.00	185	275	—
1616 IP	—	40.00	85.00	185	275	—
1617 IP	—	40.00	85.00	185	275	—
1618 IP	—	40.00	85.00	185	275	—
1619 IP	—	40.00	85.00	185	275	—
1620 IP	—	40.00	85.00	185	275	—

KM# 21 4 TARI

Silver Weight varies: 10.20-10.55g., 31 mm. **Ruler:** Filippo IV **Obv:** Armored high-collared bust to right, 4 annulets below **Obv. Legend:** +PHILIPP - IIII. D. G. **Rev:** Crowned displayed eagle, head to left, in circle, date at end of legend **Rev. Legend:** (+)REX. SICILIAE. **Note:** Ref. V-355; Sp. 1-43.

Date	Mintage	VG	F	VF	XF	Unc
1621 IP	—	50.00	100	225	400	—
1622 IP	—	50.00	100	225	400	—
1623 IP	—	50.00	100	225	400	—
1624 IP	—	50.00	100	225	400	—
1625 IP	—	50.00	100	225	400	—
1626 IP	—	50.00	100	225	400	—
1627 IP	—	50.00	100	225	400	—
1628 IP	—	50.00	100	225	400	—
1632 IP	—	50.00	100	225	400	—
1636 IP	—	50.00	100	225	400	—
1638 IP	—	50.00	100	225	400	—
1642 DF-F	—	50.00	100	225	400	—
1642 IP-MP	—	50.00	100	225	400	—
1643 IP-MP	—	50.00	100	225	400	—
1644 DF-F	—	50.00	100	225	400	—
1644 IP-MP	—	50.00	100	225	400	—
1645 IP-MP	—	50.00	100	225	400	—
1646 IP-MP	—	50.00	100	225	400	—
1647 IP-MP	—	50.00	100	225	400	—
1647 IP-MI/MP	—	50.00	100	225	400	—
1648 IP-MP	—	50.00	100	225	400	—
1649 IP-MP	—	50.00	100	225	400	—
1649 IP-P	—	50.00	100	225	400	—
1650 IP-MP	—	50.00	100	225	400	—
1650 IP-PP	—	50.00	100	225	400	—
1650 IP	—	50.00	100	225	400	—
1651 IP-PP	—	50.00	100	225	400	—
1652 IL-V	—	50.00	100	225	400	—
1653 IP-PP	—	50.00	100	225	400	—
1653 DP-PI	—	50.00	100	225	400	—
1654 IP-PP	—	50.00	100	225	400	—
1655 DG-IV	—	50.00	100	225	400	—
1656 DG-IV	—	50.00	100	225	400	—
1659 DG-IV	—	50.00	100	225	400	—
1661 DG-V	—	50.00	100	225	400	—
1662 DG-V	—	50.00	100	225	400	—
1663 DG-V	—	50.00	100	225	400	—
1664 DG-V	—	50.00	100	225	400	—
1665 DG-V	—	50.00	100	225	400	—

KM# 28 4 TARI

10.3000 g., Silver, 30 mm. **Ruler:** Filippo IV **Obv:** Armored high-collared bust to right, 4 annulets below **Obv. Legend:** PHILIPPVS. IIII. D. G. REX. **Rev:** Crowned displayed eagle, head to left, in circle, date at end of legend **Rev. Legend:** SICILIAE. ET HIERVSAL. **Note:** Ref. V-466; Sp. 44.

Date	Mintage	VG	F	VF	XF	Unc
1635 OG Rare	—	—	—	—	—	—

KM# 34 4 TARI

Silver Weight varies: 9.20-10.48g., 30 mm. **Ruler:** Carlo II **Obv:** Youthful armored bust to right in circle **Obv. Legend:** +CAROLVS. II. D(EI). GRATIA. **Rev:** Crowned displayed eagle, head to left, in circle, date at end of legend **Rev. Legend:** +REX. SICILI(AE)(Æ). **Note:** Ref. V-364; Sp. 1-6. Varieties exist.

Date	Mintage	VG	F	VF	XF	Unc
1665 DG-V	—	75.00	140	475	750	—
1666 DG-V	—	75.00	140	475	750	—
1667 DI-BV	—	100	200	675	1,000	—
1672 DI-BV	—	100	200	675	1,000	—
1674 DI-BV	—	75.00	140	475	750	—

KM# 43 4 TARI

10.3800 g., Silver, 28 mm. **Ruler:** Carlo II **Obv:** Youthful armored bust to right in circle **Obv. Legend:** +CAROLVS. II. DEI. GRATI(A). **Rev:** Crowned displayed eagle, head to left, in circle, date at end of legend **Rev. Legend:** (+)REX. SICILIAE. **Note:** Ref. V-467; Sp. 26-29.

Date	Mintage	VG	F	VF	XF	Unc
1678 RC	—	80.00	165	625	1,000	—
1679 RC	—	80.00	165	625	1,000	—

KM# 46 4 TARI

Silver Weight varies: 10.38-10.40g., 29 mm. **Ruler:** Carlo II **Obv:** Crowned and armored bust to right **Obv. Legend:** CAROLVS. (-) II. DEI. GRATIA. **Rev:** Crowned displayed eagle, head to left, in circle, date at end of legend **Rev. Legend:** +REX. SICILI(AE)(Æ). **Note:** Ref. V-471; Sp. 33-35. Varieties exist.

Date	Mintage	VG	F	VF	XF	Unc
1683 RC	—	150	325	1,200	1,900	—

KM# 53 4 TARI

10.3700 g., Silver, 31 mm. **Ruler:** Carlo II **Obv:** Large crowned high-collared bust to right **Obv. Legend:** +CAROLVS. II. DEI. GRATIA. **Rev:** Crowned displayed eagle, head to left, in circle, date at end of legend **Rev. Legend:** +REX. SICILIAE. **Note:** Ref. V-470; Sp. 36-38.

Date	Mintage	VG	F	VF	XF	Unc
1686 RC	—	150	325	1,200	1,900	—

KM# 54 4 TARI

10.4300 g., Silver, 31 mm. **Ruler:** Carlo II **Obv:** Small crowned bust to right in circle **Obv. Legend:** +CAROLVS. II. DEI. GRATIA. **Rev:** Crowned displayed eagle, head to left, in circle, date at end of legend **Rev. Legend:** +REX. SICILIAE. **Note:** Ref. V-473; Sp. 39.

Date	Mintage	VG	F	VF	XF	Unc
1686 RC	—	300	550	1,800	2,650	—

KM# 55 4 TARI

10.3400 g., Silver, 30 mm. **Ruler:** Carlo II **Obv:** Medium-sized crowned bust divides legend at top **Obv. Legend:** CAROLVS - II. D. G. **Rev:** Crowned displayed eagle, head to left, in circle, date at end of legend **Rev. Legend:** +REX. SICILIAE. **Note:** Ref. V-474; Sp. 40, 41.

Date	Mintage	VG	F	VF	XF	Unc
1686 RC	—	150	325	1,200	1,900	—

KM# 60 4 TARI

Silver Weight varies: 9.96-10.53g., 30 mm. **Ruler:** Carlo II **Obv:** Small crowned and armored bust to right in circle **Obv. Legend:** CAROLVS. II. DEI. GRATIA. **Rev:** Crowned displayed eagle, head to left, in circle, date at end of legend **Rev. Legend:** REX. SICILIAE. **Note:** Ref. V-475; Sp. 42.

Date	Mintage	VG	F	VF	XF	Unc
1693 RC	—	150	325	1,200	1,900	—

KM# 61 4 TARI

Silver Weight varies: 9.96-10.53g., 30 mm. **Ruler:** Carlo II **Obv:** Large crowned and armored bust to right breaks legend at top **Obv. Legend:** CAROLVS. II. DEI. GRATIA. **Rev:** Crowned displayed eagle, head to left, in circle, date at end of legend **Rev. Legend:** REX. SICILIAE. **Note:** Ref. V-476; Sp. 43, 44.

Date	Mintage	VG	F	VF	XF	Unc
1693 RC	—	150	325	1,200	1,900	—

KM# 67 4 TARI

10.4600 g., Silver, 28 mm. **Ruler:** Carlo II **Obv:** Large crowned and armored bust to right **Obv. Legend:** +CAROLVS - II. D. G. **Rev:** Crowned displayed eagle, head to right, in circle, date at end of legend **Rev. Legend:** REX. SICILIÆ. **Note:** Ref. V-490; Sp. 64, 65.

Date	Mintage	VG	F	VF	XF	Unc
1697 RC	—	300	550	1,800	2,650	—

KM# 14 1/2 SCUDO

Silver Weight varies: 14.66-15.76g., 33-35 mm. **Ruler:** Filippo III **Obv:** Armored high-collared bust to left **Obv. Legend:** +PHILIPPVS. III. (-) DEI. (-) GRATIA. **Rev:** Cross with flame and small crown at each end, date at end of legend **Rev. Legend:** +SICILIAE. ET. HIERVSA. REX. **Note:** Ref. V-344; Sp. 9-18. Varieties exist.

Date	Mintage	VG	F	VF	XF	Unc
1610 DC	—	70.00	150	400	750	—
1611 DC	—	70.00	150	400	750	—
1611 IP	—	70.00	150	400	750	—
1612 IP	—	80.00	165	625	1,150	—
1612 DFA	—	110	225	800	1,450	—

KM# 15 SCUDO

Silver Weight varies: 31.47-31.60g., 39-42 mm. **Ruler:** Carlo II **Obv:** Armored high-collared bust to right in circle **Obv. Legend:** +PHILIPPVS. (-) III. DEI. GRATIA. **Rev:** Crowned rhomboid shield of 4-fold arms in circle, date at end of legend **Rev. Legend:** SICILIAE. ET. HIS. REX. **Note:** Ref. V-343; Sp. 1-8; Dav. 4041. Varieties exist.

Date	Mintage	VG	F	VF	XF	Unc
1610 DC	—	150	300	750	1,500	—
1611 DC	—	150	300	750	1,500	—
1611 IP	—	150	300	750	1,500	—
1611 Rare	—	—	—	—	—	—
1612 IP	—	175	350	900	1,850	—
1612 DFA	—	200	400	1,000	2,000	—

TRADE COINAGE

KM# 68 SCUDO D'ORO

3.4500 g., Gold, 21.5 mm. **Ruler:** Carlo II **Obv:** Crowned displayed eagle with large shield of arms on breast **Obv. Legend:** CA - ROLVS. II. D. G. HISP. ET SIC. (-) REX. **Rev:** Small armored bust to right in baroque frame, large crown with 7 palm fronds above, REVI - VISCIT on ribbon band at left and right, ANNO at lower left, date at lower right, no legend **Note:** Ref. V-489; Sp. 61-63; Fr. 881. Scudo Riccio or Trionfo.

Date	Mintage	VG	F	VF	XF	Unc
1697 RC	—	850	2,100	4,900	10,500	—

PATTERNS

Including off metal strikes

KM#	Date	Mintage	Identification	Mkt Val
Pn1	1608 DC	—	4 Tari. Copper. 31 mm. KM#11.	—

SOLFERINO

A commune in the province of Mantua.

RULER

Carlo Gonzaga, 1640-1678

COMMUNE

STANDARD COINAGE

KM# 5 SESINO

0.4500 g., Billon **Obv:** Head right **Rev:** MVNI/ SESIN

Date	Mintage	VG	F	VF	XF	Unc
ND	—	65.00	120	200	400	—

KM# 6 MURAILO

1.3600 g., Billon **Obv:** Bust of Pontiff right **Rev:** St. Nicholas

Date	Mintage	VG	F	VF	XF	Unc
ND	—	70.00	125	220	425	—

KM# 7 QUATTRINO

Copper **Obv:** Armored bust right **Rev:** Ornate cross **Note:** Weight varies: 0.70-1.71 grams.

Date	Mintage	VG	F	VF	XF	Unc
ND	—	50.00	90.00	165	325	—

KM# 8 QUATTRINO

Copper **Obv:** Bust right **Rev:** Eagle **Note:** Weight varies: 0.70-1.71 grams.

Date	Mintage	VG	F	VF	XF	Unc
ND	—	30.00	70.00	140	275	—

KM# 9 QUATTRINO

Copper **Obv:** Crowned arms **Rev:** Head of saint right **Note:** Weight varies: 0.70-1.71 grams.

Date	Mintage	VG	F	VF	XF	Unc
ND	—	50.00	90.00	165	325	—

KM# 21 QUATTRINO

Copper **Obv:** MARCH/ SVL FARINI/ 1643 **Rev:** Rampant lion **Note:** Weight varies: 0.70-1.71 grams.

Date	Mintage	VG	F	VF	XF	Unc
1643	—	35.00	75.00	150	300	—

KM# 10 SOLDO

Billon **Obv:** Bust right **Rev:** Cross with sun in center **Note:** Weight varies: 1.60-1.80 grams.

Date	Mintage	VG	F	VF	XF	Unc
ND	—	40.00	80.00	150	300	—

KM# 11 SOLDO

Billon **Rev:** Radiant sun **Note:** Weight varies: 1.60-1.80 grams.

Date	Mintage	VG	F	VF	XF	Unc
ND	—	45.00	95.00	175	335	—

KM# 12 SOLDO
Billon **Rev:** Sun with long rays **Note:** Weight varies: 1.60-1.80 grams.

Date	Mintage	VG	F	VF	XF	Unc
ND	—	45.00	95.00	175	335	—

KM# 13 SOLDO
Billon **Obv:** Crowned arms **Rev:** Soldier standing **Note:** Weight varies: 1.60-1.80 grams.

Date	Mintage	VG	F	VF	XF	Unc
ND	—	40.00	80.00	150	300	—

KM# 14 SOLDO
Billon **Obv:** Head left **Rev:** Sun with rays **Note:** Weight varies: 1.60-1.80 grams.

Date	Mintage	VG	F	VF	XF	Unc
ND	—	50.00	100	175	335	—

KM# 15 SOLDO
Billon **Obv:** Crowned arms **Rev:** Tabernacle **Note:** Weight varies: 1.60-1.80 grams.

Date	Mintage	VG	F	VF	XF	Unc
ND	—	40.00	90.00	165	325	—

KM# 16 GUIGINO
Billon **Obv:** Bust right **Rev:** Saint kneeling in prayer **Note:** Weight varies: 1.54-2.45 grams.

Date	Mintage	VG	F	VF	XF	Unc
ND	—	40.00	90.00	185	350	—

KM# 20 SCUDO
31.3400 g., Silver **Obv:** Bust left **Rev:** St. Aloisius kneeling **Note:** Dav. #4174.

Date	Mintage	VG	F	VF	XF	Unc
1640 Rare	—	—	—	—	—	—

KM# 17 2 FLORIN D'ORO
7.0000 g., 0.9860 Gold 0.2219 oz. AGW **Obv:** Bust of Carlo left **Rev:** Crowned arms

Date	Mintage	VG	F	VF	XF	Unc
ND Rare	—	—	—	—	—	—

KM# 18 DUCAT
3.5000 g., 0.9860 Gold 0.1109 oz. AGW **Obv:** Carlo standing right in inner circle **Rev:** Crowned arms in Order collar in inner circle

Date	Mintage	VG	F	VF	XF	Unc
ND Rare	—	—	—	—	—	—

TASSAROLO

Countship

Tassarolo is a town of ancient origin which was already a possession of the marchese of Gavi by 1192 and, afterwards, of the Republic of Genoa. It was transferred to Alessandria in 1227, but later subjected to Genoa again and became a possession of the Spinola family in 1454. Tassarolo was erected into a countship by Emperor Ferdinand I in 1560 for the Spinolas' benefit, and received the mint right at that time. The production of coinage in Tassarolo ended in 1688.

RULERS
Augostino Spinola, 1604-1616
Filippo Spinola, 1616-1688
Livia Centurioni Oltremarini, wife of Filippo

Reference: Alberto Varesi, ***Monete Italiane Regionali: Piemonte, Sardegna, Liguria, Isola di Corsica.*** Pavia, 1996.

COUNTSHIP

STANDARD COINAGE

KM# 22 PARAGLIOLA
Billon, 22-23 mm. **Ruler:** Agostino **Obv:** Crowned displayed eagle in circle **Obv. Legend:** AVG. SPI. COM. TASS. **Rev:** St. Francis kneeling and receiving the stigmata, date in exergue **Rev. Legend:** SPES. FIRMA. **Note:** Varesi 973.

Date	Mintage	VG	F	VF	XF	Unc
1614	—	150	325	700	1,000	—

KM# 48.1 LUIGINO
Silver Weight varies: 1.41-2.16g., 20-21 mm. **Ruler:** Livia **Obv:** Bust to right **Obv. Legend:** MAR. LIV. COM. PALAT. SOW. DOM. **Rev:** Crowned shield of arms divides date, '7' at bottom **Rev. Legend:** DNS. ILLVMINAT. ET. SALVS. MEA. **Note:** Varesi 994.

Date	Mintage	VG	F	VF	XF	Unc
1658	—	60.00	100	165	250	—

KM# 48.2 LUIGINO
Silver Weight varies: 1.41-2.16g., 20-21 mm. **Ruler:** Livia **Obv:** Bust to right **Obv. Legend:** MAR. LLIV. COM. PALAT. SOW. DOM. **Rev:** Crowned shield of arms divides date, '5' at bottom **Rev. Legend:** DNS. ILLVMINAT. ET. SALVS. MEA. **Note:** Varesi 994/1.

Date	Mintage	VG	F	VF	XF	Unc
1658	—	60.00	100	165	250	—

KM# 50 LUIGINO
Silver Weight varies: 1.97-2.22g., 20 mm. **Ruler:** Filippo **Obv:** Bust to right **Obv. Legend:** PHILIPPVS. D.G. COMES. TASS. **Rev:** Crowned shield of arms, date at end of legend **Rev. Legend:** CIRCVMDEDISTI - ME. LÆTITIA. **Note:** Varesi 992/1-5.

Date	Mintage	VG	F	VF	XF	Unc
1660	—	225	385	875	1,500	—
1662	—	225	385	875	1,500	—
1663	—	225	385	875	1,500	—
1665	—	225	385	875	1,500	—
1666	—	225	385	875	1,500	—

KM# 51 LUIGINO
Silver Weight varies: 1.95-2.06g., 19-20 mm. **Ruler:** Filippo **Obv:** Bust to right **Obv. Legend:** PHILIPPVS. D.G. TASS. COMES. **Rev:** Crowned shield of arms, date above **Rev. Legend:** IN. TE. DOMINE. SPERAVI. **Note:** Varesi 993.

Date	Mintage	VG	F	VF	XF	Unc
1665	—	100	200	450	650	—

KM# 52.1 LUIGINO
Silver Weight varies: 2.06-2.13g., 21-22 mm. **Ruler:** Livia **Obv:** Bust to right **Obv. Legend:** LIV. MA. PRI. SP. COM. T. SOW. DOM. **Rev:** Crowned shield of arms divides date, 'ToA' at bottom **Rev. Legend:** DNS. ADIVTOR. ET. REDEM. MEVS. **Note:** Varesi 995.

Date	Mintage	VG	F	VF	XF	Unc
1666	—	25.00	55.00	100	175	—

KM# 52.2 LUIGINO
Silver Weight varies: 2.06-2.13g., 21-22 mm. **Ruler:** Livia **Obv:** Bust to right **Obv. Legend:** MAR. LIV. COM. PALAT. SOW. DOM. **Rev:** Crowned shield of arms divides date, 'ToA' at bottom **Rev. Legend:** DNS. ADIVTOR. ET. REDEM. MEVS. **Note:** Varesi 995/1.

Date	Mintage	VG	F	VF	XF	Unc
1666	—	45.00	80.00	135	200	—

KM# 52.3 LUIGINO
1.9800 g., Silver, 21 mm. **Ruler:** Livia **Obv:** Bust to right **Obv. Legend:** AN. MAIOV. PRINC. SOW. DE. DOM. **Rev:** Crowned shield of arms divides date, 'T' at bottom **Rev. Legend:** DNS. ADIVTOR. ET. REDEM. MEVS. **Note:** Varesi 996.

Date	Mintage	VG	F	VF	XF	Unc
1667	—	45.00	80.00	120	185	—

KM# A13 7 SOLDI
2.2500 g., Billon, 22 mm. **Ruler:** Agostino **Obv:** Bust to right, date below **Obv. Legend:** AVGVST. SPIN. COMES. TASS. **Rev:** Crowned imperial eagle, shield of Austrian arms on breast **Rev. Legend:** MONETA. DA. SOLDI. SETTE. **Note:** Varesi 972.

Date	Mintage	VG	F	VF	XF	Unc
1605 Rare	—	—	—	—	—	—

KM# 24 1/8 SCUDO
Silver Weight varies: 3.06-3.40g., 24 mm. **Ruler:** Agostino **Obv:** Half-length armored figure to right **Obv. Legend:** AVGVSTINVS. SPIN. COMES. TASS. **Rev:** Crowned imperial eagle, shield of Austrian arms on breast **Rev. Legend:** VIRTVTE. CAESAREA. DVCE. **Note:** Varesi 970.

Date	Mintage	VG	F	VF	XF	Unc
ND(1604-16)	—	120	250	600	1,500	—

KM# 25 1/8 SCUDO
3.2000 g., Silver, 24 mm. **Ruler:** Agostino **Obv:** Cross in circle **Obv. Legend:** AVGVSTINVS. SPINOLA. **Rev:** Crowned shield of arms **Rev. Legend:** COMES. TASSAROLI. **Note:** Varesi 971.

Date	Mintage	VG	F	VF	XF	Unc
ND(1604-16) Rare	—	—	—	—	—	—

KM# 53 1/8 SCUDO
2.4000 g., Silver, 21 mm. **Ruler:** Filippo **Obv:** Bust to right **Obv. Legend:** PHILIP. SPINV. TASS. COMES. **Rev:** Crowned imperial eagle, shield of arms on breast, date divided at top **Rev. Legend:** DEVS. MEVS. IN. TE. CONFIDO. **Note:** Varesi 990.

Date	Mintage	VG	F	VF	XF	Unc
1667	—	500	825	1,700	2,750	—

KM# 54 1/8 SCUDO
1.9800 g., Silver, 21 mm. **Ruler:** Filippo **Obv:** Bust to right **Obv. Legend:** PHILIP. D.G. COMES. PALAT. **Rev:** Crowned imperial eagle, shield of arms on breast, date divided at top. **Rev. Legend:** VIRT. DVCE. CES. FORTVN. **Note:** Varesi 991.

Date	Mintage	VG	F	VF	XF	Unc
1667	—	500	825	1,700	2,750	—

KM# 14 1/4 SCUDO
7.9600 g., Silver, 30-31 mm. **Ruler:** Agostino **Obv:** Armored bust to right, date below shoulder **Obv. Legend:** AVGVS. SPIN. COM. PALATIN. **Rev:** Crowned ornate shield of 4-fold arms with central shield **Rev. Legend:** NOSTRÆ. SPES - VNA. SALVTIS. **Note:** Varesi 968.

Date	Mintage	VG	F	VF	XF	Unc
1606 Rare	—	—	—	—	—	—

KM# 17 1/4 SCUDO
Silver Weight varies: 6.28-7.25g., 27-28 mm. **Ruler:** Agostino **Obv:** Half-length armored figure to right, date below, where present **Obv. Legend:** AVGVSTI(NVS). SPIN. COMES. TASS. **Rev:** Crowned imperial eagle, oval shield of Austrian arms on breast **Rev. Legend:** VIRTVTE. CAESAREA. DVCE. **Note:** Varesi 969.

Date	Mintage	VG	F	VF	XF	Unc
1607	—	125	250	650	1,100	—
ND(1607-10)	—	125	250	650	1,100	—

KM# 31 1/4 SCUDO
7.8100 g., Silver, 29-30 mm. **Ruler:** Filippo **Obv:** Armored bust to right **Obv. Legend:** PHILIPPVS. SPINVLA. **Rev:** Crowned shield of arms in baroque frame, date at end of legend **Rev. Legend:** COMES. TASSAROLI. **Note:** Varesi 988.

Date	Mintage	VG	F	VF	XF	Unc
1629	—	650	1,000	2,150	3,350	—

KM# A51 1/4 SCUDO
Silver, 30 mm. **Ruler:** Filippo **Obv:** Large armored bust to right **Obv. Legend:** PHIL. SPIN. COM. TASS. **Rev:** Imperial eagle withi shield of arms on breast, large crown above, date at end of legend **Rev. Legend:** IN. TE. DOMINE. SPERAVI. **Note:** Varesi 989.

Date	Mintage	VG	F	VF	XF	Unc
1663 Rare	—	—	—	—	—	—

KM# 8 1/2 SCUDO
14.6200 g., Silver, 35-36 mm. **Ruler:** Agostino **Obv:** Armored bust to right, date below shoulder **Obv. Legend:** AVGVSTINVS. SPINVLA. **Rev:** Shield of family arms in baroque frame, large crown above **Rev. Legend:** COMES - TASSAROLI. **Note:** Varesi 967.

Date	Mintage	VG	F	VF	XF	Unc
1604 Rare	—	—	—	—	—	—

KM# 39 1/2 SCUDO
15.7100 g., Silver, 35-36 mm. **Ruler:** Filippo **Obv:** Armored bust to right **Obv. Legend:** PHILIPPVS. SPIN. COM. TASS. **Rev:** St. George on horseback to right slaying dragon below, date in exergue **Rev. Legend:** SPES. NON. CONFVNDIT. **Note:** Varesi 987.

Date	Mintage	VG	F	VF	XF	Unc
1639	—	750	1,100	2,850	4,500	—

KM# 9 SCUDO
Silver Weight varies: 27.30-31.84g., 42 mm. **Ruler:** Agostino **Obv:** Armored bust to right, date below shoulder **Obv. Legend:** AVGVSTINVS. SPINVLA. **Rev:** Crowned shield of family arms in baroque frame **Rev. Legend:** COMES. TAS - SAROLI. **Note:** Varesi 963; Dav. 4175.

Date	Mintage	VG	F	VF	XF	Unc
1604	—	2,200	4,500	8,500	—	—

KM# 10.1 SCUDO

Silver Weight varies: 25.96-27.15g., 39-40 mm. **Ruler:** Agostino **Obv:** Armored bust to right, date below shoulder **Obv. Legend:** AVGVST. SPINVLA. COMES. TASSAR. **Rev:** Crowned shield of manifold arms, Order of Golden Fleece around **Rev. Legend:** NIL. NISI. AVGVST. AVSPICE. AVGVSTO. **Note:** Varesi 964; Dav. 4176.

Date	Mintage	VG	F	VF	XF	Unc
1604	—	1,300	2,500	4,950	8,300	—

KM# 10.2 SCUDO

Silver Weight varies: 25.96-27.15g., 39-40 mm. **Ruler:** Agostino **Obv:** Armored bust to right, date below shoulder **Obv. Legend:** AVGVSTINVS. SPINVLA. COMES. TASSAROL. **Rev:** Crowned shield of manifold arms, Order of Golden Fleece around **Rev. Legend:** NIL. NISI. AVGVST. AVSPICE. AVGVSTO. **Note:** Dav. 4176A.

Date	Mintage	VG	F	VF	XF	Unc
1604	—	1,300	2,500	4,950	8,300	—

KM# 15 SCUDO

Silver, 39 mm. **Ruler:** Agostino **Obv:** Armored bust to right, date below shoulder **Obv. Legend:** AVGVS. SPIN. COM. PALATINVS. **Rev:** Large crown above shield of 4-fold arms with central shield in baroque frame **Rev. Legend:** NOSTRÆ. SPES. - VNA. SALVTIS. **Note:** Varesi 965; Dav. 4177.

Date	Mintage	VG	F	VF	XF	Unc
1606 Rare	—	—	—	—	—	—

KM# 16.1 SCUDO

Silver Weight varies: 21.00-28.42g., 40-41 mm. **Ruler:** Agostino **Obv:** Half-length armored figure to right **Obv. Legend:** AVGVSTINVS. SPINV. COMES. TASS. **Rev:** Crowned imperial eagle, shield of Austrian arms on breast, "C.XV." below in margin **Rev. Legend:** SVB. TVVM. - PRESIDIVM. **Note:** Varesi 966; Dav. 4178.

Date	Mintage	VG	F	VF	XF	Unc
ND(1606-16)	—	500	1,000	2,500	5,000	—

KM# 16.2 SCUDO

Silver Weight varies: 21.00-28.42g., 40-41 mm. **Ruler:** Agostino **Obv:** Half-length armored figure to right **Obv. Legend:** AVGVSTINVS. SPINV. COMES. TASS. **Rev:** Crowned imperial eagle, shield of Spinola family arms on breast, "C.XV." below margin **Rev. Legend:** SVB. TVVM. - PRESIDIVM. **Note:** Varesi 966/1.

Date	Mintage	VG	F	VF	XF	Unc
ND(1606-16)	—	500	1,000	2,500	5,000	—

KM# 30 SCUDO

Silver Weight varies: 31.05-31.57g., 42-43 mm. **Ruler:** Filippo **Obv:** Armored bust to right **Obv. Legend:** PHILIPPVS. SPINVLA. **Rev:** Crowned shield of family arms in baroque frame, date at end of legend **Rev. Legend:** COMES. TASSAROLI. **Note:** Dav. #4179; Varesi 983; Dav. 4179. Varieties exist.

Date	Mintage	VG	F	VF	XF	Unc
1620 Rare	—	—	—	—	—	—
1622 Rare	—	—	—	—	—	—
1629 Rare	—	—	—	—	—	—

KM# 40 SCUDO

Silver Weight varies: 28.55-31.80g., 42-43 mm. **Ruler:** Filippo **Obv:** Armored bust to right **Obv. Legend:** PHILIPPVS. SPIN. COMES. TASS. **Rev:** St. George on horseback to right, slaying dragon below, date in exergue **Rev. Legend:** SPES. NON. - CONFVNDIT. **Note:** Varesi 984; Dav. 4180.

Date	Mintage	VG	F	VF	XF	Unc
1639	—	500	1,000	2,500	5,000	—
1640	—	500	1,000	2,500	5,000	—
1642	—	500	1,000	2,500	5,000	—

KM# 47 SCUDO

Silver Weight varies: 29.97-31.59g., 43-44 mm. **Ruler:** Agostino **Obv:** Armored bust to right **Obv. Legend:** PHILIP. SPINVLA. COM. TASSARO. **Rev:** Large crown above shield with crowned imperial eagle, shield of arms on breast, date at end of legend **Rev. Legend:** IN. TE. DOMINE. SPERAVI. **Note:** Varesi 985/1; Dav. 4181.

Date	Mintage	VG	F	VF	XF	Unc
1643 Rare	—	—	—	—	—	—

KM# 55 SCUDO

Silver Weight varies: 29.97-31.59g., 43-44 mm. **Ruler:** Filippo **Obv:** Armored bust to right **Obv. Legend:** PHILIP. SPINVLA. COM. TASSA. **Rev:** Large crown above shield in baroque frame crowned imperial eagle, shield of arms on breast, date at end of legend **Rev. Legend:** IN. TE. DOMINE. SPERAVI. **Note:** Varesi 985/2; Dav. 4182.

Date	Mintage	VG	F	VF	XF	Unc
1663 Rare	—	—	—	—	—	—

KM# 26 TALLERO (96 Soldi)

26.3500 g., Billon, 40-42 mm. **Ruler:** Filippo **Obv:** Half-length armored figure behind shield of lion arms below **Obv. Legend:** MON. DA. SOL. 96 - COM. PALAT. **Rev:** Rampant lion to left in circle **Rev. Legend:** CONFI. IN. DOM. NON. PERIB. IN. ETER. **Note:** Varesi 986; Dav. 4183. Prev. KM #5. Imitation of United Netherlands Daalder.

Date	Mintage	VG	F	VF	XF	Unc
ND(1616-88)	—	900	1,750	3,000	—	—

KM# 27 TALLERO (96 Soldi)

26.3500 g., Billon, 40-42 mm. **Ruler:** Filippo **Obv:** Half-length armored figure behind shield of lion arms below **Obv. Legend:** MO. ARG. PRO. CON - FOE. BELG. HOL. **Rev:** Rampant lion to left in circle **Rev. Legend:** CONFI. IN. DOM. NON, PERIB. IN. ETER. **Note:** Dav. 4183A. Prev. KM #6. Imitation of United Netherlands Daalder.

Date	Mintage	VG	F	VF	XF	Unc
ND(1616-88)	—	1,000	2,000	3,500	—	—

TRADE COINAGE

KM# 5 DUCATO

Gold Weight varies: 3.37-3.42g., 24 mm. **Ruler:** Agostino **Obv:** Full-length armored figure of count looking to right, holding sword pointed downwards in left hand **Obv. Legend:** AVGVSTI. SPI. COMES. TASSA. **Rev:** Crowned imperial eagle, oval shield of Austrian arms on breast **Rev. Legend:** AVGVSTINVS. SPI. COMES. TAS. **Note:** Varesi 960.

Date	Mintage	VG	F	VF	XF	Unc
ND(1604-16)	—	825	1,200	2,500	3,650	—

KM# 6 DUCATO

3.2900 g., Gold, 23-24 mm. **Ruler:** Agostino **Obv:** Full-length armored figure of count looking to right, holding sword pointed downwards in left hand **Obv. Legend:** AGV. SPI. - COM. PALA. **Rev:** Crowned imperial eagle in circle **Rev. Legend:** SVB. VMBRA. ALARVM. TVARVM. **Note:** Varesi 962.

Date	Mintage	VG	F	VF	XF	Unc
ND(1604-16)	—	825	1,200	2,500	3,650	—

KM# 12 DUCATO

3.3000 g., Gold, 22 mm. **Ruler:** Agostino **Obv:** Crowned imperial eagle, oval shield of Austrian arms on breast **Obv. Legend:** AVGVSTINVS. SPI. COMES. TAS. **Rev:** Laureate bust to right, date below shoulder **Rev. Legend:** RVDOLPHVS. II. D.G. ROM. IMP. **Note:** Varesi 956; Fr. 1175.

Date	Mintage	VG	F	VF	XF	Unc
1604 Rare	—	—	—	—	—	—

KM# 13.1 DUCATO

Gold Weight varies: 3.31-3.45g., 22-23 mm. **Ruler:** Agostino **Obv:** Full-length armored figure of count looking to right, holding sword pointed downwards in left hand **Obv. Legend:** AVGVST. SPI. - COMES. TASSA. **Rev:** Crowned imperial eagle, oval shield of family arms on breast **Rev. Legend:** VIRTVTE. CAESAREA. DVCE. **Note:** Varesi 959; Fr. 1177.

Date	Mintage	VG	F	VF	XF	Unc
ND(1604-16)	—	550	900	1,500	2,500	—

KM# 13.2 DUCATO

Gold Weight varies: 3.31-3.45g., 22-23 mm. **Ruler:** Agostino **Obv:** Full-length armored figure of count looking to right, holding sword pointed downwards in left hand **Obv. Legend:** AVGVST. SPI. - COMES. TASSA. **Rev:** Crowned imperial eagle, oval shield of Austrian arms on breast **Rev. Legend:** VIRTVTE. CAESAREA. DVCE. **Note:** Varesi 959/1. Prev. KM #13.

Date	Mintage	VG	F	VF	XF	Unc
ND(1604-16)	—	550	900	1,500	2,500	—

KM# 21 DUCATO

Gold Weight varies: 3.29-3.44g., 22-23 mm. **Ruler:** Agostino **Obv:** Full-length armored figure of count looking to right, holding sword pointed downwards in left hand **Obv. Legend:** AGVS. SPIN. - COM. PAL. **Rev:** Crowned shield of 8-fold arms in circle **Rev. Legend:** VIRTVTE. CAESAREA. DVCE. **Note:** Varesi 961; Fr. 1178.

Date	Mintage	VG	F	VF	XF	Unc
ND(1604-16)	—	825	1,200	2,500	3,650	—

KM# 20 DUCATO

Gold Weight varies: 3.35-3.38g., 23-24 mm. **Ruler:** Agostino **Obv:** 5-line inscription in ornamented square tablet **Obv. Inscription:** MO. NO. AV / ORDINI / AVG. SPI / COM. PAL / PRO. IMP. **Rev:** Full-length armored figure of count turned slightly to right, holding sword over right shoulder, divides date **Rev. Legend:** CONCORDIA. PAR - RES. CRESCV. **Note:** Varesi 958; Fr. 1176.

Date	Mintage	VG	F	VF	XF	Unc
1611	—	825	1,200	2,500	3,650	—
1612	—	825	1,200	2,500	3,650	—

KM# 23 DUCATO

Gold, 23 mm. **Ruler:** Agostino **Obv:** Madonna and child, date in exergue **Obv. Legend:** MO. NOVA. AOVS. SPICO. PAL. **Rev:** Crowned shield of 8-fold arms **Rev. Legend:** VIRTVTE. CAESAREA. DVCE. **Note:** Varesi 957; Fr. 1179.

Date	Mintage	VG	F	VF	XF	Unc
1614	—	1,650	2,750	4,950	8,800	—

KM# 36 DUCATO

3.3800 g., Gold, 21 mm. **Ruler:** Filippo **Obv:** 5-line inscription in ornamented square tablet **Obv. Inscription:** FER. IMP / SEM. AVG / PHI. SPA / COM. TAS / FIL. PER. **Rev:** Large rose in circular garland **Rev. Legend:** IN. ODOREM. CVRRVNT. QVI. DILI. **Note:** Varesi 982; Fr. 1187.

Date	Mintage	VG	F	VF	XF	Unc
ND(1616-88)	—	725	1,250	2,500	4,150	—

KM# 37.1 DUCATO

3.3500 g., Gold, 21-22 mm. **Ruler:** Filippo **Obv:** Full-length armored figure of count between two small shields of arms **Obv. Legend:** PHILIPPVS. SP. - D.G. COM. PAL. **Rev:** 5-line inscription in ornamented square tablet **Rev. Inscription:** NON. NOB / DNE. NON / NOB. SED / NOI. TVO / DA. GLAM. **Note:** Varesi 980.

Date	Mintage	VG	F	VF	XF	Unc
ND(1616-88)	—	825	1,200	2,500	3,650	—

KM# 37.2 DUCATO

Gold Weight varies: 3.34-3.50g., 21-22 mm. **Ruler:** Filippo **Obv:** 5-line inscription in ornamented square tablet **Obv. Inscription:** FER. IMP / SEM. AVG / PHI. SPA / COM. TAS / FIL. PER. **Rev:** Full-length armored figure of count holding sword pointed downwards in right hand **Rev. Legend:** PARS. MEA. DEVS. - IN. ÆTERNVM. **Note:** Varesi 981. Prev. KM #37.

Date	Mintage	VG	F	VF	XF	Unc
ND(1616-88)	—	725	1,100	2,050	3,050	—

KM# 37.3 DUCATO

Gold Weight varies: 3.34-3.50g., 21-22 mm. **Ruler:** Filippo **Obv:** 5-line inscription in ornamented square tablet **Obv. Inscription:** FER. IMP / ROM. AVG / PHI. SPA / COM. TAS / FIL. PER. **Rev:** Full-length armored figure of count holdling sword in right hand pointed downwards **Rev. Legend:** PARS. MEA. DEVS. - IN. ÆTERNVM. **Note:** Varesi 981/1.

Date	Mintage	VG	F	VF	XF	Unc
ND(1616-88)	—	725	1,100	2,050	3,050	—

KM# 38 DUCATO

Gold Weight varies: 3.32-3.35g., 21 mm. **Ruler:** Filippo **Obv:** Full-length armored figure of count between two small shields of arms **Obv. Legend:** PHILIPPVS. SP. - D.G. COM. PAL. **Rev:** Crowned imperial eagle, shield of arms on breast, date at end of legend **Rev. Legend:** SVB. VMBRA. ALAR. TVAR. PROT. **Note:** Varesi 979; Fr. 1185.

Date	Mintage	VG	F	VF	XF	Unc
1637	—	725	1,100	2,050	3,050	—

KM# 7 DOPPIA

6.8000 g., Gold, 27 mm. **Ruler:** Agostino **Obv:** Crowned imperial eagle **Obv. Legend:** AVGS. SPI. COM. PALAT. MO. NO. AV. **Rev:** Facing figure of St. Nicholas standing behind ornate shield of 4-fold arms with central shield, below in front **Rev. Legend:** SANTVS. NICOLAVS. PROTECTOR. NOV. **Note:** Varesi 955; Fr. 1180.

Date	Mintage	VG	F	VF	XF	Unc
ND(1604-16)	—	3,000	5,000	9,000	17,500	—

KM# 35 DOPPIA

6.5500 g., Gold, 25 mm. **Ruler:** Filippo **Obv:** Bust to right **Obv. Legend:** PHILIPPVS. SPINVLA. **Rev:** Crowned oval shield of family arms in baroque frame, date at end of legend **Rev. Legend:** COMES. TAS - SAROLI. **Note:** Varesi 977; Fr. 1182.

Date	Mintage	VG	F	VF	XF	Unc
1630	—	3,000	5,000	8,000	15,500	—

KM# 45 DOPPIA

6.5500 g., Gold, 25 mm. **Ruler:** Filippo **Obv:** Armored bust to right **Obv. Legend:** PHILIPPVS. COMES. TASS. **Rev:** Facing figure of San Carlo Spinola in flames, date in exergue **Rev. Legend:** P. CAROLVS. - SPIN. M. SOC. IESV. **Note:** Varesi 978; Fr. 1184.

Date	Mintage	VG	F	VF	XF	Unc
1640	—	3,000	5,000	8,000	15,500	—

KM# 11 2 DOPPIE

Gold, 30 mm. **Ruler:** Agostino **Obv:** Bust to right, date below shoulder **Obv. Legend:** AVGVSTINVS. SPINVLA. **Rev:** Crowned shield of family arms in baroque frame **Rev. Legend:** COMES. TASSAROLI. **Note:** Varesi 954; Fr. 1174.

Date	Mintage	VG	F	VF	XF	Unc
1604 Rare	—	—	—	—	—	—

KM# 28 2 DOPPIE

13.2300 g., Gold, 28 mm. **Ruler:** Filippo **Obv:** Crowned imperial eagle, shield of family arms on breast **Obv. Legend:** PHIL. SPIN. COM. PALAT. MO. AV. **Rev:** Facing figure of St. Nicholas behind shield of 4-fold arms with central shield below in front **Rev. Legend:** SANTVS. NICOLAVS. PROTECTOR. NOS. **Note:** Varesi 976; Fr. 1188.

Date	Mintage	VG	F	VF	XF	Unc
ND(1616-88) Rare	—	—	—	—	—	—

KM# 32 2 DOPPIE

Gold Weight varies: 13.0-13.14g., 29 mm. **Ruler:** Filippo **Obv:** Armored bust to right **Obv. Legend:** PHILIPPVS. SPINVLA. **Rev:** Crowned shield of family arms in baroque frame, date at end of legend **Rev. Legend:** COMES. TASSAROLI. **Note:** Varesi 974; Fr. 1181.

Date	Mintage	VG	F	VF	XF	Unc
1629 Rare	—	—	—	—	—	—

KM# 46 2 DOPPIE

Gold Weight varies: 13.06-13.10g., 31 mm. **Ruler:** Filippo **Obv:** Armored bust to right **Obv. Legend:** PHILIPPVS. COMES. TASS. **Rev:** Figure of San Carlo Spinola being burnt at the stake, date in exergue **Rev. Legend:** P. CAROLVS. - SPIN. M. SOC. IESV. **Note:** Varesi 975; Fr. 1183.

Date	Mintage	VG	F	VF	XF	Unc
1640 Rare	—	—	—	—	—	—
1645 Rare	—	—	—	—	—	—

KM# 3 5 DOPPIE

34.2700 g., Gold, 42 mm. **Ruler:** Agostino **Obv:** Armored bust to right, date below shoulder **Obv. Legend:** AVGVSTINVS. SPINVLA. **Rev:** Crowned shield of family arms in baroque frame **Rev. Legend:** COMES. TAS - SAROLI. **Note:** Varesi 953; Fr. 1173. Struck from Scudo dies, KM #9.

Date	Mintage	VG	F	VF	XF	Unc
1604 Rare	—	—	—	—	—	—

TORRIGLIA

A Doria marquisate in the mountains of Liguria from which the Princess Violante had coins struck in four years.

RULER

Violante, widow of Prince Andrea III

MARQUISATE

STANDARD COINAGE

KM# 5 LUIGINI

Silver **Ruler:** Violante **Obv:** Female head right **Obv. Legend:** VIOLANTE... **Rev:** Crowned French arms divide date **Rev. Legend:** DEVS... **Note:** Struck for the Levant.

Date	Mintage	VG	F	VF	XF	Unc
1665	—	45.00	100	300	700	—
1666	—	45.00	100	300	700	—

KM# 6 LUIGINI

Silver **Ruler:** Violante **Obv:** Head right **Obv. Legend:** DON VI... **Rev:** Crowned French arms **Rev. Legend:** DOMINVS...

Date	Mintage	VG	F	VF	XF	Unc
1665	—	45.00	100	300	700	—

KM# 7 LUIGINI

Silver **Ruler:** Violante **Obv:** Head right **Obv. Legend:** PVLCRA... **Rev:** Crowned French arms **Rev. Legend:** SIMVL...

Date	Mintage	VG	F	VF	XF	Unc
1666	—	40.00	80.00	200	500	—
1667	—	40.00	80.00	200	500	—
1668	—	40.00	80.00	200	500	—

TRESANA

Tresana, a marquisate near Massa and Carrara in Tuscany was in the possession of the Malaspina family, who were also lords of Fosdinovo. A mint was opened in 1571 and closed at Guglielmo's death in 1651.

RULER

Guglielmo II Malaspina, 1613-1651

MARQUISATE

STANDARD COINAGE

DAV# 4184 TALLERO

Silver **Obv:** Bust right dividing date **Rev:** Crowned 4-part shield

Date	Mintage	VG	F	VF	XF	Unc
1621 Rare	—	—	—	—	—	—

FR# 1192 DUCAT

3.5000 g., 0.9860 Gold 0.1109 oz. AGW **Obv:** Soldier standing divides date **Rev:** 5-line inscription in tablet

Date	Mintage	VG	F	VF	XF	Unc
1619 Rare	—	—	—	—	—	—

FR# 1190 DUCAT

3.5000 g., 0.9860 Gold 0.1109 oz. AGW **Obv:** St. Ladislaus standing in inner circle **Rev:** Madonna and child facing in inner circle

Date	Mintage	VG	F	VF	XF	Unc
1620 Rare	—	—	—	—	—	—

FR# 1191 DUCAT

3.5000 g., 0.9860 Gold 0.1109 oz. AGW **Obv:** St. Louis standing in inner circle **Rev:** Crowned eagle in inner circle

Date	Mintage	VG	F	VF	XF	Unc
ND Rare	—	—	—	—	—	—

FR# 1193 DIRHEM

Gold **Obv:** Arabic legend **Rev:** Arabic legend **Note:** Struck for trade in the Middle East.

Date	Mintage	VG	F	VF	XF	Unc
ND Rare	—	—	—	—	—	—

TRICERRO

Village

A small place in Piedmont near Vercelli, Tricerro was a feudal dependency of the Tizzone family of Desana.

RULER

Carlo Giuseppe Francesco Tizzone, 1641-1676

Reference: Alberto Varesi, ***Monete Italiane Regionali: Piemonte, Sardegna, Liguria, Isola di Corsica***. Pavia, 1996.

VILLAGE

REGULAR COINAGE

KM# 1 SOLDINO

Billon, 15-16mm mm. **Ruler:** Carlo Giuseppe Tizzoni 1641-1676 **Obv:** Bust to right in circle, date at end of legend **Obv. Legend:** CAROL. II. T.C.D.S. **Rev:** Ornate cross in circle **Rev. Legend:** MARCHIO. TRISC. ET. C. **Note:** Varesi 1031.

Date	Mintage	VG	F	VF	XF	Unc
1670 Rare	—	—	—	—	—	—

TUSCANY

Etruria

An Italian territorial division on the west-central peninsula, belonged to the Medici from 1530 to 1737, when it was given to Francis, duke of Lorraine. In 1800 the French established it as part of the Spanish dominions; from 1807 to 1809 it was a French department. After the fall of Napoleon it reverted to its pre-Napoleonic owner, Ferdinand III.

RULERS

Ferdinand I, 1587-1609
Cosimo II, 1609-1621
Ferdinand II, 1621-1670
Cosimo III, 1670-1723

MINT MARKS

FIRENZE - Florence
LEGHORN - Livorno
PISIS – Pisa

MONETARY SYSTEM

Until 1826

12 Denari = 3 Quattrini = 1 Soldo
20 Soldi = 1 Lira
10 Lire = 1 Dena
40 Quattrini = 1 Paolo
1-1/2 Paoli = 1 Lira
10 Paoli = 1 Francescone, Scudo, Tallero
3 Zecchini = 1 Ruspone = 40 Lire

GRAND DUCHY

STANDARD COINAGE

DAV# 4185 PIASTRE

Silver **Ruler:** Ferdinand I **Obv:** Bust right **Rev:** St. John baptizing Christ, date in exergue

Date	Mintage	VG	F	VF	XF	Unc
1601	—	300	600	1,250	3,250	—
1604	—	300	600	1,250	3,250	—
1608	—	300	600	1,250	3,250	—
1609	—	300	600	1,250	3,250	—

DAV# 4187 PIASTRE

Silver **Ruler:** Cosimo II **Obv:** Bust right, stars below **Rev:** Baptism scene with Christ standing, date in exergue

Date	Mintage	VG	F	VF	XF	Unc
1608 Rare	—	—	—	—	—	—
1609 Rare	—	—	—	—	—	—

DAV# 4188 PIASTRE

Silver **Ruler:** Cosimo II **Obv:** Bust right **Rev:** Christ kneeling in baptism scene, date below

Date	Mintage	VG	F	VF	XF	Unc
1609 Rare	—	—	—	—	—	—
1610 Rare	—	—	—	—	—	—

DAV# 4189 PIASTRE

Silver **Ruler:** Cosimo II **Obv:** Bust right, date below **Rev:** Christ standing in baptism scene, date below

Date	Mintage	VG	F	VF	XF	Unc
1609/1609 Rare	—	—	—	—	—	—
1610/1609 Rare	—	—	—	—	—	—
1610/1610 Rare	—	—	—	—	—	—

DAV# 4190 PIASTRE

Silver **Ruler:** Cosimo II **Obv:** Bust right **Rev:** Christ standing in baptism scene, date below

Date	Mintage	VG	F	VF	XF	Unc
1610/1610 Rare	—	—	—	—	—	—

DAV# 4191 PIASTRE

Silver **Ruler:** Cosimo II **Obv:** Bust right **Rev:** St. John standing, date below

Date	Mintage	VG	F	VF	XF	Unc
1611	—	1,850	3,750	7,500	—	—
1613	—	1,850	3,750	7,500	—	—
1615	—	1,850	3,750	7,500	—	—
1618	—	1,850	3,750	7,500	—	—

DAV# 4192 PIASTRE

Silver **Ruler:** Cosimo II **Obv:** Bust left **Rev:** St. John standing

Date	Mintage	VG	F	VF	XF	Unc
1611	—	300	1,000	2,750	6,000	—
1612	—	300	1,000	2,750	6,000	—
1613	—	300	1,000	2,750	6,000	—

DAV# 4198 PIASTRE

Silver **Ruler:** Ferdinand II **Obv:** Bust right, date below **Rev:** St. John standing

Date	Mintage	VG	F	VF	XF	Unc
1623/1623	—	1,000	2,000	4,000	7,000	—

DAV# 4199A PIASTRE

Silver **Ruler:** Ferdinand II **Obv:** Bust with ruffled collar, cape and armor right, date below **Rev:** St. John standing

Date	Mintage	VG	F	VF	XF	Unc
1624/1623	—	1,000	2,000	4,000	7,000	—

DAV# 4199 PIASTRE

Silver **Ruler:** Ferdinand II **Obv:** Bust with ruffled collar, cape and armor right **Rev:** St. John standing

Date	Mintage	VG	F	VF	XF	Unc
1625/1620	—	175	325	850	3,000	—
1625/1623	—	175	325	850	3,000	—
1625/1626	—	175	325	850	3,000	—
1628	—	175	325	850	3,000	—

DAV# 4200 PIASTRE

Silver **Ruler:** Ferdinand II **Obv:** Bust with ruffled collar and armor right **Rev:** St. John standing

Date	Mintage	VG	F	VF	XF	Unc
1629	—	175	325	850	3,000	—
1630	—	175	325	850	3,000	—
1630 Retrograde 3	—	175	325	850	3,000	—
1633	—	175	325	850	3,000	—

DAV# 4201 PIASTRE

Silver **Ruler:** Ferdinand II **Obv:** Bust with ruffled collar, mustache and armor right, date below **Rev:** St. John standing

Date	Mintage	VG	F	VF	XF	Unc
1633/1630	—	1,150	2,250	4,500	7,550	—
1633	—	1,150	2,250	4,500	7,550	—
1634	—	1,150	2,250	4,500	7,550	—
1635	—	1,150	2,250	4,500	7,550	—
1638	—	1,150	2,250	4,500	7,550	—
1641	—	1,150	2,250	4,500	7,550	—

DAV# 4202 PIASTRE

Silver **Ruler:** Ferdinand II **Obv:** Bust with ruffled collar, mustache and armor right **Rev:** St. John standing, date below

Date	Mintage	VG	F	VF	XF	Unc
1635	—	150	300	750	3,000	—
1638/1635	—	150	300	750	3,000	—
1638/1685	—	150	300	750	3,000	—
1642	—	150	300	750	3,000	—
1642/1642	—	150	300	750	3,000	—
1645/1642	—	150	300	750	3,000	—
1649/1642	—	150	300	750	3,000	—

DAV# 4207 PIASTRE

Silver **Ruler:** Ferdinand II **Obv:** Older bust right, date below

Date	Mintage	VG	F	VF	XF	Unc
1663 Rare	—	—	—	—	—	—

DAV# 4209 PIASTRE

Silver **Ruler:** Cosimo III **Obv:** Bust right, date below **Rev:** Christ standing in baptism scene

Date	Mintage	VG	F	VF	XF	Unc
1675	—	90.00	185	375	1,000	3,750
1676	—	90.00	185	375	1,000	3,750
1677	—	90.00	185	375	1,000	3,750
1678	—	90.00	185	375	1,000	3,750
1679	—	90.00	185	375	1,000	3,750

DAV# 4210 PIASTRE

Silver **Ruler:** Cosimo III **Obv:** Wide drapped bust right

Date	Mintage	VG	F	VF	XF	Unc
1680	—	350	750	1,650	3,250	—
1680/1681	—	350	750	1,650	3,250	—
ND	—	350	750	1,650	3,250	—

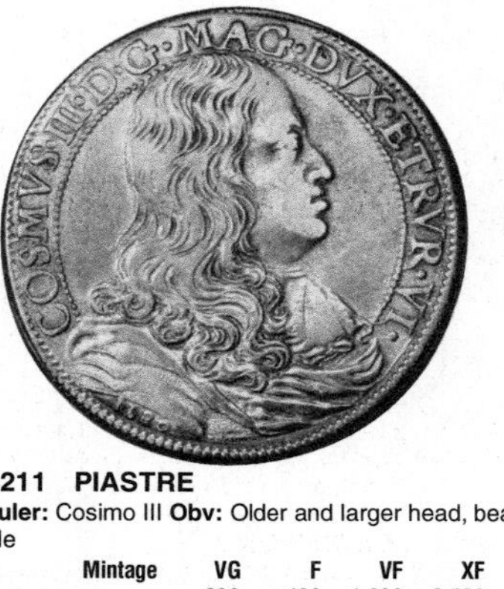

DAV# 4211 PIASTRE

Silver **Ruler:** Cosimo III **Obv:** Older and larger head, beaded inner circle

Date	Mintage	VG	F	VF	XF	Unc
1680	—	200	400	1,000	2,500	—
1680/1680	—	200	400	1,000	2,500	—

DAV# 4212 PIASTRE

Silver **Ruler:** Cosimo III **Obv:** Small bust right within linear circle, large date below

Date	Mintage	VG	F	VF	XF	Unc
1683	—	125	225	450	1,250	5,000
1684	—	125	225	450	1,250	5,000
1694	—	125	225	450	1,250	5,000

DAV# 4213 PIASTRE

Silver **Ruler:** Cosimo III **Obv:** Armored bust right **Rev:** St. John seated, lamb at left

Date	Mintage	VG	F	VF	XF	Unc
1684	—	1,500	3,000	6,500	10,000	—

FR# 314 FLORINO

Gold **Ruler:** Cosimo II **Obv:** Elaborate fleur-de-lis **Rev:** St. John the Baptist standing, date in legend

Date	Mintage	VG	F	VF	XF	Unc
1608	—	175	280	525	975	—
1610	—	175	280	525	975	—
1611	—	175	280	525	975	—
1614	—	175	280	525	975	—

FR# 319 FLORINO

Gold **Ruler:** Ferdinand II

Date	Mintage	VG	F	VF	XF	Unc
1655	—	250	400	750	1,500	—
ND	—	250	400	750	1,500	—

FR# 318 1/8 DOPPIA

0.8750 g., 0.9860 Gold 0.0277 oz. AGW **Ruler:** Cosimo II **Obv:** Crowned arms **Rev:** Ornate cross

Date	Mintage	VG	F	VF	XF	Unc
ND	—	400	800	1,600	3,500	—

FR# 321 1/8 DOPPIA

0.8750 g., 0.9860 Gold 0.0277 oz. AGW **Ruler:** Ferdinand II **Obv:** Crowned arms without legend **Rev:** Bust of St. John the Baptist facing without legend

Date	Mintage	VG	F	VF	XF	Unc
ND	—	—	—	—	—	—

FR# 311 1/4 DOPPIA

1.7500 g., 0.9860 Gold 0.0555 oz. AGW **Ruler:** Cosimo II **Obv:** Bust right, date below **Rev:** Ornate cross

Date	Mintage	VG	F	VF	XF	Unc
1609 Rare	—	—	—	—	—	—

FR# 320 1/4 DOPPIA
1.7500 g., 0.9860 Gold 0.0555 oz. AGW **Ruler:** Ferdinand II **Obv:** Crowned arms, date divided near top **Rev:** Bust of St. John the Baptist facing

Date	Mintage	VG	F	VF	XF	Unc
1663	—	750	1,200	2,000	4,500	—
1668	—	750	1,200	2,000	4,500	—

FR# 317 1/2 DOPPIA
3.5000 g., 0.9860 Gold 0.1109 oz. AGW **Ruler:** Ferdinand II **Obv:** Crowned arms **Obv. Legend:** FERD II... **Rev:** Ornate cross

Date	Mintage	VG	F	VF	XF	Unc
ND	—	750	1,250	2,250	5,000	—

FR# 324 1/2 DOPPIA
3.5000 g., 0.9860 Gold 0.1109 oz. AGW **Ruler:** Cosimo III **Obv. Legend:** COSMVS III ...

Date	Mintage	VG	F	VF	XF	Unc
ND	—	1,000	2,000	3,500	7,000	—

FR# 312 DOPPIA
7.0000 g., 0.9860 Gold 0.2219 oz. AGW **Ruler:** Cosimo II **Obv:** Crowned arms **Obv. Legend:** COS II...

Date	Mintage	VG	F	VF	XF	Unc
1608 Rare	—	—	—	—	—	—
ND	—	350	500	1,000	2,500	—

FR# 316 DOPPIA
7.0000 g., 0.9860 Gold 0.2219 oz. AGW **Ruler:** Ferdinand II **Obv. Legend:** FERDIN II...

Date	Mintage	VG	F	VF	XF	Unc
ND	—	300	500	900	1,750	—

FR# 322 2 DOPPIE
14.0000 g., 0.9860 Gold 0.4438 oz. AGW **Obv:** Crowned arms **Rev:** Ornate cross

Date	Mintage	VG	F	VF	XF	Unc
1676 Rare	—	—	—	—	—	—

URBINO

This duchy in central Italy was under Church rule in the Middle Ages. It was ceded to the Montefeltro family under whom it became a center of Renaissance culture. The Della Rovere family inherited Urbino through the feminine line. They extended its domains but moved the capital of the duchy to Pesaro. In 1626 Francesco Maria, the last of the line, abdicated and the duchy with all of its lands fell to Pope Urban VIII and was included in the Papal States.

RULER
Francesco Maria II, 1574-1624

DUCHY

STANDARD COINAGE

DAV# 4217 SCUDO (20 Grossi)
Silver **Ruler:** Francesco Maria II **Obv:** Bust right, date below **Rev:** Crowned arms in Order chain

Date	Mintage	VG	F	VF	XF	Unc
1601 Rare	—	—	—	—	—	—

DAV# 4220 SCUDO (20 Grossi)
Silver **Ruler:** Francesco Maria II **Obv:** Crowned arms **Rev:** 1621 / GROSSI / XX in baroque cartouche, L-X divided below

Date	Mintage	VG	F	VF	XF	Unc
1621 Rare	—	—	—	—	—	—

DAV# 4222 SCUDO (20 Grossi)
Silver **Ruler:** Francesco Maria II **Obv:** Crowned shield **Rev:** GROSSI / XX in frame, LX divided below

Date	Mintage	VG	F	VF	XF	Unc
ND	—	1,000	2,000	3,500	—	—

DAV# 4218 SCUDO (18 Grossi)
Silver **Ruler:** Francesco Maria II **Obv:** Bust left, Roman numeral date below **Obv. Legend:** M. SEDECINAR... **Rev:** Crowned eagle with arms

Date	Mintage	VG	F	VF	XF	Unc
1603 Rare	—	—	—	—	—	—

DAV# 4219 SCUDO (18 Grossi)
Silver **Ruler:** Francesco Maria II **Obv. Legend:** FRANCISCVS • MARIA • II • **Rev:** Crowned arms in frame **Rev. Legend:** VRBINI-DVX • VI • ET • C •

Date	Mintage	VG	F	VF	XF	Unc
1603 Rare	—	—	—	—	—	—
MDCIIII (1604) Rare	—	—	—	—	—	—

Note: Numismatica Ars Classica Auction 32, 1-06, VF realized approximately $31,750

DAV# 4219A SCUDO (18 Grossi)
Silver **Ruler:** Francesco Maria II **Rev:** Roman numeral date at bottom

Date	Mintage	VG	F	VF	XF	Unc
MDCIII (1603) Rare	—	—	—	—	—	—

DAV# 4221 SCUDO (18 Grossi)
Silver **Ruler:** Francesco Maria II **Obv:** Bust right **Rev:** Crowned arms

Date	Mintage	VG	F	VF	XF	Unc
ND Rare	—	—	—	—	—	—

FR# 1207 SCUDO D'ORO
3.5000 g., 0.9860 Gold 0.1109 oz. AGW **Ruler:** Francesco Maria II **Obv:** Bust left **Rev:** Crowned arms

Date	Mintage	VG	F	VF	XF	Unc
ND	—	1,250	2,250	3,000	5,000	—

FR# 1209 SCUDO D'ORO
3.5000 g., 0.9860 Gold 0.1109 oz. AGW **Ruler:** Francesco Maria II **Obv:** Tree in pastoral scene **Rev:** Crowned arms in Order collar in inner circle

Date	Mintage	VG	F	VF	XF	Unc
ND	—	1,500	2,500	4,000	6,500	—

FR# 1210 SCUDO D'ORO
3.5000 g., 0.9860 Gold 0.1109 oz. AGW **Ruler:** Francesco Maria II **Obv:** Crowned arms **Rev:** St. Michael standing left, holding scales of justice, spearing dragon below

Date	Mintage	VG	F	VF	XF	Unc
ND	—	800	1,600	2,750	4,750	—

FR# 1211 SCUDO D'ORO
3.5000 g., 0.9860 Gold 0.1109 oz. AGW **Ruler:** Francesco Maria II **Obv:** St. Francis of Assisi standing **Rev:** Fortress

Date	Mintage	VG	F	VF	XF	Unc
ND	—	1,850	3,250	6,000	9,000	—

FR# 1208 4 SCUDI D'ORO
14.0000 g., 0.9860 Gold 0.4438 oz. AGW **Ruler:** Francesco Maria II **Obv:** Tree in pastoral scene **Rev:** Crowned arms in Order collar in inner circle

Date	Mintage	VG	F	VF	XF	Unc
ND	—	3,000	5,000	8,500	17,000	—

VENICE

Venezia

A seaport of Venetia was founded by refugees from the Hun invasions. From that time until the arrival of Napoleon in 1797, it maintained an enormous foreign trade involving the possession of many islands in the Mediterranean while keeping a state of quasi-independence despite the antagonism of jealous Italian states and the Ottoman Turks. During the French Occupation Napoleon handed it over to Austria. Later, upon the defeat of the Austrians by Prussia in 1860, Venice then became a part of the United Kingdom of Italy.

RULERS
Marino Grimani, 1595-1605
Leonardo Donato, 1605-1612
Marcantonio Memmo, 1612-1615
Giovanni Bembo, 1615-1618
Nicolo Donato, 1618
Antonio Priuli, 1618-1623
Francesco Contarini, 1623-1624
Giovanni Corner, 1625-1629
Nicolo Contarini, 1630-1631
Francesco Erizzo, 1631-1646
Francesco Molin, 1646-1655
Carlo Contarini, 1655-1656
Francesco Corner, 1656
Bertuccio Valiero, 1656-1658
Giovanni Pesaro, 1658-1659
Domenico II Contarini, 1659-1674
Nicolo Sagredo, 1675-1676
Luigi Contarini, 1676-1684
Marcantonio Giustinian, 1684-1688
Francesco Morosini, 1688-1694
Silvestro Valiero, 1694-1700
Alvise II Mocenigo, 1700-1709

MINT MARKS
A - Vienna
F - Hall
V - Venice
ZV - Zecca Venezia - Venice
None - Venice

MINTMASTERS' INITIALS FOR SILVER

Initials	Date	Name
AB	1697-98	Gian Andrea Baffo
AB	1642-43	Anzolo Balbi
AC	1684-85	Alvise Gabriel (Cabriel)
AC	1698	Anzolo Cicogna
AC	1679	Alessandro Contarini
AC	1612-13	Antonio Contarini
AD	1666-67	Anzolo Dolfin
AD	1683-84	Antonio Dona
AF	1625-27	Andrea Falier
AG	1688	Alvise Gritti
AL	1643	Andrea Lippomano
AL	1643	Andrea Lippomano
AM	1613-14	Alvise Minio
AS	1667	Alessandro Salamon
AS	1667-68	Agustin Soranzo
AZ	1675	Agustin Zolio
AZ	1634-36	Alvise Zusto
BB	1659-60	Benetto Balbi
BB	1636	Bernardo Balbi
BC	1699	Benetto Civran
BC	1633-34	Benetto Contarini
BC	1650	Benetto Corner
BM	1612	Bernardo Morosini
BV	1656-57	Bernardino Vizzamano
CA	1649	Clandio Avogaro
CD	1621	Carlo Dona
CG	1614-15	Carlo Gritti
CP	1607-08	Constantin Pasqualigo
CZ	1609-12	Constantin Zorzi
DB	1629-30	Domenego Basadonna
DB	1637	Donato Bembo
DG	1663	Domenego Gritti
DM	1632	Domenego Michiel
DM	1609	Daniele Morosini
DM	1625	Tomaso da Mosta
DP	1685	Domenego Pizzamano
DT	1683	Domenego Trevisan

FC	1655-56	Francesco Corner
FM	1624-25	Ferigo da Molin
FM M	1624	Francesco Maria Malipiero
FP	1641-42	Francesco Pasqualigo
FR	1652-54	Francesco da Riva
FS	1612	Fantino Soranzo
FT	1693	Francesco Trevisan
FZ	1671	Fantino Zancariol
GAB	1697-98	Gian Andrea Baffo
GAB	1694-95	Gian Antonio Benzon
GB	1699-1701	Gerolamo Barbaro
GB	1632-33	Giacomo Barozzi
GBZ	1654-55	Giovan Battista Zorzi
GC	1628, 39-40, 72	Gerolamo Contarini
GD	1662-63	Gerolamo Dandolo
GD	1640-41	Gerolamo Dolfin
GD	1675	Giulio Dona
GL	1672	Gabriele Lombardo
GM	1693	Gerolamo Malipiero
GM	1681-82	Gerolamo Marcello
GM	1695	Giuseppe Minotto
GM	1691-92	Giacomo Morosini
GP IP	1627-28	Giacomo Pesaro
GR	1665-66	Giacomo da Riva
GR IR	1618-20	Giacomo Renier
GV	1685-86	Gerolamo Venier
GZ	1679-81	Gerolamo Zorzi
HZ	1620-21	Gerolamo Zorzi
IAM MAI	1627	Zan Alvise Minotto
IB	1691	Iseppo Baseggio
IBC BC ZC	1623-24	Zan Battista Contarini
IM	1659	Jacopo Malipiero
IM	1616-17	Jacopo da Molin
LF	1630-32	Luca Falier
LP	1668	Lorenzo Pisani
LP	1687-88	Lunardo Pisani
LV	1615-16	Leonardo Vendramin
MAM	1634	Marcantonio Malipiero
MAS SAM	1658-59	Marco Aurelio Soranzo
MAV MV AV	1613	Marcantonio Venier
MB	1692-93	Mattio Balbi
MB	1645-46	Marino Boldu
MM	1663	Marino da Molin
MM	1664	Marco Morosini
MQ	1678	Marchio Querini
MV	1671	Marino Vizzamano
MZ	1656	Marino Zen
MZ	1650-51	Marco Zorzi
NC	1658	Nicolo Contarini
ND	1682	Nicolo Dona
NF FN	1630	Nicolo Foscarini
OZ	1641	Ottaviano Zorzi
PB	1617	Paolo Balbi
PB	1618	Pietro Barbaro
PC	1612	Paulo Capello
PG	1649-50	Piero Gritti
PL	1675-77	Piero Lion
PM	1681	Piero Malipiero
PM	1698-99	Paolo Minotto
PM	1694	Piero Minotto
PP	1690-91	Paolo Pisani
PZ PZ60	1673	Pietro Zaguri VI
SB	1628-29	Sebastiano Badoer
SB	1677	Sebastiano Badoer
SB	1677	Stefano Barbaro
TB	1661	Tomaso Barbarigo
TB	1617-18	Tomaso Bragadin
VC	1620	Vicenzo Correr
VD	1638	Vicenzo Diedo
VE	1614	Vicenzo Emo
VM	1630	Urbano Malipiero
VV	1637-38	Valerio Valier
ZAB IAB	1646	Zan Alvise Battagia
ZAL	1686-87	Zan Andrea Loredan
ZAP	1608	Zuan Arsenio Priuli
ZAS	1651	Zan Antonio Semitecolo
ZAV	1621-22	Zan Antonio Venier
ZAZ	1647	Zan Antonio zorzi
ZB	1647-49	Zuane Barozzi
ZD	1633	Zuane Diedo
ZD ID	1622-23	Zuane Dolfin
ZL	1638-39	Zuane Loredan
ZM	1609	Zuane Marcello
ZMB	1643-44	Zan Marco Balbi
ZP	1674-75	Zuane Priuli
ZPS	1607	Zan Piero Sagredo
ZQ	1669, 1689	Zuane Querini
ZR	1693-94	Zuane da Riva
ZV	1636-37	Zaccaria Valier

MINTMASTERS' INITIALS FOR GOLD

FT	1693	Francesco Trevisan
LP	1673-75	Lorenzo Pisani

MONETARY SYSTEM

6 Denari = 1 Bezzo
12 Denari = 1 Soldo
20 Soldi = 1 Lira
30 Soldi = 1 Lirazza
124 Soldi = 1 Ducatone = 1 Ducato
140 Soldi = 1 Scudo = 1 Tallero = 1 Zecchino
160 Soldi = 1 Scudo
2 Scudi = 1 Doppia

WEIGHTS

Zechhino = 3.45 g
Doppia = 6.90 g

NOTE: Venice struck many types of gold coins using billon or silver coinage dies. They also struck many denominations from the same dies, so it is most important to check the weight to determine the proper denomination.

DIE VARIETIES

Throughout this series there is great variety in the abbreviation within the legends while various stars, dots, colons, diamonds, rosettes and other devices were used in separating them.

REPUBLIC

STANDARD COINAGE

DAV# 4267 DUCATO

23.4000 g., 0.8264 Silver 0.6217 oz. ASW **Ruler:** Domenico II Contarini **Obv:** Legend around St. Mark blessing kneeling Doge **Obv. Legend:** S • M • VEN • DOMIN • CON DVX **Rev:** Legend around lion **Rev. Legend:** DVCATVS • VENETVS **Note:** Legend varieties exist.

Date	Mintage	VG	F	VF	XF	Unc
ND(1663) MM	—	50.00	90.00	200	350	—
ND(1665) GR	—	50.00	90.00	200	350	—
ND(1666) AD	—	50.00	90.00	200	350	—
ND(1667) AS	—	50.00	90.00	200	350	—
ND(1668) LP	—	50.00	90.00	200	350	—
ND(1669) ZQ	—	50.00	90.00	200	350	—
ND(1671) FZ	—	50.00	90.00	200	350	—
ND(1671) MV	—	50.00	90.00	200	350	—
ND(1672) GC	—	50.00	90.00	200	350	—
ND(1673) PZ6o	—	50.00	90.00	200	350	—

DAV# 4270 DUCATO

23.4000 g., 0.8264 Silver 0.6217 oz. ASW **Ruler:** Nicolo Sagredo **Obv. Legend:** S • M • V • NICOLA • SAGREDO • D **Note:** Legend varieties exist.

Date	Mintage	VG	F	VF	XF	Unc
ND(1675) GD	—	150	265	450	750	—
ND(1675) AZ	—	150	265	450	750	—
ND(1675) AZ	—	150	265	450	750	—
Note: With obverse legend retrograde N						
ND(1675-76) PL	—	150	265	450	750	—

DAV# 4274 DUCATO

23.4000 g., 0.8264 Silver 0.6217 oz. ASW **Ruler:** Luigi Contarini **Obv. Legend:** S • M • V • ALOYSIVS • CONT • D **Note:** Legend varieties exist.

Date	Mintage	VG	F	VF	XF	Unc
ND(1676) AZ	—	50.00	90.00	200	350	—
ND(1676-77) PL	—	50.00	90.00	200	350	—
ND(1677) SB	—	50.00	90.00	200	350	—
ND(1679) AC	—	50.00	90.00	200	350	—
Note: Obverse legend retrograde N						
ND(1679) AC	—	50.00	90.00	200	350	—
Note: Obverse legend normal N						
ND(1679-81) GZ	—	50.00	90.00	200	350	—
Note: Obverse legend retrograde N						
ND(1679-81) GZ	—	50.00	90.00	200	350	—
Note: Obverse legend normal N						
ND(1681) PM	—	50.00	90.00	200	350	—
ND(1682) ND	—	50.00	90.00	200	350	—

DAV# 4277 DUCATO

23.4000 g., 0.8264 Silver 0.6217 oz. ASW **Ruler:** Marcantonio Giustinian **Obv. Legend:** • S • M • V • M • ANT • IVSTINIANVS • D

Date	Mintage	VG	F	VF	XF	Unc
ND(1684) AD	—	65.00	120	225	450	—
ND(1685-86) GV	—	65.00	120	225	450	—
ND(1686-87) ZAL	—	65.00	120	225	450	—

DAV# 4280 DUCATO

23.4000 g., 0.8264 Silver 0.6217 oz. ASW **Ruler:** Francesco Morosini **Obv. Legend:** • S • M • V • FRAN • MAVROC • D **Note:** Legend varieties exist.

Date	Mintage	VG	F	VF	XF	Unc
ND(1688) AG	—	50.00	90.00	200	350	—
ND(1689) ZQ	—	50.00	90.00	200	350	—
ND(1691-92) GM	—	50.00	90.00	200	350	—
ND(1692-93) MB	—	50.00	90.00	200	350	—

DAV# 4286 DUCATO

23.4000 g., 0.8264 Silver 0.6217 oz. ASW **Ruler:** Silvestro Valiero **Obv. Legend:** • S • M • V • SILV • VALERIO • DVX • V **Note:** Legend varieties exist.

Date	Mintage	VG	F	VF	XF	Unc
ND(1694) FT	—	50.00	90.00	200	350	—
ND(1698-99) PM	—	50.00	90.00	200	350	—

DAV# 1527 DUCATO

22.3700 g., 0.8264 Silver 0.5943 oz. ASW **Ruler:** Alvise II Mocenigo **Obv. Legend:** * S * M * V * ALOY * MOCENICO • DV * **Note:** Legend varieties exist.

Date	Mintage	VG	F	VF	XF	Unc
ND(1700-1709) BC	—	50.00	150	300	600	—

DAV# 4232 DUCATONE (124 Soldi)
28.1030 g., 0.9480 Silver 0.8565 oz. ASW **Ruler:** Leonardo Donato **Obv. Legend:** *S: M: VENET: LEON: DONAT. * **Note:** Four legend varieties exist.

Date	Mintage	VG	F	VF	XF	Unc
ND(1605-12) Retrograde 4	—	135	225	350	600	—
ND(1605-12) Normal 4	—	135	225	350	600	—

DAV# 4241 DUCATONE (124 Soldi)
28.1030 g., 0.9480 Silver 0.8565 oz. ASW **Ruler:** Antonio Priuli **Obv. Legend:** * S • M • VENET• ANT • PRIOL • **Note:** Legend varieties exist.

Date	Mintage	VG	F	VF	XF	Unc
ND(1618-23)	—	135	225	350	600	—

DAV# 4243 DUCATONE (124 Soldi)
28.1030 g., 0.9480 Silver 0.8565 oz. ASW **Ruler:** Francesco Contarini **Obv. Legend:** • S • M • VEN • FRANC • CONT... **Note:** Legend varieties exist.

Date	Mintage	VG	F	VF	XF	Unc
ND(1623-24)	—	135	225	350	600	—

DAV# 4245 DUCATONE (124 Soldi)
28.1030 g., 0.9480 Silver 0.8565 oz. ASW **Ruler:** Giovanni Corner **Obv. Legend:** • S • M • V • IOAN • CORNEL... **Note:** Legend varieties exist.

Date	Mintage	VG	F	VF	XF	Unc
ND(1625-29)	—	135	225	350	600	—

DAV# 4250 DUCATONE (124 Soldi)
28.1030 g., 0.9480 Silver 0.8565 oz. ASW **Ruler:** Francesco Erizzo **Obv. Legend:** • S • M • VEN • FRANC • ERIZZO DVX **Note:** Legend varieties exist.

Date	Mintage	VG	F	VF	XF	Unc
ND(1634) MAM	—	50.00	100	220	400	—

DAV# 4250A DUCATONE (124 Soldi)
28.1030 g., 0.9480 Silver 0.8565 oz. ASW **Ruler:** Francesco Erizzo **Obv:** DVX of legend in exergue

Date	Mintage	VG	F	VF	XF	Unc
ND(1634)	—	—	—	—	—	—

DAV# 4253 DUCATONE (124 Soldi)
28.1030 g., 0.9480 Silver 0.8565 oz. ASW **Ruler:** Francesco Molin **Obv. Legend:** • S • M • VEN • FRANC • MOLINO • D

Date	Mintage	VG	F	VF	XF	Unc
ND(1646) MB	—	50.00	100	220	400	—

DAV# 4255 DUCATONE (124 Soldi)
28.1030 g., 0.9480 Silver 0.8565 oz. ASW **Ruler:** Carlo Contarini **Obv. Legend:** S • M • V • CAROL • CONTAR...

Date	Mintage	VG	F	VF	XF	Unc
ND(1655) GBZ	—	55.00	110	225	400	—

DAV# 4257 DUCATONE (124 Soldi)
28.1030 g., 0.9480 Silver 0.8565 oz. ASW **Ruler:** Francesco Corner **Obv. Legend:** S • M • V • FRANC • CORNEL • D •

Date	Mintage	VG	F	VF	XF	Unc
ND(1656) FC	—	55.00	110	225	400	—

DAV# 4259 DUCATONE (124 Soldi)
28.1030 g., 0.9480 Silver 0.8565 oz. ASW **Ruler:** Bertuccio Valiero **Obv. Legend:** S•M•VEN•BERT•VALER•D•

Date	Mintage	VG	F	VF	XF	Unc
ND(1656) FC	—	100	170	325	525	—
ND(1656) FCM	—	100	170	325	525	—

DAV# 4261 DUCATONE (124 Soldi)
28.1030 g., 0.9480 Silver 0.8565 oz. ASW **Ruler:** Giovanni Pesaro **Obv. Legend:** S•M•VEN•IOAN•PISAVRO•D• **Note:** Two legend varieties exist.

Date	Mintage	VG	F	VF	XF	Unc
ND(1658) BV	—	55.00	110	225	375	—

DAV# 4265 DUCATONE (124 Soldi)
28.1030 g., 0.9480 Silver 0.8565 oz. ASW **Ruler:** Domenico II Contarini **Obv. Legend:** • S • M • VEN • DOMIN • CONT • D • **Note:** Many legend varieties exist.

Date	Mintage	VG	F	VF	XF	Unc
ND(1659) MAS	—	55.00	110	225	375	—
ND(1662-63) GD	—	55.00	110	225	375	—
ND(1663) DG	—	55.00	110	225	375	—

DAV# 4269 DUCATONE (124 Soldi)
28.1030 g., 0.9480 Silver 0.8565 oz. ASW **Ruler:** Nicolo Sagredo **Obv. Legend:** S • M • V • NICO • SAGREDO • X •

Date	Mintage	VG	F	VF	XF	Unc
ND(1675) GD	—	165	270	450	750	—

DAV# 4273 DUCATONE (124 Soldi)
28.1030 g., 0.9480 Silver 0.8565 oz. ASW **Ruler:** Luigi Contarini **Obv. Legend:** S • M • V • ALOYSIVS • CONT • D •

Date	Mintage	VG	F	VF	XF	Unc
ND(1676) AZ	—	135	225	375	650	—

DAV# 4276 DUCATONE (124 Soldi)
28.1030 g., 0.9480 Silver 0.8565 oz. ASW **Ruler:** Marcantonio Giustinian **Obv. Legend:** S • M • V • M • ANT • IVSTINIANVS •

Date	Mintage	VG	F	VF	XF	Unc
ND(1685-86) GV	—	135	225	375	650	—

DAV# 4279 DUCATONE (124 Soldi)
28.1030 g., 0.9480 Silver 0.8565 oz. ASW **Ruler:** Francesco Morosini **Obv. Legend:** S•M•V•FRANC•MAVROCENVS•D•

Date	Mintage	VG	F	VF	XF	Unc
ND(1690-91) PP	—	135	225	375	650	—

DAV# 4284 DUCATONE (124 Soldi)
28.1030 g., 0.9480 Silver 0.8565 oz. ASW **Ruler:** Silvestro Valiero **Obv. Legend:** S • M • V • SILVE • VALERIO • DVX *

Date	Mintage	VG	F	VF	XF	Unc
ND(1694) FT	—	135	225	375	650	—

DAV# 4236 REALE
28.8200 g., Silver **Ruler:** Marcantonio Memmo **Obv:** Arms within Order collar, ducal cap above **Obv. Legend:** MARCUS • ANTONINVS • MEMMO... **Rev:** St. Mark with book and lion

Date	Mintage	VG	F	VF	XF	Unc
1614	—	1,100	1,800	2,700	—	—

DAV# 4229 SCUDO (140 Soldi)
31.8290 g., 0.9480 Silver 0.9701 oz. ASW **Ruler:** Leonardo Donato **Obv:** Legend around ornate cross **Obv. Legend:** LEON • DONATO • DVX... **Rev:** Lion with shield **Note:** Legend varieties exist.

Date	Mintage	VG	F	VF	XF	Unc
ND(1605-12) AT	—	55.00	110	225	375	—
ND(1605-12) SC	—	55.00	110	225	375	—
ND(1609) ZM	—	55.00	110	225	375	—
ND(1609-12) CZ	—	55.00	110	225	375	—
ND(1609) DM	—	55.00	110	225	375	—

DAV# 4234 SCUDO (140 Soldi)
31.8290 g., 0.9480 Silver 0.9701 oz. ASW **Ruler:** Marcantonio Memmo **Obv. Legend:** M•ANTON•MEMMO•DVX•VEN **Note:** Varieties of flowers at mintmaster initials exist.

Date	Mintage	VG	F	VF	XF	Unc
ND(1612) BM	—	110	200	325	550	—
ND(1612-15) AV	—	110	200	325	550	—
ND(1613-14) AM	—	110	200	325	550	—
ND(1614) VE	—	110	200	325	550	—
ND(1614-15) CG	—	110	200	325	550	—

DAV# 4237 SCUDO (140 Soldi)
31.8290 g., 0.9480 Silver 0.9701 oz. ASW **Ruler:** Giovanni Bembo **Obv. Legend:** IOANNES • BEMBO... **Note:** Legend varieties exist.

Date	Mintage	VG	F	VF	XF	Unc
ND(1614-15) CG	—	165	270	450	750	—
ND(1615) LV	—	165	270	450	750	—

Note: With inverted "A" for "V"

Date	Mintage	VG	F	VF	XF	Unc
ND(1615) LV	—	165	270	450	750	—
ND(1616) IM	—	165	270	450	750	—

DAV# 4239 SCUDO (140 Soldi)
31.8290 g., 0.9480 Silver 0.9701 oz. ASW **Ruler:** Antonio Priuli **Obv. Legend:** ANTON • PRIOL... **Note:** Legend varieties exist.

Date	Mintage	VG	F	VF	XF	Unc
ND(1618) TB	—	55.00	110	225	375	—
ND(1618-20) GR	—	55.00	110	225	375	—
ND(1620) VC	—	55.00	110	225	375	—
ND(1620-21) HZ	—	55.00	110	225	375	—
ND(1621) CD	—	55.00	110	225	375	—
ND(1621-22) ZAV	—	55.00	110	225	375	—
ND(1622-23) ZD	—	55.00	110	225	375	—

DAV# 4238 SCUDO (140 Soldi)
31.8290 g., 0.9480 Silver 0.9701 oz. ASW **Ruler:** Nicolo Donato **Obv. Legend:** NICOL • DONATO...

Date	Mintage	VG	F	VF	XF	Unc
ND(1618) TB	—	195	325	650	1,100	—

DAV# 4242 SCUDO (140 Soldi)

31.8290 g., 0.9480 Silver 0.9701 oz. ASW **Ruler:** Francesco Contarini **Obv. Legend:** FRANC • CONT(AR)... **Note:** Legend varieties exist.

Date	Mintage	VG	F	VF	XF	Unc
ND(1623) ZD	—	55.00	110	225	375	—
ND(1623) IBC	—	55.00	110	225	375	—
ND(1624) FMM	—	55.00	110	225	375	—
ND(1624) FM	—	55.00	110	225	375	—

DAV# 4244 SCUDO (140 Soldi)

31.8290 g., 0.9480 Silver 0.9701 oz. ASW **Ruler:** Giovanni Corner **Obv. Legend:** IOAN • CORNEL... **Note:** Legend varieties exist.

Date	Mintage	VG	F	VF	XF	Unc
ND(1625) FM	—	55.00	110	225	375	—
ND(1625) DM	—	55.00	110	225	375	—
ND(1626) AF	—	55.00	110	225	375	—
ND(1627) IAM	—	55.00	110	225	375	—
ND(1627) GP	—	55.00	110	225	375	—
ND(1628) GC	—	55.00	110	225	375	—
ND(1629) NF	—	55.00	110	225	375	—
ND(1629) DB	—	55.00	110	225	375	—

DAV# 4246 SCUDO (140 Soldi)

31.8290 g., 0.9480 Silver 0.9701 oz. ASW **Ruler:** Nicolo Contarini **Obv. Legend:** NICOL • CONTAR... **Note:** Legend varieties exist.

Date	Mintage	VG	F	VF	XF	Unc
ND(1630) DB	—	55.00	110	225	375	—
ND(1630) DB	—	55.00	110	225	375	—
Note: With obverse legend CVX (error)						
ND(1630) VM	—	55.00	110	225	375	—
ND(1630) AM	—	55.00	110	225	375	—

DAV# 4249 SCUDO (140 Soldi)

31.8290 g., 0.9480 Silver 0.9701 oz. ASW **Ruler:** Francesco Erizzo **Obv. Legend:** FRANC • ERIZZO... **Note:** Legend varieties exist.

Date	Mintage	VG	F	VF	XF	Unc
ND(1631) VM	—	55.00	100	200	350	—
ND(1632) DM	—	55.00	100	200	350	—
ND(1634) MAM	—	55.00	100	200	350	—
ND(1635) AZ	—	55.00	100	200	350	—
ND(1636) BB	—	55.00	100	200	350	—
ND(1637) DB	—	55.00	100	200	350	—
ND(1638) VV	—	55.00	100	200	350	—
ND(1638-39) ZL	—	55.00	100	200	350	—
ND(1639-40) GC	—	55.00	100	200	350	—
ND(1641) OZ	—	55.00	100	200	350	—
ND(1642-43) AB	—	55.00	100	200	350	—

DAV# 4252 SCUDO (140 Soldi)

31.8290 g., 0.9480 Silver 0.9701 oz. ASW **Ruler:** Francesco Molin **Obv. Legend:** FRANC • MOLINO... **Note:** Legend varieties exist.

Date	Mintage	VG	F	VF	XF	Unc
ND(1646) MB	—	55.00	100	200	350	—
ND(1646) ZAB	—	55.00	100	200	350	—
ND(1647) ZAZ	—	55.00	100	200	350	—
ND(1649-50) PG	—	55.00	100	200	350	—
ND(1652-54) FR	—	55.00	100	200	350	—

DAV# 4254 SCUDO (140 Soldi)

31.8290 g., 0.9480 Silver 0.9701 oz. ASW **Ruler:** Carlo Contarini **Obv. Legend:** CAROL • CONTAR... **Note:** Four varieties of ornaments at value exist.

Date	Mintage	VG	F	VF	XF	Unc
ND(1655) GBZ	—	55.00	110	225	375	—

DAV# 4256 SCUDO (140 Soldi)

31.8290 g., 0.9480 Silver 0.9701 oz. ASW **Ruler:** Francesco Corner **Obv. Legend:** FRANC • CORNEL...

Date	Mintage	VG	F	VF	XF	Unc
ND(1656) FC	—	75.00	125	250	400	—

DAV# 4258 SCUDO (140 Soldi)

31.8290 g., 0.9480 Silver 0.9701 oz. ASW **Ruler:** Bertuccio Valiero **Obv. Legend:** BERTVC • VALERIO...

Date	Mintage	VG	F	VF	XF	Unc
ND(1656) FC	—	135	225	350	650	—
ND(1656-57) BV	—	135	225	350	650	—

DAV# 4260 SCUDO (140 Soldi)

31.8290 g., 0.9480 Silver 0.9701 oz. ASW **Ruler:** Giovanni Pesaro **Obv. Legend:** IOANNES • PISAVRO... **Note:** Two legend varieties exist.

Date	Mintage	VG	F	VF	XF	Unc
ND(1658) BV	—	55.00	110	225	375	—

DAV# 4263 SCUDO (140 Soldi)

31.8290 g., 0.9480 Silver 0.9701 oz. ASW **Ruler:** Domenico II Contarini **Obv. Legend:** DOMINIC • CONTAR... **Note:** Legend varieties exist.

Date	Mintage	VG	F	VF	XF	Unc
ND(1659) IM	—	55.00	110	225	375	—
ND(1659-60) BB	—	55.00	110	225	375	—
ND(1662-63) GD	—	55.00	110	225	375	—
ND(1664) MM	—	55.00	110	225	375	—
ND(1665-66) GR	—	55.00	110	225	375	—
ND(1666-67) AD	—	55.00	110	225	375	—
ND(1668) LP	—	55.00	110	225	375	—
ND(1671) MV	—	55.00	110	225	375	—
ND(1672) GL	—	55.00	110	225	375	—
ND(1673) PZ6o	—	55.00	110	225	375	—

DAV# 4268 SCUDO (140 Soldi)

31.8290 g., 0.9480 Silver 0.9701 oz. ASW **Ruler:** Nicolo Sagredo **Obv. Legend:** NICOLAVS • SAGRE • DVX • VENET * P • Z • 6° *

Date	Mintage	VG	F	VF	XF	Unc
ND(1675) PZ6o	—	210	350	600	975	—
ND(1675) ZP	—	210	350	600	975	—

DAV# 4272 SCUDO (140 Soldi)

31.8290 g., 0.9480 Silver 0.9701 oz. ASW **Ruler:** Luigi Contarini **Obv. Legend:** ALOYSIVS CONTARENDO... **Note:** Legend varieties exist.

Date	Mintage	VG	F	VF	XF	Unc
ND(1676-77) PL	—	55.00	100	200	350	—
ND(1677) SB	—	55.00	100	200	350	—
ND(1678) MQ	—	55.00	100	200	350	—
ND(1679-81) GZ	—	55.00	100	200	350	—

DAV# 4275 SCUDO (140 Soldi)

31.8290 g., 0.9480 Silver 0.9701 oz. ASW **Ruler:** Marcantonio Giustinian **Obv. Legend:** M • ANTON • IVSTINIANVS... **Note:** Legend varieties exist.

Date	Mintage	VG	F	VF	XF	Unc
ND(1684) DT	—	80.00	150	285	500	—
ND(1685) DP	—	80.00	150	285	500	—

DAV# 4278 SCUDO (140 Soldi)

31.8290 g., 0.9480 Silver 0.9701 oz. ASW **Ruler:** Francesco Morosini **Obv. Legend:** FRAN • MAVROCENVS...

Date	Mintage	VG	F	VF	XF	Unc
ND(1688) AG	—	70.00	120	250	400	—
ND(1691-92) GM	—	70.00	120	250	400	—

DAV# 4283 SCUDO (140 Soldi)

31.8290 g., 0.9480 Silver 0.9701 oz. ASW **Ruler:** Silvestro Valiero **Obv. Legend:** SILVESTER * VALERIO... **Note:** Legend varieties exist.

Date	Mintage	VG	F	VF	XF	Unc
ND(1694) FT	—	70.00	120	250	400	—
ND(1698-99) PM	—	70.00	120	250	400	—

DAV# 1524 SCUDO (140 Soldi)

31.8290 g., 0.9480 Silver 0.9701 oz. ASW **Ruler:** Alvise II Mocenigo **Obv:** Floral cross, leaves in angles, B•C below **Obv. Legend:** ALOYSIV * MOCENICO * DVX * VENET **Rev:** Winged lion holding gospel in shield above value **Rev. Legend:** SANCTVS • MARCVS • VENET •

Date	Mintage	VG	F	VF	XF	Unc
ND(1700) BC	—	70.00	120	250	400	—

DAV# 4233 SCUDO (160 Soldi)

36.3800 g., 0.9480 Silver 1.1088 oz. ASW **Ruler:** Marcantonio Memmo **Obv. Legend:** * S • M • VENETVS • M • ANT • MEMO • DV *

Date	Mintage	VG	F	VF	XF	Unc
ND(1612-13) AC	—	300	500	825	1,550	—

FR# 1457 SCUDO D'ORO
3.3310 g., 0.9170 Gold 0.0982 oz. AGW **Ruler:** Antonio Priuli **Obv. Legend:** ANT • PRIOL • DVX • VENETIAR

Date	Mintage	VG	F	VF	XF	Unc
ND(1618-23) Rare	—	—	—	—	—	—

FR# 1459 SCUDO D'ORO
3.3310 g., 0.9170 Gold 0.0982 oz. AGW **Ruler:** Francesco Contarini **Obv. Legend:** FRANC • CONTARENO • DVX • VEN

Date	Mintage	VG	F	VF	XF	Unc
ND(1623-24)	—	850	1,800	3,400	5,400	—

FR# 1461 SCUDO D'ORO
3.3310 g., 0.9170 Gold 0.0982 oz. AGW **Ruler:** Giovanni Corner **Obv. Legend:** IOAN • CORNEL • DVX • VENET

Date	Mintage	VG	F	VF	XF	Unc
ND(1625-29) Rare	—	—	—	—	—	—

FR# 1463 SCUDO D'ORO
3.3310 g., 0.9170 Gold 0.0982 oz. AGW **Ruler:** Nicolo Contarini **Obv. Legend:** NICOL CONTAR • DVX • VEN

Date	Mintage	VG	F	VF	XF	Unc
ND(1630-31) Rare	—	—	—	—	—	—

FR# 1465 SCUDO D'ORO
3.4030 g., 0.9170 Gold 0.1003 oz. AGW **Ruler:** Francesco Erizzo **Obv. Legend:** FRANC • ERIZZO • DVX • VENE

Date	Mintage	VG	F	VF	XF	Unc
ND(1631-46) Rare	—	—	—	—	—	—

FR# 1466 SCUDO D'ORO
3.4030 g., 0.9170 Gold 0.1003 oz. AGW **Ruler:** Francesco Corner **Obv. Legend:** FRANC • CORNEL • DVX • VENET

Date	Mintage	VG	F	VF	XF	Unc
ND(1656) Rare	—	—	—	—	—	—

FR# 1470 SCUDO D'ORO
3.3810 g., 0.9170 Gold 0.0997 oz. AGW **Ruler:** Silvestro Valiero **Obv. Legend:** SILVESTER • VALERIO • DVX • VE

Date	Mintage	VG	F	VF	XF	Unc
ND(1694) FT Rare	—	—	—	—	—	—

FR# 1456 2 SCUDI
6.7620 g., 0.9170 Gold 0.1994 oz. AGW **Ruler:** Antonio Priuli **Obv. Legend:** ANTON • PRIOL • DVX • VENETIAR

Date	Mintage	VG	F	VF	XF	Unc
ND(1618-23)	—	1,800	3,000	5,400	7,800	—

FR# 1458 2 SCUDI
6.7620 g., 0.9170 Gold 0.1994 oz. AGW **Ruler:** Francesco Contarini **Obv. Legend:** FRANC • CONTARENO • DVX • VENET

Date	Mintage	VG	F	VF	XF	Unc
ND(1623-24)	—	650	1,350	2,800	4,800	—

FR# 1460 2 SCUDI
6.7620 g., 0.9170 Gold 0.1994 oz. AGW **Ruler:** Giovanni Corner **Obv. Legend:** IOAN • CORNEL • DVX • VENET

Date	Mintage	VG	F	VF	XF	Unc
ND(1625-29)	—	650	1,350	2,650	4,000	—

FR# 1462 2 SCUDI
6.7620 g., 0.9170 Gold 0.1994 oz. AGW **Ruler:** Nicolo Contarini **Obv. Legend:** NICOL • CONTAR • DVX • VENE

Date	Mintage	VG	F	VF	XF	Unc
ND(1630-31)	—	700	1,500	2,750	4,500	—

FR# 1464 2 SCUDI
6.8060 g., 0.9170 Gold 0.2006 oz. AGW **Ruler:** Francesco Erizzo **Obv. Legend:** FRANC • ERIZZO • DVX • VENET

Date	Mintage	VG	F	VF	XF	Unc
ND(1631-46) Rare	—	—	—	—	—	—

FR# 1467 2 SCUDI
6.8060 g., 0.9170 Gold 0.2006 oz. AGW **Ruler:** Bertuccio Valiero **Obv. Legend:** BERTVCCIVS • VALERIO • DVX • VEN •

Date	Mintage	VG	F	VF	XF	Unc
ND(1656-58) Rare	—	—	—	—	—	—

FR# 1468 2 SCUDI
6.8060 g., 0.9170 Gold 0.2006 oz. AGW **Ruler:** Nicolo Sagredo **Obv. Legend:** NICOLAVS • SAGRE • DVX • VENE

Date	Mintage	VG	F	VF	XF	Unc
ND(1675) LP Rare	—	—	—	—	—	—

FR# 1469 2 SCUDI
6.8060 g., 0.9170 Gold 0.2006 oz. AGW **Ruler:** Silvestro Valiero **Obv. Legend:** SILVESTER • VALERIO • DVX • VEN

Date	Mintage	VG	F	VF	XF	Unc
ND(1694) FT Rare	—	—	—	—	—	—

DAV# 4282 LEONE
27.1200 g., 0.7390 Silver 0.6443 oz. ASW **Ruler:** Francesco Morosini **Obv. Legend:** FRAN • MAVROC... **Rev:** Lion holds cross and palm frond in front

Date	Mintage	VG	F	VF	XF	Unc
ND(1688-94)	—	375	750	1,500	2,500	—
ND(1691) IB	—	375	750	1,500	2,500	—

DAV# 4281 LEONE
27.1200 g., 0.7390 Silver 0.6443 oz. ASW **Ruler:** Francesco Morosini **Obv:** Legend around St. Mark standing blessing kneeling Doge **Obv. Legend:** FRAN • MAVRO... **Rev:** Legend around rearing lion holding cross behind and palm frond in front **Rev. Legend:** FIDES ET VICTORIA **Note:** Legend varieties exist.

Date	Mintage	VG	F	VF	XF	Unc
ND(1688) AG	—	375	750	1,500	2,500	—

DAV# 4287 LEONE
27.1200 g., 0.7390 Silver 0.6443 oz. ASW **Ruler:** Silvestro Valiero **Obv. Legend:** SILV • VALERIO... **Note:** Legend varieties exist.

Date	Mintage	VG	F	VF	XF	Unc
ND(1694) FT	—	350	650	1,250	2,000	—
ND(1697-98) GAB	—	350	650	1,250	2,000	—
ND(1698-99) PM	—	350	650	1,250	2,000	—
ND(1698) AC	—	350	650	1,250	2,000	—
ND(1699) AZ	—	350	650	1,250	2,000	—

FR# 1280 1/4 ZECCHINO
0.8730 g., 0.9990 Gold 0.0280 oz. AGW **Ruler:** Leonardo Donato **Obv. Legend:** LEONAR DONATO...

Date	Mintage	VG	F	VF	XF	Unc
ND(1605-12)	—	95.00	170	400	700	—

FR# 1283 1/4 ZECCHINO
0.8730 g., 0.9990 Gold 0.0280 oz. AGW **Ruler:** Marcantonio Memmo **Obv. Legend:** M ANTO MEMMO...

Date	Mintage	VG	F	VF	XF	Unc
ND(1612-15)	—	210	425	650	1,150	—

FR# 1286 1/4 ZECCHINO
0.8730 g., 0.9990 Gold 0.0280 oz. AGW **Ruler:** Giovanni Bembo **Obv. Legend:** IOAN BEMBO...

Date	Mintage	VG	F	VF	XF	Unc
ND(1615-18) Rare	—	—	—	—	—	—

FR# 1288 1/4 ZECCHINO
0.8730 g., 0.9990 Gold 0.0280 oz. AGW **Ruler:** Nicolo Donato **Obv. Legend:** NICOL DONATO...

Date	Mintage	VG	F	VF	XF	Unc
ND(1618)	—	600	1,200	2,400	4,500	—

FR# 1293 1/4 ZECCHINO
0.8730 g., 0.9990 Gold 0.0280 oz. AGW **Ruler:** Antonio Priuli **Obv. Legend:** ANTON PRIOLO...

Date	Mintage	VG	F	VF	XF	Unc
ND(1618-23)	—	110	210	350	600	—

FR# 1296 1/4 ZECCHINO
0.8730 g., 0.9990 Gold 0.0280 oz. AGW **Ruler:** Francesco Contarini **Obv. Legend:** FRANC CONTAR...

Date	Mintage	VG	F	VF	XF	Unc
ND(1623-24)	—	350	775	1,500	3,400	—

FR# 1299 1/4 ZECCHINO
0.8730 g., 0.9990 Gold 0.0280 oz. AGW **Ruler:** Giovanni Corner **Obv. Legend:** IOAN CORN...

Date	Mintage	VG	F	VF	XF	Unc
ND(1625-29)	—	350	775	1,500	3,400	—

FR# 1309 1/4 ZECCHINO
0.8730 g., 0.9990 Gold 0.0280 oz. AGW **Ruler:** Nicolo Contarini **Obv. Legend:** NICOL CONT...

Date	Mintage	VG	F	VF	XF	Unc
ND(1630-31)	—	425	850	1,900	3,900	—

FR# 1312 1/4 ZECCHINO
0.8730 g., 0.9990 Gold 0.0280 oz. AGW **Ruler:** Francesco Erizzo **Obv. Legend:** FRANC ERIZZO...

Date	Mintage	VG	F	VF	XF	Unc
ND(1631-46)	—	120	240	425	900	—

FR# 1320 1/4 ZECCHINO
0.8730 g., 0.9990 Gold 0.0280 oz. AGW **Ruler:** Francesco Molin **Obv. Legend:** FRANC MOLINO...

Date	Mintage	VG	F	VF	XF	Unc
ND(1646-55)	—	240	475	1,000	2,400	—

FR# 1323 1/4 ZECCHINO
0.8730 g., 0.9990 Gold 0.0280 oz. AGW **Ruler:** Carlo Contarini **Obv. Legend:** CAROL CONT...

Date	Mintage	VG	F	VF	XF	Unc
ND(1655-56)	—	475	950	1,800	3,600	—

FR# A1323 1/4 ZECCHINO
0.8730 g., 0.9990 Gold 0.0280 oz. AGW **Ruler:** Francesco Corner **Obv. Legend:** FRANC CORNEL...

Date	Mintage	VG	F	VF	XF	Unc
ND(1656)	—	475	950	1,800	3,600	—

FR# 1328 1/4 ZECCHINO
0.8730 g., 0.9990 Gold 0.0280 oz. AGW **Ruler:** Bertuccio Valiero **Obv. Legend:** BERTVC VALER...

Date	Mintage	VG	F	VF	XF	Unc
ND(1656-58)	—	350	650	1,200	2,400	—

FR# 1331 1/4 ZECCHINO
0.8730 g., 0.9990 Gold 0.0280 oz. AGW **Ruler:** Giovanni Pesaro **Obv. Legend:** IOANNES PISAVRO...

Date	Mintage	VG	F	VF	XF	Unc
ND(1658-59)	—	300	600	1,200	2,650	—

FR# 1334 1/4 ZECCHINO
0.8730 g., 0.9990 Gold 0.0280 oz. AGW **Ruler:** Domenico II Contarini **Obv. Legend:** DOMIN CONTAR... **Note:** Varieties exist.

Date	Mintage	VG	F	VF	XF	Unc
ND(1659-74)	—	110	180	450	900	—

FR# 1337 1/4 ZECCHINO
0.8730 g., 0.9990 Gold 0.0280 oz. AGW **Ruler:** Nicolo Sagredo **Obv. Legend:** NICOL SAGREDO...

Date	Mintage	VG	F	VF	XF	Unc
ND(1675-76) Rare	—	—	—	—	—	—

FR# 1340 1/4 ZECCHINO
0.8730 g., 0.9990 Gold 0.0280 oz. AGW **Ruler:** Luigi Contarini **Obv. Legend:** ALOYSI CONTA...

Date	Mintage	VG	F	VF	XF	Unc
ND(1676-84)	—	120	180	450	900	—

FR# 1343 1/4 ZECCHINO
0.8730 g., 0.9990 Gold 0.0280 oz. AGW **Ruler:** Marcantonio Giustinian **Obv. Legend:** M ANTON IVSTIN...

Date	Mintage	VG	F	VF	XF	Unc
ND(1684-88)	—	325	625	1,250	2,600	—

FR# 1349 1/4 ZECCHINO
0.8730 g., 0.9990 Gold 0.0280 oz. AGW **Ruler:** Francesco Morosini **Obv. Legend:** FRAN MAVROC...

Date	Mintage	VG	F	VF	XF	Unc
ND(1688-94)	—	325	650	1,300	2,600	—

FR# 1356 1/4 ZECCHINO
0.8730 g., 0.9990 Gold 0.0280 oz. AGW **Ruler:** Silvestro Valiero **Obv. Legend:** SILVEST VALERIO...

Date	Mintage	VG	F	VF	XF	Unc
ND(1694-1700)	—	325	575	1,150	2,350	—

FR# 1360 1/4 ZECCHINO
0.8730 g., 0.9990 Gold 0.0280 oz. AGW **Ruler:** Alvise II Mocenigo **Obv:** Doge kneeling before St. Mark **Obv. Legend:** ALOY • MOC... **Rev:** Christ standing in starred field **Rev. Legend:** EGO • SVM • LVX • MVN •

Date	Mintage	VG	F	VF	XF	Unc
ND(1700-09)	—	90.00	140	300	525	—

FR# 1279 1/2 ZECCHINO
1.7470 g., 0.9990 Gold 0.0561 oz. AGW **Ruler:** Leonardo Donato **Obv. Legend:** LEON DON...

Date	Mintage	VG	F	VF	XF	Unc
ND(1605-12)	—	95.00	155	325	550	—

FR# 1282 1/2 ZECCHINO
1.7470 g., 0.9990 Gold 0.0561 oz. AGW **Ruler:** Marcantonio Memmo **Obv. Legend:** M A MEMMO...

Date	Mintage	VG	F	VF	XF	Unc
ND(1612-15)	—	210	425	725	1,200	—

FR# 1285 1/2 ZECCHINO
1.7470 g., 0.9990 Gold 0.0561 oz. AGW **Ruler:** Giovanni Bembo **Obv. Legend:** IO BEMBO...

Date	Mintage	VG	F	VF	XF	Unc
ND(1615-18) Rare	—	—	—	—	—	—

FR# 1292 1/2 ZECCHINO
1.7470 g., 0.9990 Gold 0.0561 oz. AGW **Ruler:** Antonio Priuli **Obv. Legend:** ANT PRI...

Date	Mintage	VG	F	VF	XF	Unc
ND(1618-23)	—	110	170	400	700	—

FR# 1295 1/2 ZECCHINO
1.7470 g., 0.9990 Gold 0.0561 oz. AGW **Ruler:** Francesco Contarini **Obv. Legend:** FRA CONT...

Date	Mintage	VG	F	VF	XF	Unc
ND(1623-24)	—	350	775	1,600	3,600	—

FR# 1298 1/2 ZECCHINO
1.7470 g., 0.9990 Gold 0.0561 oz. AGW **Ruler:** Giovanni Corner **Obv. Legend:** IO CORN...

Date	Mintage	VG	F	VF	XF	Unc
ND(1625-29)	—	350	775	1,550	3,500	—

FR# 1308 1/2 ZECCHINO
1.7470 g., 0.9990 Gold 0.0561 oz. AGW **Ruler:** Nicolo Contarini **Obv. Legend:** NIC CONT...

Date	Mintage	VG	F	VF	XF	Unc
ND(1630-31)	—	525	1,050	2,500	5,000	—

FR# 1311 1/2 ZECCHINO
1.7470 g., 0.9990 Gold 0.0561 oz. AGW **Ruler:** Francesco Erizzo **Obv. Legend:** FRA ERI...

Date	Mintage	VG	F	VF	XF	Unc
ND(1631-46)	—	150	270	450	975	—

FR# 1319 1/2 ZECCHINO
1.7470 g., 0.9990 Gold 0.0561 oz. AGW **Ruler:** Francesco Molin **Obv. Legend:** FRANC MOL...

Date	Mintage	VG	F	VF	XF	Unc
ND(1646-55)	—	350	650	1,350	3,050	—

FR# 1322 1/2 ZECCHINO
1.7470 g., 0.9990 Gold 0.0561 oz. AGW **Ruler:** Carlo Contarini **Obv. Legend:** CAROL CON...

Date	Mintage	VG	F	VF	XF	Unc
ND(1655-56)	—	425	850	1,600	3,600	—

FR# 1325 1/2 ZECCHINO
1.7470 g., 0.9990 Gold 0.0561 oz. AGW **Ruler:** Francesco Corner **Obv. Legend:** FRANC CORN...

Date	Mintage	VG	F	VF	XF	Unc
ND(1656) Rare	—	—	—	—	—	—

FR# 1327 1/2 ZECCHINO
1.7470 g., 0.9990 Gold 0.0561 oz. AGW **Ruler:** Bertuccio Valiero **Obv. Legend:** BERT VAL...

Date	Mintage	VG	F	VF	XF	Unc
ND(1656-58)	—	600	1,200	2,550	5,100	—

FR# 1330 1/2 ZECCHINO
1.7470 g., 0.9990 Gold 0.0561 oz. AGW **Ruler:** Giovanni Pesaro **Obv. Legend:** IO PISAVR...

Date	Mintage	VG	F	VF	XF	Unc
ND(1658-59)	—	500	1,000	2,150	4,200	—

FR# 1333 1/2 ZECCHINO
1.7470 g., 0.9990 Gold 0.0561 oz. AGW **Ruler:** Domenico II Contarini **Obv. Legend:** COMIN CON...

Date	Mintage	VG	F	VF	XF	Unc
ND(1659-74)	—	110	190	350	600	—

FR# 1336 1/2 ZECCHINO
1.7470 g., 0.9990 Gold 0.0561 oz. AGW **Ruler:** Nicolo Sagredo **Obv. Legend:** NICOL SAG...

Date	Mintage	VG	F	VF	XF	Unc
ND(1675-76)	—	650	1,300	2,700	5,300	—

FR# 1339 1/2 ZECCHINO
1.7470 g., 0.9990 Gold 0.0561 oz. AGW **Ruler:** Luigi Contarini **Obv. Legend:** ALOYS CO...

Date	Mintage	VG	F	VF	XF	Unc
ND(1676-84) Rare	—	—	—	—	—	—

FR# 1342 1/2 ZECCHINO
1.7470 g., 0.9990 Gold 0.0561 oz. AGW **Ruler:** Marcantonio Giustinian **Obv. Legend:** M A IVSTIN...

Date	Mintage	VG	F	VF	XF	Unc
ND(1684-88)	—	245	500	1,050	2,300	—

FR# 1348 1/2 ZECCHINO
1.7470 g., 0.9990 Gold 0.0561 oz. AGW **Ruler:** Francesco Morosini **Obv. Legend:** FR MAVROC...

Date	Mintage	VG	F	VF	XF	Unc
ND(1688-94)	—	300	575	1,200	2,650	—

FR# 1355 1/2 ZECCHINO
1.7470 g., 0.9990 Gold 0.0561 oz. AGW **Ruler:** Silvestro Valiero **Obv. Legend:** SIL VALERI...

Date	Mintage	VG	F	VF	XF	Unc
ND(1694-1700)	—	350	650	1,400	3,000	—

FR# 1359 1/2 ZECCHINO
1.7470 g., 0.9990 Gold 0.0561 oz. AGW **Ruler:** Alvise II Mocenigo **Obv:** Doge kneeling before St. Mark **Obv. Legend:** ALOY • MOC... **Rev:** Christ standing in starred field **Rev. Legend:** * LVX * MVN * EGO * SVM *

Date	Mintage	VG	F	VF	XF	Unc
ND(1700-09)	—	110	170	300	550	—

FR# 1278 ZECCHINO
3.4940 g., 0.9990 Gold 0.1122 oz. AGW **Ruler:** Leonardo Donato **Obv. Legend:** LEON DON...

Date	Mintage	VG	F	VF	XF	Unc
ND(1605-12)	—	130	265	450	900	—

DAV# 4230 ZECCHINO
45.4700 g., 0.9480 Silver 1.3858 oz. ASW **Ruler:** Leonardo Donato **Obv:** St. Mark seated blessing kneeling Doge **Obv. Legend:** S. M. VENET: LEONARS: DONAT: DVX **Rev:** Legend around Christ standing in oval and stars **Rev. Legend:** SIT • T • XPE • DAT • Q • TV... **Note:** Two legend varieties exist.

Date	Mintage	VG	F	VF	XF	Unc
ND(1607) ZPS	—	300	525	900	1,700	—

DAV# 4231 ZECCHINO
45.4700 g., 0.9480 Silver 1.3858 oz. ASW **Ruler:** Leonardo Donato **Obv:** Legend around St. Mark standing blessing kneeling Doge **Obv. Legend:** LEONAR • DONATO... **Note:** Two legend varieties exist.

Date	Mintage	VG	F	VF	XF	Unc
ND(1607) ZPS	—	300	500	825	1,450	—
ND(1607-08) CP	—	300	500	825	1,450	—
ND(1609-12) CZ	—	300	500	825	1,450	—

DAV# 4235 ZECCHINO
45.4700 g., 0.9480 Silver 1.3858 oz. ASW **Ruler:** Marcantonio Memmo **Obv. Legend:** M • ANT • MEMO...

Date	Mintage	VG	F	VF	XF	Unc
ND(1612-13) AC	—	300	525	900	1,700	—

FR# 1281 ZECCHINO
3.4940 g., 0.9990 Gold 0.1122 oz. AGW **Ruler:** Marcantonio Memmo **Obv. Legend:** M • A • MEMMO...

Date	Mintage	VG	F	VF	XF	Unc
ND(1612-18)	—	300	800	1,200	2,000	—

FR# 1284 ZECCHINO
3.4940 g., 0.9990 Gold 0.1122 oz. AGW **Ruler:** Giovanni Bembo **Obv. Legend:** IO BEMBO...

Date	Mintage	VG	F	VF	XF	Unc
ND(1615-18)	—	500	1,000	2,000	3,500	—

FR# 1287 ZECCHINO
3.4940 g., 0.9990 Gold 0.1122 oz. AGW **Ruler:** Nicolo Donato **Obv. Legend:** NIC DONATO...

Date	Mintage	VG	F	VF	XF	Unc
ND(1618) Rare	—	—	—	—	—	—

FR# 1291 ZECCHINO
3.4940 g., 0.9990 Gold 0.1122 oz. AGW **Ruler:** Antonio Priuli **Obv. Legend:** ANT PRIOL...

Date	Mintage	VG	F	VF	XF	Unc
ND(1618-23)	—	120	220	425	850	—

DAV# 4240 ZECCHINO
45.4700 g., 0.9480 Silver 1.3858 oz. ASW **Ruler:** Antonio Priuli **Obv. Legend:** ANT: PRIOL...

Date	Mintage	VG	F	VF	XF	Unc
ND(1618-20) GR	—	300	500	825	1,450	—
ND(1620-21) HZ	—	300	500	825	1,450	—

FR# 1294 ZECCHINO
3.4940 g., 0.9990 Gold 0.1122 oz. AGW **Ruler:** Francesco Contarini **Obv. Legend:** FRANC CONT...

Date	Mintage	VG	F	VF	XF	Unc
ND(1623-24) Rare	—	—	—	—	—	—

FR# 1297 ZECCHINO
3.4940 g., 0.9990 Gold 0.1122 oz. AGW **Ruler:** Giovanni Corner **Obv. Legend:** IO CORNEL...

Date	Mintage	VG	F	VF	XF	Unc
ND(1625-29) Rare	—	—	—	—	—	—

FR# 1307 ZECCHINO
3.4940 g., 0.9990 Gold 0.1122 oz. AGW **Ruler:** Nicolo Contarini **Obv. Legend:** NIC CONT...

Date	Mintage	VG	F	VF	XF	Unc
ND(1630-31) Rare	—	—	—	—	—	—

DAV# 4247 ZECCHINO
45.4700 g., 0.9480 Silver 1.3858 oz. ASW **Ruler:** Nicolo Contarini **Obv. Legend:** NICOL • CONT...

Date	Mintage	VG	F	VF	XF	Unc
ND(1630) DB	—	300	525	900	1,700	—

FR# 1310 ZECCHINO
3.4940 g., 0.9990 Gold 0.1122 oz. AGW **Ruler:** Francesco Erizzo **Obv. Legend:** FRANC ERIZZ...

Date	Mintage	VG	F	VF	XF	Unc
ND(1631-46)	—	120	180	375	750	—

FR# 1318 ZECCHINO
3.4940 g., 0.9990 Gold 0.1122 oz. AGW **Ruler:** Francesco Molin **Obv. Legend:** FRANC MOLINO...

Date	Mintage	VG	F	VF	XF	Unc
ND(1646-55)	—	120	145	250	475	—

FR# 1321 ZECCHINO
3.4940 g., 0.9990 Gold 0.1122 oz. AGW **Ruler:** Carlo Contarini **Obv. Legend:** CAROL CONT...

Date	Mintage	VG	F	VF	XF	Unc
ND(1655-56)	—	140	280	450	900	—

FR# 1324 ZECCHINO
3.4940 g., 0.9990 Gold 0.1122 oz. AGW **Ruler:** Francesco Corner **Obv. Legend:** FRANC CORN...

Date	Mintage	VG	F	VF	XF	Unc
ND(1656)	—	2,200	3,300	6,100	9,900	—

FR# 1326 ZECCHINO
3.4940 g., 0.9990 Gold 0.1122 oz. AGW **Ruler:** Bertuccio Valiero **Obv. Legend:** BERT VALER...

Date	Mintage	VG	F	VF	XF	Unc
ND(1656-58)	—	120	150	300	600	—

FR# 1329 ZECCHINO
3.4940 g., 0.9990 Gold 0.1122 oz. AGW **Ruler:** Giovanni Pesaro **Obv. Legend:** IOAN PISAVRO...

Date	Mintage	VG	F	VF	XF	Unc
ND(1658-59)	—	150	325	625	1,150	—

FR# 1332 ZECCHINO
3.4940 g., 0.9990 Gold 0.1122 oz. AGW **Ruler:** Domenico II Contarini **Obv. Legend:** DOMIN CONT... **Note:** Varieties exist.

Date	Mintage	VG	F	VF	XF	Unc
ND(1659-74)	—	120	145	250	575	—

FR# 1335 ZECCHINO
3.4940 g., 0.9990 Gold 0.1122 oz. AGW **Ruler:** Nicolo Sagredo **Obv. Legend:** NICOL SAGREDO...

Date	Mintage	VG	F	VF	XF	Unc
ND(1675-76)	—	190	375	800	1,750	—

FR# 1338 ZECCHINO
3.4940 g., 0.9990 Gold 0.1122 oz. AGW **Ruler:** Luigi Contarini **Obv. Legend:** ALOYSIVS CONT...

Date	Mintage	VG	F	VF	XF	Unc
ND(1676-84)	—	120	145	250	575	—

FR# 1341 ZECCHINO
3.4940 g., 0.9990 Gold 0.1122 oz. AGW **Ruler:** Marcantonio Giustinian **Obv. Legend:** M ANT IVSTIN...

Date	Mintage	VG	F	VF	XF	Unc
ND(1684-88)	—	120	145	300	600	—

FR# 1347 ZECCHINO
3.4940 g., 0.9990 Gold 0.1122 oz. AGW **Ruler:** Francesco Morosini **Obv. Legend:** FRAN MABROC...

Date	Mintage	VG	F	VF	XF	Unc
ND(1688-94)	—	120	150	300	650	—

FR# 1354 ZECCHINO
3.4940 g., 0.9990 Gold 0.1122 oz. AGW **Ruler:** Silvestro Valiero **Obv. Legend:** SILV VALERIO...

Date	Mintage	VG	F	VF	XF	Unc
ND(1694-1700)	—	120	150	300	650	—

FR# 1358 ZECCHINO
3.4940 g., 0.9990 Gold 0.1122 oz. AGW **Ruler:** Alvise II Mocenigo **Obv:** Doge kneeling before St. Mark **Obv. Legend:** ALOY * MOCENI * ... **Rev:** Christ standing in starred field **Rev. Legend:** SIT • T • XPE • DAT • Q • TV REGIS • ISTE • DVCA

Date	Mintage	VG	F	VF	XF	Unc
ND(1700-09)	—	120	145	225	450	—

FR# 1290 2 ZECCHINI
6.9880 g., 0.9990 Gold 0.2244 oz. AGW **Ruler:** Antonio Priuli **Obv. Legend:** S • M • VENET • ANT • PRIOL • DVX •

Date	Mintage	VG	F	VF	XF	Unc
ND(1618-23) Rare	—	—	—	—	—	—

FR# 1306 2 ZECCHINI
6.9100 g., 0.9990 Gold 0.2219 oz. AGW **Ruler:** Nicolo Contarini **Obv. Legend:** NIC CONT... **Rev:** Christ standing in starred field

Date	Mintage	VG	F	VF	XF	Unc
ND(1630-31) Rare	—	—	—	—	—	—

FR# 1305 3 ZECCHINI
10.4820 g., 0.9990 Gold 0.3367 oz. AGW **Ruler:** Nicolo Contarini **Obv. Legend:** NIC CONT...

Date	Mintage	VG	F	VF	XF	Unc
ND(1630-31) Rare	—	—	—	—	—	—

FR# 1378 4 ZECCHINI
13.9700 g., 0.9990 Gold 0.4487 oz. AGW **Ruler:** Alvise II Mocenigo **Obv:** Doge kneeling before St. Mark **Obv. Legend:** ALOYS * MOCEN * ... **Rev:** Christ standing in starred field **Rev. Legend:** SIT * T * XPE * DAT * Q * T V ...

Date	Mintage	VG	F	VF	XF	Unc
ND(1700-09)	—	1,200	2,900	4,800	9,000	—

FR# 1289 5 ZECCHINI
17.3700 g., 0.9990 Gold 0.5579 oz. AGW **Ruler:** Antonio Priuli **Obv. Legend:** ANT PRIOL...

Date	Mintage	VG	F	VF	XF	Unc
ND(1618-23) Rare	—	—	—	—	—	—

FR# 1346 6 ZECCHINI
20.2800 g., 0.9990 Gold 0.6513 oz. AGW **Ruler:** Francesco Morosini **Obv:** Doge kneeling before St. Mark **Obv. Legend:** FRAN MAVROC... **Rev:** Christ standing in starred field **Note:** Varieties exist.

Date	Mintage	VG	F	VF	XF	Unc
ND (1688)	—	3,600	6,000	10,000	15,000	—

FR# 1317 7 ZECCHINI
24.2900 g., 0.9990 Gold 0.7801 oz. AGW **Ruler:** Francesco Molin **Obv:** Doge kneeling before St. Mark **Obv. Legend:** FRANC MOLINO... **Rev:** Christ standing in starred field

Date	Mintage	VG	F	VF	XF	Unc
ND(1646-55) Rare	—	—	—	—	—	—

FR# 1345 8 ZECCHINI
27.9400 g., 0.9990 Gold 0.8974 oz. AGW **Ruler:** Francesco Morosini **Obv:** Doge kneeling before St. Mark **Obv. Legend:** FRAN MAVROC... **Rev:** Christ standing in starred field

Date	Mintage	VG	F	VF	XF	Unc
ND(1688-94) Rare	—	—	—	—	—	—

FR# A1303 10 ZECCHINI
34.6500 g., 0.9990 Gold 1.1129 oz. AGW, 30 mm. **Ruler:** Francesco Contarini

Date	Mintage	VG	F	VF	XF	Unc
ND(1623-24) Rare	—	—	—	—	—	—

FR# 1303 10 ZECCHINI
34.6500 g., 0.9990 Gold 1.1129 oz. AGW **Ruler:** Francesco Contarini **Obv:** Doge kneeling before St. Mark

Date	Mintage	VG	F	VF	XF	Unc
ND(1623-24) Rare	—	—	—	—	—	—

FR# 1316 10 ZECCHINI
34.6500 g., 0.9990 Gold 1.1129 oz. AGW **Ruler:** Francesco Molin **Obv. Legend:** FRANC MOLINO... **Rev:** Christ standing in starred field **Note:** Varieties exist.

Date	Mintage	VG	F	VF	XF	Unc
ND(1646-55)	—	2,400	5,000	10,000	17,000	—

FR# 1344 10 ZECCHINI
34.6500 g., 0.9990 Gold 1.1129 oz. AGW **Ruler:** Francesco Morosini

Date	Mintage	VG	F	VF	XF	Unc
ND(1688-94) Rare	—	—	—	—	—	—

FR# 1353 10 ZECCHINI
34.6500 g., 0.9990 Gold 1.1129 oz. AGW **Ruler:** Silvestro Valiero **Obv. Legend:** SILV VALERIO...

Date	Mintage	VG	F	VF	XF	Unc
ND(1694-1700) Rare	—	—	—	—	—	—

FR# 1357 10 ZECCHINI
34.7500 g., 0.9990 Gold 1.1161 oz. AGW **Ruler:** Alvise II Mocenigo **Obv. Legend:** ALOY. MOCENI...

Date	Mintage	VG	F	VF	XF	Unc
ND(1700-09)	—	2,400	6,000	14,000	20,000	—

FR# 1315 12 ZECCHINI
41.8000 g., 0.9990 Gold 1.3425 oz. AGW **Ruler:** Francesco Molin **Obv:** Doge kneeling before St. Mark **Obv. Legend:** FRANC MOLINO... **Rev:** Christ standing in starred field

Date	Mintage	VG	F	VF	XF	Unc
ND(1646-55) Rare	—	—	—	—	—	—

FR# 1352 12 ZECCHINI
41.5700 g., 0.9990 Gold 1.3351 oz. AGW **Ruler:** Silvestro Valiero **Obv. Legend:** SILV VALERIO...

Date	Mintage	VG	F	VF	XF	Unc
ND(1694-1700) Rare	—	—	—	—	—	—

FR# 1351 15 ZECCHINI
52.1000 g., 0.9990 Gold 1.6733 oz. AGW **Ruler:** Silvestro Valiero **Obv:** Doge kneeling before St. Mark **Obv. Legend:** SILV VALERIO... **Rev:** Christ standing in starred field

Date	Mintage	VG	F	VF	XF	Unc
ND(1694-1700) Rare	—	—	—	—	—	—

FR# 1313 20 ZECCHINI
69.6000 g., 0.9990 Gold 2.2354 oz. AGW **Ruler:** Francesco Molin **Obv:** Doge kneeling before St. Mark **Obv. Legend:** FRANC MOLINO... **Rev:** Christ standing in starred field

Date	Mintage	VG	F	VF	XF	Unc
ND(1646-55) Rare	—	—	—	—	—	—

FR# 1494 1/2 DUCAT
1.0830 g., 0.9990 Gold 0.0348 oz. AGW **Ruler:** Leonardo Donato **Obv:** Doge kneeling before seated figure of St. Mark **Obv. Legend:** S • M • VEN • LEON • DONAT **Rev:** Lion of St. Mark in inner circle

Date	Mintage	VG	F	VF	XF	Unc
ND(1605-12)	—	300	650	1,400	2,600	—

FR# 1493 DUCAT
2.1660 g., 0.9990 Gold 0.0696 oz. AGW **Ruler:** Leonardo Donato **Obv:** Doge kneeling before seated figure of St. Mark **Obv. Legend:** S • M • VEN • LEON • DONAT • DVX **Rev:** Lion of St. Mark in inner circle

Date	Mintage	VG	F	VF	XF	Unc
ND(1605-12)	—	425	775	1,450	2,400	—

FR# 1499 DUCAT
2.1660 g., 0.9990 Gold 0.0696 oz. AGW **Ruler:** Leonardo Donato **Obv:** Doge kneeling before lion of St. Mark **Obv. Legend:** S • M • VEN • LEON • DONAT • DVX **Rev:** St. Justina standing with palm and cross in inner circle

Date	Mintage	VG	F	VF	XF	Unc
ND(1605-12) Rare	—	—	—	—	—	—

FR# 1500 DUCAT
2.1660 g., 0.9990 Gold 0.0696 oz. AGW **Ruler:** Leonardo Donato **Obv:** Doge kneeling before St. Mark **Obv. Legend:** S • M • VEN • LEONAR • DONAT • DVX **Rev:** Christ standing facing on pedestal in inner circle

Date	Mintage	VG	F	VF	XF	Unc
ND(1605-12) Rare	—	—	—	—	—	—

FR# 1495 DUCAT
2.1660 g., 0.9990 Gold 0.0696 oz. AGW **Ruler:** Nicolo Donato **Obv:** Doge kneeling before seated figure of St. Mark **Obv. Legend:** S • M • VEN • NIC • DONATO • DVX **Rev:** Lion of St. Mark in inner circle

Date	Mintage	VG	F	VF	XF	Unc
ND(1618) Rare	—	—	—	—	—	—

FR# 1496 DUCAT
2.1660 g., 0.9990 Gold 0.0696 oz. AGW **Ruler:** Antonio Priuli **Obv:** Doge kneeling before seated figure of St. Mark **Obv. Legend:** S • M • VEN • ANT • PRIOL • DVX **Rev:** Lion of St. Mark in inner circle

Date	Mintage	VG	F	VF	XF	Unc
ND(1618-23) Rare	—	—	—	—	—	—

FR# 1497 DUCAT
2.1660 g., 0.9990 Gold 0.0696 oz. AGW **Ruler:** Giovanni Corner **Obv:** Doge kneeling before seated figure of St. Mark **Obv. Legend:** S • M • VEN • IO • CORN • DVX **Rev:** Lion of St. Mark in inner circle

Date	Mintage	VG	F	VF	XF	Unc
ND(1625-29)	—	3,000	4,800	7,800	11,500	—

FR# 1492 2 DUCATS
4.3320 g., 0.9990 Gold 0.1391 oz. AGW **Ruler:** Leonardo Donato **Obv:** Doge kneeling before seated figure of St. Mark **Obv. Legend:** S • M • VEN • LEON • DONAT • DVX **Rev:** Lion of St. Mark in inner circle

Date	Mintage	VG	F	VF	XF	Unc
ND(1605-12) Rare	—	—	—	—	—	—

PATTERNS

Including off metal strikes

KM#	Date	Mintage	Identification	Mkt Val
Pn1	ND(1612) FS	—	Zecchino. Gold. 52.1500 g. Leonardo Dona. Dav. #4231.	—
Pn2	ND(1623-24)	—	Piastre. 0.9480 Silver. 26.9100 g. Francesco Contarini.	—
Pn3	ND(1623-24)	—	Reale. 0.9480 Silver. 26.7500 g. Francesco Contarini.	—
Pn4	ND(1631-46)	—	4 Soldi. Billon. 3.9850 g. Francesco Erizzo.	—
Pn5	ND(1631-46)	—	5 Soldi. Billon. 2.1700 g. Francesco Erizzo.	—
Pn6	ND(1645-46) MB	—	72 Soldi. 13.1300 g. Francesco Erizzo.	—
Pn7	1644 ZMB	—	Reale. Silver. 13.9300 g. Francesco Erizzo.	—
Pn8	ND(1639-40) GC	—	2 Scudi. Silver. 64.0000 g. Francesco Erizzo. Dav. #4248.	2,000
Pn9	ND(1641) OZ	—	2 Scudi. Silver. 64.0000 g. Francesco Erizzo. Dav. #4248.	2,000
Pn10	ND(1646) MB	—	2 Scudi. Silver. 64.0000 g. Francesco Molin. Dav. #4251.	2,000
Pn11	ND(1659-60) BB	—	2 Scudi. Silver. 64.0000 g. Domenico Contarini. Dav. #4262.	2,000
Pn12	ND(1662-63) GD	—	2 Ducatone. Silver. 56.0000 g. Domenico Contarini. Dav. #4264.	1,000
Pn13	ND(1666-67) AD	—	2 Ducato. Silver. 47.0000 g. Domenico Contarini. Dav. #4266.	1,000
Pn14	ND(1668) LP	—	2 Ducato. Silver. 47.0000 g. Domenico Contarini. Dav. #4266.	1,000
Pn15	ND(1679-81) GZ	—	2 Scudi. Silver. 64.0000 g. Alvise Contarini. Dav. #4271.	2,000
Pn16	ND(1679) AC	—	2 Ducato. Silver. 47.0000 g. Alvise Contarini. Dav. #A4274.	1,000
Pn17	ND(1694-1700) FT	—	2 Ducato. Silver. 47.0000 g. Silvestro Valier. Dav. #4285.	1,000
Pn18	ND(1700-09)	—	2 Ducato. Silver. 47.0000 g. Alvise Mociengo II; Dav.#1526.	—

VERCELLI

The town of Vercelli, located about halfway between Torino and Milan, came under the control of the dukes of Savoy in 1427. It was besieged by the Spanish under the command of Don Pedro of Toledo, governor of Milan, in 1616-17. Obsidional coinage was struck in the latter year by order of the Marchese di Caluso, commander of the defending garrison. The Spanish laid siege to the city again in 1638, during the time that Duke Francesco Giacinto of Savoy was under the regency of his mother.

REFERENCE

Cud = Sergio Cudazzo, ***Monete Italiane Regionali: Casa Savoia***, Pavia: Numismatica Varesi, 2005.

CITY

1617 SIEGE COINAGE

KM# 1 SOLDO
Copper Weight varies: 3.85-3.88g., 24 mm. **Obv:** CE monogram in circle of pellets **Rev:** 3-line inscription with date, rosette above **Rev. Inscription:** VERCEL / OBS. (date) **Note:** Ref. Cud. 692. Struck in name of Duke Carlo Emanuele I of Savoy.

Date	Mintage	VG	F	VF	XF	Unc
1617 Rare	—	—	—	—	—	—

KM# 2 2 FIORINI
Billon Weight varies: 6.69-6.78g., 30 mm. **Obv:** High-collared, draped and armored bust to right, mintmark below **Obv. Legend:** CAR. EM. D. G. DVX. SAB. P. P. **Rev:** 4-line inscription with date in square baroque frame **Rev. Inscription:** VERCEL / LIS. IN. OB / SIDIONE / (date) **Note:** Ref. Cud. 691. Prev. KM#1. Varieties exist. Struck in name of Duke Carlo Emanuele I of Savoy.

Date	Mintage	VG	F	VF	XF	Unc
1617 V	—	3,000	4,800	8,400	13,500	—

KM# 3 4 SCUDI D'ORO
13.2300 g., Gold, 30 mm. **Obv:** High-collared, draped and armored bust to right, mintmark below **Obv. Legend:** CAR. EM. D. G. DVX. SAB. P. P. **Rev:** 4-line inscription with date in square baroque frame **Rev. Inscription:** VERCELL / IS. IN. OB / SIDION / E. (date) **Note:** Ref. Cud. 689; Fr. 1521. Prev. KM#2. Struck in name of Duke Carlo Emanuele I of Savoy.

Date	Mintage	VG	F	VF	XF	Unc
1617 V Rare	—	—	—	—	—	—

SIEGE COINAGE

1638

KM# 5 1/2 SOLDO (Mezzo Soldo)
Billon Weight varies: 2.20-4.70g., 20 mm. **Obv:** Crowned shield of Savoy arms in circle **Obv. Legend:** +F. I. D. G. D. S. R. C. **Rev:** 3-line inscription in circle **Rev. Legend:** +CHR. FRAN. MATRE. REGEN. **Rev. Inscription:** VER. / ITERV. / OBS. **Note:** Ref. Cud. 733. Prev. KM#3. Struck in names of Duke Francesco Giacinto and his mother.

Date	Mintage	VG	F	VF	XF	Unc
ND(1638)	—	650	1,000	2,000	3,500	—

KM# 6.1 1/4 LIRA
Billon Weight varies: 4.24-6.45g., 29 mm. **Obv:** Crowned shield of Savoy arms divides date in circle **Obv. Legend:** +FRAN* IACINT*D*G*DVX*SAB*REX*CYPRI. **Rev:** 4-line inscription in rectangle, .S.V. below, all in circle **Rev. Legend:** +CHRIST* FRANCICA*MATRE*REGENT. **Rev. Inscription:** VERCELLÆ / .ITERVM. / .AB. HISP. / OBSESSÆ. **Note:** Ref. Cud. 729a. Struck in name of Duke Francesco Giacinto of Savoy and his mother.

Date	Mintage	VG	F	VF	XF	Unc
1638	—	1,650	3,000	6,000	—	—

KM# 6.2 1/4 LIRA
Billon Weight varies: 4.24-6.45g., 29 mm. **Obv:** Crowned shield of Savoy arms divides date in circle **Obv. Legend:** +FRAN* IACINT*D*G*DVX*SAB*REX*CYPRI. **Rev:** 4-line inscription in ornamented rectangle, • S:V • below **Rev. Legend:** +CHRIST* FRANCICA*MATRE*REGENT. **Rev. Inscription:** VERCELLÆ / .ITERVM. / .AB. HISP. / OBSESSÆ. **Note:** Ref. Cud. 729b. Prev. KM#4.1. Struck in name of Duke Francesco Giacinto of Savoy and his mother.

Date	Mintage	VG	F	VF	XF	Unc
1638	—	1,750	3,500	6,500	12,500	—

KM# 6.3 1/4 LIRA
Billon Weight varies: 4.24-6.45g., 29 mm. **Obv:** Crowned shield of Savoy arms divides date in circle, 5-petaled rosette above each part of date **Obv. Legend:** +FRAN*IACINT*D*G*DVX*SAB* REX*CYPRI. **Rev:** 4-line inscription, arabesque above, .S.V. in exergue, all in circle **Rev. Legend:** +CHRIST*FRANCICA* MATRE*REGENT. **Rev. Inscription:** VERCELLÆ / .ITERVM. / .AB. HISP. / OBSESSÆ. **Note:** Ref. Cud. 730. Struck in name of Duke Francesco Giacinto of Savoy and his mother.

Date	Mintage	VG	F	VF	XF	Unc
1638 Rare	—	—	—	—	—	—

KM# 6.4 1/4 LIRA
Billon Weight varies: 4.24-6.45g., 29 mm. **Obv:** Crowned shield of Savoy arms divides date in circle, 5-petaled rosette above each part of date **Obv. Legend:** +FRAN*IACINT*D*G*DVX* SAB*REX*CYPRI. **Rev:** 4-line inscription in plain rectangle, •S•V• below **Rev. Legend:** +CHRIST*FRANCICA*MATRE*REGENT. **Rev. Inscription:** VERCELLÆ / .ITERVM. / .AB. HISP. / OBSESSÆ. **Note:** Ref. Cud. 731. Prev. KM#4.3. Struck in name of Duke Francesco Giacinto of Savoy and his mother.

Date	Mintage	VG	F	VF	XF	Unc
1638	—	1,650	3,250	6,000	—	—

KM# 6.5 1/4 LIRA
Billon Weight varies: 5.50-5.60g., 29 mm. **Obv:** Crowned shield of Savoy arms divides date in circle **Obv. Legend:** +FRAN. IACINT. D. G. DVX. SAB. REX. CYPRI. **Rev:** 4-line inscription, arabesque above, nothing in exergue, all in circle **Rev. Legend:** +*CHRISTIANA. FRAN. MATRE. REGENTE* **Rev. Inscription:** VERCELLÆ / .ITERVM. / .AB. HISP. / OBSESSÆ. **Note:** Ref. Cud. 732. Varieties exist. In name of Duke Francesco Giacinto of Savoy and his mother.

Date	Mintage	VG	F	VF	XF	Unc
1638	—	2,500	6,000	10,000	—	—

KM# 7.1 1/4 LIRA
Billon Weight varies:4.24-6.45g., 29 mm. **Obv:** Crowned shield of Savoy arms divides date in circle **Obv. Legend:** +FRAN*I ACINT*D*G*DVX*SAB*REX*CYPRI. **Rev:** 4-line inscription, arabesque above, .5.S. in exergue, all in circle **Rev. Legend:** +CHRISTIANA*FRANCICA*MATRE*REGENT. **Rev. Inscription:** VERCELLÆ / .ITERVM. / AB. HISP. / OBSESSÆ. **Note:** Ref. Cud. 728a. Prev. KM#4.2. Struck in name of Duke Francesco Giacinto of Savoy and his mother.

Date	Mintage	VG	F	VF	XF	Unc
1638	—	1,400	2,750	6,200	—	—

KM# 7.2 1/4 LIRA
Billon Weight varies: 4.24-6.45g., 29 mm. **Obv:** Crowned shield of Savoy arms divides date in circle **Obv. Legend:** +FRA.N.* IACINT*D*G*SAB*DVX*REX*CYPRI. **Rev:** 4-line inscription, arabesque above, .5.S. in exergue, all in circle **Rev. Legend:** +CHRISTI*FRANCICA*MATRE*REGENTE. **Rev. Inscription:** VERCELLÆ / .ITERVM. / .AB. HISP. / OBSESSÆ. **Note:** Ref. Cud. 728b. Struck in name of Duke Francesco Giacinto of Savoy and his mother.

Date	Mintage	VG	F	VF	XF	Unc
1638 Rare	—	—	—	—	—	—

KM# 8 DOPPIA
Gold Weight varies: 5.50-6.76g., 29 mm. **Obv:** Crowned shield of Savoy arms divides date in circle **Obv. Legend:** +FRAN. IACINT. D. G. DVX. SAB. REX. CYPRI. **Rev:** 4-line inscription, arabesque above, nothing in exergue, all in circle **Rev. Legend:** +*CHRISTIANA. FRAN. MATRE. REGENTE* **Rev. Inscription:** VERCELLÆ / .ITERVM. / .AB. HISP. / OBSESSÆ. **Note:** Ref. Cud. 727; Fr. 1522. Struck in name of Duke Francesco Giacinto of Savoy and his mother.

Date	Mintage	VG	F	VF	XF	Unc
1638 Rare	—	—	—	—	—	—

VERGAGNI

Marquisate

Vergagni was a castle in the Valle Borbera, between Roccaforte and Mongiardino and held as a feudal possession of the Spinola family of Genoa from medieval times. In 1676, the feudal barony was raised to a marquisate by Emperor Leopold I. However, when the marchese committed an act of cowardice, Emperor Carlo VI stripped him of his possession of Vergagni and awarded it to Urbano Fieschi.

RULER
Giovanni Battista Spinola, 1676-1712

Reference: Alberto Varesi, ***Monete Italiane Regionali: Piemonte, Sardegna, Liguria, Isola di Corsica***. Pavia, 1996.

MARQUISATE

STANDARD COINAGE

KM# 1 LUIGINO
3.9800 g., Silver, 23 mm. **Ruler:** Giovanni Battista Spinola **Obv:** Armored bust to left, date below **Obv. Legend:** IO. BAPTIS. SPINVLA. **Rev:** Crowned shield of arms between two palm fronds **Rev. Legend:** MARC. S.R.I. ET. VERGAGNI. PRIM. COM. P. ET. **Note:** Varesi 1038.

Date	Mintage	VG	F	VF	XF	Unc
1680 Rare	—	—	—	—	—	—

KM# 2 2 LUIGINO
6.4000 g., Silver, 25.5 mm. **Ruler:** Giovanni Battista Spinola **Obv:** Armored bust to left, date below **Obv. Legend:** IO. BAPTIS. SPINVLA. **Rev:** Crowned shield of arms between two palm fronds **Rev. Legend:** MARC. S.R.I. ET. VERGAGNI. PRIM. COM. P. ET. **Note:** Varesi 1037.

Date	Mintage	VG	F	VF	XF	Unc
1680 Rare	—	—	—	—	—	—

KM# 3 SCUDO
26.3500 g., Silver, 41-42 mm. **Ruler:** Giovanni Battista Spinola **Obv:** Armored bust to left **Obv. Legend:** IOANNES. BAPTISTA. SPINVLA. **Rev:** Crowned imperial eagle, crowned shield of arms on breast **Rev. Legend:** MARC. S.R.I. ET VERGAGNI. PRIM. COM. P. ETc. **Note:** Varesi 1036; Dav. 4288.

Date	Mintage	VG	F	VF	XF	Unc
ND(1680) Rare	—	—	—	—	—	—

PROVAS

KM#	Date	Mintage	Identification	Mkt Val
Pr1	1697	—	Scudo. Silver. Crowned arms.	—

JAPAN

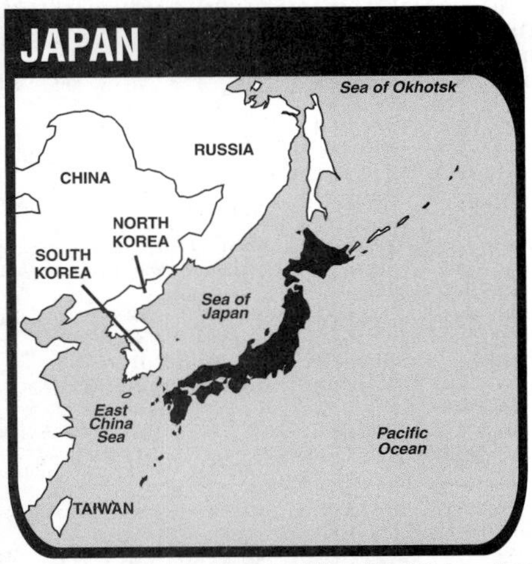

Japan, founded (so legend holds) in 660 B.C. by a direct descendant of the Sun Goddess, was first brought into contact with the west by a storm-blown Portuguese ship in 1542. European traders and missionaries proceeded to enlarge the contact until the Shogunate, sensing a military threat in the foreign presence, expelled all foreigners and restricted relations with the outside world in the 17th century. After Commodore Perry's U.S. flotilla visited in 1854, Japan rapidly industrialized, abolished the Shogunate and established a parliamentary form of government, and by the end of the 19th century achieved the status of a modern economic and military power.

Many of the provinces of Japan issued their own definitive coinage under the Shogunate.

RULERS

Shoguns
Iyeyasu Tokugawa, 1603-1605
Hidetada, 1605-1623
Iyemitsu, 1623-1651
Iyetsuna, 1651-1680
Tsunayoshi, 1680-1709

MONETARY SYSTEM

Until 1870

Prior to the Meiji currency reform, there was no fixed exchange rate between the various silver, gold and copper "cash" coins (which previously included Chinese "cash") in circulation. Each coin exchanged on the basis of its own merits and the prevailing market conditions. The size and weight of the copper coins and the weight and fineness of the silver and gold coins varied widely. From time to time the government would declare an official exchange rate, but this was usually ignored. For gold and silver, nominal equivalents were:

16 Shu = 4 Bu = 1 Ryo

MONETARY UNITS

Momme 匁　Ryo 両

Bu 分　Shu 朱　Mon 文

MINT MARKS ON MON

A - Edo (Tokyo) 文

LEGENDS

Reading top-bottom, right-left

Kan'ei Tsuho

Bunkyu-Eiho

SHOGUNATE

CAST COINAGE

KM# 5 MON
Cast Copper **Obv. Inscription:** Kei-Cho Tsu-Ho **Rev:** Plain

Date	Mintage	VG	F	VF	XF	Unc
ND(1606)	—	50.00	75.00	150	200	—

KM# 10 MON
Cast Copper **Obv. Inscription:** "Gen-Wa (Genna) Tsu-Ho" **Rev:** Character "ichi" ("one") at bottom

Date	Mintage	VG	F	VF	XF	Unc
ND(1617)	—	750	1,250	1,700	2,400	—

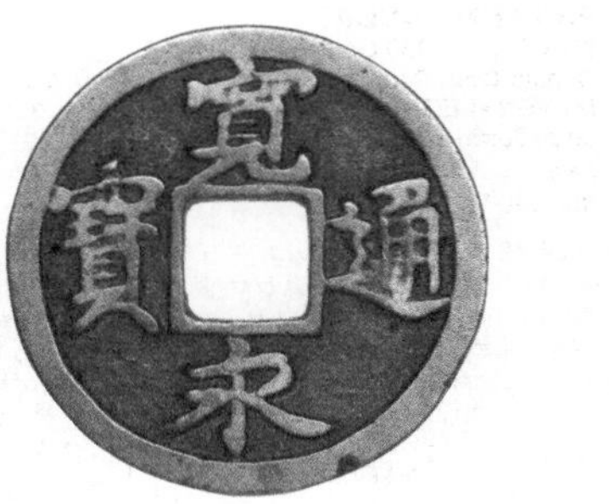

KM# 15 MON
Cast Copper **Obv:** First horizontal stroke of bottom character extends far to right of vertical **Obv. Inscription:** "Kwan-Ei (Kanei) Tsu-Ho"

Date	Mintage	VG	F	VF	XF	Unc
ND(1626)	—	300	375	550	950	—

C# 1.1 MON
Cast Copper, Bronze Or Brass **Obv. Inscription:** "Kwan-Ei (Kanei) Tsu-Ho" **Rev:** Plain **Note:** Cast at Edo (Tokyo) and Sakamoto.

Date	Mintage	VG	F	VF	XF	Unc
ND(1636-56)	—	0.25	0.50	1.00	1.50	—

C# 1.2 MON
Cast Copper, Bronze Or Brass **Rev:** "Bun" above

Date	Mintage	VG	F	VF	XF	Unc
ND(1668-1700)	—	0.25	0.50	1.00	1.50	—

BULLION COINAGE

KM# 6.1 MAMEITA GIN
0.8000 Silver **Obv:** One or more thin-line characters; without "God of Plenty" **Rev:** Chop marks **Note:** Keicho era.

Date	Mintage	VG	F	VF	XF	Unc
ND(1601-1695)	—	300	400	600	850	—

KM# 6.2 MAMEITA GIN
0.8000 Silver **Obv:** "God of Plenty" drawn with thin lines; without era designators **Note:** Keicho era.

Date	Mintage	VG	F	VF	XF	Unc
ND(1601-1695)	—	400	600	900	1,200	—

KM# 7 MAMEITA GIN
0.8000 Silver **Obv:** "God of Plenty" design, without era designators **Rev:** "God of Plenty" design, without era designators **Note:** Keicho era.

Date	Mintage	VG	F	VF	XF	Unc
ND(1601-1695) Rare	—	—	—	—	—	—

KM# 20.1 MAMEITA GIN
0.6400 Silver **Obv:** One or more characters, without "God of Plenty"; era designator "gen" between characters **Rev:** Chop marks **Note:** Genroku era.

Date	Mintage	VG	F	VF	XF	Unc
ND(1695-1706)	—	400	600	850	1,350	—

KM# 20.2 MAMEITA GIN
0.6400 Silver **Obv:** "God of Plenty" with other characters; era designator "gen" between characters and on God's belly **Note:** Genroku era.

Date	Mintage	VG	F	VF	XF	Unc
ND(1695-1706)	—	250	500	750	1,000	—

KM# 21 MAMEITA GIN
0.6400 Silver **Obv:** "God of Plenty" design, era designator on belly **Rev:** "God of Plenty" design, era designator on belly **Note:** Genroku era.

Date	Mintage	VG	F	VF	XF	Unc
ND(1695-1706)	—	250	550	800	1,250	—

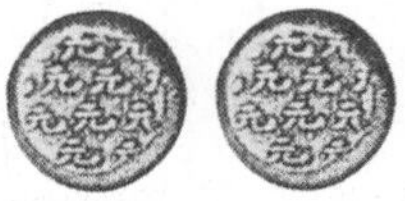

KM# 22 MAMEITA GIN
0.6400 Silver **Obv:** "God of Plenty" design, with era designator on belly **Rev:** Many small or one large character "gen" **Note:** Genroku era.

Date	Mintage	VG	F	VF	XF	Unc
ND(1695-1706)	—	1,250	1,850	2,250	3,250	—

KM# 48 CHOGIN
0.8000 Silver **Obv:** Miscellaneous characters and designs of thin strokes finely drawn throughout **Rev:** Chop marks **Note:** Keicho era. Illustration reduced by 50%.

Date	Mintage	VG	F	VF	XF	Unc
ND(1601-1695)	—	3,000	4,000	5,000	6,500	—

KM# 49.1 CHOGIN
0.8000 Silver **Obv:** Edges completely covered with 12-14 stamps, mostly of characters, a few of "God of Plenty" **Rev:** Chop marks **Note:** Keicho era.

Date	Mintage	VG	F	VF	XF	Unc
ND(1601-1695) Rare	—	—	—	—	—	—

KM# 49.2 CHOGIN
0.8000 Silver **Obv:** Edges completely covered with 12 stamps of "God of Plenty" **Rev:** Chop marks **Note:** Keicho era.

Date	Mintage	VG	F	VF	XF	Unc
ND(1601-1695) Rare	—	—	—	—	—	—

KM# 50 CHOGIN
0.6400 Silver **Obv:** Era marks at each end; miscellaneous characters and designs elsewhere **Rev:** Chop marks **Note:** Genroku era. Illustration reduced by 50%.

Date	Mintage	VG	F	VF	XF	Unc
ND(1695-1706)	—	4,500	6,000	8,000	10,000	—

KM# 51 CHOGIN
0.6400 Silver **Obv:** Edges completely covered with 12-14 stamps, mostly of characters, a few of "God of Plenty" **Rev:** Chop marks **Note:** Genroku era.

Date	Mintage	VG	F	VF	XF	Unc
ND(1695-1706) Rare	—	—	—	—	—	—

KM# 52 CHOGIN
0.6400 Silver **Obv:** Edges completely covered with 12 stamps of "God of Plenty" **Rev:** Chop marks **Note:** Genroku era.

Date	Mintage	VG	F	VF	XF	Unc
ND(1695-1706) Rare	—	—	—	—	—	—

HAMMERED COINAGE

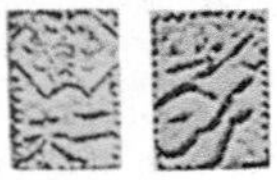

FR# 33 2 SHU (Nishu Gin)
2.2100 g., Gold And Silver .564 gold and .436 silver **Note:** Genroku era.

Date	Mintage	VG	F	VF	XF	Unc
ND(1695-1710)	—	—	1,200	1,350	2,000	—

FR# 24 BU (Ichibu)
4.4300 g., Gold And Silver **Rev:** Without characters in top corners **Note:** .857 Gold and .143 Silver. Keicho era.

Date	Mintage	VG	F	VF	XF	Unc
ND(1601-95)	—	—	550	850	1,650	—

FR# 24a BU (Ichibu)
4.4300 g., Gold And Silver **Rev:** Character in top right corner **Note:** .857 Gold and .143 Silver. Keicho era.

Date	Mintage	VG	F	VF	XF	Unc
ND(1601-95)	—	—	1,500	2,800	4,200	—

FR# 24b BU (Ichibu)
4.4300 g., Gold And Silver **Rev:** 2 characters, top right and left corners **Note:** .857 Gold and .143 Silver. Keicho era.

Date	Mintage	VG	F	VF	XF	Unc
ND(1601-95)	—	—	3,500	5,500	8,500	—

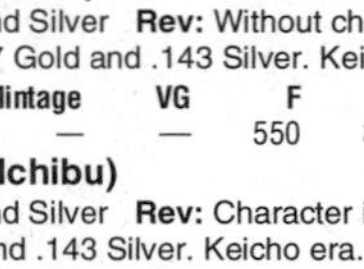

FR# 25 BU (Ichibu)
4.4600 g., Gold And Silver **Note:** .564 Gold and .436 Silver. Genroku era.

Date	Mintage	VG	F	VF	XF	Unc
ND(1695-1710)	—	—	750	1,200	2,000	—

FR# 9.1 KOBAN (1 Ryo)
17.7300 g., Gold And Silver **Obv:** Fine crenulations **Note:** .857 Gold and .143 Silver. Keicho era.

Date	Mintage	VG	F	VF	XF	Unc
ND(1601-95)	—	—	7,500	10,000	13,500	—

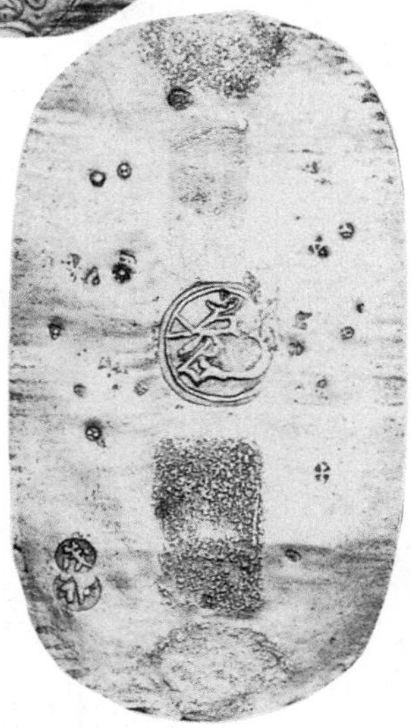

FR# 9.2 KOBAN (1 Ryo)
17.7300 g., Gold And Silver **Obv:** Coarse crenulations **Note:** .857 Gold and .143 Silver. Keicho era.

Date	Mintage	VG	F	VF	XF	Unc
ND(1602-95)	—	—	6,000	9,000	12,000	—

FR# 10 KOBAN (1 Ryo)
17.8100 g., Gold And Silver **Note:** .564 Gold and .436 Silver. Genroku era.

Date	Mintage	VG	F	VF	XF	Unc
ND(1695-1710)	13,936,000	—	7,000	10,000	17,500	—

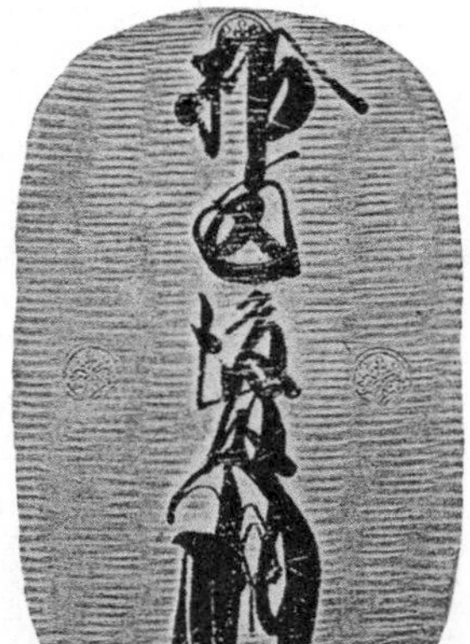

FR# A3 OBAN
165.1800 g., Gold And Silver **Note:** .672 Gold and .294 Silver. Keicho-Sasagaki era. Illustration reduced by 50%.

Date	Mintage	VG	F	VF	XF	Unc
ND(1601)	—	—	—	200,000	300,000	—

FR# 3 OBAN
165.1800 g., Gold And Silver **Note:** .672 Gold and .294 Silver. Keicho era.

Date	Mintage	VG	F	VF	XF	Unc
ND(1601)	17,000	—	—	125,000	165,000	—

FR# A4 OBAN
165.1800 g., Gold And Silver **Note:** .670 Gold and .276 Silver. Meireki era. Illustration reduced by 50%.

Date	Mintage	VG	F	VF	XF	Unc
ND(1658)	—	—	—	100,000	140,000	—

FR# 4 OBAN
164.5600 g., Gold And Silver **Note:** .521 Gold and .449 Silver. Genroku era. Illustration reduced by 50%.

Date	Mintage	VG	F	VF	XF	Unc
ND(1695-1716)	30,000	—	—	180,000	275,000	—

KOSHU

A province, (formal name Kai, now Yamanashi Prefecture), located in central Honshu west of Tokyo.

The following listings are representative of a very complex series of gold coinage. Other obscure or odd denominations may exist. This series contains many varieties. The characters usually found stamped on the reverse are hallmarks.

PROVINCE

PROVINCIAL COINAGE

KM# 90 KAKU SHU-NAKA KIN (Rectangular Half Shu Gold)
0.4000 g., Gold, 6x8 mm.

Date	Mintage	VG	F	VF	XF	Unc
ND	—	700	900	1,200	1,600	—

KM# 91 SHU-NAKA KIN (Half Shu Gold)
Gold, 8.5-9.5 mm. **Note:** Similar to Ichi-Bu KM#94. Weight varies: 0.40-0.50 grams. Size varies.

Date	Mintage	VG	F	VF	XF	Unc
ND	—	3,000	5,000	5,500	6,500	—

KM# 92 ISSHU KIN (One Shu Gold)
Gold, 11-12 mm. **Note:** Similar to Ichi-Bu KM#94. Weight varies: 0.90-1.00 grams. Size varies.

Date	Mintage	VG	F	VF	XF	Unc
ND	—	425	650	850	1,100	—

KM# 93 NISSHU KIN (Two Shu Gold)
1.9000 g., Gold, 12-13 mm. **Note:** Similar to Ichi-Bu KM#94. Size varies.

Date	Mintage	VG	F	VF	XF	Unc
ND	—	500	600	700	800	—

KM# 94 ICHI-BU KIN (One Bu Gold)
Gold, 14-17 mm. **Note:** Similar to Ichi-Bu KM#94. Weight varies: 3.70-4.00 Size varies.

Date	Mintage	VG	F	VF	XF	Unc
ND	—	600	700	900	1,100	—

KM# 95 ICHI-BU ISSHU KIN (One Bu One Shu Gold)
4.8000 g., Gold, 18 mm. **Note:** Similar to Ichi-Bu KM#94.

Date	Mintage	VG	F	VF	XF	Unc
ND Rare	—	—	—	—	—	—

KM# 96 ICHI-BU NISSHU KIN (One Bu Two Shu Gold)
5.0000 g., Gold, 16 mm. **Note:** Similar to Ichi-Bu KM#94.

Date	Mintage	VG	F	VF	XF	Unc
ND Rare	—	—	—	—	—	—

KM# 97 NI-BU KIN (Two Bu Gold)
Gold, 18-19 mm. **Note:** Similar to Ichi-Bu KM#94. Weight varies: 7.00-7.50 grams. Size varies.

Date	Mintage	VG	F	VF	XF	Unc
ND Rare	—	—	—	—	—	—

KM# 98 NI-BU ISSHU KIN (Two Bu One Shu Gold)
8.8000 g., Gold, 24 mm. **Note:** Similar to Ichi-Bu KM#94.

Date	Mintage	VG	F	VF	XF	Unc
ND Rare	—	—	—	—	—	—

KM# 99 RYO KIN (One Ryo Gold)
Gold, 16-19 mm. **Note:** Rounded "nugget" shape with stamps, similar to Ichi-Bu KM#94. Weight varies: 14.70-15.30 grams. Size varies.

Date	Mintage	VG	F	VF	XF	Unc
ND Rare	—	—	—	—	—	—

KOREA

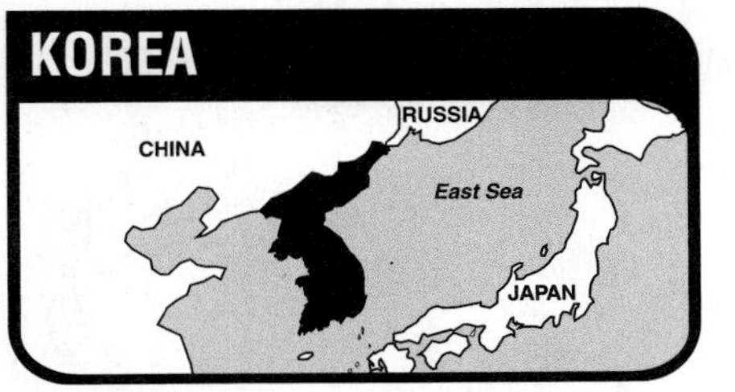

Korea, 'Land of the Morning Calm', occupies a mountainous peninsula in northeast Asia bounded by Manchuria, the Yellow Sea and the Sea of Japan.

According to legend, the first Korean dynasty, that of the House of Tangun, ruled from 2333 B.C. to 1122 B.C. It was followed by the dynasty of Kija, a Chinese scholar, which continued until 193 B.C. and brought a high civilization to Korea. The first recorded period in the history of Korea, the period of the Three Kingdoms, lasted from 57 B.C. to 935 A.D. and achieved the first political unification of the peninsula. The Kingdom of Koryo, from which Korea derived its name, was founded in 935 and continued until 1392, when it was superseded by the Yi Dynasty of King Yi. Sung Kye was to last until the Japanese annexation in 1910.

At the end of the 16th century Korea was invaded and occupied for 7 years by Japan, and from 1627 until the late 19th century it was a semi-independent tributary of China. Japan replaced China as the predominant foreign influence at the end of the Sino-Japanese War (1894-95), only to find her position threatened by Russian influence from 1896 to 1904. The Russian threat was eliminated by the Russo-Japanese War (1904-05) and in 1905 Japan established a direct protectorate over Korea. On Aug. 22,1910, the last Korean ruler signed the treaty that annexed Korea to Japan as a government-generalcy in the Japanese Empire. Japanese suzerainty was maintained until the end of World War II.

From 1633 to 1891 the monetary system of Korea employed cast coins with a square center hole. Fifty-two agencies were authorized to procure these coins from a lesser number of coin foundries. They exist in thousands of varieties. Seed, or mother coins, were used to make the impressions in the molds in which the regular cash coins were cast. Czarist-Russian Korea experimented with Korean coins when Alexiev of Russia, Korea's Financial Advisor, founded the First Asian Branch of the Russo-Korean Bank on March 1, 1898, and authorized the issuing of a set of new Korean coins with a crowned Russian-style quasi-eagle. British-Japanese opposition and the Russo-Japanese War operated to end the Russian coinage experiment in 1904.

RULERS

Yi Kweng (Sonjo Sog Yung), 1568-1609
Yi Hon (Kwang hae gun), 1609-1623
Yi Chong (Injo Honmun), 1623-1650
Yi Ho (Hyojong Sonmun), 1650-1660
Yi Yun (Hyonjong Sohyu), 1660-1675
Yi Sun (Sukjong Hyonui), 1675-1721

MONETARY UNITS

Mun	文	Yang, Niang	兩
Fun	分	Hwan, Warn	圜
Chon	錢	Won Whan, Hwan	圓

SEED COINS

Seed coins are specially prepared examples, perfectly round, with sharp characters, used in the preparation of clay or sand molds. Seed types for value 2 and 5 Mun are not included as they are very scarce and seldom are encountered in today's market.

MINT MARKS

Mark	Character	Office
Ho	戶	Treasury Department
Kong	工	Ministry of Industry
Kyong	冏	Bureau of Royal Transportation
Hyang	向	Food Supply Office
Ch'ong	摠	General Military Office
Yong	營 or 营	Special Army Unit
Hun	訓 or 訓	Military Training Command
Ch'o	抄	Commando Military Unit
Kae	開	Kaesong Township Military Office
Won	原	Wonju Township Military Office
P'yong	平	P'yongan Provincial Office
P'yong	平	P'yongan Military Fort
Sang	尙	Kyongsang Provincial Office
Sang Su	尙水	Kyongsang Naval Station
Sang U	尙右	Kyongsang Right Naval Base
Sang Chwa	尙左	Kyongsang Left Naval Base
Chon	全	Cholla Provincial Office
Chon Pyong	全兵	Cholla Military Fort
Chon U	全右	Cholla Right Naval Base
Chon Chwa	全左	Cholla Left Naval Base

NOTE: For earlier issues refer to *Cast Coinage of Korea* by the late Edgar J. Mandel.

KINGDOM

TREASURY DEPARTMENT

(Ho Jo)

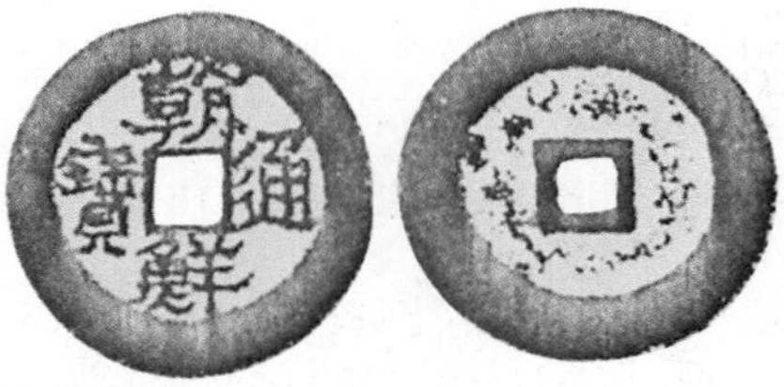

KM# 3 MUN
Cast Copper, 24 mm. **Note:** Uniface. Legend "Clerkly" characters: "Cho Son T'ong Bo".

Date	Mintage	Good	VG	F	VF	XF
ND(1625-33)	—	25.00	35.00	50.00	100	—

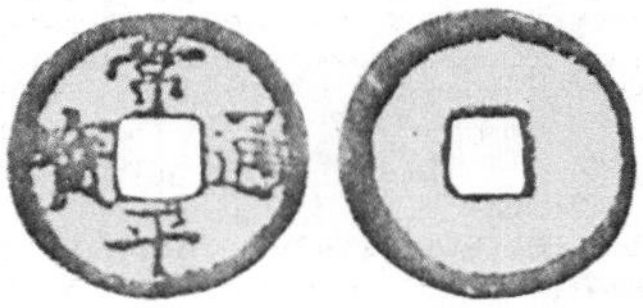

KM# 4 MUN
Cast Copper, 20 mm. **Obv. Legend:** Sang P'yong T'ong Bo

Date	Mintage	Good	VG	F	VF	XF
ND(1633)	—	225	300	450	600	—

KM# 5 MUN
Cast Copper **Note:** Size varies: 23-24 mm.

Date	Mintage	Good	VG	F	VF	XF
ND(1633)	—	225	300	450	600	—

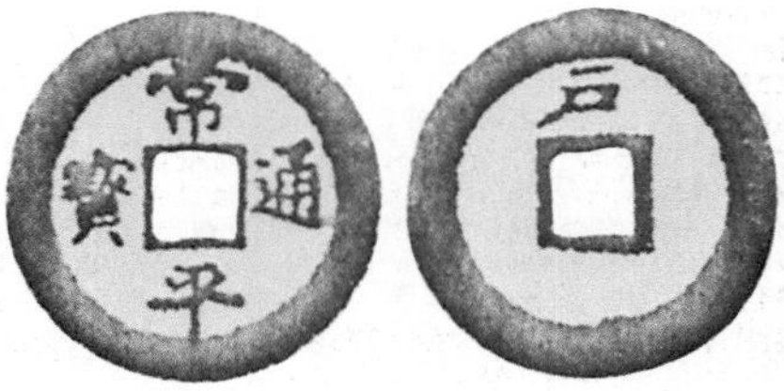

KM# 6 MUN
Cast Copper Or Bronze **Obv. Legend:** "Sang P'yong T'ong Bo" **Rev:** "Ho" at top

Date	Mintage	Good	VG	F	VF	XF
ND(1678)	—	35.00	65.00	120	180	—

KM# 6s MUN
Cast Copper Or Bronze

Date	Mintage	Good	VG	F	VF	XF
ND(1678)	—	—	—	—	—	325

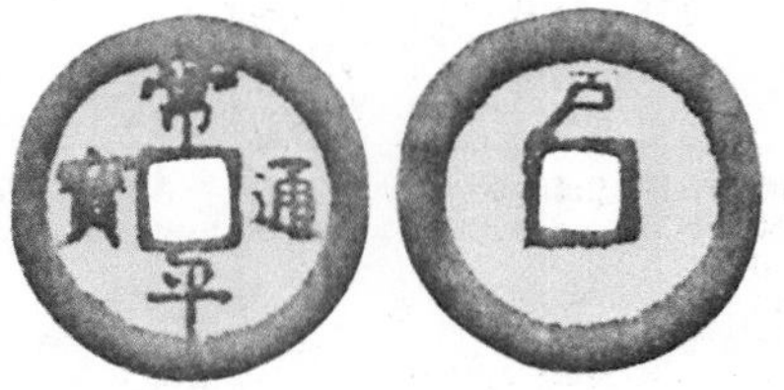

KM# 7 MUN
Cast Copper Or Bronze **Rev:** "Ho" at top in different style

Date	Mintage	Good	VG	F	VF	XF
ND(1678)	—	35.00	65.00	120	180	—

KM# 7s MUN
Cast Copper Or Bronze

Date	Mintage	Good	VG	F	VF	XF
ND(1678)	—	—	—	—	—	250

KM# 74 2 MUN
Cast Copper Or Brass **Rev:** "I" (2) at bottom **Note:** Weight varies 8.00-9.00 grams.

Date	Mintage	Good	VG	F	VF	XF
ND(1679-1752)	—	4.00	5.00	8.00	13.00	—

MINISTRY OF INDUSTRY
(Kong Jo)

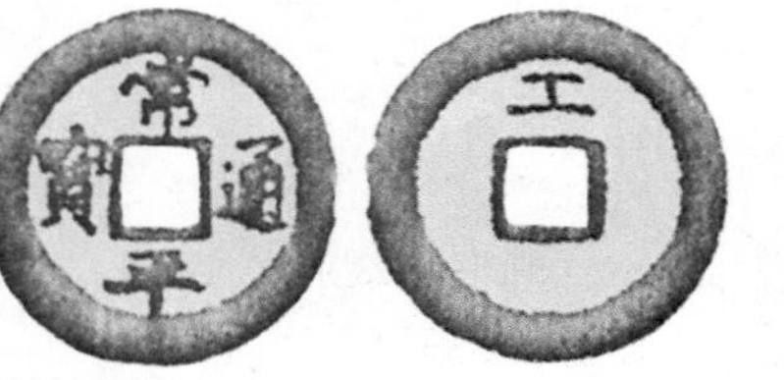

KM# 144 MUN
4.5000 g., Cast Copper **Rev:** "Kong" at top

Date	Mintage	Good	VG	F	VF	XF
ND(1685-1752) Rare	—	—	—	—	—	—

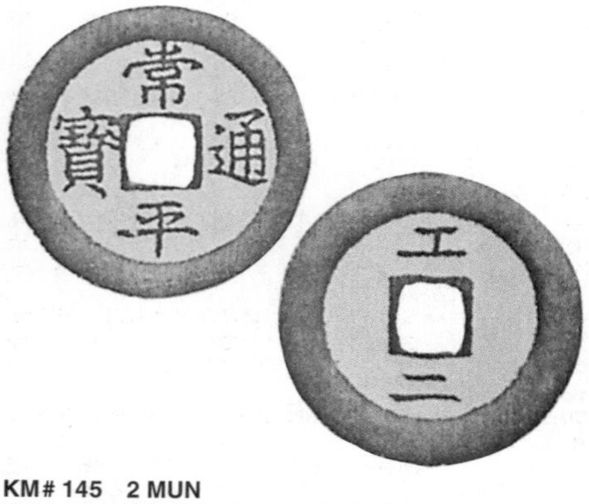

KM# 145 2 MUN
Cast Copper **Rev:** "Kong" at top, "I" (2) at bottom **Note:** Weight varies 8.00-9.00 grams.

Date	Mintage	Good	VG	F	VF	XF
ND(1685-1752)	—	3.00	5.00	8.00	15.00	—

KM# 146 2 MUN
Cast Copper **Rev:** Dot at right **Note:** Weight varies 8.00-9.00 g.

Date	Mintage	Good	VG	F	VF	XF
ND(1685-1752)	—	10.00	15.00	25.00	48.00	—

BUREAU OF ROYAL TRANSPORTATION
(Kyong Saboksi)

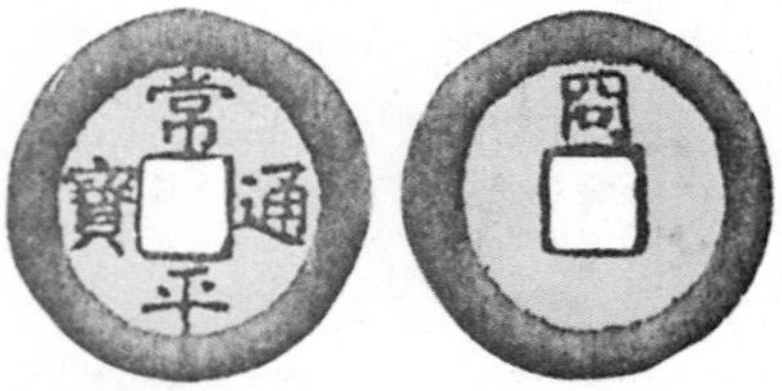

KM# 154 MUN
4.5000 g., Cast Copper **Rev:** "Kyong" at top **Note:** Small characters.

Date	Mintage	Good	VG	F	VF	XF
ND(1678-95) Rare	—	—	—	—	—	—

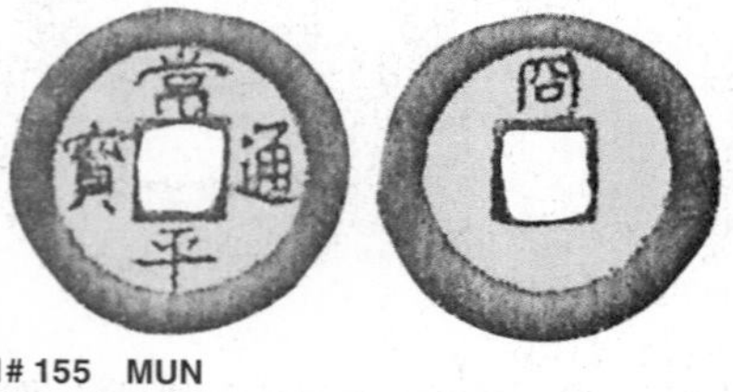

KM# 155 MUN
4.5000 g., Cast Copper **Note:** Large characters.

Date	Mintage	Good	VG	F	VF	XF
ND(1678-95) Rare	—	—	—	—	—	—

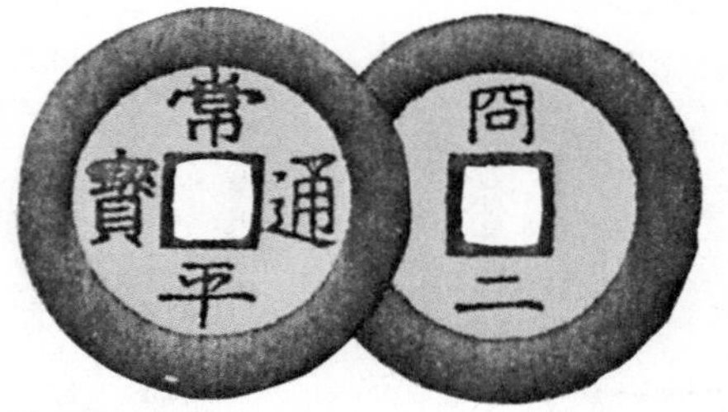

KM# 156 2 MUN
Cast Copper **Rev:** "I" (2) at bottom **Note:** Weight varies 8.00-9.00 grams.

Date	Mintage	Good	VG	F	VF	XF
ND(1679-1752) Rare	—	—	—	—	—	—

SEOUL CHARITY OFFICE
(Chinh Yu Chong)

KM# 160 2 MUN
Cast Copper **Rev:** "I" (2) at bottom **Note:** Weight varies: 8.00-9.00 grams. Inside diameter: 23-24 mm.

Date	Mintage	Good	VG	F	VF	XF
ND(1679-95)	—	4.00	7.00	12.00	15.00	—

KM# 161 2 MUN
Cast Copper **Note:** Weight varies: 8.00-9.00 grams. Inside diameter: 21 mm.

Date	Mintage	Good	VG	F	VF	XF
ND(1679-95)	—	4.00	6.00	9.00	17.00	—

KM# 161s 2 MUN
Cast Copper **Note:** Weight varies: 8.00-9.00 grams. Seed type.

Date	Mintage	Good	VG	F	VF	XF
ND(1679-95)	—	—	—	—	—	125

KM# 162 2 MUN
Cast Copper **Rev:** Dot at left **Note:** Weight varies: 8.00-9.00 grams.

Date	Mintage	Good	VG	F	VF	XF
ND(1695)	—	4.00	7.00	12.00	15.00	—

KM# 163 2 MUN
Cast Copper, 32-33 mm. **Rev:** Circle at right **Note:** Weight varies 8.00-9.00 grams. Size varies.

Date	Mintage	Good	VG	F	VF	XF
ND(1695-1742)	—	4.00	7.00	12.00	15.00	—

KM# 165 2 MUN
Cast Copper **Rev:** Circle at left **Note:** Weight varies 8.00-9.00 g.

Date	Mintage	Good	VG	F	VF	XF
ND(1695-1742)	—	10.00	25.00	35.00	70.00	—

KM# 166 2 MUN
Cast Copper, 32-33 mm. **Note:** Weight varies 8.00-9.00 grams. Size varies.

Date	Mintage	Good	VG	F	VF	XF
ND(1695-1742)	—	4.00	7.00	12.00	15.00	—

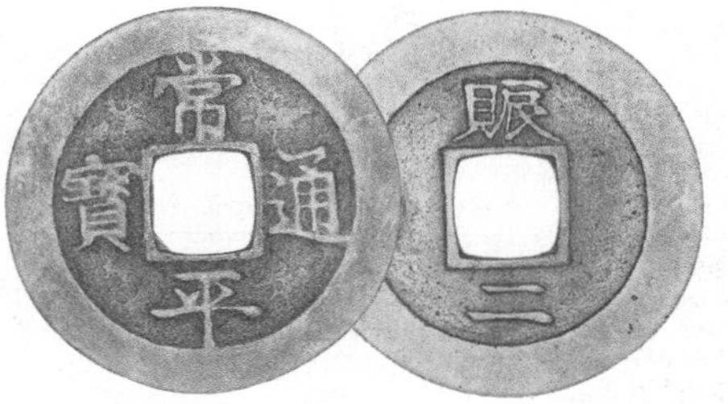

KM# 168 2 MUN
Cast Copper **Rev:** Small crescent at left **Note:** Weight varies 8.00-9.00 grams.

Date	Mintage	Good	VG	F	VF	XF
ND(1695-1742)	—	4.00	7.00	12.00	15.00	—

KM# 169 2 MUN
Cast Copper, 32-33 mm. **Rev:** Dot in crescent at left **Note:** Weight varies 8.00-9.00 grams. Size varies.

Date	Mintage	Good	VG	F	VF	XF
ND(1695-1742)	—	4.00	6.00	9.00	14.00	—

FOOD SUPPLY OFFICE
(Yang Hyang Ch'ong)

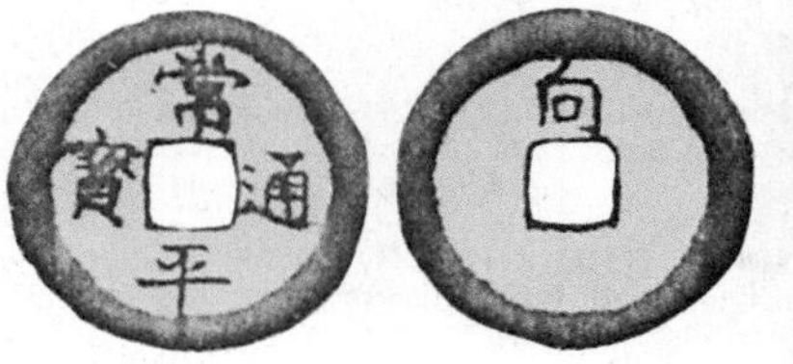

KM# 171 MUN
4.5000 g., Cast Copper **Rev:** "Hyang" at top

Date	Mintage	Good	VG	F	VF	XF
ND(1695-1742) Rare	—	—	—	—	—	—

GENERAL MILITARY OFFICE
(Ch'ong Yung Ch'ong)

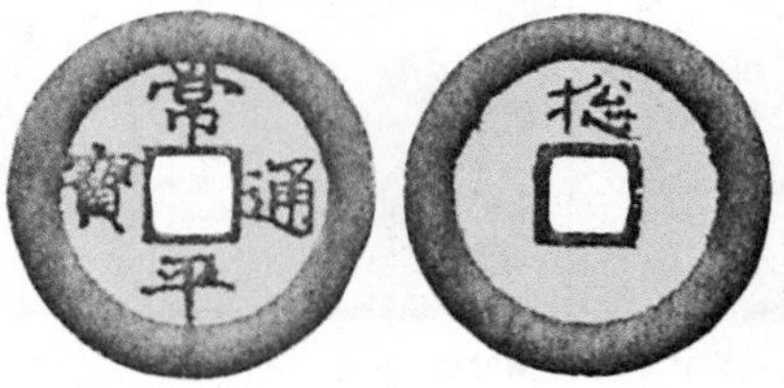

KM# 217 MUN
4.5000 g., Cast Copper **Rev:** "Ch'ong" at top

Date	Mintage	Good	VG	F	VF	XF
ND(1692) Rare	—	—	—	—	—	—

KM# 225 2 MUN
Cast Copper **Rev:** "I" (2) at bottom **Note:** Weight varies 8.00-9.00 grams.

Date	Mintage	Good	VG	F	VF	XF
ND(1692-1752)	—	4.00	6.00	9.00	14.00	—

KM# 226 2 MUN
Cast Copper **Rev:** Dot at right **Note:** Weight varies 8.00-9.00 grams.

Date	Mintage	Good	VG	F	VF	XF
ND(1692-1752)	—	13.00	25.00	39.00	65.00	—

KM# 227 2 MUN
Cast Copper **Rev:** Dot at left **Note:** Weight varies 8.00-9.00 grams.

Date	Mintage	Good	VG	F	VF	XF
ND(1692-1752)	—	18.00	30.00	48.00	75.00	—

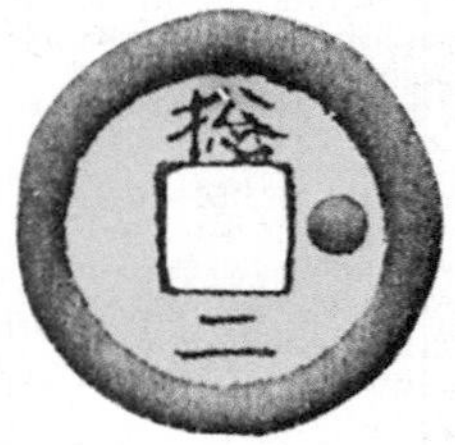

KM# 228 2 MUN
Cast Copper **Rev:** Large filled circle at right **Note:** Weight varies 8.00-9.00 grams.

Date	Mintage	Good	VG	F	VF	XF
ND(1692-1752)	—	37.50	65.00	95.00	160	—

SPECIAL ARMY UNIT
(O Yong Ch'ong)

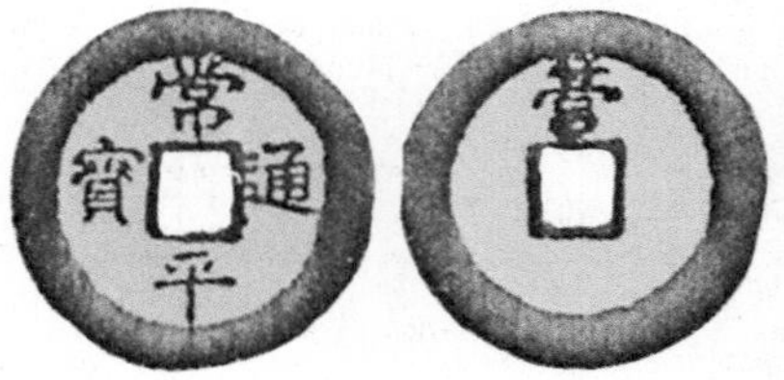

KM# 269 MUN

4.5000 g., Cast Copper **Rev:** "Yong" at top

Date	Mintage	Good	VG	F	VF	XF
ND(1678-1742) Rare	—	—	—	—	—	—

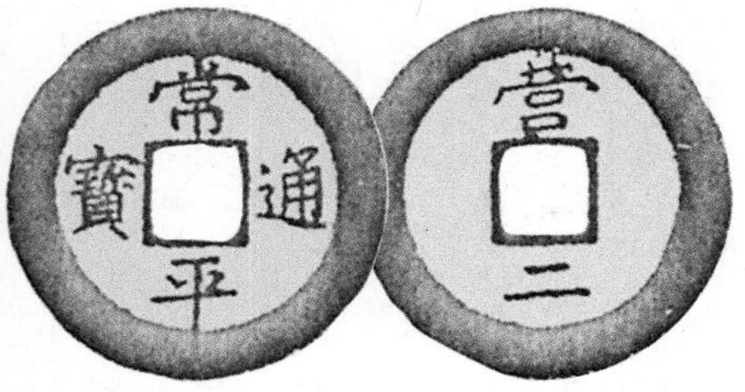

KM# 281 2 MUN

Cast Copper, 32 mm. **Rev:** "I" (2) at bottom **Note:** Weight varies: 8.00-9.00 grams. Large characters.

Date	Mintage	Good	VG	F	VF	XF
ND(1679)	—	13.00	20.00	32.00	55.00	—

MILITARY TRAINING COMMAND

(Hul Ly On Do Gam)

Obverse Character

P'yong variety I: 

P'yong variety II: 

T'ong variety I - top: 

T'ong variety II - top: 

KM# 446 MUN

4.5000 g., Cast Copper **Rev:** "Hun" at top

Date	Mintage	Good	VG	F	VF	XF
ND(1678) Rare	—	—	—	—	—	—

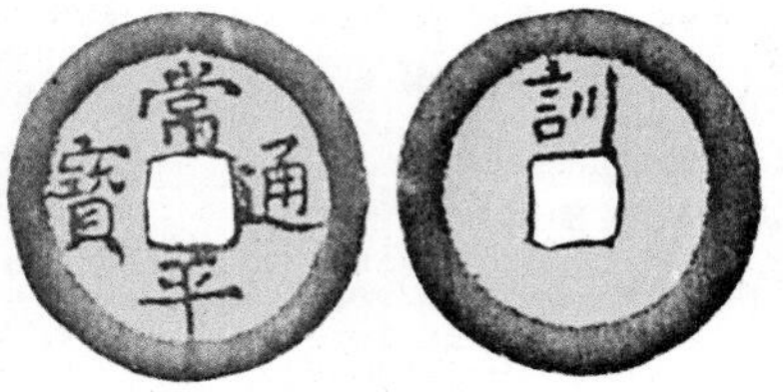

KM# 447 MUN

4.5000 g., Cast Copper **Rev:** "Hun" in different style

Date	Mintage	Good	VG	F	VF	XF
ND(1678) Rare	—	—	—	—	—	—

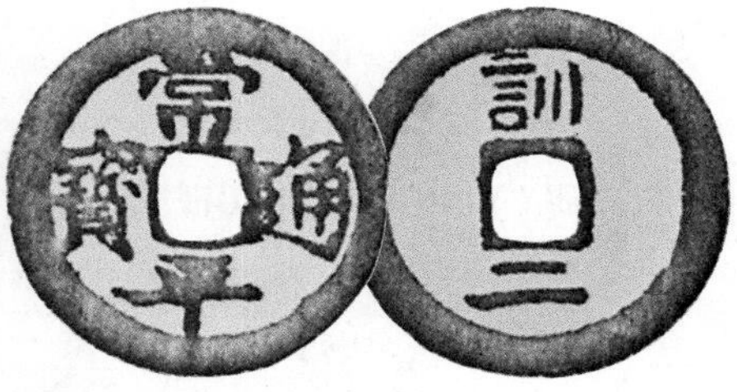

KM# 477 2 MUN

Cast Copper **Obv:** "T'ong" variety I **Rev:** "Hun" at top, "I" (2) at bottom **Note:** Weight varies: 8.00-9.00 grams. Size varies: 31.32 mm.

Date	Mintage	Good	VG	F	VF	XF
ND(1679)	—	5.00	10.00	15.00	25.00	—

KM# 477s 2 MUN

Cast Copper **Note:** Weight varies: 8.00-9.00 grams. Size varies: 31-32 mm.

Date	Mintage	Good	VG	F	VF	XF
ND(1679)	—	—	—	—	—	150

KM# 478 2 MUN

Cast Copper **Note:** Size varies: 28-30 mm.

Date	Mintage	Good	VG	F	VF	XF
ND(1679)	—	6.00	12.00	18.00	25.00	—

KM# 478s 2 MUN

Cast Copper **Note:** Size varies: 28-30 mm.

Date	Mintage	Good	VG	F	VF	XF
ND(1679)	—	—	—	—	—	150

COMMANDO MILITARY UNIT

(Chong Ch'o Ch'ong)

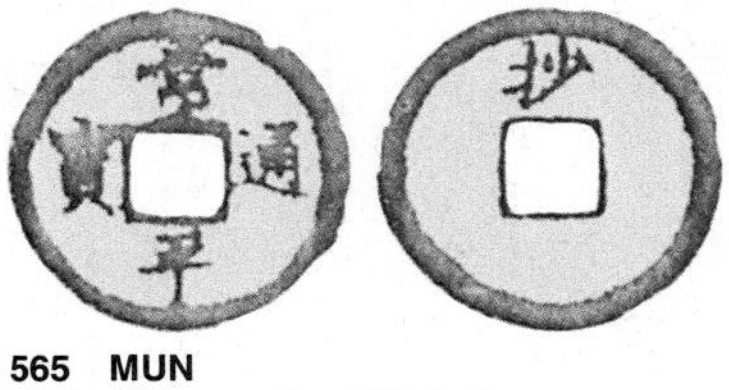

KM# 565 MUN

4.5000 g., Cast Copper **Rev:** "Ch'o" at top

Date	Mintage	Good	VG	F	VF	XF
ND(1678) Rare	—	—	—	—	—	—

KM# 566 2 MUN

Cast Copper **Rev:** "I" (2) at bottom **Note:** Weight varies: 8.00-9.00 grams.

Date	Mintage	Good	VG	F	VF	XF
ND(1679)	—	6.00	9.00	1,420	19.00	—

KM# 566a 2 MUN

Cast Copper **Obv:** "P'yong" with hooks **Note:** Weight varies: 8.00-9.00 grams.

Date	Mintage	Good	VG	F	VF	XF
ND(1679)	—	6.00	9.00	14.00	20.00	—

KAESONG TOWNSHIP MILITARY OFFICE

(Kae Song Kwal Li Yong)

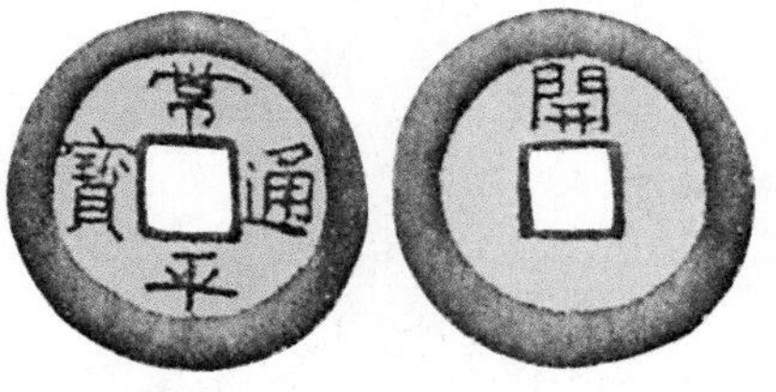

KM# 780 MUN

4.5000 g., Cast Copper Or Bronze, 26 mm. **Obv:** Large characters **Rev:** "Kae" at top

Date	Mintage	Good	VG	F	VF	XF
ND(1678-1742) Rare	—	—	—	—	—	—

KM# A780 MUN

4.5000 g., Cast Copper Or Bronze, 25 mm. **Obv:** Medium characters **Note:** Reduced size.

Date	Mintage	Good	VG	F	VF	XF
ND(1678-1742) Rare	—	—	—	—	—	—

KM# 781 MUN

4.5000 g., Cast Copper Or Bronze, 24 mm. **Obv:** Small characters **Note:** Reduced size.

Date	Mintage	Good	VG	F	VF	XF
ND(1678-1742) Rare	—	—	—	—	—	—

KM# 782 MUN

4.5000 g., Cast Copper Or Bronze **Rev:** Dot at lower right

Date	Mintage	Good	VG	F	VF	XF
ND(1678-1742) Rare	—	—	—	—	—	—

KM# 783 MUN

4.5000 g., Cast Copper Or Bronze **Rev:** Dot at bottom

Date	Mintage	Good	VG	F	VF	XF
ND(1678-1742) Rare	—	—	—	—	—	—

KM# 784 MUN

4.5000 g., Cast Copper Or Bronze **Rev:** 2 dots at bottom

Date	Mintage	Good	VG	F	VF	XF
ND(1678-1742) Rare	—	—	—	—	—	—

KM# 785 MUN

4.5000 g., Cast Copper Or Bronze **Rev:** Circle at lower right

Date	Mintage	Good	VG	F	VF	XF
ND(1678-1742) Rare	—	—	—	—	—	—

KM# 786 MUN

4.5000 g., Cast Copper Or Bronze **Rev:** Circle at left

Date	Mintage	Good	VG	F	VF	XF
ND(1678-1742) Rare	—	—	—	—	—	—

KM# 787 MUN

4.5000 g., Cast Copper Or Bronze **Rev:** 2 circles at bottom

Date	Mintage	Good	VG	F	VF	XF
ND(1678-1742) Rare	—	—	—	—	—	—

KM# 788 MUN

4.5000 g., Cast Copper Or Bronze **Rev:** Crescent at bottom

Date	Mintage	Good	VG	F	VF	XF
ND(1678-1742) Rare	—	—	—	—	—	—

KM# 789 MUN

4.5000 g., Cast Copper Or Bronze **Rev:** Circle at right, crescent at left

Date	Mintage	Good	VG	F	VF	XF
ND(1678-1742) Rare	—	—	—	—	—	—

KM# 790 MUN

4.5000 g., Cast Copper Or Bronze **Rev:** Vertical line at bottom

Date	Mintage	Good	VG	F	VF	XF
ND(1678-1742) Rare	—	—	—	—	—	—

SONG (SONG DO KWAL LI YONG)

(Song Do is another name for Kae Song)

KM# 806a 2 MUN

Cast Copper, 31 mm. **Rev:** Star at lower left **Note:** Weight varies 8.00-9.00 grams.

Date	Mintage	Good	VG	F	VF	XF
ND(1679-1752)	—	—	—	—	—	—

KM# 806b 2 MUN

Cast Copper, 30 mm. **Rev:** Star at lower left **Note:** Weight varies 8.00-9.00 grams.

Date	Mintage	Good	VG	F	VF	XF
ND(1679-1752)	—	—	—	—	—	—

KM# 807 2 MUN

Cast Copper **Rev:** Dot at right **Note:** Weight varies 8.00-9.00 g.

Date	Mintage	Good	VG	F	VF	XF
ND(1679-1752)	—	7.00	10.00	15.00	22.00	—

KM# 808 2 MUN

Cast Copper **Rev:** Circle at right **Note:** Weight varies 8.00-9.00 g.

Date	Mintage	Good	VG	F	VF	XF
ND(1679-1752)	—	7.00	10.00	15.00	22.00	—

KM# 809 2 MUN

Cast Copper **Rev:** Circle at right, crescent at left **Note:** Weight varies 8.00-9.00 grams.

Date	Mintage	Good	VG	F	VF	XF
ND(1679-1752)	—	7.00	10.00	15.00	22.00	—

KM# A809 2 MUN

Cast Copper **Rev:** Circle at right, dot at left **Note:** Weight varies 8.00-9.00 grams.

Date	Mintage	Good	VG	F	VF	XF
ND(1679-1752)	—	—	—	—	—	—

KM# 810 2 MUN

Cast Copper **Rev:** "II" (1) at right **Note:** Weight varies 8.00-9.00 g.

Date	Mintage	Good	VG	F	VF	XF
ND(1679-1752)	—	3,205	65.00	100	165	—

KM# 811 2 MUN

Cast Copper **Rev:** Vertical line at right **Note:** Weight varies 8.00-9.00 grams.

Date	Mintage	Good	VG	F	VF	XF
ND(1679-1752)	—	5.00	12.00	22.00	30.00	—

KM# 811a 2 MUN

Cast Copper **Rev:** Star at upper right **Note:** Weight varies 8.00-9.00 grams.

Date	Mintage	Good	VG	F	VF	XF
ND(1679-1752)	—	—	—	—	—	—

KM# 812 2 MUN

Cast Copper **Rev:** Vertical line at left **Note:** Weight varies 8.00-9.00 grams.

Date	Mintage	Good	VG	F	VF	XF
ND(1679-1752)	—	48.00	80.00	120	210	—

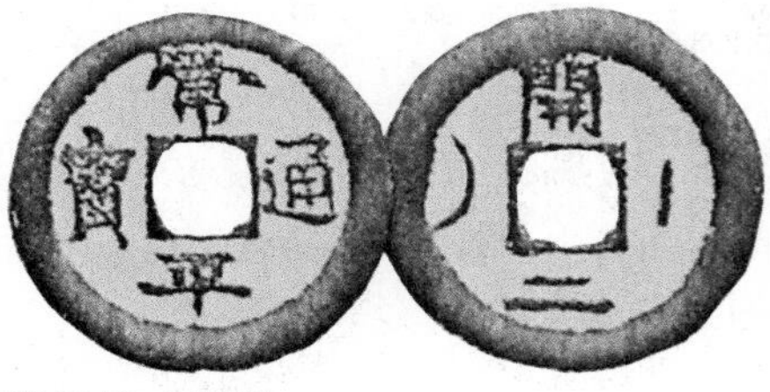

KM# 813 2 MUN

Cast Copper **Rev:** Vertical line at right, crescent at left **Note:** Weight varies 8.00-9.00 grams.

Date	Mintage	Good	VG	F	VF	XF
ND(1679-1752)	—	20.00	39.00	80.00	140	—

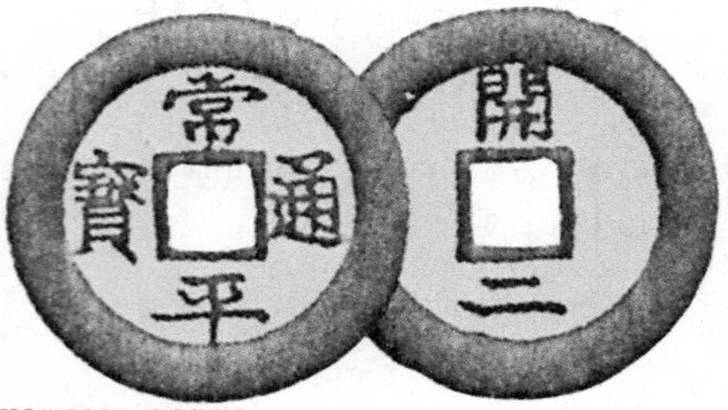

KM# 806 2 MUN
Cast Copper, 32 mm. **Rev:** "Kae" at top, "I" (2) at bottom **Note:** Weight varies 8.00-9.00 grams.

Date	Mintage	Good	VG	F	VF	XF
ND(1679-1752)	—	5.00	10.00	20.00	40.00	—

WONJU TOWNSHIP MILITARY OFFICE
(Won Ju Kwal Li Yong)

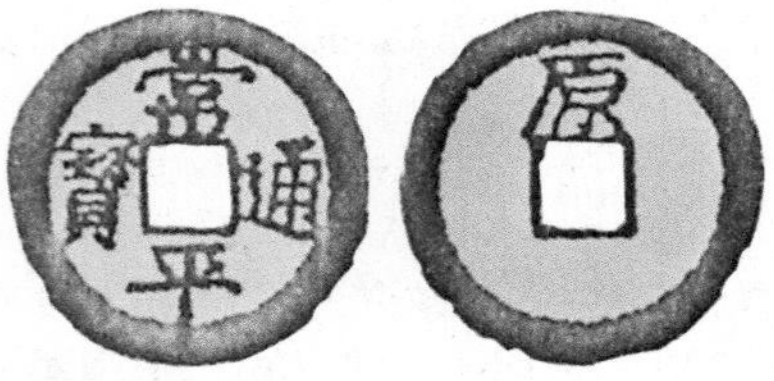

KM# 859 MUN
4.5000 g., Cast Copper **Rev:** "Won" at top **Note:** Large characters.

Date	Mintage	Good	VG	F	VF	XF
ND(1678) Rare	—	—	—	—	—	—

P'YONGAN PROVINCIAL OFFICE
(P'yong An Kam Yong)

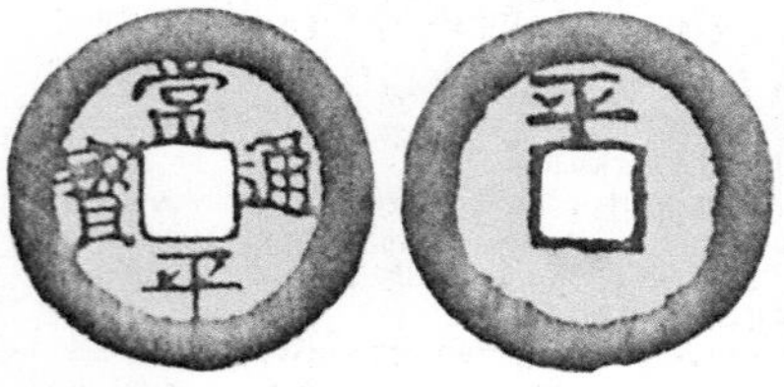

KM# 913 MUN
4.5000 g., Cast Copper **Rev:** "P'yong" at top

Date	Mintage	Good	VG	F	VF	XF
ND(1678-95) Rare	—	—	—	—	—	—

KM# 925 2 MUN
Cast Copper **Rev:** "P'yong" at top, "I" (2) at bottom **Note:** Weight varies 8.00-9.00 grams.

Date	Mintage	Good	VG	F	VF	XF
ND(1679-1742)	—	5.00	8.00	10.00	13.00	—

P'YONGAN MILITARY FORT
(P'yong An Pyong Yong)

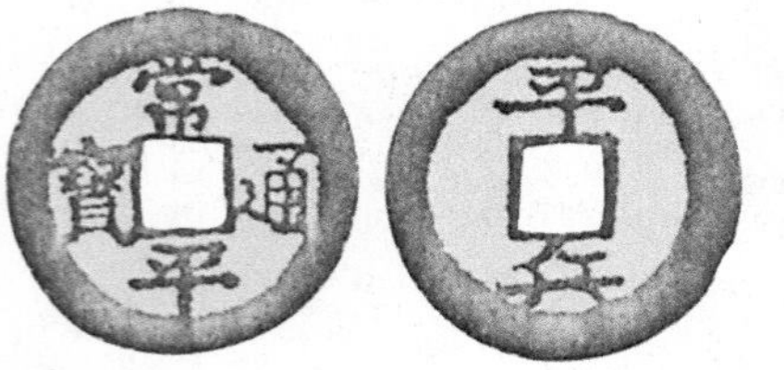

KM# 971 MUN
4.5000 g., Cast Copper **Rev:** "P'yong" at top, "Pyong" at bottom

Date	Mintage	Good	VG	F	VF	XF
ND(1678) Rare	—	—	—	—	—	—

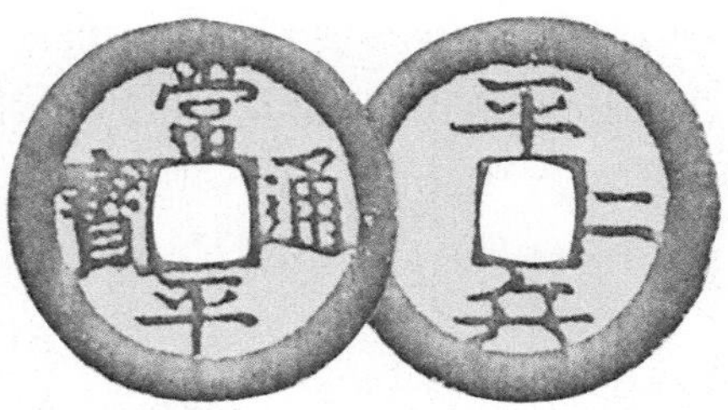

KM# 972 2 MUN
Cast Copper **Rev:** "P'yong" at top, "Pyong" at bottom, "I" (2) at right **Note:** Weight varies: 8.00-9.00 grams.

Date	Mintage	Good	VG	F	VF	XF
ND(1679)	—	85.00	125	175	250	—

KYONGSANG PROVINCIAL OFFICE
(Kyong Sang Kam Yong)

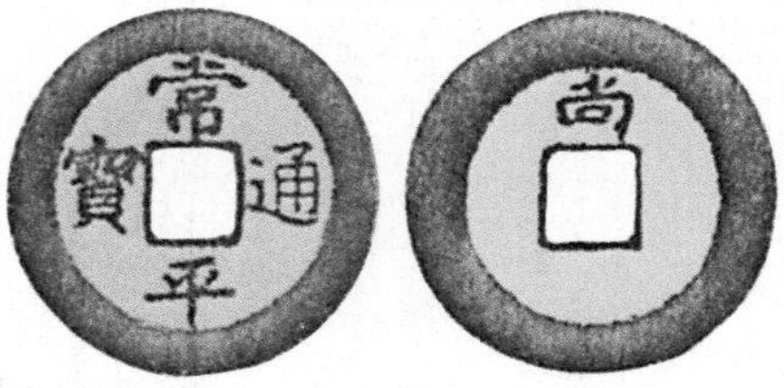

KM# 1010 MUN
4.5000 g., Cast Copper **Rev:** "Sang" at top

Date	Mintage	Good	VG	F	VF	XF
ND(1695-1727) Rare	—	—	—	—	—	—

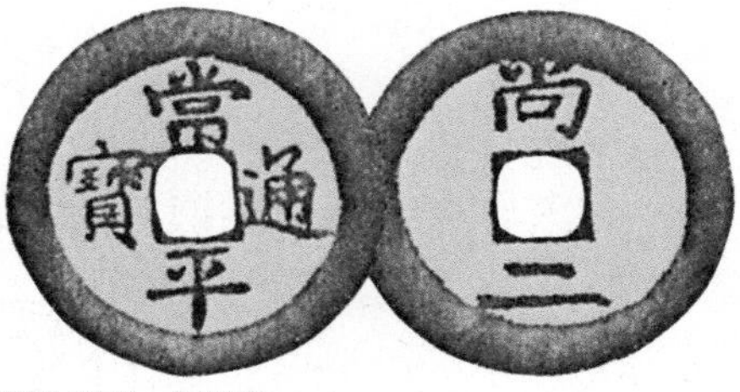

KM# 1011 2 MUN
Cast Copper **Rev:** "Sang" at top, "I" (2) a t bottom **Note:** Weight varies 8.00-9.00 grams.

Date	Mintage	Good	VG	F	VF	XF
ND(1695-1742)	—	5.00	7.00	10.00	15.00	—

KYONGSANG NAVAL STATION
(Kyong Sang Su Yong)

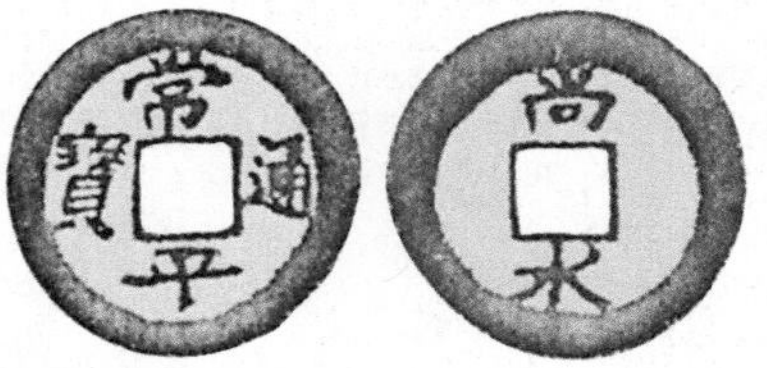

KM# 1037 MUN
4.5000 g., Cast Copper **Rev:** "Sang" at top, "Su" at bottom

Date	Mintage	Good	VG	F	VF	XF
ND(1695-1742) Rare	—	—	—	—	—	—

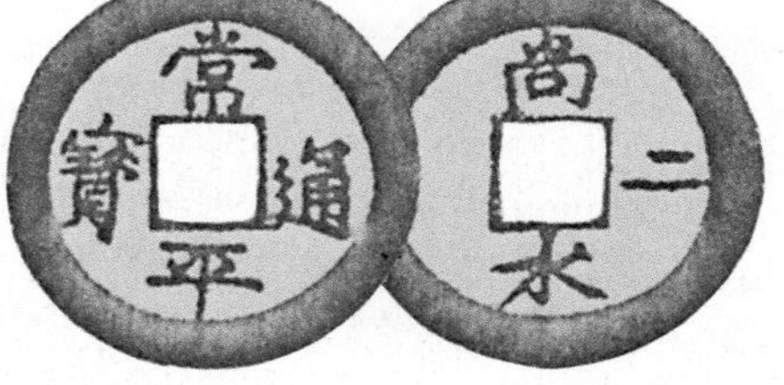

KM# 1038 2 MUN
Cast Copper **Rev:** "Sang" at top, "Su" at bottom, "I" (2) at right **Note:** Weight varies 8.00-9.00 grams.

Date	Mintage	Good	VG	F	VF	XF
ND(1695-1742) Rare	—	—	—	—	—	—

KYONGSANG RIGHT NAVAL BASE
(Kyong Sang U Yong)

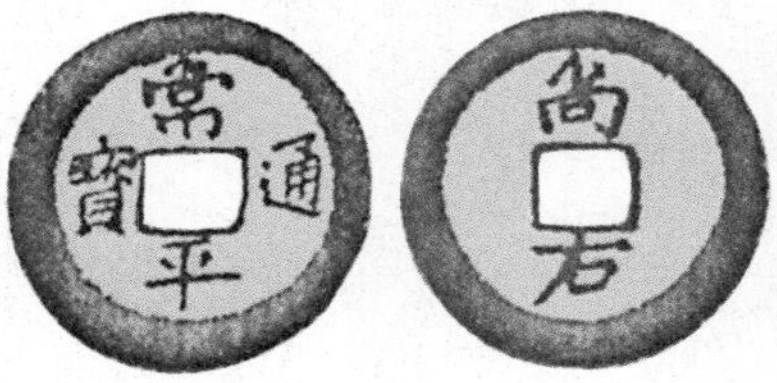

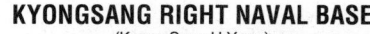

KM# 1039 MUN
4.5000 g., Cast Copper **Rev:** "Sang" at top, "U" at bottom

Date	Mintage	Good	VG	F	VF	XF
ND(1695-1742) Rare	—	—	—	—	—	—

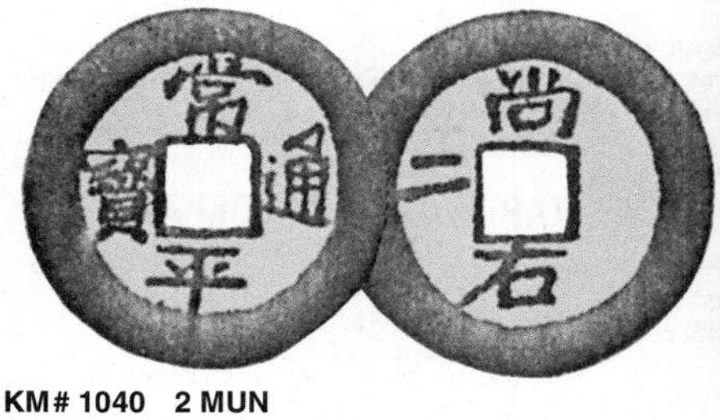

KM# 1040 2 MUN
Cast Copper **Rev:** "Sang" at top, "U" at bottom, "I" (2) at left **Note:** Weight varies 8.00-9.00 grams.

Date	Mintage	Good	VG	F	VF	XF
ND(1695-1742) Rare	—	—	—	—	—	—

KYONGSANG LEFT NAVAL BASE
(Kyong Sang Chwa Yong)

KM# 1041 MUN
4.5000 g., Cast Copper **Rev:** "Sang" at top, "Chwa" at bottom

Date	Mintage	Good	VG	F	VF	XF
ND(1695-1742) Rare	—	—	—	—	—	—

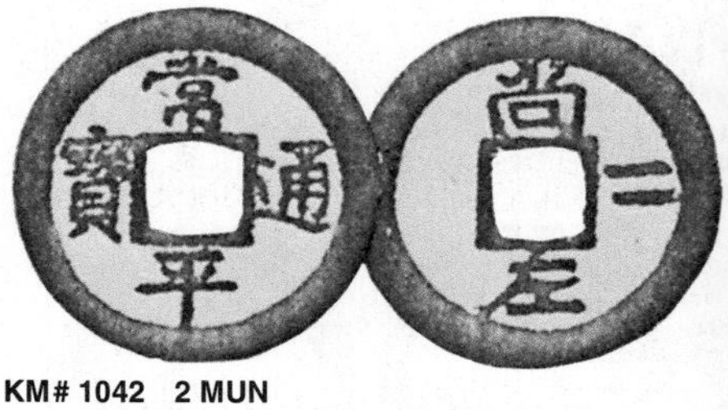

KM# 1042 2 MUN
Cast Copper **Rev:** "Sang" at top, "Chwa" at bottom, "I" (2) at right **Note:** Weight varies 8.00-9.00 grams.

Date	Mintage	Good	VG	F	VF	XF
ND(1695-1742) Rare	—	—	—	—	—	—

KM# 1043 2 MUN
Cast Copper **Rev:** "Sang" at top, "Chwa" at bottom, "I" (2) at left **Note:** Weight varies 8.00-9.00 grams.

Date	Mintage	Good	VG	F	VF	XF
ND(1695-1742) Rare	—	—	—	—	—	—

KM# 1043a 2 MUN
Cast Copper **Rev:** Star at lower left **Note:** Weight varies 8.00-9.00 grams.

Date	Mintage	Good	VG	F	VF	XF
ND(1695-1742)	—	—	—	—	—	—

CHOLLA PROVINCIAL OFFICE
(Chol La Kam Yong)

KM# 1044 MUN
4.5000 g., Cast Copper **Rev:** "Chon" at top

Date	Mintage	Good	VG	F	VF	XF
ND(1682-1727) Rare	—	—	—	—	—	—

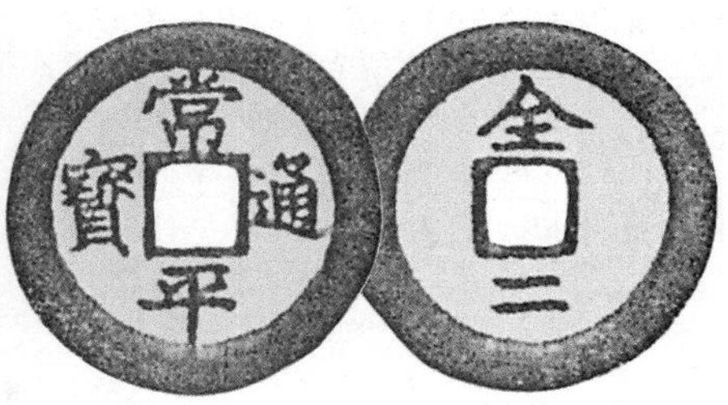

KM# 1045 2 MUN
Cast Copper **Rev:** "Chon" at top, "I" (2) at bottom **Note:** Weight varies: 8.00-9.00 grams. Size varies: 29-32 mm.

Date	Mintage	Good	VG	F	VF	XF
ND(1679-95)	—	4.00	7.00	10.00	16.00	—

KM# 1045a 2 MUN
Cast Copper, 30 mm. **Rev:** Star at lower right **Note:** Weight varies: 8.00-9.00 grams.

Date	Mintage	Good	VG	F	VF	XF
ND(1679-95)	—	—	—	—	—	—

KM# 1046 2 MUN
Cast Copper, 27 mm. **Note:** Weight varies: 8.00-9.00 grams. Reduced size.

Date	Mintage	Good	VG	F	VF	XF
ND(1679-95)	—	4.00	10.00	15.00	22.00	—

CHOLLA MILITARY FORT

(Chol La Pyong Yong)

KM# 1072 MUN
4.5000 g., Cast Copper **Rev:** "Chon" at top, "Pyong" at bottom

Date	Mintage	Good	VG	F	VF	XF
ND(1678) Rare	—	—	—	—	—	—

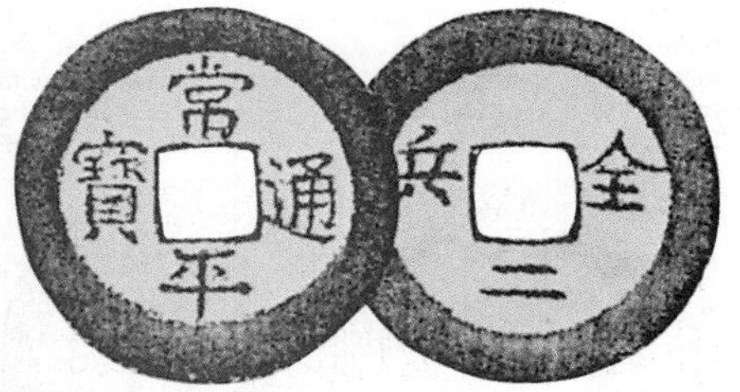

KM# 1073 2 MUN
Cast Copper **Rev:** "Chon" at right, "Pyong" at left, "I" (2) at bottom **Note:** Weight varies 8.00-9.00 grams.

Date	Mintage	Good	VG	F	VF	XF
ND(1679-1742) Rare	—	—	—	—	—	—

CHOLLA RIGHT NAVAL BASE

(Choi La U Yong)

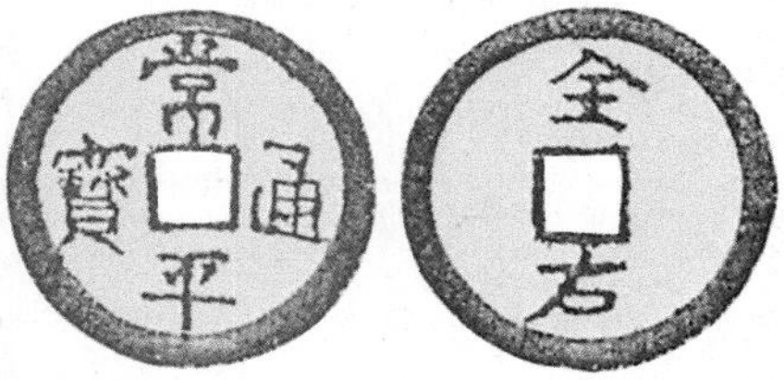

KM# 1074 MUN
4.5000 g., Cast Copper **Rev:** "Chon" at top, "U" at bottom

Date	Mintage	Good	VG	F	VF	XF
ND(1678) Rare	—	—	—	—	—	—

CHOLLA LEFT NAVAL BASE

(Chol La Chwa Yong)

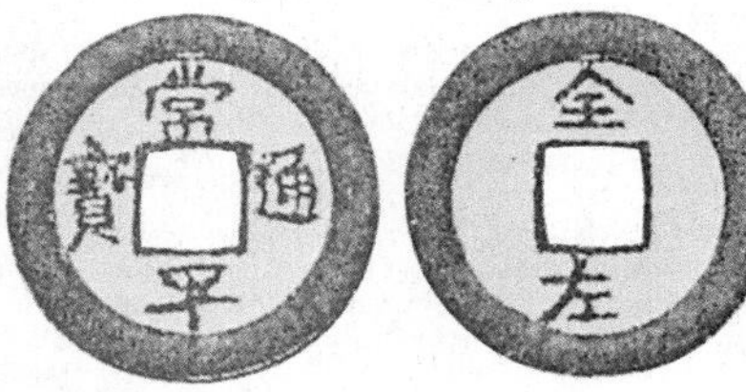

KM# 1075 MUN
4.5000 g., Cast Copper **Rev:** "Chon" at top, "Chwa" at bottom

Date	Mintage	Good	VG	F	VF	XF
ND(1678) Rare	—	—	—	—	—	—

LIBYA

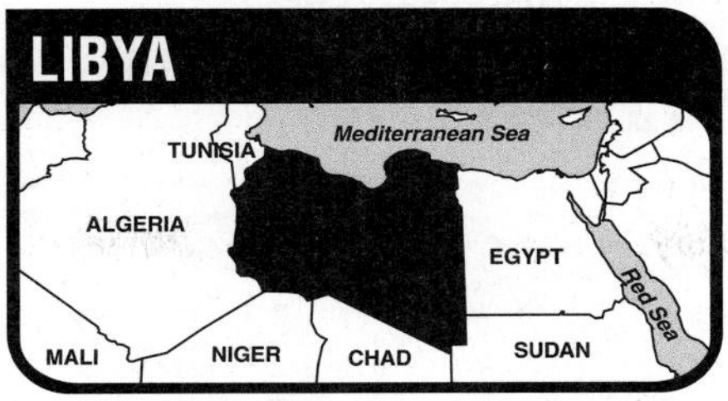

The Socialist People's Libyan Arab Jamahariya, located on the north-central coast of Africa between Tunisia and Egypt, has an area of 679,358 sq. mi. (1,759,540 sq. km.) and a population of 3.9 million. Capital: Tripoli. Crude oil, which accounts for 90 per cent of the export earnings, is the mainstay of the economy.

Libya has been subjected to foreign rule throughout most of its history, various parts of it having been ruled by the Phoenicians, Carthaginians, Vandals, Byzantines, Greeks, Romans, Egyptians, and in the following centuries the Arabs' language, culture and religion were adopted by the indigenous population. Libya was conquered by the Ottoman Turks in 1553, and remained under Turkish domination, becoming a Turkish vilayet in 1835, until it was conquered by Italy and made into a colony in 1911. The name 'Libya', the ancient Greek name for North Africa exclusive of Egypt, was given to the colony by Italy in1934

TITLES

المملكة الليبية

al-Mamlaka(t) al-Libiya(t)

الجمهورية الليبية

al-Jomhuriya(t) al-Arabiya(t) al-Libiya(t)

TRIPOLI

Tripoli (formerly Ottoman Empire Area of antique Tripolitania, 700-146 B.C.), the capital city and chief port of the Libyan Arab Jamahiriya, is situated on the North African coast on a promontory stretching out into the Mediterranean Sea. It was probably founded by Phoenicians from Sicily, but was under Roman control from 146 B.C. until 450 A.D. Invasion by Vandals and conquest by the Byzantines preceded the Arab invasions of the 11th century which, by destroying the commercial centers of Sabratha and Leptis, greatly enhanced the importance of Tripoli, an importance maintained through periods of Norman and Spanish control. Tripoli fell to the Turks, who made it the capital of the vilayet of Tripoli in 1551 and remained in their hands until 1911, when it was occupied by the Italians who made it the capital of the Italian province of Tripolitania. British forces entered the city on Jan. 23, 1943, and administered it until establishment of the independent Kingdom of Libya on Dec. 24, 1951.

RULERS

Ottoman, until 1911
refer to Turkey

MINT NAMES

طرابلس

Tarabalus

طرابلس غرب

Tarabalus Gharb = (Tripoli West)

The appellation *west* serving to distinguish it from Tripoli in Lebanon, which had been an Ottoman Mint in the 16th century. On some of the copper coins, *Gharb* is omitted; several types come both with and without *Gharb*. The mint closed between the 28th and 29th year of the reign of Mahmud II.

MONETARY SYSTEM

The monetary system of Tripoli was confused and is poorly understood. Theoretically, 40 Para were equal to one Piastre, but due to the debasement of the silver coinage, later issues are virtually pure copper, though the percentage of alloy varies radically even within a given year. The 10 Para and 20 Para pieces were a little heavier than the copper Paras, with which they could easily be confounded, except that the copper Paras were generally thicker, and bear simpler inscriptions. It is not known how many of the coppers were tariffed to the debased Piastre and its fractions. Some authorities consider the copper pieces to be Beshliks (5 Para coins).

The gold coinage came in two denominations, the Zeri Mahbub (2.4-2.5 g), and the Sultani Altin (3.3-3.4 g). The ratio of the billon Piastres to the gold coins fluctuated from day to day.

BARBARY STATE

Murad IV

OTTOMAN COINAGE

KM# 2 MANGIR
Copper **Note:** Size varies 13-16mm.

Date	Mintage	VG	F	VF	XF	Unc
AH1039	—	31.25	65.00	—	—	—
AH1041	—	31.25	65.00	—	—	—

KM# 1 SULTANI
Gold **Note:** Weight varies 3.40-3.50 grams. Size varies 22-23mm.

Date	Mintage	VG	F	VF	XF	Unc
AH1032	—	900	1,300	1,550	—	—
AH1033	—	900	1,300	1,550	—	—

Ibrahim

OTTOMAN COINAGE

KM# 3 MANGIR
Copper, 12 mm.

Date	Mintage	VG	F	VF	XF	Unc
AH(10)49	—	31.25	65.00	—	—	—

KM# 4 SULTANI
Gold **Note:** Weight varies 2.90-3.40 grams. Size varies 28-29mm.

Date	Mintage	VG	F	VF	XF	Unc
AH1049	—	900	1,300	1,550	—	—
AH1053	—	900	1,300	1,550	—	—

Mehmed IV

OTTOMAN COINAGE

KM# 7 MANGIR
Copper **Note:** Size varies 11-1/2-12-1/2mm.

Date	Mintage	VG	F	VF	XF	Unc
ND 6-pointed star	—	25.00	37.50	—	—	—
ND Hexagram ++ 40	—	25.00	37.50	—	—	—
AH(10)94	—	25.00	37.50	—	—	—
AH(10)95	—	31.25	50.00	—	—	—
AH(10)97	—	25.00	37.50	—	—	—
AH(10)98	—	25.00	37.50	—	—	—

KM# 8 PARA
Copper Weight varies: 2.46-3.60g., 13-15 mm.

Date	Mintage	VG	F	VF	XF	Unc
AH(1)076	—	25.00	43.75	65.00	—	—
AH(10)78	—	25.00	43.75	65.00	—	—
AH(10)83	—	25.00	43.75	65.00	—	—
AH(10)84	—	25.00	43.75	65.00	—	—
AH(10)87	—	25.00	43.75	65.00	—	—
AH(10)91	—	25.00	43.75	65.00	—	—
AH(10)94	—	25.00	43.75	65.00	—	—

KM# 9.1 5 PARA (Beshlik)
1.4100 g., Silver, 18 mm.

Date	Mintage	VG	F	VF	XF	Unc
AH1059	—	65.00	80.00	100	145	—

KM# 9.2 5 PARA (Beshlik)
1.5000 g., Silver

Date	Mintage	VG	F	VF	XF	Unc
AH1083	—	65.00	80.00	100	145	—

KM# 10 1/2 SULTANI
1.6000 g., Gold, 17 mm.

Date	Mintage	VG	F	VF	XF	Unc
AH1078	—	200	400	650	1,050	—
AH1098	—	200	400	650	1,050	—

KM# 11 SULTANI
3.4000 g., Gold, 23 mm.

Date	Mintage	VG	F	VF	XF	Unc
AH1078	—	—	800	1,150	1,700	—

Suleyman II

OTTOMAN COINAGE

KM# 13 MANGIR
Copper, 12-1/2 mm.

Date	Mintage	VG	F	VF	XF	Unc
AH(1)102 8-pointed star	—	37.50	55.00	100	—	—

KM# 8A PARA
0.6900 g., Silver, 15 mm. **Obv:** Sultan's names in multilobed border **Rev:** Mint and date in octagram

Date	Mintage	VG	F	VF	XF	Unc
AH1091	—	—	—	—	—	—

KM# 18 SULTANI
3.3900 g., Gold **Note:** Size varies 22-24mm.

Date	Mintage	VG	F	VF	XF	Unc
AH1099	—	—	1,600	2,700	—	—

Mustafa II

OTTOMAN COINAGE

KM# 20 MANGIR

Copper **Note:** Weight varies 1.15-1.35 grams. Size varies 12-13mm.

Date	Mintage	VG	F	VF	XF	Unc
AH118 Error for 1108	—	32.00	44.00	65.00	95.00	—

KM# 21 5 PARA (Beshlik)

1.0000 g., Billon, 19 mm.

Date	Mintage	VG	F	VF	XF	Unc
AH1108	—	100	190	270	—	—

KM# 22 10 PARA

1.5300 g., Copper, 23 mm.

Date	Mintage	VG	F	VF	XF	Unc
AH1107	—	110	210	—	—	—

Situated along the Meuse, Ourthe, and Sambre rivers, Liege was a bishopric which geographically completely divided the Austro-Spanish Netherlands.

Traditionally founded in the 7th Century by St. Lambert, Liege became a bishopric in 721 and by1000, under Bishop Notga, thrived as an intellectual hub of the west and center for Mosan art. Internal struggles between citizens' guilds and prince-bishops did not weaken Liege to self-destruction. She resisted two sacks by Charles the Bold during 15th Century Burgundian domination of the Netherlands and completely rebuilt the city upon his death in 1477.

Liege was bombarded by the French in 1691, and during the War of Spanish Succession was taken by the English in 1702. After the death of Johann Theodor (Bishop, 1744-1763) there were no coin issues of the bishops. The only coin issues were the *Sede Vacante* issues of 1763, 1771, 1784 and 1792.

Ultimately the rule of the nobles ended in 1789 by a bloodless revolution which was followed by her annexation to France in 1795 and assignment with the rest of Belgium to the Netherlands in 1815.

Since Belgium's independence in 1830, Liege is again recognized as a major river port, rail center and cosmopolitan hub for art, education and industry.

RULERS

Ernest of Bavaria, 1581-1612
Ferdinand of Bavaria, 1612-1650
Maximilian Henry of Bavaria, 1650-1688
Sede Vacante, 1688
John Louis Eldern, 1688-1694
Sede Vacante, 1694
Joseph Clement of Bavaria, 1694-1723

MONETARY SYSTEM

6 Sols = 1 Escalin
48 Sols = 1 Patagon

BISHOPRIC

STANDARD COINAGE

KM# 20 VI (6) SOLS (1/4 Liard)

Copper **Ruler:** Ferdinand **Obv:** Capped four-fold arms on crossed sword and scepter **Obv. Legend:** (Rosette) FERDINAN • ELEC • COL • EPIS • LEO **Rev:** Monument divides two shield and denomination V-I **Rev. Legend:** V • DVX • BAVARI • MAR • FRANCHT **Mint:** Liege

Date	Mintage	VG	F	VF	XF	Unc
ND(1612-50)	—	65.00	115	225	450	—

KM# 21 XII (12) SOLS (1/2 Liard)

Copper **Ruler:** Ferdinand **Obv:** Capped Bavarian arms **Obv. Legend:** FERD(I) • D • G • EP • LEO(D) **Rev:** Three shields below crown, denomination X-II divided at bottom **Mint:** Liege

Date	Mintage	VG	F	VF	XF	Unc
ND(1612-50)	—	13.00	28.00	60.00	120	—

KM# 22 XII (12) SOLS (1/2 Liard)

Copper **Ruler:** Ferdinand **Rev:** Without denomination

Date	Mintage	VG	F	VF	XF	Unc
ND(1612-50)	—	37.50	75.00	150	325	—

KM# 23 XII (12) SOLS (1/2 Liard)

Copper **Ruler:** Ferdinand **Obv:** Capped four-fold arms divide denomination X-II **Obv. Legend:** FERDINAN • ELEC • COL • EP • LE(O) • **Rev:** Large crown above three shields, date divided at bottom **Rev. Legend:** •:• MAR • FRANCHI • COMES • HORNE • (Z) **Mint:** Liege

Date	Mintage	VG	F	VF	XF	Unc
1614	—	13.00	28.00	60.00	120	—
1615	—	13.00	28.00	60.00	120	—
ND	—	13.00	28.00	60.00	120	—

KM# 55 1/3 LIARD

Copper **Ruler:** Ferdinand **Obv:** Crowned FB divides date **Obv. Legend:** (Monument) FERD • PR • ELEC(T) • COL • EP • LEOD **Rev:** Crowned arms on fleur de lis cross **Rev. Legend:** SVR • DVX • BVL • COMES • LOSS **Mint:** Liege

Date	Mintage	VG	F	VF	XF	Unc
1615	—	13.00	25.00	50.00	120	—

KM# 24 1/2 LIARD

Copper **Ruler:** Ferdinand **Obv:** Bust of Ferdinand left **Obv. Legend:** (Acorn) FERDINANDVS • DVX • BAVARIE **Rev:** Capped five-fold arms **Rev. Legend:** COMES LOSSENSIS **Mint:** Maeseyck

Date	Mintage	VG	F	VF	XF	Unc
ND(1612-50)	—	50.00	95.00	180	375	—

KM# 25 1/2 LIARD

Copper **Ruler:** Ferdinand **Obv:** Capped ornate fivd-fold arms on crossed sword and crozier **Obv. Legend:** FERD D • G • EP • LEOD **Rev:** Capped F-B divided by monument **Rev. Legend:** DV . BV . MAR . FRANC . CO . LO . **Mint:** Liege

Date	Mintage	VG	F	VF	XF	Unc
ND(1612-50)	—	43.75	80.00	155	350	—

KM# 27 1/2 LIARD

Copper **Ruler:** Ferdinand **Obv:** Bust of Ferdinand left **Obv. Legend:** (Branch) FERDI • D • G • EP • LEO • D • BVL **Rev:** Crowned five-fold arms **Rev. Legend:** • COMES • LOSSENSIS •

Date	Mintage	VG	F	VF	XF	Unc
ND(1612-50)	—	50.00	95.00	180	375	—

KM# 28 1/2 LIARD

Copper **Ruler:** Ferdinand **Obv:** Bust of Ferdinand left **Obv. Legend:** (Rosette) FERDINAND • D • G • EP • LEO •

Date	Mintage	VG	F	VF	XF	Unc
ND(1612-50)	—	50.00	95.00	180	375	—

KM# 26 1/2 LIARD

Copper **Ruler:** Ferdinand **Obv:** Capped five-fold arms on crossed sword and crozier **Obv. Legend:** FERD D • G • EP LEOD • **Rev:** Capped F ★ B, monument below **Rev. Legend:** DV . BV . MAR . FRA . CO . LO . H **Mint:** Liege

Date	Mintage	VG	F	VF	XF	Unc
1641	—	19.00	37.50	70.00	150	—
ND	—	19.00	37.50	70.00	150	—

KM# 70 1/2 LIARD

Copper **Ruler:** Maximilian Henry **Obv:** Crowned shield, titles of Maximilian **Rev:** Crown on sword and scepter above shield

Date	Mintage	VG	F	VF	XF	Unc
ND(1650-88)	—	13.00	25.00	50.00	120	—

KM# 15 LIARD

Copper **Ruler:** Ernest **Obv:** Capped bust of Ernest left **Obv. Legend:** (Monument) ERNESTVS • D • (monument) G • ARCHIEPIS • COL **Rev:** Capped four-fold arms divide date **Rev. Legend:** EPIS • LEO DIEN • V • BAVAR • DVX **Mint:** Liege **Note:** Prev. KM#11.

Date	Mintage	VG	F	VF	XF	Unc
1610	—	13.00	25.00	47.50	105	—
1611	—	13.00	25.00	47.50	105	—
1612	—	13.00	25.00	47.50	105	—

KM# A32 LIARD

Copper, 25.5 mm. **Ruler:** Ferdinand **Obv:** Crowned bust to left **Obv. Legend:** FERDINAND. D.G. ARC. COL **Rev:** Crowned four-fold arms of Bavaria-Pfalz **Rev. Legend:** PR. L. ET S. CO. P.R. D. BAV

Date	Mintage	VG	F	VF	XF	Unc
ND	—	10.00	20.00	40.00	90.00	—

KM# 30 LIARD

Copper **Ruler:** Ferdinand **Obv:** Large bust of Ferdinand left **Obv. Legend:** • FERDINANDVS • D • G • EPISCOP • LEODI **Rev:** Capped four-fold arms **Rev. Legend:** FERDINAN ELEC COL EP LEO

Date	Mintage	VG	F	VF	XF	Unc
ND(1612-50) Rare	—	10.00	20.00	40.00	90.00	—

KM# 32 LIARD

Copper **Ruler:** Ferdinand **Obv:** Bust of Ferdinand with cap left **Obv. Legend:** • FERDINANDVS • D • G • ARC • COL **Rev:** Capped four-fold arms **Rev. Legend:** • PR • L • ET • S • CO • P • R • D • BAV • **Mint:** Liege

Date	Mintage	VG	F	VF	XF	Unc
ND(1612-50)	—	9.00	19.00	37.50	85.00	—

KM# 33 LIARD

Copper **Ruler:** Ferdinand **Obv:** Bust of Ferdinand left divides legend **Obv. Legend:** • FERDINANDVS • D • G • EPISCO(P) LEO(DI) **Rev:** Capped five-fold arms **Rev. Legend:** • DVX • BVLLONIENSIS •

Date	Mintage	VG	F	VF	XF	Unc
ND(1612-50)	—	10.00	20.00	40.00	90.00	—

KM# 34 LIARD

Copper **Ruler:** Ferdinand **Obv:** Bust of Ferdinand with cap left **Obv. Legend:** ❉ FERDINAND • D • G • EPISCOPVS • LEODI **Rev. Legend:** • DVX • BVLLONIENSIS • **Mint:** Liege

Date	Mintage	VG	F	VF	XF	Unc
ND(1612-50)	—	10.00	20.00	40.00	90.00	—

KM# 40 LIARD

Copper **Ruler:** Ferdinand **Obv:** Bust of Ferdinand with cap left **Obv. Legend:** (Branch) FERDINAND • D • G • EP • LEO • D • BVL • **Rev:** Different center shield **Rev. Legend:** • COMES • LOSSENSIS • **Mint:** Hasselt

Date	Mintage	VG	F	VF	XF	Unc
ND(1612-50)	—	12.00	25.00	50.00	100	—

KM# 41 LIARD

Copper **Ruler:** Ferdinand **Obv. Legend:** h FERDINAND • D • G • EPISCOPVS • LEOD **Rev. Legend:** • COMES • LOSSENSIS • **Mint:** Hasselt

Date	Mintage	VG	F	VF	XF	Unc
ND(1612-50)	—	12.00	25.00	50.00	100	—

KM# 31 LIARD

Copper **Ruler:** Ferdinand **Obv:** Capped four-fold arms **Obv. Legend:** FERDINAN • ELEC • COL • EP(IS) • LEO(D) **Rev:** Crown above three shields, date divided below **Rev. Legend:** •:• MAR • FRANCH(I) • COMES • DE • HORNE **Mint:** Liege

Date	Mintage	VG	F	VF	XF	Unc
1614	—	8.00	15.00	32.50	80.00	—
ND	—	8.00	15.00	32.50	80.00	—

KM# 29 LIARD

Copper, 26 mm. **Ruler:** Ferdinand **Obv:** Bust of Ferdinand left **Obv. Legend:** (Rosette) FERDINAN ELEC COL EP LEO **Rev:** Capped four-fold arms dividing date **Rev. Legend:** EPIS • LEODIEN • V • BAVAR • DVX

Date	Mintage	VG	F	VF	XF	Unc
1617 Rare	—	12.00	25.00	50.00	100	—

KM# 38 LIARD

Copper **Ruler:** Ferdinand **Obv:** Bust of Ferdinand with cap left **Obv. Legend:** (Lion) FERDINAND • D • G • EPISCOP • LEO **Rev:** Capped five-fold arms **Rev. Legend:** • DVX • BVLLONIENSIS • **Mint:** Dinant

Date	Mintage	VG	F	VF	XF	Unc
ND(1640)	—	13.00	28.00	60.00	120	—

KM# 39 LIARD

Copper **Ruler:** Ferdinand **Obv:** Bust of Ferdinand with cap left **Obv. Legend:** FERDINAND • D • G • EPIS...LEOD **Rev:** Capped five-fold arms **Rev. Legend:** • DVX • BVLLONIENSIS • **Mint:** Visè

Date	Mintage	VG	F	VF	XF	Unc
ND(1640)	—	25.00	50.00	95.00	225	—

KM# 35 LIARD

Copper **Ruler:** Ferdinand **Obv:** Capped ornate five-fold arms on crossed sword and crozier divides date **Obv. Legend:** FERDINAND • D • G • EP • LEOD(IE) **Rev:** Capped *F*B*, monument below **Rev. Legend:** • DVX • BVL • MAR • FRANCH • CO • LO • HO(R) **Mint:** Liege

Date	Mintage	VG	F	VF	XF	Unc
1641	—	10.00	20.00	40.00	90.00	—

Date	Mintage	VG	F	VF	XF	Unc
1642	—	10.00	20.00	40.00	90.00	—
1643	—	10.00	20.00	40.00	90.00	—

KM# 36 LIARD

Copper **Ruler:** Ferdinand **Obv:** Crowned five-fold arms on crossed sword and crozier divides date **Obv. Legend:** FERDINAND • D • G • EP • LEO • **Rev. Legend:** DVX • BVL • MAR • FRANCH • CO • LO • (HO) **Mint:** Maeseyck

Date	Mintage	VG	F	VF	XF	Unc
1641	—	10.00	20.00	40.00	90.00	—
1642	—	10.00	20.00	40.00	90.00	—
1643	—	10.00	20.00	40.00	90.00	—

KM# 37 LIARD

Copper **Ruler:** Ferdinand **Obv:** Capped five-fold arms on crossed sword and crozier divides date **Obv. Legend:** FERDINAND • D • G • EP • LEO **Rev:** Capped monument divides F-B **Rev. Legend:** • DVX • BVL • MAR • FRANCHI • CO • LO • **Mint:** Liege

Date	Mintage	VG	F	VF	XF	Unc
1641	—	10.00	20.00	40.00	90.00	—
1642	—	10.00	20.00	40.00	90.00	—
1643	—	10.00	20.00	40.00	90.00	—
ND	—	10.00	20.00	40.00	90.00	—

KM# 42 LIARD

Copper **Ruler:** Ferdinand **Obv:** Capped five-fold arms on crossed sword and crozier divides date **Obv. Legend:** FERDINAND • D • G • EP • LEO • **Rev:** Capped monument divides • F-B • in inner circle **Rev. Legend:** ❈ DVX • BVL • MAR • FRANCH • CO • LO • HO **Mint:** Maeseyck

Date	Mintage	VG	F	VF	XF	Unc
1641	—	10.00	20.00	40.00	90.00	—
1642	—	10.00	20.00	40.00	90.00	—
1643	—	10.00	20.00	40.00	90.00	—
ND	—	10.00	20.00	40.00	90.00	—

KM# 43 LIARD

Copper **Ruler:** Ferdinand **Obv. Legend:** FERDINAND • D • G • EP • LE • **Rev. Legend:** • DVX • BVL • MAR • FRANCH • CO • LO **Mint:** Hasselt

Date	Mintage	VG	F	VF	XF	Unc
1643	—	12.00	25.00	50.00	100	—

KM# 71 LIARD

Copper, 26-27 mm. **Ruler:** Maximilian Henry **Obv:** Capped shield on crossed sword **Obv. Legend:** MAXIM • • HENRI : D. G • ARCHI • COL • **Rev:** Crowned four-fold arms **Rev. Legend:** • EPISC • ET • PRINC • LEO : D • BVL • **Mint:** Hasselt

Date	Mintage	VG	F	VF	XF	Unc
ND(1650-88)	—	25.00	55.00	110	240	—

KM# 72 LIARD

Copper, 23 mm. **Ruler:** Maximilian Henry **Obv:** Crowned Bavarian arms **Obv. Legend:** MAXIM • HEN • D • G • ARC • CO(L) **Rev:** Capped shield on crossed sword and scepter **Rev. Legend:** • EPS ET PRINC • LEO(D) • DV(X) • BV • (L) **Mint:** Hasselt

Date	Mintage	VG	F	VF	XF	Unc
ND(1650-88)	—	12.00	25.00	50.00	100	—

KM# 73 LIARD

Copper, 23 mm. **Ruler:** Maximilian Henry **Obv:** Crowned Bavarian arms without inner circle, legend with small letters **Obv. Legend:** MAX • HEN • D • G • ARC • COL • **Rev. Legend:** • EP • ET • PRIN • LEO • DVX • BVL

Date	Mintage	VG	F	VF	XF	Unc
ND(1650-88)	—	10.00	20.00	40.00	85.00	—

KM# 66 LIARD

Copper **Ruler:** Maximilian Henry **Obv:** Cap on crossed sword and crozier, date below **Obv. Legend:** MAXIM HENRI • D • G • ARC HI : COL • **Rev:** Capped arms **Rev. Legend:** EPIS • ET • PRIN : LEO • D • BVL **Edge:** Plain **Mint:** Liege

Date	Mintage	VG	F	VF	XF	Unc
1650	—	—	—	—	—	—

KM# 95 LIARD

Copper, 23-24 mm. **Obv:** Bust of St. Lambert left **Obv. Legend:** S • LAMBERT • PATRO • LEOD • **Rev:** Capped arms divides date **Rev. Legend:** (Rosette) DEC • ET • CAP • LEOD • SEDE • VACANTE **Mint:** Liege **Note:** Sede Vacante issue.

Date	Mintage	VG	F	VF	XF	Unc
1688	—	8.00	15.00	35.00	75.00	—

KM# 96 LIARD

Copper **Ruler:** John Louis **Obv:** Capped arms of Jean Louis on crossed sword and crozier, dates above **Obv. Legend:** IO • LVD • D • G • EP • ET • PRIN • LEO(D) • **Rev:** Radial cross of five shields **Rev. Legend:** DVX • BVL • MAR • FRA • COM • LOS • HOR **Mint:** Liege

Date	Mintage	VG	F	VF	XF	Unc
1688	—	8.00	15.00	35.00	75.00	—
1691	—	8.00	15.00	35.00	75.00	—
1692	—	8.00	15.00	35.00	75.00	—

KM# 97 LIARD

Copper **Ruler:** John Louis **Rev:** Shields in cross horizontally aligned **Mint:** Liege

Date	Mintage	VG	F	VF	XF	Unc
1688	—	8.00	15.00	35.00	75.00	—
1691	—	8.00	15.00	35.00	75.00	—
1692	—	8.00	15.00	35.00	75.00	—

KM# 107 LIARD

Copper, 24 mm. **Ruler:** Joseph Clement **Obv:** Crowned four-fold arms **Obv. Legend:** IOSEPH • CLEM • D • G • ARC • COL **Rev:** Without date in angles of shields **Rev. Legend:** * EP • ET • PRI • LEO • DVX • BVL • M • F • C • L • H **Mint:** Liege

Date	Mintage	VG	F	VF	XF	Unc
ND(1694-1723)	—	8.00	15.00	35.00	75.00	—

KM# 106 LIARD

Copper **Obv:** Bust of St. Lambert left **Obv. Legend:** S : LAMBERTTVS • PATRO(NVS) • LEO(D) : **Rev:** Cross of shields, date in angles **Rev. Legend:** ❈ DEC • ET • CAP • LEOD • SEDE • VACANTE **Note:** Sede Vacante issue.

Date	Mintage	VG	F	VF	XF	Unc
1694	—	25.00	50.00	110	250	—

KM# 107a LIARD

Silver, 24 mm. **Ruler:** Joseph Clement **Obv:** Crowned 4-fold arms, titles of Joseph **Rev:** Without date in angles of shields

Date	Mintage	VG	F	VF	XF	Unc
ND(1694-1723)	—	—	—	—	—	—

KM# B36 SOUVERAIN

Silver **Ruler:** Ferdinand **Obv:** Arms on floriate cross with F and B in angles **Obv. Legend:** (Rosette) FERDINANDVS • D • G • ARCHI • COL • PRINC • ELECTOR **Rev. Legend:** EPISC • ET • PRINC • LEO • VTR • BAV • ET • S • BVL • DVX **Edge:** Plain **Mint:** Liege

Date	Mintage	VG	F	VF	XF	Unc
ND(1612-50) Rare	—	—	—	—	—	—

KM# 17 TESTON (15 Sols)

Silver **Ruler:** Ernest **Obv:** Bust of Ernest left **Obv. Legend:** • ERNESTVS • D(E) • G(R) • EPICSOPVS • LEODI(E) **Rev:** Capped shield over crossed sword and crozier divides date, value XV below **Rev. Legend:** (Annulet) DVX † BVLLONIENSIS (annulet) **Edge:** Plain **Mint:** Bouillon

Date	Mintage	VG	F	VF	XF	Unc
1611	—	325	500	900	—	—
161Z	—	325	500	900	—	—

KM# 18.1 2 TESTONS

Silver **Ruler:** Ernest **Obv:** Bust of Ernest left **Obv. Legend:** (Annulet) ERNESTVS • DEI • GR • EPICSOPVS • LEODIE **Rev:** Capped shield on crossed sword and crozier, crozier divides date at upper left **Rev. Legend:** DVX :: BVILLONIENSIS :: **Edge:** Plain **Mint:** Bouillon

Date	Mintage	VG	F	VF	XF	Unc
1611	—	275	475	850	—	—

KM# 18.2 2 TESTONS

Silver **Ruler:** Ernest **Obv:** Bust of Ernest left **Obv. Legend:** (Annulet) ERNESTVS • DEI • GR • EPISC(O)PVS • LEODIE **Rev:** Capped shield over crossed sword and crozier, cap divides date **Rev. Legend:** DVX (annulet) BVILLONIENSIS **Edge:** Plain **Mint:** Bouillon

Date	Mintage	VG	F	VF	XF	Unc
1611	—	250	450	800	—	—
1612	—	250	450	800	—	—

KM# 19 4 TESTONS

Silver **Ruler:** Ernest **Obv:** Bust of Ernest left **Obv. Legend:** (Annulet) ERNESTVS • DEI • GR • EPISCOPVS • LEODIE **Rev:** Capped shield on crossed sword and crozier **Rev. Legend:** DVX (annulet) BVLLONIENSIS **Edge:** Plain **Mint:** Bouillon

Date	Mintage	VG	F	VF	XF	Unc
1611	—	375	625	1,150	—	—

KM# 48 4 TESTONS

Silver **Ruler:** Ferdinand **Obv:** Bust of Ferdinand left **Obv. Legend:** •:• FERDINANDVS • D : G • EPISCOPVS • LEODIE **Rev:** Crowned arms over crossed sword and crozier **Mint:** Bouillon **Note:** Dav. #4290.

Date	Mintage	VG	F	VF	XF	Unc
1613 Rare	—	—	—	—	—	—

KM# 44 TESTON OF 15 PATARDS

Silver **Ruler:** Ferdinand **Obv:** Bust of Ferdinand left **Obv. Legend:** (Annulet) FERDINANDVS • DEI • G • EPISCOPVS • LEODI **Rev:** Capped ornate arms on crossed sword and crozier, value XV below **Rev. Legend:** (Rosette) DVX • BVLLONIENSIS (Rosette) **Edge:** Plain **Mint:** Hasselt

Date	Mintage	VG	F	VF	XF	Unc
1612	—	75.00	125	250	500	—

KM# 45.1 2 TESTON OF 30 PATARDS

Silver **Ruler:** Ferdinand **Obv:** Bust of Ferdinand left, value XXX below **Obv. Legend:** •:• FERDINANDVS • DEI • G • EPISCOPVS • LEODI(E) **Rev:** Capped arms over crossed sword and crozier **Rev. Legend:** •:• DVX • BVLLONIENSIS **Edge:** Plain **Mint:** Bouillon

Date	Mintage	VG	F	VF	XF	Unc
161Z	—	55.00	95.00	165	385	—

KM# 45.2 2 TESTON OF 30 PATARDS

Silver **Ruler:** Ferdinand **Obv:** Bust of Ferdinand left **Obv. Legend:** •:• FERDINANDVS • DEI • G • EPISCOPVS • LEODI(E) **Rev:** Capped ornate arms over crossed sword and crozier **Rev. Legend:** •:• • DVX • BVLLONIENSIS **Edge:** Plain **Mint:** Bouillon

Date	Mintage	VG	F	VF	XF	Unc
1613	—	55.00	95.00	165	385	—

KM# D53.1 1/2 DALER OF 15 PATARDS

Silver **Ruler:** Ferdinand **Obv:** Bust of Ferdinand left **Obv. Legend:** •:• FERNANDVS • D(EI) • G • ARCHI • COL • PRI • ELE C **Rev:** Capped arms divides crowned F-B, without value or date below **Rev. Legend:** •:• EPIS • ET • PRIN(C) • LEOD • SVPR • DVX • BVLIONENSIS **Edge:** Plain **Mint:** Liege **Note:** Legend varieties exist.

Date	Mintage	VG	F	VF	XF	Unc
ND(1612-50)	—	155	325	625	—	—

KM# B53 1/2 DALER OF 15 PATARDS

Silver **Ruler:** Ferdinand **Obv:** Crowned rampant lion with sword and shield left **Obv. Legend:** (Rosette) FERDINANDUS • DEI • G • ARCHI • COL • PRIN • ELEC(T) **Rev:** Capped arms divides crowned F-B, value XV and date below **Rev. Legend:** •:• EPIS • ET • PRINC • LEOD : SVPR • DVX • BVLIONENSIS **Edge:** Plain **Mint:** Hasselt

Date	Mintage	VG	F	VF	XF	Unc
1614	—	220	375	700	—	—

KM# D53.2 1/2 DALER OF 15 PATARDS

Silver **Ruler:** Ferdinand **Obv:** Bust of Ferdinand left **Obv. Legend:**

•:• FERNANDVS • D(EI) • G • ARCHI • COL • PRI • ELE C **Rev:** Capped arms divides crowned F-B, value XV and date below **Rev. Legend:** •:• EPIS • ET • PRINC • LEOD • SVPR • DVX • BVLIONENSIS **Edge:** Plain **Mint:** Visè **Note:** Legend varieties exist.

Date	Mintage	VG	F	VF	XF	Unc
1615	—	155	325	625	—	—

KM# D53.3 1/2 DALER OF 15 PATARDS

Silver **Ruler:** Ferdinand **Obv:** Bust of Ferdinand left **Obv. Legend:** •:• FERNANDVS • D(EI) • G • ARCHI • COL • PRI • ELE C **Rev:** Capped arms divides crowned F-B, value XV and date below **Rev. Legend:** •:• EPIS • ET • PRINC • LEOD • SVPR • DVX • BVLIONENSIS **Edge:** Plain **Mint:** Liege **Note:** Legend varieties exist.

Date	Mintage	VG	F	VF	XF	Unc
1619	—	110	220	450	—	—
1625	—	110	220	450	—	—
1635	—	110	220	450	—	—

KM# 69 1/2 DALER OF 15 PATARDS

Silver **Ruler:** Ferdinand **Obv:** Bust of Ferdinand left **Obv. Legend:** (Rosette) FERDINANDVS • D • G • ARCHI • COL • PRINC • ELE C **Rev:** Capped arms divide crowned F-B, date and vlaue XXXVIII below **Rev. Legend:** EPIS • ET • PRIN • LEO • SVPRE... **Edge:** Plain **Mint:** Liege

Date	Mintage	VG	F	VF	XF	Unc
1645	—	115	235	485	—	—

KM# 68 1/2 DALER OF 15 PATARDS

Silver **Ruler:** Ferdinand **Obv:** Bust of Ferdinand left **Obv. Legend:** (Rosette) FERDINANDVS... **Rev:** Capped arms divide crowned F-B, date and vlaue XVIII below **Rev. Legend:** •:• EPIS • ET • PRINC... **Edge:** Plain **Mint:** Liege

Date	Mintage	VG	F	VF	XF	Unc
1645	—	120	235	485	—	—

KM# C53 DALER OF 30 PATARDS

Silver **Ruler:** Ferdinand **Obv:** Crowned rampoant lion with sword and shield left **Obv. Legend:** •:• FERDINANDVS • DEI G : ARCHI : COL : PRIN(C)(:)(EP)(S) : ELEC(T) **Rev:** Capped arms divides crowned F-B, value and date below **Rev. Legend:** EPIS(C) • ET • PRINC • LEOD • SVPR(E) • DVX • BVLIONENSIS **Edge:** Plain **Mint:** Hasselt

Date	Mintage	VG	F	VF	XF	Unc
1614	—	180	325	600	1,200	—

KM# 60.1 DALER OF 30 PATARDS

Silver **Ruler:** Ferdinand **Obv:** Bust of Ferdinand left **Obv. Legend:** •:•FERDINANDVS • DEI • G • ARCHI • COL • PRIN(C) • (ELEC)(T) • LEO **Rev:** Capped ornate arms divides crowned F and B, XXX - date below **Rev. Legend:** EPIS • ET • PRIN • LEOD • SUPRE • DVX • BVLIONENSIS **Edge:** Plain **Mint:** Hasselt **Note:** Dav. #4291. Reverse legend varieties exist.

Date	Mintage	VG	F	VF	XF	Unc
1614	—	115	210	400	775	—

KM# 60.2 DALER OF 30 PATARDS

Silver **Ruler:** Ferdinand **Obv:** Bust of Ferdinand left **Obv. Legend:** •:•FERDINANDVS • DEI • G • ARCHI • COL • PRIN(C) • (ELEC)(T) • LEO **Rev:** Capped ornate arms divides crowned F and B, XXX - date below **Rev. Legend:** EPIS • ET • PRIN • LEOD • SUPRE • DVX • BVLIONENSIS **Edge:** Plain **Mint:** Visè **Note:** Dav. #4291. Reverse legend varieties exist.

Date	Mintage	VG	F	VF	XF	Unc
1615	—	115	210	400	775	—

KM# 60.4 DALER OF 30 PATARDS

Silver **Ruler:** Ferdinand **Obv:** Bust of Ferdinand left **Obv. Legend:** •:•FERDINANDVS • DEI • G • ARCHI • COL • PRIN(C) • (ELEC)(T) • LEO **Rev:** Capped ornate arms divides crowned F and B, XXX - date below **Rev. Legend:** EPIS • ET • PRIN • LEOD • SUPRE • DVX • BVLIONENSIS **Edge:** Plain **Mint:** Liege **Note:** Dav. #4291. Reverse legend varieties exist.

Date	Mintage	VG	F	VF	XF	Unc
1619	—	95.00	185	325	700	—
1621	—	95.00	185	325	700	—
1622	—	95.00	185	325	700	—
1624	—	95.00	185	325	700	—
1625	—	95.00	185	325	700	—
1630	—	95.00	185	325	700	—
1634	—	95.00	185	325	700	—
1636	—	95.00	185	325	700	—
1637	—	95.00	185	325	700	—
1641	—	95.00	185	325	700	—
1645	—	95.00	185	325	700	—
1646	—	95.00	185	325	700	—

KM# 60.3 DALER OF 30 PATARDS

Silver **Ruler:** Ferdinand **Obv:** Bust of Ferdinand left **Obv. Legend:** •:•FERDINANDVS • DEI • G • ARCHI • COL • PRIN(C) • (ELEC)(T) • LEO **Rev:** Capped ornate arms divides crowned F and B, XXX - date below **Rev. Legend:** EPIS • ET • PRIN • LEOD • SUPRE • DVX • BVLIONENSIS **Edge:** Plain **Mint:** Dinant **Note:** Dav. #4291. Reverse legend varieties exist.

Date	Mintage	VG	F	VF	XF	Unc
1631 Rare	—	—	—	—	—	—
1633 Rare	—	—	—	—	—	—

KM# 64.1 1/2 ESCALIN

Silver **Ruler:** Ferdinand **Obv:** Floreate cross **Obv. Legend:** FERDINANDVS • D • G • ARCH • COL... **Rev:** Capped arms divides date **Rev. Legend:** EPIS • ET • PRIN(C) • LEO :... N • BAV • S • BVL • DVX **Edge:** Plain **Mint:** Liege

Date	Mintage	VG	F	VF	XF	Unc
1636 Rare	—	—	—	—	—	—

KM# 64.2 1/2 ESCALIN

Silver **Ruler:** Ferdinand **Obv:** Floreate cross **Obv. Legend:** FERDINANDVS • D • G • ARCH • COL... **Rev:** Capped arms divides date **Rev. Legend:** EPIS • ET • PRIN(C) • LEO • SVBR • DVX • BV... **Edge:** Plain **Mint:** Liege

Date	Mintage	VG	F	VF	XF	Unc
1636 Rare	—	—	—	—	—	—

KM# 75 1/2 ESCALIN

Silver **Ruler:** Maximilian Henry **Obv:** Floreate cross, rosette in center **Obv. Legend:** (Rosette) MAXIM • HENRI • D • G • ARCHIE • COL(LON) (BA DVX) **Rev:** Capped Bavarian arms, shield of Bouillon at center in multiple foils **Rev. Legend:** • EPISC • ET • PRIN • LEOD(I) • DVX • BVL • (LO)(NI) • **Edge:** Plain **Mint:** Bouillon

Date	Mintage	VG	F	VF	XF	Unc
1651	—	20.00	40.00	85.00	200	—
1652	—	20.00	40.00	85.00	200	—
1654	—	20.00	40.00	85.00	200	—
1656	—	20.00	40.00	85.00	200	—
1658	—	20.00	40.00	85.00	200	—
1659	—	20.00	40.00	85.00	200	—
1660	—	20.00	40.00	85.00	200	—
1662	—	20.00	40.00	85.00	200	—

KM# 59 ESCALIN

Silver **Ruler:** Ferdinand **Obv:** Rampant lion with shield left **Obv. Legend:** FERDINANDVS • D • G • ARCHI • COL • PRIN • ELEC **Rev:** Capped shield divides date in double outline **Rev. Legend:** • EPIS • ET • PRIN • LEO • VT • BA • ET •... **Edge:** Plain

Date	Mintage	VG	F	VF	XF	Unc
1633	—	—	—	—	—	—

KM# 58 ESCALIN

Silver **Ruler:** Ferdinand **Obv:** Rampant lion with sword and shield left **Obv. Legend:** FERDINANDVS • D • G • ARC(HI) • COL • P(RIN) • EL(EC) **Rev:** Capped shield on floreate cross divides date **Rev. Legend:** • EP(S) • ET • PRI(N) • • LEO • • (ET) • S • DVX • BVL • **Edge:** Plain **Mint:** Liege **Note:** Reverse legend varieties exist.

Date	Mintage	VG	F	VF	XF	Unc
1636	—	32.50	65.00	150	325	—
1637	—	32.50	65.00	150	325	—
1640	—	32.50	65.00	150	325	—
1641	—	32.50	65.00	150	325	—
1646	—	32.50	65.00	150	325	—
1650	—	32.50	65.00	150	325	—

KM# 76 ESCALIN

Silver **Ruler:** Maximilian Henry **Obv:** Rampant lion with sword and shield left **Obv. Legend:** (Rosette) MAX(IM) • HEN(RI) • D • G • ARC(HIE) • COL • (B) **Rev:** Capped arms of Bavarian, shield of Bouillon at center on floreate cross dividing legend, shield divides date **Rev. Legend:** • EPS ET • PRI NC • LEO • ET • S • BV DVX **Edge:** Plain **Mint:** Liege

Date	Mintage	VG	F	VF	XF	Unc
1651	—	35.00	75.00	150	275	—
1652	—	35.00	75.00	150	275	—
1653	—	35.00	75.00	150	275	—
1654	—	35.00	75.00	150	275	—
1656	—	35.00	75.00	150	275	—
1657	—	35.00	75.00	150	275	—
1658	—	35.00	75.00	150	275	—

KM# 77 ESCALIN

Silver **Ruler:** Maximilian Henry **Obv:** Rampant lion with sword and shield left **Obv. Legend:** (Rosette) MAXIM • HENRI • D • G • ARCHI • COL • **Rev:** Capped arms of Bavarian, shield of Bouillon at center on floreate cross dividing legend, shield divides date, cap also divides legend **Rev. Legend:** • EP • ET • P RIN • LEO ET • (S) • BV • D(V) • (X) **Edge:** Plain **Mint:** Liege

Date	Mintage	VG	F	VF	XF	Unc
1660	—	32.50	55.00	100	250	—
1661	—	32.50	55.00	100	250	—

KM# 65 DALER OF 40 PATARDS

Silver **Ruler:** Ferdinand **Obv:** Capped four-fold arms on crossed sword and crozier, capped shield at right **Rev:** St. Lambert and the Virgin with child standing **Mint:** Liege **Note:** Dav. #4293.

Date	Mintage	VG	F	VF	XF	Unc
1646 Rare	—	—	—	—	—	—

KM# 79 1/2 PATAGON

Silver **Ruler:** Maximilian Henry **Obv:** Bust of Maximlian Henry right **Obv. Legend:** MAX • HEN • D • G • ARC • COL • PRIN • EL **Rev:** Capped five-fold arms **Rev. Legend:** (Rosette) EP • ET • PRIN • LEOD • DVX • BVL • MAR • FR • LO • **Edge:** Plain **Mint:** Liege

Date	Mintage	VG	F	VF	XF	Unc
1663 Rare	—	—	—	—	—	—

KM# 61 PATAGON

Silver **Ruler:** Ferdinand **Obv:** Floriate cross with shield of Bouillon at center, crowned F's and crowned B's in angles **Obv. Legend:** FERDINANDVS • D • G • ARCHI • COL • PRINC • ELECTOR • **Rev:** Capped ornate oval Bavarian arms with shield of Bouillon at center **Rev. Legend:** • EPISC • ET • PRINC • LEO • VTR • BAV • ET • S • BVL • DVX **Note:** Dav. #4292.

Date	Mintage	VG	F	VF	XF	Unc
1635 Rare	—	—	—	—	—	—

KM# 80 PATAGON

Silver **Ruler:** Maximilian Henry **Obv:** Bust of Maximilian Henry right **Obv. Legend:** MAX • H(EA)N • D • G • ARC • COL • PRIN(C) • E(LR) • **Rev:** Capped eight-fold arms, date above **Rev. Legend:** • EP • ET • PRIN(C) • LEO(D) • DVX... **Mint:** Liege **Note:** Dav. #4294.

Date	Mintage	VG	F	VF	XF	Unc
1662	—	75.00	150	350	575	—
1663	—	75.00	150	350	575	—
1664	—	75.00	150	350	575	—
1665	—	75.00	150	350	575	—
1666	—	75.00	150	350	575	—
1667	—	75.00	150	350	575	—
1668	—	75.00	150	350	575	—
1669	—	75.00	150	350	575	—
1670	—	75.00	150	350	575	—
1671	—	75.00	150	350	575	—
1672	—	75.00	150	350	575	—

Date	Mintage	VG	F	VF	XF	Unc
1673	—	75.00	150	350	575	—
1674	—	75.00	150	350	575	—
1675	—	75.00	150	350	575	—
1676	—	75.00	150	350	575	—
1677	—	75.00	150	350	575	—
1678	—	75.00	150	350	575	—
1679	—	75.00	150	350	575	—
1680	—	75.00	150	350	575	—
1681	—	75.00	150	350	575	—
1682	—	75.00	150	350	575	—
1683	—	75.00	150	350	575	—
1685	—	75.00	150	350	575	—
1686	—	75.00	150	350	575	—

KM# 99 PATAGON

Silver **Obv:** Capped four-fold arms **Rev:** Bust of St. Lambert left **Mint:** Liege **Note:** Sede Vacante issue. Dav. #4298.

Date	Mintage	VG	F	VF	XF	Unc
1688	—	275	425	900	2,000	—

KM# 98 PATAGON

Silver **Obv:** Capped four-fold arms **Rev:** Bust of St. Lambert left in ornate oval frame **Mint:** Liege **Note:** Sede Vacante issue. Struck at Liege. Dav. #4297.

Date	Mintage	VG	F	VF	XF	Unc
1688	—	500	750	1,650	3,000	—

KM# 102 PATAGON

Silver **Ruler:** John Louis **Obv:** Bust of John Louis Eldern right **Obv. Legend:** IOAN • LVD • D • G • EP • ET • PRIN • LEO **Rev:** Capped five-fold arms with date above **Rev. Legend:** • DVX • BVL(L) • MAR • FRA • COM • LO(S) • HO(R) • **Mint:** Liege **Note:** Dav. #4300.

Date	Mintage	VG	F	VF	XF	Unc
1689	—	225	375	750	1,350	—
1690	—	225	375	750	1,350	—
1691	—	225	375	750	1,350	—
1692	—	225	375	750	1,350	—
1693	—	225	375	750	1,350	—

KM# 109 PATAGON

Silver **Ruler:** Joseph Clement **Obv:** Bust of Joseph Clement right breaking upper legend **Obv. Legend:** IOSEPH • CLE • D • G • AR • COL • P • EL • **Rev:** Capped eight-fold arms, date above **Rev. Legend:** ❋ EP • ET • PRINC • LEOD • DVX •... **Mint:** Liege **Note:** Dav. #4302.

Date	Mintage	VG	F	VF	XF	Unc
1694 Rare	—	—	—	—	—	—
1695 Rare	—	—	—	—	—	—

KM# 112.1 PATAGON

Silver **Ruler:** Joseph Clement **Obv:** Smaller bust of Joseph Clement right, legend continuous **Obv. Legend:** IOSEPH • CLEM • D • G • AR • COL • P • E(L) • **Rev:** Capped nine-fold arms, date above **Rev. Legend:** EP • ET • PRINC • LEOD • DUX • BUL • MAR • FR • CO • LO • HO. **Mint:** Liege **Note:** Dav. #4303. Varieties exist.

Date	Mintage	VG	F	VF	XF	Unc
1694	—	200	500	1,050	1,750	—
1695	—	200	500	1,050	1,750	—
1696 Rare	—	—	—	—	—	—
1698	—	125	325	700	1,150	—
1699	—	125	325	700	1,150	—
1700	—	125	325	700	1,150	—

KM# 108 PATAGON

Silver **Obv:** Capped five-fold arms with date above **Rev:** Bust of St. Lambert left **Mint:** Liege **Note:** Sede Vacante issue. Dav. #4301.

Date	Mintage	VG	F	VF	XF	Unc
1694	—	350	625	1,350	2,250	—

KM# 112.2 PATAGON

Silver **Ruler:** Joseph Clement **Rev:** Quarters of Bavaria-Palatinant in small shield reversed

Date	Mintage	VG	F	VF	XF	Unc
1700	—	250	450	950	1,600	—

KM# 84 DUCATONE

Silver **Ruler:** Maximilian Henry **Obv:** Capped bust of Maximilian Henry right **Obv. Legend:** MAX • HEN • D • G • A • C • P... **Rev:** Capped, supported five-fold arms **Rev. Legend:** SVPR(E)MV(S) BVLLONIEN SIS • DVX **Mint:** Liege **Note:** Dav. #4296.

Date	Mintage	VG	F	VF	XF	Unc
1666	—	85.00	175	350	575	—
1667	—	85.00	175	350	575	—
1668	—	85.00	175	350	575	—
1669	—	85.00	175	350	575	—
1670	—	85.00	175	350	575	—
1671	—	85.00	175	350	575	—
1673	—	85.00	175	350	575	—
1674	—	85.00	175	350	575	—
1675	—	85.00	175	350	575	—
1676	—	85.00	175	350	575	—
1677	—	85.00	175	350	575	—
1678	—	85.00	175	350	575	—
1680	—	85.00	175	350	575	—
1681	—	85.00	175	350	575	—
1682	—	85.00	175	350	575	—
1683	—	85.00	175	350	575	—

KM# 101 DUCATONE

Silver **Ruler:** John Louis **Obv:** Bust of John Louis Eldern right, date **Obv. Legend:** • IOAN • LVD • D • G • EP • PRIN • LEOD• **Rev:** Capped and supported arms **Rev. Legend:** SVPREMVS BVLLONIEN SIS • DVX **Edge:** Plain **Mint:** Liege **Note:** Dav. #4299.

Date	Mintage	VG	F	VF	XF	Unc
1689	—	250	450	950	1,600	—
1690	—	250	450	950	1,600	—
1691	—	250	450	950	1,600	—

KM# 103 DUCATONE

Silver **Ruler:** John Louis **Obv:** Similar to KM#101 **Rev:** Similar to KM#101 **Rev. Legend:** SVPREMV... **Edge Lettering:** AD PRINCIPIS GLORIAM ET POPULI SECURITATEM **Mint:** Liege **Note:** Dav. #4299A.

Date	Mintage	VG	F	VF	XF	Unc
1689	—	375	750	1,650	2,500	—

KM# 90 2 DUCATONE

Silver **Ruler:** Maximilian Henry **Obv:** Capped bust of Maximilian Henry right **Obv. Legend:** MAX • HEN • D • G • A • C • P • **Rev:** Capped, supported five-fold arms **Mint:** Liege **Note:** Struck at Liege. Dav. #4295.

Date	Mintage	VG	F	VF	XF	Unc
1671 Rare	—	—	—	—	—	—

KM# G35 2 DALER

Silver **Ruler:** Ferdinand **Obv:** Bust of Ferdinand **Obv. Legend:** (Rosette) FERDINANDVS • DEI • G • ARCHI • COL • PRINC • ELECT **Rev:** Five-fold arms with lion supporters **Rev. Legend:** (Rosette) EPISC • ET • PRIN • LEOD • VTR • BAT • ET • SVPREMVS • BVL • DVX **Edge:** Plain **Mint:** Dinant

Date	Mintage	VG	F	VF	XF	Unc
ND(1612-50) Rare	—	—	—	—	—	—

KM# E35 1/2 REAL

Silver **Ruler:** Ferdinand **Obv:** Capped five-fold arms **Obv. Legend:** FERDINANDVS • DE • GRATIA **Rev:** Long floreate cross divides legend, crosses in angles **Rev. Legend:** EPIS LEOD DVX BVLI **Edge:** Plain

Date	Mintage	VG	F	VF	XF	Unc
ND(1612-50)	—	185	375	850	—	—

KM# C35 1/2 REAL

Silver **Ruler:** Ferdinand **Obv:** Capped arms **Obv. Legend:** FERDINA • ELEC • COL • EPIS • LEO • Z **Rev:** Long floreate cross, crosses in angles, imperial eagle at center **Rev. Legend:** MATH ROMA IMPE S • AVG **Edge:** Plain **Mint:** Liege

Date	Mintage	VG	F	VF	XF	Unc
ND(1612-19)	—	185	375	850	—	—

KM# B35 1/2 REAL

Silver **Ruler:** Ferdinand **Obv:** Capped arms **Obv. Legend:** FERDINAN • ELEC • COL • EPIS • LEO : Z **Rev:** Long floreate cross, perrons in angles, imperial eagle at center **Rev. Legend:** MATH ROMA IMPE S • AVG **Edge:** Plain **Mint:** Liege

Date	Mintage	VG	F	VF	XF	Unc
ND(1612-19) Rare	—	185	375	850	—	—

KM# F35.1 1/2 REAL

Silver **Ruler:** Ferdinand **Obv:** Ornate four-fold arms **Obv. Legend:** FERD • DE • GRA • DVX • EP • LEOD • DVX • BVL • COM(E)S • LOS **Rev:** Long floreate cross divides legend, floreate ends repeated in angles, imperial eagle at center **Rev. Legend:** FERD II • ROM IMPE SEM • AV **Edge:** Plain **Mint:** Liege

Date	Mintage	VG	F	VF	XF	Unc
ND(1619-37) Rare	—	—	—	—	—	—

KM# F35.2 1/2 REAL

Silver **Ruler:** Ferdinand **Obv:** Ornate four-fold arms **Obv. Legend:** FERD • DE • G • EPS • ET • PRIN • COL **Rev:** Long floreate cross divides legend, floreate ends repeated in quarters, imperial eagle at center **Rev. Legend:** FERD II • ROM IMPE SEM • AV **Edge:** Plain **Mint:** Liege

Date	Mintage	VG	F	VF	XF	Unc
ND(1619-37) Rare	—	—	—	—	—	—

KM# A56 REAL

Silver **Ruler:** Ferdinand **Obv:** Ornate four-fold arms divides date **Obv. Legend:** FERD • D • G • EPS • ET • PRINC • LEOD • VTR • BA • ET • B • DVX **Rev:** Long floreate cross divides legend, floreate ends repeated in angles, imperial eagle at center **Rev. Legend:** FERD II • ROM IMPE SEM • AV **Edge:** Plain **Mint:** Liege

Date	Mintage	VG	F	VF	XF	Unc
1629	—	165	350	775	—	—
1630	—	165	350	775	—	—
1631	—	165	350	775	—	—

KM# A36 REAL

Silver **Ruler:** Ferdinand **Obv:** Ornate four-fold arms divides date **Obv. Legend:** FERDINANDVS • DE • G...LEO **Rev:** Long floreate cross divides legend, lis in angles **Rev. Legend:** EPI...PRI...VT • BA • ET SV • B • DVX **Edge:** Plain **Mint:** Dinant

Date	Mintage	VG	F	VF	XF	Unc
1631 Rare	—	—	—	—	—	—

KM# D35 2 PATARDS (2 Sols)

Silver **Ruler:** Ferdinand **Obv:** Capped arms divides value II-S **Obv. Legend:** FERDINAN • ELEC • COL • EPI(S) • LE(OD) • Z **Rev:** Crowned imperial eagle **Rev. Legend:** MATHIAS • ROMANO • IMPE • SEMP • AV(G) **Edge:** Plain **Mint:** Liege

Date	Mintage	VG	F	VF	XF	Unc
ND(1612-19)	—	100	200	475	—	—

KM# A35 4 PATARDS (4 Sols)

Billon **Ruler:** Ferdinand **Obv:** Capped ornate arms, value IIIS below **Obv. Legend:** FERDINAN • ELEC • COL • EPIS • LEO • Z **Rev:** Crowned imperial eagle **Rev. Legend:** MATHIAS • ROMANO • IMPE • SEM • AVG **Edge:** Plain **Mint:** Liege

Date	Mintage	VG	F	VF	XF	Unc
ND(1612-19) Rare	—	—	—	—	—	—

TRADE COINAGE

KM# A20 FLORIN D'OR

3.5000 g., 0.9860 Gold 0.1109 oz. AGW **Ruler:** Ernest **Obv:** Bust of Ernest left **Obv. Legend:** •:• ERNESTVS • D • G • EPISCOPVS • LEODIEN **Rev:** Capped arms on crossed sword and crozier, date above **Mint:** Bouillon **Note:** Fr. #210.

Date	Mintage	VG	F	VF	XF	Unc
1612	—	3,000	5,000	8,500	14,500	—

KM# 46 FLORIN D'OR

3.5000 g., 0.9860 Gold 0.1109 oz. AGW **Ruler:** Ferdinand **Obv:** Bust of Ferdinand left **Obv. Legend:** (Rosette)FERDINAN(DVS) • D • G • EPISCOPVS • LEOD(IE) **Rev:** Capped arms on crossed sword and crozier **Rev. Legend:** DVX • BV(I)LLONIENSIS **Mint:** Bouillon **Note:** Fr. #211.

Date	Mintage	VG	F	VF	XF	Unc
1612	—	1,250	2,000	4,500	—	—
1613	—	1,250	2,000	4,500	—	—

KM# 47 FLORIN D'OR

3.5000 g., 0.9860 Gold 0.1109 oz. AGW **Ruler:** Ferdinand **Obv:** Ferdinand enthroned facing in electoral robes, arms below **Obv. Legend:** •:• FERD : D : G : ARCH(I) • COL • PRIN(C) : ELE(C) •:• **Rev:** Trilobe with four-fold arms at center and F-B-D in trilobe **Mint:** Hasselt **Note:** Fr. #216.

Date	Mintage	VG	F	VF	XF	Unc
ND(1614) F-B-D	—	625	1,400	2,650	4,500	—

KM# 52 COURONNE D'OR

11.0600 g., 0.9190 Gold 0.3268 oz. AGW **Ruler:** Ferdinand **Obv:** Floreated cross with Fs in angles and crowns at ends **Obv. Legend:** •:• FERD(INAND) • D • G • ARCH(I) • COL • P(RINCEPS) **Rev:** Capped five-fold arms, date divided below **Rev. Legend:** EPISC : ET • PR : LEO : SV • (D) • BVL **Mint:** Hasselt **Note:** Fr. #215.

Date	Mintage	VG	F	VF	XF	Unc
1614	—	625	1,400	2,650	4,500	—

KM# 49 ECU D'OR

3.3600 g., 0.9520 Gold 0.1028 oz. AGW **Ruler:** Ferdinand **Obv:** Crowned arms over crossed sword and crozier **Obv. Legend:** + FERDINANDVS • D(EI) • G • EPISCOPVS • LEODIE **Rev:** Ornamental cross with B at center **Rev. Legend:** + SVPREMVS • DVX • BVLLONIENSIS **Mint:** Bouillon **Note:** Fr. #214.

Date	Mintage	VG	F	VF	XF	Unc
1613	—	575	1,250	2,100	3,750	—

KM# 53 ECU D'OR

3.3600 g., 0.9520 Gold 0.1028 oz. AGW **Ruler:** Ferdinand **Obv:** Floreated cross with F's in angles and crowns at ends **Obv. Legend:** •:• FERD • D • G • ARCHI • COL • PRINCEP(S) • ELECT **Rev:** Capped ornate spade-shaped five-fold arms on crossed sword and crozier, date divided by cap **Rev. Legend:** EPISC • ET • PRINC • LEO • SV • D • BVL **Mint:** Hasselt **Note:** Fr. #215.

Date	Mintage	VG	F	VF	XF	Unc
1614	—	575	1,250	2,100	3,750	—

KM# 54.1 ECU D'OR

3.3600 g., 0.9520 Gold 0.1028 oz. AGW **Ruler:** Ferdinand **Obv:** Floreated cross with F's in angles and crowns at ends **Obv. Legend:** FERDINANDVS • DEI • G • ARCHI • COL • PRIN • ELE **Rev:** Capped ornate spade-shaped Bavarian arms with shield of Bouillon at center, cap divides date **Rev. Legend:** EPISC • ET • PR • LEO • VTR • BA • ET • S • B • D • **Mint:** Liege

Date	Mintage	VG	F	VF	XF	Unc
1631	—	425	825	1,650	3,300	—

KM# 54.2 ECU D'OR

3.3600 g., 0.9520 Gold 0.1028 oz. AGW **Ruler:** Ferdinand **Obv:** Floreated cross with F's in angles and crowns at ends **Obv. Legend:** FERDINANDVS • D(EI) • G • ARCH(I) • COL • P(RINC) • ELE(C) **Mint:** Liege

Date	Mintage	VG	F	VF	XF	Unc
1631	—	250	550	1,150	1,950	—
1635	—	250	550	1,150	1,950	—
1636	—	250	550	1,150	1,950	—
1637	—	250	550	1,150	1,950	—
1639	—	250	550	1,150	1,950	—
1640	—	250	550	1,150	1,950	—
1641	—	250	550	1,150	1,950	—
1643	—	250	550	1,150	1,950	—
1644	—	250	550	1,150	1,950	—

KM# 62 ECU D'OR

3.3600 g., 0.9520 Gold 0.1028 oz. AGW **Ruler:** Ferdinand **Obv:** Floreated cross with F's in angles and crowns at ends **Obv. Legend:** • FERDINANDVS • D • G • ARCHI • COL • PRINC • ELEC **Rev:** Capped ornate arms divides date below **Rev. Legend:** EPS • ETPR • LEO • VT • BA • ET • S • BV • DVX • **Mint:** Liege

Date	Mintage	VG	F	VF	XF	Unc
1635 Rare	—	—	—	—	—	—

KM# 51 2 ECU D'OR

6.7200 g., 0.9520 Gold 0.2057 oz. AGW **Ruler:** Ferdinand **Obv:** Crowned arms **Obv. Legend:** •:• FERDINANDVS • D : G • EPISCOPVS • LEODI(E) **Rev:** Ornamental cross with B at center **Rev. Legend:** •:• SVPREMVS • DVX • BVILLIONIENSIS **Mint:** Bouillon

Date	Mintage	VG	F	VF	XF	Unc
1613 Rare	—	—	—	—	—	—

KM# 50 2 ECU D'OR

6.7200 g., 0.9520 Gold 0.2057 oz. AGW **Ruler:** Ferdinand **Obv:** Crowned arms over crossed sword and crozier **Obv. Legend:** FERDINANDVS • D : G • EPISCOPVS • • LEOD(IE) **Rev:** Ornamental cross with B at center **Rev. Legend:** SVPREMVS • DVX • BVILLIONIENSIS **Mint:** Bouillon **Note:** Fr. #213.

Date	Mintage	VG	F	VF	XF	Unc
1613	—	1,200	2,250	4,000	7,500	—

KM# 63 DUCAT

3.5000 g., 0.9860 Gold 0.1109 oz. AGW **Ruler:** Ferdinand **Obv:** Capped ornate four-fold arms **Obv. Legend:** FE RDI • ELEC • COL • EPS • LEO(D) • BAV(A)DV X **Rev:** Inscription in tablet, date divided at sides **Rev. Inscription:** DVCATVS / NOWS DVC / BVLLONI / ENSIS **Mint:** Liege

Date	Mintage	VG	F	VF	XF	Unc
1638	—	575	1,350	2,750	4,500	—

KM# 74 DUCAT

3.5000 g., 0.9860 Gold 0.1109 oz. AGW **Ruler:** Maximilian Henry **Obv:** Capped ornate five-fold arms **Obv. Legend:** MAX : HEN : ELEC • COL • EPS • LEO • BA(V)-D **Rev:** Tablet **Rev. Inscription:** DVCATVS / NOWS DV(C) / BVLLONI / ENSIS **Mint:** Liege

Date	Mintage	VG	F	VF	XF	Unc
1651	—	400	1,000	2,500	4,250	—
1652	—	400	1,000	2,500	4,250	—
1653	—	400	1,000	2,500	4,250	—
1654	—	400	1,000	2,500	4,250	—
1656	—	400	1,000	2,500	4,250	—
1658	—	400	1,000	2,500	4,250	—
1661	—	400	1,000	2,500	4,250	—

KM# 81 DUCAT

3.5000 g., 0.9860 Gold 0.1109 oz. AGW **Ruler:** Maximilian Henry **Obv:** Bust of Maximilian Henry right, date below **Obv. Legend:** MAX • HEN • D • G • ARC • COL • PR(•)E(L) **Rev:** Capped ornate five-fold arms **Mint:** Liege

Date	Mintage	VG	F	VF	XF	Unc
ND	—	3,000	5,500	9,500	—	—
1663	—	3,000	5,500	9,500	—	—
1664 Rare	—	—	—	—	—	—
1666 Rare	—	—	—	—	—	—
1667 Rare	—	—	—	—	—	—
1668	—	3,000	5,500	9,500	—	—
1669 Rare	—	—	—	—	—	—
1670	—	—	—	—	—	—

Date	Mintage	VG	F	VF	XF	Unc

Note: Künker Auction 181, 1-11, VF-XF realized approx. $11,640; Künker Auction 112, 6-06, XF realized approx. $16,320

1671 Rare	—	—	—	—	—	—
1672 Rare	—	—	—	—	—	—
1674 Rare	—	—	—	—	—	—

KM# 82 DUCAT

3.5000 g., 0.9860 Gold 0.1109 oz. AGW **Ruler:** Maximilian Henry **Obv:** Bust of Maximilian Henry right **Obv. Legend:** MAX • HEN • D • G • ARC • COL • PR • EL **Rev:** Capped ornate five-fold arms **Mint:** Liege

Date	Mintage	VG	F	VF	XF	Unc
1664 Rare	—	—	—	—	—	—

KM# 83 2 DUCAT

7.0000 g., 0.9860 Gold 0.2219 oz. AGW **Ruler:** Maximilian Henry **Obv:** Bust of Maximilian Henry right **Obv. Legend:** MAX • HEN • D • G • ARC • COL • PRIN • EL (dog) **Rev:** Capped ornate five-fold arms **Mint:** Liege

Date	Mintage	VG	F	VF	XF	Unc
ND(1650-88)	—	4,500	8,000	12,500	17,500	—

KM# 100 2 DUCAT

7.0000 g., 0.9860 Gold 0.2219 oz. AGW **Obv:** Crowned four-fold arms divide date **Rev:** Bust of St. Lambert left **Mint:** Liege **Note:** Sede Vacante issue.

Date	Mintage	VG	F	VF	XF	Unc
1688	—	4,500	8,000	12,500	18,500	—

KM# 105 2 DUCAT

7.0000 g., 0.9860 Gold 0.2219 oz. AGW **Ruler:** John Louis **Obv:** Bust of John Louis right **Obv. Legend:** IOZN • LVD • D • G • EP • ET • PRIN • LEO **Rev:** Crowned five-fold arms, date above **Mint:** Liege

Date	Mintage	VG	F	VF	XF	Unc
1690	—	5,500	9,000	14,500	20,000	—

KM# 110 2 DUCAT

7.0000 g., 0.9860 Gold 0.2219 oz. AGW **Obv:** Capped five-fold arms **Obv. Legend:** • MO • AVREA • CAP • LEO • SEDE • VACANTE • **Rev:** Bust of St. Lambert left **Mint:** Liege **Note:** Sede Vacante issue.

Date	Mintage	VG	F	VF	XF	Unc
1694	—	4,500	8,000	12,500	18,500	—

KM# 111 3 DUCAT

10.5000 g., 0.9860 Gold 0.3328 oz. AGW **Ruler:** Joseph Clement **Obv:** Bust of Joseph Clement right, date at lower left **Obv. Legend:** (Rosette) IOSEPH • CLEM • D • G • ARC • COL • PRIN • ELEC • **Rev:** Crowned eight-fold arms, value 3 below **Mint:** Liege

Date	Mintage	VG	F	VF	XF	Unc
1695 Rare	—	—	—	—	—	—
1700 Rare	—	—	—	—	—	—

PATTERNS

Including off metal strikes

KM#	Date	Mintage	Identification	Mkt Val
PnA1	ND(1694-1723)	—	Liard. Silver. KM#107.	—

LITHUANIA

Lithuania emerged as a grand duchy in the 14th century. In the 15th century it was a major power of central Europe, stretching from the Baltic to the Black Sea. It was joined with Poland in 1569, but lost Smolensk, Chernigovsk, and the left bank of the river Dnepr Ukraina in 1667. Following the third partition of Poland by Austria, Prussia and Russia, 1795, Lithuania came under Russian domination and did not regain its independence until shortly before the end of World War I when it declared itself a sovereign republic on Feb. 16, 1918. In fall of 1920, Poland captured Vilna (Vilnius). The republic was occupied by Soviet troops and annexed to the U.S.S.R. in 1940. Following the German occupation of 1941-44, it was retaken by Russia and reestablished as a member republic of the Soviet Union. Western countries, including the United States, did not recognize Lithuania's incorporation into the Soviet Union.

Lithuania declared its independence March 11, 1990and it was recognized by the United States on Sept. 2,1991, followed by the Soviet government in Moscow on Sept. 6. They were seated in the UN General Assembly on Sept. 17, 1991.

RULERS

Kings of Poland
Sigismund III, (Zygimantas) 1587-1632
Wladislaus, (Vladislavas) 1632-1648
Johann Casimir, (Jan II Kazimieras) 1648-1668
Michael Korybut, 1669-1673
John III Sobieski, (Jan III Sobieski) 1674-1696
Augustus II, (Augustas II) 1697-1704

MINT MARKS

LMK – Vilna

MINT OFFICIALS' INITIALS

Initial	Date	Name
LMK	1600-03	? – Vina
HT	1618-23	Jonusas Trilneris
II, I I – VE	1623-27	Jokubas Jakobsenas van Emdenas
RL (monogram)	1623-27	Rudolf Lehman
IT	1639	Jonusas Trilneris
TLB	1660-66	Titus Livijus Boratinis, Tenant
	1664-66	Brzesc. Litewski, C. Bandine, Tenant
GFH	1665-66	Georgas Fon Hornis
TZH	1665-66	Teodor Horn, Kovno

PRIVY MARKS

Mark	Date	Name
hook	1599-1604	Zacharias Boll
(a) – swan	1598-1604	Anorius Zrvisa
(b) – HW or 2 arrows	1605-18	Jeronimas Valavicius
Arrow up	1606-18	Jonusas Stypla
(c) – 2 fish	1618-30	Kristupas Narvsevicius
	1630-35	Steponas Pacas
	1636-44	Mykolas Kiska
(d) – lily	1644-52	Mykolms Georonas Tryzna
(e) – bird w/ring	1652-62	Vincentas Gonsievskis
(f) – KHPL or buck's head	1663-76	Jeronimas Kryspinas Kirsensteinas
	1676-1703	Benediktas Povilas Sapiega

GRAND DUCHY

STANDARD COINAGE

KM# 8 2 DENARI

Silver **Obv:** Crowned S monogram divides date, value below **Rev:** Vytis on horseback to left, mint mark below

Date	Mintage	VG	F	VF	XF	Unc
1606	—	100	150	175	200	—
1607	—	100	150	175	200	—
1609	—	20.00	40.00	50.00	75.00	—
1611	—	10.00	20.00	40.00	65.00	—
1612	—	10.00	20.00	40.00	65.00	—
1613	—	10.00	20.00	40.00	65.00	—
1614	—	125	175	200	225	—

KM# 15.1 2 DENARI

Silver **Rev:** H below Vytis

Date	Mintage	VG	F	VF	XF	Unc
1612 H	—	150	200	225	275	—
1614 H	—	125	175	200	245	—

KM# 15.2 2 DENARI

Silver **Note:** Without mint mark.

Date	Mintage	VG	F	VF	XF	Unc
1619	—	35.00	45.00	65.00	100	—

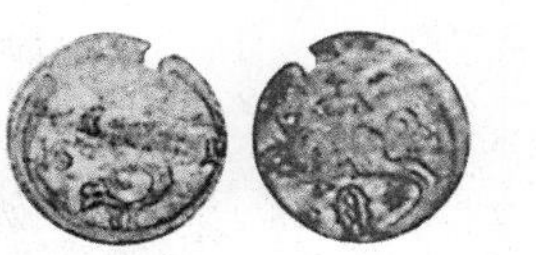

KM# 15.3 2 DENARI

Silver **Rev:** Two fish privy mark

Date	Mintage	VG	F	VF	XF	Unc
1620 (c)	—	15.00	20.00	40.00	65.00	—
1621 (c)	—	15.00	20.00	40.00	65.00	—
1622 (c) Rare	—	—	—	—	—	—
1623 (c) Rare	—	—	—	—	—	—
1626 (c) Rare	—	—	—	—	—	—

KM# 16.1 SCHILLING

Silver **Obv:** Crowned monogram divides date **Rev:** Crown above two shields

Date	Mintage	VG	F	VF	XF	Unc
(16)12 Rare	—	—	—	—	—	—
(16)14	—	15.00	30.00	50.00	100	—
(16)15	—	15.00	20.00	35.00	45.00	—
(16)16	—	15.00	20.00	35.00	45.00	—

KM# 16.2 SCHILLING

Silver **Obv:** S divides four-digit date

Date	Mintage	VG	F	VF	XF	Unc
1615	—	15.00	20.00	25.00	35.00	—
1616	—	15.00	20.00	25.00	35.00	—
1617	—	15.00	20.00	25.00	35.00	—

KM# 16.3 SCHILLING

Silver **Obv:** S divides two-digit date **Note:** Crown varieties exist.

Date	Mintage	VG	F	VF	XF	Unc
(16)17	—	15.00	20.00	35.00	45.00	—
(16)18	—	15.00	20.00	25.00	35.00	—
(16)19	—	15.00	20.00	25.00	35.00	—

KM# 25 SCHILLING

Silver **Rev:** Two-digit date in legend

Date	Mintage	VG	F	VF	XF	Unc
(16)20 Rare	—	—	—	—	—	—
(16)21 Rare	—	—	—	—	—	—
(16)22	—	15.00	20.00	25.00	35.00	—
(16)23	—	15.00	20.00	25.00	35.00	—

KM# 30 SCHILLING

Silver **Obv:** Eagle within circle **Rev:** Vytis on horse left within circle, two-digit date in legend

Date	Mintage	VG	F	VF	XF	Unc
1623	—	15.00	30.00	50.00	75.00	—
(16)23	—	15.00	30.00	50.00	75.00	—
1624	—	15.00	30.00	50.00	75.00	—

KM# 31 SCHILLING

Silver **Obv:** Crowned S monogram in inner circle **Rev:** Crown above two shields of arms in inner circle, date in legend

Date	Mintage	VG	F	VF	XF	Unc
1624	—	15.00	20.00	40.00	70.00	—

Note: Five varieties.

1625	—	15.00	20.00	40.00	70.00	—
1626	—	15.00	20.00	40.00	70.00	—
1627	—	15.00	20.00	40.00	70.00	—

KM# 41 SCHILLING

Billon **Obv:** Crowned ICR monogram in inner circle **Rev:** Vytis on horseback left in inner circle, date in legend **Note:** Legend and crown varieties exist.

Date	Mintage	VG	F	VF	XF	Unc
(16)52	—	15.00	30.00	50.00	100	—
(16)52	—	15.00	30.00	50.00	100	—
16(53)	—	15.00	30.00	50.00	100	—
1653	—	15.00	30.00	50.00	100	—
1654 Rare	—	—	—	—	—	—
1661 Rare	—	—	—	—	—	—

KM# 50 SCHILLING

Copper **Obv:** Laureate head of Johann Casimir right, TLB or GFH below head **Rev:** Vytis on horseback left, date in legend **Note:** Legend varieties exist.

Date	Mintage	VG	F	VF	XF	Unc
1660 TLB	7,000	8.00	15.00	25.00	40.00	—
1661 TLB	Inc. above	8.00	15.00	25.00	40.00	—

Date	Mintage	VG	F	VF	XF	Unc
1663 GFH	—	8.00	15.00	25.00	40.00	—
1664 GFH	—	10.00	15.00	30.00	50.00	—
1664 TLB/HKPL	Inc. above	8.00	15.00	25.00	40.00	—
1665 GFH	—	8.00	15.00	25.00	40.00	—
1665 TLB/HKPL	Inc. above	8.00	15.00	25.00	40.00	—
1666 TLB/HKPL	Inc. above	8.00	15.00	25.00	40.00	—
1666 GFH	—	8.00	15.00	25.00	40.00	—

KM# 9 GROSZ
Silver **Obv:** Crowned bust of Sigismund III right in inner circle **Obv. Legend:** SIG III D G REX PO M D L - GROS MAG DV LIT **Rev:** Vytis on horseback left in inner circle, date in legend

Date	Mintage	VG	F	VF	XF	Unc
1607 with shield under Vytis	—	30.00	50.00	80.00	100	—
1607 without shield under Vytis	—	85.00	100	175	250	—
1608	—	25.00	40.00	75.00	95.00	—

KM# 10 GROSZ
Silver **Obv:** Displayed eagle in inner circle **Note:** Legend varieties exist.

Date	Mintage	VG	F	VF	XF	Unc
1608	—	30.00	45.00	65.00	95.00	—
1609	—	30.00	45.00	65.00	95.00	—
1610	—	30.00	45.00	65.00	95.00	—
1611	—	30.00	45.00	65.00	95.00	—
1612	—	30.00	45.00	65.00	95.00	—
1613	—	30.00	45.00	65.00	95.00	—
1614	—	30.00	45.00	65.00	95.00	—
(16)15	—	30.00	45.00	65.00	95.00	—
1615	—	30.00	45.00	65.00	95.00	—

KM# 11 GROSZ
Silver **Note:** Klippe.

Date	Mintage	VG	F	VF	XF	Unc
1610 Rare	—	—	—	—	—	—

KM# 32 GROSZ
Silver **Obv:** Crowned bust of Sigismund III right **Rev:** Vytis on horseback left in inner circle, date in legend **Note:** Legend and crown varieties exist.

Date	Mintage	VG	F	VF	XF	Unc
1625	—	17.50	25.00	50.00	75.00	—
1262 Error for 1626	—	50.00	60.00	80.00	125	—
1626	—	15.00	22.00	30.00	50.00	—
1627	—	15.00	22.00	30.00	50.00	—

KM# 42 GROSZ
Silver **Obv:** Crowned bust of Johann Casimir right **Rev:** Vytis on horseback left, date in legend **Note:** Three varieties known.

Date	Mintage	VG	F	VF	XF	Unc
1652	—	60.00	80.00	125	175	—

KM# 20 1-1/2 GROSZY
Silver **Obv:** Crowned arms, titles of Sigismund III **Rev:** Orb with value within and below divides two-digit date in inner circle **Note:** Two varieties known.

Date	Mintage	VG	F	VF	XF	Unc
1619	—	75.00	100	150	200	—
1620	—	90.00	150	200	300	—

KM# 40 1-1/2 GROSZY
Silver **Obv:** Crowned arms in inner circle, titles of Johann Casimir **Rev:** Orb with value in inner circle, date in legend

Date	Mintage	VG	F	VF	XF	Unc
1650	—	75.00	150	175	250	—
1652	—	250	450	550	700	—

KM# 5 3 GROSZY
Silver **Obv:** Crowned bust right **Rev:** Value,divided date, symbols and two-line inscription between

Date	Mintage	VG	F	VF	XF	Unc
1601 W	—	75.00	125	150	200	—
1601 V	—	50.00	75.00	175	350	—
1602	—	75.00	125	200	375	—
1602 V	—	75.00	125	200	375	—
1603 V	—	125	200	400	575	—
1608	—	75.00	125	150	225	—

KM# 6 3 GROSZY
Silver **Note:** Klippe.

Date	Mintage	VG	F	VF	XF	Unc
1602 V Rare	—	—	—	—	—	—

KM# 43 3 GROSZY
Silver **Obv:** Laureate bust of Johann Casimir right in inner circle **Rev:** Value at top, divided date at bottom, three-line inscription between

Date	Mintage	VG	F	VF	XF	Unc
1652	—	150	250	350	500	—
1664 TLB/HKLP	—	100	150	225	300	—
1665 TLB/HKLP	—	125	200	275	350	—

KM# 44 6 GROSZY
Silver **Obv:** Crowned bust of Johann Casimir right in inner circle **Rev:** Vytis on horseback left, 1-5 below in inner circle, date in legend

Date	Mintage	VG	F	VF	XF	Unc
1652	—	250	375	425	500	—

KM# 51 6 GROSZY
Silver **Obv:** Crowned head reaches to edge of coin at top **Rev:** Value below Vytis

Date	Mintage	VG	F	VF	XF	Unc
1664 TLB	—	50.00	75.00	125	200	—
1665 TLB	—	50.00	75.00	125	200	—
1666 TLB	—	50.00	75.00	125	200	—
1668 TLB	—	50.00	75.00	125	200	—

KM# 52 6 GROSZY
Silver **Note:** Value as IV.

Date	Mintage	VG	F	VF	XF	Unc
1664 TLB	—	50.00	75.00	125	210	—

KM# 51.2 6 GROSZY
Silver **Obv:** Long, narrow bust

Date	Mintage	VG	F	VF	XF	Unc
1666	—	50.00	75.00	125	200	—

KM# 60 6 GROSZY
Silver **Obv:** Laureate bust right **Rev:** Crowned Vytis on horse left, value below within circle, date in legend

Date	Mintage	VG	F	VF	XF	Unc
1679 TLB Rare	—	—	—	—	—	—

KM# 53 ORT (18 Groszy; 1/2 Thaler)
Silver **Obv:** Laureate bust of Johann Casimir right, with or without inner circle **Rev:** Crowned Vytis on horseback left above value in inner circle, date in legend

Date	Mintage	VG	F	VF	XF	Unc
1664 TLB	—	250	325	400	600	—
1665 TLB	—	250	325	400	600	—

KM# 55 GULDEN (Zloty)
Silver **Obv:** Crowned ICR monogram in inner circle **Rev:** Crowned Vytis on horseback left above value XXX, date in legend

Date	Mintage	VG	F	VF	XF	Unc
1666 TLB Rare	—	—	—	—	—	—

TRADE COINAGE

KM# 54.1 1/2 DUCAT (Czerwony Zloty)
1.7500 g., 0.9860 Gold 0.0555 oz. AGW **Obv:** Laureate head of Johann Casimir right **Obv. Legend:** IOA CAS REX PO S MON AVR MAG DVC LIT

Date	Mintage	VG	F	VF	XF	Unc
1664 TLB/HKPL	—	1,200	2,500	5,000	9,000	—
1665 TLB/HKPL	—	1,200	2,500	5,000	9,000	—

KM# 54.2 1/2 DUCAT (Czerwony Zloty)
1.7500 g., 0.9860 Gold 0.0555 oz. AGW **Obv:** Smaller head **Obv. Legend:** ...MON AVREA MAG D L

Date	Mintage	VG	F	VF	XF	Unc
1665 TLB/HKPL	—	1,500	3,000	7,000	13,500	—

KM# 56 DUCAT (Dukaty)
3.5000 g., 0.9860 Gold 0.1109 oz. AGW **Obv:** Small laureate head of Johann Casimir in branches **Rev:** Rider left above HKPL monogram in branches, date in legend

Date	Mintage	VG	F	VF	XF	Unc
1666 TLB/HKPL	—	3,000	5,000	10,000	15,000	—

KM# 17 3 DUCATS
10.5000 g., 0.9860 Gold 0.3328 oz. AGW **Obv:** Crowned bust of Sigismund in inner circle **Rev:** Crowned arms in Order collar in inner circle

Date	Mintage	VG	F	VF	XF	Unc
1615 Rare	—	—	—	—	—	—

KM# 18 5 DUCATS (Dukaton)
17.5000 g., 0.9860 Gold 0.5547 oz. AGW **Obv:** Crowned bust right within circle **Obv. Legend:** SIGI SMVND III D G REX POL M D LI **Rev:** Crowned arms in Order collar in inner circle, crown divides date in legend

Date	Mintage	VG	F	VF	XF	Unc
161Z	—	—	—	—	—	—
1618	—	2,000	4,000	7,000	10,000	—

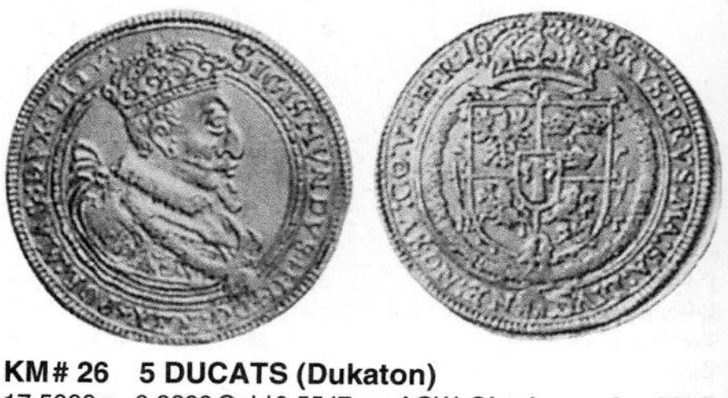

KM# 26 5 DUCATS (Dukaton)
17.5000 g., 0.9860 Gold 0.5547 oz. AGW **Obv. Legend:** ...MAG DVX LIT **Note:** Smaller planchet.

Date	Mintage	VG	F	VF	XF	Unc
1621 HT	—	6,000	9,500	14,000	20,000	—

KM# 27 5 DUCATS (Dukaton)
17.5000 g., 0.9860 Gold 0.5547 oz. AGW **Rev:** Crown divides date in inner circle

Date	Mintage	VG	F	VF	XF	Unc
1622	—	5,500	10,000	17,500	25,000	—
1623	—	5,500	10,000	17,500	25,000	—

KM# 7.1 10 DUCATS
34.6980 g., 0.9860 Gold 1.0999 oz. AGW **Obv:** Sigismund III bust facing right

Date	Mintage	VG	F	VF	XF	Unc
1604 Struck in 1614, Rare	—	—	—	—	—	—
1616 Rare	—	—	—	—	—	—
1617 Rare	—	—	—	—	—	—

KM# 7.2 10 DUCATS
34.6980 g., 0.9860 Gold 1.0999 oz. AGW **Rev:** Privy marks above crown

Date	Mintage	VG	F	VF	XF	Unc
1616	—	—	—	30,000	40,000	—

KM# 19 10 DUCATS
34.6980 g., 0.9860 Gold 1.0999 oz. AGW **Rev:** Date in legend at upper left

Date	Mintage	VG	F	VF	XF	Unc
1618	—	—	—	15,000	25,000	—

KM# 28 10 DUCATS
34.6980 g., 0.9860 Gold 1.0999 oz. AGW **Rev:** Date above shield divided by crown

Date	Mintage	VG	F	VF	XF	Unc
1621	—	—	—	30,000	50,000	—

KM# 29 10 DUCATS
34.6980 g., 0.9860 Gold 1.0999 oz. AGW **Rev:** Date in legend divided by shield

Date	Mintage	VG	F	VF	XF	Unc
1622	—	—	—	20,000	40,000	—

KM# 35 10 DUCATS
34.6980 g., 0.9860 Gold 1.0999 oz. AGW **Obv:** Crowned bust of Wladislaus half right **Rev:** Crowned arms in Order collar in inner circle

Date	Mintage	VG	F	VF	XF	Unc
1639 IT Rare	—	—	—	—	—	—

LIVONIA

A former province of Russia, now partly in Latvia and partly in southern Estonia.

The division of Livonia left the northern part governed by Russia while the southern part fell under the dominion of Poland. In 1621 it was the theatre of a war between Sweden and Poland. Being conquered by Sweden, Livonia enjoyed 25 years of milder rule.

RULERS
Polish, until 1628
Swedish, until 1720

MINT OFFICIALS' MARKS

Mark	Desc.	Date	Name
(d)= 	Dog	1647-56	Heinrich Jager
(h)= 	Helmet	1644-47	Marsilius Philipson
(o)= 	Helmet in heart outline	1644-47	Marsilius Philipson
IM		1661-97	Joachim Meinekes

RIGA
Polish Occupation

Founded in 1158, it became a bishopric in 1198 and joined the Hanseatic League in 1282. It came under Polish rule in 1581, was occupied by Sweden in 1621 and remained a Swedish possession until 1710. Ceded to Russia after the battle of Poltava, it was a part of the Treaty of Nystad in 172l. Riga is an important seaport and capital of modern Latvia.

RULERS
Polish, until 1621
Swedish, until 1721

MINT OFFICIALS' INITIALS

Initial	Date	Name
AH, GAH	1700-01	Georg Albrekt Hille
HW	1625-50	A. Winhelmann, warden
HW	1633-59	Henrik Wulff, Tenant
SD	Ca. 1645	Sebastian Dattler, engraver
IM	1652-73	Joachim Meinecke
	1652-63	As warden
	1663-68	As mintmaster
IH	1660	Jost Haltermann, mintmaster
MW	1621-33	Martin Wulff, mintmaster

STANDARD COINAGE

KM# 5 SCHILLING (Silins)
Silver **Obv:** Large S monogram divides date **Obv. Legend:** SIG III D G REX PO D LI - SOLIDVS CIVI RIGENS **Rev:** Crowned arms **Note:** Legend varieties exist.

Date	Mintage	VG	F	VF	XF	Unc
(1)601	—	6.00	12.00	20.00	35.00	—
(1)602	—	6.00	12.00	20.00	35.00	—
(1)603	—	6.00	12.00	20.00	35.00	—
(1)604	—	6.00	12.00	20.00	35.00	—
(1)605	—	6.00	12.00	20.00	35.00	—
(1)606	—	6.00	12.00	20.00	35.00	—
(1)607	—	6.00	12.00	20.00	35.00	—
(1)609	—	6.00	12.00	20.00	35.00	—
1609	—	6.00	12.00	20.00	35.00	—
(1)610	—	6.00	12.00	20.00	35.00	—
1610	—	6.00	12.00	20.00	35.00	—
(1)611	—	6.00	12.00	20.00	35.00	—
(16)12	—	6.00	12.00	20.00	35.00	—
1613	—	6.00	12.00	20.00	35.00	—
1614	—	6.00	12.00	20.00	35.00	—
1615	—	6.00	12.00	20.00	35.00	—
1616	—	6.00	12.00	20.00	35.00	—
1617	—	6.00	12.00	20.00	35.00	—
(16)18	—	6.00	12.00	20.00	35.00	—
1619	—	6.00	12.00	20.00	35.00	—
(16)20	—	6.00	12.00	20.00	35.00	—
(1)620	—	6.00	12.00	20.00	35.00	—
1620	—	6.00	12.00	20.00	35.00	—
(16)21	—	6.00	12.00	20.00	35.00	—
(16)22	—	6.00	12.00	20.00	35.00	—
ND	—	6.00	12.00	20.00	35.00	—

KM# 7 GROSCHEN (Grasis, Grosze)
Silver **Obv:** Shield of arms **Obv. Legend:** SIGIS III DG REX POL M L GROS ARGEN CIVI RIGE **Rev:** Orb, crossed keys below **Rev. Legend:** GROS AEGE (N) CIVI RIG.

Date	Mintage	VG	F	VF	XF	Unc
(16)16	—	10.00	22.00	45.00	75.00	—
(16)17	—	15.00	30.00	75.00	125	—

KM# A6 3 GROSCHEN
Silver **Obv:** Crowned bust of Sigismund III to right **Rev. Legend:** III / GR-OS / ARG. TRIP / CIVI. RI / GE.

Date	Mintage	VG	F	VF	XF	Unc
1601	—	—	—	—	—	—
1603	—	—	—	—	—	—

Date	Mintage	VG	F	VF	XF	Unc
1619	—	12.00	25.00	50.00	150	650
ND	—	10.00	20.00	40.00	130	—

KM# A9 DUCAT
Gold

Date	Mintage	VG	F	VF	XF	Unc
1619 Rare	—	—	—	—	—	—

RIGA
Swedish Occupation
STANDARD COINAGE

KM# 17 3 POLKER (3 Pelheri)
Silver **Note:** Struck at Bromberg (Bydgoszcz) Mint.

Date	Mintage	VG	F	VF	XF	Unc
1625	—	15.00	30.00	60.00	120	—

KM# 9 SOLIDUS (Schilling, Silins)
Silver **Obv:** Crowned GA monogram in inner circle **Obv. Legend:** GVSTA ADOL D G REX S SOLIDVS CIVI RIGENSIS **Rev:** Arms in cartouche in inner circle, date in legend **Note:** Legend varieties exist.

Date	Mintage	VG	F	VF	XF	Unc
1621	—	10.00	20.00	40.00	80.00	—
16Z1	—	10.00	20.00	40.00	80.00	—
162.1	—	10.00	20.00	40.00	80.00	—
1622 Rare	—	—	—	—	—	—
1623	—	—	—	—	—	—
(16)24	—	5.00	10.00	16.00	30.00	—
1625	—	5.00	10.00	16.00	30.00	—
1626	—	5.00	10.00	16.00	30.00	—
(16)27	—	5.00	10.00	16.00	30.00	—
1627 Rare	—	—	—	—	—	—
1628	—	5.00	10.00	16.00	30.00	—
1629 Rare	—	—	—	—	—	—
1630	—	5.00	10.00	16.00	30.00	—
1631	—	5.00	10.00	16.00	30.00	—
1632	—	5.00	10.00	16.00	30.00	—
(16)33	—	5.00	10.00	16.00	30.00	—
1634	—	5.00	10.00	16.00	30.00	—
ND	—	5.00	10.00	16.00	30.00	—

KM# 21 SOLIDUS (Schilling, Silins)
Silver **Obv:** Crowned C with Vasa arms within inner circle **Obv. Legend:** CHRISTINA D G DR S SOLIDUS CIVI RIGENSIS

Date	Mintage	VG	F	VF	XF	Unc
1634 Rare	—	—	—	—	—	—
1635	—	5.00	10.00	16.00	30.00	—
1636	—	5.00	10.00	16.00	30.00	—
1637	—	5.00	10.00	16.00	30.00	—
(16)83 Error for 1638	—	6.00	12.00	17.00	33.50	—
(16)38	—	5.00	10.00	18.00	30.00	—
1639	—	7.00	14.00	18.00	36.00	—
(16)40	—	7.00	14.00	18.00	36.00	—
1640	—	7.00	14.00	18.00	36.00	—
1641	—	7.00	14.00	18.00	36.00	—
(16)42	—	7.00	14.00	18.00	36.00	—
(16)43	—	7.00	14.00	18.00	36.00	—
1644	—	7.00	14.00	18.00	36.00	—
1645	—	7.00	14.00	18.00	36.00	—
1646	—	7.00	14.00	18.00	36.00	—
(16)47	—	7.00	14.00	18.00	36.00	—
(16)48	—	7.00	14.00	18.00	36.00	—
1649	—	7.00	14.00	18.00	36.00	—
(16)50	—	7.00	14.00	18.00	36.00	—
1651	—	13.00	32.00	60.00	120	—
(16)51	—	7.00	14.00	18.00	36.00	—
1652	—	13.00	32.00	60.00	120	—
(16)52	—	7.00	14.00	18.00	36.00	—
1653	—	7.00	14.00	18.00	36.00	—
1654	—	7.00	14.00	18.00	36.00	—

KM# 25 SOLIDUS (Schilling, Silins)
Silver **Rev:** Last two digits of date in Roman numerals

Date	Mintage	VG	F	VF	XF	Unc
16XL(1640)	—	10.00	25.00	50.00	100	—

KM# 50 SOLIDUS (Schilling, Silins)
Silver **Obv:** Crowned CG monogram in inner circle

Date	Mintage	VG	F	VF	XF	Unc
1654	—	7.00	15.00	30.00	60.00	—
1655	—	7.00	15.00	30.00	60.00	—
1656	—	7.00	15.00	30.00	60.00	—
1657	—	7.00	15.00	30.00	60.00	—
1658	—	7.00	15.00	30.00	60.00	—
1659	—	7.00	15.00	30.00	60.00	—
1660	—	7.00	15.00	30.00	60.00	—

KM# 53 SOLIDUS (Schilling, Silins)
Silver **Obv:** Without inner circle

Date	Mintage	VG	F	VF	XF	Unc
1657	—	16.00	40.00	90.00	180	—

KM# 55 SOLIDUS (Schilling, Silins)
Silver **Obv:** Crowned CR monogram in inner circle **Note:** 1666-68 dates are contemporary counterfeits generaly produced at Suczava.

Date	Mintage	VG	F	VF	XF	Unc
1660	—	5.00	10.00	30.00	90.00	—
1661	—	5.00	10.00	30.00	90.00	—
1662	—	5.00	10.00	30.00	90.00	—
(16)63	—	5.00	10.00	30.00	90.00	—
1664	—	5.00	10.00	30.00	90.00	—
(16)65	—	5.00	10.00	30.00	90.00	—
1666	—	5.00	10.00	30.00	90.00	—
(16)66	—	5.00	10.00	30.00	90.00	—
1668	—	5.00	10.00	30.00	90.00	—
(1)668	—	5.00	10.00	30.00	90.00	—
ND	—	5.00	10.00	30.00	90.00	—

KM# 12 1-1/2 SCHILLING
Silver **Obv:** Riga arms in inner circle **Rev:** Crossed keys divide date in inner circle

Date	Mintage	VG	F	VF	XF	Unc
(16)23	—	35.00	85.00	175	350	—

KM# 10 1/24 THALER (1/24 Dalderi, Trispelher)
Silver **Obv:** Crowned arms in inner circle **Obv. Legend:** GVST ADOLP D G REX S MON NOV CIVI RIGE **Rev:** Orb with value within divides date in inner circle

Date	Mintage	VG	F	VF	XF	Unc
(16)22	—	8.00	20.00	40.00	85.00	—
(16)23	—	7.00	15.00	30.00	65.00	—
(16)24	—	7.00	15.00	30.00	65.00	—
1625	—	7.00	15.00	30.00	65.00	—
(16)26	—	7.00	15.00	30.00	65.00	—
(16)27	—	7.00	15.00	30.00	65.00	—
(16)28	—	7.00	15.00	30.00	65.00	—
1629	—	7.00	15.00	30.00	65.00	—
1633	—	7.00	15.00	30.00	65.00	—
1634	—	7.00	15.00	30.00	65.00	—
1635	—	7.00	15.00	30.00	65.00	—

KM# 31 1/24 THALER (1/24 Dalderi, Trispelher)
Silver **Obv. Legend:** CHRISTINA D G REG SV-MON NOVA CIVI RIGE **Note:** Legend varieties exist.

Date	Mintage	VG	F	VF	XF	Unc
(16)44	—	9.00	22.50	45.00	120	—
(16)47	—	12.00	30.00	60.00	160	—
(16)48	—	9.00	22.50	45.00	120	—
(16)49	—	15.00	37.50	75.00	200	—

KM# A69 1/24 THALER (1/24 Dalderi, Trispelher)
Silver **Obv. Legend:** CHRISTINA D G R S MON NOVA LIVONI

Date	Mintage	VG	F	VF	XF	Unc
1662	—	35.00	80.00	160	300	—

KM# 69 1/24 THALER (1/24 Dalderi, Trispelher)
Silver **Obv:** Titles of Charles XI

Date	Mintage	VG	F	VF	XF	Unc
(16)69	—	35.00	70.00	140	265	—

KM# 90 1/24 THALER (1/24 Dalderi, Trispelher)
Silver **Obv:** Center shield of arms with Bavarian lozenges; Titles of Charles XII

Date	Mintage	VG	F	VF	XF	Unc
1700	—	43.75	105	210	425	—

KM# 91 1/24 THALER (1/24 Dalderi, Trispelher)
Silver **Obv:** Center shield of arms with lion

Date	Mintage	VG	F	VF	XF	Unc
1700	—	20.00	55.00	115	225	—

KM# 8 3 POLKER (1 1/2 Groschen)
Silver **Obv:** 3 at bottom **Rev:** Orb, crossed keys below, with keys and/or fox at end of legend **Rev. Legend:** MONE NOVA CIVI RIGE **Note:** Legend varieties exist.

Date	Mintage	VG	F	VF	XF	Unc
(16)Z0 fox	—	7.00	16.00	28.00	50.00	—
(16)Z0 keys	—	7.00	16.00	28.00	50.00	—
(16)Z0 fox & keys	—	8.00	20.00	30.00	60.00	—
(16)24	—	—	—	—	—	—

KM# 64 1/4 THALER
Silver **Obv:** Draped bust of Charles XI to right in inner circle **Rev:** Arms of Riga divide date in inner circle

Date	Mintage	VG	F	VF	XF	Unc
1668 IM Rare	—	—	—	—	—	—

KM# 65 1/3 THALER
Silver **Obv:** Bust of Charles XI right **Rev:** Arms of Riga divide date in inner circle

Date	Mintage	VG	F	VF	XF	Unc
1668 IM Rare	—	—	—	—	—	—

KM# 15 1/2 THALER
Silver **Note:** Similar to 1 Thaler, KM#16. Varieties exist.

Date	Mintage	VG	F	VF	XF	Unc
1629	—	3,900	6,500	11,500	—	—

KM# A15 1/2 THALER
Silver

Date	Mintage	VG	F	VF	XF	Unc
1630	—	4,550	8,500	14,500	—	—
1631 Rare	—	—	—	—	—	—

KM# A40 1/2 THALER
Silver **Note:** Similar to 1 Thaler, KM#33.

Date	Mintage	VG	F	VF	XF	Unc
1645 Rare	—	—	—	—	—	—
1648 Rare	—	—	—	—	—	—

KM# 66 1/2 THALER
Silver **Obv:** Draped bust of Charles XI right in inner circle **Rev:** Arms of Riga divide date in inner circle

Date	Mintage	VG	F	VF	XF	Unc
1668 IM Rare	—	—	—	—	—	—

KM# 14 THALER (Dalderi)
Silver **Obv:** Crowned bust of Gustavus Adolphus right in inner circle **Rev:** Arms of Riga with lion supporters divide date in inner circle **Note:** Dav. #4586.

Date	Mintage	VG	F	VF	XF	Unc
1628 MN Rare	—	—	—	—	—	—

KM# 16 THALER (Dalderi)
Silver **Note:** Dav. #4587.

Date	Mintage	VG	F	VF	XF	Unc
1629 MW	—	1,500	3,250	6,500	—	—

KM# 20 THALER (Dalderi)
Silver **Note:** Dav. #4588.

Date	Mintage	VG	F	VF	XF	Unc
1630 MW	—	1,750	3,500	6,000	9,500	—
1631 MW	—	2,000	4,000	7,000	11,500	—

KM# 23 THALER (Dalderi)
Silver **Obv:** Without lace collar **Note:** Dav. #4589.

Date	Mintage	VG	F	VF	XF	Unc
1639 HW	—	1,000	2,250	4,750	10,000	17,500

KM# 22 THALER (Dalderi)
Silver **Note:** Similar to KM#23 but with lace collar.

Date	Mintage	VG	F	VF	XF	Unc
1639 HW	—	1,000	2,250	4,750	10,000	—

KM# 26 THALER (Dalderi)
Silver **Note:** Dav. #4590. Small letters in legends.

Date	Mintage	VG	F	VF	XF	Unc
1643 HW	—	1,250	2,750	5,500	12,500	—

KM# 32.1 THALER (Dalderi)
Silver **Rev. Legend:** MON: NOVA ARGENT: CIVIT: RIGEN: **Note:** Dav. #4592. Large letters in legends.

Date	Mintage	VG	F	VF	XF	Unc
1644 HW	—	2,500	5,500	9,000	—	—

KM# 32.2 THALER (Dalderi)
Silver **Rev. Legend:** ...CIVIT: RIGENSIS: **Note:** Dav. #4592A.

Date	Mintage	VG	F	VF	XF	Unc
1644 HW Rare	—	—	—	—	—	—

Note: Künker Auction 134, 1-08, VF-XF realized approx. $19,200;ünker auction 185, 3-11, XF realized approx. $58,475

KM# 33 THALER (Dalderi)

Silver **Note:** Dav. #4594.

Date	Mintage	VG	F	VF	XF	Unc
1644 HW	—	1,750	3,750	7,000	12,500	—
1645 HW	—	2,250	4,500	8,500	15,000	—

KM# 41 THALER (Dalderi)

Silver **Obv:** Half figure of Christina right in inner circle **Note:** Dav. #4595.

Date	Mintage	VG	F	VF	XF	Unc
1646 HW	—	1,650	3,750	7,750	16,000	—
1648 HW	—	1,800	4,000	8,000	17,500	—

KM# 56.1 THALER (Dalderi)

Silver **Rev:** Towers have double pennants **Note:** Dav. #A4596.

Date	Mintage	VG	F	VF	XF	Unc
1660 IM	—	2,000	4,000	7,500	12,500	—

KM# 56.2 THALER (Dalderi)

Silver **Rev:** Towers have single pennants **Note:** Dav. #4596.

Date	Mintage	VG	F	VF	XF	Unc
1660 IM Rare	—	1,250	2,500	4,750	9,000	—

Note: Fritz Rudolf Künker Münzenhandlung Auction 134, 1-08, XF-Unc realized approximately $16,245

KM# 67 THALER (Dalderi)

Silver **Obv:** Older draped bust of Charles XI right in inner circle **Rev. Legend:** MONETA NOVA ARGENTEA CIVITATIS RIGENSIS **Note:** Dav. #4597.

Date	Mintage	VG	F	VF	XF	Unc
1668 IM Rare	—	—	—	—	—	—

KM# 75 THALER (Dalderi)

Silver **Obv:** Young armored bust of Charles XI right in inner circle **Note:** Dav. #4598.

Date	Mintage	VG	F	VF	XF	Unc
1672 IM Rare	—	—	—	—	—	—

KM# 34 2 THALER

Silver **Note:** Dav. #A4591. Similar to 1 Thaler, KM#32.

Date	Mintage	VG	F	VF	XF	Unc
1644 HW Rare	—	—	—	—	—	—

KM# 39 2 THALER

Silver **Note:** Dav. #4593. Similar to 1 Thaler, KM#33.

Date	Mintage	VG	F	VF	XF	Unc
1645 HW Rare	—	—	—	—	—	—

KM# 48 3 THALER

Silver **Note:** Dav. #4591. Similar to 1 Thaler, KM#32.

Date	Mintage	VG	F	VF	XF	Unc
1644 Rare	—	—	—	—	—	—

KM# 35 3 THALER

Silver **Note:** Dav. #B4591. Similar to 1 Thaler, KM#32.

Date	Mintage	VG	F	VF	XF	Unc
1644 HW Unique	—	—	—	—	—	—

TRADE COINAGE

KM# 13 DUCAT

3.5000 g., 0.9860 Gold 0.1109 oz. AGW **Obv:** Crowned bust of Gustavus Adolphus left **Rev:** Supported arms in inner circle, date in legend

Date	Mintage	VG	F	VF	XF	Unc
1623 Rare	—	—	—	—	—	—

KM# 27 DUCAT

3.5000 g., 0.9860 Gold 0.1109 oz. AGW **Obv:** Bust of Christina facing half left in inner circle

Date	Mintage	VG	F	VF	XF	Unc
1643 HW Rare	—	—	—	—	—	—

KM# 36 DUCAT

3.5000 g., 0.9860 Gold 0.1109 oz. AGW **Obv:** Bust of Christina left in inner circle **Obv. Legend:** CHRISTINA D G SVE GOVA Q D REG PRIN H **Rev:** Supported arms in inner circle **Rev. Legend:** MONETA AUREA CIVITATIS RIGENSIS **Note:** Legend varieties exist.

Date	Mintage	VG	F	VF	XF	Unc
1644 HW Rare	—	—	—	—	—	—

Note: Künker Auction 139, 3-08, XF-Unc realized approx. $24,935; Künker Auction 185, 3-11, XF+ realized approx. $50,120

Date	Mintage	VG	F	VF	XF	Unc
1645 HW Rare	—	—	—	—	—	—

KM# 42 DUCAT

3.5000 g., 0.9860 Gold 0.1109 oz. AGW **Obv:** Bust of Christina right

Date	Mintage	VG	F	VF	XF	Unc
1646 HW Rare	—	—	—	—	—	—

KM# 61 DUCAT

3.5000 g., 0.9860 Gold 0.1109 oz. AGW **Obv:** Bust of Charles XI right in inner circle **Rev:** Crowned arms in inner circle divide date

Date	Mintage	VG	F	VF	XF	Unc
1664 IM Rare	—	—	—	—	—	—

Note: Künker Auction 185, 3-11, nearly XF realized approx. $52,900

KM# 68 DUCAT

3.5000 g., 0.9860 Gold 0.1109 oz. AGW **Obv:** Bust of Charles XI right without inner circle

Date	Mintage	VG	F	VF	XF	Unc
1668 IM Rare	—	—	—	—	—	—

KM# 76 DUCAT

3.5000 g., 0.9860 Gold 0.1109 oz. AGW **Obv:** Large bust of Charles XI right in inner circle

Date	Mintage	VG	F	VF	XF	Unc
1673 Rare	—	—	—	—	—	—

Note: Fritz Rudolf Künker Münzenhandlung Auction 139, 3-08, nearly Unc, realized approximately $21,820

KM# 80 DUCAT

3.5000 g., 0.9860 Gold 0.1109 oz. AGW **Obv:** Large bust of Charles XI right without inner circle

Date	Mintage	VG	F	VF	XF	Unc
1681 Unique	—	—	—	—	—	—

KM# 92 DUCAT

3.5000 g., 0.9860 Gold 0.1109 oz. AGW **Obv:** Draped bust right **Obv. Legend:** CAROLVS • XII • D • G • REX • SVE • **Rev:** Crown above towers divides date within circle **Rev. Legend:** CIVITAT • RIGENSIS & MON • NOVA • AUREA

Date	Mintage	VG	F	VF	XF	Unc
1700 Rare	—	—	—	—	—	—

Note: Künker Auction 185, 3-11, VF-XF realized approx. $9,745

KM# 28 2 DUCAT

7.0000 g., 0.9860 Gold 0.2219 oz. AGW **Obv:** Bust of Christiana facing half left in inner circle **Rev:** Supported arms in inner circle, date in legend

Date	Mintage	VG	F	VF	XF	Unc
1643 HW Rare	—	—	—	—	—	—

KM# 43 2 DUCAT

7.0000 g., 0.9860 Gold 0.2219 oz. AGW **Obv:** Bust of Christiana right in inner circle **Rev:** Supported arms with date below in inner circle

Date	Mintage	VG	F	VF	XF	Unc
1646 HW Rare	—	—	—	—	—	—

Note: Künker Auction 156, 6-08, XF realized approx. $18,240

KM# 62 2 DUCAT

7.0000 g., 0.9860 Gold 0.2219 oz. AGW **Obv:** Fine style bust of Charles XI right in inner circle **Rev:** Crowned arms in inner circle divide date

Date	Mintage	VG	F	VF	XF	Unc
1664 IM Rare	—	—	—	—	—	—

KM# 63 2 DUCAT

7.0000 g., 0.9860 Gold 0.2219 oz. AGW **Obv:** Bust of Charles XI

Date	Mintage	VG	F	VF	XF	Unc
1667 IM Rare	—	—	—	—	—	—

Note: Fritz Rudolf Künker Münzenhandlung Auction 135, 1-08, nearly Unc realized approximately $44,300

KM# 29 3 DUCAT

10.5000 g., 0.9860 Gold 0.3328 oz. AGW **Obv:** Bust of Christina

Date	Mintage	VG	F	VF	XF	Unc
1643 HW Rare	—	—	—	—	—	—

KM# 37 3 DUCAT

10.5000 g., 0.9860 Gold 0.3328 oz. AGW **Obv:** Bust of Christina right in inner circle **Rev:** Supported arms with date below in inner circle

Date	Mintage	VG	F	VF	XF	Unc
1644 HW Rare	—	—	—	—	—	—

KM# A38 3 DUCAT

10.5000 g., 0.9860 Gold 0.3328 oz. AGW **Obv. Legend:** CHRISTINA D G SVE GO VAN Q REGINA & PRINCIP HAE M D F **Rev. Legend:** EX AVRO SOLIDO REGIA CIVITAS RIGENSIS FIERI F

Date	Mintage	VG	F	VF	XF	Unc
1646 HW Rare	—	—	—	—	—	—

Note: Fritz Rudolf Künker Münzenhandlung Auction 135, 1-08, XF realized approximately $38,395

KM# 44 4 DUCAT

14.0000 g., 0.9860 Gold 0.4438 oz. AGW **Obv:** Bust of Christina right in inner circle **Rev:** Supported arms with date below in inner circle

Date	Mintage	VG	F	VF	XF	Unc
1646 HW Rare	—	—	—	—	—	—

Note: Künker Auction 185, 3-11, nearly XF realized approx. $104,415

KM# 45 ROSE RYAL (4 Ducat)

14.0000 g., 0.9860 Gold 0.4438 oz. AGW **Obv:** Christina enthroned in inner circle **Rev:** Crowned arms in branches in inner circle

Date	Mintage	VG	F	VF	XF	Unc
ND Rare	—	—	—	—	—	—

KM# 40 5 DUCAT

17.5000 g., 0.9860 Gold 0.5547 oz. AGW **Obv:** Bust of Christina

Date	Mintage	VG	F	VF	XF	Unc
1645 Rare	—	—	—	—	—	—

KM# 51 5 DUCAT

17.5000 g., 0.9860 Gold 0.5547 oz. AGW **Obv:** Bust of Charles X

Date	Mintage	VG	F	VF	XF	Unc
1645(1654) Rare	—	—	—	—	—	—

Note: Künker Auction 135, 1-08, attractive example realized approx. $103,370; Künker Auction 191, 6-11, VF realized approx. $11,500; UBS Auction 85, 9-10, XF realized approx. $33,570; Künker Auction 156, 6-09, XF realized approx. $67,350

Date	Mintage	VG	F	VF	XF	Unc
1655 Rare	—	—	—	—	—	—

Note: Altered date

KM# 38 6 DUCAT

21.0000 g., 0.9860 Gold 0.6657 oz. AGW **Obv:** Bust of Christina facing half left in inner circle **Rev:** Supported arms, radiant "Jehovah" at top, date in exergue

Date	Mintage	VG	F	VF	XF	Unc
1644 HW Rare	—	—	—	—	—	—

KM# 52 6 DUCAT

21.0000 g., 0.9860 Gold 0.6657 oz. AGW **Obv:** Crowned bust of Charles right **Rev:** City of Riga in inner circle **Note:** Deleted.

Date	Mintage	VG	F	VF	XF	Unc
1645(1654) Rare	—	—	—	—	—	—

Note: Hess-Divo Auction 300, 10-04, nearly XF realized approx. $52,900

Date	Mintage	VG	F	VF	XF	Unc
1655 Rare	—	—	—	—	—	—

Note: Hess-Divo Auction 300, 10-04, XF realized approx. $24,990

KM# 11 7 DUCAT

24.5000 g., 0.9860 Gold 0.7766 oz. AGW **Obv:** Half-length figure of Gustavus Adolphus left with orb and scepter **Rev:** Supported arms in inner circle, Roman numeral date in legend

Date	Mintage	VG	F	VF	XF	Unc
1622 Unique	—	—	—	—	—	—

KM# 30 10 DUCAT

35.0000 g., 0.9860 Gold 1.1095 oz. AGW **Obv:** Christine **Rev:** Radiant "Jehovah" above supported arms

Date	Mintage	VG	F	VF	XF	Unc
1643 HW Unique	—	—	—	—	—	—
1644 HW Rare	—	—	—	—	—	—

Note: Künker Auction 185, 3-11, XF-Unc realized approx. $361,965

Date	Mintage	VG	F	VF	XF	Unc
1645 HW Rare	—	—	—	—	—	—

KM# 57 10 DUCAT

35.0000 g., 0.9860 Gold 1.1095 oz. AGW **Obv:** Child bust of Charles XI right **Rev:** Crowned arms in inner circle divide date

Date	Mintage	VG	F	VF	XF	Unc
1660 IM Rare	—	—	—	—	—	—

Note: Künker Auction 185, 3-11, VF realized approx. $97,445

LIVONIA

Swedish Occupation

STANDARD COINAGE

KM# 1 SOLIDUS (Schilling, Silins)

Silver **Obv:** Crowned CR monogram in inner circle **Rev:** Vasa arms in cartouche in inner circle, date in legend **Note:** Varieties exist.

Date	Mintage	VG	F	VF	XF	Unc
1644 Rare	—	—	—	—	—	—
1645 Rare	—	—	—	—	—	—
1645 (o) Rare	—	—	—	—	—	—

KM# 2 SOLIDUS (Schilling, Silins)

Silver **Obv:** Crowned C with Vasa arms within inner circle **Rev:** Arms in cartouche in inner circle, date in legend **Note:** Varieties exist.

Date	Mintage	VG	F	VF	XF	Unc
1645 (h)	—	25.00	50.00	100	200	—
1645 (o)	—	25.00	50.00	100	200	—
1645	—	12.00	30.00	60.00	120	—
1647	—	6.00	12.00	18.00	30.00	—
1648	—	6.00	12.00	18.00	30.00	—
1649	—	6.00	12.00	18.00	30.00	—
1650	—	6.00	12.00	18.00	30.00	—
1651	—	6.00	12.00	18.00	30.00	—
1652	—	6.00	12.00	18.00	30.00	—
1653	—	6.00	12.00	18.00	30.00	—
1654	—	6.00	12.00	18.00	30.00	—

KM# 4 SOLIDUS (Schilling, Silins)

Silver **Obv:** Crowned CG monogram inner circle

Date	Mintage	VG	F	VF	XF	Unc
1654	—	7.00	15.00	30.00	60.00	—
1655	—	7.00	15.00	30.00	60.00	—
1656	—	7.00	15.00	30.00	60.00	—
1657	—	7.00	15.00	30.00	60.00	—
1658	—	7.00	15.00	30.00	60.00	—
1659	—	7.00	15.00	30.00	60.00	—

KM# A5 SOLIDUS (Schilling, Silins)

Silver **Obv:** Crowned CR monogram inner circle **Note:** Obverse legend varieties exist.

Date	Mintage	VG	F	VF	XF	Unc
(16)60	—	7.00	15.00	30.00	60.00	—
(16)61	—	7.00	15.00	30.00	60.00	—
1662	—	7.00	15.00	30.00	60.00	—
1663	—	7.00	15.00	30.00	60.00	—
1664	—	7.00	15.00	30.00	60.00	—
1665	—	7.00	15.00	30.00	60.00	—

KM# 3 1/24 THALER (1/24 Daldieri)

Silver **Obv:** Crowned arms in inner circle, titles of Christina **Rev:** Orb with value within divides date in inner circle **Note:** Varieties exist.

Date	Mintage	VG	F	VF	XF	Unc
(16)47	—	20.00	50.00	100	200	—
(16)48	—	20.00	50.00	100	200	—
(16)48 (d)	—	10.00	20.00	40.00	80.00	—

KM# 6 1/24 THALER (1/24 Daldieri)

Silver **Obv:** Titles of Charles XI

Date	Mintage	VG	F	VF	XF	Unc
(16)69	—	16.00	40.00	80.00	160	—

PATTERNS

Including off metal strikes

KM#	Date	Mintage	Identification	Mkt Val
Pn1	1645(1654)	—	5 Ducat. Silver. KM#51.	500

MALAY PENINSULA

JOHORE

Johore (Johor) is a state with numerous small islands located between the South China Sea and the Strait of Malacca, with the capital of Johor Baharu. Ala'uddin, son of Sultan Mahmud, who fled Malacca after the Portuguese conquest of 1511, declared himself the first Sultan of Johore. Johore later was captured by Acheh, Sumatra, in 1564 and became its vassel state until the collapse of the Acheh Empire in 1641. In 1717, Raja Kechil of Siak, captured Johore, but was later defeated by Bugis forces in 1722. The Dutch defeated the Bugis forces in 1784 and subjected Johore to their control. Johore was later split by Dutch and English influence with the Anglo-Dutch Treaty of 1824. Johore came under British protection as one of the unfederated Malay States by the Anglo-Johore Treaty of 1885. By the end of January 1942 until 1945, Japanese forces occupied Johore. In April 1946, Johore joined the short-lived Malayan Union. In 1948 Johore became part of the Federation of Malaya, attained independence in 1957, and in 1963 became one of the component States of Malaysia.

REFERENCE: (SS#) – *"The Coins of Malaysia, Singapore and Brunei, 1400-1986"* by Saran Singh.

RULERS

Sultans of Johore (Malacca Royal Line)

Ala'udin Riayat Shah II, 1597-1613
Abdullah Ha'ayat Shah, 1615-1623
Abdul Jalil Shah III, 1623-1677
Ibrahim Shah, 1677-1685
Mahmud Shah II, 1685-1699

Sultans of Johore (Bendahara Line)

Abdul Jalil Riayat Shah IV, 1700-1719

MONETARY SYSTEM

25 Katun = 1 Penjuru
2 Penjuru = 1 Kupang
4 Kupang = 1 Mas

STATE

HAMMERED COINAGE

KM# 4 1/4 PENJURU

0.4500 g., Silver, 12 mm. **Ruler:** Abdul Jalil Shah III AH1033-1088/1623 - 1677AD **Obv:** Inscription in Arabic **Obv. Inscription:** "Sultan Abdul Jalil Shah" **Rev:** Inscription in Arabic **Rev. Inscription:** "Khalifatul Muminin" **Edge:** Plain **Shape:** Octagonal **Note:** SS#20a.

Date	Mintage	Good	VG	F	VF	XF
ND(1623-77)	—	200	375	650	900	—

KM# 5 KUPANG

0.6400 g., Gold, 13 mm. **Ruler:** Abdul Jalil Shah III AH1033-1088/1623 - 1677AD **Obv:** Inscription in Arabic **Obv. Inscription:** "Sultan Abdul Jalil Shah" **Rev:** Inscription in Arabic **Rev. Inscription:** "Khalifatul Muminin" **Edge:** Plain **Shape:** Octagonal **Note:** SS#14.

Date	Mintage	Good	VG	F	VF	XF
ND(1623-77)	—	150	275	450	650	—

KM# 8 KUPANG

0.6200 g., Gold **Ruler:** Mahmud Shah II AH1097-1111/1685 - 1699AD **Obv:** Inscription in Arabic **Obv. Inscription:** "Sultan Mahmud" **Rev:** Inscription in Arabic **Rev. Inscription:** "Khalifatul Muminin" **Edge:** Plain **Shape:** Octagonal **Note:** SS#16; Size varies 11 - 12 mm.

Date	Mintage	Good	VG	F	VF	XF
ND(1685-99)	—	450	850	1,350	2,000	—

KM# 2 MAS

2.6000 g., Gold, 17 mm. **Ruler:** Abdullah Ha'ayat Shah AH1024-1033/1615 - 1623AD **Obv:** Arabic inscription in octagonal border and circle of dots **Obv. Inscription:** "Sultan Abdullah Riayat Shah" **Rev:** Arabic inscription in octagonal border and circle of dots **Rev. Inscription:** "Khalifatul Muminin" **Edge:** Plain **Note:** SS#11.

Date	Mintage	Good	VG	F	VF	XF
ND(1615-1623)	—	1,350	2,750	4,500	6,500	—

KM# 6 MAS

2.4600 g., Gold, 16.8 mm. **Ruler:** Abdul Jalil Shah III AH1033-1088/1623 - 1677AD **Obv:** Inscription in Arabic **Obv. Inscription:** "Sultan Abdul Jalil Shah" **Rev:** Inscription in Arabic **Rev. Inscription:** "Khalifatul Muminin" **Edge:** Plain **Shape:** Octagonal **Note:** SS#12.

Date	Mintage	Good	VG	F	VF	XF
ND(1623-77)	—	500	1,000	1,750	2,500	—

KM# 6a MAS

1.8000 g., Copper Gilt, 16.8 mm. **Ruler:** Abdul Jalil Shah III AH1033-1088/1623 - 1677AD **Subject:** Funeral of Sultan Abdul Jalil Shah III **Obv:** Inscription in Arabic **Obv. Inscription:** "Sultan Abdul Jalil Shah" **Rev:** Inscription in Arabic **Rev. Inscription:** "Khalifatul Muminin" **Edge:** Plain **Shape:** Octagonal **Note:** SS#13.

Date	Mintage	Good	VG	F	VF	XF
ND(1677)	—	500	1,000	1,750	2,500	—

KM# 9 MAS

2.5500 g., Gold, 16 mm. **Ruler:** Mahmud Shah II AH1097-1111/1685 - 1699AD **Obv:** Inscription in Arabic **Obv. Inscription:** "Sultan Mahmud Shah" **Rev:** Inscription in Arabic **Rev. Inscription:** "Khalifatul Muminin" **Edge:** Plain **Shape:** Octagonal **Note:** SS#15.

Date	Mintage	Good	VG	F	VF	XF
ND(1685-99)	—	1,000	2,000	3,200	4,500	—

KEDAH

A state in northwestern Malaysia. Islam introduced in 15th century. Subject to Thailand from 1821-1909. Coins issued under Governor Tengku Anum.

TITLES

كداه

Kedah

SULTANS

Dhiauddin Mukarram Shah, 1661-1687
Abdullah al-Muazzam Shah I, 1698-1706

SULTANATE

HAMMERED COINAGE

KM# 3 TARRA
Copper, 30 mm. **Obv:** Inscription in Arabic **Obv. Inscription:** "Al-Sultan Dhiauddin Mukarram Shah" **Note:** Arabic legend. SS#5a.

Date	Mintage	Good	VG	F	VF	XF
ND Rare	—	—	—	—	—	—

KM# 7 TARRA
Copper, 18 mm. **Obv:** Inscription in Arabic **Obv. Inscription:** "Belanja Negeri Kedah" **Rev:** Inscription in Arabic **Rev. Inscription:** "Darul Aman Sanat" **Note:** Arabic legend. SS#6.

Date	Mintage	Good	VG	F	VF	XF
AH1110 Rare	—	—	—	—	—	—

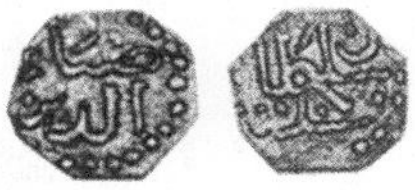

KM# 6 1/4 REAL
0.7700 g., 0.7000 Silver 0.0173 oz. ASW **Obv:** Inscription in Arabic **Obv. Inscription:** "Dhiauddin" **Rev:** Inscription in Arabic **Rev. Inscription:** "Sultan Sanat" **Note:** Arabic legend. SS#4.

Date	Mintage	Good	VG	F	VF	XF
AH1077 Rare	—	—	—	—	—	—

KM# 1 KUPANG
0.4500 g., Gold, 12 mm. **Ruler:** Dhiauddin Mukarram Shah **Obv:** Arabic inscription **Obv. Inscription:** "Sultan Abdullah Shah" **Rev:** Arabic inscription **Rev. Inscription:** "Khalifatul Muminin" **Shape:** Hexagonal

Date	Mintage	VG	F	VF	XF	Unc
ND Rare	—	—	—	—	—	—

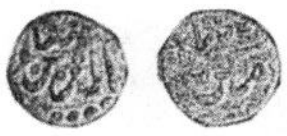

KM# 5 KUPANG
0.5000 g., Gold, 8 mm. **Obv:** Inscription in Arabic **Obv. Inscription:** "Dhiauddin" **Rev:** Inscription in Arabic **Rev. Inscription:** "Shah Mukarram" **Note:** Arabic legend

Date	Mintage	VG	F	VF	XF	Unc
ND Rare	—	—	—	—	—	—

KM# 4 KUPANG
0.5000 g., Gold, 9 mm. **Obv:** Inscription in Arabic **Obv. Inscription:** "Dar'ul-Aman" **Rev:** Inscription in Arabic **Rev. Inscription:** "Fil al-Quds"

Date	Mintage	VG	F	VF	XF	Unc
ND Rare	—	—	—	—	—	—

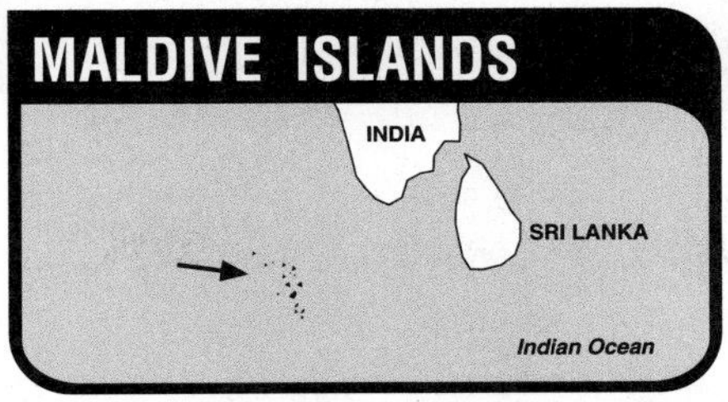

The Republic of Maldives, an archipelago of 2,000 coral islets in the northern Indian Ocean 417 miles (671 km.) west of Ceylon, has an area of 116 sq. mi. (298 sq. km.).

The Maldive Islands were visited by Arab traders and converted to Islam in 1153. After being harassed in the16th and 17th centuries by Mopla pirates of the Malabar coast and Portuguese raiders, the Maldivians voluntarily placed themselves under the suzerainty of Ceylon. In 1887 the islands became an internally self-governing British protectorate and a nominal dependency of Ceylon. Traditionally a sultanate, the Maldives became a republic in 1953 but restored the sultanate in 1954. The Sultanate of the Maldive Islands attained complete internal and external autonomy on July 26, 1965, and on Nov. 11,1968, again became a republic.

RULERS

Muhammad Imad al-Din I, AH1030-1058/1620-1648AD
Ibrahim Iskandar I bin Muhammad, AH1058-1098/1648-1687AD
Muhammad bin Ibrahim, AH1098-1102/1687-1690AD (no coinage known)
Muhammad Muhi al-Din bin Fulan, AH1102-1103/1690-1691AD
Muhammad Shams al-Din al-Hamawi, AH1103-1104/1691-1692AD
Muhammad al-Hajji bin Ali, AH1104-1112/1692-1700AD

MINT NAME

محلي

Mahle (Male)

NOTE: The metrology of the early coinage is problematical. There seem to have been three denominations: a double Larin of 8-10 g, a Larin of approximately 4.8 g, and a half Larin that varied from 1.1 to 2.4 g, known as the Bodu Larin, Larin and Kuda Larin, respectively. In some years probably when copper was cheap (AH1276 & 1294),the Kuda (1/2) Larin is found with weights as high as 3.5 g. During the rule of Muhammad Imad Al-Din II Al-Muzaffar Bin Muhammad (1704-1721AD) additional denominations in the form of the 1/4, 1/8 and 1/16 Larin (1.17 g, 0.55 g and 0.29 g) were introduced on an experimental basis. This experiment was not followed by later rulers with the exception of Muhammad Imad Al-Din IV (1835-1882AD) who struck some light weight coins of about 1.1 g which can be considered 1/4 Larins.

SULTANATE

Muhammad Imad al-Din I
AH 1030-58 / 1620-48 AD

STANDARD COINAGE

KM# 1 LARIN
Silver **Mint:** Mahle (Malé) **Note:** Countermarked bent silver wire.

Date	Mintage	Good	VG	F	VF	XF
AHxxxx Rare	—	200	300	500	750	—

Note: O.N.S. Newsletter #89, April, 1984

Ibrahim Iskandar I bin Muhammad
AH 1058-98 / 1648-87 AD

STANDARD COINAGE

KM# 2.1 LARIN
4.8000 g., Silver **Mint:** Mahle (Malé)

Date	Mintage	Good	VG	F	VF	XF
AH1070	—	7.50	12.50	18.00	25.00	—
AH1074	—	7.50	12.50	18.00	25.00	—
ND	—	7.50	12.50	18.00	25.00	—

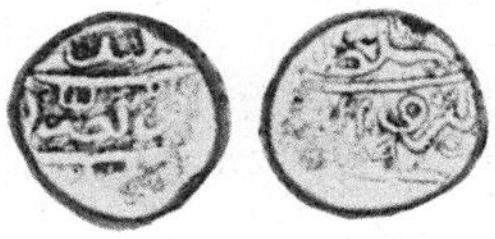

KM# 2.2 LARIN
4.8000 g., Silver **Mint:** Mahle (Malé)

Date	Mintage	Good	VG	F	VF	XF
AH1096	—	10.00	17.00	25.00	35.00	—

Muhammad Muhi al-Din bin Fulan
AH 1102-03 / 1690-91 AD

STANDARD COINAGE

KM# 6 LARIN
4.8000 g., Silver **Mint:** Mahle (Malé) **Note:** Varieties exist.

Date	Mintage	Good	VG	F	VF	XF
ND	—	13.00	22.00	32.00	45.00	—

Muhammad Shams al-Din al-Hamawi
AH 1103-04 / 1691-92 AD

STANDARD COINAGE

KM# 8 LARIN
4.8000 g., Silver **Mint:** Mahle (Malé)

Date	Mintage	Good	VG	F	VF	XF
ND	—	12.00	25.00	40.00	60.00	—

Muhammad al-Hajji bin Ali
AH 1104-12 / 1692-1700 AD

STANDARD COINAGE

KM# 9 1/2 LARIN (Kuda)
2.4000 g., Silver

Date	Mintage	Good	VG	F	VF	XF
AH1105	—	4.50	7.50	11.50	16.50	—

KM# 10 LARIN
4.8000 g., Silver **Mint:** Mahle (Malé)

Date	Mintage	Good	VG	F	VF	XF
AH1104	—	5.00	8.50	12.50	18.00	—

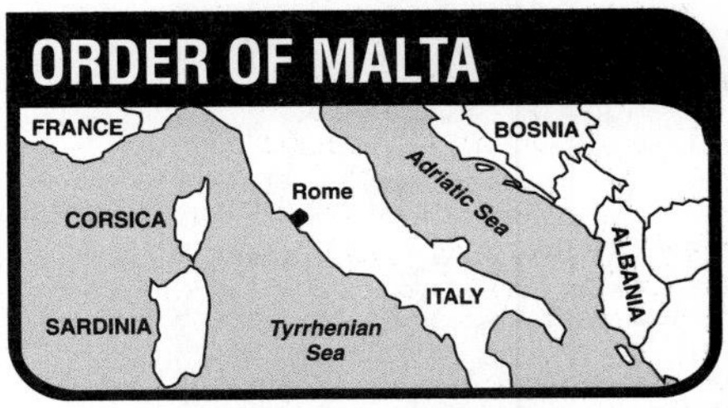

The Order of Malta, modern successor to the Sovereign Military Hospitaller Order of St. John of Jerusalem (the crusading Knights Hospitallers), derives its sovereignty from grants of extraterritoriality by Italy (1928) and the Vatican City (1953), and from its supranational character as a religious military order owing suzerainty to the Holy See. Its territory is confined to Palazzo Malta on Via Condotti, Villa Malta and the crest of the Aventine Hill, all in the city of Rome. The Order maintains diplomatic relations with about 35 governments, including Italy, Spain, Austria, State of Malta, Portugal, Brazil, Guatemala, Panama, Peru, Iran, Lebanon, Philippines, Liberia, Ethiopia, etc.

The Knights Hospitallers were founded in 1099 just before the crusaders' capture of Jerusalem. Father Gerard (died 1120) was the founder and first rector of the Jerusalem hospital. The headquarters of the Order were successively at Jerusalem 1099-1187; Acre 1187-1291; Cyprus 1291-1310; Rhodes 1310-1522; Malta 1530-1798; Trieste 1798-1799; St. Petersburg 1799-1803; Catania 1803-1825; Ferrara 1826-1834; Rome 1834-Present.

The symbolic coins issued by the Order since 1961 are intended to continue the last independent coinage of the Order on Malta in 1798. In traditional tari and scudi denominations, they are issued only in proof condition. They have a theoretical fixed exchange value with the Italian lira, but are not used in commerce.

These medallic issues are perhaps the world's last major symbolic coinage, just as their issuer is the world's last sovereign order of knighthood. Proceeds from the sale of this coinage maintain the Order's hospitals, clinics and leprosariums around the world.

RULERS

Martin Garzes, 1595-1601
Alof de Wignacourt, 1601-1622
Luis Mendes de Vasconcellos, 1622-1623
Antoine de Paule, 1623-1636
Jean-Paul Lascaris Castellar, 1636-1657
Martin de Redin, 1657-1660
Annet de Clermont Gessan, 1660
Rafael Cotoner, 1660-1663
Nicolas Cotoner, 1663-1680
Gregorio Carafa, 1680-1690
Adrien de Wignacourt, 1690-1697
Ramon Perellos y Roccaful, 1697-1720

MONETARY SYSTEM

(Until ca. 1800)

20 Grani = 1 Tari
12 Tari = 1 Scudo

SOVEREIGN ORDER

STANDARD COINAGE

KM# 5 PICCIOLO (Diniere)

Copper **Obv:** Circular arms of Alof de Wignacourt **Rev:** Maltese cross **Rev. Legend:** ORDO HOSPITALI HIERVSA

Date	Mintage	Good	VG	F	VF	XF
ND(1601-22)	—	—	50.00	200	300	—

KM# 6 PICCIOLO (Diniere)

Copper **Rev:** Maltese cross **Rev. Legend:** ORDO • OSP • S • IOA HIERV **Note:** Varieties exist.

Date	Mintage	Good	VG	F	VF	XF
ND(1602-22) Rare	—	—	50.00	200	300	—

KM# 7 PICCIOLO (Diniere)

Copper **Obv:** Circular arms **Obv. Legend:** S • JOAN BAP ORD PRO NO **Rev:** Maltese cross **Rev. Legend:** S • IOA HIERVSA **Note:** Varieties exist.

Date	Mintage	Good	VG	F	VF	XF
ND(1602-22) Unique	—	—	50.00	200	300	—

KM# 40 PICCIOLO (Diniere)

Copper **Obv:** Arms of Antoine de Paule **Rev:** Maltese cross

Date	Mintage	Good	VG	F	VF	XF
ND(1623-36)	—	—	50.00	100	200	250

KM# 61 PICCIOLO (Diniere)

Copper **Obv:** Arms of Lascaris **Rev:** Maltese cross

Date	Mintage	Good	VG	F	VF	XF
ND(1636-57)	—	—	50.00	100	200	300

KM# 125 PICCIOLO (Diniere)

Copper **Obv:** Shield of Adrien de Wignacourt in pellet circle **Rev:** Maltese cross

Date	Mintage	Good	VG	F	VF	XF
1693	—	—	50.00	100	200	300

KM# 8 3 PICCIOLI

Copper **Obv:** Circular arms of Alof de Wignacourt **Rev:** 3 in circle **Rev. Legend:** HOSPITALI HIERVSA **Note:** Varieties exist.

Date	Mintage	Good	VG	F	VF	XF
ND(1602-22)	—	—	75.00	100	150	250

KM# 35 3 PICCIOLI

Copper **Obv:** Circular arms of Vasconcellos **Rev:** 3 in circle **Rev. Legend:** HOSPITALI HIERVS

Date	Mintage	Good	VG	F	VF	XF
ND(1622-23)	—	—	75.00	100	250	—

KM# 41 3 PICCIOLI

Copper **Obv:** Arms of de Paule **Rev:** 3 in circle **Rev. Legend:** HOSPITALI HIERVSA **Note:** Legend varieties exist.

Date	Mintage	Good	VG	F	VF	XF
ND(1623-36)	—	—	50.00	100	250	300

KM# 42 3 PICCIOLI

Copper **Rev:** Maltese cross **Note:** Varieties exist.

Date	Mintage	Good	VG	F	VF	XF
ND(1623-36)	—	—	75.00	100	250	300

KM# 43 3 PICCIOLI

Copper **Obv:** 3 and small Maltese cross **Rev:** Maltese cross and four stars **Note:** Varieties exist.

Date	Mintage	Good	VG	F	VF	XF
ND(1623-36) Unique	—	—	—	—	—	—

KM# 44 3 PICCIOLI

Copper **Obv. Legend:** F DE PAULA D. WIGNACO. **Note:** Varieties exist.

Date	Mintage	Good	VG	F	VF	XF
ND(1623-36) Unique	—	—	—	—	—	—

Note: An engraver error combining names of two grand masters

KM# 62 3 PICCIOLI

Copper **Obv:** Circular arms of Lascaris **Obv. Legend:** 3 in circle, M • M • HOSPITALI • HIERVS

Date	Mintage	Good	VG	F	VF	XF
ND(1636-57)	—	—	50.00	100	150	—

KM# 9 GRANO

Copper **Obv:** Circular arms of Wignacourt **Rev:** Inner: VT / COMMO / DIVS; outer: HOSPITALIS HIERVSALEM

Date	Mintage	Good	VG	F	VF	XF
ND(1601-22)	—	—	50.00	100	150	250

KM# 36 GRANO

Copper **Obv:** Circular arms of Vasconcellos **Note:** Varieties exist.

Date	Mintage	Good	VG	F	VF	XF
ND(1622-23)	—	—	60.00	115	210	300

KM# 49 GRANO

Copper **Obv:** Arms of de Paule **Rev:** HOSPITALI HIERVSALEM around VT/COMMO/DIVS

Date	Mintage	Good	VG	F	VF	XF
ND(1623-26)	—	—	45.00	75.00	130	—

KM# 50 GRANO

Copper **Obv:** Arms of de Paule **Rev:** Plain cross of the Order, date in angles

Date	Mintage	Good	VG	F	VF	XF
1626	—	—	50.00	100	125	150
1628	—	—	50.00	100	125	150
1629	—	—	50.00	100	125	150

KM# 51 GRANO

Copper **Obv:** Legend around PVB / COMMO / DIT **Rev:** Maltese cross, date in angles

Date	Mintage	Good	VG	F	VF	XF
1629	—	—	50.00	100	150	200

KM# 70 GRANO

Copper **Obv:** Arms of Lascaris **Rev:** Maltese cross

Date	Mintage	Good	VG	F	VF	XF
1637	—	—	75.00	100	150	200
1638	—	—	75.00	100	150	200

KM# 124 GRANO

Copper **Obv:** Circular arms of Adrien Wignacourt **Rev:** Maltese cross, date in angles

Date	Mintage	Good	VG	F	VF	XF
1692	—	—	75.00	75.00	100	150
1693	—	—	75.00	75.00	100	50.00
1694	—	—	75.00	75.00	100	150
1695	—	—	75.00	75.00	100	150

KM# 10 2-1/2 GRANI (1/2 Cinquina)

Silver **Obv:** Circular arms of Alof Wignacourt **Rev:** Cross

Date	Mintage	VG	F	VF	XF	Unc
ND(1602-22)	—	120	200	400	650	—

KM# 11 V (5) GRANI (Cinquina)

Silver **Obv:** Circular arms of Alouf Wignacourt **Rev:** Arms of the Order

Date	Mintage	VG	F	VF	XF	Unc
ND(1602-22)	—	100	200	300	375	—

KM# 26 V (5) GRANI (Cinquina)

Copper **Obv:** Fleur-de-lis and two stars above arms of Vasconcellos **Rev:** Two clasped hands, V below

Date	Mintage	Good	VG	F	VF	XF
1619	—	—	100	150	200	250

KM# 52 V (5) GRANI (Cinquina)

Copper **Obv:** Fleur-de-lis above arms of de Paule **Rev:** Two clasped hands, V below

Date	Mintage	Good	VG	F	VF	XF
1629	—	—	100	120	150	200

KM# 12 X (10) GRANI (Carlino)

Silver **Obv:** Arms of Alof Wignacourt **Rev:** Arms of the Order

Date	Mintage	VG	F	VF	XF	Unc
ND(1601-22)	—	60.00	110	200	375	—

KM# 27 X (10) GRANI (Carlino)

Copper **Obv:** Crown above arms of Alof Wignacourt **Rev:** Two clasped hands, X below

Date	Mintage	Good	VG	F	VF	XF
1619	—	—	100	125	150	180

KM# 37 X (10) GRANI (Carlino)

Silver **Obv:** Arms of de Vasconcellos **Obv. Legend:** + F • L • MEN: DE VASCONCELOS • M • M • H **Rev:** Ornamental arms of the Order **Rev. Legend:** + S • IOAN • BAP • ORA • PRONOBIS

Date	Mintage	VG	F	VF	XF	Unc
ND(1622-23)	—	50.00	100	175	275	—

KM# 46 X (10) GRANI (Carlino)

Silver **Obv:** Arms of de Paule **Rev:** Shield of the Order

Date	Mintage	VG	F	VF	XF	Unc
ND(1623-36)	—	40.00	90.00	170	300	—

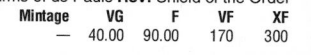

KM# 53 X (10) GRANI (Carlino)
Copper **Obv:** Crown above arms of de Paule **Rev:** Two clasped hands, X below

Date	Mintage	Good	VG	F	VF	XF
1629	—	—	100	25.00	150	200

KM# 63 X (10) GRANI (Carlino)
Silver **Obv:** Crown above arms of Lascaris **Rev:** Shield of the Order **Note:** Legend spacing varieties exist.

Date	Mintage	VG	F	VF	XF	Unc
ND(1636-57)	—	100	135	225	300	—

KM# 85 X (10) GRANI (Carlino)
Silver **Obv:** Crown above arms of de Redin **Rev:** Arms of the Order

Date	Mintage	VG	F	VF	XF	Unc
ND(1657-1660)	—	85.00	180	240	—	—

KM# 90 X (10) GRANI (Carlino)
Silver **Obv:** Crown above arms of R. Cotoner **Rev:** Shield of the Order

Date	Mintage	VG	F	VF	XF	Unc
ND(1660-1663)	—	150	200	250	300	—

KM# 99 X (10) GRANI (Carlino)
Silver **Obv:** Crown above arms of N. Cotoner **Rev:** Shield of the Order **Note:** Legend varieties exist.

Date	Mintage	VG	F	VF	XF	Unc
ND(1663-80)	—	48.00	110	180	265	—

KM# 110 X (10) GRANI (Carlino)
Silver **Obv:** Crown above arms of Carafa **Rev:** Shield of the Order

Date	Mintage	VG	F	VF	XF	Unc
ND(1680-90)	—	100	150	200	300	—

KM# 120 X (10) GRANI (Carlino)
Silver **Obv:** Crown above arms of Adrien Wignacourt **Rev:** Arms of the Order **Note:** Legend varieties exist.

Date	Mintage	VG	F	VF	XF	Unc
ND(1690-97)	—	100	150	180	240	—
1690	—	100	150	180	240	—

KM# 131 X (10) GRANI (Carlino)
Silver **Ruler:** Ramon Perellos y Roccaful **Obv:** Crown above shield of Perellos y Roccafull **Rev:** Arms of the Order

Date	Mintage	VG	F	VF	XF	Unc
ND(1697-1720)	—	120	180	240	300	—

KM# 28 TARI
Copper **Obv:** Crown above arms of Alof Wignacourt **Rev:** Two clasped hands, T I below

Date	Mintage	Good	VG	F	VF	XF
1619	—	—	75.00	100	145	240

KM# 38 TARI
Silver **Obv:** Arms of Vasconcellos **Rev:** Arms of the Order

Date	Mintage	VG	F	VF	XF	Unc
ND(1622-23)	—	75.00	120	210	325	—

KM# 71 TARI
Silver **Obv:** Crowned arms of Lascaris **Rev:** Two clasped hands, T I below **Note:** Legend varieties.

Date	Mintage	VG	F	VF	XF	Unc
1639	—	40.00	110	180	240	—

KM# 91 TARI
Silver **Obv:** Crowned arms of R. Cotoner divide TI **Rev:** Paschal Lamb with banner

Date	Mintage	VG	F	VF	XF	Unc
ND(1660-63)	—	45.00	110	210	325	—

KM# 100 TARI
Silver **Obv:** Crowned arms of N. Cotoner divide TI **Rev:** Paschal Lamb with banner

Date	Mintage	VG	F	VF	XF	Unc
ND(1663-80)	—	45.00	110	210	325	—

KM# 111 TARI
Silver **Obv:** Crowned arms of Carafa divide TI **Rev:** Arms of the Order **Note:** Variety in shield (raised or incuse lines).

Date	Mintage	VG	F	VF	XF	Unc
ND(1680-90)	—	—	—	—	—	—

Note: Reported, not confirmed

KM# 25 2 TARI
Silver **Obv:** Crowned arms of Alof Wignacourt divide T2 **Rev:** Head of St. John the Baptist in a stemmed platter

Date	Mintage	VG	F	VF	XF	Unc
1613	—	100	180	350	550	—

KM# 60 2 TARI
Silver **Obv:** Crowned arms of de Paule

Date	Mintage	VG	F	VF	XF	Unc
1634	—	150	240	475	725	—

KM# 64 2 TARI
Silver **Obv:** Crowned arms of Lascaris

Date	Mintage	VG	F	VF	XF	Unc
1636	—	100	180	350	550	—

KM# 65 2 TARI
Copper **Obv:** Crowned arms of Lascaris in legend **Rev:** Two clasped hands, date above, T2 below

Date	Mintage	Good	VG	F	VF	XF
1636	—	—	100	150	200	220
1637	—	—	100	150	200	220
1641	—	—	100	150	200	220
1642	—	—	100	150	200	220
1643	—	—	100	150	200	220

KM# 75 2 TARI
Copper **Obv:** Legend without Castellar

Date	Mintage	Good	VG	F	VF	XF
1643	—	—	200	250	450	600

KM# 13 3 TARI
Silver **Obv:** Crowned arms of Alof Wignacourt **Rev:** Maltese cross, date in angles

Date	Mintage	VG	F	VF	XF	Unc
1609	—	200	300	500	700	—
1611	—	200	300	500	700	—
1617	—	200	300	500	700	—
1620	—	200	300	500	700	—
16ZZ	—	200	300	500	700	—
ND	—	150	200	300	500	—

KM# A46 3 TARI
Silver **Obv:** Arms of Vasconcellos

Date	Mintage	VG	F	VF	XF	Unc
1623	—	220	325	650	1,100	—

KM# 47 3 TARI
Silver **Obv:** Crowned arms of de Paule

Date	Mintage	VG	F	VF	XF	Unc
1623	—	90.00	175	270	475	—
1624	—	90.00	175	270	475	—
1626	—	90.00	175	270	475	—
1627	—	90.00	175	270	475	—
1628	—	90.00	175	270	475	—
1629	—	90.00	175	270	475	—
1632	—	90.00	175	270	475	—
1635	—	90.00	175	270	475	—

KM# 66 3 TARI
Silver **Obv:** Crowned arms of Lascaris

Date	Mintage	VG	F	VF	XF	Unc
1636	—	80.00	150	240	425	—
1637	—	80.00	150	240	425	—
1638	—	80.00	150	240	425	—
1640	—	80.00	150	240	425	—
1642	—	80.00	150	240	425	—
1648	—	80.00	150	240	425	—
1649	—	80.00	150	240	425	—
1651	—	80.00	150	240	425	—

KM# 86 3 TARI
Silver **Obv:** Crowned arms of the de Redin

Date	Mintage	VG	F	VF	XF	Unc
1658	—	220	325	550	875	—

KM# 92 3 TARI
Silver **Obv:** Coronet above arms of R. Cotoner

Date	Mintage	VG	F	VF	XF	Unc
1660	—	195	300	550	875	—
1662	—	195	300	550	875	—

KM# 101 3 TARI
Silver **Obv:** Crowned arms of N. Cotoner

Date	Mintage	VG	F	VF	XF	Unc
1663/1664	—	65.00	125	220	350	—
1665	—	65.00	125	220	350	—
1666	—	65.00	125	220	350	—

KM# 112 3 TARI
Silver **Obv:** Crowned arms of Carafa

Date	Mintage	VG	F	VF	XF	Unc
1680	—	65.00	125	220	350	—

KM# 14 4 TARI

Silver **Obv:** Crowned arms of Alof Wignacourt dividing T4 **Rev:** Head of St. John the Baptist **Rev. Legend:** S IOAN... **Note:** Varieties exist.

Date	Mintage	VG	F	VF	XF	Unc
1609	—	500	600	800	1,100	—
1611	—	500	600	800	1,100	—
1619	—	500	600	800	1,100	—
16ZZ	—	500	600	800	1,100	—
16Z0	—	500	600	800	1,100	—

KM# 15 4 TARI

Silver **Rev. Legend:** PROPTER...

Date	Mintage	VG	F	VF	XF	Unc
ND	—	—	—	—	—	—

KM# 39 4 TARI

Silver **Obv:** Crowned arms of Vasconcellos

Date	Mintage	VG	F	VF	XF	Unc
16ZZ	—	1,500	2,500	15,000	20,000	—

KM# 48 4 TARI

Silver **Obv:** Crowned arms of de Paule

Date	Mintage	VG	F	VF	XF	Unc
1623	—	200	400	700	950	—
1624	—	200	400	700	950	—
1625	—	200	400	700	950	—
1626	—	200	400	700	950	—
1629	—	200	400	700	950	—
1634	—	200	400	700	950	—

KM# 67 4 TARI

Copper **Obv:** Crowned arms of Lascaris divides sun and moon; legend without CASTELLAR **Obv. Legend:** F • IOANNES • PAVLVS... **Rev:** Two clasped hands, date above, T4 below

Date	Mintage	Good	VG	F	VF	XF
1636	—	—	50.00	200	400	600
1637	—	—	50.00	200	400	600
1641	—	—	50.00	200	400	600
1642	—	—	50.00	200	400	600
1643	—	—	50.00	200	400	600
1647	—	—	50.00	200	400	600
1651	—	—	50.00	200	400	600

KM# 68 4 TARI

Copper **Obv. Legend:** F • IO:PAVLVS • LASCARIS •

Date	Mintage	Good	VG	F	VF	XF
1636	—	—	50.00	200	400	600
1637	—	—	50.00	200	400	600
1641	—	—	50.00	200	400	600
1642	—	—	50.00	200	400	600
1643	—	—	50.00	200	400	600
1647	—	—	50.00	200	400	600

KM# 69 4 TARI

Silver **Obv:** Crowned arms of Lascaris **Note:** Obv. and Rev. legend varieties exist including rotation of each starting at lower left or upper right.

Date	Mintage	VG	F	VF	XF	Unc
1637	—	200	400	500	600	—
1638	—	200	400	500	600	—
1639	—	200	400	500	600	—
1640	—	200	400	500	600	—
1642	—	200	400	500	600	—
1643	—	200	400	500	600	—
1644	—	200	400	500	600	—
1645	—	200	400	500	600	—
1646	—	200	400	500	600	—
1647	—	200	400	500	600	—
1648	—	200	400	500	600	—
1649	—	200	400	500	600	—
1650	—	200	400	500	600	—
1651	—	200	400	500	600	—
1656	—	200	400	500	600	—

KM# 87 4 TARI

Silver **Obv:** Crowned arms of de Redin **Rev:** Head of John the Baptist

Date	Mintage	VG	F	VF	XF	Unc
1658	—	1,000	2,000	3,000	5,000	—

KM# 93 4 TARI

Silver **Obv:** Crowned arms of Gessan

Date	Mintage	VG	F	VF	XF	Unc
1660	—	500	1,500	2,000	2,500	—

KM# 94 4 TARI

Silver **Obv:** Crowned arms of R. Cotoner

Date	Mintage	VG	F	VF	XF	Unc
1660	—	800	1,000	2,000	3,000	—

KM# 102 4 TARI

Silver **Obv:** Crowned arms of N. Cotoner

Date	Mintage	VG	F	VF	XF	Unc
1663	—	600	800	1,000	1,200	—
1664	—	600	800	1,000	1,200	—
1665	—	600	800	1,000	1,200	—
1666	—	600	800	1,000	1,200	—
1667	—	600	800	1,000	1,200	—
1668	—	600	800	1,000	1,200	—
1673	—	600	800	1,000	1,200	—

KM# 113 4 TARI

Silver **Obv:** Crowned arms of Carafa

Date	Mintage	VG	F	VF	XF	Unc
1680	—	500	1,000	1,500	2,000	—
1681	—	500	1,000	1,500	2,000	—
1685	—	500	1,000	1,500	2,000	—

KM# 121 4 TARI

Silver **Obv:** Crowned arms of Adrian Wignacourt

Date	Mintage	VG	F	VF	XF	Unc
1691	—	700	800	1,000	2,000	—

KM# 122 4 TARI

Silver **Obv:** Crowned shield, crown with points, the style of an Eastern crown **Note:** Varieties exist.

Date	Mintage	VG	F	VF	XF	Unc
1691	—	700	800	1,000	2,000	—

KM# 132 4 TARI

Silver **Obv:** Crowned arms of Perellos y Roccaful **Note:** Varieties with or without HH flanking shield.

Date	Mintage	VG	F	VF	XF	Unc
1697	—	1,000	2,000	3,000	4,000	—

KM# 16 ZECCHINO

3.5000 g., 0.9860 Gold 0.1109 oz. AGW **Obv:** Grand Master kneeling before St. John **Obv. Legend:** F. ALOPIVS. DE WIGNACOVRT **Rev:** Christ within stars

Date	Mintage	VG	F	VF	XF	Unc
ND(1601-22)	—	350	700	1,500	2,500	—

KM# 17 ZECCHINO

3.5000 g., 0.9860 Gold 0.1109 oz. AGW **Obv. Legend:** F. L. MENDES DE VASCONCELOS. M. M. H.

Date	Mintage	VG	F	VF	XF	Unc
ND(1622-23)	—	4,000	5,000	10,000	30,000	—

KM# 18 ZECCHINO

3.5000 g., 0.9860 Gold 0.1109 oz. AGW **Obv. Legend:** F. ANTONIUS DE PAULA. M. M. H.

Date	Mintage	VG	F	VF	XF	Unc
ND(1623-36)	—	1,000	4,000	7,000	9,000	—

KM# 19 ZECCHINO

3.5000 g., 0.9860 Gold 0.1109 oz. AGW **Obv. Legend:** F. IO. PAULUS LASC CASTELLAR. M. M. H.

Date	Mintage	VG	F	VF	XF	Unc
ND(1636-57)	—	450	725	2,200	3,300	—

KM# 20 ZECCHINO

3.5000 g., 0.9860 Gold 0.1109 oz. AGW **Obv. Legend:** F. D. GREG. CARAFA S. IO. BAPTISTA. **Rev:** Crowned arms of Grand Master

Date	Mintage	VG	F	VF	XF	Unc
ND(1680-90)	—	1,000	2,000	4,000	5,000	—

KM# 123 ZECCHINO

3.5000 g., 0.9860 Gold 0.1109 oz. AGW **Obv. Legend:** F. ADR. WIGNAC. S. 10. BAPT.

Date	Mintage	VG	F	VF	XF	Unc
1691	—	325	550	1,100	2,200	—
1694	—	325	550	1,100	2,200	—
1695	—	325	550	1,100	2,200	—
1696	—	325	550	1,100	2,200	—

KM# A133.1 ZECCHINO

3.5000 g., 0.9860 Gold 0.1109 oz. AGW **Ruler:** Ramon Perellos y Roccaful **Obv:** Crowned round shield in sprays **Obv. Legend:** (*) F (•) RAYMUNDV(S) PERELLOS (•) M • M • H • ET • S • S • HIE **Rev:** St. John standing presents Order flag to kneeling Grand Master **Rev. Legend:** PIETATE - VINCES

Date	Mintage	VG	F	VF	XF	Unc
ND(1697-1720)	—	800	1,000	2,000	3,000	—
1699	—	800	1,000	2,000	3,000	—

KM# A133.2 ZECCHINO

3.5000 g., 0.9860 Gold 0.1109 oz. AGW **Ruler:** Ramon Perellos y Roccaful **Obv:** Crowned round shield in sprays **Obv. Legend:** F RAIMUNDVS PERELLOS • M • M • H • ET • S • S • HIE **Rev:** St. John standing presents the flag of the Order to the kneeling Grand Master **Rev. Legend:** PIETATE - VINCES

Date	Mintage	VG	F	VF	XF	Unc
1699	—	800	1,000	2,000	3,000	—

KM# 21 2 ZECCHINO

7.0000 g., 0.9860 Gold 0.2219 oz. AGW **Obv:** Bust of Grand Master Castellar **Obv. Legend:** *F. 10 PAVLVS LASCARIS... **Rev:** Arms of the Grand Master

Date	Mintage	VG	F	VF	XF	Unc
ND(1636-57) Rare	—	—	—	20,000	—	—

Note: LHS Numismatic AC Auction 103, 5-09, VF-XF realized approximately $74,765.

KM# 22 2 ZECCHINO

7.0000 g., 0.9860 Gold 0.2219 oz. AGW **Ruler:** Ramon Perellos y Roccaful **Obv:** Crowned shield within sprigs **Obv. Legend:** F RAIMVNDVS PERELLOS... **Rev:** Knights of the Order holding a flag

Date	Mintage	VG	F	VF	XF	Unc
ND(1697-1720)	—	2,750	3,300	5,500	7,700	—

KM# 126 4 ZECCHINI

14.0000 g., 0.9860 Gold 0.4438 oz. AGW **Obv:** St. John presents flag to kneeling Grand Master **Obv. Legend:** F. ADR. WIGNACOURT **Rev:** Arms of Grand Master

Date	Mintage	VG	F	VF	XF	Unc
1695/4 Rare	—	—	—	—	—	—

KM# 134 4 ZECCHINI

14.0000 g., 0.9860 Gold 0.4438 oz. AGW **Ruler:** Ramon Perellos y Roccaful **Obv:** Crowned arms in palm branches **Rev:** St. John presenting banner to kneeling Grand Master

Date	Mintage	VG	F	VF	XF	Unc
1699	—	1,400	2,050	3,850	6,600	—

COUNTERMARKED COINAGE

For over a century the two and four Tari copper coins struck during the reign of Jean-Paul Lascaris Castellar were countermarked as an expedient against the prevalent forging of these coins both in Malta and Messina.

A total of eight different countermarks were utilized. As many as seven can be found on the 2 Tari and all eight different may be encountered on the 4 Tari.

COUNTERMARKS

I. Imperial eagle in circle.

Initiated May 28, 1646.

II. Head of John the Baptist in oval.

Initiated April 19, 1662.

III. Crowned fleur-de-lis.

Initiated August 27, 1696.

For more information refer to The Coinage of the Knights in Malta by Felice Restelli and Joseph C. Sammut, 1977 by Emmanuel Said Publishers, Valettta, Malta.

NOTE: Coins are properly catalogued by the latest countermark. Obviously certain coins may lack one or more countermarks having been missed during such an extensive countermarking period. Prices for this section are based on common examples, which are likely to show less detail and tend to be cupped. The images shown here are exceptional examples and command premium prices.

KM# 76 2 TARI

Copper **Countermark:** Type I **Obv. Legend:** F • IO : PAVLVS:... **Note:** Countermark on 2 Tari, KM#65.

CM Date	Host Date	Good	VG	F	VF	XF
ND(1646)	1636-43	25.00	41.25	60.00	90.00	—

KM# 77 2 TARI

Copper **Countermark:** Type I **Obv. Legend:** F • IOANNES • PAVLVS •... **Note:** Countermark on 2 Tari, KM#75.

CM Date	Host Date	Good	VG	F	VF	XF
ND(1646)	1643	25.00	41.25	60.00	90.00	—

KM# 96 2 TARI

Copper **Countermark:** Type I and Type II **Obv. Legend:** F • IOANNES • PAVLVS •... **Note:** Countermark on 2 Tari, KM#75.

CM Date	Host Date	Good	VG	F	VF	XF
ND(1662)	1643	22.50	38.50	55.00	75.00	—

KM# 95 2 TARI

Copper **Countermark:** Type I and Type II **Obv. Legend:** F • IO : PAVLVS:... **Note:** Countermark on 2 Tari, KM#65.

CM Date	Host Date	Good	VG	F	VF	XF
ND(1662)	1636-43	22.50	38.50	55.00	75.00	—

KM# 127 2 TARI

Copper **Countermark:** Type I-III **Obv. Legend:** F • IO : PAVLVS :... **Note:** Countermark on 2 Tari, KM#65.

CM Date	Host Date	Good	VG	F	VF	XF
ND(1696)	1636-43	20.00	33.00	46.75	65.00	—

KM# 128 2 TARI

Copper **Countermark:** Type I-III **Obv. Legend:** F • IOANNES • PAVLVS •... **Note:** Countermark on 2 Tari, KM#75.

CM Date	Host Date	Good	VG	F	VF	XF
ND(1696)	1643	20.00	33.00	46.75	65.00	—

KM# 78 4 TARI

Copper **Countermark:** Type I **Obv. Legend:** F • IO : PAVLVS •... **Note:** Countermark on 4 Tari, KM#67.

CM Date	Host Date	Good	VG	F	VF	XF
ND(1646)	1636-51	33.00	55.00	75.00	110	—

KM# 79 4 TARI

Copper **Countermark:** Type I **Obv. Legend:** F • IOANNES • PAVLVS •... **Note:** Countermark on 4 Tari, KM#68.

CM Date	Host Date	Good	VG	F	VF	XF
ND(1646)	1636-47	33.00	55.00	75.00	110	—

KM# 98 4 TARI

Copper **Countermark:** Type I and Type II **Obv. Legend:** F • IOANNES • PAVLVS •... **Note:** Countermark on 4 Tari, KM#68.

CM Date	Host Date	Good	VG	F	VF	XF
ND(1662)	1636-47	25.00	41.25	60.00	90.00	—

KM# 97 4 TARI

Copper **Countermark:** Type I and Type II **Obv. Legend:** F • IO : PAVLVS •... **Note:** Countermark on 4 Tari, KM#67.

CM Date	Host Date	Good	VG	F	VF	XF
ND	1636-51	25.00	41.25	60.00	90.00	—

KM# 129 4 TARI

Copper **Countermark:** Type I-III **Obv. Legend:** F • IO • PAVLVS •... **Note:** Countermark on 4 Tari, KM#67.

CM Date	Host Date	Good	VG	F	VF	XF
ND	1636-51	22.50	38.50	55.00	75.00	—

KM# 130 4 TARI

Copper **Countermark:** Type I-III **Obv. Legend:** F • IOANNES • PAVLVS •... **Note:** Countermark on 4 Tari, KM#68.

CM Date	Host Date	Good	VG	F	VF	XF
ND	1636-47	22.50	38.50	55.00	75.00	—

MEXICO

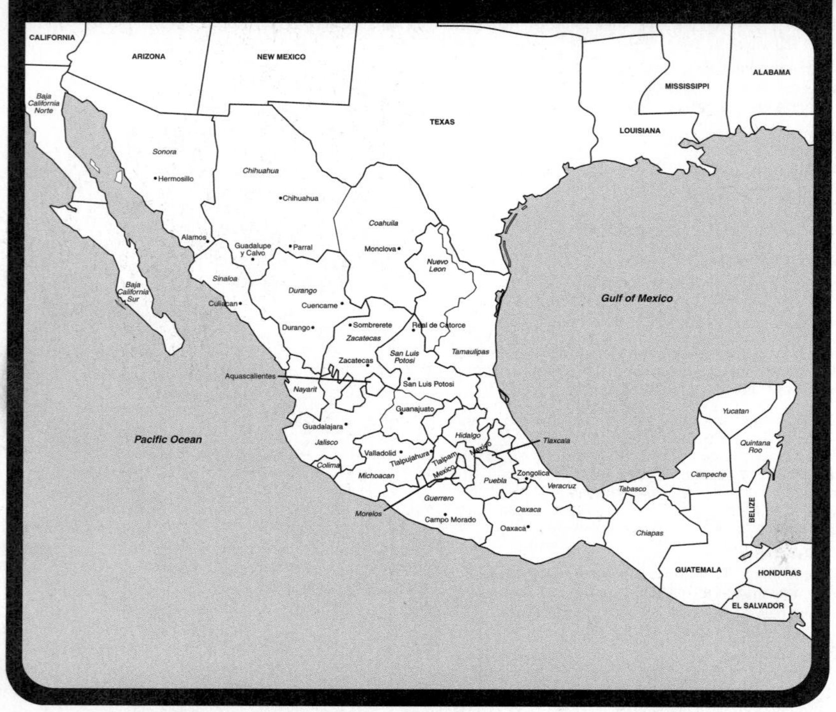

Mexico, located immediately south of the United States has an area of 759,529 sq. mi. (1,967,183 sq. km).

Mexico was the site of highly advanced Indian civilizations 1,500 years before conquistador Hernando Cortes conquered the wealthy Aztec empire of Montezuma,1519-21, and founded a Spanish colony which lasted for nearly 300 years. During the Spanish period, Mexico, then called New Spain, stretched from Guatemala to the present states of Wyoming and California, its present northern boundary having been established by the secession of Texas during 1836 and the war of 1846-48 with the United States.

Independence from Spain was declared by Father Miguel Hidalgo on Sept. 16, 1810, (Mexican Independence Day) and was achieved by General Agustin de Iturbide in 1821. Iturbide became emperor in 1822 but was deposed when a republic was established a year later. For more than fifty years following the birth of the republic, the political scene of Mexico was characterized by turmoil which saw two emperors (including the unfortunate Maximilian), several dictators and an average of one new government every nine months passing swiftly from obscurity to oblivion. The land, social, economic and labor reforms promulgated by the Reform Constitution of Feb. 5, 1917 established the basis for sustained economic development and participative democracy that have made Mexico one of the most politically stable countries of modern Latin America.

Rulers:
Philip III, 1598-1621
Philip IV, 1621-1665
Charles II, 1665-1700

Mint Marks:
M, Mo, oMo, MXo – Mexico City

Assayer's Initials

Initial	Date	Name
A	1608-09	?
F	15??-1608	?
F	1610-15 or 1616	
Ne	1611	?
D	1616 or 1617-34	?
P	1634-65	?
G	1666-77	Geronimo Becerra
L	1677-1705	Martin Lopez

SPANISH COLONY

COB COINAGE

KM# 21 1/2 REAL

1.6900 g., 0.9310 Silver 0.0506 oz. ASW **Ruler:** Philip III **Obv:** Legend around crowned PHILIPVS monogram **Rev:** Legend around cross, lions and castles **Note:** Struck at Mexico City Mint, mint mark M, Mo.

Date	Mintage	Good	VG	F	VF	XF
ND(1607-21) Date off flan	—	—	35.00	65.00	100	—
1609 A	—	—	110	185	285	—
1610 F	—	—	110	185	285	—
1614 F	—	—	110	185	285	—
1620 D	—	—	110	185	285	—

KM# 22 1/2 REAL

1.6900 g., 0.9310 Silver 0.0506 oz. ASW **Ruler:** Philip IV **Obv:** Legend around crowned PHILIPVS monogram **Rev:** Legend around cross, lions and castles **Note:** Struck at Mexico City Mint, mint mark M, Mo.

Date	Mintage	Good	VG	F	VF	XF
ND(1622-67) Date off flan	—	—	25.00	50.00	75.00	—
1622 D	—	—	110	185	285	—
1650 P	—	—	110	185	285	—
1653 P	—	—	110	185	285	—
1654 P	—	—	110	185	285	—
1656 P	—	—	110	185	285	—
1658 P	—	—	110	185	285	—
1659 P	—	—	110	185	285	—
1661 P	—	—	110	185	285	—
1662 P	—	—	110	185	285	—

KM# 23 1/2 REAL

1.6900 g., 0.9310 Silver 0.0506 oz. ASW **Ruler:** Charles II **Obv:** Legend around crowned CAROLVS monogram **Rev:** Legend around cross, lions and castles **Note:** Struck at Mexico City Mint, mark mark M, Mo.

Date	Mintage	Good	VG	F	VF	XF
ND(1668-99) Date off flan	—	—	25.00	50.00	75.00	—
1668 G	—	—	125	200	300	—
1669 G	—	—	125	200	300	—
1671 G	—	—	125	200	300	—
1673 G	—	—	125	200	300	—
1674 G	—	—	125	200	300	—
1677 L	—	—	125	200	300	—
1678 L	—	—	125	200	300	—
1681/0 L	—	—	—	—	—	—
1681 L	—	—	125	200	300	—
1682 L	—	—	125	200	300	—
1683 L	—	—	125	200	300	—
1684 L	—	—	125	200	300	—
1685 L	—	—	125	200	300	—
1687 L	—	—	125	200	300	—
1689 L	—	—	125	200	300	—
1690 L	—	—	125	200	300	—
1692	—	—	125	200	300	—
1694 L	—	—	125	200	300	—
1695 L	—	—	125	200	300	—
1697 L	—	—	125	200	300	—

KM# 27.2 REAL

3.3800 g., 0.9310 Silver 0.1012 oz. ASW **Ruler:** Philip III **Obv:** Legend and date around crowned arms **Obv. Legend:** PHILIPVS III DEI G **Rev:** Legend around cross, lions and castles **Note:** Struck at Mexico City Mint, mint mark M, Mo.

Date	Mintage	Good	VG	F	VF	XF
ND(1607-21) Date off flan	—	—	20.00	40.00	75.00	—
1607 F	—	—	110	185	285	—
1608/7 F	—	—	110	185	285	—
1608 A	—	—	110	185	285	—
1608 F	—	—	110	185	285	—
1609 A	—	—	110	185	285	—
1610/09 F	—	—	110	185	285	—
1610 F	—	—	110	185	285	—
1611/10 F	—	—	110	185	285	—
1611 F	—	—	110	185	285	—
1612/1 F	—	—	110	185	285	—
1612 F	—	—	110	185	285	—
1613 F	—	—	110	185	285	—

KM# 28 REAL

3.3800 g., 0.9310 Silver 0.1012 oz. ASW **Ruler:** Philip IV **Obv:** Legend and date around crowned arms **Obv. Legend:** PHILIPVS IIII DEI G **Note:** Struck at Mexico City Mint, mint mark M, Mo.

Date	Mintage	Good	VG	F	VF	XF
ND(1622-67) Date off flan	—	—	25.00	40.00	85.00	—
1622 D	—	—	110	185	285	—
1624/3 D	—	—	—	—	—	—
1627 D	—	—	110	185	285	—
1630 D	—	—	110	185	285	—
1632/29 D	—	—	—	—	—	—
1643 P	—	—	110	185	285	—
1651 P	—	—	110	185	285	—
1652 P	—	—	110	185	285	—
1653 P	—	—	110	185	285	—
1654 P	—	—	110	185	285	—

KM# 29 REAL

3.3800 g., 0.9310 Silver 0.1012 oz. ASW **Ruler:** Charles II **Obv:** Legend and date around crowned arms **Obv. Legend:** CAROLVS II DEI G **Note:** Struck at Mexico City Mint, mint mark M, Mo.

Date	Mintage	Good	VG	F	VF	XF
ND(1668-99) Date off flan	—	—	35.00	60.00	100	—
1668 G	—	—	300	400	500	—
1688 L	—	—	200	300	400	—
1692 L	—	—	200	300	400	—

KM# 32.2 2 REALES

6.7700 g., 0.9310 Silver 0.2026 oz. ASW **Ruler:** Philip III **Obv:** Legend around crowned arms **Obv. Legend:** PHILIPVS III DEI G **Rev:** Legend around cross, lions and castles **Note:** Struck at Mexico City Mint, mint mark M, Mo.

Date	Mintage	Good	VG	F	VF	XF
ND(1607-22) Date off flan	—	—	60.00	90.00	120	—
1607 A Rare	—	—	—	—	—	—
1607 F	—	—	150	275	400	—
1608 A	—	—	150	275	400	—
1608/9 A/F Rare	—	—	—	—	—	—
1609 A	—	—	150	275	400	—
1609 F Rare	—	—	—	—	—	—
1611 F	—	—	150	275	400	—
1613 F	—	—	150	275	400	—
1616 F	—	—	150	275	400	—

Date	Mintage	Good	VG	F	VF	XF
1620 D	—	—	150	275	400	—
1622 D (retrograde 2's)	—	—	150	275	400	—

KM# 33 2 REALES

6.7700 g., 0.9310 Silver 0.2026 oz. ASW **Ruler:** Philip IV **Obv:** Legend and date around crowned arms **Obv. Legend:** PHILIPVS IIII DEI G **Rev:** Legend around cross, lions and castles **Note:** Struck at Mexico City Mint, mint mark M, Mo.

Date	Mintage	Good	VG	F	VF	XF
ND(1622-67) Date off flan	—	—	50.00	65.00	100	—
1641 P	—	—	150	275	400	—
1653 P	—	—	150	275	400	—
1654 P	—	—	150	275	400	—
1655 P	—	—	150	275	400	—
1657 P	—	—	150	275	400	—

KM# 34 2 REALES

6.7700 g., 0.9310 Silver 0.2026 oz. ASW **Ruler:** Charles II **Obv:** Legend and date around crowned arms **Obv. Legend:** CAROLVS II DEI G **Rev:** Legend around cross, lions and castles **Note:** Struck at Mexico City Mint, mint mark M, Mo.

Date	Mintage	Good	VG	F	VF	XF
ND(1668-99) Date off flan	—	—	60.00	90.00	120	—
1668 G	—	—	300	400	600	—
1669 G	—	—	300	400	600	—
1690 L Unique	—	—	—	—	—	—
1695 L	—	—	300	400	600	—
1699 L	—	—	300	400	600	—

KM# 37.2 4 REALES

13.5400 g., 0.9310 Silver 0.4053 oz. ASW **Ruler:** Philip III **Obv:** Legend and date around crowned arms **Obv. Legend:** PHILIPVS III DEI G **Rev:** Legend around cross, lions and castles **Note:** Struck at Mexico City Mint, mint mark M, Mo.

Date	Mintage	Good	VG	F	VF	XF
ND(1607-21) Date off flan	—	—	90.00	125	250	—
1607 F	—	—	200	350	575	—
1608 A	—	—	200	350	575	—
1609/8 A Rare	—	—	—	—	—	—
1609 A	—	—	200	350	575	—
1610 F	—	—	200	350	575	—
1611 F	—	—	200	350	575	—
1612 F	—	—	200	350	575	—
1613 F	—	—	200	350	575	—
1614 F	—	—	200	350	575	—
1618 D	—	—	200	350	575	—
1620 D	—	—	200	350	575	—
1621 D	—	—	200	350	575	—

KM# 38 4 REALES

13.5400 g., 0.9310 Silver 0.4053 oz. ASW **Ruler:** Philip IV **Obv:** Legend and date around crowned arms **Obv. Legend:** PHILIPVS III DEI G **Rev:** Legend around cross, lions and castle **Note:** Struck at Mexico City Mint, mint mark M, Mo.

Date	Mintage	Good	VG	F	VF	XF
ND(1622-65) Date off flan	—	—	75.00	100	225	—
1622 D	—	—	200	350	575	—
1623/2 D	—	—	200	350	575	—
1623 D	—	—	200	350	575	—
1624 D	—	—	200	350	575	—
1629 D	—	—	200	350	575	—
1631 D	—	—	200	350	575	—
1632 D	—	—	200	350	575	—
1636 P	—	—	200	350	575	—
1639 P	—	—	200	350	575	—
1643 P	—	—	200	350	575	—
1644 P	—	—	200	350	575	—
1645 P	—	—	200	350	575	—
1648 P	—	—	200	350	575	—
1649 P	—	—	200	350	575	—
1650 P	—	—	200	350	575	—
1651 P	—	—	200	350	575	—
1652 P	—	—	200	350	575	—
1653 P	—	—	200	350	575	—
1654 P	—	—	200	350	575	—
1655 P	—	—	200	350	575	—
1656 P	—	—	200	350	575	—
1657 P	—	—	200	350	575	—
1658 P	—	—	200	350	575	—
1659/8 P	—	—	200	350	575	—
1661 P	—	—	200	350	575	—
1665 P	—	—	200	350	575	—

KM# 39 4 REALES

13.5400 g., 0.9310 Silver 0.4053 oz. ASW **Ruler:** Charles II **Obv:** Legend and date around crowned arms **Obv. Legend:** CAROLVS II DEI G **Rev:** Legend around cross, lions and castles **Note:** Struck at Mexico City Mint, mint mark M, Mo.

Date	Mintage	Good	VG	F	VF	XF
ND(1667-99) Date off flan	—	—	100	150	250	—
1678 L	—	—	500	900	1,500	—
1679 L	—	—	500	900	1,500	—
1682 L	—	—	500	900	1,500	—
1683 L	—	—	500	900	1,500	—
1685 L	—	—	500	900	1,500	—
1689 L	—	—	500	900	1,500	—
1690 L	—	—	500	900	1,500	—
1691/0 L	—	—	500	900	1,500	—
1691 L	—	—	500	900	1,500	—
1692 L	—	—	500	900	1,500	—
1694 L	—	—	500	900	1,500	—
1695 L	—	—	500	900	1,500	—
1697 L	—	—	500	900	1,500	—
1698 L	—	—	500	900	1,500	—

KM# 44.3 8 REALES

27.0700 g., 0.9310 Silver 0.8102 oz. ASW **Ruler:** Philip III **Obv:** Legend around crowned arms **Obv. Legend:** PHILIPVS III DEI G **Rev:** Legend around cross, lions and castles **Note:** Struck at Mexico City Mint, mint mark M, Mo.

Date	Mintage	Good	VG	F	VF	XF
ND(1607-21) Date off flan	—	—	100	150	200	—
1607 F Date over GRATIA	—	—	400	600	1,000	—
1607 F	—	—	300	450	900	—
1608 A/F	—	—	400	600	1,000	—
1608/7 F	—	—	500	750	1,300	—
1608 A	—	—	300	450	900	—
1608 F	—	—	500	750	1,300	—
1609 A	—	—	300	450	900	—
1609 F Rare	—	—	—	—	—	—
1610/9 F	—	—	300	450	900	—
1610 F	—	—	300	450	900	—
1611/0 F	—	—	600	850	1,650	—
1611 F	—	—	600	850	1,650	—
1612/1 F	—	—	300	450	900	—
1612 F	—	—	300	450	900	—
1613 F	—	—	600	850	1,650	—
1614 F	—	—	300	450	900	—
1615 F	—	—	300	450	900	—
1616 F Rare	—	—	—	—	—	—
1617 F Rare	—	—	—	—	—	—
1618 D/F Rare	—	—	—	—	—	—
1618 D	—	—	300	450	900	—
1619 D Rare	—	—	—	—	—	—
1620 D	—	—	300	450	900	—
1621/0 D	—	—	300	450	900	—
1621 D	—	—	300	450	900	—

KM# 45 8 REALES

27.0700 g., 0.9310 Silver 0.8102 oz. ASW **Ruler:** Philip IV **Obv:** Legend around crowned arms **Obv. Legend:** PHILIPVS IIII DEI G **Rev:** Legend around cross, lions and castles **Note:** Struck at Mexico City Mint, mint mark M, Mo.

Date	Mintage	Good	VG	F	VF	XF
ND(1621-67) Date off flan	—	—	75.00	100	150	—
1621 D	—	—	200	350	500	—
1622/1 D Rare	—	—	—	—	—	—
1622 D	—	—	200	350	500	—
1623/2 D	—	—	200	350	500	—
1623 D	—	—	200	350	500	—
1624/3 D	—	—	200	350	500	—
1624 D	—	—	200	350	500	—
1625/4 D	—	—	200	350	500	—
1625 D	—	—	200	300	500	—
1626/5 D Rare	—	—	—	—	—	—
1626 D	—	—	200	350	500	—
1627/6/5 D	—	—	200	350	500	—
1627/6 D	—	—	200	350	500	—
1627 D	—	—	200	350	500	—
1628/7	—	—	200	350	500	—
1628 D	—	—	200	350	500	—
1629 D	—	—	200	350	500	—
1630 D Rare	—	—	—	—	—	—
1631/0 D Rare	—	—	—	—	—	—
1631 D Rare	—	—	—	—	—	—
1632 D	—	—	200	350	500	—
1634 D	—	—	200	350	500	—
1634 P/D	—	—	200	350	500	—
1634 P	—	—	200	350	500	—
1635 P	—	—	200	350	500	—
1636 P	—	—	200	350	500	—
1637 P	—	—	200	350	500	—
1639/8 P	—	—	200	350	500	—
1639 P	—	—	200	350	500	—
1640/39 P	—	—	200	350	500	—
1640 P	—	—	200	350	500	—
1641/40/39 P	—	—	200	350	500	—
1641 P	—	—	200	350	500	—
1642 P	—	—	200	350	500	—
1643 P	—	—	200	350	500	—
1644 P Rare	—	—	—	—	—	—
1645 P	—	—	200	350	500	—
1646 P	—	—	200	350	500	—
1647/6 P	—	—	200	350	500	—
1647 P	—	—	200	350	500	—
1648/7 P Rare	—	—	—	—	—	—
1648 P	—	—	200	350	500	—
1649/8 P Rare	—	—	—	—	—	—
1649 P	—	—	200	350	500	—
1650 P	—	—	200	350	500	—
1651 P	—	—	175	250	350	—
1652/45 P	—	—	175	250	350	—
1652/48 P	—	—	175	250	350	—
1652/49 P	—	—	165	225	300	—
1652/0 P	—	—	165	225	300	—
1652/1 P	—	—	165	225	300	—
1652 P	—	—	165	225	300	—
1653/2 P	—	—	165	225	300	—
1653 P	—	—	165	225	300	—
1654/3 P	—	—	165	225	300	—
1654 P	—	—	165	225	300	—
1655/4 P	—	—	165	225	300	—
1655 P	—	—	165	225	300	—
1656 P	—	—	165	225	300	—
1657 P	—	—	250	400	600	—
1658/7 P	—	—	250	400	600	—
1658 P	—	—	250	400	600	—
1659 P	—	—	300	500	800	—
1660/59 P	—	—	300	500	800	—
1660 P	—	—	300	500	800	—
1661 /0P Rare	—	—	—	—	—	—
1661 P Rare	—	—	—	—	—	—
1662 P	—	—	300	500	800	—
1663 P	—	—	300	500	800	—

Date	Mintage	Good	VG	F	VF	XF
1664 P	—	—	300	500	800	—
1665 P	—	—	300	500	800	—
1666 G/P Rare	—	—	—	—	—	—
1666 G Rare	—	—	—	—	—	—

KM# 46 8 REALES

27.0700 g., 0.9310 Silver 0.8102 oz. ASW **Ruler:** Charles II **Obv:** Legend and date around crowned arms **Obv. Legend:** CAROLVS II DEI G **Rev:** Legend around cross, lions and castles **Note:** Struck at Mexico City Mint, mint mark M, Mo.

Date	Mintage	Good	VG	F	VF	XF
ND(1667-1701) Date off flan	—	—	90.00	110	150	—
1667/6 Rare	—	—	—	—	—	—
1667 G	—	—	600	900	1,500	—
1668 G	—	—	600	900	1,500	—
1669 G	—	—	600	900	1,500	—
1670 G	—	—	600	900	1,500	—
1671 G	—	—	700	1,000	1,700	—
1672 G	—	—	700	1,000	1,700	—
1673 G	—	—	700	1,000	1,700	—
1674 G	—	—	600	900	1,500	—
1675 G	—	—	600	900	1,500	—
1676/5 G	—	—	400	600	900	—
1676 G	—	—	400	600	900	—
1677 G	—	—	400	600	900	—
1678 L	—	—	400	600	900	—
1679 L	—	—	400	600	900	—
1680 L	—	—	300	400	600	—
1681 L	—	—	600	400	600	—
1682 L Rare	—	—	—	—	—	—
1683 L Rare	—	—	—	—	—	—
1684 L	—	—	600	900	1,500	—
1685 L	—	—	600	900	1,500	—
1686 L Rare	—	—	—	—	—	—
1687 L	—	—	700	1,000	1,700	—
1688 L	—	—	700	1,000	1,700	—
1689 L	—	—	600	900	1,500	—
1690 L Rare	—	—	—	—	—	—
1691 L Rare	—	—	—	—	—	—
1692 L Rare	—	—	—	—	—	—
1693 L Rare	—	—	—	—	—	—
1694 L Rare	—	—	—	—	—	—
1695 L	—	—	600	900	1,500	—
1697 L Rare	—	—	—	—	—	—
1698 L Rare	—	—	—	—	—	—
1699 L	—	—	600	900	1,500	—
1700 L	—	—	700	1,000	1,700	—

KM# 50 ESCUDO

3.3800 g., 0.9170 Gold 0.0996 oz. AGW **Ruler:** Charles II **Obv:** Legend and date around crowned arms **Obv. Legend:** CAROLVS II DEI G **Rev:** Lions and castles in angles of cross, legend around

Date	Mintage	VG	F	VF	XF	Unc
ND(1679-1701) Date off flan	—	—	1,200	1,500	2,000	—
1679MXo L Rare	—	—	—	—	—	—
1690MXo L	—	—	3,000	4,000	5,000	—
1695MXo L	—	—	3,000	4,000	5,000	—
1697MXo L	—	—	3,000	4,000	5,000	—
1698MXo L	—	—	3,000	4,000	5,000	—
1699MXo L	—	—	3,000	4,000	5,000	—
1700MXo L	—	—	3,000	4,000	5,000	—

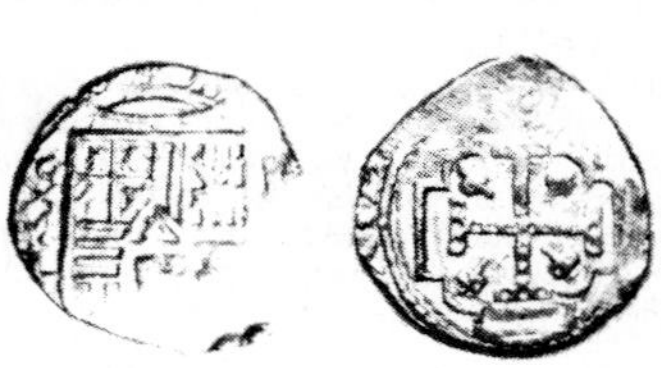

KM# 52 2 ESCUDOS

6.7700 g., 0.9170 Gold 0.1996 oz. AGW **Ruler:** Philip V **Obv:** Legend and date around crowned arms **Obv. Legend:** CAROLVS II DEI G **Rev:** Legend around cross

Date	Mintage	VG	F	VF	XF	Unc
ND(1679-1701) Date off flan	—	—	1,300	1,750	2,500	—
1680MXo L	—	—	4,000	5,000	6,000	—
1681MXo L	—	—	4,000	5,000	6,000	—
1695MXo L	—	—	4,000	5,000	6,000	—
1698MXo L	—	—	4,000	5,000	6,000	—

KM# 54 4 ESCUDOS

13.5400 g., 0.9170 Gold 0.3992 oz. AGW **Ruler:** Charles II **Obv:** Legend and date around crowned arms **Obv. Legend:** CAROLVS II DEI G **Rev:** Legend around cross

Date	Mintage	VG	F	VF	XF	Unc
ND(1679-1701) Date off flan	—	—	2,500	3,500	4,750	—
1680MXo L Rare	—	—	—	—	—	—
1681MXo L	—	—	4,500	6,000	7,500	—
1683MXo L	—	—	4,500	6,000	7,500	—
1693MXo L	—	—	4,500	6,000	7,500	—
1694MXo L	—	—	4,500	6,000	7,500	—
1695MXo L	—	—	4,500	6,000	7,500	—
1696MXo L	—	—	4,500	6,000	7,500	—
1697MXo L	—	—	4,500	6,000	7,500	—
1698MXo L	—	—	4,500	6,000	7,500	—
1699/8/7MXo L	—	—	4,500	6,000	7,500	—

KM# 56 8 ESCUDOS

27.0700 g., 0.9170 Gold 0.7981 oz. AGW **Ruler:** Philip V **Obv:** Legend and date around crowned arms **Obv. Legend:** CAROLVS II DEI G **Rev:** Legend around cross

Date	Mintage	VG	F	VF	XF	Unc
ND(1679-1701) Date off flan	—	—	4,500	6,250	7,000	—
1691MXo L	—	—	6,000	7,500	9,000	—
1694MXo L	—	—	6,000	7,500	9,000	—
1695MXo L	—	—	6,000	7,500	9,000	—
1697/6MXo L	—	—	6,000	7,500	9,000	—
1697MXo L	—	—	6,000	7,500	9,000	—
1698MXo L	—	—	6,000	7,500	9,000	—
1699MXo L	—	—	6,000	7,500	9,000	—
1700MXo L	—	—	6,000	7,500	9,000	—

ROYAL COINAGE

Struck on specially prepared round planchets using well centered dies in excellent condition to prove the quality of the minting to the Viceroy or even to the King.

KM# R28 REAL

3.3834 g., 0.9310 Silver 0.1013 oz. ASW **Ruler:** Philip IV **Obv. Legend:** PHILIPVS IIII DEI G **Note:** Struck at Mexico City Mint, mint mark Mo.

Date	Mintage	Good	VG	F	VF	XF
1643Mo P Rare	—	—	—	—	—	—

KM# R29 REAL

3.3834 g., 0.9310 Silver 0.1013 oz. ASW **Ruler:** Charles II **Obv. Legend:** CAROLVS II DEI G **Note:** Struck at Mexico City Mint, mint mark Mo.

Date	Mintage	Good	VG	F	VF	XF
1699Mo L Rare	—	—	—	—	—	—

KM# R34 2 REALES

6.7668 g., 0.9310 Silver 0.2025 oz. ASW **Ruler:** Charles II **Obv. Legend:** CAROLVS II DEI G **Note:** Struck at Mexico City Mint, mint mark Mo.

Date	Mintage	Good	VG	F	VF	XF
1668Mo G Rare	—	—	—	—	—	—

KM# R37.1 4 REALES

13.5337 g., 0.9310 Silver 0.4051 oz. ASW **Ruler:** Philip III **Obv. Legend:** PHILLIPVS III DEI GRATIA **Note:** Struck at Mexico City Mint, mint mark Mo.

Date	Mintage	Good	VG	F	VF	XF
NDMo F Rare	—	—	—	—	—	—

KM# R41 4 REALES

13.5337 g., 0.9310 Silver 0.4051 oz. ASW **Ruler:** Philip IV

Date	Mintage	Good	VG	F	VF	XF
1631Mo D Rare	—	—	—	—	—	—
1639Mo P Rare	—	—	—	—	—	—
1643Mo P Rare	—	—	—	—	—	—
1647/6Mo P Rare	—	—	—	—	—	—
1654Mo P Rare	—	—	—	—	—	—

KM# R39 4 REALES

13.5337 g., 0.9310 Silver 0.4051 oz. ASW **Ruler:** Charles II **Obv. Legend:** CAROLVS II DEI G

Date	Mintage	Good	VG	F	VF	XF
1678Mo L Rare	—	—	—	—	—	—
1682Mo L Rare	—	—	—	—	—	—
1691/0Mo L Rare	—	—	—	—	—	—
1695Mo L Rare	—	—	—	—	—	—

KM# R44.3 8 REALES

27.0674 g., 0.9310 Silver 0.8102 oz. ASW **Ruler:** Philip III **Obv. Legend:** PHILIPVS III DEI G **Note:** Struck at Mexico City Mint, mint mark Mo.

Date	Mintage	Good	VG	F	VF	XF
1607Mo F Rare	—	—	—	—	—	—
1609Mo A Rare	—	—	—	—	—	—
1610Mo F Rare	—	—	—	—	—	—
1613Mo F Rare	—	—	—	—	—	—
1614Mo F Rare	—	—	—	—	—	—
1615Mo F Rare	—	—	—	—	—	—
1617Mo F Rare	—	—	—	—	—	—
1618Mo D/F Rare	—	—	—	—	—	—

KM# R45 8 REALES

27.0674 g., 0.9310 Silver 0.8102 oz. ASW **Ruler:** Philip IV **Obv. Legend:** PHILIPVS IIII DEI G **Note:** Struck at Mexico City Mint, mint mark Mo.

Date	Mintage	Good	VG	F	VF	XF
1621Mo D Rare	—	—	—	—	—	—
1629Mo D Rare	—	—	—	—	—	—
1632Mo D Rare	—	—	—	—	—	—
1636Mo D Rare	—	—	—	—	—	—
1639Mo P Rare	—	—	—	—	—	—
1642Mo P Rare	—	—	—	—	—	—
1646Mo P Rare	—	—	—	—	—	—
1650Mo P Rare	—	—	—	—	—	—
1667Mo P Rare	—	—	—	—	—	—

KM# R46 8 REALES

27.0674 g., 0.9310 Silver 0.8102 oz. ASW **Ruler:** Charles II **Obv. Legend:** CAROLVS II DEI G **Note:** Mint mark Mo.

Date	Mintage	Good	VG	F	VF	XF
1674Mo G Rare	—	—	—	—	—	—
1678Mo L Rare	—	—	—	—	—	—
1681/0Mo L Rare	—	—	—	—	—	—
1682Mo L Rare	—	—	—	—	—	—
1685Mo L Rare	—	—	—	—	—	—
1689/8Mo L Rare	—	—	—	—	—	—
1690Mo L Rare	—	—	—	—	—	—
1691/0Mo L Rare	—	—	—	—	—	—
1691Mo L Rare	—	—	—	—	—	—
1698Mo L Rare	—	—	—	—	—	—
1699Mo L Rare	—	—	—	—	—	—
1700Mo L Rare	—	—	—	—	—	—

KM# R56 8 ESCUDOS

27.0674 g., 0.9170 Gold 0.7980 oz. AGW **Ruler:** Charles II **Note:** Fully struck sample specimens referred to as "Royal" strikes are seldom encountered.

Date	Mintage	Good	VG	F	VF	XF
1695MXo L Rare	—	—	—	—	—	—
1698MXo L Rare	—	—	—	—	—	—

MONACO

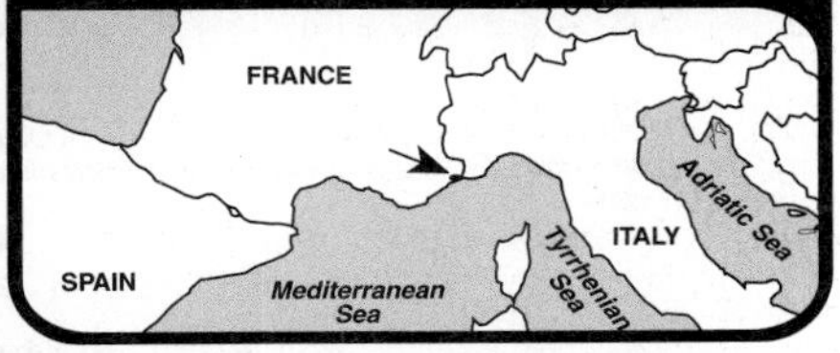

The Principality of Monaco, located on the Mediterranean coast nine miles from Nice, has an area of 0.58 sq. mi. (1.9 sq. km).

Monaco derives its name from Monoikos', the Greek surname for Hercules, the mythological strong man who, according to legend, formed the Monacan headland during one of his twelve labors. Monaco has been ruled by the Grimaldi dynasty since 1297 - Prince Rainier III, the present and 31st monarch of Monaco, is still of that line - except for a period during the French Revolution until Napoleon's downfall when the Principality was annexed to France. Since 1865, Monaco has maintained a customs union with France which guarantees its privileged position as long as the royal line remains intact. Under the new constitution proclaimed on December 17, 1962, the Prince shares his power with an 18-member unicameral National Council.

RULERS

Hercules I, 1589-1604
Honore II, 1604-1662
Louis I, 1662-1701

MINT PRIVY MARKS

(a) - Paris (privy marks only)
(ac) - Acorn, 1660-1664, 1670-1671
(b) - Bird on branch, 1678-1679
(bd) - Bird, diving, 1691
(bf) - Bird in flight, 1691-1693
(bh) - Bird, heraldic, 1683
(bs) - Bird, small, 1670-1674
C and clasped hands - Francois Cabinas, mint director, 1837-1838
(cl) - Cross, Latin, 1681
(cm) - Cross, Maltese, 1654; 1681
(d) - Daisy, stem, 1678-1679
(f) - Flower, 1673
(fb) - Flower buds, 1720
(ff) - Frame, oval with finger, 1683
(h) - Crowned H, 1701
(l) - Lily, stem, 1692-1693
(lr) - Lion, rampant, 1654-1659
(p) - Thunderbolt - Poissy
(q) - Quatrefoil, 1674-1675
(r) - Rosebud, 1648-1653
(s) - Star, 5-pointed, 1654
(sb) - Scale, balance, 1701
(sd) - Star of David, 1665-1669
(sf) - Shield with finger, 1682
(sr) - Sunface, radiant, 1681-1683
(t) - Thistle, 1672-1674

PRINCIPALITY

STANDARD COINAGE

KM# 2 2 PATACCHI (2 Patards)

Copper **Obv:** Bust of Honore II right in inner circle **Rev:** Crowned H in inner cirlce, date in legend

Date	Mintage	VG	F	VF	XF	Unc
1640	—	900	1,800	3,000	4,500	—

KM# 3 4 PATACCHI (4 Patards)

Copper **Obv:** Bust of Honore II right in inner circle **Rev:** Crowned H in inner circle, value in exergue, date in legend

Date	Mintage	VG	F	VF	XF	Unc
1640	—	250	400	750	1,400	—

KM# 52 DENIER TOURNOIS (1 Liard, 2 Deniers)

Copper **Obv:** Bust of Louis I right **Rev:** 5 groups of 3 diamonds

Date	Mintage	VG	F	VF	XF	Unc
1677 Rare	—	—	—	—	—	—

KM# 55 DENIER TOURNOIS (1 Liard, 2 Deniers)

Copper **Obv:** Louis I **Rev:** St. Devote standing, divides date

Date	Mintage	VG	F	VF	XF	Unc
1683	—	125	250	550	1,000	—

KM# 24 2 TOURNOIS

Copper **Obv:** Bust of Honore II right **Rev:** 3 diamonds in inner circle, date in legend

Date	Mintage	VG	F	VF	XF	Unc
1653 Rare	—	—	—	—	—	—

KM# 4 2 GROS

1.9000 g., Billon **Obv:** Bust of Honore II right in inner circle **Rev:** St. Devote standing, divides date

Date	Mintage	VG	F	VF	XF	Unc
1640	—	750	1,500	3,000	—	—

KM# 5 6 GROS (1/2 Florin)

3.1300 g., Billon **Obv:** Bust of Honore II right in inner circle, date in exergue **Rev:** Crowned arms in inner circle, value below in legend

Date	Mintage	VG	F	VF	XF	Unc
1640	—	900	1,800	3,750	—	—

KM# 6 12 GROS (Florin)

5.9900 g., Billon **Obv:** Bust of Honore II right in inner circle **Rev:** Crowned arms in order collar in inner circle

Date	Mintage	VG	F	VF	XF	Unc
1640	—	2,250	3,750	6,800	—	—

KM# 21 12 GROS (Florin)

5.9900 g., Billon **Obv:** Bust left

Date	Mintage	VG	F	VF	XF	Unc
1640	—	2,400	4,150	7,500	—	—

KM# 9 1-1/2 SOLS (1/2 Pezetta)

1.6500 g., Billon **Obv:** Crowned arms, titles of Honore II **Rev:** Maltese cross with diamonds in angles, date in legend

Date	Mintage	VG	F	VF	XF	Unc
1648	—	150	275	550	1,100	—

KM# 10 1-1/2 SOLS (1/2 Pezetta)

1.6500 g., Billon **Rev:** St. Devote standing, divides date

Date	Mintage	VG	F	VF	XF	Unc
1648	—	250	450	900	1,800	—

KM# 50 1-1/2 SOLS (1/2 Pezetta)

1.6500 g., Billon **Obv:** Titles of Louis I **Rev:** Maltese cross with diamonds in angles, date in legend

Date	Mintage	VG	F	VF	XF	Unc
1673 (f)	—	100	220	450	900	—
1683	—	100	220	450	900	—
1693 (bf)	—	125	250	500	1,000	—

KM# 11 3 SOLS (Pezetta)

4.5000 g., Billon **Obv:** Bust of Honore II right **Rev:** Crowned arms, date in legend

Date	Mintage	VG	F	VF	XF	Unc
1648	—	250	450	900	1,800	—

KM# 51 3 SOLS (Pezetta)

4.5000 g., Billon **Obv:** Louis I bust facing right **Rev:** Crowned arms

Date	Mintage	VG	F	VF	XF	Unc
1673 (t)	—	185	375	750	1,500	—
1683 (bh)	—	165	325	625	1,250	—

KM# 60.1 3 SOLS (Pezetta)

4.5000 g., Billon **Rev:** Cross with lozenges in angles

Date	Mintage	VG	F	VF	XF	Unc
1693 (bf//l)	—	250	450	900	1,650	—

KM# 8 5 SOLS (1/12 Ecu)

Obv: Small bust of Honore II right **Rev:** Crowned arms, date in legend at lower right

Date	Mintage	VG	F	VF	XF	Unc
1644	—	—	—	—	—	—

KM# 20 5 SOLS (1/12 Ecu)

2.2000 g., Silver **Obv:** Large bust of Honore II right **Obv. Legend:** HONORATVS II **Rev:** Crowned arms, date in legend at upper left

Date	Mintage	VG	F	VF	XF	Unc
1650 (r)	—	165	325	625	1,200	—
1651 (r)	—	165	325	625	1,200	—
1653 (r)	—	165	325	625	1,200	—

KM# 25 5 SOLS (1/12 Ecu)

2.2000 g., Silver **Obv. Legend:** HON. II

Date	Mintage	VG	F	VF	XF	Unc
1654 (s, lr)	—	150	275	550	1,000	—
1655 (lr)	—	150	275	550	1,000	—
1656 (lr)	—	150	275	550	1,000	—
1657 (lr)	—	125	225	500	950	—
1658 (lr)	—	125	225	500	950	—
16558 (lr)	—	750	1,500	3,000	—	—
16658 (lr)	—	750	1,500	3,000	—	—
1659 (lr)	—	125	225	500	950	—

KM# 35 5 SOLS (1/12 Ecu)

2.2000 g., Silver **Obv:** Draped bust of Honore II right **Rev. Legend:** DVX. VALENT.PAR $ FRANCIAE & C.

Date	Mintage	VG	F	VF	XF	Unc
1660 (ac)	—	125	225	475	950	—
1661 (ac)	—	125	225	475	950	—
1662 (ac)	—	125	225	475	950	—

KM# 36 5 SOLS (1/12 Ecu)

2.2000 g., Silver **Obv:** Young armored bust of Louis I right

Date	Mintage	VG	F	VF	XF	Unc
1662 (ac)	—	100	175	375	800	—
1663 (ac)	—	100	200	450	900	—
1664 (ac)	—	150	300	650	1,150	—

KM# 39 5 SOLS (1/12 Ecu)

2.2000 g., Silver **Obv:** Draped bust of Louis I left **Rev:** Crowned round arms with 5 vertical rows of diamonds, date in legend at left

Date	Mintage	VG	F	VF	XF	Unc
1665 (sd)	—	125	250	500	975	—

KM# 41.1 5 SOLS (1/12 Ecu)

2.2000 g., Silver **Obv:** Draped bust of Louis I **Rev:** Crowned straight-sided shield of arms with 7 vertical rows of diamonds

Date	Mintage	VG	F	VF	XF	Unc
1665 (sd)	—	90.00	185	375	800	—
1666 (sd)	—	125	275	550	1,100	—

KM# 40 5 SOLS (1/12 Ecu)

2.2000 g., Silver **Rev:** Round arms with 7 vertical rows of diamonds **Note:** Private traders produced debased 5 Sols dated 1667, 1668 and 1669 with obverse bust of Marie Louise of Dombes as well as Louis I and reverse similar to KM#40 for the Levantine trade.

Date	Mintage	VG	F	VF	XF	Unc
1665 (sd)	—	125	250	500	975	—
1666 (sd)	—	125	250	500	975	—

KM# 41.2 5 SOLS (1/12 Ecu)

2.2000 g., Silver **Obv:** Revised bust **Rev:** Crowned straight-sided shield of arms with 5 vertical rows of diamonds

Date	Mintage	VG	F	VF	XF	Unc
1674 (q)	—	200	375	750	1,400	—
1678 (d)	—	175	350	700	1,250	—

KM# 41.3 5 SOLS (1/12 Ecu)
2.2000 g., Silver

Date	Mintage	VG	F	VF	XF	Unc
1681 (cm//sr)	—	175	350	700	1,250	—

KM# 30 10 SOLS (1/6 Ecu)
4.3800 g., Silver **Obv:** Bust of Honore II right **Rev:** Crowned arms, date in legend at upper left

Date	Mintage	VG	F	VF	XF	Unc
1656 (lr)	—	450	350	1,350	2,650	—
1658 (lr)	—	400	600	1,250	2,400	—
1659 (lr)	—	400	600	1,250	2,400	—
1660 (ac)	—	400	600	1,250	2,400	—

KM# 7 1/4 ECU (15 Sols)
7.0000 g., Silver **Obv:** Bust of Honore II right **Rev:** Crowned arms in order chain

Date	Mintage	VG	F	VF	XF	Unc
1643	—	—	—	—	—	—

KM# 12 1/4 ECU (15 Sols)
7.0000 g., Silver **Obv:** Bust of Honore II right within legend **Obv. Legend:** HONORATVS... **Rev:** Crowned arms, date in legend at upper left

Date	Mintage	VG	F	VF	XF	Unc
1648 (r)	—	375	700	1,500	3,500	—
1649 (r)	—	375	700	1,500	3,500	—
1650 (r)	—	350	675	1,350	3,250	—
1651 (r)	—	350	675	1,350	3,250	—

KM# 18.1 1/4 ECU (15 Sols)
7.0000 g., Silver **Obv:** Legend begins at left **Obv. Legend:** HONO: II • D:G:...

Date	Mintage	VG	F	VF	XF	Unc
1652 (r)	—	350	675	1,350	3,250	—
1653 (r)	—	350	675	1,350	3,250	—

KM# 18.2 1/4 ECU (15 Sols)
7.0000 g., Silver **Obv. Legend:** HON • II • D:G...

Date	Mintage	VG	F	VF	XF	Unc
1654 (lr)	—	350	675	1,350	3,250	—
1655 (lr)	—	350	675	1,350	3,250	—
1656 (lr)	—	350	675	1,350	3,250	—
1657 (lr)	—	350	675	1,350	3,250	—
1658 (lr)	—	350	675	1,350	3,250	—
1660 (ac)	—	350	675	1,350	3,250	—
1661 (ac)	—	350	675	1,350	3,250	—

KM# 42.1 1/4 ECU (15 Sols)
7.0000 g., Silver **Obv:** Bust of Louis I right **Rev. Legend:** DVX.VALENT.PAR.FRANCIAE & C.

Date	Mintage	VG	F	VF	XF	Unc
1665 (sd)	—	185	375	750	1,850	—
1666 (sd)	—	200	425	875	2,150	—

KM# 42.2 1/4 ECU (15 Sols)
7.0000 g., Silver **Obv:** Divided by stars

Date	Mintage	VG	F	VF	XF	Unc
1671 (bs//ac)	—	225	450	900	2,250	—

KM# 42.3 1/4 ECU (15 Sols)
7.0000 g., Silver **Obv:** Divided by dots

Date	Mintage	VG	F	VF	XF	Unc
1673 (t)	—	250	500	1,000	2,500	—
1679 (d//b)	—	300	600	1,250	2,850	—
1683 (bh)	—	350	700	1,400	3,500	—

KM# 61 1/4 ECU (15 Sols)
7.0000 g., Silver **Rev:** Date **Rev. Legend:** AVXILIVM.MEVM.A.DOMINO

Date	Mintage	VG	F	VF	XF	Unc
1693 (bf//l)	—	500	1,000	2,000	4,250	—

KM# 13 1/2 ECU (30 Sols)
13.5500 g., Silver **Obv:** Honore II within legend **Rev:** HONORATVS • II • D • G...

Date	Mintage	VG	F	VF	XF	Unc
1648 (r)	—	375	750	1,600	3,500	—
1649 (r)	—	375	750	1,600	3,500	—
1650 (r//r)	—	375	750	1,600	3,500	—
1651 (r//r)	—	375	750	1,600	3,500	—
16648 (r)	—	375	750	1,600	3,500	—

KM# 22.1 1/2 ECU (30 Sols)
13.5500 g., Silver **Obv:** HONO:II:D:G...

Date	Mintage	VG	F	VF	XF	Unc
1652 (r)	—	350	675	1,350	3,350	—

KM# 22.2 1/2 ECU (30 Sols)
13.5500 g., Silver **Obv:** Modified portrait

Date	Mintage	VG	F	VF	XF	Unc
1653 (r)	—	350	675	1,350	3,350	—

KM# 26 1/2 ECU (30 Sols)
13.5500 g., Silver **Obv:** HON • II • D:G... **Note:** Varieties exist.

Date	Mintage	VG	F	VF	XF	Unc
1654 (cm)	—	375	750	1,600	3,500	—
1654 (lr)	—	375	750	1,600	3,500	—
1655 (lr)	—	375	750	1,600	3,500	—
1656 (lr)	—	425	800	1,650	4,000	—
1658 (lr)	—	425	800	1,650	4,000	—
1660 (ac)	—	450	850	1,750	4,500	—

KM# 43.1 1/2 ECU (30 Sols)
13.5500 g., Silver **Obv:** Louis I bust facing right

Date	Mintage	VG	F	VF	XF	Unc
1665 (sd)	—	200	400	800	2,150	—
1666 (sd)	—	175	350	700	2,100	—

KM# 43.2 1/2 ECU (30 Sols)
13.5500 g., Silver **Obv:** Legend divided by stars

Date	Mintage	VG	F	VF	XF	Unc
1674 (bs//t)	—	350	650	1,250	2,800	—

KM# 43.3 1/2 ECU (30 Sols)
13.5500 g., Silver **Obv:** Legend divided by dots with mint mark at upper left

Date	Mintage	VG	F	VF	XF	Unc
1681 (cl//sr)	—	400	750	1,350	3,350	—
1683 (ff//sr)	—	500	1,000	2,000	4,250	—

KM# 14.1 SCUDO (Ecu, 60 Sols)
27.0000 g., Silver **Obv:** Honore II within legend **Obv. Legend:** HONORATVS • II... **Note:** Dav. #4305.

Date	Mintage	VG	F	VF	XF	Unc
1648 (r//r)	—	1,300	2,700	4,950	11,500	—
1649 (r//r)	—	1,150	2,250	4,150	10,000	—
1650 (r//r)	—	1,050	2,050	3,700	9,000	—

KM# 14.2 SCUDO (Ecu, 60 Sols)
27.0000 g., Silver **Obv:** Larger modified bust **Note:** Dav. #A4305.

Date	Mintage	VG	F	VF	XF	Unc
1651 (r//r)	—	550	1,100	2,250	5,750	—

KM# 23 SCUDO (Ecu, 60 Sols)
27.0000 g., Silver **Obv:** Legend begins at left **Obv. Legend:** HONO: II... **Note:** Dav. #4306.

Date	Mintage	VG	F	VF	XF	Unc
1652 (r)	—	400	900	2,000	4,500	—
1653 (r)	—	350	800	1,850	4,000	—

KM# 32 SCUDO (Ecu, 60 Sols)
27.0000 g., Silver **Obv. Legend:** HON • II • D:G... **Note:** Dav. #4307. Varieties exist.

Date	Mintage	VG	F	VF	XF	Unc
1654 (lr)	—	400	850	1,950	4,250	—
1655 (lr)	—	450	950	2,100	4,750	—
1656 (lr)	—	600	1,150	2,500	5,500	—
1658 (lr)	—	1,000	2,000	4,150	8,500	—
1659 (lr)	—	800	1,600	3,300	6,750	—
1660 (ac)	—	900	1,750	3,600	7,250	—
1662 (ac)	—	925	1,850	3,850	7,850	—

KM# 31 SCUDO (Ecu, 60 Sols)
27.0000 g., Silver **Obv:** Honore II within legend **Obv. Legend:** HONORATVS • II... **Note:** Dav. #A4307.

Date	Mintage	VG	F	VF	XF	Unc
1654 (cm, lr)	—	650	1,250	2,500	6,250	—

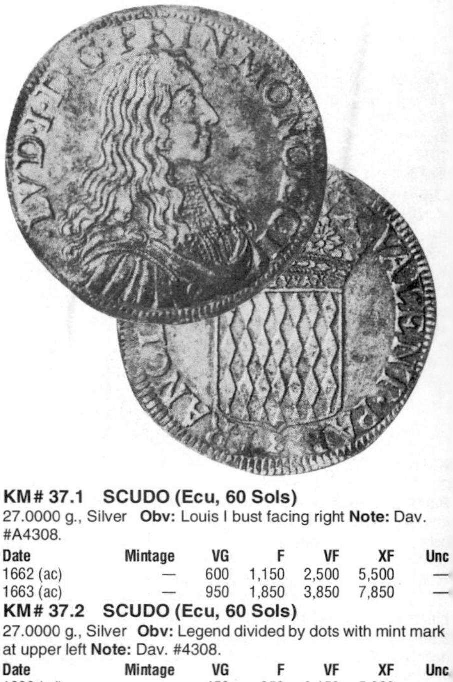

KM# 37.1 SCUDO (Ecu, 60 Sols)
27.0000 g., Silver **Obv:** Louis I bust facing right **Note:** Dav. #A4308.

Date	Mintage	VG	F	VF	XF	Unc
1662 (ac)	—	600	1,150	2,500	5,500	—
1663 (ac)	—	950	1,850	3,850	7,850	—

KM# 37.2 SCUDO (Ecu, 60 Sols)
27.0000 g., Silver **Obv:** Legend divided by dots with mint mark at upper left **Note:** Dav. #4308.

Date	Mintage	VG	F	VF	XF	Unc
1666 (sd)	—	450	950	2,150	5,000	—
1668 (sd)	—	450	950	2,150	5,000	—
1669 (sd)	—	450	950	2,150	5,000	—

KM# 37.3 SCUDO (Ecu, 60 Sols)

27.0000 g., Silver **Note:** Dav. #B4308.

Date	Mintage	VG	F	VF	XF	Unc
1670 (bs//ac)	—	600	1,150	2,500	5,500	—
1672 (bs//ac)	—	550	1,100	2,200	5,000	—
1673 (bs//t)	—	550	1,100	2,200	5,000	—
1674 (bs//t)	—	550	1,100	2,200	5,000	—
1674 (q, t)	—	550	1,100	2,200	5,000	—
1675 (q//t)	—	700	1,350	2,750	6,250	—

KM# 37.4 SCUDO (Ecu, 60 Sols)

27.0000 g., Silver **Obv:** Legend divided by dots with mint mark at upper left **Note:** Dav. #C4308.

Date	Mintage	VG	F	VF	XF	Unc
1678 (d//b)	—	600	1,150	2,500	5,500	—
1679 (d//b)	—	700	1,350	2,750	6,250	—

KM# 37.5 SCUDO (Ecu, 60 Sols)

27.0000 g., Silver **Obv:** Modified armor **Note:** Dav. #D4308.

Date	Mintage	VG	F	VF	XF	Unc
1681 (cl//sr)	—	750	1,400	2,850	6,500	—
1682 (sf//sr)	—	750	1,400	2,850	6,500	—

KM# 48 SCUDO (Ecu, 60 Sols)

27.0000 g., Silver **Rev. Legend:** AVXILIVM.MEVM... **Note:** Dav. #4309.

Date	Mintage	VG	F	VF	XF	Unc
1690	—	900	1,750	3,750	7,500	—
1691 (bf//bd)	—	1,000	2,000	4,250	8,500	—
1692 (bf//l)	—	1,000	2,000	4,250	8,500	—

KM# 27 TALLERO (28 Stuivers)

19.6100 g., Silver **Obv:** Crowned arms **Rev:** Crowned eagle with 28 in circle on breast

Date	Mintage	VG	F	VF	XF	Unc
ND	—	5,000	7,000	12,500	18,500	—

KM# 45 TALLERO (28 Stuivers)

26.1000 g., Silver **Obv:** Standing knight behind lion shield **Rev:** Rampant lion left holding shield with Grimaldi arms **Note:** Imitation of the Dutch Lion Thaler.

Date	Mintage	VG	F	VF	XF	Unc
1668 4 known	—	—	—	—	—	—

TRADE COINAGE

KM# 19 1/2 DOPPIA (1/2 Louis D'or)

3.5000 g., 0.9860 Gold 0.1109 oz. AGW **Obv:** Bust of Honore right **Rev:** Crowned H monograms in cruciform, lis in angles, date in legend

Date	Mintage	VG	F	VF	XF	Unc
1650 Rare	—	—	—	—	—	—

KM# 15 DOPPIA (Louis D' or)

7.0000 g., 0.9860 Gold 0.2219 oz. AGW **Obv:** Bust of Honore right **Rev:** Crowned H monograms in cruciform, lis in angles, date in legend

Date	Mintage	VG	F	VF	XF	Unc
1648	—	5,000	9,500	18,000	30,000	—
1649	—	5,000	9,500	18,000	30,000	—

KM# 28.1 DOPPIA (Louis D' or)

7.0000 g., 0.9860 Gold 0.2219 oz. AGW **Rev:** Crowned H in branches

Date	Mintage	VG	F	VF	XF	Unc
1654 (lr)	—	9,500	1,650	25,000	35,000	—
1656 (lr)	—	9,500	1,650	25,000	35,000	—
1657 (lr)	—	9,500	1,650	25,000	35,000	—

KM# 28.2 DOPPIA (Louis D' or)

7.0000 g., 0.9860 Gold 0.2219 oz. AGW **Rev:** Crowned H in branches

Date	Mintage	VG	F	VF	XF	Unc
1660 (ac)	—	9,500	16,500	25,000	35,000	—
1661 (ac)	—	9,500	16,500	25,000	35,000	—

KM# 16 2 DOPPIA (2 Louis D' or)

14.0000 g., 0.9860 Gold 0.4438 oz. AGW **Obv:** Honore II bust facing right

Date	Mintage	VG	F	VF	XF	Unc
1648	—	8,500	16,500	30,000	50,000	—
1649	—	8,500	16,500	30,000	50,000	—
1650	—	8,500	16,500	30,000	50,000	—

KM# 29 2 DOPPIA (2 Louis D' or)

14.0000 g., 0.9860 Gold 0.4438 oz. AGW **Obv:** Armored bust of Honore II right **Rev:** Crowned H in branches

Date	Mintage	VG	F	VF	XF	Unc
1656 (lr) Rare	—	—	—	—	—	—

KM# 38 2 DOPPIA (2 Louis D' or)

14.0000 g., 0.9860 Gold 0.4438 oz. AGW **Obv:** Louis I bust facing right

Date	Mintage	VG	F	VF	XF	Unc
1663 (ac) Rare	—	—	—	—	—	—
1664 (ac) Rare	—	—	—	—	—	—

KM# 17 5 DOPPIA (5 Louis D' or)

35.0000 g., 0.9860 Gold 1.1095 oz. AGW **Obv:** Honore II bust facing right

Date	Mintage	VG	F	VF	XF	Unc
1649 (r//r) Rare	—	—	—	—	—	—

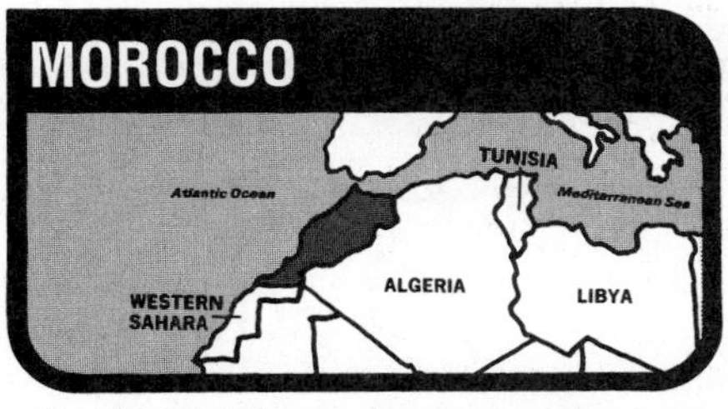

The Kingdom of Morocco, situated on the northwest corner of Africa, has an area of 275,117 sq. mi. (446,550 sq. km.).

Morocco's strategic position at the gateway to western Europe has been the principal determinant of its violent, frequently unfortunate history. Time and again the fertile plain between the rugged Atlas Mountains and the sea has echoed the battle's trumpet as Phoenicians, Romans, Vandals, Visigoths, Byzantine Greeks and Islamic Arabs successively conquered and occupied the land. Modern Morocco is a remnant of an early empire formed by the Arabs at the close of the 7th century which encompassed all of northwest Africa and most of the Iberian Peninsula. During the 17th and 18th centuries, while under the control of native dynasties, it was the headquarters of the famous Sale pirates. Morocco's strategic position involved it in the competition of 19th century European powers for political influence in Africa, and resulted in the division of Morocco into French and Spanish spheres of interest which were established as protectorates in 1912. Morocco became independent on March 2, 1956, after France agreed to end its protectorate. Spain signed similar agreements on April 7 of the same year.

TITLES

المعربية

Al-Maghribiya(t)

المملكة المغربية

Al-Mamlaka(t) al-Maghribiya(t)

المحمدية الشريفة

Al-Mohammediya(t) esh-Sherifiya(t)

RULERS

Sa'dians: Hasani Sharifs

Abu'l-'Abbas Ahmad, AH986-1012/1578-1603AD
Abu Faris 'Abd Allah al-Wathiq, AH1012-1017/1603-1608

The rival sons of Ahmad II

Abu Faris 'Abd Allah al-Wathiq (at Marrakesh), AH1012-1018/1603-1608AD
al-Nasir Zaydan, AH1012-1037/1603-1626AD
Mohammed al-Sheikh al-Ma'mun, AH1012-1022/1603-1612AD
Zaydan al-Nasir, AH1012-1037/1603-1627
Abu'l Mahally al-Mahdi, Userper, AH1021-1022/1612-1613AD
'Abd Allah al-Ghalib, AH1021-1033/1612-1624AD
'Abd al-Malik, al Mu'tasim, AH1033-1036/1623-1626AD
Abu'l-'Abbas Ahmad III, AH1037-1038/1627-1628AD
Abu Marwan 'Abd al-Malik II, AH1037-1040/1627-1629AD
al Walid, AH1040-1045/1629-1634AD
Mohammed al-Shaykh al-Saghir, AH1045-1064/1634-1654AD
Abu'l-'Abbas Ahmad IV, AH1064-1069/1654-1659AD
'Abd al-Karim, AH1069-?/1659-? AD

Filali (or 'Alawi) Sharifs

Mohammed I (at Tafilalt), AH1041-1045/1631-1635AD
Mohammed II, AH1045-1075/1635-1664AD
al-Rashid, AH1075-1082/1664-1672AD
Isma'il, AH1082-1139/1672-1727AD

EARLY COINAGE

Prior to the introduction of modern machine-struck coinage in Morocco in AH1299 (= 1882AD), a variety of primitive cast bronze coins and crudely hammered silver and gold were in circulation, together with considerable quantities of foreign coins.

The cast bronze were produced in several denominations, multiples of the basic unit, the Falus (Felous). The size of the coins is variable, and the distinction of the various denominations is not always clear, particularly on the issues of Sulaiman. The early types are varied, but beginning about AH1218, the reverse bears the seal of Solomon, and the obverse contains the date and/or mint. Several early varieties with the seal of Solomon on both sides exist. The date is inscribed in European numerals, the mint, when present, is written out in Arabic script. Many of the issues are quite barbarous, with illegible dates and mints, and occasionally light in weight. These barbarous issues may have been contemporary counterfeits, and are of little numismatic value. The bronze pieces were cast in "trees", and occasionally, entire or partial trees' are found on the market.

The silver and gold coins usually have the mintname on one side and the date on the other. The silver unit was the dirham of about 2.7 grams (but only about 2.0 grams from circa AH 1266-78), and the gold unit was the benduqi of about 3.25 grams. There were no fixed rates of exchange between coins of different metals.

Prices are for specimens with clearly legible dates and mintnames (if any). Illegible, barbarous, and defectively produced pieces are worth much less.

MINTS

فاس

Fs = Fes (Fas, Fez)

فاس حضره

FH = Fes Hazrat

الكتوه حضره

KH = al-Kitaoua Hazrat

مراكش

Mr = Marrakesh (Marakesh)

مكناس

Mk = Miknas (Meknes)

سجلماسة

Si = Sijilmasah

سوس

Sus

NOTE: Some of the above forms of the mintnames are shown as they appear on the coins, not in regular Arabic script.

The following coins are divided by reign. However, all of the coins are anonymous, and the distinction by reign is purely artificial. There is much variation within each type, and several of the subtypes overlap more than one reign. The coinage of Sulaiman II and Abd al-Rahman II are listed only by type (dates through AH1276 inclusive); those of Muhammad IV (beginning AH1277 inclusive) and those of Al Hasan I (Moulai Hasan) are broken down by mint and date. The date listings for these two rulers, however, are believed to be very incomplete.

KINGDOM

Sa'di Sharifs - Hasanid Dynasty

Abu'l-'Abbas Ahmad II

AH986-1012/1578-1603AD

HAMMERED COINAGE

Marrakesh

KM# 3 DINAR

Gold

Date	Mintage	VG	F	VF	XF	Unc
AH1010	—	325	550	900	1,400	—
AH1011	—	325	550	900	1,400	—
AH1012	—	325	550	900	1,400	—

Abu Faris 'Abd Allah al-Wathiq

Rival at Marakesh

HAMMERED COINAGE

Marrakesh

KM# 7 DINAR

Gold **Note:** 3.80-4.40 grams.

Date	Mintage	VG	F	VF	XF	Unc
AH1012	—	275	450	750	1,150	—
AH1013	—	275	450	750	1,150	—
AH1014	—	325	550	900	1,400	—
AH1015	—	325	550	900	1,400	—

Marrakesh

KM# 9 2 DINAR

Gold

Date	Mintage	VG	F	VF	XF	Unc
AH1013	—	350	600	950	1,500	—

Muhammed al-Shaykh al-Ma'mun, rival

AH1012-22/1603-12AD

HAMMERED COINAGE

Fes

KM# 10 DINAR

Gold **Note:** 3.80-4.40 grams.

Date	Mintage	VG	F	VF	XF	Unc
AH1012	—	225	350	600	850	—
AH1013	—	225	350	600	850	—

Marrakesh

KM# 11 DINAR

Gold

Date	Mintage	VG	F	VF	XF	Unc
AH1015	—	250	400	725	950	—

Zaydan al-Nasir

AH1012-37/1603-26AD

HAMMERED COINAGE

Marrakesh

KM# A13 FALUS

Copper **Obv. Legend:** Zaydan al-Nasir

Date	Mintage	VG	F	VF	XF	Unc
AH1034	—	15.00	30.00	50.00	—	—

KM# 12 DIRHAM

1.4500 g., Silver

Date	Mintage	VG	F	VF	XF	Unc
AH1015	—	30.00	75.00	125	—	—

Marrakesh

KM# 14 ECU

26.0000 g., Silver

Date	Mintage	VG	F	VF	XF	Unc
AH1016 Rare	—	—	—	—	—	—

KM# 13 DINAR

Gold **Note:** 3.80-4.40 grams.

Date	Mintage	VG	F	VF	XF	Unc
AH1016	—	200	300	475	725	—
AH1017	—	200	300	475	725	—
AH1018	—	200	300	475	725	—
AH1019	—	200	300	475	725	—
AH1020	—	200	300	475	725	—
AH1021	—	200	300	475	725	—
AH1022	—	200	300	475	725	—
AH1023	—	200	300	475	725	—
AH1024	—	200	300	475	725	—
AH1025	—	200	300	475	725	—
AH1026	—	200	300	475	725	—
AH1027	—	200	300	475	725	—
AH1028	—	200	300	475	725	—
AH1029	—	200	300	475	725	—
AH1030	—	200	300	475	725	—
AH1031	—	200	300	475	725	—

Fes

KM# B13 DINAR

Gold **Note:** 3.80-4.40 grams.

Date	Mintage	VG	F	VF	XF	Unc
AH1015	—	220	325	550	775	—

Marrakesh

KM# A15 DINAR

Gold **Obv:** Central legend in quadralobes **Rev:** Central legend in quadralobes **Note:** 3.80-4.40 grams.

Date	Mintage	VG	F	VF	XF	Unc
AH1015	—	125	150	300	475	—
AH1016	—	200	300	475	725	—
AH1017	—	200	300	475	725	—

KM# B15 DINAR

Gold **Obv:** Central legend in inner circles **Rev:** Central legend in inner circles **Note:** 3.80-4.40 grams.

Date	Mintage	VG	F	VF	XF	Unc
AH1018	—	125	150	300	475	—

KM# 15 DINAR

Gold **Note:** 3.80-4.40 grams.

Date	Mintage	VG	F	VF	XF	Unc
AH1019	—	200	300	475	725	—
AH1020	—	200	300	475	725	—
AH1021	—	200	300	475	725	—
AH1022	—	200	300	475	725	—
AH1023	—	200	300	475	725	—
AH1024	—	200	300	475	725	—
AH1025	—	200	300	475	725	—
AH1026	—	200	300	475	725	—
AH1027	—	200	300	475	725	—
AH1028	—	200	300	475	725	—
AH1029	—	200	300	475	725	—

Date	Mintage	VG	F	VF	XF	Unc
AH1030	—	200	300	475	725	—
AH1031	—	200	300	475	725	—

Sijilmasah

KM# 16 DINAR
Gold **Note:** 3.80-4.40 grams.

Date	Mintage	VG	F	VF	XF	Unc
AH1023	—	200	300	475	725	—
AH1024	—	200	300	475	725	—
AH1026	—	200	300	475	725	—
AH1027	—	200	300	475	725	—
AH1028	—	200	300	475	725	—
AH1029	—	200	300	475	725	—
AH1030	—	200	300	475	725	—
AH1031	—	200	300	475	725	—
AH1032	—	200	300	475	725	—
AH1033	—	200	300	475	725	—
AH1034	—	200	300	475	725	—

Sus

KM# 17 DINAR
Gold **Note:** 3.80-4.40 grams.

Date	Mintage	VG	F	VF	XF	Unc
AH1012	—	225	350	600	900	—

Abu' Mahally al-Mahdi, Usurper
AH1021-22/1612-13AD

HAMMERED COINAGE

KM# 18 DINAR
Gold **Note:** 3.40-4.40 grams.

Date	Mintage	VG	F	VF	XF	Unc
AH1021	—	225	350	600	850	—

Marrakesh

KM# 19 DINAR
Gold, 16.5 mm. **Note:** 3.40-4.40 grams.

Date	Mintage	VG	F	VF	XF	Unc
AH1021	—	225	350	600	850	—

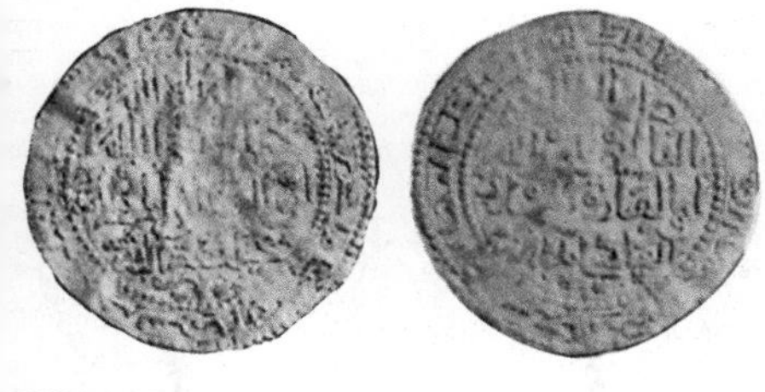

Sijilmasah

KM# A20 DINAR
Gold **Note:** 3.40-4.40 grams.

Date	Mintage	VG	F	VF	XF	Unc
AH1021	—	225	350	600	850	—

'Abd Allah al-Ghalib, in Fes
AH1021-33/1612-24AD

HAMMERED COINAGE

KM# B20 DIRHAM
Silver

Date	Mintage	VG	F	VF	XF	Unc
ND	—	25.00	60.00	100	—	—

Fes

KM# 20 DINAR
Gold **Note:** 3.40-4.40 grams.

Date	Mintage	VG	F	VF	XF	Unc
AH1021	—	225	350	600	850	—
AH1022	—	225	350	600	850	—

'Abd al-Malik, al-Mu'tasim, in Fes
AH1033-36/1623-26AD

HAMMERED COINAGE

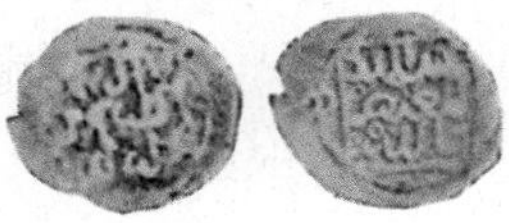

KM# 21 DIRHAM
Silver

Date	Mintage	VG	F	VF	XF	Unc
ND	—	25.00	60.00	100	—	—

Abu Marwan 'Abd al-Malik II
AH1037-40/1626-29AD

HAMMERED COINAGE

KM# A22 DIRHAM
Silver

Date	Mintage	VG	F	VF	XF	Unc
ND	—	25.00	60.00	100	—	—

Marrakesh

KM# 22 DINAR
Gold **Note:** Crescent with 2 palm trees. 3.80-4.40 grams.

Date	Mintage	VG	F	VF	XF	Unc
AH1037	—	285	425	725	1,000	—
AH1038	—	285	425	725	1,000	—
AH1039	—	285	425	725	1,000	—

Abu'l-'Abbas Ahmad III
AH1037-38/1627-28AD

HAMMERED COINAGE

Fes

KM# A21 DIRHAM
Silver **Obv. Legend:** "al-Sultan Ahmad..."

Date	Mintage	VG	F	VF	XF	Unc
ND	—	40.00	75.00	150	—	—

al-Walid
AH1040-45/1630-36AD

HAMMERED COINAGE

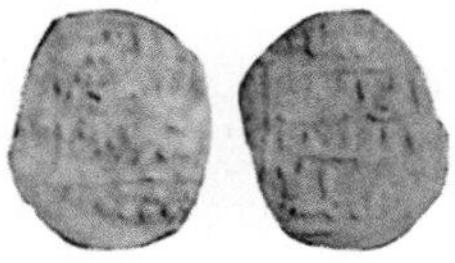

KM# 23 DIRHAM
Silver

Date	Mintage	VG	F	VF	XF	Unc
ND	—	20.00	50.00	90.00	—	—

Marrakesh

KM# 24 DINAR
Gold **Note:** 3.80-4.40 grams.

Date	Mintage	VG	F	VF	XF	Unc
AH1040	—	225	350	600	850	—
AH1041	—	225	350	600	850	—
AH1042	—	225	350	600	850	—

Muhammed al-Sheikh al-Saghir
AH1045-64/1636-54AD

HAMMERED COINAGE

Marrakesh

KM# 26 DINAR
Gold **Note:** 3.80-4.40 grams.

Date	Mintage	VG	F	VF	XF	Unc
AH1045	—	225	350	600	850	—
AH1046	—	225	350	600	850	—
AH1047	—	225	350	600	850	—
AH1048	—	225	350	600	850	—
AH1049	—	225	350	600	850	—
AH1050	—	225	350	600	850	—
AH1051	—	225	350	600	850	—
AH1052	—	225	350	600	850	—
AH1053	—	225	350	600	850	—
AH1054	—	225	350	600	850	—
AH1055	—	225	350	600	850	—
AH1056	—	225	350	600	850	—
AH1057	—	225	350	600	850	—
AH1058	—	225	350	600	850	—
AH1059	—	225	350	600	850	—
AH1060	—	225	350	600	850	—
AH1061	—	225	350	600	850	—
AH1062	—	225	350	600	850	—
AH1063	—	225	350	600	850	—
AH1064	—	225	350	600	850	—

'Abd al-Karim
AH1069+

HAMMERED COINAGE

Marrakesh

KM# 26A DIRHAM
Silver

Date	Mintage	VG	F	VF	XF	Unc
ND	—	25.00	40.00	55.00	75.00	—

KINGDOM
Filali Sharifs - Alawi Dynasty

al-Rashid
AH1075-82/1664-72AD

HAMMERED COINAGE

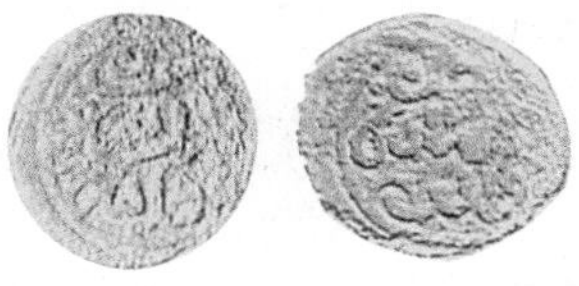

Fes

KM# A27.2 FALUS
3.9700 g., Bronze **Note:** Anonymous issues.

Date	Mintage	Good	VG	F	VF	XF
AH1081	—	20.00	40.00	80.00	—	—
AH1082	—	40.00	80.00	150	—	—

Sijilmasah

KM# A27.1 FALUS
3.9700 g., Bronze **Note:** Anonymous issues.

Date	Mintage	Good	VG	F	VF	XF
AH1081	—	40.00	80.00	150	—	—
AH1082 Rare	—	—	—	—	—	—

Fes Hazrat

KM# 27.1 MUZUNA
1.1700 g., Silver **Note:** Issues with name of ruler.

Date	Mintage	Good	VG	F	VF	XF
AH1079	—	8.00	15.00	30.00	60.00	—
AH1080	—	8.00	15.00	30.00	60.00	—
AH1081	—	25.00	45.00	70.00	120	—
AH1082	—	25.00	45.00	70.00	120	—

Marakesh Hazrat

KM# 27.2 MUZUNA

1.1700 g., Silver **Note:** Issues with name of ruler.

Date	Mintage	Good	VG	F	VF	XF
AH1082	—	8.00	15.00	30.00	60.00	—
AH1083	—	40.00	70.00	120	180	—

Rabat al-Fath

KM# 27.3 MUZUNA

1.1700 g., Silver **Note:** Issues with name of ruler.

Date	Mintage	Good	VG	F	VF	XF
AH1080	—	20.00	40.00	60.00	100	—
AH1081	—	20.00	40.00	60.00	100	—
AH1082	—	20.00	40.00	60.00	100	—

Sijilmasah

KM# 27.4 MUZUNA

1.1700 g., Silver **Note:** Issues with name of ruler.

Date	Mintage	Good	VG	F	VF	XF
AH1079	—	25.00	45.00	70.00	120	—
AH1080	—	8.00	15.00	30.00	60.00	—
AH1081	—	25.00	45.00	70.00	120	—
AH1082	—	40.00	70.00	120	180	—

Isma'il

AH1082-1139/1672-1727AD

HAMMERED COINAGE

Fes

KM# A28.2 FALUS

3.9700 g., Bronze, 18-24 mm. **Note:** Anonymous issue.

Date	Mintage	Good	VG	F	VF	XF
AHxxxx Illegible date	—	20.00	40.00	80.00	—	—
AH1088	—	25.00	50.00	100	—	—
AH1094 Rare	—	—	—	—	—	—
AH1103	—	25.00	50.00	100	—	—

Illegible Mintname

KM# 28 FALUS

3.9700 g., Copper, 18-24 mm. **Note:** Anonymous issue. Most Falus of Isma'il show Obv. and Rev. ornaments composed of interlacing lines in a circle or square with inscriptions around; some issues have octagonal or hexagonal designs besides inscriptions.

Date	Mintage	Good	VG	F	VF	XF
AHxxxx Illegible date	—	20.00	40.00	80.00	—	—

Marrakesh

KM# A28.3 FALUS

3.9700 g., Bronze, 18-24 mm. **Note:** Anonymous issue.

Date	Mintage	Good	VG	F	VF	XF
AHxxxx Illegible date	—	20.00	40.00	80.00	—	—
AH1101	—	30.00	60.00	120	—	—

Meknes Hazrat

KM# A28.4 FALUS

3.9700 g., Bronze, 18-24 mm. **Note:** Anonymous issue.

Date	Mintage	Good	VG	F	VF	XF
AHxxxx Illegible date	—	20.00	40.00	80.00	—	—

Rabat al-Fath

KM# A28.5 FALUS

3.9700 g., Bronze, 18-24 mm. **Note:** Anonymous issues.

Date	Mintage	Good	VG	F	VF	XF
AHxxxx Illegible date	—	20.00	40.00	80.00	—	—
AH1102	—	25.00	50.00	100	—	—
AH1103	—	25.00	50.00	100	—	—

Tetuan

KM# A28.6 FALUS

3.9700 g., Bronze, 18-24 mm. **Note:** Anonymous issues

Date	Mintage	Good	VG	F	VF	XF
AH108X Rare	—	—	—	—	—	—

Fes Hazrat

KM# B28.1 MUZUNA

0.9400 g., Silver **Note:** Anonymous issue.

Date	Mintage	Good	VG	F	VF	XF
AH1083	—	10.00	20.00	40.00	80.00	—
AH1084	—	8.00	15.00	30.00	60.00	—
AH1085	—	5.00	10.00	20.00	40.00	—
AH1086 Rare	—	—	—	—	—	—
AH1087	—	12.00	25.00	50.00	100	—
AH1088	—	8.00	15.00	30.00	60.00	—
AH1089	—	5.00	10.00	20.00	40.00	—
AH1090	—	8.00	15.00	30.00	60.00	—
AH1091	—	8.00	15.00	30.00	60.00	—
AH1092	—	8.00	15.00	30.00	60.00	—
AH1093	—	12.00	25.00	50.00	100	—
AH1094	—	5.00	10.00	20.00	40.00	—
AH1095	—	8.00	15.00	30.00	60.00	—
AH1096 Rare	—	—	—	—	—	—
AH1097 Rare	—	—	—	—	—	—
AH1099 Rare	—	—	—	—	—	—
AH1100 Rare	—	—	—	—	—	—
AH1101	—	8.00	15.00	30.00	60.00	—
AH1102 Rare	—	—	—	—	—	—
AH1103 Rare	—	—	—	—	—	—
AH1105	—	10.00	20.00	40.00	75.00	—
AH1106 Rare	—	—	—	—	—	—
AH1107 Rare	—	—	—	—	—	—
AH1110 Rare	—	—	—	—	—	—

Marakesh Hazrat

KM# B28.4 MUZUNA

0.9400 g., Silver **Note:** Anonymous issues.

Date	Mintage	Good	VG	F	VF	XF
AH1085	—	5.00	10.00	20.00	40.00	—
AH1086 Rare	—	—	—	—	—	—
AH1100 Rare	—	—	—	—	—	—
AH1101 Rare	—	—	—	—	—	—
AH1104 Rare	—	—	—	—	—	—

Marrakesh

KM# B28.3 MUZUNA

0.9400 g., Silver **Note:** Anonymous issues.

Date	Mintage	Good	VG	F	VF	XF
AH1088	—	5.00	10.00	20.00	40.00	—
AH1089	—	10.00	20.00	40.00	80.00	—
AH1090	—	10.00	20.00	40.00	80.00	—
AH1092	—	12.00	25.00	50.00	100	—

Meknes Hazrat

KM# B28.5 MUZUNA

0.9400 g., Silver **Note:** Anonymous issues.

Date	Mintage	Good	VG	F	VF	XF
AH1111 Rare	—	—	—	—	—	—

Rabat al-Fath

KM# B28.2 MUZUNA

0.9400 g., Silver **Note:** Anonymous issue.

Date	Mintage	Good	VG	F	VF	XF
AH1083 Rare	—	—	—	—	—	—
AH1084	—	8.00	15.00	30.00	60.00	—
AH1085	—	5.00	10.00	20.00	40.00	—
AH1086 Rare	—	—	—	—	—	—
AH1087	—	12.00	25.00	50.00	100	—
AH1088	—	8.00	15.00	30.00	60.00	—
AH1089	—	8.00	15.00	30.00	60.00	—
AH1090	—	5.00	10.00	20.00	40.00	—
AH1091	—	8.00	15.00	30.00	60.00	—
AH1092	—	12.00	25.00	50.00	100	—
AH1094	—	8.00	15.00	30.00	60.00	—
AH1105 Rare	—	—	—	—	—	—
AH1106 Rare	—	—	—	—	—	—
AH1107 Rare	—	—	—	—	—	—
AH1108 Rare	—	—	—	—	—	—
AH1111 Rare	—	—	—	—	—	—
AH1112 Rare	—	—	—	—	—	—

Sijilmasah

KM# B28.6 MUZUNA

0.9400 g., Silver **Note:** Anonymous issue.

Date	Mintage	Good	VG	F	VF	XF
AH1085	—	15.00	30.00	60.00	120	—
AH1088	—	15.00	30.00	60.00	120	—
AH1089	—	15.00	30.00	60.00	120	—
AH1090 Rare	—	—	—	—	—	—
AH1093	—	15.00	30.00	60.00	120	—
AH1094 Rare	—	—	—	—	—	—

KM# 28.3 DINAR

3.5200 g., Gold **Note:** Illegible mintname. Anonymous issues.

Date	Mintage	VG	F	VF	XF	Unc
AH1111	—	200	240	425	600	—
AH1112	—	200	240	425	600	—

Fes Hazrat

KM# 28.1 DINAR

3.5200 g., Gold **Note:** Anonymous issues.

Date	Mintage	VG	F	VF	XF	Unc
AH1089	—	200	240	425	600	—
AH1090	—	200	240	425	600	—
AH1091	—	200	240	425	600	—
AH1092	—	200	240	425	600	—
AH1093	—	200	240	425	600	—
AH1094	—	200	240	425	600	—
AH1095 Rare	—	—	—	—	—	—
AH1096	—	200	240	425	600	—
AH1097 Rare	—	—	—	—	—	—
AH1098 Rare	—	—	—	—	—	—
AH1099	—	200	240	425	600	—
AH1101 Rare	—	—	—	—	—	—
AH1108 Rare	—	—	—	—	—	—
AH1109	—	200	240	425	600	—
AH1111	—	200	240	425	600	—

Meknes Hazrat

KM# 28.2 DINAR

3.5200 g., Gold **Note:** Anonymous issues.

Date	Mintage	VG	F	VF	XF	Unc
AH1095 Rare	—	—	—	—	—	—
AH1096 Rare	—	—	—	—	—	—
AH1104 Rare	—	—	—	—	—	—
AH1106 Rare	—	—	—	—	—	—

NEPAL

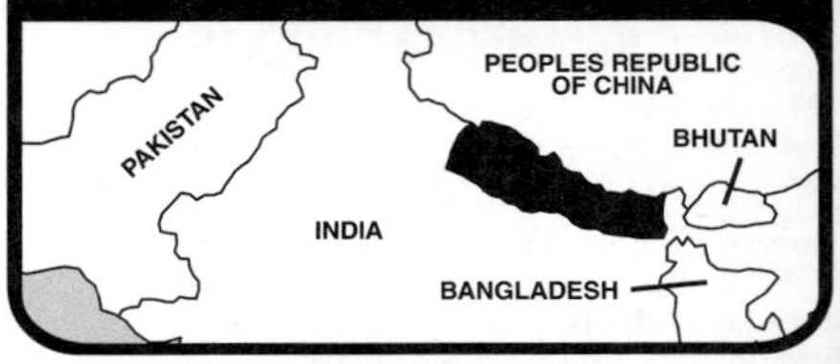

The Kingdom of Nepal, the world's only surviving Hindu kingdom, is a landlocked country occupying the southern slopes of the Himalayas. It has an area of 56,136 sq. mi. (140,800 sq. km.).

Apart from a brief Muslim invasion in the 14th century, Nepal was able to avoid the mainstream of Northern Indian politics, due to its impregnable position in the mountains. It is therefore a unique survivor of the medieval Hindu and Buddhist culture of Northern India which was largely destroyed by the successive waves of Muslim invasions.

Prior to the late 18th century, Nepal, as we know it today, was divided among a number of small states. Unless otherwise stated the term *Nepal* applies to the small fertile valley, about 4,500 ft above sea level, in which the three main cities of Kathmandu, Patan and Bhatgaon are situated.

During the reign of King Yaksha Malla (1428-1482AD), the Nepalese kingdom, with capital at Bhatgaon, was extended northwards into Tibet, and also controlled a considerable area to the south of the hills. After Yaksha Malla's death, the Kingdom was divided among his sons, so four kingdoms were established with capitals at Bhatgaon, Patan, Kathmandu and Banepa, all situated within the small valley, less than 20 miles square. Banepa was quickly absorbed within the territory of Bhatgaon, but the other three kingdoms remained until 1769. The internecine strife between the three kings effectively stopped Nepal from becoming a major military force during this period, although with its fertile land and strategic position, it was by far the wealthiest and most powerful of the Himalayan states.

Apart from agriculture, Nepal owed its prosperity to its position on one of the easiest trade routes between the great monasteries of central Tibet, and India. Nepal made full use of this, and a trading community was set up in Lhasa during the 16th century, and Nepalese coins became the accepted currency medium in Tibet.

The seeds of discord between Nepal and Tibet were sown during the first half of the 18th century, when the Nepalese debased the coinage, and the fate of the Malla kings of Nepal was sealed when Prithvi Narayan Shah, King of the small state of Gorkha, to the west of Kathmandu, was able to gain control of the trans-himalayan trade routes during the years after 1750.

Prithvi Narayan spent several years consolidating his position in hill areas before he finally succeeded in conquering the Kathmandu Valley in 1768, where he established the Shah dynasty, and moved his capital to Kathmandu.

After Prithvi Narayan's death a period of political instability ensued which lasted until the 1840's when the Rana family reduced the monarch to a figurehead and established the post of hereditary Prime Minister. A popular revolution in 1950 toppled the Rana family and reconstituted power in the throne. In 1959 King Mahendra declared Nepal a constitutional monarchy, and in 1962 a new constitution set up a system of *panchayat* (village council) democracy. In 1990, following political unrest, the king's powers were reduced. The country then adopted a system of parliamentary democracy.

DATING

Nepal Samvat Era (NS)

All coins of the Malla kings of Nepal are dated in the Nepal Samvat era (NS). Year 1 NS began in 881, so to arrive at the AD date add 880 to the NS date. This era was exclusive to Nepal, except for one gold coin of Prana Narayan of Cooch Behar.

Saka Era (SE)

Up until 1888AD all coins of the Gorkha Dynasty were dated in the Saka era (SE). To convert from Saka to AD take Saka date and add 78 to arrive at the AD date. Coins dated with this era have SE before the date in the following listing.

RULERS

KINGS OF KATHMANDU

Shiva Simha, शिवसिंह
NSc.698-740/c.1578-1620AD

Lakshmi Narasimha, लक्ष्मी नरसिंह
NS740-761/1620-1641AD

Pratap Malla, प्रताप मल्ल
NS761-794/1641-1674AD

Chakravartendra Malla, चक्रवर्तेन्द्र मल्ल
NS789/1669AD

Mahipatendra Malla, महीप तेन्द्र मल्ल
NS790/1670AD

Nripendra Malla, नृपेन्द्र मल्ल
NS794-800/1674-1680AD

Parthivendra Malla, पार्थिवेन्द्र मल्ल
NS800-807/1680-1687AD

Bhupalendra Malla, भूपालेन्द्र मल्ल
NS807-820/1687-1700AD

KINGS OF PATAN

Harihara Simha हरि हरसिंह
NSc.720-729/c.1600-1609AD

Shiva Simha, King of Kathmandu शिवसिंह
NSc.729-740/c.1609-1620AD

Siddhi Narasimha सिद्धि नरसिंह
NS740-781/1620-1661AD

Srinivasa Malla श्रीनिवास मल्ल
NS781-805/1661-1685AD

Yoga Narendra Malla, योग नरेन्द्र मल्ल
NS805-825/1685-1705AD

KINGS OF BHATGAON

Trailokya Malla and Tribhuvana Malla, joint rulers, त्रैलोक्य मल्ल
NSc.680-733/c.1560-1613AD

Jagajjotir Malla, जगज्ज्योति मल्ल
NS733-757/1613-1637AD

Naresha Malla, नरेश मल्ल
NS757-764/1637-1644AD

Jagatprakash Malla, जगत्प्रकाश मल्ल
NS764-793/1644-1673AD

Jitamitra Malla, जि तामित्र मल्ल
NS783-816/1663-1696AD

Bhupatindra Malla, भूपतीन्द्र मल्ल
NS816-842/1696-1722AD

MONETARY SYSTEM

Tanka Series, c.1560-1639AD

The main Nepalese silver coinage began soon after 1560AD with fine silver coins, struck to a tanka standard of about 10.6 g. Although the first coins were purely Hindu in design, the later issues of tankas were copied from Muslim prototypes, and although Hindu elements were included in the design, the bulk of the field was taken up by debased Arabic legends. This may have been to make the coins acceptable amongst a population used to a currency of Muslim tankas.

While some of the tankas were struck in the names of specific kings, most were anonymous, and it is not known which of the kingdoms of the Nepal Valley was responsible for their issue. However, with Kathmandu dominant at this period, (Shiva Simha being king of both Kathmandu and Patan between at least 1609 and 1620AD) it may be assumed that most of them were struck in Kathmandu.

During the early 17th century many of the tankas struck were in very debased silver. This may have been due to the fact that Ram Shah of Gorkha cut the Valley off from the Tibetan trade during part of this period.

Apart from the coin of Mahendra Malla, the tankas fall into two distinct groups, one may be called the *'Ala-ud-din* type, which has an inscription copied from the tankas of Ala-ud-din Khilji, the Sultan of Delhi, 1295-1315AD, although the inscription reads clock-wise around the coin, quite unlike the prototype. The second main type may be called the *Ghiyas-ud-din* type, as it is copied from coins of the Bengal Sultan Ghiyas-ud-din Mahmud Shah III, 1526-1532AD, although the design is inverted.

The minor denominations of this period present a problem, as surviving specimens do not readily indicate what fraction they represent of the tanka. There are many small pieces with weights ranging from about 0.04 g to 0.14 g but varying very little, if at all, in diameter. If different denominations were intended, they would have been impossible to distinguish in circulation, so they have all been included in this listing under the general term "Dam", which should be a 1/128th part of a tanka, or about 0.08 g.

After 1639AD the tanka coins seem to have been withdrawn from circulation, which probably accounts for their rarity.

Mohar Series

In about 1640 the weight standard of the Nepalese coinage was completely changed, and it is probable that all the old tanka coins were withdrawn from circulation.

The new standard coin was the Mohar, weighing about 5.4 g, or rather more than half the old tanka. The Mohar was subdivided in factors of 2, as follows:

2 Mohar (Rupee) = 10.80 g
1 Mohar = 5.40 g
1/2 Mohar = 2.70 g
1/4 Mohar (Suki) = 1.35 g
1/8 Mohar = 0.67 g
1/16 Mohar = 0.34 g
1/32 Mohar = 0.17 g
1/128 Mohar (Dam) = 0.04-0.08 g
1/512 Mohar (Jawa) = 0.01 g

The weights given above correspond to the average weight of actual specimens, rather than the theoretical weight, which has been said to be 86.4 grains, or 5.60 g.

The coinage was almost entirely of silver, with the tiny Jawa being easily the smallest coin in the world. Gold coins were struck on only one or two occasions during the Madras period, from the same dies as the silver coins, but these were probably only used for ceremonial purposes. Gold after 1777AD was struck in greater quantity.

Initially the coinage was of fine silver, in contrast to the tanka coins, which were frequently debased. During the early 18th century, however, the coins became debased, but the fineness was improved after 1753AD. The coinage was again debased in the first half of the 19th century.

Many of the mohars circulated in Tibet as well as in Nepal, and on a number of occasions coins were struck from bullion supplied by the Tibetan authorities. The smaller denominations never circulated in Tibet, but some of the mohars were cut for use as small change in Tibet.

In these listings only major changes in design have been noted. There are numerous minor varieties of ornamentation or spelling.

4 Dam = 1 Paisa
2 Paisa = 1 Dyak, Adhani

NUMERALS

Nepal has used more variations of numerals on their coins than any other nation. The most common are illustrated in the numeral chart in the introduction. The chart below illustrates some variations encompassing the last four centuries.

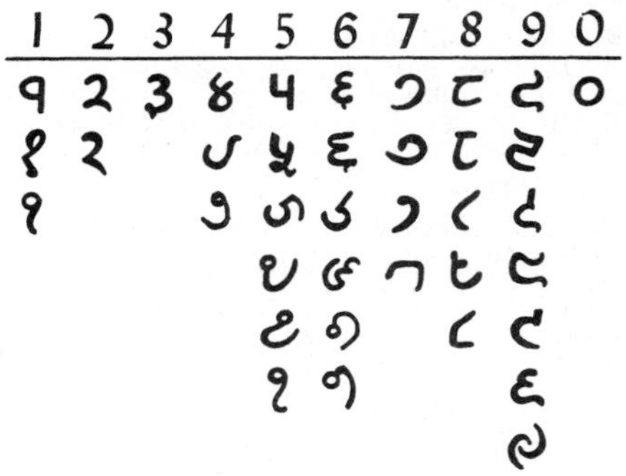

NUMERICS

Half	आधा
One	एक
Two	दुइ
Four	चार
Five	पाच
Ten	दसा
Twenty	विसा
Twenty-five	पचीसा
Fifty	पचासा
Hundred	सय

DENOMINATIONS

Paisa	पैसा
Dam	दाम
Mohar	मोहर
Rupee	रुपैयाँ
Ashrapi	असार्फी
Asarfi	अश्रफी

OBVERSE

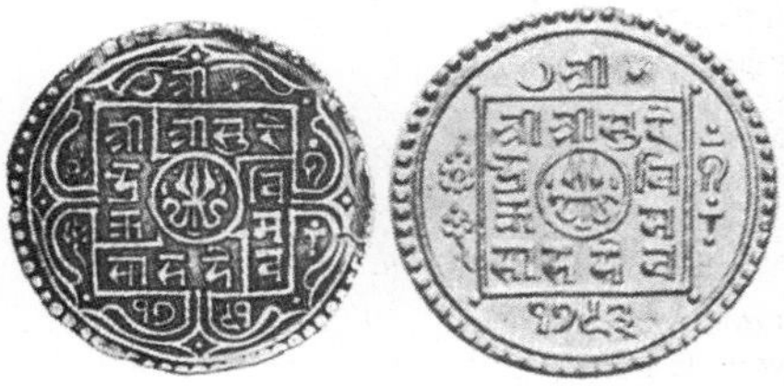

SILVER SE1791 — GOLD SE1793

LEGEND

श्री श्रीश्री सुरेन्द्र विक्रम साहदेव

Shri Shri Shri Surendra Vikrama Saha Deva (date)

REVERSE

SILVER GOLD

LEGEND
(in center)

श्री ३ भवानी

Shri 3 Bhavani
(around outer circle)

श्री श्री श्री गोरषनाथ

Shri Shri Shri Gorakhanatha

KINGDOM OF BHATGAON

KINGDOM

Jagajjotir Malla

NS733-757 / 1613-1637AD

TANKA COINAGE

KM# 35 1/128 TANKA
0.0800 g., Silver, 8 mm.

Date	Mintage	Good	VG	F	VF	XF
ND(1613-37)	—	—	—	45.00	75.00	—

Jagatprakash Malla

NS764-793 / 1644-1673AD

MOHAR COINAGE

KM# 40 1/16 MOHAR
0.3300 g., Silver

Date	Mintage	Good	VG	F	VF	XF
ND(1644-73)	—	18.00	45.00	90.00	150	—

KM# 45 1/4 MOHAR
1.3300 g., Silver

Date	Mintage	Good	VG	F	VF	XF
NS775(1655)	—	24.00	60.00	120	200	—

KM# 46 1/4 MOHAR
1.3300 g., Silver **Note:** In the name of Prime Minister, Chandra Sekhar Simha.

Date	Mintage	Good	VG	F	VF	XF
NS782(1662)	—	18.00	45.00	90.00	150	—

KM# 50 MOHAR
5.3400 g., Silver

Date	Mintage	Good	VG	F	VF	XF
NS765(1645)	—	20.00	4,705	95.00	165	—

Jaya Jitamitra Malla

NS783-816 / 1663-1696AD

MOHAR COINAGE

KM# 55 DAM
0.0400 g., Silver **Note:** Uniface.

Date	Mintage	Good	VG	F	VF	XF
ND(1663-96)	—	—	—	15.00	25.00	—

KM# 60 1/16 MOHAR
0.3300 g., Silver

Date	Mintage	Good	VG	F	VF	XF
ND(1663-96)	—	18.00	45.00	90.00	150	—

KM# 61 1/16 MOHAR
0.3300 g., Silver **Note:** In the name of Prime Minister, Jagat Chandra.

Date	Mintage	Good	VG	F	VF	XF
ND(1663-96)	—	30.00	75.00	150	250	—

KM# 63 1/8 MOHAR
0.6600 g., Silver

Date	Mintage	Good	VG	F	VF	XF
ND(1663-96)	—	24.00	60.00	120	200	—

KM# 65 1/4 MOHAR
1.3300 g., Silver

Date	Mintage	Good	VG	F	VF	XF
NS798(1678)	—	30.00	75.00	150	250	—

KM# 70 MOHAR
5.3400 g., Silver **Rev:** Coronation date, "Chaitre Sudi 9,783"

Date	Mintage	Good	VG	F	VF	XF
NS783(1663)	—	100	200	350	500	—

KM# 71 MOHAR
5.3400 g., Silver

Date	Mintage	Good	VG	F	VF	XF
NS783(1663)	—	24.00	60.00	120	200	—

Jaya Bhupatindra Malla

NS816-42 / 1696-1722AD

MOHAR COINAGE

KM# 75 DAM
0.0400 g., Silver **Obv. Inscription:** "Shri Shri Bhupa"

Date	Mintage	Good	VG	F	VF	XF
ND(1696-1722)	—	—	—	20.00	35.00	—

KM# 76 DAM
0.0400 g., Silver **Obv. Inscription:** "Shri Bhupati"

Date	Mintage	Good	VG	F	VF	XF
ND(1696-1722)	—	—	—	15.00	25.00	—

KM# 78 1/16 MOHAR
0.3300 g., Silver

Date	Mintage	Good	VG	F	VF	XF
ND(1696-1722)	—	18.00	45.00	90.00	150	—

KM# 80 1/8 MOHAR
0.6600 g., Silver

Date	Mintage	Good	VG	F	VF	XF
ND(1696-1722)	—	18.00	45.00	90.00	150	—

KM# 82 1/4 MOHAR
1.3300 g., Silver **Note:** Varieties exist.

Date	Mintage	Good	VG	F	VF	XF
NS816(1696)	—	18.00	45.00	90.00	150	—

KM# 84 1/2 MOHAR
2.6700 g., Silver **Obv:** Coronation date, "Bhadra Vadi 11,816"

Date	Mintage	Good	VG	F	VF	XF
NS816(1696)	—	85.00	170	280	400	—

KM# 86 MOHAR
5.3400 g., Silver **Obv:** Three characters in upper two lines

Date	Mintage	Good	VG	F	VF	XF
NS816(1696)	—	20.00	50.00	100	165	—

KM# 87 MOHAR
5.3400 g., Silver **Obv:** Four characters in all three lines **Note:** Varieties exist.

Date	Mintage	Good	VG	F	VF	XF
NS816(1696)	—	10.00	25.00	50.00	80.00	—

KINGDOM OF KATHMANDU

KINGDOM

Lakshmi Narasimha

NS740-761 / 1620-1641AD

TANKA COINAGE

KM# 145 1/128 TANKA
0.0800 g., Silver **Rev:** Nara and lion **Note:** Size varies: 8-9 milimeters.

Date	Mintage	Good	VG	F	VF	XF
ND(1620-41)	—	—	—	24.00	40.00	—

KM# 147 1/4 TANKA
Silver **Note:** Weight varies: 1.90-2.30 grams.

Date	Mintage	Good	VG	F	VF	XF
ND(1620-41)	—	75.00	150	250	350	—

KM# 148 1/4 TANKA
Silver **Note:** Weight varies: 1.90-2.30 grams.

Date	Mintage	Good	VG	F	VF	XF
ND(1620-41)	—	60.00	120	200	300	—

KM# 150 TANKA
Silver **Note:** Weight varies: 8.90-10.00 grams. Ala-ud-din type

Date	Mintage	Good	VG	F	VF	XF
ND(1620-41)	—	100	200	350	500	—

KM# 151 TANKA
Silver **Note:** Weight varies: 8.90-10.00 grams. Ghiyas-ud-din type.

Date	Mintage	Good	VG	F	VF	XF
ND(1620-41)	—	100	200	350	500	—

MOHAR COINAGE

KM# 158 DAM
0.0400 g., Silver **Note:** Uniface.

Date	Mintage	Good	VG	F	VF	XF
ND(1620-41)	—	—	—	15.00	25.00	—

KM# 160 MOHAR
5.3400 g., Silver **Note:** Size varies: 25-29 milimeters.

Date	Mintage	Good	VG	F	VF	XF
ND(1620-41)	—	22.00	55.00	110	185	—

Pratap Malla
NS761-794 / 1641-1674AD

MOHAR COINAGE

KM# 162 DAM
0.0400 g., Silver **Note:** Uniface.

Date	Mintage	Good	VG	F	VF	XF
ND(1641-74)	—	—	—	15.00	25.00	—

KM# 163 MOHAR
5.3400 g., Silver

Date	Mintage	Good	VG	F	VF	XF
NS761(1641)	—	15.00	35.00	75.00	145	—

KM# 164 MOHAR
5.3400 g., Silver **Obv:** Trident at center

Date	Mintage	Good	VG	F	VF	XF
NS775(1655)	—	11.00	27.00	55.00	90.00	—

KM# 166 2 MOHARS
11.1150 g., Silver **Obv:** Trident at center **Shape:** square **Note:** 27x27 mm.

Date	Mintage	Good	VG	F	VF	XF
NS781(1661)	—	165	330	550	850	—

Rupamati Devi
Queen of Pratap Malla, NS769 / 1649AD

MOHAR COINAGE

KM# 168 1/4 MOHAR
1.3300 g., Silver **Obv:** Trident at center **Obv. Inscription:** "Shri Rupamati"

Date	Mintage	Good	VG	F	VF	XF
NS769(1649)	—	18.00	45.00	90.00	150	—

KM# 169 1/4 MOHAR
1.3300 g., Silver **Obv:** Trident at center **Obv. Inscription:** "Shri Rupamati" **Rev. Inscription:** "Bihari Rajkanya"

Date	Mintage	Good	VG	F	VF	XF
NS769(1649)	—	18.00	45.00	90.00	150	—

Chakravartendra Malla
NS789 / 1669AD

MOHAR COINAGE

KM# 171 1/2 MOHAR
2.6700 g., Silver **Obv:** Trident at center

Date	Mintage	Good	VG	F	VF	XF
ND(1669)	—	27.00	67.50	135	225	—

KM# 173 MOHAR
5.3400 g., Silver **Obv:** Five arrows at left of inner circle, bow at right **Obv. Inscription:** "Shri 2 Jaya Cakra Va-" **Rev:** Noose and elephant goad in triangle **Rev. Inscription:** "rtindra Malla"

Date	Mintage	Good	VG	F	VF	XF
NS789(1669)	—	15.00	35.00	65.00	110	—

Mahipatendra Malla
NS790 / 1670AD

MOHAR COINAGE

KM# 175 1/2 MOHAR
2.6700 g., Silver

Date	Mintage	Good	VG	F	VF	XF
ND(1670)	—	45.00	110	220	325	—

KM# 177 MOHAR
5.3400 g., Silver **Obv:** Trident at center **Obv. Inscription:** "Shri Jaya Mahipa-" **Rev:** Sword at center **Rev. Inscription:** "tindra Malla Deva"

Date	Mintage	Good	VG	F	VF	XF
ND(1670)	—	22.00	55.00	110	185	—

Nripendra Malla
NS794-800 / 1674-1680AD

MOHAR COINAGE

KM# 179 DAM
0.0400 g., Silver **Note:** Uniface.

Date	Mintage	Good	VG	F	VF	XF
ND(1674-80)	—	—	—	24.00	40.00	—

KM# 181 1/16 MOHAR
0.3300 g., Silver **Note:** Uniface.

Date	Mintage	Good	VG	F	VF	XF
ND(1674-80)	—	15.00	37.50	75.00	145	—

KM# 183 1/4 MOHAR
1.3300 g., Silver

Date	Mintage	Good	VG	F	VF	XF
NS795(1675)	—	18.00	45.00	90.00	160	—

KM# 185 MOHAR
5.3400 g., Silver **Obv:** Trident at center **Rev:** Sword at center

Date	Mintage	Good	VG	F	VF	XF
NS794(1674)	—	15.00	35.00	70.00	145	—

KM# 186 MOHAR
5.3400 g., Silver **Obv:** Trident at center **Rev:** Sword at center

Date	Mintage	Good	VG	F	VF	XF
NS794(1674)	—	15.00	37.50	75.00	145	—

Parthivendra Malla
NS800-807 / 1680-1687AD

MOHAR COINAGE

KM# 188 DAM
0.0400 g., Silver **Note:** Uniface.

Date	Mintage	Good	VG	F	VF	XF
ND(1680-87)	—	—	—	15.00	25.00	—

KM# 190 1/4 MOHAR
1.3300 g., Silver

Date	Mintage	Good	VG	F	VF	XF
NS800(1680)	—	20.00	50.00	100	175	—

KM# 196 1/4 MOHAR
1.3300 g., Silver **Obv:** Trident at center **Note:** In the names of Parthivendra Malla and Queen Rajya Lakshmi.

Date	Mintage	Good	VG	F	VF	XF
NS802(1682)	—	17.00	42.50	85.00	140	—

KM# 197 1/2 MOHAR
2.6700 g., Silver **Obv:** Pedestal at center **Rev:** Sword at center **Shape:** Square, 17x17 mm **Note:** In the names of Parthivendra Malla and Queen Rajya Lakshmi.

Date	Mintage	Good	VG	F	VF	XF
ND(1680-87)	—	125	250	420	600	—

KM# 194 MOHAR
5.3400 g., Silver **Obv:** Trident at center **Note:** Size varies: 26-27 milimeters.

Date	Mintage	Good	VG	F	VF	XF
NS800(1680)	—	15.00	37.50	75.00	145	—

KM# 198 MOHAR
5.3400 g., Silver **Rev:** Vase at center **Note:** In the names of Parthivendra Malla and Queen Rajya Lakshmi. Size varies: 26-27 milimeters.

Date	Mintage	Good	VG	F	VF	XF
NS802(1682)	—	12.00	30.00	65.00	125	—

Bhupalendra Malla
NS807-820 / 1687-1700AD
MOHAR COINAGE

KM# 202 DAM
0.0400 g., Silver **Note:** Uniface.

Date	Mintage	Good	VG	F	VF	XF
ND(1687-1700)	—	—	—	15.00	25.00	—

KM# 204 1/32 MOHAR
0.1600 g., Silver **Note:** Uniface.

Date	Mintage	Good	VG	F	VF	XF
ND(1687-1700)	—	12.00	30.00	60.00	100	—

KM# 205 1/16 MOHAR
0.3300 g., Silver **Obv. Inscription:** "Shri Bhupalendra" **Note:** Uniface.

Date	Mintage	Good	VG	F	VF	XF
ND(1687-1700)	—	5.00	12.00	24.00	40.00	—

KM# 206 MOHAR
5.3400 g., Silver **Obv:** Trident at center **Rev:** Sword at center

Date	Mintage	Good	VG	F	VF	XF
NS808(1688)	—	20.00	50.00	100	175	—

KM# 207 MOHAR
5.3400 g., Silver **Obv:** Trident at center **Rev:** Sword at center

Date	Mintage	Good	VG	F	VF	XF
NS809(1689)	—	20.00	50.00	100	175	—

KM# 208 MOHAR
5.3400 g., Silver **Obv:** Trident at center **Rev:** Sword at center

Date	Mintage	Good	VG	F	VF	XF
NS812(1692)	—	8.00	20.00	40.00	70.00	—

KM# 209 MOHAR
5.3400 g., Silver **Obv:** Trident at center **Rev:** Sword at center

Date	Mintage	Good	VG	F	VF	XF
NS820(1700)	—	14.00	35.00	70.00	120	—

Riddhi Lakshmi Devi
Regent for Bhupalendra, NS808 / 1688AD
MOHAR COINAGE

KM# 200 1/4 MOHAR
1.3300 g., Silver **Obv:** Trident at center **Obv. Inscription:** "Shri 2 Hrdhi Laksmi Raje" **Rev:** Pedestal at center

Date	Mintage	Good	VG	F	VF	XF
NS808(1688)	—	8.00	20.00	40.00	65.00	—

KINGDOM OF PATAN
KINGDOM
Siddhi Narasimha
NS740-781 / 1620-1661AD
MOHAR COINAGE

KM# 295 DAM
0.0400 g., Silver **Obv:** Four characters **Note:** Uniface.

Date	Mintage	Good	VG	F	VF	XF
ND(1620-61)	—	9.00	22.50	45.00	75.00	—

KM# 296 DAM
0.0400 g., Silver **Obv:** Three characters

Date	Mintage	Good	VG	F	VF	XF
ND(1620-61)	—	5.00	12.00	24.00	40.00	—

KM# 299 1/4 MOHAR
1.3300 g., Silver, 17 mm. **Obv:** Sword at center **Obv. Inscription:** "Shri Shri Siddhi" **Rev:** Lion standing left at center **Rev. Inscription:** "Nara"

Date	Mintage	Good	VG	F	VF	XF
NS774(1654)	—	25.00	60.00	120	200	—

Note: Leather, clay, or gold coins with this design are forgeries

KM# 301 MOHAR
5.3400 g., Silver **Obv:** Sword at center **Obv. Inscription:** "Shri Shri Siddhi" at center **Rev:** Lion left at center **Rev. Inscription:** "Nara" above lion **Note:** Size varies: 26-28 milimeters.

Date	Mintage	Good	VG	F	VF	XF
NS761(1641)	—	7.50	18.00	36.00	60.00	—

TANKA COINAGE

KM# 155 TANKA
10.0000 g., Silver **Note:** Ala-ud-din type.

Date	Mintage	Good	VG	F	VF	XF
ND(1620-61)	—	150	300	500	700	—

KM# 156 TANKA
10.0000 g., Silver **Obv:** Sword at center **Obv. Inscription:** "Shri Shri Siddhi" at center **Rev:** lion left at center **Rev. Inscription:** "Nara" above lion **Note:** Ghiyas-ud-din type.

Date	Mintage	Good	VG	F	VF	XF
NS759(1639)	—	150	300	500	700	—

Srinivasa Malla
NS781-805 / 1661-1685AD
MOHAR COINAGE

KM# 302 DAM
0.0410 g., Silver **Obv. Inscription:** "Shri Nivasa" **Note:** Uniface

Date	Mintage	Good	VG	F	VF	XF
ND(1661-85)	—	—	—	45.00	75.00	—

KM# 303 1/16 MOHAR
0.3300 g., Silver **Note:** Uniface.

Date	Mintage	Good	VG	F	VF	XF
ND(1661-85)	—	—	—	—	—	—

KM# 304 1/4 MOHAR
1.3300 g., Silver

Date	Mintage	Good	VG	F	VF	XF
ND(1661-85)	—	30.00	75.00	150	250	—

KM# 310 1/4 MOHAR
1.3300 g., Silver **Obv:** Trident at center **Rev:** Sword in center of 6-pointed star **Note:** In the names of Srinivasa Malla and Queen Mrigavati.

Date	Mintage	Good	VG	F	VF	XF
ND(1661-85)	—	30.00	75.00	150	250	—

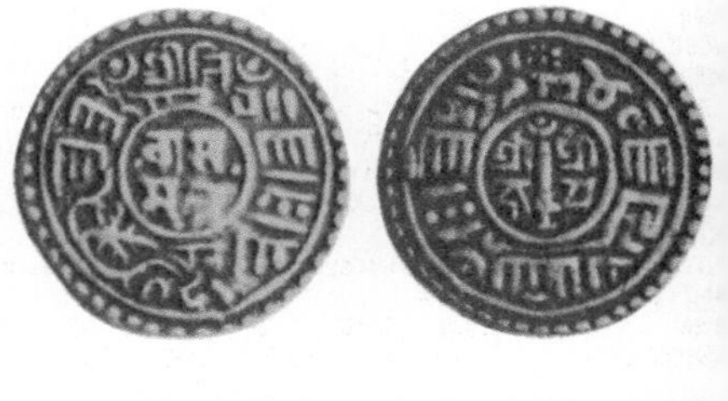

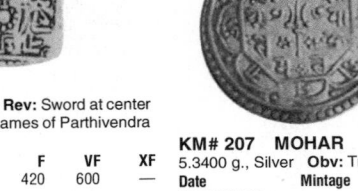

KM# 306 MOHAR
5.3400 g., Silver **Obv:** Sword in center **Obv. Inscription:** "Shri Shri Jaya" in center **Rev. Inscription:** "Shri Ni-" above, "vasa Malla" in center

Date	Mintage	Good	VG	F	VF	XF
NS781(1661)	—	15.00	36.00	72.00	120	—

KM# 307 MOHAR
5.3400 g., Silver **Obv:** Sword at lower center in 6-pointed star **Obv. Inscription:** "Shri Shri Jaya" in center, "Shri Nivasa Malla" in star points **Rev:** Staff betwen two water jugs with streamers, date below within circle **Rev. Inscription:** "Nepalesvara"

Date	Mintage	Good	VG	F	VF	XF
NS786(1666)	—	9.00	22.50	45.00	75.00	—

KM# 308 MOHAR
5.3400 g., Silver **Obv:** Sword at lower center in 6-pointed star **Obv. Inscription:** "Shri shri Jaya" in center, "Shri Nivasa Malla" in star points **Rev:** Staff between two water jugs with streamers within circle, date below **Rev. Inscription:** "Nepalesvara"

Date	Mintage	Good	VG	F	VF	XF
NS786(1666)	—	9.00	22.50	45.00	75.00	—

Yoga Narendra Malla
NS805-825 / 1685-1705AD

MOHAR COINAGE

KM# 312 DAM
0.0480 g., Silver **Obv. Inscription:** "Shri Yoga" **Note:** Uniface.

Date	Mintage	Good	VG	F	VF	XF
ND(1685-1705)	—	—	—	15.00	25.00	—

KM# 315 1/4 MOHAR
1.3830 g., Silver **Obv:** Shorter inscription

Date	Mintage	Good	VG	F	VF	XF
NS805(1685)	—	15.00	37.50	75.00	125	—

KM# 316 1/4 MOHAR
1.3830 g., Silver **Obv:** Vase, date in square **Obv. Inscription:** "Shri Shri Yoga Narendra Malla" **Rev. Inscription:** "Shri Shri Lokanatha...Shri Talejo"

Date	Mintage	Good	VG	F	VF	XF
ND(1685-1705)	—	25.00	60.00	120	200	—

KM# 317 1/4 MOHAR
1.3830 g., Silver **Obv:** Date in square **Obv. Inscription:** "Shri Yoga Narendra Malla" **Rev. Inscription:** "Shri Shri Lokanatha...Shri Taleju"

Date	Mintage	Good	VG	F	VF	XF
ND(1685-1705)	—	20.00	50.00	100	165	—

KM# 328 1/4 MOHAR
1.3830 g., Silver

Date	Mintage	Good	VG	F	VF	XF
ND(1685-1705)	—	100	200	320	450	—

KM# 314 1/4 MOHAR
1.3830 g., Silver **Obv:** Inscription, date within 4-trefoiled petals around square with staff at center **Obv. Inscription:** "Shri Shri Yoga" within, "Narendra Malla..." around square **Rev:** Curved 5-pointed star **Rev. Inscription:** "Shri Shri Shri Lokanatha...Shri Taleju Sahaya"

Date	Mintage	Good	VG	F	VF	XF
NS807(1687)	—	27.50	67.50	135	225	—

KM# 321 1/2 MOHAR
2.7600 g., Silver **Rev:** Without vase **Note:** In the names of Yoga Lakshmi and Queen Yoga Lakshmi

Date	Mintage	Good	VG	F	VF	XF
NS804(1684)	—	30.00	75.00	150	250	—

KM# 322 1/2 MOHAR
2.7600 g., Silver **Rev:** Vase **Note:** In the names of Yoga Lakshmi and Queen Yoga Lakshmi

Date	Mintage	Good	VG	F	VF	XF
NS805(1685)	—	25.00	60.00	120	200	—

KM# 330 1/2 MOHAR
2.7600 g., Silver

Date	Mintage	Good	VG	F	VF	XF
ND(1685-1705)	—	30.00	75.00	150	275	—

KM# 334 1/2 MOHAR
2.7600 g., Silver

Date	Mintage	Good	VG	F	VF	XF
ND(1685-1705)	—	30.00	75.00	150	275	—

KM# 319 3/4 MOHAR
3.9600 g., Silver **Shape:** Square **Note:** Center hole, 19x19 mm.

Date	Mintage	Good	VG	F	VF	XF
NS804(1684)	—	100	200	350	500	—

KM# 324 MOHAR
5.3400 g., Silver **Note:** In the names of Yoga Lakshmi and Queen Yoga Lakshmi

Date	Mintage	Good	VG	F	VF	XF
NS805(1685)	—	65.00	130	220	325	—

KM# 325 MOHAR
5.3400 g., Silver **Note:** In the names of Yoga Lakshmi and Queen Yoga Lakshmi

Date	Mintage	Good	VG	F	VF	XF
NS805(1685)	—	12.00	30.00	60.00	100	—

KM# 332 MOHAR
5.3400 g., Silver **Note:** In the names of Yoga Narendra Malla and Queen Jaya Lakshmi.

Date	Mintage	Good	VG	F	VF	XF
NS805(1685)	—	10.00	25.00	50.00	85.00	—

KM# 336 MOHAR
5.3400 g., Silver **Note:** In the names of Yoga Narendra Malla and Queen Narendra Lakshmi.

Date	Mintage	Good	VG	F	VF	XF
NS805(1685)	—	10.00	25.00	50.00	85.00	—

KM# 337 MOHAR
5.3400 g., Silver **Note:** In the names of Yoga Narendra Malla and Queen Narendra Lakshmi.

Date	Mintage	Good	VG	F	VF	XF
NS805(1685)	—	8.00	21.00	42.00	70.00	—

KM# 326 MOHAR
5.3400 g., Silver **Note:** In the names of Yoga Lakshmi and Queen Yoga Lakshmi

Date	Mintage	Good	VG	F	VF	XF
NS808(1688)	—	15.00	37.50	75.00	125	—

KM# 320 MOHAR
5.3400 g., Silver

Date	Mintage	Good	VG	F	VF	XF
NS820(1700)	—	12.00	30.00	60.00	100	—

NETHERLANDS

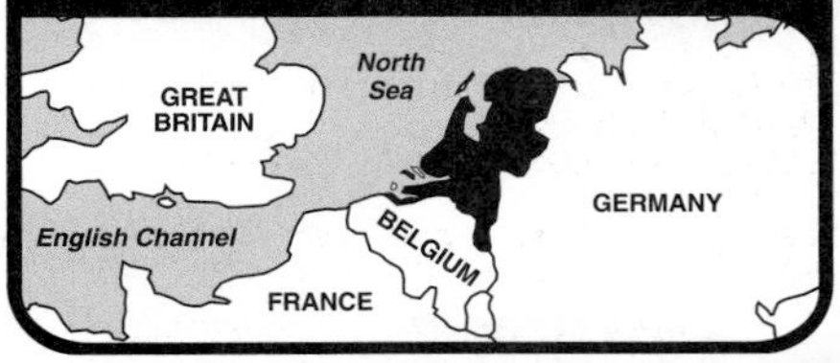

The Kingdom of the Netherlands, a country of western Europe fronting on the North Sea and bordered by Belgium and Germany, has an area of 15,770 sq. mi. (41,500 sq. km).

After being a part of Charlemagne's empire in the 8th and 9th centuries, the Netherlands came under control of Burgundy and the Austrian Hapsburgs, and finally was subjected to Spanish dominion in the 16th century. Led by William of Orange, the Dutch revolted against Spain in 1568. The seven northern provinces formed the Union of Utrecht and declared their independence in 1581, becoming the Republic of the United Netherlands. In the following century, the *Golden Age* of Dutch history, the Netherlands became a great sea and colonial power, a patron of the arts and a refuge for the persecuted. The United Dutch Republic ended in 1795 when the French formed the Batavian Republic. Napoleon made his brother Louis, the King of Holland in 1806, however he abdicated in 1810 when Napoleon annexed Holland. The French were expelled in 1813, and all the provinces of Holland and Belgium were merged into the Kingdom of the United Netherlands under William I, in 1814. The Belgians withdrew in 1830 to form their own kingdom, the last substantial change in the configuration of European Netherlands. German forces invaded in 1940 as the royal family fled to England where a government-in-exile was formed. A German High Commissioner, Arthur Seyss-Inquart, was placed in command until 1945 when the arrival of Allied military forces ended the occupation.

RULER
United Netherlands, 1543-1795

MINT PRIVY MARKS

Dordrecht (Holland)

Mark	Date
Rosette	1600-1806

Middelburg (Zeeland)

Castle	1601-1799

MONETARY SYSTEM
1 Penning = 1/2 Duit
2 Duits = 1 Oord
8 Duits = 1 Stuiver (Stiver)
6 Stuiver = 1 Schelling
20 Stuiver = 1 Gulden (Guilder or Florin)
50 Stuiver = 1 Rijksdaalder (Silver Ducat)
60 Stuiver = 1 Ducaton (Silver Rider)
14 Gulden = 1 Golden Rider

KINGDOM

COUNTERMARKED COINAGE

1693

During the late 17th century many circulating coins were found to be underweight. In 1693 coins meeting the legal requirements were countermarked with a bundle of arrows (United Netherlands) for general circulation.

KM# 2.1 6 STUIVERS
Silver **Countermark:** Bundle of arrows **Note:** Countermark on Overyssel KM#50.

CM Date	Host Date	Good	VG	F	VF	XF
ND(1693)	1680-96	—	—	—	—	—

KM# 2.2 6 STUIVERS
Silver **Countermark:** Bundle of arrows **Note:** Countermark on Utrecht KM#60.3.

CM Date	Host Date	Good	VG	F	VF	XF
ND(1693)	1679-91	—	—	—	—	—

KM# 2.3 6 STUIVERS
Silver **Countermark:** Bundle of arrows **Note:** Countermark on Zutphen KM#19.

CM Date	Host Date	Good	VG	F	VF	XF
ND(1693)	1688-91	—	—	—	—	—

KM# 3 14 STUIVERS
Silver **Countermark:** Bundle of arrows **Note:** Countermark on Deventer KM#27.

CM Date	Host Date	Good	VG	F	VF	XF
ND(1693)	1618	—	—	—	—	—

KM# 4.9 28 STUIVERS
Silver **Countermark:** Bundle of arrows **Note:** Countermark on Deventer 28 Stuivers, KM#81.1.

CM Date	Host Date	Good	VG	F	VF	XF
ND(1693)	1685	—	—	—	—	—
ND(1693)	1686	—	—	—	—	—
ND(1693)	1690	—	—	—	—	—
ND(1693)	1692	—	—	—	—	—

KM# 4.1 28 STUIVERS
Gold **Countermark:** Bundle of arrows **Note:** Countermark on Deventer KM#79.

CM Date	Host Date	Good	VG	F	VF	XF
ND(1693)	1684	—	—	—	—	—

KM# 4.10 28 STUIVERS
Silver **Countermark:** Bundle of arrows **Note:** Countermark on Friesland, KM#10.

CM Date	Host Date	Good	VG	F	VF	XF
ND(1693)	1683-84	—	60.00	100	200	—

KM# 4.2 28 STUIVERS
Silver **Countermark:** Bundle of arrows **Note:** Countermark on Groningen KM#38.

CM Date	Host Date	Good	VG	F	VF	XF
ND(1693)	1681	—	—	—	—	—

KM# 4.3 28 STUIVERS
Silver **Countermark:** Bundle of arrows **Note:** Countermark on Groningen KM#50.

CM Date	Host Date	Good	VG	F	VF	XF
ND(1693)	1690	—	—	—	—	—

KM# 4.4 28 STUIVERS
Silver **Countermark:** Bundle of arrows **Note:** Countermark on Groningen KM#52.

CM Date	Host Date	Good	VG	F	VF	XF
ND(1693)	ND	—	—	—	—	—

KM# 4.5 28 STUIVERS
Silver **Countermark:** Bundle of arrows **Note:** Countermark on Kampen KM#76.

CM Date	Host Date	Good	VG	F	VF	XF
ND(1693)	1680-86	—	—	—	—	—

KM# 4.6 28 STUIVERS
Silver **Countermark:** Bundle of arrows **Note:** Countermark on Nijmegen KM#27.

CM Date	Host Date	Good	VG	F	VF	XF
ND(1693)	1685-90	—	—	—	—	—

KM# 4.7 28 STUIVERS
Silver **Countermark:** Bundle of arrows **Note:** Countermark on Zwolle KM#78.

CM Date	Host Date	Good	VG	F	VF	XF
ND(1693)	1679-86	—	—	—	—	—

KM# 4.8 28 STUIVERS
Silver **Countermark:** Bundle of arrows **Note:** Countermark on Overijssel KM#55.

CM Date	Host Date	Good	VG	F	VF	XF
ND(1693)	1685-89	—	—	—	—	—

AMSTERDAM

CITY

STANDARD COINAGE

KM# 2.1 DUCATON
32.7800 g., Silver **Rev:** Amsterdam Arms between date below crowned shield **Note:** Dav. #4933.

Date	Mintage	Good	VG	F	VF	XF
1672	—	40.00	100	200	300	450
1673	—	40.00	100	200	300	450
1673/72	—	80.00	200	300	500	900

KM# 1 DUCATON
32.7800 g., Silver **Obv:** Knight on horseback, Holland arms below **Obv. Legend:** MON NOV ARG CONF - BELG PROV HOLLAND **Rev:** Amsterdam shield below crowned Hollard arms, date above. **Note:** Dav. #4933A.

Date	Mintage	Good	VG	F	VF	XF
1672 with roset after HOLL	1,386,230	35.00	85.00	200	350	500
1672 with star after HOLL	—	35.00	85.00	200	350	500

KM# 2.2 DUCATON
Silver **Edge Lettering:** TER NAGEDACHTENISSE... **Note:** Dav. #4933C.

Date	Mintage	Good	VG	F	VF	XF
1672	—	50.00	125	400	800	1,200
1673	—	50.00	125	400	800	1,200

KM# 2.3 DUCATON
Silver **Edge Lettering:** NERVOS REI PUBLICAE ACCIDERE FACINVS MORTE PI-A-N-D-VM **Note:** Dav. #4933c.

Date	Mintage	Good	VG	F	VF	XF
1672	—	35.00	85.00	200	350	500

KM# 3 DUCATON
Silver **Note:** Klippe. Dav. #4933D. No Inner Circle

Date	Mintage	Good	VG	F	VF	XF
1673	—	120	300	650	950	1,200

KM# 4 2 DUCATONS
Silver **Obv:** Without inner circle **Rev:** Amsterdam Arms below crowned arms, with inner circle **Note:** Dav. #4932. Weight varies 64.3 - 65.5 grams

Date	Mintage	Good	VG	F	VF	XF
1672	—	160	400	800	1,500	2,500

KM# 5 2 DUCATONS
64.5000 g., Silver **Note:** Klippe. Dav. #4932B.

Date	Mintage	Good	VG	F	VF	XF
1672	—	250	600	1,000	2,000	3,000

KM# 6.1 2 DUCATONS
Silver **Note:** Without inner circle on both sides. Dav. #4932A.

Date	Mintage	Good	VG	F	VF	XF
1673	—	160	400	750	1,200	1,850

KM# 6.2 2 DUCATONS
Silver **Edge Lettering:** TER NAGEDACHTENISSE **Note:** Dav #4932D.

Date	Mintage	Good	VG	F	VF	XF
1673	—	160	400	750	1,200	1,850

KM# 7 2 DUCATONS

65.3500 g., Silver **Obv:** Knight on horse holding sword right without inner circle **Rev:** Amsterdam arms below crowned arms **Note:** Klippe. Dav. #4932C. Illustration reduced.

Date	Mintage	Good	VG	F	VF	XF
1673	—	250	600	1,250	1,750	2,500

KM# 8 3 DUCATONS

98.2000 g., Silver **Note:** Klippe. Dav. #4932.

Date	Mintage	Good	VG	F	VF	XF
1673	—	350	900	2,000	3,000	4,000

TRADE COINAGE

KM# 10 DUCAT

3.5100 g., Gold **Obv:** 5-line inscripton in tablet, Amsterdam arms below **Rev:** Standing knight divides date

Date	Mintage	VG	F	VF	XF	Unc
1673	57,000	750	2,000	4,000	5,000	—

KM# 11 3 DUCAT

10.5000 g., 0.9860 Gold 0.3328 oz. AGW **Edge Lettering:** D GEDACHTENIS V D MUNTE V AMSTERDAM **Note:** Struck with 1 Ducat dies.

Date	Mintage	VG	F	VF	XF	Unc
1673	—	400	900	2,000	3,500	—

KM# 12 3-1/2 DUCAT

12.2500 g., 0.9860 Gold 0.3883 oz. AGW **Edge Lettering:** D GEDACHTENIS V D MUNTE V AMSTERDAM **Note:** Struck with 1 Ducat dies.

Date	Mintage	VG	F	VF	XF	Unc
1673	—	400	900	2,000	3,500	—

KM# 13 4 DUCAT

14.0000 g., 0.9860 Gold 0.4438 oz. AGW **Edge Lettering:** D GEDACHTENIS V D MUNTE V AMSTERDAM **Note:** Struck with 1 Ducat dies.

Date	Mintage	VG	F	VF	XF	Unc
1673	—	400	800	1,450	3,500	—

KM# 14 4-1/2 DUCAT

15.7500 g., 0.9860 Gold 0.4993 oz. AGW **Edge Lettering:** D GEDACHTENIS V D MUNTE V AMSTERDAM **Note:** Struck with 1 Ducat dies.

Date	Mintage	VG	F	VF	XF	Unc
1673	—	700	1,500	3,000	4,000	—

KM# 15 5 DUCAT

17.5000 g., 0.9860 Gold 0.5547 oz. AGW **Edge Lettering:** D GEDACHTENIS V D MUNTE V AMSTERDAM **Note:** Struck with 1 Ducat dies.

Date	Mintage	VG	F	VF	XF	Unc
1673	—	800	1,700	4,000	5,000	—

FRIESLAND

PROVINCE

STANDARD COINAGE

KM# 16 DUIT

2.0000 g., Copper **Obv:** Crowned shield with NISI DOMINVS or DNS NOBISCV/(M) **Rev. Inscription:** FRI/SIA/(date) in wreath

Date	Mintage	Good	VG	F	VF	XF
1604	—	4.00	10.00	20.00	40.00	100
1605	—	4.00	10.00	20.00	40.00	100
1606	—	4.00	10.00	20.00	40.00	100
1611	—	4.00	10.00	20.00	40.00	100
1612	—	4.00	10.00	20.00	40.00	100
1613/11	—	6.00	15.00	30.00	60.00	125
1613	—	4.00	10.00	20.00	40.00	100
1616	—	4.00	10.00	20.00	40.00	100
1617	—	4.00	10.00	20.00	40.00	100
1618	—	4.00	10.00	20.00	40.00	100
1619	—	4.00	10.00	20.00	40.00	100
1620	—	4.00	10.00	20.00	40.00	100

KM# 16a DUIT

2.0000 g., Copper **Obv:** Crowned shield with NISI DNS NOBISCVM mintmark **Rev. Inscription:** FRI / SIA / (date) in wreath

Date	Mintage	Good	VG	F	VF	XF
1611Lion	—	4.00	10.00	20.00	40.00	100
1612Lion	—	4.00	10.00	20.00	40.00	100
1616Lion	—	4.00	10.00	20.00	40.00	100
1617Lion	—	4.00	10.00	20.00	40.00	100
1613/11Lion	—	6.00	15.00	30.00	60.00	125
1613Lion	—	4.00	10.00	20.00	40.00	100

KM# 46 DUIT

2.0000 g., Copper, 20.2 mm. **Obv:** Wide crowned shield of arms with NISI DNS - NOBISCVM **Rev. Inscription:** FRI/SIA/(date) in wreath.

Date	Mintage	Good	VG	F	VF	XF
1626	—	1.60	4.00	10.00	20.00	40.00
1627	—	2.40	6.00	20.00	50.00	100
1629	—	1.60	4.00	10.00	20.00	40.00
1643	—	1.60	4.00	10.00	20.00	40.00
1644	—	2.40	6.00	20.00	50.00	100
1645	—	2.40	6.00	20.00	40.00	70.00
1646-4	—	4.00	10.00	30.00	70.00	120
1646	—	1.60	4.00	10.00	20.00	40.00
1647	—	1.60	4.00	10.00	20.00	40.00
1648	—	1.60	4.00	10.00	20.00	40.00
1653/48	—	1.60	4.00	10.00	20.00	40.00
1653	—	1.60	4.00	10.00	20.00	40.00
1654/48	—	1.60	4.00	10.00	20.00	40.00
1654	—	1.60	4.00	10.00	20.00	40.00
1663	—	2.40	6.00	20.00	40.00	70.00

KM# 46a DUIT

Silver **Obv:** Wide shield of arms **Note:** Weight varies 2.3 - 3.7 g.

Date	Mintage	Good	VG	F	VF	XF
1626	—	—	—	—	—	—
1627	—	—	—	—	—	—
1653	—	—	—	—	—	—

KM# 46b DUIT

3.5000 g., Gold **Obv:** Wide shield of arms **Note:** Like KM#46

Date	Mintage	Good	VG	F	VF	XF
1653	—	—	—	—	—	—

KM# 60 DUIT

Copper **Obv:** Crowned arms without legend **Rev. Inscription:** (mintmark lion) / FRISIA / (date)

Date	Mintage	Good	VG	F	VF	XF
1672Lion	—	25.00	65.00	125	250	500

KM# 61 DUIT

2.0000 g., Copper, 21 mm. **Obv:** Crowned shield **Rev. Inscription:** FRISIA/date

Date	Mintage	Good	VG	F	VF	XF
1675Lion	—	3.00	8.00	20.00	40.00	60.00
1681Lion	—	3.00	8.00	20.00	40.00	60.00
1682Lion	—	3.00	8.00	20.00	40.00	60.00
1684Lion	—	4.00	10.00	35.00	75.00	150
1685Lion	—	3.00	8.00	20.00	40.00	60.00
1686Lion	—	3.00	8.00	20.00	40.00	60.00
1688Lion	—	4.00	10.00	35.00	75.00	150
1690Lion	—	4.00	10.00	35.00	75.00	150

KM# 61a DUIT

Silver **Obv:** Crowned shield **Rev. Inscription:** FRISIA **Note:** Weight varies 2.5 - 2.8 g.

Date	Mintage	Good	VG	F	VF	XF
1675	—	—	—	—	200	300
1681	—	—	—	—	—	—
1685	—	—	—	—	—	—
1690	—	—	—	—	—	—

KM# 8 2 DUIT (Oord)

Copper **Obv:** Crowned arms on ornamental cross in inner circle with MONE NOVA ORDINVM FRISAE date. **Rev:** Frisian farmer with sword on shoulder in NISI DOMINVS NOBISCVM

Date	Mintage	Good	VG	F	VF	XF
1606	—	75.00	250	600	1,200	1,900

KM# 26 2 DUIT (Oord)

Copper **Obv:** Crowned arms on ornamental cross in inner circle **Rev:** Frisian farmer with sword on shoulder between F - O (Frisia Ordines) in inner circle

Date	Mintage	Good	VG	F	VF	XF
ND(1607)	—	4.00	10.00	30.00	60.00	100
1608/7	—	12.00	35.00	100	200	400
1608	—	3.00	8.00	25.00	40.00	75.00
1609	—	3.00	8.00	25.00	40.00	75.00
1610	—	3.00	8.00	25.00	40.00	75.00

KM# 26a 2 DUIT (Oord)

Copper **Obv:** Crowned arms on ornamental cross in inner circle **Rev:** Frisian farmer with sword on shoulder between F - O (Frisiae Ordines) in inner circle

Date	Mintage	Good	VG	F	VF	XF
1608/7	—	10.00	25.00	50.00	100	250
1608	—	6.00	20.00	40.00	80.00	200
1609	—	2.00	5.00	20.00	50.00	100
1610	—	6.00	20.00	40.00	80.00	200
1611	—	2.00	5.00	25.00	40.00	90.00
1612	—	2.00	5.00	25.00	40.00	90.00
1616	—	6.00	10.00	30.00	75.00	125

KM# 18 2 DUIT (Oord)

Copper **Obv:** Crowned arms on ornamental cross in inner circle **Rev:** Frisian farmer with longer sword crossing inner circle between F - O (Frisia Ordines)

Date	Mintage	Good	VG	F	VF	XF
1608Lion	—	2.00	5.00	25.00	60.00	100
1608	—	6.00	20.00	40.00	80.00	200

KM# 18b 2 DUIT (Oord)

Gold **Obv:** Crowned arms on ornamental cross in inner circle **Rev:** Frisian farmer with longer sword crossing inner circle **Note:** Prev. KM #26b.

Date	Mintage	Good	VG	F	VF	XF
1608	—	—	—	—	—	—

KM# 28 2 DUIT (Oord)

Silver **Obv:** Crowned arms on ornamental cross in inner circle **Rev:** Frisian farmer with sword on shoulder between F - O (Frisiae Ordines) in inner circle **Note:** Klippe. Prev. KM# 26a.2.

Date	Mintage	Good	VG	F	VF	XF
1610	—	—	—	—	—	—

KM# 27 2 DUIT (Oord)

4.2400 g., Copper **Obv:** Crowned arms on ornamental cross in inner circle with NISI DOMINVS NOBISCV(M) **Rev:** Frisian farmer with sword on shoulder between F - O (Frisiae Ordines) in inner circle and MO(N) NOVA (ARG) ORDIN(VM) FR(S) date **Note:** Varieties exist.

Date	Mintage	Good	VG	F	VF	XF
1618	—	2.00	5.00	30.00	50.00	90.00
ND(1619)	—	8.00	10.00	30.00	75.00	125
1620	—	2.00	5.00	30.00	50.00	90.00

KM# 41a 2 DUIT (Oord)

Silver **Obv:** Crowned arms on ornametal cross in inner circle, date above **Rev:** Frisian farmer with sword on shoulder between F - O (Frisiae Ordines) in inner circle

Date	Mintage	Good	VG	F	VF	XF
1620	—	—	—	—	—	—
ND(1626)	—	—	—	—	—	—
1648	—	—	—	—	—	—

KM# 43 2 DUIT (Oord)

Silver **Obv:** Crowned arms on ornamental cross in inner circle, date above **Rev:** Frisian farmer with sword on shoulder between F - O (Frisiae Ordines) in inner circle **Note:** Klippe.

Date	Mintage	Good	VG	F	VF	XF
1620	—	—	—	—	—	—

KM# 41 2 DUIT (Oord)

Copper **Obv:** Crowned arms on ornamental cross in inner circle with NISI DOMINVS NOBISCV(M) **Rev:** Frisian farmer with sword on shoulder between F - O (Frisiae Ordines) in inner circle and MO NOVA ARG ORDIN FRIS(I) date **Note:** Varieties exist.

Date	Mintage	Good	VG	F	VF	XF
1644	—	6.00	20.00	40.00	80.00	200
1646	—	6.00	20.00	40.00	80.00	200
ND(1646)	—	8.00	20.00	50.00	100	150
1647	—	6.00	20.00	40.00	80.00	200
1648	—	6.00	20.00	40.00	80.00	200
1649	—	6.00	20.00	40.00	80.00	200

KM# 19 1/2 STUIVER

1.0000 g., Silver **Obv:** Crowned arms between F - B in inner circle with MO (NE) NO(VA) ORDI(NVM) FRI(SI) mintmark. **Rev:** Ornamental cross in inner circle with F B F B. NISI - DNS - NOBI - SCVM **Note:** (or Butken)

Date	Mintage	Good	VG	F	VF	XF
ND	—	25.00	60.00	125	200	300

KM# 20 STUIVER

2.0000 g., Silver **Obv:** Crowned arms divide value in inner circle with MONE NOVA (mintmark) (ARG) ORDINVM FRISAE **Rev:** Ornamental cross in quatrefoil in inner circle and NISI - DOMI - NI - SCVM

Date	Mintage	Good	VG	F	VF	XF
ND(1601)Shield	—	30.00	75.00	200	400	600
ND(1601)Lion	—	30.00	75.00	200	400	600

KM# 42 STUIVER

1.3100 g., 0.3330 Silver 0.0140 oz. ASW **Obv. Inscription:** mintmark / FRI / SIA **Rev:** Bundle of arrows divides value in wreath **Note:** (Bezen-) Varieties exist.

Date	Mintage	VG	F	VF	XF
1619Lion	—	3.00	10.00	20.00	40.00	70.00

Date	Mintage	Good	VG	F	VF	XF
1619Lion	—	3.00	10.00	20.00	40.00	70.00
1622	—	3.00	10.00	20.00	40.00	70.00
1623	—	3.00	10.00	20.00	40.00	70.00
1627	—	3.00	10.00	20.00	40.00	70.00
1628	—	3.00	10.00	20.00	40.00	70.00
1629	—	3.00	10.00	20.00	40.00	70.00
1630	—	3.00	10.00	20.00	40.00	70.00
1650	—	3.00	10.00	20.00	40.00	70.00
1653	—	3.00	10.00	20.00	40.00	70.00
1660	—	3.00	10.00	20.00	40.00	70.00
1661	—	3.00	10.00	20.00	40.00	70.00
1664	—	3.00	10.00	20.00	40.00	70.00

KM# 5 2 STUIVERS

4.0000 g., Silver **Obv:** Crowned arms divide value in cartouche in inner circle **Obv. Legend:** NISI DOMINVS NOBISCVM 1601 **Rev:** Ornamental cross in inner circle, date in legend

Date	Mintage	Good	VG	F	VF	XF
1601Lion	—	25.00	75.00	200	450	750
1601Shield	—	25.00	75.00	200	450	750

KM# 32.2 2 STUIVERS

1.7300 g., 0.5830 Silver 0.0324 oz. ASW **Obv. Inscription:** FRI / SIA / (date) **Rev:** Crowned rampant lion left holding sword and arrows divides value 2 - S

Date	Mintage	Good	VG	F	VF	XF
1614Lion	—	2.25	7.00	20.00	45.00	90.00
1629Lion	—	1.60	5.00	15.00	40.00	80.00
1652Lion	—	1.60	5.00	15.00	40.00	80.00
1653Lion	—	1.60	5.00	15.00	40.00	80.00
1659Lion	—	1.60	5.00	15.00	40.00	80.00
1662Lion	—	1.60	5.00	15.00	40.00	80.00
1664Lion	—	1.60	5.00	15.00	40.00	80.00
1665Lion	—	1.60	5.00	15.00	40.00	80.00
1666Lion	—	1.60	5.00	15.00	40.00	80.00
1670Lion	—	1.60	5.00	15.00	40.00	80.00
1671Lion	—	1.60	5.00	15.00	40.00	80.00
1673Lion	—	1.60	5.00	15.00	40.00	80.00

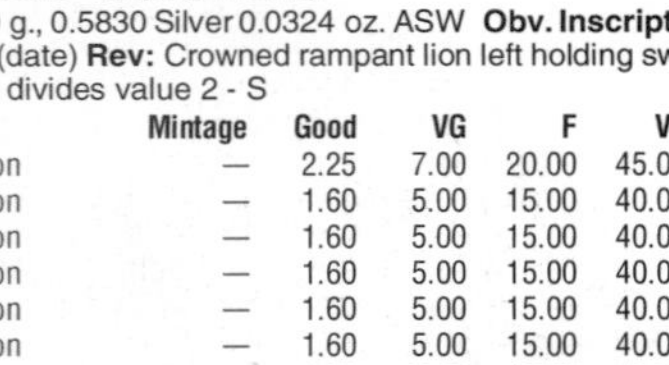

KM# 32.3 2 STUIVERS

Silver 1.5 - 1.73 grams, weight varies **Obv. Inscription:** FRI / SIA / (date) **Rev:** Rampant lion left holding sword and arrows divides value 2 - S **Note:** Mint mark: Lion between dots and rosettes. Varieties exist.

Date	Mintage	VG	F	VF	XF	Unc
1675	—	5.00	15.00	40.00	80.00	130
1675/4	—	7.00	25.00	60.00	125	170
1676	—	5.00	15.00	40.00	80.00	130
1678	—	5.00	15.00	40.00	80.00	130
1679	—	5.00	15.00	40.00	80.00	130
1680	—	5.00	15.00	40.00	80.00	130
1681	—	7.00	15.00	40.00	80.00	130
1681/76	—	7.00	25.00	60.00	125	170
1682	—	5.00	15.00	40.00	80.00	130
1683	—	5.00	15.00	40.00	80.00	130

KM# 6 3 STUIVERS (1/2 Snaphaanschelling)

3.3300 g., 0.5000 Silver 0.0535 oz. ASW **Obv:** Arms on ornamental cross **Obv. Legend:** MONE• - NOVA+ - ORDI+ - FRISI+ **Rev:** Helmeted arms **Rev. Legend:** NISI+ DOMINVS+ - NOBISCVM+

Date	Mintage	Good	VG	F	VF	XF
(16)01	—	40.00	125	225	350	500

KM# 30.1 6 STUIVERS (Snaphaanschelling)

6.6500 g., 0.5000 Silver 0.1069 oz. ASW **Obv:** Arms on ornate cross in inner circle **Obv. Legend:** MONE - NOVA• - ORDI• - FRISI• **Rev:** Knight on horseback left brandishing sword, date in exerque, in inner circle **Rev. Legend:** NISI •DOMENVS•NOBISCVM

Date	Mintage	Good	VG	F	VF	XF
1612Shield Obv. mintmark	—	20.00	60.00	120	250	500
1621Shield Obv. mintmark	—	20.00	60.00	120	250	500
1622Shield Obv. mintmark	—	20.00	60.00	120	250	500
1623Shield Obv. mintmark	—	20.00	60.00	120	250	500

KM# 30.2 6 STUIVERS (Snaphaanschelling)

6.6500 g., 0.5000 Silver 0.1069 oz. ASW **Obv:** Arms on ornate cross in inner circle **Obv. Legend:** MONE - NOVA• - ORDI• - FRISI• **Rev:** Knight on horseback left brandishing sword, date in exerque, in inner circle **Rev. Legend:** NISI •DOMENVS•NOBISCVM

Date	Mintage	Good	VG	F	VF	XF
1612Shield Rev. mintmark	—	20.00	60.00	120	250	500
1622Shield Rev. mintmark	—	20.00	60.00	120	250	500
1623Shield Rev. mintmark	—	20.00	60.00	120	250	500
1625Shield Rev. mintmark	—	20.00	60.00	120	250	500

KM# 34 6 STUIVERS (Arendschelling)

6.0000 g., 0.5000 Silver 0.0964 oz. ASW **Obv:** Crowned arms of 14 states in inner circle **Obv. Legend:** MO NOVA AR (GEN) OR(DIN) FRI(S) **Rev:** Crowned double-headed eagle in inner circle **Rev. Legend:** NISI TV DOMINE NOBISCVM FRVST (RA)

Date	Mintage	Good	VG	F	VF	XF
ND(1615-17)Lion	941,000	15.00	30.00	65.00	125	250

KM# 35 6 STUIVERS (Arendschelling)

6.0000 g., 0.5000 Silver 0.0964 oz. ASW **Obv:** Crowned arms of 11 states in inner circle **Obv. Legend:** MO(N) NOA ARGE - NT ORDIN(VM) FR(IS) **Rev:** Crowned double-headed eagle in inner circle **Rev. Legend:** NISI TV DOMINVS NOBISCVM FRVS (TRA)

Date	Mintage	Good	VG	F	VF	XF
ND(1615-1621)Lion	Inc. above	20.00	40.00	75.00	150	300

Note: 4 different states in crowned arms and with both sides a mintmark or one side only (Obv. or Rev.)

KM# 65 6 STUIVERS (RIJDERSCHELLING) (Rijderschelling)

4.9500 g., 0.5830 Silver 0.0928 oz. ASW **Obv:** Crowned arms **Rev:** Armored knight horseback right brandishing sword

Date	Mintage	Good	VG	F	VF	XF
1682	—	50.00	150	350	900	1,200
1684	—	50.00	150	350	900	1,200

KM# 7.1 7 STUIVERS (1/4 Florin)

4.3200 g., 0.7650 Silver 0.1062 oz. ASW **Obv:** Crowned arms on ornate cross in inner circle **Obv. Legend:** MONE NOVA ARGEN(TEA) ORDIN(VM) FRISI(AE) **Rev:** Frisian farmer right with sword on shoulder divides value 7 - S in inner circle, date in legend in Arabic numerals **Rev. Legend:** NISI DOMINVS NOBISCVM date in Arabic numerals

Date	Mintage	Good	VG	F	VF	XF
1601Lion	—	15.00	45.00	100	150	250

KM# 7.2 7 STUIVERS (1/4 Florin)

4.3200 g., 0.7650 Silver 0.1062 oz. ASW **Obv:** Crowned arms on ornate cross in inner circle **Obv. Legend:** MONE NOVA ORDINVM FRISI(AE) **Rev:** Frisian farmer right with sword on shoulder divides value 7 - S in inner circle, date in legend in Arabic numerals **Rev. Legend:** NISI DOMINVS NOBISCVM date in Arabic numerals

Date	Mintage	Good	VG	F	VF	XF
1601Lion	—	15.00	45.00	100	150	250

KM# 66.2 7 STUIVERS (1/4 Florin)

4.3200 g., 0.7650 Silver 0.1062 oz. ASW **Obv:** Crowned arms on ornate cross in inner circle, roset **Obv. Legend:** MONETA ARGENTEA ORDINVM FRISI(AE) **Rev:** Frisian farmer right with sword on shoulder divides value 7 - S, date in Arabic numerals **Rev. Legend:** NISI DOMINVS NOBISCVM

Date	Mintage	Good	VG	F	VF	XF
1684	—	18.00	55.00	150	350	500
1684Lion	—	18.00	55.00	150	350	500

KM# 66.1 7 STUIVERS (1/4 Florin)

4.3200 g., 0.7650 Silver 0.1062 oz. ASW **Obv:** Crowned arms on ornate cross in inner circle **Obv. Legend:** MONETA ARGENTEA ORDINVM FRISI(AE) **Rev:** Frisian farmer right with sword on shoulder divides value 7 - S, date in legend in Roman numerals, date in Roman numerals **Rev. Legend:** NISI DOMINVS NOBISCVM

Date	Mintage	Good	VG	F	VF	XF
1684cross	—	18.00	55.00	150	200	300
1684Lion	—	18.00	55.00	150	200	300

KM# 24 10 STUIVERS

5.9500 g., 0.9170 Silver 0.1754 oz. ASW **Obv:** Armored knight standing holding sword behind shield of arms, date at sides in inner circle **Obv. Legend:** MO ARG PRO CON - FOE BELG FRI **Rev:** Crowned arms divide value in inner circle **Rev. Legend:** CONCORDIA RES PARVAE CRESCVNT

Date	Mintage	Good	VG	F	VF	XF
1607Lion	—	40.00	150	500	1,000	1,800

KM# 72 10 STUIVERS (1/2 Gulden)

5.3000 g., 0.5000 Silver 0.0852 oz. ASW **Obv:** Crowned arms **Obv. Legend:** MO: ARG: ORD: FÆD: BELG: FRI: **Rev:** Dutch maiden standing with liberty cap on lance leaning on bible on column **Rev. Legend:** HAC: NITIMVR HANC. TVEMVR

Date	Mintage	Good	VG	F	VF	XF
1694	—	20.00	55.00	150	250	500
1696	—	15.00	45.00	100	150	300

KM# 9 14 STUIVERS (1/2 Florin)

8.6500 g., Silver **Obv. Legend:** MONETA. NOVA. ORDINVM. FRISIÆ. **Rev. Legend:** NISI DOMINVS NOBISC(V)M FRISIÆ

Date	Mintage	Good	VG	F	VF	XF
1601Lion	—	16.00	50.00	125	175	300

KM# A8.1 14 STUIVERS (1/2 Florin)

8.6500 g., 0.7650 Silver 0.2127 oz. ASW **Obv:** Crowned arms with ornaments at sides in inner circle **Obv. Legend:** FLORENVS • ARGENT • ORODI • FRIÆ **Rev:** Large bust of Frisian with sword on shoulder divides value in inner circle **Rev. Legend:** NISI • DOMINVS • NOBI SCVM

Date	Mintage	Good	VG	F	VF	XF
1601Lion	—	15.00	45.00	100	150	250
1601Lion	—	15.00	45.00	100	150	250
1601Shield	—	15.00	45.00	100	150	250

KM# A8.2 14 STUIVERS (1/2 Florin)

8.6500 g., 0.7650 Silver 0.2127 oz. ASW **Obv:** Crowned arms with ornaments at sides in inner circle **Obv. Legend:** FLORENVS • ARGENT • OROD(I) • FRIÆ **Rev:** Small bust of Frisian with sword on shoulder right divides value in inner circle **Rev. Legend:** NISI • DOMINVS • NOBI SCVM

Date	Mintage	Good	VG	F	VF	XF
1684Lion	—	15.00	45.00	100	150	250
1686Lion	—	15.00	45.00	100	150	250

KM# 67 14 STUIVERS (1/2 Florin)

Silver **Obv:** Crown throught the inner circle **Obv. Legend:** MONETA. ARGEN. ORD. FRIS.

Date	Mintage	Good	VG	F	VF	XF
1688	—	15.00	45.00	100	175	300

KM# 50 20 STUIVERS (1/2 Ducaton)

16.3900 g., 0.9410 Silver 0.4958 oz. ASW **Obv:** Knight horseback right brandishing sword, provincial arms below in inner circle **Rev:** Crowned arms with crowned lion supporters in inner circle, date at top in legend

Date	Mintage	Good	VG	F	VF	XF
1659	—	50.00	150	350	700	1,000
1660	—	50.00	150	350	700	1,000
1661	—	50.00	150	350	700	1,000
1662/0	—	60.00	200	450	900	1,300
1662	—	60.00	200	450	900	1,300
1668	—	60.00	200	450	900	1,300

KM# 51 20 STUIVERS (1/2 Ducaton)

Silver **Obv:** Knight horseback right brandishing sword, provincial arms below in inner circle **Rev:** Crowned arms with crowned lion supporters in inner circle, date at top in legend **Note:** Klippe.

Date	Mintage	Good	VG	F	VF	XF
1659	—	60.00	150	300	500	700

KM# 73 GULDEN (20 Stuivers)

10.6100 g., 0.9200 Silver 0.3138 oz. ASW **Obv:** Crowned lion shield divides value **Rev:** Standing female figure leaning on Bible on column, holding spear with Liberty cap, date in exerque **Note:** Varieties exist.

Date	Mintage	Good	VG	F	VF	XF
1696	—	20.00	70.00	150	300	500

KM# 12.1 24 STUIVERS (1/2 Lion Daalder)

13.8400 g., 0.7500 Silver 0.3337 oz. ASW **Obv:** Armored knight looking right above lion shield in inner circle **Obv. Legend:** MO NO ORD - FRI(S) VA(L) HO(L) **Rev:** Rampant lion left in inner circle, date at top in legend **Rev. Legend:** CONFIDENS DNO NON MOVETVR **Note:** Varieties exist.

Date	Mintage	Good	VG	F	VF	XF
1601/1599	—	20.00	60.00	150	350	600
1601	—	20.00	60.00	150	350	600
1602/1600	—	20.00	6.00	150	350	600
1602	—	200	60.00	150	350	600
1602/1599	—	20.00	60.00	150	350	600

KM# 12.2 24 STUIVERS (1/2 Lion Daalder)

13.8400 g., 0.7500 Silver 0.3337 oz. ASW **Obv:** Armored knight looking right above lion shield in inner circle **Obv. Legend:** MONE NOVA - date - ORDI(N) FRISI(AE) **Rev:** Rampant lion left in inner circle, date at top in legend **Rev. Legend:** NISI DOMINVS NOBISCVM **Note:** Varieties exist.

Date	Mintage	Good	VG	F	VF	XF
1604Lion	—	40.00	150	450	850	1,250

KM# 12.3 24 STUIVERS (1/2 Lion Daalder)

13.8400 g., 0.7500 Silver 0.3337 oz. ASW **Obv:** Armored knight looking right above lion shield in inner circle **Rev:** Rampant

Date	Mintage	Good	VG	F	VF	XF
NDLion Without mintmark	—	12.00	35.00	75.00	150	250
NDLion Mintmark both sides	—	12.00	35.00	75.00	150	250
1607Lion Without mintmark	—	12.00	40.00	80.00	160	300
1607Lion Rev. mintmark	—	12.00	40.00	80.00	160	300
1608Lion Without mintmark	—	16.00	50.00	100	200	350
1611Lion Without mintmark	—	12.00	40.00	80.00	160	300
1611Lion Rev. mintmark	—	12.00	40.00	80.00	160	300
1611Lion Obv. mintmark	—	16.00	50.00	100	200	350
1611Lion Mintmark both sides	—	16.00	50.00	100	200	350
1613Lion Obv. mintmark	—	16.00	50.00	100	200	350
1614Lion Obv. mintmark	—	16.00	50.00	100	200	350
1614Lion Without mintmark	—	12.00	40.00	80.00	160	300
1616Lion Obv. mintmark	—	16.00	50.00	100	200	350
1616Lion Rev. mintmark	—	12.00	40.00	80.00	160	300
1616Lion Mintmark both sides	—	16.00	50.00	100	200	350
1617Lion Mintmark both sides	—	16.00	50.00	100	200	350
ND1619Lion Rev. mintmark	—	12.00	35.00	75.00	150	250
1619Lion Obv. mintmark	—	16.00	50.00	100	200	350
1620Lion Mintmark both sides	—	16.00	50.00	100	200	350
1626Lion Rev. mintmark	—	15.00	45.00	125	250	400
1628Lion Without mintmark	—	16.00	50.00	100	200	350
1629/8Lion Without mintmark	—	16.00	50.00	100	200	350
1629Lion Without mintmark	—	16.00	50.00	100	200	350
1632Lion Without mintmark	—	18.00	60.00	170	300	550
1632Lion Rev. mintmark	—	15.00	45.00	125	250	400
1633Lion Obv. mintmark	—	17.00	55.00	160	275	450
1649Lion Without mintmark	—	18.00	60.00	170	300	550
1652Lion Without mintmark	—	18.00	60.00	170	300	550
1659Lion Without mintmark	—	18.00	60.00	170	300	550
1663Lion Obv. mintmark	—	18.00	60.00	170	300	550

KM# 21 24 STUIVERS (1/2 Rijksdaalder)

14.5100 g., 0.8850 Silver 0.4128 oz. ASW **Obv:** Laureate 1/2 figure holding sword and arms in inner circle **Obv. Legend:** MO AR(G) PRO - CONFOE BELG FR(ISAE) **Rev:** Crowned arms divide date in inner circle **Rev. Legend:** CONCORDIA RES PARVAE CRESCVN(T)

Date	Mintage	Good	VG	F	VF	XF
1606Lion Obv. mintmark	—	25.00	75.00	225	350	500
1607Lion Obv. mintmark	—	25.00	75.00	225	350	500
1608Lion Obv. mintmark	—	25.00	75.00	225	350	500
1609 No mintmark	—	25.00	75.00	225	350	500
1609Lion Obv. mintmark	—	25.00	75.00	225	350	500
1610 No mintmark	—	25.00	75.00	225	350	500
1610Lion Obv. mintmark	—	25.00	75.00	225	350	500
1611Lion Obv. mintmark	—	25.00	75.00	225	350	500
1619Lion Mintmark both sides	—	25.00	75.00	225	350	500
1619Lion Obv. mintmark	—	25.00	75.00	225	350	500
1620Lion Mintmark both sides	—	25.00	75.00	225	350	500
1620Lion Obv. mintmark	—	25.00	75.00	225	350	500
1621Lion Mintmark both sides	—	25.00	75.00	225	350	500
1621 No mintmark	—	25.00	75.00	225	350	500
1621Lion Obv. mintmark	—	25.00	75.00	225	350	500
1621/20Lion Obv. mintmark	—	25.00	75.00	225	350	600
1622Lion Obv. mintmark	—	25.00	75.00	225	350	500
1626Lion Obv. mintmark	—	25.00	75.00	225	350	500
1629Lion Mintmark both sides	—	25.00	75.00	225	350	500
1629Lion Obv. mintmark	—	25.00	75.00	225	350	600
1630Lion Obv. mintmark	—	25.00	75.00	225	350	600
1631Lion Obv. mintmark	—	25.00	75.00	225	350	600
1645Lion Obv. mintmark	—	25.00	75.00	225	350	600
1649Lion Obv. mintmark	—	25.00	75.00	225	350	600
1650Lion Obv. mintmark	—	25.00	75.00	225	350	600
1651Lion Obv. mintmark	—	25.00	75.00	225	350	600
1661/0Lion Obv. mintmark	—	25.00	75.00	225	350	600
1661Lion Obv. mintmark	—	25.00	75.00	225	350	600
1662Lion Obv. mintmark	—	25.00	75.00	225	350	600
1666 No mintmark	—	25.00	75.00	225	350	600
1669Lion Obv. mintmark	—	25.00	75.00	225	350	600

KM# 55 24 STUIVERS (1/2 Silver Ducat)

14.1200 g., 0.8730 Silver 0.3963 oz. ASW **Obv:** Armored knight standing holding sword behind shield of arms, date at sides in inner circle **Obv. Legend:** MO NO ARG PRO - FOE BEL(G) FRI **Rev:** Crowned arms in inner circle **Rev. Legend:** CONCORDIA RES PARVAE CRESCVNT

Date	Mintage	Good	VG	F	VF	XF
1660Lion	—	50.00	150	400	900	1,400
1672Lion	—	60.00	200	500	1,000	1,600
1673Lion	—	60.00	200	500	1,000	1,600

KM# 10 28 STUIVERS (Florin)

17.3000 g., 0.7650 Silver 0.4255 oz. ASW **Obv:** Crowned arms with ornaments **Obv. Legend:** FLORENVS • ARGENT • ORDI • FRISIÆ **Rev:** Farmer with sword **Rev. Legend:** NISI • DOMINVS • NOBISCVM •

Date	Mintage	Good	VG	F	VF	XF
1601Lion Rev. mintmark	—	16.00	50.00	150	250	400
1614Lion Mintmark both sides	—	65.00	200	300	450	700
1614/01Lion Rev. mintmark	—	65.00	200	300	450	700
1614/04Lion Rev. mintmark	—	65.00	200	300	450	700
1614Lion Rev. mintmark	—	65.00	200	300	450	700
1665/4Lion Rev. mintmark	—	25.00	85.00	200	300	500
1665Lion Rev. mintmark	—	16.00	50.00	140	220	350
1666Lion Mintmark both sides	—	25.00	75.00	150	250	400
1683Lion Rev. mintmark	—	16.00	50.00	140	220	350
1684Lion Obv. mintmark	—	25.00	75.00	150	250	400
1684Lion Rev. mintmark	—	16.00	50.00	140	220	350
1688Lion Rev. mintmark	—	16.00	50.00	140	220	350
1689Lion Rev. mintmark	—	16.00	50.00	140	220	350
1690Lion Rev. mintmark	—	16.00	50.00	140	220	350
1691Lion Rev. mintmark	—	16.00	50.00	140	220	350

KM# 71 28 STUIVERS (Florin)

19.5000 g., 0.6730 Silver 0.4219 oz. ASW **Obv:** Crowned arms **Obv. Legend:** MO: ARG: ORD: FÆD: BELG: FRI: **Rev:** Standing Dutch maiden leaning on Bible on column, holding lance with Liberty cap on top **Rev. Inscription:** HAC: NITIMVR HANC. TVEMVR

Date	Mintage	Good	VG	F	VF	XF
1694	—	—	—	—	—	—

KM# 36.1 30 STUIVERS (Arendsdaalder of 60 Groot)

20.6800 g., 0.7500 Silver 0.4986 oz. ASW **Obv:** Ornate arms with upper right shield with diagonal lines left **Obv. Legend:** MONETA ARGENT 60 ORDINVM FRISIAE **Rev:** Double-headed eagle with provincial arms on breast in inner circle **Rev. Legend:** SI DEVS NOBISCVM QVIS CON(TRA) NOS

Date	Mintage	Good	VG	F	VF	XF
1617Lion	—	25.00	80.00	200	350	650
1618Lion	—	25.00	80.00	200	350	650

KM# 36.2 30 STUIVERS (Arendsdaalder of 60 Groot)

20.6800 g., 0.7500 Silver 0.4986 oz. ASW **Obv:** Ornate arms with upper right shield with diagonal lines right **Rev:** Double-headed eagle with provincial arms on breast in inner circle

Date	Mintage	Good	VG	F	VF	XF
1617Lion	—	25.00	80.00	200	300	450
1618Lion	—	25.00	80.00	200	300	450
1619Lion	—	25.00	80.00	200	350	550

KM# A66 30 STUIVERS (Koggerdaalder)

19.1900 g., 0.7570 Silver 0.4670 oz. ASW **Obv:** Crowned arms between value **Obv. Legend:** ANTIGVA•VIRTVTE•ET • FIDE• **Rev:** Four crowned shields: Oostergo, Westergo, Sevenwolden and 11-fold with "OG - WG - SW - ST" in angles, 'OG' under "CONCOR" **Rev. Legend:** CONCOR•FRISIAE•LIBERTAS

Date	Mintage	Good	VG	F	VF	XF
1682	—	40.00	100	200	350	550

KM# A67.1 30 STUIVERS (Koggerdaalder)

Silver **Obv:** Crowned arms **Rev:** 4 crowned shields with bundle of arrows at center **Rev. Legend:** CONGO•FRISI•LIBER-TAS

Date	Mintage	Good	VG	F	VF	XF
1687	—	40.00	100	200	350	550

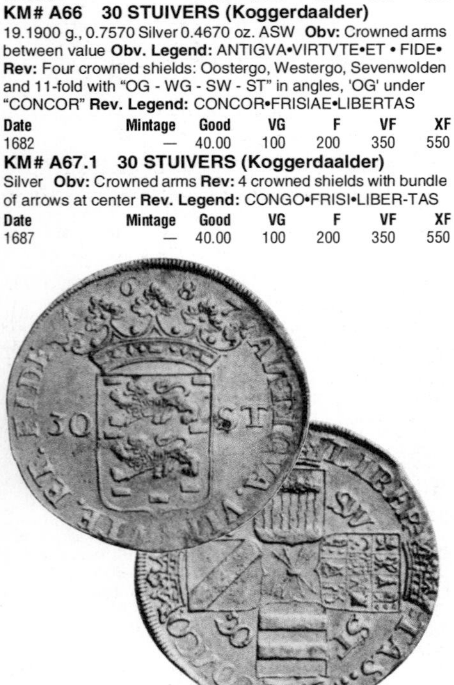

KM# A67.2 30 STUIVERS (Koggerdaalder)

Silver **Obv:** Crowned arms, legend with retrograde 'N' **Obv. Legend:** ANTIGVA VIRTVTE ET FIDE **Rev:** 4 crowned shields with bundle of arrows at center **Rev. Legend:** CONGO • DIA • FRISI • LIBER-TAS

Date	Mintage	Good	VG	F	VF	XF
1687	—	25.00	80.00	200	325	500

KM# 74 30 STUIVERS (1/2 3 Gulden)

15.9100 g., 0.9200 Silver 0.4706 oz. ASW **Obv:** Crowned arms **Obv. Legend:** MO: ARG: ORD: FÆD: BELG: FRI: **Rev:** Dutch maiden with liberty cap on lance, leaning on bible on column **Rev. Legend:** HAC: NITIMVR HANC. TVEMVR

Date	Mintage	Good	VG	F	VF	XF
1696	—	14.00	40.00	100	175	300

KM# 52 40 STUIVERS (Ducaton)

32.7800 g., 0.9410 Silver 0.9917 oz. ASW **Obv:** Knight with sword on horseback right, provincial arms below in inner circle **Obv. Legend:** MO NO ARG PRO CON - FOE BELG FRI(S) **Rev:** Crowned arms with crowned lion supporters in inner circle **Rev. Legend:** CONCORDIA RES PARVAE CRESCVNT **Note:** Dav. #4926.

Date	Mintage	Good	VG	F	VF	XF
1659	—	35.00	150	350	650	1,000
1660	—	35.00	150	350	650	1,000
1661	—	40.00	175	450	900	1,300
1662	—	40.00	175	450	900	1,300
1663	—	40.00	175	450	900	1,300
1665	—	40.00	175	450	900	1,300
1668	—	60.00	250	600	1,100	1,600

KM# 75 40 STUIVERS (2 Guilden)

21.2100 g., 0.9200 Silver 0.6273 oz. ASW **Obv:** Crowned arms divide value **Obv. Legend:** MO ARG ORD FAED BELG FRI **Rev:** Dutch maiden standing with Liberty cap on lance, leaning on bible on column

Date	Mintage	Good	VG	F	VF	XF
1696	26,796	32.00	100	250	400	550

KM# 53 48 STUIVERS (Ducat)

28.2500 g., 0.8730 Silver 0.7929 oz. ASW **Obv:** Amored knight standing holding sword behind shield of arms, date at sides in inner circle **Obv. Legend:** MO NO ARG PRO CON - FOE BEL(G) FRI **Rev:** Crowned arms in inner circle **Rev. Legend:** CONCORDIA RES PARVAE CRESCVNT **Note:** Varieties exist. Dav. #4892.

Date	Mintage	Good	VG	F	VF	XF
1659Lion	—	26.00	80.00	250	500	800
1660Lion	—	26.00	80.00	250	500	800
1661Lion	—	26.00	80.00	250	700	1,000
1662Lion	—	26.00	80.00	250	700	1,000
1663Lion	—	26.00	80.00	250	700	1,000
1672Lion	—	26.00	80.00	250	700	1,000

KM# 76 48 STUIVERS (Ducat)

Silver **Obv:** Without inner circle **Obv. Legend:** MO NO ARG PRO CON - FOE BELG FRISIAE **Rev:** Crowned arms divide date, without inner circle **Rev. Legend:** CONCORDIA RES PARVAE CRESCVNT **Note:** Dav. #4893.

Date	Mintage	Good	VG	F	VF	XF
1696	—	50.00	150	300	450	800
1698	—	50.00	150	300	450	800

KM# 22 48 STUIVERS (Dutch Rijksdaalder)

29.0300 g., 0.8850 Silver 0.8260 oz. ASW **Obv:** Laureate 1/2 figure holding sword and arms in inner circle **Obv. Legend:** MO ARG P - RO C CONFOE BELG FR - (ISIAE) **Rev:** Crowned arms divide date in inner circle **Rev. Legend:** CONCORDIA RES PARVAE CRESCVN(T) **Note:** Dav. #4829. Varieties exist.

Date	Mintage	Good	VG	F	VF	X
1606Lion Obv. mintmark	—	20.00	45.00	125	225	35
1607Lion Obv. mintmark	—	20.00	45.00	125	225	35
1608Lion Mintmark both sides	—	20.00	45.00	125	225	35
1608Lion Obv. mintmark	—	20.00	45.00	125	225	35
1609Lion Obv. mintmark	—	20.00	45.00	125	225	35
1609Lion Rev. mintmark	—	20.00	45.00	125	225	35
1610Lion Mintmark both sides	—	20.00	45.00	125	225	35
1610Lion Obv. mintmark	—	20.00	45.00	125	225	35
1611Lion Mintmark both sides	—	20.00	45.00	125	225	35
1611Lion Obv. mintmark	—	20.00	45.00	125	225	35
1611Lion Rev. mintmark	—	20.00	45.00	125	225	35
1612/1Lion Obv. mintmark	—	20.00	45.00	125	225	35
1612Lion Obv. mintmark	—	20.00	45.00	125	225	35
1613Lion Mintmark both sides	—	20.00	45.00	125	225	35
1613Lion Obv. mintmark	—	20.00	45.00	125	225	35
1617Lion Mintmark both sides	—	20.00	45.00	125	225	35
1617Lion Obv. mintmark	—	20.00	45.00	125	225	35
1618Lion Mintmark both sides	—	20.00	45.00	125	225	35
1618Lion Obv. mintmark	—	20.00	45.00	125	225	35
1619Lion Mintmark both sides	—	20.00	45.00	125	225	35
1619/2Lion Obv. mintmark	—	20.00	45.00	125	225	35
1619Lion Obv. mintmark	—	20.00	45.00	125	225	35
1620Lion Mintmark both sides	—	20.00	45.00	125	225	35
1620/19Lion Obv. mintmark	—	25.00	55.00	140	250	40
1620Lion Obv. mintmark	—	25.00	55.00	140	250	40
1621Lion Mintmark both sides	—	20.00	45.00	125	225	35
1621/10Lion Mintmark both sides	—	20.00	45.00	125	225	35
1622Lion Mintmark both sides	—	25.00	55.00	250	250	40
1622/10Lion Mintmark both sides	—	25.00	55.00	250	250	40
1626Lion Mintmark both sides	—	25.00	55.00	250	250	40
1626/3Lion Obv. mintmark	—	25.00	55.00	140	250	40
1629Lion No mintmark	—	25.00	55.00	140	250	40
1629Lion Obv. mintmark	—	25.00	55.00	140	250	40
1630Lion Obv. mintmark	—	25.00	55.00	140	250	40
1650Lion No mintmark	—	25.00	55.00	140	250	40
1651Lion Obv. mintmark	—	25.00	55.00	140	250	40
1661Lion Obv. mintmark	—	25.00	55.00	140	250	40

KM# 29 48 STUIVERS (Lion Daalder)

Obv: Armored knight looking right behind lion shield **Obv. Legend:** MO AR(G) - split dage - ORDIN FRI(S) **Rev. Legend:** CONFIDENS DNO NON MOVETVR

Date	Mintage	Good	VG	F	VF	X
1601 No mintmark (error for 1610)	—	12.00	30.00	75.00	150	25
ND1607Lion	—	12.00	30.00	75.00	150	25
1607 No mintmark	—	12.00	30.00	75.00	150	25
1607Lion	—	12.00	30.00	75.00	150	25
1608Lion	—	12.00	30.00	75.00	150	25
1608 No mintmark	—	12.00	30.00	75.00	150	25
1609Lion	—	12.00	30.00	75.00	150	25
1610Lion	—	12.00	30.00	75.00	150	25
1612Lion	—	12.00	30.00	75.00	150	25

KM# 11 48 STUIVERS (Lion Daalder)

27.6800 g., 0.7500 Silver 0.6674 oz. ASW **Obv:** Armored knight looking right above lion (of Holland) shield in inner circle, date divided at bottom **Obv. Legend:** MO + NO + ORD - FRI + VA + HOL **Rev:** Rampant lion left in inner circle **Rev. Legend:** CONFIDENS DNO NON MOVETVR **Note:** Mint mark: Lion arms. Dav. #4851.

Date	Mintage	Good	VG	F	VF	XF
1601Shield	—	20.00	45.00	125	225	350
1602/0Shield	—	20.00	45.00	125	225	350
1602/1Shield	—	20.00	45.00	125	225	350
1602Shield	—	25.00	50.00	150	300	450
1603Shield	—	25.00	50.00	150	300	450

KM# 14 48 STUIVERS (Lion Daalder)

Silver **Obv:** Friesland arms in shield (two lions) innstead of Holland **Note:** Mint mark: Arms. Dav. #4852.

Date	Mintage	Good	VG	F	VF	XF
1603Shield	—	20.00	45.00	125	225	350
1604Shield	—	20.00	45.00	125	225	350
1604 No mintmark	—	20.00	45.00	125	225	350
1604/3Shield	—	25.00	85.00	175	350	550
1605Shield	—	20.00	45.00	125	225	350
1605 No mintmark	—	20.00	45.00	125	225	350

KM# 23.1 48 STUIVERS (Lion Daalder)

Silver **Obv:** Lion shield of Holland instead of provincial Friesland arms **Obv. Legend:** MO AR(G) PR(O) CO - NFOE BEL(G) FR(IS) **Rev:** Date at top in legend **Rev. Legend:** CONFIDENS DNO NON MOVETVR **Note:** Dav. #4853.

Date	Mintage	Good	VG	F	VF	XF
NDLion	—	12.00	30.00	75.00	150	250
1606Lion	—	12.00	30.00	75.00	150	250
1607 No mintmark	—	12.00	30.00	75.00	150	250
1608 No mintmark	—	12.00	30.00	75.00	150	250
1609 No mintmark	—	12.00	30.00	75.00	150	250
1609Lion	—	12.00	30.00	75.00	150	250
1610Lion	—	12.00	30.00	75.00	150	250
1610 No mintmark	—	12.00	30.00	75.00	150	250
1601Lion Error for 1610	—	12.00	30.00	75.00	150	250
1611Lion	—	12.00	30.00	75.00	150	250
1612Lion	—	12.00	30.00	75.00	150	250
1612 No mintmark	—	12.00	30.00	75.00	150	250
1613 No mintmark	—	12.00	30.00	75.00	150	250
1613Lion	—	12.00	30.00	75.00	150	250
1614Lion	—	12.00	30.00	75.00	150	250
1614Lion Mintmark both sides	—	12.00	30.00	75.00	150	250
1614 No mintmark	—	12.00	30.00	75.00	150	250
1615 No mintmark	—	12.00	30.00	75.00	150	250
1615Lion Mintmark both sides	—	12.00	30.00	75.00	150	250
ND1615Lion Mintmark both sides	—	12.00	30.00	75.00	150	250
1615Lion	—	12.00	30.00	75.00	150	250
1616Lion	—	12.00	30.00	75.00	150	250
1616 No mintmark	—	12.00	30.00	75.00	150	250
1617Lion	—	12.00	30.00	75.00	150	250
1617Lion Mintmark both sides	—	12.00	30.00	75.00	150	250
1619/5Lion	—	20.00	45.00	125	225	350
1619/2Lion	—	20.00	45.00	125	225	350
1619Lion	—	12.00	30.00	75.00	150	250
1623Lion	—	20.00	45.00	125	225	350
1622 No mintmark	—	12.00	30.00	75.00	150	250
1625Lion Mintmark both sides	—	12.00	30.00	75.00	150	250
1625Lion	—	12.00	30.00	75.00	150	250
1626Lion	—	12.00	30.00	75.00	150	250
1628 No mintmark	—	12.00	30.00	75.00	150	250
1629 No mintmark	—	12.00	30.00	75.00	150	250
1629/8Lion	—	20.00	45.00	125	225	350
1640 No mintmark	—	12.00	30.00	75.00	150	250
1642Rosette	—	25.00	85.00	175	350	550
1643Rosette	—	25.00	85.00	175	350	550
1643Lion Mintmart between date	—	25.00	85.00	175	350	550
1649Lion Mintmart between date	—	25.00	85.00	175	350	550
1649 No mintmark	—	25.00	85.00	175	350	550
1650 No mintmark	—	25.00	85.00	175	350	550
1650Lion Mintmart between date	—	25.00	85.00	175	350	550
1653 No mintmark	—	25.00	85.00	175	350	550
1663Lion Obv. mintmark	—	20.00	45.00	125	225	350

KM# 23.2 48 STUIVERS (Lion Daalder)

Silver **Rev:** Mint mark

Date	Mintage	Good	VG	F	VF	XF
NDLion Rev. mintmark	—	12.00	30.00	75.00	150	250
1607Lion Rev. mintmark	—	12.00	30.00	75.00	150	250
1608Lion Rev. mintmark	—	12.00	30.00	75.00	150	250
1610Lion Rev. mintmark	—	12.00	30.00	75.00	150	250
1611Lion Rev. mintmark	—	12.00	30.00	75.00	150	250
1614Lion Rev. mintmark	—	12.00	30.00	75.00	150	250
1615Lion Rev. mintmark	—	12.00	30.00	75.00	150	250
1617Lion Rev. mintmark	—	12.00	30.00	75.00	150	250
1620Lion Rev. mintmark	—	12.00	30.00	75.00	150	250
1622Lion Rev. mintmark	—	12.00	30.00	75.00	150	250
1625Lion Rev. mintmark	—	20.00	45.00	125	225	350
1626Lion Rev. mintmark	—	20.00	45.00	125	225	350
1628Lion Rev. mintmark	—	20.00	45.00	125	225	350
1650Lion Rev. mintmark	—	20.00	45.00	125	225	350

KM# 33 48 STUIVERS (Lion Daalder)

Silver **Obv:** Date divided at bottom **Obv. Legend:** MO NO(VA) ARG (E) - split date - ORDIN FRI(S) **Rev. Legend:** CONFIDENS DNO NON MOVETVR **Note:** Dav. #4854.

Date	Mintage	Good	VG	F	VF	XF
1614Lion Rev. mintmark	—	12.00	30.00	75.00	150	250
1615Lion Rev. mintmark	—	12.00	30.00	75.00	150	250
1615Lion Rev. mintmark, date retrograde (5161)	—	20.00	45.00	100	225	350
1616Lion Obv. mintmark	—	12.00	30.00	75.00	150	250
1616Lion Rev. mintmark	—	12.00	30.00	75.00	150	250
1617Lion Obv. mintmark	—	12.00	30.00	75.00	150	250
1617Lion Rev. mintmark	—	12.00	30.00	75.00	150	250
1622Lion Rev. mintmark	—	12.00	30.00	75.00	150	250
ND1622Lion Mintmark on both sides	—	12.00	30.00	75.00	150	250

KM# 47 48 STUIVERS (Lion Daalder)

Silver Dav. #4853B. **Obv:** Armored knight looking right behind lion shield, date **Rev:** Rampant lion left, date

Date	Mintage	Good	VG	F	VF	XF
161-7	—	12.00	30.00	75.00	150	250
162-8	—	12.00	30.00	75.00	150	250
162-88 (error)	—	12.00	30.00	75.00	150	250
162-9	—	12.00	30.00	75.00	150	250

KM# 15 50 STUIVERS (Arendsrijksdaalder)

29.0300 g., 0.8850 Silver 0.8260 oz. ASW **Obv:** Frisian farmer with sword on shoulder in inner circle, date in legend **Obv. Legend:** NISI DOMINVS NOBISCVM - date **Rev:** Crowned double-headed eagle in inner circle **Rev. Legend:** MONET(A) NOVA ORDINVM FRISIAE **Note:** Lion arms.

Date	Mintage	Good	VG	F	VF	XF
1603/00	—	150	400	1,200	2,400	3,500
1603	—	110	300	1,000	2,000	3,000

KM# 77 60 STUIVERS (3 Gulden)

31.8200 g., 0.9200 Silver 0.9412 oz. ASW **Obv:** Crowned arms divide value **Obv. Legend:** MO ARG ORD FAED BELG FRI **Rev:** Standing female figure leaning on Bible on column, holding spear with Liberty cap, date in exergue **Rev. Legend:** HAC NITMVR - HANC TVEMVR **Note:** Dav. #4950.

Date	Mintage	Good	VG	F	VF	XF
1696	—	75.00	225	650	1,300	1,600
1697	—	75.00	225	650	1,300	1,600
1698	—	75.00	225	650	1,300	1,600

KM# 45 1/2 CAVALIER D'OR

5.0000 g., 0.9200 Gold 0.1479 oz. AGW **Obv:** Equestrian figure of knight above arms in inner circle **Obv. Legend:** MO AV® PRO CON - FOE BELG FRI(S) **Rev:** Crowned arms in inner circle, date at top **Rev. Legend:** CONCORDIA RES PARVAE CRESCVNT

Date	Mintage	VG	F	VF	XF	Unc
1620Lion	—	300	1,750	3,500	5,000	—
1620Lion Mintmark between date	—	300	1,750	3,500	5,000	—
1622Lion	—	300	1,750	3,500	5,000	—
1623Lion	—	300	1,750	3,500	5,000	—
1624Lion	—	300	1,750	3,500	5,000	—
1626Lion	—	300	1,750	3,500	5,000	—
1628Lion	—	300	1,750	3,500	5,000	—
1630Lion	—	300	1,750	3,500	5,000	—
1630 No mintmark	—	200	450	800	1,200	—
1644 No mintmark	—	200	450	800	1,200	—

KM# 48 1/2 CAVALIER D'OR

5.0000 g., 0.9200 Gold 0.1479 oz. AGW **Note:** Klippe.

Date	Mintage	F	VF	XF	Unc
1628 Proof	—	Value: 4,500			

KM# 25 CAVALIER D'OR

10.0000 g., 0.9200 Gold 0.2958 oz. AGW **Obv:** Equestrian figure of knight above arms in inner circle **Obv. Legend:** MO AV (R) PRO CON - FOE BE LG FRI (SIAE) **Rev:** Crowned arms in inner circle, date at top **Rev. Legend:** CONCORDIA RES PARVAE CRESCVNT

Date	Mintage	VG	F	VF	XF	Unc
1607Lion	—	—	2,500	4,500	7,500	—
1607 No mintmark	—	—	2,500	4,500	7,500	—
1617Lion	—	—	2,500	4,500	7,500	—
1618Lion	—	—	2,500	4,500	7,500	—
1619Lion	—	—	2,500	4,500	7,500	—
1620Lion	—	—	2,500	4,500	7,500	—
1626Lion	—	—	2,500	4,500	7,500	—
1628Lion	—	—	2,500	4,500	7,500	—

TRADE COINAGE

KM# 37 FLORIN D'OR

3.5000 g., 0.9860 Gold 0.1109 oz. AGW **Obv:** Crowned imperial eagle in inner circle **Obv. Legend:** NISI DOMINVS NOBISCVM **Rev:** 5 shields of arms in quatrefoil, date in legend **Rev. Legend:** MON AVR FRI

Date	Mintage	VG	F	VF	XF	Unc
1617Lion	—	250	1,000	2,000	3,000	—
1618Lion	—	250	1,000	2,000	3,000	—
1619Lion	—	250	1,000	2,000	3,000	—

KM# 38 FLORIN D'OR

3.5000 g., 0.9860 Gold 0.1109 oz. AGW **Obv:** Crowned imperial eagle in inner circle **Obv. Legend:** NISI DOMINVS NOBISCVM **Rev:** Helmeted arms in inner circle, date in legend **Rev. Legend:** MONE AVRA FRISTAE

Date	Mintage	VG	F	VF	XF	Unc
1617Lion Rare	—	—	—	—	—	—
1618Lion Rare	—	—	—	—	—	—
1619Lion Rare	—	—	—	—	—	—

KM# 13 DUCAT

3.5000 g., 0.9860 Gold 0.1109 oz. AGW **Obv:** Knight holding sword and a bundle of arrows between date. **Obv. Legend:** CONCORD(IA) RES - P - AR(VAE) CRES F(RI) **Rev:** 5-line inscription in tablet **Rev. Legend:** MO ORD(I)PROVI(N)/FOEDER/BELG AD/LEG IM(P)

Date	Mintage	VG	F	VF	XF	Unc
1602Lion	—	140	250	500	700	—
1603/596Lion	—	140	250	500	700	—
1603Lion	—	140	150	275	400	—
1605/4Lion	—	150	300	600	1,000	—
1605Lion	—	140	150	275	400	—
1607/3Lion	—	140	150	275	400	—
1607Lion	—	140	150	275	400	—
1608/7Lion	—	140	150	275	400	—
1608Lion	—	140	150	275	400	—
1609Lion	—	140	150	275	400	—
1610Lion	—	140	150	275	400	—
1611Lion	—	140	150	275	400	—
1612 No mintmark	—	140	250	500	700	—
1612/07Lion	—	140	150	275	400	—
1612/17Lion	—	140	—	—	—	—
1612Lion	—	140	150	275	400	—
1614/1Lion	—	140	150	275	400	—
1614Lion	—	140	150	275	400	—
1615Lion	—	140	150	275	400	—
1616Lion	—	130	200	400	500	—
1619Lion	—	140	250	500	700	—
1620Lion Rare	—	—	—	—	—	—
1626Lion	—	130	200	400	500	—
1629/8Lion	—	—	—	—	—	—
1629Lion	—	140	250	500	700	—
1630Lion	—	140	250	500	700	—
1631Lion	—	140	250	500	700	—

Date	Mintage	VG	F	VF	XF	Unc
1631 No mintmark	—	140	250	500	700	—
1633/19Lion	—	140	250	500	700	—
1633/31Lion	—	140	250	500	700	—
1633Lion	—	140	250	500	700	—
1634Lion	—	140	250	500	700	—
1634 No mintmark	—	140	250	500	700	—
1635Lion	—	140	250	500	700	—
1635 No mintmark	—	140	250	500	700	—
1636Lion	—	140	250	500	700	—
1636 No mintmark	—	140	250	500	700	—
1638/6Lion	—	140	250	500	700	—
1638Lion	—	140	250	500	700	—
1639Lion	—	140	250	500	700	—
1640/30Lion	—	140	250	500	700	—
1640/33 No mintmark	—	150	300	600	850	—
1640/33Lion	—	140	250	500	700	—
1640 No mintmark	—	140	250	500	700	—
1640Lion	—	140	250	500	700	—
1643Lion	—	140	250	500	700	—
1643 No mintmark	—	140	250	500	700	—
1644Lion	—	140	250	500	700	—
1645Lion	—	140	250	500	700	—
1645 No mintmark	—	140	250	500	700	—
1648 No mintmark	—	140	250	500	700	—
1649Lion	—	140	250	500	700	—
1649 No mintmark	—	140	250	500	700	—
1650 No mintmark	—	140	250	500	700	—
1652 No mintmark	—	140	250	500	700	—
1653 No mintmark	—	140	250	500	700	—
1654 No mintmark	—	140	250	500	700	—
1657 No mintmark	—	140	250	500	700	—
1663 No mintmark	—	140	250	500	700	—
1666 No mintmark	—	140	250	500	700	—
1668 No mintmark	—	140	250	500	700	—
1676 No mintmark	—	140	250	500	700	—
1693 No mintmark	—	140	250	500	700	—

KM# 17 DUCAT

3.5000 g., 0.9860 Gold 0.1109 oz. AGW **Obv:** Knight standing right holding sword and shield between date **Obv. Legend:** NISI DOMINV - S - NOBISCVM **Rev:** 5-line inscription in tablet **Rev. Legend:** MONETA/AVREA/ORDIN(V)/FRIS AD/LEG IMP

Date	Mintage	VG	F	VF	XF	Unc
1604Lion	—	225	500	1,000	1,500	—
1604 No mintmark	—	225	500	1,000	1,500	—
1605Lion	—	300	750	1,500	2,000	—
1605/4 No mintmark	—	500	1,000	2,000	3,000	—
1605Lion No mintmark	—	300	750	1,500	2,000	—

KM# 31 2 DUCAT

7.0200 g., 0.9860 Gold 0.2225 oz. AGW **Obv:** Knight standing right divides date **Obv. Legend:** MO ORD(I)/PROVIN/FOEDER/BELG AD/LEG IMP **Rev:** 5-line inscription in tablet. Knight holding sword and a bundle of arrows between date **Rev. Legend:** CONCORDIA) RES - P - ARVAE CRES FRI

Date	Mintage	VG	F	VF	XF	Unc
161ZLion	—	600	1,500	2,500	3,500	—
1612 No mintmark	—	600	1,500	2,500	3,500	—
1660 No mintmark	—	—	—	—	—	—
1661 No mintmark	—	—	—	—	—	—

COUNTERMARKED COINAGE

1693

During the late 17th century many circulating coins were found to be underweight. In 1693 coins meeting the legal requirements were countermarked for a specific province or city, such as a crowned shield of Friesland.

KM# 70.1 28 STUIVERS

Silver **Countermark:** Crowned shield **Note:** Countermarked on Deventer KM#81.

CM Date	Host Date	Good	VG	F	VF	XF
ND(1693)	1685-92	—	—	—	—	—

KM# 70.2 28 STUIVERS

Silver **Countermark:** Crowned shield **Note:** Countermarked on Friesland KM#10.

CM Date	Host Date	Good	VG	F	VF	XF
ND(1693)	1601-91	—	—	—	—	—

KM# 70.3 28 STUIVERS

Silver **Countermark:** Crowned shield **Note:** Countermarked on Nijmegen KM#27.

CM Date	Host Date	Good	VG	F	VF	XF
ND(1693)	1685-90	—	—	—	—	—

KM# 70.4 28 STUIVERS

Silver **Countermark:** Crowned shield **Note:** Countermarked on Overyssel KM#55.

CM Date	Host Date	Good	VG	F	VF	XF
ND(1693)	1685-89	—	—	—	—	—

PATTERNS

Including off metal strikes

KM#	Date	Mintage	Identification	Mkt Val
Pn1	1601	—	30 Stuivers. Gold. 94.0000 g.	—
Pn2	1601	—	14 Stuivers. Gold. 32.0000 g. KM#A8.2	—
Pn3	ND(1601)	—	1/2 Stuiver. Gold. KM#19	—
Pn4	1610	—	2 Ducat. Silver.	—
Pn5	1614	—	28 Stuivers. Gold. 38.6000 g. KM#10.	—
Pn6	1614/04	—	28 Stuivers. Gold. 21.2000 g. KM#10.	—
Pn7	1617	—	Duit. Silver. KM#16	—
Pn8	1618	—	30 Stuivers. Gold. 25.6000 g. KM#36.2	—
Pn9	1629	—	48 Stuivers. Gold. 38.1000 g. KM#22	—
Pn10	1652	—	30 Stuivers. Gold. 36.0000 g.	—
Pn11	1660	—	Stuiver. Gold. 5.2000 g. KM#42.	—
Pn12	1665	—	28 Stuivers. Gold. KM#10	—
Pn13	1675	—	2 Stuivers. Gold. 3.4000 g. KM#32.2.	—
Pn14	1680	—	2 Stuivers. Gold. 3.4000 g. KM#32.2.	—
Pn15	1682	—	30 Stuivers. Gold. 17.1000 g. KM#A66.	—
Pn16	1682	—	6 Stuivers. Gold. 8.7000 g. KM#65	—
Pn17	1682	—	30 Stuivers. Silver. WG under CONCOR. WG under CONCOR	5,000
Pn18	1688	—	14 Stuivers. Gold. 19.5000 g. KM#67.	—
Pn19	1688	—	28 Stuivers. Gold. 19.5000 g. KM#10.	—
Pn20	1688	—	28 Stuivers. Silver. KM#10.	—
Pn21	1694	—	2 Gulden. Gold. 23.0000 g. KM#75.	—
Pn23	1696	—	2 Gulden. Gold. 24.0000 g. KM#40	—

PIEFORTS

KM#	Date	Mintage	Identification	Mkt Val
P1	1601	—	30 Stuivers. Silver. 53.6000 g. KM#4.	2,500
P2	1601	—	30 Stuivers. Gold. KM#4.	—
P3	1601	—	7 Stuivers. Gold. KM#7	—
P4	1601	—	7 Stuivers (1/4 Florin). Silver, KM#7	
P5	1603	—	50 Stuivers. Silver. 58.0000 g. Double weight ca. KM#15	—
P6	1605	—	Duit. Silver. Double weight. KM#16	—
P7	1606	—	Duit. Silver. Double weight. KM#16	—
P8	1607	—	10 Stuivers. Silver. 3 1/5 times weight. KM#24	—
P9	1626	—	Cavalier D'Or. Gold. KM#25.	—
P10	1628	—	Cavalier D'Or. Gold. 19.8000 g. KM#25.	—
P11	1647	—	Duit. Copper. KM#47.	—
P12	1647	—	2 Duit. Silver. KM#41a.	—
P13	1652	—	2 Stuivers. Silver. Double weight on klippe. KM#32.2	—
P14	1652	—	30 Stuivers. Silver. Triple weight, 42.8-180 g.	—
P15	1652	—	30 Stuivers. Silver.	1,500
P16	1659	—	20 Stuivers. Silver. Klippe. KM#51.	—
P17	1659	—	40 Stuivers. Silver. 1 1/2 times weight. KM#52.	—
P18	1659	—	40 Stuivers. Silver. Double weight. KM#52	—
P19	1661	—	40 Stuivers. Silver. Double weight. KM#52.	—
P20	1665	—	28 Stuivers. Silver. Double weight. KM#10.	—
P21	1675	—	Duit. Silver. 7.6000 g. KM#61a.	—
P22	1684	—	28 Stuivers. Silver. Double weight. KM#10.	—
P23	1690	—	28 Stuivers. Silver. Double weight. KM#10.	—
P24	1695	—	60 Stuivers. Silver. 58.4000 g. KM#77.	—

LEEUWARDEN

A commercial and industrial city located on the Ee River. It is noted for its manufactures in gold and silver.

CITY

COUNTERMARKED COINAGE

1693

During the late 17th century many circulating coins were found to be underweight. In 1693 coins meeting the legal requirements were countermarked for a specific province or city, such as L for Leeuwarden.

KM# 5.8 28 STUIVERS

Silver **Countermark:** L **Note:** Countermark L/HOL on Deventer, KM#81.

CM Date	Host Date	Good	VG	F	VF	XF
ND(1693)	(16)85	—	—	—	—	—

KM# 5.1 28 STUIVERS

Silver **Countermark:** L **Note:** Countermark on Deventer KM#81.

CM Date	Host Date	Good	VG	F	VF	XF
ND(1693)	1685-92	—	—	—	—	—

KM# 5.2 28 STUIVERS

Silver **Countermark:** L **Note:** Countermark on Friesland KM#10.

CM Date	Host Date	Good	VG	F	VF	XF
ND(1693)	1601-91	—	—	—	—	—

KM# 5.3 28 STUIVERS

Silver **Countermark:** L **Note:** Countermark on Groningen KM#50.

CM Date	Host Date	Good	VG	F	VF	XF
ND(1693)	1690	—	—	—	—	—

KM# 5.4 28 STUIVERS

Silver **Countermark:** L **Note:** Countermark on Groningen KM#52.

CM Date	Host Date	Good	VG	F	VF	XF
ND(1693)	1692	—	—	—	—	—

KM# 5.5 28 STUIVERS

Silver **Countermark:** L **Note:** Countermark on Nijmegen KM#27.

CM Date	Host Date	Good	VG	F	VF	XF
ND(1693)	1685-90	—	—	—	—	—

KM# 5.6 28 STUIVERS

Silver **Countermark:** L **Note:** Countermark on West Friesland KM#90.

CM Date	Host Date	Good	VG	F	VF	XF
ND(1693)	1685-87	—	—	—	—	—

KM# 5.7 28 STUIVERS

Silver **Countermark:** L **Note:** Countermark on Zwolle KM#78.

CM Date	Host Date	Good	VG	F	VF	XF
ND(1693)	1679-86	—	—	—	—	—

GELDERLAND

Ducatus Gelriae

Gelder, a former duchy, was merged with the Hapsburg dominions in the Netherlands until the revolt of the Low Countries resulted in its partition. In 1579 the greater part of Gelder, comprising the quarters of Nijmegen, Arnhem, and Zutphen, became the province of Gelderland in the Dutch Republic.

PROVINCE

STANDARD COINAGE

KM# 30.1 DUIT

2.0000 g., Copper **Obv:** Provincial arms in cartouche in inner circle **Obv. Legend:** IN DEO SPES NOSTRA **Rev:** Imscription in wreath **Rev. Inscription:** DVC / GEL / (date)

Date	Mintage	Good	VG	F	VF	XF
ND1626	—	4.00	15.00	45.00	90.00	180
1626	—	2.00	7.00	20.00	45.00	90.00
1628	—	2.00	7.00	20.00	45.00	90.00
1631	115,000	2.00	7.00	20.00	45.00	90.00
1633	—	2.00	7.00	20.00	45.00	90.00
1634	—	2.00	7.00	20.00	45.00	90.00
1635	—	2.00	7.00	20.00	45.00	90.00
1636	611,000	2.00	8.00	25.00	50.00	100
1640	—	2.00	8.00	25.00	50.00	100

KM# 30.2 DUIT

2.0000 g., Copper **Obv:** Provincial arms in cartouche in inner circle **Obv. Legend:** CONCORDIA RES PAR CRES GEL

Date	Mintage	Good	VG	F	VF	XF
1633	—	4.00	15.00	45.00	90.00	180

KM# 47.1 DUIT

2.0000 g., Copper **Obv:** Crowned arms of Gelderland **Rev:** Inscription, date in wreath **Rev. Inscription:** .D. / GEL / RIÆ / (date)

Date	Mintage	Good	VG	F	VF	XF
1662	—	2.00	7.00	20.00	45.00	90.00
1663	—	2.00	7.00	20.00	45.00	90.00
1664	—	2.00	7.00	20.00	45.00	90.00
1665	—	2.00	7.00	20.00	45.00	90.00
1666	—	2.00	7.00	20.00	45.00	90.00
1668	—	4.00	15.00	45.00	90.00	180
1676	—	2.00	7.00	20.00	45.00	90.00
1678	—	2.00	7.00	20.00	45.00	90.00
1679	—	2.00	7.00	20.00	45.00	90.00
1681	—	2.00	7.00	20.00	45.00	90.00
1684	—	2.00	7.00	20.00	45.00	90.00
1690	—	2.00	7.00	20.00	45.00	90.00
1591 error for 1691	—	—	—	—	—	—
1691	—	2.00	7.00	20.00	45.00	90.00
1692	—	2.00	7.00	20.00	45.00	90.00
1693	—	2.00	7.00	20.00	45.00	90.00

KM# 47.2 DUIT

Silver **Obv:** Crowned arms of Gelderland **Rev:** Inscription, date in wreath **Rev. Inscription:** .D. / GEL / RIÆ / (date) **Note:** ca. 3.6000 - 4.7000g

Date	Mintage	Good	VG	F	VF	XF
1690	—	—	—	—	—	—
1691	—	8.00	20.00	60.00	125	250
1692	—	—	—	—	—	—
1693	—	—	—	—	—	—
1699	—	—	—	—	—	—

KM# 47.2a DUIT

2.5600 g., Silver **Obv:** Crowned arms of Gelderland **Rev:** Inscription, date in wreath **Rev. Inscription:** .D. / GEL / RIÆ / (date)

Date	Mintage	Good	VG	F	VF	XF
1691	—	8.00	20.00	60.00	125	250
1699	—	—	—	—	—	—

KM# 25 STUIVER

0.8600 g., 0.5830 Silver 0.0161 oz. ASW **Obv:** Crowned rampant lion left holding sword and arrows, value at sides **Rev. Inscription:** GEL / RIA / (date)

Date	Mintage	Good	VG	F	VF	XF
1614	222,000	2.00	10.00	45.00	100	175

KM# 35 STUIVER

1.3100 g., 0.5830 Silver 0.0246 oz. ASW **Obv:** Bundle of arrows divides value in wreath **Rev:** Inscription, date in wreath **Rev. Inscription:** GEL / RIA / (date) **Note:** Mint mrk: Lily or cross

Date	Mintage	Good	VG	F	VF	XF
1640Cross	—	3.00	10.00	25.00	50.00	100
1640Lily	—	3.00	10.00	25.00	50.00	100
1642Lily	—	3.00	10.00	25.00	50.00	100

KM# 26.1 2 STUIVERS

1.7300 g., 0.5830 Silver 0.0324 oz. ASW **Obv:** Crowned rampant lion left holding sword and arrows, value at sides **Rev. Inscription:** GEL / RIA / (date) **Note:** Mint mark: Cross

Date	Mintage	Good	VG	F	VF	XF
1614	—	2.00	7.00	20.00	45.00	90.00
1615	—	2.00	7.00	20.00	45.00	90.00
1615/4	—	3.00	9.00	30.00	65.00	130
1618	—	2.00	7.00	20.00	45.00	90.00
1619	—	2.00	7.00	20.00	45.00	90.00

KM# 26.2 2 STUIVERS

1.7300 g., 0.5830 Silver 0.0324 oz. ASW **Obv:** Crowbed rampant lion left holding sword and arrows, value at sides **Rev. Inscription:** GEL / RIA / (date) **Note:** Mint mark: Lily.

Date	Mintage	Good	VG	F	VF	XF
1646	—	2.00	7.00	20.00	45.00	90.00

KM# 26.3 2 STUIVERS

1.7300 g., 0.5830 Silver 0.0324 oz. ASW **Obv:** Crowned rampant lion left holding sword and arrows, value at sides **Rev. Inscription:** GEL / RIA / (date) **Note:** Mint mark: Dog.

Date	Mintage	Good	VG	F	VF	XF
1678	—	2.00	7.00	20.00	45.00	90.00
1679	—	2.00	7.00	20.00	45.00	90.00
1680	—	2.00	7.00	20.00	45.00	90.00

KM# 6 6 STUIVERS (Roosschelling)

5.2700 g., 0.5830 Silver 0.0988 oz. ASW **Obv:** Crowned arms in wreath in inner circle, date above crown **Obv. Legend:** MO NO DVC GEL ET COMIT ZVR **Rev:** Ornamental cross in inner circle **Rev. Legend:** ADIVTO - RIVM - NRM IN - NOE D M

Date	Mintage	Good	VG	F	VF	XF
1601Cross	—	30.00	100	250	500	900
1602/1Cross	—	30.00	100	250	500	900
1602Cross	—	40.00	125	300	600	1,000

KM# 55 6 STUIVERS (Rijderschelling)

4.9500 g., 0.5830 Silver 0.0928 oz. ASW **Obv:** Crowned arms divide value in inner circle, date above crown **Obv. Legend:** MO ORD DVC GEL ET COM ZVT **Rev:** Knight horseback right brandishing sword in inner circle **Rev. Legend:** CONCORDIA RES PARVAE CRESCUNT **Note:** Mint mark: Dog.

Date	Mintage	Good	VG	F	VF	XF
1681	—	4.00	10.00	40.00	85.00	175
1682	—	4.00	10.00	40.00	85.00	175

KM# 60 6 STUIVERS (Rijderschelling)

Silver **Obv:** Crowned arms divides date, without inner circle and between date **Obv. Legend:** MO NO ARG ORD GEL ET COM ZVT **Rev:** Knight horseback right brandishing sword, without inner circles **Rev. Legend:** CONCORDIA RES PARVAE CRESCUNT **Note:** Mint mark: Unicorn.

Date	Mintage	Good	VG	F	VF	XF
1691	—	4.00	10.00	40.00	85.00	175

KM# 12 10 STUIVERS

5.9500 g., 0.9170 Silver 0.1754 oz. ASW **Obv:** Armored knight standing holding sword behind shield of arms, date at sides in inner circle **Obv. Legend:** MO ARG PRO CON - FOE BELG GEL **Rev:** Crowned arms divide value in inner circle **Rev. Legend:** CONCORCIA RES PARVAE CRESCVNT

Date	Mintage	Good	VG	F	VF	XF
1606	405	50.00	200	500	1,000	1,500

KM# 7 20 STUIVERS (1/2 Prince Daalder)

14.5600 g., 0.8850 Silver 0.4143 oz. ASW **Obv:** Armored bust of William the Silent with sword right in inner circle, date at top in legend **Obv. Legend:** VIGILATE DEO CON - FIDENT - ES **Rev:** Helmeted arms in inner circle **Rev. Legend:** MO NO ARG DVC GELRIAE CO ZVT

Date	Mintage	Good	VG	F	VF	XF
1601Cross	—	50.00	200	550	1,100	1,600

KM# 45 20 STUIVERS (1/2 Ducaton)

16.3900 g., 0.9410 Silver 0.4958 oz. ASW **Obv:** Knight with sword on horseback to right, provincial arms below in inner circle **Obv. Legend:** MO NO ARG PRO CON - FOE BELG D GEL C Z **Rev:** Crowned arms with crowned lion supporters in inner circle, date divided in legend at top, mintmark between date **Rev. Legend:** CONCORDIA - RES PARVAE - CRESCVNT **Note:** Mint mark: Dog. Dav. #4922.

Date	Mintage	Good	VG	F	VF	XF
1661	—	50.00	150	500	750	1,000
1667	—	65.00	200	500	800	1,200
1668	—	50.00	150	500	750	1,000
1670/67	—	65.00	200	500	800	1,200
1670	—	65.00	200	500	800	1,200
1676	—	65.00	200	500	800	1,200

KM# 65.1 20 STUIVERS (Gulden)

10.6100 g., 0.9200 Silver 0.3138 oz. ASW **Obv:** Crowned arms of Gelderland divide value I-G(L) **Obv. Legend:** MO AGR ORD FAED (FOED) BEL(LG) (D) GEL (&) (ET) **Rev:** Standing female figure leaning on Bible on column, holding pole with liberty cap, date in exerque **Rev. Legend:** HAC NITIMVR - HANC TVEMVR

Date	Mintage	Good	VG	F	VF	XF
1694Unicorn	63,900	7.00	30.00	100	200	300

KM# 65.2 20 STUIVERS (Gulden)

10.6100 g., 0.9200 Silver 0.3138 oz. ASW **Obv:** Crowned arms of Gelderland divide value I-G(L) **Obv. Legend:** MO ARG ORD FAED(FOED) BE(LG) (D) GEL (&) (ET) **Rev:** Standing female figure leaning on Bible on column, holding pole with liberty cap, date in exergue **Rev. Legend:** HAC NITIMVR - HANC TVEMVR

Date	Mintage	Good	VG	F	VF	XF
1697Knight on horse	538,920	—	15.00	30.00	70.00	125
1698Knight on horse	Inc. above	—	15.00	30.00	70.00	125
1699Knight on horse	Inc. above	—	15.00	30.00	70.00	125
1700/99Knight on horse	Inc. above	—	25.00	50.00	100	150
1700Knight on horse	941,775	—	15.00	30.00	70.00	125

KM# 14 24 STUIVERS (1/2 Rijksdaalder)

14.5100 g., 0.8850 Silver 0.4128 oz. ASW **Obv:** Laureate 1/2 figure holding sword and arms in inner circle **Obv. Legend:** MO ARG PRO - CONFOE BEL(G) GEL **Rev:** Crowned arms divide date in inner circle **Rev. Legend:** CONCORDIA RES PARVAE CRESCVNT **Note:** 1/2 Netherlands Rijksdaalder

Date	Mintage	Good	VG	F	VF	XF
1606Rosette	—	22.00	70.00	200	300	500
1609Rosette	—	20.00	60.00	150	250	350
1610Rosette	—	20.00	60.00	150	250	350
1611Rosette	—	20.00	60.00	150	250	350
1612Rosette	—	20.00	60.00	150	250	350
1614/11Rosette	—	20.00	60.00	150	250	350
1614/12Rosette	—	20.00	60.00	150	250	350
1614Rosette	—	20.00	60.00	150	250	350
1616/15Rosette	—	20.00	60.00	150	250	350
1616Rosette	—	20.00	60.00	150	250	350
1618Rosette	—	20.00	60.00	150	250	250
1619/8Rosette	—	22.00	70.00	200	300	500
1619Rosette	—	20.00	60.00	150	250	350
1620Rosette	—	22.00	70.00	200	300	500
1621Rosette	—	22.00	70.00	200	300	500
1622Rosette	—	12.00	40.00	100	200	250
1624Rosette	—	20.00	60.00	150	250	350
1625Rosette	—	22.00	70.00	200	300	500
1626Rosette	—	22.00	70.00	200	300	500

KM# 9 24 STUIVERS (1/2 Lion Daalder)

13.8400 g., 0.7500 Silver 0.3337 oz. ASW **Obv:** Armored knight looking right above lion shield in inner circle, date divide at bottom **Obv. Legend:** MO NO ORDI - date - F(OE) BEL(G) GEL **Rev:** Rampant lion to left in inner circle **Rev. Legend:** CONFIDENS DNO NON MOVETVR **Note:** 1/2 Province Lion Daalder

Date	Mintage	Good	VG	F	VF	XF
1602/00Rosette	—	25.00	80.00	200	400	800
1602Rosette	—	22.00	70.00	150	350	500

KM# 13.1 24 STUIVERS (1/2 Lion Daalder)

13.8400 g., Silver **Obv:** Armored knight looking right above lion shield **Obv. Legend:** MO NO ARG PRO CON - FOE BEL (G) GEL **Rev:** Rampant lion left, date at top in legend **Rev. Legend:** CONFIDENS DNO NON MOVETVR

Date	Mintage	Good	VG	F	VF	XF
1606	—	22.00	70.00	150	300	550
1607	—	22.00	70.00	200	300	400
1608	—	32.00	100	250	400	800
1610	—	12.00	40.00	125	200	300
1611	—	12.00	40.00	125	200	300
1615/11	—	12.00	40.00	125	200	300
1615	—	12.00	40.00	125	200	300
1616	—	12.00	40.00	125	200	300
1617	—	12.00	40.00	125	200	300
1620	—	12.00	40.00	125	200	300
1622/20	—	22.00	70.00	150	300	550
1621	—	22.00	70.00	150	300	550
1622	—	12.00	40.00	125	200	300
1623	—	12.00	40.00	125	200	300
1626/16	—	22.00	70.00	150	300	550
1626	—	12.00	40.00	125	200	300
1627	—	22.00	70.00	150	300	550
1628	—	12.00	40.00	125	150	250
1632	—	12.00	40.00	125	200	300
1633	—	12.00	40.00	125	200	300
1636	—	22.00	70.00	150	300	550
1637	—	22.00	70.00	150	300	550

KM# 13.4 24 STUIVERS (1/2 Lion Daalder)

13.8400 g., Silver **Obv:** Armored knight looking right above lion shield **Obv. Legend:** MO NO ARG PRO CON - FOE BEL(G) GEL **Rev:** Rampant lion left, date at top in legend **Rev. Legend:** CONFIDENS DNO NON MOVETVR

Date	Mintage	Good	VG	F	VF	XF
1637	—	—	—	22.00	70.00	150
1638	—	—	—	22.00	70.00	150
1639	—	—	—	22.00	70.00	150

Date	Mintage	Good	VG	F	VF	XF
1640	—	—	—	12.00	40.00	125
1641	—	—	—	12.00	40.00	125
1643	—	—	—	22.00	70.00	150
1644	—	—	—	22.00	70.00	150
1645/3	—	—	—	22.00	70.00	150
1646	—	—	—	22.00	70.00	150
1647	—	—	—	22.00	70.00	150

KM# 13.3 24 STUIVERS (1/2 Lion Daalder)

Silver **Obv:** Armored knight looking right above lion shield **Rev:** Rampant lion left with tail right, date at top in legend **Note:** Mint mark: Lily.

Date	Mintage	Good	VG	F	VF	XF
1646	—	10.00	30.00	60.00	100	175

KM# 13.2 24 STUIVERS (1/2 Lion Daalder)

13.8400 g., Silver **Obv:** Armored knight looking right above lion shield **Obv. Legend:** MO NO ARG PRO CON - FOE BEL(G) GEL **Rev:** Rampant lion left with tail left, date at top in legend **Rev. Legend:** CONFIDENS DNO NON MOVETVR **Note:** Mint mark: Lily.

Date	Mintage	Good	VG	F	VF	XF
1647Lily	—	22.00	70.00	150	300	550
1648Lily	—	12.00	40.00	125	200	300
1649Lily	—	12.00	40.00	125	200	300
1650Lily	—	12.00	40.00	125	200	300
1652Lily	—	12.00	40.00	125	200	300
1653Lily	—	12.00	40.00	125	200	300

KM# 13.5 24 STUIVERS (1/2 Lion Daalder)

Silver **Obv:** Armored knight looking right above lion shield **Obv. Legend:** MO AGR PRO C - ONF BEL GEL **Rev:** Rampant lion left, date at top in legend **Rev. Legend:** CONFIDENS DNO NON MOVETVR

Date	Mintage	Good	VG	F	VF	XF
1652Dog	—	12.00	40.00	125	200	300

KM# 46 24 STUIVERS (1/2 Silver Ducat)

14.2000 g., 0.8730 Silver 0.3985 oz. ASW **Obv:** Knight standing holding sword and shield divides date **Obv. Legend:** MO.NO.AR.PRO.CON-FOE.BELG.D.GEL.C.Z **Rev:** Crowned shield **Rev. Legend:** CONCORDIA - RES - PARVAE - CRESCVNT **Note:** Similar to 48 Stuivers, KM#42.

Date	Mintage	Good	VG	F	VF	XF
1661Dog	—	40.00	125	350	600	800
1664Dog	—	40.00	125	350	600	800
1667Dog	—	40.00	125	350	600	800

KM# 62 30 STUIVERS (Daalder)

15.8800 g., 0.9060 Silver 0.4625 oz. ASW **Obv:** Standing knight with sword behind crowned arms to left, in inner circle **Rev:** Crowned double-headed eagle in inner circle

Date	Mintage	Good	VG	F	VF	XF
ND(1690-1694) Rare	—	—	—	—	—	—

KM# 61 30 STUIVERS (Daalder)

15.8800 g., Silver **Obv:** Crowned provincial arms with lion supporters, value below **Obv. Legend:** MO NO ARG OR - D GEL C Z **Rev:** Standing knight with sword behind crowned arms to left, date in legend **Rev. Legend:** IN DEO SPES - NOSTRA 1693

Date	Mintage	Good	VG	F	VF	XF
1693 Not seen	—	—	—	—	—	—

KM# 8 40 STUIVERS (Prince Daalder)

29.0300 g., 0.8850 Silver 0.8260 oz. ASW **Obv:** Armored bust of William the Silent with sword right in inner circle, date a top in legend **Obv. Legend:** VIGILATE DEO CON - FIDENT - ES **Rev:** Helmeted arms in inner circle **Rev. Legend:** MO NO ARG DVC GLERIAE CO ZVT

Date	Mintage	Good	VG	F	VF	XF
1601	—	40.00	130	350	650	1,000
1602	2,554	40.00	130	350	650	1,000
1603	1,578	40.00	130	350	650	1,000
1604	—	40.00	130	350	650	1,000

KM# 50.2 40 STUIVERS (Ducaton)

32.7800 g., Silver **Obv:** Armored knight horseback right brandishing sword shield below **Obv. Legend:** MO NO ARG PRO CON - FOE BELG D GEL C Z **Rev:** Crowned supported arms - No cartouche **Rev. Legend:** CONCORDIA - RES - PARVAE - CRCSCVNT

Date	Mintage	Good	VG	F	VF	XF
1659Dog	—	25.00	50.00	125	200	350
1660Dog	—	25.00	50.00	125	200	350
1661Dog	—	25.00	50.00	125	200	350
1662Dog	—	25.00	50.00	125	200	350
1663Dog	—	25.00	50.00	125	200	350
1664Dog	—	25.00	50.00	125	200	350
1666Dog	—	25.00	50.00	125	200	350
1667Dog	—	25.00	50.00	125	200	350
1668Dog	—	25.00	50.00	125	200	350
1668Dog No mintmark	—	25.00	50.00	125	200	350
1669Dog	—	25.00	50.00	125	250	500
1670/69Dog	—	25.00	50.00	125	250	500
1671Dog	—	25.00	50.00	125	250	500
1672Dog	—	25.00	50.00	125	250	500
1674Dog	—	25.00	50.00	125	250	500
1676Dog	—	25.00	50.00	125	250	500
1677Dog	—	25.00	50.00	125	250	500
1679Dog	—	25.00	50.00	125	250	500

KM# 50.1 40 STUIVERS (Ducaton)

32.7800 g., Silver **Obv:** Armored knight horseback right brandishing sword, shield below **Obv. Legend:** MO NO ARG PRIO CON - FOE BELG D GEL C Z **Rev:** Crowned supported arms with empty cartouche below **Rev. Legend:** CONCORDIA - RES - PARVAE CRCSCVNT **Note:** Dav. #4924.

Date	Mintage	Good	VG	F	VF	XF
1676Dog Mintmark between date	—	25.00	50.00	125	250	500
1677Dog Mintmark between date	—	25.00	50.00	125	250	500
1679/7Dog Mintmark between date	—	25.00	50.00	125	250	500
1679Dog Mintmark between date	—	25.00	50.00	125	250	500
1680Dog Mintmark between date	—	25.00	50.00	125	250	500
1681Dog Mintmark between date	—	25.00	50.00	125	250	500

KM# 67 40 STUIVERS (2 Gulden)

Silver **Obv:** Crowned Gelderland arms (with two lions) divide value 2-G, date above crown **Obv. Legend:** MO NO ARG ORD D GEL (ET) (C) Z **Rev:** Standing female figure leaning on Bible on column, holding spear with Liberty cap **Rev. Legend:** HAC NITIMVR - HANC TVEMVR

Date	Mintage	Good	VG	F	VF	XF
1694Unicorn	14,615	35.00	100	200	400	800
1696Unicorn	—	40.00	125	250	500	1,000

KM# 66 40 STUIVERS (2 Gulden)

21.2100 g., 0.9200 Silver 0.6273 oz. ASW **Obv:** Crowned shield (with lion holding sword and arrows) divides value 2-GL **Obv. Legend:** MO ARG ORD FA(A)D BELG GEL (Z) **Rev:** Date in exergue **Rev. Legend:** HAC NITIMVR - HANC TVEMVR

Date	Mintage	Good	VG	F	VF	XF
1694	—	25.00	70.00	175	350	650

KM# 69 40 STUIVERS (2 Gulden)

Gold **Note:** Without value.

Date	Mintage	Good	VG	F	VF	XF
1696	—	—	—	—	—	—

KM# 16.1 48 STUIVERS (Rijksdaalder)

29.0300 g., 0.8850 Silver 0.8260 oz. ASW **Obv:** Laureate 1/2 figure right holding sword and arms in inner circle **Obv. Legend:** MO ARG PRO - CONFOE BELG GEL **Rev:** Crowned arms divide date in inner circle **Rev. Legend:** CONCORDIA RES PARVAE CRESCVNT **Note:** Dutch Rijksdaalder. Dav. #4828.

Date	Mintage	Good	VG	F	VF	XF
1606Ornate cross Mint mark on both sides	—	30.00	80.00	175	350	50
1607Ornate cross Mint mark on both sides	—	20.00	40.00	80.00	175	30
1608Ornate cross Mint mark on both sides	—	20.00	40.00	80.00	175	30
1609Ornate cross Mint mark on both sides	—	20.00	40.00	80.00	175	30
1610/9Ornate cross Mint mark on both sides	—	28.00	60.00	120	200	40
1610Ornate cross Mint mark on both sides	—	20.00	40.00	80.00	175	30
1611/0Ornate cross Mint mark on both sides	—	20.00	40.00	80.00	175	30
1611Ornate cross Mint mark on both sides	—	20.00	40.00	80.00	175	30
1612Ornate cross Mint mark on both sides	—	20.00	40.00	80.00	175	30
1613/1Ornate cross Mint mark on both sides	—	20.00	40.00	80.00	175	30
1613/2Ornate cross Mint mark on both sides	—	20.00	40.00	80.00	175	30
1613Ornate cross Mint mark on both sides	—	20.00	40.00	80.00	175	30
1614/3Ornate cross Mint mark on both sides	—	20.00	40.00	80.00	175	30
1614Ornate cross Mint mark on both sides	—	20.00	40.00	80.00	175	30
1615Ornate cross Mint mark on both sides	—	20.00	40.00	80.00	175	30
1617/4Ornate cross Mint mark on both sides	—	20.00	40.00	80.00	175	30
1617Ornate cross Mint mark on both sides	—	25.00	50.00	100	200	35
1618/7Ornate cross Mint mark on both sides	—	20.00	40.00	80.00	175	30
1618Ornate cross Mint mark on both sides	—	20.00	40.00	80.00	175	30
1619/8Ornate cross Mint mark on both sides	—	25.00	50.00	90.00	200	33
1619Ornate cross Mint mark on both sides	—	20.00	40.00	80.00	175	30
1620Ornate cross Mint mark on both sides	—	20.00	40.00	80.00	175	30
1621/0Ornate cross Mint mark on both sides	—	25.00	50.00	90.00	200	33
1621Ornate cross Mint mark on both sides	—	20.00	40.00	80.00	175	30
1622Ornate cross Mint mark on both sides	—	25.00	50.00	90.00	200	33
16ZZOrnate cross Mint mark on both sides	—	25.00	50.00	90.00	200	33
1623Ornate cross Mint mark on both sides	—	25.00	50.00	90.00	200	33
1624Ornate cross Mint mark on both sides	—	25.00	50.00	90.00	200	33
1625Ornate cross Mint mark on both sides	—	20.00	40.00	80.00	175	30
1629/6Ornate cross Mint mark on both sides	—	20.00	40.00	80.00	175	30
1629Ornate cross Mint mark on both sides	—	20.00	40.00	80.00	175	30
1631Ornate cross Mint mark on both sides	—	30.00	80.00	175	350	50

KM# 16.5 48 STUIVERS (Rijksdaalder)

29.0300 g., 0.8850 Silver 0.8260 oz. ASW **Obv:** Laureate 1/2 length figure right holding sword and shield in inner circle **Rev:** Crowned arms divide date in inner circle **Note:** Mint mark: Diamond shape. Prev. KM#19. Dav. #4828B.

Date	Mintage	Good	VG	F	VF	X
1608	—	—	—	—	—	—

KM# 16.2 48 STUIVERS (Rijksdaalder)

29.0300 g., 0.8850 Silver 0.8260 oz. ASW **Obv:** Laureate 1/2 figure right holding sword and arms in inner circle **Obv. Legend:** MO ARG PRO - COMFOE BELG GEL **Rev:** Crowned arms divide date in inner circle **Rev. Legend:** CONCOFDIA RES PARVAE CRESCVNT **Note:** Dav. # 4828.

Date	Mintage	Good	VG	F	VF	XF
1643Lily Mintmark on both sides	—	30.00	80.00	175	350	500
1648Lily Mintmark on both sides	—	20.00	40.00	80.00	175	300
1649Lily Mintmark on both sides	—	20.00	40.00	80.00	175	300
1650Lily Mintmark on both sides	—	20.00	40.00	80.00	175	300
1651Lily Mintmark on both sides	—	20.00	40.00	80.00	175	300
1652Lily Mintmark on both sides	—	20.00	40.00	80.00	175	300
1653Lily Mintmark on both sides	—	20.00	40.00	80.00	175	300

KM# 16.3 48 STUIVERS (Rijksdaalder)

29.0300 g., 0.8850 Silver 0.8260 oz. ASW **Obv:** Laureate 1/2 figure right holding sword and arms in inner circle **Obv. Legend:** MO ARG PRO - CONFOE BELG GEL **Rev:** Crowned arms divide date in inner circle

Date	Mintage	Good	VG	F	VF	XF
1652Dog Mintmark on both sides	—	20.00	40.00	80.00	175	300
1653Dog Mintmark on both sides	—	20.00	40.00	80.00	175	30.00
1654Dog Mintmark on both sides	—	20.00	40.00	80.00	175	300
1655Dog Mintmark on both sides	—	20.00	40.00	80.00	175	300
1656Dog Mintmark on both sides	—	20.00	40.00	80.00	175	300
1657Dog Mintmark on both sides	—	20.00	40.00	80.00	175	300
1658Dog Mintmark on both sides	—	20.00	40.00	80.00	175	300
1659Dog Mintmark on both sides	—	20.00	40.00	80.00	175	300
1662Dog Mintmark on both sides	—	30.00	80.00	175	350	500
1674Dog Mintmark on both sides	—	30.00	80.00	175	350	500
1676Dog Mintmark on both sides	—	30.00	80.00	175	350	500
1680Dog Mintmark on both sides, Rare	—	—	—	—	—	—
1683Dog Mintmark on both sides	—	30.00	80.00	175	350	500

KM# 16.4 48 STUIVERS (Rijksdaalder)

29.0300 g., 0.8260 Silver 0.7709 oz. ASW **Obv:** Laureate 1/2 length figure right holding sword in inner circle **Obv. Legend:** MO ARG PRO - CONFOE BELG GEL **Rev:** Crowned arms divides date in innner circle **Rev. Legend:** CONCORDIA RES PARVAE CRESCVNT **Note:** Mint marks: Obverse Lily, reverse Dog. Dav. # 4828C.

Date	Mintage	Good	VG	F	VF	XF
1652	—	40.00	100	200	400	800
1653	—	20.00	40.00	80.00	175	300
1654	—	20.00	40.00	80.00	175	300
1655	—	20.00	40.00	80.00	175	300
1656	—	20.00	40.00	80.00	175	300

KM# 16.6 48 STUIVERS (Rijksdaalder)

Silver **Obv:** Laureate 1/2 length figure right holding sword in inner circle **Rev:** Crowned arms divide date in inner circle **Note:** Mint marks: Obverse dog, reverse Lily. Dav. # 4828.

Date	Mintage	Good	VG	F	VF	XF
1665	—	25.00	50.00	90.00	150	300

KM# 16a 48 STUIVERS (Rijksdaalder)

29.0300 g., 0.8850 Silver 0.8260 oz. ASW **Obv:** Laureate 1/2 figure right holding sword and arms in inner circle **Obv. Legend:** MO ARG PRO - CONFOE BELG GEL **Rev:** Crowned arms divide date in inner circle **Rev. Legend:** CONFIDENS DNO NON MOVETVR **Note:** Mint mark: Knight on horse. Prev. KM # 16.4.

Date	Mintage	Good	VG	F	VF	XF
1699Cross	—	30.00	80.00	175	350	500

KM# 10 48 STUIVERS (Lion Daalder)

27.6800 g., Silver **Obv:** Armored knight looking right above lion shield in inner circle, date divided at bottom **Obv. Legend:** MO NO ORDI - GEL VA HOL **Rev:** Rampant lion left in inner circle **Rev. Legend:** CONFIDENS DNO NON MOVETVR **Note:** (Province Lion Daalder) Dav. #4847.

Date	Mintage	Good	VG	F	VF	XF
160Z/0Cross	—	30.00	80.00	175	350	500
160ZCross	—	20.00	40.00	80.00	175	300

KM# 15.1 48 STUIVERS (Lion Daalder)

27.6800 g., Silver **Obv:** Armored knight looking right above lion shield **Obv. Legend:** MO ARG PRO CO(N) - CO(N) - F(OE) BEL (G) GEL **Rev:** Rampant lion left, date at top in legend **Rev. Legend:** CONFIDENS DNO NON MOVETVR **Note:** With " + " after GEL in legend. Dav. #4849.

Date	Mintage	Good	VG	F	VF	XF
1606	—	22.00	45.00	90.00	180	350
1607	—	22.00	45.00	90.00	180	350
1608	—	22.00	45.00	90.00	180	350
1609/8	—	28.00	60.00	120	200	400
1609	—	22.00	45.00	90.00	180	350
1610	—	28.00	60.00	120	200	40.00
1611	—	22.00	45.00	90.00	180	350
161Z	—	28.00	60.00	120	200	400
1613/Z	—	35.00	100	200	300	500
1613	—	22.00	45.00	90.00	180	350
1614/Z	—	28.00	60.00	120	200	400
1614	—	22.00	45.00	90.00	180	350
1615/2	—	28.00	60.00	120	200	400
1615/4	—	28.00	60.00	120	200	400
1615	—	22.00	45.00	90.00	180	350
1616/5	—	28.00	60.00	120	200	400
1616	—	22.00	45.00	90.00	180	350
1617	—	22.00	45.00	90.00	180	350
1618	—	28.00	60.00	120	200	400
1619	—	28.00	60.00	120	200	400
1622	—	22.00	45.00	90.00	180	350
1624	—	28.00	60.00	120	200	400
1626	—	22.00	45.00	90.00	180	350
1628/18	—	28.00	60.00	120	200	400
1628/2	—	28.00	60.00	120	200	400
1628	—	28.00	60.00	120	200	400
1629/7	—	28.00	60.00	120	200	400
1629	—	22.00	45.00	90.00	180	350
1630	—	28.00	60.00	120	200	400
1631	—	22.00	45.00	90.00	180	350
1632	—	22.00	45.00	90.00	180	350
1633	—	22.00	45.00	90.00	180	350
1634	—	22.00	45.00	90.00	180	350
1635	—	22.00	45.00	90.00	180	350
1636	—	22.00	45.00	90.00	180	350
1637	—	22.00	45.00	90.00	180	350
1638	—	28.00	60.00	120	200	400
1676	—	22.00	45.00	90.00	180	350

KM# 15.2 48 STUIVERS (Lion Daalder)

27.6800 g., Silver **Obv:** Armored knight looking right above lion shield **Obv. Legend:** MO ARG PRO (CO(N) - F(OE) BEL(G) GEL **Rev:** Rampant lion left **Rev. Legend:** CONFIDENS DNO NON MOVETVR **Note:** Without " + " after GEL in legend. Dav. # 4849.

Date	Mintage	Good	VG	F	VF	XF
1636	—	22.00	45.00	90.00	180	350
1637	—	22.00	45.00	90.00	180	350
1638/29	—	22.00	45.00	90.00	180	350
1638	—	22.00	45.00	90.00	180	350
1639	—	22.00	45.00	90.00	180	350
1640	—	22.00	45.00	90.00	180	350
1641	—	22.00	45.00	90.00	180	350
1642	—	22.00	45.00	90.00	180	350
1643	—	22.00	45.00	90.00	180	350
1644	—	28.00	60.00	120	200	400
1645	—	22.00	45.00	90.00	180	350
1646	—	22.00	45.00	90.00	180	350
1647	—	—	—	—	—	—

KM# 36 48 STUIVERS (Lion Daalder)

Silver **Obv:** Armored knight looking left above lion shield **Rev:** Rampant lion left **Note:** Dav. #4850.

Date	Mintage	Good	VG	F	VF	XF
1647	—	20.00	40.00	80.00	175	300
1648	—	20.00	40.00	80.00	175	300
1649	—	20.00	40.00	80.00	175	300

KM# 15.3 48 STUIVERS (Lion Daalder)

27.6800 g., Silver **Obv:** Armored knight looking right above lion shield **Obv. Legend:** MO ARG PRO CO(N) - F(OE) BEL (G) GEL **Rev:** Rampant lion left, date at top in legend **Rev. Legend:** CONFIDENS DNO NON MOVETVR **Note:** Lily. Dav. # 4849. Without "+" after GEL in legend

Date	Mintage	Good	VG	F	VF	XF
1648	—	20.00	40.00	80.00	175	300
1649/6	—	28.00	60.00	120	200	400
1649	—	20.00	40.00	80.00	175	300
1651	—	20.00	40.00	80.00	175	300
1652	—	20.00	40.00	80.00	175	300
1653	—	20.00	40.00	80.00	175	300
1654Lily	—	20.00	40.00	80.00	175	300

KM# 15.4 48 STUIVERS (Lion Daalder)

27.6800 g., Silver **Obv:** Armored knight looking right above lion shield **Obv. Legend:** MO ARG PRO CO(N) - F(OE) BEL(G) GEL **Rev:** Rampant lion left, date at top in legend **Rev. Legend:** CONFIDENS DNO NON MOVETVR **Note:** Dav. # 4849. Without "+" after GEL in legend

Date	Mintage	Good	VG	F	VF	XF
1654	—	20.00	40.00	80.00	175	300
1655	—	20.00	40.00	80.00	175	300
1657	—	20.00	40.00	80.00	175	300
1658	—	28.00	60.00	120	200	400
1661	—	28.00	60.00	120	200	400
1662	—	20.00	40.00	80.00	175	300
1663	—	20.00	40.00	80.00	157	300
1666	—	20.00	40.00	80.00	175	300
1667	—	20.00	40.00	80.00	175	300
1668	—	20.00	40.00	80.00	175	300
1674	75,855	20.00	40.00	80.00	175	300
1675	Inc. above	20.00	40.00	80.00	175	300
1676	Inc. above	20.00	40.00	80.00	175	300

KM# 15.5 48 STUIVERS (Lion Daalder)

27.6800 g., Silver **Obv:** Armored knight looking right above lion shield **Obv. Legend:** MO ARG PRO CO(N) - F(OE) BEL(G) GEL **Rev:** Rampant lion left, date at top in legend **Rev. Legend:** CONFIDENS DNO NON MOVETVR **Note:** Mint Dav. # 4849. Without "+" after GEL in legend

Date	Mintage	Good	VG	F	VF	XF
1694Knight on horse	—	20.00	40.00	80.00	175	300
1697Knight on horse	—	20.00	40.00	80.00	175	300
1699Knight on horse	—	30.00	60.00	125	250	400
1700/699Knight on horse	—	35.00	100	200	300	500

KM# 42 48 STUIVERS (Silver Ducat)

28.2500 g., 0.8730 Silver 0.7929 oz. ASW **Obv:** Knight standing holding sword and shield divides date **Obv. Legend:** MO.NO.AR.PRO.CON-FOE.BELG:D.GEL.C.Z. **Rev:** Crowned shield **Rev. Legend:** CONCORDIA:RES:PARVAE:CRESCVNT **Note:** Dav. #4890.

Date	Mintage	Good	VG	F	VF	XF
1659Dog	Inc. above	28.00	60.00	100	200	350
1660Dog	Inc. above	28.00	60.00	100	200	350
1661Dog	Inc. above	28.00	60.00	100	200	350
1662/0Dog	—	35.00	100	200	300	500
1662Dog	Inc. above	28.00	60.00	100	200	350
1663/0Dog	Inc. above	35.00	100	200	300	500
1663/62Dog	Inc. above	35.00	100	200	300	500
1663Dog	Inc. above	28.00	60.00	100	200	350
1664Dog	Inc. above	35.00	100	200	300	500
1674Dog	Inc. above	35.00	100	200	300	500
1677Dog	Inc. above	35.00	100	200	300	50.00
1680Dog	Inc. above	35.00	100	200	300	500

KM# 63.1 48 STUIVERS (Silver Ducat)

28.5000 g., Silver **Obv:** Knight standing right, crowned lion shield at feet, without inner circle **Obv. Legend:** MO ARG PRO CON - FOE BELG D GEL (&) **Rev:** Crowned arms divide date, without inner circle **Rev. Legend:** CONCORDIA RES PARVAE CRESCVNT **Note:** Mint mark: Unicorn. Dav. #4891.

Date	Mintage	Good	VG	F	VF	XF
1693Unicorn With inner circles	—	35.00	80.00	175	250	350

Date	Mintage	Good	VG	F	VF	XF
1694Unicorn	—	35.00	80.00	200	300	450
1694Unicorn With inner circles	—	35.00	80.00	200	300	450

KM# 63.2 48 STUIVERS (Silver Ducat)

28.2500 g., Silver **Obv:** Knight standing right, crowned lion shield at feet **Rev:** Crowned arms divide date, without inner circle **Note:** Mint mark: Knight horseback on reverse. Dav. #4891.

Date	Mintage	Good	VG	F	VF	XF
1695	—	35.00	80.00	200	300	450
1696	—	20.00	35.00	75.00	150	300
1698/6	—	35.00	80.00	200	300	450
1698	—	20.00	35.00	75.00	150	300
1699/8	—	35.00	80.00	200	300	450
1699	—	20.00	35.00	75.00	150	300
1700	—	20.00	35.00	75.00	150	300

KM# 70 48 STUIVERS (Silver Ducat)

Silver **Obv:** Knight standing right, crowned lion shield at feet **Rev:** Arms without crown divide date **Note:** Dav. #4891B.

Date	Mintage	Good	VG	F	VF	XF
1696	—	60.00	175	375	750	1,000

KM# 63.3 48 STUIVERS (Silver Ducat)

28.2500 g., Silver **Obv:** Knight standing right, crowned lion shield at feet **Rev:** Crowned arms divide date, without inner circle **Note:** Dav. #4891

Date	Mintage	Good	VG	F	VF	XF
1699	—	35.00	80.00	175	250	350

KM# 63.4 48 STUIVERS (Silver Ducat)

Silver **Obv:** Knight standing right, crowned lion shield at feeet. **Rev:** Crowned arms divide date, without inner circle **Note:** Without knight horseback mint mark. Dav. #4891

Date	Mintage	Good	VG	F	VF	XF
1699	—	35.00	80.00	200	300	450

KM# 63.5 48 STUIVERS (Silver Ducat)

Silver **Obv:** Knight standing right, crowned lion shield at feet **Obv. Legend:** MO ARG ORD CONFOE - BELG D GEL (&) C Z **Rev:** Crowned arms divide date, without inner circle **Note:** Dav. #4891

Date	Mintage	Good	VG	F	VF	XF
1699Knight on horse Obv. mintmark	—	35.00	80.00	200	300	450

KM# 63.6 48 STUIVERS (Silver Ducat)

Silver **Obv:** Knight standing right, crowned arms at feet **Rev:** Crowned arms divide date, without inner circle **Note:** Mint mark: Knight horseback on obverse and reverse. Dav. #4891.

Date	Mintage	Good	VG	F	VF	XF
1699	—	35.00	80.00	200	300	450

KM# 56.1 60 STUIVERS (3 Gulden)

31.8200 g., 0.9200 Silver 0.9412 oz. ASW **Obv:** Crowned provincial arms divide value 3-G date above crown **Obv. Legend:** MO NO ARG ORD D GEL C Z **Rev:** Standing female figure leaning on Bible on column, holding spear with Liberty cap **Rev. Legend:** HAC NITIMVR - HAC TVEMVR **Note:** Dav. #4948.

Date	Mintage	Good	VG	F	VF	XF
1682Dog	—	40.00	125	350	600	900
1687Dog	—	45.00	135	400	700	1,000

KM# 56.2 60 STUIVERS (3 Gulden)

31.8200 g., 0.9290 Silver 0.9504 oz. ASW **Obv:** Crowned provincial arms divide value 3-G date above crown **Obv. Legend:** MO NO ARG ORD D GEL C Z **Rev:** Standing female figure leaning on Bible on column, holding spear with Liberty cap **Rev. Legend:** HAC NITIMVR - HANC TVEMVR **Note:** Mint mark. Unicorn. Dav. #4948.

Date	Mintage	Good	VG	F	VF	XF
1694	Inc. above	40.00	125	350	600	900

KM# 68.1 60 STUIVERS (3 Gulden)

31.8200 g., Silver **Obv:** Crowned lion arms divide value: 3 - GL **Obv. Legend:** MO ARG ORD FAED (FOED) BEL(G) D GEL **Rev:** Standing female figure leaning on Bible column holding spear with Liberty cap, date in exurgue **Rev. Legend:** HAC NITIMVR - HANC TVEMVR **Note:** Mint mark: Unicorn. Dav. #4949.

Date	Mintage	Good	VG	F	VF	XF
1694	—	30.00	75.00	200	400	800

KM# 68.2 60 STUIVERS (3 Gulden)

Silver **Obv:** Crowned lion arms divide value: 3 - GL **Rev:** Standing female figure leaning on Bible column holdimg spear with Liberty cap, date in exergue **Note:** Dav. #4949.

Date	Mintage	Good	VG	F	VF	XF
1696Knight on horse	—	30.00	75.00	200	400	800
1697Knight on horse	—	30.00	75.00	200	400	800

KM# 64 1/2 GULDEN (10 Stuivers)

5.3000 g., 0.9290 Silver 0.1583 oz. ASW **Obv:** Crowned lion shield divides value **Obv. Legend:** MO ARG ORD FAED BE(L)G GEL (&) (ET) (C Z) **Rev:** Standing female figure leaning on Bible on column, holding spear with Liberty cap, date in exergue **Rev. Legend:** HAC NITIMVR - HANC TVEMVR **Note:** Diameter 27 or 31 mm.

Date	Mintage	Good	VG	F	VF	XF
1694Unicorn	44,040	15.00	40.00	125	225	350

KM# 33 DOUBLE 3 GULDEN

Silver **Obv:** Crowned double lion arms, date above **Rev:** Standing female figure leaning on Bible column holding spear with Liberty cap. **Note:** Dav. #A4948.

Date	Mintage	Good	VG	F	VF	XF
1682 Rare	—	—	—	—	—	—

KM# 41.1 DUCATON (Silver Rider)

32.7800 g., 0.9410 Silver 0.9917 oz. ASW **Obv:** Knight with sword on horseback right, provincial arms below in inner circle **Obv. Legend:** MO NO ARG PRO CON - FOE BELG D GEL C Z **Rev:** Crowned arms with crowned lion supporters in inner circle, date divided in legend at top **Rev. Legend:** CONCORDIA - RES PARVAE - CRESCVNT **Note:** Dav. #4923.

Date	Mintage	Good	VG	F	VF	XF
1659Dog	—	25.00	70.00	200	260	400
1660Dog	—	22.00	40.00	125	225	350
1661Dog	—	22.00	40.00	125	225	350
1662/1Dog	—	22.00	40.00	125	225	350
1662Dog	—	25.00	70.00	200	260	400
1663Dog	—	22.00	40.00	125	225	350
1664Dog	—	22.00	40.00	125	225	350
1666Dog	—	22.00	40.00	125	225	350
1667Dog	—	22.00	40.00	125	225	350
1668Dog	—	22.00	40.00	125	225	350
1669Dog	—	22.00	40.00	125	225	350
1670/9Dog	—	35.00	100	200	300	500
1670Dog	—	35.00	100	200	300	500
1671Dog	—	35.00	100	200	300	500
1672Dog	—	35.00	100	200	300	500
1674Dog	—	35.00	100	200	300	500
1676Dog	—	35.00	100	200	300	500
1677Dog	—	35.00	100	200	300	500
1679Dog	—	35.00	100	200	300	500

KM# 41.2 DUCATON

32.7800 g., 0.9410 Silver 0.9917 oz. ASW **Obv:** Knight with sword on horseback right, provincial arms below in inner circle **Obv. Legend:** PRO CON - FOE BELG D GEL C Z **Rev:** Crowned arms with crowned lion supporters in inner circle, date divided in legend at top. **Rev. Legend:** CONCORDIA - RES PARVAE - CRESCVNT **Note:** Empty cartouche under shield

Date	Mintage	Good	VG	F	VF	XF
1668	—	22.00	40.00	125	225	350

KM# 41.3 DUCATON

32.7800 g., 0.9410 Silver 0.9917 oz. ASW **Obv:** Knight with sword on horseback right, provincial arms below in inner circle **Obv. Legend:** MO NO ARG PRO CON - FOE BELG D GEL C Z **Rev:** Crowned arms with crowned lion supporters in inner circle, date divided in legend at top **Rev. Legend:** CONCORDIA - RES PARVAE - CRESCVNT **Note:** Empty cartouche under shield.

Date	Mintage	Good	VG	F	VF	XF
1676Dog	—	35.00	100	200	300	500
1677Dog	—	35.00	100	200	300	500
1679/7Dog	—	35.00	100	200	300	500
1679Dog	—	35.00	100	200	300	500
1680Dog	—	35.00	100	200	300	500
1681Dog	—	35.00	100	200	300	500

KM# 99.1 2 DUCATON

65.0000 g., Silver **Obv:** Inner circles **Rev:** Inner circles, date above crowned arms **Note:** Dav. #4922.

Date	Mintage	Good	VG	F	VF	XF
1659	—	—	—	—	—	—
1660 Rare	—	—	—	—	—	—
1662 Rare	—	—	—	—	—	2,500
1670/9	—	—	—	—	—	—
1670 Rare	—	—	—	—	—	—
1676 Rare	—	—	—	—	—	—
1680 Rare	—	—	—	—	—	—

KM# 99.2 2 DUCATON

Silver **Obv:** Narrow horse and rider **Rev:** Empty cartouche below crowned arms **Note:** Dav. #A4924.

Date	Mintage	Good	VG	F	VF	XF
1680 Rare	—	—	—	—	—	—

KM# 31 3 DUCATON

Silver **Obv:** Inner circles **Rev:** Inner circles, date above crowned arms **Note:** Dav. #A4922.

Date	Mintage	Good	VG	F	VF	XF
1680 Rare	—	—	—	—	—	—

KM# 28 2 SILVER DUCAT

Silver **Note:** Similar to 1 Silver Ducat, KM#27. Dav. #4889.

Date	Mintage	Good	VG	F	VF	XF
1659 Rare	—	—	—	—	—	—

KM# 29 2 SILVER DUCAT

Silver **Note:** Klippe, similar to 1 Silver Ducat, KM#27. Dav. #4889

Date	Mintage	Good	VG	F	VF	XF
1660 Rare	—	—	—	—	—	—

KM# 21 RIJKSDAALDER

Silver **Obv:** Armored half bust William the Silent right, with sword, date **Obv. Legend:** VIEILATE. DEO. CON - FIDENTES **Rev:** Helmeted small arms **Rev. Legend:** MO. NO. ARG. GELRIAE. CO ZVT **Note:** Dav. #4821.

Date	Mintage	Good	VG	F	VF	XF
1601	—	80.00	200	400	750	1,200
1604 Rare	—	—	—	—	—	—

KM# 24 2 DUTCH RIJKSDAALDER

Silver **Obv:** Half-figure with sword holding small arms **Obv. Legend:** MO. ARG. PRO. CONFOE. BE1. GEL(R) **Rev:** Crowned arms divide date **Rev. Legend:** CONCORDIA. RES. PARVAE. CRESCVNT **Note:** Klippe. Dav. #4827.

Date	Mintage	Good	VG	F	VF	XF
1608	—	—	—	—	—	—
1612	—	—	—	—	—	—
1615 Rare	—	—	—	—	—	—

KM# 23 2 DUTCH RIJKSDAALDER

Silver **Obv:** Half-figure with sword holding small arms **Obv. Legend:** MO. ARG. PRO. CONFOE. BE1. GEL(R) **Rev:** Crowned arms divide date **Rev. Legend:** CONCORDIA. RES. PARVAE. CRESCVNT **Note:** Dav. #4827.

Date	Mintage	Good	VG	F	VF	XF
1618 Rare	—	—	—	—	—	—

KM# 11 1/2 ROSE NOBLE

3.8200 g., Gold **Obv:** Ruler in ship in inner circle **Obv. Legend:** MO - AV - R DVC GEL ET (CON) ZVT **Rev:** Floriated cross with crowned lions in angles **Rev. Legend:** AVDITORIVM NRM IN NOMINE DOM **Note:** Fr. #231.

Date	Mintage	VG	F	VF	XF	Unc
ND(1601)Cross	50,361	300	750	1,000	1,600	—

KM# 17.1 1/2 CAVALIER D'OR

5.0000 g., 0.9200 Gold 0.1479 oz. AGW **Obv:** Equestrian figure of knight above arms **Obv. Legend:** MO AVR PRO CONF - OE BEL(G) GEL **Rev:** Crowned arms in inner circle, date at top **Rev. Legend:** CONCORDIA RES PARVAE CRESCVNT **Note:** Fr. #241.

Date	Mintage	VG	F	VF	XF	Unc
1606Cross	73,141	250	600	1,300	1,700	—
1607Cross	—	250	600	1,300	1,700	—
1608Cross	—	250	600	1,000	1,400	—
1613Cross	204,141	250	600	1,000	1,400	—
1614/04Cross	—	250	600	1,000	1,400	—
1614Cross	—	250	600	1,000	1,400	—
1615Cross	—	250	600	1,000	1,400	—
1616Cross	—	250	600	1,000	1,400	—
1617Cross	—	250	600	1,000	1,400	—
1618Cross	—	250	600	1,300	1,700	—
1619Cross	—	250	600	1,000	1,400	—
1620Cross	162,000	250	600	1,000	1,400	—
1621Cross	—	250	600	1,000	1,400	—
1622Cross	—	250	600	1,000	1,400	—
1623Cross	—	250	600	1,000	1,400	—
1624Cross	—	250	600	1,000	1,400	—
1625Cross	—	250	600	1,000	1,400	—
1641Cross	—	250	600	1,000	1,400	—
1644Cross	—	250	600	1,000	1,400	—

KM# 17.4 1/2 CAVALIER D'OR

5.0000 g., 0.9200 Gold 0.1479 oz. AGW **Obv:** Equestrian figure of knight above arms **Obv. Legend:** MO AVR PRO CONF - OE BEL (G) GEL **Rev:** Crowned arms in inner circle, date at top **Rev. Legend:** CONCORDIA RES PARVAE CRESCVNT

Date	Mintage	VG	F	VF	XF	Unc
1624	—	250	600	1,300	1,700	—

KM# 17.2 1/2 CAVALIER D'OR

5.0000 g., 0.9200 Gold 0.1479 oz. AGW **Obv:** Equestrian figure of knight above arms **Obv. Legend:** MO AVR PRO CONF - OE BEL(G) GEL **Rev:** Crowned arms in inner circle, date at top **Rev. Legend:** CONCORDIA RES PARVAE CRESCVNT

Date	Mintage	Good	VG	F	VF	XF
1644Lily	—	—	250	600	1,300	1,700

KM# 17.3 1/2 CAVALIER D'OR

5.0000 g., 0.9200 Gold 0.1479 oz. AGW **Obv:** Equestrian figure of knight above arms **Obv. Legend:** MO AVR PRO CONF - OE BEL(G) GEL **Rev:** Crowned arms in inner circle, date at top **Rev. Legend:** CONCORDIA RES PARVAE CRESCVNT

Date	Mintage	VG	F	VF	XF	Unc
Rosette	—	250	600	1,300	1,700	—

KM# 18 CAVALIER D'OR

10.0000 g., 0.9200 Gold 0.2958 oz. AGW **Obv:** Equestrian figure of knight above arms in inner circle **Obv. Legend:** MO AVR PRO CONFOE - BELG GEL **Rev:** Crowned arms in inner circle, date at top **Rev. Legend:** CONCORDIA RES PARVAE CRESCVNT **Note:** Fr. #240.

Date	Mintage	VG	F	VF	XF	Unc
1606Cross	22,767	500	1,500	3,000	4,000	—
1607Cross	Inc. above	350	1,000	2,000	3,000	—
1608Cross	Inc. above	350	1,000	2,000	3,000	—
1613Cross	74,207	350	1,000	2,000	3,000	—
1614Cross	Inc. above	350	1,000	2,000	3,000	—
1615Cross	Inc. above	350	1,000	2,000	3,000	—
1616Cross	Inc. above	350	1,000	2,000	3,000	—
1617Cross	Inc. above	350	1,000	2,000	3,000	—
1618Cross	Inc. above	350	1,000	200	4,000	—
1619/4Cross	Inc. above	500	1,500	3,000	4,000	—
1619/15Cross	Inc. above	500	1,500	3,000	4,000	—
1619/6Cross	Inc. above	500	1,500	3,000	4,000	—
1619Cross	Inc. above	350	1,000	2,000	3,000	—
1620Cross	66,257	350	1,000	2,000	3,000	—
1621Cross	Inc. above	500	1,500	3,000	4,000	—
1623Cross	Inc. above	350	1,000	2,000	3,000	—
1625Cross	Inc. above	350	1,000	2,000	3,000	—
1627Cross	Inc. above	500	1,500	3,000	4,000	—
1628Cross	Inc. above	500	1,500	3,000	4,000	—

KM# 5.1 DUCAT

3.5100 g., 0.9860 Gold 0.1113 oz. AGW **Obv:** Armored knight standing right holding sword on shoulder and bundle of arrows **Obv. Legend:** CONCORDIA RES - P - AR(VA) CRES GE (L) **Rev:** Ornate tablet with inscription **Rev. Legend:** MO ORDI/PROVIN/FOEDER/BELG AD/LEG IMP

Date	Mintage	VG	F	VF	XF	Unc
1637	Inc. above	140	225	400	600	—
1638/7	Inc. above	150	300	500	800	—
163-8	Inc. above	140	225	400	600	—
1638	Inc. above	140	225	400	600	—
1639	Inc. above	140	225	400	600	—
1640	178,080	140	225	400	600	—
1641	Inc. above	140	225	400	600	—
1642	Inc. above	140	225	400	600	—
1643	Inc. above	140	225	400	600	—
1644	Inc. above	140	225	400	600	—
1645	Inc. above	140	225	400	600	—
1646	722,960	140	225	400	600	—
1647	Inc. above	150	300	500	800	—
1648	Inc. above	140	225	400	600	—
1649	Inc. above	140	225	400	600	—
1650	Inc. above	140	225	400	600	—
1651	Inc. above	140	225	400	600	—
1652	Inc. above	140	225	400	600	—
1653	Inc. above	140	225	400	600	—
1654	Inc. above	140	225	400	600	—
1655	Inc. above	140	225	400	600	—
1656	Inc. above	140	225	400	600	—
1657	Inc. above	140	225	400	600	—
1658	Inc. above	140	225	400	600	—
1659	Inc. above	140	225	400	600	—
1660	Inc. above	140	225	400	600	—
1661	Inc. above	140	225	400	600	—
1662	Inc. above	140	225	400	600	—
1663	Inc. above	140	225	400	600	—
1664	Inc. above	150	300	500	800	—
1665	38,780	150	300	500	800	—
1666	Inc. above	150	300	500	800	—
1667	Inc. above	150	300	500	800	—
1686	Inc. above	150	300	500	800	—

TRADE COINAGE

KM# 5 DUCAT

3.5100 g., 0.9860 Gold 0.1113 oz. AGW **Obv:** Armored knight standing right holding sword on shoulder and bundle of arrows **Obv. Legend:** CONCORDIA RES - P - AR(VA) CRES GE (L) **Rev:** Ornate tablet with inscription **Rev. Legend:** ORD/PROVIN/FOEDER/BELG AD/LEG IMP **Note:** Fr. #237.

Date	Mintage	VG	F	VF	XF	Unc
1602/0	18,923	150	300	500	800	—
1602	Inc. above	150	300	500	800	—
1603/2	58,175	150	300	500	800	—
1603	Inc. above	140	225	400	600	—
1606	634,794	140	225	400	600	—
1607	Inc. above	140	225	400	600	—
1608	Inc. above	140	225	400	600	—
1609	121,680	140	225	400	600	—
1610	Inc. above	140	225	400	600	—
1611	Inc. above	140	225	400	600	—
1612	Inc. above	140	225	400	600	—
1613	Inc. above	140	225	400	600	—
1614/3	Inc. above	150	300	500	800	—
1617	Inc. above	150	300	500	800	—
1618	Inc. above	140	225	400	600	—
1619	Inc. above	140	225	400	600	—
1622	91,549	150	300	500	800	—
1628/23	Inc. above	150	300	500	800	—
1628	Inc. above	140	225	400	800	—
1629	Inc. above	140	225	400	600	—
1631/29	Inc. above	140	225	400	600	—
1631/23	Inc. above	140	225	400	600	—
1631	166,338	140	225	400	600	—
1632	Inc. above	140	225	400	600	—
1633	Inc. above	140	225	400	600	—
1634	Inc. above	140	225	400	600	—
1635	332,914	140	225	400	600	—
1636	Inc. above	140	225	400	600	—

KM# 40 2 DUCAT

6.9800 g., 0.9860 Gold 0.2213 oz. AGW **Obv:** Knight standing right divides date in inner circle **Obv. Legend:** CONCORDIA RES - PA - RVAE CRES GEL **Rev:** Legend in ornamental tablet **Rev. Legend:** MO AVR/PROVIN/CONFOE/BELG AD/LEG IMP **Note:** Fr. #235.

Date	Mintage	VG	F	VF	XF	Unc
1650	—	250	750	1,500	2,500	—
1656	—	250	750	1,500	2,500	—
1658	—	250	750	1,500	2,500	—
1659	—	250	750	1,500	2,500	—
1661	—	250	750	1,500	2,500	—
1662	—	250	750	1,500	2,500	—
1664	—	250	750	1,500	2,500	—

PATTERNS

Including off metal strikes

KM#	Date	Mintage	Identification	Mkt Val
Pn1	1646	—	2 Stuivers. Gold. 7.4000 g. Klippe. KM#26.2.	—
Pn2	1647	—	2 Stuivers. Gold. 7.4000 g. Klippe. KM#26.2.	—
Pn3	1662	—	Ducaton. Silver. 64.6000 g. Klippe. KM#41.	—
Pn4	1672	—	48 Stuivers. Silver. 64.6000 g. Klippe, KM#41	—
Pn6	1681	—	48 Stuivers. Gold. 20.7000 g. KM#15.4.	—
Pn7	1687	—	48 Stuivers. Gold. 20.7000 g. KM#15.4.	—
Pn8	1696	—	40 Stuivers. Gold. 21.5000 g. KM#69.	—

PIEFORTS

KM#	Date	Mintage	Identification	Mkt Val
P1	ND(1601)	—	Rose Noble. Gold.	—
P2	1608	—	48 Stuivers. Silver. 28.9000 g. Klippe. KM#14	—
P3	1608	—	48 Stuivers. Silver. 43.0000 g. KM#16.1.	—
P4	1608	—	48 Stuivers. Silver. Klippe, KM#16.1	—
P5	1612	—	48 Stuivers. Silver. Klippe, KM#16.1	—
P6	1613	—	48 Stuivers. Silver. Klippe, KM#16.1	—
P7	1615	—	48 Stuivers. Silver. Klippe, KM16.1.	—
P8	1633	—	48 Stuivers. Silver. KM15.1	1,700
P10	1643	—	Ducat. 0.9860 Gold. 13.9990 g. KM#5, Klippe. Quadruple weight.	—
P11	1646	—	2 Stuivers. Silver. 9.3000 g. Klippe, KM#26.2	—
P12	1648	—	48 Stuivers. Silver. Klippe, KM16.2	—
P13	1659	—	48 Stuivers. Silver. Double weight. KM#42.	2,000
P14	1659	—	40 Stuivers. Silver. Double weight. KM#50a	—
P15	1660	—	40 Stuivers. Silver. Double weight, KM#50a	—
P16	1660	—	40 Stuivers. Silver. KM41.	—
P17	1660	—	48 Stuivers. Silver. 57.3000 g. KM#42, Klippe.	—
P18	1662	—	40 Stuivers. Silver. Double weight. KM#50a	—
P9	1662	—	40 Stuivers. Silver. Klippe, KM#50a	—
P19	1662	—	40 Stuivers. Silver. Double weight. KM#50a	—
P20	1662	—	40 Stuivers. Silver. KM41.	—
P21	1662	—	40 Stuivers. Silver. Klippe, KM41.	—
P22	1670/69	—	40 Stuivers. Silver. Double weight. KM#50a	—
P23	1670	—	40 Stuivers. Silver. Double weight. KM#50a	—
P24	1670	—	40 Stuivers. Silver. KM41.	—
P25	1671	—	40 Stuivers. Silver. Double weight, KM#50a	—
P26	1672	—	40 Stuivers. Silver. Double weight, KM#50a	—
P27	1672	—	40 Stuivers. Silver. Klippe, KM41.	—
P28	1676	—	40 Stuivers. Silver. KM41.	—
P29	1680	—	40 Stuivers. Silver. KM50.	—
P30	1680	—	40 Stuivers. Silver. Double weight, KM50.	—
P31	1680	—	48 Stuivers. Silver. KM15.4.	—
P32	1682	—	60 Stuivers. Silver. Double weight. KM56.1.	—
P33	1693	—	30 Stuivers. Silver. 30.4 and 31.7 g. KM#61	—

'S-HEERENBERG

(Stevensweerd)

RULERS

Count Hendrik van den Bergh, 1616-1626
Herman Frederik, 1627-1631

COUNTY

STANDARD COINAGE

KM# 17 4 HELLER

Copper **Obv:** PROTECTOR/MEVS/IIII in tulip wreath **Rev:** Lion in crowned shield

Date	Mintage	VG	F	VF	XF	Unc
ND(1626-32)	—	30.00	75.00	100	250	—

KM# 36 8 HELLER

Silver **Obv:** VIII **Obv. Legend:** NVMMVS. AD. LEGEM. **Rev:** LXX/VIIII **Rev. Legend:** CVCVC. S. VALORIS 630

Date	Mintage	VG	F	VF	XF	Unc
(1)630	—	75.00	125	200	300	—

KM# 9 GIGOT (Duit)

Copper **Obv:** FRI/DER in tulip wreath with date **Rev:** Crowned arms of Friesland with lion supporters

Date	Mintage	VG	F	VF	XF	Unc
1619	—	30.00	75.00	125	300	—
1620	—	30.00	75.00	125	300	—
1621	—	30.00	75.00	125	300	—
1624	—	30.00	75.00	125	300	—

KM# 16 GIGOT (Duit)

Copper **Obv:** FRI/STA, date in tulip wreath **Rev:** Crowned arms of Friesland with lion supporters

Date	Mintage	VG	F	VF	XF	Unc
1620	—	30.00	75.00	200	400	—
1625	—	30.00	75.00	200	400	—
1626	—	30.00	75.00	200	400	—

Date	Mintage	VG	F	VF	XF	Unc
1629	—	30.00	75.00	200	400	—
1630	—	30.00	75.00	200	400	—
1631	—	30.00	75.00	200	400	—

KM# 18 GIGOT (Duit)

Copper **Obv:** FRI/STW in tulip wreath **Rev:** Crowned arms of Friesland with lion supporters

Date	Mintage	VG	F	VF	XF	Unc
ND(1626-32)	—	30.00	75.00	150	250	—

KM# 19 GIGOT (Duit)

Copper **Obv:** WER/IND/VSA in tulip wreath **Rev:** Crowned arms of Friesland with lion supporters

Date	Mintage	VG	F	VF	XF	Unc
ND(1626-32)	—	30.00	75.00	150	350	—

KM# 5 24 KREUZER

Silver **Obv:** Armored bust of Count right **Rev:** Displayed eagle with 24 in orb on breast

Date	Mintage	VG	F	VF	XF	Unc
ND	—	—	—	—	—	—

KM# 23 5 GROOT

Silver **Obv:** Man between 2 shields **Obv. Legend:** S. STEPHA/PROTH. M. **Rev:** Cross **Rev. Legend:** SIT. NOMEN. DNI. BENEDICTVM/S. ST-WER-. V. G. -ROS.

Date	Mintage	VG	F	VF	XF	Unc
ND(1627-31)	—	75.00	125	250	400	—

KM# 6 10 GROOT

Silver **Obv:** Bust of Count wearing coat right **Rev:** Crowned double-headed eagle

Date	Mintage	VG	F	VF	XF	Unc
ND	—	—	—	—	—	—

KM# 10 2 STUIVER

Silver **Obv:** INSV/LA; ST/1619 **Rev:** Lion divides 2S

Date	Mintage	VG	F	VF	XF	Unc
1619	—	100	500	1,000	1,500	—

KM# 35 8 STUIVER (Langrok)

Silver **Obv:** Mitred Saint divides VIII St **Rev:** Double-headed eagle with shield on breast **Rev. Legend:** MONETA. H. F. C. M. AD LEGEM GRONINGE

Date	Mintage	VG	F	VF	XF	Unc
1630	—	—	—	—	—	—

KM# 24 30 STUIVER

Silver

Date	Mintage	VG	F	VF	XF	Unc
1627	—	—	—	—	—	—
1627	—	—	—	—	—	—

Note: No denomination on the coin.

KM# 25 50 STUIVER

Silver **Obv:** Crowned and crested helmet above lion shield **Rev:** Crowned double-headed eagle **Note:** Dav. #5000.

Date	Mintage	VG	F	VF	XF	Unc
ND	—	—	—	—	—	—

KM# 8 1/4 SNAPHAAN

Silver **Obv:** Count on horse right **Obv. Legend:** S. P-ER-AMVSM-ELIORA **Rev:** Cross with arms on center **Rev. Legend:** MONET-A NOVA - MONT - ENSIS

Date	Mintage	VG	F	VF	XF	Unc
ND	—	75.00	225	450	900	—

KM# 7 1/2 DAALDER

Silver **Obv:** Armored bust of Count right **Rev:** Crowned and crested helmet above lion sheild

Date	Mintage	VG	F	VF	XF	Unc
ND	—	—	—	—	—	—

KM# 20 DAALDER

Silver **Ruler:** Count Hendrik van den Bergh **Obv:** Armored 1/2-length bust of Count holding baton above arms dividing date **Obv. Legend:** HENRICVS: COMES. D. - MONTE. DNS. IND. ST. W. **Rev:** Crowned and crested helmet above lion sheild **Rev. Legend:** DNS. PROTECTOR. VITAE. MEAE. QVO. TREPIDAB. **Note:** Dav. #4996.

Date	Mintage	VG	F	VF	XF	Unc
1626	—	—	—	—	—	—

KM# 21 DAALDER

Silver **Obv:** Armored bust of Count right **Note:** Dav. #4997.

Date	Mintage	VG	F	VF	XF	Unc
ND	—	40.00	—	—	—	—

KM# 22 DAALDER

Silver **Obv:** Larger bust of Count **Note:** Dav. #4999. Varieties in legend exist.

Date	Mintage	VG	F	VF	XF	Unc
ND	—	40.00	85.00	175	350	—
1628	—	40.00	85.00	175	350	—

KM# 37 DUCAT

Gold **Obv:** Crowned standing figure with halbert in right hand between H and F in inner circle **Obv. Legend:** SANCTVS OSW - A - LDVS REX **Rev:** Mary with child sitting on moonsickle in inner circle **Rev. Legend:** MARIA MATER - DIDHFCDMSW

Date	Mintage	VG	F	VF	XF	Unc
ND1635	—	—	—	—	—	—

KM# 26 FLORIN D'OR

3.5000 g., 0.9860 Gold 0.1109 oz. AGW **Obv:** Armored bust of Herman Frederik right holding helmet **Rev:** Quartered arms as 4 shields in inner circle

Date	Mintage	VG	F	VF	XF	Unc
(1632) Rare	—	—	—	—	—	—

KM# 27 FLORIN D'OR

3.5000 g., 0.9860 Gold 0.1109 oz. AGW **Obv:** Helmeted arms **Rev:** Crowned imperial eagle in inner circle

Date	Mintage	VG	F	VF	XF	Unc
(1632) Rare	—	—	—	—	—	—

KM# 28 FLORIN D'OR

3.5000 g., 0.9860 Gold 0.1109 oz. AGW **Obv:** St. Stephen **Rev:** Crowned imperial eagle in inner circle **Note:** Imitation of a Metz florin.

Date	Mintage	VG	F	VF	XF	Unc
ND	—	200	350	900	1,500	—
(16)34	—	—	—	—	—	—

BATENBURG

Free Barony

A small free barony in the duchy of Gelders, Batenburg was established as a branch of the lords of Bronckhorst in the early 14th century. Inherited Anhold (see) in the 15th century and then divided into four lines, the last Batenburg line being founded in the mid-16th century. The male line became extinct in 1641 and Batenburg passed by marriage successively to the counts of Horn, then Bentheim in 1694.

RULERS

Hermann Dietrich, 1573-1602
Maximilian, 1602-1641

ARMS

Batenburg – St. Andrew's cross, a pair of scissors with points down in each angle
Bronkhorst – lion rampant to left or right
Stein – 7 lozenges in 2 rows of three each and a single one below

Reference: K = Wilhelm Kraaz, ***Münzen der deutschen Kipperzeit***, Halle, 1924.

COUNTY

STANDARD COINAGE

KM# 1 DUIT

2.0000 g., Copper **Ruler:** Maximilian von Bronckhorst **Obv:** Lion in crowned shield **Rev:** Inscription in tulip wreath **Rev. Inscription:** BATEN / BVRV / CVSA

Date	Mintage	Good	VG	F	VF	XF
ND(1616-22)	—	5.00	15.00	40.00	100	150

KM# 2 DUIT

2.0000 g., Copper **Ruler:** Maximilian von Bronckhorst **Obv:** Lion in crowned shield **Rev:** inscription in tulip wreath **Rev. Inscription:** BAT / ENBVRG / GVM

Date	Mintage	VG	F	VF	XF	Unc
ND(1616-22)	—	30.00	75.00	100	150	—

KM# 11 GROSCHEN

1.9000 g., Silver **Ruler:** Maximilian von Bronckhorst **Obv:** In circle 24 and MATH I RO IMP 16-19 **Rev:** Climbing lion to the right in circle with MO MAX CO D BR L B.

Date	Mintage	Good	VG	F	VF	XF
ND1616-22	—	—	10.00	30.00	60.00	80.00
1619	—	50.00	125	250	400	500

KM# 5 2 STUIVERS

Silver **Ruler:** Maximilian von Bronckhorst **Obv:** Double eagle, 2S **Obv. Legend:** MO NO MAX CO D BR I B. **Rev:** Cross **Rev. Legend:** TANDEM BONA CAVSA TRIVMPHAT

Date	Mintage	VG	F	VF	XF	Unc
1620	—	60.00	150	250	400	—

KM# 5.1 2 STUIVERS

Silver **Ruler:** Maximilian von Bronckhorst **Obv:** Double eagle, 2S **Obv. Legend:** MO NO MAX CO D BR I B. **Rev:** Cross **Rev. Legend:** TANDEM BONA CAVSA TRIVMPHAT.

Date	Mintage	VG	F	VF	XF	Unc
1620	—	80.00	200	300	600	—

KM# 5.2 2 STUIVERS

2.0000 g., Silver **Ruler:** Maximilian von Bronckhorst **Obv:** Double eagle, 2S **Obv. Legend:** MO NO MAX CO D BR I B. **Rev:** Cross **Rev. Legend:** DEVS PROTECTOR MEVS.

Date	Mintage	VG	F	VF	XF	Unc
1620	—	60.00	150	250	400	—

KM# 5.3 2 STUIVERS

2.1000 g., Silver **Ruler:** Maximilian von Bronckhorst **Obv:** Lion between, 2S **Rev:** Double eagle / CI / VITAS / BAT / 1621

Date	Mintage	VG	F	VF	XF	Unc
	—	60.00	150	250	400	—

KM# 6 4 STUIVERS (Arendschelling; Kipper)

4.3000 g., Silver **Obv:** Crowned 4-fold arms, value IIII. STV. in legend. Shield between 4 - S. **Rev:** Imperial eagle, titles of Matthias

Date	Mintage	Good	VG	F	VF	XF
ND	—	25.00	60.00	125	200	350

KM# 7 4 STUIVERS (Arendschelling; Kipper)

4.3000 g., Silver **Obv:** Crowned 4-fold arms **Rev:** Imperial eagle, value IV (or III) in orb on breast, titles of Matthias

Date	Mintage	Good	VG	F	VF	XF
ND	—	25.00	60.00	125	200	350

KM# 10.1 3 KREUZER (1 Stuiver)

2.1000 g., Silver **Ruler:** Maximilian von Bronckhorst **Obv:** Arms of Bronckhorst, Batenburg and Stein with lion **Obv. Legend:** MONETA / NOVA / ARG / BAT / I / AST. **Obv. Inscription:** MONETA / NOVA / ARG / BAT / I / AST. **Rev:** Imperial eagle, value 3 **Rev. Legend:** MATH I...

Date	Mintage	Good	VG	F	VF	XF
ND	—	20.00	50.00	125	250	400

KM# 10.2 3 KREUZER (1 Stuiver)

2.1000 g., Silver **Ruler:** Maximilian von Bronckhorst **Obv:** Arms of Bronckhorst, Batenburg and Stein in centre. **Obv. Legend:** MONETA / NO(V) / ARGENT / BAT / I / ST. **Rev:** Imperial eagle, value 3 **Rev. Legend:** MATH I....

Date	Mintage	Good	VG	F	VF	XF
ND1612	—	30.00	75.00	150	300	500

KM# 20.1 ROOSSCHELLING (5 Stuiver)

5.2700 g., Silver **Ruler:** Maximilian von Bronckhorst **Obv:** Crowned arms, date **Obv. Legend:** MO. NO. AR. MAX. CO. DE. BR. BAT **Rev. Legend:** FIDE / SED / CVI / - VIDE

Date	Mintage	Good	VG	F	VF	XF
1622	—	50.00	125	350	700	900

KM# 20.2 ROOSSCHELLING (5 Stuiver)

5.2700 g., Silver **Ruler:** Maximilian von Bronckhorst **Obv:** Crowned arms, date **Obv. Legend:** MO. NO. AR. MAX. CO. DE. BR. BAT **Rev. Legend:** INSE / RVIE / NDO / NSUMUR 1622.

Date	Mintage	Good	VG	F	VF	XF
161-1622	—	—	—	—	—	—

KM# 12 ARENDSCHELLING (6 STUIVER)

6.0000 g., Silver **Ruler:** Maximilian von Bronckhorst **Obv:** Crowned double eage in circle **Obv. Legend:** MATH I D G ELEC RO IMP SEM AVG **Rev:** Crowned shield **Rev. Legend:** MO AR MAX D BR L BA - IN BATE - ET STEIN.

Date	Mintage	Good	VG	F	VF	XF
1622	—	—	—	—	—	—

KM# 8 DAALDER (ARENDSRIJKSDAALDER)

29.0300 g., Silver **Ruler:** Maximilian von Bronckhorst **Obv:** Helmeted arms **Obv. Legend:** MAXIM • CO • D: BRONCK • BAT • LI • ... **Rev:** Imperial eagle **Rev. Legend:** MATTHIAS • I • D • G • ELEC • IMP • SEM AVGVS • **Note:** Dav. # 4995.

Date	Mintage	Good	VG	F	VF	XF
1616	—	—	—	—	—	—
Note: Reported, not confirmed						
1618	—	400	1,000	2,000	3,000	5,000

KM# 9.1 DAALDER (ARENDSRIJKSDAALDER)

Silver, 45 x 45 mm. **Ruler:** Maximilian von Bronckhorst **Obv:** Helmeted arms **Obv. Legend:** MAXIM • CO • D: BRONCK • BAT • LI **Rev:** Imperial eagle **Rev. Legend:** MATTHIAS • I • D • G • ELEC • IMP • SEM AVGVS • **Note:** Klippe, illustration reduced. Dav. # A4995. Weight varies 57.9-58.8

Date	Mintage	Good	VG	F	VF	XF
1616	—	—	—	—	—	—
1618	—	—	—	—	—	—

PATTERNS

Including off metal strikes

KM#	Date	Mintage	Identification	Mkt Val
Pn1	ND(1616)	—	Duit. Silver. KM#2	—

PIEFORTS

KM#	Date	Mintage	Identification	Mkt Val
P1	ND(1616)	—	Duit. Copper. KM#2	—

ELBURG

TOWNSHIP

STANDARD COINAGE

KM# 1 1/2 DUIT

1.1000 g., Copper **Obv:** City gate with 3 towers within wreath **Rev:** Inscription **Rev. Inscription:** .1.6. / MONETA / ECCLES / ELBORG / I.S.

Date	Mintage	Good	VG	F	VF	XF
ND(1619-21)	—	7.50	30.00	75.00	150	300

KM# 2 1/2 DUIT

Copper **Obv:** Star above city gate with 3 towers within sprays **Rev:** Inscription **Rev. Inscription:** *** / MONETA / ECCLES / ELBVRG / ***

Date	Mintage	Good	VG	F	VF	XF
ND(1619-21)	—	7.50	30.00	75.00	150	300

M# 3.1 1/2 DUIT

opper **Obv:** Crowned city arms **Rev:** Inscription **Rev.**
nscription: MONE / ECCLE / ELBV

ate	Mintage	Good	VG	F	VF	XF
D(1619-21)	—	35.00	100	250	500	1,000

M# 3.2 1/2 DUIT

opper **Obv:** Crowned city arms **Rev:** Inscription **Rev.**
nscription: ... / MONE / ECCLE / ELBV / ...

ate	Mintage	Good	VG	F	VF	XF
D(1619-21)	—	7.50	30.00	75.00	150	300

M# 3.2a 1/2 DUIT

ilver **Obv:** Crowned city arms **Rev:** Inscription **Rev.**
nscription: ... / MONE / ECCLE / ELBV / ...

ate	Mintage	Good	VG	F	VF	XF
D(1619-21)	—	—	—	—	—	—

M# 5 1/2 DUIT

opper **Obv:** Arms in beaded circle **Rev:** Inscription in beaded ircle **Rev. Inscription:** MONE / ECCLE / ELBV

ate	Mintage	Good	VG	F	VF	XF
D(1619-21)	—	7.50	30.00	75.00	150	300

M# 6 1/2 DUIT

opper **Obv:** Crowned arms in branches **Rev:** Inscription in ranches **Rev. Inscription:** MONE / ECCLE / ELBV

ate	Mintage	Good	VG	F	VF	XF
D(1619-21)	—	7.50	30.00	75.00	150	300

M# 7 1/2 DUIT

opper **Obv:** Crowned arms in branches **Rev:** Inscription, date wreath **Rev. Inscription:** MON / ECCL / ELB **Note:** Weight aries 1.2000 - 1.7000g.

ate	Mintage	Good	VG	F	VF	XF
621	—	7.50	30.00	75.00	150	300

NIJMEGEN

CITY

STANDARD COINAGE

M# 3 DUIT

opper **Obv:** Inscription within tulip wreath **Obv. Inscription:** OV / IMA / GVM **Rev:** Woman with one hand raised supports hield with double eagle **Rev. Legend:** BEA. GNS. CV. DNS. PS. E.

ate	Mintage	VG	F	VF	XF	Unc
D(1618-20)	—	15.00	65.00	130	250	—

M# 5 DUIT

opper **Obv:** Inscription within tulip wreath **Obv. Inscription:** OV / IMA / GVM **Rev:** Woman with one hand raised supports hield with double eagle, all in inner circle **Rev. Legend:** BEATA GNS • CVI • DNS • SPS • EI **Note:** Legend varieties exist.

ate	Mintage	VG	F	VF	XF	Unc
6)18	—	10.00	45.00	100	150	—
6)19	—	10.00	45.00	100	150	—
6)20	—	10.00	45.00	100	150	—

M# 4 DUIT

opper **Obv:** NOV/IMA/GVM in tulip wreath **Rev:** Woman sitting fenced-in area, holding sword, one arm raised, shield with ouble eagle below **Rev. Legend:** BEA. GNS. CVIVS. DNS. SPS. IV. **Note:** Legend varieties exist.

ate	Mintage	VG	F	VF	XF	Unc
D(1618-20)	—	15.00	65.00	130	250	—

M# 6 DUIT

.0000 g., Copper **Obv:** Inscription within tulip wreath **Obv.** **egend:** NO / VIMA / GVM **Rev:** Woman with one hand raised ehind shield with double eagle **Rev. Legend:** BEA GNS.C. NS.SPS. E **Note:** Struck over Spanish Netherlands OORD of Duit of Albert and Isabella.

ate	Mintage	VG	F	VF	XF	Unc
D1620	—	15.00	75.00	150	300	—

KM# 2 2 DUIT (Oord)

Copper **Obv:** Inscription within tulip wreath **Obv. Inscription:** NO / VIMA / GVM **Rev:** Woman with one hand raised, behind shield with double eagle **Rev. Legend:** BEA.GNS.C. DNS.SPS. E. **Note:** Struck over Spanish Netherlands 2 Duit of Albert and Isabella.

Date	Mintage	VG	F	VF	XF	Unc
ND(1604)	—	15.00	65.00	130	250	—

KM# A5 1/2 STUIVER

Billon **Obv:** Crowned arms divide value in inner circle, crown divides date **Rev:** Ornate long cross with H-S-V-N in angles in inner circle

Date	Mintage	VG	F	VF	XF	Unc
1602	—	20.00	75.00	150	300	—
1603	—	20.00	75.00	150	300	—

KM# 34 1/2 STUIVER

1.0000 g., Billon **Obv:** Crowned arms divide value in inner circle, crown divides date **Obv. Legend:** MO NO CIVI NOVIM **Rev:** Ornate long cross with H-S-V-N in angles in inner circle **Rev. Legend:** BEA - GNS CV D - SPS E

Date	Mintage	VG	F	VF	XF	Unc
1620	—	20.00	75.00	150	300	—

KM# 35 STUIVER

2.0000 g., Billon **Obv:** Crowned arms divide value in inner circle, crown divides date **Obv. Legend:** MONETA NO REIPVB NOVIOMAG **Rev:** Ornamental long cross with quartrefoil around center in inner circle **Rev. Legend:** BEATA - GENS C - VI DNS - SPES EI

Date	Mintage	VG	F	VF	XF	Unc
1602	—	30.00	80.00	150	250	—

KM# 7.1 STUIVER

2.0000 g., Billon **Obv:** Crowned arms divide value in inner circle, crown divides date **Obv. Legend:** MONE NO IMP CIV NOVIM **Rev:** Ornamental long cross with quatrefoil around center **Rev. Legend:** BEA GNS CVD - SPS E

Date	Mintage	VG	F	VF	XF	Unc
1619	—	30.00	80.00	150	300	—
1620	—	30.00	80.00	150	300	—

KM# 7 STUIVER

4.0000 g., Billon **Obv:** Crowned arms divide value in inner circle, crown divides date **Rev:** Ornamental long cross with quatrefoil around center

Date	Mintage	VG	F	VF	XF	Unc
1619	—	30.00	80.00	150	300	—

KM# 15 2 STUIVERS

Silver **Obv:** Crowned arms divide value in inner circle, crown divides date **Rev:** Ornate cross in inner circle

Date	Mintage	VG	F	VF	XF	Unc
1619	—	35.00	100	200	400	—
16Z0	—	35.00	100	200	400	—

KM# 25 2 STUIVERS

1.7300 g., 0.8530 Silver 0.0474 oz. ASW **Obv:** Crowned rampant lion left holding sword and arrows, value at sides **Rev:** Inscription **Rev. Inscription:** NOVIO / MAGUM / (date) **Note:** Mint mark: Moor's head.

Date	Mintage	VG	F	VF	XF	Unc
1681	—	10.00	25.00	50.00	100	—
1685	—	10.00	25.00	50.00	100	—
1686	—	10.00	25.00	50.00	100	—
1688	—	10.00	25.00	50.00	100	—

KM# 8 3 STUIVERS (1/2 Arend-Schelling)

3.0000 g., 0.5000 Silver 0.0482 oz. ASW **Obv:** Crowned imperial eagle with arms on breast in inner circle **Rev:** Crowned arms in inner circle, crown divides date in legend **Note:** Mint mark: Pomegranate.

Date	Mintage	VG	F	VF	XF	Unc
1602	—	50.00	150	300	600	—
1604	—	60.00	200	400	800	—

KM# 9 3 STUIVERS (1/2 Arend-Schelling)

3.0000 g., Silver **Obv:** Ornate cross within circle **Rev:** Crowned double-headed eagle with arms on breast

Date	Mintage	VG	F	VF	XF	Unc
ND	—	60.00	150	300	600	—

KM# 10.1 6 STUIVERS (Arend-Schelling)

6.0000 g., 0.5000 Silver 0.0964 oz. ASW **Obv:** Crowned arms within circle, crown divides date in legend **Rev:** Crowned imperial eagle with arms on breast within circle, titles of Rudoph II **Note:** Mint mark: Pomegranate.

Date	Mintage	VG	F	VF	XF	Unc
1602	—	50.00	100	200	400	—
1603	—	50.00	100	200	400	—
1604	—	50.00	100	200	400	—
ND	—	50.00	100	200	400	—

KM# 10.2 6 STUIVERS (Arend-Schelling)

6.0000 g., 0.5000 Silver 0.0964 oz. ASW **Obv:** Titles of Matthias I **Note:** Varieties exist.

Date	Mintage	VG	F	VF	XF	Unc
1605	—	—	—	—	—	—

KM# 26.2 6 STUIVERS (Arend-Schelling)

Silver **Rev:** Sitting dog below knight

Date	Mintage	VG	F	VF	XF	Unc
1685	—	15.00	45.00	100	200	—

KM# 26.1 6 STUIVERS (Arend-Schelling)

4.9500 g., 0.5830 Silver 0.0928 oz. ASW **Obv:** Crowned arms divide value, last two digits of date right of crown **Rev:** Knight with sword on horseback right **Note:** Mint mark: Moor's head.

Date	Mintage	VG	F	VF	XF	Unc
(16)85	—	12.50	27.50	65.00	125	—
(16)86	—	12.50	27.50	65.00	125	—
(16)88/6	—	15.00	45.00	100	200	—
(16)88	—	12.50	27.50	65.00	125	—
(16)89	—	12.50	27.50	65.00	125	—
(16)90	—	12.50	27.50	65.00	125	—
(16)91	—	12.50	27.50	65.00	125	—

KM# 26.3 6 STUIVERS (Arend-Schelling)

Silver **Rev:** Eagle with one head

Date	Mintage	VG	F	VF	XF	Unc
1691	—	15.00	45.00	100	200	—

KM# 16 8 STUIVERS (Langrok)

Silver **Obv:** Standing figure of St. Stephen **Rev:** Crowned imperial eagle with arms on breast

Date	Mintage	VG	F	VF	XF	Unc
1619	—	350	1,500	3,000	4,000	—

KM# 27.1 28 STUIVERS (Florin)

19.5000 g., 0.6730 Silver 0.4219 oz. ASW **Obv:** Crowned arms **Rev:** Imperial eagle **Note:** Open crown. Mint mark: Moor's head. This coin appears with countermarks of HOL, UTR, L, G.O., arms, lion, and bundle of arrows.

Date	Mintage	VG	F	VF	XF	Unc
(16)85	48,310	50.00	140	275	550	—
(16)86	Inc. above	50.00	140	275	550	—
(16)88	Inc. above	60.00	175	350	700	—
16-90	Inc. above	50.00	140	275	550	—

KM# 27.2 28 STUIVERS (Florin)

19.5000 g., 0.6730 Silver 0.4219 oz. ASW **Obv:** Crowned arms with short date; below cartouche with 28 **Obv. Legend:** FLOR ARG CIV - NOV IOMAG mintmark **Rev:** Imperial crowned double eagle. **Rev. Legend:** FERDINA(ND) II D G ROM IMP SEM A(V) **Note:** Smaller closed crown and date between crown. Mint mark: Moor's head. This coin appears with countermarks of HOL, UTR, L, G.O., arms, lion, and bundle of arrows.

Date	Mintage	VG	F	VF	XF	Unc
16-90	Inc. above	75.00	225	450	900	—

KM# 29 GULDEN (20 Stuiver)

10.6100 g., 0.9200 Silver 0.3138 oz. ASW **Obv:** Crowned arms divide value, date above crown **Rev:** Standing female figure leaning on Bible on column, holding spear with Liberty cap **Note:** Mint mark: Moor's head.

Date	Mintage	VG	F	VF	XF	Unc
1687	69,510	25.00	70.00	110	250	—
1691	Inc. above	25.00	70.00	150	300	—
ND(1687)	Inc. above	25.00	70.00	150	300	—

KM# 28 3 GULDEN (60 Stuiver)
31.8200 g., 0.9200 Silver 0.9412 oz. ASW **Obv:** Crowned arms divide value, date above crown **Rev:** Standing knight with sword behind crowned arms left, date in legend **Note:** Dav. #4971. Mint mark: Moor's head.

Date	Mintage	VG	F	VF	XF	Unc
1686	13,860	150	300	600	1,200	—
1687	Inc. above	150	400	800	1,600	—
1689	Inc. above	150	400	800	1,600	—
1690	Inc. above	150	300	600	1,200	—

KM# 11 DAALDER (Rijks)
29.0300 g., 0.8850 Silver 0.8260 oz. ASW **Obv:** Crowned imperial eagle in inner circle **Rev:** Crowned arms with lion supporters, date below in inner circle

Date	Mintage	VG	F	VF	XF	Unc
1602	—	100	350	700	1,400	—

KM# 30 DAALDER (30 Stuivers)
15.8800 g., 0.9060 Silver 0.4625 oz. ASW **Obv:** Crowned arms with lion supporters, value below **Rev:** Standing knight with sword behind crowned arms left, date in legend **Note:** Mint mark: Moor's head.

Date	Mintage	VG	F	VF	XF	Unc
1688	94,895	60.00	125	250	500	—
1689 Closed crown	Inc. above	70.00	150	275	550	—
1689	Inc. above	70.00	150	275	550	—

KM# 32 DAALDER (Lion - 48 Stuivers)
27.6800 g., 0.7500 Silver 0.6674 oz. ASW **Obv:** Knight standing behind shield in inner circle **Rev:** Rampant lion left in inner circle, date above in legend **Note:** Dav. #4887.

Date	Mintage	VG	F	VF	XF	Unc
1692	234,325	45.00	150	350	700	—

KM# 31 60 STUIVERS 2 DAALDERS
31.7600 g., 0.9060 Silver 0.9251 oz. ASW **Obv:** Crowned arms with lion supporters, value below **Rev:** Standing knight with sword behind crowned arms left, date in legend **Note:** Dav. #4988. Mint mark: Moor's head.

Date	Mintage	VG	F	VF	XF	Unc
1688	7,735	250	500	1,000	1,750	—
1689	Inc. above	250	500	1,000	1,750	—

KM# 12 FLORIN
3.5000 g., 0.9860 Gold 0.1109 oz. AGW **Obv:** Crowned imperial eagle in inner circle, titles of Rudolf II **Rev:** Crowned arms with lion supporters, date in exergue in inner circle

Date	Mintage	VG	F	VF	XF	Unc
1602 Rare	—	—	—	—	—	—

KM# 20 FLORIN
3.5000 g., 0.9860 Gold 0.1109 oz. AGW **Obv:** Titles of Ferdinand II

Date	Mintage	VG	F	VF	XF	Unc
1620 Rare	—	—	—	—	—	—

PATTERNS

Including off metal strikes

KM#	Date	Mintage	Identification	Mkt Val
Pn1	1685	—	2 Stuivers. Gold. KM#25.	—
Pn2	1686	—	Schelling. Gold. 7.5000 g. KM#26.1.	—
Pn3	1688	—	Schelling. Gold. 7.5000 g. KM#26.1.	—
Pn4	1691	—	Gulden. Gold. KM#29	—

PIEFORTS

KM#	Date	Mintage	Identification	Mkt Val
P1	1685	—	6 Stuivers, Silver, Double weight, KM#26.1	—
P2	1685	—	28 Stuivers. Silver. Triple weight, KM27.	—
P5	1687	—	3 Gulden. Silver. Double weight. KM#28	—
P4	1688	—	28 Stuivers. Silver. Triple weight, KM27.	—
P6	1688	—	Daalder. Silver. Double weight, KM#30.	—
P7	1688	—	2 Daalder. Silver. Triple weight. KM#31	—
P3	1688/6	—	28 Stuivers. Silver. KM27.	—
P8	1692	—	Lion Daalder. Silver. Triple weight, KM32.	—

ZUTPHEN

COMMUNE

STANDARD COINAGE

KM# 4 1/4 STUIVER
Silver **Obv:** City arms in dotted circle **Obv. Legend:** + MONE. VET. VRB. ZVTPH **Rev:** Rampant lion **Rev. Legend:** FATA. VIAM. INVENIENT

Date	Mintage	VG	F	VF	XF	Unc
ND(1605)	—	125	300	600	1,100	—

KM# 2 PEERDEKE (1/4 Snaphaan)
Silver **Obv:** City arms on long cross **Obv. Legend:** MO: NE - NOVA - CIVITA - ZVTPHA **Rev:** Equestrian knight right brandishing sword **Rev. Legend:** VIAM.IN - VENIENT - FA - TA+

Date	Mintage	VG	F	VF	XF	Unc
1604	—	45.00	150	300	600	—
1605	—	45.00	150	300	600	—

KM# 10 SNAPHAAN
Silver **Obv:** Armored knight on horseback right in inner circle, date below in cartouche **Rev:** Arms on long cross in inner circle

Date	Mintage	VG	F	VF	XF	Unc
1604	—	35.00	80.00	140	200	—

KM# 3 SNAPHAAN
Silver **Obv:** City arms on long cross **Obv. Legend:** DEO * ET - VIRTVT - E* DVCI - BVS* **Rev:** Equestrian knight right brandishing sword **Rev. Legend:** + TANDEM • BONA • CAVSA • TRIVMPHAT

Date	Mintage	VG	F	VF	XF	Unc
1604	—	80.00	200	400	800	—

KM# 5 DUIT
Copper **Obv:** Crowned rampant lion left in inner circle **Rev:** 3 line inscription in wreath

Date	Mintage	VG	F	VF	XF	Unc
ND(1604-05)	—	30.00	80.00	125	250	—

KM# 16 DUIT
Copper **Obv:** Crowned arms with lion supporters with last 2 digits of date ave crown **Rev:** Inscription in cartouche **Rev. Inscription:** CIV / ZVTPHA / NIA

Date	Mintage	VG	F	VF	XF	Unc
ND	—	20.00	50.00	100	150	—
(16)87	—	20.00	50.00	100	150	—
(16)87/88	—	30.00	100	150	200	—

KM# 16a.1 DUIT
Silver **Obv:** Crowned arms with lion supporters with last 2 digits of date ave crown **Rev:** CIV/ZVTPHA/NIA in cartouche

Date	Mintage	VG	F	VF	XF	Unc
1687	—	—	—	—	—	—

KM# 16b DUIT
Gold **Obv:** Date under shield **Rev:** CIV / ZVTPHA / NIA in cartouche

Date	Mintage	VG	F	VF	XF	Unc
1687	—	—	—	—	—	—

KM# 16a.2 DUIT
Silver **Obv:** Date under shield

Date	Mintage	VG	F	VF	XF	Unc
1687	—	—	—	—	—	—

KM# 6 1/2 STUIVER
Silver **Obv:** 3 towered castle in inner circle **Rev:** Arms on long cross in inner circle

Date	Mintage	VG	F	VF	XF	Unc
ND(1604-05)	—	100	250	500	750	—

KM# 7 STUIVER
2.0000 g., Silver **Obv:** Crowned arms divide value in innr circle, crown divides date **Rev:** Ornamental long cross with arms at center in inner circle

Date	Mintage	VG	F	VF	XF	Unc
1605	—	30.00	90.00	175	350	—

KM# 8 STUIVER (1/4 Snaphaan)
Silver **Obv:** Armored knight on horseback right in inner circle, date below in cartouche **Rev:** Arms on long cross in inner circle

Date	Mintage	VG	F	VF	XF	Unc
1505 (error)	—	—	—	—	—	—
1605	—	35.00	90.00	150	210	—

KM# 9 2 STUIVERS
4.0000 g., Silver **Obv:** Crowned arms divide value in inner circle, date below **Rev:** Ornamental long cross with arms at center in inner circle

Date	Mintage	VG	F	VF	XF	Unc
1605	—	45.00	175	300	450	—

KM# 11 3 STUIVERS (1/2 Roosschelling)
2.6300 g., Silver **Obv:** Crowned arms divide value in inner circle, crown divides date **Rev:** Floreated cross with rose at center in inner circle

Date	Mintage	VG	F	VF	XF	Unc
1605	—	100	450	900	1,100	—

KM# 19 6 STUIVERS (Rijderschelling)
4.7100 g., Silver **Obv:** Crowned arms divide value, date above crown **Rev:** Armored knight on horseback right **Note:** Mint mark: Antlers.

Date	Mintage	VG	F	VF	XF	Unc
1668 (error for 1688)	—	20.00	50.00	100	200	—
1688	—	10.00	25.00	50.00	125	—
1689	—	10.00	25.00	50.00	125	—
1690	—	10.00	25.00	50.00	125	—
1691	—	10.00	25.00	50.00	125	—

KM# 25 28 STUIVERS (Florin)
19.5000 g., 0.6730 Silver 0.4219 oz. ASW **Obv:** Crowned arms, date above crown **Rev:** Crowned double-headed eagle with value on breast **Note:** Mint mark: Antlers.

Date	Mintage	VG	F	VF	XF	Unc
1660 (error)	28,920	100	350	550	900	—
1690	Inc. above	80.00	300	450	650	—

KM# 20 30 STUIVERS (Daalder)
15.8800 g., 0.9060 Silver 0.4625 oz. ASW **Obv:** Crowned arms with lion supporters, value below **Rev:** Standing knight with sword behind crowned arms to left, date in legend

Date	Mintage	VG	F	VF	XF	Unc
1688	—	100	350	650	1,000	—
1689/8	—	70.00	250	500	800	—
1689	—	70.00	250	500	800	—
1692	—	70.00	250	500	800	—

KM# 17 1/2 GULDEN (10 Stuiver)
5.3000 g., 0.9200 Silver 0.1568 oz. ASW **Note:** Mint mark: Antlers. Similar to 3 Gulden, KM#15.

Date	Mintage	VG	F	VF	XF	Unc
1687	4,460	60.00	200	400	600	—

KM# 18 GULDEN (20 Stuiver)
Silver **Note:** Mint marks: Antlers. Similar to 3 Gulden, KM#15.

Date	Mintage	VG	F	VF	XF	Unc
ND	57,935	100	250	500	1,000	—
1687	Inc. above	50.00	125	225	450	—

KM# 15 3 GULDEN (60 Stuiver)
31.8200 g., 0.9200 Silver 0.9412 oz. ASW **Note:** Mint marks: Antlers. Dav. #4972.

Date	Mintage	VG	F	VF	XF	Unc
1686	4,625	300	750	1,750	2,500	—
1687	Inc. above	175	400	800	1,750	—

KM# 26 DAALDER (Liom - 48 Stuiver)
27.6800 g., 0.7500 Silver 0.6674 oz. ASW **Obv:** Armored knight looking right above lion shield in inner circle **Rev:** Rampant lion left in inner circle, date divided at top **Note:** Mint mark: Antlers. Dav. #4888.

Date	Mintage	VG	F	VF	XF	Unc
1690	—	1,000	2,500	4,500	5,500	—
1691	—	1,000	2,500	4,500	5,500	—
1692	—	1,000	2,500	4,500	5,500	—

PATTERNS

Including off metal strikes

KM#	Date	Mintage	Identification	Mkt Val
Pn1	1690	—	Ducat D'Argent. Silver.	—

PIEFORTS

KM#	Date	Mintage	Identification	Mkt Val
P1	1604	—	Peerdeke. Silver. KM#2.	—
P2	1604	—	Snaphaan. Silver. KM#3. Klippe.	—
P3	1687	—	Gulden. Silver. KM#18.	—
P4	1687	—	Duit. Silver. KM#16a.1.	—
P5	1688	—	Daalder. Silver. Triple weight. KM#30.	—
P6	1688	—	Daalder. Silver. Quadruple weight. KM#30.	—
P7	1689	—	Daalder. Silver. Triple weight. KM#30.	—
P8	1690	—	Florin. Silver. Triple weight. KM#28.	—
P9	1690	—	3 Gulden. Silver. KM#15.	—
P10	1692	—	Daalder. Silver. Triple weight. KM#30.	—

GRONINGEN AND OMMELAND

The province of Groningen is located in northern Netherlands and is drained by numerous rivers and canals.

The early history of Groningen is chiefly one of conflict between the city and the surrounding districts known as the Ommelanden. The city remained loyal to the Spanish king while the surrounding area supported the revolt against Spain. After 1594 Groningen and Ommelanden were united into one republic but it was not until 1795 that they were merged into one province.

The Groningen Mint was closed in 1692. The following coins were struck at the Harderwyk Mint of Gelderland.

CITY

STANDARD COINAGE

KM# 12 DUIT (Plak)
0.7700 g., Billon **Obv:** Arms in inner circle, date in legend **Obv. Legend:** SIT N - ODO - BENE - date **Rev:** Double-headed eagle with arms on breast in inner circle **Rev. Legend:** MONTE(TA) NOV(VA) GRONING(ENSIS)

Date	Mintage	Good	VG	F	VF	XF
1601	—	20.00	75.00	150	300	500
1602	—	15.00	60.00	125	250	350
1604	—	15.00	60.00	125	250	350
1609	—	20.00	75.00	150	300	500
1615	—	20.00	75.00	150	300	500
1622	—	15.00	60.00	125	250	350
1623	—	15.00	60.00	125	250	350
1625	—	20.00	75.00	150	300	500
1629	—	—	—	—	—	—

KM# 45 DUIT (Plak)
2.0000 g., Copper **Obv:** Crowned arms with lion supporters, date at top **Rev:** CIV/GRONIN/GA in cartouche

Date	Mintage	Good	VG	F	VF	XF
1690	320,000	6.00	20.00	40.00	65.00	125

KM# 46 DUIT (Plak)
2.0000 g., Copper **Obv:** Crowned arms with lion supporters, date at top **Rev:** GRO/NINGA in cartouche

Date	Mintage	Good	VG	F	VF	XF
1690	Inc. above	6.00	20.00	60.00	85.00	150

KM# 8 2 PLAK
1.1700 g., Billon **Obv:** Arms on long cross in inner circle, date in legend **Obv. Designer:** SIT N - ODO - BENE - date **Rev:** Double-headed eagle with arms on breast in inner circle **Rev. Designer:** MONE(TA) NOVA GRONINGE(NSIS) **Note:** 0.083 silver.

Date	Mintage	Good	VG	F	VF	XF
1602	—	15.00	50.00	125	260	450
1608	10,732	15.00	50.00	125	260	450
1609	32,273	15.00	50.00	125	260	450
1612	3,120	20.00	75.00	150	300	500
1614	—	15.00	50.00	125	250	450
1615	—	20.00	75.00	150	300	500
1617	10,400	—	—	—	—	—
1622	6,240	20.00	75.00	150	300	500
1625	—	—	—	—	—	—
1626	6,600	15.00	50.00	125	260	450
1628	6,600	15.00	50.00	125	260	450
1635	22,000	20.00	75.00	150	300	500
1649	—	15.00	50.00	125	260	450

KM# 14.1 1/2 STUIVER (4 Plakken)
0.1770 Silver **Obv:** Crowned arms divide value in inner circle **Rev:** Ornamental long cross with S-P-Q-G in angles **Note:** Klippe of KM #10. 2.2-3.5g

Date	Mintage	Good	VG	F	VF	XF
1613	—	—	—	—	—	900
1622	—	—	—	—	—	—
1626	—	—	—	—	—	—
1629	—	—	—	—	—	900

KM# 14.2 1/2 STUIVER (4 Plakken)
0.1770 Silver **Obv:** Crowned arms divide value in inner circle **Rev:** Ornamental long cross with S-P-Q-G in angles **Note:** Klippe of KM#10. 4.6-5.9g

Date	Mintage	Good	VG	F	VF	XF
1613	—	—	—	—	—	—
1629	—	—	—	—	—	—

KM# 10 1/2 STUIVER (4 Plakken or butken)
1.1700 g., 0.1770 Silver 0.0067 oz. ASW **Obv:** Crowned double eagle in shield divide value in inner circle **Rev:** Ornamental long cross with S-P-Q-G in angles **Rev. Legend:** SI - NO D O B - date

Date	Mintage	Good	VG	F	VF	XF
1604	24,808	12.00	45.00	110	220	320
1609	20,227	12.00	45.00	110	220	320
1613	15,680	12.00	45.00	110	220	320
1614	—	16.00	60.00	150	275	450
1615	—	12.00	45.00	110	220	320
1616	—	12.00	45.00	110	220	320
1617	—	12.00	45.00	110	220	320
1620	—	12.00	45.00	110	220	320
1621	—	16.00	60.00	150	275	450
1622	—	16.00	60.00	150	275	450
1625	—	12.00	45.00	110	220	320
1626	—	12.00	45.00	110	220	320
1628	—	12.00	45.00	110	220	320
1629	—	16.00	60.00	150	275	450
1635	—	16.00	60.00	150	275	450
1649	—	16.00	60.00	150	275	450

KM# A16.1 STUIVER (8 Plakken)
Billon **Obv:** Double headed eagle with arms on breast in inner circle **Obv. Legend:** MONETA NOVA GRONINGEN(SIS) **Rev:** Ornamental long cross with I-S-B-R in angles, date in legend **Rev. Legend:** SIT N - O(M) - BEN(E) A° date **Note:** Mint mark: Quatrefoil. Klippe of KM#5.1. 9.4-10.3g.

Date	Mintage	VG	F	VF	XF	Unc
1613 ca. 2.5 g	—	—	—	—	—	1,200
1622	—	—	—	—	—	1,200

KM# 5.2 STUIVER (8 Plakken)
Billon **Obv:** Double-headed eagle with arms on breast in inner circle **Obv. Legend:** MONETA NOVA GRONINGEN(SIS) **Rev:** Ornamental long cross with I-S-B-R in angles, date in legend **Rev. Legend:** SIT NOMEN DOMINI BENED(ICTVM) **Note:** Mint mark: Double eagle.

Date	Mintage	Good	VG	F	VF	XF
1628	—	17.00	60.00	150	275	450
1630	—	15.00	20.00	125	225	350
1635	—	15.00	20.00	125	225	350

KM# A16.2 STUIVER (8 Plakken)
0.2430 Silver **Obv:** Double headed eagle with arms on breast in inner circle **Obv. Legend:** MONETA NOVA GRONINGEN(SIS) **Rev:** Ornamental long cross with I-S-B-R in angles, date in legend **Rev. Legend:** SIT N - O(M) - BEN(E) A° date **Note:** Mint mark: Double eagle. Klippe of KM #5.2.

Date	Mintage	VG	F	VF	XF	Unc
1635	—	—	—	—	—	1,200

KM# 5.1 STUIVER (8 Plakken or Brabants Stuiver)
1.9200 g., 0.2430 Silver 0.0150 oz. ASW **Obv:** Double-headed eagle with arms on breast in inner circle **Obv. Legend:** MONETA NOVA GRONINGEN(SIS) **Rev:** Ornamental long cross with I-S-B-R in angles, date in legend **Rev. Legend:** SIT N - O(M) - BEN(E) A° date **Note:** Mint mark: Quatrefoil. (ISBR: 1 Stuiver Brabants)

Date	Mintage	Good	VG	F	VF	XF
1601	—	15.00	50.00	125	225	350
1602	—	17.00	60.00	150	275	450
1604	—	15.00	50.00	125	225	350
1605	—	17.00	60.00	150	275	450
1609	—	17.00	60.00	150	275	450
1613	—	15.00	50.00	125	225	350
1615	—	17.00	60.00	150	275	450
1622	—	17.00	60.00	150	275	450
1625	—	15.00	50.00	125	225	350
1627	—	17.00	60.00	150	275	450

KM# 47 STUIVER (WEAPON)
0.8100 g., 0.5830 Silver 0.0152 oz. ASW **Obv:** Crowned arms divide value, date above crown **Rev:** Inscription **Rev. Inscription:** CIV / GRONIN / GA

Date	Mintage	Good	VG	F	VF	XF
1690	—	6.00	20.00	40.00	70.00	110
1691	—	10.00	30.00	60.00	80.00	130

KM# 47a STUIVER (WEAPON)
Gold **Obv:** Crowned arms divide value, date above crown **Rev:** Inscription **Rev. Inscription:** CIV / GRONIN / GA

Date	Mintage	Good	VG	F	VF	XF
1690	—	—	—	—	—	700

KM# 1 JAGER (2 STUIVERS)

1.9200 g., 0.4930 Silver 0.0304 oz. ASW **Obv:** Double headed eagle with arms on breast in inner circle **Obv. Legend:** *MONETA • NOVA • GRONINGENSIS • **Rev:** Ornate cross with arms at center **Rev. Legend:** DOMI - NI • BENE - DICTVM •

Date	Mintage	Good	VG	F	VF	XF
1601	—	16.00	50.00	150	225	325

KM# 11.1 JAGER (2 STUIVERS)

1.9200 g., 0.4930 Silver 0.0304 oz. ASW **Obv:** Shield of arms in inner circle, date in legend **Obv. Legend:** MONETA NOVA GRONING(ENSIS) **Rev:** Ornamental long cross in inner circle **Rev. Legend:** NOMEN DOMINI BENED(ICTVM) **Note:** Mint mark: Quatrefoil.

Date	Mintage	Good	VG	F	VF	XF
1604	44,432	16.00	50.00	150	225	300
1605	104,760	16.00	50.00	150	225	300

KM# 11.2 JAGER (2 STUIVERS)

1.9200 g., 0.4930 Silver 0.0304 oz. ASW **Obv:** Shield of arms in inner circle, date in legend **Obv. Legend:** MONETA NOVA GRONING(ENSIS) **Rev:** Ornamental long cross in inner circle **Rev. Legend:** SIT NOMEN DOMINI BENED(ICTVM)

Date	Mintage	Good	VG	F	VF	XF
1606Cross	43,898	16.00	50.00	150	225	300
1622Cross	—	16.00	50.00	150	225	300

KM# 20 JAGER (2 STUIVERS)

1.9200 g., Silver **Obv:** Crowned arms divide value **Obv. Legend:** MONETA NOVA GRONINGENSIS **Rev:** Ornamental long cross in inner circle, date in legend + SIT NOMEN DOMINI BENE

Date	Mintage	Good	VG	F	VF	XF
1622	—	15.00	50.00	125	225	350
1635	—	15.00	50.00	125	225	350

KM# 11.3 JAGER (2 STUIVERS)

1.9200 g., 0.4930 Silver 0.0304 oz. ASW **Obv:** Shield of arms in inner circle, date in legend + SIT NOMEN DOMINI BENE **Obv. Legend:** MONETA NOVA GRONING(ENSIS) **Rev:** Ornamental long cross in inner circle **Rev. Legend:** NOMEN DOMINI BENED(ICTVM) **Note:** Mint mark: Double Eagle.

Date	Mintage	Good	VG	F	VF	XF
1627	12,800	16.00	50.00	150	225	300

KM# 15 4 STUIVERS (Flabbe)

3.8400 g., Silver **Obv:** Shield of arms in inner circle, date in legend **Obv. Legend:** MONETA - NOVA AR - GEN GRO - NINGEN **Rev:** Ornamental long cross in inner circle **Rev. Legend:** SIT NOMEN DN(O) BENEDICTVM **Note:** Similar to KM#16.4 but not Klippe.

Date	Mintage	Good	VG	F	VF	XF
1625Eagle's head	—	10.00	30.00	60.00	120	200
1626Eagle's head	—	10.00	30.00	60.00	120	200
1627Eagle's head	—	10.00	30.00	60.00	120	200
1631Eagle's head	—	10.00	30.00	60.00	120	200
1635Eagle's head	—	10.00	30.00	60.00	120	200
1649Eagle's head	—	10.00	30.00	60.00	120	200

KM# 16 4 STUIVERS (Flabbe)

10.8400 g., 0.4930 Silver 0.1718 oz. ASW **Obv:** Arms with imperial eagle **Obv. Legend:** MONETA - NOVA AR - GEN GRO - NINGEN **Rev:** Ornamental long cross in inner circle **Rev. Legend:** SIT NOMEN DN(O) BENEDICTVM **Note:** Klippe.

Date	Mintage	Good	VG	F	VF	XF
1622	—	100	250	600	1,000	1,500

KM# 16a 4 STUIVERS (Flabbe)

Silver **Obv:** Arms with imperial eagle **Obv. Legend:** MONETA - NOVA AR - GEN GRO - NINGEN **Rev:** Ornamental long cross in inner circle **Rev. Legend:** SIT NOMEN DN(O) BENEDICTVM **Note:** 7.5 + 10;8 + 15.3g. Klippe.

Date	Mintage	Good	VG	F	VF	XF
1623	—	100	250	600	1,000	1,500

KM# 15a 4 STUIVERS (Flabbe)

12.4000 g., Silver **Obv:** Shield of arms in inner circle, date in legend **Obv. Legend:** MONETA - NOVA AR - GEN GRO - NINGEN **Rev:** Ornamental long cross in inner circle **Rev. Legend:** CIT NOMEN DN(O) BENEDICTVM **Note:** Similar to KM#16.2 but not Klippe.

Date	Mintage	Good	VG	F	VF	XF
1635	—	10.00	30.00	60.00	120	200

KM# 13 4 STUIVERS (Flabbe or double jager)

0.4930 Silver **Obv:** Shield of arms in inner circle, date in legend **Obv. Legend:** MONETA NOVA AR - GEN GRO - NINGEN **Rev:** Ornamental long cross in inner circle **Rev. Legend:** SIT NOMEN DN(O_ BENEDICTVM **Note:** 4.7-3.84 g

Date	Mintage	Good	VG	F	VF	XF
1604Double Eagle	—	12.00	35.00	85.00	150	200
1620	—	10.00	30.00	60.00	120	200
1622	—	10.00	30.00	60.00	120	200
1623	—	10.00	30.00	60.00	120	200

KM# 48 6 STUIVER (RYDER SCHELLING)

0.5830 Silver **Obv:** Crowned arms divide value, date above crown **Obv. Legend:** MO NO ARG CIV GRONINGAE **Rev:** Knight with sword on horseback to right **Rev. Legend:** CONCORDIA RS PARVAE CRESCUNT **Note:** 4.71-4.95 g.

Date	Mintage	Good	VG	F	VF	XF
1690Siren	—	3.00	10.00	30.00	50.00	110
1691Siren	—	3.00	10.00	30.00	50.00	110
1692Siren	—	3.00	10.00	35.00	70.00	140

KM# 17 8 STUIVERS (2 Flabbe)

7.6770 g., 0.4930 Silver 0.1217 oz. ASW **Obv:** Standing figure of St. Martin divides value in inner circle, date in legend **Obv. Legend:** SANCTVS M - ARTINVS EP(I) **Rev:** Double-headed eagle with arms on breast in inner circle **Rev. Legend:** MONETA NOVA ARGEN GRONIN

Date	Mintage	Good	VG	F	VF	XF
1626Double Eagle	—	16.00	50.00	100	200	350
1627Double Eagle	16,000	16.00	50.00	100	200	350

KM# 50 28 STUIVERS (Florin)

19.5000 g., Silver **Obv:** Crowned shield with date above in legend **Obv. Legend:** MO. NO. ARG. CIV. GRONINGAE **Rev:** Double-headed eagle in circle **Rev. Legend:** SIT NOMEN DOMINI BENEDICTVM

Date	Mintage	Good	VG	F	VF	XF
1690	—	32.00	100	200	400	800

KM# 49 28 STUIVERS (Florin)

19.5000 g., 0.6730 Silver 0.4219 oz. ASW **Obv:** Crowned arms in innr circle, date above crown **Obv. Legend:** FLOR. ARG. CIV. GRONINGAE **Rev:** Crowned double-headed eagle in inner circle **Rev. Legend:** SIT NOMEN DOMINI BENEDICTVM **Note:** Mint mark: Siren.

Date	Mintage	Good	VG	F	VF	XF
1690	—	17.00	60.00	150	275	450
1692	—	16.00	50.00	100	200	350
1962 Error 1692	—	32.00	100	300	450	600

KM# 6 RYKSDAALDER (48 Stuivers)

29.0300 g., Silver **Obv:** St. John standing facing holding Pascal lamb, date **Obv. Legend:** MONE: NOVA: ARG GRONINGENSIS **Rev:** Imperial eagle **Rev. Legend:** RVDOL • II • ROMANO: IMPE: SEMPER • AVGV **Note:** Similar to KM#7 but not Klippe. Dav. #4979.

Date	Mintage	Good	VG	F	VF	XF
1601	—	200	600	1,500	3,000	4,500
160Z	—	200	600	1,500	3,000	4,500

SIEGE COINAGE

KM# 24 6-1/4 STUIVERS

Silver **Obv:** Crowned arms **Obv. Legend:** IVRE ET TEMPORE **Note:** Uniface, Diamond Klippe.

Date	Mintage	Good	VG	F	VF	XF
1672	—	15.00	50.00	100	200	400

KM# 25 12-1/2 STUIVERS

Silver **Obv:** Crowned arms **Obv. Legend:** IVRE ET TEMPORE **Note:** Uniface. Diamond Klippe.

Date	Mintage	Good	VG	F	VF	XF
1672	—	25.00	75.00	150	300	500

KM# 26 25 STUIVERS

Silver **Obv:** Crowned arms **Obv. Legend:** IVRE ET TEMPORE **Note:** Uniface, Diamond Klippe.

Date	Mintage	Good	VG	F	VF	XF
1672	—	50.00	100	200	400	600

KM# 27.1 50 STUIVERS

Silver **Obv:** Crowned arms **Obv. Legend:** IVRE ET TEMPORE **Note:** Uniface, Klippe, large arms.

Date	Mintage	Good	VG	F	VF	XF
1672	—	25.00	150	300	500	1,00

KM# 27.2 50 STUIVERS

Silver **Obv:** Crowned arms **Obv. Legend:** IVRE ET TEMPORE **Note:** Uniface, Klippe, small arms

Date	Mintage	Good	VG	F	VF	XF
1672	—	250	275	375	500	80

PROVINCE

STANDARD COINAGE

KM# 28 DUIT

Copper ca. 2g **Obv:** Crowned arms in inner circle **Rev. Inscription:** GRON/ ET OML / (date)

Date	Mintage	Good	VG	F	VF	XF
1673	—	6.00	20.00	60.00	120	20
1674	—	3.00	10.00	30.00	60.00	90.0
1675	—	3.00	10.00	30.00	60.00	90.0
1676	—	3.00	10.00	30.00	60.00	90.0

KM# 28a DUIT

3.8000 g., Gold **Obv:** Crowned arms in inner circle **Rev. Inscription:** GRON / ET OML / (date)

Date	Mintage	Good	VG	F	VF	XF
1674	—	—	—	—	1,200	2,20
1675	—	—	—	—	1,200	2,20
1677	—	—	—	—	1,200	2,20

KM# 35 DUIT

Copper **Obv:** Crowned arms without inner circle **Rev. Inscription:** GRON / ET OML / (date)

Date	Mintage	Good	VG	F	VF	XF
1681	—	3.00	10.00	30.00	60.00	75.0
1682	—	2.00	6.00	20.00	40.00	60.0
1684	—	2.00	6.00	20.00	40.00	60.0
1685/4	—	—	—	—	—	—
1685	—	2.00	6.00	20.00	40.00	60.0
1692	—	2.00	6.00	20.00	40.00	60.0

KM# 39 1/2 STUIVER (WEAPON)

0.6100 g., 0.5830 Billon 0.0114 oz. **Obv:** Crowned arms **Rev. Inscription:** 1/2 / STUVVER / 1682

Date	Mintage	Good	VG	F	VF	XF
1682	—	25.00	90.00	250	500	70

KM# 36.1 STUIVER (WEAPON)

1.2200 g., 0.5830 Billon 0.0229 oz. **Obv:** Crowned arms divide value **Rev. Inscription:** GRON / ET OML / (date)

Date	Mintage	Good	VG	F	VF	XF
1681	—	5.00	20.00	40.00	80.00	12
1682	—	5.00	20.00	40.00	80.00	12
1683	—	5.00	20.00	40.00	80.00	12
1684	—	5.00	20.00	40.00	80.00	12

KM# 36.2 STUIVER (WEAPON)

1.2200 g., 0.5830 Billon 0.0229 oz. **Obv:** Arms under leaves divide value **Rev. Inscription:** GRON / ET OML / date

Date	Mintage	Good	VG	F	VF	XF
1681	—	—	—	—	—	—

KM# 29 6 STUIVER (RYDER SCHELLING)
4.9500 g., 0.5830 Silver 0.0928 oz. ASW **Obv:** Crowned arms divide value **Obv. Legend:** MO NO ORD GRON ET OML **Rev:** Knight with sword on horseback right, date in legend **Rev. Legend:** ADIVVANTE - DEO -

Date	Mintage	Good	VG	F	VF	XF
1673	—	8.00	25.00	50.00	100	200
1674	—	8.00	25.00	50.00	100	200
1677	—	15.00	40.00	85.00	150	350

KM# 30 6 STUIVER (RYDER SCHELLING)
Silver **Obv:** Crowned arms without value **Obv. Legend:** MO NO ORD GRON ET OML **Rev:** Knight with sword horseback right, date in legend **Rev. Legend:** ADIVVANTE - DEO -

Date	Mintage	Good	VG	F	VF	XF
1673	—	8.00	25.00	50.00	100	200

KM# 37.1 6 STUIVER (RYDER SCHELLING)
Silver 4.95-4.71g. **Obv:** Crowned arms divide value 6 - S, date above crown **Obv. Legend:** MO NO ARG ORD GRON ET OML **Rev:** Knight with sword on horseback right **Rev. Legend:** CONCORDIA RES PARVAE CRESCVNT

Date	Mintage	Good	VG	F	VF	XF
1681Rose	442,689	8.00	25.00	50.00	100	200
1682Rose	Inc. above	8.00	25.00	50.00	100	200
1683Rose	Inc. above	8.00	25.00	50.00	100	200
1684Rose	Inc. above	8.00	25.00	50.00	100	200
1685Rose	Inc. above	8.00	25.00	50.00	100	200
1686Rose	Inc. above	8.00	25.00	50.00	100	200
1687Rose	55,120	8.00	25.00	50.00	100	200

KM# A38a 6 STUIVER (RYDER SCHELLING)
Silver 14.7-15.6 g. **Obv:** Crowned arms divide value 6 - S, date above **Rev:** Knight with sword horseback right **Note:** Klippe

Date	Mintage	Good	VG	F	VF	XF
1691	—	—	—	—	—	—

KM# A38 6 STUIVER (RYDER SCHELLING)
Silver 6.2 and 9.4 g. **Obv:** Crowned arms divide value 6 - S, date above **Rev:** Knight with sword horseback right **Note:** Mint mark: Dog. Klippe.

Date	Mintage	Good	VG	F	VF	XF
1691	—	—	—	—	—	900

KM# 37.3 6 STUIVERS (Schelling)
4.7100 g., Silver **Obv:** Crowned arms divide value 6 - S, date above **Obv. Legend:** MO NO ARG ORD GRON ET OML **Rev. Legend:** CONCORDIA RES PARVAE CRESCVNT

Date	Mintage	Good	VG	F	VF	XF
1687	—	8.00	25.00	50.00	100	200

KM# 37.2 6 STUIVERS (Schelling)
4.7100 g., Silver **Obv:** Crowned arms divide value 6 - S, date above **Obv. Legend:** MO NO ARG ORD GRON ET OML **Rev:** Knight with sword on horseback right **Rev. Legend:** CONCORDIA RES PARVAE CRESCVNT **Note:** Varieties exist.

Date	Mintage	Good	VG	F	VF	XF
1691Dog	21,216	8.00	25.00	50.00	100	200
1692Dog	Inc. above	8.00	25.00	50.00	100	200

KM# 31.3 28 STUIVERS (Florin)
19.5000 g., 0.6730 Silver 0.4219 oz. ASW **Obv:** Crowned arms divide value 28 - ST without inner circle **Obv. Legend:** FLOR AREGENT ORD GRON ET OM(L) (L) (AND) **Rev:** Large 1/2 length figure of man wearing hat with sword on shoulder right divides date in inner circle **Rev. Legend:** LIBERTAS AVRO PRETIOSIOR OM (N) (n)i

Date	Mintage	Good	VG	F	VF	XF
1671	—	25.00	80.00	175	350	600
1674	—	25.00	80.00	175	350	600

KM# 31.2 28 STUIVERS (Florin)
19.5000 g., 0.6730 Silver 0.4219 oz. ASW **Obv:** Crowned arms in divide value 28 - ST in inner circle **Obv. Legend:** FLOR ARGENT ORD GRON ET OM(L) (L) (AND) **Rev:** Large 1/2-figure of man wearing hat with sword on shoulder right divides date in inner circle **Rev. Legend:** BELGICA LIBERTAS AVRO PRETIOSIOR OM (N) (n)i

Date	Mintage	Good	VG	F	VF	XF
1671	—	30.00	100	200	400	700
1673	—	25.00	80.00	175	350	600
1674	—	25.00	80.00	175	350	600
1675	—	25.00	80.00	175	350	600

KM# 31.1 28 STUIVERS (Florin)
19.5000 g., 0.6730 Silver 0.4219 oz. ASW **Obv:** Crowned arms in divide value 28 - ST in inner circle **Obv. Legend:** FLOR ARGENT ORD GRON ET OM(L) (L) (AND) **Rev:** Large 1/2-figure of man wearing hat with sword on shoulder right divides date in inner circle **Rev. Legend:** BELGICA LIBERTAS AVRO PRETIOSIOR OM (N) (n)i

Date	Mintage	Good	VG	F	VF	XF
1673Roset	—	25.00	80.00	175	350	700
1674Roset	—	25.00	80.00	175	350	700
1675Roset	—	25.00	80.00	175	350	700
1676Roset	—	25.00	80.00	175	350	700
1677Roset	—	25.00	80.00	175	350	700

KM# 32.1 28 STUIVERS (Florin)
19.5000 g., 0.6730 Silver 0.4219 oz. ASW **Obv:** Crowned arms with double headed eagle shields in 1st and 3rd quadrants divides value 28 - ST within legend **Obv. Legend:** FLOR ARGENT ORD GRON ET OM(L) (L) (AND) **Rev:** Large 1/2-figure of man wearing hat with sword on shoulder right divides date **Rev. Legend:** GELGICA LIBERTAS AVRO PRETIOSIOR OM (N) (n)i **Note:** Prev. KM #38.

Date	Mintage	Good	VG	F	VF	XF
1674	—	30.00	100	200	400	700

KM# 32.2 28 STUIVERS (Florin)
19.5000 g., 0.6730 Silver 0.4219 oz. ASW **Obv:** Crowned arms with double headed eagle in 2nd and 4th quadrants divides value 28 - ST within legend **Rev:** Large 1/2-length figure of man wearing hat with sword on shoulder right divides date

Date	Mintage	Good	VG	F	VF	XF
1674	—	25.00	80.00	175	350	600

KM# 38 28 STUIVERS (Florin)
19.5000 g., 0.7650 Silver 0.4796 oz. ASW **Obv:** Crowned arms divide value 28 - ST **Obv. Legend:** MO NO ARG ORD GRON ET OML **Rev:** Clasped hands holding two poles with hat and symbol (Gods eye) in rays **Rev. Legend:** REDDIT CONIVNCTIO TVTOS

Date	Mintage	Good	VG	F	VF	XF
1681	—	20.00	60.00	125	250	500

KM# 42 28 STUIVERS (Florin)
19.5000 g., 0.6730 Silver 0.4219 oz. ASW **Obv:** Crowned arms divide value 28 - ST **Obv. Legend:** MO NO ARG ORD GRON ET OM **Rev:** Small 1/2-figure of man wearing hat with plumes with sword on shoulderright **Rev. Legend:** PRO RELIGIONE ET LIBERTATE **Note:** Mint mark: Rose.

Date	Mintage	Good	VG	F	VF	XF
1685	—	30.00	100	200	400	700
1686	—	25.00	80.00	175	350	600

KM# 51 28 STUIVERS (Florin)
19.5000 g., 0.6730 Silver 0.4219 oz. ASW **Obv:** Crowned arms divide value 28 - ST **Obv. Legend:** MO NO ARG ORD GRON ET OML **Rev:** Small 1/2 figure of man wearing hat with plumes with sword on shoulder right **Rev. Legend:** PRO RELIGIONE ET LIBERTATE

Date	Mintage	Good	VG	F	VF	XF
1691Dog	—	100	300	650	1,250	2,000
1692Dog	—	40.00	100	200	400	600

KM# 52 28 STUIVERS (Florin)
Silver **Obv:** Crowned arms divide value 28 - ST, date above **Obv. Legend:** MO NO ARG ORD GRON ET OML **Rev:** Double headed eagle with arms on breast **Rev. Legend:** PRO RELIGIONE ET LIBERTATE

Date	Mintage	Good	VG	F	VF	XF
1692	—	25.00	75.00	150	300	400

KM# 7 ST. JANSRYKSDAALDER
35.6000 g., 0.8850 Silver 1.0129 oz. ASW **Obv:** St. John standing facing holding Pascal lamb **Obv. Legend:** MONE: NOVA: ARG GRONINGENSIS **Rev:** Imperial eagle **Rev. Legend:** RVDOL • II • ROMANO: IMPE: SEMPER • AVGV **Note:** Klippe. Dav. #4979A. Illustration reduced.

Date	Mintage	Good	VG	F	VF	XF
1601	—	—	—	—	3,500	5,500

KM# 7a ST. JANSRYKSDAALDER
40.4000 g., 0.8850 Silver 1.1495 oz. ASW **Obv:** St. John standing facing holding Pascal lamb **Obv. Legend:** MONE: NOVA: ARG GRONINGENSIS **Rev:** Imperial eagle **Rev. Legend:** RVDOL • II • ROMANO: IMPE: SEMPER • AVGV **Note:** Klippe. Dav. #4979A. Illustration reduced.

Date	Mintage	Good	VG	F	VF	XF
1601	—	—	—	—	3,500	4,500

KM# 7b ST. JANSRYKSDAALDER
41.8, 0.8850 Silver 1.1893 oz. **Obv:** St. John standing facing holding Pascal lamb **Obv. Legend:** MONE: NOVA: ARG GRONINGENSIS **Rev:** Imperial eagle **Rev. Legend:** RVDOL • II • ROMANO: IMPE: SEMPER • AVGV **Note:** Klippe. Dav. #4979A. Illustration reduced.

Date	Mintage	Good	VG	F	VF	XF
160Z	—	—	—	—	3,500	4,000

KM# 40 DUCATON (Silver Rider)
32.7800 g., 0.9410 Silver 0.9917 oz. ASW **Obv:** Crowned arms with crowned lion supporters, date in cartouche below **Obv. Legend:** MO NO - ARG - ORG GRON ET OMLAN **Rev:** Knight with sword on horseback right **Rev. Legend:** CONCORDIA RES PARVAE - CRESCVNT

Date	Mintage	Good	VG	F	VF	XF
1682Rose	570	100	375	750	1,200	2,000
1683Rose	—	100	375	750	1,200	2,000

KM# 40a DUCATON (Silver Rider)
37.1700 g., Gold **Obv:** Crowned arms with crowned lion supporters, date in cartouche below **Rev:** Knight with sword on horseback right

Date	Mintage	Good	VG	F	VF	XF
1682 Rare	—	—	—	—	—	—

Note: Stack's International sale 3-88 AU realized $8,800

KM# 41 SILVER DUCAT
28.2500 g., 0.8730 Silver 0.7929 oz. ASW **Obv:** Armored knight standing holding sword and shield of arms **Rev:** Crowned arms, date above crown

Date	Mintage	Good	VG	F	VF	XF
1683	—	100	250	500	1,000	1,500

COUNTERMARKED COINAGE

1693

During the late 17th century many circulating coins were found to be underweight. In 1693 coins meeting the legal requirements were countermarked for a specific province or city, such as G.O. for Groningen and Ommeland.

KM# 53.1 28 STUIVERS
Silver **Countermark:** G.O. **Note:** Countermark on Deventer KM#81.

CM Date	Host Date	Good	VG	F	VF	XF
ND(1693)	1685-92	—	—	—	—	—

KM# 53.2 28 STUIVERS
Silver **Countermark:** G.O. **Note:** Countermark on Friesland KM#10.

CM Date	Host Date	Good	VG	F	VF	XF
ND(1693)	1601-91	—	—	—	—	—

KM# 53.3 28 STUIVERS
Silver **Countermark:** G.O. **Note:** Countermark on Groningen & Ommeland KM#38.

CM Date	Host Date	Good	VG	F	VF	XF
ND(1693)	1681	—	—	—	—	—

KM# 53.4 28 STUIVERS
Silver **Countermark:** G.O. **Note:** Countermark on Groningen & Ommeland KM#50.

CM Date	Host Date	Good	VG	F	VF	XF
ND(1693)	1690	—	—	—	—	—

KM# 53.5 28 STUIVERS
Silver **Countermark:** G.O. **Note:** Countermark on Groningen & Ommeland KM#52.

CM Date	Host Date	Good	VG	F	VF	XF
ND(1693)	1692	—	—	—	—	—

KM# 53.6 28 STUIVERS
Silver **Countermark:** G.O. **Note:** Countermark on Groningen & Ommeland KM#31.

CM Date	Host Date	Good	VG	F	VF	XF
ND(1693)	1673-77	—	—	—	—	—

KM# 53.7 28 STUIVERS
Silver **Countermark:** G.O. **Note:** Countermark on Groningen & Ommeland KM#32.

CM Date	Host Date	Good	VG	F	VF	XF
ND(1693)	1674	—	—	—	—	—

KM# 53.8 28 STUIVERS
Silver **Countermark:** G.O. **Note:** Countermark on Kampen KM#76.

CM Date	Host Date	Good	VG	F	VF	XF
ND(1693)	1680-86	—	—	—	—	—

KM# 53.9 28 STUIVERS
Silver **Countermark:** G.O. **Note:** Countermark on Nijmegen KM#27.

CM Date	Host Date	Good	VG	F	VF	XF
ND(1693)	1685-90	—	—	—	—	—

KM# 53.10 28 STUIVERS
Silver **Countermark:** G.O. **Note:** Countermark on Overyssel KM#55.

CM Date	Host Date	Good	VG	F	VF	XF
ND(1693)	1685-90	—	—	—	—	—

KM# 53.11 28 STUIVERS
Silver **Countermark:** G.O. **Note:** Countermark on West Friesland KM#90.

CM Date	Host Date	Good	VG	F	VF	XF
ND(1693)	1685-87	—	—	—	—	—

KM# 53.12 28 STUIVERS
Silver **Countermark:** G.O. **Note:** Countermark on Zwolle KM#78.

CM Date	Host Date	Good	VG	F	VF	XF
ND(1693)	1679-86	—	—	—	—	—

PATTERNS

Including off metal strikes

KM#	Date	Mintage	Identification	Mkt Val
Pn2	1609	—	2 Plak. Silver. Klippe, KM#8.	1,200
Pn3	1615	—	2 Plak. Silver. 4.1000 g. Klippe. KM#8	—
Pn4	1625	—	2 Plak. Silver. 4.1000 g. Klippe, KM#8.	—
Pn5	1626	—	2 Plak. Silver. Klippe, KM#8.	1,200
Pn6	1626Roset	—	2 Plak. Silver. 1.9000 g. Klippe. KM#8	1,200
Pn7	1627	—	8 Stuivers. Gold. 6.6000 g. KM#17.	—
Pn8	1635	—	4 Stuivers. Gold. 6.7000 g. KM#15.2.	—
Pn9	1649	—	4 Plakken. Copper. Uniface klippe. KM#10	1,000
Pn10	1672	—	6 Stuivers. Gold. 9.0000 g. KM#29.	—
Pn11	1673	—	28 Stuivers. Gold. 14.7500 g. KM#31.1	—
Pn12	1673	—	6 Stuivers. Gold. 9.0000 g. KM#29.	—
Pn13	1675	—	28 Stuivers. Gold. 15.5000 g. KM#31.1	—
Pn14	1676	—	28 Stuivers. Gold. 15.2500 g. KM#31.1	—
Pn15	1677	—	28 Stuivers. Gold. 15.4000 g. KM#31.	—
Pn16	1680	—	Duit. Copper. Klippe.	—
Pn17	1683	—	Ducat. Copper-Silver. 27.9000 g. Klippe. KM#41	—
Pn18	1690	—	6 Stuivers. Gold. 9.9000 g. KM#48.	—
Pn19	1691	—	6 Stuivers. Gold. 7.0000 g. KM#37.2.	—

PIEFORTS

KM#	Date	Mintage	Identification	Mkt Val
P1	1601	—	48 Stuivers. Silver. Double weight. KM#6.	4,500
P2	1602	—	48 Stuivers. Silver. Double weight. KM#6	4,500
P3	1611	—	28 Stuivers. Silver. W/o value.	—
P4	1626	—	8 Stuivers. Silver. 19.1000 g. Klippe, KM17.	3,000
P5	1626	—	8 Stuivers. Silver. Klippe. Weight 11.2 - 15.2. KM#17	—
P6	1626	—	8 Stuivers. Silver. 7.9000 g. Double weight. KM#17	—
P7	1627	—	8 Stuivers. Silver. Klippe, KM#17	—
P8	1627	—	8 Stuivers. Silver. Klippe. Weight 11.2 - 15.2g. KM#17	—
P9	1672	—	6-1/4 Stuivers. Gold. 7.7000 g. KM#29	—
P10	1673	—	6 Stuivers. Gold. 7.7000 g. KM#29	—
P11	1681	—	Duit. Copper. Klippe.	—
P12	1682	—	Duit. Copper. Klippe.	—
P13	1683	—	Ducaton. Silver. Double weight. KM#40	—
P14	1683	—	Ducaton. Silver. KM#40.	—
P15	1683	—	Silver Ducat. Double weight. KM#41.	2,800
P16	1690	—	Duit. Copper. 3.4000 g. KM46.	—
P17	1690	—	28 Stuivers. Silver. 76.0000 g. 4x weight. Triple weight, KM49.	—
P18	1690	—	6 Stuiver (Ryder Schelling). Silver. .4 x weight. KM#48	—
P19	1691	—	28 Stuivers. Silver. Triple weight, KM49.	—
P20	1691	—	28 Stuivers. Silver. KM#51.	—
P21	1691	—	6 Stuiver (Ryder Schelling). Silver. KM#48	750
P22	1691	—	6 Stuiver (Ryder Schelling). Silver. Double weight. KM#37.2	850
P23	1691	—	28 Stuivers. Silver. KM49 with value.	1,000
P24	1691	—	28 Stuivers. Silver, 28.500g, KM#51	3,500
P25	1692	—	28 Stuivers. Silver. Double weight, KM51	2,500
P26	1692	—	28 Stuivers. Silver. Quintuple weight, KM50.	—
P27	1692	—	28 Stuivers. Silver. Quadruple weight, KM52.	5,000
P28	1692	—	28 Stuivers. Silver.	3,500
P29	1692	—	28 Stuivers. Silver. 36.8300 g. KM49.	1,500
P30	1692	—	28 Stuivers. Silver. KM52.	2,500

HOLLAND

Hollandia

Holland, a Dutch maritime province fronting on the North Sea, is the most important region of the Netherlands. It is a leader in maritime activities and in efficient agriculture. During the period of Spanish domination, Holland was the bulwark of the Protestant faith in the Netherlands and the focus of the resistance to Spanish tyranny.

MINT MARKS

Rose - Dordrecht

State Arms - Amsterdam

PROVINCE

STANDARD COINAGE

KM# 13 DUIT

2.9300 g., Copper **Obv:** Maiden sitting in enclosed fence with right hand raised, date in legend **Obv. Legend:** AVX NOS IN NOM DOM **Rev:** Inscription in wreath **Rev. Inscription:** HOL / LAN / DIA

Date	Mintage	Good	VG	F	VF	XF
1604	—	3.00	10.00	30.00	85.00	200
1605	—	3.00	10.00	30.00	85.00	200

KM# 13a DUIT

2.7000 g., Silver **Obv:** Maiden sitting in enclosed fence with right hand raised **Obv. Legend:** AVX NOS IN NOM DOM **Rev:** Inscription in wreath **Rev. Inscription:** HOL / LAN / DIA

Date	Mintage	Good	VG	F	VF	XF
1605	—	—	—	—	—	—

KM# 30 DUIT

2.9300 g., Copper **Obv:** Maiden sitting in enclosed fence with right hand raised **Obv. Legend:** AVX NOS IN NOM DOM **Rev:** Inscription in wreath **Rev. Inscription:** HOL / LANDIA / (date)

Date	Mintage	Good	VG	F	VF	XF
1626	—	6.00	20.00	40.00	80.00	175
1627	—	6.00	20.00	40.00	80.00	175

KM# 30b DUIT

2.1000 g., Silver **Obv:** Maiden sitting in enclosed fence with right hand raised **Obv. Legend:** AVX NOS IN NOM DOM **Rev:** Inscription in wreath **Rev. Inscription:** HOL / LANDIA / (date)

Date	Mintage	VG	F	VF	XF	Unc
1626	—	—	80.00	150	250	—

KM# 30a DUIT

1.4000 g., Silver **Obv:** Maiden sitting in enclosed fence with right hand raised. **Obv. Legend:** AVX NOS IN NOM DOM **Rev:** Inscription in wreath **Rev. Inscription:** HOL / LANDIA / (date)

Date	Mintage	Good	VG	F	VF	XF
1627	—	—	—	—	—	—

KM# 26 STUIVER

0.8600 g., 0.5830 Silver 0.0161 oz. ASW **Obv:** Crowned rampant lion left holding sword and arrows, value at sides **Rev. Inscription:** HOL / LAN / DIA / (date)

Date	Mintage	Good	VG	F	VF	XF
1614	—	3.00	10.00	30.00	50.00	90.00
1616/4	—	8.00	25.00	50.00	90.00	150
1618	—	3.00	10.00	30.00	50.00	90.00
1628	—	3.00	10.00	30.00	50.00	90.00

KM# 28 STUIVER

1.3100 g., 0.3330 Silver 0.0140 oz. ASW **Obv:** Bundle of arrows divides value in wreath **Rev:** Inscription in wreath **Rev. Inscription:** rose / HOL / LANDIA / (date)

Date	Mintage	Good	VG	F	VF	XF
1619	—	3.00	10.00	20.00	50.00	90.00
1628	—	3.00	10.00	20.00	50.00	90.00

KM# 5 2 STUIVERS (1/3 Roosschelling)

1.7600 g., 0.5830 Silver 0.0330 oz. ASW **Obv:** Crowned arms divide value in enclosed fence in inner circle, date at top **Obv. Legend:** MO NO COM HOLLANDIAE mintmark (rose) **Rev:** Ornamental cross with rose at center in inner circle **Rev. Legend:** VIGILA - TE.DEO - CONFID_ENTES

Date	Mintage	Good	VG	F	VF	XF
1601	—	32.00	100	250	450	750

KM# 27 2 STUIVERS (Double Stuiver)

1.7300 g., 0.5830 Silver 0.0324 oz. ASW **Obv:** Crowned rampant lion left holding sword and arrows, value at sides **Rev. Inscription:** rose / HOL / LAN / DIA / (date)

Date	Mintage	Good	VG	F	VF	XF
1614	—	2.00	8.00	20.00	40.00	75.00
1615	—	2.00	8.00	20.00	40.00	75.00
1616	—	2.00	8.00	20.00	40.00	75.00
1617	—	2.00	8.00	20.00	40.00	75.00
1618	—	2.00	8.00	20.00	40.00	75.00
1619	—	2.00	8.00	20.00	40.00	75.00
1620	—	2.00	8.00	20.00	40.00	75.00
1628	—	2.00	10.00	25.00	50.00	90.00
1670	—	6.00	20.00	40.00	100	250

KM# 48 2 STUIVERS (Double Wapenstuiver)

1.6200 g., 0.5830 Silver 0.0304 oz. ASW, 19.6 mm. **Obv:** Crowned arms of Holland divides value **Rev. Inscription:** HOL/ LAN /DIA / (date)

Date	Mintage	VG	F	VF	XF	Unc
1672	—	3.00	20.00	45.00	75.00	—
1675	—	3.00	20.00	45.00	75.00	—
1676	—	3.00	20.00	45.00	75.00	—
1677	—	3.00	10.00	15.00	40.00	—
1678	—	3.00	10.00	15.00	40.00	—
1680/70	—	4.00	25.00	50.00	90.00	—
1680	—	3.00	10.00	15.00	40.00	—
1683	—	3.00	10.00	15.00	40.00	—
1697	—	3.00	10.00	15.00	40.00	—
1698	—	3.00	10.00	15.00	40.00	—
1699	—	3.00	10.00	15.00	40.00	—
1700	—	3.00	10.00	15.00	40.00	—

KM# 6 3 STUIVERS (1/2 Roosschelling)

2.6300 g., 0.5830 Silver 0.0493 oz. ASW **Obv:** Crowned arms divide value in enclosed fence in inner circle, date at top **Obv. Legend:** MO NO COM HOLLANDIAE mintmark rose **Rev:** Ornamental cross with rose at center in inner circle **Rev. Legend:** VIGILA - TE.DEO - CONFID - ENTES

Date	Mintage	Good	VG	F	VF	XF
1601	—	25.00	75.00	200	450	900

KM# 70 5 STUIVERS (Province 1/4 Guilden)

2.6500 g., 0.9200 Silver 0.0784 oz. ASW **Obv:** Crowned arms divide value, date above crown **Rev:** Standing female figure leaning on Bible on column, holding spear with Liberty cap

Date	Mintage	Good	VG	F	VF	XF
1692	—	25.00	75.00	175	250	325

KM# 7 6 STUIVERS (Roosschelling)

5.2700 g., 0.5830 Silver 0.0988 oz. ASW **Obv:** Crowned arms inside garden with railing. **Obv. Legend:** MO NO COM HOLLANDIAE rose and date **Rev:** Ornate short cross **Rev. Legend:** VIGILA - TE DEO - CONFID - ENTES

Date	Mintage	Good	VG	F	VF	XF
1601	—	10.00	30.00	80.00	125	200

KM# 45.2 6 STUIVERS (Scheepjesschelling)

4.9500 g., 0.5830 Silver 0.0928 oz. ASW **Obv:** With denomination 6 - S

Date	Mintage	Good	VG	F	VF	XF
1671	—	5.00	15.00	35.00	70.00	140
1674	—	5.00	15.00	35.00	70.00	140
1675	—	5.00	15.00	35.00	70.00	140
1677	—	5.00	15.00	35.00	70.00	140
1679	—	5.00	15.00	35.00	70.00	140
1680	—	5.00	15.00	35.00	70.00	140
1688	—	5.00	15.00	35.00	70.00	140
1700	—	5.00	15.00	35.00	70.00	140

KM# 45a.2 6 STUIVERS (Scheepjesschelling)

Gold **Obv:** With denomination 6 - S

Date	Mintage	Good	VG	F	VF	XF
1671	—	—	—	—	—	—
1674	—	—	—	—	—	1,200
1684	—	—	—	—	—	1,200

KM# 45.1 6 STUIVERS (Design of a Scheepjesschelling by Chr. Adolph)

4.9500 g., 0.5830 Silver 0.0928 oz. ASW **Obv:** Crowned arms without denomination 6 - S **Obv. Legend:** MO NO ORD HOLL ET WESTFR 1670 **Rev:** Ship moves right **Rev. Legend:** VIGILATE DEO CONFIDENTES

Date	Mintage	Good	VG	F	VF	XF
1670	—	—	—	—	500	1,000

KM# 14 10 STUIVERS

5.9500 g., 0.9170 Silver 0.1754 oz. ASW **Obv:** Knight standing right with sword on shoulder, left hand on lion shield divides date **Rev:** Crowned arms divide value X - S

Date	Mintage	Good	VG	F	VF	XF
1606	—	40.00	125	350	750	1,100
1607	—	40.00	125	350	750	1,100

KM# 15 10 STUIVERS

5.9500 g., 0.9170 Silver 0.1754 oz. ASW **Obv:** Knight standing right holding bow in left hand

Date	Mintage	Good	VG	F	VF	XF
1606	—	40.00	125	350	750	1,100

KM# 59 10 STUIVERS

5.3000 g., 0.9200 Silver 0.1568 oz. ASW **Obv:** Crowned arms divide value, date above **Rev:** Standing female figure leaning on Bible on column holding spear with Liberty cap

Date	Mintage	Good	VG	F	VF	XF
1681	142,900	20.00	60.00	170	350	600
1682	Inc. above	20.00	60.00	170	350	600
1688/1	Inc. above	26.00	80.00	200	400	800
1688	Inc. above	26.00	80.00	200	400	800
1692	Inc. above	40.00	110	225	450	900

KM# 59a 10 STUIVERS

Gold **Obv:** Crowned arms divide value, date above **Rev:** Standing female figure leaning on Bible on column holding spear with Liberty cap **Note:** Weight varies 6.90-10.30 g.

Date	Mintage	Good	VG	F	VF	XF
1688	—	—	—	—	5,000	6,000
1689	—	—	—	—	5,000	6,000

KM# 71 28 STUIVERS (Florin)
19.5000 g., 0.6730 Silver 0.4219 oz. ASW **Obv:** Crowned arms of the 7 provinces **Rev:** Standing female figure leaning on Bible on column, holding spear with Liberty cap divides value, date in exergue

Date	Mintage	Good	VG	F	VF	XF
1694	—	—	—	—	2,500	4,000

KM# 71a 28 STUIVERS (Florin)
17.2000 g., Gold **Obv:** Crowned arms of the 7 provinces **Rev:** Standing female figure leaning on Bible on column, holding spear with Liberty cap divides value, date in exergue

Date	Mintage	Good	VG	F	VF	XF
1694	—	—	—	10,000	15,000	20,000

KM# 65 1/2 GULDEN (10 Stuivers)
Silver **Obv:** Without value 10 - S

Date	Mintage	Good	VG	F	VF	XF
1682	—	—	—	—	400	800

KM# 65a 1/2 GULDEN (10 Stuivers)
10.3000 g., Gold **Obv:** Without value 10 - S , with value 1/2 - GL

Date	Mintage	Good	VG	F	VF	XF
1682	—	—	—	—	4,000	6,000

KM# 72 1/2 GULDEN (10 Stuivers)
5.3000 g., 0.9200 Silver 0.1568 oz. ASW **Obv:** Standing female figure leaning on Bible column, holding spear with Liberty cap **Rev:** Crowned arms divide value

Date	Mintage	Good	VG	F	VF	XF
1694	—	30.00	80.00	175	350	700

KM# 55 GULDEN (20 Stuiver)
10.6100 g., 0.9200 Silver 0.3138 oz. ASW **Obv:** Rampant lion left **Rev:** Crowned arms divide value I - G

Date	Mintage	Good	VG	F	VF	XF
1680	—	—	—	—	1,500	2,000

KM# 56 GULDEN (20 Stuiver)
10.6100 g., 0.9200 Silver 0.3138 oz. ASW **Rev:** Standing female figure holding lion shield and spear with Liberty cap, date in exergue

Date	Mintage	Good	VG	F	VF	XF
1680	—	—	—	—	1,700	3,000

KM# 60 GULDEN (20 Stuiver)
Silver **Obv:** Crowned arms divide value I - G **Rev:** Standing female figure leaning on Bible column, holding spear with Liberty cap

Date	Mintage	Good	VG	F	VF	XF
1681	—	26.00	80.00	250	350	700
1682	—	32.00	100	300	450	800

KM# 61 GULDEN (20 Stuiver)
Silver **Obv:** Crowned arms without value **Rev:** Standing female figure leaning on Bible column, holding spear with Liberty cap

Date	Mintage	Good	VG	F	VF	XF
1681	—	50.00	150	350	550	1,000

KM# 61a GULDEN (20 Stuiver)
Gold **Obv:** Crowned arms without value **Rev:** Standing female figure leaning on Bible column, holding spear with Liberty cap **Note:** Weight varies 13.80-17.30 g.

Date	Mintage	Good	VG	F	VF	XF
1681	—	—	—	—	5,000	10,000

KM# 73 GULDEN (20 Stuiver)
10.6100 g., 0.9200 Silver 0.3138 oz. ASW **Obv:** Crowned arms of Holland divides value I - G **Obv. Legend:** MO: ARG : ORD: FÆD: BELG : HOLL : **Rev:** Standing figure leaning on column, holding pole with cap, date below **Rev. Legend:** HANCTVEMVR HAC NITIMVR **Edge:** Plain, from 1762 edge: reeded

Date	Mintage	VG	F	VF	XF	Unc
1694	—	20.00	60.00	100	200	—

KM# 73a GULDEN (20 Stuiver)
Gold 13.8-17.2 grams, weight varies **Obv:** Crowned arms of Holland divides value **Rev:** Standing figure leaning on column, holding pole with cap, date below

Date	Mintage	VG	F	VF	XF	Unc
1694 Rare	—	—	—	—	—	—
1696 Rare	—	—	—	—	—	—

KM# 74 1/2 3 (1-1/2) GULDEN
15.9100 g., 0.9200 Silver 0.4706 oz. ASW **Obv:** Crowned arms divide value (1/2 - 3GL) **Rev:** Standing female figure leaning on Bible on column holding spear with Liberty cap

Date	Mintage	Good	VG	F	VF	XF
1694	—	125	500	1,000	2,000	3,000

KM# 74a 1/2 3 (1-1/2) GULDEN
Gold **Obv:** Crowned arms divide value 1/2 - 3GL **Rev:** Standing female figure leaning on Bible on column holding spear with Liberty cap **Note:** Weight varies 17.20-20.60 g.

Date	Mintage	VG	F	VF	XF	Unc
1694	—	—	—	—	8,000	10,000
1698	—	—	—	—	10,000	15,000

KM# 57 2 GULDEN
21.2100 g., 0.9200 Silver 0.6273 oz. ASW **Obv:** Rampant lion left **Rev:** Crowned arms

Date	Mintage	Good	VG	F	VF	XF
1680	—	—	—	—	1,500	2,000

KM# 62 2 GULDEN
21.2100 g., 0.9200 Silver 0.6273 oz. ASW **Obv:** Crowned arms divides value 2 - G **Rev:** Standing female figure leaning on Bible column, holding spear with Liberty cap

Date	Mintage	Good	VG	F	VF	XF
1681	8,150	80.00	200	400	700	1,40
1682	—	80.00	200	400	700	1,40
1687	—	80.00	200	400	700	1,40

KM# 75 2 GULDEN
Silver **Obv:** Value 2 - GL **Rev:** Date in exergue

Date	Mintage	Good	VG	F	VF	XF
1694	—	80.00	200	400	700	1,40

KM# 58 3 GULDEN (60 Stuiver)
31.8200 g., 0.9200 Silver 0.9412 oz. ASW **Obv:** Rampant lion laft **Rev:** Crowned arms divide value 3 - G **Note:** Dav. #4951.

Date	Mintage	Good	VG	F	VF	XF
1680	—	—	—	1,000	1,700	2,50

KM# 63 3 GULDEN (60 Stuiver)
31.8200 g., 0.9200 Silver 0.9412 oz. ASW **Obv:** Crowned arms

divide value 3 - G **Rev:** Standing female figure leaning on Bible column holding spear with Liberty cap **Note:** Dav. #4952.

Date	Mintage	Good	VG	F	VF	XF
1681	—	40.00	150	350	600	1,000
1682	—	40.00	150	350	600	1,000
1694/82	—	60.00	200	450	800	1,200
1694	—	60.00	200	450	800	1,200

KM# 64 3 GULDEN (60 Stuiver)

31.8200 g., 0.9200 Silver 0.9412 oz. ASW **Obv:** Crowned arms without value **Rev:** Standing female figure leaning on Bible column holding spear with Liberty cap **Note:** Dav. #4952A.

Date	Mintage	Good	VG	F	VF	XF
1681	—	60.00	200	800	1,300	1,800
1682	—	60.00	200	800	1,300	1,800

KM# 66 3 GULDEN (60 Stuiver)

31.8200 g., 0.9200 Silver 0.9412 oz. ASW **Obv:** Rampant lion left without value in inner circle **Rev:** Standing female figure leaning on Bible column holding spear with Liberty cap **Note:** Dav. #4953.

Date	Mintage	VG	F	VF	XF	Unc
1684	—	—	—	1,000	2,000	2,600

KM# 152 3 GULDEN (60 Stuiver)

Silver **Obv:** Crowned lion with sword arms divide value 3 - GL **Obv. Legend:** MO: ARG: ORD: FAED: BELG: HOLL **Rev:** Standing female figure leaning on Bible column holding spear with Liberty cap, date below **Note:** Dav. #4954.

Date	Mintage	Good	VG	F	VF	XF
1694	—	30.00	90.00	250	400	750

KM# 40 1/2 DUCATON

Silver **Obv:** Knight with sword on horseback right, provincial arms below in inner circle **Rev:** Crowned arms with crowned lion supporters in inner circle, date at top in legend

Date	Mintage	Good	VG	F	VF	XF
1659	—	50.00	125	300	600	800

KM# 41 DUCATON

32.7800 g., 0.9410 Silver 0.9917 oz. ASW **Obv:** Knight horseback right brandishing sword **Rev:** Crowned arms with lion supporters **Note:** Similar to KM#46 but cruder style. Dav. #4928.

Date	Mintage	Good	VG	F	VF	XF
1659	—	20.00	40.00	100	175	265
1660	—	20.00	40.00	100	200	400
1661/0	—	25.00	55.00	125	250	500
1661	—	20.00	40.00	100	200	400
1662	—	20.00	40.00	100	200	400
1666	—	25.00	55.00	125	250	500
1668	—	20.00	40.00	100	200	400

KM# 46 DUCATON

Silver **Obv:** Knight horseback right holding sword upright **Rev:** Crowned arms with lion supporters **Edge:** Lettered **Note:** Dav. #4931.

Date	Mintage	VG	F	VF	XF	Unc
1671	—	—	—	1,800	2,200	—
1672	—	—	—	2,000	2,500	—

KM# 93 DUCATON

Silver **Obv:** Knight horseback right brandishing sword **Rev:** Crowned arms with lion supporters **Note:** Dav. #4929.

Date	Mintage	Good	VG	F	VF	XF
1672	—	—	—	—	1,500	2,000
1673	—	—	—	—	1,500	2,000
1673/2	—	—	—	—	—	—
1674	—	—	—	—	1,500	2,000
1675	—	—	—	—	2,000	2,500
1676	—	—	—	—	1,500	2,000
1678	—	—	—	—	1,500	2,000
1678/6	—	—	—	—	1,500	2,000
1679	—	—	—	—	2,000	2,500
1679/6	—	—	—	—	1,500	2,000
1680 Rare	—	—	—	—	2,000	2,500
1687	—	—	—	—	2,000	2,500
1693	—	—	—	—	1,000	1,650

KM# 51 DUCATON

32.7800 g., 0.9410 Silver 0.9917 oz. ASW **Obv:** Knight on horseback right holds sword upright, crowned arms below **Obv. Legend:** BELG : PRO : HOLLAND : MO : NO : ARG : CONFOE **Rev:** Crowned arms of Holland, with supporters, date in cartouche below **Rev. Legend:** * CONCORDIA RES PARVAE CRESCUNT : **Note:** Dav. #4930. Similar to KM#90.

Date	Mintage	Good	VG	F	VF	XF
1672	—	30.00	65.00	130	250	350
1673/2	—	35.00	90.00	175	300	400
1673	—	30.00	65.00	130	250	350
1674	—	30.00	65.00	130	250	350
1675	—	30.00	65.00	130	250	350
1676	—	30.00	65.00	130	250	350
1679/69	—	30.00	65.00	130	250	350
1679/6	—	35.00	90.00	175	300	400
1679	—	35.00	90.00	175	300	400
1680	—	30.00	65.00	130	250	350
1687	—	30.00	65.00	130	250	350
1692	—	30.00	65.00	130	250	350
1693	—	30.00	65.00	130	250	350
1694	—	30.00	65.00	130	250	350

KM# 42 1/2 DUCAT (24 Stuivers)

14.1200 g., 0.8730 Silver 0.3963 oz. ASW **Obv:** Knight standing right with sword on shoulder, left hand on lion shield **Rev:** Crowned arms

Date	Mintage	Good	VG	F	VF	XF
1659	—	45.00	150	300	600	1,200

KM# 43 DUCAT (48 Stuivers)

28.2500 g., 0.8730 Silver 0.7929 oz. ASW **Obv:** Knight standing right with sword on shoulder, left hand on lion shield **Rev:** Crowned arms **Note:** Dav. #4896.

Date	Mintage	Good	VG	F	VF	XF
1659	594,275	20.00	50.00	100	150	300
1660/59	Inc. above	25.00	80.00	175	250	400
1660	Inc. above	20.00	50.00	100	150	300
1661	Inc. above	20.00	50.00	100	150	300
1662/0	Inc. above	20.00	50.00	100	150	300
1662/1	Inc. above	20.00	50.00	100	150	300
1662	Inc. above	20.00	50.00	100	200	300
1663	Inc. above	20.00	50.00	100	200	300
1664/2	Inc. above	20.00	50.00	100	150	300
1664	Inc. above	20.00	50.00	100	150	300
1665	Inc. above	25.00	80.00	175	250	400
1666/5	Inc. above	25.00	80.00	175	250	400
1666	Inc. above	25.00	80.00	175	250	400
1668	Inc. above	35.00	80.00	175	250	400
1670	Inc. above	35.00	80.00	175	250	400

KM# 52.1 DUCAT (48 Stuivers)

Silver **Obv:** Standing armored Knight with crowned shield at feet **Obv. Legend:** BELG : .. : HOL : MONO : ARG : PRO : CONFOE : **Rev:** Crowned arms of Holland divides date **Rev. Legend:** CONCORDIA RES PAR.... **Note:** Dav. #4898 and #1840.

Date	Mintage	VG	F	VF	XF	Unc
1672	—	35.00	100	200	300	—
1673	—	35.00	100	200	300	—
1674	—	35.00	100	200	300	—
1679	—	40.00	100	200	300	—
1680/79	—	50.00	125	250	400	—
1680	—	40.00	100	200	300	—
1683	—	60.00	125	250	400	—
1684	46,595	40.00	100	200	300	—
1693	—	40.00	100	200	300	—
1694/3	—	40.00	100	200	300	—
1694	—	40.00	100	200	300	—
1695/4	—	40.00	100	200	300	—
1695	—	50.00	125	250	400	—

KM# 108 2 DUCAT

Silver **Obv:** Armored knight standing right holding bow in left hand **Rev:** Crowned arms divides date **Note:** Dav. #4897.

Date	Mintage	Good	VG	F	VF	XF
1673	—	—	—	—	1,800	2,300
1674	—	—	—	—	1,800	2,300
1683	—	—	—	—	1,800	2,300
1693	—	—	—	—	1,800	2,300
1694	—	—	—	—	1,800	2,300

KM# 8 1/2 DAALDER (Prince 20 Stuiver)

14.5100 g., 0.8850 Silver 0.4128 oz. ASW **Obv:** Armoured bust of William the Silent with sword right in inner circle, date at top in legend **Rev:** Helmeted arms in inner circle

Date	Mintage	Good	VG	F	VF	XF
1601	—	70.00	300	600	850	1,400
1602	—	70.00	300	600	850	1,400

KM# 9 1/2 DAALDER (Lion 24 Stuiver)

13.8400 g., 0.7500 Silver 0.3337 oz. ASW **Obv:** Armored knight looking right above lion shield, date divided at bottom **Rev:** Rampant lion left in inner circle

Date	Mintage	Good	VG	F	VF	XF
1601/89	—	20.00	60.00	125	300	600
1601/99	—	20.00	60.00	125	300	600
1601/0	—	20.00	60.00	125	300	600
1601	—	15.00	50.00	100	250	500
1602/1	—	20.00	60.00	125	300	600
1602	—	15.00	50.00	100	250	500
1604	—	15.00	50.00	100	250	500
1605/4	—	20.00	60.00	125	300	600
1605	—	15.00	50.00	100	250	500

KM# 16 1/2 DAALDER (Lion 24 Stuiver)

Silver **Rev:** Date at top in legend

Date	Mintage	Good	VG	F	VF	XF
1606	—	25.00	65.00	130	225	500
1607	—	25.00	65.00	130	225	500
1608	—	25.00	65.00	130	225	500
1609	—	25.00	65.00	130	225	500
1610	—	25.00	65.00	130	225	500
1611	—	25.00	65.00	130	225	500
1615/3	—	25.00	65.00	130	225	500
1616	—	20.00	50.00	100	175	350
1617	—	20.00	50.00	100	175	350
1618	—	20.00	50.00	100	175	350
1622	—	20.00	50.00	100	175	350
1623/2	—	20.00	65.00	130	225	500
1623	—	25.00	65.00	130	225	500
1624/2	—	25.00	65.00	130	225	500
1624/3	—	25.00	65.00	130	225	500
1624	—	25.00	65.00	130	225	500
1626	—	25.00	65.00	130	225	500
1632	—	25.00	65.00	130	225	500
1633	—	25.00	65.00	130	225	500
1634	—	25.00	65.00	130	225	500
1636	—	25.00	65.00	130	225	500
1637	—	25.00	65.00	130	225	500
1640	—	25.00	65.00	130	225	500
1641/0	—	25.00	65.00	130	225	500
1641	—	25.00	65.00	130	225	500
1643	—	25.00	65.00	130	225	500
1645	—	25.00	65.00	13.00	225	500
1647	—	25.00	65.00	130	225	500
1648/7	—	20.00	50.00	100	175	350
1648	—	20.00	50.00	100	175	350
1649	—	25.00	75.00	150	300	600
1650	—	20.00	50.00	100	175	350
1651/0	—	20.00	50.00	100	175	350
1652	—	20.00	50.00	100	175	350
1653/2	—	20.00	75.00	150	300	600
1653	—	20.00	50.00	100	175	350

KM# 25 1/2 DAALDER (Rijks)

14.5100 g., 0.8850 0.4128 oz. **Obv:** Laureate 1/2 figure holding sword and arms in inner circle **Rev:** Crowned arms divide date in inner circle

Date	Mintage	Good	VG	F	VF	XF
1606	—	25.00	65.00	130	225	500
1610	—	20.00	60.00	125	200	400
1611	—	20.00	60.00	125	200	400
1612	—	20.00	60.00	125	200	400
1614	—	20.00	60.00	125	200	400
1620/7	—	25.00	65.00	130	225	500
1620	—	20.00	60.00	125	200	400
1621	—	20.00	60.00	125	200	400
1622	—	20.00	60.00	125	200	400
1623/2	—	20.00	60.00	125	200	400
1623	—	20.00	60.00	125	200	400
1624	—	20.00	60.00	125	200	400
1625/4	—	20.00	60.00	125	200	400
1625	—	20.00	60.00	125	200	400
1628	—	20.00	60.00	125	200	400
1629	—	20.00	60.00	125	200	400
1630	—	25.00	65.00	130	225	500
1632	—	25.00	65.00	130	225	500
1640	—	25.00	65.00	130	225	500
1648	—	20.00	65.00	125	200	400
1649	—	20.00	60.00	125	200	400
1650	—	20.00	60.00	125	200	400
1654	—	20.00	60.00	125	200	400
1657/4	—	20.00	60.00	125	200	400
1657	—	20.00	60.00	125	200	400
1659	—	20.00	60.00	125	200	400

KM# 10 DAALDER (Prince 40 Stuivers)

29.0300 g., 0.8850 Silver 0.8260 oz. ASW **Obv:** Helmeted arms in inner circle **Rev:** Armored half figure of William the Silent with sword right in inner circle, date at top in legend **Note:** Dav. #4822.

Date	Mintage	Good	VG	F	VF	XF
1601	—	60.00	175	400	800	1,300
1602	—	60.00	175	400	800	1,300

KM# 11 DAALDER (Lion - 48 Stuivers)

27.6300 g., 0.7500 Silver 0.6662 oz. ASW **Obv:** Armored knight looking right above lion shield, date divided at bottom **Rev:** Rampant lion to left in inner circle **Note:** Dav. #4856.

Date	Mintage	Good	VG	F	VF	XF
1601/1589	—	20.00	40.00	100	200	400
1601/1594	—	20.00	40.00	100	200	400
1601/0/1599	—	20.00	40.00	100	200	400
1601/0	—	16.00	30.00	75.00	160	300
1601	—	16.00	30.00	75.00	160	300
1602/1	—	20.00	40.00	100	200	400
1602	—	16.00	30.00	75.00	160	300
1604	—	16.00	30.00	75.00	160	300
1605	—	20.00	40.00	100	200	400

KM# 17 DAALDER (Lion - 48 Stuivers)

Silver **Obv:** Armored knight left looking backwards holding bow and resting hand on shield **Rev:** Rampant lion left, date at top in legend **Note:** Dav. #4858.

Date	Mintage	Good	VG	F	VF	XF
1606	—	18.00	35.00	75.00	150	300
1607	—	18.00	35.00	70.00	125	250
1608/6	—	18.00	35.00	70.00	125	250
1608	—	16.00	30.00	75.00	150	300
1609/8	—	16.00	30.00	75.00	150	300
1609	—	18.00	35.00	70.00	125	250
1610	—	18.00	35.00	75.00	150	300
1611/0	—	18.00	35.00	70.00	125	250
1611	—	18.00	35.00	70.00	125	250
1612	—	18.00	35.00	75.00	150	300
1614	—	18.00	35.00	75.00	150	300
1616/3	—	16.00	30.00	75.00	150	300
1616	—	16.00	30.00	75.00	150	300
1617	—	16.00	30.00	75.00	150	300
1621	—	18.00	35.00	75.00	150	300
1622	—	18.00	35.00	75.00	150	300
1623/17	—	18.00	35.00	75.00	150	300
1623/19	—	18.00	35.00	75.00	150	300
1623/22	—	18.00	35.00	75.00	150	300
1623	—	18.00	35.00	75.00	150	300
1624/23/22	—	18.00	35.00	75.00	150	300
1624	—	18.00	35.00	70.00	125	250
1625	—	18.00	35.00	70.00	125	250
1626	—	18.00	35.00	70.00	125	250
1627/6	—	18.00	35.00	70.00	125	250
1627	—	18.00	35.00	70.00	125	250
1628	—	18.00	35.00	70.00	125	250
1629	—	18.00	35.00	75.00	150	300
1631/31	—	18.00	35.00	75.00	150	300
1632	—	18.00	35.00	70.00	125	250
1633	—	18.00	35.00	70.00	125	250
1634/3	—	18.00	35.00	70.00	125	250
1634	—	18.00	35.00	70.00	125	250
1635	—	18.00	35.00	70.00	125	250
1636	—	18.00	35.00	70.00	125	250
1637	—	18.00	35.00	70.00	125	250
1638	—	18.00	35.00	70.00	125	250
1639	—	18.00	35.00	70.00	125	250
1641/0	—	25.00	75.00	150	300	600
1640	—	18.00	35.00	70.00	125	250
1641	—	18.00	35.00	75.00	150	300
1643	—	18.00	35.00	70.00	125	250
1644	—	18.00	35.00	75.00	150	300
1645	—	18.00	35.00	75.00	150	300
1647	—	18.00	35.00	70.00	125	250
1648	—	18.00	35.00	70.00	125	250
1649	—	18.00	35.00	70.00	125	250
1650/49	—	18.00	35.00	70.00	125	250
1650	—	18.00	35.00	70.00	125	250
1651	—	18.00	35.00	70.00	125	250
1652	—	18.00	35.00	70.00	125	250
1653	—	18.00	35.00	75.00	150	300
1654	—	18.00	35.00	75.00	150	300
1655	—	18.00	35.00	75.00	150	300
1658	—	18.00	35.00	75.00	150	300
1659	—	18.00	35.00	75.00	150	300
1661	—	18.00	35.00	75.00	150	300
1662/52	—	25.00	50.00	125	250	500
1662	—	18.00	35.00	75.00	150	300
1663	—	18.00	35.00	75.00	150	300
1664	—	18.00	35.00	75.00	150	300
1665	—	18.00	35.00	75.00	150	300
1666	—	18.00	35.00	75.00	150	300
1668	—	18.00	35.00	75.00	150	300
1674	—	18.00	35.00	75.00	150	300
1675	—	18.00	35.00	75.00	150	300
1676	—	18.00	35.00	75.00	150	300
1679	—	18.00	35.00	75.00	150	300
1680	—	18.00	35.00	75.00	150	300
1683	—	18.00	35.00	75.00	150	300
1684	—	18.00	35.00	75.00	150	300
1685	—	18.00	35.00	75.00	150	300
1687	—	18.00	35.00	75.00	150	300
1697	—	22.00	45.00	110	200	350

KM# 18 DAALDER (Rijks)

28.2500 g., 0.8730 Silver 0.7929 oz. ASW **Obv:** Laureate 1/2 figure holding sword and arms in inner circle **Obv. Legend:** * MO: ARG: PRO• - CONFOE: BELG: C: HOL• **Rev:** Crowned arms divide date **Rev. Legend:** CONCORDIA RES PARVAE CRESCUNT **Note:** Dav. #4831.

Date	Mintage	Good	VG	F	VF	XF
1606	—	20.00	40.00	75.00	150	300
1607	—	20.00	40.00	75.00	150	300
1609	—	20.00	40.00	75.00	150	300
1610	—	22.00	45.00	90.00	175	350
1611	—	20.00	40.00	75.00	150	300
1612	—	20.00	40.00	75.00	150	300
1614	—	20.00	40.00	75.00	150	300
1619/8	—	20.00	40.00	75.00	150	300
1619	—	20.00	40.00	75.00	150	300
1620	—	20.00	40.00	75.00	150	300
1621/0	—	22.00	45.00	90.00	175	350
1621	—	20.00	40.00	75.00	150	300
1622	—	20.00	40.00	75.00	150	300
1623/2	—	22.00	45.00	90.00	175	350
1623	—	20.00	40.00	75.00	150	300
1624/3/2	—	22.00	45.00	90.00	175	350
1624/2	—	20.00	40.00	75.00	150	300
1624/3	—	20.00	40.00	75.00	150	300
1624	—	20.00	40.00	75.00	150	300
1625	—	20.00	40.00	75.00	150	300
1626	—	20.00	40.00	75.00	150	300
1628	—	22.00	45.00	90.00	175	350
1629	—	20.00	40.00	75.00	150	300
1631/28	—	20.00	40.00	75.00	150	300
1631	—	20.00	40.00	75.00	150	300
1634	—	20.00	40.00	75.00	150	300
1636	—	20.00	40.00	75.00	150	300
1640	—	20.00	40.00	75.00	150	300
1644	—	20.00	40.00	75.00	150	300
1648	—	20.00	40.00	75.00	150	300
1649	—	20.00	40.00	75.00	150	300
1650	—	20.00	40.00	75.00	150	300
1651	—	20.00	40.00	75.00	150	300
1652	—	20.00	40.00	75.00	150	300
1653	—	20.00	40.00	75.00	150	300
1656	—	20.00	40.00	75.00	150	300
1657/6	—	20.00	40.00	75.00	150	300
1657	—	20.00	40.00	75.00	150	300
1658	—	20.00	40.00	75.00	150	300
1659	—	20.00	40.00	75.00	150	300
1662	—	20.00	40.00	75.00	150	300
1674	—	20.00	40.00	75.00	150	300
1675	—	20.00	40.00	75.00	150	300
1676	—	20.00	40.00	75.00	150	300
1683	—	20.00	40.00	75.00	150	300
1684/3	—	20.00	40.00	75.00	150	300
1684	—	22.00	45.00	90.00	175	350
1687	—	22.00	45.00	90.00	175	350
1693	—	22.00	45.00	90.00	175	350

KM# 88 2 DAALDERS (Lion)

Silver **Obv:** Armored knight left looking backwards holding bow and lion shield **Rev:** Rampant lion left, date above in legend **Note:** Dav. #4857.

Date	Mintage	Good	VG	F	VF	XF
1636	—	—	—	—	1,750	2,750
1640	—	—	—	—	1,750	2,750
1641	—	—	—	—	1,750	2,750
1645	—	—	—	—	1,750	2,750
1674	—	—	—	—	1,750	2,750
1676/4	—	—	—	—	1,750	2,750
1676	—	—	—	—	1,750	2,750

KM# 86 2 DAALDERS (Rijks)

Silver **Obv:** Armored knight right with sword on shoulder holding bow **Rev:** Crowned arms divides date **Note:** Dav. #4830.

Date	Mintage	Good	VG	F	VF	XF
1631 Rare	—	—	—	—	—	—
1649 Rare	—	—	—	—	—	—
1674 Rare	—	—	—	—	—	—
1687 Rare	—	—	—	—	—	—

KM# 87 2 DAALDERS (Rijks)

Silver **Obv:** Armored knight with sword on shoulder holding bow **Rev:** Crowned arms divides date **Note:** Klippe. Dav. #4830A.

Date	Mintage	Good	VG	F	VF	XF
1631 Rare	—	—	—	—	—	—

KM# 20 1/2 CAVALIER D'OR

5.0000 g., 0.9200 Gold 0.1479 oz. AGW **Obv:** Knight horseback right brandishing sword **Rev:** Crowned arms, date above **Note:** Fr. # 252.

Date	Mintage	VG	F	VF	XF	Unc
1606	—	220	450	900	1,500	—
1607	—	220	450	900	1,500	—
1608	—	220	450	900	1,500	—
1617	—	220	450	900	1,500	—
1621	—	270	625	1,250	1,750	—
1622	—	220	450	900	1,500	—
1623	—	220	450	900	1,500	—
1632/22	—	270	625	1,250	1,750	—
1632/31	—	270	625	1,250	1,750	—
1634	—	300	750	1,500	2,000	—
1635	—	300	750	1,500	2,000	—
1638	—	300	750	1,500	2,000	—
1644/38/35	—	300	750	1,500	2,000	—
1644	—	220	450	900	1,500	—
1645	—	220	450	900	1,500	—

KM# 19 CAVALIER D'OR

10.0000 g., 0.9200 Gold 0.2958 oz. AGW **Obv:** Knight horseback right brandishing sword **Rev:** Crowned arms, date above **Note:** Fr. # 251.

Date	Mintage	VG	F	VF	XF	Unc
1606	—	450	1,300	2,500	3,600	—
1607	—	450	1,300	2,500	3,600	—
1608	—	450	1,300	2,500	3,600	—
1621	—	450	1,300	2,500	3,600	—
1622	—	450	1,300	2,500	3,600	—
1623/22	—	500	1,750	3,000	4,000	—
1623	—	450	1,300	2,500	3,600	—
1624	—	450	1,300	2,500	3,600	—
1625	—	450	1,300	2,500	3,600	—
1629/28	—	500	1,750	3,000	4,000	—
1629	—	450	1,300	2,500	3,600	—
1632	—	450	1,300	2,500	3,600	—

TRADE COINAGE

KM# 12.1 DUCAT

3.4900 g., Gold **Obv:** Knight standing right divides date within inner circle **Obv. Legend:** CONCORDIA. RES. PAR. CRES. HOL **Rev:** 5-line inscription on tablet **Note:** Fr. #249, 250.

Date	Mintage	VG	F	VF	XF	Unc
1603	—	160	250	350	500	—
1604	—	180	300	500	700	—
1605	—	160	250	350	500	—
1606	—	160	250	350	500	—
1608	—	160	250	350	500	—
1609/7	—	210	325	475	725	—
1609	—	160	250	350	500	—
1610	—	160	250	350	500	—
1611	—	160	250	350	500	—
1612	—	180	300	500	700	—
1614	—	180	300	500	700	—
1621	—	210	325	475	725	—
1622	—	210	325	475	725	—
1631/23	—	180	300	500	700	—
1631/24	—	180	300	500	700	—
1631	—	160	250	350	500	—
1632	—	160	250	350	500	—
1633	—	160	250	350	500	—
1634	—	160	250	350	500	—
1634/3	—	160	250	350	500	—
1635	—	160	250	350	500	—
1636	—	160	250	350	500	—
1637	—	160	250	350	500	—
1638	—	160	250	350	500	—
1639	—	160	250	350	500	—
1640	—	210	300	475	725	—
1641	—	160	250	350	500	—
1642	—	160	250	350	500	—
1643	—	160	250	350	500	—
1644	—	160	250	350	500	—
1645	—	160	250	350	500	—
1646	—	160	250	350	500	—
1646/5	—	210	425	725	950	—
1647	—	160	250	350	500	—
1648	—	210	425	725	950	—
1649/42	—	180	300	500	700	—
1649	—	160	250	350	500	—
1650	—	160	250	350	500	—
1651	—	160	250	350	500	—
1651/0	—	160	250	350	500	—
1652	—	160	250	350	500	—
1653	—	160	250	350	500	—
1654	—	160	250	350	500	—
1655	—	160	250	350	500	—
1657	—	210	425	725	950	—
1658	—	210	425	725	950	—
1659	—	180	300	500	700	—
1659/5	—	160	250	350	500	—
1660	—	160	250	350	500	—
1661	—	210	425	725	950	—

Date	Mintage	VG	F	VF	XF	Unc
1662	—	170	240	475	725	—
1663	—	210	425	725	950	—
1664	—	210	425	725	950	—
1665	—	210	425	475	725	—
1666	—	180	300	500	700	—
1668	—	210	425	725	950	—

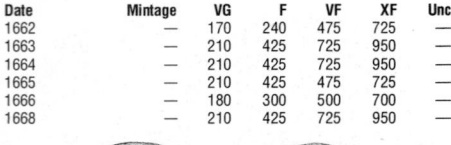

KM# 12.2 DUCAT
3.4900 g., 0.9860 Gold 0.1106 oz. AGW **Obv:** Armored, standing Knight holding bundle of arrows divides date without inner circle **Obv. Legend:** CONCORDIA • RES PAR • CRES • HOL • **Rev:** Inscription within ornamented square **Rev. Inscription:** MO:ORD:/ PROVIN./ FOEDER BELGAD/ LEGIMP. **Note:** Fr. #249, 250.

Date	Mintage	VG	F	VF	XF	Unc
1672	—	160	250	350	500	—
1673	—	160	250	350	500	—
1674/3	—	180	300	500	700	—
1674	—	160	250	350	500	—
1683	—	160	250	350	500	—
1685	—	210	425	725	950	—
1686	—	160	250	350	500	—
1688	—	160	250	350	500	—
1691	—	160	250	350	500	—
1692	—	160	250	350	500	—
1693	—	160	250	350	500	—
1694/1	—	160	250	350	500	—
1694	—	180	300	500	700	—
1698	—	210	425	725	950	—
1699	—	160	250	350	500	—

KM# 35 2 DUCAT
6.9800 g., 0.9860 Gold 0.2213 oz. AGW **Obv:** Standing knight wearing helmet **Rev:** Tablet with five line inscription **Note:** Fr. #247.

Date	Mintage	VG	F	VF	XF	Unc
1645	—	250	350	700	1,400	—
1646	—	250	350	700	1,400	—
1647	—	250	350	700	1,400	—
1648	—	250	350	700	1,400	—
1649	—	250	350	700	1,400	—
1650	—	250	350	700	1,400	—
1651	—	250	350	700	1,400	—
1652	—	250	350	700	1,400	—
1653	—	250	350	700	1,400	—
1654	—	250	375	750	1,500	—
1655/4	—	250	375	750	1,500	—
1655	—	250	350	700	1,400	—
1656	—	250	400	800	1,600	—
1657/0	—	250	375	750	1,500	—
1657	—	250	350	700	1,400	—
1658	—	250	400	800	1,600	—
1659	—	250	350	700	1,400	—
1660	—	250	350	700	1,400	—
1661	—	250	350	700	1,400	—
1662	—	250	350	700	1,400	—
1663	—	250	400	800	1,600	—

KM# 47.1 2 DUCAT
6.9800 g., 0.9860 Gold 0.2213 oz. AGW **Obv:** Standing, armored knight holding bundle of arrows, divides date within broken circle **Obv. Legend:** CONCORDIA • RES PAR • CRES • HOL • **Rev:** Inscription within ornamented square **Rev. Inscription:** MO:ORD:/ PROVIN./ FOEDER/ BELG•AD/ LEG•IMP• **Edge:** Plain

Date	Mintage	VG	F	VF	XF	Unc
1671	—	350	600	1,200	1,800	—
1672	—	350	600	1,200	1,800	—
1673	—	350	600	1,200	1,800	—

Date	Mintage	VG	F	VF	XF	Unc
1674	—	350	600	1,200	1,800	—
1687	—	400	800	1,600	2,400	—
1694	—	450	900	1,800	2,700	—

COUNTERMARKED COINAGE

1693

During the late 17th century many circulating coins were found to be underweight. In 1693 coins meeting the legal requirements were countermarked for a specific province or city, such as HOL for Holland.

KM# 68 14 STUIVERS
Silver **Countermark:** HOL **Note:** Countermark on Friesland KM#67.

CM Date	Host Date	Good	VG	F	VF	XF
ND(1693)	1688	—	—	—	—	—

KM# 69.18 28 STUIVERS
Silver **Countermark:** HOL **Note:** Countermarked on Deventer 28 Stuivers KM # 81.2.

CM Date	Host Date	Good	VG	F	VF	XF
ND(1693)	1685	—	—	—	—	—

KM# 69.1 28 STUIVERS
Silver **Countermark:** HOL **Note:** Countermark on Deventer KM#79.

CM Date	Host Date	Good	VG	F	VF	XF
ND(1693)	1684	—	—	—	—	—

KM# 69.2 28 STUIVERS
Silver **Countermark:** HOL **Note:** Countermark on Deventer KM#81.

CM Date	Host Date	Good	VG	F	VF	XF
ND(1963)	1685-92	—	—	—	—	—

KM# 69.3 28 STUIVERS
Silver **Countermark:** HOL **Note:** Countermark on Friesland KM#10.

CM Date	Host Date	Good	VG	F	VF	XF
ND(1693)	1601-91	30.00	60.00	100	200	—

KM# 69.6 28 STUIVERS
Silver **Countermark:** HOL **Note:** Countermark on Groningen & Ommeland KM#31.

CM Date	Host Date	Good	VG	F	VF	XF
ND(1693)	1673-77	—	—	200	—	—

KM# 69.7 28 STUIVERS
Silver **Countermark:** HOL **Note:** Countermark on Groningen & Ommeland KM#33.

CM Date	Host Date	Good	VG	F	VF	XF
ND(1693)	1674	—	—	—	—	—

KM# 69.19 28 STUIVERS

Silver **Countermark:** HOL **Note:** Countermark on Groningen & Ommeland 28 Stuiver, KM#42.

CM Date	Host Date	Good	VG	F	VF	XF
ND(1693)	1685-86	—	—	—	—	—

KM# 69.8 28 STUIVERS

Silver **Countermark:** HOL **Note:** Countermark on Groningen & Ommeland KM#47.

CM Date	Host Date	Good	VG	F	VF	XF
ND(1693)	1685-86	75.00	150	250	—	—

KM# 69.4 28 STUIVERS

Silver **Countermark:** HOL **Note:** Countermark on Groningen & Ommeland KM#49.

CM Date	Host Date	Good	VG	F	VF	XF
ND(1693)	1690-92	—	—	—	—	—

KM# 69.5 28 STUIVERS

Silver **Countermark:** HOL **Note:** Countermark on Groningen & Ommeland KM#50.

CM Date	Host Date	Good	VG	F	VF	XF
ND(1693)	1690	—	—	—	—	—

KM# 69.9 28 STUIVERS

Silver **Countermark:** HOL **Note:** Countermark on Groningen & Ommeland KM#52.

CM Date	Host Date	Good	VG	F	VF	XF
ND(1693)	1692	—	—	100	—	—

KM# 69.10 28 STUIVERS

Silver **Countermark:** HOL **Note:** Countermark on Kampen KM#23.

CM Date	Host Date	Good	VG	F	VF	XF
ND(1693)	1616-19	—	—	—	—	—

KM# 69.11 28 STUIVERS

Silver **Countermark:** HOL **Note:** Countermark on Kampen KM#76.

CM Date	Host Date	Good	VG	F	VF	XF
ND(1693)	1680-86	—	—	—	—	—

KM# 69.12 28 STUIVERS

Silver **Countermark:** HOL **Note:** Countermark on Nijmegen KM#27.

CM Date	Host Date	Good	VG	F	VF	XF
ND(1693)	1685-90	—	—	—	—	—

KM# 69.13 28 STUIVERS

Silver **Countermark:** HOL **Note:** Countermark on Overyssel KM#55.

CM Date	Host Date	Good	VG	F	VF	XF
ND(1693)	1685-89	—	—	—	—	—

KM# 69.14 28 STUIVERS

Silver **Countermark:** HOL **Note:** Countermark on West Friesland KM#90.

CM Date	Host Date	Good	VG	F	VF	XF
ND(1693)	1685-87	—	—	—	—	—

KM# 69.17 28 STUIVERS

Silver, 37 mm. **Countermark:** HOL **Note:** c/m on West Friesland, 28 Stuivers.

CM Date	Host Date	Good	VG	F	VF	XF
ND(1693)	ND	60.00	120	200	300	—

KM# 69.15 28 STUIVERS

Silver **Countermark:** HOL **Note:** Countermark on Zutphen KM#25.

CM Date	Host Date	Good	VG	F	VF	XF
ND(1693)	1690	—	—	—	—	—

KM# 69.16 28 STUIVERS

Silver **Countermark:** HOL **Note:** Countermark on Zwolle KM#78.

CM Date	Host Date	Good	VG	F	VF	XF
ND(1693)	1679-86	—	—	—	—	—

PATTERNS

Including off metal strikes

KM#	Date	Mintage	Identification	Mkt Val
Pn1	1670	—	6 Stuivers. Gold. 7.0000 g. KM#45.1	—
Pn2	1670	—	6 Stuivers. Gold. 3.5000 g. KM#45.1	—
Pn3	1670	—	6 Stuivers. Gold. 7.0000 g. KM#45.2.	—
Pn4	1671	—	6 Stuivers. Gold. 7.0000 g. KM#45.2.	—
Pn5	1672	—	Ducaton. Gold. 34.7000 g. KM#51.	—
Pn6	1672	—	Ducaton. Gold. 62.3000 g. KM#51.	—
Pn7	1672	—	Ducaton. Gold. 40.8000 g. KM#49.1.	—
Pn8	1672	—	Ducaton. Gold. 38.3000 g. KM#51.	20,000
Pn9	1673	—	Ducaton. Gold. 30.5000 g. KM#49.1.	—
Pn10	1674	—	6 Stuivers. Gold. 7.0000 g. KM#45.2.	—
Pn11	1680	—	Ducaton. Gold. 38.3000 g.	—
Pn12	1681	—	Ducaton. Gold. 38.4000 g. KM#63.	—
Pn13	ND	—	2 Gulden. Gold. 27.6000 g. KM#62.	—
Pn14	1681	—	3 Gulden. Gold. 34.9000 g. KM#64	10,000
Pn15	1681	—	3 Gulden, Gold, 38.4000 g. KM#84	10,000
Pn16	1684	—	Daalder. Gold. 35.0000 g. KM#17.	—
Pn17	1684	—	6 Stuivers. Gold. 7.0000 g. KM#45.2.	—
Pn18	1684	—	3 Gulden. Gold. 35.0000 g. KM#66.	—
Pn19	1687	—	Ducaton. Gold. 34.5000 g. KM#51.	18,000
Pn20	1687	—	Daalder. Gold. 34.5000 g. KM#18.	35,000
Pn21	1692	—	Gulden. Gold. 13.8000 g. KM#61.	—
Pn22	1692	—	5 Stuivers. Gold. KM#70.	2,000
Pn23	1694	—	1/2 Gulden. Gold. 10.3000 g. KM#72.	—
Pn24	1694	—	3 Gulden, Gold, 34.5000 g. KM#152 with edge legend, KM#152	
Pn25	1696	—	1/2 Gulden. Gold. 10.3000 g. KM#65a.	—
Pn26	1697	—	3 Gulden. Gold. 34.5000 g. KM#152 with edge legend	—
Pn27	1697	—	2 Gulden. Gold. 27.5000 g. KM#75.	—
Pn28	1697	—	2 Stuivers. Gold. 1697.0000 g. KM#48a.	—
Pn29	1697	—	2 Gulden. Gold. KM#62.	—
Pn30	1698	—	1/2 3 (1-1/2) Gulden. Gold. 20.6000 g. KM#74a.	—
Pn31	1698	—	1/2 Gulden. Gold. 10.3000 g. KM#65a.	—

PIEFORTS

KM#	Date	Mintage	Identification	Mkt Val
P1	1631	—	Daalder. Silver. KM18.	—
P2	1631	—	Daalder. Silver. Klippe, KM18.	—
P3	1636	—	Lion Daalder. Silver. KM17.	—
P4	1640	—	Lion Daalder. Silver. KM17.	—
P5	1645	—	Lion Daalder. Silver. KM17.	—
P6	1649	—	Daalder. Silver. KM18.	—
P7	1672	—	Ducaton. Silver. KM49.	700
PA8	1672	—	Ducaton. Silver. Klippe, KM49.2.	—
P8	1672	—	Ducaton. Silver. Klippe, KM50.	—
P9	1672	—	Ducaton. Silver. KM51.	1,500
P10	1673	—	Ducaton. Silver. KM49.	—
P11	1673	—	Ducaton. Silver. Klippe, KM50.	—
P12	1673	—	Ducaton. Silver. Klippe, triple weight, KM50.	—
P13	1673	—	Ducaton. Silver. KM51.	2,000
P14	1673	—	Silver Ducat. KM52.	2,000
PA15	1674	—	6 Stuivers. Silver. Double weight. KM#45.2, KM#17	—
P15	1674	—	Ducaton. Silver. KM51.	1,500
P16	1674	—	Silver Ducat. KM52.	—
P17	1674	—	Lion Daalder. Silver. KM17.	—
P18	1674	—	Daalder. Silver. KM18.	1,500
P19	1675	—	Ducaton. Silver. KM51.	—
P20	1676	—	Ducaton. Silver. KM51.	—
P21	1676/4	—	Lion Daalder. Silver. KM17.	—
P22	1676	—	Lion Daalder. Silver. KM17.	—

KM#	Date	Mintage	Identification	Mkt Val
P23	1678/6	—	Ducaton. Silver. KM51.	2,000
P24	1678	—	Ducaton. Silver. KM51.	—
P25	1679/6	—	Ducaton. Silver. KM51.	2,000
P26	1679	—	Ducaton. Silver. KM51.	—
P27	1680	—	Ducaton. Silver. KM51.	—
PA27	1680	—	6 Stuivers. Silver. Double weight. KM45.2	650
P28	1682	—	3 Gulden. Silver. Double weight. KM63, Dav.#A4952.	2,000
P29	1683	—	Silver Ducat. KM52.	2,500
P30	1684	—	3 Gulden. Silver. Double weight. KM66, Dav.#A4953.	3,000
P31	1687	—	Ducaton. Silver. KM51.	—
PA31	1687	—	Daalder. Gold. KM#18, Rare.	—
PB31	1687	—	Ducaton. Gold. KM#51.	2,000
P32	1692	—	5 Stuivers. Gold.	2,000
P33	1693	—	Ducaton. Silver. KM51.	2,500
P34	1693	—	Silver Ducat. KM52.	2,000
P35	1694	—	Silver Ducat. KM52.	2,000
P36	1697	—	2 Stuivers. Silver. Double weight. KM#48	600

OVERIJSSEL

Overijsel, Transisulania

Overijssel is a province in northeastern Netherlands whose name means *beyond the Issel*, a tributary of the Rhine. Originally known as the lordship of Oversticht it was a part of the holdings of the bishops of Utrecht. It was sold to Charles V in 1527 and made a part of the Habsburg domain. Three of its cities - Kampen, Deventer and Zwolle were important Hanseatic towns of the medieval period.

PROVINCE

STANDARD COINAGE

KM# 22 DUIT

2.0000 g., Copper **Obv:** Crowned arms with rampant lion facing to right **Rev:** Four line inscription TRANNN(S) / INSLV/NIA in wreath.

Date	Mintage	VG	F	VF	XF	Unc
ND (1607)	—	5.00	20.00	40.00	80.00	—
1619	—	6.00	40.00	75.00	150	—
1626	—	6.00	40.00	75.00	150	—
1628	—	5.00	20.00	40.00	80.00	—
1629	—	6.00	40.00	75.00	150	—
1633	—	5.00	20.00	40.00	80.00	—
1635	—	6.00	40.00	75.00	150	—

KM# 22a DUIT

5.2500 g., Gold **Rev. Inscription:** TRANS / SISVLA / NIA / date in wreath

Date	Mintage	VG	F	VF	XF	Unc
1628 Rare	—	—	—	—	—	—

KM# 18 2 DUIT (Oord)

Copper **Obv:** Bust of Rudolph II left **Obv. Legend:** MONE • NOVA - ORDI • TRAS **Rev:** Crowned arms

Date	Mintage	VG	F	VF	XF	Unc
1607/6 Rare	—	—	—	—	—	—
1607	—	10.00	50.00	100	200	—

KM# 103 1 1/2 STUIVER ((Quarter Snaphaanschelling))

2.1600 g., Silver **Obv:** Crowned arms with rampant lion on cross in inner circle **Obv. Legend:** SPER - AMVS - MELI - ORA **Rev:** Knight with sword on horseback to right, below. N.R.O.T. **Rev. Legend:** DEO DV-CE VIRTVT-E COMITE

Date	Mintage	VG	F	VF	XF	Unc
ND1607-1611	—	100	300	600	1,250	—

KM# 23.1 STUIVER

1.3100 g., 0.3330 Silver 0.0140 oz. ASW **Obv:** Bundle of arrows divides value in wreath, value outside bow **Rev:** TRA/ISVLA/NIA(date) in wreath

Date	Mintage	VG	F	VF	XF	Unc
1619	243,040	10.00	20.00	45.00	100	—
1621	Inc. above	4.00	10.00	25.00	50.00	—
1625	Inc. above	4.00	10.00	25.00	50.00	—
1628	Inc. above	5.00	15.00	32.50	65.00	—
1629	Inc. above	10.00	20.00	45.00	100	—
1633	Inc. above	4.00	10.00	25.00	50.00	—
1634	Inc. above	30.00	80.00	150	300	—

KM# 24 STUIVER

Billon **Obv:** Value inside bow

Date	Mintage	VG	F	VF	XF	Unc
1619	Inc. above	4.00	10.00	25.00	50.00	—
1628	Inc. above	4.00	10.00	25.00	50.00	—
1653	Inc. above	4.00	10.00	25.00	50.00	—
1665	132,440	4.00	10.00	25.00	50.00	—
1666	Inc. above	4.00	10.00	25.00	50.00	—

KM# 23.2 STUIVER

1.3100 g., 0.3330 Silver 0.0140 oz. ASW **Obv:** Bundle of arrows divides value in wreath, value outside bow **Rev:** TRA/ISVLA/NIA(date) in wreath **Note:** Mintmark: Lily

Date	Mintage	VG	F	VF	XF	Unc
	Inc. above	10.00	20.00	45.00	100	—
	Inc. above	5.00	15.00	32.50	65.00	—

KM# 19.1 2 STUIVERS

1.7300 g., 0.5830 Silver 0.0324 oz. ASW **Obv:** Crowned rampant lion left holding sword and arrows divides value 2 - S **Rev:** Inscription. date **Rev. Inscription:** TRS / ISS / VLA or TRAS / ISVLA / • NIA •

Date	Mintage	VG	F	VF	XF	Unc
1612Kampen	4,978,347	10.00	25.00	50.00	100	—
1614Kampen	Inc. above	10.00	25.00	50.00	100	—
1615Kampen	Inc. above	10.00	25.00	50.00	100	—
1616Lily	Inc. above	6.00	15.00	50.00	100	—
1616Kampen	Inc. above	10.00	25.00	50.00	100	—
1616Zwolle	Inc. above	10.00	25.00	50.00	100	—
1616	Inc. above	10.00	25.00	50.00	100	—
1617Lily	Inc. above	6.00	15.00	50.00	100	—
1617	Inc. above	10.00	25.00	50.00	100	—
1618Lily	Inc. above	6.00	15.00	50.00	100	—
1618Zwolle	Inc. above	10.00	25.00	50.00	100	—
1619Lily	Inc. above	6.00	15.00	50.00	100	—
1619Zwolle	Inc. above	10.00	25.00	50.00	100	—
1619	Inc. above	10.00	25.00	50.00	100	—
1620Lily	Inc. above	—	—	—	—	—
1622Lily	Inc. above	—	—	—	—	—
1622	Inc. above	10.00	25.00	50.00	100	—
1627Lily	317,770	6.00	15.00	50.00	100	—
1628Lily	Inc. above	6.00	15.00	50.00	100	—
1629Lily	Inc. above	—	—	—	—	—
1630Lily	Inc. above	—	—	—	—	—
1631Lily	Inc. above	—	—	—	—	—
1632Lily	Inc. above	6.00	15.00	50.00	100	—
1633Lily	Inc. above	6.00	15.00	50.00	100	—
1634Lily	Inc. above	6.00	15.00	50.00	100	—

KM# 25 2 STUIVERS

Billon **Obv:** Rampant lion left holding sword and arrows **Rev:** Inscription, date **Rev. Inscription:** TRAS / ISVLA / • NIA • **Note:** Klippe.

Date	Mintage	VG	F	VF	XF	Unc
1619	—	—	—	175	300	—

KM# 48 2 STUIVERS

1.6200 g., 0.5830 Silver 0.0304 oz. ASW **Obv:** Crowned shield with rampant lion left holding sword and arrows divides value 2 - S **Rev:** Inscription, date **Rev. Inscription:** TRAS / ISVLA / NIA **Note:** Mint marks: lion, lily or cross,

Date	Mintage	VG	F	VF	XF	Unc
1673	3,106,053	10.00	25.00	50.00	100	—
1677	Inc. above	10.00	25.00	50.00	100	—
1678	Inc. above	10.00	25.00	50.00	100	—
1679	Inc. above	10.00	25.00	50.00	100	—
1680	Inc. above	10.00	25.00	50.00	100	—
1681	Inc. above	10.00	25.00	50.00	100	—

KM# 30 6 STUIVERS (Roosschelling)

5.2700 g., 0.5830 Billon 0.0988 oz. **Obv:** Crowned arms in inner circle, date above crown **Rev:** Floreated cross in inner circle

Date	Mintage	VG	F	VF	XF	Unc
1639	—	50.00	150	250	500	—

KM# 47 6 STUIVERS (Rijderschelling)

4.9500 g., 0.5830 Billon 0.0928 oz. **Obv:** Crowned arms divide value in inner circle, date above crown **Rev:** Knight with sword on horseback to right

Date	Mintage	VG	F	VF	XF	Unc
1679	143,111	15.00	40.00	75.00	120	—
1680	Inc. above	15.00	40.00	75.00	100	—
1681	Inc. above	15.00	40.00	75.00	100	—

KM# 50 6 STUIVERS (Rijderschelling)

Billon **Note:** Mint mark: Rose. Small planchet

Date	Mintage	VG	F	VF	XF	Unc
1680	—	15.00	40.00	75.00	100	—
1681	—	15.00	40.00	75.00	100	—
1682	—	15.00	40.00	75.00	100	—
1683	—	15.00	40.00	75.00	100	—
1684	—	15.00	40.00	75.00	100	—
1685	—	15.00	40.00	75.00	100	—
1686	—	15.00	40.00	75.00	100	—
1688	—	15.00	40.00	75.00	100	—
1689/8	—	20.00	60.00	100	170	—
1689	—	15.00	40.00	75.00	100	—
1690	—	15.00	40.00	75.00	100	—
1691	—	15.00	40.00	75.00	100	—
1696	—	15.00	40.00	75.00	100	—

KM# 55a 28 STUIVERS (Florin)

30.5000 g., Gold **Obv:** Crowned arms in inner circle, date at top above crown **Rev:** Crowned double-headed eagle with value in orb on breast in inner circle **Note:** Mint mark: Rose.

Date	Mintage	VG	F	VF	XF	Unc
1685	—	—	—	5,000	7,000	—

KM# 55 28 STUIVERS (Florin)

19.5000 g., 0.6730 Silver 0.4219 oz. ASW **Obv:** Crowned arms in inner circle, date at top above crown **Rev:** Crowned double-headed eagle with value in orb on breast in inner circle **Note:** Mint mark: Rose. This coin appears with countermarks of HOL, FRI, UTR, TRAN and G.O.

Date	Mintage	VG	F	VF	XF	Unc
1685	228,000	60.00	120	200	400	—
1686	Inc. above	60.00	120	200	400	—
1688	Inc. above	70.00	160	250	500	—
1689	Inc. above	60.00	120	200	400	—

KM# 56 30 STUIVERS (1 Daalder)

15.8800 g., 0.9060 Silver 0.4625 oz. ASW **Obv:** Standing knight with sword behind crowned arms to left **Rev:** Crowned arms of Deventer, Zwolle and Kampen in triangle in inner circle, value and date in angles **Note:** Mint mark: Rose.

Date	Mintage	VG	F	VF	XF	Unc
1685	352,827	30.00	80.00	150	300	—
1686	Inc. above	30.00	80.00	150	300	—
1689	Inc. above	30.00	80.00	150	300	—
1690	Inc. above	30.00	80.00	150	300	—
1691	Inc. above	30.00	80.00	150	300	—
1692	Inc. above	40.00	100	175	350	—

KM# 56a 30 STUIVERS (1 Daalder)

27.7600 g., Gold **Obv:** Standing knight with sword behind crowned arms to left **Rev:** Crowned arms of Deventer, Zwolle and Kampen in triangle in inner circle, value and date in angles

Date	Mintage	VG	F	VF	XF	Unc
1690 1 known	—	—	—	—	14,000	—

KM# 63.1 GULDEN

10.6100 g., 0.9200 Silver 0.3138 oz. ASW **Obv:** Crowned arms of Overyssel divide value **Rev:** Standing female figure leaning on Bible on column, holding spear with Liberty cap, date below figure **Note:** Mint mark: Rose.

Date	Mintage	VG	F	VF	XF	Unc
1698	88,170	15.00	30.00	75.00	150	—

KM# 62 2 GULDEN
21.2100 g., 0.9200 Silver 0.6273 oz. ASW **Obv:** Crowned arms divide value **Rev:** Standing female figure leaning on Bible on column, holding spear with Liberty cap, date below figure

Date	Mintage	VG	F	VF	XF	Unc
1697	—	100	250	450	750	—

KM# 52 3 GULDEN (60 Stuiver)
Silver **Rev:** Figure divides date **Note:** Dav. #4956.

Date	Mintage	VG	F	VF	XF	Unc
1681	Inc. above	70.00	200	400	750	—
1682	Inc. above	70.00	200	400	750	—
1683	Inc. above	70.00	200	400	750	—
1684	Inc. above	150	300	750	1,400	—

KM# 51 3 GULDEN (60 Stuiver)
31.8200 g., 0.9200 Silver 0.9412 oz. ASW **Obv:** Crowned arms divide value, date above **Rev:** Standing female figure leaning on Bible column, holding spear with Liberty cap **Note:** Mint mark: Rose. Dav. #4955.

Date	Mintage	VG	F	VF	XF	Unc
1681	215,697	70.00	200	400	600	—
1682	Inc. above	70.00	200	400	600	—
1683	Inc. above	70.00	200	400	600	—
1684	Inc. above	150	300	750	1,100	—

KM# 54 3 GULDEN (60 Stuiver)
31.8200 g., 0.9200 Silver 0.9412 oz. ASW **Note:** Date on obverse and reverse.

Date	Mintage	VG	F	VF	XF	Unc
1682	Inc. above	125	350	700	900	—

KM# 60 3 GULDEN (60 Stuiver)
31.8200 g., Silver **Obv:** Crowned arms of Overyssel divide value **Rev:** Standing female figure leaning on Bible on column, holding spear with Liberty cap, date below figure **Note:** Mint mark: Rose. Dav. #4957.

Date	Mintage	VG	F	VF	XF	Unc
1694/1594	Inc. above	50.00	200	350	600	—
1694	Inc. above	40.00	150	250	450	—
1695	Inc. above	40.00	150	250	450	—
1697/96	Inc. above	50.00	200	350	600	—
1697	Inc. above	40.00	150	250	450	—

KM# 46 1/2 DUCATON ((20 Stuiver))
16.3000 g., 0.9410 Silver 0.4931 oz. ASW **Obv:** Knight with sword on horseback right, provincial arms below in inner circle **Rev:** Crowned arms with crowned lion supporters in inner circle, date at top in legend

Date	Mintage	VG	F	VF	XF	Unc
1677	—	150	450	825	1,650	—

KM# 35 DUCATON (40 Stuiver)
32.7800 g., 0.9410 Silver 0.9917 oz. ASW **Obv:** Knight with sword on horseback right, provincial arms below in inner circle **Rev:** Crowned arms with crowned lion supporters in inner circle, date at top in legend **Note:** Mint mark: Sun. Dav. #4935.

Date	Mintage	VG	F	VF	XF	Unc
1659	—	50.00	100	200	375	—
1660	—	50.00	100	200	375	—
1661	—	50.00	100	200	375	—
1662	—	40.00	80.00	200	375	—
1663/2	—	80.00	225	450	800	—
1663	—	40.00	80.00	200	375	—
1664	—	40.00	80.00	200	375	—
1665	—	60.00	150	250	500	—
1666	—	40.00	80.00	200	375	—
1668	—	40.00	80.00	200	375	—
1669	—	60.00	150	250	500	—

KM# 41.1 DUCATON (40 Stuiver)
Silver **Obv:** Smaller knight and horse with crowned arms below **Rev:** Date in Cartouche **Note:** Mint mark: Rose. Dav. #4936.

Date	Mintage	VG	F	VF	XF	Unc
1675	—	60.00	130	275	550	—
1676	—	60.00	120	240	475	—
1677	—	60.00	120	240	475	—

KM# 41.2 DUCATON (40 Stuiver)
Silver **Obv:** Smaller knight and horse with crowned arms below **Rev:** Date at top in legend **Note:** Mintmark: Rose. Dav.#4936

Date	Mintage	VG	F	VF	XF	Unc
1675	—	60.00	120	240	475	—
1676	—	60.00	120	240	475	—
1677	—	60.00	120	240	475	—
1678	—	60.00	120	240	475	—
1679	—	60.00	120	240	475	—
1680	—	60.00	120	240	475	—
1682	5,923	80.00	225	450	800	—

KM# 36.1 DUCAT (48 Stuiver)
28.2500 g., 0.8730 Silver 0.7929 oz. ASW **Obv:** Armoured knight standing holding sword behind shield of arms, date at sides in inner circle **Rev:** Crowned arms in inner circle **Note:** Mint mark: Sun. Dav. #4899.

Date	Mintage	VG	F	VF	XF	Unc
1659	156,397	40.00	125	200	400	—
1660	Inc. above	40.00	125	200	400	—
1661	Inc. above	50.00	175	250	450	—
1662	Inc. above	40.00	125	200	400	—
1663	Inc. above	50.00	175	250	450	—
1664	Inc. above	50.00	175	250	450	—

KM# 36.2 DUCAT (48 Stuiver)
Silver **Obv:** Armoured knight standing holding sword behind shield of arms, date at sides in inner circle **Rev:** Crowned arms in inner circle **Note:** Mint mark: Rose. Varieties exist.

Date	Mintage	VG	F	VF	XF	Unc
1676	96,335	50.00	175	250	350	—
1677	Inc. above	50.00	175	300	500	—
1679	Inc. above	50.00	175	250	350	—
1680	Inc. above	50.00	175	250	350	—
1681	Inc. above	50.00	175	300	500	—
1683	Inc. above	50.00	175	250	350	—

KM# 61 DUCAT (48 Stuiver)
28.2500 g., Silver **Obv:** Standing, armored knight with crowned shield at feet **Rev:** Crowned arms of Overyssel divides date **Note:** Mint mark: Rose. Dav. #4900.

Date	Mintage	VG	F	VF	XF	Unc
1695/65 Error	506,773	70.00	150	300	600	—
1695	Inc. above	60.00	120	200	400	—
1698	Inc. above	60.00	120	200	400	—
1699/5	Inc. above	60.00	130	250	500	—
1699	172,202	60.00	120	200	400	—
1700	Inc. above	60.00	120	200	400	650

KM# 10.1 1/2 DAALDER (Dutch Rijks - 24 Stuiver)
14.5100 g., 0.8850 Silver 0.4128 oz. ASW **Obv:** Laureate 1/2 figure holding sword and arms in inner circle **Obv. Legend:** MO ARG PRO - CONFOE BEL(G) TRAN(SIS) **Rev:** Crowned arms divide date in inner circle **Rev. Legend:** CONCORDIA RES PARVAE CRESCVNT mintmark or cross **Note:** Mintmark: Rose

Date	Mintage	VG	F	VF	XF	Unc
1606	—	55.00	150	300	400	—
1610	—	45.00	100	200	300	—
1612	—	45.00	100	200	300	—
1613	—	45.00	100	200	300	—
1614	—	45.00	100	200	300	—
1614/13	—	55.00	150	300	400	—
1616	—	45.00	100	200	300	—
1618	—	45.00	100	200	350	—
1619	—	45.00	100	200	350	—
1620	—	45.00	100	200	300	—
1621	—	45.00	100	200	300	—
1623	—	45.00	100	200	300	—
1628	—	45.00	100	200	300	—
1629	—	45.00	100	200	300	—

KM# 10.2 1/2 DAALDER (Dutch Rijks - 24 Stuiver)
14.5100 g., 0.8850 Silver 0.4128 oz. ASW **Obv:** Laureate 1/2 figure holding sword and arms in inner circle **Obv. Legend:** MO ARG PRO - CONFOE BEL(G) TRAN(SIS) **Rev:** Crowned arms divide date in inner circle **Rev. Legend:** CONCORDIA RES PARVAE CRESCVNT mintmark or cross **Note:** Mintmark: Rose on both sides

Date	Mintage	VG	F	VF	XF	Unc
1606	—	55.00	150	300	400	—
1610	—	45.00	100	200	300	—
1612	—	45.00	100	200	300	—
1614	—	45.00	100	200	300	—
1614/13	—	55.00	150	300	400	—

KM# 10.4 1/2 DAALDER (Dutch Rijks - 24 Stuiver)
14.5100 g., 0.8850 Silver 0.4128 oz. ASW **Obv:** Laureate 1/2 figure holding sword and arms in inner circle. Mintmark cross. **Obv. Legend:** MO ARG PRO - CONFOE BEL(G) TRAN(SIS) **Rev:** Crowned arms divide date in inner circle. Mintmark rose. **Rev. Legend:** CONCORDIA RES PARVAE CRESCVNT mintmark or cross

Date	Mintage	VG	F	VF	XF	Unc
1618	—	80.00	200	400	600	—
1620	—	80.00	200	400	600	—

KM# 10.5 1/2 DAALDER (Dutch Rijks - 24 Stuiver)
14.5100 g., 0.8850 Silver 0.4128 oz. ASW **Obv:** Laureate 1/2 figure holding sword and arms in inner circle. Mintmark rose. **Obv. Legend:** MO ARG PRO - CONFOE BEL(G) TRAN(SIS) **Rev:** Crowned arms divide date in inner circle **Rev. Legend:** CONCORDIA RES PARVAE CRESCVNT mintmark or cross

Date	Mintage	VG	F	VF	XF	Unc
1619	—	45.00	100	200	300	—

KM# 10.3 1/2 DAALDER (Dutch Rijks - 24 Stuiver)
14.5100 g., 0.8850 Silver 0.4128 oz. ASW **Obv:** Laureate 1/2 figure holding sword and arms in inner circle **Obv. Legend:** MO ARG PRO - CONFOE BEL(G) TRAN(SIS) **Rev:** Crowned arms divide date in inner circle **Rev. Legend:** CONCORDIA RES PARVAE CRESCVNT mintmark or cross **Note:** Mintmark: Obv. Rose, Rev. Cross

Date	Mintage	VG	F	VF	XF	Unc
1620	—	45.00	100	200	300	—
1621	—	45.00	100	200	300	—

KM# 11.1 1/2 DAALDER (Lion - 24 Stuiver)
13.8400 g., 0.7500 Silver 0.3337 oz. ASW **Obv:** Armoured knight looking to right above lion shield in inner circle **Rev:** Rampant lion to left in inner circle, date at top in legend

Date	Mintage	VG	F	VF	XF	Unc
1606	—	35.00	80.00	150	250	—
1608	—	35.00	80.00	150	250	—
1610	—	35.00	80.00	150	250	—
1611	—	35.00	80.00	150	250	—
1612	—	35.00	80.00	150	250	—
1613/2	—	50.00	100	200	375	—
1613	—	35.00	80.00	150	250	—
1614	—	35.00	80.00	150	250	—
1615	—	35.00	80.00	150	250	—
1615/2	—	50.00	100	200	375	—
1616	—	50.00	100	200	375	—
1616/Z	—	50.00	100	200	375	—
1617	—	35.00	80.00	150	250	—
1622	—	35.00	80.00	150	250	—
1629	—	35.00	80.00	150	250	—
1629/8	—	35.00	80.00	150	250	—
1633	—	35.00	80.00	150	250	—
1637	—	35.00	80.00	150	250	—
1639	—	35.00	80.00	150	250	—
1640	—	35.00	80.00	150	250	—
1641	—	50.00	100	200	375	—
1643	—	50.00	100	200	375	—

KM# 11.2 1/2 DAALDER (Lion - 24 Stuiver)
13.8400 g., 0.7500 Silver 0.3337 oz. ASW **Obv:** Armoured knight looking to right above lion shield looking right **Rev:** Rampant lion to left in inner circle, date at top in legend

Date	Mintage	VG	F	VF	XF	Unc
1614	—	60.00	165	325	650	—
1615/12	—	60.00	165	325	650	—
1616	—	60.00	165	325	650	—
1616/12	—	60.00	165	325	650	—
1617	—	60.00	165	325	650	—

KM# 12 DAALDER (Lion - 24 Stuiver)
27.6800 g., 0.7500 Silver 0.6674 oz. ASW **Rev:** Date at top in legend

Date	Mintage	VG	F	VF	XF	Unc
1606	—	40.00	100	175	450	—
1607	—	25.00	75.00	125	350	—
1608/7	—	40.00	100	175	450	—
1608	—	25.00	75.00	125	350	—
1610	—	25.00	75.00	125	350	—
1611/08	—	40.00	100	175	450	—
1611	—	25.00	75.00	125	350	—
1612	—	25.00	75.00	125	350	—
1613/1	—	40.00	100	175	450	—
1613/2	—	40.00	100	175	450	—
1613	—	25.00	75.00	125	350	—
1614	—	25.00	75.00	125	350	—
1615/2/08	—	40.00	100	175	450	—
1615/2	—	40.00	100	175	450	—
1615	—	40.00	100	175	450	—
1616/2	—	40.00	100	175	450	—
1616/3	—	40.00	100	175	450	—
1616	—	40.00	100	175	450	—
1617/6	—	40.00	100	175	450	—
1617	—	40.00	100	175	450	—
1619	—	40.00	100	175	450	—
1621/13	—	40.00	100	175	450	—
16ZZ	—	25.00	75.00	125	350	—
1622	—	25.00	75.00	125	350	—
1623/1	—	40.00	100	175	450	—
1623/2	—	40.00	100	175	450	—
1623	—	40.00	100	175	450	—
1628/2	—	40.00	100	175	450	—
1628	—	40.00	100	175	450	—
1629/16	—	40.00	100	175	450	—
1629/2	—	40.00	100	175	450	—
1629/7	—	40.00	100	175	450	—
1629/8/2	—	40.00	100	175	450	—
1629/8	—	40.00	100	175	450	—
1629	—	40.00	100	175	450	—
1631	—	40.00	100	175	450	—
1632	—	40.00	100	175	450	—
1633/23	—	25.00	75.00	125	350	—
1633	—	25.00	75.00	125	350	—
1634	—	25.00	75.00	125	350	—
1636	—	25.00	75.00	125	350	—
1637	—	25.00	75.00	125	350	—
1639	—	25.00	75.00	125	350	—
1640	—	25.00	75.00	125	350	—
1641	—	25.00	75.00	125	350	—
1642	—	25.00	75.00	125	350	—
1643/2	—	40.00	100	175	450	—
1643	—	25.00	75.00	125	350	—
1644	—	40.00	100	175	450	—
1645	—	40.00	100	175	450	—
1647	—	40.00	100	175	450	—
1656	—	40.00	100	175	450	—
1663	—	40.00	100	175	450	—
1666	—	40.00	100	175	450	—
1683	—	40.00	100	175	450	—
1684	—	40.00	100	175	450	—

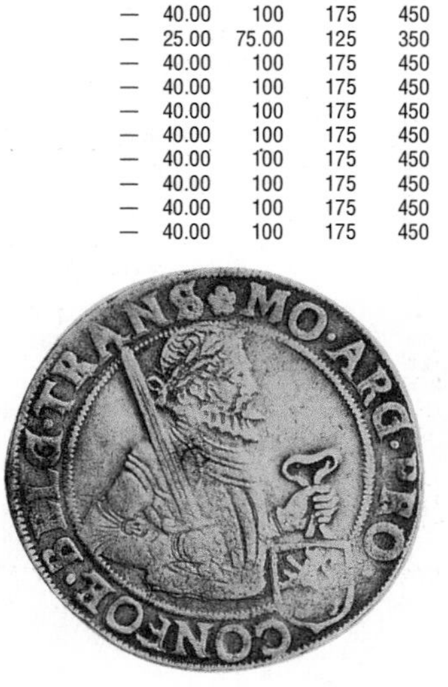

KM# 13 DAALDER (Rijks)
29.0300 g., 0.8850 Silver 0.8260 oz. ASW **Obv:** Laureate 1/2 figure holding sword and arms in inner circle **Rev:** Crowned arms divide date **Note:** Mint mark: Rose.

Date	Mintage	VG	F	VF	XF	Unc
1606	—	50.00	110	200	300	—
1607	—	35.00	80.00	125	250	—
1610/07	—	35.00	80.00	125	250	—
1610	—	35.00	80.00	125	250	—
1611/0	—	75.00	150	250	450	—
1612/11	—	—	—	—	—	—
1612	—	35.00	80.00	125	250	—
1614/2	—	50.00	110	200	300	—
1614	—	50.00	110	200	300	—
1616/4	—	50.00	110	200	300	—
1616	—	50.00	110	200	300	—
1617	—	75.00	150	250	450	—
1618/17	—	50.00	110	200	300	—
1618	—	35.00	80.00	125	250	—
1619	—	35.00	80.00	125	250	—
1620	—	35.00	80.00	125	250	—
1621	—	35.00	80.00	125	250	—
1622	—	50.00	110	175	350	—
1623/2	—	100	200	200	300	—
1623	—	50.00	110	200	300	—
1628	—	50.00	110	175	300	—
1629	—	75.00	150	250	350	—
1651	—	—	—	—	—	—

KM# 44.4 DAALDER (Rijks)
29.0300 g., 0.8850 Silver 0.8260 oz. ASW **Obv:** Laureate 1/2 figure holding sword and arms in inner circle **Rev:** Crowned arms divide date. Mintmark cross.

Date	Mintage	VG	F	VF	XF	Unc
1607	—	35.00	80.00	125	250	—
1612	—	35.00	80.00	125	250	—
1614	—	35.00	80.00	125	250	—
1614/2	—	50.00	110	200	300	—
1618	—	35.00	80.00	125	250	—

KM# 44.3 DAALDER (Rijks)
Silver **Obv:** Laureate 1/2 figure holding sword and arms in inner circle. **Rev:** Crowned arms divide date. Rev. rose

Date	Mintage	VG	F	VF	XF	Unc
1618	—	35.00	80.00	125	250	—
1619	—	35.00	80.00	125	250	—
1620	—	35.00	80.00	125	250	—

KM# 44.1 DAALDER (Rijks)
Silver **Rev:** Date at top in legend **Note:** Varieties exist.

Date	Mintage	VG	F	VF	XF	Unc
1676	42,130	70.00	200	375	750	—
1677	Inc. above	70.00	200	375	750	—

KM# 44.2 DAALDER (Rijks)
Silver **Rev:** Date at top in legend

Date	Mintage	VG	F	VF	XF	Unc
1688	14,750	70.00	200	375	750	—

KM# 64 DAALDER (Rijks)
Silver **Obv:** Laureate 1/2 figure holding sword and arms in inner circle **Obv. Legend:** MO NO ARG CON(FOE) - BELG PRO TRANS **Rev:** Crowned arms divide date. With or without inner circle. **Note:** Mintmark rose. Dav. #4861.

Date	Mintage	VG	F	VF	XF	Unc
1699	9,830	80.00	250	400	750	—

:M# 42.1 DAALDER (Lion)

7.6800 g., 0.7500 Silver 0.6674 oz. ASW **Obv:** Knight without lume in helmet **Note:** Mint mark: Rose.

ate	Mintage	VG	F	VF	XF	Unc
675/4	216,531	40.00	100	175	450	—
675	Inc. above	25.00	75.00	125	350	—
676	Inc. above	25.00	75.00	125	350	—
677	Inc. above	25.00	75.00	125	350	—
678	Inc. above	40.00	100	175	450	—
679	Inc. above	25.00	75.00	125	350	—
680	Inc. above	25.00	75.00	125	350	—
681	Inc. above	25.00	75.00	125	350	—
682	Inc. above	25.00	75.00	125	350	—
683	Inc. above	25.00	75.00	125	350	—
684	Inc. above	40.00	100	175	450	—
685	Inc. above	40.00	100	175	450	—
688	Inc. above	25.00	75.00	125	350	—
689/8	Inc. above	25.00	75.00	125	350	—
689	Inc. above	25.00	75.00	125	350	—
690	Inc. above	40.00	100	175	450	—
692	Inc. above	40.00	100	175	450	—
697	330,489	25.00	75.00	125	350	—
698	Inc. above	40.00	100	175	450	—
699	Inc. above	40.00	100	175	450	—
700	Inc. above	25.00	75.00	125	350	—

:M# 42.2 DAALDER (Lion)

ilver **Obv:** Knight without plume in helmet **Note:** Without mint ark.

ate	Mintage	VG	F	VF	XF	Unc
676	Inc. above	25.00	75.00	125	350	—
683	Inc. above	25.00	75.00	125	350	—
684	Inc. above	25.00	75.00	125	350	—

M# 5 DAALDER (Lion - 48 Stuivers)

ilver **Obv:** Armored knight looking to right above lion shield in ner circle, date divided at bottom **Rev:** Rampant lion to left in ner circle

ate	Mintage	VG	F	VF	XF	Unc
602	—	50.00	125	250	500	—

:M# 6 DAALDER (Leicester - 48 Stuivers)

9.2400 g., 0.8880 Silver 0.8348 oz. ASW **Obv:** Laureate bust Leicester holding sword and arrows in inner circle. **Rev:** Shield arms of the 7 provinces with date above in inner circle

ate	Mintage	VG	F	VF	XF	Unc
603	—	350	1,000	2,000	3,000	—

M# 14 1/2 CAVALIER D'OR

.0000 g., 0.9200 Gold 0.1479 oz. AGW **Obv:** Equestrian knight ght above arms in inner circle **Rev:** Crowned arms in inner circle, ate at top **Note:** Fr. #272.

ate	Mintage	VG	F	VF	XF	Unc
606	—	225	450	900	1,600	—
067 (error)	23,480	225	450	900	1,600	—
607	Inc. above	225	450	900	1,600	—
609	—	225	450	900	1,600	—
610	—	225	450	900	1,600	—
616	—	225	450	900	1,600	—

:M# 16.1 CAVALIER D'OR

0.0000 g., 0.9200 Gold 0.2958 oz. AGW **Obv:** Equestrian night above arms in inner circle **Rev:** Crowned arms in inner rcle, date at top **Note:** FR. #271.

ate	Mintage	VG	F	VF	XF	Unc
067 (error)	—	450	900	1,800	2,600	—
607	—	450	800	1,600	2,400	—
616/07	—	450	900	1,800	2,600	—
617	—	450	800	1,600	2,400	—
620	—	450	800	1,600	2,400	—

M# 16.2 CAVALIER D'OR

0.0000 g., 0.9200 Gold 0.2958 oz. AGW **Obv:** Equestrian night above arms in inner circle **Rev:** Crowned arms in inner rcle, shield between date

ate	Mintage	VG	F	VF	XF	Unc
616	—	450	800	1,600	2,400	—

:M# 16.3 CAVALIER D'OR

0.0000 g., 0.9200 Gold 0.2958 oz. AGW **Obv:** Equestrian night above arms in inner circle **Rev:** Crowned arms in inner rcle, date at top **Note:** Mintmark rose.

ate	Mintage	VG	F	VF	XF	Unc
620	—	450	800	1,600	2,400	—

TRADE COINAGE

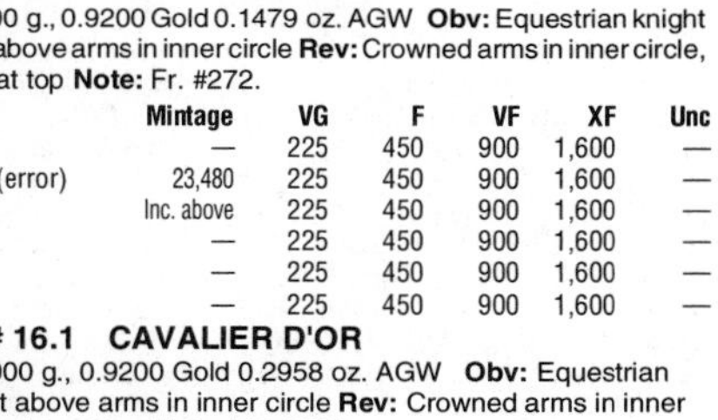

M# 7 DUCAT

.5000 g., 0.9860 Gold 0.1109 oz. AGW **Obv:** Knight standing ght divides date in inner circle **Rev:** 5-line inscripton on tablet ote: Fr. #268.

ate	Mintage	VG	F	VF	XF	Unc
603	49,000	135	250	350	650	—
604	Inc. above	120	150	200	400	—
606	187,250	120	150	200	400	—
607	Inc. above	120	150	200	400	—
608/7	252,490	125	210	300	550	—
608	Inc. above	120	150	200	400	—

Date	Mintage	VG	F	VF	XF	Unc
1610	Inc. above	125	210	300	550	—
1611	96,250	135	250	350	650	—
1612	Inc. above	120	150	200	400	—
1613/2	Inc. above	120	150	200	400	—
1613	Inc. above	120	150	200	400	—
1614/3	Inc. above	125	210	300	550	—
1614	Inc. above	120	150	200	400	—
1616	Inc. above	120	150	200	400	—
1630	Inc. above	125	250	350	650	—
1631/16	Inc. above	125	210	300	550	—
1631/0	Inc. above	125	210	300	550	—
1631	Inc. above	120	150	200	400	—
1633/11	Inc. above	125	210	300	550	—
1633	Inc. above	120	150	200	400	—
1634	Inc. above	135	250	350	650	—
1635	Inc. above	135	250	350	650	—
1636/1	Inc. above	135	250	350	650	—
1636/3	Inc. above	135	250	350	650	—
1636	Inc. above	135	250	350	650	—
1637	Inc. above	120	150	200	400	—
1638	Inc. above	135	250	350	650	—
1640	Inc. above	135	250	350	650	—
1646	21,319	135	250	350	650	—
1660	Inc. above	135	250	350	650	—
1662	Inc. above	135	250	350	650	—
1664	Inc. above	135	250	350	650	—
1666	Inc. above	135	250	350	650	—

KM# 21 DUCAT

3.5000 g., 0.9860 Gold 0.1109 oz. AGW **Note:** Klippe. Fr. # 268a.

Date	Mintage	VG	F	VF	XF	Unc
1615	—	—	—	—	4,000	6,000
1616	—	—	—	—	4,000	6,000

KM# 40 DUCAT

3.5000 g., 0.9860 Gold 0.1109 oz. AGW **Rev:** Rosette in small shield below tablet

Date	Mintage	VG	F	VF	XF	Unc
1673	41,393	150	325	600	1,000	—
1675	Inc. above	150	325	600	1,000	—
1676	Inc. above	150	325	600	1,000	—
1678	Inc. above	150	325	600	1,000	—

KM# 53 DUCAT

3.5000 g., 0.9860 Gold 0.1109 oz. AGW **Obv:** Knight standing right divides date, without inner circle **Rev:** 5-line inscription on tablet **Note:** Fr. #268.

Date	Mintage	VG	F	VF	XF	Unc
1681	—	125	250	400	600	—
1688	—	125	250	400	600	—
1689/8	—	125	250	400	600	—

KM# 104 2 DUCAT

7.0200 g., Gold **Obv:** Knight standing right divides date in inner circle **Obv. Legend:** CONCORDIA RES - PA - RVAE CRES TRAN - S. **Rev:** 5-line inscription on tablet **Rev. Legend:** MO AVR/PROVIN/CONFOE/BELG AD/LEG IMP **Note:** FR. #268

Date	Mintage	VG	F	VF	XF	Unc
1607	—	—	—	—	—	—
1660	—	—	—	—	—	—

PATTERNS

Including off metal strikes

KM#	Date	Mintage	Identification	Mkt Val
Pn1	1606	—	Ducat, Silver, 6.2000 g. Klippe, KM#7	
Pn2	ND(1607)	—	Duit, Silver, 3.4000 g. KM#22	
Pn3	1616	—	24 Stuivers, Silver, Klippe, Double weight, KM#11	
Pn4	1617	—	2 /styuversm /sukverm 7,3999 g, Jkuooem JN#18	600
Pn5	1619	—	2 Stuivers, 3.7000 g. Klippe, KM#19	600
Pn6	1628	—	Duit. Gold. 5.2500 g. KM#22.	—
Pn7	1628	—	Duit. Copper. KM#22. Klippe. Weight 4.4 / 5.5 / 8 or 9.5g.	250
Pn8	1631	—	2 Stuivers. Gold. 6.9000 g. KM#19	—
Pn9	1679	—	6 Stuivers. Gold. 10.5000 g. KM#47.	—

PIEFORTS

KM#	Date	Mintage	Identification	Mkt Val
P1	1607	—	2 Ducat, Gold, 27.3000 g. KM#104	
P2	1607	—	Ducat. Gold. 7.3000 g. KM#7.	—
P3	1616	—	Ducat. Gold. KM#7. Klippe.	6,000
P4	1616	—	Cavalier D'Or. Gold. KM16	—
P5	1620	—	24 Stuivers. Silver. Klippe. Double weight. KM#10.3	2,000
P6	1620	—	Daalder. Silver. Klippe. Double weight. KM#13	—
P7	1620	—	Daalder. Silver. 28.6000 g. Klippe. Double weight. KM#13	—
P8	1628	—	Duit. Copper. Klippe, KM22.	—
P9	1633	—	Daalder. Silver. KM12. Klippe.	—
P10	1660	—	Ducaton. Silver. KM35	—
P11	1660	—	Ducat. Silver. Double weight. KM#36.1.	2,000
P12	1661	—	Ducaton. Silver. KM35	—
P13	1668	—	Ducaton. Silver. KM35.	3,000
P14	1680	—	Ducaton. Silver. Double weight. KM#41	3,000
P15	1686	—	6 Stuivers. Silver. Double weight. KM#50	800

DEVENTER

CITY

STANDARD COINAGE

KM# 7 DUIT

Copper **Obv:** Crowned arms on cross **Rev:** Inscription in sprays **Rev. Inscription:** DA / VEN / TRIA / date **Note:** (Or 1/8 Stuiver)

Date	Mintage	Good	VG	F	VF	XF
1602	—	6.00	15.00	40.00	80.00	120
1605	—	6.00	15.00	40.00	80.00	120
1615	—	12.00	30.00	60.00	100	200
1617	—	6.00	15.00	40.00	80.00	120
1618	—	12.00	30.00	60.00	100	200

KM# 47 DUIT

3.5000 g., Copper **Obv:** Crowned city arms **Rev:** Inscription **Rev. Inscription:** DA / VEN / TRIA

Date	Mintage	Good	VG	F	VF	XF
ND(1628)	200,000	3.00	10.00	30.00	55.00	70.00

KM# 47b DUIT

5.9000 g., Silver **Obv:** Crowned city arms **Rev:** Inscription **Note:** Prev. KM#7a

Date	Mintage	Good	VG	F	VF	XF
ND(1628)	—	15.00	40.00	125	200	300

KM# 47a DUIT

Silver **Obv:** Crowned city arms. **Rev:** Inscription **Rev. Inscription:** DA / VEN / TRIA **Note:** Prev. KM #7a.

Date	Mintage	Good	VG	F	VF	XF
ND(1628)	—	10.00	25.00	75.00	125	200

KM# 66 DUIT

1.9000 g., Copper **Obv:** Crowned arms in sprays **Rev:** Inscription in sprays **Rev. Inscription:** DA / VEN / TRIA / date

Date	Mintage	Good	VG	F	VF	XF
1663	—	4.00	10.00	30.00	50.00	80.00

KM# 66a DUIT

7.0000 g., Silver **Obv:** Crowned arms in sprays **Rev:** Inscription in sprays **Rev. Inscription:** DA / VEN / TRIA / date **Note:** Klippe.

Date	Mintage	Good	VG	F	VF	XF
1663	—	—	—	—	—	—

KM# 4 1/8 STUIVER

Silver (Or 1/8 Stuiver) **Obv:** 4-fold arms **Obv. Inscription:** DAV. **Note:** Uniface.

Date	Mintage	Good	VG	F	VF	XF
ND(1602)	—	100	300	800	2,000	3,500

KM# 60 1/2 STUIVER

1.0000 g., Billon **Obv:** Crowned arms divide value in inner circle, crown divides date **Rev:** Ornate long cross with H-S-D-E in angles in inner circle

Date	Mintage	Good	VG	F	VF	XF
ND(1629)	192,650	8.00	20.00	50.00	100	150

KM# 61 STUIVER

1.7000 g., Billon **Obv:** Crowned arms divide value in inner circle **Rev:** Ornamental long cross with quatrefoil around center

Date	Mintage	Good	VG	F	VF	XF
ND	16,900	25.00	75.00	150	300	400
1663	Inc. above	25.00	75.00	150	300	400

KM# 83c STUIVER

15.8800 g., 0.9060 Silver 0.4625 oz. ASW **Obv:** Crowned arms **Rev:** Standing knight, between 30 - ST, with sword behind crowned arms to left, date in legend. **Note:** Value on both sides

Date	Mintage	Good	VG	F	VF	XF
1685Sitting dog	—	25.00	60.00	125	200	350

KM# 90 STUIVER (WEAPON)

1.3000 g., 0.5830 Silver 0.0244 oz. ASW **Obv:** Crowned arms divide value in sprays **Rev. Inscription:** DAVEN / TRIA / date

Date	Mintage	Good	VG	F	VF	XF
1691	490,000	6.00	15.00	35.00	70.00	140

KM# 8 2 STUIVERS

1.8000 g., Billon **Obv:** Arms in inner circle and MON NO CIVIT IMPER DAV(E) **Rev:** Orb divides date in inner circle and RVDOL II ROM IMP SEM AV

Date	Mintage	Good	VG	F	VF	XF
1602	—	16.00	60.00	150	300	500

KM# 77 2 STUIVERS

1.7300 g., 0.5830 Silver 0.0324 oz. ASW **Obv:** Crowned rampant lion left holding sword and arrows, value at sides **Rev:** DAVEN/TRIA/(date) **Note:** Mint mark: Sitting dog.

Date	Mintage	VG	F	VF	XF	Unc
1683	290,000	7.50	25.00	50.00	80.00	—

Date	Mintage	VG	F	VF	XF	Unc
1685	61,000	7.50	25.00	50.00	80.00	—
1687	—	7.50	25.00	40.00	50.00	—

KM# 31 5 STUIVERS (1/10 Arendsrijksdaalder)
2.9000 g., 0.8850 Silver 0.0825 oz. ASW **Obv:** Crowned double-headed eagle with value on breast in inner circle **Rev:** Sheild of arms with plumed helmet above

Date	Mintage	Good	VG	F	VF	XF
ND(1619) w/o value	109,000	60.00	150	250	600	1,200

KM# 6 6 STUIVERS (Roosschelling)
5.2700 g., 0.5830 Silver 0.0988 oz. ASW **Obv:** Crowned arms in wreath in inner circle, date at top in legend, titles of Rudolph II **Rev:** Ornamental cross in inner circle

Date	Mintage	Good	VG	F	VF	XF
1601	—	16.00	40.00	100	200	300

KM# 32 6 STUIVERS (Roosschelling)
5.2800 g., Silver **Obv:** Crowned arms in wreath in inner circle, date at top in legend, titles of Ferdinand II **Rev:** Ornamental cross in inner circle

Date	Mintage	Good	VG	F	VF	XF
ND(1623)	37,000	12.00	20.00	50.00	80.00	150

KM# 78 6 STUIVERS (Rijderschelling)
0.5830 Silver **Obv:** Crowned arms divide value, date above crown **Rev:** Knight with sword on horseback right **Note:** Mint mark: Sitting dog. Varieties exist. Weight varies 4.71 - 4.95 g.

Date	Mintage	Good	VG	F	VF	XF
1683	16,000	4.00	10.00	30.00	50.00	90.00
1684	—	3.00	7.50	20.00	40.00	60.00
1685	364,000	3.00	7.50	20.00	40.00	60.00
1686	520,000	3.00	7.50	20.00	40.00	60.00
1688	2,000,000	3.00	7.50	20.00	40.00	60.00
1689	350,000	3.00	7.50	20.00	40.00	60.00
1690	764,000	3.00	7.50	20.00	40.00	60.00
1691	540,000	3.00	7.50	20.00	40.00	60.00

KM# 26 8 STUIVERS
8.0000 g., Silver **Obv:** Crowned eagle in inner circle **Rev:** Standing figure of St. Lubvinus divides value in inner circle, date at top in legend **Note:** (Or Langrok). Mint mark: Shamrock.

Date	Mintage	Good	VG	F	VF	XF
1618	105,000	40.00	125	300	600	900

KM# 40 8 STUIVERS
7.7000 g., Silver **Obv:** Crowned quartered arms **Rev:** Crowned imperial eagle

Date	Mintage	Good	VG	F	VF	XF
ND(1620)	32,000	40.00	125	300	600	900

KM# 41 8 STUIVERS
7.7000 g., Silver **Obv:** Mitred bust of St. Lubvinus left **Rev:** Crowned imperial eagle

Date	Mintage	Good	VG	F	VF	XF
ND(1620)	136,000	40.00	125	300	650	1,000

KM# 23 10 STUIVERS (1/5 Arendsrijksdaalder)
5.8000 g., 0.8850 Silver 0.1650 oz. ASW **Obv:** Crowned imperial eagle with value on breast **Rev:** Shield of arms with plumed helmet above

Date	Mintage	Good	VG	F	VF	XF
ND(1617)	—	60.00	150	250	600	1,200
1617	—	60.00	150	250	600	1,200
1620	—	—	—	—	—	—

KM# 27 14 STUIVERS (1/2 Florin)
10.2500 g., 0.6730 Silver 0.2218 oz. ASW **Obv:** Crowned imperial eagle **Rev:** Crowned arms with date below in inner circle **Note:** Mint mark: Shamrock.

Date	Mintage	Good	VG	F	VF	XF
1618	3,700	200	400	800	1,500	2,250

KM# 28 14 STUIVERS (1/2 Florin)
10.2500 g., 0.6730 Silver 0.2218 oz. ASW **Obv:** Date between crown and top of sheild

Date	Mintage	Good	VG	F	VF	XF
1618	Inc. above	200	400	800	1,500	2,250

KM# A66 20 STUIVERS (1/2 Ducaton)
16.3900 g., 0.9410 Silver 0.4958 oz. ASW **Obv:** Knight with sword on horseback right, city arms below in inner circle **Rev:** Crowned arms with crowned lion supporters in inner circle, date at top in legend **Note:** Mint mark: Sitting dog or head.

Date	Mintage	Good	VG	F	VF	XF
1666	—	50.00	125	350	800	1,500

KM# 75 20 STUIVERS (Gulden)
10.6100 g., 0.9200 Silver 0.3138 oz. ASW **Obv:** Crowned eagle arms divide value, date above crown **Rev:** Standing female figure leaning on Bible on column, holding spear with Libertry cap

Date	Mintage	Good	VG	F	VF	XF
1682	—	10.00	25.00	50.00	100	200
1686	—	10.00	25.00	50.00	100	200
1687	116,000	10.00	25.00	50.00	100	200

KM# 91 20 STUIVERS (Gulden)
Silver **Obv:** Crowned lion arms divide value **Rev:** Date at sides

Date	Mintage	Good	VG	F	VF	XF
1698	345,050	12.00	30.00	60.00	120	200

KM# 50 24 STUIVERS (1/2 Lion Daalder)
13.8400 g., 0.7500 Silver 0.3337 oz. ASW **Obv:** Armored knight looking right above eagle shield **Rev:** Rampant lion left in inner circle **Note:** Mint mark: Lily.

Date	Mintage	Good	VG	F	VF	XF
1640Lily	—	20.00	50.00	150	250	400

KM# A51 24 STUIVERS (1/2 Lion Daalder)
Silver **Obv:** Armored knight looking right above eagle shield **Rev:** Rampant lion left in circle **Note:** Klippe. Mint mark: Lily.

Date	Mintage	Good	VG	F	VF	XF
1640Lily	—	—	—	—	1,500	2,500

KM# 67 24 STUIVERS (1/2 Silver Ducat)
14.1200 g., 0.8730 Silver 0.3963 oz. ASW **Obv:** Armored knight standing holding sword behind shield of arms, date at sides in inner circle **Rev:** Crowned arms in inner circle **Note:** Mint mark: Sitting dog.

Date	Mintage	Good	VG	F	VF	XF
1666	—	50.00	125	350	750	1,500

KM# 14 25 STUIVERS (1/2 Arendsrijksdaalder)
Silver **Note:** 10.6 - 14.4g. Klippe. See KM#13

Date	Mintage	Good	VG	F	VF	XF
ND(1622)	—	—	—	—	—	—

KM# 13 25 STUIVERS (1/2 Arendsrijksdaalder)
14.5100 g., 0.8850 Silver 0.4128 oz. ASW **Obv:** Shield of arms with plumed helmet above in inner circle **Rev:** Crowned imperial eagle with orb on breast in inner circle

Date	Mintage	Good	VG	F	VF	XF
ND	—	—	—	400	800	1,200

KM# 25 28 STUIVERS (Florin)
20.5100 g., 0.6730 Silver 0.4438 oz. ASW **Obv:** Date between crown and top of shield **Obv. Legend:** FLOR • ARG • CI - • IMP • DAVENT **Rev:** Crowned imperial eagle with orb on breast in inner circle **Rev. Legend:** MATTH • I • D • G • ROM • IMP • ...

Date	Mintage	Good	VG	F	VF	XF
1617	—	12.00	30.00	80.00	125	250
1618/7	—	16.00	40.00	100	150	300
1618	390,000	12.00	30.00	80.00	125	250
1619	—	12.00	30.00	80.00	125	250
1621	—	12.00	30.00	80.00	125	250

KM# 24 28 STUIVERS (Florin)
20.5100 g., Silver **Obv:** Crowned arms in inner circle, date above crown, value at bottom **Obv. Legend:** FLOR x ARG x CIV x IMP x DAVENT x **Rev:** Crowned imperial eagle in inner circle, titles of Matthias **Rev. Legend:** MATH. 1 . I. D.G. ROM. IMP. SEM. AVG. **Note:** Mint mark: Shamrock.

Date	Mintage	Good	VG	F	VF	XF
1.6.1.7	—	32.00	80.00	220	400	800
1619	—	20.00	50.00	150	275	400

KM# 29 28 STUIVERS (Florin)
Silver **Rev:** Value "Z8" in orb

Date	Mintage	Good	VG	F	VF	XF
1618	—	16.00	40.00	80.00	125	250

KM# 30 28 STUIVERS (Florin)
41.6000 g., Silver **Rev:** Value "Z8" in orb **Note:** Klippe

Date	Mintage	Good	VG	F	VF	XF
1618	—	—	—	—	—	—

KM# 43.1 28 STUIVERS (Florin)
20.5100 g., Silver **Obv:** Crowned arms **Obv. Legend:** FLOR • ARG • CI - • IMP • DAVEN **Rev:** Crowned imperial eagle with "Z8 in orb on breast **Rev. Legend:** FERDNAND • II • ROM • IMP • ...

Date	Mintage	Good	VG	F	VF	X
1619	440,000	14.00	35.00	60.00	120	25
1621	170,000	14.00	35.00	60.00	120	25

KM# 43.2 28 STUIVERS (Florin)
20.5100 g., Silver **Obv:** Crowned arms **Obv. Legend:** FLOR • ARG • CI - IMP • DAVEN **Rev:** Crowned inperial eagle with error "8Z' in orb on breast **Rev. Legend:** FERDNAND • II • ROM • IMP •

Date	Mintage	Good	VG	F	VF	X
1619	—	40.00	100	170	280	40

KM# 79 28 STUIVERS (Florin)
19.6300 g., Silver **Obv:** Crowned arms divide denomination, date at top, titles of Leopold I **Obv. Legend:** FLOR. ARG. CIV DAVENTRIAE. **Rev:** Crowned imperial eagle with orb on breas **Rev. Legend:** LEOP. IGN. D.G. ELEC. ROM. IMP. SEM. AVG **Note:** Mint mark: Sitting dog.

Date	Mintage	Good	VG	F	VF	X
1684	460,000	20.00	50.00	100	220	35

KM# 81.1 28 STUIVERS (Florin)
19.6300 g., Silver **Obv:** Crowned arms in inner circle, date abov crown, titles of Ferdinand II **Obv. Legend:** FLOR. ARG. CIV. DAVENTRIAE. **Rev:** Crowned imperial eagle in inner circle, valu "28" below in cartouche **Rev. Legend:** FERDINAND. II. D.G. ROM. IMP. SEM. AVG. **Note:** Prev. KM#81. This coin appears with countermarks of HOL, FRI, UTR, and G.O.

Date	Mintage	Good	VG	F	VF	X
(16)85	364,000	10.00	20.00	50.00	100	20
(16)86	378,000	10.00	20.00	50.00	100	20
1690	—	10.00	20.00	50.00	100	20
1692	152,000	10.00	20.00	50.00	100	20

KM# 81.2 28 STUIVERS (Florin)
Silver **Obv:** Crowned arms in inner circle, date above crown, titles of Ferdinand II **Obv. Legend:** FLOR. ARG. DIV. DAVENTRIAE. **Rev:** Crowned imperial eagle in inner circle, erro value "8Z" below in cartouche

Date	Mintage	Good	VG	F	VF	X
1685	—	16.00	40.00	100	150	30

KM# 82 30 STUIVERS (Daalder)
15.8800 g., Silver **Obv:** Crowned arms with lion supporters **Rev** Standing knight with sword divides value, date in legend **Note** Mint mark: Sitting dog. Varieties exist.

Date	Mintage	Good	VG	F	VF	X
1685	387,000	25.00	60.00	125	200	35

KM# 83 30 STUIVERS (Daalder)
15.8800 g., 0.9060 Silver 0.4625 oz. ASW **Obv:** Value below arms **Rev:** Standing knight with sword behind crowned arms to left, date in legend **Note:** Varieties exist.

Date	Mintage	Good	VG	F	VF	X
1685Sitting dog	—	16.00	40.00	100	150	30
1686Sitting dog	—	16.00	40.00	100	150	30
1686Sitting dog no mintmark	—	16.00	40.00	100	150	30
1687Sitting dog	—	16.00	40.00	100	150	30
1688Sitting dog	—	16.00	40.00	100	150	30

KM# 83b 30 STUIVERS (Daalder)
15.8800 g., 0.9060 Silver 0.4625 oz. ASW **Obv:** Crowned arm **Rev:** Standing knight between 30 - ST, with sword behind crowned arms to left, date in legend. **Note:** Varieties exist.

Date	Mintage	Good	VG	F	VF	X
1685Sitting dog	—	16.00	40.00	100	150	30
1686Sitting dog	—	16.00	40.00	100	150	30
1686Sitting dog no mintmark	—	16.00	40.00	100	150	30
1687Sitting dog	—	16.00	40.00	100	150	30
1688Sitting dog	—	16.00	40.00	100	150	30

KM# 62.1 40 STUIVERS (Ducaton)

32.7800 g., 0.9410 Silver 0.9917 oz. ASW **Obv:** Knight with sword on horseback right, city arms below in inner circle **Rev:** Crowned arms with crowned lion supporters in inner circle, date at top in legend **Note:** Mint mark: Moor's head. Dav. #4944.

Date	Mintage	Good	VG	F	VF	XF
1662	—	30.00	75.00	150	300	500
1662 no mintmark	—	30.00	75.00	150	300	500
1663	—	30.00	75.00	150	300	500
1664	13,000	30.00	75.00	150	300	500

KM# 62.2 40 STUIVERS (Ducaton)

32.7800 g., 0.9410 Silver 0.9917 oz. ASW **Obv:** Knight on horseback right, city arms below in inner circle **Rev:** Crowned arms with crowned lion supporters in inner circle, date at top in legend. **Note:** Mint mark: Sitting dog. Varieties exist. Dav. #4944.

Date	Mintage	Good	VG	F	VF	XF
1664	Inc. above	30.00	75.00	150	300	500
1665	—	30.00	75.00	150	300	500
1666	—	30.00	75.00	150	300	500
1667	—	30.00	75.00	150	300	500
1668	—	30.00	75.00	150	300	500

KM# 51 48 STUIVERS (Lion Daalder)

27.6800 g., 0.7500 Silver 0.6674 oz. ASW **Obv:** Rampant lion left in inner circle **Rev:** Armored knight left in inner circle **Note:** Mint mark: Lily. Dav. #4873.

Date	Mintage	Good	VG	F	VF	XF
1640	7,000	30.00	75.00	150	300	500

KM# 52 48 STUIVERS (Lion Daalder)

27.9000 g., Silver **Obv:** Rampant lion left in inner circle **Rev:** Armored knight left in inner circle **Note:** Klippe. Mint mark: Lily.Dav. #A4873.

Date	Mintage	Good	VG	F	VF	XF
1640	—	30.00	75.00	150	300	500

KM# 63.1 48 STUIVERS (Lion Daalder)

27.6800 g., Silver **Obv:** Armored knight looking right above lion shield **Rev:** Rampant lion left **Note:** Mint mark: Moor's head. Dav. #4875.

Date	Mintage	Good	VG	F	VF	XF
1662	7,800	16.00	30.00	80.00	150	250
1663	38,000	16.00	30.00	80.00	150	250
1664	—	16.00	30.00	80.00	150	250

KM# 63.2 48 STUIVERS (Lion Daalder)

Silver **Obv:** Armored knight looking right above lion shield **Rev:** Rampant lion left **Note:** Mint mark: Sitting dog. Dav. #4875.

Date	Mintage	Good	VG	F	VF	XF
1664	20,000	16.00	30.00	80.00	150	250
1666	21,000	16.00	30.00	80.00	150	250

Date	Mintage	Good	VG	F	VF	XF
1667	4,400	16.00	30.00	80.00	150	250
1668	20,000	18.00	40.00	100	175	275

KM# 80 48 STUIVERS (Lion Daalder)

27.6800 g., Silver **Obv:** Armored knight looking right without plume in knight's helmet. MO ARG CIV IMP BEL(G). **Rev:** Rampant lion left, divided date in legend **Note:** Dav. #4876.

Date	Mintage	Good	VG	F	VF	XF
(16)84	—	16.00	30.00	80.00	150	250
(16)85	6,000	16.00	30.00	80.00	150	250
1687	200,000	16.00	30.00	80.00	150	250
1688/7	146,000	18.00	40.00	100	175	300
1688	Inc. above	16.00	30.00	80.00	150	250
1691	17,000	18.00	40.00	100	175	300

KM# 80b 48 STUIVERS (Lion Daalder)

Silver **Obv:** Armored knight looking right without plume in knight's helmet. MO ARG PRO CON - FOE BELG CIV DAV **Rev:** Rampant lion left, divided date in legend **Note:** Dav. #4876

Date	Mintage	Good	VG	F	VF	XF
1698	17,450	16.00	30.00	80.00	150	250

KM# 64.1 48 STUIVERS (Silver Ducat)

28.2500 g., 0.8730 Silver 0.7929 oz. ASW **Obv:** Armored knight looking right **Rev:** Crowned lion shield **Note:** Mint mark: Moor's head. Varieties exist. Dav. #4916.

Date	Mintage	Good	VG	F	VF	XF
1662	21,000	22.00	50.00	120	250	400
1663	2,600	22.00	50.00	120	250	400
1666	9,300	22.00	50.00	120	250	400

KM# 64.2 48 STUIVERS (Silver Ducat)

28.2500 g., 0.8730 Silver 0.7929 oz. ASW **Obv:** Armored knight looking right **Rev:** Crowned lion shield **Note:** Mint mark: Sitting dog.

Date	Mintage	Good	VG	F	VF	XF
1662	Inc. above	30.00	75.00	150	275	450
1663	Inc. above	22.00	50.00	120	250	400
1666	Inc. above	22.00	50.00	120	250	400

KM# 92 48 STUIVERS (Silver Ducat)

28.2500 g., Silver **Obv:** Armored knight looking right, without inner circle **Rev:** Crowned lion shield divides date, without inner circle **Note:** Dav. #4917.

Date	Mintage	Good	VG	F	VF	XF
1698	126,000	22.00	50.00	120	250	400

KM# 9 50 STUIVERS (Arendsrijksdaalder)

29.0300 g., 0.8850 Silver 0.8260 oz. ASW **Obv:** Arms of Deventer and Oversticht below plumed helmet, date in legend **Rev:** Similar to KM#11 **Note:** Dav. #4974.

Date	Mintage	Good	VG	F	VF	XF
1603	—	250	500	1,000	1,500	2,000

KM# 10 50 STUIVERS (Arendsrijksdaalder)

29.0300 g., Silver **Obv:** Shield divided with arms of Deventer and Oversticht below plumed helmet in inner circle **Note:** Dav. #4975.

Date	Mintage	Good	VG	F	VF	XF
ND(1620)	80,000	80.00	200	600	1,000	1,600

KM# 11.1 50 STUIVERS (Arendsrijksdaalder)

29.0300 g., Silver **Obv:** Arms of Deventer below plumed helmet in inner circle **Rev:** Crowned imperial eagle **Rev. Legend:** FERDINAND • II • ROM - IMP • SEM • AV • **Note:** Mint mark: Clover leaf. Dav. #4976.

Date	Mintage	Good	VG	F	VF	XF
ND(1622)	80,000	80.00	200	600	1,000	1,600

KM# 11.2 50 STUIVERS (Arendsrijksdaalder)

29.0300 g., Silver **Obv:** Arms of Deventer below plumed helmet in inner circle **Rev:** Crowned imperial eagle **Rev. Legend:** FERDINAND • II • ROM - IMP • SEM • AV • **Note:** Mint mark: Lily.

Date	Mintage	Good	VG	F	VF	XF
ND(1627)	15,000	80.00	200	600	1,000	1,600

KM# 84 60 STUIVERS (Double Daalder)

31.7600 g., 0.9060 Silver 0.9251 oz. ASW **Obv:** Crowned arms with lion supporters, value below **Rev:** Standing knight with sword behind crowned arms to left, date in legend **Note:** Mint mark: Sitting dog. Dav. #4978.

Date	Mintage	Good	VG	F	VF	XF
1689	15,500	32.00	80.00	200	400	800

KM# 76 60 STUIVERS (3 Gulden)

31.8200 g., 0.9200 Silver 0.9412 oz. ASW **Obv:** Crowned eagle arms divide value, date above crown **Rev:** Standing female figure leaning on Bible on column, holding spear with Liberty cap **Note:** Dav. #4967. Eagle's head in arms may face left or right.

Date	Mintage	Good	VG	F	VF	XF
1682/1	8,000	80.00	200	400	800	1,200
1682	Inc. above	80.00	200	400	800	1,200
1683	—	80.00	200	400	800	1,200
1686	—	80.00	200	400	800	1,200
1687	—	80.00	200	400	800	1,200

KM# 93 60 STUIVERS (3 Gulden)
31.8200 g., Silver **Obv:** Crowned lion shield divides value **Rev:** Female figure seated, date below **Edge Lettering:** TE DOMNE CONFUNDAR IN AETERNUM **Note:** Dav. #4968. Varieties exist.

Date	Mintage	Good	VG	F	VF	XF
1698	128,000	30.00	70.00	170	300	450
1698	—	35.00	80.00	200	400	800

TRADE COINAGE

KM# 20 FLORIN D'OR
3.5000 g., 0.9860 Gold 0.1109 oz. AGW **Obv:** Helmeted arms in inner circle **Rev:** Crowned imperial eagle in inner circle, date in legend, titles of Matthias as emperor

Date	Mintage	VG	F	VF	XF	Unc
ND(1612-19)	Est. 100,000	150	250	350	500	900

KM# 21 FLORIN D'OR
3.5000 g., 0.9860 Gold 0.1109 oz. AGW **Rev:** Titles of Matthias as king of Hungary and Bohemia

Date	Mintage	VG	F	VF	XF	Unc
ND(1612-19)	—	250	400	650	1,000	1,500

KM# 22 FLORIN D'OR
7.0000 g., 0.9860 Gold 0.2219 oz. AGW **Note:** Klippe. Like KM#21

Date	Mintage	VG	F	VF	XF	Unc
ND(1618)	—	—	—	—	—	—

KM# 33 FLORIN D'OR
3.5000 g., 0.9860 Gold 0.1109 oz. AGW **Rev:** Titles of Ferdinand II **Note:** Mintmark clover or lilly

Date	Mintage	VG	F	VF	XF	Unc
ND(1619-29)Lily	—	250	400	650	1,000	1,500

KM# 12 DUCAT
3.5000 g., 0.9860 Gold 0.1109 oz. AGW **Obv:** 5-line inscription in tablet: MON NO / AVREA / DAVENT / CIVITATIS / IMPERI **Rev:** Rudolf II D G R - I - VNG BO REX. Standing knight divides date

Date	Mintage	VG	F	VF	XF	Unc
1603	—	150	300	500	850	1,200
1604	—	150	300	500	850	1,200
1605	—	150	300	500	850	1,200

KM# 15 DUCAT
3.5000 g., 0.9860 Gold 0.1109 oz. AGW **Obv:** 5-line inscription in tablet. MON NO / AVREA / DAVENT / CIVITATIS / IMPERI **Rev:** MATTHIAS D G - R I - VGN BO (R(EC) Standing right divides date

Date	Mintage	VG	F	VF	XF	Unc
1615	—	250	400	650	1,000	1,500

KM# 45 DUCAT
3.5000 g., 0.9860 Gold 0.1109 oz. AGW **Obv:** 5-line inscription in tablet: MONET / AVERA / CIVITATIS / DAVENT. **Rev:** FERD II D G RO - IMP SEM AV(G). Standing knight divides date

Date	Mintage	VG	F	VF	XF	Unc
1632Lily	—	150	300	400	750	1,100
1633Lily	12,000	150	300	400	750	1,100
1634Lily	38,000	150	300	400	750	1,100
1635Lily	18,000	150	300	400	750	1,100
1636Lily	6,000	150	300	400	750	1,100
1637Lily	—	150	300	400	750	1,100
1639Lily	—	150	300	400	750	1,100
1640Lily	—	150	300	400	750	1,100
1641Lily	—	150	300	400	750	1,100
1642Lily	—	175	400	600	1,000	1,500
1643Lily	—	150	300	400	750	1,100

KM# 65 DUCAT
3.5000 g., 0.9860 Gold 0.1109 oz. AGW **Obv:** 5-line inscription in tablet: MO VOC / AREA / CIVITA / IMPER / DAVENT. **Rev:** LEOPOLD(U)S D G ROM IMP S AV G. Standing knight divides date **Note:** Titles of Leopold I.

Date	Mintage	VG	F	VF	XF	Unc
1662	1,000	250	400	650	1,000	1,500
1663	—	250	400	650	1,000	1,500
1665	1,300	250	400	650	1,000	1,500
1666	8,000	250	400	650	1,000	1,500

KM# 55 2 DUCAT
7.0000 g., 0.9860 Gold 0.2219 oz. AGW **Obv:** 5-line inscription in tablet **Rev:** Leopold I standing knight divides date

Date	Mintage	VG	F	VF	XF	Unc
1656	—	300	1,000	1,750	2,500	3,500
1662	500	300	1,000	1,750	2,500	3,500
1666	2,000	300	1,000	1,750	2,500	3,500

SIEGE COINAGE

KM# 70 1/8 DAALDER
Silver **Obv:** Crowned eagle, date **Note:** Uniface klippe.

Date	Mintage	Good	VG	F	VF	XF
1672	—	100	250	500	1,000	1,500

KM# 71 1/4 DAALDER
Silver **Obv:** Crowned eagle, date **Note:** Uniface klippe.

Date	Mintage	Good	VG	F	VF	XF
1672	—	100	250	500	1,000	1,500

KM# 72 1/2 DAALDER
Silver **Obv:** Crowned eagle, date **Note:** Uniface klippe.

Date	Mintage	Good	VG	F	VF	XF
1672	—	150	350	650	1,250	2,000

KM# 73 DAALDER
Silver **Obv:** Crowned eagle, date **Note:** Uniface klippe.

Date	Mintage	Good	VG	F	VF	XF
1672	—	175	375	750	1,500	2,500

PATTERNS

Including off metal strikes

KM#	Date	Mintage	Identification	Mkt Val
Pn1	1615	—	Ducat. Gold Plated Silver. Klippe, KM#15	—
Pn9	1615	—	Ducat. Silver. Double weight. KM#15	—
Pn2	ND1619-1623	—	Florin D'Or. Copper. KM#33	—
Pn6	1628	—	Duit. Gold. 5.25 g.	—
Pn8	1662	—	2 Ducat.	—
Pn3	1683	—	2 Stuivers. Gold. KM#77	2,500
Pn4	1685	—	Schelling. Gold. 7.6000 g. Knight on horse.	—
Pn5	1687	—	Florin. Gold. 13.6000 g.	5,000
Pn7	1688	—	6 Stuivers. Gold. KM#78.	3,000

PIEFORTS

KM#	Date	Mintage	Identification	Mkt Val
P10	1618	—	28 Stuivers. Silver. Klippe, KM#29.	—
P11	ND(1629)	—	1/2 Stuiver. Silver. 6.3000 g. Klippe, KM#60	—
P12	1640	—	48 Stuivers. Silver. Triple weight. Klippe.	—
P13	1640	—	40 Stuivers. Silver. Klippe, (triple weight), KM#52.	—
P14	1660	—	40 Stuivers. Silver. Double weight. KM#64.1	—
P15	1662	—	40 Stuivers. Silver. Double weight. KM#62.1	—
P23	1662	—	48 Stuivers. Silver. KM#63.1.	—
P25	1662	—	48 Stuivers. Silver. KM#64.2.	1,20
P26	1662	—	48 Stuivers. Silver. KM#64.1.	—
P28	1663	—	48 Stuivers. Silver. KM#64.1.	1,20
P29	1664	—	48 Stuivers. Silver. KM#63.1.	1,75
P24	1664	—	48 Stuivers. Silver. KM#63.2	—
P16	1664	—	40 Stuivers. Silver. Double weight. KM#62.1	—
P18	1664	—	40 Stuivers. Silver. Double weight. KM#62.2	—
P19	1666	—	40 Stuivers. Silver. Double weight, KM#62.2	—
P20	1666	—	Ducat. Gold. Klippe, KM#65	—
P30	1666	—	48 Stuivers. Silver. KM#64.2.	1,75
P31	1666	—	Ducat. Gold. Klippe, KM#65.	7,50
P21	1667	—	40 Stuivers. Silver. Double weight. KM#62.2	—
P17	1668	—	40 Stuivers. Silver. Klippe, KM#62.2.	—
P22	1668	—	40 Stuivers. Silver. Double weight. KM#62.2	—
P32	1682	—	60 Stuivers. Silver. KM#76.	—
P33	1683	—	2 Stuivers. Silver. KM#77.	—
P34	1684	—	28 Stuivers. Silver. KM#79.	—
P35	1685	—	28 Stuivers. Silver. (Triple weight), KM#81.1.	—
P36	1685	—	28 Stuivers. Silver. Five times weight. KM#81.1	—
P37	1685	—	30 Stuivers. Silver. Triple weight, KM#82.	—
P38	1688	—	30 Stuivers. Silver. Triple weight, KM#83.	3,00
P39	1689	—	60 Stuivers. Silver. Triple weight. KM#84.	—
P40	1689	—	60 Stuivers. Silver. KM#84.	2,00

HUISSEN

COMMUNE

STANDARD COINAGE

KM# 10 16 HELLER
1.2000 g., Silver **Obv:** Crowned double eagle in inner circle **Obv. Legend:** MATTH I ROM IMP SEM AVG **Rev:** Crowned arems with 6 shields in inner circle **Rev. Legend:** mintmark MO NO AR POSSI PRI

Date	Mintage	Good	VG	F	VF	XF
ND1611-1613	—	10.00	75.00	250	600	90

KM# 5 DUIT
1.8250 g., Copper, 21 mm. **Obv:** Crowned arms **Obv. Legend:** MO : POSS. - PRIN : CIP **Rev:** Legend in wreath **Rev. Legend:** *IN* / HVES / SEN

Date	Mintage	Good	VG	F	VF	XF
ND(1611-13)	663,151	10.00	25.00	70.00	110	15

KM# 6 DUIT
Copper **Obv:** Crowned arms **Rev:** Inscription in wreath **Rev. Inscription:** CVSA / HVNS / SIÆ

Date	Mintage	Good	VG	F	VF	XF
ND(1611-13)	Inc. above	10.00	25.00	70.00	110	15

KM# 7 2 DUIT (Oord)
Copper **Obv:** Crowned arms **Obv. Legend:** IVSTITIA . THRONVM . FIR **Rev:** Cross, date **Rev. Legend:** MO: POSS: PRIN IVL. E. MON

Date	Mintage	Good	VG	F	VF	XF
1609	44,496	25.00	60.00	100	150	20
1611	Inc. above	5.00	15.00	35.00	70.00	10

ꓘM# 8 STUIVER
.7000 g., Silver **Obv:** Crowned shield in 6 parts in circle divides 'alue **Obv. Legend:** MO NO (AR) POSS(I) PRI N **Rev:** Cross vith lily in centre in inner circle **Rev. Legend:** 56 DVC - IVLIE - ꓛLI E(T) - MONT

ate	Mintage	Good	VG	F	VF	XF
1611-1613)	—	15.00	40.00	90.00	150	200

ꓘM# 8.1 STUIVER
.7000 g., Silver **Obv:** Crowned shield in 6 parts in circle **Obv. .egend:** NVMVS CLIVENSIS (Coin of Kievs - Germany) **Rev:** ꓛross with lily in centre in inner circle **Rev. Legend:** MON - ARG CVS(S) - HVS(S)

ate	Mintage	Good	VG	F	VF	XF
611-1613	—	15.00	40.00	100	200	350

ꓘM# 8.2 STUIVER
.7000 g., Silver **Obv:** Crown shield in 6 parts in circle divides 'alue **Obv. Legend:** NVMMVS CLIVENSIS (Coin of Kleve - ɜermany) **Rev:** Cross with lily in center in inner circle **Rev. .egend:** MON - ARG - CVS(S) - HVS(S)

ate	Mintage	Good	VG	F	VF	XF
611-1613	—	15.00	40.00	100	200	350

ꓘM# 14 DAALDER
.7000 g., Silver **Obv:** Arms with 76 shields in inner circle **Obv. .egend:** MO NO ARGEN DVC IVLIAE CLI MONT POSS PRIN **ꓤev:** In inner cirlce 6 lines +/NASCITVR/ANNO 1562/28 MAI ꓠOC HO/I MORTIVR Ao/1609 25 MAR/VESP HO 7/+ **Note:** ꟽintmark lily

ate	Mintage	Good	VG	F	VF	XF
609	—	—	—	—	—	—

ꓘM# 11 ARENDSCHELLING
ꓢilver **Obv:** Crowned double eagle in inner circle. **Obv. Legend:** ꓤVDOL II D G ELEC RO IM(P) SE(M) AVGV(S) **Rev:** Crowned .rms with 6 shields **Rev. Legend:** Mintmark MO(N) mintmark AR) - (NO) POSS PRIN IV - L CL(I) E(T) M - ON(T) **Note:** 4.5 - ɡ. Mintmark lily

ate	Mintage	Good	VG	F	VF	XF
ꓷD1611-1613	—	30.00	60.00	100	200	400

ꓘM# 12 ARENDSCHELLING
ꓢilver **Obv:** Crowned double eagle in inner circle **Obv. Legend:** ꟽATH I D G ELEC RO(M) IMP SEM(P) AVGV(S) **Rev:** Crowned .rms with 6 shields in inner circle **Rev. Legend:** (mintmark) (star) ꟽO - (NO) POSS(I) PRIN IV(IE) CLU E MN **Note:** Mintmark lily. .9 - 5.1g

ate	Mintage	Good	VG	F	VF	XF
ꓷD1611-1613	—	30.00	60.00	100	200	400

ꓘM# 9 ARENDSCHELLING
.7000 g., Silver **Obv:** Crowned double eagle in inner circle **ꓷbv. Legend:** RVDOL II D G ELEC RO IMP SEM AVGS(T) **Rev:** ꓛrowned arms with 6 shields in inner circle **Rev. Legend:** MO ɿintmark (NO) ARG POS(I) (PR) DV(C) IV(LI) ET **Note:** Titles f Rudolph II. Mintmark lily

ate	Mintage	Good	VG	F	VF	XF
ꓷD (1611-1613	—	30.00	60.00	100	200	400

ꓘM# 13 SCHELLING
8.5000 g., Silver **Obv:** Arms with 5 shields in inner circle **Obv. .egend:** (mintmark) MONETA NO ARGEN POSS PRINCIP **Rev:** ı inner circle 6 lines +/NASCITVR/ANNO 1562/28 MAI NOC HO/I ꟽORTIVR Ao/1609 25 MAR/VESP HO 7/+ **Note:** Mintmark lily

ate	Mintage	Good	VG	F	VF	XF
609	—	—	—	—	—	—

KAMPEN

CITY

STANDARD COINAGE

ꓘM# 36 DUIT
ꓛopper **Obv:** Arms in beaded circle **Rev:** CAM/PEN/1639 in ʌreath

ate	Mintage	VG	F	VF	XF	Unc
639	—	15.00	50.00	100	130	—

ꓘM# 36a DUIT
2.6000 g., Silver **Obv:** Arms in beaded circle **Rev:** ꓛAM/PEN/1639 in wreath

ate	Mintage	VG	F	VF	XF	Unc
639	—	—	—	—	—	—

ꓘM# 40 DUIT
ꓛopper **Obv:** Arms in wreath

ate	Mintage	VG	F	VF	XF	Unc
644	—	10.00	25.00	50.00	100	—

ꓘM# 40a DUIT
ɜold **Obv:** Arms in wreath

ate	Mintage	VG	F	VF	XF	Unc
644	—	—	—	—	—	—

KM# 41 DUIT
Copper **Obv:** CAM/DEN, date below in ornamental circle **Rev:** Rampant lion left in wreath

Date	Mintage	VG	F	VF	XF	Unc
1644	—	30.00	100	175	250	—

KM# 51 DUIT
Copper **Obv:** City arms in wreath **Rev:** CAM/DEN(date) in ornamental circle **Note:** Varieties exist.

Date	Mintage	VG	F	VF	XF	Unc
1655	—	15.00	25.00	55.00	90.00	—
1658	—	15.00	25.00	55.00	90.00	—
1659	—	15.00	25.00	55.00	90.00	—
1660	—	15.00	25.00	55.00	90.00	—
1661	—	15.00	25.00	55.00	90.00	—
1662	—	15.00	25.00	55.00	90.00	—
1663	—	15.00	25.00	55.00	90.00	—
1664	—	15.00	25.00	55.00	90.00	—
1665	—	15.00	25.00	55.00	90.00	—
1666	—	15.00	25.00	55.00	90.00	—
1668	—	15.00	25.00	55.00	90.00	—
1669	—	15.00	25.00	55.00	90.00	—
1670	—	15.00	25.00	55.00	90.00	—
1671	—	15.00	25.00	55.00	90.00	—

KM# 53 DUIT
Copper **Obv:** Crowned city arms

Date	Mintage	VG	F	VF	XF	Unc
1658	—	15.00	30.00	60.00	85.00	—
1659	—	15.00	30.00	60.00	85.00	—
16660 Error	—	25.00	60.00	100	150	—
1660	—	15.00	30.00	60.00	85.00	—

KM# 51a DUIT
Silver **Obv:** City arms in wreath **Rev:** CAM/DEN(date) in ornamental circle

Date	Mintage	VG	F	VF	XF	Unc
1659	—	—	—	—	—	—

KM# 5 STUIVER
2.0000 g., Billon **Obv:** Crowned arms divide value in inner circle **Rev:** Ornamental long cross with quatrefoil around center **Note:** Varieties exist.

Date	Mintage	VG	F	VF	XF	Unc
ND(ca.1621)	—	15.00	55.00	110	160	—

KM# 71 2 STUIVERS
1.7300 g., 0.5830 Silver 0.0324 oz. ASW **Obv:** Crowned rampant lion left holding sword and arrows, value at sides **Rev:** CAM/PEN/(date)

Date	Mintage	VG	F	VF	XF	Unc
1677	—	7.50	20.00	40.00	100	—
1678	—	7.50	20.00	40.00	100	—
1679	—	7.50	20.00	40.00	100	—
1680	—	7.50	20.00	40.00	100	—
1681	—	7.50	20.00	40.00	100	—

KM# 6 3 STUIVERS (1/2 Schelling)
3.0000 g., 0.5000 Silver 0.0482 oz. ASW **Obv:** Crowned arms in inner circle **Rev:** Crowned double-headed eagle in inner circle

Date	Mintage	VG	F	VF	XF	Unc
ND	—	50.00	150	300	500	—

KM# 7 6 STUIVERS (Schelling)
6.0000 g., 0.5000 Silver 0.0964 oz. ASW **Obv:** Crowned arms within circle **Rev:** Crowned double-headed imperial eagle within circle, titles of Rudolf II

Date	Mintage	VG	F	VF	XF	Unc
ND	—	15.00	30.00	50.00	100	—

KM# 22 6 STUIVERS (Schelling)
Silver **Obv:** Titles of Matthias I

Date	Mintage	VG	F	VF	XF	Unc
ND	—	15.00	50.00	100	150	—

KM# 45 6 STUIVERS (Schelling)
Silver **Obv:** Titles of Ferdinand III

Date	Mintage	VG	F	VF	XF	Unc
ND	—	20.00	70.00	125	175	—

KM# 67 6 STUIVERS (Schelling)
Silver **Obv:** Titles of Leopold I

Date	Mintage	VG	F	VF	XF	Unc
1675	—	20.00	75.00	150	225	—

KM# 75 6 STUIVERS (Schelling)
Silver **Obv:** Crowned arms with lion supporters in inner circle, date at top **Rev:** Knight with sword on horseback right **Note:** Mint mark: Rider.

Date	Mintage	VG	F	VF	XF	Unc
1680	—	15.00	60.00	125	200	—

KM# 77 6 STUIVERS (Schelling)
4.9500 g., 0.5830 Silver 0.0928 oz. ASW **Obv:** Crowned arms divide value, date above crown **Rev:** Knight with sword on horseback right, crowned arms below horse

Date	Mintage	VG	F	VF	XF	Unc
1681	—	7.50	30.00	55.00	85.00	—
1682	—	7.50	30.00	55.00	85.00	—
1683	—	15.00	40.00	75.00	150	—
1684	—	15.00	40.00	75.00	150	—
1686	—	7.50	30.00	55.00	85.00	—
1688	—	15.00	40.00	75.00	150	—
1689	—	7.50	30.00	55.00	85.00	—
1690	—	7.50	30.00	55.00	85.00	—
1691	—	7.50	30.00	55.00	85.00	—

KM# 23 28 STUIVERS (Florin)
19.5000 g., 0.6730 Silver 0.4219 oz. ASW **Obv:** Crowned arms within circle, date above crown, value below **Rev:** Crowned double-headed imperial eagle within circle, titles of Matthias **Note:** Mint mark: Rosette.

Date	Mintage	VG	F	VF	XF	Unc
ND	—	40.00	100	200	300	—
1618	—	40.00	100	200	300	—
1619	—	50.00	125	250	350	—

KM# 30 28 STUIVERS (Florin)
Silver **Obv:** Titles of Ferdinand II

Date	Mintage	VG	F	VF	XF	Unc
1628	—	40.00	100	200	300	—

KM# 76 28 STUIVERS (Florin)
Silver **Obv:** Titles of Matthias I **Note:** Mint mark: Rider.

Date	Mintage	VG	F	VF	XF	Unc
(16)80/60	90,314	25.00	70.00	150	300	—
1680	Inc. above	25.00	70.00	150	300	—
(16)81	Inc. above	25.00	70.00	150	300	—
1682	Inc. above	25.00	60.00	125	250	—
(16)82	553,356	20.00	60.00	125	250	—
(16)83	Inc. above	20.00	60.00	125	250	—
(16)84	Inc. above	20.00	60.00	125	250	—
(16)85	Inc. above	20.00	60.00	125	250	—
(16)86	Inc. above	20.00	60.00	125	250	—

KM# 64 1/2 DUCATON
16.8900 g., 0.9410 Silver 0.5110 oz. ASW

Date	Mintage	VG	F	VF	XF	Unc
1670	—	75.00	200	350	600	—

KM# 54 DUCATON (40 Stuiver - Silver Rider)
32.7800 g., 0.9410 Silver 0.9917 oz. ASW **Note:** Mint mark: Lily

Date	Mintage	VG	F	VF	XF	Unc
1659	128,518	50.00	125	250	400	—
1660	Inc. above	50.00	125	250	400	—
1661	Inc. above	50.00	125	250	400	—
1662	Inc. above	50.00	125	250	400	—
1663	Inc. above	50.00	125	250	400	—
1664/3	79,420	70.00	175	300	500	—
1664	Inc. above	50.00	125	250	400	—

KM# 61.1 DUCATON (40 Stuiver - Silver Rider)
Silver **Obv:** Smaller knight, city arms below in inner circle **Note:** Dav. #4945. Mint mark: Moor's head.

Date	Mintage	VG	F	VF	XF	Unc
1664	—	50.00	125	200	350	—
1665	—	60.00	125	250	400	—
1666	—	50.00	125	200	350	—
1667	—	60.00	125	250	400	—
1668	—	50.00	125	200	350	—
1669	—	60.00	125	250	400	—
1670	—	50.00	125	200	350	—
1675	—	50.00	125	200	350	—

KM# 61.2 DUCATON (40 Stuiver - Silver Rider)
Silver **Obv:** Smaller knight, city arms below in inner circle **Note:** Dav. #4945. Mint mark: Rider. Varieties exist.

Date	Mintage	VG	F	VF	XF	Unc
1676	155,515	40.00	150	250	400	—
1677	Inc. above	40.00	150	250	400	—
1678	Inc. above	40.00	150	250	400	—
1679/6	Inc. above	60.00	200	350	500	—
1679	Inc. above	40.00	150	250	400	—
1680/79	Inc. above	60.00	200	350	500	—
1680	Inc. above	40.00	150	250	400	—
1682	Inc. above	40.00	150	250	400	—

KM# 78 3 GULDEN (60 Stuiver)
31.8200 g., 0.9200 Silver 0.9412 oz. ASW **Obv:** Crowned arms divide value, date above crown **Rev:** Standing female figure leaning on Bible on column, holding spear with Liberty cap **Note:** Dav. #4969. Mint mark: Rider

Date	Mintage	VG	F	VF	XF	Unc
1682	193,695	90.00	200	400	750	—
1862 error	Inc. above	150	600	1,000	1,350	—
1683	Inc. above	90.00	200	400	750	—
1686	Inc. above	90.00	200	400	750	—
1687	Inc. above	90.00	200	400	750	—

KM# 55.1 DUCAT (48 Stuiver)
28.2500 g., 0.8730 Silver 0.7929 oz. ASW **Note:** Dav. #4918. Mint mark: Lily.

Date	Mintage	VG	F	VF	XF	Unc
1659	—	30.00	90.00	160	325	—
1660	—	30.00	90.00	160	325	—
1661	—	30.00	90.00	160	325	—
1662	—	50.00	160	300	450	—
1662/1	—	30.00	90.00	160	325	—
1663	—	200	400	800	1,500	—
1664	—	50.00	160	300	450	—

KM# 55.2 DUCAT (48 Stuiver)
28.2500 g., 0.8730 Silver 0.7929 oz. ASW **Rev:** Lion without sword and arrows **Note:** Dav. #4918. Mint mark: Lily.

Date	Mintage	VG	F	VF	XF	Unc
1659	—	40.00	80.00	175	425	—

KM# 68 DUCAT (48 Stuiver)
Silver **Obv:** Armored knight standing behind shield looking right with sword on shoulder **Rev:** Crowned lion shield divides date **Note:** Dav. #4919. Mint mark: Rider.

Date	Mintage	VG	F	VF	XF	Unc
1676	15,820	50.00	150	300	450	—
1677	Inc. above	50.00	150	300	450	—

KM# 79 DUCAT (48 Stuiver)
Silver **Obv:** Armored knight standing behind shield looking right with sword on shoulder **Rev:** Crowned lion shield, date above **Note:** Dav. #4920.

Date	Mintage	VG	F	VF	XF	Unc
1679	7,810	50.00	100	200	400	—
1684	Inc. above	50.00	100	200	400	—

KM# 87 DUCAT (48 Stuiver)
Silver **Obv:** Armored knight standing behind shield looking right with sword on shoulder and ribbon bow in other hand **Rev:** Crowned lion shield divides date

Date	Mintage	VG	F	VF	XF	Unc
1693	13,439	70.00	200	400	550	—

KM# 2 1/5 DAALDER (Philip - 10 Stuiver)
6.8500 g., 0.8330 Silver 0.1834 oz. ASW **Obv:** Crowned arms on ornamental cross in inner circle **Rev:** Bust of Rudolph II left in inner circle

Date	Mintage	VG	F	VF	XF	Unc
ND(1601)	—	250	600	1,500	3,000	—

KM# 3 1/2 DAALDER (Philip - 25 Stuiver)
17.1300 g., 0.8330 Silver 0.4587 oz. ASW **Obv:** Crowned arms on ornamental cross in inner circle **Rev:** Bust of Rudolph II left in inner circle

Date	Mintage	VG	F	VF	XF	Unc
ND(1601)	—	—	—	—	—	—

KM# 43 1/2 DAALDER (Lion - 24 Stuiver)
13.8400 g., 0.7500 Silver 0.3337 oz. ASW **Obv:** Armored knigh looking to right above lion shield **Rev:** Rampant lion left in inne circle, date divided at top **Note:** Mint mark: Lily

Date	Mintage	VG	F	VF	XF	Un
1646/43	—	70.00	180	275	400	-
1646	—	60.00	160	250	350	-
1647	—	60.00	160	250	350	-
1648	—	70.00	180	275	400	-
1657	—	60.00	160	250	350	-

KM# 8 DAALDER (Philip - 50 Stuiver)
34.2770 g., 0.9180 Silver 0.9180 oz. ASW **Obv:** Crownd arms on ornamental cross in inner circle **Rev:** Bust of Rudolph II left in inner circle **Note:** Dav. #4984.

Date	Mintage	VG	F	VF	XF	Un
ND(1601)	—	—	—	—	—	—

KM# 34.4 DAALDER ((Arendsrijks - 48 Stuiver))
29.0300 g., 0.8260 Silver 0.7709 oz. ASW **Obv:** City arms wit digits of date between towers in inner circle **Obv. Legend:** MONE NO CIVITATIS IMPE CAMPENSIS mintmark (Lily) **Rev:** Crowned double-headed eagle in inner circle, titles of Ferdinan III **Rev. Legend:** FER(DINAND) III D G ELEC RO IMP SEM AVG(VS) **Note:** One mintmark. Dav.#4880

Date	Mintage	VG	F	VF	XF	Ur
1649	—	80.00	150	300	600	-
1653	—	80.00	150	300	600	-

KM# 34.2 DAALDER ((Arendsrijks - 48 Stuiver))
29.0300 g., 0.8260 Silver 0.7709 oz. ASW **Obv:** City arms wit digits of date between towers in inner circle **Obv. Legend:** MONE NO CIVITATIS IMPR CAMPENSIS mintmark (Lily) **Rev:** Crowned double-headed eagle in inner circle, titles of Ferdinan III **Rev. Legend:** FER(DINAND) III D G ELEC RO IMP SEM AVG(VS) mintmark (castle) **Note:** Two mintmarks

Date	Mintage	VG	F	VF	XF	Ur
1649	—	80.00	150	300	600	-
1651	—	80.00	150	300	600	-
1653	—	80.00	150	300	600	-

KM# 34.3 DAALDER ((Arendsrijks - 48 Stuiver))
29.0300 g., 0.8260 Silver 0.7709 oz. ASW **Obv:** City arms wit digits of date between towers in inner circle **Obv. Legend:** MONE NO CIVITATIS IMPE CAMPENSIS mintmark (Lily) **Rev:** Crowned double-headed eagle in inner circle, titles of Ferdinan III **Rev. Legend:** FER(DINAND) III D G ELEC RO IMP SEM AVG(VS) mintmark (city gate) **Note:** Two mintmarks

Date	Mintage	VG	F	VF	XF	Ur
1654	—	80.00	150	300	600	-

KM# 21 DAALDER (Arendsrijks 50 Stuiver)
Silver **Obv:** City arms with digits of date between towers in inne circle **Rev:** Crowned double-headed eagle in inner circle, titles of Matthias **Note:** Dav. #4980.

Date	Mintage	VG	F	VF	XF	Un
1614	—	100	350	700	1,000	-
1615	—	100	350	700	1,000	-

M# 35.1 DAALDER (Lion - 48 Stuiver)
7.6800 g., 0.7500 Silver 0.6674 oz. ASW **Obv:** Armored knight oking right behind lion shield **Rev:** Rampant lion left **Note:** Dav. 4879. Without mint mark.

ate	Mintage	VG	F	VF	XF	Unc
637	—	30.00	100	175	250	—
642	—	30.00	100	175	250	—
643	—	30.00	100	175	250	—
656	—	90.00	225	450	600	—
671	—	30.00	80.00	150	300	—
688	—	30.00	100	175	250	—

M# 42.1 DAALDER (Lion - 48 Stuiver)
7.6800 g., 0.7500 Silver 0.6674 oz. ASW **Obv:** Armored knight oking left behind lion shield **Rev:** Rampant lion left **Note:** Vithout mint mark. Dav. # 4879.

ate	Mintage	VG	F	VF	XF	Unc
644	—	60.00	120	200	400	—
646	—	30.00	100	175	250	—
656	—	75.00	150	300	600	—

M# 42.2 DAALDER (Lion - 48 Stuiver)
7.6800 g., 0.7500 Silver 0.6674 oz. ASW **Obv:** Armored knight oking left behind lion shield **Rev:** Rampant lion left **Note:** Mint ark: Lily. Dav. # 4879.

ate	Mintage	VG	F	VF	XF	Unc
646/3	—	40.00	80.00	175	350	—
646	—	30.00	60.00	125	275	—
647/4	—	30.00	60.00	125	275	—
647	—	30.00	60.00	125	275	—
648/7	—	30.00	60.00	125	275	—
648	—	30.00	60.00	125	275	—
649	—	30.00	60.00	125	275	—
650	—	30.00	60.00	125	275	—

M# 35.2 DAALDER (Lion - 48 Stuiver)
7.6800 g., 0.7500 Silver 0.6674 oz. ASW **Obv:** Armored knight oking right behind lion shield **Rev:** Rampant lion left **Note:** Dav. 4879. Mint mark: Lily.

ate	Mintage	VG	F	VF	XF	Unc
646	—	30.00	70.00	140	200	—
650	—	30.00	70.00	140	200	—
651	—	30.00	70.00	140	200	—
652	—	30.00	70.00	140	200	—
653	—	30.00	70.00	140	200	—
654	—	35.00	80.00	150	300	—
655	—	35.00	80.00	150	300	—
657	—	35.00	80.00	150	300	—
662	—	35.00	80.00	150	300	—
664	—	35.00	80.00	150	300	—

M# 35.3 DAALDER (Lion - 48 Stuiver)
7.6800 g., 0.7500 Silver 0.6674 oz. ASW **Note:** Dav. #4879. nt mark: Moor's head.

ate	Mintage	VG	F	VF	XF	Unc
664	—	25.00	70.00	140	200	—
666	—	55.00	100	250	400	—
667	—	25.00	70.00	140	200	—
672	—	25.00	70.00	140	200	—
688	—	—	—	—	—	—

M# 35.5 DAALDER (Lion - 48 Stuiver)
7.6800 g., 0.7500 Silver 0.6674 oz. ASW **Obv:** Armored knight oking right behind lion shield

ate	Mintage	VG	F	VF	XF	Unc
671Moor's head	—	55.00	100	250	400	—
672Moor's head	—	55.00	100	250	400	—

KM# 35.4 DAALDER (Lion - 48 Stuiver)
27.6800 g., 0.7500 Silver 0.6674 oz. ASW **Note:** Dav. #4879. Mint mark: Rider.

Date	Mintage	VG	F	VF	XF	Unc
1675	—	35.00	80.00	140	225	—
1676	—	30.00	70.00	110	175	—
1677	—	25.00	60.00	80.00	175	—
1679	—	30.00	70.00	110	175	—
1681	—	25.00	60.00	80.00	175	—
1682/1	—	35.00	80.00	140	225	—
1682	—	25.00	60.00	80.00	175	—
1683	—	25.00	60.00	80.00	175	—
1684	—	25.00	60.00	80.00	175	—
1685	—	25.00	60.00	80.00	175	—
1686	—	25.00	60.00	80.00	175	—
1687	—	25.00	70.00	140	225	—
1688	—	25.00	80.00	140	225	—
1689	—	30.00	80.00	140	225	—
1690	—	30.00	80.00	140	225	—
1691	—	30.00	70.00	130	150	—
1692	—	25.00	60.00	80.00	175	—
1693	—	25.00	60.00	80.00	175	—

KM# 34.1 DAALDER (Rijks - 48 Stuiver)
29.0300 g., 0.8850 Silver 0.8260 oz. ASW **Obv:** City arms with digits of date between towers in inner circle **Obv. Legend:** MONE NO CIVITATIS IMPE CAMPENSIS mintmark (Lily) **Rev:** Crowned double-headed eagle in inner circle, titles of Ferdinand I **Rev. Legend:** FERDIN(AND) I D G ELEC RO IMP SEM AVG(VS) **Note:** Dav. #4983.

Date	Mintage	VG	F	VF	XF	Unc
1633	—	100	325	650	1,100	—
1649	—	100	325	650	1,100	—

KM# 52 DAALDER (Rijks - 48 Stuiver)
29.0300 g., 0.8850 Silver 0.8260 oz. ASW **Note:** Dav. #4985.

Date	Mintage	VG	F	VF	XF	Unc
1655	—	50.00	150	300	600	—
1657	—	50.00	150	300	600	—

KM# 65 DAALDER (Lion)
Silver **Obv:** Armored knight right holding shield with city arms **Note:** Dav. #4880.

Date	Mintage	VG	F	VF	XF	Unc
1671	—	40.00	100	200	400	—
1672	—	40.00	100	200	400	—

KM# 70 DAALDER (Rijks)
29.0300 g., 0.8850 Silver 0.8260 oz. ASW **Note:** Dav. #4845. Without inner circle.

Date	Mintage	VG	F	VF	XF	Unc
1676	8,420	200	500	1,000	2,000	—

KM# 85 DAALDER (30 Stuiver)
Silver **Obv:** Crowned arms with lion supporters, value below. **Rev:** Standing knight with sword behind crowned arms to left, date in legend

Date	Mintage	VG	F	VF	XF	Unc
1690	—	80.00	275	550	1,000	—
1692	32,209	40.00	150	250	500	—

KM# 10 1/2 NOBLE
Gold **Obv:** Ruler in ship in inner circle **Rev:** Floriated cross with crowned lions in angles **Note:** Fr. 152a.

Date	Mintage	VG	F	VF	XF	Unc
ND	—	500	700	800	1,250	—

KM# 12 NOBLE
Gold **Obv:** Ruler in ship in inner circle **Rev:** Floriated cross with crowned lions in angles **Note:** Fr. 151a.

Date	Mintage	VG	F	VF	XF	Unc
ND	—	600	1,000	1,500	2,000	—

KM# 20.2 FLORIN D'OR
3.2500 g., 0.9860 Gold 0.1030 oz. AGW **Obv:** Crowned double-headed eagle in inner circle, titles of Matthias I **Obv. Legend:** MATTHI I D G ELEC RO IMP SEM AVG **Rev:** Orb in trilobe in inner circle **Rev. Legend:** MO NO - CI IMP - CAMPE

Date	Mintage	VG	F	VF	XF	Unc
ND1613-17	—	175	300	500	1,000	—

SIEGE COINAGE

Struck after the city was under siege by Christoph Bernard von Galen, the Bishop of Munster

KM# 66 DAALDER
Obv: City arms with CAMPEN below **Rev:** NE / CESSITAS / ALTERA / 1672 **Note:** Dav. #4987.

Date	Mintage	VG	F	VF	XF	Unc
1672	—	—	800	1,500	2,000	—

TRADE COINAGE

KM# 20.1 FLORIN D'OR
3.2500 g., 0.9860 Gold 0.1030 oz. AGW **Obv:** Three shields with tops touching in inner circle **Obv. Legend:** MON AVR IMPERI CI(VI) CAMP(E) **Rev:** Orb in trilobe, titles of Matthias **Rev. Legend:** MATH I D G ELEC RO OMP SEM AV(GVST) **Note:** Fr. #158.

Date	Mintage	VG	F	VF	XF	Unc
ND(1612-19)	—	175	300	500	1,000	—

KM# 4 DUCAT
3.5000 g., 0.9860 Gold 0.1109 oz. AGW **Rev:** Titles of Rudolph II **Note:** Fr. #161.

Date	Mintage	VG	F	VF	XF	Unc
1601/599	—	130	250	350	600	—
1601	—	125	175	250	500	—
1602	—	125	175	250	500	—
1603/597	—	130	250	350	600	—
1603/02	—	130	250	350	600	—
1603	—	125	175	250	500	—

KM# 24 DUCAT
3.5000 g., 0.9860 Gold 0.1109 oz. AGW **Obv:** Matthias standing right divides date **Rev:** 5-line inscription in tablet

Date	Mintage	VG	F	VF	XF	Unc
1616	—	125	250	425	850	—
1619	—	125	250	425	850	—

KM# 44 DUCAT
3.5000 g., 0.9860 Gold 0.1109 oz. AGW **Obv:** Inscription within ornamented square **Rev:** Ferdinand III, armored standing figure divides date

Date	Mintage	VG	F	VF	XF	Unc
1646	—	125	175	300	600	—
1647	—	125	175	300	600	—
1648	—	125	175	300	600	—
1649	—	125	175	300	600	—
1650	—	150	275	350	750	—
1651	—	125	175	300	600	—
1652/1/0	—	150	275	300	600	—
1652	—	125	175	300	600	—
1653	—	125	175	300	600	—
1654	—	125	175	300	600	—
1655	—	125	175	300	600	—
1656	—	150	275	350	750	—
1658	—	125	175	300	600	—
1659	—	125	175	300	600	—
1660	—	125	175	300	600	—

KM# 60 DUCAT
3.5000 g., 0.9860 Gold 0.1109 oz. AGW **Obv:** Leopold standing right divides date

Date	Mintage	VG	F	VF	XF	Unc
1662	—	125	175	300	600	—
1664	—	125	175	300	600	—
1666	—	150	250	500	1,000	—
1668	17,000	125	175	300	600	—
1675	—	125	175	300	600	—
1676	3,640	125	175	300	600	—

KM# 50 2 DUCAT
7.0000 g., 0.9860 Gold 0.2219 oz. AGW **Obv:** Inscription within ornamented square **Rev:** Ferdinand III standing right, divides date **Note:** FR. #160.

Date	Mintage	VG	F	VF	XF	Unc
1650	—	300	500	800	1,200	—
1655	—	300	500	800	1,200	—
1656	—	300	500	800	1,200	—
1657	—	300	500	800	1,200	—
1658	—	300	500	800	1,200	—

PATTERNS

Including off metal strikes

KM#	Date	Mintage	Identification	Mkt Val
Pn1	ND	—	2 Rose Noble. Gold. 61.0000 g. KM#14	50,000
Pn2	ND	—	2 Rose Noble. Gold. 20.4400 g. KM#14	30,000
Pn3	ND	—	3 Stuivers. Silver. KM#6	—
Pn4	ND	—	3 Stuivers. Silver. KM#7	—
Pn5	ND	—	6 Stuivers. Gold. 7.0000 g. KM#7	—
Pn6	ND	—	6 Stuivers. Silver. Klippe. 11.9 - 15.8g. KM#22	—
Pn7	ND	—	6 Stuivers. Silver. 15.5000 g. KM#22	3,000
Pn8	ND	—	6 Stuivers. Gold. 6.2000 g. KM#22	5,000
Pn9	ND	—	6 Stuivers. Silver. 9.0000 g. Klippe. KM#45	2,750
Pn10	1615	—	Rijksdaalder. Gold. 6.5000 g. Eagle. KM#21	—
Pn11	1618	—	28 Stuivers. Silver. Klippe. KM#23.	—
Pn12	ND(1621)	—	6 Stuivers. Silver. Klippe. KM#22.	500
Pn13	ND(1621)	—	6 Stuivers. Silver. Octagonal klippe. KM#22.	1,250
Pn14	ND(1621)	—	Stuiver. Gold. 3.4400 g. KM#5.	4,000
Pn15	1639	—	Duit. Tin. 2.0000 g. KM#36.	—
Pn16	1639	—	Duit. Silver. 12.3000 g. Klippe. KM#36	—
Pn17	ND	—	6 Stuivers. Gold. 6.6500 g. KM#7.	5,000
Pn18	1644	—	Duit. Gold.	—
Pn19	1647	—	1/2 Lion Daalder. Silver. Klippe. KM#43	—
Pn20	1667	—	1/2 Daalder. Silver. Klippe. KM#63.	—
Pn21	1689	—	Lion Daalder. Gold.	—
Pn22	1653	—	Duit. Silver. KM#53	—

PIEFORTS

KM#	Date	Mintage	Identification	Mkt Val
P1	ND(1600)	—	4 Noble. Gold. KM#12. (4 Sovereign weight).	—
P2	ND	—	Noble. Gold. Cross. KM#12.	—
P3	ND	—	6 Stuivers. Silver.	—
P4	1614	—	Daalder. Silver. Towered building facade, towers divide date. Crowned double-headed imperial eagle, orb on breast. Klippe. Weight between 29 and 41g. KM#21.	1,750
P5	1614	—	Daalder. Silver. Klippe. Double weight. KM#21	—
P6	1615	—	Daalder. Silver. Klippe, Weight between 29 and 41g. KM#21.	—
P7	1615	—	Daalder. Silver. Klippe. Double weight. KM#21	—
P8	1616/15	—	Daalder. Silver. Klippe, Weight between 29 and 41g. KM#21	—
P9	1616	—	Daalder. Silver. Towered building facade, towers divide date. Imperial double-headed eagle, titles of Ferdinand I. Klippe, KM#21.	—
P10	1618	—	28 Stuivers. Silver. KM23.	—
P11	1618	—	28 Stuivers. Silver. Diamond planchet, KM23.	—
P12	ND	—	28 Stuivers. Silver. Crowned ornate shield. Crowned double-headed imperial eagle, orb on breast. KM23.	—
P13	1618	—	28 Stuivers. Silver. 20.4000 g. Klippe. Square planchet, KM23.	1,750
P14	1618	—	28 Stuivers. Silver. 37.1000 g. Klippe. KM#23	2,250
P15	1618	—	28 Stuivers. Silver. Double weight. KM#23	—
P16	1634	—	Daalder. Silver. Klippe, titles of Ferdinand I, KM34.	—
P17	1634	—	Daalder. Silver. KM#34.	—
P18	1639	—	Duit. Copper. 5.3000 g. KM#36. Klippe.	1,000
PA10	1639	—	Duit. Copper. KM36.	—
P19	1647	—	Lion Daalder. Silver. KM#35.2.	3,000
P20	1647	—	Lion Daalder. Silver. Double weight. KM#42.1	2,500
P21	1648	—	Lion Daalder. Silver. Klippe. Double weight. KM#42.2	3,0
P22	1648	—	Lion Daalder. Silver. Klippe, KM35.2.	4,0
P23	1649	—	Daalder. Silver. KM#45.	—
P24	1649	—	Daalder. Silver. Double weight. KM#34.2	—
P25	1650	—	Lion Daalder. Silver. Klippe, KM42.2	—
P26	1652	—	Ducat. Gold. 7.0300 g. KM#44.	—
P27	1659	—	Ducaton. Silver. KM54.	2,0
P28	1659	—	Silver Ducat. KM#55.1	2,5
P29	1661	—	Ducaton. Silver. KM#54.	3,0
P30	1664	—	1/2 Ducaton. Silver. Klippe. Double weight. KM#64	—
P31	1664	—	Ducaton. Silver. KM54.	2,5
P32	1669	—	Ducaton. Silver. KM61.	—
P33	1670	—	Ducaton. Silver. KM61.	—
P34	1670	—	Ducaton. Silver. Klippe, KM61.	—
P35	1671	—	Duit. Copper. 4.6000 g. Klippe, KM51.	—
P36	1677	—	Stuiver. Silver. Triple weight. KM#77	—
P37	1672	—	28 Stuivers. Silver. Double weight. KM#66	—
P38	1679	—	Lion Daalder. Silver. KM#36.6.	—
P39	1680	—	28 Stuivers. Silver. Triple weight, KM76.	—
P40	1681	—	28 Stuivers. Silver. 39.8000 g. KM#76.	—
P41	1682	—	28 Stuivers. Silver. Triple weight, KM76.	—
P42	1682	—	3 Gulden. Silver. KM78.	—
P43	1682	—	28 Stuivers. Silver. 39.8000 g. KM76.	1,5
P44	1682	—	28 Stuivers. Silver. 61.3000 g. KM#76	3,0
P45	1682	—	3 Gulden. Silver. KM#78. Klippe.	5,0
P46	1682	—	3 Gulden. Silver. Double weight. KM#78	—
P47	1689	—	Lion Daalder. Silver. KM36.6.	—
P48	1689	—	Lion Daalder. Gold. 18.0000 g. KM#35.4	—
P49	1689	—	Ryderschelling. Silver. 12.6000 g. KM#77.	1,0
P50	1689	—	Ryderschelling. Silver. 16.4000 g. KM#77	1,6

ZWOLLE

COMMUNE

STANDARD COINAGE

KM# 21 DUIT
Copper **Obv:** Shield of Zwolle arms (St. Michael holding swor and shield) **Rev:** ZW/OLLAE/1 (shield) 8 in wreath

Date	Mintage	VG	F	VF	XF	Unc
1618	—	10.00	25.00	50.00	100	

KM# 37 DUIT
Copper **Obv:** Shield of Zwolle arms **Obv. Legend:** DEVS.REFVGIVM. NOSTRVM. **Rev:** ZW/OLLAE/3 (shield) 9 wreath

Date	Mintage	VG	F	VF	XF	Unc
(16)36	—	25.00	50.00	100	200	
(16)39	—	10.00	25.00	50.00	100	

KM# 69 DUIT
Copper **Obv:** Shield of Zwolle arms in wreath **Rev:** ZW/OLLAE (shield) 3 in wreath

Date	Mintage	VG	F	VF	XF	Unc
1663	—	15.00	40.00	60.00	100	

KM# 7 2 STUIVERS
Billon **Obv:** Orb with value divides date in inner circle **Rev:** Arm with St. Michael above in inner circle

Date	Mintage	VG	F	VF	XF	Unc
1601	—	50.00	125	250	400	
1602	—	50.00	125	250	400	

KM# 76 2 STUIVERS
1.7300 g., 0.5830 Silver 0.0324 oz. ASW **Obv:** Crowned rampant lion left divides value **Rev:** ZW/OLLA/ (date divided b arms)

Date	Mintage	VG	F	VF	XF	Unc
1672	—	10.00	50.00	100	150	

ate	Mintage	VG	F	VF	XF	Unc
674	—	10.00	50.00	100	150	—
677	—	10.00	50.00	100	150	—
678	—	10.00	50.00	100	150	—
679	—	10.00	50.00	100	150	—

KM# 8 3 STUIVERS (1/2 Arendschelling)

3illon **Obv:** Crowned imperial eagle in inner circle **Rev:** Shield f arms with elaborate helmet above in inner circle

ate	Mintage	VG	F	VF	XF	Unc
ID	—	75.00	225	450	700	—

KM# 70 1/2 SCHELLING

ilver **Obv:** Crowned city arms **Obv. Legend:** MONETA. RGENTEA. CIVIT. ZW **Rev:** Laureate male right **Rev. Legend:** A. PAC. Domin. IN. DIEB. NOS

ate	Mintage	VG	F	VF	XF	Unc
662	—	90.00	225	450	800	—
664	—	90.00	225	450	800	—

KM# 15 6 STUIVERS (Arendschelling)

illon **Obv:** Crowned arms in inner circle **Rev:** Crowned imperial agle in inner circle, titles of Rudolph II

ate	Mintage	VG	F	VF	XF	Unc
D(1601)	—	15.00	30.00	50.00	100	—

KM# 15a 6 STUIVERS (Arendschelling)

.0400 g., Gold **Obv:** Crowned arms in inner circle **Rev:** rowned imperial eagle, titles of Rudolph II

ate	Mintage	VG	F	VF	XF	Unc
D(1601)	—	—	—	3,000	6,000	—

KM# 16 6 STUIVERS (Arendschelling)

illon **Rev:** Titles of Matthias

ate	Mintage	VG	F	VF	XF	Unc
D(1613)	—	15.00	25.00	40.00	75.00	—
618	—	15.00	25.00	40.00	65.00	—
678 (error for 1618)	—	20.00	40.00	60.00	100	—

KM# 75 6 STUIVERS (Arendschelling)

illon **Rev. Legend:** Da: DAC: DOM: IN: DIEB: NOST

ate	Mintage	VG	F	VF	XF	Unc
670	—	15.00	40.00	75.00	100	—
675	—	25.00	50.00	100	150	—
678	—	20.00	45.00	90.00	120	—
679	—	14.00	40.00	75.00	100	—

KM# 85 6 STUIVERS (Rijderschelling)

.9500 g., 0.5830 Billon 0.0928 oz. **Obv:** Crowned arms divide alue **Rev:** Knight with sword on horseback to right, crowned rms below horse, date with Arabic numerals in legend

ate	Mintage	VG	F	VF	XF	Unc
680	—	10.00	25.00	55.00	85.00	—
681	—	10.00	25.00	55.00	85.00	—
682	—	10.00	25.00	55.00	85.00	—
683	—	10.00	25.00	55.00	85.00	—
691	—	10.00	25.00	55.00	85.00	—

KM# 87 6 STUIVERS (Rijderschelling)

.7100 g., 0.5830 Billon 0.0883 oz. **Obv:** Crowned arms divide alue **Rev:** Date in Roman style numerals

ate	Mintage	VG	F	VF	XF	Unc
685	—	20.00	40.00	75.00	150	—
686	—	15.00	30.00	50.00	100	—
687	—	15.00	30.00	50.00	100	—
688	—	15.00	30.00	50.00	100	—
689	—	15.00	30.00	50.00	100	—
690	—	15.00	30.00	50.00	100	—

KM# 17 28 STUIVERS (Florin)

19.5000 g., 0.6730 Silver 0.4219 oz. ASW **Obv:** Crowned arms in inner circle, date at top above crown **Rev:** Crowned imperial eagle with value in orb on breast in inner circle

Date	Mintage	VG	F	VF	XF	Unc
1619	—	30.00	70.00	140	250	—
1620 (error, value "82")	—	—	—	—	—	—
1620	—	30.00	70.00	140	250	—
1621	—	40.00	70.00	140	250	—
1626	—	30.00	70.00	140	250	—
1628	—	30.00	70.00	140	250	—
ND(1650-65)	—	30.00	70.00	140	250	—

KM# 22 28 STUIVERS (Florin)

Silver **Obv:** Crowned arms in inner circle, date above **Rev:** Crowned imperial eagle with value in orb on breast in inner circle **Note:** Klippe.

Date	Mintage	VG	F	VF	XF	Unc
1619	—	—	—	—	—	—

KM# 78.1 28 STUIVERS (Florin)

Silver **Obv:** Crowned arms in inner circle **Obv. Legend:** FLOR • ARG • CIVITA • IMP • ZWOLLÆ **Rev:** Crowned imperial eagle with orb on breast in inner circle, partial date at upper left **Rev. Legend:** DA • PAC • DOM • IN • DIEB • NOSTRIS •

Date	Mintage	VG	F	VF	XF	Unc
(16)79	70,020	25.00	75.00	150	250	—
(16)80	Inc. above	25.00	75.00	150	250	—

KM# 78.2 28 STUIVERS (Florin)

Silver **Obv:** Crowned arms in inner circle, partial date above **Obv. Legend:** FLOR • ARG • CIVITA • IMP • ZWOLLÆ **Rev:** Crowned imperial eagle with orb on breast with value 28 **Rev. Legend:** DA • PAC • DOM • IN • DIEB • NOSTRIS •

Date	Mintage	VG	F	VF	XF	Unc
1680	Inc. above	—	25.00	75.00	150	250
1683/0	Inc. above	—	25.00	75.00	150	250
1683	Inc. above	—	25.00	75.00	150	250
1685	Inc. above	—	25.00	75.00	150	250

KM# 78.3 28 STUIVERS (Florin)

Silver **Obv:** Crowned arms, date above **Obv. Legend:** FLOR • ARG • CIVITA • IMP • ZWOLLÆ **Rev:** Crowned imperial eagle with orb on breast with value 28 **Rev. Legend:** DA • PAC • DOM • IN • DIEB • NOSTRIS •

Date	Mintage	VG	F	VF	XF	Unc
1684	Inc. above	25.00	75.00	150	250	—
1685	Inc. above	25.00	75.00	150	250	—
1686	Inc. above	15.00	50.00	75.00	150	—

KM# 88 30 STUIVERS (Daalder)

15.8800 g., 0.9610 Silver 0.4906 oz. ASW **Obv:** Crowned arms divide value, date in legend **Rev:** Standing knight with sword behind crowned arms to left **Note:** Mint mark: Rosette.

Date	Mintage	VG	F	VF	XF	Unc
1685	91,650	120	300	600	800	—

KM# 89 30 STUIVERS (Daalder)

Silver **Obv:** Crowned quartered arms divide value, date in legend

Date	Mintage	VG	F	VF	XF	Unc
1686	—	40.00	85.00	160	300	—
1688	—	40.00	85.00	160	300	—
1692/1	—	80.00	150	300	450	—
1692	—	40.00	85.00	160	300	—

KM# 90 GULDEN

10.6100 g., 0.9200 Silver 0.3138 oz. ASW **Obv:** Crowned arms divide value, date above crown **Rev:** Standing female figure leaning on Bible on column, holding spear with Liberty cap

Date	Mintage	VG	F	VF	XF	Unc
1687	21,555	125	400	900	1,400	—

KM# 86 3 GULDEN (60 Stuiver)

31.8200 g., 0.9200 Silver 0.9412 oz. ASW **Obv:** Crowned arms divide value, date above crown **Rev:** Standing female figure leaning on Bible on column, holding spear with Liberty cap **Note:** Mint mark: Rosette. Dav. #4970.

Date	Mintage	VG	F	VF	XF	Unc
1682	40,595	100	250	500	1,000	—
1686	Inc. above	75.00	200	400	800	—
1687	Inc. above	75.00	200	400	800	—
1689	Inc. above	75.00	200	400	800	—
1690	Inc. above	75.00	200	400	800	—

KM# 18 1/2 DAALDER (Arendsrijks - 25 Stuiver)

14.5100 g., 0.8850 Silver 0.4128 oz. ASW **Obv:** Shield of arms with elaborate helmet above in inner circle **Rev:** Crowned imperial eagle with orb on breast in inner circle, titles of Rudolph II

Date	Mintage	VG	F	VF	XF	Unc
1612	—	175	500	900	1,300	—

KM# 19 1/2 DAALDER (Arendsrijks - 25 Stuiver)

Silver **Rev:** Titles of Matthias

Date	Mintage	VG	F	VF	XF	Unc
ND	—	150	500	1,000	1,500	—
1612	—	150	500	1,000	1,500	—
1620	—	150	500	1,000	1,500	—
1647	—	150	500	1,000	1,500	—

KM# 50 1/2 DAALDER (Arendsrijks - 25 Stuiver)

Silver **Rev:** Titles of Ferdinand III

Date	Mintage	VG	F	VF	XF	Unc
1647	—	—	—	—	—	—
1649	—	175	500	900	1,400	—

KM# 31 1/2 DAALDER (Lion - 24 Stuiver)

27.6800 g., 0.7500 Silver 0.6674 oz. ASW **Obv:** Armored knight looking right above lion sheild in inner circle **Rev:** Rampant lion left divides date in inner circle

Date	Mintage	VG	F	VF	XF	Unc
1633	—	75.00	200	450	850	—

KM# 35 1/2 DAALDER (Lion - 24 Stuiver)

Silver **Obv:** Armored knight looking right above Zwolle arms in inner circle

Date	Mintage	VG	F	VF	XF	Unc
1637	—	35.00	100	150	250	—
1639	—	35.00	100	150	250	—
1641	—	35.00	100	150	250	—
1642	—	35.00	100	150	250	—
1644	—	35.00	100	150	250	—

KM# 45 1/2 DAALDER (Lion - 24 Stuiver)

Silver **Rev:** Date in legend

Date	Mintage	VG	F	VF	XF	Unc
1641	—	35.00	100	250	400	—
1642	—	35.00	100	200	400	—
1644	—	35.00	100	200	400	—
1646	—	35.00	100	200	400	—
1648	—	35.00	100	200	400	—
1649	—	35.00	100	200	400	—
1650	—	35.00	100	200	400	—
1651	—	35.00	100	200	400	—
1652	—	35.00	100	200	400	—

KM# 57 1/2 DAALDER (Rijks)

14.5100 g., 0.8850 Silver 0.4128 oz. ASW **Obv:** Laureate 1/2 figure holding sword and arms in inner circle **Rev:** Crowned arms divide date in inner circle

Date	Mintage	VG	F	VF	XF	Unc
1653	—	—	—	—	—	—

KM# 10 DAALDER (Arendsrijks - 50 Stuiver)

29.0300 g., 0.8850 Silver 0.8260 oz. ASW **Obv:** Shield of arms with elaborate helmet above in inner circle, divided at bottom **Rev:** Crowned imperial eagle with orb on breast in inner circle, titles of Rudolph II **Note:** Dav. #4989.

Date	Mintage	VG	F	VF	XF	Unc
ND	—	70.00	200	400	800	—
1601	—	70.00	200	400	800	—
1612	—	125	250	500	1,000	—
1613	—	125	250	500	1,000	—

KM# 20 DAALDER (Arendsrijks - 50 Stuiver)

Silver **Rev:** Titles of Matthias **Note:** Dav. #4990.

Date	Mintage	VG	F	VF	XF	Unc
ND	—	125	450	900	1,300	—
1613	—	125	450	900	1,300	—
1620	—	125	450	900	1,300	—

KM# 25.1 DAALDER (Arendsrijks - 50 Stuiver)

Silver **Obv:** Shield of arms with elaborate helmet above in inner circle, date near helmet **Rev:** Crowned imperial eagle with orb on breast in inner circle, titles of Ferdinand II **Note:** Dav. #4991.

Date	Mintage	VG	F	VF	XF	Unc
ND	—	—	—	—	—	—
1628	—	150	450	900	1,200	—
1629	—	150	450	900	1,200	—
1631	—	175	500	1,250	2,500	—
1636	—	175	500	1,250	2,500	—

KM# 32 DAALDER (Arendsrijks - 50 Stuiver)

Silver **Rev:** Titles of Ferdinand III (or 3) in legend **Note:** Dav. #4992.

Date	Mintage	VG	F	VF	XF	Unc
ND	—	150	450	900	1,200	—
1646	—	150	450	900	1,200	—
1647	—	150	450	900	1,200	—
1649	—	150	450	900	1,200	—
1652	—	150	450	900	1,200	—
1653	—	150	450	900	1,200	—

KM# 25.2 DAALDER (Arendsrijks - 50 Stuiver)

Silver **Obv:** Shield of arms with elaborate helmet above in inner circle **Rev:** Crowned imperial eagle with orb on breast in inner circle, date in legend, titles of Ferdinand II

Date	Mintage	VG	F	VF	XF	Unc
1636	—	250	750	1,750	2,500	—

KM# 33 DAALDER (Lion - 48 Stuiver)

27.6800 g., 0.7500 Silver 0.6674 oz. ASW **Obv:** Similar to KM#36 but with lion on sheild **Rev:** Similar to KM#36 but smaller sheild on lion's side **Note:** Dav. #4881.

Date	Mintage	VG	F	VF	XF	Unc
1633	—	40.00	125	250	450	—

KM# 36 DAALDER (Lion - 48 Stuiver)

Silver **Obv:** Shield with St. Michael **Rev:** Larger shield on lion's side **Note:** Dav. #4882.

Date	Mintage	VG	F	VF	XF	Unc
1637	—	35.00	125	250	500	—
1639	—	30.00	100	225	450	—

KM# 38 DAALDER (Lion - 48 Stuiver)

Silver **Obv:** Shield with St. Michael **Rev:** Without shield on lion's side **Note:** Dav. #4883.

Date	Mintage	VG	F	VF	XF	Unc
1639	—	30.00	100	200	275	—
1640	—	30.00	100	200	275	—
1641	—	30.00	100	200	275	—
1642	—	30.00	100	200	275	—
1644	—	30.00	100	200	275	—
1646	—	30.00	100	200	275	—

KM# 46 DAALDER (Lion - 48 Stuiver)

Silver **Rev:** Date in legend **Note:** Varieties exist. Dav. #4885.

Date	Mintage	VG	F	VF	XF	Unc
1641	—	30.00	70.00	140	250	—
1642	—	30.00	70.00	140	250	—
1644	—	30.00	70.00	140	250	—
1646	—	30.00	70.00	140	250	—
1647	—	30.00	70.00	140	250	—
1648	—	30.00	70.00	140	250	—
1649	—	30.00	70.00	140	250	—
1650	—	30.00	70.00	140	250	—
1651	—	30.00	70.00	140	250	—
1652	—	30.00	70.00	140	250	—
1653	—	30.00	70.00	140	250	—
1654/1	—	40.00	100	200	350	—
1654	—	30.00	70.00	140	250	—
1655	—	30.00	70.00	140	250	—

KM# 48 DAALDER (Lion - 48 Stuiver)

Silver **Rev:** Date behind lion **Note:** Dav. #4884.

Date	Mintage	VG	F	VF	XF	Unc
1642	—	50.00	150	300	500	—
1644	—	50.00	150	300	500	—

KM# 56 DAALDER (Rijks)

29.0300 g., 0.8850 Silver 0.8260 oz. ASW **Obv:** Crowned lion shield divides date **Obv. Legend:** MONETA • ARG • CIVITATES • ZWOL(L) • **Rev:** 1/2 length armored knight right **Rev. Legend:** FERDINA III - • DG • RO... **Note:** Dav. #4993.

Date	Mintage	VG	F	VF	XF	Un
1650	—	80.00	175	350	650	–
1652	—	80.00	175	350	650	–
1654	—	80.00	175	350	650	–
1655	—	80.00	175	350	650	–
1656	—	80.00	175	350	650	–

KM# 55 DAALDER (Rijks)

Silver **Obv:** Crowned bust of Ferdinand III **Note:** Mint mark: Flower. Dav. #4994.

Date	Mintage	VG	F	VF	XF	Un
1650	—	150	500	1,000	2,000	–

KM# 77 DAALDER (Rijks)

Silver **Obv:** Laureate 1/2 figure holding sword and arms **Rev:** Crowned arms divide date in inner circle **Note:** Dav. #4846.

Date	Mintage	VG	F	VF	XF	Un
1676	63,960	125	300	550	750	–

KM# 66 DAALDER (Lion)

Silver **Note:** Dav. #4886.

Date	Mintage	VG	F	VF	XF	Un
1661	—	35.00	90.00	175	225	–
1662	—	35.00	90.00	175	225	–
1663	—	35.00	90.00	175	225	–
1664	—	35.00	90.00	175	225	–
1665	—	35.00	90.00	175	225	–
1666	—	35.00	90.00	175	225	–
1667	—	35.00	90.00	175	225	–
1674	—	45.00	110	225	300	–
1676	—	45.00	110	225	300	–
1677	—	35.00	90.00	175	225	–
1679	—	45.00	110	225	300	–
1685/7	—	45.00	110	225	300	–
1685	—	35.00	90.00	175	225	–
1688/7	—	45.00	110	225	300	–
1692	—	75.00	150	300	500	–

KM# 59 SILVER DUCAT

28.2500 g., 0.8730 Silver 0.7929 oz. ASW **Note:** Mint mark: Flower.

Date	Mintage	VG	F	VF	XF	Un
1656 (error, inverted 9)	443,655	80.00	225	400	600	–
1659	—	60.00	175	275	450	–
1660	—	60.00	175	275	450	–

KM# 60 SILVER DUCAT
Silver **Rev. Legend:** CONCORDIA. RES. PARVAE. CRESCVNT. **Note:** Dave. #4921.

Date	Mintage	VG	F	VF	XF	Unc
1659	—	60.00	175	250	400	—
1660	—	60.00	175	250	475	—
1661	—	60.00	175	250	475	—
1662	—	60.00	175	250	475	—
1664	—	150	350	500	900	—
1667	—	60.00	175	250	475	—
1668	—	60.00	175	250	475	—
1669	—	60.00	175	250	475	—

KM# 67 1/2 DUCATON (20 Stuiver)
16.3900 g., 0.9410 Silver 0.4958 oz. ASW **Obv:** Knight with sword on horseback right, city arms below in inner circle **Rev:** Crowned arms with crowned lion supporters in innr circle, date at top in legend

Date	Mintage	VG	F	VF	XF	Unc
1661	—	150	300	600	1,000	—

KM# 61 DUCATON (40 Stuiver)
32.7800 g., 0.9410 Silver 0.9917 oz. ASW **Obv:** Knight with sword on horseback right, city arms below in inner circle **Rev:** Crowned arms with crowned lion supporters in innr circle, date at top in legend **Note:** Mint mark: Flower. Dav. #4946.

Date	Mintage	VG	F	VF	XF	Unc
1659	262,695	40.00	150	300	600	—
1660	Inc. above	40.00	150	300	600	—

KM# 65.1 DUCATON (40 Stuiver)
Silver **Rev. Legend:** CONCORDIA. RES. PARVAE. CRESCVNT. **Note:** Dav. #4947. Varieties exist.

Date	Mintage	VG	F	VF	XF	Unc
1660	—	45.00	175	325	500	—
1661	—	40.00	150	300	450	—
1662	—	40.00	150	300	450	—
1663	—	40.00	150	300	450	—
1664	—	25.00	100	200	300	—
1665	—	25.00	100	200	300	—
1666	—	25.00	100	200	300	—
1667	—	25.00	100	200	300	—
1668	—	35.00	140	225	350	—
1669	—	45.00	175	325	500	—
1670	—	45.00	175	325	500	—
1671	—	45.00	175	325	500	—
1674	—	45.00	175	325	500	—
1675	—	40.00	150	300	450	—
1676	—	40.00	150	300	450	—
1677	—	35.00	140	225	350	—
1682	—	40.00	150	300	450	—
1686	—	45.00	175	325	500	—

KM# 65.2 DUCATON (40 Stuiver)
Silver **Rev. Legend:** CONCORDIA - RES - PARVAE - CRESCVNT **Note:** Struck with special dies by C. Adolphi.

Date	Mintage	VG	F	VF	XF	Unc
1662 Proof	—	—	—	—	2,000	2,500

KM# 49 1/2 CAVALIER D'OR
5.0000 g., 0.9200 Gold 0.1479 oz. AGW **Obv:** Equestrian figure of knight above arms in inner circle **Rev:** Crowned arms in inner circle, date at top **Note:** Fr. #215.

Date	Mintage	VG	F	VF	XF	Unc
1644	—	650	1,500	3,000	7,000	—

KM# 51 CAVALIER D'OR
10.0000 g., 0.9200 Gold 0.2958 oz. AGW **Note:** FR. # 214.

Date	Mintage	VG	F	VF	XF	Unc
1644	—	—	—	10,000	15,000	—

TRADE COINAGE

KM# 30 DUCAT
3.5000 g., 0.9860 Gold 0.1109 oz. AGW **Obv:** 5-line inscription in tablet **Rev:** Titles of Ferdinand II **Note:** Fr. #213.

Date	Mintage	VG	F	VF	XF	Unc
1630	—	180	300	450	600	—
1631	—	180	300	450	600	—
1632	—	180	300	450	600	—
1633	—	180	300	450	600	—
1634	—	180	300	450	600	—
1636	—	180	300	450	600	—
1637	—	180	300	450	600	—
1638	—	180	300	450	600	—

KM# 34 DUCAT
3.5000 g., 0.9860 Gold 0.1109 oz. AGW **Obv:** 4-line inscription in tablet

Date	Mintage	VG	F	VF	XF	Unc
1633	—	180	300	450	600	—
1634	—	180	300	450	600	—
1636	—	180	300	450	600	—
1638	—	180	300	450	600	—
1639	—	180	300	450	600	—
1640	—	180	300	450	600	—
1641/1461	—	250	400	600	800	—
1641	—	180	300	450	600	—
1642	—	180	300	450	600	—
1644	—	180	300	450	600	—
1645	—	180	300	450	600	—
1646	—	180	300	450	600	—
1647	—	180	300	450	600	—
1648	—	180	300	450	600	—
1649	—	180	300	450	600	—
1650	—	180	300	450	600	—
1652	—	180	300	450	600	—
1653	—	180	300	450	600	—
1654	—	180	300	450	600	—
1655	—	180	300	450	600	—
1656	—	180	300	450	600	—
1659	—	180	300	450	600	—
1660/50	—	180	300	450	600	—
1660	—	180	300	450	600	—
1661	—	180	300	450	600	—
1662	—	180	300	450	600	—
1676/5	—	—	—	—	—	—
1676	—	200	400	700	1,200	—

KM# 68 DUCAT
3.5000 g., 0.9860 Gold 0.1109 oz. AGW **Rev:** Titles of Ferdinand III, date in legend **Note:** Fr. # 213.

Date	Mintage	VG	F	VF	XF	Unc
1662	—	200	300	500	800	—
1664	—	200	300	500	800	—
1666	—	200	300	500	800	—
1668	—	200	300	500	800	—
1674	—	200	300	500	800	—

KM# 58.1 2 DUCAT
7.0000 g., 0.9860 Gold 0.2219 oz. AGW **Obv:** 5-line inscription in tablet **Rev:** Standing figure of knight to right divides date in inner circle **Note:** Fr. # 212.

Date	Mintage	VG	F	VF	XF	Unc
1655	—	325	600	1,600	2,800	—
1656	—	325	600	1,600	2,800	—
1662	—	325	600	1,600	2,800	—

KM# 58.2 2 DUCAT
7.0000 g., 0.9860 Gold 0.2219 oz. AGW **Obv:** 4-line inscription in tablet **Rev:** Standing figure of knight to right divides date in inner circle **Note:** Fr. #212.

Date	Mintage	VG	F	VF	XF	Unc
1662	—	325	600	1,600	2,800	—

KM# 47 10 DUCAT (Portugaleser)
35.0000 g., 0.9860 Gold 1.1095 oz. AGW **Obv:** Crowned arms in inner circle, double circled legend **Rev:** Cross in inner circle

Date	Mintage	VG	F	VF	XF	Unc
1641 Rare	—	—	—	—	—	—

PATTERNS

Including off metal strikes

KM#	Date	Mintage	Identification	Mkt Val
Pn1	ND(1601)	—	Arendschelling. Silver. KM#15. Klippe.	800
Pn2	1677	—	Schelling. Gold. 14.0000 g. KM#75.	—

PIEFORTS

KM#	Date	Mintage	Identification	Mkt Val
P1	1637	—	Lion Daalder. Silver. KM#36.	—
PA2	(16)39	—	Duit. Copper. KM37	—
P2	1648	—	Lion Daalder. Silver. KM#46. Klippe.	3,000
P3	1650	—	Rijksdaalder. Silver. KM#55.	3,000
P4	1653	—	Rijksdaalder. Silver. KM#55.	—
P5	1660	—	Silver Ducat. KM#60.	—
P6	1664	—	Ducaton. Silver. KM#65.1.	—
P7	1682	—	3 Gulden. Silver. KM#86.	3,000
P8	1685	—	Ryderschelling. KM#87. Klippe.	900

STAATS / BRABANT

A marquisate in medieval time. In 1578 Don John of Austria, the hero of Lepanto, died here. The area and town were much fought over even into modern times.

BREDA

Breda is a town on the Merk River, 14 miles (23 km) west of Tilburg. It received a municipal charter in 1252 when it was a heavily fortified city. The Dutch and Spanish kept taking and retaking the town thru much of the 16th and 17th centuries. Compromise of Breda was signed 1566 by the Dutch and Spanish, retaken by duke of Parma 1581 only to be retaken again by Maurice of Nassau in 1590. The Spanish laid a year-long siege to Breda before the inhabitants surrendered in 1625. The Dutch re-couped their hold in 1637. An amnesty proclamation (Declaration of Breda) was issued in 1660 by exiled Charles II of England. Peace Treaties were concluded in 1667 between Britain, France and the Netherlands.

Breda remained an important city in wars of the French Revolution, 1793-95.

SIEGE COINAGE

KM# 1 STUIVER
1.8600 g., Copper, 14 x 14 mm. **Obv:** B/date/shield divides divides 1 - S **Note:** Uniface klippe.

Date	Mintage	Good	VG	F	VF	XF
1625	—	40.00	100	175	250	400
1625 dot before date	—	60.00	150	250	350	500

KM# 2 2 STUIVERS
4.8000 g., Copper **Obv:** Shield divides date, 3-line inscription **Obv. Inscription:** II / BREDA / OBSESSA **Note:** Uniface klippe.

Date	Mintage	Good	VG	F	VF	XF
1625	—	40.00	100	175	250	400

KM# 3 20 STUIVERS
5.0000 g., Silver, 20 x 20 mm. **Obv:** Date around shield **Obv. Legend:** BREDA • OBSES • **Note:** Uniface klippe.

Date	Mintage	Good	VG	F	VF	XF
1625	—	64.00	160	320	500	850

KM# 5 40 STUIVERS

9.8800 g., Silver, 24 x 25 mm. **Obv:** Date at left of crowned shield **Obv. Legend:** BREDA • OBSESSA **Note:** Uniface klippe.

Date	Mintage	Good	VG	F	VF	XF
1625	—	100	350	700	1,250	2,000

KM# 4 40 STUIVERS

Silver **Obv:** Date around rampant lion with sword **Obv. Legend:** BREDA • OBSESSA **Note:** Uniface klippe. Diameter round die 20 or 22mm.

Date	Mintage	Good	VG	F	VF	XF
1625	—	100	375	900	2,000	3,000

KM# 6.1 60 STUIVERS

Silver, 28 x 29 mm. **Obv:** Rampant lion with sword between 2 shield countermarks, rosette countermark below, value 60 above **Obv. Legend:** BREDA • OBSESSA **Note:** Uniface klippe. Diameter round die 20 or 22mm.

Date	Mintage	Good	VG	F	VF	XF
1625	—	—	—	850	1,150	1,650

KM# 6.2 60 STUIVERS

Silver **Obv:** Legend, date **Obv. Legend:** BREDA • BSESSA **Note:** Uniface klippe.

Date	Mintage	Good	VG	F	VF	XF
1625	—	—	—	850	1,150	1,650

THORN

TOWN

STANDARD COINAGE

KM# 10 DUIT

Copper **Ruler:** Anna van der Marck **Obv:** Crowned arms of Friesland in wreath **Obv. Legend:** NISI DNS NOBISCVM **Rev:** INscription in wreath **Rev. Inscription:** TORN / GVSA /.../arms

Date	Mintage	VG	F	VF	XF	Unc
ND(1613-14)	—	25.00	75.00	150	300	—

KM# 11 2 DUIT

Copper **Ruler:** Anna van der Marck **Obv:** Crowned arms of • March in wreath **Rev:** Inscription within wreath **Rev. Inscription:** IN / THEO / REN CV / SVS

Date	Mintage	VG	F	VF	XF	Unc
ND(1613-14) Lily	—	25.00	75.00	150	300	—

KM# 12 3 DUITS

Copper **Ruler:** Anna van der Marck **Obv:** Crowned arms of Marck in wreath

Date	Mintage	VG	F	VF	XF	Unc
ND(1613-1614)	—	25.00	75.00	150	300	—

KM# 13 OORD

Copper **Ruler:** Anna van der Marck **Obv:** Crowned shield with 5 arms in circle **Obv. Legend:** ANNA D MARCK AB THO **Rev:** Crowned arms of Marck on cross, divised date

Date	Mintage	VG	F	VF	XF	Unc
1613	—	25.00	75.00	150	300	—
1614	—	25.00	75.00	150	300	—

KM# 14 OORD

Copper **Ruler:** Anna van der Marck **Obv:** Crowned shield with 5 arms in inner circle **Obv. Legend:** ANNA DEMARCK AB THOR **Rev:** Crowned arms of Marck on cross, divided date **Rev. Legend:** SIT NO DOMIMI BENEDI

Date	Mintage	VG	F	VF	XF	Unc
ND	—	25.00	75.00	150	300	—
1613	—	—	—	—	—	—
1614	—	—	—	—	—	—

KM# 15 OORD

Copper **Ruler:** Anna van der Marck **Obv:** Crowned shield with 6 arms in inner circle **Obv. Legend:** ANNA DEMARCK AB THOR **Rev:** Crowned arms of Marck on cross, divides date **Rev. Legend:** SIT NO DONIMI BENEDI(CT)

Date	Mintage	VG	F	VF	XF	Unc
1613	—	25.00	75.00	150	300	—

KM# 16 OORD

Copper **Ruler:** Anna van der Marck **Obv:** Corwned shield with arms in inner circle **Obv. Legend:** ANNA D MARCK AB THOR **Rev:** Crowned arms of marck on cross divide date **Rev. Legend:** SIT NO DO - MI - NI BENEDI

Date	Mintage	VG	F	VF	XF	Unc
	—	25.00	75.00	150	300	—
1614	—	25.00	75.00	150	300	—

KM# 17 OORD

Copper **Ruler:** Anna van der Marck **Obv:** Crowned shield with arms in inner circle **Obv. Legend:** ANNA D MARCK AB THOR **Rev:** Crowned arms of Marck on cross, divide date **Rev. Legend:** SIT NO DO - MI - NI BENEDI

Date	Mintage	VG	F	VF	XF	Unc
1613	—	25.00	75.00	150	300	—

KM# 5 3 KREUTZER

Silver **Ruler:** Anna van der Marck **Obv:** Crowned shield with 5 arms on cross in inner circle **Obv. Legend:** ANNA D G ABBA IN THOR C D M (I ST) **Rev:** Crowned double headed eagle with 3 in orb in inner circle **Rev. Legend:** MATH I ELEC RO IMP SEM AV

Date	Mintage	VG	F	VF	XF	Unc
ND Lily	—	—	—	—	—	—

KM# 6 3 KREUTZER

Silver **Ruler:** Anna van der Marck **Obv:** Three arms in inner circle **Obv. Legend:** ANNA D G ABB IN THOR C D M **Rev:** Crowned double headed eagle with 3 in orb, in inner circle **Rev. Legend:** MATH I ELEC RO IMP SEM

Date	Mintage	VG	F	VF	XF	Unc
ND Lily	—	—	—	—	—	—

KM# 8 4 STUIVERS

Silver **Ruler:** Anna van der Marck **Obv:** Crowned shield with 5 arms on cross **Obv. Legend:** AN NA D G AB IN THOR EN CO D **Rev:** Crowned double headed eagle **Rev. Legend:** MATH I D G ELEC ROM IMP SEM AV IV

Date	Mintage	VG	F	VF	XF	Unc
ND(1610)	—	60.00	150	300	500	—

KM# 7 STUIVER

Silver **Ruler:** Anna van der Marck **Obv:** Crowned shield with 5 arms, value 1-S flanking **Obv. Legend:** ANNA C A M AB D THOR **Rev:** Decorated cross **Rev. Legend:** MON - AR - THO - REN

Date	Mintage	VG	F	VF	XF	Unc
ND(1610) Lily	—	—	—	—	—	—

KM# 19 STUIVER

Silver **Ruler:** Anna van der Marck **Obv:** Crowned sheild with 5 arms, value 1-S flanking **Obv. Legend:** ANNA C A MARCK AB THOR **Rev:** Decorated cross, shield at center **Rev. Legend:** MO NO AR TH OREN SIS

Date	Mintage	VG	F	VF	XF	Unc
ND(1612-1619) Lily	—	—	—	—	—	—

KM# 18 STUIVER

Silver **Ruler:** Anna van der Marck **Obv:** Crowned shield with 5 arms **Obv. Legend:** ANNA D MARCA ABBA IN THOR **Rev:** Cross with lily's on ends, shield at center **Rev. Legend:** MATH ELEC ROMA IMPE

Date	Mintage	VG	F	VF	XF	Unc
ND(1612)	—	—	—	—	—	—

KM# 20 RIJKSDAALDER

48.0000 g., Silver **Ruler:** Anna van der Marck **Obv:** Crowned shield with 5 arms on cross **Obv. Legend:** ANNA DEI GRA ABBA IN THOR C D M **Rev:** Crowned double headed eagle **Rev. Legend:** MATHIAS DEI GRA ROM IMP SEM P AVG

Date	Mintage	VG	F	VF	XF	Unc
1614	—	—	—	—	—	—

KM# 21 RIJKSDAALDER

Silver **Ruler:** Anna van der Marck **Obv:** Crowned shield on cross **Obv. Legend:** ANNA D G ABBA THOR P IMP CO A MAR **Rev:** Crowned double headed eagle **Rev. Legend:** FERDINANDVS II D G RO IM S AVG

Date	Mintage	VG	F	VF	XF	Unc
1627	—	—	—	—	—	—

PIEFORTS

KM#	Date	Mintage	Identification	Mkt Val
P1	1614	—	Rijksdaalder. Silver. KM#20	—
P2	1627	—	Rijksdaalder. Silver.	—

UTRECHT

Trajectum

Utrecht (Trajectum), the smallest Netherlands province, represents the bulk of a see founded in 722. It was one of the seven provinces that signed the Union of Utrecht against Spain, a treaty regarded as the foundation of the Dutch Republic and later kingdom of the Netherlands.

CITY

STANDARD COINAGE

KM# 22 DUIT

2.0000 g., Copper **Obv:** Shield of arms on floral long cross **Rev:** TRA/IEC/TVM/(date) in wreath

Date	Mintage	VG	F	VF	XF	Unc
1617 (error)	—	10.00	35.00	70.00	150	—
1619	—	5.00	20.00	50.00	100	—
1622	—	5.00	20.00	50.00	100	—
1625	—	4.00	12.50	20.00	60.00	—
1626	—	6.00	20.00	40.00	70.00	—
1627	—	5.00	20.00	50.00	100	—
1628	—	6.00	20.00	40.00	70.00	—
1631	—	6.00	20.00	50.00	100	—
1634	—	4.00	20.00	50.00	100	—
1637	—	4.00	12.50	20.00	40.00	—
1637/4	—	6.00	20.00	40.00	70.00	—
1654 (error)	—	—	—	—	—	—

KM# 43.1 DUIT

Copper **Obv:** Crowned arms with lion supporters, CIV • TRA below **Rev:** U/TRECHT and date in quatrefoil

Date	Mintage	VG	F	VF	XF	Unc
1657	—	10.00	40.00	80.00	130	—

KM# 43.2 DUIT

Copper **Obv:** UTRECHT below **Rev:** CIV/TRAIECT/1657

Date	Mintage	VG	F	VF	XF	Unc
1657	—	10.00	40.00	60.00	90.00	—
1659	—	15.00	60.00	90.00	120	—

KM# 43.2a DUIT

3.5000 g., Silver **Obv:** UTRECHT below **Rev:** CIV/TRAIECT/1657

Date	Mintage	VG	F	VF	XF	Unc
1657	—	—	—	225	450	—

KM# 44 DUIT

Copper **Obv:** Crowned arms with horizontal stripes

Date	Mintage	VG	F	VF	XF	Unc
1657	—	5.00	15.00	30.00	60.00	—
1659	—	5.00	15.00	30.00	60.00	—
1661	—	5.00	15.00	20.00	40.00	—
1663	—	5.00	15.00	20.00	40.00	—
1664	—	5.00	15.00	20.00	40.00	—
1665	—	5.00	15.00	20.00	40.00	—
1666	—	5.00	15.00	20.00	40.00	—
1667	—	5.00	15.00	20.00	40.00	—
1668	—	5.00	15.00	20.00	40.00	—
1670	—	5.00	15.00	20.00	40.00	—
1671	—	5.00	15.00	20.00	40.00	—
1676	—	5.00	15.00	20.00	40.00	—
1677	—	5.00	15.00	20.00	40.00	—
1681	—	5.00	15.00	20.00	40.00	—
1683	—	5.00	15.00	20.00	40.00	—
1684	—	5.00	15.00	20.00	40.00	—
1685	—	6.00	20.00	40.00	80.00	—
1687	—	10.00	25.00	50.00	100	—

KM# 44a DUIT

3.3000 g., Silver **Obv:** Crowned arms with horizontal stripes

Date	Mintage	VG	F	VF	XF	Unc
1659/7	—	—	—	—	—	—
1659	—	—	—	200	400	—
1663	—	—	—	—	—	—
1665	—	—	—	—	—	—
1671	—	—	—	—	—	—
1676	—	—	—	—	—	—
1681	—	—	—	—	—	—

KM# 44b DUIT

3.5000 g., Gold **Obv:** Crowned arms with horizontal stripes

Date	Mintage	VG	F	VF	XF	Unc
1659 Rare	—	—	—	—	—	—
1678 Rare	—	—	—	—	—	—
1680	—	—	—	—	—	—

KM# 43.2b DUIT

3.5000 g., Gold **Obv:** UTRECHT below **Rev:** CIV / TRAIECT / 1657

Date	Mintage	VG	F	VF	XF	Unc
1659	—	—	—	750	1,200	2,400

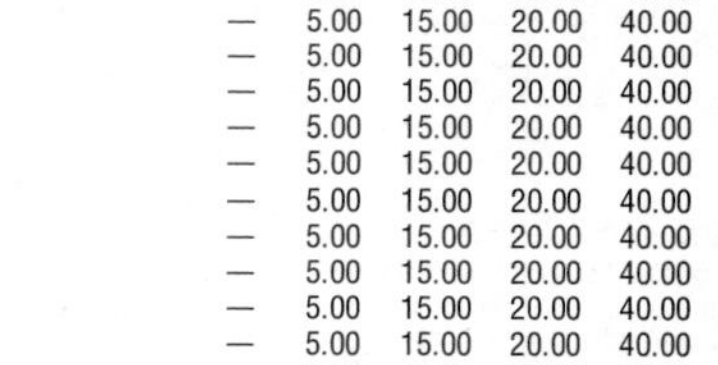

KM# 66 DUIT

Copper **Obv:** Vertical stripes in arms

Date	Mintage	VG	F	VF	XF	Unc
1681	—	10.00	25.00	50.00	100	—

ate	Mintage	VG	F	VF	XF	Unc
383	—	10.00	25.00	50.00	100	—
384	—	6.00	20.00	40.00	80.00	—
386	—	6.00	20.00	40.00	80.00	—
387	—	5.00	15.00	30.00	60.00	—
389	—	5.00	15.00	30.00	60.00	—
390	—	—	—	—	—	—

M# 66b DUIT

.5000 g., Gold **Obv:** Vertical stripes in arms

ate	Mintage	VG	F	VF	XF	Unc
387	—	—	—	800	1,200	1,800
389	—	—	—	—	—	—
390	—	—	—	800	1,200	1,800
91	—	—	—	—	—	—

M# 66a DUIT

1500 g., Silver **Obv:** Vertical stripes in arms

ate	Mintage	VG	F	VF	XF	Unc
87	—	—	—	150	300	450
390	—	—	—	150	300	450
391	—	—	—	—	—	—

M# 25 1/2 STUIVER

0000 g., Billon **Obv:** Crowned arms, date at top **Rev:** rnamental cross

ate	Mintage	VG	F	VF	XF	Unc
27	—	50.00	175	350	550	—

M# 26 STUIVER

5000 g., Billon **Obv:** Crowned arms divide value, date at top **ev:** Cross in ornamental cartouche

ate	Mintage	VG	F	VF	XF	Unc
27	—	30.00	60.00	125	250	—

M# 50 STUIVER

3000 g., Billon **Note:** Reduced size.

te	Mintage	VG	F	VF	XF	Unc
65	—	25.00	75.00	150	300	—
66	—	25.00	75.00	150	300	—

PROVINCE

STANDARD COINAGE

M# 20 STUIVER

3600 g., 0.5830 Silver 0.0161 oz. ASW **Obv:** Crowned mpant lion left holding sword and arrows, value at sides **Rev. scription:** TRA / IEC / TVM / date

te	Mintage	VG	F	VF	XF	Unc
14	—	8.00	15.00	45.00	90.00	—
15	—	35.00	50.00	100	150	—
18	—	8.00	15.00	45.00	90.00	—

M# 21 2 STUIVERS

7300 g., 0.5830 Silver 0.0324 oz. ASW **Obv:** Crowned mpant lion left holding sword and arrows, value at sides **Rev. scription:** TRA / IC / TVM / date

te	Mintage	VG	F	VF	XF	Unc
14	—	10.00	20.00	40.00	100	—
15	—	10.00	20.00	40.00	100	—
16	—	10.00	20.00	40.00	100	—
17	—	10.00	20.00	40.00	100	—
18	—	10.00	20.00	40.00	100	—
19	—	—	—	—	—	—

M# 55 2 STUIVERS

ver **Obv:** Rampant lion without crown and weapons

te	Mintage	VG	F	VF	XF	Unc
46	—	20.00	40.00	80.00	200	—
74	116,078	10.00	20.00	40.00	100	—
75	Inc. above	10.00	20.00	40.00	100	—

M# 27 3 STUIVERS (1/2 Roosschelling)

5300 g., 0.5830 Silver 0.0493 oz. ASW **Obv:** Crowned arms nner circle, date above crown **Rev:** Ornamental quatrefoil with se at center, in inner circle

te	Mintage	VG	F	VF	XF	Unc
27	—	60.00	200	400	800	—

M# 8 6 STUIVERS (Roosschelling)

2700 g., 0.5830 Silver 0.0988 oz. ASW **Obv:** Crowned arms nner circle, date above crown **Rev:** Ornamental quatrefoil with se at center, in inner circle

te	Mintage	VG	F	VF	XF	Unc
)1	292,790	30.00	85.00	175	250	—

Date	Mintage	VG	F	VF	XF	Unc
1627	Inc. above	40.00	125	250	350	—
1629/7	Inc. above	50.00	150	300	500	—
1629	Inc. above	40.00	125	250	350	—
1630	Inc. above	40.00	125	250	350	—
1631	Inc. above	40.00	125	250	350	—
1632	Inc. above	40.00	125	250	350	—

KM# 60.1 6 STUIVERS (Rijderschelling)

4.9500 g., 0.5830 Silver 0.0928 oz. ASW **Obv:** Crowned quartered arms divide value in branches, date above crown **Rev:** Knight with sword on horseback to right **Note:** Mint mark: Agnus Dei on obverse.

Date	Mintage	VG	F	VF	XF	Unc
1675	132,830	15.00	50.00	100	200	—

KM# 60.2 6 STUIVERS (Rijderschelling)

4.9500 g., 0.5830 Silver 0.0928 oz. ASW **Rev:** Mint mark **Note:** Mint mark: Agnus Dei on reverse.

Date	Mintage	VG	F	VF	XF	Unc
1676	Inc. above	15.00	50.00	100	200	—
1677	Inc. above	15.00	50.00	100	200	—
1678	Inc. above	15.00	50.00	100	200	—

KM# 60.3 6 STUIVERS (Rijderschelling)

Silver **Note:** Mint mark: Rosette. Varieties exist.

Date	Mintage	VG	F	VF	XF	Unc
1679	713,280	10.00	25.00	40.00	80.00	—
1680	705,970	10.00	25.00	40.00	80.00	—
1681	Inc. above	10.00	25.00	40.00	80.00	—
1682	Inc. above	10.00	30.00	50.00	110	—
1686/81	920,855	15.00	35.00	65.00	150	—
1686	Inc. above	10.00	15.00	40.00	80.00	—
1691	376,885	10.00	25.00	40.00	80.00	—

KM# 80 6 STUIVERS (Scheepjesschelling)

4.9500 g., 0.5830 Silver 0.0928 oz. ASW **Obv:** Crowned quartered arms with center shield divide value, branches below arms **Rev:** Ship sailing to right, date in legend

Date	Mintage	VG	F	VF	XF	Unc
1700	1,569,870	15.00	30.00	75.00	125	250

KM# 69 10 STUIVERS (1/2 Gulden)

5.3000 g., 0.9200 Silver 0.1568 oz. ASW

Date	Mintage	VG	F	VF	XF	Unc
1682	8,815	40.00	100	200	450	—

KM# 67 GULDEN

10.6100 g., 0.9200 Silver 0.3138 oz. ASW **Obv:** Crowned quartered arms divide value 1 - G **Rev:** Standing female figure leaning on Bible on column, holding spear with Liberty cap, date on column

Date	Mintage	VG	F	VF	XF	Unc
1681	—	125	350	600	900	—

KM# 70 GULDEN

Silver **Obv:** Date above crown

Date	Mintage	VG	F	VF	XF	Unc
1682	—	45.00	125	225	350	—
1683	—	45.00	125	225	350	—
1684	—	45.00	125	225	350	—
1687	—	45.00	125	225	350	—

KM# 76 GULDEN

Silver

Date	Mintage	VG	F	VF	XF	Unc
1697/4	63,275	15.00	30.00	60.00	125	—
1697	Inc. above	15.00	30.00	60.00	125	—
1698	Inc. above	15.00	30.00	60.00	125	—

KM# 68 3 GULDEN (60 Stuiver)

31.8200 g., 0.9200 Silver 0.9412 oz. ASW **Obv:** Crowned arms divide value **Rev:** Standing female figure leaning on Bible on column, holding spear with Liberty cap, date on column **Note:** Dav. #4958.

Date	Mintage	VG	F	VF	XF	Unc
1681	287,099	125	400	700	1,000	—

KM# 71 3 GULDEN (60 Stuiver)

Silver **Obv:** Date above crown **Note:** Dav. #4959.

Date	Mintage	VG	F	VF	XF	Unc
1682	432,085	60.00	150	250	550	—
1683	Inc. above	60.00	150	250	550	—
1684	Inc. above	60.00	150	250	550	—
1685	Inc. above	60.00	150	250	550	—
1686	Inc. above	60.00	150	250	550	—
1687	Inc. above	60.00	150	250	550	—
1689/7	Inc. above	—	—	—	—	—
1689	Inc. above	60.00	150	250	550	—

KM# 75 3 GULDEN (60 Stuiver)

Silver **Rev:** Date in exergue **Note:** Dav. #4960.

Date	Mintage	VG	F	VF	XF	Unc
1693	—	50.00	100	200	400	—
1694	222,836	50.00	100	200	400	—
1695	Inc. above	50.00	100	200	400	—
1696	266,882	50.00	100	200	300	—
1697	Inc. above	50.00	100	200	400	—

KM# 45 1/2 DUCATON (20 Stuiver)

16.3900 g., 0.9410 Silver 0.4958 oz. ASW **Obv:** Knight on horseback right brandishing sword jumps over arms of Ultricht in inner circle **Obv. Legend:** MO NO ARG PRO CON - FOE BELG TRAI **Rev:** Crowned arms with lion supporters, in inner circle. **Rev. Legend:** CONCORDIA - RES PARVAE - CRESCVNT date **Note:** Similar to 1 Ducaton, KM#46.1

Date	Mintage	VG	F	VF	XF	Unc
1659	—	90.00	200	350	500	—
1660	—	90.00	200	400	600	—
1661	—	90.00	200	400	600	—
1662	—	90.00	200	350	500	—
1663	—	90.00	200	400	600	—
1664	—	90.00	200	400	600	—
1666	—	90.00	200	400	600	—
1667	—	90.00	200	400	600	—
1668	—	90.00	200	350	500	—
1669	—	90.00	200	400	600	—
1670	—	90.00	200	400	600	—
1671	—	90.00	200	350	500	—
1672	—	90.00	200	400	600	—

KM# 56.1 1/2 DUCATON (20 Stuiver)

Silver **Obv:** Knight on horseback right brandishing sword jumps over arms of Ultricht in inner circle **Obv. Legend:** MO NO ARG PRO CON - FOE BELG TRAI **Rev:** Crowned arms with lion supporters, in inner circle. **Rev. Legend:** CONCORDIA - RES PARVAE - CRESCVNT date **Note:** Without inner circles on both sides. Mint mark: Agnus Dei.

Date	Mintage	VG	F	VF	XF	Unc
1674	—	90.00	200	400	600	—
1675	—	90.00	200	350	500	—
1676	—	90.00	200	350	500	—

KM# 56.2 1/2 DUCATON (20 Stuiver)

Silver **Obv:** Knight on horseback right brandishing sword jumps over arms of Ultricht in inner circle **Obv. Legend:** MO NO ARG PRO CON - FOE BELG TRAI **Rev:** Crowned arms with lion supporters, in inner circle. **Rev. Legend:** CONCORDIA - RES PARVAE - CRESCVNT date **Note:** Mint mark between date Rosette. Varieties exist with or without inner circles on both sides.

Date	Mintage	VG	F	VF	XF	Unc
1679	—	90.00	200	350	500	—
1680	—	90.00	200	350	500	—

KM# 56.3 1/2 DUCATON (20 Stuiver)

Silver **Obv:** Knight on horseback right brandishing sword jumps over arms of Ultricht in inner circle **Obv. Legend:** MO NO ARG PRO CON - FOE BELG TRAI **Rev:** Crowned arms with lion supporters, in inner circle. **Rev. Legend:** CONCORDIA - RES PARVAE - CRESCVNT date **Note:** No mintmark

Date	Mintage	VG	F	VF	XF	Unc
1679	—	90.00	200	350	500	—

KM# 46.1 DUCATON (60 Stuiver - Silver Rider)

32.7800 g., 0.9410 Silver 0.9917 oz. ASW **Note:** Dav. #4937.

Date	Mintage	VG	F	VF	XF	Unc
1659	—	40.00	100	200	400	—
1660	—	40.00	100	200	400	—
1661	—	50.00	150	300	600	—
1662	—	50.00	150	300	600	—
1664	—	50.00	150	300	600	—
1665	—	40.00	100	300	400	—
1666	—	30.00	70.00	150	300	—
1667	—	30.00	70.00	150	300	—
1668	—	30.00	70.00	150	300	—
1669	—	50.00	150	300	600	—
1670	—	30.00	70.00	110	300	—
1671	—	40.00	100	200	400	—
1672	—	40.00	100	200	400	—
1673	—	40.00	100	200	400	—

KM# 46.2 DUCATON (60 Stuiver - Silver Rider)

32.7800 g., 0.9410 Silver 0.9917 oz. ASW **Note:** Mint mark: Agnus Dei. Without inner circles.

Date	Mintage	VG	F	VF	XF	Unc
1674	63,450	50.00	130	250	500	—
1675	Inc. above	50.00	130	250	500	—
1676	Inc. above	50.00	150	250	500	—

KM# 63 DUCATON (60 Stuiver - Silver Rider)

Silver **Rev:** Date in cartouche below arms **Note:** Mint mark: Rossette. Dav. #4938.

Date	Mintage	VG	F	VF	XF	Unc
1679	—	50.00	100	200	400	—
1680	—	50.00	100	200	400	—
1681	—	50.00	100	200	400	—
1682	—	50.00	100	200	400	—
1692	—	50.00	100	200	400	—

KM# 47 1/2 SILVER DUCAT (24 Stuiver)

14.1200 g., 0.8730 Silver 0.3963 oz. ASW **Obv:** Armored knight standing, holding sword behind shield of arms, date at sides in inner circle **Rev:** Crowned arms in inner circle

Date	Mintage	VG	F	VF	XF	Unc
1659	—	75.00	200	400	800	—
1660	—	75.00	200	400	800	—
1661	—	75.00	200	400	800	—
1662	—	75.00	200	400	800	—
1663	—	75.00	200	400	800	—
1664	—	75.00	200	400	800	—
1669/4	—	—	—	—	—	—
1669	—	75.00	200	400	800	—
1673	—	75.00	200	400	800	—

KM# 58 1/2 SILVER DUCAT (24 Stuiver)

Silver **Note:** Without inner circles on both sides. Mint mark: Agnus Dei.

Date	Mintage	VG	F	VF	XF	Unc
1674	—	100	300	500	900	—

KM# 48.1 SILVER DUCAT (48 Stuiver)

28.2500 g., 0.8730 Silver 0.7929 oz. ASW **Obv:** Armored knight standing holding sword behind shield of arms, date at sides in inner circle **Rev:** Crowned arms in inner circle **Note:** Dav. #4902.

Date	Mintage	VG	F	VF	XF	Unc
1659	353,865	50.00	100	200	400	—
1660	Inc. above	50.00	100	200	400	—
1661	Inc. above	50.00	100	200	400	—
1662	Inc. above	50.00	100	200	400	—
1663	Inc. above	60.00	125	250	500	—
1664	Inc. above	50.00	100	200	400	—
1668	Inc. above	60.00	125	250	500	—
1669	Inc. above	60.00	125	250	500	—
1671	Inc. above	70.00	140	280	550	—
1672	Inc. above	70.00	140	280	550	—
1673	—	70.00	140	280	550	—
1674	—	80.00	160	320	600	—

KM# 48.2 SILVER DUCAT (48 Stuiver)

28.2500 g., 0.8730 Silver 0.7929 oz. ASW **Note:** Mint mark: Agnus Dei.

Date	Mintage	VG	F	VF	XF	Unc
1674	—	80.00	225	400	600	—

KM# 65 SILVER DUCAT (48 Stuiver)

Silver **Note:** Without inner circles on both sides. Mint mark: Rosette. Dav. #4904.

Date	Mintage	VG	F	VF	XF	Unc
1679	1,702,895	70.00	175	325	450	—
1680	Inc. above	70.00	175	325	450	—
1681	Inc. above	40.00	100	200	350	—
1682	Inc. above	35.00	75.00	125	250	—
1683	Inc. above	35.00	75.00	125	250	—
1684	Inc. above	35.00	75.00	125	250	—
1687	Inc. above	35.00	75.00	150	300	—
1688	Inc. above	70.00	150	300	500	—
1692	Inc. above	35.00	75.00	150	300	—
1693/33	Inc. above	80.00	200	400	600	—
1693	Inc. above	35.00	75.00	150	300	—
1694	Inc. above	35.00	75.00	150	300	—
1695	Inc. above	35.00	75.00	150	300	—
1696/5	Inc. above	70.00	150	300	500	—
1696	Inc. above	70.00	150	300	500	—
1697	Inc. above	35.00	75.00	150	300	—
1698	Inc. above	35.00	75.00	150	300	—
1699	Inc. above	35.00	75.00	150	300	—

KM# 11.1 1/2 DAALDER (Rijks - 24 Stuiver)

14.5100 g., 0.8850 Silver 0.4128 oz. ASW **Obv:** Laureate 1/2 figure holding sword and arms in inncer circle **Obv. Legend:** MO ARG PRO - CONFOE BEL(G) TRA(IEC) mintmark **Rev:** Crowned arms divide date in inner circle **Rev. Legend:** CONCORDIA RES PARVAE CRESCVNT **Note:** Similar to 1 Dutch Rijksdaalder, KM#14. With dotted inner circles on both sides.

Date	Mintage	VG	F	VF	XF	Unc
1606	—	65.00	150	250	350	—
1607	—	60.00	200	300	400	—
1610	—	65.00	150	250	350	—
1611/08	—	65.00	150	250	350	—
1611	—	65.00	150	250	350	—
1612	—	65.00	150	250	350	—
1613	—	65.00	150	250	350	—
1617	—	65.00	150	250	350	—
1618	—	65.00	150	250	350	—
1619	—	40.00	100	175	275	—
1620	—	40.00	100	175	275	—
1621	—	40.00	100	175	275	—
1622	—	40.00	100	175	275	—
1623	—	65.00	150	250	350	—
1624	—	40.00	100	175	275	—
1625	—	65.00	150	250	350	—
1626	—	40.00	100	175	275	—
1629	—	40.00	100	175	275	—
1645	—	65.00	150	250	350	—
1650	—	—	—	—	—	—

KM# 11.2 1/2 DAALDER (Rijks - 24 Stuiver)

14.5100 g., 0.8850 Silver 0.4128 oz. ASW **Obv:** Laureate 1/2 figure holding sword and arms in inncer circle **Obv. Legend:** MO ARG PRO - CONFOE BEL(G) TRA(IEC) mintmark **Rev:** Crowned arms divide date in inner circle **Rev. Legend:** CONCORDIA RES PARVAE CRESCVNT **Note:** With solid inner circles on both sides.

Date	Mintage	VG	F	VF	XF	Unc
1650	—	65.00	150	250	350	—
1651	—	65.00	150	250	350	—
1654	—	40.00	100	175	275	-
1656	—	40.00	100	175	275	-
1657	—	40.00	100	175	275	-
1658	—	40.00	100	175	275	-
1663	—	40.00	100	175	275	-
1668	—	40.00	100	175	275	-

KM# 11.3 1/2 DAALDER (Rijks - 24 Stuiver)

14.5100 g., 0.8850 Silver 0.4128 oz. ASW **Obv:** Laureate 1/2 figure holding sword and arms in inncer circle **Obv. Legend:** MO ARG PRO - CONFOE BEL(G) TRA(IEC) mintmark **Rev:** Crowned arms divide date in inner circle **Rev. Legend:** CONCORDIA RES PARVAE CRESCVNT **Note:** No inner circles on both sides. Mint mark: Agnus Dei.

Date	Mintage	VG	F	VF	XF	Unc
1675	—	80.00	200	300	400	-

KM# 12 1/2 DAALDER (Lion)

13.8400 g., 0.7500 Silver 0.3337 oz. ASW **Note:** Similar to 1 Daalder, KM#30. With dotted inner circles on both sides.

Date	Mintage	VG	F	VF	XF	Unc
1606	—	40.00	100	200	400	-
1607	—	40.00	100	200	400	-
1608	—	40.00	100	200	400	-
1609	—	40.00	100	200	400	-
1610	—	40.00	100	200	400	-
1613	—	65.00	150	275	550	-
1614/13	—	45.00	125	250	500	-
1614	—	40.00	100	200	400	-
1616	—	20.00	50.00	100	200	-
1617	—	20.00	50.00	100	200	-
1618	—	20.00	50.00	100	400	-
1626	—	20.00	50.00	100	200	-
1628	—	40.00	100	200	400	-
1629/1	—	40.00	100	200	400	-
1629/8	—	40.00	100	200	400	-
1629	—	20.00	50.00	100	200	-
1633	—	40.00	100	200	400	-
1634	—	40.00	100	200	400	-
1636	—	20.00	50.00	100	200	-
1637	—	20.00	50.00	100	200	-
1639	—	30.00	75.00	125	250	-
1640	—	20.00	50.00	100	200	-
1641	—	20.00	50.00	100	200	-
1642/1	—	20.00	50.00	100	200	-
1642	—	30.00	75.00	200	400	-
1643	—	20.00	50.00	100	200	-
1644/3	—	20.00	50.00	100	200	-
1644	—	40.00	100	200	400	-
1645	—	40.00	100	200	400	-
1646	—	30.00	75.00	200	400	-
1647	—	20.00	50.00	100	200	-
1648	—	20.00	50.00	100	200	-
1649	—	20.00	50.00	100	200	-
1650	—	20.00	50.00	100	200	-

KM# 31 1/2 DAALDER (Lion)

Silver **Rev:** Crowned lion

Date	Mintage	VG	F	VF	XF	Unc
1636	—	40.00	100	200	400	-
1640	—	30.00	75.00	150	300	-
1642/1	—	40.00	100	200	400	-
1644	—	40.00	100	200	400	-
1646/5	—	40.00	100	200	400	-
1646	—	40.00	100	200	400	-

KM# 35.1 1/2 DAALDER (Lion)

Silver **Rev:** Lion without crown **Note:** With solid inner circles on both sides.

Date	Mintage	VG	F	VF	XF	Unc
1644	—	40.00	100	20.00	400	
1645	—	40.00	100	20.00	400	
1646	—	30.00	75.00	150	300	
1647	—	30.00	75.00	150	300	
1648	26,610	30.00	75.00	150	300	

ate	Mintage	VG	F	VF	XF	Unc
649	—	30.00	75.00	150	300	—
650	—	30.00	75.00	150	300	—
654	—	40.00	100	200	400	—
658/4	—	40.00	100	200	400	—
660	—	30.00	75.00	150	300	—
661	—	30.00	75.00	150	300	—
663	—	30.00	75.00	150	300	—
664	—	40.00	100	200	400	—
667	—	30.00	75.00	150	300	—

KM# 35.2 1/2 DAALDER (Lion)

Silver **Note:** Mint mrk: Agnus Dei. With solid inner circles on both sides.

ate	Mintage	VG	F	VF	XF	Unc
674	—	75.00	175	250	500	—
676	—	75.00	175	250	500	—

KM# 41 1/2 DAALDER (Rijks)

4.5100 g., 0.8850 Silver 0.4128 oz. ASW **Note:** Without solid inner circles on both sides. Similar to 1 Daalder, KM#14.

ate	Mintage	VG	F	VF	XF	Unc
650	—	50.00	125	200	400	—
651	—	50.00	125	200	400	—
654	—	50.00	125	200	400	—
656	—	50.00	125	200	400	—
657	—	50.00	125	200	400	—
658	—	50.00	125	200	400	—
659	—	50.00	125	200	400	—
663	—	50.00	125	200	400	—
668	—	50.00	125	200	400	—

KM# 61 1/2 DAALDER (Rijks)

Silver **Note:** Without inner circles on both sides.

ate	Mintage	VG	F	VF	XF	Unc
675	—	60.00	150	225	450	—

KM# 9 DAALDER (Prince - 40 Stuiver)

9.0300 g., 0.8850 Silver 0.8260 oz. ASW **Obv:** Helmeted arms in inner circle. **Rev:** Armored bust of William the Silent with sword to right in inner circle, date divided at top **Note:** Dav. #4823.

ate	Mintage	VG	F	VF	XF	Unc
601/0	—	90.00	300	600	1,000	—
601	—	70.00	250	500	900	—
603/1	—	90.00	300	600	1,000	—
603/2	—	90.00	300	600	1,000	—
603	—	90.00	300	600	1,000	—

M# 10 DAALDER (Lion - 48 Stuiver)

7.6800 g., 0.7500 Silver 0.6674 oz. ASW **Note:** Similar to M#30 but date divided at bottom on obverse. Dav. #4862.

ate	Mintage	VG	F	VF	XF	Unc
601/1598	—	30.00	60.00	200	400	—
601	—	30.00	60.00	200	400	—
602	—	30.00	60.00	200	400	—
603	—	30.00	60.00	200	400	—

M# 13 DAALDER (Lion - 48 Stuiver)

7.6800 g., 0.7500 Silver 0.6674 oz. ASW **Rev:** Lion shield ithout crown **Note:** Similar to KM#30. Dav. #4863.

ate	Mintage	VG	F	VF	XF	Unc
606	—	25.00	60.00	100	200	—
607/06	—	25.00	60.00	100	200	—
607	—	25.00	60.00	100	200	—
608/7	—	25.00	60.00	100	200	—
608	—	25.00	60.00	100	200	—
609	—	25.00	60.00	100	200	—
610	—	25.00	60.00	100	200	—
611/0	—	35.00	75.00	150	300	—
612/08	—	35.00	80.00	175	350	—
612/09	—	30.00	70.00	150	300	—
612/0	—	35.00	80.00	175	350	—

Date	Mintage	VG	F	VF	XF	Unc
1612	—	35.00	80.00	175	350	—
1613	—	25.00	60.00	100	200	—
1614/3	—	25.00	60.00	100	200	—
1614	—	25.00	60.00	100	200	—
1615	—	25.00	60.00	100	200	—
1616/5	—	25.00	60.00	100	200	—
1616	—	25.00	60.00	100	200	—
1617/4	—	30.00	70.00	150	300	—
1617/5	—	30.00	70.00	150	300	—
1617/6	—	30.00	70.00	150	300	—
1617	—	25.00	60.00	100	200	—
1618/6	—	55.00	100	200	400	—
1618/7	—	30.00	70.00	150	300	—
1618	—	25.00	60.00	100	200	—
1623	—	35.00	75.00	150	300	—
1626/3	—	25.00	60.00	100	200	—
1626	—	25.00	60.00	100	200	—
1627/5	—	35.00	75.00	150	300	—
1627/6	—	35.00	75.00	150	300	—
1628	—	25.00	60.00	100	200	—
1629/6	—	25.00	60.00	100	200	—
1629/8	—	25.00	60.00	100	200	—
1629	—	25.00	60.00	100	200	—
1632/29	—	25.00	60.00	100	200	—
1632	—	25.00	60.00	100	200	—
1633	—	35.00	75.00	150	300	—
1634/3	—	35.00	75.00	150	300	—
1634	—	35.00	75.00	150	300	—

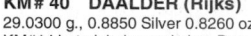

KM# 14 DAALDER (Rijks)

29.0300 g., 0.8850 0.8260 oz. **Note:** Dav. #4836.

Date	Mintage	VG	F	VF	XF	Unc
1606	—	40.00	150	200	300	—
1607/06	—	40.00	150	200	300	—
1607	—	40.00	150	200	300	—
1608	—	50.00	170	225	350	—
1609	—	40.00	150	200	300	—
1610	—	40.00	150	200	300	—
1611/0	—	40.00	150	200	300	—
1611	—	40.00	150	200	300	—
1612	—	30.00	75.00	100	200	—
1613	—	40.00	150	200	300	—
1614/3	—	40.00	150	200	300	—
1614	—	30.00	75.00	100	200	—
1616/3	—	40.00	150	200	300	—
1616	—	50.00	170	225	350	—
1617	—	40.00	150	200	300	—
1618	—	30.00	75.00	100	200	—
1619/8	—	30.00	75.00	100	200	—
1619	—	30.00	75.00	100	200	—
1620	—	30.00	75.00	100	200	—
1621	—	30.00	75.00	100	200	—
1622	—	30.00	75.00	100	200	—
1623	—	30.00	75.00	100	200	—
1624	—	30.00	75.00	100	200	—
1625	—	30.00	75.00	100	200	—
1626	—	30.00	75.00	100	200	—
1629/28	—	40.00	150	200	300	—
1629/28/24	—	40.00	150	200	300	—
1629/24	—	30.00	75.00	100	200	—
1629/25	—	30.00	75.00	100	200	—
1629/3	—	30.00	75.00	100	350	—
1629	—	30.00	75.00	100	200	—
1631	—	50.00	170	225	350	—
1648	—	40.00	150	200	300	—
1652	—	40.00	150	200	300	—
1687/3	—	40.00	150	200	300	—
1688	—	40.00	150	200	300	—

KM# 40 DAALDER (Rijks)

29.0300 g., 0.8850 Silver 0.8260 oz. ASW **Note:** Similar to KM#14 but plain inner circles. Dav. #4838.

Date	Mintage	VG	F	VF	XF	Unc
1650	—	50.00	125	175	250	—
1651	—	50.00	125	175	250	—
1652	—	60.00	150	250	350	—
1653	—	50.00	125	175	250	—
1654	—	50.00	125	175	250	—
1655	—	50.00	125	175	250	—
1656	—	50.00	125	175	250	—
1657/0	—	50.00	125	175	250	—
1657	—	50.00	125	175	250	—
1658	—	50.00	125	175	250	—
1659/6/4	—	60.00	130	225	300	—
1659	—	50.00	125	175	250	—
1661	—	60.00	50.00	125	250	—
1668	—	50.00	125	175	250	—
1683/77	—	60.00	130	225	300	—
1683	—	55.00	125	200	275	—
1687/3	—	55.00	125	200	275	—
1687	—	55.00	125	200	275	—
1688	—	55.00	125	200	275	—
1693/82	—	55.00	125	200	275	—
1693/86	—	80.00	175	250	350	—
1693/2	—	80.00	175	250	350	—
1693	—	80.00	175	250	350	—
1694	—	55.00	125	200	275	—
1695	—	55.00	125	200	275	—
1700	—	60.00	130	225	300	—

KM# A41 DAALDER (Rijks)

28.5600 g., Silver **Obv:** 1/2-length figure of knight right holding sword upright **Obv. Legend:** MO • ARG • PRO • CONFOE • BEL • TRA **Rev:** Crowned shield **Rev. Legend:** + CONCORDIA RES PARVAE CRESCVNT **Note:** Klippe.

Date	Mintage	Good	VG	F	VF	XF
1656	—	—	—	—	—	—

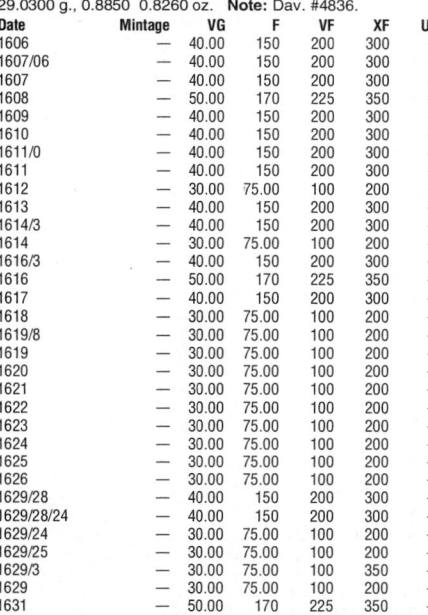

KM# 119 DAALDER (Rijks)

28.0300 g., Silver **Obv:** 1/2-length figure of Prince William III right holding sword upright and in left hand arms of Ultrecht **Obv. Legend:** MO • ARG • PRO - CONF • BEL - TRA **Rev:** Crowned shield in inner circle **Rev. Legend:** + CONCORDIA RES PARVAE CRESCVNT. Date between two roses **Note:** Proof made by Chr. Adolphi. (not an official coin but to show his quality as a die engraver for a function at the Mint) Pattern

Date	Mintage	VG	F	VF	XF	Unc
1673	—	—	—	2,000	5,000	6,500

KM# 62 DAALDER (Rijks)

Silver **Note:** Mint mark: Agnus Dei. Similar to KM#14 but without inner circles. Dav. #4839.

Date	Mintage	VG	F	VF	XF	Unc
1675	—	60.00	130	225	300	—
1676	—	60.00	130	225	300	—

KM# 30 DAALDER (Lion)

27.6800 g., 0.7500 Silver 0.6674 oz. ASW **Rev:** Crowned lion shield in inner circle **Note:** Dav. #4863.

Date	Mintage	VG	F	VF	XF	Unc
1635	—	15.00	60.00	150	325	—
1636	—	10.00	50.00	125	250	—
1637	—	10.00	50.00	125	250	—
1638	—	10.00	50.00	125	250	—
1639/7	—	25.00	50.00	125	250	—
1639	—	10.00	50.00	125	250	—
1640	—	10.00	50.00	125	250	—
1641	—	10.00	50.00	125	250	—
1642/1	—	25.00	50.00	125	250	—
1642	—	10.00	50.00	125	250	—
1643/1	—	25.00	50.00	125	250	—
1643	—	10.00	50.00	125	250	—
1644/04	—	10.00	50.00	125	250	—
1644/3	—	10.00	50.00	125	250	—
1644	—	10.00	50.00	125	250	—
1645/4	—	10.00	50.00	125	250	—
1645	—	25.00	70.00	175	350	—
1646/5	—	25.00	70.00	175	350	—
1646	—	15.00	60.00	150	325	—
1647	—	40.00	125	250	500	—
1648	—	10.00	50.00	125	250	—
1649	—	10.00	50.00	125	250	—
1650	—	10.00	50.00	125	250	—
1651	—	10.00	50.00	125	250	—
1652	—	10.00	50.00	125	250	—

KM# 32.1 DAALDER (Lion)

Silver **Obv:** Armored knight behind lion shield in inner dotted circle **Rev:** Rampant lion left in inner dotted circle **Note:** Mint mark: Rosette.

Date	Mintage	VG	F	VF	XF	Unc
1636	—	—	—	—	—	—
1641	—	10.00	50.00	80.00	160	—
1645	—	35.00	50.00	200	400	—
1647	—	10.00	50.00	80.00	160	—
1648	—	10.00	40.00	80.00	160	—
1649/8	—	10.00	40.00	80.00	160	—
1649	—	10.00	40.00	80.00	160	—
1650	—	10.00	40.00	80.00	160	—
1651	—	10.00	40.00	80.00	160	—
1652	—	10.00	40.00	80.00	160	—
1653	—	10.00	40.00	80.00	160	—
1654	—	10.00	40.00	80.00	160	—
1655	—	10.00	40.00	80.00	160	—
1656	—	10.00	40.00	80.00	160	—
1658	—	10.00	40.00	80.00	160	—
1659	—	10.00	40.00	80.00	160	—
1660	—	10.00	40.00	80.00	160	—
1661	—	10.00	40.00	80.00	160	—
1662	—	10.00	40.00	80.00	160	—
1663	—	10.00	40.00	80.00	160	—
1664	—	10.00	40.00	80.00	160	—
1666	—	25.00	70.00	150	300	—
1667	—	25.00	70.00	150	300	—
1668/7	—	20.00	50.00	100	200	—
1669/86/67	—	40.00	90.00	180	400	—

KM# 32.2 DAALDER (Lion)

27.6800 g., 0.7500 Silver 0.6674 oz. ASW **Obv:** Crowned lion shield in inner circle **Note:** Dav. #4863. No mintmark

Date	Mintage	VG	F	VF	XF	Unc
1640	—	10.00	40.00	80.00	160	—
1641	—	10.00	40.00	80.00	160	—
1642/1	—	25.00	60.00	150	300	—
1642	—	10.00	60.00	80.00	160	—

KM# 59.1 DAALDER (Lion)

Note: Mint mrk: Agnus Dei. Similar to kM#30 but without inner circles. Dav. #4838.

Date	Mintage	VG	F	VF	XF	Unc
1674	—	30.00	75.00	175	400	—
1675	—	30.00	75.00	175	400	—
1676	—	30.00	75.00	175	400	—

KM# 72 DAALDER (Lion)

Silver **Obv:** Without plume on knight's helmet **Note:** Similar to KM#30. Dav. #4866.

Date	Mintage	VG	F	VF	XF	Unc
1679	—	45.00	100	150	300	—
1680	—	45.00	100	150	300	—
1681	—	45.00	100	150	300	—
1682	—	45.00	100	150	300	—
1683	—	25.00	60.00	100	200	—
1685/83	—	45.00	100	150	300	—
1685	—	25.00	60.00	100	200	—
1686	—	25.00	60.00	100	200	—
1687	—	25.00	60.00	100	200	—
1688	—	25.00	60.00	100	200	—
1689	—	25.00	60.00	100	200	—
1690	—	65.00	125	225	350	—
1690/81	—	65.00	125	225	350	—
1690/86	—	65.00	125	225	350	—
1696	—	25.00	60.00	100	200	—
1697	—	25.00	60.00	100	200	—
1698	—	25.00	60.00	100	200	—
1700	—	25.00	60.00	100	200	—

KM# 59.2 DAALDER (Lion)

Silver **Obv:** Armored knight looking right behind lion shield **Rev:** Rampant lion left **Note:** Mint mark: Rosette. Varieties exist.

Date	Mintage	VG	F	VF	XF	Unc
1679	—	30.00	75.00	100	250	—
1680/79	—	30.00	75.00	125	300	—
1680	—	30.00	75.00	100	250	—
1681	—	30.00	75.00	100	250	—
1682/80	—	30.00	75.00	100	250	—
1682	—	30.00	75.00	125	300	—
1683	—	30.00	75.00	125	300	—

KM# 73 DAALDER (30 Stuiver)

15.8800 g., 0.9060 Silver 0.4625 oz. ASW

Date	Mintage	VG	F	VF	XF	Unc
1685	808,295	30.00	70.00	150	250	—
1686	Inc. above	30.00	70.00	150	250	—
1687	Inc. above	30.00	70.00	150	250	—
1688/6	Inc. above	30.00	70.00	150	250	—
1688	Inc. above	30.00	70.00	150	250	—
1689	376,885	30.00	70.00	150	250	—
1690	Inc. above	60.00	150	250	350	—
1691	Inc. above	30.00	70.00	150	250	—
1692	Inc. above	30.00	70.00	150	250	—

KM# 16 1/2 CAVALIER D'OR

5.0000 g., 0.9200 Gold 0.1479 oz. AGW **Obv:** Knight on horseback right above arms **Rev:** Crowned arms, date above **Note:** fr. #287.

Date	Mintage	VG	F	VF	XF	Unc
1606	—	200	350	700	1,400	—
1607/6	—	200	400	800	1,600	—
1607	—	200	350	700	1,400	—
1608	—	200	350	700	1,400	—
1614/06	—	200	400	800	1,600	—
1614/07	—	200	400	800	1,600	—
1614	—	200	350	700	1,400	—
1615/4	—	200	400	800	1,600	—
1615	—	200	350	700	1,400	—
1616	—	200	350	700	1,400	—
1617/07	—	200	400	800	1,600	—
1617	—	200	350	700	1,400	—
1618	—	200	350	700	1,400	—
1622	—	200	350	700	1,400	—
1629	—	200	350	700	1,400	—
1639	—	200	350	700	1,400	—
1644	—	200	350	700	1,400	—

KM# 15 CAVALIER D'OR

10.0000 g., 0.9200 Gold 0.2958 oz. AGW **Note:** Fr. #286.

Date	Mintage	VG	F	VF	XF	Unc
1606	—	400	600	1,100	2,200	—
1607/6	—	400	650	1,250	2,500	—
1607	—	400	600	1,100	2,200	—
1608	—	400	600	1,100	2,200	—
1614/06	—	400	600	1,100	2,200	—
1614	—	400	600	1,100	2,200	—
1615/4	—	400	600	1,100	2,200	—
1615	—	400	600	1,100	2,200	—
1616	—	400	650	1,250	2,500	—
1617/0	—	400	650	1,250	2,500	—
1617/6	—	400	650	1,250	2,500	—
1617	—	400	650	1,250	2,500	—
1618	—	400	600	1,100	2,200	—
1619	—	400	600	1,100	2,200	—
1620/19	—	400	600	1,100	2,200	—
1620	—	400	650	1,250	2,500	—
1621	—	400	600	1,100	2,200	—
1622	—	400	600	1,100	2,200	—
1623	—	400	600	1,100	2,200	—
1624	—	400	600	1,100	2,200	—
1625	—	400	600	1,100	2,200	—
1627	—	425	700	1,350	2,700	—

TRADE COINAGE

KM# 7.1 DUCAT
3.5100 g., 0.9860 Gold 0.1113 oz. AGW **Obv:** Standing, armored knight holding bundle of arrows, divides date **Obv. Legend:** CONCORDIA RES - P- AR(V) CRES TRA mintmark **Rev:** Inscription within ornamented tablet **Rev. Legend:** MO ORD(I)/PROVIN/FOEDER/BELG AD/LEG IMP **Rev. Inscription:** MO/ ORD/ PROVIN/ FOEDER/ BELGAD/ LEGIMP **Note:** Fr. #284. Mintmark: City of arms of Ultrecht

Date	Mintage	VG	F	VF	XF	Unc
1602	—	125	175	250	500	750
1603	—	125	175	250	500	750
1604/3	—	—	—	—	—	—
1604	—	125	150	225	400	500
1605	—	125	150	225	400	500
1606/5	—	125	175	250	500	750
1606	—	125	175	250	500	750
1607/5	—	—	—	—	—	—
1607/6	—	125	150	225	400	500
1607	—	125	150	225	400	500
1608/3	—	125	150	225	400	500
1608/7	—	125	150	225	400	500
1608	—	125	150	225	400	500
1609	—	125	150	225	400	500
1610	—	125	150	225	400	500
1611/09	—	125	150	225	400	500
1611	—	125	150	225	400	500
1612	—	125	150	225	400	500
1613/0	—	125	175	250	500	750
1613	—	125	150	225	400	500
1614/3	—	125	150	225	400	500
1614	—	125	150	225	400	500
1615/3	—	125	175	250	500	750
1615/4	—	125	175	250	500	750
1615	—	125	175	250	500	750
1616	—	125	150	225	400	500
1618/07	—	125	150	225	400	500
1620	—	125	175	250	500	750
1622	—	125	175	250	500	750
1623/14	—	125	150	225	400	500
1623/19	—	125	150	225	400	500
1623	—	125	150	225	400	500
1624	—	125	175	250	500	750
1629/7	—	125	175	250	500	750
1629	—	125	175	250	500	750
1630/24	—	—	—	—	—	—
1630/29	—	125	175	250	500	750
1630	—	125	150	225	400	500
1631/20	—	125	175	250	500	50.00
1631	—	125	175	250	500	750
1632	—	125	175	250	500	750
1633/2	—	125	175	250	500	750
1633	—	—	—	—	—	—
1634	—	125	150	225	400	500
1635	—	125	150	225	400	500
1636	—	125	150	225	400	500
1637	—	125	150	225	400	500
1638/7	—	125	150	225	450	650
1638	—	125	150	225	400	500
1639	—	125	175	250	500	750
1640/36	—	125	150	225	400	500
1640	—	125	150	225	400	500
1641	—	125	150	225	400	500
1642	—	125	175	250	500	750
1643/34	—	—	—	—	—	—
1643/0	—	—	—	225	400	500
1643	—	125	150	170	500	750
1644	—	125	175	250	500	750
1645/3	—	125	175	225	400	500
1645	—	125	150	225	400	500
1646	—	125	150	225	400	500
1647	—	125	150	225	400	500
1648	—	125	150	225	400	500

KM# 7.2 DUCAT
3.5100 g., 0.9860 Gold 0.1113 oz. AGW **Obv:** Standing, armored knight holding bundle of arrows, divides date, in plain inner circle **Obv. Legend:** CONCORDIA RES - P- AR(V) CRES TRA mintmark **Rev:** Inscription within ornamented tablet **Rev. Legend:** MO ORD(I)/PROVIN/FOEDER/BELG AD/LEG IMP **Rev. Inscription:** MO/ ORD/ PROVIN/ FOEDER/ BELGAD/ LEGIMP **Note:** Fr. #284. Mintmark: City of arms of Ultrecht

Date	Mintage	VG	F	VF	XF	Unc
1649	—	125	150	200	400	500
1650	—	125	175	250	500	750
1651	—	125	175	250	500	750
1652	—	125	150	200	400	500
1653	—	125	175	250	500	750
1654	—	125	175	250	500	750
1656/55	—	125	175	250	500	750
1656	—	125	175	250	500	750
1657	—	125	175	250	500	750
1658	—	125	150	200	500	750
1659	—	125	175	250	500	750
1660	—	125	175	250	500	750
1661	—	125	150	200	400	500
1662	—	125	150	200	400	500
1663	—	125	150	200	400	500
1664	—	125	150	200	400	500
1666	—	125	150	200	400	500
1667	—	125	150	200	400	500
1668	—	125	150	200	400	500
1669	—	125	150	200	400	500
1670	—	125	150	200	400	500
1671	—	125	150	200	400	500
1672	—	125	175	250	500	750
1673	—	125	150	200	400	500
1674	—	125	150	200	500	750

KM# 7.3 DUCAT
3.5000 g., 0.9860 Gold 0.1109 oz. AGW **Obv:** Standing, armored knight holding bundle of arrows, divides date. Without inner circle **Obv. Legend:** CONCORDIARES ... **Rev:** Inscription within ornamented tablet **Rev. Inscription:** MO/ ORD/ PROVIN/ FOEDER/ BELGAD/ LEGIMP **Note:** Fr. #284. Mintmark mastersign: Agnus Dei

Date	Mintage	VG	F	VF	XF	Unc
1674	—	125	175	250	500	750
1675	—	125	175	200	400	500
1676/5	—	—	—	—	—	—
1676	—	125	175	250	500	750

KM# 7.4 DUCAT
3.5100 g., 0.9860 Gold 0.1113 oz. AGW **Obv:** Standing, armored knight holding bundle of arrows, divides date. Without inner circle **Obv. Legend:** CONCORDIARES ... **Rev:** Inscription within ornamented tablet **Rev. Inscription:** MO/ ORD/ PROVIN/ FOEDER/ BELGAD/ LEGIMP **Edge:** Cable **Note:** Fr. #284. Mint mastersign: rose

Date	Mintage	VG	F	VF	XF	Unc
1679	—	125	150	200	400	500
1680	—	125	175	250	500	750
1681/0	—	125	175	250	500	750
1681	—	125	175	250	500	750
1682/0	—	125	175	250	500	750
1682	—	125	175	250	500	750
1683	—	125	150	200	400	500
1684	—	125	150	200	400	500
1685	—	125	150	200	400	500
1686	—	125	150	200	400	500
1687	—	125	150	200	400	500
1688	—	125	150	200	400	500
1689	—	125	150	200	400	500
1690	—	125	150	200	400	500
1691	—	125	175	250	500	750
1692	—	125	150	200	400	500
1693/88	—	125	175	250	500	750
1693	—	125	150	200	400	500
1694	—	125	175	250	500	750
1695	—	125	150	200	400	500
1696/2	—	125	175	250	500	750
1696	—	125	175	250	500	750
1697	—	125	175	250	500	750
1698	—	125	175	250	500	750
1699	—	125	175	250	500	750
1700	—	125	200	350	600	800

KM# 42.1 2 DUCAT
7.0200 g., 0.9860 Gold 0.2225 oz. AGW **Obv:** Standing, armored knight holding bundle of arrows, divides date within plain broken circle **Obv. Legend:** CONCORDIA RES PAR• CRESTRA• mintmark (city arms of Ultrecht) **Rev:** Inscription within ornamented square **Rev. Inscription:** MO:ORD/PROVIN/FOEDER:/BELGAD/LEG.IMP **Note:** Fr. #282.

Date	Mintage	VG	F	VF	XF	Unc
1650	—	300	650	1,200	2,400	3,000
1652	—	300	750	1,350	2,700	35,000
1653	—	300	650	1,200	2,400	3,000
1654	—	300	650	1,200	2,400	3,000
1655	—	300	650	1,200	2,400	3,000
1656	—	300	650	1,200	2,400	3,000
1657	—	300	650	1,200	2,400	3,000
1658	—	300	750	1,350	2,700	3,500

KM# 42.2 2 DUCAT
7.2000 g., 0.9860 Gold 0.2282 oz. AGW **Obv:** Standing, armored knight with scarf, divides date within plain broken circle. No inner circle and mintmaster sign (rose) between leggs **Obv. Legend:** CONCORDIA RES PAR• CRESTRA• **Rev:** Inscription within ornamented square **Rev. Inscription:** MO:ORD/PROVIN/FOEDER:/BELGAD/LEG.IMP **Note:** Fr. #282.

Date	Mintage	VG	F	VF	XF	Unc
1660	—	300	650	1,200	2,400	3,000
1666	—	300	650	1,200	2,400	3,000
1669	—	300	750	1,350	2,700	3,500
1683	—	300	605	1,200	2,400	3,000
1684	—	250	750	1,350	2,700	3,500
1688	—	300	750	1,350	2,700	3,500
1690	—	300	650	1,200	2,400	3,000
1691	—	300	650	1,200	2,400	3,000
1692	—	300	650	1,200	2,400	3,000
1693	—	300	750	1,350	2,700	3,500
1694	—	300	750	1,350	2,700	3,500
1695	—	300	750	1,350	2,700	3,500
1696	—	300	750	1,350	2,700	3,500
1697	—	300	750	1,350	2,700	3,500
1699/66	—	300	750	1,350	2,700	3,500
1699	—	300	750	1,350	2,700	3,500

COUNTERMARKED COINAGE

1693

During the late 17th century many circulating coins were found to be underweight. In 1693 coins meeting the legal requirements were countermarked for a specific province or city, such as UTR for Utrecht.

KM# 74.1 28 STUIVERS
Silver **Countermark:** UTR **Note:** Countermark on Deventer KM#79.

CM Date	Host Date	Good	VG	F	VF	XF
ND(1693)	1684	—	—	—	—	—

KM# 74.2 28 STUIVERS
Silver **Countermark:** UTR **Note:** Countermark on Deventer KM#81.

CM Date	Host Date	Good	VG	F	VF	XF
ND(1693)	1685-92	—	—	—	—	—

KM# 74.3 28 STUIVERS
Silver **Countermark:** UTR **Note:** Countermark on Friesland KM#10.

CM Date	Host Date	Good	VG	F	VF	XF
ND(1693)	1601-91	—	—	—	—	—

KM# 74.4 28 STUIVERS
Silver **Countermark:** UTR **Note:** Countermark on Groningen KM#50.

CM Date	Host Date	Good	VG	F	VF	XF
ND(1693)	1690	—	—	—	—	—

KM# 74.5 28 STUIVERS
Silver **Countermark:** UTR **Note:** Countermark on Groningen and Ommeland KM#52.

CM Date	Host Date	Good	VG	F	VF	XF
ND(1693)	1692	—	—	—	—	—

KM# 74.6 28 STUIVERS
Silver **Countermark:** UTR **Note:** Countermark on Groningen and Ommeland KM#31.

CM Date	Host Date	Good	VG	F	VF	XF
ND(1693)	1673-77	—	—	—	—	—

KM# 74.7 28 STUIVERS

Silver **Countermark:** UTR **Note:** Countermark on Nijmegen KM#27.

CM Date	Host Date	Good	VG	F	VF	XF
ND(1693)	1685-90	—	—	—	—	—

KM# 74.8 28 STUIVERS

Silver **Countermark:** UTR **Note:** Countermark on Overyssel KM#55.

CM Date	Host Date	Good	VG	F	VF	XF
ND(1693)	1685-89	—	—	—	—	—

KM# 74.9 28 STUIVERS

Silver **Countermark:** UTR **Note:** Countermark on West Friesland KM#90.

CM Date	Host Date	Good	VG	F	VF	XF
ND(1693)	1685-87	—	—	—	—	—

KM# 74.10 28 STUIVERS

Silver **Countermark:** UTR **Note:** Countermark on Zwolle KM#78.

CM Date	Host Date	Good	VG	F	VF	XF
ND(1693)	1679-86	—	—	—	—	—

KM# 74.11 28 STUIVERS

Silver **Countermark:** UTR **Note:** Countermark on Groningen and Ommeland KM#50

CM Date	Host Date	Good	VG	F	VF	XF
ND(1693)	1690	—	—	—	—	—

PATTERNS

Including off metal strikes

KM#	Date	Mintage	Identification	Mkt Val
Pn1	1627	—	3 Stuivers. Lead. KM#27	—
Pn2	1673	—	Rijksdaalder. Silver. 35.1000 g. Prince William III	—
Pn3	1681	—	Gulden. Gold. 17.5000 g. KM#69	—
Pn4	1682	—	Gulden. Gold. 17.5000 g. KM#70	—
Pn5	1682	—	Gulden. Gold. 13.8000 g. KM#70	3,750
Pn6	1682	—	1/2 Gulden. Gold. 10.4000 g. KM#69.	2,000
Pn7	1682	—	Gulden. Gold. 13.8000 g. KM#70.	4,750
Pn8	1684	—	3 Gulden. Gold. 41.8000 g. KM#71.	—
Pn9	1685	—	Daalder. Gold. 21.8000 g. KM#73.	17,500
Pn10	1687	—	Daalder. Gold. 21.8000 g. KM#73.	—
Pn11	1700	—	6 Stuivers. Gold. 7.0000 g. KM#80	—

PIEFORTS

KM#	Date	Mintage	Identification	Mkt Val
P1	1606	—	Cavalier D'Or. Gold. 19.9000 g. KM15.	—
P2	1617	—	Daalder. Silver. Double weight. KM#13	3,000
P3	1620	—	Ducat. Gold. 19.2000 g. KM#7.1	—
P4	1620	—	Cavalier D'Or. Gold. 19.9000 g. KM#15	—
P5	1629	—	Cavalier D'Or. Gold. 19.9000 g. KM15.	—
P6	1642	—	Daalder. Silver. Double weight. KM#32.2	—
P7	1653	—	Rijksdaalder. Silver. KM40	2,000
P8	1656	—	Rijksdaalder. Silver. KM40, not klippe	2,000
P9	1657	—	Duit. Copper. KM43.2	—
P10	1657	—	Duit. Copper. Double weight. KM#44	—
P12	1659	—	Silver Ducat. Silver. KM48.1, Dav. #4901.	—
P13	1659	—	1/2 Daalder. Silver. Klippe. KM#41	—
P14	1659	—	1/2 Ducaton. Silver. Double weight. KM#45	—
P15	1659	—	Ducaton. Silver. KM46.1, round version.	1,200
P16	1660	—	1/2 Ducaton. Silver. Klippe. KM#45	—
P17	1660	—	1/2 Ducaton. Silver. Klippe. Double weight. KM#45	—
P18	1660	—	1/2 Ducaton. Silver. Double weight. KM#45	—
P19	1660	—	Silver Ducat. KM48.1, Dav. #4901.	—
P20	1660	—	Ducaton. Silver. KM48.1, round version.	—
P21	1660	—	Ducaton. Silver. Klippe, KM46.1	2,000
P22	1661	—	Ducaton. Silver. KM46.1, round version	1,000
P23	1661	—	1/2 Ducaton. Silver. Klippe. KM#45	—
P24	1661	—	1/2 Ducaton. Silver. Double weight. KM#45	—
P25	1661	—	Ducaton. Silver. Klippe, KM46.1.	1,200
P26	1662	—	1/2 Ducaton. Silver. Klippe. KM#45	—
P27	1662	—	Silver Ducat. KM48.1, Dav. #4901.	—
P28	1662	—	Ducaton. Silver. KM46.1, round version	—
P29	1662	—	Ducaton. Silver. Klippe, KM46.1	—
P30	1664	—	Ducaton. Silver. KM46.1, but not Klippe	—
P31	1664	—	1/2 Ducaton. Silver. Double weight, KM#45	—
P32	1664	—	Silver Ducat. Double weight, KM48.1, Dav. #4901.	1,300
P33	1668	—	Ducaton. Silver. 65.1100 g. KM46 but not Klippe	2,000
P34	1668	—	1/2 Ducaton. Silver. Double weight, KM#45	2,500
P35	1669	—	2 Ducat. Gold. KM42	—
P36	1670	—	Ducaton. Silver. KM46.2	2,500
P37	1672	—	Ducaton. Silver. KM46.2	—
P38	1679	—	Ducaton. Silver. KM63.	—
P39	1680	—	Ducaton. Silver. KM63.	—
P40	1681	—	6 Stuivers. Silver. Double weight. KM#60.3	—
P41	1682	—	1/2 Gulden. Gold. 7.1000 g. KM#69	3,000
P42	1682	—	1/2 Gulden. Gold. 10.5000 g. KM69	4,000
P43	1687	—	Daalder. Silver. Double weight. KM#73	—
P44	1687	—	Silver Ducat. KM65, Dav. #4903.	—
P45	1689	—	Duit. Copper. KM66#	—
P46	1692	—	Ducaton. Silver. KM63.	—
P-A24	1693	—	2 Ducat. Gold. 13.8300 g. KM42.	—

WEST FRIESLAND

West Frisia

West Friesland (West Frisia), also known as North Holland, is part of the province of Holland, and is not associated with the province of Friesland.

PROVINCE

STANDARD COINAGE

KM# 10 DUIT

2.0000 g., Copper **Obv:** Crowned arms **Rev:** WEST/FRISIAE/(date) in wreath

Date	Mintage	VG	F	VF	XF	Unc
ND(1603)	—	10.00	25.00	55.00	100	—
1604	779,490	5.00	15.00	35.00	70.00	—
1605	Inc. above	8.00	20.00	45.00	90.00	—

KM# 40a DUIT

Silver **Note:** Klippe. KM#29. Weight varies 3 - 8g.

Date	Mintage	VG	F	VF	XF	Unc
1626	—	—	—	450	900	—
1627	—	—	—	—	—	—
1645	—	—	—	450	900	—
1645	—	—	—	450	900	—
1645	—	—	—	—	—	—
1658	—	—	—	350	700	—
1660	—	—	—	—	—	—
1663	—	—	—	450	900	—
1665	—	—	—	450	900	—

KM# 40 DUIT

Copper **Note:** Klippe. Weight varies 4-12 grams.

Date	Mintage	VG	F	VF	XF	Unc
1626	—	—	—	—	—	—
1645	—	—	—	—	—	—
1658	—	—	—	—	600	—
1660	—	—	—	—	—	—
1661	—	—	—	—	—	—
1663	—	—	—	—	600	—
1665	—	—	—	—	—	—

KM# 29 DUIT

Copper **Obv:** Crowned arms **Rev:** Larger wreath **Note:** Varieties exist.

Date	Mintage	VG	F	VF	XF	Unc
1626	3,182,560	8.00	20.00	45.00	90.00	—
1627	Inc. above	8.00	20.00	45.00	90.00	—
1645	Inc. above	15.00	50.00	100	250	—
1658	Inc. above	8.00	20.00	45.00	90.00	—
1659	Inc. above	15.00	50.00	100	250	—
1660	Inc. above	8.00	20.00	45.00	90.00	—
1663	Inc. above	8.00	20.00	45.00	90.00	—
1664	Inc. above	8.00	20.00	45.00	90.00	—

KM# 29a DUIT

Silver **Note:** Weight varies 2 - 6g.

Date	Mintage	VG	F	VF	XF	Unc
1645	—	—	—	—	—	—
1645	—	—	—	—	200	—
1658	—	—	—	—	—	—
1660	—	—	—	350	700	—

KM# 45 DUIT

2.0000 g., Copper **Obv:** Arms of Enkhuizen, Hoorn and Medemblik **Obv. Legend:** DEVS. FORTI. E. SP. NOS.

Date	Mintage	VG	F	VF	XF	Unc
1658	—	15.00	35.00	75.00	150	—

KM# 45a DUIT

Silver

Date	Mintage	VG	F	VF	XF	Unc
1658	—	—	—	—	250	—
1660	—	—	—	—	250	—

KM# 45b DUIT

3.5000 g., Gold **Obv:** Crowned shield **Obv. Legend:** DEVS. FORT. ET. SP. NOS. **Rev:** 3 shields of Enkhuizen, Hoorn and Medemblik

Date	Mintage	VG	F	VF	XF	Unc
1658	—	—	—	—	—	—
1660	—	—	—	—	—	—

KM# 11 2 DUIT

Copper **Obv:** Crowned arms **Rev. Inscription:** WEST / FRISIAE / date in wreath

Date	Mintage	VG	F	VF	XF	Unc
1604	—	6.00	20.00	35.00	70.00	—

KM# 20 STUIVER

0.8600 g., 0.3330 Silver 0.0092 oz. ASW **Obv:** Crowned rampant lion to left holding sword and arrows, value at sides **Rev:** W/FRISIA/(date)

Date	Mintage	VG	F	VF	XF	Unc
1614	—	10.00	30.00	70.00	130	—
1615	—	10.00	30.00	70.00	130	—
1628	149,050	15.00	50.00	100	150	—

KM# 38 STUIVER

1.3190 g., 0.3330 Silver 0.0141 oz. ASW **Obv:** Bundle of arrows divides value in wreath **Rev:** W/FRI/SIA/(date) in wreath

Date	Mintage	VG	F	VF	XF	Unc
1639	—	7.00	20.00	40.00	60.00	—
1641/39	—	10.00	25.00	45.00	90.00	—
1641	—	7.00	20.00	40.00	60.00	—

KM# 60 STUIVER

Silver **Obv:** Crowned rampant lion to left holding sword and arrows **Rev:** Small shield with 3 herrings at top **Rev. Inscription:** WEST / FRISIA / 1 STUIVER / (date) **Note:** Struck at private mint of Dirk Bosch in Enkhuizen.

Date	Mintage	VG	F	VF	XF	Unc
1673	—	125	250	500	750	—

KM# 69 STUIVER

Silver **Obv:** Crowned rampant lion to left holding sword and arrows **Rev. Inscription:** W / FRISIA / 1 STUIVER / BANKG / (date) **Note:** Struck at private mint of Dirk Bosch in Enkhuizen.

Date	Mintage	VG	F	VF	XF	Unc
1675	—	50.00	200	400	750	—

KM# 71 STUIVER

Silver **Obv:** Crowned arms divide B-P (Bank Payment) **Rev. Inscription:** WEST / FRISIA / 1 STUIVER / BANKG / (date) **Note:** Struck at private mint of Dirk Bosch in Enkhuizen.

Date	Mintage	VG	F	VF	XF	Unc
1676	—	12.00	25.00	40.00	80.00	12[illegible]
1677	—	15.00	40.00	75.00	110	17[illegible]

KM# 74 STUIVER

Silver **Obv:** Crowned arms divides value **Rev. Inscription:** WEST / FRISIA / (date) **Note:** Struck at private mint of Dirk Bosch in Enkhuisen.

Date	Mintage	VG	F	VF	XF	Unc
1677	—	8.00	40.00	70.00	120	—
1678	—	8.00	40.00	70.00	120	—

KM# 21.1 2 STUIVERS

Silver **Obv:** Crowned rampant lion to left holding sword and arrows, value at sides **Rev. Inscription:** W / FRI / SIA / (date) **Note:** Mint mark: Lily.

Date	Mintage	VG	F	VF	XF	Unc
1614	—	5.00	20.00	40.00	80.00	—
1615	—	5.00	20.00	40.00	80.00	—
1616	—	5.00	20.00	40.00	80.00	—
1639	—	5.00	20.00	40.00	80.00	—
1641/39	—	8.00	25.00	50.00	100	—
1641	—	5.00	20.00	40.00	80.00	—
1646/1	—	10.00	25.00	50.00	100	—
1646	—	5.00	20.00	40.00	80.00	—

KM# 21.2 2 STUIVERS

1.7300 g., 0.5830 Silver 0.0324 oz. ASW **Obv:** Crowned rampant lion to left holding sword and arrows, value at sides **Rev. Inscription:** W / FRI / SIA / (date) **Note:** Mint mark: Rosette.

Date	Mintage	VG	F	VF	XF	Unc
1625	—	10.00	25.00	50.00	100	—
1628	—	10.00	25.00	50.00	100	—

KM# 21.3 2 STUIVERS

1.7300 g., 0.5830 Silver 0.0324 oz. ASW **Obv:** Crowned rampant lion to left holding sword and arrows, value at sides **Rev. Inscription:** W / FRI / SIA / (date) **Note:** Mint mark: Cinquefoil. Varieties exist.

Date	Mintage	VG	F	VF	XF	Unc
1653	—	10.00	25.00	50.00	100	—
1670	—	10.00	25.00	50.00	100	—
1671	—	5.00	20.00	40.00	80.00	—
1672	—	5.00	20.00	40.00	80.00	—
1673	—	5.00	20.00	40.00	80.00	—
1674	—	5.00	20.00	40.00	80.00	—
1675	—	10.00	25.00	50.00	100	—
1677	—	5.00	20.00	40.00	80.00	—
1678	—	5.00	20.00	40.00	80.00	—
1679	—	5.00	20.00	40.00	80.00	—
1685	—	75.00	150	200	275	—
1699	—	5.00	20.00	40.00	80.00	—
1700	—	5.00	20.00	40.00	80.00	—

KM# 61 2 STUIVERS

Silver **Note:** Struck at private mint of Dirk Bosch in Enkhuisen.

Date	Mintage	VG	F	VF	XF	Unc
1673	—	100	250	550	750	—

KM# 65 2 STUIVERS

Silver **Obv:** Provincial arms of West Friesland **Note:** Struck at private mint of Dirk Bosch in Enkhuisen.

Date	Mintage	VG	F	VF	XF	Unc
1674	—	100	400	600	1,000	—

KM# 70 2 STUIVERS

Silver **Obv:** Crowned rampant lion to left holding sword and arrows **Rev:** WEST/FRISIA/II STUIVERS/BANKGELT/1675 **Note:** Struck at private mint of Dirk Bosch in Enkhuizen.

Date	Mintage	VG	F	VF	XF	Unc
1675	—	80.00	250	500	750	—

KM# 72 2 STUIVERS

Silver **Obv:** Crowned arms divide B - P (Bank Payment) **Rev:** WEST/FRISIA/2 STUIVERS/ (date) **Note:** Struck at private mint of Dirk Bosch in Enkhuizen.

Date	Mintage	VG	F	VF	XF	Unc
1676	—	25.00	75.00	100	170	—
1677	—	25.00	75.00	100	170	—

KM# 79 1/2 ROOSSCHELLING (3 Stuivers)

5.2700 g., Silver **Obv:** Crowned provincial arms, date above within dotted circle **Rev:** Ornate cross with rosette at center

Date	Mintage	VG	F	VF	XF	Unc
1682	—	80.00	150	300	600	—

KM# 66 6 STUIVERS (Lion Schelling)

3.3000 g., 0.8750 Silver 0.0928 oz. ASW **Note:** Struck at private mint of Dirk Bosch in Enkhuisen.

Date	Mintage	VG	F	VF	XF	Unc
1674	—	100	400	600	1,000	—
1676	—	100	400	600	1,000	—

KM# 5.1 6 STUIVERS (Roosschelling)

5.2700 g., 0.5830 Silver 0.0988 oz. ASW **Obv:** Crowned arms in branches in inner circle, date above crown **Obv. Legend:** MO NO ORDIN WESTFRISAE **Rev:** Ornamental cross with rose at center in inner circle **Rev. Legend:** DEVS - FORTI - ET - NOS(TR)

Date	Mintage	VG	F	VF	XF	Unc
1601	—	20.00	75.00	150	300	—
1629	—	25.00	100	200	400	—
1653	—	15.00	45.00	75.00	125	—
1680	—	15.00	45.00	75.00	125	—

KM# 5.4 6 STUIVERS (Roosschelling)

5.2700 g., 0.5830 Silver 0.0988 oz. ASW **Obv:** Crowned arms in branches no inner circle, date above crown. **Rev:** Ornamental cross with rose at center in inner circle

Date	Mintage	VG	F	VF	XF	Unc
1680	—	25.00	100	200	400	—

KM# 5.2 6 STUIVERS (Roosschelling)

5.2700 g., 0.5830 Silver 0.0988 oz. ASW **Obv:** Crowned arms in branches in inner circle, date above crown **Rev:** Ornamental cross with rose at center in inner circle **Note:** Mint mark: Bull. Varieties exist.

Date	Mintage	VG	F	VF	XF	Unc
1682	—	25.00	75.00	125	250	—
1683	—	25.00	75.00	125	250	—

KM# 62 6 STUIVERS (Scheepjesschelling)

3.3000 g., 0.8750 Silver 0.0928 oz. ASW **Obv:** Crowned arms divide date **Rev:** Sailing ship to right **Note:** Struck at private mint of Dirk Bosch in Enkhuizen.

Date	Mintage	VG	F	VF	XF	Unc
1673	—	125	400	800	1,200	—

KM# 77 6 STUIVERS (Scheepjesschelling)

3.3900 g., Silver **Obv:** Rampant lion left holding sword and bundle of arrows **Obv. Legend:** MONET•NO ORD•FOEDERATÆ•BELG• **Rev. Inscription:** rosette / WEST / FRISIA / VI • STUIVERS / BANKGELD / (date) **Note:** Struck at the private mint of Dirk Bosch in Enkhuizen.

Date	Mintage	VG	F	VF	XF	Unc
1674	—	100	200	350	500	—
1676	—	100	200	350	500	700

KM# 77a 6 STUIVERS (Scheepjesschelling)

3.2000 g., Gold **Obv:** Rampant lion left holding sword and bundle of arrows **Obv. Legend:** MONET• NO ORD•FOEDERATÆ•BELG• **Rev. Inscription:** WEST / FRISIA / VI • STUIVERS / BANKGELD / (date) **Note:** Struck at the private mint of Dirk Bosch in Enkhuizen.

Date	Mintage	VG	F	VF	XF	Unc
1674	—	—	—	—	—	2,750

KM# 73 6 STUIVERS (Scheepjesschelling)

3.3900 g., 0.8750 Silver 0.0954 oz. ASW **Obv:** Crowned arms divide value 6 - S and B - P (Bank Payment) **Obv. Legend:** MO(NE) (NO) ORDIN WE(T)FRISA(E) date **Rev:** Sailing ship to right **Rev. Legend:** DEVS FORT(ITVDO) ET SP(ED) NOST(RA) **Note:** Struck at private mint of Dirk Bosch in Enkhuizen.

Date	Mintage	VG	F	VF	XF	Unc
1676	—	60.00	200	350	700	—
1677	—	60.00	200	350	700	—

KM# 73a 6 STUIVERS (Scheepjesschelling)

3.5000 g., Gold **Obv:** Crowned arms divide value 6 - s and B - P (Bank Payment) **Rev:** Sailing ship **Note:** Struck at private mint of Dirk Bosch in Enkhuizen.

Date	Mintage	VG	F	VF	XF	Unc
1676	—	—	—	—	—	—
1677	—	—	—	—	—	—

KM# 73b 6 STUIVERS (Scheepjesschelling)

7.0000 g., Gold **Obv:** Crowned arms divide value 6 - s and B - P (Bank Payment) **Rev:** Sailing ship **Note:** Struck at private mint of Dirk Bosch in Enkhuizen.

Date	Mintage	VG	F	VF	XF	Unc
1677	—	—	—	—	—	—

KM# 73c 6 STUIVERS (Scheepjesschelling)

8.5000 g., Gold **Obv:** Crowned arms divide value 6 - s and B - P (Bank Payment) **Rev:** Sailing ship **Note:** Struck at private mint of Dirk Bosch in Enkhuizen.

Date	Mintage	VG	F	VF	XF	Unc
1677	—	—	—	—	—	—

KM# 76 6 STUIVERS (Scheepjesschelling)

3.3000 g., 0.8750 Silver 0.0928 oz. ASW **Obv:** Without B-P **Rev:** Sailing ship to right **Note:** Struck at private mint of Dirk Bosch in Enkhuizen.

Date	Mintage	VG	F	VF	XF	Unc
1677	—	15.00	50.00	100	175	—
1678/7	—	15.00	50.00	100	175	—
1678	—	8.00	20.00	45.00	90.00	—
1679	—	8.00	20.00	45.00	90.00	—

KM# 3 10 STUIVERS

5.9500 g., Silver **Obv:** Armored knight standing behind shield with sword on shoulder **Obv. Legend:** MO•ARG•PRO•CON - FOE•BELG•WESTF **Rev:** Crowned lion shield divides value X - S **Rev. Legend:** +CON CORDIA • RES • PARVÆ • CRESCVNT•

Date	Mintage	VG	F	VF	XF	Unc
1606	—	—	—	—	—	—

KM# 80 10 STUIVERS (1/2 Gulden)

5.3000 g., 0.9200 Silver 0.1568 oz. ASW **Obv:** Crowned arms divide value 10 - S, date above crown **Rev:** Standing female figure leaning on Bible on column, holding spear with Liberty cap

Date	Mintage	VG	F	VF	XF	Unc
1682	—	60.00	175	350	700	—

KM# 81 GULDEN

10.6100 g., 0.9200 Silver 0.3138 oz. ASW

Date	Mintage	VG	F	VF	XF	Unc
1682	Inc. below	175	350	700	1,500	—
1687	26,240	60.00	175	350	700	—

KM# 97.1 GULDEN

10.6100 g., 0.9200 Silver 0.3138 oz. ASW **Obv:** Crowned arms of Friesland divide value **Obv. Legend:** MO: ARG: ORD: FÆD: ... **Rev:** Standing figure leaning on column with cap on pole, date in exergue below **Rev. Legend:** HAC NITIMVR HANCTVEMVR **Note:** Mint mark: Cinquefoil. Similar to 3 Gulden, KM#141.

Date	Mintage	VG	F	VF	XF	Unc
1699	—	12.50	30.00	60.00	100	—

KM# 83 2 GULDEN (40 Stuiver)
Silver **Obv:** Crowned W-Friesland arms divide value 2 - G, date above crown **Obv. Legend:** MO NO ARGENT ORDIN WESTF date **Rev:** Standing female figure leaning on Bible on column, holding spear with Liberty cap. **Rev. Legend:** HAC NITIMVR - HANC TVEMVR **Note:** Klippe. Weight varies 31 - 37g.

Date	Mintage	VG	F	VF	XF	Unc
1682	—	—	—	—	—	—

KM# 83a 2 GULDEN (40 Stuiver)
Silver **Obv:** Crowned W-Friesland arms divide value 2 - G, date above crown **Obv. Legend:** MO NO ARGENT ORDIN WESTF date **Rev:** Standing female figure leaning on Bible on column, holding spear with Liberty cap. **Rev. Legend:** HAC NITIMVR - HANC TVEMVR **Note:** Klippe. Weight varies 55.5 - 56.5g.

Date	Mintage	VG	F	VF	XF	Unc
1682	—	—	—	—	2,500	—

KM# 82 2 GULDEN (40 Stuiver)
21.2100 g., Silver **Note:** Similar to KM#83 but not Klippe.

Date	Mintage	VG	F	VF	XF	Unc
1682	—	150	450	900	1,800	—

KM# 84 3 GULDEN (60 Stuiver)
31.8200 g., 0.9200 Silver 0.9412 oz. ASW **Obv:** Crowned arms of West Friesland divide value, date above crown **Rev:** Standing female figure leaning on Bible on column, holding spear with Liberty cap **Note:** Dav. #4961.

Date	Mintage	VG	F	VF	XF	Unc
1682	77,420	100	300	500	800	—
1687	Inc. above	125	350	700	1,000	—
1687/2	Inc. above	150	400	600	900	—

KM# 95.1 3 GULDEN (60 Stuiver)
31.8200 g., 0.9200 Silver 0.9412 oz. ASW **Rev:** Date in exergue **Note:** Mint mark: Ship. Dav. #4963.

Date	Mintage	VG	F	VF	XF	Unc
1694	—	50.00	125	200	300	—

KM# 95.2 3 GULDEN (60 Stuiver)
31.8200 g., 0.9200 Silver 0.9412 oz. ASW **Obv:** Crowned arms of United Netherlands **Note:** Mint mark: Cinquefoil. Similar to KM#141.

Date	Mintage	VG	F	VF	XF	Unc
1695/4	—	50.00	125	200	300	—
1695	—	30.00	60.00	100	200	—
1696	—	30.00	60.00	100	200	—
1697	—	30.00	60.00	100	200	—
1698/7	—	—	—	—	—	—
1698	—	30.00	60.00	100	200	—
1700	—	30.00	60.00	100	250	350

KM# 51 1/2 DUCATON (20 Stuiver)
16.3900 g., 0.9410 Silver 0.4958 oz. ASW **Note:** Mint mark: Cinquefoil. Similar to 1 Ducaton, KM#46.

Date	Mintage	VG	F	VF	XF	Unc
1660	—	75.00	175	300	600	—
1661/0	—	100	200	350	700	—
1661	—	75.00	175	300	600	—
1662	—	75.00	175	300	600	—
1663	—	75.00	175	300	600	—
1664	—	75.00	175	300	600	—
1666	—	75.00	175	300	600	—
1667	—	75.00	175	300	600	—
1669	—	100	200	350	700	—
1670	—	75.00	175	300	600	—
1672	—	75.00	175	300	600	—
1673	—	75.00	175	300	600	—
1674	—	75.00	175	300	600	—
1679	—	100	200	350	700	—

KM# 57 1/2 DUCATON (20 Stuiver)
Silver **Note:** Klippe.

Date	Mintage	VG	F	VF	XF	Unc
1664	—	—	—	—	—	—

KM# 67 1/2 DUCATON (20 Stuiver)
Silver **Obv:** Without inner circle **Rev:** Date above crown in inner circle

Date	Mintage	VG	F	VF	XF	Unc
1674	—	100	250	450	600	—
1679	—	75.00	150	250	400	—

KM# 46.1 DUCATON
32.7800 g., 0.9410 Silver 0.9917 oz. ASW **Obv:** Knight on horseback right brandishing sword jumps over arms of West-Frieslandin inner circle. **Obv. Legend:** MO NO ARG PRO CON - FOE BELG WESTF mintmark **Rev:** Crowned arms of the United Netherlans with lion supporters, in inner circle **Rev. Legend:** CONCORDIA - RES PARVAE - CRESCVNT date **Note:** Dotted or plain inner circles. Mint mark: Cinquefoil. Dav. #4939.

Date	Mintage	VG	F	VF	XF	Unc
1659	—	30.00	90.00	150	300	—
1660/59	—	45.00	125	200	400	—
1660	—	30.00	90.00	160	325	—
1661/0	—	35.00	100	160	325	—
1661	—	35.00	100	160	325	—
1662	—	30.00	90.00	150	300	—
1663/2	—	35.00	100	160	325	—
1663	—	30.00	90.00	150	300	—
1664	—	30.00	90.00	150	300	—
1665	—	30.00	90.00	150	300	—
1666	—	30.00	90.00	150	300	—
1668	—	30.00	90.00	150	300	—
1669	—	30.00	90.00	150	300	—
1670	—	20.00	75.00	125	250	—
1671	—	45.00	125	200	400	—
1672	—	30.00	90.00	150	300	—
1673	—	30.00	90.00	150	300	—
1674	—	45.00	125	200	400	—

KM# 68 DUCATON
32.7800 g., Silver **Obv:** Knight on horseback right brandishing sword jumps over crowned arms of West-Friesland **Obv. Legend:** MO NO ARG (PRO) CON - FOE BELG WEST(FI) mintmark **Rev:** Crowned arms of the United Netherlands with lion supporters with date in cartouche **Rev. Legend:** CONCORDIA - RES PARVAE - CRESCVNT mintmark **Note:** Dav. #4940. Mint mark: Cinquefoil. Similar to KM#107.1.

Date	Mintage	VG	F	VF	XF	Unc
1672	499,170	—	—	—	—	—
1674	Inc. above	30.00	100	200	400	—
1675	Inc. above	35.00	125	250	500	—
1676	Inc. above	30.00	100	200	400	—
1677	Inc. above	30.00	100	200	400	—
1678	Inc. above	30.00	100	200	400	—
1679	Inc. above	30.00	100	200	400	—
1692Star	Inc. above	85.00	125	250	500	—

KM# 46.2 DUCATON
32.7800 g., 0.9410 Silver 0.9917 oz. ASW **Obv:** Knight on horseback right brandishing sword jumps over arms of West-Friesland. no inner circle. **Obv. Legend:** MO NO ARG PRO CON - FOE BELG WESTF mintmark **Rev:** Crowned arms of the United Netherlans with lion supporters, in inner circle **Rev. Legend:** CONCORDIA - RES PARVAE - CRESCVNT date **Note:** Dotted or plain inner circles. Mint mark: Cinquefoil. Dav. #4939.

Date	Mintage	VG	F	VF	XF	Unc
1673	—	35.00	100	160	325	—
1674	—	45.00	125	225	450	—

KM# 63.1 DUCATON
32.7800 g., 0.9410 Silver 0.9917 oz. ASW **Rev:** Small arms of Enkhuisen (3 herrings) below shield **Note:** Struck at a private mint of Dirk Hosch in Enkhuizen. Dav. #4941.

Date	Mintage	VG	F	VF	XF	Unc
1673	—	250	700	1,500	2,100	—

KM# 63.2 DUCATON
32.7800 g., 0.9410 Silver 0.9917 oz. ASW **Edge:** Lettered **Note:** Struck at private mint of Dirk Bosch in Enkhuizen.

Date	Mintage	VG	F	VF	XF	Unc
1673	—	—	1,400	2,500	4,000	—

KM# 55 1/2 SILVER DUCAT

Silver **Shape:** Klippe

Date	Mintage	VG	F	VF	XF	Unc
1660	—	—	—	—	—	—
1662	—	—	—	—	—	—
1665	—	—	—	—	—	—

KM# 52 1/2 SILVER DUCAT

14.1200 g., 0.8730 Silver 0.3963 oz. ASW **Note:** Mint mark: Cinquefoil. Similar to 1 Silver Ducat, KM#47.

Date	Mintage	VG	F	VF	XF	Unc
1660	—	100	250	400	600	—
1661	—	100	250	400	600	—
1662	—	100	250	400	600	—
1663/2	—	100	250	500	800	—
1664	—	100	250	500	800	—
1665	—	100	250	400	600	—
1672	—	100	250	400	600	—
1673/2	—	100	300	600	900	—
1673	—	100	250	400	600	—

KM# 47 SILVER DUCAT

28.2500 g., 0.8730 Silver 0.7929 oz. ASW **Obv:** Knight standing facing right holding broad sword upwards and shield **Rev:** Crowned shield **Note:** Mint mark: Cinquefoil. Dav. #4906.

Date	Mintage	VG	F	VF	XF	Unc
1659	—	30.00	75.00	125	250	—
1660	—	30.00	75.00	125	250	—
1661	—	30.00	75.00	125	250	—
1662	—	30.00	75.00	125	250	—
1663/2	—	40.00	100	200	400	—
1663	—	30.00	75.00	125	250	—
1664	—	30.00	75.00	125	250	—
1665	—	40.00	100	200	400	—
1666	—	30.00	75.00	125	250	—
1668	—	30.00	75.00	125	250	—
1669/8/2	—	40.00	100	200	400	—
1669	—	40.00	100	200	400	—
1672	—	30.00	75.00	125	250	—
1673	—	30.00	75.00	125	250	—
1674	—	30.00	75.00	125	250	—
1675	—	40.00	100	200	400	—
1687	—	40.00	100	200	400	—

KM# 54 SILVER DUCAT

Silver **Shape:** Klippe **Note:** Weight 42.4 grams, heavier 1662 exists at 56.5 grams.

Date	Mintage	VG	F	VF	XF	Unc
1661	—	—	—	—	—	—
1662	—	—	—	—	—	—

KM# 64.2 SILVER DUCAT

Silver **Obv:** Knight standing facing right holding broad sword downwards and shield **Rev:** Crowned shield **Edge:** Lettered **Note:** Struck at private mint of Dirk Bosch in Enkhuizen. Prev. KM #62.3.

Date	Mintage	VG	F	VF	XF	Unc
1673	—	400	1,500	2,500	3,000	—
1673 Edge lettered	—	—	—	—	—	—
1678	—	400	1,500	2,500	3,000	—

KM# 64.1 SILVER DUCAT

28.2500 g., Silver **Obv:** Knight standing facing right holding broad sword downwards and shield **Obv. Legend:** MO • NO • ARG • PRO - CONFOE • BEL • WES **Rev:** Crowned shield **Note:** Struck at the private mint of Dirk Hosch in Enkhuizen. Dav. #4910.

Date	Mintage	VG	F	VF	XF	Unc
1673	—	250	500	1,000	1,500	—
1676	—	175	300	500	750	—
1677	—	175	300	500	750	—
1678	—	175	300	500	750	—

KM# 85.1 SILVER DUCAT

Silver **Rev:** Crowned arms divide date **Note:** Mint mark: Bull. Without inner circles. Dav. #4908.

Date	Mintage	VG	F	VF	XF	Unc
1683	54,205	60.00	175	275	425	—
1687/3	Inc. above	60.00	175	275	425	—
1687/6	Inc. above	60.00	175	275	425	—
1687	Inc. above	50.00	125	225	350	—

KM# 85.2 SILVER DUCAT

Silver **Note:** Mint mark: Rosette.

Date	Mintage	VG	F	VF	XF	Unc
1683	—	60.00	175	275	425	—
1687/3	—	60.00	175	275	425	—
1687	—	60.00	175	275	425	—
1688	—	60.00	175	275	425	—
1692	5,487	60.00	175	275	425	—

KM# 85.3 SILVER DUCAT

Silver **Note:** Mint mark: Ship.

Date	Mintage	VG	F	VF	XF	Unc
1693/2	126,774	50.00	125	225	350	—
1693	Inc. above	30.00	75.00	125	250	—
1694	Inc. above	30.00	75.00	125	250	—
1695	Inc. above	30.00	75.00	125	250	—

KM# 85.4 SILVER DUCAT

28.2500 g., Silver **Obv:** Standing armored knight with crowned shield at feet **Obv. Legend:** MO: NO: ARG: TRO: CONFOE: .... **Rev:** Crowned arms of Friesland divide date **Rev. Legend:** CONCORDIA RESPARVÆ ... **Note:** Mint mark: Cinquefoil. Similar to KM#128. Varieties exist.

Date	Mintage	VG	F	VF	XF	Unc
1695	143,767	30.00	75.00	125	250	—
1696/5	Inc. above	60.00	150	250	350	—
1696	Inc. above	60.00	150	250	350	—
1698	Inc. above	30.00	75.00	125	250	—
1699	Inc. above	30.00	75.00	125	250	—

KM# 90 FLORIN (28 Stuiver)

19.5000 g., 0.6730 Silver 0.4219 oz. ASW **Obv:** Crowned arms in inner circle, date above crown, value at bottom **Rev:** Crowned double-headed eagle in inner circle

Date	Mintage	VG	F	VF	XF	Unc
1685	49,375	100	250	400	700	—
1686	Inc. above	100	250	400	700	—
1687/6	Inc. above	125	300	500	800	—

KM# 91 FLORIN (28 Stuiver)

Silver **Shape:** Diamond klippe

Date	Mintage	VG	F	VF	XF	Unc
1685	—	—	—	—	—	—

KM# 92 FLORIN (28 Stuiver)

Silver **Shape:** Octagonal klippe

Date	Mintage	VG	F	VF	XF	Unc
1686	—	—	—	—	—	—

KM# 9 1/2 DAALDER (Lion - 24 Stuiver)

13.8400 g., 0.7500 Silver 0.3337 oz. ASW **Note:** Similar to 1 Daalder, KM#12.

Date	Mintage	VG	F	VF	XF	Unc
1603	—	70.00	200	300	600	—
1604/3	—	80.00	225	400	750	—
1604	—	50.00	150	200	400	—
1605	—	50.00	150	200	400	—
1605/4	—	70.00	200	300	600	—

KM# 22.4 1/2 DAALDER (Lion - 24 Stuiver)

13.8400 g., Silver **Note:** Without mint mark.

Date	Mintage	VG	F	VF	XF	Unc
1606	—	50.00	100	200	400	—
1608	—	100	200	400	700	—
1609	—	—	—	—	—	—
1612	—	100	200	400	700	—
1613/2	—	100	200	400	700	—
1613	—	100	200	400	700	—
1616	—	50.00	100	200	400	—
1617	—	50.00	100	200	400	—
1618/6	—	50.00	100	200	400	—
1618	—	50.00	100	200	400	—
1622	—	75.00	150	300	600	—
1623	—	50.00	100	200	400	—
1624	—	100	200	400	700	—
1625	—	50.00	100	200	400	—
1626	—	50.00	100	200	400	—
1627/6	—	50.00	100	200	400	—
1629	—	75.00	150	300	600	—
1643	—	50.00	100	200	400	—
1650	—	50.00	100	200	400	—

KM# 22.1 1/2 DAALDER (Lion - 24 Stuiver)

13.8400 g., 0.7500 Silver 0.3337 oz. ASW **Note:** Mintmark: Lily. Similar to KM#35.1 but not Klippe

Date	Mintage	VG	F	VF	XF	Unc
1616	—	35.00	100	175	350	—
1617	—	35.00	100	175	350	—
1618/16	—	60.00	150	300	600	—
1618	—	40.00	110	225	450	—
1623	—	35.00	100	175	350	—
1629/8	—	70.00	200	300	550	—
1629	—	35.00	100	175	350	—
1631	—	40.00	120	250	500	—
1632	—	35.00	100	175	350	—
1633/1	—	35.00	100	175	350	—
1633	—	35.00	100	175	350	—
1634	—	60.00	150	300	600	—
1635	—	60.00	150	300	600	—
1636	—	60.00	150	300	600	—
1637	—	35.00	100	175	350	—
1638	—	35.00	100	175	350	—
1639	—	35.00	100	175	350	—
1640	—	35.00	100	175	350	—
1641	—	35.00	100	175	350	—
1642	—	35.00	100	175	350	—
1643	—	35.00	100	175	350	—
1644	—	35.00	100	175	350	—
1645/1	—	60.00	150	300	600	—
1645	—	35.00	100	175	350	—
1646/3	—	60.00	150	300	600	—
1646	—	60.00	150	300	600	—
1647/6	—	60.00	150	300	600	—
1647	—	35.00	100	175	350	—
1648	—	35.00	100	175	350	—

KM# 22.3 1/2 DAALDER (Lion - 24 Stuiver)

13.8400 g., 0.7500 Silver 0.3337 oz. ASW **Note:** Mintmark: Cinquefoil. Varieties exist.

Date	Mintage	VG	F	VF	XF	Unc
1629	—	60.00	150	300	600	—
1650	—	35.00	100	175	350	—
1651	—	45.00	125	200	450	—
1652	—	45.00	125	200	450	—
1654	—	45.00	125	200	450	—
1661	—	45.00	125	200	450	—
1662	—	45.00	125	200	450	—
1663/1	—	60.00	150	300	600	—
1664	—	45.00	125	200	450	—
1666	—	45.00	125	200	450	—
1668	—	45.00	125	200	450	—

KM# 35.1 1/2 DAALDER (Lion - 24 Stuiver)

20.7600 g., Silver **Note:** Mint mark: Lily. Klippe.

Date	Mintage	VG	F	VF	XF	Unc
1632	—	—	—	1,200	2,000	—
1634	—	—	—	1,200	2,000	—
1635	—	—	—	1,200	2,000	—
1637	—	—	—	1,200	2,000	—
1638	—	—	—	1,200	2,000	—
1639	—	—	—	1,200	2,000	—
1640	—	—	—	1,200	2,000	—
1641	—	—	—	1,200	2,000	—
1642	—	—	—	1,200	2,000	—
1645	—	—	—	1,200	2,000	—
1646	—	—	—	1,200	2,000	—
1649	—	—	—	1,200	2,000	—

KM# 35.2 1/2 DAALDER (Lion - 24 Stuiver)
20.7600 g., Silver **Note:** Mint mark: Cinquefoil. Klippe.

Date	Mintage	VG	F	VF	XF	Unc
1666	—	—	—	—	—	—

KM# 13.1 1/2 DAALDER (Rijks)
14.5100 g., 0.8850 Silver 0.4128 oz. ASW **Note:** Mintmark: Rosette. Similar to 1 Daalder, KM#15.

Date	Mintage	VG	F	VF	XF	Unc
1606	—	30.00	100	225	450	—
1607	—	30.00	100	225	450	—
1609	—	30.00	100	225	450	—
1610	—	30.00	100	225	450	—
1611	—	40.00	130	275	550	—
1612	—	30.00	100	225	450	—
1613	—	80.00	250	500	900	—
1614	—	30.00	100	225	450	—
1615	—	30.00	100	225	450	—
1616	—	40.00	130	275	550	—
1618	—	20.00	75.00	150	300	—
1619	—	20.00	75.00	150	300	—
1620	—	20.00	75.00	150	300	—
1621	—	20.00	75.00	150	300	—
1622	—	20.00	75.00	150	300	—
1623	—	20.00	75.00	150	300	—
1624	—	20.00	75.00	150	300	—
1625	—	30.00	100	225	450	—

KM# 13.2 1/2 DAALDER (Rijks)
14.5100 g., 0.8850 Silver 0.4128 oz. ASW **Note:** Mintmark: Lily. Similar to 1 Daalder, KM#15.

Date	Mintage	VG	F	VF	XF	Unc
1618	—	20.00	75.00	150	300	—
1619	—	20.00	75.00	150	300	—
1644/22	—	30.00	100	200	400	—
1644	—	20.00	75.00	150	300	—
1646/5	—	30.00	100	200	400	—
1648	—	20.00	75.00	150	300	—
1649	—	20.00	75.00	150	300	—

KM# 28 1/2 DAALDER (Rijks)
Silver **Note:** Klippe.

Date	Mintage	VG	F	VF	XF	Unc
1623	—	—	—	1,200	2,200	—
1636	—	—	—	1,200	2,200	—
1638	—	—	—	1,200	2,200	—
1646	—	—	—	1,200	2,200	—

KM# 13.3 1/2 DAALDER (Rijks)
14.5100 g., 0.8850 Silver 0.4128 oz. ASW **Note:** Mint mark: Cinquefoil. Similar to 1 Daalder, KM#15. Varieties exist.

Date	Mintage	VG	F	VF	XF	Unc
1649	—	20.00	75.00	150	300	—
1650	—	20.00	75.00	150	300	—
1651	—	20.00	75.00	150	300	—
1656	—	20.00	75.00	150	300	—
1657	—	20.00	75.00	150	300	—
1658	—	20.00	75.00	150	300	—
1659	—	20.00	75.00	150	300	—
1662	—	20.00	75.00	150	300	—

KM# 6 DAALDER (Prince - 40 Stuiver)
29.0300 g., 0.8850 Silver 0.8260 oz. ASW **Obv:** Armored bust of William the Silent with sword to right in inner circle, date at top in legend **Rev:** Helmeted arms in inner circle **Note:** Dav. #4824.

Date	Mintage	VG	F	VF	XF	Unc
1601	—	100	300	550	1,100	—

KM# 7 DAALDER (Lion - 48 Stuiver)
27.6800 g., 0.7500 Silver 0.6674 oz. ASW **Note:** Similar to KM#12 but date divided below shield. Dav. #4867.

Date	Mintage	VG	F	VF	XF	Unc
ND	—	45.00	125	225	450	—
1601	—	45.00	125	225	450	—
1603	268,860	45.00	125	225	450	—
1609/3	—	45.00	125	250	500	—

KM# 12 DAALDER (Lion - 48 Stuiver)
27.6800 g., 0.7500 Silver 0.6674 oz. ASW **Obv:** Date at sides of shield **Note:** Province Liondaalder. Dav. #4868.

Date	Mintage	VG	F	VF	XF	Unc
1604	—	20.00	75.00	175	400	—
1605/4	—	25.00	100	225	500	—
1605	—	20.00	75.00	175	400	—

KM# 14.1 DAALDER (Lion - 48 Stuiver)
27.6800 g., 0.7500 Silver 0.6674 oz. ASW **Rev:** Date at top in legend **Note:** Without mint mark. Dav. #4870.

Date	Mintage	VG	F	VF	XF	Unc
1606	—	25.00	75.00	150	300	—
1608	—	25.00	75.00	150	300	—
1609/6	—	25.00	60.00	125	250	—
1609/8	—	25.00	60.00	125	250	—
1609	—	25.00	75.00	150	300	—
1610	—	25.00	60.00	125	250	—
1611	—	25.00	60.00	125	250	—
1612/09	—	25.00	60.00	125	250	—
1612	—	25.00	60.00	125	250	—
1613/2	—	25.00	60.00	125	250	—
1613	—	25.00	60.00	125	250	—
1614	—	25.00	60.00	125	250	—
1615	—	25.00	60.00	125	250	—
1618	—	25.00	60.00	125	250	—
1618/7	—	25.00	60.00	125	250	—
1621	—	25.00	60.00	125	250	—
1622	—	25.00	60.00	125	250	—
1623/2	—	25.00	75.00	150	300	—
1623	—	25.00	60.00	125	250	—
1624/2	—	25.00	75.00	150	300	—
1624/3	—	25.00	60.00	125	250	—
1624	—	25.00	60.00	125	250	—
1625	—	25.00	60.00	125	250	—
1627	—	25.00	60.00	125	250	—
1628/7	—	25.00	60.00	125	250	—
1628	—	25.00	60.00	125	250	—
1630	—	25.00	60.00	125	250	—
1650	—	25.00	60.00	125	250	—

KM# 14.2 DAALDER (Lion - 48 Stuiver)
27.6800 g., 0.7500 Silver 0.6674 oz. ASW **Rev:** Date at top in legend **Note:** Mint mark: Lily.

Date	Mintage	VG	F	VF	XF	Unc
1616	—	15.00	45.00	100	200	—
1617	—	15.00	45.00	100	200	—
1631	—	15.00	45.00	100	200	—
1632	—	15.00	45.00	100	200	—
1633	—	15.00	45.00	100	200	—
1634	—	15.00	45.00	100	200	—
1635/3	—	15.00	45.00	100	200	—
1635	—	15.00	45.00	100	200	—
1636	—	15.00	45.00	100	200	—
1637	—	15.00	45.00	100	200	—
1638	—	15.00	45.00	100	200	—
1639	—	15.00	45.00	100	200	—
1640	—	15.00	45.00	100	200	—
1641	—	15.00	45.00	100	200	—
1642	—	15.00	45.00	100	200	—
1643/1	—	15.00	45.00	100	200	—
1643	—	15.00	45.00	100	200	—
1644/2	—	20.00	70.00	160	325	—
1644	—	15.00	45.00	100	200	—
1645	—	20.00	70.00	160	325	—
1646/3	—	20.00	70.00	160	325	—
1646	—	15.00	45.00	100	200	—
1647	—	15.00	45.00	100	200	—
1648/7	—	20.00	70.00	160	325	—
1648	—	15.00	45.00	100	200	—
1649	—	20.00	70.00	160	325	—

KM# 14.5 DAALDER (Lion - 48 Stuiver)
27.6800 g., 0.7500 Silver 0.6674 oz. ASW **Rev:** Date at top in legend **Note:** Mint mark: Rosette.

Date	Mintage	VG	F	VF	XF	Unc
1616	—	15.00	60.00	150	300	—
1622/13	—	15.00	75.00	175	350	—
1622	—	20.00	75.00	175	350	—
1623/2	—	25.00	60.00	150	300	—
1623	—	15.00	60.00	150	300	—
1624	—	15.00	60.00	150	300	—
1624/3	—	25.00	60.00	150	300	—
1624/2	—	—	—	—	—	—
1624/3	—	25.00	90.00	200	400	—
1626	—	15.00	60.00	150	300	—
1627/6	—	—	—	—	—	—
1627	—	25.00	90.00	200	400	—
1628/7	—	15.00	45.00	100	200	—
1628	—	15.00	45.00	100	200	—
1629	—	15.00	60.00	150	300	—

KM# 37 DAALDER (Lion - 48 Stuiver)
27.6800 g., 0.7500 Silver 0.6674 oz. ASW **Note:** Klippe.

Date	Mintage	VG	F	VF	XF	Unc
1637	—	—	—	—	—	—
1638	—	—	—	—	—	—
1639	—	—	—	—	2,000	—
1650	—	—	—	—	1,500	2,00
1652	—	—	—	—	—	—
1667	—	—	—	—	—	—

KM# 14.3 DAALDER (Lion - 48 Stuiver)
27.6800 g., 0.7500 Silver 0.6674 oz. ASW **Rev:** Date at top in legend **Note:** Mint mark: Cinquefoil.

Date	Mintage	VG	F	VF	XF	Unc
1649/0	—	25.00	75.00	150	300	—
1649	—	25.00	75.00	150	300	—
1650/49	—	25.00	75.00	150	300	—
1650	—	15.00	50.00	100	200	—
1651	—	15.00	50.00	100	200	—
1652	—	15.00	50.00	100	200	—
1654/3	—	15.00	50.00	100	200	—
1654	—	15.00	50.00	100	200	—
1655	—	25.00	80.00	175	350	—
1657	—	25.00	80.00	175	350	—
1658	—	25.00	80.00	175	350	—
1661	—	25.00	80.00	175	350	—
1662	—	15.00	50.00	100	200	—
1663	—	25.00	80.00	175	350	—
1664	—	25.00	80.00	175	350	—
1665	—	15.00	75.00	150	300	—
1666	—	15.00	75.00	150	300	—
1667	—	40.00	75.00	150	300	—
1668/7	—	25.00	80.00	175	350	—
1668	—	15.00	75.00	150	300	—
1670	—	15.00	75.00	150	300	—
1671	132,620	15.00	75.00	150	300	—
1672	Inc. above	15.00	75.00	150	300	—
1674	Inc. above	15.00	75.00	150	300	—
1675	Inc. above	15.00	75.00	150	300	—
1676	Inc. above	25.00	80.00	175	350	—
1677	Inc. above	15.00	75.00	150	300	—
1678	Inc. above	15.00	75.00	150	300	—
1679	Inc. above	15.00	75.00	150	300	—
1697	263,735	25.00	80.00	175	350	—
1698	Inc. above	25.00	80.00	175	350	—
1699	Inc. above	25.00	80.00	175	350	—
1700	Inc. above	25.00	80.00	175	350	—

KM# 14.4 DAALDER (Lion - 48 Stuiver)
27.6800 g., 0.7500 Silver 0.6674 oz. ASW **Rev:** Date at top in legend **Note:** Mint mark: Bull. Varieties exist.

Date	Mintage	VG	F	VF	XF	Unc
1682	30,630	25.00	100	200	400	—
1687	Inc. above	50.00	125	250	500	—

KM# 86 DAALDER (30 Stuivers)
15.8800 g., 0.9060 Silver 0.4625 oz. ASW **Obv:** Three opposed crowned shields **Rev:** Knight standing behind shield brandishing sword, with inner circle

Date	Mintage	VG	F	VF	XF	Unc
1684	—	60.00	125	250	500	—

KM# 87 DAALDER (30 Stuivers)
15.8800 g., 0.9060 Silver 0.4625 oz. ASW **Obv:** Three opposed crowned shields **Rev:** Knight standing behind shield looking left brandishing sword **Note:** Klippe.

Date	Mintage	VG	F	VF	XF	Unc
1684	—	—	—	—	—	—

KM# 89 DAALDER (30 Stuivers)
15.8800 g., 0.9060 Silver 0.4625 oz. ASW **Obv:** Three opposed crowned shields **Rev:** Knight standing behind shield looking right brandishing sword **Note:** Klippe.

Date	Mintage	VG	F	VF	XF	Unc
1684	—	—	—	—	—	—

KM# 88.2 DAALDER (30 Stuivers)
15.8800 g., 0.9060 Silver 0.4625 oz. ASW **Obv:** Three opposed crowned shields **Rev:** Knight standing behind left brandishing sword **Note:** Mint mark: Cinquefoil.

Date	Mintage	VG	F	VF	XF	Unc
1684	—	35.00	100	150	300	—
1685	—	35.00	100	150	300	—
1686	—	35.00	100	150	300	—
1687	—	35.00	100	150	300	—

KM# 88.3 DAALDER (30 Stuivers)
15.8800 g., 0.9060 Silver 0.4625 oz. ASW **Obv:** Three opposed crowned shields **Rev:** Knight standing behind shield brandishing sword **Note:** Mint mark: Shield of Medenblik.

Date	Mintage	VG	F	VF	XF	Unc
1684	—	35.00	100	150	300	—
1685	—	35.00	100	150	300	—

KM# 88.1 DAALDER (30 Stuivers)
15.8800 g., 0.9060 Silver 0.4625 oz. ASW **Obv:** Three opposed crowned shields **Rev:** Knight standing behind shield brandishing sword **Note:** Without mint mark.

Date	Mintage	VG	F	VF	XF	Unc
1684	—	35.00	100	150	300	—
1685	—	35.00	100	150	300	—

KM# 15.1 DAALDER (Rijks)
29.0300 g., 0.8850 Silver 0.8260 oz. ASW **Note:** Mint mark: Rosette. Dav. #4842.

Date	Mintage	VG	F	VF	XF	Unc
1607	—	30.00	80.00	160	325	—
1608	—	30.00	80.00	160	325	—
1609/8	—	40.00	100	150	300	—
1609	—	30.00	65.00	140	275	—
1610	—	30.00	65.00	140	275	—
1611	—	30.00	65.00	140	275	—
1612/1	—	30.00	65.00	140	275	—
1612	—	30.00	65.00	140	275	—
1613	—	30.00	65.00	140	275	—
1614/1	—	30.00	65.00	140	275	—
1614	—	30.00	65.00	140	275	—
1615/3	—	30.00	65.00	140	275	—
1615	—	30.00	65.00	140	275	—
1616	—	30.00	65.00	140	275	—
1618	—	30.00	65.00	140	275	—
1619	—	30.00	65.00	140	275	—
1620	—	30.00	65.00	140	275	—
1621	—	30.00	65.00	140	275	—
1622	—	30.00	65.00	140	275	—

Date	Mintage	VG	F	VF	XF	Unc
1623	—	30.00	65.00	140	275	—
1624/2	—	40.00	100	150	300	—
1624/3	—	40.00	100	150	300	—
1624	—	30.00	65.00	140	275	—
1625	—	30.00	65.00	140	275	—
1626	—	40.00	100	150	300	—
1628	—	40.00	100	150	300	—
1629	—	40.00	100	150	300	—

KM# 15.2 DAALDER (Rijks)
29.0300 g., 0.8850 Silver 0.8260 oz. ASW **Note:** Mint mark: Lily.

Date	Mintage	VG	F	VF	XF	Unc
1616	—	30.00	65.00	140	275	—
1619	—	30.00	65.00	140	275	—
1644	—	30.00	65.00	140	275	—
1646	—	30.00	65.00	140	275	—
1649	—	30.00	65.00	140	275	—

KM# 25 DAALDER (Rijks)
Silver **Note:** Klippe.

Date	Mintage	VG	F	VF	XF	Unc
1620	—	—	—	—	—	—
1626	—	—	—	—	—	—

KM# 15.4 DAALDER (Rijks)
Silver **Note:** Without mint mark.

Date	Mintage	VG	F	VF	XF	Unc
1622	—	30.00	50.00	140	275	—
1623	—	30.00	50.00	140	275	—

KM# 15.3 DAALDER (Rijks)
29.0300 g., 0.8850 Silver 0.8260 oz. ASW **Note:** Mint mark: Cinquefoil. Varieties exist.

Date	Mintage	VG	F	VF	XF	Unc
1649	—	25.00	80.00	140	275	—
1650	—	25.00	80.00	140	275	—
1651	—	25.00	80.00	140	275	—
1652	—	65.00	125	275	450	—
1653	—	25.00	80.00	140	275	—
1654/3	—	30.00	85.00	140	275	—
1654	—	25.00	80.00	140	275	—
1655/1	—	65.00	125	275	450	—
1655	—	30.00	85.00	140	275	—
1656	—	25.00	80.00	140	275	—
1657	—	25.00	80.00	140	275	—
1658	—	25.00	80.00	140	275	—
1659	—	25.00	80.00	140	275	—
1668	—	65.00	125	275	450	—
1675	—	25.00	80.00	140	275	—
1683	—	65.00	125	275	450	—
1693	—	65.00	125	275	450	—

KM# 26 1/2 CAVALIER D'OR
5.0000 g., 0.9200 Gold 0.1479 oz. AGW **Obv:** Equestrian figure of knight above arms in inner circle **Rev:** Crowned arms in inner circle, date at top **Note:** Fr. #297.

Date	Mintage	VG	F	VF	XF	Unc
1621	3,300	350	1,000	2,000	3,000	—
1626	—	350	1,000	2,000	3,000	—
1632	—	250	700	1,300	2,600	—
1644	—	500	1,400	2,500	3,500	—

KM# 27 CAVALIER D'OR
10.0000 g., 0.9200 Gold 0.2958 oz. AGW **Obv:** Equestrian figure of knight above arms in inner circle **Rev:** Crowned arms in inner circle, date at top **Note:** Fr. #296.

Date	Mintage	VG	F	VF	XF	Unc
1621	—	350	1,000	2,000	3,000	—
1623	—	350	1,000	2,100	3,250	—
1627	—	350	1,000	2,000	3,000	—

TRADE COINAGE

KM# 8 DUCAT
3.5000 g., 0.9860 Gold 0.1109 oz. AGW **Obv:** Ruler standing divides date in inner circle **Rev:** Crowned arms in inner circle, date at top **Note:** Fr. #294.

Date	Mintage	VG	F	VF	XF	Unc
1601	327,600	160	250	500	750	—
1603	Inc. above	200	450	750	1,000	—
1604	Inc. above	150	225	450	650	—
1605/1	Inc. above	160	250	500	750	—
1605	Inc. above	150	225	450	650	—

KM# 16 DUCAT
3.5000 g., 0.9860 Gold 0.1109 oz. AGW **Obv:** Ruler standing facing divides date in dotted inner circle. **Obv. Legend:** CONCORDIA RES PAR - VAE - CRES(CVNT) WEST(F) **Rev:** Inscription within ornamental tablet **Rev. Legend:** MO ORDI / ROVIN / FOE DER / BELG AD / LEG IMP **Note:** Varieties exist. Fr. #294, 295. After 1671 plain inner circle.

Date	Mintage	VG	F	VF	XF	Unc
1607	180,880	150	200	300	500	—
1608	Inc. above	150	200	300	500	—
1609	Inc. above	150	200	300	500	—
1610/09	Inc. above	150	200	300	500	—
1610	Inc. above	200	350	500	700	—
1611	Inc. above	150	200	300	500	—
1612	Inc. above	150	200	300	500	—
1619	30,480	150	200	300	500	—
1622Lily	Inc. above	150	200	300	500	—
1624Lily	15,409	150	200	300	500	—
1631Lily	363,020	150	200	300	500	—
1632Lily	Inc. above	150	200	300	500	—
1633Lily	Inc. above	150	200	300	500	—
1634/3Lily	Inc. above	200	350	500	700	—
1634Lily	Inc. above	150	200	300	500	—
1635Lily	Inc. above	150	200	300	500	—
1636Lily	Inc. above	150	200	300	500	—
1637Lily	351,050	150	200	300	500	—
1638Lily	Inc. above	150	200	300	500	—
1639Lily	Inc. above	150	200	300	500	—
1640Lily	Inc. above	150	200	300	500	—
1641Lily	Inc. above	150	200	300	500	—
1642Lily	Inc. above	150	200	300	500	—
1643Lily	442,120	150	200	300	500	—
1644Lily	Inc. above	150	200	300	500	—
1645Lily	Inc. above	150	200	300	500	—
1646Lily	Inc. above	150	200	300	500	—
1647/6Lily	Inc. above	200	350	500	700	—
1647Lily	Inc. above	150	200	300	500	—
1648Lily	Inc. above	150	200	300	500	—
1649Lily	Inc. above	150	200	300	500	—
1649Cinquefoil	396,200	200	350	500	700	—
1650Cinquefoil	Inc. above	200	350	500	700	—
1651Cinquefoil	Inc. above	200	350	500	700	—
1652Cinquefoil	Inc. above	150	200	300	500	—
1653/2Cinquefoil	Inc. above	150	200	300	500	—
1653Cinquefoil	Inc. above	150	200	300	500	—
1654Cinquefoil	Inc. above	150	200	300	500	—
1655Cinquefoil	Inc. above	150	200	300	500	—
1656Cinquefoil	Inc. above	150	200	300	500	—
1657Cinquefoil	Inc. above	150	200	300	500	—
1658Cinquefoil	Inc. above	150	200	300	500	—
1659Cinquefoil	Inc. above	200	250	500	700	—
1661Cinquefoil	Inc. above	150	200	300	500	—
1662Cinquefoil	Inc. above	150	200	300	500	—
1664Cinquefoil	Inc. above	200	350	500	700	—
1666Cinquefoil	Inc. above	200	350	500	700	—
1667Cinquefoil	Inc. above	200	350	500	700	—
1668Cinquefoil	Inc. above	150	250	400	600	—
1669Cinquefoil	Inc. above	200	350	500	700	—
1670Cinquefoil	Inc. above	200	350	500	700	—
1671Cinquefoil	Inc. above	150	200	300	500	—
1672Cinquefoil	Inc. above	150	200	300	500	—
1673Cinquefoil	Inc. above	150	200	300	500	—
1674Cinquefoil	Inc. above	150	200	300	500	—
1675Cinquefoil	Inc. above	150	200	300	500	—

KM# 36 DUCAT
0.9860 Gold **Obv:** Knight standing right with sword and bundle of arrows **Rev:** Tablet with five-line inscription **Note:** Klippe. Struck with 1 Ducat dies, KM#16. Weight varies 6.76 - 7.02 grams.

Date	Mintage	VG	F	VF	XF	Unc
1635	—	—	—	2,750	3,350	—
1637	—	—	—	2,750	3,350	—
1638	—	—	—	2,750	3,350	—
1662	—	—	—	—	—	—

KM# 93.1 DUCAT
3.5100 g., 0.9860 Gold 0.1113 oz. AGW **Obv:** Standing armored knight divides date **Obv. Legend:** CONCO(RDIAK) RES PAR - CRES W(ESTFR) **Rev:** 5 lines incription within ornamented square **Rev. Legend:** MO:ORD/PRO.FOE/BEL.AD/LEG.IM **Rev. Inscription:** MO:ORD/PROVIN/FOEDER/BELGAD/LEG IMP **Note:** Fr. #295. Mintmark rosette

Date	Mintage	VG	F	VF	XF	Unc
1683	—	—	—	—	—	—
1684	—	150	275	450	650	950
1686/5/4	—	150	250	400	600	900
1686	—	150	250	400	600	900
1689	—	200	350	500	700	1,000
1690	—	200	350	500	700	1,000
1692	5,355	150	250	400	900	900
1693/2	—	200	350	500	700	1,000
1693	—	150	250	400	600	900
1694	—	200	350	500	700	1,000

KM# 93.2 DUCAT

3.5100 g., 0.9860 Gold 0.1113 oz. AGW **Obv:** Standing armored knight divides date **Obv. Legend:** CONCO(RDIA) RED PAR - CRES W(ESTFRI) **Rev:** 4 Lines incription within ornamented square **Rev. Legend:** MO.ORD/PRO.FOE/BEL.AD/LEG.IM **Rev. Inscription:** MO: ORD / PROVIN / FOEDER / BELGAD / LEG IMP **Note:** Fr. #295, Mint mark: Turnip

Date	Mintage	VG	F	VF	XF	Unc
1696	—	150	250	400	600	900
1697	—	200	350	500	700	1,000

KM# 53.1 2 DUCAT

7.0200 g., 0.9860 Gold 0.2225 oz. AGW **Obv:** Standing armored knight holding bundle of arrows divides date within broken circle **Obv. Legend:** CONCORDIA RES PAR CRES • WF • **Rev:** Inscription within ornamented square **Rev. Inscription:** MO:ORD/PROVIN/FOEDER/BELG•AD/LEG•IMP **Note:** Fr. #292, Mint mark: Turnip

Date	Mintage	VG	F	VF	XF	Unc
1660	—	350	750	1,500	2,500	3,500
1661	—	400	1,000	2,000	3,000	4,000
1662	—	350	750	1,500	2,500	3,500
1663/1	—	350	750	1,500	2,500	3,500
1664	—	350	750	1,500	2,500	3,500
1666	—	350	750	1,500	2,500	3,500
1672	—	250	650	1,250	2,000	3,000
1673	—	250	650	1,250	2,000	3,000

KM# 53.2 2 DUCAT

7.0200 g., 0.9860 Gold 0.2225 oz. AGW **Obv:** Armored knight standing holding bundle of arrows, divides date within broken circle **Obv. Legend:** CONCORDIA RES PAR CRES • WF • **Rev:** Inscription on ornamented tablet **Rev. Inscription:** MO: ORD / PROVIN / FOEDER / BELG • AD / LEG • IMP **Note:** Mint mark: Cinquefoil. Fr. #292.

Date	Mintage	VG	F	VF	XF	Unc
1662	—	350	750	1,500	2,500	3,500
1666	—	350	750	1,500	2,500	3,500
1672	—	350	750	1,500	2,500	3,500

KM# 94 2 DUCAT

7.0200 g., 0.9860 Gold 0.2225 oz. AGW **Obv:** Knight standing holding bundle of arrows divides date **Obv. Legend:** CONCORDIA RES PAR CRES • WF • **Rev:** Inscription on ornamented tablet **Rev. Inscription:** MO: ORD / PROVIN / FOEDER / BELG • AD / LEG • IMP **Note:** Without mint mark. Fr. #293.

Date	Mintage	VG	F	VF	XF	Unc
1684	—	350	750	1,500	2,500	3,500
1694	—	350	750	1,500	2,500	3,500
1694/84	—	400	1,000	2,000	3,000	4,000
1696	—	350	750	1,500	2,500	3,500

PATTERNS

Including off metal strikes

KM#	Date	Mintage	Identification	Mkt Val
Pn1	1639	—	Stuiver. Gold. Klippe, KM#39.	2,000
Pn2	1673	—	Ducaton. Gold. 45.6300 g. KM#63.1	—
Pn3	1674	—	6 Stuivers. Gold. 3.5100 g. KM#66	—
Pn4	1674	—	6 Stuivers. Gold. 12.3000 g. KM#66	—
Pn5	1677	—	6 Stuivers. Gold. 5.2400 g. KM#76	—
Pn6	1682	—	6 Stuivers. Gold. 6.9300 g. KM#5.2	4,000
Pn7	1682	—	10 Stuivers. Gold. 6.9000 g. KM#80	4,000
Pn8	1682	—	10 Stuivers. Gold. 10.4500 g. KM#80	5,000
Pn9	1682	—	Gulden. Gold. 10.3500 g. KM#81.	5,000
Pn10	1682	—	Gulden. Gold. 13.9000 g. KM#81.	6,000
Pn11	1682	—	Gulden. Gold. 17.2000 g. KM#81.	—
Pn12	1682	—	2 Gulden. Gold. 27.8000 g. KM#82	—
Pn13	1683	—	Gulden. Gold. 13.9000 g. KM#81.	—
Pn14	1683	—	Gulden. Gold. 17.2000 g. KM#81.	—
Pn15	1684	—	Daalder. Gold. 13.8600 g. KM#88.2.	10,000
Pn16	1684	—	Daalder. Gold. 17.2900 g. KM#88.2.	—
Pn17	1686	—	Ducaton. Gold. 41.7300 g. KM#68.	—

PIEFORTS

KM#	Date	Mintage	Identification	Mkt Val
P1	1609	—	Lion Daalder. Silver. KM14.1.	—
PA2	1609/8	—	Daalder. Silver.	—
PB2	1633	—	Daalder. Silver. 41.5000 g.	—
PC2	1639	—	Daalder. Silver. 41.5000 g.	—
PD2	1639	—	Stuiver. Gold. 4.0400 g. KM 38, Klippe	2,000
PE2	1645	—	Duit. Silver. 6.0000 g. KM#29.	300
P2	1646	—	Rijks Daalder. Silver. KM15.2	—
P3	1649	—	Lion Daalder. Silver. Km14.1	—
P4	1650	—	Rijks Daalder. Silver. Klippe, KM15.3.	—
P5	1651	—	Rijks Daalder. Silver. Quadruple weight, KM15.3.	—
PA6	1652	—	Daalder. Silver. 55.3600 g. KM#14.1.	—
PB6	1658	—	Duit. Copper. Klippe, KM29.	—
P6	1659	—	Ducaton. Silver. KM#46.	—
P7	1659	—	Ducaton. Silver. Klippe, KM#46.	—
PA8	1660	—	Duit. Copper. Klippe, KM29.	—
PB8	1661	—	Duit. Copper. Klippe, KM29.	—
P9	1662	—	Silver Ducat. Silver. Klippe, KM47.	—
P8	1662	—	1/2 Ducaton. Silver. KM51.	1,400
PA10	1663	—	Duit. Copper. KM29.	—
PB10	1663	—	Duit. Copper. Klippe, KM29.	—
P10	1665	—	Ducaton. Silver. KM#46.	1,300
P11	1666	—	Ducaton. Silver. KM#46.	1,500
PA12	1667	—	Daalder. Silver. 55.3600 g. KM14.1.	—
P12	1668	—	Ducaton. Silver. Km#46.	—
P14	1670	—	Ducaton. Silver. Klippe, KM#46.	—
P13	1670	—	Ducaton. Silver. Km#46.	1,250
P15	1672	—	1/2 Ducaton. Silver. Klippe, KM51.	—
P16	1673	—	Ducaton. Silver. KM46.	—
P18	1674	—	Ducaton. Silver. KM46.	—
P19	1674	—	Ducaton. Silver. KM#68.	—
P17	1674	—	1/2 Ducaton. Silver. Klippe, KM57.	—
P21	1677	—	Silver Ducat. Silver. KM47.	—
P20	1677	—	Ducaton. Silver. KM68.	1,500
PA26	1679	—	Ducaton. Silver. KM#68.	2,000
P26	1682	—	Silver Ducat. Silver. KM85.	—
P24	1682	—	2 Gulden. Silver. Klippe, KM83.	—
P25	1682	—	3 Gulden. Silver. KM84.	—
P22	1682	—	Gulden. Gold. KM81.	—
P23	1682	—	2 Gulden. Silver. KM82.	1,500
PA24	1682	—	2 Gulden. Silver. Klippe, KM#82.	1,700
P27	1693	—	Silver Ducat. Silver. Klippe, KM85.	—
P28	1694	—	Silver Ducat. Silver. KM85.	—
P29	1694	—	Silver Ducat. Silver. Klippe, KM85.	—
P30	1696	—	3 Gulden. Silver. KM95.	—
P31	1696	—	2 Ducat. Gold. KM#94.	—
P32	1697	—	Lion Daalder. Silver. 55.3600 g. KM#14.1.	—

ZEELAND

Zelandia

Zeeland (Zelandia), the southernmost maritime province of the Netherlands, consists of a strip of the Flanders mainland and six islands.

MINT MARK

Castle

PROVINCE

STANDARD COINAGE

KM# 14a 1/2 DUIT

1.5000 g., Silver **Obv:** Inscription within wreath **Obv. Inscription:** ZE / LAN / DIA **Rev:** Maiden standing within sprays, shield below

Date	Mintage	VG	F	VF	XF	Unc
ND	—	—	—	—	—	—
1626	—	—	—	—	—	—
1632	—	—	—	—	—	—
1637	—	—	—	—	—	—

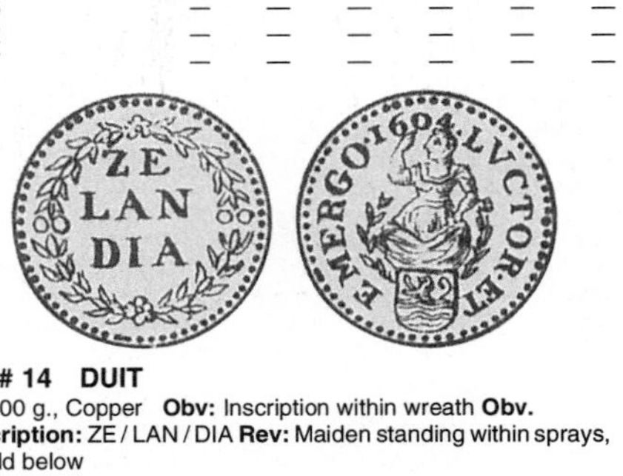

KM# 14 DUIT

2.0400 g., Copper **Obv:** Inscription within wreath **Obv. Inscription:** ZE / LAN / DIA **Rev:** Maiden standing within sprays, shield below

Date	Mintage	VG	F	VF	XF	Unc
1601	—	8.00	45.00	90.00	160	—
1604	—	6.00	25.00	55.00	100	—
1609	—	8.00	35.00	70.00	120	—
1626	—	6.00	25.00	55.00	100	—
1632	—	6.00	30.00	80.00	160	—
1636	—	5.00	30.00	60.00	120	—
1637	—	60.00	100	150	225	—

KM# 14b DUIT

3.5000 g., Gold **Obv:** Inscription within wreath **Rev:** Maiden standing within sprays, shield below **Rev. Inscription:** ZE / LAN / DIA

Date	Mintage	VG	F	VF	XF	Unc
1637 Rare	—	—	—	—	—	—

KM# 33 DUIT

2.0400 g., Copper **Obv:** Inscripion within wreath **Obv. Inscription:** ZEE / LAN / DIA **Rev:** Maiden seated within fence, crowned shield below

Date	Mintage	VG	F	VF	XF	Unc
1641	—	5.00	40.00	90.00	130	—
1642/1	—	8.00	20.00	40.00	100	—
1642	—	5.00	15.00	30.00	80.00	—
1643	—	8.00	40.00	90.00	130	—
1645	—	5.00	15.00	30.00	80.00	—
1647	—	5.00	15.00	30.00	80.00	—
1648	—	5.00	15.00	30.00	80.00	—
1649	—	5.00	15.00	30.00	80.00	—
1653	—	5.00	15.00	30.00	80.00	—
1654	—	8.00	40.00	90.00	130	—
1657	—	5.00	15.00	35.00	95.00	—
1658	—	8.00	40.00	90.00	160	—
1663	—	5.00	15.00	30.00	80.00	—
1664	—	5.00	15.00	30.00	80.00	—
1665	—	8.00	20.00	40.00	100	—
1669	—	5.00	40.00	90.00	160	—
1670	—	6.00	17.50	35.00	80.00	—

KM# 33a DUIT

1.5000 g., Silver **Obv:** Inscription within wreath **Obv. Inscription:** ZEE / LAN / DIA **Rev:** Maiden seated within fence, crowned shield below

Date	Mintage	VG	F	VF	XF	Unc
1641	—	—	—	—	—	—
1647	—	—	—	—	—	—

KM# 33b DUIT

3.5000 g., Gold **Obv:** Inscription within wreath **Obv. Inscription** ZEE / LAN / DIA **Rev:** Maiden seated within fence

Date	Mintage	VG	F	VF	XF	Unc
1647 Rare	—	—	—	—	—	—

KM# 33c DUIT

4.8000 g., Silver **Note:** Similar to #33.

Date	Mintage	F	VF	XF	Unc	BU
1663	—	—	—	400	—	—

KM# 55 DUIT

Copper **Obv:** Inscription in wreath **Obv. Inscription:** ZEE / LAN / DIA / date **Rev:** Figure seated within fence, shield below

Date	Mintage	VG	F	VF	XF	Unc
1680	1,279,445	5.00	15.00	35.00	70.00	—
1681	Inc. above	5.00	15.00	35.00	70.00	—
1683	960,010	5.00	15.00	35.00	70.00	—
1684	Inc. above	5.00	15.00	35.00	70.00	—
1685	Inc. above	5.00	15.00	35.00	70.00	—
1686	Inc. above	5.00	25.00	50.00	100	—
1686/5	Inc. above	6.00	17.50	35.00	70.00	—
1689	960,000	5.00	15.00	35.00	70.00	—

KM# 55b DUIT

3.5000 g., Gold **Obv:** ZEE / LAN / DIA / date in wreath

Date	Mintage	VG	F	VF	XF	Unc
1681 Rare	—	—	—	—	—	—
1684 Rare	—	—	—	—	—	—
1686 Rare	—	—	—	—	1,500	2,00
1689	—	—	—	—	1,500	2,00

KM# 55a DUIT

5.5000 g., Silver **Obv:** ZEE/LAN/DIA/(date) in wreath **Rev:** Figure seated

Date	Mintage	VG	F	VF	XF	Unc
1683	—	—	—	—	—	—

KM# 5 OORD (2 Duit)

5.1000 g., Copper **Obv:** Bust of Prince William of Orange righ **Rev:** Crowned arms of Zeeland, castle divides date above crow

Date	Mintage	VG	F	VF	XF	Unc
1601	—	7.00	30.00	65.00	130	—
1602	—	7.00	30.00	65.00	130	—
1603	—	15.00	60.00	125	250	—

KM# 15.1 OORD (2 Duit)

4.3000 g., Copper **Obv:** Bust of Prince Maurice right **Rev:** Crowned shield, crown divides date

Date	Mintage	VG	F	VF	XF	Unc
1604	—	7.00	22.50	90.00	120	—
1608	—	15.00	55.00	125	200	—
1626	—	7.00	22.50	100	130	—
1636	—	7.00	22.50	100	130	—
1637	—	15.00	55.00	125	200	—

KM# 15.2 OORD (2 Duit)

4.3000 g., Copper **Obv:** Bust of Prince Maurice right **Obv. Legend:** NON NOVA COMIT ZELANDIAE (rosette) **Rev:** Crowned shield, crown with dots deivded date **Rev. Legend:** LVICTOR ET EMER(G)O

Date	Mintage	VG	F	VF	XF	Unc
1641	—	7.00	45.00	100	200	—
1642	—	7.00	25.00	70.00	140	—

Date	Mintage	VG	F	VF	XF	Unc
1643	—	7.00	25.00	70.00	140	—
1645	—	7.00	25.00	70.00	140	—
1649	—	7.00	25.00	70.00	140	—
1653/43	—	7.00	45.00	100	200	—
1653	—	7.00	25.00	70.00	140	—
1655	—	7.00	25.00	70.00	140	—

KM# 15.3 OORD (2 Duit)

3.9000 g., Copper **Obv:** Bust of Prince Maurice right **Rev:** Crowned shield, crown with dots divides date

Date	Mintage	VG	F	VF	XF	Unc
1657/3	—	7.00	25.00	70.00	140	—
1657/5	—	7.00	25.00	70.00	140	—
1657	—	7.00	25.00	70.00	140	—
1659	—	7.00	25.00	70.00	140	—
1663	—	7.00	22.50	60.00	120	—

KM# 15.4 OORD (2 Duit)

3.9000 g., Copper **Obv:** Bust of Prince Maurice right **Obv. Legend:** MON NOVA COMIT ZELANDIAE (castle) **Rev:** Crowned shield, crown with lily's divides date **Rev. Legend:** LVCTOR ET EMERGO

Date	Mintage	VG	F	VF	XF	Unc
1669	—	9.00	30.00	70.00	140	—
1671	—	15.00	55.00	110	220	—

KM# 8 STUIVER

1.3000 g., 0.3000 Silver 0.0125 oz. ASW **Obv:** Crowned arms divide value in inner circle **Rev:** Ornate cross with castle at center in quatrefoil in inner circle

Date	Mintage	VG	F	VF	XF	Unc
1602	—	50.00	200	350	500	—

KM# 27 STUIVER

0.8600 g., 0.5830 Silver 0.0161 oz. ASW **Obv:** ZEE/LAN/DIA/(date) **Rev:** Crowned rampant lion left holding sword and arrows, value at sides

Date	Mintage	VG	F	VF	XF	Unc
1614	—	15.00	50.00	100	200	—
1615	—	15.00	50.00	100	200	—

KM# 58 STUIVER

0.8600 g., 0.2710 Silver 0.0075 oz. ASW **Obv:** Arms of Zeeland **Rev:** Inscription above date **Rev. Inscription:** ZEE/LAN/DIA

Date	Mintage	VG	F	VF	XF	Unc
1681	344,697	6.00	15.00	50.00	100	—
1682	279,038	6.00	15.00	50.00	100	—
1683	968,992	6.00	15.00	40.00	85.00	—
1684	Inc. above	6.00	15.00	40.00	85.00	—
1685	Inc. above	6.00	15.00	40.00	85.00	—

KM# 28 STUIVER (Bezem)

0.8600 g., 0.5830 Silver 0.0161 oz. ASW **Obv:** Bundle of arrows divide value within wreath **Rev:** Inscription above date **Rev. Inscription:** ZEE/LAN/DIA • **Note:** Varieties exist.

Date	Mintage	VG	F	VF	XF	Unc
1614	—	6.00	25.00	50.00	90.00	—
1619	—	6.00	25.00	50.00	90.00	—
1628	—	6.00	25.00	50.00	90.00	—
1691 Error	—	6.00	25.00	50.00	90.00	—
1629	—	6.00	25.00	50.00	90.00	—

KM# 29 2 STUIVER

1.7300 g., 0.5830 Silver 0.0324 oz. ASW **Obv:** ZEE/LAN/DIA/(date) **Rev:** Crowned rampant lion left holding sword and arrow, value at sides

Date	Mintage	VG	F	VF	XF	Unc
1614	—	6.00	20.00	40.00	80.00	—
1615	—	6.00	20.00	40.00	80.00	—
1616	—	6.00	20.00	40.00	80.00	—
1617	—	6.00	20.00	40.00	80.00	—
1618	—	6.00	20.00	40.00	80.00	—
1619	—	6.00	20.00	40.00	80.00	—
1622	—	6.00	20.00	40.00	80.00	—
1624	—	6.00	20.00	40.00	80.00	—
1625	—	6.00	20.00	40.00	80.00	—
1626	—	6.00	20.00	40.00	80.00	—
1627	—	6.00	20.00	40.00	80.00	—
1628	—	6.00	20.00	40.00	80.00	—
1637	—	6.00	20.00	40.00	80.00	—
1639	1,054,009	6.00	20.00	40.00	80.00	—
1640	Inc. above	6.00	20.00	40.00	80.00	—
1641	Inc. above	6.00	20.00	40.00	80.00	—
1646	221,583	6.00	20.00	40.00	80.00	—
1653	40,818	6.00	20.00	40.00	80.00	—
1669	7,326,523	6.00	20.00	40.00	80.00	—
1670	Inc. above	6.00	20.00	40.00	80.00	—

Date	Mintage	VG	F	VF	XF	Unc
1672	268,974	6.00	20.00	40.00	80.00	—
1675	Inc. above	6.00	20.00	40.00	80.00	—

KM# 59 2 STUIVER

1.6200 g., 0.5830 Silver 0.0304 oz. ASW **Obv:** Crowned arms of Zeeland divide value **Rev:** Inscription above date **Rev. Inscription:** ZEE/LAN/DIA

Date	Mintage	VG	F	VF	XF	Unc
1681	118,983	2.00	7.00	20.00	35.00	—
1683	442,906	2.00	7.00	20.00	35.00	—
1684	Inc. above	2.00	7.00	20.00	35.00	—
1686	Inc. above	2.00	7.00	20.00	35.00	—
1690	Inc. above	2.00	7.00	20.00	35.00	—
1695	Inc. above	2.00	7.00	20.00	35.00	—
1696	314,837	2.00	7.00	20.00	35.00	—
1699	1,552,122	2.00	7.00	20.00	35.00	—
1700	5,673,627	2.00	6.00	15.00	30.00	—

KM# 9 2-1/2 STUIVER (1/12 Arendsdaalder)

1.7200 g., 0.7500 Silver 0.0415 oz. ASW **Obv:** Garnished arms with date above in inner circle **Rev:** Doulbe-headed eagle with arms on breat in inner circle

Date	Mintage	VG	F	VF	XF	Unc
1602	—	80.00	200	400	850	—

KM# 6 3 STUIVERS (1/2 Roosschelling)

2.6300 g., 0.5830 Silver 0.0493 oz. ASW **Obv:** Crowned Zeeland arms in inner circle, date above crown **Rev:** Ornate cross in inner circle with castle at center

Date	Mintage	VG	F	VF	XF	Unc
1601	14,515	40.00	100	200	400	—
1603	—	40.00	100	200	400	—
1614	—	40.00	100	200	400	—

KM# 10 5 STUIVERS (1/6 Arendsdaalder)

3.4500 g., 0.7500 Silver 0.0832 oz. ASW **Obv:** Garnished arms with date above in inner circle **Rev:** Double-headed eagle with arms on breast in inner circle

Date	Mintage	VG	F	VF	XF	Unc
1602	—	80.00	250	500	1,000	—

KM# 7 6 STUIVERS (Roosschelling)

5.2700 g., 0.5830 Silver 0.0988 oz. ASW **Obv:** Crowned Zeeland arms in inner circle, date above crown **Rev:** Ornate cross in inner circle with castle at center

Date	Mintage	VG	F	VF	XF	Unc
1601	—	40.00	100	200	300	—
1603	—	40.00	100	200	300	—
1613	—	40.00	100	200	300	—
1614	—	40.00	100	200	300	—
1615	—	40.00	100	200	300	—
1646	—	40.00	100	200	300	—
1653 Rev: w/o castle	—	40.00	100	200	300	—

KM# 47 6 STUIVERS (Snaphaanschilling)

6.5300 g., 0.5000 Silver 0.1050 oz. ASW **Obv:** Armored knight standing holding sword behind shield of arms, date divided at top **Rev:** Ornate cross in inner circle with castle at center

Date	Mintage	VG	F	VF	XF	Unc
1669	371,800	30.00	100	250	400	—
1670	Inc. above	30.00	100	250	400	—

KM# 50 6 STUIVERS (Hoedjesschelling)

4.9500 g., 0.5830 Silver 0.0928 oz. ASW **Obv:** Crowned arms of Zeeland divide date **Rev:** Reclining lion holding pole with cap

Date	Mintage	VG	F	VF	XF	Unc
1672	130,000	10.00	35.00	80.00	160	—
1677	91,139	10.00	35.00	80.00	160	—
1678	Inc. above	10.00	35.00	80.00	160	—
1680	426,853	10.00	35.00	80.00	160	—
1681	88,374	10.00	35.00	80.00	160	—
1682	487,630	10.00	35.00	80.00	160	—
1683	Inc. above	10.00	35.00	80.00	160	—
1684	Inc. above	10.00	35.00	80.00	160	—
1685	Inc. above	10.00	35.00	80.00	160	—
1687	Inc. above	10.00	35.00	80.00	160	—
1692	Inc. above	10.00	35.00	80.00	160	—
1699	328,125	10.00	35.00	80.00	160	—
1700	Inc. above	10.00	35.00	80.00	160	—

KM# 50b 6 STUIVERS (Hoedjesschelling)

17.0000 g., Gold **Obv:** Crowned arms divide date **Rev:** Reclining lion to left holding spear with Liberty cap **Note:** Prev. KM#50c. Weight varies, 1681 - 14.4 grams, 1687 - 10.5 grams.

Date	Mintage	VG	F	VF	XF	Unc
1681 Rare	—	—	—	—	—	—
1687	—	—	—	—	—	—

KM# 50a 6 STUIVERS (Hoedjesschelling)

6.8000 g., Gold **Obv:** Crowned arms of Zeeland divide date **Rev:** Reclining lion holding pole with cap

Date	Mintage	VG	F	VF	XF	Unc
1684 Rare	—	—	—	—	—	—
1685	—	—	—	—	2,500	3,500

KM# 26 10 STUIVERS

5.9500 g., 0.9170 Silver 0.1754 oz. ASW **Obv:** Armored knight standing behind shield with sword on shoulder **Rev:** Crowned arms divide value X - S

Date	Mintage	VG	F	VF	XF	Unc
1613	1,653	75.00	300	600	1,200	1,700

KM# 11 10 STUIVERS (1/3 Arendsdaalder)

6.9000 g., 0.7500 Silver 0.1664 oz. ASW **Obv:** Garnished arms with date above in inner circle **Rev:** Double-headed eagle with arms on breast in iner circle

Date	Mintage	VG	F	VF	XF	Unc
1602	—	40.00	150	350	600	—

KM# 12 30 STUIVERS (Arendsdaalder of 60 Groot)

20.6800 g., 0.7500 Silver 0.4986 oz. ASW **Obv:** Garnished arms with date above in inner circle **Rev:** Double-headed eagle with arms on breast in inner circle

Date	Mintage	VG	F	VF	XF	Unc
1602	859,190	40.00	80.00	160	350	—
1618/02	246,033	60.00	175	350	600	—
1618	Inc. above	40.00	80.00	160	350	—
1619	Inc. above	40.00	80.00	160	350	—

KM# 53 30 STUIVERS (Daalder)

15.8800 g., 0.9060 Silver 0.4625 oz. ASW **Obv:** Armored knight standing holding sword behind crowned shield of arms **Obv. Legend:** LVCTOR ET EMERGO (castle) **Rev:** Garnished arms with 9 shields and value above. Date in Legend **Rev. Legend:** MO NO ARG ORDIN ZELANDIAE

Date	Mintage	VG	F	VF	XF	Unc
1676	422,670	35.00	90.00	175	350	—
1677	Inc. above	35.00	90.00	175	350	—
1678	Inc. above	35.00	90.00	175	350	—
1679	725,540	35.00	90.00	175	350	—
1680	Inc. above	35.00	90.00	175	350	—
1681	Inc. above	35.00	90.00	175	350	—
1682/0	147,793	35.00	100	200	400	—
1682	Inc. above	35.00	90.00	175	350	—

KM# 60 30 STUIVERS (Daalder)

15.8800 g., 0.9060 Silver 0.4625 oz. ASW

Date	Mintage	VG	F	VF	XF	Unc
1682	—	35.00	90.00	175	350	—
1683	—	35.00	90.00	175	350	—
1684/3	—	35.00	90.00	175	350	—
1684	—	35.00	90.00	175	350	—
1685/3	—	50.00	100	200	400	—
1685	—	35.00	90.00	175	350	—
1686/2	—	50.00	100	200	400	—
1686/5	—	50.00	100	200	400	—
1686	—	35.00	90.00	175	350	—

KM# 64 30 STUIVERS (5 Schelling = 1 Daalder)

15.8500 g., 0.9060 Silver 0.4617 oz. ASW **Obv:** Value appears as 5 - SC

Date	Mintage	VG	F	VF	XF	Unc
1685	—	60.00	150	250	450	—
1686	138,059	50.00	125	200	400	—
1687	Inc. above	60.00	150	275	500	—

KM# A70 3 GULDEN

31.8200 g., 0.9200 Silver 0.9412 oz. ASW **Obv:** 6 Shields around center shield, between 5-G **Obv. Legend:** MO NO ARG ORDIN ZEELANDIAE (date) **Rev:** Armored knight standing holding sword behind crowned shield of arms **Rev. Legend:** LUCTOR ET - EMERGO (castle) **Note:** Similar to KM#64

Date	Mintage	F	VF	XF	Unc	BU
1685	—	—	—	—	—	—

KM# 70 3 GULDEN

Silver **Obv:** Crowned arms of Zeeland **Note:** Dav. #4965.

Date	Mintage	VG	F	VF	XF	Unc
1694	84,689	150	350	500	800	—

KM# 71 3 GULDEN

31.8200 g., 0.9200 Silver 0.9412 oz. ASW **Obv:** Different crowned lion shield divides value 3 - GL **Rev:** Date in exergue **Note:** Dav. #4966.

Date	Mintage	VG	F	VF	XF	Unc
1694	—	125	300	400	650	—
1698	—	125	325	450	750	—

KM# 66 15 GULDEN

10.2000 g., Gold **Obv:** Crowned arms divide date **Obv. Legend:** MO. NO. AUR... **Rev:** Reclining lion to left holding spear with Liberty cap **Note:** Previously listed as 6 Stuiver, KM50b, gold strike.

Date	Mintage	VG	F	VF	XF	Unc
1687	—	—	—	—	—	20,000

KM# A65 30 GULDEN

20.8000 g., Gold **Obv:** 6 shields around center shield, between 30-G. **Obv. Legend:** MO. NO. AUR. ORDIN. ZEELANDIAE *1684* **Rev:** Armored standing knight, looking to right, holding sword, behind shield of arms

Date	Mintage	VG	F	VF	XF	Unc
1684	—	—	—	—	25,000	—
1686	—	—	—	—	25,000	—
1687	—	—	—	—	25,000	—

KM# B65 30 GULDEN

20.8000 g., Gold **Obv:** Without denominatjon

Date	Mintage	VG	F	VF	XF	Unc
1687 Rare	—	—	—	—	—	30,000

KM# 65 60 GULDEN

34.4000 g., Gold **Obv:** Circle of shields flanked by denomination **Rev:** Standing knight holding sword, behind arms

Date	Mintage	VG	F	VF	XF	Unc
1684 Rare	—	—	—	—	—	—

KM# 25 1/2 DAALDER (Rijks - 24 Stuiver)

14.5100 g., 0.8850 Silver 0.4128 oz. ASW **Obv:** Laureate 1/2 figure holding sword and arms in inner circle **Rev:** Crowned arms divide date in inner circle

Date	Mintage	VG	F	VF	XF	Unc
1609	—	120	300	450	600	—
1601 (error for 1610))	—	130	325	550	1,000	—
1610	—	100	250	400	500	—
1612	—	65.00	175	300	400	—
1613	—	65.00	175	300	400	—
1619/3	—	65.00	175	300	400	—
1619/6	—	65.00	175	300	400	—
1619	—	65.00	175	300	400	—
1620	—	65.00	175	300	400	—
1621	—	65.00	175	300	400	—
1622	—	65.00	175	300	400	—
1623	—	65.00	175	300	400	—
1625	—	100	250	400	500	—
1626	—	100	250	400	500	—
1628	—	100	250	400	500	—
1629	—	100	250	400	500	—
1631	—	65.00	175	300	400	—
1634	—	65.00	175	300	400	—
1635	—	65.00	175	300	400	—
1646/3	—	65.00	175	300	400	—
1646	—	65.00	175	300	400	—
1647	—	65.00	175	300	400	—
1648	—	65.00	175	300	400	—
1649	—	65.00	175	300	400	—
1650	—	65.00	175	300	400	—
1651	—	65.00	175	300	400	—
1652	—	65.00	175	300	400	—
1653	—	65.00	175	300	400	—
1655/2	—	65.00	175	300	400	—
1655	—	65.00	175	300	400	—
1656	—	65.00	175	300	400	—

Date	Mintage	VG	F	VF	XF	Unc
1657	—	65.00	175	300	400	—
1658	—	65.00	175	300	400	—
1659	—	65.00	175	300	400	—
1660	—	65.00	175	300	400	—
1661	—	65.00	175	300	400	—
1662/1	—	65.00	175	300	400	—
1662	—	65.00	175	300	400	—

KM# 30 1/2 DAALDER (1/2 Lion)

13.8400 g., 0.7500 Silver 0.3337 oz. ASW **Obv:** Armoured knight looking right above lion shield in inner circle **Rev:** Rampant lion left in inner circle, date at top in legend

Date	Mintage	VG	F	VF	XF	Unc
1609	—	65.00	175	350	600	—
1614	—	50.00	125	250	500	—
1615	—	50.00	125	250	500	—
1616	—	50.00	125	250	500	—
1617	—	50.00	125	250	500	—
1618	—	50.00	125	250	500	—
1619	—	50.00	125	250	500	—
1623	—	50.00	125	250	500	—
1625/4	—	65.00	175	350	700	—
1628	—	50.00	125	250	500	—
1632/0	—	65.00	175	350	700	—
1633	—	75.00	200	400	800	—
1634	—	75.00	200	400	800	—
1635	—	75.00	200	400	800	—
1637	—	65.00	175	350	700	—
1638	—	50.00	125	250	500	—
1639	—	75.00	200	400	800	—
1640	—	65.00	125	250	500	—
1641	—	75.00	200	400	800	—
1645	—	65.00	125	250	500	—
1647	—	65.00	125	250	500	—
1648	—	65.00	125	250	500	—
1649/8	—	75.00	200	400	800	—
1649	—	65.00	175	350	700	—
1650	—	50.00	125	250	500	—
1651	—	50.00	125	250	500	—
1652	—	50.00	125	250	500	—
1653	—	50.00	125	250	500	—

KM# 17.1 DAALDER

29.0300 g., 0.8850 Silver 0.8260 oz. ASW **Obv:** Laureate 1/2 figure holding sword and arms in dotted inner circle **Obv. Legend:** MO ARG PRO(V)-CONFOE BELG ZD(L) (castle) **Rev:** Crowned arms divide date in dotted inner circle **Rev. Legend:** CONCORDIE RES PARVAE CRESCVNT (castle) **Note:** Similar to KM#17 but no mintmark

Date	Mintage	VG	F	VF	XF	Unc
1652	—	40.00	100	150	400	—
1653	—	60.00	150	200	400	—
1654	—	40.00	100	150	400	—
1655	—	40.00	100	150	400	—
1656	—	40.00	100	150	400	—
1657	—	40.00	100	150	400	—
1658	—	40.00	100	150	400	—
1659	—	40.00	100	150	400	—
1660	—	40.00	100	150	400	—
1661	—	40.00	100	150	400	—
1662	—	40.00	100	150	400	—
1664	—	60.00	150	200	400	—
1671	—	60.00	150	200	400	—

KM# 13 DAALDER (Prince - 40 Stuiver)

29.0300 g., 0.8850 Silver 0.8260 oz. ASW **Obv:** Armored bust of Prince Maurice with sword right in inner circle, date at top **Rev:** Helmeted provincial arms in inner circle **Note:** Dav. #4825.

Date	Mintage	VG	F	VF	XF	Unc
1603	2,410	100	300	600	1,000	1,500

KM# 16 DAALDER (Lion)

27.6800 g., 0.7500 Silver 0.6674 oz. ASW **Obv:** Armored knight looking right above lion shield in inner circle **Rev:** Rampant lion left in inner circle, date at top in legend **Note:** Dav. #4872.

Date	Mintage	VG	F	VF	XF	Unc
1606	46,770	25.00	75.00	150	300	—
1607	—	45.00	100	200	400	—
1609/7	—	45.00	85.00	175	350	—
1609	—	45.00	85.00	175	350	—

Date	Mintage	VG	F	VF	XF	Unc
1611	—	45.00	85.00	175	350	—
1612	—	25.00	75.00	150	300	—
1613	—	25.00	75.00	150	300	—
1614	—	25.00	75.00	150	300	—
1615	—	25.00	75.00	150	300	—
1616	—	25.00	75.00	150	300	—
1617	—	25.00	75.00	150	300	—
1618	—	45.00	100	200	400	—
16222 (error)	—	—	—	—	—	—
1623	—	25.00	75.00	150	300	—
1624	—	45.00	100	200	400	—
1627/5	—	45.00	100	200	400	—
1628	—	35.00	85.00	175	350	—
1629	—	45.00	100	200	400	—
1631/0	—	55.00	120	230	450	—
1633	—	25.00	75.00	150	300	—
1634	—	45.00	85.00	175	350	—
1635	—	45.00	100	200	400	—
1636	—	45.00	85.00	175	350	—
1637	—	45.00	85.00	175	350	—
1638	—	45.00	85.00	175	350	—
1640/30	—	25.00	75.00	150	300	—
1640	—	25.00	75.00	150	300	—
1644	—	40.00	100	200	400	—
1645/3	—	40.00	100	200	400	—
1645	—	40.00	100	200	400	—
1646	—	40.00	85.00	175	350	—
1647	—	40.00	100	200	400	—
1648	—	25.00	75.00	150	300	—
1649	—	25.00	75.00	150	300	—
1650/49	—	25.00	75.00	150	300	—
1650	—	25.00	75.00	150	300	—
1651	—	25.00	75.00	150	300	—
1652	—	25.00	75.00	150	300	—
1653	—	40.00	100	200	400	—
1655	—	70.00	175	250	500	—
1658	—	25.00	75.00	150	300	—

KM# 17 DAALDER (Rijks)

29.0300 g., 0.8850 Silver 0.8260 oz. ASW **Obv:** Laureate 1/2 figure holding sword and arms in inner circle **Rev:** Crowned arms divide date in inner circle **Note:** 1606-51 mint mark: castle; 1652-71 without mint mark. Dav. #4844.

Date	Mintage	VG	F	VF	XF	Unc
1606	—	40.00	100	150	300	—
1607	—	40.00	100	150	300	—
1610	—	60.00	150	200	400	—
1612/1	—	60.00	150	200	400	—
1612	—	40.00	100	150	300	—
1613	—	40.00	100	150	300	—
1616	—	40.00	100	150	300	—
1617	—	40.00	100	150	300	—
1619	—	40.00	100	150	300	—
1620	—	40.00	100	150	300	—
1621	—	40.00	100	150	300	—
1622	—	40.00	100	150	300	—
1623	—	40.00	100	150	300	—
1624	—	40.00	100	150	300	—
1625	—	40.00	100	150	300	—
1626	—	40.00	100	150	300	—
1628/6	—	40.00	100	150	300	—
1629	—	40.00	100	150	300	—
1630	—	40.00	100	150	300	—
1631/0	—	40.00	100	150	300	—
1631	—	40.00	100	150	300	—
1635	—	75.00	175	250	500	—
1638	—	40.00	100	150	300	—
1642	—	40.00	100	150	300	—
1643	—	75.00	175	250	500	—
1644	—	40.00	100	150	300	—
1646	—	40.00	100	150	300	—
1647	—	40.00	100	150	300	—
1648	—	40.00	100	150	300	—
1649	—	40.00	100	150	300	—
1650	—	40.00	100	150	300	—
1651	—	40.00	100	150	300	—

KM# 63 2 DAALDERS (60 Stuiver - 10 Schelling, Escalins)

31.7600 g., 0.9060 Silver 0.9251 oz. ASW **Note:** Dav. #4973.

Date	Mintage	VG	F	VF	XF	Unc
1685	—	75.00	150	250	500	—
1685 Proof	—	—	—	—	—	—
1687	495,837	75.00	150	250	500	—
1688	104,307	100	250	400	600	—
1689/7	619,171	100	250	400	600	—
1689/8	Inc. above	75.00	150	250	500	—
1689	Inc. above	50.00	125	200	400	—
1690	57,990	50.00	125	200	400	—
1692	Inc. above	50.00	125	200	400	—
1693	Inc. above	75.00	150	250	500	—

KM# 45 1/2 SILVER DUCAT

14.1200 g., 0.8730 Silver 0.3963 oz. ASW **Obv:** Armored knight standing holding sword behind shield o f arms, date at sides in dotted inner circle **Rev:** Crowned arms in inner circle

Date	Mintage	VG	F	VF	XF	Unc
1659	—	100	250	400	600	—
1660	—	100	250	400	600	—
1661/0	—	100	275	450	700	—
1661	—	100	250	400	600	—
1662/1	—	100	275	450	700	—
1662	—	100	250	400	600	—
1663	—	100	250	400	600	—
1664	—	100	250	400	600	—
1668	—	100	275	450	700	—

KM# 51.1 1/2 SILVER DUCAT

14.1200 g., 0.8730 Silver 0.3963 oz. ASW **Obv:** Standing armored knight with crowned shield at feet **Obv. Legend:** MON • NOV • ARG • PRO • CONFOED • BELG • COM • ZEL • **Rev:** Crowned arms of Zeeland divide date **Rev. Legend:** CONCORDIA RES PARVÆ CRESCUNT

Date	Mintage	VG	F	VF	XF	Unc
1672	—	40.00	100	200	400	—
1673	—	40.00	100	200	400	—
1675	—	40.00	100	200	400	—

KM# 40 SILVER DUCAT

28.2500 g., 0.8730 Silver 0.7929 oz. ASW **Obv:** Armored kniht standing holding sword behind shield of arms, date at sides in inner circle **Rev:** Crowned arms in inner circle **Note:** Dav. #4912.

Date	Mintage	VG	F	VF	XF	Unc
1659	—	55.00	125	175	350	—
1660	—	55.00	125	175	350	—
1661/0	—	55.00	125	175	350	—
1661	—	55.00	125	175	350	—
1662	—	55.00	125	175	350	—
1663	—	55.00	125	175	350	—
1664	—	95.00	200	300	500	—
1667	—	55.00	125	175	350	—
1668	—	95.00	200	300	500	—

KM# 52.1 SILVER DUCAT

28.2500 g., 0.8730 Silver 0.7929 oz. ASW **Obv:** Standing armored Knight with crowned shield at feet **Obv. Legend:** MO • NO • ARG • PRO : CON • FOE • BELG • COM • ZEEL • **Rev:** Crowned arms of Zeeland divide date **Rev. Legend:** CONCORDIA • RES • PARVÆ • CRESCUNT **Note:** Dav. #4914.

Date	Mintage	VG	F	VF	XF	Unc
ND	—	40.00	150	300	600	—
1672	—	20.00	75.00	150	300	—
1673	—	20.00	75.00	150	300	—
1674	—	20.00	75.00	150	300	—
1675/3	—	20.00	75.00	150	300	—
1675	—	20.00	75.00	150	300	—
1676	—	20.00	75.00	150	300	—
1677	—	20.00	85.00	175	350	—
1678	—	20.00	75.00	150	300	—
1679/6	—	20.00	75.00	150	300	—
1679	—	20.00	75.00	150	300	—
1680	—	20.00	75.00	150	300	—
1693	—	20.00	85.00	175	350	—
1694/73	—	20.00	85.00	175	350	—
1694/93	—	20.00	85.00	175	350	—
1694	—	20.00	75.00	150	300	—
1695	—	20.00	75.00	150	300	—
1695/4	—	20.00	85.00	175	350	—
1696	—	20.00	75.00	150	300	—
1697/5	—	20.00	75.00	150	300	—
1697/6	—	20.00	75.00	150	300	—
1697	—	20.00	75.00	150	300	—
1698	—	20.00	75.00	150	300	—
1699	—	20.00	85.00	175	350	—
1700	—	20.00	75.00	150	300	400

KM# 46 1/2 DUCATON (20 Stuiver)

16.3900 g., 0.9410 Silver 0.4958 oz. ASW **Obv:** Knight with sword on horseback right, provincial arms below in inner circle **Rev:** Crowned arms with crowned lion supporters in inner circle, date at top in legend

Date	Mintage	VG	F	VF	XF	Unc
1660	—	90.00	200	400	600	—
1661	—	90.00	200	400	600	—
1662	—	90.00	200	400	600	—
1663	—	90.00	200	400	600	—
1664	—	100	250	450	700	—
1670	—	100	250	450	700	—
1671	—	110	265	475	750	—
1672	—	110	265	475	750	—
1673	—	110	265	475	750	—

KM# 41.1 DUCATON (40 Stuiver)

32.7800 g., 0.9410 Silver 0.9917 oz. ASW **Obv:** Knight with sword on horseback right, provincial arms below in inner circle **Rev:** Crowned arms with crowned lion supporters in inner circle, date at top in legend **Note:** Dotted inner circle 1659-66; solid inner circle 1668-72. Dav. #4942.

Date	Mintage	VG	F	VF	XF	Unc
1659	—	60.00	150	250	400	—
1660	—	70.00	200	325	500	—
1661	—	60.00	150	250	400	—
1662/0	—	70.00	200	275	500	—
1662	—	60.00	150	250	400	—
1663	—	60.00	150	250	400	—
1664/3	—	70.00	200	325	500	—
1664	—	60.00	150	250	400	—
1666	—	60.00	150	250	400	—
1668	—	60.00	150	250	400	—
1670	—	60.00	150	250	400	—
1671	—	70.00	200	325	500	—
1672	—	70.00	200	325	500	—

KM# 41.2 DUCATON (40 Stuiver)

32.7800 g., 0.9410 Silver 0.9917 oz. ASW **Obv:** Knight with sword on horseback right, provincial arms below in inner circle **Rev:** Crowned arms with crowned lion supporters in inner circle, date at top in legend **Edge:** Lettered **Edge Lettering:** LVCT(OR) ET.EMERGO.

Date	Mintage	VG	F	VF	XF	Unc
1670	—	—	—	—	—	—
1672	—	—	—	—	—	—

KM# 56 DUCATON (40 Stuiver)

Silver **Obv:** Without ground under the horse's legs **Note:** Dav. #4943.

Date	Mintage	VG	F	VF	XF	Unc
1680	15,705	100	275	550	1,100	—
1683	2,027	—	—	—	—	—

KM# 57.1 DUCATON (Silver Rider)

32.7800 g., 0.9410 Silver 0.9917 oz. ASW **Obv:** Armored Knight on horse above crowned shield **Obv. Legend:** MON: NOV: ARG: PRO: CON FOED: BELG: COM: ZEL • **Rev:** Crowned arms of Zeeland with supporters, date in cartouche below **Rev. Legend:** CONCORDIA RES • PARVÆ • CRESCUNT •

Date	Mintage	VG	F	VF	XF	Unc
1670	—	100	225	450	900	—
1671	—	100	225	450	900	—
1672	—	100	225	450	900	—
1675	—	100	225	450	900	—
1680	—	100	225	450	900	—
1683	—	100	225	500	1,000	—

KM# 3 1/2 ROSE NOBLE

3.8200 g., Gold **Obv:** Ruler in ship facing holding sword upright and provincial shield **Obv. Legend:** ... COMITAT • ZELAN **Rev:** Radiant sun surrounded by crowned lions and lis **Note:** FR#303.

Date	Mintage	Good	VG	F	VF	XF
ND(1591-1602)	—	—	400	900	1,750	2,500

KM# 4 ROSE NOBLE

7.6400 g., Gold **Obv:** Ruler in ship facing holding sword upright and provincial shield **Obv. Legend:** ... COMITAT • ZELAN **Rev:** Radiant sun surrounded by crowned lions and lis **Note:** FR.#302.

Date	Mintage	Good	VG	F	VF	XF
ND(1591-1602)	—	—	500	1,250	2,500	3,500

KM# 19 1/2 CAVALIER D'OR

5.0000 g., 0.9200 Gold 0.1479 oz. AGW **Note:** Date divided by mint mark 1645-48. Fr. #312.

Date	Mintage	VG	F	VF	XF	Unc
1609	—	275	500	1,000	1,500	—
1610	—	275	500	1,000	1,500	—
1611	—	275	500	1,000	1,500	—
1614	—	275	500	1,000	1,500	—
1615	—	250	400	650	1,200	—
1617	—	250	400	650	1,200	—
1618	—	250	450	800	1,400	—
1621	—	250	400	650	1,200	—
1622	—	250	400	650	1,200	—
1623	—	250	400	650	1,200	—
1625	—	250	400	650	1,200	—
1626	—	275	500	1,000	1,500	—
1627	—	250	400	650	1,200	—
1628	—	275	500	900	1,500	—
1629	—	250	400	650	1,200	—
1630	—	250	400	650	1,200	—
1631	—	275	500	1,000	1,500	—
1634	—	275	500	1,000	1,500	—
1635	—	275	500	1,000	1,500	—
1638	—	250	400	650	1,200	—
1639	—	250	400	650	1,200	—
1640	—	250	400	650	1,200	—
1641	—	250	400	650	1,200	—
1644	—	250	400	650	1,200	—
1645	—	250	400	650	1,200	—
1647	—	250	400	650	1,200	—
1648	—	250	400	650	1,200	—

KM# 18 CAVALIER D'OR

10.0000 g., 0.9200 Gold 0.2958 oz. AGW **Obv:** Equestrian figure of knight above arms in inner circle **Rev:** Crowned arms in inner circle, date at top **Note:** Fr. #311.

Date	Mintage	VG	F	VF	XF	Unc
1606	—	500	1,100	2,200	3,300	—
1615	—	500	1,100	2,200	3,300	—
1621	—	500	1,100	2,200	3,300	—
1624	—	500	1,100	2,200	3,300	—
1630	—	700	1,750	3,500	4,000	—
1638	—	500	1,100	2,200	3,300	—
1644/38	—	500	1,100	2,200	3,300	—
1644	—	500	1,100	2,200	3,300	—

TRADE COINAGE

KM# 20 DUCAT

3.5000 g., 0.9860 Gold 0.1109 oz. AGW **Obv:** 5-line inscription in tablet **Rev:** Standing figure of knight to right divides date in inner circle **Note:** Fr. #307.

Date	Mintage	VG	F	VF	XF	Unc
1609	3,640	140	175	300	450	—
1621	—	140	175	300	450	—
1631	114,680	140	175	300	450	—
1632	Inc. above	140	175	300	450	—
1635	Inc. above	175	300	550	700	—
1638	80,815	140	175	300	450	—
1641	Inc. above	140	175	300	450	—
1642	Inc. above	140	175	300	450	—
1643	Inc. above	140	175	300	450	—
1645	—	200	400	600	800	—
1648	—	200	400	600	800	—
1649	—	140	175	300	450	—
1650	—	200	400	600	800	—
1651	—	200	400	600	800	—
1654	—	140	175	300	450	—
1658	—	140	175	300	450	—
1659	—	140	175	300	450	—

KM# 62 DUCAT

3.5000 g., 0.9860 Gold 0.1109 oz. AGW **Obv:** Knight standing to right divides date within inner circle **Rev:** Tablet on full-blown rose **Note:** Fr. #307.

Date	Mintage	VG	F	VF	XF	Unc
1682	—	175	300	500	650	—
1683	—	175	300	500	650	—
1686	—	200	400	600	800	—
1687/3	—	175	300	500	650	—
1687	—	175	300	500	650	—
1690	—	175	300	500	650	—

KM# 35 2 DUCAT

7.0000 g., 0.9860 Gold 0.2219 oz. AGW **Obv:** Knight standing right divides date in inner circle **Rev:** 5-line inscription in tablet **Note:** FR. #306.

Date	Mintage	VG	F	VF	XF	Unc
1645	—	350	800	1,500	2,500	—
1646	—	300	700	1,300	2,000	—
1647/6	—	350	800	1,500	2,500	—
1647	—	300	700	1,300	2,000	—
1648	—	300	700	1,300	2,000	—
1649	—	300	700	1,300	2,000	—
1649/7	—	350	800	1,500	2,500	—
1650	—	300	700	1,300	2,000	—
1651	—	300	700	1,300	2,000	—
1652	—	300	700	1,300	2,000	—
1653	—	300	700	1,300	2,000	—
1654	—	300	700	1,300	2,000	—
1655	—	300	700	1,300	2,000	—
1656	—	300	700	1,300	2,000	—
1658	—	300	700	1,300	2,000	—
1658/6	—	350	800	1,500	2,500	—
1659	—	350	800	1,500	2,500	—
1660	—	300	700	1,300	2,000	—
1661	—	350	800	1,500	2,500	—
1662	—	300	700	1,300	2,000	—
1668	—	350	800	1,500	2,500	—
1672	—	350	800	1,500	2,500	—
1673	—	400	1,000	2,000	3,000	—

KM# 61 2 DUCAT

7.0000 g., 0.9860 Gold 0.2219 oz. AGW **Obv:** Without inner circle **Rev:** Tablet on full blown rose **Note:** FR. #306.

Date	Mintage	VG	F	VF	XF	Unc
1673	—	400	1,000	2,000	3,000	—
1682	—	400	1,000	2,000	3,000	—
1683	—	400	1,000	2,000	3,000	—
1684	—	400	1,000	2,000	3,000	—
1689	—	400	1,000	2,000	3,000	—
1690	—	400	1,000	2,000	3,000	—

COPIED COINAGE

KM# 15.5 OORD (2 Duit)

3.1000 g., Copper, 25 mm. **Obv:** Bust of Prince Maurice right **Rev:** Crowned shield, crown divides date **Edge:** Plain **Note:** Contemporary copy of similar but altered design.

Date	Mintage	F	VF	XF	Unc	BU
1657	—	—	—	—	—	—

PATTERNS

Including off metal strikes

KM#	Date	Mintage	Identification	Mkt Va
Pn3	1682	—	Daalder. Gold. 34.6000 g. KM#17.	—
Pn6	1684	—	Daalder. Gold. 34.6000 g. KM#17.	—
Pn7	1685/3	—	30 Gulden. Silver.	—
Pn8	1685/3	—	30 Stuivers. Silver. 30St over 30G, ARG over AUR.	—
Pn10	1686	—	Daalder. Gold. 42.0000 g. KM#17.	—
Pn11	1687	—	Daalder. Silver. 36.6000 g. KM#52.1.	—
Pn12	1687	—	2 Daalders. Gold. 35.0000 g. KM#63.	—
Pn13	1687	—	2 Daalders. Gold. 21.0000 g. KM#63.	—
Pn14	1689	—	Stuiver. Gold. 3.4000 g. KM#58.	—
Pn15	1689	—	2 Stuiver. Gold. 3.4500 g. KM#59a.	—

PIEFORTS

KM#	Date	Mintage	Identification	Mkt Va
P3	1627	—	2 Stuiver.	20(
P4	1659	—	Ducaton, Silver, KM#41.1	1,20(
P5	1660	—	Ducaton. KM#41.1.	1,50(
P6	1661	—	Ducaton.	—
P7	1662	—	Ducaton.	—

KM#	Date	Mintage	Identification	Mkt Val
P8	1663	—	Ducaton.	—
P9	1664	—	Ducaton.	—
P10	1666	—	Ducaton. KM#61.1.	1,500
P11	1668	—	Ducaton. KM#61.1.	1,500
P12	1669	—	Duit. Copper. KM14.	—
P13	1676	—	10 Stuivers.	—
P14	1676	—	Daalder. Silver. KM#53.	—
P15	1683	—	10 Stuivers. Silver.	1,500
P16	1683	—	30 Gulden. Gold. 42.0000 g.	3,000
P17	1683	—	Daalder. Silver. KM#60.	1,500
P18	1683	—	Ducaton. KM#57.	—
P19	1683	—	2 Ducaton.	2,250
P20	1685	—	Daalder. Silver. KM#60.	1,500
P21	1687	—	30 Stuivers.	—
P22	1687	—	Daalder. Silver. KM#64.	900
P23	1687	—	2 Daalders. KM#63.	1,750
P24	1688	—	2 Daalders. Silver. KM#63.	1,750
P25	1690	—	2 Daalders. Silver. KM#63.	1,750
PA26	1690	—	2 Daalders. Silver. KM#63. Triple weight.	—
P26	1693	—	2 Daalders. KM#63.	1,750
P27	1694	—	3 Gulden. Silver. KM#70.	3,000
P28	1694	—	3 Gulden. Silver. KM#71.	—

ANHOLT

MANOR

STANDARD COINAGE

KM# 5 DUIT

2.0000 g., Copper **Obv:** Crowned arms of Bronkhorst with lion left in wreath **Rev:** Inscription in wreath **Rev. Inscription:** CI / CITAS / ANH / (LT)

Date	Mintage	VG	F	VF	XF	Unc
(1615)	—	50.00	120	250	350	—

KM# 6 DUIT

2.0000 g., Copper **Obv:** Crowned arms of Bronkhorst with lion right in wreath **Rev:** Inscription in wreath **Rev. Inscription:** CVS / ANHO / LT

Date	Mintage	VG	F	VF	XF	Unc
(1615)	—	50.00	120	250	350	—

KM# 7 DUIT

2.0000 g., Copper **Obv:** Crowned arms of Bronkhorst with lion right in wreath **Rev:** Inscription within wreath **Rev. Inscription:** CVS / ANH

Date	Mintage	VG	F	VF	XF	Unc
(1615)	—	80.00	300	500	700	—

KM# 8 STUIVER

1.9000 g., Silver **Obv:** Lion of Bronkhorst left in dotted inner circle **Obv. Legend:** T CO D BR L BA D B I A **Rev:** Cross above 24 within circle **Rev. Legend:** FERDI II D G R I S

Date	Mintage	VG	F	VF	XF	Unc
ND(1620)	—	—	—	—	—	—

KM# 15 1/8 DAALDER

3.6000 g., Silver **Obv:** Shield with arms of Bronkhorst and Batenburg with arms in center, date divided **Obv. Legend:** TH CO D CRONC L BA(R) D BAT IN ANH **Rev:** Arms and ornaments

Date	Mintage	VG	F	VF	XF	Unc
1620	—	—	—	—	—	—

KM# 16 1/2 DAALDER

14.5000 g., Silver **Obv:** Crowned arms in dotted inner circle **Obv. Legend:** TH CO D BRON L BAR D B I ANH **Rev:** Crowned double headed eagle **Rev. Legend:** FERDINAND II D G RO IMP S AVG

Date	Mintage	VG	F	VF	XF	Unc
ND(1620)	—	—	—	—	—	—

KM# 17 DAALDER

29.0300 g., Silver **Obv:** Arms with four helmets above **Obv. Legend:** TH CO D BRON L BAR D B I ANH **Rev:** Crowned double headed eagle **Rev. Legend:** FERDINAND II D G RO IMP S AVG

Date	Mintage	VG	F	VF	XF	Unc
ND(1620)	—	—	—	—	—	—

NORWAY

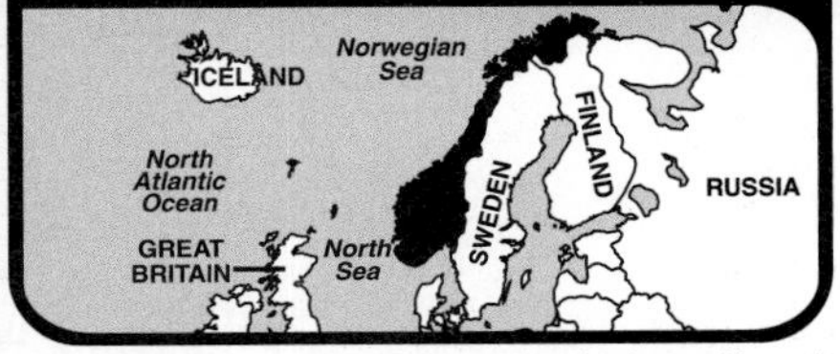

The Kingdom of Norway (*Norge, Noreg*) is located in northwestern Europe, has an area of 150,000sq. mi. (324,220 sq. km.), including the island territories of Spitzbergen (Svalbard) and Jan Mayen

A united Norwegian kingdom was established in the 9th century, the era of the indomitable Norse Vikings who ranged far and wide, visiting the coasts of northwestern Europe, the Mediterranean, Greenland and North America. In the 13th century the Norse kingdom was united briefly with Sweden, then passed through inheritance in 1380 to the rule of Denmark which was maintained until 1814. In 1814 Norway fell again under the rule of Sweden. The union lasted until 1905 when the Norwegian Parliament arranged a peaceful separation and invited a Danish prince (King Haakon VII) to ascend the throne of an independent Kingdom of Norway.

RULER

Danish, until 1814

MINT MARK

(h) - Crossed hammers – Kongsberg

MINT OFFICIALS' INITIALS

Christiania, 1628-1695

Initial	Date	Name
FG, bottle (b)	1651-59	Frederik Gruner
FG, clover leaf on hill (c)	1659-94	Frederik Gruner
PG, clover leaf on hill	1643-50	Peter Gruner
(C) Clover leaf	1628-42	Anders Pedersen
(R) Rose	1643	Anders Pedersen

Kongsberg, 1686-

HCM plus Flower (f)	1687-1718	Henning Christofer Meyer
IAR		Angrid Austlid Rise, engraver

Lettered Edges for Kongsberg Mint

Number	Edges
1	HAEC BOREAS CYMBRO FERT ORNAMENTO LABORUM
2	DET KLIPPERNE YDER VOR BERGMAND UDBRYDER HVA HYTTEN DA GYDER AF MYNTEN VI NYDER
3	DANNER KONGIS NORDSKE FIELDE SLIGE FRUGTER HAR I VAELDE
4	I DETTE ANSIGT DANNEMARK OG NORGE SKUER SIN MONARK
5	NICHT AUS SILBER-SUCHT DIESE NORDENS-FRUCHT WIRD ZU GOTTES EHR GESUCHT
6	STORE KONGE NORDENS AERE LAD DE FRUGTER YNDIG VAERE SOM DIG NORSKE KLIPPER BAERE VAERE SOM DIG NORSKE
7	SAADAN NORDENS SKAT GUD GIEMTE TIL KONG CHRISTIAN DEND FEMTE

MONETARY SYSTEM

Until 1794

96 Skilling = 1 Speciedaler

KINGDOM

STANDARD COINAGE

KM# 133 1/2 SKILLING

0.7500 g., 0.1250 Silver 0.0030 oz. ASW **Obv:** Lion **Rev:** 1/2 SKILING/DANSKE/ year

Date	Mintage	VG	F	VF	XF	Unc
1676	262,000	150	300	500	1,100	—

KM# 149 1/2 SKILLING

0.7300 g., 0.1250 Silver 0.0029 oz. ASW **Obv:** Lion **Rev:** 1 HAL SKILING/DANSKE/ year

Date	Mintage	VG	F	VF	XF	Unc
1682	64,000	400	700	1,200	3,000	—

KM# 23 SKILLING

0.9200 g., 0.1560 Silver 0.0046 oz. ASW **Obv:** Crowned lion **Obv. Legend:** CHRISTIAN... **Rev:** 1/SKILI/NGDA/NSK **Note:** Legend varieties exist.

Date	Mintage	VG	F	VF	XF	Unc
1643 (c)	207,000	90.00	200	350	700	—
1644 (c)	205,000	90.00	200	350	700	—
1645 (c) Unique	—	—	—	—	—	—
1646 (c)	47,000	80.00	150	300	600	—
1647 (c)	123,000	80.00	150	300	600	—
1648 (c)	255,000	80.00	150	300	600	—

KM# 29 SKILLING

0.9200 g., 0.1560 Silver 0.0046 oz. ASW **Rev. Legend:** NOR GOT REX...

Date	Mintage	VG	F	VF	XF	Unc
1649 (c)	1,074,000	30.00	50.00	140	400	—
1650 (c)	Inc. above	30.00	50.00	140	400	—
1651 (b)	Inc. above	30.00	50.00	140	400	—
1652 (b)	372,000	30.00	50.00	140	400	—
1653 (b)	419,000	30.00	50.00	140	400	—
1654 (b)	262,000	30.00	50.00	140	400	—
1655 (b)	484,000	30.00	50.00	140	400	—
1656 (b)	554,000	30.00	50.00	140	400	—
1657 (b)	368,000	30.00	50.00	140	400	—
1658 (b)	475,000	30.00	50.00	140	400	—
1659 (b) Rare	—	—	—	—	—	—
1659	359,000	30.00	50.00	140	400	—
1660	376,000	30.00	50.00	140	400	—
1661	259,000	30.00	50.00	140	400	—
1662	211,000	—	50.00	140	400	—
1663	229,000	30.00	50.00	140	400	—
1664	305,000	30.00	50.00	140	400	—
1665	175,000	30.00	50.00	140	400	—
1666	157,000	30.00	50.00	140	400	—
1667	175,000	30.00	50.00	140	400	—
1668	112,000	30.00	50.00	140	400	—
1669	208,000	30.00	50.00	140	400	—
1670 Rare; only 3 known	55,000	—	—	—	—	—

KM# 90 SKILLING

0.9200 g., 0.1560 Silver 0.0046 oz. ASW **Obv:** Lion **Rev:** NOR/VAN/GOT/REX.

Date	Mintage	VG	F	VF	XF	Unc
1670	31,000	130	200	500	1,000	—

KM# 91 SKILLING

0.8100 g., 0.1560 Silver 0.0041 oz. ASW **Obv:** Lion **Rev:** DAN/NOR/VAN/GOT

Date	Mintage	VG	F	VF	XF	Unc
1670	Inc. above	200	450	1,000	1,800	—

KM# 130 SKILLING

0.8100 g., 0.2500 Silver 0.0065 oz. ASW **Rev:** 1/SKILLING/ DANSKE/ year

Date	Mintage	VG	F	VF	XF	Unc
1675 (ch)	402,000	60.00	100	200	500	—
1682 PG	26,000	400	700	1,250	—	—

KM# 152 SKILLING

1.1100 g., 0.1880 Silver 0.0067 oz. ASW **Obv:** Crowned C5 monogram

Date	Mintage	VG	F	VF	XF	Unc
1686	14,000	250	500	1,200	2,400	—
1687	77,000	150	300	700	1,500	—

KM# 159 SKILLING

1.1100 g., 0.1880 Silver 0.0067 oz. ASW **Obv:** Crowned script C5 monogram

Date	Mintage	VG	F	VF	XF	Unc
1687	Inc. above	100	225	450	900	—
1688	41,000	90.00	190	425	825	—

KM# 173 SKILLING

1.1100 g., 0.1880 Silver 0.0067 oz. ASW

Date	Mintage	VG	F	VF	XF	Unc
1688	Inc. above	75.00	150	375	750	—
1690	23,000	75.00	150	375	750	—
1691	72,000	55.00	115	300	600	—
1692	15,000	150	300	650	1,100	—
1693	18,000	55.00	115	300	600	—
1694	10,000	75.00	150	375	750	—
1695	26,000	75.00	150	375	750	—
1696	36,000	75.00	150	375	750	—
1697	20,000	150	300	650	1,100	—
1698	12,000	75.00	150	375	750	—
1699	40,000	75.00	150	375	750	—

KM# 205 SKILLING

1.1100 g., 0.1880 Silver 0.0067 oz. ASW **Obv:** Crowned monogram **Rev:** Value, crossed hammers divide date below

Date	Mintage	VG	F	VF	XF	Unc
1700	21,000	115	300	650	1,200	—

KM# 20 2 SKILLING

0.5900 g., 0.8750 Silver 0.0166 oz. ASW **Obv:** Crowned lion **Rev:** II/SKILIN/G:DANS/year **Note:** Legend varieties exist.

Date	Mintage	VG	F	VF	XF	Unc
1641 (f)	13,000	115	230	425	1,000	—
1642 (f)	91,000	65.00	130	265	500	—

KM# 24 2 SKILLING

1.3000 g., 0.2810 Silver 0.0117 oz. ASW **Rev:** II/SKILI/NGDA /NSK in inner circle **Note:** Legend varieties exist.

Date	Mintage	VG	F	VF	XF	Unc
1643 (c)	60,000	60.00	120	240	525	—
1644 (c)	170,000	55.00	105	210	450	—
1646 (c)	17,000	60.00	120	240	525	—
1647 (c)	245,000	45.00	90.00	180	350	—
1648 (c)	302,000	45.00	90.00	180	350	—

KM# 30 2 SKILLING

1.3000 g., 0.2810 Silver 0.0117 oz. ASW **Obv. Legend:** FRIDERIC III... **Note:** Legend varieties exist.

Date	Mintage	VG	F	VF	XF	Unc
1649 (c)	913,000	13.00	37.00	100	280	—
1650 (c)	Inc. above	13.00	37.00	100	280	—
1651 (b)	Inc. above	13.00	37.00	100	280	—
1651 (c)	Inc. above	46.25	140	280	775	—
1652 (b)	244,000	13.00	37.00	100	280	—
1653 (b)	247,000	13.00	37.00	100	280	—
1654 (b)	421,000	13.00	37.00	100	280	—
1655 (b)	336,000	13.00	37.00	100	280	—
1656 (b)	286,000	13.00	37.00	100	280	—
1657 (b)	332,000	13.00	37.00	100	280	—

Date	Mintage	VG	F	VF	XF	Unc
1658 (b)	299,000	13.00	37.00	100	280	—
1659 (b)	—	185	425	—	—	—
1659 (b+ch)	—	185	425	—	—	—
1659 (ch)	283,000	13.00	37.00	100	280	—
1660	351,000	13.00	37.00	100	280	—
1660 (ch)	Inc. above	13.00	37.00	100	280	—
1661	479,000	13.00	37.00	100	280	—
1662	554,000	13.00	37.00	100	280	—
1663	634,000	13.00	37.00	100	280	—
1664	497,000	13.00	37.00	100	280	—
1665	473,000	13.00	37.00	100	280	—
1666	440,000	13.00	37.00	100	280	—
1667	496,000	13.00	37.00	100	280	—

KM# 82 2 SKILLING

1.3000 g., 0.2810 Silver 0.0117 oz. ASW **Obv:** Crowned lion with shield

Date	Mintage	VG	F	VF	XF	Unc
1667	Inc. above	1,050	1,800	3,650	7,300	—
1668	Inc. above	1,050	1,800	3,650	7,300	—

KM# 85 2 SKILLING

1.2200 g., 0.2810 Silver 0.0110 oz. ASW **Obv:** Crowned lion in inner circle **Note:** Legend varieties exist.

Date	Mintage	VG	F	VF	XF	Unc
1668	491,000	14.00	45.00	100	250	—
1669	708,000	14.00	45.00	100	250	—
1670	116,000	14.00	45.00	100	250	—

KM# 92 2 SKILLING

1.2200 g., 0.2810 Silver 0.0110 oz. ASW **Obv. Legend:** CHRISTIAN... **Rev:** II/SKILL/INGDA/NSK in inner circle

Date	Mintage	VG	F	VF	XF	Unc
1670	88,000	27.50	55.00	165	500	—
1671	—	55.00	145	325	875	—
1672 Rare	—	—	—	—	—	—

KM# 114 2 SKILLING

1.3000 g., 0.2810 Silver 0.0117 oz. ASW **Rev:** II/SKILLING/DANSKE/year

Date	Mintage	VG	F	VF	XF	Unc
1673 (ch)	43,000	120	250	550	1,100	—
1673 FG	195,000	140	280	600	1,200	—

KM# 115 2 SKILLING

1.0900 g., 0.4060 Silver 0.0142 oz. ASW **Obv:** Crowned C5 monogram **Rev:** II/SKILLING/DANSKE/year divided by lion

Date	Mintage	VG	F	VF	XF	Unc
1673	151,000	30.00	100	250	650	—

KM# 116 2 SKILLING

1.0900 g., 0.4060 Silver 0.0142 oz. ASW **Rev:** Lion

Date	Mintage	VG	F	VF	XF	Unc
1673 Rare	—	—	—	—	—	—

KM# 131 2 SKILLING

1.0900 g., 0.4060 Silver 0.0142 oz. ASW

Date	Mintage	VG	F	VF	XF	Unc
1675 (ch)	272,000	14.00	45.00	100	280	—
1676 (ch)	95,000	14.00	45.00	100	280	—
1677 (ch)	89,000	20.00	55.00	150	300	—
1678 (ch)	370,000	14.00	45.00	100	280	—
1679 (ch)	499,000	20.00	55.00	150	280	—
1680 (ch)	528,000	14.00	45.00	100	280	—
1681 (ch)	441,000	14.00	45.00	100	280	—
1682 (ch)	331,000	14.00	45.00	100	280	—
1682 PG	Inc. above	20.00	55.00	150	300	—
1683 PG	246,000	14.00	45.00	100	280	—

KM# 135 2 SKILLING

2.7800 g., 0.1250 Silver 0.0112 oz. ASW **Obv:** Crowned C5 monogram

Date	Mintage	VG	F	VF	XF	Unc
1677 (ch)	89,000	150	400	650	1,500	—

KM# 151 2 SKILLING

1.2200 g., 0.3440 Silver 0.0135 oz. ASW **Rev:** II/SKILLING/DANSKE/year divided by lion

Date	Mintage	VG	F	VF	XF	Unc
1684 PG	214,000	12.00	30.00	110	300	—
1685 PG	586,000	12.00	30.00	110	300	—
1686 PG	231,000	18.00	36.00	130	325	—

KM# 153 2 SKILLING

1.2200 g., 0.3440 Silver 0.0135 oz. ASW **Obv:** Crowned double C5 monogram **Rev:** Crowned arms in rectangular shield dividing date **Note:** Varieties exist.

Date	Mintage	VG	F	VF	XF	Unc
1686	—	140	275	925	2,550	—
1687	503,000	70.00	140	275	925	—

KM# 160 2 SKILLING

1.2200 g., 0.3440 Silver 0.0135 oz. ASW **Obv:** Crowned double CV monogram **Note:** Varieties exist.

Date	Mintage	VG	F	VF	XF	Unc
1687	Inc. above	80.00	200	700	2,400	—
1688	660,000	70.00	160	550	1,600	—

KM# 161 2 SKILLING

1.2200 g., 0.3440 Silver 0.0135 oz. ASW **Obv:** Crowned double CV monogram, date below

Date	Mintage	VG	F	VF	XF	Unc
1687	Inc. above	325	900	2,100	4,000	—

KM# 174 2 SKILLING

1.2200 g., 0.3440 Silver 0.0135 oz. ASW **Obv:** Crowned ornate double C5 monogram **Rev:** Lion in circle **Note:** Varieties exist.

Date	Mintage	VG	F	VF	XF	Unc
1688	Inc. above	60.00	120	300	900	—
1689	728,000	40.00	80.00	220	700	—
1690	898,000	40.00	80.00	200	600	—
1691	959,000	40.00	80.00	160	550	—
1692	334,000	40.00	80.00	200	600	—
1693	306,000	50.00	80.00	220	700	—
1694	370,000	40.00	120	300	900	—
1695	357,000	50.00	80.00	200	600	—
1696	371,000	40.00	120	300	900	—
1697	455,000	40.00	80.00	220	700	—
1698	396,000	40.00	80.00	200	600	—
1699	483,000	40.00	80.00	200	600	—

KM# 206 2 SKILLING

1.2200 g., 0.3440 Silver 0.0135 oz. ASW **Obv:** Crowned double F4 monogram

Date	Mintage	VG	F	VF	XF	Unc
1700	613,000	40.00	90.00	260	1,200	—

KM# 21.1 4 SKILLING

1.1800 g., 0.8750 Silver 0.0332 oz. ASW **Obv:** Crowned lion **Rev:** IIII / SKILI / NGDA / NS

Date	Mintage	Good	VG	F	VF	XF
1641 (f)	12,000	100	170	525	1,050	—
1642 (f)	90,000	50.00	100	325	675	—

KM# 21.2 4 SKILLING

1.1800 g., 0.8750 Silver 0.0332 oz. ASW **Rev:** SCKILING DANSK

Date	Mintage	Good	VG	F	VF	XF
1641 (f)	Inc. above	—	—	—	—	—

KM# 21.1a 4 SKILLING

1.1700 g., 0.7500 Silver 0.0282 oz. ASW **Note:** Mint mark: Cloverleaf.

Date	Mintage	Good	VG	F	VF	XF
1643 (c) Rare	—	—	—	—	—	—

KM# 136 4 SKILLING

5.8500 g., 0.1250 Silver 0.0235 oz. ASW **Obv:** Crowned C5 monogram **Rev:** IIII/SKILLING/DANSKE/year

Date	Mintage	VG	F	VF	XF	Unc
1677	128,000	110	190	425	1,100	—

KM# 22 8 SKILLING (1/2 Mark)

2.3900 g., 0.8750 Silver 0.0672 oz. ASW **Note:** Similar to KM#26.1. Legend varieties exist.

Date	Mintage	VG	F	VF	XF	Unc
1641 (f)	3,100	350	775	1,650	3,500	—
1642 (f)	17,000	255	500	975	2,350	—

KM# 22a 8 SKILLING (1/2 Mark)

2.3400 g., 0.7500 Silver 0.0564 oz. ASW

Date	Mintage	VG	F	VF	XF	Unc
1643 (c)	42,000	90.00	225	450	1,200	—

KM# 26.1 8 SKILLING (1/2 Mark)

2.3400 g., 0.7500 Silver 0.0564 oz. ASW **Obv:** Mintmaster's initials

Date	Mintage	VG	F	VF	XF	Unc
1644 (c)	80,000	800	1,600	2,800	—	—

KM# 26.2 8 SKILLING (1/2 Mark)

2.3400 g., 0.7500 Silver 0.0564 oz. ASW **Obv:** Mintmaster's initials **Rev:** Mintmaster's initials

Date	Mintage	VG	F	VF	XF	Unc
1644 (c)	Inc. above	450	1,000	2,000	—	—

KM# 26.3 8 SKILLING (1/2 Mark)

2.3400 g., 0.7500 Silver 0.0564 oz. ASW **Rev:** Mintmaster's initials **Note:** Legend varieties exist.

Date	Mintage	VG	F	VF	XF	Unc
1644 (c)	Inc. above	100	200	500	1,200	—

KM# 31 8 SKILLING (1/2 Mark)

2.7800 g., 0.6720 Silver 0.0601 oz. ASW

Date	Mintage	VG	F	VF	XF	Unc
1649 (c)	—	325	650	1,650	3,750	—
1650 (c)	—	650	1,300	2,600	5,200	—
1651 (c)	—	325	650	1,650	3,750	—
1651 (b)	—	325	650	1,650	3,750	—
1652 (b)	—	325	650	1,650	3,750	—
1653 (b)	—	425	825	1,650	3,900	—
1654 (b)	—	425	825	1,650	3,900	—
1655 (b)	—	425	825	1,650	3,900	—
1656 (b)	—	425	825	1,650	3,900	—
1657 (b)	—	725	1,450	2,950	5,200	—
1658 (b)	—	260	650	1,650	3,750	—
1659 (ch)	—	295	525	1,300	3,250	—
1660 (ch)	—	295	575	1,300	3,250	—
Note: Crown breaks inner circle						
1660 (ch)	—	295	575	1,200	2,600	—
Note: Crown within inner circle						
1661	—	295	650	1,650	2,950	—
1661	—	295	575	1,650	2,950	—
1663 (ch)	—	575	975	1,950	4,250	—
1665	—	325	650	1,300	3,250	—
1668	—	825	1,650	3,600	7,800	—

KM# 93 8 SKILLING (1/2 Mark)

2.6600 g., 0.6670 Silver 0.0570 oz. ASW **Obv:** Crowned C5 monogram within inner circle **Rev:** Crowned lion within inner circle, date in legend

Date	Mintage	VG	F	VF	XF	Unc
1670	—	100	225	450	900	—

KM# 93a 8 SKILLING (1/2 Mark)

2.7800 g., 0.6720 Silver 0.0601 oz. ASW

Date	Mintage	VG	F	VF	XF	Unc
1672	—	700	1,550	3,450	8,300	—
1675	—	875	1,750	3,450	8,300	—

KM# 145 8 SKILLING (1/2 Mark)

2.7800 g., 0.6720 Silver 0.0601 oz. ASW **Obv:** Crowned C5 monogram divides date **Rev:** Lion within branches **Note:** Varieties exist.

Date	Mintage	VG	F	VF	XF	Unc
1681	—	450	875	1,750	4,000	—
1682 PG	—	425	825	1,750	4,000	—
1683 PG	—	425	825	1,450	3,500	—
1685 PG	—	825	1,650	3,250	7,000	—
1689 PG	—	1,000	2,000	4,000	8,800	—

KM# 207 8 SKILLING (1/2 Mark)

3.0600 g., 0.5620 Silver 0.0553 oz. ASW **Obv:** Bust of Frederic IV, right **Rev:** Crown

Date	Mintage	VG	F	VF	XF	Unc
1700 (f)	423,000	50.00	125	275	675	—

KM# 27 16 SKILLING (1 Mark)

5.5700 g., 0.5930 Silver 0.1062 oz. ASW **Obv:** Crowned C4 monogram **Rev:** IUSTUS/"Jehovah"/IUDEX

Date	Mintage	VG	F	VF	XF	Unc
1644 (c)	45,000	245	500	1,250	3,000	—
1645 (c)	48,000	325	625	1,400	3,150	—
1646 (c)	9,475	325	625	1,400	3,150	—
1647 (c)	7,707	350	700	1,600	3,700	—

KM# 32.1 16 SKILLING (1 Mark)

5.5700 g., 0.6720 Silver 0.1203 oz. ASW **Obv. Legend:** ...DANSK

Date	Mintage	VG	F	VF	XF	Unc
1648 Unique	—	—	—	—	—	—
1649 (c)	—	210	425	875	2,100	—
1650 (c)	—	210	425	875	2,100	—
1651 (b)	—	210	425	875	2,100	—
1651 (c)	—	450	900	1,750	4,050	—
1652 (b)	—	210	425	875	2,100	—
1653 (b)	—	210	425	875	2,100	—
1654 (b)	—	210	425	875	2,100	—
1655 (b)	—	210	425	875	2,100	—
1656 (b)	—	210	425	875	2,100	—
1657 (b)	—	210	425	875	2,100	—
1658 (b)	—	210	425	875	2,100	—
1659 (b)	—	450	900	2,100	4,550	—
1659 (ch)	—	325	625	1,250	3,000	—
1660 (ch)	—	325	625	1,250	3,000	—
1660	—	325	625	1,250	3,000	—
1661	—	325	625	1,250	3,000	—

KM# 32.2 16 SKILLING (1 Mark)

5.5700 g., 0.6720 Silver 0.1203 oz. ASW **Obv. Legend:** ...DANSKE

Date	Mintage	VG	F	VF	XF	Unc
1648 Unique	—	—	—	—	—	—
1663 (ch)	—	450	900	1,750	4,050	—
1663 Rare	—	—	—	—	—	—
Note: Inverted N in DOMINVS						
ND(1663)	—	1,250	2,450	4,900	10,500	—
1665 (ch)	—	245	500	975	2,450	—

Date	Mintage	VG	F	VF	XF	Unc
1666 (ch) PROUIDEBIT	—	245	500	975	2,450	—
1667 (ch)	—	245	500	975	2,450	—
1668 (ch)	—	245	500	975	2,450	—
1669 (ch)	—	280	550	1,100	2,800	—

KM# 94 16 SKILLING (1 Mark)

5.3100 g., 0.6670 Silver 0.1139 oz. ASW

Date	Mintage	VG	F	VF	XF	Unc
1670	—	700	1,750	3,350	8,400	—

KM# 94a 16 SKILLING (1 Mark)

5.5700 g., 0.6720 Silver 0.1203 oz. ASW

Date	Mintage	VG	F	VF	XF	Unc
1671	—	875	1,750	3,500	7,700	—
1673	—	875	1,750	3,500	7,700	—
1674	—	6,300	9,100	16,000	—	—
1675	—	525	1,050	2,100	5,300	—
1676	—	525	1,050	2,100	5,300	—
1679	—	875	1,750	3,000	6,700	—

KM# 146 MARK (16 Skilling)

5.5700 g., 0.6720 Silver 0.1203 oz. ASW **Obv:** Crowned C5 monogram divides date **Rev:** Crowned lion between laurel branches

Date	Mintage	VG	F	VF	XF	Unc
1681	—	400	700	1,700	3,800	—
1681 PG Unique	—	—	—	—	—	—
1682 PG	—	400	700	1,700	3,800	—
1683 PG	—	650	1,400	2,800	4,800	—
1684	—	400	700	1,700	3,800	—
1685 PG	—	650	1,400	2,800	4,800	—
1686 PG	—	650	1,400	2,800	4,800	—

KM# 155 MARK (16 Skilling)

5.5700 g., 0.6720 Silver 0.1203 oz. ASW **Obv:** Crowned, more ornate monogram

Date	Mintage	VG	F	VF	XF	Unc
1686 Rare	—	—	—	—	—	—

KM# 154 MARK (16 Skilling)

5.5700 g., 0.6720 Silver 0.1203 oz. ASW **Obv:** Crowned double C5 monogram **Rev:** Crowned lion in shield with rectangular sides **Note:** Varieties exist.

Date	Mintage	VG	F	VF	XF	Unc
1686	—	500	1,000	2,000	4,000	—

KM# 162 MARK (16 Skilling)

5.5700 g., 0.6720 Silver 0.1203 oz. ASW **Rev:** Crowned lion in shield with oval sides divides HC M **Note:** Varieties exist.

Date	Mintage	VG	F	VF	XF	Unc
1687 HCM	—	500	1,000	2,000	4,000	—

KM# 175 MARK (16 Skilling)

5.5700 g., 0.6720 Silver 0.1203 oz. ASW **Rev:** Crowned lion, smaller shield

Date	Mintage	VG	F	VF	XF	Unc
1688 HCM	—	700	1,400	2,800	5,600	—

KM# 176 MARK (16 Skilling)

5.5700 g., 0.6720 Silver 0.1203 oz. ASW **Obv:** More ornate monogram **Rev:** Crowned lion within laurel branches, HCM inside branches

Date	Mintage	VG	F	VF	XF	Unc
1688 HCM	—	1,600	3,200	6,400	14,000	—

KM# 185.1 MARK (16 Skilling)

5.5700 g., 0.6720 Silver 0.1203 oz. ASW **Rev:** HCM outside branches **Edge:** Plain

Date	Mintage	VG	F	VF	XF	Unc
1689 HCM	—	1,300	2,600	5,200	10,500	—
1690 HCM Rare	—	—	—	—	—	—

KM# 185.2 MARK (16 Skilling)

5.5700 g., 0.6720 Silver 0.1203 oz. ASW **Edge:** Milled **Note:** Edge varieties exist.

Date	Mintage	VG	F	VF	XF	Unc
1691 HCM	—	700	1,400	2,800	5,600	—
1692 HCM	—	350	700	1,400	2,800	—
1693 HCM Rare	—	—	—	—	—	—
1694 HCM	—	400	800	1,600	3,400	—
1695 HCM	—	400	800	1,600	3,400	—
1697 HCM	—	350	700	1,400	2,800	—
1698 HCM	—	350	700	1,400	2,800	—
1699 HCM Rare	—	—	—	—	—	—

KM# 197 MARK (16 Skilling)

4.5000 g., 0.8330 Silver 0.1205 oz. ASW **Obv:** Portrait of Christian V **Rev:** Crown

Date	Mintage	VG	F	VF	XF	Unc
1699 HCM(f)	—	600	1,200	2,400	4,800	—

KM# 28 2 MARK

11.1400 g., 0.5930 Silver 0.2124 oz. ASW **Obv:** Crowned C4 monogram **Rev:** IUSTUS/"Jehova"/IUDEX

Date	Mintage	VG	F	VF	XF	Unc
1644 WM	—	90.00	180	450	1,050	—
1644 (c)	—	90.00	140	400	900	—
1645 (c)	—	100	200	500	1,100	—
1646 (c)	—	140	280	600	1,400	—
1647 (c)	—	150	300	600	1,550	—

KM# 33 2 MARK

11.1400 g., 0.6720 Silver 0.2407 oz. ASW

Date	Mintage	VG	F	VF	XF	Unc
1649 (c)	—	125	245	500	1,250	—
1650 (c)	—	125	245	500	1,250	—
1651 (c)	—	195	375	800	1,750	—
1651 (b)	—	125	245	500	1,250	—
1652 (b)	—	125	245	500	1,250	—
1653 (b)	—	125	245	500	1,250	—
1654 (b)	—	125	245	500	1,250	—
1655 (b)	—	125	245	500	1,250	—
1656 (b)	—	125	245	500	1,250	—
1657 (b)	—	125	245	500	1,250	—
1657 (b) Rare; MAARK	—	—	—	—	—	—
1658 (b)	—	125	245	500	1,250	—
1659 (b)	—	125	245	500	1,250	—
1659	—	140	280	525	1,250	—
1659 AO before date	—	140	280	525	1,250	—
1660	—	140	280	525	1,250	—
1660 Rosette	—	140	280	525	1,250	—
1661 Rare	—	—	—	—	—	—
1661 Rosette	—	140	210	500	1,000	—
1661 (ch)	—	245	500	1,050	2,100	—
1661 (ch) before DOMINUS	—	105	195	425	775	—
1662 Rosette Rare	—	—	—	—	—	—
1662 (ch) before DOMINUS	—	105	195	425	775	—
1662 PRVIDEBIT Rare	—	—	—	—	—	—

KM# 95 2 MARK

11.1400 g., 0.6720 Silver 0.2407 oz. ASW

Date	Mintage	VG	F	VF	XF	Unc
1670 (ch)	—	200	400	700	1,400	—

KM# 95a 2 MARK

10.6300 g., 0.6670 Silver 0.2279 oz. ASW

Date	Mintage	VG	F	VF	XF	Unc
1670 (ch)	—	400	700	1,400	1,800	—
1671 (ch)	—	—	—	—	—	—

KM# 105 2 MARK

10.6300 g., 0.6670 Silver 0.2279 oz. ASW **Note:** Similar to KM#105a.

Date	Mintage	VG	F	VF	XF	Unc
1671	—	325	650	1,300	2,600	—

KM# 105a 2 MARK

11.1400 g., 0.6720 Silver 0.2407 oz. ASW

Date	Mintage	VG	F	VF	XF	Unc
1672	—	270	550	1,000	2,300	—
1673 Rare	—	—	3,000	4,600	—	—
Note: Four known						
1674 Rare	—	—	3,300	5,000	—	—
Note: Two known						

KM# 147 2 MARK

11.1400 g., 0.6720 Silver 0.2407 oz. ASW **Obv:** Crowned C5 monogram divides date **Rev:** Lion between laurel branches

Date	Mintage	VG	F	VF	XF	Unc
1681	—	1,000	1,900	4,000	7,000	—

KM# 150 2 MARK

11.1400 g., 0.6720 Silver 0.2407 oz. ASW **Rev:** Lion divides PG

Date	Mintage	VG	F	VF	XF	Unc
1682 PG Rare	—	—	3,500	5,600	—	—
Note: Three known						
1683 PG Rare	—	—	3,500	5,600	—	—
Note: Three known						
1685 PG	—	1,800	3,000	4,600	9,000	—

KM# 156 2 MARK

11.1400 g., 0.6720 Silver 0.2407 oz. ASW **Obv:** Crowned double monogram **Rev:** Crowned arms in rectangular shield **Note:** Varieties exist.

Date	Mintage	VG	F	VF	XF	Unc
1686	—	750	1,500	3,150	6,300	—

KM# 165 2 MARK

11.1400 g., 0.6720 Silver 0.2407 oz. ASW **Obv:** Ornate double monogram **Rev:** Crossed hammers mint mark **Note:** Varieties exist.

Date	Mintage	VG	F	VF	XF	Unc
1687 HCM	—	500	1,300	2,500	5,000	—

KM# 163 2 MARK

11.1400 g., 0.6720 Silver 0.2407 oz. ASW **Rev:** Crowned arms in shield with bowed sides divide HCM

Date	Mintage	VG	F	VF	XF	Unc
1687 HCM Rare	—	—	—	—	—	—

KM# 164 2 MARK

11.1400 g., 0.6720 Silver 0.2407 oz. ASW **Rev:** Crowned arms in smaller shield

Date	Mintage	VG	F	VF	XF	Unc
1687 HCM Rare	—	—	—	—	—	—

KM# 166 2 MARK

11.1400 g., 0.6720 Silver 0.2407 oz. ASW **Rev:** Without mint mark

Date	Mintage	VG	F	VF	XF	Unc
1687 HCM Rare	—	—	—	—	—	—

KM# 177 2 MARK

11.1400 g., 0.6720 Silver 0.2407 oz. ASW **Rev:** Star instead of rosette

Date	Mintage	VG	F	VF	XF	Unc
1688 HCM Rare	—	—	—	—	—	—

KM# 178 2 MARK

11.1400 g., 0.6720 Silver 0.2407 oz. ASW **Obv:** Crowned more ornate double monogram **Rev:** Crowned lion with HCM inside laurel branches

Date	Mintage	VG	F	VF	XF	Unc
1688 HCM	—	—	—	—	—	—

KM# 179.1 2 MARK

11.1400 g., 0.6720 Silver 0.2407 oz. ASW **Rev:** HCM outside laurel branches **Edge:** Milled

Date	Mintage	VG	F	VF	XF	Unc
1688 HCM Rare	—	—	—	—	—	—
1689 HCM	—	1,200	2,400	5,000	8,000	—
1693 HCM	—	1,200	2,400	5,000	8,000	—
1695 HCM	—	1,000	2,000	4,000	7,500	—
1697 HCM	—	1,000	2,000	4,000	7,500	—
1698 HCM	—	1,200	2,400	5,000	8,000	—
1699 HCM	—	1,200	2,400	5,000	8,000	—

KM# 179.2 2 MARK

11.1400 g., 0.6720 Silver 0.2407 oz. ASW **Edge:** Plain

Date	Mintage	VG	F	VF	XF	Unc
1690 HCM Rare	—	—	—	—	—	—
1691 HCM Rare	—	—	—	—	—	—
1692 HCM	—	1,000	2,000	4,000	7,500	—
1693 HCM	—	700	1,400	3,000	6,000	—
1694 HCM	—	1,000	2,000	4,000	7,500	—
1696 HCM	—	1,200	2,400	5,000	8,000	—

KM# 198 2 MARK

8.9900 g., 0.8330 Silver 0.2408 oz. ASW **Obv:** Portrait of Christian V **Rev:** Crown

Date	Mintage	VG	F	VF	XF	Unc
1699 HCM(f)	—	300	600	1,200	2,400	—

KM# 208 2 MARK

8.9900 g., 0.8330 Silver 0.2408 oz. ASW

Date	Mintage	VG	F	VF	XF	Unc
1700 (f)	—	400	850	1,900	3,600	—

KM# 96 4 MARK (1 Krone)
22.2700 g., 0.6720 Silver 0.4811 oz. ASW **Note:** Dav. #3662. Edge varieties exist.

Date	Mintage	VG	F	VF	XF	Unc
1669 FG	—	3,600	7,000	3,350	26,000	—
1670 FG	—	200	400	200	1,600	—
1670 EG 3 known	—	2,600	4,000	1,500	—	—
1671 FG	—	200	400	200	1,600	—
1671 Rare	—	3,000	4,600	1,850	—	—
1672 FG	—	200	400	200	1,600	—
1673 FG	—	200	400	200	1,600	—
1674 FG	—	350	725	350	2,800	—
1676 PG	—	400	800	400	3,400	—
1677 PG	—	270	550	325	2,400	—
1678 PG	—	170	350	200	1,350	—
1679 PG	—	170	350	200	1,350	—
1680 PG	—	170	350	200	1,350	—

KM# 96a 4 MARK (1 Krone)
21.2600 g., 0.6720 Silver 0.4593 oz. ASW

Date	Mintage	VG	F	VF	XF	Unc
1670 FG Rare	—	—	—	—	—	—
1671 FG Rare	—	—	—	—	—	—

KM# 148.1 4 MARK (1 Krone)
22.2700 g., 0.6720 Silver 0.4811 oz. ASW **Note:** Dav. #3663.

Date	Mintage	VG	F	VF	XF	Unc
1681 PG	—	150	300	600	1,200	—
1682 PG	—	150	300	600	1,200	—
1683 PG	—	150	300	600	1,200	—
1684 PG	—	150	300	600	1,200	—
1685 PG	—	270	550	1,050	2,100	—
1686 PG	—	500	975	1,950	4,300	—
1687 PG	—	195	400	750	1,750	—
1688 PG	—	195	400	750	1,750	—
1689 PG	—	165	350	675	1,300	—
1690 PG	—	165	350	675	1,300	—
1691 PG	—	165	350	675	1,300	—
1692 PG	—	195	400	750	1,750	—
1693 PG	—	150	300	600	1,350	—
1694 PG	—	150	300	600	1,350	—
1695 PG	—	—	5,400	8,400	—	—

KM# 148.2 4 MARK (1 Krone)
11.1400 g., 0.6720 Silver 0.2407 oz. ASW **Obv:** Crowned C5 in cartouche, lions **Rev:** Cross

Date	Mintage	VG	F	VF	XF	Unc
1683 PG	—	350	1,000	1,800	4,000	—

KM# A148.2 4 MARK (1 Krone)
22.2700 g., 0.6720 Silver 0.4811 oz. ASW **Obv:** Crowned C5 monogram in inner circle

Date	Mintage	VG	F	VF	XF	Unc
1683 PG	—	90.00	180	325	850	—

KM# 158 4 MARK (1 Krone)
22.2700 g., 0.6720 Silver 0.4811 oz. ASW **Obv:** More ornate double monogram

Date	Mintage	VG	F	VF	XF	Unc
1686	—	575	1,150	2,200	4,400	—

KM# 157 4 MARK (1 Krone)
22.2700 g., 0.6720 Silver 0.4811 oz. ASW **Obv:** Crowned double C5 monogram **Rev:** Crowned lion in shield with rectangular sides **Note:** Varieties exist.

Date	Mintage	VG	F	VF	XF	Unc
1686	56,000	300	600	1,100	2,200	—

KM# 167 4 MARK (1 Krone)
22.2700 g., 0.6720 Silver 0.4811 oz. ASW **Note:** Varieties exist.

Date	Mintage	VG	F	VF	XF	Unc
1687	44,000	300	600	1,100	2,300	—

KM# 168 4 MARK (1 Krone)
22.2700 g., 0.6720 Silver 0.4811 oz. ASW **Obv:** Star before "PIETATE" **Note:** Dav. #3665. Edge varieties exist.

Date	Mintage	VG	F	VF	XF	Unc
1687 Rare	—	—	—	—	—	—

KM# 169 4 MARK (1 Krone)
22.2700 g., 0.6720 Silver 0.4811 oz. ASW **Obv:** Smaller shield dividing HC M **Note:** Dav. #3665A. Varieties exist.

Date	Mintage	VG	F	VF	XF	Unc
1687 HCM	—	350	700	1,000	1,800	—
1688 HCM Rare	—	—	—	—	—	—

KM# 170 4 MARK (1 Krone)
22.2700 g., 0.6720 Silver 0.4811 oz. ASW **Obv:** Star before "PIETATE"

Date	Mintage	VG	F	VF	XF	Unc
1687 HCM Rare	—	—	—	—	—	—

KM# 171 4 MARK (1 Krone)
22.2700 g., 0.6720 Silver 0.4811 oz. ASW **Rev:** Crowned Danish coat of arms

Date	Mintage	VG	F	VF	XF	Unc
1687 Rare	—	—	—	—	—	—

KM# 182 4 MARK (1 Krone)
22.2700 g., 0.6720 Silver 0.4811 oz. ASW **Obv:** Point instead of mint mark

Date	Mintage	VG	F	VF	XF	Unc
1688 HCM Rare	—	—	—	—	—	—

KM# 180 4 MARK (1 Krone)
22.2700 g., 0.6720 Silver 0.4811 oz. ASW **Obv:** More ornate double monogram, flower after "JUSTITIA"

Date	Mintage	VG	F	VF	XF	Unc
1688 HCM Rare	26,000	—	—	—	—	—

KM# 183 4 MARK (1 Krone)
22.2700 g., 0.6720 Silver 0.4811 oz. ASW **Rev:** Divided HCM outside laurel branches **Note:** Dav. #3666.

Date	Mintage	VG	F	VF	XF	Unc
1688 HCM(f) Rare	—	—	—	—	—	—
1689 HCM(f)	19,000	375	775	1,500	3,050	—
1690 HCM(f)	14,000	375	775	1,500	3,050	—
Note: Edge varieties exist						
1691 HCM(f)	16,000	975	1,950	3,850	7,700	—
1692 HCM(f)	19,000	500	975	1,950	4,400	—
Note: Edge varieties exist						
1693 HCM(f)	25,000	350	700	1,400	3,300	—
1694 HCM(f)	27,000	350	700	1,400	3,300	—
1695 HCM(f)	29,000	375	775	1,500	3,300	—
Note: Edge varieties exist						
1696 HCM(f)	45,000	350	700	1,400	2,900	—
1697 HCM(f)	76,000	350	700	1,400	2,900	—
1698 HCM(f)	65,000	350	700	1,400	2,900	—
1699 HCM(f)	56,000	375	775	1,500	3,050	—

KM# 181 4 MARK (1 Krone)
22.2700 g., 0.6720 Silver 0.4811 oz. ASW **Rev:** Crowned lion and HCM within laurel branches **Note:** Vareieties exist.

Date	Mintage	VG	F	VF	XF	Unc
1688 HCM	—	550	1,000	1,900	3,700	—

KM# 199 4 MARK (1 Krone)
17.9900 g., 0.8330 Silver 0.4818 oz. ASW **Obv:** Portrait of Christian V **Rev:** Crown **Note:** Dav. #3648.

Date	Mintage	VG	F	VF	XF	Unc
1699 HCM(f)	—	750	1,500	2,700	4,500	—

KM# 200.1 4 MARK (1 Krone)
17.9900 g., 0.8330 Silver 0.4818 oz. ASW **Rev:** Swedish, Danish, and Norwegian arms in ovals **Edge Lettering:** ET NORDENS LYYS GIK UD. ET ANDET TAENDTE GUD

Date	Mintage	VG	F	VF	XF	Unc
1699 (f)	—	1,800	3,900	7,800	15,000	—
1700 (f)	—	—	—	—	—	—

KM# 200.2 4 MARK (1 Krone)
17.9900 g., 0.8330 Silver 0.4818 oz. ASW **Edge Lettering:** SERVANT ET DECORANT

Date	Mintage	VG	F	VF	XF	Unc
1700 (F)	17,000	750	1,650	3,300	6,600	—

KM# 5 1/8 SPECIE DALER
3.2500 g., 0.9690 Silver 0.1012 oz. ASW **Obv:** Crowned portrait **Rev:** Lion **Note:** See 1 Specie daler, KM#8 for mintage information

Date	Mintage	VG	F	VF	XF	Unc
1628 (f)	—	825	1,500	2,750	5,000	—
1629 (f)	—	575	1,150	2,000	3,750	—

KM# 9 1/8 SPECIE DALER
3.6500 g., 0.8820 Silver 0.1035 oz. ASW **Note:** Varieties exist.

Date	Mintage	VG	F	VF	XF	Unc
1629 (f)	—	550	1,050	2,050	4,200	—
1630 (f)	—	425	850	1,950	4,200	—
1631 (f)	—	425	850	1,950	4,200	—
1632 (f)	—	425	850	1,950	4,200	—
1633 (f) Unique	—	—	—	—	—	—
1634 (f)	—	—	3,100	6,200	—	—
1635 (f) Unique	—	—	—	—	—	—
1636 (f)	—	—	3,100	6,200	—	—
1637 (f)	—	—	3,100	6,200	—	—
1638 (f)	—	—	3,100	6,200	—	—
1639 (f)	—	425	1,100	2,650	3,500	—
1640 (f)	—	850	900	1,800	4,500	—
1641 (f)	—	450	1,700	2,650	4,050	—
1642 (f)	—	850	1,100	1,950	5,300	—
1643 (c) before FAC	—	500	1,100	1,950	4,200	—
1643 (c) after FAC Rare	—	—	—	—	—	—
1643 (c) Rare	—	—	—	—	—	—
1646 PG(c)	—	—	3,100	6,200	—	—
1647 (PG(c)	—	—	3,100	6,200	—	—

KM# 34 1/8 SPECIE DALER
3.5900 g., 0.8750 Silver 0.1010 oz. ASW, 27 mm. **Rev:** Lion with two tails **Note:** Larger planchet.

Date	Mintage	VG	F	VF	XF	Unc
1649 PG(c) Rare	—	—	—	—	—	—
1650 PG(c) Rare	—	—	—	—	—	—

KM# 49 1/8 SPECIE DALER
3.6000 g., 0.8750 Silver 0.1013 oz. ASW, 25 mm. **Rev:** Lion in smaller circle **Note:** Smaller planchet.

Date	Mintage	VG	F	VF	XF	Unc
1654 FG(b) Rare	—	—	—	—	—	—

KM# 60 1/8 SPECIE DALER
3.6000 g., 0.8750 Silver 0.1013 oz. ASW **Obv:** Crowned facing portrait without inner circle **Rev:** Lion with one tail within laurel branches

Date	Mintage	VG	F	VF	XF	Unc
1660 FG Rare	—	—	—	—	—	—

KM# 62 1/8 SPECIE DALER
3.6000 g., 0.8750 Silver 0.1013 oz. ASW **Obv:** Different crowned facing portrait in inner circle **Rev:** Lion in inner circle

Date	Mintage	VG	F	VF	XF	Unc
1661 FG	—	1,250	2,150	5,000	7,500	—

KM# 63 1/8 SPECIE DALER
3.6000 g., 0.8750 Silver 0.1013 oz. ASW **Rev:** Lion within laurel branches

Date	Mintage	VG	F	VF	XF	Unc
1661 FG Rare	—	—	—	—	—	—

KM# 68 1/8 SPECIE DALER
3.6000 g., 0.8750 Silver 0.1013 oz. ASW

Date	Mintage	VG	F	VF	XF	Unc
1663 FG	—	1,000	2,400	4,400	7,500	—

KM# 71 1/8 SPECIE DALER
3.6000 g., 0.8750 Silver 0.1013 oz. ASW **Rev:** Lion within crowned oval shield

Date	Mintage	VG	F	VF	XF	Unc
1665	—	875	1,750	3,500	6,300	—

KM# 104 1/8 SPECIE DALER
3.6100 g., 0.8750 Silver 0.1016 oz. ASW **Obv:** Laureate bust of Christian V **Rev:** Lion in crowned shield

Date	Mintage	VG	F	VF	XF	Unc
1671	—	1,000	2,000	4,000	8,000	—

KM# 6 1/4 SPECIE DALER

6.5000 g., 0.9690 Silver 0.2025 oz. ASW **Note:** See 1 Specie daler, KM#8 for mintage information.

Date	Mintage	VG	F	VF	XF	Unc
1628 (f)	—	1,150	2,800	5,700	11,500	—
1629 (f)	—	1,600	3,150	6,800	13,500	—

KM# 10 1/4 SPECIE DALER

7.3100 g., 0.8820 Silver 0.2073 oz. ASW **Note:** Varieties exist.

Date	Mintage	VG	F	VF	XF	Unc
1629 (f)	—	825	1,650	3,350	6,700	—
1630 (f)	—	825	1,650	3,350	6,700	—
1631 (f)	—	825	1,650	3,550	7,600	—
1632 (f)	—	825	1,650	3,550	7,600	—
1633 (f)	—	825	1,650	3,550	7,600	—
1634 (f)	—	825	1,650	3,350	6,700	—
1635 (f)	—	825	1,650	3,350	6,700	—
1636 (f)	—	825	1,650	3,350	7,600	—
1637 (f)	—	825	1,650	3,350	7,600	—
1638 (f)	—	825	1,650	3,350	6,700	—
1639 (f)	—	825	1,650	3,350	6,700	—
1640 (f)	—	825	1,650	3,350	6,700	—
1641 (f)	—	825	1,650	3,350	6,700	—
1642 (f)	—	825	1,650	3,350	6,700	—
1643 (f)	—	1,650	2,400	4,300	9,500	—
1643 (c)	—	1,050	2,150	4,300	9,500	—
1646 PG(c)	—	1,050	2,150	4,300	9,500	—
1647 PG(c)	—	1,050	2,150	4,300	9,500	—

KM# 10a 1/4 SPECIE DALER

7.1800 g., 0.8750 Silver 0.2020 oz. ASW

Date	Mintage	VG	F	VF	XF	Unc
1648 PG(c)	—	875	1,650	2,750	6,000	—
1648 PG	—	875	1,650	2,750	6,000	—

KM# 35 1/4 SPECIE DALER

7.1800 g., 0.8750 Silver 0.2020 oz. ASW **Obv:** Crowned bust of Frederick III **Rev:** Crowned lion with two tails whithin inner circle

Date	Mintage	VG	F	VF	XF	Unc
1649 PG(c)	—	3,300	5,200	9,600	19,500	—
1650 PG(c)	—	3,300	5,200	9,900	19,500	—
1651 FG(b)	—	3,300	5,200	9,900	19,500	—

KM# 45.1 1/4 SPECIE DALER

7.1800 g., 0.8750 Silver 0.2020 oz. ASW **Obv:** Small bust wtih drapery **Obv. Legend:** ...DG DA NO VA

Date	Mintage	VG	F	VF	XF	Unc
1652 FG(b)	—	3,300	4,950	9,900	19,500	—
1653 FG(b)	—	3,300	4,950	9,900	19,500	—
1654 FG(b) 2 known	—	—	—	—	—	—

KM# 45.2 1/4 SPECIE DALER

7.1800 g., 0.8750 Silver 0.2020 oz. ASW **Obv. Legend:** ...DG DA NO V G REX

Date	Mintage	VG	F	VF	XF	Unc
1655 FG(b) 3 known	—	—	—	—	—	—
1656 FG(b) 2 known	—	—	—	—	—	—

KM# 69 1/4 SPECIE DALER

7.1800 g., 0.8750 Silver 0.2020 oz. ASW **Obv:** Large bust **Rev:** Lion with one tail within laurel branches

Date	Mintage	VG	F	VF	XF	Unc
1663 FG Unique	—	—	—	—	—	—

KM# 106 1/4 SPECIE DALER

7.2200 g., 0.8750 Silver 0.2031 oz. ASW **Obv:** Laureate bust **Rev:** Lion in crowned oval shield divides date

Date	Mintage	VG	F	VF	XF	Unc
1671 FG	—	9,900	16,500	25,000	41,500	—
1675 FG 4 known	—	—	—	—	—	—

KM# 7 1/2 SPECIE DALER

12.9900 g., 0.9690 Silver 0.4047 oz. ASW **Note:** Similar to KM#11 but without legend in inner circle around bust. See 1 Specie daler, KM#8 for mintage information.

Date	Mintage	VG	F	VF	XF	Unc
1628 (f)	—	6,100	9,900	18,000	25,000	—
1629 (f) Rare	—	—	—	—	—	—

KM# 11 1/2 SPECIE DALER

14.6200 g., 0.8820 Silver 0.4146 oz. ASW

Date	Mintage	VG	F	VF	XF	Unc
1629 (f)	—	3,600	5,500	11,000	18,000	—
1630 (f)	—	3,600	5,500	11,000	18,000	—
1631 (f)	—	3,600	5,500	11,000	18,000	—
1632 (f) Rare	—	—	—	—	—	—
1633 (f)	—	3,600	5,500	11,000	18,000	—
1634 (f)	—	3,600	5,500	11,000	18,000	—
1635 (f)	—	3,600	5,500	11,000	18,000	—
1636 (f) Rare	—	—	—	—	—	—
1637 (f)	—	3,600	5,500	11,000	18,000	—
1638 (f)	—	3,600	5,500	11,000	18,000	—
1639 (f)	—	3,600	5,500	11,000	18,000	—
1640 (f)	—	3,600	5,500	11,000	18,000	—
1641 (f) DANI NOR Rare	—	—	—	—	—	—
1641 (f) DAN NOR Rare	—	—	—	—	—	—
1642 (f)	—	3,850	6,600	12,000	20,500	—
1643 (f) Rare	—	—	—	—	—	—
1644 (f) Rare	—	—	—	—	—	—
1644 PG(c) Rare	—	—	—	—	—	—
1645 PG(c) Rare	—	—	—	—	—	—
1646 PG(c)	—	—	—	11,000	—	—
1646 PG Rare	—	3,300	5,500	11,000	19,500	—
1647 PG	—	3,300	5,500	11,000	19,500	—
1647 PG(c) Rare	—	3,300	5,500	11,000	19,500	—

KM# 11a 1/2 SPECIE DALER

14.3600 g., 0.8750 Silver 0.4040 oz. ASW

Date	Mintage	VG	F	VF	XF	Unc
1648 PG(c)	—	3,300	5,500	11,000	19,500	—
1648 PG	—	3,300	5,500	11,000	19,500	—

KM# 36 1/2 SPECIE DALER

14.3600 g., 0.8750 Silver 0.4040 oz. ASW **Obv:** Bust of Frederic III **Rev:** Lion with two tails **Note:** Varieties exist.

Date	Mintage	VG	F	VF	XF	Unc
1649 PG(c)	—	6,100	11,500	19,500	28,000	—
1650 PG(c)	—	6,100	11,500	19,500	28,000	—
1651 FG(b)	—	6,100	11,500	19,500	28,000	—
1651 FG(b)	—	6,100	11,500	19,500	28,000	—
1652 FG(b)	—	6,100	11,500	19,500	28,000	—
1653 FG(b)	—	6,100	11,500	19,500	28,000	—

KM# 47 1/2 SPECIE DALER

14.3600 g., 0.8750 Silver 0.4040 oz. ASW **Obv:** Larger bust **Note:** Varieties exist.

Date	Mintage	VG	F	VF	XF	Unc
1653 FG(b)	—	6,100	11,500	19,500	28,000	—
1654 FG(b)	—	6,100	11,500	19,500	28,000	—
1655 FG(b)	—	6,100	11,500	19,500	28,000	—
1656 FG(b)	—	6,100	11,500	19,500	28,000	—
1657 FG(b)	—	6,100	11,500	19,500	28,000	—
1658 FG(b)	—	6,100	11,500	19,500	28,000	—

KM# 53 1/2 SPECIE DALER

14.3900 g., 0.8750 Silver 0.4048 oz. ASW **Rev:** Lion with one tail

Date	Mintage	VG	F	VF	XF	Unc
1659 FG	—	7,700	13,000	24,500	35,000	—
1660 FG	—	7,700	13,000	24,500	35,000	—

KM# 72 1/2 SPECIE DALER

14.3900 g., 0.8750 Silver 0.4048 oz. ASW **Obv:** Laureate and cuirassed bust **Rev:** Lion within crowned oval shield **Note:** Varieties exist.

Date	Mintage	VG	F	VF	XF	Unc
1665 FG	—	7,000	12,500	21,000	33,500	—
1667 FG	—	7,000	12,500	21,000	33,500	—

KM# 87 1/2 SPECIE DALER

14.3900 g., 0.8750 Silver 0.4048 oz. ASW **Obv:** Draped bust

Date	Mintage	VG	F	VF	XF	Unc
1669 FG	—	7,000	12,500	21,000	33,500	—

KM# 107 1/2 SPECIE DALER

14.4500 g., 0.8750 Silver 0.4065 oz. ASW **Obv:** Laureate bust of Christian V

Date	Mintage	VG	F	VF	XF	Unc
1671 FG Rosettes	—	7,000	12,500	21,000	33,500	—
1673 FG Stars	—	7,000	12,500	21,000	33,500	—
1674 FG Stars, Rare	—	—	—	—	—	—

KM# 191 1/2 SPECIE DALER

14.4500 g., 0.8750 Silver 0.4065 oz. ASW **Rev:** National arms amid eight provincial arms

Date	Mintage	VG	F	VF	XF	Unc
1693 HCM	—	2,450	4,200	6,300	11,500	—

KM# 4 LION DALAR

Silver **Obv:** Knight behind arms **Rev:** Lion on battle axe **Note:** Dav. #3515. This has come to be considered a Danish coin

Date	Mintage	VG	F	VF	XF	Unc
1608 Rare	—	—	—	—	—	—

KM# 8 SPECIE DALER

25.9800 g., 0.9690 Silver 0.8093 oz. ASW **Note:** Dav. #3529. Mintage figures reflect combined totals of KM#5-8, 1/8 Speciedaler through 1 Speciedaler respectively.

Date	Mintage	VG	F	VF	XF	Unc
1628	Est. 43,000	1,500	2,550	4,500	9,000	—
1629	Est. 78,000	2,100	3,750	7,500	16,500	—

KM# 12 SPECIE DALER

29.2300 g., 0.8820 Silver 0.8288 oz. ASW **Ruler:** Christian IV **Obv:** Bust right **Rev:** Lion left on battle axe divides date **Note:** Dav. #3534. Varieties exist in the king's bust and the lion.

Date	Mintage	VG	F	VF	XF	Unc
1629	—	825	1,400	1,750	3,350	—
1630	—	825	1,400	1,750	3,350	—
1631	53,000	825	1,400	1,750	3,350	—
1632	32,000	825	1,400	1,750	3,350	—
1633	33,000	825	1,400	1,750	3,350	—
1634	39,000	825	1,400	1,750	3,350	—
1635	50,000	825	1,400	1,750	3,350	—
1636	50,000	825	1,400	1,750	3,350	—
1637	57,000	825	1,400	1,750	3,350	—

Date	Mintage	VG	F	VF	XF	Unc
1638	50,000	825	1,400	1,750	3,350	—
1639	52,000	825	1,400	1,750	3,350	—
1640	50,000	825	1,400	1,750	3,350	—
1641	45,000	825	1,400	1,750	3,350	—
1642	38,000	825	1,400	1,750	3,350	—
1643	7,834	825	1,500	1,850	3,500	—
1643 (c)	6,206	825	1,500	1,850	3,500	—
1644 P(c)G	14,000	875	1,550	2,600	4,800	—
1644 PG	—	875	1,550	2,600	4,800	—
1645 PG	21,000	825	1,400	1,750	3,500	—
1646 PG	55,000	825	1,400	1,750	3,500	—
1647 PG	62,000	825	1,400	1,750	3,500	—
1648 PG	62,000	825	1,200	1,750	2,800	—

KM# 12a SPECIE DALER

28.7200 g., 0.8750 Silver 0.8079 oz. ASW **Obv:** Frederick III

Date	Mintage	VG	F	VF	XF	Unc
1648 PG Rare	55,000	—	—	—	—	—

KM# 37 SPECIE DALER

28.7200 g., 0.8750 Silver 0.8079 oz. ASW **Obv:** Crowned bust of Frederick III **Note:** Dav. #3583.

Date	Mintage	VG	F	VF	XF	Unc
1649 PG(c)	—	750	1,650	2,600	4,250	—
1650 PG(c)	45,000	750	1,650	2,600	4,250	—
1651 PG(c) Rare	—	—	—	—	—	—

KM# 40 SPECIE DALER

28.7200 g., 0.8750 Silver 0.8079 oz. ASW **Obv:** Crowned bust of Frederick III with longer hair **Note:** Dav. #3590. Varieties exist.

Date	Mintage	VG	F	VF	XF	Unc
1651 FG(b)	—	1,400	3,150	4,900	8,100	—
1652 FG(b)	15,000	1,400	3,150	4,900	8,100	—

KM# A46 SPECIE DALER

28.7800 g., 0.8750 Silver 0.8096 oz. ASW **Note:** Dav. #3592. Varieties exist.

Date	Mintage	VG	F	VF	XF	Unc
1652 FG(b) Rare	15,000	—	—	—	—	—
1653 FG(b)	Inc. above	1,200	2,700	4,200	6,600	—

KM# 48 SPECIE DALER

28.7800 g., 0.8750 Silver 0.8096 oz. ASW **Obv:** Higher crown **Note:** Dav. #3595.

Date	Mintage	VG	F	VF	XF	Unc
1653 FG(b)	—	1,150	2,450	3,900	6,200	—
1654 FG(b)	23,000	1,150	2,450	3,900	6,200	—
1655 FG(b)	20,000	1,150	2,450	3,900	6,200	—
1656 FG(b)	18,000	1,650	3,100	4,550	8,100	—

KM# A41 SPECIE DALER

28.7800 g., 0.8750 Silver 0.8096 oz. ASW **Obv:** Smaller bust in circle, continuous legend **Note:** Dav. #3597.

Date	Mintage	VG	F	VF	XF	Unc
1655 Unique	—	—	—	—	—	—
1656	—	1,050	2,250	3,600	5,700	—
1657	—	1,350	2,700	3,900	6,600	—

KM# A42 SPECIE DALER

28.7800 g., 0.8750 Silver 0.8096 oz. ASW **Rev:** Smaller lettering, flowers at top **Note:** Dav. #3601. Varieties exist.

Date	Mintage	VG	F	VF	XF	Unc
1657 FG(b)	17,000	1,500	2,250	3,450	5,400	—
1658 FG(b)	18,000	1,650	2,400	3,750	6,000	—

KM# A43 SPECIE DALER

28.7800 g., 0.8750 Silver 0.8096 oz. ASW **Obv:** Small bust in inner circle **Rev:** Frame border around lion with tail **Note:** Dav. #3603.

Date	Mintage	VG	F	VF	XF	Unc
1658	—	3,000	4,400	7,200	13,000	—

KM# 51 SPECIE DALER

28.7800 g., 0.8750 Silver 0.8096 oz. ASW **Rev:** Lion with one tail **Note:** Dav. #3604. Varieties exist.

Date	Mintage	VG	F	VF	XF	Unc
1658 (b)	15,000	1,500	2,200	4,000	7,000	—
1659 FG(b) Rare	—	—	—	—	—	—
1659 FG(f)	—	1,500	2,200	4,000	7,000	—
1659 FG	—	1,500	2,200	4,000	7,000	—

KM# 54 SPECIE DALER

28.7800 g., 0.8750 Silver 0.8096 oz. ASW **Note:** Dav. #3607. Varieties exist.

Date	Mintage	VG	F	VF	XF	Unc
1659 FG	—	1,100	1,800	3,600	5,000	—
1660 FG	18,000	1,100	1,800	3,600	5,000	—
1661 FG	22,000	1,100	1,800	3,600	5,000	—
1662 FG	24,000	1,100	1,800	3,600	5,000	—

KM# 64 SPECIE DALER

28.7800 g., 0.8750 Silver 0.8096 oz. ASW **Subject:** Akershus Castle in Oslo **Note:** Dav. #3609.

Date	Mintage	VG	F	VF	XF	Unc
ND(1661) Rare	—	—	—	—	—	—

KM# 56 SPECIE DALER

28.7800 g., 0.8750 Silver 0.8096 oz. ASW **Obv:** Large crowned bust **Rev:** Lion in wreath **Note:** Dav. #3611.

Date	Mintage	VG	F	VF	XF	Unc
1661 Unique	—	—	—	—	—	—
1662	—	1,000	1,700	3,200	5,700	—

KM# A57 SPECIE DALER

28.7800 g., 0.8750 Silver 0.8096 oz. ASW **Obv:** Bust with bow knot on back and armored sleeve **Note:** Dav. #3614.

Date	Mintage	VG	F	VF	XF	Unc
1662	—	—	—	—	—	—
1663	—	—	—	—	—	—
1664	—	—	—	—	—	—

KM# 58 SPECIE DALER

28.7800 g., 0.8750 Silver 0.8096 oz. ASW **Obv:** Crowned armored bust right in laurel border **Note:** Dav. #3615.

Date	Mintage	VG	F	VF	XF	Unc
1662 Unique	—	—	—	—	—	—

KM# 67 SPECIE DALER

28.7800 g., 0.8750 Silver 0.8096 oz. ASW **Note:** Dav. #3617. Varieties exist.

Date	Mintage	VG	F	VF	XF	Unc
1662 FG	—	1,700	3,400	6,900	12,500	—
1663 FG	24,000	1,700	3,400	6,900	12,500	—
1664 FG	—	1,700	3,400	6,900	12,500	—

KM# 70 SPECIE DALER

28.7800 g., 0.8750 Silver 0.8096 oz. ASW **Obv:** Laureate bust with angels holding crown above **Note:** Dav. #3618.

Date	Mintage	VG	F	VF	XF	Unc
1664 FG	23,000	3,600	8,300	13,000	19,500	—

KM# 59 SPECIE DALER

28.7800 g., 0.8750 Silver 0.8096 oz. ASW **Obv:** Laureate bust without angels, leafy inner circle **Rev:** Crowned Norwegian lion on cross **Note:** Dav. #3619.

Date	Mintage	VG	F	VF	XF	Unc
1665	—	—	—	—	—	—

KM# 73 SPECIE DALER

28.7800 g., 0.8750 Silver 0.8096 oz. ASW **Obv:** Laureate bust within laurel branches **Rev:** Lion in crowned rectangular shield within laurel branches **Note:** Dav. #3621. Varieties exist.

Date	Mintage	VG	F	VF	XF	Unc
1665 FG	19,000	3,600	8,300	13,000	19,500	—

KM# 74 SPECIE DALER

28.7800 g., 0.8750 Silver 0.8096 oz. ASW **Obv:** Laureate and cuirassed bust **Rev:** Lion in crowned oval shield **Note:** Dav. #3623. Varieties exist.

Date	Mintage	VG	F	VF	XF	Unc
1665 FG	—	1,500	2,850	5,400	9,000	—
1666 FG	—	—	—	—	—	—
1667 FG	18,000	1,500	2,850	5,400	9,000	—

KM# 83 SPECIE DALER

28.7800 g., 0.8750 Silver 0.8096 oz. ASW **Obv:** Laureate, draped bust **Note:** Dav. #3625.

Date	Mintage	VG	F	VF	XF	Unc
1667 FG	32,000	1,500	2,850	5,400	9,000	—
1668 FG	12,000	1,500	2,850	5,400	9,000	—
1669 FG	13,000	1,500	2,850	5,400	9,000	—

KM# 97 SPECIE DALER

28.7800 g., 0.8750 Silver 0.8096 oz. ASW **Obv:** Crowned bust in armor **Rev:** Lion in crowned oval shield, date in legend **Note:** Dav. #3650. Varieties exist.

Date	Mintage	VG	F	VF	XF	Unc
1670 FG	3,149	4,200	8,400	16,000	28,500	—

KM# 98 SPECIE DALER

28.7800 g., 0.8750 Silver 0.8096 oz. ASW **Rev:** Date divided by shield **Note:** Dav. #3650A.

Date	Mintage	VG	F	VF	XF	Unc
1670 FG Rare	—	—	—	—	—	—

KM# 99 SPECIE DALER

28.7800 g., 0.8750 Silver 0.8096 oz. ASW **Obv:** Laureate bust **Rev:** Date in legend **Note:** Dav. #3651.

Date	Mintage	VG	F	VF	XF	Unc
1670 FG 3 known	—	—	—	—	—	—

KM# 108 SPECIE DALER

28.8900 g., 0.8750 Silver 0.8127 oz. ASW **Rev:** Motto within legend **Note:** Dav. #3653.

Date	Mintage	VG	F	VF	XF	Unc
1671 FG	7,728	3,000	3,900	8,100	15,000	—
1672 FG	7,728	2,100	3,600	6,600	10,500	—

KM# 109 SPECIE DALER

28.7800 g., 0.8750 Silver 0.8096 oz. ASW **Obv:** Laureate bust, Roman style **Rev:** Crown divides rosettes **Note:** Dav. #3656.

Date	Mintage	VG	F	VF	XF	Unc
1671 FG Rare	7,728	2,400	4,500	9,000	13,500	—
1672 FG	10,000	1,500	2,850	6,600	11,000	—
1674 FG	35,000	1,500	2,250	5,400	9,600	—

KM# 132 SPECIE DALER

28.7800 g., 0.8750 Silver 0.8096 oz. ASW **Obv:** Draped bust

Date	Mintage	VG	F	VF	XF	Unc
1675 PG	29,000	1,950	3,300	5,700	11,000	—
1676 PG	31,000	1,950	3,300	5,700	11,000	—
1677 PG	18,000	2,700	4,500	9,000	16,500	—
1678 PG	12,000	2,250	3,900	8,100	15,000	—
1679 PG	16,000	2,700	4,500	9,000	16,500	—
1680 PG Rare	13,000	—	—	—	—	—

KM# 172 SPECIE DALER

28.8900 g., 0.8750 Silver 0.8127 oz. ASW **Obv:** Cuirassed bust **Rev:** Crowned national arms amid eight provincial arms **Note:** Dav. #3657.

Date	Mintage	VG	F	VF	XF	Unc
1687 HCM 2 known, (1)	—	—	—	—	—	—

KM# 184 SPECIE DALER

28.8900 g., 0.8750 Silver 0.8127 oz. ASW **Obv:** Roman style portrait with long hair **Note:** Dav. #3658.

Date	Mintage	VG	F	VF	XF	Unc
1688 HCM 3 known, (1)	126	—	—	—	—	—
1690 HCM 3 known, (1)	44	—	—	—	—	—

KM# 190 SPECIE DALER

28.8900 g., 0.8750 Silver 0.8127 oz. ASW **Obv:** Laureate Roman style portrait **Note:** Dav. #3659.

Date	Mintage	VG	F	VF	XF	Unc
1692 HCM (1)	—	800	1,400	2,400	4,500	—
1692 HCM (2)	—	800	1,400	2,400	4,500	—
1692 HCM (3)	13,000	800	1,400	2,400	4,500	—
1692 HCM (4), Rare	—	—	—	—	—	—
1692 HCM (5), 2 known	—	—	—	—	—	—
1692 HCM (6)	—	800	1,400	2,400	4,500	10,500
1693 HCM (1)	22,000	800	1,400	2,400	4,500	10,500
1693 HCM (2)	—	800	1,400	2,400	4,500	10,500
1693 HCM (3)	—	800	1,400	2,400	4,500	10,500
1693 HCM (4), 2 known	—	—	—	—	—	—
1693 HCM (6), 2 known	—	—	—	—	—	—

KM# 192 SPECIE DALER

28.8900 g., 0.8750 Silver 0.8127 oz. ASW **Rev:** Crowned arms within Order of the Elephant **Note:** Dav. #3660.

Date	Mintage	VG	F	VF	XF	Unc
1693 HCM (1)	—	3,000	5,000	10,000	15,000	—
1693 HCM (2)	—	3,000	5,000	10,000	15,000	—
1693 HCM (3)	—	3,000	5,000	10,000	15,000	—

KM# 193 SPECIE DALER

28.8900 g., 0.8750 Silver 0.8127 oz. ASW **Obv:** Draped portrait without Order of the Elephant **Note:** Dav. #3661.

Date	Mintage	VG	F	VF	XF	Unc
1693 HCM Unique, (1)	—	—	—	—	—	—
1693 HCM Unique, (2)	—	—	—	—	—	—
1693 HCM Unique, (3)	—	—	—	—	—	—
1694 HCM (1)	—	700	1,500	2,600	5,000	—
1694 HCM (2)	—	700	1,500	2,600	5,000	—
1694 HCM (3)	—	700	1,500	2,600	5,000	—
1694 HCM 4 known, (6)	—	—	—	—	—	—

KM# 194 SPECIE DALER

28.8900 g., 0.8750 Silver 0.8127 oz. ASW **Obv:** Draped portrait with Order of the Elephant

Date	Mintage	VG	F	VF	XF	Unc
1694 HCM (1)	—	500	1,000	1,700	2,600	—
1694 HCM (2)	—	500	1,000	1,700	2,600	—
1694 HCM (3)	—	500	1,000	1,700	2,600	—
1694 HCM (7)	—	500	1,000	1,700	2,600	—
1694 HCM 3 known, (4)	—	—	—	—	—	—
1694 HCM 4 known, (6)	—	—	—	—	—	—
1694 HCM Unique, (5)	—	—	—	—	—	—
1695 HCM (1)	—	500	1,000	1,700	2,600	—
1695 HCM (2)	—	500	1,000	1,700	2,600	—
1695 HCM (3)	—	500	1,000	1,700	2,600	—
1695 HCM (7)	—	500	1,000	1,700	2,600	—
1695 HCM 2 known, (5)	—	—	—	—	—	—
1695 HCM 3 known, (4)	—	—	—	—	—	—
1695 HCM Unique, (6)	—	—	—	—	—	—
1696 HCM (1)	16,000	500	1,000	1,700	2,600	—
1696 HCM (2)	Inc. above	500	1,000	1,700	2,600	—
1696 HCM (3)	Inc. above	500	1,000	1,700	2,600	—
1696 HCM 3 known, (4)	Inc. above	—	—	—	—	—
1696 HCM 3 known, (6)	Inc. above	—	—	—	—	—
1696 HCM 4 known, (5)	Inc. above	—	—	—	—	—
1696 HCM Rare, (7)	Inc. above	500	1,000	1,700	2,600	—

KM# 16 1 1/2 SPECIE DALER

Silver **Note:** Similar to 1 Specie Daler, KM#12.

Date	Mintage	VG	F	VF	XF	Unc
1630	—	—	—	—	—	—

KM# 13 2 SPECIE DALER

58.4600 g., 0.8820 Silver 1.6577 oz. ASW **Obv:** Crowned portrait of Christian IV **Rev:** Lion with two tails **Note:** Dav. #3532.

Date	Mintage	VG	F	VF	XF	Unc
1629 (f) Unique	—	—	—	—	—	—
1630 (f) Unique	—	—	—	—	—	—

Date	Mintage	VG	F	VF	XF	Unc
1631 (f) Rare	—	—	—	—	—	—
1632 (f) Rare	—	—	—	—	—	—
1633 (f) Unique	—	—	—	—	—	—
1634 (f) Unique	—	—	—	—	—	—
1635 (f) Unique	—	—	—	—	—	—
1636 (f) Rare	—	—	—	—	—	—
1637 (f) Rare	—	—	—	—	—	—
1638 (f) Rare	—	—	—	—	—	—
1639 (f) Unique	—	—	—	—	—	—
1640 (f) Unique	—	—	—	—	—	—
1641 (f) Rare	—	—	—	—	—	—
1642 (f) Rare	—	—	—	—	—	—
1644 PG(c) Rare	—	—	—	—	—	—
1645 PG(c) Rare	—	—	—	—	—	—
1646 PG(c)	—	5,300	10,500	22,500	45,000	—
1647 PG(c)	—	5,300	10,500	22,500	45,000	—

KM# 13a 2 SPECIE DALER

57.4300 g., 0.8750 Silver 1.6155 oz. ASW

Date	Mintage	VG	F	VF	XF	Unc
1648 PG(c)	—	6,000	12,000	22,500	45,000	—

KM# 38 2 SPECIE DALER

57.4300 g., 0.8750 Silver 1.6155 oz. ASW **Obv:** Bust of Frederick III **Note:** Dav. #3587. Similar to 1 Specie Daler, KM#37.

Date	Mintage	VG	F	VF	XF	Unc
1649 PG(c)	—	9,000	19,500	33,000	49,500	—
1650 PG(c)	—	9,000	19,500	33,000	49,500	—

KM# 44 2 SPECIE DALER

57.4300 g., 0.8750 Silver 1.6155 oz. ASW **Note:** Dav. #3589. Similar to 1 Specie Daler, KM#37. Varieties exist.

Date	Mintage	VG	F	VF	XF	Unc
1651 FG(b) 3 known	—	—	—	—	—	—
1652 FG(b)	—	9,000	19,500	33,000	49,500	—

KM# 46 2 SPECIE DALER

57.4300 g., 0.8750 Silver 1.6155 oz. ASW **Note:** Dav. #3591. Similar to 1 Specie Daler, KM#A46.

Date	Mintage	VG	F	VF	XF	Unc
1653 Rare	—	—	—	—	—	—

KM# 38a 2 SPECIE DALER

57.5500 g., 0.8750 Silver 1.6189 oz. ASW **Obv:** Large bust breaking legend at top **Note:** Dav. #3594. Similar to 1 Specie Daler, KM#48.

Date	Mintage	VG	F	VF	XF	Unc
1653 FG(b) Unique	—	—	—	—	—	—
1654 FG(b) 2 known	—	—	27,000	42,000	60,000	—
1655 FG(b) Unique	—	—	—	—	—	—
1656 FG(b) 2 known	—	—	27,000	42,000	60,000	—

KM# 41 2 SPECIE DALER

57.5500 g., 0.8750 Silver 1.6189 oz. ASW **Note:** Dav. #3596. Similar to 1 Specie Daler, KM#A41.

Date	Mintage	VG	F	VF	XF	Unc
1656 FG(b) Unique	—	—	—	—	—	—
1657 FG(b) Unique	—	—	—	—	—	—

KM# 42 2 SPECIE DALER

57.5500 g., 0.8750 Silver 1.6189 oz. ASW **Note:** Dav. #3600. Similar to 1 Specie Daler, KM#A42. Varieties exist.

Date	Mintage	VG	F	VF	XF	Unc
1657 FG(b) 2 known	—	—	—	—	—	—
1658 FG(b) 7 known	—	—	—	—	—	—

KM# B52 2 SPECIE DALER

57.5500 g., 0.8750 Silver 1.6189 oz. ASW **Obv:** Small bust in inner circle **Rev:** Frame border around lion with one tail **Note:** Dav. #3602.

Date	Mintage	VG	F	VF	XF	Unc
1658 (b) 4 known	—	—	—	—	—	—

KM# A52 2 SPECIE DALER

57.5500 g., 0.8750 Silver 1.6189 oz. ASW **Note:** Dav. #3606. Similar to 1 Specie Daler, KM#54.

Date	Mintage	VG	F	VF	XF	Unc
1659 FG 5 known	—	—	—	—	—	—
1660 FG 3 known	—	—	—	—	—	—
1661 FG 2 known	—	—	—	—	—	—
1662 FG Unique	—	—	—	—	—	—

KM# 65 2 SPECIE DALER

57.5500 g., 0.8750 Silver 1.6189 oz. ASW **Subject:** Akershus Castle in Oslo **Note:** Dav. #3608. Similar to 1 Specie Daler, KM#64.

Date	Mintage	VG	F	VF	XF	Unc
ND(1661) 3 known	—	—	—	—	—	—

KM# 89 2 SPECIE DALER

57.5500 g., 0.8750 Silver 1.6189 oz. ASW **Obv:** Large crowned bust **Rev:** Lion in wreath **Note:** Dav. #3610.

Date	Mintage	VG	F	VF	XF	Unc
1662 Rare	—	—	—	—	—	—

KM# 57 2 SPECIE DALER

57.5500 g., 0.8750 Silver 1.6189 oz. ASW **Note:** Dav. #3613. Similar to 1 Specie Daler, KM#A57.

Date	Mintage	VG	F	VF	XF	Unc
1662 Rare	—	—	—	—	—	—
1663 Rare	—	—	—	—	—	—
1664 Rare	—	—	—	—	—	—

KM# 52 2 SPECIE DALER

57.5500 g., 0.8750 Silver 1.6189 oz. ASW **Note:** Dav. #3613. Similar to 1 Specie Daler, KM#67.

Date	Mintage	VG	F	VF	XF	Unc
1663 FG Rare	—	—	—	—	—	—
1664 FG Rare	—	—	—	—	—	—

KM# 76 2 SPECIE DALER

57.5500 g., 0.8750 Silver 1.6189 oz. ASW **Obv:** Cuirrassed bust **Rev:** Lion within oval shield **Note:** Dav. #3622. Similar to 1 Specie Daler, KM#74.

Date	Mintage	VG	F	VF	XF	Unc
1665 FG Rare	—	—	—	—	—	—
1666 FG Rare	—	—	—	—	—	—
1667 FG Rare	—	—	—	—	—	—

KM# 75 2 SPECIE DALER

57.5500 g., 0.8750 Silver 1.6189 oz. ASW **Rev:** Lion within crowned shield

Date	Mintage	VG	F	VF	XF	Unc
1665 FG Rare	—	—	—	—	—	—

KM# 84 2 SPECIE DALER

57.5500 g., 0.8750 Silver 1.6189 oz. ASW **Obv:** Draped bust **Note:** Dav. #3624. Similar to 1 Specie Daler, KM#83.

Date	Mintage	VG	F	VF	XF	Unc
1667 FG	—	13,000	21,000	37,500	54,000	—
1668 FG	—	13,000	21,000	37,500	54,000	—
1669 FG Unique	—	—	—	—	—	—

KM# 100 2 SPECIE DALER

57.5500 g., 0.8750 Silver 1.6189 oz. ASW **Obv:** Crowned bust of Christian V in armor **Rev:** Lion in crowned oval shield, date in legend **Note:** Dav. #3649.

Date	Mintage	VG	F	VF	XF	Unc
1670 FG 2 known	—	—	—	—	—	—

KM# 101 2 SPECIE DALER

57.5500 g., 0.8750 Silver 1.6189 oz. ASW **Rev:** Lion in oval shield divides date **Note:** Dav. #3649A.

Date	Mintage	VG	F	VF	XF	Unc
1670 FG 2 known	—	—	—	—	—	—

KM# 102 2 SPECIE DALER

57.5500 g., 0.8750 Silver 1.6189 oz. ASW **Obv:** Cuirassed and laureate bust **Rev:** Date in legend

Date	Mintage	VG	F	VF	XF	Unc
1670 FG Unique	—	—	—	—	—	—

KM# A110 2 SPECIE DALER

57.5500 g., 0.8750 Silver 1.6189 oz. ASW **Rev:** Motto around crowned shield within legend **Note:** Dav. #3652. Similar to 1 Specie Daler, KM#108.

Date	Mintage	VG	F	VF	XF	Unc
1671 FG Unique	—	—	—	—	—	—
1672 FG Unique	—	—	—	—	—	—

KM# 110 2 SPECIE DALER

57.5500 g., 0.8750 Silver 1.6189 oz. ASW **Note:** Dav. #3655. Similar to 1 Specie Daler, KM#109. Varieties exist.

Date	Mintage	VG	F	VF	XF	Unc
1672 FG 2 known	—	12,500	22,000	37,500	52,500	—
1674 FG 4 known	—	12,500	22,000	37,500	52,500	—
1675 PG Unique	—	—	—	—	—	—
1676 PG Unique	—	—	—	—	—	—
1677 PG Rare	—	10,500	21,000	37,500	52,500	—
1678 PG 2 known	—	12,500	22,000	37,500	52,500	—
1679 PG 2 known	—	12,500	22,000	37,500	52,500	—
1680 PG Unique	—	—	—	—	—	—

KM# 25 3 SPECIE DALER

87.7000 g., 0.8820 Silver 2.4868 oz. ASW **Obv:** Crowned portrait of Christian IV **Rev:** Lion **Note:** Dav. #3531. Similar to 1 Specie Daler, KM#12.

Date	Mintage	VG	F	VF	XF	Unc
1643 (f) Unique	—	—	—	—	—	—
1644 PG(c) Unique	—	—	—	—	—	—

KM# A39 3 SPECIE DALER

86.1500 g., 0.8750 Silver 2.4235 oz. ASW **Obv:** Crowned portrait of Frederick III **Rev:** Lion with two tails within circle **Note:** Dav. #3586

Date	Mintage	VG	F	VF	XF	Unc
1649 PG(c) 3 known	—	—	—	—	—	—
1650 PG(c) 3 known	—	—	—	—	—	—

KM# 39 3 SPECIE DALER

86.1500 g., 0.8750 Silver 2.4235 oz. ASW **Note:** Dav. #A3589. Similar to 1 Specie Daler, KM#40. Varieties exist.

Date	Mintage	VG	F	VF	XF	Unc
1651 FG(b) Unique	—	—	—	—	—	—
1652 FG(b) Unique	—	—	—	—	—	—

KM# A39a 3 SPECIE DALER

86.3200 g., 0.8750 Silver 2.4282 oz. ASW **Note:** Dav. #A3591. Similar to 1 Specie Daler, KM#A46.

Date	Mintage	VG	F	VF	XF	Unc
1652 FG(b) Unique	—	—	—	—	—	—

KM# B39a 3 SPECIE DALER

86.3200 g., 0.8750 Silver 2.4282 oz. ASW **Note:** Dav. #3593. Similar to 1 Specie Daler, KM#48.

Date	Mintage	VG	F	VF	XF	Unc
1654 FG(b) 4 known	—	—	—	—	—	—
1655 FG(b) Unique	—	—	—	—	—	—
1656 FG(b) Unique	—	—	—	—	—	—

KM# 39a 3 SPECIE DALER

86.3200 g., 0.8750 Silver 2.4282 oz. ASW **Note:** Dav. #3599. Similar to 1 Specie Daler, KM#A42. Varieties exist.

Date	Mintage	VG	F	VF	XF	Unc
1657 FG(b) Unique	—	—	—	—	—	—
1658 FG(b) 2 known	—	—	—	—	—	—

KM# A55 3 SPECIE DALER

86.3200 g., 0.8750 Silver 2.4282 oz. ASW **Rev:** Lion with one tail **Note:** Dav. #3605. Similar to 1 Specie Daler, KM#54.

Date	Mintage	VG	F	VF	XF	Unc
1659 FG(b) 2 known	—	—	—	—	—	—
1660 FG 2 known	—	—	—	—	—	—

KM# 55 3 SPECIE DALER

86.3200 g., 0.8750 Silver 2.4282 oz. ASW **Note:** Dav. #3612. Similar to 1 Specie Daler, KM#A57.

Date	Mintage	VG	F	VF	XF	Unc
1663 FG Unique	—	—	—	—	—	—
1664 FG 2 known	—	—	—	—	—	—

KM# A67 3 SPECIE DALER

86.3200 g., 0.8750 Silver 2.4282 oz. ASW **Note:** Dav. #A3616. Similar to 1 Specie Daler, KM#67.

Date	Mintage	VG	F	VF	XF	Unc
1663 2 known	—	—	—	—	—	—

KM# 79 3 SPECIE DALER

86.3200 g., 0.8750 Silver 2.4282 oz. ASW **Obv:** Laureate bust **Rev:** Crowned lion in shield

Date	Mintage	VG	F	VF	XF	Unc
1666 FG Unique	—	—	—	—	—	—
1667 FG Unique	—	—	—	—	—	—
1668 FG Unique	—	—	—	—	—	—

KM# 128 3 SPECIE DALER

86.6800 g., 0.8750 Silver 2.4384 oz. ASW **Obv:** Christian V **Note:** Dav. #3654. Similar to 1 Specie Daler, KM#109.

Date	Mintage	VG	F	VF	XF	Unc
1674 FG Unique	—	—	—	—	—	—
1678 PG Unique	—	—	—	—	—	—
1679 PG 2 known	—	—	—	—	—	—
1680 PG 3 known	—	—	—	—	—	—

KM# 15 4 SPECIE DALER

116.9300 g., 0.8820 Silver 3.3156 oz. ASW **Obv:** Christian IV **Rev:** Lion **Note:** Dav. #3530. Similar to 1 Specie Daler, KM#12

Date	Mintage	VG	F	VF	XF	Unc
1634 (f) Unique	—	—	—	—	—	—
1644 PG(c) 3 known	—	—	—	—	—	—
1645 PG(c) Unique	—	—	—	—	—	—

KM# 15a 4 SPECIE DALER

114.8800 g., 0.8750 Silver 3.2317 oz. ASW

Date	Mintage	VG	F	VF	XF	Unc
1648 PG Unique	—	—	—	—	—	—

KM# A50 4 SPECIE DALER

115.1000 g., 0.8750 Silver 3.2378 oz. ASW **Obv:** Portrait of Frederick III **Rev:** Lion with two tails within circle **Note:** Dav. #A3596. Similar to 1 Specie Daler, KM#A41.

Date	Mintage	VG	F	VF	XF	Unc
1656 FG(b) 2 known	—	—	—	—	—	—

KM# 50 4 SPECIE DALER
115.1000 g., 0.8750 Silver 3.2378 oz. ASW **Note:** Dav. #A3596. Similar to 1 Specie Daler, KM#A42.

Date	Mintage	VG	F	VF	XF	Unc
1657 FG(b) 2 known	—	—	—	—	—	—
1658 FG(b) Unique	—	—	—	—	—	—

KM# 66 4 SPECIE DALER
115.1000 g., 0.8750 Silver 3.2378 oz. ASW **Rev:** Lion with one tail within laurel wreath

Date	Mintage	VG	F	VF	XF	Unc
1661 FG Unique	—	—	—	—	—	—

KM# 129 4 SPECIE DALER
115.5700 g., 0.8750 Silver 3.2511 oz. ASW **Obv:** Portrait of Christian V **Rev:** Crowned lion in shield **Note:** Dav. #A3654.

Date	Mintage	VG	F	VF	XF	Unc
1674 FG Unique	—	—	—	—	—	—
1678 PG Unique	—	—	—	—	—	—
1679 PG Unique	—	—	—	—	—	—
1680 PG 3 known	—	—	—	—	—	—

KM# A119 2 DUCAT
6.9900 g., 0.9790 Gold 0.2200 oz. AGW **Obv:** Laureate bust of Frederik III right **Rev:** Crown above orb between sword and scepter **Note:** Small planchet.

Date	Mintage	VG	F	VF	XF	Unc
1670	—	10,000	20,000	30,000	40,000	—

TOKEN COINAGE

KM# Tn1 12 SKILLING
4.1800 g., 0.6720 Silver 0.0903 oz. ASW **Subject:** Summer Transport Token

Date	Mintage	VG	F	VF	XF	Unc
1689	—	750	1,450	2,750	4,750	—

KM# Tn2 16 SKILLING
5.5700 g., 0.6720 Silver 0.1203 oz. ASW **Subject:** Winter Transport Token

Date	Mintage	VG	F	VF	XF	Unc
1689	—	600	1,200	2,250	3,850	—

TRADE COINAGE

KM# 80 1/2 DUCAT
1.4900 g., 0.9790 Gold 0.0469 oz. AGW **Obv:** Draped, laureate bust of Frederick right **Rev:** Crowned arms mounted on cross **Note:** Struck at Christiania Mint.

Date	Mintage	VG	F	VF	XF	Unc
1666 3 known	—	—	—	—	—	—

KM# 103 1/2 DUCAT
1.4900 g., 0.9790 Gold 0.0469 oz. AGW **Obv:** Laureate bust of Christian right

Date	Mintage	VG	F	VF	XF	Unc
ND Rare	—	—	—	—	—	—

KM# 81 1/2 DUCAT
1.4900 g., 0.9790 Gold 0.0469 oz. AGW **Obv:** Roman style bust of Frederick III right

Date	Mintage	VG	F	VF	XF	Unc
ND(f) Rare	—	—	—	—	—	—

KM# 61 DUCAT
3.4900 g., 0.9790 Gold 0.1098 oz. AGW **Obv:** Crowned bust right of Frederick **Note:** Struck at Christiania Mint.

Date	Mintage	VG	F	VF	XF	Unc
1660 FG Unique	—	—	—	—	—	—

KM# 77 DUCAT
3.4900 g., 0.9790 Gold 0.1098 oz. AGW **Obv:** Frederick

Date	Mintage	VG	F	VF	XF	Unc
1665 3 known, Rare	—	—	—	—	—	—

KM# 86 DUCAT
3.4900 g., 0.9790 Gold 0.1098 oz. AGW **Obv:** Draped bust of Frederick right

Date	Mintage	VG	F	VF	XF	Unc
1668 Unique	—	—	—	—	—	—

KM# 88 DUCAT
3.4900 g., 0.9790 Gold 0.1098 oz. AGW **Obv:** Large Roman bust of Frederick right **Rev:** Crowned arms mounted on cross, date below

Date	Mintage	VG	F	VF	XF	Unc
1669 FG(ch) Unique	—	—	—	—	—	—

KM# 117 DUCAT
3.4900 g., 0.9790 Gold 0.1098 oz. AGW **Obv:** Laureate bust of Christian V right **Rev:** Crowned arms mounted on cross, date divided below

Date	Mintage	VG	F	VF	XF	Unc
1673 Unique	—	—	—	—	—	—
ND 2 known	—	—	—	—	—	—

KM# 118 DUCAT
3.4900 g., 0.9790 Gold 0.1098 oz. AGW **Rev:** Crowned arms mounted on cross **Note:** Small planchet.

Date	Mintage	VG	F	VF	XF	Unc
ND Unique	—	—	—	—	—	—

KM# 195 DUCAT
3.4900 g., 0.9790 Gold 0.1098 oz. AGW **Obv:** Bust of Christian V right **Rev:** Six-line inscription **Note:** Struck at Kongsberg Mint.

Date	Mintage	VG	F	VF	XF	Unc
1697 HCM 2 known	—	—	—	—	—	—

KM# 78 2 DUCAT
6.9800 g., 0.9790 Gold 0.2197 oz. AGW **Obv:** Armored bust of Frederick right **Obv. Legend:** FREDERIC: III: D: G: DAN: NOR: **Rev:** Crowned arms mounted on cross, date in legend **Rev. Legend:** VANDAL: GOTO: REX:

Date	Mintage	VG	F	VF	XF	Unc
1665 2 known, Rare	—	—	—	—	—	—

KM# 119 2 DUCAT
6.9800 g., 0.9790 Gold 0.2197 oz. AGW **Obv:** Laureate bust of Christian V right **Rev:** Crowned arms mounted on cross, date divided below

Date	Mintage	VG	F	VF	XF	Unc
1673 Unique	—	—	—	—	—	—
ND 2 known	—	—	—	—	—	—

KM# 121 2 DUCAT
6.9800 g., 0.9790 Gold 0.2197 oz. AGW **Obv:** Equestrian figure of Christian V

Date	Mintage	VG	F	VF	XF	Unc
1673 Rare	—	—	—	—	—	—

KM# 122 2 DUCAT
6.9800 g., 0.9790 Gold 0.2197 oz. AGW **Obv:** Laureate head of Christian V right, date below

Date	Mintage	VG	F	VF	XF	Unc
1673 Rare	—	—	—	—	—	—

KM# 123 2 DUCAT
6.9800 g., 0.9790 Gold 0.2197 oz. AGW **Rev:** Three C5 monograms among six crowns at border

Date	Mintage	VG	F	VF	XF	Unc
1673 Rare	—	—	—	—	—	—

KM# 120 2 DUCAT
6.9800 g., 0.9790 Gold 0.2197 oz. AGW **Rev:** Crowned arms mounted on cross **Note:** Small thick planchet.

Date	Mintage	VG	F	VF	XF	Unc
ND 3 known	—	—	—	—	—	—

KM# 137 2 DUCAT
6.9800 g., 0.9790 Gold 0.2197 oz. AGW **Obv:** Larger head of Christian

Date	Mintage	VG	F	VF	XF	Unc
1678 Unique	—	—	—	—	—	—

KM# 138 2 DUCAT
6.9800 g., 0.9790 Gold 0.2197 oz. AGW **Obv:** Draped bust of Christian right

Date	Mintage	VG	F	VF	XF	Unc
ND Unique	—	—	—	—	—	—

KM# 196 2 DUCAT
6.9800 g., 0.9790 Gold 0.2197 oz. AGW **Obv:** Bust of Christian V right **Rev:** Six-line inscription **Note:** Struck at Kongsberg Mint.

Date	Mintage	VG	F	VF	XF	Unc
1697 HCM 2 known	—	—	—	—	—	—

KM# 111 3 DUCAT
10.4700 g., 0.9790 Gold 0.3295 oz. AGW **Obv:** Laureate bust of Christian V right **Rev:** Crowned arms mounted on cross divide date **Note:** Struck at Christiania Mint.

Date	Mintage	VG	F	VF	XF	Unc
1671 FB Unique	—	—	—	—	—	—

KM# 124 3 DUCAT
10.4700 g., 0.9790 Gold 0.3295 oz. AGW **Rev:** Crowned arms mounted on cross, date divided below

Date	Mintage	VG	F	VF	XF	Unc
1673 Unique	—	—	—	—	—	—

KM# 125 3 DUCAT
10.4700 g., 0.9790 Gold 0.3295 oz. AGW **Obv:** Equestrian figure of Christian V left **Rev:** Crowned arms, date in legend

Date	Mintage	VG	F	VF	XF	Unc
1673 4 known	—	—	—	—	—	—

KM# 126 3 DUCAT
10.4700 g., 0.9790 Gold 0.3295 oz. AGW **Obv:** Equestrian figure of Christian V right **Rev:** Elephant with arms on side cloth, date in exergue

Date	Mintage	VG	F	VF	XF	Unc
1673 Unique	—	—	—	—	—	—

KM# 127 3 DUCAT
10.4700 g., 0.9790 Gold 0.3295 oz. AGW **Obv:** Three C5 monograms among six crowns at border

Date	Mintage	VG	F	VF	XF	Unc
1673 Rare	—	—	—	—	—	—

KM# 139 3 DUCAT
10.4700 g., 0.9790 Gold 0.3295 oz. AGW **Obv:** Three C5 monograms among six crowns at border

Date	Mintage	VG	F	VF	XF	Unc
1678 3 known	—	—	—	—	—	—

KM# A140 3-3/8 DUCAT
11.8500 g., 0.9790 Gold 0.3730 oz. AGW

Date	Mintage	VG	F	VF	XF	Unc
1684 Rare	—	—	—	—	—	—

KM# 112 4 DUCAT
13.9600 g., 0.9790 Gold 0.4394 oz. AGW **Obv:** Christian V

Date	Mintage	VG	F	VF	XF	Unc
1671 FG Unique	—	—	—	—	—	—

LARGESSE COINAGE

KM# A107.1 1/4 SPECIE DALER
7.2200 g., 0.8750 Silver 0.2031 oz. ASW **Subject:** Royal Visti to Norway **Obv. Legend:** CVRDNVG IN MEMORIAM

Date	Mintage	VG	F	VF	XF	Unc
1685 Rare	—	—	—	—	—	—

KM# A107.2 1/4 SPECIE DALER
7.2200 g., 0.8750 Silver 0.2031 oz. ASW **Obv. Legend:** CVRDNVG TERPAMARI

Date	Mintage	VG	F	VF	XF	Unc
1685 Rare	—	—	—	—	—	—

PATTERNS

Including off metal strikes

KM#	Date	Mintage	Identification	Mkt Val
Pn1	ND	—	12 Skilling. 0.6720 Silver. King on horseback, crowned C5 monogram	600
Pn2	ND	—	1/2 Ducat. 0.9790 Gold. Head of king, crowned arms.	—
Pn3	ND	—	Ducat. Gold. King on horseback, knight and lion.	—
Pn4	ND	—	Ducat. Silver. King on horseback, knight and lion.	300
Pn5	ND	—	Ducat. Gold. King on horseback, crowned monograms.	—
Pn6	ND	—	Ducat. Silver. King on horseback, lion.	300
Pn7	ND	—	Ducat. Gold. Head of king, crowned arms.	—
Pn8	ND	—	Ducat. Silver. Head of king, crowned arms.	—
Pn9	ND	—	2 Ducat. Silver. King on horseback, arms.	500
Pn10	ND	—	2 Ducat. Gold. King on horseback, crowned monograms.	—
Pn11	ND	—	2 Ducat. Silver. King on horseback, crowned monograms.	200
Pn12	ND	—	2 Ducat. Gold. King on horseback, crowned monograms.	—
Pn13	ND	—	2 Ducat. Silver. King on horseback, crowned monograms.	—
Pn14	ND	—	2 Ducat. Silver. Head of king, crowned monograms.	—
Pn15	ND	—	2 Ducat. Silver. Head of king, crowned monograms.	—
Pn16	ND	—	2 Ducat. Gold. Head of king, crowned monograms.	—
Pn17	ND	—	4 Ducat. Gold. King on horseback, crowned monograms.	—
Pn18	ND	—	4 Ducat. Silver. King on horseback, crowned monograms.	750
PnA19	ND	—	10 Ducat. 35.5000 Gold.	—
PnB19	1644	—	4 Skilling. Copper. IIII/SKL/D	—
PnC19	1660	—	1/8 Specie Daler. Gold. KM#60.	—
Pn19	1660	—	Ducat. Gold. KM#61.	—
PnA20	1664	—	10 Ducat. 35.0000 Gold. Struck with Specidaler dies, KM#10.	—
PnB20	1665	—	7-7/8 Ducat. 28.0000 Gold. Struck with Speciedaler dies, KM#73.	—
PnC20	1665	—	10 Ducat. 33.8000 Gold. Struck with Speciedaler dies, KM#74.	—
PnD20	1668	—	10 Ducat. 35.5000 Gold. Struck with Speciedaler dies, KM#83.	—
PnE20	1669	—	12 Ducat. 40.7000 Gold. Struck with Speciedaler dies, KM#83.	—
Pn20	1673	—	2 Ducat. 40.7000 Silver. Laureate head.	1,200
Pn21	1673	—	2 Ducat. 40.7000 Silver. C5 monograms.	1,000
Pn22	1673	—	3 Ducat. 40.7000 Silver. Equestrian figure.	800
PnA23	1674	—	5 Ducat. 17.5000 Gold. Struck with Speciedaler dies, KM#109.	—
PnB23	1675	—	4-3/16 Ducat. 14.6500 Gold. Struck with Speciedaler dies, KM#132.	—
Pn23	1678	—	2 Ducat. Gold. Head of king, monograms and crowns.	—
Pn24	1678	—	2 Ducat. Gold. Head of king, elephant.	—
Pn25	1678	—	3 Ducat. Silver. C5 monograms.	—
Pn26	1678	—	3 Ducat. Gold. Head of king, elephant.	—
Pn27	1681	—	12 Skilling. Head of king, lion in branches.	—
Pn28	1683	—	4 Mark. Monogram and lion, Dannenbrog cross.	2,500
Pn29	1684	—	Mark. Monogram and lion, Dannebrog cross.	1,300
Pn30	1685	—	1/2 Mark. Monogram and lion; Dannebrog cross.	550
PnA31	1685	—	16-5/8 Ducat. 58.0000 Gold. Struck with Speciedaler dies.	—
PnB31	1690	—	12 Ducat. 58.0000 Gold. Struck with Speciedaler dies, KM#184.	—
Pn31	1697 HCM	—	Ducat. Silver.	—
Pn34	ND	—	8 Skilling. Head of King/lion and lift on mountain.	—

PERU

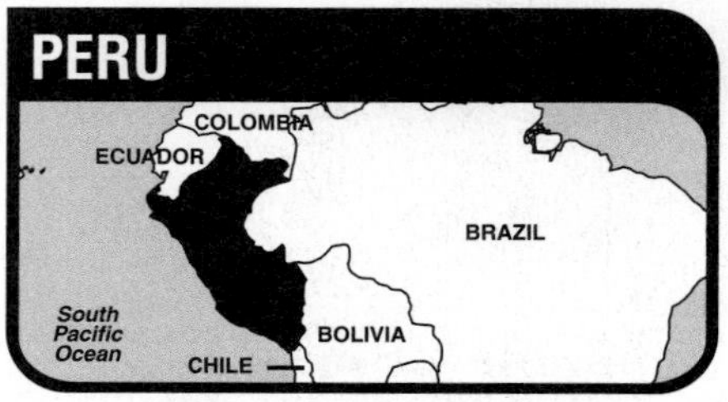

The Republic of Peru, located on the Pacific coast of South America, has an area of 496,225 sq. mi. (1,285,220sq. km).

Once part of the great Inca Empire that reached from northern Ecuador to central Chile, the conquest of Peru by Francisco Pizarro began in 1531. Desirable as the richest of the Spanish viceroyalties, it was torn by warfare between avaricious Spaniards until the arrival in 1569 of Francisco de Toledo, who initiated 2-1/2 centuries of efficient colonial rule, which made Lima the most aristocratic colonial capital and the stronghold of Spain's American possessions. Jose de San Martin of Argentina proclaimed Peru's independence on July 28, 1821;Simon Bolivar of Venezuela secured it in December, 1824 when he defeated the last Spanish army in South America. After several futile attempts to re-establish its South American empire, Spain recognized Peru's independence in 1879.

Andres de Santa Cruz, whose mother was a high-ranking Inca, was the best of Bolivia's early presidents, and temporarily united Peru and Bolivia 1836-39, thus realizing his dream of a Peruvian/Bolivian confederation. This prompted the separate coinages of North and South Peru. Peruvian resistance and Chilean intervention finally broke up the confederation, sending Santa Cruz into exile. A succession of military strongman presidents ruled Peru until Marshall Castilla revitalized Peruvian politics in themid-19th century and repulsed Spain's attempt to reclaim its one-time colony. Subsequent loss of southern territory to Chile in the War of the Pacific, 1879-81, and gradually increasing rejection of foreign economic domination, combined with recent serious inflation, affected the country numismatically.

As a result of the discovery of silver at Potosi in 1545, a mint was eventually authorized in 1565 with the first coinage taking place in 1568. The mint had an uneven life span during the Spanish Colonial period from 1568-72. It was closed from 1573-76, reopened from 1577-88. It remained closed until 1659-1660 when an unauthorized coinage in both silver and gold were struck. After being closed in 1660, it remained closed until 1684 when it struck cob style coins until 1752.

RULER
Spanish until 1822

MINT MARKS
AREQUIPA, AREQ = Arequipa
AYACUCHO = Ayacucho
(B) = Brussels
CUZCO (monogram), Cuzco, Co. Cuzco
L, LIMAE (monogram), Lima
(monogram), LIMA = Lima
(L) = London
PASCO (monogram), Pasco, Paz, Po= Pasco
P, (P) = Philadelphia
S = San Francisco
(W) = Waterbury, CT, USA

NOTE: The LIMAE monogram appears in three forms. The early LM monogram form looks like a dotted L with M. The later LIMAE monogram has all the letters of LIMAE more readily distinguishable. The third form appears as an M monogram during early Republican issues.

MINT ASSAYERS' INITIALS

Initial	Date	Name
H, Ho	1696-1705,	?
M	1694	?
N	1699-1706	Joaquin Negrow
R	1698-1701	
V	1659-60	Francesco Villegas
V	1684, 1689-90	
V	1692-93	

The letter(s) following the dates of Peruvian coins are the assayer's initials appearing on the coins. They generally appear at the 11 o'clock position on the Colonial coinage and at the 5 o'clock position along the rim on the obverse or reverse on the Republican coinage.

MONETARY SYSTEM
16 Reales = 2 Pesos = 1 Escudo

SPANISH COLONY

COLONIAL COB COINAGE

KM# 14 1/2 REAL
1.6917 g., 0.9310 Silver 0.0506 oz. ASW **Ruler:** Philip IV **Obv:** PHILIPPVS momgram **Rev:** Cross of Jerusalem. lions and castles in quarters, date in legend

Date	Mintage	Good	VG	F	VF	XF
ND(1659)	—	100	200	350	500	—
1659 Rare	—	—	—	—	—	—

KM# 22 1/2 REAL
1.6917 g., 0.9310 Silver 0.0506 oz. ASW **Ruler:** Charles II **Obv:** CAROLVS monogram, date below **Rev:** Cross of Jerusalem, lions and castles in quarters

Date	Mintage	Good	VG	F	VF	XF
ND(1684-1700) Date off flan	—	25.00	30.00	40.00	50.00	—
1684L	—	30.00	50.00	70.00	110	—
1685L	—	30.00	50.00	70.00	110	—
1686L	—	30.00	50.00	70.00	110	—
1687L	—	30.00	50.00	70.00	110	—
1688L	—	30.00	50.00	70.00	110	—
1689L	—	30.00	50.00	70.00	110	—
1690L	—	30.00	50.00	70.00	110	—
1691L	—	30.00	50.00	70.00	110	—
1692L	—	30.00	50.00	70.00	110	—
1693L	—	30.00	50.00	70.00	110	—
1694L	—	30.00	55.00	70.00	110	—
1695L	—	30.00	55.00	70.00	110	—
1696L	—	30.00	50.00	70.00	110	—
1697L	—	30.00	50.00	70.00	110	—
1698L	—	32.00	50.00	70.00	110	—
1699L	—	30.00	50.00	75.00	135	—
1700L	—	38.00	55.00	95.00	155	—

KM# 15 REAL
3.3834 g., 0.9310 Silver 0.1013 oz. ASW **Ruler:** Philip IV **Obv:** Pillars and waves, star above mint mark and date **Obv. Legend:** PHILIPPVS IIII DEI

Date	Mintage	Good	VG	F	VF	XF
1659L*M V	—	125	200	350	525	—
1660L*M V	—	200	300	500	800	—

KM# 20 REAL
3.3834 g., 0.9310 Silver 0.1013 oz. ASW **Ruler:** Charles II **Obv:** Cross of Jerusalem, lions and castles in quarters **Rev:** Pillars and waves

Date	Mintage	Good	VG	F	VF	XF
ND(1684-1700)L Date off flan	—	25.00	30.00	40.00	50.00	—
1684L V	—	35.00	50.00	80.00	125	—
1685L R	—	35.00	50.00	80.00	125	—
1686L R	—	35.00	50.00	80.00	125	—
1687L R	—	35.00	50.00	80.00	125	—
1688L R	—	35.00	50.00	80.00	125	—
1689L V	—	35.00	50.00	80.00	125	—
1690L V	—	35.00	50.00	80.00	125	—
1690L R	—	35.00	50.00	80.00	125	—
1691L R	—	35.00	50.00	80.00	125	—
1692L V	—	35.00	50.00	80.00	125	—
1693L V	—	35.00	50.00	80.00	125	—
1694L M	—	35.00	50.00	80.00	125	—
1695L R	—	35.00	50.00	80.00	125	—
1696L H	—	35.00	50.00	80.00	125	—
1697L H	—	35.00	50.00	80.00	125	—
1698L H	—	35.00	50.00	80.00	125	—
1699L R	—	35.00	50.00	80.00	125	—
1700L H	—	35.00	50.00	80.00	125	—

KM# 16 2 REALES
6.7668 g., 0.9310 Silver 0.2025 oz. ASW **Obv. Legend:** PHILIPPVS IIII DEI. G

Date	Mintage	Good	VG	F	VF	XF
1659L*M V Rare	—	—	—	—	—	—
1659LI*M V Rare	—	—	—	—	—	—
1660L*M V Rare	—	—	—	—	—	—

KM# 21 2 REALES

6.7668 g., 0.9310 Silver 0.2025 oz. ASW **Obv:** Cross of Jerusalem, lions and castles in quarters, mint mark **Obv. Legend:** CAROLVS II D • G • HISPANIARVM REX **Rev:** Pillars, assayer's initial, date, PLVS VLTRA within

Date	Mintage	Good	VG	F	VF	XF
ND(1684-1700)L Date off flan	—	50.00	60.00	75.00	100	—
1684L V	—	60.00	90.00	150	250	—
1685L R	—	60.00	90.00	150	250	—
1686L R	—	60.00	90.00	150	250	—
1687L R	—	60.00	90.00	150	250	—
1688L R	—	60.00	90.00	150	250	—
1689L V	—	60.00	90.00	150	250	—
1690L R	—	60.00	90.00	150	250	—
1691L R	—	60.00	90.00	150	250	—
1692L V	—	60.00	90.00	150	250	—
1693L V	—	60.00	90.00	150	250	—
1694L M	—	60.00	90.00	150	250	—
1695L R	—	60.00	90.00	150	250	—
1696L H	—	60.00	90.00	150	250	—
1696L Ho Rare	—	—	—	—	—	—
1697L H	—	60.00	90.00	150	250	—
1698L H	—	60.00	90.00	150	250	—
1699L R	—	60.00	90.00	150	250	—
1700L H	—	60.00	90.00	150	250	—

KM# 17 4 REALES

13.5337 g., 0.9310 Silver 0.4051 oz. ASW **Obv:** Pillars and waves, star above mint mark and date **Obv. Legend:** PHILIPPVS IIII DEI. G **Rev. Inscription:** ...PLVS/• * •/VLTRA/660.

Date	Mintage	Good	VG	F	VF	XF
1659LIMA V Star above mint mark, rare	—	—	—	—	—	—
1659L*M V Rare	—	—	—	—	—	—
(1)660L V Rare	—	—	—	—	—	—
1660L*M V Rare	—	—	—	—	—	—

KM# 23 4 REALES

13.5337 g., 0.9310 Silver 0.4051 oz. ASW **Obv:** Cross of Jerusalem, lions and castles in quarters **Obv. Legend:** CAROLVS II D • G • HISPANIARVM REX **Rev:** Pillars with mint mark, value and assayer's initial between

Date	Mintage	Good	VG	F	VF	XF
ND(1684-1700)L Date off flan	—	75.00	100	125	200	—
1684L V	—	125	200	350	550	—
1685L R	—	110	180	285	480	—
1686L R	—	110	180	285	480	—
1687L R	—	110	180	285	480	—
1688L R	—	110	180	285	480	—
1689L V Rare	—	—	—	—	—	—
1689L R	—	—	—	—	—	—
Note: Reported, not confirmed						
1690L R Rare	—	—	—	—	—	—
1691L R	—	125	200	350	550	—
1692L V	—	125	200	350	550	—
1693L V	—	125	200	350	550	—
1695L R Rare	—	—	—	—	—	—
1696L H	—	125	220	400	580	—
1697L H	—	110	170	270	435	—
1698L H	—	110	170	270	435	—
1699L H	—	—	—	—	—	—
Note: Reported, not confirmed						
1699L R Rare	—	—	—	—	—	—
1700L H	—	110	170	270	435	—

KM# 18.1 8 REALES

27.0674 g., 0.9310 Silver 0.8102 oz. ASW **Obv:** Pillars and waves, star above mint mark and date **Obv. Legend:** PHILIPPVS IIII DEI. G **Note:** Struck at Lima.

Date	Mintage	Good	VG	F	VF	XF
1659LIMA V LIMA 8 V left and right; Rare	—	—	—	—	—	—
Note: Swiss Bank Coins of Peru Auction #20 9-88 VF realized $13,400.						
1659LIMA V Lima V left, 8 right	—	900	1,500	2,500	3,500	—
1659L*M V 8-pointed star	—	900	1,500	2,500	3,500	—

KM# 18.2 8 REALES

27.0674 g., 0.9310 Silver 0.8102 oz. ASW **Obv:** PLVS/ • * • /VLTRA/660 between pillars **Obv. Legend:** PHILIPPVS IIII DEI. G

Date	Mintage	Good	VG	F	VF	XF
660 (1) 660 • * • 6-pointed star	—	2,000	3,000	4,000	5,000	—

Note: Clear, sharply struck examples of KM#18.1 and KM#18.2, along with other denominations of the Star of Lima coinage, have been known to bring much higher prices for examples which may exceed a VF grade

KM# 24 8 REALES

27.0674 g., 0.9310 Silver 0.8102 oz. ASW **Ruler:** Charles II **Obv:** Cross of Jerusalem, lions and castles in quarters **Rev:** PLV/ SVL/ TRA between pillars

Date	Mintage	Good	VG	F	VF	XF
ND(1684-1701)L Date off flan	—	125	150	175	200	—
1684L V	—	150	250	350	500	—
1685L R	—	150	250	350	500	—
1685L V Rare	—	—	—	—	—	—
1686/5L R Rare	—	—	—	—	—	—
1686L R	—	150	250	350	500	—
1687L R	—	150	250	350	500	—
1688L R	—	150	250	350	500	—
1689L V	—	150	250	350	500	—
1690L V	—	150	250	350	500	—
1690L R	—	150	250	350	500	—
1691L R	—	150	250	350	500	—
1692L V	—	150	250	350	500	—
1693L V	—	150	250	350	500	—
1694L M	—	175	275	375	575	—
1695L R	—	150	250	350	500	—
1696L H	—	150	250	350	500	—
1696L Ho Rare	—	—	—	—	—	—
1697L H	—	150	250	350	500	—
1698L H	—	150	250	350	500	—
1699L R	—	150	250	350	500	—
1700L H	—	150	250	350	500	—

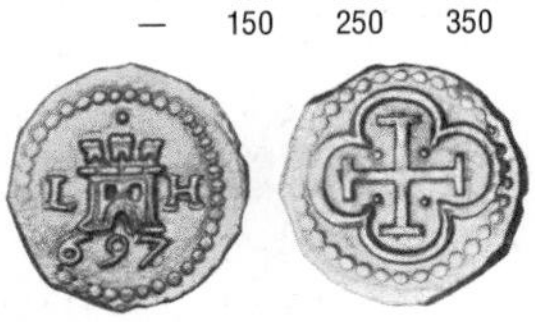

KM# 27 ESCUDO

3.3834 g., 0.9170 Gold 0.0997 oz. AGW **Ruler:** Charles II **Obv:** Castle divides L H, date as 698 below **Rev:** Cross of Jerusalem, dots in quarters **Note:** See pattern section of 1696 date.

Date	Mintage	VG	F	VF	XF	Unc
ND(1696-1700)L Date off flan	—	—	2,000	2,500	4,000	—
1697/6L H	—	—	3,000	4,000	6,000	—
1698L H	575	—	3,000	4,000	6,000	—
1698L R	Inc. above	—	3,000	4,000	6,000	—
1699L R	748	—	3,000	4,000	6,000	—
1700L R	427	—	3,000	4,000	6,000	—

KM# A27 ESCUDO

3.3834 g., 0.9170 Gold 0.0997 oz. AGW **Obv:** Castle **Rev:** Cross of Jerusalem, X's in quarters

Date	Mintage	VG	F	VF	XF	Unc
ND(1698)C M Date off flan	—	—	3,000	3,500	5,000	—
1698C M	—	—	5,000	7,000	10,000	—

KM# 29 2 ESCUDOS

6.7668 g., 0.9170 Gold 0.1995 oz. AGW **Ruler:** Charles II **Obv:** Cross of Jerusalem with lions and castles in quarters **Obv. Legend:** C • II D • G • HISPANIARVM **Rev:** Pillars and waves

Date	Mintage	VG	F	VF	XF	Unc
ND(1696-1701)L Date off flan	—	—	1,500	2,500	3,500	—
1696L H	32,979	—	4,000	5,000	7,000	—
1697L H	39,472	—	4,000	5,000	7,000	—
1698L H	912	—	4,000	5,000	7,000	—
1699L H	1,788	—	4,000	5,000	7,000	—
1699L R	Inc. above	—	4,000	5,000	7,000	—
1700L H	6,315	—	4,000	5,000	7,000	—

KM# 28 2 ESCUDOS

6.7668 g., 0.9170 Gold 0.1995 oz. AGW **Ruler:** Charles II **Obv:** Cross of Jerusalem with lions and castles in quarters **Obv. Legend:** C • II D • G • HISPANIARVM **Rev:** Pillars, PVA and date, mintmark

Date	Mintage	VG	F	VF	XF	Unc
ND(1698)	—	—	1,500	2,500	3,500	—
1698C M	—	—	3,500	5,000	7,500	—

KM# 25 4 ESCUDOS

13.5337 g., 0.9170 Gold 0.3990 oz. AGW **Ruler:** Charles II **Obv:** Cross of Jerusalem with castles and lions in quarters **Obv. Legend:** C • II D • G • HISPANIARVM **Rev:** Pillars and waves

Date	Mintage	VG	F	VF	XF	Unc
ND(1696-1701)L Date off flan	—	—	5,000	6,250	7,500	—
1696L H	—	—	9,000	12,000	15,000	—
1697L H	—	—	9,000	12,000	15,000	—
1698L H	1,260	—	9,000	12,000	15,000	—
1699L R	1,636	—	9,000	12,000	15,000	—
1700L H	2,006	—	9,000	12,000	15,000	—

KM# 19 8 ESCUDOS

27.0674 g., 0.9170 Gold 0.7980 oz. AGW **Obv:** Arms, pillars **Obv. Legend:** PHILIPPVS IIII D • G • HISPANIARVM **Rev:** Cross of Jerusalem, legend and date around

Date	Mintage	VG	F	VF	XF	Unc
1659L V Rare	1,617	—	—	—	—	—
1660L V Rare	846	—	—	—	—	—

KM# 26.2 8 ESCUDOS

27.0674 g., 0.9170 Gold 0.7980 oz. AGW **Ruler:** Charles II **Obv:** Cross of Jerusalem, lions and castles in quarters **Obv. Legend:** C • II D • G • HISPANIARVM **Rev:** Pillars, PVA, date and mint mark

Date	Mintage	VG	F	VF	XF	Unc
ND(1696-1701)L Date off flan	—	—	5,000	6,250	7,500	—
1696L H	—	—	8,000	10,000	12,500	—
1697L H	—	—	8,000	10,000	12,500	—
1698L H	—	—	8,000	10,000	12,500	—
1699L R	Inc. above	—	8,000	10,000	12,500	—
1700L H	10,350	—	8,000	10,000	12,500	—

KM# 26.1 8 ESCUDOS

27.0674 g., 0.9170 Gold 0.7980 oz. AGW **Ruler:** Charles II **Obv:** Cross of Jerusalem with castles and lions in quarters **Obv. Legend:** C•II D•G•HISPANIARVM **Rev:** Pillars, P. V. A., date and mint mark

Date	Mintage	VG	F	VF	XF	Unc
1697L H	—	—	8,000	10,000	12,000	—
1698L H	5,898	—	8,000	10,000	12,000	—
1699L R	15,656	—	8,000	10,000	12,000	—

ROYAL COINAGE

KM# R21 2 REALES

6.7668 g., 0.9310 Silver 0.2025 oz. ASW **Ruler:** Charles II **Note:** Struck at Lima.

Date	Mintage	Good	VG	F	VF	XF
1685L R Rare	—	—	—	—	—	—

KM# R18 8 REALES

27.0674 g., 0.9310 Silver 0.8102 oz. ASW

Date	Mintage	Good	VG	F	VF	XF
1659 Rare	—	—	—	—	—	—

KM# R24 8 REALES

Ruler: Charles II **Note:** Struck at Lima.

Date	Mintage	Good	VG	F	VF	XF
1684L V Rare	—	—	—	—	—	—
1686L R Rare	—	—	—	—	—	—
1687L R Rare	—	—	—	—	—	—
1688L R Rare	—	—	—	—	—	—
1689L V Rare	—	—	—	—	—	—
1691L R Rare	—	—	—	—	—	—
1692L V Rare	—	—	—	—	—	—
1693L V Rare	—	—	—	—	—	—
1694L M Rare	—	—	—	—	—	—
1695L R Rare	—	—	—	—	—	—
1697L H Rare	—	—	—	—	—	—

PATTERNS

Including off metal strikes

KM#	Date	Mintage	Identification	Mkt Val
PnA1	ND(1696)	—	Escudo. Gold.	—

POLAND

The Republic of Poland, located in central Europe, has an area of 120,725 sq. mi. (312,680 sq. km).

Poland began as a Slavic duchy in the 10th century and reached its peak of power between the 14th and 16th centuries. In the 17th century it has had a turbulent history of invasion, occupation or partition by Mongols (13th century), Turkey (14th century), Transylvania, Sweden (17th century), Austria, Prussia and Russia (18th century) .

RULERS

Zygmunt III Waza, 1587-1632
Wladyslaw IV Waza, 1633-1648
Jan II Kazimierz Waza, 1649-1668
Michal Korybut Wisniowiecki, 1669-1673
Jan III Sobieski, 1674-1696
August II Mocny Wettin, 1697-1733

MINT MARKS

MW - Moneta Wschovensis, 1650-1655

Other letters appearing with date denote the Mintmaster at the time the coin was struck.

Mintmasters' Initials, Marks and Symbols

Mintmasters' initials usually appear flanking the shield or by the date.

BYDGOSZCZ MINT
(Bromberg)

Initial	Date	Name
B		Bydgoszcz mint
(u)= 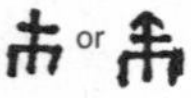 or SC	1594-1601	Stanislaw Cikowski, mint contractor
VI	1595-?	Walenteg (Valentin Jahns, mint contractor
(v)= 	Ca.1614	Stanislaw Koniecpolski, mintmaster
AS or SA	1614-17	Samuel Amman, die-cutter
CG	1650-52	Christoph Guttman
DS	1622	Daniel Seiler
GG	1640-44	Gabriel Gorloff
II or II-VE	1616-24	Jacob Jacobson van Emden
MH	1671-85	Michael Haderman
MRVM	1639	Mathias Rippers von Meiningen
MS	1640-42	Melchior Schirmer, mint official
BS	Ca. 1640-44	Benedykt Stefani, die-cutter
TT	1660	Thomas Timpf
EPH	1693-1714	Ernst Peter Hecht

ELBLAG MINT
(Elbing)

MP	1628-35	Marek (Marsilius) Philippson, mint contractor
BS	Ca. 1631-36	Benedykt Stefani, die-cutter
WVE or VE	1650-52	Wilhelm von Eck, mintmaster
NH	1652-65	Mikolaj Hennig, mintmaster
IP	1665-67	Jan Paulson, mintmasster
CS	1671-73	Chrystian Schultz, mintmaster

GDANSK MINT
(Danzig)

(x) = arm holding dagger	1582-1610	Philipp Klüwer, mintmaster
PK (in ligature)		
(w)= bear paw or DC	1608-18	Daniel Klüwer, mintmaster
FB	Ca. 1610	Unknown die-cutter
SA	1613-21	Samuel Amman, medailleur and die-cutter
SB or BS	1618-35	Stanislaw Berman, mintmaster
DG	Ca. 1623	Unknown mint official
KHW	Ca. 1623	Unknown mint official
II or II-VE	1630-39	Jakub Jakobson van Emden, mint contractor
CS	1636-60	Chrystian Schirmer, Sr., warden
GR	1639-56	Gerard Rogge, mintmaster
IH/h	Ca. 1644-58	Jan Hoehn, die-cutter
DL	1656-85	Daniel Lesse, mintmaster
CS	1664-91	Chrystian Schirmer, Jr., warden

KRAKOW MINT
(Cracow)

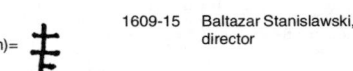

(p) = lion rampant left or IF	1590-1609	Jan Firlej, royal mint director
(s)=  or HR	1595-1601	Hermann Rüdiger, royal mint contractor
(m)= 	1609-15	Baltazar Stanislawski, royal mint director
TKA/TA	1614-24	Tomasz Altenberger, royal mint contractor
W	1614-16	Stanislaw Warszycki, royal mint director
(o)= 	1616-24	Nikolaus Danillowicz, royal mint director
SA	1621	Samuel Amman, die-cutter
(n) = donkey head	1624-32	Hermolaus Ligeza, royal mint director
II or II-VE	1624-30	Jakub Jacobson van Emden, mint contractor
(y)= 	1632-50	Jan Danillowicz, royal mint director
CDC	1644-46	Claudius de Canotti
GP	1647-50	Gerhard Pyrami
(aa) = ox head facing	1650-59	Boguslaw Leszczynski, royal mint director
AT or ACPT	1650-67	Andrzej Tymf, royal mint contractor
SCH	1655-58	Stanislaw Chrzastowski, mint administrator
IT	1655-61	Jan Thamm, mintmaster & warden
IC	1656	Jakub Chamer, mintmaster
TLB	1658-87	Tytus Liwiusz Boratini, mintmaster
(z) = bird on horseshoe	1659-68	Jan Kazimierz Krasinski, royal mint director
(bb)= 	1668-83	Jan Andrzej Morsztyn, royal mint director
(cc)= 	1683-89	Marcin Zamojski, royal mint director
B	Ca. 1685	Gotfryd Bartsch, mint contractor
(dd)= 	1689-92	Markus Matczynski, royal mint director
(ee)= 	1692-1702	August Lubomirski, royal mint director

LOBZENICA MINT
(Lobsenz)

L		Lobzenica mint
AK	1612	Andrzej Krotoski, mintmaster
	1612-15	Jan Beker, mintmaster

LWÓW Mint
(Lvov in Ukraine, Ger. Lemberg)

GBA or BGA	1661-63	Giovanni Battista Amuretti, mint contractor

OLKUSZ MINT

(i) = clover	Ca. 1680	Unknown

POZNAN
(Posen)

RL (usually ligature)	1599-1601	Rudolph Lehmann, medailleur and warden
GC	Ca. 1610	Unknown moneyer
AT	1650-60	Andrzej Tymp (Tümfe, Tümpfe) mint contractor
NG	1660-62	Mikolaj (Nicolaus) Gille, mint administrator

TORUN MINT
(Thorn)

HH	1629-31	Henryk Hema, warden
HL	1630	Jan (Hans) Lippe, mintmaster
II or II-VE	1630-39	Jakub Jakobson van Emden, mint contractor
MS	1640-42	Melchior Schirmer, mintmaster
GR	1643-49	Gerard Rogge, mintmaster
HDL	1649-69	Jan (Hans) Dawid Lauer, mint contractor
HIL	1653-55	Jan (Hans) Jakub Lauer, mintmaster
HS	1668-72	Henryk Sievert, mintmaster

UJAZDOW MINT

TLB	1659-65	Tytus Liwiusz Boratini, mintmaster

WSCHOWA MINT
(Fraustadt)

HR	1595-1601	Herman Rüdiger
RL (usually ligature)	1599-1603	Rudolph Lehmann, medailleur and warden

ARMS

as Found on Coins of Poland

Batory dynasty – wolf's jawbone with 3 teeth
Elblag – shield divided horizontally with cross in each half, lower half shaded
Gdansk – crown over 2 crosses, 1 above the other
Jagiellon dynasty – double-barred cross
Lithuania – knight on horseback to left
Prussia – eagle usually holding sword over head with claw
Torun – triple-towered city gate
Waza dynasty – sheaf of grain
Wschowa – double-barred cross, annulet to either side between bar

MONETARY SYSTEM

Until 1815

1 Solidus = 1 Schilling
3 Solidi = 2 Poltura = 1 Grosz
3 Poltura = 1-1/2 Grosze = 1 Polturak
6 Groszy = 1 Szostak
18 Groszy = 1 Tympf = 1 Ort
30 Groszy = 4 Silbergroschen = 1 Zloty
1 Talar = 1 Zloty
6 Zlotych = 1 Reichsthaler
8 Zlotych = 1 Speciesthaler
5 Speciesthaler = 1 August D'or
3 Ducats = 1 Stanislaus D'or

KINGDOM

STANDARD COINAGE

KM# 34 DENAR (Solidus, Obol, Halerz)

Silver **Ruler:** Sigismund III **Obv:** Crowned large S **Rev:** Three shields

Date	Mintage	Good	VG	F	VF	XF
(16)12	—	—	—	—	—	—
(16)18	—	36.00	70.00	140	—	—
(16)19	—	41.50	85.00	170	—	—
(16)20	—	41.50	85.00	170	—	—
(16)21	—	36.00	70.00	140	—	—
(16)ZZ	—	36.00	70.00	140	—	—
(16)22	—	36.00	70.00	140	—	—
(16)Z3	—	20.00	41.50	85.00	—	—
(16)23	—	—	—	—	—	—
(16)Z4	—	20.00	41.50	85.00	—	—
(16)24	—	—	—	—	—	—

KM# 1 DENAR (Solidus, Obol, Halerz)

Silver **Ruler:** Sigismund III **Obv:** Three shields

Date	Mintage	Good	VG	F	VF	XF
ND	—	17.00	30.00	60.00	—	—

KM# 3 3 DENAR (Trzeciak, Ternar)

Silver **Ruler:** Sigismund III **Obv:** Large S, shield at center **Rev:** Three shields, crown above

Date	Mintage	Good	VG	F	VF	XF
1601 Rare	—	—	—	—	—	—

KM# 4 SOLIDUS (Szelag, Schilling)

Silver **Ruler:** Sigismund III **Obv:** Crowned large S, dividing date and initials **Rev:** Crown above two or three shields **Note:** Struck at Bromberg, Fraustadt, Marborg, Krakow and Poznan mints.

Date	Mintage	Good	VG	F	VF	XF
1601 Inverted F	—	7.00	20.00	41.50	85.00	—
1601 F	—	7.00	20.00	41.50	85.00	—
1601	—	7.00	20.00	41.50	85.00	—
1601 BB	—	11.00	20.00	41.50	85.00	—
1601 B	—	7.00	14.00	27.50	60.00	—
1601 B-B	—	11.00	20.00	41.50	85.00	—
1601 FF	—	4.00	8.00	17.00	27.50	—
1601 C	—	4.00	8.00	17.00	27.50	—
1601 D	—	4.00	8.00	17.00	27.50	—
1601 G	—	4.00	8.00	17.00	27.50	—
1601 K	—	4.00	8.00	17.00	36.00	—
1601 M	—	4.00	8.00	17.00	27.50	—
1601 N	—	4.00	8.00	17.00	27.50	—
1613	—	4.00	7.00	14.00	25.00	—
1616 F	—	4.00	7.00	14.00	25.00	—
1616 P	—	4.00	7.00	14.00	25.00	—
1619 F	—	4.00	7.00	14.00	25.00	—

KM# 25 SOLIDUS (Szelag, Schilling)

Silver **Ruler:** Sigismund III **Obv:** Crowned large SR **Rev:** Legend and date **Note:** Varieties exist.

Date	Mintage	Good	VG	F	VF	XF
1601K	—	—	—	—	—	—
1616K	—	4.00	11.00	20.00	36.00	—
1622K	—	4.00	11.00	20.00	36.00	—
16ZZK	—	4.00	11.00	20.00	36.00	—
1623K	—	4.00	11.00	20.00	36.00	—
1624K	—	4.00	11.00	20.00	36.00	—
1625K	—	4.00	11.00	20.00	36.00	—
1626K	—	2.75	7.00	14.00	25.00	—
1627K	—	7.00	20.00	41.50	85.00	—
1631K Unique	—	—	—	—	—	—
NDK	—	4.00	11.00	20.00	36.00	—

KM# 16 SOLIDUS (Szelag, Schilling)

Silver **Ruler:** Sigismund III **Obv:** Eagle with shield on breast **Rev:** Crowned large S, shield at center dividing date **Note:** Legend varieties exist.

Date	Mintage	Good	VG	F	VF	XF
(16)13	—	4.00	8.00	17.00	27.50	—
(1)614	—	4.00	8.00	17.00	27.50	—
(16)14 Rare	—	—	—	—	—	—
1616 SR	—	8.00	17.00	33.00	70.00	—
(16)16	—	4.00	8.00	17.00	27.50	—
(16)17	—	—	—	—	—	—
(16)19	—	14.00	41.50	100	210	—
(16)21 Rare	—	—	—	—	—	—
(16)25	—	4.00	8.00	17.00	27.50	—

KM# 24 SOLIDUS (Szelag, Schilling)

Silver **Ruler:** Sigismund III **Obv:** Three shields **Rev:** Crowned large S, shield at center dividing date

Date	Mintage	Good	VG	F	VF	XF
1616	—	—	—	—	—	—

KM# 28 SOLIDUS (Szelag, Schilling)

Silver **Ruler:** Sigismund III **Rev:** Three-line inscription

Date	Mintage	Good	VG	F	VF	XF
1617	—	4.00	8.00	17.00	27.50	—

KM# 36 SOLIDUS (Szelag, Schilling)

Silver **Ruler:** Sigismund III **Obv:** Eagle with shield on breast **Rev:** Large crown

Date	Mintage	Good	VG	F	VF	XF
1620	—	5.00	10.00	19.00	36.00	—
1621	—	5.00	10.00	19.00	36.00	—

KM# A37 SOLIDUS (Szelag, Schilling)

Silver **Ruler:** Sigismund III **Obv:** Five-fold arms in inner circle **Obv. Legend:** SIGIS•III•D•G•REX•POLONIA• **Rev:** Crowned S with shield in center divides date **Rev. Legend:** SOLIDVS REGNI POLO

Date	Mintage	Good	VG	F	VF	XF
(16)25	—	6.00	11.00	22.50	44.00	—
(16)26	—	6.00	11.00	22.50	44.00	—

KM# 83 SOLIDUS (Szelag, Schilling)

Copper **Ruler:** Johann Casimir **Obv:** Crowned JCR monogram **Rev:** Inscription, date below

Date	Mintage	Good	VG	F	VF	XF
1650	—	70.00	95.00	170	350	—

KM# 84 SOLIDUS (Szelag, Schilling)

Copper **Ruler:** Johann Casimir **Obv:** Crowned JCR monogram in circle **Rev:** Crowned eagle with shield on breast

Date	Mintage	Good	VG	F	VF	XF
1650	—	70.00	95.00	170	350	—

KM# 100 SOLIDUS (Szelag, Schilling)

Copper **Ruler:** Johann Casimir **Obv:** Crowned eagle with shield on breast **Rev:** Crowned large S, shield in center

Date	Mintage	Good	VG	F	VF	XF
1652 Rare	—	—	—	—	—	—
1653 Rare	—	—	—	—	—	—

KM# 110 SOLIDUS (Szelag, Schilling)

Copper **Ruler:** Johann Casimir **Obv:** Bust right **Rev:** Crowned eagle with shield on breast

Date	Mintage	Good	VG	F	VF	XF
1659	—	2.75	6.00	12.00	27.50	—
1660	—	2.75	6.00	12.00	25.00	—
1661	—	2.75	6.00	12.00	25.00	—
1665	—	2.75	6.00	12.00	25.00	—

KM# 20 3 POLKER (3 Poltorak - 1 Kruzierz)

Silver **Ruler:** Sigismund III **Obv:** Eagle with shield on breast **Rev:** 24 within orb dividing date **Note:** Varieties exist.

Date	Mintage	Good	VG	F	VF	XF
(16)14 W	—	14.00	27.50	48.25	70.00	—

KM# 41 3 POLKER (3 Poltorak - 1 Kruzierz)

Silver **Ruler:** Sigismund III **Obv:** Crowned shield **Rev:** 24 within orb dividing date **Note:** Varieties exist.

Date	Mintage	Good	VG	F	VF	XF
(16)14	—	7.00	22.50	46.00	70.00	—
1614	—	3.00	14.00	30.00	46.00	—
1615	—	3.00	14.00	30.00	46.00	—
(16)15	—	3.00	14.00	30.00	46.00	—
(16)16	—	3.00	14.00	30.00	46.00	—
(16)17	—	3.00	14.00	30.00	46.00	—
(16)18	—	3.00	14.00	30.00	46.00	—
(16)19	—	3.00	14.00	30.00	46.00	—
16Z0	—	2.25	7.00	14.00	22.50	—
(16)20	—	2.25	7.00	14.00	22.50	—
(16)21	—	2.25	6.00	12.00	17.00	—
(16)22	—	1.25	3.00	7.00	12.00	—
(16)23	—	1.25	3.00	7.00	12.00	—
(16)24	—	1.25	3.00	7.00	12.00	—
(16)25	—	1.25	3.00	7.00	12.00	—
(16)26	—	1.25	3.00	7.00	12.00	—
16Z7	—	1.75	3.00	7.00	12.00	—
(16)27	—	1.25	3.00	7.00	12.00	—
16Z8	—	12.00	22.50	60.00	85.00	—
(16)28	—	12.00	22.50	60.00	85.00	—
ND	—	6.00	12.00	22.50	40.25	—

KM# 105 3 POLKER (3 Poltorak - 1 Kruzierz)

Silver **Ruler:** Johann Casimir **Obv:** Crowned shield **Rev:** 60 within orb **Note:** Varieties exist with 60 or 61 in orb.

Date	Mintage	Good	VG	F	VF	XF
(16)54 Rare	—	—	—	—	—	—
(16)58 Rare	—	—	—	—	—	—
(16)59	—	48.25	120	240	400	—
(16)61	—	36.00	70.00	140	240	—
(16)62	—	27.50	41.50	70.00	140	—
(16)66 Rare	—	—	—	—	—	—

KM# 23 3 KREUZER

Silver **Ruler:** Sigismund III **Obv:** Crowned bust right **Rev:** Crowned shield **Note:** Varieties exist.

Date	Mintage	Good	VG	F	VF	XF
1615	—	14.00	27.50	60.00	90.00	—
1616	—	14.00	27.50	60.00	90.00	—
1617	—	14.00	27.50	60.00	90.00	—
1618	—	25.00	34.00	80.00	160	—

KM# 5 GROSCHEN (1/24 Thaler, 7-1/2 Groszy, Srebrnik)

Silver **Ruler:** Sigismund III **Obv:** Crowned half-length bust right, lion in shield below **Rev:** Crown above three shields, eagle **Note:** Varieties exist.

Date	Mintage	Good	VG	F	VF	XF
1601	—	18.00	34.00	80.00	130	—
1603	—	18.00	34.00	80.00	130	—
1604	—	12.00	25.00	34.00	80.00	—
1605	—	12.00	25.00	34.00	80.00	—
1605	—	12.00	25.00	34.00	80.00	—
Note: Legend error: G POSSVS...						
1606	—	12.00	25.00	34.00	80.00	—
1607	—	12.00	25.00	34.00	80.00	—
1607	—	12.00	25.00	34.00	80.00	—
Note: Legend error: ...POLONI/ND...						

KM# 11 GROSCHEN (1/24 Thaler, 7-1/2 Groszy, Srebrnik)

Silver **Ruler:** Sigismund III **Obv:** Large crown above legend **Rev:** Eagle with shield on breast, lion in shield below **Note:** Varieties exist.

Date	Mintage	Good	VG	F	VF	XF
1601 Error 10	—	60.00	90.00	180	350	—
1603	—	60.00	90.00	180	350	—
1604	—	12.00	25.00	45.00	70.00	—
1605	—	12.00	25.00	45.00	70.00	—
1606	—	12.00	25.00	45.00	70.00	—
1607	—	12.00	25.00	45.00	70.00	—
1608	—	60.00	90.00	180	350	—
1609	—	12.00	25.00	45.00	70.00	—
1610	—	12.00	25.00	45.00	70.00	—
1611	—	12.00	25.00	45.00	70.00	—
1612	—	12.00	25.00	45.00	70.00	—
1613	—	12.00	25.00	45.00	70.00	—
1614	—	12.00	25.00	45.00	70.00	—
1615	—	12.00	25.00	45.00	70.00	—
1616	—	—	—	—	—	—
1617	—	—	—	—	—	—
1621 Error 12	—	—	—	—	—	—
1623	—	5.00	12.00	25.00	60.00	—
1624	—	5.00	12.00	25.00	60.00	—
1625	—	5.00	12.00	25.00	60.00	—
1626	—	5.00	12.00	25.00	60.00	—
1627	—	5.00	12.00	25.00	60.00	—
ND	—	25.00	45.00	80.00	150	—

KM# 8 GROSCHEN (1/24 Thaler, 7-1/2 Groszy, Srebrnik)

Silver **Ruler:** Sigismund III **Obv:** Crowned bust left **Rev:** Eagle with shield on breast, lion in shield below **Note:** Varieties exist.

Date	Mintage	Good	VG	F	VF	XF
1604	—	14.00	27.50	60.00	90.00	—
1607	—	10.00	18.00	45.00	85.00	—
1608	—	10.00	18.00	45.00	85.00	—

KM# 85 GROSCHEN (1/24 Thaler, 7-1/2 Groszy, Srebrnik)

Silver **Ruler:** Johann Casimir **Obv:** Crowned eagle with shield on breast **Rev:** Crown above date and legend **Note:** Struck at Krakow and Bydgoszcz; Varieties exist.

Date	Mintage	Good	VG	F	VF	XF
1650 Rare	—	—	—	—	—	—
1666 Rare	—	—	—	—	—	—

KM# 86 2 GROSCHEN (1/12 Thaler, 15 Groszy, Polzlotek)

Silver **Ruler:** Johann Casimir **Obv:** Crowned eagle with shield on breast **Rev:** Crown above legend and date

Date	Mintage	Good	VG	F	VF	XF
1650 CG	—	20.00	41.50	85.00	170	—

KM# 97 2 GROSCHEN (1/12 Thaler, 15 Groszy, Polzlotek)

Silver **Ruler:** Johann Casimir **Rev:** Crown above value, legend and date **Note:** Varieties exist.

Date	Mintage	Good	VG	F	VF	XF
1651 CG	—	—	20.00	41.50	100	210
1652	—	—	27.50	70.00	140	275
1654 Rare	—	—	—	—	—	—

KM# 88.1 18 GROSZY (Tympf)

Silver **Ruler:** Johann Casimir **Obv:** Laureate bust right **Rev:** Crowned shield dividing 18 **Note:** Numerious varieties exist.

Date	Mintage	Good	VG	F	VF	XF
1650 CGDAL Rare	—	—	—	—	—	—
1650 CG/BA Rare	—	—	—	—	—	—
1650 GP Rare	—	—	—	—	—	—
1650 CG Rare	—	—	—	—	—	—
1650	—	22.50	35.00	85.00	175	—
1651 MW	—	22.50	35.00	85.00	175	—
1651 MW (monogram)	—	19.00	30.00	80.00	150	—
1651 CG	—	22.50	45.25	120	265	—

Date	Mintage	Good	VG	F	VF	XF
1651 AT	—	39.50	80.00	180	375	—
1652	—	22.50	35.00	85.00	175	—
1652 MW	—	22.50	35.00	85.00	175	—
1652 CG Rare	—	—	—	—	—	—
1652 AT	—	22.50	45.25	90.00	265	—
1653 MW	—	22.50	35.00	85.00	175	—
1653 MW (monogram)	—	19.00	30.00	80.00	150	—
1653 AT	—	19.00	35.00	85.00	175	—
1654 MW	—	22.50	35.00	85.00	150	800
1654 MW (monogram)	—	22.50	35.00	85.00	175	—
1654 AT	—	22.50	45.25	110	175	—
1655 MW (monogram)	—	19.00	25.00	75.00	175	—
1655 IT	—	19.00	25.00	75.00	210	—
1655 AT	—	22.50	35.00	85.00	160	—
1655 SCH	—	19.00	25.00	75.00	160	—

KM# 88.2 18 GROSZY (Tympf)

Silver **Ruler:** Johann Casimir **Rev:** 22 flanking shield

Date	Mintage	Good	VG	F	VF	XF
1650 CG	—	70.00	115	215	365	—

KM# 88.3 18 GROSZY (Tympf)

Silver **Ruler:** Johann Casimir **Rev:** 21 flanking shield

Date	Mintage	Good	VG	F	VF	XF
1650 CG	—	70.00	115	215	365	—

KM# A94 18 GROSZY (Tympf)

Silver **Ruler:** Johann Casimir **Obv:** Crowned portraitbust right **Rev:** Crowned shield **Note:** Numerious varieties exist. Prev. KM#88.4.

Date	Mintage	Good	VG	F	VF	XF
1651 AT	—	34.50	75.00	145	295	—
1652 AT	—	17.00	40.25	85.00	180	—
1653 AT	—	17.00	40.25	85.00	180	—
1654 AT	—	17.00	40.25	75.00	150	—
1655 IT	—	14.00	20.00	40.25	90.00	200
1655 AT	—	17.00	30.00	50.00	105	250
1656 AT	—	34.50	85.00	175	355	—
1656 IT/IC	—	17.00	30.00	50.00	105	250
1656 IDV/IC Rare	—	—	—	—	—	—
1656 Lion	—	60.00	115	175	355	—
1657 AT	—	14.00	20.00	30.00	90.00	200
1657 IT/SCH	—	14.00	20.00	40.25	90.00	200
1657 Lion	—	—	—	—	—	—
1658 AT, "18"	—	14.00	20.00	100	205	—
1658	—	17.00	34.50	70.00	180	—
1658 AT	—	14.00	20.00	70.00	120	—
1658 "18"	—	14.00	20.00	70.00	120	—
1658 IT/SCH	—	14.00	20.00	80.00	145	—
1658 TLB/IT	—	17.00	30.00	70.00	120	—
1658 TLB	—	14.00	20.00	70.00	120	—
1659 AT	—	14.00	20.00	70.00	120	—
1659 TLB	—	14.00	20.00	70.00	120	—
1660 GBA Rare	—	—	—	—	—	—
1660 Lion Rare	—	—	—	—	—	—
1663 AT	—	14.00	20.00	70.00	120	—
1664 AT	—	14.00	20.00	70.00	120	—
1667 TLB	—	14.00	20.00	70.00	120	—
1668 TLB	—	14.00	20.00	70.00	120	275

KM# 126 18 GROSZY (Tympf)

Silver **Ruler:** Johann III Sobieski **Obv:** Laureate armored bust right **Rev:** Crowned shield, 18 flanking shield **Note:** For previously listed 18 Groszy, KM#134, see 1/4 Thaler, KM#677, Saxony-German States.

Date	Mintage	Good	VG	F	VF	XF
1677	—	22.50	46.00	105	180	—
1677 SB	—	12.00	20.00	70.00	130	—
1677 MH	—	17.00	30.00	80.00	145	—
1678	—	12.00	20.00	70.00	130	—
1678 SB	—	17.00	30.00	80.00	145	—
1678 MN Rare	—	—	—	—	—	—
1679	—	17.00	30.00	80.00	145	—
1679 TLB	—	17.00	30.00	80.00	155	—
1680	—	30.00	60.00	115	180	—
1684 TLB	—	12.00	20.00	70.00	120	—
1685	—	46.00	70.00	145	180	—
1686	—	60.00	85.00	175	295	—

KM# 32 ORT (18 Groszy - 1/4 Thaler)

Silver **Ruler:** Sigismund III **Obv:** Crowned half-length figure right **Rev:** Crowned shield within fleece collar

Date	Mintage	Good	VG	F	VF	XF
1618 Rare	—	—	—	—	—	—

KM# 37 ORT (18 Groszy - 1/4 Thaler)

Silver **Ruler:** Sigismund III **Rev:** Crowned shield **Note:** Varieties exist.

Date	Mintage	Good	VG	F	VF	XF
1620 IIVE Rare	—	—	—	—	—	—
1620/21	—	—	—	—	—	—
1621 IIVE	—	—	—	—	—	—
1622	—	14.00	25.00	46.00	80.00	—
1623	—	12.00	17.00	30.00	70.00	—
1624	—	12.00	17.00	30.00	70.00	—
1625 Rare	—	—	—	—	—	—
1628 11 Rare	—	—	—	—	—	—
ND	—	—	—	—	—	—

KM# A6 3 GROSCHEN

Silver **Ruler:** Sigismund III **Obv:** Large crowned bust right **Rev:** Value and armorials above inscription, date

Date	Mintage	Good	VG	F	VF	XF
1601 K	—	12.00	25.00	50.00	125	—

KM# 6 3 GROSCHEN

Silver **Ruler:** Sigismund III **Obv:** Crowned bust right **Rev:** Value and armorial above legend, date and mintmaster below **Note:** Varieties exist.

Date	Mintage	Good	VG	F	VF	XF
1601 K	—	13.00	25.00	45.00	90.00	175
1601 FI	—	22.50	30.50	60.00	125	—
1601 P	—	11.00	22.50	40.50	90.00	—
1601 F	—	11.00	22.50	40.50	90.00	—
1601 B	—	11.00	22.50	40.50	90.00	—
1601 L/IF	—	22.50	30.50	60.00	125	—
1601 L Rare	—	—	—	—	—	—
1601 IF Rare	—	—	—	—	—	—
1602 K	—	30.50	70.00	155	300	—
1603 K	—	30.50	70.00	155	300	—
1604 K	—	13.00	25.00	45.00	90.00	—
1605 K	—	13.00	25.00	45.00	90.00	—
1606 K	—	40.50	85.00	160	350	—
1607 K	—	13.00	25.00	45.00	75.00	—
1608 Rare	—	—	—	—	—	—
1614 TKA Rare	—	—	—	—	—	—
ND	—	22.50	30.50	60.00	125	—

KM# 31 3 GROSCHEN

Silver **Ruler:** Sigismund III **Rev:** Value, armorials and date above legend **Note:** Varieties exist.

Date	Mintage	Good	VG	F	VF	XF
1618	—	11.00	22.50	40.50	75.00	—
1619	—	11.00	22.50	40.50	75.00	—
1620	—	11.00	22.50	40.50	75.00	—
1621	—	11.00	22.50	40.50	75.00	—
1622	—	11.00	22.50	40.50	75.00	—
1623	—	11.00	22.50	40.50	75.00	—
1624	—	11.00	22.50	40.50	75.00	—
ND	—	22.50	30.50	60.00	135	—

KM# 87 3 GROSCHEN

Silver **Ruler:** Johann Casimir **Obv:** Bust of Johann Casimir right **Rev:** Crown dividing date above value and legend

Date	Mintage	Good	VG	F	VF	XF
1650 CG Rare	—	—	—	—	—	—
Note: Künker Auction 188, 6-11, XF realized approx. $22,890.						
1657 Rare	—	—	—	—	—	—
1658 Rare	—	—	—	—	—	—

KM# 114 3 GROSCHEN

Silver **Ruler:** Johann Casimir **Obv:** Crowned bust right **Rev:** Value above armorials, date and legend **Note:** Varieties exist.

Date	Mintage	Good	VG	F	VF	XF
1660 Rare	—	—	—	—	—	—
1661 AT Rare	—	—	—	—	—	—
1662 AT	—	60.00	115	220	425	—
1665 AT Rare	—	—	—	—	—	—

KM# 130 3 GROSCHEN

Silver **Ruler:** Johann Casimir **Obv:** Laureate bust of Johann III Sobieski right **Rev:** Value and armorials above legend and date

Date	Mintage	Good	VG	F	VF	XF
1684 C	—	50.00	105	220	425	—
1684 B	—	—	—	—	—	—
1685 B	—	50.00	105	220	425	—

KM# 7.1 6 GROSCHEN

Silver **Ruler:** Sigismund III **Obv:** Crowned bust right **Rev:** Value and armorials above legend and date

Date	Mintage	Good	VG	F	VF	XF
1601 (P)	—	34.00	80.00	150	280	—

KM# 7.2 6 GROSCHEN

Silver **Ruler:** Sigismund III

Date	Mintage	Good	VG	F	VF	XF
1601 (P)-M	—	34.00	80.00	150	280	—

KM# 42 6 GROSCHEN

Silver **Ruler:** Sigismund III **Rev:** Crown above three shields **Note:** Varieties exist.

Date	Mintage	Good	VG	F	VF	XF
1623	—	16.00	32.00	60.00	130	—
1624	—	16.00	32.00	60.00	130	—
1625	—	16.00	32.00	60.00	130	—
1626	—	16.00	32.00	60.00	130	—
1627	—	16.00	32.00	60.00	130	—
ND	—	20.00	34.00	70.00	150	—

KM# 91 6 GROSCHEN

Silver **Ruler:** Johann Casimir **Obv:** Large crowned bust right in linear circle **Rev:** Crown above three shields **Note:** Varieties exist.

Date	Mintage	Good	VG	F	VF	XF
1650	—	48.25	90.00	175	350	—
1656 IT	—	8.00	17.00	38.75	70.00	—
1657 IT	—	8.00	17.00	38.75	70.00	—
1658 IT Rare	—	—	—	—	—	—
1658 TLB	—	36.00	70.00	140	275	—
1659	—	8.00	17.00	38.75	70.00	—
1660	—	8.00	17.00	38.75	70.00	—
1660 GBA	—	8.00	17.00	38.75	70.00	—
1660 TT	—	8.00	17.00	38.75	70.00	—
1660 TLB	—	8.00	17.00	38.75	70.00	—
1660 LT	—	8.00	17.00	38.75	70.00	—
1661 TLB	—	8.00	17.00	38.75	70.00	—
1661 GBA	—	8.00	17.00	38.75	70.00	—
1661 NG	—	8.00	17.00	38.75	70.00	—
1661 AT	—	8.00	17.00	38.75	70.00	—
1661 TT	—	8.00	17.00	38.75	70.00	—
1662 AT	—	8.00	17.00	38.75	70.00	—
1662 ACPT	—	14.00	27.50	55.00	120	—
1662 NG	—	8.00	17.00	38.75	70.00	—
1662 TT	—	8.00	17.00	38.75	70.00	—
1662	—	8.00	17.00	38.75	70.00	—
1662 BGA	—	14.00	27.50	55.00	120	—
1662 GBA	—	8.00	17.00	38.75	70.00	—
1663 AT	—	8.00	17.00	38.75	70.00	—
1663 ACPT	—	14.00	27.50	55.00	120	—
1664 AT	—	8.00	17.00	38.75	70.00	—
1664 ACPT Rare	—	—	—	—	—	—
1664 TLB Rare	—	—	—	—	—	—
1665 AT	—	7.00	17.00	38.75	70.00	—
1666 AT	—	7.00	17.00	38.75	70.00	—
1666 TLB Rare	—	—	—	—	—	—
1667 TLB	—	14.00	27.50	55.00	110	—

KM# 89 6 GROSCHEN

Silver **Ruler:** Johann Casimir **Obv:** Small bust of Johann Casimir right **Rev:** Crown above three shields

Date	Mintage	Good	VG	F	VF	XF
1650	—	—	—	—	—	—

KM# 90 6 GROSCHEN
Silver **Ruler:** Johann Casimir **Obv:** Large bust right **Rev:** Crowned eagle with shield on breast

Date	Mintage	Good	VG	F	VF	XF
1650 CG	—	75.00	160	300	500	—

KM# 121 6 GROSCHEN
Silver **Ruler:** Johann Casimir **Obv:** Crowned bust within pellet circle

Date	Mintage	Good	VG	F	VF	XF
1667 TLB	—	14.00	27.50	65.00	120	—
1667 AT	—	14.00	27.50	65.00	120	—
1668 TLB	—	14.00	27.50	65.00	120	—
ND TLB	—	34.00	60.00	100	200	—
ND AT	—	34.00	60.00	100	200	—

KM# 122 6 GROSCHEN
Silver **Ruler:** Johann III Sobieski **Obv:** Crowned bust right **Rev:** Crown above three shields **Note:** Varieties exist.

Date	Mintage	Good	VG	F	VF	XF
1677	—	8.00	20.00	44.00	85.00	—
1677 SB Rare	—	—	—	—	—	—
1677 TLB Rare	—	—	—	—	—	—
1678	—	8.00	20.00	44.00	85.00	—
1679 TLB	—	8.00	20.00	44.00	85.00	—
1680 TLB/C	—	14.00	27.50	55.00	120	—
1680 K Rare	—	—	—	—	—	—
1680 IT Rare	—	—	—	—	—	—
1681 TLB	—	8.00	20.00	44.00	85.00	—
1681 TLB/C	—	8.00	20.00	44.00	85.00	—
1682 TLB without C	—	8.00	20.00	44.00	85.00	—
1682 C with TLB only	—	20.00	41.50	85.00	170	—

KM# 128 6 GROSCHEN
Silver **Ruler:** Johann III Sobieski **Obv:** Laureate armored bust right

Date	Mintage	Good	VG	F	VF	XF
1682 TLB	—	8.00	20.00	48.25	90.00	—
1683 TLB/C	—	8.00	20.00	48.25	90.00	—
1683 C	—	8.00	20.00	48.25	90.00	—
1684 TLB	—	8.00	20.00	48.25	90.00	—
1684 SVP	—	20.00	36.00	60.00	120	—
1684 SP	—	8.00	20.00	48.25	95.00	—
1684 C	—	20.00	36.00	60.00	120	—
1685 B	—	8.00	20.00	48.25	95.00	—
1686 TLB	—	36.00	70.00	140	350	—
1687 TLB	—	36.00	70.00	140	350	—

KM# 135 6 GROSCHEN
Silver **Ruler:** August II **Obv:** Small crowned bust of August II right **Rev:** Crown above three shields

Date	Mintage	VG	F	VF	XF	Unc
1698EPH Rare	—	—	—	—	—	—

KM# 120 GULDEN (30 Groschen - 1/3 Thaler - Tympf)
Silver **Ruler:** Johann Casimir **Obv:** Crowned monogram **Rev:** Crowned shield, XXX GRO on shield

Date	Mintage	VG	F	VF	XF	Unc
1633 AT Rare, error 63	—	—	—	—	—	—
1661 Rare	—	—	—	—	—	—
1663	—	25.00	50.00	80.00	160	—
1663 AT	—	25.00	50.00	80.00	160	—
1664 AT	—	25.00	50.00	80.00	160	—
1665 AT	—	25.00	50.00	80.00	160	—
1665/1665	—	25.00	50.00	80.00	160	—
1666 AT	—	25.00	50.00	80.00	160	—

KM# 123 GULDEN (30 Groschen - 1/3 Thaler - Tympf)
Silver **Ruler:** Johann Casimir **Obv:** Laureate bust of Michael Korybut right **Rev:** Crowned shield, date divided by crown, 1/3 in shield below

Date	Mintage	VG	F	VF	XF	Unc
1671 MH Rare	—	—	—	—	—	—

KM# 38 1/2 THALER (4 Zlotych - 1/2 Talar)
Silver **Ruler:** Sigismund III **Obv:** Crowned half-length figure right **Rev:** Crowned shield within fleece collar **Rev. Legend:** SAM LIV NE NO SVE GOT VAD Q HRI REX **Note:** Varieties exist.

Date	Mintage	VG	F	VF	XF	Unc
1620 IIVE Rare	—	—	—	—	—	—
1622 IIVE Rare	—	—	—	—	—	—
1628	—	230	350	900	1,950	—
1628 11	—	230	450	1,050	2,100	—
1629 II	—	230	450	1,050	2,100	—
1630	—	230	350	900	1,950	—
1631 II	—	230	350	900	1,950	—
1632 II Rare	—	—	—	—	—	—

KM# 55 1/2 THALER (4 Zlotych - 1/2 Talar)
Silver **Ruler:** Wladislaus IV **Obv:** Crowned bust right **Obv. Legend:** VLADISLS IIII D G REX POL M D L LIT RVS PRVS MAS **Rev:** Crowned arms within fleece collar **Note:** Varieties exist.

Date	Mintage	VG	F	VF	XF	Unc
1633 Rare	—	—	—	—	—	—
1634 Rare	—	—	—	—	—	—
1640 GG Rare	—	—	—	—	—	—
1640 BS Rare	—	—	—	—	—	—
1641 GG Rare	—	—	—	—	—	—
1642 GG Rare	—	—	—	—	—	—
164Z BS Rare	—	—	—	—	—	—
1644 CDC Rare	—	—	—	—	—	—
1645 CDC Rare	—	—	—	—	—	—
1646 CDC Rare	—	—	—	—	—	—
1646 GGT Rare	—	—	—	—	—	—
1647 GP Rare	—	—	—	—	—	—

KM# 70 1/2 THALER (4 Zlotych - 1/2 Talar)
Silver **Ruler:** Wladislaus IV **Obv:** Large laureate bust of Johann Casimir right **Rev:** Crowned oval shield

Date	Mintage	VG	F	VF	XF	Unc
1649 GP Rare	—	—	—	—	—	—
1649 GR Rare	—	—	—	—	—	—
1651 Rare	—	—	—	—	—	—
1652 MW Rare	—	—	—	—	—	—

KM# 71 1/2 THALER (4 Zlotych - 1/2 Talar)
Silver **Ruler:** Wladislaus IV **Obv:** Smaller crowned bust right **Rev:** Crowned shield **Note:** For previously listed 1/2 Thaler, KM#158, see KM#928, Saxony-German States.

Date	Mintage	VG	F	VF	XF	Unc
ND1652 GP Rare	—	—	—	—	—	—

KM# 17 THALER
Silver **Ruler:** Sigismund III **Rev:** Crowned arms in fleece collar **Note:** Dav. #4311.

Date	Mintage	VG	F	VF	XF	Unc
ND Rare	—	—	—	—	—	—
1613 Rare	—	—	—	—	—	—
1614 Rare	—	—	—	—	—	—
1616 Rare	—	—	—	—	—	—

KM# A17 THALER
Silver **Ruler:** Sigismund III **Obv:** Bust of Sigismund III right **Rev:** Crowned arms in ornate frame **Note:** Dav. #A4310.

Date	Mintage	VG	F	VF	XF	Unc
1612 Rare	—	—	—	—	—	—

KM# 18 THALER
Silver **Ruler:** Sigismund III **Note:** Klippe. Dav.#4311A.

Date	Mintage	VG	F	VF	XF	Unc
1613 Rare	—	—	—	—	—	—
1614 Rare	—	—	—	—	—	—
Note: Gorny & Mosch Giessener Münzhandlung Auction 127, 10-03, XF realized approximately $16,375.						
1616 Rare	—	—	—	—	—	—
1617 SA Rare	—	—	—	—	—	—
1617 IIVE Rare	—	—	—	—	—	—
1617 MS Rare	—	—	—	—	—	—
1617 AS Rare	—	—	—	—	—	—

KM# 33.1 THALER
Silver **Ruler:** Sigismund III **Obv:** Crowned half-length figure right **Rev:** Crowned shield above 6-0 dividing date **Note:** Dav. #4313.

Date	Mintage	VG	F	VF	XF	Unc
1618 MS Unique	—	—	—	—	—	—
1620	—	2,250	4,500	8,500	—	—
1620 IIVE	—	2,250	4,500	8,500	—	—
1621 IIVE	—	2,250	4,500	8,500	—	—

KM# 33.2 THALER
Silver **Ruler:** Sigismund III **Rev:** Crowned shield above 3-0 dividing date **Note:** Legend varieties exist.

Date	Mintage	VG	F	VF	XF	Unc
1621 IIVE Rare	—	—	—	—	—	—
1622 IIVE	—	3,500	7,000	12,500	—	—
1623 IIVE	—	3,500	7,000	12,500	—	—

KM# 43 THALER
Silver **Ruler:** Sigismund III **Rev:** Crowned shield with ornamented sides above divided date **Note:** Dav. #4314.

Date	Mintage	VG	F	VF	XF	Unc
1623 IIVE	—	1,750	3,450	6,900	9,600	—
1624 IIVE	—	1,750	3,450	6,900	9,600	—

KM# 44 THALER

Silver **Ruler:** Sigismund III **Note:** Dav. #4315.

Date	Mintage	VG	F	VF	XF	Unc
1625 IIVE	—	1,750	3,450	6,900	9,600	—
1625 Crowned STR Rare	—	—	—	—	—	—
1626 IIVE	—	1,750	3,450	6,900	9,600	—
1626 STR Rare	—	—	—	—	—	—
1627 Crowned STR Rare	—	—	—	—	—	—
1627 IIVE	—	240	550	1,150	3,150	—
1627	—	240	550	1,150	3,150	—
1628	—	—	—	—	—	—
1629	—	—	—	—	—	—

KM# 48.1 THALER

Silver **Ruler:** Sigismund III **Obv:** Similar but with small bull's head shield (of treasurer, Hormolaus Lipezy) in legend at six o'clock **Note:** Dav. #4316.

Date	Mintage	VG	F	VF	XF	Unc
1627 IIVE	—	270	600	1,300	3,500	—
1627 II	—	270	600	1,300	3,500	—
1627	—	270	600	1,300	3,500	—
1628 II	—	270	600	1,300	3,500	—
1629 II	—	270	600	1,300	3,500	—
1629 Crowned STR Rare	—	—	—	—	—	—
1630 II	—	270	600	1,400	4,400	—
1631 II	—	270	600	1,300	3,500	—

KM# 48.5 THALER

Silver **Ruler:** Sigismund III **Obv:** Bust with ornamentation on armor and bull's head shield at six o'clock **Rev:** Without small bull's head shield **Note:** Crown, portrait and legend varieties exist.

Date	Mintage	VG	F	VF	XF	Unc
1630 II	—	270	600	1,300	2,500	—
1630	—	270	600	1,300	2,500	—
1631 II	—	270	600	1,300	2,500	—
1632 II	—	270	600	1,300	2,500	—
16xx II	—	270	600	1,300	2,500	—
1633 II	—	270	600	1,300	2,500	—
ND	—	750	1,750	4,600	11,000	—

KM# 48.2 THALER

Silver **Ruler:** Sigismund III **Rev:** Small bull's head shield below arms

Date	Mintage	VG	F	VF	XF	Unc
1630 II	—	270	600	1,300	2,500	—

KM# 48.3 THALER

Silver **Ruler:** Sigismund III **Obv:** Small bull's head shield **Rev:** Small bull's head shield

Date	Mintage	VG	F	VF	XF	Unc
1630 II	—	270	600	1,300	2,500	—

KM# 48.4 THALER

Silver **Ruler:** Sigismund III **Obv:** Without small bull's head shield **Rev:** Without small bull's head shield

Date	Mintage	VG	F	VF	XF	Unc
1630 II	—	270	600	1,300	2,500	—

KM# 52 THALER

Silver **Ruler:** Sigismund III **Obv:** Bare-headed bust **Note:** Dav. #4322.

Date	Mintage	VG	F	VF	XF	Unc
ND Rare	—	—	—	—	—	—

KM# 54 THALER

Silver **Ruler:** Wladislaus IV **Obv:** Crowned half-figure of Ladislaus IV **Note:** Dav. #4326. Legend and crown varieties exist.

Date	Mintage	VG	F	VF	XF	Unc
1633 II	—	375	750	1,800	3,500	—
1634 II	—	375	750	1,800	3,500	—
1635 II	—	375	750	1,800	3,500	—
1636 II	—	375	750	1,800	3,500	—
1637 II	—	375	750	1,800	3,500	—
1638 II Rare	—	—	—	—	—	—
1639 II Rare	—	—	—	—	—	—
1640 BS	—	575	975	2,300	5,800	—

KM# 58 THALER

Silver **Ruler:** Wladislaus IV **Obv:** Bust right **Rev:** Crowned oval shield within fleece collar, cupid supporters **Note:** Dav. #4327.

Date	Mintage	VG	F	VF	XF	Unc
1635	—	825	1,550	2,800	4,400	—

KM# 59 THALER

Silver **Ruler:** Wladislaus IV **Rev:** Crowned oval shield without cupid supporters **Note:** Dav. #4328.

Date	Mintage	VG	F	VF	XF	Unc
1636 II	—	950	1,700	3,050	4,700	—
1636 IH	—	950	1,700	3,050	4,700	—

KM# 62 THALER

Silver **Ruler:** Wladislaus IV **Obv:** Crowned bust right **Note:** Dav. #4329.

Date	Mintage	VG	F	VF	XF	Unc
ND GGBS	—	—	—	—	—	—
1640 GGBS	—	1,000	2,000	3,500	7,000	—
1641 GGBS	—	1,000	2,000	3,500	7,000	—
164Z GGBS	—	1,000	2,000	3,500	7,000	—
1642 GGBS	—	1,000	2,000	3,500	7,000	—
1643 GGBS	—	1,000	2,000	3,500	7,000	—
1644 GG	—	1,850	3,500	7,500	—	—
1644 CDC-FS	—	1,250	2,750	5,500	9,500	—
1644 DC-BS	—	1,250	2,750	5,500	9,500	—
1644 DC-BL	—	1,250	2,750	5,500	9,500	—
1644 CDC-BL	—	1,250	2,750	5,500	9,500	—
1645 CDC-BS	—	1,250	2,750	5,500	9,500	—
1645 CDC-BS	—	1,250	2,750	5,500	9,500	—
1646 CDC Rare	—	—	—	—	—	—

Note: WAG Auction 41, 3-07, nearly XF realized approx. $10,900

Date	Mintage	VG	F	VF	XF	Unc
1646 GP-BS	—	1,250	2,750	5,500	9,500	—
1647 GP	—	1,250	2,750	5,500	9,500	—

KM# 64 THALER

Silver **Ruler:** Wladislaus IV **Obv:** Smaller crowned bust right in inner circle **Note:** Dav. #4330.

Date	Mintage	VG	F	VF	XF	Unc
1640 GG	—	2,000	4,000	7,500	12,500	—
1641 GG	—	2,000	4,000	7,500	12,500	—
1642 GG	—	2,000	4,000	7,500	12,500	—

KM# 68 THALER

Silver **Ruler:** Wladislaus IV **Rev:** Shield between vertical date **Note:** Dav. #4332.

Date	Mintage	VG	F	VF	XF	Unc
1644 CDC Rare	—	—	—	—	—	—

KM# 67 THALER

Silver **Ruler:** Wladislaus IV **Obv:** Crowned half-length figure, 3/4 facing **Rev:** Crowned shield in fleece collar **Note:** Dav. #4331. Varieties exist.

Date	Mintage	VG	F	VF	XF	Unc
1644 BS Rare	—	—	—	—	—	—
1644 BL Rare	—	—	—	—	—	—
1644 CDC Rare	—	—	—	—	—	—
1645 CDC Rare	—	—	—	—	—	—
1645 BS Rare	—	—	—	—	—	—
1645 BL Rare	—	—	—	—	—	—

KM# 74 THALER

Silver **Ruler:** Johann Casimir **Obv:** Tall crowned half-length bust right **Rev. Legend:** SA • LI • SM • SEV • CZE ... **Note:** Dav. #4335. Varieties exist.

Date	Mintage	VG	F	VF	XF	Unc
1649 GP Rare	—	—	—	—	—	—

Note: Künker Auction 154, 6-09, VF realized approx. $23,595.

Date	Mintage	VG	F	VF	XF	Unc
1650 GP Rare	—	—	—	—	—	—

KM# 76 THALER

Silver **Ruler:** Johann Casimir **Obv:** Large crowned bust right **Rev. Legend:** PM S(A) S (E) CZN ... **Note:** Dav. #4336. Varieties exist.

Date	Mintage	VG	F	VF	XF	Unc
1649 GP	—	750	1,500	3,150	6,600	—
1650 CP	—	750	1,500	3,150	6,600	—

KM# 77 THALER

Silver **Ruler:** Johann Casimir **Rev. Legend:** P • M • S • CZ • NE • N... **Note:** Dav. #4337.

Date	Mintage	VG	F	VF	XF	Unc
1649 GP	—	975	1,750	3,450	6,800	—
1650 CP	—	975	1,750	3,450	6,800	—

KM# 78 THALER

Silver **Ruler:** Johann Casimir **Rev. Legend:** P • M • L • SA(SE) • CZ(E)N ... **Note:** Dav. #4338.

Date	Mintage	VG	F	VF	XF	Unc
1649 GP	—	1,150	1,900	4,350	9,500	—
1650 CP	—	1,150	1,900	4,350	9,500	—

KM# 72 THALER

Silver **Ruler:** Johann Casimir **Obv:** Tall crowned half-length bust of Johann Casimir right with scepter and orb **Rev. Legend:** SA: SE • CZ ... **Note:** Dav. #4333.

Date	Mintage	VG	F	VF	XF	Unc
1649 GP	—	750	1,500	3,150	6,600	—

KM# 73 THALER

Silver **Ruler:** Johann Casimir **Rev. Legend:** SM(O) • SE(V) • CZ(E) (R)... **Note:** Dav. #4334

Date	Mintage	VG	F	VF	XF	Unc
1649 GP Rare	—	—	—	—	—	—

Note: Künker Auction 184, 3-11, VF/XF realized approximately $50,310.

KM# 75 THALER

Silver **Ruler:** Johann Casimir **Rev. Legend:** SM • SE • CZ • NEC ... **Note:** Dav. #A4336.

Date	Mintage	VG	F	VF	XF	Unc
1649 GP	—	1,750	3,250	6,000	—	—

KM# 93 THALER

Silver **Ruler:** Johann Casimir **Rev:** Small arms below shield **Note:** Dav. #4339.

Date	Mintage	VG	F	VF	XF	Unc
1650 GP Rare	—	—	—	—	—	—
1650 CP Rare	—	—	—	—	—	—

KM# 98 THALER

Silver **Ruler:** Johann Casimir **Obv:** Laureate, armored bust of Johann Casimir right **Rev:** Crowned shield **Note:** Dav. #4340.

Date	Mintage	VG	F	VF	XF	Unc
1651 Rare	—	—	—	—	—	—

KM# 99 THALER

Silver **Ruler:** Johann Casimir **Rev:** Crowned oval shield **Note:** Dav. #4341. Varieties exist.

Date	Mintage	VG	F	VF	XF	Unc
1651 Rare	—	—	—	—	—	—
1652 Rare	—	—	—	—	—	—

KM# 101 THALER

Silver **Ruler:** Johann Casimir **Obv:** Small crowned bust right

Date	Mintage	VG	F	VF	XF	Unc
1652 AT Rare	—	—	—	—	—	—

KM# A115 THALER
Silver **Ruler:** Johann Casimir **Rev:** Crowned ornate oval arms **Note:** Dav. #4342.

Date	Mintage	VG	F	VF	XF	Unc
1661 Rare	—	—	—	—	—	—

Note: Künker Auction 46, 2-08, VF realized approx. $14,355.

KM# B115 THALER
Silver **Ruler:** Johann Casimir **Obv:** Crowned ornate arms **Note:** Dav. #4343.

Date	Mintage	VG	F	VF	XF	Unc
1661 Rare	—	—	—	—	—	—

KM# 115 THALER
Silver **Ruler:** Johann Casimir **Obv:** Large crowned bust right **Rev:** Crowned oval shield, ornate border **Note:** Dav. #4344.

Date	Mintage	VG	F	VF	XF	Unc
1661 GBA Rare	—	—	—	—	—	—

KM# 131 THALER
Silver **Ruler:** Johann III Sobieski **Obv:** Laureate bust of Johann III Sobieski right **Rev:** Crowned shield **Note:** Dav. #4345.

Date	Mintage	VG	F	VF	XF	Unc
ND(1684) Rare	—	—	—	—	—	—

KM# 21 1-1/2 THALER
Silver **Ruler:** Sigismund III **Note:** Similar to 1 Thaler, KM#50. Dav. #A4311. Klippe.

Date	Mintage	VG	F	VF	XF	Unc
1614 Rare	—	—	—	—	—	—

KM# 22 2 THALER
Silver **Ruler:** Sigismund III **Obv:** Bust of Sigismund III right **Rev:** Crowned arms in collar of the Golden Fleece **Note:** Dav. #4310.

Date	Mintage	VG	F	VF	XF	Unc
1614 Rare	—	—	—	—	—	—

KM# 29 2 THALER
Silver **Ruler:** Sigismund III **Obv:** Bust with tall collar right **Rev:** Crowned ornate arms dividing date at top **Note:** Dav. #4312.

Date	Mintage	VG	F	VF	XF	Unc
1617 Rare	—	—	—	—	—	—

KM# A30 2 THALER
Silver **Ruler:** Sigismund III **Obv:** Armored bust right **Rev:** Crowned arms **Rev. Legend:** MAGNVS•DUX•LITVA... **Note:** Dav. #A4313.

Date	Mintage	VG	F	VF	XF	Unc
ND Rare	—	—	—	—	—	—

KM# 30 2 THALER
Silver **Ruler:** Sigismund III **Obv:** Large bust right **Rev:** Crowned arms divide II-VI at center **Note:** Dav. #4323.

Date	Mintage	VG	F	VF	XF	Unc
ND Rare	—	—	—	—	—	—

KM# 56 2 THALER
Silver **Ruler:** Wladislaus IV **Note:** Dav. #4325. Similar to 1 Thaler, KM#58.

Date	Mintage	VG	F	VF	XF	Unc
1633 Rare	—	—	—	—	—	—
1634 Rare	—	—	—	—	—	—
1635 Rare	—	—	—	—	—	—
1636 Rare	—	—	—	—	—	—

KM# 65 2 THALER
Silver **Ruler:** Wladislaus IV **Note:** Dav. #A4329. Similar to 1 Thaler, KM#61.

Date	Mintage	VG	F	VF	XF	Unc
1641 Rare	—	—	—	—	—	—
1643 Rare	—	—	—	—	—	—
1647 Rare	—	—	—	—	—	—

TRADE COINAGE

KM# 104 1/2 DUCAT (1/2 Czerwenego Zlotego)
1.7500 g., 0.9860 Gold 0.0555 oz. AGW **Ruler:** Johann Casimir **Obv:** Crowned bust of Johann Casimir right **Rev:** Crowned displayed eagle, date in legend

Date	Mintage	VG	F	VF	XF	Unc
1653 MW	—	750	1,350	2,650	5,300	—
1654 MW	—	750	1,350	2,650	5,300	—
ND IC	—	750	1,350	2,650	5,300	—

KM# 109 1/2 DUCAT (1/2 Czerwenego Zlotego)
1.7500 g., 0.9860 Gold 0.0555 oz. AGW **Ruler:** Johann Casimir **Rev:** Crowned arms, date in legend

Date	Mintage	VG	F	VF	XF	Unc
1657 IT	—	750	1,350	2,650	5,300	—

KM# 112 1/2 DUCAT (1/2 Czerwenego Zlotego)
1.7500 g., 0.9860 Gold 0.0555 oz. AGW **Ruler:** Johann Casimir **Obv:** Head laureate right **Rev:** Eagle **Note:** Reverse legend varieties exist.

Date	Mintage	VG	F	VF	XF	Unc
1660 TLB	—	750	1,350	2,650	5,300	—
1661 TLB	—	750	1,350	2,650	5,300	—
1662 AT	—	750	1,350	2,650	5,300	—
ND MW	—	750	1,350	2,650	5,300	—

KM# 9 DUCAT
3.5000 g., 0.9860 Gold 0.1109 oz. AGW **Ruler:** Sigismund III **Obv:** Large crowned bust right **Rev:** Crowned arms within fleece collar

Date	Mintage	VG	F	VF	XF	Unc
1609	—	1,300	2,550	5,300	8,400	—
1610	—	1,300	2,550	5,300	8,400	—
1611	—	1,300	2,550	5,300	8,400	—
1612	—	1,300	2,550	5,300	8,400	—

KM# 19 DUCAT
3.5000 g., 0.9860 Gold 0.1109 oz. AGW **Ruler:** Sigismund III **Obv:** Smaller bust right

Date	Mintage	VG	F	VF	XF	Unc
1613 IIVE	—	1,300	2,550	5,300	8,400	—
1623 II/VE	—	1,300	2,550	5,300	8,400	—

KM# 47 DUCAT
3.5000 g., 0.9860 Gold 0.1109 oz. AGW **Ruler:** Sigismund III **Obv:** Crowned longer bust right

Date	Mintage	VG	F	VF	XF	Unc
1628 II	—	1,350	2,650	5,800	9,500	—

KM# 49 DUCAT
3.5000 g., 0.9860 Gold 0.1109 oz. AGW **Ruler:** Sigismund III **Rev:** Five shields above date in inner circle

Date	Mintage	VG	F	VF	XF	Unc
1630	—	1,350	2,650	5,800	9,500	—

KM# 50 DUCAT
3.5000 g., 0.9860 Gold 0.1109 oz. AGW **Ruler:** Sigismund III **Rev:** Four-line inscription in tablet

Date	Mintage	VG	F	VF	XF	Unc
ND	—	1,350	2,650	5,800	9,500	—

KM# 61 DUCAT
3.5000 g., 0.9860 Gold 0.1109 oz. AGW **Ruler:** Wladislaus IV **Obv:** Crowned bust right in inner circle **Rev:** Crowned arms in inner circle, crown divides date at top

Date	Mintage	VG	F	VF	XF	Unc
1639 MR-VM	—	1,150	2,400	4,750	8,000	—
1640 GG-BS	—	1,150	2,400	4,750	8,000	—
1641 GG-BS	—	1,150	2,400	4,750	8,000	—
1642 GG-BS	—	1,150	2,400	4,750	8,000	—
1644 C-DC	—	1,150	2,400	4,750	8,000	—

KM# 69 DUCAT
3.5000 g., 0.9860 Gold 0.1109 oz. AGW **Ruler:** Wladislaus IV **Obv:** Heavier crowned bust right **Rev:** Crowned arms in Order collar in inner circle

Date	Mintage	VG	F	VF	XF	Unc
1647 GP	—	1,150	2,400	4,750	8,000	—
ND	—	1,150	2,400	4,750	8,000	—

KM# 79 DUCAT
3.5000 g., 0.9860 Gold 0.1109 oz. AGW **Ruler:** Johann Casimir **Obv:** Laureate bust right

Date	Mintage	VG	F	VF	XF	Unc
1649 GP	—	1,050	2,100	4,200	6,800	—

KM# 80 DUCAT
3.5000 g., 0.9860 Gold 0.1109 oz. AGW **Ruler:** Johann Casimir **Obv:** Johann standing in inner circle **Note:** Varieties exist, including an obverse legend error.

Date	Mintage	VG	F	VF	XF	Unc
1649 GP	—	2,850	5,800	11,500	19,000	—

KM# 81 DUCAT
3.5000 g., 0.9860 Gold 0.1109 oz. AGW **Ruler:** Johann Casimir **Obv:** Crowned bust right in inner circle

Date	Mintage	VG	F	VF	XF	Unc
1649 GP	—	1,050	2,100	4,200	6,800	—

KM# 95 DUCAT
3.5000 g., 0.9860 Gold 0.1109 oz. AGW **Ruler:** Johann Casimir **Obv:** Laureate bust right **Rev:** Crowned displayed eagle, date divided at top **Note:** Legend varieties exist.

Date	Mintage	VG	F	VF	XF	Unc
1650	—	1,050	2,100	4,200	6,800	—
1651 AT	—	1,050	2,100	4,200	6,800	—
1651 CG	—	1,050	2,100	4,200	6,800	—
1651 MW	—	1,050	2,100	4,200	6,800	—

KM# 102 DUCAT
3.5000 g., 0.9860 Gold 0.1109 oz. AGW **Ruler:** Johann Casimir **Obv:** Crowned bust right in inner circle, finer style **Rev:** Crowned arms in inner circle, date in legend **Note:** Legend varieties exist.

Date	Mintage	VG	F	VF	XF	Unc
1652 AT	—	1,050	2,100	4,200	6,800	—
1652 MW	—	1,050	2,100	4,200	6,800	—
1653 AT	—	1,050	2,100	4,200	6,800	—
1653 MW	—	1,050	2,100	4,200	6,800	—
1654 AT	—	1,050	2,100	4,200	6,800	—
1654 MW	—	1,050	2,100	4,200	6,800	—
1655 MW	—	1,050	2,100	4,200	6,800	—
1655 IT/SCH	—	1,050	2,100	4,200	6,800	—

KM# 108 DUCAT
3.5000 g., 0.9860 Gold 0.1109 oz. AGW **Ruler:** Johann Casimir **Obv:** Coarse crowned bust right

Date	Mintage	VG	F	VF	XF	Unc
1655 SCH	—	1,050	2,100	4,200	6,800	—
1657 IT	—	1,050	2,100	4,200	6,800	—
1658 IT/SCH	—	1,050	2,100	4,200	6,800	—
1658 TLB	—	1,050	2,100	4,200	6,800	—
1659 TLB	—	1,050	2,100	4,200	6,800	—

KM# 107 DUCAT
3.5000 g., 0.9860 Gold 0.1109 oz. AGW **Ruler:** Johann Casimir **Obv:** Crowned bust right, without inner circle **Rev:** Crowned shield, without inner circle

Date	Mintage	VG	F	VF	XF	Unc
1656 IT/IC	—	1,050	2,100	4,200	6,800	—

KM# 113 DUCAT
3.5000 g., 0.9860 Gold 0.1109 oz. AGW **Ruler:** Johann Casimir **Obv:** Older crowned bust right **Note:** Legend varieties exist.

Date	Mintage	VG	F	VF	XF	Unc
1660 TLB	—	1,050	2,100	4,200	6,800	—
1660 NG	—	1,050	2,100	4,200	6,800	—
1661 TT	—	1,050	2,100	4,200	6,800	—
1661 GBA	—	1,050	2,100	4,200	6,800	—
1662 AT	—	1,050	2,100	4,200	6,800	—
1668	—	1,050	2,100	4,200	6,800	—

KM# 124 DUCAT
3.5000 g., 0.9860 Gold 0.1109 oz. AGW **Ruler:** Michael Korybut **Obv:** Laureate bust right in inner circle **Rev:** Crowned arms within scroll

Date	Mintage	VG	F	VF	XF	Unc
1671 MH	—	1,650	3,250	5,800	10,500	—

KM# 127 DUCAT
3.5000 g., 0.9860 Gold 0.1109 oz. AGW **Ruler:** Johann III Sobieski **Obv:** Laureate bust right **Rev:** Crowned arms in inner circle, date in legend **Note:** Legend varieties exist.

Date	Mintage	VG	F	VF	XF	Unc
1681	—	1,300	2,650	4,800	9,000	—
1682	—	1,050	2,100	4,500	8,400	—
1685 BIC	—	1,050	2,100	4,500	8,400	—

KM# 129 DUCAT
3.5000 g., 0.9860 Gold 0.1109 oz. AGW **Ruler:** Johann III Sobieski **Rev:** Crowned shield, without inner circle

Date	Mintage	VG	F	VF	XF	Unc
1683 TLB	—	1,050	2,100	4,500	8,400	—

KM# A129 DUCAT

3.5000 g., 0.9860 Gold 0.1109 oz. AGW **Ruler:** August II **Subject:** Coronation of August II **Obv. Inscription:** PRO REGNO, ID-DG / AUGUSTUS II / CORON IN REG / POLON & MDL / I SEPT / 1697

Date	Mintage	VG	F	VF	XF	Unc
1697 Rare	—	—	—	—	—	—

KM# 10 2 DUCAT

7.0000 g., 0.9860 Gold 0.2219 oz. AGW **Ruler:** Sigismund III **Obv:** Crowned bust right in inner circle **Rev:** Crowned arms in Order collar in inner circle, date in legend

Date	Mintage	VG	F	VF	XF	Unc
1609 Rare	—	—	—	—	—	—
1610	—	6,300	12,500	20,000	32,500	—

KM# 96 2 DUCAT

7.0000 g., 0.9860 Gold 0.2219 oz. AGW **Ruler:** Johann Casimir **Obv:** Large laureate bust of Johann Casimir right **Note:** Legend varieties exist.

Date	Mintage	VG	F	VF	XF	Unc
1650	—	80.00	80.00	80.00	80.00	—
1651 MW	—	80.00	80.00	80.00	80.00	—
1652 AT	—	80.00	80.00	80.00	80.00	—
1652 MW	—	80.00	80.00	80.00	80.00	—
1653 MW	—	80.00	80.00	80.00	80.00	—
1654	—	80.00	80.00	80.00	80.00	—
1655 IT	—	80.00	80.00	80.00	80.00	—

KM# 106 2 DUCAT

7.0000 g., 0.9860 Gold 0.2219 oz. AGW **Ruler:** Johann Casimir **Obv:** Crowned bust of Johann Casimir right in inner circle **Rev:** Crowned arms in Order collar in inner circle, date in legend **Note:** Legend varieties exist.

Date	Mintage	VG	F	VF	XF	Unc
1654	—	2,000	3,900	8,400	17,000	—
1654 AT	—	2,000	3,900	8,400	17,000	—
1654 MW	—	2,200	4,200	9,000	18,000	—
1655 AT	—	2,000	3,900	8,400	17,000	—
1655 IT/SCH	—	2,000	3,900	8,400	17,000	—
1656 IT/IC	—	2,000	3,900	8,400	17,000	—
1657 IT/SCH Rare	—	—	—	—	—	—
1657 IT/IC Rare	—	—	—	—	—	—
1658 AT	—	2,000	3,400	6,800	14,000	—
1658 TLB	—	2,000	3,400	6,800	14,000	—
1658 IT/SCH	—	2,000	3,400	6,800	14,000	—

KM# 111.2 2 DUCAT

7.0000 g., 0.9860 Gold 0.2219 oz. AGW **Ruler:** Johann Casimir **Rev:** Different arms **Note:** Legend varieties and inner circle varieties (dotted, plain) exist.

Date	Mintage	VG	F	VF	XF	Unc
1659 TLB	—	2,500	4,800	9,800	19,500	—

KM# 111.1 2 DUCAT

7.0000 g., 0.9860 Gold 0.2219 oz. AGW **Ruler:** Johann Casimir **Rev:** Without Order collar

Date	Mintage	VG	F	VF	XF	Unc
1659 TLB	—	1,800	3,500	7,600	15,000	—
1659 AT	—	1,800	3,500	7,600	15,000	—
1660 TLB	—	1,800	3,050	5,000	10,000	—
1660 TT	—	1,800	3,050	5,000	10,000	—
1660 GBA	—	2,000	3,800	7,600	15,000	—
1661 TLB	—	1,800	3,050	7,600	15,000	—
1661 GBA	—	1,800	3,050	7,600	15,000	—
1661 NG	—	1,800	3,050	7,600	15,000	—
1661 AT	—	2,000	3,800	7,600	15,000	—

KM# 116 2 DUCAT

7.0000 g., 0.9860 Gold 0.2219 oz. AGW **Ruler:** Johann Casimir **Obv:** Laureate bust of Johann Casimir right **Rev:** Crowned eagle displayed with four-fold arms on breast in inner circle, date in legend **Rev. Legend:** ARCUS FORTIUM...

Date	Mintage	VG	F	VF	XF	Unc
1661 NG	—	2,250	4,300	8,800	17,500	—
1662 NG	—	2,250	4,300	8,800	17,500	—

KM# 117 2 DUCAT

7.0000 g., 0.9860 Gold 0.2219 oz. AGW **Ruler:** Johann Casimir **Rev:** Without inner circle, date at sides of eagle **Rev. Legend:** NON EST FORTIS...

Date	Mintage	VG	F	VF	XF	Unc
1661 NG	—	2,250	4,300	8,800	17,500	—

KM# 119 2 DUCAT

7.0000 g., 0.9860 Gold 0.2219 oz. AGW **Ruler:** Johann Casimir **Obv:** Crowned bust of Johann Casimir right **Rev:** Crowned arms in order collar **Note:** Legend varieties exist.

Date	Mintage	VG	F	VF	XF	Unc
1662 NG	—	3,750	6,300	12,500	25,000	—
1662 AT	—	3,750	6,300	12,500	25,000	—
1663 AT	—	3,750	6,300	12,500	25,000	—
1664 AT	—	3,750	6,300	12,500	25,000	—
1666 AT	—	3,750	6,600	14,500	29,500	—
1667 TLB Rare	—	—	—	—	—	—

KM# 125 2 DUCAT

7.0000 g., 0.9860 Gold 0.2219 oz. AGW **Ruler:** Michael Korybut **Obv:** Bust of Michael Korybut right **Rev:** Crowned arms

Date	Mintage	VG	F	VF	XF	Unc
1671 MH Rare	—	—	—	—	—	—

KM# 132 2 DUCAT

7.0000 g., 0.9860 Gold 0.2219 oz. AGW **Ruler:** Michael Korybut **Obv:** Crowned bust of Johann Sobieski right **Rev:** Crowned arms divides date

Date	Mintage	VG	F	VF	XF	Unc
1681 TB	—	6,300	10,500	17,500	29,500	—
1683	—	6,300	10,500	17,500	29,500	—
1685 B	—	6,300	10,500	17,500	29,500	—

KM# 133 2 DUCAT

7.0000 g., 0.9860 Gold 0.2219 oz. AGW **Ruler:** Johann III Sobieski **Obv:** Laureate head of Johann Sobieski right in inner circle

Date	Mintage	VG	F	VF	XF	Unc
ND	—	6,300	10,500	17,500	29,500	—

KM# 14 3 DUCAT

10.5000 g., 0.9860 Gold 0.3328 oz. AGW **Ruler:** Sigismund III **Obv:** Crowned bust right in inner circle **Rev:** Crowned arms in Order collar in inner circle, date in legend

Date	Mintage	VG	F	VF	XF	Unc
1612	—	5,300	9,500	17,000	29,500	—

KM# 15 4 DUCAT

14.0000 g., 0.9860 Gold 0.4438 oz. AGW **Ruler:** Sigismund III **Obv:** Crowned bust right in inner circle **Rev:** Crowned arms in Order collar in inner circle, date in legend

Date	Mintage	VG	F	VF	XF	Unc
1611	—	8,400	14,500	25,000	40,500	—
1612	—	8,400	14,500	25,000	40,500	—

KM# A97 4 DUCAT

14.0000 g., 0.9860 Gold 0.4438 oz. AGW **Ruler:** Johann Casimir

Date	Mintage	VG	F	VF	XF	Unc
1650 Rare	—	—	—	—	—	—

KM# A126 4 DUCAT

14.0000 g., 0.9860 Gold 0.4438 oz. AGW **Ruler:** Johann III Sobieski **Subject:** January 3 Commemorative

Date	Mintage	VG	F	VF	XF	Unc
1677 Rare	—	—	—	—	—	—

KM# 12 5 DUCAT

17.5000 g., 0.9860 Gold 0.5547 oz. AGW **Ruler:** Sigismund III **Subject:** January 3 Commemorative

Date	Mintage	VG	F	VF	XF	Unc
1611 Rare	—	—	—	—	—	—

Note: Künker Auction 191, 6-11, XF-Unc realized approximately $100,605.

Date	Mintage	VG	F	VF	XF	Unc
1612 Rare	—	—	—	—	—	—
1613 Rare	—	—	—	—	—	—
1614 Rare	—	—	—	—	—	—

KM# 26 5 DUCAT

17.5000 g., 0.9860 Gold 0.5547 oz. AGW **Ruler:** Sigismund III

Date	Mintage	VG	F	VF	XF	Unc
1616 Rare	—	—	—	—	—	—

KM# 45 5 DUCAT

17.5000 g., 0.9860 Gold 0.5547 oz. AGW **Ruler:** Sigismund III **Obv:** Crowned bust right with sword and orb in inner circle **Rev:** Crowned arms divides date in Order collar and inner circle

Date	Mintage	VG	F	VF	XF	Unc
1623 Rare	—	—	—	—	—	—
ND Rare	—	—	—	—	—	—

KM# 57 5 DUCAT

17.5000 g., 0.9860 Gold 0.5547 oz. AGW **Ruler:** Wladislaus IV **Obv:** Bust right **Rev:** Crowned arms in order chain **Note:** Fr. #85.

Date	Mintage	VG	F	VF	XF	Unc
1633 Rare	—	—	—	—	—	—
1642 GG Rare	—	—	—	—	—	—
1644 CDC Rare	—	—	—	—	—	—
1645 CDC Rare	—	—	—	—	—	—
1646 CDC Rare	—	—	—	—	—	—
1647 GP Rare	—	—	—	—	—	—

KM# 13 10 DUCAT

35.0000 g., 0.9860 Gold 1.1095 oz. AGW **Ruler:** Sigismund III **Obv:** Crowned bust right in inner circle **Rev:** Crowned arms in inner circle, date in legend

Date	Mintage	VG	F	VF	XF	Unc
1611 Rare	—	—	—	—	—	—
1612 Rare	—	—	—	—	—	—

KM# 27 10 DUCAT

35.0000 g., 0.9860 Gold 1.1095 oz. AGW **Ruler:** Sigismund III

Date	Mintage	VG	F	VF	XF	Unc
1616 Rare	—	—	—	—	—	—
1617 Rare	—	—	—	—	—	—
1617 SA Rare	—	—	—	—	—	—
1618 SA Rare	—	—	—	—	—	—
1620 SA Rare	—	—	—	—	—	—
1622 Rare	—	—	—	—	—	—

KM# 35 10 DUCAT

35.0000 g., 0.9860 Gold 1.1095 oz. AGW **Ruler:** Sigismund III **Obv:** Bust of sigismund right without inner circle **Note:** Varieties exist.

Date	Mintage	VG	F	VF	XF	Unc
ND Rare	—	—	—	—	—	—

KM# 60 10 DUCAT

35.0000 g., 0.9860 Gold 1.1095 oz. AGW **Ruler:** Wladislaus IV

Date	Mintage	VG	F	VF	XF	Unc
1636 II Rare	—	—	—	—	—	—

KM# 103 10 DUCAT
35.0000 g., 0.9860 Gold 1.1095 oz. AGW **Ruler:** Johann Casimir **Obv:** Laureate bust of Casimir inside outer laurel border **Rev:** Crowned oval arms in ornamental frame, half Order collar below outside laurel border

Date	Mintage	VG	F	VF	XF	Unc
1652 Rare	—	—	—	—	—	—

KM# 118 10 DUCAT
35.0000 g., 0.9860 Gold 1.1095 oz. AGW **Ruler:** Johann Casimir **Obv:** Crowned bust of Johann Casimir in Order collar **Rev:** Crowned oval arms in ornamental frame, crown divides date

Date	Mintage	VG	F	VF	XF	Unc
1661 TT Rare	—	—	—	—	—	—

KM# A42 20 DUCAT
70.0000 g., 0.9860 Gold 2.2190 oz. AGW **Ruler:** Sigismund III

Date	Mintage	VG	F	VF	XF	Unc
1614 Rare	—	—	—	—	—	—
1617 AS Rare	—	—	—	—	—	—
1621 II VE Rare	—	—	—	—	—	—
1621 SA Rare	—	—	—	—	—	—
1622 DS Rare	—	—	—	—	—	—

KM# A43 30 DUCAT
105.0000 g., 0.9860 Gold 3.3284 oz. AGW **Ruler:** Sigismund III

Date	Mintage	VG	F	VF	XF	Unc
1621 II VE Rare	—	—	—	—	—	—
1621 SA Rare	—	—	—	—	—	—

KM# B43 40 DUCAT
140.0000 g., 0.9860 Gold 4.4379 oz. AGW, 68.5 mm. **Ruler:** Sigismund III **Note:** Illustration reduced.

Date	Mintage	VG	F	VF	XF	Unc
1621 II VE Rare	—	—	—	—	—	—
1621 SA Rare	—	—	—	—	—	—

KM# C43 50 DUCAT
175.0000 g., 0.9860 Gold 5.5474 oz. AGW **Ruler:** Sigismund III

Date	Mintage	VG	F	VF	XF	Unc
1621 II AE Rare	—	—	—	—	—	—
1621 SA Rare	—	—	—	—	—	—
1621 Rare	—	—	—	—	—	—

KM# D43 60 DUCAT
210.0000 g., 0.9860 Gold 6.6569 oz. AGW **Ruler:** Sigismund III

Date	Mintage	VG	F	VF	XF	Unc
1621 II AE Rare	—	—	—	—	—	—
1621 SA Rare	—	—	—	—	—	—

KM# E43 70 DUCAT
245.0000 g., 0.9860 Gold 7.7663 oz. AGW **Ruler:** Sigismund III

Date	Mintage	VG	F	VF	XF	Unc
1621 II AE Rare	—	—	—	—	—	—
1621 SA Rare	—	—	—	—	—	—

KM# F43 80 DUCAT
280.0000 g., 0.9860 Gold 8.8758 oz. AGW **Ruler:** Sigismund III

Date	Mintage	VG	F	VF	XF	Unc
1621 II AE Rare	—	—	—	—	—	—
1621 SA Rare	—	—	—	—	—	—

KM# G43 90 DUCAT
315.0000 g., 0.9860 Gold 9.9853 oz. AGW **Ruler:** Sigismund III

Date	Mintage	VG	F	VF	XF	Unc
1621 II VE Rare	—	—	—	—	—	—
1621 SA Rare	—	—	—	—	—	—

KM# H43 100 DUCAT
350.0000 g., 0.9860 Gold 11.094 oz. AGW **Ruler:** Sigismund III

Date	Mintage	VG	F	VF	XF	Unc
1621 II VE Rare	—	—	—	—	—	—
1621 SA Rare	—	—	—	—	—	—

PATTERNS

Including off metal strikes

KM#	Date	Mintage	Identification	Mkt Val
Pn1	1601	—	3 Groschen. Klippe.	—
Pn2	1609	—	2 Ducaton.	—
Pn3	1610	—	2 Ducaton.	—
Pn4	1613	—	Thaler. Klippe.	—
Pn5	1614	—	Thaler. Weight of 2 Thaler.	—
Pn6	1614	—	Thaler. Klippe.	—
Pn7	1614	—	Thaler. Gold.	—
Pn8	1616	—	Thaler. Klippe.	—
Pn9	1617	—	2 Thaler. Gold.	—
Pn10	1620	—	Thaler. Gold.	—
Pn11	1621	—	Orte. Klippe.	—
Pn12	1621	—	Thaler. Gold.	—
Pn13	1622	—	Schilling. Gold.	—
Pn14	1622	—	Schilling. Klippe.	—
Pn15	1622	—	Thaler. Gold.	—
Pn16	1624	—	Thaler. Gold.	—
Pn17	1628	—	Thaler. Gold. Gedenk.	—
Pn18	1629	—	Thaler. Gold. Gedenk.	—
Pn19	1633	—	Thaler. Weight of 2 Thaler.	—
Pn20	1635	—	3 Groschen.	—
Pn21	1635	—	6 Groschen.	—
Pn22	1635	—	Ort.	—
Pn23	1642	—	1/2 Thaler. Gold.	—
Pn24	1643	—	Thaler. Weight of 2 Thaler.	—
Pn25	1645	—	1/2 Thaler. Gold.	—
Pn26	1647	—	1/2 Thaler. Gold.	—
Pn27	1647	—	Thaler. Weight of 2 Thaler.	—
Pn28	1649	—	1/2 Thaler. Gold.	—
Pn29	1651	—	Thaler. Gold.	—
Pn30	ND	—	1/2 Thaler. Gold.	—
Pn31	1652	—	1/2 Thaler. Gold.	—
Pn32	1652 AT	—	Thaler. Gold.	—
Pn33	1661 TT	—	Thaler. Gold. Weight of 5 Dukat.	—
Pn34	1661 TT	—	Thaler. Gold. Weight of 10 Dukat.	—
Pn35	1668	—	Dukat. Silver. Fr. 20, Casimer	—

BROMBERG

North of Poznan by about 67 mi., Bromberg originated as a commercial center for the Teutonic Knights. It was under Prussian rule from 1772-1919 and thrived during the reign of Frederik the Great.

ORDER

STANDARD COINAGE

KM# 1 THALER
Silver **Obv:** DEVS PROVIDEBIT above crown, crossed sword and scepter, orb below **Rev:** Crowned arms divide date **Rev. Legend:** SAM • LIV • NE • SVE-GOT • VAD • Q • HR • REX **Note:** Dav. #4346.

Date	Mintage	VG	F	VF	XF	Unc
1632	—	1,500	2,850	5,300	8,700	—

KM# 2 THALER
Silver **Obv:** Laureate bust right **Obv. Legend:** IOAN CASIM D G POL & SUEC REX M D L RUS PR. **Rev:** Crowned arms **Rev. Legend:** MON ARGENT CIVIT BIDGOSTIENS **Note:** Dav. #4347.

Date	Mintage	VG	F	VF	XF	Unc
1650 Rare	—	—	—	—	—	—

DANZIG

Danzig is an important seaport on the northern coast of Poland with access to the Baltic Sea. It has at different times belonged to the Teutonic Knights, Pomerania, Russia, and Prussia. It was part of the Polish Kingdom from 1587-1772.

Danzig (Gdansk) was a free city from 1919 to 1939 during which most of its modern coinage was made.

MONETARY SYSTEM

Until 1923
100 Pfennig = 1 Mark

Commencing 1923
100 Pfennig = 1 Gulden

KINGDOM

STANDARD COINAGE

KM# 10 TERNAR (3 Denarii - 1 Pfennig)
Silver **Obv:** Oval arms divide date, value above **Rev:** Prussian eagle

Date	Mintage	VG	F	VF	XF	Unc
1613	—	15.00	30.00	60.00	—	—
1616 SA	—	22.50	55.00	120	—	—

KM# 57 SZELAG (12 Danarii)
Silver **Obv:** ICR monogram divides date in inner circle **Rev:** Oval arms in cartouche in inner circle, date in legend

Date	Mintage	VG	F	VF	XF	Unc
1657	—	40.00	80.00	140	—	—

KM# 58 SZELAG (12 Danarii)
Silver **Obv:** Crowned ICR monogram

Date	Mintage	VG	F	VF	XF	Unc
1657	—	18.00	36.00	70.00	—	—
1658	—	18.00	36.00	70.00	—	—

KM# 70 SZELAG (12 Danarii)
Silver **Obv:** Crowned MR monogram

Date	Mintage	VG	F	VF	XF	Unc
1670	—	25.00	70.00	145	—	—

KM# 77 SZELAG (12 Danarii)
Silver **Obv:** Crowned I3R monogram

Date	Mintage	VG	F	VF	XF	Unc
1688	128,000	18.00	36.00	70.00	—	—

KM# 11 GROSZ
Silver **Obv:** Crowned bust of Sigismund III right **Rev:** Oval arms in inner circle, date in legend **Note:** Varieties exist.

Date	Mintage	VG	F	VF	XF	Unc
1623 SB	—	16.00	31.25	55.00	—	—
1623	—	31.25	65.00	125	—	—
1624	—	16.00	31.25	55.00	—	—
1625	—	16.00	31.25	55.00	—	—
1626	—	16.00	31.25	55.00	—	—
1627	—	16.00	31.25	55.00	—	—

KM# 45 2 GROSZE
Silver **Subject:** Johann Casimir **Note:** Varieties exist.

Date	Mintage	VG	F	VF	XF	Unc
1651 GR	—	22.50	43.75	80.00	150	—
1652 GR	—	31.25	95.00	190	450	—
1653 GR Rare	—	—	—	—	—	—

KM# 6 ORT (1/4 Thaler - 10 Groszy)
Silver **Ruler:** Sigismund III **Obv:** Sigismund III in ruff collar

Date	Mintage	VG	F	VF	XF	Unc
1608 Rare	—	—	—	—	—	—
1609	—	27.50	55.00	110	180	—
1610	—	27.50	65.00	180	270	—
1611	—	65.00	125	250	450	—
1612	—	65.00	125	250	450	—
1613	—	27.50	55.00	110	180	—
1614	—	27.50	55.00	110	180	—
1615 SA	—	18.00	45.00	110	180	—
1616 SA	—	18.00	45.00	110	180	—

KM# 14 ORT (1/4 Thaler - 10 Groszy)
Silver **Obv:** Sigismund III without ruff collar

Date	Mintage	VG	F	VF	XF	Unc
1617 SA	—	16.00	37.50	70.00	115	—
1618 SA/SB	—	16.00	37.50	70.00	115	—
1618 SB	—	16.00	37.50	70.00	115	—
1619 SA/SB	—	16.00	37.50	70.00	115	—
1619 SB/SA	—	16.00	37.50	70.00	115	—
1620 SA	—	16.00	37.50	70.00	115	—
1621 SB/SA	—	19.00	40.75	75.00	125	—

KM# 15.1 ORT (1/4 Thaler - 10 Groszy)
Silver **Obv:** Sigismund III in ruff collar divides 1-6 **Rev:** Date repeated in legend

Date	Mintage	VG	F	VF	XF	Unc
1623	—	27.50	55.00	115	190	—

KM# 15.2 ORT (1/4 Thaler - 10 Groszy)
Silver, 29 mm. **Obv:** Sigismund III in ruff collar divides 1-6

Date	Mintage	VG	F	VF	XF	Unc
1623	—	16.00	35.00	70.00	105	—
1623 (SB) Rare	—	—	—	—	—	—
1623 SA Rare	—	—	—	—	—	—
1624/35	—	16.00	35.00	70.00	105	—
1624 SA	—	13.00	35.00	70.00	105	—
1625 SA	—	13.00	35.00	70.00	105	—
1626/55A	—	19.00	37.50	75.00	125	—
1626 SA	—	13.00	35.00	70.00	105	—

KM# 46 ORT (1/4 Thaler - 10 Groszy)
Silver **Subject:** Johann Casimir

Date	Mintage	VG	F	VF	XF	Unc
1650 GR Rare	—	—	—	—	—	—
1651 GR	—	50.00	100	225	600	—

KM# 54 ORT (1/4 Thaler - 10 Groszy)
Silver **Obv:** Inner circles added **Rev:** Inner circles added

Date	Mintage	VG	F	VF	XF	Unc
1652 GR	—	150	250	625	1,800	—
1654 GR Rare	—	—	—	—	—	—
1655 GR	—	100	200	375	900	—
1656 GR	—	100	200	375	900	—
1657 DL	—	50.00	90.00	190	500	—
1658 DL	—	50.00	90.00	190	500	—
1659 DL	—	50.00	90.00	190	600	—
1660 DL	—	50.00	90.00	190	600	—
1661 DL	—	50.00	90.00	190	500	—
1662 DL	—	50.00	90.00	190	500	—
1663 DL	—	50.00	90.00	190	500	—
1664 DL	—	50.00	90.00	190	500	—
1666 DL	—	100	200	500	1,600	—
1667 DL Rare	—	—	—	—	—	—

KM# 26.1 1/2 THALER
Silver **Subject:** Wladislaus IV

Date	Mintage	VG	F	VF	XF	Unc
1639 GR	—	1,250	2,500	—	—	—
1640 GR	—	1,250	2,500	—	—	—
1641 GR	—	1,250	2,500	—	—	—
1646 GR	—	1,250	2,500	—	—	—

KM# 26.2 1/2 THALER
Silver **Obv:** Smaller bust **Obv. Legend:** ...PRUS

Date	Mintage	VG	F	VF	XF	Unc
1640 GR Rare	—	—	—	—	—	—
1641 GK Rare	—	—	—	—	—	—

KM# 39 1/2 THALER
Silver **Obv:** Crowned bust of Johann Casimir right in inner circle

Date	Mintage	VG	F	VF	XF	Unc
1649 GR	—	2,750	4,750	—	—	—
Note: Künker Auction 165, 8-10, VF realized approx. $12,930						
1650 GR	—	2,250	4,500	7,500	—	—

KM# 48 1/2 THALER
Silver **Note:** Octagonial klippe.

Date	Mintage	VG	F	VF	XF	Unc
1650 GR Rare	—	—	—	—	—	—

KM# 22 THALER
Silver **Rev:** Date divided in legend at top **Note:** Dav. #4350.

Date	Mintage	VG	F	VF	XF	Unc
1636 II	—	2,200	4,500	7,500	—	—
1637 II/CS	—	2,200	4,500	7,500	—	—

KM# 21 THALER
Silver **Subject:** Wladislaus IV **Note:** Dav. #4351.

Date	Mintage	VG	F	VF	XF	Unc
1636 II	—	1,750	3,500	6,500	—	—

KM# 23 THALER
Silver **Rev:** Date divided below shield **Note:** Dav. #4352.

Date	Mintage	VG	F	VF	XF	Unc
1638 II	—	2,000	4,000	7,000	—	—
Note: WAG Auction 41, 3-07, VF-XF realized approx. $21,140						

KM# 24 THALER
Silver **Obv:** Crowned bust of Wladislaus IV right in inner circle **Rev:** Date in cartouche below arms **Note:** Dav. #4353.

Date	Mintage	VG	F	VF	XF	Unc
1638 II	—	750	1,600	3,500	—	—
1639 II	—	650	1,250	2,750	6,750	—
1639 GR	—	600	1,200	2,500	6,500	—
1640 GR	—	700	1,500	3,000	—	—

KM# 27 THALER

Silver **Note:** Dav. #4356. Varieties exist.

Date	Mintage	VG	F	VF	XF	Unc
1640 GR	—	250	625	1,450	4,000	—
1641 GR	—	200	500	1,000	3,500	—
1642 GR	—	200	500	1,000	3,500	—
1643 GR	—	700	1,250	2,400	6,500	—
1644 GR	—	700	1,250	2,400	6,500	—
1645 GR	—	900	2,250	4,150	9,600	—
1646 GR	—	800	1,650	2,750	7,700	—
1647 GR Rare	—	—	—	—	—	—
1648 GR	—	300	625	1,750	4,250	—

KM# 38 THALER

Silver **Rev:** Cherubs above city view of Danzig, date **Note:** Dav. #4357.

Date	Mintage	VG	F	VF	XF	Unc
1643 GR Rare	—	—	—	—	—	—

KM# 40 THALER

Silver **Subject:** Johann Casimir **Note:** Dav. #4358. Varieties exist.

Date	Mintage	VG	F	VF	XF	Unc
1649 GR	—	350	850	2,250	6,500	—

KM# 49 THALER

Silver **Rev. Legend:** MON... **Note:** Dav. #4360.

Date	Mintage	VG	F	VF	XF	Unc
1650 GR	—	250	750	2,000	6,250	—
1651 GR Rare	—	—	—	—	—	—
1652 GR Rare	—	—	—	—	—	—
1655 GR Rare	—	—	—	—	—	—

KM# 76 THALER

Silver **Subject:** Johann III Sobieski **Note:** Dav. #4361.

Date	Mintage	VG	F	VF	XF	Unc
1685 DL	2,000	4,000	8,000	14,500	24,500	—

Note: Stack's Tallent & Belzberg Collections, 4-08, choice AU realized $40,000

KM# 28 2 THALER

Silver **Obv:** Crowned bust of Wladislaus IV right in inner circle **Rev:** Similar to KM#50 **Note:** Dav. #4355.

Date	Mintage	VG	F	VF	XF	Unc
1639 GR Rare	—	—	—	—	—	—

KM# 50 2 THALER

Silver **Subject:** Johann Casimir **Note:** Dav. #4359.

Date	Mintage	VG	F	VF	XF	Unc
1650 GR	—	6,500	10,000	16,500	—	—

TRADE COINAGE

KM# 5.1 DUCAT

3.5000 g., 0.9860 Gold 0.1109 oz. AGW

Date	Mintage	VG	F	VF	XF	Unc
1601	—	1,600	3,950	7,900	10,500	—

KM# 5.2 DUCAT

3.5000 g., 0.9860 Gold 0.1109 oz. AGW **Obv:** Bust divides legend between DG and REX

Date	Mintage	VG	F	VF	XF	Unc
1609	—	1,600	3,400	8,000	11,500	—

KM# 5.3 DUCAT

3.5000 g., 0.9860 Gold 0.1109 oz. AGW **Obv:** Bust divides legend between D and G

Date	Mintage	VG	F	VF	XF	Unc
1610	—	1,000	2,250	4,500	8,000	—

KM# 5.4 DUCAT

3.5000 g., 0.9860 Gold 0.1109 oz. AGW

Date	Mintage	VG	F	VF	XF	Unc
1610 FB	—	800	1,350	2,700	5,000	11,500
1610 PK	—	800	1,350	2,700	5,000	11,500
1611	—	800	1,350	2,700	5,000	11,500
1612	—	800	1,350	2,700	5,000	11,500
1614 PK with angel head Rare	—	—	—	—	—	—

KM# 5.5 DUCAT

3.5000 g., 0.9860 Gold 0.1109 oz. AGW **Obv:** Tall, smaller bust, closed crown

Date	Mintage	VG	F	VF	XF	Unc
1614 S-A	—	800	2,050	5,100	10,000	—
1619 S-B Rare	—	—	—	—	—	—
1621 S-B	—	800	2,400	6,100	12,000	—
1622 S-B	—	800	2,050	4,050	8,100	—
1623 S-B	—	800	2,050	5,100	10,000	22,500
1623 DG/S-B	—	800	2,050	5,100	10,000	—
1623 DG Rare	—	—	—	—	—	—
1625 S-B	—	800	2,050	4,050	8,100	—
1626 S-B	—	1,350	3,400	7,400	11,500	—
1627 S-B Rare	—	—	—	—	—	—
1628 S-B	—	1,350	3,400	7,400	11,500	—
1629 S-B	—	800	1,800	3,100	5,400	—
1630 S-B	—	800	1,350	2,550	4,750	—
1631 S-B	—	800	1,350	2,550	4,750	8,500

KM# 5.6 DUCAT

3.5000 g., 0.9860 Gold 0.1109 oz. AGW **Obv:** Open crown

Date	Mintage	VG	F	VF	XF	Unc
ND	—	—	1,250	3,000	5,500	—
1632 S-B	—	—	1,250	3,000	5,500	—

KM# 20.1 DUCAT

3.5000 g., 0.9860 Gold 0.1109 oz. AGW **Subject:** Wladislaus IV **Obv:** Larger tall, thin bust

Date	Mintage	VG	F	VF	XF	Unc
1633 SB	—	800	1,650	4,150	7,800	—
1634 SB	—	800	1,650	4,150	7,800	—
1635 SB	—	800	1,650	4,150	7,800	—

KM# 20.2 DUCAT

3.5000 g., 0.9860 Gold 0.1109 oz. AGW

Date	Mintage	VG	F	VF	XF	Unc
1636 CS	—	800	1,650	3,550	7,100	—
1638 II	—	800	1,900	5,800	13,500	—
1639 II	—	800	1,650	4,550	10,000	—

KM# 20.3 DUCAT

3.5000 g., 0.9860 Gold 0.1109 oz. AGW **Obv:** Small, short, fat bust

Date	Mintage	VG	F	VF	XF	Unc
1639 GR	—	800	1,350	3,250	6,100	13,500
1640 GR Rare	—	—	—	—	—	—
1641 GR	—	800	2,050	5,400	11,000	—
1642 GR	—	800	1,350	2,850	5,400	—
1643 GR	—	800	1,350	3,250	6,100	—
1644 GR	—	800	2,050	5,400	11,000	—
1645 GR	—	800	1,350	3,250	6,100	—
1646 GR	—	800	2,050	5,400	11,000	—
1647 GR	—	800	1,350	2,850	5,400	—

KM# 20.4 DUCAT

3.5000 g., 0.9860 Gold 0.1109 oz. AGW **Obv:** Small head

Date	Mintage	VG	F	VF	XF	Unc
1642 GR Rare	—	—	—	—	—	—

KM# 41.1 DUCAT

3.5000 g., 0.9860 Gold 0.1109 oz. AGW **Subject:** Johann Casimir

Date	Mintage	VG	F	VF	XF	Unc
1649 GR	—	800	1,350	2,700	5,000	—
1650 GR	—	800	1,350	2,700	5,000	—
1651 GR	—	800	1,350	2,700	5,000	—
1652 GR	—	800	1,350	4,050	8,000	—
1653 GR	—	800	1,350	3,750	6,750	—
1655 GR	—	800	1,350	2,700	5,000	—
1656 GR	—	800	1,350	2,700	5,000	—
1657 DL	—	800	1,350	2,700	5,000	—

KM# 53 DUCAT

3.5000 g., 0.9860 Gold 0.1109 oz. AGW **Rev:** Date below arms

Date	Mintage	VG	F	VF	XF	Unc
1651 GR	—	850	1,850	3,600	7,500	—

KM# 41.2 DUCAT

3.5000 g., 0.9860 Gold 0.1109 oz. AGW **Obv:** No knot at shoulder

Date	Mintage	VG	F	VF	XF	Unc
1658 DL	—	800	1,500	3,400	8,000	—
1659 DL	—	1,050	3,000	7,500	18,000	—
1660 DL	—	800	1,900	3,750	8,100	—
1661 DL	—	800	1,500	2,850	5,800	12,500
1662 DL	—	800	1,500	2,850	5,800	—
1663 DL	—	800	1,500	2,850	5,800	15,000

KM# 41.3 DUCAT

3.5000 g., 0.9860 Gold 0.1109 oz. AGW **Obv:** Knot at shoulder

Date	Mintage	VG	F	VF	XF	Unc
1666 DL	—	625	1,200	2,300	5,300	—
1667 DL	—	625	1,200	2,300	5,300	—
1668 DL	—	625	1,200	2,400	5,600	—

KM# 71.1 DUCAT

3.5000 g., 0.9860 Gold 0.1109 oz. AGW **Subject:** Michael Korybut

Date	Mintage	VG	F	VF	XF	Unc
1670 DL	—	1,500	3,600	9,000	—	—

Note: Künker Auction 181, 1-11, XF realized approx. $23,280

KM# 71.2 DUCAT

3.5000 g., 0.9860 Gold 0.1109 oz. AGW

Date	Mintage	VG	F	VF	XF	Unc
1672 DL	—	750	1,650	3,250	7,750	—
1673 DL	—	750	1,650	3,250	7,750	—
ND	—	750	1,650	3,250	7,750	—

KM# 72.1 DUCAT

3.5000 g., 0.9860 Gold 0.1109 oz. AGW **Subject:** Johann III Sobieski

Date	Mintage	VG	F	VF	XF	Unc
1676 DL	—	900	1,900	5,200	12,000	—

KM# 72.2 DUCAT

3.5000 g., 0.9860 Gold 0.1109 oz. AGW

Date	Mintage	VG	F	VF	XF	Unc
1677 DL	—	750	1,500	2,950	7,200	—
1682 DL	—	750	1,500	3,750	8,600	—

KM# 75.1 DUCAT

3.5000 g., 0.9860 Gold 0.1109 oz. AGW

Date	Mintage	VG	F	VF	XF	Unc
1683 DL	—	550	900	2,150	4,200	8,400
1688/6	—	550	900	2,150	4,200	—
1688	—	550	900	2,150	4,200	—

KM# 75.2 DUCAT

3.5000 g., 0.9860 Gold 0.1109 oz. AGW

Date	Mintage	VG	F	VF	XF	Unc
1692	—	575	975	2,550	5,700	—

KM# 83 DUCAT

3.5000 g., 0.9860 Gold 0.1109 oz. AGW **Subject:** August II

Date	Mintage	VG	F	VF	XF	Unc
1698	—	1,550	3,050	5,900	10,000	—

KM# 84 DUCAT

3.5000 g., 0.9860 Gold 0.1109 oz. AGW **Obv:** Small bust of Augustus II with continuous legend

Date	Mintage	VG	F	VF	XF	Unc
1698	—	1,550	3,050	5,900	10,000	—

KM# A21 1-1/2 DUCAT

Gold **Obv:** Crowned bust of Wladislaus IV in inner circle **Rev:** City of Danzig in inner circle, date and arms in exergue **Note:** Fr#21c

Date	Mintage	VG	F	VF	XF	Unc
1647	—	—	7,500	13,500	22,500	—

Note: Leipziger-Höhn Auction 62, 9-08, XF realized approximately $23,000

KM# 59 1-1/2 DUCAT

Gold **Subject:** Johann Casimir

Date	Mintage	VG	F	VF	XF	Unc
1658 DL Rare	—	—	—	—	—	—
1661 DL Rare	—	—	—	—	—	—

Note: Künker Auction 171, 6-10, XF realized approx. $36,850

KM# 35 2 DUCAT

7.0000 g., 0.9860 Gold 0.2219 oz. AGW **Obv:** Crowned bust of Wladislaus IV in inner circle **Rev:** City of Danzig in inner circle, date and arms in exergue **Note:** Fr#21a

Date	Mintage	VG	F	VF	XF	Unc
1642 GR Rare	—	—	—	—	—	—
1647 GR Rare	—	—	—	—	—	—

Note: Rauch Auction 84, 5-09, XF, realized approx. $19,245

KM# 56.1 2 DUCAT

7.0000 g., 0.9860 Gold 0.2219 oz. AGW **Subject:** Johann Casimir

Date	Mintage	VG	F	VF	XF	Unc
1651 Rare	—	—	—	—	—	—
1655 DL	—	—	5,500	9,500	16,000	—
1658 DL	—	—	5,500	9,500	16,000	—
1661 DS	—	—	5,500	9,500	16,000	—

KM# 56.2 2 DUCAT

7.0000 g., 0.9860 Gold 0.2219 oz. AGW

Date	Mintage	VG	F	VF	XF	Unc
ND GR Rare	—	—	—	—	—	—

KM# 65 2 DUCAT

7.0000 g., 0.9860 Gold 0.2219 oz. AGW **Subject:** Michael Korybut

Date	Mintage	VG	F	VF	XF	Unc
ND Rare	—	—	—	—	—	—

KM# 80.1 2 DUCAT

7.0000 g., 0.9860 Gold 0.2219 oz. AGW **Subject:** Johann III Sobieski

Date	Mintage	VG	F	VF	XF	Unc
1692	—	—	9,500	16,500	27,500	—
ND DL	—	—	9,500	16,500	27,500	—

KM# 80.2 2 DUCAT
7.0000 g., 0.9860 Gold 0.2219 oz. AGW

Date	Mintage	VG	F	VF	XF	Unc
ND	—	—	9,500	16,500	27,500	—

KM# 81 2 DUCAT
7.0000 g., 0.9860 Gold 0.2219 oz. AGW **Obv:** Laureate bust of Johann III Sobieski right

Date	Mintage	VG	F	VF	XF	Unc
ND DL	—	—	9,500	16,500	27,500	—

KM# 85 2 DUCAT
7.0000 g., 0.9860 Gold 0.2219 oz. AGW **Subject:** August II

Date	Mintage	VG	F	VF	XF	Unc
1698 Rare	—	—	—	—	—	—
1699 Rare	—	—	—	—	—	—

KM# 34 2-1/2 DUCAT
8.7500 g., 0.9860 Gold 0.2774 oz. AGW

Date	Mintage	VG	F	VF	XF	Unc
1645 GR Rare	—	—	—	—	—	—

KM# 16 3 DUCAT
10.5000 g., 0.9860 Gold 0.3328 oz. AGW

Date	Mintage	VG	F	VF	XF	Unc
1617 Rare	—	—	—	—	—	—

Note: Hess-Divo Auction 309, 4-08, VF realized approximately $36,760.

KM# 36 3 DUCAT
10.5000 g., 0.9860 Gold 0.3328 oz. AGW **Subject:** Wladislaus IV

Date	Mintage	VG	F	VF	XF	Unc
1634	—	—	4,500	9,500	15,000	—
1640	—	—	4,500	9,500	15,000	—
1641	—	—	4,500	9,500	15,000	—
1642	—	—	4,500	9,500	15,000	—
1647 GR	—	—	4,500	9,500	15,000	—

KM# 51.1 3 DUCAT
10.5000 g., 0.9860 Gold 0.3328 oz. AGW **Ruler:** Johann Casimir **Obv:** Laureate bust right in inner circle **Rev:** City view, arms below

Date	Mintage	VG	F	VF	XF	Unc
ND(1649-68)	—	—	7,400	14,000	24,000	—
1650	—	—	7,400	14,000	24,000	—
1658	—	—	7,400	14,000	24,000	—

KM# 51.2 3 DUCAT
10.5000 g., 0.9860 Gold 0.3328 oz. AGW **Ruler:** Johann Casimir **Obv:** Laureate bust right without inner circle **Rev:** City view, arms below, without value 3 at top

Date	Mintage	VG	F	VF	XF	Unc
ND(1649-68) Rare	—	—	—	—	—	—

KM# A66 3 DUCAT
10.5000 g., 0.9860 Gold 0.3328 oz. AGW **Ruler:** Michael Korybut **Obv:** Laureate bust right without inner circle **Rev:** City view, arms below, without value 3 at top

Date	Mintage	VG	F	VF	XF	Unc
ND(1669-73) Rare	—	—	—	—	—	—

Note: Stack's Belzberg Sale 4-08, Choice AU realized $75,000.

KM# 37 4 DUCAT
14.0000 g., 0.9860 Gold 0.4438 oz. AGW **Obv:** Crowned bust of Wladislaus IV in inner circle **Rev:** City of Danzig in inner circle, arms below **Note:** Legend varieties exist.

Date	Mintage	VG	F	VF	XF	Unc
1641	—	—	4,500	9,500	15,000	—
1642	—	—	4,500	9,500	15,000	—
1643	—	—	4,500	9,500	15,000	—
1644	—	—	4,500	9,500	15,000	—
1645	—	—	4,500	9,500	15,000	—

KM# 44 4 DUCAT
14.0000 g., 0.9860 Gold 0.4438 oz. AGW **Subject:** Johann Casimir

Date	Mintage	VG	F	VF	XF	Unc
1650 GR	—	—	3,500	7,500	12,500	—
ND GR	—	—	3,500	7,500	12,500	—

KM# A59 4 DUCAT
14.0000 g., 0.9860 Gold 0.4438 oz. AGW, 37 mm. **Ruler:** Johann Casimir **Obv:** Crowned bust right **Rev:** Hebrew and script in sunburst over city view, supported arms below **Note:** Fr. #29.

Date	Mintage	Good	VG	F	VF	XF
ND(1648-69) IH Rare	—	—	—	—	—	—

Note: WAG Auction 41, 3-07, Unc realized approx. $22,460

KM# 82 4 DUCAT
14.0000 g., 0.9860 Gold 0.4438 oz. AGW **Subject:** Johann Sobieski

Date	Mintage	VG	F	VF	XF	Unc
1692	—	—	12,500	22,500	37,500	—

KM# 7 5 DUCAT (1/2 Portugaloser)
16.8620 g., 0.9860 Gold 0.5345 oz. AGW **Subject:** Sigismund III

Date	Mintage	VG	F	VF	XF	Unc
ND(1614)	—	—	12,500	22,500	37,500	75,000

Note: Hess-Divo Aution 309, 4-08, XF realized approx. $37,785

KM# 55.1 5 DUCAT (1/2 Portugaloser)
16.8620 g., 0.9860 Gold 0.5345 oz. AGW **Subject:** Johann Casimir

Date	Mintage	VG	F	VF	XF	Unc
1649 GR Rare	—	—	—	—	—	—
1654 GR Rare	—	—	—	—	—	—

KM# 55.2 5 DUCAT (1/2 Portugaloser)
16.8620 g., 0.9860 Gold 0.5345 oz. AGW **Rev:** 5 added above all seeing eye above modified city view

Date	Mintage	VG	F	VF	XF	Unc
1656 GR Rare	—	—	—	—	—	—

KM# A33 6 DUCAT
Gold **Subject:** Wladislaus IV

Date	Mintage	VG	F	VF	XF	Unc
1644	—	—	8,500	15,000	25,000	—
1645	—	—	8,500	15,000	25,000	—

KM# B33 7 DUCAT
Gold **Subject:** Wladislaus IV

Date	Mintage	VG	F	VF	XF	Unc
1644	—	—	9,000	16,500	27,000	—
1645	—	—	9,000	16,500	27,000	—

KM# 12 8 DUCAT
28.0000 g., 0.9860 Gold 0.8876 oz. AGW **Subject:** Sigismund III **Note:** Struck from 5 Ducat dies.

Date	Mintage	VG	F	VF	XF	Unc
1614	—	—	12,500	25,000	45,000	—

KM# C33 8 DUCAT
28.0000 g., 0.9860 Gold 0.8876 oz. AGW **Subject:** Wladislaus IV

Date	Mintage	VG	F	VF	XF	Unc
1644 Rare	—	—	—	—	—	—
Note: Meister & Soantag Auction 7, 4-09 good VF realized approximately $21,450.						
1645 Rare	—	—	—	—	—	—

KM# 4 10 DUCAT
35.0000 g., 0.9860 Gold 1.1095 oz. AGW **Subject:** Sigismund III

Date	Mintage	VG	F	VF	XF	Unc
1613//1614 Rare	—	—	—	—	—	—

Note: Stack's Belzberg Sale 4-09, VF realized $62,500.

KM# 33 10 DUCAT
35.0000 g., 0.9860 Gold 1.1095 oz. AGW **Subject:** Wladislaus IV

Date	Mintage	VG	F	VF	XF	Unc
1644 GR Rare	—	—	—	—	—	—

Note: Künker Auction 181, 1-11, VF realized approx. $30,125

KM# 52 10 DUCAT
35.0000 g., 0.9860 Gold 1.1095 oz. AGW **Subject:** Johann Casimir

Date	Mintage	VG	F	VF	XF	Unc
1650 GR Rare	—	—	—	—	—	—
1651 GR Rare	—	—	—	—	—	—
ND	—	—	—	—	—	—

KM# A53 12 DUCAT
Gold **Subject:** Johann Casimir

Date	Mintage	VG	F	VF	XF	Unc
1650 GR Rare	—	—	—	—	—	—

Note: Stack's Belzberg Sale 4-08 about XF realized $75,000.

KM# 13 15 DUCAT
52.5000 g., 0.9860 Gold 1.6642 oz. AGW **Subject:** Sigismund III

Date	Mintage	VG	F	VF	XF	Unc
ND(1614) Rare	—	—	—	—	—	—

KM# 17 20 DUCAT
69.7400 g., 0.9860 Gold 2.2107 oz. AGW **Subject:** Sigismund III

Date	Mintage	VG	F	VF	XF	Unc
1613//1614 Rare	—	—	—	—	—	—

Note: Stack's Belzberg sale 4-08, VF realized $110,000. Bowers and Merena Guia sale 3-88 VF realized $14,300

PIEFORTS

KM#	Date	Mintage	Identification	Mkt Val
P1	1616	—	Orte. Silver.	—

PATTERNS

Including off metal strikes

KM#	Date	Mintage	Identification	Mkt Val
Pn1	1613	—	Ternar. Gold. KM#10.	—
Pn2	1640	—	1/2 Thaler. Gold. KM#26.	—
Pn3	1641	—	1/2 Thaler. Gold. KM#26. Weight of 2 Ducat.	—
Pn4	1641	—	1/2 Thaler. Gold. KM#26. Weight of 3 Ducat.	—
Pn5	1641	—	1/2 Thaler. Gold. KM#26. Weight of 4 Ducat.	—
Pn6	1657	—	Schilling. Gold. KM#57.	—
Pn7	1659 DL	—	Ducat. Silver. KM#41.	200
Pn8	1661 DL	—	Ducat. Lead. KM#41.	150

ELBING

Elbing is an important industrial city and seaport in northern Poland and was founded in 1237 (Elblag). They later joined the Hanseatic League. The city was under Polish control from 1454-1772 when it was annexed to Prussia. They produced their own coinage from 1454-1763.

RULERS
Polish, 1454-1626, 1636-1655, 1660-
Swedish, 1626-1636, 1655-1660

MINT OFFICIALS' INITIALS

Initials or Mark	Desc.	Date	Name
CS		1671-73	Christian Schultz
IP		1665-67	Jan Paulson
WVE		1650-52	Wilhelm von Eck
	MP, (ha) – Heart with crossed arrows		
	(he) – Helmet above crescent		
	(hf) – Heart with flag	1628-35	Marsilius Philipsen
NH		1656-60	Nicholaus Henning
Without mint mark		1631	Benedikt Steffen

MONETARY SYSTEM
1-1/2 Groschen (Grosze) = Poltorak (1630-1633)

POLISH AUTHORITY

STANDARD COINAGE

KM# 5 SOLIDUS (Schilling)
Silver **Obv:** Crowned large S monogram

Date	Mintage	VG	F	VF	XF	Unc
(16)14	—	—	—	—	—	—

KM# 86 SOLIDUS (Schilling)
Silver **Obv:** Crowned ICR monogram divides date **Rev. Legend:** SOLID / CIVITAT / ELBIN

Date	Mintage	VG	F	VF	XF	Unc
1666	—	41.50	70.00	125	210	—

KM# 90 SOLIDUS (Schilling)
Silver **Obv:** Crowned MR monogram with date **Rev. Legend:** SOLID / CIVITAT / ELBINGE, arms below

Date	Mintage	VG	F	VF	XF	Unc
1671	—	85.00	170	350	550	—
1672	—	36.00	70.00	140	275	—
1673	—	19.00	44.25	75.00	160	—
ND	—	19.00	44.25	75.00	160	—

KM# 54 2 GROSCHEN (2 Groschen = 1 Poltorak)
Silver **Subject:** John Casimir **Obv:** Crowned bust right **Obv. Legend:** IO • CAS • DG • R • P • :&SMDL • R • PR **Rev:** Arms with II above **Rev. Legend:** GROS • DVP • L • CIVELBING

Date	Mintage	VG	F	VF	XF	Unc
1651 WE	—	65.00	125	225	350	—
1651 WVE	—	65.00	125	225	350	—

KM# 50 ORTE
Silver **Subject:** John Casimir

Date	Mintage	VG	F	VF	XF	Unc
650 WVE Rare	—	—	—	—	—	—
651 WVE Rare	—	—	—	—	—	—

KM# 51 ORTE
Silver **Note:** Klippe.

Date	Mintage	VG	F	VF	XF	Unc
650 WVE Rare	—	—	—	—	—	—

KM# 53 ORTE
Silver **Note:** Klippe.

Date	Mintage	VG	F	VF	XF	Unc
651 WVE	—	—	—	—	—	—

KM# 52 ORTE
Silver **Rev:** 1-8 at top of arms

Date	Mintage	VG	F	VF	XF	Unc
651 WVE	—	700	1,450	2,750	4,500	—
660 WVE	—	300	600	1,150	2,350	—
661 NH	—	300	600	1,150	2,350	—

KM# 85 ORTE
Silver **Subject:** John Casimir **Obv:** Crowned bust right **Rev:** Oval arms at center

Date	Mintage	VG	F	VF	XF	Unc
662 NH	—	300	600	1,150	2,350	—
665 IP	—	400	800	1,750	3,500	—
666 IP	—	400	800	1,750	3,500	—
667 IP Rare	—	—	—	—	—	—

KM# A52 1/2 THALER
Silver **Subject:** John Casimir

Date	Mintage	VG	F	VF	XF	Unc
650 WVE Rare	—	—	—	—	—	—
651 WVE Rare	—	—	—	—	—	—

KM# 48 THALER
Silver **Obv:** Facing bust of Wladislaus IV in inner circle **Rev:** Oval arms in wreath, date at top **Note:** Dav. #4362.

Date	Mintage	VG	F	VF	XF	Unc
635 II	—	2,000	5,000	8,000	—	—
636/5 II	—	3,000	7,000	12,000	—	—
636 II	—	2,000	5,000	8,000	—	—

KM# 55 THALER
Silver **Subject:** John Casimir **Note:** Dav. #4364.

Date	Mintage	VG	F	VF	XF	Unc
651 WVE	—	4,000	7,000	12,500	20,000	—

KM# 91 THALER
Silver **Subject:** Michael Korybut **Note:** Dav. #4365.

Date	Mintage	VG	F	VF	XF	Unc
1671 CS Rare	—	—	—	—	—	—

KM# 92 THALER
Silver **Note:** Weight of 1/2 Thaler. Dav. #4365A.

Date	Mintage	VG	F	VF	XF	Unc
1671 CS Rare	—	—	—	—	—	—

KM# 56 1-1/2 THALER
43.2600 g., Silver **Note:** Dav. #4364A.

Date	Mintage	VG	F	VF	XF	Unc
1651 WVE Rare	—	—	—	—	—	—

KM# B57 2 THALER
57.6800 g., Silver **Note:** Dav. #4364B.

Date	Mintage	VG	F	VF	XF	Unc
1651 WVE Rare	—	—	—	—	—	—

KM# A57 2 THALER
Silver **Note:** Similar to 1 Tharler, KM#55. Dav. #4563.

Date	Mintage	VG	F	VF	XF	Unc
1651 WVE Rare	—	—	—	—	—	—

TRADE COINAGE

KM# 76 DUCAT
3.5000 g., 0.9860 Gold 0.1109 oz. AGW **Subject:** John Casimir

Date	Mintage	VG	F	VF	XF	Unc
1658 NH Rare	—	—	—	—	—	—
1660 Rare	—	—	—	—	—	—
1661 Rare	—	—	—	—	—	—
1663 Rare	—	—	—	—	—	—

KM# 93 DUCAT
3.5000 g., 0.9860 Gold 0.1109 oz. AGW **Subject:** Michael Korybut

Date	Mintage	VG	F	VF	XF	Unc
1671 CS Rare	—	—	—	—	—	—
1672 CS Rare	—	—	—	—	—	—

KM# 94 2 DUCAT
7.0000 g., 0.9860 Gold 0.2219 oz. AGW **Subject:** Michael Korybut

Date	Mintage	VG	F	VF	XF	Unc
1672 CS Rare	—	—	—	—	—	—

SWEDISH AUTHORITY

STANDARD COINAGE

KM# 23 SOLIDUS (Schilling)
Silver **Obv:** Crowned GA monogram, titles of Gustavus Adolphus

Date	Mintage	VG	F	VF	XF	Unc
1629 Rare	—	—	—	—	—	—
1630	—	9.00	17.00	30.00	80.00	—
1631	—	9.00	17.00	30.00	80.00	—
1632	—	9.00	17.00	30.00	80.00	—

KM# 38 SOLIDUS (Schilling)
Silver **Obv:** Crowned GA monogram in inner circle

Date	Mintage	VG	F	VF	XF	Unc
1632 MP	—	14.00	30.00	50.00	125	—
1633 MP	—	20.00	40.25	75.00	185	—

KM# 46 SOLIDUS (Schilling)
Silver **Obv:** Crowned CR monogram in inner circle, titles of Christina

Date	Mintage	VG	F	VF	XF	Unc
1633 Rare	—	—	—	—	—	—
1634	—	12.00	22.50	45.00	120	—
1635	—	12.00	22.50	45.00	120	—

KM# 45 SOLIDUS (Schilling)
Silver **Note:** Posthumous issue.

Date	Mintage	VG	F	VF	XF	Unc
1633	—	9.00	17.00	30.00	80.00	—
1634	—	17.00	34.00	70.00	150	—

KM# 57 SOLIDUS (Schilling)
Silver **Obv:** Crowned CG monogram in inner circle **Rev:** Three crowns, two above one, in inner circle; date in legend

Date	Mintage	VG	F	VF	XF	Unc
1656 Rare	—	—	—	—	—	—
1657 Rare	—	—	—	—	—	—

KM# 65 SOLIDUS (Schilling)
Silver **Obv:** Crowned CG monogram in inner circle, titles of Charles X **Rev:** Arms in carotuche in inner circle, date in legend **Rev. Legend:** SOLIDVS PRUSSIAE

Date	Mintage	VG	F	VF	XF	Unc
1657 Rare	—	—	—	—	—	—

KM# 66 SOLIDUS (Schilling)
Silver **Rev. Legend:** SOLIDVS ELBING

Date	Mintage	VG	F	VF	XF	Unc
1657 Rare	—	—	—	—	—	—

KM# 10 GROSCHEN (Grosz)
Silver **Obv:** Crown above three-line inscription **Rev:** Oval arms in inner circle, date in legend

Date	Mintage	VG	F	VF	XF	Unc
1628	—	1,000	2,000	3,500	—	—

KM# 24 GROSCHEN (Grosz)
Silver **Obv:** Crowned bust of Gustavus Adolphus right

Date	Mintage	VG	F	VF	XF	Unc
1629	—	17.00	40.25	80.00	165	—
(16)29	—	17.00	34.50	60.00	125	—
1630	—	17.00	34.50	60.00	125	—

KM# 39 GROSCHEN (Grosz)
Silver **Obv:** Crowned bust of Gustavus Adolphus right in inner circle

Date	Mintage	VG	F	VF	XF	Unc
1632	—	50.00	100	200	450	—

KM# 30 3 GROSCHEN

Silver **Obv:** Crowned bust of Gustavus Adolphus right **Rev:** Value and date above three-line inscription **Note:** Varieties exist.

Date	Mintage	VG	F	VF	XF	Unc
1631 (ha)	—	45.00	75.00	150	300	—
1631 (hc)	—	20.00	45.00	95.00	175	—
1632 Rare	—	—	—	—	—	—

KM# 40 3 GROSCHEN

Silver **Obv:** Crowned bust of Gustav Adolf II right **Rev:** Supported arms divide date, three-line inscription below

Date	Mintage	VG	F	VF	XF	Unc
1632	—	20.00	45.00	95.00	175	—
1633	—	60.00	125	200	350	—

KM# 73 6 GROSCHEN

Silver **Obv:** Crowned bust of Charles X right in inner circle **Rev:** Value above Elbing arms in inner circle, date in legend

Date	Mintage	VG	F	VF	XF	Unc
1658	—	85.00	175	350	700	—
1659	—	70.00	140	275	550	—

KM# 58 18 GROSCHEN

Silver **Obv:** Laureate bust of Charles X left **Rev:** Rampant lion surrounded by three crowns, without value

Date	Mintage	VG	F	VF	XF	Unc
ND(1656)	—	100	210	425	850	—

KM# 62 18 GROSCHEN

Silver **Obv:** Laureate bust of Charles X right **Rev:** Oval arms in cartouche divides value, date in legend

Date	Mintage	VG	F	VF	XF	Unc
1656 NH	—	115	235	475	950	—

KM# 63 18 GROSCHEN

Silver **Obv:** Laureate bust of Charles X right **Rev:** Angel above oval arms divides value in inner circle, date in legend

Date	Mintage	VG	F	VF	XF	Unc
1656 Rare	—	—	—	—	—	—

KM# 64 18 GROSCHEN

Silver **Obv:** Bust in inner circle **Rev:** Without inner circle

Date	Mintage	VG	F	VF	XF	Unc
1656 Rare	—	—	—	—	—	—
1657	—	200	400	700	—	—
1658/7 Rare	—	—	—	—	—	—

KM# 59 18 GROSCHEN

Silver **Rev:** Value added

Date	Mintage	VG	F	VF	XF	Unc
ND(1656)	—	100	210	425	850	—
ND(1656) NH	—	85.00	170	325	650	—

KM# 60 18 GROSCHEN

Silver **Obv:** Laureate bust of Charles X left in inner circle

Date	Mintage	VG	F	VF	XF	Unc
ND(1656) NH	—	90.00	180	350	725	—

KM# 61 18 GROSCHEN

Silver **Obv:** Laureate bust of Charles X right in inner circle

Date	Mintage	VG	F	VF	XF	Unc
ND(1656)	—	100	210	425	850	—

KM# 69 18 GROSCHEN

Silver **Obv:** S • G • V at end of legend

Date	Mintage	VG	F	VF	XF	Unc
1657	—	85.00	170	325	650	—

KM# 67 18 GROSCHEN

Silver **Note:** Inner circles on both sides.

Date	Mintage	VG	F	VF	XF	Unc
1657	—	70.00	140	275	550	—

KM# 68 18 GROSCHEN

Silver **Note:** Klippe.

Date	Mintage	VG	F	VF	XF	Unc
1657 Rare	—	—	—	—	—	—

KM# 11 1/24 THALER

Silver **Obv:** Crowned arms in inner circle, titles of Gustavus Adolphus **Rev:** Orb with value within divides date in inner circle **Note:** City issue.

Date	Mintage	VG	F	VF	XF	Unc
(16)28	—	39.00	80.00	150	300	—
(16)29	—	18.00	39.00	80.00	150	—
(16)30	—	18.00	39.00	80.00	150	—
(16)31	—	18.00	39.00	80.00	150	—
(16)32	—	18.00	39.00	80.00	150	—

KM# 42 1/24 THALER

Silver **Note:** Error: 60 instead of 24 as value.

Date	Mintage	VG	F	VF	XF	Unc
1632	—	80.00	150	300	575	—

KM# 43 1/24 THALER

Silver **Obv:** Titles of Christina

Date	Mintage	VG	F	VF	XF	Unc
1632 Rare	—	—	—	—	—	—
1634	—	30.00	60.00	115	240	—
1635	—	30.00	60.00	115	240	—

KM# 41 1/24 THALER

Silver **Obv:** Crowned arms, titles of Gustav Adolf II **Rev:** Orb with value within divides two-digit date **Note:** Royal issue.

Date	Mintage	VG	F	VF	XF	Unc
(16)32	—	22.50	44.75	90.00	180	—
(16)33	—	30.00	60.00	115	240	—
(16)34 Unique	—	—	—	—	—	—
(16)35 Rare	—	—	—	—	—	—

KM# 47 1/24 THALER

Silver **Note:** Posthumous issue.

Date	Mintage	VG	F	VF	XF	Unc
(16)33 Rare	—	—	—	—	—	—

KM# 70 1/24 THALER

Silver **Obv:** Titles of Charles X

Date	Mintage	VG	F	VF	XF	Unc
1657	—	—	—	—	—	—
1658	—	—	275	550	900	—

KM# 12 1/4 THALER

Silver **Obv:** Crowned Swedish arms in inner circle **Rev:** Oval arms in cartouche divides date in inner circle

Date	Mintage	VG	F	VF	XF	Unc
1628 Rare	—	—	—	—	—	—

KM# 31 1/4 THALER

Silver **Obv:** Crowned bust of Gustavus Adolphus right in inner circle **Rev:** Oval arms with lion supporters in inner circle, date in legend

Date	Mintage	VG	F	VF	XF	Unc
1631 MP Rare	—	—	—	—	—	—

KM# 32 1/4 THALER

Silver **Obv:** Bust divides 1-6 within linear circle **Rev:** 24 above lion supported arms

Date	Mintage	VG	F	VF	XF	Unc
1631 Rare	—	—	—	—	—	—

KM# 13 1/2 THALER

Silver **Obv:** Crowned Swedish arms with lion supporters **Rev:** Angel above oval arms in cartouche, date above legend

Date	Mintage	VG	F	VF	XF	Unc
1628 Rare	—	—	—	—	—	—

KM# 15 THALER

Silver **Note:** Date on both sides. Dav. #4565.

Date	Mintage	VG	F	VF	XF	Unc
1628	—	1,350	2,750	5,000	8,500	—

KM# 14 THALER

Silver **Obv:** Crowned Swedish arms with lion supporters **Rev:** Angel above oval arms in cartouche, date above angel **Note:** Dav. #4567.

Date	Mintage	VG	F	VF	XF	Unc
1628 Rare	—	—	—	—	—	—

KM# 16 THALER

Silver **Note:** Klippe. Dav. #4565A. Struck wtih 1/2 Thaler dies, KM#13.

Date	Mintage	VG	F	VF	XF	Unc
1628 Rare	—	—	—	—	—	—

KM# 74 THALER

Silver **Obv:** Crowned bust of Charles X right in inner circle **Rev:** Angel above arms in inner circle, date in legend **Note:** Dav. #4369.

Date	Mintage	VG	F	VF	XF	Unc
1658 Rare	—	—	—	—	—	—

KM# 75 1-1/4 THALER

Silver **Obv:** Crowned bust of Charles X right in inner circle **Rev:** Angel above arms in inner circle, date in legend **Note:** Klippe. Dav. #4568.

Date	Mintage	VG	F	VF	XF	Unc
1658 Rare	—	—	—	—	—	—

KM# 17 1-1/2 THALER

Silver **Obv:** Crowned Swedish arms in inner circle **Rev:** Angel above oval arms in cartouche, date divided above angel **Note:** Dav. #4562.

Date	Mintage	VG	F	VF	XF	Unc
1628 Rare	—	—	—	—	—	—

KM# 18 1-1/2 THALER

Silver **Obv:** Crowned Swedish arms with lion supporters **Note:** Dav. #4564.

Date	Mintage	VG	F	VF	XF	Unc
1628 Rare	—	—	—	—	—	—

KM# 19 2 THALER

Silver **Obv:** Crowned Swedish arms with lion supporters **Rev:** Angel above oval arms in cartouche, date divided above angel **Note:** Dav. #4563.

Date	Mintage	VG	F	VF	XF	Unc
1628 Rare	—	—	—	—	—	—

KM# 20 3 THALER

Silver **Obv:** Crowned Swedish arms in inner circle **Rev:** Angel above oval arms in cartouche, date divided above angel **Note:** Dav. #A4562.

Date	Mintage	VG	F	VF	XF	Unc
1628 Unique	—	—	—	—	—	—

KM# 21 3 THALER

Silver **Obv:** Crowned Swedish arms with lion supporters **Note:** Dav. #A4563.

Date	Mintage	VG	F	VF	XF	Unc
1628 Unique	—	—	—	—	—	—

TRADE COINAGE

KM# 71 DUCAT

3.5000 g., 0.9860 Gold 0.1109 oz. AGW **Obv:** Crowned bust of Charles right in inner circle **Rev:** Garnished arms in inner circle

Date	Mintage	VG	F	VF	XF	Unc
1657 NH Rare	—	—	—	—	—	—
1658 NH Rare	—	—	—	—	—	—

KM# 72 DUCAT

3.5000 g., 0.9860 Gold 0.1109 oz. AGW **Rev:** Garnished arms without inner circle

Date	Mintage	VG	F	VF	XF	Unc
ND Rare	—	—	—	—	—	—

KM# 77 1-1/2 DUCAT

0.9860 Gold **Obv:** Crowned bust of Charles right in inner circle **Rev:** Arms held by angel above, date in legend

Date	Mintage	VG	F	VF	XF	Unc
1658 NH Rare	—	—	—	—	—	—

KM# 78 2 DUCAT

7.0000 g., 0.9860 Gold 0.2219 oz. AGW **Obv:** Crowned bust of Charles right in inner circle **Rev:** Arms held by angel above, date in legend

Date	Mintage	VG	F	VF	XF	Unc
1658 Rare	—	—	—	—	—	—
ND Rare	—	—	—	—	—	—

KM# 33 3 DUCAT

10.5000 g., 0.9860 Gold 0.3328 oz. AGW **Obv:** Crowned bust of Gustavus Adolphus right **Rev:** Supported arms in inner circle, date in legend

Date	Mintage	VG	F	VF	XF	Unc
1631 MP Rare	—	—	—	—	—	—

Note: Künker Auction 185, 3-11, nearly XF realized approximately $118,335.

KM# 34 3 DUCAT

10.5000 g., 0.9860 Gold 0.3328 oz. AGW **Obv:** Crowned draped bust of Gustavus Adolphus right

Date	Mintage	VG	F	VF	XF	Unc
1631 MP Unique	—	—	—	—	—	—

KM# 22 4 DUCAT

14.0000 g., 0.9860 Gold 0.4438 oz. AGW **Obv:** Crowned Swedish arms in inner circle **Rev:** Garnished Elbing arms, date divided at top

Date	Mintage	VG	F	VF	XF	Unc
1628 Rare	—	—	—	—	—	—

KM# 35 4 DUCAT

13.8000 g., 0.9860 Gold 0.4375 oz. AGW **Obv:** Crowned bust of Gustavus Adolphus right **Rev:** Supported arms in inner circle, date in legend

Date	Mintage	VG	F	VF	XF	Unc
1631 MP Unique	—	—	—	—	—	—

KM# 36 5 DUCAT

17.5000 g., 0.9860 Gold 0.5547 oz. AGW **Obv:** Crowned bust of Gustavus Adolphus right **Rev:** Supported arms in inner circle, date in legend

Date	Mintage	VG	F	VF	XF	Unc
1631 Rare	—	—	—	—	—	—

KM# 37 5 DUCAT

17.5000 g., 0.9860 Gold 0.5547 oz. AGW **Obv:** Crowned draped bust of Gustavus Adolphus right

Date	Mintage	VG	F	VF	XF	Unc
1631 Rare	—	—	—	—	—	—

KM# 79 5 DUCAT

17.5000 g., 0.9860 Gold 0.5547 oz. AGW **Obv:** Crowned bust of Charles right **Rev:** Arms held by angel above in inner circle, date in legend

Date	Mintage	VG	F	VF	XF	Unc
1658 Rare	—	—	—	—	—	—

KM# 44 10 DUCAT

35.0000 g., 0.9860 Gold 1.1095 oz. AGW **Obv:** Bust of Gustavus Adolphus facing half-right in inner circle **Rev:** Ornamental Swedish arms divide date

Date	Mintage	VG	F	VF	XF	Unc
1632 Rare	—	—	—	—	—	—

KM# 80 10 DUCAT

35.0000 g., 0.9860 Gold 1.1095 oz. AGW **Obv:** Crowned bust of Charles right **Rev:** Arms held by angel above in inner circle, date in legend

Date	Mintage	VG	F	VF	XF	Unc
1658 Rare	—	—	—	—	—	—

Note: Künker Auction 156, 6-09, F-VF realized approximatley $45,600.

PATTERNS

Including off metal strikes

KM#	Date	Mintage	Identification	Mkt Val
PnA1	1630	—	Ducat. Silver. Klippe.	—
Pn1	1631	—	3 Groschen. Gold. KM#30.	—
Pn2	1632	—	Solidus. Gold. KM#38. Weight of 1/2 Ducat.	—
Pn3	1635	—	1/24 Thaler. Gold. KM#43. Weight of 3/4 Ducat.	—
PnA5	1658	—	Ducat. Silver. Klippe.	—
Pn4	1658	—	18 Groschen. Gold. KM#67. Weight of 3 Ducat.	—

FRAUSTADT

(Wschowa)

MINT MARK

W - Wschowa (Fraustadt)

MINT OFFICIALS' INITIALS

Initial or Mark	Date	Name
(a) rose	1595-1601	Herman Rudiger
(b)	1599-1603	Rudolf Lehman

CITY

STANDARD COINAGE

KM# 5 DENARE

Silver **Obv:** Crowned displayed eagle **Rev:** Crowned arms divide date, CW above

Date	Mintage	VG	F	VF	XF	Unc
(1)60Z Rare	—	—	—	—	—	—
160Z	—	30.00	50.00	85.00	—	—
(16)03	—	120	240	600	—	—
(16)04	—	150	300	750	—	—

KM# 6 DENARE

Silver **Note:** Uniface. Two shields of arms, date above, W below.

Date	Mintage	VG	F	VF	XF	Unc
1608	—	125	250	600	—	—
1609	—	100	200	550	—	—

KM# 7 DENARE

Silver **Obv:** Crowned displayed eagle **Rev:** Crowned arms divide two-digit date, W above

Date	Mintage	VG	F	VF	XF	Unc
(16)10	—	120	240	600	—	—
(16)11	—	125	250	650	—	—
(16)1Z	—	120	240	600	—	—

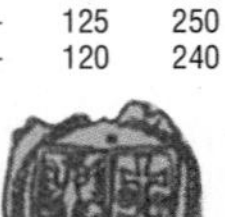

KM# 8 DENARE

Silver **Note:** Uniface. Two shields of arms, W below.

Date	Mintage	VG	F	VF	XF	Unc
ND(1608-10) Rare	—	—	—	—	—	—

LOBSENZ

(Lobzenica)

MINT MARK

L - Lobsenz (Lobzenica)

MINT OFFICIALS' INITIALS

Initial	Date	Name
AK crowned	1612-30	Andrzej Krotoski
(b)	1612-16	Jan Beker

CITY

STANDARD COINAGE

KM# 5 DENAR

Silver

Date	Mintage	VG	F	VF	XF	Unc
(16)12 Rare	—	—	—	—	—	—
(16)13 Rare	—	—	—	—	—	—
(16)14 Rare	—	—	—	—	—	—

KM# 6 DENAR

Silver

Date	Mintage	VG	F	VF	XF	Unc
(16)13 Rare	—	—	—	—	—	—
(16)15L Rare	—	—	—	—	—	—

KM# 7 DENAR

Silver

Date	Mintage	VG	F	VF	XF	Unc
(16)22	—	135	275	450	—	—
(16)23	—	100	200	350	—	—
(16)24	—	125	250	425	—	—
ND	—	—	—	—	—	—

KM# 8 DENAR

Silver **Note:** Klippe.

Date	Mintage	VG	F	VF	XF	Unc
(16)23 Rare	—	—	—	—	—	—
ND Rare	—	—	—	—	—	—

KM# 9 TERNAR (3 Denarii, Pfennig = 1/6 Grosy)

Silver

Date	Mintage	VG	F	VF	XF	Unc
1623	—	75.00	185	400	—	—

KM# 10 TERNAR (3 Denarii, Pfennig = 1/6 Grosy)

Silver **Note:** Varieties exist.

Date	Mintage	VG	F	VF	XF	Unc
1624	—	65.00	175	375	—	—
16Z4	—	65.00	125	225	—	—
1625	—	65.00	125	225	—	—
16Z5	—	65.00	125	225	375	—
1626	—	65.00	125	225	—	—
16Z6	—	65.00	125	225	—	—

KM# 11 TERNAR (3 Denarii, Pfennig = 1/6 Grosy)

Silver **Note:** Legend varieties exist.

Date	Mintage	VG	F	VF	XF	Unc
1626L	—	65.00	125	225	—	—
16Z6	—	65.00	125	225	—	—
1627L	—	65.00	125	225	—	—
16Z7	—	65.00	125	225	—	—
1630	—	65.00	125	225	—	—

KM# 12 TERNAR (3 Denarii, Pfennig = 1/6 Grosy)

Silver

Date	Mintage	VG	F	VF	XF	Unc
1627	—	65.00	125	225	—	—
16Z7	—	65.00	125	225	—	—
1628	—	65.00	125	225	—	—
16Z8	—	65.00	125	225	—	—
16Z9	—	65.00	125	225	—	—
1630	—	65.00	125	225	—	—

POSEN

Posen was part of Poland until 1793, then a province of Prussia from 1793-1918. It became part of the Grand Duchy of Warsaw (Warszawa). Returned to Prussia after the Congress of Vienna (1815). A special coin issue was made as a provincial issue for the Grand Duchy (Frederich August, Grand Duke) of Posen by Prussia immediately after repossession.

RULER

Sigisimund III (of Poland), 1587-1632

MINT MARK

B - Breslau

KINGDOM

STANDARD COINAGE

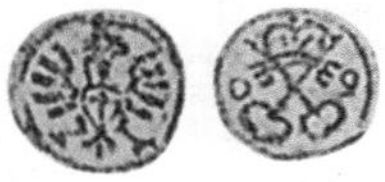

KM# 5 DENAR

Silver

Date	Mintage	VG	F	VF	XF	Unc
(16)01 Unique	—	—	—	—	—	—
(16)02 Rare	—	—	—	—	—	—
(16)03	—	35.00	90.00	220	—	—
1603	—	50.00	125	325	—	—
(16)04 Rare	—	—	—	—	—	—
(16)05	—	35.00	90.00	220	—	—
(16)06	—	40.00	100	250	—	—
(16)07	—	27.50	75.00	190	—	—
(16)08	—	35.00	90.00	220	—	—
(16)09	—	27.50	75.00	190	—	—
(16)10	—	27.50	75.00	190	—	—
(16)11	—	35.00	90.00	220	—	—
(16)12	—	27.50	75.00	190	—	—
(16)1Z	—	—	—	—	—	—
(16)13	—	35.00	90.00	220	—	—
(16)14 Rare	—	—	—	—	—	—
ND Rare	—	—	—	—	—	—

KM# 6 TERNAR (3 Denarii - Pfennig)

Silver **Obv:** Large S monogram

Date	Mintage	VG	F	VF	XF	Unc
(16)03 Rare	—	—	—	—	—	—

KM# 7 TERNAR (3 Denarii - Pfennig)

Silver **Obv:** Displayed eagle

Date	Mintage	VG	F	VF	XF	Unc
1603	—	—	—	—	—	—
(16)03 Rare	—	—	—	—	—	—
(16)04 Rare	—	—	—	—	—	—

KM# 8 TERNAR (3 Denarii - Pfennig)

Silver **Obv:** Large S monogram divides date **Rev:** Three shields of arms

Date	Mintage	VG	F	VF	XF	Unc
(16)03 P Rare	—	—	—	—	—	—

KM# 9 TERNAR (3 Denarii - Pfennig)

Silver **Note:** Varieties exist.

Date	Mintage	VG	F	VF	XF	Unc
(16)05 P	—	60.00	140	290	—	—
(16)05	—	60.00	140	290	—	—
(16)06 P	—	60.00	140	290	—	—
(16)06	—	60.00	140	290	—	—
(16)08 P	—	60.00	140	290	—	—
(16)08	—	60.00	140	290	—	—
(16)09 P Rare	—	—	—	—	—	—
(16)10	—	60.00	140	290	—	—
(16)10 GC	—	80.00	175	400	—	—
(16)11	—	60.00	140	290	—	—
(16)13 Rare	—	—	—	—	—	—
(16)15	—	60.00	140	290	—	—
(16)16	—	60.00	140	290	—	—

KM# 15 TERNAR (3 Denarii - Pfennig)

Silver

Date	Mintage	VG	F	VF	XF	Unc
(16)16	—	60.00	140	290	—	—
(16)17	—	—	—	—	—	—
(16)18	—	—	—	—	—	—
(16)19	—	30.00	70.00	150	300	—

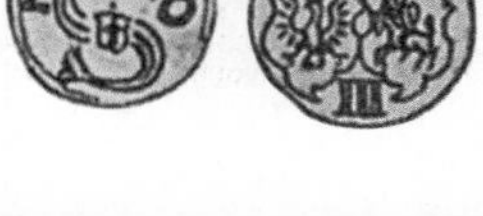

KM# 20 TERNAR (3 Denarii - Pfennig)
Silver

Date	Mintage	VG	F	VF	XF	Unc
(16)20	—	—	—	—	—	—

KM# 21 TERNAR (3 Denarii - Pfennig)
Silver **Obv:** Displayed eagle **Rev:** Crossed keys divide two-digit date

Date	Mintage	VG	F	VF	XF	Unc
(16)Z4	—	46.00	115	230	—	—

KM# 22 TERNAR (3 Denarii - Pfennig)
Silver **Note:** Varieties exist.

Date	Mintage	VG	F	VF	XF	Unc
1624	—	46.00	115	230	—	—
1626	—	46.00	115	230	—	—

KM# 23 TERNAR (3 Denarii - Pfennig)
Silver

Date	Mintage	VG	F	VF	XF	Unc
1626	—	46.00	115	230	—	—
1627	—	30.00	70.00	140	—	—

KM# 25 THALER
Silver **Subject:** Johann Casimir **Note:** Dav. #4366.

Date	Mintage	VG	F	VF	XF	Unc
1652 (aa)-AT Rare	—	—	—	—	—	—

THORN

Thorn is an industrial city in north-central Poland which was founded in 1231. They became a member of the Hanseatic League. The city came under Polish suzerainty (Torun) in 1454 and remained until they were absorbed by Prussia in 1793, except for brief periods of Swedish Occupation from1655-58 and during the Great Northern War (1703) when they were ruled by Sweden.

The city of Thorn was the birthplace of the astronomer, Copernicus. The last city coinage was struck in 1765.

RULERS

Sigismund III, 1587-1632
Wladislaus IV, 1632-1648
Johann Casimir, 1648-1655, 1658-1668
Swedish, 1655-1658
Michael Korybut, 1669-1673
August II of Saxony, 1697-1733

MINT OFFICIALS' INITIALS

Initial	Date	Name
GR	1643-49	Gerhard Rogge, tenant
HDL	1649-68	Hans Daniel Lauer, tenant during Swedish Occupation
HH	1629-31	Jenryk Hema, warden
HIL	1653-55	Hans Jacob Lauer
HL	1630	Hans Lippe, tenant
HS	1668-72	Heinrich Sievert
II	1630	Jacob Jacobson van Emden
MS	1640-42	Melchior Schirmer, tenant

CITY

STANDARD COINAGE

KM# 46 SOLIDUS
Silver **Obv:** Bust of Carl X Gustavus left, crowned ICR monogram divides date **Rev:** 3 crowns of Sweden **Rev. Legend:** SOLIDVS / CIVITATIS / THORVN

Date	Mintage	VG	F	VF	XF	Unc
1665 Rare	—	—	—	—	—	—
1666	—	15.00	32.00	65.00	120	—
1668	—	15.00	32.00	65.00	120	—

KM# 50 SOLIDUS
Silver **Obv:** Crowned MR monogram

Date	Mintage	VG	F	VF	XF	Unc
1671	—	20.00	45.00	90.00	175	—
ND(ca.1673)	—	20.00	45.00	90.00	175	—

KM# 36 2 GROSCHEN (2 Grosze)
Silver **Subject:** John Casimir

Date	Mintage	VG	F	VF	XF	Unc
1651 HDL	—	35.00	75.00	150	250	—

KM# 35 18 GROSZY (Ort)
Silver **Subject:** John Casimir

Date	Mintage	VG	F	VF	XF	Unc
1650 HDL	—	80.00	180	375	1,150	—
1651 HDL	—	55.00	140	275	800	—
1653 HDL	—	39.00	90.00	180	525	—
1654 HDL	—	39.00	90.00	180	525	—
1655 HDL	—	22.50	50.00	90.00	230	—
1655 HIL	—	39.00	90.00	180	525	—
1659 HDL	—	25.00	55.00	100	260	—
1660 HDL	—	22.50	50.00	90.00	230	—
1661 HDL	—	22.50	50.00	90.00	230	—
1662 HDL	—	22.50	50.00	90.00	230	—
1663 HDL	—	22.50	50.00	90.00	230	—
1664 HDL	—	22.50	50.00	90.00	230	—
1665 HDL	—	30.00	85.00	160	450	—
1666 HDL	—	30.00	85.00	160	450	—
1667 HDL	—	80.00	180	375	1,050	—
1668 HDL Unique	—	—	—	—	—	—
1668 HS Rare	—	—	—	—	—	—

KM# 38 18 GROSZY (Ort)
Silver **Ruler:** Carl X Gustavus **Note:** Swedish Occupation.

Date	Mintage	VG	F	VF	XF	Unc
ND(1656) Rare	—	—	—	—	—	—

KM# 15 1/4 THALER (Ort)
Silver **Subject:** Sigismund III

Date	Mintage	VG	F	VF	XF	Unc
1630 HL Rare	—	—	—	—	—	—

KM# 16 1/2 THALER (1/2 Talar)
Silver **Note:** Similar to 1/4 Thaler, KM#15.

Date	Mintage	VG	F	VF	XF	Unc
1629 HH Rare	—	—	—	—	—	—
1630 HL Rare	—	—	—	—	—	—
1630 II Rare	—	—	—	—	—	—
Note: Künker Auction 170, 6-10, nearly XF realized approximately $44,565.						
1631 II Rare	—	—	—	—	—	—
1632 II Rare	—	—	—	—	—	—

KM# 30 1/2 THALER (1/2 Talar)
Silver **Note:** Similar to 1 Thaler, KM#24.

Date	Mintage	VG	F	VF	XF	Unc
1640 MS Rare	—	—	—	—	—	—
1642 MS Rare	—	—	—	—	—	—

KM# 8 THALER
Silver **Rev:** Without angel behind arms

Date	Mintage	VG	F	VF	XF	Unc
1629 Rare	—	—	—	—	—	—

KM# 5 THALER
Silver **Note:** Seige Thaler. Dav. #4367.

Date	Mintage	VG	F	VF	XF	Unc
1629 HL Rare	—	—	—	—	—	—
Note: Künker Auction 145, 10-08, nearly XF realized approximately $96,865. Hess-Divo Auction 300, 10-04, gVF realized approximatley $28,325						

KM# 6 THALER
Silver **Obv:** City of Torn in flames in inner circle **Rev:** Angel holding arms with decorations at sides above six-line inscription **Note:** Seige Thaler. Dav. #4368.

Date	Mintage	VG	F	VF	XF	Unc
1629 HH//HL Rare	—	—	—	—	—	—

KM# 9 THALER
Silver **Obv:** Small angel holding oval city arms above 7-line inscription with ornamentation **Rev:** Two small angels above city of Thorn in flames in inner circle **Note:** Seige Thaler. Dav. #4370.

Date	Mintage	VG	F	VF	XF	Unc
1629 Rare	—	—	—	—	—	—

KM# 7.2 THALER
Silver **Obv:** Large angel holding city arms above 7-line inscription **Rev:** City of Thorn in flames, ten ships in river in inner circle **Rev. Legend:** ...PROBATA:* **Note:** Siege Thaler Dav.#4369A.

Date	Mintage	VG	F	VF	XF	Unc
1629 Rare	—	—	—	—	—	—
Note: Künker Auction 184, 3-11, nearly XF realized approximately $22,360						

KM# 7.1 THALER

Silver **Obv:** Small angel holding city arms above 7-line inscription **Rev:** City of Thorn in flames, twelve ships in river and canal in inner circle **Rev. Legend:** ...PROBATA* **Note:** Siege Thaler. Dav. #4369.

Date	Mintage	VG	F	VF	XF	Unc
1629	—	1,800	3,250	6,000	10,000	17,500

KM# 17 THALER

Silver **Subject:** Sigismund III **Note:** Dav. #4371.

Date	Mintage	VG	F	VF	XF	Unc
1630 HL/HH	—	275	550	1,000	1,650	—
1631 HH	—	275	550	1,000	1,650	—

KM# 18 THALER

Silver **Rev:** Amgel holding city arms divides date in inner circle **Note:** Dav. #4372.

Date	Mintage	VG	F	VF	XF	Unc
1630 II	—	175	350	725	1,350	—
1631 II	—	175	350	725	1,350	—
1632 II	—	175	350	675	1,250	—

KM# 20 THALER

Silver **Note:** Interregnum Issue. Dav. #4373.

Date	Mintage	VG	F	VF	XF	Unc
1632 II Rare	—	—	—	—	—	—

KM# 21 THALER

Silver **Subject:** Wladislaus IV **Note:** Dav. #4374.

Date	Mintage	VG	F	VF	XF	Unc
1633 II	—	300	525	1,000	2,000	—
1634 II	—	375	650	1,150	2,400	—
1635 II	—	300	525	925	1,850	—
1636 II	—	425	725	1,400	2,650	—
1637 II	—	260	520	900	1,550	—
1638 II	—	260	520	900	1,550	—

KM# 24 THALER

Silver **Subject:** Wladislaus IV **Note:** Dav. #4375.

Date	Mintage	VG	F	VF	XF	Unc
1638 II	—	525	1,200	2,000	2,600	—
1639 II	—	525	1,200	2,000	2,600	—
1640 MS	—	575	1,350	2,250	3,150	—
1641 MS	—	450	1,050	1,750	2,450	—
1642 MS	—	450	1,050	1,750	2,300	—

KM# 31 THALER

Silver **Obv:** Crowned bust of Wladislaus IV right in inner circle **Note:** Dav. #4376.

Date	Mintage	VG	F	VF	XF	Unc
1643 GR	—	260	450	875	1,650	—
1644 GR Rare	—	—	—	—	—	—
1645 GR Rare	—	—	—	—	—	—
1646 GR Rare	—	—	—	—	—	—
1647 GR Rare	—	—	—	—	—	—
1648 GR	—	260	450	875	1,650	—

KM# 32 THALER

Silver **Subject:** John Casimir **Note:** Dav. #4377.

Date	Mintage	VG	F	VF	XF	Unc
1649 GR	—	775	1,350	2,650	4,950	—
1649 HDL	—	575	975	1,900	3,450	—
1650 HDL	—	575	1,200	2,500	3,900	—
1659 HDL	—	575	975	1,900	3,750	—
1663 HDL Rare	—	—	—	—	—	—

KM# 23 2 THALER

Silver **Obv:** Crowned half-figure of Wladislaus IV right holding orb and sword in inner circle **Rev:** Angel holding oval city arms divides date in inner circle **Note:** Dav. #A4374.

Date	Mintage	VG	F	VF	XF	Unc
1637 II Rare	—	—	—	—	—	—
1639 II Rare	—	—	—	—	—	—

KM# 25 2 THALER

Silver **Note:** Dav. #B4374. Klippe.

Date	Mintage	VG	F	VF	XF	Unc
1639 II Rare	—	—	—	—	—	—

KM# 49 2 DUCAT

7.0000 g., 0.9860 Gold 0.2219 oz. AGW **Obv:** Bust right, crown breaks circle **Rev:** City view, arms divide date below

Date	Mintage	VG	F	VF	XF	Unc
1670 HS Rare	—	—	—	—	—	—

Note: Künker Auction 191, 6-11, nearly VF realized approx. $31,620

TRADE COINAGE

KM# 19 DUCAT (Dukat)

3.5000 g., 0.9860 Gold 0.1109 oz. AGW **Subject:** Sigismund

Date	Mintage	VG	F	VF	XF	Unc
1630 HL	—	4,200	7,800	14,000	24,000	—
1630 II	—	4,200	7,800	14,000	24,000	—

KM# 22.1 DUCAT (Dukat)

3.5000 g., 0.9860 Gold 0.1109 oz. AGW **Subject:** Wladislaus IV **Note:** Small bust.

Date	Mintage	VG	F	VF	XF	Unc
1633 II	—	2,000	3,950	7,500	13,000	—
1634 II	—	1,650	3,300	6,600	12,000	—
1635 II	—	1,650	3,300	6,600	12,000	—
1637 II	—	1,650	3,300	6,600	12,000	—
1638 II	—	1,650	3,300	6,600	12,000	—
1639 II	—	1,650	3,650	7,300	12,500	—

KM# 22.2 DUCAT (Dukat)

3.5000 g., 0.9860 Gold 0.1109 oz. AGW **Note:** Medium bust.

Date	Mintage	VG	F	VF	XF	Unc
1640 MS	—	1,950	3,900	7,800	13,000	25,000
1641 MS	—	1,950	3,900	7,800	13,000	25,000
1642 MS	—	1,950	3,900	7,800	13,000	25,000

KM# 22.3 DUCAT (Dukat)

3.5000 g., 0.9860 Gold 0.1109 oz. AGW **Note:** Large bust.

Date	Mintage	VG	F	VF	XF	Unc
1643 GR Rare	—	—	—	—	—	—
1645 GR	—	1,900	3,750	7,500	12,500	—
1646 GR Rare	—	—	—	—	—	—

Note: Baldwin's Auction 65, 5-10, ch XF realized approx. $36,275

Date	Mintage	VG	F	VF	XF	Unc
1647 GR	—	2,250	4,500	8,600	14,000	—
1648 GR	—	1,900	3,750	7,500	12,500	—

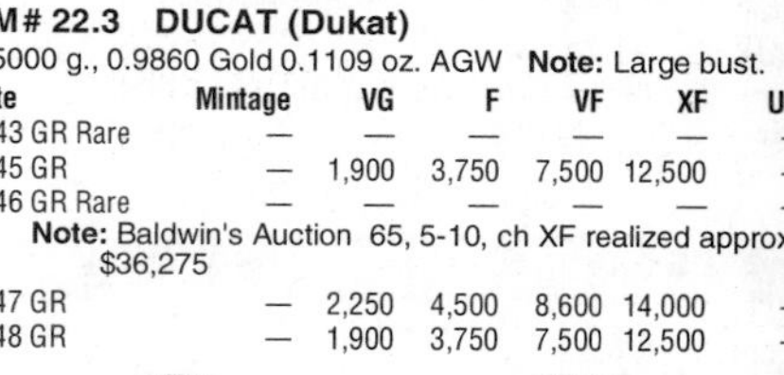

KM# 33 DUCAT (Dukat)

3.5000 g., 0.9860 Gold 0.1109 oz. AGW **Subject:** Johann Casimir

Date	Mintage	VG	F	VF	XF	Unc
1649 GR	—	2,450	4,800	9,000	15,000	—
1649 HDL	—	2,250	4,500	8,600	14,000	—
1650 HDL	—	1,900	3,750	7,500	12,500	—
1651 HDL	—	1,900	3,750	7,500	12,500	—
1653 HIL, HDL	—	1,900	3,750	7,500	12,500	—
1654 HIL	—	1,900	4,200	8,100	13,000	—
1655 HIL	—	1,900	3,750	7,500	12,500	—
1655 HDL	—	1,900	3,750	7,500	12,500	—
1659 HDL	—	1,900	3,750	7,500	12,500	—
1660 HDL	—	1,900	3,750	7,500	12,500	—
1661 HDL	—	1,900	3,750	7,500	12,500	—
1666 HDL	—	2,250	4,500	8,600	14,000	—
1667 HDL	—	3,050	5,700	10,500	17,500	—
1668 HS Rare	—	—	—	—	—	—

KM# 45 2 DUCAT
7.0000 g., 0.9860 Gold 0.2219 oz. AGW **Subject:** Johann Casimir **Note:** Legend varieties exist.

Date	Mintage	VG	F	VF	XF	Unc
1660 HDL	—	2,150	4,300	8,600	16,000	—
1662 HDL	—	2,150	4,300	8,600	16,000	—
1663 HDL	—	2,150	4,300	8,600	16,000	—
1664 HDL	—	2,150	4,300	8,600	16,000	—
1665 HDL	—	2,150	4,300	8,600	16,000	—
1667 HDL	—	2,150	4,300	8,600	16,000	—
1668 HS	—	2,600	4,900	9,800	19,000	—

KM# 52 2 DUCAT
7.0000 g., 0.9860 Gold 0.2219 oz. AGW **Obv:** Laureate bust of Michael Korybut right in inner circle **Rev:** City of Thorn

Date	Mintage	VG	F	VF	XF	Unc
ND(ca.1670) HDL Rare	—	—	—	—	—	—

Note: Baldwin's Auction 65, 5-10, about Unc realized approx. $30,230

KM# 51 2 DUCAT
7.0000 g., 0.9860 Gold 0.2219 oz. AGW **Subject:** Michael Korybut

Date	Mintage	VG	F	VF	XF	Unc
1671 HS Rare	—	—	—	—	—	—

KM# 10 3 DUCAT
10.5000 g., 0.9860 Gold 0.3328 oz. AGW **Subject:** Siege of Thorn in 1629 **Obv:** Burning city of Thorn in inner circle **Rev:** Five-line inscription and Roman numeral date, arms above

Date	Mintage	VG	F	VF	XF	Unc
1629 HH Rare	—	—	—	—	—	—
1630 HH Rare	—	—	—	—	—	—
1631 HH Rare	—	—	—	—	—	—

KM# 37 3 DUCAT
10.5000 g., 0.9860 Gold 0.3328 oz. AGW **Subject:** Johann Casimir

Date	Mintage	VG	F	VF	XF	Unc
1655	—	2,650	4,950	9,100	16,000	—

KM# 39 3 DUCAT
10.5000 g., 0.9860 Gold 0.3328 oz. AGW

Date	Mintage	VG	F	VF	XF	Unc
1659 H Rare	—	—	—	—	—	—

Note: Künker Auction 186, 3-11, XF realized approx. $36,200

KM# 53 3 DUCAT
10.5000 g., 0.9860 Gold 0.3328 oz. AGW **Obv:** Laureate bust of Michael Korybut right **Rev:** Arms of Thorn with angel above in inner circle, date in legend

Date	Mintage	VG	F	VF	XF	Unc
1671 HS Rare	—	—	—	—	—	—

KM# 40 4 DUCAT
14.0000 g., 0.9860 Gold 0.4438 oz. AGW

Date	Mintage	VG	F	VF	XF	Unc
1655 HL	—	4,150	6,800	11,500	20,000	—
1659 HL	—	4,150	6,800	11,500	20,000	—

KM# 41 5 DUCAT
17.5000 g., 0.9860 Gold 0.5547 oz. AGW

Date	Mintage	VG	F	VF	XF	Unc
1655 HL	—	6,000	9,000	14,500	22,500	—
1659 HL	—	6,000	9,000	14,500	22,500	—

KM# 44 6 DUCAT
21.0000 g., 0.9860 Gold 0.6657 oz. AGW, 38 mm. **Ruler:** Johann Casimir **Obv:** Crowned bust right **Rev:** City, harbor view **Note:** Fr. #61.

Date	Mintage	Good	VG	F	VF	XF
1659	—	—	—	—	15,000	25,000

PATTERNS

Including off metal strikes

KM#	Date	Mintage	Identification	Mkt Val
Pn2	1629	—	Thaler. Gold. KM#7.	—
Pn1	1629 HH/HL	—	Thaler. Gold. KM#6.	16,500

PORTUGAL

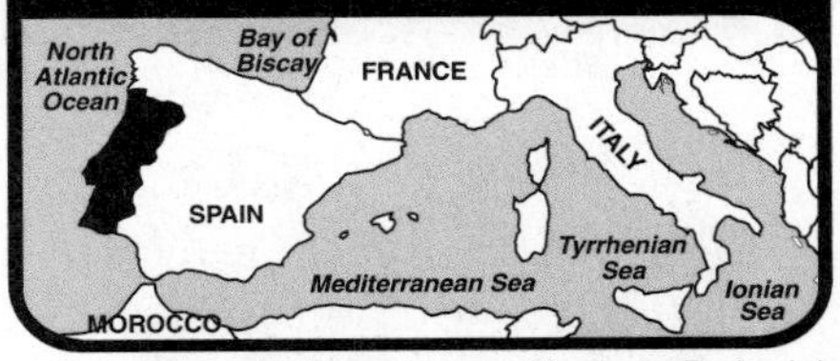

Portugal, located in the western part of the Iberian Peninsula in southwestern Europe, has an area of 35,553 sq. mi. (92,080 sq. km

After centuries of domination by Romans, Visigoths and Moors, Portugal emerged in the 12th century as an independent kingdom financially and philosophically prepared for the great period of exploration that would soon follow. Attuned to the inspiration of Prince Henry the Navigator (1394-1460), Portugal's daring explorers of the 15th and 16th centuries roamed the world's oceans from Brazil to Japan in an unprecedented burst of energy and endeavor that culminated in 1494 with Portugal laying claim to half the transoceanic world. Unfortunately for the fortunes of the tiny kingdom, the Portuguese population was too small to colonize this vast territory. Less than a century after Portugal laid claim to half the world, English, French and Dutch trading companies had seized the lion's share of the world's colonies and commerce, and Portugal's place as an imperial power was lost forever. The monarchy was overthrown in 1910 and a republic was established.

RULERS

Philip II (Philip III of Spain), 1598-1621
Philip III (Philip IV of Spain), 1621-1640
John IV, 1640-1656
Alfonso VI, 1656-1683
Peter, as Prince Regent, (for Alfonso VI), 1667-1683
Peter II, 1683-1706

NOTE: The coins of Philip II and Philip III are so similar that it is not possible to give an absolute attribution. Portuguese authorities rely on legend variants and many times these are lacking in certainty. The "Philippvs" name is attributed to both rulers but it is likely that "Philipvs" is only Philip III.

MINT MARKS

E - Evora
L - Lisbon
P - Porto
No Mint mark – Lisbon

MONETARY SYSTEM

Until 1825

20 Reis = 1 Vintem
100 Reis = 1 Tostao
480 Reis = 24 Vintens = 1 Cruzado
1600 Reis = 1 Escudo
6400 Reis = 4 Escudos = 1 Peca

NOTE: The primary denomination was the Peca, weighing14.34 g, tariffed at 6400 Reis until 1825, and at 7500 Reis after 1826. The weight was not changed.

KINGDOM

DUMP COINAGE

KM# 25 1-1/2 REIS
Copper **Obv:** Crowned arms **Obv. Legend:** IOANNES IIII... **Rev:** 1-1/2 within circle **Note:** Varieties exist.

Date	Mintage	VG	F	VF	XF	Unc
ND(1640-56)	—	40.00	65.00	110	230	—

KM# 95 1-1/2 REIS
Copper **Obv. Legend:** PETRVS... **Note:** Varieties exist.

Date	Mintage	VG	F	VF	XF	Unc
1670	—	—	—	—	—	—
1673	—	65.00	145	350	725	—
1674	—	65.00	145	350	725	—
1675	—	65.00	145	350	725	—
1676	—	30.00	60.00	105	210	—
1677	—	30.00	60.00	105	210	—
1678	—	65.00	145	350	725	—

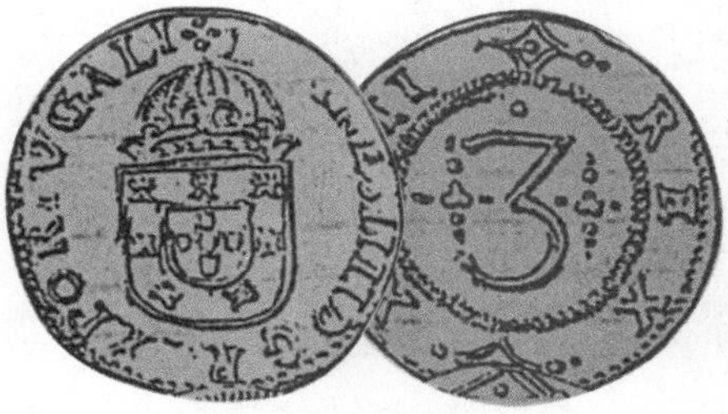

KM# 26 3 REIS
Copper **Obv:** Crowned arms **Obv. Legend:** IOANNES IIII... **Rev:** 3 within circle **Note:** Varieties exist.

Date	Mintage	VG	F	VF	XF	Unc
ND(1640-56)	—	44.00	90.00	145	300	—

KM# 96 3 REIS
Copper **Obv:** Crowned arms **Obv. Legend:** PETRVS... **Rev:** 3 within circle

Date	Mintage	VG	F	VF	XF	Unc
1675	—	60.00	110	290	550	—
1676	—	30.00	60.00	105	210	—
1677	—	30.00	60.00	95.00	190	—

KM# 27 5 REIS
Copper **Obv:** Crowned arms **Obv. Legend:** IOANNES IIII... **Rev:** V within circle **Note:** Varieties exist.

Date	Mintage	VG	F	VF	XF	Unc
ND(1640-56)	—	36.00	65.00	110	240	—

KM# 97 5 REIS
Copper **Obv:** Crowned arms **Obv. Legend:** PETRVS... **Rev:** V within circle

Date	Mintage	VG	F	VF	XF	Unc
1675	—	48.00	95.00	290	550	—
1676	—	32.00	90.00	145	270	—
1677	—	30.00	60.00	105	210	—

KM# 28 10 REIS (1/2 Vinten)
Silver **Obv:** 4 shields in cruciform **Obv. Legend:** IOANNES... **Rev:** Cross of Jerusalem with dots in angles **Note:** Varieties exist.

Date	Mintage	VG	F	VF	XF	Unc
ND(1640-56)	—	500	825	1,400	2,200	—

KM# 65 10 REIS (1/2 Vinten)
Silver **Obv:** 4 shields in cruciform **Obv. Legend:** ALPHONSVS... **Rev:** Without dots **Note:** Varieties exist.

Date	Mintage	VG	F	VF	XF	Unc
ND(1656-83)	—	300	500	775	1,300	—

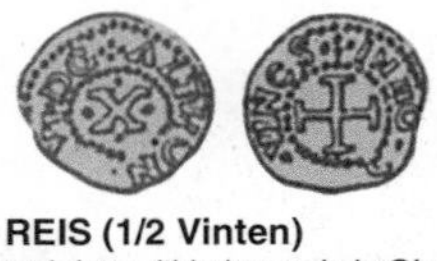

KM# 66 10 REIS (1/2 Vinten)

Silver **Obv:** X and dots within inner circle **Obv. Legend:** ALPHONSVS... **Rev:** Without dots **Note:** Varieties exist.

Date	Mintage	VG	F	VF	XF	Unc
ND(1656-83)	—	250	450	725	1,100	—

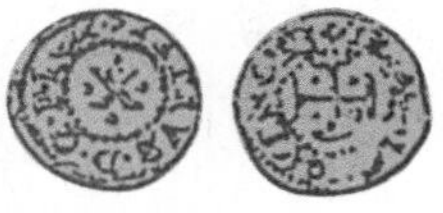

KM# 98 10 REIS (1/2 Vinten)

Silver **Obv:** X and dots within inner circle **Obv. Legend:** PETRVS... **Rev:** Cross of Jerusalem with dots in angles **Note:** Varieties exist.

Date	Mintage	VG	F	VF	XF	Unc
ND(1663)	—	325	550	875	1,650	—

KM# 99 10 REIS (1/2 Vinten)

Copper **Obv:** Crowned arms **Obv. Legend:** PETRVS... **Rev:** X and annulets within inner circle

Date	Mintage	VG	F	VF	XF	Unc
1675	—	37.50	75.00	225	450	—
1676	—	22.50	48.25	80.00	165	—
1677	—	19.00	45.00	75.00	150	—

KM# 15 20 REIS (Vinten)

Silver **Obv:** Crowned arms **Obv. Legend:** PHILIPVS... **Rev:** F above XX **Note:** Struck at Lisbon.

Date	Mintage	VG	F	VF	XF	Unc
ND	—	48.00	100	215	350	—

KM# 29 20 REIS (Vinten)

Silver **Obv:** Crowned arms **Obv. Legend:** IOANNES... **Rev:** I above XX **Note:** Varieties exist.

Date	Mintage	VG	F	VF	XF	Unc
ND	—	30.00	60.00	115	215	—

KM# 30 20 REIS (Vinten)

Silver **Obv:** Crowned arms **Obv. Legend:** IOANNES... **Rev:** I above XPX **Note:** Varieties exist.

Date	Mintage	VG	F	VF	XF	Unc
ND	—	42.00	90.00	195	325	—

KM# 31 20 REIS (Vinten)

Silver **Obv:** Crowned arms **Obv. Legend:** IOANNES... **Rev:** I/XX/E **Note:** Varieties exist.

Date	Mintage	VG	F	VF	XF	Unc
ND	—	60.00	120	255	400	—

KM# 67 20 REIS (Vinten)

Silver **Obv:** A above XX **Obv. Legend:** ALPHONSVS... **Rev:** Crowned arms **Note:** Varieties exist.

Date	Mintage	VG	F	VF	XF	Unc
ND	—	48.00	110	235	400	—

KM# 32 20 REIS (Vinten)

Silver **Obv:** I above XX **Obv. Legend:** IOANNES... **Rev:** Crowned arms **Rev. Legend:** ALPHONSVS...

Date	Mintage	VG	F	VF	XF	Unc
ND	—	145	290	550	—	—

KM# 68 20 REIS (Vinten)

Silver **Obv:** XX within circle **Rev:** Cross of Jerusalem in inner circle **Note:** Varieties exist.

Date	Mintage	VG	F	VF	XF	Unc
ND	—	25.00	48.00	90.00	170	—

KM# 100 20 REIS (Vinten)

Silver **Obv:** XX within circle **Obv. Legend:** PETRVS... **Rev:** Dots in angles of cross **Note:** Varieties exist.

Date	Mintage	VG	F	VF	XF	Unc
ND	—	25.00	36.00	70.00	130	—

KM# 33 40 REIS (2 Vintens)

Silver **Obv:** Crown above JO IIII / XXXX **Rev:** Annulets, fleur de lis or dots in angles of St. George cross **Note:** Varieties exist.

Date	Mintage	VG	F	VF	XF	Unc
ND	—	25.00	48.00	90.00	215	—

KM# 34 40 REIS (2 Vintens)

Silver **Obv:** Crown above JO IIII / XXXX **Rev:** P in angles of cross **Note:** Varieties exist.

Date	Mintage	VG	F	VF	XF	Unc
NDP	—	36.00	70.00	30.00	30.00	—

KM# 35 40 REIS (2 Vintens)

Silver **Obv:** Crown above JO IIII / XXXX **Rev:** E in angles of cross **Note:** Varieties exist.

Date	Mintage	VG	F	VF	XF	Unc
ND	—	70.00	145	295	725	—

KM# 69 40 REIS (2 Vintens)

Silver **Obv:** Crown above AL. VI / XXXX **Rev:** Cross of St. George with dots in angles

Date	Mintage	VG	F	VF	XF	Unc
ND	—	1,200	2,000	3,250	—	—

KM# 70 40 REIS (2 Vintens)

Silver **Obv:** Crown above XXXX **Obv. Legend:** ALPHONSVS... **Rev:** Cross of Jerusalem with dots in angles **Note:** Varieties exist.

Date	Mintage	VG	F	VF	XF	Unc
ND	—	36.00	60.00	125	255	—

KM# 101 40 REIS (2 Vintens)

Silver **Obv:** Crown above XXXX **Obv. Legend:** PETRVS... **Rev:** Cross of Jerusalem with dots in angles **Note:** Varieties exist.

Date	Mintage	VG	F	VF	XF	Unc
ND	—	25.00	42.00	90.00	215	—

KM# 16 50 REIS (1/2 Tostao)

Silver **Obv:** 4 shields in cruciform within beaded circle **Obv. Legend:** PHILIPVS... **Rev:** Cross with or without dots in angles **Note:** Varieties exist.

Date	Mintage	VG	F	VF	XF	Unc
ND	—	25.00	48.00	90.00	215	—

KM# 36 50 REIS (1/2 Tostao)

Silver **Obv:** Design in angles of cruciform **Obv. Legend:** JOANNES IIII... **Rev:** Cross with date in bottom angles, annulets in top angles **Note:** Varieties exist.

Date	Mintage	VG	F	VF	XF	Unc
1641	—	35.00	75.00	140	325	—

KM# 37 50 REIS (1/2 Tostao)

Silver **Obv:** Design in angles of cruciform **Obv. Legend:** JOANNES IIII... **Rev:** Cross with date in angles

Date	Mintage	VG	F	VF	XF	Unc
1641	—	25.00	42.00	90.00	230	—
1642	—	25.00	42.00	90.00	230	—

KM# 38 50 REIS (1/2 Tostao)

Silver **Obv:** Design in angles of cruciform **Obv. Legend:** JOANNES IIII... **Rev:** Cross with P in angles **Note:** Varieties exist Struck at Porto.

Date	Mintage	VG	F	VF	XF	Unc
ND	—	30.00	55.00	110	265	—

KM# 39 50 REIS (1/2 Tostao)

Silver **Obv:** Design in angles of cruciform **Obv. Legend:** JOANNES IIII... **Rev:** Cross with E in angles **Note:** Varieties exist

Date	Mintage	VG	F	VF	XF	Unc
ND	—	30.00	48.00	100	325	—

KM# 71 50 REIS (1/2 Tostao)

Silver **Obv:** Design in angles of cruciform **Obv. Legend:** ALPHONSVS... **Rev:** Dots in angles of cross

Date	Mintage	VG	F	VF	XF	Unc
ND	—	215	400	725	—	—

KM# 72 50 REIS (1/2 Tostao)

Silver **Obv:** Crowned arms in baroque frame **Obv. Legend:** ALPHONSVS... **Rev:** Cross of Jerusalem **Note:** Varieties exist

Date	Mintage	VG	F	VF	XF	Unc
ND	—	18.00	38.50	80.00	180	—

KM# 102 50 REIS (1/2 Tostao)

Silver **Obv:** Crowned arms in baroque frame **Obv. Legend:** PETRVS... **Rev:** Cross of Jerusalem with dots in angles

Date	Mintage	VG	F	VF	XF	Unc
ND	—	25.00	48.00	90.00	215	—

KM# 40 80 REIS (4 Vintens)

Silver **Obv:** Crown above JO IIII / LXXX **Rev:** Annulets, fleur de lis or dots in angles of St. George cross **Note:** Varieties exist.

Date	Mintage	VG	F	VF	XF	Unc
ND	—	25.00	45.00	90.00	165	—

KM# 41 80 REIS (4 Vintens)

Silver **Obv:** Crown above JO IIII / LXXX **Rev:** P in angles of cross **Note:** Varieties exist.

Date	Mintage	VG	F	VF	XF	Unc
ND	—	90.00	190	375	725	—

KM# 42 80 REIS (4 Vintens)

Silver **Obv:** Crown above JO IIII / LXXX **Rev:** E in angles of cross **Note:** Varieties exist.

Date	Mintage	VG	F	VF	XF	Unc
ND	—	120	240	450	850	—

KM# 73 80 REIS (4 Vintens)

Silver **Obv:** Crown above AL. VI / LXXX **Rev:** Annulets in angles of cross **Note:** Varieties exist.

Date	Mintage	VG	F	VF	XF	Unc
ND	—	1,200	2,400	3,900	—	—

KM# 74 80 REIS (4 Vintens)

Silver **Obv:** Crown above LXXX **Rev:** Cross of Jerusalem with or without dots in angles **Note:** Varieties exist.

Date	Mintage	VG	F	VF	XF	Unc
ND	—	42.00	70.00	145	265	—

KM# 103 80 REIS (4 Vintens)

Silver **Obv:** Crown above LXXX **Obv. Legend:** PETRVS... **Rev:** Cross of Jerusalem with or without dots in angles

Date	Mintage	VG	F	VF	XF	Unc
ND	—	36.00	60.00	125	235	—

KM# 17 100 REIS (Tostao)

Silver **Obv:** Crowned arms with mintmark at left and right **Obv. Legend:** PHILIPPVS... **Rev:** Cross of Jerusalem in inner circle with five dots in each angle **Note:** Varieties exist.

Date	Mintage	VG	F	VF	XF	Unc
ND LB	—	125	275	500	925	—

KM# 43 100 REIS (Tostao)

Silver **Obv:** Crowned arms with or without fleur de lis or dots **Obv. Legend:** JOANNES IIII... **Rev:** Cross of St. George with or without dots in angles

Date	Mintage	VG	F	VF	XF	Unc
ND(1640)INCM LC	—	250	500	850	1,650	—
ND(1640)INCM LS	—	650	1,200	2,000	3,850	—

KM# 44 100 REIS (Tostao)

Silver **Obv:** Crowned arms with or without annulets **Obv. Legend:** JOANNES IIII... **Rev:** P in angles of cross **Note:** Varieties exist.

Date	Mintage	VG	F	VF	XF	Unc
ND(1640)	—	45.00	90.00	160	325	—

KM# 45 100 REIS (Tostao)

Silver **Obv:** Crowned arms with or without annulets **Obv. Legend:** JOANNES IIII... **Rev:** E in angles of cross **Note:** Varieties exist.

Date	Mintage	VG	F	VF	XF	Unc
ND(1640)	—	100	200	350	725	—

KM# 46 100 REIS (Tostao)

Silver **Obv:** Crowned arms with or without annulets **Obv. Legend:** JOANNES IIII... **Rev:** Cross of Jerusalem with or without dots in angles **Note:** Varieties exist.

Date	Mintage	VG	F	VF	XF	Unc
1641	—	350	750	1,200	2,200	—

KM# 47 100 REIS (Tostao)

Silver **Obv:** Crowned arms with mint mark at left and right **Obv. Legend:** JOANNES IIII... **Rev:** Cross of Jerusalem with date in bottom of angles **Note:** Varieties exist.

Date	Mintage	VG	F	VF	XF	Unc
1641 LC	—	450	900	1,500	2,750	—
1641	—	30.00	50.00	100	220	—
1642	—	35.00	60.00	120	300	—

KM# 48 100 REIS (Tostao)

Silver **Obv:** Crowned arms with or without fleur de lis or dots **Obv. Legend:** JOANNES IIII... **Rev:** Cross of St. George with or without dots **Note:** Varieties exist.

Date	Mintage	VG	F	VF	XF	Unc
ND	—	30.00	60.00	120	300	—

KM# 75 100 REIS (Tostao)

Silver **Obv:** Crowned arms **Obv. Legend:** ALPHONSVS... **Rev:** Cross with dots in angles **Note:** Varieties exist.

Date	Mintage	VG	F	VF	XF	Unc
ND	—	300	550	1,050	—	—

KM# 76 100 REIS (Tostao)

Silver **Obv:** Crowned arms in baroque frame **Obv. Legend:** ALPHONSVS... **Rev:** Cross of Jerusalem in inner circle **Note:** Varieties exist.

Date	Mintage	VG	F	VF	XF	Unc
ND	—	20.00	40.00	75.00	165	—

KM# 104 100 REIS (Tostao)

Silver **Obv:** Crowned arms in baroque frame **Obv. Legend:** PETRVS... **Rev:** Cross of Jerusalem in inner circle

Date	Mintage	VG	F	VF	XF	Unc
ND	—	750	1,250	2,200	—	—

KM# 49 200 REIS (1/2 Cruzado)

Silver **Obv:** Crowned arms, value at right **Obv. Legend:** IOANNES... **Rev:** Cross of Jerusalem with dots in angles **Note:** Varieties exist.

Date	Mintage	VG	F	VF	XF	Unc
ND	—	40.00	85.00	150	325	—

KM# 50 200 REIS (1/2 Cruzado)

Silver **Obv:** Crowned arms, value at right **Obv. Legend:** IOANNES... **Rev:** Cross with P in angles **Note:** Varieties exist.

Date	Mintage	VG	F	VF	XF	Unc
ND	—	75.00	165	325	600	—

KM# 51 200 REIS (1/2 Cruzado)

Silver **Obv:** Crowned arms, value at right **Obv. Legend:** IOANNES... **Rev:** Cross with E in angles **Note:** Varieties exist.

Date	Mintage	VG	F	VF	XF	Unc
ND	—	125	250	450	825	—

KM# 77 200 REIS (1/2 Cruzado)

Silver **Obv:** Crowned arms, value at right **Obv. Legend:** ALPHONSVS... **Rev:** Dots in angles of cross **Note:** Varieties exist.

Date	Mintage	VG	F	VF	XF	Unc
ND	—	150	275	550	—	—

KM# 82 200 REIS (1/2 Cruzado)

Silver **Obv:** Crowned arms, value at right **Obv. Legend:** ALPHONSVS... **Rev:** Date in angles of cross

Date	Mintage	VG	F	VF	XF	Unc
1663	—	20.00	40.00	90.00	220	—
1664	—	22.00	45.00	100	250	—
1665	—	25.00	55.00	125	275	—
1666	—	30.00	65.00	150	350	—

KM# 105 200 REIS (1/2 Cruzado)

Silver **Obv:** Crowned arms, value at right **Obv. Legend:** PETRVS... **Rev:** Date in angles of cross

Date	Mintage	VG	F	VF	XF	Unc
1676	—	—	—	—	—	—

Note: Reported, not confirmed.

KM# 52 400 REIS (Cruzado)
Silver **Obv:** Crowned arms, value at right **Obv. Legend:** JOANNES... **Rev:** Cross of Jerusalem with dots in angles **Note:** Dav. #4380. Varieties exist.

Date	Mintage	VG	F	VF	XF	Unc
ND	—	75.00	150	285	575	—

KM# 53 400 REIS (Cruzado)
Silver **Obv:** Crowned arms, value at right **Obv. Legend:** JOANNES... **Rev:** Cross with P in angles **Note:** Dav. #4381. Varieties exist.

Date	Mintage	VG	F	VF	XF	Unc
ND	—	125	250	450	925	—

KM# 54 400 REIS (Cruzado)
Silver **Obv:** Crowned arms, value at right **Obv. Legend:** JOANNES... **Rev:** Cross with E in angles **Note:** Dav. #4382. Varieties exist.

Date	Mintage	VG	F	VF	XF	Unc
ND	—	400	900	2,250	4,950	—

KM# 78 400 REIS (Cruzado)
Silver **Obv:** Crowned arms, value at right **Obv. Legend:** ALPHONSVS... **Rev:** Dots in angles of cross **Note:** Dav. #4383

Date	Mintage	VG	F	VF	XF	Unc
ND	—	2,500	4,500	7,000	—	—

KM# 83 400 REIS (Cruzado)
Silver **Obv:** Crowned arms, value at right **Obv. Legend:** ALPHONSVS... **Rev:** Date in angles of cross **Note:** Dav. #4384

Date	Mintage	VG	F	VF	XF	Unc
1663	—	80.00	200	550	1,100	—
1664	—	100	250	650	1,300	—
1665	—	100	250	650	1,300	—
1666	—	80.00	200	550	1,100	—

KM# 84 1000 REIS
3.0600 g., 0.9170 Gold 0.0902 oz. AGW **Obv:** Crowned arms with date and value at sides, titles of Alphonso VI **Rev:** Jerusalem cross with annulets in angles in inner circle

Date	Mintage	VG	F	VF	XF	Unc
1663 Rare	—	—	—	—	—	—
1666 Rare	—	—	—	—	—	—

KM# 87 1100 REIS (1/4 Moeda)
3.0600 g., 0.9170 Gold 0.0902 oz. AGW **Obv:** Crowned arms with date and value at sides, titles of Peter as Prince Regent **Rev:** Jerusalem cross in quatrefoil in inner circle

Date	Mintage	VG	F	VF	XF	Unc
1668 Rare	—	—	—	—	—	—
Note: Sotheby's Geneva Sale 11-86 Fine realized $23,750						
1671 Rare	—	—	—	—	—	—

KM# 85 2000 REIS (1/2 Moeda)
6.1200 g., 0.9170 Gold 0.1804 oz. AGW **Obv:** Crowned arms with date and value at sides, titles of Alphonso VI **Rev:** Jerusalem cross with annulets in angles

Date	Mintage	VG	F	VF	XF	Unc
1663 Rare	—	—	—	—	—	—
1666 Rare	—	—	—	—	—	—

KM# 88 2200 REIS
6.1200 g., 0.9170 Gold 0.1804 oz. AGW **Obv:** Crowned arms with date and value at sides, titles of Peter as Prince Regent **Rev:** Jerusalem cross in quatrefoil in inner circle

Date	Mintage	VG	F	VF	XF	Unc
1668 Rare	—	—	—	—	—	—
1669 Rare	—	—	—	—	—	—
Note: Sotheby's Geneva Sale 11-86 Fine realized $22,450						
1671 Rare	—	—	—	—	—	—
1674 Rare	—	—	—	—	—	—

KM# 86 4000 REIS
12.2400 g., 0.9170 Gold 0.3608 oz. AGW **Obv:** Crowned arms with date and value at sides, titles of Alphonso VI **Rev:** Jerusalem cross with annulets in angles in inner circle

Date	Mintage	VG	F	VF	XF	Unc
1663 Rare	—	—	—	—	—	—
1664 Rare	—	—	—	—	—	—
1665 Rare	—	—	—	—	—	—
1666 Rare	—	—	—	—	—	—

KM# 89 4400 REIS (Moeda)
12.2400 g., 0.9170 Gold 0.3608 oz. AGW **Obv:** Crowned arms with date and value at sides, titles of Peter as Prince Regent **Rev:** Jerusalem cross in quatrefoil in inner circle

Date	Mintage	VG	F	VF	XF	Unc
1668 Rare	—	—	—	—	—	—
1669 Rare	—	—	—	—	—	—
Note: Sotheby's Geneva Sale 11-86 Fine realized $22,450						
1670 Rare	—	—	—	—	—	—
1671 Rare	—	—	—	—	—	—
1672 Rare	—	—	—	—	—	—
1673 Rare	—	—	—	—	—	—
1674 Rare	—	—	—	—	—	—

KM# 55 CRUZADO
3.0600 g., 0.9170 Gold 0.0902 oz. AGW **Obv:** Crowned arms with large crown, titles of John IV **Rev:** Cross of St. George with date in angles, center turned 90 degrees

Date	Mintage	VG	F	VF	XF	Unc
1642 Rare	—	—	—	—	—	—

KM# 58 CRUZADO
3.0600 g., 0.9170 Gold 0.0902 oz. AGW **Obv:** Small crown on arms **Rev:** Cross of St. George with date in angles, center turned 90 degrees

Date	Mintage	VG	F	VF	XF	Unc
1642 Rare	—	—	—	—	—	—
1647 Rare	—	—	—	—	—	—

KM# 56 2 CRUZADOS
6.1200 g., 0.9170 Gold 0.1804 oz. AGW **Obv:** Crowned arms, titles of John VI **Rev:** Cross of St. George with date in angles, center turned 90 degrees **Note:** Varieties exist with large and small crowns.

Date	Mintage	VG	F	VF	XF	Unc
1642 Rare	—	—	—	—	—	—

KM# 59 2 CRUZADOS
Obv: Small crown on arms

Date	Mintage	VG	F	VF	XF	Unc
1642 Rare	—	—	—	—	—	—
1646 Rare	—	—	—	—	—	—
1647 Rare	—	—	—	—	—	—

KM# 80 2 CRUZADOS
6.1200 g., 0.9170 Gold 0.1804 oz. AGW **Obv:** Titles of Alphonso VI **Rev:** Cross of St. George with date in angles, center turned 90 degrees

Date	Mintage	VG	F	VF	XF	Unc
1660 Rare	—	—	—	—	—	—

KM# 18 4 CRUZADOS
12.2400 g., 0.9220 Gold 0.3628 oz. AGW **Ruler:** Philip III **Obv:** Crowned arms. **Obv. Legend:** PHILIPVS... **Rev:** Cross of St. George in inner circle, 5 dots in each angle **Note:** Varieties exist.

Date	Mintage	VG	F	VF	XF	Unc
ND L Rare	—	—	—	—	—	—
ND LB Rare	—	—	—	—	—	—

KM# 60 4 CRUZADOS
12.2400 g., 0.9170 Gold 0.3608 oz. AGW **Ruler:** John IV **Obv:** Crowned arms, titles of John IV **Rev:** Cross of St. George with date in angles in inner circle **Note:** Varieties exist.

Date	Mintage	VG	F	VF	XF	Unc
1642 Rare	—	—	—	—	—	—
1645 Rare	—	—	—	—	—	—
1646 Rare	—	—	—	—	—	—
1647 Rare	—	—	—	—	—	—
1648 Rare	—	—	—	—	—	—
1652 Rare	—	—	—	—	—	—

KM# 57 4 CRUZADOS
12.2400 g., 0.9170 Gold 0.3608 oz. AGW **Ruler:** John IV **Obv:** Crowned arms flanked by quatrefoils, titles of John IV **Rev:** Cross of St. George with date in angles, center turned 90 degrees

Date	Mintage	VG	F	VF	XF	Unc
1642 Rare	—	—	—	—	—	—

KM# 9.1 4 CRUZADOS
12.2400 g., 0.9220 Gold 0.3628 oz. AGW **Ruler:** Philip II **Obv:** Crowned arms with mint mark at left and value at right **Obv. Legend:** PHILIPPVS... **Rev:** Cross of St. George in inner circle, 5 dots in each angle

Date	Mintage	VG	F	VF	XF	Unc
ND LB Rare	—	—	—	—	—	—
ND L Rare	—	—	—	—	—	—

KM# 81 4 CRUZADOS
12.2400 g., 0.9170 Gold 0.3608 oz. AGW **Ruler:** Alfonso VI **Obv:** Crowned arms with date and value at sides, titles of Alfonso VI **Rev:** Jerusalem cross with date in angles in inner circle **Note:** Varieties exist.

Date	Mintage	VG	F	VF	XF	Unc
1660 Rare	—	—	—	—	—	—
1663 Rare	—	—	—	—	—	—

KM# A82 4 CRUZADOS
12.2400 g., 0.9170 Gold 0.3608 oz. AGW **Ruler:** Alfonso VI **Obv:** 4000 Reis KM#86 **Rev:** 4 Cruzados KM#81 **Note:** Mule.

Date	Mintage	VG	F	VF	XF	Unc
1663 Rare	—	—	—	—	—	—

MILLED COINAGE

KM# 128 1-1/2 REIS
Copper **Obv:** Crowned shield in baroque frame **Obv. Legend:** PETRVS... **Rev:** 1-1/2 in cartouche, date above

Date	Mintage	VG	F	VF	XF	Unc
1683	—	240	475	900	1,500	—

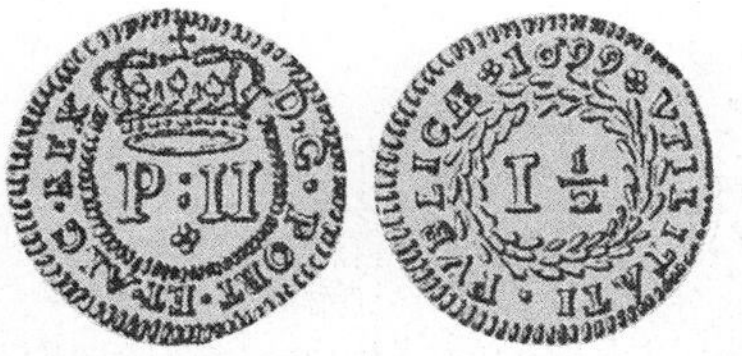

KM# 165 1-1/2 REIS
Copper **Ruler:** Peter II **Obv:** Crown above P:II within wreath **Obv. Legend:** D • G • PORT • ET • ALG • REX **Rev:** Value within wreath, date above **Rev. Legend:** VTILITATI • PVBLICÆ **Note:** Varieties exist with center turned 180 degrees.

Date	Mintage	VG	F	VF	XF	Unc
1699	—	12.00	25.00	55.00	110	—

KM# 132 20 REIS (Vinten)
Silver **Obv:** Globe **Rev:** Cross of Jerusalem with quatrefoils in angles

Date	Mintage	VG	F	VF	XF	Unc
ND(1686)INCM	—	48.00	95.00	180	300	—

KM# 129 3 REIS (III)
Copper **Obv:** Crowned arms on baroque frame

Date	Mintage	VG	F	VF	XF	Unc
1683	—	60.00	120	250	550	—

KM# 166 3 REIS (III)
Copper **Ruler:** Peter II **Obv:** Crown above PII within wreath **Rev:** Value within wreath **Note:** Varieties exist.

Date	Mintage	VG	F	VF	XF	Unc
1699	—	10.00	25.00	50.00	120	—

KM# 130 5 REIS (V)
Copper **Obv:** Crowned shield in baroque frame

Date	Mintage	VG	F	VF	XF	Unc
1683	—	70.00	150	300	650	—

KM# 167 5 REIS (V)
Copper **Ruler:** Peter II **Obv:** Crown above P II within wreath **Obv. Legend:** D • G • PORT • ET • ALG • REX **Rev:** Value within wreath, date above **Rev. Legend:** PVBLICÆ ....

Date	Mintage	VG	F	VF	XF	Unc
1699	—	10.00	25.00	50.00	120	—

KM# 131 10 REIS (X; 1/2 Vinten)
Copper **Obv:** Crowned shield in baroque frame

Date	Mintage	VG	F	VF	XF	Unc
1683	—	100	200	400	850	—

KM# 168 10 REIS (X; 1/2 Vinten)
Copper **Ruler:** Peter II **Obv:** Crowned PII within broken rope wreath **Obv. Legend:** D • G • PORT ET • ALG • REX **Rev:** Value (X) within wreath, date above **Rev. Legend:** VTILITATI .... **Note:** Varieties exist.

Date	Mintage	VG	F	VF	XF	Unc
1699	—	10.00	25.00	55.00	130	—

KM# 133 20 REIS (Vinten)
Silver **Obv:** Globe **Rev:** Cross with P in angles **Note:** Varieties exist.

Date	Mintage	VG	F	VF	XF	Unc
ND(1688)P	—	14.00	25.00	45.50	100	—

KM# 118 40 REIS (Pataco)
Silver **Obv:** Crown above XXXX **Obv. Legend:** PETRVS... **Rev:** Cross with rosettes in angles **Note:** Varieties exist.

Date	Mintage	VG	F	VF	XF	Unc
ND	—	15.00	30.00	85.00	175	—
(1)679	—	300	550	1,150	2,100	—

KM# 134 40 REIS (Pataco)
Silver **Obv:** Crown above XXXX **Obv. Legend:** PETRVS II... **Rev:** Cross with rosettes in angles **Note:** Varieties exist.

Date	Mintage	VG	F	VF	XF	Unc
ND	—	9.00	18.00	39.00	85.00	—

KM# 110 50 REIS (1/2 Tostao)
Silver **Obv:** Crowned arms **Obv. Legend:** PETRVS... **Rev:** Cross of Jerusalem with dots in angles **Note:** Varieties exist.

Date	Mintage	VG	F	VF	XF	Unc
ND(1667-83)	—	30.00	60.00	145	295	—

KM# 135 50 REIS (1/2 Tostao)
Silver **Obv:** Crowned arms **Obv. Legend:** PETRVS II... **Rev:** Cross of Jerusalem with dots in angles **Note:** Varieties exist.

Date	Mintage	VG	F	VF	XF	Unc
ND(1683-1706)	—	25.00	20.00	110	230	—

KM# 136 50 REIS (1/2 Tostao)
Silver **Obv:** Value: XXXX, crown above **Obv. Legend:** PETRVS II... **Rev:** Cross of St. George with quatrefoils in angles **Note:** Varieties exist.

Date	Mintage	VG	F	VF	XF	Unc
ND(1683-1706)	—	12.00	25.00	60.00	115	—

KM# 137 50 REIS (1/2 Tostao)
Silver **Obv:** Value: XXXX, crown above **Obv. Legend:** PETRVS II... **Rev:** Cross with P in angles **Note:** Varieties exist.

Date	Mintage	VG	F	VF	XF	Unc
ND(1683-1706)P	—	12.00	25.00	60.00	115	—

KM# 138 60 REIS (3 Vintens)
Silver **Obv:** Crowned arms **Obv. Legend:** PETRVS II... **Rev:** Cross of Jerusalem with quatrefoils or rosettes in angles **Note:** Varieties exist.

Date	Mintage	VG	F	VF	XF	Unc
ND	—	12.00	30.00	65.00	130	—

KM# 139 60 REIS (3 Vintens)
Silver **Obv:** Crowned arms **Obv. Legend:** PETRVS II... **Rev:** Cross with P in angles **Note:** Varieties exist.

Date	Mintage	VG	F	VF	XF	Unc
ND	—	12.00	30.00	65.00	130	—

KM# 111 80 REIS
Silver **Obv:** Crown with LXXX below **Obv. Legend:** PETRVS... **Rev:** Cross of St. George with rosettes in angles **Note:** Varieties exist.

Date	Mintage	VG	F	VF	XF	Unc
ND(1667-83)	—	25.00	48.00	110	230	—

KM# 140 80 REIS
Silver **Obv:** Crown with LXXX below **Obv. Legend:** PETRVS II... **Rev:** Cross of St. George with rosettes in angles **Note:** Varieties exist.

Date	Mintage	VG	F	VF	XF	Unc
ND(1676-1706)	—	25.00	48.00	110	230	—

KM# 112 80 REIS (LXXX; Tostao)
Silver **Obv:** Crowned arms **Obv. Legend:** PETRVS... **Rev:** Cross of Jerusalem with quatrefoils in angles **Note:** Worth 100 Reis, though marked LXXX = 80 Reis. Varieties exist.

Date	Mintage	VG	F	VF	XF	Unc
ND(1663-83)	—	30.00	60.00	130	260	—
1681	—	350	650	1,300	2,400	—

KM# 141 80 REIS (LXXX; Tostao)
Silver **Obv:** Crowned arms **Obv. Legend:** PETRVS II. D G. REX. PORTVOA **Rev:** Rosettes in angles of cross

Date	Mintage	VG	F	VF	XF	Unc
ND(1683-1706)	—	25.00	48.00	110	230	—

KM# 142 80 REIS (LXXX; Tostao)
Silver **Obv:** Crowned above LXXX **Obv. Legend:** PETRVS II. D G. PORT. ET. AL. REX **Rev:** Cross of St. George with rosettes in angles of cross **Note:** Varieties exist.

Date	Mintage	VG	F	VF	XF	Unc
ND(1683-1706)	—	14.00	30.00	70.00	145	—

KM# 157 80 REIS (LXXX; Tostao)
Silver **Ruler:** Peter II **Obv:** Crown above LXXX, date below **Obv. Legend:** • PETRVS • II • D • G • REX • PORTVG • **Rev:** Cross with P in angles **Rev. Legend:** IN HOC SIGNO VINCES **Note:** Varieties exist.

Date	Mintage	VG	F	VF	XF	Unc
1689	—	8.00	18.00	41.50	100	—
1690	—	8.00	18.00	41.50	100	—
1691	—	8.00	18.00	41.50	100	—
1692	—	14.00	30.00	65.00	130	—
1693	—	18.00	36.00	80.00	155	—
1696	—	25.00	48.00	110	260	—
1697	—	25.00	48.00	110	260	—
1699	—	70.00	145	325	575	—
1700	—	8.00	18.00	41.50	100	—

KM# 143 120 REIS (6 Vintens)
Silver **Obv:** Crowned arms **Obv. Legend:** PETRVS II... **Rev:** Jerusalem cross with rosettes in angles

Date	Mintage	VG	F	VF	XF	Unc
ND(1673-1706)	—	25.00	48.00	110	230	—

KM# 158 120 REIS (6 Vintens)
Silver **Obv:** Crowned arms **Obv. Legend:** PETRVS II... **Rev:** P in angles of cross

Date	Mintage	VG	F	VF	XF	Unc
1689	—	20.00	36.00	65.00	125	—
1690	—	20.00	36.00	65.00	125	—
1691	—	25.00	42.00	70.00	145	—
1693	—	30.00	48.00	85.00	165	—
1698	—	36.00	60.00	130	295	—

KM# 113 200 REIS (1/2 Cruzado)
Silver **Obv:** Crowned arms, value at left, date at right **Obv. Legend:** PETRVS... **Rev:** Cross of Jerusalem with rosettes in angles **Note:** Varieties exist.

Date	Mintage	VG	F	VF	XF	Unc
1677	—	650	1,400	2,700	5,100	—
1679	—	550	1,200	2,400	4,800	—
1681	—	150	300	600	1,150	—
1682	—	350	775	1,500	3,000	—

KM# 144 200 REIS (1/2 Cruzado)
Silver **Obv:** Crowned arms, value at left, date at right **Obv. Legend:** PETRVS II... **Rev:** Cross of Jerusalem with rosettes in angles **Note:** Varieties exist.

Date	Mintage	VG	F	VF	XF	Unc
1683	—	350	750	1,500	2,700	—
1684	—	325	700	1,400	2,600	—

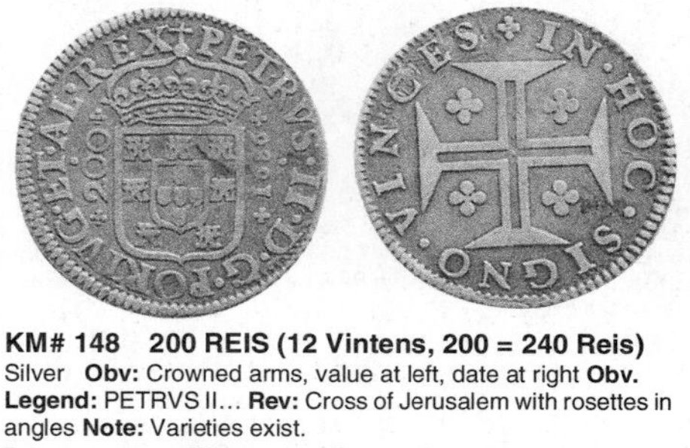

KM# 148 200 REIS (12 Vintens, 200 = 240 Reis)
Silver **Obv:** Crowned arms, value at left, date at right **Obv. Legend:** PETRVS II... **Rev:** Cross of Jerusalem with rosettes in angles **Note:** Varieties exist.

Date	Mintage	VG	F	VF	XF	Unc
1686	—	37.50	90.00	190	425	—
1687	—	22.50	55.00	115	300	—
1688	—	22.50	55.00	115	300	—
1689	—	22.50	55.00	115	300	—
1690	—	60.00	130	265	525	—
1691	—	60.00	130	265	525	—
1692	—	180	350	650	1,400	—
1693	—	350	775	1,600	3,000	—
1696	—	105	225	450	825	—
1697	—	130	265	525	900	—

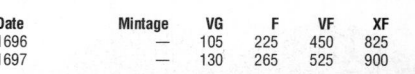

KM# 153 200 REIS (12 Vintens, 200 = 240 Reis)
Silver **Obv:** Crowned arms, value at left, date at right **Obv. Legend:** PETRVS II... **Rev:** Cross of Jerusalem, P in angles **Note:** Varieties exist.

Date	Mintage	VG	F	VF	XF	Unc
1688	—	75.00	150	350	675	—
1689	—	27.50	55.00	115	225	—
1690	—	30.00	70.00	135	280	—
1699 Rare	—	—	—	—	—	—

KM# 114.1 400 REIS (Cruzado)
Silver **Obv:** Crowned arms, value at left, date at right **Obv. Legend:** PETRVS... **Rev:** Cross of St. George with rosettes in angles **Note:** Dav. #4386

Date	Mintage	VG	F	VF	XF	Unc
1677 Rare	—	—	—	—	—	—
1679 Rare	—	—	—	—	—	—
1681	—	2,000	3,600	6,000	11,000	—

KM# 114.2 400 REIS (Cruzado)
Silver **Obv:** Dots or rosettes before and after date and value **Obv. Legend:** PETRVS... **Rev:** Cross of St. George with rosettes in angles **Note:** Varieties exist.

Date	Mintage	VG	F	VF	XF	Unc
1681	—	550	1,150	2,200	3,900	—
1682	—	550	1,150	2,200	3,900	—
1683	—	550	1,150	2,200	3,900	—

KM# 145.1 400 REIS (Cruzado)
Silver **Obv:** Prince's crown above arms **Obv. Legend:** PETRVS II... **Rev:** Cross of St. George with rosettes in angles **Note:** Dav. #4388

Date	Mintage	VG	F	VF	XF	Unc
1683	—	475	950	2,100	4,200	—
1684	—	350	775	1,900	4,000	—
1686	—	1,200	2,400	4,200	6,600	—

KM# 145.2 400 REIS (Cruzado)
Silver **Obv:** Arms with King's crown above **Obv. Legend:** PETRVS II... **Rev:** Cross of St. George with rosettes in angles **Note:** Dav. #4389. Varieties exist.

Date	Mintage	VG	F	VF	XF	Unc
1686	—	180	350	775	1,500	—
1687	—	55.00	115	225	525	—

Λ# 154.2 400 REIS (Cruzado Novo, 400 = 480 ›is)

ver **Obv:** Crowned arms, value at left, date at right **Obv.** **gend:** PETRVS II... **Rev:** Cross of St. George with rosettes in gles **Note:** Dav. #4390

e	Mintage	VG	F	VF	XF	Unc
8INCM	—	70.00	150	300	700	—
9	—	70.00	150	300	700	—
0	—	110	250	500	1,000	—
1	—	625	1,250	2,500	5,000	—
2	—	500	1,150	2,200	4,400	—
3 Rare	—	—	—	—	—	—

 # 154.1 400 REIS (Cruzado Novo, 400 = 480 is)

er **Obv:** Crowned arms, value at left, date at right **Obv.** **end:** PETRVS II... **Rev:** Cross of St. George with P in angles **e:** Dav. #4392; 1702 is Dav. #1625.

	Mintage	VG	F	VF	XF	Unc
3	—	240	475	1,050	2,000	—
9	—	48.00	110	200	400	—
)	—	48.00	110	200	400	—
	—	55.00	120	215	450	—
2	—	120	240	475	950	—
3	—	145	280	550	1,100	—
4	—	160	325	650	1,350	—
5	—	550	1,200	2,400	4,000	—
	—	160	325	650	1,350	—
	—	200	400	800	1,500	—
	—	200	400	800	1,500	—
Rare	—	—	—	—	—	—

 # 154.3 400 REIS (Cruzado Novo, 400 = 480 s)

r **Ruler:** Peter II **Obv:** Crowned arms, flanked by vertical date value **Obv. Legend:** PETRVS • II • ... **Rev:** Maltese cross, refoil in angles **Rev. Legend:** • IN HOC SIGNO VINCES • **Note:** #4391; 1700s are Dav. #1627. Varieties exist.

Mintage	VG	F	VF	XF	Unc
—	270	550	1,150	2,200	—
—	775	1,500	3,300	5,400	—

 # 115 1000 REIS (Quartinho, 1200 Reis)

00 g., 0.9170 Gold 0.0793 oz. AGW **Obv:** Crowned arms value at side, titles of Peter as Prince Regent **Rev:** Jerusalem s with quatrefoils in angles, date at top

Mintage	VG	F	VF	XF	Unc
—	775	1,600	3,250	5,200	—
—	325	650	1,300	2,600	—
—	475	950	1,950	3,250	—
—	475	950	1,950	3,250	—

 # 146 1000 REIS (Quartinho, 1200 Reis)

00 g., 0.9170 Gold 0.0793 oz. AGW **Obv:** Crowned narrow d with value at side, titles of Peter II **Rev:** Jerusalem cross quatrefoils in angles, date at top

Mintage	VG	F	VF	XF	Unc
—	1,400	2,700	4,900	9,100	—

KM# 155 1000 REIS (Quartinho, 1200 Reis)

2.6900 g., 0.9170 Gold 0.0793 oz. AGW **Ruler:** Peter II **Obv:** Crowned arms with vertical value at left side, titles of Peter II at right **Obv. Legend:** PETRVS • II • ... **Rev:** Jerusalem cross, quatrefoil in angles, date above **Rev. Legend:** IN HOC SIGNO VINCES

Date	Mintage	VG	F	VF	XF	Unc
1688	—	300	600	1,200	2,150	—
1689	—	200	400	775	1,450	—
1690	—	235	500	1,000	1,800	—
1691	—	170	325	575	1,050	—
1698	—	235	500	1,000	1,800	—
1699	—	200	400	775	1,450	—

KM# 116 2000 REIS

5.3800 g., 0.9170 Gold 0.1586 oz. AGW **Obv:** Crowned arms with value at side, titles of Peter as Prince Regent **Rev:** Jerusalem crown with quatrefoils in angles **Note:** Varieties exist.

Date	Mintage	VG	F	VF	XF	Unc
1677	—	1,100	2,100	3,950	6,400	—
1678	—	600	1,250	2,550	4,300	—
1680	—	600	1,250	2,550	4,300	—
1681	—	600	1,250	2,550	4,300	—
1682	—	725	1,450	2,850	5,000	—

KM# 147 2000 REIS

5.3800 g., 0.9170 Gold 0.1586 oz. AGW **Ruler:** Peter II **Obv:** Crowned arms with vertical value at left, titles of Peter II at right **Rev:** Jerusalem cross with quatrefoils in angles **Note:** Similar to 4000 Reis, KM#156. Varieties exist.

Date	Mintage	VG	F	VF	XF	Unc
1683	—	2,100	3,950	5,800	9,400	—
1684	—	1,750	3,200	5,000	8,600	—
1688	—	600	1,150	1,850	3,200	—
1689	—	350	650	1,150	1,950	—
1690	—	350	650	1,150	1,950	—
1691	—	425	850	1,350	2,350	—
1692	—	285	575	950	1,700	—
1699	—	425	850	1,350	2,350	—

KM# 117 4000 REIS

10.7600 g., 0.9170 Gold 0.3172 oz. AGW **Obv:** Crowned arms, value at sides, titles of Peter as Prince Regent **Rev:** Jerusalem cross with quatrefoils in angles **Note:** Varieties exist.

Date	Mintage	VG	F	VF	XF	Unc
1677	—	1,100	2,200	4,200	7,800	—
1678	—	1,250	2,500	4,500	8,400	—
1680/78	—	1,100	2,200	4,200	7,800	—
1680	—	1,100	2,200	4,200	7,800	—
1681	—	1,100	2,200	4,200	7,800	—
1682	—	1,100	2,200	4,200	7,800	—

KM# 156 4000 REIS

10.7600 g., 0.9170 Gold 0.3172 oz. AGW **Ruler:** Peter II **Obv:** Crowned arms, vertical value at left, titles of Peter II at right **Obv. Legend:** PETRVS • II • D • G • PORT • E • TALG • REX **Rev:** Jerusalem cross with quatrefoils in angles, date above **Rev. Legend:** IN HOC SIGNO VINCES

Date	Mintage	VG	F	VF	XF	Unc
1683 Rare	—	—	—	—	—	—
1688	—	625	1,250	2,500	4,000	—
1689	—	625	1,050	1,700	2,500	—
1690	—	BV	625	1,150	1,850	—
1691	—	625	1,250	2,500	4,000	—
1692/90	—	—	—	—	—	—
1692	—	BV	625	1,150	1,850	—
1693	—	600	1,050	1,700	2,500	—
1694	—	600	1,050	1,700	2,500	—
1695	—	BV	625	1,150	1,850	—
1696	—	BV	625	1,150	1,850	—
1697	—	BV	625	1,150	1,850	—

COUNTERMARKED COINAGE

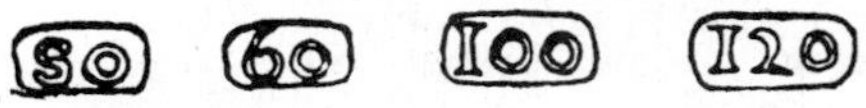

Countermarked Type I

Countermarked Type II

Countermarked Type III

Countermarked Type IV

Countermarked Type V

Countermarked Type VII

KM# 416 50 REIS

Silver **Countermark:** 50 in rectangle **Note:** Countermark Type I on Portugal 40 Reis, KM#34.

CM Date	Host Date	Good	VG	F	VF	XF
ND(1642)	ND(1642)	38.50	70.00	140	250	—

KM# 420.3 60 REIS

Silver **Countermark:** 60 in rectangle **Note:** Countermark on Type I on Spain 1 Real of Philip II.

CM Date	Host Date	Good	VG	F	VF	XF
ND(1642)	ND(1556-98)	35.00	65.00	125	225	—

KM# 420.4 60 REIS

Silver **Countermark:** 60 in rectangle **Note:** Countermark Type I on Spain 1 Real, KM#52.

CM Date	Host Date	Good	VG	F	VF	XF
ND(1642)	ND(1598-1620)	35.00	—	65.00	125	225

KM# 420.1 60 REIS

Silver **Countermark:** 60 in rectangle **Note:** Countermark on Portugal 1/2 Tostao, KM#16.

CM Date	Host Date	Good	VG	F	VF	XF
ND(1642)	ND	33.00	65.00	120	185	—

KM# 420.2 60 REIS

Silver **Countermark:** 60 in rectangle **Note:** Countermark Type I on Portugal 1/2 Tostao, KM#36.

CM Date	Host Date	Good	VG	F	VF	XF
ND(1642)	ND	38.50	70.00	140	250	—

KM# 429.3 120 REIS

Silver **Countermark:** 120 in rectangle **Note:** Countermark Type I on Spain 2 Reales of Philip II.

CM Date	Host Date	Good	VG	F	VF	XF
ND(1642)	ND(1587-98)	35.00	65.00	125	225	—

KM# 429.4 120 REIS

Silver **Countermark:** 120 in rectangle **Note:** Countermark Type I on Spain 2 Reales, KM#17.

CM Date	Host Date	Good	VG	F	VF	XF
ND(1642)	1601-21	35.00	65.00	125	225	—

KM# 429.1 120 REIS

Silver **Countermark:** 120 in rectangle **Note:** Countermark Type I on Portugal 100 Reis, 1 Tostao, KM#17.

CM Date	Host Date	Good	VG	F	VF	XF
ND(1642)	ND	38.50	70.00	140	250	—

KM# 429.2 120 REIS

Silver **Countermark:** 120 in rectangle **Note:** Countermark Type I on Portugal 100 Reis, 1 Tostao, KM#43.

CM Date	Host Date	Good	VG	F	VF	XF
ND(1642)	ND	150	300	600	1,100	—

COUNTERMARKED COINAGE

Type III

KM# 417.1 50 REIS

Silver **Countermark:** 50 in crowned square **Note:** Countermark Type III on Portugal 40 Reis, KM#33.

CM Date	Host Date	Good	VG	F	VF	XF
ND(1663)	ND	49.50	100	165	250	—

KM# 417.2 50 REIS

Silver **Countermark:** 50 in crowned square **Note:** Countermark Type III on Portugal 40 Reis, KM#35.

CM Date	Host Date	Good	VG	F	VF	XF
ND(1663)	ND	55.00	110	195	300	—

KM# 417.3 50 REIS

Silver **Countermark:** 50 in crowned square **Note:** Countermark Type III on Portugal 40 Reis, KM#34.

CM Date	Host Date	Good	VG	F	VF	XF
ND(1663)	ND	38.50	70.00	120	185	—

KM# 417.4 50 REIS
Silver **Countermark:** 50 in crowned square **Note:** Countermark Type III on Portugal 40 Reis, KM#69.

CM Date	Host Date	Good	VG	F	VF	XF
ND(1663)	ND	220	500	1,000	1,650	—

KM# 426.1 100 REIS
Silver **Countermark:** 100 in crowned rectangle **Note:** Countermark Type III on Portugal 80 Reis, KM#40.

CM Date	Host Date	Good	VG	F	VF	XF
ND(1663)	ND	49.50	100	165	250	—

KM# 426.2 100 REIS
Silver **Countermark:** 100 in crowned rectangle **Note:** Countermark Type III on Portugal 80 Reis, KM#42.

CM Date	Host Date	Good	VG	F	VF	XF
ND(1663)	ND	55.00	110	195	300	—

KM# 426.3 100 REIS
Silver **Countermark:** 100 in crowned rectangle **Note:** Countermark Type III on Portugal 80 Reis, KM#41.

CM Date	Host Date	Good	VG	F	VF	XF
ND(1663)	ND	49.50	100	165	250	—

KM# 426.4 100 REIS
Silver **Countermark:** 100 in crowned rectangle **Note:** Countermark Type III on Portugal 80 Reis, KM#73.

CM Date	Host Date	Good	VG	F	VF	XF
ND(1663)	ND	195	425	825	1,400	—

KM# 434.1 250 REIS
Silver **Countermark:** 250 in crowned rectangle **Note:** Countermark Type III on Portugal 200 Reis, KM#49.

CM Date	Host Date	Good	VG	F	VF	XF
ND(1663)	ND	55.00	110	180	270	—

KM# 434.2 250 REIS
Silver **Countermark:** 250 in crowned rectangle **Note:** Countermark Type III on Portugal 200 Reis, KM#51.

CM Date	Host Date	Good	VG	F	VF	XF
ND(1642)	ND	90.00	180	300	475	—

KM# 434.3 250 REIS
Silver **Countermark:** 250 in crowned rectangle **Note:** Countermark Type III on Portugal 200 Reis, KM#50.

CM Date	Host Date	Good	VG	F	VF	XF
ND(1663)	ND	60.00	120	210	325	—

KM# 434.4 250 REIS
Silver **Countermark:** 250 in crowned rectangle **Note:** Countermark Type III on Portugal 200 Reis, KM#77.

CM Date	Host Date	Good	VG	F	VF	XF
ND(1642)	ND	70.00	145	240	425	—

KM# 437.1 500 REIS
Silver **Countermark:** 500 in crowned rectangle **Note:** Countermark Type III on Portugal 400 Reis, KM#52.

CM Date	Host Date	Good	VG	F	VF	XF
ND(1663)	ND	85.00	160	270	425	—

KM# 437.2 500 REIS
Silver **Countermark:** 500 in crowned rectangle **Note:** Countermark Type III on Portugal 400 Reis, KM#54.

CM Date	Host Date	Good	VG	F	VF	XF
ND(1663)	ND	300	650	1,200	2,000	—

KM# 437.3 500 REIS
Silver **Countermark:** 500 in crowned rectangle **Note:** Countermark Type III on Portugal 400 Reis, KM#53.

CM Date	Host Date	Good	VG	F	VF	XF
ND(1663)	ND	120	240	400	650	—

KM# 437.4 500 REIS
Silver **Countermark:** 500 in crowned rectangle **Note:** Countermark Type III on Portugal 400 Reis, KM#78.

CM Date	Host Date	Good	VG	F	VF	XF
ND(1663)	ND Rare	—	—	—	—	—

COUNTERMARKED COINAGE

Type IV

KM# 418.1 50 REIS
Silver **Countermark:** 50 in crowned square **Note:** Countermark Type IV on Portugal 40 Reis, KM#33.

CM Date	Host Date	Good	VG	F	VF	XF
ND(1663)	ND	44.00	75.00	130	220	—

KM# 418.2 50 REIS
Silver **Countermark:** 50 in crowned square **Note:** Countermark Type IV on Portugal 40 Reis, KM#35.

CM Date	Host Date	Good	VG	F	VF	XF
ND(1663)	ND	55.00	110	195	300	—

KM# 418.3 50 REIS
Silver **Countermark:** 50 in crowned square **Note:** Countermark Type IV on Portugal 40 Reis, KM#34.

CM Date	Host Date	Good	VG	F	VF	XF
ND(1663)	ND	49.50	100	165	250	—

KM# 418.4 50 REIS
Silver **Countermark:** 50 in crowned square **Note:** Countermark Type IV on Portugal 40 Reis, KM#69.

CM Date	Host Date	Good	VG	F	VF	XF
ND(1663)	ND	220	500	1,000	1,650	—

KM# 427.1 100 REIS
Silver **Countermark:** 100 in crowned rectangle **Note:** Countermark Type IV on Portugal 80 Reis, KM#40.

CM Date	Host Date	Good	VG	F	VF	XF
ND(1663)	ND	49.50	100	165	250	—

KM# 427.2 100 REIS
Silver **Countermark:** 100 in crowned rectangle **Note:** Countermark Type IV on Portugal 80 Reis, KM#42.

CM Date	Host Date	Good	VG	F	VF	XF
ND(1663)	ND	65.00	130	220	350	—

KM# 427.3 100 REIS
Silver **Countermark:** 100 in crowned rectangle **Note:** Countermark Type IV on Portugal 80 Reis, KM#41.

CM Date	Host Date	Good	VG	F	VF	XF
ND(1663)	ND	49.50	100	165	250	—

KM# 427.4 100 REIS
Silver **Countermark:** 100 in rectangle **Note:** Countermark Type IV on Portugal 80 Reis, KM#73.

CM Date	Host Date	Good	VG	F	VF	XF
ND(1663)	ND	195	425	825	1,400	—

KM# 435.1 250 REIS
Silver **Countermark:** 250 in crowned rectangle **Note:** Countermark Type IV on Portugal 200 Reis, KM#49.

CM Date	Host Date	Good	VG	F	VF	XF
ND(1663)	ND	49.50	100	165	250	—

KM# 435.2 250 REIS
Silver **Countermark:** 250 in crowned rectangle **Note:** Countermark Type IV on Portugal 200 Reis, KM#51.

CM Date	Host Date	Good	VG	F	VF	XF
ND(1663)	ND	85.00	165	275	450	—

KM# 435.3 250 REIS
Silver **Countermark:** 250 in crowned rectangle **Note:** Countermark Type IV on Portugal 200 Reis, KM#50.

CM Date	Host Date	Good	VG	F	VF	XF
ND(1663)	ND	55.00	110	195	300	—

KM# 435.4 250 REIS
Silver **Countermark:** 250 in crowned rectangle **Note:** Countermark Type IV on Portugal 200 Reis, KM#82.

CM Date	Host Date	Good	VG	F	VF
ND(1663)	ND	100	200	350	600

KM# 438.1 500 REIS
Silver **Countermark:** 500 in crowned rectangle **Note:** Countermark Type IV on Portugal 400 Reis, KM#52.

CM Date	Host Date	Good	VG	F	VF
ND(1663)	ND	90.00	175	300	500

KM# 438.2 500 REIS
Silver **Countermark:** 500 in crowned rectangle **Note:** Countermark Type IV on Portugal 400 Reis, KM#54.

CM Date	Host Date	Good	VG	F	VF
ND(1663)	ND	375	775	1,400	2,500

KM# 438.3 500 REIS
Silver **Countermark:** 500 in crowned rectangle **Note:** Countermark Type IV on Portugal 400 Reis, KM#53.

CM Date	Host Date	Good	VG	F	VF
ND(1663)	ND	120	225	400	650

KM# 438.4 500 REIS
Silver **Countermark:** 500 in crowned rectangle **Note:** Countermark Type IV on Portugal 400 Reis, KM#83.

CM Date	Host Date	Good	VG	F	VF
ND(1663)	ND	775	1,300	2,200	3,850

COUNTERMARKED COINAGE

Type II

Authorized by Decree of November 20, 1662 on Po guese coins of John IV and Alfonso VI.

KM# 450.1 1000 REIS
3.0600 g., 0.9170 Gold 0.0902 oz. AGW **Countermark:** Crowned 1 in square frame **Note:** Countermark Type II on 1 Cruzado, KM#55.

CM Date	Host Date	Good	VG	F	VF
ND(1662)	1642 Rare	—	—	—	—

KM# 450.2 1000 REIS
3.0600 g., 0.9170 Gold 0.0902 oz. AGW **Countermark:** Crowned 1 in square frame **Note:** Countermark Type II on 1 Cruzado, KM#58.

CM Date	Host Date	Good	VG	F	VF
ND(1662)	1642, 1647 Rare	—	—	—	—

KM# 451.1 2000 REIS
6.1200 g., 0.9170 Gold 0.1804 oz. AGW **Countermark:** Crowned 1, 2, or 4 in square frame **Note:** Countermark Typ on 2 Cruzados, KM#59.

CM Date	Host Date	Good	VG	F	VF
ND(1662)	1642, 1646, 1647 Rare	—	—	—	—

KM# 451.2 2000 REIS
6.1200 g., 0.9170 Gold 0.1804 oz. AGW **Countermark:** Crowned 1, 2, or 4 in square frame **Note:** Countermark Typ on 2 Cruzados, KM#80.

CM Date	Host Date	Good	VG	F	VF
ND(1662)	1660 Rare	—	—	—	—

KM# 452.1 4000 REIS
12.2400 g., 0.9170 Gold 0.3608 oz. AGW **Countermark:** Crowned 4 in square frame **Note:** Countermark Type II on 4 Cruzados of Philip I.

CM Date	Host Date	Good	VG	F	VF
ND(1662)	ND Rare	—	—	—	—

KM# 452.2 4000 REIS
12.2400 g., 0.9170 Gold 0.3608 oz. AGW **Countermark:** Crowned 4 in square frame **Note:** Countermark Type II on 4 Cruzados, KM#9.

CM Date	Host Date	Good	VG	F	VF
ND(1662)	ND Rare	—	—	—	—

KM# 452.3 4000 REIS
12.2400 g., 0.9170 Gold 0.3608 oz. AGW **Countermark:** Crowned 4 in square frame **Note:** Countermark Type II on Cruzados, KM#18.

CM Date	Host Date	Good	VG	F	VF
ND(1662)	ND Rare	—	—	—	—

M# 452.4 4000 REIS
.2400 g., 0.9170 Gold 0.3608 oz. AGW **Countermark:** owned 4 in square frame **Note:** Countermark Type II on 4 uzados, KM#60.

Date	Host Date	Good	VG	F	VF	XF
(1662)	1642-1652 Rare	—	—	—	—	—

M# 452.5 4000 REIS
.2400 g., 0.9170 Gold 0.3608 oz. AGW **Countermark:** owned 4 in square frame **Note:** Countermark Type II on 4 uzados, KM#81.

Date	Host Date	Good	VG	F	VF	XF
(1662)	1660, 1663 Rare	—	—	—	—	—

COUNTERMARKED COINAGE

Type V

Authorized by Decree of April 12, 1668 on Portuguese ins of John IV and Alfonso VI.

Countermark: Crowned 1100, 2200, or 4400 in rectangle.

 # 453.1 1100 REIS
600 g., 0.9220 Gold 0.0907 oz. AGW **Countermark:** owned 1100 in rectangle **Note:** Countermark Type V on 1 uzado, KM58.

Date	Host Date	Good	VG	F	VF	XF
(1668)	1642 Rare	—	—	—	—	—
(1668)	1647 Rare	—	—	—	—	—

 # 453.2 1100 REIS
600 g., 0.9220 Gold 0.0907 oz. AGW **Countermark:** owned 1100 in rectangle **Note:** Countermark Type V on 1000 is, KM#450.2.

Date	Host Date	Good	VG	F	VF	XF
(1668)	1642, 1647 Rare	—	—	—	—	—

 # 453.3 1100 REIS
600 g., 0.9170 Gold 0.0902 oz. AGW **Countermark:** owned 1100 in rectangle **Note:** Countermark Type V on 1000 s, KM#84.

Date	Host Date	Good	VG	F	VF	XF
1668)	1663, 1666 Rare	—	—	—	—	—

 # 454.1 2200 REIS
200 g., 0.9170 Gold 0.1804 oz. AGW **Countermark:** wned 2200 in rectangle **Note:** Countermark Type V on 2 zados, KM#59.

Date	Host Date	Good	VG	F	VF	XF
1668)	1642, 1646, 1647 Rare	—	—	—	—	—

 # 454.2 2200 REIS
200 g., 0.9170 Gold 0.1804 oz. AGW **Countermark:** wned 2200 in rectangle **Note:** Countermark Type V on 2000 s, KM#451.1

Date	Host Date	Good	VG	F	VF	XF
1668)	1642, 1646, 1647 Rare	—	—	—	—	—

 # 454.3 2200 REIS
200 g., 0.9170 Gold 0.1804 oz. AGW **Countermark:** wned 2200 in rectangle **Note:** Countermark Type V on 2000 s, KM#451.2.

Date	Host Date	Good	VG	F	VF	XF
1668)	1660 Rare	—	—	—	—	—

 # 454.4 2200 REIS
200 g., 0.9170 Gold 0.1804 oz. AGW **Countermark:** wned 2200 in rectangle **Note:** Countermark Type V on 2 zados, KM#80.

Date	Host Date	Good	VG	F	VF	XF
1668)	1660 Rare	—	—	—	—	—

KM# 454.5 2200 REIS
6.1200 g., 0.9170 Gold 0.1804 oz. AGW **Countermark:** Crowned 2200 in rectangle **Note:** Countermark Type V on 2000 Reis, KM#85.

CM Date	Host Date	Good	VG	F	VF	XF
ND(1668)	1663, 1666 Rare	—	—	—	—	—

KM# 455.1 4400 REIS
12.2400 g., 0.9220 Gold 0.3628 oz. AGW **Countermark:** Crowned 4400 in rectangle **Note:** Countermark Type V on 4 Cruzados, KM#60.

CM Date	Host Date	Good	VG	F	VF	XF
ND(1668)	1642-1652 Rare	—	—	—	—	—

KM# 455.2 4400 REIS
12.2400 g., 0.9220 Gold 0.3628 oz. AGW **Countermark:** Crowned 4400 in rectangle **Note:** Countermark Type V on 4000 Reis, KM#452.1.

CM Date	Host Date	Good	VG	F	VF	XF
ND(1668)	ND Rare	—	—	—	—	—

KM# 455.3 4400 REIS
12.2400 g., 0.9220 Gold 0.3628 oz. AGW **Countermark:** Crowned 4400 in rectangle **Note:** Countermark Type V on 4000 Reis, KM#452.2.

CM Date	Host Date	Good	VG	F	VF	XF
ND(1668)	ND Rare	—	—	—	—	—

KM# 455.4 4400 REIS
12.2400 g., 0.9220 Gold 0.3628 oz. AGW **Countermark:** Crowned 4400 in rectangle **Note:** Countermark Type V on 4000 Reis, KM#452.3.

CM Date	Host Date	Good	VG	F	VF	XF
ND(1668)	ND Rare	—	—	—	—	—

KM# 455.5 4400 REIS
12.2400 g., 0.9220 Gold 0.3628 oz. AGW **Countermark:** Crowned 4400 in rectangle **Note:** Countermark Type V on 4000 Reis, KM#452.4.

CM Date	Host Date	Good	VG	F	VF	XF
ND(1668)	1642-1652 Rare	—	—	—	—	—

KM# 455.6 4400 REIS
12.2400 g., 0.9220 Gold 0.3628 oz. AGW **Countermark:** Crowned 4400 in rectangle **Note:** Countermark Type V on 4000 Reis, KM#452.5.

CM Date	Host Date	Good	VG	F	VF	XF
ND(1668)	ND Rare	—	—	—	—	—

KM# 455.7 4400 REIS
12.2400 g., 0.9220 Gold 0.3628 oz. AGW **Countermark:** Crowned 4400 in rectangle **Note:** Countermark Type V on 4 Cruzados, KM#81.

CM Date	Host Date	Good	VG	F	VF	XF
ND(1668)	1660, 1663 Rare	—	—	—	—	—

KM# 455.8 4400 REIS
12.2400 g., 0.9170 Gold 0.3608 oz. AGW **Countermark:** Crowned 4400 in rectangle **Note:** Countermark Type V on 4000 Reis, KM#86.

CM Date	Host Date	Good	VG	F	VF	XF
ND(1668)	1663-1666 Rare	—	—	—	—	—

COUNTERMARKED COINAGE

Type VII

Authorized by Decree of August 9, 1686 on Portuguese coins of Alfonso IV and Peter as Prince Regent.

Countermark: Crowned globe.

KM# 456 CRUZADO
3.0600 g., 0.9170 Gold 0.0902 oz. AGW **Countermark:** Crowned globe **Note:** Countermark Type VII on 1000 Reis, KM#84.

CM Date	Host Date	Good	VG	F	VF	XF
ND(1686)	1663, 1666 Rare	—	—	—	—	—

KM# 456.2 CRUZADO
3.0600 g., 0.9170 Gold 0.0902 oz. AGW **Countermark:** Crowned globe **Note:** Countermark Type VII on 1100 Reis, KM#453.2.

CM Date	Host Date	Good	VG	F	VF	XF
ND(1686)	1642 Rare	—	—	—	—	—

KM# 456.3 CRUZADO
3.0600 g., 0.9220 Gold 0.0907 oz. AGW **Countermark:** Crowned globe **Note:** Countermark Type VII on 1100 Reis, KM#453.3.

CM Date	Host Date	Good	VG	F	VF	XF
ND(1686)	1663, 1666 Rare	—	—	—	—	—

KM# 456.4 CRUZADO
3.0600 g., 0.9170 Gold 0.0902 oz. AGW **Countermark:** Crowned globe **Note:** Countermark Type VII on 1100 Reis, KM#87.

CM Date	Host Date	Good	VG	F	VF	XF
ND(1686)	1668, 1671 Rare	—	—	—	—	—

KM# 457.1 2 CRUZADOS
6.1200 g., 0.9170 Gold 0.1804 oz. AGW **Countermark:** Crowned globe **Note:** Countermark Type VII on 2000 Reis, KM#85.

CM Date	Host Date	Good	VG	F	VF	XF
ND(1686)	1663, 1666 Rare	—	—	—	—	—

KM# 457.2 2 CRUZADOS
6.1200 g., 0.9170 Gold 0.1804 oz. AGW **Countermark:** Crowned globe **Note:** Countermark Type VII on 2200 Reis, KM#454.3.

CM Date	Host Date	Good	VG	F	VF	XF
ND(1686)	1642 Rare	—	—	—	—	—

KM# 457.3 2 CRUZADOS
6.1200 g., 0.9170 Gold 0.1804 oz. AGW **Countermark:** Crowned globe **Note:** Countermark Type VII on 2200 Reis, KM#454.5.

CM Date	Host Date	Good	VG	F	VF	XF
ND(1686)	1663, 1666 Rare	—	—	—	—	—

KM# 457.4 2 CRUZADOS
6.1200 g., 0.9170 Gold 0.1804 oz. AGW **Countermark:** Crowned globe **Note:** Countermark Type VII on 2200 Reis, KM#88.

CM Date	Host Date	Good	VG	F	VF	XF
ND(1686)	1668-1674 Rare	—	—	—	—	—

KM# 458.1 4 CRUZADOS
12.2400 g., 0.9170 Gold 0.3608 oz. AGW **Countermark:** Crowned globe **Note:** Countermark Type VII on 4000 Reis, KM #86.

CM Date	Host Date	Good	VG	F	VF	XF
ND(1686)	1663, 1666 Rare	—	—	—	—	—

KM# 458.2 4 CRUZADOS
12.2400 g., 0.9170 Gold 0.3608 oz. AGW **Countermark:** Crowned globe **Note:** Countermark Type VII on 4400 Reis, KM#455.1

CM Date	Host Date	Good	VG	F	VF	XF
ND(1686)	1642-1652 Rare	—	—	—	—	—

KM# 458.3 4 CRUZADOS
12.2400 g., 0.9170 Gold 0.3608 oz. AGW **Countermark:** Crowned globe **Note:** Countermark Type VII on 4400 Reis, KM#455.2.

CM Date	Host Date	Good	VG	F	VF	XF
ND(1686)	ND Rare	—	—	—	—	—

KM# 458.4 4 CRUZADOS
12.2400 g., 0.9170 Gold 0.3608 oz. AGW **Countermark:** Crowned globe **Note:** Countermark Type VII on 4400 Reis, KM#455.3.

CM Date	Host Date	Good	VG	F	VF	XF
ND(1686)	ND Rare	—	—	—	—	—

KM# 458.5 4 CRUZADOS
12.2400 g., 0.9170 Gold 0.3608 oz. AGW **Countermark:** Crowned globe **Note:** Countermark Type VII on 4400 Reis, KM#455.4.

CM Date	Host Date	Good	VG	F	VF	XF
ND(1686)	ND Rare	—	—	—	—	—

KM# 458.6 4 CRUZADOS
12.2400 g., 0.9170 Gold 0.3608 oz. AGW **Countermark:** Crowned globe **Note:** Countermark Type VII on 4400 Reis, KM#455.5.

CM Date	Host Date	Good	VG	F	VF	XF
ND(1686)	1642-1652 Rare	—	—	—	—	—

KM# 458.7 4 CRUZADOS
12.2400 g., 0.9170 Gold 0.3608 oz. AGW **Countermark:** Crowned globe **Note:** Countermark Type VII on 4400 Reis, KM#455.7.

CM Date	Host Date	Good	VG	F	VF	XF
ND(1686)	1663-1666 Rare	—	—	—	—	—

KM# 458.8 4 CRUZADOS
12.2400 g., 0.9170 Gold 0.3608 oz. AGW **Countermark:** Crowned globe **Note:** Countermark Type VII on 4400 Reis, KM#455.8.

CM Date	Host Date	Good	VG	F	VF	XF
ND(1686)	ND Rare	—	—	—	—	—

KM# 458.9 4 CRUZADOS
12.2400 g., 0.9170 Gold 0.3608 oz. AGW **Countermark:** Crowned globe **Note:** Countermark Type VII on 4400 Reis, KM#89.

CM Date	Host Date	Good	VG	F	VF	XF
ND(1686)	1668-1674 Rare	—	—	—	—	—

PATTERNS

Including off metal strikes

KM#	Date	Mintage	Identification	Mkt Val
Pn1	1650	—	2 Cruzados. Copper.	—
Pn2	1660	—	1000 Reis. Silver. Similar to KM#84.	1,400
Pn3	1682	—	3 Reis. Copper.	3,300
Pn4	1682	—	5 Reis. Copper.	2,700
Pn5	1682	—	10 Reis. Copper.	2,700
Pn7	1688	—	3 Reis. Copper.	1,100
Pn8	1688	—	5 Reis. Copper.	850
Pn9	1688	—	10 Reis. Copper.	1,500
Pn10	1688	—	Cruzado. Copper.	—
Pn11	1696	—	4000 Reis. Copper. As KM156.	—

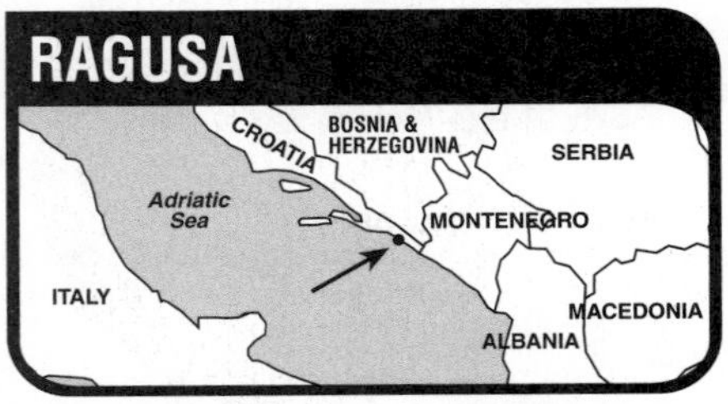

A port city in Croatia on the Dalmatian coast of the Adriatic Sea. Ragusa was once a great mercantile power, the merchant fleets of which sailed as far abroad as India and America.

Refugees from the destroyed Latin communities of Salona and Epidaurus, and a colony of Slavs colonized the island rock of Ragusa during the 7th century. For four centuries Ragusa successfully defended itself against attacks by foreign powers, but from 1205 to 1358 recognized Venetian suzeranity. From 1358 to 1526, Ragusa was a vassal state of Hungary. The fall of Hungary in 1526 freed Ragusa, permitting it to become one of the foremost commercial powers of the Mediterranean and a leader in the development of literature and art. After this period its importance declined, due in part to the discovery of America, which reduced the importance of Mediterranean ports. A measure of its former economic importance was regained during the Napoleonic Wars when the republic, by adopting a policy of neutrality (1800-1805), became the leading carrier of the Mediterranean. This favored position was terminated by French seizure in 1805. In 1814 Ragusa was annexed by Austria, remaining a part of the Austrian Empire until its incorporation in the newly formed state of Yugoslavia in 1918. Croatia proclaimed its independence in 1991.

MONETARY SYSTEM

6 Soldi = 1 Grosetto
12 Grosetti = 1 Perpero
3 Perpero = 1 Scudo
36 Grosetti = 1 Scudo
40 Grosetti = 1 Ducato
60 Grosetti = 1 Tallero
5 Perpero = 1 Tallero

REPUBLIC

STANDARD COINAGE

KM# 6 SOLDO

Copper **Obv:** Bust of Saint, facing above brick-like design **Rev:** Christ flanked by designs within circle of stars **Note:** Varieties exist.

Date	Mintage	VG	F	VF	XF	Unc
1678	—	12.00	25.00	55.00	140	—
1682	—	12.00	25.00	55.00	140	—
1689	—	12.00	25.00	55.00	140	—

KM# 5 GROSETTO

Billon **Obv:** St. Blaze **Rev:** Christ within stars **Note:** Varieties exist.

Date	Mintage	VG	F	VF	XF	Unc
1626	—	10.00	20.00	35.00	75.00	—
1627	—	10.00	20.00	35.00	75.00	—
1628	—	10.00	20.00	35.00	75.00	—
1629	—	10.00	20.00	35.00	75.00	—
1630	—	10.00	20.00	35.00	75.00	—
1631	—	10.00	20.00	35.00	75.00	—
1635	—	10.00	20.00	35.00	75.00	—
1642	—	10.00	20.00	35.00	75.00	—
1643	—	10.00	20.00	35.00	75.00	—
1644	—	10.00	20.00	35.00	75.00	—
1645	—	10.00	20.00	35.00	75.00	—
1646	—	10.00	20.00	35.00	75.00	—
1647	—	10.00	20.00	35.00	75.00	—
1648	—	10.00	20.00	35.00	75.00	—
1649	—	10.00	20.00	35.00	75.00	—
1650	—	10.00	20.00	35.00	75.00	—
1651	—	10.00	20.00	35.00	75.00	—
1652	—	10.00	20.00	35.00	75.00	—
1653	—	10.00	20.00	35.00	75.00	—
1654	—	10.00	20.00	35.00	75.00	—
1655	—	10.00	20.00	35.00	75.00	—
1656	—	10.00	20.00	35.00	75.00	—
1657	—	10.00	20.00	35.00	75.00	—
1658	—	10.00	20.00	35.00	75.00	—
1659	—	10.00	20.00	35.00	75.00	—
1660	—	10.00	20.00	35.00	75.00	—
1661	—	10.00	20.00	35.00	75.00	—
1662	—	10.00	20.00	35.00	75.00	—
1663	—	10.00	20.00	35.00	75.00	—
1664	—	10.00	20.00	35.00	75.00	—
1665	—	10.00	20.00	35.00	75.00	—
1666	—	10.00	20.00	35.00	75.00	—
1667	—	10.00	20.00	35.00	75.00	—
1676	—	10.00	20.00	35.00	75.00	—
1677	—	10.00	20.00	35.00	75.00	—
1678	—	10.00	20.00	35.00	75.00	—
1679	—	10.00	20.00	35.00	75.00	—
1680	—	10.00	20.00	35.00	75.00	—
1681	—	10.00	20.00	35.00	75.00	—
1682	—	10.00	20.00	35.00	75.00	—
1683	—	10.00	20.00	35.00	75.00	—
1684	—	10.00	20.00	35.00	75.00	—
1685	—	10.00	20.00	35.00	75.00	—
1686	—	10.00	20.00	35.00	75.00	—
1687	—	10.00	20.00	35.00	75.00	—
1688	—	10.00	20.00	35.00	75.00	—
1689	—	10.00	20.00	35.00	75.00	—
1690	—	10.00	20.00	35.00	75.00	—
1691	—	10.00	20.00	35.00	75.00	—
1692	—	10.00	20.00	35.00	75.00	—
1694	—	10.00	20.00	35.00	75.00	—
1695	—	10.00	20.00	35.00	75.00	—
1696	—	10.00	20.00	35.00	75.00	—
1697	—	10.00	20.00	35.00	75.00	—
1698	—	10.00	20.00	35.00	75.00	—
1699	—	10.00	20.00	35.00	75.00	—
1700	—	10.00	20.00	35.00	75.00	—

KM# 4 3 GROSETTI (Alltilucho)

1.1200 g., Billon **Obv:** Head of Saint, right **Obv. Legend:** S BLASIVS • RAGVSII **Rev:** Legend **Rev. Legend:** GROS • ARG / TRIP / CIVI / RAGV **Note:** Varieties exist.

Date	Mintage	VG	F	VF	XF	U
1627	—	30.00	60.00	125	275	
1628	—	30.00	60.00	125	275	
1629	—	30.00	60.00	125	275	
1630	—	30.00	60.00	125	275	
1631	—	30.00	60.00	125	275	
1632	—	30.00	60.00	125	275	
1633	—	30.00	60.00	125	275	
1635	—	30.00	60.00	125	275	
1642	—	30.00	60.00	125	275	
1643	—	30.00	60.00	125	275	
1644	—	30.00	60.00	125	275	
1645	—	30.00	60.00	125	275	
1646	—	30.00	60.00	125	275	
1647	—	30.00	60.00	125	275	
1648	—	30.00	60.00	125	275	
1649	—	30.00	60.00	125	275	
1654	—	30.00	60.00	125	275	
1675	—	30.00	60.00	125	275	
1683	—	30.00	60.00	125	275	
1684	—	30.00	60.00	125	275	
1685	—	30.00	60.00	125	275	
1686	—	30.00	60.00	125	275	
1692	—	30.00	60.00	125	275	

KM# 7 PERPERO

Billon **Obv:** St. Blaze divides date and S B **Obv. Legend:** PR • RAEIP • RHAGVSINAE **Rev:** Christ within stars

Date	Mintage	VG	F	VF	XF
1683	—	25.00	50.00	100	200
1692	—	25.00	50.00	100	200

Russia, formerly the central power of the Union of Soviet Socialist Republics and now of the Commonwealth of Independent States occupies the northern part of Asia and the eastern part of Europe, has an area of 17,075,400 sq. km. Capital: Moscow.

The first Russian dynasty was founded in Novgorod by the Viking Rurik in 862 A.D. under Yaroslav the Wise (1019-54). The subsequent Kievan state became one of the great commercial and cultural centers of Europe before falling to the Mongols of the Batu Khan, 13th century, who were suzerains of Russia until late in the 15th century when Ivan III threw off the Mongol yoke. T Russian Empire was enlarged, solidified and Westernized dur the reigns of Ivan the Terrible, Peter the Great and Catherine Great, and by 1881 extended to the Pacific and into Central As Contemporary Russian history began in March of 1917 wh Tsar Nicholas II abdicated under pressure and was replaced a provisional government composed of both radical and c servative elements. This government rapidly lost ground to Bolshevik wing of the Socialist Democratic Labor Party wh

tained power following the Bolshevik Revolution which began Nov. 7, 1917. After the Russian Civil War, the regional gov- nments, national states and armies became federal republics the Russian Socialist Federal Soviet Republic. These auton- nous republics united to form the Union of Soviet Socialist epublics that was established as a federation under the pre- ership of Lenin on Dec. 30, 1922.

EMPIRE

JLERS

oris Godunov, 1598-1605
dor II, 1605
nitri, 1605-1606
chael I, 1613-1645
eksei, 1645-1676
dor III, 1676-1682
an V, 1682-1689
ter I (The Great), 1689-1725

NT MARKS

M – Moscow, Dvor Zamoskvoretsky,
Naval Mint, 1700

ONETARY SYSTEM

4 Kopek = Polushka ПОЛУШКА
2 Kopek = Denga, Denezhka ДЕНГА, ДЕНЕЖКА
pek = КОП_ИКА
3 & 4) Kopeks КОП_ИКИ
and up) Kopeks КОП_ЕКЪ
924 – 5 and up) Kopeks КОПЕЕК
Kopeks = Poltina, Poltinnik ПОЛТИНА,...ПОЛРУБЛЪ
0 Kopeks = Rouble, Ruble РУБЛЪ
Roubles = Imperial ИМПЕРІАЛЪ
Roubles = Chervonetz ЧЕРВОНЕЦ

NOTE: For silver or gold coins with Zlotych, Kopek or Ruble nominations, see Poland.

NOTE: Gold coins of 1 Ducat or Chervonetz denomination h both multiples and fractions are known before Peter I. Most ssian authorities agree that these pieces were not meant to be ns but were only made as awards for the military. The higher rank of the individual the larger the gold piece. Thus the range s from a gold denga for a common soldier to a "Portugal" or 10 cat size for a high ranking officer.

GENDS

Peter i

Obverse with full title:
ЦРЬ И ВЕЛИКИИ КНЗЬ ПЕТРЬ АЛЕЗІЕВИЧЪ
"Tsar and Grand Duke Peter Alexievich"
Obverse with short title:
ЦРЬ ПЕТРЬ АЛЕЗІЕВИЧЪ
"Tsar Peter Alexievich"
Reverse with full title:
ВСЕА ВЕЛІКІА И МЛЫА И ВЕЛЫА РОСИИ САМОДЕРЖЕЦЪ
"of All Great, Little & White Russias Autocrat"
Reverse with short title:
ВСЕА РОСИИ САМОДЕРЖЕЦЪ
"of All Russias Autocrat"
ВСЕА РОСИИ ПОВЕЛИТЕЛЬ
"of All Russias Ruler"

GE INSCRIPTIONS

Peter 1

МАНЭТЪНАГО ДЕНЕЖЪНАГО ДВОРА 1701
МОСКОВЪСКАА КАПЕИКА Х МАНЕТНОГО ДЕНЕЖНОГО ДВОРА
КОПЕИКА МАНЕТНОГО ДЕНЕЖЪНАГО ДВОРА 1710
КОПЕИКА МАНЕТНОГО . . . ДЕНЕЖЪНАГО ДВОРА
КОПЕИКА МАНЕТНОГО ДЕНЕЖНОГО ДВРОА

KINGDOM

STANDARD COINAGE

1# 51 DENGA (1/2 Kopek)
300 g., Silver **Ruler:** Dmitri

e	Mintage	VG	F	VF	XF	Unc
1605-6)	—	100	170	250	400	—

1# 54 DENGA (1/2 Kopek)
400 g., Silver **Ruler:** Aleksei **Obv. Legend:** CZAR I VELIKIY YAZ ALEKSEY MIKHAILOVICH VSEYA RUSI

e	Mintage	VG	F	VF	XF	Unc
1645-76)	—	40.00	60.00	150	450	—

1# 53 KOPEK
000 g., Silver **Ruler:** Michael I **Obv. Legend:** CZAR I IKIY KNYAZ MIKHAIL

e	Mintage	VG	F	VF	XF	Unc
1613-45)	—	25.00	40.00	50.00	200	—

1# 55 KOPEK
300 g., Silver **Ruler:** Aleksei **Obv. Legend:** CZAR I VELIKIY YAZ ALEKSEY MIKHAILOVICH VSEYA RUSI

	Mintage	VG	F	VF	XF	Unc
1645-76)	—	25.00	40.00	50.00	200	—

KM# 55a KOPEK
0.4800 g., Gold **Ruler:** Aleksei **Obv. Legend:** CZAR I VELIKIY KNYAZ ALEKSEY MIKHAILOVICH VSEYA RUSI **Note:** as an Award.

Date	Mintage	VG	F	VF	XF	Unc
ND(1645-76)	—	1,000	1,600	2,250	3,250	—

KM# 40 POLUSHKA (1/4 Kopek)
0.4290 g., Gold **Ruler:** Aleksei

Date	Mintage	VG	F	VF	XF	Unc
ND(1645-76)	—	550	1,200	2,500	3,850	—

KM# 102 DENGA (1/2 Kopek)
6.4000 g., Copper **Ruler:** Peter I **Obv:** Crowned double-headed eagle, legend around **Obv. Legend:** CZAR PETER ALEXIEVITCH **Rev:** Value, date withinn circle, legend around **Rev. Legend:** AUTOCRAT OF ALL THE RUSSIAS

Date	Mintage	VG	F	VF	XF	Unc
ND(1700)	—	50.00	85.00	170	325	—

KM# 22 KOPEK
0.5650 g., Gold **Ruler:** Fedor II

Date	Mintage	VG	F	VF	XF	Unc
ND(1606-10)	—	700	1,525	3,250	5,000	—

TRADE COINAGE

FR# 43 DUCAT
3.5000 g., 0.9860 Gold 0.1109 oz. AGW **Ruler:** Fedor III

Date	Mintage	VG	F	VF	XF	Unc
ND(1676-82)	—	700	1,500	2,700	4,550	—

COUNTERMARKED COINAGE

In 1654 the Ukraine was united to Russia under Czar Alexis; this was the pretext for a Russo-Polish war that lasted several years. It was decided to countermark European thalers with the figure of the czar on horseback and the date, for use primarliy in the Ukraine. The value was set at 64 Kopeks. About 800,000 of these thalers were issued in 1655, the majority of which were from German mints, although many were from the Netherlands. Others were countermarked on thalers of Austria, the Scandinavian states, and Switzerland. A few are known from other European regions, such as Poland and the Italian states. Their legal tender status was abrogated by Czar Alexis in 1659; most existing specimens derive from hoards found in the Ukraine in the nineteenth century.

KM# 440 TALER
Silver **Ruler:** Aleksei **Series:** Swiss Thaler **Countermark:** Czar horseback right in dotted circle, date in rectangle **Note:** Countermark on Saint Gall Thaler, KM#61; Dav. #4677.

CM Date	Host Date	Good	VG	F	VF	XF
1655	1645-76	1,375	2,275	3,285	4,500	—

KM# 407 YEFIMOK
Silver **Ruler:** Aleksei **Series:** French State Thaler **Countermark:** Czar horseback right in dotted circle, date in rectangle **Note:** Countermark on Alsace Thaler; Dav. #3346.

CM Date	Host Date	Good	VG	F	VF	XF
1655	1621-25	1,000	1,750	2,300	3,500	—

KM# 434 YEFIMOK
Silver **Ruler:** Aleksei **Series:** French Local Issue Thaler **Countermark:** Czar horseback right in dotted circle, date in rectangle **Note:** Countermark on Alsace-Metz Thaler, Dav. #5583A.

CM Date	Host Date	Good	VG	F	VF	XF
1655	1638-41, 43, 45-47, 50	2,250	3,750	5,500	8,000	—

KM# 424 YEFIMOK
Silver **Ruler:** Aleksei **Series:** Spanish Netherlands Patagon **Countermark:** Czar horseback right in dotted circle, date in rectangle **Note:** Countermark on Brabant Patagon, Dav. #4432.

CM Date	Host Date	Good	VG	F	VF	XF
1655	1612-21	900	1,500	2,150	3,250	—

KM# 425 YEFIMOK

Silver **Ruler:** Aleksei **Series:** Spanish Netherlands Patagon **Countermark:** Czar horseback right in dotted circle, date in rectangle **Note:** Countermark on Brabant Patagon, Dav. #4462.

CM Date	Host Date	Good	VG	F	VF	XF
1655	1621-53	675	1,100	1,575	3,000	—

KM# 423 YEFIMOK

Silver **Ruler:** Aleksei **Series:** Germanic Thaler **Countermark:** Czar horseback right in dotted circle, date in rectangle **Note:** Countermark on Brunswick-Luneberg-Celle Thaler, Dav. #6521.

CM Date	Host Date	Good	VG	F	VF	XF
1655	1649-53	1,000	1,700	2,350	4,000	—

KM# 400 YEFIMOK

Silver **Ruler:** Aleksei **Series:** Germanic Thaler **Countermark:** Czar horseback right in dotted circle, date in rectangle **Note:** Countermark on Brunswick-Wolfenbuttel Thaler, Dav. #6303.

CM Date	Host Date	Good	VG	F	VF	XF
1655	1613-28	1,275	2,000	2,800	3,850	—

KM# 410 YEFIMOK

Silver **Ruler:** Aleksei **Series:** Spanish Netherlands Patagon **Countermark:** Czar horseback right in dotted circle, date in rectangle **Note:** Countermark on Flanders Patagon, Dav. #4464.

CM Date	Host Date	Good	VG	F	VF	XF
1655	1622-53	700	1,100	1,550	2,350	—

KM# 431 YEFIMOK

Silver **Ruler:** Aleksei **Series:** Germanic Thaler **Countermark:** Czar horseback right in dotted circle, date in rectangle **Note:** Countermark on Frankfurt Thaler, Dav. #5296.

CM Date	Host Date	Good	VG	F	VF	XF
1655	1647	1,375	2,350	3,450	5,000	—

KM# 421 YEFIMOK

Silver **Ruler:** Aleksei **Series:** United Netherlands Lion and Rijksdaalder **Countermark:** Czar horseback right in dotted circle, date in rectangle **Note:** Countermark on Gelderland Lion Daalder, Dav. #4829.

CM Date	Host Date	Good	VG	F	VF	XF
1655	1606-53	750	1,300	1,825	2,750	—

KM# 420 YEFIMOK

Silver **Ruler:** Aleksei **Series:** United Netherlands Lion and Rijksdaalder **Countermark:** Czar horseback right in dotted circ date in rectangle **Note:** Countermark on Gelderland Rijksdaald Dav. #4828.

CM Date	Host Date	Good	VG	F	VF
1655	1606-53	675	1,200	1,800	2,500

KM# 429 YEFIMOK

Silver **Ruler:** Aleksei **Series:** Netherlands Free City Rijksdaalc **Countermark:** Czar horseback right in dotted circle, date in rectangle **Note:** Countermark on Kampen Rijksdaalder, Dav. #49

CM Date	Host Date	Good	VG	F	VF
1655	1633-58	1,350	2,250	3,250	4,750

KM# 432 YEFIMOK

Silver **Ruler:** Aleksei **Series:** Germanic Thaler **Counterma** Czar horseback right in dotted circle, date in rectangle **Note:** Countermark on Lubeck Thaler, Dav. #5438.

CM Date	Host Date	Good	VG	F	VF
1655	1606-07	1,500	2,500	3,500	5,000

/I# 403 YEFIMOK

/er **Ruler:** Aleksei **Series:** Germanic Thaler **Countermark:** ar horseback right in dotted circle, date in rectangle **Note:** untermark on Lubeck Thaler, Dav.#9405.

Date	Host Date	Good	VG	F	VF	XF
5	1549	1,850	2,250	3,250	5,000	—

1# 405 YEFIMOK

'er **Ruler:** Aleksei **Series:** Germanic Thaler **Countermark:** ar horseback right in dotted circle, date in rectangle **Note:** untermark on Nurnberg Thaler, KM#52; Dav. #5636.

Date	Host Date	Good	VG	F	VF	XF
1655)	1621-28	1,600	2,750	4,000	5,500	—

 # 426 YEFIMOK

er **Ruler:** Aleksei **Series:** United Netherlands Lion and sdaalder **Countermark:** Czar horseback right in dotted circle, in rectangle **Note:** Countermark on Overijssel Rijksdaalder, . #4832.

Date	Host Date	Good	VG	F	VF	XF
5	1606-29	700	1,200	1,650	2,375	—

 # 401 YEFIMOK

er **Ruler:** Aleksei **Series:** Germanic Thaler **Countermark:** r horseback right in dotted circle, date in rectangle **Note:** ntermark on Saxony Thaler, Dav. #7601.

ate	Host Date	Good	VG	F	VF	XF
	1620-38	1,150	1,900	2,750	3,900	—

KM# 436 YEFIMOK

Silver **Ruler:** Aleksei **Series:** Germanic Thaler **Countermark:** Czar horseback right in dotted circle, date in rectangle **Note:** Countermark on Saxony Thaler, Dav. #7612.

CM Date	Host Date	Good	VG	F	VF	XF
1655	1638-56	1,100	1,750	2,500	3,500	—

KM# 430 YEFIMOK

Silver **Ruler:** Aleksei **Series:** Polish Thaler **Countermark:** Czar horseback right in dotted circle, date in rectangle **Note:** Countermark on Thorn Thaler, Dav. #4374.

CM Date	Host Date	Good	VG	F	VF	XF
1655	1633-38	3,000	5,000	6,500	9,500	—

KM# 435 YEFIMOK

Silver **Ruler:** Aleksei **Series:** Spanish Netherlands Patagon **Countermark:** Czar horseback right in dotted circle, date in rectangle **Note:** Countermark on Tournai Patagon, Dav. #4470.

CM Date	Host Date	Good	VG	F	VF	XF
1655	1621-26, 28-37, 41, 43-65	150	250	400	650	—

KM# 439 YEFIMOK

Silver **Series:** United Netherlands Lion and Rijksdaalder **Countermark:** Czar on horseback in circle, date in rectangle **Note:** Countermark on Utrecht Rijksdaalder, KM#40; Dav. #4838.

CM Date	Host Date	Good	VG	F	VF	XF
1655	1650-51	650	1,000	1,500	2,400	—

KM# 422 YEFIMOK

Silver **Ruler:** Aleksei **Series:** United Netherlands Lion and Rijksdaalder **Countermark:** Czar horseback right in dotted circle, date in rectangle **Note:** Countermark on West Friesland Rijksdaalder, Dav. #4829.

CM Date	Host Date	Good	VG	F	VF	XF
1655	1606-53	650	1,000	1,500	2,250	—

KM# 427 YEFIMOK

Silver **Ruler:** Aleksei **Series:** United Netherlands Lion and Rijksdaalder **Countermark:** Czar horseback right in dotted circle, date in rectangle **Note:** Countermark on Zeeland Rijksdaalder, Dav. #4844.

CM Date	Host Date	Good	VG	F	VF	XF
1655	1606-53	750	1,250	1,750	2,500	—

KM# 428 YEFIMOK

Silver **Ruler:** Michael I **Series:** Netherlands Free City Rijksdaalder **Countermark:** Czar horseback right in dotted circle, date in rectangle **Note:** Countermark on Zwolle Rijksdaalder, Dav. #4992.

CM Date	Host Date	Good	VG	F	VF	XF
1655	1636-53	1,400	2,500	3,500	5,000	—

KM# 406 JEFIMOK

Silver **Ruler:** Aleksei **Series:** Germanic Thaler **Countermark:** Czar horseback right in dotted circle, date in rectangle **Note:** Countermark on Nürnberg Thaler; Dav. #5654.

CM Date	Host Date	Good	VG	F	VF	XF
1655	1635-37	3,000	5,000	6,500	9,000	—

KM# 408 JEFIMOK

Silver **Ruler:** Aleksei **Series:** Germanic Thaler **Countermark:** Czar horseback right in dotted circle, date in rectangle **Note:** Countermark on Strasburg Thaler; Dav. #5842.

CM Date	Host Date	Good	VG	F	VF	XF
1655	ND(1617)	2,000	3,250	4,500	6,500	—

NOVODELS

KM#	Date	Mintage	Identification	Mkt Val
N-AA1	1654	—	Poltina.	—
N-AA2	ND(1654)	—	Rouble.	—
N-A1	ND(1685)	—	3 Kopeks. Silver.	—
N-A2	ND(1697)	—	3 Kopeks. Silver.	—
N-A3	ND(1698)	—	3 Kopeks. Silver.	—
N-A4	ND(1699)	—	3 Kopeks. Silver.	—
N-A5	ND(1700)	—	Denga. Copper. Portrait.	—
N-A6	ND(1700)	—	Denga. Copper. Eagle.	—

PATTERNS

Including off metal strikes

KM#	Date	Mintage	Identification	Mkt Val
PnA1	1699	—	1/2 Rouble. Silver.	—

SCOTLAND

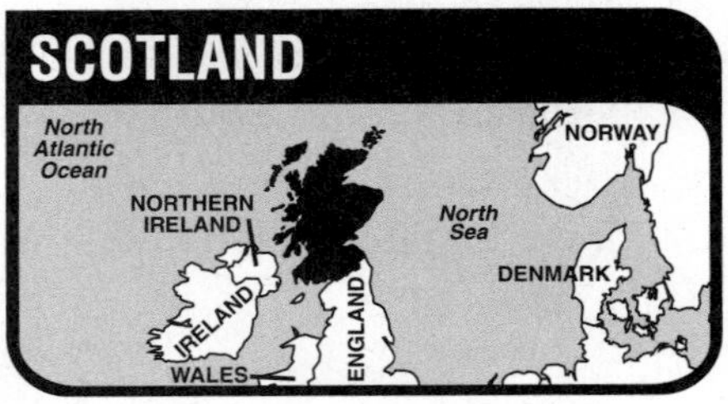

Scotland is located on the northern part of the island of Great Britain. It has an area of 30,414 square miles (78,772 sq. km.

Scotland was the traditional home of the Picts in ancient times. The Romans invaded the area after 80 A.D. and Hadrian's Wall was built from 122-126 A.D. to keep the Picts from the Roman settlements to the south. In the 5th century Scotland had 4 kingdoms: Northumbria (Anglo-Saxon), Picts, Scots (of Irish extraction) and Strathclyde. St. Columba converted the Picts to Christianity in the late 6th century. Norse invasions started in the late 8th century. The Picts conquered the Scots in the 9th century and under Malcolm II (1005-1034) the Scottish kingdoms were united. The Scottish King became a vassal of the English king in 1174 (a circumstance that was to lead to many disputes). The Scots gained independence in 1314 at Bannockburn under Robert Bruce. From 1371-1714 it was ruled by the Stuarts, and in 1603 when James VI of Scotland succeeded Elizabeth I as James I, King of England, a personal union of the two kingdoms was formed. Parliamentary Act in 1707 made final union of the two kingdoms.

RULERS

James IV, 1488-1513
James V, 1513-1542
Mary, 1542-1567
Mary and Henry Darnley, 1565-1567
James VI (I), 1567-1625
Charles I, 1625-1649
Charles II, 1649-1685
James VII (II), 1685-1689
William and Mary, 1689-1694
William II (III), 1694-1702

MINTS

Edinburgh
Holyrood
Stirling

MINT OFFICIALS' INITIALS

Initial	Date	Name
A		Acheson, mintmaster
IG	1553	Jacobus Gubernator, Earl of Arran, Regent

KINGDOM

HAMMERED COINAGE

KM# 22 1/2 CROWN

1.1250 g., 0.9170 Gold 0.0332 oz. AGW **Ruler:** James VI (I) **Obv:** Crowned bust right **Rev:** Crowned arms, Scottish arms in 1st and 4th quarters **Note:** S#5470.

Date	Mintage	Good	VG	F	VF	XF
ND(1609-29)	—	185	350	750	1,650	2,750

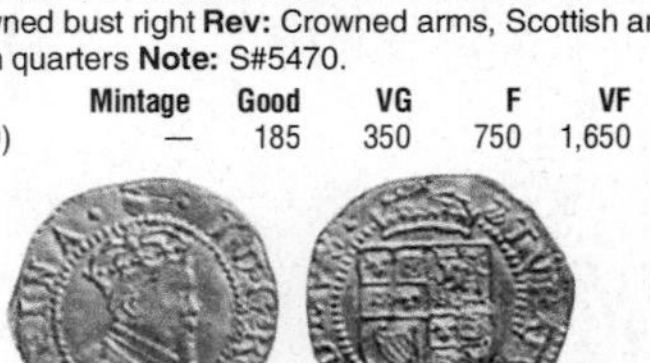

KM# 21 1/2 CROWN

1.1250 g., 0.9170 Gold 0.0332 oz. AGW **Ruler:** James VI (I) **Obv:** Crowned bust of King James VI right **Rev:** Crowned arms, English arms in 1st and 4th quarters **Note:** S#5469.

Date	Mintage	Good	VG	F	VF	XF
ND(1604-09)	—	325	600	1,150	2,250	3,500

KM# 48 BRITAIN 1/2 CROWN

1.1250 g., 0.9170 Gold 0.0332 oz. AGW **Ruler:** Charles I **Obv:** Crowned head of Charles left **Rev:** Crowned arms, B above crown **Note:** S#5538.

Date	Mintage	Good	VG	F	VF	XF
ND(1637-42)	—	185	350	775	1,850	3,000

KM# 49 BRITAIN 1/2 CROWN

1.1250 g., 0.9170 Gold 0.0332 oz. AGW **Ruler:** Charles I **Ob** B below crowned head **Rev:** Crowned arms **Note:** S#5539.

Date	Mintage	Good	VG	F	VF	
ND(1637-42)	—	200	375	800	2,000	3,

KM# 23 BRITAIN CROWN

2.2500 g., 0.9170 Gold 0.0663 oz. AGW **Ruler:** James VI (**Obv:** Crowned bust of James VI right **Rev:** Crowned arms, English arms in 1st and 4th quarters **Note:** S#5467.

Date	Mintage	Good	VG	F	VF	
ND(1604-09)	—	475	925	1,950	3,850	7,

KM# 24 BRITAIN CROWN

2.2500 g., 0.9170 Gold 0.0663 oz. AGW **Ruler:** James VI (**Obv:** Crowned bust of King James VI **Rev:** Crowned arms, Scottish arms in 1st and 4th quarters **Note:** S#5470.

Date	Mintage	Good	VG	F	VF	
ND(1609-25)	—	195	350	725	1,400	2,

KM# 50 BRITAIN CROWN

2.2500 g., 0.9170 Gold 0.0663 oz. AGW **Ruler:** Charles I **Ob** Crowned bust of Charles right **Rev:** Crowned arms **Note:** S#55

Date	Mintage	Good	VG	F	VF
ND(1625-36)	—	1,250	2,250	4,500	8,500

KM# 51 BRITAIN CROWN

2.2500 g., 0.9170 Gold 0.0663 oz. AGW **Ruler:** Charles I **O** Crowned bust of King Charles left, B at end of legend **Rev:** Crowned arms **Note:** S#5536.

Date	Mintage	Good	VG	F	VF	
ND(1637-40)	—	650	1,250	2,500	4,750	9

KM# 52 BRITAIN CROWN

2.2500 g., 0.9170 Gold 0.0663 oz. AGW **Ruler:** Charles I **O** Crowned bust left, B at beginning of legend **Rev:** Crowned ar **Note:** S#5537.

Date	Mintage	Good	VG	F	VF	
ND(1637-42)	—	700	1,350	2,650	5,000	9

KM# 26 DOUBLE CROWN

4.5000 g., 0.9170 Gold 0.1327 oz. AGW **Ruler:** James VI **Obv:** Crowned bust of James VI right **Rev:** Crowned arms, English arms in 1st and 4th quarters **Note:** S#5465.

Date	Mintage	Good	VG	F	VF	
ND(1604-09)	—	900	1,500	3,000	5,400	10,

KM# 27.1 DOUBLE CROWN

4.5000 g., 0.9170 Gold 0.1327 oz. AGW **Ruler:** James VI **Obv:** Crowned bust of King James VI right **Obv. Legend:** IA G… **Rev:** Crowned arms, Scottish arms in 1st and 4th quart **Note:** S#5466.

Date	Mintage	Good	VG	F	VF	
ND(1609-25)	—	500	925	1,950	3,850	7

M# 27.2 DOUBLE CROWN

5000 g., 0.9170 Gold 0.1327 oz. AGW **Ruler:** James VI (I) **Obv:** owned bust right **Obv. Legend:** IACOBVS. D. G... **Rev:** Crowned ms, Scottish arms in 1st and 4th quarters **Note:** S#5466v.

te	Mintage	Good	VG	F	VF	XF
(1609-25)	—	550	1,050	2,050	4,150	7,800

M# 53 DOUBLE CROWN

ld, 20 mm. **Ruler:** Charles I **Obv:** Crowned bust of Charles ght **Rev:** Crowned arms **Note:** Britain Crown. S#5529.

te	Mintage	Good	VG	F	VF	XF
(1625-36)	—	3,500	6,500	10,000	—	—

M# 25 THISTLE CROWN

500 g., 0.9170 Gold 0.0663 oz. AGW **Ruler:** James VI (I) **v:** Crowned rose **Rev:** Crowned thistle **Note:** S#5471.

te	Mintage	Good	VG	F	VF	XF
(1604-25)	—	150	320	650	1,350	2,500

M# 17 1/2 RIDER (50 Shillings)

450 g., 0.9170 Gold 0.0603 oz. AGW **Ruler:** James VI (I) **v:** King in armor with raised sword, right on horseback **Obv. gend:** IACOBVS • 6 • D • G • R... **Rev:** Crowned shield **Rev. gend:** SPERO • MELIORA **Note:** Seventh Coinage. S#5459.

e	Mintage	Good	VG	F	VF	XF
)1	—	275	550	1,100	2,400	—

M# 19 1/2 SWORD & SCEPTRE

450 g., 0.9170 Gold 0.0603 oz. AGW **Ruler:** James VI (I) **v:** Crowned arms **Rev:** Crown over crossed sword and scepter **te:** S#5462.

e	Mintage	Good	VG	F	VF	XF
1	—	115	230	450	925	2,250
)2	—	145	260	525	1,050	2,500
)3	—	400	800	1,750	3,450	5,600
)4	—	175	350	700	1,400	2,800

M# 18 RIDER (100 Shillings)

900 g., 0.9170 Gold 0.1501 oz. AGW **Ruler:** James VI (I) **v:** King in armor with raised sword, right on horseback **Obv. gend:** IACOBVS•6•D•G•R... **Rev:** Crowned shield **Rev. gend:** SPERO•MELIORA **Note:** Seventh Coinage; Similar to Rider, KM#17; S#5458.

e	Mintage	Good	VG	F	VF	XF
1	—	425	800	1,600	5,600	—

KM# 20 SWORD AND SCEPTRE

5.0900 g., 0.9170 Gold 0.1501 oz. AGW **Ruler:** James VI (I) **Obv:** Crossed arms **Note:** S#5460.

Date	Mintage	Good	VG	F	VF	XF
1601	—	175	350	700	1,450	2,850
1602	—	175	350	700	1,400	2,750
1603	—	300	475	950	1,900	4,550
1604	—	300	475	1,000	2,000	4,700

KM# 54 1/2 UNIT

Gold **Ruler:** Charles I **Obv:** Crowned bust of Charles I left, B below bust **Rev:** Crowned arms **Note:** Briot Coinage. S#5534.

Date	Mintage	Good	VG	F	VF	XF
ND(1637-42)	—	450	900	1,800	3,750	6,000

KM# 55 1/2 UNIT

Gold **Ruler:** Charles I **Obv:** Crowned bust of Charles I left, F at end of legend **Rev:** Crowned arms **Note:** Falconer Coinage. S#5535.

Date	Mintage	Good	VG	F	VF	XF
ND(1637-42)	—	2,000	3,500	6,500	10,000	—

KM# 28 UNIT

9.0000 g., 0.9170 Gold 0.2653 oz. AGW **Ruler:** James VI (I) **Obv:** Crowned 1/2-length figure of James VI right with scepter and orb in inner circle **Rev:** Crowned arms, English arms in 1st and 4th quarters **Note:** S#5463.

Date	Mintage	Good	VG	F	VF	XF
ND(1604-09)	—	325	600	1,100	2,150	5,400

KM# 29 UNIT

9.0000 g., 0.9170 Gold 0.2653 oz. AGW **Ruler:** James VI (I) **Obv:** Crowned 1/2-length figure of James VI right with scepter and orb in inner circle **Rev:** Cowned arms, Scottish arms in 1st and 4th quarters **Note:** S#5464.

Date	Mintage	Good	VG	F	VF	XF
ND(1609-25)	—	265	425	925	1,850	4,750

KM# 56 UNIT

9.0000 g., 0.9170 Gold 0.2653 oz. AGW **Ruler:** Charles I **Obv:** Crowned 1/2-length figure of Charles I right with scepter and orb in inner circle **Rev:** Crowned arms **Note:** S#5527.

Date	Mintage	Good	VG	F	VF	XF
ND(1625-49)	—	500	900	1,750	3,250	6,500

KM# 57 UNIT

9.0000 g., 0.9170 Gold 0.2653 oz. AGW **Ruler:** Charles I **Obv:** Fine style crowned 1/2-length figure of Charles right with scepter and orb, thistle and B after legend **Note:** Briot Coinage. S#5531.

Date	Mintage	Good	VG	F	VF	XF
ND(1637-42)	—	425	775	1,600	2,850	6,000

KM# 58 UNIT

9.0000 g., 0.9170 Gold 0.2653 oz. AGW **Ruler:** Charles I **Obv:** Crowned 1/2-length figure of Charles I right with scepter and orb, B at beginning of legend and thistle at end **Rev:** Crowned arms **Note:** S#5532.

Date	Mintage	Good	VG	F	VF	XF
ND(1637-42)	—	1,450	2,400	4,000	7,000	—

KM# 59 UNIT

9.0000 g., 0.9170 Gold 0.2653 oz. AGW **Ruler:** Charles I **Obv:** Crowned 1/2-length figure of Charles I right with scepter and orb, thistle and F after legend **Rev:** Crowned arms **Note:** S#5533.

Date	Mintage	Good	VG	F	VF	XF
ND(1637-42)	—	2,200	4,150	7,750	12,500	—

STERLING COINAGE

KM# 36 PENNY

Copper **Obv:** Three thistles in inner circle **Obv. Legend:** IACOBV5. DEI... **Rev:** Crowned rampant lion left, pellet behind in inner circle **Rev. Legend:** FRANCIE ET HIBERNIE REX

Date	Mintage	VG	F	VF	XF	Unc
ND(1614)	—	35.00	65.00	250	—	—

KM# 40 PENNY

Copper **Rev. Legend:** FRAN & HIB REX

Date	Mintage	VG	F	VF	XF	Unc
ND(1623)	—	40.00	75.00	275	—	—

KM# 60 PENNY

Copper, 13.5 mm. **Obv:** Three thistles in inner circle **Obv. Legend:** CAROLVS... **Rev:** Crowned rampant lion left, pellet behind in inner circle

Date	Mintage	VG	F	VF	XF	Unc
ND(1629)	—	60.00	150	375	—	—

KM# 37 2 PENCE

Copper, 18 mm. **Obv:** Three thistles in inner circle **Obv. Legend:** JACOBVS... **Rev:** Crowned rampant lion left, two pellets behind in inner circle **Rev. Legend:** FRANCIE ET HIBERNIE REX

Date	Mintage	VG	F	VF	XF	Unc
ND(1614)	—	20.00	40.00	100	—	—

KM# 41 2 PENCE

Copper **Rev. Legend:** FRAN & HIB REX

Date	Mintage	VG	F	VF	XF	Unc
ND(1623)	—	20.00	35.00	85.00	—	—

KM# 61 2 PENCE
Copper **Obv:** Three thistles in inner circle **Obv. Legend:** CAROLVS... **Rev:** Crowned rampant lion left, two pellets behind in inner circle

Date	Mintage	VG	F	VF	XF	Unc
ND(1629)	—	20.00	40.00	90.00	—	—

KM# 65 2 PENCE
Copper **Obv:** "English" crown above C. II. R in inner circle **Rev:** Thistle in inner circle

Date	Mintage	VG	F	VF	XF	Unc
ND(1632-39)	—	20.00	35.00	65.00	—	—

KM# 66 2 PENCE
Copper **Obv:** Scottish crown (jeweled band and arches)

Date	Mintage	VG	F	VF	XF	Unc
ND(1632-39)	—	20.00	40.00	90.00	—	—

KM# 67 2 PENCE
Copper **Obv:** Scottish crown (plain band and arches)

Date	Mintage	VG	F	VF	XF	Unc
ND(1632-39)	—	20.00	40.00	90.00	—	—

KM# 68 2 PENCE
Copper **Obv:** Crown with five crosses

Date	Mintage	VG	F	VF	XF	Unc
ND(1632-39)	—	20.00	40.00	90.00	—	—

KM# 69 2 PENCE
Copper **Obv:** Crowned C.R in inner circle **Note:** Varieties exist.

Date	Mintage	VG	F	VF	XF	Unc
ND(1642-50)	—	20.00	40.00	90.00	—	—

KM# 100 2 PENCE
Copper **Obv:** Crowned C.R with II at right in inner circle

Date	Mintage	VG	F	VF	XF	Unc
ND(1663)	—	25.00	45.00	100	200	—

KM# 114 2 PENCE
Copper **Obv:** Crown above crossed sword and scepter **Rev:** Thistle in inner circle, date at top in legend **Note:** Various misspellings occur.

Date	Mintage	VG	F	VF	XF	Unc
1677	—	75.00	135	325	—	—
1678	—	75.00	135	325	—	—
1679	—	75.00	135	325	—	—

KM# 130 2 PENCE
Copper **Obv:** Crowned script W M monogram **Rev:** Crowned thistle, date in legend at upper left

Date	Mintage	VG	F	VF	XF	Unc
1691	—	25.00	45.00	110	350	—
1692	—	25.00	45.00	110	350	—
1693	—	25.00	45.00	110	350	—
1694	—	25.00	45.00	110	350	—

KM# 137 2 PENCE
Copper **Obv:** Crown above sword and secpter, crossed at flat angle **Rev:** Crowned large thistle

Date	Mintage	VG	F	VF	XF	Unc
1695	—	30.00	50.00	185	450	—
1696	—	30.00	50.00	185	450	—

KM# 138 2 PENCE
Copper **Obv:** Sword and scepter crossed at right angles **Rev:** Crowned small thistle

Date	Mintage	VG	F	VF	XF	Unc
1695	—	30.00	50.00	185	450	—
1696	—	30.00	50.00	185	450	—
1697	—	30.00	50.00	185	450	—

KM# 115 6 PENCE
Copper, 25 mm. **Obv:** Laureate bust of Charles II left **Rev:** Crowned thistle, date in legend at upper left **Note:** Varieties exist.

Date	Mintage	VG	F	VF	XF	Unc
1677	—	40.00	60.00	275	650	—
1678	—	40.00	60.00	220	550	—
1679	—	40.00	60.00	185	450	—

KM# 131 6 PENCE
Copper **Obv:** Conjoined laureate busts of William and Mary left **Note:** Varieties exist.

Date	Mintage	VG	F	VF	XF	Unc
1691	—	45.00	65.00	220	550	—
1692	—	45.00	65.00	275	650	—
1693	—	45.00	65.00	220	550	—
1694	—	45.00	65.00	220	550	—

KM# 139 6 PENCE
Copper **Obv:** Laureate bust of William III left **Note:** Varieties exist.

Date	Mintage	VG	F	VF	XF	Unc
1695	—	60.00	120	500	1,250	—
1696	—	60.00	120	500	1,250	—
1697	—	70.00	150	650	1,500	—

KM# 5 SHILLING
Silver **Obv:** Displayed rose in inner circle **Obv. Legend:** I. D. G... **Rev:** Thistle in inner circle **Note:** Mint mark: Thistle.

Date	Mintage	VG	F	VF	XF	Unc
ND(1605)	—	50.00	90.00	250	—	—

KM# 42 SHILLING
Silver **Obv:** C above I in legend **Note:** First Coinage (1625-1634).

Date	Mintage	VG	F	VF	XF	Unc
ND(1625)	—	150	250	450	—	—

KM# 70 20 PENCE
Silver **Obv:** Crowned bust of Charles I left with value behind head in inner circle **Rev:** Crowned thistle in inner circle **Note:** Second Coinage (Briot's hammered 1636).

Date	Mintage	VG	F	VF	XF	Unc
ND(1636)	—	35.00	100	275	—	—

KM# 73 20 PENCE
Silver **Obv:** Bust to edge of coin **Note:** Third Coinage, 1637-1642. Briot's issue.

Date	Mintage	VG	F	VF	XF	Unc
ND(1637)	—	25.00	40.00	90.00	—	—

KM# 74 20 PENCE
Silver **Obv:** Bust breaks inner circle **Note:** Third Coinage, 1637-1642. Falconer's Second issue.

Date	Mintage	VG	F	VF	XF	Unc
ND(1637)	—	25.00	50.00	100	—	—

KM# 75 20 PENCE
Silver **Obv:** Bust within inner circle

Date	Mintage	VG	F	VF	XF	Unc
ND(1637)	—	30.00	60.00	120	—	—

KM# 3 30 PENCE
1.5000 g., 0.9160 Silver 0.0442 oz. ASW, 17 mm. **Obv:** Armored bust right **Obv. Legend:** IACOBVS • 6 • D • G • R... **Rev:** Crown over triple-headed thistle **Rev. Legend:** NEMO ME IMPUNE LACESSET **Note:** Seventh Coinage, 1593-1601

Date	Mintage	VG	F	VF	XF	Unc
1601	—	250	650	1,150	—	—

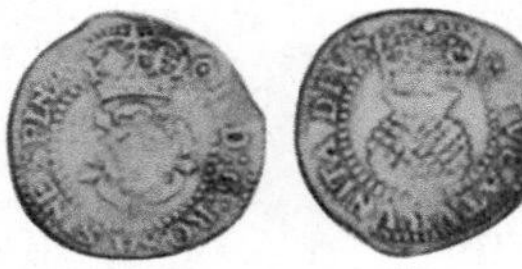

KM# 6 2 SHILLINGS
Silver, 17 mm. **Obv:** Crowned displayed rose **Obv. Legend:** I.D.G. ROSA SINE SPINA **Rev:** Crowned thistle **Rev. Legend:** TVEATVR **Note:** Mint mark: Thistle.

Date	Mintage	VG	F	VF	XF	Unc
ND(1605)	—	35.00	65.00	150	—	—

KM# 43 2 SHILLINGS
Silver **Obv. Legend:** C.D.G...

Date	Mintage	VG	F	VF	XF	Unc
ND(1625)	—	55.00	100	250	—	—

KM# 95 2 SHILLINGS
Silver **Obv:** Crowned bust of Charles I left with value behind head in inner circle **Rev:** Crowned arms in inner circle

Date	Mintage	VG	F	VF	XF	Unc
ND(1642)	—	30.00	65.00	165	—	—

KM# 96 3 SHILLING
Silver **Obv:** Crowned bust of Charles I left iwth thistle behind head in inner circle **Rev:** Crowned arms in inner circle **Note:** Fourth Coinage.

Date	Mintage	VG	F	VF	XF	Unc
ND(1642)	—	35.00	85.00	325	—	—

KM# 71 40 PENCE
Silver, 20 mm. **Obv:** Crowned bust of Charles I left with thistle behind head in inner circle **Rev:** Crowned thistle in inner circle **Note:** Second Coinage (Briot's hammered issue 1636).

Date	Mintage	VG	F	VF	XF	Unc
ND(1636)	—	35.00	70.00	175	—	—

KM# 76 40 PENCE
Silver **Rev:** B above crown **Note:** Third Coinage 1637-1642. Briot's issue.

Date	Mintage	VG	F	VF	XF
ND(1637)	—	40.00	90.00	225	—

KM# 77 40 PENCE
Silver **Rev:** F above crown **Note:** Falconer's First Issue. Varieti exist.

Date	Mintage	VG	F	VF	XF
ND(1637)	—	25.00	60.00	150	—

KM# 4 5 SHILLINGS
2.9900 g., 0.9160 Silver 0.0881 oz. ASW, 25 mm. **Obv:** Armor bust right **Obv. Legend:** IA COBVS • 6 • D • G • R... **Rev:** Crov over triple-headed thistle **Rev. Legend:** NEMO ME IM PUNE LACESSET **Note:** Seventh Coinage, 1596-1601.

Date	Mintage	VG	F	VF	XF
1601	—	700	1,500	2,500	—

KM# 132 5 SHILLINGS
2.9900 g., 0.9160 Silver 0.0881 oz. ASW, 19 mm. **Obv:** Conjoined laureate busts of William and Mary left **Rev:** Crown script W M monogram with value below

Date	Mintage	VG	F	VF	XF
1691	—	60.00	200	650	1,350

KM# 136 5 SHILLINGS
2.9900 g., 0.9160 Silver 0.0881 oz. ASW **Obv:** Value below bu

Date	Mintage	VG	F	VF	XF
1694	—	40.00	120	375	900

KM# 140 5 SHILLINGS
Silver, 19 mm. **Ruler:** William II (III) **Obv:** Laureate bust left value below **Rev:** Crown above 3 thistles, date in legend at upp left **Note:** Varieties exist.

Date	Mintage	VG	F	VF	XF
1695	—	40.00	120	325	—
1696	—	36.00	80.00	175	—
1697	—	40.00	120	325	—
1699	—	60.00	160	500	—
1700	—	50.00	140	400	—

KM# 30 6 SHILLING
Silver **Obv:** Crowned bust of James I right, with value behir head in inner circle **Rev:** Shield with arms of England in 1st a 4th quarters, date above in inner circle

Date	Mintage	VG	F	VF	XF
1605	—	400	800	1,800	—
1606	—	350	700	1,600	—
1609/7	—	350	700	1,600	—

KM# 35 6 SHILLING
Silver **Rev:** Arms of Scotland in 1st and 4th quarters

Date	Mintage	VG	F	VF	XF
1610	—	300	600	1,250	—
1611	—	300	600	1,250	—
1612	—	300	600	1,250	—
1613	—	300	600	1,250	—
1614	—	300	600	1,250	—
1615	—	300	600	1,250	—
1616	—	325	650	1,500	—
1617	—	325	650	1,500	—
1618	—	325	650	1,500	—
1619	—	250	500	1,200	—
1622	—	250	500	1,200	—

KM# 44 6 SHILLING
Silver **Obv:** Crowned bust of Charles I right, value behind he in inner circle **Rev:** Shield of arms with date above in inner circ **Note:** First Coinage (1625-1634).

Date	Mintage	VG	F	VF	XF
1625	—	200	525	1,500	—
1626	—	200	525	1,500	—
1627	—	200	525	1,500	—
1628	—	200	525	1,500	—
1630	—	200	525	1,500	—
1631	—	200	525	1,500	—
1632	—	200	525	1,500	—
1633	—	200	525	1,500	—
1634	—	200	525	1,500	—

KM# 78 6 SHILLING
Silver **Obv:** Crowned bust of Charles I left, value behind he in inner circle, bust to edge of coin **Rev:** Crowned arms divide R in inner circle **Note:** Third Coinage (1637-1642) Briot's iss

Date	Mintage	VG	F	VF	XF
ND(1637-42)	—	45.00	110	350	—

KM# 81 6 SHILLING
Silver **Obv:** New narrow bust of Charles I **Note:** Falconer's Anonymous Issue (without F).

Date	Mintage	VG	F	VF	XF
ND(1637-42)	—	45.00	110	350	750

KM# 79 6 SHILLING
Silver **Rev:** F above crown **Note:** Falconer's First Issue.

Date	Mintage	VG	F	VF	XF
ND(1637-42)	—	50.00	120	375	—

KM# 80 6 SHILLING
Silver **Obv:** Bust within inner circle **Note:** Falconer's Secon Issue.

Date	Mintage	VG	F	VF	XF
ND(1637-42)	—	45.00	110	350	—

M# A5 10 SHILLINGS
9800 g., 0.9160 Silver 0.1761 oz. ASW, 25 mm. **Obv:** Armored ıst right **Obv. Legend:** IACOBVS • 6 • D • G • R... **Rev:** Crown ver triple-headed thistle **Rev. Legend:** NEMO ME IMPUNE ACESSET **Note:** Seventh Coinage, 1593-1601.

te	Mintage	VG	F	VF	XF	Unc
01	—	400	1,000	2,250	—	—

M# 121 10 SHILLINGS
9800 g., 0.9160 Silver 0.1761 oz. ASW **Obv:** Laureate bust James VII right, value below bust **Rev:** Cruciform arms divided St. Andrew's cross, date divided at top

te	Mintage	VG	F	VF	XF	Unc
87	—	48.00	120	550	—	—
88	—	65.00	220	875	—	—

M# 124 10 SHILLINGS
9800 g., 0.9160 Silver 0.1761 oz. ASW **Obv:** Conjoined ureate busts of William and Mary left, value below busts **Rev:** nglish crown on small shield, date in legend at upper left

te	Mintage	VG	F	VF	XF	Unc
89	—	160	475	—	—	—
90	—	95.00	215	550	—	—

M# 133 10 SHILLINGS
9800 g., 0.9160 Silver 0.1761 oz. ASW **Rev:** Scottish crown large shield **Note:** Varieties exist.

te	Mintage	VG	F	VF	XF	Unc
91	—	85.00	200	450	—	—
92	—	100	295	650	—	—
94	—	90.00	265	875	—	—

M# 141 10 SHILLINGS
9800 g., 0.9160 Silver 0.1761 oz. ASW **Obv:** William III, value low bust

te	Mintage	VG	F	VF	XF	Unc
95	—	43.75	115	375	—	—
96	—	43.75	115	375	—	—
97	—	43.75	115	375	—	—
98	—	43.75	115	375	—	—
99	—	65.00	190	625	—	—

M# 7 12 SHILLING
ver, 31 mm. **Obv:** Bust of James VI right, value behind head inner circle **Rev:** Shield of arms with English arms in 1st and h quarters, in inner circle

te	Mintage	VG	F	VF	XF	Unc
(1603)	—	100	250	600	—	—

M# 8 12 SHILLING
ver **Rev:** Scottish arms in 1st and 4th quarters

te	Mintage	VG	F	VF	XF	Unc
(1603)	—	100	250	600	—	—

M# 45 12 SHILLING
ver, 31 mm. **Obv:** Crowned bust of Charles I right, value hind head in inner circle **Rev:** Shield of arms in inner circle **te:** First Coinage 1625-1634

te	Mintage	VG	F	VF	XF	Unc
(1625-34)	—	75.00	180	525	—	—

KM# 86 12 SHILLING
Silver **Obv:** Bust completely within inner circle

Date	Mintage	VG	F	VF	XF	Unc
ND(1637-42)	—	45.00	165	475	—	—

KM# A84 12 SHILLING
Silver **Obv:** Bust left **Rev:** F above crown

Date	Mintage	VG	F	VF	XF	Unc
ND1637-42	—	40.00	150	400	—	—

KM# 84 12 SHILLING
Silver **Rev:** F above crown, thistle begins legend **Note:** Falconer's First Issue.

Date	Mintage	VG	F	VF	XF	Unc
ND(1637-42)	—	40.00	150	400	—	—

KM# 85 12 SHILLING
Silver **Obv:** Bust breaks bottom of inner circle, F after legend **Note:** Falconer's Second Issue.

Date	Mintage	VG	F	VF	XF	Unc
ND(1637-42)	—	35.00	125	375	—	—

KM# 83 12 SHILLING
Silver **Rev:** Thistle above crown **Note:** Intermediate issue.

Date	Mintage	VG	F	VF	XF	Unc
ND(1637-42)	—	45.00	165	475	—	—

KM# 82 12 SHILLING
Silver **Obv:** Charles I, small B at end of legend **Rev:** Small B at end of legend **Note:** Third Coinage 1637-1642, Briot's issue.

Date	Mintage	VG	F	VF	XF	Unc
ND(1637-42)	—	40.00	150	400	1,600	—

KM# 13 1/8 MERK
0.0850 g., 0.9160 Silver 0.0025 oz. ASW, 15 mm. **Obv:** Crowned shield **Rev:** Crowned thistle

Date	Mintage	VG	F	VF	XF	Unc
1601	—	30.00	90.00	260	—	—
1602	—	28.00	75.00	220	—	—
1603	—	75.00	185	—	—	—

KM# 14 1/4 MERK
1.7000 g., 0.9160 Silver 0.0501 oz. ASW, 20 mm. **Obv:** Crowned shield **Rev:** Crowned thistle

Date	Mintage	VG	F	VF	XF	Unc
1601	—	25.00	80.00	250	—	—
1602	—	25.00	70.00	200	—	—
1603	—	35.00	175	450	—	—
1604	—	45.00	350	500	—	—

KM# 116 1/4 MERK
1.7000 g., 0.9160 Silver 0.0501 oz. ASW **Obv:** Laureate bust of Charles II left **Rev:** Crown on St. Andrew's cross with national emblems in angles, date in legend at upper left

Date	Mintage	VG	F	VF	XF	Unc
1677	—	60.00	215	450	—	—
1678/7	—	70.00	170	500	—	—
1679/7 Rare	—	—	—	—	—	—
1680	—	180	425	1,150	—	—
1680	—	210	475	1,300	—	—
1681	—	85.00	210	575	—	—

KM# 15 1/2 MERK
3.4000 g., 0.9160 Silver 0.1001 oz. ASW, 28 mm. **Obv:** Crowned shield **Rev:** Crowned thistle

Date	Mintage	VG	F	VF	XF	Unc
1601	—	30.00	75.00	250	—	—
1602	—	30.00	75.00	250	—	—
1603	—	40.00	110	275	—	—
1604	—	50.00	225	550	—	—

KM# 72 1/2 MERK
3.4000 g., 0.9160 Silver 0.1001 oz. ASW **Obv:** Crowned bust of Charles I left, value VI behind head in inner circle **Rev:** Crowned arms in inner circle **Note:** Second Coinage (1636) Briot's Hammered Issue.

Date	Mintage	VG	F	VF	XF	Unc
ND(1636)	—	35.00	90.00	325	—	—

KM# 93 1/2 MERK
3.4000 g., 0.9160 Silver 0.1001 oz. ASW **Rev:** Crowned arms divide C-R in inner circle, B after legend **Note:** Third Coinage (1637-42) Briot's Issue.

Date	Mintage	VG	F	VF	XF	Unc
ND(1637-42)	—	40.00	105	245	—	—

KM# 101 1/2 MERK
3.4000 g., 0.9160 Silver 0.1001 oz. ASW **Obv:** Laureate bust of Charles II right **Rev:** Cruciform arms with value at center, crowned linked C's in angles, date in legend at upper right **Note:** Varieties exist.

Date	Mintage	VG	F	VF	XF	Unc
1664	—	155	325	—	—	—
1664 Rare	—	—	—	—	—	—
Note: Stamped 1665						
1665	—	155	325	—	—	—
1666	—	185	400	—	—	—
1667	—	155	325	—	—	—
1668	—	130	265	575	—	—
1669	—	110	210	525	—	—
1670	—	110	210	525	—	—
1671	—	110	210	525	—	—
1672	—	120	240	550	—	—
1673	—	120	240	550	—	—
1675	—	130	265	575	—	—

KM# 105 1/2 MERK
3.4000 g., 0.9160 Silver 0.1001 oz. ASW **Rev:** Arms of England and Ireland transposed **Note:** Error.

Date	Mintage	VG	F	VF	XF	Unc
1665	—	180	450	1,450	—	—
1666 Rare	—	325	775	—	—	—

KM# 112 1/2 MERK
3.4000 g., 0.9160 Silver 0.1001 oz. ASW **Obv:** Charles II **Note:** Second Coinage.

Date	Mintage	VG	F	VF	XF	Unc
1676	—	48.50	160	500	—	—
1677	—	60.00	190	525	—	—
1678/7 Rare	—	—	—	—	—	—
1679	—	210	550	1,550	—	—
1680	—	60.00	190	525	—	—
1682	—	210	550	1,550	—	—

KM# 120 1/2 MERK

3.4000 g., 0.9160 Silver 0.1001 oz. ASW **Rev:** Arms of Scotland and France transposed **Note:** Error.

Date	Mintage	VG	F	VF	XF	Unc
1680	—	325	800	2,300	—	—

KM# 16 MERK

6.7900 g., 0.9160 Silver 0.2000 oz. ASW, 32 mm. **Obv:** Crowned shield **Rev:** Crowned thistle

Date	Mintage	VG	F	VF	XF	Unc
1601	—	45.00	150	400	—	—
1602	—	35.00	130	375	—	—
1603	—	35.00	130	375	—	—
1604	—	50.00	200	500	—	—

KM# 102.1 MERK

6.7900 g., 0.9160 Silver 0.2000 oz. ASW, 25 mm. **Obv:** Charles II, thistle below bust **Note:** First Coinage. Varieties exist.

Date	Mintage	VG	F	VF	XF	Unc
1664	—	95.00	215	500	—	—
1665	—	95.00	270	575	—	—
1666	—	110	300	750	—	—
1668	—	95.00	205	500	—	—
1669	—	95.00	205	450	—	—
1670	—	95.00	205	450	—	—
1671	—	95.00	205	450	—	—
1672	—	95.00	205	450	—	—
1673	—	95.00	205	450	—	—
1674	—	110	270	750	—	—

KM# 102.2 MERK

6.7900 g., 0.9160 Silver 0.2000 oz. ASW **Obv:** F below bust

Date	Mintage	VG	F	VF	XF	Unc
1674	—	120	325	975	—	—
1675	—	110	280	850	—	—

KM# 102.3 MERK

6.7900 g., 0.9160 Silver 0.2000 oz. ASW **Obv:** Plain below bust

Date	Mintage	VG	F	VF	XF	Unc
1675	—	180	450	1,500	—	—

KM# 110.1 MERK

6.7900 g., 0.9160 Silver 0.2000 oz. ASW **Obv:** Laureate bust of Charles II left **Rev:** Cruciform arms with linked C's at center, thistles in angles, date divided at top **Note:** Second Coinage.

Date	Mintage	VG	F	VF	XF	Unc
1675	—	130	350	900	—	—
1676	—	115	245	550	—	—
1677/6	—	115	280	—	—	—
1677	—	115	300	550	—	—
1678	—	115	300	725	—	—
1679	—	115	245	550	—	—
1680	—	115	245	550	—	—
1681	—	115	245	550	—	—
1682	—	115	265	625	—	—

KM# 110.2 MERK

6.7900 g., 0.9160 Silver 0.2000 oz. ASW **Rev:** Arms of Ireland in 1st shield

Date	Mintage	VG	F	VF	XF	Unc
1682	—	210	550	1,650	—	—

KM# 103.2 2 MERKS

Silver **Obv:** Thistle below bust

Date	Mintage	VG	F	VF	XF	Unc
1664	—	270	650	2,150	—	—
1670	—	180	450	1,500	—	—
1673	—	170	425	1,450	—	—
1674	—	210	550	1,800	—	—

KM# 103.1 2 MERKS

Silver, 33 mm. **Obv:** Laureate bust of Chalres II right, thistle above head **Rev:** Cruciform arms with value at center, crowned linked C's in angles, date in legend at upper left **Note:** First Coinage.

Date	Mintage	VG	F	VF	XF	Unc
1664	—	220	550	1,750	—	—

KM# 103.4 2 MERKS

Silver **Obv:** F below bust

Date	Mintage	VG	F	VF	XF	Unc
1673 Rare	—	—	—	—	—	—

Date	Mintage	VG	F	VF	XF	Unc
1674	—	240	475	1,550	—	—
1675	—	190	400	1,500	—	—

KM# 111 2 MERKS

Silver **Obv:** Laureate bust of Charles II left **Rev:** Cruciform arms with linked C's at center, thistles in angles, date divided at top **Note:** Second Coinage.

Date	Mintage	VG	F	VF	XF	Unc
1675	—	240	475	1,300	—	—
1676	—	450	900	2,150	—	—
1681	—	245	500	1,150	—	—

KM# 104.2 4 MERKS

Silver **Obv:** Thistle below bust

Date	Mintage	VG	F	VF	XF	Unc
1664	—	450	1,600	—	—	—
1665 Rare	—	—	—	—	—	—
1670	—	400	950	2,300	—	—
1673	—	400	950	2,300	—	—

KM# 104.1 4 MERKS

Silver, 38 mm. **Obv:** Laureate bust of Charles II right, thistle above head **Rev:** Cruciform arms with value at center, crowned linked C's in angles, date in legend at upper left **Note:** First Coinage.

Date	Mintage	VG	F	VF	XF	Unc
1664	—	775	1,500	2,950	—	—

KM# 104.3 4 MERKS

Silver **Obv:** F below bust

Date	Mintage	VG	F	VF	XF	Unc
1674	—	350	900	2,150	—	—
1675	—	775	1,500	—	—	—

KM# 113 4 MERKS

Silver **Obv:** Charles II **Note:** Second Coinage.

Date	Mintage	VG	F	VF	XF	Unc
1676	—	300	775	2,400	—	—
1679	—	270	650	2,150	—	—
1680	—	425	1,000	3,600	—	—
1681	—	300	775	2,400	—	—
1682	—	220	550	1,950	—	—

KM# 135 20 SHILLINGS

Silver, 28.5 mm. **Obv:** William and Mary, value below busts

Date	Mintage	VG	F	VF	XF	Unc
1693	—	175	400	1,250	—	—
1694	—	400	800	2,500	—	—

KM# 142 20 SHILLINGS

Silver **Obv:** Laureate bust of William III left, value below bust

Date	Mintage	VG	F	VF	XF	Unc
1695	—	100	350	675	—	—
1696	—	100	350	675	—	—
1697	—	150	550	—	—	—
1698	—	110	325	750	—	—
1699	—	130	325	—	—	—

KM# 9 30 SHILLINGS

Silver, 35 mm. **Obv:** James VI on horseback with sword on shoulder right in inner circle **Rev:** Shield of arms with English arms in 1st and 4th quarters, in inner circle

Date	Mintage	VG	F	VF	XF	U
ND(1603)	—	45.00	170	450	—	

KM# 10 30 SHILLINGS

Silver **Rev:** Scottish arms in 1st and 4th quarters

Date	Mintage	VG	F	VF	XF	U
ND(1603)	—	45.00	170	450	—	

KM# 46 30 SHILLINGS

Silver **Obv:** Charles I **Rev:** Scottish arms in 1st and 4th quarte **Note:** First Coinage 1625-1634.

Date	Mintage	VG	F	VF	XF	U
ND(1625-34)	—	65.00	230	500	—	

KM# 88 30 SHILLINGS

Silver **Obv:** Without B **Rev:** Without B **Note:** Intermediate issu

Date	Mintage	VG	F	VF	XF	U
ND(1637-42)	—	35.00	110	275	675	

KM# 87 30 SHILLINGS

Silver **Obv:** Charles I on horseback with sword erect left in inne circle, B and rosette at top **Rev:** Crowned arms in inner circle, B a thistle before legend **Note:** Third Coinage 1637-1642, Briot's Issu

Date	Mintage	VG	F	VF	XF	U
ND(1637-42)	—	35.00	110	275	675	

KM# 90.1 30 SHILLINGS

Silver **Obv:** Horse on rough ground, F under horse's rear raised h

Date	Mintage	VG	F	VF	XF	U
ND(1637-42)	—	35.00	110	275	675	

KM# 90.2 30 SHILLINGS

Silver **Obv:** Charles I on horseback on rough ground **Rev:** F over the crown

Date	Mintage	VG	F	VF	XF	U
ND(1637-42)	—	100	200	500	1,250	

/I# 91 30 SHILLINGS
/er **Obv:** Without F **Obv. Legend:** CAROLVS • D:G • MAG •
IT • FRAN • & • HIB • REX **Note:** Falconer's Anonymous Issue.

e	Mintage	VG	F	VF	XF	Unc
(1637-42)	—	85.00	110	275	675	—

/I# 89 30 SHILLINGS
/er **Obv:** Horse on smooth ground, F under raised rear hoof
te: Falconer's Second Issue.

e	Mintage	VG	F	VF	XF	Unc
(1637-42)	—	100	200	500	1,250	3,500

1# 122 40 SHILLING
/er, 35 mm. **Obv:** Laureate bust of James VII right, value
ow bust **Rev:** Crowned arms, crown divides date **Note:**
ieties exist.

e	Mintage	VG	F	VF	XF	Unc
7	—	110	300	750	1,300	—
8	—	150	450	900	—	—

1# 125 40 SHILLING
er **Obv:** Conjoined laureate busts of William and Mary left,
ue below busts **Rev:** Crowned arms, date in legend at upper
Note: Varieties exist.

e	Mintage	VG	F	VF	XF	Unc
9	—	175	350	875	—	—
0	—	110	265	800	—	—
1	—	100	245	625	—	—
2	—	110	265	800	—	—
3	—	145	300	475	—	—
4	—	195	400	550	—	—

1# 143 40 SHILLING
er **Obv:** William III **Note:** Varieties exist.

e	Mintage	VG	F	VF	XF	Unc
5	—	120	280	750	—	—
6	—	110	270	700	—	—
7	—	130	300	825	—	—
8	—	100	270	650	—	—
9	—	150	325	475	—	—
0 Rare	—	—	—	—	—	—

KM# 11 60 SHILLING
Silver, 42 mm. **Obv:** James VI **Rev:** English arms in 1st and 4th quarters

Date	Mintage	VG	F	VF	XF	Unc
ND(1603)	—	175	550	1,450	3,000	—

KM# 12 60 SHILLING
Silver **Rev:** Scottish arms in 1st and 4th quarters

Date	Mintage	VG	F	VF	XF	Unc
ND(1603)	—	200	700	1,600	3,300	—

KM# 47 60 SHILLING
Silver **Obv:** Charles I **Rev:** Scottish arms in 1st and 4th quarters **Note:** First Coinage 1625-1634.

Date	Mintage	VG	F	VF	XF	Unc
ND(1625-34)	—	325	900	2,350	5,000	—

KM# 92 60 SHILLING
Silver **Obv:** Charles I **Note:** Third Coinage 1637-1642. Briot's Issue.

Date	Mintage	VG	F	VF	XF	Unc
ND(1637-42)	—	150	475	1,500	3,250	—

KM# 134 60 SHILLING
Silver **Obv:** William and Mary

Date	Mintage	VG	F	VF	XF	Unc
1691	—	375	700	2,150	4,500	—
1692	—	225	450	1,500	3,750	—

KM# 134a 60 SHILLING
Copper

Date	Mintage	VG	F	VF	XF	Unc
1691 Rare	—	—	—	—	—	—

PATTERNS

Including off metal strikes

KM#	Date	Mintage	Identification	Mkt Val
Pn1	ND	—	2 Pence. Copper. Crowned C-R. Thistle.	—
Pn2	ND	—	3 Pence. Silver. Crowned C-R. Thistle.	—
Pn3	ND	—	3 Pence. Silver. Bust of Charles I. Thistle.	—
Pn4	ND	—	20 Pence. Silver. Bust of Charles I. Crowned thistle, C-R.	—
Pn5	ND	—	40 Pence. Silver. Bust of Charles I. Crowned thistle, C-R.	—
Pn6	1636	—	1/2 Merk. Silver. Bust of Charles I. Crowned thistle, C-R.	—

The Spanish State, forming the greater part of the Iberian Peninsula of southwest Europe, has an area of 195,988 sq. mi. (504,714 sq. km.) and a population of 39.4 million including the Balearic and the Canary Islands. Capital: Madrid. The economy is based on agriculture, industry and tourism. Machinery, fruit, vegetables and chemicals are exported.

It isn't known when man first came to the Iberian Peninsula - the Altamira caves off the Cantabrian coast approximately 50 miles west of Santander were fashioned in Paleolithic times. Spain was a battleground for centuries before it became a united nation, fought for by Phoenicians, Carthaginians, Greeks, Celts, Romans, Vandals, Visigoths and Moors. Ferdinand and Isabella destroyed the last Moorish stronghold in 1492, freeing the national energy and resources for the era of discovery and colonization that would make Spain the most powerful country in Europe during the 16th century. After the destruction of the Spanish Armada, 1588, Spain never again played a major role in European politics.

RULERS

Philip III, 1598-1621
Philip IV, 1621-1665
Charles II, 1665-1700

HOMELAND MINT MARKS

Until 1851

B - Burgos

B, BA – Barcelona

(c) - Scalloped shell – Coruna

C, CA (monogram) – Cuenca

G – Granada

MD - M - M̃

M, crowned M, ligate MD – Madrid

S, SL – Seville

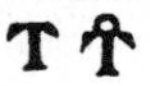

T, To (monogram) – Toledo

VD, VDL, VL, VLL – Valladolid

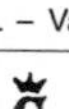

Crowned C – Cadiz

Aqueduct – Segovia

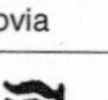

(f) Flags - Valladolid

MINTMASTERS' INITIALS

BURGOS MINT

A	1650-51	Pedro Arce
BR	1651	Bernardo de Pedrera y Negrete
R	1661-64	?

CUENCA MINT

CA	1651	?
E	1628-33	?
I	1600-02	?
JJ	1725	Juan Jose Garcia Caballero

MADRID MINT

A	1650-51, 1660-61	Agustin Mayens
AI	1651	Agustin Mayens and Ipolito de Santo Domingo
G	1620	?
IB	1644-45	Ipolito de Santo Domingo
M	1632, 1638	?
OP	1639	Oracio Levanto
P	1630-37	?
S	1660-64	?
TR	1661, 1680, 1686	?
C	1621-27	?
V+	1642	?
Y	1660-64	?

SEGOVIA MINT

A	1617	?
A+	1616-21	Andres de Pedrera
AR	1614	?
B	1613, 31	?
BR	1659-91	Bernardo de Pedrera y Negrete
Castle Tower (t)	1599-1619	Melchor Rodriquez del Castillo
C	1599-1611	Melchor Rodriquez del Castillo
CA	1610	Melchor Rodriquez del Castillo
F	1699	Francisco de Pedrera y Negrete
I	1651	Ipolito de Santo Domingo
P	1625-30	Esteban de Pedrera
R	1632-39	Rafael Salvan
S	1660-64	?
X	1655	?

SEVILLE MINT

B	1592-1611	Juan Vicente Bravo
D	1612	?
G	1615-21	Gaspar de Talavera
M	1668-70, 1673-74	Manuel Duarte
M	1686-1703, 1707-19	?
R	1621-65	?
V	1613-16	?

TOLEDO MINT

C	1593-1601	Melchor Rodriquez del Castillo
C	1663-64	?
M	1663-64	?
P	1619-35	?
V	1611-18	?
Y	1651-55	?

MONETARY SYSTEM

34 Maravedi = 1 Real (of Silver)
16 Reales = 1 Escudo

NOTE: The early coinage of Spain is listed by denomination based on a system of 16 Reales de Plata (silver) = 1 Escudo (gold).

KINGDOM

HAMMERED COINAGE

KM# 1.2 BLANCA

Billon **Ruler:** Philip III **Obv:** King's monogram crowned, date below **Rev:** Castle between mint mark and assayer mark **Mint:** Segovia

Date	Mintage	VG	F	VF	XF	Unc
1601 tower/castle	—	25.00	40.00	60.00	—	—
1602 tower/castle	—	25.00	40.00	60.00	—	—

KM# 1.1 BLANCA

Billon **Ruler:** Philip III **Obv:** King's monogram crowned, date below **Rev:** Castle between mint mark and value **Mint:** Cuenca

Date	Mintage	VG	F	VF	XF	Unc
1602C	—	60.00	100	200	—	—

KM# 2.2 MARAVEDI

Billon **Ruler:** Philip III **Obv:** Castle between mint mark and assayer mark **Rev:** Lion, date in legend **Mint:** Cuenca

Date	Mintage	VG	F	VF	XF	Unc
1601C	—	10.00	15.00	30.00	—	—
1602C	—	10.00	15.00	30.00	—	—

KM# 2.1 MARAVEDI

Billon **Ruler:** Philip III **Obv:** Castle between mint mark and assayer mark **Rev:** Lion, date in legend **Mint:** Cuenca **Note:** Mint mark: Star above chalice.

Date	Mintage	VG	F	VF	XF	Unc
1601	—	10.00	15.00	35.00	—	—

KM# 2.3 MARAVEDI

Billon **Ruler:** Philip III **Obv:** Castle between value and assayer mark **Rev:** Lion, date in legend **Mint:** Segovia

Date	Mintage	VG	F	VF	XF	Unc
1602 Tower/castle	—	20.00	30.00	45.00	—	—

KM# 3.3 2 MARAVEDIS

Billon **Ruler:** Philip III **Obv:** Castle between mint mark and assayer mark **Rev:** Lion, date in legend **Mint:** Cuenca **Note:** M mark: Star above chalice.

Date	Mintage	VG	F	VF	XF
1601	—	10.00	15.00	25.00	—
1602	—	10.00	15.00	25.00	—

KM# 3.2 2 MARAVEDIS

Bronze **Ruler:** Philip III **Obv:** Castle between mint mark and value **Rev:** Lion, date in wreath **Mint:** Coruna **Note:** Mint ma Scallop shell.

Date	Mintage	VG	F	VF	XF
ND	—	25.00	45.00	90.00	—
1602	—	35.00	75.00	150	—
1603	—	35.00	75.00	150	—
1604	—	35.00	75.00	150	—

KM# 3.10 2 MARAVEDIS

Bronze **Ruler:** Philip III **Obv:** Castle between mint mark and value, within circle **Rev:** Lion within circle **Mint:** Valladolid **Note:** Mint mark: Flags

Date	Mintage	VG	F	VF	XF
1602Flags	—	12.00	20.00	30.00	—
1603Flags	—	12.00	20.00	30.00	—
1604Flags	—	12.00	20.00	30.00	—

KM# 3.1 2 MARAVEDIS

Bronze **Ruler:** Philip III **Obv:** Castle between mint mark and value **Rev:** Lion, date in legned **Mint:** Burgos

Date	Mintage	VG	F	VF	XF
1602B	—	8.00	15.00	25.00	—
1603B	—	8.00	15.00	25.00	—
1604B	—	8.00	15.00	25.00	—
1605B	—	8.00	15.00	25.00	—
1606B	—	8.00	15.00	25.00	—

KM# 3.4 2 MARAVEDIS

Bronze **Ruler:** Philip III **Obv:** Castle between mint mark and value, within circle **Rev:** Lion within circle **Mint:** Cuenca

Date	Mintage	VG	F	VF	XF
1602C	—	10.00	15.00	25.00	—
1603C	—	10.00	15.00	25.00	—
1604C	—	10.00	15.00	25.00	—
1605C	—	10.00	15.00	25.00	—
1606C	—	10.00	15.00	25.00	—
1607C	—	10.00	15.00	25.00	—
1608C	—	10.00	15.00	25.00	—
1618C	—	10.00	20.00	35.00	—
1619C	—	10.00	20.00	35.00	—
1620C	—	10.00	20.00	35.00	—

KM# 3.5 2 MARAVEDIS

Bronze **Ruler:** Philip III **Obv:** Castle between mint mark above assayer and value, within circle **Rev:** Lion within circle **Mint:** Granada

Date	Mintage	VG	F	VF	XF
1602G M	—	12.00	25.00	40.00	—
1603G M	—	12.00	25.00	40.00	—
1604G M	—	12.00	25.00	40.00	—

KM# 3.8 2 MARAVEDIS

Bronze **Ruler:** Philip III **Obv:** Castle between mint mark and value **Rev:** Lion, date in legend **Mint:** Seville

Date	Mintage	VG	F	VF	XF
1602S	—	20.00	45.00	80.00	—
1603S	—	20.00	45.00	80.00	—

KM# 3.9 2 MARAVEDIS

Bronze **Ruler:** Philip III **Obv:** Castle between mint mark and value, within circle **Rev:** Lion within circle **Mint:** Toledo

Date	Mintage	VG	F	VF	XF
1602T	—	12.00	30.00	45.00	—
1603T	—	12.00	30.00	45.00	—
1604T	—	12.00	30.00	45.00	—

KM# 3.7 2 MARAVEDIS

Bronze **Ruler:** Philip III **Obv:** Castle between value and mint mark with assayer above **Rev:** Lion, date in legend **Mint:** Segovi **Note:** Mint mark: Aqueduct.

Date	Mintage	VG	F	VF	XF
1603Aqueduct	—	20.00	30.00	45.00	—
1603Aqueduct Mint mark at left	—	20.00	30.00	45.00	—

KM# 3.6 2 MARAVEDIS

Bronze **Ruler:** Philip III **Obv:** Castle between mint mark and vlaue **Rev:** Lion, date in legend **Mint:** Madrid

Date	Mintage	VG	F	VF	XF
1618MD	—	10.00	15.00	30.00	—
1619MD	—	10.00	15.00	30.00	—
1620MD	—	10.00	15.00	30.00	—

KM# 4.4 2 MARAVEDIS

Bronze **Ruler:** Philip IV **Obv:** Castle between mint mark and value **Rev:** Lion, date in legend **Mint:** Madrid

Date	Mintage	VG	F	VF	XF
1621MD	—	15.00	30.00	75.00	—
1622MD	—	15.00	30.00	75.00	—
1623MD	—	15.00	30.00	75.00	—
1624MD	—	15.00	30.00	75.00	—

te	Mintage	VG	F	VF	XF	Unc
25MD	—	15.00	30.00	75.00	—	—
26MD	—	15.00	30.00	75.00	—	—

M# 4.2 2 MARAVEDIS

onze **Ruler:** Philip IV **Obv:** Castle between mint mark and lue within circle **Rev:** Lion within circle **Mint:** Cuenca

te	Mintage	VG	F	VF	XF	Unc
21C	—	10.00	15.00	30.00	—	—
22C	—	10.00	15.00	30.00	—	—
23C	—	10.00	15.00	30.00	—	—
24C	—	10.00	15.00	30.00	—	—
25C	—	10.00	15.00	30.00	—	—
26C	—	10.00	15.00	30.00	—	—

M# 4.1 2 MARAVEDIS

onze **Ruler:** Philip IV **Obv:** Castle between mint mark and lue **Rev:** Lion, date in legend **Mint:** Burgos

te	Mintage	VG	F	VF	XF	Unc
21B	—	12.00	18.00	30.00	—	—
22B	—	12.00	18.00	30.00	—	—
23B	—	12.00	18.00	30.00	—	—
24B	—	12.00	18.00	30.00	—	—
25B	—	12.00	18.00	30.00	—	—
26B	—	12.00	18.00	30.00	—	—

M# 4.7 2 MARAVEDIS

onze **Ruler:** Philip III **Obv:** Castle between mint mark and lue, within circle **Rev:** Lion within circle **Mint:** Toledo

te	Mintage	VG	F	VF	XF	Unc
21T	—	8.00	20.00	35.00	—	—
22T	—	8.00	20.00	35.00	—	—
23T	—	8.00	20.00	35.00	—	—
24T	—	8.00	20.00	35.00	—	—
25T	—	8.00	20.00	35.00	—	—
26T	—	8.00	20.00	35.00	—	—

M# 4.6 2 MARAVEDIS

onze **Ruler:** Philip IV **Obv:** Castle between mint mark and lue **Rev:** Lion, date in legend **Mint:** Seville

te	Mintage	VG	F	VF	XF	Unc
21S	—	10.00	20.00	40.00	—	—
22S	—	10.00	20.00	40.00	—	—
23S	—	10.00	20.00	40.00	—	—
24S	—	10.00	20.00	40.00	—	—
25S	—	10.00	20.00	40.00	—	—
26S	—	10.00	20.00	40.00	—	—

M# 4.3 2 MARAVEDIS

onze **Ruler:** Philip IV **Obv:** Castle between mint mark and lue, within circle **Rev:** Lion within circle **Mint:** Granada

te	Mintage	VG	F	VF	XF	Unc
21G	—	10.00	15.00	30.00	—	—
22G	—	10.00	15.00	30.00	—	—
23G	—	10.00	15.00	30.00	—	—
24G	—	10.00	15.00	30.00	—	—
25G	—	10.00	15.00	30.00	—	—
26G	—	10.00	15.00	30.00	—	—

M# 4.5 2 MARAVEDIS

onze **Ruler:** Philip IV **Obv:** Castle between mint mark and lue **Rev:** Lion, date in legend **Mint:** Segovia **Note:** Mint mark: ueduct.

te	Mintage	VG	F	VF	XF	Unc
21Aqueduct	—	60.00	150	400	—	—
22Aqueduct	—	60.00	150	400	—	—

M# 4.8 2 MARAVEDIS

onze **Ruler:** Philip IV **Obv:** Castle between mint mark and lue **Rev:** Lion, date in legend **Mint:** Valladolid **Note:** Mint mark: gs

te	Mintage	VG	F	VF	XF	Unc
21Flags	—	10.00	30.00	45.00	—	—
22Flags	—	10.00	30.00	45.00	—	—
23Flags	—	10.00	30.00	45.00	—	—
24Flags	—	10.00	30.00	45.00	—	—
25Flags	—	10.00	30.00	45.00	—	—
26Flags	—	10.00	30.00	45.00	—	—

M# 5.4 2 MARAVEDIS

onze **Ruler:** Charles II **Obv:** Shield of Castle between mint rk and value **Rev:** Shield of Leon, date at right **Mint:** Granada te: Mint mark: Pomegranate.

te	Mintage	VG	F	VF	XF	Unc
30	—	10.00	20.00	35.00	—	—
31	—	10.00	20.00	35.00	—	—
35	—	10.00	20.00	35.00	—	—
36 inverted int mark	—	15.00	30.00	65.00	—	—

M# 5.2 2 MARAVEDIS

onze **Ruler:** Charles II **Obv:** Shield of Castle between mint d value **Rev:** Shield of Leon, date at right **Mint:** Coruna **Note:** nt mark: Scallop shell.

te	Mintage	VG	F	VF	XF	Unc
30	—	10.00	15.00	35.00	—	—
31	—	10.00	15.00	35.00	—	—
32	—	10.00	15.00	35.00	—	—
33	—	10.00	15.00	35.00	—	—
34	—	10.00	15.00	35.00	—	—
35	—	10.00	15.00	35.00	—	—
36	—	10.00	15.00	50.00	—	—
94	—	10.00	15.00	35.00	—	—
95	—	10.00	15.00	35.00	—	—
96	—	10.00	15.00	35.00	—	—

KM# 5.3 2 MARAVEDIS

Bronze **Ruler:** Charles II **Obv:** Shield of Castle between mint mark and value **Rev:** Shield of Leon, date at right **Mint:** Cuenca **Note:** Mint mark: Star above chalice.

Date	Mintage	VG	F	VF	XF	Unc
1680	—	10.00	15.00	30.00	—	—
1680 Inverted mint mark	—	15.00	25.00	50.00	—	—
1680 Mint mark at right	—	15.00	25.00	45.00	—	—
1681	—	10.00	15.00	30.00	—	—

KM# 5.8 2 MARAVEDIS

Bronze **Ruler:** Charles II **Obv:** Shield of Castle between mint mark and value **Rev:** Shield of Leon, date at right **Mint:** Seville

Date	Mintage	VG	F	VF	XF	Unc
1680S	—	8.00	15.00	30.00	—	—
1681S	—	8.00	15.00	30.00	—	—
1682S	—	8.00	15.00	30.00	—	—
1683S	—	8.00	15.00	30.00	—	—
1684S	—	8.00	15.00	30.00	—	—
1685S	—	8.00	15.00	30.00	—	—

KM# 5.9 2 MARAVEDIS

Bronze **Ruler:** Charles II **Obv:** Shield of Castle between mint mark and value **Rev:** Shield of leon, date at right **Mint:** Toledo

Date	Mintage	VG	F	VF	XF	Unc
1680T	—	8.00	15.00	35.00	—	—
1681T	—	8.00	15.00	35.00	—	—
1682T	—	8.00	15.00	35.00	—	—
1683T	—	8.00	15.00	35.00	—	—
1684T	—	8.00	15.00	35.00	—	—
1685T	—	8.00	15.00	35.00	—	—

KM# 5.10 2 MARAVEDIS

Bronze **Ruler:** Charles II **Obv:** Shield of Castile between mint mark and value **Rev:** Shield of Leon, date at right **Mint:** Trujillo

Date	Mintage	VG	F	VF	XF	Unc
1680TR	—	—	15.00	25.00	45.00	—
1681TR	—	—	15.00	25.00	45.00	—
1682TR	—	—	15.00	25.00	45.00	—
1683TR	—	—	15.00	25.00	45.00	—
1684TR	—	—	15.00	25.00	45.00	—
1685TR	—	—	15.00	25.00	45.00	—
1686TR	—	—	15.00	25.00	45.00	—

KM# 5.11 2 MARAVEDIS

Bronze **Ruler:** Charles II **Obv:** Shield of Castile between mint mark and value **Rev:** Shield of Leon between assayer mark and date **Mint:** Valladolid

Date	Mintage	VG	F	VF	XF	Unc
1680VD L	—	20.00	35.00	45.00	—	—
1681VD L	—	20.00	35.00	45.00	—	—

KM# 5.12 2 MARAVEDIS

Bronze **Ruler:** Charles II **Obv:** Shield of Castile between mint mark and value **Rev:** Shield of Leon between assayer mark and date **Mint:** Valladolid

Date	Mintage	VG	F	VF	XF	Unc
1680VLL L	—	20.00	35.00	50.00	—	—
1681VLL L	—	20.00	35.00	50.00	—	—
1682VLL L	—	20.00	35.00	50.00	—	—
1683VLL L	—	20.00	35.00	50.00	—	—
1684VLL L	—	20.00	35.00	50.00	—	—
1685VLL L	—	20.00	35.00	50.00	—	—
1686VLL L	—	20.00	35.00	50.00	—	—

KM# 5.1 2 MARAVEDIS

Bronze **Ruler:** Charles II **Obv:** Shield of Castle between mint mark and value **Rev:** Shield of Leon, date at right **Mint:** Burgos

Date	Mintage	VG	F	VF	XF	Unc
1680B	—	10.00	15.00	40.00	—	—
1681B	—	10.00	15.00	40.00	—	—
1682B	—	10.00	15.00	40.00	—	—

KM# 5.6 2 MARAVEDIS

Bronze **Ruler:** Charles II **Obv:** Shield of Castle between mint mark and value **Rev:** Shield of Leon, date at right **Mint:** Madrid

Date	Mintage	VG	F	VF	XF	Unc
1680MD	—	15.00	20.00	35.00	—	—
1681MD	—	15.00	20.00	35.00	—	—
1682MD	—	15.00	20.00	35.00	—	—
1683MD	—	15.00	20.00	35.00	—	—
1684MD	—	15.00	20.00	35.00	—	—
1686MD	—	15.00	20.00	35.00	—	—

KM# 5.7 2 MARAVEDIS

Bronze **Ruler:** Charles II **Obv:** Shield of Castle between mint mark and value **Rev:** Shield of Leon, date at right **Mint:** Segovia

Date	Mintage	VG	F	VF	XF	Unc
1680Aqueduct	—	10.00	15.00	30.00	—	—
1681Aqueduct	—	10.00	15.00	30.00	—	—
1682Aqueduct	—	10.00	15.00	30.00	—	—
1683Aqueduct	—	10.00	15.00	30.00	—	—
1684Aqueduct	—	10.00	15.00	30.00	—	—
1685Aqueduct	—	10.00	15.00	30.00	—	—
1691Aqueduct	—	20.00	35.00	75.00	—	—

KM# 5.13 2 MARAVEDIS

Bronze **Ruler:** Charles II **Obv:** Shield of Castile between assayer and value **Rev:** Shield of Leon between mint mark and date **Mint:** Valladolid

Date	Mintage	VG	F	VF	XF	Unc
168xFlags	—	20.00	35.00	50.00	—	—
1681Flags	—	20.00	35.00	50.00	—	—
1686Flags	—	20.00	35.00	50.00	—	—

KM# 5.5 2 MARAVEDIS

Bronze **Ruler:** Charles II **Obv:** Shield of Castle between mint mark and value **Rev:** Shield of Leon, date at right **Mint:** Linares

Date	Mintage	VG	F	VF	XF	Unc
1692L	—	15.00	25.00	40.00	—	—
1693L	—	15.00	25.00	40.00	—	—
1694L	—	15.00	25.00	40.00	—	—
1694L date in two places	—	25.00	35.00	60.00	—	—
1695L	—	15.00	25.00	40.00	—	—
1696L	—	15.00	25.00	40.00	—	—
1697L	—	15.00	25.00	40.00	—	—
1698L	—	15.00	25.00	40.00	—	—
1699L	—	15.00	25.00	40.00	—	—
1700L	—	15.00	25.00	40.00	—	—

KM# 4 4 MARAVEDIS

Billon **Ruler:** Philip III **Obv:** Castle between mint mark and assayer mark **Rev:** Lion, date in legend **Mint:** Cuenca **Note:** Mint mark: Star above chalice.

Date	Mintage	VG	F	VF	XF	Unc
1601	—	18.00	30.00	45.00	—	—
1602	—	18.00	30.00	45.00	—	—

KM# 6.1 4 MARAVEDIS

Bronze **Ruler:** Philip III **Obv:** Castle between mint mark and value **Rev:** Lion, date in legend **Mint:** Burgos

Date	Mintage	VG	F	VF	XF	Unc
1602B	—	8.00	15.00	25.00	—	—
1603B	—	8.00	15.00	25.00	—	—
1604B	—	8.00	15.00	25.00	—	—
1605B	—	8.00	15.00	25.00	—	—
1606B	—	8.00	15.00	25.00	—	—
1607B	—	8.00	15.00	25.00	—	—
1608B	—	8.00	15.00	25.00	—	—
1618B	—	8.00	15.00	25.00	—	—
1619B	—	8.00	15.00	25.00	—	—

KM# 6.3 4 MARAVEDIS

Bronze **Ruler:** Philip III **Obv:** Castle between mint mark and value **Rev:** Lion, date in legend **Mint:** Cuenca

Date	Mintage	VG	F	VF	XF	Unc
1602C	—	8.00	15.00	20.00	—	—
1603C	—	8.00	15.00	20.00	—	—
1604C	—	8.00	15.00	20.00	—	—
1605C	—	8.00	15.00	20.00	—	—
1606C	—	8.00	15.00	20.00	—	—
1607C	—	8.00	15.00	20.00	—	—
1608C	—	8.00	15.00	20.00	—	—
1618C	—	10.00	20.00	35.00	—	—
1619C	—	10.00	20.00	35.00	—	—
1620C	—	10.00	20.00	35.00	—	—

KM# 6.6 4 MARAVEDIS

Bronze **Ruler:** Philip III **Obv:** Castle between mint mark and value **Rev:** Lion, date in legend **Mint:** Toledo

Date	Mintage	VG	F	VF	XF	Unc
1602T	—	8.00	15.00	25.00	—	—
1603T	—	8.00	15.00	25.00	—	—
1604T	—	8.00	15.00	25.00	—	—
1605T	—	8.00	15.00	25.00	—	—
1606T	—	8.00	15.00	25.00	—	—
1607T	—	8.00	15.00	25.00	—	—
1608T	—	8.00	15.00	25.00	—	—
1618T	—	8.00	15.00	25.00	—	—
1619T	—	8.00	15.00	25.00	—	—
1620T	—	10.00	20.00	40.00	—	—

KM# 6.7 4 MARAVEDIS

Bronze **Ruler:** Philip III **Obv:** Castle between mint mark and value **Rev:** Lion and date within circle **Mint:** Valladolid

Date	Mintage	VG	F	VF	XF	Unc
1602Flags	—	8.00	15.00	25.00	—	—
1603Flags	—	8.00	15.00	25.00	—	—
1604Flags	—	8.00	15.00	25.00	—	—
1605Flags	—	8.00	15.00	25.00	—	—
1606Flags	—	8.00	15.00	25.00	—	—
1618Flags	—	8.00	15.00	25.00	—	—
1619Flags	—	8.00	15.00	25.00	—	—
1620Flags	—	8.00	15.00	25.00	—	—

KM# 6.5 4 MARAVEDIS

Bronze **Ruler:** Philip III **Obv:** Castle between mint mark and value **Rev:** Lion, date in legend **Mint:** Segovia **Note:** Horizontal mint mint of aqueduct, but for 1618 and possibly 1604.

Date	Mintage	VG	F	VF	XF	Unc
1604Aqueduct	—	10.00	18.00	25.00	—	—
1605Aqueduct	—	10.00	18.00	25.00	—	—
1606Aqueduct	—	12.00	20.00	30.00	—	—
1607Aqueduct	—	12.00	20.00	30.00	—	—
1608Aqueduct	—	12.00	20.00	30.00	—	—
1609Aqueduct	—	12.00	20.00	30.00	—	—
1610Aqueduct	—	15.00	25.00	35.00	—	—
1618Aqueduct	—	25.00	50.00	65.00	—	—
1618Aqueduct Vertical aqueduct	—	15.00	30.00	45.00	—	—
1619Aqueduct	—	10.00	18.00	25.00	—	—
1620Aqueduct	—	10.00	18.00	25.00	—	—

KM# 6.4 4 MARAVEDIS

Bronze **Ruler:** Philip III **Obv:** Castle between mint mark and value **Rev:** Lion, date in legend **Mint:** Madrid

Date	Mintage	VG	F	VF	XF	Unc
1618MD	—	8.00	15.00	25.00	—	—
1619MD	—	8.00	15.00	25.00	—	—
1620MD	—	8.00	15.00	25.00	—	—

KM# 7.5 4 MARAVEDIS

Bronze **Ruler:** Philip IV **Obv:** Castle between mint mark and value **Rev:** Lion, date in legend **Mint:** Madrid

Date	Mintage	VG	F	VF	XF	Unc
1621MD	—	8.00	15.00	25.00	—	—
1622MD	—	8.00	15.00	25.00	—	—
1623MD	—	8.00	15.00	25.00	—	—
1624MD	—	8.00	15.00	25.00	—	—
1625MD	—	8.00	15.00	25.00	—	—
1626MD	—	8.00	15.00	25.00	—	—

KM# 7.3 4 MARAVEDIS

Bronze **Ruler:** Philip IV **Obv:** Castle between mint mark and value **Rev:** Lion, date in legend **Mint:** Cuenca

Date	Mintage	VG	F	VF	XF	Unc
1621C	—	8.00	10.00	20.00	—	—
1622C	—	8.00	10.00	20.00	—	—
1623C	—	8.00	10.00	20.00	—	—
1624C	—	8.00	10.00	20.00	—	—
1625C	—	8.00	10.00	20.00	—	—
1626C	—	8.00	10.00	20.00	—	—

KM# 7.1 4 MARAVEDIS

Bronze **Ruler:** Philip IV **Obv:** Castle between mint mark and value **Rev:** Lion, date in legend **Mint:** Burgos

Date	Mintage	VG	F	VF	XF	Unc
1621B	—	12.00	25.00	40.00	—	—
1622B	—	8.00	15.00	25.00	—	—
1623B	—	8.00	15.00	25.00	—	—
1624B	—	8.00	15.00	25.00	—	—
1625B	—	8.00	15.00	25.00	—	—
1626B	—	8.00	15.00	25.00	—	—

KM# 7.9 4 MARAVEDIS

Bronze **Ruler:** Philip IV **Obv:** Castle between mint mark and value **Rev:** Lion, date in legend **Mint:** Valladolid

Date	Mintage	VG	F	VF	XF	Unc
1621Flags	—	10.00	15.00	25.00	—	—
1622Flags	—	10.00	15.00	25.00	—	—
1623Flags	—	10.00	15.00	25.00	—	—
1624Flags	—	10.00	15.00	25.00	—	—
1625Flags	—	10.00	15.00	25.00	—	—
1626Flags	—	10.00	15.00	25.00	—	—

KM# 7.8 4 MARAVEDIS

Bronze **Ruler:** Philip IV **Obv:** Castle between mint mark and value **Rev:** Lion, date in legend **Mint:** Toledo

Date	Mintage	VG	F	VF	XF	Unc
1621T	—	10.00	20.00	45.00	—	—
1622T	—	10.00	20.00	45.00	—	—
1623T	—	10.00	20.00	45.00	—	—
1624T	—	10.00	20.00	45.00	—	—
1625T	—	10.00	20.00	45.00	—	—
1626T	—	10.00	20.00	45.00	—	—

KM# 7.4 4 MARAVEDIS

Bronze **Ruler:** Philip IV **Obv:** Castle between mint mark and value **Rev:** Lion, date in legend **Mint:** Granada

Date	Mintage	VG	F	VF	XF	Unc
1621G	—	8.00	15.00	35.00	—	—
1622G	—	8.00	15.00	35.00	—	—
1623G	—	8.00	15.00	35.00	—	—
1624G	—	8.00	15.00	35.00	—	—
1625G	—	8.00	15.00	35.00	—	—
1626G	—	8.00	15.00	35.00	—	—

KM# 7.7 4 MARAVEDIS

Bronze **Ruler:** Philip IV **Obv:** Castle between mint mark and value **Rev:** Lion, date in legend **Mint:** Seville

Date	Mintage	VG	F	VF	XF	Unc
1621S	—	8.00	12.00	20.00	—	—
1622S	—	8.00	12.00	20.00	—	—
1623S	—	8.00	12.00	20.00	—	—
1624S	—	8.00	12.00	20.00	—	—
1625S	—	8.00	12.00	20.00	—	—
1626S	—	8.00	12.00	20.00	—	—

KM# 7.6 4 MARAVEDIS

Bronze **Ruler:** Philip IV **Obv:** Castle between mint mark and value **Rev:** Lion, date in legend **Mint:** Segovia **Note:** Varieties exist.

Date	Mintage	VG	F	VF	XF	Unc
1621Aqueduct	—	8.00	15.00	25.00	—	—
1622Aqueduct	—	8.00	15.00	25.00	—	—
1623Aqueduct	—	8.00	15.00	25.00	—	—
1624Aqueduct	—	8.00	15.00	25.00	—	—
1625Aqueduct	—	8.00	15.00	25.00	—	—
1626Aqueduct	—	8.00	15.00	25.00	—	—

KM# 8.2 4 MARAVEDIS

Bronze **Ruler:** Philip IV **Obv:** King's bust right **Rev:** Castle between assayer mark and mint mark. Date above, value below **Mint:** Madrid

Date	Mintage	VG	F	VF	XF	Unc
1660MD A	—	30.00	50.00	75.00	—	—
1661MD A	—	30.00	50.00	75.00	—	—

KM# 8.3 4 MARAVEDIS

Bronze **Ruler:** Philip IV **Obv:** King's bust right **Rev:** Crowned arms between mint mark and assayer mark. Date in legend **Mint:** Segovia

Date	Mintage	VG	F	VF	XF	Unc
1661Aqueduct S	—	85.00	200	400	—	—

KM# 8.1 4 MARAVEDIS

Bronze **Ruler:** Philip IV **Obv:** King's head to right **Rev:** Castle between assayer and mint mark **Mint:** Cuenca

Date	Mintage	VG	F	VF	XF	Unc
1661C CA	—	90.00	165	280	—	—

KM# 8.4 4 MARAVEDIS

Bronze **Ruler:** Philip IV **Obv:** King's bust right **Rev:** Castle between assayer mark and mint mark. Date above, value below **Mint:** Trujillo

Date	Mintage	VG	F	VF	XF	Unc
1661TR M	—	150	300	450	—	—

KM# 8.5 4 MARAVEDIS

Bronze **Ruler:** Philip IV **Obv:** King's bust right **Rev:** Castle between assayer mark and mint mark. Date above, value below **Mint:** Valladolid

Date	Mintage	VG	F	VF	XF	Unc
1661Flags M	—	95.00	300	450	—	—

KM# 7.2 4 MARAVEDIS

Bronze **Ruler:** Philip IV **Obv:** King's head right **Rev:** Castle between mint mark and assayer, date above and value below **Mint:** Coruna **Note:** Mint mark: Scallop.

Date	Mintage	VG	F	VF	XF	Unc
1661 R Rare	—	—	—	—	—	—

KM# 9.2 8 MARAVEDIS

Bronze **Ruler:** Philip III **Obv:** Crowned shield of Castile between mint mark and value **Rev:** Crowned shield of Leon **Mint:** Cuenca

Date	Mintage	VG	F	VF	XF	Unc
1602C	—	15.00	25.00	35.00	—	—
1603C	—	15.00	25.00	35.00	—	—
1604C	—	10.00	20.00	30.00	—	—
1605C	—	10.00	20.00	30.00	—	—
1606C	—	10.00	20.00	30.00	—	—
1607C	—	10.00	20.00	30.00	—	—
1618C	—	10.00	20.00	30.00	—	—
1619C	—	15.00	25.00	35.00	—	—
1620C	—	15.00	25.00	30.00	—	—

KM# 9.6 8 MARAVEDIS

Bronze **Ruler:** Philip III **Obv:** Crowned shield of Castile between mint mark and value **Rev:** Crowned shield of Leon between mint mark and date **Mint:** Toledo

Date	Mintage	VG	F	VF	XF	Unc
1602To	—	15.00	30.00	50.00	—	—
1603To	—	15.00	30.00	50.00	—	—
1604To	—	10.00	20.00	35.00	—	—
1605To	—	10.00	20.00	35.00	—	—
1606To	—	10.00	20.00	35.00	—	—
1607To	—	10.00	20.00	35.00	—	—
1608To	—	10.00	20.00	35.00	—	—
1618To	—	10.00	20.00	35.00	—	—
1619To	—	10.00	20.00	35.00	—	—

KM# 9.7 8 MARAVEDIS

Bronze **Ruler:** Philip III **Obv:** Crowned shield of Castile between mint mark and value **Rev:** Crowned shield of Leon between mint mark and date **Mint:** Valladolid

Date	Mintage	VG	F	VF	XF	Unc
1602Flags	—	15.00	30.00	40.00	—	—
1603Flags	—	15.00	30.00	40.00	—	—
1604Flags	—	15.00	30.00	40.00	—	—
1605Flags	—	15.00	30.00	40.00	—	—
1606Flags	—	15.00	30.00	40.00	—	—
1618Flags	—	10.00	15.00	25.00	—	—
1619Flags	—	10.00	15.00	25.00	—	—
1620Flags	—	10.00	15.00	25.00	—	—

KM# 9.1 8 MARAVEDIS

Bronze **Ruler:** Philip III **Obv:** Shield of Castile between mint mark and value **Rev:** Shield of Leon between mint mark and date **Mint:** Burgos

Date	Mintage	VG	F	VF	XF	Unc
1602B	—	10.00	15.00	25.00	—	—
1603B	—	10.00	15.00	25.00	—	—
1603B	—	10.00	15.00	25.00	—	—
Note: Date in field and in legend.						
1604B	—	10.00	15.00	25.00	—	—
1605B	—	10.00	15.00	25.00	—	—
1606B	—	10.00	15.00	25.00	—	—
1607B	—	10.00	15.00	25.00	—	—
1608B	—	10.00	15.00	25.00	—	—
1609B	—	10.00	15.00	25.00	—	—
1614B	—	15.00	25.00	40.00	—	—
1618B	—	10.00	15.00	25.00	—	—
1619B	—	10.00	15.00	25.00	—	—

KM# 9.5 8 MARAVEDIS

Bronze **Ruler:** Philip III **Obv:** Crowned shield of Castile between mint mark and value **Rev:** Crowned shield of Leon, date at right **Mint:** Segovia **Note:** Varieties exist.

Date	Mintage	VG	F	VF	XF	Unc
1604Aqueduct	—	10.00	—	25.00	35.00	—
1618Aqueduct	—	10.00	—	20.00	30.00	—
1619Aqueduct	—	10.00	—	20.00	30.00	—

KM# 9.3 8 MARAVEDIS

Bronze **Ruler:** Philip III **Obv:** Crowned shield of Castile betwee mint mark and value **Rev:** Crowned shield of Leon, date at rig **Mint:** Granada

Date	Mintage	VG	F	VF	XF
1616G	—	50.00	100	165	—

KM# 9.4 8 MARAVEDIS

Bronze **Ruler:** Philip III **Obv:** Crowned shield of Castile betwee mint mark and value **Rev:** Crowned shield of Leon, date at rig **Mint:** Madrid

Date	Mintage	VG	F	VF	XF
1618MD	—	8.00	15.00	25.00	—
1618MD Horizontal mint mark	—	15.00	20.00	35.00	—
1619MD	—	8.00	15.00	25.00	—
1620MD	—	8.00	15.00	25.00	—
1621MD	—	15.00	20.00	35.00	—

KM# 10.4 8 MARAVEDIS

Bronze **Ruler:** Philip IV **Obv:** Crowned shield of Castile betwee mint mark and value **Rev:** Crowned shield of Leon, date at rig **Mint:** Madrid

Date	Mintage	VG	F	VF	XF
1621MD	—	8.00	20.00	35.00	—
1622MD	—	8.00	20.00	35.00	—
1623MD	—	8.00	20.00	35.00	—
1624MD	—	8.00	20.00	35.00	—
1625MD	—	8.00	20.00	35.00	—
1626MD	—	8.00	20.00	35.00	—

KM# 10.3 8 MARAVEDIS

Bronze **Ruler:** Philip IV **Obv:** Crowned shield of Castile betwe mint mark and value **Rev:** Crowned shield of Leon, date at rig **Mint:** Granada

Date	Mintage	VG	F	VF	XF
1621G	—	12.00	25.00	40.00	—
1622G	—	10.00	20.00	35.00	—
1623G	—	10.00	20.00	35.00	—
1624G	—	10.00	20.00	35.00	—
1625G	—	10.00	20.00	35.00	—
1626G	—	10.00	20.00	35.00	—

KM# 10.6 8 MARAVEDIS

Bronze **Ruler:** Philip IV **Obv:** Crowned shield of Castile betwe mint mark and value **Rev:** Crowned shield of Leon, date at rig **Mint:** Segovia

Date	Mintage	VG	F	VF	XF
1621S	—	10.00	25.00	40.00	—
1622S	—	10.00	25.00	40.00	—
1623S	—	10.00	25.00	40.00	—
1624S	—	10.00	25.00	40.00	—
1625S	—	10.00	25.00	40.00	—
1626S	—	10.00	25.00	40.00	—

KM# 10.2 8 MARAVEDIS

Bronze **Ruler:** Philip IV **Obv:** Crowned shield of Castile betwe mint mark and value **Rev:** Crowned shield of leon, date at rig **Mint:** Cuenca

Date	Mintage	VG	F	VF	XF
1621C	—	12.00	25.00	50.00	—
1622C	—	12.00	25.00	50.00	—
1623C	—	12.00	25.00	50.00	—
1624C	—	12.00	25.00	50.00	—

KM# 10.1 8 MARAVEDIS

Bronze **Ruler:** Philip IV **Obv:** Shield of Castile between min mark and value **Rev:** Shield of Leon, date at right **Mint:** Burg

Date	Mintage	VG	F	VF	XF
1621B	—	8.00	12.00	20.00	—
1622B	—	8.00	12.00	20.00	—
1623B	—	8.00	12.00	20.00	—
1624B	—	8.00	12.00	20.00	—
1625B	—	8.00	12.00	20.00	—
1626B	—	8.00	12.00	20.00	—

KM# 10.5 8 MARAVEDIS

Bronze **Ruler:** Philip IV **Obv:** Crowned shield of Castile betwe mint mark and value **Rev:** Crowned shield of Leon, date at le **Mint:** Segovia **Note:** Varieties exist.

Date	Mintage	VG	F	VF	XF
1261 (sic)Aqueduct	—	35.00	80.00	135	—
1621Aqueduct	—	10.00	25.00	45.00	—
1622Aqueduct	—	10.00	25.00	45.00	—
1622Aqueduct	—	80.00	100	200	—
Note: Without value or mint mark.					
1623Aqueduct	—	10.00	25.00	45.00	—
1624Aqueduct	—	10.00	25.00	45.00	—
1625Aqueduct	—	10.00	25.00	45.00	—
1626Aqueduct	—	10.00	25.00	45.00	—

KM# 10.8 8 MARAVEDIS

Bronze **Ruler:** Philip IV **Obv:** Crowned shield of Castile betwe mint mark and value **Rev:** Crowned shield of Leon between m mark and date **Mint:** Valladolid

Date	Mintage	VG	F	VF	XF
1621Flags	—	12.00	20.00	40.00	—
1622Flags	—	12.00	20.00	40.00	—
1623Flags	—	12.00	20.00	40.00	—
1624Flags	—	12.00	20.00	40.00	—
1625Flags	—	12.00	20.00	40.00	—
1626Flags	—	12.00	20.00	40.00	—

KM# 10.7 8 MARAVEDIS

Bronze **Ruler:** Philip III **Obv:** Crowned shield of Castile betwe mint mark and value **Rev:** Crowned shield of Leon between m mark and date **Mint:** Toledo

Date	Mintage	VG	F	VF	XF
1621To	—	12.00	30.00	45.00	—
1622To	—	12.00	30.00	45.00	—

te	Mintage	VG	F	VF	XF	Unc
23To	—	12.00	30.00	45.00	—	—
24To	—	12.00	30.00	45.00	—	—
25To	—	12.00	30.00	45.00	—	—
26To	—	12.00	30.00	45.00	—	—

M# 13 8 MARAVEDIS

8078 g., 0.9306 Silver 0.0242 oz. ASW **Ruler:** Philip IV **Obv:** alue, mint mark below **Rev:** Crowned arms of Castile-Leon **int:** Madrid

te	Mintage	VG	F	VF	XF	Unc
4xMD B Rare	—	—	—	1,000	—	—

M# 14 8 MARAVEDIS

8078 g., 0.9306 Silver 0.0242 oz. ASW **Ruler:** Philip IV **Obv:** ng's bust right between value and mint mark **Rev:** Crowned ms of Castile-Leon **Mint:** Madrid

te	Mintage	VG	F	VF	XF	Unc
43MD B Rare	—	—	—	1,500	—	—

M# 11.1 8 MARAVEDIS

onze **Ruler:** Philip IV **Obv:** King's bust right **Rev:** Value tween pillars of Hercules, mint mark below **Mint:** Burgos

te	Mintage	VG	F	VF	XF	Unc
60B	—	—	—	—	1,500	—

Note: Some authorities define this as a pattern, however, other mints also struck this type.

M# 11.2 8 MARAVEDIS

onze **Ruler:** Philip IV **Obv:** King's bust right **Rev:** Pillars of ercules, value at left, mint mark inbetween, date at right **Mint:** adrid

te	Mintage	VG	F	VF	XF	Unc
60MD Rare	—	—	—	—	—	—

M# 11.3 8 MARAVEDIS

onze **Ruler:** Philip IV **Obv:** King's bust right, date above in gend **Rev:** Pillars of Hercules with value between, mint mark low **Note:** Mint: Palencia?

te	Mintage	VG	F	VF	XF	Unc
60 P Rare	—	—	—	—	—	—

M# 11.4 8 MARAVEDIS

onze **Ruler:** Philip IV **Obv:** King's bust right, date in legend **v:** Pillars of Hercules, value and mint mark below **Mint:** Seville

te	Mintage	VG	F	VF	XF	Unc
60S Rare	—	—	—	—	950	—

M# 12.1 8 MARAVEDIS

onze **Ruler:** Philip IV **Obv:** King's bust right **Rev:** Crowned ms between mint mark / assayer mark and value **Mint:** Burgos

te	Mintage	VG	F	VF	XF	Unc
61B	—	90.00	150	350	—	—

M# 12.2 8 MARAVEDIS

onze **Ruler:** Philip IV **Obv:** King's bust right **Rev:** Crowned ms between mint mark and value **Mint:** Cuenca

te	Mintage	VG	F	VF	XF	Unc
61C	—	50.00	130	280	—	—

M# 12.3 8 MARAVEDIS

onze **Ruler:** Philip IV **Obv:** King's bust right **Rev:** Crowned ms between mint mark / assayer and value **Mint:** Granada

te	Mintage	VG	F	VF	XF	Unc
61G	—	60.00	100	280	—	—

M# 12.4 8 MARAVEDIS

onze **Ruler:** Philip IV **Obv:** King's head to right **Rev:** Crowned ms between assayer and value. Date in legend **Mint:** Madrid

te	Mintage	VG	F	VF	XF	Unc
61 A	—	75.00	250	400	—	—

M# 12.5 8 MARAVEDIS

onze **Ruler:** Philip IV **Obv:** King's bust right **Rev:** Crowned ms between mint mark / assayer mark and date **Mint:** Segovia

te	Mintage	VG	F	VF	XF	Unc
61Aqueduct S	—	75.00	150	350	—	—

M# 12.6 8 MARAVEDIS

onze **Ruler:** Philip IV **Obv:** King's bust right **Rev:** Crowned ms between mint mark and value **Mint:** Seville

te	Mintage	VG	F	VF	XF	Unc
61S Rare	—	—	—	450	—	—
61S R Rare	—	—	—	600	—	—

Note: Assayer initial behind bust.

M# 12.7 8 MARAVEDIS

onze **Ruler:** Philip IV **Obv:** King's bust right **Rev:** Crowned ms of Castile-Leon betwen mint mark and value **Mint:** Toledo

te	Mintage	VG	F	VF	XF	Unc
61To	—	120	300	425	—	—
61To	—	120	300	425	—	—

Note: Variety with reversed shield as Leon-Castle.

M# 12.8 8 MARAVEDIS

onze **Ruler:** Philip IV **Obv:** King's bust right **Rev:** Crowned ms between assayer mark and value. Mint mark below, date ove **Mint:** Trujillo

te	Mintage	VG	F	VF	XF	Unc
61TR	—	120	300	450	—	—

M# 12.9 8 MARAVEDIS

onze **Ruler:** Philip IV **Obv:** King's bust right **Rev:** Crowned ms between assayer mark and mint mark. Date above, value low **Mint:** Valladolid

te	Mintage	VG	F	VF	XF	Unc
61Flags M	—	90.00	225	425	—	—

M# 215 8 MARAVEDIS

onze **Ruler:** Charles II **Obv:** Crowned king's monogram, date ove **Rev:** Crowned arms between mint mark and value **Mint:** adrid

te	Mintage	VG	F	VF	XF	Unc
91MD	—	175	300	450	—	—

KM# 20.6 1/2 REAL

3.4335 g., 0.9306 Silver 0.1027 oz. ASW **Ruler:** Philip III **Obv:** Crowned shield of royal arms between mint mark above assayer mark and value **Rev:** Quartered arms of Castile-Leon **Mint:** Toledo

Date	Mintage	VG	F	VF	XF	Unc
1601To C	—	40.00	65.00	160	—	—
1605To C	—	40.00	65.00	160	—	—
1606To C	—	40.00	65.00	160	—	—
1609To C	—	40.00	65.00	160	—	—
1609To 0	—	45.00	80.00	220	—	—
1612To C	—	40.00	65.00	160	—	—
1615To C	—	40.00	65.00	160	—	—
1616To C	—	40.00	65.00	160	—	—
1620To P	—	45.00	80.00	220	—	—
1621To P	—	45.00	80.00	220	—	—

KM# 15.1 1/2 REAL

1.7167 g., 0.9306 Silver 0.0514 oz. ASW **Ruler:** Philip III **Obv:** Crowned monogram **Rev:** Quartered arms of Castile-Leon, date in legend **Mint:** Segovia **Note:** Assayer mark: Tower/Castle.

Date	Mintage	VG	F	VF	XF	Unc
1602	—	65.00	150	300	—	—
1610 A	—	65.00	15.00	300	—	—

Note: With aqueduct mint mark.

KM# 15.2 1/2 REAL

1.7167 g., 0.9306 Silver 0.0514 oz. ASW **Ruler:** Philip III **Obv:** Monogram between mint mark and assayer mark **Rev:** Quartered arms of Castile-Leon, date above **Mint:** Seville

Date	Mintage	VG	F	VF	XF	Unc
1609S B	—	75.00	180	300	—	—
1610S B	—	30.00	45.00	85.00	—	—
1611S B	—	35.00	65.00	110	—	—
1612S V	—	35.00	65.00	110	—	—
1615S V	—	35.00	65.00	110	—	—
1615S G	—	60.00	110	250	—	—
1620S R	—	75.00	180	300	—	—
1621S R	—	75.00	180	300	—	—

KM# 15.3 1/2 REAL

1.7167 g., 0.9306 Silver 0.0514 oz. ASW **Ruler:** Philip III **Obv:** Crowned monogram, mint mark above assayer mark at left **Rev:** Quartered arms of Castile-Leon **Mint:** Toledo

Date	Mintage	VG	F	VF	XF	Unc
1612To C	—	95.00	200	375	—	—

KM# 16.1 1/2 REAL

1.7167 g., 0.9306 Silver 0.0514 oz. ASW **Ruler:** Philip IV **Obv:** Crowned monogram, mint mark at right **Rev:** Quartered arms of Castile-Leon **Mint:** Granada

Date	Mintage	VG	F	VF	XF	Unc
1621G	—	200	400	950	—	—
1651G	—	200	400	950	—	—

Note: Mint mark below anagram.

KM# 16.2 1/2 REAL

1.7167 g., 0.9306 Silver 0.0514 oz. ASW **Ruler:** Philip IV **Obv:** Crowned monogram, mint mark and assayer at left or below **Rev:** Quartered arms of Castile-Leon, date above in legend **Mint:** Madrid

Date	Mintage	VG	F	VF	XF	Unc
1627MD	—	120	280	500	—	—
1651MD	—	95.00	190	400	—	—

Note: Crowned arms of Leon-Castle.

KM# 16.3 1/2 REAL

1.7167 g., 0.9306 Silver 0.0514 oz. ASW **Ruler:** Philip IV **Obv:** Crowned monogram betweek assayer and mint mark **Rev:** Quartered arms of Castile-Leon, date above in legend **Mint:** Seville

Date	Mintage	VG	F	VF	XF	Unc
1627S D	—	65.00	100	250	—	—
1627S R	—	65.00	100	250	—	—

KM# 18 1/2 REAL

1.7167 g., 0.9306 Silver 0.0514 oz. ASW **Ruler:** Philip IV **Obv:** Crowned shield of royal arms, mint mark and assayer at left **Rev:** Quartered arms of Castile-Leon **Mint:** Seville

Date	Mintage	VG	F	VF	XF	Unc
NDS D	—	65.00	100	250	—	—

KM# 16.4 1/2 REAL

1.7167 g., 0.9306 Silver 0.0514 oz. ASW **Ruler:** Philip IV **Obv:** Crowned monogram between mint mark and assayer mark **Rev:** Quartered arms of Castile-Leon **Mint:** Toledo

Date	Mintage	VG	F	VF	XF	Unc
NDTo M	—	80.00	150	350	—	—

KM# 17 1/2 REAL

1.7167 g., 0.9306 Silver 0.0514 oz. ASW **Ruler:** Philip IV **Obv:** King's bust right between assayer mark and value **Rev:** Quartered arms fo Castile-Leon, date above in legend **Mint:** Madrid **Note:** 17 Marvaedis.

Date	Mintage	VG	F	VF	XF	Unc
1643MD B	—	150	325	750	—	—

KM# 19 1/2 REAL

1.7167 g., 0.9306 Silver 0.0514 oz. ASW **Ruler:** Charles II **Obv:** Crowned shield of Castile-Leon between mint mark and assayer mark **Rev:** Cross above MARIA monogram, date below in legend **Mint:** Madrid

Date	Mintage	VG	F	VF	XF	Unc
1691MD BR	—	180	420	750	—	—
1699MD BR	—	180	420	750	—	—

KM# 20.1 REAL

3.4335 g., 0.9306 Silver 0.1027 oz. ASW **Ruler:** Philip III **Obv:** Crowned shield of royal arms, mint mark and assayer mark at left **Rev:** Quartered arms of Castile-Leon, date above in legend **Mint:** Granada

Date	Mintage	VG	F	VF	XF	Unc
1601G M	—	50.00	120	260	—	—
1612G M	—	50.00	120	260	—	—
1614G M	—	65.00	160	380	—	—

KM# 20.4 REAL

3.4335 g., 0.9306 Silver 0.1027 oz. ASW **Ruler:** Philip III **Obv:** Crowned shield of royal arms between mint mark above assayer mark and value **Rev:** Quartered arms of Castile-Leon, date in legend **Mint:** Seville

Date	Mintage	VG	F	VF	XF	Unc
1601S B	—	30.00	80.00	150	—	—
1602S B	—	30.00	80.00	150	—	—
1603S B	—	30.00	80.00	150	—	—
1604S B	—	30.00	80.00	150	—	—
1605S B	—	30.00	80.00	150	—	—
1607S B	—	30.00	80.00	150	—	—
1608S B	—	30.00	80.00	150	—	—
1609S B	—	30.00	80.00	150	—	—
1610S B	—	30.00	80.00	150	—	—
1611S B	—	30.00	80.00	150	—	—
1612S B	—	30.00	80.00	150	—	—
1612S D	—	45.00	100	220	—	—
1613S V	—	40.00	85.00	180	—	—
1614S B	—	30.00	80.00	150	—	—
1615S B	—	30.00	80.00	150	—	—
1615S V	—	40.00	85.00	180	—	—
1618S G	—	45.00	100	220	—	—
1619S R	—	45.00	100	220	—	—
1620S B	—	30.00	80.00	150	—	—

KM# 20.8 REAL

3.4335 g., 0.9306 Silver 0.1027 oz. ASW **Ruler:** Philip III **Obv:** Crowned shield of royal arms between mint mark with assayer mark above and value **Rev:** Quartered arms of Castile-Leon **Mint:** Valladolid **Note:** Varieties exist.

Date	Mintage	VG	F	VF	XF	Unc
1603Flags Do	—	80.00	200	450	—	—
1609Flags Do	—	80.00	200	450	—	—

KM# 20.3 REAL

3.4335 g., 0.9306 Silver 0.1027 oz. ASW **Ruler:** Philip III **Obv:** Crowned shield of royal arms between assayer mark, mint mark and value **Rev:** Quartered arms of Castile-Leon, date above in legend **Mint:** Segovia

Date	Mintage	VG	F	VF	XF	Unc
1612Aqueduct A	—	90.00	200	350	—	—

KM# 20.2 REAL

3.4335 g., 0.9306 Silver 0.1027 oz. ASW **Ruler:** Philip III **Obv:** Crowned shield of royal arms, assayer mark and mint mark at left **Rev:** Quartered arms of Castile-Leon, date above in legend **Mint:** Madrid

Date	Mintage	VG	F	VF	XF	Unc
1616MD G	—	180	450	1,200	—	—

KM# 22.3 REAL

3.4335 g., 0.9306 Silver 0.1027 oz. ASW **Ruler:** Philip IV **Obv:** Crowned shield of royal arms between mint mark, assayer mark below and value **Rev:** Quartered arms of Castile-Leon, date above in legend **Mint:** Toledo

Date	Mintage	VG	F	VF	XF	Unc
1621To P	—	40.00	110	325	—	—
1627To P	—	40.00	110	325	—	—

KM# 22.4 REAL
3.4335 g., 0.9306 Silver 0.1027 oz. ASW **Ruler:** Philip IV **Obv:** Crowned shield of royal arms between mint mark, assayer mark below and value **Rev:** Quartered arms of Castile-Leon, date above in legend **Mint:** Valladolid

Date	Mintage	VG	F	VF	XF	Unc
1622Flags Y Rare	—	—	—	—	—	—

KM# 22.2 REAL
3.4335 g., 0.9306 Silver 0.1027 oz. ASW **Ruler:** Philip IV **Obv:** Crowned shield of royal arms between mint mark, assayer mark below and value **Mint:** Seville

Date	Mintage	VG	F	VF	XF	Unc
1625S R	—	40.00	85.00	200	—	—
1627S D	—	40.00	85.00	200	—	—
1627S R	—	40.00	85.00	200	—	—
1628S R	—	40.00	85.00	200	—	—
1635S R	—	40.00	85.00	200	—	—

KM# 21 REAL
3.4335 g., 0.9306 Silver 0.1027 oz. ASW **Ruler:** Philip IV **Obv:** King's monogram with mint mark and assayer mark below **Rev:** Quartered arms of Castile-Leon **Mint:** Madrid

Date	Mintage	F	VF	XF	Unc	BU
1627MD V	—	80.00	240	600	—	—
1628MD V	—	80.00	240	600	—	—
1642MD B	—	80.00	240	600	—	—
1651MD A	—	80.00	240	600	—	—

KM# 22.1 REAL
3.4335 g., 0.9306 Silver 0.1027 oz. ASW **Ruler:** Philip IV **Obv:** Crowned shield of royal arms betyween mint mark, assayer mark and value **Rev:** Quartered arms of Castile-Leon **Mint:** Madrid

Date	Mintage	VG	F	VF	XF	Unc
1628MD V	—	60.00	220	500	—	—
1642MD B retrograde	—	60.00	220	500	—	—
1651MD A	—	60.00	220	500	—	—

Y# 23 REAL
3.4335 g., 0.9306 Silver 0.1027 oz. ASW **Ruler:** Philip IV **Obv:** King's bust right between mint mark, assayer mark and value **Rev:** Quartered arms of Castile-Leon, date above in legend **Mint:** Madrid **Note:** Varieties exist.

Date	Mintage	VG	F	VF	XF	Unc
1643MD B	—	200	425	650	—	—

KM# 23.2 REAL
3.4335 g., 0.9306 Silver 0.1027 oz. ASW **Ruler:** Charles II **Obv:** Crowned shield of royal arms between mint mark, assayer mark and value **Rev:** Quartered arms of Castile-Leon, date in legend **Mint:** Madrid

Date	Mintage	VG	F	VF	XF	Unc
1681MD M	—	100	350	900	—	—

KM# 25 REAL
3.4335 g., 0.9306 Silver 0.1027 oz. ASW **Ruler:** Charles II **Obv:** Crowned shield of royal arms between mint mark and assayer mark **Rev:** Cross above MARIA monogram, value above and date below **Mint:** Seville

Date	Mintage	VG	F	VF	XF	Unc
1689S M	—	100	220	600	—	—
1690S M	—	100	220	600	—	—

KM# 24.2 REAL
3.4335 g., 0.9306 Silver 0.1027 oz. ASW **Ruler:** Charles II **Obv:** Crowned shield of Castile-Leon between mint mark and assayer mark **Rev:** Cross above MARIA monogram, value above, date below **Mint:** Seville

Date	Mintage	VG	F	VF	XF	Unc
1690S M	—	80.00	200	480	—	—
1691S M	—	80.00	200	480	—	—
1692S M	—	80.00	200	480	—	—
1693S M	—	80.00	200	480	—	—
1694S M	—	80.00	200	480	—	—
1699S M	—	80.00	200	480	—	—

KM# 24.1 REAL
3.4335 g., 0.9306 Silver 0.1027 oz. ASW **Ruler:** Charles II **Obv:** Crowned shield of Castile-Leon between mint mark and assayer mark **Rev:** Cross above MARIA monogram. Value above, date below **Mint:** Madrid

Date	Mintage	VG	F	VF	XF	Unc
1691MD BR	—	80.00	320	800	—	—
1699MD BR	—	80.00	320	800	—	—

KM# A25 REAL
3.4335 g., 0.9306 Silver 0.1027 oz. ASW **Ruler:** Philip V **Obv:** Crowned shield of royal arms between mint mark with assayer mark below adn value **Rev:** Quartered arms of Castile-Leon, date above in legend **Mint:** Madrid

Date	Mintage	VG	F	VF	XF	Unc
1700MD F/I	—	250	600	1,200	—	—

KM# 26.7 2 REALES
6.8670 g., 0.9306 Silver 0.2054 oz. ASW **Ruler:** Philip III **Obv:** Crowned shield of royal arms between mint mark with assayer below and date **Rev:** Quartered arms of Castile-Leon **Mint:** Seville

Date	Mintage	VG	F	VF	XF	Unc
1601S B	—	45.00	60.00	180	—	—

KM# 27.2 2 REALES
6.8670 g., 0.9306 Silver 0.2054 oz. ASW **Ruler:** Philip III **Obv:** Crowned shield of royal arms between mint mark with assayer below and value **Rev:** Quartered arms of Castile-Leon, date in legend **Mint:** Toledo

Date	Mintage	VG	F	VF	XF	Unc
1601To C	—	80.00	115	200	—	—
1602To C	—	80.00	115	200	—	—

KM# 26.1 2 REALES
6.8670 g., 0.9306 Silver 0.2054 oz. ASW **Ruler:** Philip III **Obv:** Crowned shield of royal arms between mint mark and value with assayer mark below **Rev:** Quartered arms of Castile-Leon, date above in legend **Mint:** Burgos **Note:** Assayer mark: Castle, may be above or below the value.

Date	Mintage	VG	F	VF	XF	Unc
1601B (c)	—	180	420	725	—	—
1602B (c)	—	180	420	725	—	—

KM# 26.3 2 REALES
6.8670 g., 0.9306 Silver 0.2054 oz. ASW **Ruler:** Philip III **Obv:** Crowned shield of royal arms between value and mint mark with assayer mark above **Rev:** Quartered arms of Castile-Leon, date above in legend **Mint:** Granada **Note:** Varieties exist in the position of the value, mintmark and assayer mark.

Date	Mintage	VG	F	VF	XF	Unc
1601G M	—	70.00	160	350	—	—
1602G M	—	70.00	160	350	—	—
1603G M	—	70.00	160	350	—	—
1604G M	—	70.00	160	350	—	—
1605G M	—	70.00	160	350	—	—
1606G M	—	70.00	160	350	—	—
1608G M	—	70.00	160	350	—	—
1609G M	—	70.00	160	350	—	—

KM# 26.9 2 REALES
6.8670 g., 0.9306 Silver 0.2054 oz. ASW **Ruler:** Philip III **Obv:** Crowned shield of royal arms between mint mark with assayer mark below and value **Rev:** Quartered arms of Castile-Leon, date above in legend **Mint:** Valladolid

Date	Mintage	VG	F	VF	XF	Unc
1602Flags	—	115	325	780	—	—
1605Flags	—	115	325	780	—	—
1606Flags	—	115	325	780	—	—
1611Flags	—	115	325	780	—	—
1613Flags	—	115	325	780	—	—
1621Flags	—	115	325	780	—	—

KM# 27.1 2 REALES
6.8670 g., 0.9306 Silver Varieties exist. 0.2054 oz. ASW **Ruler:** Philip III **Obv:** Crowned shield of royal arms between mint mark with assayer mark below and value **Rev:** Quartered arms of Castile-Leon , date above in legend **Rev. Legend:** OMNIVM... **Mint:** Seville

Date	Mintage	VG	F	VF	XF	Unc
1602S B	—	40.00	90.00	180	—	—
1603S B	—	40.00	90.00	180	—	—
1604S B	—	40.00	90.00	180	—	—
1605S B	—	40.00	90.00	180	—	—
1607S B	—	40.00	90.00	180	—	—
1609S B	—	45.00	100	200	—	—
1611S B	—	40.00	90.00	180	—	—
1612S B	—	40.00	90.00	180	—	—
1612S D	—	40.00	90.00	180	—	—
1612S V	—	40.00	90.00	180	—	—
1613S V/D	—	40.00	90.00	180	—	—
1613S V	—	40.00	90.00	180	—	—
1614S V	—	40.00	90.00	180	—	—
1615S D	—	40.00	90.00	180	—	—
1615S V	—	40.00	90.00	180	—	—
1616S D	—	40.00	90.00	180	—	—
1617S D	—	40.00	90.00	180	—	—
1618S D	—	45.00	110	220	—	—
1618S R	—	55.00	135	235	—	—
1619S G	—	60.00	150	290	—	—
1619S R	—	55.00	135	230	—	
1620S D	—	45.00	95.00	200	—	

KM# 26.2 2 REALES
6.8670 g., 0.9306 Silver 0.2054 oz. ASW **Ruler:** Philip III **Ob** Crowned shield of royal arms between mint mark with assaye mark above and value **Rev:** Quartered arms of Castile-Leon, da above in legend **Mint:** Cuenca

Date	Mintage	VG	F	VF	XF
1603C I	—	180	400	1,200	—

KM# 26.8 2 REALES
6.8670 g., 0.9306 Silver 0.2054 oz. ASW **Ruler:** Philip III **Ob** Crowned shield of royal arms between mint mark with assaye mark below and value **Rev:** Quartered arms of Castile-Leon, da above in legend **Mint:** Toledo

Date	Mintage	VG	F	VF	XF
1603To C	—	60.00	95.00	185	—
1604To C	—	60.00	95.00	185	—
1605To C	—	60.00	95.00	185	—
1607To C	—	60.00	95.00	185	—
1609To C	—	70.00	100	200	—
1610To C	—	60.00	95.00	185	—
1612To C	—	60.00	95.00	185	—
1613To C	—	60.00	95.00	185	—
1614To C	—	60.00	95.00	185	—
1617 V	—	90.00	150	275	—
1618To P	—	115	200	340	—
1618To V	—	90.00	150	275	—
1619To V	—	90.00	150	275	—
1620To P	—	115	150	340	—

KM# 26.5 2 REALES
6.8670 g., 0.9306 Silver 0.2054 oz. ASW **Ruler:** Philip III **Ob** Crowned shield of royal arms between mint mark with assaye and value **Rev:** Quartered arms of Castile-Leon, date above i legend **Mint:** Segovia

Date	Mintage	VG	F	VF	XF
1608Aqueduct tree	—	180	350	1,250	—
1611Aqueduct A	—	90.00	200	550	—
1613Aqueduct B	—	90.00	200	550	—
1614/0Aqueduct AR	—	110	240	480	—

KM# 26.4 2 REALES
6.8670 g., 0.9306 Silver 0.2054 oz. ASW **Ruler:** Philip III **Ob** Crowned shield of royal arms between mint mark with assaye below and value **Rev:** Quartered arms of Castile-Leon, date above in legend **Mint:** Madrid

Date	Mintage	VG	F	VF	XF
1609MD V	—	120	325	850	—
1620MD Go	—	120	325	850	—
1621MD V	—	120	325	850	—

KM# 29.5 2 REALES
6.8670 g., 0.9306 Silver 0.2054 oz. ASW **Ruler:** Philip IV **Ob** Crowned shield of royal arms between mint mark with assaye mark below and value **Rev:** Quartered arms of Castile-Leon, da above in legend **Mint:** Toledo

Date	Mintage	VG	F	VF	XF
1621To P	—	35.00	90.00	185	—
1622To P	—	35.00	90.00	185	—
1623To P	—	35.00	90.00	185	—
1626To P	—	45.00	135	280	—
1627To P	—	45.00	135	280	—
1628To P	—	35.00	90.00	185	—
1635To P	—	35.00	90.00	185	—
1641To C	—	35.00	90.00	185	—
1651To Y	—	35.00	90.00	185	—
1652To Y	—	65.00	160	300	—
1657To Y	—	65.00	160	300	—

KM# 29.3 2 REALES
6.8670 g., 0.9306 Silver 0.2054 oz. ASW **Ruler:** Philip IV **Ob** Crowned shield of royal arms between mint mark with assaye mark and value **Rev:** Quartered arms of Castile-Leon, date abo in legend **Mint:** Segovia

Date	Mintage	VG	F	VF	XF
1623Aqueduct R	—	180	400	900	—
1625Aqueduct R	—	180	400	900	—

KM# 29.4 2 REALES
6.8670 g., 0.9306 Silver 0.2054 oz. ASW **Ruler:** Philip IV **Ob** Crowned shield of royal arms between mint mark with assaye mark below and value **Rev:** Quartered arms of Castile-Leon, da above in legend **Mint:** Seville

Date	Mintage	VG	F	VF	XF
1627S D	—	40.00	90.00	165	—
1627S R	—	40.00	90.00	165	—
1628S R	—	40.00	90.00	165	—
1629S R	—	40.00	90.00	165	—
1633S R	—	40.00	90.00	165	—
1634S R	—	40.00	90.00	165	—
1636S R	—	40.00	90.00	165	—

KM# 29.2 2 REALES
6.8670 g., 0.9306 Silver 0.2054 oz. ASW **Ruler:** Philip IV **Ob** Crowned shield of royal arms between mint mark with assaye mark below and value **Rev:** Quartered arms of Castile-Leon, da above in legend **Mint:** Madrid

Date	Mintage	VG	F	VF	XF
1628MD V	—	210	550	1,200	—
1629MD BI	—	260	400	780	—
1629MD M	—	170	290	625	—
1630MD BI	—	170	290	625	—
1634MD BI	—	170	290	625	—
1639MD BI	—	170	290	625	—

te	Mintage	VG	F	VF	XF	Unc
41MD B	—	170	290	625	—	—
42MD B	—	250	400	780	—	—
49MD B	—	125	280	500	—	—
50MD A	—	100	220	425	—	—
51MD A	—	100	220	425	—	—
54MD A	—	100	220	425	—	—

M# A30 2 REALES

670 g., 0.9306 Silver 0.2054 oz. ASW **Ruler:** Philip IV **Obv:** g's bust to right, mint mark, assayer mark and value **Rev:** artered arms of Castile-Leon, date above in legend **Mint:** drid

e	Mintage	VG	F	VF	XF	Unc
43MD B	—	280	475	750	—	—
43MD IB	—	300	600	900	—	—

M# 29.1 2 REALES

670 g., 0.9306 Silver 0.2054 oz. ASW **Ruler:** Philip IV **Obv:** owned shield of royal arms between mint mark with assayer rk below and value **Rev:** Quartered arms of Castile-Leon, date ove in legend **Mint:** Burgos

e	Mintage	VG	F	VF	XF	Unc
51B BR	—	115	325	850	—	—

M# 31 2 REALES

670 g., 0.9306 Silver 0.2054 oz. ASW **Ruler:** Charles II **Obv:** owned shield of royal arms between mint mark with assayer rk below and value **Rev:** Quartered arms of Castile-Leon, date egend **Mint:** Madrid

e	Mintage	VG	F	VF	XF	Unc
1MD M	—	120	300	650	—	—
1MD BR	—	200	525	1,200	—	—
2MD BR	—	200	525	1,200	—	—
4MD BR	—	200	525	1,200	—	—

M# 33.4 4 REALES

7341 g., 0.9306 Silver 0.4109 oz. ASW **Ruler:** Philip III **Obv:** owned shield of royal arms between mint mark with assayer rk below and value **Rev:** Quartered arms of Castile-Leon, date ove in legend **Mint:** Seville

e	Mintage	VG	F	VF	XF	Unc
1S B	—	90.00	220	500	—	—
2S B	—	90.00	220	500	—	—
3S B	—	125	275	600	—	—
4S B	—	125	275	600	—	—
0S B	—	90.00	220	500	—	—
1S B	—	90.00	220,220	500	—	—
1S D	—	90.00	185	500	—	—
2S B	—	70.00	190	340	—	—
2S D	—	80.00	210	380	—	—
2S V	—	90.00	190	400	—	—
3S D	—	80.00	190	380	—	—
3S V/D	—	80.00	190	380	—	—
3S V	—	80.00	190	380	—	—
4S V	—	80.00	275	380	—	—
5S B	—	125	190	600	—	—
5S D	—	80.00	190	380	—	—
5S V	—	80.00	190	380	—	—
6S D	—	80.00	190	380	—	—
6S V	—	90.00	220	500	—	—
7S D	—	80.00	190	380	—	—
7S G	—	90.00	220	500	—	—
8S D	—	90.00	220	500	—	—
8S G	—	90.00	220	500	—	—
9S G	—	90.00	220	500	—	—
0S G	—	90.00	220	500	—	—
1S G	—	90.00	220	500	—	—

 # 33.5 4 REALES

7341 g., 0.4109 Silver 0.1814 oz. ASW **Ruler:** Philip III **Obv:** wned shield of royal arms between mint mark with assayer k below and value **Rev:** Quartered arms of Castile-Leon, date ve in legend **Mint:** Toledo

e	Mintage	VG	F	VF	XF	Unc
2To C	—	110	280	650	—	—
9To C	—	110	280	650	—	—
0To C	—	110	280	650	—	—
1To C	—	110	280	650	—	—
1To V/C	—	110	280	650	—	—
2To C	—	130	345	800	—	—
3To C	—	110	280	650	—	—
3To V	—	110	280	650	—	—

Date	Mintage	VG	F	VF	XF	Unc
1614To C	—	130	345	800	—	—
1614To V	—	110	280	650	—	—
1615To C	—	130	345	800	—	—
1615To V	—	110	280	650	—	—
1616To V	—	110	280	650	—	—
1617To V	—	110	280	650	—	—
1618To P	—	85.00	200	500	—	—
1618To V	—	110	280	650	—	—
1619To P	—	85.00	200	500	—	—
1620To P	—	85.00	200	500	—	—
1621/0To P	—	85.00	200	500	—	—
1621To P	—	85.00	200	500	—	—

KM# 33.1 4 REALES

13.7341 g., 0.9306 Silver 0.4109 oz. ASW **Ruler:** Philip III **Obv:** Crowned shield of royal arms between mint mark above assayer mark and value **Rev:** Quartered arms of Castile-Leon, date above in legend **Mint:** Granada

Date	Mintage	VG	F	VF	XF	Unc
1609G M	—	200	550	1,200	—	—
1610G M	—	200	550	1,200	—	—
1611G M	—	170	400	725	—	—
1612G M	—	170	400	725	—	—
1613G M	—	170	400	725	—	—
1614G M	—	170	400	725	—	—
1615G M	—	170	400	725	—	—
1621G M	—	170	400	725	—	—

KM# 33.3 4 REALES

13.7341 g., 0.9306 Silver 0.4109 oz. ASW **Ruler:** Philip III **Obv:** Crowned shield of royal arms between mint mark with assayer mark below and value **Rev:** Quartered arms of Castile-Leon, date above in legend **Mint:** Segovia

Date	Mintage	VG	F	VF	XF	Unc
1611Aqueduct A	—	190	425	1,100	—	—
1612Aqueduct A	—	240	650	1,400	—	—
1613Aqueduct TB	—	190	425	1,100	—	—

KM# 33.6 4 REALES

13.7341 g., 0.9306 Silver 0.4109 oz. ASW **Ruler:** Philip III **Obv:** Crowned shield of royal arms between mint mark with assayer mark below and value **Rev:** Quartered arms of Castile-Leon, date above in legend **Mint:** Valladolid

Date	Mintage	VG	F	VF	XF	Unc
1611Flags H	—	250	625	1,500	—	—
1612Flags F	—	250	625	1,500	—	—
1613/2Flags F	—	250	625	1,500	—	—

KM# 33.2 4 REALES

13.7341 g., 0.9306 Silver 0.4109 oz. ASW **Ruler:** Philip III **Obv:** Crowned shield of royal arms between mint mark with assayer mark below and value **Rev:** Quartered arms of Castile-Leon, date above in legend **Mint:** Madrid

Date	Mintage	VG	F	VF	XF	Unc
1615MD Go	—	190	520	1,200	—	—
1620MD Go	—	190	520	1,200	—	—
1621MD V	—	190	520	1,200	—	—

KM# 35.7 4 REALES

13.7341 g., 0.9306 Silver 0.4109 oz. ASW **Ruler:** Philip IV **Obv:** Crowned shield of royal arms between mint mark with assayer mark below and value **Rev:** Quartered arms of Castile-Leon, date above in legend **Mint:** Toledo

Date	Mintage	VG	F	VF	XF	Unc
1621To P	—	70.00	150	350	—	—
1622To P	—	70.00	150	350	—	—
1623To P	—	70.00	150	350	—	—
1624To P	—	70.00	150	350	—	—
1626To P	—	70.00	150	350	—	—
1627To P	—	70.00	150	350	—	—
1628To P	—	70.00	150	350	—	—
1630To P	—	165	325	750	—	—
1632To P	—	130	280	600	—	—

Note: Value to left, mint mark and assayer mark at right

Date	Mintage	VG	F	VF	XF	Unc
1632To P	—	70.00	150	350	—	—
1635To P	—	70.00	150	350	—	—
1640To P	—	165	325	750	—	—
1651To Y	—	130	280	600	—	—

Date	Mintage	VG	F	VF	XF	Unc
1652To Y	—	165	325	750	—	—
1655To Y	—	130	280	600	—	—

KM# 35.3 4 REALES

13.7341 g., 0.4109 Silver 0.1814 oz. ASW **Ruler:** Philip IV **Obv:** Crowned shield of royal arms between mint mark with assayer below and value **Rev:** Quartered arms of Castile-Leon **Mint:** Granada **Note:** Mint mark: Pomegranate

Date	Mintage	VG	F	VF	XF	Unc
1621 N	—	480	1,350	3,800	—	—
1652/1 N	—	480	1,350	3,800	—	—
1652 N	—	480	1,350	3,800	—	—

KM# 35.5 4 REALES

13.7341 g., 0.9306 Silver 0.4109 oz. ASW **Ruler:** Philip IV **Obv:** Crowned shield of royal arms between mint mark with assayer mark below and value **Rev:** Quartered arms of Castile-Leon **Mint:** Segovia **Note:** Varieties exist.

Date	Mintage	VG	F	VF	XF	Unc
1624Aqueduct R	—	200	550	1,200	—	—
1626Aqueduct R	—	200	550	1,200	—	—
1627Aqueduct R	—	200	550	1,200	—	—
1643Aqueduct R	—	200	550	1,200	—	—
1644Aqueduct BR	—	200	550	1,200	—	—
1659Aqueduct M	—	200	550	1,200	—	—
1662Aqueduct BR	—	200	550	1,200	—	—

KM# 35.6 4 REALES

13.7341 g., 0.9306 Silver 0.4109 oz. ASW **Ruler:** Philip IV **Obv:** Crowned shield of royal arms between mint mark with assayers mark below and value **Rev:** Quartered arms of Castile-Leon, date above in legend **Mint:** Seville

Date	Mintage	VG	F	VF	XF	Unc
1624S R	—	60.00	145	350	—	—
1625S R	—	60.00	145	350	—	—
1627S R	—	60.00	145	350	—	—
1628S R	—	60.00	145	350	—	—
1629S R	—	60.00	145	350	—	—
1631S R	—	60.00	145	350	—	—
1632S R	—	60.00	145	350	—	—
1633S R	—	60.00	145	350	—	—
1634S R	—	60.00	145	350	—	—
1636S R	—	60.00	145	350	—	—
1637S R	—	60.00	145	350	—	—
1641S R	—	60.00	145	350	—	—
1642S R	—	60.00	145	350	—	—
1643S R	—	60.00	145	350	—	—
1644S R	—	60.00	145	350	—	—
1648S R	—	60.00	145	350	—	—

KM# 35.4 4 REALES

13.7341 g., 0.9306 Silver 0.4109 oz. ASW **Ruler:** Philip IV **Obv:** Crowned shield of royal arms between mint mark with assayer below and value **Rev:** Quartered arms of Castile-Leon, date above in legend **Mint:** Madrid

Date	Mintage	VG	F	VF	XF	Unc
1626MD V	—	200	550	1,200	—	—
1627MD V	—	200	550	1,200	—	—
1628MD V	—	200	550	1,200	—	—
1639MD B	—	200	550	1,200	—	—
1639MD BI	—	200	550	1,200	—	—
1640MD B	—	200	550	1,200	—	—
1641MD B	—	200	550	1,200	—	—
1642MD B	—	200	550	1,200	—	—
1643MD B	—	200	550	1,200	—	—
1644MD B	—	200	550	1,200	—	—
1644 IB	—	200	550	1,200	—	—
1649MD BI	—	200	550	1,200	—	—
1650MD BI	—	200	550	1,200	—	—
1650MD A	—	200	550	1,200	—	—
1651MD A/BI	—	200	550	1,200	—	—
1651MD A	—	200	550	1,200	—	—
1659MD BI	—	200	550	1,200	—	—
1662MD A	—	200	550	1,200	—	—
16xxMD M	—	200	550	1,200	—	—

KM# 35.1 4 REALES

13.7341 g., 0.9306 Silver 0.4109 oz. ASW **Ruler:** Philip IV **Obv:** Crowned shield of royal arms between mint mark with assayer mark below and value **Rev:** Quartered arms of Cstile-Leon, date above in legend **Mint:** Burgos

Date	Mintage	VG	F	VF	XF	Unc
1651B BR	—	300	750	1,800	—	—

KM# 35.2 4 REALES

13.7341 g., 0.9306 Silver 0.4109 oz. ASW **Ruler:** Philip IV **Obv:** Crowned shield of royal arms between mint mark with assayer mark below, and value **Rev:** Quartered arms of Castile-Leon, date above in legend **Mint:** Cuenca

Date	Mintage	VG	F	VF	XF	Unc
1651C CA	—	900	1,800	4,500	—	—

KM# 35.8 4 REALES

13.7341 g., 0.9306 Silver 0.4109 oz. ASW **Ruler:** Philip IV **Obv:** Crowned shield of royal arms between mint mark with assayers mark below and value **Rev:** Quartered arms of Castile-Leon, date above in legend **Mint:** Valladolid

Date	Mintage	VG	F	VF	XF	Unc
1651Flags Y Rare	—	—	—	—	—	—

KM# 36.1 4 REALES

13.7341 g., 0.9306 Silver 0.4109 oz. ASW **Ruler:** Charles II **Obv:** Crowned shield of royal arms between mint mark and assayer **Rev:** Cross atop MARIA monogram between value **Mint:** Madrid

Date	Mintage	VG	F	VF	XF	Unc
1689MD BR	—	300	800	1,750	—	—
1690MD BR	—	300	800	1,750	—	—
1693MD BR	—	300	800	1,750	—	—

KM# 36.2 4 REALES

13.7341 g., 0.9306 Silver 0.4109 oz. ASW **Ruler:** Charles II **Obv:** Crowned shiedl of royal arms between mint mark and assayer mark **Rev:** Cross atop MARIA monogram, between value **Mint:** Seville

Date	Mintage	VG	F	VF	XF	Unc
1689S M	—	270	800	1,750	—	—
1692S M	—	270	800	1,750	—	—

KM# 38.1 8 REALES

27.4682 g., 0.9306 Silver 0.8218 oz. ASW **Ruler:** Philip III **Obv:** Crowned shield of royal arms between mint mark with assayer mark below and value **Rev:** Quartered arms of Catile-Leon, date in legend **Rev. Legend:** OMNIVM... **Mint:** Seville

Date	Mintage	VG	F	VF	XF	Unc
1601S B	—	95.00	200	400	—	—
1602S B	—	95.00	200	400	—	—
1603S B	—	290	650	1,400	—	—
1604S B	—	290	650	1,400	—	—
1607S B	—	95.00	200	400	—	—
1608S B	—	95.00	200	400	—	—
1609S B	—	95.00	200	400	—	—
1613S B	—	190	400	850	—	—

KM# 37.4 8 REALES

27.4682 g., 0.9306 Silver 0.8218 oz. ASW **Ruler:** Philip III **Obv:** Crowned shield of royal arms between mint mark with assayer mark below and value **Rev:** Quartered arms of Castile-Leon, date above in legend **Mint:** Toledo

Date	Mintage	VG	F	VF	XF	Unc
1601To C	—	600	1,250	2,900	—	—
1607To C	—	600	1,250	2,900	—	—
1608To C	—	480	1,100	2,400	—	—
1609To C	—	480	1,100	2,400	—	—
1615To P	—	120	290	625	—	—
1620To P	—	120	290	625	—	—
1621To P	—	120	290	625	—	—

KM# 37.5 8 REALES

27.4682 g., 0.9306 Silver 0.8218 oz. ASW **Ruler:** Philip III **Obv:** Crowned shield of royal arms between mint mark with assayer mark above and value **Rev:** Quartered arms of Castile-Leon, date above in legend **Mint:** Valladolid **Note:** The obverse die is one for Philip II.

Date	Mintage	VG	F	VF	XF	Unc
1601Flags Do	—	1,000	3,000	6,800	—	—

KM# 38.2 8 REALES

27.4682 g., 0.9306 Silver 0.8218 oz. ASW **Ruler:** Philip III **Obv:** Crowned shield of royal arms between mint mark with assayer mark below and value **Rev:** Quartered arms of Castile-Leon, date above in legend **Rev. Legend:** OMNIVM... **Mint:** Toledo

Date	Mintage	VG	F	VF	XF	Unc
1605To C	—	550	1,200	2,500	—	—

KM# 37.3 8 REALES

27.4682 g., 0.9306 Silver 0.8218 oz. ASW **Ruler:** Philip III **Obv:** Crowned shield of royal arms between mint mark with assayers mark below and value **Rev:** Quartered arms of Castile-Leon, date above in legend **Mint:** Seville

Date	Mintage	VG	F	VF	XF	Unc
1611S B	—	85.00	200	425	—	—
1612S B	—	85.00	200	425	—	—
1612S D	—	85.00	200	425	—	—
1614S D	—	180	400	900	—	—
1615S D	—	120	300	650	—	—
1617/5S D/V	—	225	550	1,200	—	—
1618S D	—	120	300	650	—	—
1619S D/V	—	225	550	1,200	—	—
1620S D	—	120	300	6,500	—	—
1620S G	—	225	630	1,200	—	—
1621S D	—	120	300	650	—	—
1621S G	—	220	600	1,000	—	—

KM# 37.2 8 REALES

27.4682 g., 0.9306 Silver 0.8218 oz. ASW **Ruler:** Philip III **Obv:** Crowned shield of royal arms between mint mark with assayer mark above and value **Rev:** Quartered arms of Castile-Leon, date above in legend **Mint:** Segovia

Date	Mintage	VG	F	VF	XF	Unc
1619Aqueduct tower	—	1,200	3,500	7,500	—	—

Note: Value at left, mint mark and assayer mark at right.

KM# 37.1 8 REALES

27.4682 g., 0.9306 Silver 0.8218 oz. ASW **Ruler:** Philip III **Obv:** Crowned shield of royal arms between mint mark with assayer mark below and value **Rev:** Quartered arms of Catile-Leon, date above in legend **Mint:** Madrid

Date	Mintage	VG	F	VF	XF	Unc
1620MD Go	—	750	1,650	3,500	—	—
1621MD V	—	750	1,650	3,500	—	—

KM# 39.5 8 REALES

27.4682 g., 0.9306 Silver 0.8218 oz. ASW **Ruler:** Philip IV **Obv:** Crowned shield of royal arms between mint mark with assayer below and value **Rev:** Quartered arms of Castile-Leon, date above in legend **Mint:** Segovia

Date	Mintage	VG	F	VF	XF	Unc
NDAqueduct P	—	400	900	2,200	—	—
1621Aqueduct R	—	500	1,100	2,500	—	—
1623Aqueduct R	—	750	1,800	4,200	—	—
1623Aqueduct R Arms reversed	—	750	1,800	4,200	—	—
1623Aqueduct R	—	500	1,100	2,500	—	—
1623Aqueduct R	—	500	1,100	2,500	—	—
Note: King's name on reverse.						
1624/3Aqueduct R	—	500	1,100	2,500	—	—
1624Aqueduct R	—	500	1,100	2,500	—	—
1624Aqueduct R	—	500	1,100	2,500	—	—
1625Aqueduct R	—	500	1,100	2,500	—	—
Note: Reversed arms Leon-Castile						
1627Aqueduct R	—	500	1,100	2,500	—	—
1628Aqueduct R	—	500	1,100	2,500	—	—
1659Aqueduct M	—	500	1,100	2,500	—	—
1660Aqueduct BR	—	500	1,100	2,500	—	—
1661Aqueduct B	—	500	1,100	2,500	—	—
1662Aqueduct B	—	500	1,100	2,500	—	—
1662Aqueduct BR	—	500	1,100	2,500	—	—
1662Aqueduct BR	—	500	1,100	2,500	—	—
Note: King's name on reverse						

KM# 39.4 8 REALES

27.4682 g., 0.9306 Silver 0.8218 oz. ASW **Ruler:** Philip IV **Obv:** Crowned shield of royal arms between mint mark with assayer mark below and value **Rev:** Quartered arms of Castile-Leon, date above in legend **Mint:** Madrid **Note:** Varieties exist.

Date	Mintage	VG	F	VF	XF	Unc
1621MD V Horizontal mm, Value VIII	—	750	1,800	3,900	—	—
1627/0MD V Vertical mm, Value VIII	—	850	1,900	4,200	—	—
1627MD M Horizontal mm, Value VIII	—	750	1,800	3,900	—	—
1627MD V Horizontal mm, Value VIII	—	550	1,200	2,800	—	—
1631MD M Horizontal mm, Value VIII	—	550	1,200	2,800	—	—
1633MD M Horizontal mm, Value VIII	—	550	1,200	2,800	—	—
1635MD M Horizontal mm, Value VIII	—	550	1,200	2,800	—	—
1639MD BI Vertical mm, Value VIII	—	550	1,200	2,800	—	—
1639MD VI Vertical mm, Value VIII	—	750	1,800	3,900	—	—
1641 B Vertical mm, Value 8	—	325	675	1,500	—	—
1641MD B Vertical mm, Value VIII	—	550	1,200	2,800	—	—
1642 B Vertical mm, Value 8	—	325	675	1,500	—	—
1642MD B Vertical mm, Value VIII	—	550	1,200	2,800	—	—
1642MD B Vertical mm, Value 8	—	400	950	2,000	—	—
1642MD B Vertical mm, Value 8	—	400	950	2,000	—	—

Date	Mintage	VG	F	VF	XF
1643MD B Vertical mm, Value 8	—	325	675	1,500	—
1643MD B Vertical mm, Value 8	—	400	950	2,000	—
Note: Retrograde 4 and B.					
1643MD B Vertical mm, Value 8	—	325	675	1,500	—
Note: Retrograde B.					
1644/3MD B Vertical mm, Value 8	—	325	675	1,500	—
1644MD B Vertical mm, Value 8	—	325	675	1,500	—
Note: Retrograde B.					
1644MD IB Vertical mm, Value 8	—	350	700	1,650	—
Note: I instead of 4.					
1649MD IB Vertical mm, Value 8	—	325	700	1,650	—
1650MD A Vertical mm, Value 8	—	325	675	1,500	—
1650MD A Vertical mm, Value VIII	—	750	1,800	3,900	—
1651MD A Vertical mm, Value 8	—	325	675	1,500	—
16xxMD M Horizontal mm, Value VIII	—	400	800	1,500	—
Note: Obverse and reverse legends switched.					
1659MD A Vertical mm, Value 8	—	325	675	1,500	—
1661/59MD A Vertical mm, Value 8	—	350	700	1,650	—
1662MD A Vertical mm, Value 8	—	350	700	1,650	—

KM# 39.6 8 REALES

27.4682 g., 0.9306 Silver 0.8218 oz. ASW **Ruler:** Philip IV **Ob** Crowned shield of royal arms between mint mark with assay mark below and value **Rev:** Quartered arms of Castile-Leon, da above in legend **Mint:** Seville

Date	Mintage	VG	F	VF	XF
1622S D	—	150	350	750	—
1623/2S D	—	110	225	500	—
1624S D	—	100	200	400	—
1625S D	—	100	200	400	—
1625S R	—	100	200	400	—
1627/6S R	—	100	200	400	—
1628S D	—	325	700	1,500	—
1628S R	—	100	200	400	—
1629S R	—	100	200	400	—
1630S R	—	100	200	400	—
1631S R	—	250	600	1,200	—
1632S R	—	110	225	500	—
1633S R	—	110	225	500	—
1634S R	—	150	325	700	—
1635S R	—	110	225	500	—
1636S R	—	300	625	1,350	—
1637S R	—	110	225	500	—
1638/7S R	—	100	200	400	—
1638S R	—	150	325	700	—
1640S R	—	250	600	1,200	—
1642S R	—	100	200	400	—
1643S R	—	100	200	400	—
1644S R	—	100	200	400	—
1651S R	—	100	200	400	—
1653S R	—	150	325	700	—
1655S R	—	100	200	400	—
1656S R	—	150	325	700	—
1657S R	—	100	200	400	—
1659S R	—	100	200	400	—
1660S R	—	250	600	1,200	—
1662S R	—	100	200	400	—
1663S R Rare	—	—	—	—	—

KM# 39.7 8 REALES

27.4682 g., 0.9306 Silver 0.8218 oz. ASW **Ruler:** Philip IV **O** Crowned shield of royal arms between mint mark with assay below and value **Rev:** Quartered arms of Castile-Leon, date above in legend **Mint:** Toledo

Date	Mintage	VG	F	VF	XF
1630To P	—	400	850	1,750	—
1631/0To P	—	300	700	1,450	—
1631To P	—	250	475	1,100	—
1632To P	—	250	475	1,100	—
1634To P	—	250	475	1,100	—
1635To P	—	250	475	1,100	—
1639To P	—	250	475	1,100	—
1651To Y	—	250	475	1,100	—
1651To Y Value as 8	—	300	700	1,450	—
1652To Y	—	300	700	1,450	—

ate	Mintage	VG	F	VF	XF	Unc
555To Y	—	300	700	1,450	—	—
559To CA	—	900	2,000	4,250	—	—
560/59To Y	—	250	475	1,100	—	—
562To CA	—	900	2,000	4,250	—	—
562To CA/Y	—	900	2,000	4,250	—	—
562To Y	—	250	475	1,100	—	—

M# 39.8 8 REALES

.4682 g., 0.9306 Silver 0.8218 oz. ASW **Ruler:** Philip IV **Obv:** rowned shield of royal armb between mint mark with assayer ark below and value **Rev:** Quartered arms of Castile-Leon, date ove in legend **Mint:** Valladolid

ate	Mintage	VG	F	VF	XF	Unc
51 F Rare	—	—	—	—	—	—

M# 39.1 8 REALES

.4682 g., 0.9306 Silver 0.8218 oz. ASW **Ruler:** Philip IV **Obv:** rowned shield of royal arms between mint mark with assayer low and value **Rev:** Quartered arms of Castile-Leon, date ove in legend **Mint:** Burgos

te	Mintage	VG	F	VF	XF	Unc
51B BR Rare	—	—	—	—	—	—

M# 39.2 8 REALES

.4682 g., 0.9306 Silver 0.8218 oz. ASW **Ruler:** Philip IV **Obv:** owned shield of royal arms between mint mark with assayer ark below and value **Rev:** Quartered arms of Castile-Leon, date ove in legend **Mint:** Cuenca

te	Mintage	VG	F	VF	XF	Unc
51C CA	—	1,650	3,500	8,000	—	—

M# 39.3 8 REALES

.4682 g., 0.9306 Silver 0.8218 oz. ASW **Ruler:** Philip IV **Obv:** owned shield of royal arms between mint mark with assayer ark below and value **Rev:** Quartered arms of Castile-Leon, date ove in legend **Mint:** Granada **Note:** Mint mark: Pomegranate.

te	Mintage	VG	F	VF	XF	Unc
51 N	—	1,400	3,000	3,500	—	—

M# 40.3 8 REALES

.4682 g., 0.9306 Silver 0.8218 oz. ASW **Ruler:** Charles II **v:** Crowned shield of royal arms between mint mark with sayer mark below and value **Rev:** Quartered arms of Castile-on, date below in legend **Mint:** Madrid

te	Mintage	VG	F	VF	XF	Unc
66 R	—	1,600	3,900	8,500	—	—
70MD R	—	1,200	2,700	6,300	—	—
73MD BR	—	1,200	2,700	6,300	—	—

M# 40.4 8 REALES

.4682 g., 0.9306 Silver 0.8218 oz. ASW **Ruler:** Charles II **v:** Crowned shield of royal arms between mint mark with sayer below and value **Rev:** Quartered arms of Castile-Leon, te above in legend **Mint:** Seville

te	Mintage	VG	F	VF	XF	Unc
68S M	—	225	500	1,100	—	—
70S M	—	300	650	1,400	—	—
71S M	—	300	650	1,400	—	—
73S M	—	300	650	1,400	—	—
80S S	—	300	650	1,400	—	—
xxS G	—	225	500	1,100	—	—

KM# 40.2 8 REALES

27.4682 g., 0.9306 Silver 0.8218 oz. ASW **Ruler:** Charles II **Obv:** Crowned shield of royal arms between mint mark and value as 8 **Rev:** Quartered arms of Castile-Leon, date above in legend **Mint:** Granada

Date	Mintage	VG	F	VF	XF	Unc
1679G Rare	—	—	—	—	—	—

KM# 40.1 8 REALES

27.4682 g., 0.9306 Silver 0.8218 oz. ASW **Ruler:** Charles II **Obv:** Crowned shield of royal arms between mint mark and value **Rev:** Quartered arms of Castile-Leon, date above **Mint:** Burgos

Date	Mintage	VG	F	VF	XF	Unc
1680B Rare	—	—	—	—	—	—

KM# 41.2 8 REALES

27.4682 g., 0.9306 Silver 0.8218 oz. ASW **Ruler:** Charles II **Obv:** Crowned shield of royal arms between mint mark and assayer mark **Rev:** Cross between value R-8 atop MARIA monogram. Date below in legend **Mint:** Seville

Date	Mintage	VG	F	VF	XF	Unc
1686S M	—	140	350	800	—	—
1689S M	—	140	350	800	—	—
1690S M	—	140	350	800	—	—
1691/81S M	—	140	350	800	—	—
1691S M	—	180	380	925	—	—
1691S M value as 8-R	—	160	370	875	—	—
1692S M	—	180	380	920	—	—
169ZS M	—	160	370	875	—	—
1693S M	—	180	380	925	—	—
1694S M	—	180	380	925	—	—
1697S M	—	140	350	800	—	—
1698S M	—	180	380	925	—	—
1699/8S M	—	180	380	925	—	—
16xxS J	—	300	650	1,400	—	—

KM# 41.1 8 REALES

27.4682 g., 0.9306 Silver 0.8218 oz. ASW **Ruler:** Charles II **Obv:** Crowned shield of royal arms between mint mark and assayer mark **Rev:** Cross atop MARIA, value flanking, date below **Mint:** Madrid

Date	Mintage	VG	F	VF	XF	Unc
1689MD BR value R8	—	800	1,850	3,800	—	—
1699MD NR value 8R	—	500	1,200	3,600	—	—

KM# 42.1 ESCUDO

3.4335 g., 0.9167 Gold 0.1012 oz. AGW **Ruler:** Philip III **Obv:** Crowned shield of royal arms between mint mark with assayer mark below and value **Rev:** Cross in quatrefoil, date above in legend **Mint:** Madrid

Date	Mintage	VG	F	VF	XF	Unc
NDMD G	—	300	700	1,500	—	—

KM# 42.2 ESCUDO

3.4335 g., 0.9167 Gold 0.1012 oz. AGW **Ruler:** Philip III **Obv:** Crowned shield of royal arms between mint mark with assayer mark below and value **Rev:** Cross in quatrefoil, date above in legend **Mint:** Seville

Date	Mintage	VG	F	VF	XF	Unc
1610S B	—	300	600	1,350	—	—
1611S V	—	300	600	1,350	—	—
1614S V	—	300	600	1,350	—	—
1615S V	—	300	600	1,350	—	—
1617S G	—	300	600	1,350	—	—
1618S D	—	300	600	1,350	—	—

KM# 44.2 ESCUDO

3.4335 g., 0.9167 Gold 0.1012 oz. AGW **Ruler:** Philip IV **Obv:** Crowned shield of royal arms between mint mark with assayer mark below and value **Rev:** Cross in quatrefoil, date above in legend **Mint:** Seville

Date	Mintage	VG	F	VF	XF	Unc
1623S C	—	300	750	1,700	—	—
1623S D	—	225	500	1,100	—	—
1623S R	—	225	500	1,100	—	—

Date	Mintage	VG	F	VF	XF	Unc
1628S D	—	225	500	1,100	—	—
1646S D	—	600	1,200	2,500	—	—

Note: Shield without the escutcheons of Portugal and Habsburgs

Date	Mintage	VG	F	VF	XF	Unc
1659S R	—	225	500	1,100	—	—

KM# 44.1 ESCUDO

3.4335 g., 0.9167 Gold 0.1012 oz. AGW **Ruler:** Philip IV **Obv:** Crowned shield of royal arms between mint mark with assayer mark below and value **Rev:** Cross in quatrefoil, date above in legend **Mint:** Madrid

Date	Mintage	VG	F	VF	XF	Unc
1627MD V	—	1,200	2,800	4,000	—	—
1639MD R	—	1,200	2,800	4,000	—	—

KM# 43 ESCUDO

3.4335 g., 0.9167 Gold 0.1012 oz. AGW **Ruler:** Philip IV **Obv:** Crowned royal arms between mint mark as B-A **Rev:** Cross in quatrefoil, date above in legend **Mint:** Barcelona

Date	Mintage	VG	F	VF	XF	Unc
1662BA	—	1,400	3,000	7,000	—	—

KM# 45 ESCUDO

3.4335 g., 0.9167 Gold 0.1012 oz. AGW **Ruler:** Charles II **Obv:** Crowned shield of royal arms **Rev:** Cross in quatrefoil, date above in legend **Mint:** Barcelona

Date	Mintage	VG	F	VF	XF	Unc
1672	—	1,000	2,000	4,200	—	—
1674	—	1,000	2,000	4,200	—	—

KM# 46.2 ESCUDO

3.4335 g., 0.9167 Gold 0.1012 oz. AGW **Ruler:** Charles II **Obv:** Crowned shield of royal arms between mint mark with assayer mark below and value **Rev:** Cross in quatrefoil, date above in legend **Mint:** Seville

Date	Mintage	VG	F	VF	XF	Unc
1672S M	—	200	400	900	—	—
1675S M	—	200	400	900	—	—
1687S M	—	190	300	700	—	—

KM# 46.1 ESCUDO

3.4335 g., 0.9167 Gold 0.1012 oz. AGW **Ruler:** Charles II **Obv:** Crowned shield of royal arms between mint mark with assayer mark below and value **Rev:** Cross in quatrefoil, date above in legend **Mint:** Madrid

Date	Mintage	VG	F	VF	XF	Unc
1679MD BR	—	1,000	2,000	4,200	—	—
1689MD M	—	1,000	2,000	4,200	—	—
1689MD M	—	1,000	2,000	4,200	—	—

Note: Assayer to right of arms

Date	Mintage	VG	F	VF	XF	Unc
16xxMD R	—	650	1,500	3,400	—	—

KM# 47 ESCUDO

3.4335 g., 0.9167 Silver 0.1012 oz. ASW **Ruler:** Charles II **Obv:** Crowned shield of royal arms between mint mark with assayer mark below and value **Rev:** Quartered arms of Castile-Leon, date above in legend **Mint:** Seville

Date	Mintage	VG	F	VF	XF	Unc
1686S G	—	325	700	1,450	—	—

KM# 46.3 ESCUDO

3.4335 g., 0.9167 Gold 0.1012 oz. AGW **Ruler:** Charles II **Obv:** Crowned shield of Castile-Leon between mint mark and assayer mark **Rev:** Cross in quatrefoil, date above in legend **Mint:** Seville

Date	Mintage	VG	F	VF	XF	Unc
1691S M	—	900	2,000	4,200	—	—

KM# 224 ESCUDO

3.4335 g., 0.9167 Gold 0.1012 oz. AGW **Ruler:** Philip V **Obv:** Crowned shield of royal arms between mint mark with assayer mark below and value **Rev:** Quartered arms of Castile-Leon, date above in legend **Mint:** Madrid

Date	Mintage	VG	F	VF	XF	Unc
1700MD F/I	—	450	1,000	2,200	—	—

KM# 48.1 2 ESCUDOS

6.8670 g., 0.9167 Gold 0.2024 oz. AGW **Ruler:** Philip III **Obv:** Crowned shield of royal arms between value and mint mark with assayer mark below **Rev:** Cross in quatrefoil, date above in legend **Mint:** Granada

Date	Mintage	VG	F	VF	XF	Unc
1605/598G M	—	950	2,100	4,800	—	—
1606G M	—	950	2,100	4,800	—	—
1611G M	—	950	2,100	4,800	—	—

KM# 48.4 2 ESCUDOS

6.8670 g., 0.9167 Gold 0.2024 oz. AGW **Ruler:** Philip III **Obv:** Crowned shield of royal arms between mint mark with assayer mark below and value **Rev:** Cross in quatrefoil, date above in legend **Mint:** Toledo

Date	Mintage	VG	F	VF	XF	Unc
1608To C	—	850	1,800	4,000	—	—
1613To P	—	850	1,800	4,000	—	—
1614To P	—	600	1,200	3,000	—	—
1614To V	—	850	1,800	4,000	—	—

KM# 48.3 2 ESCUDOS

6.8670 g., 0.9167 Gold 0.2024 oz. AGW **Ruler:** Philip III **Obv:** Crowned shield of royal arms between mint mark with assayer mark below and value **Rev:** Cross in quatrefoil, date above in legend **Mint:** Seville

Date	Mintage	VG	F	VF	XF	Unc
1610S B	—	375	750	1,500	—	—
1611S B	—	375	750	1,500	—	—
1611S D	—	375	750	1,500	—	—
1611S V	—	375	750	1,500	—	—
1612S B	—	375	750	1,500	—	—
1612S D	—	375	750	1,500	—	—
1612S V	—	375	750	1,500	—	—
1613S V	—	375	750	1,500	—	—
1614S V	—	375	750	1,500	—	—
1615S D	—	375	750	1,500	—	—
1615S V	—	375	750	1,500	—	—
1617S D	—	375	750	1,500	—	—
1617S G	—	375	750	1,500	—	—
1618S G	—	375	750	1,500	—	—
1619S G	—	375	750	1,500	—	—
1620S G	—	375	750	1,500	—	—
1621S G	—	375	750	1,500	—	—
NDS B	—	650	1,400	3,100	—	—

Note: Error: Value 1 from escudo die.

Y# 49 2 ESCUDOS

6.8670 g., 0.9167 Gold 0.2024 oz. AGW **Ruler:** Philip III **Obv:** Crowned shield of royal arms between mint mark with assayer mark below and value **Rev:** Cross in quatrefoil, date above in legend **Mint:** Seville **Note:** Round presentation strike - Royal

Date	Mintage	F	VF	XF	Unc	BU
1610S B	—	—	—	15,000	—	—
1612S B	—	—	—	—	—	—

KM# 48.2 2 ESCUDOS

6.8670 g., 0.9167 Gold 0.2024 oz. AGW **Ruler:** Philip III **Obv:** Crowned shield of royal arms bwteen mint mark with assayer mark above and value **Rev:** Cross in quatrefoil, date above in legend **Mint:** Madrid

Date	Mintage	VG	F	VF	XF	Unc
1615MD G	—	2,000	4,000	8,000	—	—
Note: The 1615 expamles have the assayer below the mint mark and appear to be round presentation examples. Seldom seen.						
1616MD G	—	1,500	3,100	6,900	—	—
1620MD G	—	1,500	3,100	6,900	—	—

KM# 48.5 2 ESCUDOS

6.8670 g., 0.9167 Gold 0.2024 oz. AGW **Ruler:** Philip III **Obv:** Crowned shield of royal arms between mint mark with assayer mark abbove and value **Rev:** Cross in quatrefoil **Mint:** Valladolid

Date	Mintage	VG	F	VF	XF	Unc
NDFlags Do	—	800	1,800	4,000	—	—

KM# 51.3 2 ESCUDOS

6.8670 g., 0.9167 Gold 0.2024 oz. AGW **Ruler:** Philip IV **Obv:** Crowned shield of royal arms between mint mark with assayer mark below and value **Rev:** Cross in quatrefoil, date above in legend **Mint:** Seville

Date	Mintage	VG	F	VF	XF	Unc
1622S R	—	350	550	1,200	—	—
1623S D	—	350	550	1,200	—	—
1623S R	—	325	425	800	—	—
1628S R	—	350	550	1,200	—	—
1629S R	—	352	425	800	—	—
1634S R	—	352	425	800	—	—
1640S D	—	350	500	1,100	—	—
1641S D	—	375	750	1,400	—	—
Note: Shield without the escutcheon of Portugal and Habsburg						
1644S R	—	325	450	800	—	—
1645S R	—	350	600	1,100	—	—
1651S R	—	350	750	1,400	—	—
1652S C	—	375	750	1,400	—	—
Note: Value to left of shield, mint and assayer to right. Shield without the escutcheon of Portugal and Habsburg						
1661S C	—	375	750	1,400	—	—
Note: Shield without the escutcheon of Portugal and Habsburg						

KM# 51.2 2 ESCUDOS

6.8670 g., 0.9167 Gold 0.2024 oz. AGW **Ruler:** Philip IV **Obv:** Crowned shield of royal arms between mint mark with assayer below and value **Rev:** Cross in quatrefoil, date above in legend **Mint:** Madrid **Note:** Mint mark is horizontal on first three dates, vertical on others.

Date	Mintage	VG	F	VF	XF	Unc
1625MD V	—	1,200	2,600	5,500	—	—
1627MD V	—	1,200	2,600	5,500	—	—
1628MD V	—	1,200	2,600	5,500	—	—
1638MD Po	—	1,200	2,600	5,500	—	—
1644MD A	—	1,200	2,600	5,500	—	—
1645MD B	—	1,200	2,600	5,500	—	—
1646MD A	—	1,200	2,600	5,500	—	—

KM# 51.1 2 ESCUDOS

6.8670 g., 0.9167 Gold 0.2024 oz. AGW **Ruler:** Philip IV **Obv:** Crowned shield of royal arms between value and mint mark above assayer mark **Rev:** Cross in quatrefoil, date above in legend **Mint:** Granada

Date	Mintage	VG	F	VF	XF	Unc
1651G M	—	1,250	3,000	6,700	—	—

KM# 50 2 ESCUDOS

6.8670 g., 0.9167 Gold 0.2024 oz. AGW **Ruler:** Philip IV **Obv:** Crowned shield of royal arms between B-A **Rev:** Cross in quatrefoil, date above in legend **Mint:** Barcelona

Date	Mintage	VG	F	VF	XF	Unc
1653BA	—	1,600	3,500	8,000	—	—
1655BA	—	1,600	3,500	8,000	—	—
1656BA	—	1,600	3,500	8,000	—	—
1660BA	—	1,600	3,500	8,000	—	—
1660BA	—	1,900	4,000	9,500	—	—
Note: Without A of mint mark, some authors place this as a Burgos issue, which had no gold issues at this time.						

KM# 52 2 ESCUDOS

6.8670 g., 0.9167 Gold 0.2024 oz. AGW **Ruler:** Charles II **Obv:** Crowned shield of royal arms between B-A **Rev:** Cross in quatrefoil, date above in legend **Mint:** Barcelona **Note:** Varieties exist.

Date	Mintage	VG	F	VF	XF	Unc
1673BA	—	1,200	2,500	5,000	—	—
1685BA	—	1,200	2,500	5,000	—	—

Y# 53.1 2 ESCUDOS

6.8670 g., 0.9167 Gold 0.2024 oz. AGW **Ruler:** Charles II **Obv:** Crowned shield of royal arms between mint mark with assayer mark below and date **Rev:** Cross in quatrefoil **Mint:** Granada **Note:** Mint mark: Pomegranate

Date	Mintage	VG	F	VF	XF	Unc
ND G	—	2,200	4,000	8,000	—	—

KM# 53.2 2 ESCUDOS

6.8670 g., 0.9167 Gold 0.2024 oz. AGW **Ruler:** Charles II **Obv:** Crowned royal shield between mint mark with assayer mark below and value **Rev:** Cross in quatrefoil, date above in legend **Mint:** Madrid

Date	Mintage	VG	F	VF	XF	Unc
1678MD BR	—	1,200	2,300	5,000	—	—
1686MD M	—	1,200	2,300	5,000	—	—
Note: Without the escutcheon of Portugal						

KM# 53.3 2 ESCUDOS

6.8670 g., 0.9167 Gold 0.2024 oz. AGW **Ruler:** Charles II **Obv:** Crowned royal shield between mint mark with assayer mark below and value **Rev:** Cross in quatrefoil **Mint:** Seville

Date	Mintage	VG	F	VF	XF	Unc
NDS G	—	350	425	850	—	—
1689S M	—	400	800	1,600	—	—
1690S M	—	400	800	1,600	—	—

KM# 54 4 ESCUDOS

13.7341 g., 0.9167 Gold 0.4048 oz. AGW **Ruler:** Philip III **Obv:** Crowned shield of royal arms between mint mark with assayer mark below and value **Rev:** Cross in quatrefoil, date above in legend **Mint:** Seville

Date	Mintage	VG	F	VF	XF	Unc
1609S B	—	4,000	6,000	12,000	—	—

KM# 55 4 ESCUDOS

13.7341 g., 0.9167 Gold 0.4048 oz. AGW **Ruler:** Philip IV **Obv:** Crownd shield of royal arms between BA **Rev:** Cross in quatrefoil **Mint:** Barcelona

Date	Mintage	VG	F	VF	XF	Unc
NDBA	—	1,100	2,300	5,000	—	—

KM# 56.1 4 ESCUDOS

13.7341 g., 0.9167 Gold 0.4048 oz. AGW **Ruler:** Philip IV **Obv** Crowned shield of royal arms between mint mark with assaye mark below and value **Rev:** Cross in quatrefoil, date above in legend **Mint:** Madrid

Date	Mintage	VG	F	VF	XF	U
1629/8MD V	—	2,600	5,000	9,000	—	
1630MD R	—	2,600	5,000	9,000	—	
1631MD V	—	2,600	5,000	9,000	—	
1632MD V	—	2,600	5,000	9,000	—	
1636MD Ro	—	2,600	5,000	9,000	—	
1638MD A/Po	—	2,600	5,000	9,000	—	
1641MD B	—	2,600	5,000	9,000	—	
1642MD V	—	2,600	5,000	9,000	—	
1644MD B	—	2,600	5,000	9,000	—	
1645MD A	—	2,600	5,000	9,000	—	
1645MD V	—	2,600	5,000	9,000	—	
1646MD A	—	2,600	5,000	9,000	—	
1651MD A	—	2,600	5,000	9,000	—	
1655MD A	—	2,600	5,000	9,000	—	
1660MD A/Ro	—	2,600	5,000	9,000	—	
1664MD A	—	2,600	5,000	9,000	—	
1665MD A/V	—	2,600	5,000	9,000	—	
NDMD M	—	2,600	5,000	9,000	—	

KM# 56.2 4 ESCUDOS

13.7341 g., 0.9167 Gold 0.4048 oz. AGW **Ruler:** Philip IV **Ob** Crowned shield of royal arms between mint mark with assaye mark below and value **Rev:** Cross in quatrefoil, date above in legend **Mint:** Seville

Date	Mintage	VG	F	VF	XF	U
1630S R	—	850	1,600	2,200	—	
1631S R	—	850	1,600	2,200	—	
1632S R	—	850	1,600	2,200	—	
1633S R	—	850	1,600	2,200	—	
1636S R	—	1,200	2,000	3,400	—	
1637S R	—	850	1,600	2,200	—	
1639S R	—	850	1,600	2,200	—	
1641S R	—	850	1,200	2,300	—	
1644S R	—	850	1,200	2,600	—	
Note: Assayer mark above mint mark.						
1645/4S R	—	850	1,200	2,300	—	
1647S R	—	850	1,200	2,300	—	
1655S R	—	850	1,200	2,300	—	
1664/3S R	—	1,000	1,800	4,000	—	

KM# 58.1 4 ESCUDOS

13.7341 g., 0.9167 Gold 0.4048 oz. AGW **Ruler:** Charles II **Ob** Crowned shiedl of royal arms between mint mark with assaye mark below and value **Rev:** Cross in quatrefoil, date above in legend **Mint:** Madrid

Date	Mintage	VG	F	VF	XF	U
1672MD R	—	2,000	4,000	8,500	—	
168xMD M	—	2,000	4,000	8,500	—	
1689MD BR	—	2,000	4,000	8,500	—	

KM# 57 4 ESCUDOS

13.7341 g., 0.9167 Gold 0.4048 oz. AGW **Ruler:** Charles II **Ob** Crowned shield of royal arms between B-A **Rev:** Cross in quatrifoil, date above in legend **Mint:** Barcelona

Date	Mintage	VG	F	VF	XF	U
1676BA	—	3,000	5,000	10,000	—	
1679BA	—	3,000	5,000	10,000	—	
1684BA	—	3,000	5,000	10,000	—	
1697BA	—	3,000	5,000	10,000	—	
1699BA	—	3,000	5,000	10,000	—	

KM# 58.2 4 ESCUDOS

13.7341 g., 0.9167 Gold 0.4048 oz. AGW **Ruler:** Charles II **Ob** Crowned shield of royal arms between mint mark with assaye mark below and value **Rev:** Cross in quatrefoil, date above in legend **Mint:** Seville

Date	Mintage	VG	F	VF	XF	U
NDS S	—	950	1,500	2,500	—	
1689S M	—	1,300	2,200	4,000	—	
1699S M	—	1,300	2,200	4,000	—	

KM# 59.2 8 ESCUDOS

27.4682 g., 0.9167 Gold 0.8095 oz. AGW **Ruler:** Philip IV **Ob** ʳowned shield of royal arms between mint mark with assayer ark below and value **Rev:** Cross in quatrefoil, date above in gend **Mint:** Seville

te	Mintage	VG	F	VF	XF	Unc
31S R	—	1,800	3,000	6,000	—	—
32S R	—	1,800	3,000	6,000	—	—
33S R	—	1,800	3,000	6,000	—	—
34S R	—	2,000	4,500	9,000	—	—
Note: Inner fringe on reverse						
34S R	—	2,000	4,000	7,000	—	—
Note: Inner fringe on both sides, Assayer mark above mint mark						
37S R	—	2,000	4,000	7,000	—	—
38/7S R	—	2,000	4,000	7,000	—	—
39/29S R	—	2,000	4,000	7,000	—	—
39/3S R	—	1,800	3,000	6,000	—	—
39S R	—	1,800	3,000	6,000	—	—
40S R	—	1,800	3,000	6,000	—	—
42S R	—	1,800	3,000	6,000	—	—
42S R	—	1,800	3,000	6,000	—	—
Note: Assayer mark above mint mark						
44S R	—	1,800	3,000	6,000	—	—
45/2S R	—	1,800	3,000	6,000	—	—
45S R	—	1,800	3,000	6,000	—	—
46S R	—	1,800	3,000	6,000	—	—
47S R	—	1,800	3,000	6,000	—	—
49S R	—	1,800	3,000	6,000	—	—
53S R	—	1,800	3,000	6,000	—	—
55S R	—	1,800	3,000	6,000	—	—
57S R	—	1,800	3,000	6,000	—	—
59S R	—	1,800	3,000	6,000	—	—
60S A	—	1,800	3,000	6,000	—	—
60S A/C	—	1,800	3,000	6,000	—	—
61S BR	—	2,000	4,000	7,000	—	—
63/2S R	—	2,000	4,000	7,000	—	—
63S R	—	1,800	3,000	6,000	—	—
64S R	—	1,600	2,800	5,000	—	—
65S R	—	1,800	3,000	6,000	—	—

M# 136.1 8 ESCUDOS

.4682 g., 0.9167 Gold 0.8095 oz. AGW **Ruler:** Philip IV **Obv:** owned shield of royal arms between mint mark with assayers ark below and value **Rev:** Cross in quatrefoil, date above in gend **Mint:** Madrid **Note:** Value as VIII

te	Mintage	VG	F	VF	XF	Unc
31MD M Rare	—	—	—	—	—	—
32MD PM Rare	—	—	—	—	—	—
33MD M Rare	—	—	—	—	—	—
35MD M	—	6,000	12,000	25,000	—	—
37MD M	—	6,000	12,000	25,000	—	—
39MD P	—	8,000	18,000	35,000	—	—
50MD A	—	8,000	18,000	35,000	—	—
Note: Horizontal mint mark						
51MD A	—	8,000	18,000	35,000	—	—
54MD A	—	8,000	18,000	35,000	—	—
Note: Horizontal mint mark						
61MD A	—	8,000	18,000	35,000	—	—
62MD A	—	8,000	18,000	35,000	—	—
63/2MD A	—	8,000	18,000	35,000	—	—

M# 136.2 8 ESCUDOS

Ruler: Philip IV **Obv:** Crowned shiedl of royal arms between nt mark with assayer mark below and value **Rev:** Cross in atrefoil, date above in legend **Mint:** Madrid **Note:** Value as 8

te	Mintage	VG	F	VF	XF	Unc
40MD B	—	9,000	16,000	35,000	—	—
41MD B	—	9,000	16,000	35,000	—	—
41MD B etrograde	—	9,000	16,000	35,000	—	—
42MD B	—	5,000	11,000	24,000	—	—
43MD B	—	9,000	16,000	35,000	—	—
44/3MD B	—	5,000	11,000	24,000	—	—
44MD B	—	5,000	11,000	24,000	—	—
45/3MD B	—	5,000	11,000	24,000	—	—
45/3MD V/IB	—	9,000	16,000	35,000	—	—
45MD B	—	5,000	11,000	24,000	—	—
45MD IB	—	5,000	11,000	24,000	—	—
46/3MD A/V	—	5,000	11,000	24,000	—	—
46MD A	—	5,000	11,000	24,000	—	—
48/0MD A/B	—	6,500	12,000	27,000	—	—
48/7MD A	—	6,500	12,000	27,000	—	—
48MD A	—	6,500	12,000	27,000	—	—
49MD A	—	6,500	12,000	27,000	—	—

M# 59.3 8 ESCUDOS

.4682 g., 0.9167 Gold 0.8095 oz. AGW **Ruler:** Philip IV **Obv:** owned shield of royal arms between mint mark with assayer ark below and value **Rev:** Cross in quatrefoil, date above in gend **Mint:** Toledo

te	Mintage	VG	F	VF	XF	Unc
65To CA monogram Rare	—	—	—	—	—	—

M# 59.4 8 ESCUDOS

.4682 g., 0.9167 Gold 0.8095 oz. AGW **Ruler:** Philip IV **Obv:** owned shield of royal arms, between mint mark with assayer ark below and value **Rev:** Cross in quatrefoil, date above in gend **Mint:** Valladolid

te	Mintage	VG	F	VF	XF	Unc
Flags M Rare	—	—	—	—	—	—
Note: Date is usually off-flan or unreadable.						

M# 61.1 8 ESCUDOS

.4682 g., 0.9167 Gold 1.1042 oz. AGW **Ruler:** Charles II **Obv:** owned shield of royal arms between mint mark with assayer ark below and value **Rev:** Cross in quatrefoin, date above in gend **Mint:** Madrid

te	Mintage	VG	F	VF	XF	Unc
66MD A	—	9,000	20,000	35,000	—	—

Date	Mintage	VG	F	VF	XF	Unc
1668MD A	—	9,000	20,000	35,000	—	—
1669/8MD A	—	9,000	20,000	35,000	—	—
1669MD A	—	9,000	20,000	35,000	—	—
1685MD M	—	9,000	20,000	35,000	—	—
Note: Without escutcheon of Portugal						
1687MD M	—	9,000	20,000	35,000	—	—
Note: Without escutcheon of Portugal						
1696MD BR	—	9,000	20,000	35,000	—	—
1696MD BR	—	9,000	20,000	35,000	—	—
Note: Without escutcheon of Portugal and reversed arms in shield (Lion-Castle)						

KM# 61.2 8 ESCUDOS

27.4682 g., 0.9167 Gold 0.8095 oz. AGW **Ruler:** Charles II **Obv:** Crowned shield of royal arms between mint mark with assayer mark below and value **Rev:** Cross in quatrefoil, date above in legend **Mint:** Seville

Date	Mintage	VG	F	VF	XF	Unc
1666S R	—	1,900	3,000	7,000	—	—
1666S M	—	1,900	3,000	7,000	—	—
1667S M	—	1,900	3,000	7,000	—	—
1668S M	—	1,900	2,800	6,000	—	—
1669S M	—	1,900	2,800	6,000	—	—
1670S M	—	1,900	2,800	6,000	—	—
1673S M	—	1,900	2,800	6,000	—	—
1674S M	—	1,900	2,800	6,000	—	—
1675/4S M	—	1,900	2,800	6,000	—	—
1676/5S S	—	1,900	3,000	7,000	—	—
1676S M	—	1,900	2,800	6,000	—	—
1678S M	—	1,900	3,000	7,000	—	—
1679S M	—	1,900	3,000	7,000	—	—
1680/78S M	—	1,900	3,000	7,000	—	—
1683S S	—	1,900	3,000	7,000	—	—
1684/3S S	—	1,900	3,000	7,000	—	—
1684S L	—	2,000	4,000	8,000	—	—
1685/84S M/L	—	1,900	3,000	7,000	—	—
1685S S	—	1,900	3,000	7,000	—	—
1686S S	—	1,900	3,000	7,000	—	—
1686S G	—	1,900	2,800	6,000	—	—
1687S M	—	1,900	3,000	7,000	—	—
1687S M/G	—	1,900	3,000	7,000	—	—
1687S G	—	1,900	3,000	7,000	—	—
1688/78S G	—	1,900	3,000	7,000	—	—
1688S G	—	1,900	3,000	7,000	—	—
1688S M	—	1,900	2,800	6,000	—	—
1689/8S M	—	1,900	2,800	6,000	—	—
1689S M/S	—	1,900	2,800	6,000	—	—
1690S M	—	1,900	2,800	6,000	—	—
1691/0S M	—	1,900	2,800	6,000	—	—
1691S M	—	1,900	2,800	6,000	—	—
1692/0S M/S	—	1,900	3,000	7,000	—	—
1692/0S M	—	1,900	3,000	7,000	—	—
1692S M	—	1,900	3,000	7,000	—	—
1694/3S M	—	1,900	3,000	7,000	—	—
1698/7S M	—	1,900	2,800	6,000	—	—
1698S M	—	1,900	2,800	6,000	—	—
1699/3S M	—	1,900	2,800	6,000	—	—
1699/8S M	—	1,900	2,800	6,000	—	—
1699S M	—	1,900	2,800	6,000	—	—

KM# A60 8 ESCUDOS

27.4682 g., 0.9167 Gold 0.8095 oz. AGW **Ruler:** Charles II **Obv:** Crowned shield of royal arms between B-A **Rev:** Cross in quatrefoil, date above in legend **Mint:** Barcelona

Date	Mintage	VG	F	VF	XF	Unc
1693BA	—	10,000	20,000	50,000	—	—
1694BA	—	10,000	20,000	50,000	—	—
1695BA	—	10,000	20,000	50,000	—	—
1698BA	—	10,000	20,000	50,000	—	—

KM# A62 8 ESCUDOS

27.4682 g., 0.9167 Gold 0.8095 oz. AGW **Ruler:** Charles II **Obv:** Crowned shield of Castile-Leon between mint mark and assayer mark **Rev:** Cross in quatrefoil, date above in legend **Mint:** Seville

Date	Mintage	VG	F	VF	XF	Unc
1694/3S M	—	5,000	12,000	30,000	—	—

MILLED REAL COINAGE

KM# 103 1/2 MARAVEDI

Copper **Ruler:** Philip IV **Obv:** Crowned PHILIPPVS monogram, date below **Rev:** Castle and lions **Mint:** Segovia

Date	Mintage	VG	F	VF	XF	Unc
1631	—	205	375	825	1,500	—

KM# 104 1/2 MARAVEDI

Copper **Ruler:** Philip IV **Obv:** Crowned PHILIPPVS monogram, date below **Rev:** BI-ON / CA, facing lion **Mint:** Segovia

Date	Mintage	VG	F	VF	XF	Unc
1631	—	115	235	475	875	—

KM# 105 MARAVEDI

Copper **Ruler:** Philip IV **Obv:** Castle in quatrolobe **Rev:** Lion rampant left in quatrolobe **Mint:** Segovia

Date	Mintage	VG	F	VF	XF	Unc
1631	—	110	225	425	800	—

KM# 154.2 2 MARAVEDIS

Copper **Ruler:** Philip IV **Obv:** Bust of Philip IV right **Rev:** Crowned shield of Leon **Mint:** Seville

Date	Mintage	VG	F	VF	XF	Unc
1661 R	—	60.00	115	240	450	—
1662 R	—	60.00	115	240	450	—
1663 R	—	60.00	115	240	450	—
1664 R	—	60.00	115	240	450	—

KM# 154.3 2 MARAVEDIS

Copper **Ruler:** Philip IV **Obv:** Bust of Philip IV right **Rev:** Crowned shield of Leon **Mint:** Trujillo

Date	Mintage	VG	F	VF	XF	Unc
1661 M	—	55.00	100	195	350	—
1662 M	—	55.00	100	195	350	—
1663 M	—	47.25	90.00	175	325	—
1664 M	—	55.00	100	195	350	—

KM# 155.1 2 MARAVEDIS

Copper **Ruler:** Philip IV **Obv:** Bust of Philip IV right in inner circle **Rev:** Crowned shield of Leon **Mint:** Toledo

Date	Mintage	VG	F	VF	XF	Unc
1661 M	—	60.00	100	195	350	—
1662 M	—	60.00	100	195	350	—
1663 M	—	60.00	100	195	350	—
1664 M	—	60.00	100	195	350	—

KM# 154.1 2 MARAVEDIS

Copper **Ruler:** Philip IV **Obv:** Bust right of Philip IV **Rev:** Crowned shield of Leon **Mint:** Segovia **Note:** Mint mark: Aqueduct.

Date	Mintage	VG	F	VF	XF	Unc
1661 S	—	95.00	190	375	675	—
1662 S	—	95.00	190	375	675	—
1663 BR	—	70.00	135	270	475	—
1664 BR	—	95.00	190	375	675	—

KM# 155.2 2 MARAVEDIS

Copper **Ruler:** Philip IV **Obv:** Bust of Philip IV right in inner circle **Rev:** Crowned shield of Leon **Mint:** Valladolid

Date	Mintage	VG	F	VF	XF	Unc
1662 M	—	47.25	90.00	175	325	—
1663 M	—	55.00	110	220	400	—
1664 M	—	47.25	90.00	175	325	—

KM# 169.1 2 MARAVEDIS

Copper **Ruler:** Philip IV **Obv:** Bust of Philip IV right in circle **Rev:** Crowned shield of Leon **Mint:** Burgos

Date	Mintage	VG	F	VF	XF	Unc
1662 R	—	47.25	90.00	175	325	—
1663 R	—	47.25	90.00	175	325	—
1664 R	—	55.00	100	195	350	—

KM# 169.2 2 MARAVEDIS

Copper **Ruler:** Philip IV **Obv:** Bust of Philip IV right in circle **Rev:** Crowned shield of Leon **Mint:** Coruna

Date	Mintage	VG	F	VF	XF	Unc
1662 R	—	47.25	90.00	175	325	—
1661 R	—	47.25	90.00	175	325	—
1663 R	—	47.25	90.00	175	325	—
1664 R	—	47.25	90.00	175	325	—

KM# 169.3 2 MARAVEDIS

Copper **Ruler:** Philip IV **Obv:** Bust of Philip IV right in circle **Rev:** Crowned shield of Leon **Mint:** Cuenca

Date	Mintage	VG	F	VF	XF	Unc
1662	—	47.25	90.00	175	325	—
1663	—	47.25	90.00	175	325	—
1664	—	47.25	90.00	175	325	—

KM# 169.4 2 MARAVEDIS

Copper **Ruler:** Philip IV **Obv:** Bust of Philip IV right in circle **Rev:** Crowned shield of Leon **Mint:** Granada

Date	Mintage	VG	F	VF	XF	Unc
1662 M	—	70.00	135	255	450	—
1661 M	—	70.00	135	255	450	—
1663 M	—	47.25	90.00	175	325	—

KM# 174 2 MARAVEDIS

Copper **Ruler:** Philip IV **Obv:** Bust of Philip IV right **Rev:** Crowned shield of Leon **Mint:** Granada

Date	Mintage	VG	F	VF	XF	Unc
1663 M	—	47.25	90.00	175	325	—

KM# 175 2 MARAVEDIS

Copper **Ruler:** Philip IV **Obv:** Small head of Philip IV right **Rev:** Crowned shield of Castile **Mint:** Madrid

Date	Mintage	VG	F	VF	XF	Unc
1663 S	—	40.50	80.00	160	290	—
1663 Y	—	40.50	80.00	160	290	—
1664 S	—	40.50	80.00	160	290	—
1664 Y	—	40.50	80.00	160	290	—

KM# 72.7 4 MARAVEDIS

Copper **Ruler:** Philip IV **Obv:** Castle with IIII at right, mint mark at left **Rev:** Rampant lion left **Mint:** Segovia **Note:** Milled coinage.

Date	Mintage	VG	F	VF	XF	Unc
1622	—	12.00	25.00	40.50	70.00	—
1625	—	33.75	60.00	115	265	—
1626	—	16.00	33.75	60.00	105	—

KM# 151 4 MARAVEDIS

Copper **Ruler:** Philip IV **Obv:** Bust of Philip IV right **Rev:** Crowned shield of Castile **Mint:** Segovia

Date	Mintage	VG	F	VF	XF	Unc
1660 S	—	16.00	33.75	60.00	105	—
1661 S	—	14.00	27.50	50.00	95.00	—

Date	Mintage	VG	F	VF	XF	Unc
1662 S	—	25.00	47.25	80.00	145	—
1663 S	—	25.00	47.25	80.00	145	—
1663 BR	—	16.00	33.75	60.00	105	—
1664 BR	—	20.00	40.50	65.00	110	—

KM# 159 4 MARAVEDIS

Copper **Ruler:** Philip IV **Obv:** Head of Philip IV right **Rev:** Castle **Mint:** Toledo

Date	Mintage	VG	F	VF	XF	Unc
1661 M	—	33.75	60.00	115	265	—
1662 M	—	33.75	60.00	115	265	—
1663 M	—	33.75	60.00	115	265	—
1664 M	—	33.75	60.00	115	265	—

KM# 160 4 MARAVEDIS

Copper **Ruler:** Philip IV **Obv:** Tall bust of Philip IV right **Rev:** Castle, value below **Mint:** Toledo

Date	Mintage	VG	F	VF	XF	Unc
1661 M	—	19.00	37.75	65.00	120	—
1662 M	—	19.00	37.75	65.00	120	—
1663 M	—	19.00	37.75	65.00	120	—
1664 M	—	19.00	37.75	65.00	120	—

KM# 156.1 4 MARAVEDIS

Copper **Ruler:** Philip IV **Obv:** Bust of Philip IV right in inner circle, legend around **Rev:** Crowned shield of Castile

Date	Mintage	VG	F	VF	XF	Unc
1661B R	—	14.00	27.50	60.00	95.00	—
1662B R	—	14.00	27.50	60.00	95.00	—
1663B R	—	16.00	33.75	65.00	105	—
1963B R (error)	—	20.00	40.50	75.00	130	—
1664B R	—	16.00	33.75	65.00	105	—

KM# 156.3 4 MARAVEDIS

Copper **Ruler:** Philip IV **Obv:** Bust of Philip IV right in inner circle, legend around **Rev:** Crowned shield of Castile **Mint:** Cuenca

Date	Mintage	VG	F	VF	XF	Unc
1662	—	20.00	40.50	75.00	135	—
1663	—	16.00	33.75	60.00	105	—
1664	—	16.00	33.75	60.00	105	—

KM# 156.4 4 MARAVEDIS

Copper **Ruler:** Philip IV **Obv:** Bust of Philip IV right in inner circle, legend around **Rev:** Crowned shield of Castile **Mint:** Madrid

Date	Mintage	VG	F	VF	XF	Unc
1663 S	—	19.00	37.75	65.00	120	—
1663 Y	—	19.00	37.75	65.00	120	—
1664 S	—	16.00	33.75	60.00	105	—
1664 Y	—	16.00	33.75	60.00	105	—

KM# 156.5 4 MARAVEDIS

Copper **Ruler:** Philip IV **Obv:** Bust of Philip IV right in inner circle, legend around **Rev:** Crowned shield of Castile **Mint:** Seville

Date	Mintage	VG	F	VF	XF	Unc
1661 R	—	20.00	40.50	75.00	130	—
1662 R	—	27.50	50.00	85.00	160	—
1663 R	—	20.00	40.50	75.00	130	—
1664 R	—	27.50	50.00	85.00	160	—

KM# 156.6 4 MARAVEDIS

Copper **Ruler:** Philip IV **Obv:** Bust of Philip IV right in inner circle, legend around **Rev:** Crowned shield of Castile **Mint:** Valladolid

Date	Mintage	VG	F	VF	XF	Unc
1661 M	—	30.00	55.00	95.00	175	—
1662 M	—	30.00	55.00	95.00	175	—
1663 M	—	30.00	55.00	95.00	175	—
1664 M	—	30.00	55.00	95.00	175	—

KM# 156.2 4 MARAVEDIS

Copper **Ruler:** Philip IV **Obv:** Bust of Philip IV right in inner circle, legend around **Rev:** Crowned shield of Castile **Note:** Mint mark: Crown.

Date	Mintage	VG	F	VF	XF	Unc
1661 R	—	19.00	37.75	65.00	110	—
1662 R	—	16.00	33.75	60.00	105	—
1663 R	—	16.00	33.75	60.00	105	—
1664 R	—	19.00	37.75	65.00	110	—

KM# 158 4 MARAVEDIS

Copper **Ruler:** Philip IV **Obv:** Bust of Philip IV right in inner circle **Rev:** IIII below castle in inner circle **Mint:** Granada

Date	Mintage	VG	F	VF	XF	Unc
1661 N	—	16.00	33.75	65.00	110	—
1662 N	—	16.00	33.75	60.00	105	—
1663 N	—	20.00	40.50	75.00	120	—
1664 N	—	25.00	47.25	80.00	145	—

KM# 157 4 MARAVEDIS

Copper **Ruler:** Philip IV **Obv:** Bust of PHilip IV right **Rev:** IIII below castle **Mint:** Cuenca

Date	Mintage	VG	F	VF	XF	Unc
1661	—	55.00	105	175	325	—

KM# 170 4 MARAVEDIS

Copper **Ruler:** Philip IV **Obv:** Tall bust of Philip IV right in circle **Rev:** Crowned shield of Castile **Mint:** Trujillo

Date	Mintage	VG	F	VF	XF	Unc
1662 M	—	14.00	27.50	50.00	90.00	—
1664 M	—	40.50	80.00	145	295	—

KM# 176 4 MARAVEDIS

Copper **Ruler:** Philip IV **Obv:** Tall bust of Philip IV right **Rev:** Crowned shield of Castile **Mint:** Trujillo

Date	Mintage	VG	F	VF	XF	Unc
1663 M	—	14.00	27.50	50.00	90.00	—

KM# 16 8 MARAVEDIS

Copper **Ruler:** Philip III **Obv:** Crowned shield of Castile **Rev:** Crowned shield of Leon **Mint:** Segovia **Note:** Milled coinage; Mint mark varieties of 3 or 4 arches in aqueduct exist. Mint mark: Aqueduct.

Date	Mintage	VG	F	VF	XF	Unc
1600	—	15.00	32.00	55.00	95.00	—
1601	—	15.00	30.00	50.00	90.00	—
1602	—	15.00	30.00	50.00	90.00	—
1603	—	17.00	36.25	60.00	95.00	—
1604	—	13.00	25.00	46.50	80.00	—
1605	—	13.00	25.00	46.50	80.00	—
1606	—	13.00	25.00	46.50	80.00	—
1607	—	13.00	25.00	46.50	80.00	—
1608	—	13.00	25.00	46.50	80.00	—
1609	—	17.00	36.25	60.00	95.00	—
1610	—	22.50	43.50	75.00	130	—
1611	—	25.00	50.00	80.00	145	—
1612	—	13.00	25.00	46.50	80.00	—
1613	—	15.00	32.00	50.00	90.00	—
1614	—	15.00	32.00	50.00	90.00	—
1615	—	13.00	25.00	46.50	80.00	—
1616	—	13.00	25.00	46.50	80.00	—
1617	—	13.00	25.00	46.50	80.00	—
1618/7	—	15.00	32.00	50.00	90.00	—
1618	—	13.00	25.00	46.50	80.00	—
1619	—	13.00	25.00	46.50	80.00	—
1620	—	17.00	36.25	60.00	95.00	—

KM# 163 8 MARAVEDIS

Copper **Ruler:** Philip IV **Obv:** Bust of Philip IV right within legend **Rev:** Crowned shield of Castile and Leon **Mint:** Seville **Note:** Milled.

Date	Mintage	VG	F	VF	XF	Unc
1661 R	—	14.00	27.50	46.50	80.00	—
1662 R	—	14.00	27.50	46.50	80.00	—
1663 R	—	14.00	27.50	46.50	90.00	—
1664 R	—	14.00	27.50	46.50	90.00	—

KM# 171.1 8 MARAVEDIS

Copper **Ruler:** Philip IV **Obv:** Bust of Philip IV right within circle **Rev:** Crowned shield of Spain, 8 at right **Mint:** Burgos

Date	Mintage	VG	F	VF	XF	Unc
1662B R	—	14.00	27.50	46.50	80.00	—
1663B R	—	14.00	27.50	46.50	90.00	—
1664B R	—	14.00	27.50	46.50	90.00	—

KM# 171.3 8 MARAVEDIS

Copper **Ruler:** Philip IV **Obv:** Bust of Philip IV right within circle **Rev:** Crowned shield of Spain, 8 at right

Date	Mintage	VG	F	VF	XF	Unc
1661 N	—	11.00	22.50	40.50	65.00	—
1662 N	—	11.00	22.50	40.50	65.00	—
1663 N	—	11.00	22.50	40.50	65.00	—
1664 N	—	14.00	27.50	46.50	80.00	—

KM# 165 8 MARAVEDIS

Copper **Ruler:** Philip IV **Obv:** Small bust of Philip IV right within circle **Rev:** Crowned shield of Castile and Leon **Mint:** Cuenca **Note:** Milled coinage.

Date	Mintage	VG	F	VF	XF	Unc
1661 R	—	12.00	25.00	43.50	70.00	—
1662 R	—	11.00	22.50	40.50	65.00	—
1663 R	—	11.00	22.50	40.50	65.00	—
1664 R	—	11.00	22.50	40.50	65.00	—

KM# 164.3 8 MARAVEDIS

Copper **Ruler:** Philip IV **Obv:** Bust of Philip IV right within legend **Rev:** Crowned shield of Castile and Leon **Mint:** Valladolid **Note:** Milled.

Date	Mintage	VG	F	VF	XF	Unc
1662 M	—	20.00	40.50	75.00	130	—
1663 M	—	16.00	33.75	60.00	95.00	—
1664 M	—	16.00	33.75	60.00	95.00	—

KM# 162 8 MARAVEDIS

Copper **Ruler:** Philip IV **Obv:** Bust of Philip IV right within legend **Rev:** Crowned shield of Castile and Leon **Mint:** Segovia **Note:** Value as 8.

Date	Mintage	VG	F	VF	XF	Unc
1661M S	—	11.00	22.50	40.50	65.00	—
Note: A variety of 1661 exists with lions and castles switched in the reverse						
1662M S	—	14.00	30.00	50.00	90.00	—
1663M S	—	12.00	25.00	43.50	70.00	—
1663M BR	—	12.00	25.00	43.50	70.00	—
1664M S	—	14.00	30.00	50.00	90.00	—
1664M BR	—	14.00	30.00	50.00	90.00	—

KM# 171.5 8 MARAVEDIS

Copper **Ruler:** Philip IV **Obv:** Bust of Philip IV right within circle **Rev:** Crowned shield of Spain, VIII at right **Mint:** Madrid **Note:** Value as VIII.

Date	Mintage	VG	F	VF	XF	Unc
1660MD A	—	14.00	27.50	46.50	80.00	—
1661MD	—	14.00	27.50	50.00	90.00	—
1661MD Y	—	14.00	27.50	46.50	80.00	—
1662MD A	—	16.00	33.75	60.00	95.00	—
1662MD Y	—	14.00	27.50	46.50	80.00	—
1663MD Y	—	14.00	27.50	50.00	90.00	—
1664MD Y	—	14.00	27.50	46.50	80.00	—

KM# 171.4 8 MARAVEDIS

Copper **Ruler:** Philip IV **Obv:** Bust of Philip IV right within circ **Rev:** Crowned shield of Spain, 8 at right **Mint:** Madrid **Note:** Varieties exist with 8 vertical or horizontal.

Date	Mintage	VG	F	VF	XF	U
1662M S	—	16.00	33.75	60.00	95.00	
1662M Y	—	14.00	27.50	50.00	90.00	
1663M S	—	14.00	27.50	50.00	90.00	
1663M Y	—	14.00	27.50	50.00	90.00	
1664M S	—	14.00	27.50	46.50	80.00	
1664M Y	—	14.00	27.50	46.50	80.00	

KM# 161.2 8 MARAVEDIS

Copper **Ruler:** Philip IV **Obv:** Bust of Philip IV right within circ **Rev:** Crowned shield of Spain, VIII to right **Mint:** Madrid **Note** Milled, large flan.

Date	Mintage	VG	F	VF	XF	U
1664 Y	—	80.00	160	290	475	

KM# 164.1 8 MARAVEDIS

Copper **Ruler:** Philip IV **Obv:** Bust of Philip IV right within leger **Rev:** Crowned shield of Castile and Leon **Mint:** Toledo **Note:** Milled.

Date	Mintage	VG	F	VF	XF	U
1662 M	—	14.00	27.50	46.50	80.00	
1663 M	—	14.00	27.50	46.50	80.00	
1664 M	—	14.00	27.50	46.50	80.00	

KM# 164.2 8 MARAVEDIS

Copper **Ruler:** Philip IV **Obv:** Bust of Philip IV right within leger **Rev:** Crowned shield of Castile and Leon **Mint:** Trujillo **Note:** Milled.

Date	Mintage	VG	F	VF	XF	U
1662 M	—	14.00	30.00	50.00	90.00	
1663 M	—	14.00	30.00	50.00	90.00	
1664 M	—	14.00	30.00	50.00	90.00	

KM# 171.2 8 MARAVEDIS

Copper **Ruler:** Philip IV **Obv:** Bust of Philip IV right within circl **Rev:** Crowned shield of Spain, 8 at right **Mint:** Cuenca

Date	Mintage	VG	F	VF	XF	U
1662	—	14.00	27.50	50.00	90.00	
1663	—	14.00	27.50	50.00	90.00	
1664	—	14.00	27.50	50.00	90.00	

KM# 153.1 16 MARAVEDIS

Copper **Ruler:** Philip IV **Obv:** Large bust of Philip IV right **Re** Crowned shield, 16 at right **Mint:** Madrid

Date	Mintage	VG	F	VF	XF	U
1960MD A (error)	—	12.00	25.00	50.00	110	
1660MD A	—	9.00	20.00	36.25	70.00	
1661MD A	—	9.00	20.00	36.25	70.00	
1661MD Y	—	9.00	20.00	36.25	70.00	

KM# 153.2 16 MARAVEDIS

Copper **Ruler:** Philip IV **Obv:** Large bust of Philip IV right **Re** Crowned shield, 16 at right **Mint:** Trujillo

Date	Mintage	VG	F	VF	XF	U
1661 F	—	80.00	160	290	475	

KM# 172.1 16 MARAVEDIS

Copper **Ruler:** Philip IV **Obv:** Smaller bust of Philip IV right **Re** Crowned arms, 16 at right **Mint:** Burgos

Date	Mintage	VG	F	VF	XF	U
1662B R	—	5.00	11.00	22.50	55.00	
1663B R	—	5.00	11.00	22.50	55.00	
1664B R	—	5.00	11.00	22.50	55.00	

KM# 172.4 16 MARAVEDIS

Copper **Ruler:** Philip IV **Obv:** Smaller bust of Philip IV right **Re** Crowned arms, 16 at right **Mint:** Granada

Date	Mintage	VG	F	VF	XF	U
1661 N	—	12.00	25.00	50.00	105	
1662 N	—	5.00	11.00	22.50	55.00	
1663 N	—	5.00	11.00	22.50	55.00	
Note: Coin dated 1663 also exists with N inverted						
1664 N	—	5.00	11.00	22.50	55.00	

KM# 172.6 16 MARAVEDIS

Copper **Ruler:** Philip IV **Obv:** Smaller bust of Philip IV right **Re** Crowned arms, 16 at right **Mint:** Segovia

Date	Mintage	VG	F	VF	XF	U
1661 S	—	5.00	11.00	22.50	55.00	
1661 BR	—	7.00	14.00	30.00	65.00	
1662 S	—	5.00	11.00	22.50	55.00	
1662 BR	—	7.00	14.00	30.00	65.00	
1663 S	—	7.00	14.00	30.00	65.00	
1663 BR	—	5.00	11.00	22.50	55.00	
1664 S	—	7.00	14.00	30.00	65.00	
1664 BR	—	5.00	11.00	22.50	55.00	

KM# 172.7 16 MARAVEDIS

Copper **Ruler:** Philip IV **Obv:** Smaller bust of Philip IV right **Re** Crowned arms, 16 at right **Mint:** Seville

Date	Mintage	VG	F	VF	XF	U
1661 R	—	5.00	11.00	22.50	55.00	
1662 R	—	5.00	11.00	22.50	55.00	
1663 R	—	5.00	11.00	22.50	55.00	

Date	Mintage	VG	F	VF	XF	Unc
1664 R	—	7.00	11.00	22.50	55.00	—
1664 R	—	9.00	16.00	36.25	70.00	—
Reversed 4						

KM# 172.8 16 MARAVEDIS

Copper **Ruler:** Philip IV **Obv:** Smaller bust of Philip IV right **Rev:** Crowned arms, 16 at right **Mint:** Toledo

Date	Mintage	VG	F	VF	XF	Unc
1661 M	—	9.00	19.00	40.50	90.00	—
1662 M	—	9.00	19.00	40.50	90.00	—
1663	—	7.00	14.00	30.00	65.00	—
1663 M	—	7.00	14.00	30.00	65.00	—
1664 M	—	7.00	14.00	30.00	65.00	—

KM# 172.10 16 MARAVEDIS

Copper **Ruler:** Philip IV **Obv:** Smaller bust of Philip IV right **Rev:** Crowned arms, 16 at right **Mint:** Valladolid

Date	Mintage	VG	F	VF	XF	Unc
1661 M	—	16.00	33.75	65.00	135	—
1662 M	—	14.00	27.50	60.00	120	—
1663 M	—	20.00	40.50	80.00	160	—
1963 M Error	—	16.00	33.75	65.00	135	—
1664 M	—	14.00	27.50	60.00	120	—

KM# 172.2 16 MARAVEDIS

Copper **Ruler:** Philip IV **Obv:** Smaller bust of Philip IV right **Rev:** Crowned arms, 16 at right **Mint:** Coruna **Note:** Mint mark: Scalloped shell.

Date	Mintage	VG	F	VF	XF	Unc
1661 R	—	7.00	14.00	30.00	70.00	—
1662 R	—	5.00	11.00	22.50	55.00	—
1663 R	—	5.00	11.00	22.50	55.00	—
1664 R	—	5.00	11.00	22.50	55.00	—

KM# 172.3 16 MARAVEDIS

Copper **Ruler:** Philip IV **Obv:** Smaller bust of Philip IV right **Rev:** Crowned arms, 16 at right **Mint:** Cuenca **Note:** Mint mark: Star above chalice.

Date	Mintage	VG	F	VF	XF	Unc
1661	—	8.00	16.00	36.25	80.00	—
1662	—	5.00	11.00	22.50	55.00	—
1663	—	5.00	11.00	22.50	55.00	—
1664	—	5.00	11.00	22.50	55.00	—

KM# 172.5 16 MARAVEDIS

Copper **Ruler:** Philip IV **Obv:** Smaller bust of Philip IV right **Rev:** Crowned arms, 16 at right **Mint:** Madrid **Note:** Varieties exist.

Date	Mintage	VG	F	VF	XF	Unc
1662M S	—	5.00	11.00	22.50	55.00	—
1662M Y	—	7.00	14.00	30.00	65.00	—
1663M S	—	7.00	14.00	30.00	70.00	—
1663M Y	—	7.00	14.00	30.00	65.00	—
1664M S	—	5.00	11.00	22.50	55.00	—
1664M Y	—	5.00	11.00	22.50	55.00	—

KM# 172.9 16 MARAVEDIS

Copper **Ruler:** Philip IV **Obv:** Smaller bust of Philip IV right **Rev:** Crowned arms, 16 at right **Mint:** Trujillo **Note:** Varieties exist.

Date	Mintage	VG	F	VF	XF	Unc
1661 M	—	7.00	14.00	30.00	65.00	—
1662 M	—	8.00	16.00	36.25	80.00	—
1663 M	—	8.00	16.00	36.25	80.00	—
1664 M	—	8.00	16.00	36.25	80.00	—

KM# 23 1/2 REAL (1/2 Croat)

1.7167 g., 0.9306 Silver 0.0514 oz. ASW **Ruler:** Philip III **Obv:** Crowned PHILIPPVS monogram **Rev:** Cross with castles and lions in quarters **Mint:** Segovia

Date	Mintage	VG	F	VF	XF	Unc
1602	—	40.50	70.00	145	325	—
1609 C	—	40.50	70.00	145	325	—
1611 C	—	40.50	70.00	220	475	—
1611 A/C	—	70.00	135	175	400	—
1613 AR	—	55.00	110	240	550	—
1614 AR	—	19.00	37.75	75.00	160	—
1620	—	19.00	37.75	75.00	160	—
1621/0	—	14.00	27.50	60.00	130	—
1621	—	19.00	37.75	75.00	160	—

KM# 46 1/2 REAL (1/2 Croat)

1.7167 g., 0.9306 Silver 0.0514 oz. ASW **Ruler:** Philip III **Obv:** Crowned PHILIPPVS monogram, mintmaster's mark below **Rev:** Cross with castles and lions in quarters **Mint:** Seville **Note:** Hammered.

Date	Mintage	VG	F	VF	XF	Unc
1609 B	—	47.25	90.00	175	325	—
1610 B	—	20.00	40.50	75.00	145	—
1611 B	—	27.50	47.25	85.00	160	—

KM# 88 1/2 REAL (1/2 Croat)

1.7167 g., 0.9306 Silver 0.0514 oz. ASW **Ruler:** Philip IV **Obv:** Crowned PHILIPPVS monogram **Rev:** Cross with castle and lions in angles **Mint:** Segovia **Note:** Milled, mint mark: Aqueduct.

Date	Mintage	VG	F	VF	XF	Unc
1622 A	—	40.50	70.00	130	240	—
1623 A	—	55.00	95.00	180	325	—
1627 A	—	16.00	33.75	65.00	120	—
1627 P	—	14.00	27.50	50.00	90.00	—
1631 R	—	33.75	55.00	110	200	—
1632 R	—	60.00	110	195	350	—
1633 R	—	55.00	95.00	180	325	—
1651 BR	—	16.00	33.75	65.00	120	—
1651 I	—	33.75	55.00	100	190	—
1691 I (Error)	—	55.00	95.00	180	325	—
1652 BR	—	16.00	33.75	65.00	120	—
1652 BB	—	70.00	115	220	400	—
1653 BB	—	27.50	47.25	85.00	160	—
1654 BR	—	90.00	170	325	600	—
1659 BR	—	14.00	27.50	50.00	90.00	—
1663 BR	—	16.00	33.75	65.00	120	—
1664 BR	—	27.50	47.25	85.00	160	—

KM# 87 1/2 REAL (1/2 Croat)

1.7167 g., 0.9306 Silver 0.0514 oz. ASW **Ruler:** Philip IV **Obv:** Crowned PHILIPPVS monogram **Rev:** Cross with castles and lions in angles **Mint:** Seville **Note:** Hammered.

Date	Mintage	VG	F	VF	XF	Unc
1627 D	—	60.00	115	220	475	—
1627 R	—	60.00	115	220	475	—

KM# 89 1/2 REAL (1/2 Croat)

1.7167 g., 0.9306 Silver 0.0514 oz. ASW **Ruler:** Philip IV **Obv:** Crowned PHILIPPVS monogram **Rev:** Cross with castles and lions in angles **Mint:** Segovia **Note:** Milled.

Date	Mintage	VG	F	VF	XF	Unc
1627 P	—	255	475	800	1,550	—

KM# 203 1/2 REAL (1/2 Croat)

1.7167 g., 0.9306 Silver 0.0514 oz. ASW **Ruler:** Charles II **Obv:** Crowned arms **Obv. Legend:** CAROLVS • II • D • G **Rev:** Cross with castles and lions in angles **Mint:** Segovia **Note:** Varieties exist in shape of crown.

Date	Mintage	VG	F	VF	XF	Unc
1685 BR	—	47.25	90.00	180	350	—
1686 BR	—	47.25	90.00	180	350	—

KM# 27 REAL (Croat)

3.4335 g., 0.9306 Silver 0.1027 oz. ASW **Ruler:** Philip III **Obv:** Crowned Spanish shield **Obv. Legend:** PHILIPPVS • III • D • G • **Rev:** Arms of Castile and Leon in octolobe **Mint:** Segovia **Note:** Milled. Mint mark: Aqueduct.

Date	Mintage	VG	F	VF	XF	Unc
1607 C	—	22.50	47.25	85.00	200	—
1608 C	—	27.50	55.00	100	240	—
1612 AR	—	37.75	75.00	145	325	—
1613 AR	—	47.25	90.00	175	400	—
1614 AR	—	37.75	75.00	145	325	—
1617	—	30.00	55.00	115	265	—
1621	—	33.75	60.00	125	280	—

KM# 52.1 REAL (Croat)

3.4335 g., 0.9306 Silver 0.1027 oz. ASW **Ruler:** Philip III **Obv:** Crowned arms **Rev:** Cross with castles and lions in angles in octolobe **Mint:** Granada **Note:** Milled.

Date	Mintage	VG	F	VF	XF	Unc
1611 M	—	27.50	55.00	110	265	—
1612 M	—	27.50	55.00	110	265	—
1614 M	—	120	235	475	950	—

KM# 92 REAL (Croat)

3.4335 g., 0.9306 Silver 0.1027 oz. ASW **Ruler:** Philip IV **Obv:** Crowned arms **Obv. Legend:** PHILIPPVS • IIII • D • G • **Rev:** Cross with castles and lions in angles in octolobe **Mint:** Segovia **Note:** Milled, Mint mark: Aqueduct.

Date	Mintage	VG	F	VF	XF	Unc
1627 A	—	20.00	37.75	65.00	145	—
1627 P	—	16.00	27.50	50.00	110	—
1628 A	—	19.00	37.75	75.00	160	—
1628 A/BR	—	33.75	70.00	130	290	—
1628 P	—	14.00	25.00	46.50	105	—
1629 P	—	14.00	27.50	50.00	110	—
1651 I	—	90.00	170	290	550	—
1652 BR	—	20.00	37.75	65.00	145	—
1653 BR	—	20.00	37.75	75.00	160	—
1659 BR	—	20.00	37.75	65.00	145	—
1660 BR	—	22.50	43.25	85.00	190	—
1660	—	135	270	500	950	—

KM# 183 REAL (Croat)

3.4335 g., 0.9306 Silver 0.1027 oz. ASW **Ruler:** Charles II **Obv:** Crowned arms **Rev:** Cross with castles and arms in octolobe **Rev. Legend:** CARLOS SECVNDO... **Mint:** Segovia

Date	Mintage	VG	F	VF	XF	Unc
1675 BR	—	60.00	110	220	475	—

KM# 193 REAL (Croat)

3.4335 g., 0.9306 Silver 0.1027 oz. ASW **Ruler:** Charles II **Obv:** Crowned shield of Castile and Leon **Obv. Legend:** CAROLVS • II • D • G • **Rev:** Crowned CAROLVS monogram **Mint:** Segovia

Date	Mintage	VG	F	VF	XF	Unc
1681 R	—	95.00	180	325	725	—

KM# 198 REAL (Croat)

3.4335 g., 0.9306 Silver 0.1027 oz. ASW **Ruler:** Charles II **Obv:** Crowned Spanish shield **Obv. Legend:** CAROLVS • II • D • G • **Rev:** Cross with castles and lions in angles in octolobe **Mint:** Segovia

Date	Mintage	VG	F	VF	XF	Unc
1683 BR	—	55.00	100	220	475	—

KM# 202 REAL (Croat)

3.4335 g., 0.9306 Silver 0.1027 oz. ASW **Ruler:** Charles II **Obv:** Shield with arms of Portugal **Obv. Legend:** CAROLVS • II • D • G • **Rev:** Cross with castles and lions in angles in octolobe **Mint:** Segovia

Date	Mintage	VG	F	VF	XF	Unc
1684 BR	—	55.00	100	220	475	—
1685 BR	—	70.00	135	290	650	—

KM# 204.1 REAL (Croat)

3.4335 g., 0.9306 Silver 0.1027 oz. ASW **Ruler:** Charles II **Obv:** Crowned shield of Castile and Leon **Obv. Legend:** CAROLVS • II • D • G • **Rev:** Cross above AM monogram **Mint:** Segovia

Date	Mintage	VG	F	VF	XF	Unc
1686 BR	—	75.00	150	300	600	—
1687 BR	—	180	290	475	1,100	—

KM# 204.2 REAL (Croat)

3.4335 g., 0.9306 Silver 0.1027 oz. ASW **Ruler:** Charles II **Obv:** Crowned arms **Obv. Legend:** CAROLVS • II • D • G • **Rev:** Cross above AM monogram **Mint:** Seville

Date	Mintage	VG	F	VF	XF	Unc
1690 M	—	110	220	400	750	—
1691 M	—	110	220	400	750	—
1692 M	—	110	220	400	750	—
1694 M	—	110	220	400	750	—
1699 M	—	110	220	400	750	—

KM# 240 REAL (Croat)

3.4335 g., 0.9306 Silver 0.1027 oz. ASW **Ruler:** Charles II **Obv:** Crowned shield of Castile and Leon **Obv. Legend:** CAROLVS II **Rev:** Cross above AM monogram **Mint:** Seville **Note:** Milled. Two varieties exist: one uses a dot, the other rossetes in the inner circle legends.

Date	Mintage	VG	F	VF	XF	Unc
1700 M	—	115	225	425	750	—

KM# 241 REAL (Croat)

3.4335 g., 0.9306 Silver 0.1027 oz. ASW **Ruler:** Charles II **Obv:** Crowned shield of Castile and Leon **Rev:** Circle around cross and monogram **Mint:** Seville **Note:** Milled, Cross above AM monogram in inner circle in legends.

Date	Mintage	VG	F	VF	XF	Unc
1700 M	—	115	225	375	675	—

KM# 32 2 REALES

6.8670 g., 0.9306 Silver 0.2054 oz. ASW **Ruler:** Philip III **Obv:** Crowned arms, II at right **Obv. Legend:** PHILIPPVS • III • D • G **Rev:** Cross with castles and lions in angles in octolobe **Mint:** Segovia **Note:** Large regular flan. Mint mark: Aqueduct.

Date	Mintage	VG	F	VF	XF	Unc
1608 C	—	70.00	135	255	450	—
1611 A	—	55.00	100	220	400	—
1614 AR	—	60.00	120	240	450	—
1620 AR	—	70.00	135	255	450	—
1621/08	—	55.00	110	220	400	—
1621/08 A/C	—	55.00	110	220	400	—
1621/09 A/C	—	55.00	110	220	400	—
1621/11	—	55.00	110	220	400	—
1621/14	—	47.25	90.00	180	350	—

KM# 60 2 REALES

6.8670 g., 0.9306 Silver 0.2054 oz. ASW **Ruler:** Philip III **Obv:** Crowned arms, II at right **Rev:** Cross with castles and lions in angles in octolobe **Note:** Small irregular flan. Mint mark: Aqueduct.

Date	Mintage	VG	F	VF	XF	Unc
1614/10 AR	—	265	425	750	1,300	—
1614 S	—	225	400	725	1,250	—

KM# 93.1 2 REALES

6.8670 g., 0.9306 Silver 0.2054 oz. ASW **Ruler:** Philip IV **Obv:** Crowned arms **Rev:** Cross with castles and lions in angles in octolobe **Mint:** Segovia **Note:** Milled.

Date	Mintage	VG	F	VF	XF	Unc
1627	—	55.00	110	195	400	—
1627 P	—	33.75	60.00	125	265	—
1628 P	—	27.50	55.00	110	230	—
1652/20 BR	—	25.00	47.25	85.00	190	—
1652/22 BR	—	25.00	47.25	85.00	190	—
1652/29 BR	—	27.50	47.25	95.00	215	—
1652 BR	—	25.00	43.25	80.00	175	—
1659/28 BR	—	25.00	43.25	80.00	175	—
1659/29 BR	—	27.50	47.25	95.00	215	—
1659 BR	—	27.50	55.00	100	240	—

KM# 184 2 REALES

6.8670 g., 0.9306 Silver 0.2054 oz. ASW **Ruler:** Charles II **Obv:** Crowned arms **Obv. Legend:** CARLOS SECVNDO... **Rev:** Cross with castles and lions in angles in octolobe **Mint:** Segovia

Date	Mintage	VG	F	VF	XF	Unc
1675 BR	—	115	225	400	750	—

KM# 195 2 REALES

6.8670 g., 0.9306 Silver 0.2054 oz. ASW **Ruler:** Charles II **Obv:** Cross with castles and lions in angles in octolobe **Rev:** Crowned CAROLVS monogram **Mint:** Segovia

Date	Mintage	VG	F	VF	XF	Unc
1682 M	—	16.00	27.50	50.00	120	—

KM# 199 2 REALES

6.8670 g., 0.9306 Silver 0.2054 oz. ASW **Ruler:** Charles II **Obv:** Crowned arms **Obv. Legend:** CAROLVS II... **Rev:** Cross with castles and lions in angles in octolobe **Mint:** Segovia **Note:** Varieties exist.

Date	Mintage	VG	F	VF	XF	Unc
1683 BR	—	16.00	27.50	50.00	120	—
1684 BR	—	16.00	27.50	50.00	120	—
1685 BR	—	16.00	27.50	50.00	120	—
1686 BR	—	16.00	27.50	50.00	120	—

Y# 32.2 2 REALES

6.8670 g., 0.9306 Silver 0.2054 oz. ASW **Ruler:** Charles II **Obv:** Crowned shield of Castile-Leon between mint mark and assayer mark **Rev:** Cross above MARIA monogram, 2-R flanking **Mint:** Seville

Date	Mintage	VG	F	VF	XF	Unc
1686S M	—	125	300	750	—	—
1694S M	—	125	300	750	—	—

Note: Value as R-2.

KM# 208 2 REALES

6.8670 g., 0.9306 Silver 0.2054 oz. ASW **Ruler:** Charles II **Obv:** Crowned arms of Castile and Leon **Rev:** Cross above AM monogram **Mint:** Segovia

Date	Mintage	VG	F	VF	XF	Unc
1687 BR	—	135	270	475	925	—

Y# 32.1 2 REALES

6.8670 g., 0.9306 Silver 0.2054 oz. ASW **Ruler:** Charles II **Obv:** Crowned shield of Castile-Leon, mint mark to left over dotted cross **Rev:** Cross above MARIA monogram, between value and assayer mark **Mint:** Madrid

Date	Mintage	VG	F	VF	XF	Unc
1691MD BR	—	190	425	1,200	—	—
1694MD M	—	190	425	1,200	—	—
1699MD BR	—	190	425	1,200	—	—

KM# 242 2 REALES

6.8670 g., 0.9306 Silver 0.2054 oz. ASW **Ruler:** Charles II **Obv:** Crowned arms of Castile and Leon **Rev:** Cross above AM monogram **Mint:** Madrid **Note:** Small flan. Varieties exist with and without pellets in circle on reverse.

Date	Mintage	VG	F	VF	XF	Unc
1700S M	—	180	300	625	1,100	—

KM# 62 4 REALES

13.7341 g., 0.9306 Silver 0.4109 oz. ASW **Ruler:** Philip III **Obv:** Crowned arms, IIII vertical at right **Obv. Legend:** PHILIPPVS • III • D • G **Rev:** Cross with castles **Mint:** Segovia **Note:** Milled. Mint mark: Aqueduct.

Date	Mintage	VG	F	VF	XF	Unc
1614 AR	—	425	750	1,600	3,300	—
1616	—	240	400	725	1,650	—
1617	—	290	475	875	1,900	—
1620	—	240	400	750	1,800	—
1621	—	290	475	875	1,900	—

KM# 98 4 REALES

13.7341 g., 0.9306 Silver 0.4109 oz. ASW **Ruler:** Philip IV **Obv:** Crowned arms **Obv. Legend:** PHILIPPVS • IIII • D • G **Rev:** Cross with castles and lions in fields **Mint:** Segovia **Note:** Milled. Mint mark: Aqueduct.

Date	Mintage	VG	F	VF	XF	Unc
1621 A	—	220	375	650	1,300	—
1625 P	—	145	290	500	950	—
1628 P	—	110	195	375	650	—
1630 P	—	110	195	375	700	—
1632 R	—	145	290	500	950	—
1633 R	—	145	290	500	950	—
1635 R	—	145	255	475	900	—
1635 R/1625 P	—	180	375	650	1,250	—
1636 R	—	145	255	475	900	—
1651 I	—	145	325	625	1,100	—
1659 BR	—	145	290	500	950	—
1660 BR	—	145	290	500	1,000	—

KM# 200 4 REALES

13.7341 g., 0.9306 Silver 0.4109 oz. ASW **Ruler:** Charles II **Obv:** Crowned Spanish shield **Rev:** Arms of Castile and Leon in octolobe **Mint:** Segovia **Note:** Mint mark varieties of 3 or 4 arches exist. Mint mark: Aqueduct.

Date	Mintage	VG	F	VF	XF	Unc
1683 BR	—	205	350	650	1,200	—
1684 BR	—	135	235	550	1,050	—
1684/3 BR	—	135	270	575	1,100	—
1684/63 BR	—	270	475	950	1,850	—
1685 BR	—	160	270	625	1,100	—
1685/4 BR	—	180	375	725	1,300	—

KM# 209 4 REALES

13.7341 g., 0.9306 Silver 0.4109 oz. ASW **Ruler:** Charles II **Obv:** Crowned shield of Castile and Leon **Rev:** Cross above AM monogram **Mint:** Segovia **Note:** Mint mark: Aqueduct.

Date	Mintage	VG	F	VF	XF	Unc
1687 BR	—	270	500	975	2,000	—
1691 BR	—	550	1,000	1,950	3,600	—
1699 BR	—	350	600	1,200	2,650	—

KM# 230 4 REALES

13.7341 g., 0.9306 Silver 0.4109 oz. ASW **Ruler:** Charles II **Obv:** Crowned shield of Castile and Leon **Rev:** Cross above AM monogram **Mint:** Seville **Note:** Milled.

Date	Mintage	VG	F	VF	XF	Unc
1699 M	—	700	1,250	2,400	4,400	—

KM# 243 4 REALES

13.7341 g., 0.9306 Silver 0.4109 oz. ASW **Ruler:** Charles II **Obv:** Crowned shield of Castile and Leon **Rev:** Cross above AM monogram in pellet border **Mint:** Seville **Note:** Milled.

Date	Mintage	VG	F	VF	XF	Unc
1700 M	—	675	1,200	2,250	4,250	—

KM# 28.1 8 REALES

27.4682 g., 0.9306 Silver 0.8218 oz. ASW **Ruler:** Philip III **Obv:** Crowned Spanish shield, narrow crown **Obv. Legend:** PHILIPPVS • III • D • G **Rev:** Arms of Castile and Leon, letter J used for 1 in date **Mint:** Segovia **Note:** Dav. #4394. Mint mark: Aqueduct.

Date	Mintage	VG	F	VF	XF	Unc
1607 C	—	575	1,100	1,600	2,700	—
1608 C	—	575	1,200	1,700	2,900	—
1610 C	—	725	1,450	2,000	3,400	—

KM# 28.3 8 REALES

27.4682 g., 0.9306 Silver 0.8218 oz. ASW **Ruler:** Philip III **Obv:** Crowned Spanish shield, wide crown **Obv. Legend:** PHILIPPVS • III • D • G **Rev:** Arms of Castile and leon, Roman numeral Is in date **Mint:** Segovia **Note:** Mint mark: Aqueduct.

Date	Mintage	VG	F	VF	XF	Unc
1610 C	—	650	1,300	1,800	3,000	—
1611/09 C	—	575	1,150	1,700	2,700	—
1611 C	—	500	1,100	1,500	2,400	—
1613 AR	—	575	1,250	1,700	2,800	—
1614/07 AR/C	—	475	1,000	1,450	2,400	—
1614 AR	—	375	750	1,000	1,750	—
1617 A+ Punctuated date	—	400	800	1,100	1,800	—
1617 A+	—	325	575	900	1,500	—
1618 A+	—	290	500	725	1,200	—
1620 A+ V in HISPANIARVM inverted A	—	290	500	725	1,200	—
1620 A+ V in PHILIPAVS inverted A	—	290	500	725	1,200	—
1620 A+ Inverted A on obverse and reverse	—	325	575	900	1,500	—
1620 A+	—	290	500	725	1,200	—
1621 A+	—	2,200	3,650	4,800	7,800	—

M# 76 8 REALES

.4682 g., 0.9306 Silver 0.8218 oz. ASW **Ruler:** Philip IV **Obv:** rowned Spanish shield, mint mark vertical **Obv. Legend:** HILIPPVS • IIII • D • G • **Rev:** Arms of Castile and Leon **Rev. egend:** HISPANIARVM • REX • **Mint:** Segovia **Note:** Dav. 408. Mint mark: Aqueduct.

ite	Mintage	VG	F	VF	XF	Unc
21 A	—	1,100	2,250	3,350	5,100	—
30 P	—	280	500	850	1,600	—
51 I	—	280	550	950	1,850	—
59 BR	—	280	525	900	1,750	—
60 BR	—	350	700	1,100	2,100	—

M# 111 8 REALES

.4682 g., 0.9306 Silver 0.8218 oz. ASW **Ruler:** Philip IV **Obv:** rowned Spanish shield, 2-tier, 4-arch aqueduct, denomination 8 **Obv. Legend:** PHILIPPVS • IIII • D • G • **Rev:** Arms of Castile d Leon **Rev. Legend:** HISPANIARVM • REX • **Mint:** Segovia **ote:** Dav. #4409. Mint mark: Aqueduct.

ite	Mintage	VG	F	VF	XF	Unc
32 R	—	280	525	900	1,500	—
33 R	—	325	600	1,000	1,450	—
35 R HILIPXXS	—	625	1,250	1,800	3,000	—
35 R ISPANIARAM	—	350	625	1,100	1,800	—
35 R ISPANIARVM	—	280	500	800	1,400	—
36/5 R	—	280	550	925	1,600	—
51 I	—	280	525	900	1,500	—
52 BR	—	350	700	1,200	2,100	—
59/32 BR	—	280	525	900	1,500	—
59/35 BR	—	280	550	950	1,700	—
59/56 BR	—	350	625	1,100	1,800	—
59 BR rosses eparate legend	—	425	850	1,450	2,400	—
59 BR	—	350	625	1,100	1,800	—
59 I	—	625	1,250	1,800	3,000	—
60 BR rosses eparate legend	—	280	500	850	1,450	—
60 BR rosses flank 8	—	280	525	900	1,500	—

M# 210.2 8 REALES

.4682 g., 0.9306 Silver 0.8218 oz. ASW **Ruler:** Charles II **ov:** Crowned shield of Castile and Leon in collar of The Golden eece **Obv. Legend:** PHILIPPVS • IIII • D • G • **Rev:** Cross above A monogram **Rev. Legend:** HISPANIARVM • REX • **Mint:** ledo **Note:** Dav. #4419. Mint mark: Aqueduct.

te	Mintage	VG	F	VF	XF	Unc
87 BR	—	350	675	1,000	1,800	—
Note: Several varieties of 1687 exist						
91 BR	—	775	1,600	2,400	4,200	—

KM# 227 8 REALES

27.4682 g., 0.9306 Silver 0.8218 oz. ASW **Ruler:** Charles II **Obv:** Crowned Spanish shield, Portugal shield removed **Obv. Legend:** PHILIPPVS • IIII • D • G • **Rev:** Arms of Castile and Leon **Rev. Legend:** HISPANIARVM • REX • **Mint:** Segovia **Note:** Dav. #4416. Mint mark: Aqueduct.

Date	Mintage	VG	F	VF	XF	Unc
1697/82 F/M	—	450	875	1,200	2,400	—
1697 F 4 lines in first quarter of arms of Sicily	—	850	1,400	2,100	3,600	—
1697 F	—	450	875	1,200	2,400	—

KM# 37 50 REALES

170.0000 g., 0.9306 Silver 5.0861 oz. ASW **Ruler:** Philip III **Obv:** Crowned Spanish shield in inner circle **Rev:** Arms of Castile and Leon **Mint:** Segovia **Note:** Dav. #LS566. Mint mark: Aqueduct.

Date	Mintage	VG	F	VF	XF	Unc
1609 C Rare. 2 known	—	—	—	—	—	—
1610 C Rare. 3 known	—	—	—	—	—	—
1613 AR Rare. 2 known	—	—	—	—	—	—
1614 AR Rare. 3 known	—	—	—	—	—	—

KM# 65 50 REALES

170.0000 g., 0.9306 Silver 5.0861 oz. ASW **Ruler:** Philip III **Obv:** Crowned Spanish shield overlaps inner circle **Rev:** Arms of Castile and Leon **Mint:** Segovia **Note:** Dav. #LS566. Mint mark: Aqueduct. Illustration reduced.

Date	Mintage	VG	F	VF	XF	Unc
1617 A+ Rare	—	—	—	—	—	—
1618/7 A+ Rare	—	—	—	—	—	—
1620 A+ Rare	—	—	—	—	—	—

KM# 81.1 50 REALES

170.0000 g., 0.9306 Silver 5.0861 oz. ASW **Ruler:** Philip IV **Obv:** Crowned Spanish shield overlaps inner circle **Obv. Legend:** PHILIPPVS • IIII • D • G • **Rev:** Arms of Castile and Leon **Mint:** Segovia **Note:** Dav. #LS567. Mint mark: Aqueduct.

Date	Mintage	VG	F	VF	XF	Unc
1622 A+ Unique	—	—	—	—	—	—
1623 A+ Rare	—	—	—	—	—	—

KM# 81.2 50 REALES

170.0000 g., 0.9306 Silver 5.0861 oz. ASW **Ruler:** Philip IV **Obv:** Crowned Spanish shield, floral crown, floral stops **Obv. Legend:** PHILIPPVS • IIII • D • G • **Rev:** Arms of Castile and Leon, floral stops in legend **Mint:** Segovia **Note:** Dav. #LS567. Mint mark: Aqueduct.

Date	Mintage	VG	F	VF	XF	Unc
1626 A+ Rare	—	—	—	—	—	—
1628 A+ Rare	—	—	—	—	—	—
Note: UBS Gold & Numismatics Auction 55, 9-02, VF realized approximately $7,945						
1631 A+ Rare	—	—	—	—	—	—

KM# 81.3 50 REALES

170.0000 g., 0.9306 Silver 5.0861 oz. ASW **Ruler:** Philip IV **Obv:** Crowned Spanish shield, 2-tier, 6-arch aqueduct mint mark **Obv. Legend:** PHILIPPVS • IIII • D • G • **Rev:** Arms of Castile and Leon, floral stops in legend **Mint:** Segovia **Note:** Dav. #LS567. Mint mark: Aqueduct.

Date	Mintage	VG	F	VF	XF	Unc
1632 R Rare	—	—	—	—	—	—
1633/32 R Rare	—	—	—	—	—	—

KM# 81.4 50 REALES

170.0000 g., 0.9306 Silver 5.0861 oz. ASW **Ruler:** Philip IV **Obv:** 2-tier, 4-arch aqueduct mint mark **Obv. Legend:** PHILIPPVS • IIII • D • G • **Rev:** Floral stops **Mint:** Segovia **Note:** Dav. #LS567. Mint mark: Aqueduct.

Date	Mintage	VG	F	VF	XF	Unc
1633 R Rare	—	—	—	—	—	—

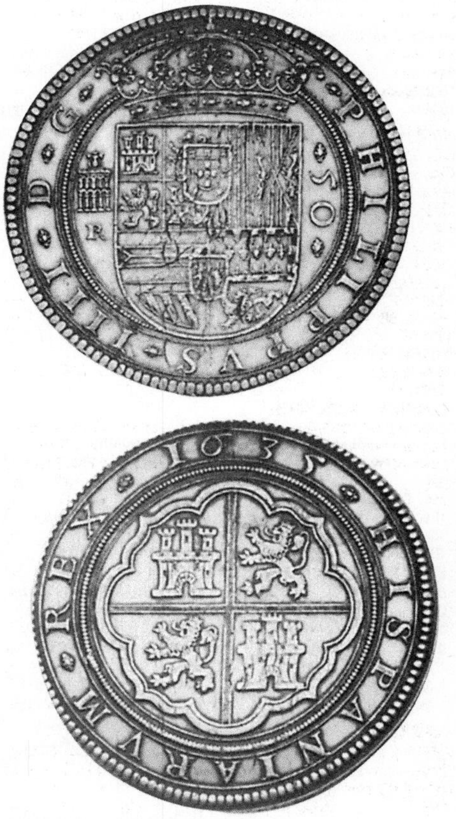

KM# 81.5 50 REALES

170.0000 g., 0.9306 Silver 5.0861 oz. ASW **Ruler:** Philip IV **Obv:** Crowned Spanish shield, 2-tier, 8-arch aqueduct mint mark **Obv. Legend:** PHILIPPVS • IIII • D • G • **Rev:** Arms of Castile and Leon, floral stops in legend **Mint:** Segovia **Note:** Dav. #LS567. Mint mark: Aqueduct. Illustration reduced.

Date	Mintage	VG	F	VF	XF	Unc
1635 R Rare, 12 known	—	—	—	—	—	—
Note: Ira & Larry Goldberg Coins & Collectibles Auction 46 - The Millennia Collection, 5-08, MS-60 realized $57,500						
1636 R Rare, 6-8 known	—	—	—	—	—	—
Note: Akers J. J. Pittman sale 8-99 VF realized $143,750						
1651 I Rare	—	—	—	—	—	—
1652 BR Rare, 3 known	—	—	—	—	—	—
1659/32 BR	—	—	—	—	—	—
Note: The 1659 BR has been reported as 1659/31, 1659/51 and 1659/36 by various authorities						

KM# 196 50 REALES

170.0000 g., 0.9306 Silver 5.0861 oz. ASW **Ruler:** Charles II **Subject:** Titles of Charles II **Obv:** 2-tier, 8-arch aqueduct mint mark **Obv. Legend:** PHILIPPVS • IIII • D • G • **Rev:** Floral stops **Mint:** Segovia

Date	Mintage	VG	F	VF	XF	Unc
1682 M Rare	—	—	—	—	—	—

KM# 29 ESCUDO
3.4335 g., 0.9167 Gold 0.1012 oz. AGW **Ruler:** Philip III **Obv:** Crowned arms **Rev:** Cross in quatrefoil **Mint:** Segovia **Note:** Mint mark: Aqueduct.

Date	Mintage	VG	F	VF	XF	Unc
1607 C	—	500	900	1,400	2,000	—
1608 C	—	500	900	1,400	2,000	—

KM# 231.1 ESCUDO
3.4335 g., 0.9167 Gold 0.1012 oz. AGW **Ruler:** Charles II **Obv:** Crowned arms **Obv. Legend:** ...GRAC **Rev:** Cross in quatrefoil, date at top **Mint:** Seville **Note:** Mint mark: S, S/L.

Date	Mintage	VG	F	VF	XF	Unc
1699 M	—	650	1,400	2,200	3,700	—

KM# 231.2 ESCUDO
3.4335 g., 0.9167 Gold 0.1012 oz. AGW **Ruler:** Charles II **Obv:** Crowned arms **Obv. Legend:** ...GRAT **Rev:** Cross in quatrefoil, date at top **Mint:** Seville

Date	Mintage	VG	F	VF	XF	Unc
1699S M	—	600	1,300	2,200	3,700	—

KM# 245 ESCUDO
3.4335 g., 0.9167 Gold 0.1012 oz. AGW **Ruler:** Philip V **Obv:** Crowned arms, pointed bottom **Rev:** Cross is quatrefoil, date at top **Mint:** Seville

Date	Mintage	VG	F	VF	XF	Unc
1700S M	—	550	1,150	2,000	3,300	—

KM# 30 2 ESCUDOS
6.8670 g., 0.9167 Gold 0.2024 oz. AGW **Ruler:** Philip III **Obv:** Crowned arms in inner circle **Rev:** Cross in quatrefoil in inner circle, date at top **Mint:** Segovia **Note:** Mint mark: Aqueduct.

Date	Mintage	VG	F	VF	XF	Unc
1607 C	—	1,750	3,500	6,100	8,800	—
1610 A	—	1,750	3,500	6,100	8,800	—
1610 C	—	1,750	3,500	6,100	8,800	—
1610 CA	—	1,750	3,500	6,100	8,800	—

KM# 135 2 ESCUDOS
6.8670 g., 0.9167 Gold 0.2024 oz. AGW **Ruler:** Philip IV **Obv:** Crowned arms in inner circle **Rev:** Cross in quatrefoil in inner circle, date at top **Mint:** Segovia **Note:** Mint mark: Aqueduct.

Date	Mintage	VG	F	VF	XF	Unc
1651 I	—	1,100	2,700	4,500	6,800	—

KM# 137 2 ESCUDOS
6.8670 g., 0.9167 Gold 0.2024 oz. AGW **Ruler:** Philip IV **Obv:** Crowned arms without inner circle **Rev:** Cross in quatrefoil in inner circle, date at top **Mint:** Segovia **Note:** Mint mark: Aqueduct.

Date	Mintage	VG	F	VF	XF	Unc
1652 BR	—	1,100	2,700	4,500	6,800	—

KM# 201 2 ESCUDOS
6.8670 g., 0.9167 Gold 0.2024 oz. AGW **Ruler:** Charles II **Obv:** Crowned arms without inner circle **Rev:** Cross in quatrefoil, date at top **Mint:** Segovia **Note:** Mint mark: Aqueduct.

Date	Mintage	VG	F	VF	XF	Unc
1683 BR	—	1,250	2,900	4,950	7,700	—

KM# 207 2 ESCUDOS
6.8670 g., 0.9167 Gold 0.2024 oz. AGW **Ruler:** Charles II **Obv:** Crowned arms without inner circle **Rev:** Cross in quatrefoil, date at top **Mint:** Segovia **Note:** Mint mark: Aqueduct.

Date	Mintage	VG	F	VF	XF	Unc
1686 M	—	700	1,400	2,400	3,700	—
1693 B	—	700	1,400	2,400	3,700	—

KM# 108 4 ESCUDOS
13.7341 g., 0.9167 Gold 0.4048 oz. AGW **Ruler:** Philip IV **Obv:** Bust of Philip VI right in inner circle **Rev:** Crowned arms **Mint:** Pamplona

Date	Mintage	VG	F	VF	XF	Unc
NDPA	—	2,650	6,200	9,600	14,000	—

KM# 136 4 ESCUDOS
13.7341 g., 0.9167 Gold 0.4048 oz. AGW **Ruler:** Philip IV **Obv:** Crowned arms **Rev:** Cross in quatrefoil in inner circle, date at top **Mint:** Segovia **Note:** Mint mark: Aqueduct.

Date	Mintage	VG	F	VF	XF	Unc
1651 I Rare	—	—	—	—	—	—
1655 BR Rare	—	—	—	—	—	—

KM# 185.2 4 ESCUDOS
13.7341 g., 0.9167 Gold 0.4048 oz. AGW **Ruler:** Charles II **Obv:** Crowned arms in order collar **Rev:** Cross in quatrefoil in inner collar, date at top **Mint:** Seville **Note:** Mint mark: Aqueduct.

Date	Mintage	VG	F	VF	XF	Unc
1683 BR Rare	—	—	—	—	—	—
1686 BR Rare	—	—	—	—	—	—
1687/6 BR	—	2,800	6,000	9,100	13,000	—
1687 BR	—	2,100	4,550	6,700	9,600	—
1699 M	—	800	1,400	2,450	3,500	—
1700 M Rare	—	—	—	—	—	—

KM# 232.1 4 ESCUDOS
13.7341 g., 0.9167 Gold 0.4048 oz. AGW **Ruler:** Charles II **Obv:** Crowned arms **Obv. Legend:** ...GRAT **Rev:** Cross in quatrefoil in inner collar, date at top **Mint:** Seville

Date	Mintage	VG	F	VF	XF	Unc
1699S M	—	1,200	2,000	3,600	5,800	—
1700S M	—	1,200	2,000	3,600	5,800	—

KM# 232.2 4 ESCUDOS
13.7341 g., 0.9167 Gold 0.4048 oz. AGW **Ruler:** Charles II **Obv:** Crowned arms **Obv. Legend:** ...GRAC **Rev:** Cross in quatrefoil in inner collar, date at top **Mint:** Seville

Date	Mintage	VG	F	VF	XF	Unc
1699S M	—	2,200	3,400	6,000	8,600	—

KM# 49 8 ESCUDOS
27.4682 g., 0.9167 Gold 0.8095 oz. AGW **Ruler:** Philip III **Obv:** Crowned arms in inner circle **Rev:** Cross in quatrefoil in inner circle, date at top **Mint:** Segovia **Note:** Mint mark: Aqueduct.

Date	Mintage	VG	F	VF	XF	Unc
1610 CA Monogram; Rare	—	—	—	—	—	—
1611 C Rare	—	—	—	—	—	—
1614 AR Ligate, Rare	—	—	—	—	—	—
1615 A	—	3,500	7,000	9,600	15,000	—

KM# 95 8 ESCUDOS
27.4682 g., 0.9167 Gold 0.8095 oz. AGW **Ruler:** Philip IV **Obv:** Crowned arms in inner circle, 2 arches in mint mark **Rev:** Cross in quatrefoil in inner circle, date at top **Mint:** Segovia **Note:** Mint mark: Aqueduct.

Date	Mintage	VG	F	VF	XF	Unc
1627 A Rare	—	—	—	—	—	—
1632 R Rare	—	—	—	—	—	—
1633 R Rare	—	—	—	—	—	—
1635 R Rare	—	—	—	—	—	—
1636 R Rare	—	—	—	—	—	—
1637 R Rare	—	—	—	—	—	—
1638 R Rare	—	—	—	—	—	—
1639 R Rare	—	—	—	—	—	—
1651 I Rare	—	—	—	—	—	—
1652 BR Rare	—	—	—	—	—	—

KM# 96 8 ESCUDOS
27.4682 g., 0.9167 Gold 0.8095 oz. AGW **Ruler:** Philip IV **Obv:** Crowned arms in inner circle **Rev:** Cross in quatrefoil **Mint:** Seville

Date	Mintage	VG	F	VF	XF	Unc
1627S R	—	—	—	—	—	—
Note: Reported, not confirmed						
1631S R	—	—	—	—	—	—
Note: Reported, not confirmed						

KM# 138 8 ESCUDOS
27.4682 g., 0.9167 Gold 0.8095 oz. AGW **Ruler:** Philip IV **Obv:** Crowned arms of Navarre in inner circle **Rev:** Cross in ornamental cartouche in inner circle, date in legend **Mint:** Pamplona

Date	Mintage	VG	F	VF	XF	Unc
1652PA AP Rare	—	—	—	—	—	—

KM# 139 8 ESCUDOS
27.4682 g., 0.9167 Gold 0.8095 oz. AGW **Ruler:** Philip IV **Obv** Crowned arms in inner circle, 3 arches in mint mark **Rev:** Cros in quatrefoil in inner circle, date at top **Mint:** Seville **Note:** Min mark: Aqueduct. Varieties exist.

Date	Mintage	VG	F	VF	XF	U
1655 BRx	—	—	—	62,500	—	-

KM# 197 8 ESCUDOS
27.4682 g., 0.9167 Gold 0.8095 oz. AGW **Ruler:** Charles II **Obv** Crowned arms **Rev:** Cross in quatrefoil **Mint:** Segovia **Note:** Mi mark: Aqueduct.

Date	Mintage	VG	F	VF	XF	U
1682 M Rare	—	—	—	—	—	-
1683 BR Rare	—	—	—	—	—	-
1687/3 BR	—	2,250	5,300	8,300	13,500	-
1687 BR	—	2,250	5,300	8,300	13,500	-
1688 BR Rare	—	—	—	—	—	-

KM# 233.1 8 ESCUDOS
27.4682 g., 0.9167 Gold 0.8095 oz. AGW **Ruler:** Charles II **Ob** Crowned arms in order collar **Obv. Legend:** CAROLVS II • DE • GRAT **Rev:** Cross in quatrefoil, date at top **Rev. Legend:** HISPANIARVM • REX **Mint:** Seville

Date	Mintage	VG	F	VF	XF	U
1699S M	—	2,250	4,750	7,000	12,000	-
1699S M DEI.GRAC (error)	—	2,250	4,750	7,000	12,000	-

KM# 233.2 8 ESCUDOS
27.4682 g., 0.9167 Gold 0.8095 oz. AGW **Ruler:** Charles II **Ob** Crowned arms in order collar **Obv. Legend:** ...GRAC **Rev:** Cro in quatrefoil **Mint:** Seville

Date	Mintage	VG	F	VF	XF	U
1699S M	—	2,300	4,900	7,000	12,500	

KM# 233.3 8 ESCUDOS
27.4682 g., 0.9167 Gold 0.8095 oz. AGW **Ruler:** Charles II **Ob** Crowned arms in order collar **Obv. Legend:** CAROLVS II • DE • GRAT **Rev:** Cross in quatrefoil within inner circle **Mint:** Sevi

Date	Mintage	VG	F	VF	XF	U
1700S M	—	2,250	4,750	7,000	12,000	

KM# 38 100 ESCUDOS
0.9167 Gold **Ruler:** Philip III **Obv:** Crowned arms in inner circ **Rev:** Cross in quatrefoil in inner circle, date at top **Mint:** Segov **Note:** Mint mark: Aqueduct.

Date	Mintage	VG	F	VF	XF	U
1609 C Rare	—	—	—	—	—	
1618 AR Rare	—	—	—	—	—	

KM# 84 100 ESCUDOS
.9167 Gold **Ruler:** Philip IV **Obv:** Crowned arms in inner circle, arches in mint mark **Rev:** Cross in quatrefoil in inner circle, date at top **Mint:** Segovia **Note:** Mint mark: Aqueduct.

ate	Mintage	VG	F	VF	XF	Unc
623 AR Unique	—	—	—	—	—	—

KM# 113 100 ESCUDOS
.9167 Gold **Ruler:** Philip IV **Obv:** Crowned arms in inner circle, 0 arches in mint mark **Rev:** Cross in quatrefoil in inner circle, ate at top **Mint:** Segovia **Note:** Mint mark: Aqueduct.

ate	Mintage	VG	F	VF	XF	Unc
633 R Rare	—	—	—	—	—	—

PATTERNS

Including off metal strikes

M#	Date	Mintage	Identification	Mkt Val
n1	1631	—	Maravedi. Copper. Monogram: PH-IL-P-P-V-S. Castle and lion.	—
n3	1631	—	2 Maravedis. Copper. Castle in circle. Lion in circle.	—
n2	1631	—	Maravedi. Copper. Castle in quatrefoil. Lion in quatrefoil.	1,150
n4	1660	—	8 Maravedis. Copper. MD between crowned pillars	—
n5	1660	—	8 Maravedis. Copper. VIII between crowned pillars	—
n6	1660	—	8 Maravedis. Copper. VIII between crowned pillars	—
n7	1663S	—	8 Reales. Silver.	—
n8	1663S	—	8 Reales. Silver.	—
n9	1663S	—	8 Reales. Silver.	—

SPAIN-Local

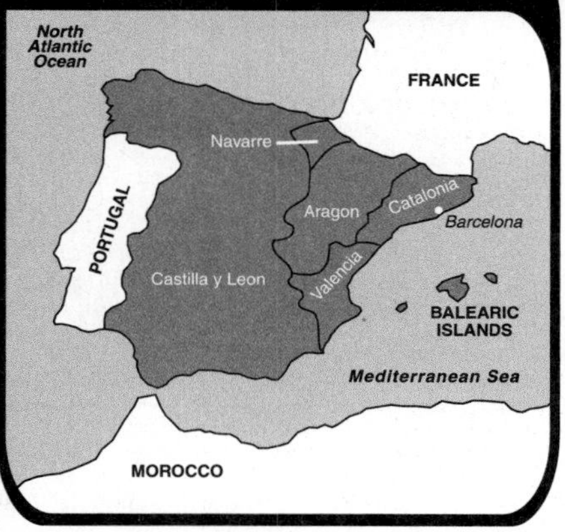

ARAGON

Aragon, bordered by Navarre on the west and Catalonia on he east, was an influential Christian Kingdom in Northern Spain. ven after unification the main city of Zaragoza, name of the mint, etained its prominence in the region.

ULERS
hilip III, 1598-1621
hilip IV, 1621-1665
harles II, 1665-1700
hilip V, 1700-1746

INT MARKS
, CA, Z – Zaragoza

PROVINCE

STANDARD COINAGE

KM# 6 DINERO
opper **Obv:** Large head left **Rev:** Crowned arms of Aragon **lint:** Granollers

ate	Mintage	VG	F	VF	XF	Unc
601	—	17.00	28.00	55.00	110	—
602	—	17.00	28.00	55.00	110	—
616	—	17.00	28.00	55.00	110	—

KM# 25 DINERO
opper **Obv:** Bust of Philip IV right **Rev:** Diamond-shaped shield **lint:** Perpinan

ate	Mintage	VG	F	VF	XF	Unc
632	—	—	—	—	—	—

KM# 50 DINERO
opper **Obv:** Crowned bust of Charles II left **Rev:** Cross in inner ircle, date in legend

ate	Mintage	VG	F	VF	XF	Unc
670CA	—	12.00	20.00	45.00	75.00	—
671CA	—	12.00	20.00	45.00	75.00	—
672CA	—	12.00	20.00	45.00	75.00	—
673CA	—	12.00	20.00	45.00	75.00	—
674CA	—	12.00	20.00	45.00	75.00	—
675CA	—	12.00	20.00	45.00	75.00	—
676CA	—	12.00	20.00	45.00	75.00	—
677CA	—	12.00	20.00	45.00	75.00	—
678CA	—	12.00	20.00	45.00	75.00	—

Date	Mintage	VG	F	VF	XF	Unc
1679CA	—	12.00	20.00	45.00	75.00	—
1680CA	—	12.00	20.00	45.00	75.00	—

KM# 15 3 DINEROS (Ternet)
Copper **Obv:** PP monogram **Rev:** St. John the Baptist with lamb **Mint:** Perpinan

Date	Mintage	VG	F	VF	XF	Unc
1611	—	70.00	140	275	—	—

KM# 55 5 DINEROS (Cinquen)
Copper **Obv:** Crowned bust right **Rev:** Crowned diamond-shaped shield **Mint:** Ibiza

Date	Mintage	VG	F	VF	XF	Unc
1686	—	55.00	90.00	190	—	—

KM# 8 6 DINEROS
Copper **Obv:** Bust right **Rev:** Castle **Mint:** Ibiza **Note:** Legend varieties exist.

Date	Mintage	VG	F	VF	XF	Unc
ND	—	37.50	75.00	150	—	—

KM# 19 1/2 REAL
Silver **Obv:** Crowned shield **Rev:** Tree, cross above, date in legend **Mint:** Zaragoza

Date	Mintage	VG	F	VF	XF	Unc
1612	—	95.00	155	250	375	—

KM# 35 1/2 REAL
Silver **Obv:** Crowned shield **Rev:** Cross above bush

Date	Mintage	VG	F	VF	XF	Unc
1651	—	155	250	475	825	—

KM# 16 REAL
Silver **Obv:** Crowned shield of Aragon **Rev:** Head in each quarter round arms, date in legend **Mint:** Zaragoza

Date	Mintage	VG	F	VF	XF	Unc
1611CA	—	125	190	325	525	—
1612CA	—	125	190	325	525	—
161ZCA	—	100	175	300	500	—

KM# 36 REAL
Silver **Obv:** Crowned shield **Rev:** Zaragoza Arms **Note:** Round flan, with complete legends, struck milled style

Date	Mintage	VG	F	VF	XF	Unc
1651	—	375	675	1,200	—	—

KM# 37 REAL
Silver **Obv:** Crowned Shield **Rev:** Zaragoza arms **Note:** Trimmed flan, legends mostly missing, struck cob style

Date	Mintage	VG	F	VF	XF	Unc
1651	—	150	300	575	—	—

KM# 38 2 REALES
Silver **Obv:** Crowned shield of Aragon in plain field **Rev:** Zaragoza arms in plain field, date in legend **Mint:** Zaragoza

Date	Mintage	VG	F	VF	XF	Unc
1651	—	265	525	1,150	—	—

KM# 39 2 REALES
Silver **Obv:** Dotted inner circle around shield **Rev:** Dotted inner circle around arms

Date	Mintage	VG	F	VF	XF	Unc
1651	—	265	525	1,150	—	—

KM# 40 2 REALES
Silver

Date	Mintage	VG	F	VF	XF	Unc
1651	—	225	425	825	—	—
1652	—	265	450	900	—	—

KM# 45 2 REALES
Silver **Obv:** Crowned shield **Rev:** Zaragoza arms

Date	Mintage	VG	F	VF	XF	Unc
1669 Rare	—	—	—	—	—	—

KM# 17 4 REALES
Silver **Mint:** Zaragoza **Note:** Similar to 8 Reales, KM#18

Date	Mintage	VG	F	VF	XF	Unc
1611	—	—	—	—	—	—

Note: Reported, not confirmed

KM# 41 4 REALES
Silver **Note:** Similar to 8 Reales, KM#42. Exists as a cob or a round coin.

Date	Mintage	VG	F	VF	XF	Unc
1651	—	975	1,900	3,000	—	—

KM# 18.1 8 REALES
Silver **Obv:** Crowned ornamental arms of Aragon, denomination as VIII **Obv. Legend:** PHILIPPVS • II • DEI • G **Rev:** Ornamental quartered arms with crowned heads **Rev. Legend:** ARAGONVM • REX • **Mint:** Zaragoza

Date	Mintage	Good	VG	F	VF	XF
1611CA Rare	—	—	—	—	—	—

KM# 18.2 8 REALES
Silver **Obv:** Crowned ornamental arms of Aragon, denomination as VII, dot in center of arms **Obv. Legend:** PHILIPPVS • II • DEI • G **Rev:** Ornamental quartered arms with crowned heads **Rev. Legend:** ARAGONVM • REX • **Mint:** Zaragoza **Note:** Dav. #4399.

Date	Mintage	Good	VG	F	VF	XF
1611CA Rare	—	—	—	—	—	—

KM# 42 8 REALES
Silver **Obv:** Crowned plain arms, denomination 8 **Obv. Legend:** PHILIPPVS • IV • DEI • G **Rev:** Plain quartered arms **Mint:** Zaragoza

Date	Mintage	Good	VG	F	VF	XF
1651	—	1,250	2,500	5,000	7,500	—
1652	—	1,550	3,150	5,600	8,250	—

BARCELONA

Barcelona was a maritime province located in northeast Spain. The city was the provincial capital of Barcelona. Barcelona is a major port and commercial center.

RULERS
Philip III, 1598-1621
Philip IV, 1621-1665
French Occupation
Louis XIII, 1641-1643
Louis XIV, 1643-1659
Charles II, 1665-1700

MINT MARK
Ba - Barcelona

PROVINCE

HAMMERED COINAGE

KM# 5 1/3 TRENTIN

Gold, 16-17 mm. **Ruler:** Philip III **Obv:** Bust of Philip III right **Obv. Legend:** PHILIPP.D GRAT **Rev:** Crowned shield of Barcelona within inner circle **Rev. Legend:** CIVIT **Mint:** Barcelona **Note:** Size varies.

Date	Mintage	VG	F	VF	XF	Unc
1618B	—	300	600	1,150	2,250	—

KM# A14 1/3 TRENTIN

Gold, 15-16 mm. **Ruler:** Philip IV **Obv:** Bust of Philip IV left **Obv. Legend:** PHILIPP.D GRATIA **Rev:** Crowned shield of Barcelona within inner circle **Rev. Legend:** AR...CIV... **Mint:** Barcelona **Note:** Size varies.

Date	Mintage	VG	F	VF	XF	Unc
16Z3B	—	725	1,450	2,750	4,650	—
16Z5B	—	625	1,150	2,550	4,250	—
16Z5	—	900	1,800	3,800	6,650	—

KM# 15.1 1/2 TRENTIN

3.5000 g., Gold, 24 mm. **Ruler:** Philip IV **Obv:** Facing busts of Ferdinand and Isabella, star between **Obv. Legend:** FERNANDVS ET ISABET DG RGS **Rev:** Crowned arms **Rev. Legend:** SVBVM BRA **Note:** Imitation of Spanish 1 Excelente of 1476-1516.

Date	Mintage	VG	F	VF	XF	Unc
16Z3	—	650	1,300	2,500	4,650	—
16Z5	—	650	1,300	2,500	4,650	—
16Z6	—	650	1,300	2,500	4,650	—

KM# 16.2 1/2 TRENTIN

3.5000 g., Gold, 24 mm. **Ruler:** Philip IV **Obv:** Facing busts of Ferdinand and Isabella, mint mark between **Obv. Legend:** FERNAN DVS ELISABET **Rev:** Crowned arms **Rev. Legend:** SVBVMBRA **Note:** Imitation of Spanish 1 Excelente of 1476-1516.

Date	Mintage	VG	F	VF	XF	Unc
1626B	—	650	1,300	2,500	4,650	—
1627B	—	725	1,450	2,750	5,200	—
1630B	—	650	1,300	2,500	4,650	—
1631B	—	650	1,300	2,500	4,650	—
1632B	—	650	1,300	2,500	4,650	—

KM# 17.1 TRENTIN

7.0000 g., Gold, 29 mm. **Ruler:** Philip IV **Obv:** Facing busts of Ferdinand and Isabella, star above and between **Obv. Legend:** FERNANDVS ET ELISABET REGES **Rev:** Eagle with wings spread behind crowned arms **Rev. Legend:** SVBVMBRA **Note:** Imitation of Spanish 2 Excellentes of 1476-1516.

Date	Mintage	VG	F	VF	XF	Unc
1622	—	475	950	1,850	3,250	—
1625	—	475	950	1,850	3,250	—
1626	—	475	950	1,850	3,250	—
1627	—	675	1,300	2,600	4,250	—
1628	—	475	950	1,850	3,250	—

KM# 17.2 TRENTIN

7.0000 g., Gold, 29 mm. **Ruler:** Philip IV **Obv:** Facing busts of Ferdinand and Isabella, star above, mint mark between **Obv. Legend:** FERNANDVS ET ELISABET REGES **Rev:** Eagle with wings spread behind crowned arms **Rev. Legend:** SVBVMBRA **Note:** Imitation of Spanish 2 Excellentes of 1476-1516.

Date	Mintage	VG	F	VF	XF	Unc
16ZZ	—	550	1,100	2,250	3,750	—
1628	—	550	1,100	2,250	3,750	—
1629	—	550	1,100	2,250	3,750	—
1630	—	600	1,200	2,500	4,150	—
1631	—	550	1,100	2,250	3,750	—
1632	—	550	1,100	2,250	3,750	—
1633	—	550	1,100	2,250	3,750	—

COUNTERMARKED COINAGE

KM# 18 TRENTIN

7.0000 g., Gold, 29 mm. **Countermark:** "B" mint mark between facing busts **Note:** Countermark on Trentin, KM#17.1.

CM Date	Host Date	Good	VG	F	VF	XF
ND(1622-40)	1622B	—	800	1,600	1,650	6,750
ND(1635-40)	1626B	—	625	1,250	2,850	5,850

KM# 19 TRENTIN

7.0000 g., Gold **Ruler:** Philip IV **Countermark:** Barcelona diamond shield between facing busts **Note:** Countermarked on Spanish 2 Excellentes.

CM Date	Host Date	Good	VG	F	VF	XF
ND(1622-40)	ND	—	700	1,500	2,850	—

STANDARD COINAGE

KM# 14 DINERO (Menut)

Silver **Obv:** Bust of Philip III left **Rev:** Cross with dots and annulets in angles **Mint:** Barcelona **Note:** Varieties exist.

Date	Mintage	VG	F	VF	XF	Unc
1615	—	10.00	20.00	39.25	75.00	—
1616	—	18.00	35.00	55.00	105	—
1617	—	10.00	20.00	39.25	75.00	—
1618	—	10.00	20.00	39.25	75.00	—
1619	—	10.00	20.00	39.25	75.00	—
162 Error	—	10.00	20.00	39.25	75.00	—
1621	—	10.00	20.00	39.25	75.00	—

KM# 20 DINERO (Menut)

Silver **Obv:** Bust of Philip IV left **Mint:** Barcelona **Note:** Titles of Philip IV

Date	Mintage	VG	F	VF	XF	Unc
1622	—	18.00	35.00	55.00	105	—
1623	—	20.00	42.00	70.00	140	—
1625	—	8.00	17.00	35.00	70.00	—
1628	—	8.00	17.00	35.00	70.00	—
1629	—	8.00	17.00	35.00	70.00	—
1632	—	8.00	17.00	35.00	70.00	—
1633	—	8.00	17.00	35.00	70.00	—
1634	—	8.00	17.00	35.00	70.00	—
1635	—	8.00	17.00	35.00	70.00	—

KM# 13 ARDITE

Copper **Obv:** Bust of Philip III left between A - R **Rev:** Quartered diamond arms in inner circle **Mint:** Barcelona **Note:** Prev. KM#16.

Date	Mintage	VG	F	VF	XF	Unc
1612 AR	—	18.00	35.00	55.00	105	—
1613 AR	—	8.00	17.00	35.00	70.00	—
1614 AR	—	8.00	17.00	35.00	70.00	—
1615 AR	—	8.00	17.00	35.00	70.00	—
1616 AR	—	8.00	17.00	35.00	70.00	—
1617 AR	—	11.00	20.00	42.00	75.00	—
1618 AR	—	8.00	22.50	44.75	85.00	—
1619 AR	—	14.00	27.50	49.00	100	—
1620 AR	—	14.00	27.50	49.00	100	—
1621 AR	—	27.50	55.00	85.00	170	—

KM# 21 ARDITE

Copper **Obv:** Bust of Philip IV left between A - R

Date	Mintage	VG	F	VF	XF	Unc
1622	—	20.00	42.00	70.00	140	—
1623	—	20.00	42.00	70.00	140	—
1624	—	8.00	17.00	35.00	70.00	—
1625	—	8.00	17.00	35.00	70.00	—
1626	—	8.00	17.00	35.00	70.00	—
1627	—	8.00	17.00	35.00	70.00	—
1628	—	8.00	17.00	35.00	70.00	—
1629	—	8.00	17.00	35.00	70.00	—
1630	—	8.00	17.00	35.00	70.00	—
1631	—	8.00	17.00	35.00	70.00	—
1632	—	8.00	17.00	35.00	70.00	—
1633	—	8.00	17.00	35.00	70.00	—
1634	—	8.00	17.00	35.00	70.00	—
1635	—	8.00	17.00	35.00	70.00	—
1653	—	8.00	17.00	35.00	70.00	—
1654	—	8.00	17.00	35.00	70.00	—
1655	—	8.00	17.00	35.00	70.00	—

KM# 33 SEISENO

Copper **Obv:** Bust of Philip IV left in inner circle **Rev:** Diamond arms in inner circle, date in legend **Mint:** Barcelona

Date	Mintage	VG	F	VF	XF	Unc
1640 SI	—	17.00	35.00	65.00	120	—
1640	—	17.00	35.00	65.00	120	—
1641 SI	—	17.00	35.00	65.00	120	—
1641	—	20.00	42.00	70.00	140	—
1642	—	20.00	42.00	70.00	140	—

KM# 12 1/4 REAL (1/4 Croat)

Silver **Obv:** Bust of Philip III left in inner circle

Date	Mintage	VG	F	VF	XF	Unc
1611	—	—	—	—	—	—

KM# 3 1/2 REAL (1/2 Croat)

Silver **Obv:** Head of Philip III left in inner circle **Rev:** Long cross with dots and annulets in angles, date in legend **Mint:** Barcelona **Note:** Prev. KM#5.

Date	Mintage	VG	F	VF	XF	Unc
1609	—	125	190	350	575	—
1611	—	125	190	350	575	—
1620	—	125	220	375	625	—

KM# 11 1/2 REAL (1/2 Croat)

Silver **Obv:** Bust of Philip III left in inner circle **Note:** Varieties exist.

Date	Mintage	VG	F	VF	XF	Unc
1611	—	17.00	35.00	65.00	105	—
1612	—	17.00	35.00	65.00	105	—
1613	—	27.50	55.00	105	175	—
1614	—	100	195	350	525	—
1615	—	35.00	70.00	140	230	—
1617	—	27.50	55.00	105	175	—
1618	—	20.00	42.00	75.00	140	—
1619	—	20.00	42.00	75.00	140	—

KM# 22 1/2 REAL (1/2 Croat)

Silver **Obv:** Titles of Philip IV

Date	Mintage	VG	F	VF	XF	Unc
1626	—	20.00	42.00	70.00	140	—
ND	—	20.00	42.00	70.00	140	—

KM# 25 1/2 REAL (1/2 Croat)

Silver **Obv:** Bust of Philip III

Date	Mintage	VG	F	VF	XF	Unc
1632	—	20.00	42.00	70.00	140	—

KM# 26 1/2 REAL (1/2 Croat)

Silver **Obv:** Bust of Philip IV left in inner circle **Rev:** Cross with dots and annulets in angles in inner circle, date in legend

Date	Mintage	VG	F	VF	XF	Unc
1632	—	49.00	105	170	280	—
1633	—	49.00	105	170	280	—
1635	—	49.00	105	170	280	—

KM# 4 REAL (Croat)

0.9310 g., Silver **Obv:** Bust of Philip III left in inner circle **Rev:** Long cross with dots and annulets in angles in inner circle, date in legend **Mint:** Barcelona **Note:** Prev. KM#6.

Date	Mintage	VG	F	VF	XF	Unc
1607	—	49.00	105	210	425	—
1609	—	35.00	70.00	120	280	—
1610	—	49.00	105	210	425	—
1611	—	49.00	105	210	425	—

Date	Mintage	VG	F	VF	XF	Unc
1612	—	49.00	105	210	425	—
1613	—	49.00	105	210	425	—
1620	—	35.00	70.00	120	280	—
16NO	—	42.00	85.00	140	325	—
1621	—	49.00	105	210	425	—

KM# 23.2 REAL (Croat)

0.9310 Silver **Obv:** Bust of Philip IV left in inner circle **Obv. Legend:** PHILIPP **Rev. Legend:** BARCINO CIVI, date **Note:** Titles of Philip IV.

Date	Mintage	VG	F	VF	XF	Unc
1626	—	25.00	44.75	75.00	155	—
1630	—	25.00	49.00	85.00	170	—
1631	—	25.00	44.75	75.00	155	—
1632	—	25.00	44.75	75.00	155	—
1633	—	25.00	44.75	75.00	155	—
1636	—	25.00	44.75	75.00	155	—
1637	—	25.00	44.75	75.00	155	—
1637 Date on both sides	—	35.00	70.00	140	280	—
1638	—	25.00	44.75	75.00	155	—
1639	—	25.00	44.75	75.00	155	—
1640	—	25.00	44.75	75.00	155	—
1653	—	27.50	55.00	100	175	—
1654	—	25.00	44.75	75.00	155	—
1655	—	25.00	49.00	85.00	170	—
1658	—	25.00	49.00	85.00	170	—

KM# 23.1 REAL (Croat)

Silver **Obv:** Bust of Philip IV left in inner circle **Obv. Legend:** PHILIPUS

Date	Mintage	VG	F	VF	XF	Unc
1626	—	25.00	49.00	85.00	170	—

KM# 28 REAL (Croat)

0.9310 Silver **Obv:** Bust of Philip IV left **Rev:** Long cross, circle and 3 pellets in angles **Rev. Legend:** BARCINO CIVITAS, date **Note:** Bust of Philip II.

Date	Mintage	VG	F	VF	XF	Unc
1630	—	—	—	—	—	—
1632	—	65.00	120	245	400	—
1633	—	65.00	120	245	400	—
1635	—	35.00	55.00	105	175	—
1636	—	49.00	90.00	175	325	—

KM# 40 REAL (Croat)

Silver **Obv:** Small crude bust of Charles II left in inner circle **Rev:** Long cross with dots and annulets in angles, date in legend **Note:** Varieties exist

Date	Mintage	VG	F	VF	XF	Unc
1667	—	49.00	90.00	175	280	—
1674	—	49.00	90.00	175	280	—
1675	—	25.00	49.00	85.00	155	—
1677	—	25.00	49.00	85.00	155	—
1682	—	25.00	49.00	85.00	155	—
1687	—	55.00	100	190	375	—
1688	—	25.00	49.00	85.00	155	—

KM# 45 REAL (Croat)

0.9310 Silver **Ruler:** Charles II **Obv:** Large crude bust of Charles II to left **Obv. Legend:** CAROL. II. D. G. HIS. REX. **Rev:** Long cross with alternating groups of 3 pellets and single annulets in angles, date at end of legend **Rev. Legend:** BAR - CINO - CIVI -(date) **Mint:** Barcelona

Date	Mintage	VG	F	VF	XF	Unc
1687	—	30.00	55.00	90.00	160	—
1698	—	30.00	55.00	90.00	160	—

KM# 50 REAL (Croat)

0.9310 Silver **Obv:** Finer style bust of Chalres II left **Obv. Legend:** CARLOS II **Rev:** Cross above AM monogram

Date	Mintage	VG	F	VF	XF	Unc
1693	—	20.00	35.00	65.00	125	—
1698	—	27.50	49.00	85.00	155	—

FRENCH OCCUPATION

STANDARD COINAGE

KM# 34 MENUT

Copper **Ruler:** Louis XIV French Occupation **Obv:** Laureate bust right **Obv. Legend:** L9 - D • G **Rev:** Cross, circles and dots in angles **Rev. Legend:** BAR - CINO - CIVI

Date	Mintage	Good	VG	F	VF	XF
1644	—	15.00	30.00	60.00	125	—

KM# 36 MENUT

Copper **Ruler:** Louis XIV French Occupation **Obv:** Laureate bust right **Obv. Legend:** LVD • XIIII • D • G • **Rev:** Cross, circles and dots in angles **Rev. Legend:** BAR - CIN - CIVI

Date	Mintage	Good	VG	F	VF	XF
1645	—	15.00	30.00	60.00	125	—

KM# 35 1/2 SEIZAIN

Copper **Ruler:** Louis XIV French Occupation **Obv:** Bust right divides A-R **Rev:** Diamond Catalonian shield **Rev. Legend:** BARCINO - CIVI

Date	Mintage	Good	VG	F	VF	XF
1644	—	12.00	25.00	50.00	110	—

KM# 37 SEIZAIN

Copper **Ruler:** Louis XIV French Occupation **Obv:** Laureate bust right **Obv. Legend:** LVD • XIII • D • G • R • F • ET • CO • B **Rev:** Diamond Catalonian shield on cross, head of St. Eulalie above, lis below **Rev. Legend:** BARCINO - CIVI

Date	Mintage	Good	VG	F	VF	XF
1645	—	10.00	20.00	40.00	85.00	—
1648	—	10.00	20.00	40.00	85.00	—

KM# 38 SEIZAIN

Copper **Ruler:** Louis XIV French Occupation **Obv:** Laureate bust right with pearl necklace **Obv. Legend:** LVD•XIII•D•G•R•F•ET•CO•B **Rev:** Diamond Catalonian shield on cross, head of St. Eulalie above, lis below **Rev. Legend:** BARCINO - CIVI

Date	Mintage	Good	VG	F	VF	XF
1648	—	12.00	25.00	45.00	95.00	—

SIEGE

KM# 39 10 REALES

Silver **Ruler:** Louis XIV French Occupation **Obv:** Laureate bust right divides value X-R **Obv. Legend:** LVD • XIIII • D • G • R • F • C • B • **Rev:** Short cross with circles and dots in angles **Rev. Legend:** BARCINO CIVIT OBSESSA

Date	Mintage	Good	VG	F	VF	XF
1652	—	225	450	900	1,500	2,500

FRENCH OCCUPATION - VICH

STANDARD COINAGE

KM# 6 1/2 SEIZAIN

Copper **Ruler:** Louis XIV French Occupation **Obv:** Laureate bust right **Obv. Legend:** + LVDOVIC • D • G • R • FRANC **Rev:** Diamond shield **Rev. Legend:** CIVITAS • VICEN •

Date	Mintage	Good	VG	F	VF	XF
1644	—	35.00	70.00	150	275	—

CATALONIA

Catalonia, a triangular territory forming the northeast corner of the Iberian Peninsula, was formerly a province of Spain and also formerly a principality of Aragon. In1833 the region was divided into four provinces, Barcelona, Gerona, Lerida and Tarragona.

RULERS

Philip III of Spain, 1598-1621
Philip IV of Spain, 1621-1665
Louis XIII of France,
As Count of Barcelona, 1641-1643

MINT MARK

C – Catalonia

MONETARY SYSTEM

12 Ardites (Dineros) = 8 Ochavos =
4 Quartos = 1 Sueldo
6 Sueldos = 1 Peseta
5 Pesetas = 1 Duro

FRENCH OCCUPATION

STANDARD COINAGE

KM# 5 DINERO

Copper **Obv:** Head right **Rev:** Long cross with pellets and circles in angles **Mint:** Agramont

Date	Mintage	VG	F	VF	XF	Unc
164x	—	110	215	375	—	—
1641	—	110	215	375	—	—
1642	—	100	185	350	—	—
1643	—	100	185	350	—	—
1646	—	120	230	425	—	—

KM# 6 DINERO

Copper **Obv:** Head left **Mint:** Agramont

Date	Mintage	VG	F	VF	XF	Unc
164x	—	110	215	375	—	—
1642	—	110	215	375	—	—

KM# 8 DINERO

Copper **Obv:** Bust right **Rev:** Long cross with pellets and circles in angles **Mint:** Cervera

Date	Mintage	VG	F	VF	XF	Unc
164x	—	60.00	120	220	—	—
1641	—	80.00	160	300	—	—
1642	—	70.00	140	250	—	—
ND	—	36.00	70.00	120	—	—

KM# 9 DINERO

Copper **Obv:** Bust left **Mint:** Cervera

Date	Mintage	VG	F	VF	XF	Unc
164x	—	75.00	155	300	—	—
ND	—	75.00	155	300	—	—

KM# 7 DINERO

Copper **Obv:** Bust right **Mint:** Barcelona **Note:** The 1640 date uses bust of Philip IV, 1642-43 uses bust of Luis XIII, a second 1643 uses name of Luis XIV and the 1646 and 1648 use bust of Luis XIV.

Date	Mintage	VG	F	VF	XF	Unc
1640	—	75.00	155	300	—	—
1642	—	37.50	75.00	140	250	—
1643	—	45.00	90.00	150	275	—
1646	—	25.00	50.00	90.00	190	—
1648	—	25.00	50.00	90.00	190	—

KM# 10 DINERO

Copper **Obv:** Bust right **Rev:** Shield **Mint:** Olot

Date	Mintage	VG	F	VF	XF	Unc
ND	—	60.00	120	215	—	—

KM# 22 DINERO

Copper **Obv:** Crowned arms divide date **Rev:** Long cross with pellets and pebbles in angles **Mint:** Cervera

Date	Mintage	VG	F	VF	XF	Unc
1641	—	80.00	160	300	—	—
1642	—	70.00	140	250	—	—

KM# 23 DINERO

Copper **Obv:** Head left **Rev:** Shield **Mint:** Puigcerda

Date	Mintage	VG	F	VF	XF	Unc
1641	—	30.00	65.00	115	215	—

KM# 24 DINERO

Copper **Obv:** Head left, date at top **Rev:** Long cross with pellets and circles in angles **Mint:** Solsona

Date	Mintage	VG	F	VF	XF	Unc
1641	—	30.00	65.00	115	215	—
1643	—	35.00	70.00	140	250	—

KM# 25 DINERO

Copper **Rev:** Long cross with two bars **Mint:** Solsona

Date	Mintage	VG	F	VF	XF	Unc
1641	—	30.00	65.00	115	215	—
1651	—	35.00	70.00	140	250	—

KM# 26 DINERO

Copper **Obv:** Bust left **Rev:** Castle above waves **Mint:** Tarrega

Date	Mintage	VG	F	VF	XF	Unc
1641	—	90.00	165	300	500	—
1642	—	65.00	100	190	375	—

KM# 76 DINERO

Copper **Obv:** Crowned shield **Rev:** Saint bust facing **Mint:** Camprodon

Date	Mintage	VG	F	VF	XF	Unc
1642	—	120	230	375	—	—

KM# 77 DINERO

Copper **Obv:** Bust right **Rev:** Long cross, pellets and circles in angles **Mint:** Oliana

Date	Mintage	VG	F	VF	XF	Unc
1642	—	120	230	375	—	—

KM# 78 DINERO

Copper **Obv:** Shield **Rev:** Fleur de Lis **Mint:** Puigcerda

Date	Mintage	VG	F	VF	XF	Unc
1642	—	70.00	150	250	—	—
1644	—	70.00	150	250	—	—

KM# 79 DINERO

Copper **Obv:** Bust right **Rev:** Long cross **Mint:** Tarrega

Date	Mintage	VG	F	VF	XF	Unc
1642	—	65.00	100	190	375	—

KM# 80 DINERO

Copper **Obv:** Bust right **Rev:** Diamond shield **Mint:** Vic

Date	Mintage	VG	F	VF	XF	Unc
1642	—	35.00	70.00	125	250	—
1643	—	35.00	70.00	125	250	—
1644	—	35.00	70.00	125	250	—
1645	—	35.00	70.00	125	250	—
1646	—	35.00	70.00	125	250	—

KM# 97 DINERO

Copper **Ruler:** Louis XIV of France **Obv:** Fleur de lis **Obv. Legend:** ACRIMONI **Rev:** Short cross with circles and dots in angles **Mint:** Agramont

Date	Mintage	VG	F	VF	XF	Unc
1643	—	110	215	375	—	—
1645	—	—	—	—	—	—

KM# 98 DINERO

Copper **Obv:** Bust right **Rev:** 3-leaf plant **Mint:** Lerida

Date	Mintage	VG	F	VF	XF	Unc
1643	—	255	475	775	—	—

KM# A97 DINERO

Copper **Ruler:** Louis XIV of France **Obv:** Bust of Louis XIV right **Obv. Legend:** LVDOVIC. D. G. FRA. **Rev:** Crowned oval arms of Catalonia **Rev. Legend:** VILL. AGRANV **Mint:** Agramont

Date	Mintage	Good	VG	F	VF	XF
ND(1643-59)	—	—	—	—	—	—

KM# 99 DINERO

Copper **Obv:** Bust facing **Rev:** Arms **Mint:** Perpinya

Date	Mintage	VG	F	VF	XF	Unc
1644	—	30.00	65.00	115	215	—
1645	—	30.00	65.00	115	215	—
1646	—	30.00	65.00	115	215	—
1647	—	30.00	65.00	115	215	—
1648	—	30.00	65.00	115	215	—
1654	—	30.00	65.00	115	215	—

KM# A100 DINERO

Copper **Ruler:** Louis XIV of France **Obv:** Lis **Rev:** Long cross wtih two annulets in first and fourth quarters, three circles in second and third quarters **Mint:** Agramont

Date	Mintage	Good	VG	F	VF	XF
1645	—	—	—	—	—	—

KM# 11 ARDITE

Copper **Obv:** Bust left dividing A - R **Rev:** Diamond shield **Mint:** Barcelona

Date	Mintage	VG	F	VF	XF	Unc
1640	—	9.00	18.00	35.00	70.00	—

KM# 100 ARDITE

Copper **Obv:** Bust right dividing A - R **Mint:** Barcelona

Date	Mintage	VG	F	VF	XF	Unc
1644	—	25.00	50.00	100	150	—
1647	—	25.00	50.00	100	150	—
1648	—	25.00	50.00	100	150	—

KM# 101 SUELDO

Copper **Obv:** Facing figure **Rev:** Crowned shield **Mint:** Perpinya

Date	Mintage	VG	F	VF	XF	Unc
1644	—	30.00	65.00	115	215	—
1645	—	25.00	55.00	100	200	—
1647	—	65.00	100	190	350	—

KM# 102 2 SUELDOS

Copper **Obv:** Saint standing **Rev:** Crowned diamond shield **Mint:** Perpinya

Date	Mintage	VG	F	VF	XF	Unc
1644	—	25.00	55.00	100	200	—
Note: 1644 date has value as 2 or II						
1645	—	25.00	55.00	100	200	—
1646	—	25.00	55.00	100	200	—
1647	—	25.00	55.00	100	200	—
1648	—	25.00	55.00	100	200	—
1654	—	30.00	65.00	115	215	—

KM# 13 SEISENO

Copper **Obv:** Small bust left **Rev:** Crowned diamond shield

Date	Mintage	VG	F	VF	XF	Unc
1640	—	35.00	70.00	125	225	—
1641	—	30.00	55.00	100	200	—

Note: 1641 with and without SI on reverse

KM# 14 SEISENO

Copper **Obv:** Crowned Catalonian arms in inner circle **Rev:** Diamond arms, date in legend **Mint:** Girona **Note:** Varieties exist.

Date	Mintage	VG	F	VF	XF	Unc
1640	—	25.00	50.00	90.00	175	—
1641	—	25.00	50.00	90.00	175	—
1642	—	25.00	50.00	90.00	175	—

KM# 34 SEISENO

Copper **Obv:** Crowned Catalonian arms in inner circle **Rev:** Diamond arms in inner circle, date in legend **Mint:** Tarrasa **Note:** Legend varieties exist.

Date	Mintage	VG	F	VF	XF	Unc
ND	—	30.00	65.00	115	215	—
1641	—	30.00	65.00	115	215	—
1642	—	30.00	65.00	115	215	—

KM# 27 SEISENO

Copper **Obv:** Large bust right in circle of dots **Rev:** Diamond arms in inner circle, date in legend **Mint:** Barcelona

Date	Mintage	VG	F	VF	XF	Unc
1641	—	42.00	85.00	150	255	—
1642	—	42.00	85.00	150	255	—
1643	—	30.00	60.00	105	210	—
1644	—	20.00	40.00	75.00	125	—
1645	—	20.00	40.00	75.00	125	—
1646	—	20.00	40.00	75.00	125	—
1647	—	20.00	40.00	75.00	125	—
1648	—	20.00	40.00	75.00	125	—
1649	—	20.00	40.00	75.00	125	—
1650	—	20.00	40.00	75.00	125	—
1651	—	20.00	40.00	75.00	125	—
1652	—	45.00	90.00	165	270	—
165x	—	20.00	40.00	75.00	125	—

KM# 28 SEISENO

Copper **Rev:** Large bust right

Date	Mintage	VG	F	VF	XF	Unc
1641	—	30.00	65.00	115	215	—
1642	—	25.00	50.00	90.00	175	—

KM# 29 SEISENO

Copper **Obv:** Crowned Catalonian arms **Rev:** Cross of Lorraine in inner circle, date in legend **Mint:** Besalu

Date	Mintage	VG	F	VF	XF	Unc
1641	—	65.00	100	190	350	—

KM# 30 SEISENO

Copper **Rev:** Cross of Lorraine on left half of shield

Date	Mintage	VG	F	VF	XF	Unc
1641	—	65.00	100	190	350	—
1642	—	65.00	125	225	400	—

KM# 31 SEISENO

Copper **Obv:** Crowned Catalonian arms in inner circle **Rev:** Diamond arms in inner circle, date in legend **Mint:** Caldas

Date	Mintage	VG	F	VF	XF	Unc
1641	—	100	175	300	525	—

KM# 32 SEISENO

Copper **Obv:** Crowned Catalonian arms in inner circle **Rev:** Diamond shield **Mint:** Solsona

Date	Mintage	VG	F	VF	XF	Unc
1641	—	37.50	75.00	140	225	—
1642	—	65.00	125	200	350	—

KM# 33 SEISENO

Copper **Obv:** Bust right **Rev:** Diamond shield

Date	Mintage	VG	F	VF	XF	Unc
1641	—	37.50	75.00	140	225	—

KM# 35 SEISENO

Copper **Mint:** Tarrega

Date	Mintage	VG	F	VF	XF	Unc
1641	—	45.00	90.00	150	250	—

KM# 36 SEISENO

Copper **Obv:** Laureate head right

Date	Mintage	VG	F	VF	XF	Unc
1641	—	50.00	100	190	325	—

KM# 81 SEISENO

Copper **Obv:** Laureate head right **Rev:** Diamond shield **Mint:** Bellpuig

Date	Mintage	VG	F	VF	XF	Unc
1642	—	70.00	125	225	425	—

KM# 82 SEISENO

Copper **Obv:** Head right **Mint:** Girona

Date	Mintage	VG	F	VF	XF	Unc
1642	—	30.00	55.00	100	200	—
1643	—	30.00	55.00	100	200	—
1646	—	125	250	450	700	—

KM# 83 SEISENO

Copper **Obv:** Bust left

Date	Mintage	VG	F	VF	XF	Unc
1642	—	375	725	1,200	—	—

KM# 84 SEISENO

Copper **Obv:** Narrow crowned Catalonian arms **Rev:** Narrow diamond arms, date in legend **Mint:** Manresa

Date	Mintage	VG	F	VF	XF	Unc
1642	—	50.00	100	190	—	—

KM# 85 SEISENO

Copper **Obv:** Wider arms **Rev:** Wider arms

Date	Mintage	VG	F	VF	XF	Unc
1642	—	35.00	70.00	140	—	—

KM# 86 SEISENO

Copper **Obv:** Laureate head right **Rev:** Diamond shield **Mint:** Sanahuja

Date	Mintage	VG	F	VF	XF	Unc
1642	—	115	200	350	—	—

KM# 87 SEISENO

Copper **Obv:** Bust right **Rev:** Diamond shield on long cross **Mint:** Vallis

Date	Mintage	VG	F	VF	XF	Unc
1642	—	155	300	500	—	—

KM# 88 SEISENO

Copper **Obv:** Laureate bust of Louis XIII right divides 5 - E in inner circle **Rev:** Crowned Catalonian arms in inner circle, date in legend **Mint:** Vila Franca del Penedes

Date	Mintage	VG	F	VF	XF	Unc
1642	—	115	215	350	575	—

KM# 89 SEISENO

Copper **Obv:** Bust right **Rev:** Diamond shield

Date	Mintage	VG	F	VF	XF	Unc
1642	—	140	250	450	725	—

M# 37 1/2 CROAT
lver **Obv:** Bust right **Rev:** Short cross with pellets and circles angles **Mint:** Vich **Note:** Legend varieties exist.

te	Mintage	VG	F	VF	XF	Unc
41	—	500	900	1,600	2,800	—
42	—	350	625	1,200	2,100	—

M# 15 CROAT
lver **Obv:** Bust of Felipe IV right **Rev:** Long cross with pellets ıd circles in angles **Mint:** Barcelona

te	Mintage	VG	F	VF	XF	Unc
40	—	125	250	450	750	—

M# 16 CROAT
lver **Obv:** Bust left **Mint:** Ileida

te	Mintage	VG	F	VF	XF	Unc
40	—	1,050	1,900	3,150	—	—

M# 18 5 SOUS
lver **Obv:** Crowned shield **Rev:** Long cross with pellets and cle in angle **Mint:** Girona

te	Mintage	VG	F	VF	XF	Unc
40	—	1,100	2,100	3,850	—	—
41	—	700	1,250	2,450	—	—

M# 17 5 SOUS
lver **Obv:** Crowned arms dividing V - S **Rev:** Long cross with llets and circles in angles, date in legend **Mint:** Barcelona **Note:** gend varieties exist.

te	Mintage	VG	F	VF	XF	Unc
40	—	500	900	1,700	—	—
41	—	625	1,200	2,100	—	—

M# 39 5 SOUS
ver **Rev:** Long cross with diamond shield of city at juncture **nt:** Banyoles **Note:** Legend varieties exist.

te	Mintage	VG	F	VF	XF	Unc
41	—	875	1,600	3,150	—	—

M# 52 5 SOUS
ver **Rev:** Long cross with diamond shield of city at juncture **ote:** Legend varieties exist.

te	Mintage	VG	F	VF	XF	Unc
41	—	900	1,750	3,150	—	—

M# 41 5 SOUS
ver **Obv:** Bust of Louis XIII right dividing V - S **Rev:** Long oss with diamond shield of city at juncture **Mint:** Barcelona **te:** Legend and design varieties exist for 1642 and 1643 date ins.

te	Mintage	VG	F	VF	XF	Unc
41	—	900	1,700	3,500	—	—
42	—	525	950	1,750	—	—
43	—	675	1,250	2,450	—	—

M# 38 5 SOUS
ver **Obv:** Crowned Catalonian arms dividing V - S **Rev:** Long oss with pellets and circles in angle **Mint:** Balaguer

te	Mintage	VG	F	VF	XF	Unc
41	—	875	1,650	3,300	—	—

M# 40 5 SOUS
ver **Rev:** Long cross with diamond shield of city at Juncture

te	Mintage	VG	F	VF	XF	Unc
41	—	1,250	2,300	4,200	—	—

M# 42 5 SOUS
ver **Obv:** Crowned arms dividing V - S **Rev:** Long cross with llets and circles in angles **Mint:** Berga

te	Mintage	VG	F	VF	XF	Unc
41	—	875	1,650	3,300	—	—

KM# 43 5 SOUS
Silver **Rev:** Long cross with diamond shield of city at juncture **Mint:** Bisbal

Date	Mintage	VG	F	VF	XF	Unc
1641	—	875	1,600	3,150	—	—

KM# 44 5 SOUS
Silver **Rev:** Long cross with pellets and circles in angles **Mint:** Cervera

Date	Mintage	VG	F	VF	XF	Unc
1641	—	1,100	2,100	4,000	—	—

KM# 45 5 SOUS
Silver **Obv:** Bust right

Date	Mintage	VG	F	VF	XF	Unc
1641	—	1,350	2,450	4,550	—	—

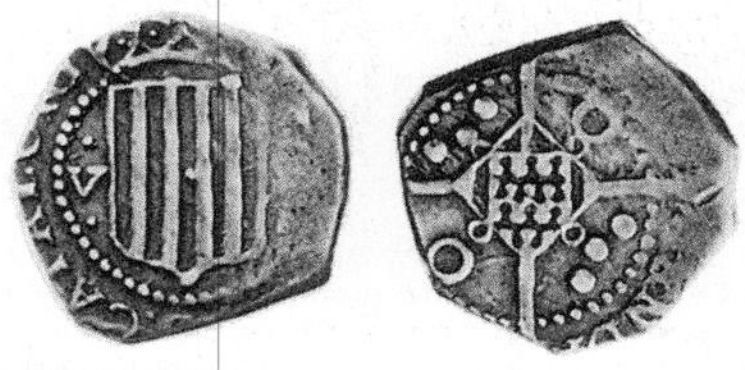

KM# 46 5 SOUS
Silver **Obv:** Crowned arms **Rev:** Long cross with diamond shield of city at juncture **Mint:** Girona

Date	Mintage	VG	F	VF	XF	Unc
1641	—	500	900	1,750	—	—

KM# 47 5 SOUS
Silver **Rev:** Long cross with pellets and circle in angles **Mint:** Manresa

Date	Mintage	VG	F	VF	XF	Unc
1641	—	1,250	2,300	4,200	—	—

KM# 48 5 SOUS
Silver **Mint:** Olot

Date	Mintage	VG	F	VF	XF	Unc
1641	—	1,350	2,450	4,550	—	—

KM# 49 5 SOUS
Silver **Rev:** Pellets around circles in angles

Date	Mintage	VG	F	VF	XF	Unc
1641	—	1,250	2,300	4,200	—	—

KM# 50 5 SOUS
Silver **Rev:** Long cross with pellets and circle in angles **Mint:** Puigcerda

Date	Mintage	VG	F	VF	XF	Unc
1641	—	875	1,600	3,150	—	—

KM# 51 5 SOUS
Silver **Mint:** Vich

Date	Mintage	VG	F	VF	XF	Unc
1641	—	900	1,700	3,500	—	—

KM# 90 5 SOUS
Silver **Rev:** Long cross with pellets and circles in angles **Mint:** Besalu

Date	Mintage	VG	F	VF	XF	Unc
1642	—	900	1,750	3,150	—	—

KM# 91 5 SOUS
Silver **Mint:** Camprodon

Date	Mintage	VG	F	VF	XF	Unc
1642	—	1,550	3,000	6,000	—	—

KM# 92 5 SOUS
Silver **Mint:** Vich **Note:** Louis XIII.

Date	Mintage	VG	F	VF	XF	Unc
1642	—	1,100	2,300	4,200	—	—

KM# 20 5 REAL (1/2 Libra)
Silver **Rev:** Long cross with diamond city shield at juncture **Mint:** Bisbal

Date	Mintage	VG	F	VF	XF	Unc
164x	—	1,250	2,300	3,850	—	—
1641	—	900	1,700	3,150	—	—

KM# 19 5 REAL (1/2 Libra)
Silver **Obv:** Crowned shield dividing V - R **Obv. Legend:** PHILIPP, D.G. R HISP **Rev:** Long cross with pellets and circle in angles **Rev. Legend:** BARC INO.C IVITAS **Mint:** Barcelona **Note:** Legend and design varieties exist.

Date	Mintage	VG	F	VF	XF	Unc
1640	—	375	675	1,250	—	—
1641	—	325	525	950	—	—
1642	—	325	550	975	—	—

KM# 21 5 REAL (1/2 Libra)
Silver **Mint:** Girona **Note:** Philip II. Legend and design varieties exist.

Date	Mintage	VG	F	VF	XF	Unc
1640	—	350	625	1,200	—	—
1641	—	280	500	900	—	—

KM# 53 5 REAL (1/2 Libra)
Silver **Obv:** Crowned shield of Catalongia-Aragon **Obv. Legend:** PRINCIPAT VS CATALONIE **Rev:** Long cross with pellets and circle in angles **Rev. Legend:** SITNO MIRCA ALLIV **Mint:** Agramont **Note:** Legend varieties exist for 1641 dates.

Date	Mintage	VG	F	VF	XF	Unc
1461 Error for 1641	—	675	1,250	2,300	—	—
1642	—	625	1,200	2,200	—	—

KM# 75 5 REAL (1/2 Libra)
Silver **Rev:** Long cross with pellets and circle in angles **Mint:** Vila Franca del Penedes **Note:** Legend varieties exist with 1642.

Date	Mintage	VG	F	VF	XF	Unc
1641	—	1,700	2,800	4,550	—	—
1642	—	1,350	2,450	4,200	—	—

KM# 61 5 REAL (1/2 Libra)
Silver **Mint:** Cervera **Note:** Legend varieties exist.

Date	Mintage	VG	F	VF	XF	Unc
1641	—	280	525	1,000	—	—

KM# 63 5 REAL (1/2 Libra)
Silver **Obv:** Crowned shield dividing V - R **Mint:** Figueres **Note:** Legend varieties exist.

Date	Mintage	VG	F	VF	XF	Unc
1641	—	850	1,550	3,250	—	—

KM# 66 5 REAL (1/2 Libra)
Silver **Mint:** Igualada **Note:** Legend varieties exist.

Date	Mintage	VG	F	VF	XF	Unc
1641	—	325	600	1,150	—	—
1642	—	325	625	1,200	—	—

KM# 54 5 REAL (1/2 Libra)
Silver **Rev:** Long cross with pellets and circles in angles **Mint:** Balaguer **Note:** Legend and design varieties exist.

Date	Mintage	VG	F	VF	XF	Unc
1641	—	450	850	1,600	—	—

KM# 68 5 REAL (1/2 Libra)
Silver **Mint:** Mataro **Note:** Legend and design varieties exist.

Date	Mintage	VG	F	VF	XF	Unc
1641	—	280	525	1,150	—	—
1642	—	450	875	1,650	—	—

KM# 72 5 REAL (1/2 Libra)
Silver **Mint:** Tarrasa **Note:** Legend and design varieties exist.

Date	Mintage	VG	F	VF	XF	Unc
1641	—	775	1,400	2,600	—	—
1642	—	280	550	1,200	—	—

KM# 73 5 REAL (1/2 Libra)
Silver **Mint:** Vich **Note:** Legend and design varieties exist.

Date	Mintage	VG	F	VF	XF	Unc
1641	—	425	850	1,600	—	—

KM# A53 5 REAL (1/2 Libra)
Silver **Obv:** Crowned shield of Catalonia-Arzgon **Obv. Legend:** PHILIPP. D • G R HISPANIA **Rev:** Long cross with pellets and circles in angles **Rev. Legend:** VILLA-AGRIM-ONST

Date	Mintage	VG	F	VF	XF	Unc
1641	—	625	1,200	2,200	—	—

KM# B53 5 REAL (1/2 Libra)
Silver **Obv:** Crowned shield of Catalonia-Aragon **Obv. Legend:** PRINCIPAT VS CATALONI (A)E **Rev:** Long cross with pellets and circles in angles **Rev. Legend:** VILLA ACRIM ONSTS

Date	Mintage	VG	F	VF	XF	Unc
1641	—	550	1,100	2,150	—	—

KM# 70 5 REAL (1/2 Libra)
Silver **Mint:** Puigcerda **Note:** Design varieties exist.

Date	Mintage	VG	F	VF	XF	Unc
1641	—	1,050	1,750	3,000	—	—

KM# 58 5 REAL (1/2 Libra)
Silver **Obv:** Bust of Luis XIII right dividing V- R **Mint:** Barcelona **Note:** Legend and bust varieties exist.

Date	Mintage	VG	F	VF	XF	Unc
1641	—	375	750	1,400	—	—
1642	—	325	625	1,150	2,750	—
1643	—	325	625	1,150	2,750	—

KM# 55 5 REAL (1/2 Libra)
Silver **Mint:** Banyoles

Date	Mintage	VG	F	VF	XF	Unc
1641	—	525	950	1,700	—	—

KM# 56 5 REAL (1/2 Libra)
Silver **Rev:** Long cross with diamond city shield at juncture

Date	Mintage	VG	F	VF	XF	Unc
1641	—	625	1,200	2,100	—	—

KM# 57 5 REAL (1/2 Libra)
Silver **Obv. Legend:** PRINCIPATV S CATALONIE **Rev. Legend:** BARC INOC IVITAS **Mint:** Barcelona

Date	Mintage	VG	F	VF	XF	Unc
1641	—	300	600	1,250	2,500	—

KM# 59 5 REAL (1/2 Libra)
Silver **Obv:** Crowned shield dividing V - R **Rev:** Long cross with pellets and circles in angles **Mint:** Berga

Date	Mintage	VG	F	VF	XF	Unc
1641	—	1,000	1,900	3,700	—	—

KM# 60 5 REAL (1/2 Libra)
Silver **Mint:** Besalu

Date	Mintage	VG	F	VF	XF	Unc
1641	—	1,250	2,300	3,850	—	—
1642	—	425	850	1,550	—	—

KM# 62 5 REAL (1/2 Libra)
Silver **Obv:** Bust of Louis XIII right

Date	Mintage	VG	F	VF	XF	Unc
1641	—	500	1,000	1,800	—	—
1642	—	400	850	1,600	—	—

KM# 64 5 REAL (1/2 Libra)
Silver **Rev:** Long cross with diamond city shield at juncture **Mint:** Girona

Date	Mintage	VG	F	VF	XF	Unc
1641	—	280	550	1,150	—	

KM# 65 5 REAL (1/2 Libra)
Silver **Rev:** Long cross with pellets and circle in angles **Mint:** Granollers

Date	Mintage	VG	F	VF	XF	Unc
1641	—	550	975	1,750	—	
1642	—	850	1,550	2,650	—	

KM# 67 5 REAL (1/2 Libra)
Silver **Mint:** Manresa

Date	Mintage	VG	F	VF	XF	Unc
1641	—	350	700	1,350	—	

KM# 69 5 REAL (1/2 Libra)
Silver **Mint:** Olot

Date	Mintage	VG	F	VF	XF	Unc
1641	—	850	1,700	2,800	—	

KM# 71 5 REAL (1/2 Libra)
Silver **Mint:** Tarrega

Date	Mintage	VG	F	VF	XF	Unc
1641	—	850	1,700	2,800	—	
1642	—	550	975	2,000	—	

KM# 74 5 REAL (1/2 Libra)
Silver **Rev:** Long cross with diamond city arms at center

Date	Mintage	VG	F	VF	XF	Unc
1641	—	1,250	2,300	3,850	—	—

KM# 94 5 REAL (1/2 Libra)
Silver **Rev:** Long cross with pellets and circles in angles **Mint:** Argentona **Note:** Legend and design varieties exist.

Date	Mintage	VG	F	VF	XF	Unc
1642	—	500	900	1,650	—	—

KM# 95 5 REAL (1/2 Libra)
Silver **Rev:** Pellets around circles in angles **Mint:** Besalu **Note:** Legend varieties exist.

Date	Mintage	VG	F	VF	XF	Unc
1642	—	425	775	1,450	—	—

KM# 96 5 REAL (1/2 Libra)
Silver **Mint:** Vich **Note:** Titles of Luis XIII.

Date	Mintage	VG	F	VF	XF	Unc
1642	—	1,250	2,250	3,700	—	—

KM# 103 5 REAL (1/2 Libra)
Silver **Obv:** Bust of Louis XIV right dividing V - R **Rev:** Long cross with diamond city shield **Mint:** Barcelona

Date	Mintage	VG	F	VF	XF	Unc
1644	—	1,250	2,300	3,850	—	—

KM# 104 5 REAL (1/2 Libra)
Silver **Rev:** Pellets around circles in angles **Mint:** Olot

Date	Mintage	VG	F	VF	XF	Unc
1646	—	850	1,700	2,800	—	—

KM# 110 5 REAL (1/2 Libra)
Silver **Obv:** Crowned shield of Spain **Rev:** Bust left **Mint:** Girona

Date	Mintage	VG	F	VF	XF	Unc
1653 Rare	—	—	—	—	—	—

KM# 106 10 REALES
Silver **Obv:** Bust of Louis XIIII right **Obv. Legend:** LVD • XIIII • D • G • R • F • C • B **Rev:** Cross with pellets and circles in angles **Rev. Legend:** BARCINO CIVIT OBBESSA

Date	Mintage	VG	F	VF	XF	Unc
1652/1	—	350	700	1,250	—	—
1652	—	325	625	1,150	—	—

KM# 121 LOUIS D'OR
Gold **Ruler:** Louis XIII of France **Obv:** Laureate head **Obv. Legend:** LVD•XIII•D•G - FR•ET•NAV•REX **Rev:** Crowned cruciform double L monograms with lys in angles, date in legend **Rev. Legend:** CATA-LONIS-

Date	Mintage	VG	F	VF	XF	Unc
1642 Rare	—	—	—	—	—	—

KM# 109 1/12 ECU
Silver, 20.5 mm. **Ruler:** Louis XIII of France **Obv:** Laureate bust right **Obv. Legend:** LVDOVICVS•XIII•D•G•FR•ET NAV•REX **Rev:** Crowned arms **Rev. Legend:** CATALONIAE • COMES

Date	Mintage	VG	F	VF	XF	Unc
1642 Rare	—	—	—	—	—	—

KM# 111 1/4 ECU
Silver, 26 mm. **Ruler:** Louis XIII of France **Obv:** Laureate bust right **Obv. Legend:** LVDOVICVS•XIII•D•G•FR•ET NAV•REX **Rev:** Crowned arms **Rev. Legend:** CATALONIAE • COMES

Date	Mintage	VG	F	VF	XF	Unc
1642 Rare	—	—	—	—	—	—

KM# 112 1/2 ECU
Silver, 31.2 mm. **Ruler:** Louis XIII of France **Obv:** Laureate bust right **Obv. Legend:** LVDOVICVS•XIII•D•G•FR•ET NAV•REX **Rev:** Crowned arms **Rev. Legend:** CATALONIAE • COMES

Date	Mintage	VG	F	VF	XF	Unc
1642 Rare	—	—	—	—	—	—

KM# 113 ECU
Silver, 37.5 mm. **Ruler:** Louis XIII of France **Obv:** Laureate bust right **Obv. Legend:** LVDOVICVS•XIII•D•G•FR•ET NAV•REX **Rev:** Crowned arms **Rev. Legend:** CATALONIAE • COMES

Date	Mintage	VG	F	VF	XF	Unc
1642 Rare	—	—	—	—	—	—

KM# 114 ECU
Silver, 39 mm. **Ruler:** Louis XIII of France **Obv:** Laureate bust right **Obv. Legend:** LVDOVICVS•XIII•D•G•FR•ET NAV•REX **Rev:** Crowned arms of France, Navarre and Catalonia **Rev. Legend:** CATALONIAE PRINCEPS **Note:** Possibly a pattern.

Date	Mintage	VG	F	VF	XF	Unc
1642 Rare	—	—	—	—	—	—

PROVINCE

COUNTERMARKED COINAGE

KM# 1.2 1/3 TRENTIN
Gold **Countermark:** Diamond-shaped shield **Note:** Countermark on Barcelona, KM#14.

CM Date	Host Date	Good	VG	F	VF	XF
ND(1640-59)	16Z5	—	975	1,900	3,400	6,000

KM# 1.1 1/3 TRENTIN
Gold **Countermark:** Diamond-shaped shield **Note:** Countermark on Barcelona, KM#5.

CM Date	Host Date	Good	VG	F	VF	XF
ND(1640-59)	1618B	—	900	1,800	3,000	5,300

KM# 2.4 1/2 TRENTIN
Gold **Countermark:** Diamond-shaped shield **Note:** Countermark on Barcelona, KM#.

CM Date	Host Date	Good	VG	F	VF	XF
ND(1640-59)	1631B	—	750	1,500	3,000	5,300

KM# 2.3 1/2 TRENTIN
Gold **Countermark:** Diamond-shaped shield **Note:** Countermark on Barcelona, KM#15.

CM Date	Host Date	Good	VG	F	VF	XF
ND(1640-59)	1623	—	750	1,500	3,000	5,300

KM# 2.1 1/2 TRENTIN
Gold **Countermark:** Diamond-shaped shield **Note:** Countermark on Barcelona, KM#6.1.

CM Date	Host Date	Good	VG	F	VF	XF
ND(1640-59)	ND(1598-1621)	—	950	1,900	3,750	6,400

KM# 2.2 1/2 TRENTIN
Gold **Countermark:** Diamond-shaped shield **Note:** Countermark on Barcelona, KM#6.2.

CM Date	Host Date	Good	VG	F	VF	XF
ND(1640-59)	ND(1598-1621)	—	950	1,900	3,750	6,400

KM# 3.3 TRENTIN
Gold **Countermark:** Diamond-shaped shield **Note:** Countermark on Barcelona, KM#17.1.

CM Date	Host Date	Good	VG	F	VF	XF
ND(1640-59)	1625	—	900	1,850	3,500	5,750
ND(1640-59)	1626	—	900	1,850	3,500	5,750
ND(1640-59)	1628	—	900	1,850	3,500	5,750

KM# 3.4 TRENTIN
Gold **Countermark:** Diamond-shaped shield **Note:** Countermark on Barcelona, KM#17.2.

CM Date	Host Date	Good	VG	F	VF	XF
ND(1640-59)	1628	—	900	1,850	3,500	5,750
ND(1640-59)	1629	—	900	1,850	3,500	5,750
ND(1640-59)	1632	—	900	1,850	3,500	5,750
ND(1640-59)	1633	—	900	1,850	3,500	5,750

KM# 3.1 TRENTIN
Gold **Countermark:** Diamond-shaped shield **Note:** Countermark on Barcelona, KM#7.

CM Date	Host Date	Good	VG	F	VF	XF
ND(1640-59)	ND(1598-1621)	—	1,100	2,150	4,250	7,000

KM# 3.2 TRENTIN
Gold **Countermark:** Diamond-shaped shield **Note:** Countermark on Barcelona, KM#8.

CM Date	Host Date	Good	VG	F	VF	XF
ND(1640-59)	ND(1598-1621)	—	1,100	2,150	4,250	7,000

KM# 3.5 TRENTIN
Gold **Countermark:** Diamond-shaped shield **Note:** Countermark on Segovia 2 Excellente of Ferdinand and Isabel.

CM Date	Host Date	Good	VG	F	VF	XF
ND(1640-59)	ND(1474-1504)	—	2,350	3,850	6,250	11,500

PATTERNS

Including off metal strikes

KM#	Date	Mintage	Identification	Mkt Val
Pn1	ND(ca 1643)	—	2 Louis D'Or. Gold. Struck at Barcelona Mint.	—

PROOF SETS

KM#	Date	Mintage	Identification	Issue Price	Mkt Val
XPS1	1993c (5)	100	X17-21	—	10,150

MAJORCA

(Yslas Baleares)
Majorca

The Balearic Islands, an archipelago located in the Mediterranean Sea off the east coast of Spain including Majorca, Minorca, Cabrera, Ibiza, Formentera and a number of islets. Majorca, largest of the Balearic Islands is famous for its 1,000-year-old olive trees.

RULERS
Philip III of Spain, 1598-1621
Philip IV of Spain, 1621-1665
Charles II, 1665-1700
Philip V, 1700-1746
Louis I, 1723-1726
Pretender, Charles III, 1700-1720
Ferdinand (Fernando) VII, 1808-1833

MONETARY SYSTEM
12 Dineros = 6 Doblers = 1 Sueldo (Sou)
30 Sueldos = 1 Duro

PROVINCE

STANDARD COINAGE

KM# 33 DINAR
Copper, 12 mm. **Ruler:** Philip V **Obv:** Small bust of Philip V left, "I" behind **Rev:** Cross with castles and lions in angles **Mint:** Palma de Mallorca

Date	Mintage	VG	F	VF	XF	Unc
ND(1700-1746)	—	50.00	95.00	175	—	—

KM# 32 DINAR

Copper **Ruler:** Philip V **Obv:** Large bust of Philip V left **Rev:** Cross, "II" at lower right **Mint:** Palma de Mallorca **Note:** Size varies 14-15 mm.

Date	Mintage	VG	F	VF	XF	Unc
ND(1700-1746)	—	43.75	80.00	160	280	—

KM# 11 DOBLER

Copper **Ruler:** Philip IV of Spain **Obv:** Crowned bust of Philip IV left **Rev:** Cross **Mint:** Palma de Mallorca **Note:** Size varies 15-16 mm.

Date	Mintage	VG	F	VF	XF	Unc
ND(1621-1665)	—	31.25	55.00	120	—	—

KM# 18 DOBLER

Copper **Ruler:** Charles II **Obv:** Crowned bust of Charles II right **Rev:** Cross **Mint:** Palma de Mallorca **Note:** Size varies 15-16 MM.

Date	Mintage	VG	F	VF	XF	Unc
ND(1665-1700)	—	18.00	35.00	65.00	—	—

KM# 19 DOBLER

Copper **Ruler:** Charles II **Obv:** Crowned bust of Charles II right **Rev:** Cross **Mint:** Palma de Mallorca **Note:** Size varies 15-16 mm.

Date	Mintage	VG	F	VF	XF	Unc
ND(1665-1700)	—	19.00	37.50	70.00	—	—

KM# 34 DOBLER

Copper **Ruler:** Philip V **Obv:** Bust of Philip V left **Rev:** Cross with figure at lower left, "II" at lower right **Mint:** Palma de Mallorca **Note:** Size varies 14-15 mm.

Date	Mintage	VG	F	VF	XF	Unc
ND(1700-1746)	—	55.00	100	190	325	—

KM# 35.1 DOBLER

Copper, 14 mm. **Ruler:** Philip V **Obv:** Bust of Philip V left, "2" behind **Rev:** Crowned shield of Castile and Leon, fleur-de-lis at center **Mint:** Palma de Mallorca

Date	Mintage	VG	F	VF	XF	Unc
ND(1700-1746)	—	37.50	75.00	140	250	—

KM# 20 1/2 REAL

Silver, 16 mm. **Ruler:** Charles II **Obv:** Crowned bust of Charles II IV left **Rev:** Diamond-shaped shield **Mint:** Palma de Mallorca

Date	Mintage	VG	F	VF	XF	Unc
ND(1665-1700)	—	205	375	700	—	—

KM# 21 1/2 REAL

Silver, 16 mm. **Ruler:** Charles II **Obv:** Crowned bust of Charles II right **Rev:** Diamond-shaped shield **Mint:** Palma de Mallorca

Date	Mintage	VG	F	VF	XF	Unc
ND(1665-1700)	—	190	350	675	—	—

KM# 12 REAL (Croat)

Silver **Ruler:** Philip IV of Spain **Obv:** Crowned bust of Philip IV left **Obv. Legend:** PHILIPPVS REX... **Rev:** Diamond-shaped shield within inner circle **Rev. Legend:** MALORICARVM CATOLICVS **Mint:** Palma de Mallorca **Note:** Size varies 21-22 mm.

Date	Mintage	VG	F	VF	XF	Unc
ND(1621-1665)	—	250	500	1,050	1,750	—

KM# 9 REAL

Silver **Ruler:** Philip IV of Spain **Obv:** Crowned bust of Philip III right **Obv. Legend:** PHILIPPVS REX ARAGONVM **Rev:** Diamond - shaped shield within inner circle **Rev. Legend:** MAIORICARVM...VS **Mint:** Palma de Mallorca **Note:** Size varies 18-19 mm.

Date	Mintage	VG	F	VF	XF	Unc
1617	—	375	700	1,350	—	—

KM# 13 2 REAL

Silver **Ruler:** Philip IV of Spain **Obv:** Crowned bust of Philip IV left **Obv. Legend:** PHILIPPVS... **Rev:** Diamond-shaped shield within inner circle **Rev. Legend:** MALORICARVM CATOLIC **Mint:** Palma de Mallorca **Note:** Size varies 23-25 mm.

Date	Mintage	VG	F	VF	XF	Unc
ND(1621-1665)	—	170	350	700	—	—

KM# 22 2 REAL

Ruler: Charles II **Obv:** Short crowned bust of Charles II IV left **Obv. Legend:** CAROLVS•II•ARAGONVM **Rev:** Diamond-shaped shield **Rev. Legend:** MALORICARVM CATOLICVS **Mint:** Palma de Mallorca **Note:** Size varies 24-25 mm.

Date	Mintage	VG	F	VF	XF	Unc
ND(1665-1700)	—	350	625	1,250	2,100	—

KM# 23 2 REAL

Silver **Ruler:** Charles II **Obv:** Tall crowned bust of Charles II left **Rev:** Diamond-shaped shield **Mint:** Palma de Mallorca **Note:** Size varies 28-29 mm.

Date	Mintage	VG	F	VF	XF	Unc
ND(1665-1700)	—	500	950	1,900	3,150	—

KM# 6.1 4 REAL

Silver **Ruler:** Philip III of Spain **Obv:** Crowned bust of Philip III right **Obv. Legend:** PHILIPPVS REX ARAGONVM **Rev:** Diamond-shaped shield within inner circle **Rev. Legend:** MALORICARVM CATOLIC **Mint:** Palma de Mallorca **Note:** Size varies 30-31 mm.

Date	Mintage	VG	F	VF	XF	Unc
1607	—	975	1,800	3,000	—	—

KM# 6.2 4 REAL

Silver **Ruler:** Philip III of Spain **Obv:** Crowned bust of Philip III right **Obv. Legend:** PHILIPPVS REX ARAGONMD **Rev:** Diamond-shaped shield within inner circle **Rev. Legend:** MALORICARVM CATOLIC **Mint:** Palma de Mallorca **Note:** Size varies 30-31 mm.

Date	Mintage	VG	F	VF	XF	Unc
1617	—	975	1,800	3,000	—	—

KM# 14 4 REAL

Silver, 32 mm. **Ruler:** Philip IV of Spain **Obv:** Crowned bust of Philip IV left **Obv. Legend:** PHILIPPVS...REX ARAGONVM... **Rev:** Diamond-shaped shield within inner circle **Rev. Legend:** MALORICARVM...CVTO **Mint:** Palma de Mallorca

Date	Mintage	VG	F	VF	XF	Unc
ND(1621-1665)	—	1,150	2,250	4,150	6,800	—
1633	—	1,150	2,250	4,150	6,800	—
1648	—	1,150	2,250	4,150	6,800	—

KM# 24 4 REAL

Silver **Ruler:** Charles II **Obv:** Crowned bust of Charles II right **Obv. Legend:** CAROLVS... **Rev:** Diamond-shaped shield **Rev. Legend:** MAIORICARVM CATOLICVS **Mint:** Palma de Mallorca **Note:** Size varies 30-31 mm.

Date	Mintage	VG	F	VF	XF	Unc
ND(1665-1700)	—	1,500	3,000	5,300	9,000	—

KM# 25 4 REAL

Silver **Ruler:** Charles II **Obv:** Crowned bust of Charles II IV left **Rev:** Diamond-shaped shield **Mint:** Palma de Mallorca **Note:** Size varies 33-34 mm.

Date	Mintage	VG	F	VF	XF	Unc
ND(1665-1700)	—	2,250	4,500	7,500	11,500	—

KM# 26 1/2 ESCUDO

1.6917 g., 0.9170 Gold 0.0499 oz. AGW **Ruler:** Charles II **Obv:** Crowned arms divide date **Rev:** Diamond-shaped shield **Note:** Previous Fr.#67.

Date	Mintage	VG	F	VF	XF	Unc
1695	—	600	1,200	2,250	3,750	—

KM# 40 1/2 ESCUDO

1.6917 g., 0.9170 Gold 0.0499 oz. AGW **Ruler:** Philip V **Obv:** Bust of Philip V right, legend at right **Obv. Legend:** PHILIPVS... **Rev:** Diamond shield topped by cross **Rev. Legend:** MAIORIC - ARVM CA **Note:** Previous Fr.#71.

Date	Mintage	VG	F	VF	XF	Unc
ND(1700-1746)	—	1,300	2,650	3,750	5,300	—

KM# 27 ESCUDO

3.3834 g., 0.9170 Gold 0.0997 oz. AGW **Ruler:** Charles II **Obv:** Crowned arms in inner circle, date in legend **Rev:** Diamond-shaped shield **Note:** Previous Fr.#66.

Date	Mintage	VG	F	VF	XF	Unc
1698	—	700	1,300	2,000	3,500	—

KM# 41 ESCUDO

3.3834 g., 0.9170 Gold 0.0997 oz. AGW **Ruler:** Philip V **Obv:** Large bust of Philip V right **Obv. Legend:** PHILIPVS... **Rev:** Crowned arms, tree at left **Mint:** Palma de Mallorca **Note:** Fr.#7

Date	Mintage	VG	F	VF	XF	Unc
ND(1700-1746)	—	500	950	1,700	2,750	—

KM# 42 ESCUDO

3.3834 g., 0.9170 Gold 0.0997 oz. AGW **Ruler:** Philip V **Obv:** Small bust of Philip V right **Rev:** Crowned arms, tree at left **Mint:** Palma de Mallorca **Note:** Fr.#70a.

Date	Mintage	VG	F	VF	XF	Unc
ND(1700-1746)	—	500	1,000	1,650	2,750	—

KM# 15 2 ESCUDOS

6.7667 g., 0.9170 Gold 0.1995 oz. AGW **Ruler:** Philip IV of Spai **Obv:** Crowned arms in inner circle, titles of Philip IV **Rev:** Diamond-shaped shield **Mint:** Palma de Mallorca

Date	Mintage	VG	F	VF	XF	Unc
1660	—	2,150	4,150	7,500	13,500	—

KM# 28 2 ESCUDOS

6.7667 g., 0.9170 Gold 0.1995 oz. AGW **Ruler:** Charles II **Obv:** Crowned arms in ornamental cartouche in inner circle, date in legend **Note:** Previous Fr.#65.

Date	Mintage	VG	F	VF	XF	Unc
1678	—	1,700	3,300	5,500	8,400	—
1689	—	1,600	3,000	4,500	7,000	—
1695	—	1,900	3,600	6,000	10,000	—
1698	—	1,900	3,600	6,000	10,000	—

KM# 8 4 ESCUDOS

13.5334 g., 0.9170 Gold 0.3990 oz. AGW **Ruler:** Philip III of Spain **Obv:** Crowned arms in inner circle, titles of Philip III **Rev:** Diamond shield in inner circle **Note:** Previous Fr.#58.

Date	Mintage	VG	F	VF	XF	Unc
1607 Rare	—	—	—	—	—	—

KM# 16 4 ESCUDOS

13.5334 g., 0.9170 Gold 0.3990 oz. AGW **Ruler:** Philip IV of Spain **Obv:** Titles of Philip IV **Note:** Previous Fr.#61.

Date	Mintage	VG	F	VF	XF	Unc
1648 Rare	—	—	—	—	—	—

KM# 29 4 ESCUDOS

13.5334 g., 0.9170 Gold 0.3990 oz. AGW **Ruler:** Charles II **Obv:** Titles of Charles II **Note:** Previous Fr.#64.

Date	Mintage	VG	F	VF	XF	Unc
1698	—	2,250	3,750	6,800	11,500	—

KM# 30 8 ESCUDOS

27.0674 g., 0.9170 Gold 0.7980 oz. AGW **Ruler:** Charles II **Obv:** Crowned arms in ornamental cartouche in inner circle, date in legend **Obv. Legend:** CAROLVS III **Rev:** Diamond shield in inne circle, cross on top **Note:** Previous Fr.#63.

Date	Mintage	VG	F	VF	XF	Unc
1689 Rare	—	—	—	—	—	—

NAVARRE

Navarre, a frontier province of northern Spain and a forme kingdom lies on the western end of the border between Franc and Spain. From the 10th through the 12th centuries Navarre wa a solid power in the region. After 1234 the kingdom fell unde French dominance. In 1516 Ferdinand annexed Navarre to Spai and it was under this vice royalty that coinage was struck at th mint in Pamplona.

The Kingdom of Navarre was ultimately divided an absorbed by France and Spain.

RULERS

Philip III of Spain, 1598-1621
Philip IV of Spain, 1621-1665
Charles II of Spain, 1665-1700
Philip V of Spain, 1700-1746

MINT MARK

P - Pamplona

PROVINCE

STANDARD COINAGE

KM# 5 DINERO

Copper **Obv:** Crowned bust right **Rev:** Diamond shield of Banolas **Mint:** Banyoles **Note:** Legend varieties exist.

Date	Mintage	VG	F	VF	XF	Unc
ND	—	20.00	45.00	85.00	180	—

KM# 6 4 CORNADOS

Copper **Obv:** Crowned FI monogram, value below in inner circl titles of Philip III **Rev:** Crowned arms in inner circle **Mint:** Pamplona **Note:** Varieties exist.

Date	Mintage	VG	F	VF	XF	Unc
1608	—	14.00	27.50	60.00	120	—
168 Error	—	17.00	33.50	75.00	140	—
169 Error	—	17.00	33.50	75.00	140	—
16x Error	—	14.00	30.00	70.00	125	—
1610	—	14.00	27.50	60.00	120	—

Date	Mintage	VG	F	VF	XF	Unc
1611	—	14.00	27.50	60.00	120	—
1611 PA	—	14.00	27.50	60.00	120	—
1612	—	14.00	27.50	60.00	120	—
1613	—	14.00	27.50	60.00	120	—
1614	—	14.00	27.50	60.00	120	—
1615 P	—	14.00	27.50	60.00	120	—
1615 PA	—	14.00	27.50	60.00	120	—
1616 PA	—	14.00	27.50	60.00	120	—
1617 PA	—	14.00	27.50	60.00	120	—
1618 PA	—	14.00	27.50	60.00	120	—
1619 PA	—	14.00	27.50	60.00	120	—
1620 PA	—	14.00	27.50	60.00	120	—
1621 PA	—	17.00	33.50	75.00	140	—

KM# 10 4 CORNADOS

Copper **Note:** Without inner circle.

Date	Mintage	VG	F	VF	XF	Unc
1611	—	18.00	37.50	70.00	125	—

KM# 11 4 CORNADOS

Copper **Obv:** Crowned FI monogram in inner circle, titles of Philip IV **Rev:** Crowned pointed arms in inner circle **Mint:** Pamplona

Date	Mintage	VG	F	VF	XF	Unc
NDPP PP	—	125	210	375	—	—

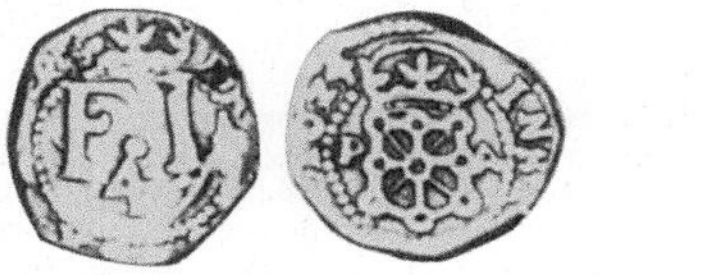

KM# 20 4 CORNADOS

Copper **Obv:** Crowned FI monogram, value 4 between, in pellet circle **Rev:** Crowned arms of Navarre in pellet circle

Date	Mintage	VG	F	VF	XF	Unc
1622	—	27.50	55.00	100	180	—
1624	—	25.00	48.00	90.00	150	—
1625	—	27.50	55.00	100	180	—
1626	—	27.50	55.00	100	180	—
1627	—	25.00	48.00	90.00	150	—
1641	—	25.00	48.00	90.00	150	—

KM# 30 4 CORNADOS

Copper **Rev:** Without pellet circles

Date	Mintage	VG	F	VF	XF	Unc
1641	—	30.00	60.00	110	200	—
1644	—	27.50	55.00	100	180	—
1645	—	27.50	55.00	100	180	—
1650	—	25.00	48.00	90.00	150	—
1651	—	30.00	60.00	110	200	—
1652	—	30.00	60.00	110	200	—
1653	—	30.00	60.00	110	200	—

KM# 31 4 CORNADOS

Copper **Obv:** Crowned Philip monogram **Rev:** Crowned arms of Navarre

Date	Mintage	VG	F	VF	XF	Unc
1644	—	38.50	80.00	140	220	—
1645	—	38.50	80.00	140	220	—
1646	—	38.50	80.00	140	220	—
1649	—	38.50	80.00	140	220	—
1650	—	38.50	80.00	140	220	—
1653	—	38.50	80.00	140	220	—
1654	—	38.50	80.00	140	220	—
1655	—	38.50	80.00	140	220	—
1659	—	38.50	80.00	140	220	—
1663	—	38.50	80.00	140	220	—
1664	—	38.50	80.00	140	220	—
1665	—	55.00	110	210	325	—

KM# 12 8 CORNADOS

Copper **Obv:** Crowned FI monogram in inner circle, titles of Philip IV **Rev:** Crowned pointed arms in inner circle **Mint:** Pamplona

Date	Mintage	VG	F	VF	XF	Unc
ND PP	—	140	265	425	—	—

KM# 13 REAL

Silver **Obv:** Crowned arms of Navarre, 1 at right **Rev:** Cross in cartouche

Date	Mintage	VG	F	VF	XF	Unc
1611 P	—	275	450	750	1,500	—
1612 P	—	325	500	875	1,800	—

KM# 35 REAL

Silver **Obv:** Crowned arms of Navarre in inner circle dividing P - I **Rev:** Cross in cartouche, circles in angles, date in legend **Mint:** Pamplona

Date	Mintage	VG	F	VF	XF	Unc
1651P A	—	175	325	525	950	—
1652P A	—	175	325	525	950	—

KM# 14 2 REALES

Silver **Obv:** Crowned arms in inner circle, titles of Philip III **Rev:** Cross in cartouche, date in legend **Mint:** Pamplona

Date	Mintage	VG	F	VF	XF	Unc
1611 P	—	400	650	1,150	2,200	—
1612 PA	—	450	700	1,250	2,400	—

KM# 36 2 REALES

Silver **Obv:** Titles of Philip IV **Mint:** Pamplona

Date	Mintage	VG	F	VF	XF	Unc
1651 PA	—	285	500	750	1,300	—
1652 PA	—	285	500	800	1,350	—

KM# 15 4 REALES

Silver **Obv:** Crowned arms of Navarre, IIII vertical at left **Rev:** Short cross in cartouche, pellets and ovals in quarters, date in legend **Mint:** Pamplona

Date	Mintage	VG	F	VF	XF	Unc
1612 Rare	—	—	—	—	—	—

KM# 41 4 REALES

Silver **Obv:** Crowned eight equal part shield **Rev:** Cross divides date in lower quadrants **Mint:** Pamplona

Date	Mintage	Good	VG	F	VF	XF
1659 Rare	—	—	—	—	—	—

KM# 37 8 REALES

Silver **Obv:** Crowned eight equal part shield **Obv. Legend:** PHILIPPVS • D • GRACIA • REX • **Rev:** Cross, ovals at corners **Rev. Legend:** CASTELLE • ET • NAVARRE

Date	Mintage	VG	F	VF	XF	Unc
1651 A Rare	—	—	—	—	—	—

KM# 38 8 REALES

Silver **Obv. Legend:** PHILIPPVS • VI • D • GRACIA **Rev:** Cross, ovals at corners **Rev. Legend:** NAVARRE • REX

Date	Mintage	Good	VG	F	VF	XF
1652 A Rare	—	—	—	—	—	—

KM# 40 8 REALES

Silver **Obv:** Similar to KM#37 **Rev:** Similar to KM#38

Date	Mintage	Good	VG	F	VF	XF
1658 Rare	—	—	—	—	—	—

KM# 39 50 REALES

Silver **Obv:** Crowned arms of Navarre dividing PA - 50 **Rev:** Cross with ovals in angles, date in legend

Date	Mintage	Good	VG	F	VF	XF
1652 Rare	—	—	—	—	—	—

Note: This is a cast coin and forgeries are known to exist

ROUSSILLON

SPANISH OCCUPATION - PERPIGNAU

STANDARD COINAGE

KM# 5 MENUT

Copper **Ruler:** Philip III **Obv:** Double "P" monogram **Rev:** St. John the Baptist standing facing

Date	Mintage	Good	VG	F	VF	XF
1611	—	80.00	160	350	—	—

KM# 15 TRENET (3 Deneros)

Copper **Ruler:** Philip III **Obv:** Double P monogram, A above **Rev:** St. John the Babtist standing facing, divides date

Date	Mintage	Good	VG	F	VF	XF
1611	—	60.00	120	250	—	—

FRENCH OCCUPATION - PERPIGNAU

STANDARD COINAGE

KM# 14 MENUT

Copper **Ruler:** Louis XIV **Obv:** Double "P" monogram **Obv. Legend:** LVDOVICVS •-• XIIII **Rev:** St. John the Baptist standing facing **Rev. Legend:** + ECCE * AGNVS • DELx

Date	Mintage	Good	VG	F	VF	XF
1648	—	25.00	50.00	100	200	—

KM# 11 SOL

Billon **Ruler:** Louis XIV **Obv:** Crowned diamond arms divides date **Obv. Legend:** PERPINIANI VILE **Rev:** St. John the Baptist standing facing, lis below, retrograde value "2" at left **Rev. Legend:** + INTER NATOS - MVLIERVM

Date	Mintage	Good	VG	F	VF	XF
1644	—	15.00	25.00	50.00	90.00	—

KM# 13 SOL

Billon **Ruler:** Louis XIV **Obv:** Crowned arms with lis at center divides date **Obv. Legend:** PERPINIANI * VILLE **Rev:** St. John the Baptist standing facing, value "1" at left **Rev. Legend:** + INTER NATOS. MVLIERVM

Date	Mintage	Good	VG	F	VF	XF
1645	—	15.00	25.00	50.00	90.00	—

KM# 12.1 2 SOLS

Billon **Ruler:** Louis XIV **Obv:** Crowned diamond arms divides date **Obv. Legend:** PERPINIANI VILE **Rev:** St. John the Baptist standing facing, lis below, value "2" at left **Rev. Legend:** + INTER NATOS - MVLIERVM

Date	Mintage	Good	VG	F	VF	XF
1644	—	20.00	40.00	75.00	150	—

KM# 12.2 2 SOLS

Billon **Ruler:** Louis XIV **Obv:** Crowned diamond arms divides date **Obv. Legend:** PERPINIANI VILE **Rev:** St. John the Baptist standing facing, lis below, retrograde value "2" at left **Rev. Legend:** + INTER NATOS - MVLIERVM

Date	Mintage	Good	VG	F	VF	XF
1644	—	20.00	35.00	65.00	145	—

VALENCIA

Valencia is a maritime province of eastern Spain with a capital city of Valencia. Once a former kingdom, Valencia included the present provinces of Castellon de la Plana and Alicante.

RULERS

Philip III of Spain, 1598-1621
Philip IV of Spain, 1621-1665
Charles II of Spain, 1665-1700
Philip V of Spain, 1700-1746

PROVINCE

STANDARD COINAGE

KM# 5 DINERO (Menudo, Menut)

Copper **Obv:** Bust of Philip right in inner circle **Rev:** Lily plant in center circle, date in legend **Mint:** Valencia

Date	Mintage	VG	F	VF	XF	Unc
1610	—	16.00	32.00	60.00	120	—

KM# 16 DINERO (Menudo, Menut)

Copper **Obv:** Crowned bust right in inner circle **Mint:** Valencia

Date	Mintage	VG	F	VF	XF	Unc
1624	—	36.00	65.00	120	200	—
1634	—	25.00	50.00	90.00	160	—
1646	—	25.00	50.00	90.00	160	—
1651	—	20.00	40.00	70.00	140	—
1652	—	16.00	32.00	60.00	130	—
1653	—	16.00	32.00	60.00	130	—
1654	—	16.00	32.00	60.00	130	—
1655	—	16.00	32.00	60.00	130	—
1660	—	16.00	32.00	100	200	—
1661	—	20.00	40.00	70.00	140	—
1662	—	20.00	40.00	70.00	140	—
1663	—	16.00	32.00	60.00	130	—
1664	—	16.00	32.00	60.00	130	—
1665	—	16.00	32.00	60.00	130	—

KM# 35 DINERO (Menudo, Menut)

Copper **Obv:** Crowned bust of Charles II left in inner circle **Mint:** Valencia

Date	Mintage	VG	F	VF	XF	Unc
1667	—	16.00	30.00	50.00	100	—
1668	—	12.00	25.00	40.00	80.00	—
1669	—	12.00	25.00	40.00	80.00	—
1670	—	12.00	25.00	40.00	80.00	—
1671	—	12.00	25.00	40.00	80.00	—
1672	—	12.00	25.00	40.00	80.00	—
1673	—	12.00	25.00	40.00	80.00	—
1680	—	18.00	36.00	60.00	120	—
1681	—	12.00	25.00	40.00	80.00	—
1682	—	12.00	25.00	40.00	80.00	—
1683	—	14.00	25.00	44.00	90.00	—
1684	—	12.00	25.00	40.00	80.00	—
1685	—	14.00	25.00	44.00	90.00	—
1686	—	14.00	25.00	44.00	90.00	—
1687	—	14.00	25.00	44.00	90.00	—
1688	—	12.00	25.00	40.00	80.00	—
1689	—	14.00	25.00	44.00	90.00	—
1690	—	12.00	25.00	40.00	80.00	—
1691	—	12.00	25.00	40.00	80.00	—
1692	—	12.00	25.00	40.00	80.00	—
1693	—	12.00	25.00	40.00	80.00	—
1694	—	12.00	25.00	40.00	80.00	—
1695	—	12.00	25.00	40.00	80.00	—
1696	—	12.00	25.00	40.00	80.00	—
1697	—	12.00	25.00	40.00	80.00	—
1698	—	12.00	25.00	40.00	80.00	—
1699	—	12.00	25.00	40.00	80.00	—

KM# 6 1/2 REAL

Silver **Obv:** Crowned facing bust of Philip III in inner circle **Rev:** Arms divide date in inner circle **Mint:** Valencia

Date	Mintage	VG	F	VF	XF	Unc
1610	—	70.00	140	250	450	—

KM# 17 1/2 REAL

Silver **Obv:** Crowned facing bust of Philip IV

Date	Mintage	VG	F	VF	XF	Unc
1624	—	265	450	800	—	—
1650	—	265	450	800	—	—

KM# 45 1/2 REAL

Silver **Obv:** Crowned facing bust of Charles II **Rev:** Crowned arms with value, divide date

Date	Mintage	VG	F	VF	XF	Unc
1681	—	120	200	350	550	—
1682	—	60.00	120	180	350	—

KM# 48 1/2 REAL

Silver **Rev:** Without value

Date	Mintage	VG	F	VF	XF	Unc
1682	—	44.00	90.00	150	300	—
1684	—	120	200	350	550	—

KM# 7 REAL

Silver **Obv:** Crowned facing bust of Philip III **Rev:** Crowned arms, date divided near top **Mint:** Valencia **Note:** Varieties exist.

Date	Mintage	VG	F	VF	XF	Unc
1610	—	40.00	80.00	140	280	—
1616	—	40.00	80.00	150	300	—
1618	—	40.00	80.00	130	260	—
1619	—	40.00	80.00	130	260	—
1620	—	40.00	80.00	140	280	—

KM# 15 REAL

Silver **Obv:** Crowned facing bust of Philip IV **Note:** Varieties exist.

Date	Mintage	VG	F	VF	XF	Unc
1621	—	25.00	60.00	100	200	—
1622	—	25.00	60.00	100	200	—
1623	—	25.00	60.00	100	200	—
1624/2	—	25.00	70.00	120	240	—
1624	—	25.00	60.00	100	200	—
1625	—	80.00	160	290	500	—
1638	—	100	200	350	550	—
1639	—	100	200	350	550	—
1640	—	70.00	140	260	400	—
1641	—	30.00	60.00	100	200	—
1642	—	30.00	60.00	100	200	—
1643	—	36.00	70.00	120	240	—
1644	—	30.00	60.00	100	200	—
1645	—	36.00	70.00	120	240	—
1646	—	36.00	70.00	120	240	—
1647	—	70.00	140	260	400	—
1648	—	30.00	60.00	100	200	—
1649	—	30.00	60.00	100	200	—
1650	—	30.00	60.00	100	200	—
1651	—	30.00	60.00	100	200	—
1652	—	30.00	60.00	100	200	—
1653	—	30.00	60.00	100	200	—
1654	—	70.00	140	280	450	—
1655	—	90.00	180	325	525	—
1656	—	120	240	400	700	—
1657	—	120	240	400	700	—
1658	—	120	240	400	700	—
1659	—	70.00	140	260	400	—

KM# 46 REAL

Silver **Obv:** Crowned bust of Charles II right **Note:** Varieties exist.

Date	Mintage	VG	F	VF	XF	Unc
1681	—	225	450	825	1,450	—
1682	—	300	600	1,150	1,900	—
1683	—	265	525	975	1,650	—
1686	—	265	525	975	1,650	—
1687	—	265	525	1,000	1,750	—

KM# 47 REAL

Silver **Obv:** Crowned facing bust of Charles II **Note:** Varieties exist.

Date	Mintage	VG	F	VF	XF	Unc
1681	—	30.00	60.00	100	200	—
1682	—	30.00	60.00	100	200	—
1683	—	36.00	70.00	120	240	—
1684	—	30.00	60.00	100	200	—
1685	—	36.00	70.00	120	240	—
1686	—	36.00	70.00	120	240	—
1687	—	30.00	60.00	100	200	—
1688	—	30.00	60.00	100	200	—
1689	—	30.00	60.00	100	200	—
1690	—	55.00	100	180	350	—
1691	—	55.00	100	180	350	—
1692	—	30.00	60.00	100	200	—
1695	—	60.00	120	200	400	—
1697	—	60.00	120	200	400	—
1698	—	120	240	400	750	—
1699	—	80.00	160	300	600	—

KM# 49 2 REALES

Silver **Obv:** Crowned bust of Charles II right, shield below **Rev:** Crowned arms **Mint:** Valencia

Date	Mintage	VG	F	VF	XF	Unc
1683	—	950	1,600	2,800	4,550	—

KM# 51 ESCUDO

3.3834 g., 0.9170 Gold 0.0997 oz. AGW **Obv:** Crowned diamond shield with vertical stripes, L at each side in inner circle **Rev:** Cross in quadrolobe in inner circle, titles of Philip IV

Date	Mintage	VG	F	VF	XF	Unc
ND	—	325	575	1,150	2,150	—

KM# 52 ESCUDO

3.3834 g., 0.9170 Gold 0.0997 oz. AGW **Rev:** Titles of Charles II

Date	Mintage	VG	F	VF	XF	Unc
1688	—	325	625	1,250	2,250	—
1693	—	325	600	1,150	2,150	—
1694	—	325	625	1,250	2,250	—
1695	—	325	575	1,050	1,950	—
1700	—	400	825	1,550	2,700	—

KM# 53 ESCUDO

3.3834 g., 0.9170 Gold 0.0997 oz. AGW **Rev:** Dragon on helmet

Date	Mintage	VG	F	VF	XF	Unc
1688	—	625	1,250	2,500	4,400	—

SPANISH NETHERLANDS

The Netherlands as an entity perhaps came into being when Philip the Good, duke of Burgundy (1419-1467) called all the Burgundian states together for a common session at Bruges in 1464. Charles the Bold continued to add to the territory and consolidated his power, which, however reverted to the States General at his death in 1477. His daughter Mary married the Austrian archduke Maximilian, and was succeeded by her only son, Philip the Handsome (1494-1506). He married Joanna of Spain, daughter of Ferdinand and Isabella, and their oldest son, Charles V, became king of Aragon and Castile in 1520, head of the Austrian house of Habsburg, and Holy Roman Emperor. The Netherlands passed under the regency of his aunts Margaret of Austria (1519-30) and Mary of Hungary (1531-55). Philip II (1556-98) was a Spaniard and resented by many of the Netherlanders, especially the Protestants and the higher nobility and clergy. The ruthless savagery of his governor the duke of Alba led to continued revolts, and finally to the Pacification of Ghent 1576, a union which was short lived. By the Union of Utrecht (1579) the northern provinces to all intents and purposes were separated from the southern ones.

The Spanish under Farnese, the duke of Parma, gradually regained supremacy in the southern provinces. Philip gave the provinces as dowry when his daughter, Isabella, married the archduke Albert of Austria in 1598. The Spanish Netherlands was to be an independent state based on Catholicism as the only recognized religion, and strong central government. Albert died in 1621 and Isabella in 1633, childless, and the provinces reverted to Philip IV of Spain. War with the United Netherlands and France followed until by the Peace Westphalia, concluding the Thirty Years War in1648, Philip recognized the independence of the northern states. By the Peace of the Pyrenes in 1659 and the Peace of Aix-la-Chapelle in 1668 Louis XIV of France acquired Artois and other border districts. On the death of Charles II in 1700 the southern Netherlands passed to the new Bourbon king of Spain, the French duke Philip of Anjou. In 1701, Louis XIV compelled his grandson to turn the territory over to France, but by the Treaty of Utrecht concluding the War of the Spanish Succession, the provinces were given to Austria.

ARTOIS

(Aire-sur-la-Lys)

A town in north France on the Lys, lies in a low and marshy area at the junction of 3 canals.

In the middle ages, Artois belonged to the counts of Flanders and a charter of 1188 is still extant. It was given to France by the peace of Utrecht in 1713. In World War I, it was one of the headquarters of the British Army Expeditionary Forces.

RULER

Spanish

MINT MARK

Rat - Arras

NOTE: See also France-Aire.

COUNTY

HAMMERED COINAGE

KM# 6 GIGOT

Copper **Obv:** St. Andrew's cross, crown above, fleece below **Rev:** Crowned shield of Philip IV **Rev. Legend:** ...DVX BVRG CO ART Z

Date	Mintage	Good	VG	F	VF	XF
1627	—	12.00	30.00	60.00	150	275
1628	—	12.00	30.00	60.00	150	275
1638	—	12.00	30.00	60.00	150	275
1639	—	12.00	30.00	60.00	150	275
1640	—	12.00	30.00	60.00	150	275

KM# 7 LIARD

Copper **Obv:** Crowne and shields of Burgundy, Brabant, and Breda **Rev:** Crowned shield divides date **Rev. Legend:** ...DVX BVRG CO ART Z

Date	Mintage	Good	VG	F	VF	XF
1627	—	6.00	15.00	25.00	40.00	70.00
1628	—	6.00	15.00	25.00	40.00	70.00
1629	—	8.00	20.00	35.00	55.00	95.00

KM# 1 LIARD

Copper **Obv:** Philip IV

Date	Mintage	VG	F	VF	XF	Unc
ND	—	20.00	40.00	75.00	—	—

KM# 19 LIARD

Copper **Obv:** Bust of Philip IV right **Rev:** Crowned shield of Artois

Date	Mintage	Good	VG	F	VF	XF
1636	—	12.00	30.00	55.00	110	205
1637	—	10.00	25.00	45.00	90.00	160
1638	—	10.00	25.00	45.00	90.00	160
1639	—	10.00	25.00	45.00	90.00	160
1640	—	10.00	25.00	45.00	90.00	160

KM# 2 ESCALIN

5.2600 g., 0.5820 Silver 0.0984 oz. ASW **Obv:** Lion **Rev:** St. Andrew's cross of Bourgogne

Date	Mintage	Good	VG	F	VF	XF
ND	—	12.00	30.00	60.00	120	—

KM# 3 ESCALIN

5.2600 g., 0.5820 Silver 0.0984 oz. ASW **Obv:** Lion rampant left with sword and shield **Rev:** Crowned shield of Philip IV on St. Andrew's cross **Rev. Legend:** ...DVX BVR C ART Zc

Date	Mintage	Good	VG	F	VF	XF
1623	—	8.00	20.00	40.00	85.00	150
1624	—	10.00	25.00	50.00	100	195
1625	—	8.00	20.00	40.00	85.00	150
1626	—	10.00	25.00	50.00	100	195
1627	—	7.50	18.00	35.00	70.00	130
1628	—	8.00	20.00	40.00	85.00	150
1631	—	10.00	25.00	50.00	100	195
1634	—	10.00	25.00	50.00	100	195
1635	—	9.00	22.00	45.00	90.00	180

KM# 5 1/4 PATAGON

7.0300 g., 0.8750 Silver 0.1978 oz. ASW **Obv:** St. Andrew's cross, shield at center, crown above, fleece below, divides date **Rev:** Crowned shield of Philip IV in collar of the Golden Fleece **Rev. Legend:** ...DVX BVRG CO ART Zc

Date	Mintage	Good	VG	F	VF	XF
1624	—	50.00	125	250	500	925
1625	—	60.00	150	300	600	1,100
1626	—	60.00	150	300	600	1,100
1634	—	50.00	125	250	500	925
1635	—	60.00	150	300	600	1,100

KM# 8 1/2 PATAGON

14.0500 g., 0.8750 Silver 0.3952 oz. ASW **Obv:** St. Andrew's cross, shield at center, crown above, fleece below, divides date **Rev:** Crowned shield of Philip IV in collar of the Golden Fleece **Rev. Legend:** ...DVX BVRG CO ART Zc

Date	Mintage	Good	VG	F	VF	XF
1627	—	50.00	125	250	500	925
1628	—	60.00	150	300	600	1,100
1629	—	60.00	150	300	600	1,100
1634	—	70.00	175	350	700	1,250
1635	—	70.00	175	350	700	1,250

KM# 4 PATAGON

28.1000 g., 0.8750 Silver 0.7905 oz. ASW **Obv:** St. Andrew's cross, crown above, fleece below, divides pair of crowned double C monograms **Rev:** Crowned shield in collar of the Golden Fleece **Rev. Legend:** ...DVX BVRG CO ART Zc **Note:** Dav. #4466.

Date	Mintage	Good	VG	F	VF	XF
1623	—	50.00	115	225	450	850
1624	—	60.00	135	270	550	1,000
1625	—	60.00	135	270	550	1,000
1627	—	35.00	75.00	160	325	600
1628/7	—	45.00	105	205	400	700
1629	—	50.00	115	225	450	850
1634	—	60.00	135	270	550	1,000
1635	—	60.00	135	270	550	1,000

KM# 9 2 PATAGON

56.2000 g., 0.8750 Silver 1.5809 oz. ASW **Obv:** St. Andrew's cross, crown above, fleece below, divides pair of crowned double C monograms **Rev:** Crowned shield in collar of the Golden Fleece **Rev. Legend:** ... DVX BVRG CO ART Zc **Note:** Dav. #4465.

Date	Mintage	Good	VG	F	VF	XF
1623	1,623	—	—	—	—	—
1624	—	—	—	—	—	—
1634	—	—	—	—	—	—

KM# 16 1/2 DUCATONE

16.2400 g., 0.9440 Silver 0.4929 oz. ASW **Obv:** Bust of Philip IV right in ruffled collar **Rev:** Crowned shield with lion supporters **Rev. Legend:** ...DVX BVRG CO ART Zc

Date	Mintage	Good	VG	F	VF	XF
1635	—	250	450	850	1,750	2,850

KM# 17 DUCATONE

32.4800 g., 0.9440 Silver 0.9857 oz. ASW **Obv:** Bust of Philip IV right in ruffled collar; mint mark divides date in top legend **Rev:** Lions support crowned shield **Rev. Legend:** ...DVX BVRG CO ART Z **Note:** Dav. #4448.

Date	Mintage	Good	VG	F	VF	XF
1635	—	110	280	550	1,200	2,250

KM# 18 2 DUCATONE

Silver **Note:** Similar to KM#17. Dav. #4447.

Date	Mintage	Good	VG	F	VF	XF
1635 Rare	—	—	—	—	—	—

KM# 15 2 SOUVERAIN D'OR

22.1200 g., 0.9190 Gold 0.6535 oz. AGW **Obv:** Crowned bust of Philip IV in ruffled collar in inner circle; date at top **Rev:** Crowned arms in collar of the Golden Fleece

Date	Mintage	Good	VG	F	VF	XF
1632 Rare	—	—	—	—	—	—
1634 Rare	—	—	—	—	—	—

SIEGE COINAGE

1641

NOTE: OBS = Obsessa, Obsidione (Obsidional)

KM# 25 REAL

3.5000 g., Silver **Obv:** Inscription in six lines **Obv. Inscription:** PHIL. IIII / REX / PATER / PATRIAE / ARIA OBS / 1641 **Note:** Uniface.

Date	Mintage	Good	VG	F	VF	XF
1641	—	400	550	850	1,250	1,900

KM# 26 2 REALES

6.2000 g., Silver **Obv:** Inscription in six lines **Obv. Inscription:** PHIL. IIII / REX / PATER / PATRIAE / ARIA OBS / 1641.II. **Note:** Uniface.

Date	Mintage	Good	VG	F	VF	XF
1641	—	450	750	1,250	1,850	2,500

KM# 27 4 REALES

Silver **Obv:** Inscription in six lines **Obv. Inscription:** PHIL. IIII. / REX / PATER • / PATRIAE. / ARIA OBSESSA./1641.VIII.

Date	Mintage	Good	VG	F	VF	XF
ND(1641)	—	1,200	2,000	3,500	5,500	8,000

BRABANT

A marquisate in medieval time. In 1578 Don John of Austria, the hero of Lepanto, died here. The area and town were much fought over even into modern times.

RULERS

Spanish

Albert and Elizabeth, 1598-1621
Philip IV, 1621-1665
Charles II, 1665-1700
Philip V, 1700-1712

MINT MARKS

Hand - Anvers
Angel face - Brussels
Star - Maastricht
Tree - 's Hertogenbosch (Bois-le-Duc)

SPANISH RULE

STANDARD COINAGE

KM# 28 DENIER (4 Mites)

Copper **Obv:** Crowned AE monogram **Rev:** Crowned shield of Austria and Bourgonne on St. Andrews's cross **Mint:** Antwerp

Date	Mintage	VG	F	VF	XF	Unc
1606	—	10.00	20.00	60.00	200	—
1607	—	10.00	20.00	60.00	200	—

Note: Legend varieties exist for 1607

KM# 29 2 DENIER (8 Mites)

Copper **Obv:** Crowned AE monogram **Obv. Legend:** Ends: BVRG ET. BRA. **Rev:** Crowned shield of Austria and Bourgonne on St. Andrew's cross **Mint:** Antwerp

Date	Mintage	VG	F	VF	XF	Unc
1606	—	10.00	15.00	20.00	65.00	—
1607	—	10.00	15.00	20.00	65.00	—

KM# 23 1/2 LIARD (6 Mites, Gigot)

Copper **Obv:** Crowned shield of Albert and Elizabeth **Rev:** Shield of 's Hertogenbosch **Mint:** s Hertogenbosch

Date	Mintage	VG	F	VF	XF	Unc
1602	—	15.00	30.00	100	300	—
1603	—	20.00	40.00	125	350	—
1604	—	20.00	40.00	125	350	—
1605	—	20.00	40.00	125	350	—
1607	—	25.00	50.00	175	525	—

KM# 32.1 1/2 LIARD (6 Mites, Gigot)

Copper **Obv:** Crowned shield of Austria and Burgundy, lion at center **Obv. Legend:** ...BVRG ET B **Rev:** St. Andrew's cross, crown on top, fleece below **Mint:** Antwerp

Date	Mintage	VG	F	VF	XF	Unc
1608	—	10.00	15.00	25.00	75.00	—
1609	—	10.00	15.00	25.00	75.00	—
1615	—	10.00	15.00	20.00	75.00	—
1616	—	10.00	15.00	20.00	55.00	—
1618	—	10.00	15.00	35.00	130	—
1619	—	10.00	15.00	35.00	130	—

KM# 32.2 1/2 LIARD (6 Mites, Gigot)

Copper **Obv. Legend:** Ends: BVRG Z **Mint:** Brabant

Date	Mintage	VG	F	VF	XF	Unc
1615	—	10.00	15.00	25.00	65.00	—
1616	—	10.00	15.00	25.00	65.00	—

KM# 32.3 1/2 LIARD (6 Mites, Gigot)

Copper **Obv. Legend:** ...BVRG ET B. Z. **Mint:** s Hertogenbosch

Date	Mintage	VG	F	VF	XF	Unc
1615	—	10.00	20.00	50.00	150	—
1616	—	20.00	35.00	95.00	300	—

KM# 32.4 1/2 LIARD (6 Mites, Gigot)

Copper **Obv. Legend:** ...BVRG BRA Z **Mint:** Maastricht

Date	Mintage	VG	F	VF	XF	Unc
1616	—	10.00	15.00	45.00	135	—
1617	—	10.00	15.00	35.00	100	—
1618	—	10.00	15.00	35.00	110	—
1619	—	10.00	15.00	40.00	120	—

KM# 55.2 1/2 LIARD (6 Mites, Gigot)

Copper **Mint:** Maastricht

Date	Mintage	VG	F	VF	XF	Unc
1624	—	35.00	65.00	200	600	—
1625	—	45.00	90.00	275	825	—
1626	—	45.00	90.00	275	825	—

KM# 55.3 1/2 LIARD (6 Mites, Gigot)

Copper **Mint:** Brabant

Date	Mintage	VG	F	VF	XF	Unc
1626	—	25.00	50.00	150	450	—
1650	—	20.00	35.00	100	300	—
1655	—	15.00	30.00	90.00	275	—

KM# 55.1 1/2 LIARD (6 Mites, Gigot)

Copper **Obv:** St. Andrew's cross, crown above, fleece below **Rev:** Crowned shield of Philippe IV **Rev. Legend:** ...DVX BVRG BRAB Z **Mint:** Antwerp

Date	Mintage	VG	F	VF	XF	Unc
1626	—	15.00	30.00	75.00	225	—
1628	—	30.00	60.00	175	525	—
1644	—	—	—	—	—	—
1646	—	—	—	—	—	—
1650	—	25.00	45.00	125	350	—
1654	—	30.00	55.00	175	475	—
1656	—	20.00	40.00	90.00	275	—

KM# 100.1 1/2 LIARD (6 Mites, Gigot)

Copper **Obv:** Fleece separates date **Rev:** Crowned shield of Austria and Burgundy, small lion at center **Rev. Legend:** ...DVX BVRG BRAB Z **Mint:** Antwerp

Date	Mintage	VG	F	VF	XF	Unc
1681	—	25.00	45.00	100	200	—
1685	—	20.00	30.00	60.00	125	—
1686	—	25.00	45.00	100	200	—

KM# 100.2 1/2 LIARD (6 Mites, Gigot)

Copper **Mint:** Brabant

Date	Mintage	VG	F	VF	XF	Unc
1685	—	35.00	70.00	175	450	—
1688	—	75.00	150	375	875	—

KM# 118 1/2 LIARD (6 Mites, Gigot)

Copper **Rev:** Crowned shield separates date **Rev. Legend:** ...DVX BVRG BRAB Z **Mint:** Antwerp

Date	Mintage	VG	F	VF	XF	Unc
1696	—	10.00	12.50	15.00	25.00	—
1700	—	10.00	12.50	15.00	25.00	—

KM# 24.1 LIARD (12 Mites)

Copper **Obv:** Crowned shield of Albert and Elizabeth **Rev:** Shield of 's Hertogenbosch, date above **Mint:** s Hertogenbosch

Date	Mintage	VG	F	VF	XF	Unc
1602	—	15.00	25.00	60.00	175	—
1603	—	15.00	25.00	60.00	175	—
1604	—	15.00	30.00	90.00	250	—
1605	—	—	—	—	—	—

KM# 24.2 LIARD (12 Mites)

Copper **Mint:** Maastricht

Date	Mintage	VG	F	VF	XF	Unc
1603	—	10.00	15.00	40.00	85.00	—
1604	—	10.00	15.00	35.00	65.00	—
1605	—	10.00	15.00	40.00	80.00	—
1606	—	10.00	15.00	40.00	85.00	—
1607	—	10.00	15.00	30.00	75.00	—
1608	—	10.00	15.00	35.00	65.00	—
1609	—	10.00	15.00	45.00	80.00	—

Date	Mintage	VG	F	VF	XF	Unc
1611	—	10.00	15.00	40.00	80.00	—
1612	—	10.00	15.00	30.00	60.00	—
1613	—	10.00	20.00	50.00	95.00	—
1614	—	10.00	15.00	35.00	65.00	—
1615	—	10.00	15.00	35.00	65.00	—

KM# 30 LIARD (12 Mites)

Copper **Rev:** Shield of 's Hertogenbosch on St. Andrew's cross divides date **Mint:** s Hertogenbosch

Date	Mintage	VG	F	VF	XF	Unc
1607	—	10.00	20.00	55.00	150	—
1609	—	10.00	20.00	55.00	150	—

KM# 33.1 LIARD (12 Mites)

Copper **Obv:** Crowned shield of Albert and Elizabeth **Obv. Legend:** ...BVRG ET B **Rev:** Crown and shields of Austria, Burgundy and Brabant **Mint:** Antwerp

Date	Mintage	VG	F	VF	XF	Unc
1608	—	10.00	15.00	20.00	65.00	—
1610	—	10.00	12.50	15.00	55.00	—
1617	—	15.00	30.00	90.00	250	—

KM# 40 LIARD (12 Mites)

Billon **Obv:** Crowned shield of Austria and Burgundy **Rev:** Cross floree **Mint:** Antwerp **Note:** Legend varieties exist.

Date	Mintage	VG	F	VF	XF	Unc
1614	—	275	450	875	1,750	—

KM# 62.1 LIARD (12 Mites)

Copper **Obv:** Crown and shields of Austria, Burgundy and Brabant **Rev:** Crowned shield divides date **Mint:** Antwerp

Date	Mintage	VG	F	VF	XF	Unc
1626	—	—	—	—	—	—
1643	—	10.00	12.50	15.00	45.00	—
1650	—	10.00	15.00	30.00	80.00	—
1652	—	10.00	15.00	20.00	50.00	—
1653	—	10.00	15.00	25.00	65.00	—
1654	—	10.00	15.00	20.00	50.00	—
1656	—	10.00	15.00	20.00	50.00	—

KM# 63 LIARD (12 Mites)

Copper **Obv:** Crown and shields of Austria, Brabant and Breda **Mint:** Antwerp

Date	Mintage	VG	F	VF	XF	Unc
1626	—	—	—	—	—	—

KM# 62.2 LIARD (12 Mites)

Copper **Mint:** Maastricht

Date	Mintage	VG	F	VF	XF	Unc
1629	—	10.00	15.00	30.00	95.00	—
1630	—	10.00	15.00	20.00	65.00	—
1632	—	10.00	15.00	20.00	65.00	—

KM# 62.3 LIARD (12 Mites)

Copper **Mint:** Brabant

Date	Mintage	VG	F	VF	XF	Unc
1643	—	10.00	12.50	15.00	50.00	—
1644	—	10.00	12.50	15.00	50.00	—
1647	—	10.00	15.00	25.00	80.00	—
1648	—	10.00	15.00	25.00	80.00	—
1650	—	10.00	15.00	30.00	95.00	—
1652	—	10.00	15.00	20.00	55.00	—
1653	—	10.00	15.00	25.00	80.00	—
1654	—	10.00	15.00	25.00	80.00	—
1655	—	10.00	15.00	30.00	95.00	—
1656	—	10.00	15.00	25.00	80.00	—

KM# 91.1 LIARD (12 Mites)

Copper **Obv:** Crown and shields of Austria, Burgundy and Brabant **Rev:** Crowned shield of Charles II divides date **Rev. Legend:** ...DVX BVRG BRAB Z **Mint:** Antwerp

Date	Mintage	VG	F	VF	XF	Unc
1679	—	10.00	15.00	30.00	65.00	—
1680	—	10.00	15.00	20.00	45.00	—
1683	—	15.00	30.00	75.00	160	—
1685	—	10.00	12.50	15.00	35.00	—

KM# 91.2 LIARD (12 Mites)

Copper **Mint:** Brabant

Date	Mintage	VG	F	VF	XF	Unc
1685	—	10.00	12.50	15.00	35.00	—
1690	—	10.00	12.50	15.00	35.00	—
1691	—	10.00	15.00	25.00	55.00	—

KM# 93.2 LIARD (12 Mites)

Copper **Mint:** Brabant

Date	Mintage	VG	F	VF	XF	Unc
1690	—	10.00	12.50	15.00	35.00	—
1691	—	10.00	12.50	15.00	35.00	—
1692	—	10.00	12.50	15.00	35.00	—
1693	—	10.00	12.50	15.00	35.00	—

KM# 93.3 LIARD (12 Mites)

Copper **Rev. Legend:** ARC D...

Date	Mintage	VG	F	VF	XF	Unc
1691	—	—	—	—	—	—

KM# 93.1 LIARD (12 Mites)

Copper **Obv:** Crown divides date in legend **Obv. Legend:** Ends: ...DVX BVRG BRAB Z **Mint:** Antwerp

Date	Mintage	VG	F	VF	XF	Unc
1692	—	10.00	12.50	15.00	35.00	—
1693	—	10.00	12.50	15.00	35.00	—
1695	—	—	—	—	—	—
1698	—	—	—	—	—	—

KM# 41.1 1/2 PATARD

Billon **Obv:** Cross floree, AE monogram **Rev:** Crowned shield of Albert and Elizabeth **Rev. Legend:** ...BVRG BR(AB) Z **Mint:** Antwerp

Date	Mintage	VG	F	VF	XF	Unc
ND(1614-19)	—	30.00	50.00	100	300	—
1614	—	45.00	75.00	150	300	—
1615	—	45.00	75.00	150	300	—
1616	—	45.00	75.00	150	300	—

KM# 41.3 1/2 PATARD

Billon **Mint:** s Hertogenbosch

Date	Mintage	VG	F	VF	XF	Unc
1614	—	35.00	65.00	150	275	—
1616	—	35.00	65.00	150	275	—
1617	—	35.00	65.00	150	275	—
1618	—	35.00	65.00	150	275	—
1619	—	35.00	65.00	150	275	—

KM# 41.2 1/2 PATARD

Billon **Mint:** Brabant **Note:** Legend varieties exist.

Date	Mintage	VG	F	VF	XF	Unc
1614	—	35.00	50.00	75.00	200	—
1618	—	25.00	45.00	90.00	175	—
1619	—	25.00	45.00	90.00	175	—

KM# 42.1 PATARD

Billon **Obv:** Cross floree, AE monogram **Rev:** Crowned shield of Albert and Elizabeth divides date **Rev. Legend:** ...BVRG BR Z **Mint:** Antwerp

Date	Mintage	VG	F	VF	XF	Unc
ND(1613-16)	—	25.00	45.00	90.00	175	—
1614	—	25.00	45.00	90.00	175	—
1615	—	30.00	60.00	125	250	—
1616	—	25.00	45.00	90.00	175	—

KM# 42.2 PATARD

Billon **Mint:** Brabant

Date	Mintage	VG	F	VF	XF	Unc
1614	—	—	—	—	—	—
1615	—	25.00	35.00	65.00	150	—
1616	—	25.00	35.00	65.00	150	—

KM# 42.3 PATARD

Billon **Mint:** s Hertogenbosch

Date	Mintage	VG	F	VF	XF	Unc
1614	—	25.00	35.00	65.00	150	—
1615	—	30.00	50.00	100	200	—
1616	—	—	—	—	—	—
1617	—	30.00	50.00	100	200	—
1618	—	30.00	50.00	100	200	—
1619	—	30.00	50.00	100	200	—
1620	—	30.00	50.00	100	200	—
1621	—	30.00	50.00	100	200	—

KM# 70.2 PATARD

Billon **Mint:** Brabant

Date	Mintage	VG	F	VF	XF	Unc
1631	—	40.00	75.00	150	300	—
1633	—	90.00	150	275	550	—

KM# 70.1 PATARD

Billon **Obv:** Linear cross **Rev:** Crowned shield of Philip IV divides date **Rev. Legend:** ...DVX BVRG BRAB Z **Mint:** Antwerp

Date	Mintage	VG	F	VF	XF	Unc
1632	—	40.00	75.00	150	300	—
1646	—	75.00	125	225	450	—

KM# 92.2 PATARD

Billon **Obv:** Long, linear cross, mint mark at center **Rev:** Crowned shield divides date **Rev. Legend:** ...DVX BRAB Zc **Mint:** Antwerp

Date	Mintage	VG	F	VF	XF	Unc
1679	—	40.00	75.00	200	400	—

KM# 92.3 PATARD

Billon **Mint:** Brabant

Date	Mintage	VG	F	VF	XF	Unc
1679	—	20.00	40.00	100	200	—

KM# 120 2 PATARDS

2.4500 g., 0.3850 Silver 0.0303 oz. ASW **Obv:** Linear cross with lion in center, lion and crown in angles **Rev:** Crowned shield divides date **Mint:** Antwerp

Date	Mintage	VG	F	VF	XF	Unc
1698	—	350	575	1,150	2,300	—

KM# 45.1 3 PATARDS

2.6300 g., 0.5820 Silver 0.0492 oz. ASW **Obv:** Cross floree, lion at center **Rev:** Crowned shield in octolobe **Rev. Legend:** ...BVR BRAB Z **Mint:** Antwerp

Date	Mintage	VG	F	VF	XF	Unc
1616	—	18.00	30.00	60.00	125	—
1617	—	15.00	25.00	50.00	100	—
1620	—	10.00	18.00	40.00	75.00	—
1621	—	10.00	18.00	40.00	75.00	—

KM# 45.3 3 PATARDS

2.6300 g., 0.5820 Silver 0.0492 oz. ASW **Mint:** Brabant

Date	Mintage	VG	F	VF	XF	Unc
1616	—	15.00	25.00	45.00	90.00	—
1617	—	10.00	18.00	40.00	75.00	—
1618	—	10.00	18.00	40.00	75.00	—
1619	—	10.00	18.00	40.00	75.00	—
1620	—	—	—	—	—	—

KM# 45.4 3 PATARDS

2.6300 g., 0.5820 Silver 0.0492 oz. ASW **Mint:** s Hertogenbosch

Date	Mintage	VG	F	VF	XF	Unc
1616	—	30.00	55.00	125	225	—
1617	—	30.00	55.00	125	225	—
1618	—	35.00	65.00	150	275	—
1619	—	35.00	65.00	150	275	—
1620	—	25.00	45.00	90.00	175	—
1621	—	25.00	45.00	90.00	175	—

KM# 45.2 3 PATARDS

2.6300 g., 0.5820 Silver 0.0492 oz. ASW **Mint:** Maastricht

Date	Mintage	VG	F	VF	XF	Unc
1617	—	525	875	1,750	3,450	—

KM# 45.5 3 PATARDS

2.6300 g., 0.5820 Silver 0.0492 oz. ASW **Rev. Legend:** ...DVX BVRG BRAB Z **Mint:** Brabant

Date	Mintage	VG	F	VF	XF	Unc
1623	—	—	—	—	—	—

KM# 121 4 PATARDS

4.9000 g., 0.3850 Silver 0.0606 oz. ASW **Obv:** St. Andrew's cross divides date, crown above, fleece below **Rev:** Crowned shield **Rev. Legend:** ...DVX BVRG BRAB Z **Mint:** Antwerp

Date	Mintage	VG	F	VF	XF	Unc
1698	—	50.00	95.00	220	375	—
1700	—	125	175	350	650	—

KM# 26.1 1/4 REAL

1.7400 g., 0.3960 Silver 0.0222 oz. ASW **Obv:** Crowned shield of Albert and Elizabeth **Rev:** Crowned shield divides date **Rev. Legend:** ...BVRG ET BRAB Z **Mint:** Antwerp

Date	Mintage	VG	F	VF	XF	Unc
1604	—	35.00	65.00	150	275	—
1605	—	25.00	45.00	90.00	175	—

KM# 26.2 1/4 REAL

1.7400 g., 0.3960 Silver 0.0222 oz. ASW **Mint:** s Hertogenbosch

Date	Mintage	VG	F	VF	XF	Unc
1609	—	150	250	475	925	—

KM# 31 1/2 REAL

3.4800 g., 0.3960 Silver 0.0443 oz. ASW **Obv:** Crowned shield of St. Andrew's cross divides date **Obv. Legend:** ...BVRG ET BRA **Rev:** Crowned shield **Mint:** Antwerp **Note:** Legend varieties exist.

Date	Mintage	VG	F	VF	XF	Unc
1607	—	40.00	80.00	175	325	—
1609	—	40.00	80.00	175	325	—

KM# 25.1 REAL

3.0600 g., 0.8960 Silver 0.0881 oz. ASW **Obv:** Crowned shield in collar of the Golden Fleece **Rev:** St. Andrew's cross, crown above, fleece below **Rev. Legend:** ...DVCES BVRG ET BRAB Z **Mint:** Antwerp

Date	Mintage	VG	F	VF	XF	Unc
ND(1603-07)	—	18.00	30.00	60.00	125	—

KM# 25.2 REAL

3.0600 g., 0.8960 Silver 0.0881 oz. ASW **Obv. Legend:** ...DVCES BVRG ET B **Mint:** Maastricht

Date	Mintage	VG	F	VF	XF	Unc
ND(1603-10)	—	90.00	150	300	600	—

KM# 25.3 REAL

3.0600 g., 0.8960 Silver 0.0881 oz. ASW **Obv. Legend:** ...DVCES BVRG ET BRAB **Mint:** s Hertogenbosch

Date	Mintage	VG	F	VF	XF	Unc
ND(1606-09)	—	275	450	875	1,750	—

KM# 20 1/4 FLORIN

4.2700 g., 0.6670 Silver 0.0916 oz. ASW **Obv:** Confronted busts of Albert and Elizabeth, crown above, V below **Rev:** Crowned shield in collar of the Golden Fleece **Mint:** Brabant

Date	Mintage	VG	F	VF	XF	Unc
1601	—	525	875	1,750	3,450	—

KM# 47.2 ESCALIN

5.2600 g., 0.5820 Silver 0.0984 oz. ASW **Mint:** Brabant

Date	Mintage	VG	F	VF	XF	Unc
ND(1612-21)	—	15.00	30.00	90.00	400	—
1618	—	35.00	65.00	200	700	—
1620	—	15.00	25.00	75.00	350	—
1621	—	15.00	25.00	75.00	350	—

KM# 47.3 ESCALIN

5.2600 g., 0.5820 Silver 0.0984 oz. ASW **Mint:** s Hertogenbosch

Date	Mintage	VG	F	VF	XF	Unc
1617	—	300	500	1,000	2,000	—

KM# 47.1 ESCALIN

5.2600 g., 0.5820 Silver 0.0984 oz. ASW **Obv:** Eagle with shield of Austria, Burgundy on breast **Rev:** Crowned shield of Albert and Elizabeth on St. Andrew's cross **Rev. Legend:** ...BVRG ET BR Z **Mint:** Antwerp

Date	Mintage	VG	F	VF	XF	Unc
ND(1619-21)	—	15.00	30.00	90.00	400	—
1620	—	35.00	65.00	200	700	—
1621	—	25.00	45.00	150	475	—

KM# 52.1 ESCALIN

5.2600 g., 0.5820 Silver 0.0984 oz. ASW **Obv:** Lion rampant left with sword and shield **Rev:** Crowned shield of Philip IV on St. Andrew's cross **Rev. Legend:** ...DVX BVRG BR Zc **Mint:** Antwerp

Date	Mintage	VG	F	VF	XF	Unc
1621	—	40.00	65.00	125	375	—
1622	—	15.00	25.00	45.00	125	—
1623	—	15.00	25.00	45.00	125	—
1624	—	15.00	25.00	45.00	125	—
1625	—	15.00	25.00	45.00	125	—
1626	—	25.00	45.00	90.00	275	—
1627	—	40.00	80.00	175	475	—
1628	—	15.00	25.00	45.00	125	—
1629	—	18.00	30.00	60.00	175	—
1630	—	18.00	30.00	60.00	175	—
1631	—	30.00	60.00	125	350	—
1637	—	30.00	45.00	90.00	275	—
1638	—	—	—	—	—	—
1639	—	18.00	30.00	60.00	175	—
1641	—	30.00	45.00	90.00	275	—
1644	—	18.00	30.00	60.00	175	—
1645	—	15.00	25.00	45.00	125	—
1650	—	18.00	30.00	60.00	175	—
1651	—	18.00	30.00	60.00	175	—
1652	—	30.00	60.00	125	350	—
1654	—	40.00	80.00	175	475	—
1657	—	30.00	60.00	125	350	—

KM# 52.3 ESCALIN

5.2600 g., 0.5820 Silver 0.0984 oz. ASW **Mint:** Brabant

Date	Mintage	VG	F	VF	XF	Unc
1621	—	18.00	30.00	55.00	150	—
1622	—	18.00	30.00	55.00	150	—
1623	—	15.00	25.00	45.00	125	—
1624	—	15.00	25.00	45.00	125	—
1625	—	15.00	25.00	45.00	125	—
1626	—	30.00	50.00	100	300	—
1628	—	15.00	25.00	45.00	125	—
1629	—	15.00	25.00	45.00	125	—
1630	—	25.00	40.00	75.00	225	—
1637	—	25.00	40.00	75.00	225	—
1641	—	75.00	125	225	650	—
1643	—	30.00	60.00	125	350	—
1645	—	25.00	35.00	65.00	200	—
1646	—	30.00	50.00	100	300	—
1650	—	30.00	60.00	125	350	—
1651	—	30.00	45.00	90.00	275	—
1652	—	40.00	65.00	125	375	—

KM# 52.4 ESCALIN

5.2600 g., 0.5820 Silver 0.0984 oz. ASW **Mint:** s Hertogenbosch

Date	Mintage	VG	F	VF	XF	Unc
1622	—	55.00	90.00	175	525	—
1623	—	30.00	50.00	100	300	—
1624	—	30.00	60.00	125	350	—

KM# 52.2 ESCALIN

5.2600 g., 0.5820 Silver 0.0984 oz. ASW **Mint:** Maastricht

Date	Mintage	VG	F	VF	XF	Unc
1623	—	—	—	—	—	—
1624	—	125	175	325	950	—
1625	—	90.00	150	300	875	—
1628	—	60.00	100	200	600	—
1629	—	75.00	125	250	775	—
1632	—	125	200	275	1,100	—

KM# 119.1 ESCALIN

5.2600 g., 0.5820 Silver 0.0984 oz. ASW **Obv:** Lion rampant left wtih sword, shield of Austria-Burgundy **Rev:** Crowned shield of Charles II divides date over St. Andrew's cross **Rev. Legend:** ...DVX BVRG BRAB Z **Mint:** Antwerp

Date	Mintage	VG	F	VF	XF	Unc
1698	—	45.00	75.00	150	300	—
1699	—	75.00	125	250	475	—

KM# 119.2 ESCALIN

5.2600 g., 0.5820 Silver 0.0984 oz. ASW **Rev:** Cross above crown **Rev. Legend:** ...DVX BVRG BRAB Z **Mint:** Antwerp

Date	Mintage	VG	F	VF	XF	Unc
1700	—	60.00	100	200	550	—

KM# 21.1 1/2 FLORIN

8.5300 g., 0.6670 Silver 0.1829 oz. ASW **Obv:** Confronted busts of Albert and Elizabeth, crown above, date below **Rev:** St. Andrew's cross, crown above, X below **Mint:** Antwerp

Date	Mintage	VG	F	VF	XF	Unc
1601	—	90.00	150	275	550	—
1602	—	125	200	400	775	—

KM# 21.3 1/2 FLORIN

8.5300 g., 0.6670 Silver 0.1829 oz. ASW **Mint:** Brabant

Date	Mintage	VG	F	VF	XF	Unc
ND(1601)	—	125	200	400	775	—
1601	—	125	175	325	650	—

KM# 21.2 1/2 FLORIN

8.5300 g., 0.6670 Silver 0.1829 oz. ASW **Mint:** Maastricht

Date	Mintage	VG	F	VF	XF	Unc
1603	—	750	1,250	2,450	5,000	—

KM# 34.2 1/4 PATAGON

7.0300 g., 0.8750 Silver 0.1978 oz. ASW **Mint:** Brabant

Date	Mintage	VG	F	VF	XF	Unc
ND(1612-16)	—	25.00	40.00	75.00	150	—

KM# 34.1 1/4 PATAGON

7.0300 g., 0.8750 Silver 0.1978 oz. ASW **Obv:** St. Andrew's cross, crown above, fleece below **Rev:** Crowned shield in collar of the Golden Fleece **Rev. Legend:** ...BVRG ET BRAB Z **Mint:** Antwerp **Note:** Legend varieties exist.

Date	Mintage	VG	F	VF	XF	Unc
ND(1613-20)	—	25.00	35.00	65.00	150	—
1616	—	30.00	60.00	125	250	—
1617	—	25.00	40.00	80.00	175	—

KM# 34.3 1/4 PATAGON

7.0300 g., 0.8750 Silver 0.1978 oz. ASW **Mint:** s Hertogenbosch

Date	Mintage	VG	F	VF	XF	Unc
ND(1614-19)	—	300	500	1,000	2,000	—
1617	—	275	450	900	1,800	—
1620	—	300	575	1,150	2,300	—

KM# 54.1 1/4 PATAGON

7.0300 g., 0.8750 Silver 0.1978 oz. ASW **Rev. Legend:** ...DVX BVRG BRAB Zc **Mint:** Antwerp

Date	Mintage	VG	F	VF	XF	Unc
1623	—	50.00	95.00	200	375	—
1631	—	—	—	—	—	—
1632	—	125	175	350	650	—
1633	—	—	—	—	—	—
1645	—	40.00	75.00	150	300	—
1656	—	75.00	125	225	450	—

KM# 54.3 1/4 PATAGON

7.0300 g., 0.8750 Silver 0.1978 oz. ASW **Mint:** Brabant

Date	Mintage	VG	F	VF	XF	Unc
1623	—	40.00	80.00	175	325	—
1624	—	90.00	150	300	575	—
1626	—	40.00	80.00	175	325	—
1627	—	75.00	125	225	450	—
1628	—	75.00	125	225	450	—
1629	—	125	200	375	725	—
1631	—	40.00	80.00	175	325	—
1632	—	225	375	725	1,450	—
1634	—	—	—	—	—	—
1635	—	—	—	—	—	—
1645	—	40.00	80.00	175	325	—
1654	—	200	325	650	1,300	—
1655	—	150	250	475	950	—
1656	—	—	—	—	—	—
1660	—	225	375	725	1,450	—

KM# 54.2 1/4 PATAGON

7.0300 g., 0.8750 Silver 0.1978 oz. ASW **Mint:** Maastricht

Date	Mintage	VG	F	VF	XF	Unc
1625	—	800	1,300	2,600	5,200	—

KM# 27 3 REAL

9.1900 g., 0.8960 Silver 0.2647 oz. ASW **Obv:** Busts of Albert and Elizabeth conjoined left **Obv. Legend:** ...DVCES BVRG ET BRABAN **Rev:** Crowned shield on St. Andrew's cross **Mint:** Antwerp

Date	Mintage	VG	F	VF	XF	Unc
1605	—	125	200	400	800	—
1606	—	90.00	150	300	575	—
1607	—	125	175	325	650	—
1608	—	90.00	150	300	575	—
1610	—	125	200	400	800	—

KM# 7.1 FLORIN

13.5400 g., 0.8330 Silver 0.3626 oz. ASW **Obv:** Confronted busts of Albert and Elizabeth **Rev:** Crowned shield in collar of the Golden Fleece **Mint:** Antwerp

Date	Mintage	VG	F	VF	XF	Unc
1601	—	225	375	725	1,450	—

KM# 14 FLORIN DE 20 SOLS

13.5400 g., 0.8750 Silver 0.3809 oz. ASW **Obv:** Bust of Philip IV right **Rev:** Lin seated facing with sword and sceptre behind crowned shield **Mint:** Brabant

Date	Mintage	VG	F	VF	XF	Unc
1631	—	2,200	3,600	7,200	14,250	—

KM# 46.1 1/2 PATAGON

14.0500 g., 0.8750 Silver 0.3952 oz. ASW **Obv:** St. Andrew's cross, crown above, fleece below **Rev:** Crowned shield in collar of the Golden Fleece **Rev. Legend:** ...BVRG (ET) BRAB Z **Mint:** Antwerp

Date	Mintage	VG	F	VF	XF	Unc
ND(1612-21)	—	25.00	40.00	75.00	150	—
1616	—	30.00	60.00	125	250	—
1617	—	30.00	50.00	95.00	200	—
1618	—	30.00	60.00	125	250	—
1619	—	25.00	40.00	80.00	175	—

KM# 46.2 1/2 PATAGON

14.0500 g., 0.8750 Silver 0.3952 oz. ASW **Mint:** Brabant

Date	Mintage	VG	F	VF	XF	Unc
ND(1612-21)	—	30.00	50.00	100	200	—
1616	—	35.00	65.00	150	275	—
1617	—	40.00	75.00	150	300	—
1620	—	30.00	50.00	100	200	—
1621	—	30.00	50.00	95.00	200	—

KM# 46.3 1/2 PATAGON

14.0500 g., 0.8750 Silver 0.3952 oz. ASW **Mint:** s Hertogenbosch

Date	Mintage	VG	F	VF	XF	Unc
ND(1614-21)	—	675	1,100	2,150	4,300	—
1617	—	875	1,450	2,900	5,750	—
1619	—	875	1,450	2,900	5,750	—

KM# 46.6 1/2 PATAGON

14.0500 g., 0.8750 Silver 0.3952 oz. ASW **Mint:** Brabant

Date	Mintage	VG	F	VF	XF	Unc
1622	—	70.00	115	205	450	—
1623	—	270	425	850	1,900	—
1628	—	180	270	525	1,150	—
1631	—	115	160	325	700	—
1632	—	70.00	115	205	450	—
1633	—	80.00	135	250	500	—
1634	—	70.00	115	205	450	—
1635	—	70.00	115	205	450	—
1636	—	115	160	325	700	—
1645	—	270	425	850	1,900	—
1651	—	180	270	525	1,150	—
1652	—	180	270	525	1,150	—
1653	—	160	250	450	1,000	—
1654	—	135	205	400	875	—
1655	—	—	—	—	—	—
1656	—	—	—	—	—	—

KM# 46.4 1/2 PATAGON

14.0500 g., 0.8750 Silver 0.3952 oz. ASW **Rev. Legend:** ...DVX BVRG BRAB Zc **Mint:** Antwerp

Date	Mintage	VG	F	VF	XF	Unc
1623	—	45.00	85.00	180	375	—
1625	—	—	—	—	—	—
1627	—	115	160	325	650	—
1628	—	205	325	325	1,300	—
1629	—	—	—	—	—	—
1631	—	45.00	85.00	180	375	—
1632	—	45.00	85.00	180	375	—
1633	—	70.00	115	205	450	—
1635	—	70.00	115	205	450	—
1636	—	80.00	135	250	500	—
1637	—	80.00	135	250	500	—
1639	—	115	160	325	650	—
1645	—	80.00	135	250	500	—
1649	—	—	—	—	—	—
1651	—	80.00	135	250	500	—
1652	—	—	—	—	—	—
1653	—	80.00	135	250	500	—
1655	—	160	250	500	1,100	—
1656	—	—	—	—	—	—

KM# 46.5 1/2 PATAGON

14.0500 g., 0.8750 Silver 0.3952 oz. ASW **Mint:** Maastricht

Date	Mintage	VG	F	VF	XF	Unc
1625	—	—	—	—	—	—
1627	—	—	—	—	—	—
1628	—	—	—	—	—	—
1629	—	—	—	—	—	—
1630	—	—	—	—	—	—
1631	—	—	—	—	—	—
1632	—	—	—	—	—	—

KM# 78.2 1/2 PATAGON

14.0500 g., 0.8750 Silver 0.3952 oz. ASW **Mint:** Brabant

Date	Mintage	VG	F	VF	XF	Unc
1666	—	—	—	—	—	—
1671	—	350	550	1,100	2,150	—
1672	—	350	550	1,100	2,150	—
1673	—	225	375	725	1,450	—
1679	—	200	300	575	1,150	—
1685	—	300	500	1,000	2,000	—

KM# 78.1 1/2 PATAGON

14.0500 g., 0.8750 Silver 0.3952 oz. ASW **Obv:** St. Andrew's cross divides date, crown above, fleece below **Rev:** Crowned shield of Charles II in collar of the Golden Fleece **Rev. Legend:** ...DVX BVRG BRAB Zc **Mint:** Antwerp

Date	Mintage	VG	F	VF	XF	Unc
1672	—	200	325	625	1,250	—
1673	—	300	500	1,000	2,000	—
1677	—	400	650	1,300	2,600	—

KM# A117.1 1/2 PATAGON

14.0500 g., 0.8750 Silver 0.3952 oz. ASW **Ruler:** Charles II **Obv:** St. Andrew's cross, crown above, fleece below divides pair of crowned C monograms **Rev. Legend:** ...BVRG BRABAN Z **Mint:** Antwerp

Date	Mintage	VG	F	VF	XF	Unc
1694	—	300	500	1,000	2,000	—
1698	—	1,050	1,750	3,300	6,600	—

KM# 48.1 1/2 DUCATON

16.2400 g., 0.9440 Silver 0.4929 oz. ASW **Obv:** Busts of Albert and Elizabeth conjoined right **Rev:** Lions supporting crowned shield **Mint:** Antwerp

Date	Mintage	VG	F	VF	XF	Unc
1618	—	500	800	1,600	3,150	—
1619	—	350	575	1,150	2,300	—

KM# 48.2 1/2 DUCATON

16.2400 g., 0.9440 Silver 0.4929 oz. ASW **Mint:** Brabant

Date	Mintage	VG	F	VF	XF	Unc
1618	—	500	800	1,600	3,150	—
1619	—	450	750	1,450	2,900	—
1621	—	450	750	1,450	2,900	—

KM# 60.2 1/2 DUCATON

16.2400 g., 0.9440 Silver 0.4929 oz. ASW **Mint:** Brabant

Date	Mintage	VG	F	VF	XF	Unc
1624	—	875	1,450	2,750	5,450	—
1631	—	600	1,000	2,000	4,000	—
1632	—	400	650	1,300	2,600	—
1633	—	225	350	650	1,300	—
1634	—	525	875	1,750	3,450	—
1635	—	275	525	1,100	2,150	—
1636	—	225	375	725	1,450	—
1637	—	—	—	—	—	—

KM# 60.1 1/2 DUCATON

16.2400 g., 0.9440 Silver 0.4929 oz. ASW **Obv:** Bust of Philip IV right in ruffled collar **Rev:** Lions supporting crowned shield **Rev. Legend:** ...DVX BVRG BRAB Zc **Mint:** Antwerp

Date	Mintage	VG	F	VF	XF	Unc
1628	—	525	950	1,900	3,750	—
1631	—	350	650	1,300	2,600	—
1632	—	225	400	800	1,600	—
1633	—	205	375	725	1,450	—
1634	—	180	300	575	1,150	—
1635	—	115	175	350	1,250	—
1636	—	135	250	500	975	—
1637	—	180	300	600	1,200	—

KM# 73.1 1/2 DUCATON

16.2400 g., 0.9440 Silver 0.4929 oz. ASW **Obv:** Date below bust of Philip IV **Rev:** One lion with swords behind crowned shield **Rev. Legend:** ...DVX BVRG BRAB Zc **Mint:** Antwerp

Date	Mintage	VG	F	VF	XF	Unc
1637	—	135	225	475	925	—
1638	—	135	225	475	925	—
1639	—	115	160	325	650	—
1640	—	135	205	450	875	—
1643	—	250	400	875	1,750	—
1646	—	135	225	475	925	—
1647	—	135	225	475	925	—
1648	—	270	425	950	1,900	—
1649	—	115	180	375	725	—
1650	—	135	225	475	925	—
1651	—	180	295	625	1,250	—
1652	—	180	270	575	1,150	—
1654	—	135	225	475	925	—
1656	—	160	250	550	1,100	—
1658	—	205	350	725	1,400	—
1659	—	135	225	475	925	—
1660	—	135	205	450	875	—
1661	—	205	350	725	1,450	—
1662	—	135	205	450	875	—
1663	—	160	250	550	1,100	—
1665	—	135	205	450	875	—

KM# 73.2 1/2 DUCATON

16.2400 g., 0.9440 Silver 0.4929 oz. ASW **Mint:** Brabant

Date	Mintage	VG	F	VF	XF	Unc
1637	—	275	450	875	1,750	—
1639	—	225	350	650	1,300	—
1640	—	400	650	1,300	2,600	—
1642	—	—	—	—	—	—
1649	—	225	375	725	1,450	—
1650	—	350	550	1,100	2,150	—
1652	—	300	475	950	1,900	—
1654	—	275	450	875	1,750	—
1658	—	275	450	875	1,750	—
1661	—	275	450	875	1,750	—
1662	—	275	450	875	1,750	—
1664	—	275	450	875	1,750	—
1665	—	300	475	950	1,900	—
1666	—	300	475	950	1,900	—

KM# 102 1/2 DUCATON

16.2400 g., 0.9440 Silver 0.4929 oz. ASW **Obv:** Youthful bust of Charles II right with long hair and cravat **Mint:** Brabant

Date	Mintage	VG	F	VF	XF	Unc
1682	—	3,000	5,000	10,000	20,000	—

KM# 104.1 1/2 DUCATON

16.2400 g., 0.9440 Silver 0.4929 oz. ASW **Obv:** Youthful bust of Charles II with long hair and court robe **Rev. Legend:** ...DVX BRAB Z **Mint:** Antwerp

Date	Mintage	VG	F	VF	XF	Unc
1684	—	1,900	3,150	6,150	12,150	—

KM# 104.2 1/2 DUCATON

16.2400 g., 0.9440 Silver 0.4929 oz. ASW **Mint:** Brabant

Date	Mintage	VG	F	VF	XF	Unc
1684	—	1,900	3,150	6,150	12,150	—

KM# 9.1 2 FLORIN

27.0800 g., 0.8330 Silver 0.7252 oz. ASW **Obv:** Confronted busts of Albert and Elizabeth **Obv. Legend:** ...DEI GRA **Rev:** Crowned shield in collar of the Golden Fleece **Mint:** Antwerp **Note:** Dav. #4422.

Date	Mintage	VG	F	VF	XF	Unc
1601	—	—	—	—	—	—

KM# 9.2 2 FLORIN

27.0800 g., 0.8330 Silver 0.7252 oz. ASW **Obv. Legend:** ...DEI • GRATIA **Mint:** Antwerp

Date	Mintage	VG	F	VF	XF	Unc
1602	—	—	—	—	—	—

KM# 9.3 2 FLORIN

27.0800 g., 0.8330 Silver 0.7252 oz. ASW **Mint:** Maastricht **Note:** Dav. #4425.

Date	Mintage	VG	F	VF	XF	Unc
1603	—	2,800	4,650	9,300	18,600	—
1604	—	3,250	5,400	10,750	21,450	—
1605	—	3,250	5,400	10,750	21,450	—

KM# 35.1 PATAGON

28.1000 g., 0.8750 Silver 0.7905 oz. ASW **Obv:** St. Andrew's cross, crown above, fleece below divide pairs of crowned C monograms **Rev:** Crowned shield in collar of the Golden Fleece **Rev. Legend:** ...BVRG ET BRAB (Zc) **Mint:** Antwerp

Date	Mintage	VG	F	VF	XF	Unc
ND(1612-21)	—	50.00	90.00	175	350	—
1612	—	85.00	150	300	575	—
1616	—	55.00	100	200	400	—
1617	—	45.00	95.00	200	375	—
1618	—	70.00	125	225	450	—
1619	—	70.00	125	225	450	—
1620	—	85.00	95.00	200	375	—
1621	—	—	—	—	—	—

KM# 35.2 PATAGON

28.1000 g., 0.8750 Silver 0.7905 oz. ASW **Mint:** Maastricht

Date	Mintage	VG	F	VF	XF	Unc
ND(1612-21)	—	2,800	4,650	9,300	18,600	—

KM# 35.3 PATAGON

28.1000 g., 0.8750 Silver 0.7905 oz. ASW **Mint:** Brabant

Date	Mintage	VG	F	VF	XF	Unc
ND(1612-21)	—	35.00	65.00	150	300	—
1616	—	45.00	80.00	175	350	—
1617	—	45.00	80.00	175	350	—
1618	—	45.00	80.00	175	350	—
1619	—	45.00	80.00	175	350	—
1620	—	45.00	80.00	175	350	—
1621	—	30.00	70.00	175	325	—

KM# 35.4 PATAGON

28.1000 g., 0.8750 Silver 0.7905 oz. ASW **Mint:** s Hertogenbosch

Date	Mintage	VG	F	VF	XF	Unc
ND(1614-21)	—	3,000	5,000	10,000	20,000	—
1617	—	3,900	6,450	12,900	25,750	—

KM# 53.3 PATAGON

28.1000 g., 0.8750 Silver 0.7905 oz. ASW **Mint:** Brabant

Date	Mintage	VG	F	VF	XF	Unc
1621	—	115	200	375	725	—
1622	—	80.00	150	275	500	—
1623	—	115	175	350	650	—
1624	—	80.00	150	275	500	—
1625	—	115	175	350	650	—
1628	—	215	350	650	1,300	—
1629	—	240	400	800	1,600	—
1630	—	80.00	150	300	575	—
1631	—	80.00	150	300	575	—
1632	—	115	200	400	800	—
1633	—	80.00	150	300	575	—
1634	—	80.00	150	275	500	—
1635	—	80.00	150	275	500	—
1636	—	140	225	450	875	—
1637	—	115	200	375	725	—
1638	—	265	450	875	1,750	—
1639	—	115	175	350	650	—
1645	—	115	200	400	800	—
1647	—	215	350	650	1,300	—
1649	—	140	225	450	875	—
1651	—	80.00	150	300	575	—
1652	—	215	350	650	1,300	—
1653	—	115	175	350	650	—
1654	—	80.00	150	300	575	—
1655	—	115	200	400	800	—
1657	—	115	175	350	650	—
1660	—	240	400	800	1,600	—

KM# 53.1 PATAGON

28.1000 g., 0.8750 Silver 0.7905 oz. ASW **Obv:** Crowned shield of Philip IV in fleece collar **Rev. Legend:** ...DVX BVRG BRAB Zc **Mint:** Antwerp

Date	Mintage	VG	F	VF	XF	Unc
1622	—	80.00	150	275	500	—
1623	—	80.00	150	275	500	—
1624	—	115	175	350	650	—
1625	—	115	175	350	650	—
1626	—	115	200	400	800	—
1627	—	115	175	350	650	—
1628	—	140	250	475	950	—
1629	—	—	—	—	—	—
1630	—	—	—	—	—	—
1631	—	80.00	150	275	500	—
1632	—	80.00	150	275	500	—
1633	—	80.00	150	300	575	—
1634	—	80.00	150	275	500	—
1635	—	80.00	150	275	500	—
1636	—	80.00	150	275	500	—
1637	—	140	225	450	875	—
1638	—	80.00	150	275	500	—
1639	—	115	200	375	725	—
1645	—	240	400	800	1,600	—
1646	—	80.00	150	300	575	—
1647	—	115	200	375	725	—
1648	—	290	475	950	1,900	—
1649	—	115	200	375	725	—
1650	—	165	275	550	1,100	—
1651	—	80.00	150	300	575	—
1652	—	115	200	375	725	—
1653	—	115	175	350	650	—
1654	—	80.00	150	275	500	—
1655	—	140	225	450	875	—
1656	—	115	175	350	650	—
1657	—	140	250	475	950	—
1658	—	115	200	375	725	—
1661	—	165	275	550	1,100	—
1663	—	140	250	475	950	—
1664	—	240	400	800	1,600	—
1665	—	115	200	400	800	—

KM# 53.2 PATAGON

28.1000 g., 0.8750 Silver 0.7905 oz. ASW **Mint:** Maastricht

Date	Mintage	VG	F	VF	XF	Unc
1624	—	—	—	—	—	—
1625	—	350	550	1,100	2,150	—
1626	—	275	450	875	1,750	—
1627	—	275	450	875	1,750	—
1628	—	300	500	1,000	2,000	—
1629	—	275	450	875	1,750	—
1630	—	300	500	1,000	2,000	—
1631	—	350	575	1,150	2,300	—
1632	—	—	—	—	—	—

KM# 81.2 PATAGON

28.1000 g., 0.8750 Silver 0.7905 oz. ASW **Mint:** Brabant

Date	Mintage	VG	F	VF	XF	Unc
1669	—	270	475	950	1,900	—
1670	—	160	275	550	1,100	—
1671	—	160	275	550	1,100	—
1672	—	325	550	1,100	2,150	—
1673	—	115	200	375	725	—
1675	—	325	550	1,100	2,150	—
1676	—	205	375	725	1,450	—
1677	—	400	725	1,450	2,900	—
1678	—	160	275	550	1,100	—

Date	Mintage	VG	F	VF	XF	Unc
1679	—	400	725	1,450	2,900	—
1680	—	350	650	1,300	2,600	—
1681	—	400	725	1,450	2,900	—
1682	—	205	375	725	1,450	—
1685	—	205	375	725	1,450	—

KM# 81.1 PATAGON

28.1000 g., 0.8750 Silver 0.7905 oz. ASW **Obv:** St. Andrew's cross, crown above, fleece below, divides date **Rev:** Crowned shield of Charles II **Rev. Legend:** ...DVX BVRG BRAB Zc **Mint:** Antwerp

Date	Mintage	VG	F	VF	XF	Unc
1670	—	—	—	—	—	—
1671	—	—	—	—	—	—
1672	—	115	200	375	725	—
1673	—	115	200	375	725	—
1676	—	325	550	1,100	2,150	—
1677	—	160	275	550	1,100	—
1680	—	—	—	—	—	—
1684	—	205	375	725	1,450	—
1686	—	400	725	1,450	2,900	—

KM# 107.2 PATAGON

28.1000 g., 0.8750 Silver 0.7905 oz. ASW **Mint:** Brabant

Date	Mintage	VG	F	VF	XF	Unc
1686	—	725	1,150	2,600	5,150	—
1687	—	350	5,900	1,300	2,600	—
1688	—	550	900	2,000	4,000	—
1692	—	525	850	1,900	3,750	—
1694	—	350	575	1,300	2,600	—
1695	—	—	—	—	—	—

KM# 115 PATAGON

28.1000 g., 0.8750 Silver 0.7905 oz. ASW **Rev. Legend:** ...DVX BVRGVN BRABAN Zc **Mint:** Brabant

Date	Mintage	VG	F	VF	XF	Unc
1691	—	—	—	—	—	—

KM# 81.3 PATAGON

28.1000 g., 0.8750 Silver 0.7905 oz. ASW **Rev. Legend:** ...DVX BVRGVN BRABAN Zc **Mint:** Brabant

Date	Mintage	VG	F	VF	XF	Unc
1691	—	2,000	3,600	7,150	14,300	—

KM# 107.1 PATAGON

28.1000 g., 0.8750 Silver 0.7905 oz. ASW **Obv:** St. Andrew's cross, crown above, fleece below, divides pair of double crowned C monograms **Rev:** Crowned shield in collar of the Golden Fleece divides date **Rev. Legend:** ...DVX BVRG BRABAN Zc **Mint:** Antwerp

Date	Mintage	VG	F	VF	XF	Unc
1694	—	—	—	—	—	—
1695	—	270	450	1,000	2,000	—
1698	—	—	—	—	—	—
1699	—	600	1,000	2,150	4,300	—
1700	—	400	650	1,450	2,900	—

KM# 49.2 DUCATON

32.4800 g., 0.9440 Silver 0.9857 oz. ASW **Mint:** Brabant

Date	Mintage	VG	F	VF	XF	Unc
1618	—	350	600	1,250	2,600	—
1619	—	350	600	1,250	2,600	—
1620	—	300	525	1,100	2,300	—
1621	—	300	500	1,050	2,150	—

KM# 49.1 DUCATON

32.4800 g., 0.9440 Silver 0.9857 oz. ASW **Obv:** Busts of Albert and Elizabeth conjoined right, mint mark divides date above **Rev:** Lions support crowned shield **Rev. Legend:** ...BVRG BRAB Zc **Mint:** Antwerp **Note:** Dav. #4428.

Date	Mintage	VG	F	VF	XF	Unc
1618	—	350	600	1,250	2,600	—
1619	—	300	525	1,100	2,300	—

KM# 49.3 DUCATON

32.4800 g., 0.9440 Silver 0.9857 oz. ASW **Mint:** s Hertogenbosch

Date	Mintage	VG	F	VF	XF	Unc
1619	—	—	—	—	—	—

KM# 56.1 DUCATON

32.4800 g., 0.9440 Silver 0.9857 oz. ASW **Obv:** Bust of Phillip IV in ruffled collar, mint mark divides date above **Rev:** Lions supporting crowned shield **Rev. Legend:** ...DVX BVRG BRAB Zc **Mint:** Antwerp

Date	Mintage	VG	F	VF	XF	Unc
1622	—	—	—	—	—	—
1623	—	—	—	—	—	—
1631	—	200	350	700	1,450	—
1632	—	150	250	500	1,050	—
1633	—	150	250	500	1,050	—
1634	—	150	250	500	1,050	—
1635	—	125	200	425	575	—
1636	—	100	175	350	725	—

KM# 56.2 DUCATON

32.4800 g., 0.9440 Silver 0.9857 oz. ASW **Mint:** Brussels

Date	Mintage	VG	F	VF	XF	Unc
1624	—	425	700	1,400	2,900	—
1629	—	—	—	—	—	—
1631	—	275	450	875	1,800	—
1633	—	150	250	500	1,100	—
1634	—	125	200	400	875	—
1636	—	125	200	400	875	—

KM# 72.2 DUCATON

32.4800 g., 0.9440 Silver 0.9857 oz. ASW **Mint:** Brussels

Date	Mintage	VG	F	VF	XF	Unc
1636	—	100	175	325	675	—
1637	—	100	175	350	750	—
1638	—	100	175	350	750	—
1640	—	100	175	350	750	—
1642	—	150	250	450	1,050	—
1644	—	150	250	450	1,050	—
1645	—	200	325	600	1,250	—
1648	—	100	175	350	750	—
1649	—	100	175	325	675	—
1650	—	125	200	400	825	—
1651	—	100	175	325	675	—
1652	—	100	175	325	825	—
1653	—	100	175	350	675	—
1654	—	125	225	425	675	—
1655	—	150	250	450	750	—
1656	—	125	200	400	900	—
1657	—	125	200	400	950	—
1658	—	150	250	450	825	—
1659	—	100	175	350	825	—
1660	—	125	200	400	950	—
1661	—	100	175	350	750	—
1662	—	100	175	325	675	—
1663	—	125	225	425	900	—
1664	—	100	175	325	675	—
1665	—	125	225	425	900	—

KM# 72.1 DUCATON

32.4800 g., 0.9440 Silver 0.9857 oz. ASW **Obv:** Bust of Philip IV in thin collar right **Mint:** Antwerp **Note:** Dav. #4454.

Date	Mintage	VG	F	VF	XF	Unc
1636	—	100	150	275	600	—
1637	—	65.00	125	225	500	—
1638	—	65.00	125	225	500	—
1639	—	100	175	325	700	—
1640	—	100	175	325	700	—
1641	—	100	175	325	700	—
1642	—	150	250	500	1,050	—
1644	—	125	225	425	900	—
1647	—	100	175	325	700	—
1648	—	65.00	125	225	500	—
1649	—	100	150	300	650	—
1650	—	100	150	300	650	—
1651	—	100	175	325	700	—
1652	—	100	175	325	700	—
1653	—	65.00	125	225	500	—
1654	—	100	175	325	700	—
1655	—	100	175	325	700	—
1656	—	125	200	400	825	—
1657	—	100	175	350	750	—
1658	—	125	200	400	825	—
1659	—	100	150	275	600	—
1660	—	125	200	400	825	—
1661	—	100	175	325	675	—
1662	—	125	200	400	825	—
1663	—	100	175	350	750	—
1664	—	100	175	325	700	—
1665	—	100	175	325	700	—

KM# 79.1 DUCATON

32.4800 g., 0.9440 Silver 0.9857 oz. ASW **Obv:** Child's bust of Charles II right **Rev:** Crowned shield of Charles II with lion supporters **Rev. Legend:** ...DVX BVRG BRAB Z **Mint:** Antwerp

Date	Mintage	VG	F	VF	XF	Unc
1665	—	—	—	—	—	—
1666	—	175	275	600	1,200	—
1667	—	175	275	600	1,200	—
1668	—	150	250	550	1,100	—
1670	—	200	325	700	1,400	—
1671	—	175	275	600	1,200	—
1672	—	200	325	700	1,400	—
1673	—	150	250	550	1,100	—
1676	—	250	375	875	1,750	—

KM# 79.2 DUCATON

32.4800 g., 0.9440 Silver 0.9857 oz. ASW **Mint:** Brabant

Date	Mintage	VG	F	VF	XF	Unc
1666	—	225	350	725	1,450	—
1667	—	275	450	975	1,950	—
1668	—	175	275	550	1,100	—
1670	—	100	200	600	1,200	—
1673	—	175	275	550	1,100	—
1676	—	295	475	1,050	2,100	—
1677	—	350	550	1,200	2,350	—
1678	—	—	—	—	—	—
1679	—	175	275	550	1,100	—
1680	—	650	1,100	2,350	4,750	—

KM# 103.2 DUCATON

32.4800 g., 0.9440 Silver 0.9857 oz. ASW **Mint:** Brabant

Date	Mintage	VG	F	VF	XF	Unc
1682	—	1,300	2,150	4,300	8,600	—
1683	—	700	1,150	2,300	4,600	—
1684	—	875	1,450	2,900	5,750	—

KM# 103.1 DUCATON

32.4800 g., 0.9440 Silver 0.9857 oz. ASW **Obv:** Youthful bust of Charles II right with long hair and large cravat **Rev. Legend:** ...DVX BVRG BRAB Zc **Mint:** Antwerp

Date	Mintage	VG	F	VF	XF	Unc
1683	—	800	1,300	2,600	5,000	—
1684	—	675	1,100	2,150	4,300	—

KM# 105.1 DUCATON

32.4800 g., 0.9440 Silver 0.9857 oz. ASW **Obv:** Youthful bust of Charles II in court robes **Mint:** Antwerp

Date	Mintage	VG	F	VF	XF	Unc
1684	—	675	1,100	2,150	4,300	—
1700	—	—	—	—	—	—

KM# 105.2 DUCATON

32.4800 g., 0.9440 Silver 0.9857 oz. ASW **Mint:** Brabant

Date	Mintage	VG	F	VF	XF	Unc
1684	—	1,050	1,750	3,450	6,900	—

KM# 106.1 DUCATON

32.4800 g., 0.9440 Silver 0.9857 oz. ASW **Obv:** Mature bust right **Rev. Legend:** ...DVX BVRG BRABAN Zc **Mint:** Antwerp

Date	Mintage	VG	F	VF	XF	Unc
1684	—	—	—	—	—	—
1700	—	—	—	—	—	—

KM# 106.2 DUCATON

32.4800 g., 0.9440 Silver 0.9857 oz. ASW **Mint:** Brabant

Date	Mintage	VG	F	VF	XF	Unc
1686	—	1,750	2,900	5,750	11,450	—
1687	—	2,200	3,600	7,150	14,300	—
1689	—	1,750	2,900	5,750	11,450	—
1692	—	—	—	—	—	—
1693	—	2,200	3,600	7,150	14,300	—
1694	—	1,950	3,250	6,450	12,900	—
1698	—	—	—	—	—	—

KM# 50.1 2 DUCATON

Silver **Mint:** Antwerp **Note:** Similar to 1 Ducaton, KM#49.1.

Date	Mintage	VG	F	VF	XF	Unc
1618	—	—	—	—	—	—

KM# 50.2 2 DUCATON

Silver **Mint:** Brabant **Note:** Similar to 1 Ducaton, KM#49.2.

Date	Mintage	VG	F	VF	XF	Unc
1618	—	—	—	—	—	—
1619	—	—	—	—	—	—
1620	—	—	—	—	—	—

KM# 57.1 2 DUCATON

Silver **Mint:** Antwerp **Note:** Similar to 1 Ducaton, KM#56.1. Dav. #4453.

Date	Mintage	VG	F	VF	XF	Unc
1623	—	500	900	1,750	3,000	—
1628	—	500	900	1,750	3,000	—
1631	—	500	900	1,750	3,000	—
1632	—	500	900	1,750	3,000	—
1633	—	500	900	1,750	3,000	—
1634	—	500	900	1,750	3,000	—
1635	—	500	900	1,750	3,000	—
1636	—	500	900	1,750	3,000	—

KM# 57.2 2 DUCATON

Silver **Mint:** Brabant **Note:** Similar to 1 Ducaton, KM#56.2.

Date	Mintage	VG	F	VF	XF	Unc
1623	—	550	1,000	1,850	3,250	—
1624	—	550	1,000	1,850	3,250	—
1631	—	550	1,000	1,850	3,250	—
1632	—	550	1,000	1,850	3,250	—
1633	—	550	1,000	1,850	3,250	—
1634	—	550	1,000	1,850	3,250	—
1635	—	550	1,000	1,850	3,250	—
1636	—	550	1,000	1,850	3,250	—

KM# 75.1 2 DUCATON

Silver **Ruler:** Philip IV **Mint:** Antwerp **Note:** Similar to 1 Ducaton, KM#72.1, Dav. #4454.

Date	Mintage	VG	F	VF	XF	Unc
1636	—	450	850	1,650	2,850	—
1640	—	450	850	1,650	2,850	—
1642	—	450	850	1,650	2,850	—
1644	—	450	850	1,650	2,850	—
1645	—	450	850	1,650	2,850	—
1646	—	450	850	1,650	2,850	—
1647	—	450	850	1,650	2,850	—
1648	—	450	850	1,650	2,850	—
1650	—	450	850	1,650	2,850	—
1651	—	450	850	1,650	2,850	—
1652	—	450	850	1,650	2,850	—
1654	—	450	850	1,650	2,850	—
1656	—	450	850	1,650	2,850	—
1658	—	450	850	1,650	2,850	—
1662	—	450	850	1,650	2,850	—

KM# 75.2 2 DUCATON

Silver **Ruler:** Philip IV **Mint:** Brabant **Note:** Similar to 1 Ducaton, KM#72.2, Dav. #4454.

Date	Mintage	VG	F	VF	XF	Unc
1636	—	500	900	1,750	3,000	—
1638	—	500	900	1,750	3,000	—
1639	—	500	900	1,750	3,000	—
1640	—	500	900	1,750	3,000	—
1644	—	500	900	1,750	3,000	—
1645	—	500	900	1,750	3,000	—
1646	—	500	900	1,750	3,000	—
1647	—	500	900	1,750	3,000	—
1648	—	500	900	1,750	3,000	—
1649	—	500	900	1,750	3,000	—
1650	—	500	900	1,750	3,000	—
1653	—	500	900	1,750	3,000	—
1654	—	500	900	1,750	3,000	—
1655	—	500	900	1,750	3,000	—
1658	—	500	900	1,750	3,000	—
1659	—	500	900	1,750	3,000	—
1662	—	500	900	1,750	3,000	—
1664	—	500	900	1,750	3,000	—
1673	—	500	900	1,750	3,000	—

KM# A75.2 2 DUCATON

Silver **Ruler:** Philip IV **Mint:** Brabant **Note:** Similar to 1 Ducaton, KM#72.2, Dav. #4454.

Date	Mintage	VG	F	VF	XF	Unc
1636	—	—	—	—	—	—
1638	—	—	—	—	—	—
1646	—	—	—	—	—	—
1648	—	—	—	—	—	—
1658	—	—	—	—	—	—

KM# B75.2 2 DUCATON

Silver **Ruler:** Philip IV **Mint:** Brabant **Note:** Similar to 1 Ducaton, KM#72.2, Dav. #4454.

Date	Mintage	VG	F	VF	XF	Unc
1636	—	—	—	—	—	—
1662	—	—	—	—	—	—

KM# A75.1 2 DUCATON

Silver **Ruler:** Philip IV **Mint:** Antwerp **Note:** Similar to 1 Ducaton, KM#72.1, Dav. #4454.

Date	Mintage	VG	F	VF	XF	Unc
1637	—	—	—	—	—	—
1638	—	—	—	—	—	—
1639	—	—	—	—	—	—

Date	Mintage	VG	F	VF	XF	Unc
1640	—	—	—	—	—	—
1642	—	—	—	—	—	—
1648	—	—	—	—	—	—
1650	—	—	—	—	—	—
1653	—	—	—	—	—	—
1657	—	—	—	—	—	—

KM# B75.1 2 DUCATON

Silver **Ruler:** Philip IV **Mint:** Antwerp **Note:** Similar to 1 Ducaton, KM#72.1, Dav. #4454.

Date	Mintage	VG	F	VF	XF	Unc
1637 Rare	—	—	—	—	—	—
1639 Rare	—	—	—	—	—	—
1640 Rare	—	—	—	—	—	—
1648 Rare	—	—	—	—	—	—
1649 Rare	—	—	—	—	—	—
1650 Rare	—	—	—	—	—	—
1653 Rare	—	—	—	—	—	—

KM# C75.1 2 DUCATON

Silver **Ruler:** Philip IV **Mint:** Antwerp **Note:** Similar to 1 Ducaton, KM#72.1, Dav. #4454.

Date	Mintage	VG	F	VF	XF	Unc
1638 Rare	—	—	—	—	—	—

KM# 51.1 3 DUCATON

Silver **Mint:** Antwerp **Note:** Similar to 1 Ducaton, KM#49.1.

Date	Mintage	VG	F	VF	XF	Unc
1619	—	—	—	—	—	—

KM# 51.2 3 DUCATON

Silver **Mint:** Brabant **Note:** Similar to 1 Ducaton, KM#49.2.

Date	Mintage	VG	F	VF	XF	Unc
1619	—	—	—	—	—	—
1620	—	—	—	—	—	—

KM# 58.1 3 DUCATON

Silver **Mint:** Antwerp **Note:** Similar to 1 Ducaton, KM#56.1.

Date	Mintage	VG	F	VF	XF	Unc
1623	—	—	—	—	—	—
1631	—	—	—	—	—	—
1632	—	—	—	—	—	—
1633	—	—	—	—	—	—
1634	—	—	—	—	—	—

KM# 58.2 3 DUCATON

Silver **Mint:** Brabant **Note:** Similar to 1 Ducaton, KM#56.2.

Date	Mintage	VG	F	VF	XF	Unc
1633	—	—	—	—	—	—
1634	—	—	—	—	—	—
1635	—	—	—	—	—	—
1636	—	—	—	—	—	—

KM# 59.1 4 DUCATON

Silver **Mint:** Antwerp **Note:** Similar to 1 Ducaton, KM#56.1.

Date	Mintage	VG	F	VF	XF	Unc
1623 Rare	—	—	—	—	—	—
1631 Rare	—	—	—	—	—	—
1634 Rare	—	—	—	—	—	—

KM# 59.2 4 DUCATON

Silver **Mint:** Brabant **Note:** Similar to 1 Ducaton, KM#56.2.

Date	Mintage	VG	F	VF	XF	Unc
1633	—	—	—	—	—	—
1634	—	—	—	—	—	—

KM# 71 5 DUCATON

Silver **Mint:** Antwerp **Note:** Similar to 1 Ducaton, KM#56.1.

Date	Mintage	VG	F	VF	XF	Unc
1632 Rare	—	—	—	—	—	—
1633 Rare	—	—	—	—	—	—

KM# 8.2 ALBERTIN (2/3 Ducat, Corona)

2.9200 g., 0.7920 Gold 0.0743 oz. AGW **Obv:** Crowned arms in collar of the Golden Fleece **Rev:** Crowned floral St. Andrew's cross; date at sides, Golden Fleece at bottom **Mint:** Maastricht **Note:** Mint mark: Star.

Date	Mintage	VG	F	VF	XF	Unc
1601	—	325	575	975	1,650	—
1603	—	325	575	975	1,650	—
1604	—	325	575	975	1,650	—
1605	—	325	575	975	1,650	—

KM# 10.3 2 ALBERTIN (4/3 Ducat)

5.1500 g., 0.8950 Gold 0.1482 oz. AGW **Mint:** Brussels **Note:** Mint mark: Angel face.

Date	Mintage	VG	F	VF	XF	Unc
1601	15,000	475	800	1,250	2,150	—

KM# 10.1 2 ALBERTIN (4/3 Ducat)

5.1500 g., 0.8950 Gold 0.1482 oz. AGW **Obv:** Crowned shield in collar of the Golden Fleece **Rev:** St. Andrew's cross, crown above, fleece below **Mint:** Antwerp **Note:** Mint mark: Hand.

Date	Mintage	VG	F	VF	XF	Unc
1601	Inc. above	280	425	650	925	—
1602	356,000	280	425	650	925	—
1603	173,000	280	425	650	925	—
1604	235,000	280	425	650	925	—
1605	195,000	280	425	650	925	—
1606	Inc. above	280	425	650	925	—
1607	66,000	280	425	650	925	—
1608	32,000	280	475	775	1,250	—
1609	16,000	350	650	925	1,450	—

KM# 10.2 2 ALBERTIN (4/3 Ducat)

5.1500 g., 0.8950 Gold 0.1482 oz. AGW **Mint:** Maastricht **Note:** Mint mark: Star.

Date	Mintage	VG	F	VF	XF	Unc
1601	Inc. above	325	650	1,000	1,450	—
1602	69,000	275	550	875	1,300	—
1603	Inc. above	275	550	875	1,300	—
1607 Rare	924	—	—	—	—	—
1608 Rare	Inc. above	—	—	—	—	—

KM# 36.1 1/2 SOUVERAIN OU LION D'OR

2.8000 g., 0.9190 Gold 0.0827 oz. AGW **Obv:** Crowned arms of Austria-Burgundy in inner circle **Rev:** Crowned imperial arms between crowned AE monograms in inner circle **Mint:** Antwerp **Note:** Mint mark: Hand.

Date	Mintage	VG	F	VF	XF	Unc
ND(1613) Rare	840	—	—	—	—	—

KM# 36.2 1/2 SOUVERAIN OU LION D'OR

2.8000 g., 0.9190 Gold 0.0827 oz. AGW **Mint:** Brussels **Note:** Mint mark: Angel face.

Date	Mintage	VG	F	VF	XF	Unc
ND1613 Rare	1,433	—	—	—	—	—

KM# 65 1/2 SOUVERAIN OU LION D'OR

2.8000 g., 0.9190 Gold 0.0827 oz. AGW **Rev:** Crowned monograms replaced by crowned clasps

Date	Mintage	VG	F	VF	XF	Unc
ND Rare	Inc. above	—	—	—	—	—

KM# 38 SOUVERAIN OU LION D'OR

5.1600 g., 0.9880 Gold 0.1639 oz. AGW **Obv:** Conjoined half figures of Albert and Elizabeth right **Rev:** Crowned arms in collar of the Golden Fleece **Mint:** Brussels **Note:** Mint mark: Angel face.

Date	Mintage	VG	F	VF	XF	Unc
ND Rare	2,630	—	—	—	—	—

KM# 77.1 SOUVERAIN OU LION D'OR

5.1600 g., 0.9880 Gold 0.1639 oz. AGW **Obv. Legend:** PHIL IIII... **Mint:** Antwerp

Date	Mintage	VG	F	VF	XF	Unc
1648	40,000	225	300	575	1,250	—
1649/8	—	300	425	825	1,300	—
1649	35,000	300	425	825	1,300	—
1650	31,000	300	425	825	1,300	—
1651	10,000	300	425	825	1,300	—
1652	9,000	300	425	825	1,300	—
1653	31,000	300	425	825	1,300	—
1655	20,000	300	425	825	1,300	—
1656	44,000	300	425	825	1,300	—
1657	55,000	300	425	825	1,300	—
1658	64,000	300	425	825	1,300	—
1659	31,000	300	425	825	1,300	—
1660	Inc. above	300	425	825	1,300	—
1662	10,000	300	425	825	1,300	—
1663	—	750	1,200	2,200	3,300	—
1664	9,000	300	425	825	1,300	—
1665	Inc. above	525	625	975	1,600	—

KM# 77.2 SOUVERAIN OU LION D'OR

5.1600 g., 0.9880 Gold 0.1639 oz. AGW **Mint:** Brussels

Date	Mintage	VG	F	VF	XF	Unc
1648	5,631	300	425	825	1,300	—
1649	23,000	300	425	825	1,300	—
1650	49,000	300	425	825	1,300	—
1651	37,000	300	425	825	1,300	—
1652	110,000	300	425	825	1,300	—
1653	Inc. above	300	425	825	1,300	—
1654	Inc. above	300	425	825	1,300	—
1655	37,000	300	425	825	1,300	—
1656	33,000	300	425	825	1,300	—
1657	22,000	300	425	825	1,300	—
1658	42,000	300	425	825	1,300	—
1659	21,000	300	425	825	1,300	—
1661	23,000	300	425	825	1,300	—
1662	11,000	300	425	825	1,300	—
1663	Inc. above	300	425	825	1,300	—
1664	10,000	300	425	825	1,300	—
1665	Inc. above	300	425	825	1,300	—

KM# 80.1 SOUVERAIN OU LION D'OR

5.1600 g., 0.9880 Gold 0.1639 oz. AGW **Mint:** Antwerp

Date	Mintage	VG	F	VF	XF	Unc
1666	9,145	650	1,200	2,250	5,000	—
1684	1,005	800	1,500	3,000	6,000	—
1694	3,976	750	1,300	2,500	5,500	—

KM# 80.2 SOUVERAIN OU LION D'OR

5.1600 g., 0.9880 Gold 0.1639 oz. AGW **Note:** Mint mark: Angel face.

Date	Mintage	VG	F	VF	XF	Unc
1666	4,125	650	1,200	2,250	5,000	—
1667	Inc. above	650	1,200	2,250	5,000	—
1676	4,663	650	1,200	2,250	5,000	—
1681	4,631	650	1,200	2,250	5,000	—
1684	Inc. above	650	1,200	2,250	5,000	—
1686	1,793	800	1,500	2,500	5,500	—
1691	2,222	1,500	2,500	4,000	7,000	—

Note: Machine struck

KM# 43.2 COURONNE D'OR

3.3100 g., 0.9190 Gold 0.0978 oz. AGW **Mint:** Brussels **Note:** Mint mark: Angel face.

Date	Mintage	VG	F	VF	XF	Unc
1614	—	625	1,250	2,000	4,500	—
1616	2,261	625	1,250	2,000	4,500	—
ND	5,442	625	1,250	2,000	4,500	—

KM# 43.1 COURONNE D'OR

3.3100 g., 0.9190 Gold 0.0978 oz. AGW **Obv:** Cruciform crowned AE monograms in inner circle **Rev:** Crowned arms in inner circle, date at top **Mint:** Antwerp **Note:** Mint mark: Hand.

Date	Mintage	VG	F	VF	XF	Unc
1614	38,000	525	1,200	1,850	4,250	—
1616	Inc. above	525	1,200	1,850	4,250	—

KM# 43.3 COURONNE D'OR

3.3100 g., 0.9190 Gold 0.0978 oz. AGW **Mint:** s Hertogenbosch **Note:** Mint mark: Tree.

Date	Mintage	VG	F	VF	XF	Unc
1617 Rare	284	—	—	—	—	—

KM# A57.1 COURONNE D'OR

3.3100 g., 0.9190 Gold 0.0978 oz. AGW **Obv:** Floreated cross in inner circle; date in legend **Rev:** Crowned arms in inner circle **Mint:** Brussels **Note:** Mint mark: Angel face.

Date	Mintage	VG	F	VF	XF	Unc
1622	4,784	350	675	950	1,650	—
1623	11,000	350	675	950	1,650	—
1624	10,000	350	675	950	1,650	—
1625 Rare	3,308	—	—	—	—	—
1629	7,881	350	675	950	1,650	—
1630 Rare	25,000	—	—	—	—	—
1631	Inc. above	350	675	950	1,650	—
1632	14,000	350	675	950	1,650	—
1633	25,000	350	675	950	1,650	—
1635	1,155	350	675	950	1,650	—
1637	4,963	350	675	950	1,650	—
1639	13,000	350	675	950	1,650	—

KM# A57.2 COURONNE D'OR

3.3100 g., 0.9190 Gold 0.0978 oz. AGW **Mint:** Antwerp **Note:** Mint mark: Hand.

Date	Mintage	VG	F	VF	XF	Unc
1623	2,195	350	675	950	1,650	—
1624	3,375	350	675	950	1,650	—
1625	1,121	350	675	950	1,650	—

Date	Mintage	VG	F	VF	XF	Unc
1627	2,370	350	675	950	1,650	—
1631	12,000	350	675	950	1,650	—
1634	1,979	350	675	950	1,650	—
1637	35,000	350	675	950	1,650	—
1638	11,000	350	675	950	1,650	—
1639	19,000	350	675	950	1,650	—

KM# 57.3 COURONNE D'OR

3.3100 g., 0.9190 Gold 0.0978 oz. AGW **Mint:** s Hertogenbosch **Note:** Mint mark: Tree.

Date	Mintage	VG	F	VF	XF	Unc
1623 Rare	1,056	—	—	—	—	—

KM# 90.1 DUCATON D'OR

0.9480 Gold **Obv:** Child's bust of Charles II right **Rev:** Lions supporting crowned shield of Charles II **Rev. Legend:** ...DVX BVRG BRAB Zc **Mint:** Antwerp

Date	Mintage	VG	F	VF	XF	Unc
1676 Rare	—	—	—	—	—	—

KM# 90.2 DUCATON D'OR

0.9480 Gold **Mint:** Brussels

Date	Mintage	VG	F	VF	XF	Unc
1676 Rare	—	—	—	—	—	—

KM# 109.2 DUCATON D'OR

0.9480 Gold **Mint:** Brabant

Date	Mintage	VG	F	VF	XF	Unc
1687 Rare	—	—	—	—	—	—
1689 Rare	—	—	—	—	—	—
1692 Rare	—	—	—	—	—	—
1694 Rare	—	—	—	—	—	—

KM# 109.1 DUCATON D'OR

0.9480 Gold **Obv:** Mature bust right **Rev. Legend:** ...DVX BVRG BRABAN Zc **Mint:** Antwerp

Date	Mintage	VG	F	VF	XF	Unc
1693 Rare	—	—	—	—	—	—
1698 Rare	—	—	—	—	—	—

KM# 37 2/3 SOUVERAIN D'OR

7.7334 g., 0.9190 Gold 0.2285 oz. AGW **Obv:** Albert and Elizabeth walking right **Rev:** Crowned arms in collar of the Golden Fleece **Mint:** Brussels **Note:** Mint mark: Angel face.

Date	Mintage	VG	F	VF	XF	Unc
ND Rare	168	—	—	—	—	—

KM# 39.1 2 SOUVERAIN D'OR

11.0600 g., 0.9190 Gold 0.3268 oz. AGW **Mint:** Brussels **Note:** Mint mark: Angel face.

Date	Mintage	VG	F	VF	XF	Unc
ND	7,919	875	1,800	3,700	6,600	—
1612	993	900	1,850	3,850	6,900	—
1613	572	925	1,850	4,050	7,400	—
1614	—	900	1,850	3,850	6,900	—
1615	1,809	875	1,800	3,700	6,600	—
1616 Rare	342	—	—	—	—	—
1617 Rare	—	—	—	—	—	—
1618	2,393	875	1,800	3,700	6,600	—
1619	3,226	925	1,850	4,050	7,400	—
1620	Inc. above	875	1,800	3,700	6,600	—

KM# 39.3 2 SOUVERAIN D'OR

11.0600 g., 0.9190 Gold 0.3268 oz. AGW **Mint:** Maastricht **Note:** Mint mark: Star.

Date	Mintage	VG	F	VF	XF	Unc
1612 Rare	59	—	—	—	—	—
1613 Rare	Inc. above	—	—	—	—	—

KM# 39.2 2 SOUVERAIN D'OR

11.0600 g., 0.9190 Gold 0.3268 oz. AGW **Note:** Mint mark: Hand.

Date	Mintage	VG	F	VF	XF	Unc
ND	8,843	725	1,400	3,000	6,200	—
1614 Rare	1,640	—	—	—	—	—

KM# 64.1 2 SOUVERAIN D'OR

11.0600 g., 0.9190 Gold 0.3268 oz. AGW **Obv:** Philip IV in ruffled collar **Mint:** Brussels **Note:** Mint mark: Angel face.

Date	Mintage	VG	F	VF	XF	Unc
1626	930	725	1,650	3,050	5,500	—
1627	4,360	600	1,300	2,500	5,200	—
1629	4,987	600	1,300	2,500	5,200	—
1634	3,464	600	1,300	2,500	5,200	—
1635	4,003	600	1,300	2,500	5,200	—
1636	5,389	600	1,300	2,500	5,200	—

KM# 64.2 2 SOUVERAIN D'OR

11.0600 g., 0.9190 Gold 0.3268 oz. AGW **Mint:** Antwerp **Note:** Mint mark: Hand.

Date	Mintage	VG	F	VF	XF	Unc
1628	1,352	600	1,300	2,500	5,200	—
1629	—	600	1,300	2,500	5,200	—
1636	25,000	600	1,300	2,500	5,200	—
1637	Inc. above	600	1,300	2,500	5,200	—

KM# 74.1 2 SOUVERAIN D'OR

11.0600 g., 0.9190 Gold 0.3268 oz. AGW **Obv:** Philip IV in flat collar **Mint:** Antwerp **Note:** Mint mark: Hand.

Date	Mintage	VG	F	VF	XF	Unc
1637	40,000	600	900	1,650	3,000	—
1638	33,000	600	900	1,650	3,000	—
1639	29,000	600	900	1,650	3,000	—
1640	42,000	600	900	1,650	3,000	—
1641	35,000	600	900	1,650	3,000	—
1642	82,000	600	900	1,650	3,000	—
1643	Inc. above	600	900	1,650	3,000	—
1644	Inc. above	600	900	1,650	3,000	—
1645	138,000	600	900	1,650	3,000	—
1646	Inc. above	600	900	1,650	3,000	—
1647	Inc. above	600	900	1,650	3,000	—

KM# 74.2 2 SOUVERAIN D'OR

11.0600 g., 0.9190 Gold 0.3268 oz. AGW **Mint:** Brussels **Note:** Mint mark: Angel face.

Date	Mintage	VG	F	VF	XF	Unc
1637	23,000	600	900	1,650	3,000	—
1638	20,000	600	900	1,650	3,000	—
1640	8,000	600	900	1,650	3,000	—
1641	39,000	600	900	1,650	3,000	—
1642	17,000	600	900	1,650	3,000	—
1643	47,000	600	900	1,650	3,000	—
1644	Inc. above	600	900	1,650	3,000	—
1645	14,000	600	900	1,650	3,000	—
1646	Inc. above	600	900	1,650	3,000	—
1647	Inc. above	600	900	1,650	3,000	—

KM# 82.2 2 SOUVERAIN D'OR

11.0600 g., 0.9190 Gold 0.3268 oz. AGW **Mint:** Brussels **Note:** Mint mark: Angel face.

Date	Mintage	VG	F	VF	XF	Unc
1667	2,076	1,500	3,000	5,300	9,000	—
1668	Inc. above	1,500	3,000	5,300	9,000	—
1671	3,374	1,500	3,000	5,300	9,000	—
1673	2,002	1,500	3,000	5,300	9,000	—
1686	3,098	1,500	3,000	5,300	9,000	—
1687	Inc. above	1,500	3,000	5,300	9,000	—

KM# 82.1 2 SOUVERAIN D'OR

11.0600 g., 0.9190 Gold 0.3268 oz. AGW **Obv:** Crowned child bust of Charles II right in inner circle, date below **Mint:** Antwerp **Note:** Mint mark: Hand.

Date	Mintage	VG	F	VF	XF	Unc
1667	1,836	1,250	2,500	4,400	7,500	—
1669	1,252	1,250	2,500	4,400	7,500	—
1671	1,623	1,250	2,500	4,400	7,500	—
1675	3,248	1,250	2,500	4,400	7,500	—
1681 Rare	394	—	—	—	—	—
1684 Rare	538	—	—	—	—	—
1694	11,000	1,250	2,500	4,400	7,500	—

KM# 101.1 2 SOUVERAIN D'OR

11.0600 g., 0.9190 Gold 0.3268 oz. AGW **Obv:** Large crowned bust of Charles II right, mint mark below **Rev:** Crowned arms in collar of the Golden Fleece, divided date at top **Mint:** Brussels **Note:** Mint mark: Angel face.

Date	Mintage	VG	F	VF	XF	Unc
1689	15,000	1,100	2,150	3,800	6,800	—
1690	Inc. above	1,100	2,150	3,800	6,800	—
1691	Inc. above	1,100	2,150	3,800	6,800	—
1692	7,096	1,100	2,150	3,800	6,800	—
1693	Inc. above	1,100	2,150	3,800	6,800	—
1694	Inc. above	1,100	2,150	3,800	6,800	—

KM# 101.2 2 SOUVERAIN D'OR

11.0600 g., 0.9190 Gold 0.3268 oz. AGW **Obv:** Crowned bust of Charles II right, mint mark below **Mint:** Antwerp **Note:** Mint mark: Hand.

Date	Mintage	VG	F	VF	XF	Unc
1697	—	1,200	2,400	4,200	7,500	—
1699	14,000	1,200	2,400	4,200	7,500	—
1700	5,711	1,200	2,400	4,200	7,500	—

KM# 70 4 SOUVERAIN D'OR
Gold **Note:** Similar to 2 Souverain d'Or, KM#64.1.

Date	Mintage	VG	F	VF	XF	Unc
1628 Rare	—	—	—	—	—	—
1636 Rare	—	—	—	—	—	—

KM# A76 4 SOUVERAIN D'OR
Gold **Note:** Similar to 2 Souverain d'Or, KM#64.2.

Date	Mintage	VG	F	VF	XF	Unc
1644 Rare	—	—	—	—	—	—

KM# 90 4 SOUVERAIN D'OR
Gold **Note:** Similar to 2 Souverain d'Or, KM#101.2.

Date	Mintage	VG	F	VF	XF	Unc
1697	—	—	—	—	—	—

Note: Reported, not confirmed

KM# 45 6 SOUVERAIN D'OR
Gold

Date	Mintage	VG	F	VF	XF	Unc
1616 Rare	—	—	—	—	—	—

KM# 117.1 8 SOUVERAIN D'OR
14.0500 g., 0.8750 Silver 0.3952 oz. ASW **Obv:** Bust right **Obv. Legend:** CAROL • II • D•G• HISP • ET • INDIAR • REX **Rev:** Crowned supported arms **Rev. Legend:** ...ARCHID • AVST. - DVX • BURG - BRABANT **Mint:** Brussels **Note:** Mint mark: Angel face. Fr.#114.

Date	Mintage	VG	F	VF	XF	Unc
1687 Rare	—	—	—	—	—	—
1689 Rare	—	—	—	—	—	—
1692 Rare	—	—	—	—	—	—
1694 Rare	—	—	—	—	—	—

KM# 117.2 8 SOUVERAIN D'OR
44.3600 g., Gold **Ruler:** Charles II **Obv:** Bust right **Obv. Legend:** CAROL • II • D • G • HISP • ET • INDIAR • REX **Rev:** Crowned supported arms **Rev. Legend:** ARCHID • AVST • DVX • BURG BRABANT **Mint:** Antwerp **Note:** Fr. #115.

Date	Mintage	VG	F	VF	XF	Unc
1693 Rare	—	—	—	—	—	—

Note: Bowers and Marena Guia sale 3-88 AU realized $17,600.

Date	Mintage	VG	F	VF	XF	Unc
1698 Rare	—	—	—	—	—	—

PIEFORTS

KM#	Date	Mintage	Identification	Mkt Val
P1	1624	—	1/2 Ducaton. KM#60.2.	—
P2	1631	—	1/2 Ducaton. KM#60.2.	—
P3	1637	—	1/2 Ducaton. KM#60.2.	—
P4	1643	—	1/2 Ducaton. KM#73.1.	—
P5	1648	—	1/2 Ducaton. KM#73.1.	—
P6	1657	—	1/2 Ducaton. KM#73.1. 48.72g.	—

FLANDERS

A coastal county of modern Belgium first mentioned in 862 which by the Renaissance had become the industrial and commercial center of northern Europe. It was the target of dynastic maneuvering between Burgundy, Spain and France.

RULERS
Albert and Elizabeth, 1598-1621
Philip IV, 1621-1665
Charles II, 1665-1700

MINT MARK
Lis - Bruges (Flanders)

COUNTY

STANDARD COINAGE

KM# 7 DENIER (4 Mites)
Copper **Obv:** Crowned AE monogram **Rev:** Crowned shield of Austria and Burgundy on St. Andrew's cross

Date	Mintage	VG	F	VF	XF	Unc
1607	—	16.00	32.00	60.00	100	—
1608	—	16.00	32.00	60.00	100	—
1609	—	16.00	32.00	60.00	100	—
1610	—	16.00	32.00	60.00	100	—
1615	—	14.00	28.00	50.00	85.00	—
1616	—	14.00	28.00	50.00	85.00	—

KM# 38 GIGOT (6 Mites)
Copper **Obv:** St. Andrew's cross, crown above, fleece below **Rev:** Crowned shield of Philip IV **Rev. Legend:** ...DVX BVR(G) ET CO FL(AN) Z

Date	Mintage	VG	F	VF	XF	Unc
1625	—	28.00	55.00	100	175	—
1626	—	32.00	65.00	120	200	—
1627	—	32.00	65.00	120	200	—
1645	—	40.00	80.00	150	250	—
1655	—	32.00	65.00	120	200	—

KM# 101 GIGOT (6 Mites)
Copper **Rev:** Crowned shield of Austria and Burgundy, small lion in center **Rev. Legend:** ...DVX BVRG C(O) FLAN Z

Date	Mintage	VG	F	VF	XF	Unc
1700	—	10.00	16.00	30.00	55.00	—

KM# 6 2 DENIER (8 Mites)
Copper **Obv:** Crowned AE monogram **Rev:** Crowned shield of Austria and Burgundy on St. Andrew's cross **Rev. Legend:** ...BVRG Z CO(M) F(LA)

Date	Mintage	VG	F	VF	XF	Unc
1606	—	10.00	15.00	25.00	45.00	—
1607	—	10.00	15.00	20.00	35.00	—
1608	—	10.00	20.00	40.00	65.00	—
1609	—	10.00	20.00	40.00	65.00	—
1610	—	10.00	15.00	30.00	50.00	—
1615	—	10.00	15.00	20.00	35.00	—
1616	—	10.00	15.00	20.00	30.00	—

KM# 36 LIARD (12 Mites)
Copper **Obv:** Crown and shields of Austria, Burgundy, and Flanders **Rev. Legend:** ...BVRG ET CO FL(AN) Z (variations exist)

Date	Mintage	VG	F	VF	XF	Unc
1623	—	10.00	15.00	28.00	45.00	—
1633	—	10.00	20.00	40.00	65.00	—
1643	—	10.00	15.00	20.00	35.00	—
1644	—	10.00	15.00	20.00	35.00	—
1645	—	10.00	15.00	20.00	35.00	—
1650	—	10.00	15.00	30.00	50.00	—
1653	—	10.00	15.00	20.00	35.00	—
1654	—	10.00	15.00	20.00	35.00	—
1655	—	10.00	15.00	20.00	35.00	—
1656	—	10.00	15.00	20.00	35.00	—
1657	—	10.00	15.00	20.00	35.00	—
1658	—	10.00	15.00	20.00	35.00	—
1659	—	10.00	15.00	20.00	35.00	—

KM# 81.1 LIARD (12 Mites)
Copper **Rev. Legend:** ...DVX BVRG C(O) FLAN Z

Date	Mintage	VG	F	VF	XF	Unc
1680	—	10.00	15.00	25.00	35.00	—
1681	—	10.00	20.00	40.00	65.00	—
1685	—	10.00	15.00	25.00	35.00	—
1686	—	10.00	15.00	25.00	35.00	—

KM# 81.2 LIARD (12 Mites)
Copper **Rev. Legend:** ...DVX BVRG C(O) FL(AN Z)

Date	Mintage	VG	F	VF	XF	Unc
1691	—	10.00	15.00	20.00	30.00	—
1692	—	10.00	15.00	20.00	30.00	—
1693	—	10.00	15.00	20.00	30.00	—
1694	—	10.00	15.00	20.00	30.00	—
1695	—	10.00	15.00	20.00	30.00	—
1696	—	10.00	15.00	28.00	45.00	—
1698	—	10.00	15.00	20.00	30.00	—
1699	—	10.00	15.00	20.00	30.00	—
1700	—	10.00	15.00	20.00	30.00	—

KM# 19 1/2 PATARD (1/2 Sol)
Billon **Obv:** Cross floree, AE monogram at center **Rev:** Crowned shield of Albert and Elizabeth **Rev. Legend:** ...BVRG CO FL(A) Z

Date	Mintage	VG	F	VF	XF	Unc
1615	—	30.00	60.00	110	200	—

KM# 17 PATARD
Billon **Obv:** Cross floree, AE monogram at center **Rev:** Crowned shield of Albert and Elizabeth divides dates **Rev. Legend:** ...BVRG CO F(L) Z

Date	Mintage	VG	F	VF	XF	Unc
1614	—	12.50	25.00	50.00	85.00	—
1615	—	12.50	25.00	50.00	85.00	—
1616	—	15.00	30.00	60.00	100	—
ND	—	15.00	30.00	60.00	100	—

KM# 47.1 PATARD
Billon **Obv:** Linear cross **Rev:** Crowned shield of Philip IV divides date **Rev. Legend:** ...HISP. INDIAR Z

Date	Mintage	VG	F	VF	XF	Unc
1633	—	70.00	135	250	400	—

KM# 47.2 PATARD
Billon **Rev. Legend:** ...HIS. INDIA Z

Date	Mintage	VG	F	VF	XF	Unc
1644	—	80.00	150	270	450	—

KM# 75 PATARD
Billon **Obv:** Long cross, mintmark in center **Rev:** Crowned shield divides date **Rev. Legend:** ...DVX BVRG CO FL(AN) Zc

Date	Mintage	VG	F	VF	XF	Unc
1679	—	18.00	35.00	70.00	125	—
1680	—	28.00	55.00	100	175	—

KM# 5 1/4 REAL
1.7400 g., 0.3960 Silver 0.0222 oz. ASW **Obv:** Crowned shield of Albert and Elizabeth in fleece collar **Rev:** Crowned shield divides date **Rev. Legend:** ...BVRG COM FL(A)

Date	Mintage	VG	F	VF	XF	Unc
1603	—	225	400	650	1,000	—
1604	—	120	225	425	700	—
1605	—	165	300	500	800	—
1606	—	275	500	1,000	1,650	—
1611 Rare	—	—	—	—	—	—

KM# 9 1/2 REAL
3.4800 g., 0.3960 Silver 0.0443 oz. ASW **Obv:** Crowned shield on St. Anthony's cross divides date **Rev:** Crowned shield with fleece below **Rev. Legend:** ...BVRG Z COM FLA

Date	Mintage	VG	F	VF	XF	Unc
1609	—	325	675	1,250	2,000	—
1610	—	450	900	1,600	2,500	—
ND	—	265	525	950	1,500	—

KM# 1 STOTER (1/8 Florin)
3.4200 g., 0.4170 Silver 0.0458 oz. ASW **Obv:** Crowned shield in fleece collar **Rev:** Cross floree, lion and crown in angles

Date	Mintage	VG	F	VF	XF	Unc
1601	—	225	400	650	1,000	—

KM# 21 3 PATARDS
2.6300 g., 0.5820 Silver 0.0492 oz. ASW **Obv:** Cross floree, lion at center **Rev:** Crowned shield in octolobe **Rev. Legend:** ...BVRG Z CO FL

Date	Mintage	VG	F	VF	XF	Unc
1616	—	15.00	25.00	40.00	60.00	—
1617	—	15.00	25.00	45.00	75.00	—
1620	—	15.00	25.00	40.00	60.00	—

KM# 94 4 PATARDS
4.9000 g., 0.3850 Silver 0.0606 oz. ASW **Obv:** St. Andrew's cross, crown above, fleece below, divides date **Rev:** Crowned shield **Rev. Legend:** ...DVX BVRG C FLAND Z

Date	Mintage	VG	F	VF	XF	Unc
1698	—	25.00	45.00	80.00	135	—
1700	—	35.00	65.00	120	200	—

KM# 23 ESCALIN
5.2600 g., 0.5820 Silver 0.0984 oz. ASW **Obv:** Eagle with shield of Austria, Burgundy on breast **Rev:** Crowned shield of Albert and Elizabeth on St. Andrew's cross **Rev. Legend:** ...BVRG Z CO FL(A) (Z)

Date	Mintage	VG	F	VF	XF	Unc
1619	—	50.00	100	185	300	—
1620	—	15.00	25.00	40.00	65.00	—
1621	—	15.00	25.00	40.00	65.00	—
ND	—	15.00	25.00	40.00	65.00	—

KM# 31 ESCALIN
5.2600 g., 0.5820 Silver 0.0984 oz. ASW **Obv:** Lion rampant left with sword and shield **Rev:** Crowned shield of Philip IV on St. Andrew's cross **Rev. Legend:** ...DVX BVR CO FL(A) Zc

Date	Mintage	VG	F	VF	XF	Unc
1621	—	50.00	100	185	300	—
1622	—	15.00	25.00	40.00	65.00	—
1623	—	15.00	25.00	40.00	65.00	—
1624	—	35.00	75.00	150	250	—
1625	—	15.00	30.00	60.00	100	—
1628	—	50.00	100	185	300	—
1633	—	70.00	140	275	450	—
1646	—	40.00	85.00	165	275	—
1658	—	135	250	425	650	—

KM# 95 ESCALIN
5.2600 g., 0.5820 Silver 0.0984 oz. ASW **Obv:** Lion rampant left with sword, paw on globe **Rev:** Crowned shield on St. Andrew's cross of Charles II **Rev. Legend:** ...DVX BVRG C FLAN (D) Z

Date	Mintage	VG	F	VF	XF	Unc
1698	—	28.00	55.00	100	175	—

KM# 102 ESCALIN
5.2600 g., 0.5820 Silver 0.0984 oz. ASW **Rev. Legend:** ...DVX BVRG C FLAN Z

Date	Mintage	VG	F	VF	XF	Unc
1700	—	135	250	425	650	—

KM# 15 1/4 PATAGON
7.0300 g., 0.8750 Silver 0.1978 oz. ASW **Obv:** St. Andrew's cross, crown above, fleece below divides pair of crowned triple C monograms **Rev:** Crowned shield in fleece collar **Rev. Legend:** ...BVRG ET CO(M) FL(A) Z

Date	Mintage	VG	F	VF	XF	Unc
1612	—	150	300	550	950	—
1620	—	125	250	500	850	—

KM# 37 1/4 PATAGON

7.0300 g., 0.8750 Silver 0.1978 oz. ASW **Obv:** St. Andrew's cross, crown above, fleece below divides date **Rev:** Crowned shield of Philip IV in fleece collar **Rev. Legend:** ...DVX BVRG ET CO FL(AN) Z

Date	Mintage	VG	F	VF	XF	Unc
1624	—	32.00	65.00	120	200	—
1625	—	80.00	165	300	500	—
1628	—	100	200	350	600	—
1629	—	135	265	475	800	—
1631	—	32.00	65.00	120	200	—
1632	—	40.00	80.00	150	250	—
1638	—	110	220	400	650	—
1640	—	65.00	135	250	400	—
1644	—	80.00	165	300	500	—
1654	—	50.00	100	180	300	—
1655	—	50.00	100	180	300	—
1657	—	80.00	165	300	500	—
1660	—	55.00	110	200	350	—
1663	—	100	200	350	600	—

KM# 8 3 REAL (15 Sols)

9.1900 g., 0.8960 Silver 0.2647 oz. ASW **Obv:** Busts of Albert and Elizabeth conjoined left **Rev:** Crowned arms with fleece below covers St. Andrew's cross and divides date **Rev. Legend:** ...DVCES BVRG ET COM FLAN

Date	Mintage	VG	F	VF	XF	Unc
1607	—	1,000	2,000	3,500	6,000	—
1608	—	1,000	2,000	3,500	6,000	—

KM# 3 FLORIN

13.8700 g., 0.8330 Silver 0.3714 oz. ASW **Obv:** Busts of Albert and Elizabeth confronted **Rev:** Crowned shield within fleece collar

Date	Mintage	VG	F	VF	XF	Unc
1602 Rare	—	—	—	—	—	—

KM# 30 1/2 PATAGON (24 Sols)

14.0500 g., 0.8750 Silver 0.3952 oz. ASW **Obv:** St. Andrew's cross, crown above, fleece below, divides pair of crowned triple C monograms **Rev:** Crowned shield in fleece collar **Rev. Legend:** ...BVRG ET CO FL Z

Date	Mintage	VG	F	VF	XF	Unc
1620 Rare	—	—	—	—	—	—
ND Rare	—	—	—	—	—	—

KM# 33 1/2 PATAGON (24 Sols)

14.0500 g., 0.8750 Silver 0.3952 oz. ASW **Obv:** St. Andrew's cross, crown above, fleece below, divides date **Rev:** Crowned shield of Philip IV in fleece collar **Rev. Legend:** ...DVX BVRG ET CO FL(AN) Zc

Date	Mintage	VG	F	VF	XF	Unc
1622	—	100	200	350	600	—
1623	—	100	200	350	600	—
1631	—	55.00	110	200	350	—
1633	—	40.00	80.00	150	250	—
1635	—	65.00	135	250	400	—
1641	—	100	200	350	600	—
1646	—	75.00	150	275	450	—
1647	—	65.00	135	250	400	—
1648	—	45.00	90.00	165	275	—
1649	—	100	200	350	600	—
1652	—	50.00	100	180	300	—
1653	—	65.00	135	250	400	—
1655	—	65.00	135	250	400	—
1657	—	110	220	400	650	—
1658	—	150	300	575	950	—
1660	—	135	265	475	800	—
1662	—	100	200	350	600	—
1663	—	100	200	350	600	—
1664	—	110	220	400	650	—
1665	—	50.00	100	180	300	—

KM# 66 1/2 PATAGON (24 Sols)

14.0500 g., 0.8750 Silver 0.3952 oz. ASW **Obv:** St. Andrew's cross, crown above, fleece below, divides date **Rev:** Crowned shield of Charles II in fleece collar **Rev. Legend:** ...DVX BVRG C FLAN(D) Z

Date	Mintage	VG	F	VF	XF	Unc
1667	—	85.00	165	300	500	—
1669	—	110	220	400	650	—
1672	—	85.00	165	300	500	—
1673	—	65.00	135	250	400	—
1674	—	110	220	400	650	—
1675	—	85.00	165	300	500	—
1680	—	85.00	165	300	500	—
1686	—	85.00	165	300	500	—
1687	—	100	200	350	600	—
1689	—	85.00	165	300	500	—

KM# 90 1/2 PATAGON (24 Sols)

14.0500 g., 0.8750 Silver 0.3952 oz. ASW **Ruler:** Charles II **Obv:** St. Andrew's cross, crown above, fleece below, divides pair of crowned double C monograms **Rev. Legend:** ...DVX BVRG C FLAN(D) Zc

Date	Mintage	VG	F	VF	XF	Unc
1694 Rare	—	—	—	—	—	—
1695 Rare	—	—	—	—	—	—
1696 Rare	—	—	—	—	—	—
1699 Rare	—	—	—	—	—	—
1700	—	80.00	175	275	400	—

KM# 45 1/2 DUCATON

16.2400 g., 0.9440 Silver 0.4929 oz. ASW **Obv:** Bust of Philip IV right in ruffled collar **Rev:** Crowned shield supported by lions **Rev. Legend:** ...DVX BVRG CO FLAN Zc

Date	Mintage	VG	F	VF	XF	Unc
1632	—	180	350	575	900	—
1633	—	240	450	725	1,150	—
1636	—	220	400	650	1,000	—

KM# 49 1/2 DUCATON

16.2400 g., 0.9440 Silver 0.4929 oz. ASW **Obv:** Bust of Philip IV right in thin collar, date divided by mint mark in exergue **Rev:** Lion with swords behind crowned shield **Rev. Legend:** ...DVX BVRG CO FLAN Zc

Date	Mintage	VG	F	VF	XF	Unc
1637	—	240	450	725	1,150	—
1639	—	265	475	775	1,200	—
1644	—	265	475	775	1,200	—
1652	—	110	190	325	475	—
1654	—	130	240	400	600	—
1660	—	220	400	650	1,000	—
1662	—	150	270	475	725	—

KM# 67 1/2 DUCATON

16.2400 g., 0.9440 Silver 0.4929 oz. ASW **Obv:** Child's bust of Charles II right **Rev:** Crowned shield supported by lions **Rev. Legend:** ...DVX BVRG CO FLAN Zc

Date	Mintage	VG	F	VF	XF	Unc
1668	—	100	200	350	600	—
1670	—	85.00	170	300	500	—
1673	—	70.00	145	265	450	—

KM# 83 1/2 DUCATON

16.2400 g., 0.9440 Silver 0.4929 oz. ASW **Obv:** Youthful bust of Charles II with long hair and court robe **Rev. Legend:** ...DVX BVRG CO FLAN Zc

Date	Mintage	VG	F	VF	XF	Unc
1687 Rare	—	—	—	—	—	—

KM# 22 PATAGON

28.1000 g., 0.8750 Silver 0.7905 oz. ASW **Obv:** St. Andrew's cross, crown above, fleece below, divides pair of crowned CCAV monograms **Rev:** Crowned shield in fleece collar **Rev. Legend:** ...BVRG ET CO FLA (Z) **Note:** Legend varieties exist. Dav. #4435.

Date	Mintage	VG	F	VF	XF	Unc
1616	—	55.00	115	205	450	—
1617	—	43.75	80.00	155	425	—
1618	—	43.75	80.00	155	425	—
1619	—	50.00	95.00	170	425	—
1620	—	43.75	80.00	155	425	—
1621	—	55.00	105	190	425	—
ND	—	37.50	75.00	155	425	—

KM# 34 PATAGON

28.1000 g., 0.8750 Silver 0.7905 oz. ASW **Obv:** St. Andrew's cross, crown above, fleece below, divides date **Rev:** Crowned shield of Philip IV in fleece collar **Rev. Legend:** ...DVX BVRG ET CO FL(AN) Zc **Note:** Dav. #4464.

Date	Mintage	VG	F	VF	XF	Unc
1622	—	55.00	115	220	450	—
1623	—	80.00	155	280	600	—
1626	—	190	375	725	1,450	—
1628	—	220	400	750	1,500	—
1631	—	65.00	125	225	500	—
1632	—	80.00	155	280	600	—
1633	—	50.00	95.00	170	425	—
1636	—	65.00	125	225	500	—
1638	—	95.00	190	350	725	—
1639	—	115	220	400	875	—
1640	—	140	275	500	1,000	—
1641	—	155	325	575	1,150	—
1642	—	95.00	190	350	725	—
1644	—	125	250	450	950	—
1645	—	65.00	125	225	500	—
1646	—	65.00	125	225	500	—
1647	—	80.00	170	325	650	—
1648	—	80.00	170	325	650	—
1649	—	50.00	95.00	170	425	—
1650	—	80.00	170	450	650	—
1651	—	55.00	105	190	425	—
1652	—	50.00	95.00	170	425	—
1653	—	80.00	155	280	600	—
1654	—	65.00	125	225	500	—
1655	—	80.00	170	325	650	—
1656	—	100	195	350	750	—
1657	—	70.00	140	250	525	—
1658	—	80.00	170	325	650	—
1659	—	140	275	500	1,000	—
1660	—	100	195	350	750	—
1661	—	110	220	375	800	—
1663	—	110	220	375	800	—
1664	—	140	275	500	1,000	—
1665	—	100	195	350	750	—

KM# 63 PATAGON

28.1000 g., 0.8750 Silver 0.7905 oz. ASW **Obv:** St. Andrew's cross, crown above, fleece below, divides date **Rev:** Crowned shield of Charles II in fleece collar **Rev. Legend:** ...DVX BVRG CO FLAN Zc **Note:** Dav. #4494.

Date	Mintage	VG	F	VF	XF	Unc
1666	—	55.00	110	190	425	—
1667	—	70.00	140	250	525	—
1668	—	55.00	110	190	425	—
1669	—	55.00	110	190	425	—
1670	—	70.00	140	250	525	—
1671	—	70.00	140	250	525	—
1672	—	40.00	80.00	155	375	—
1673	—	65.00	125	225	500	—
1674	—	65.00	125	225	500	—
1675	—	70.00	140	250	525	—
1676	—	70.00	140	250	525	—
1677	—	70.00	140	250	525	—
1678	—	40.00	80.00	155	375	—
1679	—	55.00	110	190	425	—
1680	—	55.00	110	190	425	—
1683	—	110	220	375	800	—
1684	—	90.00	170	325	650	—
1685	—	55.00	110	190	425	—
1686	—	65.00	125	225	500	—
1687	—	55.00	110	190	425	—
1688	—	90.00	170	325	650	—
1689	—	70.00	140	250	525	—
1690	—	70.00	140	250	525	—
1691	—	125	250	450	950	—
1692	—	90.00	170	325	650	—

KM# 91 PATAGON

28.1000 g., 0.8750 Silver 0.7905 oz. ASW **Obv:** St. Andrew's cross, crown above, fleece below, divides pair of crowned double C monograms **Rev:** Crowned shield of Charles II in fleece collar **Rev. Legend:** ...DVX BVRG C FLAND Z **Note:** Dav. #4500.

Date	Mintage	VG	F	VF	XF	Unc
1694	—	200	400	650	1,000	—
1699	—	275	550	950	1,450	—
1700	—	250	475	800	1,250	—

KM# 35 DUCATON

32.4800 g., 0.9440 Silver 0.9857 oz. ASW **Obv:** Bust of Philip IV in ruffled collar, mint mark divides date in legend **Rev:** Lions supporting crowned shield **Rev. Legend:** ...DVX BVRG ET CO FL(AN) Zc **Note:** Dav. #4446.

Date	Mintage	VG	F	VF	XF	Unc
1622 Rare	—	—	—	—	—	—
1631	—	175	350	600	1,200	—
1632	—	175	350	600	1,200	—
1633	—	120	225	400	825	—
1634	—	120	225	400	825	—
1635	—	150	265	475	1,000	—
1636	—	175	350	600	1,200	—

KM# 50 DUCATON

32.4800 g., 0.9440 Silver 0.9857 oz. ASW **Obv:** Bust of Philip IV in thin collar **Rev:** Lions supporting crowned shield **Rev. Legend:** ...DVX BVRG ET CO FL(AN) Zc **Note:** Dav. #4457.

Date	Mintage	VG	F	VF	XF	Unc
1636	—	80.00	165	325	650	—
1637	—	100	210	400	775	—
1638	—	90.00	190	350	725	—
1639	—	115	240	450	900	—
1641	—	75.00	155	300	600	—
1642	—	80.00	165	325	650	—
1644	—	80.00	165	325	650	—
1648	—	80.00	165	325	650	—
1649	—	90.00	190	350	725	—
1650	—	55.00	125	250	475	—
1651	—	65.00	140	275	550	—
1652	—	55.00	125	250	475	—
1653	—	75.00	155	300	600	—
1654	—	55.00	125	250	475	—
1655	—	55.00	125	250	475	—
1656	—	75.00	155	300	600	—
1657	—	55.00	125	250	475	—
1658	—	75.00	155	300	600	—
1659	—	75.00	155	300	600	—
1660	—	75.00	155	300	600	—
1662	—	75.00	155	300	600	—
1664	—	55.00	125	250	475	—
1665	—	55.00	125	250	475	—

KM# 64 DUCATON

32.4800 g., 0.9440 Silver 0.9857 oz. ASW **Obv:** Child's bust of Charles II right **Rev:** Crowned shield supported by lions **Rev. Legend:** ...DVX BVRG CO FLAN Zc **Note:** Dav. #4479.

Date	Mintage	VG	F	VF	XF	Unc
1666	—	85.00	175	325	600	—
1667	—	85.00	175	325	600	—
1668	—	85.00	175	325	600	—
1669	—	95.00	190	350	650	—
1670	—	60.00	125	250	500	—
1672	—	60.00	125	250	500	—
1673	—	60.00	125	250	500	—
1676	—	120	245	450	850	—

KM# 82 DUCATON

32.4800 g., 0.9440 Silver 0.9857 oz. ASW **Obv:** Youthfull bust of Charles II with long hair and large cravat **Rev. Legend:** ...DVX BVRG CO FLAN Z **Note:** Dav. #4482.

Date	Mintage	VG	F	VF	XF	Unc
1684 Rare	—	—	—	—	—	—
1687 Rare	—	—	—	—	—	—
1689 Rare	—	—	—	—	—	—

KM# 84 DUCATON

32.4800 g., 0.9440 Silver 0.9857 oz. ASW **Obv:** Mature bust of Charles II right **Rev. Legend:** ...DVX BVRG C FLAND Zc **Note:** Dav. #4488.

Date	Mintage	VG	F	VF	XF	Unc
1694 Rare	—	—	—	—	—	—

KM# 46 2 DUCATON

Silver **Note:** Similar to 1 Ducaton, KM#50.

Date	Mintage	VG	F	VF	XF	Unc
1632	—	550	1,000	1,750	2,750	—
1634	—	550	1,000	1,750	2,750	—
1639	—	450	800	1,750	2,750	—
1645	—	450	800	1,750	2,750	—
1650	—	450	800	1,750	2,750	—
1652	—	450	800	1,750	2,750	—
1654	—	450	800	1,750	2,750	—
1664	—	450	800	1,750	2,750	—

KM# A84 2 DUCATON

64.9800 g., 0.9440 Silver 1.9721 oz. ASW **Ruler:** Charles II **Obv:** Mature bust of Charles II right **Rev. Legend:** ...DVX BVRG C FLAND Zc **Note:** Dav. #4487.

Date	Mintage	VG	F	VF	XF	Unc
1694	—	—	—	2,250	3,750	5,500

KM# 62 3 DUCATON

Silver **Note:** Similar to 1 Ducaton, KM#50.

Date	Mintage	VG	F	VF	XF	Unc
1665 Rare	—	—	—	—	—	—

KM# 61 4 DUCATON

Silver **Note:** Similar to 1 Ducaton, KM#50.

Date	Mintage	VG	F	VF	XF	Unc
1662 Rare	—	—	—	—	—	—

KM# 4 ALBERTIN (Corona)

2.9200 g., 0.7920 Gold 0.0743 oz. AGW **Obv:** Crowned arms in collar of the Golden Fleece **Rev:** crowned floral St. Andrew's cross, date at sides, Golden Fleece at bottom

Date	Mintage	VG	F	VF	XF	Unc
1602	19,000	350	675	1,150	1,950	—

KM# 39 COURONNE D'OR

3.4100 g., 0.8820 Gold 0.0967 oz. AGW **Obv:** Cross of four crowned monograms, lions and crowns in angles **Rev:** Crowned shield of Albert and Isabella divides pair of crowned monograms **Rev. Legend:** ...BVRG CO FL Z

Date	Mintage	VG	F	VF	XF	Unc
1615	9,203	1,150	2,250	4,400	7,500	—
1620	3,519	1,150	2,250	4,400	7,500	—

KM# 40 COURONNE D'OR

3.4100 g., 0.8820 Gold 0.0967 oz. AGW **Obv:** Cross floree **Rev:** Crowned shield of Philip IV divides pair of crowned monograms **Rev. Legend:** ...DVX BVRG CO FL Zc

Date	Mintage	VG	F	VF	XF	Unc
1627	834	600	1,200	2,400	3,600	—
1628	Inc. above	600	1,200	2,400	3,600	—
1631	13,000	350	750	1,500	2,400	—
1632	Inc. above	350	750	1,500	2,400	—
1640	15,000	350	750	1,500	2,400	—
1642	Inc. above	350	750	1,500	2,400	—

KM# 2.1 2 ALBERTINS

5.1500 g., 0.8950 Gold 0.1482 oz. AGW **Obv:** Crowned arms in collar of the Golden Fleece **Rev:** Crowned floral St. Andrew's cross, date at sides, Golden Fleece at bottom

Date	Mintage	VG	F	VF	XF	Unc
1601	21,000	500	1,000	2,000	3,200	—
1602	Inc. above	500	1,000	2,000	3,200	—
1603	Inc. above	500	1,000	2,000	3,200	—
1607	3,496	500	1,000	2,000	3,200	—

KM# 2.2 2 ALBERTINS

5.1500 g., 0.8950 Gold 0.1482 oz. AGW **Rev. Legend:** ...COM FLAN

Date	Mintage	VG	F	VF	XF	Unc
1601	—	500	1,000	2,000	3,200	—

KM# 32 SOUVERAIN D'OR (Lion d'Or)

5.5400 g., 0.9470 Gold 0.1687 oz. AGW **Obv:** Crowned lion with sword and shield left **Rev:** Crowned shield of Philip IV in fleece collar **Rev. Legend:** ...BVRG. CO. FLAN. Z.

Date	Mintage	VG	F	VF	XF	Unc
1621 Rare	—	—	—	—	—	—
1625	—	300	425	800	1,450	—
1644	12,000	300	425	800	1,450	—
1648	48,000	300	425	800	1,450	—
1649	Inc. above	300	425	800	1,450	—
1650	Inc. above	300	425	800	1,450	—

Date	Mintage	VG	F	VF	XF	Unc
1651	—	300	425	800	1,450	—
1652	—	300	425	800	1,450	—
1653	17,000	300	425	800	1,450	—
1654	Inc. above	300	425	800	1,450	—
1655	14,000	300	425	800	1,450	—
1656	27,000	300	425	800	1,450	—
1657	Inc. above	300	425	800	1,450	—
1658	Inc. above	300	425	800	1,450	—
1660	22,000	300	425	800	1,450	—
1662	7,000	300	425	800	1,450	—
1663	Inc. above	300	425	800	1,450	—
1664	5,000	300	425	800	1,450	—

KM# 65 SOUVERAIN D'OR (Lion d'Or)

5.5400 g., 0.9470 Gold 0.1687 oz. AGW **Obv:** Crowned lion with sword, paw on globe set on pedestal, date in exergue **Rev:** Crowned shield of Charles II in fleece collar **Rev. Legend:** ...DVX BVRG CO FL(AN) Z

Date	Mintage	VG	F	VF	XF	Unc
1666	3,014	1,500	3,000	5,000	7,500	—
1668	2,940	1,500	3,000	5,000	7,500	—
1669	2,676	1,500	3,000	5,000	7,500	—
1672	2,513	1,500	3,000	5,000	7,500	—
1673	Inc. above	1,500	3,000	5,000	7,500	—
1674	1,067	1,500	3,000	5,000	7,500	—
1675	3,148	1,500	3,000	5,000	7,500	—
1685	2,663	1,500	3,000	5,000	7,500	—

KM# 103 SOUVERAIN D'OR (Lion d'Or)

5.5400 g., 0.9470 Gold 0.1687 oz. AGW, 25 mm. **Rev. Legend:** ...DVX BVRG C FLAN (D) Zc **Note:** Machine struck.

Date	Mintage	VG	F	VF	XF	Unc
1700	1,938	1,000	2,250	3,750	6,000	—

KM# 16 2 SOUVERAIN D'OR

11.0800 g., 0.9470 Gold 0.3373 oz. AGW **Obv:** Albert and Elizabeth, seated facing on thrones, date in exergue **Rev:** Crowned shield in fleece collar **Rev. Legend:** ...ET COM(IT) FLA(Z)

Date	Mintage	VG	F	VF	XF	Unc
ND	—	725	1,500	2,850	5,300	—
1612	3,059	850	1,600	3,200	5,800	—
1613	Inc. above	725	1,500	2,850	5,300	—
1614	6,090	775	1,550	3,050	5,500	—
1615	Inc. above	725	1,500	2,850	5,300	—
1616	5,730	725	1,500	2,850	5,300	—
1617	Inc. above	850	1,600	3,200	5,800	—
1618	Inc. above	775	1,550	3,050	5,500	—
1620 Rare	176	—	—	—	—	—

KM# 48 2 SOUVERAIN D'OR

11.0800 g., 0.9470 Gold 0.3373 oz. AGW **Obv:** Crowned bust of Philip IV in ruffled collar right **Rev:** Crowned shield in fleece collar **Rev. Legend:** ...DVX BVRG ET CO FL(AN) Zc

Date	Mintage	VG	F	VF	XF	Unc
1634 Rare	9,035	—	—	—	—	—
1635 Rare	Inc. above	—	—	—	—	—
1636	Inc. above	1,000	2,000	4,500	6,500	—

KM# 51 2 SOUVERAIN D'OR

11.0800 g., 0.9470 Gold 0.3373 oz. AGW **Obv:** Older bust of Philip IV in flat collar

Date	Mintage	VG	F	VF	XF	Unc
1638	19,000	625	825	1,850	3,250	—
1639	Inc. above	625	825	1,850	3,250	—
1640	Inc. above	625	825	1,850	3,250	—
1642	36,000	625	825	1,850	3,250	—
1643	Inc. above	625	825	1,850	3,250	—
1644	Inc. above	625	825	1,850	3,250	—
1645	Inc. above	625	825	1,850	3,250	—
1646	41,000	625	825	1,850	3,250	—
1647	Inc. above	625	825	1,850	3,250	—

KM# 68 2 SOUVERAIN D'OR

11.0800 g., 0.9470 Gold 0.3373 oz. AGW **Obv:** Child's bust of Charles II crowned, right **Rev:** Crowned shield in fleece collar **Rev. Legend:** ...DBX BVRG CO FLAN Zc

Date	Mintage	VG	F	VF	XF	Unc
1668 Unique	508	—	—	—	—	—

KM# 104 2 SOUVERAIN D'OR

11.0800 g., 0.9470 Gold 0.3373 oz. AGW **Obv:** Mature bust of Charles II crowned, right

Date	Mintage	VG	F	VF	XF	Unc
1700 Rare	260	—	—	—	—	—

KM# 93 1/2 DUCATON D'OR (4 Souverain)

0.9480 Gold **Obv:** Mature bust of Charles II right **Rev:** Crowned shield of Charles II, supported by lions

Date	Mintage	VG	F	VF	XF	Unc
1696 Rare	—	—	9,500	15,000	25,000	—
1700 Rare	—	—	9,500	15,000	25,000	—

KM# 92 DUCATON D'OR (8 Souverain)

0.9480 Gold **Obv:** Mature bust of Charles II right **Rev:** Crowned shield of Charles II **Rev. Legend:** ...DVX BVRG C FLAND Zc

Date	Mintage	VG	F	VF	XF	Unc
1694 Rare	—	—	8,500	13,500	22,500	—

Note: Stack's International sale 3-88 AU realized $13,750

PIEFORTS

KM#	Date	Mintage	Identification	Mkt Val
P1	1614	—	2 Souverain D'Or. Gold. Double	—
P2	1615	—	2 Souverain D'Or. Gold. Triple	—
P3	1644	—	2 Souverain. Gold.	—
P4	1646	—	2 Souverain. Gold.	—

LUXEMBOURG

Founded about 963, Luxembourg was a prominent country of the Holy Roman Empire; one of its sovereigns became Holy Roman Emperor as Henry VII, 1308. After being made a duchy by Emperor Charles IV, 1354, Luxembourg passed under the domination of burgundy, Spain, Austria and France, 1443-1815.

DUCHY

Spanish Rule

STANDARD COINAGE

KM# 13 ESCALIN

Silver **Ruler:** Philip IV **Obv:** Rampant lion with sword and shield left **Obv. Legend:** PHIL. IIII. D. G. HISP. ET. INDIAR. REX **Rev:** Crowned arms **Rev. Legend:** ARCHID • AVST • DVX • BVRG • LVXEM • Zc

Date	Mintage	Good	VG	F	VF	XF
1637	—	35.00	85.00	175	250	—

KM# 15 1/4 PATAGON

Silver **Ruler:** Philip IV **Obv:** St. Andrew's cross, crown above divides date **Obv. Legend:** PHIL. IIII. D. G. HISP. ET. INDIAR. REX **Rev:** Crowned arms in Order collar **Rev. Legend:** ARCHID • AVST • DVX • BVRG • LVXEM. Zc

Date	Mintage	Good	VG	F	VF	XF
1632	—	200	550	900	1,300	—

KM# 16 1/2 PATAGON

Silver **Ruler:** Philip IV **Obv:** St. Andrew's cross with crown above divides date **Obv. Legend:** PHIL. IIII. D. G. HISP. ET. INDIAR. REX **Rev:** Crowned arms in order collar **Rev. Legend:** ARCHID • AVST • DVX • BVRG • LUVXEM. Zc

Date	Mintage	Good	VG	F	VF	XF
1632	—	200	550	900	1,350	—
1633	—	200	550	900	1,350	—
1634	—	200	550	900	1,350	—
1635	—	200	550	900	1,350	—
1636	—	200	550	900	1,350	—
1639	—	200	550	900	1,350	—

KM# 10 PATAGON

Silver **Ruler:** Albert and Elizabeth **Obv:** St. Andrew's cross with crown above, crowned monograms at left and right, Order of Golden Fleece below **Obv. Legend:** • ALBERTVS • ET • ELISABET • DEI • GRATIA **Rev:** Crowned arms in Order colla **Rev. Legend:** • ARCHID • AVST • DVCES • BURG • ET • LUXENE • **Note:** Mint mark: Lion.

Date	Mintage	Good	VG	F	VF	XF
ND(1616-19)	—	—	—	—	—	—

KM# 17 PATAGON

Silver **Ruler:** Philip IV **Obv:** St. Andrew's cross with crown above divides date **Obv. Legend:** PHIL. IIII. D. G. HISP. ET. INDIAR REX **Rev:** Crowned arms in Order collar **Rev. Legend:** ARCHID • AVXT • DVX • BVRG • LVXEM. Zc **Note:** Dav. #4468.

Date	Mintage	Good	VG	F	VF	XF
1632	—	200	500	850	1,250	2,50
1633	—	200	500	850	1,250	2,50
1634	—	200	500	850	1,250	2,50
1635	—	200	500	850	1,250	2,50
1636	—	200	500	850	1,250	2,50
1637	—	200	500	850	1,250	2,50
1639	—	200	500	850	1,250	2,50
1643	—	200	500	850	1,250	2,50

KM# 18 2 PATAGON

Silver **Ruler:** Philip IV **Obv:** St. Andrew's cross with crown above divides date **Obv. Legend:** PHIL. IIII. D. G. HISP. ET. INDIAR REX **Rev:** Crowned arms **Rev. Legend:** ARCHID • AVST • DVX • BVRG. LVXEM. Zc **Note:** Dav. #4467.

Date	Mintage	Good	VG	F	VF	XF
1632	—	—	—	—	—	—
1633	—	—	—	—	—	—
1634	—	—	—	—	—	—
1636	—	—	—	—	—	—
1643	—	—	—	—	—	—

KM# 19 COURONNE D'OR

Gold **Ruler:** Philip IV **Obv:** Rampant lion with sword and shield left **Obv. Legend:** PHIL. IIII. D. G. HISP. ET. INDIAR. REX **Rev:** Crowned arms **Rev. Legend:** ARCHID • AVST • DVX • BVRG LVXEM. Zc **Note:** Fr. #11.

Date	Mintage	Good	VG	F	VF	XF
1632 Rare	—	—	—	—	—	—

NAMUR

Became an independent duchy in the late 12th century. Divided in 1609- the north becoming part of the United Netherlands, the south staying as Spanish (and later Austrian) Netherlands. Became part of Belgium after 1830.

RULER

Philip V of Spain, 1700-1711

MINT MARK

Lion rampant - Namur

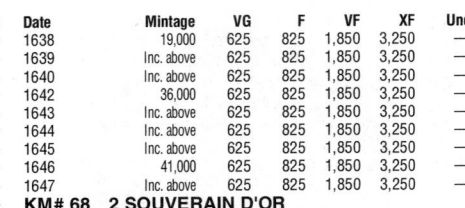

DUCHY

MILLED COINAGE

KM# 1 LIARD

Copper **Obv:** Crowned briquet with arms of Austria, Burgundy and Brabant at sides and below, titles of Charles II **Rev:** Crowned arms **Note:** Imitation of Liards of Brabant.

Date	Mintage	VG	F	VF	XF	Unc
1692	—	45.00	90.00	150	250	—

TOURNAI

Tournai, a city in Hainaut made an episcopal see in 6th century, came under French rule and received its charter in 1187. In the early 16th century it was an English possession for a few years and Henry VIII sold it to Francis I. In 1521 the Count of Nassau took it for Spain. It was frequently besieged in wars in the sixteenth through eighteenth centuries. It was severely damaged during World War 1, being captured by the Germans in 1914 and held until 1918.

RULERS

Albert and Elisabeth, 1599-1621

Philip IV, 1621-1665

MINT MARK

Tower - Tournai

COUNTY

STANDARD COINAGE

KM# 29 DENIER (4 Mites)

Copper **Obv:** Crowned AE monogram **Rev:** Crowned shield of Austria-Burgundy on St. Andrew's cross

Date	Mintage	VG	F	VF	XF	Unc
1616	—	11.50	22.50	40.00	65.00	—
1617	—	11.50	22.50	40.00	65.00	—

KM# 12 2 DENIER

Copper **Obv:** Crowned AE monogram **Rev:** Crowned shield of Austria-Burgundy on St. Andrew's cross **Rev. Legend:** ...BVR(G) DOM TOR(NA Z)

Date	Mintage	VG	F	VF	XF	Unc
1607	—	10.00	20.00	40.00	65.00	—
1608	—	10.00	15.00	28.00	45.00	—
1609	—	10.00	15.00	22.50	35.00	—
1615	—	10.00	20.00	40.00	65.00	—
1616	—	10.00	15.00	22.50	35.00	—
1617	—	20.00	40.00	75.00	125	—

KM# 20 1/2 LIARD (Gigot, 6 Mites)

Copper **Obv:** Crowned shield of Austria and Burgundy, lion at center **Rev:** St. Andrew's cross, crown above, fleece below **Rev. Legend:** ...BVR. DOM TOR (N Z)

Date	Mintage	VG	F	VF	XF	Unc
1610	—	14.00	28.00	50.00	85.00	—
1611	—	10.00	15.00	22.50	35.00	—

KM# 54 1/2 LIARD (Gigot, 6 Mites)

Copper **Obv:** St. Andrew's cross, crown above, fleece below, divides date **Rev:** Crowned shield of Philip IV **Rev. Legend:** ..DVX BVR D TOR Zc

Date	Mintage	VG	F	VF	XF	Unc
1638	—	65.00	135	250	400	—
1640	—	65.00	135	250	400	—
1646	—	32.00	65.00	120	200	—
1647	—	40.00	80.00	150	250	—
1648	—	40.00	80.00	150	250	—
1649	—	32.00	65.00	120	200	—
1650	—	40.00	80.00	150	250	—
1651	—	40.00	80.00	150	250	—
1652	—	32.00	65.00	120	200	—
1653	—	28.00	55.00	100	175	—
1654	—	50.00	100	185	300	—
1655	—	40.00	80.00	150	250	—
1656	—	50.00	100	185	300	—
1657	—	50.00	100	185	300	—
1658	—	50.00	100	185	300	—
1659	—	50.00	100	185	300	—

KM# 21 LIARD (12 Mites)

Copper **Obv:** Crowned shield of Albert and Elizabeth **Rev:** Crown and shields of Austria, Burgundy, and Brabant **Rev. Legend:** ..BVRG DOM TOR

Date	Mintage	VG	F	VF	XF	Unc
1610	—	10.00	20.00	40.00	65.00	—
1611	—	10.00	15.00	28.00	45.00	—

KM# 53 LIARD (12 Mites)

Copper **Obv:** Philip IV bust right **Rev:** Crowned shield of Philip IV

Date	Mintage	VG	F	VF	XF	Unc
1637	—	25.00	50.00	90.00	150	—
1638	—	25.00	50.00	90.00	150	—
1639	—	25.00	50.00	90.00	150	—
1640	—	25.00	50.00	90.00	150	—
1641	—	25.00	50.00	90.00	150	—

KM# 61 LIARD (12 Mites)

Copper **Obv:** Crown and shields of Austria, Burgundy, and Brabant **Rev:** Crowned shield divides date **Rev. Legend:** ...DVX BVR D TOR Z

Date	Mintage	VG	F	VF	XF	Unc
1644	—	10.00	15.00	20.00	35.00	—
1645	—	10.00	15.00	20.00	35.00	—
1649	—	10.00	15.00	20.00	35.00	—
1650	—	10.00	15.00	20.00	35.00	—
1651	—	10.00	15.00	22.00	45.00	—
1652	—	10.00	15.00	22.00	45.00	—
1653	—	10.00	15.00	20.00	35.00	—
1654	—	10.00	15.00	20.00	35.00	—
1655	—	10.00	15.00	20.00	35.00	—
1656	—	10.00	15.00	20.00	35.00	—
1657	—	10.00	15.00	20.00	35.00	—
1658	—	10.00	15.00	20.00	35.00	—
1659	—	10.00	15.00	20.00	35.00	—
1660	—	10.00	15.00	20.00	35.00	—
1664	—	10.00	15.00	20.00	35.00	—
1665	—	10.00	15.00	22.00	45.00	—
1666	—	10.00	16.00	30.00	55.00	—

KM# 27 1/2 PATARD (1/2 Sol)

Billon **Obv:** Cross flores, AE monogram at center **Rev:** Crowned shield of Albert and Elizabeth **Rev. Legend:** ...BVRG DOM TOR

Date	Mintage	VG	F	VF	XF	Unc
ND(1612-18)	—	18.00	35.00	60.00	100	—
1615	—	20.00	40.00	75.00	125	—
1616	—	25.00	50.00	90.00	145	—
1618	—	30.00	60.00	110	175	—

KM# 25 PATARD

Billon **Obv:** AE monogram in center of octolobe design **Rev:** Crowned shield of Albert and Elizabeth divides date **Rev. Legend:** ...BVRG DOM TOR(N) Z

Date	Mintage	VG	F	VF	XF	Unc
ND(1612-18)	—	15.00	25.00	40.00	65.00	—
1614	—	15.00	28.00	50.00	85.00	—
1615	—	15.00	25.00	40.00	65.00	—
1616	—	15.00	25.00	40.00	65.00	—
1617	—	15.00	25.00	40.00	65.00	—
1618	—	15.00	35.00	60.00	100	—

KM# 60 PATARD

Billon **Obv:** Linear cross **Rev:** Crowned shield of Philip IV divides date **Rev. Legend:** ...DVX BVRG D TOR Z

Date	Mintage	VG	F	VF	XF	Unc
1641	—	45.00	90.00	165	275	—
1643	—	32.00	65.00	120	200	—
1644	—	50.00	100	180	300	—

KM# 9 1/4 REAL (1-1/4 Sol)

1.7400 g., 0.3960 Silver 0.0222 oz. ASW **Obv:** Crowned shield of Albert and Elizabeth **Rev:** Crowned shield **Rev. Legend:** ...BVRG DOM TOR

Date	Mintage	VG	F	VF	XF	Unc
1603	—	32.00	65.00	120	200	—
1604	—	30.00	60.00	110	185	—
1605	—	25.00	50.00	90.00	150	—
1606	—	30.00	60.00	110	185	—
1611	—	—	—	—	—	—

KM# 13 1/2 REAL (2-1/2 Sol)

3.4800 g., 0.3960 Silver 0.0443 oz. ASW **Obv:** Crowned shield on St. Andrew's cross divides date **Rev:** Crowned shield **Rev. Legend:** ...DVCE. BVRG. DOM.

Date	Mintage	VG	F	VF	XF	Unc
1607	—	65.00	135	250	400	—
1608	—	60.00	115	200	350	—
1609	—	50.00	100	180	300	—
1610	—	60.00	115	200	350	—
1611	—	65.00	135	250	400	—

KM# 1 STOTER (2-1/2 Sols)

3.4200 g., 0.4170 Silver 0.0458 oz. ASW **Obv:** Crowned shield in fleece collar **Rev:** Cross floree, lion and crown in angles

Date	Mintage	VG	F	VF	XF	Unc
1601	—	30.00	60.00	110	185	—
1602	—	28.00	55.00	100	165	—

KM# 30 3 PATARDS

2.6300 g., 0.5820 Silver 0.0492 oz. ASW **Obv:** Cross floree, lion at center **Rev:** Crowned shield in octolobe **Rev. Legend:** ...BVRG DOM TOR(N) Z

Date	Mintage	VG	F	VF	XF	Unc
1616	—	15.00	25.00	45.00	75.00	—
1617	—	15.00	25.00	45.00	75.00	—
1618	—	18.00	35.00	60.00	100	—
1619	—	15.00	25.00	35.00	60.00	—
1620	—	15.00	25.00	35.00	60.00	—

KM# 11 REAL

3.0600 g., 0.8960 Silver 0.0881 oz. ASW **Obv:** Crowned shield in fleece collar **Rev:** St. Andrew's cross, crown above, fleece below **Rev. Legend:** ...DVCES BVRG ET DOM TOR

Date	Mintage	VG	F	VF	XF	Unc
ND(1604-08)	—	35.00	70.00	125	285	—
1606	—	—	—	—	—	—

KM# 2 1/4 FLORIN (5 Sols)

4.2700 g., 0.6670 Silver 0.0916 oz. ASW **Obv:** Bust of Albert and Elizabeth confronted, crown above, V below **Rev:** Crowned shield in fleece collar

Date	Mintage	VG	F	VF	XF	Unc
1601	—	750	1,350	2,250	3,500	—

KM# 40 ESCALIN (6 Sols)

5.2600 g., 0.5820 Silver 0.0984 oz. ASW **Obv:** Eagle with shield of Austria-Burgundy on breast **Rev:** Crowned shield of Albert and Elizabeth on St. Andrew's cross **Rev. Legend:** ...BVRG DOM TOR(N) Z

Date	Mintage	VG	F	VF	XF	Unc
ND(1612-21)	—	15.00	30.00	60.00	125	—
1621	—	28.00	55.00	100	175	—

KM# 41 ESCALIN (6 Sols)

5.2600 g., 0.5820 Silver 0.0984 oz. ASW **Obv:** Lion rampant left with shield and sword **Rev:** Crowned shield of Philip IV on St. Andrew's cross **Rev. Legend:** ...DVX BVRG D TOR(N) Z

Date	Mintage	VG	F	VF	XF	Unc
1621	—	15.00	25.00	50.00	90.00	—
1622	—	15.00	25.00	50.00	90.00	—
1623	—	15.00	27.50	50.00	90.00	—
1624	—	18.00	35.00	65.00	115	—
1625	—	28.00	55.00	100	165	—
1626	—	18.00	35.00	65.00	115	—
1627	—	22.00	45.00	80.00	135	—
1628	—	15.00	25.00	50.00	90.00	—
1629	—	15.00	25.00	50.00	90.00	—
1630	—	15.00	30.00	60.00	100	—
1636	—	35.00	65.00	120	200	—
1637	—	15.00	25.00	50.00	90.00	—
1638	—	22.00	45.00	80.00	135	—
1640	—	15.00	30.00	60.00	100	—
1642	—	28.00	55.00	100	165	—
1643	—	22.00	45.00	80.00	135	—
1644	—	28.00	55.00	100	165	—
1645	—	20.00	40.00	70.00	120	—
1646	—	35.00	65.00	120	200	—
1649	—	40.00	80.00	150	250	—
1651	—	35.00	65.00	120	200	—
1652	—	28.00	55.00	100	165	—
1659	—	60.00	120	200	350	—
1662	—	75.00	150	250	400	—
1663	—	75.00	150	250	400	—

KM# 3 1/2 FLORIN

8.5300 g., 0.6670 Silver 0.1829 oz. ASW **Obv:** Busts of Albert and Isabella confronted, crown above, date below **Rev:** St. Andrew's cross, crown above, X below **Note:** Legend varieties exist.

Date	Mintage	VG	F	VF	XF	Unc
1601	—	135	275	500	850	—
1602	—	135	275	500	850	—
1603 Rare	—	—	—	—	—	—

KM# 10 3 REALS (15 Sols)

9.1900 g., 0.8960 Silver 0.2647 oz. ASW **Obv:** Conjoined busts of Albert and Elizabeth left **Rev:** Crowned shield, St. Andrew's cross in back **Note:** Legend varieties exist.

Date	Mintage	VG	F	VF	XF	Unc
1605	—	75.00	150	275	450	—
1606	—	75.00	150	275	450	—
1607	—	75.00	150	275	450	—
1608	—	75.00	150	275	450	—
1609	—	100	200	350	600	—
1610 Rare	—	—	—	—	—	—

KM# 44 1/2 DUCATON

16.2400 g., 0.9440 Silver 0.4929 oz. ASW **Obv:** Bust of Philip IV right in ruffled collar **Rev:** Crowned shield supported by lions **Rev. Legend:** ...DUX BVRG DOM TOR Z

Date	Mintage	VG	F	VF	XF	Unc
1623	—	550	1,000	1,650	2,500	—

KM# 42 1/2 DUCATON

16.2400 g., 0.9440 Silver 0.4929 oz. ASW **Obv:** Bust of Philip IV right in thin collar right **Rev:** Lion with two swords supports crowned shield **Rev. Legend:** ...DVX BVRG DOM TOR Zc

Date	Mintage	VG	F	VF	XF	Unc
1647	—	200	400	750	1,250	—
1648	—	200	400	750	1,250	—
1649	—	225	450	800	1,350	—
1651	—	185	375	700	1,150	—
1664 Rare	—	—	—	—	—	—
1665 Rare	—	—	—	—	—	—

KM# 47 1/4 PATAGON

Silver, 33 mm. **Ruler:** Albert and Elisabeth **Obv:** St. Andrew's cross, crown above divides date **Obv. Legend:** • PHIL • IIII • D • G • HISP • ET • **Rev:** Crowned arms in order collar **Rev. Legend:** • ARCHID • AVST • DVX • BVRG • DOM • TORN • Zc **Note:** Mint mark: Tower.

Date	Mintage	VG	F	VF	XF	Unc
1626	—	25.00	50.00	100	—	—
1630	—	25.00	50.00	100	—	—
1631	—	25.00	50.00	100	—	—
1632	—	25.00	50.00	100	—	—
1633	—	25.00	50.00	100	—	—
1634	—	25.00	50.00	100	—	—
1635	—	25.00	50.00	100	—	—
1654	—	25.00	50.00	100	—	—

KM# 48 1/2 PATAGON

Silver, 36 mm. **Ruler:** Philip IV **Obv:** St. Andrew's cross, crown above divides date **Obv. Legend:** • PHIL • IIII • D • G • HISP • ET • INDIAR • REX **Rev:** Crowned arms in order collar **Rev. Legend:** • ARCHID • AVST • BVRG • DOM • TORN • Zc **Note:** Mint mark: Tower

Date	Mintage	VG	F	VF	XF	Unc
1626	—	45.00	95.00	175	—	—
1630	—	175	325	650	—	—
1631	—	45.00	95.00	175	—	—
1633	—	45.00	95.00	175	—	—
1634	—	45.00	95.00	175	—	—
1635	—	45.00	95.00	175	—	—
1636	—	65.00	125	250	—	—
1645	—	45.00	95.00	175	—	—
1646	—	45.00	95.00	175	—	—
1647	—	45.00	95.00	175	—	—
1648	—	45.00	95.00	175	—	—
1652	—	45.00	95.00	175	—	—
1653	—	45.00	95.00	175	—	—
1655	—	45.00	95.00	175	—	—
1657	—	45.00	95.00	175	—	—
1658	—	45.00	95.00	175	—	—
1660	—	45.00	95.00	175	—	—
1663	—	45.00	95.00	175	—	—
1665	—	45.00	95.00	175	—	—

KM# 31 PATAGON (48 Sols)

28.1000 g., 0.8750 Silver 0.7905 oz. ASW **Obv:** St. Andrew's cross, crown above, fleece below, divides pair of crowned monograms **Rev:** Crowned shield in fleece collar **Rev. Legend:** ...DVCES DOM TOR(NA Z) **Note:** Dav. #4438.

Date	Mintage	VG	F	VF	XF	Unc
ND(1612-21)	—	50.00	80.00	150	300	—
1616	—	50.00	80.00	150	300	—
1618	—	50.00	80.00	150	300	—
1620	—	50.00	80.00	150	300	—
1621	—	50.00	80.00	150	300	—

KM# A42 PATAGON (48 Sols)

28.1000 g., 0.8750 Silver 0.7905 oz. ASW **Obv:** Date divided by St. Andrew's cross, crown above **Rev:** Crowned shield of Philip IV in fleece collar **Rev. Legend:** ...DVX BVRG DOM TOR(N) Zc **Note:** Dav. #4470.

Date	Mintage	VG	F	VF	XF	Unc
1621	—	—	—	—	—	—
1622	—	50.00	75.00	145	285	—
1623	—	50.00	75.00	145	285	—
1624	—	55.00	110	220	385	—
1625	—	50.00	75.00	145	285	—
1626	—	50.00	75.00	150	300	—
1628	—	50.00	75.00	145	285	—
1630	—	50.00	75.00	150	300	—
1631	—	50.00	75.00	145	285	—
1632	—	50.00	75.00	145	285	—
1633	—	50.00	75.00	145	285	—
1634	—	50.00	75.00	145	285	—
1635	—	50.00	75.00	145	285	—
1636	—	50.00	75.00	145	285	—
1637	—	—	—	—	—	—
1641	—	—	—	—	—	—
1643	—	50.00	75.00	170	325	—
1644	—	50.00	75.00	170	325	—
1645	—	50.00	75.00	145	285	—
1646	—	50.00	75.00	145	285	—
1647	—	50.00	75.00	145	285	—
1648	—	50.00	75.00	145	285	—
1649	—	50.00	75.00	150	300	—
1650	—	50.00	75.00	145	285	—
1651	—	50.00	80.00	170	325	—
1652	—	50.00	75.00	145	285	—
1653	—	50.00	75.00	145	285	—
1654	—	50.00	75.00	145	285	—
1655	—	50.00	75.00	145	285	—
1656	—	50.00	75.00	145	285	—
1657	—	50.00	100	200	350	—
1658	—	50.00	75.00	145	285	—
1659	—	50.00	75.00	145	285	—
1661	—	50.00	80.00	170	325	—
1662	—	50.00	80.00	170	325	—
1663	—	80.00	145	275	485	—
1664	—	80.00	145	275	485	—
1665	—	80.00	145	275	485	—

KM# 70 PATAGON (48 Sols)

28.1000 g., 0.8750 Silver 0.7905 oz. ASW **Obv:** St. Andrew's cross, crown above, fleece divides date **Rev:** Crowned shield of Charles II in fleece collar **Rev. Legend:** ...DVX BRVG DOM TOR Z **Note:** Dav. #4495.

Date	Mintage	VG	F	VF	XF	Unc
1666	—	125	250	425	750	—
1667	—	125	250	425	750	—

KM# 32 DUCATON

32.4800 g., 0.9440 Silver 0.9857 oz. ASW **Obv:** Conjoined busts of Albert and Elisabeth right **Rev:** Lions supporting crowned shield **Rev. Legend:** ...BVRG DOM TORN Z **Note:** Dav. #4430

Date	Mintage	VG	F	VF	XF	Un
1618	—	1,800	3,000	5,100	7,800	—
1620	—	2,000	3,300	5,500	8,400	—

KM# 50 DUCATON

32.4800 g., 0.9440 Silver 0.9857 oz. ASW **Obv:** Bust of Philip IV in ruffled collar right **Rev:** Lions supporting crowned shield **Rev. Legend:** ...DVX BVRG DOM TOR Zc **Note:** Dav. #4450.

Date	Mintage	VG	F	VF	XF	Un
1631	—	125	275	600	1,100	—
1632	—	100	200	450	850	—
1633	—	150	300	700	1,250	—
1634	—	100	200	450	850	—
1635	—	150	300	700	1,250	—
1636	—	125	275	600	1,100	—

KM# 52 DUCATON

32.4800 g., 0.9440 Silver 0.9857 oz. ASW **Obv:** Bust of Philip IV in thin collar right **Rev. Legend:** ...DVX BVRG DOM TOR Zc **Note:** Dav. #4458.

Date	Mintage	VG	F	VF	XF	Un
1636	—	120	240	500	950	—
1638	—	120	240	500	950	—
1647	—	95.00	210	425	850	—
1648	—	120	240	500	950	—
1649	—	120	240	500	950	—
1650	—	120	240	500	950	—
1651	—	120	240	500	950	—
1652	—	150	325	725	1,300	—
1664	—	180	350	850	1,500	—
1665	—	180	350	850	1,500	—

KM# A5 ALBERTIN

2.9200 g., 0.7920 Gold 0.0743 oz. AGW **Obv:** Crowned arms in collar of the Golden Fleece **Rev:** Crowned floral St. Andrew's cross, date at side, Golden Fleece at bottom

Date	Mintage	VG	F	VF	XF	Un
1601	—	225	375	675	1,150	—
1603	—	225	375	675	1,150	—

KM# 22 1/2 SOUVERAIN D'OR

2.7700 g., 0.9200 Gold 0.0819 oz. AGW **Obv:** Crowned shield of Austria-Burgundy on cross floree **Rev:** Crowned shield of Albert and Isabella divides pair of crowned monograms **Rev. Legend:** ...BVRG DOM TORN (Z)

Date	Mintage	VG	F	VF	XF	Un
ND(1612-13) Rare	5,188	—	—	—	—	—

KM# 26 COURONNE D'OR

3.4100 g., 0.8820 Gold 0.0967 oz. AGW **Obv:** Cross of four crowned monograms, lions and crowns in angles **Rev:** Crowned shield of Albert and Elizabeth divides pair of crowned monograms **Rev. Legend:** ...BVRG DOM TORN Z

Date	Mintage	VG	F	VF	XF	Un
1614	9,082	450	875	1,850	3,500	—
1615	Inc. above	450	875	1,850	3,500	—
1616	—	450	875	1,850	3,500	—
1620	—	450	875	1,850	3,500	—
1621	5,914	450	875	1,850	3,500	—

KM# 43 COURONNE D'OR

3.4100 g., 0.8820 Gold 0.0967 oz. AGW **Obv:** Cross floree **Rev:** Crowned shield of Philip IV **Rev. Legend:** ...DVX BVRG D TOR Z

Date	Mintage	VG	F	VF	XF	Un
1622 Rare	214	—	—	—	—	—
1629	5,905	250	500	1,000	1,850	—

ate	Mintage	VG	F	VF	XF	Unc
630	94,000	250	500	1,000	1,850	—
631	11,000	250	500	1,000	1,850	—
632	5,000	250	500	1,000	1,850	—
633	Inc. above	250	500	1,000	1,850	—
636	7,000	250	500	1,000	1,850	—
640	20,000	250	500	1,000	1,850	—
641	—	250	500	1,000	1,850	—
642	—	250	500	1,000	1,850	—
643	22,000	250	500	1,000	1,850	—
644	Inc. above	250	500	1,000	1,850	—
645	—	250	500	1,000	1,850	—
646	9,000	250	500	1,000	1,850	—
647	48,000	250	500	1,000	1,850	—
648	Inc. above	250	500	1,000	1,850	—
649	Inc. above	250	500	1,000	1,850	—

KM# 6 2 ALBERTIN (Corona)
.1500 g., 0.8950 Gold 0.1482 oz. AGW **Obv:** St. Andrew's ross, crown above, fleece below, divides date **Obv. Legend:** .COM TOR **Rev:** Crowned shield in fleece collar

ate	Mintage	VG	F	VF	XF	Unc
601	—	400	600	1,150	1,950	—
602	—	400	600	1,150	1,950	—
603	—	400	600	1,150	1,950	—
604	84,000	400	600	1,150	1,950	—
605	Inc. above	400	600	1,150	1,950	—
606	13,000	400	600	1,150	1,950	—
607	—	400	600	1,150	1,950	—
610	3,003	400	600	1,150	1,950	—

M# 28 2/3 SOUVERAIN D'OR
4900 g., 0.9800 Gold 0.1100 oz. AGW **Obv:** Figures of Albert nd Isabella standing right **Rev:** Crowned shield in fleece collar **ev. Legend:** ...BVRG DOM TOR Z **Note:** Legend varieties xist.

ate	Mintage	VG	F	VF	XF	Unc
D(1615-18) Rare	2,582	—	—	—	—	—
616 Rare	Inc. above	—	—	—	—	—

M# 51 SOUVERAIN OU LION D'OR
.5400 g., 0.9470 Gold 0.1687 oz. AGW **Obv:** Crowned lion left ith sword and shield **Rev:** Crowned shield of Philip IV in fleece ollar **Rev. Legend:** ...DVX BVRG DOM TOR Zc

ate	Mintage	VG	F	VF	XF	Unc
633	—	450	425	850	1,500	—
634	—	450	425	850	1,500	—
641	—	450	425	850	1,500	—
644	—	450	425	850	1,500	—
645	—	450	425	850	1,500	—
648	74,000	450	425	850	1,500	—
649	—	450	425	850	1,500	—
650	Inc. above	450	425	850	1,500	—
651	22,000	450	425	850	1,500	—
652	Inc. above	450	425	850	1,500	—
653	Inc. above	450	425	850	1,500	—
654	17,000	450	425	850	1,500	—
655	14,000	450	425	850	1,500	—
656	Inc. above	450	425	850	1,500	—
657	—	450	425	850	1,500	—
658	Inc. above	450	425	850	1,500	—
659	16,000	450	425	850	1,500	—
660	Inc. above	450	425	850	1,500	—
661	—	450	425	850	1,500	—
662	—	450	425	850	1,500	—
663	Inc. above	450	425	850	1,500	—
665	2,020	450	425	850	1,500	—

KM# 23.2 2 SOUVERAIN D'OR
11.0800 g., 0.9470 Gold 0.3373 oz. AGW **Obv:** Date added below throne **Note:** Legend varieties exist.

Date	Mintage	VG	F	VF	XF	Unc
1612 Rare	5,618	—	—	—	—	—
1613	Inc. above	675	1,200	2,200	3,850	—
1616	23,000	675	1,200	2,200	3,850	—
1617	Inc. above	600	1,000	1,950	3,300	—
1618	12,000	675	1,200	2,200	3,850	—
1619	Inc. above	600	1,000	1,950	3,300	—
1620	2,219	750	1,300	2,500	4,250	—

KM# 45 2 SOUVERAIN D'OR
11.0800 g., 0.9470 Gold 0.3373 oz. AGW **Obv:** Young crowned bust of Philip IV in ruffled collar right, date above **Rev:** Crowned arms in collar of the Golden Fleece in inner circle **Rev. Legend:** ...DVX BVRG DOM TOR Zc

Date	Mintage	VG	F	VF	XF	Unc
1623	1,950	1,150	1,650	3,200	6,000	—
1626 Rare	533	—	—	—	—	—
1630	—	—	—	—	—	—
1632	—	—	—	—	—	—
1637	1,811	1,150	1,650	3,200	6,000	—

KM# 55 2 SOUVERAIN D'OR
11.0800 g., 0.9470 Gold 0.3373 oz. AGW **Obv:** Older bust of Philip IV in flat collar

Date	Mintage	VG	F	VF	XF	Unc
1638	5,145	600	900	1,875	3,250	—
1643	40,000	600	900	1,875	3,250	—
1644	Inc. above	600	900	1,875	3,250	—
1645	Inc. above	600	900	1,875	3,250	—
1646	16,000	600	900	1,875	3,250	—
1647	Inc. above	600	900	1,875	3,250	—
1650	25,000	600	900	1,875	3,250	—
1651	Inc. above	600	900	1,875	3,250	—
1657	—	600	900	1,875	3,250	—

KM# 24.1 4 SOUVERAIN D'OR
22.1000 g., 0.9190 Gold 0.6530 oz. AGW **Note:** Similar to 2 Souverain D'or, KM#23.1.

Date	Mintage	VG	F	VF	XF	Unc
ND Rare	—	—	—	—	—	—

KM# 24.2 4 SOUVERAIN D'OR
22.1000 g., 0.9190 Gold 0.6530 oz. AGW **Note:** Similar to 2 Souverain D'or, KM#23.2.

Date	Mintage	VG	F	VF	XF	Unc
1613 Rare	—	—	—	—	—	—
1617 Rare	—	—	—	—	—	—
1619 Rare	—	—	—	—	—	—
1620 Rare	—	—	—	—	—	—

KM# 46 4 SOUVERAIN D'OR
Gold **Ruler:** Philip IV **Obv:** Young crowned bust in ruffled collar right, date above **Rev:** Crowned arms in collar of the Golden Fleece in inner circle **Rev. Legend:** ... DVX BURG DOM TOR Zc **Note:** Prev. KM#P6.

Date	Mintage	VG	F	VF	XF	Unc
1623 Rare	—	—	—	—	—	—

PIEFORTS

KM#	Date	Mintage	Identification	Mkt Val
P1	ND	—	2 Souverain D'Or. Gold.	—
P2	1613	—	2 Souverain D'Or. Gold.	—
P3	1617	—	2 Souverain D'Or. Gold.	—
P4	1619	—	2 Souverain D'Or. Gold.	—
P5	1620	—	2 Souverain D'Or. Gold.	—
P6	1623	—	2 Souverain D'Or. Gold.	—

SWEDEN

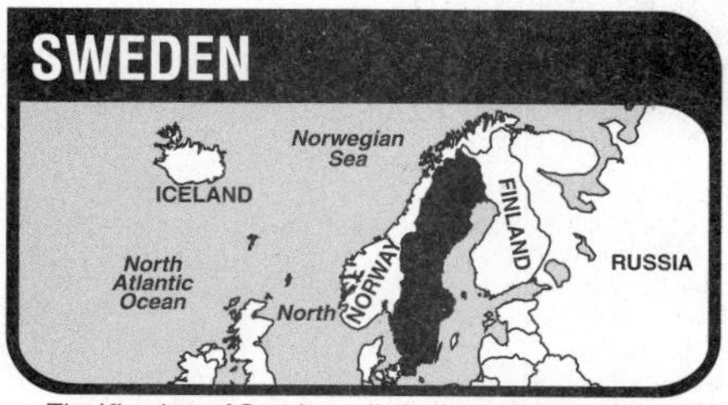

The Kingdom of Sweden, a limited constitutional monarchy located in northern Europe between Norway and Finland, has an area of 173,732 sq. mi. (449,960 sq. km).

Sweden was founded as a Christian stronghold by Olaf Skottkonung late in the 10th century. After conquering Finland late in the 13th century, Sweden, together with Norway, came under the rule of Denmark, 1397-1523, in an association known as the Union of Kalmar. Modern Sweden had its beginning in 1523 when Gustaf Vasa drove the Danes out of Sweden and was himself chosen king. Under Gustaf Adolphus II and Charles XII, Sweden was one of the great powers of 17th century Europe – until Charles invaded Russia in 1708, and was defeated at the Battle of Pultowa in June, 1709

RULERS

Carl IX, regent, 1598-1604
Carl IX, 1604-1611
John, Duke of Ostergotland, 1606-1618
Gustaf II Adolphus, 1611-1632
Christina, 1632-1654
Carl X Gustavus, 1654-1660
Carl XI, 1660-1697
Carl XII, 1697-1718

MINT OFFICIALS' INITIALS

Initial	Date	Name
AG	1641-45	Anthony Grooth d.y.
AG	1645-46	Anna Grooth f. Skytte
AS	1684-99	Anders Strommer
DF, D	1672-83	Daniel Faxell
DK	1646-50	Daniel Markusson Kock
GW	1658-64	Goran Wagner
	1663-64	Johan Fredrik Herman
IK	1664-65	Isak Kock
MK	1633-39	Markus Kock
(ca) Crossed axes	1652-58	Michael Hack
(as) Arrow between 2 stars	1665-68	Abraham Kock
(monogram FIRST)	1669-72	Christopher Conradi

KINGDOM

STANDARD COINAGE

KM# 5 FYRK
Silver **Obv:** Three large crowns in inner circle **Rev:** "Jehovah" in radiant circle **Mint:** Stockholm

Date	Mintage	VG	F	VF	XF	Unc
1601	—	45.00	95.00	175	—	—

KM# 6 FYRK
Silver **Obv:** Three smaller crowns in inner circle **Mint:** Stockholm

Date	Mintage	VG	F	VF	XF	Unc
1601	—	70.00	150	300	—	—

KM# 103.1 FYRK
7.1000 g., Copper **Obv:** Sheaf with letters G.A.R. **Rev:** Three crowns, date, value **Mint:** Sater **Note:** Klippe.

Date	Mintage	VG	F	VF	XF	Unc
1624	—	100	225	350	—	—

KM# 103.2 FYRK
7.1000 g., Copper **Mint:** Nykoping and Sater

Date	Mintage	VG	F	VF	XF	Unc
1625 Rare	—	—	—	—	—	—

KM# 110 FYRK
7.1000 g., Copper **Mint:** Arboga

Date	Mintage	VG	F	VF	XF	Unc
1627	—	40.00	85.00	200	—	—

KM# 120 FYRK

7.1000 g., Copper **Obv:** Sheaf with value **Rev:** Crossed arrows, date **Mint:** Sater

Date	Mintage	VG	F	VF	XF	Unc
1628	—	750	—	—	—	—

KM# 121 FYRK

7.1000 g., Copper **Obv:** Sheaf with value **Rev:** Griffin, date above left **Mint:** Nykoping

Date	Mintage	VG	F	VF	XF	Unc
1628	—	125	250	700	—	—
1629	—	85.00	225	550	—	—

KM# 126 FYRK

Copper **Rev:** Date between feet of griffin

Date	Mintage	VG	F	VF	XF	Unc
1629	—	50.00	150	300	—	—

KM# 254 1/6 ORE (S.M.)

Copper **Obv:** Three crowns with letters C.R.S. and date **Rev:** Griffin below crown, value and mint mark **Mint:** Avesta

Date	Mintage	VG	F	VF	XF	Unc
1666 S.M.	35,040,000	70.00	130	450	825	—
1666 S.m.	Inc. above	8.00	25.00	39.00	90.00	—
1667	4,512,000	8.00	30.00	46.50	100	—
1668/67	—	14.00	42.25	90.00	230	—
1668	2,846,000	9.00	32.50	50.00	110	—
1669/68	—	14.00	42.25	90.00	230	—
1669	7,137,000	10.00	32.50	60.00	115	—
1670	14,478,000	8.00	30.00	46.50	100	—
1671	12,881,000	8.00	30.00	46.50	100	—
1672	2,858,000	9.00	32.50	50.00	110	—
1673	6,355,000	10.00	32.50	65.00	130	—
Note: Without star in date						
1673	Inc. above	8.00	30.00	46.50	100	—
Note: With star in date						
1674	1,862,000	8.00	30.00	46.50	100	—
1675	1,229,000	10.00	32.50	50.00	110	—
1676	6,123,000	8.00	30.00	46.50	100	—
1677	9,811,000	8.00	25.00	39.00	90.00	—
1680/77	—	17.00	50.00	110	245	—
1680	2,090,000	10.00	42.25	60.00	145	—
1681	Inc. above	8.00	30.00	46.50	100	—
1682/81	—	14.00	46.50	85.00	180	—
1682	597,000	10.00	32.50	50.00	110	—
1683/82	—	14.00	46.50	85.00	180	—
1683	2,057,000	8.00	30.00	46.50	100	—
1686/83	—	13.00	46.50	80.00	165	—
1686	1,708,000	8.00	25.00	39.00	90.00	—

KM# 297 1/6 ORE (S.M.)

Copper **Note:** Klippe.

Date	Mintage	VG	F	VF	XF	Unc
1686	—	—	—	—	—	—

KM# 152.1 1/4 ORE

10.6000 g., Copper **Obv:** Three crowns, letters C.R.S. **Rev:** Sheaf on shield below crown divide value and date **Mint:** Nykoping **Note:** Varieties exist.

Date	Mintage	VG	F	VF	XF	Unc
1633	1,971,000	22.50	60.00	170	425	—
1634	37,734,000	14.00	42.25	105	230	—

KM# 152.2 1/4 ORE

10.6000 g., Copper **Mint:** Nykoping and Sater

Date	Mintage	VG	F	VF	XF	Unc
1634	—	20.00	45.50	85.00	130	—
1635 Mint mark	59,827,200	20.00	45.50	85.00	130	—
1635 Rose	Inc. above	41.50	80.00	165	550	—
1636	40,488,960	27.50	60.00	100	155	—

KM# 160 1/4 ORE

12.9000 g., Copper **Mint:** Sater

Date	Mintage	VG	F	VF	XF	Unc
1637	54,502,400	10.00	42.25	85.00	180	—
1638	5,068,800	10.00	42.25	85.00	180	—
1640	—	17.00	80.00	170	375	—
1641	13,981,449	13.00	105	105	220	—
1642	7,138,560	14.00	65.00	145	325	—

KM# 188 1/4 ORE

12.9000 g., Copper **Mint:** Avesta **Note:** Varieties exist.

Date	Mintage	VG	F	VF	XF	Unc
1644	4,224,000	10.00	32.50	50.00	115	—
1644/45	—	43.50	130	255	550	—
1645	940,000	10.00	32.50	50.00	115	—
1653	445,400	10.00	32.50	50.00	115	—
1654	1,750,400	10.00	32.50	60.00	155	—

KM# 211 1/4 ORE

12.9000 g., Copper **Obv:** Three crowns with letters C.R.S. **Rev:** Griffin with date, crown and value

Date	Mintage	VG	F	VF	XF	Unc
1654 Rare	—	—	—	—	—	—
1655	1,729,600	22.50	48.75	170	500	—
1656	1,024,000	18.00	39.00	130	425	—
1657	819,200	22.50	48.75	170	500	—
1658	6,144,000	22.50	48.75	170	500	—
1658 Rose	Inc. above	85.00	195	550	—	—
1659	—	18.00	39.00	130	425	—
1660	Inc. above	60.00	150	375	900	—

KM# 7 1/2 ORE

1.6201 g., 0.2030 Silver 0.0106 oz. ASW **Obv:** Three crowns in crowned rectangular shield **Rev:** "Jehovah" in inner circle **Mint:** Stockholm

Date	Mintage	VG	F	VF	XF	Unc
1601	—	48.75	100	195	—	—
1602	—	48.75	100	195	—	—

KM# 65 1/2 ORE

1.6200 g., 0.2030 Silver 0.0106 oz. ASW **Obv:** Three crowns and value **Rev:** Sheaf with letters G.A.R. **Mint:** Stockholm

Date	Mintage	VG	F	VF	XF	Unc
1615	—	65.00	115	255	550	—

KM# 104.1 1/2 ORE

16.2000 g., Copper **Obv:** Sheaf with letters G.A.R. **Rev:** Crossed arrows below crown, value, date **Mint:** Sater **Note:** Klippe.

Date	Mintage	VG	F	VF	XF	Unc
1624	—	135	775	1,250	2,650	—

KM# 123 1/2 ORE

14.1000 g., Copper **Note:** Klippe.

Date	Mintage	VG	F	VF	XF	Unc
1625	—	135	295	400	1,000	—

KM# 104.2 1/2 ORE

14.1000 g., Copper **Mint:** Nykoping and Sater

Date	Mintage	VG	F	VF	XF	Unc
1625	—	85.00	175	400	950	—
1626 Value as 1/2	—	55.00	170	375	875	—
1626 Value as 2/1	—	—	—	—	—	—
1627 Value as 1/2	—	100	190	500	1,250	—
1627 Value as 2/1	—	—	—	—	—	—

KM# 111 1/2 ORE

14.1000 g., Copper **Rev:** Crossed arrows below crown, value

Date	Mintage	VG	F	VF	XF	Unc
1627	—	110	400	725	—	—
1628	—	2,200	—	—	—	—
1629	—	135	500	825	—	—

KM# 122 1/2 ORE

14.1000 g., Copper **Obv:** Asterisks in field beside shield

Date	Mintage	VG	F	VF	XF	Unc
1627	—	275	—	—	—	—
1628	—	85.00	195	400	825	—
1629	—	65.00	150	350	775	—
1630	—	65.00	150	350	775	—
1631	—	115	245	450	900	—

KM# 112 1/2 ORE

14.1000 g., Copper **Obv:** Similar to KM#111 **Rev:** Griffin, value date **Mint:** Nykoping

Date	Mintage	VG	F	VF	XF	Unc
1627	—	110	295	725	1,550	—
1628	—	220	—	—	—	—
1629	—	130	350	825	1,650	—

KM# 113 1/2 ORE

14.1000 g., Copper **Obv:** Three crowns in oval below large crown or crowned arms **Rev:** Eagle **Mint:** Arboga

Date	Mintage	VG	F	VF	XF	Unc
1627	—	155	400	1,000	2,200	—

KM# 124 1/2 ORE

14.1000 g., Copper **Obv:** Crowned rectangular shield **Mint:** Arboga

Date	Mintage	VG	F	VF	XF	Unc
1628 Rare	—	—	—	—	—	—

KM# 127 1/2 ORE

14.1000 g., Copper **Obv:** Crowned ornate arms **Rev:** Griffin **Mint:** Nykoping

Date	Mintage	VG	F	VF	XF	Unc
1629 Rare	—	—	—	—	—	—

KM# 247 1/2 ORE

Silver **Obv:** C.R. below crown **Rev:** Value, date **Mint:** Stockholm

Date	Mintage	VG	F	VF	XF	Unc
1665 Rare	—	—	—	—	—	—

M# 231 1/2 ORE (K.M.)
9000 g., Copper **Obv:** Three crowns, letters CRS, date **Rev:** rown above lion rampant, value **Mint:** Avesta

te	Mintage	VG	F	VF	XF	Unc
61	—	85.00	175	300	650	—
62	—	65.00	135	260	550	—
63/2	—	65.00	135	260	550	—
63	—	85.00	175	300	650	—
64	—	85.00	175	300	650	—

M# 8 ORE
7353 g., 0.2500 Silver 0.0220 oz. ASW **Obv:** Three crowns crowned rectangular shield **Rev:** "Jehovah" in radiant circle **nt:** Stockholm

te	Mintage	VG	F	VF	XF	Unc
01	—	115	255	375	—	—
02	—	220	450	850	—	—
03	—	110	235	350	—	—

M# 31 ORE
6201 g., 0.2500 Silver 0.0130 oz. ASW **Obv:** Sheaf separating ters C R **Rev:** Lion rampant **Mint:** Stockholm

te	Mintage	VG	F	VF	XF	Unc
09	—	35.75	60.00	90.00	210	—
10	—	35.75	60.00	90.00	210	—
11	—	41.00	70.00	105	235	—
(1611) Rare	—	—	—	—	—	—
12 Rare	—	—	—	—	—	—

M# 32 ORE
6201 g., 0.2500 Silver 0.0130 oz. ASW **Obv:** Value in legend **nt:** Gothenburg

te	Mintage	VG	F	VF	XF	Unc
09	—	230	500	950	1,900	—
10	—	135	245	375	850	—

M# 33 ORE
6201 g., 0.2500 Silver 0.0130 oz. ASW **Obv:** Value in field **nt:** Gothenburg

te	Mintage	VG	F	VF	XF	Unc
09	—	155	295	450	975	—
10	—	135	245	350	750	—
11	—	155	275	375	850	—

M# 50 ORE
6201 g., 0.2500 Silver 0.0130 oz. ASW **Note:** "1010" error te variety.

te	Mintage	VG	F	VF	XF	Unc
10 Rare	—	135	245	425	825	—
10 error date	—	135	245	425	825	—

M# 58 ORE
6201 g., 0.2500 Silver 0.0130 oz. ASW **Obv:** Lion rampant, lue below **Rev:** GAR around three crown shield **Mint:** Vadstena d Soderkoping

te	Mintage	VG	F	VF	XF	Unc
(1611-17)	—	55.00	115	200	425	—

M# 59 ORE
6201 g., 0.2500 Silver 0.0130 oz. ASW **Obv:** Value at lion's le **Mint:** Vadstena and Soderkoping

te	Mintage	VG	F	VF	XF	Unc
(1611-17)	—	70.00	150	235	500	—

M# 60 ORE
6201 g., 0.2500 Silver 0.0130 oz. ASW **Obv:** Without value **nt:** Vadstena and Soderkoping

te	Mintage	VG	F	VF	XF	Unc
(1611-17)	—	85.00	155	245	500	—

KM# 70 ORE
1.6201 g., 0.2500 Silver 0.0130 oz. ASW **Obv:** Three crowns with value **Rev:** Sheath with date and letters G.A.R. **Mint:** Stockholm

Date	Mintage	VG	F	VF	XF	Unc
1613	—	45.50	115	220	450	—

KM# 71.1 ORE
1.6201 g., 0.2500 Silver 0.0130 oz. ASW **Obv:** Lion rampant **Rev:** Sheath with date and letters G.A.R. **Mint:** Stockholm

Date	Mintage	VG	F	VF	XF	Unc
1615	—	45.50	130	220	450	—
1616	—	35.75	100	170	375	—
1617	—	35.75	100	170	375	—
1618	—	35.75	100	170	375	—
1619	—	35.75	100	170	375	—
1620	—	35.75	100	170	375	—
1621	—	35.75	100	170	375	—
1622	—	35.75	100	170	375	—
x622	—	45.50	150	200	450	—
xx22	—	45.50	150	200	450	—
1623	—	35.75	100	170	375	—
1624	—	32.50	80.00	145	325	—
1625 Rare	—	—	—	—	—	—
ND(1625) Rare	—	—	—	—	—	—

KM# 73 ORE
1.6201 g., 0.2500 Silver 0.0130 oz. ASW **Obv:** Without value **Mint:** Soderkoping

Date	Mintage	VG	F	VF	XF	Unc
(16)17	—	90.00	195	300	575	—

KM# 72 ORE
1.6201 g., 0.2500 Silver 0.0130 oz. ASW **Obv:** Lion rampant, value below **Mint:** Soderkoping

Date	Mintage	VG	F	VF	XF	Unc
1617	—	70.00	150	255	550	—
(16)17	—	85.00	170	300	650	—
1671 Error, rare	—	—	—	—	—	—

KM# 71.2 ORE
1.6201 g., 0.2500 Silver 0.0130 oz. ASW **Mint:** Kalmar **Note:** Varieties of placement of mint marks exist.

Date	Mintage	VG	F	VF	XF	Unc
1623 Rare	—	—	—	—	—	—
1624	—	110	235	350	725	—
1625	—	110	235	350	725	—
1626	—	—	—	—	—	—
1627	—	—	—	—	—	—

KM# 71.3 ORE
1.6201 g., 0.2500 Silver 0.0130 oz. ASW **Mint:** Gothenburg **Note:** Both dates also known on square planchets.

Date	Mintage	VG	F	VF	XF	Unc
1625	—	115	235	375	825	—
1626 Rare	180,000	—	—	—	—	—

KM# 106.1 ORE
28.3000 g., Copper **Mint:** Sater

Date	Mintage	VG	F	VF	XF	Unc
1625	—	115	245	425	900	—
1626	—	110	195	350	825	—
1627	—	155	350	625	1,250	—

KM# 106.2 ORE
28.3000 g., Copper **Mint:** Nykoping and Sater

Date	Mintage	VG	F	VF	XF	Unc
1625	—	35.00	85.00	250	550	—
1625 Rare	—	—	—	—	—	—
Note: "S" on reverse						
1626	—	50.00	125	250	850	—
1627	—	90.00	200	400	1,200	—

KM# 114 ORE
28.3000 g., Copper **Obv:** Three crowns, date **Rev:** Griffin, value **Mint:** Arboga

Date	Mintage	VG	F	VF	XF	Unc
1626 Rare	—	—	—	—	—	—
1627	—	1,400	2,800	5,500	—	—

KM# 71.4 ORE
1.6201 g., 0.2500 Silver 0.0130 oz. ASW **Mint:** Norrkoping **Note:** Varieties exist, including a square planchet.

Date	Mintage	VG	F	VF	XF	Unc
1626	—	525	875	1,750	3,200	—

KM# 115 ORE
28.3000 g., Copper **Obv:** Crown above crossed arrows, value, date in legend **Rev:** Crowned arms **Mint:** Sater **Note:** Varieties of crown types exist.

Date	Mintage	VG	F	VF	XF	Unc
1627	—	40.00	90.00	220	700	—
1628 MDCXXVIII	—	27.50	75.00	160	550	—
1628 DCXXVIII	—	210	525	950	1,950	—
1629	—	27.50	75.00	130	425	—
1630	—	—	—	—	—	—
1631	—	—	—	—	—	—

KM# 118 ORE
28.3000 g., Copper, 44 mm. **Obv:** Crown above arms **Rev:** Eagle, value, date **Mint:** Arboga

Date	Mintage	VG	F	VF	XF	Unc
1627	—	100	190	500	975	—

KM# 119 ORE
28.3000 g., Copper, 41 mm. **Mint:** Arboga

Date	Mintage	VG	F	VF	XF	Unc
1627	—	100	255	40.50	1,050	—
1628	—	95.00	205	40.50	950	—

KM# 116 ORE
28.3000 g., Copper **Obv:** Arms below crown, sheaf in center **Rev:** Griffin with wings down, value, date **Mint:** Nykoping

Date	Mintage	VG	F	VF	XF	Unc
1627 MDCXXV2 Rare	—	—	—	—	—	—
1627 MDCXXVII	—	115	205	400	775	—
1627 Rare, date in field	—	—	—	—	—	—
1627 MDCXX7	—	15.00	33.00	85.00	275	—

KM# 125 ORE

28.3000 g., Copper **Rev:** Value at griffin's sides **Mint:** Sater

Date	Mintage	VG	F	VF	XF	Unc
1628	—	265	550	1,550	2,700	—

KM# 117 ORE

28.3000 g., Copper **Rev:** Griffin with wings up **Mint:** Nykoping **Note:** Varieties exist.

Date	Mintage	VG	F	VF	XF	Unc
1628 MDCXXVIII	—	85.00	185	325	1,500	—
1628 DCXXVIII Rare	—	—	—	—	—	—
1629 MDCXXVIIII Rare	—	—	—	—	—	—
1629 MDCXXIX	—	85.00	185	325	1,500	—

KM# 153 ORE

1.2317 g., 0.3750 Copper 0.0148 oz. **Obv:** Sheaf on shield below crown, date **Rev:** Three crowns on shield, value **Mint:** Stockholm

Date	Mintage	VG	F	VF	XF	Unc
1633 CHRISTINA	683,000	42.75	85.00	155	270	—
1633 CHRITINA	—	165	295	500	975	—
1634	3,216,000	42.75	85.00	155	270	—
1635	1,238,000	38.75	75.00	125	265	—
1636	1,395,000	42.75	85.00	155	270	—
1637	—	38.75	75.00	130	265	—
1650	—	75.00	115	240	500	—
1653	404,000	38.75	75.00	125	265	—

KM# 154 ORE

1.2317 g., 0.3750 Copper 0.0148 oz. **Obv:** Shield with ornaments at sides **Mint:** Stockholm

Date	Mintage	VG	F	VF	XF	Unc
1633 Rare	—	—	—	—	—	—

KM# 159 ORE

1.2317 g., 0.3750 Copper 0.0148 oz. **Obv:** Date above shield **Rev:** Griffin **Mint:** Gothenburg

Date	Mintage	VG	F	VF	XF	Unc
1635	—	75.00	180	475	850	—
1636 RE.SVE.	—	70.00	165	325	775	—
1636 REC.SV.	—	110	280	725	1,200	—

KM# 161 ORE

51.5000 g., Copper **Mint:** Sater

Date	Mintage	VG	F	VF	XF	Unc
1638	12,471,000	65.00	165	300	575	—
1639	12,612,000	65.00	165	325	650	—
1640	8,835,000	75.00	185	350	700	—
1641	Inc. above	550	1,950	3,900	6,500	—

KM# 162.1 ORE

51.5000 g., Copper **Obv:** Without ornamentation at sides of arms **Mint:** Sater

Date	Mintage	VG	F	VF	XF	Unc
1638	Inc. above	75.00	170	300	675	—

KM# 162.2 ORE

51.5000 g., Copper **Mint:** Avesta

Date	Mintage	VG	F	VF	XF	Unc
1644 MDCXLIV	2,798,400	295	525	1,250	2,950	—
1644 MDCXL4	Inc. above	70.00	160	325	700	—
1645	9,929,600	55.00	125	275	600	—
1646	6,893,200	60.00	140	300	625	—
1647	2,622,400	70.00	160	325	700	—
1648	1,780,400	100	210	375	775	—
1649	1,914,800	70.00	160	325	700	—
1650	356,400	60.00	140	300	625	—
1651	733,600	70.00	160	375	775	—
1652	542,880	70.00	160	325	700	—
1653	256,000	100	210	375	775	—
1653 Small crown	Inc. above	215	525	900	1,750	—

KM# 212 ORE

1.2317 g., 0.3750 Silver 0.0148 oz. ASW **Obv:** Griffin in shield below crown, date **Rev:** Three crowns in shield, value **Mint:** Stockholm **Note:** Three mint mark varieties exist.

Date	Mintage	VG	F	VF	XF	Unc
1654	315,000	105	210	425	775	—
1655	145,000	75.00	170	275	525	—
1656	167,000	75.00	170	275	525	—
1657	361,000	75.00	170	275	525	—
1659*	83,000	75.00	170	275	525	—
1660	75,000	90.00	190	325	625	—

KM# 230 ORE

1.2317 g., 0.3750 Silver 0.0148 oz. ASW **Obv. Legend:** CAROLVS ... **Mint:** Stockholm **Note:** Similar to KM#212.

Date	Mintage	VG	F	VF	XF	Unc
1660 Rare	—	—	—	—	—	—
1661	37,000	70.00	180	325	725	—
1662 GW	59,000	70.00	180	325	725	—
1662 Rare	Inc. above	—	160	—	600	—
1663 GW	35,000	105	210	425	875	—
1663	—	100	210	375	775	—
1664 GW	431,000	100	210	375	775	—
1664 IK	—	60.00	160	275	600	—
1664	—	49.00	105	180	400	—

KM# 248 ORE

1.2317 g., 0.3130 Silver 0.0124 oz. ASW **Obv:** Crowned CRS monogram **Rev:** Three crowns, date, value **Mint:** Stockholm

Date	Mintage	VG	F	VF	XF	Unc
1665 IK	857,000	49.00	120	205	450	—
1665 Arrow	Inc. above	75.00	210	375	775	—

KM# 249 ORE

1.2317 g., 0.3130 Silver 0.0124 oz. ASW **Obv:** Crowned double C monogram **Mint:** Stockholm

Date	Mintage	VG	F	VF	XF	Unc
1665 Rare	Inc. above	—	—	—	—	—
1697	Inc. below	38.50	100	155	350	—

KM# 250 ORE

1.2317 g., 0.3130 Silver 0.0124 oz. ASW **Mint:** Stockholm

Date	Mintage	VG	F	VF	XF	Unc
1665	—	35.00	75.00	140	295	—
1666/65	—	27.50	65.00	120	245	—
1666	1,864,000	25.00	55.00	90.00	195	—
1667/66	—	35.00	75.00	140	295	—
1667	1,556,000	25.00	55.00	90.00	195	—
1668	3,058,000	25.00	55.00	90.00	195	—
1669	Inc. above	25.00	55.00	90.00	195	—
1669 FIRST	283,000	35.00	75.00	125	295	—

Date	Mintage	VG	F	VF	XF	U
1670	606,000	25.00	55.00	90.00	195	
1671	598,000	27.50	65.00	100	240	
1672 FIRST	1,341,000	25.00	55.00	90.00	195	
1672 DF	Inc. above	27.50	65.00	100	240	
1673	438,000	25.00	55.00	90.00	195	
1674	379,000	25.00	55.00	90.00	195	
1675	Inc. above	27.50	65.00	110	245	
1677	378,000	25.00	55.00	90.00	195	
1681	204,000	25.00	55.00	90.00	195	
1682/81	—	35.00	75.00	145	350	
1682	377,000	20.00	42.00	85.00	175	
1683	599,000	20.00	42.00	85.00	175	
1684	726,000	20.00	42.00	85.00	175	
1685	583,000	20.00	42.00	85.00	175	

KM# 250a ORE

1.2317 g., 0.2500 Silver 0.0099 oz. ASW **Ruler:** Carl XII **Ob** XII within C and sprigs, crown above **Rev:** 3 Crowns, divided date, initials and value **Mint:** Stockholm

Date	Mintage	VG	F	VF	XF	U
1686/85	—	38.50	55.00	145	—	
1686	408,000	18.00	46.25	90.00	170	
1687	335,000	18.00	46.25	85.00	170	
1688	324,000	20.00	46.25	85.00	170	
1689	337,000	20.00	46.25	85.00	170	
1690	329,000	18.00	46.25	70.00	170	
1691	323,000	25.00	46.25	85.00	170	
1692	333,000	20.00	46.25	85.00	170	
1693	319,000	18.00	46.25	85.00	170	
1694	333,000	18.00	46.25	85.00	170	
1695	328,000	18.00	46.25	85.00	170	
1696	422,000	18.00	46.25	85.00	170	
1697	329,000	35.00	46.25	85.00	170	
1698	328,000	27.50	46.25	85.00	170	
1698/7	—	27.50	46.25	85.00	170	
1699	322,000	27.50	46.25	85.00	170	
1700	418,000	27.50	46.25	85.00	170	

KM# 264 ORE (S.M.)

49.4000 g., Copper **Mint:** Avesta

Date	Mintage	VG	F	VF	XF	U
1669 Rose	1,983,000	105	230	425	875	
1673 Rose	3,219,000	125	265	450	975	
1673 Large star	Inc. above	70.00	160	245	525	
1673 Small star	Inc. above	75.00	170	275	600	
1673 Fleur-de-lis	—	—	—	—	—	

KM# 264a ORE (S.M.)

42.5000 g., Copper **Mint:** Avesta

Date	Mintage	VG	F	VF	XF
1675	1,728,000	48.25	105	200	425
1676	1,595,000	40.25	85.00	180	400
1677/76	—	55.00	120	225	500
1677	3,286,000	40.25	85.00	180	400
1678	1,469,000	44.25	100	190	400
1679	269,000	100	205	400	900
1680	630,000	44.25	100	180	400

KM# 264b ORE (S.M.)

40.5000 g., Copper **Mint:** Avesta

Date	Mintage	VG	F	VF	XF
1683	336,000	37.75	80.00	155	325
1684/83	—	70.00	150	255	550
1684	277,000	44.00	95.00	195	350
1685	551,000	37.75	80.00	155	325
1686	578,000	34.75	75.00	130	295

KM# 232.1 ORE (K.M.)
7.7000 g., Copper **Obv:** C.R.S. above crowned ornamented shield **Mint:** Avesta **Note:** Prev. KM#232.

Date	Mintage	VG	F	VF	XF	Unc
1661 Without square by crown	—	48.25	105	200	400	—
1661 Square over arrow	—	50.00	130	245	525	—
1661 Two squares by crown	—	85.00	190	350	775	—
1662	—	48.25	105	200	400	—
1663	—	48.25	105	200	400	—
1664/63	—	80.00	175	325	725	—
1664	—	55.00	120	245	575	—

KM# 232.2 ORE (K.M.)
7.7000 g., Copper **Obv:** Crowned plain shield **Mint:** Avesta **Note:** Prev. KM#233.

Date	Mintage	VG	F	VF	XF	Unc
1661 Rare	—	—	—	—	—	—

KM# 9 2 ORE
2.9254 g., 0.5000 Silver 0.0470 oz. ASW **Mint:** Stockholm

Date	Mintage	VG	F	VF	XF	Unc
1602	—	425	725	1,450	—	—

KM# 16 2 ORE
1.8805 g., 0.5000 Silver 0.0302 oz. ASW **Obv:** Crown above sheaf, C D R below **Rev:** Three crowns, value, date **Mint:** Stockholm

Date	Mintage	VG	F	VF	XF	Unc
1605 Rare	—	—	—	—	—	—

KM# 28 2 ORE
1.8805 g., 0.5000 Silver 0.0302 oz. ASW **Obv:** Sheaf in shield below crown, date **Rev:** Three crowns in shield, value **Mint:** Stockholm **Note:** Struck at Stockholm Mint.

Date	Mintage	VG	F	VF	XF	Unc
1608	—	65.00	140	275	600	—
1609	—	60.00	125	240	500	—
1610	—	60.00	125	240	500	—
1611	—	70.00	145	300	625	—

KM# 34 2 ORE
1.8805 g., 0.5000 Silver 0.0302 oz. ASW **Obv:** Shield with ornaments **Mint:** Stockholm

Date	Mintage	VG	F	VF	XF	Unc
1609	—	140	325	500	1,250	—

KM# 35 2 ORE
1.8805 g., 0.5000 Silver 0.0302 oz. ASW **Obv:** Sheaf in shield below crown, date **Rev:** Lion rampant in shield, value **Mint:** Gothenburg

Date	Mintage	VG	F	VF	XF	Unc
1609	—	500	975	1,950	3,450	—
1610 Rare	—	—	—	—	—	—

KM# 51 2 ORE
1.8805 g., 0.5000 Silver 0.0302 oz. ASW **Mint:** Gothenburg **Note:** Square planchet.

Date	Mintage	VG	F	VF	XF	Unc
1610 Rare	—	—	—	—	—	—

KM# A67 2 ORE
4.8418 g., 0.6250 Silver 0.0973 oz. ASW **Obv:** Hebrew "Jehovah" above crowned bust of Gustaf II Adolf left **Rev:** Crown above three shields **Mint:** Stockholm

Date	Mintage	VG	F	VF	XF	Unc
1618 Rare	—	—	—	—	—	—

KM# 102 2 ORE
1.8805 g., 0.5000 Silver 0.0302 oz. ASW **Mint:** Kalmar **Note:** Square planchet.

Date	Mintage	VG	F	VF	XF	Unc
1623 Rare	—	—	—	—	—	—

KM# 101 2 ORE
1.8805 g., 0.5000 Silver 0.0302 oz. ASW **Obv:** Sheaf in shield below crown, date **Rev:** Three crowns in shield, value **Mint:** Kalmar

Date	Mintage	VG	F	VF	XF	Unc
1623	—	275	450	1,100	1,950	—
1624	—	400	725	1,400	2,450	—
1625 Rare	—	—	—	—	—	—

KM# 107 2 ORE
58.6000 g., Copper **Obv:** Crown above G A R, S below **Rev:** Sheaf, value, date **Mint:** Säter and Nyköping

Date	Mintage	VG	F	VF	XF	Unc
1625	—	600	1,600	—	—	—
1626	1,020,000	400	1,250	—	—	—
1627	—	700	2,150	—	—	—

KM# 108 2 ORE
58.6000 g., Copper **Mint:** Nykoping and Sater

Date	Mintage	VG	F	VF	XF	Unc
1626	—	350	525	1,000	1,950	—
1627	—	525	950	1,750	3,450	—

KM# 241.1 2 ORE
1.7551 g., 0.4440 Silver 0.0251 oz. ASW **Obv:** Crown above C R S, wreath around **Rev:** Three crowns, date, value **Mint:** Stockholm

Date	Mintage	VG	F	VF	XF	Unc
1664 IK, 2	2,639,000	27.50	65.00	120	245	—
1664 IAK	576,000	55.00	100	245	425	—
1664 IK, II	Inc. above	27.50	65.00	120	245	—
1664 IK, II	Inc. above	25.00	42.00	85.00	195	—
1665/65	—	25.00	55.00	100	215	—
1665 IK, 2	Inc. above	25.00	55.00	100	215	—
1665 With arrow	Inc. above	25.00	55.00	100	215	—
1666	2,087,000	20.00	42.00	90.00	195	—
1667	1,313,000	25.00	55.00	100	215	—
1669	39,000	44.00	105	180	400	—

KM# 241.3 2 ORE
1.7551 g., 0.4440 Silver 0.0251 oz. ASW **Obv:** CXI **Mint:** Stockholm

Date	Mintage	VG	F	VF	XF	Unc
1666 Rare	Inc. above	—	—	—	—	—

KM# 241.2 2 ORE
1.7551 g., 0.4440 Silver 0.0251 oz. ASW **Mint:** Landskrone

Date	Mintage	VG	F	VF	XF	Unc
1675	—	120	265	500	1,100	—
1675	—	250	550	1,000	1,950	—
1676	—	195	425	725	1,550	—

KM# 234.2 2 ORE (K.M.)
35.4000 g., Copper **Obv:** Crowned plain shield **Mint:** Avesta

Date	Mintage	VG	F	VF	XF	Unc
1661	—	—	—	—	—	—

KM# 234.1 2 ORE (K.M.)
35.4000 g., Copper **Obv:** C R S above crowned ornamented shield, date **Rev:** Crown above shield with three crowns, value **Mint:** Avesta **Note:** Prev. KM#234.

Date	Mintage	VG	F	VF	XF	Unc
1661	—	60.00	120	235	500	—
Note: Shield with ornaments						
1662	—	95.00	205	425	900	—
1663/62	—	75.00	170	325	700	—
1663	—	44.00	95.00	195	400	—
1664/63	—	75.00	160	325	700	—
1664	—	44.00	95.00	175	375	—
1665	—	75.00	170	205	450	—

KM# 235 2-1/2 ORE (K.M.)
44.3000 g., Copper **Obv:** C. R. S. above crowned shield **Rev:** Value above threee crowns **Mint:** Avesta

Date	Mintage	VG	F	VF	XF	Unc
1661	—	900	1,600	3,200	5,600	—

KM# 10 4 ORE (1/2 Mark)
4.8418 g., 0.6250 Silver 0.0973 oz. ASW **Mint:** Stockholm

Date	Mintage	VG	F	VF	XF	Unc
1602	—	325	725	1,150	—	—
1603	—	260	575	850	—	—

KM# 17 4 ORE (1/2 Mark)
4.8418 g., 0.6250 Silver 0.0973 oz. ASW **Obv:** Crown above shield with three crowns, sheaf and lion, value **Rev:** Hebrew "Jehovah", date in outer circle **Mint:** Stockholm

Date	Mintage	VG	F	VF	XF	Unc
1605 Rare	—	—	—	—	—	—
1606	—	160	280	475	925	—

KM# 21 4 ORE (1/2 Mark)
4.8418 g., 0.6250 Silver 0.0973 oz. ASW **Obv:** Hebrew "Jehovah" above crowned bust of Carl IX left **Rev:** Crowned arms, value, date **Mint:** Stockholm

Date	Mintage	VG	F	VF	XF	Unc
1607	—	140	245	400	850	—
1608	—	160	325	475	1,000	—
1609	—	160	325	475	1,000	—

KM# 66 4 ORE (1/2 Mark)

4.8418 g., 0.6250 Silver 0.0973 oz. ASW **Obv:** Hebrew "Jehovah" above bust of Gustaf II Adolf left **Rev:** Crown above three shields, lion, value, date **Mint:** Stockholm

Date	Mintage	VG	F	VF	XF	Unc
1615	—	1,300	1,900	2,700	4,600	—
1617	—	1,150	1,550	1,900	3,350	—

KM# 251 4 ORE (1/2 Mark)

3.5103 g., 0.4440 Silver 0.0501 oz. ASW **Obv:** Doubled C monogram below crown **Rev:** Three crowns, date, value **Mint:** Stockholm

Date	Mintage	VG	F	VF	XF	Unc
1665 Rare	—	—	—	—	—	—
1666 Rare	—	—	—	—	—	—

KM# 257 4 ORE (1/2 Mark)

2.9252 g., 0.3750 Silver 0.0353 oz. ASW **Ruler:** Carl XII **Obv:** Crowned C **Rev:** Three crowns **Note:** Varieties exist.

Date	Mintage	VG	F	VF	XF	Unc
1667	473,000	40.50	85.00	160	295	—
1668	1,102,000	25.00	48.50	110	210	—
1669	1,023,000	25.00	48.50	110	210	—
1669 AO before date	Inc. above	33.00	65.00	120	250	—
1669 Without mm	Inc. above	33.00	65.00	120	250	—
x669	Inc. above	55.00	120	325	600	—
1670	4,197,000	20.00	40.50	95.00	210	—
x670	Inc. above	55.00	120	325	600	—
1671	3,627,000	25.00	48.50	110	230	—
1672	1,055,000	25.00	48.50	110	230	—
1672 DF	Inc. above	36.50	70.00	130	295	—
1673	1,052,000	33.00	65.00	120	250	—
1674	356,000	25.00	48.50	110	205	—
1675	560,000	25.00	48.50	110	205	—
1676	1,196,000	25.00	48.50	110	205	—
1677	1,047,000	20.00	40.50	85.00	170	—
1678	1,258,000	20.00	40.50	85.00	170	—
1679/76	—	33.00	65.00	120	250	—
1679	978,000	25.00	48.50	110	230	—
1680	103,554	20.00	40.50	85.00	170	—
1681	458,000	25.00	48.50	115	250	—
1682	197,000	40.50	85.00	160	325	—
1683	202,000	33.00	65.00	130	270	—
1684	137,000	48.50	95.00	190	400	—

KM# 310 5 ORE (S.M.)

3.5103 g., 0.4440 Silver 0.0501 oz. ASW **Obv:** Crown above doubled large C monogram, date **Rev:** Three crowns, value **Mint:** Stockholm

Date	Mintage	VG	F	VF	XF	Unc
1690	1,678,000	19.00	40.50	90.00	185	—
1691	2,563,000	19.00	40.50	90.00	185	—
1692	1,857,000	27.50	48.50	110	230	—
1693/92	—	36.50	65.00	145	295	—
1693	2,368,000	19.00	40.50	90.00	185	—
1694	2,257,000	19.00	40.50	90.00	185	—
1699	1,271,000	19.00	40.50	90.00	185	—
1700	2,195,000	19.00	40.50	90.00	185	—

KM# 158 8 ORE (1 Mark)

5.2004 g., 0.7500 Silver 0.1254 oz. ASW **Obv:** Christina seated holding book and orb **Rev:** Crowned arms divide value **Mint:** Stockholm

Date	Mintage	VG	F	VF	XF	Unc
1634	105,000	280	475	950	1,700	—

KM# 13 MARK (8 Ore)

4.9363 g., 0.0210 Silver 0.0033 oz. ASW **Obv:** Crowned arms divide date **Rev:** Hebrew "Jehovah" in rays at center, value **Mint:** Stockholm

Date	Mintage	VG	F	VF	XF	Unc
1604	—	205	425	900	1,700	—
1605	—	140	280	450	1,000	—
1606	—	130	245	350	750	—

KM# 22 MARK (8 Ore)

4.9363 g., 0.0210 Silver 0.0033 oz. ASW **Obv:** Hebrew "Jehovah" above half-length crowned figure of Carl IX left **Rev:** Crowned arms divide date **Mint:** Stockholm

Date	Mintage	VG	F	VF	XF	Unc
1607	—	120	205	325	425	—
1608	—	95.00	190	295	350	—
1609	—	120	205	325	450	—
1610	—	130	245	450	850	—
1610 CARLOS	—	205	475	950	1,850	—
1611	—	160	110	600	450	—

KM# 61 MARK (8 Ore)

4.9363 g., 0.0210 Silver 0.0033 oz. ASW **Obv:** Hebrew "Jehovah" above laureate bust of Gustaf II Adolf left **Rev:** Triple shield, three crowns, lion, sheaf, date, value **Mint:** Stockholm

Date	Mintage	VG	F	VF	XF	Unc
1613 Rare	—	—	—	—	—	—
1614	—	1,150	1,600	2,350	5,500	—
1615	—	775	1,150	1,600	2,950	—
1616 Rare	—	—	—	—	—	—
1617	—	700	1,150	1,500	2,900	—
1617/19	—	775	1,150	1,600	2,950	—

KM# 74 MARK (8 Ore)

4.9363 g., 0.0210 Silver 0.0033 oz. ASW **Obv:** Crowned bust of Gustaf II Adolf left **Rev:** Crowned amrs divide value **Mint:** Stockholm

Date	Mintage	VG	F	VF	XF	Unc
1617 Rare	—	—	—	—	—	—
1618	—	1,300	1,600	2,100	4,200	—

KM# 181 MARK (8 Ore)

5.5063 g., 0.7500 Silver 0.1328 oz. ASW **Obv:** Bust of Queen Christina right **Rev:** Crowned arms divide value **Mint:** Stockholm

Date	Mintage	VG	F	VF	XF	Unc
1641	—	—	575	1,450	—	—
1642 Rare	—	—	—	—	—	—
1646 Rare	—	—	—	—	—	—
1647	—	85.00	245	650	1,300	—
1648	—	180	325	950	2,100	—

KM# 191 MARK (8 Ore)

5.2004 g., 0.7500 Silver 0.1254 oz. ASW **Rev:** Curved shield **Mint:** Stockholm

Date	Mintage	VG	F	VF	XF	Unc
1648	—	160	550	1,300	2,350	—

KM# 181a MARK (8 Ore)

5.2004 g., 0.7500 Silver 0.1254 oz. ASW **Obv:** Bust of Christina right **Rev:** Crowned arms **Mint:** Stockholm

Date	Mintage	VG	F	VF	XF	Unc
1649	—	95.00	245	575	1,000	—
1650	—	95.00	245	575	1,000	—
1651	—	110	270	575	1,100	—

KM# 182 MARK (8 Ore)

5.2004 g., 0.7500 Silver 0.1254 oz. ASW **Rev:** Three crowns **Mint:** Stockholm

Date	Mintage	VG	F	VF	XF	Unc
ND No mintmark	—	120	270	575	1,250	—
ND (ca) No value	—	85.00	230	550	1,150	—

KM# 219 MARK (8 Ore)

5.2004 g., 0.7500 Silver 0.1254 oz. ASW **Obv:** Bust of King Ca X Gustaf left **Rev:** Three crowns, value, date **Mint:** Stockholm

Date	Mintage	VG	F	VF	XF	Ur
1655	—	1,000	1,450	2,050	4,600	-
1656	—	1,000	1,450	2,050	4,600	-
1658	—	1,300	1,800	2,450	5,500	-
ND	—	1,200	1,600	2,300	5,000	-

KM# 240 MARK (8 Ore)

5.2004 g., 0.6940 Silver 0.1160 oz. ASW **Obv:** Bust of Carl X left **Rev:** Three crowns **Mint:** Stockholm **Note:** Varieties exist.

Date	Mintage	VG	F	VF	XF	Ur
1663	73,000	500	1,000	2,550	5,800	-
1664 GW	—	350	675	2,050	4,250	-
1664	—	400	825	2,300	5,300	-
1664 IK	—	300	700	1,600	3,550	-
1664 IAK	—	400	775	2,300	4,250	-
1665	—	350	800	1,300	3,300	-
1669	—	400	975	2,300	5,300	-
1671	—	375	800	1,550	4,100	-
1671	—	400	925	1,550	5,300	-
Note: Error, Carolvs IX						
1672 Rare	—	—	—	—	—	-
1673	—	575	1,300	2,700	5,300	-
1674	—	400	975	2,300	5,300	-

KM# 295 MARK (8 Ore)

5.2004 g., 0.6940 Silver 0.1160 oz. ASW **Obv:** Bust of Carl X right **Rev:** Three crowns **Mint:** Stockholm

Date	Mintage	VG	F	VF	XF	U
1683	—	95.00	190	475	1,000	-
1684	—	85.00	160	450	925	-
1685	—	55.00	120	280	600	-
1686/5	—	65.00	130	295	625	-
1686	—	55.00	120	280	600	-
1687	—	55.00	120	280	600	-
1688	—	48.50	110	245	500	-
1689	—	48.50	110	245	500	-
1690	—	48.50	110	245	500	-
1691	—	48.50	110	245	500	-
1692	—	48.50	110	245	500	-
1693	—	48.50	110	245	500	-
1694	—	48.50	110	245	500	-
1695	—	48.50	110	245	500	-
1696	—	48.50	110	245	500	-
1697	—	115	210	550	1,100	-

KM# 313 MARK (8 Ore)

0.6940 Silver **Ruler:** Carl XII **Obv:** Bust right **Obv. Inscription** CAROLVS • XII • D • G • REX • SVE • **Rev:** Three crowns, divide date, value **Mint:** Stockholm

Date	Mintage	VG	F	VF	XF	U
1697	—	160	325	850	1,500	-
1698	24,000	85.00	160	425	750	-
1699	52,000	55.00	120	350	650	-
1700	46,000	55.00	120	350	650	-

KM# 11 2 MARK

Silver **Obv:** Crowned "CDS" **Rev:** Crowned sheaf, dates in corners **Mint:** Kalmar

Date	Mintage	VG	F	VF	XF	U
1603	—	325	650	1,050	2,050	-
1604	—	425	1,150	1,900	3,000	-

.M# 14 2 MARK

.8726 g., 0.8210 Silver 0.2606 oz. ASW **Obv:** Crowned arms ivides date **Rev:** Hebrew "Jehovah" in rays **Mint:** Stockholm

ate	Mintage	VG	F	VF	XF	Unc
604	—	245	475	950	1,700	—

Note: An incorrect coat-of-arms is reported dated 1604 and is rare

ate	Mintage	VG	F	VF	XF	Unc
605	—	245	475	950	1,700	—
606	—	215	425	775	1,300	—

.M# 23 2 MARK

.8726 g., 0.8210 Silver 0.2606 oz. ASW **Obv:** Hebrew Jehovah" above half-length crowned figure of Carl IX left **Rev:** rowned arms divides date **Mint:** Stockholm

ate	Mintage	VG	F	VF	XF	Unc
607	—	450	800	1,300	2,050	—
608	—	450	800	1,300	2,050	—
609	—	550	1,150	1,800	2,500	—
610	—	450	950	1,550	2,350	—
611 Rare	—	—	—	—	—	—

.M# 67 2 MARK

8726 g., 0.8210 Silver 0.2606 oz. ASW **Obv:** Hebrew ehovah" above laureate bust of King Gustaf II Adolf **Rev:** Triple hield, three crowns, lion, sheaf, value, date **Mint:** Stockholm

ate	Mintage	VG	F	VF	XF	Unc
615	—	1,400	1,900	2,550	4,400	—
617	—	1,150	1,500	2,150	3,950	—
618 Rare	—	—	—	—	—	—
619 Rare	—	—	—	—	—	—

.M# 163 2 MARK

1.0126 g., 0.7500 Silver 0.2655 oz. ASW **Obv:** 3/4-figure ueen Christina **Rev:** Crowned arms, value, date **Mint:** tockholm

ate	Mintage	VG	F	VF	XF	Unc
638	—	170	400	1,300	2,200	—

.M# 183 2 MARK

1.0126 g., 0.7500 Silver 0.2655 oz. ASW **Obv:** Facing bust of hristina **Mint:** Stockholm

ate	Mintage	VG	F	VF	XF	Unc
641	—	165	350	1,150	2,650	—
642	—	500	1,200	2,650	3,950	—
646 Rare	—	—	—	—	—	—

.M# 192 2 MARK

1.0126 g., 0.7500 Silver 0.2655 oz. ASW **Obv:** Laureate bust f Christina with long hair right **Mint:** Stockholm

ate	Mintage	VG	F	VF	XF	Unc
647 Rare	—	—	—	—	—	—
648	—	450	950	2,200	—	—

M# 195 2 MARK

0.4009 g., 0.7500 Silver 0.2508 oz. ASW **Obv:** Laureate bust f Christina with short hair right **Mint:** Stockholm

ate	Mintage	VG	F	VF	XF	Unc
649	—	160	325	600	1,250	—
650 REG	—	75.00	145	270	400	—
650 REGI	—	75.00	150	270	475	—
650 REGIN	—	90.00	170	350	625	—

Date	Mintage	VG	F	VF	XF	Unc
1650 REGINA	—	90.00	165	270	525	—
1651	—	90.00	170	350	475	—

KM# 210 2 MARK

10.4008 g., 0.7500 Silver 0.2508 oz. ASW **Obv:** Head of Christina right **Rev:** Three crowns **Mint:** Stockholm

Date	Mintage	VG	F	VF	XF	Unc
ND(1651) (ca)	—	75.00	150	450	875	—
ND(1651) II M	—	90.00	170	500	1,050	—
ND(1651) 2 M Rare	—	—	—	—	—	—

KM# 213 2 MARK

10.4008 g., 0.7500 Silver 0.2508 oz. ASW **Obv:** Bust of Carl X Gustaf left **Rev:** Three crowns **Mint:** Stockholm

Date	Mintage	VG	F	VF	XF	Unc
ND(1655)	—	140	240	375	775	—
ND(1655)	—	150	255	450	875	—

Note: Bust with epaulet

Date	Mintage	VG	F	VF	XF	Unc
1656	—	170	295	500	1,050	—
1657	—	215	350	625	1,300	—
1658	—	170	295	500	1,050	—
1659	—	170	295	500	1,050	—
1660	62,000	255	375	700	1,400	—

KM# 236 2 MARK

10.4008 g., 0.7500 Silver 0.2508 oz. ASW **Obv:** Bust of Carl XI left **Rev:** Three crowns **Mint:** Stockholm

Date	Mintage	VG	F	VF	XF	Unc
1661	154,000	170	375	850	1,750	—

KM# 237 2 MARK

10.4008 g., 0.7500 Silver 0.2508 oz. ASW **Obv:** Longer laureate bust of Carl XI left **Rev:** Three crowns, value: II M: **Mint:** Stockholm

Date	Mintage	VG	F	VF	XF	Unc
1661	Inc. above	260	525	1,150	2,300	—
1662	171,000	110	225	550	1,200	—
1663 GW	14,000	150	295	725	1,300	—
1663 IFH	Inc. above	225	450	1,150	2,300	—
1663	Inc. above	225	450	1,050	2,150	—

KM# 237a 2 MARK

10.4008 g., 0.6940 Silver 0.2321 oz. ASW **Obv:** Half-length figure of Carl XI left **Rev:** Three crowns **Mint:** Stockholm

Date	Mintage	VG	F	VF	XF	Unc
1664 IK	—	44.50	100	200	375	—
1664 IAK	—	44.50	100	200	375	—
1665 IK	—	44.50	100	200	450	—
1665 IAK	—	44.50	100	200	450	—
1665 (as)	—	44.50	100	200	450	—
1666	494,000	37.25	90.00	185	300	—
1667	438,000	37.25	90.00	185	300	—
1668	—	37.25	90.00	185	300	—
1669	—	37.25	90.00	185	300	—

KM# 243 2 MARK

10.4008 g., 0.6940 Silver 0.2321 oz. ASW **Obv:** Youthful draped laureate bust of Carl XI right **Rev:** Three crowns **Mint:** Stockholm

Date	Mintage	VG	F	VF	XF	Unc
1664 IK	—	235	500	1,050	—	—

KM# 242 2 MARK

10.4008 g., 0.6940 Silver 0.2321 oz. ASW **Obv:** Youthful laureate bust of Carl XI left **Rev:** Three crowns, value: 2. - M: **Mint:** Stockholm **Note:** Varieties exist.

Date	Mintage	VG	F	VF	XF	Unc
1664 IK	—	—	—	—	—	—
1665 (as)	—	—	—	—	—	—
1665 IK	—	—	—	—	—	—
1669 FIRST	—	—	—	—	—	—
1670	802,000	37.25	90.00	185	325	—
1671	—	37.25	90.00	185	300	—
1671 Reversed 2	—	75.00	165	325	700	—
1672	—	44.50	100	185	350	—
1674	—	44.50	100	185	300	—
1675	240,000	44.50	100	185	350	—
1676	115,000	44.50	100	185	350	—
1677	76,000	60.00	150	270	550	—

KM# 260 2 MARK

10.4008 g., 0.6940 Silver 0.2321 oz. ASW **Obv:** Young laureate bust of Carl XI right **Mint:** Stockholm

Date	Mintage	VG	F	VF	XF	Unc
1668	—	37.25	85.00	175	350	—
1673	—	37.25	85.00	175	350	—
1674	—	37.25	85.00	200	425	—

KM# 282.2 2 MARK

10.4008 g., 0.6940 Silver 0.2321 oz. ASW **Mint:** Landskrone **Note:** Prev. KM#282a.2.

Date	Mintage	VG	F	VF	XF	Unc
1675	—	—	—	—	—	—

KM# 282.1 2 MARK

10.4008 g., 0.6940 Silver 0.2321 oz. ASW **Obv:** Mature bust of Carl XI right **Rev:** Three crowns **Mint:** Stockholm

Date	Mintage	VG	F	VF	XF	Unc
1677	Inc. above	90.00	175	375	800	—
1678	35,000	125	280	600	1,200	—
1679	36,000	125	280	600	1,200	—
1680	73,000	65.00	145	295	600	—
1680 with epaulet	—	125	280	600	1,200	—
1681	—	65.00	145	350	775	—
1682	153,000	44.50	85.00	230	500	—
1683	—	44.50	85.00	260	550	—
1684	—	50.00	100	275	575	—
1685	—	50.00	100	295	600	—
1686	—	44.50	85.00	185	375	—
1687	—	37.25	75.00	175	350	—
1688	—	30.25	65.00	165	325	—
1689	—	30.25	65.00	165	325	—
1690	—	30.25	65.00	165	325	—
1691	—	30.25	65.00	165	325	—
1692	—	30.25	60.00	150	300	—
1693	—	30.25	60.00	150	300	—
1694	—	30.25	60.00	150	300	—
1695	—	30.25	60.00	150	300	—
1696	—	30.25	60.00	150	300	—
1697	—	90.00	175	850	1,850	—

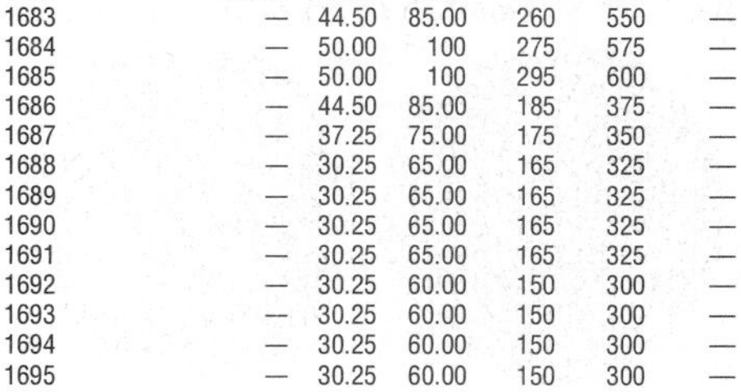

KM# 314 2 MARK

10.4000 g., 0.6940 Silver 0.2320 oz. ASW **Ruler:** Carl XII **Obv:** Bust right **Obv. Legend:** CAROLVS • XII • D • G • REX • SVE • **Rev:** Three crowns, value **Mint:** Stockholm

Date	Mintage	VG	F	VF	XF	Unc
1697	—	50.00	225	450	925	—
1698	41,000	65.00	150	325	775	—

Date	Mintage	VG	F	VF	XF	Unc
1699	365,000	37.25	125	260	575	—
1700	518,000	30.25	110	225	475	—

KM# 12 4 MARK

Silver **Obv:** Crowned "CDS" **Rev:** Crowned sheaf, date in corners **Mint:** Kalmar

Date	Mintage	VG	F	VF	XF	Unc
1603	—	325	625	1,000	2,000	—
1604	—	425	950	1,900	3,150	—

KM# 15.1 4 MARK

19.7453 g., 0.8210 Silver 0.5212 oz. ASW **Obv:** Half-figure of Charles IX above arms divides date **Rev:** Hebrew "Jehovah" in rays at center **Mint:** Stockholm

Date	Mintage	VG	F	VF	XF	Unc
1604	—	235	450	750	1,400	—
1605	—	205	425	650	1,250	—
1606	—	220	450	700	1,300	—

KM# 15.2 4 MARK

19.7453 g., 0.8210 Silver 0.5212 oz. ASW **Obv:** Shield with lions and crowns incorrectly placed **Mint:** Stockholm

Date	Mintage	VG	F	VF	XF	Unc
1604 Rare	—	—	—	—	—	—

KM# 24 4 MARK

19.7453 g., 0.8210 Silver 0.5212 oz. ASW **Obv:** Hebrew "Jehovah" above half-length crowned figure of Carl IX left **Rev:** Crowned arms divide date **Mint:** Stockholm

Date	Mintage	VG	F	VF	XF	Unc
1607 3 varieties	—	205	350	650	1,250	—
1608 GOLATIM	—	290	525	1,200	2,400	—
1608 GOLATIVN	—	195	300	625	1,200	—
1609	—	205	350	650	1,250	—
1610 MEVM	—	195	300	625	1,200	—
1610 MVEM	—	235	425	700	1,550	—
1611	—	205	350	700	1,550	—

KM# 62 4 MARK

19.7453 g., 0.8210 Silver 0.5212 oz. ASW **Obv:** Half-figure of John, Duke of Ostergotland right, date **Rev:** Triform arms below Hebrew "Jehovah", value **Mint:** Vadstena

Date	Mintage	VG	F	VF	XF	Unc
1613	—	—	—	—	—	—

KM# 63.1 4 MARK

19.7453 g., 0.8210 Silver 0.5212 oz. ASW **Obv:** Bust of John, Duke of Ostergotland left **Rev:** Triform arms below Hebrew "Jehovah" **Mint:** Vadstena

Date	Mintage	VG	F	VF	XF	Unc
1613 Rare	—	—	—	—	—	—
1614	—	1,450	2,400	5,000	9,700	—

KM# 64 4 MARK

19.7453 g., 0.8210 Silver 0.5212 oz. ASW **Obv:** Hebrew "Jehovah" above laureate bust of Gustaf II Adolfus left **Rev:** Three crowned shields **Mint:** Stockholm

Date	Mintage	VG	F	VF	XF	Unc
1613	—	525	875	1,250	2,450	—
1614 GLORIA	—	300	550	650	1,400	—
1614 GLORIA	—	300	550	650	1,400	—
1614 GLORA	—	400	700	975	2,000	—
1614 Reversed 4	—	400	575	875	1,800	—
1615	—	300	550	650	1,400	—
1616	—	350	550	800	1,800	—
1617	—	300	550	750	1,550	—
1618	—	425	700	900	1,850	—
1619 Rare	—	—	—	—	—	—
1620 Rare	—	—	—	—	—	—
1626	—	1,400	2,700	4,650	8,100	—

KM# 63.2 4 MARK

19.7453 g., 0.8210 Silver 0.5212 oz. ASW **Mint:** Soderkoping

Date	Mintage	VG	F	VF	XF	Unc
1617 Rare	—	—	—	—	—	—

KM# 164 4 MARK

22.0252 g., 0.7500 Silver 0.5311 oz. ASW **Obv:** Christina seate left **Rev:** Crowned arms **Mint:** Stockholm

Date	Mintage	VG	F	VF	XF	U
1638 Large Collar	—	185	375	1,000	2,250	-
1638 Over date: III/II Small Collar legend ends ER:HE	—	400	775	1,550	4,050	-
1638 Small Collar Legend ends PR: HE	—	195	400	1,850	3,200	-
1638 Small Collar Legend ends ER:HE	—	350	750	2,200	4,050	-

KM# 184 4 MARK

22.0252 g., 0.7500 Silver 0.5311 oz. ASW **Obv:** Facing bust o Queen Christina **Rev:** Crowned arms, date, value **Mint:** Stockholm

Date	Mintage	VG	F	VF	XF	U
1641	—	425	575	1,150	—	-
1642	—	1,050	1,750	3,500	—	-
1646 Rare	—	—	—	—	—	-

KM# 193 4 MARK

22.0252 g., 0.7500 Silver 0.5311 oz. ASW **Obv:** Bust of Christir right **Rev:** Crowned arms divide date **Mint:** Stockholm **Note:** Varieties exist.

Date	Mintage	VG	F	VF	XF	U
1647	—	195	375	950	2,000	-
1647 Small bust	—	265	525	1,350	2,750	-
1648 WAN	—	375	375	950	2,000	-
1648 WAND	—	220	425	1,150	2,350	-
1649 MDCXLIX	—	265	525	1,450	3,450	-
1649 MDCXLVIIII	—	130	265	975	2,000	-

KM# 244 4 MARK

20.8016 g., 0.6940 Silver 0.4641 oz. ASW **Obv:** Laureate bus of Carl XI left **Rev:** Crowned shield, sprays below **Mint:** Stockhol

ate	Mintage	VG	F	VF	XF	Unc
664 IK	—	300	875	1,750	4,100	—
664 IAK	—	265	650	1,450	3,650	—
664 Carolvs Rex	—	350	575	1,250	3,450	—
664 Seven dots below collar	—	450	625	1,300	3,600	—

KM# 261 4 MARK

.8016 g., 0.6940 Silver 0.4641 oz. ASW **Obv:** Bust of Carl XI ft **Rev:** Cruciform of crowned arms **Mint:** Stockholm

ate	Mintage	VG	F	VF	XF	Unc
668 Rare	—	—	—	—	—	—

M# 262 4 MARK

.8016 g., 0.6940 Silver 0.4641 oz. ASW **Obv:** Laureate bust Carl XI left **Rev:** Crowned arms **Mint:** Stockholm

ate	Mintage	VG	F	VF	XF	Unc
668	—	265	525	1,100	2,750	—
669	—	295	575	1,150	2,950	—

M# 279 4 MARK

.8016 g., 0.6940 Silver 0.4641 oz. ASW **Obv:** Laureate bust Carl XI right **Rev:** Crowned interlocked "C's" with three crowns **int:** Stockholm

ate	Mintage	VG	F	VF	XF	Unc
673	—	265	575	1,150	2,350	—
674 Reversed 4	—	265	575	1,150	2,350	—

M# 296 4 MARK

.8016 g., 0.6940 Silver 0.4641 oz. ASW **Obv:** Mature bust of arl XI right **Rev:** Crowned shield divides value **Mint:** Stockholm

ate	Mintage	VG	F	VF	XF	Unc
683	—	95.00	185	400	825	—
683 DF	—	85.00	175	350	725	—
84/83	—	60.00	115	230	475	—
84	—	60.00	115	230	475	—
685	—	60.00	115	230	475	—
686/85	—	60.00	115	230	475	—
686	—	60.00	115	230	475	—
87	—	50.00	100	230	475	—
88	—	50.00	100	230	475	—

Date	Mintage	VG	F	VF	XF	Unc
1689	—	50.00	100	230	475	—
1690	—	50.00	100	210	425	—
1691	—	50.00	100	210	425	800
1692/1	—	50.00	100	200	425	—
1692	—	46.75	95.00	200	425	—
1693	—	46.75	95.00	200	425	—
1694/93	—	46.75	95.00	200	425	—
1695	—	46.75	95.00	200	425	—
1696	—	50.00	100	215	450	—

KM# 315 4 MARK

Silver **Ruler:** Carl XII **Obv:** Bust right **Obv. Legend:** CAROLVS • XII • D • G • REX • SVE • **Rev:** Crowned shield divides value **Rev. Legend:** DOMINVS • PROTECTOR • MEVS • **Mint:** Stockholm

Date	Mintage	VG	F	VF	XF	Unc
1697	—	140	285	575	1,150	—
1698/7	—	115	215	400	900	—
1698	28,000	115	215	425	950	—
1699	91,000	105	180	375	750	—
1700	208,000	85.00	160	375	725	—

KM# 52 5 MARK

1.6365 g., 0.8700 Gold 0.0458 oz. AGW **Obv:** Crowned wheat sheaf divides C-R and U-M **Rev:** Radiant "Jehovah", date in corners **Mint:** Stockholm **Note:** Klippe. Fr. #23.

Date	Mintage	VG	F	VF	XF	Unc
1610 Rare	—	—	—	—	—	—
1611 Rare	—	—	—	—	—	—
1612 Rare	—	—	—	—	—	—

KM# 36 6 MARK

1.8600 g., Gold **Obv:** Hebrew "Jehovah" above crowned bust of Carl IX right

Date	Mintage	VG	F	VF	XF	Unc
1609	—	1,200	2,150	4,200	8,500	—

KM# 37 6 MARK

29.6179 g., 0.8210 Silver 0.7818 oz. ASW **Obv:** Half-figure of Carl IX, with arms and sword **Rev:** Lion rampant in shield in two circles of legends **Mint:** Stockholm **Note:** Dav. #4513.

Date	Mintage	VG	F	VF	XF	Unc
1609	—	850	1,400	2,850	6,000	—

KM# 53 6 MARK

1.8584 g., 0.9790 Gold 0.0585 oz. AGW **Obv:** Hebrew "Jehovah" above crowned bust of Carl IX left **Rev:** Arms of Goteborg in cartouche and inner circle **Mint:** Gothenburg **Note:** Fr. #24.

Date	Mintage	VG	F	VF	XF	Unc
1610 Rare	—	—	—	—	—	—

KM# A11 8 MARK

Gold **Ruler:** Carl IX, Regent **Obv:** Crowned wheat sheaf divides date **Rev:** Three crowns, value **Mint:** Stockholm **Note:** Fr.#14. Klippe.

Date	Mintage	VG	F	VF	XF	Unc
1603 Rare	—	—	—	—	—	—

KM# 29 8 MARK

39.4905 g., 0.8210 Silver 1.0423 oz. ASW **Obv:** Half-figure of Carl IX, with arms and sword left **Rev:** Lion rampant with three crowns **Mint:** Stockholm **Note:** Dav. #4512.

Date	Mintage	VG	F	VF	XF	Unc
1608	—	850	1,700	3,000	6,300	—

KM# 75 8 MARK

39.4905 g., 0.8210 Silver 1.0423 oz. ASW **Rev:** Crowned three shields **Mint:** Stockholm **Note:** Dav. #4518.

Date	Mintage	VG	F	VF	XF	Unc
1617	—	425	925	2,050	4,400	—

KM# 76 8 MARK

39.4905 g., 0.8210 Silver 1.0423 oz. ASW **Obv:** Hebrew "Jehovah" above standing figure of Gustaf II Adolphus **Rev:** Rectangular shield in two circle of shields **Mint:** Stockholm

Date	Mintage	VG	F	VF	XF	Unc
ND(1617)	—	1,000	1,400	2,250	4,250	—

KM# 77 8 MARK

39.4905 g., 0.8210 Silver 1.0423 oz. ASW **Rev:** Crowned heart-shaped four-fold arms **Mint:** Stockholm

Date	Mintage	VG	F	VF	XF	Unc
ND(1617) Rare	—	—	—	—	—	—

KM# 245 8 MARK

31.3475 g., 0.9220 Silver 0.9292 oz. ASW **Obv:** Laureate bust of Carl XI left **Rev:** Crowned arms divide date **Mint:** Stockholm **Note:** Dav. #4529.

Date	Mintage	VG	F	VF	XF	Unc
1664 IK	1,362	400	900	1,800	3,300	—

KM# 252 8 MARK
31.3475 g., 0.9220 Silver 0.9292 oz. ASW **Mint:** Stockholm **Note:** Dav. #4530.

Date	Mintage	VG	F	VF	XF	Unc
1665	1,801	425	1,000	2,000	3,750	—

KM# 253 8 MARK
31.3475 g., 0.9220 Silver 0.9292 oz. ASW **Mint:** Stockholm **Note:** Dav. #4531.

Date	Mintage	VG	F	VF	XF	Unc
1666	6,237	295	750	1,650	3,100	—

KM# 255 8 MARK
31.3475 g., 0.9220 Silver 0.9292 oz. ASW **Obv:** Thinner bust, divided legend **Mint:** Stockholm **Note:** Dav. #4532.

Date	Mintage	VG	F	VF	XF	Unc
1666	Inc. above	295	750	1,650	3,100	—

KM# 258 8 MARK
31.3475 g., 0.9220 Silver 0.9292 oz. ASW **Mint:** Stockholm **Note:** Dav. #4533.

Date	Mintage	VG	F	VF	XF	Unc
1667	2,046	450	1,000	2,100	4,300	—

KM# 259 8 MARK
31.3475 g., 0.9220 Silver 0.9292 oz. ASW **Obv:** Revised bust **Obv. Legend:** DEI GRATIA **Rev:** Interlocking C's between crowned shields in cruciform **Mint:** Stockholm **Note:** Dav. #4534.

Date	Mintage	VG	F	VF	XF	Unc
1667 Rare	Inc. above	—	—	—	—	—

KM# 275 8 MARK
31.3475 g., 0.9220 Silver 0.9292 oz. ASW **Obv:** Laureate bust of Carl XI right **Rev:** Crowned shields in cruciform **Mint:** Stockholm **Note:** Dav. #4535.

Date	Mintage	VG	F	VF	XF	Unc
1670	4,223	295	750	1,500	2,700	—

KM# 276 8 MARK
31.3475 g., 0.9220 Silver 0.9292 oz. ASW **Obv:** Laureate bust of Carl XI right **Rev:** Crowned double C monogram, three crowns in field **Mint:** Stockholm **Note:** Dav. #4536. Both lettered edge and plain edge with small bust and broken legend are known.

Date	Mintage	VG	F	VF	XF	Unc
1670	Inc. above	325	875	2,000	3,450	—

KM# 278 8 MARK
31.3475 g., 0.9220 Silver 0.9292 oz. ASW **Obv:** Wide bust **Rev. Legend:** IMPERIO SVSCEPTO **Mint:** Stockholm **Note:** Dav. #4537.

Date	Mintage	VG	F	VF	XF	Unc
1672	2,024	260	650	1,300	2,700	—

KM# 311 8 MARK
31.3475 g., 0.9220 Silver 0.9292 oz. ASW **Obv:** Draped armored bust of Carl XI right **Mint:** Stockholm **Note:** Dav. #4539. Minor variations in the harness and crown exist.

Date	Mintage	VG	F	VF	XF	Unc
1692 AS	51,000	150	325	700	1,450	—
1693 AS	52,000	150	325	700	1,450	—
1694/3 AS	51,000	165	325	750	1,550	—
1694 AS	Inc. above	150	295	650	1,400	—
1695 AS	24,000	185	425	825	1,700	—
1696 AS	8,000	225	450	975	1,950	—

KM# 316 8 MARK
31.3475 g., 0.9220 Silver 0.9292 oz. ASW **Obv:** Draped armored bust of Carl XII right, curved shoulder armor **Rev:** Crowned shield **Mint:** Stockholm **Note:** Dav. #4540.

Date	Mintage	VG	F	VF	XF	Unc
1697 AS	4,714	1,650	4,350	8,700	17,500	—
1698 AS	6,448	1,450	3,650	7,100	13,000	—

KM# 317 8 MARK
31.3475 g., 0.9220 Silver 0.9292 oz. ASW **Ruler:** Carl XII **Obv** Armored bust right **Obv. Legend:** CAROLVS • XII • D • G • RE • SVE • **Rev:** Crowned shield divides value **Rev. Legend:** DOMINVS ... **Note:** Dav. #4541, 1712.

Date	Mintage	VG	F	VF	XF	U
1697 AS	Inc. above	375	825	1,700	3,450	

KM# 320 8 MARK
31.3475 g., 0.9220 Silver 0.9292 oz. ASW **Obv:** Ornate harnes **Mint:** Stockholm **Note:** Dav. #4541A.

Date	Mintage	VG	F	VF	XF	U
1698 AS	Inc. above	375	875	1,700	3,100	
1700 HZ	6,284	375	900	1,850	3,450	

KM# 319 8 MARK
31.3475 g., 0.9220 Silver 0.9292 oz. ASW **Obv:** Draped armored bust of Carl XII right, straight shoulder armour **Mint:** Stockholm **Note:** Dav. #4540A.

Date	Mintage	VG	F	VF	XF	U
1698 AS	—	—	—	—	—	
Note: Reported, not confirmed						
1699 AS	6,100	325	850	1,750	3,400	

KM# 54 10 MARK
3.2728 g., 0.8700 Gold 0.0915 oz. AGW **Obv:** Crowned whe sheaf divides C-R and X-M **Rev:** Radiant "Jehovah", date in corners **Mint:** Stockholm **Note:** Klippe. Fr.#22.

Date	Mintage	VG	F	VF	XF	U
1610	—	2,550	5,300	12,500	—	

KM# 109 10 MARK
3.2728 g., 0.8700 Gold 0.0915 oz. AGW **Obv:** Crowned whe sheaf divides G-A and X-M, R below **Rev:** Radiant "Jehovah" date in corners **Mint:** Stockholm **Note:** Fr.#29.

Date	Mintage	VG	F	VF	XF	U
16Z6	—	4,400	7,300	11,500	17,000	

KM# 18 16 MARK

.9557 g., 0.9790 Gold 0.1560 oz. AGW **Obv:** Laureate bust of ;arl IX left with radiant "Jehovah" above **Rev:** Crowned arms ivide date **Mint:** Stockholm **Note:** Fr.#18.

ate	Mintage	VG	F	VF	XF	Unc
606 Rare	—	—	—	—	—	—

KM# 25 16 MARK

.9557 g., 0.9790 Gold 0.1560 oz. AGW **Obv:** Crowned bust of ;arl IX left in inner circle, radiant "Jehovah" at top **Rev:** Crowned rms divide date in inner circle **Mint:** Stockholm **Note:** Fr.#19.

ate	Mintage	VG	F	VF	XF	Unc
607	—	2,150	4,000	9,200	16,000	—
608	—	2,150	4,000	9,200	16,000	—
610	—	2,150	4,000	9,200	16,000	—
611 Rare	—	—	—	—	—	—

KM# 68 16 MARK

.9557 g., 0.9790 Gold 0.1560 oz. AGW **Obv:** Laureate bust of ustaf II Adolf left in inner circle **Rev:** Crown above three shields inner circle, date in legend **Mint:** Stockholm **Note:** Fr.#28.

ate	Mintage	VG	F	VF	XF	Unc
615 Rare	—	—	—	—	—	—

Note: Swiss Bank/Spink & Son Zurich Coins of Sweden sale Part I 12-89 two examples, XF and GVF each realized $27,750

KM# 105 16 MARK

.9557 g., 0.9790 Gold 0.1560 oz. AGW **Obv:** Crowned bust of ustaf II Adolf left **Rev:** Crown above three shields **Mint:** tockholm **Note:** Fr.#28.

ate	Mintage	VG	F	VF	XF	Unc
6Z4 Rare	—	—	—	—	—	—
Z4 Rare	—	—	—	—	—	—

Note: Swiss Bank/Spink & Sons Zurich Coins of Sweden sale Part I 12-89 VF realized $26,500

KM# A19 20 MARK

3.7260 g., 0.8210 Silver 2.6058 oz. ASW **Obv:** Carl IX standing acing left holding sword and orb, crown at right on table **Obv. Legend:** VERM left of Hebrew "Jehovah" above **Rev:** Crowned ve-fold arms surrounded by fifteen shields **Mint:** Stockholm

ate	Mintage	VG	F	VF	XF	Unc
606	—	1,750	2,950	5,200	9,200	—

KM# 19 20 MARK

98.7264 g., 0.8210 Silver 2.6058 oz. ASW **Obv:** Crowned Carl IX standing facing left holding sword and orb **Obv. Legend:** REX left of Hebrew "Jehovah" above **Mint:** Stockholm **Note:** Dav. #LS574.

Date	Mintage	VG	F	VF	XF	Unc
1606 Unique	—	—	—	—	—	—
1607 Rare	—	—	—	—	—	—
1608	—	3,500	4,500	6,500	10,000	—
1611 Rare	—	—	—	—	—	—

KM# 79 20 MARK

98.7264 g., 0.8210 Silver 2.6058 oz. ASW **Rev:** Crowned heart-shaped shield in two circle legend **Mint:** Stockholm

Date	Mintage	VG	F	VF	XF	Unc
ND(1617) Rare	—	—	—	—	—	—

KM# 78 20 MARK

98.7264 g., 0.8210 Silver 2.6058 oz. ASW **Obv:** Hebrew "Jehovah" above Gustaf II Adolf standing with sword and crown **Mint:** Stockholm

Date	Mintage	VG	F	VF	XF	Unc
1617 Rare	—	—	—	—	—	—
ND(1617) Rare	—	—	—	—	—	—

KM# 80 40 MARK

Silver **Obv:** Hebrew "Jehovah" above Gustaf II Adolf standing with sword and crown, value **Rev:** Similar to 20 Mark, KM#19

Date	Mintage	VG	F	VF	XF	Unc
1617 Unique	—	—	—	—	—	—

KM# 1 1/4 DALER (Ort)

Silver, 32-33 mm. **Ruler:** Carl IX, Regent **Obv:** Half-length bust of Carl IX left holding crowned shield **Obv. Legend:** CAROLVS • D : G • HAER - E •... **Rev:** "Jehovah" in radiant circle **Mint:** Stockholm

Date	Mintage	VG	F	VF	XF	Unc
1603 Rare	—	—	—	—	—	—

KM# 180 1/4 RIKSDALER

7.1926 g., 0.8780 Silver 0.2030 oz. ASW **Obv:** Bust of Queen Christina with hair drawn back facing **Rev:** The Savior with globe, crowned shields at lower left, date **Mint:** Stockholm

Date	Mintage	VG	F	VF	XF	Unc
1640	—	210	450	1,000	1,650	—
1641	—	325	675	1,750	3,150	—

KM# 185 1/4 RIKSDALER

7.1926 g., 0.8780 Silver 0.2030 oz. ASW **Obv:** Hair hanging long **Mint:** Stockholm

Date	Mintage	VG	F	VF	XF	Unc
1641	—	265	525	1,150	255	—
1641 Divided date	—	265	525	1,150	255	—
1642	—	210	450	1,000	2,100	—
1642 Divided date, Rare	—	—	—	—	—	—
1643	—	265	525	1,150	2,550	—
1644	—	180	400	975	2,100	—
1645	—	325	675	1,750	3,700	—
1646 AG	—	265	525	1,150	2,550	—
1646	—	180	400	975	2,100	—
1646 MDCXLVI	—	160	375	875	1,900	—

KM# 2 1/2 DALER

Silver, 35-36 mm. **Ruler:** Carl IX, Regent **Obv:** Half-length bust of Carl IX left holding crowned shield **Obv. Legend:** CAROLVS • D : G • HAER - E •... **Rev:** "Jehovah" in radiant circle **Mint:** Stockholm

Date	Mintage	VG	F	VF	XF	Unc
1601 Rare	—	—	—	—	—	—
1603 Rare	—	—	—	—	—	—

KM# 20 1/2 RIKSDALER

Silver **Obv:** Bust of Carl IX below Hebrew "Jehovah", date **Rev:** Arms below crown **Mint:** Stockholm **Note:** Struck with dies used for 16 Marks in gold, but with not value given.

Date	Mintage	VG	F	VF	XF	Unc
1606 Rare	—	—	—	—	—	—

KM# 140 1/2 RIKSDALER

14.6261 g., 0.8750 Silver 0.4114 oz. ASW **Obv:** Half-figure of Gustaf II Adolf with mace and globe, ornamentation at shoulder **Rev:** The Savior with globe, triform arms left, date **Mint:** Stockholm

Date	Mintage	VG	F	VF	XF	Unc
MDCXXXI (1631) Rare	—	—	—	—	—	—

KM# 141 1/2 RIKSDALER

14.6261 g., 0.8750 Silver 0.4114 oz. ASW **Obv:** Without ornamentation at shoulder **Obv. Legend:** GOTT • MIT • UNS **Rev:** Crowned ornate arms in sprays **Mint:** Stockholm

Date	Mintage	VG	F	VF	XF	Unc
1631	—	825	1,800	3,450	7,100	—
1632	—	950	1,900	3,750	7,400	—

KM# 165 1/2 RIKSDALER

14.3852 g., 0.8780 Silver 0.4061 oz. ASW **Obv:** 3/4-length figure of Christina **Rev:** The Savior standing facing holding orb, crowned shields at left **Mint:** Stockholm

Date	Mintage	VG	F	VF	XF	Unc
1639 MDCXXXVIIII	—	325	675	1,350	2,950	—
1639 MDCXXIX	—	425	900	1,900	3,700	—
1640 Small crown	—	375	750	1,500	3,150	—
1640 Large crown	—	375	750	1,500	3,150	—
1641 Small crown Rare	—	325	675	1,450	3,100	—

KM# 186 1/2 RIKSDALER

14.3852 g., 0.8780 Silver 0.4061 oz. ASW **Obv:** Bust of Christina facing **Mint:** Stockholm

Date	Mintage	VG	F	VF	XF	Unc
1641	—	525	1,200	2,800	5,300	—
1642	—	285	650	1,300	2,650	—
1643	—	210	525	1,150	2,550	—

KM# 186a 1/2 RIKSDALER

14.6261 g., 0.8780 Silver 0.4129 oz. ASW **Mint:** Stockholm

Date	Mintage	VG	F	VF	XF	Unc
1644	—	195	375	850	1,850	—
1645	—	195	375	850	1,850	—
1646	—	195	375	850	1,850	—
1647	—	230	500	1,000	2,150	—
1652	—	230	500	1,000	2,150	—

KM# 3 RIKSDALER

Silver **Ruler:** Carl IX, Regent **Obv:** 1/2-length figure holding crowned shield **Rev:** "Jehovah" in rays at center **Mint:** Stockholm **Note:** Dav. #4510.

Date	Mintage	VG	F	VF	XF	Unc
1601 Rare	—	—	—	—	—	—
1603 M IHEHOVA	—	325	650	1,300	2,350	—
1603 VM IHEHOVA	—	325	575	1,150	2,150	—
1603 M IEHOVA	—	425	800	1,550	3,050	—

KM# 26 RIKSDALER

29.2523 g., 0.8750 Silver 0.8229 oz. ASW **Obv:** Hebrew "Jehovah" above crowned Carl IX standing facing left holding sword and orb, three shields at his fett **Rev:** The Savior, date **Mint:** Stockholm **Note:** Dav. #4511.

Date	Mintage	VG	F	VF	XF	Unc
ND(1607) Rare	—	—	—	—	—	—
1608	—	275	425	2,100	4,400	—
1610 MEV M	—	180	325	1,250	2,500	—
1610 ME VM	—	160	350	1,600	3,350	—
1610 MEVM	—	205	425	1,700	3,550	—
1610 N OS	—	160	350	1,600	3,350	—
1610 NO S	—	160	350	1,550	3,200	—
1611	—	280	425	1,900	4,000	—

KM# 69 RIKSDALER

29.2523 g., 0.8750 Silver 0.8229 oz. ASW **Obv:** Hebrew "Jehovah" above half-length figure of Gustaf II Adolf holding scepter **Rev:** The Savior standing facing holding orb, crowned shields at left **Mint:** Stockholm **Note:** Dav. #4515.

Date	Mintage	VG	F	VF	XF	Unc
1615 HAE	—	255	575	1,650	3,450	—
1615 HAER	—	350	725	1,900	4,000	—
1615 HAERE	—	255	575	1,700	3,650	—
1616	—	295	600	1,700	3,650	—

KM# 82 RIKSDALER

29.2523 g., 0.8750 Silver 0.8229 oz. ASW **Mint:** Stockholm **Note:** Dav. #4516.

Date	Mintage	VG	F	VF	XF	Unc
1617 VANDALOR	—	300	600	1,600	3,300	—
1617 VANDAL	—	350	675	1,750	3,850	—

KM# 83 RIKSDALER

29.2523 g., 0.8750 Silver 0.8229 oz. ASW **Mint:** Sala and Stockholm **Note:** Dav. #4517.

Date	Mintage	VG	F	VF	XF	Unc
1617	—	600	1,450	2,950	—	—
1618	—	350	725	2,400	—	—
1619	—	350	725	2,400	—	—

KM# 81.2 RIKSDALER

29.2523 g., 0.8750 Silver 0.8229 oz. ASW **Obv:** Small head **Mint:** Soderkoping

Date	Mintage	VG	F	VF	XF	Unc
1617 Rare	—	—	—	—	—	—

KM# 81.1 RIKSDALER

29.2523 g., 0.8750 Silver 0.8229 oz. ASW **Obv:** Half-figure of John, Duke of Ostergotland, large head, date **Rev:** Hebrew "Jehovah" above crowned shields **Mint:** Soderkoping **Note:** Dav. #4514. Prev. KM#81.

Date	Mintage	VG	F	VF	XF	Unc
1617 Large head	—	2,950	5,700	11,000	—	—
1617 Small head	—	2,950	5,700	11,000	—	—

KM# 144 RIKSDALER

29.2523 g., 0.8750 Silver 0.8229 oz. ASW **Obv:** Scepter far away **Mint:** Sala and Stockholm **Note:** Dav. #A4520.

Date	Mintage	VG	F	VF	XF	Unc
1631	—	525	1,000	2,050	3,850	—

KM# 142 RIKSDALER

29.2523 g., 0.8750 Silver 0.8229 oz. ASW **Mint:** Sala and Stockholm **Note:** Dav. #4519.

Date	Mintage	VG	F	VF	XF	Unc
1631	—	525	1,000	2,050	4,350	—

KM# 143 RIKSDALER

29.2523 g., 0.8750 Silver 0.8229 oz. ASW **Obv:** Scepter near **Rev:** Roman numeral date **Mint:** Sala and Stockholm **Note:** Dav. #4520.

Date	Mintage	VG	F	VF	XF	Unc
MDCXXXI (1631)	—	300	600	1,600	3,300	—
MDCXXXII (1632)	—	525	1,000	2,050	4,350	—

KM# 146 RIKSDALER

29.2523 g., 0.8750 Silver 0.8229 oz. ASW **Obv:** Without shoulder bow **Rev:** Christ without robes **Mint:** Sala and Stockholm **Note:** Dav. #4521.1.

Date	Mintage	VG	F	VF	XF	Unc
1631 Rare	—	—	—	—	—	—

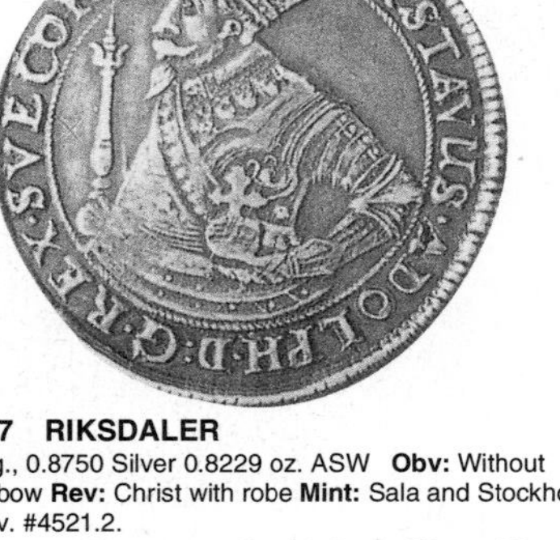

KM# 147 RIKSDALER

29.2523 g., 0.8750 Silver 0.8229 oz. ASW **Obv:** Without shoulder bow **Rev:** Christ with robe **Mint:** Sala and Stockholm **Note:** Dav. #4521.2.

Date	Mintage	VG	F	VF	XF	Unc
MDCXXXII (1632)	—	450	900	1,750	3,300	—

KM# 148 RIKSDALER

29.2523 g., 0.8750 Silver 0.8229 oz. ASW **Obv:** Narrow bust **Mint:** Sala and Stockholm **Note:** Dav. #A4521.

Date	Mintage	VG	F	VF	XF	Unc
MDCXXXII (1632)	—	525	1,000	2,050	3,850	—

KM# 145 RIKSDALER

29.2523 g., 0.8750 Silver 0.8229 oz. ASW **Rev:** Christ with textured robe **Mint:** Sala and Stockholm **Note:** Dav. #B4520.

Date	Mintage	VG	F	VF	XF	Unc
MDCXXXII (1632)	—	1,500	2,550	4,050	—	—

KM# 155 RIKSDALER

29.2523 g., 0.8750 Silver 0.8229 oz. ASW **Mint:** Sala and Stockholm **Note:** Dav. #4522.

Date	Mintage	VG	F	VF	XF	Unc
MDCXXXIII (1633) Rare	—	—	—	—	—	—

Note: Swiss Bank/Spink & Sons Zurich Coins of Sweden sale Part I 12-89 GVF realized $11,300

:M# 168 RIKSDALER
8.7703 g., 0.8780 Silver 0.8121 oz. ASW **Obv:** Large bust, rnate gown, broken inner circle **Mint:** Sala and Stockholm **Note:** av. #4523.1.

ate	Mintage	VG	F	VF	XF	Unc
:DC:XXXIX (1639)	—	600	1,200	2,250	4,800	—

:M# 169 RIKSDALER
3.7703 g., 0.8780 Silver 0.8121 oz. ASW **Obv:** Small bust, rnate gown, unbroken inner circle **Mint:** Sala and Stockholm **ote:** Dav. #4523.2. Numerous varieties in legend punctuation, own and jewelry exist for Dav. #4523.

ate	Mintage	VG	F	VF	XF	Unc
:DC:XXXIX (1639)	—	725	1,450	2,700	5,800	—
540 REGI	—	625	1,200	1,550	3,250	—
540 REG	—	550	900	1,400	2,900	—
540 RE	—	475	900	1,400	2,900	—
541	—	475	850	1,200	2,600	—

M# 167 RIKSDALER
3.7703 g., 0.8780 Silver 0.8121 oz. ASW **Obv:** Simple gown, ngle-edged lace on skirt **Mint:** Sala and Stockholm **Note:** Dav. 34523.

ate	Mintage	VG	F	VF	XF	Unc
IDCXXXVIIII (1639)	—	500	1,000	1,500	3,150	—

M# 166 RIKSDALER
3.7703 g., 0.8780 Silver 0.8121 oz. ASW **Obv:** Simple gown, ouble-edged lace on skirt **Mint:** Sala and Stockholm **Note:** Dav. A4523.

ate	Mintage	VG	F	VF	XF	Unc
DCXXXVIIII (1639)	—	1,000	1,650	2,400	5,300	—

KM# 187 RIKSDALER
28.7703 g., 0.8780 Silver 0.8121 oz. ASW **Obv:** Bust of Christina left **Mint:** Sala and Stockholm **Note:** Dav. #4525. Variations in Christina's gown occur beginning with the 1646 issue.

Date	Mintage	VG	F	VF	XF	Unc
M.DC.XLI (1641)	—	325	650	1,000	2,100	—
MDCXLII (1642) AG	—	575	900	1,400	2,750	—
1642 M	—	775	1,300	1,900	4,200	—
1642	—	280	475	725	1,550	—
MDCXLIII (1643) AG	—	280	475	725	1,550	—
MDCXLIV (1644) AG	—	280	475	800	1,750	—
Note: Large or small date varieties						
MDCXLIII (1644) AG	—	850	1,600	2,750	5,200	—
M+DC+XLV (1645) AG	—	325	575	800	1,750	—
1646 SALUATOR SALUA	—	400	650	1,200	2,450	—
1646 AG	—	325	575	900	1,900	—
1646	—	325	575	900	1,900	—
1647	—	325	575	900	1,900	—
1652	—	400	650	1,150	2,450	—
1653	11,000	2,300	3,250	4,850	10,500	—

KM# 194 RIKSDALER
28.7703 g., 0.8780 Silver 0.8121 oz. ASW **Obv:** Bust of Christina right **Mint:** Sala and Stockholm **Note:** Dav. #4526.

Date	Mintage	VG	F	VF	XF	Unc
1647 Rare	—	—	—	—	—	—

KM# 214 RIKSDALER
28.7703 g., 0.8780 Silver 0.8121 oz. ASW **Obv:** Charles X Gustavus **Mint:** Sala and Stockholm **Note:** Dav. #4528.

Date	Mintage	VG	F	VF	XF	Unc
1654	4,000	850	1,650	2,250	4,550	—

KM# 215 RIKSDALER
28.7703 g., 0.8780 Silver 0.8121 oz. ASW **Mint:** Sala and Stockholm **Note:** Klippe.

Date	Mintage	VG	F	VF	XF	Unc
1654 Rare	—	—	—	—	—	—

KM# 280 RIKSDALER
29.2523 g., 0.8780 Silver 0.8257 oz. ASW **Obv:** Carl XI **Mint:** Sala and Stockholm **Note:** Dav. #4538. Klippe.

Date	Mintage	VG	F	VF	XF	Unc
1676	791	1,700	3,800	7,100	—	—
1676	—	—	400	1,000	—	—
Note: 19th Century restrike						
1676	—	—	350	850	—	—
Note: Restrike of 1909						

KM# 196 1-1/2 RIKSDALER
Silver **Obv:** Bust of Christina, right **Rev:** Arms below crown, date **Mint:** Stockholm **Note:** Dav. #4527.

Date	Mintage	VG	F	VF	XF	Unc
1649 Rare	—	—	—	—	—	—
Note: Swiss Bank/Spink & Son Zurich Coins of Sweden sale part I 12-89 GXF realized $25,850						

KM# 27 2 RIKSDALER
Silver **Obv:** Full figure of Carl IX with sword and globe below Hebrew legend **Rev:** Arms below crown, double circle of shields, date **Mint:** Stockholm **Note:** Struck with 20 Mark dies.

Date	Mintage	VG	F	VF	XF	Unc
1607 Unique	—	—	—	—	—	—
1611 Unique	—	—	—	—	—	—

KM# 38 2 RIKSDALER
Silver **Obv:** Half-figure of Carl IX with sword and arms below Hebrew legend, date **Rev:** Arms with three cronws in field **Mint:** Stockholm

Date	Mintage	VG	F	VF	XF	Unc
1609 Unique	—	—	—	—	—	—

KM# 55 2 RIKSDALER

Silver **Subject:** Founding of Gothenburg **Obv:** Carl IX with sword below Hebrew legend **Rev:** Panorama with ships and buildings in foreground, tree in background **Mint:** Gothenburg

Date	Mintage	VG	F	VF	XF	Unc
1610	—	1,600	4,050	7,700	16,500	—

KM# 84 2 RIKSDALER

Silver **Obv:** Full figure of Gustaf II Adolf, laurel head **Rev:** Arms below crown, double circle of shields **Mint:** Stockholm

Date	Mintage	VG	F	VF	XF	Unc
1617	—	1,450	2,750	5,400	11,500	—

KM# 85 2 RIKSDALER

Silver **Obv:** Full figure of Gustaf II Adolf, crowned head **Mint:** Stockholm

Date	Mintage	VG	F	VF	XF	Unc
ND	—	1,450	2,750	5,600	11,500	—

KM# 156 2 RIKSDALER

Silver **Obv:** Gustaf II Adolf, mounted **Rev:** Arms below crown, single circle of shields **Mint:** Stockholm **Note:** Illustration reduced.

Date	Mintage	VG	F	VF	XF	Unc
1633	—	975	1,950	4,050	6,900	—

KM# 189 2 RIKSDALER

Silver **Obv:** Bust of Christina **Rev:** The Savior with globe, arms at left, date **Mint:** Stockholm **Note:** Dav. #4524.

Date	Mintage	VG	F	VF	XF	Unc
1644 Rare	—	—	—	—	—	—
1645 Rare	—	—	—	—	—	—
Note: Swiss Bank/Spink & Sons Zurich Coins of Sweden sale Part I 12-89 GVF realized $13,250						
1646 Rare	—	—	—	—	—	—
1647 Rare	—	—	—	—	—	—

KM# 197 2 RIKSDALER

Silver **Obv:** Christina bust right **Rev:** Arms below crown, date **Mint:** Stockholm

Date	Mintage	VG	F	VF	XF	Unc
1649 Rare	—	—	—	—	—	—

KM# 216 2 RIKSDALER

Silver **Obv:** Carl X Gustaf **Rev:** Arms below crown, lions rampant at sides, date **Mint:** Stockholm **Note:** Dav. #A4528.

Date	Mintage	VG	F	VF	XF	Unc
1654 Rare	—	—	—	—	—	—

KM# 56 2-1/2 RIKSDALER

Silver **Subject:** Founding of Gothenburg **Obv:** Charles IX with sword below Hebrew legend **Rev:** Panorama with ships and buildings in foreground, tree in background **Mint:** Gothenburg

Date	Mintage	VG	F	VF	XF	Unc
1610 Rare	—	—	—	—	—	—

KM# 30 3 RIKSDALER

Silver **Obv:** Carl IX with sword and orb below Hebrew legend **Rev:** The Savior with cross and orb, date **Mint:** Stockholm **Note:** Dav. #A4511.

Date	Mintage	VG	F	VF	XF	Unc
1608 Unique	—	—	—	—	—	—

KM# 39 3 RIKSDALER

Silver **Obv:** Carl IX with sword below Hebrew legend **Rev:** The Savior, date **Mint:** Stockholm **Note:** Dav. #B4511.

Date	Mintage	VG	F	VF	XF	Unc
1609 Unique	—	—	—	—	—	—

KM# 57 3 RIKSDALER

Silver **Subject:** Founding of Gothenburg **Obv:** Carl IX with swor below Hebrew legend **Rev:** Panorama with ships and building in foreground, tree in background **Mint:** Gothenburg

Date	Mintage	VG	F	VF	XF	U
1610	—	1,600	4,050	8,100	—	-

KM# 86 3 RIKSDALER

Silver **Obv:** Gustaf II Adolf with sword and orb below Hebrew legend **Rev:** Arms below crown, rings of multiple shields **Mint:** Sala and Stockholm

Date	Mintage	VG	F	VF	XF	U
1617 Rare	—	—	—	—	—	-

KM# 87 3 RIKSDALER

Silver **Rev:** Arms below crown, circle by legends **Mint:** Sala an Stockholm

Date	Mintage	VG	F	VF	XF	U
ND(1617) Rare	—	—	—	—	—	-

KM# 88 3 RIKSDALER

Silver **Obv:** Gustaf II Adolf with sword and orb below Hebrew legend **Rev:** Arms below crown, rings of multiple shields **Mint:** Stockholm

Date	Mintage	VG	F	VF	XF	U
ND(1617)	—	—	—	—	—	-

KM# 150 3 RIKSDALER

Silver **Obv:** Gustaf II Adolf mounted **Rev:** Arms below crown ring of shields, date beside crown **Mint:** Stockholm

Date	Mintage	VG	F	VF	XF	U
1632 Rare	—	—	—	—	—	-

KM# 151 3 RIKSDALER

Silver **Obv:** City view behind rearing horse **Mint:** Stockholm

Date	Mintage	VG	F	VF	XF	U
1632 Rare	—	—	—	—	—	-

KM# 149 3 RIKSDALER

Silver **Obv:** Gustaf II Adolf mounted **Rev:** Arms below crown ring of multiple shields **Mint:** Sala and Stockholm

Date	Mintage	VG	F	VF	XF	U
1632 Rare	—	—	—	—	—	-

KM# 157 3 RIKSDALER

Silver **Rev:** Crowned rectangular shield **Mint:** Stockholm

Date	Mintage	VG	F	VF	XF	U
1633	—	2,300	4,050	6,900	—	-

KM# 190 3 RIKSDALER

Silver **Obv:** Queen Christina **Rev:** The Savior, arms at lower left, date **Mint:** Sala and Stockholm **Note:** Dav. #A4524.

Date	Mintage	VG	F	VF	XF	U
1646 Rare	—	—	—	—	—	-

PLATE MONEY

The Kingdom of Sweden issued copper plate mone heavy and cumbersome square or rectangular coins ran ing in size up to about 13 by 25 inches down to less than by 3 inches, from 1644 to 1776. The kingdom was poor silver and gold but had rich copper resources. The coi were designed to contain copper bullion in the value of th silver coins they replaced, and were denominated as on two, four, etc. dalers in silver mint or silver coin.

Although sometimes classed with odd and curious mo ey these were legal tender coins of the realm and althoug used and exported as bullion, they circulated domestica and were essential in the commerce of Sweden and Finlar for more than a century.

They are widely collected, not only in Scandinavia b around the world.

Each denomination is catalogued under the name of th issuing monarch and by the mint mark and or source of th copper. The latter are important in the rarity and thus price of the coins. The pieces are identified by the center stam with the denomination, mint mark, etc., and four identic corner stamps, with the insignia of the king and date.

Many are extremely rare, with only a single specimen two known, often only a unique survivor in a major museur

KM# PM15 1/2 DALER S.M.

Copper **Subject:** Charles XI **Mint:** Avesta **Note:** Corner stamp Crowned C R S, date. Center stamp: 1/2 Daler Solff:Myt, three sta

Date	Mintage	VG	F	VF	XF	U
1681	—	600	1,200	2,100	—	-
1682 Rare	—	600	1,200	2,100	—	-
1683 Rare	—	—	—	—	—	-
1685 Rare	—	—	—	—	—	-
1686 Rare	—	—	—	—	—	-
1687 Rare	—	—	—	—	—	-
1689 Rare	—	—	—	—	—	-
1691 Rare	—	—	—	—	—	-

KM# PM1 DALER S.M.

Copper **Subject:** Queen Christina **Mint:** Avesta **Note:** Corne stamps: Crown above date, legend: CHRISTINA... Center stam 1 Daler Solff:Mnt, M K.

Date	Mintage	VG	F	VF	XF	U
1649	—	650	2,400	2,650	—	-
1650	—	550	1,100	2,150	—	-
1651	—	—	—	—	—	-
1652	—	650	1,300	2,650	—	-
1653	—	600	1,200	2,400	—	-
1654	—	650	1,300	2,650	—	-

KM# PM10 DALER S.M.

Copper **Subject:** Carl X Gustaf **Mint:** Avesta **Note:** Corner stamps: Legend: CAROLUS GUSTAVUS...

Date	Mintage	VG	F	VF	XF	Unc
655	—	850	1,750	2,500	—	—
656	—	725	1,500	2,150	—	—
657	—	650	1,400	2,050	—	—
658	—	650	1,300	1,900	—	—
659	—	650	1,750	2,500	—	—
660 Rare	—	950	2,300	3,000	—	—

M# PM16 DALER S.M.

Copper **Subject:** Carl XI **Mint:** Avesta **Note:** Corner stamps: Legend: CAROLUS... Cemter stamp: 1 DALER Solff:Myt.

Date	Mintage	VG	F	VF	XF	Unc
660	—	725	1,500	3,000	—	—
661	—	600	1,250	2,500	—	—
662	—	650	1,350	2,700	—	—
663	—	600	1,250	2,500	—	—
664	—	650	1,350	2,700	—	—
667	—	725	1,450	3,000	—	—
668	—	725	1,450	2,900	—	—
669	—	1,100	2,200	4,200	—	—
672	—	775	1,600	3,100	—	—
673 R/L	—	650	1,400	2,700	—	—
674	—	650	1,400	2,700	—	—
674 G	—	650	1,400	2,700	—	—
675	—	650	1,400	2,700	—	—
675 K	—	650	1,400	2,700	—	—
676	—	500	1,150	2,400	—	—
677	—	600	1,250	2,500	—	—
678	—	600	1,250	2,500	—	—
679	—	600	1,250	2,500	—	—
680	—	600	1,250	2,500	—	—
681	—	775	1,600	3,100	—	—
682	—	950	2,000	3,850	—	—
683	—	1,000	2,150	4,200	—	—
684	—	900	1,850	3,600	—	—
685	—	900	1,850	3,600	—	—
686	—	775	1,600	3,600	—	—
689	—	650	1,400	2,650	—	—
690	—	650	1,400	2,650	—	—
691	—	725	1,500	3,000	—	—

M# PM17 DALER S.M.

Copper **Note:** Copper from Garpenberg.

Date	Mintage	VG	F	VF	XF	Unc
674 Rare	—	—	—	—	—	—

M# PMA18 DALER S.M.

Copper **Mint:** Kengis **Note:** Center stamp: AIR monogram below denomination.

Date	Mintage	VG	F	VF	XF	Unc
675	—	725	1,450	2,900	—	—

M# PM2 2 DALER S.M.

Copper **Obv:** Queen Christina **Mint:** Avesta **Note:** Center stamp: DALER Solff:Mnt, M.K.

Date	Mintage	VG	F	VF	XF	Unc
649	—	1,450	3,600	7,200	—	—
650 Rare	—	—	—	—	—	—
651 Rare	—	—	—	—	—	—
652 Rare	—	—	—	—	—	—
653 Rare	—	—	—	—	—	—
654 Rare	—	—	—	—	—	—

M# PM11 2 DALER S.M.

Copper **Obv:** Carl X Gustaf **Mint:** Avesta **Note:** Corner stamps: Crown above date; legend: CAROLUS GUSTAVUS. Center stamp: 2 DALER Solff:Mnt.

Date	Mintage	VG	F	VF	XF	Unc
658 Rare	—	—	—	—	—	—
659 Rare	—	—	—	—	—	—

M# PM18 2 DALER S.M.

Copper **Obv:** Carl XI **Mint:** Avesta **Note:** Corner stamps: Crown above date; legend: CAROLUS... Center stamp: 2 DALER Solff:Myt, shield or rose between stars or lilies, or three stars.

Date	Mintage	VG	F	VF	XF	Unc
660	—	725	1,500	2,900	—	—
661	—	950	1,900	3,850	—	—
662	—	950	1,900	3,850	—	—
663	—	600	1,200	2,400	—	—
664	—	950	1,900	3,850	—	—
667	—	775	1,550	3,100	—	—
668	—	900	1,850	3,600	—	—
669	—	725	1,500	2,900	—	—
672	—	725	1,500	2,900	—	—
673	—	475	950	1,900	—	—
674	—	550	1,150	2,150	—	—
675	—	450	875	1,700	—	—
676	—	400	775	1,550	—	—
677	—	900	925	1,800	—	—
678	—	900	925	1,800	—	—
679	—	650	1,300	2,650	—	—
680	—	475	950	1,900	—	—
681	—	475	950	1,900	—	—
682	—	425	850	1,700	—	—
683	—	425	850	1,700	—	—
684	—	425	850	1,700	—	—
685	—	425	850	1,700	—	—
686	—	425	850	1,700	—	—
687	—	900	1,750	3,350	—	—
689	—	425	850	1,700	—	—
690	—	650	1,250	2,400	—	—
691	—	550	1,100	2,150	—	—

KM# PM19 2 DALER S.M.

Copper **Mint:** Avesta **Note:** Center stamp: Star between lilies below denomination. Copper from Garpenberg.

Date	Mintage	VG	F	VF	XF	Unc
1673 Rare	—	—	—	—	—	—
1674 Rare	—	550	1,150	2,300	—	—

KM# PM20 2 DALER S.M.

Copper **Mint:** Kengis **Note:** Center stamp: Monogram AIR below denomination.

Date	Mintage	VG	F	VF	XF	Unc
1693 Rare	—	—	—	—	—	—

KM# PM41 2 DALER S.M.

Copper **Ruler:** Carl XII **Obv:** Corner stamps: Crown above date, legend CAROLUS... Center stamp: Daler Sölff: Myt, AIR monogram. **Mint:** Kengis

Date	Mintage	VG	F	VF	XF	Unc
1700 Rare	—	—	—	—	—	—

KM# PM21 3 DALER S.M.

Copper **Obv:** Carl XI **Mint:** Avesta **Note:** Corner stamps: Date below crown; legend: CAROLUS XI... Center stamp: 3 DALER Solff:Myt, three stars.

Date	Mintage	VG	F	VF	XF	Unc
1674 Rare	—	—	—	—	—	—

KM# PM3 4 DALER S.M.

Copper **Obv:** Queen Christina **Mint:** Avesta **Note:** Corner stamps: Crown above date; legend: CHRISTINA...Center stamp: 4 DALER Solff:Mnt, MK.

Date	Mintage	VG	F	VF	XF	Unc
1649 Rare	—	—	—	—	—	—
1652 Rare	—	—	—	—	—	—
1653 Rare	—	—	—	—	—	—

KM# PM12 4 DALER S.M.

Copper **Obv:** Carl X Gustaf **Mint:** Avesta **Note:** Corner stamps: Crown above date; legend: CAROLUS... Center stamp: 4 DALER Solff:Mnt, M.K.

Date	Mintage	VG	F	VF	XF	Unc
1656 Rare	—	—	—	—	—	—
1657 Rare	—	—	—	—	—	—
1658 Rare	—	—	—	—	—	—
1659 Rare	—	—	—	—	—	—

KM# PM22 4 DALER S.M.

Copper **Obv:** Carl XI **Mint:** Avesta **Note:** Corner stamps: Crown above date; legend: CAROLUS... Center stamp: 4 DALER Solff:Mnt, M K.

Date	Mintage	VG	F	VF	XF	Unc
1663	—	—	—	—	—	—

KM# PM23 5 DALER S.M.

Copper **Obv:** Carl XI **Mint:** Avesta **Note:** Corner stamps: Crown above date; legend: CAROLUS XI... Center stamp: 5 DALER Solff:Myt, three stars.

Date	Mintage	VG	F	VF	XF	Unc
1674 Rare	—	—	—	—	—	—

KM# PM4 8 DALER S.M.

Copper **Obv:** Queen Christina **Mint:** Avesta **Note:** Corner stamps: Crown above date; legend: CHRISTINA... Center stamp: 8 DALER Solff:Mnt, M K.

Date	Mintage	VG	F	VF	XF	Unc
1652 Rare	—	—	—	—	—	—
1653 Rare	—	—	—	—	—	—

KM# PM13 8 DALER S.M.

Copper **Obv:** Carl X Gustaf **Mint:** Avesta **Note:** Corner stamps: Crown above date; legend: CAROLUS GUSTAVUS. Center stamp: 8 DALER Solff:Mnt, shield between roses.

Date	Mintage	VG	F	VF	XF	Unc
1656 Rare	—	—	—	—	—	—
1657 Rare	—	—	—	—	—	—
1658 Rare	—	—	—	—	—	—
1659	—	30,000	63,500	—	—	—

KM# PM24.1 8 DALER S.M.

Copper **Obv:** Carl XI Gustaf **Mint:** Avesta **Note:** Corner stamps: Crown above date; legend: CAROLUS... Center stamp: 8 DALER Solff:mnt, roses.

Date	Mintage	VG	F	VF	XF	Unc
1660	—	15,000	23,000	45,000	—	—
1661	—	15,000	23,000	45,000	—	—
1662	—	15,000	23,000	45,000	—	—
1663	—	15,000	23,000	45,000	—	—
1674	—	15,000	23,000	45,000	—	—

KM# PM24.2 8 DALER S.M.

Copper **Mint:** Avesta **Note:** Center stamp: 8 DALER Solff:myt, three stars.

Date	Mintage	VG	F	VF	XF	Unc
1681 Rare	—	—	—	—	—	—
1682 Rare	—	—	—	—	—	—

KM# PM5 10 DALER S.M.

Copper **Obv:** Queen Christina **Mint:** Avesta **Note:** Corner stamps: C R S around crown above date. Center stamp: X DALER Solff:Mnt, shield.

Date	Mintage	VG	F	VF	XF	Unc
1644 Rare	—	—	—	—	—	—
1645 Rare	—	—	—	—	—	—

TRADE COINAGE

KM# 312 1/4 DUCAT

0.8703 g., 0.9760 Gold 0.0273 oz. AGW **Obv:** Bust of Carl XI right **Rev:** Crowned double C monogram divides date, value below **Note:** Fr. #46.

Date	Mintage	VG	F	VF	XF	Unc
1692	—	550	775	1,200	—	—

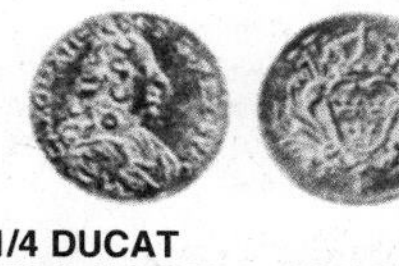

KM# 330 1/4 DUCAT

0.8703 g., 0.9760 Gold 0.0273 oz. AGW **Obv:** Crowned bust of Carl XII right **Rev:** Crowned arms **Note:** Fr. #52.

Date	Mintage	VG	F	VF	XF	Unc
1700	—	425	550	875	—	—

KM# 217 DUCAT

3.4386 g., 0.9720 Gold 0.1075 oz. AGW **Obv:** Bust of Carl X right, legend begins at bottom **Rev:** Crowned arms divides date near top **Note:** Fr. #36.

Date	Mintage	VG	F	VF	XF	Unc
1654 Rare	—	5,900	9,200	14,500	—	—
ND Rare	—	—	—	—	—	—

KM# 218 DUCAT

3.4386 g., 0.9720 Gold 0.1075 oz. AGW **Obv:** Bust of Carl X Gustavus right **Rev:** Legend begins at top **Note:** Fr. #36.

Date	Mintage	VG	F	VF	XF	Unc
1654 Rare	—	—	—	—	—	—

Note: Swiss Bank/Spink & Son Zurich Coins of Sweden sale Part I 12-89 VF realized $15,750

Date	Mintage	VG	F	VF	XF	Unc
ND(1654)	3,649	4,000	7,900	18,500	—	—
1656	2,184	4,000	7,900	18,500	—	—
1657 Rare	1,466	—	—	—	—	—

KM# 220 DUCAT

3.4386 g., 0.9720 Gold 0.1075 oz. AGW **Obv:** Modified bust and legend **Note:** Fr. #36.

Date	Mintage	VG	F	VF	XF	Unc
1658	2,664	5,000	7,900	18,500	—	—

Note: Swiss Bank/Spink & Son Zurich Coins of Sweden sale Part I 12-89 nearly XF realized $20,800

Date	Mintage	VG	F	VF	XF	Unc
1660 Rare	423	—	—	—	—	—

KM# 238 DUCAT

3.4386 g., 0.9720 Gold 0.1075 oz. AGW **Obv:** Laureate bust of Carl XI right **Note:** Fr. #40.

Date	Mintage	VG	F	VF	XF	Unc
1662/0 GW Rare	4,255	—	—	—	—	—
1662 GW Rare	Inc. above	—	—	—	—	—

Note: Swiss Bank/Spink & Son Zurich Coins of Sweden sale Part I 12-89 GVF realized $12,600

KM# 246 DUCAT

3.4813 g., 0.9720 Gold 0.1088 oz. AGW **Obv:** Laureate bust of Carl XI left **Note:** Fr. #41.

Date	Mintage	VG	F	VF	XF	Unc
1664	380	2,300	4,250	9,200	—	—
1665 Rare	4,293	—	—	—	—	—

KM# 256 DUCAT

3.4813 g., 0.9720 Gold 0.1088 oz. AGW **Obv:** Finer style bust of Carl XI left **Rev:** Crowned cruciform arms with entwined C's at bottom **Note:** Varieties exist. Fr. #42.

Date	Mintage	VG	F	VF	XF	Unc
1666	4,222	1,850	3,400	11,000	—	—

Date	Mintage	VG	F	VF	XF	Unc
1667	—	1,400	2,650	11,000	—	—
1668	4,484	1,250	2,400	9,000	—	—

KM# 263 DUCAT
3.4813 g., 0.9720 Gold 0.1088 oz. AGW **Obv:** Laureate head of Carl XI left **Note:** Varieties exist. Fr. #42.

Date	Mintage	VG	F	VF	XF	Unc
1668 Rare	—	—	—	—	—	—
1669	6,395	1,000	2,050	7,000	—	—
1670	4,649	1,250	2,450	9,000	—	—

KM# 277 DUCAT
3.4813 g., 0.9720 Gold 0.1088 oz. AGW **Note:** Varieties exist. Fr. #43.

Date	Mintage	VG	F	VF	XF	Unc
1671 Rare	3,861	—	—	—	—	—
1672	5,058	1,600	3,050	5,900	12,000	—
1673	Inc. above	1,300	2,400	4,500	9,000	—
1674 Rare	16,000	—	—	—	—	—
1675	Inc. above	1,300	2,400	4,500	9,000	—
ND(1675)	Inc. above	1,300	2,400	4,500	9,000	—
1676	Inc. above	1,300	2,400	4,500	9,000	—

KM# 281 DUCAT
3.4813 g., 0.9720 Gold 0.1088 oz. AGW **Obv:** Armored bust of Carl XI left **Rev:** Crowned double C monogram, three crowns in field **Note:** Varieties exist. Fr. #44.

Date	Mintage	VG	F	VF	XF	Unc
1676	—	1,250	2,450	5,000	10,000	—
1677	14,000	1,250	2,450	5,000	10,000	—

KM# 283 DUCAT
3.4813 g., 0.9720 Gold 0.1088 oz. AGW **Obv:** Draped bust of Carl XI right **Note:** Varieties exist. Fr. #45.

Date	Mintage	VG	F	VF	XF	Unc
1677	Inc. above	1,050	2,350	4,400	7,700	—
1678	9,001	925	2,150	3,850	6,700	—
1679	16,000	925	2,150	3,850	6,700	—
1680	13,000	925	2,150	3,850	6,700	—
1681	12,000	925	2,150	3,850	6,700	—
1682 Rare	2,617	—	—	—	—	—
1683	11,000	925	2,150	3,850	6,700	—
1684 Rare	3,943	—	—	—	—	—
1685	12,000	925	2,150	3,850	6,700	—
1686	6,312	1,550	2,900	5,100	4,600	—
1687	9,473	1,550	2,900	5,100	4,600	—
1688 Rare	5,513	—	—	—	—	—
1689	3,809	925	2,350	3,850	6,700	—
1690	—	925	2,350	4,400	7,700	—
1691	5,897	925	2,350	4,400	7,700	—
1692	2,385	925	2,350	4,400	7,700	—
1694	3,755	925	2,350	4,400	7,700	—
1695	1,683	925	2,350	4,400	7,700	—

KM# 318 DUCAT
3.5000 g., 0.9760 Gold 0.1098 oz. AGW **Ruler:** Carl XII **Obv:** Draped bust right **Obv. Legend:** CAROLVS • XII • D • G • REX • ... **Rev:** Crowned double C monogram, date below **Note:** Fr. #49.

Date	Mintage	VG	F	VF	XF	Unc
1697	4,781	1,250	2,500	6,600	13,000	—
1699	6,152	1,000	1,900	3,650	7,800	—
1700	5,840	1,250	2,500	6,600	13,000	—

KM# 239 3 DUCAT
10.3158 g., 0.9760 Gold 0.3237 oz. AGW **Obv:** Laureate bust of Carl XI left **Rev:** Three crowns divide date **Note:** Fr. #39.

Date	Mintage	VG	F	VF	XF	Unc
1662 GW Unique	—	—	—	—	—	—

KM# 100 5 DUCAT
17.5000 g., 0.9760 Gold 0.5491 oz. AGW **Obv:** Half-figure of Gustaf II Adolf right in inner circle, radiant "Jehovah" at top **Rev:** Crowned arms with lion supporters, date below in inner circle **Note:** Fr. #30.

Date	Mintage	VG	F	VF	XF	Unc
1620 Rare	—	—	—	—	—	—

KM# A195 5 DUCAT
17.5000 g., 0.9760 Gold 0.5491 oz. AGW, 39 mm. **Ruler:** Christina **Obv:** Bust of Christina right **Obv. Legend:** CHRISTINA • D : G • SVE • GOT •... **Rev:** Crowned supported five-fold arms **Mint:** Stockholm **Note:** Fr. #34.

Date	Mintage	VG	F	VF	XF	Unc
1649 Unique	—	—	—	—	—	—

KM# A21 6 DUCAT
20.6316 g., 0.9760 Gold 0.6474 oz. AGW, 50 mm. **Ruler:** Carl IX, Regent **Obv:** Laureate Carl IX standing facing left holding sword and orb, crown on table at right **Rev:** Crowned five-fold arms surrounded by two rows of shields **Mint:** Stockholm **Note:** Fr. #16.

Date	Mintage	VG	F	VF	XF	Unc
1606 Unique	—	—	—	—	—	—

KM# A28 6 DUCAT
20.6316 g., 0.9760 Gold 0.6474 oz. AGW, 51 mm. **Ruler:** Carl IX, Regent **Obv:** Crowned Carl IX standing facing left holding sword and orb **Rev:** Crowned five-fold arms surrounded by two rows of shields **Mint:** Stockholm **Note:** Fr. #16.

Date	Mintage	VG	F	VF	XF	Unc
1607 Unique	—	—	—	—	—	—

KM# 40 6 DUCAT
20.6316 g., 0.9760 Gold 0.6474 oz. AGW, 46 mm. **Ruler:** Carl IX, Regent **Obv:** Half-length figure of Carl IX holding sword and shield in inner circle **Rev:** Lion shield surrounded by three crowns **Mint:** Stockholm **Note:** Fr. #17.

Date	Mintage	VG	F	VF	XF	Unc
1608 Rare	—	—	—	—	—	—

KM# 41 6 DUCAT
20.6316 g., 0.9760 Gold 0.6474 oz. AGW, 43 mm. **Ruler:** Carl IX **Obv:** Hebrew "Jehovah" above crowned half-length figure of Carl IX holding sword and shield (no inner circle) **Rev:** Lion shield surrounded by three crowns **Mint:** Stockholm **Note:** Fr. #17.

Date	Mintage	VG	F	VF	XF	Unc
1609 Rare	—	—	—	—	—	—

KM# 93 6 DUCAT
20.6316 g., 0.9760 Gold 0.6474 oz. AGW, 50 mm. **Ruler:** Carl IX **Obv:** Hebrew "Jehovah" above uncrowned Gustaf II Adolf standing facing left holding sword, crown, and orb **Rev:** Crowned five-fold arms surrounded by two rows of shields **Mint:** Stockholm **Note:** Fr. #27.

Date	Mintage	VG	F	VF	XF	Unc
1617 Rare	—	—	—	—	—	—

KM# 94 10 DUCAT
35.0000 g., 0.9760 Gold 1.0982 oz. AGW, 52 mm. **Ruler:** Carl IX **Obv:** Hebrew "Jehovah" above uncrowned Gustaf II Adolf standing facing left holding sword and orb, crown on table at right **Rev:** Crowned five-fold arms surrounded by two rows of shields **Mint:** Stockholm **Note:** Fr. #26.

Date	Mintage	VG	F	VF	XF	Unc
1617 Unique	—	—	—	—	—	—

KM# 95 10 DUCAT
35.0000 g., 0.9760 Gold 1.0982 oz. AGW, 53 mm. **Ruler:** Carl IX **Obv:** Hebrew "Jehovah" above crowned Gustaf II Adolf standing facing left holding sword and orb **Rev:** Crowned five-fold arms surrounded by two rows of shields **Mint:** Stockholm **Note:** Fr. #26.

Date	Mintage	VG	F	VF	XF	Unc
ND(ca.1618) Unique	—	—	—	—	—	—

KM# A219 10 DUCAT
35.0000 g., 0.9760 Gold 1.0982 oz. AGW, 43 mm. **Ruler:** Carl X Gustavus **Obv:** Bust of Carl X Gustaf left **Obv. Legend:** CAROLUS•GUSTAVUS•DECIMUS•D:G:REX•SVECORUM **Rev:** Crowned supported arms **Mint:** Stockholm **Note:** Fr. #35.

Date	Mintage	VG	F	VF	XF	Unc
MDCLIV (1654) Unique	—	—	—	—	—	—

KM# 96 12 DUCAT
42.0000 g., 0.9760 Gold 1.3179 oz. AGW, 52 mm. **Obv:** Hebrew "Jehovah" above uncrowned Gustaf II Adolf standing facing left holding sword and orb, crown on table at right **Rev:** Crowned five-fold arms surrounded by two rows of shields **Mint:** Stockholm **Note:** Fr. #25.

Date	Mintage	VG	F	VF	XF	Unc
ND(ca.1618) Unique	—	—	—	—	—	—

PATTERNS

Including off metal strikes

KM#	Date	Mintage	Identification	Mkt Val
Pn1	1606	—	3 Penningar. Silver.	—
Pn2	16Z5	—	Fyrk. Copper. Klippe.	—
Pn3	(16)Z5	—	1/2 Ore. Copper. Klippe.	—
Pn4	16Z5	—	Ore. Copper. Klippe.	2,000
Pn5	16Z5	—	Ore. Copper. Round planchet.	—
Pn6	16Z9	—	1/2 Ore. Copper. Struck at Nyköping Mint.	750
Pn7	16Z9	—	Ore. Copper. Struck at Sater Mint. Large crowns.	500
Pn8	16Z9	—	Ore. Copper. Small crowns.	750
Pn9	1648	—	Ore. Copper. Date in Roman numerals.	750
Pn10	ND(1660)	—	4 Ore. Silver. Large bust. Struck at Stockholm Mint.	500
Pn11	ND(1660)	—	4 Ore. Silver. Small bust. Struck at Stockholm Mint.	—
Pn12	1665	—	1/2 Ore. Silver. Struck at Stockholm Mint.	—
Pn13	1681	—	4 Mark. Copper. Struck at Stockholm Mint.	—

KRISTIANSTAD

(Christianstad)

Situated in the southwest of Sweden, Kristianstad is a sea port and trade center. Founded in 1614 by Denmark's Christia IV, it was ceded to Sweden in 1658. The Danes occupied th region briefly from 1676 to 1678.

DANISH OCCUPATION

SIEGE COINAGE

KM# 5 2 SKILLING
Copper **Obv:** Crowned C5 monogram in circle **Rev:** Crown above value, date below

Date	Mintage	VG	F	VF	XF	Ur
1677 Rare	—	—	—	—	—	-

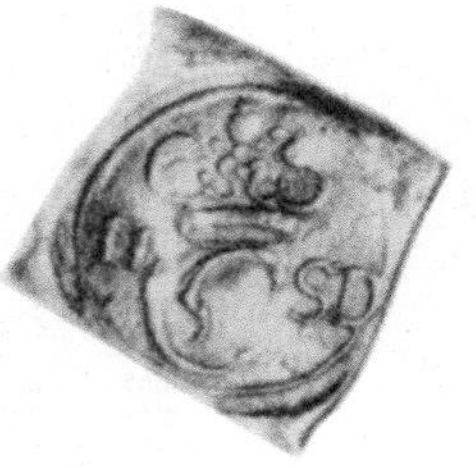

KM# 6 2 SKILLING
Copper **Obv:** Value flanking crowned monogram

Date	Mintage	VG	F	VF	XF	U
ND(1677-78)	—	375	650	1,150	—	-

KM# 7 4 SKILLING
Copper **Obv:** Value flanking crowned C5 monogram **Note:** Uniface.

Date	Mintage	VG	F	VF	XF	U
ND(1677-78)	—	450	750	1,250	—	-

KM# 8 8 SKILLING
Copper **Note:** Uniface.

Date	Mintage	VG	F	VF	XF	U
ND(1677-78)	—	350	600	1,000	—	-

KM# 9 MARK
Copper **Obv:** Value flanking crowned C5 monogram **Note:** Uniface.

Date	Mintage	VG	F	VF	XF	U
ND(1677-78) Rare	—	—	—	—	—	

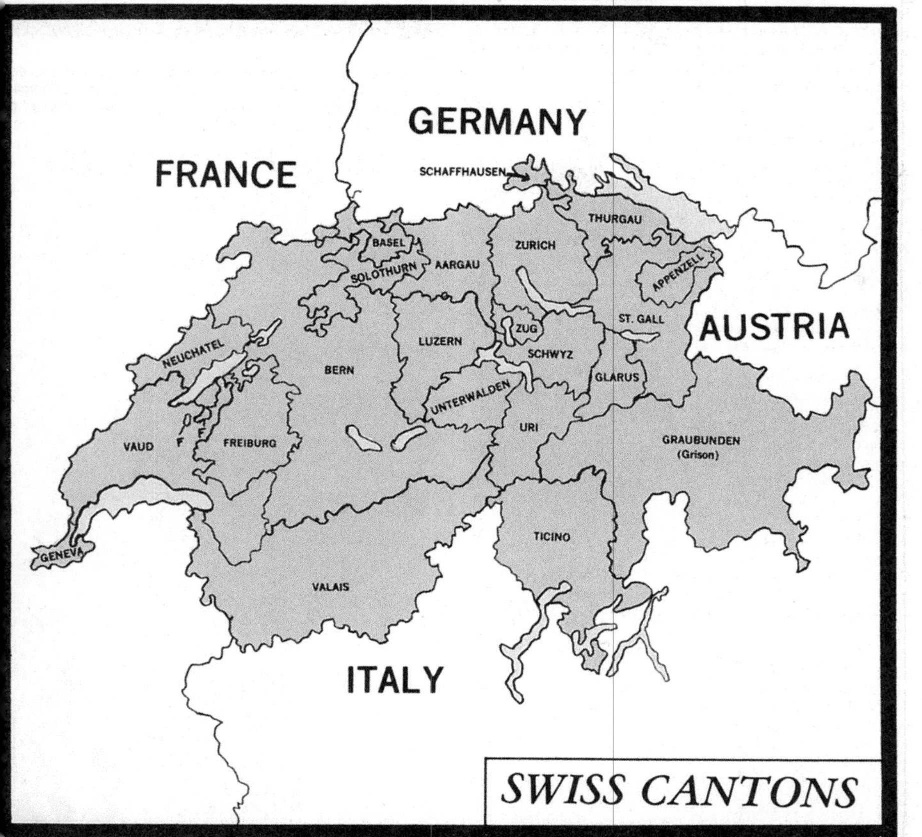

In Switzerland, canton is the name given to each of the 23 ates comprising the Swiss Federation. The origin of the cantons rooted in the liberty-loving instincts of the peasants of Helvetia.

After the Romans departed Switzerland to defend Rome jainst the barbarians, Switzerland became, in the Middle Ages, federation of fiefs of the Holy Roman Empire. In 888 it was again nited by Rudolf of Burgundy, a minor despot, and for 150 years witzerland had a king. Upon the death of the last Burgundian ng, the kingdom crumbled into a loose collection of feudal fiefs led by bishops and ducal families who made their own laws and vied their own taxes. Eventually this division of rule by arbitrary espots became more than the freedom-loving and resourceful easants could bear. The citizens living in the remote valleys of ri, Schwyz (from which Switzerland received its name) and nterwalden decided to liberate themselves from all feudal obli- ations and become free.

On Aug. 1, 1291, the elders of these three small states met n a tiny heath known as the Rutli on the shores of the Lake of ucerne and negotiated an eternal pact' which recognized their ght to local self-government, and pledged one another assis- nce against any encroachment upon these rights. The pact was e beginning of the Everlasting League' and the foundation of the wiss Confederation.

BASEL

A bishopric in northwest Switzerland, founded in the 5th cen- ry. The first coinage was c.1000AD. During the Reformation asel became Protestant and the bishop resided henceforth in e town of Porrentruy. The Congress of Vienna gave the ter- ories of the Bishopric to Bern. Today they form the Canton Jura d the French speaking part of Bern.

ULERS

hann Franz von Schonau, 1651-1656

hann Conrad von Roggenbach, 1656-1693

ONETARY SYSTEM

Kreuzer = 1 Batzen

BISHOPRIC

STANDARD COINAGE

M# 8 RAPPEN (Vierer)

llon **Obv:** Round arms **Obv. Legend:** WILHEL. EPISCO. ASILIENSIS. **Rev:** Cruciform in inner circle, date **Rev. Legend:** RMA. NOMEN. DOMINI. **Note:** Uniface.

te	Mintage	VG	F	VF	XF	Unc
22 Rare	—	—	—	—	—	—

M# 11 RAPPEN (Vierer)

llon **Obv:** Arms on shield, date **Obv. Legend:** WILHEL: EPS: ASI: **Rev:** Cruciform of flowers **Rev. Legend:** FIRMA: MEV: OM: DNI.

Date	Mintage	VG	F	VF	XF	Unc
1623	—	75.00	200	750	—	—
1624	—	125	300	1,000	2,500	—

KM# 13 BATZEN

Billon **Obv:** Four-fold arms in cartouche, 1 in circle above **Rev:** Standing Madonna and child

Date	Mintage	VG	F	VF	XF	Unc
1624	—	400	1,000	25,000	—	—

KM# 17 BATZEN

Billon **Obv:** Four-fold arms on shield, 1 in oval above

Date	Mintage	VG	F	VF	XF	Unc
1654	—	100	250	1,000	—	—
1655	—	100	250	1,000	—	—

KM# 21 BATZEN

Billon **Rev:** Half-length standing Madonna and child

Date	Mintage	VG	F	VF	XF	Unc
1655	—	50.00	150	600	—	—
1657	—	65.00	250	1,000	—	—
1658	—	65.00	250	1,000	—	—
1659	—	45.00	100	400	—	—
1660	—	45.00	100	400	—	—
1661	—	45.00	100	400	—	—
1662	—	45.00	100	400	—	—
1663	—	45.00	100	400	—	—

KM# 7 2 BATZEN

Billon **Obv:** Four-fold arms in cartouche, Z in circle above **Rev:** Madonna standing, facing with child

Date	Mintage	VG	F	VF	XF	Unc
1621 Rare	—	—	—	—	—	—
1624	—	200	500	1,200	—	—
1625	—	200	500	1,200	—	—

KM# 18 2 BATZEN

Billon **Obv:** Four-fold arms in ornate cartouche, 2 in oval above

Date	Mintage	VG	F	VF	XF	Unc
1654 Rare	—	—	—	—	—	—

KM# 9 1/2 SCHILLING

Billon **Obv:** Two-fold arms in cartouche **Rev:** Saint standing holding a book and flower

Date	Mintage	VG	F	VF	XF	Unc
1622	—	75.00	200	750	—	—

KM# 10 SCHILLING

Billon **Obv:** Four-fold arms **Rev:** Saint standing holding a book and flower

Date	Mintage	VG	F	VF	XF	Unc
1622	—	75.00	200	750	—	—
1623	—	25.00	50.00	200	—	—
1624	—	25.00	50.00	200	—	—

KM# 12 1/4 THALER

Silver **Obv:** Four-fold arms in cartouche **Rev:** Crowned imperial eagle

Date	Mintage	VG	F	VF	XF	Unc
1623	—	3,000	8,000	20,000	—	—

KM# 15 1/2 THALER

Silver **Obv:** Four-fold arms in front of Kaiser Heinrich II **Rev:** Crowned imperial eagle

Date	Mintage	VG	F	VF	XF	Unc
1625 Rare	—	—	—	—	—	—

KM# 14 THALER

Silver **Obv:** Four-fold arms in front of Kaiser Heinrich II **Rev:** Crowned imperial eagle **Note:** Dav. #4657.

Date	Mintage	VG	F	VF	XF	Unc
1624 Rare	—	—	—	—	—	—
1625	—	1,800	3,000	15,000	—	—

KM# 19 THALER

Silver **Obv:** Different four-fold arms **Rev:** Larger eagle **Note:** Dav. #4658.

Date	Mintage	VG	F	VF	XF	Unc
1654	—	2,000	4,000	10,000	20,000	—

KM# 16 2 THALER

Silver **Note:** Dav. #4656. Similar to 1 Thaler, KM#14.

Date	Mintage	VG	F	VF	XF	Unc
1624	—	—	—	—	—	—
1625	—	—	—	—	—	—

KM# A17 2 THALER

Silver **Note:** Klippe.

Date	Mintage	VG	F	VF	XF	Unc
1625	—	—	—	—	—	—

TRADE COINAGE

KM# 20 DUCAT

3.5000 g., 0.9860 Gold 0.1109 oz. AGW **Obv:** Inscription in shield, date divided below **Obv. Inscription:** IOHA / FRAN • D: G / EPIS • BASI / LIEN / SIS **Rev:** St. Heinrich standing with church and scepter in inner circle **Note:** Fr. #88.

Date	Mintage	VG	F	VF	XF	Unc
1654 Rare	—	—	—	—	—	—

KM# 22 DUCAT

3.5000 g., 0.9860 Gold 0.1109 oz. AGW **Obv:** Inscription in shield **Note:** Fr. #89.

Date	Mintage	VG	F	VF	XF	Unc
1659	—	7,000	15,000	40,000	—	—
1662	—	7,000	15,000	40,000	—	—

KM# B17 3 DUCAT

10.5000 g., 0.9860 Gold 0.3328 oz. AGW **Obv:** Four-fold arms in front of Kaiser Heinrich II **Rev:** Crowned imperial eagle **Note:** Struck with 1/2 Thaler dies, KM#15.

Date	Mintage	VG	F	VF	XF	Unc
1625 Rare	—	—	—	—	—	—

CITY

A city in northwest Switzerland, it was founded in 374 by the Roman Emperor Valentinian. It became a Burgundian Mint in the 10th century and obtained the mint right in 1373. It was admitted to the Swiss Confederation in 1501. Developed into a canton.

MONETARY SYSTEM

Until 1798

8 Rappen = 1 Batzen

30 Batzen = 2 Gulden = 1 Thaler

Dicken = 24 Kreuzer

STANDARD COINAGE

KM# 5 STEBLER

Billon, 12.8 mm. **Obv:** Arms on shield, low relief in circle of dots **Note:** Uniface.

Date	Mintage	VG	F	VF	XF	Unc
ND Rare	—	—	—	—	—	—

KM# 6 STEBLER

Billon, 17 mm. **Obv:** Arms on shield, high relief in circle of dots **Note:** Uniface.

Date	Mintage	VG	F	VF	XF	Unc
ND	—	20.00	50.00	200	500	—

KM# 55 STEBLER

Billon **Obv:** Arms on shield, small ornaments on top and sides in inner circle, small pearls at edge **Note:** Uniface.

Date	Mintage	VG	F	VF	XF	Unc
ND	—	25.00	40.00	170	450	—

KM# 57 RAPPEN (Vierer)

Billon **Obv:** Arms on shield within circle **Obv. Legend:** MONETA NO BASILIE **Rev:** Floreate cross within circle **Rev. Legend:** DA PACEM DOMINE

Date	Mintage	VG	F	VF	XF	Unc
ND	—	10.00	20.00	50.00	150	—

KM# 110 ASSIS

Billon **Obv:** Shield **Obv. Legend:** MONETA • NOVA • BASILEENSIS **Rev:** Value, date in center **Rev. Legend:** DOMINE • CONSERVA • NOS • IN • PACE

Date	Mintage	VG	F	VF	XF	Unc
1663	—	5.00	9.00	60.00	120	200
1695	—	5.00	9.00	60.00	120	200
1697	—	5.00	9.00	60.00	120	200
1698	—	5.00	9.00	60.00	120	200

KM# 74 2 ASSIS

Billon **Note:** Similar to 1 Assis KM#135.

Date	Mintage	VG	F	VF	XF	Unc
ND	—	9.00	25.00	100	—	—
1623	—	9.00	25.00	100	—	—
1624	—	9.00	25.00	1,000	—	—
1634	—	50.00	250	1,000	—	—
1638	—	50.00	250	1,000	—	—

KM# A75 2 ASSIS

Billon **Note:** Klippe.

Date	Mintage	VG	F	VF	XF	Unc
1624	—	—	—	—	—	—

KM# 74a 2 ASSIS

Billon **Obv:** Shield **Obv. Legend:** MONETA • NOVA • BASILEENSIS **Rev:** Value, date in center **Rev. Legend:** DOMINE • CONSERVA • NOS • IN • PACE **Note:** Klippe.

Date	Mintage	VG	F	VF	XF	Unc
1624	—	—	—	—	—	—

KM# 58 10 KREUZER (1/6 Thaler)

Silver **Obv:** Arms on shield, ornamentation in field within inner circle, legend around **Rev:** Crowned imperial eagle with 10 on breast

Date	Mintage	VG	F	VF	XF	Unc
1606 Rare	—	—	—	—	—	—

KM# 61 12 KREUZER (Zwolfer)

Silver **Obv:** Arms on shield, flourishes in field within circle, legend around **Rev:** Crowned imperial eagle within inner circle, 12 in circle on breast

Date	Mintage	VG	F	VF	XF	Unc
ND	—	150	400	1,000	2,000	—
1621	—	100	250	600	1,200	—

KM# 63 12 KREUZER (Zwolfer)

Silver **Obv:** Arms on ornate shield within inner circle

Date	Mintage	VG	F	VF	XF	Unc
ND Rare	—	—	—	—	—	—

KM# 75 12 KREUZER (Zwolfer)

Silver

Date	Mintage	VG	F	VF	XF	Unc
1622	—	200	550	1,000	1,500	—

KM# 77 12 KREUZER (Zwolfer)

Silver **Obv:** Date in legend at top

Date	Mintage	VG	F	VF	XF	Unc
1622	—	250	600	1,500	3,000	—

KM# 76 12 KREUZER (Zwolfer)

Silver **Note:** Additional ornamentation in fields within circles.

Date	Mintage	VG	F	VF	XF	Unc
1622	—	250	600	1,500	3,000	—

KM# 62 12 KREUZER (Zwolfer)

Silver **Note:** Klippe.

Date	Mintage	VG	F	VF	XF	Unc
ND Rare	—	—	—	—	—	—

KM# 81 12 KREUZER (Zwolfer)

Silver

Date	Mintage	VG	F	VF	XF	Unc
1623	—	60.00	150	350	600	—

KM# 59 60 KREUZER (Guldenthaler)

Silver **Obv:** Arms on shield divide ornamentations, date divided on sides **Obv. Legend:** ✠ MONETA • NOVA • VRBIS • BASILIENSIS **Rev:** Crowned imperial eagle with 60 in orb on breast **Rev. Legend:** ✠ DOMINE • CONSERVA • NOS • IN • PACE **Note:** Dav. #159.

Date	Mintage	VG	F	VF	XF	Unc
1616 Rare	—	2,200	5,000	12,000	25,000	—

KM# 64 DICKEN

Silver **Note:** Klippe. Similar to KM#82.

Date	Mintage	VG	F	VF	XF	Unc
1621 Rare	—	—	—	—	—	—

KM# 82 DICKEN

Silver

Date	Mintage	VG	F	VF	XF	Unc
1623	—	60.00	200	500	1,000	—
1632	—	60.00	200	500	1,000	—
1633	—	25.00	60.00	150	1,000	—
1634	—	25.00	60.00	150	300	—
1635	—	25.00	60.00	150	300	—
1636	—	25.00	60.00	150	300	—

KM# 88 DICKEN

Silver **Obv:** Arms dividing date in cartouche **Rev:** Eagle facing left with 1/4 on breast in circle

Date	Mintage	VG	F	VF	XF	Unc
1640	—	125	300	750	1,500	—

KM# 65 1/2 THALER

Silver **Obv:** Arms divide date in inner circle **Rev:** Eagle facing left in inner circle

Date	Mintage	VG	F	VF	XF	Unc
1621 Rare	—	—	—	—	—	—

KM# 83 1/2 THALER

Silver

Date	Mintage	VG	F	VF	XF	Unc
1623	—	125	300	750	1,500	—
1624	—	150	350	900	1,800	—
1638	—	125	300	750	1,500	—
1639	—	150	350	900	1,800	—

KM# 89 1/2 THALER

Silver

Date	Mintage	VG	F	VF	XF	Unc
1640	—	100	200	500	1,000	—

KM# 90 1/2 THALER

Silver **Obv:** MONET: /NOVA/REIPVBL:/BASIL: within ornamentation **Rev:** Arms within round cartouche, legend around

Date	Mintage	VG	F	VF	XF	Unc
ND	—	175	400	1,000	2,000	—

KM# 123 1/2 THALER

Silver

Date	Mintage	VG	F	VF	XF	Unc
ND	—	75.00	200	400	900	—

KM# 124 1/2 THALER

Silver

Date	Mintage	VG	F	VF	XF	Unc
ND	—	75.00	200	400	900	—

KM# A66 THALER

Silver **Obv:** Arms divide date **Rev:** Eagle left **Note:** Dav. #45

Date	Mintage	VG	F	VF	XF	Unc
16Z1	—	60.00	150	400	750	—

KM# 66 THALER

Silver **Obv:** Arms divide date, border of arcs within inner circle **Rev:** Eagle left within inner circle **Note:** Dav. #4601.

Date	Mintage	VG	F	VF	XF	Unc
1621	—	250	600	1,500	3,000	—

KM# 68 THALER

Silver **Note:** Klippe.

Date	Mintage	VG	F	VF	XF	Unc
16Z1 Rare	—	—	—	—	—	

KM# 80 THALER

Silver **Note:** Klippe.

Date	Mintage	VG	F	VF	XF	Unc
16ZZ	—	—	—	—	—	
16ZZ Rare	—	—	—	—	—	

KM# 67 THALER

Silver **Obv:** Arms supported by two basilisks, date in legend **Note:** Dav. #4603.

Date	Mintage	VG	F	VF	XF	Unc
16ZZ	—	65.00	150	400	750	

KM# 79.1 THALER

Silver **Obv:** Arms in quatrefoil, four inward lis at angles **Obv. Legend:** + MONETA + NOVA + VRBIS + BASILIEN(SIS) **Rev:** Eagle left **Rev. Legend:** (Flower bud) DOMINE + CONSERVA + NOS + IN + PACE **Edge:** Plain **Note:** Dav. #4604.

Date	Mintage	VG	F	VF	XF	Unc
16ZZ	—	50.00	125	300	600	
1623	—	45.00	100	250	575	

KM# 79.2 THALER

ilver **Obv:** Arms in quatrefoil, four inward lis at angles **Obv. egend:** + MONETA + NOVA + VRBIS + BASILIENSIS **Rev:** agle left **Rev. Legend:** (Flower bud) DOMINE + CONSERVA NOS + IN + PACE **Edge:** Plain **Note:** Dav. #4604.

ate	Mintage	VG	F	VF	XF	Unc
623	—	50.00	100	250	500	—
624	—	50.00	125	300	600	—
638	—	250	6,000	1,500	3,000	—
639	—	100	200	500	1,200	—

M# 84 THALER

ilver **Obv:** Eagle head right **Note:** Dav. #4605.

ate	Mintage	VG	F	VF	XF	Unc
624	—	65.00	150	400	750	—

M# A94 THALER

3.4200 g., Silver **Obv:** Arms in thick ornamental frame, cherub's ead at top with full wings **Obv. Legend:** MONETA * NOVA * RBIS * BASILIENSIS **Rev:** Eagle left **Rev. Legend:** DOMINE CONSERVA * NOS * IN * PACE **Edge:** Plain **Note:** Dav. #4606.

ate	Mintage	VG	F	VF	XF	Unc
640	—	60.00	150	400	800	—

M# B94.1 THALER

ilver **Obv:** Arms in thin ornamental frame, cherub's head at p, wings fold downward **Obv. Legend:** MONETA * NOVA * RBIS * BASILIENSIS **Rev:** Eagle left **Rev. Legend:** DOMINE CONSERVA * NOS * IN * PACE **Edge:** Plain **Note:** Dav. #4607.

ate	Mintage	VG	F	VF	XF	Unc
640	—	60.00	150	400	750	—

M# 94 THALER

lver **Obv:** Arms in thick ornamental frame, cherub's head at p, wings drawn upwards **Obv. Legend:** MONETA * NOVA * RBIS * BASILEESIS **Rev:** Eagle left **Rev. Legend:** DOMINE * ONSERVA * NOS * IN * PACE **Edge:** Plain **Note:** Dav. #4608.

te	Mintage	VG	F	VF	XF	Unc
40	—	125	300	750	1,500	—

M# B94.2 THALER

lver **Obv:** Similar to KM#B94.1 **Obv. Legend:** MONETA * OVA * VRBIS * BASILIENSIS **Rev:** Similar to KM#B94.1 **Rev. egend:** DOMINE * CONSERVA * NOS * IN * PACE **Edge:** Plain ote: Dav. #4609.

te	Mintage	VG	F	VF	XF	Unc
40	—	125	300	750	1,500	—

M# B94.3 THALER

lver **Obv:** Similar to KM#B94.1 **Obv. Legend:** MONETA * OVA * VRBIS * BASILIEESIS **Rev:** Similar to KM#B94.1 **Rev. egend:** DOMINE * CONSERVA * NOS * IN * PACE **Edge:** Plain ote: Dav. #4610.

te	Mintage	VG	F	VF	XF	Unc
40	—	125	300	750	1,500	—

M# A95 THALER

lver **Obv:** Arms at center surrounded by eight shields **Obv. egend:** MONETA + NOVA + VRBIS + BASILENSIS **Rev:** perial eagle **Rev. Legend:** DOMINE + CONSERVA + NOS + + PACE **Edge:** Plain

te	Mintage	VG	F	VF	XF	Unc
(1640)	—	175	350	600	850	—

KM# 127 THALER

Silver **Obv:** City view below banner **Rev:** Arms of Basel with dragon supporters **Rev. Legend:** DOMINE • CONSERVA • NOS • IN • PACE **Note:** Dav. #1744.

Date	Mintage	VG	F	VF	XF	Unc
ND	—	160	315	525	1,000	—

KM# 128 THALER

Silver **Obv:** BASILEA above city view **Rev:** Winged dragon with arms of Basel at lower left **Rev. Legend:** DOMINE • CONSERVA • NOS • IN • PACE **Note:** Dav. #1747.

Date	Mintage	VG	F	VF	XF	Unc
ND	—	125	300	750	1,500	2,100

KM# 129 THALER

Silver **Obv:** BASILEA in cartouche above city view **Rev:** Winged dragon with arms of Basel in center of assorted shields at lower left **Rev. Legend:** DOMINE • CONSERVA • NOS • IN • PACE **Note:** Dav. #1743.

Date	Mintage	VG	F	VF	XF	Unc
ND	—	125	300	750	1,500	2,100

KM# 111 THALER

Silver **Obv:** Ornate cartouche around legend, date divided at bottom **Obv. Legend:** MONETA. NOVA/REIPVBLICAE/BASILIENSIS **Rev:** Basilisk left holding pointed shield with arms **Note:** Dav. #4612.

Date	Mintage	VG	F	VF	XF	Unc
1668 Rare	—	—	—	—	—	—

KM# 112 THALER

Silver **Obv:** Date not divided at bottom **Rev:** Arms in ornate circle **Note:** Dav. #4613.

Date	Mintage	VG	F	VF	XF	Unc
1669	—	150	350	900	1,800	—
1676	—	250	600	1,500	—	—

KM# 118 THALER

Silver **Obv:** Date divided at bottom **Rev:** Arms in ornate cartouche, basilisks at both sides **Note:** Dav. #4614.

Date	Mintage	VG	F	VF	XF	Unc
1694	—	175	400	1,000	2,000	—

KM# A69 1-1/2 THALER

Silver **Obv:** Arms supported by two basillisks **Obv. Legend:** + MONETA + NOVA + VRBIS + BASILIEN : **Rev:** Eagle left **Rev. Legend:** + DOMINE + CONSERVA + NOS + IN + PACE **Edge:** Plain **Note:** Dav. #A4603. Klippe.

Date	Mintage	VG	F	VF	XF	Unc
1621 Rare	—	—	—	—	—	—

KM# A71 1-1/2 THALER

Silver **Note:** Dav. #A4603. Similar to 1 Thaler, KM#67.

Date	Mintage	VG	F	VF	XF	Unc
16Z1 Rare	—	—	—	—	—	—
16Z1 Rare	—	—	—	—	—	—
16ZZ Rare	—	—	—	—	—	—

KM# 70 2 THALER

Silver **Obv:** Arms divide date, border of arcs within inner circle **Note:** Dav. #4600.

Date	Mintage	VG	F	VF	XF	Unc
1621 Rare	—	3,000	8,000	20,000	40,000	—

KM# 69 2 THALER

Silver **Obv:** Two basilisks leaning on shield with arms in inner circle **Rev:** Eagle left in inner circle **Note:** Dav. #4602.

Date	Mintage	VG	F	VF	XF	Unc
1621 Rare	—	2,500	7,000	18,000	36,000	—

KM# 78 2 THALER

Silver **Obv:** 2 basilisks leaning over small shield with arms **Rev:** Large, full eagle **Note:** Dav. #4602.

Date	Mintage	VG	F	VF	XF	Unc
1621	—	250	500	1,500	2,500	—

TRADE COINAGE

KM# 95 1/2 GOLDGULDEN

3.8200 g., 0.9000 Gold 0.1105 oz. AGW **Obv:** Basilisk right holding shield **Rev:** Similar to 1 Goldgulden, KM#132

Date	Mintage	VG	F	VF	XF	Unc
ND(1640)	—	225	500	1,000	1,500	2,200

KM# 73 GOLDGULDEN

7.6400 g., 0.9000 Gold 0.2211 oz. AGW **Note:** Varieties exist. Fr. #21.

Date	Mintage	VG	F	VF	XF	Unc
1621	—	800	1,750	3,500	6,000	—
1622	—	800	1,750	3,500	6,000	—
1623	—	2,000	4,500	9,000	15,000	—

KM# 100 GOLDGULDEN

7.6400 g., 0.9000 Gold 0.2211 oz. AGW **Note:** Fr. 25a.

Date	Mintage	VG	F	VF	XF	Unc
ND(1640) Rare	—	—	—	—	—	—

KM# 96 GOLDGULDEN

7.6400 g., 0.9000 Gold 0.2211 oz. AGW **Obv:** Similar to KM#100 **Rev:** Eagle right

Date	Mintage	VG	F	VF	XF	Unc
ND(1640) Rare	—	—	—	—	—	—

KM# 99 GOLDGULDEN

7.6400 g., 0.9000 Gold 0.2211 oz. AGW

Date	Mintage	VG	F	VF	XF	Unc
ND(1648)	—	350	750	1,500	2,500	4,000

KM# 132 GOLDGULDEN

7.6400 g., 0.9000 Gold 0.2211 oz. AGW

Date	Mintage	VG	F	VF	XF	Unc
ND(1648)	—	500	1,000	2,200	3,500	5,000

KM# 98 2 GOLDGULDEN

15.2800 g., 0.9000 Gold 0.4421 oz. AGW

Date	Mintage	VG	F	VF	XF	Unc
ND(ca.1645)	—	1,500	3,000	5,000	8,500	12,500

KM# 109 2 GOLDGULDEN

15.2800 g., 0.9000 Gold 0.4421 oz. AGW

Date	Mintage	VG	F	VF	XF	Unc
ND(1648)	—	1,000	2,000	4,500	7,500	10,000

KM# 116 1/2 DUCAT

1.7500 g., 0.9860 Gold 0.0555 oz. AGW **Obv:** Basilisk right holding shield with arms **Rev:** Legend in cartouche **Rev. Legend:** MONETA / NOVA / REIPVB / BASILE / ENSIS

Date	Mintage	VG	F	VF	XF	Unc
ND(1680)	—	2,000	4,000	8,000	—	—

KM# 97 DUCAT

3.5000 g., 0.9860 Gold 0.1109 oz. AGW **Obv:** Oval arms in cartouche, date divided in arms **Rev:** Crowned imperial eagle

Date	Mintage	VG	F	VF	XF	Unc
1640	—	850	1,700	3,000	5,000	—

KM# 86 DUCAT

3.5000 g., 0.9860 Gold 0.1109 oz. AGW **Note:** Fr. #46.

Date	Mintage	VG	F	VF	XF	Unc
ND(1640)	—	600	1,200	2,500	4,000	—

KM# 105 DUCAT

3.5000 g., 0.9860 Gold 0.1109 oz. AGW **Obv:** Basilisk holding different shield with arms **Rev:** Legend in curved lines in smaller cartouche **Note:** Fr. #52.

Date	Mintage	VG	F	VF	XF	Unc
ND(1650)	—	400	750	1,500	2,500	—

KM# 102 DUCAT

3.5000 g., 0.9860 Gold 0.1109 oz. AGW **Obv:** Legend in tablet **Rev:** Oval arms in cartouche

Date	Mintage	VG	F	VF	XF	Unc
ND(1650) Rare	—	—	—	—	—	—

KM# 103 DUCAT

3.5000 g., 0.9860 Gold 0.1109 oz. AGW **Obv:** Basilisk right holding shield with arms **Rev:** Legend in curved line in cartouche

Date	Mintage	VG	F	VF	XF	Unc
ND(1650)	—	400	750	1,500	2,500	—

KM# 104 DUCAT

3.5000 g., 0.9860 Gold 0.1109 oz. AGW **Rev:** Legend in straight lines in cartouche

Date	Mintage	VG	F	VF	XF	Unc
ND(1650)	—	450	900	1,800	3,000	—

KM# 107 DUCAT

3.5000 g., 0.9860 Gold 0.1109 oz. AGW **Rev:** Legend in laurel wreath

Date	Mintage	VG	F	VF	XF	Unc
1653 Rare	—	—	—	—	—	—

KM# 106 DUCAT

3.5000 g., 0.9860 Gold 0.1109 oz. AGW **Obv:** Date added to legend **Note:** Fr. #51.

Date	Mintage	VG	F	VF	XF	Unc
1653	—	850	1,700	3,000	5,000	—

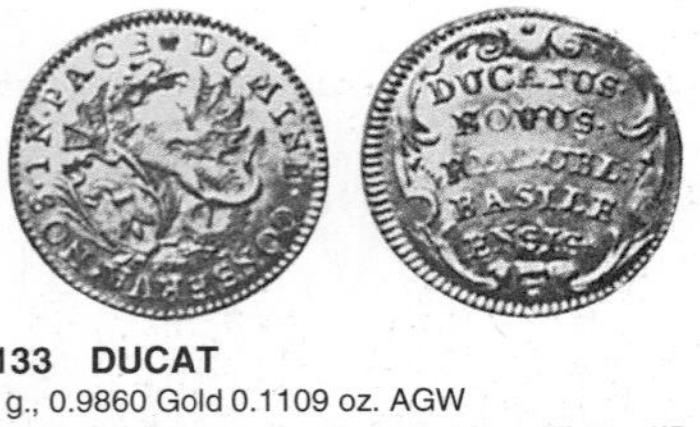

KM# 133 DUCAT

3.5000 g., 0.9860 Gold 0.1109 oz. AGW

Date	Mintage	VG	F	VF	XF	Unc
ND(ca.1700)	—	250	475	900	2,400	—

KM# 114 2 DUCAT

7.0000 g., 0.9860 Gold 0.2219 oz. AGW **Obv:** Basilisk right holding shield with arms **Rev:** Inscription in cartouche, small oval at bottom **Rev. Inscription:** MONETA / NOVA...

Date	Mintage	VG	F	VF	XF	Unc
ND(1675)	—	2,500	5,000	10,000	—	—

BERN

A city and canton in west central Switzerland. It was founded as a military post in 1191 and became an imperial city with the mint right in 1218. It was admitted to the Swiss Confederation as a canton in 1353.

MINTMASTERS' INITIALS

Initial	Date	Name
BF	1680	
D	1681-84	

MONETARY SYSTEM

Until 1798

8 Vierer = 4 Kreuzer = 1 Batzen

40 Batzen = 1 Thaler

CITY

STANDARD COINAGE

KM# 5 PFENNIG

Billon **Obv:** Bear left, eagle above **Note:** Uniface.

Date	Mintage	VG	F	VF	XF	Unc
ND	—	300	600	1,500	—	—

KM# 10 1/2 KREUZER

Billon **Note:** Similar to 1 Kreuzer, KM#8.

Date	Mintage	VG	F	VF	XF	Unc
ND	—	5.00	10.00	40.00	100	—
1617 Rare	—	—	—	—	—	—
1618 Rare	—	—	—	—	—	—
1619 Rare	—	—	—	—	—	—
1620	—	60.00	150	350	1,000	—
1621	—	60.00	150	350	1,000	—
1622	—	60.00	150	350	1,000	—
1623	—	60.00	150	350	1,000	—
1624 Rare	—	—	—	—	—	—

KM# 11 1/2 KREUZER

Billon **Note:** Without inner circle.

Date	Mintage	VG	F	VF	XF	Unc
ND	—	5.00	10.00	40.00	100	—

KM# 41 1/2 KREUZER

Billon

Date	Mintage	VG	F	VF	XF	Unc
ND	—	5.00	10.00	40.00	100	—
1680	—	20.00	40.00	150	400	—
1684	—	5.00	10.00	40.00	100	—
1699	—	20.00	40.00	150	400	—

KM# 40 1/2 KREUZER

Billon **Rev:** Double B's in cruciform, lilies in angles

Date	Mintage	VG	F	VF	XF	Unc
1679 Rare	—	—	—	—	—	—

KM# 39 1/2 KREUZER

Billon **Obv:** Bern arms **Rev:** Thicker cross

Date	Mintage	VG	F	VF	XF	Unc
1679	—	8.00	20.00	80.00	200	—

KM# 58 1/2 KREUZER

Billon **Rev:** Anchor crosses in angles of cross

Date	Mintage	VG	F	VF	XF	Unc
1684	—	9.00	20.00	80.00	200	—

KM# 8 KREUZER

Billon

Date	Mintage	VG	F	VF	XF	Unc
1612	—	8.00	20.00	60.00	250	—
1613	—	50.00	100	400	—	—
1614	—	50.00	100	400	—	—
1617	—	200	450	1,000	—	—
1618	—	5.00	10.00	40.00	100	—
1619	—	5.00	10.00	40.00	100	—
1620	—	5.00	10.00	40.00	100	—
1621	—	5.00	10.00	40.00	100	—
1622	—	25.00	60.00	200	500	—
1623	—	—	—	—	—	—

KM# 25 10 KREUZER

Silver **Obv:** Arms in oval cartouche, date in legend **Rev:** Legend in laurel wreath, 10 below **Rev. Legend:** DEVX / PROVIDE / BIT

Date	Mintage	VG	F	VF	XF	Unc
1656	—	35.00	75.00	150	300	600

KM# 26 10 KREUZER

Silver **Rev:** Crowned imperial eagle with 10 in circle on breas

Date	Mintage	VG	F	VF	XF	U
1656	—	22.00	50.00	100	200	4
1658	—	22.00	50.00	100	200	4
1669	—	520	1,000	2,500	—	-

KM# 35 10 KREUZER

Silver **Rev:** 10 at top above heads

Date	Mintage	VG	F	VF	XF	U
1669	—	22.00	50.00	100	200	4

KM# 42 10 KREUZER

Silver **Obv:** Value below arms **Rev:** Legend, date and mintmaster's initials in laurel wreath, 10 below ribbon **Rev. Inscription:** DEVS / PROVIDE / BIT

Date	Mintage	VG	F	VF	XF	U
1679	—	25.00	60.00	125	250	5

KM# 17 12 KREUZER

Silver **Note:** 3 Batzen, 1/2 Dicken.

Date	Mintage	VG	F	VF	XF	U
1620	—	100	200	500	1,000	[illegible]
1621	—	75.00	150	350	700	[illegible]

KM# 27 20 KREUZER

Silver

Date	Mintage	VG	F	VF	XF	U
1656	—	25.00	50.00	100	200	4
1658	—	35.00	75.00	200	400	7
1659	—	25.00	50.00	100	200	4

KM# 43 20 KREUZER

Silver **Obv:** Value below arms **Obv. Legend:** MONETA. REIPVBLICAE. BERNENSIS. **Rev:** Cruciform of intertwined B 20 in square in center

Date	Mintage	VG	F	VF	XF	U
1679	—	35.00	75.00	200	400	7

KM# 28 30 KREUZER (1/2 Gulden)

Silver **Note:** 1/4 Taler.

Date	Mintage	VG	F	VF	XF	[illegible]
ND	—	30.00	60.00	150	300	6
1657	—	40.00	80.00	200	400	8
1680	—	40.00	80.00	200	400	8

M# 9 1/2 BATZEN

illon **Obv:** Arms on shield, eagle above, date in legend **Rev:** ross in inner circle

ate	Mintage	VG	F	VF	XF	Unc
614	—	75.00	150	600	—	—

M# 15 BATZEN

illon **Obv:** Date above cartouche

ate	Mintage	VG	F	VF	XF	Unc
D	—	10.00	20.00	60.00	250	—
617	—	10.00	20.00	60.00	250	—
618	—	8.00	20.00	60.00	250	—
619	—	50.00	100	175	350	—
620	—	8.00	20.00	60.00	250	—
621	—	8.00	20.00	60.00	250	—
622	—	7.00	15.00	50.00	150	—
623	—	7.00	15.00	50.00	150	—

M# 13 BATZEN

illon **Obv:** Arms on shield with decorative flourishes divide date **ev:** Crowned imperial eagle, breast orb above

ate	Mintage	VG	F	VF	XF	Unc
617	—	3,530	750	2,500	—	—

M# 14 BATZEN

illon **Obv:** Arms on shield in cartouche **Rev:** Crowned imperial agle, date in legend

ate	Mintage	VG	F	VF	XF	Unc
617	—	200	400	1,500	—	—

M# 23 BATZEN

illon **Note:** Klippe.

ate	Mintage	VG	F	VF	XF	Unc
622	—	—	—	—	—	—

M# 18 3 BATZEN

lver **Obv:** Bear walking left, eagle above, 3 in oval below **Rev:** ross in inner circle, date divided at bottom

te	Mintage	VG	F	VF	XF	Unc
20	—	100	200	500	1,000	—
21	—	75.00	150	350	700	—

M# 19 1/2 DICKEN

ver **Obv:** Bear walking left, eagle above **Rev:** Cross in inner cle

te	Mintage	VG	F	VF	XF	Unc
20	—	100	200	500	1,000	—

M# A20 1/2 DICKEN

ver **Obv:** Ornate arms **Rev:** Imperial eagle

te	Mintage	VG	F	VF	XF	Unc
21	—	75.00	150	350	700	—

KM# 12 DICKEN

Silver **Obv:** Arms in cartouche, date in upper legend **Rev:** Crowned imperial eagle in inner circle

Date	Mintage	VG	F	VF	XF	Unc
1617	—	600	1,200	3,000	—	—
1618	—	750	1,500	3,500	—	—
1620	—	200	400	1,000	2,000	—
1621	—	500	1,100	3,000	—	—

KM# 21 DICKEN

Silver **Obv:** Bear walking left, eagle above **Rev:** Cross with ornamentation in angles

Date	Mintage	VG	F	VF	XF	Unc
1620	—	1,250	2,500	6,000	—	—
1621 Rare	—	—	—	—	—	—
ND(1623)	—	—	—	—	—	—

KM# 20 DICKEN

Silver **Note:** Klippe.

Date	Mintage	VG	F	VF	XF	Unc
1620	—	—	—	—	—	—

KM# 22 DICKEN

Silver **Note:** Klippe.

Date	Mintage	VG	F	VF	XF	Unc
1620	—	—	—	—	—	—

KM# 51 1/4 THALER

Silver **Obv:** Arms in cartouche within inner circle **Rev:** Cross with flowery ornaments in angles, date in legend above and value 1/4 in legend below

Date	Mintage	VG	F	VF	XF	Unc
ND	—	25.00	60.00	150	300	500
1657	—	35.00	80.00	200	400	750
1680	—	35.00	80.00	200	400	750

KM# 44 1/2 THALER

Silver **Note:** Similar to 1 Thaler, KM#46.

Date	Mintage	VG	F	VF	XF	Unc
1679	—	50.00	100	250	600	—
1680	—	300	600	1,500	—	—

KM# 37 THALER

Silver **Obv:** Shield with ornamental flourishes **Rev:** Cross with ornamentation in angles **Note:** Dav. #4615.

Date	Mintage	VG	F	VF	XF	Unc
ND(1670)	—	1,200	2,400	4,000	6,000	—

KM# 38 THALER

Silver **Rev:** Bust of the duke of Zahringen right divides date **Rev. Legend:** -:- BERCHT. DVS • ZERING (:) COND. VRB. BERN **Note:** Dav. #4616.

Date	Mintage	VG	F	VF	XF	Unc
ND Rare	—	4,000	8,000	20,000	—	—
1671 Rare	—	—	—	—	—	—

KM# 46.1 THALER

Silver **Obv:** Oval shield in ornate frame **Rev:** Date x1679x **Note:** Dav. #4618.

Date	Mintage	VG	F	VF	XF	Unc
1679 V Small date	—	150	300	750	1,500	2,500

KM# 46.2 THALER

Obv: Similar to KM#46.6 **Note:** Dav. #4618A.

Date	Mintage	VG	F	VF	XF	Unc
1679 V	—	150	300	750	1,500	2,500

KM# 46.3 THALER

Silver **Obv:** Oval shield with vertical lines in upper and lower fields **Note:** Dav. #4619.

Date	Mintage	VG	F	VF	XF	Unc
1679 V	—	150	300	750	1,500	2,500

KM# 46.4 THALER

Silver **Obv:** Similar shield to KM#46.3 with P and rosette above **Note:** Dav. #4619A.

Date	Mintage	VG	F	VF	XF	Unc
1679 V	—	150	300	750	1,500	2,500

KM# 46.5 THALER

Silver **Obv:** Similar shield to KM#46.3 with rosette and P above **Note:** Dav. #4619B.

Date	Mintage	VG	F	VF	XF	Unc
1679	—	150	300	750	1,500	2,500

KM# 46.6 THALER

Silver **Obv:** Shield with ornamentation in upper and lower fields **Rev:** Rosettes in angles of monogram **Note:** Dav. #4620.

Date	Mintage	VG	F	VF	XF	Unc
1679 C	—	300	700	1,750	—	—

KM# 46.7 THALER

Silver **Obv:** Similar shield to KM#46.3 **Note:** Dav. #4620A.

Date	Mintage	VG	F	VF	XF	Unc
1679 V	—	350	700	1,750	—	—

KM# 45 THALER

Silver **Rev. Legend:** DOMINVS. PROVIDEBIT. **Note:** Similar to KM#46. Dav. #4617.

Date	Mintage	VG	F	VF	XF	Unc
1679 V	—	35.00	700	1,750	—	—

TRADE COINAGE

KM# 6 1/2 DUCAT

1.7500 g., 0.9860 Gold 0.0555 oz. AGW **Rev:** St. Vincent

Date	Mintage	VG	F	VF	XF	Unc
1601	—	700	1,500	3,000	5,000	7,500
1623 Rare	—	—	—	—	—	—

KM# 29 DUCAT

3.5000 g., 0.9860 Gold 0.1109 oz. AGW **Note:** Fr. #123.

Date	Mintage	VG	F	VF	XF	Unc
1658	—	900	1,500	3,500	6,000	9,000
ND(1658) Rare	—	—	—	—	—	—

KM# 47 DUCAT

3.5000 g., 0.9860 Gold 0.1109 oz. AGW **Rev:** Value and date in branches **Note:** Fr. #126.

Date	Mintage	VG	F	VF	XF	Unc
1679	—	750	1,500	3,000	5,000	7,500

KM# 48 DUCAT
3.5000 g., 0.9860 Gold 0.1109 oz. AGW **Rev:** Value and date in cartouche **Note:** Fr. #127.

Date	Mintage	VG	F	VF	XF	Unc
1679	—	3,000	5,000	10,000	—	—

KM# 59 DUCAT
3.5000 g., 0.9860 Gold 0.1109 oz. AGW **Obv:** Bear and lion supporting oval arms **Rev:** Similar to KM#61

Date	Mintage	VG	F	VF	XF	Unc
1684 Rare	—	—	—	—	—	—

KM# 61 DUCAT
3.5000 g., 0.9860 Gold 0.1109 oz. AGW

Date	Mintage	VG	F	VF	XF	Unc
1696	—	900	1,800	3,500	6,000	9,000

KM# 62 DUCAT
3.5000 g., 0.9860 Gold 0.1109 oz. AGW **Obv:** Crowned, ornate oval arms of Bern **Obv. Legend:** BENEDICTUS • SIT • IEHOVA • DEUS • **Rev:** Inscription, value and date within partial frame flanked by 1/2 figures above **Rev. Inscription:** REIPUBLICA / BERNENSIS / DUCAT **Note:** Fr. #139.

Date	Mintage	F	VF	XF	Unc	BU
1697	—	1,000	2,000	3,200	5,000	6,500

KM# A32 2 DUCAT
Note: Fr. #122.

Date	Mintage	VG	F	VF	XF	Unc
ND(1645-65)	—	1,600	3,000	6,000	10,000	15,000

KM# A30 2 DUCAT
7.0000 g., 0.9860 Gold 0.2219 oz. AGW **Obv:** Ornate arms **Rev:** Imperial eagle **Note:** Struck with 1 Ducat dies, KM#29.

Date	Mintage	VG	F	VF	XF	Unc
1658	—	1,600	3,000	6,000	10,000	15,000

KM# 30 2 DUCAT
7.0000 g., 0.9860 Gold 0.2219 oz. AGW **Note:** Fr. #121.

Date	Mintage	VG	F	VF	XF	Unc
ND(1658-59)	—	1,600	3,000	6,000	10,000	15,000

KM# 31 2 DUCAT
7.0000 g., 0.9860 Gold 0.2219 oz. AGW **Note:** Varieties exist. Fr. #121.

Date	Mintage	VG	F	VF	XF	Unc
1659 Rare	—	—	—	—	—	—

KM# 49 2 DUCAT
7.0000 g., 0.9860 Gold 0.2219 oz. AGW **Note:** Fr. #125.

Date	Mintage	VG	F	VF	XF	Unc
1679	—	1,300	2,500	5,000	8,000	12,000

KM# 64 2 DUCAT
7.0000 g., 0.9860 Gold 0.2219 oz. AGW **Obv:** Crowned oval arms **Rev:** Man and woman holding drapery, value and date on drapery **Note:** Fr. #138.

Date	Mintage	VG	F	VF	XF	Unc
1698	—	1,300	2,500	5,000	8,000	12,000

KM# 32 3 DUCAT
10.5000 g., 0.9860 Gold 0.3328 oz. AGW **Obv:** Arms in cartouche, date in legend **Rev:** Crowned imperial eagle **Note:** Fr. #120.

Date	Mintage	VG	F	VF	XF	Unc
1659	—	1,800	4,500	9,000	15,000	22,000

KM# 52 3 DUCAT
10.5000 g., 0.9860 Gold 0.3328 oz. AGW **Rev. Inscription:** BENEDICTUS/ • SIT • / • IEHOVA • / • DEUS • **Note:** Fr. #132.

Date	Mintage	VG	F	VF	XF	Unc
1680	—	1,600	4,500	9,000	15,000	22,000
1684	—	1,600	4,500	9,000	15,000	22,000
1697	—	1,600	4,500	9,000	15,000	22,000

KM# 63 3 DUCAT
10.5000 g., 0.9860 Gold 0.3328 oz. AGW **Rev. Inscription:** MONEDA / NOVA **Note:** Fr. #133.

Date	Mintage	VG	F	VF	XF	Unc
1697	—	1,600	3,000	6,000	10,000	15,000

KM# 65 3 DUCAT
10.5000 g., 0.9860 Gold 0.3328 oz. AGW **Obv:** Single crowned shield of arms **Note:** Fr. #134.

Date	Mintage	VG	F	VF	XF	Unc
1699	—	1,600	3,000	6,000	10,000	15,000

KM# 33 4 DUCAT
14.0000 g., 0.9860 Gold 0.4438 oz. AGW **Obv:** Arms in cartouche, date in legend **Rev:** Crowned imperial eagle

Date	Mintage	VG	F	VF	XF	Unc
1659 Rare	—	—	—	—	—	—

KM# 53 4 DUCAT
14.0000 g., 0.9860 Gold 0.4438 oz. AGW **Obv:** Crowned supported arms **Note:** Fr. #131.

Date	Mintage	VG	F	VF	XF	Unc
1680 BF	—	1,800	3,500	9,000	12,000	18,000
1684 D	—	2,100	4,000	8,000	14,000	20,000

KM# 50 5 DUCAT
17.5000 g., 0.9860 Gold 0.5547 oz. AGW **Note:** Similar to 10 Ducat, KM#54.

Date	Mintage	VG	F	VF	XF	Unc
ND(1680) Rare	—	—	—	—	—	—

KM# 55 8 DUCAT
28.0000 g., 0.9860 Gold 0.8876 oz. AGW **Obv:** Crowned arms, palm branches above, being held by lion and bear, garland of flowers below **Rev:** Chain ring on outside, wreath of crosses and flowers around cartouche which contains legend, value and date **Note:** Fr. #130.

Date	Mintage	VG	F	VF	XF	Unc
1681 D Rare	—	—	—	—	—	—

KM# 54 10 DUCAT
35.0000 g., 0.9860 Gold 1.1095 oz. AGW **Obv:** Crowned arms with bear and lion supporters **Rev:** Ctiy of Bern with arms above

Date	Mintage	VG	F	VF	XF	Unc
ND(1680) Rare	—	—	—	—	—	—

KM# 56 10 DUCAT
35.0000 g., 0.9860 Gold 1.1095 oz. AGW **Obv:** Crowned arms palm branches above, being held by lion and bear, garland of flowers below **Rev:** Chain ring on outside, wreath of crosses an flowers around cartouche which contains legend, value and dat **Note:** Fr. #129; Similar to 20 Ducat, KM#60.

Date	Mintage	VG	F	VF	XF	Ur
1681 D	—	—	15,000	30,000	50,000	75,00

KM# 57 12 DUCAT
42.0000 g., 0.9860 Gold 1.3314 oz. AGW **Obv:** Crowned arms palm branches above, being held by lion and bear, garland of flowers below **Rev:** Chain ring on outside, wreath of crosses an flowers around cartouche containing legend, value and date **Note:** Fr. #128.

Date	Mintage	VG	F	VF	XF	Ur
1681 D	—	—	17,500	35,000	60,000	90,00

KM# 60 20 DUCAT
70.0000 g., 0.9860 Gold 2.2190 oz. AGW **Note:** Fr. #127a.

Date	Mintage	VG	F	VF	XF	Ur
1681 D Rare	—	—	3,500	70,000	10,000	180,00

CHUR

A former bishopric now part of the canton Graubunden. Th mint right was given from 959 until about 1798.

BISHOPRIC

RULERS
Johann V Flugi von Aspermont, 1601-1627
Joseph Mohr von Zernetz, 1627-1635
Johann VI Flugi von Aspermont, 1636-1661
Ulrich VI von Mont, 1661-1692
Ulrich VII von Federspiel, 1692-1728

STANDARD COINAGE

KM# 6 PFENNIG
Billon **Obv:** Bishop's arms with three swan heads right on shiel IEC around within barley corn circle **Note:** Uniface.

Date	Mintage	VG	F	VF	XF	U
ND(1601)	—	32.50	65.00	100	200	-

KM# 7 PFENNIG
Billon **Obv:** Three roses around shield **Note:** Uniface.

Date	Mintage	VG	F	VF	XF	U
ND(1601)	—	32.50	65.00	100	200	

KM# 8 PFENNIG
Billon **Obv:** Bishop's family arms on shield with four fields, lette IEC around within pearl circle **Note:** Uniface.

Date	Mintage	VG	F	VF	XF	U
ND(1601)	—	32.50	65.00	100	200	

KM# 9 PFENNIG
Billon **Obv:** Without letters around shield **Note:** Uniface.

Date	Mintage	VG	F	VF	XF	U
ND(1601)	—	35.00	70.00	125	250	

KM# 10 PFENNIG
Billon **Obv:** Bishop's family arms on four-fold shield with swa necks in two fields, IEC around, within crude pearl circle **Note** Uniface.

Date	Mintage	VG	F	VF	XF	U
ND(1601)	—	32.50	65.00	100	200	

KM# 5 PFENNIG
Billon **Obv:** Bishop's arms with three swan heads left on shiel IEC around within pearl circle **Note:** Uniface. Schussel type.

Date	Mintage	VG	F	VF	XF	U
ND(1601)	—	10.00	20.00	40.00	80.00	

KM# 105 PFENNIG
Billon **Obv:** Bishop's arms with unicorn on shield, letters VE around within barley corn circle **Note:** Uniface.

Date	Mintage	VG	F	VF	XF	U
ND(1661)	—	25.00	60.00	150	300	

KM# 106 PFENNIG
Billon **Obv:** Bishop's arms with unicorn on shield, circle arour broken by letters VEC within barley corn circle **Note:** Uniface

Date	Mintage	VG	F	VF	XF	U
ND(1661)	—	10.00	20.00	40.00	80.00	

KM# 107 PFENNIG
Billon **Obv:** Bishop's arms with unicorn on shield, VEC abov flowers at sides within barley corn circle **Note:** Uniface.

Date	Mintage	VG	F	VF	XF	
ND(1661) Rare	—	—	—	—	—	

KM# 108 PFENNIG
Billon **Obv:** Bishop's arms with unicorn on curved shield, VE around within barley corn circle **Note:** Uniface.

Date	Mintage	VG	F	VF	XF	U
ND(1661)	—	10.00	20.00	40.00	80.00	

KM# 128 PFENNIG
Billon **Obv:** Arms of Bishopric with Ibex right on curved shie VEC around **Note:** Uniface.

Date	Mintage	VG	F	VF	XF	
ND(1692)	—	10.00	20.00	40.00	80.00	

KM# 129 PFENNIG
Billon **Obv:** Ibex left **Note:** Uniface.

Date	Mintage	VG	F	VF	XF	
ND(1692)	—	15.00	40.00	100	200	

KM# 11 2 PFENNIG
illon **Obv:** Three shields, one with swan necks, one with Ibex, ne with eagle, 2 in center **Note:** Uniface.

ate	Mintage	VG	F	VF	XF	Unc
D(1601)	—	10.00	20.00	40.00	80.00	—

KM# 12 2 PFENNIG
illon **Obv:** Three shields with dot in center **Note:** Uniface.

ate	Mintage	VG	F	VF	XF	Unc
D(1601)	—	10.00	20.00	40.00	80.00	—

KM# 13 2 PFENNIG
illon **Obv:** Three shields with two dots in center, 2 below **Note:** niface.

ate	Mintage	VG	F	VF	XF	Unc
D(1601)	—	10.00	20.00	40.00	80.00	—

M# 14 2 PFENNIG
llon **Obv:** Three shields, two roses and one eagle in fields etween, 2 in center **Note:** Uniface.

ate	Mintage	VG	F	VF	XF	Unc
)(1601)	—	10.00	20.00	40.00	80.00	—

M# 15 2 PFENNIG
illon **Obv:** Three shields joined at center, eagle, rose and 2 in elds **Note:** Uniface.

ate	Mintage	VG	F	VF	XF	Unc
)(1601)	—	15.00	30.00	80.00	—	—

M# 16 2 PFENNIG
llon **Obv:** Three shields joined at center, eagle at top, bishop's ms at left, Bishopric arms at right, 2 below **Note:** Uniface.

ate	Mintage	VG	F	VF	XF	Unc
601	—	3.00	5.00	15.00	40.00	—

M# 17 2 PFENNIG
llon **Obv:** Bishopric arms at left, Bishop's arms at right **Note:** niface.

ate	Mintage	VG	F	VF	XF	Unc
)(1601)	—	10.00	20.00	40.00	80.00	—

M# 109 2 PFENNIG
llon **Obv:** Three shields, eagle at top, unicorn at left, Ibex at ght, 2 below **Note:** Uniface.

ate	Mintage	VG	F	VF	XF	Unc
(1661)	—	15.00	30.00	75.00	80.00	—

M# 110 2 PFENNIG
llon **Obv:** Ibex at left, unicorn at right **Note:** Uniface.

ate	Mintage	VG	F	VF	XF	Unc
(1661)	—	8.00	15.00	40.00	80.00	—

M# 130 2 PFENNIG
llon **Obv:** 1/2 stamped on blank reverse **Note:** Uniface.

ate	Mintage	VG	F	VF	XF	Unc
)(1692)	—	8.00	20.00	50.00	100	—

M# 18 BLUZGER
lon **Obv:** Wide anchor cross in pearl circle, legend around ev: Bishopric arms with Ibex right on ornamental shield in pearl cle, legend around

te	Mintage	VG	F	VF	XF	Unc
(1602) Rare	—	500	1,200	3,000	—	—

M# 19 BLUZGER
lon **Obv:** Dots at sides and in angles of cross **Rev:** Bust of adonna holding child, both with halos

te	Mintage	VG	F	VF	XF	Unc
(1601)	—	20.00	40.00	200	—	—

M# 20 BLUZGER
lon **Obv:** Maltese cross

te	Mintage	VG	F	VF	XF	Unc
(1601)	—	20.00	40.00	200	—	—

M# 21 BLUZGER
lon **Obv:** Cross with prongs at end

te	Mintage	VG	F	VF	XF	Unc
(1601)	—	20.00	40.00	200	—	—

M# 52 BLUZGER
lon **Obv:** Cross with ornamentation at ends **Rev:** Madonna d child, date in legend

te	Mintage	VG	F	VF	XF	Unc
10 Rare	—	500	1,000	2,500	—	—
16	—	200	400	1,000	—	—
23	—	75.00	150	400	—	—
24	—	20.00	100	300	—	—

M# 118 BLUZGER
on **Obv:** Four-fold arms in oval cartouche in inner circle **Rev:** chor cross in inner circle

e	Mintage	VG	F	VF	XF	Unc
30	—	175	350	800	—	—

M# 120 BLUZGER
on **Obv:** Without inner circles **Rev:** Without inner circles

e	Mintage	VG	F	VF	XF	Unc
34	—	100	200	500	—	—
31	—	175	350	800	—	—

M# 131 BLUZGER
on **Ruler:** Ulrich VII **Obv:** 4-fold arms in oval cartouche in cle of pearls **Rev:** Anchor cross with ornamentation on arms

e	Mintage	VG	F	VF	XF	Unc
03	—	8.00	15.00	40.00	75.00	—
34	—	8.00	15.00	40.00	75.00	—

KM# 65 KREUZER
Billon

Date	Mintage	VG	F	VF	XF	Unc
1623	—	250	600	1,500	—	—

KM# 73 KREUZER
Billon

Date	Mintage	VG	F	VF	XF	Unc
1627	—	350	800	2,000	—	—

KM# 77 KREUZER
Billon **Obv:** Crowned imperial eagle, one in circle on breast, date below **Rev:** Ibex shield in inner circle **Rev. Legend:** IOSEP...

Date	Mintage	VG	F	VF	XF	Unc
1628	—	125	300	750	—	—

KM# 97 KREUZER
Billon **Obv:** Bust right dividing S-L **Obv. Legend:** IOAN.... **Rev:** Legend, date. **Rev. Legend:** FER.III...

Date	Mintage	VG	F	VF	XF	Unc
1643	—	8.00	20.00	60.00	120	—
1644	—	7.00	15.00	50.00	100	—
1645	—	8.00	20.00	60.00	120	—
1646	—	8.00	20.00	60.00	120	—
1649 Rare	—	—	—	—	—	—
1650	—	16.00	40.00	100	—	—
1652	—	35.00	80.00	200	—	—

KM# 69 2 KREUZER (1/2 Batzen)
Billon **Obv:** Four-fold arms on shield in inner circle, legend, date **Obv. Legend:** MO.NO... **Rev:** Imperial orb w/2 in inner circle

Date	Mintage	VG	F	VF	XF	Unc
1624 Rare	—	—	—	—	—	—

KM# 71 2 KREUZER (1/2 Batzen)
Billon **Obv:** Legend, date **Obv. Legend:** IOAN. D. G. E. P. CVR

Date	Mintage	VG	F	VF	XF	Unc
1625	—	50.00	120	250	—	—
1626	—	50.00	120	250	—	—

KM# 99 2 KREUZER (1/2 Batzen)
Billon **Obv:** Four-fold arms on round, with indented sides, shield in inner circle **Obv. Legend:** IOAN. D. G. EPIS. **Rev:** Imperial orb w/2 in center in inner circle, date **Rev. Legend:** FER. III. D.G. R. IM. S.

Date	Mintage	VG	F	VF	XF	Unc
1646	—	8.00	20.00	60.00	120	—

KM# 100 2 KREUZER (1/2 Batzen)
Billon **Obv:** Four-fold arms on oval shield in inner circle **Obv. Legend:** IOANNES. D. G. EPIS **Rev:** Legend, date **Rev. Legend:** ...ROM. IM. SEM. A.

Date	Mintage	VG	F	VF	XF	Unc
1648	—	16.00	30.00	100	—	—
1649	—	35.00	80.00	200	—	—

KM# 101 2 KREUZER (1/2 Batzen)
Billon **Rev:** Legend, date **Rev. Legend:** MONE. NO. CVRIAE. RETIC.

Date	Mintage	VG	F	VF	XF	Unc
1649	—	90.00	200	500	—	—

KM# 103 2 KREUZER (1/2 Batzen)
Billon **Obv:** Four-fold arms on round with indented sides, shield in inner circle **Rev:** Legend, date **Rev. Legend:** LEOPOLD. I. D. G...

Date	Mintage	VG	F	VF	XF	Unc
1659	—	45.00	100	250	—	—

KM# 111 2 KREUZER (1/2 Batzen)
Billon **Obv. Legend:** VDAL. D. G. EPIS. CVR. S. R. I. P.

Date	Mintage	VG	F	VF	XF	Unc
1663	—	16.00	40.00	100	200	—

KM# 119 2 KREUZER (1/2 Batzen)
Billon **Obv:** Arms in oval cartouche **Obv. Legend:** ...EP. CVR. D. IN. FV... **Rev. Legend:** LEOPOLDVS...

Date	Mintage	VG	F	VF	XF	Unc
1680	—	250	600	1,500	—	—

KM# 121 2 KREUZER (1/2 Batzen)
Billon **Obv:** Legend, date **Obv. Legend:** D. I. FV. E. G. E. **Rev:** Four-fold arms on ornate shield **Rev. Legend:** LEOPOLD. D. G. R. IM. S. A.

Date	Mintage	VG	F	VF	XF	Unc
1686	—	250	600	1,500	—	—

KM# 22 3 KREUZER (1 Groschen)
Silver **Rev. Legend:** SI DEVS PRO NOB Q CON NOS

Date	Mintage	VG	F	VF	XF	Unc
ND(1601)	—	150	300	750	—	—

KM# 23 3 KREUZER (1 Groschen)
Silver **Rev. Legend:** DO. CONSER. NOS. IN. PAC.

Date	Mintage	VG	F	VF	XF	Unc
ND(1601)	—	300	600	1,500	—	—

KM# 24 3 KREUZER (1 Groschen)
Silver **Obv:** Without bishopric arms in legend

Date	Mintage	VG	F	VF	XF	Unc
ND(1601) Rare	—	—	—	—	—	—

KM# 25 3 KREUZER (1 Groschen)
Silver **Obv:** Without inner circle

Date	Mintage	VG	F	VF	XF	Unc
ND(1601)	—	150	300	750	—	—

KM# 26 3 KREUZER (1 Groschen)
Silver **Obv:** Four-fold arms on ornate shield **Obv. Legend:** IOANNES. DEI... **Rev. Legend:** MATHIAS II D: G. RO. IM. SE. AV. H. B. RE.

Date	Mintage	VG	F	VF	XF	Unc
ND(1601) Rare	—	—	—	—	—	—

KM# 28 3 KREUZER (1 Groschen)
Silver **Obv:** Quartered arms **Obv. Legend:** IOANNES. D. G. EPISC. CVRI **Rev. Legend:** DO. CONSER. NOS. IN. PAC.

Date	Mintage	VG	F	VF	XF	Unc
ND(1601)	—	400	800	2,000	—	—

KM# 29 3 KREUZER (1 Groschen)
Silver **Rev. Legend:** SI DEVS PRO NOB Q CON NOS

Date	Mintage	VG	F	VF	XF	Unc
ND(1601) Rare	—	—	—	—	—	—

KM# 27 3 KREUZER (1 Groschen)
Silver **Note:** Klippe.

Date	Mintage	VG	F	VF	XF	Unc
ND(1601) Rare	—	—	—	—	—	—

KM# 74 3 KREUZER (1 Groschen)
Silver **Obv:** Bust right dividing date in inner circle, 3 in oval shield in legend **Rev:** Three shields, rosette in center within inner circle **Rev. Legend:** DOMI. CONS...

Date	Mintage	VG	F	VF	XF	Unc
1627	—	60.00	120	350	—	—

KM# 75 3 KREUZER (1 Groschen)
Silver **Rev:** Dot at center of shields **Rev. Legend:** DOMINE: CONSER:...

Date	Mintage	VG	F	VF	XF	Unc
1627	—	100	200	500	—	—

KM# 78 3 KREUZER (1 Groschen)
Silver **Obv:** 4-fold arms in inner circle **Obv. Legend:** IOSEPHVS. DEI. G... **Rev:** Crowned imperial eagle, 3 on breast, date below

Date	Mintage	VG	F	VF	XF	Unc
1628 Rare	—	650	1,200	3,000	—	—

KM# 79 3 KREUZER (1 Groschen)
Silver **Obv:** Three shields with lily decorations between in inner circle **Rev:** Imperial orb w/3 on breast of imperial eagle

Date	Mintage	VG	F	VF	XF	Unc
1628	—	50.00	100	250	500	—
1631 Rare	—	—	—	—	—	—

KM# 87 3 KREUZER (1 Groschen)
Silver **Rev:** Different shields

Date	Mintage	VG	F	VF	XF	Unc
1633	—	75.00	150	400	—	—

KM# 80 10 KREUZER
Silver **Obv:** Four-fold arms on shield with ornamentation **Rev:** Similar to KM#84

Date	Mintage	VG	F	VF	XF	Unc
1628	—	50.00	100	250	500	800
1629	—	40.00	80.00	200	400	600
1630	—	40.00	80.00	200	400	600

KM# 84 10 KREUZER
Silver **Obv:** Capped arms **Rev:** Crowned imperial eagle

Date	Mintage	VG	F	VF	XF	Unc
1630	—	25.00	50.00	120	250	400
1632	—	30.00	60.00	150	300	500
1633	—	50.00	100	250	500	—
1634	—	40.00	80.00	200	400	600
1635	—	50.00	100	250	500	800
1636 Rare	—	—	—	—	—	—

KM# 93 10 KREUZER
Silver **Obv:** Quartered arms, bishop's cap above

Date	Mintage	VG	F	VF	XF	Unc
1637 Rare	—	—	—	—	—	—

KM# 94 10 KREUZER
Silver **Obv:** Half-length figure right, bishop's arms in oval shield at bottom **Rev:** Date in legend divided by crown

Date	Mintage	VG	F	VF	XF	Unc
1637 Rare	—	—	—	—	—	—

KM# 92 10 KREUZER
Silver **Obv:** Bishop's cap above **Note:** Similar to KM#84.

Date	Mintage	VG	F	VF	XF	Unc
1637 Rare	—	—	—	—	—	—

KM# 30 12 KREUZER (1/2 Dicken)
Silver **Obv:** Four-fold mantled arms in inner circle **Rev:** Crowned imperial eagle, 12 on breast

Date	Mintage	VG	F	VF	XF	Unc
ND(1601)	—	650	1,200	3,000	—	—

KM# 31 12 KREUZER (1/2 Dicken)
Silver **Obv:** Half-length figure right holding scepter and imperial orb **Rev:** 1Z on breast of eagle

Date	Mintage	VG	F	VF	XF	Unc
ND(1601)	—	200	400	1,000	—	—

KM# 32 12 KREUZER (1/2 Dicken)
Silver **Obv:** Figure divides S-L

Date	Mintage	VG	F	VF	XF	Unc
ND(1601)	—	75.00	150	400	750	—

KM# 122 15 KREUZER
Silver **Obv:** Bust right with bare head in inner circle **Rev:** Similar to KM#135

Date	Mintage	VG	F	VF	XF	Unc
1688	—	40.00	80.00	200	400	—
1689	—	75.00	150	400	—	—
1690	—	100	200	500	—	—

KM# 85 20 KREUZER
Silver **Obv:** Bust right dividing S-L **Rev:** Crowned imperial eagle, 20 in orb on breast, date below

Date	Mintage	VG	F	VF	XF	Unc
1631 Rare	—	—	—	—	—	—

KM# 66 24 KREUZER (1 Dicken)
Silver **Obv:** Mantled four-fold arms, bishop's mitre above **Obv. Legend:** MO. NO... **Rev:** Crowned imperial eagle, 24 on breast, date below

Date	Mintage	VG	F	VF	XF	Unc
1623 Rare	—	—	—	—	—	—
1624 Rare	—	—	—	—	—	—

KM# 70 24 KREUZER (1 Dicken)
Silver **Obv:** 24 in shield below arms **Obv. Legend:** IOANNE...

Date	Mintage	VG	F	VF	XF	Unc
1624 Rare	—	—	—	—	—	—

KM# 86 24 KREUZER (1 Dicken)
Silver **Obv:** Half-length saint right with crozier **Rev:** Half-length saint right with crozier

Date	Mintage	VG	F	VF	XF	Unc
1632 Rare	—	1,250	2,500	6,000	—	—

KM# 88 24 KREUZER (1 Dicken)
Silver **Obv:** 24 below crozier **Rev:** 24 below crozier

Date	Mintage	VG	F	VF	XF	Unc
1633 Rare	—	—	—	—	—	—

KM# 33 BATZEN
Billon **Obv:** Shield with Ibex left, eagle above **Obv. Legend:** IOANNES... **Rev:** Anchor corss **Rev. Legend:** MONETA: NOVA: CVRIE

Date	Mintage	VG	F	VF	XF	Unc
ND(1601)	—	75.00	150	400	—	—

KM# 34 BATZEN
Billon **Obv. Inscription:** IOANNES D G EPIS CVR **Rev. Legend:** MONETA NOVA CVR

Date	Mintage	VG	F	VF	XF	Unc
ND(1601) Rare	—	400	800	2,000	—	—

KM# 35 DICKEN
Silver **Obv:** Half-length figure right divides SI-PEC, shield below **Rev:** Crowned imperial eagle, crown above in legend

Date	Mintage	VG	F	VF	XF	Unc
ND(1601)	—	300	600	1,500	—	—

KM# 36 DICKEN
Silver **Obv:** Smaller figure right, without letters in field

Date	Mintage	VG	F	VF	XF	Unc
ND(1601)	—	65.00	125	350	700	—

KM# 37 DICKEN
Silver **Rev:** Two shields below figure

Date	Mintage	VG	F	VF	XF	Unc
ND(1601)	—	250	500	1,200	—	—

KM# 38 DICKEN
Silver **Obv:** Shield below eagle

Date	Mintage	VG	F	VF	XF	Unc
ND(1601)	—	250	500	1,200	—	—

KM# 39 DICKEN
Silver

Date	Mintage	VG	F	VF	XF	Unc
ND(1601)	—	75.00	150	350	750	—

KM# 40 DICKEN
Silver **Obv:** Without shield below figure **Rev:** Shield below eagle

Date	Mintage	VG	F	VF	XF	Unc
ND(1601)	—	75.00	150	350	750	—

KM# 41 DICKEN
Silver **Obv:** Half-length figure divides S-L, shield below

Date	Mintage	VG	F	VF	XF	Unc
ND(1601)	—	75.00	150	350	750	—

KM# 42 DICKEN
Silver **Rev:** Without shield below eagle

Date	Mintage	VG	F	VF	XF	Unc
ND(1601)	—	60.00	125	350	700	—

KM# 59 DICKEN
Silver **Obv:** W/o S-L **Note:** Similar to KM#58.

Date	Mintage	VG	F	VF	XF	Unc
ND	—	250	500	1,200	—	—
1620	—	200	400	1,000	—	—
1621	—	250	500	1,200	—	—

KM# 58 DICKEN
Silver **Obv:** 1/2-length figure of Johann V Flugi von Aspermont right **Rev:** Crowned imperial eagle

Date	Mintage	VG	F	VF	XF	Unc
1621	—	150	300	750	—	—
1623 Rare	—	—	—	—	—	—

KM# 63 DICKEN
Silver **Note:** Klippe.

Date	Mintage	VG	F	VF	XF	Unc
1622	—	300	600	1,500	—	—

KM# 43 SCHILLING
Billon **Obv:** Standing figure of saint in inner circle **Rev:** Standing Ibex left in inner circle

Date	Mintage	VG	F	VF	XF	Unc
ND(1601) Rare	—	—	—	—	—	—

KM# 125 1/3 THALER (1/2 Gulden)
Silver **Obv:** Armored bust right **Rev:** Crowned imperial eagle, value in oval shield below

Date	Mintage	VG	F	VF	XF	Unc
1689 Rare	—	1,500	3,000	7,500	—	—

KM# 124 2/3 THALER (1 Gulden)
Silver **Obv:** Bust of Ulrich VI von Mont right **Rev:** Crowned imperial eagle

Date	Mintage	VG	F	VF	XF
1688	—	125	225	500	900
1689 Rare	—	—	—	—	—
1690	—	65.00	150	400	700

KM# 123 2/3 THALER (1 Gulden)
Silver **Note:** Similar to KM#124 but without inner circles.

Date	Mintage	VG	F	VF	XF
1688	—	150	300	700	1,000

KM# 126 2/3 THALER (1 Gulden)
Silver **Obv:** 1/2-length figure right **Rev:** Crowned imperial eag

Date	Mintage	VG	F	VF	XF
1689	—	60.00	120	300	500
1690	—	60.00	120	300	500

KM# 60 THALER
Silver **Obv:** Capped arms **Rev:** Bishop seated facing **Note:** Da #4661.

Date	Mintage	VG	F	VF	XF
ND	—	200	400	1,500	3,000

KM# 61 THALER
Silver **Rev:** Crowned imperial eagle **Note:** Dav. #4660, 466

Date	Mintage	VG	F	VF	XF
ND(1621) Rare	—	1,600	3,000	7,500	—
1622 Rare	—	—	—	—	—

KM# 67 THALER
Silver **Obv:** Larger, more ornate shield, large mitre divides da **Rev:** Fully displayed eagle, larger crown above **Note:** Dav. #4663.

Date	Mintage	VG	F	VF	XF
1623	—	600	1,200	3,000	—

KM# 72 THALER
Silver **Obv:** Small four-fold arms divide date, shorter mantle **Note:** Dav. #4664.

Date	Mintage	VG	F	VF	XF
1625	—	750	1,500	4,000	—
1626	—	500	1,000	2,500	5,000

KM# 82 THALER
Silver **Obv:** Oval arms with bust left in two folds of arms, in ornate cartouche **Rev. Legend:** FERDINANDVS II D G ROM IMP SEM AV **Note:** Dav. #4665.

Date	Mintage	VG	F	VF	XF
MDCXXVIII (1628)	—	2,250	4,000	10,000	20,000

KM# 81 THALER
Silver **Obv:** Date in Roman numerals in legend, oval arms w half-length figure in two folds of arms, in cartouche **Note:** Da #4666.

Date	Mintage	VG	F	VF	XF
1628	—	850	1,800	4,500	9,000

KM# 89 THALER
Silver **Obv:** Simpler cartouche **Rev:** Legend, date **Rev. Inscription:** DOMINE... **Note:** Dav. #4667.

Date	Mintage	VG	F	VF	XF
1633	—	1,100	2,000	5,000	—

KM# 90 THALER
Silver **Obv. Legend:** Legend, date **Rev. Legend:** FERDINANDVS: II: D: G... **Note:** Dav. #4668.

Date	Mintage	VG	F	VF	XF
1634	—	850	1,600	4,000	8,000

KM# 96 THALER
Silver **Obv:** Helmeted arms in inner circle **Note:** Dav. #466

Date	Mintage	VG	F	VF	XF
1642	—	2,250	4,000	10,000	20,000

KM# A62 1-1/2 THALER
Silver **Obv:** Similar to 1 Thaler KM#60 **Rev:** Crowned impe eagle **Note:** Dav. #A4660.

Date	Mintage	VG	F	VF	XF
ND(1621) Rare	—	—	—	—	—

KM# 62 2 THALER
Silver **Obv:** Similar to 1 Thaler, KM#60 **Rev:** Crowned impe eagle **Note:** Dav. #4659.

Date	Mintage	VG	F	VF	XF
ND(1621) Rare	—	3,500	6,000	15,000	—

TRADE COINAGE

M# 44 GOLDGULDEN

5000 g., 0.9860 Gold 0.1109 oz. AGW **Obv:** St. Luke **Obv. egend:** ...CVR: **Rev. Legend:** MATH. D. G. R. **Note:** Fr. #196.

ate	Mintage	VG	F	VF	XF	Unc
)(1601)	—	500	1,000	2,000	3,500	—

M# 45 GOLDGULDEN

5000 g., 0.9860 Gold 0.1109 oz. AGW **Obv:** St. Luke divides ·L **Obv. Legend:** CVRIEN

ate	Mintage	VG	F	VF	XF	Unc
)(1601)	—	900	1,800	3,500	6,000	—

M# 46 GOLDGULDEN

5000 g., 0.9860 Gold 0.1109 oz. AGW **Rev. Legend:** FERDI: G: RO:... **Note:** Fr. #197.

ate	Mintage	VG	F	VF	XF	Unc
)(1601)	—	600	1,200	2,500	4,000	—

M# 47 GOLDGULDEN

5000 g., 0.9860 Gold 0.1109 oz. AGW **Obv:** Bishop standing hind family arms

ate	Mintage	VG	F	VF	XF	Unc
Rare	—	—	—	—	—	—

M# 76 DUCAT

5000 g., 0.9860 Gold 0.1109 oz. AGW **Obv:** Shield w/bishop's tre, crozier and stole above **Rev:** Crowned imperial eagle, arms breast, Order of the Golden Fleece around **Note:** Fr. #202.

ate	Mintage	VG	F	VF	XF	Unc
)(1627) Rare	—	—	—	—	—	—

M# 91 DUCAT

5000 g., 0.9860 Gold 0.1109 oz. AGW **Obv:** Arms in oval rtouche, titles of Johann VI **Rev:** Crowned imperial eagle in ner circle **Note:** Fr. #204.

te	Mintage	VG	F	VF	XF	Unc
36	—	6,000	12,000	24,000	—	—
49	—	3,000	6,000	12,000	18,000	—
52	—	3,000	6,000	12,000	18,000	—

M# 112.1 DUCAT

5000 g., 0.9860 Gold 0.1109 oz. AGW **Obv:** Arms on shield, namentation on corners **Rev:** W/o inner circle **Note:** Fr. #208.

te	Mintage	VG	F	VF	XF	Unc
64	—	3,750	7,500	15,000	25,000	—

M# 112.2 DUCAT

old **Obv:** Arms on shield, ornamentation on corners **Rev:** W/o ner circle **Note:** Fr. #209.

te	Mintage	VG	F	VF	XF	Unc
91 Rare	—	—	—	—	—	—

M# 132 DUCAT

5000 g., 0.9860 Gold 0.1109 oz. AGW **Obv:** Shield of arms **v:** Crowned imperial eagle, date divided at top **Note:** Fr. #212.

te	Mintage	VG	F	VF	XF	Unc
93 Rare	—	—	—	—	—	—

M# 133 DUCAT

5000 g., 0.9860 Gold 0.1109 oz. AGW **Obv:** Ornate oval arms **v:** St. Luke

e	Mintage	VG	F	VF	XF	Unc
97	—	3,500	7,500	15,000	25,000	—

M# 48 2 DUCAT

000 g., 0.9860 Gold 0.2219 oz. AGW **Obv:** 4-fold arms in er circle **Obv. Legend:** IOANNES... **Rev:** Crowned imperial gle in inner circle **Rev. Legend:** RODL. II...

e	Mintage	VG	F	VF	XF	Unc
(1601)	—	3,000	6,000	12,000	20,000	—

M# 49 2 DUCAT

000 g., 0.9860 Gold 0.2219 oz. AGW **Obv:** Arms in inner cle **Rev:** Crowned imperial eagle in inner circle, titles of dolph II

e	Mintage	VG	F	VF	XF	Unc
	—	3,000	6,000	12,000	20,000	—

M# 50 2 DUCAT

000 g., 0.9860 Gold 0.2219 oz. AGW **Rev:** Titles of Matthias **te:** Fr. #201.

e	Mintage	VG	F	VF	XF	Unc
	—	3,750	7,500	15,000	25,000	—

M# 68 2 DUCAT

000 g., 0.9860 Gold 0.2219 oz. AGW **Obv:** Legend, date **v. Legend:** MO NO AVR EPIS CVR **Rev. Legend:** FER II RO SEM AVG **Note:** Fr. #199.

e	Mintage	VG	F	VF	XF	Unc
3 Rare	—	—	—	—	—	—

KM# 64 4 DUCAT

14.0000 g., 0.9860 Gold 0.4438 oz. AGW **Obv:** Arms in inner circle **Rev:** Crowned imperial eagle in inner circle **Note:** Fr. #198.

Date	Mintage	VG	F	VF	XF	Unc
ND Rare	—	—	—	—	—	—
1623 Rare	—	—	—	—	—	—

KM# A132 4 DUCAT

14.0000 g., 0.9860 Gold 0.4438 oz. AGW **Obv:** Bust of Ulrich VI von Mont right **Rev:** Crowned imperial eagle **Note:** Struck with 2/3 Thaler dies, KM#124. Fr. #210.

Date	Mintage	VG	F	VF	XF	Unc
1689 Rare	—	—	—	—	—	—

KM# 53 5 DUCAT

17.5000 g., 0.9860 Gold 0.5547 oz. AGW **Note:** Similar to 7 Ducat, KM#55. Fr. #193.

Date	Mintage	VG	F	VF	XF	Unc
1613 Rare	—	—	—	—	—	—

KM# 98 5 DUCAT

17.5000 g., 0.9860 Gold 0.5547 oz. AGW **Obv:** Facing bust of bishop, date **Obv. Legend:** IO EPS CVR DNS... **Rev:** Crowned, helmeted small shield w/arms **Rev. Legend:** DOMINVS... **Note:** Fr. #203.

Date	Mintage	VG	F	VF	XF	Unc
1644 Rare	—	—	—	—	—	—

KM# 113 5 DUCAT

17.5000 g., 0.9860 Gold 0.5547 oz. AGW **Obv:** Larger facing bust of bishop **Obv. Legend:** VDAL: D: G: EP:... **Rev:** Crowned imperial eagle **Rev. Legend:** LEOPOLDUS:... **Note:** Fr. #207.

Date	Mintage	VG	F	VF	XF	Unc
1664 Rare	—	—	—	—	—	—

KM# 114 6 DUCAT

21.0000 g., 0.9860 Gold 0.6657 oz. AGW **Obv:** Facing bust of bishop **Obv. Legend:** VDAL: D: G: EP:... **Rev:** Crowned imperial eagle **Rev. Legend:** LEOPOLDVS:... **Note:** Fr. #205.

Date	Mintage	VG	F	VF	XF	Unc
1664 Rare	—	—	—	—	—	—

KM# 54 7 DUCAT

24.5000 g., 0.9860 Gold 0.7766 oz. AGW **Obv:** 1/2-length figure of St. Luke **Rev:** Crowned imperial eagle **Note:** Fr. #190.

Date	Mintage	VG	F	VF	XF	Unc
ND(1613)	—	1,750	3,500	7,000	12,000	—

KM# 55 7 DUCAT

24.5000 g., 0.9860 Gold 0.7766 oz. AGW **Rev:** Date divided by crowned imperial eagle **Note:** Fr. #191.

Date	Mintage	VG	F	VF	XF	Unc
1613	—	2,250	4,500	8,000	15,000	—

KM# 56 7 DUCAT

24.5000 g., 0.9860 Gold 0.7766 oz. AGW **Obv:** 1/2-length figure of St. Luke divides date **Rev:** Crowned imperial eagle **Note:** Fr. #194.

Date	Mintage	VG	F	VF	XF	Unc
1615	—	4,250	8,500	17,000	25,000	—

KM# 57 10 DUCAT

35.0000 g., 0.9860 Gold 1.1095 oz. AGW **Note:** Similar to 7 Ducat, KM#56. Fr. #193.

Date	Mintage	VG	F	VF	XF	Unc
1615 Rare	—	—	—	—	—	—

KM# 115 10 DUCAT

35.0000 g., 0.9860 Gold 1.1095 oz. AGW **Obv:** Facing bust of bishop **Obv. Legend:** VDAL: D:G: EP:... **Rev:** Crowned imperial eagle **Rev. Legend:** LEOPOLDVS:... **Note:** Fr. #205.

Date	Mintage	VG	F	VF	XF	Unc
1664 Rare	—	—	—	—	—	—

CITY

STANDARD COINAGE

KM# 200 PFENNIG

Billon **Obv:** Arms with Ibex left, CVR at top and sides **Note:** Uniface. Schussel type.

Date	Mintage	VG	F	VF	XF	Unc
ND(1601)	—	10.00	20.00	50.00	100	—

KM# 201 PFENNIG

Billon **Obv:** Arms without CVR **Note:** Uniface.

Date	Mintage	VG	F	VF	XF	Unc
ND(1601) Rare	—	—	—	—	—	—

KM# 202 PFENNIG

Billon **Obv:** Larger arms, CVR at top and sides, large pearl circles around **Note:** Uniface.

Date	Mintage	VG	F	VF	XF	Unc
ND(1601)	—	10.00	20.00	50.00	100	—

KM# 203 PFENNIG

Billon **Obv:** Arms without CVR **Note:** Uniface.

Date	Mintage	VG	F	VF	XF	Unc
ND(1601)	—	10.00	20.00	50.00	100	—

KM# 204 PFENNIG

Billon **Obv:** Arms with CVR at top and sides, barley corn circle around **Note:** Uniface.

Date	Mintage	VG	F	VF	XF	Unc
ND(1601)	—	8.00	20.00	50.00	700	—

KM# 205 PFENNIG

Billon **Obv:** Small arms, Ibex right, CVR at top and sides, barley corn circle around **Note:** Uniface.

Date	Mintage	VG	F	VF	XF	Unc
ND(1601)	—	10.00	20.00	50.00	100	—

KM# 206 PFENNIG

Billon **Obv:** Larger arms, Ibex left, CVR at top and sides, inner circle, barley corn circle around **Note:** Uniface.

Date	Mintage	VG	F	VF	XF	Unc
ND(1601)	—	10.00	20.00	50.00	100	—

KM# 261 PFENNIG

Billon **Obv:** CUR at top and sides of shield, without inner circle **Note:** Uniface.

Date	Mintage	VG	F	VF	XF	Unc
ND(1700)	—	10.00	20.00	50.00	100	—

KM# 262 PFENNIG

Billon **Obv:** CVR at top and sides of shield with Ibex right, without inner circle **Note:** Uniface.

Date	Mintage	VG	F	VF	XF	Unc
ND(1700)	—	10.00	20.00	50.00	100	—

KM# 217 BLUZGER

Billon **Obv:** Tall, narrow arms, Ibex left in inner circle **Rev:** Cross in inner circle, date **Rev. Legend:** ...REGNV

Date	Mintage	VG	F	VF	XF	Unc
1624	—	15.00	30.00	100	—	—

KM# 224 BLUZGER

Billon **Obv:** City arms with Ibex facing either right or left in inner circle **Rev:** Cross in inner circle, date in legend **Rev. Legend:** DOMINI.EST.REGN

Date	Mintage	VG	F	VF	XF	Unc
1628 Rare	—	—	—	—	—	—
1632	—	7.50	15.00	40.00	75.00	—
1633	—	25.00	50.00	125	250	—
1634 Rare	—	—	—	—	—	—
1636	—	20.00	40.00	100	200	—
1637	—	30.00	60.00	150	300	—
1638	—	7.50	15.00	40.00	75.00	—
1639	—	15.00	35.00	80.00	150	—
1642	—	3.00	5.00	15.00	30.00	60.00
1643	—	15.00	35.00	80.00	150	—
1644	—	3.00	5.00	15.00	30.00	60.00
1645	—	25.00	50.00	125	—	—
1652	—	3.00	5.00	15.00	30.00	60.00
1660	—	3.00	5.00	15.00	30.00	60.00
1674	—	8.00	15.00	40.00	75.00	—
1676	—	50.00	100	250	—	—
1677	—	10.00	20.00	50.00	100	—
1678	—	10.00	20.00	50.00	100	—
1679	—	10.00	20.00	50.00	100	—
1680	—	15.00	30.00	75.00	150	—
1684	—	25.00	50.00	125	250	—
1691	—	25.00	50.00	125	—	—
1693	—	5.00	10.00	20.00	50.00	100
1694	—	10.00	20.00	50.00	100	—

KM# 240 KREUZER

Billon **Obv:** Arms in round border on cross, legend underneath **Rev:** Crowned imperial eagle with halos in inner circle

Date	Mintage	VG	F	VF	XF	Unc
ND(1641) Rare	—	600	1,200	3,000	—	—

KM# 242 KREUZER
Billon **Obv:** Double cross, arms on shield at center in inner circle **Rev:** Crowned imperial eagle, 1 in orb on breast in inner circle

Date	Mintage	VG	F	VF	XF	Unc
1642 Rare	—	250	500	1,250	—	—
1643	—	60.00	120	300	—	—
1650	—	60.00	120	300	600	—

KM# 243 KREUZER
Billon **Obv:** Armored bust of St. Luke right in inner circle **Rev:** Crowned imperial eagle, 1 in orb on breast in inner circle

Date	Mintage	VG	F	VF	XF	Unc
1643	—	20.00	40.00	125	250	—

KM# 218 2 KREUZER (1/2 Batzen)
Silver **Obv:** Large imperial orb w/2 in inner circle **Rev:** Crowned imperial eagle in inner circle

Date	Mintage	VG	F	VF	XF	Unc
1624	—	35.00	80.00	200	400	—
1625	—	30.00	60.00	450	300	—
1626	—	35.00	80.00	200	400	—

KM# 245 2 KREUZER (1/2 Batzen)
Billon **Obv:** Smaller imperial orb, date **Obv. Legend:** MONE. NO. CVRIAE. **Rev. Legend:** FER. III. D. G. ROM. IM. SEM. AVG.

Date	Mintage	VG	F	VF	XF	Unc
1648	—	15.00	30.00	100	200	—

KM# 246 2 KREUZER (1/2 Batzen)
Billon **Rev:** Legend, date **Rev. Legend:** FER. III. D. G. ROM. IM. SEM. A.

Date	Mintage	VG	F	VF	XF	Unc
1649	—	150	300	750	—	—

KM# 249 2 KREUZER (1/2 Batzen)
Billon **Obv:** Arms with Ibex left in oval ornate cartouche **Rev:** Large imperial orb with 2, date above

Date	Mintage	VG	F	VF	XF	Unc
1659	—	40.00	80.00	200	400	—
1663	—	22.00	50.00	125	250	—
1686 Rare	—	—	—	—	—	—

KM# 207 3 KREUZER (1 Groschen)
Billon **Obv:** 1/2-length St. Luke right in inner circle **Obv. Legend:** MONETA. C-VRI. **Rev:** Crowned imperial eagle, 3 in orb on breast in inner circle **Rev. Inscription:** DOMIN...

Date	Mintage	VG	F	VF	XF	Unc
ND(1601) Rare	—	—	—	—	—	—

KM# 208 3 KREUZER (1 Groschen)
Billon **Obv. Legend:** DOMINE: E-ST: REGNVM **Rev. Legend:** FER II DEI G ROM IM SEM A

Date	Mintage	VG	F	VF	XF	Unc
ND(1601) Rare	—	—	—	—	—	—

KM# 225 3 KREUZER (1 Groschen)
Silver **Obv. Legend:** MONETA. C-VRIAE: RET. **Rev:** Crowned imperial eagle, orb with 3 on breast, date below **Rev. Legend:** DOMINI-EST. REGN.

Date	Mintage	VG	F	VF	XF	Unc
1628	—	125	250	500	—	—

KM# 226 3 KREUZER (1 Groschen)
Silver **Obv:** Ornamentation on top and sides of shield. **Rev. Legend:** DOMI: CON.-NOS. IN. PA. **Note:** Similar to KM#232.

Date	Mintage	VG	F	VF	XF	Unc
1629	—	35.00	80.00	200	450	—

KM# 231 3 KREUZER (1 Groschen)
Silver **Note:** Similar to KM#232 but ornamentation on top and sides of shield.

Date	Mintage	VG	F	VF	XF	Unc
1631	—	75.00	150	400	—	—

KM# 232 3 KREUZER (1 Groschen)
Silver

Date	Mintage	VG	F	VF	XF	Unc
1631	—	12.00	25.00	50.00	100	250
1633	—	20.00	50.00	125	250	—
1634 Rare	—	—	—	—	—	—
1635 Rare	—	—	—	—	—	—

KM# 237 3 KREUZER (1 Groschen)
Silver **Obv:** Half-length of St. Luke right in inner circle **Obv. Legend:** MONE. NOVA... **Rev. Legend:** FERD. III...

Date	Mintage	VG	F	VF	XF	Unc
1637 Rare	—	—	—	—	—	—
1638 Rare	—	—	—	—	—	—

KM# 228 10 KREUZER
Silver **Obv:** 1/2-length figure of St. Luke right **Rev:** Crowned imperial eagle

Date	Mintage	VG	F	VF	XF	Unc
1629	—	16.00	40.00	100	200	350
1630	—	16.00	40.00	100	200	350
1631	—	16.00	40.00	100	200	350
1632	—	16.00	35.00	80.00	150	275
1633	—	25.00	60.00	150	300	500
1634	—	16.00	40.00	100	200	350
1635	—	16.00	40.00	100	200	350
1636	—	22.00	50.00	125	250	400
1637	—	275	600	1,200	2,500	—

KM# 227 10 KREUZER
Silver **Obv:** Ornate shield **Rev:** Crowned imperial eagle

Date	Mintage	VG	F	VF	XF	Unc
1629	—	500	1,000	2,500	5,000	—

KM# 209 12 KREUZER (1/2 Dicken)
Billon **Obv:** 1/2-length St. Luke right in inner circle **Rev:** Crowned imperial eagle with 1Z on round shield on breast

Date	Mintage	VG	F	VF	XF	Unc
ND(1601)	—	400	800	2,000	—	—

KM# 219 24 KREUZER (1 Dicken)
Silver **Obv:** St. Martin riding right, w/o halo **Rev:** Crowned imperial eagle, imperial orb with 24 on breast, date below

Date	Mintage	VG	F	VF	XF	Unc
1624 Rare	—	750	1,500	4,500	7,000	—

KM# 220 24 KREUZER (1 Dicken)
Silver **Obv:** Large halo behind St. Martin's head **Rev:** Crowned imperial eagle without orb on breast, shield divides date below

Date	Mintage	VG	F	VF	XF	Unc
1624 Rare	—	900	1,800	4,500	—	—

KM# 230 24 KREUZER (1 Dicken)
Silver **Obv:** 1/2-length figure of St. Luke right, shield below **Rev:** Crowned imperial eagle, imperial orb with 24 on breast

Date	Mintage	VG	F	VF	XF	Unc
1630 Rare	—	1,000	2,000	5,000	—	—
1632	—	600	1,200	3,000	6,000	—
1633	—	375	750	1,500	3,000	—
1638 Rare	—	—	—	—	—	—

KM# 213 DICKEN
Silver **Obv:** 1/2-length figure of St. Luke right in inner circle, date **Obv. Legend:** DOMINI. EST-RENGNVM **Rev:** Crowned imperial eagle in inner circle **Rev. Legend:** MONETA: CVRIAE: RETICAE.

Date	Mintage	VG	F	VF	XF	Unc
ND(1619)	—	125	250	600	—	—
1620	—	500	1,000	2,500	—	—
1621	—	250	500	1,250	—	—

KM# 214 DICKEN
Silver **Obv:** Without halo behind St. Luke's head, arms without shield below figure

Date	Mintage	VG	F	VF	XF	Unc
ND(1619)	—	125	250	600	—	—

KM# 221 SCHILLING
Billon **Obv:** Standing saint in inner circle **Rev:** Crowned imperial eagle, arms on shield divide date below

Date	Mintage	VG	F	VF	XF	Unc
1624	—	125	250	600	1,200	—

KM# 216 1/2 THALER
Silver **Obv:** Standing angel in inner circle **Rev:** Crowned imperial eagle, arms on shield divide date below

Date	Mintage	VG	F	VF	XF	Unc
1623 Rare	—	6,000	12,000	30,000	—	—

KM# 223 THALER
Silver **Rev:** Ornaments or date at left of crown **Note:** Dav. #467

Date	Mintage	VG	F	VF	XF	U
1620	—	—	—	—	—	
ND(1625)	—	150	300	750	1,500	
1626	—	750	1,500	3,500	—	

KM# A217 THALER
Silver **Obv:** 3/4-length figure of St. Lucius with sceptre and o right **Obv. Legend:** MONETA NOVA CVRIAE RETICE **Rev:** Crowned imperial eagle **Note:** Dav. #4673.

Date	Mintage	VG	F	VF	XF	U
1623	—	—	—	—	—	

KM# 222 THALER
Silver **Obv:** 1/2-length St. Luke in inner circle, crown divides date above **Rev:** Crowned imperial eagle in inner circle **Note** Dav. #4674.

Date	Mintage	VG	F	VF	XF
1624	—	1,650	3,000	7,500	—

KM# 233 THALER
Silver **Obv:** Ornate oval shield **Rev:** Crowned imperial eagl **Rev. Legend:** FERDINANDVS • II • D: G: ROM: **Note:** Dav. #4675.

Date	Mintage	VG	F	VF	XF	
1633	—	185	350	800	1,800	3,
1638/3	—	—	—	—	—	
1638	—	1,000	2,000	5,000	10,000	

TRADE COINAGE

KM# 211 GOLDGULDEN
3.5000 g., 0.9860 Gold 0.1109 oz. AGW **Obv:** St. Luke sea facing **Rev:** Crowned imperial eagle **Rev. Legend:** MATTIAS:

Date	Mintage	VG	F	VF	XF
1618	—	2,000	4,000	8,000	—

KM# 212 GOLDGULDEN

.5000 g., 0.9860 Gold 0.1109 oz. AGW **Obv:** St. Luke **Rev:** rowned imperial eagle **Rev. Legend:** FERDINANDVS: II... **ote:** Fr. #226.

ate	Mintage	VG	F	VF	XF	Unc
D(1618-37) Rare	—	—	—	—	—	—

KM# 236 DUCAT

.5000 g., 0.9860 Gold 0.1109 oz. AGW **Rev:** Crowned imperial agle **Rev. Legend:** FERDINAND II... **Note:** Fr. #230.

ate	Mintage	VG	F	VF	XF	Unc
634	—	800	1,800	3,500	6,000	—
636	—	800	1,800	3,500	6,000	—
637	—	800	1,800	3,500	6,000	—
638 Rare	—	—	—	—	—	—

KM# 238 DUCAT

5000 g., 0.9860 Gold 0.1109 oz. AGW **Rev. Legend:** ERDINAND III...

ate	Mintage	VG	F	VF	XF	Unc
639	—	1,250	2,500	5,000	—	—

KM# 241 DUCAT

.5000 g., 0.9860 Gold 0.1109 oz. AGW **Obv:** Modified state hield **Note:** Fr. #231.

ate	Mintage	VG	F	VF	XF	Unc
641	—	1,250	2,500	5,000	—	—
642 Rare	—	—	—	—	—	—

KM# 244 DUCAT

.5000 g., 0.9860 Gold 0.1109 oz. AGW **Obv:** Modified state hield **Note:** Fr. #231.

ate	Mintage	VG	F	VF	XF	Unc
644	—	1,250	2,500	5,000	—	—
645 Rare	—	—	—	—	—	—

KM# 248 DUCAT

5000 g., 0.9860 Gold 0.1109 oz. AGW **Obv:** Modified state hield **Note:** Fr. #231.

ate	Mintage	VG	F	VF	XF	Unc
652 Rare	—	—	—	—	—	—

M# 251 DUCAT

.5000 g., 0.9860 Gold 0.1109 oz. AGW **Rev. Legend:** EOPOLDBS. I... **Note:** Fr. #231a.

ate	Mintage	VG	F	VF	XF	Unc
664 Rare	—	—	—	—	—	—

KM# 234 2 DUCAT

.0000 g., 0.9860 Gold 0.2219 oz. AGW **Obv:** Standing knight armor with shield in inner circle **Rev:** Crowned imperial eagle inner circle **Note:** Fr. #228.

ate	Mintage	VG	F	VF	XF	Unc
D Rare	—	—	—	—	—	—

KM# 235 2 DUCAT

.0000 g., 0.9860 Gold 0.2219 oz. AGW **Obv:** Arms in cartouche inner circle **Rev:** Crowned imperial eagle in inner circle **Rev. egend:** FERDINAND: II... **Note:** Fr. #229.

ate	Mintage	VG	F	VF	XF	Unc
633	—	3,700	7,500	15,000	—	—

FREIBURG

Friburg, Fribourg, Freyburg

A canton and city located in western Switzerland. The city as founded in 1178 and obtained the mint right in 1422. It joined e Swiss Confederation in 1481. During the Helvetian Republic eriod it was known as Sarine Et Broye but changed the name ack to Freiburg in 1803.

ONETARY SYSTEM

Until 1798

6 Denier = 8 Vierer = 4 Kreuzer = 1 Batzen
6 Kreuzer = 8 Piecette = 1 Gulden
4 Piecette = 1 Thaler

CITY

STANDARD COINAGE

KM# 16 KREUZER

Billon **Obv:** Crowned imperial eagle with shield arms on breast **Rev:** Blossoms in angles of cross

Date	Mintage	VG	F	VF	XF	Unc
ND	—	100	200	800	—	—
1622	—	15.00	30.00	125	—	—
1623	—	15.00	30.00	125	—	—
1624	—	15.00	30.00	125	—	—
1625	—	30.00	80.00	250	—	—
1630	—	25.00	60.00	150	—	—
1636	—	25.00	60.00	150	—	—
1650	—	25.00	60.00	150	—	—
1656	—	10.00	20.00	75.00	—	—

CANTON

STANDARD COINAGE

KM# 20 1/2 KREUZER (Vierer)

Billon **Obv:** Tower arms **Obv. Legend:** MO:FRIBVRG **Rev:** Cross, S. NICOLA, date

Date	Mintage	VG	F	VF	XF	Unc
ND	—	500	1,000	2,500	—	—
1623 Rare	—	1,000	2,000	5,000	—	—

KM# 8 KREUZER

Billon **Obv:** Tower arms **Rev:** Cross with prongs

Date	Mintage	VG	F	VF	XF	Unc
ND	—	100	200	800	—	—
1610	—	37.50	75.00	250	—	—
1612	—	125	250	1,000	—	—
1613	—	37.50	75.00	250	—	—
1614	—	37.50	75.00	250	—	—
1615	—	37.50	75.00	250	—	—
1616	—	125	250	1,000	—	—

KM# 9 KREUZER

Billon **Note:** Klippe.

Date	Mintage	VG	F	VF	XF	Unc
ND	—	—	—	—	—	—

KM# 13 12 KREUZER (1/2 Dicken)

Silver **Obv:** Crowned imperial eagle with halos, 12 on breast, tower arms below **Rev:** St. Nicholas bust facing slightly right, holding crozier

Date	Mintage	VG	F	VF	XF	Unc
1620	—	400	800	2,000	—	—
1621 Rare	—	600	1,200	3,000	—	—

KM# 22 12 KREUZER (1/2 Dicken)

Silver **Obv:** Crown above eagle **Rev:** Date below saint

Date	Mintage	VG	F	VF	XF	Unc
1635	—	750	1,500	4,000	—	—

KM# 25 20 KREUZER (1/2 Dicken)

Silver **Obv:** Tower arms divide value: 2-0, ealge above, ring below **Rev:** Bust of saint wearing mitre facing forward

Date	Mintage	VG	F	VF	XF	Unc
1658	—	650	1,250	2,500	—	—

KM# 10 BATZEN

Billon **Obv:** Tower arms **Rev:** Cross with flowers in angles

Date	Mintage	VG	F	VF	XF	Unc
ND	—	200	400	1,500	—	—
1618 Rare	—	—	—	—	—	—
1619 Rare	—	—	—	—	—	—

KM# 14 BATZEN

Billon **Obv:** 20 in legend **Rev:** Nothing in angles of cross

Date	Mintage	VG	F	VF	XF	Unc
1620	—	37.50	75.00	300	—	—

KM# 15 BATZEN

Billon **Rev:** Date in legend

Date	Mintage	VG	F	VF	XF	Unc
ND	—	200	400	1,500	—	—
1621	—	50.00	100	400	—	—
1622	—	50.00	100	400	—	—

KM# 17 BATZEN

Billon **Obv:** Tower of arms on shield on top of cross **Rev:** Saint facing forward, date in legend

Date	Mintage	VG	F	VF	XF	Unc
1622	—	50.00	100	400	—	—
1623	—	10.00	20.00	75.00	200	—
1630	—	10.00	20.00	75.00	200	—
1631	—	10.00	20.00	75.00	200	—
1639 Rare	—	—	—	—	—	—
1641	—	10.00	20.00	75.00	200	—
1648	—	10.00	20.00	75.00	200	—

KM# 5 1/2 DICKEN

Billon **Obv:** Tower arms **Rev:** Half-length saint right divides date 60-8

Date	Mintage	VG	F	VF	XF	Unc
1608	—	750	1,500	4,000	—	—

KM# 6 DICKEN

Silver

Date	Mintage	VG	F	VF	XF	Unc
1608	—	400	800	2,000	—	—

TRADE COINAGE

KM# 11 GOLDGULDEN

3.5000 g., 0.9860 Gold 0.1109 oz. AGW **Note:** Similar to 1 Duplone, KM#18. Fr. #238.

Date	Mintage	VG	F	VF	XF	Unc
1619 Rare	—	—	—	—	—	—
1620 Rare	—	—	—	—	—	—

KM# 18.1 DUPLONE (Pistole)

7.6400 g., 0.9000 Gold 0.2211 oz. AGW **Note:** Fr. #245.

Date	Mintage	VG	F	VF	XF	Unc
1622 Rare	—	—	—	—	—	—
1623 Rare	—	—	—	—	—	—
1635	—	2,500	5,000	11,000	18,000	—

KM# 18.2 DUPLONE (Pistole)

7.6400 g., 0.9000 Gold 0.2211 oz. AGW **Note:** Fr. #246

Date	Mintage	VG	F	VF	XF	Unc
1635	—	2,500	5,000	11,000	18,000	—

KM# 19 2 DUPLONE (Quadrupla)

15.2800 g., 0.9000 Gold 0.4421 oz. AGW **Note:** Similar to 1 Duplone, KM#18. Fr. #244.

Date	Mintage	VG	F	VF	XF	Unc
1622 Rare	—	—	—	—	—	—

PATTERNS

Including off metal strikes

KM#	Date	Mintage	Identification	Mkt Val
PnA1	1610	—	Kreuzer. Gold. KM#8.	—

GENEVA

A canton and city in southwestern Switzerland. The city became a bishopric c.400 AD and was part of the Burgundian Kingdom for 500 years. They became completely independent in 1530. In 1798 they were occupied by France but became independent again in 1813. They joined the Swiss Confederation in 1815.

MINT OFFICIALS' INITIALS

Initial	Date	Name
A-B	1652-55	Augustin Hurtebinet
A-B		Auguste Bovet
AC	1656-64	Andre Capitel
AE	1665-67, 71-76	Andre Emery
AD, D and AD, DS, SE	1641-43	Ami Deneria and Daniel Sardes
AE, IE	1677-87	Paul Marcet
B	1644-46	Augustin Baccuet
B		Binet
BG	1638-40	David Guainier and Augustin Baccuet
C	1612-17	Pierre Caille
CL	1692	David Camp and J.A. Lullin
D	1610-12	Jacques Dansse
G, X	1621	Jean Gringalet
G	1621-22, 46-49	Joseph Gringalet
G		Girod
G		Gresset
GR, RG	1622-25	Jean, Richard and Francois Grenus
H		Hoyer
HC	1625-33	Jerome Capitel
IE, Sgr, Srie	1687-89	Jean Emery
IG		Jacques Gresset
JG		Jean Gresset
M	1601-02	Gedeon Morlot
M	1649-51	Jean Mussard
M	1651-52	Augustin Baccuet
NP, NPG	1617-21	Nicolas and Pierre Girard
PB		Paul Binet
PM	1633-37	Pierre du Meurier
TB		Theodore Benneton
W		Charles Wielandy

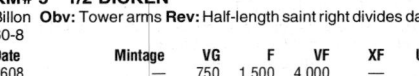

MONETARY SYSTEM

Until 1794

12 Deniers = 4 Quarts = 1 Sol
12 Sols = 1 Florin
12 Florins, 9 Sols = 1 Thaler
35 Florins = 1 Pistole

CANTON

STANDARD COINAGE

KM# 5 DENIER

Copper **Obv:** Arms **Rev:** I in center **Rev. Legend:** POUR. VN. DENIER.

Date	Mintage	VG	F	VF	XF	Unc
ND	—	37.50	75.00	250	500	—

KM# 16 DENIER

Copper **Obv:** Arms, legend, date **Obv. Legend:** GENEVA. CIVITAS **Rev:** I at center, flowers at sides, dots above and below **Rev. Legend:** POUR. VN. DENIER.

Date	Mintage	VG	F	VF	XF	Unc
1609 Rare	—	—	—	—	—	—

KM# 6 2 DENIERS

Copper **Obv:** Arms **Rev:** II at center, dot above, flower below **Rev. Legend:** POUR. DEUX. DENIERS.

Date	Mintage	VG	F	VF	XF	Unc
ND	—	37.50	75.00	250	500	—

KM# 17 2 DENIERS

Copper **Obv:** Arms, legend, date **Obv. Legend:** GENEVA CIVITAS **Rev:** .I.I. at center, flowers above and below, legend around

Date	Mintage	VG	F	VF	XF	Unc
1609 Rare	—	—	—	—	—	—

KM# 7 3 DENIERS (1 Quart)

Billon **Obv:** Arms, legend, date **Obv. Legend:** GENEVA CIVITAS **Rev:** Ornate cross **Rev. Legend:** POST. TENEBRAS. LVX.

Date	Mintage	VG	F	VF	XF	Unc
1601	—	10.00	20.00	60.00	150	—
1606	—	10.00	20.00	60.00	150	—
1608 Rare	—	—	—	—	—	—
1609	—	10.00	20.00	60.00	150	—
1610 D	—	50.00	100	350	800	—
1615	—	10.00	20.00	60.00	150	—
1616	—	10.00	20.00	60.00	150	—
1617 NPG	—	10.00	20.00	60.00	150	—
1619 NPG	—	10.00	20.00	60.00	150	—
1621	—	10.00	20.00	60.00	150	—

KM# 7a 3 DENIERS (1 Quart)

Gold **Obv:** Arms, legend, date **Obv. Legend:** GENEVA CIVITAS **Rev:** Ornate cross **Rev. Legend:** POST • TENEBRAS • LUX •

Date	Mintage	VG	F	VF	XF	Unc
1621 M Rare	—	—	—	—	—	—

KM# 21 4 DENIERS

Billon **Obv:** Arms on shield, legend and date around **Rev:** Inscription at center, legend around **Rev. Inscription:** POVR / IIII / DEN

Date	Mintage	VG	F	VF	XF	Unc
1617	—	50.00	100	400	1,000	—

KM# 12 6 DENIERS (2 Quarts)

Billon **Obv:** IHS in center of radiant sun in inner circle, date in legend **Rev:** Arms on shield, date above, legend around

Date	Mintage	VG	F	VF	XF	Unc
1603	—	10.00	20.00	60.00	150	—
1604	—	10.00	20.00	60.00	150	—
1610 C	—	10.00	20.00	60.00	150	—
1612 C	—	10.00	20.00	60.00	150	—
1613 C	—	10.00	20.00	60.00	150	—
1614 C	—	10.00	20.00	60.00	150	—
1615 C	—	10.00	20.00	60.00	150	—
1616 C	—	10.00	20.00	60.00	150	—
1617 NPG	—	10.00	20.00	60.00	150	—
1618 NPG	—	10.00	20.00	60.00	150	—
1619 NPG	—	10.00	20.00	60.00	150	—
1619 NP	—	10.00	20.00	60.00	150	—
1620 NPG	—	10.00	20.00	60.00	150	—
1620 PG	—	10.00	20.00	60.00	150	—
1621 Rare	—	—	—	—	—	—
1645 B	—	10.00	20.00	60.00	150	—
1646 B	—	10.00	20.00	60.00	150	—
1648 G	—	10.00	20.00	60.00	150	—
1649 G	—	25.00	60.00	200	500	—
1650 M	—	8.00	16.00	50.00	125	—
1651 M	—	8.00	16.00	50.00	125	—
1652 M	—	8.00	16.00	50.00	125	—
1653 AB	—	8.00	16.00	50.00	125	—
1654 C	—	8.00	16.00	50.00	125	—
1654 AB Rare	—	—	—	—	—	—
1677 AE	—	8.00	16.00	50.00	125	—
1678 AE	—	8.00	16.00	50.00	125	—
1687 IE	—	8.00	16.00	50.00	125	—
1688 IE	—	8.00	16.00	50.00	125	—

KM# 12a 6 DENIERS (2 Quarts)

Silver

Date	Mintage	VG	F	VF	XF	Unc
1655 AB Rare	—	—	—	—	—	—
1687 IE	—	8.00	16.00	50.00	125	—
1688 IE	—	8.00	16.00	50.00	125	—

KM# 49 6 DENIERS (2 Quarts)

Billon **Rev:** Inscription in center, legend around **Rev. Inscription:** SIX / DENI / ERS

Date	Mintage	VG	F	VF	XF	Unc
1674 AE	—	20.00	40.00	150	350	—

KM# 22 8 DENIERS

Billon **Obv:** Arms on shield, legend and date around **Rev:** Inscription in center, legend around **Rev. Inscription:** POVR / VI. II / DEN:

Date	Mintage	VG	F	VF	XF	Unc
1617	—	20.00	40.00	150	350	—
1618	—	20.00	40.00	150	350	—
1620	—	20.00	40.00	150	350	—

KM# 8 9 DENIERS (3 Quarts)

Billon **Obv:** Anchor cross within quatrefoil **Rev:** Arms, crowned imperial eagle above, date in legend

Date	Mintage	VG	F	VF	XF	Unc
1601 G Rare	—	—	—	—	—	—
1612 C Rare	—	—	—	—	—	—
1613 C	—	20.00	40.00	150	350	—
1614 Rare	—	—	—	—	—	—
1616	—	20.00	40.00	150	350	—
1617	—	20.00	40.00	150	350	—
1619 NP Rare	—	40.00	100	400	—	—
1634	—	20.00	40.00	150	350	—
1636	—	20.00	45.00	200	500	—
1637	—	20.00	45.00	200	500	—

KM# 50 9 DENIERS (3 Quarts)

Billon **Obv:** Arms in inner circle, date in legend

Date	Mintage	VG	F	VF	XF	Unc
1678 IE	—	20.00	40.00	150	350	—

KM# 34 18 DENIERS (6 Quarts)

Billon **Obv:** Arms in inner circle, legend and date around **Rev:** Cross of flowers in inner circle, mintmaster's initials above

Date	Mintage	VG	F	VF	XF	Unc
1633 PM	—	25.00	50.00	200	550	—
1634 PM	—	20.00	40.00	150	350	—

KM# 51 18 DENIERS (6 Quarts)

Billon **Rev:** Crowned imperial eagle above arms

Date	Mintage	VG	F	VF	XF	Unc
1678 IE	—	20.00	40.00	150	350	—

KM# 13 UN (1) SOL

Billon **Obv:** Arms on shield, imperial eagle above **Rev:** Anchor cross, flower or mintmaster's initials above

Date	Mintage	VG	F	VF	XF	Unc
1603 Rare	—	—	—	—	—	—
1604	—	35.00	80.00	300	—	—
1605	—	35.00	80.00	300	—	—
1606	—	35.00	80.00	300	—	—
1609	—	35.00	80.00	300	—	—
1611 D	—	18.00	40.00	150	350	—
1612 C	—	18.00	40.00	150	350	—
1619 NP	—	27.00	60.00	200	400	—
1619 NP. G	—	27.00	60.00	200	400	—
1621 G	—	27.00	60.00	200	400	—
1622 G	—	18.00	40.00	150	350	—
1622 RG	—	18.00	40.00	150	350	—

KM# 13a UN (1) SOL

Gold **Obv:** Arms on shield, crowned imperial eagle above **Rev:** Anchor cross, flower or mintmaster's initials above

Date	Mintage	VG	F	VF	XF	Unc
1622 RG Rare	—	—	—	—	—	—

KM# 14 3 SOLS

Silver **Obv:** Arms on shield, date above, flower at top **Rev:** POVR / III / SOLS in inner circle, legend around

Date	Mintage	VG	F	VF	XF	Unc
1604	—	110	250	600	—	—

KM# 15 3 SOLS

Silver **Obv:** Crowned imperial eagle above arms on shield, date in legend

Date	Mintage	VG	F	VF	XF	Unc
1607	—	65.00	150	400	—	—

KM# 23 3 SOLS

Billon **Obv:** Date above arms on shield **Rev:** Cross on quatrefoil in inner circle

Date	Mintage	VG	F	VF	XF	Unc
1619 NP. G	—	12.00	30.00	100	300	—
1620 NP. G	—	12.00	30.00	100	300	—
1621 G	—	12.00	30.00	100	300	—
1622 G Rare	—	—	—	—	—	—
1624 RG Rare	—	—	—	—	—	—
1633 PM	—	8.00	20.00	75.00	250	—
1634 PM	—	8.00	20.00	75.00	250	—
1636 PM	—	8.00	20.00	75.00	250	—
1637 PM	—	8.00	20.00	75.00	250	—
1638 GB	—	8.00	20.00	75.00	250	—
1638 BG	—	8.00	20.00	75.00	250	—
1639 GB	—	8.00	20.00	75.00	250	—
1639 BG	—	8.00	20.00	75.00	250	—
1640 GB	—	8.00	20.00	75.00	250	—
1640 BG	—	8.00	20.00	75.00	250	—
1641 DS	—	8.00	20.00	75.00	250	—
1641 SD	—	8.00	20.00	75.00	250	—
1641 AD.D.	—	8.00	20.00	75.00	250	—
1642 DS	—	8.00	20.00	75.00	250	
1642 SD	—	8.00	20.00	75.00	250	
1643 DS	—	8.00	20.00	75.00	250	
1643 SD	—	8.00	20.00	75.00	250	
1644 B	—	8.00	20.00	75.00	250	
1645 B	—	8.00	20.00	75.00	250	
1646 B	—	8.00	20.00	75.00	250	
1661 Rare	—	—	—	—	—	

KM# 35 3 SOLS

Billon **Obv:** Arms on shield, flower divides date above **Rev:** Radiant sun in inner circle, IHS in circle at center

Date	Mintage	VG	F	VF	XF	U
1633 Rare	—	—	—	—	—	

KM# 52 3 SOLS

Billon

Date	Mintage	VG	F	VF	XF	U
1689 SRG	—	22.00	50.00	150	400	
1689 RGS	—	32.00	75.00	200	500	
1689 SRIE	—	40.00	100	300	750	

KM# 19 4 SOLS

Silver **Obv:** Arms in shield, radiant sun above, date in legen
Rev: Inscription, D above in legend **Rev. Inscription:** POVR II.II / SOLS

Date	Mintage	VG	F	VF	XF	U
1610 D	—	110	250	600	—	

KM# 9 6 SOLS

Silver **Obv:** Arms on shield, crowned imperial eagle above, da in legend **Rev:** Inscription in center, legend around **Rev. Inscription:** POVR / SIX / SOLS

Date	Mintage	VG	F	VF	XF	U
1602	—	18.00	40.00	100	300	

KM# 10 6 SOLS

Silver **Rev:** Inscription in center **Rev. Inscription:** POVR / V SOLS

Date	Mintage	VG	F	VF	XF	U
1602 Rare	—	—	—	—	—	
1603	—	25.00	60.00	150	400	
1611 D Rare	—	—	—	—	—	

KM# 29 6 SOLS

Silver **Obv:** Arms in inner circle, 6-S above **Rev:** Crowned imperial eagle, mintmaster's initials above

Date	Mintage	VG	F	VF	XF	U
1624 GR Rare	—	—	—	—	—	

KM# 33 6 SOLS

Billon **Obv:** Arms on shield, VI. S, date above **Rev:** Decorat cross in center, mintmaster's initials above

Date	Mintage	VG	F	VF	XF	U
1632 PM Rare	—	—	—	—	—	
1633 PM	—	18.00	40.00	100	—	
1634 PM	—	18.00	40.00	100	—	
1635 PM	—	45.00	100	250	—	
1638 GB	—	45.00	100	250	—	
1639 GB	—	45.00	100	250	—	
1639 BG	—	45.00	100	250	—	
1640 BG	—	45.00	100	250	—	
1641 DS	—	45.00	100	250	—	
1678 AE	—	18.00	40.00	100	—	
1678 IE	—	18.00	40.00	100	—	

KM# 33a 6 SOLS

Silver

Date	Mintage	VG	F	VF	XF	U
1678 IE	—	—	—	—	—	

KM# 20 8 SOLS

Silver **Obv:** Arms on shield, radiant sun above, date in lege **Rev:** Inscription in inner circle, legend around **Rev. Inscriptic** POVR / VIII / SOLS

Date	Mintage	VG	F	VF	XF	U
1610 D	—	450	1,000	2,500	—	

KM# 30 10 SOLS (Achtelthaler)

Silver **Obv:** Arms in inner circle, date in legend **Rev:** Crown imperial eagle, mintmaster's initials above

Date	Mintage	VG	F	VF	XF	U
1624 GR	—	50.00	100	250	—	
1624 RG	—	75.00	150	400	—	
1625 GR	—	75.00	150	400	—	
1625 HC	—	50.00	100	250	—	
1626 HC	—	75.00	150	400	—	
1628 HC Rare	—	—	—	—	—	

M# 11 12 SOLS (1 Gulden)
ilver

ate	Mintage	VG	F	VF	XF	Unc
502	—	85.00	175	400	1,000	—
503	—	60.00	125	300	800	—

M# 38 12 SOLS (1 Gulden)
lver **Obv:** Arms on shield, imperial eagle above, 12 S below
ev: IHS in center of radiant sun in inner circle, date in legend

ate	Mintage	VG	F	VF	XF	Unc
535 PM	—	225	500	1,200	3,000	—

M# 45 12 SOLS (1 Gulden)
lver **Obv:** Inscription in center, mintmaster's initials above
bv. Inscription: POVR / XII / SOLS **Rev:** W/o value, date in
gend

ate	Mintage	VG	F	VF	XF	Unc
554 AB	—	18.00	40.00	100	250	—

M# 36 24 SOLS (2 Guldens)
lver

ate	Mintage	VG	F	VF	XF	Unc
34 PM	—	135	300	750	—	—
35 PM	—	70.00	150	400	—	—
36 PM	—	115	250	600	—	—

M# 41 24 SOLS (2 Guldens)
ver

te	Mintage	VG	F	VF	XF	Unc
44 B	—	115	250	600	—	—
45 B	—	115	250	600	—	—
47 G Rare	—	—	—	—	—	—

M# 48 24 SOLS (2 Guldens)
ver **Obv:** Arms **Obv. Legend:** * GENEVA * CIVITAS * **Rev:**
owned imperial eagle

te	Mintage	VG	F	VF	XF	Unc
57	—	115	250	600	—	—

M# A30 1/16 THALER
ver

te	Mintage	VG	F	VF	XF	Unc
24	—	185	400	1,000	—	—

M# 24 1/4 THALER
ver **Obv:** Arms in inner circle, flower above, date in legend
v: Crowned imperial eagle in inner circle, mintmaster's initials
ove

te	Mintage	VG	F	VF	XF	Unc
9 NPG Rare	—	—	—	—	—	—
20 NPG Rare	—	—	—	—	—	—
24 RG	—	450	1,000	2,500	—	—

KM# 28 1/4 THALER
Silver

Date	Mintage	VG	F	VF	XF	Unc
1623 RG	—	275	600	1,500	—	—
1625 HC	—	450	1,000	2,500	—	—
1627 HC	—	450	1,000	2,500	—	—
1633 PM Rare	—	—	—	—	—	—

KM# 27 1/2 THALER
Silver **Obv:** Arms in inner circle, IHS in radiant sun above, divides date **Rev:** Crowned imperial eagle in inner circle, mintmaster's initials divided by crown

Date	Mintage	VG	F	VF	XF	Unc
1621 GI	—	700	1,500	3,500	—	—
1622 GI Rare	—	—	—	—	—	—
1622 RG	—	225	500	1,200	—	—
1622 GR	—	450	1,000	2,500	—	—
1623 RG	—	350	750	1,700	—	—
1625 HC	—	800	1,750	4,000	—	—
1626 HC Rare	—	—	—	—	—	—
1627 HC Rare	—	—	—	—	—	—
1629 HC Rare	—	—	—	—	—	—
1630 HC Rare	—	—	—	—	—	—
1633 PM Rare	—	—	—	—	—	—
1638 GB Rare	—	—	—	—	—	—
1640 GB Rare	—	—	—	—	—	—
1641 SD Rare	—	—	—	—	—	—
1641 D-AD	—	350	750	1,700	—	—
1657 AC	—	425	1,000	2,500	—	—
1659 AC	—	425	1,000	2,500	—	—

KM# 26 THALER
Silver **Obv:** Arms in inner circle, IHS in radiant sun divide date **Rev:** Crowned imperial eagle in inner circle, mintmaster's initials divided by crown **Note:** Dav. #4621.

Date	Mintage	VG	F	VF	XF	Unc
1620 NPG	—	900	2,000	5,200	—	—
1621 G	—	325	800	2,000	—	—
1622 GI	—	625	1,500	3,500	—	—
1622 GR	—	85.00	200	500	1,500	—
1622 RG	—	135	300	750	—	—
1623 RG	—	85.00	200	600	1,800	—
1625 HC	—	325	750	1,800	—	—
1626 HC	—	325	750	1,800	—	—
1627 HC	—	325	750	1,800	—	—
1628 HC Rare	—	—	—	—	—	—
1629 HC Rare	—	—	—	—	—	—
1630 G-B	—	800	1,750	4,000	—	—
1633 G-B	—	800	1,750	4,000	—	—
1635 G-B	—	800	1,750	4,000	—	—
1638 BG Rare	—	—	—	—	—	—
1638 GB	—	800	1,750	4,000	—	—
1639 GB Rare	—	—	—	—	—	—
1640 GB	—	100	2,500	6,000	—	—
1641 SD	—	100	2,500	6,000	—	—
1641 D-AD	—	1,000	2,500	6,000	—	—
1642 DS	—	100	2,500	6,000	—	—
1642 SD	—	100	2,500	6,000	—	—
1657 AC no overdate	—	—	—	—	—	—
1657 AC over 1642	—	900	2,000	5,500	10,000	—
1659 AC no overdate	—	—	—	—	—	—
1659 AC over 1642 or 1657	—	900	2,000	5,500	—	—

KM# 32 ECU-PISTOLET
0.9170 Gold **Obv:** Radiant sun in inner circle **Rev:** Crowned imperial eagle with shield of arms on breast **Note:** Fr. #250, 251.

Date	Mintage	VG	F	VF	XF	Unc
1622 Rare	—	—	—	—	—	—
1630 RG Rare	—	—	—	—	—	—
1634 PM Rare	—	—	—	—	—	—
1638 BG Rare	—	—	—	—	—	—
1639 BG Rare	—	—	—	—	—	—
1640	—	—	—	—	—	—
1641	—	—	—	—	—	—
1642 BD Rare	—	—	—	—	—	—
1644	—	—	—	—	—	—

KM# 39 QUADRUPLA ECU PISTOLET
15.2800 g., 0.9000 Gold 0.4421 oz. AGW **Obv:** Radiant sun in inner circle **Rev:** Crowned imperial eagle with shield of arms on breast **Note:** Fr. #247, 248.

Date	Mintage	VG	F	VF	XF	Unc
1635 PM	—	4,000	10,000	20,000	35,000	—
1637 PM	—	4,000	10,000	20,000	35,000	—
1638 BG	—	3,500	9,000	18,000	30,000	—
1638 GB Rare	—	—	—	—	—	—
1640 GB Rare	—	—	—	—	—	—
1641 SD	—	3,500	7,500	15,000	25,000	—
1642 SD	—	3,500	7,500	15,000	25,000	—
1644 B Rare	—	—	—	—	—	—
1645 B Rare	—	—	—	—	—	—
1646 B Rare	—	—	—	—	—	—
1647 G Rare	—	—	—	—	—	—

KM# 37 PISTOLE
7.6400 g., 0.9000 Gold 0.2211 oz. AGW **Obv:** Radiant sun in inner circle **Rev:** Crowned imperial eagle with shield of arms on breast **Note:** Fr. #252.

Date	Mintage	VG	F	VF	XF	Unc
1630	—	—	—	—	—	—
1634 PM Rare	—	—	—	—	—	—
1636 PM Rare	—	—	—	—	—	—
1637 PM Rare	—	—	—	—	—	—
1638 BG Rare	—	—	—	—	—	—
1639 BG Rare	—	—	—	—	—	—
1640 GB Rare	—	—	—	—	—	—
1641 SD Rare	—	—	—	—	—	—
1642 SD Rare	—	—	—	—	—	—

TRADE COINAGE

KM# 42 DUCAT
3.5000 g., 0.9860 Gold 0.1109 oz. AGW **Note:** Varieties exist. Fr. #256, 257.

Date	Mintage	VG	F	VF	XF	Unc
1644 B	—	800	2,000	4,000	—	—
1645 B Rare	—	—	—	—	—	—
1646 B	—	800	2,000	4,000	—	—
1647 G Rare	—	—	—	—	—	—
1648 G	—	1,000	2,500	5,000	—	—
1649 G	—	1,200	3,000	6,000	—	—
1650 M	—	1,200	3,000	6,000	—	—
1651 M	—	1,200	3,000	6,000	—	—
1652 M Rare	—	—	—	—	—	—
1654 AB Rare	—	—	—	—	—	—
1657 DS Rare	—	—	—	—	—	—
1677	—	—	—	—	—	—

KM# 46 2 DUCAT
7.0000 g., 0.9860 Gold 0.2219 oz. AGW **Note:** Varieties exist. Fr. #254, 255.

Date	Mintage	VG	F	VF	XF	Unc
1654 AB Rare	—	—	—	—	—	—
1655 AC Rare	—	—	—	—	—	—
1656 AC	—	1,500	3,500	7,000	12,000	—
1657 AC	—	1,500	3,500	7,000	12,000	—
1658 AC Rare	—	—	—	—	—	—
1659 AC Rare	—	—	—	—	—	—
1660 AC Rare	—	—	—	—	—	—
1662 AC Rare	—	—	—	—	—	—
1663 AC Rare	—	—	—	—	—	—
1664 AC Rare	—	—	—	—	—	—
1665 AE Rare	—	—	—	—	—	—
1666 AE Rare	—	—	—	—	—	—
1674 AE Rare	—	—	—	—	—	—
1690 CL Rare	—	—	—	—	—	—
ND AE Rare	—	—	—	—	—	—

GLARUS

A canton in eastern Switzerland. Independence was gained in c.1390 but from 1798-1803 it was occupied by the French. They rejoined the Swiss Confederation in 1803.

MONETARY SYSTEM
3 Rappen = 1 Schilling
100 Rappen = 1 Frank

CANTON

STANDARD COINAGE

KM# 5 SCHILLING
Billon **Obv:** Standing saint wearing mantle, holding Bible and cane **Rev:** Crowned imperial eagle, cross between heads

Date	Mintage	VG	F	VF	XF	Unc
ND	—	1,200	2,500	9,000	—	—
1617	—	1,400	3,000	10,000	—	—

KM# 6 SCHILLING
Billon **Note:** Klippe.

Date	Mintage	VG	F	VF	XF	Unc
ND	—	—	—	—	—	—

HALDENSTEIN

Haldenstein was an area in the canton of Graubunden. The rulers were barons who held various estates. They received the mint right in 1612. The property of the barons was mediatized during the French invasion of Graubunden in 1798 and 1799.

RULERS
Thomas I, 1609-1628
Julius Otto, 1628-1666
Georg Philip, 1666-1695

BARONY

STANDARD COINAGE

KM# 91 2 PFENNIG (1/2 Kreuzer)
Billon **Obv:** Crowned five-fold arms on round shield in cartoucne within barley corn circle **Note:** Uniface.

Date	Mintage	VG	F	VF	XF	Unc
ND	—	250	500	1,000	—	—

KM# 10 BLUZGER
Billon **Obv:** Crowned five-fold arms of Haldenstein-Schauenstein on a Spanish shield between palm branches, value: 1/2 below **Note:** Uniface.

Date	Mintage	VG	F	VF	XF	Unc
ND	—	40.00	100	250	—	—

CANTON

STANDARD COINAGE

KM# 6 BLUZGER
Billon **Obv:** Large five-fold arms on Spanish shield in inner circle **Rev:** Plain cross in pearl circle, legend around

Date	Mintage	VG	F	VF	XF	Unc
ND	—	125	300	750	—	—

KM# 7 BLUZGER
Billon **Obv. Legend:** THOMAS. L. B. AB. EREN. **Rev. Legend:** DOMINVS. IN. HALDEN

Date	Mintage	VG	F	VF	XF	Unc
ND(1609-20)	—	150	350	900	—	—

KM# 8 BLUZGER
Billon **Obv. Legend:** IVLIVS. OTTO. L. B. AB. EHRE. D. I. H. **Rev. Legend:** MON. NOVA. HALDENSTA.

Date	Mintage	VG	F	VF	XF	Unc
ND(1628-66)	—	50.00	120	300	—	—

KM# 9 BLUZGER
Billon **Obv:** Arms larger **Rev:** Cross with all four sides broken from center

Date	Mintage	VG	F	VF	XF	Unc
ND	—	90.00	200	500	—	—

KM# 59 BLUZGER
Billon **Obv:** Five-fold arms in oval decorative cartouche **Obv. Legend:** GEORG. PHLIP. L. B. AB. EHRF. D. I H **Rev:** Cross without inner circle, date in legend

Date	Mintage	VG	F	VF	XF	Unc
1684	—	125	700	750	—	—
1687	—	20.00	40.00	100	200	—

KM# 73 BLUZGER
Billon **Obv:** Five-fold arms on Spanish shield in inner circle **Rev:** Cross in inner circle

Date	Mintage	VG	F	VF	XF	Unc
ND	—	40.00	100	250	—	—
1693	—	20.00	40.00	100	200	—

KM# 45 2 KREUZER (1/2 Batzen)
Billon **Obv:** 2 on imperial orb in inner circle **Rev:** Crowned imperial eagle with halos in inner circle

Date	Mintage	VG	F	VF	XF	Unc
1624 Rare	—	—	—	—	—	—

KM# 51 2 KREUZER (1/2 Batzen)
Billon **Obv:** Five-fold arms on round shield with indented sides **Rev:** 2 on imperial orb

Date	Mintage	VG	F	VF	XF	Unc
1648	—	800	2,000	5,000	—	—

KM# 48 3 KREUZER (1 Groschen)
Silver **Obv:** Bust right **Obv. Legend:** IVLIVS. OTTO. L. B. AB. EHREN **Rev:** Crowned imperial eagle, 3 on imperial orb on breast, date below **Note:** Klippe.

Date	Mintage	VG	F	VF	XF	Unc
1638 Rare	—	—	—	—	—	—

KM# 11 3 KREUZER (1 Groschen)
Silver **Obv:** Three decorated Spanish shields in cloverleaf form in inner circle **Rev:** Crowned double-headed eagle with cross and halo, 3 on breast of eagle

Date	Mintage	VG	F	VF	XF	Unc
ND	—	800	1,750	4,000	—	—

KM# 60 6 KREUZER
Billon **Obv:** Bust right, VI in oval shield below **Rev:** Crowned imperial eagle with crown dividing legend, date in legend

Date	Mintage	VG	F	VF	XF	Unc
1687	—	110	250	750	—	—

KM# 61 6 KREUZER
Billon **Obv:** Date in legend at top **Rev:** Crowned imperial eagle withn circle

Date	Mintage	VG	F	VF	XF	Unc
1687 Rare	—	—	—	—	—	—

KM# 63 6 KREUZER
Billon **Obv:** Bust right **Rev:** Crowned five-fold arms on shield between palm branches, date above

Date	Mintage	VG	F	VF	XF	Unc
1688	—	275	600	1,500	—	—

KM# 12 12 KREUZER (1/2 Dicken)
Silver **Obv:** Five-fold arms of Lichtenstein, Grottenstein, Haldenstien, and Herzschild Schauenstein **Rev:** Crowned imperial eagle, 1Z in imperial orb on breast

Date	Mintage	VG	F	VF	XF	Unc
ND	—	150	300	750	—	—

KM# 13 12 KREUZER (1/2 Dicken)
Silver **Rev:** Without orb on breast

Date	Mintage	VG	F	VF	XF	Unc
ND Rare	—	—	—	—	—	—

KM# 44 12 KREUZER (1/2 Dicken)
Silver **Obv:** 1/2-length figure right in innere circle **Rev:** Crowned imperial eagle, 1Z in circle on breast

Date	Mintage	VG	F	VF	XF	Unc
ND	—	100	200	500	—	—
1623 Rare	—	—	—	—	—	—

KM# 62 15 KREUZER (1/4 Gulden)
Silver **Obv:** Bust of Georg Philip right **Rev:** Crowned imperia eagle

Date	Mintage	VG	F	VF	XF	Unc
1687	—	100	200	400	800	

KM# 64 15 KREUZER (1/4 Gulden)
Silver **Obv:** Taller figure right **Rev:** Larger shield on eagle's breast, XV in shield below

Date	Mintage	VG	F	VF	XF	Unc
1689	—	100	200	400	800	

KM# 65 15 KREUZER (1/4 Gulden)
Silver **Obv:** Larger bust right **Rev:** Larger eagle

Date	Mintage	VG	F	VF	XF	Unc
1689	—	100	300	400	800	
1690	—	60.00	125	300	600	
1691	—	300	600	1,500	—	

KM# 66 30 KREUZER (1/2 Gulden)
Silver **Obv:** Bust right in inner circle **Rev:** Crowned five-fold arms between branches, 30 in shield at bottom

Date	Mintage	VG	F	VF	XF	Unc
1689	—	750	1,500	3,500	7,000	

KM# 14 BATZEN
Billon **Obv:** 1/2-length figure of Thomas I right

Date	Mintage	VG	F	VF	XF
ND	—	175	400	1,000	—

KM# 15 BATZEN
Billon **Obv:** Similar to KM#14 reverse **Rev:** Cross in inner cir

Date	Mintage	VG	F	VF	XF
ND	—	350	800	2,000	—

KM# 16 BATZEN
Billon **Obv:** Smaller cross in inner circle **Rev:** Smaller five-fc shield, crowned imperial eagle above

Date	Mintage	VG	F	VF	XF
ND	—	225	500	1,200	—

KM# 17 BATZEN
Billon **Obv:** 5-fold Spanish shield in inner circle **Rev:** Crown imperial eagle on spanish shield, crosses on both sides, top, a bottom of shield

Date	Mintage	VG	F	VF	XF
ND	—	350	1,200	3,000	—

KM# 18 BATZEN
Billon **Obv:** Five-fold arms in inner circle **Rev:** Cross in inne circle

Date	Mintage	VG	F	VF	XF
ND	—	275	600	1,500	—

KM# A19 1/2 DICKEN
Silver

Date	Mintage	VG	F	VF	XF
ND	—	90.00	200	500	—
1623 Rare	—	—	—	—	—

KM# 19 DICKEN
Silver **Obv:** 1/2-length figure right in inner circle **Rev:** Crown imperial eagle with shield on breast

Date	Mintage	VG	F	VF	XF
ND	—	225	500	1,200	—

KM# 20 DICKEN
Silver **Rev:** Large shield on eagle

Date	Mintage	VG	F	VF	XF
ND	—	125	250	600	1,200

KM# 21 DICKEN
Silver **Obv:** 1/2-length figure right behind large five-fold shie **Rev:** W/o shield on eagle

Date	Mintage	VG	F	VF	XF
ND	—	275	600	1,200	—

 # 22 DICKEN
ilver **Obv:** Taller figure with head breaking into legend **Rev:** arrow legend around larger eagle

ate	Mintage	VG	F	VF	XF	Unc
D	—	550	1,200	3,000	—	—

M# 23 DICKEN
ilver **Obv:** Arms slanting in front of figure

ate	Mintage	VG	F	VF	XF	Unc
D Rare	—	—	—	—	—	—

M# 24 DICKEN
ilver **Obv:** Shield with two trout in legend below figure

ate	Mintage	VG	F	VF	XF	Unc
D	—	200	400	750	1,300	—

M# 25 DICKEN
ilver **Obv:** 1/2-length figure left wearing cardinal's hat

ate	Mintage	VG	F	VF	XF	Unc
D	—	200	400	800	1,600	—

M# 26 DICKEN
ilver **Obv:** 1/2-length figure right wearing cardinal's hat

ate	Mintage	VG	F	VF	XF	Unc
D Rare	—	—	—	—	—	—

M# 27 DICKEN
ilver **Obv:** 1/2-length figure left wearing cardinal's hat **Rev:** nperial eagle w/o crown

ate	Mintage	VG	F	VF	XF	Unc
)	—	200	400	800	1,600	—

M# 35 DICKEN
ilver **Obv:** Bare-headed 1/2-length figure left, date in legend **ev:** Crowned imperial eagle

ate	Mintage	VG	F	VF	XF	Unc
)	—	125	250	600	1,200	—
317	—	700	1,500	—	—	—

M# 41 DICKEN
ilver **Obv:** Bare-headed 1/2-length figure right, date in legend

ate	Mintage	VG	F	VF	XF	Unc
320	—	225	550	1,200	—	—
321	—	175	350	800	—	—
323	—	550	1,200	3,000	—	—

M# 42 1/2 THALER
lver **Obv:** 1/2-length figure of Thomas I right **Rev:** Crowned nperial eagle

ate	Mintage	VG	F	VF	XF	Unc
320	—	1,400	3,000	7,500	—	—

M# 67 60 KREUZER (1 Gulden; 2/3 Thaler)
lver **Obv:** Bust right in inner circle **Rev:** Crowned imperial agle, five-fold shield on breast, 60 in oval shield below

ate	Mintage	VG	F	VF	XF	Unc
389	—	175	400	1,000	—	—

M# 68 60 KREUZER (1 Gulden; 2/3 Thaler)
lver **Obv:** Larger, closer bust right **Rev:** Five-fold shield on artouche, 60 in oval shield below

ate	Mintage	VG	F	VF	XF	Unc
89	—	275	600	1,500	—	—
90	—	175	400	1,000	—	—

KM# 70 2/3 THALER
Silver **Obv:** Bust of Georg Philip right **Rev:** 5-fold arms, 2/3 in oval shield below

Date	Mintage	VG	F	VF	XF	Unc
1690	—	75.00	150	350	600	—
1691	—	150	300	750	—	—
1692	—	125	250	600	—	—

KM# 71 2/3 THALER
Silver **Obv:** Bust of Georg Philip right **Rev:** Crowned imperial eagle, 2/3 in oval shield below

Date	Mintage	VG	F	VF	XF	Unc
1690	—	75.00	150	350	600	—
1691	—	75.00	150	350	600	—
1692	—	85.00	175	400	700	—

KM# 43.1 THALER
Silver **Obv:** Bare-headed 1/2-length figure right, date in legend above head **Rev:** Crowned imperial eagle **Note:** Dav. #46789.

Date	Mintage	VG	F	VF	XF	Unc
1621	—	450	1,000	2,500	—	—

KM# 43.2 THALER
Silver **Obv:** Bare-headed 1/2-length figure right looking up, date in legend to left of head **Note:** Dav. #4679.

Date	Mintage	VG	F	VF	XF	Unc
1623	—	300	650	1,500	—	—

KM# 47 2 THALER
Silver **Obv:** 1/2-length figure right, helmet and Spanish shield in lower margin **Rev:** Crowned imperial eagle, date in legend

Date	Mintage	VG	F	VF	XF	Unc
1637 Rare	—	9,500	20,000	40,000	75,000	—

TRADE COINAGE

KM# 29 GOLDGULDEN
3.5000 g., 0.9860 Gold 0.1109 oz. AGW **Obv:** Shield on eagle's chest **Note:** Several varieties exist, all ar rare.

Date	Mintage	VG	F	VF	XF	Unc
1618	—	4,500	10,000	20,000	—	—
ND	—	2,500	5,000	—	—	—

KM# 28 GOLDGULDEN
3.5000 g., 0.9860 Gold 0.1109 oz. AGW **Obv:** Orb on eagle's chest **Note:** Legend varieties exist.

Date	Mintage	VG	F	VF	XF	Unc
ND	—	500	1,000	2,000	3,000	—

KM# 49 DUCAT
3.5000 g., 0.9860 Gold 0.1109 oz. AGW **Obv:** Julius Otto standing **Rev:** Crowned imperial eagle **Note:** Fr. #279.

Date	Mintage	VG	F	VF	XF	Unc
1638	—	3,500	7,500	15,000	—	—
1642 Rare	—	—	—	—	—	—
1648 Rare	—	—	—	—	—	—
1649	—	3,500	7,500	15,000	—	—

KM# 55 DUCAT
3.5000 g., 0.9860 Gold 0.1109 oz. AGW **Obv:** 1/2-length figure facing 3/4 front with long hair **Rev:** Crowned imperial eagle w/shield on breast **Note:** Fr. #275.

Date	Mintage	VG	F	VF	XF	Unc
1667 Rare	—	—	—	—	—	—

KM# 36 2 DUCAT
7.0000 g., 0.9860 Gold 0.2219 oz. AGW **Obv:** 1/2-length figure of Thomas I left **Rev:** Crowned imperial eagle **Note:** Fr. #268.

Date	Mintage	VG	F	VF	XF	Unc
1617	—	3,500	7,500	15,000	25,000	—

KM# 37 2 DUCAT
7.0000 g., 0.9860 Gold 0.2219 oz. AGW **Obv:** Shield **Rev:** Crowned imperial eagle **Note:** Fr. #269.

Date	Mintage	VG	F	VF	XF	Unc
ND	—	4,500	10,000	20,000	35,000	—

KM# 72 2 DUCAT
7.0000 g., 0.9860 Gold 0.2219 oz. AGW **Obv:** Bust right w/long hair **Obv. Legend:** GEORG. PHIL. L. B... **Rev:** Crowned imperial eagle, shield on bust **Note:** Fr. #276.

Date	Mintage	VG	F	VF	XF	Unc
1690 Rare	—	—	—	—	—	—

KM# 38 4 DUCAT
14.0000 g., 0.9860 Gold 0.4438 oz. AGW **Obv:** Bust of Thomas left **Rev:** Crowned imperial eagle **Note:** Fr. #267.

Date	Mintage	VG	F	VF	XF	Unc
1617 Rare	—	—	—	—	—	—

KM# 39 7 DUCAT
24.5000 g., 0.9860 Gold 0.7766 oz. AGW **Obv:** 1/2-length figure of Thomas I right **Rev:** Crowned imperial eagle **Note:** Fr. #266.

Date	Mintage	VG	F	VF	XF	Unc
1617	—	4,000	9,000	18,000	30,000	—

LAUFENBURG

A city in northern Switzerland in the canton of Aargau. They received their coinage rights in the early 16th century.

CITY

STANDARD COINAGE

KM# 5 VIERER
Billon **Obv:** Round arms with standing lion in inner circle **Rev:** Floreate cross in inner circle

Date	Mintage	VG	F	VF	XF	Unc
ND Rare	—	—	—	—	—	—

KM# 6 SCHILLING
Billon **Obv:** Arms on shield in inner circle **Rev:** Bust of saint right, lamb in front

Date	Mintage	VG	F	VF	XF	Unc
ND Rare	—	—	—	—	—	—

KM# 7 PLAPPART
Billon **Obv:** Oval arms in cartouche in inner circle **Rev:** Standing saint holding lamb in arms

Date	Mintage	VG	F	VF	XF	Unc
ND Rare	—	—	—	—	—	—

KM# 10 PLAPPART
Billon **Rev:** Half-length figure of saint holding lamb in arms, 1 in circle divides date below

Date	Mintage	VG	F	VF	XF	Unc
1623	—	500	1,000	4,000	—	—

KM# 11 PLAPPART
Billon **Rev:** Standing saint in long robe holding lamb in arms, 1 in shield divides date below

Date	Mintage	VG	F	VF	XF	Unc
1623	—	500	1,000	4,000	—	—

KM# 9 2 PLAPPART
Billon **Obv:** Standing lion arms on shield, leaf decorations around in inner circle **Rev:** Standing saint in long robe holding lamb and cross divides date in field, Z below

Date	Mintage	VG	F	VF	XF	Unc
1622 Rare	—	—	—	—	—	—

KM# 12 2 PLAPPART
Billon **Obv:** Oval arms in cartouche

Date	Mintage	VG	F	VF	XF	Unc
1623	—	—	—	—	—	—

KM# 13 4 PLAPPART
Billon **Obv:** Oval standing lion arms in cartouche **Rev:** Lamb with halo and cross on round shield, script SVRR - EXIT - IOAN - BAPT in center legend

Date	Mintage	VG	F	VF	XF	Unc
1623 Rare	—	—	—	—	—	—

LUZERN

Lucerne

A canton and city in central Switzerland. The city grew around the Benedictine Monastery which was founded in 750. They joined the Swiss Confederation as the 4th member in 1332. Few coins were issued before the1500s.

MINT OFFICIAL'S INITIALS

Initial	Date	Name
LV	1622	?

MONETARY SYSTEM

Until 1798

240 Angster = 120 Rappen = 40 Schillinge = 1 Gulden
10 Rappen = 1 Batzen
4 Kreuzer = 1 Batzen
10 Batzen = 1 Frank
40 Batzen = 3 Gulden = 1 Thaler
4 Franken = 1 Thaler
12 Gulden = 1 Duplone

CITY

STANDARD COINAGE

KM# 5 HELLER
Billon **Obv:** Plain bishop's mitre above form with hollow cheeks, dots missing in mitre **Note:** Uniface.

Date	Mintage	VG	F	VF	XF	Unc
ND	—	12.00	25.00	50.00	200	—

KM# A8 ANGSTER (Rappen)
Billon **Note:** Uniface.

Date	Mintage	VG	F	VF	XF	Unc
ND	—	12.00	25.00	50.00	200	—

KM# 6 ANGSTER (Rappen)
Billon **Obv:** Bishop's mitre above composed form with hollow cheeks, dots in mitre **Note:** Uniface.

Date	Mintage	VG	F	VF	XF	Unc
ND	—	12.00	25.00	50.00	200	—

KM# 8 SCHILLING
Billon **Obv:** Crowned imperial eagle above arms on shield **Rev:** Bust of saint wearing a mitre

Date	Mintage	VG	F	VF	XF	Unc
1601	—	18.00	40.00	120	—	—
1603	—	18.00	40.00	120	—	—
1604 Rare	—	—	—	—	—	—
1605	—	12.00	25.00	80.00	200	—

KM# 13 SCHILLING
Billon **Obv:** Larger eagle, date below, small shield of arms in legend at bottom

Date	Mintage	VG	F	VF	XF	Unc
ND	—	22.00	50.00	150	—	—
1609	—	12.00	25.00	80.00	200	—
1610	—	12.00	25.00	80.00	200	—
1611	—	12.00	25.00	80.00	200	—

KM# 17 SCHILLING
Billon **Obv:** Date in legend

Date	Mintage	VG	F	VF	XF	Unc
1611	—	12.00	25.00	80.00	200	—
1612	—	12.00	25.00	80.00	200	—
1613	—	12.00	25.00	80.00	200	—
1614	—	12.00	25.00	80.00	200	—
1615	—	18.00	25.00	100	250	—
1616	—	32.00	70.00	150	400	—
1617	—	32.00	70.00	150	400	—
1618	—	32.00	70.00	150	400	—
1619	—	32.00	70.00	150	400	—
1620	—	32.00	70.00	150	400	—
1621	—	12.00	25.00	80.00	200	—
1622	—	12.00	25.00	80.00	200	—

KM# 25 SCHILLING
Billon

Date	Mintage	VG	F	VF	XF	Unc
1623	—	12.00	25.00	80.00	200	—
1634	—	12.00	25.00	80.00	200	—
1638	—	12.00	25.00	80.00	200	—
1639 Rare	—	—	—	—	—	—
1647	—	12.00	25.00	80.00	200	—

KM# 9 3 KREUZER (1 Groschen)
Silver **Obv:** Large shield in inner circle, date in legend **Rev:** Crowned imperial eagle, imperial orb with 3 on breast

Date	Mintage	VG	F	VF	XF	Unc
1601	—	10.00	20.00	40.00	100	—
1602	—	10.00	20.00	40.00	100	—
1603	—	10.00	20.00	40.00	100	—
1604	—	10.00	20.00	40.00	100	—
1605	—	10.00	20.00	40.00	100	—
1606	—	10.00	20.00	40.00	100	—
1613 Rare	—	—	—	—	—	—

KM# 22 BATZEN-10 RAPPEN
Billon **Obv:** Arms, eagle above, with or without L-V at sides of arms, date in legend **Rev:** Cross, fleur-de-lis in angles

Date	Mintage	VG	F	VF	XF	Unc
1622 LV	—	7.00	115	50.00	125	—
1622	—	9.00	20.00	60.00	150	—

KM# 29 BATZEN-10 RAPPEN
Billon **Obv:** Large shield in inner circle, date below **Rev:** Large cross in inner circle

Date	Mintage	VG	F	VF	XF	Unc
1638	—	7.00	15.00	50.00	125	—

KM# 21 1/2 DICKEN
Silver **Obv:** Crowned imperial eagle above shield dividing date **Rev:** 1/2-length St. Mauritius in armor right holding swords

Date	Mintage	VG	F	VF	XF	Unc
1620 Rare	—	—	—	—	—	—
1621 Rare	—	—	—	—	—	—
1622 Rare	—	—	450	1,000	2,500	—

KM# 23 1/2 DICKEN
Silver **Obv:** Large eagle above small shield **Rev:** Bust of Saint wearing mitre, right

Date	Mintage	VG	F	VF	XF	Unc
1622 Rare	—	—	450	1,000	2,500	—

KM# 26 1/2 DICKEN
Silver **Obv:** Large shield in inner circle, date below **Rev:** Half-length saint in armor right holding sword

Date	Mintage	VG	F	VF	XF	Unc
1623	—	45.00	100	250	600	—

KM# 15 DICKEN
Silver

Date	Mintage	VG	F	VF	XF	Unc
1610	—	350	800	2,000	—	—

KM# 16 DICKEN
Silver **Obv:** Smaller shield, date divided by eagle's tail **Rev:** Similar to KM#19

Date	Mintage	VG	F	VF	XF	Unc
1610	—	450	1,000	2,500	—	—
1611	—	45.00	100	250	600	—
1612	—	45.00	100	250	600	—

KM# 18 DICKEN
Silver **Obv:** Without date **Rev:** Similar to KM#19

Date	Mintage	VG	F	VF	XF	Unc
1612	—	45.00	100	250	600	—
1613	—	45.00	100	250	600	—
1614	—	45.00	100	250	600	—
1615	—	45.00	100	250	600	—
1616	—	45.00	100	250	600	—

KM# 19 DICKEN
Silver

Date	Mintage	VG	F	VF	XF	Unc
1617	—	90.00	200	500	—	—
1618	—	225	500	1,200	—	—
1619	—	350	600	1,500	—	—
1620	—	70.00	150	350	750	—
1621	—	70.00	150	350	750	—
1622	—	70.00	150	350	750	—

KM# 27 DICKEN
Silver

Date	Mintage	VG	F	VF	XF	Unc
1623	—	45.00	100	250	600	—
1647	—	175	700	1,000	2,000	—
1656	—	275	600	1,500	—	—

KM# 10 THALER
Silver **Obv:** Eighteen shields of district arms encircle crown above three shields, lion on each side of shields **Rev:** Scene depicting legend of the blinding St. Leodegar **Note:** Dav. #462

Date	Mintage	VG	F	VF	XF	Unc
1603 Rare	—	—	—	—	—	—

KM# 24 THALER

ilver **Obv:** Crowned imperial eagle **Rev:** St. Leodegar standing acing **Note:** Dav. #4624.

ate	Mintage	VG	F	VF	XF	Unc
622	—	100	250	500	—	—

KM# 40 THALER

ilver **Obv:** Ornate oval shield **Rev:** St. Leodegar standing facing **ote:** Dav. #4625.

ate	Mintage	VG	F	VF	XF	Unc
698	—	275	600	1,500	3,000	4,500

KM# 11 2 THALER

ilver **Obv:** Eighteen shields of district arms encircle crown bove three shields, lion on each side of shields **Rev:** Scene epicting the blinding of the saint **Note:** Dav. #4622.

ate	Mintage	VG	F	VF	XF	Unc
603 Rare	—	3,750	8,000	20,000	40,000	—

KM# 41 2 THALER

ilver **Note:** Similar to 1 Thaler, KM#40. Dav. #A4625.

ate	Mintage	VG	F	VF	XF	Unc
698 Rare	—	2,750	6,000	15,000	25,000	—

TRADE COINAGE

KM# 36 DUCAT

.5000 g., 0.9860 Gold 0.1109 oz. AGW **Obv:** Inscription in artouche **Rev:** Sts. Leodegar and Maurice standing **Note:** Fr. #302.

ate	Mintage	VG	F	VF	XF	Unc
D(1695-1700) Rare	—	—	—	—	—	—

KM# 12 2 DUCAT

.0000 g., 0.9860 Gold 0.2219 oz. AGW **Obv:** Shield of arms with agle above **Rev:** Facing bust of St. Leodegar **Note:** Fr. #288.

ate	Mintage	VG	F	VF	XF	Unc
603 Rare	—	—	—	—	—	—

KM# 34 2 DUCAT

.0000 g., 0.9860 Gold 0.2219 oz. AGW **Obv:** Crowned arms **ev:** St. Leodegar with church at side **Note:** Fr. #304.

ate	Mintage	VG	F	VF	XF	Unc
675 Rare	—	—	—	—	—	—

KM# 37 2 DUCAT

.0000 g., 0.9860 Gold 0.2219 oz. AGW **Obv:** Soldier **Rev:** St. .eodegar **Note:** Fr. #307.

ate	Mintage	VG	F	VF	XF	Unc
695	—	4,000	9,000	15,000	25,000	—

KM# A37 2 DUCAT

.0000 g., 0.9860 Gold 0.2219 oz. AGW **Obv:** Inscription in artouche **Rev:** Sts. Leodegar and Maurice standing **Note:** Fr. #301.

ate	Mintage	VG	F	VF	XF	Unc
D(1695-1700) Rare	—	—	—	—	—	—

KM# 14 4 DUCAT

4.0000 g., 0.9860 Gold 0.4438 oz. AGW **Obv:** Crowned mperial eagle over shield **Rev:** Bust of St. Leodegar facing **Note:** Struck with 1 Dicken dies, KM#15. Fr. #287.

ate	Mintage	VG	F	VF	XF	Unc
610 Rare	—	—	—	—	—	—

KM# 20 4 DUCAT

14.0000 g., 0.9860 Gold 0.4438 oz. AGW **Obv:** Crowned imperial eagle over shield **Rev:** Bust of St. Leodegar right **Note:** Struck with 1 Dicken dies, KM#19. Fr. #292.

Date	Mintage	VG	F	VF	XF	Unc
1619 Rare	—	—	—	—	—	—

KM# 38 4 DUCAT

14.0000 g., 0.9860 Gold 0.4438 oz. AGW **Obv:** Soldier seated beside shield **Rev:** St. Leodegar seated **Note:** Fr. #306.

Date	Mintage	VG	F	VF	XF	Unc
1695 Rare	—	—	—	—	—	—

KM# A42 4 DUCAT

14.0000 g., 0.9860 Gold 0.4438 oz. AGW **Obv:** Ornate oval arms **Rev:** St. Leodegar standing facing **Note:** Struck with 1 Thaler dies, KM#40. Fr. #300.

Date	Mintage	VG	F	VF	XF	Unc
1698 Rare	—	—	—	—	—	—

KM# 39 5 DUCAT

17.5000 g., 0.9860 Gold 0.5547 oz. AGW **Obv:** Soldier seated beside shield **Rev:** St. Leodegar seated **Note:** Fr. #305.

Date	Mintage	VG	F	VF	XF	Unc
1695	—	5,500	12,000	25,000	40,000	—

KM# B42 5 DUCAT

17.5000 g., 0.9860 Gold 0.5547 oz. AGW **Obv:** Ornate oval arms **Rev:** St. Leodegar standing facing **Note:** Struck with 1 Thaler dies. KM#40. Fr. #299.

Date	Mintage	VG	F	VF	XF	Unc
1698 Rare	—	—	—	—	—	—

KM# A15 6 DUCAT

21.0000 g., 0.9860 Gold 0.6657 oz. AGW **Obv:** Eighteen shields of district arms encircle crown above three shields with lion on each **Rev:** Scene depicting legend of the blinding of St. Leodegar **Note:** Struck with 1 Thaler dies. KM#10. Fr. 290.

Date	Mintage	VG	F	VF	XF	Unc
1603 Rare	—	—	—	—	—	—

KM# C42 6 DUCAT

21.0000 g., 0.9860 Gold 0.6657 oz. AGW **Obv:** Ornate oval arms **Rev:** St. Leodegar standing facing **Note:** Struck with 1 Thaler dies. KM#40. Fr. #298.

Date	Mintage	VG	F	VF	XF	Unc
1698 Rare	—	—	—	—	—	—

KM# B15 10 DUCAT

35.0000 g., 0.9860 Gold 1.1095 oz. AGW **Obv:** Eighteen shields of district arms encircle crown above three shields with lion on each side **Rev:** Scene depicting legend of the blinding of St. Leodegar **Note:** Struck with 1 Thaler dies. KM#10. Fr. #289.

Date	Mintage	VG	F	VF	XF	Unc
1603 Rare	—	—	—	—	—	—

KM# A25 10 DUCAT

35.0000 g., 0.9860 Gold 1.1095 oz. AGW **Obv:** Crowned imperial eagle **Obv. Legend:** MONETA + NOVA + LVCERNENSIS * **Rev:** St. Leodegar standing facing with crook and borer **Rev. Legend:** SANCTVS * LEODIGARIVS * P * **Note:** Struck with 1 Thaler dies. KM#24. Fr. #291.

Date	Mintage	VG	F	VF	XF	Unc
1622 Rare	—	—	—	—	—	—

KM# 42 10 DUCAT

35.0000 g., 0.9860 Gold 1.1095 oz. AGW **Obv:** Ornate oval arms **Rev:** St. Leodegar standing facing **Note:** Struck with 1 Thaler dies. KM#40. Fr. #297.

Date	Mintage	VG	F	VF	XF	Unc
1698 Rare	—	—	—	—	—	—

PATTERNS

Including off metal strikes

KM#	Date	Mintage	Identification	Mkt Val
Pn1	1621	—	Schilling. Gold. KM#17.	2,000
Pn2	1621	—	1/2 Dicken. Gold. Weight of 2 Goldgulden, KM#21.	—
Pn3	1622	—	1/2 Dicken. Gold. Weight of 1 Goldgulden, KM#21.	—
Pn4	1638	—	Batzen. Gold. 6.6000 g. KM#29.	2,500
Pn5	1639	—	Batzen. Gold. KM#25.	2,000

NEUCHATEL

Nuenberg

A canton on the west central border of Switzerland. The first coins (bracteates) were struck in the 11th century. They were under Prussian rule from 1707 to 1806. France occupied the canton from 1806-1815. They reverted to Prussia until 1857, when they became a full member of the Swiss Confederation.

NOTE: For coins previously listed here dated 1707-1806, see German States, Prussia.

RULERS

Henri II, 1595-1663
Jean Louis, 1663-1671
Charles Paris, 1671-1673
Marie de Orleans-Nemours, 1672-1707

MONETARY SYSTEM

4 Kreuzer = 1 Batzen
7 Kreuzer = 1 Piecette
21 Batzen = 1 Gulden
2 Gulden = 1 Thaler

CANTON

Prussian Administration

STANDARD COINAGE

KM# 24 1/2 KREUZER

Billon

Date	Mintage	VG	F	VF	XF	Unc
1617 Rare	—	—	—	—	—	—
ND(1666)	—	65.00	150	600	—	—

KM# 6 KREUZER

Billon **Obv:** Crowned four-fold arms divide date **Rev:** Cross wtih forked ends in inner circle

Date	Mintage	VG	F	VF	XF	Unc
1606	—	27.00	60.00	250	—	—
1610	—	27.00	60.00	250	—	—
1611	—	45.00	100	350	—	—
1613	—	45.00	100	350	—	—
1614	—	45.00	100	350	—	—
1615 Rare	—	—	—	—	—	—
1616	—	27.00	60.00	250	—	—
1617	—	27.00	60.00	250	—	—
1618	—	27.00	60.00	250	—	—
1619 Rare	—	—	—	—	—	—

KM# 11 KREUZER

Billon **Obv:** Four fields of arms connected

Date	Mintage	VG	F	VF	XF	Unc
ND	—	27.00	60.00	250	—	—
1621	—	27.00	60.00	250	—	—
1622	—	27.00	60.00	250	—	—
1629	—	27.00	60.00	250	—	—

KM# 15 KREUZER

Billon **Obv:** Crowned two-fold arms divide date **Rev:** Cross with fleur-de-lis in angles

Date	Mintage	VG	F	VF	XF	Unc
1630	—	20.00	42.00	150	—	—
1631	—	20.00	42.00	150	—	—
1640	—	20.00	42.00	150	—	—

KM# 21 10 KREUZER

Silver **Obv:** Armored and draped bust right **Rev:** Crowned two-fold arms

Date	Mintage	VG	F	VF	XF	Unc
ND(1648)	—	45.00	100	350	—	—

KM# 25 10 KREUZER

Silver **Obv:** Draped bust with long hair right **Rev:** Crowned two-fold arms divide date

Date	Mintage	VG	F	VF	XF	Unc
1668	—	1,500	4,000	8,000	—	—

KM# 27 16 KREUZER

Silver

Date	Mintage	VG	F	VF	XF	Unc
1694	—	25.00	50.00	150	250	400

KM# 28 20 KREUZER

Silver **Obv:** Bust of Marie right **Rev:** Crowned arms

Date	Mintage	VG	F	VF	XF	Unc
1694 Rare	—	—	—	—	—	—
1695	—	45.00	100	250	500	—

KM# 8 1/2 BATZEN

Billon **Obv:** Crowned four-fold arms divide date **Rev:** Cross with prongs at end in inner circle

Date	Mintage	VG	F	VF	XF	Unc
ND Rare	—	—	—	—	—	—
1615 Rare	—	—	—	—	—	—
1619 Rare	—	—	—	—	—	—

KM# 22 1/2 BATZEN

Billon **Obv:** Crowned two-fold arms divide date **Rev:** Cross with prongs at end, fleur-de-lis in angles

Date	Mintage	VG	F	VF	XF	Unc
1648	—	24.00	50.00	200	—	—
1649	—	24.00	50.00	200	—	—

KM# 12 BATZEN

Billon **Obv:** Crowned four-fold arms in inner circle **Rev:** Cross with prongs in inner circle

Date	Mintage	VG	F	VF	XF	Unc
1621 Rare	—	—	—	—	—	—

KM# 13 BATZEN

Billon **Rev:** Date divided by bottom of cross

Date	Mintage	VG	F	VF	XF	Unc
1622	—	25.00	50.00	200	—	—

KM# 9 TESTON (1 Dicken)

Silver **Obv:** Bust left **Obv. Legend:** HEN. DVX. LONGAVIL. CO. S. NEOC. **Rev:** Crowned four-fold arms dividing date **Rev. Legend:** OCVLI. DOMINI. SVPER. IVSTOS.

Date	Mintage	VG	F	VF	XF	Unc
1618 Rare	—	—	—	—	—	—

KM# 16 TESTON (1 Dicken)

Silver **Obv:** Draped bust right **Rev:** Crowned two-fold arms, date below

Date	Mintage	VG	F	VF	XF	Unc
1631	—	4,500	10,000	25,000	—	—

KM# 17 TESTON (1 Dicken)

Silver **Shape:** 8-sided **Note:** Klippe.

Date	Mintage	VG	F	VF	XF	Unc
1631 Rare	—	—	—	—	—	—

KM# 29 1/4 THALER (1/4 Ecu)

Silver **Obv:** Draped bust right **Rev:** Crowned four-fold arms

Date	Mintage	VG	F	VF	XF	Unc
1694	—	375	800	2,000	4,000	—

KM# 19 THALER (1 Ecu)

Silver **Obv:** Draped bust right **Rev:** Crowned two-fold arms divide date **Note:** Dav. #4626.

Date	Mintage	VG	F	VF	XF	Unc
163Z Rare	—	—	—	—	—	—

KM# 5.1 2 PISTOLES

15.2800 g., 0.9000 Gold 0.4421 oz. AGW **Obv:** Bust of Henri II left **Rev:** Crowned arms **Note:** Fr. #335.

Date	Mintage	VG	F	VF	XF	Unc
1603	—	—	25,000	50,000	—	—

KM# 5.2 2 PISTOLES

15.2800 g., 0.9000 Gold 0.4421 oz. AGW **Obv:** Bust of Henri II left **Rev:** Crowned arms **Note:** Fr. #336.

Date	Mintage	VG	F	VF	XF	Unc
1618 Rare	—	—	—	—	—	—

KM# 18 2 PISTOLES

15.2800 g., 0.9000 Gold 0.4421 oz. AGW **Obv:** Bust of Henri II right **Note:** Fr. #337.

Date	Mintage	VG	F	VF	XF	Unc
1631 Rare	—	—	—	—	—	—

KM# 30 2 PISTOLES

15.2800 g., 0.9000 Gold 0.4421 oz. AGW **Obv:** Bust of Marie right **Rev:** Crowned 4-fold arms **Note:** Fr. #339.

Date	Mintage	VG	F	VF	XF	Unc
1694	—	—	12,000	24,000	40,000	—

Note: Bowers and Merena Guia sale 3-88 XF realized $28,600

KM# 31 4 PISTOLES

30.5600 g., 0.9000 Gold 0.8842 oz. AGW **Obv:** Bust of Marie right **Rev:** Crowned 4-fold arms **Note:** Fr. #338.

Date	Mintage	VG	F	VF	XF	Unc
1694 Unique	—	—	—	—	—	—

PATTERNS

Including off metal strikes

KM#	Date	Mintage	Identification	Mkt Val
Pn2	1618	—	Teston. Gold. 13.8700 g. KM#9.	—
Pn1	1618	—	Teston. Gold. 12.7500 g. KM#9.	—
Pn4	1631	—	Teston. Gold. 13.3500 g. KM#16.	—
Pn3	1631	—	Teston. Gold. 8.4500 g. KM#16.	—

SAINT GALL

ABBEY

An abbey in northeast Switzerland, established in c.720. They obtained the mint right in 947 but the first coins were not made until about 100 years later. The power of the abbey dwindled until the last Abbot resigned in 1805.

STANDARD COINAGE

KM# 8 THALER

Silver **Obv:** Crowned imperial eagle, four-fold arms on shield below **Rev:** Half-length saint with bread and staff

Date	Mintage	VG	F	VF	XF	Unc
1622	—	350	800	2,000	4,000	—

KM# 9 THALER

Silver **Note:** Klippe.

Date	Mintage	VG	F	VF	XF	Unc
1622 Rare	—	—	—	—	—	—

KM# 10 2 THALER

Silver **Obv:** Crowned imperial eagle, four-fold arms on shield below **Rev:** Half-length saint with bread and staff

Date	Mintage	VG	F	VF	XF	Unc
1622 Rare	—	4,500	10,000	25,000	—	—

KM# 11 2 THALER

Silver **Note:** Klippe.

Date	Mintage	VG	F	VF	XF	Unc
1622 Rare	—	—	—	—	—	—

CITY

A city located in northeast Switzerland which was built to protect the abbey. It became a free city in 1311 and gained independence from the Abbots in 1457. The first coins were struck in the 1400s and the last ones in 1790.

MINT OFFICIALS' INITIALS

Initials	Date	Name
A		
A-H		
G		
H.G.Z., Z		Hans Georg Zolli Kofer
Z		

STANDARD COINAGE

KM# A51 PFENNIG

Billon **Note:** Uniface.

Date	Mintage	VG	F	VF	XF	Unc
ND	—	20.00	50.00	150	300	—

KM# 51 3 KREUZER

Billon **Obv:** Standing bear left in inner circle **Rev:** Crowned imperial eagle with 3 in circle on breast **Note:** Groschen.

Date	Mintage	VG	F	VF	XF	Unc
1618	—	85.00	200	500	1,000	—
1619	—	85.00	200	500	1,000	—

KM# 52 3 KREUZER

Billon **Note:** Klippe.

Date	Mintage	VG	F	VF	XF	Unc
1618 Rare	—	—	—	—	—	—

KM# 66 4 KREUZER (1 Batzen)

Billon, 26 mm. **Obv:** Bear standing left divides date, value in oval shield below **Rev:** Eagle on shield on long cross

Date	Mintage	VG	F	VF	XF	Unc
1621	—	70.00	160	475	1,200	—

KM# 67 4 KREUZER (1 Batzen)

Billon, 22 mm. **Obv:** Bear standing left divides value, date below

Date	Mintage	VG	F	VF	XF	Unc
1621	—	35.00	75.00	250	—	—
1622	—	40.00	100	300	—	—

KM# 68 4 KREUZER (1 Batzen)

Billon **Note:** Klippe.

Date	Mintage	VG	F	VF	XF	Unc
1621	—	—	—	—	—	—
1622	—	—	—	—	—	—

KM# 56 3 BATZEN (1/2 Dicken)

Silver **Obv:** Bear standing left, date below **Rev:** Crowned imperial eagle in inner circle, 3 below

Date	Mintage	VG	F	VF	XF	Unc
1619	—	100	250	600	—	—
1620	—	60.00	125	300	—	—
1621	—	25.00	60.00	150	—	—
1622	—	25.00	60.00	150	—	—
1624	—	25.00	60.00	150	—	—

KM# 58 3 BATZEN (1/2 Dicken)

Silver **Note:** Klippe.

Date	Mintage	VG	F	VF	XF	Unc
1619	—	—	—	—	—	—
1620	—	—	—	—	—	—
1621	—	—	—	—	—	—
1622	—	—	—	—	—	—

KM# 53 1/2 DICKEN

Silver **Obv:** Bear standing left, date in legend **Rev:** Crowned imperial eagle in inner circle

Date	Mintage	VG	F	VF	XF	Unc
1618	—	1,400	3,000	1,500	—	—
1619 Rare	—	900	2,000	5,000	—	—

KM# 70 24 KREUZER (6 Batzen - 1 Dicken)

Silver **Obv:** Bear standing left **Rev:** Imperial eagle

Date	Mintage	VG	F	VF	XF	Unc
1631	—	175	400	1,000	—	—
1633	—	225	500	1,200	—	—

KM# 54 DICKEN (6 Batzen)

Silver **Note:** Similar to 1/2 Thaler, KM#59.

Date	Mintage	VG	F	VF	XF	Unc
1618	—	90.00	200	400	—	—
1619	—	75.00	150	350	—	—
1620	—	50.00	100	250	—	—
1621	—	40.00	85.00	200	—	—

KM# 57 DICKEN (6 Batzen)

Silver **Note:** Klippe.

Date	Mintage	VG	F	VF	XF	Unc
1619	—	—	—	—	—	—
1620	—	—	—	—	—	—
1621 Rare	—	—	—	—	—	—
1622 Rare	—	—	—	—	—	—

KM# 59 1/2 THALER

Silver **Obv:** Bear standing left **Obv. Legend:** Crowned imperial eagle

Date	Mintage	VG	F	VF	XF	Unc
1620	—	150	300	750	1,500	—

KM# 60 1/2 THALER
Silver **Note:** Klippe. Illustration reduced.

Date	Mintage	VG	F	VF	XF	Unc
1620	—	—	—	—	—	—

KM# 62 THALER
Silver **Note:** Klippe. Dav. #4677A.

Date	Mintage	VG	F	VF	XF	Unc
1620	—	—	—	—	—	—
1621	—	—	—	—	—	—
1622	—	—	—	—	—	—
1623	—	—	—	—	—	—

KM# 61 THALER
Silver **Note:** Similar to 1/2 Thaler, KM#59. Dav. #4677.

Date	Mintage	VG	F	VF	XF	Unc
1620	—	45.00	100	250	—	—
1621	—	45.00	100	250	—	—
1622	—	45.00	100	250	—	—
1623	—	45.00	100	250	—	—
1624	—	70.00	150	350	—	—

KM# 64 2 THALER
Silver **Obv:** Bear standing left **Rev:** Crowned imperial eagle **Note:** Klippe. Dav. #4676A.

Date	Mintage	VG	F	VF	XF	Unc
1620 Rare	—	—	—	—	—	—
1621 Rare	—	—	—	—	—	—
1622 Rare	—	—	—	—	—	—

KM# 63 2 THALER
Silver **Obv:** Bear standing left **Rev:** Crowned imperial eagle **Note:** Similar to 1/2 Thaler, KM#59. Dav. #4676.

Date	Mintage	VG	F	VF	XF	Unc
1620 Rare	—	—	—	—	—	—
1621	—	1,200	2,500	6,000	—	—

TRADE COINAGE

KM# A55 2 DUCAT
7.0000 g., 0.9860 Gold 0.2219 oz. AGW **Obv:** Bear standing walking left **Rev:** Imperial eagle **Note:** Fr. #361.

Date	Mintage	VG	F	VF	XF	Unc
1618 Rare	—	—	—	—	—	—
1619 Rare	—	—	—	—	—	—

KM# 69 2 DUCAT
7.0000 g., 0.9860 Gold 0.2219 oz. AGW **Obv:** Bear walking left in inner circle, date in legend **Rev:** Imperial eagle **Note:** Fr. #362.

Date	Mintage	VG	F	VF	XF	Unc
1621	—	1,500	3,000	6,000	10,000	—

KM# 55 3 DUCAT
10.5000 g., 0.9860 Gold 0.3328 oz. AGW **Obv:** Bear walking left in inner circle, date in legend **Rev:** Imperial eagle **Note:** Fr. #360.

Date	Mintage	VG	F	VF	XF	Unc
1618 Unique	—	—	—	—	—	—
1619 Unique	—	—	—	—	—	—

KM# 65 4 DUCAT
14.0000 g., 0.9860 Gold 0.4438 oz. AGW **Obv:** Bear walking left in inner circle, date in legend **Rev:** Crowned imperial eagle **Note:** Klippe. Fr. #359.

Date	Mintage	VG	F	VF	XF	Unc
1620 Unique	—	—	—	—	—	—

PATTERNS

Including off metal strikes

KM#	Date	Mintage	Identification	Mkt Val
PnA1	1621	—	1/2 Dicken. Klippe.	—
Pn1	ND	—	Pfennig. Gold. KM#5	—
Pn2	1621	—	2 Ducat. Silver. 6.9500 g. KM#69	500

SCHAFFHAUSEN

A canton located on the north central border of Switzerland. The first coins, which were issued in the 13th century were known as "Ram Bracteates". It joined the Swiss Confederation in 1501.

MONETARY SYSTEM
4 Kreuzer = 1 Batzen

CANTON

STANDARD COINAGE

KM# 5 HELLER
Billon **Note:** Uniface. Schussel type. Ram leaping over town gate.

Date	Mintage	VG	F	VF	XF	Unc
ND	—	225	500	2,000	—	—

KM# 6 4 HELLER (Vierer)
Billon **Obv:** Ram leaping over town gate, three hills above **Rev:** Eagle facing right

Date	Mintage	VG	F	VF	XF	Unc
ND	—	50.00	200	600	1,500	—

KM# 7 4 HELLER (Vierer)
Billon **Rev:** Eagle facing left

Date	Mintage	VG	F	VF	XF	Unc
ND	—	90.00	300	600	1,500	—
1610 Rare	—	—	—	—	—	—
(16)16 Rare	—	—	—	—	—	—

KM# 8 4 HELLER (Vierer)
Billon **Note:** Klippe.

Date	Mintage	VG	F	VF	XF	Unc
ND Rare	—	—	—	—	—	—
(16)16 Rare	—	—	—	—	—	—

KM# 9 4 HELLER (Vierer)
Billon **Rev:** 4 on round shield on eagle's breast

Date	Mintage	VG	F	VF	XF	Unc
ND	—	35.00	75.00	250	600	—
1626	—	40.00	100	400	—	—
1627	—	40.00	100	400	—	—
1628	—	40.00	100	400	—	—
1630 Rare	—	—	—	—	—	—

KM# 10 PFENNIG
Billon **Note:** Ram jumping out of town gate over grassy bush.

Date	Mintage	VG	F	VF	XF	Unc
ND	—	25.00	50.00	200	500	—

KM# 11 PFENNIG
Billon **Note:** Ram jumping out of town gate over three hills.

Date	Mintage	VG	F	VF	XF	Unc
ND	—	70.00	150	600	—	—

KM# 12 PFENNIG
Billon **Note:** Upright ram standing left.

Date	Mintage	VG	F	VF	XF	Unc
ND	—	45.00	100	400	1,000	—

KM# 13 KREUZER
Billon **Obv:** Ram standing left **Rev:** Crowned imperial eagle, 1 in round shield on breast

Date	Mintage	VG	F	VF	XF	Unc
ND Rare	—	—	—	—	—	—

KM# 41 2 KREUZER (1/2 Batzen)
Billon **Obv:** Ram jumping from town gate over grassy bush **Rev:** Crowned imperial eagle with 2 on breast

Date	Mintage	VG	F	VF	XF	Unc
1626	—	90.00	200	750	—	—
1698	—	110	250	1,000	2,000	4,000

KM# 59 2 KREUZER (1/2 Batzen)
Billon **Note:** Klippe.

Date	Mintage	VG	F	VF	XF	Unc
1698 Rare	—	—	—	—	—	—

KM# 15 3 KREUZER (1 Groschen)
Silver **Obv:** Ram jumping left from town gate over three hills **Rev:** Crowned imperial eagle with 3 on round shield on breast

Date	Mintage	VG	F	VF	XF	Unc
1605 Rare	—	—	—	—	—	—
1609 Rare	—	—	—	—	—	—
1611	—	12.00	25.00	75.00	150	—
(16)16	—	25.00	50.00	150	250	—
1619	—	45.00	100	250	500	—
161x	—	45.00	100	250	500	—

KM# 17 3 KREUZER (1 Groschen)
Silver **Note:** Klippe.

Date	Mintage	VG	F	VF	XF	Unc
1607 Rare	—	—	—	—	—	—
1611 Rare	—	—	—	—	—	—
1619 Rare	—	—	—	—	—	—

KM# 27 3 KREUZER (1 Groschen)
Billon **Rev:** Crowned imperial eagle on anchor cross, arms extend into legend

Date	Mintage	VG	F	VF	XF	Unc
ND	—	25.00	60.00	150	250	—
1622	—	35.00	75.00	200	400	—

KM# 28 3 KREUZER (1 Groschen)
Billon **Note:** Klippe.

Date	Mintage	VG	F	VF	XF	Unc
1622	—	—	—	—	—	—

KM# 35 3 KREUZER (1 Groschen)
Silver **Rev:** 3 in round shield divides date at bottom

Date	Mintage	VG	F	VF	XF	Unc
1623	—	25.00	60.00	175	300	—

KM# 36 3 KREUZER (1 Groschen)
Silver **Obv:** Date in legend **Rev:** 3 between ornaments below eagle

Date	Mintage	VG	F	VF	XF	Unc
1624	—	24.00	50.00	150	250	—
1625	—	30.00	75.00	200	400	—
1626	—	20.00	40.00	100	200	—
1627	—	20.00	40.00	100	200	—

Date	Mintage	VG	F	VF	XF	Unc
1628	—	20.00	40.00	100	200	—
1629	—	20.00	40.00	100	200	—
1633	—	20.00	40.00	100	200	—
1634	—	20.00	40.00	100	200	—

KM# 37 3 KREUZER (1 Groschen)
Silver **Note:** Klippe.

Date	Mintage	VG	F	VF	XF	Unc
1624	—	—	—	—	—	—

KM# 48 4 KREUZER (1 Batzen)
Billon, 23 mm. **Obv:** Crowned ram walking left **Rev:** Crowned imperial eagle with 4 on breast

Date	Mintage	VG	F	VF	XF	Unc
1657	—	25.00	50.00	200	—	—

KM# 50 4 KREUZER (1 Batzen)
Billon, 26 mm.

Date	Mintage	VG	F	VF	XF	Unc
1657	—	35.00	75.00	250	—	—
1658	—	40.00	100	400	—	—

KM# 49 4 KREUZER (1 Batzen)
Billon **Note:** Klippe.

Date	Mintage	VG	F	VF	XF	Unc
1657	—	—	—	—	—	—

KM# 51 4 KREUZER (1 Batzen)
Billon **Note:** Klippe.

Date	Mintage	VG	F	VF	XF	Unc
1657	—	—	—	—	—	—

KM# 21 12 KREUZER (1/2 Dicken - Zwolfer)
Silver **Obv:** Ram standing right, date in legend **Rev:** Crowned imperial eagle with 1Z on breast

Date	Mintage	VG	F	VF	XF	Unc
(16)16	—	150	300	750	—	—
1619	—	150	300	750	—	—
1620	—	100	200	500	—	—
1621	—	125	250	600	—	—

KM# 22 12 KREUZER (1/2 Dicken - Zwolfer)
Silver **Note:** Klippe.

Date	Mintage	VG	F	VF	XF	Unc
(16)16	—	—	—	—	—	—
1619	—	—	—	—	—	—
1621	—	—	—	—	—	—

KM# 31 12 KREUZER (1/2 Dicken - Zwolfer)
Billon **Note:** Klippe.

Date	Mintage	VG	F	VF	XF	Unc
1622	—	—	—	—	—	—

KM# 29 12 KREUZER (1/2 Dicken - Zwolfer)
Billon **Obv:** Ram jumping from town gate over three hills, date above **Rev:** Crowned imperial eagle with 12 on breast

Date	Mintage	VG	F	VF	XF	Unc
1622	—	20.00	40.00	150	—	—

KM# 30 12 KREUZER (1/2 Dicken - Zwolfer)
Billon **Rev:** Date above eagle

Date	Mintage	VG	F	VF	XF	Unc
1622	—	20.00	40.00	150	—	—

KM# 43 12 KREUZER (1/2 Dicken - Zwolfer)
Billon **Obv:** Ram jumping right over three hills **Rev:** Crowned imperial eagle with 12 on breast, date below

Date	Mintage	VG	F	VF	XF	Unc
1627	—	750	1,500	3,500	—	—

KM# 52 15 KREUZER (Ortli)
Silver **Rev:** Value "XV"

Date	Mintage	VG	F	VF	XF	Unc
ND	—	200	400	900	—	—

KM# 53 15 KREUZER (Ortli)
Silver **Obv:** Without ornamentation in legend **Rev:** Without ornamentation in legend, 15 on breast of eagle

Date	Mintage	VG	F	VF	XF	Unc
1657	—	70.00	60.00	150	—	—
1658	—	150	300	700	—	—

KM# 54 15 KREUZER (Ortli)
Silver **Obv. Legend:** DEVS SPES NOSTRA EST **Rev. Legend:** DEVS SPES NOSTRA EST

Date	Mintage	VG	F	VF	XF	Unc
ND	—	150	300	750	—	—

KM# 38 24 KREUZER (1 Dicken)
Silver **Obv:** Ram jumping from town gate over three hills, date in legend **Rev:** Crowned imperial eagle, 24 on round shield on breast

Date	Mintage	VG	F	VF	XF	Unc
1624	—	275	600	1,500	—	—

KM# 39 24 KREUZER (1 Dicken)
Silver **Note:** Klippe.

Date	Mintage	VG	F	VF	XF	Unc
1624	—	—	—	—	—	—

KM# 18 DICKEN
Silver **Rev:** Imperial eagle

Date	Mintage	VG	F	VF	XF	Unc
1611	—	35.00	75.00	200	—	—
1614	—	25.00	50.00	125	—	—
(16)16	—	350	800	2,000	—	—
1617	—	35.00	75.00	200	—	—
1620	—	125	300	750	—	—
1621	—	125	300	750	—	—

KM# 23 DICKEN
Silver **Note:** Klippe.

Date	Mintage	VG	F	VF	XF	Unc
1617	—	—	—	—	—	—
1620	—	—	—	—	—	—
1621	—	—	—	—	—	—

KM# 40 DICKEN
Silver **Obv:** Similar to KM#18 **Rev:** Similar to KM#42

Date	Mintage	VG	F	VF	XF	Unc
1624//1631 Rare	—	—	—	—	—	—

KM# 42 DICKEN
Silver

Date	Mintage	VG	F	VF	XF	Unc
1626	—	700	1,500	3,500	—	—
1627	—	700	1,500	3,500	—	—
1631	—	40.00	100	250	500	—
1632	—	40.00	100	250	500	—
1633	—	40.00	100	250	500	—
1634	—	40.00	100	205	500	—
1635 Rare	—	—	—	—	—	—

KM# 45 DICKEN
Silver **Note:** Klippe.

Date	Mintage	VG	F	VF	XF	Unc
1633	—	—	—	—	—	—

KM# 26 1/2 THALER
Silver **Rev:** Imperial eagle

Date	Mintage	VG	F	VF	XF	U
1621	—	175	350	800	—	

KM# 25 THALER
Silver **Obv:** Similar to 1/2 Thaler, KM#26 **Rev:** Imperial eagl
Note: Dav. #4627.

Date	Mintage	VG	F	VF	XF	U
1620	—	40.00	100	250	—	
1621	—	40.00	100	250	—	
1622	—	40.00	100	250	—	
1623	—	40.00	100	250	—	
1624 Rare	—	—	—	—	—	

KM# 47 THALER
Silver **Obv:** Similar to 1/2 Thaler, KM#26 but date divided at to
Rev: Crowned imperial eagle **Note:** Dav. #4628.

Date	Mintage	VG	F	VF	XF	U
1656 HMA	—	1,200	2,500	6,000	—	

COUNTERSTAMPED COINAGE

KM# 55 15 KREUZER
Silver **Countermark:** Crowned ram head in circle **Note:** Counterstamp on KM#52.

CS Date	Host Date	Good	VG	F	VF
ND(1657)	1657	—	30.00	60.00	150
ND	1658	—	150	300	750

KM# 56 15 KREUZER
Silver **Countermark:** Crowned ram head in circle **Note:** Counterstamp on KM#54.

CS Date	Host Date	Good	VG	F	VF
	ND	—	125	250	600

TRADE COINAGE

KM# 32 GOLDGULDEN
3.5000 g., 0.9860 Gold 0.1109 oz. AGW **Obv:** Ram leaping left from doorway in inner circle **Obv. Legend:** MO NO AVREA **Rev:** Crowned imperial eagle in inner circle **Note:** Fr. #368.

Date	Mintage	VG	F	VF	XF	U
1622	—	2,400	5,000	10,000	—	

KM# 33 GOLDGULDEN
3.5000 g., 0.9860 Gold 0.1109 oz. AGW **Obv. Legend:** MONETA NOVA... **Note:** Fr. #368.

Date	Mintage	VG	F	VF	XF	U
1622 Rare	—	—	—	—	—	
1633 Rare	—	—	—	—	—	

KM# 34 1/2 DUCAT
1.7500 g., 0.9860 Gold 0.0555 oz. AGW **Obv:** Shield of arm in inner circle **Rev:** Crowned imperial eagle in inner circle **Not** Fr. #370.

Date	Mintage	VG	F	VF	XF	U
ND Rare	—	—	—	—	—	

KM# 19 DUCAT
3.5000 g., 0.9860 Gold 0.1109 oz. AGW **Rev:** Crowned imper eagle with two heads **Note:** Fr. #369.

Date	Mintage	VG	F	VF	XF	U
1614 Rare	—	—	—	—	—	

KM# 20 DUCAT
3.5000 g., 0.9860 Gold 0.1109 oz. AGW **Rev:** Crowned imper eagle with one head **Note:** Fr. #369.

Date	Mintage	VG	F	VF	XF	
1614 Rare	—	—	—	—	—	
1618 Rare	—	—	—	—	—	

KM# 46 DUCAT
3.5000 g., 0.9860 Gold 0.1109 oz. AGW **Obv:** Modified shield **Note:** Fr. #370.

Date	Mintage	VG	F	VF	XF	Unc
1633	—	600	1,200	2,500	4,000	—
1657/33	—	1,100	2,200	4,500	7,500	—

KM# 57 DUCAT
3.5000 g., 0.9860 Gold 0.1109 oz. AGW **Note:** Fr. #370.

Date	Mintage	VG	F	VF	XF	Unc
ND(1658)	—	700	1,400	2,700	4,500	—

KM# A41 3 DUCAT
10.5000 g., 0.9860 Gold 0.3328 oz. AGW **Obv:** Ram jumping from town gate **Rev:** Imperial eagle with 24 on breast **Note:** Struck with 24 Kreuzer dies, KM#38.

Date	Mintage	VG	F	VF	XF	Unc
1624 Rare	—	—	—	—	—	—

KM# 44 3 DUCAT
10.5000 g., 0.9860 Gold 0.3328 oz. AGW **Obv:** Ram jumping from town gate **Rev:** Imperial eagle, date in exergue **Note:** Struck with 1 Dicken dies, KM#42.

Date	Mintage	VG	F	VF	XF	Unc
1632 Rare	—	—	—	—	—	—

KM# 24 5 DUCAT
17.5000 g., 0.9860 Gold 0.5547 oz. AGW **Obv:** Ram jumping from town gate **Rev:** Imperial eagle **Note:** Struck with 1/2 Thaler dies, KM#26.

Date	Mintage	VG	F	VF	XF	Unc
1621 Rare	—	—	—	—	—	—

KM# A48 20 DUCAT
70.0000 g., 0.9860 Gold 2.2190 oz. AGW **Obv:** Ram jumping from town gate **Rev:** Crowned imperial eagle **Note:** Struck with 1 Thaler dies, KM#47.

Date	Mintage	VG	F	VF	XF	Unc
1656 Rare	—	—	—	—	—	—

PATTERNS

Including off metal strikes

KM#	Date	Mintage	Identification	Mkt Val
Pn1	ND(1630)	—	4 Heller. Gold. Eagle facing right, KM#6.	—
Pn2	ND(1630)	—	4 Heller. Gold. Eagle facing left, klippe, KM#8.	—
Pn3	ND(1630)	—	4 Heller. Gold. 4 on eagle's breast, KM#9.	—
Pn4	ND	—	Pfennig. Gold. KM#10.	—
Pn5	1611	—	Dicken. Gold. Klippe, KM#18.	25,000
Pn6	(16)16	—	12 Kreuzer. Gold. KM#21.	10,000

SCHWYZ

Schwytz, Suitensis

A canton in central Switzerland. In 1291 it became one of the three cantons that would ultimately become the Swiss Confederation and were known as the "Everlasting League". The first coinage was issued in1624.

MONETARY SYSTEM

Until 1798

240 Angster = 120 Rappen
= 40 Schillinge = 1 Gulden
4 Kreuzer = 1 Batzen
40 Batzen = 3 Gulden = 1 Thaler
12 Gulden = 1 Duplone

CANTON

STANDARD COINAGE

KM# 5 RAPPEN
Billon **Obv:** Square-cornered arms. **Note:** Angster. Uniface.

Date	Mintage	VG	F	VF	XF	Unc
ND(1650)	—	20.00	50.00	200	500	—

KM# 6 RAPPEN
Billon **Obv:** Curved and arched double arms. **Note:** Angster. Uniface.

Date	Mintage	VG	F	VF	XF	Unc
ND(1675)	—	15.00	30.00	125	250	—

KM# 7 RAPPEN
Billon **Obv:** Small arched and curved arms. **Note:** Angster. Uniface.

Date	Mintage	VG	F	VF	XF	Unc
ND(1695)	—	15.00	40.00	150	300	—

KM# 8 SCHILLING
Billon **Obv:** Crowned imperial eagle, shield divides I-T at bottom **Rev:** Bust of Saint facing forward

Date	Mintage	VG	F	VF	XF	Unc
ND	—	5.00	10.00	50.00	150	—

KM# 15 SCHILLING
Billon **Obv:** Shield divides date at bottom

Date	Mintage	VG	F	VF	XF	Unc
1623	—	5.00	10.00	50.00	150	—
1624	—	5.00	10.00	50.00	150	—
1629	—	5.00	10.00	50.00	150	—
1630	—	5.00	10.00	50.00	150	—
1633	—	5.00	10.00	50.00	150	—
1653	—	5.00	10.00	50.00	150	—
1654	—	5.00	10.00	50.00	150	—
1655	—	5.00	10.00	50.00	150	—
1656	—	12.00	30.00	100	250	—
1673	—	20.00	50.00	150	350	—

KM# 12 BATZEN
Billon **Obv:** Spanish shield on anchor cross **Rev:** Crowned imperial eagle

Date	Mintage	VG	F	VF	XF	Unc
1622	—	55.00	120	300	—	—

KM# 13 BATZEN
Billon **Obv:** Curved and arched shield on anchor cross

Date	Mintage	VG	F	VF	XF	Unc
1622	—	45.00	100	250	—	—

KM# 14 BATZEN
Billon **Obv:** Square-cornered shield on anchor cross

Date	Mintage	VG	F	VF	XF	Unc
1622	—	35.00	80.00	200	—	—

KM# 16 BATZEN
Billon **Obv:** Plain square-cornered shield on anchor corss, date below

Date	Mintage	VG	F	VF	XF	Unc
1623	—	15.00	40.00	100	—	—

KM# 17 BATZEN
Billon **Obv:** Ornamentation on shield

Date	Mintage	VG	F	VF	XF	Unc
1623	—	15.00	40.00	100	—	—

KM# 18 BATZEN
Billon **Obv:** Plain curved and arched shield on anchor cross, date below

Date	Mintage	VG	F	VF	XF	Unc
1623	—	25.00	60.00	150	—	—
1624	—	12.00	30.00	75.00	—	—

KM# 20 BATZEN
Billon **Obv:** Ornamentation on shield

Date	Mintage	VG	F	VF	XF	Unc
1624	—	12.00	30.00	75.00	—	—

KM# 27 4 BATZEN (Ortli)
Silver **Obv:** Square-cornered shield on anchor corss, date in legend **Rev:** Crowned, small imperial eagle

Date	Mintage	VG	F	VF	XF	Unc
1672 Rare	—	800	2,000	4,500	—	—

KM# 28 4 BATZEN (Ortli)
Silver **Obv:** Ornamental arms, rosette on each side

Date	Mintage	VG	F	VF	XF	Unc
1672	—	65.00	150	400	—	—

KM# 29 4 BATZEN (Ortli)
Silver

Date	Mintage	VG	F	VF	XF	Unc
1672	—	65.00	150	400	—	—
1674	—	125	300	800	—	—

KM# 19 DICKEN
Silver

Date	Mintage	VG	F	VF	XF	Unc
1623	—	500	1,200	3,000	—	—
1629	—	800	2,000	4,500	—	—
1656	—	700	1,750	4,000	—	—

KM# 22 DICKEN
Silver **Rev:** Bust of St. Martin left wearing long robe

Date	Mintage	VG	F	VF	XF	Unc
1630	—	800	2,000	4,500	—	—

KM# 25 1/2 THALER
Silver **Obv:** Crowned imperial eagle, shield divides date below **Rev:** Similar to 1 Dicken, KM#19

Date	Mintage	VG	F	VF	XF	Unc
1656	—	1,200	3,000	7,000	—	—

KM# 24 THALER
Silver **Obv:** Crowned imperial eagle, shield below, date in legend **Rev:** Similar to 1 Dicken, KM#19 **Note:** Dav. #4629.

Date	Mintage	VG	F	VF	XF	Unc
1653	—	250	600	1,500	—	—

TRADE COINAGE

KM# 11.1 DUCAT
3.5000 g., 0.9860 Gold 0.1109 oz. AGW **Obv:** St. Martin on horseback **Obv. Legend:** Madonna standing with child **Note:** Fr. #377.

Date	Mintage	VG	F	VF	XF	Unc
ND(1621)	—	1,200	3,000	6,000	10,000	—
1653	—	1,200	3,000	6,000	10,000	—

KM# 11.2 DUCAT
3.5000 g., 0.9860 Gold 0.1109 oz. AGW **Obv:** St. Martin on horseback **Rev:** Madonna standing with child **Note:** Fr. #378

Date	Mintage	VG	F	VF	XF	Unc
1674 Rare	—	—	—	—	—	—

SITTEN

A canton which was founded in 580 that comprises most of the canton of Valais. Sitten was a Burgundian mint in the 9th century with the first Episcopal coinage being struck c. 1496. They joined the Swiss Confederation as Valais in 1815.

RULER
Hildebrand, 1565-1604

MINT OFFICIAL'S INITIALS

Initial	Date	Name
D-S		David Stedelin

CANTON

STANDARD COINAGE

KM# 5 QUART (Vierer)
Billon **Obv:** X with stars in angles **Rev:** Cross, date in legend

Date	Mintage	VG	F	VF	XF	Unc
1623 Rare	—	—	—	—	—	—
1627 Rare	—	—	—	—	—	—

KM# 23 QUART (Vierer)
Billon **Obv:** Clover in center, ADR and stars around **Rev:** Arms at center, W above, 8-5 at sides

Date	Mintage	VG	F	VF	XF	Unc
1685	—	35.00	75.00	300	750	—

KM# 6 KREUZER
Billon **Obv:** Mitre above crossed sword and crozier **Rev:** Cross in inner circle, date in legend

Date	Mintage	VG	F	VF	XF	Unc
1623	—	40.00	100	400	—	—
1624	—	40.00	100	400	—	—
1625	—	100	250	1,000	—	—

KM# 7 KREUZER
Billon **Obv:** Mitre above shield with clover leaves on crossed sword and crozier **Rev:** Eagle left above shield with seven stars

Date	Mintage	VG	F	VF	XF	Unc
ND	—	15.00	40.00	200	—	—

KM# 8 KREUZER
Billon **Obv:** Without sword and crozier

Date	Mintage	VG	F	VF	XF	Unc
ND Rare	—	—	—	—	—	—

KM# 9 1/2 BATZEN
Billon **Obv:** Shield with X in center, stars in field on crossed sword and crozier **Rev:** Anchor cross with beams in angles, date in legend

Date	Mintage	VG	F	VF	XF	Unc
1623	—	50.00	100	400	—	—
1624	—	50.00	100	400	—	—
1625	—	100	350	1,000	—	—
1627	—	50.00	100	400	—	—

KM# 15 1/2 BATZEN
Billon **Obv:** Mitre above shield with clover leaves and stars on crossed sword and crozier **Rev:** Eagle above shield with seven stars dividing date

Date	Mintage	VG	F	VF	XF	Unc
1644	—	20.00	40.00	200	—	—
1645	—	20.00	40.00	200	—	—
1646	—	20.00	40.00	200	—	—

KM# 18 1/2 BATZEN
Billon **Note:** Klippe.

Date	Mintage	VG	F	VF	XF	Unc
1646	—	—	—	—	—	—

KM# 20 1/2 BATZEN
Billon **Rev:** Crowned imperial eagle above shield

Date	Mintage	VG	F	VF	XF	Unc
1683	—	12.00	25.00	100	—	—
1684	—	12.00	25.00	100	—	—
1685	—	12.00	25.00	100	—	—

KM# 10 BATZEN
Billon **Obv:** Mitre above shield with X and stars on crossed sword and crozier **Rev:** Bust of saint left wearing mitre and holding sword and crozier

Date	Mintage	VG	F	VF	XF	Unc
1623	—	50.00	120	500	—	—
1624	—	50.00	120	500	—	—
1625 Rare	—	300	750	2,000	—	—
1627	—	50.00	120	500	—	—

KM# 16 BATZEN
Billon **Obv:** Mitre above shield with clover leaves on crossed sword and crozier **Rev:** Eagle above shield with seven stars dividing date

Date	Mintage	VG	F	VF	XF	Unc
1644	—	25.00	50.00	250	—	—

KM# 17 BATZEN
Billon **Note:** Klippe.

Date	Mintage	VG	F	VF	XF	Unc
1644	—	—	—	—	—	—

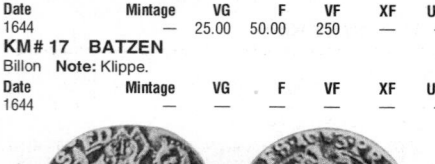

KM# 21 BATZEN
Billon

Date	Mintage	VG	F	VF	XF	Unc
1683	—	50.00	100	400	—	—

KM# 22 BATZEN
Billon **Rev:** Arms divide date in field

Date	Mintage	VG	F	VF	XF	Unc
1683	—	50.00	100	400	—	—
1684	—	15.00	30.00	150	—	—
1685	—	15.00	30.00	150	—	—

KM# 11 1/4 THALER (1 Teston)
Silver **Obv:** Mitre above shield with X in center, stars in field on sword and crozier **Rev:** Standing saint holding sword and crozier with foot on devil holding bell

Date	Mintage	VG	F	VF	XF	Unc
1624	—	2,000	4,000	10,000	—	—

KM# 12 1/2 THALER
Silver **Obv:** Mitre above shield with X in center, stars in field on sword and crozier **Rev:** Standing saint holding sword and crozier with foot on devil holding bell

Date	Mintage	VG	F	VF	XF	Unc
1624	—	2,500	5,000	12,000	—	—

TRADE COINAGE

KM# 13 SCUDO D'ORO
3.5000 g., 0.9860 Gold 0.1109 oz. AGW **Obv:** Ornate cross in inner circle **Rev:** St. Theodolus above arms in inner circle **Note:** Fr. #381.

Date	Mintage	VG	F	VF	XF	Unc
ND(1565-1604)	—	7,500	15,000	30,000	—	—

REPUBLIK WALLIS
1627-1630

STANDARD COINAGE

KM# 40 KREUZER
Billon **Obv:** Eagle above shield with seven stars **Rev:** Cross in inner circle, date in legend

Date	Mintage	VG	F	VF	XF	Unc
1628	—	45.00	85.00	225	—	—

KM# 41 KREUZER
Silver **Note:** Klippe.

Date	Mintage	VG	F	VF	XF	Unc
1628	—	—	—	—	—	—

KM# 42 1/2 BATZEN
Billon **Obv:** Eagle above shield with seven stars **Rev:** Anchor cross with fleur-de-lis in angles

Date	Mintage	VG	F	VF	XF	Unc
1628	—	20.00	45.00	100	—	—

KM# 43 DICKEN
Silver **Obv:** Shield with seven stars in cartouche in inner circle **Rev:** Crowned imperial eagle in inner circle, date below

Date	Mintage	VG	F	VF	XF	Unc
1628 Rare	—	6,000	12,000	30,000	—	—

PATTERNS

Including off metal strikes

KM#	Date	Mintage	Identification	Mkt Val
Pn1	ND	—	Kreuzer. Gold. Sword and crozier, KM#7.	—
Pn2	ND	—	Kreuzer. Silver. Without sword and crozier, KM#8.	—
Pn3	ND	—	Kreuzer. Gold. Without sword and crozier, KM#8.	—
Pn4	1644	—	Batzen. Silver. KM#16.	—
Pn5	1646	—	1/2 Batzen. Silver. KM#15.	—
Pn6	1684	—	Batzen. Gold. KM#22.	5,000

SOLOTHURN

Solodornensis, Soleure

A canton in northwest Switzerland. Bracteates were struck in the 1300s even though the mint right was not officially granted until 1381. They joined the Swiss Confederation in 1481.

MINT OFFICIAL'S INITIALS

Initials	Date	Name
T		Thiebaud

MONETARY SYSTEM

Until 1798

2 Vierer = 1 Kreuzer
4 Kreuzer = 1 Batzen
40 Batzen = 2 Gulden = 1 Thaler

CANTON

STANDARD COINAGE

Commencing 1804

10 Rappen = 4 Kreuzer = 1 Batzen; 10 Batzen = 1 Frank

KM# 5 1/2 KREUZER (Vierer)
Billon **Obv:** Eagle looking left above state arms **Rev:** Cross with prongs at end in inner circle

Date	Mintage	VG	F	VF	XF	Unc
ND	—	100	250	750	—	—
1622	—	400	1,000	3,000	—	—
1623	—	400	1,000	3,000	—	—
1624	—	225	500	1,500	—	—

KM# 4 KREUZER
Billon **Obv:** Arms divide S-O, Eagle above **Obv. Legend:** MONETA: SOLODORENSIS **Rev:** Short cross with prongs on ends, plain fields **Rev. Legend:** * SANCTVS * SVRBUS * **Note:** Klippe. Previous KM#7.

Date	Mintage	VG	F	VF	XF	Un
1622	—	20.00	40.00	150	—	—

KM# 3 KREUZER
Billon **Obv:** Arms divide S-O, Eagle above **Obv. Legend:** MON: NO: SLODO **Rev:** Short cross with prongs on ends, plain fields in quarters **Rev. Legend:** SANCT: VRBVS **Note:** Previous KM#6

Date	Mintage	VG	F	VF	XF	Un
1622	—	20.00	40.00	150	—	—

KM# 6 KREUZER
Billon **Obv:** Curved, arched arms divide S-O, eagle above **Rev:** Cross with prongs on ends, fleur-de-lis in angles **Note:** Varieites exist.

Date	Mintage	VG	F	VF	XF	Unc
1623	—	10.00	25.00	100	250	—
1624	—	10.00	25.00	100	250	—
1627	—	15.00	40.00	150	300	—
1628	—	10.00	25.00	100	250	—
1629	—	10.00	25.00	100	250	—
1637	—	20.00	50.00	250	400	—
1640	—	10.00	25.00	100	250	—

KM# 10 1/2 BATZEN (2 Kreuzer)
Billon **Obv:** Curved and arched arms, eagle looking left above **Rev:** Bust of saint right, date in legend

Date	Mintage	VG	F	VF	XF	Unc
1623	—	15.00	40.00	150	350	—
1624	—	15.00	40.00	150	350	—

KM# 11 1/2 BATZEN (2 Kreuzer)
Billon **Note:** Klippe.

Date	Mintage	VG	F	VF	XF	Unc
1623	—	—	—	—	—	—

KM# 8 BATZEN
Billon **Obv:** Arms on cross in inner circle **Rev:** Bust of saint right dividing date

Date	Mintage	VG	F	VF	XF	Unc
16ZZ	—	200	500	2,000	—	—

KM# 9 BATZEN
Billon **Obv:** Eagle looking left above curved and arched arms **Rev:** Large cross with ornamentation in angles, date in legend

Date	Mintage	VG	F	VF	XF	Unc
16ZZ	—	400	1,000	4,000	—	—
16Z3	—	35.00	75.00	250	600	—
16Z4	—	40.00	100	300	750	—
1630	—	25.00	50.00	200	500	—
1631	—	15.00	30.00	120	300	—
1632	—	25.00	50.00	200	500	—
1637	—	40.00	100	300	750	—
1638	—	40.00	100	300	750	—
1642	—	15.00	30.00	120	300	—

KM# 12 BATZEN
Billon **Note:** Klippe.

ate	Mintage	VG	F	VF	XF	Unc
623	—	—	—	—	—	—
624	—	—	—	—	—	—

KM# 15 1/2 DICKEN
ilver **Obv:** Eagle looking left above arms dividing S-O **Rev:** rmored bust of saint right, date below

ate	Mintage	VG	F	VF	XF	Unc
624 Rare	—	—	—	—	—	—

KM# 25 1/2 DICKEN
ilver **Obv:** Arms dividing S-O **Rev:** Crowned imperial eagle, ate below

ate	Mintage	VG	F	VF	XF	Unc
642 Rare	—	—	—	—	—	—

KM# 16 DICKEN
ilver **Obv:** Eagle looking left above arms dividing date **Rev:** ust of saint in armor right

ate	Mintage	VG	F	VF	XF	Unc
624 Rare	—	—	—	—	—	—

KM# 20 DICKEN
ilver **Obv:** Eagle looking left above arms dividing S-O, date elow **Rev:** Half-length saint armored right

ate	Mintage	VG	F	VF	XF	Unc
632 Rare	—	2,250	5,000	12,000	22,000	—

Note: Leu Numismatik Auction 66 5-96 XF realized $15,010

KM# 21 DICKEN
ilver **Obv:** Crowned imperial eagle, date below **Rev:** Half-length aint armored right, arms below

ate	Mintage	VG	F	VF	XF	Unc
632	—	1,750	4,000	10,000	20,000	—

KM# 22 DICKEN
ilver **Obv:** Imperial eagle with arms on breast, date below **Rev:** rmored bust of saint right

ate	Mintage	VG	F	VF	XF	Unc
633	—	650	1,500	4,000	7,500	—

KM# 26 DICKEN
ilver **Obv:** Arms on floreate cross **Rev:** Crowned imperial eagle, ate below

ate	Mintage	VG	F	VF	XF	Unc
642	—	1,150	2,500	5,000	9,000	—

KM# 27 DICKEN
Silver **Obv:** Arms with ornamentation around **Rev:** Imperial eagle

Date	Mintage	VG	F	VF	XF	Unc
1642	—	1,000	2,000	4,000	8,000	—

KM# 13 1/2 THALER
Silver **Obv:** Arms with crowned imperial eagle above divide date and S-O **Rev:** Standing saint in armor

Date	Mintage	VG	F	VF	XF	Unc
1623	—	1,750	4,000	8,000	—	—

KM# 14 THALER
Silver **Obv:** Standing saint in armor **Rev:** Crowned imperial eagle, date in legend **Note:** Dav. #4630.

Date	Mintage	VG	F	VF	XF	Unc
1623 Rare	—	—	—	—	—	—

TRADE COINAGE

KM# 18 1/2 DUCAT
1.7500 g., 0.9860 Gold 0.0555 oz. AGW **Obv:** Arms of Solothurn divides S-O, topped by date in inner circle **Rev:** St. Ursus standing in elongated inner circle **Note:** Fr. #387.

Date	Mintage	VG	F	VF	XF	Unc
1630	—	—	—	—	—	—

Note: Leu Numismatik Auction 66 5-96 VF-XF realized $12,640

KM# 19 DUCAT
3.5000 g., 0.9860 Gold 0.1109 oz. AGW **Obv:** Arms of Solothurn divides S-O below date in inner circle **Rev:** St. Ursus standing in elongated inner circle **Note:** Fr. #386.

Date	Mintage	VG	F	VF	XF	Unc
1630 Rare	—	—	—	—	—	—

KM# 23 DUCAT
3.5000 g., 0.9860 Gold 0.1109 oz. AGW **Obv:** Imperial eagle and arms **Rev:** St. Ursus standing facing **Note:** Fr. #388.

Date	Mintage	VG	F	VF	XF	Unc
ND(ca.1635)	—	5,000	12,000	24,000	40,000	—

Note: Leu Numismatik Auction 66 5-96 VF-XF realized $23,700

PATTERNS
Including off metal strikes

KM#	Date	Mintage	Identification	Mkt Val
Pn1	1623	—	Kreuzer. Gold. Klippe. KM#6.	9,500
Pn2	1624	—	Kreuzer. Gold. KM#6.	3,000
Pn3	1628	—	Kreuzer. Gold. KM#6.	3,000
Pn4	1642	—	Batzen. Gold. KM#9.	3,500

URI

Uranie

A canton in central Switzerland. It is one of the three original cantons which became the Swiss Confederation in 1291. They had their own coinage from the early 1600s until 1811.

MONETARY SYSTEM
10 Rappen = 1 Batzen
10 Batzen = 1 Frank

CANTON

STANDARD COINAGE

KM# 23 KREUZER
Copper **Obv:** Arms in inner circle, date in legend **Rev:** Anchor cross in inner circle

Date	Mintage	VG	F	VF	XF	Unc
1622	—	40.00	100	250	600	—
1624	—	40.00	100	250	600	—
1627	—	40.00	100	250	600	—

KM# 5 SCHILLING
Billon **Obv:** Crowned imperial eagle, arms below, date in legend **Rev:** St. Martin standing facing forward

Date	Mintage	VG	F	VF	XF	Unc
1605	—	12.00	30.00	120	300	—
1608	—	12.00	30.00	120	300	—
1609	—	12.00	30.00	120	300	—
1610	—	12.00	30.00	120	300	—
1611	—	12.00	30.00	120	300	—
1612	—	10.00	25.00	100	250	—
1613	—	10.00	25.00	100	250	—
1614	—	10.00	25.00	100	250	—
1615	—	10.00	25.00	100	250	—
1616 Rare	—	—	—	—	—	—
1618 Rare	—	—	—	—	—	—
1619	—	10.00	25.00	100	250	—
1620 Rare	—	—	—	—	—	—
1621	—	40.00	100	300	750	—

KM# 24 SCHILLING
Billon **Obv:** Large arms in inner circle

Date	Mintage	VG	F	VF	XF	Unc
1622 Rare	—	—	—	—	—	—

KM# 25 SCHILLING
Billon **Obv:** Crowned double-headed eagle, date below **Rev:** St. Martin standing facing forward in long robe

Date	Mintage	VG	F	VF	XF	Unc
1623	—	9.00	20.00	75.00	200	—
1624	—	9.00	20.00	75.00	200	—
1627	—	9.00	20.00	75.00	200	—

Date	Mintage	VG	F	VF	XF	Unc
1629	—	9.00	20.00	75.00	200	—
1630	—	9.00	20.00	75.00	200	—
1633	—	9.00	20.00	75.00	200	—
1639 Rare	—	—	—	—	—	—
1641	—	35.00	100	400	1,000	—

KM# 20 1/2 BATZEN
Billon **Obv:** Crowned imperial eagle, arms below, date in legend **Rev:** Cross in inner circle

Date	Mintage	VG	F	VF	XF	Unc
1618 Rare	—	—	—	—	—	—

KM# 6 BATZEN-10 RAPPEN
Billon **Obv:** Large arms on Spanish shield, eagle above **Rev:** Anchor cross in inner circle, date in legend

Date	Mintage	VG	F	VF	XF	Unc
1607	—	600	1,200	3,000	—	—

KM# 15 BATZEN-10 RAPPEN
Billon **Obv:** Crowned imperial eagle above arms **Rev:** Large cross with fleur-de-lis in angles, date in legend

Date	Mintage	VG	F	VF	XF	Unc
1615 Rare	—	—	—	—	—	—

KM# 16 BATZEN-10 RAPPEN
Billon **Obv:** Ornamentation around arms **Rev:** Large cross on plain field

Date	Mintage	VG	F	VF	XF	Unc
1615 Rare	—	—	—	—	—	—
1616 Rare	—	750	1,500	4,000	—	—

KM# 22 BATZEN-10 RAPPEN
Billon **Obv:** Small shield with arms at center of anchor cross, date in legend **Rev:** Crowned imperial eagle

Date	Mintage	VG	F	VF	XF	Unc
1621	—	65.00	150	600	—	—
1622	—	18.00	40.00	150	—	—

KM# 26 BATZEN-10 RAPPEN
Billon **Obv:** Date below cross

Date	Mintage	VG	F	VF	XF	Unc
1624	—	24.00	50.00	200	—	—

KM# 27 BATZEN-10 RAPPEN
Billon **Obv:** Large arms, small eagle above **Rev:** Wide anchor cross in inner circle, date below

Date	Mintage	VG	F	VF	XF	Unc
1624	—	85.00	175	500	—	—

KM# 9 1/2 DICKEN
Silver **Obv:** Crowned imperial eagle above shield of arms divides date **Rev:** Bust of St. Martin in long robe right

Date	Mintage	VG	F	VF	XF	Unc
1610	—	750	1,500	4,000	—	—
1611 Rare	—	—	—	—	—	—

KM# 17 1/2 DICKEN
Silver **Obv:** Large crowned imperial eagle above small arms, date in legend

Date	Mintage	VG	F	VF	XF	Unc
1615 Rare	—	—	—	—	—	—

KM# 28 1/2 DICKEN
Silver **Obv:** Crowned imperial eagle, date below divided by arms

Date	Mintage	VG	F	VF	XF	Unc
1624 Rare	—	—	—	—	—	—

KM# 7 DICKEN
Silver **Obv:** Crowned imperial eagle, arms below divide date **Rev:** Bust of St. Martin in robe right

Date	Mintage	VG	F	VF	XF	Unc
1608 Rare	—	—	—	—	—	—
1610	—	500	1,000	2,500	—	—
1611 Rare	—	—	—	—	—	—

KM# 10 DICKEN
Silver **Obv:** Similar to KM#18 but without shield below eagle **Rev:** Similar to KM#18 but with shield below saint

Date	Mintage	VG	F	VF	XF	Unc
1612 Rare	—	—	—	—	—	—
1614	—	110	250	600	1,200	—

KM# 18 DICKEN
Silver

Date	Mintage	VG	F	VF	XF	Unc
1615	—	110	250	600	1,200	—
1616	—	110	250	600	1,200	—
1617	—	110	250	600	1,200	—

KM# 19 DICKEN
Silver **Obv:** Imperial eagle

Date	Mintage	VG	F	VF	XF	Unc
1617	—	110	250	600	1,200	—
1618	—	110	250	600	1,200	—
1619	—	800	1,750	4,000	—	—
1620	—	150	350	500	—	—
1621	—	125	300	700	—	—
1622	—	850	2,000	5,000	—	—

KM# 11 PISTOLE
7.6400 g., 0.9000 Gold 0.2211 oz. AGW **Obv:** Floriated cross with sceptres in angles **Obv. Legend:** MON: AV:... **Rev:** St. Martin on horseback and the beggar **Note:** Fr. #397.

Date	Mintage	VG	F	VF	XF	Unc
ND(1613-16) Rare	—	4,000	9,000	18,000	30,000	45,000

KM# 14 PISTOLE
7.6400 g., 0.9000 Gold 0.2211 oz. AGW **Obv:** Floriated cross with sceptres in angles **Obv. Legend:** MO AVREA... **Rev:** St. Martin on horseback and the beggar **Note:** Fr. #397.

Date	Mintage	VG	F	VF	XF	Unc
1613 Rare	—	—	—	—	—	—
1616 Rare	—	—	—	—	—	—

KM# 29 PISTOLE
7.6400 g., 0.9000 Gold 0.2211 oz. AGW **Obv:** Arms on cross **Obv. Legend:** DVO: AV:... **Rev:** St. Martin standing **Note:** Fr. #399.

Date	Mintage	VG	F	VF	XF	Unc
1624 Rare	—	—	—	—	—	—

KM# 31 PISTOLE
7.6400 g., 0.9000 Gold 0.2211 oz. AGW **Obv:** Cross above date **Obv. Legend:** MON: NOVA:... **Rev:** St. Martin on horseback **Note:** Fr. #400.

Date	Mintage	VG	F	VF	XF	Unc
1633 Rare	—	—	—	—	—	—

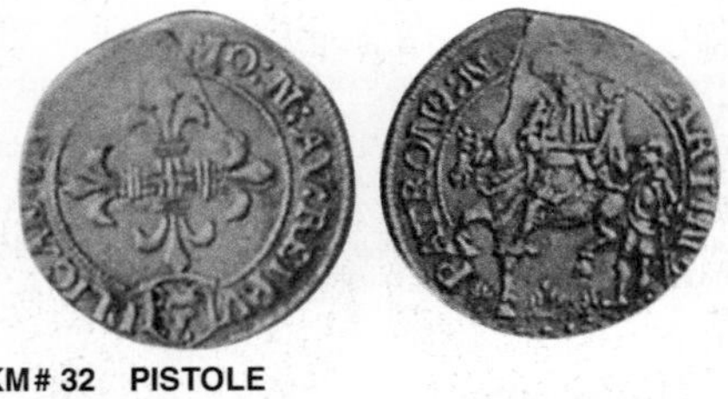

KM# 32 PISTOLE
7.6400 g., 0.9000 Gold 0.2211 oz. AGW **Obv:** Floriated cross **Obv. Legend:** MO: N(o): AV: REIPV-PLICAE: VRANIE **Rev. Legend:** PATRONS: **Note:** Fr. #398.

Date	Mintage	VG	F	VF	XF	Unc
ND(1635)	—	800	1,800	3,600	6,000	10,000

TRADE COINAGE

KM# 12 1/2 DUCAT
1.7500 g., 0.9860 Gold 0.0555 oz. AGW **Obv:** Imperial eagle **Rev:** St. Martin standing **Note:** Fr. #402.

Date	Mintage	VG	F	VF	XF	Unc
ND Rare	—	—	—	—	—	—

KM# 13 DUCAT
3.5000 g., 0.9860 Gold 0.1109 oz. AGW **Obv:** Imperial eagle **Rev:** St. Martin standing **Note:** Fr. #401.

Date	Mintage	VG	F	VF	XF	Unc
1612 Rare	—	—	—	—	—	—

ZUG

Tugium, Tugiensis

A canton in central Switzerland which joined the Swiss Confederation in 1352 and had their own coinage from 1564 to 1805.

MONETARY SYSTEM
6 Angster = 3 Rappen = 1 Schilling = 1 Assis

CANTON

STANDARD COINAGE

KM# 36 RAPPEN
Billon **Note:** Uniface

Date	Mintage	VG	F	VF	XF	Unc
ND	—	25.00	60.00	250	600	—

KM# 37 SCHILLING
Billon **Obv:** Crowned imperial eagle, date divided by arms below **Rev:** Bust of saint wearing mitre facing forward

Date	Mintage	VG	F	VF	XF	Unc
1691	—	20.00	50.00	200	500	—
1692	—	12.00	30.00	120	300	—
1693	—	12.00	30.00	120	300	—

KM# 18 10 SCHILLING
Silver **Obv:** Crowned imperial eagle above arms divide date **Rev:** Standing saint, 10 in legend above

Date	Mintage	VG	F	VF	XF	Unc
1602	—	450	1,000	2,500	5,000	—

KM# 17 3 KREUZER (1 Groschen)
Billon

Date	Mintage	VG	F	VF	XF	Unc
1601	—	10.00	20.00	50.00	175	—
160Z	—	10.00	20.00	50.00	175	—
1603	—	10.00	20.00	50.00	175	—
1604	—	10.00	20.00	50.00	175	—
1605	—	50.00	120	400	—	—
1606	—	10.00	20.00	50.00	175	—
1608	—	15.00	30.00	75.00	200	—

KM# 19 3 KREUZER (1 Groschen)
Billon **Note:** Klippe.

Date	Mintage	VG	F	VF	XF	Unc
1604	—	—	—	—	—	—
1606	—	—	—	—	—	—

KM# 38 3 KREUZER (1 Groschen)
Billon **Obv:** Crowned imperial eagle with arms on breast **Rev:** Armored bust of saint right, 3 in oval below

Date	Mintage	VG	F	VF	XF	Unc
1691	—	550	1,200	3,000	6,000	—

KM# 47 10 KREUZER
Silver **Obv:** Oval arms in ornate cartouche **Rev:** Crowned imperial eagle, 10 in oval on breast

Date	Mintage	VG	F	VF	XF	Unc
1693	—	200	400	1,000	—	—
1694	—	250	600	1,500	—	—

KM# 27 12 KREUZER (1/2 Dicken)
Silver

Date	Mintage	VG	F	VF	XF	Unc
1620	—	100	200	500	1,000	—
1621	—	100	200	500	1,000	—

KM# 30 BATZEN
Billon

Date	Mintage	VG	F	VF	XF	Unc
1621	—	20.00	40.00	165	400	—
1622	—	20.00	40.00	165	400	—

KM# 33 BATZEN
Billon **Obv:** Arms with ornamentation, date below **Rev:** Cross with prongs on end, lilies in angles

Date	Mintage	VG	F	VF	XF	Unc
1623	—	18.00	40.00	150	500	—
1624	—	18.00	40.00	150	500	—
1692	—	350	750	2,500	—	—

KM# 20 DICKEN
Silver

Date	Mintage	VG	F	VF	XF	U
ND	—	100	200	750	1,500	
1609	—	45.00	100	250	500	
1610	—	45.00	100	250	500	
1611	—	45.00	100	250	500	
1612	—	45.00	100	250	500	
1613	—	175	400	1,000	2,000	
1615	—	25.00	5.00	150	300	
1616	—	25.00	50.00	150	300	
1617	—	25.00	50.00	150	300	
1618	—	25.00	50.00	150	300	
1619	—	90.00	200	500	1,000	
1620	—	90.00	200	500	1,000	
1621	—	80.00	175	400	800	
1622	—	120	400	1,000	2,000	

KM# 22 DICKEN
Silver **Note:** Klippe.

Date	Mintage	VG	F	VF	XF	U
1612	—	—	—	—	—	

KM# 34 DICKEN
Silver **Rev:** Date below eagle

Date	Mintage	VG	F	VF	XF	U
1623	—	300	600	1,500	3,000	
1624	—	250	500	1,000	2,000	

KM# 40 20 KREUZER
Silver **Obv:** Oval arms in ornate cartouche, date in legend **Re** Crowned imperial eagle, 10 in oval on breast

Date	Mintage	VG	F	VF	XF	U
1692	—	300	600	1,500	—	
1694	—	250	500	1,200	—	

KM# 41 1/6 THALER (20 Kreuzers)
Silver **Obv:** Oval arms in cartouche, date in legend **Rev:** Crowned imperial eagle, 1/6 in oval on breast

Date	Mintage	VG	F	VF	XF	U
1692	—	400	800	2,000	—	

KM# 25 1/2 THALER
Silver **Obv:** Half-length armored St. Oswald right with scepte and raven, date in legend **Rev:** Crowned imperial eagle in circ

Date	Mintage	VG	F	VF	XF	U
1617 Rare	—	—	—	—	—	

KM# 28 1/2 THALER
Silver **Obv:** Angel holds shield **Rev:** Imperial eagle

Date	Mintage	VG	F	VF	XF	U
1620	—	50.00	100	250	600	
1621	—	35.00	75.00	200	500	
1622	—	125	250	600	1,200	

KM# 31 1/2 THALER
Silver **Note:** Klippe.

Date	Mintage	VG	F	VF	XF	U
1621	—	—	—	—	—	

KM# 43 1/2 THALER
Silver **Note:** Klippe.

Date	Mintage	VG	F	VF	XF	U
1692	—	—	—	—	—	

KM# 42 1/2 THALER
Silver **Obv:** Archangel Michael standing holding oval arms **Re** Crowned imperial eagle, date in legend

Date	Mintage	VG	F	VF	XF	U
1692	—	1,750	4,000	10,000	—	

KM# 29 THALER
ilver **Note:** Similar to KM#32 but date in legend on obverse. Dav. #4631.

ate	Mintage	VG	F	VF	XF	Unc
620	—	175	400	1,000	2,000	—
621 Rare	—	—	—	—	—	—

KM# 32 THALER
ilver **Obv:** Angel holds shield **Rev:** Crowned impereial eagle **ote:** Dav. #4633.

ate	Mintage	VG	F	VF	XF	Unc
621	—	75.00	150	400	800	—
622	—	75.00	150	400	800	—

KM# 35 THALER
ilver **Obv:** Legend, date **Obv. Legend:** MONETA.NOVA. VGIENSI **Note:** Dav. #4635, 4636.

ate	Mintage	VG	F	VF	XF	Unc
623	—	110	250	650	1,250	—
624	—	350	800	2,000	4,000	—

TRADE COINAGE

KM# 23 GOLDGULDEN
.5000 g., 0.9860 Gold 0.1109 oz. AGW **Obv:** Bust of St. Oswald ight **Rev:** Crowned imperial eagle and arms **Note:** Fr. #416.

ate	Mintage	VG	F	VF	XF	Unc
615 Unique	—	—	—	—	—	—

KM# 44 1/4 DUCAT
.8750 g., 0.9860 Gold 0.0277 oz. AGW **Note:** Similar to 1/2 Ducat, KM#45. Fr. #421.

ate	Mintage	VG	F	VF	XF	Unc
692	—	2,500	6,000	12,000	20,000	—

KM# 45 1/2 DUCAT
.7500 g., 0.9860 Gold 0.0555 oz. AGW **Note:** Fr. #420.

ate	Mintage	VG	F	VF	XF	Unc
692	—	1,750	4,000	9,000	15,000	—

KM# 24 DUCAT
.5000 g., 0.9860 Gold 0.1109 oz. AGW **Obv:** Crowned imperial eagle **Rev:** 1/2 bust of St. Oswald right

ate	Mintage	VG	F	VF	XF	Unc
615 Rare	—	—	—	—	—	—

KM# 39 DUCAT
3.5000 g., 0.9860 Gold 0.1109 oz. AGW **Obv:** Bust of St. Oswald right **Rev:** Crowned imperial eagle and arms **Note:** Fr. #415.

Date	Mintage	VG	F	VF	XF	Unc
1691 Rare	—	—	—	—	—	—

KM# 46 1-1/2 DUCAT (Pistole)
5.2500 g., 0.9860 Gold 0.1664 oz. AGW **Obv:** Arms of Zug **Rev:** Seven-line inscription **Note:** Fr. #419.

Date	Mintage	VG	F	VF	XF	Unc
1692 Rare	—	—	20,000	40,000	70,000	—

KM# A48 3 DUCAT
10.5000 g., 0.9860 Gold 0.3328 oz. AGW **Obv:** Archangel Michael standing facing holding oval arms **Rev:** Crowned imperial eagle **Note:** Struck with 1/2 Thaler dies, KM#42. Fr. #418.

Date	Mintage	VG	F	VF	XF	Unc
1692 Rare	—	—	—	—	—	—

KM# 48 6 DUCAT
21.0000 g., 0.9860 Gold 0.6657 oz. AGW **Obv:** Archangel Michael standing facing holding oval arms **Rev:** Crowned imperial eagle **Note:** Struck with 1/2 Thaler dies, KM#42. Fr. #417.

Date	Mintage	VG	F	VF	XF	Unc
1692 Rare	—	—	—	—	—	—

PATTERNS

Including off metal strikes

KM#	Date	Mintage	Identification	Mkt Val
Pn1	1609	—	Dicken. Gold. KM#20.	25,000
Pn2	1609	—	Dicken. Copper. KM#20.	1,000
Pn3	ND	—	Rappen. Gold. KM#7.	2,000

ZURICH

Thicurinae, Thuricensis, Ticurinae, Turicensis

A canton in north central Switzerland which was the mint for the dukes of Swabia in the 10th and 11th centuries. The mint right was obtained in 1238. The first coinage struck there were bracteates and the last coins were struck in 1848. It joined the Swiss Confederation in 1351.

MINT OFFICIALS' INITIALS

B - Bruckmann
AV - A. Vorster

MONETARY SYSTEM

Until 1798
12 Haller = 4 Rappen = 1 Schilling
72 Schillinge = 2 Gulden = 1 Thaler

CANTON

STANDARD COINAGE

KM# 5 HELLER
Billon **Obv:** Arms in Spanish shield, Z above, rosettes at sides **Note:** Uniface.

Date	Mintage	VG	F	VF	XF	Unc
ND	—	7.00	15.00	30.00	80.00	175

KM# 7 ANGSTER
Billon **Obv:** Large arms on Spanish shield, Z above, half moons on both sides

Date	Mintage	VG	F	VF	XF	Unc
ND	—	4.00	10.00	20.00	50.00	100

KM# 8 ANGSTER
Billon **Obv:** Mirror image of arms on Spanish shield on clover leaf **Rev:** Eagle in inner circle

Date	Mintage	VG	F	VF	XF	Unc
ND	—	20.00	40.00	85.00	150	—

KM# 9 ANGSTER
Billon **Rev:** Crowned imperial eagle in inner circle

Date	Mintage	VG	F	VF	XF	Unc
ND	—	4.00	10.00	40.00	100	200

KM# A12 RAPPEN
Billon **Rev:** Single-headed eagle and double-headed eagle

Date	Mintage	VG	F	VF	XF	Unc
ND	—	30.00	100	300	600	—
Note: single-head eagle						
ND	—	15.00	40.00	150	400	800
Note: double-headed eagle						

KM# B12 SECHSER
Billon **Obv:** Arms **Rev:** Double-headed eagle

Date	Mintage	VG	F	VF	XF	Unc
ND	—	20.00	50.00	200	500	—

KM# 12 SCHILLING
Billon **Obv:** Arms on Spanish shield, four tulip blossoms at top and bottom and sides **Rev:** Crowned imperial eagle in inner circle

Date	Mintage	VG	F	VF	XF	Unc
ND	—	3.00	5.00	30.00	75.00	150

KM# 13 SCHILLING
Billon **Note:** Klippe.

Date	Mintage	VG	F	VF	XF	Unc
ND	—	—	—	—	—	—

KM# 14 SCHILLING
Billon **Obv:** Arms on Spanish shield on long armed cross, ornaments on cross arms in inner circle **Rev:** Eagle in inner circle

Date	Mintage	VG	F	VF	XF	Unc
ND	—	3.00	5.00	30.00	75.00	150

KM# 49 SCHILLING
Billon **Obv:** Arms on spanish shield, tulip blossoms at top, bottom, and sides **Rev:** Crowned imperial eagle

Date	Mintage	VG	F	VF	XF	Unc
1639	—	4.00	10.00	40.00	100	250
1640	—	4.00	10.00	40.00	100	250
1641	—	4.00	10.00	40.00	100	250

KM# 55 SCHILLING
Billon **Note:** Klippe.

Date	Mintage	VG	F	VF	XF	Unc
1640	—	—	—	—	—	—

KM# 85 5 SCHILLINGS
Billon **Obv:** Standing lion holding arms in Spanish shield **Rev:** Inscription, date in circle with six indentations with ornaments **Rev. Inscription:** PRO / DEO Et PA / TRIA

Date	Mintage	VG	F	VF	XF	Unc
1656	—	45.00	100	250	500	—

KM# 110 5 SCHILLINGS
Silver **Obv:** Oval arms in cartouche within palm branches **Rev:** S.P.Q.T., date above shield with 5 within laurel branches

Date	Mintage	VG	F	VF	XF	Unc
1693	—	15.00	30.00	75.00	150	400
1694	—	15.00	30.00	75.00	150	400
1697	—	15.00	30.00	75.00	150	400

KM# 115 5 SCHILLINGS
Silver **Obv:** Standing lion holding arms and sword **Rev:** Inscription in ornamented ring **Rev. Inscription:** PRO DEO / ET / PATRIA / (date)

Date	Mintage	VG	F	VF	XF	Unc
1697	—	25.00	60.00	150	300	800
1699	—	15.00	30.00	75.00	150	400
1700	—	15.00	30.00	75.00	150	400

KM# 86 10 SCHILLINGS (1/4 Gulden - Oertli)
Silver **Obv:** Curved, arched arms, roses at sides in inner circle **Rev:** Inscription in ornamented ring **Rev. Inscription:** PRO / DEO / ET PA / TRIA / (date)

Date	Mintage	VG	F	VF	XF	Unc
ND	—	15.00	30.00	75.00	200	400
1656	—	15.00	30.00	75.00	200	400
1677	—	15.00	30.00	75.00	200	400
1700	—	15.00	30.00	75.00	200	400

KM# 15 20 SCHILLINGS (1/2 Gulden)
Silver

Date	Mintage	VG	F	VF	XF	Unc
ND	—	25.00	50.00	100	200	500

KM# 28 BATZEN
Billon **Obv:** Large arms on Spanish shield, eagle above **Rev:** Anchor cross in inner circle, date in legend

Date	Mintage	VG	F	VF	XF	Unc
1606	—	15.00	30.00	100	300	—
1607	—	10.00	20.00	75.00	250	—
1608	—	10.00	20.00	75.00	250	—

KM# 29 BATZEN
Billon **Note:** Klippe.

Date	Mintage	VG	F	VF	XF	Unc
1607	—	—	—	—	—	—

KM# 36 BATZEN
Billon **Obv:** Smaller arms on Spanish shield, eagle above, roses on sides **Rev:** Anchor cross with small flowers in angles

Date	Mintage	VG	F	VF	XF	Unc
1621	—	5.00	10.00	30.00	200	—
1622	—	5.00	10.00	30.00	200	—

KM# 40 BATZEN
Billon

Date	Mintage	VG	F	VF	XF	Unc
1623	—	5.00	10.00	30.00	200	—
1624	—	5.00	10.00	30.00	200	—
1633	—	12.00	25.00	80.00	200	—

KM# 41 BATZEN
Billon **Note:** Klippe.

Date	Mintage	VG	F	VF	XF	Unc
1623	—	—	—	—	—	—
1624	—	—	—	—	—	—
1633	—	—	—	—	—	—

KM# 51 BATZEN
Billon **Note:** Klippe.

Date	Mintage	VG	F	VF	XF	Unc
1639	—	—	—	—	—	—

KM# 50 BATZEN
Billon **Obv. Legend:** MO-NET-ANO-VA **Rev:** Legend, date **Rev. Legend:** THVRICENSIS

Date	Mintage	VG	F	VF	XF	Unc
1639	—	5.00	10.00	30.00	100	—
1640	—	5.00	10.00	30.00	100	—
1641	—	5.00	10.00	30.00	100	—

KM# A30 1/2 DICKEN
Silver **Obv:** Lion facing left **Rev:** Double-headed eagle, 12 on breast

Date	Mintage	VG	F	VF	XF	Unc
1608 Rare	—	—	—	—	—	—
1620	—	50.00	100	350	700	—
1621	—	50.00	100	350	700	—
1622	—	25.00	50.00	150	300	—

KM# 30 DICKEN (1/4 Thaler)
Silver

Date	Mintage	VG	F	VF	XF	Unc
1608 Rare	—	—	—	—	—	—
1620	—	60.00	125	300	600	—
1621	—	60.00	125	300	600	—
1622	—	65.00	150	400	750	—

KM# 32 DICKEN (1/4 Thaler)
Silver

Date	Mintage	VG	F	VF	XF	Unc
1620	—	60.00	125	300	600	—
1621	—	60.00	125	300	600	—
1622	—	65.00	150	400	750	—

KM# 33 DICKEN (1/4 Thaler)
Silver **Note:** Klippe.

Date	Mintage	VG	F	VF	XF	Unc
1620	—	—	—	—	—	—
1621	—	—	—	—	—	—

KM# 45 DICKEN (1/4 Thaler)
Silver **Note:** Klippe.

Date	Mintage	VG	F	VF	XF	Unc
1629	—	—	—	—	—	—

KM# 44 DICKEN (1/4 Thaler)
Silver **Obv:** Similar to KM#30 **Rev:** Crowned imperial eagle in inner circle, date below

Date	Mintage	VG	F	VF	XF	Unc
1629	—	50.00	100	250	500	—

KM# 80 1/4 THALER (1/2 Gulden)
Silver, 35 mm.

Date	Mintage	VG	F	VF	XF	Unc
1652	—	75.00	150	400	750	—

KM# 81 1/4 THALER (1/2 Gulden)
Silver, 31 mm.

Date	Mintage	VG	F	VF	XF	Unc
1652	—	75.00	150	400	750	—

KM# 100 1/4 THALER (1/2 Gulden)
Silver **Obv:** Standing lion holding arms and sword **Rev:** Inscription in two laurel branches **Rev. Inscription:** DOMINE / CONSERVA / NOS IN / PACE

Date	Mintage	VG	F	VF	XF	Unc
ND	—	75.00	150	400	750	—

KM# 101 1/4 THALER (1/2 Gulden)
Silver

Date	Mintage	VG	F	VF	XF	Unc
1673	—	75.00	150	400	750	—
1674	—	75.00	150	400	750	—

KM# 34 1/2 THALER (1 Gulden - 36 Schillings)
Silver

Date	Mintage	VG	F	VF	XF	Unc
1620	—	75.00	150	400	750	—

KM# 35 1/2 THALER (1 Gulden - 36 Schillings)
Silver

Date	Mintage	VG	F	VF	XF	Unc
ND Rare	—	450	1,000	2,500	5,000	—
1622	—	75.00	150	400	750	—

KM# 70 1/2 THALER (1 Gulden - 36 Schillings)

Silver **Obv:** Arms on Spanish shield between two standing lions holding a laurel wreath above **Rev:** Cherub's head above DOMINE / CONSERVA / NOS IN / PACE, date in ornamental cartouche

Date	Mintage	VG	F	VF	XF	Unc
1647	—	50.00	100	250	500	—
1649	—	50.00	100	250	500	—

KM# 82 1/2 THALER (1 Gulden - 36 Schillings)

Silver

Date	Mintage	VG	F	VF	XF	Unc
1652	—	50.00	100	250	500	—

KM# 102 1/2 THALER (1 Gulden - 36 Schillings)

Silver **Obv:** Similar to KM#35 but shield curved, 1/2 below lion **Rev:** Cherub's head above inscription in sweeping ornamentation **Rev. Inscription:** DOMINE / CONSERVA / NOS IN PACE / (date)

Date	Mintage	VG	F	VF	XF	Unc
1673	—	100	200	450	900	—
1674 Rare	—	—	—	—	—	—
1690	—	65.00	125	300	600	—

KM# 37 THALER

Silver **Obv:** Lion standing left with arms on Spanish shield and sword, date above **Rev:** Crowned imperial eagle **Note:** Dav. #4638.

Date	Mintage	VG	F	VF	XF	Unc
1622	—	75.00	150	400	750	—
1624	—	100	200	500	1,000	—
1645	—	125	250	600	1,200	—

KM# 56 THALER

Silver **Obv:** Two lions standing holding arms and laurel wreath above, date divided below **Note:** Dav. #4639.

Date	Mintage	VG	F	VF	XF	Unc
1640	—	125	250	600	1,200	—
1645	—	1,500	3,000	7,000	—	—

KM# 66 THALER

Silver **Obv:** Two pentagonal-shaped arms between two standing lions holding a sword and palm branch **Rev:** Inscription in laurel wreath **Rev. Inscription:** DOMINE / CONSERVA / NOS IN / PACE / (date) **Note:** Dav. #4640.

Date	Mintage	VG	F	VF	XF	Unc
1646	—	100	200	500	1,000	—

KM# 71 THALER

Silver **Rev:** Legend in cartouche, cherub's head at top **Note:** Dav. #4641.

Date	Mintage	VG	F	VF	XF	Unc
1647	—	100	200	500	1,000	—

KM# 72 THALER

Silver **Obv:** Lions holding laurel wreath above arms **Note:** Dav. #4643.

Date	Mintage	VG	F	VF	XF	Unc
1649	—	150	300	750	1,500	—

KM# 75 THALER

Silver **Obv:** Lion with sword, orb, and shield on flowered background **Obv. Legend:** MONETA * NOVA * REIPVBLICAE * TIGVRINAE * **Rev:** Inscription within cartouche, cherub head at top **Rev. Inscription:** DOMINE / CONSER- / VA. NOS. / IN. PACE. / (date) **Note:** Dav. #4647.

Date	Mintage	VG	F	VF	XF	Unc
1651	—	150	300	750	1,500	—
1652	—	150	300	750	1,500	—

KM# 76 THALER

Silver **Rev:** View of port city **Note:** Vogelitaler. Dav. #4645.

Date	Mintage	VG	F	VF	XF	Unc
MDCLI (1651)	—	300	600	1,500	3,000	—

KM# 88 THALER

Silver **Obv:** Large crowned arms in laurel branches **Obv. Legend:** + MONETA NOVA REIPVBLICAE TIGVRINAE **Rev:** Legend on banner, inscription in center with lily **Rev. Legend:** DOMINE CONSERVA NOS IN PACE **Rev. Inscription:** MDC / LX **Note:** Wasertaler. Dav. #4648.

Date	Mintage	VG	F	VF	XF	Unc
MDCLX (1660)	—	200	400	1,000	2,000	3,500

KM# 89.1 THALER

Silver **Note:** Dav. #4649.

Date	Mintage	VG	F	VF	XF	Unc
1661	—	125	250	600	1,200	—
1662	—	125	250	600	1,200	—
1663	—	125	250	600	1,200	—
1665	—	100	200	500	1,000	—

KM# 103 THALER

Silver **Note:** Dav. #4651.

Date	Mintage	VG	F	VF	XF	Unc
1673	—	100	200	500	1,000	—
1676	—	100	200	500	1,000	—
1677	—	100	200	500	1,000	—
1694	—	50.00	100	250	600	—

KM# 113 THALER

Silver **Obv:** Lion holding oval shield and sword **Rev:** City view **Note:** Dav. #4655.

Date	Mintage	VG	F	VF	XF	Unc
ND(ca.1680)	—	250	500	1,000	2,000	—

KM# 89.2 THALER

Silver **Obv:** Without inner circle **Note:** Dav. #4652.

Date	Mintage	VG	F	VF	XF	Unc
1691	—	75.00	150	400	800	—
1693	—	125	250	600	1,200	—
1694	—	50.00	80.00	200	425	—

KM# 112 THALER

Silver **Rev:** Similar to KM#89.1 but lion head at top, palm branches at bottom **Note:** Dav. #4653.

Date	Mintage	VG	F	VF	XF	Unc
1695	—	125	250	600	1,200	—

KM# 38 2 THALER

Silver **Obv:** Lion standing left with arms on Spanish shield and sword, date above **Rev:** Crowned imperial eagle **Note:** Dav. #4637.

Date	Mintage	VG	F	VF	XF	Unc
1622	—	500	1,000	2,500	5,000	9,000
1624	—	500	1,000	2,500	5,000	9,000

KM# 57 2 THALER

Silver **Obv:** Two lions standing holding arms and laurel wreath above, date divided below **Note:** Dav. #A4639.

Date	Mintage	VG	F	VF	XF	Unc
1640	—	1,200	2,400	6,000	12,000	—

KM# 67 2 THALER

Silver **Obv:** Two pentagonal-shaped arms between two standing lions holding a sword and palm branch **Obv. Inscription:** DOMINE / CONSERVA / NOS IN / PACE / (date) **Rev:** Inscription in laurel wreath **Note:** Dav. #A4640.

Date	Mintage	VG	F	VF	XF	Unc
1646	—	1,000	2,000	5,000	10,000	—

KM# 73 2 THALER

Silver **Rev:** Legend in cartouche, cherub's head at top **Note:** Dav. #4642.

Date	Mintage	VG	F	VF	XF	Unc
1649	—	2,500	5,000	12,000	—	—

KM# 78 2 THALER

Silver **Rev:** View of port city **Note:** Dav. #4644.

Date	Mintage	VG	F	VF	XF	Unc
MDCLI (1651) Rare	—	—	—	—	—	—

KM# 77 2 THALER

Silver **Note:** Dav. #4646. Similar to 1 Thaler, KM#75.

Date	Mintage	VG	F	VF	XF	Unc
1651	—	2,000	4,000	10,000	—	—
1652 Rare	—	—	—	—	—	—

KM# 111 2 THALER

Silver **Note:** Dav. #4650. Similar to 1 Thaler, KM#103.

Date	Mintage	VG	F	VF	XF	Unc
1694	—	1,000	2,000	4,500	9,000	—

KM# 114 2 THALER

Silver **Obv:** Similar to 1 Thaler, KM#103. **Rev:** Similar to 1 Thaler, KM#89. **Note:** Dav. #4653.

Date	Mintage	VG	F	VF	XF	Unc
1695	—	1,000	2,000	4,500	9,000	—

KM# 16 1/2 KRONE

Gold **Obv:** Arms on Spanish shield on breast of crowned imperial eagle **Rev:** Floreate cross in inner circle

Date	Mintage	VG	F	VF	XF	Unc
—	—	—	—	—	—	—

KM# 48 KRONE

Gold **Obv:** Large curved shield of arms in front of crowned imperial eagle in inner circle **Rev:** Floreate cross in inner circle **Note:** Fr. #429.

Date	Mintage	VG	F	VF	XF	Unc
1631	—	2,500	5,000	10,000	—	—

TRADE COINAGE

FR# 433 1/2 GOLDGULDEN

1.7500 g., 0.9860 Gold 0.0555 oz. AGW **Obv:** Eagle with shield or arms on breast in inner circle **Rev:** Enthroned figure of Charlemagne in inner circle

Date	Mintage	VG	F	VF	XF	Unc
ND(ca. 1600)	—	3,000	6,000	12,000	20,000	—

FR# 431 GOLDGULDEN

3.5000 g., 0.9860 Gold 0.1109 oz. AGW **Obv:** Eagle with shield or arms on breast in inner circle **Rev:** Enthroned figure of Charlemagne in inner circle

Date	Mintage	VG	F	VF	XF	Unc
ND	—	2,500	5,000	9,500	15,000	—

KM# 39 GOLDGULDEN

3.5000 g., 0.9860 Gold 0.1109 oz. AGW **Obv:** Shield of arms in quatrefoil in inner circle **Rev:** Crowned imperial eagle in inner circle **Note:** Fr. #434.

Date	Mintage	VG	F	VF	XF	Unc
1622	—	1,100	2,200	4,500	7,500	—

KM# 52 1/4 DUCAT

0.8750 g., 0.9860 Gold 0.0277 oz. AGW **Obv:** Standing knight facing **Rev:** Three-line legend and date in branches **Note:** Fr. # 449.

Date	Mintage	VG	F	VF	XF	Unc
1639	—	1,200	2,400	5,000	8,000	—

KM# 58 1/4 DUCAT

0.8750 g., 0.9860 Gold 0.0277 oz. AGW **Obv:** Lion holding shield of arms **Rev:** Four-line legend and date in branches **Note:** Varieties exist. Fr. #466.

Date	Mintage	VG	F	VF	XF	Unc
1641	—	125	250	500	750	1,200
1645	—	100	200	400	600	900
1649	—	100	200	400	600	900
1651	—	100	200	400	600	900
1670	—	75.00	150	300	500	800
1671	—	75.00	150	300	500	800

KM# 83 1/4 DUCAT

0.8750 g., 0.9860 Gold 0.0277 oz. AGW **Note:** Similar to 1/2 Ducat, KM#84. Fr. #475.

Date	Mintage	VG	F	VF	XF	Unc
1654	—	100	200	400	600	900
1662	—	100	200	400	600	900

KM# 91 1/4 DUCAT

0.8750 g., 0.9860 Gold 0.0277 oz. AGW **Obv:** Lion holding shield of arms and sword **Rev:** Inscription, date in ornamental border **Rev. Inscription:** MONE / TA NOVA / REIPVB / TIGVRIN /

Date	Mintage	VG	F	VF	XF	Unc
1666	—	75.00	150	300	500	800

KM# 98 1/4 DUCAT

0.8750 g., 0.9860 Gold 0.0277 oz. AGW **Obv:** Lion holding arms and palm branch **Rev:** Inscription, date in laurel wreath **Rev. Inscription:** ANNO / DOMINI / **Note:** Fr. #468.

Date	Mintage	VG	F	VF	XF	Unc
1671	—	75.00	150	300	500	800
1677	—	75.00	150	300	500	800
1692	—	65.00	100	200	400	600

KM# 19 1/2 DUCAT

1.7500 g., 0.9860 Gold 0.0555 oz. AGW **Obv:** Crowned imperial eagle in inner circle **Rev:** Charlemagne standing with sword in inner circle **Note:** Fr. #438.

Date	Mintage	VG	F	VF	XF	Unc
ND(1570) Rare	—	—	—	—	—	—

KM# 20 1/2 DUCAT

1.7500 g., 0.9860 Gold 0.0555 oz. AGW **Obv:** Single-headed eagle **Note:** Fr. #436.

Date	Mintage	VG	F	VF	XF	Unc
ND(ca. 1600)	—	1,500	3,200	5,200	6,500	—

KM# 53 1/2 DUCAT

1.7500 g., 0.9860 Gold 0.0555 oz. AGW **Note:** Fr. #448.

Date	Mintage	VG	F	VF	XF	Unc
1639	—	600	1,200	2,500	4,000	—

KM# 59 1/2 DUCAT

1.7500 g., 0.9860 Gold 0.0555 oz. AGW **Obv:** Lion holding shield and palm branch **Rev:** Date in laurel branches **Rev. Inscription:** MON. / NO. THV / RICEN / SIS **Note:** Fr. #465.

Date	Mintage	VG	F	VF	XF	Unc
1641	—	125	250	500	800	1,250
1645	—	125	250	500	800	1,250
1649	—	125	250	500	800	1,250
1651	—	125	250	500	800	1,250
1670	—	110	200	400	700	1,100
1671	—	110	200	400	700	1,100

KM# 84 1/2 DUCAT

1.7500 g., 0.9860 Gold 0.0555 oz. AGW **Note:** Fr. #474.

Date	Mintage	VG	F	VF	XF	Unc
1654	—	125	250	500	800	1,250
1662	—	125	250	500	800	1,250

KM# 92 1/2 DUCAT

1.7500 g., 0.9860 Gold 0.0555 oz. AGW **Obv:** Lion holding shield and sword **Rev:** Inscription, date in wide ornate edge **Rev. Inscription:** MONE / TA NOVA / REIPVB / TIGVRIN **Note:** Fr. #465.

Date	Mintage	VG	F	VF	XF	Unc
1666	—	110	200	400	700	1,100

KM# 97 1/2 DUCAT

1.7500 g., 0.9860 Gold 0.0555 oz. AGW **Rev:** Inscription, date in laurel branches **Rev. Inscription:** MON. / NO. THV / RICEN SIS **Note:** Fr. #465.

Date	Mintage	VG	F	VF	XF	Unc
1670	—	110	200	400	700	1,10

KM# 99 1/2 DUCAT

1.7500 g., 0.9860 Gold 0.0555 oz. AGW **Note:** Fr. #467.

Date	Mintage	VG	F	VF	XF	Unc
1671	—	110	200	400	700	1,10
1677	—	110	200	400	700	1,10
1692	—	110	200	400	700	1,10

KM# 21 DUCAT

3.5000 g., 0.9860 Gold 0.1109 oz. AGW **Obv. Inscription:** S.P.Q. /THVRICEN/SIS **Rev:** Charlemagne enthroned **Note:** Fr #442.

Date	Mintage	VG	F	VF	XF	Un
ND(ca. 1620)	—	1,000	1,600	2,500	4,000	—

KM# 22 DUCAT

3.5000 g., 0.9860 Gold 0.1109 oz. AGW **Obv:** Charlemagne enthroned in inner circle **Rev:** Sts. Regula and Felix standing facing holding their heads **Note:** Fr. #440.

Date	Mintage	VG	F	VF	XF	Un
ND(ca. 1580)	—	1,600	3,000	6,000	10,000	—

KM# 23 DUCAT

3.5000 g., 0.9860 Gold 0.1109 oz. AGW **Obv:** Shield of arms on crowned imperial eagle in inner circle **Rev:** Charlemagne standing left with raised sword in inner circle **Note:** Fr. #437.

Date	Mintage	VG	F	VF	XF	Un
ND(ca. 1570) Rare	—	—	—	—	—	—

KM# 24 DUCAT

3.5000 g., 0.9860 Gold 0.1109 oz. AGW **Obv:** Shield of arms on crowned imperial eagle in inner circle **Rev:** Charlemagne standing right with sword and orb in inner circle **Note:** Fr. #435

Date	Mintage	VG	F	VF	XF	Un
ND(ca. 1600)	—	750	1,500	3,000	5,000	—

KM# 60 DUCAT

3.5000 g., 0.9860 Gold 0.1109 oz. AGW **Obv:** Oval arms with lion supporters **Rev:** Four-line legend and date in branches **Note:** Fr. #458.

Date	Mintage	VG	F	VF	XF	Unc
1641	—	450	900	1,800	3,000	4,20
1643	—	450	900	1,800	3,000	4,20

KM# 65 DUCAT

3.5000 g., 0.9860 Gold 0.1109 oz. AGW **Obv:** Standing lion holding shield and palm branch **Rev:** Inscription, date in laurel wreath **Rev. Inscription:** DVCATVS / NOVVS / REIPVBLI / THURICENS / IS **Note:** Fr. #464.

Date	Mintage	VG	F	VF	XF	Unc
1645	—	600	1,200	2,500	4,000	6,00

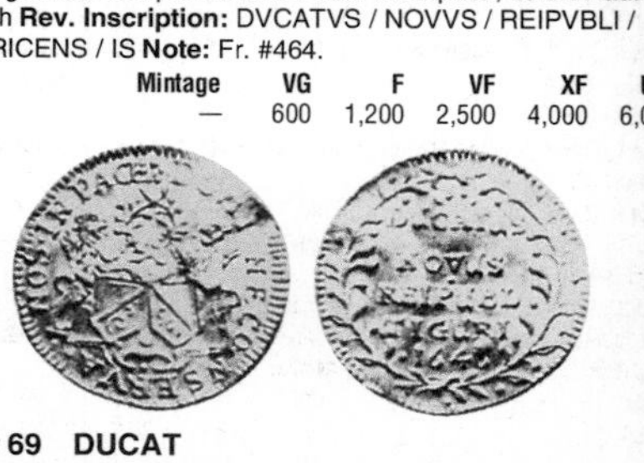

KM# 69 DUCAT

3.5000 g., 0.9860 Gold 0.1109 oz. AGW **Note:** Fr. #459.

ate	Mintage	VG	F	VF	XF	Unc
646	—	400	900	1,800	3,000	4,200
648	—	400	900	1,800	3,000	4,200
649	—	400	900	1,800	3,000	4,200
650	—	600	1,200	2,500	4,000	6,000

:M# 68 DUCAT

5000 g., 0.9860 Gold 0.1109 oz. AGW **Obv:** Two pentagonal-haped arms between two standing lions holding a sword and alm branch **Rev:** Inscription, date in laurel wreath **Rev. nscription:** DUCATUS / NOVUS / REIPUBL / TIGURI /

ate	Mintage	VG	F	VF	XF	Unc
646	—	450	900	1,800	3,000	4,200

:M# 79 DUCAT

.5000 g., 0.9860 Gold 0.1109 oz. AGW **Note:** Fr. #473.

ate	Mintage	VG	F	VF	XF	Unc
651	—	400	800	2,000	3,200	4,800
660 Rare	—	—	—	—	—	—

:M# A90 DUCAT

.5000 g., 0.9860 Gold 0.1109 oz. AGW **Obv:** Arms **Obv. .egend:** DOMINE • CONSERVA • NOS • IN • PACE **Rev:** Ornate ame with fruit at bottom **Rev. Inscription:** DVCATUS / NOVV REIPVBL / TIGVRI **Note:** Prev. KM#90. Fr.#464.

ate	Mintage	VG	F	VF	XF	Unc
ID(c.1660)	—	600	1,200	2,400	4,000	—

:M# 90 DUCAT

.5000 g., 0.9860 Gold 0.1109 oz. AGW **Obv:** Arms **Obv. .egend:** * DOMINE • CONSERVA • NOS • IN • PACE * **Rev:** Ornate frame **Rev. Inscription:** DVCATUS / NOVVS / REIPVBL TIGVRI **Note:** Fr.#464.

Date	Mintage	VG	F	VF	XF	Unc
1661	—	500	1,000	2,100	3,500	5,000
1662	—	500	1,000	2,100	3,500	5,000

KM# 105.1 DUCAT

3.5000 g., 0.9860 Gold 0.1109 oz. AGW **Note:** Varieties exist. Fr. #464.

Date	Mintage	VG	F	VF	XF	Unc
1673	—	1,350	2,700	4,500	10,000	—
1676	—	1,350	2,700	4,500	10,000	—
1679	—	1,350	2,700	4,500	10,000	—
1680	—	500	1,000	2,100	3,500	5,000
1684	—	500	1,000	2,100	3,500	5,000
1693	—	500	1,000	2,100	3,500	5,000

KM# 104 DUCAT

3.5000 g., 0.9860 Gold 0.1109 oz. AGW **Rev:** Similar to KM#90 but different legend **Rev. Inscription:** JUSTICIA / ET / CONCORDIA

Date	Mintage	VG	F	VF	XF	Unc
1673 Rare	—	—	—	—	—	—

KM# 105.2 DUCAT

Gold **Obv:** Redesigned lion with sword and shield left **Note:** Fr. #464a.

Date	Mintage	VG	F	VF	XF	Unc
1697	—	500	1,000	2,100	3,500	5,000

KM# 42 2 DUCAT

7.0000 g., 0.9860 Gold 0.2219 oz. AGW **Obv:** Standing lion with orb holding shield in inner circle, date in legend **Rev:** Crowned imperial eagle in inner circle **Note:** Fr. #446.

Date	Mintage	VG	F	VF	XF	Unc
1624	—	1,500	3,000	6,000	10,000	—

KM# 46 2 DUCAT

7.0000 g., 0.9860 Gold 0.2219 oz. AGW **Rev:** Date in exergue **Note:** Fr. #447.

Date	Mintage	VG	F	VF	XF	Unc
1629	—	1,600	3,000	4,000	6,000	—

KM# 25 2 DUCAT

7.0000 g., 0.9860 Gold 0.2219 oz. AGW **Obv:** Inscription in wreath **Obv. Inscription:** S.P.Q / THURICEN / SIS **Rev:** Charlemagne enthroned in ornamented inner circle **Note:** Fr. #441.

Date	Mintage	VG	F	VF	XF	Unc
ND(ca. 1620) Rare	—	—	—	—	—	—

KM# 26 2 DUCAT

7.0000 g., 0.9860 Gold 0.2219 oz. AGW **Obv:** Charlemagne enthroned in inner circle **Rev:** Sts. Regula and Felix standing facing holding their heads **Note:** Fr. #439.

Date	Mintage	VG	F	VF	XF	Unc
ND(ca. 1580) Rare	—	3,750	7,500	15,000	—	—

KM# 61 2 DUCAT

7.0000 g., 0.9860 Gold 0.2219 oz. AGW **Obv:** Laurel wreath above oval arms supported by two standing lions **Note:** Fr. #457.

Date	Mintage	VG	F	VF	XF	Unc
1641	—	1,500	3,000	6,000	10,000	—

KM# 106 2 DUCAT

7.0000 g., 0.9860 Gold 0.2219 oz. AGW **Obv:** Standing lion with sword holding shield in inner circle, date in legend **Rev:** Value in cartouche **Note:** Fr. #463.

Date	Mintage	VG	F	VF	XF	Unc
1673	—	1,500	3,000	6,000	10,000	—

KM# 108 2 DUCAT

7.0000 g., 0.9860 Gold 0.2219 oz. AGW **Note:** Similar to 1 Ducat, KM#90. Fr. #463.

Date	Mintage	VG	F	VF	XF	Unc
1683	—	2,500	5,000	10,000	17,000	—

KM# 62 3 DUCAT

10.5000 g., 0.9860 Gold 0.3328 oz. AGW **Note:** Similar to 2 Ducat, KM#61. Fr. #456.

Date	Mintage	VG	F	VF	XF	Unc
1641	—	1,750	3,500	7,500	12,500	—

KM# 93 3 DUCAT

10.5000 g., 0.9860 Gold 0.3328 oz. AGW **Obv:** Standing lion with sword in inner circle, legend within laurel wreath **Obv. Legend:** DOMINE CONSERVA NOS IN PACE **Rev:** Inscription, date in baroque frame in laurel wreath **Rev. Inscription:** MONE / TA NOVA / REIPVB / TIGVRIN / **Note:** Fr. #462.

Date	Mintage	VG	F	VF	XF	Unc
1666	—	5,000	10,000	20,000	35,000	—

KM# 31 4 DUCAT

14.0000 g., 0.9860 Gold 0.4438 oz. AGW **Obv:** Standing lion holding sword and shield **Rev:** Imperial eagle **Note:** Struck with 1/2 Thaler dies, KM#35. Fr. #444.

Date	Mintage	VG	F	VF	XF	Unc
1622 Rare	—	—	—	—	—	—

KM# 43 4 DUCAT

14.0000 g., 0.9860 Gold 0.4438 oz. AGW **Obv:** Standing lion with orb holding shield in inner circle, date in legend **Rev:** Crowned imperial eagle in inner circle **Note:** Struck with 1 Thaler dies, KM#37. Fr. #443.

Date	Mintage	VG	F	VF	XF	Unc
1624	—	6,000	12,000	25,000	40,000	—

KM# 47 4 DUCAT

14.0000 g., 0.9860 Gold 0.4438 oz. AGW **Obv:** Lion standing holding sword and shield **Rev:** Crowned imperial eagle, date in exergue **Note:** Struck with 2 Ducat dies, KM#46. Fr. #445.

Date	Mintage	VG	F	VF	XF	Unc
1629	—	4,500	7,500	12,500	18,000	—

KM# A63 4 DUCAT

14.0000 g., 0.9860 Gold 0.4438 oz. AGW **Note:** Similar to 4 Ducat, KM#63. Struck with 1 Thaler dies, KM#56.

Date	Mintage	VG	F	VF	XF	Unc
1640	—	—	—	—	—	—

KM# 63 4 DUCAT

14.0000 g., 0.9860 Gold 0.4438 oz. AGW **Obv:** Laurel wreath above oval arms at center supported by two standing lions

Date	Mintage	VG	F	VF	XF	Unc
1641	—	2,500	5,000	11,000	18,000	—

KM# 94 4 DUCAT

14.0000 g., 0.9860 Gold 0.4438 oz. AGW **Obv:** Standing lion with sword in inner circle, legend within laurel wreath **Obv. Legend:** DOMINE CONSERVA NOS IN PACE **Rev:** Inscription, date in baroque frame in laurel wreath **Rev. Inscription:** MONE / TA NOVA / REIPVB / TIGVRIN / **Note:** Fr. #461.

Date	Mintage	VG	F	VF	XF	Unc
1666 Rare	—	—	12,000	24,000	40,000	—

KM# 64 5 DUCAT

17.5000 g., 0.9860 Gold 0.5547 oz. AGW **Obv:** Two standing lions holding oval arms at bottom dividing date and laurel wreath at top **Rev:** Crowned imperial eagle in inner circle **Note:** Klippe. Fr. #454.

Date	Mintage	VG	F	VF	XF	Unc
1641 Rare	—	—	—	—	—	—

KM# 95 5 DUCAT

17.5000 g., 0.9860 Gold 0.5547 oz. AGW **Obv:** Standing lion with sword in inner circle **Obv. Legend:** DOMINE CONSERVA NOS IN PACE all within laurel wreath **Rev:** Inscription, date in baroque frame in laurel wreath **Rev. Inscription:** MONE / TA NOVA / REIPVB / TIGVRIN / **Note:** Fr. #460.

Date	Mintage	VG	F	VF	XF	Unc
1666 Rare	—	—	—	—	—	—

KM# A44 6 DUCAT

Gold **Obv:** Lion with sword and shield left **Rev:** Crowned imperial eagle **Note:** Struck with 1 Thaler dies, KM#37. Fr. #442a.

Date	Mintage	VG	F	VF	XF	Unc
1624 Rare	—	—	—	—	—	—

KM# A70 6 DUCAT

21.0000 g., 0.9860 Gold 0.6657 oz. AGW **Obv:** Two pentagonal-shaped arms between two standing lions holding a sword and palm branch **Rev:** Inscription, date in laurel wreath **Rev. Inscription:** DOMINE / CONSERVA / NOS IN / PACE / **Note:** Struck wtih 1 Thaler dies, KM#66. Fr. #472.

Date	Mintage	VG	F	VF	XF	Unc
1646 Rare	—	—	—	—	—	—

KM# 74 6 DUCAT

21.0000 g., 0.9860 Gold 0.6657 oz. AGW **Obv:** Two lions standing holding laurel wreath above arms **Note:** Struck wtih 1 Thaler dies, KM#72. Fr. #472.

Date	Mintage	VG	F	VF	XF	Unc
1649 Rare	—	—	—	—	—	—

KM# A75 7 DUCAT

24.5000 g., 0.9860 Gold 0.7766 oz. AGW **Note:** Similar to 6 Ducat, KM#74. Struck with 1 Thaler dies, KM#72. Fr. #471.

Date	Mintage	VG	F	VF	XF	Unc
1649 Rare	—	—	—	—	—	—

KM# B70 8 DUCAT

28.0000 g., 0.9860 Gold 0.8876 oz. AGW **Note:** Similar to 6 Ducat, KM#A70. Struck with 1 Thaler dies, KM#66. Fr. #470.

Date	Mintage	VG	F	VF	XF	Unc
1646 Rare	—	—	—	—	—	—

KM# B75 8 DUCAT

28.0000 g., 0.9860 Gold 0.8876 oz. AGW **Note:** Similar to 6 Ducat, KM#74. Struck with 1 Thaler dies, KM#72. Fr. #470.

Date	Mintage	VG	F	VF	XF	Unc
1649 Rare	—	—	—	—	—	—

KM# 107 10 DUCAT

35.0000 g., 0.9860 Gold 1.1095 oz. AGW **Obv:** Lion standing holding sword and shield **Rev:** City view **Note:** Struck with 1 Thaler dies, KM#113. Fr. #476.

Date	Mintage	VG	F	VF	XF	Unc
ND(ca.1680) Rare	—	—	—	—	—	—

KM# C75 15 DUCAT

52.5000 g., 0.9860 Gold 1.6642 oz. AGW **Note:** Similar to 8 Ducat, KM#B75. Struck with 1 Thaler dies, KM#72. Fr. #469.

Date	Mintage	VG	F	VF	XF	Unc
1649 Rare	—	—	—	—	—	—

CITY

STANDARD COINAGE

KM# 6 3 HALLER (1 Rappen)
Billon **Obv:** Oval arms between palm and laurel branches **Rev:** Value: 3/Haller in baroque frame

Date	Mintage	VG	F	VF	XF	Unc
ND	—	3.00	5.00	10.00	15.00	25.00

KM# 10 RAPPEN
Billon **Obv:** Arms on Spanish shield on clover leaf, three leaves in field **Rev:** Inscription in palm and laurel branches **Rev. Inscription:** MONETA / NOVA / TIGURI / NA

Date	Mintage	VG	F	VF	XF	Unc
ND	—	3.00	5.00	20.00	50.00	150

KM# 11 RAPPEN
Billon **Obv:** Arms of Zurich within sprigs **Rev:** Inscription within palm and laurel branches **Rev. Inscription:** MONETA / TIGURI / NA

Date	Mintage	VG	F	VF	XF	Unc
ND	—	3.00	5.00	10.00	20.00	50.00

PATTERNS

Including off metal strikes

KM#	Date	Mintage	Identification	Mkt Val
Pn1	1620	—	Dicken. Silver. 14.9900 g. KM#32.	—
Pn4	1624	—	Batzen. Gold. KM#41.	3,000
Pn2	ND	—	Angster. Gold. 0.8400 g. KM#7.	1,100
Pn3	ND	—	Schilling. Gold. KM#13. Klippe.	1,500
Pn5	1694	—	Thaler. Silver.	—

SYRIA

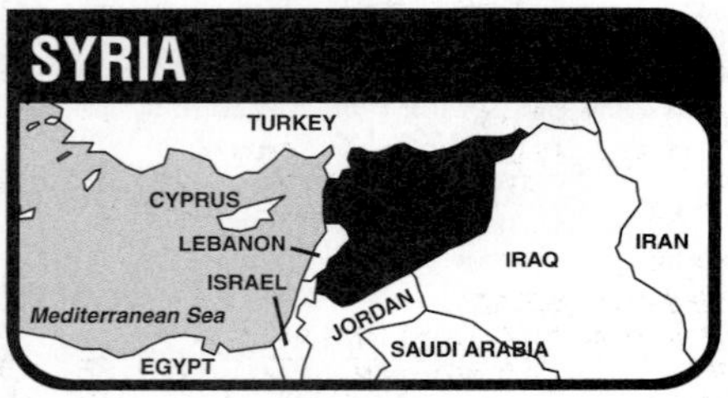

The Syrian Arab Republic, located in the Near East at the eastern end of the Mediterranean Sea, has an area of 71,498 sq. mi. (185,180 sq. km.).

Ancient Syria, a land bridge connecting Europe, Africa and Asia, has spent much of its history in thrall to the conqueror's whim. Its subjection by Egypt about 1500 B.C. was followed by successive conquests by the Hebrews, Phoenicians, Babylonians, Assyrians, Persians, Macedonians, Romans, Byzantines and finally, in 636 A.D., by the Moslems. The Arabs made Damascus, one of the oldest continuously inhabited cities of the world, the trade center and capital of an empire stretching from India to Spain. In 1516, following the total destruction of Damascus by the Mongols of Tamerlane, Syria fell to the Ottoman Turks and remained a part of Turkey until the end of World War I.

TITLES

الجمهورية السورية

Al-Jumhuriya(t) al-Suriya(t)

RULER
Ottoman, until 1918

MINT NAME

دمشق

Damascus (Dimask)

بلب

Haleb (Aleppo)

MONETARY SYSTEM
100 Piastres (Qirsh) = 1 Pound (Lira)

OTTOMAN EMPIRE

Ahmed I

AH1012-26/1603-17AD

HAMMERED COINAGE

Haleb

KM# 11 MANGIR
1.9000 g., Copper

Date	Mintage	Good	VG	F	VF	XF
AH1012	—	37.50	43.75	65.00	95.00	—

Damascus

KM# 14 AKCE
0.2200 g., Silver

Date	Mintage	Good	VG	F	VF	XF
AH1012	—	22.50	31.25	37.50	65.00	—

Haleb

KM# 15 AKCE
0.2200 g., Silver

Date	Mintage	Good	VG	F	VF	XF
AH1012	—	10.00	13.00	18.00	31.25	—

Haleb

KM# 12 MEDIN
Silver **Note:** Weight varies: 1.25-1.30 grams.

Date	Mintage	Good	VG	F	VF	XF
AH1012	—	13.00	25.00	50.00	75.00	—

Damascus

KM# 16 DIRHEM
Silver **Rev:** Legend in three lines **Note:** Reduced weight varies: 2.10-2.30 grams. Previous KM #17.

Date	Mintage	Good	VG	F	VF	XF
AH1012	—	30.00	34.50	46.00	80.00	—

KM# 13 DIRHEM
2.9100 g., Silver **Note:** Size varies: 14-16 millimeters.

Date	Mintage	Good	VG	F	VF	XF
AH1012	—	30.00	40.00	55.00	100	—

Haleb

KM# 17 DIRHEM
Silver **Obv:** Toughra **Rev:** 3-line inscription with date **Note:** Weight varies: 2.10-2.18 grams. Previous KM #16.

Date	Mintage	Good	VG	F	VF	XF
AH1012	—	19.00	25.00	31.25	50.00	—

KM# 18 DIRHEM
Silver **Obv:** Toughra **Rev:** Legend around six-pointed star **Note:** Weight varies: 2.10-2.30 grams.

Date	Mintage	Good	VG	F	VF	XF
AH1012	—	20.00	25.00	32.50	50.00	—

Damascus

KM# 21 SULTANI
3.4500 g., Gold **Rev. Inscription:** Darib al-Nasr...

Date	Mintage	VG	F	VF	XF	Unc
AH1012	—	185	250	325	500	—

KM# 22 SULTANI
3.4500 g., Gold **Rev. Inscription:** Sultan al-Barrain....

Date	Mintage	VG	F	VF	XF	Un
AH1012	—	195	275	350	550	-

Haleb

KM# 24 SULTANI
3.4500 g., Gold

Date	Mintage	VG	F	VF	XF	Un
AH1012	—	175	225	325	500	-
AH10012 Error	—	200	300	400	600	-

Mustafa I

AH1026-27/1617-18AD First Reign

HAMMERED COINAGE

Damascus

KM# A25 AKCE
0.3600 g., Silver, 13 mm.

Date	Mintage	Good	VG	F	VF
AH1026 Rare	—	—	—	—	—

Haleb

KM# 25 MEDIN
1.2500 g., Silver

Date	Mintage	Good	VG	F	VF
AH1026 Rare	—	—	—	—	—

Haleb

KM# 28 SULTANI
3.4500 g., Gold

Date	Mintage	Good	VG	F	VF
AH1026 Rare	—	—	—	—	—

Osman II

AH1027-31/1618-22AD

HAMMERED COINAGE

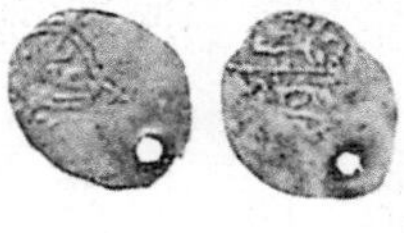

Damascus

KM# 30 AKCE
0.3500 g., Silver

Date	Mintage	Good	VG	F	VF
AH1027	—	40.00	45.00	60.00	100

Haleb

KM# 31 AKCE
0.3500 g., Silver

Date	Mintage	Good	VG	F	VF
AH1027	—	15.00	20.00	25.00	50.00

Haleb

KM# 34 MEDIN
1.2500 g., Silver

Date	Mintage	Good	VG	F	VF
AH1027	—	20.00	25.00	30.00	60.00

Haleb

KM# 32 DIRHEM
Silver **Note:** Weight varies: 2.10-2.18 grams.

Date	Mintage	Good	VG	F	VF
AH1027	—	50.00	60.00	75.00	125

Haleb

KM# 33 ONLUK

.9000 g., Silver **Note:** The Dirham and the Onluk may refer to the same type.

Date	Mintage	Good	VG	F	VF	XF
AH1027	—	50.00	60.00	75.00	125	—

Damascus

KM# 36 SULTANI

.4500 g., Gold **Note:** Size varies 21-22 mm.

Date	Mintage	Good	VG	F	VF	XF
AH1027	—	—	275	425	600	800

Haleb

KM# 38 SULTANI

.4500 g., Gold **Note:** Size varies 21-22 mm.

Date	Mintage	Good	VG	F	VF	XF
AH1027	—	—	275	425	625	850

KM# 39 SULTANI

.4500 g., Gold, 19.5 mm.

Date	Mintage	Good	VG	F	VF	XF
AH1029	—	—	185	250	325	500

Mustafa I

AH1031-32/1622-23AD Second Reign

HAMMERED COINAGE

Haleb

KM# 26 DIRHEM

.7900 g., Silver, 22 mm.

Date	Mintage	Good	VG	F	VF	XF
AH1031	—	70.00	80.00	100	175	—

Damascus

KM# 27 SULTANI

.4500 g., Gold

Date	Mintage	Good	VG	F	VF	XF
AH1031 Rare	—	—	—	—	—	—

Murad IV

AH1032-49/1623-40AD

HAMMERED COINAGE

Damascus

KM# 40 MANGIR

Copper **Note:** Weight varies: 1.50-3.00 grams.

Date	Mintage	Good	VG	F	VF	XF
AH1032	—	40.00	45.00	55.00	100	—

Haleb

KM# 41 MANGIR

Copper **Note:** Weight varies: 1.50-3.00 grams.

Date	Mintage	Good	VG	F	VF	XF
AH1032	—	7.00	18.00	36.00	60.00	—

Damascus

KM# 43 AKCE

Silver **Note:** Weight varies: 0.35-0.40 grams.

Date	Mintage	Good	VG	F	VF	XF
AH1032	—	25.00	30.00	35.00	60.00	—

Haleb

KM# 42 AKCE

Silver **Note:** Weight varies: 0.35-0.40 grams.

Date	Mintage	Good	VG	F	VF	XF
AH1032	—	10.00	15.00	20.00	40.00	—

Damascus

KM# 45 MEDIN

1.7000 g., Silver

Date	Mintage	Good	VG	F	VF	XF
AH1032	—	30.00	50.00	90.00	150	—

Haleb

KM# 44 MEDIN

1.2000 g., Silver

Date	Mintage	Good	VG	F	VF	XF
AH1032	—	30.00	50.00	90.00	150	—

Damascus

KM# 48 DIRHEM

Silver **Note:** Weight varies: 1.79-1.98 grams.

Date	Mintage	Good	VG	F	VF	XF
AH1032	—	40.00	60.00	100	150	—

Haleb

KM# 46 DIRHEM

2.0600 g., Silver **Note:** Several legend varieties exist.

Date	Mintage	Good	VG	F	VF	XF
AH1032	—	40.00	50.00	60.00	85.00	—

Mehmed IV

AH1058-99/1648-87AD

HAMMERED COINAGE

Damascus

KM# 54 MANGIR

2.8100 g., Copper, 14 mm.

Date	Mintage	Good	VG	F	VF	XF
AH1058	—	25.00	30.00	40.00	80.00	—

Damascus

KM# 52 AKCE

Silver **Note:** Weight varies: 0.25-0.28 grams. Varieties exist.

Date	Mintage	Good	VG	F	VF	XF
AH1058	—	30.00	35.00	40.00	75.00	—

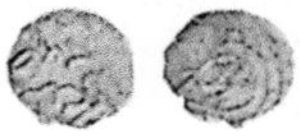

Haleb

KM# 53 AKCE

Silver **Note:** Weight varies: 0.25-0.28 grams.

Date	Mintage	Good	VG	F	VF	XF
AH1058	—	35.00	40.00	50.00	75.00	—

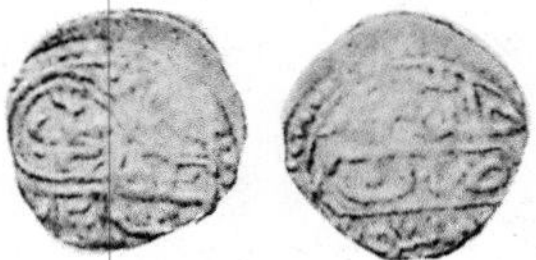

Haleb

KM# 56 MEDIN

0.7800 g., Silver

Date	Mintage	Good	VG	F	VF	XF
AH1058	—	45.00	60.00	70.00	110	—

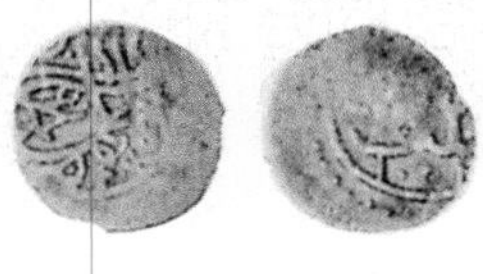

Damascus

KM# 59 BESLIK

Silver **Note:** Weight varies: 1.27-1.35 grams.

Date	Mintage	Good	VG	F	VF	XF
AH1058	—	20.00	25.00	35.00	75.00	—

Haleb

KM# 60 BESLIK

Silver **Note:** Weight varies: 1.27-1.35 grams.

Date	Mintage	Good	VG	F	VF	XF
AH1058	—	22.50	27.50	40.00	80.00	—

Haleb

KM# 62 DIRHEM

2.2800 g., Silver

Date	Mintage	Good	VG	F	VF	XF
AH1058	—	30.00	35.00	40.00	85.00	—

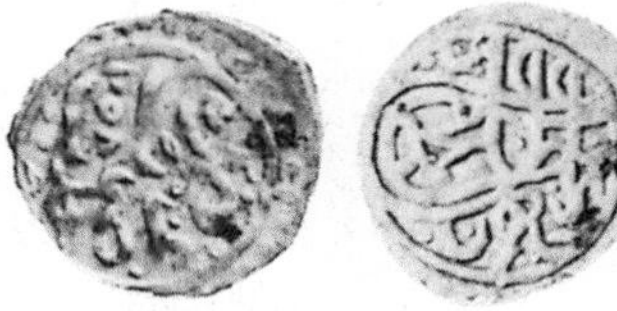

KM# 63 DIRHEM

2.2800 g., Silver

Date	Mintage	Good	VG	F	VF	XF
AH1058	—	30.00	35.00	40.00	85.00	—

Ibrahim

AH1040-58/1640-48AD

HAMMERED COINAGE

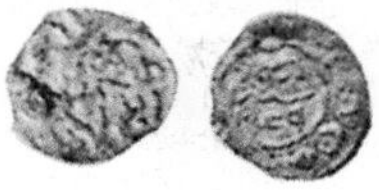

Damascus

KM# 50 AKCE

Silver **Note:** Weight varies: 0.28-0.32 grams.

Date	Mintage	Good	VG	F	VF	XF
AH1049	—	25.00	30.00	40.00	75.00	—

Damascus

KM# 51 BESLIK

Silver **Note:** Weight varies: 1.50-1.55 grams.

Date	Mintage	Good	VG	F	VF	XF
AH1049	—	40.00	60.00	100	150	—

Haleb

KM# A51 BESLIK

Silver **Note:** Weight varies: 1.50-1.55 grams.

Date	Mintage	Good	VG	F	VF	XF
AH1049	—	30.00	35.00	45.00	75.00	—

TRANSYLVANIA

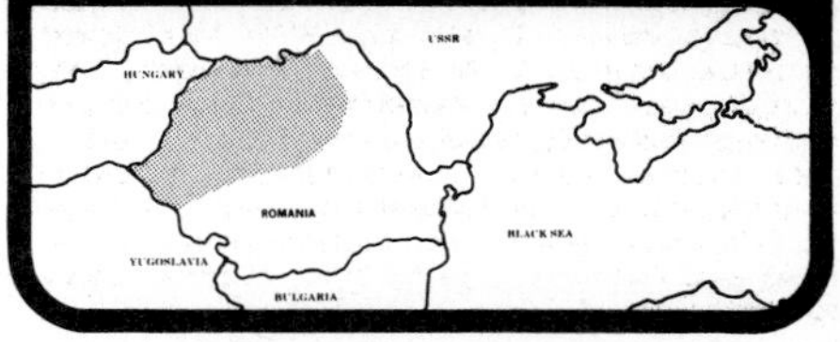

Transylvania (Cibin, Siebenburgen) is the plateau region of northwestern Romania, formerly part of Ancient Dacia, a region occupied by the Romans under Emperor Trajan in 100 AD and abandoned to the Goths in 271 AD under Aurelianus. The Romanized population maintained its Latin speech and Christian identity.

In 896 the Hungarians settled into the Carpathian basin, this included Transylvania. While the region remained an autonomous principality, mercenary Saxons enforced the suzerainty of the King of Hungary in exchange for land. When the Hungarian army was defeated by the advancing Turks at Monacs in 1526, the country was divided into three parts under protection of the Sultan. The center was occupied by the Turks, the West by the Hungary Kingdom under the Hapsburgs and Transylvania in the East which became a principality in 1540. Holy Roman Emperor Rudolf II seized control of the territory in 1604 after the murder of Michael the Brave of Wallachia, who had briefly united the Romanian principalities. In 1605 the Diet elected Stephen Bocskaias prince. After George Rakoczi II was defeated in war with Poland, the Turks were able to intervene, deposing the prince and appointing their own vassals. After the defeat of the Ottoman Turks in 1683, the Transylvanian princes then looked to Austria for guidance and protection.

The last Turkish vassal abdicated in 1697, and with the Orthodox Romanians recognizing the authority of the Pope, the Greek-Catholic, or Uniate Church is created. Under these circumstances, and the treaty of Szatmar in 1711, Transylvania was absorbed into the vast Holy Roman Empire. Transylvania continued to be a part of Hungary until the end of World War I. In 1918, Romania occupied Transylvania.

RULERS

Austrian
Michael the Brave of Wallachia, 1601
no monetary issues
Austrian Commissaries, 1602-1603, 1604
no monetary issues
Sigismund Bathori, 1601-1602
coinage of Kronstad
Francis Rakoczi, 1652-1676
no monetary issues
Francis Rhedei, 1657-1658
no monetary issues
George Bannfy I, 1691-1708
Governor and Count of Losoncz
Leopold I, 1690-1705

Local Princes

Moses Szekely, 1603
Stephan Bocskai, 1604-1606
(postmortem issues 1607-1609)
Sigismund Rakoczi, 1606-1608
Gabriel Bathori, 1608-1613
Gabriel Bethlen, 1613-1629
Catherine of Brandenburg, 1629-1630
widow of Gabriel Bethlen
Stephan Bethlen, 1630
George Rakoczi I, 1630-1648
George Rakoczi II, 1648-1660
John Kemeny, 1661-1662

Turkish Vassals

Achatius Barcsai, 1658-1660
Michael Apafi, 1661-1690
Emeric Tokely, 1682-1690
Michael Apafi II, 1690
no monetary issues

MINT MARKS

A-B - Abrud, 1661
A-C - (Arx Claudiopolis), Klausenburg, Cluj, Kolosvar, 1671-1673
AF - (Arx Fogarasch), 1668-89
AI - (Alba Iulia), Karlsburg, 1610-83 (Wissenburg) until 1716
AL-IV - (Alba Iulia), Karlsburg, 1611-13
AZ - (Arx Zalathna), Zlatna
BE \ V - (Besztercze Varos), Bistritz, Bistrita, 1673
BEZ - (Besztercze), Bistritz, Bistrita, 1673
BF – Opole, Polen, 1622-23
BN - Nagybanya
BT - (Besztercze), Bistritz, Bistrita, 1672-73
C - Civitas (Brassoviensis), 1614
CB - (Cibinium), Hermannstadt, 1672
CB - (Claudiolopolis), Klausenburg, Kolosvar, Cluj, 1604-1605
CB - (Civitas Brassoviensis), Kronstadt, Brasov, 1612-60
CB \ crowned roots, 1662-1675
crowned roots, 1601-1674
C-B - (Cibiniu-Sibiu), 1673-1674
CC - (Camera Cassoviensis), Cassovia, Koschice, 1625-1629 (Kaschau), 1574-83, 1693-98, 1705-07
CF - (Civitas Fogarasch), (w/3 fish) Fagaras, 1677
CI, CI-BI, CIBIN, C-B - (Cibinium), Hermannstadt, Sibiu, 1611-13, 1660, 1672
Cor. - (Corona), Kronstadt
CM - (Cibiniensis moneta), Hermannstadt
CM - (Cassoviensis moneta), Cassovia, Koshice, (Kaschau), 1619, 1623-27
CV - (Colosvar), Klausenburg, Cluj, 1636-94
Cor. - (Cibinium), Hermannstadt
D-K – Sibin, 1671
FB - (Felso Banya), Baia Sprie
Fog. - (Fogarasch)
FT - (?), Klausenberg, 1696-1697
HS - Hermannstadt, Sibiu, 1606
KB - (Kormoczbanya), Kremnitz, Kremnica, 1620-22
KO - (Kolosvar), Klausenburg, Cluj, 1613
KS - (Kis-Selyk), Seica-Mica, 1610
KV - (Kolosvar), Klausenburg, Cluj, 1693-1707
M - (Mediasch)
MC - (Moneta Cibiniensis), Hermannstadt, Sibiu, 1672
MC - (Moneta Cassoviensis), Cassovia, Kaschau, Kosice, Slovakia, 1619, 1626-1627
M-M - (Moneta-Munkacsiensis), Mukachiv, Ukraine, 1623
MO \ COM \ N-E - (Moneta Comitatus), Nagy-Enyed, Aiud, 1673-75
MR - Hermannstadt, Sibiu, 1671-72
NB - Nagybanya, Baia-Mare, 1589-1659
NE - Nagy-Enyed, Aiud, 1672
O - (Oravita), Orawitza Banat, 1783, 1812, 1816
P-S – Sibin, 1673
SB - Schassburg, Sighisoara, 1433-1435, 1661, 1664, 1666-1673
SV - Szeben-Varos, Hermannstadt, Sibiu, 1673
SV - Szasz Varos, Orastie, 1672-1675
ZB - Zalathna Banya, Zlatna

Root of the tree under crown – Brasov, 1601-74

HERMANNSTADT MINT OFFICIALS' INITIALS

Initial	Date	Name
A-HR	1605	Anton Huet
GS		Georg Schuler
IR	1660	Johann Ruckinsattel
MR	1671-72	Unknown
PS	1673	Unknown

MONETARY SYSTEM

1 Denar = 2 Obols
1 Kreuzer = 2 Denars
1 Poltura = 3 Denars
1 Groschen = 3 Kreuzer
1 Sechser = 6 Denars
1 Zwolfer = 12 Denars
1 Gulden = 60 Kreuzer
1 Thaler = 2 Gulden

NOTE: Refer also to Austrian listings for common circulation types struck at mints listed above.

PRINCIPALITY

STANDARD COINAGE

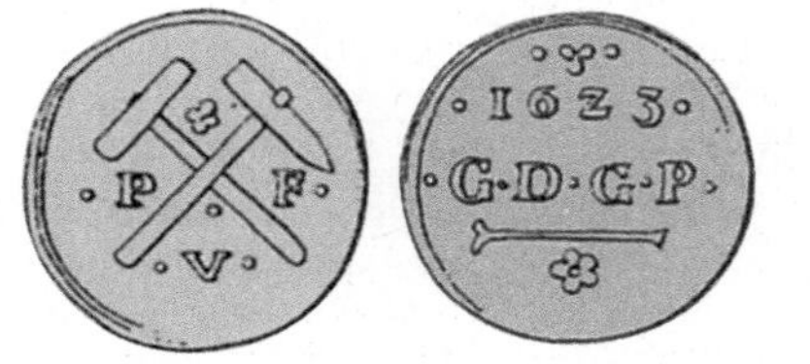

KM# 152 MINING PFENNIG (Bergwerkspfennig)
Copper

Date	Mintage	VG	F	VF	XF	Unc
1623	—	90.00	115	150	275	—

KM# 166 MINING PFENNIG (Bergwerkspfennig)
Copper

Date	Mintage	VG	F	VF	XF	Unc
1626 F-B - A-Z	—	70.00	90.00	140	250	—

KM# 197 MINING PFENNIG (Bergwerkspfennig)
Copper

Date	Mintage	VG	F	VF	XF	Unc
1628 I-L - F-K	—	70.00	90.00	140	250	—
1628 Z-B - F-K	—	70.00	90.00	140	250	—

KM# 220 MINING PFENNIG (Bergwerkspfennig)
Copper

Date	Mintage	VG	F	VF	XF	Unc
1630	—	90.00	115	150	275	—

KM# 230 MINING PFENNIG (Bergwerkspfennig)
Copper

Date	Mintage	VG	F	VF	XF	Unc
1634 Z-B	—	90.00	115	150	275	—

KM# 246 MINING PFENNIG (Bergwerkspfennig)
Copper, 25 mm. **Obv:** W.

Date	Mintage	VG	F	VF	XF	Unc
1643	—	90.00	115	150	275	—

KM# 248 MINING PFENNIG (Bergwerkspfennig)
Copper **Obv:** V

Date	Mintage	VG	F	VF	XF	Unc
1643	—	90.00	115	150	275	—

KM# 247 MINING PFENNIG (Bergwerkspfennig)
Copper, 14 mm. **Note:** Reduced size.

Date	Mintage	VG	F	VF	XF	Unc
1643	—	90.00	115	150	275	—

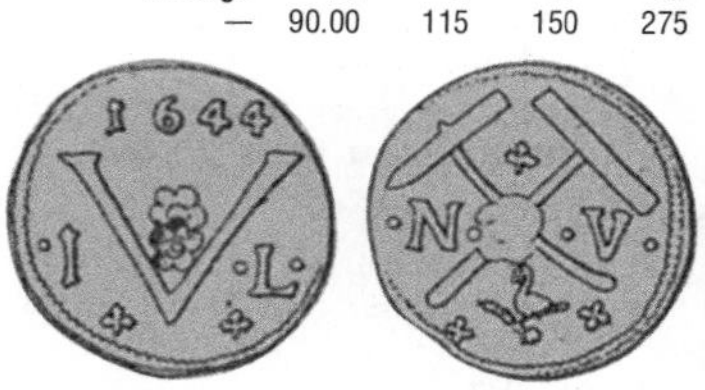

KM# 249 MINING PFENNIG (Bergwerkspfennig)
Copper

Date	Mintage	VG	F	VF	XF	Unc
1644	—	90.00	115	150	275	—

KM# 250 MINING PFENNIG (Bergwerkspfennig)
Copper **Note:** Varieties exist.

Date	Mintage	VG	F	VF	XF	Unc
1663NB Rare	—	150	350	750	1,500	—

KM# 130 OBOL
0.3000 g., Silver, 11 mm. **Obv:** Date above arms

Date	Mintage	VG	F	VF	XF	Unc
1621KB	—	60.00	90.00	140	250	—

KM# 131 OBOL
0.3000 g., Silver

Date	Mintage	VG	F	VF	XF	Unc
1621NB	—	60.00	90.00	140	250	—
1622KB	—	60.00	90.00	140	250	—

KM# 167 OBOL
0.3000 g., Silver **Obv:** Crowned arms **Rev:** Madonna divides date

Date	Mintage	VG	F	VF	XF	Unc
1626KB	—	60.00	90.00	140	250	—

KM# 76 DENAR
0.5000 g., Silver **Obv:** Hermannstadt arms **Note:** Varieties exist.

Date	Mintage	VG	F	VF	XF	Unc
1611CI	—	34.50	70.00	115	250	—

KM# 87 DENAR
0.5000 g., Silver **Obv:** Different shaped shield with Hermannstadt arms **Note:** Varieties exist.

Date	Mintage	VG	F	VF	XF	Unc
1612CI	—	34.50	70.00	115	250	—

KM# 93 DENAR
0.5000 g., Silver **Obv:** Hermannstadt arms

Date	Mintage	VG	F	VF	XF	Unc
1613CI	—	35.00	70.00	125	250	—

KM# 106 DENAR
0.5000 g., Silver **Obv:** Hermannstadt arms on shield

Date	Mintage	VG	F	VF	XF	Unc
1614	—	35.00	70.00	125	250	—

KM# 107 DENAR
0.5000 g., Silver **Obv:** Hermannstadt arms in center

Date	Mintage	VG	F	VF	XF	Unc
1614	—	35.00	70.00	125	250	—

KM# 120 DENAR
0.5000 g., Silver **Obv:** Hungarian arms **Note:** Varieties exist.

Date	Mintage	VG	F	VF	XF	Unc
1620KB	—	12.00	22.50	45.00	75.00	—
1621 KA	—	12.00	22.50	45.00	75.00	—
1621AI	—	12.00	22.50	45.00	75.00	—
1621KB	—	12.00	22.50	45.00	75.00	—
1621NB	—	12.00	22.50	45.00	75.00	—
1622KB	—	12.00	22.50	45.00	75.00	—
1623CM	—	12.00	22.50	45.00	75.00	—
1623NB	—	12.00	22.50	45.00	75.00	—
1623ZB	—	12.00	22.50	45.00	75.00	—
1624NB	—	12.00	22.50	45.00	75.00	—

KM# 162 DENAR
0.5000 g., Silver **Obv:** Crowned Hungarian arms **Note:** Varieties exist.

Date	Mintage	VG	F	VF	XF	Unc
1625NB	—	12.00	22.50	45.00	75.00	—
1626NB	—	12.00	22.50	45.00	75.00	—
1626CC	—	12.00	22.50	45.00	75.00	—

KM# 168 DENAR
Billon

Date	Mintage	VG	F	VF	XF	Unc
1626NB	—	9.00	18.00	35.00	65.00	—
1627NB	—	9.00	18.00	35.00	65.00	—

KM# 210 DENAR
Billon

Date	Mintage	VG	F	VF	XF	Unc
1629NB	—	12.00	22.50	45.00	75.00	—

KM# 288 DENAR
Silver **Obv:** Crowned Hungarian arms **Rev:** Madonna in flame circle

Date	Mintage	VG	F	VF	XF	Unc
1653NB	—	12.00	22.50	45.00	75.00	—

KM# 231 DREI (3) POLKER (= 3 Grosze)
1.2000 g., Silver **Note:** Varieties exist.

Date	Mintage	VG	F	VF	XF	Unc
1636CV	—	40.25	75.00	140	275	—
1637	—	40.25	75.00	140	275	—
1638	—	40.25	75.00	140	275	—

KM# 518 3 KREUZER (Groschen)
Silver **Obv:** Laureate bust of Leopold I right in inner circle, value below **Rev:** Crowned imperial eagle in inner circle, crown divides date **Note:** Varieties exist. Weight varies: 0.80-1.10 grams.

Date	Mintage	VG	F	VF	XF	Unc
1696 FT	—	22.50	50.00	85.00	170	—
1697 FT	—	22.50	50.00	85.00	170	—

KM# 519 3 KREUZER (Groschen)
Silver **Note:** Varieties exist. Weight varies: 0.80-1.10 grams.

Date	Mintage	VG	F	VF	XF	Unc
1696 FT	—	30.00	60.00	110	200	—

KM# 153 24 KREUZER
2.7000 g., Silver **Note:** Varieties exist.

Date	Mintage	VG	F	VF	XF	Unc
1623ZB	—	40.25	85.00	175	290	—
1623BN	—	40.25	85.00	175	290	—

KM# 434 SECHSER
Silver **Rev:** Small Hermannstadt arms

Date	Mintage	VG	F	VF	XF	Unc
1673 PS	—	115	200	375	750	—

KM# 435 SECHSER
Silver **Obv:** Larger bust

Date	Mintage	VG	F	VF	XF	Unc
1673CB	—	115	200	375	750	—

KM# 436 SECHSER
Silver **Rev:** Date quartered by arms

Date	Mintage	VG	F	VF	XF	Unc
1673CB	—	115	200	375	750	—

KM# 438 SECHSER
Silver **Rev:** Circle with MO • CO • M at bottom replacing small city arms

Date	Mintage	VG	F	VF	XF	Unc
1673NE	—	115	200	375	750	—

KM# 437 SECHSER
Silver **Rev:** Small arms of Kronstadt **Note:** Varieties exist.

Date	Mintage	VG	F	VF	XF	Unc
1673	—	115	200	375	750	—
1673NE	—	115	200	375	750	—

KM# 455 SECHSER
Silver **Rev:** Circle with MO-C at bottom

Date	Mintage	VG	F	VF	XF	Unc
1674NE	—	115	200	375	750	—

KM# 456 SECHSER
Silver **Rev:** Small Hermannstadt arms **Note:** Varieties exist.

Date	Mintage	VG	F	VF	XF	Unc
1674	—	115	200	375	750	—
1674CI	—	115	200	375	750	—
1674CB	—	115	200	375	750	—

KM# 461 SECHSER
Silver

Date	Mintage	VG	F	VF	XF	Unc
1675 NF	—	115	200	375	750	—

KM# 421 ZWOLFER
Silver **Rev:** Small Kronstadt arms at bottom center **Note:** Varieties exist. Weight varies: 2.60-2.90 grams.

Date	Mintage	VG	F	VF	XF	Unc
1672	—	85.00	145	250	600	—

KM# 417 ZWOLFER
Silver **Note:** Weight varies: 2.60-2.90 grams.

Date	Mintage	VG	F	VF	XF	Unc
1672CI-BI	—	75.00	140	250	600	—

KM# 418 ZWOLFER
Silver **Rev:** Small Hermannstadt arms at bottom **Note:** Weight varies: 2.60-2.90 grams.

Date	Mintage	VG	F	VF	XF	Unc
1672	—	60.00	115	225	600	—

KM# 420 ZWOLFER
Silver **Note:** Weight varies: 2.60-2.90 grams.

Date	Mintage	VG	F	VF	XF	Unc
1672NE Retrograde 2	—	60.00	115	225	600	—

KM# 419 ZWOLFER
Silver **Note:** Varieties exist. Weight varies: 2.60-2.90 grams.

Date	Mintage	VG	F	VF	XF	Unc
1672MC	—	60.00	115	225	600	—
1672NE	—	60.00	115	225	600	—

KM# 441 ZWOLFER
Silver **Note:** Varieties exist. Weight varies: 2.60-2.90 grams.

Date	Mintage	VG	F	VF	XF	Unc
1673SV	—	60.00	115	225	600	—

KM# 443 ZWOLFER
Silver Plated Copper **Rev:** Quartered date

Date	Mintage	VG	F	VF	XF	Unc
1673	—	70.00	115	225	600	—

KM# 444 ZWOLFER
Silver Plated Copper **Rev:** PE-V replacing small Kronstadt arms, date quartered

Date	Mintage	VG	F	VF	XF	Unc
1673 PEV	—	75.00	150	300	700	—

KM# 442 ZWOLFER
Silver **Rev:** Small Hermannstadt arms **Note:** Varieties exist. Weight varies: 2.60-2.90 grams.

Date	Mintage	VG	F	VF	XF	Unc
1673	—	75.00	140	250	600	—
1637 Error	—	75.00	140	250	600	—

KM# 439 ZWOLFER
Silver **Rev:** Small Hermannstadt arms **Note:** Varieties exist. Weight varies: 2.60-2.90 grams.

Date	Mintage	VG	F	VF	XF	Unc
1673	—	60.00	115	225	600	—
1673CI	—	60.00	115	225	600	—
1673SV	—	60.00	115	225	600	—

KM# 440 ZWOLFER
Silver **Rev:** Different Hermannstadt arms **Note:** Varieties exist. Weight varies: 2.60-2.90 grams.

Date	Mintage	VG	F	VF	XF	Unc
1673SV	—	60.00	115	225	600	—
1673SV Inverted date	—	60.00	115	225	600	—
1673 XX	—	60.00	115	225	600	—

KM# 457 ZWOLFER
Silver Plated Copper **Rev:** Small Hermannstadt arms

Date	Mintage	VG	F	VF	XF	Unc
1674	—	65.00	125	275	700	—

KM# 458 ZWOLFER
Silver Plated Copper **Rev:** Small Kronstadt arms, quartered date

Date	Mintage	VG	F	VF	XF	Unc
1674	—	85.00	175	400	800	—

KM# 48 GROSCHEN
Silver **Obv:** Heraldic Transylvanian eagle **Rev:** Fur hat above seven castle towers **Note:** Varieties exist. Weight varies: 1.40-2.20 grams.

Date	Mintage	VG	F	VF	XF	Unc
1608NB	—	25.00	46.00	80.00	150	—
1609NB	—	25.00	46.00	80.00	150	—

KM# 54 GROSCHEN
Silver **Note:** Weight varies: 1.40-2.20 grams.

Date	Mintage	VG	F	VF	XF	Unc
1609NB	—	25.00	46.00	80.00	150	—

KM# 70 GROSCHEN
Silver **Rev:** Five-part arms **Note:** Weight varies: 1.40-2.20 grams.

Date	Mintage	VG	F	VF	XF	Unc
1610NB	—	25.00	50.00	95.00	200	—

KM# 71 GROSCHEN
Silver **Rev:** Four-part arms **Note:** Varieties exist. Weight varies: 1.40-2.20 grams.

Date	Mintage	VG	F	VF	XF	Unc
1610NB	—	25.00	50.00	95.00	200	—

KM# 72 GROSCHEN
Silver **Obv:** Crown above three-line inscription and date **Rev:** Heraldic eagle right **Note:** Varieties exist. Weight varies: 1.40-2.20 grams.

Date	Mintage	VG	F	VF	XF	Unc
1610NB	—	25.00	45.00	95.00	200	—
1611NB	—	25.00	45.00	95.00	200	—
1611	—	25.00	45.00	95.00	200	—
1612NB	—	25.00	45.00	95.00	200	—
1613NB	—	25.00	45.00	95.00	200	—

KM# 109 GROSCHEN
1.9000 g., Silver **Note:** Klippe. Varieties exist.

Date	Mintage	VG	F	VF	XF	Unc
1617 Rare	—	—	—	—	—	—

KM# 110 GROSCHEN
Silver **Note:** Round version of KM#109. Varieties exist.

Date	Mintage	VG	F	VF	XF	Unc
1617	—	45.00	80.00	150	350	—

KM# 112 GROSCHEN
Silver **Note:** Varieties exist.

Date	Mintage	VG	F	VF	XF	Unc
1619	—	25.00	50.00	95.00	225	—

KM# 121 GROSCHEN
Silver **Rev:** Madonna holding child on right side

Date	Mintage	VG	F	VF	XF	Unc
16Z0NB	—	25.00	50.00	95.00	225	—

KM# 122 GROSCHEN
Silver **Rev:** Madonna holding child on left side

Date	Mintage	VG	F	VF	XF	Unc
1620	—	25.00	50.00	95.00	225	—

KM# 123 GROSCHEN
.4000 g., Silver

Date	Mintage	VG	F	VF	XF	Unc
1620	—	25.00	50.00	95.00	225	—

KM# 132 GROSCHEN
Silver **Obv:** Arms **Rev:** Madonna and child **Note:** Varieties exist.

Date	Mintage	VG	F	VF	XF	Unc
1621NB	—	25.00	50.00	95.00	225	—
1622NB	—	25.00	50.00	95.00	225	—
1623CM	—	25.00	50.00	95.00	225	—
1623NB	—	25.00	50.00	95.00	225	—

KM# 161 GROSCHEN
Silver **Obv:** Hungarian arms **Rev:** Madonna and child **Note:** Varieties exist.

Date	Mintage	VG	F	VF	XF	Unc
1624CM	—	25.00	50.00	95.00	350	—
1624 MM	—	25.00	50.00	95.00	350	—
1624NB	—	25.00	50.00	95.00	350	—
1624	—	25.00	50.00	95.00	350	—
1625CM	—	25.00	50.00	95.00	350	—
1625NB	—	25.00	50.00	95.00	350	—

KM# 163 GROSCHEN
Silver **Obv:** Madonna and child **Rev:** Crowned Hungarian arms **Note:** Varieties exist.

Date	Mintage	VG	F	VF	XF	Unc
1625NB	—	25.00	50.00	95.00	225	—
1625CC	—	25.00	50.00	95.00	225	—

KM# 164 GROSCHEN
Silver **Note:** Varieties exist.

Date	Mintage	VG	F	VF	XF	Unc
1625	—	25.00	46.00	90.00	220	—
1625NB	—	25.00	46.00	90.00	220	—
1625CC	—	25.00	46.00	90.00	220	—

KM# 169 GROSCHEN
Silver **Obv:** Crowned Hungarian arms **Rev:** Madonna and child **Note:** Varieties exist.

Date	Mintage	VG	F	VF	XF	Unc
1626CC	—	25.00	50.00	95.00	225	—
1626NB	—	25.00	50.00	95.00	225	—
1627MC	—	25.00	50.00	95.00	225	—
1627NB	—	25.00	50.00	95.00	225	—
1628NB	—	25.00	50.00	95.00	225	—
1629NB	—	25.00	50.00	95.00	225	—

KM# 174 GROSCHEN
Silver **Obv:** Transylvania arms **Rev:** Crown above three-line inscription

Date	Mintage	VG	F	VF	XF	Unc
1627 MC	—	25.00	50.00	125	300	—

KM# 211 2 GROSCHEN
Silver **Note:** Similar to 1 Groschen, KM#169.

Date	Mintage	VG	F	VF	XF	Unc
1629MC	—	40.00	75.00	175	400	—

KM# 8 3 GROSCHEN
Silver **Note:** Varieties exist. Weight varies: 2.00-2.60 grams.

Date	Mintage	VG	F	VF	XF	Unc
1605	—	40.00	75.00	175	450	—
1606	—	40.00	75.00	175	450	—

KM# 39 3 GROSCHEN
Silver **Note:** Varieties exist. Weight varies: 2.00-2.60 grams.

Date	Mintage	VG	F	VF	XF	Unc
1607	—	50.00	100	250	600	—

KM# 38 3 GROSCHEN
Silver **Note:** Klippe. Weight varies: 2.00-2.60 grams.

Date	Mintage	VG	F	VF	XF	Unc
1607 Rare	—	—	—	—	—	—

KM# 49 3 GROSCHEN
Silver **Note:** Varieties exist. Weight varies: 2.00-2.60 grams.

Date	Mintage	VG	F	VF	XF	Unc
1608	—	25.00	50.00	125	300	—
1609	—	25.00	50.00	125	300	—

KM# 50 3 GROSCHEN
Silver **Note:** Weight varies: 2.00-2.60 grams.

Date	Mintage	VG	F	VF	XF	Unc
1608	—	25.00	50.00	125	300	—

KM# 56 3 GROSCHEN
Silver **Note:** Weight varies: 2.00-2.60 grams.

Date	Mintage	VG	F	VF	XF	Unc
1609	—	25.00	50.00	125	300	—

KM# 57 3 GROSCHEN
Silver **Note:** Varieties exist. Weight varies: 2.00-2.60 grams.

Date	Mintage	VG	F	VF	XF	Unc
1609	—	25.00	50.00	125	300	—
1610	—	25.00	50.00	125	300	—

KM# 55 3 GROSCHEN
Silver **Note:** Klippe. Weight varies: 2.00-2.60 grams.

Date	Mintage	VG	F	VF	XF	Unc
1609 Rare	—	—	—	—	—	—

KM# 77 3 GROSCHEN
Silver **Obv:** Bust of Gabriel Bathori right. **Rev:** Value III above shield divides CI-BI and date. **Note:** Klippe. Weight varies: 2.00-2.60 grams.

Date	Mintage	VG	F	VF	XF	Unc
1611 Rare	—	—	—	—	—	—

KM# 78 3 GROSCHEN
Silver **Note:** Thick Groschen. Weight varies: 8.40-10.00 grams.

Date	Mintage	VG	F	VF	XF	Unc
1611 Rare	—	—	—	—	—	—

KM# 79 3 GROSCHEN
2.5000 g., Silver **Note:** Varieties exist.

Date	Mintage	VG	F	VF	XF	Unc
1611	—	25.00	50.00	125	300	—

KM# A77 3 GROSCHEN
Silver **Obv:** Bust of Gabriel Bathori right **Rev:** Value III above shield divides CI-BI and date. **Note:** Weight varies, 2.00-2.60 g.

Date	Mintage	VG	F	VF	XF	Unc
1611	—	25.00	50.00	120	185	—

KM# 80 3 GROSCHEN
Silver **Obv:** Bust of Gabriel Bathori right. **Rev:** Value III above shield divides AL-IV and date.

Date	Mintage	VG	F	VF	XF	Unc
1611	—	25.00	50.00	125	300	—
1612	—	25.00	50.00	125	300	—
1613	—	25.00	50.00	125	300	—

KM# 94 3 GROSCHEN

Silver

Date	Mintage	VG	F	VF	XF	Unc
1613	—	25.00	50.00	125	300	—

KM# 233 3 GROSCHEN

1.7000 g., Silver **Obv:** Bust of George Rakoczi I in fur hat

Date	Mintage	VG	F	VF	XF	Unc
1637	—	45.00	75.00	150	350	—

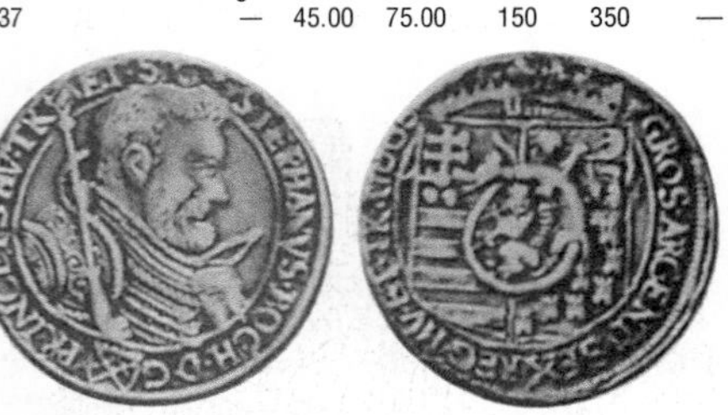

KM# 20 6 GROSCHEN

7.0000 g., Silver

Date	Mintage	VG	F	VF	XF	Unc
1606	—	125	250	650	1,000	—

KM# 21 6 GROSCHEN

4.5000 g., Silver **Note:** Varieties exist.

Date	Mintage	VG	F	VF	XF	Unc
1606	—	100	200	600	900	—

KM# 234 6 GROSCHEN

2.9000 g., Silver **Rev:** Three coats of arms

Date	Mintage	VG	F	VF	XF	Unc
1637	—	45.00	95.00	175	375	—

KM# 235 6 GROSCHEN

2.9000 g., Silver **Rev:** Four coats of arms

Date	Mintage	VG	F	VF	XF	Unc
1637	—	45.00	95.00	175	375	—

KM# 236 1/2 GULDEN

6.8500 g., Silver

Date	Mintage	VG	F	VF	XF	Unc
1637	—	200	400	800	1,250	—

KM# 237 1/2 GULDEN

6.8500 g., Silver

Date	Mintage	VG	F	VF	XF	Unc
1637	—	250	450	900	1,350	—

KM# 251 1/2 GULDEN

6.8500 g., Silver

Date	Mintage	VG	F	VF	XF	Unc
1645NB	—	250	500	1,000	2,000	—

KM# 252 1/2 GULDEN

6.8500 g., Silver

Date	Mintage	VG	F	VF	XF	Unc
1645NB	—	250	500	1,000	2,000	—

KM# 285 1/2 GULDEN

7.2000 g., Silver **Obv:** Armored portrait with fur hat and scepter **Rev:** Crowned Transylvania arms

Date	Mintage	VG	F	VF	XF	Unc
1651NB	—	—	—	—	—	—

KM# 292 1/2 GULDEN

7.4000 g., Silver

Date	Mintage	VG	F	VF	XF	Unc
1656NB	—	350	750	1,500	2,750	—

KM# 5 GULDEN

Silver **Obv:** Two lions holding sword through crown **Rev:** Three-line inscription within legend

Date	Mintage	VG	F	VF	XF	Unc
1603	—	450	900	1,800	3,000	—

KM# 9 GULDEN

Silver **Obv:** Armored portrait right wearing fur hat **Rev:** Arm from clouds holding sword through coiled ribbon

Date	Mintage	VG	F	VF	XF	Unc
1605	—	450	900	1,800	3,000	—

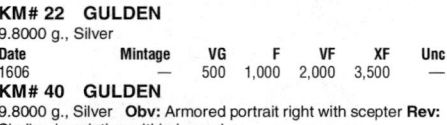

KM# 22 GULDEN

9.8000 g., Silver

Date	Mintage	VG	F	VF	XF	Unc
1606	—	500	1,000	2,000	3,500	—

KM# 40 GULDEN

9.8000 g., Silver **Obv:** Armored portrait right with scepter **Rev:** Six-line inscription within legend

Date	Mintage	VG	F	VF	XF	Unc
ND(1607)	—	450	900	1,800	3,000	—

KM# 51 GULDEN

15.1000 g., Silver

Date	Mintage	VG	F	VF	XF	Unc
1608	—	450	900	1,800	3,500	—

KM# 58 GULDEN

14.8000 g., Silver **Obv:** Without helmet right of portrait

Date	Mintage	VG	F	VF	XF	Unc
1609	—	450	900	1,800	3,000	—

KM# 81 GULDEN

14.2000 g., Silver, 40 mm. **Obv:** Crowned arms within circled dragon and legend **Rev:** Five-line inscription

Date	Mintage	VG	F	VF	XF	Unc
1611	—	600	1,200	2,500	4,500	—

KM# 82 GULDEN

14.3000 g., Silver, 33 mm. **Obv:** Bear claw arms within dragon and legend **Note:** Uniface.

Date	Mintage	VG	F	VF	XF	Unc
1611	—	400	750	1,150	2,250	—

KM# 113 GULDEN

16.1000 g., Silver **Obv:** Bust right wearing cape and fur hat **Rev:** Crown wtih two supporting lions above three coats of arms

Date	Mintage	VG	F	VF	XF	Unc
1619CM	—	—	—	—	—	—

KM# 145 GULDEN

16.1000 g., Silver **Obv:** Bust right **Rev:** Coat of arms

Date	Mintage	VG	F	VF	XF	Unc
1622NB	—	—	—	—	—	—

KM# 175 GULDEN

14.1000 g., Silver **Obv:** Armored bust right **Rev:** Crowned arms

Date	Mintage	VG	F	VF	XF	Unc
1627MC	—	—	—	—	—	—

KM# 176 GULDEN

13.9000 g., Silver

Date	Mintage	VG	F	VF	XF	Unc
1627NB	—	600	1,200	2,500	5,000	—

KM# 177 GULDEN

13.9000 g., Silver **Obv:** Different portrait **Rev:** Different arms

Date	Mintage	VG	F	VF	XF	Unc
1627NB	—	575	925	1,500	3,000	—

‹M# 198 GULDEN
ilver **Obv:** Armored bust right **Note:** Weight varies: 12.40-14.60 rams.

ate	Mintage	VG	F	VF	XF	Unc
628CC	—	750	1,500	3,000	5,500	—
629CC	—	750	1,500	3,000	5,500	—

‹M# 264 GULDEN
ilver **Obv:** Armored bust right in fur hat **Note:** Weight varies: 2.40-14.60 grams.

ate	Mintage	VG	F	VF	XF	Unc
647NB	—	500	1,000	2,200	4,000	—

‹M# 289 GULDEN
4.4000 g., Silver **Rev:** Crude crown above arms

ate	Mintage	VG	F	VF	XF	Unc
654NB	—	—	—	—	—	—

‹M# 293 GULDEN
4.0000 g., Silver

ate	Mintage	VG	F	VF	XF	Unc
656NB	—	—	—	—	—	—

‹M# 314 GULDEN
4.0000 g., Silver **Obv:** Barcsais bust right with scepter **Rev:** Crowned arms

ate	Mintage	VG	F	VF	XF	Unc
659CV	—	700	1,350	2,750	5,000	—

KM# 313 GULDEN
14.0000 g., Silver **Obv:** Bust right **Rev:** Crowned arms **Note:** Varieties exist.

Date	Mintage	VG	F	VF	XF	Unc
1659NB	—	700	1,350	2,750	5,000	—

KM# 325 GULDEN
14.0000 g., Silver **Obv:** Crowned arms in legend **Rev:** Three-line inscription within double legend **Note:** Octagonal klippe.

Date	Mintage	VG	F	VF	XF	Unc
1660 Rare	—	—	—	—	—	—

KM# 326 GULDEN
14.0000 g., Silver **Note:** Round version of KM#325.

Date	Mintage	VG	F	VF	XF	Unc
1660 Rare	—	—	—	—	—	—
1661	—	—	—	—	—	—

KM# 344 GULDEN
13.8000 g., Silver **Obv:** Crowned arms and legend **Rev:** Angel head above inscription, tree trunk below

Date	Mintage	VG	F	VF	XF	Unc
1661CB	—	650	1,250	2,250	5,000	—

KM# 361 GULDEN
Silver **Rev:** Crowned arms with Kronstadt arms at bottom

Date	Mintage	VG	F	VF	XF	Unc
1662CB Rare	—	—	—	—	—	—

KM# 360 GULDEN
Silver **Note:** Round version of KM#359.

Date	Mintage	VG	F	VF	XF	Unc
1662	—	700	1,350	2,400	5,000	—

KM# 359 GULDEN
Silver **Obv:** Armored bust right with fur hat and scepter **Rev:** Crowned arms, small Hermannstadt arms at bottom **Shape:** Hexagonal. **Note:** Klippe.

Date	Mintage	VG	F	VF	XF	Unc
1662 Rare	—	—	—	—	—	—

KM# 362 GULDEN
Silver **Note:** Varieties exist.

Date	Mintage	VG	F	VF	XF	Unc
1662CB	—	—	—	—	—	—
1663CB	—	—	—	—	—	—

KM# 374 GULDEN
Silver **Note:** Varieties exist.

Date	Mintage	VG	F	VF	XF	Unc
1663CB	—	650	1,250	2,500	4,500	—
1664CB	—	650	1,250	2,500	4,500	—
1665CB	—	650	1,250	2,500	4,500	—
1666	—	650	1,250	2,500	4,500	—

KM# 386 GULDEN
Silver **Rev:** Small Hermannstadt arms at bottom **Shape:** Hexagon **Note:** Klippe.

Date	Mintage	VG	F	VF	XF	Unc
1667 Rare	—	—	—	—	—	—

KM# 387 GULDEN
Silver **Rev:** Crowned arms, small Kronstadt arms at bottom

Date	Mintage	VG	F	VF	XF	Unc
1667 Rare	—	—	—	—	—	—

KM# 410 GULDEN
14.0000 g., Silver **Obv:** Bust right **Rev:** Crowned arms

Date	Mintage	VG	F	VF	XF	Unc
1670KV	—	—	—	—	—	—

KM# 412 GULDEN
14.0000 g., Silver **Obv:** Bust right **Rev:** Crowned arms

Date	Mintage	VG	F	VF	XF	Unc
1671KV	—	—	—	—	—	—

KM# 413 GULDEN
14.0000 g., Silver **Rev:** Crowned arms, small Hermannstadt arms at bottom

Date	Mintage	VG	F	VF	XF	Unc
1671 CT	—	—	—	—	—	—

KM# 422 GULDEN
14.0000 g., Silver **Rev:** Crowned arms above small castle

Date	Mintage	VG	F	VF	XF	Unc
1672	—	—	—	—	—	—

KM# 445 GULDEN
14.0000 g., Silver **Rev:** Crowned arms, small Kronstadt arms at bottom

Date	Mintage	VG	F	VF	XF	Unc
1673	—	—	—	—	—	—

KM# 446 GULDEN
Silver **Note:** Irregular klippe.

Date	Mintage	VG	F	VF	XF	Unc
1673 CW Rare	—	—	—	—	—	—

KM# 496 GULDEN
Silver

Date	Mintage	VG	F	VF	XF	Unc
1689AF	—	—	—	—	—	—

KM# 23 2 GULDEN
27.5000 g., Silver, 33 mm. **Obv:** Armored bust right **Rev:** Crowned arms **Note:** Varieties exist.

Date	Mintage	VG	F	VF	XF	Unc
1606	—	—	—	—	—	—

KM# 179 2 GULDEN
Silver **Note:** Klippe with rounded corners.

Date	Mintage	VG	F	VF	XF	Unc
1627MC	—	1,000	2,000	4,000	75,000	—

KM# 178 2 GULDEN
28.5000 g., Silver **Note:** Klippe.

Date	Mintage	VG	F	VF	XF	Unc
1627MC	—	1,000	2,000	4,000	7,500	—

KM# 199 2 GULDEN
28.3000 g., Silver **Note:** Klippe.

Date	Mintage	VG	F	VF	XF	Unc
1628 Rare	—	—	—	—	—	—

KM# 201 2 GULDEN
Silver **Note:** Reduced size.

Date	Mintage	VG	F	VF	XF	Unc
1628	—	—	—	—	—	—

KM# 200 2 GULDEN
28.9000 g., Silver **Note:** Round version on KM#199.

Date	Mintage	VG	F	VF	XF	Unc
1628	—	—	—	—	—	—

KM# 24 3 GULDEN
42.5000 g., Silver **Obv:** Armored bust right **Rev:** Crowned arms

Date	Mintage	VG	F	VF	XF	Unc
1606 Rare	—	—	—	—	—	—

KM# 180 3 GULDEN
42.5000 g., Silver **Note:** Klippe.

Date	Mintage	VG	F	VF	XF	Unc
1627MC Rare	—	—	—	—	—	—

KM# 202 3 GULDEN
43.0000 g., Silver **Note:** Klippe. Varieties exist.

Date	Mintage	VG	F	VF	XF	Unc
1628CC Rare	—	—	—	—	—	—

KM# 203 4 GULDEN
57.2000 g., Silver **Note:** Klippe.

Date	Mintage	VG	F	VF	XF	Unc
1628CC Rare	—	—	—	—	—	—

KM# 212 4 GULDEN
56.0000 g., Silver **Note:** Klippe.

Date	Mintage	VG	F	VF	XF	Unc
1629 Rare	—	—	—	—	—	—

KM# 294 1/4 THALER
Silver **Obv:** Armored bust right with scepter and fur hat **Rev:** Crowned arms

Date	Mintage	VG	F	VF	XF	Unc
1656NB Rare	—	—	—	—	—	—

KM# A83 1/2 THALER
Silver **Note:** Struck with 1 Thaler dies, KM#83.

Date	Mintage	VG	F	VF	XF	Unc
1611CIBIN	—	450	900	1,750	3,500	—

KM# A390 1/2 THALER
14.4500 g., Silver **Note:** Struck with 1 Thaler dies, KM#390.

Date	Mintage	VG	F	VF	XF	Unc
1671AC	—	1,000	2,000	4,000	8,500	—

KM# 6 THALER
Silver **Obv:** Two lions holding sword through crown within legend **Rev. Legend:** Center: DOMINVS / PROTECToR / MEVS **Note:** Dav. #4685.

Date	Mintage	VG	F	VF	XF	Unc
1603 Rare	—	—	—	—	—	—

KM# 10 THALER
29.7000 g., Silver **Obv. Legend:** STEPHANVS: DEI: GRATIA:... **Rev:** Crowned lion on helmet above three coats of arms **Note:** Varieties exist. Dav. #4689.

Date	Mintage	VG	F	VF	XF	Unc
1605	—	700	1,350	2,750	5,500	—

KM# 12 THALER
29.7000 g., Silver **Obv:** Coat of arms and date within dragon and legend **Rev:** Madonna and child within legend **Note:** Varieties exist. Dav. #4691.

Date	Mintage	VG	F	VF	XF	Unc
1605NB	—	400	800	1,600	3,750	—

KM# 11 THALER
29.7000 g., Silver **Obv:** Bust right with fur hat **Obv. Legend:** STEPHANVS. BOCHKAY. D: G... **Rev:** Arm from clouds holding sword throught coiled ribbon **Note:** Varieties exist. Dav. #4692.

Date	Mintage	VG	F	VF	XF	Unc
1605 Rare	—	—	—	—	—	—

KM# 12A THALER
29.7000 g., Silver **Obv. Legend:** *STE. BOCHKAY. D: G:... **Note:** Varieties exist. Dav. #4694.

Date	Mintage	VG	F	VF	XF	Unc
1605	—	325	575	1,050	1,750	—

KM# A25 THALER
27.2000 g., Silver **Obv. Legend:** *STEPHANVS. BOCH:. D. G... **Rev:** Crowned ornamented arms **Note:** Dav. #4696.

Date	Mintage	VG	F	VF	XF	Unc
1606HS Rare	—	—	—	—	—	—

KM# B25 THALER
27.2000 g., Silver **Rev:** Crowned arms without ornaments **Rev. Legend:** ...EICZ **Note:** Dav. #4696A.

Date	Mintage	VG	F	VF	XF	Unc
1606HS Rare	—	—	—	—	—	—

KM# C25 THALER
27.2000 g., Silver **Rev:** Legend divided with small city arms below **Rev. Legend:** C - OMES. ET... **Note:** Dav. #4696B.

Date	Mintage	VG	F	VF	XF	Unc
1606HS Rare	—	—	—	—	—	—

KM# D25 THALER
27.2000 g., Silver **Rev:** Large mint mark **Note:** Dav. #4696C.

Date	Mintage	VG	F	VF	XF	Unc
1606HS Rare	—	—	—	—	—	—

KM# 25 THALER
27.2000 g., Silver **Rev:** Crowned arms without ornaments **Rev. Legend:** ...ETCZ **Note:** Dav. #4696D.

Date	Mintage	VG	F	VF	XF	Unc
1606HS Rare	—	—	—	—	—	—

KM# 26 THALER

27.2000 g., Silver **Obv. Legend:** STEPHANVS: D: G: HVNGARIAE... **Note:** Dav. #4698.

Date	Mintage	VG	F	VF	XF	Unc
1606 Rare	—	—	—	—	—	—

KM# 41 THALER

27.2000 g., Silver **Obv. Legend:** SIGISMVNDVS RAKOCII: D: G: PR:... **Rev:** Six-line inscription within legend **Note:** Dav. #4699.

Date	Mintage	VG	F	VF	XF	Unc
MDCVII Rare	—	—	—	—	—	—

KM# 52 THALER

27.2000 g., Silver **Obv. Legend:** *:GABRIEL: BATHORY: D: G:... **Note:** Dav. #4700.

Date	Mintage	VG	F	VF	XF	Unc
1608	—	275	550	1,100	3,500	—
1609	—	275	550	1,100	3,500	—

KM# A52 THALER

27.2000 g., Silver **Note:** Dav. #4700A. Rosettes replace colons in legends.

Date	Mintage	VG	F	VF	XF	Unc
1608	—	275	550	1,100	3,500	—
1609	—	275	550	1,100	3,500	—

KM# A53.1 THALER

27.2000 g., Silver **Rev:** Crowned shield of arms **Note:** Dav. #4702.

Date	Mintage	VG	F	VF	XF	Unc
1609NB	—	275	550	1,100	3,500	—

KM# A53.2 THALER

27.2000 g., Silver **Note:** Dav. #4702A. Retrograde "N's" in legends.

Date	Mintage	VG	F	VF	XF	Unc
1609NB	—	200	400	800	2,000	—

KM# 83.1 THALER

28.6000 g., Silver **Obv. Legend:** ...ET: SI(C). COMES **Note:** Dav. #4703.

Date	Mintage	VG	F	VF	XF	Unc
1611CIBIN	—	350	700	1,500	4,000	—

KM# 85 THALER

Silver **Note:** Dav. #4703A. Uniface. Varieties exist in diameter and thickness.

Date	Mintage	VG	F	VF	XF	Unc
1611CIBIN	—	350	700	1,500	4,000	—

KM# 83.2 THALER

28.6000 g., Silver **Obv. Legend:** ...ET: SI. COM: **Note:** Dav. #4703B.

Date	Mintage	VG	F	VF	XF	Unc
1611CIBIN	—	350	700	1,500	4,000	—

KM# 83.3 THALER

28.6000 g., Silver **Obv. Legend:** ...ET • SI: COMES **Note:** Dav. #4704.

Date	Mintage	VG	F	VF	XF	Unc
1611	—	350	700	1,500	4,000	—

KM# 84 THALER

Silver **Note:** Dav. #4705. Uniface.

Date	Mintage	VG	F	VF	XF	Unc
1611CIBIN	—	350	700	1,500	4,000	—

KM# 88.1 THALER

Silver **Obv. Legend:** GABRIEL. D. G. PRIN: TRAN:... **Rev:** Date in Latin in legend **Rev. Legend:** Central: PRO / PATRIA / ARIS • ET / FOCIS **Note:** Dav. #4706.

Date	Mintage	VG	F	VF	XF	Unc
ND(1612)CIBIN	—	500	1,000	2,000	5,000	—

KM# 88.2 THALER

Silver **Note:** Dav. #4707. Similar to KM#88.1.

Date	Mintage	VG	F	VF	XF	Unc
ND(1613)CIBIN	—	400	900	1,800	5,000	—

KM# 95.1 THALER

Silver **Rev:** Rosette below 1613 **Note:** Dav. #4708.

Date	Mintage	VG	F	VF	XF	Unc
1613	—	400	900	1,800	5,000	—

KM# 95.2 THALER

Silver **Rev:** Without rosette below 16.13 **Note:** Dav. #4708A.

Date	Mintage	VG	F	VF	XF	Unc
16.13	—	400	900	1,800	5,000	—

KM# 114 THALER

29.6000 g., Silver **Obv. Legend:** *GABRIEL BETH... **Rev:** Crowned arms **Note:** Dav. #4709. Possibly a medallic issue.

Date	Mintage	VG	F	VF	XF	Unc
1619 CM	—	500	1,000	2,100	5,000	—

KM# 115 THALER

22.2000 g., Silver **Note:** Dav. #4709A. Possibly a medallic issue. Reduced weight.

Date	Mintage	VG	F	VF	XF	Unc
1619 CM	—	500	1,000	2,100	5,000	—

KM# 124 THALER

Silver **Obv. Legend:** *GABRIEL-Madonna-D. G. EL... **Rev. Legend:** TRANS. PRINCEPS. ET... **Note:** Dav. #4710.

Date	Mintage	VG	F	VF	XF	Unc
1620KB	—	400	900	1,800	3,750	—

KM# 125 THALER

20.6000 g., Silver **Obv:** Large armored bust right with fur hat with plume

Date	Mintage	VG	F	VF	XF	Unc
1620AI	—	350	700	1,500	3,750	—

KM# 134 THALER

28.6000 g., Silver **Note:** Dav. #4710. Varieties exist. Similar to KM#124.

Date	Mintage	VG	F	VF	XF	Unc
1621KB	—	300	600	1,200	2,750	—
1622KB	—	300	600	1,200	2,750	—

KM# 135 THALER

28.6000 g., Silver **Obv. Legend:** * GABRIEL - Madonna - D:G. EL. HVN... **Note:** Dav. #4711. Varieties exist.

Date	Mintage	VG	F	VF	XF	Unc
1621NB	—	300	600	1,200	2,750	—

KM# 136 THALER

28.6000 g., Silver **Obv:** Similar to KM#135 **Obv. Legend:** Ends: DROA-arms-SCL A. REX **Rev:** Modified crowned arms **Note:** Dav. #4712.

Date	Mintage	VG	F	VF	XF	Unc
1621NB	—	300	600	1,200	2,750	—

KM# 137 THALER

28.6000 g., Silver **Obv:** Large bust **Note:** Dav. #4713. Varieties exist.

Date	Mintage	VG	F	VF	XF	Unc
16Z1NB	—	350	700	1,500	3,000	—
16ZZNB	—	350	700	1,500	3,000	—

KM# 146 THALER

28.6000 g., Silver **Obv:** Similar to KM#137, date behind shoulder **Note:** Dav. #4714.

Date	Mintage	VG	F	VF	XF	Unc
16ZZNB	—	350	700	1,500	3,000	—

KM# 147 THALER

Silver **Obv:** Harnassed bust with scepter **Note:** Dav. #4715. Varieties exist.

Date	Mintage	VG	F	VF	XF	Unc
16ZZNB	—	300	600	1,200	2,750	—

KM# 170 THALER

Silver **Obv. Legend:** :GABR.D: G. SA. R. IMP... **Note:** Varieties exist. Dav. #4717.

Date	Mintage	VG	F	VF	XF	Unc
1626 CC	—	300	600	1,200	2,750	—

KM# 182 THALER

Silver **Obv. Legend:** GAB. D. G. SA. RO. IM(P):-.ET... **Note:** Varieties exist. Dav. #4720.

Date	Mintage	VG	F	VF	XF	Unc
1627NB	—	300	650	1,400	3,000	—
1628NB	—	300	650	1,400	3,000	—

KM# 181 THALER

Silver **Obv. Legend:** *GABR. D. G. SA. R. IMP. ET... **Note:** Varieties exist. Dav. #4721.

Date	Mintage	VG	F	VF	XF	Unc
1627NB	—	1,250	2,500	5,000	9,500	—

KM# 183 THALER

Silver **Obv:** Divided legend **Obv. Legend:** *GABR. D. G. S(A)R... **Note:** Dav. #4719.

Date	Mintage	VG	F	VF	XF	Unc
1627 MC	—	350	700	1,400	2,750	—

KM# A183 THALER

Silver **Obv:** Continuous legend **Note:** Dav. #4719A.

Date	Mintage	VG	F	VF	XF	Unc
1627 MC	—	350	700	1,400	2,750	—

M# A204 THALER

ilver **Obv:** Bare-headed armored bust with scepter **Note:** Dav. 4723.

ate	Mintage	VG	F	VF	XF	Unc
628 CC	—	350	700	1,400	2,750	—

(M# B204 THALER

ilver **Obv:** Similar to KM#204 **Obv. Legend:** GABRIEL. D: G. A. RO. IMP... **Note:** Dav. #4725.

ate	Mintage	VG	F	VF	XF	Unc
628NB	—	350	700	1,400	2,750	—

(M# 204 THALER

ilver **Obv:** Armored bust right with fur hat with plume and cepter **Obv. Legend:** GAB. D: G. SA. RO. IM... **Rev:** Crowned rms **Note:** Varieties exist. Dav. #4724.

ate	Mintage	VG	F	VF	XF	Unc
628NB	—	350	700	1,500	3,000	—
6Z9NB	—	350	700	1,500	3,000	—

KM# C204 THALER

Silver **Obv. Legend:** *GABR*D: G: S*R*IMP*... **Note:** Dav. #4727.

Date	Mintage	VG	F	VF	XF	Unc
1629	—	500	1,000	2,000	3,500	—

KM# 240.1 THALER

Silver **Obv:** Knight left looking back, shield with lion below **Obv. Legend:** MONE • ARGEN • PRO • REG • TRAN **Rev:** Rampant lion left **Rev. Legend:** * CONFIDENS: DOM • NON • MOVETVR • **Note:** Imitation of Netherlands-Overyssel Daalder.

Date	Mintage	VG	F	VF	XF	Unc
1638	—	—	—	—	—	—

KM# 240.2 THALER

Silver **Obv. Legend:** MONE • ARGEN • PRO • REG • TRA **Rev. Legend:** * CONFIDENS • DNO • NON • MOVETVR **Note:** Imitation of Netherlands-Overyssel Daalder.

Date	Mintage	VG	F	VF	XF	Unc
1.6.3.8.	—	—	—	—	—	—
1.638	—	—	—	—	—	—
1638	—	—	—	—	—	—

KM# 254 THALER

Silver **Note:** Dav. #4729. Round version of KM#253. Varieties exist.

Date	Mintage	VG	F	VF	XF	Unc
1645NB	—	500	1,000	2,100	4,000	—
1646NB	—	500	1,000	2,100	4,000	—

KM# 253 THALER

Silver **Note:** Dav. #4729C. Klippe.

Date	Mintage	VG	F	VF	XF	Unc
1645NB Rare	—	—	—	—	—	—
1646NB Rare	—	—	—	—	—	—

KM# 255 THALER

Silver **Note:** Dav. #4730.

Date	Mintage	VG	F	VF	XF	Unc
1645NB	—	600	1,200	2,200	4,000	—

KM# 259 THALER

Silver **Obv:** Similar to 1 Thaler, KM#255. **Rev. Legend:** .PAR. REG. HVNG. DOM. ET. SI. COMES. **Note:** Dav. #4731.

Date	Mintage	VG	F	VF	XF	Unc
1645 NB	—	600	1,200	2,200	4,000	—

KM# 260 THALER

Silver **Obv. Legend:** GEORG. RAKO-.D: G. PRI. TRA **Note:** Dav. #4732. Varieties exist.

Date	Mintage	VG	F	VF	XF	Unc
1646NB	—	375	750	1,500	3,500	—
1647NB	—	375	750	1,500	3,500	—
1648NB	—	375	750	1,500	3,500	—

KM# A265 THALER

Silver **Obv:** Bust right divides legend at top and bottom with left hand on sword hilt **Note:** Dav. #4734. Varieties exist.

Date	Mintage	VG	F	VF	XF	Unc
1646NB	—	375	750	1,500	3,500	—
1647NB	—	375	750	1,500	3,500	—
1648NB	—	375	750	1,500	3,500	—

KM# A270 THALER

Silver **Obv:** Small bust right divides legend at top with left hand on sword hilt **Note:** Dav. #4736. Varieties exist.

Date	Mintage	VG	F	VF	XF	Unc
1646NB	—	375	750	1,500	3,500	—
1647NB	—	375	750	1,500	3,500	—
1648NB	—	375	750	1,500	3,500	—

KM# A271 THALER

Silver **Obv:** Similar to KM#A265 **Rev:** Crowned ornate shield with mint mark below **Note:** Dav. #A4735.

Date	Mintage	VG	F	VF	XF	Unc
1647NB	—	500	1,000	2,000	3,500	—

KM# A269 THALER

Silver **Obv. Legend:** .GEORG: RAKO-: D: G: PRIN: TRA **Note:** Dav. #4742.

Date	Mintage	VG	F	VF	XF	Unc
1648NB	—	300	600	1,200	2,750	—
1649NB	—	300	600	1,200	2,750	—

KM# B269 THALER

Silver **Obv:** Similar to 1 Thaler, KM#269 **Rev:** Similar to 1 Thaler, KM#269C **Note:** Dav. #4742A.

Date	Mintage	VG	F	VF	XF	Unc
1648NB	—	300	600	1,200	2,750	—
1649NB	—	300	600	1,200	2,750	—

KM# C269 THALER

Silver **Obv. Legend:** .GEOR: RAKO-. D. G: P: TRA **Rev. Legend:** ...SIC. COM(ES) **Note:** Dav. #4743.

Date	Mintage	VG	F	VF	XF	Unc
1649NB	—	300	600	1,200	2,750	—
1650NB	—	300	600	1,200	2,750	—

KM# D269 THALER

Silver **Obv. Legend:** .GEORGIVS.-RAKO: D: G: P: T **Rev:** Wheel in center of crowned arms **Note:** Dav. #4744.

Date	Mintage	VG	F	VF	XF	Unc
1649NB	—	300	600	1,200	2,750	—

KM# E269 THALER

Silver **Obv:** Similar to 1 Thaler, KM#269C **Rev:** Bird in center of crowned arms **Note:** Dav. #4744A.

Date	Mintage	VG	F	VF	XF	Unc
1649NB	—	300	600	1,200	2,750	—

KM# 269 THALER

Silver **Obv. Legend:** GEORGIVS: RA.- D: G: PRI: TRA **Rev:** Wheel in center of crowned arms **Note:** Dav. #4745.

Date	Mintage	VG	F	VF	XF	Unc
1649NB	—	300	600	1,200	2,750	—

KM# A282 THALER

Silver **Obv. Legend:** .GEOR(G) : RAKO-D. G. P. TRA(N) **Note:** Dav. #4746. Varieties exist.

Date	Mintage	VG	F	VF	XF	Unc
1650NB	—	300	600	1,200	2,750	—
1651NB	—	300	600	1,200	2,750	—

KM# A281 THALER

Silver **Obv. Legend:** .GEORGIVS. -RA: D: G: P: T: **Note:** Dav. #4747. Varieties exist.

Date	Mintage	VG	F	VF	XF	Unc
1650NB	—	300	600	1,200	2,750	—

KM# B281 THALER

Silver **Obv. Legend:** GEORGIVS. - RAKO: D:G: P: T: **Note:** Dav. #4747A.

Date	Mintage	VG	F	VF	XF	Unc
1650NB	—	300	600	1,200	2,750	—

KM# C281 THALER

Silver **Obv. Legend:** .GEOR: RAKO-: D:G: PRIN: TRA **Rev:** Wheel in center of crowned arms **Note:** Dav. #4748.

Date	Mintage	VG	F	VF	XF	Unc
1650NB	—	300	600	1,200	2,750	—

KM# 281 THALER

Silver **Obv:** Similar to 1 Thaler, KM#281B **Rev:** Bird on wheel in center of crowned arms **Note:** Dav. #4748A.

Date	Mintage	VG	F	VF	XF	Unc
1650NB	—	300	600	1,200	2,750	—

KM# 280 THALER

Silver **Obv. Legend:** .GEOR: RAKO-. D: G: P: TRA **Note:** Dav. #4749. Square klippe. Illustration reduced.

Date	Mintage	VG	F	VF	XF	Unc
1650NB	—	1,800	3,500	6,500	10,500	—

KM# 282 THALER

Silver **Obv. Legend:** .GEORGIVS.-RA: D: G: P: T: **Rev:** Bird on wheel in center of crowned arms **Note:** Dav. #4750.

Date	Mintage	VG	F	VF	XF	Unc
1650NB	—	300	600	1,200	2,750	—
1651NB	—	300	600	1,200	2,750	—

KM# 286 THALER

Silver **Obv. Legend:** .GEOR: RAKO... **Note:** Dav. #4751. Varieties exist.

Date	Mintage	VG	F	VF	XF	Unc
1651NB	—	300	600	1,200	2,750	—
1652NB	—	300	600	1,200	2,750	—
1653NB	—	300	600	1,200	2,750	—
1654NB	—	300	600	1,200	2,750	—
1655NB	—	300	600	1,200	2,750	—
1656NB	—	300	600	1,200	2,750	—

KM# B287 THALER

Silver **Note:** Dav. #4752. Round version of KM#A287.

Date	Mintage	VG	F	VF	XF	Unc
1656NB	—	300	600	1,200	2,750	—
1657NB	—	300	600	1,200	2,750	—
1658NB	—	300	600	1,200	2,750	—

KM# C287 THALER

Silver **Obv. Legend:** .GEOR:RAKO-: D: G. P. T. **Rev:** Similar to 1 Thaler, KM#286 **Note:** Dav. #4753.

Date	Mintage	VG	F	VF	XF	Unc
1656NB	—	300	600	1,200	2,750	—

KM# 297 THALER

27.3000 g., Silver **Note:** Dav. #4754. Round version of KM#296A. Varieties exist.

Date	Mintage	VG	F	VF	XF	Unc
1657NB Rare	—	—	—	—	—	—

KM# 296 THALER

Silver **Obv. Legend:** GEORGIVS RAKOCI... **Note:** Dav. #4754B. Octagonal klippe.

Date	Mintage	VG	F	VF	XF	Unc
1657NB Rare	—	—	—	—	—	—

KM# 296A THALER

Silver **Note:** Dav. #4754C. Square klippe.

Date	Mintage	VG	F	VF	XF	Unc
1657NB Rare	—	—	—	—	—	—

KM# A287 THALER

Silver **Obv. Legend:** .GEORGIVS... **Shape:** Square **Note:** Dav. #4752A. Klippe.

Date	Mintage	VG	F	VF	XF	Unc
1657ND Rare	—	—	—	—	—	—

KM# 311 THALER

Silver **Note:** Dav. #4755. Round version of KM#309. Varieties exist.

Date	Mintage	VG	F	VF	XF	Unc
1658NB	—	300	600	1,200	3,000	—
1659NB	—	300	600	1,200	3,000	—

KM# 309 THALER

27.3000 g., Silver **Obv. Legend:** GEORGI.-RA • D:G • P.T. **Note:** Dav. #4755A. Klippe with Denar strikings in three corners

Date	Mintage	VG	F	VF	XF	Unc
1658NB Rare	—	—	—	—	—	—

KM# 310 THALER

26.5800 g., Silver **Note:** Dav. #4755B. Klippe without Denar strikings.

Date	Mintage	VG	F	VF	XF	Unc
1658NB	—	2,500	4,500	8,500	12,000	—

ːM# 311A THALER
ilver **Obv:** Armored bust right with scepter **Obv. Legend:** ·EOR: RA-D: G: P. TR. **Rev:** Ornate crowned arms **Rev. ·egend:** • PAR • REG • HVN • DOM • ET • SIC • COM • **Note:** ·av. #4756.

ate	Mintage	VG	F	VF	XF	Unc
659NB	—	350	700	1,500	3,500	—
660NB	—	350	700	1,500	3,500	—

ːM# 320 THALER
ilver **Note:** Dav. #4758. Round version of KM#319. Legend arieties exist.

ate	Mintage	VG	F	VF	XF	Unc
659CV	—	350	700	1,500	3,500	—
660CV	—	350	700	1,500	3,500	—

ːM# 319 THALER
ilver **Obv. Legend:** ACHA:BAR-D.G.PR.TR. **Note:** Dav. 4758A. Hexagonal klippe.

ate	Mintage	VG	F	VF	XF	Unc
659CV Rare	—	—	—	—	—	—

ːM# 329.1 THALER
ilver **Obv:** Crowned arms **Obv. Legend:** ACHATIVS ARCSAI. D.G... **Rev. Legend:** Center: *SERVA/NOSQ VIA / ERIMVS* / SCHESBVRGI **Note:** Dav. #4759. Size varies: 39-3mm.

ate	Mintage	VG	F	VF	XF	Unc
660	—	900	1,800	3,500	7,000	—

ːM# 329.2 THALER
ilver **Obv. Legend:** .A CHAT. BAR. D. G. PRI... **Rev. Legend:** ..SCHESSBVRGI **Note:** Dav. #4760.

ate	Mintage	VG	F	VF	XF	Unc
660	—	900	1,800	3,500	7,000	—

KM# A330 THALER
Silver **Rev. Legend:** DEVS / PROVI / DEBIT **Note:** Dav. #4761.

Date	Mintage	VG	F	VF	XF	Unc
1660 IR	—	900	1,800	3,500	7,000	—

KM# 330.1 THALER
Silver **Obv:** Moon face to left in shield **Rev:** Central legend in small cartouche **Note:** Dav. #4762.

Date	Mintage	VG	F	VF	XF	Unc
1660CB	—	900	1,800	3,500	7,500	—

KM# 330.2 THALER
Silver **Obv:** Moon face to right in shield **Rev:** Central legend in large cartouche **Note:** Dav. #4763.

Date	Mintage	VG	F	VF	XF	Unc
1660CB	—	900	1,800	3,500	7,500	—

KM# 330.3 THALER
Silver **Obv:** Moon face to left in shield **Rev:** Without cartouche; blossoms before and after SERVA **Note:** Dav. #4764.

Date	Mintage	VG	F	VF	XF	Unc
1660CB	—	900	1,800	3,500	7,500	—

KM# 330.4 THALER
Silver **Obv:** Moon face to right **Rev:** Without cartouche; without blossoms before and after SERVA **Note:** Dav. #4765.

Date	Mintage	VG	F	VF	XF	Unc
1660CB	—	900	1,800	3,500	7,500	—

KM# 328 THALER
Silver **Note:** Dav. #4757. Round version of KM#327. Varieties exist.

Date	Mintage	VG	F	VF	XF	Unc
1660CV	—	300	650	1,400	3,000	—

KM# 327 THALER
Silver **Note:** Dav. #4757A. Hexagonal klippe.

Date	Mintage	VG	F	VF	XF	Unc
1660CV Rare	—	—	—	—	—	—

KM# A345 THALER
Silver **Obv. Legend:** IOAN: KEMENY... **Note:** Dav. #4766.

Date	Mintage	VG	F	VF	XF	Unc
1661	—	1,800	3,500	7,000	12,000	—

KM# 345 THALER
Silver **Obv. Legend:** IOANNES: KE... **Note:** Dav. #4767. Varieties exist.

Date	Mintage	VG	F	VF	XF	Unc
1661CV	—	700	1,300	3,000	7,500	—

KM# 346 THALER
Silver **Obv. Legend:** IOANNES. KEM... **Note:** Dav. #4768.

Date	Mintage	VG	F	VF	XF	Unc
1661SB	—	900	1,500	2,750	5,500	—

KM# 347 THALER

Silver **Obv. Legend:** *IOHAN: KEMENY*... **Note:** Dav. #4769. Varieties exist.

Date	Mintage	VG	F	VF	XF	Unc
1661SB Rare	—	—	—	—	—	—

KM# 346A THALER

Silver **Obv:** Similar to 1 Thaler, KM#346 with date below bust **Note:** Dav. #4770.

Date	Mintage	VG	F	VF	XF	Unc
1661SB Rare	—	—	—	—	—	—

KM# 366 THALER

Silver **Note:** Dav. #4771. Round version of KM#365. Varieties exist.

Date	Mintage	VG	F	VF	XF	Unc
1662	—	250	500	1,100	2,750	—
1663	—	250	500	1,100	2,750	—

KM# 364 THALER

Silver **Shape:** Hexagonal **Note:** Dav. #4771A. Klippe with rounded corners.

Date	Mintage	VG	F	VF	XF	Unc
1662	—	1,850	3,750	7,500	12,000	—

KM# 363 THALER

Silver **Obv. Legend:** MICHA • APAFI.-D. G. PR. TR. **Shape:** Hexagonal **Note:** Dav. #4771A. Klippe.

Date	Mintage	VG	F	VF	XF	Unc
1662	—	1,250	2,500	5,000	10,500	—
1663	—	1,250	2,500	5,000	10,500	—

KM# 365 THALER

Silver **Shape:** Square **Note:** Dav. #4771B. Klippe. Varieties in size exist - 43x42mm and 45x45mm. Illustration reduced.

Date	Mintage	VG	F	VF	XF	Unc
1662	—	1,250	2,500	5,000	10,500	—

KM# A375 THALER

Silver **Obv. Legend:** MI. APA. D. G.-PRIN. TRA(N)* **Note:** Dav. #4772.

Date	Mintage	VG	F	VF	XF	Unc
1663CB	—	250	500	1,100	2,750	—

KM# 375 THALER

Silver **Rev:** Small Kronstadt arms at bottom **Note:** Dav. #4773. Varieties exist.

Date	Mintage	VG	F	VF	XF	Unc
1663CB Rare	—	—	—	—	—	—

KM# A377 THALER

Silver **Obv. Legend:** * MI * APA * D.G * **Note:** Dav. #4775.

Date	Mintage	VG	F	VF	XF	Unc
1664CB	—	250	500	1,100	2,750	—

KM# 377 THALER

Silver **Obv. Legend:** MICHA. APAFI... **Rev:** Kronstadt arms at bottom **Note:** Dav. #4777. Varieties exist.

Date	Mintage	VG	F	VF	XF	Unc
1664	—	250	500	1,100	2,750	—
1665	—	250	500	1,100	2,750	—
1667	—	250	500	1,100	2,750	—

KM# B377 THALER

Silver **Obv. Legend:** *MICHA + APAFI + D +... **Rev. Legend** PAR + REG + HVN + DOM + ET... **Note:** Dav. #4778.

Date	Mintage	VG	F	VF	XF	Unc
1664SB	—	250	500	1,100	2,750	—

KM# A383 THALER

Silver **Obv. Legend:** *MI. APA. D: G*... **Rev. Legend:** .PAR. REG. HV(N). DO(M)... **Note:** Dav. #4780.

Date	Mintage	VG	F	VF	XF	Unc
1665CB	—	250	500	1,100	2,750	—
1666CB	—	250	500	1,100	2,750	—

KM# B383 THALER

Silver **Obv. Legend:** MIC. APA. D. G... **Rev. Legend:** + PAR REG. HV(N). DO +... **Note:** Dav. #4782.

Date	Mintage	VG	F	VF	XF	Unc
1665	—	250	500	1,100	2,750	—
1666	—	250	500	1,100	2,750	—
1667	—	250	500	1,100	2,750	—

KM# 383 THALER

Silver **Obv. Legend:** *MICH: APAFII... **Note:** Dav. #4783.

Date	Mintage	VG	F	VF	XF	Unc
1666SB	—	250	500	1,100	2,750	—

KM# 388 THALER

Silver **Obv. Legend:** *MIC. APA. D. G... **Rev:** Crowned arms, small Hermannstadt arms at bottom **Note:** Dav. #4785. Varieties exist.

Date	Mintage	VG	F	VF	XF	Unc
1667	—	250	500	1,100	2,750	—

KM# 389 THALER

Silver **Obv. Legend:** MICHA. APAFI... **Rev:** Small Kronstadt arms at bottom **Note:** Dav. #4788. Varieties exist.

Date	Mintage	VG	F	VF	XF	Unc
1667	—	250	500	1,100	2,750	—

KM# B390 THALER

Silver **Obv. Legend:** *MI(C). APA. D. G. flower... **Rev. Legend:** PAR. REG. HV. DO flower... **Note:** Dav. #4789. Prev. KM#A390.

Date	Mintage	VG	F	VF	XF	Unc
1667	—	250	500	1,100	2,750	—

KM# C390 THALER

Silver **Obv. Legend:** Flower MICHA • APAFI... **Rev:** Legend continuous **Note:** Dav. #4790. Prev. KM#B390.

Date	Mintage	VG	F	VF	XF	Unc
1667	—	250	500	1,100	2,750	—

KM# 391 THALER
Silver **Obv. Legend:** *MICH: APAFI… **Note:** Dav. #4791.

Date	Mintage	VG	F	VF	XF	Unc
667SB	—	250	500	1,100	2,750	—

KM# 390 THALER
Silver **Obv. Legend:** *MICHAEL. APAFI. D. G… **Note:** Dav. #4793.

Date	Mintage	VG	F	VF	XF	Unc
667KV	—	250	500	1,100	2,750	—
668KV	—	250	500	1,100	2,750	—
669KV	—	250	500	1,100	2,750	—
670KV	—	250	500	1,100	2,750	—
671AC	—	250	500	1,100	2,750	—

KM# 414 THALER
Silver **Obv. Legend:** MICHA. APAFI… **Note:** Dav. #4794. Varieties exist.

Date	Mintage	VG	F	VF	XF	Unc
671 CT	—	250	500	1,100	2,750	—
671 MR	—	250	500	1,100	2,750	—
671 DK	—	250	500	1,100	2,750	—
672	—	250	500	1,100	2,750	—

KM# 415 THALER
Silver **Obv. Legend:** *MICHA: APAFI: D: G:… **Note:** Dav. #4795. Varieties exist.

Date	Mintage	VG	F	VF	XF	Unc
671 CT	—	250	500	1,100	2,750	—

KM# 423 THALER
Silver **Obv. Legend:** *MIC. APA. D. G. PRINCEPS… **Note:** Dav. #4796. Varieties exist.

Date	Mintage	VG	F	VF	XF	Unc
67Z/6ZCB	—	250	500	1,100	2,750	—

KM# 426 THALER
Silver **Obv. Legend:** MICA. APAFI. DE. GRA… **Note:** Dav. #4797. Varieties exist.

Date	Mintage	VG	F	VF	XF	Unc
672	—	250	500	1,100	2,750	—

KM# 425 THALER
Silver **Obv. Legend:** + MICH. APAFI. D. G. PRIN… **Rev. Legend:** + PAR. REG. HV. DO… **Note:** Dav. #4798.

Date	Mintage	VG	F	VF	XF	Unc
1672AC	—	250	500	1,100	2,750	—

KM# 427 THALER
Silver **Obv. Legend:** MICH: APAFI.-D: G: PR: TR: **Note:** Dav. #4799.

Date	Mintage	VG	F	VF	XF	Unc
1672	—	250	500	1,100	2,750	—

KM# 428 THALER
Silver **Obv. Legend:** x MICH x APAFI x - D:G: PR + TR **Note:** Dav. #4800. Varieties exist.

Date	Mintage	VG	F	VF	XF	Unc
167ZSB	—	500	1,000	2,000	3,500	—

KM# 430 THALER
Silver **Obv. Legend:** :MIC: APA: D:G: - .PRIN. TRA. **Note:** Dav. #4804.

Date	Mintage	VG	F	VF	XF	Unc
167ZBT	—	500	1,000	2,000	4,000	—

KM# 430A THALER
Silver **Obv. Legend:** *MIC APA: D: G: -:PRIN: TRAN: **Note:** Dav. #4805.

Date	Mintage	VG	F	VF	XF	Unc
1672	—	500	1,000	2,000	4,000	—

KM# 429 THALER
Silver **Obv. Legend:** *MICHA: APAFI: *D: G: *PRIN: TRANSIL **Note:** Dav. #4806.

Date	Mintage	VG	F	VF	XF	Unc
167ZBT	—	300	650	1,400	3,000	—

KM# 430B THALER
Silver **Obv. Legend:** :MICH: APAFI: D: G:-:PRIN: TRAN* **Note:** Dav. #4807.

Date	Mintage	VG	F	VF	XF	Unc
1672	—	300	650	1,400	3,000	—

KM# 424 THALER
Silver **Obv:** Similar to KM#415 **Rev. Legend:** *PAR: REG: HV: DO… **Note:** Dav. #A4796.

Date	Mintage	VG	F	VF	XF	Unc
1672CIBI	—	400	800	1,600	3,500	—

KM# 428A THALER
Silver **Obv. Legend:** *MIC. APA. D. G.-PRIN. TRAN. **Note:** Similar to 2 Thaler klippe, KM#431. Dav. #4802.

Date	Mintage	VG	F	VF	XF	Unc
1672	—	275	600	1,200	2,750	—

KM# 448 THALER
Silver **Note:** Dav. #4809. Round version of KM#447.

Date	Mintage	VG	F	VF	XF	Unc
1673	—	275	600	1,200	2,750	—

KM# 447 THALER
Silver **Obv. Legend:** MICHA. APAFI.-D: G. PR. TR. **Note:** Dav. #4809A.

Date	Mintage	VG	F	VF	XF	Unc
1673 Rare	—	—	—	—	—	—

KM# 449 THALER
Silver **Obv. Legend:** MICH: APAFI.-D: G: PR: TR: **Note:** Dav. #4810.

Date	Mintage	VG	F	VF	XF	Unc
1673SB	—	300	650	1,400	3,000	—

KM# 450 THALER
Silver **Obv. Legend:** *MICH: APAFI.-*:D: G. PRI: TRA **Note:** Dav. #4811.

Date	Mintage	VG	F	VF	XF	Unc
1673BT Rare	—	—	—	—	—	—

KM# 459 THALER
Silver **Obv. Legend:** MICHAEL * APAFI. D. G. PRIN * TRAN **Rev. Legend:** PAR. REG. HVN. DOM... **Note:** Dav. #4812.

Date	Mintage	VG	F	VF	XF	Unc
1674 Rare	—	—	—	—	—	—

KM# 459A THALER
Silver **Obv. Legend:** MICH. APAFI-D. G. P. T. **Note:** Dav. #4813. Varieties exist.

Date	Mintage	VG	F	VF	XF	Unc
1675 Rare	—	—	—	—	—	—

KM# 465 THALER
Silver **Obv. Legend:** MIC: APAFI-D: G: P: TR: **Note:** Dav. #4814.

Date	Mintage	VG	F	VF	XF	Unc
1677CF	—	275	650	1,300	3,000	—

KM# 465A THALER
Silver **Obv. Legend:** MIC: APAFI-D: G: P: T: **Note:** Dav. #4815.

Date	Mintage	VG	F	VF	XF	Unc
1677AI	—	275	650	1,300	3,000	—

KM# 465B THALER
Silver **Obv. Legend:** MICH: APAFI*-D*-G: PRIN: TR: **Note:** Dav. #4816.

Date	Mintage	VG	F	VF	XF	Unc
1678AI	—	275	650	1,300	3,000	—

KM# 474 THALER
Silver **Obv. Legend:** MIC: APAFI-*D: G: P: T: **Rev. Legend:** ...DO:& SI: COM **Note:** Dav. #4817.

Date	Mintage	VG	F	VF	XF	Unc
1678AI	—	275	650	1,300	3,000	—

KM# 474A THALER
Silver **Rev. Legend:** ...:DO-ET. SIC. COM(ES) **Note:** Dav. #4818. Similar to KM#474. Varieties exist.

Date	Mintage	VG	F	VF	XF	Unc
1678AI	—	275	650	1,300	3,000	—
1679AI	—	275	650	1,300	3,000	—
1680AI	—	275	650	1,300	3,000	—

KM# 492 THALER
Silver **Note:** Dav. #4820. Round version of KM#490.

Date	Mintage	VG	F	VF	XF	Unc
1681AI	—	450	900	1,800	4,000	—
1683AI	—	450	900	1,800	4,000	—
1684AI	—	450	900	1,800	4,000	—
1686AI	—	450	900	1,800	4,000	—
1687AF	—	450	900	1,800	4,000	—

KM# 490 THALER
Silver **Shape:** Hexagon **Note:** Dav. #4820A. Klippe.

Date	Mintage	VG	F	VF	XF	Unc
1681AI	—	1,250	2,500	4,500	8,000	—
1683AI	—	1,250	2,500	4,500	8,000	—
1684AI	—	1,250	2,500	4,500	8,000	—
1686AI	—	1,250	2,500	4,500	8,000	—

KM# A490 THALER
Silver **Obv. Legend:** MICHAEL•APAFI. DEI. GRATIA... **Shape:** Square **Note:** Dav. #4820B. Klippe.

Date	Mintage	VG	F	VF	XF	Unc
1681AI	—	1,250	2,500	4,500	8,000	—

KM# 491 THALER
Silver **Shape:** Hexagon **Note:** Klippe - clipped nearly round.

Date	Mintage	VG	F	VF	XF	Unc
1686AI	—	2,750	5,000	9,000	15,000	—

KM# 510 THALER
Silver **Subject:** Leopold I **Note:** Dav. #3277.

Date	Mintage	VG	F	VF	XF	Unc
1694KV Rare	—	—	—	—	—	—
1696KV Rare	—	—	—	—	—	—

:M# 13 1-1/2 THALER
6.2000 g., Silver **Obv:** Shield with lion **Obv. Legend:** ;TEPHANVS... **Rev:** Madonna and child **Note:** Dav. #4690. 'arieties exist.

ate	Mintage	VG	F	VF	XF	Unc
605NB Rare	—	—	—	—	—	—

:M# 59 1-1/2 THALER
6.2000 g., Silver **Note:** Dav. #4701. Klippe. Similar to 1 Thaler, :M#A53.1.

ate	Mintage	VG	F	VF	XF	Unc
609NB Rare	—	—	—	—	—	—

KM# 184 1-1/2 THALER
42.5000 g., Silver **Obv. Legend:** GABR. D. G... **Note:** Dav. #4718C. Klippe.

Date	Mintage	VG	F	VF	XF	Unc
1627MC	—	1,500	2,750	5,000	8,500	—

KM# 185 1-1/2 THALER
36.2000 g., Silver **Obv:** Crowned arms **Rev:** Madonna and child **Note:** Klippe. Struck using 1 Denar (ducat) dies, KM#192.

Date	Mintage	VG	F	VF	XF	Unc
1627NB	—	—	—	—	—	—

KM# 205 1-1/2 THALER
43.0000 g., Silver **Note:** Dav. #4722D. Varieties exist. 46 x 44mm.

Date	Mintage	VG	F	VF	XF	Unc
1628CC	—	1,800	3,000	5,500	10,000	—

KM# 270 1-1/2 THALER
42.7000 g., Silver **Note:** Dav. #4735. Similar to 1 Thaler, KM#A270.

Date	Mintage	VG	F	VF	XF	Unc
1648 Rare	—	—	—	—	—	—

KM# 14 2 THALER
56.5000 g., Silver **Note:** Dav. #4693. Similar to 1 Thaler, KM#12A.

Date	Mintage	VG	F	VF	XF	Unc
1605 Rare	—	—	—	—	—	—

KM# 27 2 THALER
Silver **Note:** Dav. #4695. Similar to 1 Thaler, KM#25.

Date	Mintage	VG	F	VF	XF	Unc
1606 Rare	—	—	—	—	—	—

KM# 138 2 THALER
57.0000 g., Silver **Obv:** Bare headed half-length armored bust right with scepter **Rev:** Crowned arms **Note:** Dav. #A4710. Varieties exist.

Date	Mintage	VG	F	VF	XF	Unc
1621KB Rare	—	—	—	—	—	—

KM# 171.1 2 THALER
58.0000 g., Silver **Obv:** Legend separated at top **Note:** Dav. #4716A. Klippe.

Date	Mintage	VG	F	VF	XF	Unc
1626CC	—	1,500	2,750	5,000	9,500	—

KM# 172.1 2 THALER
57.3000 g., Silver **Note:** Dav. #4716B. Round version of KM#171.1.

Date	Mintage	VG	F	VF	XF	Unc
1626CC Rare	—	—	—	—	—	—

KM# 171.2 2 THALER
Silver **Obv:** Legend separated at top and bottom **Note:** Dav. #4718B. Klippe.

Date	Mintage	VG	F	VF	XF	Unc
1627	—	1,800	3,000	5,500	10,500	—

KM# 172.2 2 THALER
Silver **Note:** Dav. #4718E. Round version of KM#171.2.

Date	Mintage	VG	F	VF	XF	Unc
1627 Rare	—	—	—	—	—	—

KM# 205B 2 THALER
Silver **Note:** Dav. #4722D. Round version of KM#205A.

Date	Mintage	VG	F	VF	XF	Unc
1628CC Rare	—	—	—	—	—	—

KM# 205A 2 THALER
Silver **Note:** Dav. #4722E. Klippe. Illustration reduced.

Date	Mintage	VG	F	VF	XF	Unc
1628CC	—	1,800	3,000	5,500	10,500	—

KM# A207 2 THALER
Silver **Note:** Dav. #4726A. Klippe. Varieties exist. Illustration reduced.

Date	Mintage	VG	F	VF	XF	Unc
1629CC	—	1,800	2,000	5,500	10,500	—

KM# 213 2 THALER
Silver **Note:** Dav. #4728.

Date	Mintage	VG	F	VF	XF	Unc
1629 HL	—	2,000	3,500	6,500	12,000	—

KM# 265 2 THALER
Silver **Obv:** Half-length armored bust right with fur hat and scepter **Rev:** Crowned arms **Note:** Dav. #4733.

Date	Mintage	VG	F	VF	XF	Unc
1647 Rare	—	—	—	—	—	—

KM# 291 2 THALER
Silver **Obv. Legend:** GEOR: RAKO... **Note:** Dav. #A4751.

Date	Mintage	VG	F	VF	XF	Unc
1655NB Rare	—	—	—	—	—	—

KM# D287 2 THALER
Silver **Obv:** Legend with two 1 Denar stampings **Obv. Legend:** GEORGIVS-RAKO. D: G: P. T. **Rev:** Legend with two 1 Denar stampings **Rev. Legend:** PAR • REG • HVN... **Shape:** Rectangular **Note:** Dav. #A4752. Klippe, 95 x 42mm. Prev. KM#C287.

Date	Mintage	VG	F	VF	XF	Unc
1658NB Rare	—	—	—	—	—	—

KM# 348 2 THALER
Silver **Obv. Legend:** IOAN: KEMENY... **Note:** Dav. #A4766.

Date	Mintage	VG	F	VF	XF	Unc
1661CV Rare	—	—	—	—	—	—

KM# 379 2 THALER
55.5000 g., Silver **Shape:** Hexagon **Note:** Klippe. 43mm. Varieties exist.

Date	Mintage	VG	F	VF	XF	Unc
1664CB Rare	—	—	—	—	—	—
1665CB Rare	—	—	—	—	—	—
1667CB Rare	—	—	—	—	—	—

KM# 378 2 THALER
56.5000 g., Silver **Obv:** Half-length armored bust right with fur hat and scepter **Rev:** Crowned arms with small Kronstadt arms at bottom **Shape:** Square **Note:** Dav. #4774. Klippe. 44 x 45mm. Varieties exist.

Date	Mintage	VG	F	VF	XF	Unc
1664CB Rare	—	—	—	—	—	—
1665CB Rare	—	—	—	—	—	—
1667CB Rare	—	—	—	—	—	—

KM# 392 2 THALER
Silver **Note:** Dav. #4784. Round version of KM#379.

Date	Mintage	VG	F	VF	XF	Unc
1667CB Rare	—	—	—	—	—	—

KM# 395 2 THALER
Silver **Note:** Dav. #4792.

Date	Mintage	VG	F	VF	XF	Unc
1668AF Rare	—	—	—	—	—	—

KM# 411 2 THALER
56.5000 g., Silver **Obv:** Half-length armored bust right **Rev:** Crowned arms **Shape:** Hexagon **Note:** Klippe.

Date	Mintage	VG	F	VF	XF	Unc
1670KV Rare	—	—	—	—	—	—

KM# 431 2 THALER
56.2000 g., Silver **Obv:** Half-length bust right **Rev:** Crowned arms with small Kronstadt arms at bottom **Shape:** Square **Note:** Dav. #4801. Klippe. 45 x 46mm. Illustration reduced.

Date	Mintage	VG	F	VF	XF	Unc
1672 Rare	—	—	—	—	—	—

KM# 432 2 THALER
56.7000 g., Silver, 43 mm. **Note:** Dav. #4803. Similar to KM#431.

Date	Mintage	VG	F	VF	XF	Unc
1672 Rare	—	—	—	—	—	—

KM# 451 2 THALER
57.5000 g., Silver **Shape:** Hexagon **Note:** Dav. #4808. Klipp

Date	Mintage	VG	F	VF	XF	Ur
1673AC Rare	—	—	—	—	—	-

KM# 483 2 THALER
Silver **Obv:** Half-length bust right **Rev:** Crowned arms **Shape** Hexagon **Note:** Dav. #4819. Klippe.

Date	Mintage	VG	F	VF	XF	U
1683AI Rare	—	—	—	—	—	-

KM# 186 2-1/2 THALER
71.3000 g., Silver **Obv:** Armored bust right **Rev:** Crowned arm **Note:** Dav. #4718A. Klippe.

Date	Mintage	VG	F	VF	XF	U
1627MC Rare	—	—	—	—	—	-

KM# A205B 2-1/2 THALER
71.3000 g., Silver **Note:** Klippe. Dav. #4722B. Prev. KM#205

Date	Mintage	VG	F	VF	XF	U
1628CC Rare	—	—	—	—	—	-

KM# 187 3 THALER
Silver **Obv:** Armored bust right **Rev:** Crowned arms **Note:** Dav #4718. Klippe. Weight varies: 86.5-87.5 grams.

Date	Mintage	VG	F	VF	XF	U
1627MC Rare	—	—	—	—	—	-

KM# 188 3 THALER
Silver **Note:** Dav. #4718. Round version of KM#187. Weight varies: 86.5-87.5 grams.

Date	Mintage	VG	F	VF	XF	U
1627MC Rare	—	—	—	—	—	-

KM# 205C 3 THALER
Silver **Note:** Dav. #4722A. Klippe. Weight varies: 86.5-87.5 grams.

Date	Mintage	VG	F	VF	XF	U
1628CC Rare	—	—	—	—	—	-

KM# 205D 3 THALER
Silver **Note:** Dav. #4722E. Round version of KM#205C. Weigh varies: 86.5-87.5 grams.

Date	Mintage	VG	F	VF	XF	U
1628CC Rare	—	—	—	—	—	-

KM# B207 3 THALER
Silver **Note:** Dav. #4726. Klippe. Weight varies: 86.5-87.5 gram

Date	Mintage	VG	F	VF	XF	U
1629CC Rare	—	—	—	—	—	-

:M# C207 3 THALER

ilver **Note:** Dav. #4726B. Round version of KM#B207. Weight aries: 86.5-87.5 grams.

ate	Mintage	VG	F	VF	XF	Unc
629CC Rare	—	—	—	—	—	—

:M# A492 3 THALER

3.4700 g., Silver **Obv:** 3/4-length figure of Michael Apafi holding ceptre right **Obv. Legend:** MICHAEL * APAFI. DEI. GRATIA... ev: Crowned ornate arms **Rev. Legend:** . PAR: REG: VNGARIAE... **Note:** Struck with 1 Thaler dies, KM#492.

ate	Mintage	VG	F	VF	XF	Unc
681 AI	—	—	—	—	—	—

M# 173 4 THALER

17.0000 g., Silver **Note:** Dav. #4716. Klippe. Illustration educed.

ate	Mintage	VG	F	VF	XF	Unc
626CC Rare	—	—	—	—	—	—

:M# 206 4 THALER

14.1000 g., Silver **Note:** Dav. #4722.

ate	Mintage	VG	F	VF	XF	Unc
628CC Rare	—	—	—	—	—	—

TRADE COINAGE

:M# 28 1/4 DUCAT

.8750 g., 0.9860 Gold 0.0277 oz. AGW **Obv:** Arms of Hungary bv. Legend: STEPH. DG HVN TRAN... **Rev:** Madonna and hild facing, date below

ate	Mintage	VG	F	VF	XF	Unc
606	—	125	270	625	1,250	—

KM# 53 1/4 DUCAT

0.8750 g., 0.9860 Gold 0.0277 oz. AGW **Obv:** Ams of Hungary and Dalmetia **Obv. Legend:** SIG: RAKOCY. D. G. P. TRAN.

Date	Mintage	VG	F	VF	XF	Unc
1608	—	125	270	625	1,250	—

KM# 60 1/4 DUCAT

0.8750 g., 0.9860 Gold 0.0277 oz. AGW **Obv:** Coat of arms **Rev:** Madonna and child

Date	Mintage	VG	F	VF	XF	Unc
1609	—	125	270	625	1,250	—
1610	—	125	270	625	1,250	—

KM# 73 1/4 DUCAT

0.8750 g., 0.9860 Gold 0.0277 oz. AGW **Obv. Legend:** GABRI. D. G. PRIN. TRAN. ET. **Rev:** Madonna and child facing on half moon without inner circle

Date	Mintage	VG	F	VF	XF	Unc
1610	—	125	245	500	1,050	—

KM# 89 1/4 DUCAT

0.8750 g., 0.9860 Gold 0.0277 oz. AGW **Obv:** Date in legend

Date	Mintage	VG	F	VF	XF	Unc
1612	—	125	245	500	1,050	—

KM# 96 1/4 DUCAT

0.8750 g., 0.9860 Gold 0.0277 oz. AGW **Obv:** Last two digits of date at sides of arms

Date	Mintage	VG	F	VF	XF	Unc
1613	—	125	245	500	1,050	—

KM# 116 1/4 DUCAT

0.8750 g., 0.9860 Gold 0.0277 oz. AGW **Obv:** Oval arms of Transylvania in cartouche in inner circle **Rev:** Madonna and child facing on half moon divide A-I in inner circle, date in legend

Date	Mintage	VG	F	VF	XF	Unc
1619	—	125	245	500	1,050	—
1620	—	125	245	500	1,050	—

KM# 148 1/4 DUCAT

0.8750 g., 0.9860 Gold 0.0277 oz. AGW **Obv:** Arms of Hungary divide N-B in inner circle

Date	Mintage	VG	F	VF	XF	Unc
1622	—	125	245	500	1,050	—
1623	—	125	245	500	1,050	—
1624	—	125	245	500	1,050	—
1626	—	125	245	500	1,050	—

KM# 190 1/4 DUCAT

0.8750 g., 0.9860 Gold 0.0277 oz. AGW **Obv:** Crowned oval arms **Rev:** Madonna and child in circle of flames

Date	Mintage	VG	F	VF	XF	Unc
1627	—	125	245	500	1,050	—

KM# 189 1/4 DUCAT

0.8750 g., 0.9860 Gold 0.0277 oz. AGW **Obv:** Crowned shield-shaped arms **Note:** Varieties exist.

Date	Mintage	VG	F	VF	XF	Unc
1627NB	—	125	245	500	1,050	—
1628NB	—	125	245	500	1,050	—

KM# 245 1/4 DUCAT

0.8750 g., 0.9860 Gold 0.0277 oz. AGW **Obv:** Crowned arms of Hungary divide N-B in inner circle **Obv. Legend:** GEOR. RAKO. D. G. PRI. TRAN **Rev:** Madonna and child facing on half moon with flames below in inner circle

Date	Mintage	VG	F	VF	XF	Unc
1642NB	—	125	245	500	1,050	—
1647NB	—	125	245	500	1,050	—

KM# 283 1/4 DUCAT

0.8750 g., 0.9860 Gold 0.0277 oz. AGW **Obv:** Titles of Georg Rakoczi II

Date	Mintage	VG	F	VF	XF	Unc
1650NB	—	125	245	500	1,050	—
1653NB	—	125	245	500	1,050	—

KM# 29 1/2 DUCAT

1.7500 g., 0.9860 Gold 0.0555 oz. AGW **Obv:** Arms of Hungary **Obv. Legend:** DG HVN TRAN... **Rev:** Madonna and child facing, date below

Date	Mintage	VG	F	VF	XF	Unc
1606	—	350	700	1,100	2,100	—

KM# 90 1/2 DUCAT

1.7500 g., 0.9860 Gold 0.0555 oz. AGW **Obv:** Arms of Hungary and Dalmatia **Rev:** Madonna and child facing on half moon, date in legend

Date	Mintage	VG	F	VF	XF	Unc
1612	—	280	550	1,000	1,750	—

KM# 97 1/2 DUCAT

1.7500 g., 0.9860 Gold 0.0555 oz. AGW **Obv:** Last two digits of date at sides of arms

Date	Mintage	VG	F	VF	XF	Unc
1613	—	210	425	750	1,300	—

KM# 16 DUCAT

3.5000 g., 0.9860 Gold 0.1109 oz. AGW **Obv:** St. Ladislaus

Date	Mintage	VG	F	VF	XF	Unc
1605 SL	—	290	575	1,050	2,200	4,250
1606 SL	—	290	575	1,050	2,200	4,250
1607 SL	—	290	575	1,050	2,200	4,250

KM# 15 DUCAT

3.5000 g., 0.9860 Gold 0.1109 oz. AGW **Rev:** St. Ladislaus

Date	Mintage	VG	F	VF	XF	Unc
1605	—	290	575	1,050	2,200	4,250

KM# 30 DUCAT

3.5000 g., 0.9860 Gold 0.1109 oz. AGW **Rev:** Bocskai arms

Date	Mintage	VG	F	VF	XF	Unc
1606	—	375	750	1,450	3,150	6,250

KM# 31 DUCAT
3.5000 g., 0.9860 Gold 0.1109 oz. AGW

Date	Mintage	VG	F	VF	XF	Unc
1606	—	500	950	1,900	3,700	7,250

KM# 42 DUCAT
3.5000 g., 0.9860 Gold 0.1109 oz. AGW **Obv:** Sigismund Rakoczi **Rev:** AQV ILA and seven towers below in inner circle

Date	Mintage	VG	F	VF	XF	Unc
1607	—	525	1,050	2,350	4,750	9,500
1608	—	525	1,050	2,350	4,750	9,500

KM# 61 DUCAT
3.5000 g., 0.9860 Gold 0.1109 oz. AGW **Obv:** St. Ladislaus standing divides N-B in inner circle **Rev:** Madonna and child facing on half moon in inner circle, date in legend **Note:** Varieties exist.

Date	Mintage	VG	F	VF	XF	Unc
1609	—	350	675	1,300	2,650	5,250
1610	—	350	675	1,300	2,650	5,250

KM# 62 DUCAT
3.5000 g., 0.9860 Gold 0.1109 oz. AGW **Obv:** Gabriel Bathori **Rev:** Crowned Bathori arms **Note:** Varieties exist.

Date	Mintage	VG	F	VF	XF	Unc
1609	—	500	950	1,900	3,700	7,250
1610	—	500	950	1,900	3,700	7,250
1611/0	—	500	950	1,900	3,700	7,250
1611	—	500	950	1,900	3,700	7,250
161Z	—	500	950	1,900	3,700	7,250
ND	—	500	950	1,900	3,700	7,250

KM# 74 DUCAT
3.5000 g., 0.9860 Gold 0.1109 oz. AGW **Obv:** Armored bust of Gabriel Bathori right **Rev:** Eagle with Barhori arms on breast **Note:** Varieties exist.

Date	Mintage	VG	F	VF	XF	Unc
1610	—	500	950	1,900	3,700	7,250
1611	—	500	950	1,900	3,700	7,250
1612	—	500	950	1,900	3,700	7,250
1613	—	500	950	1,900	3,700	7,250

KM# 102 DUCAT
3.5000 g., 0.9860 Gold 0.1109 oz. AGW **Obv:** Gabriel Bethlen **Rev:** Bethlen arms

Date	Mintage	VG	F	VF	XF	Unc
1613	—	375	750	1,450	3,150	6,250
1614	—	375	750	1,450	3,150	6,250
1615	—	375	750	1,450	3,150	6,250
1616	—	375	750	1,450	3,150	6,250
1618	—	375	750	1,450	3,150	6,250

KM# 98 DUCAT
3.5000 g., 0.9860 Gold 0.1109 oz. AGW **Obv:** Gabriel Bathori **Rev:** Crowned Bathori arms **Note:** Struck at Klausenburg.

Date	Mintage	VG	F	VF	XF	Unc
1613 KO	—	525	1,050	2,100	4,650	9,500

KM# 99 DUCAT
3.5000 g., 0.9860 Gold 0.1109 oz. AGW **Obv:** Armored bust of Gabriel Bathori right in inner circle **Rev:** Bathori arms with CIBINI in dragon circle in inner circle, date in legend

Date	Mintage	VG	F	VF	XF	Unc
1613	—	525	1,050	2,100	4,650	9,500

KM# 100 DUCAT
3.5000 g., 0.9860 Gold 0.1109 oz. AGW **Rev:** Bathori arms divide C-I in dragon circle in inner circle

Date	Mintage	VG	F	VF	XF	Unc
1613CI	—	525	1,050	2,100	4,650	9,500

KM# 101 DUCAT
3.5000 g., 0.9860 Gold 0.1109 oz. AGW

Date	Mintage	VG	F	VF	XF	Unc
ND(1613)CV	—	500	950	2,050	4,200	8,500

KM# 111 DUCAT
3.5000 g., 0.9860 Gold 0.1109 oz. AGW **Obv:** Gabriel Bethlen **Rev:** Crowned Bethlen arms

Date	Mintage	VG	F	VF	XF	Unc
1618	—	375	750	1,450	3,150	6,250
1619	—	375	750	1,450	3,150	6,250
1620	—	375	750	1,450	3,150	6,250

KM# 128 DUCAT
3.5000 g., 0.9860 Gold 0.1109 oz. AGW **Obv:** Gabriel Bethlen

Date	Mintage	VG	F	VF	XF	Unc
1620	—	375	750	1,450	3,150	6,250
1621	—	375	750	1,450	3,150	6,250
1622	—	375	750	1,450	3,150	6,250

KM# 126 DUCAT
3.5000 g., 0.9860 Gold 0.1109 oz. AGW

Date	Mintage	VG	F	VF	XF	Un
1620AI	—	500	950	1,900	3,700	7,25

KM# 127 DUCAT
3.5000 g., 0.9860 Gold 0.1109 oz. AGW **Note:** Similar to KM#101.

Date	Mintage	VG	F	VF	XF	Un
1620AI	—	400	800	1,600	3,450	7,00

KM# 139 DUCAT
3.5000 g., 0.9860 Gold 0.1109 oz. AGW **Obv:** Gabriel Bethlen **Note:** Struck at Nagybanya.

Date	Mintage	VG	F	VF	XF	Un
1621	—	375	750	1,450	3,150	6,25
1622	—	375	750	1,450	3,150	6,25

KM# 140 DUCAT
3.5000 g., 0.9860 Gold 0.1109 oz. AGW

Date	Mintage	VG	F	VF	XF	Un
1621NB	—	375	750	1,450	3,150	6,25
1622NB	—	375	750	1,450	3,150	6,25

KM# 149 DUCAT
3.5000 g., 0.9860 Gold 0.1109 oz. AGW **Obv:** Gabriel Bethlen **Rev:** Crowned arms of Oppeln, Ratibor, and Transylvania

Date	Mintage	VG	F	VF	XF	Un
1622	—	375	750	1,450	3,150	6,25

KM# 160 DUCAT
3.5000 g., 0.9860 Gold 0.1109 oz. AGW **Note:** Varieties exist

Date	Mintage	VG	F	VF	XF	Un
1623	—	375	750	1,450	3,150	6,25
1624	—	375	750	1,450	3,150	6,25
1625	—	375	750	1,450	3,150	6,25
1626	—	375	750	1,450	3,150	6,25
1627	—	375	750	1,450	3,150	6,25

KM# 165 DUCAT
3.5000 g., 0.9860 Gold 0.1109 oz. AGW

Date	Mintage	VG	F	VF	XF	Unc
1625CC	—	350	675	1,300	2,650	5,25

KM# 191 DUCAT

3.5000 g., 0.9860 Gold 0.1109 oz. AGW

Date	Mintage	VG	F	VF	XF	Unc
1627	—	375	750	1,450	3,150	6,250
1629	—	375	750	1,450	3,150	6,250

KM# 192 DUCAT

3.5000 g., 0.9860 Gold 0.1109 oz. AGW **Note:** Struck with 1 Denar dies.

Date	Mintage	VG	F	VF	XF	Unc
1627NB	—	285	575	1,150	2,400	4,750

KM# 193 DUCAT

3.5000 g., 0.9860 Gold 0.1109 oz. AGW **Note:** Struck with 1 Denar dies.

Date	Mintage	VG	F	VF	XF	Unc
1627	—	285	575	1,150	2,400	4,750

KM# 207 DUCAT

3.5000 g., 0.9860 Gold 0.1109 oz. AGW **Obv:** Bareheaded armored bust right **Obv. Legend:** GAB • D : G • SA • RO • IM • - • ET • TRAN • PRIN **Rev:** Crowned arms **Rev. Legend:** PAR • R • HVN • DOM • SIG - COM • OP • R • DVX • 16Z9 **Note:** Varieties exist.

Date	Mintage	VG	F	VF	XF	Unc
16Z8	—	375	750	1,450	3,150	6,250
16Z9/8	—	375	750	1,450	3,150	6,250
16Z9	—	375	750	1,450	3,150	6,250

KM# 214 DUCAT

3.5000 g., 0.9860 Gold 0.1109 oz. AGW **Obv:** Bust of Gabriel Bethlen in fur hat with plume right divides A-I in inner circle **Rev:** Crowned arms of Hungary and Transylvania in inner circle

Date	Mintage	VG	F	VF	XF	Unc
ND(1629)	—	400	800	1,600	3,450	7,000

KM# 221 DUCAT

3.5000 g., 0.9860 Gold 0.1109 oz. AGW **Subject:** Catherine Bethlen

Date	Mintage	VG	F	VF	XF	Unc
1630	—	3,700	7,400	10,500	13,500	27,500

KM# 222 DUCAT

3.5000 g., 0.9860 Gold 0.1109 oz. AGW

Date	Mintage	VG	F	VF	XF	Unc
1630	—	4,200	8,000	12,500	16,000	32,500

KM# 223 DUCAT

3.5000 g., 0.9860 Gold 0.1109 oz. AGW **Subject:** Stephen Bethlen **Obv:** Crowned Bethlen arms

Date	Mintage	VG	F	VF	XF	Unc
1630CV	—	825	1,750	3,700	5,300	10,500

KM# 224 DUCAT

3.5000 g., 0.9860 Gold 0.1109 oz. AGW **Obv:** Bust of George Rakoczi I with mace right in inner circle **Rev:** Crowned eagle with sword left, AQV ILA and seven towers below in inner circle

Date	Mintage	VG	F	VF	XF	Unc
MDCXXXI (1631)	—	650	1,050	2,050	3,900	7,750

KM# 225 DUCAT

3.5000 g., 0.9860 Gold 0.1109 oz. AGW **Rev:** Arabic date in legend **Note:** Varieties exist.

Date	Mintage	VG	F	VF	XF	Unc
1631	—	650	1,050	2,050	3,900	7,750
1632	—	650	1,050	2,050	3,900	7,750
1633	—	650	1,050	2,050	3,900	7,750
1635	—	650	1,050	2,050	3,900	7,750
1636	—	650	1,050	2,050	3,900	7,750
1637	—	650	1,050	2,050	3,900	7,750

KM# 238 DUCAT

3.5000 g., 0.9860 Gold 0.1109 oz. AGW

Date	Mintage	VG	F	VF	XF	Unc
1639	—	650	1,050	2,050	3,900	7,750

KM# 256 DUCAT

3.5000 g., 0.9860 Gold 0.1109 oz. AGW **Subject:** George Rakoczi I **Note:** Varieties exist.

Date	Mintage	VG	F	VF	XF	Unc
1645	—	650	1,050	2,050	3,900	7,750

KM# 261 DUCAT

3.5000 g., 0.9860 Gold 0.1109 oz. AGW **Note:** Varieties exist.

Date	Mintage	VG	F	VF	XF	Unc
1646	—	650	1,050	2,050	3,900	7,750

KM# 262 DUCAT

3.5000 g., 0.9860 Gold 0.1109 oz. AGW **Obv:** Fur hat with plume added **Note:** Varieties exist.

Date	Mintage	VG	F	VF	XF	Unc
1646	—	650	1,050	2,050	3,900	7,750
1648	—	650	1,050	2,050	3,900	7,750

KM# 266 DUCAT

3.5000 g., 0.9860 Gold 0.1109 oz. AGW **Obv:** Similar but bust divides lower legend

Date	Mintage	VG	F	VF	XF	Unc
1647NB	—	650	1,050	2,050	3,900	7,750

KM# 271 DUCAT

3.5000 g., 0.9860 Gold 0.1109 oz. AGW **Note:** Varieties exist.

Date	Mintage	VG	F	VF	XF	Unc
1648NB	—	650	1,050	2,050	3,900	7,750

KM# 272 DUCAT

3.5000 g., 0.9860 Gold 0.1109 oz. AGW

Date	Mintage	VG	F	VF	XF	Unc
1648NB	—	650	1,050	2,050	3,900	7,750

KM# 274 DUCAT

3.5000 g., 0.9860 Gold 0.1109 oz. AGW **Subject:** George Rakoczi II **Note:** Varieties exist.

Date	Mintage	VG	F	VF	XF	Unc
1649NB	—	650	1,050	2,050	3,900	7,750
1650NB	—	650	1,050	2,050	3,900	7,750
1651NB	—	650	1,050	2,050	3,900	7,750
1653NB	—	650	1,050	2,050	3,900	7,750
1654NB	—	650	1,050	2,050	3,900	7,750
1655NB	—	650	1,050	2,050	3,900	7,750
1656NB	—	650	1,050	2,050	3,900	7,750

KM# 298 DUCAT

3.5000 g., 0.9860 Gold 0.1109 oz. AGW

Date	Mintage	VG	F	VF	XF	Unc
1657NB	—	650	1,050	2,050	3,900	7,750

KM# 299 DUCAT

3.5000 g., 0.9860 Gold 0.1109 oz. AGW **Subject:** George Rakoczi II **Rev:** AZV-ILA and seven towers below

Date	Mintage	VG	F	VF	XF	Unc
1657	—	675	1,150	2,100	4,200	8,500

KM# A300 DUCAT

3.5000 g., 0.9860 Gold 0.1109 oz. AGW

Date	Mintage	VG	F	VF	XF	Unc
1657AI	—	500	950	2,050	3,700	7,250

KM# 300 DUCAT

3.5000 g., 0.9860 Gold 0.1109 oz. AGW **Note:** Hexagonal klippe.

Date	Mintage	VG	F	VF	XF	Unc
1657AI	—	950	1,750	3,450	5,300	10,500

KM# 315 DUCAT

3.5000 g., 0.9860 Gold 0.1109 oz. AGW **Obv:** Bust of Achatius Barcsai with fur hat holding scepter right in inner circle **Rev:** Crowned Triune arms in inner circle

Date	Mintage	VG	F	VF	XF	Unc
1659CV	—	1,050	2,100	4,450	10,000	20,000

KM# 316 DUCAT

3.5000 g., 0.9860 Gold 0.1109 oz. AGW **Obv:** Without fur hat

Date	Mintage	VG	F	VF	XF	Unc
1659 G	—	1,150	2,350	4,500	10,000	20,500

KM# 331 DUCAT

3.5000 g., 0.9860 Gold 0.1109 oz. AGW

Date	Mintage	VG	F	VF	XF	Unc
1660CIBI	—	825	1,650	3,450	5,300	10,500

KM# 349 DUCAT

3.5000 g., 0.9860 Gold 0.1109 oz. AGW **Obv. Legend:** IO KEMEN... **Rev:** Crowned arms **Shape:** Hexagon **Note:** Klippe.

Date	Mintage	VG	F	VF	XF	Unc
1661 Rare	—	—	—	—	—	—

KM# 350 DUCAT

3.5000 g., 0.9860 Gold 0.1109 oz. AGW **Note:** Round version of KM#349.

Date	Mintage	VG	F	VF	XF	Unc
1661	—	500	950	2,350	4,750	9,500

KM# 351 DUCAT

3.5000 g., 0.9860 Gold 0.1109 oz. AGW **Obv. Legend:** IOAN • KEM...

Date	Mintage	VG	F	VF	XF	Unc
1661	—	500	950	2,350	4,750	9,500

KM# 352 DUCAT

3.5000 g., 0.9860 Gold 0.1109 oz. AGW **Note:** Similar but reverse with oval center arms.

Date	Mintage	VG	F	VF	XF	Unc
1661	—	500	950	2,350	4,750	9,500

KM# 353 DUCAT

3.5000 g., 0.9860 Gold 0.1109 oz. AGW **Obv:** John Kemeny **Rev:** Crowned Triune arms

Date	Mintage	VG	F	VF	XF	Unc
1661	—	500	950	2,350	4,750	9,500

KM# 367 DUCAT

3.5000 g., 0.9860 Gold 0.1109 oz. AGW **Obv:** Armored bust of Michael Apafi with fur hat holding scepter right in inner circle **Rev:** Crowned Triune arms in cartouche in inner circle, date in legend

Date	Mintage	VG	F	VF	XF	Unc
1662	—	500	950	2,350	4,750	9,500
1663	—	500	950	2,350	4,750	9,500

KM# 368 DUCAT

3.5000 g., 0.9860 Gold 0.1109 oz. AGW **Shape:** Hexagon **Note:** Klippe.

Date	Mintage	VG	F	VF	XF	Unc
1662	—	400	800	1,650	3,700	7,250
1663	—	400	800	1,650	3,700	7,250

KM# 384 DUCAT

3.5000 g., 0.9860 Gold 0.1109 oz. AGW **Rev:** Triune arms

Date	Mintage	VG	F	VF	XF	Unc
1666AF	—	400	800	1,650	3,700	7,250

KM# 393 DUCAT

3.5000 g., 0.9860 Gold 0.1109 oz. AGW **Rev:** Triune arms with large Apafi shield

Date	Mintage	VG	F	VF	XF	Unc
1667	—	400	800	1,650	3,700	7,250

KM# 396 DUCAT

3.5000 g., 0.9860 Gold 0.1109 oz. AGW **Rev:** Triune arms with large Apafi shield, divided A-F in exergue of inner circle

Date	Mintage	VG	F	VF	XF	Unc
1668AF	—	400	800	1,650	3,700	7,250

KM# 397 DUCAT

3.5000 g., 0.9860 Gold 0.1109 oz. AGW **Shape:** Hexagon **Note:** Klippe.

Date	Mintage	VG	F	VF	XF	Unc
1668AF	—	1,750	3,000	5,000	10,000	—

KM# 452 DUCAT

3.5000 g., 0.9860 Gold 0.1109 oz. AGW **Rev:** Crowned Triune arms, A-F in exergue in inner circle, date in legend

Date	Mintage	VG	F	VF	XF	Unc
1673AF	—	525	1,000	2,100	4,200	8,500
1675AF	—	525	1,000	2,100	4,200	8,500
1676AF	—	525	1,000	2,100	4,200	8,500
1676AI	—	525	1,000	2,100	4,200	8,500
1677	—	525	1,000	2,100	4,200	8,500

KM# 476 DUCAT

3.5000 g., 0.9860 Gold 0.1109 oz. AGW **Note:** Varieties exist.

Date	Mintage	VG	F	VF	XF	Unc
1678AF	—	525	1,000	2,100	4,200	8,500
1680AF	—	525	1,000	2,100	4,200	8,500
1681AF	—	525	1,000	2,100	4,200	8,500
1682	—	525	1,000	2,100	4,200	8,500
1683	—	525	1,000	2,100	4,200	8,500

KM# 505 DUCAT

3.5000 g., 0.9860 Gold 0.1109 oz. AGW **Note:** Varieties exist.

Date	Mintage	VG	F	VF	XF	Unc
1684AF	—	525	1,000	2,100	4,200	8,500
1685	—	525	1,000	2,100	4,200	8,500
1686	—	525	1,000	2,100	4,200	8,500
1687AF	—	525	1,000	2,100	4,200	8,500
1687	—	525	1,000	2,100	4,200	8,500
1688	—	525	1,000	2,100	4,200	8,500
1689AF	—	525	1,000	2,100	4,200	8,500
1690	—	525	1,000	2,100	4,200	8,500

KM# 485 DUCAT

3.5000 g., 0.9860 Gold 0.1109 oz. AGW **Shape:** Hexagon **Note:** Klippe. Varieties exist.

Date	Mintage	VG	F	VF	XF	Unc
1684AF	—	1,750	3,000	6,000	11,000	—
1685	—	1,750	3,000	6,000	11,000	—
1687AF	—	1,750	3,000	6,000	11,000	—
1688	—	1,750	3,000	6,000	11,000	—
1689AF	—	1,750	3,000	6,000	11,000	—

M# 506 DUCAT
5000 g., 0.9860 Gold 0.1109 oz. AGW **Obv:** Emeric Tokely
ev: Triune arms, with helmet and lion crests in inner circle

te	Mintage	VG	F	VF	XF	Unc
90 Rare	—	—	—	—	—	—

M# 508 DUCAT
5000 g., 0.9860 Gold 0.1109 oz. AGW **Obv:** Titles of Leopold
Rev: Crowned arms of Transylvania

te	Mintage	VG	F	VF	XF	Unc
92	—	750	1,550	3,400	7,000	11,500

M# 509 DUCAT
5000 g., 0.9860 Gold 0.1109 oz. AGW **Subject:** Leopold I
ev: Crowned imperial eagle with Transylvania arms on breast
te: Varieties exist.

te	Mintage	VG	F	VF	XF	Unc
93CV	—	450	775	1,550	4,900	7,350
94CV	—	450	775	1,550	4,900	7,350
95KV	—	450	775	1,550	4,900	7,350
96KV	—	450	775	1,550	4,900	7,350
97KV	—	450	775	1,550	4,900	7,350
98KV	—	450	775	1,550	4,900	7,350
99KV	—	450	775	1,550	4,900	7,350
00KV	—	450	775	1,550	4,900	7,350

M# 515 DUCAT
5000 g., 0.9860 Gold 0.1109 oz. AGW **Shape:** Hexagon **Note:** ppe.

te	Mintage	VG	F	VF	XF	Unc
95	—	2,500	5,000	10,000	15,000	—

M# 522 DUCAT
5000 g., 0.9860 Gold 0.1109 oz. AGW **Shape:** Octagon **Note:** ppe.

te	Mintage	VG	F	VF	XF	Unc
99	—	2,500	5,000	10,000	15,000	—

M# 32 2 DUCAT
0000 g., 0.9860 Gold 0.2219 oz. AGW **Obv:** Stephan Bocskai
v: Bocskai arms **Note:** Struck from 1 Ducat dies.

te	Mintage	VG	F	VF	XF	Unc
06 Rare	—	—	—	—	—	—

M# 33 2 DUCAT
0000 g., 0.9860 Gold 0.2219 oz. AGW **Rev:** Crown above ossed swords

te	Mintage	VG	F	VF	XF	Unc
06H Rare	—	—	—	—	—	—

KM# 43 2 DUCAT
7.0000 g., 0.9860 Gold 0.2219 oz. AGW **Subject:** Sigismund Rakoczi

Date	Mintage	VG	F	VF	XF	Unc
1607CV Rare	—	—	—	—	—	—

KM# 75 2 DUCAT
7.0000 g., 0.9860 Gold 0.2219 oz. AGW **Obv:** Bust of Gabriel Bathori right with mace divides C-V in inner circle **Rev:** Crowned Bathori arms in dragon circle in inner circle, date in legend **Note:** Varieties exist.

Date	Mintage	VG	F	VF	XF	Unc
1610 Rare	—	—	—	—	—	—

KM# 91 2 DUCAT
7.0000 g., 0.9860 Gold 0.2219 oz. AGW **Obv:** Half-length armored bust **Note:** Varieties exist.

Date	Mintage	VG	F	VF	XF	Unc
1612 Rare	—	—	—	—	—	—

KM# 103 2 DUCAT
7.0000 g., 0.9860 Gold 0.2219 oz. AGW **Obv:** Gabriel Bethlen **Rev:** Crowned Bethel arms **Note:** Struck from 1 Ducat dies.

Date	Mintage	VG	F	VF	XF	Unc
1613 Rare	—	—	—	—	—	—
1615 Rare	—	—	—	—	—	—

KM# 194 2 DUCAT
7.0000 g., 0.9860 Gold 0.2219 oz. AGW **Obv:** Armored bust of Gabriel Bethlen **Rev:** Madonna and child in radiance

Date	Mintage	VG	F	VF	XF	Unc
1627 Rare	—	—	—	—	—	—
1628 Rare	—	—	—	—	—	—

KM# 229 2 DUCAT
7.0000 g., 0.9860 Gold 0.2219 oz. AGW **Obv:** Bust of George Rakoczi I in fur hat with plume right in inner circle **Rev:** Crowned eagle with sword left, AZV ILA and seven towers below in inner circle, Arabic date in legend

Date	Mintage	VG	F	VF	XF	Unc
1632 Rare	—	—	—	—	—	—

KM# 301 2 DUCAT
7.0000 g., 0.9860 Gold 0.2219 oz. AGW **Obv:** Half-length armored bust right **Rev:** Crowned arms

Date	Mintage	VG	F	VF	XF	Unc
1657AI Rare	—	—	—	—	—	—

KM# 317 2 DUCAT
7.0000 g., 0.9860 Gold 0.2219 oz. AGW **Obv:** Achativs Barcsai **Rev:** Crowned Triune arms **Note:** Struck from 1 Ducat dies.

Date	Mintage	VG	F	VF	XF	Unc
1659 Rare	—	—	—	—	—	—

KM# 318 2 DUCAT
7.0000 g., 0.9860 Gold 0.2219 oz. AGW **Obv:** Without fur hat

Date	Mintage	VG	F	VF	XF	Unc
1659 Rare	—	—	—	—	—	—

KM# 354 2 DUCAT
7.0000 g., 0.9860 Gold 0.2219 oz. AGW **Obv:** Bust of John Kemeny in fur hat with scepter right in inner circle **Note:** Struck from 1 Ducat dies.

Date	Mintage	VG	F	VF	XF	Unc
1661 Rare	—	—	—	—	—	—

KM# 355 2 DUCAT
7.0000 g., 0.9860 Gold 0.2219 oz. AGW **Shape:** Hexagonal **Note:** Klippe.

Date	Mintage	VG	F	VF	XF	Unc
1661 Rare	—	—	—	—	—	—

KM# 369 2 DUCAT
7.0000 g., 0.9860 Gold 0.2219 oz. AGW **Subject:** Michael Apafi **Shape:** Hexagon **Note:** Klippe. Struck from 1 Ducat dies. Varieties exist.

Date	Mintage	VG	F	VF	XF	Unc
1662	—	2,500	5,000	10,000	15,000	—
1668	—	2,500	5,000	10,000	15,000	—
1689	—	—	—	—	—	—

KM# 399 2 DUCAT
7.0000 g., 0.9860 Gold 0.2219 oz. AGW **Note:** 8-pointed star.

Date	Mintage	VG	F	VF	XF	Unc
1668 AF Rare	—	—	—	—	—	—

KM# 400 2 DUCAT
7.0000 g., 0.9860 Gold 0.2219 oz. AGW

Date	Mintage	VG	F	VF	XF	Unc
1668 AF	—	2,500	5,000	10,000	15,000	—

KM# 481 2 DUCAT
7.0000 g., 0.9860 Gold 0.2219 oz. AGW **Obv:** Half-length armored bust right with hat and scepter **Rev:** Crowned arms

Date	Mintage	VG	F	VF	XF	Unc
1682 AF	—	2,500	5,000	10,000	15,000	—

KM# 486 2 DUCAT
7.0000 g., 0.9860 Gold 0.2219 oz. AGW **Note:** Klippe.

Date	Mintage	VG	F	VF	XF	Unc
1684 AF	—	2,500	5,000	10,000	15,000	—

KM# 497 2 DUCAT
7.0000 g., 0.9860 Gold 0.2219 oz. AGW **Shape:** Hexagon **Note:** Klippe.

Date	Mintage	VG	F	VF	XF	Unc
1689 AF	—	2,500	5,000	10,000	15,000	—

KM# 516 2 DUCAT
7.0000 g., 0.9860 Gold 0.2219 oz. AGW **Obv:** Armored bust of Leopold I right in inner circle **Rev:** Crowned imperial eagle with Transylvania arms on breast, date divided at top **Shape:** Hexagon **Note:** Klippe. Struck from 1 Ducat dies.

Date	Mintage	VG	F	VF	XF	Unc
1695	—	1,250	2,800	6,000	10,500	—
1696	—	1,250	2,800	6,000	10,500	—

KM# 195 3 DUCAT
10.5000 g., 0.9860 Gold 0.3328 oz. AGW

Date	Mintage	VG	F	VF	XF	Unc
1627NB Rare	—	—	—	—	—	—

KM# 302 3 DUCAT
10.5000 g., 0.9860 Gold 0.3328 oz. AGW **Obv:** Bust right with hat and scepter **Rev:** Crowned eagle holding sword

Date	Mintage	VG	F	VF	XF	Unc
1657AI Rare	—	—	—	—	—	—

KM# 356 3 DUCAT
10.5000 g., 0.9860 Gold 0.3328 oz. AGW **Obv:** John Kemeny **Rev:** Crowned Triune arms **Note:** Struck from 1 Ducat dies.

Date	Mintage	VG	F	VF	XF	Unc
1661 Rare	—	—	—	—	—	—

KM# 376 3 DUCAT
10.5000 g., 0.9860 Gold 0.3328 oz. AGW **Obv:** Armored bust of Michael Apafi in fur hat iwth scepter right in inner circle **Rev:** Crowned Triune arms in cartouche in inner circle, date in legend **Note:** Struck from 1 Ducat dies. Klippe. Varieties exist.

Date	Mintage	VG	F	VF	XF	Unc
1663 Rare	—	—	—	—	—	—
1684 Rare	—	—	—	—	—	—

KM# 466 3 DUCAT
10.5000 g., 0.9860 Gold 0.3328 oz. AGW **Shape:** Star **Note:** Klippe.

Date	Mintage	VG	F	VF	XF	Unc
1677AF Rare	—	—	—	—	—	—

KM# 507 3 DUCAT
10.5000 g., 0.9860 Gold 0.3328 oz. AGW **Obv:** Half-length bust right **Rev:** Two lions above crowned arms

Date	Mintage	VG	F	VF	XF	Unc
1690 Rare	—	—	—	—	—	—

KM# 521 3 DUCAT
10.5000 g., 0.9860 Gold 0.3328 oz. AGW **Obv:** Laureate bust of Leopold I right in inner circle **Rev:** Crowned imperial eagle with Transylvanian arms on breast, date in legend **Note:** Varieties exist.

Date	Mintage	VG	F	VF	XF	Unc
1697 Rare	—	—	—	—	—	—
1698 Rare	—	—	—	—	—	—

KM# 196 4 DUCAT
14.0000 g., 0.9860 Gold 0.4438 oz. AGW **Obv:** Portrait right **Rev:** Crowned arms

Date	Mintage	VG	F	VF	XF	Unc
1627 NB Rare	—	—	—	—	—	—

KM# 382 4 DUCAT
14.0000 g., 0.9860 Gold 0.4438 oz. AGW **Obv:** Half-length bust right with hat and scepter **Rev:** Crowned arms, small Kronstadt arms at bottom

Date	Mintage	VG	F	VF	XF	Unc
1665	—	3,500	6,500	10,000	20,000	—

KM# B403 4 DUCAT
14.0000 g., 0.9860 Gold 0.4438 oz. AGW **Note:** Similar to 10 Ducat, KM#403.

Date	Mintage	VG	F	VF	XF	Unc
1668 AF	—	—	—	—	35,000	—

KM# 467 4 DUCAT
14.0000 g., 0.9860 Gold 0.4438 oz. AGW **Obv:** Bust right **Rev:** Crowned arms

Date	Mintage	VG	F	VF	XF	Unc
1677 CF Rare	—	—	—	—	—	—

KM# 477 4 DUCAT
14.0000 g., 0.9860 Gold 0.4438 oz. AGW **Subject:** Michael Apafi **Rev:** Crowned Triune arms **Shape:** 8-pointed star **Note:** Struck from 1 Ducat dies.

Date	Mintage	VG	F	VF	XF	Unc
1678 Rare	—	—	—	—	—	—

KM# 484 4 DUCAT
14.0000 g., 0.9860 Gold 0.4438 oz. AGW **Subject:** Emeric Tokely

Date	Mintage	VG	F	VF	XF	Unc
1683	—	2,500	5,000	10,000	16,000	—

KM# 484A 4 DUCAT
14.0000 g., 0.9860 Gold 0.4438 oz. AGW **Note:** Klippe.

Date	Mintage	VG	F	VF	XF	Unc
1683	—	4,000	7,500	15,000	20,000	—

KM# 498 4 DUCAT
14.0000 g., 0.9860 Gold 0.4438 oz. AGW **Obv:** Half-length bust of Apafi right **Rev:** Crowned arms

Date	Mintage	VG	F	VF	XF	Unc
1689 AF	—	4,500	7,700	15,500	22,000	—

KM# 520 4 DUCAT
14.0000 g., 0.9860 Gold 0.4438 oz. AGW **Subject:** Leopold I **Shape:** Hexagon **Note:** Klippe. Varieties exist.

Date	Mintage	VG	F	VF	XF	Unc
1696	—	2,000	6,000	10,000	25,000	—
1697	—	2,000	6,000	10,000	25,000	—
1698	—	2,000	6,000	10,000	25,000	—

KM# 34 5 DUCAT
17.0000 g., Gold **Obv:** Armored bust right with secpter **Rev:** Crowned arms

Date	Mintage	VG	F	VF	XF	Unc
1606 Rare	—	—	—	—	—	—

KM# 150 5 DUCAT
17.0000 g., Gold **Subject:** Gabriel Bethlen **Note:** Struck from Gulden dies.

Date	Mintage	VG	F	VF	XF	U
16ZZNB Rare	—	—	—	—	—	

KM# 226 5 DUCAT
17.0000 g., 0.9860 Gold 0.5389 oz. AGW **Subject:** George Rakoczi **Note:** Varieties exist.

Date	Mintage	VG	F	VF	XF	U
1631	—	5,500	9,500	14,500	24,000	
1637	—	5,500	9,500	14,500	24,000	
1639	—	5,500	9,500	14,500	24,000	

KM# 332 5 DUCAT
17.0000 g., 0.9860 Gold 0.5389 oz. AGW

Date	Mintage	VG	F	VF	XF	
1660 Rare	—	—	—	—	—	

KM# 333 5 DUCAT
17.0000 g., 0.9860 Gold 0.5389 oz. AGW **Note:** Round versi of KM#332.

Date	Mintage	VG	F	VF	XF	
1660 Rare	—	—	—	—	—	

KM# 357 5 DUCAT
17.0000 g., 0.9860 Gold 0.5389 oz. AGW **Obv:** Half-length armored portrait right **Rev:** Crowned arms

Date	Mintage	VG	F	VF	XF	
1661CV Rare	—	—	—	—	—	

M# 370 5 DUCAT
7.0000 g., 0.9860 Gold 0.5389 oz. AGW **Obv. Legend:** ICHA. APAFI-D • G • PR • TR

ate	Mintage	VG	F	VF	XF	Unc
362	—	3,250	6,000	10,000	19,000	—

M# 370A 5 DUCAT
7.0000 g., 0.9860 Gold 0.5389 oz. AGW **Obv. Legend:** + MI APA + D. G* - PRIN + TRA(N)

ate	Mintage	VG	F	VF	XF	Unc
363CV	—	3,250	6,000	10,000	19,000	—

M# 370B 5 DUCAT
7.0000 g., 0.9860 Gold 0.5389 oz. AGW **Obv. Legend:** *MI. PA. D: G*-PRIN. TRAN(S)*

ate	Mintage	VG	F	VF	XF	Unc
364CV	—	3,250	6,000	10,000	19,000	—

M# 370C 5 DUCAT
7.0000 g., 0.9860 Gold 0.5389 oz. AGW **Obv. Legend:** *MI. PA. D: G*-PRIN. TRAN(S)*

ate	Mintage	VG	F	VF	XF	Unc
365CV	—	3,250	6,000	10,000	19,000	—

M# 370D 5 DUCAT
7.0000 g., 0.9860 Gold 0.5389 oz. AGW **Obv. Legend:** MIC. PA. D. G. -PRIN. TRAN* **Note:** Varieties exist.

ate	Mintage	VG	F	VF	XF	Unc
366	—	3,250	6,000	10,000	19,000	—

M# 453 5 DUCAT
7.0000 g., 0.9860 Gold 0.5389 oz. AGW **Obv:** Half-length bust ght **Rev:** Crowned arms, small Kronstadt arms at bottom

ate	Mintage	VG	F	VF	XF	Unc
373	—	3,500	6,500	10,000	19,000	—

M# 468 5 DUCAT
7.0000 g., 0.9860 Gold 0.5389 oz. AGW **Rev:** Crowned arms, nall Fogarasch arms at bottom

ate	Mintage	VG	F	VF	XF	Unc
377CF	—	5,000	8,500	13,500	20,500	—

M# 494 5 DUCAT
7.0000 g., 0.9860 Gold 0.5389 oz. AGW **Rev:** Crowned arms

ate	Mintage	VG	F	VF	XF	Unc
387AI	—	5,000	8,500	13,500	20,500	—

M# 499 5 DUCAT
7.0000 g., 0.9860 Gold 0.5389 oz. AGW **Shape:** Hexagon **ote:** Klippe.

ate	Mintage	VG	F	VF	XF	Unc
389AI Rare	—	—	—	—	—	—

KM# 511 5 DUCAT
17.0000 g., 0.9860 Gold 0.5389 oz. AGW **Subject:** Leopold I **Obv:** Crowned imperial eagle with Transylvanian arms on breast

Date	Mintage	VG	F	VF	XF	Unc
1694	—	4,000	7,000	11,500	17,500	—

KM# 512 5 DUCAT
17.0000 g., 0.9860 Gold 0.5389 oz. AGW **Shape:** Octagon **Note:** Klippe.

Date	Mintage	VG	F	VF	XF	Unc
1694KV	—	6,500	11,000	22,000	40,000	—

KM# 104 6 DUCAT
21.0000 g., 0.9860 Gold 0.6657 oz. AGW **Obv:** Armored bust of Gabriel Bathori right in inner circle **Rev:** Displayed eagle with Bathori arms on breast in inner circle, date in legend **Note:** Struck from 1 Ducat dies.

Date	Mintage	VG	F	VF	XF	Unc
1613NB Rare	—	—	—	—	—	—

KM# 267 6 DUCAT
21.0000 g., 0.9860 Gold 0.6657 oz. AGW

Date	Mintage	VG	F	VF	XF	Unc
1647NB	—	6,500	10,500	16,500	23,500	—

KM# 402 6 DUCAT
21.0000 g., 0.9860 Gold 0.6657 oz. AGW **Subject:** Michael Apafi **Shape:** Hexagon **Note:** Klippe. Struck from 1 Ducat dies.

Date	Mintage	VG	F	VF	XF	Unc
1668AF Rare	—	—	—	—	—	—

KM# 469 6 DUCAT
21.0000 g., 0.9860 Gold 0.6657 oz. AGW **Obv:** Half-length bust right with hat and scepter **Rev:** Crowned arms **Shape:** Star **Note:** Klippe.

Date	Mintage	VG	F	VF	XF	Unc
1677AF Rare	—	—	—	—	—	—

KM# 493 6 DUCAT
21.0000 g., 0.9860 Gold 0.6657 oz. AGW **Obv:** Half-length armored bust right **Rev:** Crowned arms **Shape:** Hexagon **Note:** Klippe.

Date	Mintage	VG	F	VF	XF	Unc
1686AI Rare	—	—	—	—	—	—

KM# 290 7 DUCAT
24.5000 g., 0.9860 Gold 0.7766 oz. AGW **Subject:** George Rakoczi II

Date	Mintage	VG	F	VF	XF	Unc
1654	—	7,500	11,500	19,000	31,500	—

KM# 334 7 DUCAT
24.5000 g., 0.9860 Gold 0.7766 oz. AGW **Obv:** Crowned arms within legend **Rev:** Three-line inscription within double legend

Date	Mintage	VG	F	VF	XF	Unc
1660	—	6,000	9,000	14,500	21,500	—

KM# 92 8 DUCAT
0.9860 Gold **Obv:** Crown above three coats of arms **Rev:** Four-line inscription within legend

Date	Mintage	VG	F	VF	XF	Unc
1612 CIBIN Rare	—	—	—	—	—	—

KM# 335 9 DUCAT
0.9860 Gold **Obv:** Crowned arms within legend **Rev:** Legend within double legends **Rev. Legend:** DEVS PROVI • DEBIT •

Date	Mintage	VG	F	VF	XF	Unc
1660 Rare	—	—	—	—	—	—

KM# A371 9 DUCAT
0.9860 Gold **Subject:** Michael Apafi

Date	Mintage	VG	F	VF	XF	Unc
1662	—	5,000	8,500	14,000	25,000	—

KM# 7 10 DUCAT
35.0000 g., 0.9860 Gold 1.1095 oz. AGW

Date	Mintage	VG	F	VF	XF	Unc
1603	—	15,000	27,500	42,000	59,000	—

KM# 17 10 DUCAT
35.0000 g., 0.9860 Gold 1.1095 oz. AGW **Subject:** Stephan Bocskai

Date	Mintage	VG	F	VF	XF	Unc
1605 Rare	—	—	—	—	—	—

KM# 18 10 DUCAT
35.0000 g., 0.9860 Gold 1.1095 oz. AGW **Obv. Legend:** STE: BOCHKAY. D: G. HVNGA. TRAN...

Date	Mintage	VG	F	VF	XF	Unc
1605	—	4,500	7,250	12,500	22,000	—

KM# 19 10 DUCAT
35.0000 g., 0.9860 Gold 1.1095 oz. AGW **Obv. Legend:** STEPHANVS BOCHKAY. D: G...

Date	Mintage	VG	F	VF	XF	Unc
1605	—	4,250	7,250	12,500	22,000	—

KM# 35 10 DUCAT
35.0000 g., 0.9860 Gold 1.1095 oz. AGW

Date	Mintage	VG	F	VF	XF	Unc
1606HS Rare	—	—	—	—	—	—

KM# 36 10 DUCAT
35.0000 g., 0.9860 Gold 1.1095 oz. AGW

Date	Mintage	VG	F	VF	XF	Unc
1606 Rare	—	—	—	—	—	—

KM# 37 10 DUCAT
35.0000 g., 0.9860 Gold 1.1095 oz. AGW

Date	Mintage	VG	F	VF	XF	Unc
1606	—	7,500	12,500	20,000	30,000	—

KM# 44 10 DUCAT
35.0000 g., 0.9860 Gold 1.1095 oz. AGW **Subject:** Sigimund Rakoczi

Date	Mintage	VG	F	VF	XF	Unc
1607	—	6,500	10,500	19,000	31,500	—

KM# 63 10 DUCAT
35.0000 g., 0.9860 Gold 1.1095 oz. AGW **Obv:** Half-length armored bust right **Rev:** Crowned arms circled by dragon

Date	Mintage	VG	F	VF	XF	Unc
1609	—	6,500	10,500	19,000	31,500	—

KM# 86 10 DUCAT
35.0000 g., 0.9860 Gold 1.1095 oz. AGW

Date	Mintage	VG	F	VF	XF	Unc
1611CIBIN	—	8,500	14,500	24,000	40,500	—
1612CIBIN	—	8,500	14,500	24,000	40,500	—
1613CIBIN	—	8,500	14,500	24,000	40,500	—

KM# 105 10 DUCAT
35.0000 g., 0.9860 Gold 1.1095 oz. AGW

Date	Mintage	VG	F	VF	XF	Unc
1613CIBIN	—	8,500	14,500	24,000	40,500	—

M# 108 10 DUCAT
5.0000 g., 0.9860 Gold 1.1095 oz. AGW **Subject:** Gabriel ethlen

ate	Mintage	VG	F	VF	XF	Unc
516	—	6,000	8,500	14,500	25,000	—

M# 117 10 DUCAT
5.0000 g., 0.9860 Gold 1.1095 oz. AGW **Subject:** Gabriel ethlen **Rev:** Crowned Triune arms

ate	Mintage	VG	F	VF	XF	Unc
519	—	6,500	12,500	19,000	31,000	—

M# 129 10 DUCAT
5.0000 g., 0.9860 Gold 1.1095 oz. AGW

ate	Mintage	VG	F	VF	XF	Unc
520AI	—	6,000	12,500	20,500	33,000	—

KM# 141 10 DUCAT
35.0000 g., 0.9860 Gold 1.1095 oz. AGW **Subject:** Gabriel Bethlen **Obv. Legend:** ...• DAL • CR shield...

Date	Mintage	VG	F	VF	XF	Unc
1621	—	5,500	11,000	17,000	29,500	—

KM# 142 10 DUCAT
35.1000 g., 0.9860 Gold 1.1126 oz. AGW **Obv. Legend:** ...• DAL • CR shield...

Date	Mintage	VG	F	VF	XF	Unc
1621KB	—	6,000	12,000	18,500	40,000	—

KM# 151 10 DUCAT
35.1000 g., 0.9860 Gold 1.1126 oz. AGW

Date	Mintage	VG	F	VF	XF	Unc
16ZZNB	—	6,000	9,500	16,500	30,000	—

KM# 208 10 DUCAT
35.1000 g., 0.9860 Gold 1.1126 oz. AGW **Subject:** Gabriel Bethlen

Date	Mintage	VG	F	VF	XF	Unc
16Z8	—	5,000	8,500	13,500	25,000	—

KM# 209 10 DUCAT
35.1000 g., 0.9860 Gold 1.1126 oz. AGW **Obv:** Gabriel Bethlen

Date	Mintage	VG	F	VF	XF	Unc
16Z8NB	—	7,000	12,500	22,000	35,000	—

KM# 227 10 DUCAT
35.1000 g., 0.9860 Gold 1.1126 oz. AGW **Subject:** George Rakoczi

Date	Mintage	VG	F	VF	XF	Unc
1631 Rare	—	—	—	—	—	—

KM# 228 10 DUCAT
35.1000 g., 0.9860 Gold 1.1126 oz. AGW

Date	Mintage	VG	F	VF	XF	Unc
1631CV	—	7,000	10,000	18,000	30,000	—

KM# 232.1 10 DUCAT
35.1000 g., 0.9860 Gold 1.1126 oz. AGW **Subject:** George Rakoczi I **Rev. Legend:** ...ANNO*DOM 1636

Date	Mintage	VG	F	VF	XF	Unc
1636	—	8,000	13,500	25,000	40,000	—

KM# 232.2 10 DUCAT
35.1000 g., 0.9860 Gold 1.1126 oz. AGW **Rev. Legend:** ...ANNO * DO 1637

Date	Mintage	VG	F	VF	XF	Unc
1637CV	—	7,600	12,500	21,000	33,500	—

KM# 232.3 10 DUCAT
35.1000 g., 0.9860 Gold 1.1126 oz. AGW **Rev. Legend:** ...ANNO * DOMINI 1639

Date	Mintage	VG	F	VF	XF	Unc
1639CV	—	7,600	12,500	21,000	33,500	—

KM# 257 10 DUCAT
35.1000 g., 0.9860 Gold 1.1126 oz. AGW **Obv:** Half-length armored bust right **Rev:** Crowned arms

Date	Mintage	VG	F	VF	XF	Unc
1645NB	—	7,600	12,500	23,000	38,000	—

KM# 263 10 DUCAT
35.1000 g., 0.9860 Gold 1.1126 oz. AGW

Date	Mintage	VG	F	VF	XF	Unc
1646NB	—	7,600	12,500	23,000	38,000	—

KM# 268 10 DUCAT
35.1000 g., 0.9860 Gold 1.1126 oz. AGW **Obv:** Armored bust right **Rev:** Crowned arms

Date	Mintage	VG	F	VF	XF	Unc
1647NB	—	7,600	12,500	23,000	38,000	—

KM# 273 10 DUCAT
35.1000 g., 0.9860 Gold 1.1126 oz. AGW **Obv:** Armored bust right **Rev:** Crowned arms

Date	Mintage	VG	F	VF	XF	Unc
1648NB	—	7,600	12,500	23,000	38,000	—

KM# 275 10 DUCAT
35.1000 g., 0.9860 Gold 1.1126 oz. AGW **Obv:** Half-length armored bust right **Rev:** Crowned arms **Note:** Varieties exist.

Date	Mintage	VG	F	VF	XF	Unc
1649NB	—	5,500	9,000	18,000	27,500	—

KM# 284 10 DUCAT
35.1000 g., 0.9860 Gold 1.1126 oz. AGW

Date	Mintage	VG	F	VF	XF	Unc
1650NB	—	5,000	8,000	15,000	30,000	—
1651NB	—	5,000	8,000	15,000	30,000	—

KM# 287 10 DUCAT
35.1000 g., 0.9860 Gold 1.1126 oz. AGW **Obv. Legend:** • GEOR • RAKO... **Note:** Varieties exist.

Date	Mintage	VG	F	VF	XF	Unc
165Z	—	5,000	8,000	15,000	30,000	—
1653	—	5,000	8,000	15,000	30,000	—
1654	—	5,000	8,000	15,000	30,000	—
1655	—	5,000	8,000	15,000	30,000	—

KM# 295 10 DUCAT
35.1000 g., 0.9860 Gold 1.1126 oz. AGW

Date	Mintage	VG	F	VF	XF	Unc
1656NB	—	5,000	8,000	15,000	30,000	—

KM# 304 10 DUCAT
35.1000 g., 0.9860 Gold 1.1126 oz. AGW **Note:** 4-sided klipp

Date	Mintage	VG	F	VF	XF	Unc
1657AI Rare	—	—	—	—	—	—

KM# 303 10 DUCAT
35.1000 g., 0.9860 Gold 1.1126 oz. AGW **Note:** Hexagonal klippe.

Date	Mintage	VG	F	VF	XF	Unc
1657AI Rare	—	—	—	—	—	—

M# 305 10 DUCAT

.1000 g., 0.9860 Gold 1.1126 oz. AGW **Note:** Round version KM#303.

te	Mintage	VG	F	VF	XF	Unc
57AI	—	6,000	9,000	14,500	25,000	—

M# 312 10 DUCAT

.1000 g., 0.9860 Gold 1.1126 oz. AGW **Obv:** Bust right **Rev:** owned arms

te	Mintage	VG	F	VF	XF	Unc
58NB	—	6,000	9,000	14,500	25,000	—
59NB	—	6,000	9,000	14,500	25,000	—

M# 322 10 DUCAT

.1000 g., 0.9860 Gold 1.1126 oz. AGW

te	Mintage	VG	F	VF	XF	Unc
59CV	—	6,500	10,000	17,000	27,500	—
60CV	—	6,500	10,000	17,000	27,500	—

M# 323 10 DUCAT

.1000 g., 0.9860 Gold 1.1126 oz. AGW **Note:** Hexagonal ppe of KM#322.

te	Mintage	VG	F	VF	XF	Unc
59CV	—	8,000	13,500	25,000	40,000	—
59CV Restrike	—	—	—	16,000	21,000	—

KM# 340 10 DUCAT

35.1000 g., 0.9860 Gold 1.1126 oz. AGW **Note:** Varieties exist.

Date	Mintage	VG	F	VF	XF	Unc
1660CB	—	11,000	17,000	31,000	47,000	—

KM# 338 10 DUCAT

35.1000 g., 0.9860 Gold 1.1126 oz. AGW **Note:** Round version of KM#336.

Date	Mintage	VG	F	VF	XF	Unc
1660CV	—	5,900	10,000	17,000	25,000	—

KM# 343 10 DUCAT

35.1000 g., 0.9860 Gold 1.1126 oz. AGW **Note:** Round version of KM#342.

Date	Mintage	VG	F	VF	XF	Unc
1660	—	6,700	11,000	18,500	30,000	—

KM# 337 10 DUCAT

35.1000 g., 0.9860 Gold 1.1126 oz. AGW **Note:** Klippe with rounded corners.

Date	Mintage	VG	F	VF	XF	Unc
1660CV Rare	—	—	—	—	—	—

KM# 339 10 DUCAT

35.1000 g., 0.9860 Gold 1.1126 oz. AGW

Date	Mintage	VG	F	VF	XF	Unc
1660	—	6,500	12,000	20,000	35,000	—

KM# 341 10 DUCAT

35.1000 g., 0.9860 Gold 1.1126 oz. AGW

Date	Mintage	VG	F	VF	XF	Unc
1660CB	—	7,000	12,500	20,500	35,000	—

KM# 342 10 DUCAT

35.1000 g., 0.9860 Gold 1.1126 oz. AGW

Date	Mintage	VG	F	VF	XF	Unc
1660 Rare	—	—	—	—	—	—

KM# 336 10 DUCAT

35.1000 g., 0.9860 Gold 1.1126 oz. AGW

Date	Mintage	VG	F	VF	XF	Unc
1660CV Rare	—	—	—	—	—	—

KM# 358 10 DUCAT

35.1000 g., 0.9860 Gold 1.1126 oz. AGW **Note:** Varieties exist.

Date	Mintage	VG	F	VF	XF	Unc
1661CV	—	8,400	13,000	23,000	38,000	—

KM# 371 10 DUCAT

35.1000 g., 0.9860 Gold 1.1126 oz. AGW

Date	Mintage	VG	F	VF	XF	Unc
1662	—	7,000	10,000	18,000	35,000	—
1663	—	7,000	10,000	18,000	35,000	—

KM# 373 10 DUCAT

35.1000 g., 0.9860 Gold 1.1126 oz. AGW **Obv:** Half-length armored bust right **Rev:** Crowned arms above small Kronstadt arms

Date	Mintage	VG	F	VF	XF	Unc
1662CB	—	7,000	10,000	18,000	35,000	—
1663CV	—	7,000	10,000	18,000	35,000	—

KM# 372 10 DUCAT

35.1000 g., 0.9860 Gold 1.1126 oz. AGW **Note:** 4-sided klippe. 44 x 44mm.

Date	Mintage	VG	F	VF	XF	Unc
1662	—	7,000	10,000	18,000	35,000	—

KM# 380 10 DUCAT

35.1000 g., 0.9860 Gold 1.1126 oz. AGW **Obv:** Half-length bust right **Rev:** Crowned arms

Date	Mintage	VG	F	VF	XF	Unc
1664CB	—	7,000	10,000	18,000	35,000	—
1665CB	—	7,000	10,000	18,000	35,000	—

KM# 381 10 DUCAT

35.1000 g., 0.9860 Gold 1.1126 oz. AGW

Date	Mintage	VG	F	VF	XF	Unc
1664SB	—	7,000	10,000	18,000	35,000	—

KM# 385 10 DUCAT

35.1000 g., 0.9860 Gold 1.1126 oz. AGW **Subject:** Michael Apafi **Note:** Struck at Kronstadt.

Date	Mintage	VG	F	VF	XF	Unc
1666	—	8,000	12,000	22,000	40,000	—

KM# 394 10 DUCAT

35.1000 g., 0.9860 Gold 1.1126 oz. AGW

Date	Mintage	VG	F	VF	XF	Unc
1667KV	—	8,000	12,000	22,000	40,000	—

KM# 403 10 DUCAT

35.1000 g., 0.9860 Gold 1.1126 oz. AGW **Note:** Round versi of KM#A403.

Date	Mintage	VG	F	VF	XF	U
1668AF	—	7,200	12,000	17,000	27,000	
1669AF	—	7,200	12,000	17,000	27,000	
1670AF	—	7,200	12,000	17,000	27,000	
1671AF	—	7,200	12,000	17,000	27,000	

KM# A403 10 DUCAT

35.1000 g., 0.9860 Gold 1.1126 oz. AGW **Obv. Legend:** MICHAEL. APAFI. D. G... **Shape:** Hexagon **Note:** Klippe.

Date	Mintage	VG	F	VF	XF	U
1668AF	—	—	—	8,000	12,500	

Note: Believed to be a later strike

KM# A416 10 DUCAT

35.1000 g., 0.9860 Gold 1.1126 oz. AGW **Obv. Legend:** MIC • APAFI - D. G. P. T.

Date	Mintage	VG	F	VF	XF	U
1671	—	6,000	9,500	17,000	27,500	

M# 416 10 DUCAT

5.1000 g., 0.9860 Gold 1.1126 oz. AGW

ate	Mintage	VG	F	VF	XF	Unc
571 CT	—	6,000	9,500	17,000	27,500	—

M# 433 10 DUCAT

5.1000 g., 0.9860 Gold 1.1126 oz. AGW **Note:** Varieties exist.

ate	Mintage	VG	F	VF	XF	Unc
572CIBI	—	7,800	12,500	18,000	30,000	—

M# 454 10 DUCAT

5.1000 g., 0.9860 Gold 1.1126 oz. AGW **Obv. Legend:** ICHA. APAFI-DG • PR • TR

ate	Mintage	VG	F	VF	XF	Unc
673AC	—	5,000	8,000	14,000	27,500	—
673	—	5,000	8,000	14,000	27,500	—
674	—	5,000	8,000	14,000	27,500	—

KM# 462 10 DUCAT

35.1000 g., 0.9860 Gold 1.1126 oz. AGW **Obv. Legend:** *MICHA: APAFI-D. G: PR • TR*

Date	Mintage	VG	F	VF	XF	Unc
1675 AF Rare	—	—	—	—	—	—

KM# 463 10 DUCAT

35.1000 g., 0.9860 Gold 1.1126 oz. AGW **Obv. Legend:** MICH • APAFI - D.G. P. T. **Note:** Varieties exist.

Date	Mintage	VG	F	VF	XF	Unc
1675 AF	—	5,600	8,500	14,000	24,000	—

KM# 471 10 DUCAT

35.1000 g., 0.9860 Gold 1.1126 oz. AGW **Note:** Round version of KM#470.

Date	Mintage	VG	F	VF	XF	Unc
1677AI	—	5,600	8,500	14,000	24,000	—
1678AI	—	5,600	8,500	14,000	24,000	—
1679AI	—	5,600	8,500	14,000	24,000	—
1680AI	—	5,600	8,500	14,000	24,000	—

KM# 470 10 DUCAT

35.1000 g., 0.9860 Gold 1.1126 oz. AGW **Shape:** Hexagon **Note:** Klippe.

Date	Mintage	VG	F	VF	XF	Unc
1677AI Rare	—	—	—	—	—	—

KM# 480 10 DUCAT

35.1000 g., 0.9860 Gold 1.1126 oz. AGW

Date	Mintage	VG	F	VF	XF	Unc
1681AI	—	5,900	8,900	14,500	25,000	—
1683AI	—	5,900	8,900	14,500	25,000	—

KM# 487 10 DUCAT

35.1000 g., 0.9860 Gold 1.1126 oz. AGW **Subject:** Emeric Tokely

Date	Mintage	VG	F	VF	XF	Unc
1683	—	14,000	23,000	40,000	65,000	—

KM# 488 10 DUCAT
35.1000 g., 0.9860 Gold 1.1126 oz. AGW **Shape:** Hexagon **Note:** Klippe.

Date	Mintage	VG	F	VF	XF	Unc
1684AI	—	8,400	13,500	25,000	35,000	—
1689AF	—	8,400	13,500	25,000	35,000	—

KM# 489 10 DUCAT
35.1000 g., 0.9860 Gold 1.1126 oz. AGW **Note:** Round version of KM#488.

Date	Mintage	VG	F	VF	XF	Unc
1684AI	—	4,900	7,000	11,500	23,000	—
1686AI	—	4,900	7,000	11,500	23,000	—
1687AI	—	4,900	7,000	11,500	23,000	—
1689AF	—	4,900	7,000	11,500	23,000	—

KM# 523 10 DUCAT
35.1000 g., 0.9860 Gold 1.1126 oz. AGW **Obv:** Bust of Leopold I **Rev:** Crowned imperial eagle

Date	Mintage	VG	F	VF	XF	Unc
1694 Rare	—	—	—	—	—	—

KM# 517 10 DUCAT
34.3400 g., 0.9860 Gold 1.0886 oz. AGW **Subject:** Leopold I **Note:** Struck from 1 Thaler dies, KM#510.

Date	Mintage	VG	F	VF	XF	Unc
1695	—	9,500	14,500	22,000	35,000	—
1696	—	9,500	14,500	22,000	35,000	—

KM# 306 12 DUCAT
42.0000 g., 0.9860 Gold 1.3314 oz. AGW **Obv:** Armored bust right with hat and scepter **Rev:** Crowned arms **Note:** Klippe.

Date	Mintage	VG	F	VF	XF	Unc
1657AI Rare	—	—	—	—	—	—

KM# 307 13 DUCAT
45.5000 g., 0.9860 Gold 1.4423 oz. AGW **Obv:** Armored bust right with hat and scepter **Rev:** Crowned arms **Note:** Klippe.

Date	Mintage	VG	F	VF	XF	Unc
1657AI Rare	—	—	—	—	—	—

KM# A227 20 DUCAT
70.0000 g., 0.9860 Gold 2.2190 oz. AGW **Subject:** George Rakoczi I **Note:** Klippe.

Date	Mintage	VG	F	VF	XF	Unc
1631	—	—	—	6,500	12,000	—

Note: Believed to be a later strike as the 20 Ducat weight is uncommon to Transylvanian coinage

KM# 287A 20 DUCAT
70.0000 g., 0.9860 Gold 2.2190 oz. AGW **Subject:** George Rakoczi II

Date	Mintage	VG	F	VF	XF	Ur
1652NB	—	—	—	8,000	13,000	-

Note: Believed to be a later strike as the 20 Ducat weigh is uncommon to Transylvanian coinage

KM# 308 25 DUCAT
87.5000 g., 0.9860 Gold 2.7737 oz. AGW **Note:** Round versio of 12 Ducat, KM#306.

Date	Mintage	VG	F	VF	XF	Ur
1657AI Rare	—	—	—	—	—	-

KM# 472 50 DUCAT
175.0000 g., 0.9860 Gold 5.5474 oz. AGW **Note:** Similar to 10 Ducat, KM#473.

Date	Mintage	VG	F	VF	XF	Ur
1677AF Rare	—	—	—	—	—	-

KM# 473 100 DUCAT
350.0000 g., 0.9860 Gold 11.094 oz. AGW, 83 mm. **Subject:** Michael Apafi **Note:** Illustration reduced.

Date	Mintage	VG	F	VF	XF	Un
1677AF Rare	—	—	—	—	—	-

PATTERNS

Inlcuding off metal strikes

KM#	Date	Mintage	Identification	Mkt V
Pn1	1606	—	6 Groschen. Gold. 14.0000 g. 4 Ducat.	-
Pn2	1610	—	Groschen. Gold. Broad. 4 Ducat.	-
Pn3	1610	—	Groschen. Gold. Broad. 5 Ducat.	-
Pn4	1620	—	Groschen. Copper. KM#122.	22
Pn5	1630	—	Ducat. Silver. 9.0000 g.	26
Pn6	1657AI	—	10 Ducat. Silver Gilt. 34.5000 g. KM#305.	-
Pn7	1668	—	Zwolfer. Silver. 1.4000 g. 1 Ducat.	-
Pn8	1677	—	100 Ducat. Silver. 90.8000 g. KM#473.	-
Pn9	1692	—	Ducat. Silver. Leopold I	20

HERMANNSTADT

ɹermanstadt (Sibiu), a city located 220 miles northwest of ucharest, north of the Transylvanian Alps. Originally a Roman olony, refounded by Saxon settlers in the 12th century, became nperial in 1699.

Occupied by imperial troops - Occupation issues in the name Rudolph II.

INT

T - Hermannstadt

INTMASTER'S INITIALS

itial	Date	Name
Crowned AHR monogram	1605	Albertus Hutter

CITY

SIEGE COINAGE

1612-1614

M# 1 GULDEN

.0000 g., Silver **Note:** Similar to 1 Thaler, KM#2.2.

ate	Mintage	VG	F	VF	XF	Unc
05 H	—	1,000	1,800	2,500	3,600	—

M# 2.2 THALER

3.5000 g., Silver **Rev:** Legend with rosette **Rev. Legend:** .ANO 1605

ate	Mintage	VG	F	VF	XF	Unc
605 H	—	1,500	2,500	4,000	8,000	—

M# 2.3 THALER

3.5000 g., Silver **Rev:** Legend with Maltese cross **Rev. egend:** ...ANO 1605

ate	Mintage	VG	F	VF	XF	Unc
05 H	—	1,500	2,500	3,750	7,500	—

M# 2.4 THALER

3.5000 g., Silver **Rev:** Legend with Maltese cross **Rev. egend:** ...ANNO 1605

ate	Mintage	VG	F	VF	XF	Unc
605 H	—	1,700	2,800	4,500	8,500	—

M# 2.5 THALER

3.5000 g., Silver **Rev:** Legend with pointed cross **Rev. Legend:** .ANNO 1605

ate	Mintage	VG	F	VF	XF	Unc
605 H	—	1,500	2,500	3,750	7,500	—

M# 2.1 THALER

3.5000 g., Silver **Obv:** Crowned imperial eagle, titles of Rudolf **Rev:** Crowned swords, legend with rosettes **Rev. Legend:** .ANNO 1605 **Note:** Dav. #4688.

ate	Mintage	VG	F	VF	XF	Unc
605 H	—	1,500	2,500	3,750	7,500	—

M# 3 1-1/2 THALER

ilver **Note:** Similar to 1 Thaler, KM#2.2. Dav. #4687.

ate	Mintage	VG	F	VF	XF	Unc
605 H Rare	—	—	—	—	—	—

KM# 4 2 THALER

57.0000 g., Silver **Note:** Similar to 1 Thaler, KM#2.2. Dav. #4686.

Date	Mintage	VG	F	VF	XF	Unc
1605 H Rare	—	—	—	—	—	—

KM# 5 DUCAT

3.5000 g., 0.9860 Gold 0.1109 oz. AGW **Obv:** Crowned swords **Rev:** Crowned imperial eagle, titles of Rudolf II **Note:** Fr. #304.

Date	Mintage	VG	F	VF	XF	Unc
1605 H	—	—	5,500	9,500	15,000	—

KM# 6.1 5 DUCAT

17.5000 g., 0.9860 Gold 0.5547 oz. AGW **Rev:** Legend wtih Maltese cross **Rev. Legend:** ...ANNO 1605 **Note:** Similar to 10 Ducats, KM#8.1. Fr. #303.

Date	Mintage	VG	F	VF	XF	Unc
1605 H Rare	—	—	—	—	—	—

KM# 7.2 5 DUCAT

17.5000 g., 0.9860 Gold 0.5547 oz. AGW **Rev:** Legend wtih rosette **Rev. Legend:** ...ANO 1605 **Note:** Similar to 10 Ducats, KM#8.2.

Date	Mintage	VG	F	VF	XF	Unc
1605 H Rare	—	—	—	—	—	—

KM# 8.1 10 DUCAT

35.0000 g., 0.9860 Gold 1.1095 oz. AGW **Obv:** Legend with Maltese cross **Obv. Legend:** ...ANNO 1605 **Rev:** Crowned imperial eagle, titles of Rudolf II **Note:** Fr. #302.

Date	Mintage	VG	F	VF	XF	Unc
1605 H Rare	—	—	—	—	—	—

KM# 8.2 10 DUCAT

35.0000 g., 0.9860 Gold 1.1095 oz. AGW **Obv:** Legend wtih rosette **Obv. Legend:** ...ANO 1605 **Rev:** Crowned imperial eagle **Note:** Fr. #302.

Date	Mintage	VG	F	VF	XF	Unc
1605 H Rare	—	—	—	—	—	—
1605 H Restrike	—	—	—	—	10,000	—

KRONSTADT

Brasov, Brasso

A city located in the foothills of the Transylvanian Alps founded by the Teutonic Order in 1211AD. A leader in Reformation in Transylvania in the 16th century.

Issues of 1601

Struck in support of Sigismund Bathori.

CITY

STANDARD COINAGE

KM# 5 GULDEN

14.1000 g., Silver **Note:** Similar to 1 Thaler, KM#6. Klippe. 36 x 35 millimeters.

Date	Mintage	VG	F	VF	XF	Unc
1601 Rare	—	—	—	—	—	—

KM# 6 THALER

Silver **Obv. Legend:** SIGIS. TRA. NS. ET... **Note:** Dav. #4682. Square klippe. Size varies: 33-38 millimeters. Weight varies: 27.60-28.40 grams.

Date	Mintage	VG	F	VF	XF	Unc
1601	—	1,200	2,500	5,000	12,500	—

KM# 7 THALER

Silver **Note:** Dav. #4682A. Thick flan, smaller dies. Weight varies: 27.60-28.40 grams.

Date	Mintage	VG	F	VF	XF	Unc
1601	—	1,200	2,500	5,000	12,500	—

KM# 11 2 THALER

57.2000 g., Silver **Note:** Dav. #4681. Similar to 1 Thaler, KM#6. 39x38 millimeters.

Date	Mintage	VG	F	VF	XF	Unc
1601 Rare	—	—	—	—	—	—

SIEGE COINAGE

1612-1614

KM# 17 GULDEN

15.8000 g., Silver **Note:** Similar to 1 Thaler, KM#18.

Date	Mintage	VG	F	VF	XF	Unc
161ZCB	—	—	—	—	—	—

KM# 18 THALER

28.7000 g., Silver **Obv:** City arms **Obv. Legend:** NOS IN NOM: DOM... **Rev. Legend:** • ILLE • INEQVIS ET **Note:** Dav. #4684.

Date	Mintage	VG	F	VF	XF	Unc
1612CB	—	1,250	2,200	4,500	10,000	—

KM# 21 2 THALER
56.0000 g., Silver, 45 mm.

Date	Mintage	VG	F	VF	XF	Unc
161ZCB	—	1,500	2,500	5,000	12,500	—

KM# 20 2 THALER
56.5000 g., Silver, 40 mm. **Note:** Dav. #4683. Round version of KM#19.

Date	Mintage	VG	F	VF	XF	Unc
161ZCB	—	1,500	2,500	5,000	12,500	—

KM# 19 2 THALER
57.5000 g., Silver **Note:** Dav. #4683A. Similar to 1 Thaler, KM#18. 45x45mm Hexagonal klippe.

Date	Mintage	VG	F	VF	XF	Unc
161ZCB Rare	—	—	—	—	—	—

KM# 15 GROSCHEN
1.5000 g., Silver **Obv:** Crowned city arms **Rev:** Crowned heraldic eagle

Date	Mintage	VG	F	VF	XF	Unc
161Z	—	175	350	650	1,000	—
161ZCB	—	175	350	650	1,000	—

KM# 16 GROSCHEN
1.5000 g., Silver **Rev:** Heraldic eagle without crown

Date	Mintage	VG	F	VF	XF	Unc
161Z	—	175	350	650	1,000	—

KM# 25 GROSCHEN
1.5000 g., Silver **Rev:** Non-heraldic eagle

Date	Mintage	VG	F	VF	XF	Unc
1613	—	175	350	650	1,000	—
1613CB	—	175	350	650	1,000	—
1614CB	—	175	350	650	1,000	—

KM# 29 GROSCHEN
1.5000 g., Silver **Rev:** P on shield

Date	Mintage	VG	F	VF	XF	Unc
1613	—	175	350	650	1,000	—

KM# 30 GROSCHEN
1.5000 g., Silver **Rev:** Uncrowned heraldic eagle with S on shield

Date	Mintage	VG	F	VF	XF	Unc
1613	—	175	350	650	1,000	—

KM# 31 GROSCHEN
1.5000 g., Silver **Rev:** Crowned heraldic eagle with dot on shield

Date	Mintage	VG	F	VF	XF	Unc
1613	—	175	350	650	1,000	—
1613CB	—	175	350	650	1,000	—
1614C	—	175	350	650	1,000	—

KM# 27 GROSCHEN
1.5000 g., Silver **Rev:** Crowned heraldic eagle with empty heart-shaped shield

Date	Mintage	VG	F	VF	XF	Unc
1613	—	175	350	650	1,000	—

KM# 28 GROSCHEN
1.5000 g., Silver **Rev:** H on shield

Date	Mintage	VG	F	VF	XF	Unc
1613	—	175	350	650	1,000	—
1613CB	—	175	350	650	1,000	—

KM# 26 GROSCHEN
1.5000 g., Silver **Rev:** Crowned heraldic eagle with S on shield

Date	Mintage	VG	F	VF	XF	Unc
1613	—	175	350	650	1,000	—
1613B	—	175	350	650	1,000	—
1613CB	—	175	350	650	1,000	—
1613C	—	175	350	650	1,000	—

KM# 31a GROSCHEN
Copper

Date	Mintage	VG	F	VF	XF	Unc
1614C	—	—	—	—	—	—

KM# 33 GROSCHEN
Silver **Note:** Klippe of KM#31.

Date	Mintage	VG	F	VF	XF	Unc
1614CB Rare	—	—	—	—	—	—

KM# 34 GROSCHEN
Silver Plated Copper **Rev:** Heraldic eagle with S on shield

Date	Mintage	VG	F	VF	XF	Unc
1615CB 5 an inverted 2	—	350	750	1,250	2,250	—

TRADE COINAGE

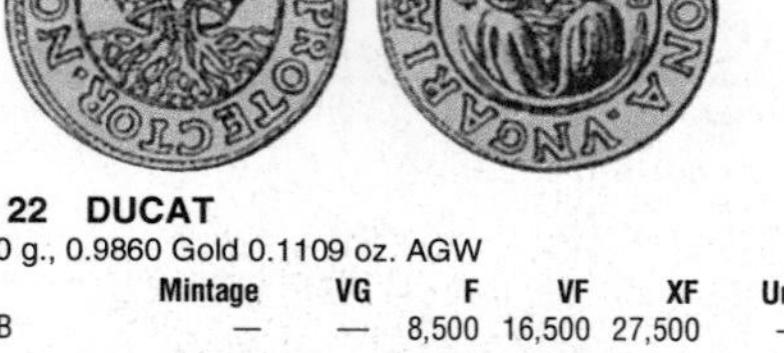

KM# 22 DUCAT
3.5000 g., 0.9860 Gold 0.1109 oz. AGW

Date	Mintage	VG	F	VF	XF	Unc
161ZCB	—	—	8,500	16,500	27,500	—

KM# 32 DUCAT
3.5000 g., 0.9860 Gold 0.1109 oz. AGW

Date	Mintage	VG	F	VF	XF	Unc
1613CB	—	—	8,500	16,500	27,500	—

KM# 23 10 DUCATS
34.8000 g., Gold **Note:** Struck with 1 Thaler dies, KM#18.

Date	Mintage	VG	F	VF	XF	Un
161ZCB Rare	—	—	—	—	—	-

PROVAS

KM#	Date	Mintage	Identification	Mkt V
Pr1	1612CB	—	10 Ducats. Gold. 59.7000 g. Klippe. KM#23. 45x45 millimeters.	-

TUNISIA

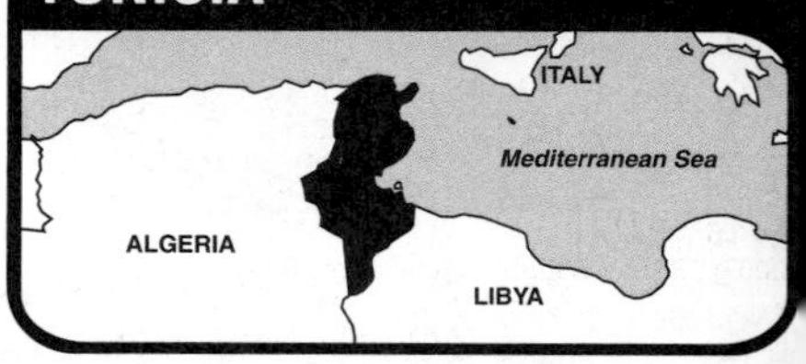

The Republic of Tunisia, located on the northern coast o Africa between Algeria and Libya, has an area of 63,170 sq. mi (163,610 sq. km.) and a population of *7.9 million. Capital: Tunis Agriculture is the backbone of the economy. Crude oil, phos phates, olive oil, and wine are exported.

Tunisia, settled by the Phoenicians in the 12th century B.C. was the center of the seafaring Carthaginian Empire. After th total destruction of Carthage, Tunisia became part of Rome's African province. It remained a part of the Roman Empire (excep for the 439-533 interval of Vandal conquest) until taken by the Arabs, 648, who administered it until the Turkish invasion o 1570. Under Turkish control, the public revenue was heavil dependent upon the piracy of Mediterranean shipping, a endeavor that wasn't abandoned until 1819 when a coalition o powers threatened appropriate reprisal. Deprived of its majo source of income, Tunisia underwent a financial regression tha ended in bankruptcy, enabling France to establish a protectorat over the country in 1881.

TUNIS

Tunis, the capital and major seaport of Tunisia, existed in th Carthaginian era, but its importance dates only from the Mosler conquest, following which it became a major center of Arab powe and prosperity. Spain seized it in 1535, lost it in 1564, retook it i 1573 and ceded it to the Turks in 1574. Thereafter the history o Tunis merged with that of Tunisia.

RULER
Ottoman, until 1881

MINT

تونس

Tunis

With exceptions noted in their proper place, all coins wer struck at Tunis prior to AH1308/1891AD. Thereafter, all coin were struck at Paris with mint mark A until 1928, symbols of th mint from 1929-1957.

MONETARY SYSTEM

Until 1891
6 Burben (Bourbine) = 1 Burbe (Bourbe)
2 Burbe (Bourbe) = 1 Nasri
13 Burbe = 1 Kharub (Caroub)
16 Kharub (Caroub) = 1 Piastre (Rial Sebili)

Arabic name	French name	Value
Qafsi of Falls Raqiq	Bourbine	1/12 Nasri
Fals	Bourbe	6 Qafsi or 1/2 Nasri
Nasri	Asper	1/52 Riyal
Kharub	Caroub	1/16 Riyal
1/8 Riyal	1/8 Piastre	1 Kharub
1/4 Riyal	1/4 Piastre	4 Kharub
1/2 Riyal	1/2 Piastre	8 Kharub
Riyal	Piastre	16 Kharub

Ahmed I

AH1012-1026/1603-1617AD

HAMMERED COINAGE

M# 5 DIRHAM

5200 g., Silver **Mint:** Tunis **Note:** Square; 12.5 x 12.5 mm.

te	Mintage	VG	F	VF	XF	Unc
(1603-17)	—	18.00	45.00	80.00	120	—

M# 7 SULTANI

5000 g., Gold, 19 mm. **Mint:** Tunis

te	Mintage	VG	F	VF	XF	Unc
1013	—	700	1,200	2,000	3,000	—
1015 Rare	—	—	—	—	—	—

Mustafa I

AH1031-1032/1622-1623AD

HAMMERED COINAGE

M# 10 BURBE

9000 g., Copper **Mint:** Tunis

te	Mintage	Good	VG	F	VF	XF
1031	—	35.00	50.00	75.00	100	—

Murad IV

AH1032-1049/1623-1640AD

HAMMERED COINAGE

M# 15 BURBE

0100 g., Copper **Mint:** Tunis

te	Mintage	Good	VG	F	VF	XF
1033	—	20.00	30.00	50.00	70.00	—
1049	—	—	—	—	—	—

M# 16 NASRI

3000 g., Silver **Shape:** Square **Mint:** Tunis

te	Mintage	Good	VG	F	VF	XF
1033	—	30.00	40.00	80.00	150	—

Ibrahim

AH1049-1058/1640-1648AD

HAMMERED COINAGE

M# 17 BURBE

0000 g., Copper **Mint:** Tunis

te	Mintage	Good	VG	F	VF	XF
(10)49	—	15.00	25.00	40.00	60.00	—

M# A17 NASRI

7500 g., Silver **Shape:** Square **Mint:** Tunis

te	Mintage	VG	F	VF	XF	Unc
1049	—	—	—	—	—	—

KM# 18 SULTANI

3.6700 g., Gold **Mint:** Tunis

Date	Mintage	VG	F	VF	XF	Unc
AH1049	—	225	375	550	800	—

Mehmed IV

AH1058-1099/1648-1687AD

HAMMERED COINAGE

KM# 22 3 BURBEN

Copper **Mint:** Tunis

Date	Mintage	Good	VG	F	VF	XF
AH1058	—	10.00	20.00	30.00	50.00	—
AH1060	—	2.50	7.50	20.00	40.00	—
AH1066	—	10.00	20.00	30.00	50.00	—
AH1067	—	10.00	20.00	30.00	50.00	—
AH1068	—	2.50	7.50	20.00	40.00	—
AH1080	—	10.00	20.00	30.00	50.00	—
AH1085	—	10.00	20.00	30.00	50.00	—
AH1086	—	10.00	20.00	30.00	50.00	—
AH1088	—	10.00	20.00	30.00	50.00	—
AH1089	—	10.00	20.00	30.00	50.00	—
AH1090	—	10.00	20.00	30.00	50.00	—
AH1092	—	10.00	20.00	30.00	50.00	—
AH1095	—	10.00	20.00	30.00	50.00	—

KM# 23 NASRI

0.6300 g., Silver **Mint:** Tunis

Date	Mintage	Good	VG	F	VF	XF
AH1059	—	40.00	80.00	150	180	—

KM# 24 ONLUK

2.9800 g., Silver **Mint:** Tunis

Date	Mintage	Good	VG	F	VF	XF
AH1066	—	—	—	—	800	—

KM# 25 SULTANI

Gold **Mint:** Tunis **Note:** Weight varies: 3.20-3.35 grams.

Date	Mintage	VG	F	VF	XF	Unc
AH1058	—	500	1,000	1,500	2,000	—
AH1061	—	500	1,000	1,500	2,000	—
AH1068	—	500	1,250	1,650	3,000	—
AH1076	—	175	300	450	600	—
AH1087	—	175	300	450	600	—
AH1091	—	1,000	1,500	2,500	3,500	—

Suleyman II

AH1099-1102/1687-1691AD

HAMMERED COINAGE

KM# 28 SULTANI

3.4000 g., Gold **Mint:** Tunis

Date	Mintage	VG	F	VF	XF	Unc
AH1099	—	200	400	600	900	—
AH1100	—	200	400	600	900	—
AH1101	—	200	400	600	900	—
AH1102	—	200	400	600	900	—

Mustafa II

AH1106-15/1695-1703AD

HAMMERED COINAGE

KM# 30 3 BURBEN

Copper **Mint:** Tunis **Note:** Weight varies: 2.44-2.79 grams.

Date	Mintage	Good	VG	F	VF	XF
ND	—	5.00	8.00	25.00	45.00	—
AH1112	—	12.00	18.00	35.00	60.00	—

KM# 31 SULTANI

3.2200 g., Gold, 23 mm. **Mint:** Tunis

Date	Mintage	VG	F	VF	XF	Unc
AH1108	—	175	225	400	600	—
AH1109	—	195	285	450	800	—
AH1111	—	195	285	450	800	—

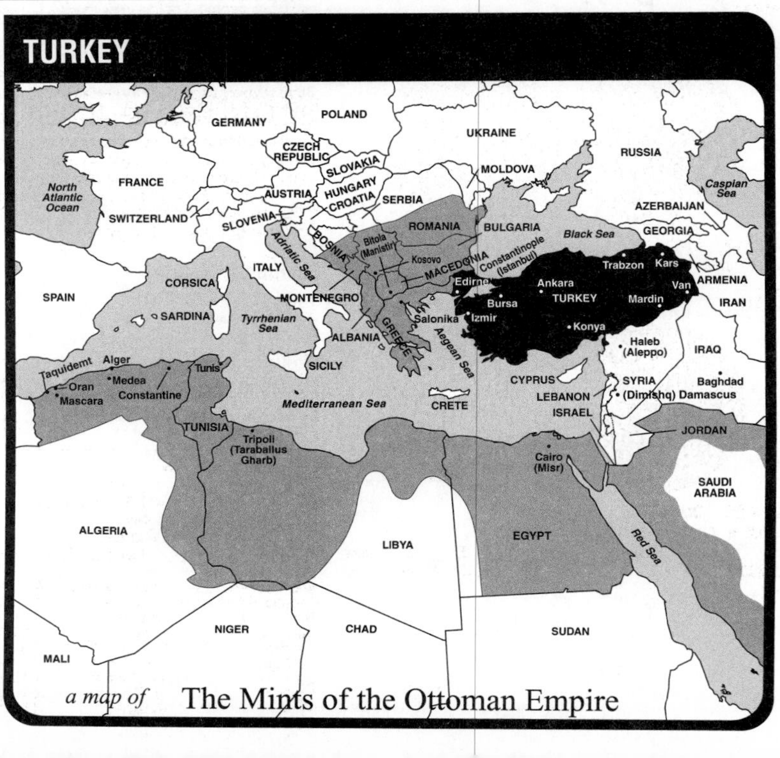

Turkey, located partially in Europe and partially in Asia between the Black and the Mediterranean Seas, has an area of 301,382 sq. mi. (780,580 sq. km).

The Ottoman Turks, a tribe from Central Asia, first appeared in the early 13th century, and by the 17th century had established the Ottoman Empire which stretched from the Persian Gulf to the southern frontier of Poland, and from the Caspian Sea to the Algerian plateau. The defeat of the Turkish navy by the Holy League in 1571, and of the Turkish forces besieging Vienna in 1683, began the steady decline of the Ottoman Empire which, accelerated by the rise of nationalism, contracted its European border, and by the end of World War I deprived it of its Arab lands. The present Turkish boundaries were largely fixed by the Treaty of Lausanne in 1923. The sultanate and caliphate, the political and spiritual ruling institutions of the old empire, were separated and the sultanate abolished in 1922. On Oct. 29, 1923, Turkey formally became a republic.

RULERS

Mehmed III, AH1003-1012/1595-1603AD
Ahmed I, AH1012-1026/1603-1617AD
Mustafa I,
First reign, AH1026-1027/1617-1618AD
Second reign, AH1031-1032/1622-1623AD
Osman II, AH1027-1031/1618-1622AD
Murad IV, AH1032-1049/1623-1640AD
Ibrahim, AH1040-1058/1640-1648AD
Mehmed IV, AH1058-1099/1648-1687AD
Suleyman II, AH1099-1102/1687-1691AD
Ahmed II, AH1102-1106/1691-1695AD
Mustafa II, AH1106-1115/1695-1703AD

MINT NAMES

اماسية

Amasiah

آمد
Amid
Diarbakar
Kara Amid

انگورية انقرية انقرة
Ankara (Anguriyah)

انگوريه
Ayasulik

آزاق آزق
Azak

بغداد
Baghdad - See Iraq-Mesopotamia

بنگالور
Belgrad

بسولے بسولي
Bitlis (Bidlis)

بوسنة سراي
Bosnasaray Saray

كنسا
Canca or Chaniche Gumushhane

قسطنطنية
Constantinople (Qustantiniyah)

Diarbakar - See Amid

ادرنه
Edirne (Adrianople)

روان
Erevan (Erewan, Revan, Yerevan) - See Armenia

ارزروم
Erzerum

فيليپ فلبه
Filibe (Philipopolis - Plovdiv)

گليبولی
Gelibolu (Gallipoli)

كنجه
Genje (Azerbaijan)

گمشخانه
Gumushhane or (Canca)

بلب
Halab (Aleppo) - See Syria

اسلامبول
Islambul or Istanbul

ازمير ازمر
Izmir (Smyrna)

قسطمونی
Kastamonu

(قبريس) قبرس
bris (Cyprus)

قونية
hanja)

ماردين
Mardin

نخجوان
Nackhchawan - See Azerbaijan

نگبولو
Nigbolu

نوابرده
Novabirda Novar

اوخرى
Ohri

اردو همايون
Ordu-yu Humayun

قراطوه
Qaratova

سكيز ساقز
Sakiz (Scio)

سلانيك
Salonika (Selanik, Saloniki)

بوسنة سراي
Saray Bosnasarzy

سرز سريز
Serez (Siroz)

شماخي شماخه
Shamakhi - See Azerbaijan

شيراز
Shirvan - See Azerbaijan

بسدره قپسى
Sidrekapsi

سيواس
Sivas

صوفية
Sofia

تيره
Tire

توقاط توقات
Tokat

طرابزون طرابزن
Trebizond Trabzon

تونس
Tunis - See Tunisia-Tunis

اسكوپ
Uskub

وان
Van (Wan) - Until AH1032. AH1133-34

ينكى شهر
Yenishehir

زبيد
Zabid - See Yemen

MONETARY EQUIVALENTS

3 Akche = 1 Para
5 Para = Beshlik (Beshparalik)
10 Para = Onluk
20 Para = Yirmilik
30 Para = Zolota
40 Para = Kurush (Piastre)
1-1/2 Kurush (Piastres) = Altmishlik

MONETARY SYSTEM

Silver Coinage
40 Para = 1 Kurush (Piastre)
2 Kurush (Piastres) = 1 Ikilik
2-1/2 Kurush (Piastres) = Yuzluk
3 Kurush (Piastres) = Uechlik
5 Kurush (Piastres) = Beshlik
6 Kurush (Piastres) = Altilik

Gold Coinage
100 Kurush (Piastres) = 1 Turkish Pound (Lira)

This system has remained essentially unchanged since i introduction by Ahmad III in 1688, except that the Asper and Pa have long since ceased to be coined. The Piastre, established a a crown-sized silver coin approximately equal to the French Ec of Louis XIV, has shrunk to a tiny copper coin, worth about 1/1 of a U.S. cent. Since the establishment of the Republic in 192 the Turkish terms, Kurus and Lira, have replaced the Europea names Piastres and Turkish Pounds.

OTTOMAN EMPIRE

Ahmed I

AH1012-26/1603-17AD

HAMMERED COINAGE

Amid

KM# 13.11 AKCE

0.2700 g., Silver

Date	Mintage	VG	F	VF	XF	Unc
AH1012	—	8.00	12.00	20.00	30.00	-

Belgrad

KM# 13.1 AKCE

0.2700 g., Silver

Date	Mintage	VG	F	VF	XF	Unc
AH1012	—	7.00	15.00	25.00	35.00	-

Bursa

KM# 13.2 AKCE

0.2700 g., Silver

Date	Mintage	VG	F	VF	XF	Unc
AH1012	—	3.00	6.00	10.00	20.00	-

Canca

KM# 13.17 AKCE

0.2700 g., Silver

Date	Mintage	VG	F	VF	XF	Unc
AH1013	—	—	—	—	—	—

Constantinople

KM# 13.3 AKCE

0.2700 g., Silver

Date	Mintage	VG	F	VF	XF	Unc
AH1012	—	3.00	6.00	10.00	20.00	-
AH1013	—	10.00	20.00	30.00	50.00	-

Edirne

KM# 13.4 AKCE

0.2700 g., Silver

Date	Mintage	VG	F	VF	XF	Unc
AH1012	—	3.00	6.00	10.00	20.00	-

Erzerum

KM# 13.12 AKCE

0.2700 g., Silver

Date	Mintage	VG	F	VF	XF	Unc
AH1012	—	15.00	20.00	30.00	50.00	-

Filibe

KM# 13.5 AKCE

0.2700 g., Silver

Date	Mintage	VG	F	VF	XF	Unc
AH1012	—	12.00	25.00	35.00	50.00	-

Gelibolu

KM# 13.6 AKCE

0.2700 g., Silver

Date	Mintage	VG	F	VF	XF	Unc
AH1012	—	18.00	35.00	60.00	100	-

enje

M# 13.13 AKCE

2700 g., Silver

ate	Mintage	VG	F	VF	XF	Unc
H1012	—	80.00	120	200	300	—

uzelhisar

M# 13.14 AKCE

2700 g., Silver

ate	Mintage	VG	F	VF	XF	Unc
H1012	—	150	200	300	500	—

ibris

M# 13.15 AKCE

2700 g., Silver

ate	Mintage	VG	F	VF	XF	Unc
H1012	—	30.00	50.00	80.00	150	—

onya

M# 13.7 AKCE

2700 g., Silver

ate	Mintage	VG	F	VF	XF	Unc
H1012	—	14.00	28.00	40.00	60.00	—

ovabirda

M# 13.8 AKCE

.2700 g., Silver

ate	Mintage	VG	F	VF	XF	Unc
H1012	—	3.00	6.00	10.00	20.00	—

erez

M# 13.9 AKCE

2700 g., Silver

ate	Mintage	VG	F	VF	XF	Unc
H1012	—	3.00	6.00	10.00	20.00	—

idrekapsi

M# 13.18 AKCE

.2700 g., Silver

ate	Mintage	VG	F	VF	XF	Unc
H1012	—	12.00	25.00	35.00	55.00	—

ukat

M# 13.10 AKCE

.2700 g., Silver

ate	Mintage	VG	F	VF	XF	Unc
H1012	—	20.00	35.00	50.00	75.00	—

skub

M# 13.19 AKCE

.2700 g., Silver

ate	Mintage	VG	F	VF	XF	Unc
H1012	—	10.00	20.00	30.00	50.00	—

an

M# 13.16 AKCE

.2700 g., Silver

ate	Mintage	VG	F	VF	XF	Unc
H1012	—	80.00	120	200	300	—

enje

M# 15.2 DIRHAM

ilver **Note:** Prev. KM#15; Weight varies 2.1 - 3 grams.

ate	Mintage	VG	F	VF	XF	Unc
H1012	—	BV	30.00	75.00	110	—

M# 14 DIRHAM

ilver **Note:** Weight varies 2.1 - 3 grams.

ate	Mintage	VG	F	VF	XF	Unc
H1012	—	BV	30.00	75.00	110	—

mid

M# A14.4 PARA

ilver **Obv:** Toughra **Rev:** Mint in central lozenge, date in circular egend

ate	Mintage	VG	F	VF	XF	Unc
H1012	—	10.00	20.00	35.00	50.00	—

Kara Amid

KM# A14.3 PARA

1.0200 g., Silver **Obv:** Toughra **Rev:** 3-line inscription with mint and date

Date	Mintage	VG	F	VF	XF	Unc
AH1012	—	28.00	50.00	85.00	125	—

Canca

KM# A14.1 BESHLIK

0.9400 g., Silver

Date	Mintage	VG	F	VF	XF	Unc
AH1012	—	—	—	—	—	—

Erzerum

KM# A14.2 BESHLIK

1.3300 g., Silver

Date	Mintage	VG	F	VF	XF	Unc
AH1014	—	—	—	—	—	—

Amid

KM# 16.1 ALTIN

3.2000 g., Gold

Date	Mintage	VG	F	VF	XF	Unc
AH1012	—	175	300	500	800	—

Canca

KM# 16.2 ALTIN

3.2000 g., Gold

Date	Mintage	VG	F	VF	XF	Unc
AH1013	—	175	300	500	800	—

Constantinople

KM# 16.3 ALTIN

3.2000 g., Gold

Date	Mintage	VG	F	VF	XF	Unc
AH1012	—	BV	220	300	400	—

KM# 19 ALTIN

3.2000 g., Gold

Date	Mintage	VG	F	VF	XF	Unc
AH1012	—	BV	220	300	450	—

Erzerum

KM# 16.4 ALTIN

3.2000 g., Gold

Date	Mintage	VG	F	VF	XF	Unc
AH1012	—	250	400	600	1,000	—

Sakiz

KM# 17 ALTIN

3.2000 g., Gold

Date	Mintage	VG	F	VF	XF	Unc
AH1012	—	200	350	500	900	—

Trebizum

KM# 16.5 ALTIN

3.2000 g., Gold

Date	Mintage	VG	F	VF	XF	Unc
AH1012	—	325	550	900	1,500	—

Tukat

KM# 16.6 ALTIN

3.2000 g., Gold

Date	Mintage	VG	F	VF	XF	Unc
AH1012	—	220	400	600	1,100	—

KM# 18 ALTIN

3.2000 g., Gold

Date	Mintage	VG	F	VF	XF	Unc
AH1013	—	BV	350	500	750	—

Van

KM# 16.7 ALTIN

3.2000 g., Gold

Date	Mintage	VG	F	VF	XF	Unc
AH1012	—	1,000	1,800	3,000	5,000	—

Mustafa I, 1st reign

AH1026-27/1617-18AD

HAMMERED COINAGE

Amid

KM# 22.6 AKCE

Silver Weight varies: 0.27-0.28g.

Date	Mintage	VG	F	VF	XF	Unc
AHxxxx	—	12.00	30.00	60.00	100	—

Belgrad

KM# 22.1 AKCE

Silver **Note:** Weight varies: 0.27-0.28 grams.

Date	Mintage	VG	F	VF	XF	Unc
AHxxxx	—	30.00	50.00	75.00	125	—

Bursa

KM# 22.2 AKCE

Silver **Note:** Weight varies: 0.27-0.28 grams.

Date	Mintage	VG	F	VF	XF	Unc
AHxxxx	—	6.00	12.00	25.00	40.00	—

Constantinople

KM# 22.3 AKCE

Silver **Note:** Weight varies: 0.27-0.28 grams.

Date	Mintage	VG	F	VF	XF	Unc
AHxxxx	—	6.00	12.00	25.00	40.00	—

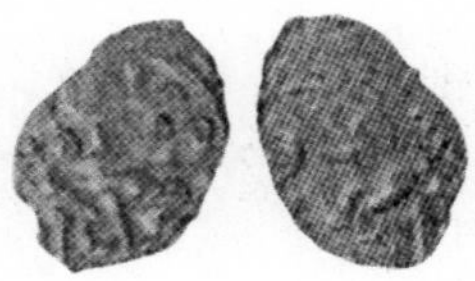

Edirne

KM# 22.7 AKCE
Silver **Note:** Weight varies: 0.27-0.28 grams. Previous KM #23.

Date	Mintage	VG	F	VF	XF	Unc
AHxxxx	—	8.00	15.00	30.00	45.00	—

Tukat

KM# 22.4 AKCE
Silver **Note:** Weight varies: 0.27-0.28 grams.

Date	Mintage	VG	F	VF	XF	Unc
AHxxxx	—	9.00	18.00	35.00	60.00	—

Yenishehir

KM# 22.5 AKCE
Silver **Note:** Weight varies: 0.27-0.28 grams.

Date	Mintage	VG	F	VF	XF	Unc
AHxxxx	—	6.00	12.00	25.00	40.00	—

Osman II
AH1027-31/1618-22AD
HAMMERED COINAGE

KM# 34 MANGIR
Copper

Date	Mintage	Good	VG	F	VF	XF
AHxxxx	—	4.00	8.00	15.00	25.00	—

KM# 35 MANGIR
Copper

Date	Mintage	Good	VG	F	VF	XF
AH1027	—	6.00	12.00	20.00	35.00	—

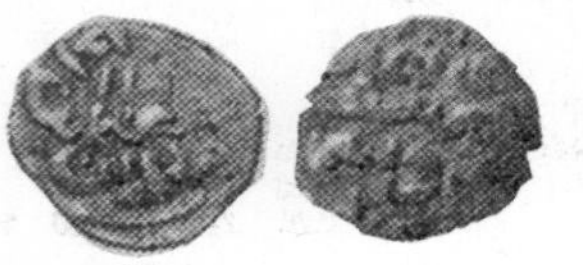

Constantinople

KM# 33 MANGIR
Copper

Date	Mintage	Good	VG	F	VF	XF
AH102x	—	6.00	12.00	20.00	35.00	—

Amasiah

KM# 38.12 AKCE
0.3000 g., Silver

Date	Mintage	VG	F	VF	XF	Unc
AH1027	—	7.00	15.00	30.00	50.00	—

Amid

KM# 38.17 AKCE
0.3000 g., Silver

Date	Mintage	VG	F	VF	XF	Unc
AH1027	—	30.00	55.00	75.00	110	—

Belgrad

KM# 38.1 AKCE
0.3000 g., Silver

Date	Mintage	VG	F	VF	XF	Unc
AH1027	—	8.00	15.00	25.00	30.00	—

Bursa

KM# 38.2 AKCE
0.3000 g., Silver

Date	Mintage	VG	F	VF	XF	Unc
AH1027	—	8.00	15.00	30.00	50.00	—

Canca

KM# 38.3 AKCE
0.3000 g., Silver

Date	Mintage	VG	F	VF	XF	Unc
AH1027	—	5.00	10.00	15.00	20.00	—

Constantinople

KM# 38.4 AKCE
0 g., Silver

	Mintage	VG	F	VF	XF	Unc
	—	4.00	7.00	12.00	20.00	—

Edirne

KM# 38.18 AKCE
0.3000 g., Silver

Date	Mintage	VG	F	VF	XF	Unc
AH1027	—	20.00	35.00	50.00	85.00	—

Konya

KM# 38.5 AKCE
0.3000 g., Silver

Date	Mintage	VG	F	VF	XF	Unc
AH1027	—	9.00	18.00	35.00	60.00	—

Novabirda

KM# 38.16 AKCE
Silver

Date	Mintage	Good	VG	F	VF	XF
AH1027	—	—	9.00	18.00	35.00	60.00

Ohri

KM# 38.6 AKCE
0.3000 g., Silver

Date	Mintage	VG	F	VF	XF	Unc
AH1027	—	9.00	18.00	35.00	60.00	—

Serez

KM# 38.7 AKCE
0.3000 g., Silver

Date	Mintage	VG	F	VF	XF	Unc
AH1027	—	4.00	7.00	12.00	20.00	—

Sofia

KM# 38.8 AKCE
0.3000 g., Silver

Date	Mintage	VG	F	VF	XF	Unc
AH1027	—	7.00	15.00	30.00	50.00	—

Tire

KM# 38.15 AKCE
0.3000 g., Silver

Date	Mintage	VG	F	VF	XF	Unc
AH1027	—	—	—	—	—	—

Tokat

KM# 38.13 AKCE
0.3000 g., Silver

Date	Mintage	VG	F	VF	XF	Unc
AH1027	—	18.00	35.00	60.00	85.00	—

Ushkub

KM# 38.10 AKCE
0.3000 g., Silver

Date	Mintage	VG	F	VF	XF	Unc
AH1027	—	5.00	8.00	15.00	25.00	—

Van

KM# 38.14 AKCE
0.3000 g., Silver

Date	Mintage	VG	F	VF	XF	Unc
AH1027	—	60.00	100	150	200	—

Yenishehir

KM# 38.11 AKCE
0.3000 g., Silver

Date	Mintage	VG	F	VF	XF	Unc
AH1027	—	5.00	8.00	15.00	25.00	—

Amid

KM# 39.1 PARA
Silver Weight varies: 0.95-1.10g. **Obv:** Toughra **Rev:** 3-line inscription with mint and date

Date	Mintage	VG	F	VF	XF	Unc
AH1027	—	10.00	20.00	32.00	60.00	—

KM# 40.1 PARA
Silver Weight varies: 0.95-1.15g, 16 mm. **Obv:** Sultan's name in circle, inscription around **Rev:** Mint in circle, inscription with date around

Date	Mintage	VG	F	VF	XF	Unc
AH1027	—	—	—	—	—	—

Canca

KM# 39.2 PARA
Silver Weight varies: 0.95-1.10g. **Obv:** Toughra **Rev:** 3-line inscription with mint and date

Date	Mintage	VG	F	VF	XF	Unc
AH1027	—	10.00	20.00	32.00	60.00	—

Canca

KM# 42.1 ONLUK
Silver **Note:** Weight varies: 2.60-2.75 grams.

Date	Mintage	VG	F	VF	XF	Unc
AH1027	—	20.00	60.00	85.00	120	—

Constantinople

KM# 41 ONLUK
Silver **Note:** Weight varies: 2.60-2.75 grams.

Date	Mintage	VG	F	VF	XF	Un
AH1027	—	BV	60.00	75.00	110	–

Edirne

KM# 42.2 ONLUK
Silver **Note:** Weight varies: 2.60-2.75 grams.

Date	Mintage	VG	F	VF	XF	Un
AH1027	—	20.00	60.00	80.00	120	–

Constantinople

KM# 45 SULTANI
3.4000 g., Gold

Date	Mintage	VG	F	VF	XF	Un
AH1027	—	225	450	700	1,100	–

Mustafa I, 2nd reign
AH1031-32/1622-23AD
HAMMERED COINAGE

Belgrad

KM# 27.4 ONLUK
Silver **Note:** Weight varies: 2.48-2.68 grams.

Date	Mintage	VG	F	VF	XF	Un
AH1031	—	60.00	100	150	200	–

Canca

KM# 27.1 ONLUK
Silver **Rev:** Date within inner circle **Note:** Weight varies: 2.48-2.68 grams.

Date	Mintage	VG	F	VF	XF	Unc
AH1031 Rare	—	—	—	—	—	—

Constantinople

KM# 26 ONLUK
Silver **Note:** Weight varies: 2.48-2.68 grams.

Date	Mintage	VG	F	VF	XF	Unc
AHxxxx	—	BV	40.00	75.00	120	—

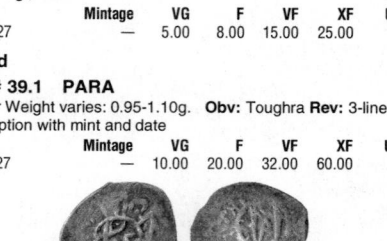

M# 27.2 ONLUK
ilver **Note:** Weight varies: 2.48-2.68 grams.

ate	Mintage	VG	F	VF	XF	Unc
H1031	—	BV	40.00	75.00	120	—

dirne

M# 27.5 ONLUK
ilver **Note:** Weight varies: 2.48-2.68 grams.

ate	Mintage	VG	F	VF	XF	Unc
H1031	—	BV	50.00	75.00	140	—

rzerum

M# 27.3 ONLUK
ilver **Note:** Weight varies: 2.48-2.68 grams.

ate	Mintage	VG	F	VF	XF	Unc
H1031	—	—	—	—	—	—

ofia

M# 27.6 ONLUK
ilver **Note:** Weight varies: 2.48-2.68 grams.

ate	Mintage	VG	F	VF	XF	Unc
H1031	—	60.00	150	200	300	—

okat

M# 27.7 ONLUK
ilver **Note:** Weight varies: 2.48-2.68 grams.

ate	Mintage	VG	F	VF	XF	Unc
H1031	—	BV	60.00	85.00	150	—

onstantinople

M# 30 ALTIN
.3000 g., Gold

ate	Mintage	VG	F	VF	XF	Unc
H1031	—	550	1,200	1,750	2,500	—

Murad IV
AH1032-49/1623-40AD
HAMMERED COINAGE

nkara

M# A48.1 AKCE
.3300 g., Silver

ate	Mintage	VG	F	VF	XF	Unc
H1032	—	40.00	70.00	120	200	—

elgrad

M# 48.1 AKCE
.3300 g., Silver

ate	Mintage	VG	F	VF	XF	Unc
H1032	—	7.00	15.00	25.00	40.00	—

Bursa

KM# 48.2 AKCE
0.3300 g., Silver

Date	Mintage	VG	F	VF	XF	Unc
AH1032	—	4.00	8.00	12.00	20.00	—

Canca

KM# 48.3 AKCE
0.3300 g., Silver

Date	Mintage	VG	F	VF	XF	Unc
AH1032	—	4.00	8.00	12.00	20.00	—

Constantinople

KM# 48.4 AKCE
0.3300 g., Silver

Date	Mintage	VG	F	VF	XF	Unc
AH1032	—	4.00	8.00	12.00	20.00	—

Edirne

KM# 48.5 AKCE
0.3300 g., Silver

Date	Mintage	VG	F	VF	XF	Unc
AH1032	—	4.00	8.00	12.00	20.00	—

Erzerum

KM# 48.6 AKCE
0.3300 g., Silver

Date	Mintage	VG	F	VF	XF	Unc
AH1032	—	18.00	35.00	60.00	100	—

Karatova

KM# 48.9 AKCE
0.3300 g., Silver

Date	Mintage	VG	F	VF	XF	Unc
AH1032	—	4.50	9.00	15.00	25.00	—

Kibris

KM# 48.7 AKCE
0.3300 g., Silver

Date	Mintage	VG	F	VF	XF	Unc
AH1032	—	125	200	450	600	—

Konya

KM# 48.8 AKCE
0.3300 g., Silver

Date	Mintage	VG	F	VF	XF	Unc
AH1032	—	25.00	50.00	90.00	150	—

Nigbolu

KM# 48.10 AKCE
0.3300 g., Silver

Date	Mintage	VG	F	VF	XF	Unc
AH1032	—	25.00	50.00	90.00	150	—

Novabirda

KM# 48.11 AKCE
0.3300 g., Silver

Date	Mintage	VG	F	VF	XF	Unc
AH1032	—	12.00	25.00	40.00	70.00	—

Saray

KM# 48.12 AKCE
0.3300 g., Silver

Date	Mintage	VG	F	VF	XF	Unc
AH1032	—	5.00	10.00	18.00	30.00	—

Selanik

KM# 48.13 AKCE
0.3300 g., Silver

Date	Mintage	VG	F	VF	XF	Unc
AH1032	—	12.00	25.00	40.00	70.00	—

Sidrekapsi

KM# 48.14 AKCE
0.3300 g., Silver

Date	Mintage	VG	F	VF	XF	Unc
AH1032	—	4.00	8.00	12.00	20.00	—

Sofia

KM# 48.15 AKCE
0.3300 g., Silver

Date	Mintage	VG	F	VF	XF	Unc
AH1032	—	9.00	18.00	30.00	50.00	—

Tire

KM# 48.16 AKCE
0.3300 g., Silver

Date	Mintage	VG	F	VF	XF	Unc
AH1032	—	—	—	—	—	—

Tokat

KM# 48.17 AKCE
0.3300 g., Silver

Date	Mintage	VG	F	VF	XF	Unc
AH1032	—	18.00	35.00	60.00	100	—

Ushkub

KM# 48.18 AKCE
0.3300 g., Silver

Date	Mintage	VG	F	VF	XF	Unc
AH1032	—	18.00	35.00	60.00	100	—

Van

KM# 48.20 AKCE
0.3300 g., Silver

Date	Mintage	VG	F	VF	XF	Unc
AH1032 Rare	—	—	—	—	—	—

Yenishehir

KM# 48.19 AKCE
0.3300 g., Silver

Date	Mintage	VG	F	VF	XF	Unc
AH1032	—	5.00	10.00	18.00	30.00	—

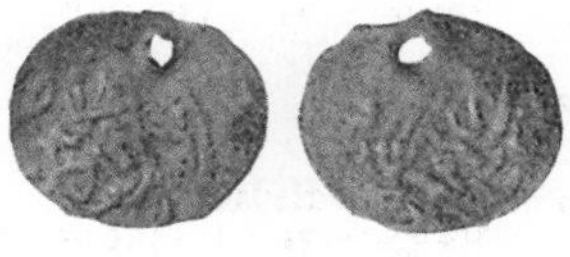

Amid

KM# 49 PARA
Silver **Note:** Weight varies: 0.86-1.28 grams.

Date	Mintage	VG	F	VF	XF	Unc
AH1032	—	10.00	20.00	30.00	50.00	—

KM# 50.1 PARA
Silver **Obv:** Toughra **Note:** Weight varies: 0.86-1.28 grams.

Date	Mintage	VG	F	VF	XF	Unc
AH1032	—	10.00	20.00	30.00	50.00	—

Canca

KM# 50.2 PARA
Silver **Note:** Weight varies: 0.86-1.28 grams.

Date	Mintage	VG	F	VF	XF	Unc
AH1032	—	10.00	20.00	30.00	50.00	—

KM# 51 PARA
Silver **Note:** Weight varies: 0.86-1.28 grams.

Date	Mintage	VG	F	VF	XF	Unc
AH1032	—	—	—	—	—	—

Constantinople

KM# 50.3 PARA
Silver **Note:** Weight varies: 0.86-1.28 grams.

Date	Mintage	VG	F	VF	XF	Unc
AH1032	—	10.00	20.00	30.00	50.00	—

Tokat

KM# 52 PARA
Silver **Note:** Weight varies: 0.86-1.28 grams.

Date	Mintage	VG	F	VF	XF	Unc
AH1032	—	60.00	100	150	200	—

Constantinople
KM# 54 ONLUK
2.5000 g., Silver

Date	Mintage	VG	F	VF	XF	Unc
AH1032	—	20.00	35.00	60.00	85.00	—

Constantinople
KM# 57 ALTIN
3.4000 g., Gold

Date	Mintage	VG	F	VF	XF	Unc
AH1032	—	BV	220	300	500	—

Ibrahim
AH1040-58/1640-48AD
HAMMERED COINAGE

Constantinople
KM# 60 MANGIR
1.4500 g., Copper **Obv:** Toughra

Date	Mintage	Good	VG	F	VF	XF
AHxxxx	—	6.00	10.00	20.00	35.00	—

KM# 61 MANGIR
1.4500 g., Copper **Obv:** Toughra

Date	Mintage	Good	VG	F	VF	XF
AH1049	—	6.00	10.00	20.00	35.00	—

KM# 62 MANGIR
1.4500 g., Copper **Obv:** Toughra

Date	Mintage	Good	VG	F	VF	XF
AH1054	—	6.00	10.00	20.00	35.00	—

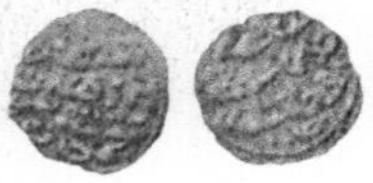

Constantinople
KM# 65.1 AKCE
0.3200 g., Silver

Date	Mintage	VG	F	VF	XF	Unc
AH1049	—	6.00	12.00	25.00	50.00	—

Kara Amid
KM# 65.2 AKCE
0.3000 g., Silver

Date	Mintage	VG	F	VF	XF	Unc
AHxxxx	—	—	—	—	—	—

Constantinople
KM# 68 PARA
0.6000 g., Silver

Date	Mintage	VG	F	VF	XF	Unc
AHxxxx	—	25.00	50.00	100	150	—

Amid
KM# 71.1 BESHLIK
Silver **Note:** Weight varies: 1.48-1.52 grams.

Date	Mintage	VG	F	VF	XF	Unc
AH1049 Rare	—	—	—	—	—	—

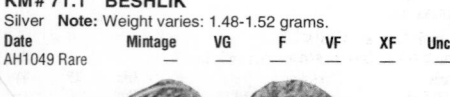

Constantinople
KM# 71.2 BESHLIK
Silver **Note:** Weight varies: 1.48-1.52 grams.

Date	Mintage	VG	F	VF	XF	Unc
AH1049	—	BV	20.00	50.00	100	—

Constantinople
KM# 74 ONLUK
3.0500 g., Silver

Date	Mintage	VG	F	VF	XF	Unc
AHxxxx	—	20.00	50.00	75.00	120	—

Mehmed IV
AH1058-99/1648-87AD
HAMMERED COINAGE

Constantinople
KM# 77 MANGIR
Copper

Date	Mintage	Good	VG	F	VF	XF
AH(1)061	—	6.00	12.00	20.00	40.00	—

Van
KM# 78 MANGIR
Copper

Date	Mintage	VG	F	VF	XF	Unc
AHxxxx	—	—	—	—	—	—

Constantinople
KM# 80 AKCE
0.3200 g., Silver

Date	Mintage	VG	F	VF	XF	Unc
AH1058	—	4.00	8.00	12.00	25.00	—

Constantinople
KM# 82.1 DIRHAM
Silver **Note:** Prev. KM#82

Date	Mintage	VG	F	VF	XF	Unc
AH1058	—	—	—	—	—	—

Halab
KM# 82.2 DIRHAM
Silver

Date	Mintage	VG	F	VF	XF	Unc
AH1058	—	BV	35.00	60.00	85.00	—

Constantinople
KM# 83 ALTIN
Gold **Note:** Weight varies: 3.45-3.55 grams.

Date	Mintage	VG	F	VF	XF	Unc
AH1058	—	225	425	750	1,000	—

KM# 84 ALTIN
Gold **Note:** Weight varies: 3.45-3.55 grams.

Date	Mintage	VG	F	VF	XF	Unc
AH1058	—	225	425	750	1,000	—

Suleyman II
AH1099-1102/1687-91AD
HAMMERED COINAGE

Bosnasaray
KM# 87.1 MANGIR
Copper

Date	Mintage	Good	VG	F	VF	XF
AH1099	—	—	—	—	—	

Constantinople
KM# 87.2 MANGIR
Copper

Date	Mintage	Good	VG	F	VF	XF
AH1099	—	2.00	4.00	6.00	12.00	—

Saray
KM# 89 MANGIR
Copper

Date	Mintage	VG	F	VF	XF	Unc
AH1100	—	—	—	—	—	—

Van
KM# 91 MANGIR
Copper

Date	Mintage	VG	F	VF	XF	Unc
AHxxxx	—	—	—	—	—	—

Constantinople
KM# 88 AKCE
Silver

Date	Mintage	VG	F	VF	XF	Unc
AH1099	—	200	300	500	800	—

Constantinople
KM# 90 CEYREK KURUS
6.2500 g., Silver **Note:** Struck at Constantinople.

Date	Mintage	VG	F	VF	XF	Unc
AH1099	—	750	1,000	1,500	2,000	—

Constantinople
KM# 93 YARIM KURUS
9.4000 g., Silver

Date	Mintage	VG	F	VF	XF	Unc
AH1099	—	250	450	750	1,500	—

onstantinople

M# 96 KURUS

.3800 g., Silver **Note:** Dav. #314.

te	Mintage	VG	F	VF	XF	Unc
1099	—	60.00	150	250	350	—

onstantinople

M# 100 SHERIFI ALTIN

4500 g., Gold

te	Mintage	VG	F	VF	XF	Unc
1099	—	BV	250	500	750	—

M# 99 SHERIFI ALTIN

2500 g., Gold, 27 mm.

te	Mintage	VG	F	VF	XF	Unc
xxxx	—	BV	250	500	750	—

Ahmed II
AH1102-1106/1691-95AD
HAMMERED COINAGE

onstantinople

M# 103 MANGIR

3000 g., Copper

ate	Mintage	Good	VG	F	VF	XF
H1102	—	15.00	30.00	50.00	100	—

onstantinople

M# 105 AKCE

3200 g., Silver

ate	Mintage	VG	F	VF	XF	Unc
H1102	—	300	400	550	700	—

onstantinople

M# 107 YARIM KURUS

3500 g., Silver

ate	Mintage	VG	F	VF	XF	Unc
H1102	—	180	250	450	600	—

Constantinople

KM# 110 KURUS

18.7000 g., Silver **Note:** Dav. #316.

Date	Mintage	VG	F	VF	XF	Unc
AH1102	—	100	200	350	500	—

Constantinople

KM# 113 SHERIFI ALTIN

3.4000 g., Gold

Date	Mintage	VG	F	VF	XF	Unc
AH1102	—	250	600	1,000	1,500	—

Mustafa II
AH1106-15/1695-1703AD
HAMMERED COINAGE

Constantinople

KM# 115 PARA

Silver

Date	Mintage	VG	F	VF	XF	Unc
AH1106	—	150	200	300	500	—

Constantinople

KM# 116 YARIM KURUS

9.4300 g., Silver

Date	Mintage	VG	F	VF	XF	Unc
AH1106	—	BV	25.00	40.00	75.00	—

KM# 116A YARIM KURUS

9.4300 g., Silver **Note:** Without "KAF" in the Mulkehu.

Date	Mintage	VG	F	VF	XF	Unc
AH1106	—	20.00	30.00	60.00	110	—

Edirne

KM# 117.1 YARIM KURUS

9.6200 g., Silver

Date	Mintage	VG	F	VF	XF	Unc
AH1106	—	20.00	60.00	120	150	—

Erzerum

KM# 117.2 YARIM KURUS

9.6200 g., Silver

Date	Mintage	VG	F	VF	XF	Unc
AH1106 Rare	—	550	1,000	1,800	2,500	—

Izmir

KM# 117.3 YARIM KURUS

9.6200 g., Silver

Date	Mintage	VG	F	VF	XF	Unc
AH1106	—	75.00	150	250	400	—

KM# 117.3A YARIM KURUS

9.6200 g., Silver **Note:** Without "KAF" in the Mulkehu.

Date	Mintage	VG	F	VF	XF	Unc
AH1106 Rare	—	—	—	—	—	—

Constantinople

KM# 120 KURUS

18.6200 g., Silver **Note:** Dav. #317.

Date	Mintage	VG	F	VF	XF	Unc
AH1106	—	BV	30.00	60.00	95.00	—

Edirne

KM# 121.1 KURUS

20.0500 g., Silver **Note:** Dav. #318.

Date	Mintage	VG	F	VF	XF	Unc
AH1106	—	20.00	50.00	95.00	150	—

Erzerum

KM# 121.2 KURUS

20.0500 g., Silver **Note:** Dav. #319A.

Date	Mintage	VG	F	VF	XF	Unc
AH1106	—	200	400	600	850	—

Izmir

KM# 121.3 KURUS

20.0500 g., Silver **Note:** Dav. #319.

Date	Mintage	VG	F	VF	XF	Unc
AH1106	—	75.00	100	250	400	—

Constantinople

KM# 124 SHERIFI ALTIN

3.3500 g., Gold

Date	Mintage	VG	F	VF	XF	Unc
AH1106	—	BV	220	300	400	—

Constantinople

KM# 128 ASHRAFI

3.4500 g., Gold

Date	Mintage	VG	F	VF	XF	Unc
AH1106	—	BV	200	300	350	—

KM# 130 TEK

3.3500 g., Gold, 29 mm.

Date	Mintage	VG	F	VF	XF	Unc
AH1106	—	—	—	—	—	—

Constantinople

KM# 127 TEK

3.3500 g., Gold, 20.5 mm.

Date	Mintage	VG	F	VF	XF	Unc
AH1106	—	BV	200	300	400	—

Edirne

KM# 129 TEK

3.4500 g., Gold

Date	Mintage	VG	F	VF	XF	Unc
AH1106	—	BV	200	300	400	—

Izmir

KM# 131 TEK

3.4500 g., Gold

Date	Mintage	VG	F	VF	XF	Unc
AH1106 Rare	—	—	—	—	—	—

Ordu-yu Humayun

KM# A131 TEK

3.4500 g., Gold

Date	Mintage	VG	F	VF	XF	Unc
AH1106 Rare	—	—	—	—	—	—

Constantinople

KM# 132 CIFTE

.5000 g., Gold

	Mintage	VG	F	VF	XF	Unc
06 Rare	—	—	—	—	—	—

UNITED STATES - COLONIAL

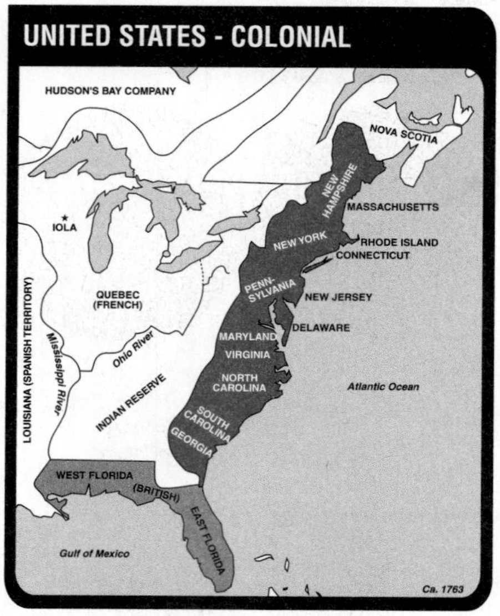

The United States of America as politically organized under the Articles of Confederation consisted of 13 former British-American colonies: New Hampshire, Massachusetts, Rhode Island, Connecticut, New York, New Jersey, Pennsylvania, Delaware, Maryland, Virginia, North Carolina, South Carolina, and Georgia. They were clustered along the eastern seaboard of North America between the forests of Maine (then part of Massachusetts) and the marshes of Georgia.

North America was explored by the Vikings, but it was not until the age of Discovery, that vast colonization began – by the French, Spanish, Dutch, English and Portuguese.

The Spanish would be strongest in Central and South America, taking that whole continent except for Brazil which went to Portugal. The Spanish also would be in Florida, Texas, and California.

The French would settle in the Mississippi River Delta, from New Orleans northward to St. Louis, then east to the Ohio River basin, and west to the Rockies; they would also be to the north, in the St. Lawrence River area in Canada; Quebec and Montreal being their principal cities.

The English would be on the east coast of the United States, from Georgia north to Maine, and east of the Allegheny and Appalachian Mountains. To the north in Canada, they would be in Nova Scotia, Newfoundland, and north of the French in Quebec, Ontario, and with the explorers of the Hudson Bay Company, westward on the plains and to the Pacific.

The Dutch had a presence from the 1620s through 1664, mainly in the New York region, but lost that territory to the English, and never again gained a stronghold on the mainland during this period.

MINT MARK

P – Philadelphia, PA, 1793-present

MONETARY SYSTEM

12 Pence = 1 Shilling
5 Shillings = 1 Crown
21 Shillings = 1 Guinea

EARLY AMERICAN TOKENS

American Plantations

KM# Tn5.1 1/24 REAL

Tin **Obv. Legend:** ET HIB REX

Date	AG	Good	VG	Fine	VF	XF	Unc
ND(1688)	125	200	300	450	850	2,000	—

KM# Tn5.3 1/24 REAL

Tin **Rev:** Horizontal 4

Date	AG	Good	VG	Fine	VF	XF	Unc
ND91688)	275	400	900	1,750	4,250	6,750	—

KM# Tn5.4 1/24 REAL

Tin **Obv. Legend:** ET HB REX

Date	AG	Good	VG	Fine	VF	XF	Unc
ND(1688)	—	250	450	850	1,900	3,250	11,500

KM# Tn6 1/24 REAL

Tin **Rev:** Arms of Scotland left, Ireland right

Date	AG	Good	VG	Fine	VF	XF	Unc
ND(1688)	450	750	1,250	2,150	5,000	7,700	—

EARLY AMERICAN TOKENS

Elephant

KM# Tn2 UNKNOWN DENOMINATION

Copper **Rev:** Diagonals tie shield

Date	AG	Good	VG	Fine	VF	XF	
ND(1664)	250	450	650	2,250	7,000	11,500	35,(

KM# Tn3 UNKNOWN DENOMINATION

Copper **Rev:** Sword right side of shield

Date	AG	Good	VG	Fine	VF	XF
ND(1664) 3 known	—	—	—	—	25,000	—

Note: Norweb $1,320

KM# Tn1.1 UNKNOWN DENOMINATION

15.5500 g., Copper **Note:** Thick planchet.

Date	AG	Good	VG	Fine	VF	XF	U
ND(1664)	125	200	300	550	1,000	1,750	4,5

KM# Tn1.2 UNKNOWN DENOMINATION

Copper **Note:** Thin planchet.

Date	AG	Good	VG	Fine	VF	XF	U
ND(1664)	175	300	500	900	3,000	5,500	12,5

KM# Tn4 UNKNOWN DENOMINATION

Copper **Rev. Legend:** LON DON

Date	AG	Good	VG	Fine	VF	XF	U
ND(1684)	340	650	1,000	2,250	4,200	8,000	20,0

KM# Tn7 UNKNOWN DENOMINATION

Copper **Rev. Legend:** NEW ENGLAND

Date	AG	Good	VG	Fine	VF	XF	U
ND(1664) 2 known	—	—	55,000	85,000	110,000	160,000	

Note: Norweb $25,300

KM# Tn8.1 UNKNOWN DENOMINATION

Copper **Rev. Legend:** CAROLINA (PROPRIETORS)

Date	AG	Good	VG	Fine	VF	XF	U
ND(1694)	—	—	4,750	7,500	15,000	25,000	

Note: Norweb $35,200

KM# Tn8.2 UNKNOWN DENOMINATION

Copper **Rev. Legend:** CAROLINA (PROPRIETORS, O over E

Date	AG	Good	VG	Fine	VF	XF	Un
1694	1,300	2,500	4,500	7,000	12,500	20,000	-

Note: Norweb $17,600

EARLY AMERICAN TOKENS

New Yorke

KM# Tn9 UNKNOWN DENOMINATION

Brass **Obv. Legend:** NEW.YORK.IN.AMERICA

Date	AG	Good	VG	Fine	VF	XF	Un
CA1700	1,800	3,750	7,000	15,000	27,500	55,000	-

KM# Tn9a UNKNOWN DENOMINATION

White Metal **Obv. Legend:** NEW.YORK.IN.AMERICA

Date	AG	Good	VG	Fine	VF	XF	Un
CA1700 4 known	—	—	7,500	20,000	32,000	75,000	-

MARYLAND

COLONIAL COINAGE

Lord Baltimore

M# 1 PENNY (Denarium)

opper **Obv. Legend:** CAECILIVS Dns TERRAE MARIAE

ate	AG	Good	VG	Fine	VF	XF	Unc
)(1659)	—	—	—	65,000	120,000	200,000	—

known

Note: Stack's Auction 5-04, Proof realized $241,500

M# 2 4 PENCE (Groat)

ilver **Obv:** Large bust **Obv. Legend:** CAECILIVS Dns TERRAE ARIAE **Rev:** Large shield

ate	AG	Good	VG	Fine	VF	XF	Unc
)(1659)	1,250	1,950	3,500	6,250	13,500	22,000	—

M# 3 4 PENCE (Groat)

ilver **Obv:** Small bust **Obv. Legend:** CAECILIVS Dns TERRAE ARIAE **Rev:** Small shield

ate	AG	Good	VG	Fine	VF	XF	Unc
)(1659)	—	—	—	—	—	—	—

Jnique

Note: Norweb $26,400

M# 4 6 PENCE

ilver **Obv:** Small bust **Obv. Legend:** CAECILIVS Dns TERRAE IARIAE **Note:** Known in two other rare small-bust varieties and vo rare large-bust varieties.

ate	AG	Good	VG	Fine	VF	XF	Unc
D(1659)	850	1,400	2,400	5,000	9,500	15,000	—

KM# 6 SHILLING

ilver **Obv. Legend:** CAECILIVS Dns TERRAE MARIAE **Note:** 'arieties exist; one is very rare.

ate	AG	Good	VG	Fine	VF	XF	Unc
D(1659)	1,100	1,850	3,250	6,000	13,500	20,000	—

MASSACHUSETTS

COLONIAL COINAGE

New England

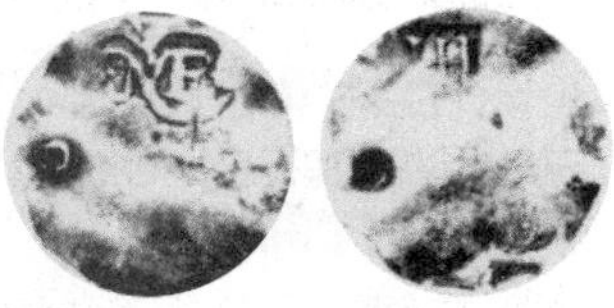

KM# 1 3 PENCE

Silver **Obv:** NE **Rev:** III

Date	Good	VG	Fine	VF	XF	Unc
ND(1652) Unique	—	—	—	—	—	—

Note: Massachusetts Historical Society specimen

KM# 2 6 PENCE

Silver **Obv:** NE **Rev:** VI

Date	AG	Good	VG	Fine	VF	XF
ND(1652) 8 known	—	28,000	60,000	115,000	225,00	—

Note: Garrett $75,000

KM# 3 SHILLING

Silver **Obv:** NE **Rev:** XII

Date	AG	Good	VG	Fine	VF	XF	Unc
ND(1652)	—	37,500	75,000	150,000	250,000	—	—

COLONIAL COINAGE

Willow Tree

KM# 4 3 PENCE

Silver

Date	AG	Good	VG	Fine	VF	XF	Unc
1652 3 known	—	—	—	—	—	—	—

KM# 5 6 PENCE

Silver

Date	AG	Good	VG	Fine	VF	XF
1652 14 known	9,500	18,500	30,000	60,000	135,000	225,000

KM# 6 SHILLING

Silver

Date	AG	Good	VG	Fine	VF	XF	Unc
1652	10,000	20,000	35,000	85,000	165,000	250,000	—

COLONIAL COINAGE

Oak Tree

KM# 7 2 PENCE

Silver **Note:** Small 2 and large 2 varieites exist

Date	AG	Good	VG	Fine	VF	XF	Unc
1662		500	900	2,000	3,850	6,500	15,000

KM# 8 3 PENCE

Silver **Note:** Two types of legends.

Date	AG	Good	VG	Fine	VF	XF	Unc
1652	350	650	1,250	3,000	6,500	12,000	

KM# 9 6 PENCE

Silver **Note:** Three types of legends.

Date	AG	Good	VG	Fine	VF	XF	Unc
1652	400	900	1,350	3,500	8,000	17,500	35,000

KM# 10 SHILLING

Silver **Note:** Two types of legends.

Date	AG	Good	VG	Fine	VF	XF	Unc
1652	375	750	1,250	3,000	6,000	11,500	27,500

COLONIAL COINAGE

Pine Tree

KM# 11 3 PENCE

Silver **Obv:** Tree without berries

Date	AG	Good	VG	Fine	VF	XF	Unc
1652	250	500	750	1,650	3,250	6,500	18,500

KM# 12 3 PENCE

Silver **Obv:** Tree with berries

Date	AG	Good	VG	Fine	VF	XF	Unc
1652	250	500	750	1,650	3,500	6,750	19,500

KM# 13 6 PENCE

Silver **Obv:** Tree without berries; "spiney tree"

Date	AG	Good	VG	Fine	VF	XF	Unc
1652	400	700	1,400	2,000	4,000	7,000	22,000

KM# 14 6 PENCE

Silver **Obv:** Tree with berries

Date	AG	Good	VG	Fine	VF	XF	Unc
1652	300	600	1,000	1,850	3,750	6,500	20,000

KM# 15 SHILLING

Silver **Note:** Large planchet. Many varieties exist; some are very rare.

Date	AG	Good	VG	Fine	VF	XF	Unc
1652	375	700	1,100	2,200	4,500	7,750	22,500

KM# 16 SHILLING

Silver **Note:** Small planchet; large dies. All examples are thought to be contemporary fabrications.

Date	AG	Good	VG	Fine	VF	XF	Unc
1652	—	—	—	—	—	—	—

SHILLING

Note: Small planchet; small dies. Many varieties exist; ome are very rare.

Date	AG	Good	VG	Fine	VF	XF	Unc
1652	285	550	850	1,750	3,750	7,250	25,000

NEW JERSEY

COLONIAL COINAGE

St. Patrick or Mark Newby

KM# 1 FARTHING

Copper **Obv. Legend:** FLOREAT REX **Rev. Legend:** QUIESCAT PLEBS

Date	AG	Good	VG	Fine	VF	XF	Unc
ND(1682)	70	125	285	775	3,750	6,500	—

Note: One very rare variety is known with reverse legend: QUIESAT PLEBS

KM# 1a FARTHING

Silver **Obv. Legend:** FLOREAT REX **Rev. Legend:** QUIESCAT PLEBS

Date	AG	Good	VG	Fine	VF	XF	Unc
ND(1682)	800	1,750	2,750	5,500	9,500	17,500	—

KM# 2 HALFPENNY

Copper **Obv. Legend:** FLOREAT REX **Rev. Legend:** ECCE GREX

Date	AG	Good	VG	Fine	VF	XF	Unc
ND(1682)	180	365	850	1,650	4,000	12,500	—

VIET NAM

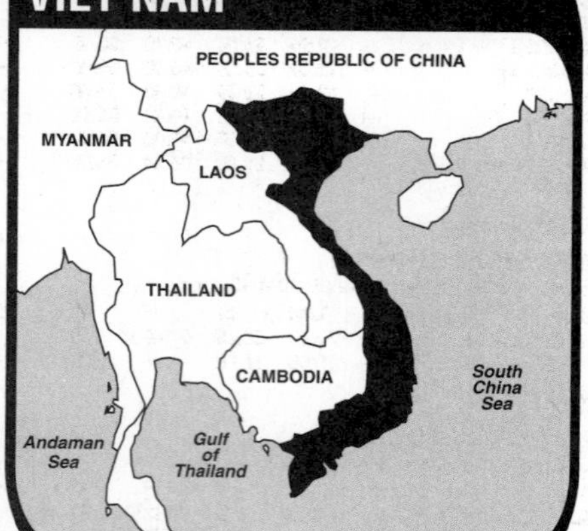

In 207 B.C. a Chinese general set up the Kingdom of Nam-Viet on the Red River. This passed to direct Chinese control under the Han and Tang lasting until 968. From that time native clans and dynasties ruled.

In 1407 China again invaded. Forces coalescing around resistance leader Le Loi ousted the Chinese in 1428, founding the Le dynasty. Its capital was Hanoi. Within a century three generals, each at the head of a clan, had splintered off their own rival territories. The Mac were in the north, the Nguyen in the south. The lords Trinh came to dominate the Le kings as puppets, deposing many, but never completely usurping the line.

The weak Le kings, controlled by a virtually parallel Trinh military dynasty, were engaged in constant wars during the 16th century. The Macs occupied nearly the entire country in 1527, claimed the throne and began issuing coins with their own reign titles. Yet by 1593 they had been fought back to two provinces on the Chinese border. Their last kings were permitted by China to make necessity money only. These used the common inscriptions *An-phap nguyen-bao* and *Tai-binh thong-bao.* The scarce Mac An-phap cash can only be differentiated from others by small details. Their Tai-binh cash cannot be attributed at all. The Macs were extinguished in 1667.

In 1599 the Le general Trinh was given the princely title Binh-An-Vuong by the Chinese, and his own sovereignty over 3 former Mac provinces. Coins inscribed Binh-An thong-bao have been attributed to him, but are Japanese trade cash.

In the 1600's the Nguyen clan expanded north and west, establishing their capital at Hue, and annexing Cambodia. While cash were almost certainly cast by them, they were not in their own names. Issues of the Nguyen are not attributable until the 1700's. During this period private casting of cash imitating Chinese and older Vietnamese coins accelerated. Mining and coining licenses were sold by local rulers to Chinese merchants, who then exported the cash in exchange for goods. (Such trade cash were made also in Java, South China and Japan.) Coins formerly attributed to two 17th century Le dynasty kings are now recognized as issues of the Nguyen duke's large mint establishment in the mid 1700's. The Le and Trinh were overturned in the 1780's by the Tayson rebellion. In 1801 a member of the Nguyen triumphed as founder of a new dynasty.

EMPERORS

Thinh Duc, 1653-1658 盛德

Vinh Tho, 1658-1662 永壽

Vinh Tri, 1676-1680 永治

Chinh Hoa, 1680-1705 政和

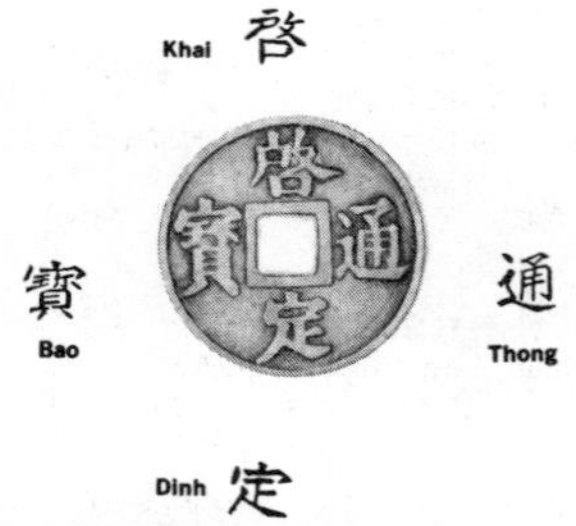

CHARACTER IDENTIFICATION

The Vietnamese used Chinese-style characters for official documents and coins and bars. Some were modified to their liking and will sometimes not match the Chinese character for the same word. The above identification and this table will translate most of the Vietnamese characters (Chinese-style) on their coins and bars described herein.

Chinese/French
Vietnamese/English

An Nam = name of the French protectorate

Dai Nam = name of the country under Gia Long's Nguyen dynasty

Viet Nam = name used briefly During Minh Mang's reign and became the modern name of the country

DAI VIET

CAST COINAGE

KM# 5 PHAN

Copper Or Brass **Ruler:** Thinh Duc **Obv:** Conventional script with Thong Bao **Rev:** Plain **Note:** Only rubbings, drawings and fakes are known of this coin.

Date	Mintage	F	VF	XF	Unc	BU
ND(1653-58) Reported, not confirmed	—	—	—	—	—	—

KM# 10 PHAN

Cast Copper **Ruler:** Vinh Tho **Obv:** Conventional script inscription **Obv. Inscription:** Vinh-tho Thong-bao **Rev:** Plain

Date	Mintage	Good	VG	F	VF	XF
ND(1658-62)	—	3.50	5.50	12.50	20.00	—

KM# 11 PHAN

Cast Copper **Ruler:** Vinh Tho **Obv:** Conventional script inscription **Obv. Inscription:** Vinh-tho Thong-bao **Rev:** Double rim

Date	Mintage	Good	VG	F	VF	XF
ND(1658-62)	—	5.00	7.50	15.00	25.00	—

KM# 12 PHAN

Cast Copper **Ruler:** Vinh Tho **Obv:** Grassy, cursive and conventional inscription **Obv. Inscription:** Vinh-tho Thong-bao"

Date	Mintage	Good	VG	F	VF	XF
ND(1658-62)	—	6.00	12.50	20.00	35.00	—

KM# 14 PHAN

Cast Copper **Ruler:** Vinh Tho **Obv:** Semi-seal script inscription **Obv. Inscription:** Vinh-tho Thong-bao

Date	Mintage	Good	VG	F	VF	XF
ND(1658-62) Rare	—	—	—	—	—	—

KM# 13 PHAN

Cast Copper **Ruler:** Vinh Tho **Obv:** Cursive inscription **Obv. Inscription:** Vinh-tho Thong-bao **Note:** Numerous script variations may be encountered among "Ving-tho Thong-bao" coins, particularly in the character "VINH".

Date	Mintage	Good	VG	F	VF	X
ND(1658-62) Rare	—	—	—	—	—	—

KM# 15 PHAN

Zinc **Ruler:** Vinh Tri **Obv:** Conventional script **Rev:** Blank

Date	Mintage	Good	VG	F	VF	X
ND(1663-71)	—	35.00	50.00	60.00	85.00	—

KM# 25 PHAN

Zinc **Ruler:** Vinh Tri **Obv:** Conventional script with Chi Bao

Date	Mintage	Good	VG	F	VF	X
ND(1676-80)	—	17.50	30.00	45.00	60.00	—

KM# 19 PHAN

Zinc **Ruler:** Vinh Tri **Obv. Inscription:** Vin-tri Nguyen-bao **Note:** Similar to KM#20.

Date	Mintage	Good	VG	F	VF	X
ND(1676-80)	—	—	—	—	—	—

KM# 20 PHAN

Cast Copper **Ruler:** Vinh Tri **Obv:** Semi-seal inscription **Obv. Inscription:** Vinh-tri Nguyen-bao

Date	Mintage	Good	VG	F	VF	XF
ND(1676-80)	—	5.00	7.50	15.00	25.00	—

KM# 21 PHAN

Cast Copper **Ruler:** Vinh Tri **Obv:** Seal script with Nguyen Bao **Obv. Inscription:** "Vinh-tri Nguyen-bao" **Rev:** Crescent right, dot left

Date	Mintage	Good	VG	F	VF	XF
ND(1676-80)	—	4.00	6.50	12.50	22.50	—

KM# 22 PHAN

Cast Copper Or Brass **Ruler:** Vinh Tri **Obv:** Conventional script inscription **Obv. Inscription:** Vinh-tri Nguyen-bao

Date	Mintage	Good	VG	F	VF	XF
ND(1676-80)	—	5.00	8.00	17.50	27.50	—

DAI VIET

Capital: Tay Do (Hanoi)

CAST COINAGE

KM# 31 PHAN

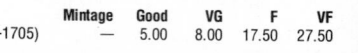

Zinc **Ruler:** Chinh Hoa **Obv:** Conventional script with 5-stroke Chanh with Thong Bao **Obv. Inscription:** "Chinh-hoa Thong-bao"

Date	Mintage	Good	VG	F	VF	XF
ND(1676-1705)	—	5.00	8.00	17.50	27.50	—

.M# A33 PHAN
inc **Ruler:** Chinh Hoa **Note:** Similar to KM#32.

ate	Mintage	Good	VG	F	VF	XF
D(1676-1705)	—	—	—	—	—	—

.M# 32 PHAN
inc **Ruler:** Chinh Hoa **Obv:** Convention script with 5-stroke hanh with Thong Bao **Obv. Inscription:** Chinh-hoa Thong-bao **ev:** Crescent right. **Note:** Only the 5-stroke Chanh of the above hanh Hoa Thong Bao coins is attributed to the Vietnamese. hose with the 9-stroke Chanh are only copies, of indeterminate ate, of chinese Northern Sung coins. Some Vietnamese Chanh oa coins may also exist in copper or brass.

ate	Mintage	Good	VG	F	VF	XF
D(1680-1705)	—	5.00	8.00	17.50	27.50	—

YEMEN

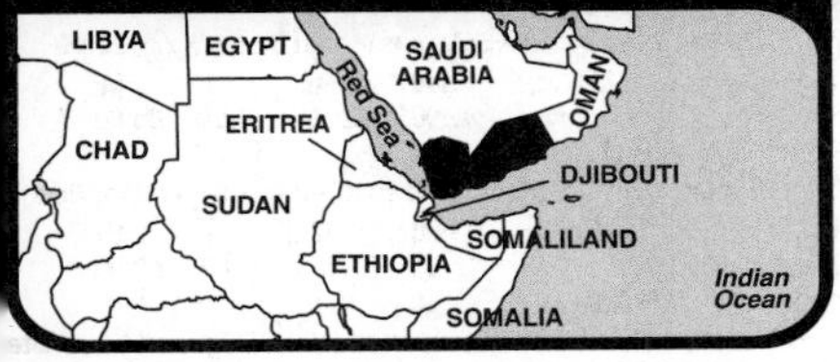

One of the oldest centers of civilization in the Middle East, emen was once part of the Minaean Kingdom and of the ancient ingdom of Sheba, after which it was captured successively by :gyptians, Ethiopians and Romans. It was converted to Islam in 28 A.D. and administered as a caliphate until 1538, when it came nder Ottoman occupation in 1849. The second Ottoman occu-ation which began in 1872 was maintained until 1918 when utonomy was achieved through revolution.

ULERS
)ttoman, until 1625

INT NAMES

l-Damigh	الدامغ
dan	عدن
hamar	ذمار ذمر
b	ايب
awkaban	كوكبان
Rada'	راداء
San'a	صنعاء
Zabid	زبيد

OTTOMAN OCCUPATION

Ahmed I
AH1012-1026 / 1603-1617AD

HAMMERED COINAGE

KM# 110 'UTHMANI
0.6000 g., Silver

Date	Mintage	Good	VG	F	VF	XF
ND Rare	—	—	—	—	—	—

Osman II
AH1027-1031 / 1618-1622AD

HAMMERED COINAGE

KM# 115 'UTHMANI
0.6000 g., Silver

Date	Mintage	Good	VG	F	VF	XF
ND Rare	—	—	—	—	—	—

Mustafa I
2nd reign, AH1031-1032 / 1622-1623AD

HAMMERED COINAGE

KM# 120 'UTHMANI
0.6000 g., Silver

Date	Mintage	Good	VG	F	VF	XF
ND Rare	—	—	—	—	—	—

Murad IV
in the Yemen, AH1032-1045 / 1623-1635AD

HAMMERED COINAGE

Sana'a

KM# 125 MANGIR
Copper

Date	Mintage	Good	VG	F	VF	XF
AH1032	—	75.00	125	225	500	—

KM# 130 'UTHMANI
0.6000 g., Silver

Date	Mintage	Good	VG	F	VF	XF
ND Date off flan; Rare	—	50.00	100	200	400	—

KINGDOM

al-Mu'ayyad Muhammad I
AH1009-1054 / 1602-1644AD

HAMMERED COINAGE

Dhamar

KM# 140.1 FALS
Copper **Note:** Weight varies: 0.30-0.50 grams.

Date	Mintage	Good	VG	F	VF	XF
ND Date off flan	—	20.00	35.00	60.00	100	—

Ibb

KM# 140.2 FALS
Copper **Note:** Weight varies: 0.30-0.50 grams.

Date	Mintage	Good	VG	F	VF	XF
AH1039	—	45.00	75.00	125	—	—

Al-Damigh

KM# 141.1 BUQSHA
Silver **Obv:** "Muhammad" in circle, titles around **Rev:** Mint and date **Note:** Weight varies: 0.30-0.50 grams.

Date	Mintage	Good	VG	F	VF	XF
ND Date off flan	—	15.00	28.00	45.00	70.00	—
AH1046	—	25.00	50.00	80.00	135	—
AH1047	—	25.00	50.00	80.00	135	—
AH1048	—	25.00	50.00	80.00	135	—
AH1049	—	25.00	50.00	80.00	135	—

Dhamar

KM# 141.2 BUQSHA
Silver **Note:** Weight varies: 0.30-0.50 grams.

Date	Mintage	Good	VG	F	VF	XF
ND Date off flan	—	10.00	18.00	30.00	50.00	—
AH1049	—	16.00	32.00	55.00	90.00	—
AH1050	—	16.00	32.00	55.00	90.00	—
AH1051	—	16.00	32.00	55.00	90.00	—

Ibb

KM# 141.3 BUQSHA
Silver **Note:** Weight varies: 0.30-0.50 grams.

Date	Mintage	Good	VG	F	VF	XF
ND Date off flan	—	8.00	15.00	25.00	40.00	—
AH1039	—	15.00	28.00	45.00	70.00	—
AH1041	—	15.00	28.00	45.00	70.00	—
AH1047	—	15.00	28.00	45.00	70.00	—
AH1048	—	15.00	28.00	45.00	70.00	—
AH1050	—	15.00	28.00	45.00	70.00	—

Kawkaban

KM# 141.4 BUQSHA
Silver **Note:** Weight varies: 0.30-0.50 grams.

Date	Mintage	Good	VG	F	VF	XF
ND Date off flan	—	12.00	25.00	40.00	65.00	—
AH1036	—	25.00	45.00	70.00	120	—

Sana'a

KM# 141.5 BUQSHA
Silver **Note:** Weight varies: 0.30-0.50 grams.

Date	Mintage	Good	VG	F	VF	XF
ND Date off flan	—	15.00	30.00	50.00	85.00	—
AH1047	—	25.00	50.00	80.00	135	—
AH1048	—	25.00	50.00	80.00	135	—

al-Mutawakkil Isma'il
AH1054-1087 / 1644-1676AD

HAMMERED COINAGE

Dhamarmar

KM# 145.1 FALS
Copper

Date	Mintage	Good	VG	F	VF	XF
ND Date off flan	—	16.00	30.00	50.00	80.00	—
AH1083	—	20.00	35.00	60.00	100	—

Sa'da

KM# 145.2 FALS
Copper

Date	Mintage	Good	VG	F	VF	XF
ND Date off flan	—	16.00	30.00	50.00	80.00	—
AH1070	—	20.00	35.00	60.00	100	—

Shihara

KM# 145.3 FALS
Copper

Date	Mintage	Good	VG	F	VF	XF
ND Date off flan	—	16.00	30.00	50.00	80.00	—
AH1064	—	20.00	35.00	60.00	100	—

Al-Damigh

KM# 155.1 BUQSHA
Silver **Obv:** "Isma'il" usually in oval, titles around **Rev:** Mint and date **Note:** Weight varies: 0.20-0.40 grams.

Date	Mintage	Good	VG	F	VF	XF
ND Date off flan	—	8.00	15.00	25.00	40.00	—
AH1069	—	16.00	30.00	50.00	80.00	—

Al-Rawda

KM# 155.2 BUQSHA
Silver **Note:** Weight varies: 0.20-0.40 grams.

Date	Mintage	Good	VG	F	VF	XF
ND Date off flan	—	12.00	25.00	40.00	65.00	—
AH1064	—	35.00	45.00	75.00	125	—
AH1079	—	35.00	45.00	75.00	125	—

Dhamar

KM# 155.3 BUQSHA
Silver **Note:** Weight varies: 0.20-0.40 grams.

Date	Mintage	Good	VG	F	VF	XF
ND Date off flan	—	8.00	15.00	25.00	40.00	—
AH1060	—	12.00	25.00	40.00	65.00	—
AH1062	—	12.00	25.00	40.00	65.00	—
AH1063	—	12.00	25.00	40.00	65.00	—
AH1065	—	12.00	25.00	40.00	65.00	—
AH1066	—	12.00	25.00	40.00	65.00	—
AH1022 Error for 66	—	12.00	25.00	40.00	65.00	—

Dhamarmar

KM# 155.4 BUQSHA
Silver **Note:** Weight varies: 0.20-0.40 grams.

Date	Mintage	Good	VG	F	VF	XF
ND Date off flan	—	20.00	35.00	60.00	100	—
AH1077	—	30.00	60.00	100	175	—

Ibb

KM# 155.9 BUQSHA
Silver Weight varies: 0.20-0.40g.

Date	Mintage	VG	F	VF	XF	Unc
AH1055	—	30.00	50.00	70.00	110	—
AH1056	—	25.00	45.00	65.00	100	—
ND	—	20.00	35.00	55.00	80.00	—

Kawkaban

KM# 155.5 BUQSHA
Silver **Note:** Weight varies: 0.20-0.40 grams.

Date	Mintage	Good	VG	F	VF	XF
ND Date off flan	—	7.00	12.00	20.00	30.00	—
AH1055	—	10.00	20.00	35.00	60.00	—
AH1056	—	10.00	20.00	35.00	60.00	—
AH1057	—	10.00	20.00	35.00	60.00	—
AH1058	—	10.00	20.00	35.00	60.00	—
AH1064	—	10.00	20.00	35.00	60.00	—
AH1065	—	10.00	20.00	35.00	60.00	-
AH1066	—	10.00	20.00	35.00	60.00	-

KM# 155.6 BUQSHA

Silver **Note:** Weight varies: 0.20-0.40 grams.

Date	Mintage	Good	VG	F	VF	XF
ND Date off flan	—	7.00	12.00	20.00	45.00	—
AH1070	—	20.00	35.00	60.00	100	—

Sana'a

KM# 155.7 BUQSHA

Silver Weight varies: 0.20-0.40g.

Date	Mintage	Good	VG	F	VF	XF
ND Date off flan	—	6.00	10.00	18.00	30.00	—
AH1054	—	10.00	20.00	35.00	60.00	—
AH1055	—	10.00	20.00	35.00	60.00	—
AH1056	—	10.00	20.00	35.00	60.00	—
AH1057	—	10.00	20.00	35.00	60.00	—
AH1058	—	10.00	20.00	35.00	60.00	—
AH1059	—	10.00	20.00	35.00	60.00	—
AH1064	—	10.00	20.00	35.00	60.00	—
AH1065	—	10.00	20.00	35.00	60.00	—
AH1066	—	10.00	20.00	35.00	60.00	—
AH1022 error for 1066	—	15.00	30.00	50.00	80.00	—
AH1067	—	10.00	20.00	35.00	60.00	—
AH1069	—	10.00	20.00	35.00	60.00	—
AH1074	—	10.00	20.00	35.00	60.00	—
AH1075	—	10.00	20.00	35.00	60.00	—
AH1078	—	10.00	20.00	35.00	60.00	—
AH1079	—	10.00	20.00	35.00	60.00	—

Shihara

KM# 155.8 BUQSHA

Silver **Note:** Weight varies: 0.20-0.40 grams.

Date	Mintage	Good	VG	F	VF	XF
ND Date off flan	—	15.00	20.00	45.00	70.00	—
AH1056	—	25.00	45.00	75.00	125	—
AH1057	—	25.00	45.00	75.00	125	—

Dhamar

KM# 150.1 KHUMS KABIR

Silver **Note:** Weight varies: 0.80-1.20 grams.

Date	Mintage	Good	VG	F	VF	XF
ND Date off flan	—	12.00	22.00	35.00	60.00	—
AH1071	—	20.00	35.00	60.00	100	—

Kawkaban

KM# 150.2 KHUMS KABIR

Silver **Note:** Weight varies: 0.80-1.20 grams.

Date	Mintage	Good	VG	F	VF	XF
ND Date off flan	—	10.00	20.00	30.00	50.00	—
AH1074	—	16.00	30.00	50.00	80.00	—

Rada'

KM# 150.3 KHUMS KABIR

Silver **Note:** Weight varies: 0.80-1.20 grams.

Date	Mintage	Good	VG	F	VF	XF
ND Date off flan	—	15.00	25.00	45.00	75.00	—
AH1070	—	25.00	45.00	75.00	125	—

Sana'a

KM# 150.4 KHUMS KABIR

Silver **Note:** Weight varies: 0.80-1.20 grams.

Date	Mintage	Good	VG	F	VF	XF
ND Date off flan	—	8.00	16.00	28.00	45.00	—
AH1066	—	—	—	—	—	—
Note: Reported, not confirmed						
AH1070	—	15.00	28.00	45.00	70.00	—
AH1074	—	15.00	28.00	45.00	70.00	—
AH1075	—	15.00	28.00	45.00	70.00	—

al-Mahdi Ahmad

AH1087-1092 / 1676-1681AD

HAMMERED COINAGE

'Ayyan

KM# 162.1 BUQSHA

000 g., Silver

Date	Mintage	Good	VG	F	VF	XF
e off flan	—	35.00	70.00	120	200	—

2 BUQSHA

ver

Date	Mintage	Good	VG	F	VF	XF
	—	25.00	45.00	75.00	125	—

San'a

KM# 162.3 BUQSHA

Silver **Note:** Weight varies: 1.00-2.00 grams.

Date	Mintage	Good	VG	F	VF	XF
ND	—	—	—	—	80.00	—

KM# 165 BUQSHA (Undetermined denomination)

Gold

Date	Mintage	Good	VG	F	VF	XF
ND Date off flan; Rare	—	—	—	—	—	—

Dhamarmar

KM# 160.1 KHUMS KABIR

Silver **Note:** Weight varies: 0.80-1.00 grams.

Date	Mintage	Good	VG	F	VF	XF
ND Date off flan	—	15.00	28.00	45.00	75.00	—
AH1087	—	28.00	55.00	90.00	150	—

Kawkaban

KM# 160.2 KHUMS KABIR

Silver **Note:** Weight varies: 0.80-1.00 grams.

Date	Mintage	Good	VG	F	VF	XF
ND Date off flan	—	12.00	25.00	45.00	80.00	—
AH1088	—	20.00	35.00	60.00	100	—

al-Mu'ayyad Muhammad II

AH1092-1097 / 1681-1686AD

HAMMERED COINAGE

Rada'

KM# 170 KHUMS KABIR

Silver **Note:** Weight varies: 0.80-1.00 grams.

Date	Mintage	Good	VG	F	VF	XF
ND Date off flan	—	30.00	60.00	100	175	—
AH1093	—	35.00	70.00	120	200	—

al-Nasir Muhammad

First reign AH1098-1105 / 1687-1693AD

HAMMERED COINAGE

Al-Ghiras

KM# 175.1 1/2 FALS

Copper

Date	Mintage	Good	VG	F	VF	XF
ND Date off flan	—	60.00	120	200	350	—

Rada'

KM# 175.2 1/2 FALS

Copper

Date	Mintage	Good	VG	F	VF	XF
ND Date off flan	—	12.00	25.00	40.00	65.00	—
AH1102	—	18.00	35.00	60.00	100	—
AH1103	—	18.00	35.00	60.00	100	—

Rahban

KM# 175.3 1/2 FALS

Copper

Date	Mintage	Good	VG	F	VF	XF
AH1097	—	60.00	120	200	350	—

Al-Hadra'

KM# 180.1 FALS

Copper

Date	Mintage	Good	VG	F	VF	XF
ND Date off flan	—	30.00	60.00	100	175	—

Rada'

KM# 180.2 FALS

Copper

Date	Mintage	Good	VG	F	VF	XF
ND Date off flan	—	9.00	15.00	30.00	40.00	—
AH1101	—	18.00	35.00	60.00	—	—
AH1102	—	18.00	35.00	60.00	—	—
AH1103	—	18.00	35.00	60.00	—	—
AH1104	—	18.00	35.00	60.00	—	—
AH1105	—	18.00	35.00	60.00	—	—

Al-Hadra'

KM# 185.1 KHUMS KABIR

Silver **Note:** Weight varies: 0.80-1.00 grams.

Date	Mintage	Good	VG	F	VF	XF
ND Date off flan	—	20.00	35.00	60.00	100	—
AH1105	—	30.00	60.00	100	175	—

Unknown Mint

KM# 185.2 KHUMS KABIR

Silver **Note:** Probably struck at San'a. Weight varies: 0.80-1.00 gram.

Date	Mintage	Good	VG	F	VF	XF
ND Date off flan	—	12.00	25.00	40.00	65.00	—
AH1102	—	28.00	55.00	90.00	150	—

al-Nasir Muhammad

Second reign as al-Hadi Muhammad AH1105-1109 / 1693-1697AD

HAMMERED COINAGE

Unknown Mint

KM# 190 1/2 FALS

Copper **Note:** Probably struck at San'a.

Date	Mintage	Good	VG	F	VF	XF
ND Date off flan	—	25.00	45.00	75.00	125	—
AH1108	—	25.00	45.00	75.00	125	—

Al-Hadra'

KM# 195 FALS

Copper

Date	Mintage	Good	VG	F	VF	XF
ND Date off flan	—	25.00	45.00	75.00	125	—

Al-Hadra'

KM# 200.1 KHUMS KABIR

Silver **Note:** Weight varies: 0.80-1.00 grams.

Date	Mintage	Good	VG	F	VF	XF
ND Date off flan	—	16.00	32.00	55.00	90.00	—
AH110x	—	30.00	60.00	100	175	—

Unknown Mint

KM# 200.2 KHUMS KABIR

Silver **Note:** Probably struck at San'a. Weight varies: 0.80-1.00 gram.

Date	Mintage	Good	VG	F	VF	XF
ND Date off flan	—	16.00	32.00	55.00	90.00	—

al-Nasir Muhammad

Third reign as al-Madhi Muhammad AH1109-1130 / 1697-1718AD

HAMMERED COINAGE

San'a

KM# 215 BUQSHA

Silver **Note:** Weight varies: 0.15-0.20 grams.

Date	Mintage	Good	VG	F	VF	XF
ND Date off flan	—	10.00	20.00	35.00	55.00	—
AH1110	—	15.00	28.00	45.00	75.00	—

San'a

KM# 210 KHUMS KABIR

Silver **Note:** Weight varies: 2.00-3.00 grams.

Date	Mintage	Good	VG	F	VF	XF
ND Date off flan	—	10.00	18.00	30.00	50.00	—
AH1111	—	15.00	28.00	45.00	100	—